THE ENCYCLOPEDIA OF
WORLD HISTORY

THE ENCYCLOPEDIA OF WORLD HISTORY

ANCIENT, MEDIEVAL, and MODERN
CHRONOLOGICALLY ARRANGED

PETER N. STEARNS, General Editor

SIXTH EDITION

A COMPLETELY REVISED
AND UPDATED EDITION
of the
CLASSIC REFERENCE WORK
originally compiled and edited by

WILLIAM L. LANGER

HOUGHTON MIFFLIN COMPANY
BOSTON   NEW YORK
2001

Copyright © 2001 by Houghton Mifflin Company

For information about permission to reproduce selections from this book, write to
Permissions, Houghton Mifflin Company, 215 Park Avenue South,
New York, New York 10003.

Visit our Web site: www.houghtonmifflinbooks.com.

Library of Congress Cataloging-in-Publication Data

The encyclopedia of world history : ancient, medieval, and modern,
chronologically arranged / Peter N. Stearns, general editor. — 6th ed.,
[rev. and expanded]
    p. cm.
    "A completely revised and updated edition of the classic reference
work originally compiled and edited by William L. Langer."
    Includes index.
    ISBN 0-395-65237-5
    1. History — Outlines, syllabi, etc.   2. History — Encyclopedias.
I. Stearns, Peter N.   II. Langer, William L. (William Leonard),
1896–1977. Encyclopedia of world history.

D21 .E578   2001
902'.02 — dc21   2001024479

Book design by Anne Chalmers

Maps by Mary Reilly. Copyright © 2001 by Houghton Mifflin Company
Additional contributors to the Sixth Edition: Elizabeth Armstrong, Steven Beaudoin, Max
Bilson, Liping Bu, Derek Coryell, Alexander Dawson, Kathleen Dickson, Brian Fagan, Bill
Gammage, Steve Gish, James Grehan, David Duoblas Haldane, Joan Judge, Miriam Lang,
Ancella Livers, Thomas McClendon, Miles McDonnell, Magdalena Chocan Mena, Mont-
serrat Miller, Jodie Minor, Jonathan Roth, Denise Spellberg, and Plamen Tsevtkov.

Printed in the United States of America

QUM 10 9 8 7 6 5 4 3 2 1

CONTRIBUTING EDITORS
TO THE SIXTH EDITION

Joshua A. Fogel
Sandria Freitag
William Harris
Bennett Hill
Brij V. Lal
Abraham Marcus
Richard Roberts
Joseph W. Trotter
John Voll
Barbara Weinstein

CONTRIBUTING EDITORS
TO EARLIER EDITIONS

Crane Brinton
Geoffrey Brunn
George Busalla
Robert S. Chamberlain
Carleton Coon
Paul P. Cram
Frank M. Cross, Jr.
Sterling Dow
Robert H. Dyson, Jr.
John K. Fairbank
Charles S. Gardner
Hans W. Gatzke
Marija Gimbutas
Madeleine Gleason
Mason Hammond
Carol R. Harting

Stephen N. Hay
James B. Hedges
Halil Inalcik
Michael Karpovich
Melvin Kranzberg
William L. Langer
Dwight E. Lee
Derwood Lockard
Donald C. McKay
Robert H. Pfeiffer
Edwin O. Reischauer
Penfield Roberts
Robert O. Schlaifer
William Thomson
J. A. B. Van Buitenen
Lauriston Ward

PREFACE TO THE SIXTH EDITION

The history of this encyclopedia is one of the most interesting in American (and German) publishing, with a lineage going back well over a century. My colleagues and I, as editors of this new edition, have been conscious of our responsibility in dealing with probably the most revered reference work in our discipline. I myself knew and used what we called the "Langer encyclopedia," after its distinguished editor, William L. Langer, throughout my professional education and career. My copy was a gift from my father, and all the more cherished as a result.

The present edition takes up the encyclopedia's heritage with that combination of change and continuity that any historian will recognize as a standard of human endeavor. We have kept the style of most references, as well as many specific entries from what was a marvelous compendium. We have retained the emphasis on periodization as an organizing device for the historian's craft. But in seeking to match the earlier editors' commitment to thoroughness and to an up-to-date rendition of history as a discipline, we have also made significant changes. Two of these warrant brief comment by way of orientation, and two others deserve more complete explanation.

First, the present edition changes the format a bit, in that it sets out highlights before taking up the major periods and areas in detail. This arrangement is partly for convenience and partly to help readers see the forest before they engage the trees. Not all major developments, after all, fall into neat year-by-year categories, yet they must be conveyed. Purely event-based history is less satisfactory now than it was a generation ago.

Second, the book has been updated chronologically from the early 1970s, where the previous edition left off, to the end of the second millennium in the Christian, or Common Era, calendar. This update captures a host of specific developments, but particularly the unfolding of history in the many new or renewed nations of Asia, Africa, and the Pacific; the trends of increasing globalization; the revival of key religions; and the end of the cold war around 1989.

Two other changes, each of which required a major recasting of the encyclopedia and some reduction of previous coverage of Western Europe, reflect the twin revolutions in historical study during the past generation. The past has been redefined, and now this venerable encyclopedia has been as well.

Historians now take very seriously the history of ordinary people and of facets of life apart from the great events of politics, diplomacy, and high culture. Shifts in the relationships between men and women, developments in leisure, demographic currents, and many other topics are now part of the historical mainstream. They draw attention both because they are important in their own right — workers, minority groups, and crime patterns have serious histories of their own, without which current social patterns cannot be understood — and because they have major impacts on politics, war, and high culture. Groups of ordinary people are historical actors, not just acted upon. Social and cultural history, largely ignored in the previous editions, is now given consistent attention, so that major trends can be traced and evaluated alongside the more familiar parade of statesmen and scientists. Aspects of this newer approach to history are still a knowledge frontier, and major discoveries continue to occur; but there is abundant material that can be conveyed in a standard reference work of this sort.

The final change in the new edition reflects the explosion of knowledge about the histories of regions outside of Western Europe and North America and about larger, crosscutting global trends. The sections dealing with Africa, the Middle East, South Asia, and Latin America are almost unrecognizable when juxtaposed with their counterparts in the previous edition. They are much more extensive, with a host of data included that was absent before. And their tone is different, in conveying significant histories that go well beyond the chronicling of the impact of the West. The histories of the world's regions outside of Europe are elaborate and complex, in premodern centuries as well as in modern times.

A related change is the focus on trends that cannot be captured through the coverage of a single nation or even a single region, particularly in the sections on international patterns that preface each major chronological divide. Here are details about the diffusion of technologies or the impacts of migration, disease, and trade; and here, in the more contemporary eras, is coverage of international governmental and commercial organizations.

Simply put, this is a volume that has always intended to convey the key features of world history. The world we know historically has greatly changed. The revisions that animate this edition celebrate this change, benefiting from the labors of countless venturesome scholars over the past several decades.

— PETER N. STEARNS

PREFACE TO THE FIRST EDITION

This *Epitome of History* itself has a long and interesting history. More than seventy years ago Dr. Karl Ploetz, in his time a well-known German teacher, published an *Auszug aus der alten, mittleren und neueren Geschichte*, intended as a factual handbook for the use of students and for the convenience of the general reader. That his compilation filled a real need is attested by the fact that within a few years it went through seven editions, and by the further fact that to date more than twenty editions have appeared in Germany, revised and edited by noted scholars. The book has easily held its own despite competition of numerous similar books.

Ploetz's *Epitome* was translated into English by William H. Tillinghast and published by Houghton Mifflin Company in this country in 1883. The translator, recognizing that the original was designed particularly to meet the needs of the German student and that therefore the history of central Europe was weighted against the history of France, England, and America, took the opportunity to enlarge a number of sections and to add others. No less a scholar than Edward Channing contributed the new sections on modern England and the United States. Furthermore, Tillinghast first added brief sections on the Middle and Far Eastern countries, which had been completely omitted from the German version. The book appeared under the title *An Epitome of Ancient, Medieval, and Modern History,* and proved so popular that no less than twenty-four printings were necessary before 1905. Occasional revisions were made and in 1915 the title was changed to *A Handbook of Universal History.*

Since historical knowledge and historical conceptions are notoriously fluid, it is not to be wondered at that even so sound and reliable a book as the old Ploetz-Tillinghast *Epitome* should ultimately have fallen behind the times. After the First World War the publishers therefore commissioned Dr. Harry Elmer Barnes to overhaul the book and bring it up to date. The new editor, with a number of collaborators, left the kernel of the old work (the Greek and Roman history, the medieval sections, and the early modern parts) as it was, judging quite rightly that in the large it was not so badly out of line as to justify rewriting and resetting. But the sections dealing with the early Near East, of which little was known in Ploetz's day, were completely redone, and a great deal of material on the period from 1883 to 1923 was added. The *Epitome,* thus revised, was published in 1925 as *A Manual of Universal History.* Like the preceding versions it has been widely used by students and laymen alike.

But despite revisions of one kind or another, it became increasingly clear that sooner or later the original book would require drastic changes if it were to keep abreast of modern knowledge and meet contemporary requirements. It stands to reason that in seventy years our command of the facts and our views of even those subjects best treated by Ploetz and Tillinghast have changed substantially. Above all, the past fifty years have witnessed the expansion of western influence over the entire globe and, as a result, there is now a much greater need to know something of the past of non-European countries and cultures, and a much livelier interest in formerly neglected fields. To fill the new requirements no amount of revision of the old book would do, for the original author wrote as a German and treated European history primarily as it touched his own country's develpment. Tillinghast attempted to give the English translation a somewhat more Anglo-American slant, and Dr. Barnes did what was humanly possible to adapt the old text to a more world-wide approach. But the point had been definitely reached where adaptations and adjustments would no longer suffice. The publishers therefore invited me to undertake a complete rewriting of the entire book, securing the aid of collaborators qualified to treat of special fields where it seemed desirable. It was my great good fortune to be able to interest fifteen of my colleagues to take over particular sections and to secure from them the most whole-hearted co-operation in what, after all, was an enterprise of some magnitude. Their names, with the sections for which they made themselves responsible, are listed above.

When embarking upon this project I still had hope that considerable parts of the old book might yet be salvaged and that a thoroughgoing revision would prove adequate for the ancient, medieval, and early modern sections. But it soon became apparent to all of us engaged in the work that the whole plan and approach required rethinking and that, consequently, there was but little use in trying to adhere to the old text. Here and there a few pages (thoroughly emended) have been retained, but they are relatively so few in number as to be hardly worth mentioning. Almost nothing of the substance of the old book remains; every single section has been gone over in thorough fashion, reduced or expanded and, above all, brought into line with present-day knowledge. Many other sections, naturally, have been newly written, so that I think we can honestly say that the book is no longer a manual of European history with some perfunctory reference to other countries, but genuine world history, in which the geographical divisions are dealt with on their merits.

In the course of rewriting we have, however, stuck by

Ploetz's original conception. That is, we have tried to compile a handbook of historical facts, so arranged that the dates stand out while the material itself flows in a reasonably smooth narrative. Individual judgments have been kept in the background and divergent interpretations have been adduced only where they seem to be indispensable. The great diversity of type which had crept into the old book has been done away with and we have broken the uniformity of the print only by the use of small and capital boldface and very occasional employment of italics. The number of genealogical charts has been much increased: new tables have been added for some of the non-European dynasties and all charts have been brought up to date. Furthermore, a considerable number of maps has been included, not with the idea of supplying a complete historical atlas, but simply for the convenience of the user who, when he is checking one event or another, cannot be expected to have always at hand the necessary map material.

In the preface to the 1925 edition Dr. Barnes referred to the growing interest in non-political aspects of history and to his attempt to expand sections dealing with economic and cultural developments. Though deeply interested in these phases of history, Dr. Barnes felt obliged to recognize that the majority of those who would use the book would come seeking information on political, military, and diplomatic history and that therefore those angles would have to be primarily considered. I subscribe entirely to this view, but I take this opportunity to point out further that cultural history does not lend itself readily to the method of treatment upon which this particular work is based. The backbone of this book is chronology which, in the case of general economic trends, religious and artistic movements, and intellectual currents, is both hard to define and of relatively less significance. For methodological reasons, if for no other, we could therefore give but slight emphasis to these aspects of history. In addition we had to consider the further difficulties presented by space limitation: obviously anything like adequate treatment of literature, art, science, and economics would have taken us so far afield that the results could not possibly have been enclosed within two covers. In some sections the reader will find brief summaries of cultural activities, in others not; but in any case we offer them only for what they may be worth, as a matter of convenience, without any thought of sufficiency, much less exhaustiveness. And these remarks apply equally to the special sections at the beginning of the nineteenth century,

entitled *Social Thought and Social Movements, Scientific Thought and Progress,* and *Mechanical Inventions and Technical Achievements.* * The material we adduce in these sections appeared to us indispensable for an understanding of nineteenth-century development. It cannot be suitably included under one country, for its application is general. We could not aim or hope for completeness; hence our only objective in these sections has been to bring together an irreducible minimum of pertinent information.

Each successive editor of this *Handbook* has come away from his task impressed with the difficulties of attaining accuracy in dealing with so vast a number of dates covering so wide a range of time and territory. I am no exception to the rule and am far from being arrogant enough to suppose that this new book is even more free from error than the old. There is some consolation, however, in the thought that we collaborators have all done what we reasonably could to guard against blunders and that, as a matter of fact, many dates are so uncertain or disputed that they will probably never be satisfactorily fixed.

The success of the *Epitome of History* over a period of more than two generations is ample proof of the need for a manual of this type. In the revised and extended form here presented, it ought to be more valuable than ever. Its use for students of history is obvious enough, but it ought to prove as helpful to many others. Students of the history of literature and of art should find a concise guide to political history a great boon and all readers of historical novels or biographies should welcome a book of reference to events of the past, to genealogical relationships, and so on. My own experience with the old book was that I used it more as I became better acquainted with it. Nothing would please me more than to have the new edition find a secure place on the shelves of all book-lovers.

In presenting the new *Epitome* I cannot refrain from expressing my profound gratitude to all the contributors and also to Professors Walter Clark and Vincent Scramuzza, to Professor Sterling Dow, Mr. Eugene Boardman, and to Miss Katharine Irwin for the ready help they gave in reading proof. My secretaries, Mrs. Elizabeth Fox and Mrs. Rosamund Chapman, took care of countless loose ends and deserve more than a little credit for whatever merit the book may have.

— WILLIAM L. LANGER

---

*In the present edition these sections are entitled *Philosophical, Religious, and Social Thought; Science and Learning; Technological Achievements.*

CONTENTS

I. PREHISTORIC TIMES

II. ANCIENT AND CLASSICAL PERIODS, 3500 B.C.E.–500 C.E.

III. THE POSTCLASSICAL PERIOD, 500–1500

IV. THE EARLY MODERN PERIOD, 1500–1800

V. THE MODERN PERIOD, 1789–1914

VI. THE WORLD WARS AND THE INTERWAR PERIOD, 1914–1945

VII. THE CONTEMPORARY PERIOD, 1945–2000

APPENDIXES

MAPS

GENEALOGICAL TABLES

I. PREHISTORIC TIMES

A. INTRODUCTION

1. HISTORY AND PREHISTORY

Human beings have flourished on Earth for at least 2.5 million years. The study of history in its broadest sense is a record of humanity and its accomplishments from its earliest origins to modern times. This record of human achievement has reached us in many forms, as written documents, as oral traditions passed down from generation to generation, and in the archaeological record—sites, artifacts, food remains, and other surviving evidence of ancient human behavior. The earliest written records go back about 5,000 years in the Near East, in Mesopotamia, and the Nile Valley. Elsewhere, written history begins much later: in Greece, about 3,500 years ago; in China, about 2,000 years ago; and in many other parts of the world, after the 15th century C.E. with the arrival of Western explorers and missionaries. Oral histories have an even shorter compass, extending back only a few generations or centuries at the most.

History, which remains primarily though not exclusively the study of written documents, covers only a tiny fraction of the human past. **Prehistory,** the span of human existence before the advent of written records, encompasses the remainder of the past 2.5 million years. **Prehistorians,** students of the prehistoric past, rely mainly on archaeological evidence to study the origins of humanity, the peopling of the world by humans, and the beginnings of agriculture and urban civilization.

Archaeology is the study of the human past based on the material remains of human behavior. These remains come down to us in many forms. They survive as archaeological sites, ranging from the mighty pyramids of Giza built by ancient Egyptian pharaohs to insignificant scatters of stone tools and animal bones abandoned by very early humans in East Africa. Then there are caves and rock shelters adorned with ancient paintings and engravings, and human burials that can provide vital information, not only on biological makeup but also on ancient diet and disease and social rankings.

Modern scientific archaeology has three primary objectives: to study the basic culture history of prehistoric times, to reconstruct ancient lifeways, and to study the processes by which human cultures and societies changed over long periods of time. Archaeology is unique among all scientific disciplines in its ability to chronicle human biological and cultural change over long periods of time. The development of this sophisticated approach to the human past ranks as one of the major scientific achievements of this century.

Archaeology, by its very nature, is concerned more with the material and the environmental. It is basically an anonymous science, dealing with generalities about human cultures derived from artifacts, buildings, and food remains rather than with the individuals who appear in many of the historians' archives. But by using complex theoretical models and carefully controlled analogies from living societies, it is sometimes possible for the archaeologist to gain insights into prehistoric spiritual and religious life, and into the great complexities of ancient human societies living in worlds remote from our own.

2. THE STUDY OF PREHISTORY

a. ARCHAEOLOGY AS ANTHROPOLOGY AND HISTORY

In contrast to classicists and historians, prehistoric archaeologists deal with an enormous time scale of human biological and cultural evolution that extends back at least 2.5 million years. Prehistoric archaeology is the primary source of information on 99 percent of human history. Prehistoric archaeologists investigate how early human societies all over the world came into being, how they differed from one another, and, in particular, how they changed through time.

No one could possibly become an expert in all periods of human prehistory. Some specialists deal with the earliest human beings, working closely with geologists and anthropologists concerned with human biological evolution. Others are experts on stone toolmaking, the early peopling of the New and Old Worlds, or on many other topics, such as the origins of agriculture in the Near East. All of this specialist expertise means that archaeologists, whatever time period they are working on, draw on scientists from many other disciplines—botanists, geologists, physicists, zoologists.

Prehistoric archaeologists consider themselves a special type of anthropologist. Anthropologists study humanity in the widest possible sense, and archaeological anthropologists study human societies of the past that are no longer in existence. Their ultimate research objectives are the same as those of anthropologists studying living societies. Instead of using informants, however, they use the material remains of long-vanished societies to reach the same general goals. Prehistorians also share many objectives with historians, but work with artifacts and food remains rather than documents. In some parts of the world, such as tropical Africa, for example, prehistoric archaeology is the primary way of writing history, since oral traditions extend back only a few centuries, and in many places written records appear no earlier than the 19th century C.E.

b. CULTURE AND CONTEXT

Anthropology, and archaeology as part of it, is unified by one common thread, the concept of **culture.** Everyone lives within a cultural context—middle-class Americans, Romans, and Kwakiutl Indians of northwestern North America. Each culture has its own recognizable cultural style, which shapes the behavior of its members, their political and judicial institutions, and their morals.

Human culture is unique because much of its content is transmitted from generation to generation by sophisticated communication systems. Formal education, religious beliefs, and daily social intercourse all transmit culture and allow societies to develop complex and continuing adaptations to aid their survival. Culture is a potential guide to human behavior created through generations of human experience. Human beings are the only animals that use culture as their primary means of adapting to the environment. While biological evolution has protected animals like the arctic fox from bitterly cold winters, only human beings make thick clothes in cold latitudes and construct light thatched shelters in the Tropics.

Culture is an adaptive system, an interface between ourselves, the environment, and other human societies. Throughout the long millennia of prehistory, human culture became more elaborate, for it is our only means of adaptation and we are always adjusting to environmental, technological, and societal change.

The great Victorian anthropologist Sir Edward Tylor described culture as "that complex whole which includes knowledge, belief, art, morals, law, custom, and any other capabilities and habits acquired by man as a member of society." Prehistoric archaeologists prefer to define culture as the primary nonbiological means by which people adapt to their environment. They consider it as representing the cumulative intellectual resources of human societies, passed down by the spoken word and by example.

Human cultures are made up of many different parts, such as language, technology, religious beliefs, ways of obtaining food, and so on. These elements interact with one another to form complex and ever-changing cultural systems, systems that adjust to long- and short-term environmental change.

Archaeologists work with the tangible remains of ancient cultural systems, typically such durable artifacts as stone tools or clay pot fragments. Such finds are a patterned reflection of the culture that created them. Archaeologists spend much time studying the linkages between past cultures and their archaeological remains. They do so within precise contexts of time and space.

c. TIME AND SPACE

Archaeologists date the past and study the ever-changing distributions of ancient cultures across the world by studying the context of archaeological finds, whether sites, food remains, or artifacts, in time and space. This is the study of **culture history,** the description of human cultures as they extend back thousands of years.

1. TIME

Human prehistory has a time scale of more than 2.5 million years and a vast landscape of archaeological sites that were occupied for long and short periods of time. Some, like the Aztec capital, Tenochtitlán, in the Valley of Mexico, were occupied for a few centuries. Others, like Olduvai Gorge in East Africa, were visited repeatedly over hundreds of thousands of years. The chronology of prehistory is made up from thousands of careful excavations and many types of dating tests. These have created hundreds of local sequences of prehistoric cultures and archaeological sites throughout the world.

Historical records provide a chronology for about 5,000 years of human history in Egypt and Mesopotamia, less time in other regions. For earlier times, archaeologists rely on both relative and absolute dating methods to develop chronological sequences.

Relative dating is based on a fundamental principle of stratigraphic geology, the Law of Superposition, which states that underlying levels are earlier than those that cover them. Thus any object found in a lower level is from an earlier time than any from upper layers. Manufactured artifacts are the fundamental data that archaeologists use to study human behavior. These artifacts have changed in radical ways with passing time. One has only to look at the simple stone choppers and flakes made by the first humans and compare them with the latest luxury automobile to get the point. By combining the study of changes in artifact forms with observations of their contexts in stratified layers in archaeological sites, the prehistorian can develop relative chronologies for artifacts, sites, and cultures in any part of the world.

The story of prehistory has unfolded against a backdrop of massive world climatic change during the Great Ice Age (p. 5). Sometimes, when human artifacts come to light in geological strata dating to the Ice Age, one can place them in a much broader geological context. But in such cases, as with relative chronologies from other archaeological sites, determining the actual date of these sites and artifacts in years is a matter of guesswork, or of applying absolute dating methods.

Absolute chronology is the process of dating in calendar years. A whole battery of chronological methods have been developed to date human prehistory, some of them frankly experimental, others well established and widely used. The following are the best known ones.

a. Historical Records and Objects of Known Age

Historical documents can sometimes be used to date events, such as the death of an ancient Egyptian pharaoh or the Spanish conquest of Mexico in 1519–21 C.E. Clay tablet records in Mesopotamia and ancient Egyptian papyri provide dates going back to about 3000 B.C.E.

The early Near Eastern civilizations traded many of their wares, such as pottery or coins with precise dates, over long distances. These objects can be used to date sites in, say, temperate Europe, far from literate civilization at the time.

b. Dendrochronology

Dendrochronology, the science of tree-ring dating, was first developed by astronomer A. E. Douglass in the southwestern United States as a way of dating climatic changes. It is based on the fact that certain tree species display annual growth rings that fluctuate in thickness from year to year depending on rainfall and other factors. Sequences of rings from living and ancient trees can be matched with one another to provide long master tree-ring sequences so accurate that wood fragments from prehistoric sites can sometimes be matched with them. Archaeological tree-ring chronologies extend back to 322 B.C.E. in the American Southwest and to as early as 9000 B.C.E. in Ireland and Germany, providing an accurate chronology for early farming in Europe and parts of North America.

c. Radiocarbon

Radiocarbon (C-14) dating provides dates for archaeological sites dating from about 1500 C.E. to at least 40,000 years ago, and sometimes earlier. Developed by Willard F. Libby of the University of Chicago, radiocarbon dating is based on the fact that carbon isotope carbon-14 enters the carbon dioxide of the atmosphere with carbon-12, ordinary carbon (c). Living vegetation builds up its own organic matter by photosynthesis and by using atmospheric carbon dioxide. Thus, the ratio of carbon-12 to carbon-14 in living vegetation and the animals that eat it is the same as that in the atmosphere. As soon as an organism dies, no further radiocarbon is incorporated into it and the carbon-14 left therein disintegrates at a known rate, only half remaining after 5,730 years.

The C-14 atoms in radiocarbon samples taken from tiny samples of bone, charcoal, shell, wood, and other organic substances found in archaeological sites are counted by accelerator mass spectrometry, resulting in age determinations that are statistical approximations of the date of the sample. The margin of statistical error can be as high as 2,000 years or more.

Radiocarbon dates from about 9000 B.C.E. can be calibrated with tree-ring chronologies, which are absolutely precise. This calibration is essential, because the concentration of radiocarbon in the atmosphere has varied considerably over time.

d. Potassium-Argon Dating

So far, we lack accurate methods for dating prehistoric time between about 50,000 and 500,000 years ago. The potassium-argon method is sometimes useful for dating very early prehistory. Geologists use it to date rocks as early as 4 to 5 billion years old and some as recent as 100,000 years old.

Potassium (K), one of the most abundant elements in the earth's crust, is present in nearly every mineral. In its natural form, it contains a small proportion of radioactive 40K atoms. For every 100 40K atoms that decay, 11 percent become 40Ar, an inactive gas that escapes from its parent material by diffusion when lava and other molten rocks are formed. By using a spectrometer, it is possible to measure the concentration of 40Ar that has accumulated since the rock formed.

Many early archaeological sites like Koobi Fora and Olduvai Gorge in East Africa were formed during periods of intense volcanic activity. Potassium-argon dates from lavas and volcanic ashes stratified above and below places where early human artifacts and bones occur date early human activity between 2.5 million and 500,000 years ago.

Radiocarbon and potassium-argon dating techniques are especially important, for they enable archaeologists to date widely separated archaeological sites and to compare, say, the dates for early agriculture in the Peruvian Andes with those in sub-Saharan Africa. They have made possible the writing of a truly global prehistory of humankind.

2. SPACE

We humans leave telltale clues about our behavior in the artifacts, abandoned houses, and food remains we leave behind us. The archaeologist studies the patternings of such finds—finds like a scatter of stone tools and animal bones at the site of a big-game kill 20,000 years ago. Such spatial analyses are based on another fundamental law, the Law of Association, which provides the second dimension of archaeological context.

The Law of Association states that an artifact is contemporary with the other objects found in the precise archaeological layer in which it is found. For instance, the mummy of the Egyptian pharaoh Tutankhamen was associated with an astonishing array of household possessions and magnificent ceremonial objects. This association provided unique information on ancient Egyptian life in 1323 B.C.E.

Association is of great importance when studying prehistoric burials and changing artifact styles. The lavish ornaments and possessions buried with, say, Moche warrior-priests from coastal Peru give us invaluable information on social ranking in prehistoric societies.

Archaeologists also use associations of artifacts to study prehistoric human behavior. For example, a grindstone, some seeds, and a mortar lying where they were abandoned near a hearth can provide much information on women's activities in an early farming household.

In recent years, archaeologists have paid close attention to changing distributions of prehistoric sites on ancient landscapes, within well-defined regions like the basin of Mexico or coastal river valleys in Peru. In studying changing settlement patterns, they pay close attention to evidence for environmental change, distributions of plants and animals, people's economic practices, and changing technological skills. Perhaps the most remarkable study of this type comes from the basin of Mexico, where a team of archaeologists surveyed the entire highland region and chronicled changes in land usage over more than 3,000 years, right up to the Spanish conquest of the Aztec civilization in 1519–21 C.E.

The concepts of culture, time, and space in archaeology are inseparable, for, in the final analysis, archaeology is the study of the interrelations between the form of artifacts found in a site and their date and spatial location. The account of human prehistory which follows below is based on the two critical concepts of time and space that make up the archaeological context.

d. FINDING AND DIGGING UP THE PAST

The finding and excavating of archaeological sites is a meticulous process of uncovering and recording the finite archives that make up the archaeological record. The sites, large and small, that make up this record are finite resources. Once destroyed and the context of their artifact contents disturbed, they are gone forever.

Although the destruction wrought by early archaeologists and treasure hunters was devastating, that of modern industrial development, deep plowing, professional looters, and amateur pothunters has been far worse. In some parts of North America, experts estimate that less than 5 percent of the archaeological record of prehistoric times remains intact. In recent years, massive efforts have been made to stem the tide of destruction and to preserve important sites using federal and state laws and regulations. While some progress has been made in such **cultural resource management,** the recent archaeological record of human prehistory is a shadow of its former self and in many parts of the world is doomed to near-total destruction.

1. FINDING ARCHAEOLOGICAL SITES

Many archaeological sites come to light by accident: during highway or dam construction, through industrial activity and mining, or as a result of natural phenomena such as wind erosion. For example, the famous early human sites at Olduvai Gorge in Tanzania, East Africa, were exposed in the walls of the gorge as a result of an ancient earthquake that cut a giant fissure through the surrounding plains. Well-designed archaeological field surveys provide vital information on ancient settlement patterns and site distributions.

Increasingly, archaeologists are relying on **remote sensing techniques,** such as aerial photography, satellite imagery (digital images of the earth recorded by satellites), or side-scan radar (airplane-based radar used to penetrate ground cover). These allow them to identify likely areas, even to spot sites without ever going into the field. The latest approach involves the use of **Geographic Information Systems** (mapping systems based on satellite imagery that inventory environmental data). The combination of satellite imagery with myriad environmental, climatic, and other data provides a backdrop for interpreting distributions of archaeological sites. For instance, in Arkansas, archaeologists have been able to study the locations of river valley farming villages and establish that they were founded close to easy routes to the uplands, where deer could be hunted in winter.

2. EXCAVATION

The process of excavation begins with a formal research design, for no investigation is undertaken without specific hypotheses to be tested, questions to be asked. Small-scale excavation may involve small test pits or vertical trenches designed to establish the stratigraphy of a site and the sequence of occupation. Larger-scale excavations often require exposing considerable horizontal areas, perhaps several farmers' huts, the foundations of a city wall, perhaps even an entire market precinct or a set of workers' cottages.

The same principles of excavation apply to all archaeological sites, however simple or complex: precise recording and testing of the hypotheses before a spade is placed in the ground, analysis of the sequence of events that occurred at the site, and lastly, reconstruction of how the site was formed. For example, many Near Eastern cities were occupied over thousands of years, gradually accumulating a large mound of occupation debris, known to archaeologists as a **tell** (Arabic for "small hill."). Excavating such a city would involve not only recording the sequence of occupation, but the many factors that led to the buildup of the mound, everything from major fires that swept through closely packed buildings to a complex sequence of rebuilding events on a temple.

The process of excavation ends with the analysis of the finds from the dig and their publication as a permanent record of the research. Without such publication, the site is effectively destroyed. The archaeologist's report is a vital, and unique, archive of the prehistoric past.

e. ANALYSIS AND INTERPRETATION

For every month of excavation there is at least six months' laboratory analysis—a long process of classifying, analyzing, and interpreting the finds from the dig. Such finds come in many forms. Stone tools, clay potsherds, and other artifacts tell us much about the technology of our forebears. Broken animal bones, seeds, shells, and other food remains, even desiccated human feces, are a mine of information on ancient subsistence, and sometimes diet. All of these finds are combined to produce a reconstruction of human behavior at the site.

1. ANALYSIS OF ARTIFACTS

Human artifacts come in many forms. The most durable are stone tools and clay vessels, while those in wood and bone often perish in the soil. Archaeologists have developed elaborate methods for classifying artifacts of all kinds, classifications based on distinctive features like the shapes of clay vessels, painted decoration on the pot, methods of stone flaking, and so on. Once they have worked out a classification of artifact types, the experts use various arbitrary units to help order groups of artifacts in space and time.

These units include the **assemblage,** which is a diverse group of artifacts found in one site that reflect the shared activities of a community. Next is the **component,** a physically bounded portion of a site that contains a distinct assemblage. The social equivalent of an archaeologist's component is a **community.** Obviously a site can contain several components, stratified one above another. The final unit is the **culture,** a cultural unit represented by like components on different sites or at different levels of the same site, although always within a well-defined chronological bracket.

Archaeological "cultures" are concepts designed to assist in the ordering of artifacts in time and space. They are normally named after a key site where characteristic artifacts of the culture are found. For instance, the Acheulian culture of early prehistory is named after the northern French town of St. Acheul, where the stone hand axes so characteristic of this culture are found.

2. FOOD REMAINS

How did prehistoric peoples make their living? The answer comes not only from artifacts like stone axes and digging sticks, but from food remains of all kinds. Animal bones provide valuable information on hunting practices, on herding and management of domesticated animals, and on butchery techniques. For example, a band of Paleo-Indian hunters drove a large bison herd into a gully at Olsen-Chubbock, Colorado, in 6000 B.C.E. By analyzing the thousands of bison bones in the gully, archaeologists have managed to reconstruct the standardized butchery techniques the Indians used after the hunt.

Plant remains survive at many sites and can be recovered by using flotation techniques, that is, floating soil samples through water and fine screens and collecting the light seeds from the surface while the residue falls away. Ancient seeds show us that foraging for wild plant foods was of vital importance to human societies from the earliest times. They also provide insights into ancient agricultural techniques, into the cereal and root crops that sustained early farming societies and early industrial civilizations for thousands of years. Fish bones, freshwater shells, and seashells, as well as artifacts and ancient rock paintings, tell us much about prehistoric subsistence patterns.

Reconstructing actual prehistoric diets is much harder, for differential preservation of food remains causes many foods to be underrepresented in the archaeological record. Desiccated human feces found in dry caves in western North America have told us much about prehistoric Indian diets as early as 6,000 years ago. Sophisticated carbon isotope analyses use the ratios between two stable carbon isotopes—C-12 and C-13—in animal tissues to establish the diets of prehistoric populations as they switched from wild plant foods to a predominantly cereal diet.

3. INTERPRETATION

Interpretation of artifacts and food remains provides clues as to ancient human behavior. Archaeologists use three major approaches to interpretation: **ethnographic analogy, ethnoarchaeology,** and **controlled experimentation.**

Sometimes analogies between living societies and those of the prehistoric past can yield fruitful insights. Such difficult analogies must be carried out under carefully controlled conditions. For example, comparisons of present Inuit harpoons from the Canadian Arctic can sometimes give insights into prehistoric bone artifacts from the same region, even those manufactured a thousand years earlier.

Some archaeologists have employed ethnoarchaeology, living for long periods among surviving hunter-gatherer and subsistence-farming societies like the San hunter-gatherers of the Kalahari Desert in southern Africa. Such studies provide data for controlled interpretation of the dynamics of ancient hunter-gatherer life or early agriculture.

Controlled experimentation with ancient technology can yield valuable information. For instance, by replicating the stoneworking techniques used by prehistoric peoples, some prehistorians have been able to reconstruct minute details of ancient stone technology, even establishing that some very early humans were left handed!

f. SUBDIVIDING PREHISTORIC TIMES

The 2.5 million years of human prehistory have seen a brilliant diversity of human societies, both simple and complex, flourish at different times throughout the world. Ever since the early 19th century, archaeologists have tried with varying degrees of success to subdivide prehistory into meaningful general subdivisions.

The most durable subdivisions of the prehistoric past were devised by Danish archaeologist Christian Jurgensen Thomson in 1806. His **Three Age System,** based on finds from prehistoric graves, subdivided prehistory into three ages based on technological achievement: the **Stone Age,** the **Bronze Age,** and the **Iron Age.** This scheme has been proven to have some general validity in the Old World and is still used as a broad label to this day. However, the term Stone Age has little

more than technological significance, for it means that a society does not have the use of metals of any kind. Stone Age has no chronological significance, for although societies without metal vanished in the Near East after 4000 B.C., some still flourish in New Guinea to this day. We only use the Three Age System in the most general way here.

Sometimes, the three ages are subdivided further. The Stone Age, for example, is conventionally divided into three periods: the **Palaeolithic,** or Old Stone Age (Greek: from *palaios,* old; and from *lithos,* stone), which applies to societies who used chipped-stone technology; the **Mesolithic** (Middle Stone Age), which is a transitional period; and the **Neolithic** (New Stone Age), when people used polished stone artifacts and were farmers. However, only the term Palaeolithic remains in common use, as Mesolithic and Neolithic have proved increasingly meaningless, even if they occasionally appear in specialist and popular literature.

New World archaeologists have never used the Three Age System, largely because in the Americas, metallurgy of any kind had limited distribution. They tend to use more local terms, defined at intervals in these pages.

In recent years, archaeologists have tried to classify prehistoric societies on the basis of political and social development. They subdivide all human societies into two broad categories: **prestate** and **state-organized societies.**

Prestate societies are invariably small-scale, based on the community, band, or village. Many prestate societies are **bands,** associations of families that may not exceed 25 to 60 people, the dominant form of social organization for most hunter-gatherers from the earliest times up to the origins of farming. Clusters of bands linked by clans, groups of people linked by common ancestral ties, are labeled **tribes. Chiefdoms** are societies headed by individuals with unusual ritual, political, or entrepreneurial skills, and are often hard to distinguish from tribes. Such societies are still kin-based, but power is concentrated in the hands of powerful kin leaders responsible for redistributing food and other commodities through society.

Chiefdoms tend to have higher population densities and vary greatly in their elaboration. For example, Tahitian chiefs in the Society Islands of the South Pacific presided over elaborate, constantly bickering chiefdoms, frequently waging war against their neighbors.

State-organized societies operate on a large scale, with a centralized political and social organization, distinct social and economic classes, and large food surpluses created by intensive farming, often employing irrigation agriculture. Such complex societies were ruled by a tiny elite class, who held monopolies over strategic resources and used force and religious power to enforce their authority. Such social organization was typical of the world's **preindustrial civilizations,** civilizations that functioned with technologies that did not rely on fossil fuels like coal.

g. THEORETICAL APPROACHES TO PREHISTORY

Archaeologists study human prehistory within broad theoretical frameworks. Such theoretical approaches are a means for looking beyond the facts and material objects from archaeological sites for explanations of cultural developments and changes that took place during the remote past.

Two broad theoretical approaches dominate interpretative thinking:

1. CULTURE HISTORY

Culture-historical approaches are based on systematic descriptions of sites, artifacts, and entire cultural sequences. Culture history is based on studies of archaeological context in time and space. Such studies are the backbone of all archaeological research and provide us with the chronology of human prehistory. They also give us data on the broad distributions of human cultures through the Old and the New World over more than 2.5 million years. No more sophisticated theoretical approaches can exist without this culture-historical background.

2. CULTURE AS ADAPTATION

This common approach thinks of human cultures as cultural systems interacting with their natural environments—environmental systems of which they are part. Culture as adaptation is concerned not only with the evolution of prehistoric cultures but also with reconstructing ancient environments and ways in which past cultures made their living.

At the core of this paradigm is the notion of **multilinear cultural evolution,** multiple-branched evolution that saw highly diverse human societies evolve from the simple to the more complex in many different ways. It is also based on the doctrines of **cultural ecology,** which think of human cultures as systems interacting with other human cultures, the biotic community, and the physical environment over long periods of time.

Proponents of culture-as-adaptation theories argue that each human society pursues its own evolutionary course, determined by the long-term success of its adaptation, via technology and social institutions, to the natural environment.

Culture as adaptation is now widely accepted as a general framework for the study of human prehistory.

3. NEW THEORETICAL DIRECTIONS

Intense controversy surrounds new generations of archaeological theory that draw on evolutionary biology, behavioral ecology, and studies that focus on the acts of individuals rather than impersonal cultural processes.

New, highly sophisticated evolutionary theories that combine ecological models with biological and cultural developments are likely to dominate the study of early prehistory. As far as later prehistory is concerned, we can expect a new emphasis on research into changing gender roles in ancient societies and into ethnic diversity in complex societies.

Of concern, also, are the different ways in which Western and non-Western societies conceive of archaeology and the past, for fundamental cultural and ideological differences can affect the ways in which one interprets the archaeological record.

B. PREHISTORY AND THE GREAT ICE AGE

The biological and cultural evolution of humankind unfolded against a complex backdrop of constant climatic change. For most of geological time, the world's climate was warmer and more homogeneous than it is today. The first signs of glacial cooling occurred in Antarctica about 35 million years ago. There was a major drop in world temperatures between 14 and 11 million years ago, and another about 3.2 million years ago, when glaciers first formed in northern latitudes. Then, just as humans first appeared, about 2.5 million years ago, the glaciation intensified and the earth entered its present period of constantly fluctuating climate.

Humans evolved during the period of relatively minor climatic oscillations. Between 4 and 2 million years ago, the world climate was somewhat warmer and more stable than it became in later times. The African savanna, where humans originated, supported many mammal species, large and small, including a great variety of the order Primates, to which we belong.

About 1.6 million years ago, at the beginning of the **Pleistocene** (commonly called the **Great Ice Age**), the world's climatic changes intensified. Global climates constantly fluctuated between warm and intensely cold. For long stretches of time, the northern parts of both Europe and North America were mantled with great ice sheets, the last retreating only some 15,000 years ago. While glaciers covered northern areas, world sea levels fell as much as 300 feet below modern shorelines, joining Alaska to Siberia, Britain to the Continent, and exposing vast continental shelves off ocean coasts. The glacial periods brought drier conditions to tropical regions. The Sahara and northern Africa became very arid, and rain forests shrank.

Fluctuations of warm and cold temperatures were relatively minor until about 800,000 years ago. Since then, periods of intense cold have recurred about every 90,000 years, perhaps triggered by long-term changes in Earth's orbit around the Sun. Core samples taken from the sea floor tell us that there have been at least nine cold periods in the last 800,000 years, each of them characterized by a gradual cooling that

took tens of thousands of years and a subsequent rapid warming up that saw glaciers retreat and world sea levels rise with remarkable speed.

Few of these oscillations are well documented, except for the last interglacial and glacial cycle, which began about 128,000 years ago. During the last interglacial, Europe, Eurasia, and North America were warmer than today. But a gradual cooling set in about 118,000 years ago, as the last glaciation, **Würm,** set in. (The term Würm comes from a river in the Alps where the glaciation was first identified.) Glacial conditions were especially intense about 75,000 years ago, when the archaic Neanderthal people were flourishing in Europe and when the Americas were still uninhabited. After a brief milder interval about 40,000 years ago, the cold intensified again, peaking about 18,000 years ago. A rapid amelioration began about 15,000 years ago, and the world's climate reached near-modern conditions by 6000 B.C.E.

By using **pollen analysis,** microscopic and statistical analyses of fossilized plant pollens found in geological deposits, scientists have chronicled dramatic changes in the world's environment during the Würm glaciation, changes that also took hold much earlier in the Ice Age. During the height of the Würm, most of western and central Europe and Eurasia was open steppe-tundra, while Scandinavia and much of Britain were under ice. The Balkans were joined to Turkey, the Sahara was extremely arid, and snow levels on the world's mountains were hundreds of feet lower. Rain forests shrank, and the Southeast Asian mainland was joined to the offshore islands. Only narrow straits separated the mainland from New Guinea and Australia, which formed a single landmass. Alaska and Siberia were joined by a low-lying land bridge. Most of Canada and the United States were covered with vast ice sheets, as far south as Seattle, the Great Lakes, and Nova Scotia. The 90,000 years of the Würm glaciation witnessed dramatic changes in human life, which unfolded in a world very different from our own.

C. HUMAN ORIGINS (4 MILLION TO 1.8 MILLION YEARS AGO)

All humans are members of the order **Primates.** There are two suborders: **Anthropoids** (apes, humans, and monkeys) and Prosimians (lemurs, tarsiers, and other "premonkeys"). We also belong in the family **Hominidae,** which includes modern humans, earlier human subspecies, and their direct ancestors. Our closest primate relatives are the

Pongidae, the so-called anthropoid apes, including the chimpanzee and the gorilla. The research of more than a century has shown that the many similarities in behavior and physical characteristics between Hominidae (hominids) and Pongidae can be explained by identical characteristics that each group inherited millions of years ago from a common ancestor. Nearly all scientists agree that tropical Africa was the cradle of humankind, simply because this is where our closest living primate relatives still live.

According to biochemists Vincent Sarich and Alan Wilson, apes and Old World monkeys diverged about 23 million years ago, and the chimpanzee, the gorilla, and humans last shared a common ancestor about 7 to 6 million years ago. Unfortunately, this divergence occurred at a moment in geological time for which fossil-bearing beds in Africa are very rare. There is what has been called a "black hole" in primate evolution between about 15 and 4 million years ago. But this was a critical time when the Africa forest and savanna were densely populated by many primate species. Some of these primates were flourishing in small groups, probably walking upright, and adopting daily behaviors different from their tree-dwelling relatives nearby.

To understand early human evolution means identifying the ecological problems faced by our earliest ancestors at a time of constant climatic change. The first humans were descended from a yet unidentified nonhuman primate, who lived both in forests and, increasingly, on the open African savanna. Early hominids adapted to open country not only by adopting a more mobile, wide-ranging lifeway, but also by walking upright.

An **upright posture** and **bipedal gait** are characteristic of hominids. Walking upright frees the hands for other tasks like toolmaking, while bipedalism favors endurance and the covering of long distances, vital for hominids living in open country. Our remote ancestors may have first "come down from the trees" about 10 million years ago. Relying as they now did on food supplies scattered over large areas, they not only became more mobile, but began scavenging meat from predator kills, even hunting down small animals when the opportunity arose. Among mammal species, these characteristics are associated with a trend toward larger brain size.

The earliest fossil evidence for these anatomical and behavioral changes comes from the **Middle Awash** and **Hadar** areas of Ethiopia. Here physical anthropologists—Don Johanson, Tim White, and others—have uncovered primates dating back to close to the time, between 4 and 5 million years ago, when the ancestors of living apes and humans split off from one another. *Australopithecus ramidus,* from Hadar, was a small, upright-walking primate who displayed many apelike features and might have been the ancestor of later hominids. Another small primate, which Johanson and White nicknamed "Lucy," lived during a somewhat later time than *ramidus.* She was between three and a half and four feet tall and was 19 to 21 years old when she died. A gracile, lightly built hominid, she was fully bipedal, with arms slightly longer than the arms of modern humans. Johanson and White also recovered the remains of other contemporary hominids. All had ape-shaped heads, brains the size of chimpanzees, and forward-thrusting jaws. Potassium-argon dates for the Hadar fossil beds are between 3.75 and 3 million years ago. Johanson and White believe that all the Hadar specimens are members of the species **Australopithecus afarensis** ("southern ape-man of the Afar") and that they are the common ancestor of all later hominids, including the first humans.

Australopithecus ("southern ape-man") was first identified by anatomist Raymond Dart in 1924, when he described the fossil skull of an immature primate from the Taung limestone quarry in South Africa. Dart realized that the Taung skull was not that of an ape; it had more humanlike teeth and other features that set it apart from chimpanzees. He named it **Australopithecus africanus,** a small, graceful creature that stood upright, and announced it was an ancestor of modern humans. Dart's claim was greeted with derision by the fossil experts of the day. Only one scholar, Robert Broom, realized Dart was right. He found more *Australopithecus* fossils in caverns in northern South Africa. These included not only *Australopithecus africanus,* but also a much more robust form, massively built with a crested skull. Broom named this australopithecine **Australopithecus robustus.** The South African *Australopithecus* finds date to between 3 million and 800,000 years ago.

The South African finds showed there was great variability among early hominids, but no stone tools or other artifacts were found with these fossils. Most of them have come from the sites of ancient hyena kills. Who, then, was the ancestor of humanity? In 1959, Louis and Mary Leakey announced the discovery of an *Australopithecus robus-*

tus fossil (named **Zinjanthropus boisei**) in the lowermost bed of **Olduvai Gorge** in northern Tanzania.

Olduvai is a great natural gash in the Serengeti Plain, where hundreds of feet of ancient lakebeds have been exposed by earthquake action. Olduvai transects the shores of a long-dried-up, shallow lake where game and hominids came to drink. The Leakeys found small scatters of stone tools and debris, also animal bones, in the lakebeds. The robust australopithecine came from one such scatter and was potassium-argon dated to about 1.75 million years ago. A year later, the Leakeys found the skull bones of a much lighter, more human-looking hominid at a slightly lower level in the gorge, again associated with animal bones and flaked-stone artifacts. Louis Leakey did not believe this was an australopithecine, so he named it **Homo habilis** ("handy person") and claimed that this was the earliest toolmaking human being.

Even earlier than Olduvai are the rich fossil beds at **East Turkana** in northern Kenya. They have yielded fragments not only of gracile and robust australopithecines, but also of *Homo habilis* as well. These discoveries showed that there was great variability among the hominid populations of eastern Africa between 4 and 2 million years ago. This complicates the study of early human evolution greatly, but makes it certain that there was no direct, linear progression from *Australopithecus afarensis* at Hadar to *Homo habilis* at East Turkana and Olduvai Gorge. Instead, it is best to think in terms of a branching bush, with numerous parallel and highly varied evolutionary lines that reflect a great diversity of hominid populations on the savanna between 4 and 1.5 million years ago.

Most likely, however, *Homo habilis* was the earliest toolmaking hominid, and, in general terms, the ancestor of all humankind. *Homo habilis* was a graceful, fairly human-looking primate that stood about 4 feet 3 inches tall and weighed about 80 pounds. *Homo habilis* looked less apelike around the face and skull, with a taller forehead and a large brain size. These hominids walked upright, but their upper and lower arm bones were of almost equal length and their powerful hands were more curved than ours. These features enabled them to grip branches and swing in the tress, a sign that our earliest ancestors spent considerable periods of time off the ground.

The earliest archaeological evidence for toolmaking, the appearance of rudimentary human culture, comes from the **Koobi Fora** area of East Turkana and is potassium-argon dated to about 2.5 million years ago. Excavations at both Koobi Fora and Olduvai Gorge give us a tantalizing portrait of very early human behavior, tantalizing because it is incomplete.

Originally, the Leakeys and others assumed that *Homo habilis* was a hunter and a plant food forager, who behaved just like today's hunter-gatherers. But microscopic examination of the stone artifacts and food remains from the scatters at Koobi Fora and Olduvai paint a picture of a much more apelike lifeway.

Archaeologist Nicholas Toth has replicated the simple **Oldowan** (named after Olduvai Gorge) stone technology used by *Homo habilis* so thoroughly that he has even been able to show that some of the toolmakers were left-handed. He discovered this was an opportunistic technology. The hominids could carry around convenient lumps of lava with them, then strike off simple stone flakes with a hammerstone when they needed them to split tough hide, to cut up an animal carcass, or to break open a bone for its marrow.

Homo habilis lived a highly mobile life, ranging over large territories in search of meat and plant foods. Undoubtedly, fruit, seeds, and tubers played a vital role in the diet, for they come into season on the savanna throughout the year. Our earliest ancestors also scavenged meat from the kills of lions and other predators, chasing away the animals, seizing limbs and other body parts, and running away. They may also have run down and killed some smaller antelope themselves.

Once the precious meat was in hand, they would find a convenient spot in the shade to butcher and eat the flesh and marrow. These places comprised the bone and stone scatters uncovered at Olduvai and Koobi Fora. One Koobi Fora band camped in a dry watercourse about 1.8 million years ago, where they found the carcass of a hippopotamus. Carrying in some of their tools from nearly 9 miles away, they gathered around and then removed bones and meat from the carcass with small stone flakes.

Much of this life is not that different from that of chimpanzees, who hunt small game and break open bones and nuts. Two important differences separated the first humans from their other primate relatives in Africa. First, they were fully bipedal, a posture far more efficient for carrying objects of all kinds. Second, they were adapted to savanna living, where they had to organize and cover far larger territories in open country than their relatives in the forest. At the same time, our ancestors became more and more dependent on technology and on one another, a development that led to better communication skills and, eventually and much later, to fully articulate speech.

By a million years ago, the hominid line had been pruned to the extent that one lineage, *Homo*, remained. Judging from the abundance of hominid fossils at Koobi Fora, these highly varied populations were about as common as baboons on the East African savanna. The adoption of a wider-based diet with a food-sharing social group would have placed many more acute demands on the hominids' ability to cope with the complex and unpredictable. They had to become more and more socially adept, living as they did in a world far more complex and demanding than that of *Australopithecus*. The increased complexity of human social interactions was a powerful force in the evolution of the hominid brain and led to the appearance of more advanced human forms after 1.8 million years ago.

D. *HOMO ERECTUS* AND THE FIRST PEOPLING OF THE WORLD (1.8 MILLION TO 250,000 YEARS AGO)

By 1.8 million years ago, new, anatomically more advanced humans had evolved from earlier hominids in tropical Africa. These were the first of two waves of humans to move out of Africa and settle in other parts of the Old World. The second wave, modern humans, followed.

1. *HOMO ERECTUS*

In the 1890s, Dutch physician Eugene Dubois discovered the remains of a primitive-looking human in the gravels of the **Solo River** in Java. He claimed that the bones were those of the so-called missing link between apes and humans. His claims were greeted with skepticism. It was not until the discovery of closely similar fossils in northern China in the 1920s that Dubois was vindicated. The Chinese and Javanese fossils are grouped under a general human form named **Homo erectus.**

Today, *Homo erectus* is known to have lived over a wide area of the Old World. The fossils from **Zhoukoudian Cave** in northern China provide a portrait of a very variable human form. These hominids had a brain capacity between 775 and 1,300 cc, showing much variation. Their vision was excellent, and they were probably capable of exten-

sive thought. Their skulls were more rounded than those of earlier hominids, with conspicuous brow ridges and a sloping forehead. The jaw was massive. Limbs and hips were fully adapted to an upright posture but more robust than those of modern humans.

Homo erectus stood about 5 feet 6 inches tall and had hands fully capable of precision gripping and many kinds of toolmaking. Although we cannot be sure, it seems possible that *Homo erectus* had lost the dense hair covering characteristic of nonhuman primates. *Homo erectus* also had abundant sweat glands, and presumably, in common with most tropical primates and humans, relatively dark skin. These humans were certainly capable of a far more complex and varied life than their predecessors.

2. FIRE

The earliest *Homo erectus* fossils come from East Africa and date to around 1.8 million years ago. By this time, the savanna was drier and human settlement intensified as *Homo erectus* developed efficient technologies and lifeways. *Homo erectus* now tamed fire, presumably by using brands from a natural conflagration. This discovery was a revolution in human history, for it enabled people to protect themselves against predators—they could move into more open country, where trees were much rarer, and camp in the open or in caves or rock shelters where hostile animals lurked. They could also increase their home range and cook food, as well as cope with harsh winters. It may be no coincidence that the first human settlement of Europe and Asia occurred after *Homo erectus* mastered fire.

3. OUT OF AFRICA

There was a widespread interchange of mammals between Africa and Europe between 1.8 million and 700,000 years ago. Hippopotamuses, forest elephants, and other herbivores and carnivores migrated north, crossing the Sahara when rainfall was higher and the region could support animal life. Human predators shared many ecological characteristics with these mammals and radiated out of Africa with this familiar mammalian community.

The earliest recorded human settlement of Europe and the Near East dates to about 700,000 years ago. By the same time, tiny *Homo erectus* populations were flourishing in south and Southeast Asia and were widespread by half a million years ago. Apparently, however, *Homo erectus* lacked the technology to settle in anything more than tropical and temperate latitudes, for it was not until the very end of the Ice Age that humans mastered arctic and periglacial environments in Europe and northern Asia, or ventured on boats to New Guinea and Australia.

Half a million years ago, the world's population was no more than a few thousand people, scattered in temperate and tropical environments. In Africa, Europe, the Near East, and south Asia, *Homo erectus* exploited more open country, subsisting on plant foods and game of all sizes. The bands used simple tool kits that revolved around multipurpose stone axes and cleavers with sharp edges and points. They used such hand axes for butchering, digging up roots, and many other purposes, such as woodworking and fashioning fire-hardened spears. Their hunting methods were simple and involved not only scavenging predator kills, but also careful stalking of their prey to get close enough to kill or wound with a spear. Like their predecessors, *Homo erectus* hunted and foraged for plant foods, but in more effective ways than earlier hominids. At **Ambrona** and **Torralba** in central Spain, bands of hunters drove elephants into swamps, killed the mired animals, and butchered them where they lay. Similar kill sites have come from eastern and southern Africa, but we can be sure that wild plant foods were still of great importance in the diet.

The dense tropical forests of Southeast and eastern Asia provided a quite different challenge, for game was rare. *Homo erectus* lived off small animals like monkeys and a multitude of plant foods. Instead of hand axes and cleavers, the bands relied on wooden tools and bamboo artifacts. They had no need of any stone tools other than crude flakes and choppers for woodworking.

For hundreds of thousands of years, archaic humans, loosely classified as *Homo erectus,* lived in the tropical and temperate regions of the Old World. Except for an overall increase in brain size, *Homo erectus* remained remarkably stable in evolutionary terms for more

than a million years, until less than 500,000 years ago. During these long millennia, they developed improved language and communication skills. With enhanced language skills and more advanced technology, it became possible for people to achieve better cooperation in foraging, storing food, and hunting. These people depended on cooperative activity by every individual in the band. The secret of individual success was group success.

E. EARLY *HOMO SAPIENS* (c. 250,000 TO c. 35,000 YEARS AGO)

Eventually, *Homo erectus* evolved into a more advanced form, known to anthropologists as **early *Homo sapiens,*** but we do not know when or where the transition began or how it took place. Some researchers believe it took place more than 400,000 years ago; others believe it was much later, some time around or after 200,000 years ago. Throughout the Old World, there was a general evolutionary trend toward larger

brain size and more enhanced intellectual capacities. Human populations displayed increased variability, partly in response to their adaptations to increasingly varied natural environments. Unfortunately, we still know little of early *Homo sapiens,* but there was great human variability throughout the Old World.

1. THE NEANDERTHALS

The best-known early *Homo sapiens* populations are the so-called **Neanderthals,** named after the **Neanderthal Cave** in Germany, where the first Neanderthal fossil came to light in 1856. Once dismissed as brutal, primitive savages—the cave people of popular cartoon fame—the Neanderthals are now recognized as being tough, adaptable people capable of flourishing in very harsh climates indeed.

Neanderthals *(Homo sapiens neanderthalensis)* probably evolved from earlier *Homo sapiens* populations in Europe and Eurasia at least 150,000 years ago, perhaps earlier. They were nimble, squat people, standing about 5 feet high, with forearms that were somewhat shorter than those of modern people. Heavily built, beetle-browed hunter-gatherers, the Neanderthals of western Europe were robust men and women, well adapted to the arctic cold of the early Würm glaciation of 100,000 years ago. Their relatives in the Near East were more lightly built and displayed much more anatomical variation.

The Neanderthals of Europe and Eurasia lived in caves and rock shelters during the winter months and ranged more widely during summer. They used a more specialized technology for hunting and foraging, one that made use of composite tools, with stone spearheads bound to wooden shafts. They made thousands of scrapers and woodworking

tools using more or less standardized flakes struck off from carefully prepared stone blanks. This **Mousterian** technology, named after the Le Moustier cave in southwestern France, was highly versatile and used in various forms over a wide area of Europe, Eurasia, North Africa, and the Near East. The Neanderthals were expert foragers who were not afraid to hunt the largest animals, including bison. Success in the hunt meant expert stalking, enabling the hunter to thrust a spear into the prey's heart, a high-risk way of obtaining food. Somewhat similar technologies were used by early *Homo sapiens* populations throughout the western portions of the Old World after 150,000 years ago.

The Neanderthals were the first humans to bury their dead, and, presumably, to believe in an afterlife. Single burials are most common, usually accompanied by a few stone tools or some game meat. Group sepulchers are also known. Some western European groups engaged in elaborate rituals involving cave bears, the most formidable of all Ice Age prey. We find in the Neanderthals and their culture the first roots of our own complicated beliefs, societies, and religious sense. But they were an evolutionary dead end, supplanted in their homeland by more modern humans between 40,000 and 25,000 years ago.

F. THE ORIGINS OF MODERN HUMANS (c. 150,000 TO 100,000 YEARS AGO)

Homo sapiens sapiens means "wise person." We are the clever people, animals capable of intelligent thought, of manipulation, of subtlety. A great biological and cultural chasm separates us from archaic humans. This chasm comes from our ability to speak fluently, to pass on knowledge and ideas through the medium of language. Consciousness, self-awareness, foresight, and the ability to express one's emotions—all are the consequence of articulate speech. These qualities can be linked to our capacity for symbolic and spiritual thought. We modern humans are concerned not only with subsistence and technology, but with defining the boundaries of existence and the relationship between the individual, the group, and the universe. Fluent speech, the full flowering of human creativity expressed in art and religion, expert tool-making—these are some of the hallmarks of anatomically modern humans. With these abilities, humankind eventually colonized not only temperate and tropical environments, but the entire globe. We are now concerned with people biologically identical to ourselves, with the same intellectual abilities and potential as ourselves.

One of the great controversies of archaeology surrounds the origins of *Homo sapiens sapiens.* One group of scholars believes that *Homo erectus* populations throughout the world evolved independently, first into early *Homo sapiens,* then into fully modern humans. Thus, the modern geographic populations (races) of the world would have been separated for a long time, perhaps a million years. Most experts take a diametrically opposite view. They hypothesize that *Homo sapiens sapiens* evolved in Africa sometime between 200,000 and 100,000 years ago, then spread to other parts of the Old World. Under this model, modern geographic populations are less than 100,000 years old.

These two models represent extremes, which pit advocates of anatomical continuity against those who believe there was population replacement. Each model is based on the minute study of human fossil remains, but the replacement theory also relies on studies of **mitochondrial DNA (mtDNA).**

Molecular biologists like Alan Wilson and Rebecca Cann have studied the human family tree using this form of DNA, which is inherited through the female line without being diluted with paternal DNA. Thus, they argue, it provides a unique tool for studying ancestral populations. They compared mtDNA from Africans, Asians, Europeans, and Southeast Asians and found that the differences between them were small. They formed two groups: one was the Africans, the other the remainder. Wilson and Cann concluded that all modern humans derive from a primordial African population, from which populations migrated to the rest of the Old World with little or no interbreeding with existing archaic human groups.

By calculating the rate of mtDNA mutations, they argue that archaic *Homo sapiens* evolved from *Homo erectus* in Africa by about 200,000 years ago. Then *Homo sapiens sapiens*, anatomically modern humans, appeared some 140,000 years ago.

Mitochondrial DNA is still controversial, but there is some archaeological evidence from Africa that supports the biologists' scenario. Highly varied, early *Homo sapiens* populations flourished in sub-Saharan Africa between 200,000 and 150,000 years ago, some of them displaying some anatomically modern features. At the **Klasies River Caves** on the Indian Ocean coast of South Africa, anatomically modern human remains date to between 125,000 and 95,000 years ago. They are associated with sophisticated, versatile tool kits that were, if anything, superior to those used by the Neanderthals in Europe at the time.

Many scientists believe that *Homo sapiens sapiens*, modern humans, did indeed evolve in tropical Africa sometime after 150,000 years ago, as the geneticists argue. Ecologist Robert Foley has theorized that modern humans evolved in a mosaic of constantly changing tropical environments, which tended to isolate evolving human populations for considerable periods of time. Some groups living in exceptionally rich areas may have developed unusual hunting and foraging skills, using a new technology so effective that they could prey on animals from a distance with finely made projectiles. With efficient technology, more planning, and better organization of both hunting and foraging, our ancestors could have reduced the risks of living in unpredictable environments in dramatic ways. And, when climatic conditions changed, and hitherto isolated populations mingled with others, the process of biological and cultural evolution accelerated.

G. THE SPREAD OF MODERN HUMANS IN THE OLD WORLD (100,000 TO 12,000 YEARS AGO)

About 100,000 years ago, the Sahara was cooler and wetter than today and capable of supporting sparse hunter-gatherer populations. It may have been then that modern humans spread to North Africa and the Near East. We know they were living at **Qafzeh Cave** in Israel by 90,000 years ago. For the next 45,000 years, they flourished in the Near East alongside highly varied Neanderthal populations. Then, some 45,000 years ago, *Homo sapiens sapiens* hunted and foraged out of the Near East into south Asia and also much harsher northern environments.

1. EUROPE

As the Near East became increasingly dry and less productive during the Würm glaciation, some of the newcomers responded to population pressure and food shortages by moving across the wide land bridge that joined Turkey to southeastern Europe 45,000 years ago, spreading into the game-rich steppe-tundras of central and western Europe and Eurasia.

The first anatomically modern Europeans were the robust **Cro-Magnons,** who showed no signs of having evolved from local Neanderthal populations. They lived alongside their predecessors for about 10,000 years, using a distinctive and highly specialized stone technology based on fine blades. Expert stoneworkers used carefully shaped cylindrical lumps of flint and antler, bone, or wood punches to produce dozens of standard stone blades. These long, parallel-sided, thin blades could be made into scrapers, woodworking tools, and, above all, fine graving tools. A good analogy is the Swiss Army Knife with its strong hinges, which allows one to carry around a variety of different blades for specific uses.

The graving tool, or burin, was of critical importance, for it enabled people to cut strips of fresh reindeer antler to manufacture specialized tools. These included needles for tailoring fitted, layered clothing, essential for survival in the nine-month winters of the late Ice Age. Technological innovations like the needle enabled modern humans to master arctic environments for the first time, to expand and adapt into new landscapes.

By 30,000 years ago, the last Neanderthals had vanished from Europe and Eurasia. Over 15,000 years, up to the end of the Ice Age, the Cro-Magnons enjoyed an increasingly elaborate hunting and foraging culture, wintering in deep river valleys in western and central Europe, following reindeer migrations in spring and fall. All manner of arctic game, many plant foods, and salmon were among the foods taken by these people.

By 30,000 years ago, the Cro-Magnons had developed elaborate art traditions, rock engravings and paintings. They also carved and engraved fine bone and antler artifacts. The artists painted naturalistic depictions of mammoth, bison, wild ox, and other now long-extinct animals, sometimes using natural protrusions on the rock to give relief to a figure. Experts believe that the art had a deeply symbolic meaning, connected with the intricate relationships between humans and the animal and spiritual worlds. But we cannot, at a distance of 18,000 years, hope to understand this symbolism. The Cro-Magnon paintings are among the earliest-known human art, but Australians and South Africans may have been painting at the same period.

2. EURASIA AND SIBERIA

To the east, other late Ice Age people adapted to life on the open steppe-tundra, relying on mammoth bones, skins, and sod to build dome-shaped, semisubterranean houses. The late Ice Age population of Eurasia, between central Europe and Lake Baikal in Siberia, was never large. Most bands lived on the edges of river valleys like the Dnepr and Don in the Ukraine, subsisting on mammoth and other gregarious big game, as well as fish and plant foods in the spring, summer, and fall.

Eighteen thousand years ago, some bands along the Dnepr were trading raw materials and ornaments like seashells over distances of more than 100 miles.

Perhaps as early as 30,000 years ago, and certainly by 20,000, late Ice Age bands were hunting and foraging to the east of Lake Baikal. But it was not until after 18,000 years ago that people ventured farther east, into extreme northeast Asia.

3. SOUTH AND SOUTHEAST ASIA

While the Cro-Magnons and other northern groups were mastering arctic climates, other modern humans moved into tropical south and Southeast Asia, probably by at least 45,000 years ago, if not earlier. For thousands of years, forest bands exploited small game and plant foods, using increasingly smaller and more specialized tool kits. At the time, the exposed continental shelf joined offshore islands like Borneo to the Asian mainland. This Ice Age land, known to geologists as **Sunda,** was separated from New Guinea and Australia (**Sahul**) by only a narrow strait of open water.

Homo sapiens sapiens built rafts or canoes to cross deep water by at least 40,000 years ago, for artifacts of this age have been found in southern New Guinea. By 32,000 years ago, people were living on the islands of the Bismarck Archipelago in the southwestern Pacific, and by 28,000 years ago people had reached the Solomon Islands. Line-of-sight, island-to-island voyaging was all that was needed to colonize these landmasses. It was to be many thousands of years before the peoples of the southwestern Pacific developed the agriculture, outrig-ger canoes, and the navigation skills needed to reach islands much farther offshore.

The first human settlement of Australia came at least 35,000 years ago, perhaps somewhat earlier: the dating is controversial. Hunter-gatherer groups, the ancestors of the modern aboriginal population, were dwelling as far south as Tasmania before 31,000 years ago. At the time, Tasmania was joined to the Australian mainland by a land bridge. Late Ice Age Tasmanians were hunting wallabies in an open landscape that became dense forest at least 20,000 years ago.

These late Ice Age Australian populations continued to evolve without interruption into recent times, developing increasingly more elaborate cultures that are remarkable for their sophisticated art traditions, social organization, and ritual life. The highly diverse and sophisticated Australian aboriginal cultures encountered by Dutch and English explorers in the 17th and 18th centuries C.E. are the direct result of more than 30,000 years of continuous cultural evolution in an isolated, remote landmass.

H. THE FIRST SETTLEMENT OF THE AMERICAS (c. 15,000 YEARS AGO)

Dental morphology, genetics, and archaeology show that the biological and cultural roots of the Native Americans lie in northern China and extreme northeast Asia.

We do not know when modern humans first settled in China. Although Chinese archaeologists claim that *Homo sapiens sapiens* evolved independently in the Far East, they have yet to put forward convincing evidence for such a hypothesis. Anatomically modern people were hunting and foraging in the Ordos area of Mongolia by 35,000 years ago. Ten thousand years later, a vast area between Mongolia in the west and the Pacific coast in the east supported a highly varied population of hunter-gatherers exploiting game and plant foods as well as coastal resources. As time went on, their tool kits became progressively smaller and more refined. They produced tiny stone blades used as lethal spear barbs and small scrapers; they also relied on artifacts made of wood and bone. This so-called microblade technology spread widely in northeast Asia, offshore to Japan, and north into Siberia.

The earliest human settlement of extreme northeast Siberia, from Lake Baikal eastward, took place late in the Ice Age. This was after the last glacial climax 18,000 years ago, when warmer conditions opened up hitherto uninhabited steppe-tundra. The first settlers were few in number, living off big game, plant foods, and perhaps fish and sea mammals. The middle Aldan River Valley began to support bands of late Ice Age people using microblade technology 15,000 years ago, perhaps earlier. These same people settled as far northeast as the Bering Strait.

A low-lying land bridge joined Siberia to Alaska during the entire Würm glaciation, from about 100,000 to 15,000 years ago. During glacial maxima, the land bridge was a wide, poorly drained plain, swept by arctic winds. The climate was dry and intensely cold, with only a two-month summer. Low scrub covered the landscape, except in shallow river valleys where some trees and lush grasses grew in spring and summer. During warmer intervals, sea levels rose, flooding much of the plain, leaving but an isthmus between Old World and New. This was the route by which humans settled the Americas.

Great controversy surrounds the first settlement of the New World. While everyone agrees that the first settlers crossed the Bering land bridge, some archaeologists believe the crossing dates to at least 40,000 years ago. Others favor a much later date, at the very end of the Ice Age, or soon afterward.

Claims of very early settlement are based on a series of cave and rock shelter finds in South America. There are affirmations of humans occupying **Boqueirao de Pedra Furada** in northeastern Brazil at least 40,000 years ago. Only a few scholars accept this claim or other much heralded occupations said to have occurred between 40,000 and 25,000 years ago.

The most widely accepted scenario has small numbers of hunter-gatherers from northeast Asia crossing into Alaska as the land bridge began to flood at the end of the Ice Age some 15,000 years ago. This was not a journey of exploration but rather part of an age-old hunter-gatherer lifeway that had people following migrating game and searching for new clumps of scarce plant foods.

The earliest archaeological evidence for human settlement in Alaska—nothing more than small scatters of stones and bones—dates to about 11,500 years ago. From that date onward, there has been continuous human occupation in the Arctic into modern times.

During the height of the Würm glaciation (called the **Wisconsin** in the New World), northern North America was mantled by two vast ice sheets that extended from Greenland to British Columbia. There may have been a narrow, ice-free corridor between them, but it would not have supported animal or plant life. Most likely, people from Alaska hunted and foraged their way south onto the Great Plains as the ice sheets receded rapidly after 13,000 years ago.

Despite occasional occurrences of 12,000-year-old artifacts in North America, the first widespread settlement of the Americas as a whole dates with great consistency to about 11,000 years ago (9000 B.C.E.). Within a few centuries, perhaps no more than 500 years, hunter-gatherer groups had colonized the entire Americas, from ice-free Nova Scotia in the north to Patagonia in the south.

The **Clovis** people (named after a site near Clovis, New Mexico) are best known for their characteristic stone projectile points, fluted at the base for mounting in a wooden shaft. These people preyed on game of every size and also foraged plant foods. They hunted large Ice Age animals like the mammoth, mastodon, and large steppe bison, sometimes camping close to a kill while they butchered the carcass. Clovis artifacts have been found throughout North America and deep into Central America, with variants on this culture farther south.

It appears that humans literally exploded into the New World, living off a fauna that was unused to such formidable predators. As a result, the human population rose rapidly, then stabilized, as people adapted to a great variety of natural environments, everything from rocky coasts to desert and dense rainforest.

By 8800 B.C.E., most large late Ice Age animals except for the bison were extinct, probably as a result of rapid climate change and drought. Some experts believe that human predators helped in the process of extinction by exploiting slow-breeding mammals like the mammoth and mastodon. Whatever the cause of extinction, the disappearance of big game fostered greater cultural diversity among Paleo-Indian groups. They adapted to a rapidly changing world that was not to stabilize to near-modern conditions until about 4000 B.C.E.

I. AFTER THE ICE AGE: HOLOCENE HUNTER-GATHERERS (12,000 YEARS AGO TO MODERN TIMES)

Global warming began in earnest after about 15,000 years ago. The great ice sheets retreated irregularly from northern latitudes, ushering in **Holocene** times. Dramatic climatic and geographic changes ensued, as glaciers melted and sea levels rose irregularly toward modern levels. The Bering land bridge was severed by rising water, and the Baltic Sea and Scandinavia emerged from beneath vast ice sheets. The Southeast Asian islands were isolated from the nearby mainland. Thick temperate forests covered much of Europe, while familiar Ice Age animals like the mammoth became extinct by 9000 B.C.E. The Sahara enjoyed slightly higher rainfall and supported semiarid grasslands and shallow lakes, ending millennia of isolation for tropical Africans.

By this time, the world's human population numbered perhaps 5 million, scattered over the Old World and New. All hunter-gatherers were faced with the problem of adapting to constant climatic change and often acute environmental uncertainty. In response, they developed ever more specialized tool kits and intensified their food quest. They often specialized in a few resources, like fish and sea mammals on newly exposed Scandinavian coasts or annual nut harvests in the North American Midwest.

The intensification of hunting and foraging was marked by two long-term trends. The first was a gradual shrinking of tool kits, the second, the development of highly sophisticated artifacts and weapons designed for exploitation of specific food resources like acorns or sea mammals. Among these was the bow and arrow, first developed in Europe, Africa, and the Near East perhaps by 15,000 years ago. It enabled the hunter to shoot at his quarry from a distance.

As people adapted to the challenges of local environments, human culture became greatly diversified. Human populations were rising gradually, so the world's hunting and foraging grounds were filling up, given that only the most favored environments could support more than one human being per square mile. Reduced mobility, rising local populations, and new strategies for dealing with unpredictable climatic change—these problems were common to postglacial hunter-gatherers in every part of the world. A few of these societies, especially those living in areas with rich and diverse food resources that included fish and sea mammals, achieved a high degree of social complexity, with, for the first time, some signs of social ranking.

1. AFRICAN HUNTER-GATHERERS

For thousands of years during the Würm glaciation, sub-Saharan Africans lived in isolation from the rest of the late Ice Age world. The arid Sahara was uninhabitable for much of the Würm. African savannas and grasslands supported a rich mammalian fauna and many species of plant foods. The hunter-gatherers who subsisted on these diverse resources developed ever more efficient ways of hunting and foraging.

After the Ice Age, these cultures became more specialized, with the densest populations concentrated in large river valleys like the Zam-

bezi, or near lakes, where fishing became of great importance. The Sahara now supported a sparse population of hunter-gatherers adapted to arid, open country. The people of the Nile Valley lived much of the year in permanent base camps, subsisting off a bounty of game, plant foods, and river fish. The ancestry of the **San** of the Kalahari Desert and other living African hunter-gatherer peoples can be traced back to extinct groups that flourished on the savanna thousands of years earlier in prehistory.

2. ASIAN HUNTER-GATHERERS

Intensely conservative hunter-gatherer cultures continued to flourish in Asia after the Ice Age. In the more open country of the north, the microblade traditions of millennia earlier continued to diversify into ever more specialized hunting and foraging economies, as well as into emerging seacoast economies. The peoples of the tropical forests of Southeast Asia continued to rely heavily on bamboo and wood technology, and their simple culture was little changed from much earlier times, except for a gradual trend toward more diminutive, specialized tool kits. These tool kits reflect much more varied adaptations by these peoples to local environments, adaptations subsumed under the archaeological label **Hoabhinian Tradition.**

Offshore, in New Guinea and Australia, more specialized local cultures now appeared, many of them oriented toward the exploitation of specific foods like fish, sea mammals, and small game. In the New Guinea highlands, there are signs that people began to deliberately clear forests and plant wild yams after the Ice Age to enhance their food supplies as best they could. Human settlement was still confined to the islands of the extreme southwestern Pacific, for Asians still lacked the necessary boats and foods to navigate far offshore.

3. MESOLITHIC HUNTER-GATHERERS IN EUROPE

European environments changed dramatically as Alpine and Scandinavian ice sheets retreated for the last time. Sea levels rose, flooding the North Sea, while the Baltic Sea formed at the foot of northern glaciers. Dense forests spread over formerly open country. Europeans now adapted to hunting and foraging in forest environments, camping in clearings and in more open woodland environments. Much human settlement was confined to riverbanks, lakeshores, and seacoasts. Here people found a bounty of fish, sea mammals, and bird life, supple-

menting this diet with plant foods and forest game. These **Mesolithic** cultures (*Mesolithic*, meaning "Middle Stone Age," describes post–Ice Age European hunter-gatherers) achieved some degree of social complexity in Scandinavia, where richly decorated individuals were buried in cemeteries by 5500 B.C.E. These same cultures were the indigenous societies of Europe, farmers who first spread north and west across central Europe from the Balkans after 4500 B.C.E.

4. NEAR EASTERN HUNTERS AND FORAGERS

In the Near East, the end of the Ice Age brought drier conditions, although the climate was somewhat wetter than today. The densest human settlement was confined to major river valleys, especially places where open steppe, woodland, and floodplain environments intersected.

One such location was **Abu Hureyra,** by the Euphrates River in Syria, where a sedentary community of hunter-gatherers flourished between 10,500 and 9000 B.C.E. About 300 to 400 people lived in a small village settlement of pit dwellings with thatched roofs. Each spring, they killed thousands of migrating gazelle, a small desert antelope from the south. Eventually deteriorating climatic conditions and deforestation due to heavy firewood consumption caused abandonment of the settlement. Sedentary villages like these, located at the margins of several environmental zones, were the places where agriculture and animal domestication first took hold in the Near East, and, indeed, in the world.

5. PALEO-INDIAN AND ARCHAIC NORTH AMERICANS

Holocene times ushered in major climatic change in the Americas. As the ice sheets of the north retreated, more temperate vegetational zones spread north. Ice Age big game had vanished, except for the bison, which flourished on the short grass of the Great Plains. Here Paleo-Indian, and later, more sophisticated **Archaic** big-game hunting cultures diversified over a period of more than 10,000 years, right into modern times. First the bow and arrow, which arrived in the first millennium B.C.E., and then the horse, introduced by Spanish conquistadors in 1543 C.E., enriched Plains hunting cultures. They had already achieved a high degree of elaboration as a result of chronic warfare and competition when European settlers reached the Plains.

The West Coast and interior of North America became progressively drier, resulting in great environmental diversity. In the desert interior, Paleo-Indian and Archaic cultures developed a remarkable expertise with wild plant foods. These were highly mobile cultures, except in favored areas near lakes and marshes, where people preyed on waterfowl, freshwater fish, and plant foods for much of the year.

As Ice Age sea levels rose and flooded estuaries and bays, the Pacific coast of North America supported a great, and predictable, bounty of fish and sea mammals. These predictable food supplies supported sedentary hunter-gatherer cultures in southeast Alaska and the Pacific Northwest, in the San Francisco Bay area and interior, and along the southern California coast.

After about 4000 B.C.E., when sea levels stabilized, many of these societies enjoyed periods of remarkable social and political sophistication. In the Santa Barbara Channel region, for example, some **Chumash** people lived in settlements of more than 1,000 people headed by a hereditary chief. The famous **Ozette** whale-hunting settlement on Washington's Olympic Peninsula chronicles the history of an ancestral Makah Indian community from at least 1000 C.E. to the 18th century.

The first human settlement of the shores of the Arctic Ocean and of the Canadian Arctic Archipelago dates to about 2000 B.C.E. The **Pre-Dorset** and **Dorset** people were fisherfolk and caribou hunters, with the simplest of material culture. In the western Arctic, elaborate hunter-gatherer societies that can be attributed to ancestral Eskimo developed after 1000 B.C.E. in the Bering Strait area. They became specialized sea mammal hunters, trading walrus ivory, iron, and other commodities between Asia and Alaska and farther south. The **Thule** people from the west colonized the Canadian Arctic Archipelago as far east as Greenland in about 1000 C.E., just as **Norse** voyagers were pressing west to Labrador.

The eastern woodlands of North America supported a great diversity of hunter-gatherer groups after 8000 B.C.E., many of them concentrated in large river valleys where plant foods and fish were abundant. Some of these societies, especially in the Midwest and Southeast, developed highly specialized cultures that exploited bountiful nut harvests and river fish. By 4000 B.C.E., many of them lived in permanent base camps and competed for floodplain land. This competition was one of the factors that led to food production in North America.

6. CENTRAL AND SOUTH AMERICANS

We still know little of the postglacial hunter-gatherer societies of Central and South America, except for those of coastal Peru, where, in later millennia, important civilizations were to flourish. The **Paloma** site and other fishing settlements at the mouths of coastal rivers flourished from the remarkable bounty of the nearby Pacific after 8000 B.C.E. Offshore currents brought deep-water species inshore, while shoals of anchovies and other small fish provided sustenance year-round. The same communities also exploited plant foods nourished by coastal fogs. Such Archaic hunter-gatherer societies developed increasing complexity over many centuries. Fish and sea mammals remained a vital resource for coastal Peruvians long after agriculture developed along the coast after 2000 B.C.E. and civilizations prospered.

Elsewhere in Central and South America, late Paleo-Indian and Archaic hunter-gatherers adapted to every kind of Holocene environment imaginable, from cold, oceanic coastlines in the far south to the dense rain forest in the Amazon basin and high-altitude plateaux in the Andes Mountains. It was here, in the high Andes, that the inhabitants of **Guitarrero Cave** in Peru began the deliberate cultivation of beans as early as 8000 B.C.E. In doing so, they laid the foundation for the brilliant expertise of Native Americans with cultivated native plants of every kind in later millennia.

J. THE ORIGINS OF FOOD PRODUCTION

For more than 99 percent of human existence, our forebears lived by hunting and foraging, tied to the season of plant foods and the movements of game, fish, and sea mammals. Food production, the deliberate cultivation of cereal grasses and edible root plants, is a phenomenon of the last 10,000 years of human existence. It is in large part responsible for the rapidly accelerating rates of population growth and culture change throughout the world during the past ten millennia.

The great Old World archaeologist Vere Gordon Childe (1892–1957) wrote of two great developments in prehistoric times, a **Neolithic Rev-** **olution** and an **Urban Revolution.** The Neolithic Revolution saw the development of agriculture and animal domestication in the Near East during a period of prolonged drought in the Near East. The Urban Revolution coincided with the appearance of the first cities, writing, and literate civilization in Mesopotamia and Egypt. Childe developed his revolution theory during the 1930s, when much less was known about world prehistory.

Child's theory is too simplistic, for it has long been surpassed by more sophisticated formulations, based on a much more detailed knowledge of ancient societies. In one respect, however, Childe was correct. The deliberate cultivation of the soil and the domestication of animals were not, in themselves, revolutionary developments, for every hunter-gatherer was familiar with the germination of seeds and the taming of animals. But the consequences of the new economies were indeed revolutionary, for they were the catalyst for lasting, and dramatic, culture changes.

Thanks to radiocarbon dating, we know that agriculture appeared in widely separated areas of the world over several thousand years: in the Near East, China, south and Southeast Asia, and the Americas. Modern theories are based on the realization that many postglacial hunter-gatherer societies were preadapted to food production before anyone started planting wild cereal grasses or penning animals. They were already exploiting such resources intensively, local populations were rising, and there were occasional food shortages in areas like the Near East, where the most favored areas were already at the limits of their carrying capacity.

Hunter-gatherers spend much of their time "managing" risk, the risk of starvation, of drought, of sudden changes in animal migration habits. They do so by acting very conservatively, responding to different risks by either moving away or developing new storage technologies for fish, plants, and other foods, and by drying foods like pounded bison or salmon. A straightforward solution to rising populations, occasional food shortages, and unpredictable environments may have been to go one step further, to cultivate familiar plants and domesticate common prey so that people could draw on familiar "stored" resources in scarce months.

This process has been documented by archaeologist Kent Flannery at **Guila Naquitz** cave in Mexico. A small group of hunters and foragers visited this small cave six times over a period of 2,000 years after 8750 B.C.E. Using a sophisticated computer model, Flannery and his colleagues have shown that the local people learned how to schedule foraging for different plant species over the seasons. They lived in an area with unpredictable rainfall, so collective memory based on experience was vital to them. The seeds found in the cave showed that the band used one set of seeds in wet years, another in dry. They tried to manage risk by experimenting with the planting of wild beans in wet years, when the chance of starvation was lower. When this strategy worked, they began planting every year. In time, they relied even more heavily on beans, maize, and squash for their subsistence, to the point where cultivation became more important than foraging.

The new food-producing economies proved dramatically successful. People cultivated an extraordinary range of cereal and root crops, many of them for food, others for medicinal, even hallucinogenic purposes. They domesticated animals ranging in size from the ox and the camel to guinea pigs. Ten thousand years ago, virtually everybody in the world lived by hunting and gathering. By 2,000 years ago, most people were farmers or herders and only a minority were still hunter-gatherers.

The spread of food-producing economies throughout the world only took about 8,000 years. It spread everywhere except where an environment with extreme aridity or heat or cold rendered agriculture or herding impossible, or where people chose to remain hunters and foragers. In some places, food production was the economic base for urbanization and literate civilization.

K. EARLY FOOD PRODUCTION IN THE OLD WORLD (c. 10,000 B.C.E. AND LATER)

1. FIRST FARMERS IN THE NEAR EAST

In 10,000 B.C.E., most human settlement in the Near East was confined to the Levant (the easternmost Mediterranean shoreline) and to the Zagros Mountains of Iran and Iraq and their western foothills. Some locations, like the Jordan Valley and the Middle Euphrates Valley, were more densely populated, often by large hunter-gatherer communities located at the margins of several ecological zones. They foraged on wooded hill slopes for cereal grasses and nuts, hunting game on open grasslands and floodplains.

One such settlement was at **Abu Hureyra** in the Middle Euphrates Valley, where a permanent hunter-gatherer base camp exploited gazelle migrations between 10,500 and 9000 B.C.E. About 8500 B.C.E., a new settlement appeared on the same site, this time a permanent village of rectangular mud-brick houses connected by narrow alleyways. At first the inhabitants hunted gazelle intensively. About 8000 B.C.E., they switched abruptly to domestic sheep and goats and to growing einkorn, pulses, and other cereal crops.

Abu Hureyra was not, of course, unique. Contemporary farming settlements have come to light in Syria and the Levant, most of them on low ground close to fertile soils. By 6500 B.C.E., farming communities were trading with each other, passing such exotic materials as obsidian (fine-grained volcanic glass for toolmaking) from village to village over long distances. Obsidian contains distinctive trace elements, which have enabled archaeologists to track even tiny fragments of this much-prized volcanic glass back to sources in central Turkey and elsewhere.

Some settlements, notably **Jericho** in the Jordan Valley, reached an impressive size. By 6500 B.C.E., Jericho covered nine acres, its small beehive-shaped houses clustered behind massive stone walls. It was a small town, perhaps in constant fear of marauders after its large grain stocks and stored trade goods, bartered from the coast and interior deserts.

By 6000 B.C.E., farmers were living throughout the Zagros Mountains of Iran and Iraq in small permanent villages of mud-brick houses. Below, other cultivators dwelt by the edges of the low-lying plains of central and southern Mesopotamia. By at least 8000 B.C.E. some farmers settled at **Ali Kosh**, north of the confluence of the Tigris and Euphrates Rivers. As time went on, Ali Kosh grew until it became a substantial village, with wide lanes and rectangular houses. The people herded sheep and goats, perhaps driving them to the nearby highlands in the hot summer months. They relied on hunting and fishing in nearby marshes and were using irrigation to grow cereal crops by at least 6000 B.C.E. Such irrigation techniques were to prove of vital importance for early civilization in Mesopotamia (p. 25).

2. EARLY EUROPEAN FARMERS

Near Eastern cereal grains like emmer and bread wheat and domesticated animals were introduced into southeastern Europe and Greece by at least 6000 B.C.E. The local people were already heavily dependent on wild cereal grasses and may have been planting some of them. The first farmers lived in compact villages on river floodplains, occupying the same sites for many generations.

After 4500 B.C.E. farming based on cattle herding combined with spring-sown crops like wheat and barley spread over enormous areas of continental Europe. The expansion of farming was a stop-and-go process, coinciding with favorable rainfall cycles and dependent on the distribution of lighter soils easily turned with stone and wood artifacts. These cultivators, known to archaeologists as the **Bandkeramik Com-**

plex, lived in hamlets of rectangular houses, made of timber and thatch. As each settlement grew, companion villages were founded nearby, gradually filling in vacant land.

By 4000 B.C.E., cereal crops and domesticated animals were widely used throughout much of Europe, including Britain. Eventually, farmers settled on heavier soils, and indigenous hunter-gatherer groups gradually adopted the new economies. This was a time when more

elaborate burial customs developed throughout Europe, as ancestor cults came into fashion, with their close ties to ancestral farming land.

In western Europe, groups of villages built communal stone tombs, often called **megaliths**, where important kin leaders and people with genealogical ties to kin group ancestors were buried. Those who supervised the building of shrines and communal tombs, and led the rituals conducted there, assumed increasing political and social power in new, nonegalitarian European societies.

3. EGYPT AND SUB-SAHARAN AFRICA

The Nile Valley was a rich environment for hunter-gatherers throughout the late Ice Age and for many millennia afterward. Such was the bounty of game, fish, and plant foods that hunter-gatherer groups could live in permanent base camps for much of the year. It was not until as late as 6000 B.C.E. that wheat and barley were farmed along the Nile.

By this time, people living on the semiarid grasslands of the Sahara were herding both cattle and goats or sheep. Some experts believe that cattle were domesticated from wild oxen independently in North Africa or the Sahara as early as they were in the Near East. As the Sahara dried up after 6000 B.C., some of these nomadic herders moved into the Nile Valley and became absorbed into the indigenous population.

Two thousand years later, small farming villages flourished from the Nile Delta upstream as far as Aswan at the First Cataract and deep into Nubia (modern Sudan). The farmers took advantage of the annual Nile floods to grow winter crops, grazing their animals at water's edge. This indigenous farming tradition was the foundation of later Ancient Egyptian civilization (p. 29).

By 3500 B.C.E., cattle herders were grazing their herds far upstream, in what is now the Sudan. Fifteen hundred years later, some of these herders had moved as far southward as the East African highlands and are ultimately the ancestors of cattle-herding peoples like the Masai

who live there today. This movement, and others to the west, were responses to the increasing aridity of the Sahara. Many of these groups cultivated summer rainfall crops domesticated from indigenous cereals like finger millet and sorghum, as did fisherfolk living by lakes and rivers. These crops were to become the staples of tropical African agriculture.

Cereal agriculture was practiced on the southern fringes of the Sahara by at least 2000 B.C.E. For thousands of years, peoples living at the fringes of the West and central African rain forests cut off the tops of wild yams and replanted them. This form of vegeculture gave way to more formal root agriculture in the West African forest by 2000 B.C.E., where people lived alongside riverbanks and in clearings.

Cereal agriculture did not spread to the savanna regions of east, central, and southern Africa until about 2,000 years ago. This event coincided with the spread of iron-using farmers from West Africa across much of the continent. Iron technology enabled Africans to clear woodland on a large scale. Within a few centuries, iron-using farmers had crossed the Zambezi and Limpopo Rivers into southern Africa. Their distant descendants were still expanding southward when European farmers expanded into South Africa's eastern Cape Province in the 18th century C.E.

4. ASIAN FARMERS

We do not know if cereal agriculture developed independently in India and Pakistan. Farmers were living at **Mehrgarh** west of the Indus River by 6000 B.C.E. Cereal crops, humped cattle, pig, and water buffalo were domesticated by local south Asian populations in this region. The new economies spread rapidly in northwest Pakistan and into other areas. By 5000 B.C.E., the Mehrgarh people were cultivating locally domesticated cotton, which became a vital trade commodity in later centuries, one of the foundations of later urban civilization in the Indus River Valley.

There are signs of intensive exploitation of wild plant foods in the Southeast Asian highlands, and perhaps even domestication of wild yams and other root plants as early as 8000 B.C.E., but the evidence is very controversial. The rices and Asian millets ancestral to modern rice were first domesticated somewhere between northeast India, Southeast Asia, and southern China. The initial process of domestication probably took place in an alluvial swamp area where there was plenty of seasonal flooding to stimulate crop growth. The earliest records of cultivated rice come from China's Middle Yangzi River Valley, dating from as early as 7000 B.C.E., but it is likely that similar early dates will come from the Ganges Plain and other regions in the future.

By 6500 B.C.E., Southeast Asians were moving from the hills onto river plains and into lowland areas, where intensive cultivation and

irrigation permitted rice agriculture. Rice soon became the vital staple of farmers throughout southern and Southeast Asia, but its spread is not well documented. At **Homutu** in coastal southern China, a community of rice farmers lived in a marshy area between 5000 and 4000 B.C.E. Their village of beautifully made wooden houses was surrounded by forests and was close to a great diversity of food resources. The women of Homutu made a distinctive type of cord-decorated pottery, which was also widespread in Southeast Asia, Taiwan, and Japan.

North Chinese farmers relied not on rice, but on local cereals and seeded plants such as millets, sorghum, and the mulberry planted on river valley soils. Again, agriculture was a local development. The earliest farming villages date to about 5000 B.C.E., perhaps earlier. For the next 2,000 years, the **Yangshao** farming culture flourished in the Yellow River Basin, an area as large as the early centers of agriculture in Egypt or Mesopotamia. Each Yangshao community was self-contained, overlooking a fertile river valley. By 3000 B.C.E., Yangshao people were enjoying a characteristic and thoroughly Chinese culture with its own naturalistic art style. The roots of Chinese cuisine and language may date from Yangshao times.

During these 2,000 years, many distinctive farming cultures developed throughout China. They became the **Longshanoid** cultures, which were the founder societies of early Chinese civilization.

L. THE ORIGINS OF FOOD PRODUCTION IN THE AMERICAS (c. 5000 B.C.E. AND LATER)

The Native Americans were remarkable for their expertise with native plants. They domesticated not only staples like maize and beans, but

also hundreds of varieties of potato, amaranth, and other crops that are now international staples. In contrast to the Old World, only a few animals were available for domestication, among them the guinea pig, llama, and turkey. Potential beasts of burden had become extinct at the end of the Ice Age.

As in the Old World, experimentation with native plants began early, especially in the Andean area of South America, where people strove constantly to expand the range of wild plants into marginal environments. In North America, hunter-gatherer societies in major Midwestern river valleys were planting such native plants as goosefoot and marsh elder to supplement wild stands as early as 2500 B.C.E. And the Guila Naquitz excavations in central Mexico show that hunter-gatherers in Central America also experimented with bean and squash cultivation as a means of surviving dry years in an unpredictable environment as early as 7000 B.C.E.

Maize (Zea mays) was the staple cereal crop for many Native American societies when Christopher Columbus landed in the New World in 1492. It was cultivated from Argentina and Chile northward to Canada, from sea level to high in the Andes, in low-lying swamp environments, and in arid lands. Hundreds of races of domesticated maize evolved over the millennia, each with a special adaptation to local conditions. The wild ancestor of maize is thought to be teosinte, a wild grass that grows over much of Central America. Teosinte was transformed into a primitive maize through human selection that was much easier to harvest. The earliest known maize cobs date to about 2750 B.C.E. in the **Tehuacán Valley** in southern Mexico and from the Valley of Mexico in the highlands.

By 1700 B.C.E., the inhabitants of the Tehuacán Valley were growing amaranth, gourds, and maize to the point that agriculture was the dominant part of the subsistence economy. Tehuacán is by no means unique, for many groups throughout Central America were turning to agriculture by this time. In time, a primitive form of domesticated maize with kernels in eight rows was the ancestral crop, which spread thousands of miles from its original homeland after 2700 B.C.E.

In South America, people living in the Andean highlands of Peru were cultivating potatoes, maize, beans, and squash by 2500 B.C.E., some of these crops, especially potatoes, beans, and quinoa, much earlier. Llamas were domesticated by at least 2500 B.C.E. Maize agriculture probably spread south from Central America to the highlands, then to the arid Peruvian coast by 800 B.C.E., where maize was grown in large-scale irrigation schemes in river valleys. This intensive agriculture was the staple of the coastal civilizations that developed by the Pacific after 800 B.C.E.

Maize agriculture spread into the North American Southwest by about 1500 B.C.E., where cold winters and arid conditions made cereal agriculture difficult. Nevertheless, maize and bean agriculture became the basis of the sedentary **Pueblo Indian cultures** that developed in the Southwest after 2,000 years ago. The well known **Anasazi, Hohokam,** and **Mogollon** cultural traditions of the Southwest were the ancestral foundations of modern Southwest Indian society. Between the 10th and 13th centuries C.E., some Anasazi pueblos, notably in **Chaco Canyon,** New Mexico, and **Mesa Verde,** Colorado, housed hundreds of people, especially during important seasonal ceremonials. Southwestern Pueblo societies were successful, highly flexible adaptations to unpredictable, semiarid environments. As such, they never achieved the degree of social complexity found further east in North America.

By 2500 B.C.E., hunter-gatherer societies in the eastern woodlands of North America were planting native plants on a regular basis. Maize crossed the southern Plains into eastern North America during the first millennium C.E., but did not become well established until after 800 C.E. By this time, many eastern societies were living in sizable, sedentary communities, presided over by powerful kin leaders.

M. LATER OLD WORLD PREHISTORY (3000 B.C.E. AND AFTERWARD)

1. STATE-ORGANIZED SOCIETIES

Within 5,000 years of the appearance of farming villages in the Near East, state-organized societies developed in Egypt and Mesopotamia. Subsequently, other preindustrial civilizations of great complexity emerged—not only in the Near East, but also in south Asia, Southeast Asia, and China. They also flourished in Central America and the Andean region of South America (p. 19). Such state-organized societies operated on a large scale with centralized political and social organization. They were marked by class stratification, intensive agriculture, and were based on assumptions of social inequality. All had complex government bureaucracies and were often ruled by despotic leaders who governed as divine monarchs.

State formation was not a universal phenomenon. Many archaeologists theorize that states emerged because they were beneficial as a way of organizing both food supplies increased through intensified agriculture and trade, and external relations with neighbors. They believe states emerged in environmental settings with severe population problems or shortages of agricultural land. Effective, centralized management of trade monopolies, and of food production, through state-organized irrigation systems and other means, could bring ecological imbalance under control. For example, both Ancient Egyptian pharaohs and Aztec rulers in Mexico employed hundreds of officials to ensure that all available land was cultivated efficiently.

2. WEBS OF RELATIONS

For all their complexity and sophistication, the early civilizations ruled over relatively small geographical areas by modern standards. But their insatiable demands for exotic raw materials—for gold, copper, iron ore, even such prosaic items as timber or textiles—brought them into contact with dozens of prehistoric, nonliterate societies that lived on the margins of, or outside, their boundaries. The last 5,000 years of prehistory are remarkable for the ever-expanding tentacles of interconnectedness that linked hundreds of prehistoric societies with one another, and with more complex literate civilizations many miles away.

This web of relations began to expand as early as 7000 B.C.E. in the Near East, when the obsidian trade linked small farming settlements seeking fine toolmaking stone. In time, these small regional trading networks became well-traveled caravan routes that linked Mesopotamia with the Mediterranean and the Nile Valley to the Levant.

During the fourth millennium B.C.E., long-distance trade exploded throughout the Near East, linking societies all the way from the Indus Valley in Pakistan and Iran with Mesopotamia, the Levant, Anatolia, and the Nile Valley. This rapidly evolving "world system" transformed human life. A millennium later, it embraced not only the Near East, but Cyprus, the Aegean, and mainland Greece as well. It developed because of an insatiable demand for nonlocal raw materials in different ecological regions where societies were developing along very similar lines. The Sumerians of Mesopotamia, for example, lived in a largely treeless environment with no metals. Yet they produced large grain surpluses, which they traded for timber and metals with the highlands by boat and across the desert by donkey camels. Nowhere did this emerging world economic system have a greater impact than in Africa.

3. LATER AFRICAN PREHISTORY

a. EGYPT AND NUBIA

Ancient Egyptian civilization began with the unification of Upper and Lower Egypt by the pharaoh Narmer in about 3100 B.C.E. This long-lived civilization was an entirely indigenous development, its homeland a favored river oasis surrounded by desert. But Ancient Egypt was far from isolated, for from early times the Nile Valley was part of interregional trade networks that linked Mesopotamia and the Levant with the Nile. These relationships involved not only commerce, but occasionally frontier wars in distant lands like Syria. Egypt's relationship with lands upstream was just as important. The pharaohs traded for vital raw materials outside the narrow confines of their kingdom. They prospected for gold in the Sinai and in Nubia, the **Land of Kush** upstream of the First Nile Cataract. Despite many centuries of trading and occasional military expeditions, Ancient Egypt's cultural contribution to later African history was probably negligible, if nothing else because of the realities of Nile geography.

Nubia provided Egypt with gold, copper, and ivory, with semiprecious stones and slaves, and with mercenaries for the royal armies. It was so vital to Egyptian interests that the Middle Kingdom pharaohs garrisoned Lower Nubia in about 1800 B.C.E., specifically so they could control the gold trade.

Nubia itself was ruled by black African chiefs, who became wealthy on the Egyptian trade. Although the pharaohs colonized Nubia for a while during the New Kingdom, they never fully controlled the long river reaches upstream. As Egypt weakened after 1000 B.C.E., the Nubians became more powerful. A dynasty of Nubian rulers from Napata far upstream actually ruled Egypt for a short time in the 8th century B.C.E.

The Nubian state controlled caravan routes along the Nile and across the Eastern Desert. About 6000 B.C.E., the Nubian rulers moved their capital from **Napata** far upstream to **Meroë**, on a fertile floodplain between the Nile and Atbara Rivers in what is now the Sudan. The Meroitic state flourished for nine centuries, ruled by African kings who imitated many of the customs of Egyptian pharaohs. Their capital lay at a strategic point on the Nile, where desert trading routes from the Red Sea to the east intersected with trails leading west along the southern margins of the Sahara and upstream along the Nile. Meroë maintained at least sporadic contacts with the classical world but was never conquered by Rome, for the strategic obstacles were too great.

Meroë owed its prosperity to the gold, copper, iron, ivory, and slave trade, and even supplied war elephants for Roman armies. But, above all, its importance can be attributed to the introduction of the camel from Arabia in the closing centuries of the first millennium B.C.E. The Arabs called the camel "the ship of the desert," an appropriate metaphor, for this tough beast of burden opened up the Sahara and tropical Africa to the outside world.

b. WEST AFRICAN STATES

The Roman colonies in North Africa were in constant conflict with the Berber nomads of the desert. But they never opened regular trading routes across the Sahara with the black people who lived on its southern margins. By the time the Arabs conquered North Africa in the 7th century C.E., camel caravans were crossing the desert regularly, bringing West African gold to the north in exchange for cake salt, mined in the heart of the Sahara. Salt was so prized by the salt-starved West Africans that they sometimes paid for it in its equivalent weight of gold.

In the 7th century C.E., small towns devoted to the gold and salt trade ruled by entrepreneurial African chiefs dotted the southern margins of the western Sahara. The most important was the **Kingdom of Ghana,** which flourished well before the 8th century C.E. Ghana started as a network of smaller chiefdoms and rose to prominence because it controlled gold sources near the Senegal River. This state, and its successors, came into being as a result of both indigenous cultural developments and because of links with the growing web of relations that was drawing the western Sudan into a much wider commercial and political world.

West Africa came into contact with Islamic merchants and religious reformers in the 11th century C.E. Islamic forces captured Ghana in 1076, and the kingdom soon dissolved into its constituent parts. From this time onward, the savanna regions south of the Sahara were part of the vast caravan routes that linked the Islamic world. Later, West African states such as Mali and Songhay were ruled by Islamic kings and were familiar to Arab geographers.

c. EAST AND SOUTHERN AFRICA

Meroë was part of a vast trade network that linked Nubia with Arabia and the Mediterranean world. So was the kingdom of **Axum** on the Ethiopian highlands to the southeast. This state competed with Meroë, then overthrew it. Axum's Christian kings exchanged gold, ivory, and slaves for luxuries from the Mediterranean world, and from distant India throughout the late first millennium C.E. They were an outlying part of another great web of interconnected, and diverse, trading societies that extended not only to Arabia, but far across the Indian Ocean and beyond.

The catalyst for this trade was the monsoon winds of the Indian Ocean. They allowed downwind sailing vessels to travel from India to Africa and back in the course of a year. India had an insatiable demand for soft, easily carved African elephant ivory, and for gold. This ocean trade developed nearly 2,000 years ago, bringing foreign merchants not only to Arabia and the Red Sea, but to the East African coast. The same winds brought Islam to the Africans of the coast, their partners in the trade. By 1000 C.E., a string of small trading communities dotted the Kenya and Tanzanian coasts. They formed an indigenous trading culture linked both with the outside world and with suppliers of gold, ivory, and slaves in the far interior, especially up the Zambezi River.

The **Karanga** people living in the inland plateau south of the Zambezi were cattle herders and farmers, who controlled rich gold and copper outcrops. Their leaders ruled over small, volatile kingdoms and used their religious powers to monopolize the gold and ivory trade with the coast. In return, they received cotton cloth, glass beads, Chinese porcelain, glass vessels, and other cheap trinkets, which had high prestige value in the interior. The greatest Karanga chief lived at **Great Zimbabwe,** a complex of stone enclosures built between 1100 and 1550 C.E.

4. EUROPE AFTER 3500 B.C.E.

By 3500 B.C.E., Europe was peopled by small, egalitarian Stone Age farming communities. They had cleared vast acreages of land and lived in highly organized landscapes of small hamlets, homesteads, and farmlands. By this time, copper and gold metallurgy were well established in the Balkans; indeed, metallurgy may have developed independently in this region.

Initially, copper and gold were used as decorative metals, fashioned into luxury ornaments that were traded throughout Europe. The same trade networks carried distinctive bell-shaped beakers throughout much of western Europe. By 2000 B.C.E., European smiths had learned how to alloy copper and tin to make bronze. The result was tough-edged artifacts that could be used to fell trees and work with wood. The trade in these weapons, as well as control of ore outcrops, lay in the hands of local chiefs. For the first time, European society showed signs of social ranking. Surplus food supplies were channeled into erecting majestic religious monuments, of which **Stonehenge** in southern Britain is best known. Important religious ceremonies took place at such shrines, perhaps at the winter and summer solstices.

The Bronze Age, the period when bronze technology came into use throughout Europe, was a period of political instability and intense competition for land. Now warrior chiefs presided over warlike tribes, as plows and more consolidated forms of agriculture produced higher crop yields. Some of these European groups raided the eastern Mediterranean world in about 1200 B.C.E., destroying **Mycenae** in Greece and overthrowing the **Hittite empire.** These were formidable fighters, who used horse-drawn vehicles and devastating slashing swords, far more effective than the cutting weapons of earlier centuries.

After 1000 B.C.E., iron technology spread rapidly across Europe. Iron-working originated in the Mitanni area of Anatolia in the mid-second millennium B.C.E. Hittite monarchs guarded the secret for some time, for they were well aware of the strategic advantages of iron. But mercenaries in their armies took the metallurgy home with them, and the secret was out. Europeans embraced the new technology with enthusiasm. By this time, the most coherent political unit was a loose confederacy of tribes formed in time of war, or temporarily under a char-

ismatic chieftain. This native form of government was to survive for centuries beyond Roman frontiers.

The **Hallstatt** people were expert bronze and iron workers who colonized former Urnfield areas of central and western Europe in the early first millennium B.C.E. Celtic speakers with a distinctive and highly sophisticated **La Tene** technology spread north from the Rhine and Danube Valleys into the Low Countries and Britain in the 4th century B.C.E. The Celts were formidable warriors, who built large hill forts and introduced the Romans to the short sword, sacking Rome itself in about 390 B.C.E.

The last three centuries C.E. saw the appearance of coinage and the founding of small states and fortified towns. These were the people defeated by Julius Caesar in Gaul in 56 B.C.E. And these were the warrior groups who eventually sacked Rome and sacked its provinces in later centuries.

5. EURASIAN NOMADS

To the east, the rolling grasslands from the Ukraine to China were unable to support high population densities. Nomadic herders settled there at an unknown date, domesticating the horse as early as 4000 B.C.E. They lived in felt tents and subsisted mostly on horse milk and cheese, also off game and plant foods. The **Pazyryk** burial mounds in Siberia contain the bodies of elaborately tattooed chiefs, who wore leather and woolen clothing and traveled in beautifully decorated horse-drawn chariots.

Scythian nomads, descended from these earlier groups, menaced the northern frontiers of the Mediterranean world for many centuries, as sedentary colonists impinged on their lands and threatened a lifeway that required enormous areas of land for survival. Eurasian nomads continued to flourish during the closing centuries of prehistory.

6. ASIA

The later prehistory of Asia is still little known, especially that of humbler village societies rather than spectacular civilizations.

a. SOUTII ASIA

By about 3500 B.C.E., hundreds of small farming villages dotted the Indus floodplain in northwest Pakistan. Many of these settlements boasted of fortifications and planned streets. Many villages and small towns practiced intensive agriculture and were built just above river flood level. The stone and mud-brick houses of **Kot Diji** were clustered behind massive stone flood dikes and defense walls, for neighboring communities quarreled constantly about the control of prime agricultural land. As the valley population rose, so did pressure on the land. Forests were denuded for firewood used in brick making, sheep and goats stripped the natural vegetation. The need for communal irrigation and flood control works led to the emergence of the **Harappan Civilization** in the Indus Valley by 3000 B.C.E. The Harappans traded with Sumerian city-states and highland Iran over many centuries.

The Harappan Civilization declined after 2000 B.C.E., a development that led to a massive expansion of village settlement in Gujerat to the south. In about 1500 B.C.E., Aryan nomads swept south over India. A few centuries later, iron technology arrived in the subcontinent, enabling farmers to break up the hard soils of the Ganges plain in the east. This region was to become the heartland of later Indian empires. India was invaded by King Darius in 516 B.C.E. and by Alexander the Great two centuries later.

The period between 200 B.C.E. and 300 C.E. saw India linked by regular trading routes, not only to Arabia and the Red Sea, but also to Southeast Asia, as Buddhism and Hinduism spread over enormous areas of the eastern world.

b. CHINA

By 3000 B.C.E., agriculture had taken such a hold in China that population densities rose rapidly, as most available land was taken under cultivation. At the same time, rice agriculture expanded in lowland areas where irrigation was easy. Those villages fortunate enough to possess irrigable lands soon turned into larger, much more permanent

settlements, often protected with earthen walls to guard against floods and marauding neighbors. Even these larger communities were part of a self-regulating folk society in which kinship loyalties and the extended family were all important and age was deeply revered. The family ancestors were the conduit to the gods who controlled the harmony of the world.

By this time, too, a new social order was coming into being. Important kin leaders became warrior rulers, often men of great spiritual authority who interceded with the ancestors. Soon they became the aristocratic nobility of early Chinese civilization, represented by the **Shang Civilization** of northern China and other states. But these political and social developments would never have been possible without the unswerving conservatism of the village farmer, who accepted the new and emerging social order that imposed an almost alien, wealthy, and very privileged society on their shoulders. They did so because of putative kin ties that obligated the farmer to provide food and labor for their rulers.

Early Chinese states rose and fell with rapidity for centuries, until the Emperor Shi Huangdi unified China in 221 B.C.E. In later centuries, Chinese trading activities in Southeast Asia played a pivotal role in the development of indigenous states there. The Chinese were also linked to the Indian Ocean trade, indeed sailed as far as the East African coast in the sixth century C.E.

c. JAPAN

The later prehistory of Japan is dominated by the Jomon culture, a common cultural tradition that linked many ethnic groups in the archipelago and flourished from 10,500 B.C.E. to 300 C.E. Jomon people were hunters and fisherfolk, remarkable for their fine clay vessels, the earliest in the world. They developed an elaborate technology for processing and storing huge stocks of nuts, an activity that may have combined with the cultivation of milletlike plants.

The basis for what was to become traditional Japanese society was formed during the **Yayoi Period,** which began after 300 C.E., when large-scale rice agriculture and new technologies spread through the archipelago. Japan was unified into a single state in about 600 C.E., by which time stratified, complex societies were commonplace.

d. SOUTHEAST ASIA

Rice cultivators flourished throughout Southeast Asia by 3000 B.C.E. Bronze technology came into widespread use in about 1500 B.C.E. The **Dong Son** culture of Vietnam represents the culmination of bronze working and ironworking in prehistoric times. **Co Loa** near Hanoi was a fortified and moated settlement, ruled by local chieftains called **Lac Lords,** Keepers of the Drums. Intensive rice cultivation, use of the plow, and careful water control produced enormous food surpluses. The region became part of a Chinese protectorate in 43 C.E.

For centuries, Southeast Asia was dominated, at least tangentially, by two foreign presences—China to the north and India to the south. By the time of Christ, southerly towns were being incorporated into the oceanic trade routes that stretched from China in the east to the shores of the Red Sea and the east coast of Africa in the west. No one people controlled this vast trade, another nascent "world system," like that of the Mediterranean and Classical worlds.

Beyond India, Indian merchants traded as far as the South China Sea and with tribal societies of the mainland and islands. Metal and spices were the big attractions. Within a few centuries, kingdoms appeared with governments run according to Hindu or Buddhist ideas of social order. Eventually, these tribal chieftains became divine kings. Expanding mercantile empires like **Funan** in Vietnam's Mekong Delta dominated long-distance trade between the 3rd and 6th centuries C.E. Funan was the first of the great Southeast Asian civilizations.

7. OFFSHORE SETTLEMENT IN THE PACIFIC

By 2000 B.C.E., a myriad of stone-using farming cultures flourished by Southeast Asian rivers and coasts. Canoes played a major role in intervalley trade. Commodities like clay vessels, stone axes, and tool-making stone were exchanged through trade networks that linked small communities from Taiwan in the north to New Guinea and the southwestern Pacific islands in the south.

Yams and taro, both root crops, were cultivated in the New Guinea highlands by at least 7000 B.C.E. Agriculture became a staple throughout the southwestern Pacific by 2500 B.C.E. The new economies enabled offshore navigators to carry storable foods as well as cultigens, even edible dogs, chickens, and pigs, on long open-water voyages.

By 1500 B.C.E., the **Lapita people** of the Bismarck Archipelago in the southwestern Pacific had developed oceangoing, double-hulled canoes and mastered simple navigational techniques using the stars that enabled them to sail to islands far over the horizon. The Lapita people were expert traders. They voyaged as far east as Fiji, Tonga, and Samoa during the first millennium B.C.E.

From there, much longer distances entailed voyages of nearly 600 open-water miles. From Melanesia, canoes voyaged to Micronesia about 2,000 years ago. Polynesian culture originated in the west; then small groups settled the Marquesas by 400 C.E. and the Society Islands and Tahiti by 800 C.E.

By the time French and British explorers visited Tahiti in the mid-18th century, the Tahitians were ruled by a powerful hierarchy of chiefs and nobles. Canoes arrived on Hawaii before 700 C.E. and on Easter Island 200 years earlier. Finally, Polynesians voyaged southward to colonize New Zealand around 750 C.E. After 1400 C.E., Classic Maori culture developed, based on sweet potato agriculture and ruled by a flamboyant, warlike elite.

With the colonization of the Pacific Islands, the prehistoric human settlement of the Old World was complete.

N. CHIEFDOMS AND STATES IN THE AMERICAS (c. 1500 B.C.E.–1532 C.E.)

When Europeans landed in the New World, they encountered an astounding diversity of Native American societies. Some, like the Inuit of the Canadian Arctic or the Shoshone of the Great Basin, were simple hunter-gatherers living in small bands. Some lived in small farming villages, others in elaborate pueblos or small towns that housed several hundred people. Then there was the Aztec capital, Tenochtitlán, a city of some 200,000 people with a market that rivaled that of Constantinople or Seville. Archaeologists believe that these great variations in cultural and social complexity were the result, in part, of local environmental conditions as well as technological innovation. It was only in a few areas of exceptional resource diversity like Mesoamerica and Peru that fully fledged preindustrial civilizations developed.

1. NORTH AMERICAN CHIEFDOMS

Some of the most complex hunter-gatherer societies on Earth developed in North America. However, the climate was too harsh for the kinds of intensive maize and bean agriculture that would support urban civilizations.

By the time maize and beans reached eastern North America, local societies had been evolving toward more complexity for many centuries. After 2000 B.C.E., such societies developed a preoccupation with elaborate mortuary cults that celebrated the ancestors. Village kin groups erected large burial mounds and earthworks in which they interred kin leaders and other clan members, often adorned with badges of rank and fine heirlooms like soapstone pipes, acquired from afar. First the **Adena** culture developed in about 500 B.C.E. to be followed by the **Hopewell** complex two-and-a-half centuries later. These cults' rituals were reflected in prolonged burials. The Hopewell cult in particular developed great elaboration in the Ohio Valley and other parts of the Midwest. It involved, among other activities, complex gift exchanges that validated extensive long-distance trade. This brought commodities like obsidian from Yellowstone Park in the west to the Hopewell heartland.

The arrival of maize and bean agriculture transformed societies that relied heavily on hunting and foraging, as well as on the cultivation of native plants. River valley populations rose rapidly, trading and religious activity intensified, and an ever-changing mosaic of complex **Mississippian** chiefdoms developed throughout the southern Midwest and the Southeast. The greatest Mississippian chiefdoms were based on **Cahokia,** near East St. Louis, and **Moundville,** Alabama. Both were large towns, with imposing sacred precincts of pyramids and plazas. The Mississippian was an indigenous North American culture that went into decline in the 15th century, just before the Spanish landed in Florida. Within two centuries of European contact, the southeastern Indians were decimated by disease, their chiefdoms in tatters.

2. MESOAMERICAN CIVILIZATIONS

By 2000 B.C.E. sedentary village farmers were common in most of Mesoamerica. These societies became more complex as time passed, as groups of villages formed alliances and long-distance trade routes linked the lowlands and the Gulf of Mexico with the highlands inland. Small shrines appeared in larger villages, as social ranking became commonplace in Mesoamerican society.

a. OLMEC

This trend toward social complexity took hold throughout the region, but the most famous of these newly more complex societies is that of the Olmec on the Mexican south Gulf Coast. Olmec culture flourished from about 1500 to 500 B.C.E., a society of tropical farmers who traded extensively with one another and peoples on the highlands. Major ceremonial centers at **La Venta** and **San Lorenzo** boasted of earthen mounds, temples, and plazas, and a distinctive art style of snarling jaguars and animal humans.

Olmec society was a manifestation of a much more complex social and political order. It comprised a series of chiefdoms who maintained contacts with other lowland and highland societies. Art motifs, religious symbols, and ritual beliefs were shared with many other Mesoamerican peoples. This complex process of interaction over many centuries produced the complex and sophisticated traditions of Mesoamerican civilization in later centuries.

b. TEOTIHUACÁN

In the highlands, village populations rose sharply after 1000 B.C.E., leading to more intensive agriculture and increasingly sophisticated trade networks. By 200 B.C.E., the effects of this intensified economic activity led to the founding of the city of Teotihuacán in the Valley of Mexico. A century later, Teotihuacán expanded rapidly. Its streets, pyramids, and plazas covered eight square miles by 500 C.E. The city grew according to a master plan that was followed for six centuries.

Bisected by the Avenue of the Dead, Teotihuacán was dominated by the 210-foot-high Pyramid of the Sun. At least 120,000 people lived in the city during its heyday, ruled by a tiny elite of powerful, militaristic nobles. It was the dominant economic and religious state over much of highland Mexico until 750 C.E., when it collapsed suddenly. The collapse may have resulted from a combination of many factors, among them overexploitation of the commoners by the elite and a series of drought cycles that may have forced the population to disperse into smaller communities.

Maya Civilization developed in the Mesoamerican lowlands by 600 B.C.E. At **Nakbe** and **El Mirador,** the Maya erected elaborate ceremonial centers of stone and stucco buildings standing on pyramids and platforms. Even as El Mirador prospered, other important centers like **Tikal** and **Uaxactún** grew in importance, ushering in the Classic Period of Maya Civilization from 300 C.E. to 900. Maya life was governed by an intricate calendar system and a recently deciphered hieroglyphic script. Their writings tell us of a lowland civilization ruled by powerful lords, who presided over small city-states. Each state competed constantly with its neighbors, as different centers like Tikal, **Palenque,** and **Copán** vied for control of key trade routes and for political and religious prestige.

Maya lords considered themselves intermediaries between the living and spiritual worlds. A small nobility controlled Maya society. Their power base gave way suddenly in about 900 C.E., probably as a result of partial ecological collapse as farmlands became exhausted. Nevertheless, Maya Civilization continued to flourish in the northern Yucatán until the Spanish Conquest in the 16th century C.E.

In the highlands, the **Toltecs** held brief sway over the Valley of Mexico from about 900 C.E. to 1200, ruling their state from **Tula,** north of the valley. They may also have had some influence over lowland politics, for there is strong Toltec influence at **Chichén Itzá,** a great ceremonial center in the northern Yucatán. Political chaos followed the collapse of Toltec civilization in the 13th century. Eventually, the **Aztecs,** once nomadic farmers, rose to power in the Valley of Mexico.

3. ANDEAN CIVILIZATIONS

Andean states developed in every kind of environment imaginable, everything from mountain valleys high in the Andes to arid coastal plains. In this region, different ecological zones were "stacked" one above the other from sea level high into the mountains, and the inhabitants of each zone depended on others for vital resources. Thus, Andean civilization pursued many evolutionary paths, which came together in a remarkable mosaic of states that depended on one another for survival.

a. BEGINNINGS

The introduction of maize and cotton to the coast in about 2000 B.C.E. was a catalyst for civilization. So was the existence of dense populations and sedentary settlements. The formation of states both on the coast and in the highlands was also fostered by continuous interchange between coast and interior. Highland farmers needed dried fish, salt, and seaweed, the latter to combat endemic goiter. Carbohydrate foods like oca, ullucu, and white potatoes could not be grown in the lowlands. The two regions became closely interdependent.

Andean Civilization began in about 1900 B.C.E., a time when large ceremonial centers first appeared on the coast. The oldest is **El Paraíso,** a U-shaped complex of square buildings surrounded by tiers of platforms. These centers reflected new religious beliefs that used smoke and water to bridge the layers of the cosmos, to establish communication with the spiritual world.

b. CHAVIN

A thousand years later, an intricate religious iconography born at **Chavín de Huantar** in the Andes foothills of central Peru spread widely

over the coast and highlands. Chavin itself was a revered shrine and trading center. The terraced temple was a honeycomb of narrow passages and rooms that led to a central chamber with a carving of a jaguarlike human. Chavin art is dominated by animal and human forms. Jaguar motifs predominate; humans, gods, and animals have jaguarlike fangs or limbs. Snakes flow from the bodies of many figures. The art reflects new religious beliefs and shamanistic practices that were to underpin centuries of Andean civilization.

c. MOCHE

In later centuries, the Andean region witnessed an extraordinary array of state-organized societies with great diversity of culture, art, organization, and religious beliefs. By 200 B.C.E., the Moche state had emerged in northern coastal Peru, flourishing for 800 years. The Moche were maize farmers and fisherfolk, skilled artisans and priests, who traded cotton textiles and other goods with the highlands. They were ruled by militaristic warrior-priests, part of a small, wealthy elite. The undisturbed Moche royal tombs at **Sipan** have revealed the burials of two warrior-priests, wearing golden masks, surrounded by sacrificial victims and clay pots, and wearing magnificent, finely crafted copper and gold ornaments.

The Moche were expert metalworkers, who hammered and annealed gold and copper, the first Native Americans to master metallurgy. Their rulers taxed their subjects for labor, to build and maintain vast irrigation systems and vast monumental platforms and temples.

d. TIWANAKU

The Moche state was a multivalley kingdom, which collapsed in about 600 C.E. In the southern highlands, at the other end of the Andean world, Tiwanaku rose to power after 200 C.E. Tiwanaku itself was an important copper-working and trade center near Lake Titicaca. Its enclosures and platforms housed an important shrine to the creator god and nurtured a religious ideology that spread widely before Tiwanaku collapsed in about 1200 C.E.

e. CHIMU

On the north coast, the Chimu kingdom based on the Moche Valley filled the vacuum left by collapsing Moche after 850 C.E. The Chimu capital, **Chan Chan,** at the mouth of the Chicama River, housed the adobe compounds of aristocratic rulers. Each enclosure became the burial place of its royal builder, for new rulers inherited the title, but not the material possessions, of their predecessors. Thus, it was incumbent on a new leader to acquire more land, extra subjects, and fresh wealth, by expanding the empire. The same institutions of split inheritance, of reverence for royal ancestors, were to fuel later Andean civilization. The Chimu state extended far south with each river valley linked by carefully maintained roads. But the empire was vulnerable to attack and fell to Inca invaders in the 1460s.

O. THE END OF PREHISTORY (1500 C.E. TO MODERN TIMES)

The end of prehistory varied widely from one area to the next. It ended about 5,000 years ago in the Near East, with the Olmecs of 3,000 years ago, and then with the Mayans of 2,000 years ago in Central America, and with the Chimu of 650 years ago in the Andean region. Parts of central Africa and many remote Pacific islands did not come in contact with literate societies and emerge from what is technically prehistory until the late 19th century.

Between the 15th and 19th centuries, the European age of discovery linked societies in all parts of the world in ever more intricate webs of relations, which resulted in major adjustments in human societies everywhere. Extensive contacts with Europeans brought catastrophic culture changes. Infectious diseases such as smallpox and influenza killed off millions of native Americans who had no resistance to Old World viruses. European colonists with their firearms and sophisticated technology took over tribal lands and pushed back indigenous peoples into marginal areas on all continents. The process of contact and colonization continues in remote areas of the Amazon basin and highland New Guinea, where rain forests are felled and age-old lifeways evaporate in the face of exploitative industrial civilization. Despite these centuries of sustained contact and disruption, much survives of indigenous culture, religious beliefs, and values, often blended with new elements introduced from outside. Humankind is as biologically and culturally diverse as it has always been.

II. ANCIENT AND CLASSICAL PERIODS, 3500 B.C.E.–500 C.E.

A. GLOBAL AND COMPARATIVE DIMENSIONS

1. ORIGINS OF CIVILIZATIONS, 4000–2000 B.C.E.

In a few areas, **Neolithic** settlements grew in size and complexity, acquiring social organization commonly called **civilization.** This life is characterized by (1) large concentrations of people, usually cities, in central areas (even though the majority of settlements remained rural); (2) hierarchical social and political structures, usually with states and priesthoods; (3) economic specialization and organized societal division of labor; and (4) formal methods of permanent record keeping using some form of writing.

a. EMERGENCE OF FIRST CIVILIZATIONS

The first known civilizations developed in three river valley systems in Eurasia: (1) **the Tigris-Euphrates Valley** (Mesopotamia); (2) **the Nile Valley** (Egypt); and (3) **the Indus Valley.** Changing environmental conditions, population pressures, and the evolution of available technologies are possible reasons for the emergence of civilized societies. Each society experienced a long transition during which techniques of maintaining large-scale societies were developed. Remains of **temples** and palaces reflect the emergence of priestly and political managerial classes. These societies utilized technologies of **irrigation** to manage water resources and skills in metallurgy made new materials like **bronze** available.

The earliest civilization was in the region of **SUMER** in southern Mesopotamia. By 3000 B.C.E., the first cities controlled relatively large areas and built great temple structures called **ziggurats.** In **EGYPT,** the **protodynastic** unification of the northern and southern regions occurred by about 3000 B.C.E. **INDUS VALLEY** civilization began somewhat later, but by 2500 B.C.E., the two great cities of **Harappa** and **Mohenjo-Daro** were well established.

b. LATER PRIMARY CIVILIZATIONS

In other regions, civilized societies developed independently but later than the early river valley civilizations. The origins of **CHINESE CIVILIZATION** are in the agricultural societies in the northern Chinese **YELLOW RIVER VALLEY.** The **loess soil** of the region provided a fertile basis for agriculture using labor-intensive methods of garden cultivation. Irrigation was not a major element, but flood control was a significant activity. Civilized life developed out of expanding Neolithic villages around 2500–2000 B.C.E. Chinese tradition describes this time as an era of rule by five Heavenly Emperors who were succeeded by the human rulers of the **Xia dynasty** (p. 46). Scholars assume that some formal state existed by 2000 B.C.E., but little direct evidence of the Xia exists. The **Shang dynasty,** which controlled northern China by the 1500s B.C.E., is the first for which clear archeological evidence exists. Its capital, **Anyang,** was a major city by 1300 B.C.E.

MESOAMERICAN CIVILIZATIONS in the areas of modern Mexico and Guatemala and **ANDEAN CIVILIZATIONS** started in complex agricultural communities that developed possibly as early as 2500 B.C.E. Distinctive crops, especially corn, and, in the Andes, potatoes, along with the absence of major domesticated draft animals made the emerging civilizations quite different in character from those in the Eastern Hemisphere. The **OLMECS** created the first major Mesoam-erican urban society by c. 1200 B.C.E., with large stone structures and statues and ceremonial centers with some urban functions (p. 19). Olmec civilization disappears from the historical record by 400 B.C.E. but its heritage may have influenced the **MAYA CIVILIZATION** which flourished from c. 200–800 C.E., followed by a long decline (p. 19).

In the Andes region in Peru, the **Chavin** developed a powerful urban-based state by c. 1000 B.C.E. which flourished until c. 200 C.E. This was followed by division of the region into smaller states that were not brought together again until the **Inca Empire** in the 15th century C.E.

c. EARLY, COMPLEX NONURBAN SOCIETIES

The development of agricultural productivity and complexity did not inevitably lead to the emergence of civilizations. In many areas, complex, hierarchically organized societies developed that did not create cities or develop formal writing systems. They are not formally identifiable as civilizations but are more developed than the simple Neolithic agricultural settlements. In Southeast Asia, in the **Khorat Plateau** region of modern Thailand, archeological evidence from **Ban Chiang** and **Non Nok Tha** shows that by c. 2000 B.C.E. villagers were producing sophisticated ceramics and cast bronze tools, as well as developing techniques of rice paddy cultivation, which may have influenced the later evolution of agriculture in Chinese civilization.

In continental North America, large **mound builder societies** began by c. 1500 B.C.E. in the lower Mississippi Valley (p. 18). The great ceremonial center and cluster of villages at **Poverty Point,** in Louisiana, may have contained more than 5000 inhabitants by 1000 B.C.E.

d. COMPARISONS

Civilized societies show many similarities and differences.

Civilizations and river valleys. Origins of civilization were frequently identified with river valleys in early modern historical scholarship. Some scholars felt that irrigation was the necessary catalyst for creating a hierarchical society of dominant managers. While this may have been true for the cases of the three earliest civilizations, further study of early **Chinese civilization** shows that irrigation-based agriculture did not play a major role in developing hierarchical institutions, and the absence of major river valleys in **Mesoamerica** and the region of the **Andes civilization** brought an end to the old "river valley theory" of the origins of civilization.

Cities took different forms in ancient societies but were distinguished from the agricultural village. Cities were generally significantly larger and contained a cosmopolitan population consisting of more than a cluster of kinship-defined clans. The city had a clearly defined nucleus of settlement, often marked with a wall, that separated it from its related agricultural hinterland. It had institutions that are identified with the city as a unit, and these municipal institutions in ancient cities included temples and grand monuments, palaces, markets, and the defense structures like walls. Cities in **Sumer** and the **Indus Valley** most completely fit this definition, while the large population centers in ancient **Egypt** were more palace-temple complexes and had structures that were less clearly municipal. In **China,** there is no evidence of true cities until the **Shang dynasty** (p. 46), but the Shang capital, Anyang, was a major city of the ancient world. In early **Mesoamerican** and **Andean civilizations,** the major population centers were similar to those in Egypt, being more ceremonial centers of power than true urban areas. At the extreme, clusters of villages around ceremonial monuments distinguished the early **mound builder societies** and showed their character as complex, nonurban societies.

Agriculture provided another area of diversity among the early civilizations, with each being associated with a distinctive cluster of products and methods. **Sumer, Egypt,** and the **Indus Valley** society were similar in terms of the basic crops grown, which were standard grains like wheat and barley, and the field method of cultivation using plows.

Irrigation in Sumer and the Indus Valley required utilization of canals and levees to control and distribute river waters that could otherwise cause significant damage. In Egypt, **basin irrigation** simply channeled water into fields because Nile floods were less violent and in cycle with the growing season. In **China,** the primary early crop was millet, with rice being introduced later. The basic method for garden cultivation did not include the use of a plow or draft animals and gave a distinctive tone to Chinese society. In the Western Hemisphere, the lack of available draft animals and cattle for domestication gave increased importance to distinctive crops like corn and potatoes. In Mesoamerica, water control involved creating fields from swamps by building raised plots or **chiampas,** and in the larger areas, older methods of slash-and-burn agriculture were continued.

2. THE GROWTH OF CIVILIZATIONS, 2000–300 B.C.E.

Periodization of world history, after the formative period of agricultural civilizations, focuses mainly on the **integration of larger regional units,** based in turn on **commercial, cultural, and political interactions.** The stages of integration in the Eastern Hemisphere mark the main periods of ancient history from 2000 B.C.E. onward, culminating in the great classical empires. Subsidiary themes in periodization involve the main civilizations spreading influence and the major centers making commercial and cultural contacts from China to the Mediterranean.

a. THE CREATION OF REGIONALLY UNIFIED SOCIETIES

The civilizations in the Eastern Hemisphere interacted with their surrounding societies through **trade, conquest,** and **migrations of peoples.** Civilizations grew from smaller temple- or city-states into regional empires. Egypt (p. 29) was unified by 3100 B.C.E. by the conquests of **Narmer,** and the state remained concentrated in the Nile Valley during the **Old Kingdom** (to 2200 B.C.E.) and **Middle Kingdom** (c. 2100–1800 B.C.E.). In the **New Kingdom** (c. 1570–1050 B.C.E.), however, Egyptian rulers expanded into Southwest Asia, as well as farther south into East Africa. In **Mesopotamia** around 2350 B.C.E., **Sargon I of Akkad** conquered the city-states of the Tigris-Euphrates Valley, creating a unified regional empire (p. 26). His empire was short-lived but others followed, maintaining broader regional unity under increasingly large and better organized empires. In the **Indus Valley** (p. 41), the political structure is not clear from the surviving evidence, but the similarities of the great cities of **Harappa** and **Mohenjo-daro** indicate significant cultural uniformity if not political unity. However, this regional society declined and collapsed as a result of natural changes and disasters and nomadic invasions in 1600–1200 B.C.E. The regional civilization was replaced by a society dominated by **ARYAN** herding peoples. They established a society with regional cultural unity under temples and a priestly **Brahman** class by c. 800 B.C.E. but did not achieve political unity. **SHANG** rulers established a regional empire in northern China (c. 1800–1122 B.C.E.), and expansion into southern China continued under the early (western) **Zhou** dynasty (1122–c. 770 B.C.E.). Trade and movements of peoples also expanded the civilized lifestyle into new areas. The **MINOAN CIVILIZATION** (p. 57) emerged on the island of Crete by c. 3000 B.C.E. as a result of contacts with Egypt and Mesopotamia. Its capital, **Knossos,** became the capital of a sea-based trade empire which brought civilization to the mainland of Greece and elsewhere in the Mediterranean.

b. CIVILIZATIONS AND NONURBAN SOCIETIES

Commercial and military contacts with surrounding peoples resulted in the formation of distinctive societies. "Barbarians" often successfully invaded civilized states, and this interaction was part of the expansion of civilization into new regions.

1700–1300 B.C.E. War Chariot invasions. The development of the two-wheeled war chariot among "barbarians" around 1700 B.C.E. resulted in conquests of major civilized societies. **HYKSOS** charioteers conquered Egypt (p. 30) and ruled it from 1730–1570 B.C.E. **Kassite** (p. 27) charioteer invaders successfully invaded Mesopotamia around

1700 B.C.E. and formed the first of a series of **charioteer empires** there. In China, the **Shang dynasty** used war chariots as they established control. The **Aryan** invaders of India were also charioteers. The end of the Minoan civilization around 1400 B.C.E. opened the way for the chariot warriors of **Mycenae,** on the Greek mainland, to emerge as the dominant force in that region.

c. 1000 B.C.E. New migrations and conquests. Charioteer dominance was broken by new peoples with new technologies in many areas. In the Middle East, often in association with the development of **iron tools and weapons,** new peoples conquered much of the region. **Hittites** in Anatolia and groups like the **Philistines** in the eastern Mediterranean coastal areas established powerful states, while old centers of civilization in Egypt and Mesopotamia experienced repeated invasions. The climax came with the establishment by 665 B.C.E. of the new **ASSYRIAN EMPIRE** (p. 28). Many of these groups were **INDO-EUROPEAN,** coming from central Eurasia and migrating into Europe and South Asia as well as the Middle East. These included the **Aryans** in India and the **Dorians** in Greece. The **Zhou** conquerors of China in the 11th century B.C.E. came from Central Asia, and may have been forced out by Indo-European migrations.

c. THE AXIAL PERIOD

Increasing interregional trade, development of political institutions capable of ruling large areas, and emergence of new world-views transformed the ancient civilized societies of the Eastern Hemisphere. The result was the existence by 300 B.C.E. of distinctive regional civilizations in China, South Asia, the Middle East, and the Mediterranean basin.

The transformation of ancient societies was accompanied by important redefinitions of world-views in the civilized regions. Thinkers created the "axes" around which philosophical and religious thought revolved for the next two thousand years.

Ethical monotheism in the **Middle East** was developed especially by **ZARATHUSTRA** or **Zoroaster** in eastern Persia, probably about 600 B.C.E. but possibly earlier; Zoroastrianism (p. 39) spread in the **Persian Empire** starting in the 6th century B.C.E. Ethical monotheism also arose among the **HEBREW PROPHETS** in **Palestine** (p. 34), starting in the 8th century B.C.E. and spreading as Jewish people migrated in later classical empires.

HINDU traditions of belief and social organization developed in the emerging Aryan society of India, with the early sacred hymns or **Vedas** and the **Brahman** priesthood providing the foundations by 700–500 B.C.E. The composition in the 8th to the 4th centuries B.C.E. of the **Upanishads** (p. 42) provided systematic interpretation of the Vedas and are the foundation for much of later Indian philosophical thought.

BUDDHISM (p. 42) developed in India in these same centuries, beginning with the teaching career of **GAUTAMA SIDDHARTHA, the BUDDHA** (c. 542–483 B.C.E.), as a rejection of Brahman dominance and the caste system. The development of Hinduism and Buddhism created the distinctive world-views of Indian civilization by the end of the Axial era.

CONFUCIUS (p. 48) lived during the 6th century B.C.E. in China, in a time of great political instability as the **Zhou dynasty's** control disintegrated. His teachings provided a philosophical base for social loyalty and obedience. At this same time, other world-view alternatives were defined. Among them were **DAOISM** (p. 48), which is usually traced to the legendary teacher **Laozi** who lived around 600 B.C.E., the egalitarian teachings of **Mo-Zi** (c. 471–391 B.C.E.), and the authoritarian **LEGALISM**, most fully articulated by the later **Han Fei** (d. 233 B.C.E.).

GREEK PHILOSOPHY represents the intellectual culmination of the transformations in the eastern Mediterranean societies of the Mycenaeans and Dorians. **Socrates** (469–399 B.C.E.), **Plato** (427–327 B.C.E.), and **Aristotle** (384–322 B.C.E.) provided the basis for the main traditions of Greek philosophy emerging from the Axial age (p. 63).

3. CLASSICAL CIVILIZATIONS, 300 B.C.E.–500 C.E.

300 B.C.E.–200 C.E. THE ECUMENE, a continuous belt of urban societies and networks of trade and ideas, emerged in the Eastern Hemisphere. Important features of this ecumene were the great empires, which provided large, secure areas for trade and the wealth and power necessary for basic economic development and political stability.

300 B.C.E.–500 C.E. GREAT CLASSICAL EMPIRES. Regional civilizations in the Eastern Hemisphere were politically unified by major imperial systems in the classical era. Commercial and technological developments had made such large political systems feasible, while shared cultures both facilitated and benefited from the empires. These empires provided a foundation in most regions for a sense of civilizational identity.

a. THE MIDDLE EAST

The Middle East was the first region to be brought under the control of a single empire, and a long imperial tradition of regional control was established.

935–612 B.C.E. ASSYRIAN EMPIRE gained control of both Mesopotamia and Egypt by 665 B.C.E.

550–330 B.C.E. PERSIAN EMPIRE, established by **Cyrus the Great** (556–530 B.C.E.), reestablished full regional control after the end of the Assyrian Empire. The empire was defeated by **Alexander the Great** (356–323 B.C.E.), whose conquests laid the foundations for a number of imperial states in Greece, the Middle East, and central Asia.

330–30 B.C.E. ALEXANDER'S SUCCESSOR STATES. The **Seleucid** successors to Alexander's generals controlled most of the Middle East, except for Egypt from 305–64 B.C.E. Egypt was ruled by the descendants of Alexander's general, **PTOLEMY** (367–283 B.C.E.), until the Roman victory in 30 B.C.E.

312 B.C.E.–651 C.E. PERSIAN EMPIRES.

312 B.C.E.–226 C.E. Parthian Empire (p. 74) was established in the eastern regions of the Middle East after the death of Alexander the Great; it expanded until it controlled most of the region except for Egypt and the Mediterranean coastal societies, which by the end of the 1st century B.C.E. had come under Roman control.

226–651 C.E. Sassanid Empire (p. 100) replaced the declining Parthian state and reestablished effective regional control until falling to the **Muslim** conquests in the 7th century.

b. THE MEDITERRANEAN BASIN

Imperial unification of the Mediterranean basin came gradually and was associated with a single imperial system.

The **ROMAN EMPIRE** (p. 78) began as a republican city-state in Italy around 500 B.C.E. By the end of the 2nd century B.C.E. it had gained control of all of Italy, Greece, and the Iberian Peninsula. By the 1st century C.E. it controlled all of the Mediterranean basin and much of western Europe. This unity lasted until the fall of Rome to nomadic invaders in the fifth century, although this invasion had been preceded by a long period of loss of control in many areas and a formal division of the Empire into eastern and western sections. The tradition of Roman unity provided a strong sense of identity to western civilization but also contributed to ideas of empire in eastern Europe.

c. CHINESE IMPERIAL UNITY

In 221 B.C.E., **Shi Huangdi** of the **QIN** dynasty conquered all of the rival states that had emerged in the later **Zhou Empire.** Qin control did not survive Shi Huangdi's death, but imperial unification was reestablished in 202 B.C.E. by the **HAN dynasty.** By the time the Han

Empire disintegrated in the 3rd century C.E., a clear sense of Chinese unity had been established, and it survived nearly four centuries of division until the reunification of China under the **SUI dynasty** in 589 C.E.

d. INDIAN EMPIRES

Hinduism (p. 24) provided a strong basis for the social order in India that was less identified with imperial political structures than in the other regional civilizations. Temple organizations and the **caste system** were effective alternatives to the control of kings. However, India did experience major imperial unifications (p. 42).

322–184 B.C.E. MAURYAN EMPIRE. The defeat of local states by Alexander in 327–324 B.C.E. opened the way for unification of northern India by imperial conquest.

322–298 B.C.E. CHANDRAGUPTA MAURYA conquered much of northern India, creating the basis for the Mauryan Empire.

268–232 B.C.E. REIGN OF ASHOKA, Chandragupta's grandson, represented the high point of Mauryan power and a time of official support for Buddhism. After Ashoka's death, dynastic rivalries, civil unrest, and a revival of Hinduism led to five centuries of political disunity.

78–180 C.E. KUSHAN EMPIRE was the strongest state in the era of instability. Based in central Asia and modern Afghanistan, it controlled northern India under **Kanishka** (r. 78–96 C.E.), who aided the expansion of **Buddhism** in central Asia.

320–535 C.E. GUPTA EMPIRE (p. 43) revived Indian imperial unity. Gupta rulers gave support to Brahmans and Hinduism. The empire disintegrated in the face of invasions from central Asia, especially in 500–535 C.E.

e. EXPANSION OF THE ECUMENE

The zone of urban societies, trade networks, and large states expanded beyond the core regions of the major civilizations in the classical era. Some of this was the result of imperial conquests, but more was the result of expanding trade networks and the growing communities based on the great religions of the Axial era.

1. AFRICA

1000–591 B.C.E. KUSH. New Kingdom Egyptian expansion south in the Nile Valley created the Nubian state of Kush. Kush became independent around 950 B.C.E. and then conquered Egypt where Kushites ruled as the **25th Dynasty** (751–656 B.C.E.). After the Assyrian conquest of Egypt, the Kushite Empire continued in Nubia, developing a distinctive culture and urban society with its capital in **Napata.**

591 B.C.E.–350 C.E. MEROË (p. 32), the successor to Napata, was the center of a state which engaged actively in trade with the Mediterranean world and was a major producer of iron implements in a developing trade in Africa.

1ST TO 6TH CENTURIES C.E. KINGDOM OF AXUM (p. 32) developed in the Ethiopian highlands. Trade with India and Mediterranean areas and Greek and Arabian cultural influences created a prosperous state which conquered Meroë. The conversion of the king to Christianity around 350 C.E. laid the basis for the long-lasting Ethiopian Christian culture.

2. CENTRAL EURASIA

Central Eurasia witnessed the development of strong herding societies all along the northern regions of the ecumene. The migrations of these peoples and their invasions of the urban societies are a major theme in the history of classical civilizations.

5TH CENTURY B.C.E.–5TH CENTURY C.E. XIONGNU AND HUNS developed as strong herding societies in the central Asian borderlands of China. **Maodun** (ruled 209–174 B.C.E.) created a large confederation which threatened the Han dynasty and opened central Eurasia to increasing commercial and military interactions. The confederation disintegrated by the 1st century C.E., but the **HUN** descendants of the Xiongnu affected all the civilizations of the ecumene. In the 5th century C.E. they gained control of much of eastern Europe under the leadership of **ATTILA** (d. 453), and Hun invaders were a major cause of the collapse of the Gupta Empire in India.

3. THE SILK ROADS

The movements of herding peoples were part of the creation of a whole belt of societies stretching from northern China to central Europe, through which peoples, goods, and ideas could move. Because **SILK** was an important product in these trade networks, the whole system of economic interchange has become known as "the **SILK ROADS.**" The stability provided by the great empires and growing demand for goods helped to create an economic network in which textiles, precious stones, glass, horses, and other products passed from one side of the Eastern Hemisphere to the other on a regular basis.

4. THE SPREAD OF RELIGIONS, 300 B.C.E.–500 C.E.

Many of the world-views that emerged during the Axial period spread across the boundaries of civilizations, creating new communities with shared ideals. These new-style communities combined urban and herding societies and spread throughout the Eastern Hemisphere, providing new bases for interregional relations.

a. THE SPREAD OF HELLENISM

Hellenism's spread outward from the Greek city-states received a major impetus from the conquests of **Alexander the Great** (p. 69) late in the 4th century B.C.E. From the Mediterranean basin to northern India, Alexander's forces aided the spread of Hellenistic ideas, urban structures, and political concepts. For three centuries, the successor states to Alexander's empire developed Hellenistic institutions and ideas in the Middle East, making them an important part of the general cultural framework in that region. In northern India and central Asia, Greek themes blended with local traditions creating distinctive cultural syntheses. This blend, which was reflected in art and sculpture, reached a high point in the Buddhist sculpture of **Gandhara** in the 1st century C.E. Hellenistic artistic influence has been traced as far east as China.

509–44 B.C.E. The **ROMAN REPUBLIC** emerged as the dominant force in the Mediterranean basin. Roman culture was strongly influenced by Hellenism, especially after the Roman conquest of Greece in the 2nd century B.C.E. In general terms, the Roman Empire was a distinctive but clearly Hellenistic society by the 1st century B.C.E. Hellenism provided at least some important artistic and cultural themes for societies all across the Eastern Hemisphere.

b. BUDDHISM

Buddhism (p. 45) spread both north and south from India. Official support from the Mauryan ruler **Ashoka** in the 3rd century B.C.E. and the active sending of missionaries encouraged the spread of Buddhism.

200 B.C.E.–500 C.E. THERAVADA BUDDHISM was the early Buddhist form, and it spread to southern India, Sri Lanka, and ultimately to the mainland territories and islands of Southeast Asia.

1ST CENTURY C.E. MAHAYANA BUDDHISM developed as a distinctive form of the faith in central Eurasia and later China (p. 52). Buddhist merchants and teachers interacted with Greeks and Persians in central Asia and the Middle East, and Buddhism spread through diaspora communities of merchants in many regions along the **Silk Roads.** It was brought to China by the 1st century C.E., gradually winning converts and becoming very powerful following the collapse of the Han

dynasty. By 500 C.E., Buddhism was an important force throughout more than half of the Eastern Hemisphere.

c. HINDUISM

Hinduism successfully transformed itself in the face of social change in India and competition from other world-views, especially Buddhism. By 500 C.E. Hinduism was the dominant world-view in India (p. 42). Although it was not formally a missionary religion, its concepts and rituals spread with Indian merchants into Southeast Asia where by 500 C.E. it became an important part of the world-views of royal courts in Cambodia, Java, and elsewhere in the region (p. 46).

d. THE EXPANSION OF CHRISTIANITY

Christianity began in the eastern Mediterranean at the heart of the Hellenistic world among Jewish communities and in the context of the **Roman Empire.** It spread throughout the Mediterranean basin and in Roman western Europe, competing with a variety of other popular religions. As Christianity spread, it took a number of distinctive forms.

312–395 C.E. ROMAN WESTERN CHRISTIANITY received official toleration and support from emperors, leading to the Roman Empire becoming formally Christian. The Western Church was centered in **Rome** where the Bishop of Rome as **Pope** claimed authority over all Christians. The Roman-led Church expanded into western Europe and became the dominant world-view in the whole region by the 7th to 8th centuries.

330–451 C.E. EASTERN ORTHODOX CHRISTIANITY developed in the older cities in the eastern Mediterranean and had its center in Constantinople, proclaimed the capital of the **Eastern Roman Empire** in 330 C.E. The Eastern Church did not accept the primacy of the Bishop of Rome and developed doctrinally distinctive positions. It was the official church of the Byzantine Empire and spread through missionary activity into the Middle East and the Balkans. By the 6th century C.E. the Eastern Church was the dominant church in those regions.

451 C.E. NESTORIAN CHURCH emerged as the independent tradition after the **Council of Chalcedon.** This was part of the development of distinctive Christian church traditions in Egypt and Ethiopia in Africa, in the territories of the Sassanid Empire, and eventually in central Eurasia.

200 C.E.–500 C.E. THE CLASSICAL ECUMENE developed as an interacting set of empires, religious communities, trade networks, and migrating peoples. Although imperial systems collapsed in many areas by 500 C.E., the broader ecumene continued to expand.

B. KINGDOMS OF WESTERN ASIA AND AFRICA, TO 323 B.C.E.

1. PERIODIZATION

The early civilizations of western Asia and northeast Africa took shape in the 4th millennium B.C.E. Two major centers arose in Mesopotamia and Egypt, each with quite different characteristics but recurrent contacts in war, trade, and culture. Mesopotamian history was marked by recurrent invasions plus the formation of new empires and smaller kingdoms; societies in contact with this civilization center fanned out in North Africa (Carthage) and Asia Minor. The long period in the histories of both western Asia and Egypt extends from the formation of civilizations to the conquests first of the **Persians,** then of **Alexander the Great.**

2. MESOPOTAMIA, c. 3500–539 B.C.E.

a. GEOGRAPHY

Mesopotamia lay between and around the Euphrates and Tigris Rivers. The region reaches from the **Taurus Mountains** to the Persian Gulf and from the Syrian Desert to the **Zagros Mountains** and splits into Upper and Lower Mesopotamia at the point where the rivers come closest together, near ancient Babylon and modern Baghdad. **Upper Mesopotamia** is a large piedmont zone flanked by semiarid highlands. In the west, the **Balikh** and the **Khabur** flow south to the Euphrates, and in the east, the **Great Zab** and the **Little Zab** flow west from the Zagros into the Tigris. **Lower Mesopotamia** is an alluvial plain, and the Tigris and Euphrates form frequent lakes and marshes. The ancient shoreline of the **Persian Gulf** probably lay farther north than at present.

b. ECONOMY, TECHNOLOGY, SOCIETY, AND CULTURE

The **staple crops** in Mesopotamia were wheat and barley, along with the date palm. Drainage canals and irrigation works made the interior plain of Lower Mesopotamia **highly productive,** but irrigation led to **salinization** of the soil and decreased arable land. In Upper Mesopotamia the rivers flow through deep valleys, and irrigation of the interior was not possible. Agriculture was confined to the river valleys, and the interior was used primarily for **pastoralism** (p. 13). The region had few natural resources, except **bitumen,** but finished goods, such as textiles and metalwork, were exported. Originally, economic activity centered around **temples,** but eventually, kings and private individuals engaged in large-scale agriculture and trade.

Technological advances in Mesopotamia during the early civilization period (by 3000–2500 B.C.E.) included the **use of bronze** for tools and weapons. Copper had been introduced earlier, but mixing it with tin for bronze created much stronger equipment; bronze use also prompted wider trade relations to gain access to metal ores. The **introduction of plows** increased crop yields. The **wheel** was probably imported by migrants from central Asia like the early Hurrians (p. 27). The **potter's wheel,** invented by 6000 B.C.E., was further improved, an early sign of craft specialization.

Architecture was sophisticated, but since most building was done in **mud-brick,** examples have not survived as well as stone counterparts in Egypt and Greece. Immense **ziggurats** (stepped temple platforms) and large palaces were built, and even private houses had drainage systems. **Writing** first developed in Mesopotamia. Its origins lay in clay **tokens,** used to count cattle as early as the 8th millennium. True writing (as opposed to pictographs) appeared around 3500 B.C.E. Writing was done on clay with sharp reeds, producing the wedgelike **cuneiform** script. Originally used to write Sumerian, cuneiform was later adapted to Akkadian, Elamite, Hittite, Hurrian, Eblaite, Ugaritic (Canaanite), and Old Persian. Many Sumerian and Akkadian myths survive, the best known being the **Gilgamesh Epic,** describing the legendary exploits of a king of Uruk, fragments of which go back to the early second millennium. The **King Lists** provide important historical material, running, with some gaps, from around 2700 down to the 1st century B.C.E. Economic and legal texts, letters, and scholarly works such as dictionaries, grammar books, and mathematical texts also survive. Mathematical texts contain tables of cube roots, exponential functions, and **Pythagorean numbers.** The Sumerians and Akkadians normally used a **sexagesimal** numbering system, the basis of our division of the hour and minute into 60 units.

Mesopotamian society was organized around **city-states.** In early Sumerian times, a priest-king *(en)* ruled as a representative of the city's god, assisted by an assembly of citizens or elders. Later, as multicity states formed, a king (Sumerian *lugal,* Akkadian *sharrum*) reigned, and each individual city was administered by a governor *(ensi* or *ishiakkum).* Sumerian and Akkadian religion eventually formed a **common pantheon,** and most gods had both a Sumerian and an Akkadian name. **An** (Akkadian **Anu**) was the first king of the gods, later replaced by the Lord of the Air, **Enlil,** and ultimately by **Marduk,** the city god of Babylon. Other major gods were **Enki (Ea),** god of wisdom; **Ninmah,** mother of all life; **Nanna (Sin)** the moon; **Utu (Shamash)** the sun; **Inanna (Ishtar)** the star Venus; her husband, the shepherd god **Dumuzi (Tammuz);** and **Ninurta (Adad),** the god of war. During the five-day New Year's festival (Sumerian *zagmuk,* Akkadian *akitu*), a **sacred marriage** was performed between Enlil (later Marduk), in the person of the king, and a priestess representing Inanna/Ishtar, ensuring fertility and the return of spring.

c. THE SUMERIANS AND THE AKKADIANS

c. 3500–2900. THE PROTOLITERATE PERIOD.

c. 3500–3100. THE URUK CULTURE. It is uncertain whether the **Sumerians** were native to Mesopotamia or if they migrated into the region from the east or south sometime after 4000 B.C.E. In any case, **Semitic** (Akkadian) elements in the earliest texts suggest an early mixing of ethnic groups. In the **Uruk period,** the population of Sumer was probably several hundred thousand, with some settlements large enough to be called cities (over 10,000 in population). The stepped temple platform **(ziggurat)** and **cylinder seals** so characteristic of Mesopotamian culture developed. The **first known writing,** a small limestone tablet, comes from Kish and is dated to c. 3500. At Uruk several hundred clay tablets have been found, most dating to c. 3200–3100. These, like the tablet from Kish, are too primitive to be read, but appear to be **economic documents.**

c. 3100–2900. THE JEMDET NASR CULTURE (Early Bronze Age). Tablets from Jemdet Nasr sites are clearly written in **Sumerian,** and almost all are economic texts. **Bronze** was first utilized in Mesopotamia and there is evidence of **extensive overseas trade.** Mesopotamian influence appeared in predynastic Upper Egypt, the so-called **Mesopotamian Stimulation** (p. 29).

c. 2900–2370. THE EARLY DYNASTIC PERIOD.

2900–2700. EARLY DYNASTIC I. The **Sumerian King List** names eight antediluvian kings who reigned for tens of thousands of years, but it is not known if these names have any **historical basis.** The **royal tombs of Ur** contain the graves of **Meskalamdug** and **Akalamdug,** among others, which probably date to this period.

2700–2600. EARLY DYNASTIC II. According to the King Lists, the first dynasty after the Great Flood (recorded in the **Gilgamesh Epic**) was the

1st Dynasty of Kish. The last two kings, **Enmebaragesi** and his son **Agga,** are the first rulers attested in contemporary inscriptions. According to the King List, "kingship" *(namlugal)* then passed to the **1st Dynasty of Uruk,** which included **Enmerkar, Lugalbanda,** and **Gilgamesh,** heroes of epic tradition, and finally to the **1st Dynasty of Ur.** Epigraphic evidence, however, shows that these dynasties (and a dynasty at Mari) were all contemporary and date to c. 2700–2600 B.C.E. Many rulers known from contemporary inscriptions are not found in the King Lists.

2600–2370. EARLY DYNASTIC III. The King Lists record eleven more dynasties before **Sargon of Akkad,** but, except for the **3rd dynasty of Uruk,** little is known of them, and many were probably contemporaneous. The **1st Dynasty of Lagash** (Telloh) is well known from inscriptions, though not mentioned in the King List. It started with **Mesilim** (c. 2600), but it was **Eannatum** (c. 2500) who conquered much of Sumer, extending Lagash's power into Elam and Mari. **Uru-inim-gina** of Lagash (2378–2371) was the earliest known social reformer: he established **"freedom"** *(amargi),* the first recorded use of the term in a political sense. The **3rd Dynasty of Uruk** had only one king: **Lugal-zagesi** (2371–2347). Beginning his career as Governor **(ensi)** of Umma, he defeated Lagash and took the title **King of Uruk.** Lugal-zagesi claimed to rule from the Persian Gulf to the Mediterranean, though this is doubtful. Under his rule, Akkadians began to rise to high positions in government. The **population of Mesopotamia** probably reached half a million in this period.

2371–2190. THE DYNASTY OF AKKAD. Sargon the Great (Sharru-kin, 2371–2316) rose from obscure origins to become cupbearer to **Ur-zababa,** king of Kish. Rebelling, he built the city of Agade or **Akkad** (whose site has not been located) and proclaimed himself king. After defeating **Lugal-zagesi of Uruk** (c. 2347), he conquered the rest of Sumer. Sargon installed his daughter **Enheduanna** as high priestess at Ur. Enheduanna's hymns to Inanna have survived, making her history's **first known author.** Sargon went on to conquer Upper Mesopotamia, the **Amorites** (Amurru or "Westerners") in Syria, Elam, and Subartu (Assyria). Later legends fancifully describe conquests of Anatolia and Crete, but Sargon's empire certainly ranged from the Persian Gulf to the Mediterranean. Sargon's sons **Rimush** (2315–2307) and **Manishtushu** (2306–2292) faced constant revolts: both died in palace coups. **Naram-Sin** (2291–2255) brought the kingdom of Akkad to its zenith. He was the first Mesopotamian king to claim divinity, as well as the first to be called **"King of the Four Quarters"** (that is, the World). Defeating the powerful state of **Ebla** in Syria, he extended his empire to Anatolia. Under **Shar-kali-sharri** (2254–2230), **Gutian tribes** from the Zagros began raiding into Mesopotamia. Shar-kali-sharri was assassinated, and after him came a period of anarchy. An independent **4th Dynasty of Uruk** broke away and ruled parts of Lower Mesopotamia. Around 2190, Akkad fell to the Gutians.

c. 2230–2114. THE GUTIANS. The King List records 21 Gutian kings, though most of them were probably local chiefs with only limited authority. Some cities, such as **Lagash** and **Uruk,** became independent, though their rulers retained the title of governor *(ensi).* **Gudea** of Lagash left inscriptions which contain the most important texts in **classical Sumerian.** Around 2114, **Utu-Hegal** of Uruk (2120–2114), drove the Gutians out of Sumer but died soon after.

2113–2004. 3rd DYNASTY OF UR: The Sumerian Renaissance. Ur-nammu (2113–2096) of Ur proclaimed himself king and soon conquered all of **Sumer and Akkad.** He built and renovated many public buildings, including the enormous **temple of Nanna** at Ur, best preserved of Mesopotamian ziggurats. Ur-nammu, whose stated purpose was to establish **"justice in the land,"** is best known for his law code. The reestablishment of central control led to a rise in **population:** Mesopotamia probably had about one million inhabitants at the beginning of the second millennium. **Shulgi** (2095–2048) brought the empire of Ur III to its height. He conquered Elam and Upper Mesopotamia and, like the Akkadian kings, proclaimed himself the divine **"King of the Four Quarters."** **Shu-Sin** (2038–2030) built a 150-mile-long wall between the rivers to defend against the encroaching **Amorites.** Nevertheless, in the reign of **Ibbi-Sin** (2029–2006) the Amorites invaded and established independent states in Lower Mesopotamia. In 2025, **Larsa** became autonomous under Naplanum, and in 2017 Ishbi-Erra established a dynasty at **Isin.** Eshnunna and Elam also broke away. In 2004, the Elamites attacked and destroyed Ur (p. 39).

d. THE AMORITE KINGDOMS

2004–1763. THE ISIN-LARSA PERIOD.
2017–1794. THE DYNASTY OF ISIN. Late in his reign, **Ishbi-Erra** (2017–1985), king of Isin, drove the Elamites from Ur. **Ishme-Dagan** (1953–1935) was a social reformer, and **Lipit-Ishtar** (1934–1924) left behind an important early **law code.** After nine more kings, **Damiq-ilishu** (1816–1794) ruled as the last king of Isin.
2025–1763. THE DYNASTY OF LARSA. Naplanum was king of Larsa from 2025–2005, but it was **Samium** (1976–1942) who established Larsa as a rival power to Isin. After a dynasty of ten more kings, **Rimsin** (1822–1763) brought Larsa to its largest extent, defeating Damiq-ilishu of Isin and **unifying Lower Mesopotamia.**
c. 2000–1763. Amorite and Elamite Dynasties. While not mentioned in the King List, inscriptions show an **independent dynasty at Eshnunna,** some with Elamite names. Indeed, under **Naram-Sin** (c. 1830), Eshnunna and Assyria may have been united. Other independent Amorite dynasties ruled in Kazallu, Sippar, Uruk, Kish, Marad, and, most importantly, at **Babylon.**
c. 1900–1741. OLD ASSYRIAN PERIOD.
c. 1900–1813. THE DYNASTY OF PUZUR-ASHUR. The Assyrians probably originated as a nomadic tribe. The city of **Ashur** (Qalat Sharquat) is first mentioned in the reign of Sargon of Akkad (c. 2350). Around 1950 **Puzur-Ashur I** built the city's wall, and c. 1900, an Assyrian **trading colony** *(karum)* was established at **Kanesh** in Anatolia, where tens of thousands of cuneiform tablets have been discovered. The Assyrian king **Naram-Sin** (c. 1830) may be the same as a contemporaneous king **Naram-Sin of Eshnunna,** and the two kingdoms may have united under him. In any case, Naram-Sin expanded Assyria's rule to the west. In 1813, an Amorite prince, **Shamshi-Adad,** overthrew Erishum II (c. 1814) to become king of Assyria.
1813–1741. THE DYNASTY OF SHAMSHI-ADAD. Shamshi-Adad I (1813–1781) conquered **Mari** and expanded Assyrian power to the west. His son, **Ishme-Dagan** (1780–1741), invaded Babylonia, in alliance with Elam, Eshnunna, and the Gutians but was defeated by **Hammurapi the Great.** After Ishme-Dagan's death came a series of usurpations, and Assyria declined into **400 years of obscurity.**
1830–1531. 1ST DYNASTY OF BABYLON (Old Babylonian Empire). The **1st Dynasty of Babylon** was established under **Sumu-abum** (1894–1881). By the reign of **Sin-muballit** (1812–1793) the city controlled a region running for 60 miles along the Euphrates. **Hammurapi the Great** (1792–1750) took Uruk and Isin soon after his accession to the throne. For over 20 years, he concentrated on building and irrigation projects, organized a centralized administration, and issued the famous **Law Code of Hammurapi.** In 1764, Babylon was attacked by a coalition of Elam, Assyria, the Gutians, and Eshnunna, but Hammurapi defeated the coalition, annexed Eshnunna and Elam, and **expanded the empire** to the borders of Assyria and the Zagros. The Babylonian king then took **Larsa,** made it his southern capital, and in 1759 defeated **Mari** and tore down its walls. In 1757–1755, Hammurapi defeated another **Assyrian invasion,** and when Eshnunna revolted it was destroyed. Hammurapi now controlled all of Mesopotamia, with the exception of Assyria. In this period the Amorites completely **assimilated** into Akkadian culture, adopting their language, religion, and culture. Two dialects of Akkadian were spoken, **Babylonian** in the south, and **Assyrian** in the north—Sumerian survived only in **scholarly writing. Marduk,** god of Babylon, replaced Enlil as king of the gods. The Marduk temple complex in Babylon was expanded, including the great ziggurat **E-temen-an-ki** ("House of the Foundation of Heaven and Earth"): the biblical **Tower of Babel** (Gen. 11:1–9).
1749–1595. Decline of the Babylonian Empire. In the reign of **Samsu-iluna** (1749–1712), the **Kassites** (Kassu) made their first inroads into Babylonia, and the **Sealands** (the coastal region on the Persian Gulf) broke away from the empire. Under Abieshu' (1711–1684) and Ammiditana (1683–1647), the Kassites again attacked Babylon, but were driven off. **Ammisaduqa** (1646–1626) made internal reforms, forgiving debt and freeing debt-slaves. **Samsuditana** (1625–1595) ruled for 30 years in relative peace, but in 1595 the Hittite King **Mursilis** marched

into Mesopotamia and captured and plundered Babylon (p. 37). The Hittites did not remain, but Babylonian authority was broken, allowing the **Kassite seizure of power.**

e. THE KASSITES, THE HURRIANS, AND THE ARAMEANS

c. 1700–1600. KASSITE INVASIONS. In the 17th century, the **Kassites** (*Kassu*) gradually moved into Babylonia from the northeast. After the Hittite raid on Babylon in 1595, the Kassites took the city.

1595–1150. THE KASSITE DYNASTY. Burnaburiash I (c. 1500) signed a treaty with **Puzur-Ashur III** (1521–1498) of Assyria, fixing their common boundaries. From this time, Upper Mesopotamia was known as **Assyria** and Lower Mesopotamia as **Babylonia.** Ulamburiash (c. 1450) took over the **Sealands** and **Kurigalzu I** (c. 1400), the strongest of the Kassites, conquered Elam and entered into an alliance with **Amenophis III** of Egypt (p. 30). During the reign of **Kashtiliash IV** (1242–1235), Babylonia was conquered by the Assyrians, but after seven years, its independence was recovered. In 1160, the Assyrians conquered the Lower Zab region, and the Elamites took Babylon itself, carrying off spoils, including the **Code of Hammurapi** to Susa. Enlil-nadin-ahhi (1159–1139) was the last Kassite king of Babylon.

1156–1025. 2nd DYNASTY OF ISIN. After the Kassite defeat, a new dynasty arose in Isin under **Marduk-kabit-ahheshu** (1156–1139) which eventually retook Babylon. **Nebuchadnezzar I** (Nabu-kudduri-usur, 1124–1103) even conquered Elam. **Tiglath-Pileser I** of Assyria defeated Marduk-nadin-ahhe (1098–1081) and conquered Babylonia (p. 27). By the end of the second millennium, the population of Mesopotamia was probably around 1.25 million.

c. 1700–1500. THE HURRIAN INVASION. The **Hurrians** had lived in Mesopotamia in small numbers from the late 3rd millennium, but the major Hurrian invasion of the region began around 1700. By 1500, they had penetrated into all of Mesopotamia, as well as Syria-Palestine and eastern Anatolia. There are indications that they had been influenced by **Aryans** somewhere outside the Near East. The Hurrians worshiped gods later associated with the Iranians and Indians (such as **Mithra** and **Varuna**) (p. 39)—the names of some Hurrian rulers and certain technical expressions in Hurrian texts (particularly in connection with the chariot) are **Indo-European.** The Hurrians adopted Mesopotamian religion and culture, utilizing Babylonian as an administrative language and cuneiform script to write the Hurrian language. Despite the large number of surviving texts, the Hurrian language remains undeciphered.

c. 1550–1250. THE KINGDOM OF MITANNI. Sudarna I (c. 1550) created the Hurrian **Kingdom of Mitanni** with its capital at **Washukanni** on the Khabur River. **Saustatar** (c. 1500) expanded the kingdom, and eventually, the kings of Mitanni ruled all of Upper Mesopotamia and much of Syria, from the Orontes to the Little Zab. In 1475, **Tuthmosis III** conquered Syria and pillaged Mitanni, but Egyptian control did not extend east of the Euphrates (p. 30). Both **Artadama I** (c. 1450) and **Sudarna II** (c. 1400) made marriage alliances with the Egyptians. After Sudarna's death, a civil war broke out between his two sons, **Tushratta** (c. 1390–1370) and **Artadama II**, and was continued by their sons **Matiwaza** and **Sudarna III.** This infighting, and the **plundering of Washukanni** by the Hittites (p. 37), led to the kingdom's decline. Finally, Ashur-uballit I of Assyria attacked Mitanni and pillaged it. Shalmeneser I defeated the last Hurrian king, **Shattuara II**, and the Hurrians were absorbed into the Assyrian Empire around 1270.

1365–1078. THE MIDDLE ASSYRIAN EMPIRE. Ashur-uballit I (1365–1330) expanded the Assyrian domain to the north and west and corresponded with **Amenophis IV** (Akhenaten) of Egypt as an equal (p. 30). **Adad-Nirari I** (1307–1275) defeated the Babylonians and conquered the Hurrian city-states. **Shalmaneser I** (1275–1245) continued his predecessors' energetic campaigns of conquest, fighting in the far north against Urartu and again crushing the Hurrians, annexing their lands. He conquered the lands up to Carchemish, but an **Egyptian-Hittite** treaty signed in 1283, which divided Syria between them, frustrated the Assyrians' westward movement. **Tukulti-Ninurta I** (1244–1208), the biblical **Nimrod** (Gen. 10:8–12), conquered Babylon, but only held it for seven years. Tukulti-Ninurta also promulgated the **Middle Assyrian law-code**, a continuation of the Sumerian and Baby-

lonian legal tradition and built a new capital, **Kar-Tukulti-Ninurta** (Tulul el-Aqir), across the Tigris from Ashur. Tukulti-Ninurta was murdered by his son in a palace coup, and Assyria entered into an 85-year **period of weakness.** When the invasion of the Sea Peoples around 1200 destroyed the Hittite Empire and pushed the Egyptians out of Asia, and created a power vacuum in the region, **Tiglath-Pileser I** (Tukulti-apal-eser, 1115–1077) quickly took advantage of the situation. In a series of campaigns, he conquered **a large empire** from the Zagros to the Mediterranean, and from Babylon north to Urartu. Tiglath-Pileser initiated the policy of ruthless warfare, mass executions, and the deportation of civilian populations, which became characteristic of Assyrian conquest.

1078–977. THE ARAMEAN INVASIONS. In the 11th century, Aramean tribes from the Syrian desert, including the **Chaldeans** (Kaldu), invaded Mesopotamia. The Assyrians were driven back into Assyria proper, and Babylonia was overrun and broken up into **small tribal states.** The coastal region retained its independence from 1024–1004 under the **2nd Scaland Dynasty,** but subsequently this area was conquered by the Chaldeans, who ruled southernmost Babylonia.

f. THE NEO-ASSYRIANS AND THE NEO-BABYLONIANS

934–824. THE ESTABLISHMENT OF THE NEO-ASSYRIAN EMPIRE. Ashurdan II (934–912) built up a new Assyrian Empire. Further conquests were carried out by **Adad-nirari II** (911–890), **Tukulti-Ninurta II** (890–884), and **Ashur-nasir-apli II** (883–859), by which time the Assyrians again ruled from the Tigris to the Mediterranean, and from Lake Van to the borders of Babylonia. **Ashur-nasir-apli** was the chief architect of the Neo-Assyrian Empire, developing its centralized bureaucracy and building **Kalah** (Nimrud) as a capital. Its palaces and temples combined traditional Mesopotamian mud-brick architecture with monumental stone sculptures and wall-reliefs.

858–824. THE REIGN OF SHALMENESER III. Shalmeneser III began integrating conquered areas into the empire as provinces. Vassals, who could not yet be wholly subjugated, paid tribute. Shalmeneser moved west to conquer the Aramean kingdoms of Syria. Though initially stopped at the **Battle of Qarqar** (853) by a coalition of Hamath, Damascus, and Israel, in 842 Shalmeneser captured Damascus and received tribute from Tyre and from Israel (p. 34). He defeated **Kizzuwatna** (Cilicia) and **Urartu**, "washing his weapons" in Lake Van. After Shalmeneser's death, there was a civil war between two of his sons, which led to a period of **Urartian domination.**

824–745. URARTIAN DOMINATION OF ASSYRIA. Shamshi-Adad V (823–811) took the throne after defeating his brother, though parts of the empire were lost. He was succeeded by his minor son, **Adad-nirari III** (810–783). For the first four years of the child's reign, his mother **Sammuramat** (Greek **Semiramis**) ruled as regent. Adad-nirari briefly reimposed tribute on the western states, including Israel, but increasingly Assyria retreated before Urartu. Commagene and Melitene in southern Anatolia and Carchemish in Syria came under Urartian control, and Assyria became practically a **vassal of Urartu.**

745–626. THE HEIGHT OF THE NEO-ASSYRIAN EMPIRE.

744–727. THE REIGN OF TIGLATH-PILESER III. The youngest son of Adad-nirari III, **Tiglath-Pileser III** introduced the last and greatest period of the Neo-Assyrian Empire. In the years 743–738, the Urartians and their Neo-Hittite allies were defeated at the **Battle of Arpad**, as was a coalition of Aramean kings under the leadership of Judah. In 735, Tiglath-Pileser III defeated the Urartians again and annexed the region around Lake Urmia. He then subdued **Damascus** and **Israel**, annexing all of Damascus's territory and the Israelite provinces of Gilead and Galilee, all of which were made into Assyrian provinces (p. 34). In 731, a revolt broke out in Babylonia, and after crushing it, Tiglath-Pileser named himself **king of Babylon.**

726–705. SHALMENESER V AND SARGON II. Upon taking the throne, **Shalmeneser V** (726–722) was immediately faced with a new rebellion in the west. Both Tyre and Samaria, the capital of Israel, were besieged. Samaria fell late in 722 after a three-year siege (shortly before the death of Shalmeneser), but Tyre held out. When **Sargon II** (721–705) mounted the throne, another revolt broke out in Babylon under **Merodach-Baladan II**, which Sargon failed to quell initially. In 720, Sargon moved west, reconquering Hamath, Samaria, Ekron, and Gaza. **King Ahaz of Judah** paid tribute and Tyre finally capitulated after a five-year siege (p. 35). In 717–716, Sargon took and annexed **Carchemish** and defeated the Egyptians at Raphia, the farthest west the Assyrians had yet penetrated. Urartu was again crushed in 714, and in 712 the Assyrians took Ashdod and annexed Philistia. Finally, in 709, the revolt in Babylon was suppressed, and Merodach-Baladan went into exile in Elam. Sargon built a new capital, which he named **Dur-Sharrukin** (Khorsabad).

704–681. THE REIGN OF SENNACHERIB (Sin-ahhi-eriba). In 703 **Merodach-Baladan II** again seized power in Babylon, and though Sennacherib quickly put down the revolt, resistance continued for the next 13 years. Sennacherib campaigned to the north, taking tribute from the Medes, then west, defeating the Egyptians at the **Battle of Elteqeh** in 701. Next it was Judah's turn and Sennacherib besieged **Jerusalem.** But when King Hezekiah paid tribute, the Assyrians broke off the siege (p. 35). In 689, Babylon revolted again, with Elamite assistance, but was sacked and burnt to the ground. Sennacherib transformed **Nineveh,** on the east bank of the Tigris, into a city of unparalleled splendor, and it remained the Assyrian capital until the end of the empire. In the 7th century, the **population of Mesopotamia** reached a height (until modern times) of around 2 million inhabitants. Sennacherib's eldest son had died before him, so he designated his youngest son **Esarhaddon** as heir. This led to a revolt by his older sons, and the king's assassination.

680–669. THE REIGN OF ESARHADDON. With the active assistance of his mother, **Naqia** (Greek **Nitocris**), Esarhaddon put down the revolt by his brothers. He then rebuilt Babylon and made one of his sons **Shamash-shum-ukin** its king; he gave another son, **Ashurbanipal,** the title king of Assyria. While Scythian and Cimmerian tribes appeared on Assyria's northern border, Esarhaddon was preoccupied with plans to **conquer Egypt.** The first Assyrian invasion of Egypt (674–673) was unsuccessful, but Esarhaddon struck with full force in 671, routed the Pharaoh Taharka, and took Memphis (p. 31). In 669, Esarhaddon went to Egypt to prepare for an invasion of Ethiopia, but he fell sick and died.

668–627. THE REIGN OF ASHURBANIPAL. Ashurbanipal was both a great military commander and a patron of arts and letters. His palace reliefs are among the finest examples of Assyrian art, and he gathered a great library of tablets, which remains one of our main sources for knowledge of Sumero-Akkadian literature. The king boasted he could read and write the cuneiform script. Ashurbanipal attacked Egypt and, in two campaigns (667–666 and 664–663), defeated **Pharaoh Taharka** and his son **Tenuatamun** and extended Assyrian power as far south as Thebes (p. 31). In 652, Shamash-shuma-ukin tried to overthrow his brother with Elamite help, and civil war raged until 648, when Shamash-shuma-ukin finally surrendered in Babylon. **Susa** was taken and sacked in 639, but the civil wars had revealed Assyria's weakness to its enemies.

626–609. THE LAST DAYS OF ASSYRIA. The Assyrian Empire collapsed quickly. There was apparently a revolt on Ashurbanipal's death, and his son **Ashur-etil-ilani** (626) ruled only a few months. The usurper, **Sin-shum-lishar** (626), also kept the throne only a short period. At this point, the Chaldean **Nabopolassar** declared himself king of Babylon. **Sin-shar-ishkun** (626–612), another son of Ashurbanipal, took back the throne of Assyria and stabilized the internal situation. Soon, however, **Cyaxares, king of the Medes,** and the **Babylonian king, Nabopolassar,** joined forces to attack Assyria. After a protracted struggle, **Nineveh** fell in 612 and was completely destroyed. An Assyrian noble, **Ashur-uballit II** (611–609) proclaimed himself king at Harran in Syria. The Babylonians took Harran in 610, however, and an attempt by the Assyrians, now allied to the Egyptians, to retake the city failed. Ashur-uballit died in obscurity.

977–626. 8TH AND 9TH DYNASTIES OF BABYLON. After a period of political confusion, **Nabu-mukin-apli** (977–942) reestablished an 8th Dynasty of Babylon, though his rule did not extend far beyond the city itself. While unimportant politically, Babylon continued to be a cultural and intellectual center. Under **Nabonassar** (Nabu-nasir, 747–734) an important **calendar reform** was instituted in which the monthly lunar cycle was reconciled with the solar year, a standard system still used in the Jewish calendar. In 731 an Aramean dynasty came to power under **Nabu-mukin-zeri** (731–729), and the **first use of Aramaic** is attested in Babylonian documents. The Assyrians conquered Babylon in 728, but the Chaldean King **Merodach-Baladan II** (Marduk-apal-iddina) drove them out. From 710 to 626, Chaldean kings, often supported by Elam, alternated with Assyrian rulers (p. 40).

626–539. THE CHALDEAN or NEO-BABYLONIAN EMPIRE.

626–604. THE RISE OF THE NEO-BABYLONIAN EMPIRE. The **Chaldeans,** an Aramean tribe, entered Lower Mesopotamia around 1000, and became the dominant ethnic group in Babylon in Neo-Assyrian times. Babylonian gave way to **Aramaic** as a spoken tongue, though Babylonian and Sumerian both continued to be used as **scholarly languages** until Seleucid times. **Nabopolassar** (Nabu-apal-usur, 626–605), the Chaldean king of the Sealand, rebelled from the Assyrians and in 626 took the archaic title **king of Akkad.** In 612, he allied himself with Cyaxares of Media and destroyed Nineveh. Nabopolassar then marched west and defeated the remnants of the Assyrians at **Harran.** Meanwhile, the Egyptians had taken Palestine and were driving into Syria, but they were defeated by the Babylonians at the decisive **Battle of Carchemish** in 605 (p. 35).

604–562. THE REIGN OF NEBUCHADNEZZAR II. Nabopolassar's son, **Nebuchadnezzar II** (604–562) took the Babylonian throne in 604. He marched **against Egypt** in 601, but after an indecisive battle fought on the frontier, both sides withdrew. In 598–7, Nebuchadnezzar defeated Judah and placed a vassal king, **Zedekiah,** on its throne (p. 35). After he returned to Babylon to quell a revolt, Tyre and Judah rebelled, and in 588 Jerusalem suffered a second siege. **Jerusalem finally fell** in July of 586; the city and Solomon's Temple were laid waste and Judah became a Babylonian province (p. 35). **Tyre,** an island city with control of the sea, was besieged for 13 years. Nebuchadnezzar spent much of his enormous wealth on the **city of Babylon,** which became a byword for urban splendor.

561–539. THE END OF THE NEO-BABYLONIAN EMPIRE. After Nebuchadnezzar's death the Babylonian Empire quickly declined. **Evil-Merodach** (Awil-Marduk 561–560) was assassinated by his brother-in-law **Neriglissar** (Nergal-shar-usur, 559–556), who took power. In 555, a usurper, **Nabonidus** (Nabu-na'id 555–539) became king. Nabonidus worshiped **the moon-god Sin,** whom he attempted to promote over Babylon's god Marduk, alienating Marduk's powerful priesthood. Shunning the city and leaving his son **Belshazzar** (Bel-shar-usur) as regent, Nabonidus spent many years at **Teima** in north Arabia, 480 miles from Babylon (p. 40). Meanwhile, **Cyrus the Great** (p. 41) had united the Medes and Persians and defeated the Lydians (547). In 539 Cyrus marched on Babylonia and took the country almost without a struggle. Nabonidus fled and **Babylon opened its gates** to the Persians, probably with the connivance of the priests of Marduk.

539–332. MESOPOTAMIA UNDER PERSIAN RULE. Cyrus appointed a Persian **satrap,** or governor, to rule both Assyria and Babylonia, but left the native religious and political institutions intact. **Cuneiform script** continued to be used, and it is in this period that astrology developed in Babylonia and spread to the west. **Alexander the Great** defeated the Persian army under Darius III at the **Battle of Arbela** (331) in Upper Mesopotamia (p. 70). He then marched to Babylon where he was invested as **king of Babylon** at the temple of Marduk, which he restored. After a long campaign in the east, Alexander returned to Babylon, where he died of fever in 323. *(To p. 70)*

3. EGYPT, c. 3500–332 B.C.E.

a. GEOGRAPHY

EGYPT consisted of two parts: Upper (southern) and Lower (northern) Egypt. **Upper Egypt** was made up of a long and narrow strip of land, no more than 13 miles wide, on both banks of the Nile River. It stretched for 750 miles from Lake Moeris and the Fayum Depression upriver to the **First Cataract** (waterfall), the border with Nubia. The major cities of Upper Egypt were Nennusu (**Heracleopolis**), Khmun (**Hermopolis**),

Abydos, and **Thebes.** A dry riverbed, the **Wadi Hammamat,** extended overland from Upper Egypt to the Red Sea. **Lower Egypt** was the Nile Delta formed by the seven branches of the river which flowed into the Mediterranean. The Delta contained two-thirds of Egypt's arable land and was where most of the principal cities of Lower Egypt lay: **Avaris, Tanis** (later Pi-Ramses), **Sais,** and **Bubastis.** Lower Egypt did contain a small portion of the Nile itself, including the cities of On **(Heliopolis)** and **Memphis.**

b. ECONOMY, TECHNOLOGY, SOCIETY, AND CULTURE

Egypt receives virtually no rainfall, and agriculture depended on **the annual flood of the Nile,** which deposited fertile mud on the fields and provided water for irrigation. This ensured a large and fairly constant surplus of crops, though famines were not unknown. The main staple was barley, which provided both bread and beer. A wide variety of fruits and vegetables were raised, and flax was grown to produce linen, while cattle and sheep furnished meat. **Mines in the Sinai** provided copper, those in Nubia gold, and marble was quarried in the Eastern Desert. The Nile provided **easy communication,** both with the Mediterranean and along the length of the country; the Wadi Hammamat connected the country with the Red Sea. As a result, Egypt was an entrepôt for trade to and from East Africa, Arabia, the eastern Mediterranean, and western Asia.

Public architecture was in stone from an early period, but most houses were built of mud-brick. The earliest examples of Egyptian **hieroglyphic** writing, recently discovered, date to 3300–3200 B.C.E. Starting in the Middle Kingdom, a cursive form of writing was developed called **hieratic.** In the late period an even more cursive writing came into use, called **demotic,** or "popular" writing. Much of **Egyptian writing** survives carved or painted on the walls of tombs, but the dry climate has also preserved texts on **papyrus.** In addition to administrative documents and letters, considerable Egyptian literature has survived: quasi historical tales (such as the **Tale of Sinuhe**), mythological and religious works, books of prophecy and wisdom literature, mathematical and scientific texts, even pornography. Historical texts include both monumental inscriptions and king lists, such as the **Palermo Stone** and the **Turin Canon.** In addition, a continuous, though not always accurate, **king list** is provided by **Manetho,** who wrote a history of Egypt in Greek around 250 B.C.E. It was Manetho who divided the kings into "dynasties."

Egyptian government was **highly centralized** and society **strictly hierarchical:** proper order in the kingdom, expressed by the term *ma'at,* was thought to ensure national well-being. The Egyptian king was considered the link between the gods and his people. The king was identified with the god Horus (and had a **Horus name** in addition to his personal name), but when he died became the god **Osiris,** lord of the underworld. By the 5th Dynasty, the king was also considered the son of Ra, the sun god. The title *"pharaoh"* only came to refer to the Egyptian king in the New Kingdom. Although the institution of the monarchy was divine, **popular literature** often portrayed the king in an irreverent way. The king technically owned all the land in Egypt, and the palace administered the economy as well as political affairs. The **vizier,** a sort of prime minister, headed a vast bureaucracy which administered the country down to the village level. Upper and Lower Egypt each had their own governors, and the land was further subdivided into **nomes** or districts: 20 in Lower Egypt and 22 in Upper Egypt. Wealth and power were generally hereditary, though commoners could rise in the **scribal bureaucracy** and the army. **Egyptian women** had a very high degree of independence compared to other ancient societies: they could own property, make contracts, and divorce their husbands by a simple act of repudiation.

Religion was also centrally organized and headed by an **"Overseer of all the Prophets of the Gods,"** a post sometimes held by the vizier and sometimes by the High Priest of Amun. **The temples** controlled large tracts of land and were important economic centers. Each region had its own patron deity, but eventually the Egyptians placed local gods in a hierarchy and developed a common religion. Religion was closely tied to politics: when **Memphis** was the capital, its god **Ptah** was paramount; the rising importance of **Heliopolis** gave **Ra** his importance; and finally, the ascendancy of **Thebes** is reflected in the New Kingdom emphasis on **Amun.** Egyptian gods commonly had mixed human and animal form: the ibis-headed god **Thoth,** falcon-headed god **Horus,** and jackal-headed god **Anubis** are examples. Under Amenophis IV, who renamed himself **Akhenaten,** the sun disk **Aten** was worshipped as the only god, but this **solar monotheism** was abandoned soon after Akhenaten's death. The worship of **Isis,** originally the deified throne, but later a mother-goddess, became popular only in the Late Dynastic Period.

c. THE OLD KINGDOM AND THE FIRST INTERMEDIATE PERIOD (1ST–11TH DYNASTIES)

c. 3500–3100. THE GERZEAN CULTURE. Gerzean sites are found in both Lower and Upper Egypt (p. 14). Both copper and pottery were in common use, and tomb wall paintings appear for the first time. **Irrigation-based agriculture** was introduced, and this is reflected in a dramatic **growth in population:** from approximately 200,000 at the beginning of the period to over a million at its end. **Egyptian art, architecture, and hieroglyphic writing** developed in their earliest forms. These advances were influenced, to some extent, by contacts with the Sumerian culture—the **Mesopotamian Stimulation** (p. 25). At the beginning of the period, the various nomes were probably independent states, but by the end there were two kingdoms: **Lower Egypt** with a capital at **Pe** in the northwest Delta and **Upper Egypt** ruled either from **Nekhen** (Hierakonpolis) or **This** (near Abydos). At some point, **King Scorpion** of Upper Egypt conquered part of the Delta region.

c. 3100–2686. THE PROTODYNASTIC PERIOD.

c. 3100–2890. 1st Dynasty. Menes, whose Horus name was **Narmer,** was the king of Upper Egypt who conquered Lower Egypt, **united the two lands** and built the city of **Memphis,** near the border, as his capital. A **palace bureaucracy** developed, and artists and craftsmen were employed by the royal court. Other 1st Dynasty kings were **Djer, Djet, Den, Aha** (who invaded Nubia), and a queen, **Merneith.**

c. 2890–2686. 2nd Dynasty. Virtually nothing is known of this dynasty except the names of its kings, and it is unclear what divided it from the previous dynasty. **Hetep** was the first king of the 2nd Dynasty, and **Khasekhemwy** was the last. The latter was the first king to have a **stone burial chamber** in his tomb.

c. 2686–2181. THE OLD KINGDOM.

c. 2686–2613. 3rd Dynasty. What divided the 2nd and 3rd Dynasties is also unclear—the 3rd Dynasty's first king **Nebka** may have been related to the previous rulers. Inscriptions of Nebka have been found at **Byblos** in Phoenicia, indicating overseas trade (p. 36). The most famous king of this dynasty was **Djoser,** who built the famous **Step Pyramid at Saqqara.** The architect of this edifice was **Imhotep,** who was later worshipped as a god. The kings of the 3rd Dynasty campaigned in the **Sinai,** defeating the nomadic chieftains who ruled there.

c. 2613–2494. 4th Dynasty. Snefru fought successful wars against the Nubians and Libyans, further developed the **sea trade in cedar** with Byblos, and began the serious exploitation of turquoise from the Sinai. His successor, Khufru **(Cheops)** was best known for building the **Great Pyramid** at Giza. Originally 481.4 ft. high, it covered an area of about 13 acres and contained 2,300,000 blocks of stone, each weighing an average of 2.5 tons. Khafre **(Chephren)** built the second pyramid at Giza (473.5 ft. high), as well as the enormous human-headed lion, the **Sphinx,** called **Herakhte** ("Horus of the Horizon") by the Egyptians. Menkaure **(Mycerinus)** built the third pyramid of Giza (219.5 ft. high). In the 3rd and 4th Dynasties the idea of **divine kingship** developed, as did the classical Egyptian canons of art and architecture. There were remarkable advances in **mathematics** and **medicine,** the latter including diagnostic techniques and systematic treatment. In the Old Kingdom the **population of Egypt** was between 1.5 and 2 million.

c. 2494–2345. 5th Dynasty. The 5th Dynasty witnessed the rise of the **Heliopolitan priesthood of Ra:** its nine kings regularly assumed the title "son of Ra" and built obelisk temples dedicated to the sun god. **Sahurre** defeated the Libyans and organized **trading expeditions** to **Punt** (Somalia) and the "Turquoise Land" in **the Sinai.** Under **Unas,** the last king of the dynasty, the first **Pyramid Texts** appear, although they contain much earlier material, some dating from predynastic times.

c. 2345–2181. 6th Dynasty. Uni, a general of **Pepy I,** campaigned in Palestine, perhaps as far north as Mount Carmel (p. 33), and **Merenre I** took the homage of Nubian chiefs south of the **First Cataract.** Especially after the reign of **Pepy II,** the rulers of the nomes assumed more independence and often ruled as **feudal lords.** The eighth and last ruler of the dynasty was **Queen Nitokerti (Nitocris),** the sister and widow of Merenre II.

c. 2181–2133. THE FIRST INTERMEDIATE PERIOD. According to Manetho, the **7th Dynasty** (c. 2181–2173) had 70 kings in 70 days, obviously a fiction but representative of the unstable conditions of the **First Intermediate Period.** For much of this period there was strife between nobles of **Heracleopolis** (Nennesu) in Lower Egypt and **Thebes** (Waset) in Upper Egypt. The **8th Dynasty** (c. 2173–2160), comprised of six kings, still ruled from Memphis. In the **9th Dynasty** (c. 2160–2130), the capital moved to Heracleopolis, althoughthe kings were still buried at Memphis. Toward the end of the 9th Dynasty, the country was divided in two, the **10th Dynasty** (c. 2130–2040) ruling in Heracleopolis and the **11th Dynasty** (c. 2133–1191) in Thebes. **Central authority was weak,** banditry became common, and commerce with overseas interrupted. Despite the civil unrest, literature flourished: notable are the *Admonitions of Ipuwer,* and the *Instructions for King Merikare.* The idea of a **life after death** began to include persons other than the royal family.

d. THE MIDDLE KINGDOM AND THE SECOND INTERMEDIATE PERIOD (11TH–17TH DYNASTIES)

2040–1786. THE MIDDLE KINGDOM.

c. 2133–1991. 11th Dynasty. The fifth ruler of the 11th Dynasty, **Mentuhotep II** (2060–2010), defeated Heracleopolis around 2040 and **reunited Upper and Lower Egypt.** A powerful ruler, Mentuhotep suppressed the power of the nobles; reinstituted a strong central government; campaigned in Libya, Nubia, and western Asia; and extended Egypt's boundaries. Under **Mentuhotep III** (2009–1998), trade with the Red Sea via the Wadi Hammamat was resumed. **Mentuhotep IV** (1997–1991) was a weak ruler, and on his death his vizier, **Amenemhet,** took the throne.

1991–1786. 12th Dynasty. Amenemhet I (1991–1962) was a commoner who attributed his rise to the god **Amun.** This deity rose in national prominence. Amenemhet built a new royal capital, **Itj-towy** (site unidentified), near the border of Upper and Lower Egypt. He also conquered **Lower Nubia** and undertook a punitive campaign against the **Asiatic nomads.** Amenemhet made his eldest son, **Sesostris** (Senusret) his coregent, a practice which persisted through the dynasty. **Sesostris I** (1971–1928) extended Egyptian rule to the Second Cataract, and it is during his reign that the quasi-historical **Story of Sinuhue** is set. **Sesostris II** (1897–1878) began irrigation and land reclamation operations in the Fayum Depression west of the Nile. **Sesostris III** (1878–1843) marched into central Palestine, but made no attempt to establish permanent control (p. 33). **Amenemhet III** (1842–1797) completed the Fayum irrigation project and expanded turquoise mining in the Sinai. Amenemhet built the enormous palace and mortuary temple later called the **Labyrinth.** In addition to the **Story of Sinuhe,** Middle Kingdom literature includes the **Instructions of King Amenemhet,** the **Tale of the Shipwrecked Sailor,** and the **Coffin Texts,** giving instructions for obtaining eternal life.

1786–1552. SECOND INTERMEDIATE PERIOD. The **13th Dynasty** (1786–1633) was a period of **declining power** for Egypt, and increasing pressure from invaders from western Asia. The sixty kings of this dynasty ruled a disintegrating kingdom from Memphis and Itj-towy. Already in the beginning of the period, the kings of the **14th Dynasty** (1786–c. 1603) ruled an independent state from **Xois** (Sakha) in the western Delta. Some of these Xoian rulers had Semitic names and may have been Amorites or Canaanites. Under **Dudimose I** (Tutimaios, c. 1674) of the 13th Dynasty, most of Egypt fell to the **Hyksos** (from Egyptian **Heqa-Khoswe,** "chiefs of the foreign lands") who invaded from Syria-Palestine. The Hyksos were probably Amorites or Canaanites from Syria-Palestine (p. 33). They introduced the horse, chariot, and com-

pound bow into Egypt and are said to have worshipped Seth, who apparently represented the god **Baal.** The **15th Dynasty** (1674–1552) was made up of Hyksos who established control over Lower Egypt, with their capital at **Avaris** in the eastern Delta. The remaining kings of the 13th Dynasty were their vassals. Hyksos rule reached its height under **Apophis I,** who ruled more than 40 years. The **16th Dynasty** (c. 1684–1552), contemporary to the 14th and 15th, was made up of independent Hyksos chieftains who had established themselves somewhere in the Delta. The **17th Dynasty** (c. 1650–1552) was originally the Egyptian vassal kings in Thebes, who gradually won their independence from the Hyksos. One of these Theban kings, **Seqenenre Tao II,** is the hero of a folk tale, **"The Contending of Apophis and Seqenenre."** His successor, **Kamose,** left a stele (an upright slab with an inscribed surface) describing wars with the Hyksos king **Apophis II.**

e. THE NEW KINGDOM AND THE THIRD INTERMEDIATE PERIOD (18TH–24TH DYNASTIES)

Note: For the 18th to 20th Dynasties, there is a high and a low chronology, differing by some 10 to 20 years. The low chronology is used here.

1567–1320. 18th Dynasty. Amosis (Ahmose, 1552–1527) drove the **Hyksos** out of the country and reestablished the power of the central government. Rather than remaining in a single capital, the 18th-Dynasty kings divided their time between Thebes and Memphis. The worship of the **Theban god Amun** became increasingly important, and the priesthood of Amun became a political force. **Amenophis I** (Amenhotep, 1527–1506) secured the Nubian and Libyan borders. Nubia was administered by a viceroy called the **"King's Son of Kush." Tuthmosis I** (Tuthmose, 1506–1494) and **Tuthmosis II** (1494–1490) both fought successful campaigns in Nubia and Syria-Palestine (p. 32).

1490–1426. THE REIGNS OF HATSHEPSUT AND TUTHMOSIS III. Tuthmosis II associated his wife (and half-sister), **Hatshepsut,** (1490–1468) with him in his reign, and when he died at an early age, Hatshepsut seized power. At first she acted as regent of **Tuthmosis III** (1490–1436), but in 1489 Hatshepsut proclaimed herself "king" and thereafter depicted herself as a man. Meanwhile, Tuthmosis grew up in the army. In 1468 he took power: the fate of Hatshepsut is unknown. Tuthmosis immediately invaded Syria-Palestine, and at the first **Battle of Megiddo** (1468) defeated a coalition of Canaanite states under the leadership of the king of Qadesh (p. 35). In a further series of campaigns, Tuthmosis III established an empire stretching to the Euphrates. He even crossed the river and pillaged **Washukanni,** the capital of the Hurrian kingdom of Mitanni (p. 27). In **Nubia,** he moved the border to the Fourth Cataract and founded a fortified town at Napata (p. 31). The title **pharaoh** (per'o, "Great House"), previously used to refer to the royal palace, was now used to refer to the king himself.

1402–1364. THE REIGN OF AMENOPHIS III. Under **Amenophis III** Egypt enjoyed **unparalleled wealth and peace.** Amenophis built an enormous mortuary temple at Thebes, including two enormous statues of himself, the **Colossi of Memnon** (65.6 ft. high). He also built the gigantic temple to Amun at **Luxor** and founded a new city in Nubia called Gematen ("finding Aten"), which reflected the rising importance of this god. Although Amenophis made diplomatic marriages with two daughters of Mitannian kings, his chief wife was **Queen Tiy,** the daughter of a Nubian general.

1364–1347. THE REIGN OF AMENOPHIS IV (AKHENATEN). Amenophis IV and his wife, **Nefertiti,** introduced an anomalous Egyptian monotheism. The god of the solar disk, **Aten,** was now worshipped as the only deity. The king changed his name to **Akhenaten** ("Pleasing to Aten") and built a new capital at **Akhetaten** ("Horizon of Aten," modern **Tell al-'Amarna**), halfway between Memphis and Thebes. Here were found the **Amarna letters,** correspondence with the kings of Babylonia, Mitanni, the Hittites, and others written on clay tablets in Akkadian, the *lingua franca* of the period. **Egypt's empire began to disintegrate.** Some areas of Syria-Palestine broke away, and others were taken over by the Hittites (p. 37).

1347–1305. THE END OF THE 18TH DYNASTY. After Akhenaten's death, his son-in-law **Tutankhaten** (1347–1337) abandoned the Aten cult, changed his name to **Tutankhamen,** and moved the government back to Memphis and Thebes. He is chiefly known for this tomb, which yielded fantastic treasures when discovered in 1922 C.E. The last king of the 18th Dynasty was a usurper, **Horemheb** (1333–1305), who had worked his way up from a scribe to become chief commander of the army. A capable ruler, Horemheb took steps to suppress graft and corruption, particularly in tax collection, restored the temples of Amun, and undertook a campaign in Asia, which reached **Carchemish** in Syria (p. 32).

1305–1186. 19th Dynasty. Horemheb was succeeded by another military man, **Ramses I** (1305–1303), whose family came from Tanis. His son, **Seti I** (1303–1289) set out to reconquer western Asia. He was successful in Palestine and southern Syria, extending control as far as **Qadesh on the Orontes** (p. 38). Seti built a great temple at Abydos and continued work on the great Hypostyle Hall in **Karnak.**

1289–1224. THE REIGN OF RAMSES THE GREAT. Ramses II spent much of his reign on military campaigns. In **Libya** he defeated the Tehenu and built a series of fortifications guarding the western frontier. He also subdued the **Nubian tribes** and built a temple at **Abu Simbel** between the First and Second Cataracts, which included colossal statues 70 ft. high. The main military activity of Ramses II was a long struggle with the Hittite Empire. In 1286 he fought the **Battle of Qadesh** against **King Muwatallis**—the Egyptians claimed victory, but the Hittites actually won (p. 38). Further fighting ensued, until in 1270 Ramses signed a peace treaty with the new Hittite king, **Hattusilis.** Tanis was rebuilt as a new capital and called **Pi-Ramses,** the biblical "store-city of Ramses" (Exodus 1:11). Ramses II completed the **Hypostyle Hall** at Karnak.

1224–1186. THE END OF THE 19TH DYNASTY. Merneptah (1224–1204) defeated an incursion of Libu (Libyans) and **Sea Peoples** at the **Battle of Piyer** (1220). Some of these Sea Peoples, who had destroyed the Hittite Empire and ravaged the Near East, might be identified with later Mediterranean peoples: the Akiyawash (Achaeans), Turush (Etruscans), Luku (Lycians), and Sharden (Sardinians). The **Merneptah Stele** records a successful campaign in Palestine which defeated, among others, the **people of Israel,** their first datable mention in history. The 19th Dynasty ended in a series of short, confused reigns. The final ruler was a woman, **Queen Tawosre** (1194–1186), who took the throne with the name **Sitre** ("Daughter of Ra").

1186–1069. 20th Dynasty. After a short interregnum, order was restored by a military figure, **Sethnakhte** (1186–1184), whose son took the name **Ramses III** (1184–1153). Ramses III defeated the Libyans and in his 8th year overcame another coalition of Sea Peoples: Peleset (Philistines), Tjeker (Sicels?), Danuna (Danaoi?), Sharden (Sardinians), Weshwesh, and Shakrusha. The scenes of Ramses III's victory are shown on the walls of the mortuary temple at **Medinet Habu.** In general, Egypt was stable and prosperous under Ramses III, but in the closing years of his reign there were signs of unrest, including the **first known strike in history,** by funerary artisans in Thebes. After the death of Ramses III, there was a **series of weak kings,** Ramses IV–XI (1153–1069), and the central government declined into impotence. In the time of **Ramses XI** (1099–1069), **Herihor,** the high priest of Amun-Ra at Karnak, ruled Upper Egypt from Thebes. Much of the Delta was controlled by a local official, **Smendes** (Nesbenebdeb). The **Tale of Wenamun,** another quasi-historical story, reflects the unsettled conditions of Egypt, and its lack of international stature. During the New Kingdom, **the cult of the dead** and the availability of the afterlife extended even to relatively minor officials and private persons. **Tomb paintings** show naturalistic scenes of everyday life. While drawing on earlier material, the **Book of the Dead** was compiled during this period. By the end of the New Kingdom, **the population of Egypt** had risen to some 4.5 million.

1069–715. THIRD INTERMEDIATE PERIOD.

1069–945. 21st (Tanite) Dynasty. After the death of Ramses XI, **Smendes** (Nesbenebdeb, 1069–1043) claimed the kingship and ruled from **Pi-Ramses** (Tanis). The hereditary **high priests of Amun-Ra,** descendants of **Herihor,** governed Upper Egypt as a theocracy, and the viceroy of Nubia **(King's Son of Kush)** (p. 32) ruled independently in the south, although both recognized the 21st Dynasty pharaohs as titular rulers. The rise of the Kingdom of Israel created a powerful state in Palestine. It was probably **Siamun** (978–959) who married his daughter to King Solomon (1 Kings 11:1). **The Instruction of Amunemope,** one of the most famous of Egyptian books of wisdom, was written around this time. The Book of Proverbs quotes a number of its precepts (Prov. 15: 16, 17:1, 22:17–24:22).

945–715. 22nd (Bubastite) Dynasty. Sheshonq I (945–924), from a Libyan family, took the throne and appointed one of his sons as the **high priest of Amun-Ra,** reunifying Egypt. The dynasty ruled from both **Tanis** and **Bubastis** in the eastern Delta. Sheshonq made the first additions to the temple at Karnak in centuries. In 926, he invaded both **Israel and Judah,** sacked a number of cities, but did not try to establish permanent control (p. 34). Under his successors, central control broke down and many nomes (provinces) were controlled by local dynasts. By the reign of **Osorkon II** (874–850), the high priests of Amun-Ra had reestablished independence. Egypt allied itself with Israel and Syrian kings to oppose the rising power of Assyria, but sent only 1,000 soldiers to fight at the **Battle of Qarqar** in 853 (p. 34). Under **Pedubast I** (818–793), a branch of the royal family broke away and ruled independently in **Leontopolis** as the **23rd Dynasty. Tefnakhte I** (727–720) established a short-lived **24th Dynasty** at Sais.

f. THE LATE DYNASTIC PERIOD (25TH–31ST DYNASTIES)

747–656. 25th (Kushite) Dynasty. The **25th Dynasty** began as a line of Kushite kings, operating from their capital at **Napata** (p. 30). **Piankhy** (751–716) sacked Memphis, but did not establish permanent control of Egypt. His brother **Shabako** (716–702) defeated the last king of the 22nd Dynasty, **Osorkon IV;** of the 23rd, **Sheshonq IV** (720–715); of the 24th, **Bakenref** (Bochchoris, 720–715); and reunited the country. Shabako established his capital at Thebes. The next king, **Taharka** (690–664) defeated an invading Assyrian army led by Esarhaddon (674), but in 672, the Assyrians returned and captured Memphis. Esarhaddon set up **Necho I** (672–664), the governor of Sais, as a client king, establishing the **26th Dynasty.** When Taharka died, his son **Tenuatamun** (664–656) continued the resistance to the Assyrians, but in 663 **Ashurbanipal** finally defeated Tenuatamun and drove him back to Napata (p. 30).

664–525. 26th (Saite) Dynasty. After the final defeat of Tenuatamun, the Assyrians placed **Psammetichus I** (Psamtek, 664–610) on the throne. The family of Psammetichus stemmed from Sais, but he made Memphis the capital. Toward the end of his long reign, the collapse of the Assyrian Empire allowed Psammetichus to establish his independence and reassert central authority. He used **Greek and Carian mercenaries** sent by Gyges of Lydia to suppress local dynasts (p. 38). Political independence produced the **Saite revival** in painting, architecture, literature, and religion, a nostalgic attempt to recreate the forms and styles of the Old Kingdom. **Necho II** (610–595) marched north to aid the last remnant of the Assyrians, fighting in Syria against the Babylonians. On his way, he defeated King Josiah at the second **Battle of Megiddo** (609), and Judah became an Egyptian vassal (p. 35). Later, Necho II suffered a crushing defeat at the Battle of Carchemish (605) at the hands of Nebuchadnezzar. The Egyptians were driven from Syria-Palestine, but in 601 they stopped the Babylonians at the border of Egypt (p. 28). Herodotus describes **the successful circumnavigation of Africa** by Phoenician sailors sent by Necho. **Apries** (589–570, biblical Hophra) attempted unsuccessfully to drive the Babylonians from Judah and was defeated by the Greeks in Cyrene when he attempted to aid his Libyan allies. Apries was deposed by **Amasis** ('Ahmose-si-neit, 570–526), a commoner from the Delta who had risen in the military. Amasis allied himself with Babylonia and Lydia against **the rising power of the Persians,** but saw his allies defeated in turn by Cyrus the Great. Psammetichus III (526–525) ruled only for six months, before the Persians invaded (p. 40).

525–404. 27th (Persian) Dynasty. The Persians defeated the Egyptians at the **Battle of Pelusium** (525). The Persian King **Cambyses** (525–521) ruled Egypt as pharaoh. Although Herodotus says he suppressed Egyptian religion, according to hieroglyphic inscriptions Cambyses carried out the pharaoh's ritual functions. **Darius I** (521–485) certainly treated the Egyptians with respect and had **Egyptian law codified,** both in demotic and Aramaic. He assigned a priest, **Udjahorresenet,** to reestablish the **Houses of Life,** which copied sacred writings. Darius placed Egypt, along with Libya and Cyrenaica, in the **sixth satrapy** (province) with the satrap (governor) at Memphis. The Egyptians revolted in the last years of Darius, and the uprising was not suppressed until the reign of **Xerxes** (485–464). Persian rule became harsher after the revolt. **Greek and Jewish minorities** grew considerably in the Persian period. Around 450, Herodotus visited the country. When Darius II (423–404) died, there was another revolt, this time successful (p. 40).

404–399. 28th Dynasty. Amyrtaeus (404–399), probably a Libyan, ruled the entire country but was the 28th Dynasty's only king.

399–380. 29th (Mendesian) Dynasty. Nepherites (Nef'aurud, 399–393) from Mendes (Djed) in Lower Egypt formed an alliance with the **Spartans,** the most powerful state in the eastern Mediterranean (p. 68). In 386, Persia and Sparta signed a peace accord, and **Artaxerxes II** invaded Egypt (385–383). **Achoris** (Hakor, 393–380) allied himself with Evagoras, king of Salamis in Cyprus, and defeated the Persians (p. 40).

His son, **Nepherites II** (380) ruled only four months before being overthrown by Nectanebo.

380–343. 30th (Sebennytic) Dynasty. Nectanebo I (Nakhtnebef, 380–362) from Tjeb-neter (**Sebennytus**) drove off a Persian invasion (371) and built and restored many monuments throughout Egypt. His son, **Teos** (Djeho, 362–360) attempted an invasion of Phoenicia and Syria but was defeated. The army rebelled and replaced Teos with his son **Nectanebo II** (Nakhthorhebe, 369–342), the last native pharaoh. In 343–342, **Artaxerxes III** led a successful invasion, Nectanebo fled to Ethiopia, and Egypt was again made a Persian satrapy.

343–332. 31st (Persian) Dynasty. The second period of Persian rule lasted only ten years. In 332, **Alexander the Great** entered the country, and the satrap Mazaces surrendered the country to him without resistance (p. 38). *(To p. 74)*

4. EAST AFRICA, c. 2000–332 B.C.E.

a. GEOGRAPHY

Nubia, or **Kush,** began at the Nile's **First Cataract** (waterfall), where the island of Elephantine (Yeb) was located, although the political boundary was often farther upriver. As one moved upriver, the Nile flowed over six more cataracts, before the river split into the **White and Blue Niles.** Between these two points lay the massive Egyptian temples at **Abu Simbel,** now inundated by the Aswan Dam, as well as the three capitals of the region: **Kerma, Napata,** and **Meroë.** Around 500,000 people lived in the area of modern Sudan around 2000 B.C.E., and nearly 1 million by 1500, though Kush comprised only a portion of this region. The region between the Nile and the Red Sea was not heavily populated before the 5th century B.C.E. The Somalian and Eritrean coast, however, was an important center for trade, known to the Egyptians as **Punt.**

b. ECONOMY, TECHNOLOGY, SOCIETY, AND CULTURE

From c. 7000–3500, a common material culture existed from Nubia to Middle Egypt, but after 3500, **Nubian and Egyptian cultures diverge.** Nubia remained primarily pastoral, but traded with Egypt, exporting gold, ivory, ebony, and exotic animals. Kerma period architecture is autochthonous, but Kush came under increasing **Egyptian influence.** After the Egyptians gained control of the region, they began exploiting its mineral resources. Under Napata and Meroë, a syncretistic architectural style developed. From the 8th century the Nubians utilized Egyptian hieroglyphics. It is not until 170 B.C.E. that the native language, **Meroitic,** was written. Meroitic has not yet been deciphered, and its relation to other African languages is unknown.

c. KUSH AND PUNT

c. 2000–1069. KUSH.

c. 2000–1506. THE KINGDOM OF KUSH arose around 2000 and was centered around **Kerma,** near the Third Cataract. It flourished during Egypt's Second Intermediate Period (1786–1552) (p. 30). Kerma contains the remains of a **brick palace** and large *tumuli* or **burial mounds.** Hieroglyphic inscriptions are found only on Egyptian imports, and none of the Kushite kings of this period is known.

1506–1069. EGYPTIAN KUSH. Tuthmosis I conquered Nubia past the Fourth Cataract (p. 30). The Egyptians built large temple complexes in Nubia, for example at **Buhen** (Hatshepsut) and at **Abu Simbel** (Ramses II). **Amenophis III** built the city of **Gematen,** opposite modern Dongola, and **Thutmose III** founded **Napata,** on the Fourth Cataract. Nubia was administered by an elaborate bureaucracy headed by the viceroy ("King's Son of Kush"). Local chiefs were also used in the administration, and an **ongoing Egyptianization** occurred. The **population of Egyptian Kush** was probably around 100,000. After the reign of **Ramses XI** (p. 31) nothing is known of Kush until the 8th century.

c. 2500–1150. THE LAND OF PUNT. From the 5th Dynasty (c. 2494–2345) the Egyptians sent ships to **Punt** to obtain the **myrrh** grown there and the **frankincense** from south Arabia. The expedition of Queen Hatshepsut is the best known. No reference to Punt survives after the reign of **Ramses III.** The introduction of camel caravans in Arabia around 1000 probably ended the Puntine trade (p. 41).

d. THE KINGDOMS OF NAPATA AND MEROË

c. 780–591. THE KINGDOM OF NAPATA. Alara (c. 780–760) founded an independent Kushite dynasty with its capital at **Napata.** Under **Piankhy** (or Peye, 747–716) the Kushites sacked Memphis, and **Shabako** (716–702) conquered Egypt, founding the 25th (Kushite) Dynasty (747–656), which ruled from the Sixth Cataract to the Mediterranean (p. 31). **Taharka** (690–664) did extensive building at Napata and campaigned as far east as Palestine. **Tenuatamum** (664–656) was driven from Egypt by the Assyrians, but the dynasty continued to rule in Napata. **Anlamani** (623–593) campaigned against the nomadic Blemmyes and was succeeded by **Aspelta** (593–568). In 591, Psamtek II (595–589) invaded Kush and captured Napata (p. 31), and Aspelta moved the capital south to Meroë, near the Sixth Cataract.

591 B.C.E.–350 C.E. THE KINGDOM OF MEROË. Between 591 and 270 B.C.E. **Meroë** became the political capital, but Meroitic rulers continued to be buried at **Napata** (which was recaptured) to the end of the fourth century. The Kushites worshiped Amun in the form of the lion god **Apedemak.** Stone temples, pyramids, and obelisks were built, and a native Meroitic building style developed. The **kingdom's population** was probably around 500,000. Around 525 B.C.E., Cambyses unsuccessfully attempted to conquer the kingdom (p. 31). In the fourth century three kings left inscriptions: **Ammanoteyeriké, Harsiotef,** and **Nastasen.** The kingdom finally collapsed in the third century C.E. under the assault of the nomadic Blemmyes and by the fourth century had been absorbed by the newer kingdom of Axum. *(To p. 142)*

5. SYRIA-PALESTINE, c. 3500–323 B.C.E.

a. GEOGRAPHY

Syria-Palestine has three geographic zones: a **coastal area** along the Mediterranean, a **desert fringe** along the Syrian Desert, and a double mountain chain from the **central steppe,** which divides the other two zones. In the third millennium the major cities were **Mari** (Tell Hariri), located where the Euphrates met the road to the Mediterranean, and **Ebla** (Tell Mardikh) near the Orontes River. The second millennium saw the development of Canaanite cities: **Ugarit, Byblos, Sidon,** and **Tyre** along the coast; **Damascus, Aleppo (Halab), Carchemish, Yamhad, Qatna,** and **Qadesh** in the central steppe; and **Hazor, Gezer,** and **Shechem** (among others) in Palestine. After 1200, the region is divided into **Palestine** (Philistia, Israel, and Judah), **Aram** (Syria), and **Phoenicia** (discussed separately). The **population of Syria-Palestine** rose from approximately 250,000 in 3000 B.C.E. to about 800,000 by 1000 B.C.E.

b. ECONOMY, TECHNOLOGY, SOCIETY, AND CULTURE

Syria-Palestine was originally **heavily forested,** and home to panthers, lions, and even elephants. Deforestation and overgrazing, however, destroyed much of the woodland even in antiquity, though the **cedars of Lebanon** were a valuable item of trade. The desert fringe was the home to **pastoralists,** who used donkeys for transport until the domestication of the camel around 1000 B.C.E. In the steppe region wheat, barley, olives, and grapes were grown. The coastal area relied on **trade:** routes from Anatolia, Mesopotamia, and Arabia led to the Mediterranean coast and were linked by ship to Cyprus, Greece, and Egypt. The coastal cities also produced a famous **purple dye** made from the *murex* sea-mollusk.

Cuneiform texts from **Ebla** are the earliest writing in Syria and included historical texts, lexicons (including a massive Eblaite-Sumerian dictionary), mathematical texts, administrative documents, and letters, as well as literary and mythological texts. By 1400 B.C.E. scribes at **Ugarit** (Ras Shamra) developed a cuneiform alphabet in which was preserved Canaanite literature, including legal, historical, religious, and mythological texts. It is unclear whether the alphabet known as "Phoenician" developed before or after Ugaritic, but it was sometime in the mid-second millennium. Around 750 the Greeks borrowed this **alphabet** from the Phoenicians (p. 35).

At Ebla and Mari the main deity was **Dagan**—other gods were **Ishtar, Baal, Rasap,** and **Adad.** The chief gods of the Canaanite pantheon were **El** (God), creator of heaven and earth; **Asherah,** El's consort and the mother-goddess; their son **Baal Haddu** (or Lord Storm); **'Anat,** goddess of love and war; and **Dagan,** a grain god. The course of the development of the **monotheistic worship of Yahweh** by the Israelites is problematic. Some scholars see monotheism as an early element of Hebrew religion; others think it a much later development from an earlier polytheism. A Hebrew inscription of the 9th century suggests **Yahweh** had a consort named **Asherah.**

c. EBLA AND MARI

c. 3500–1600. EBLA.
c. 3500–2400. EARLY EBLA. Urban culture began around the same time as the Mesopotamian Uruk Culture (3500–3100), but the first large palace dates to c. 2700–2400. **Eblaite** was a west Semitic language, possibly an early version of **Canaanite.**
c. 2400–2000. THE KINGDOM OF EBLA. At its height **Ebla** controlled the region, from the Orontes to Mari as far north as Carchemish, and held hegemony over a much larger area, from Kanesh in Anatolia to the northern border of Palestine. Ebla's king *(malikum),* was originally **the elected head of an oligarchy** made up of the provincial governors, who were the real power in the land. **Ibrium** (c. 2300) instituted a hereditary, and apparently absolute, monarchy. The kingdom had a **sophisticated economy** controlled by an elaborate palace bureaucracy. Women enjoyed a high position and a freedom unusual in ancient societies. **Sargon of Akkad** campaigned against Ebla, and his grandson, **Naram-Sin** destroyed the city (p. 26). Ebla recovered, although little is known of its history except that it suffered another destruction around 2000.
2000–1600. AMORITE EBLA. After a period of subservience to the kings of Ur III (2112–2004), **Ibbit-Lim** founded the **2nd (Amorite) Dynasty.** Amorite Ebla was much reduced from its third millennium height, but it was still the most important city in northern Syria. The Eblaites traded with **the Assyrian colony at Kanesh** (p. 26). The city was finally destroyed between 1700 and 1600, probably by the Hittites.
c. 2900–1759. MARI.
c. 2900–2370. EARLY DYNASTIC MARI. Mari flourished in the Early Dynastic Period (2900–2370), and the **1st Dynasty of Mari** is cataloged in the Sumerian King Lists. At some point Mari became tributary to **Ebla,** but when that city fell it recovered its independence.
c. 1900–1759. AMORITE MARI. In the early 19th century, Mari was

ruled by an Amorite, **Yaggid-Lim,** who was succeeded by his son, **Yahdun-Lim.** The Assyrian Shamshi-Adad I (1813–1781) conquered Mari and made his son Yasmah Addu its ruler (p. 26). **Zimri-Lim,** (c. 1791–1759), a descendant of Yahdun-Lim, drove out the Assyrians. The **palace at Mari** covered eight acres and contained a library of some 20,000 cuneiform tablets, almost all in Akkadian. Mari was destroyed by Hammurapi in 1759 (p. 26), but continued to be a city-state. It was abandoned in the 8th century.

d. THE LAND OF CANAAN

c. 3100–2000. EARLY BRONZE AGE CANAAN. City-states developed in Syria-Palestine around 3100, serving as mediators between the protoliterate culture of Mesopotamia and the Gerzean culture of Egypt. In the mid-third millennium the region was dominated by **Ebla.** Egyptian inscriptions begin at Byblos with **Nebka** c. 2686, and there are close trade relations throughout the period. Around 2300, **Uni,** a general of Pepy I, led an expedition which may have reached Mt. Carmel (p. 30). Mesopotamian culture also exerted influence, and **Sargon the Great** (2370–2316) conquered parts of northern Syria, reaching the Mediterranean (p. 23).
c. 2100–1800. FIRST PERIOD OF EGYPTIAN DOMINATION. The **Amorite invasion** into Syria-Palestine, c. 2000, caused much dislocation, a decline in urbanism, and a return to nomadism in the Transjordan and parts of the central steppe. The **Execration Texts** from the Middle Kingdom Period (2040–1786) establish that **Egypt exercised political control** over southern Syria-Palestine, ruling through local vassal kings at Ashkelon, Beth-Shean, Shechem, Akko, Hazor, and Jerusalem. An inscription of **Sesostris III** (1878–1843) records a campaign which reached Shechem (p. 30).
c. 1800–1450. THE GOLDEN AGE OF CANAAN. By the 18th century, urban culture was reestablished and the Canaanite cities, many with Amorite rulers, **prospered through trade.** Yantin'ammu ruled in an affluent **Byblos; Ugarit** rose in prominence; and **Hazor, Qatna,** and **Aleppo** were great centers of power. The rise of the **Hyksos,** apparently Amorites or Canaanites, is obscure, but in the 17th century they began building an **empire in the west.** Hyksos sites are characterized by enormous fortifications of earthen-work *(terre pisée).* The Hyksos 15th Dynasty (1650–1552) in Egypt exercised feudal authority in both Palestine and Egypt (p. 30). In the 16th century **Hurrians** (biblical **Horites**) migrated into Palestine. By the end of the period, the Amorites had completely assimilated.
c. 1450–1365. SECOND PERIOD OF EGYPTIAN DOMINATION. Tuthmosis III (p. 30) reestablished Egyptian political control over Syria, placing a garrison in Ugarit. Egyptian power loosened under **Akehnaten** (1364–1347), and the Hittite Empire exerted increasing control on the region. The **Amarna Letters,** written by vassal kings in Palestine to the Egyptian pharaohs, give some information on political and social history. The society was **feudal,** with a nobility of chariot warriors and serfs beneath. One segment of the population became outlaws and mercenaries, the so-called **Hapiru,** who often attacked and even took over Canaanite cities. A connection with the later **Hebrews** is possible, but problematic. In the late 14th century, the **Akhlamu,** possible forerunners of the **Arameans,** began to enter Syria (p. 30). In 1270, Egypt and the Hittites divided Syria by treaty, with the boundary at the **Eleutheris River** (Nahr el-Kebir) (p. 31).
c. 1200. THE INVASION OF THE SEA PEOPLES. Around 1200, after having demolished the Hittite Empire, the **Sea Peoples** entered the region, and destroyed Ugarit and Tyre (p. 31). Around 1180, one of the Sea Peoples, the **Philistines** (Peleset), settled on the coastal plain of Palestine. They formed a **league of five city states** (Gaza, Gath, Ashkelon, Ashdod, and Ekron), each governed by a "tyrant" *(seren).* After the fall of the Hittite Empire, Hittites and Luwians moved into northern Syria and formed the **Neo-Hittite Kingdoms.** There was a northern group under the hegemony of **Carchemish** and a southern group consisting of Ya'diya, Hattina, Arpad, Til Barsip, and Hamath. **Neo-Hittite art and architecture** is a mix of their traditional style with Hurrian, Assyrian, and Aramean traditions. A number of **Canaanite enclaves** (such as the Jebusites at Jerusalem) remained in the interior, but most of the Canaanites retreated to the narrow strip of coastal land from

Tyre northward to Arvad. This region is subsequently called **Phoenicia** (p. 35).

e. ISRAEL AND JUDAH

c. 1300–1020. ISRAELITE TRIBAL PERIOD.

c. 1300–1200. THE CONQUEST OF CANAAN. The biblical tradition traces the tribes of Israel back to the time of the **patriarchs** (Abraham, Isaac, and Jacob), who came from Mesopotamia to Canaan, living there as seminomads. Some scholars place the patriarchs in the context of the **Amorite invasions** in the 19th and 18th centuries, others in the **Aramean migrations** of the 14th to 11th centuries. Another biblical tradition details the migration of the Israelites from serfdom in the eastern Delta of Egypt under **Moses** and **Aaron.** The relationship of these two traditions to each other, and to the archaeological record, is problematic, and the history of Israel obscure, until the **Conquest of Canaan** sometime in the 13th century. It is unclear if the Israelite conquest was a **sudden invasion** or a **gradual infiltration.** In any case, the Israelites adopted the local Canaanite language, and to some extent, religion and customs. The first dated attestation of the People of Israel in Canaan is the **Merneptah Stele** (c. 1220) (p. 31).

c. 1200–1020. THE PERIOD OF THE JUDGES. The Book of **Judges** records a story of conflicts between the Israelites and the surrounding Canaanites, Midianites and Ammonites, in which the **Israelite tribes** joined together under a judge *(shophet)*, primarily a military position. In the course of the 11th century, the **Philistines united** under the king of Gath and began an aggressive campaign of conquest against Israel. These attacks culminated around 1050, when the central shrine of the Israelites at Shiloh was destroyed and the **Ark of the Covenant** taken as booty. Around 1020, the last of the judges, **Samuel,** was anointed **Saul** as king of Israel in order to better resist the Philistines.

c. 1020–930. THE UNITED KINGDOM OF ISRAEL.

c. 1020–1000. THE REIGN OF KING SAUL. Saul's kingship was limited, and his main title was not *melech* "king" but *nagid* "military commander." Saul's authority was more **charismatic** than **institutional,** and the tribal elders and the prophets *(nabi'im)* sometimes opposed him. Saul was successful for a time in his wars against the Philistines but was defeated and killed by them at the **Battle of Gilboa** (c. 1000). Saul's son **Ishbaal** ruled for a short period but was then assassinated, perhaps at the instigation of the next king, **David.**

c. 1000–965. THE REIGN OF KING DAVID. A minor noble from the tribe of Judah, **David** fought in Saul's army but quarreled with the king and withdrew with his clan into the Judean desert. There he operated as a **bandit-chief** and eventually became a **vassal** of the Philistine king of Gath. After the death of Saul, he ruled **Judah** from Hebron for seven years, and when Ishbaal was assassinated, David was elected **king of Israel** by a tribal assembly. Conquering **Jerusalem** from the Jebusites, David made it both a **religious center,** transferring the Ark of the Covenant there, and the **royal residence.** A royal bureaucracy was developed. The **cult of Yahweh was centralized** and used to support the validity of his dynasty. David conquered the northern and Transjordanian tribes, incorporating them into Israel. The Philistines and the Aramean state of Zobah to the north were defeated and made vassals. He entered into a treaty with **Hiram,** king of Sidon and Tyre (969–936). **The earliest Hebrew writings,** including some **Psalms** and historical annals, possibly date to the reign of David.

c. 965–931. THE REIGN OF KING SOLOMON. After David's death, Solomon killed his rival half-brother **Adonijah** and took power. With Phoenician help, Solomon built a **Temple** to Yahweh, as well as a magnificent palace and a citadel, in Jerusalem. Solomon reorganized the **administration** and expanded the royal **bureaucracy** and the **standing army.** Diplomatic marriages were made with surrounding powers, including one to the daughter of Pharaoh **Siamun** of Egypt. In partnership with **Hiram of Tyre,** Solomon organized **shipping** for trade in the Mediterranean and on the Red Sea; with Cilicia and Egypt, he developed a cartel in horses and chariots; and he arranged with the **Queen of Sheba** (Saba) for trade in **frankincense and myrrh** from south Arabia (p. 41). The population of Solomon's kingdom was probably between 300,000 and 500,000. On Solomon's death, his son **Rehoboam** took the throne, but a revolt broke out under **Jeroboam I** who became king of the bulk of the country. **Rehoboam** retained only Jerusalem and Judah.

931–722. THE (NORTHERN) KINGDOM OF ISRAEL.

931–909. THE DYNASTY OF JEROBOAM. Jeroboam I (931–910) established Israel's political capital at **Shechem** and fought a five-year war with Judah, which ended only with the invasion of Pharaoh **Sheshonq I (Shishak)** in 926 (p. 31). The Egyptians devastated much of Israel. Jeroboam's son **Nadab** (910–909) was assassinated by a general, **Baasha.**

909–885. THE DYNASTY OF BAASHA. Baasha (909–886) fought both with Judah and Damascus. **Ben Hadad I** of Damascus defeated Israel and annexed Bashan, north of the Yarmuk River (p. 35). Apparently in response to this, Baasha moved the capital to **Tirzah,** whose site is not known. Baasha's son **Elah** (886–885) ruled only two years before he was assassinated by one of his generals. A three-year civil war broke out in which another general, **Omri,** was finally successful.

885–841. THE DYNASTY OF OMRI. Omri (885–874) established a new capital at Samaria, which he fortified, and married his son Ahab to Jezebel, daughter of **King Ittobaal of Tyre.** Omri attacked and subdued Moab in the Transjordan and also fought against the Judeans, but without much success. **Ahab** (874–853) made peace with Judah, marrying his daughter **Athaliah** to Jehoram, son of Jehoshaphat. In the **Battle of Qarqar** in 853, Ahab, along with the kings of Damascus and Hamath, temporarily stopped the Assyrians (p. 27). The coalition did not last, and Ahab lost his life fighting against Damascus. Jezebel attempted to **suppress the worship of Yahweh,** in favor of Baal, but was boldly resisted by the prophet **Elijah the Tishbite.** On Ahab's death he was succeeded by his two sons **Ahaziah** (853–852) and **Jehoram** (Joram, 852–841).

841–752. THE DYNASTY OF JEHU. Jehoram was killed in a rebellion by one of his generals, **Jehu** (841–814), supported by the prophet **Elisha.** In the revolt, Jezebel was murdered and the **priests of Baal massacred.** Jehu's foreign policy was weak: he paid tribute to Assyria, and Hazael of Damascus took Transjordan from Israel. Indeed, under Jehu's son, Joahaz (814–798), Israel became a **dependency of Damascus** (p. 35). Joash (798–782) was more successful, leading Israel in a series of wars against Ben Hadad II in which he recovered Israel's lost territories. Later Joash turned against Judah and defeated Amaziah, took Jerusalem, looted the temple, and reduced the southern kingdom to vassals. Joash's son, **Jeroboam II** (782–753), ruled a wealthy and powerful Israel: Damascus and Hamath were defeated, and perhaps annexed. The prophets **Amos** and **Hosea** opposed oppression and corruption in the kingdom. **Zechariah** (753–752) was the fifth and last king of Jehu's dynasty.

752–722. THE LAST DAYS OF ISRAEL. Zechariah was assassinated by **Shallum** (752), but after only one month's rule, he in turn was killed by **Menahem** (752–742), who paid an enormous tribute of 1,000 talents of silver to Tiglath-Pileser III of Assyria to avoid conquest. This submission was unpopular and Menahem's son **Pekahiah** (742–740) was assassinated by an anti-Assyrian party led by **Pekah** (740–732). Israel joined forces with Damascus against Assyria, but **Tiglath-Pileser III** came west in 734–732 and laid waste to both kingdoms. The Galilee was taken from Israel and turned into an Assyrian province, and Hoshea (732–722) was placed on the throne as a client-king. About 725, Hoshea revolted, seeking an alliance with **"So, King of Egypt"** (either Osorkon IV or Tefnahkte) (p. 31). The Assyrians managed to seize Hoshea, and Samaria fell in 722 after a three-year siege. According to Sargon II, 27,290 Israelites were deported from the country, and Israel was made an Assyrian province called **Samaria.**

931–586. THE (SOUTHERN) KINGDOM OF JUDAH.

931–768. PERIOD OF ISRAELITE DOMINATION. The **descendants of David** ruled Judah for its entire history, except for the reign of Queen Athaliah, the daughter of Ahab of Israel and Jezebel of Tyre. **Rehoboam** (931–913) died shortly after the raid by Sheshonq I (Shishak) of Egypt (p. 31), but the **war between Judah and Israel** continued intermittently through the reigns of Abijah (913–911) and Asa (911–870). **Jehoshaphat** (870–848) made peace with Ahab of Israel and joined him in war against Damascus. After the death of Jehoram (848–841) and Ahaziah (841), Jehoram's wife, **Athaliah** (841–835) seized power in Judah. With the backing of the **high priest,** Athaliah was deposed and killed, and Ahaziah's son **Jehoash** (835–796) was enthroned, but he was forced to pay heavy tribute to Damascus. Amaziah (796–768) lost a war with Joash and became a vassal of Israel.

768–715. THE REIGNS OF UZZIAH AND AHAZ. Uzziah (Azariah, 768–740) won military victories against Philistia, Edom, and northern Arabia and **restored Judah to political strength. Uzziah** became the head of the western anti-Assyrian coalition, but he was defeated by Tiglath-Pileser III in 738, although (unlike its Aramean allies) Judah managed to keep its independence (p. 27). **Ahaz** (734–715) came to the throne in time to face attack from a **coalition of Israel and Damascus.** Against the advice of the prophet **Isaiah,** he appealed to Assyria and the destruction of Damascus and Israel by Assyria soon followed.

715–640. PERIOD OF ASSYRIAN DOMINATION. Hezekiah (715–687) instituted a number of **religious reforms** and suppressed pagan practices, such as destroying a bronze serpent in the temple attributed to Moses. He organized a **coalition of Phoenicia, Philistia, and Egypt** to oppose the Assyrians, but in 701 Sennacherib crushed it (p. 27). Sennacherib accepted heavy tribute and did not take Jerusalem. **Manasseh** (687–642) and his son Amon (642–640) ruled as mere puppets of Assyria.

640–609. THE REIGN OF JOSIAH. Amon was murdered in a palace coup, but popular unrest put his son, **Josiah,** (640–609) on the throne. In 627, around the time of Ashurbanipal's death, Josiah reasserted Judah's independence and expanded the kingdom's borders. He moved into the old territory of Israel, annexing the Assyrian provinces of Samaria, Gilead, and Galilee, and **briefly reunited Judah and Israel. A law book,** the nucleus of the book of Deuteronomy, was found in the temple and made the basis of a religious reform: foreign and pagan cults were extirpated and worship was centralized in Jerusalem. The **Deuteronomic history** was compiled during Josiah's reign. Josiah was killed at the second **Battle of Megiddo** (609) opposing Pharaoh Necho II's march into Syria, and Judah briefly became an Egyptian vassal (p. 31).

609–586. PERIOD OF BABYLONIAN DOMINATION. During the reign of **Jehoiakim** (609–598), Nebuchadnezzar (p. 31) defeated the Egyptians at the **Battle of Carchemish** (605), and Judah became a Babylonian client-state. Around 601, Jehoiakim revolted against **Nebuchadnezzar** but died just before the Babylonian army arrived at Jerusalem. His son, **Jehoiachin** (597) reigned three months and then surrendered. He and about 10,000 Jews were taken captive into **Babylonian exile.** Nebuchadnezzar placed the king's uncle **Zedekiah** (597–586) on the throne. Despite the protests of the prophet **Jeremiah,** Zedekiah joined Egypt in a revolt, and Nebuchadnezzar besieged Jerusalem a second time. The city fell in 586, **Solomon's Temple** was razed, and a second group of captives was taken into **Babylonian captivity** (p. 28).

586–331. THE PROVINCE OF JUDAH.

586–539. JUDAH UNDER BABYLONIAN RULE. A Jewish governor, **Gedaliah,** was appointed, but he was soon assassinated in a nationalist revolt, which was suppressed. After this event, the focus of the biblical text turns to **the exiled community in Babylon,** and events in the province of Judah are obscure. The exile community, under the leadership of the former royal family, prospered. The prophets **Ezekiel** and **Deutero-Isaiah** operated in Babylonia. The Deuteronomic history was re-edited, and the priestly edition of the Pentateuch written. The last Babylonian governor was **Shesh-bazzar,** probably a member of the royal family.

539–332. JUDAH UNDER PERSIAN RULE. Cyrus (p. 28) confirmed Shesh-bazzar as governor and allowed him to begin construction of the **Second Temple.** It was the next governor, **Zerubbabel** (c. 520–516), the grandson of King Jehoiachin, who completed the structure. Zerubbabel's rebuff to the "people of the land" (that is, Jews who had remained in Judah and Israel) was the beginning of the split between **Samaritans** and **Jews.** Around 445, **Nehemiah,** the Jewish cupbearer to King Artaxerxes I (464–424), was appointed governor of Judah and rebuilt the walls of Jerusalem. **Ezra** served both as governor of Judah and as the religious authority for all Jews in the western Persian empire. His **cultic and legal reforms** had far-reaching effects on the development of post-exilic Judaism. The date of his mission is problematic: 457, 437, or 398 are all possible dates. Little is known about the subsequent

history of Judah until the conquest by **Alexander the Great** (see p. 69). When Alexander was besieging Tyre in 333, the high priest **Jaddua** submitted to him. The stories of Alexander visiting Jerusalem are probably apocryphal.

f. THE LAND OF ARAM (SYRIA)

1300–1200. EARLY ARAMEAN MOVEMENTS. The **Akhlamu,** mentioned in late 14th-century cuneiform records, may be the forerunners of the Arameans. It is certain that **two major movements of Aramaic speakers,** one west into Syria and another into Upper Mesopotamia and Babylonia (the Chaldeans), occurred in the course of the 12th century.

1000–900. EARLY ARAM. By 1000, the Arameans had become dominant in the region of **Damascus** and **Zobah** (the valleys of the Anti-Lebanon, south of modern Homs). These **southern Aramean states** were already in conflict with Saul. Hadadezer, king of Zobah, led a **coalition of Aramean kings** into the Transjordan, but was defeated by David. David later counterattacked, and Zobah came under **Israelite domination** (p. 34). One of Hadadezer's general's, **Rezon,** set up a kingdom north of Zobah and continued resistance to Israel. In the course of the 10th century, the Arameans took over and replaced some of the Neo-Hittite states in Syria. Til Barsip became known as **Bit Adini** around 1000, Sam'al became Ya'diya around 920, and Arpad turned into Bit Argusi around 900. These, with Qarqar, Hamath, and others, became the **northern Aramean states.** The population of Aram was probably around 600,000 in 1000 B.C.E.

859–855. THE ASSYRIAN CONQUEST OF NORTHERN ARAM. Shalmeneser III engaged a **coalition of northern Aramean kings,** Khayan of Ya'diya (Sam'al) and Akhuni of Bit Adini, and the Hittite states of Carchemish and Khattina. At the **Battle of Lutibu** (858) the Aramean-Hittite forces were defeated but not broken. In a second series of campaigns (857–855) Shalmeneser III conquered Bit Adini, the strongest of the northern Aramean states and turned it into an **Assyrian province** (p. 27).

900–806. THE RISE OF DAMASCUS. Damascus became the major Aramean state under the long reign of **Ben Hadad I** (also called Hadadezer, 880–842). In 878, Ben Hadad **defeated Israel** and annexed the territory of Bashan north of the Yarmuk. Ben Hadad again invaded Israel around 855 but was defeated by Ahab at the **Battle of Aphek.** When Shalmeneser, having broken the northern coalition, turned south, Ben Hadad allied himself with Ahab and King Ikhuleni of Hamath. At the **Battle of Qarqar** (853), the Aramean-Israelite coalition defeated Shalmeneser, who retired to Assyria. Ben Hadad subsequently absorbed all the small southern Aramean states. The **Assyrians returned,** however, and in a series of four campaigns Shalmeneser defeated Ben Hadad and took Damascus (842) (p. 27). Ben Hadad was murdered and a commoner, **Hazael** (842–806), seized the throne. The Assyrians did not remain in the region, and Hazael was left free to pursue his imperial ambitions. He **subjugated Israel** and much of Philistia and **laid tribute on Judah.**

806–732. THE DECLINE OF ARAM. Hazael's son, **Ben Hadad II** (806–750) was unable to hold together the Aramean Empire. Early in his reign he attacked Zakir, king of Hamath, but failed to subdue him. Joash of Israel fought free of Damascene control; indeed under Jeroboam II, Damascus as well as Hamath may have been annexed by Israel. With the **decline of Damascus,** the northern Aramean state of Arpad (Bit Argusi) came to the fore. In 755, King Matiel of Arpad allied himself with Urartu (p. 27) against the Assyrians, but they were defeated by Tiglath-Pileser III in 743. After a three-year siege, **Arpad itself fell.** Rezin, the son of Ben Hadad II, allied himself with Israel in an anti-Assyrian coalition. In 732 Tiglath-Pileser defeated the Aramean-Israelite coalition, and Aram, including Damascus, was divided into **Assyrian provinces,** collectively known as **Aram Naharain** (p. 27). This was the effective end of Aram as a political entity, although the Aramaic language subsequently became the **lingua franca** of western Asia and replaced Hebrew as the spoken language in Palestine.

6. PHOENICIA, CARTHAGE, AND THE PHOENICIAN COLONIES, c. 1200–322 B.C.E.

a. GEOGRAPHY

Phoenicia is the long narrow strip of land along the Mediterranean from the mouth of the Orontes in the north to Mount Carmel in the south. Its eastern boundary, the Lebanon chain, is rarely more than 12 miles from the coast. The most important cities were **Arvad**, Gubal or **Byblos, Sidon,** and **Tyre;** other cities were Marathus, Berytus (Beirut), and Ecdippa. By an arbitrary change of terminology, the Canaanites are called **Phoenicians** after 1200.

b. ECONOMY, TECHNOLOGY, SOCIETY, AND CULTURE

The **arable land** around the Phoenician cities was fertile, but limited, and wheat, grapes, figs, and date palms were staple crops. The Carthaginians developed a highly **systematized agriculture** in North Africa and wrote technical manuals on the subject. The main industry of Phoenicia was the manufacture of purple dye from the *murex* sea-mollusk, but weaving, glassmaking, metalworking, and ivory-working were also important. The famous **cedars of Lebanon** were exported to Egypt and elsewhere. The Phoenicians were famous **traders** and traveled widely from an early period all over the Mediterranean, and eventually as far as West Africa and Britain.

The **Phoenician script** reached its completed form around 1200 B.C.E. Though some inscriptions exist, little Phoenician literature survives, mainly a few translated fragments of the historian **Dius** and the philosopher **Sanchuniathon.** The Phoenicians created a **synthesis** of Egyptian and Mesopotamian culture and were the agents for passing much of Near Eastern civilization on to the Greeks.

The **Phoenician city-states** generally controlled only a small territory around them and rarely attempted to enlarge their land holdings. Generally, the city-states were ruled by hereditary kings assisted by advisory councils of nobles. **Carthage** also originally had a monarchy, but by the fourth century, the government was republican, with two annually elected magistrates (**sufetes**), a senate of 300 (which served for life), and a Council of 104, which had some sort of executive function. It is unclear when the republic replaced the monarchy: Carthaginian leaders are often called "kings," which might be meant literally or as a translation of *sufet,* literally "judge." In their late period other Phoenician cities were ruled by elected **sufetes** and senates.

The chief god of Tyre and its colonies was **Melqart,** and Sidon's main deity was **Eshmun.** Both worshiped Resheph (Apollo), Dagon, Astarte, and Tanit. The Phoenicians also worshiped Egyptian deities, especially Isis and Bes. The Carthaginians worshiped **Baal Hammon,** an assimilation of Baal with the Egyptian Amun, perhaps in a Libyan form. Archaeological evidence has confirmed that the Phoenicians and Carthaginians practiced child sacrifice.

c. PHOENICIA

1200–627. THE SIDONIAN STATE.
1200–1000. The Rise of Sidon. Sidon and **Byblos** were the chief city-states at the beginning of the 12th century. **Tyre** had been destroyed by the Sea Peoples but was refounded by Sidonians in the 12th century. It was **well protected**, located on an island off the coast, and became the capital of the Sidonian state, which by 1000 dominated Phoenicia. By this time the population of Phoenicia had reached approximately 200,000.
1000–888. The Dynasty of Abibaal. Under **Abibaal** (c. 1000), Tyre was transformed into a superb harbor and Abibaal's son **Hiram I** (969–935) entered into an alliance with David of Israel, which continued in the time of Solomon (p. 34). Phoenician artisans designed and built the temple of Solomon, and joint Phoenician-Israelite fleets sailed in the Mediterranean and the Indian Ocean. Hiram I unified all of Phoenicia from Mount Carmel to Arvad, though vassal dynasties continued to rule at Byblos and Arvad under Sidonian suzerainty. Little is known

of Hiram's successors other than their names and dates: Baalmazzar I (935–919), Abd'ashtart (918–910), Ashtart (909–898), and 'Astartrom (897–889). The last king of Abibaal's dynasty, Pilles (888) was assassinated by the high priest of Astarte, Ittobaal, who founded a new dynasty.
887–627. The Dynasty of Ittobaal. Ittobaal (887–856) married his daughter Jezebel to Ahab, the son of Omri of Israel, and may also have linked his house by marriage to Ben Hadad I of Damascus. **Baalmazzar II** (849–830) paid tribute to Shalmeneser in 842 and was succeeded by Mittin (829–821) and then by Pu'mayton (**Pygmalion**, 821–774). Pygmalion's sister **Elissa** or **Dido** is credited with founding the city of **Carthage** in 814. **Hiram II** (774–c. 730) paid tribute to Tiglath-Pileser III in 738, but his successor **Luli** (c. 730–701) joined with the Egyptians and Judah in an unsuccessful rebellion against the Assyrians and fled to Cyprus. Sennacherib appointed **Ittobaal II** as king. The next Assyrian vassal king, 'Abdmilkot, rebelled against Esarhaddon, who defeated the Phoenicians, razed Sidon to the ground, and built a new city opposite it called Kar-Esarhaddon. 'Abdmilkot was executed and what was left of Sidon became an Assyrian province.
627–573. THE ASCENDANCE OF TYRE. The destruction of Sidon left Tyre as the leading city of Phoenicia. **Baalu** (c. 680) rebelled in the reign of Esarhaddon but soon capitulated: his mainland territories were taken from him, and he paid tribute. After the decline of the Assyrian Empire, the Phoenicians enjoyed a brief period of independence, though they never regained their former position, as Greek colonization had ended their near monopoly of trade in the Mediterranean (p. 62).
573–332. BABYLONIAN AND PERSIAN PHOENICIA.
573–539. Babylonian domination. Nebuchadnezzar (p. 28) invested Tyre in 587, during the reign of Ittobaal III. The siege lasted 13 years; the city probably surrendered in 573. At first, Tyre was ruled by judges (*sufetes*) under Babylonian domination, but after a short time the monarchy was restored.
539–332. Phoenicia under Persian Rule. When Cyrus came to power in Babylon (539) Phoenicia was bloodlessly absorbed into the Persian Empire (p. 40). It was designated as the fifth satrapy, but vassal kings continued to rule in Sidon, Tyre, Arvad, and Byblos. Phoenician fleets played an important part in Persia's wars against Greece. In c. 350, **Tennes** led a revolt against the Persians in Sidon, which was crushed by Artaxerxes III with great loss of life. When Alexander invaded Phoenicia, Tyre was the only city to resist under its last king, **Azemilkos.** The siege lasted from January to August 332. Alexander built an enormous mole across to the island city, which permanently connected it to the mainland. (To p. 40)

d. CARTHAGE AND THE WESTERN PHOENICIAN COLONIES

1100–600. The Foundation of the Western Colonies. The Phoenicians founded merchant colonies as early as the 11th century (at Hazor and Gaza in Palestine, Memphis in Egypt, and Kition [Latarkia] in Cyprus), but these were all quarters within established cities rather than separate settlements. Literary sources place the foundation of Phoenician colonies at **Lixus** (on the Atlantic coast of Africa), **Gades** (on the Atlantic coast of Spain), and **Utica** (in North Africa) at around 1100, but these dates have not been confirmed archaeologically. These three early colonies were probably settled by late 10th or early 9th centuries. Around 850, the settlement at Kition moved out of the native town and established itself as an independent town called Qart Hadasht—New City. The next Phoenician colony to be founded became the most famous—**Carthage.** The city's Phoenician name was the same as Kition's: **Qart-Hadasht** (Greek **Carchedon** and Latin **Carthago**). Several versions of its founding exist: one has **Elissa** (Dido) fleeing from Tyre and founding the city of Carthage in the 7th year of Pu'mayton (814), but another source gives the foundation date as 751. No archaeological remains have been uncovered at Carthage before the 8th century, but both dates remain possible. The colony of **Sexi** in Spain was also founded in the 8th century, probably in response to a growing Greek colonization movement. In the 7th century, the Tyrians established settlements at **Lepcis Magna** and Hadrumetum in North Africa; **Motya** in Sicily; and Sulcis, Caralis, Nora, and Tharros in Sardinia. Around the same time, **Mogador** was founded on an island on the West African coast, 450 miles south of the Strait of Gibralter. Carthage established **Ibiza,** off the east coast of Spain, 160 years after its own founding, in 654 or 591.

600–322. The Rise of Carthage. Around 600, Carthage tried unsuccessfully to prevent the Phocaean Greeks from founding Massilia (Marseilles) (p. 60), and in the 6th century, open war broke out between the Greeks and an alliance of the Etruscans and Carthaginians. The Carthaginians under **Malchus** defeated the Greeks in Sicily around 550. In 535, the Carthaginian-Etruscan alliance crushed the Phocaeans in the sea **Battle of Alalia** in Corsica. From the mid-sixth to fourth centuries, **Mago** and his descendants dominated Carthage, either as mon-

archs or as political strongmen. By this time, the population of Carthage was probably around half a million—about 20 percent Phoenician and the rest native Berbers. In 508, the Carthaginians signed a treaty with the new Roman state. While Xerxes was invading Greece, in 480 (p. 40), the Carthaginians invaded Sicily but were defeated at the **Battle of Himera** by the forces of Syracuse and Agrigentum. Around this time the Carthaginians turned inland, taking over the city's fertile Libyan hinterland. In the fifth century the **voyage of Hanno** occurred down the African coast, as far as Sierra Leone and perhaps Nigeria, as well as the **voyage of Himilco,** which may have reached Britain or Ireland. Around 409, war broke out again between Syracuse and Carthage: in a seesaw struggle Dionysius sacked Motya in 398 and the Carthaginians besieged Syracuse unsuccessfully in 396. The Syracusans ultimately won this war, but fighting between the Carthaginians and Syracusans continued through much of the fourth century. In 348, a second treaty was signed with Rome, and the subsequent history of Carthage is part of Roman history (p. 78).

7. ASIA MINOR, c. 3000–333 B.C.E.

a. GEOGRAPHY

Asia Minor, or Anatolia, is a peninsula stretching westward from the Armenian mountains to the Aegean Sea, with the Black Sea to the north and the Mediterranean to the south. **Western Anatolia** contained four fertile river valleys, was called Arzawa and Assuwa in Hittite times, and later contained Troas, Mysia, and Lydia. In the southern part of the peninsula lay the Lukka Lands (Lycia) and to the east Kizzuwatna, later Cilicia. The northern Pontic coast was home of the warlike Kaska peoples. Most of Asia Minor is dominated by the **central plateau.** In its western part was Phrygia; in the center, south of the great Salt Lake (Tuz Göl), was the fertile Konya plain; and to the east of the Halys river was Hatti, the center of the Hittite Empire. In the southeast of the peninsula, Cappadocia was located in the **Anti-Taurus range.** In easternmost Anatolia, the mountains rise to the high peaks of Armenia. It was the most populous region of ancient western Asia, with a **population** of some 3 million through the Bronze Age.

b. ECONOMY, TECHNOLOGY, SOCIETY, AND CULTURE

In the fertile valleys of the west, as well as the Konya valley and Cilicia, grain, olives, and grapes were grown. Raising stock was important in the more mountainous regions. Both the Taurus and southwest Anatolia had mines, which provided copper, silver, iron, and gold. Since the peninsula lay on the land bridge to Europe and was the sea route from the Mediterranean to the Black Sea, trade was always a large part of the economy. The earliest writings in Asia Minor are 19th-century B.C.E. records of the Assyrian merchant colony at Kanesh in Cappadocia (p. 26). In a later period, both **Hattic** and **Hittite** were written in cuneiform. After the fall of the Hittite Empire, so-called **hieroglyphic** Hittite was used to write inscriptions in the Luwian language. The Phrygians used an alphabet borrowed from the Phoenicians, but their language remains untranslatable.

The Hittite Empire adopted the palace bureaucracy of the Mesopotamian kingdoms along with the cuneiform script. Although the Hittite king was called the Sun and served as military leader, high priest, and judge, the Hittite state was not centralized, but feudal. Chariot-riding nobility were allotted serfs for their support in exchange for military service. The city-states of the west and south generally were ruled by kings, and some regions, like the Pontic coast, remained tribal in organization.

The Hattians worshipped the sun goddess Wurusemu and the storm god Taru; the Hurrians, Teshup and Hepat; and the Luwians, Tarkhunt. The **Hittite religion** was peculiarly syncretistic and mixed Hattic, Hurrian, Luwian, Akkadian, and Sumerian gods with native Hittite deities such as the sun goddess Arinna. The chief deities of the Phrygians were **Cybele** (or **Ma**, the Great Mother) and **Attis**, a god who died

and was resurrected. Little is known about the religion of the Lydians: the gods **Santas** and **Baki** (Bacchus) were named in their inscriptions.

c. THE HATTIANS AND THE HITTITES

c. 3000–2000. THE HATTIANS AND THE LUWIANS. The **Hattians** inhabited central Asia Minor in the third millennium. Their language, known from Hittite religious texts, is without known affinities. They appear to have been absorbed by the Hittites. Sometime after 2300, the **Luwians,** an Indo-European-speaking people, settled in southern Anatolia.

c. 2000–1200. THE HITTITES.

2000–1700. THE HITTITE INVASION OF ASIA MINOR. The Indo-European-speaking Hittites migrated into central Anatolia from Europe sometime around 2000. Around 1800, the Hittite King **Pitkhana** of Kussara and his successor **Anitta** defeated the Hattic rulers of Hattusas and Kanesh. They sacked **Hattusas,** but used **Kanesh** as the capital of a Hittite state.

c. 1680–1500. THE OLD KINGDOM. Labarnas I (c. 1680–1610) founded what is known as the Old Hittite Kingdom or **Hatti. Hattusilis I** (c. 1660–1620) moved the capital to Hattusas (modern Boghazköy), located in the bend of the Halys River. He conquered the area of the Konya plain, which became the center of the Hittite empire, then overcame Alalakh in northern Syria and campaigned against Arzawa in the far west. His successor **Mursilis I** (c. 1620–1595) defeated a Hurrian army, destroyed Aleppo, and then boldly marched south into Mesopotamia. The Hittites took Babylon, pillaged it, and brought down the 1st Dynasty of Babylon (1595) (p. 26). Political disturbances brought Mursilis back to Hattusas where he was assassinated in a coup d'état. After his death a series of petty kings ruled, and the Old Kingdom declined in power. The Hurrians (p. 26) took the North Syrian region, which they named **Hanigalbat** and Cilicia, now called **Kizzuwatna.** When **Telepinus** (c. 1520) came to the throne he halted the kingdom's decline of Hatti, pushing back the Hurrians. Telepinus issued an edict on the law of succession that stabilized the crown. The Hittite law code also dates from this general period.

c. 1420–1200. THE HITTITE EMPIRE.

c. 1420–1375. THE EARLY KINGS. Tudhaliyas II (c. 1420) established a new dynasty, but in the reigns of Arnuwandas I (c. 1425), Hattusilis II (c. 1400), and Tudhaliyas III (c. 1420–1375), the Hittite state was almost destroyed. The Hurrian kingdom of Mitanni attacked on the east, and Arzawa, now important enough to correspond with the Egyptian pharaoh, pressed from the west. The Kaska tribes from the north succeeded in taking and sacking Hattusas. The Hittites faced a desperate situation, when Tudhaliyas's son, who had served as commander of the army, took the throne.

c. 1375–1345. THE REIGN OF SUPPILULIUMAS. Suppiluliumas rebuilt Hattusas, expanding the city and fortifying it with a four-mile-long wall of stone and brick. He also reorganized the home territories and then marched against the Hurrians. His first encounter with Tush-rata of Mitanni resulted in a severe defeat for the Hittites, but, with the help of Artadama II, the rival to Tushrata for the throne of Mitanni, Suppiluliumas was able to conquer the capital Washukkani and Mitanni was turned into a vassal (p. 27). The Hittites then attacked the Amorite kingdoms of northern Syria, and the two largest, Aleppo and Carchemish, were taken and given Hittite princes as kings (p. 27). The wealthy coastal city-state of Ugarit paid tribute. Suppiluliumas also campaigned against the Kaska peoples, keeping them under control. Suppiluliumas fell victim to a plague, and his son, Arnuwandas II (1345–1344), died after only a year.

c. 1344–1250. THE HEIGHT OF THE HITTITE EMPIRE. In the early part of the reign of **Mursilis II** (1344–c.1310), Ashur-Uballit I took Mitanni and annexed it to Assyria. Mursilis had more success against Arzawa in the west, defeating and killing its king. A revolt in Carchemish was pacified, and for many years he fought almost annual campaigns against the Kaska. **Muwatallis** (c. 1310–1280) inherited a powerful, well-organized empire from his father, but Ramses II was ambitious to regain Egypt's Syrian possessions and the inevitable battle was fought at **Qadesh on the Orontes** in 1286 (p. 31). Ramses claimed a victory but probably falsely, as Muwatallis continued his advance as far as Damascus, and the Hittites retained firm control of northern Syria. During the king's absence in Syria, the **Kaska** again sacked Hattusas, and, perhaps as a result, Muwatillis moved his official residence to **Tarhuntassa**, somewhere in the Taurus Mountains. **Urhiteshup** (c. 1280), Muwatallis's oldest son by a royal concubine, was shortly deposed by his uncle **Hattusilis III** (c. 1280–1250). In 1270, Hattusilis signed an important treaty with Ramses II, setting a boundary between the Hittite and Egyptian Empires. The treaty was probably made to counter the growing threat of Assyria under Shalmeneser I (p. 27). Hattusilis married Puduhepa, the daughter of a Hurrian priest from Kizzuwatna, and the couple issued edicts jointly. Hurrian influence appears in sculpture, particularly on the **reliefs of Yazilikaya,** with their enormous processions of gods.

c. 1250–1200. THE FALL OF THE HITTITE EMPIRE. Tudhaliyas IV (c. 1250–1225) was almost continuously at war in western Anatolia: fighting the kings of Arzawa, as well as the **Ahhiyawa** (probably Achaeans from the Greek mainland). He conquered the island of Cyprus (Alashiya) to obtain control of its copper deposits. In the reign of Arnuwandas III (c. 1225–1220), the situation in the western provinces abruptly worsened, and in the reign of Suppiluliumas II (c. 1220–1200) the final waves of the **Sea Peoples** (p. 31) and Phrygians destroyed the empire.

d. THE PHRYGIANS AND THE LYDIANS

c. 1200–1000. THE PHRYGIAN INVASION. The Indo-European-speaking Phrygians came from Thrace about 1200 and occupied the whole of Asia Minor from the Sea of Marmara to the border of Assyria. They were divided into two groups of tribes, **Mushki** (biblical Meshech, perhaps the Mysians) and **Tabal** (biblical Tubal).

c. 1000–700. THE KINGDOM OF PHRYGIA arose in the western part of the central plateau, with its capital at Gordium, not far from modern Ankara. Since the Phrygian inscriptions cannot be read, almost nothing is known of their history. Greek legend speaks of a King **Midas** of the Phrygians, whose touch turned objects to gold, but, ironically, a royal burial that was discovered unplundered in 1955, while quite elaborate, contained no gold whatsoever. **Midas** might be the individual

called Mita of Mushku mentioned in the inscriptions of Sargon II (c. 715). The **Cimmerians** invaded Phrygia and devastated the kingdom, but the Phrygian nation remained independent until its conquest by Cyrus in 547 (p. 40).

c. 800–685. THE LYDIAN KINGDOM. Little is known about the early history of the Lydian kingdom. Its capital Sardis was located on the Magnesia River between the Ionian cities of the coast and Phrygia. Lydia survived the devastation of the Cimmerians c. 695, which destroyed Phrygia. Herodotus relates the story of King Candaules' overthrow by his closest friend and advisor, Gyges.

685–547. THE DYNASTY OF THE MERMNADAE. Gyges (680–652) was the founder of the Mermnadae dynasty and defeated the nomadic Cimmerian tribes, extending the borders of his kingdom. A tablet recording an embassy of Gyges to Ashurbanipal of Assyria survives, but Gyges sent Carian and Ionian mercenaries to aid Psammetichus I in driving the Assyrians out of Egypt (p. 31). In 652, the Cimmerians renewed their attack on Lydia, and Gyges fell in battle. Gyges' successor **Ardys** (652–625) overcame the Cimmerian menace and then turned to fight the Greek cities along the coast of Asia Minor. The **Lydians invented coinage** in the 7th century using **electrum,** a natural alloy of gold and silver.

609–560. THE REIGN OF ALYATTES. Under Alyattes, the Greek cities of the coast (except Miletus) were conquered. In 590, **Alyattes** began a war with Cyaxares of Media which lasted for five years. After a battle, which can be dated by a solar eclipse to May 28, 585, a treaty was signed. Alyattes' daughter married Astyages, son of the Median king. The enormous tumulus tomb of Alyattes was described by Herodotus and is still to be seen near the ruins of Sardis.

560–546. THE REIGN OF CROESUS. Croesus brought the Lydian kingdom to its height. He controlled all of Asia Minor west of the Halys except Cilicia and Lycia. Under Croesus, pure gold coins were minted for the first time. In 547, Croesus went to war with Cyrus of Persia (p. 40) but was completely outmaneuvered. The Persians routed the Lydians in a pitched battle at Sardus, and Croesus was taken prisoner. A Lydian noble named Pactyas took the throne and continued resistance but was defeated.

e. PERSIAN ASIA MINOR

Asia Minor was divided into four satrapies. Lydia and Mysia, plus all of the cities along the western coast, were ruled from Sardis. A second province, Phrygia, with its capital at Daskylion, extended to the Halys River. The satrapy of Cilicia was ruled from Adana, and that of Cappadocia from Mazaca. The Royal Road connected Sardis to Susa, 1677 miles away. By this time the population of Asia Minor was probably around 4 million, including some 250,000 Greeks. The Greek cities revolted against the Persians from 499–494, and in 498, Sardis was burnt by the Ionians and Athenians. The army that Xerxes sent to Greece gathered somewhere in Cappadocia and wintered in Sardis from 481–480. In 407, Cyrus, the brother of Artaxerxes III, was appointed satrap of all Asia Minor. From there he planned and organized the revolt which culminated in his death at the **Battle of Cunaxa** (401). Asia Minor was the first part of the Persian Empire invaded by Alexander the Great (p. 69). He defeated the Persians in decisive battles in the region, first at **Granicus** (334), near the Sea of Marmara, then at Issus in **Cilicia.** From here he went on to conquer all the Persian Empire.

8. ARMENIA, c. 1300–331 B.C.E.

a. GEOGRAPHY

Armenia is a mountainous region lying between the Black and Caspian Seas. The mountains of Kurdistan separate it from Mesopotamia, and its northern border is the Kura River. The region contains three great lakes: Van, Urmia, and Sevan. In the Urartian period, the main cities were **Tushpa, Erebuni,** and **Rusahinili.** The only major city in the Armenian period under discussion was **Armavir.**

b. ECONOMY, TECHNOLOGY, SOCIETY, AND CULTURE

Farming was excellent in the fertile river valleys, and fine wine was produced. Husbandry was also highly developed: Urartian cattle and sheep were famous for their high quality, and superb horses were raised. At its height, the **Kingdom of Urartu** had a technology and culture equivalent to any in western Asia. Urartian architecture is noteworthy for the quality of its masonry, and its mountain-fortresses are impressive feats of construction. The Urartians also built formidable **hydraulic works:** an aqueduct brought fresh water 47 miles to Tushpa. After the invasion of the Armenians in the 6th century, the material culture regressed considerably and little survived of the Urartian civilization. In the Urartian period, a native hieroglyphic script was used alongside cuneiform. In Persian Armenia, Iranian written with Aramaic characters was utilized. The chief Urartian deity was **Haldi,** a warrior god; the storm god was **Teisheba** (Hurrian Teshup) and his wife was **Huba** (Hebat). After the Armenians arrived in the region, they adopted the **Zoroastrian** religion of the Persians (p. 39). *(To p. 39)*

c. URARTU (VAN)

c. 1300–c. 850. THE EARLY HISTORY OF URARTU. The Urartians were related to the Hurrians and moved into the region sometime in the second millennium. In the time of Shalmeneser I (1275–1246), the region was divided into a number of small kingdoms and subsequently became tributary to the Assyrians. The Aramean invasions of the 11th century drove the Assyrians back to their homeland (p. 27), and at some point afterward the kingdom of Urartu was established around Lake Van, with its capital at **Tushpa.**

c. 850–584. THE KINGDOM OF URARTU (VAN). Shalmeneser III defeated the first known king of Urartu, **Aramu** in 856. Sarduri I (c. 834) and Ishpuini (c. 822) also fought the Assyrians. **Menua** (c. 800) increased Urartian power, occupying the entire Armenian highland area, and built the walls and aqueduct of Tushpa. Argishti I (786–764) built the city of Erebuni as a royal capital. **Sarduri II** (764–735) reorganized the army along Assyrian lines and extended Urartian power as far as northern Syria. In 743, however, Tiglath-Pileser III defeated the Urar-

tians and reestablished Assyrian control over north Syria. The Assyrians attacked Urartu itself in 735, annexed Urmia, and besieged Tushpa (unsuccessfully). In 714 Sargon II launched a carefully planned attack against **Rusa I** (735–714) and defeated the Urartian army. Although defeated by marauding Cimmerians in 707, **Argishti II** (714–685) kept the Assyrians at bay and built a number of new fortresses and irrigation works. Such projects were continued by his son **Rusa II** (685–645), who completed a new capital **Rusahinili** (Toprakkale). After the death of Rusa II, the Urartian kingdom declined. Sometime after 584, the Medes defeated King Rusa IV and destroyed Rusahinili.

d. ARMENIA

612–559. ARMENIA UNDER MEDIAN RULE. Around the time that the Medians took over Urartu, the Armenians arrived in the region. The Armenians spoke an Indo-European language, but their origins are obscure. They may have originated in Phrygia, or even farther west, or may have arrived with Iranian tribes north of the Black Sea.

559–331. ARMENIA UNDER PERSIAN RULE. When Cyrus took over Astyages' kingdom in 559, the region was absorbed into the Persian Empire. Darius I (522–486) (p. 40) made Armenia the 13th satrapy of his reorganized empire. It is in an inscription of Darius that the Armenians are first explicitly mentioned (519). In 401, Xenophon and the Ten Thousand arrived in the region, fleeing from the Persians (p. 40). The satrap of Armenia at the time was Orontes I (c. 401–366). His son and successor, Orontes II (366–331) was killed fighting Alexander the Great at Arbela (p. 70). Alexander appointed Orontes II's son, **Mithanes,** to be the satrap. The dynasty, the **Orontids,** eventually became kings and ruled Armenia until 200 B.C.E.

9. IRAN, c. 2700–330 B.C.E.

a. GEOGRAPHY

Iran, or Persia, extends from the Zagros Mountains to the Indus Valley, and from the Persian Gulf to the Caspian Sea. The southwestern region was the site of the Elamite cities **Anshan** (Malyan), **Simashki** and **Susa,** and later the homeland of the Persians. The highland area was urbanized very late; the Median cities of **Ecbatana** (Hamadan) and **Rhagae** and the Persian **Persepolis** and **Parsargadae** were built only in the first millennium. In 1000 B.C.E. the population was around 2 million.

b. ECONOMY, TECHNOLOGY, SOCIETY, AND CULTURE

In the southwest urban life based around the temple and the royal palace flourished from an early period, but groups in the highlands usually remained tribal in organization. A hieroglyphic script (**Proto-Elamite**) was used as early as 2900 B.C.E., but around 2230 the Elamites adopted the cuneiform script, which was used as late as the Persian period. Though a large number of tablets have been found, Elamite still cannot be translated. The Persians also used cuneiform to write their language in monumental inscriptions.

The religion of Elam, like Mesopotamia, had an organized priesthood and the use of ziggurat temples. The main gods of the Elamites were **Humban,** the sun god **Nahhunte,** and **Inshushinak,** the god of Susa, but Sumerian deities such as Inanna and Nanna were also worshipped. The original religion of the Medes and Persians was similar to that of the Vedic Indians, with many gods, including **Mithra** and **Varuna,** in common. The Median religious reformer **Zoroaster** (Zarathustra, c. 630–550) introduced monotheism. **Zoroastrianism** banned the sacrifice of animals and the use of intoxicants and introduced the idea of individual salvation through the free choice of God (**Ahura Mazda**) over the Spirit of Evil (Angro-mainyu or **Ahriman**). The priests of the religion were known as **Magi,** originally a Median tribe.

c. THE ELAMITES

c. 2700–2230. EARLY DYNASTIC ELAM.
c. 2700–2550. THE FIRST DYNASTY OF AWAN was contemporary to

the Mesopotamian Early Dynastic Period, though none of the kings are known. The first mention of Elam is in the Sumerian King List: Enmebaragesi (c. 2700) "carried off the arms of the land of Elam as booty." Eannatum of Lagash also raided Elam, and temple records from Lagash (c. 2300) speak of an Elamite raid on Sumer. A state of more or less constant warfare existed between Sumer and Elam throughout the 3rd millennium (p. 26).

c. 2550–2230. THE SECOND DYNASTY OF AWAN was founded by **Peli** and ruled from Susa. The king ruled through a viceroy, often the king's brother, and the monarchy appears to have been elective. The provincial governors had considerable independence. Sargon of Akkad (2371–2316) defeated **Hishap-Resher** and sacked Susa. Under Naram-Sin (2291–2255) a treaty (the earliest known) was made with the king of Elam who was made a vassal. The last king of the dynasty **Kutik-in-shushinak** (c. 2240–2230) threw off the yoke of Akkad and took the title "King of the Four Quarters." He did a great deal of building in the sacred acropolis at Susa. The Dynasty of Awan, like that of Akkad, fell victim to Gutian incursions (p. 26).

2230–c. 1400. THE OLD ELAMITE KINGDOM.
2230–c. 1925. THE DYNASTY OF SIMASHKI. Shulgi of Ur (2095–2048) conquered Susa, where he did considerable building, including a temple to Inshushinak. The Sumerians set up a frontier force made up of mercenary Elamites, commanded by a *sukkal-mah,* or Great Regent. Independent kings ruled in **Simashki** to the north of Susa. In 2021, the fifth king of Simashki, **Enpi-luhhan** attacked Elam and took Susa. Ibbi-Sin of Ur counterattacked and captured the Elamite king, but despite another invasion in 2017, the Sumerians were unable to maintain control of Elam. Soon afterwards, in alliance with tribes from the Zagros, the new king of Elam, probably **Hutran-tempti,** attacked and destroyed Ur itself. Royal succession in the Simashki dynasty was through the king's sister (and wife), who was called the "reverend mother" *(amma hashtuk).* In 1993, Ishbi-Erra (2017–1985) drove the Elamites from Ur, but the kings of Simashki continued to rule Elam. The end of the dynasty is obscure; its last certain king was **Indattu II** (c. 1925).

c. 1925–1400. THE DYNASTY OF EPARTI began around the same time the Awan dynasty ended. Its kings styled themselves "Great Regent," after the military title of the Ur III period, as well as "King of Anshan and Susa." The dynasty reached its height under **Kutur-Nahhunte I** (c.

1752) who conquered southern Babylonia. Texts from Elam indicate large Akkadian and Amorite minorities in the country. Kurigalzu I, the Kassite king of Babylonia, conquered Elam around 1400 (p. 27).

c. 1350–1110. THE MIDDLE ELAMITE KINGDOM.

c. 1350–c. 1200. THE DYNASTY OF IGI-HALKI. Elam regained its independence in the 14th century under Igi-Halki, who took the title "King of Elam." Untash-napir-risha (c. 1250) founded a new capital **Dur-Untash** (Tchogha-Zambil), with a large ziggurat temple. The last king of this dynasty was Kiten-Hutran.

c. 1200–1110. THE DYNASTY OF HULLUTUSH-INSHUSHINAK. Around 1200, Hullutush-Inshushinak I founded a new dynasty. Around 1160, **Shutruk-nahhunte** invaded Mesopotamia and took Babylon. He brought back spoils, including the Code of Hammurapi, to Susa and placed his son, Kutir-Nahhunte III, on the throne of Babylon. On his father's death, Kutir-Nahhunte III (1155–1150) became king of Elam but lost Babylon. **Shilak-Inshushinak I** (c. 1150–1120), one of the greatest kings of Elam, conquered large areas in the highlands and parts of Mesopotamia, but Hutelush-Inshushinak (c. 1120–1110) lost Anshan to Nebuchadnezzar I of Babylon (p. 27). After his reign, records cease and the end of the kingdom is obscure.

c. 820–640. THE NEO-ELAMITE KINGDOM. Early in the 9th century, Humban-Tahrah founded a new dynasty, with its capital at Susa. Humban-nikash (743–717) joined forces with Merodoch-Baladan II and defeated Sargon II at the **Battle of Der** (721). The next king, **Shutruk-Nahhunte II** (717–699), conquered a considerable area to the northwest. Hallushu-Inshushinak (699–693) deposed his brother, raided Mesopotamia, and carried off Sennacherib's son, who was reigning as king of Babylon. Humban-numena (692–687), allied with the Arameans and Persians, defeated Sennacherib at the **Battle of Halule** (691). There was further fighting between Elam and Assyria over the next 40 years. Ashurbanipal defeated and killed **Tempt-Humban-Inshushinak** (Tuemman, 663–653) and made Elam an Assyrian vassal. The Assyrians invaded again in 647 and sacked Susa (p. 28). Humban-haltash II (648–644) fled but was turned over to Ashurbanipal and executed. Elam regained its independence but was absorbed into the Persian Empire in 538.

d. THE MEDES AND THE PERSIANS

c. 1500–559. THE MEDES.

c. 1500–850. THE ARYAN INVASION OF IRAN. The Medes were an **Aryan** (Indo-Iranian) people who entered the Iranian plateau around 1500 along with the Persians, Parthians, Bactrians, and Arachosians, while other Aryan tribes went on to conquer northern India. The Medes themselves were divided into six tribes (one of which was called the **Magi**). Nothing certain is known of Median history until their first mention in the Assyrian records of Shalmeneser III (859–825) (p. 27).

701–625. MEDIA UNDER ASSYRIAN RULE. Sometime during the 8th century B.C.E., the Medes established a capital at **Ecbatana** (Hamadan) on the mountainous eastern fringes of Babylonia. The Dahyauka mentioned in Assyrian sources as a Median chieftain around 715 might be **Deioces**, who Herodotus says founded the Median dynasty. **Sennacherib** (705–682) made the Medes tributary in 701, but a revolt broke out in 674 under Khshathrita (possibly Herodotus's **Phraortes**), who ruled an independent Media for some time. Zoroaster (c. 630–550) introduced his religious reforms in Media. After a period of Scythian domination, **Cyaxares** (Huvakhshtara, 624–585) became king of Media and reorganized the army along Assyrian lines. The Medians took and sacked Ashur in 614. Cyaxares then allied himself to Nabopolassar of Babylon and, in 612 the Medians and Babylonians destroyed the Assyrian capital Nineveh (p. 28). Cyaxares and Nabopolassar divided the Assyrian Empire between them. In 609, the Medes conquered Urartu. Between 590 and 585, Cyaxares fought a war with the Lydians, which ended with a marriage alliance. Little is known of the subsequent history of the empire until its fall under **Astyages** (Arshit-vega, 584–549).

c. 850–549. THE RISE OF THE PERSIANS. Sometime in the 9th century, another Aryan tribe, the **Persians,** settled in Anshan to the south of Susa. In the early 7th century, one of their chiefs, Achaemenes (Hakhamanish) founded a dynasty, the **Achaemenids,** and won independence from the Neo-Elamite kings. His son, **Teispes** (Chishpish), took the title "King of Anshan" and allied himself with the Elamites in their war against Sennacherib. When Ashurbanipal sacked Susa in 646, **Cyrus I** (Kurush) became an Assyrian vassal. After the rise of Cyaxares, Persia became a Median dependency. Around 560, the Median King Astyages arranged for his daughter to marry the Persian King Cambyses I. Their son Cyrus II served as a commander in the Median army.

e. THE PERSIAN EMPIRE

556–530. THE REIGN OF CYRUS THE GREAT. On the death of his father, Cyrus II became the king of the Persians. In 553, Cyrus led a revolt against his grandfather Astyages. Although he suffered some early defeats, the Median army eventually went over to Cyrus, and he took Ecbatana in 549. Cyrus now ruled the entire Median Empire. In 546 Cyrus conquered Lydia, adding much of Asia Minor to his realm. Cyrus then defeated King Nabonidus, entered Babylon in 539, and took over all the Babylonian Empire: Mesopotamia, Phoenicia, and Syria-Palestine.

c. 530–521. THE REIGN OF CAMBYSES. Cyrus was succeeded by **Cambyses** (Kambujiya) who, to ensure the throne, had his brother **Smerdis** (Bardiya) killed. Cambyses defeated Psammetichus III and by the summer of 525 had taken control of all of Egypt, but he was unsuccessful in an attempt to conquer the Kushite kingdom of Meroë (p. 32). In 522, a pretender named Gaumata seized the throne, claiming to be the dead Smerdis. Cambyses died on his way to deal with the revolt.

c. 522–486. THE REIGN OF DARIUS I. A member of another branch of the Achaemenid family, **Darius I** (Darayavaush) defeated Gaumata's revolt as well as other revolts in Babylonia and the eastern provinces. Darius's commemoration of his achievements, the **Behistun inscription,** written in Old Persian, Elamite, and Akkadian, became the key to the modern decipherment of cuneiform. Darius later added the Indus Valley and Libya to his empire, now the largest the world had ever known. He reorganized the administration and divided the empire into 20 **satrapies,** as well as introducing a standard gold coinage, the **daric.** At its height, the Persian Empire probably contained around 15 to 16 million inhabitants, with some 4 million in Persia proper. There were royal residences at Susa, Persepolis, Ecbatana, and Babylon, and good roads, with stations for royal messengers, which made possible regular communications within the vast realm. After 513, Darius started expanding into Europe and led an expedition which crossed the Danube. In 499, the Ionian Greeks in Asia Minor revolted but were suppressed after a six-year war. The Athenians had aided the rebels, and to punish them Darius sent the expedition which was defeated at the **Battle of Marathon** (490) (p. 64).

c. 586–330. THE DECLINE AND FALL OF THE PERSIAN EMPIRE. The next king, **Xerxes I** (Khshayarsa, 486–465), undertook a major invasion of Greece but was defeated at sea in the **Battle of Salamis** (480) and on land at **Plataea** and **Mycale** (479). After Xerxes' murder in a palace coup, **Artaxerxes I Longimanus** (Rtaxshaca, 465–424) took the throne. Athens took the offensive against Persia by sending troops to aid a revolt in Egypt (456–454) and by attacking Cyprus (450), but finally readied a peace agreement with Persia in 448 (p. 66). The empire suffered a series of coups d'état: **Xerxes II (424–404)** was assassinated by his brother Sogdianus (424), who in turn fell at the hands of **Darius II Nothus** (424–404). **Artaxerxes II Mnemon (404–358)** faced the rebellion of his brother Cyrus, who raised an army in Anatolia which included ten thousand Greek mercenaries. The rebel army won the **Battle of Cunaxa** (401) near Babylon, but Cyrus was killed. The Greeks marched back to the Black Sea under the leadership of Xenophon, who wrote the **Anabasis** ("March Upcountry") about the experience. Another insurrection broke out in Asia Minor under Datames, the satrap of Cappadocia, and spread to the western satrapies (366–360). Egypt won its independence in 404. **Artaxerxes III Ochus (358–338)** succeeded through energetic measures in reconstituting the empire but faced the growing power of **Philip of Macedon,** who had unified the Greeks under his rule (p. 69). Both Artaxerxes III and his weak son, Arses (338–336), were assassinated, and it was **Darius III Codomannus** (336–330) who met the invasion of Philip's son, **Alexander the Great.** Alexander defeated the Persians at the battles of Granicus (334), Issus (333), and Gaugamela, near Arbela (331). The next year, Darius, fleeing from the Macedonians, was killed by some of his nobles (p. 70).

(To p. 100)

10. ARABIA, c. 850–332 B.C.E.

a. GEOGRAPHY

Arabia is divided into northern and southern regions. The north is mainly flat desert dotted by oases, while in the southwest the Sarat Mountains rise up to 10,000 feet and receive generous rainfall. The main trade route ran through **Yathrib** (Medina), with a western branch running through Dedan to Ma'in to Gaza and an eastern branch through **Teima** to **Qedar** (Duma) to Mesopotamia. The population was around 100,000 in 2000 B.C.E., rising to around 500,000 by the end of the second millennium.

b. ECONOMY, TECHNOLOGY, SOCIETY, AND CULTURE

The **domestication of the camel,** around 1000 B.C.E., made possible a Northern Arabian nomadic culture based on goat-herding and sheep-herding. Some oases supported permanent settlements, which combined stock raising with date cultivation. The use of the camel also led to overland trade with South Arabia. In South Arabia, the mountainous terrain was cultivated on a network of terraces. Arabia controlled the long-distance trade in spices and raw silk from the Far East and, in addition, produced **frankincense and myrrh,** resins used in religious rituals throughout the Mediterranean world. The frankincense tree grew only in Dhofar (in modern Oman) and myrrh was harvested around the peninsula (especially in Ma'in).

In this period Aramaic was the written language of North Arabia, but native **Sabean and Minean scripts** developed in the south. The polytheistic religion of Northern Arabia lacked a structure or priesthood, but Southern Arabian religion was temple-based. Each Southern Arabian tribal state was under the patronage of a god, but there was a common pantheon. Major deities were **Athtar, Ilmaqa,** and **Wadd.**

c. NORTHERN ARABIA

c. 850–700. NORTHERN ARAB TRIBES. Tiglath-Pileser III (745–727) received 30,000 camels as tribute from Samsi, an Arabian queen, and Sennacherib (704–681) defeated a Queen Iati'e of the Arabs (pp. 27 and 28). These "Queens" were probably tribal leaders, and the Assyrians did not establish political control in the region. Tribes such as the **Abdeel** and **Nebaioth** roamed near Palestine.
c. 700–400. THE KINGDOM OF QEDAR. The Qedarites were the most organized of the Northern Arabian tribes, and at its height in the 6th century, the organization controlled a large region from the Persian Gulf to the Sinai. Ashurbanipal allied himself with the King **Yauta'** (676–652), though he later helped depose him in favor of **Abiyate** (652–644). After this, nothing is known of Qedar until the 5th century, when an Aramaic inscription names Geshem and Qainu as kings. The "Geshem the Arab" mentioned in the Book of Nehemiah is possibly this person (Neh. 2:19, 6:1).
c. 550–332. BABYLONIAN AND PERSIAN DOMINATION. It was Nabonidus (555–539) who first conquered Northern Arabia (p. 28). The purpose behind his mysterious ten-year sojourn in the oasis of Teima is unknown, but he subdued most of Northern Arabia during his stay. The region was peacefully absorbed into the Persian Empire in 539, and units of Arabs on camels took part in Xerxes' campaign in 480. After Alexander defeated the Persians, Northern Arabia regained its independence.

d. SOUTHERN ARABIA

c. 1000–420. THE SOUTHERN ARABIAN KINGDOMS. From about 1000, the **Hadrami** tribe ruled the Wadi Hadramaut from Shabwa and controlled the production of frankincense. The **Mineans** lived along the eastern foothills of the Sarat Mountains, with a capital at **Ma'in.** Minean edicts were issued in the name of both their king (malik) and a council of nobles and priests. **Saba** was the wealthiest and most advanced of the South Arabian kingdoms. At its capital **Marib,** as well as at Sirwah, Yithil, and Sana, there were palaces and temples to the tribal god Ilmaqa. The king had more power than at Ma'in, although there was a tribal council. Some scholars connect the **Queen of Sheba** (1 Kings 10:1–13) with a Saba in the north, but the consensus is that she came from Southern Arabia. Sargon II (721–706) received tribute from King Ita'amra and Sennacherib from **Karib'il** (685).
c. 420–332. THE SABEAN EMPIRE. The greatest Sabean king was **Karib'il Watar** (c. 420), who conquered Ma'in, Hadramaut, Awsan, and Qataban and took the title mukarrib, something like "emperor." The succeeding mukarribs engaged in massive building projects, like the stone dam at Ma'rib, which distributed the waters of the Wadi Dhana for agriculture. The Sabean kingdom declined in the 3rd century and control over the desert trade shifted north to the Kingdom of Nabatea.

(To p. 107)

C. EARLY CIVILIZATIONS AND CLASSICAL EMPIRES OF SOUTH AND EAST ASIA

1. SOUTH ASIA, TO 72 B.C.E.

An early urban civilization in the Indus Valley produced the polished stone, metals, incised seals, and pictographs excavated since 1920 at Harappa and Mohenjo-Daro. Harappan civilization began in the middle of the third millennium B.C.E. It generated a writing system that has yet to be deciphered. It was anchored in two great cities along the Indus River, Harappa itself and Mohenjo-Daro, each carefully laid out in a gridlike pattern. Extensive building suggests a strong governing elite capable of organizing forts, city walls, and extensive urban sewage systems. Trade was conducted with the Middle East, China and Southeast Asia, but military technology lagged, with scant use of bronze. Priests figured prominently in a polytheistic religion, with abundant artistic expression of goddesses and sacred animals. The civilization declined by the second millennium B.C.E. and was thereafter open to nomadic invasions.

A good deal more is known about the civilization that emerged much later with invasion from the Iranian plateau by **Aryans** of uncertain antecedents, who gradually conquered, pushed back, or absorbed the earlier **Dravidian** and Austro-Asiatic **Munda** populations. The conquest is variously placed at 2000–1200 B.C.E.
1200–c. 800. The Indian Aryans worshiped nature-gods. The chief gods were **Indra,** god of the air and of the storm; **Agni,** the sacrificial fire; and **Soma,** the intoxicant used for libations. **Varuna** was worshiped as guardian of cosmic regularity, including individual human acts. The oldest sacrificial hymns, composed in north India west of the Ganges (perhaps 1200), are contained in the *Rigveda,* which dates from c. 1000 B.C.E., possibly two centuries prior to the related *Gathas* in the *Avesta* of Iran; the *Samaveda,* which contains antiphonal selections from the Rig; the *Yajurveda,* hymns and sacrificial prose; and the *Atharvaveda,* a repertory of magical formulae. The *Rigveda* reveals an Indo-European hieratic literary language remarkable for clarity of structure and

wealth of inflection, which was originally transmitted orally. This normative text depicts a patriarchal society, engaged in cattle raising and agriculture, characterized by usual monogamy, adult marriage, and normal widowhood. The Aryan tribes were frequently at war among themselves and with indigenous tribes. Their attitude toward life was vigorous and objective; the doctrine of reincarnation and the correlated aspiration to release are absent.

800–c. 550. A transition period during which the Aryans expanded eastward through Magadha (modern Bihar) is known chiefly from the *Brahmanas*, prose commentaries upon the *Vedas* (c. 800–600), and the earlier *Upanishads* or confidential teachings (c. 600–300). These texts include the first religious justifications for a hierarchical structuring of society, asserting the Vedic division of Aryan society into three honorable classes: priests *(brahman)*, noble warriors *(kshatriya)*, and commonalty *(vaisya)*, including both farmers and artisans. These "twice-born" castes were augmented by a fourth group, the slaves *(sudra)*, consisting of non-Aryans with whom the twice-born classes had no ritual community. Progressive **evolution of the concept of caste** in these normative texts may be traced to desire of priest and noble to perpetuate supremacy, to diversification of specialized occupation, to indigenous rules of endogamy, and to absorption of the sudras, many of whom improved their servile status. The relationship between normative prescriptions and actual social practice is, however, debatable. It is clear that successful military campaigns brought to power men with varied social antecedents who then claimed kshatriya status. Significant social mobility made the textual definition of the caste hierarchy more theoretical than real. Continual elaboration by the priesthood of an already laborious ritual had become devoid of religious significance. The doctrine of continuous rebirth *(samsara)*, conditioned by the inescapable results of former acts *(karma)*, was first expressed in the early *Upanishads* (c. 600–550). The *Upanishads*, too, teach that the soul may escape from the suffering inherent in individual existence only by the realization of its identity with an impersonal cosmic soul. Union with the latter is possible through knowledge, but not through Brahman ritual.

550–321. The north Indian area was divided among many petty states. These divisions suggest a much larger pattern characteristic of the subcontinent throughout much of its history: an ongoing tension between localized rule (increasingly clustered around distinct regional cultures) and larger kingdoms or empires. Sixteen small states are enumerated in an early list. **Kosala** (King Prasenajit, contemporary of the Buddha) was the largest, extending from Nepal to the Ganges, including modern Oudh. **Magadha** was its small neighbor on the east, south of the Ganges. The King of Avanti ruled at Ujjain. The capital of the Vamsas (King Sedayama) was at Kosambi (on the Jumna below Agra). Ten tribal republics are named in the oldest Pali records.

A general estimate of **population** at the end of the 4th century B.C.E. puts it around 100 million, a figure calculated partly from the size of the Indian army as described in Greek sources discussing Alexander of Macedon's campaign in north India. (Another estimate for the early 17th century C.E. uses the same figure, suggesting relatively little absolute population growth before the modern period, although there would have been important ebbs and flows in the intervening centuries, brought on by famine, drought, and disease and countered during periods of good trade and agrarian production, as well as immigration patterns.)

Dissent from Brahmanism, to abolish authority of its scriptures and rites, was found in many schools, among them the Jina ("Victorious"); followers of the Jina ("Victorious"); Vardhamana Mahavira (?540–468?), who elaborated the doctrines of an earlier prophet **Parsva;** and in Magadha under Kings Bimbisara (?543–491?) and his parricide son Ajatasatru (?491–459?). Parsva had enjoined four vows: to injure no life, to be truthful, not to steal, and to possess no property. **Mahavira** added chastity and rigid asceticism as a means to a free man's immortal soul from bondage to the material world.

BUDDHISM was founded in the same period and region by **Siddhartha** (?563–483?) of the clan of Gautama and the hill tribe of Sakya, who attained "illumination" *(bodhi)* at Bodh-Gaya after he had convinced himself that Brahman doctrine and asceticism were alike ineffective. He taught the means of escape from the world of suffering and rebirth to **Nirvana,** a state of peaceful release from rebirth, through a twofold way of life, withdrawal for meditation and personal religious

experience, combined with strict morality and self-sacrificial altruism. Shortly after the Buddha's death, 500 disciples met at Rajagriha to rehearse together his doctrine *(dharma)* and his code of discipline *(sangha)* which he founded. That community served as the instrument for propagation of his religion, which, like Christianity, offers salvation to all who accept the simple doctrine and ethics and seek for personal religious experience. A second **council at Vaisali** a century after the Buddha's death was concerned with the *vinaya*. About this time were formed the four *Nikayas*, earliest extant anthologies from more primitive collections *(Pratimoksa,* and so on).

517–509. Darius I of Achaemenid Persia seized Gandhara from the disunited Aryans and sent his Greek admiral Skylax to explore the Indus. *Kharoshthi* script, used in northwestern India (5th century), is based on Aramaic of the Persian scribes. It remained confined to the northwest.

The *Sutras* (c. 6th–2nd century B.C.E.), "Threads" through the **Brahmanas,** compendious manuals designed to be learned by heart, prescribe rules of conduct of various Vedic schools, regions, and periods, for sacrifice and incidentally, for daily life and describe a society in which plural marriage is permitted and child marriage recommended, while numerous taboos mark the beginning of an elaborate theory of caste defilement. **Panini** (c. 400) gives in his *Sutra* the earliest extant Sanskrit grammar, with a wealth of illustration which is augmented by the *Varttikas* or supplementary rules of Katyayana (c. 180) and the rich *Mahabhashya* (Great Commentary) of Patanjali (c. 150).

327–325. Alexander the Great (p. 70) invaded the Punjab, crossed the Indus (Feb. 326), was welcomed to the rich and cultured city of Takshasila (Taxila), won a battle on the banks of the Jhelum, and withdrew on demand of his troops, sending Nearchus with a fleet by sea. Important **cultural contacts** took place between Hellenistic and Indian civilizations.

c. 321–c. 184. The **MAURYA DYNASTY** was founded by **Chandragupta** (c. 321–c. 297), who first united north India from Herat to the Ganges Delta with his capital at Pataliputra (Patna) and who defended it against Seleucus Nicator (c. 305). The emperor ruled with aid of a privy council and an elaborate official hierarchy, paid army, and secret service. Administration of public works embraced highways and irrigation, important underpinnings for the expanded trade characteristic of this period.

A Jain high priest **Bhadrabahu** led a portion of his community south into the Carnatic to escape a 12-year famine in Bengal. On their return (c. 300) the still resident monks in church council at Pataliputra undertook to collect the Jain scriptures but were unable to record some of the older *purvas.* The canon of the Svetambara sect, the *Siddhanta*, written in its present form at the council of Valabhi (5th or early 6th century C.E.), is consequently incomplete. The returning monks maintained a stricter rule, avoided the council, and, as the **Digambara sect,** have steadily maintained that the true canon is lost. The **Jain** community had then already begun a westward migration to Ujjain and Mathura.

Despite the vagaries of political rule, a continuity of strong **trading relationships** provided coherence and consistency for society. In particular, merchants became increasingly wealthy, powerful, and influential. Indeed, it was merchant patronage that ensured the expansion of both Jainism and Buddhism in this period. **Merchant guilds** shaped much of urban life, influencing public opinion and organizing production.

Artisans, too, participated in guilds that set standards for quality and rules for work. The guilds had to be registered in the locality; some of the leading guilds including potters, metalworkers, and carpenters. (Given the fact that sons usually followed the trade of their fathers, guilds also became associated with caste. If an occupation underwent a transition, however, this triangulated relationship between work, social status, and economic organization was disrupted.)

c. 274–c. 236. ASHOKA'S EMPIRE, extended by conquest of Kalinga (Orissa with the Circars, c. 262), embraced two-thirds of the peninsula. As a devout convert he ruled at home and abroad in accordance with Buddhist law. This ideological connection between kingship and religion also served Ashoka well in positioning his kingdom to support trade and merchants, and the strong political support he received from traders was an important aspect of his rule.

Besides many pious foundations, he engraved on rocks and pillars throughout his empire in true Achaemenid-style edicts in vernacular Prakrit exhorting respect for animal life, reverence, and truth, and appointed censors to enforce these injunctions. He sent Buddhist missions to Syria, Egypt, Cyrene, Macedonia, and Epirus, and with much greater success to Burma and Ceylon (c. 251–246; Aryan conquest of Ceylon, traditional date 485 B.C.E.). The Punjab and Gandhara became a stronghold of the liberal Mahasanghikas, who developed a canonical tradition enriched by legends to bring the life of the Buddha into that region. The canon was then or in the 2nd century expanded in Kausambhi, Sanchi, and Malwa and fixed in Pali to form the *Tripitaka* ("Three Baskets"): *stura* (doctrine), *vinaya* (monastic code), and *abhidharma* (philosophical discussion). The Pali tradition, which was carried to Ceylon and there preserved intact, says a third church council was held at Pataliputra under Ashoka.

The west remained the chief stronghold of **Brahman doctrine** which now reasserted itself. The gradual absorption of substratum cults within the formal brahmanistic framework under the tutelage of the Brahmans gave rise to the complex system of beliefs and practices, characterized as the two main sects of **Saivism** (worship of Siva) and **Vaishnavism** (worship of Visnu and his avatars or incarnations). Major gods arose: **Siva**, personification of cosmic forces of destruction and reproduction implicit in all change; **Vishnu**, god of the sacrifice who was recognized as incarnate in **Krishna**, a hero presented by popular legend at Mathura as romantic lover of cowherd-girls, and on the west coast as a somber warrior. A second avatar or reincarnation of Vishnu was **Rama**, symbol of conjugal devotion. To Vishnu as Preserver and Siva as Destroyer was added **Brahma** the Creator, a personification of the Brahman principle of the *Upanishads*.

The *Mahabharata*, an epic poem composed by several generations of bards, seems to have taken form about the 4th century B.C.E., although probably revised early in our era. The original 9,000 verses were swelled to 100,000 by later accretions, including myths, legends, popular philosophy, and moralizing narratives. It recounts a feud between the wily Kurus and the fierce Pandus. Krishna takes prominent part in the struggle as counselor of Arjuna, the Pandu chief. Noteworthy within the epic is the *Bhagavadgita* ("Song of the Lord"), which first urges personal love and devotion *(bhakti)* to Krishna. The *Ramayana*, although traditionally ascribed to Valmiki (?6th century B.C.E.), is, in its present form, later than the *Mahabharata*. It recounts the trials of Rama in rescuing, with an army of apes, his wife, Sita, from a fiend. Both epics are composed in a popular form of Sanskrit.

The **increasing prosperity and resulting influence of merchants** suggests a society that departed from the normative theories put forward in these texts. Indeed, Ashoka's pleas for social harmony suggest that those labeled vaisyas and placed third in the hierarchy persistently challenged Brahmans and kshatriyas through their patronage of the heterodox sects of Buddhism and Jainism and through their support of the ruler. Social and economic tension undoubtedly was mirrored in religious life.

One way to ease this tension lay in giving the king increasing power by seeing him as the connecting point for various communities in the realm. Ashoka elaborated this connection through a new interpretation of **dhamma** (or **dharma**), which assigned to the king the duty of enabling each caste to fulfill its own dharma. The polity thus was seen as a congeries of distinct groups, each with its own duties or social responsibilities to fulfill, integrated by the figure of the king. To effect such a political theory, Mauryan government created a centralized **bureaucracy**, dependent especially on the treasurer and chief (tax revenue) collector; Mauryan fiscal accounts were carefully kept. Ashoka also traveled extensively to stay in touch with, and to influence, public opinion. He elaborated, as well, the use of spies into an **espionage system** that brought him regular news of his far-flung empire.

206. Antiochus III of Syria occupied Gandhara but shortly lost it to the Greek (Yavana) King Demetrius of Bactria, who (c. 185) seized the Punjab also. Eastward expansion of the Yavanas was halted (after c. 162) by civil war between the houses of Euthydemus, represented especially by the warrior-philosopher Menander, and Eucratides.

c. 184–c. 72. The **SUNGA DYNASTY** was founded in the Ganges Valley and in Malwa by **Pushyamitra,** who overthrew the Maurya and repulsed the Yavanas under Menander, and by a Brahman reaction that may have stimulated Buddhist emigration to Bharhut, Sanchi, and Mathura. The dynasty in its later years was overshadowed if not actually displaced by its line of Brahman advisers, the **Kanvas.**

At the same time (c. 100 B.C.E.–50 C.E.) flourished in Gandhara a school of sculpture which created a Buddha image based on the Greek Apollo. Only a few decadent monuments (mostly 1st century C.E.) bear dates (318, 356, 384 with coin of Kadphises, 399) by reference to a Mauryan era (?322 B.C.E.) or more probably the Seleucid era of 312 B.C.E. Stylistic influence of the art of Gandhara was exerted chiefly in Afghanistan (frescoes of Bamiyan and Dukhtar-i-Nushirwan), where it was fused with Sassanian influences, eastern Turkestan, China of the North Wei dynasty, and Japan. But its iconographic formulae were accepted by the entire Buddhist world. Meanwhile, in western India (near Bombay) were cut in rocky cliffs Buddhist *chaityas* or temple halls, of which the earliest (c. 125–100 B.C.E.) are at Bhaja, Kondane, Pitalkhora, and Ajanta (cave 10); the largest, finest, and latest (1st century C.E.) at Karli. Jain caves in the Udayagiri hills of Orissa are of similar date.

2. SOUTH ASIA, 72 B.C.E.–500 C.E.

By the end of this period, the **rule of the Guptas (c. 300–700 C.E.)** over much of north India provided an integrative pattern taken by later historians as representative of a "classical civilization." The characteristics of Gupta rule, in which some centralization and some rise in the standard of living (especially for elite groups) took place, were taken as establishing certain norms for a broad-based empire ruling over much of the subcontinent. At the same time, and in tension with this characterization of a political "norm," a series of regional politico-cultural clusters began to solidify that provided alternative bases for state formations. In particular, based on the very different geographical and agrarian patterns in the north and south, these halves of the subcontinent tended to foster different sizes and forms of polities.

(To p. 131)

a. NORTH INDIA: PUNJAB AND THE GANGETIC PLAIN

1st century B.C.E. Dating of the known Saka rulers, the **"Great King Moga"** or Maues, Azes, and Azilises, raises a complex chronological problem affecting the whole epoch from 100 B.C.E. to 200 C.E. It springs from multiplicity of eras, which are hardly ever explicitly identified.

The **Pahlavas** (Parthians closely related to the Scythians) under Vonones and his brother Spalirises became independent in eastern Iran with the title of "King of Kings" sometime (c. 30? B.C.E.) after the death of Mithridates II (88 B.C.E., supposed by L. de la Vallée Poussin to begin a Pahlava era). **Azes II,** son of Spalirises, succeeded the Sakas in the Punjab. Pacores was the last to rule as suzerain, although others probably continued as satraps.

The Kushana **Kujula Kadphises** forcibly united the five tribes of Yüeh-chih in Bactria (end 1st century B.C.E.) and seized from the Pahlavas the Kabul Valley and adjacent regions. His son **Vima Kadphises** conquered northwestern India and ruled it by deputy till his death at 80. An inscription near Panjtar speaks of a "Gushana Great King" under date "122" which is 64 or 34 C.E. by the Azes or Pahlava systems. The inscriptions of "136" similarly belong to 78 or 48 C.E.

c. 78–176+ C.E. A **second Kushana dynasty** was founded by

c. 78–96+ C.E. KANISHKA, who extended his rule from Benares and Kabul to the Vindhyas, and established his capital at Peshawar. Whether or not the era he founded is the "Saka" era of 78 C.E., he probably came to the throne near that date.

Kanishka appears to have been tolerant in religion and built a great stupa at Peshawar over relics of the Buddha. A fourth church council, unknown to the Pali sources, was apparently convoked at Jalandhara in the Punjab by the powerful Sarvastivadin, a realist sect of the conservative **Theravada** (Hinayana, p. 44). It probably supervised translation into Sanskrit of the canon which had been fixed in Prakrit in Mathura, the Punjab, and Kashmir in the last centuries B.C.E. The earliest and most vigorous classical Sanskrit is found in Asvaghosha's

Saundarananda ("Conversion of Nanda") and the *Buddhacharita*, an artistic versified life of the Buddha, together with a work long supposed to be his *Sutralamkara*, which is now identified as the *Kalpanamanditika* of Kumaralata, a junior contemporary.

2nd century C.E. Kanishka's successors with their inscriptions (dated in terms of his reign) are: his son Vasishka (24, 28, 29); the latter's son Kanishka II (41); his younger brother Huvishka (29 or 33–60); Vasushka, son of Kanishka II (68, 74); and Vasudeva (76–98).

Ujjayini (Ujjain) became a center of Sanskrit learning and was taken as meridian by Indian astronomers. At Mathura, where sculpture early resembled that of Bharhut and Sañchi, and later imitated the forms of Gandhara, the heavy drapery of the Hellenistic school was rendered transparent and schematized in decorative ridges, creating the so-called *Udayana Buddha* carried to China and Japan.

The Buddhist community was now divided between two means to salvation: the **Hinayana,** or Lesser Vehicle, which retained much of the primitive simplicity of the *Dharma*, "Law" by which Buddhism was then named; and the **Mahayana,** or Great Vehicle, which emphasized personal devotion to Sakyamuni and exalted **Bodhisattva** (future Buddhas) as saviors. Although practically deified in the *Lalitavistara* (2nd century ?, Chinese trans. 308) and *Saddharma-pundarika-sutra*, "Lotus of the Good Law" (Chinese trans., 265–316), Buddha is regarded as but the human representative *(manushi-buddha)*, for the current epoch, of an infinite series of buddhas. Popular bodhisattvas are Avalokitesvara (*Lotus Sutra*, ch. 24), Manjusri (*Avatamsaka-sutra*, 2nd–3rd centuries, Chinese trans. 317–420), Samantabhadra, and Kshitigarbha, all of whom have deferred their own illumination to succor struggling mankind. The goal of effort is no longer sainthood or final absorption in nirvana, but direct attainment of buddhahood or rebirth to indefinite residence in a celestial paradise. Nagarjuna (2nd century), founder of the *Madhyamika Sutra*, teaches that all sensory and mental experience is illusion and comments on the *Prajñaparamita*, "Perfect Wisdom" (Chinese trans. 160), which consists in recognition of the Buddhist law as sole reality.

Already before this era Indian writers recognized and wrote treatises about three phases of human existence: **dharma,** religious and moral duty; **artha,** politics and practical life; and **kama,** love. The *Artha-sastra* (compounded from earlier materials c. 300–330) aims to teach a prince the whole science of successful rule according to accepted principles. It assumes autocratic monarchy, justification of all means by the end (personal aggrandizement), and chronic war. It advocates use of spies in all quarters; deception, intimidation, false witness, and confiscation to obtain money; cunning; and assassination. Virtuous rule is described because it is desirable to win affection of a conquered people. The *Kamasutra* ("Laws of Love") by Vatsyayana Mallanaga (c. 4th century or later) imitates the *Artha-sastra* in both form and morals.

320–c. 535. The **GUPTA DYNASTY** united north India after five centuries' division.

320–c. 330. Chandragupta I ruled from Pataliputra (Patna), having strengthened his position by marriage into the ancient Lichchavi tribe.

c. 330–c. 375. Samudragupta, his son, completed the conquest of the north (Aryavarta) and won glory by traversing Telugu lands to force homage of the Pallava. He claimed to receive tribute from southeastern Bengal; Assam; and Nepal; with presents from the Kushan "son of Heaven and king of kings" (now actually vassal of the Sassanids) in Kabul-Kapisa-Gandhara; the satrap of Ujjain; and the King Meghavanna (352–379) of Ceylon (who founded a monastery at Gaya for his subjects). He revived the Vedic horse-sacrifice which sanctified claim to the title of "universal monarch." He was a patron of poetry and music.

c. 375–c. 415. Chandragupta II Vikramaditya (on throne in 379) ended the satrapy of Ujjain by conquest of Malwa, Gujerat, and Surashtra (between 388 and 401). He moved his capital to Ayodhya (in Awadh) and then to Kausambi on the Jumna.

c. 415–455. Kumaragupta I probably founded the monastic community at Nalanda which was the principal Buddhist seminary till it burned c. 988.

455–c. 467. Skandagupta repulsed the White Huns, as heir apparent and as emperor (455).

477–495+. Budhagupta, one of the last emperors of the dynasty, ruled from northern Bengal to eastern Malwa, perhaps to Surashtra. After c. 500 the chief branch of his house ruled as kings of Magadha till the 8th century.

The **Brahman legal writers** defined the social structure and ritual obligations. The *Dharma Sastra* of **Manu** (1st century B.C.E.?) was respected and freely utilized by later writers. The *Dharma Sutra* of **Vishnu** (3rd century C.E.), like the epics, recognized *suttee*, widow burning, though it was not yet recommended. The days of the week were named from Greek sources. **Yanjavalkya** (4th century) admitted documentary evidence and recommended use of ordeals of ploughshare, scales, and poison in addition to Manu's fire and water. **Narada** (5th century) first omitted religious and moral precepts from legal discussion. **Brihaspati** (c. 600 or 700) cited nine ordeals. Punishments, such as impalement, hanging, burning, mutilation, fines, and outcasting, were adjusted to caste. A plaintiff might enforce justice by fasting to death on a debtor's premises. Fa-hsien, pioneer Chinese Buddhist pilgrim at the height of Gupta power, stated that fines were usually imposed and that mutilation was reserved for brigands and rebels. He was enthusiastic about the peace and happiness of north India (401–409) and Ceylon (410–411).

Six **schools of Hindu philosophy** (or rationalized religion) developed during the first centuries before and after Christ. They enjoy orthodox status in that all recognize the primordial and eternal character of the *Veda*, although in fact they do not derive from it. None is concerned primarily with ethics, but all seek freedom from bondage through deeds to rebirth. Escape for the soul is found in knowledge and cessation of thought.

Vasubandhu (c. 300–350), leading philosopher of Hinayana Buddhism, in his *Abhidharmakosa sastra* gave a classic summary of the Vibhasha and of the Vaibhashika school based upon it, with illuminating comments on the competing Sautrantika school founded by Kumaralabdha (c. 150–200) and developed by Harivarman.

Literary studies at Ujjain blossomed under the Guptas into the **golden age of classical Sanskrit.** Arya Sura in the *Jatakamala* (Chinese trans. 428) put into elegant *kavya* verse tales of former births of the Buddha which had been best known through the *Divyavadana* (Chinese trans. in part, 265). Secular fables gathered into the *Panchatantra* passed through Pehlvi (531–570), Syriac (570), and Arabic (750) into the languages of Europe. The *Sakuntala* and *Vikramorvasi* of **Kalidasa** (c. 400–455) rank first among Indian dramas (Greek influence), with his *Meghaduta* equally high as a lyric poem, while his *Kumarasambhava* and *Raghuvamsa* mark the apogee of *Kavya*, scholarly epic poetry. Literary taste survived the Gupta Empire: witness **Sudraka's** drama *Mrichchakatika* ("Little Clay Cart") and **Dandin's** romance *Dasakumaracharita* (both 6th century) and **Santideva's** brilliant poem of Mahayanist altruism, *Bodhicharyavatara* (late 7th century).

As in literature, so in **art** the Gupta period is one of dignity, restraint, and refinement, characteristics attributed to classicism. The sophisticated treatment of surface detail and explication of the concepts and motifs elaborated in the texts produced in this period would be used by later historians to exemplify a pure "Hindu" high culture untouched by Islamic or European influence.

Indian medicine largely paralleled the Greek but was limited, and surgery atrophied, by objection to dissection. An ethical code like the Hippocratic oath appeared in works of Charaka and Susruta (prior to 4th century, though present texts date from 8th and 11th). Greek origin is clear for many astronomical ideas in the (4th century?) treatises, but many Indian inconsistencies suggest that Greek astronomy was known imperfectly, perhaps through rule-of-thumb manuals. **Aryabhata** (499) taught rotation of the Earth and the value of π as 3.1416 (epic value 3.5). **Brahmagupta** (b. 598) systematized the rules of astronomy, arithmetic, algebra, and geometry. His integral solution of an indeterminate equation, with another method given by **Bhaskara** in his *Siddhantasiromani* (1150), is called by Hankel the finest thing in numerical theory before Lagrange (1736–1813). The abacus was described in the *Abhidharmakosa* from 1st-century sources, long before its use in China (1303–1383). More important, the zero (actually a superscribed dot) is attested in Indian literature (600), and the decimal position appeared in a Sanskrit inscription in Cambodia (604) before they passed to the Arabs of Syria (662) and thence to the Europeans.

(To p. 131)

b. THE DECCAN

The **DECCAN** was dominated (from c. 100 B.C.E. to c. 225 C.E.) by a dynasty called **Andhra** by the late *Puranas* but **Satavahana** or **Satakani** in their own Prakrit inscriptions. Founded by Simuka on the ruins of the Sunga-Kanva power, with its capital at Pratishthana (Paithan) on the upper Godavari, its early conquests to the north and northwest were appropriated by the Saka satraps. A Saka satrap **Bhumaka** established Scythian power on the northwest coast (c. 70 C.E.). Nahapana, junior to him, ruled many years over Surashtra (Kathiawar) and the adjacent coast with a capital probably at Junnar, east of Bombay. Named Mambanos in the *Periplus* (c. 89), his inscriptions are dated "41–46" (?119–124 C.E.), probably with reference to the Saka era of 78.

c. 109–132+. Gotamiputa Siri Satakani conquered Surashtra from Nahapana and in an inscription at Nasik (18th year of his reign, c. 126) claimed not only the Deccan from the Vindhyas to Banavasi, but less probably Malwa as well. Very likely by this epoch the Satakani had extended control over the properly Andhra Teluga (Dravidian) lands of the Godavari and Kistna deltas. The Prakrit poems of the *Sattasai* in part date from this time. Liberal toward all religions, the Satakani especially exalted the Brahmans.

Sculptures about the great Buddhist stupa of Amaravati on the lower Kistna reveal union of Hindu traditional style with its crowding and naturalism, already more refined than at Bharhut and Sanchi, with Greco-Buddhist motifs which were borrowed from Gandhara and in turn transmitted to Malaya, Sumatra-Java, Cambodia, and Champa.

c. 120–c. 395. A DYNASTY OF WESTERN SATRAPS of Ujjain in Malwa was founded by Bhumaka's son Chashtana (Tiastanes of Ptolemy, c. 150).

c. 170. Rudradaman, Chashtana's grandson, in a Sanskrit inscription at Girnar in Kathiawar, records repair of a dam which broke in 150 C.E., defeat of northern tribesmen, and repeated rout of the southern Satakani.

(To p. 132)

c. SOUTH INDIA

The whole Indian peninsula south of the Vindhyas, save for a part of Maharashtra (Nasik and Pratishthana) easily accessible from Malwa and already Aryanized, was occupied by **Dravidians:** Canarese-speakers on the northwest, Telugu-speakers on the east, and Tamil-speakers in the Carnatic. Jainism, brought to Sravana Belgola in Mysore under Chandragupta (end 4th century B.C.E.), flourished in the Digambara, "naked clergy," form which the north rejected. Buddhism with its stupas and sculpture was brought to Amaravati and Mysore under Ashoka. Sanskrit culture and Hindu culture were carried from the south to Cambodia about the opening of our era. Sanskrit influence is clear in the early Tamil grammar *Tolkappiyam* and in the *Kural* of Tiruvalluvar, lofty songs of a priest of pariahs (2nd–3rd centuries C.E.). Brahman colonies with Saivite and Vaishnava sectarianism and the caste system were at various periods imported from the Ganges Valley and endowed by local rulers, as was done also in Bengal.

The south, however, placed its own impress on what it received and developed linga-worship, *bhakti* devotion to Vishnu and Siva, organization of Saiva monasteries and laymen, occasional violent religious intolerance, especially between adherents of Vishnu and Siva, and municipal and corporate life with a sacrificial spirit of personal loyalty.

In search of the great profits on spices sold to the Romans, merchants on west and south coasts began to sail eastward to Java, Sumatra, and Bali. Their sharply increased wealth helped to fund expanding urbanism and the spread of Buddhism and Jainism.

2nd century C.E. Ashoka's inscriptions name three **Tamil states** in the Carnatic: Pandya (extreme south), Chola (southeast), and Chera or Kerala (southwest coast, chief port Muziris). These competed with Maesolia at the mouth of the Kistna and especially with the rich western port of Barygaza (Broach) in thriving trade with the Roman Empire. An embassy to Augustus (c. 22 B.C.E.) was sent by a king "Pandion" who may have been a Pandya. Strabo (d. 21 C.E.) speaks of fleets of 120 ships from Egypt to India, and Pliny (23–79) values annual imports from India at 50 million sesterces.

100–200. King Karikalan of early Tamil poems is credited with construction of a great irrigation dam on the Kaveri River, east of Trichinopoly.

c. 225. Breakup of the Satakani Empire led to establishment, in Maharashtra near Nasik, of a

c. 250–c. 500. Traikutaka dynasty, probably founded by chiefs of the pastoral Abhira tribe.

c. 300–888. The Pallava warrior dynasty of foreign (Pahlava?) origin, using Prakrit and later Sanskrit, held from Kanchi (near Madras) hegemony of the Deccan, which it disputed with the Chalukyas of Vatapi (550–753), the Rashtrakutas of Malkhed (753–973), and the Chalukyas of Vengi (611–1078).

c. 300–c. 500. The Vakatakas, extended their power from the fortress of Gawilgarh in northern Berar to Nagpur, Bundelkhand, and Kuntala, probably limiting Gupta expansion to the south.

Farther south the **Chutu branch of the Satakani,** called Andhrabhrityas in the Puranas, ruled at Banavasi (c. 200–c. 250) where they were succeeded by

c. 350–c. 500. The Kadamba dynasty, founded by a Brahman rebel from the Pallava. His great-grandson **Kakutsthavarman** (c. 435–475) married his daughters to a Gupta, a Vakataka (445), and a Ganga of Mysore.

In the Telugu lands, the Andhras were succeeded by the **Ikshvaku dynasty** (3rd century), notable for donations to a Buddhist stupa on the Nagarjunikonda (hill), on the Kistna above Amaravati; by the

c. 300–450. Salankayana of Vengi; and by the

c. 400–611. Vishnukundins, a dynasty of at least ten kings at the same place.

(To p. 132)

d. CEYLON (SRI LANKA)

Ceylon traditionally received Buddhism from Ashoka under

?247–?207 B.C.E. Devanampiya Tissa, who founded the Mahavihara or Great Monastery at his capital Anuradhapura. The Pali *Tripitaka,* which reflects Theravadin tradition, was written under

89 B.C.E.–40 C.E. or 29 B.C.E.–?17 C.E. Vattagamani, who founded the rival Abhayagiri Monastery. His epoch is supported by the geography (c. 90–200 C.E.) of the *Mahaniddesa,* a commentary admitted late to the Canon.

412–434. Mahanaman, Buddhaghosha of Magadha, author of the *Visuddhimagga* or "Way of Purity," recorded in Pali Singhalese traditions.

(To p. 138)

3. SOUTHEAST ASIA, c. 500 B.C.E.–500 C.E.

For both the Malay Archipelago and the mainland areas of Southeast Asia, the main characteristic during this period was of scattered centers of civilization with widely divergent linguistic patterns (p. 46). What has been called the *mandala* pattern organized space and the polities within it (often this meant an unstable political situation in a vaguely definable geographical area without fixed boundaries; these boundaries expanded and contracted regularly); within these mandalas would reside several tributary rulers. Typical of the entire Southeast Asia area, between the 3rd and the 13th centuries C.E., was the appearance of hundreds of Indic kingdoms *(negara)*, in which rulers adopted the Indic models of kingship and social order.

Demography. Characteristic of this period, in areas where there was surplus food production—resulting primarily from the development of wet rice production—there would be a tendency to have **more dense population growth,** but this increase in population was offset by patterns of warfare and plunder during this period. The scarcity of labor in relation to available land meant a pattern of competition for resources in which additional labor was more valued than additional land. As different centers of power vied for control, an area would be stripped of its inhabitants and they would be forced to relocate to the territory of the victorious ruler. This pattern of warfare, though not particularly high in casualties, severely disrupted agricultural patterns so that **sustained population growth patterns did not occur until after the 1500s.**

Around 500 B.C.E. beginning with the establishment of wet rice cultivation, socially stratified villages relatively autonomous from one another developed. Common to most lowland areas was cognatic kinship (descent reckoned equally through males and females) and, thus, the downgrading of the importance of lineage. The development of town life and, especially, the emergence of entrepôts (established to facilitate the growing trade between India and China) were among the greatest changes. The entrepôts became centers for the spread of Indian civilization in Southeast Asia, a process of cultural synthesis often referred to as the "Indianization" of the states of mainland Southeast Asia, or the "Hinduizing" of belief systems, beginning about 200 B.C.E.

These early civilizations centered around the major river valleys and the Great Lake of Cambodia. At the same time, the emergence of peasant societies underscored the increasing differentiation between hill (tribal cultures) and lowland peoples. Hill peoples became incorporated into social systems dominated by lowland peoples, a relationship symbolized by various ceremonials in which the hill peoples paid tribute, often situated in gift exchanges.

This period witnessed the expansion of trade between China and India via Southeast Asia. Accompanying this expansion was the movement of Brahman priestly specialists, Buddhist monks, and other scholars. The Southeast Asian rulers played a leading role in the Indianization of their societies.   *(To p. 134)*

a. FUNAN

The polity termed by the Chinese "Funan" is the first known polity to emerge in Southeast Asia, usually dated in the **1st century C.E.,** with its capital near present-day Ba Phnom in Cambodia's province of Prei Veng. Because of its location on the then-existent trade route, which included an overland segment, and its access to sufficient agricultural production to support the needs of traders, it greatly benefited from the growth of maritime trade, which resulted during the century when Roman demand for Asian goods increased dramatically.

By the 2nd or 3rd century, Funan was a center with Indians, Chinese, Persian Gulf, and Malay traders. Its fortunes of wealth and power appear to have peaked in the **4th century.**

By the 5th century, competition from the Malay traders and the competition of an all-sea route from India to China that went through the Straits of Melaka undermined its position.

By the 6th century, its position had been so undermined that it was taken over by the **Khmer** people who lived in the middle sections of the Mekong River.

b. CHAMPA

The peoples of Champa, located in the region between the Mekong Delta and the Hue, are ethnolinguistically Malay. The Cham monarchs during this era evidently did not have access to a broad plain providing enough wet rice production to support an elaborate political structure or power base and could not maintain dominance over other Cham monarchs for any extended period of time. As a result, the center or capital of Cham authority would shift over time to various locations as one Cham ruler would lose his dominance to other rulers. As a result of the failure to have a secure economic base either through agricultural production or trade activities, the Cham ruler relied on plunder from raids on neighboring areas, including Khmer territories to the west and Vietnamese territories to the north. In addition, the Cham rulers used local and Indian cultural symbols and their spiritual relationship with the ancestors as defined by religious cults. Also part of the ideological mix were Indian traditions of the king's divinity as the basis for their authority.   *(To p. 134)*

c. BURMA (PAGAN)

From early times Burma came under Indian influence. By the **3rd century C.E.,** expanding Hindu peoples had established commercial settlements on the Tenasserim coast and at the principal river mouths, which developed small kingdoms in contact with the Tibeto-Burman tribes of the Irrawaddy Valley. Commercial relations with China were less influential, although an embassy from a Burmese state reached Ch'ang An in 802.   *(To p. 139)*

4. CHINA, TO 221 B.C.E.

The Chinese people are now considered part of the larger Mongoloid race. The Chinese language is related to Thai and Vietnamese, all of which are part of the larger Sino-Tibetan group. The importance of family to Chinese society and culture dates far back into Chinese prehistory. Family organization and family names are extremely old in China, and families were unified by worship of common ancestors. The "Chinese," or Han people, began in the north China plain and then spread south. Early people of the south include the Man and the Tai. Southerners were linguistically and racially kin, though in the north people were racially kin but linguistically diverse.

Periodization. Early Chinese history is derived from archaeological evidence and (with due caution) later legend. More systematic history begins with the Shang and particularly the Zhou dynasties. This early political period, vital in Chinese cultural development, ends in 221 B.C.E. with the establishment of a more powerful state.

Legendary rulers. Chinese texts speak of three great rulers and three sage kings, all mythical, of high antiquity. The former include:

2852–2737 B.C.E. Reign of Fuxi who domesticated animals and instituted the family.

2737–2697 B.C.E. Reign of Shennong who invented farm tools and sedentary agriculture.

2697 B.C.E.–? Reign of Huangdi, the Yellow Emperor, who created Chinese writing, silk cloth, and the bow and arrow—he was a heroic figure as well.

The latter three include:

2357–2256 B.C.E. Reign of YAO, who is credited with the calendar for managing agriculture, for beginning centralized government, and for using ritual to foster morality. He sagaciously ignored his own incompetent son to pass the reigns of state to **SHUN (r. 2255–2205 B.C.E.),** a poor peasant but a filial son. Shun similarly passed the throne to **YU**

(r. 2205–2198 B.C.E.), because the latter had controlled China's flood waters by dredging to the sea, thus creating north China's major river systems. Yu picked an able successor, but the people allegedly opted instead for his son and so was instituted the **XIA dynasty (trad. 2205–1966).** The last ruler of the Xia was the evil Jie, who was deposed by Tang, who founded the **SHANG dynasty (1766–1122).** Details of the Xia from historical and literary texts are difficult to corroborate. It was probably in present-day Shanxi Province.

The oldest Chinese **archaeological evidence** comes from Zhoukoudian (near Beijing); between 200,000 and 500,000 years old, **Beijing Man (Peking Man)** (p. 7) of the Old Stone Age was found here with certain Mongoloid characteristics. Mongoloid *homo sapiens* appear c. 20,000 years ago, using Stone Age techniques. Agriculture and ceramics emerge in China c. 12,000 years ago (in the transition from paleolithic to neolithic eras) in the Yellow River region. There is also archaeological evidence for rice agriculture in the Yangzi Valley from prehistoric times. Neolithic or **Yangshao** culture is associated with painted clay pottery; people lived in small villages, mainly harvested millet, hunted with bows and arrows, domesticated pigs and dogs, used numerous tools made of stone and bone, engaged in fertility rites, and showed respect for their dead through burial. This culture reached its apex c. 3000 B.C.E. and was gradually replaced by **Longshan** culture, characterized by black, unpainted pottery crafted on wheels. Longshan society was less mobile, more sedentary than before, with walled communities. People harvested rice and millet, domesticated cows and sheep (as well as dogs and pigs), had more buildings and agricultural implements, used a more stratified system of professions and for burial rites, practiced ancestor worship, and divined by means of **"oracle bones."** It reached its apex c. 2000 B.C.E.

Shang rulers, about thirty in all, came from one branch of Longshan culture centered in present-day Henan province. They covered from the Yellow River plain in the west to as far as Shandong in the east. There were numerous capitals, the last of which was at **Yin** (or **Anyang**) where the last twelve kings ruled from c. 1395 B.C.E. The Shang is thus often called the Yin. Capital cities were unprecedentedly large in scale. There were developments in bronze technology and the emergence of horse-drawn chariots. Also new was the **earliest form of written ideographic Chinese:** oracle bones (made of turtle shells and the clavicles of oxen) were inscribed, placed in a fire, and the cracks were read by diviners. Shang also used elaborate, inscribed bronzes for ceremonies.

Shang state and society witnessed the origins of the patrilineal family and ancestor worship, as well as increasing differentiation in social and status roles from earlier times. There were three principal classes in Shang times: hereditary nobles and their families, commoners, and slaves (often sacrificially buried) who were largely war captives. The Shang state was a centralized monarchy. While Shang times saw the further development of settled agriculture, hunting remained important.

c. 1133 B.C.E. King Wu, song of King Wen who hatched a plot to break with their erstwhile ally, the Shang, came to power. He erected a new capital at Hao (near present-day Xi'an) and invaded Shang unsuccessfully in 1124 B.C.E.

1122?–771 B.C.E. The **WESTERN ZHOU** was, like the Shang, descended from Longshan civilization and settled in the Wei River valley of Shaanxi.

1122 B.C.E. The second attack defeated the Shang under the rule of the last "evil" Shang king, Shou. According to tradition, Wen was a wise, kind ruler, while Wu was a strong and tough one.

1116 B.C.E. Wu died at Hao. Tradition has it that he had wanted to sack Yin but was prevailed upon by his brother, the **Duke of Zhou,** who is credited (as regent to the boy ruler Cheng) with giving the Zhou longevity and a firm institutional basis, especially after crushing a rebellion of the last Shang heir and bringing the Yellow River plain under Zhou hegemony. The Duke of Zhou was later revered. Zhou built a city at Luoyang on the opposite side of the Yellow River plain to balance Hao. Yin was destroyed. Cheng died in 1079 B.C.E. by which point Zhou institutions were soundly in place.

771 B.C.E. King You (r. 781–771) was killed and Hao pillaged by northern border peoples. Hao was thereafter abandoned by Zhou descendants for the new capital at Luoyang. End of western Zhou.

The **state system of the western Zhou** was less centralized with small city-states and graded (feudal) rankings. Zhou lords and vassals were unified via bonds of kinship or marriage. The Zhou king was simultaneously the political leader and the paterfamilias of a large extended family. Over time the ties of the regional states to the Zhou loosened, and they acquired characteristics of their own. By the 8th century B.C.E., there were about 200 such states. There were also non-Zhou peoples on the borders and in the large **state of Chu** south of the Zhou in the Yangzi Delta. From the 9th century, there were interstate troubles and clashes with border peoples increasingly.

Western Zhou culture, religion, and society showed marked developments. Two major works describe this era, though both were written much later: *Zhouli (Rites of Zhou),* traditionally believed to depict state organization, and *Yili (Propriety and Rites),* depicting proper behavior for the cultivated gentleman. The *Zhouli* pictures a centralized feudal system with fiefs (or states) probably centered on walled towns where the lords lived, the surrounding terrain falling to their control. The "central states" (later the term for "China") were considered the most culturally advanced. Lords paid personal homage to the Zhou king, offered military support, had their heir confirmed by the king, paid taxes, and kept local order. The king was responsible for peace in the entire realm, maintained through garrison forces throughout the land. There were countless bureaucratic titles which are now difficult to understand. Originally tied to Zhou religious beliefs, the idea of a **"mandate of heaven"** emerges; omnipotent heaven rules through the men upon whom it confers its mandate, and it can withdraw same. Victory over a dynasty in battle was used *ex post facto* to prove a change in heaven's will. Rulers were rigorously obliged to listen to able ministers, for governments ruled to keep peace and social order and for the welfare of the common people. To ignore the latter's feelings was conceived of as tantamount to betraying heaven. While Zhou elite society was organized around common ancestors, commoners lived in

nuclear families. From early on, government service was considered the highest calling; **scholarship was revered and early became an avenue into public service.** Farmers were esteemed in theory as the basic producers. Social mobility in the western Zhou is still a moot point, but there was less "slavery" than in the Shang. The economy was based on settled agriculture of a manorial sort. Barter exchange remained, and hunting declined. There was also population growth through expansion and greater stress on agriculture.

770–256 B.C.E. The **EASTERN ZHOU** marked the end of centralized control by the Zhou king and the commencement of increasingly strong regional powers. The **state of Qin,** initially a semi-Sinic state like Chu, was given control over northern Shaanxi, homeland of the Zhou, and gradually became extremely strong in the west. The states of Jin in the north and Qi in the east (Shandong) were also quite powerful.

c. 700 B.C.E. Qin, Jin, Qi, and the semi-Sinic state of Chu in the south were the most important regimes. Honors continued to be paid by all to the Zhou in Luoyang, but the latter had little real power.

722–481 B.C.E. The **Spring and Autumn period,** named after the *Spring and Autumn Annals* (p. 49), continued the earlier fractiousness and decentralization.

680s B.C.E. In response to continued incursions north by Chu, Duke Huan (r. 685–643 B.C.E.), ruler of Qi, was approached by other states to ally. He turned to his administrative advisor **Guan Zhong** (d. 654 B.C.E.).

681–678 B.C.E. An alliance was thus forged in the north with Huan as hegemon *(ba)* to repel Chu and other border invaders, which lasted for about two centuries under many subsequent hegemons, mostly from Jin in Shanxi.

6th cent. B.C.E. Qin entered the fray to beat back Chu.

453 B.C.E. Wracked by domestic strife, Jin broke up into three states, leaving only three major powers (Chu in the south, Qin and Qi in the north).

5th cent. B.C.E. A major civil war erupted between the states leading to the next era.

403–221 B.C.E. The **WARRING STATES period** (named for an ancient text, *Intrigues of the Warring States*) began with the Zhou king's formal acceptance (403 B.C.E.) of Jin's dismemberment. There were seven principal players in the subsequent fighting: Qin in the west, Qi in the east, and Chu in the south were the major powers; with a second rung of Yan in the Beijing area and the three substates of Jin (Han, Zhao, and Wei). All sought political unification as in the early Zhou.

335 B.C.E. The feudal lords started adopting the title of "king" *(wang)* for themselves.

c. 300 B.C.E. Incessant fighting brought developments in hardware and strategy. Chariot warfare was replaced by infantry fighting on a massive scale and by cavalries.

297 B.C.E. Qin captured the ruler of Chu and began the process of conquering Chu. In turn, other states began aligning to halt Qin.

285 B.C.E. All states aligned to crush Qi.

260 B.C.E. Qin defeated Zhao (in Shanxi) and brutally annihilated the entire Zhao military force of allegedly 400,000.

256 B.C.E. Qin deposed the last Zhou ruler and seized its lands.

231–221 B.C.E. Qin emerged victor over the other states and unified the realm (221 B.C.E.).

Qin rulers had frequently employed advisors from different states to help reform and strengthen the region. The most famous was **Gongson Yang** (d. 338 B.C.E.) from Wei, also known as **Lord Shang,** who served as high counselor to the Qin, 356–338 B.C.E. His **Legalist** policies (p. 49) helped strengthen Qin: he made the peasants freeholders who remitted taxes, built a bureaucratic administration, organized the populace into mutual surveillance groups, and instituted stringent laws. **Lü Buwei** (d. 238 b.c.e.) from Henan served as the Qin's chief counselor, 250–238 B.C.E.; and **LI SI (d. 208 B.C.E.)** from Chu became an important advisor from 237 B.C.E. He later became chief counselor and a major figure in building the Qin's Legalist state system. The Qin unifier, later to become known as **QIN SHI HUANGDI (259–210, r. 247–210 B.C.E.)** or "First Emperor of the Qin," coined the term *huangdi* for "emperor."

Society in the eastern Zhou was organized around nuclear families and stressed worship of ancestors, but warfare in the Spring and Autumn period and Warring States period brought about a decline of the older feudal order. By the Spring and Autumn period, the stress on lineage overcame the elite's earlier aristocratic roots. In the later Zhou centuries, great clans took up political roles, but these clans were largely destroyed in the Warring States period with the Qin later delivering the coup de grâce. The Qin sought complete central control over the entire realm and divided the country up into nuclear families who spied on one another, thus ensuring loyalty to the regime. With the decline of the great clans, commoners and non-natives found their way into high posts, such as the merchant Lü Buwei and the commoner Shen Buhai, indicating a trend that stressed individual merit over birth. **China's population reached 50–60 million in this era;** one record gives a population of 70,000 households for the state of Qi. Rulers needed satisfied troops for this era of warfare and were thus less rigid about class rankings than earlier and less harsh in land tenure arrangements. They also needed experts in administrative management and the like. This spawned generations of itinerant intellectuals, the **Hundred Schools** with their numerous responses to China's troubles.

As for the **economy,** the Zhou feudal manorial system had disintegrated by the later centuries of eastern Zhou. The Qin sought uniform standards for the whole populace. The size of "China" grew throughout the Zhou with new lands reclaimed and territorial expansion. The major irrigation projects date from mid-Zhou, as did such innovations in agriculture as the horse-drawn plow. Iron implements were introduced into agriculture and weaponry in the 5th century B.C.E. In the Warring States period, large foundries for casting iron produced a wealthy merchant class. **Cities** in the Spring and Autumn period and Warring States period became not only administrative centers, but **industrial and commercial centers** as well. Money grew in importance, although a barter economy remained largely intact; money was used for interregional trade. Cast-iron coins—in use from no later than the 5th century B.C.E.—were of many sorts and regionally minted. It was apparently so confusing that the Qin abolished them all for a standard currency.

a. SCHOOLS OF CLASSICAL CHINESE THOUGHT

In response to the chaotic, changing world of the late Spring and Autumn period and Warring States period, many schools (frequently dubbed the "Hundred Schools") emerged usually surrounding an individual, an itinerant thinker seeking to offer advice to the feudal lords. The following schools are among the most famous:

1. CONFUCIANISM

Confucians shared a belief in a heaven that guided all matters in the cosmos and that men were most happy when they were ruled in accordance with the **Way (dao).** To live a moral, virtuous life was to live in harmony with the *dao.* **Rites (li)** were manifestations of proper conduct. Proper behavior required wisdom gained through rigorous study, which all were capable of acquiring, by learning from the sage kings and through the lessons of history. All humankind and human society itself was perfectible. Each of the **five human relationships**—father-son, ruler-subject, brother-brother, husband-wife, and friend-friend—was nurtured by a distinct virtue, and all bonds were reciprocal.

a. Confucius (551–479 B.C.E.)

Born Kong Qiu in the state of Lu (in Shandong), Confucius taught students about proper behavior in government and life, traveling widely to get a hearing at regional states but without success. His **Lunyu (Analects),** compiled by his disciples, is a collection of his thoughts and didactic stories usually in question-answer form with the disciples. Human beings were central to his thinking. He argued that people should seek to be the best they could, for goodness itself was its own reward. He stressed the role of the **gentleman *(junzi)*** or moral exemplar who should rule. He also placed emphasis on ritual as the embodiment of proper behavior. **The Way** was the correct sociomoral manner in which human life and politics need be conducted, and the *junzi* lived in full accord with it. "Do not do to others what you would not want others to do to you." His government would be one ruled by moral

men, not abstract laws; he was a self-proclaimed transmitter of the institutions and practices of the Duke of Zhou, not their creator.

b. Mencius (372?–289? B.C.E.)

Confucius's best-known follower, Mencius was from the state of Zou near Lu. He too had many students and traveled to many of the feudal states. His work, ***Mengzi* (The Mencius)** is also an anecdotal collection of chats with his disciples, a masterpiece of classical Chinese prose. He stressed **benevolence *(ren)*** in government, noting that the best rulers knew to treat the people well, for then the latter would support the ruler always and without compulsion. He articulated a **"right of revolution"** whereby regicide in the case of an evil sovereign was not, properly speaking, regicide, because a bad ruler forfeited his right to govern. He emphasized that everyone innately possessed the roots of goodness and must try to recapture them from the perverting forces of greed. Rulers had a responsibility to establish the basis for the people to cultivate goodness and proper behavior.

c. Xunzi (Xun Qing, c. 300–235 B.C.E.)

Another disciple of Confucius, Xunzi was born in Zhao and traveled less than he or Mencius. He was an extreme rationalist and utilitarian, arguing that men were innately evil and had to study goodness to attain it. His systematic tract, the ***Xunzi,*** covers many themes, such as the proper behavior of ministers, military matters, kingly rule, and music. He argued that all men could become *junzi* but it required much hard work; he was not as kindhearted as Mencius but more authoritarian in his ideas regarding the need to follow a teacher strictly. He laid great stress on ritual, because the sage kings had created it, he argued, to guide men in proper behavior. He railed against sacrifices to the spirits which he deemed irrational. He shared Mencius's ideas on good governance to aid the people and on the importance of education.

2. MOZI (MO DI, c. 470–391 B.C.E.)

Mozi hailed from the state of Song and lived in the century between Confucius and Mencius. His work, entitled the ***Mozi,*** is extremely logical, systematic, and utilitarian. He supported maximizing whatever helped the people, made their lives better, and increased the peace. Everything that worked against this he deemed jibberish. He believed that an authoritarian social organization with obedience to superiors was absolutely necessary, and rulers were to be obedient to heaven in almost a religious sense. He vilified the human relationships prized so highly by the Confucians, because they only separated people. Instead, he called for **"universal love" (jian'ai)** in which all respected all without reference to family. He despised war so much that he trained his followers in defensive strategies and put them at the service of beleaguered states.

3. DAOISM

In general, Daoism was a philosophy that rejected the organized political and social institutions of this world. **Yang Zhu** (c. 440–c. 360 B.C.E.), from whom no writings remain, was condemned by Mencius for pure hedonism and self-centeredness, for showing no concern for the world. He is considered a predecessor of the major Daoist thinkers.

a. *Laozi* (trad. 5th cent. B.C.E.)

The putative author of the ***Daode jing* (Classic of the Way and Virtue,** also simply known as the *Laozi*) was said to have come from Chu. The text was probably the work of several hands, compiled in the 3rd century B.C.E. It is extremely vague, aphoristic, open to widely different interpretations, purposefully cryptic. "The Dao [Way] that can be named is not the true Dao." "Those who understand do not speak, those who speak do not understand."

b. Zhuangzi (c. 369–c. 286 B.C.E.)

Zhuangzi hailed from the state of Wei. His work, known as the ***Zhuangzi,*** is brilliantly argued, using anecdotes to elucidate his points. He was stingingly critical of all other schools, especially the Confucians and Mozi. Zhuangzi believed in living in accord with the flow of nature, or the Dao, acting spontaneously, not planning and structuring life. All organized structures were figments, he argued, antithetical to human nature; he sought escape into an ever-changing nature. As soon as we have labeled something, we have distorted its true place in the cosmic order. He did not oppose activity as such, just purposive action, and he despised all governments.

4. LEGALISM

Legalism preached rule by law, not the moral suasion of Confucianism or the antiauthoritarianism of Daoism. It was concerned with how to make the state prosper and continue expanding until the realm was unified. It was a mixture of extreme rationalism, antihumanitarianism, and totalitarianism. Some Legalists stressed administrative bureaucracy, others strict laws.

a. Guan Zhong (7th cent. B.C.E.) author of the *Guanzi*, pioneered in bureaucratic reforms in the state of Qi.

b. Shen Buhai (d. 337 B.C.E.) served as chief counselor in the state of Han. Fragments of his works remain, dealing with personnel issues; he opposed draconian punishments.

c. *The Book of Lord Shang* was a work by Gongson Yang (p. 47), chief counselor of Qin, who built the Qin's bureaucratic system in the 4th century B.C.E. He believed in rule by law, not by men.

d. Han Fei (d. 233 B.C.E.) author of the *Han Fei zi*, came to Qin from the state of Han. His ideas were implemented by Li Si who later put Han Fei to death. He called for an extreme authoritarianism; power was far more important than morality, virtue, or talent. A ruler can be brilliant, he claimed, but without authoritarian powers, nothing will ever be accomplished. He placed no trust in government or society as such, only in laws, for no one could be trusted. He sought rule by strict laws with harsh punishments and rewards for service to the ruler.

5. SUN WU (SUNZI, "MASTER SUN," C. 4TH CENTURY B.C.E.)

Sun Wu was said to be a general hailing from the state of Qi. In his ***Bingfa (Art of War)***, he devised strategies for war and political organization needed to support it; he discussed such topics as topography, psychology, and the exploitation of human weaknesses in battle. He was especially attentive to deception and how to use minimal conflict to attain victory. His work extremely influenced 20th-century theorists of guerrilla warfare.

6. GONGSON LONG (320–250 B.C.E.)

Gongson Long from Zhao was author of a master work of logic and categorical speculation which bears his name, ***Gongzon Longzi.*** His most famous line, "A white horse is not a horse," deals with the important distinction between "horse," "white," and "white horse."

The major literary and historical texts of the golden age of antiquity are the **Five Classics:** (a) *Yijing (Classic of Change)*, a work used in divination, was later commented on extensively and thus became seen as a work on cosmology; (b) *Shujing* or *Shangshu (Classic of Documents)*, a collection of "documents" spanning a long period of time into the early Zhou, though much of it is now considered spurious; (c) *Shijing (Classic of Poetry)*, considered the greatest literary work of high antiquity; (d) *Chunqiu (Spring and Autumn Annals)*, a chronicle of the state of Lu for the years 772–481 B.C.E., traditionally attributed to Confucius; early on it acquired three famous commentaries of which the *Zuo Zhuan (Zuo Commentary)* adds much to the text; and (e) three ritual texts, Zhouli, Yili, and *Liji (Records of Rites)*. In addition, another work of poetry, **Chuci** *(Songs of the South)*, attributed to **Qu Yuan (d. late 3rd cent. B.C.E.)**, represents a different poetic tradition from that of the *Shijing.*

In artwork, the Shang and early Zhou left magnificent bronzes which were used both for household and ritual use. From the mid-Zhou, bronzes became solely decorative pieces.

5. CHINA, 221 B.C.E.–589 C.E.

The year 221 B.C.E. marked the emergence of East Asia's first unified empire, that of the Qin in China, followed soon thereafter by the Han. Han expansionism in all directions, but especially to the northeast, south, and southeast, brought Chinese civilization to what is now Korea and Vietnam. There was still, at this time, minimal contact with Japan. The notion of an East Asian or Sinitic sphere began to take shape. Despite the breakup of the Han Empire in 220 C.E., this East Asian region continued to retain its overall form, and, in the subsequent Three Kingdoms period in China, Japan established contact with the state of Wei. The Period of Division from 220 C.E. through reunification of China in 589 marked the major second subdivision of the larger period. By the late 6th century, East Asia as a unit was firmly in place.

221–206 B.C.E. QIN DYNASTY (or Qin Empire). Originally a feudal state to the west of the ruling Zhou house, the Qin had weathered a long history of military conflicts with non-Sinic tribes along its borders. In the process, it developed an ironhanded political tradition. It was the first truly unified Chinese dynasty to control a region all of which was considered to be "China." Although the size and shape of "China" would change over the subsequent centuries, Qin laid the foundations of a government structure and bureaucratic administration for all later dynasties.

247–210 B.C.E. The **reign of SHI HUANGDI,** "China's first unifier," was an era in which the very idea of a Chinese dynasty as such came into being. The "feudal" decentralized form of the Zhou was transformed into a centralized governmental structure with a bureaucracy; former feudal states were abolished and incorporated into the new regime. The political map of China was redrawn into a system of districts and prefectures for levels of local administration with a strict chain of command. Precedents for this system can be found in the work of Guan Zhong (7th cent. B.C.E., state of Qi), Shen Buhai (d. 337 B.C.E., Han), and Long Shang (d. 338 B.C.E., Qin). Qin standardized weights, measures, coins, wheel-axle widths, even variant Chinese writing in an

effort to overcome the plethora of regional systems in use till then. Qin also sought to standardize thought by ending the philosophical debates popular in the late Zhou, so as to forestall criticism of the Qin state and its tough policies.

221, 219, 213 B.C.E. Former great families and their dependents (numbering in the tens of thousands) were removed to the capital where they could be watched.

213 B.C.E. The **great book burning** proscribed all writings other than official state documents, texts on agriculture and medicine, and some writings on divination.

212 B.C.E. The **execution of 460 scholars** was ordered by the emperor in a draconian effort to standardize thought as he was doing with weights and measures. A new palace was constructed in the rebuilt capital at Xi'an, and Shi Huangdi made grand tours throughout his realm. He also began construction on his own huge tomb. He undertook massive public works projects: a network of uniform-width roads, better waterways, a canal linking the Yangzi River to south China so as to facilitate the movement of goods to armies in the south, and a linking of the walls built by some of the northern states along the northern border into the first **Great Wall of China.** All of these projects cost many lives. Harsh Qin laws, inspired by Legalism, supported these labor drives and the forced labor of criminals. There was also continued fighting with states south of the core Zhou homeland.

210 B.C.E. By the time of Shi Huangdi's death, Qin conquests in the south reached as far as the Hanoi area of Vietnam. In the process, all former city walls were destroyed; all weapons were seized and melted down for the Qin imperial palace. Late in life, Shi Huangdi sought a Daoist elixir to attain immortality, and **Li Si** took over affairs of state. Shi Huangdi had earlier banished his eldest son and heir, leaving a will that he succeed him, but Li Si hid the will after the emperor's death, forged an edict demanding this son commit suicide, and placed the second son on the Qin throne.

208 B.C.E. Li Si was imprisoned by a fellow schemer and executed.

207 B.C.E. The weak second Qin emperor was poisoned.

206 B.C.E. Qin surrendered to rebel forces.

Qin state and society were built on a strict brand of Legalism. While this enabled the regime to rise rapidly, it ultimately undid it as well. In an effort to abolish the Zhou social order and nobility, Qin eliminated heredity as grounds for bureaucratic recruitment; only service to the state mattered, and only rewards and punishments were meted out. Qin also began using eunuchs more extensively than earlier as the emperor's personal attendants to watch over the harem. Conflicts between regional bureaucrats and eunuchs became endemic. Merchants were particularly despised, and many were banished to the far south. Legalism was respected at the expense of almost all other schools of Zhou thought.

207–206 B.C.E. The many rebellious groups that arose in late Qin boiled down to **Xiang Yu (232–202 B.C.E.)** of Chu noble stock and **Liu Bang (c. 256–195 B.C.E.)** of poor peasant stock. They had worked together to bring down the Qin. After the Qin capital surrendered, Xiang destroyed it, angering Liu who had accrued a popular following among the rebels for his evenhandedness. Xiang, a brilliant strategian, lost out in the struggle and committed suicide.

202 B.C.E.–9 C.E. The **FORMER OR WESTERN HAN DYNASTY** was founded by Liu Bang (posthumous temple name [Han] **Gaozu, r. 202–195 B.C.E.**), who had been Prince of Han since 206 B.C.E., the first time a peasant rose all the way to become emperor. He relied on advisers for civil and military matters and rewarded them accordingly; he relaxed Qin authoritarian controls of state, so that government could serve the populace. He realized that one "can conquer the realm on horseback, but one must dismount to rule." Taxes were lowered on farmers. While the basic Qin bureaucratic structure was retained, Gaozu gave to his major supporters hereditary fiefs in the eastern half of the Han Empire, realizing that he could not maintain the Qin centralization and keep order.

201 B.C.E. The **Xiongnu**, a nomadic, tribal people living along the northern and western border of China, having formed an empire in Mongolia in the previous decade, attacked and encircled Gaozu for a week. The emperor gained his freedom by offering tribute payments. Subsequent emperors also paid them off.

195 B.C.E. Upon Gaozu's death, his wife, the Empress Lü effectively ruled as regent for the next 15 years.

180–157 B.C.E. The reign of their son, Wendi, kept the regime intact, as did their grandson, Jingdi (r. 157–141 B.C.E.). Most high posts through these years were in the hands of Gaozu's former advisers and generals. Aside from a revolt of seven princes in 154 B.C.E. that was crushed, this was an era of peace, during which the population and the economy grew; taxes were further cut in half by Jingdi to about 1/30 of a crop yield, and the state granaries and treasury remained well stocked.

141–87 B.C.E. The **reign of Wudi (b. 159)**, the "Martial Emperor," was a period of widespread imperial activism. Wudi moved to stem the growth of class polarization, to reduce the powers of enfeoffed princes, and to centralize authority. In 114 B.C.E., he returned 104 fiefdoms to the state, and they were incorporated into the districts and prefectures; and he demanded they divide all holdings among all male heirs, not just the eldest, to ensure parcellation of power. He moved to eradicate abuses of a now freer merchant class and taxed them to bring more money to the central government and reduce their power; they were also forbidden from owning land. He began the **"ever-normal granary" system** to ensure state control over the grain supply, and he instituted state monopolies on iron, salt, and liquor.

140 B.C.E. Dong Zhongshu (c. 179–140 B.C.E.) advocated Confucian training for civil service and making Confucianism state orthodoxy, effectively outfitting it for the structure of the Legalist state. He also urged limitations on private landholdings and servants so as to counteract the growing imbalance of wealth.

139 B.C.E. In an effort to forge an alliance with the Yuezhi (an Indo-European people driven out of Gansu to the west by the Xiongnu into Yili) against the Xiongnu, Wudi sent **Zhang Qian (d. 114)** to find them. Zhang was captured by the Xiongnu, among whom he married and settled. Ten years later he escaped to continue the search, finding the Yuezhi in the Pamir Mountains of northern Pakistan.

136 B.C.E. Doctors (or Erudites) of the Five Classics were established at court by Wudi, each expert in one of the Five Classics.

133 B.C.E. Wudi began attacks on the Xiongnu, first in the Ordos region north of the Han capital at Chang'an.

127 B.C.E. Victorious, the Han armies spread farther to drive the Xiongnu out of the north and northwest generally. Han then established military colonies from Gansu into central Asia with 700,000 colonists. Subservient central Asian states sent tribute to Wudi to acknowledge China's nominal suzerainty.

126 B.C.E. Captured again on his return trip, Zhang Qian ultimately arrived back in the capital with much new information on the lands and peoples to China's west and southwest.

124 B.C.E. A **National University** was created to train civil officials in Confucian principles and texts. Examinations began, too. Great families still continued to have much social, political, and economic power.

122 B.C.E. Death of **Liu An,** prince of Huainan who directed the compilation of a compendium, the *Huainanzi*, primarily of Daoist philosophical interest.

111–110 B.C.E. As Wudi's armies continued their conquests of small states along the Han's north, northeast, south, and southeast borders, they attacked and conquered Minyue (in present-day Fujian province) and Nanyue (Viet Nam in Vietnamese, in the Guangzhou [Canton] region), bringing Han control to this area of south China and Vietnam.

110 B.C.E. Wudi inaugurated the sacrifice to Heaven, subsequently the primary imperial prerogative and responsibility of the emperor.

109–108 B.C.E. Southern Manchuria and much of Korea fell and were divided into commanderies with Han garrison forces, a process that led to the Sinification of these regions.

104–102 B.C.E. Contacts were established over the Pamirs into Russian Turkestan.

73 B.C.E. The Xiongnu groups were further broken up, so that one group submitted to the Han in 51 B.C.E., and a leader of the other major group was killed in battle in 36 B.C.E.

Imperial finances, depleted by wars, were replenished by the sale of military titles (123 B.C.E.), the salt and iron monopolies (119 B.C.E.), forced contributions by the nobility (112 B.C.E.), and commutations of judicial sentences by fines (97). They were inflated by the debasement of currency (119).

9–23 C.E. WANG MANG (45 B.C.E.–23 C.E.), after serving as regent for several child emperors, Wang Mang seized the throne and established the short-lived **Xin dynasty.** Wang, a highly moral Confucian official with a spotless reputation, was pushed into usurpation, and his reign was a series of failed efforts at radical reform on the model of the Zhou. He returned powers to the old feudal nobles, made many administrative posts hereditary, strengthened the laws against merchants, outlawed transactions for slaves and tried to assist them, confiscated large tracts of land from the great landowning families and redistributed them through state allotment to able-bodied males, and strengthened the ever-normal granary system and state monopolies. To halt usury, loans were offered free for up to 90 days for funerals, and at 3 percent a month or 10 percent a year for productive purposes. The dislocations caused by these reforms alienated many. There was also a string of natural disasters during Wang's reign: floods, bad harvests, and a change in the course of the Yellow River in 11 C.E. with untold casualties.

18. The **Red Eyebrows** rebel band formed among the poor, vagrant masses.

22. Members of the Former Han royal house joined the rebels and took the capital (23) and killed Wang Mang.

25–220. LATER OR EASTERN HAN DYNASTY reconstituted the Han house under a collateral imperial relative, **Emperor Guangwu (6 B.C.E.–57, r. 25–57).** The capital was established at Luoyang to the east of Chang'an. A stable state and society were reorganized under Guangwu, as well as his successors, Mingdi (r. 57–75) and Zhangdi (r. 75–88). Peace and less intrusive state policies allowed the Chinese economy to bounce back. Culture and scholarship were revived.

43. Ma Yuan (14 B.C.E.–49 C.E.) conquered Tonkin and Annam, most of which remained under Chinese control until 939.

74–94. Ban Chao (32–102) used personal diplomacy and strategy to compel the small states of Turkestan to submit to the Han, opening the way for extensive trade with the Roman Empire. His lieutenant Gan Ying reached the Persian Gulf in 97.

82. Empress Dou, during the reign of Zhangdi, altered the succession and ruled as dowager (88–97) with her family.

105. Paper was invented by this date, if not earlier.

105–121. Empress Deng ruled as dowager for her infant son and his boy successor until her death, when her most prominent relatives chose suicide.

144–150. Empress Liang ruled for three young emperors until her death, with a younger empress of the same family ruling until 159.

159. A eunuch group under **Huandi (b. 133, r. 146–167)** wiped out the family of Empress Liang and took its land and powers for themselves.

166. Anti-eunuch protests led to a repression of over 200 officials and scholars. When the same opposition erupted in 169, there was another suppression, leading to prison deaths of over 100 critics of state, known as the **suppression of cliques.**

Early 180s. Two major rebel bands influenced by **religious Daoism** with large numbers of followers arose: the **Yellow Turbans** in the east and the **Five Pecks of Rice** in Sichuan. Less state control in society and the economy eventually caused peasant emiseration and allowed great families to amass huge fortunes and retinues of laborers and private armies. In addition, natural disasters—for example, floods and locusts in 175, epidemics in 173 and 179—caused further rural deprivation and fueled the growth of religious Daoist groups.

184. The Yellow Turbans rose in rebellion. Among the factors to be counted as background to the rebellion were a weakened center with no major, charismatic figures; a self-indulgent elite; excessive powers fallen into the extra-bureaucratic hands of eunuchs who worked as a group as well as inner-court relatives; and large-scale student demonstrations (said to number as many as 30,000 students) at the National University against the decline in government morality.

190. General Dong Zhuo, after putting down the Yellow Turbans, took the capital of Luoyang, deposed the emperor, placed a puppet on the throne (Xiandi), and massacred a large number of eunuchs. In the face of growing opposition, Dong fled to the west where he was killed in 192. The emperor came under the control of **CAO CAO (155–220),** who finally crushed the last of the Yellow Turbans.

200. With Cao Cao's death, his son **Cao Pi (187–226)** received the abdication of the last Han emperor and installed the **Wei dynasty,** ending four centuries of Han rule.

Han **government** basically carried on the Qin administrative structure with the imperial institution at the top of a pyramidal organization. The highest official was a prime minister or chief counselor who ran the bureaucracy and presided over the council of state, with ministers in charge of various high-level functions (for example, the military, courts, taxation). While the emperor retained final decision-making powers, Gaozu instituted a policy of placing trust in the prime minister. With time, **the bureaucracy** was outflanked by the **inner court** (palace ladies, their families, servants, and eunuchs). In the Later Han era, governmental administration was divided into three bodies: **department of state affairs, secretariat,** and **chancellory.** The declining authority of the top bureaucrats led to factional strife and demonstrations. Cao Cao, as the effective ruler in the Han's last years, tried to rebuild the institution of the prime ministership.

The Han retained the Qin's system of districts and prefectures with a considerable delegation of authority to local magistrates. Wudi went further and regularized this by eliminating many fiefs; he divided the realm into 13 **circuits,** each with a circuit inspector sent by the censorate to report to the center, and these inspectors became more powerful over time.

The ideal of **bureaucratic recruitment** based more on merit than birth was curtailed after the Qin collapse, and there was a return to a measure of hereditary principles. Han did begin the effort to lay out **objective, meritocratic criteria** for bureaucratic recruitment and evaluation. 195 B.C.E. is the first known date of a call to local officials to offer recommendations of "worthy and talented" men for bureaucratic positions. In 165 B.C.E. all officials were called upon to recommend able men, who were then examined by the emperor. Two distinct Han systems thus emerged: **recommendations** and **confirming examinations.** In 125 B.C.E. local officials were called on to recommend brilliant talents to study one of the Five Classics with a famed teacher, which became the basis for the **National University.** There were initially 50 such students; by the end of the 1st century B.C.E., the number

reached 3000; by the height of the Later Han, there were some 30,000. Thus, all officials were literate and well respected locally.

Local village headmen in the Han reported regularly to the county magistrate on **population** and landownership. Because these were the bases of taxation, the claimed population figures tended to be intrinsically inaccurate. The **first national census in China of 1** C.E. gave a population of just under 60 million; the 140 census registered just under 50 million; the 156 census came in at over 56 million. With the fall of the Han, there was a great population decline. In addition, there were large population shifts east and south through the Han dynasty, and people moved into the Sichuan and Beijing–southern Manchuria areas.

The **biggest city of the Former Han** was Chang'an, with a population of 246,200. It had walls 16 miles in circumference with a grid pattern of large streets within. Luoyang in the Later Han was roughly the same size, probably larger in the 2nd century.

Great families or clans remained extremely prominent in **Han society.** They differed from the Zhou elite who owed their position to noble birth; the Han elite acquired status only partly via heredity, as many commoners rose through individual merit (especially in the military) which they then transformed into hereditary privilege for their descendants; and it worked in reverse for downward social mobility as well. Whereas the Zhou elite was a hereditary nobility, the Han elite was an aristocracy of wealth (through land) and sociopolitical power (through military control). The Han elite had immense estates, and laborers and tenants who worked the land were under their control; while the latter could in theory work their way to freedom, the great wealth in private hands led to frequent impoverishment. People who hit hard times often went into tenancy to wealthier holders, a further tendency toward class polarization. **Wang Mang** attempted to **nationalize** all lands and divide up the great estates among the poor, and that plan proved a dismal failure. The Later Han just continued the trend.

Commerce, distrusted in both Confucian and Legalist theory, came under close state scrutiny in the Han. **Merchants** were taxed heavily, sometimes arbitrarily as Wudi did to support his military campaigns. Wudi ended private profiteering in salt, iron, and grain, and he set up a fiscal administration to keep check on the markets: the ever-normal granary system, designed to keep the supply and price of grains stable and to eliminate speculation; and state monopolies, whereby the state licensed the producers and the distributors of salt and iron. Both systems were completed under **Sang Hongyang (143–80 B.C.E.)** and led to big profits for the state. In 81 B.C.E., some 60 scholars discussed the government's commercial role in the *Discourses on Salt and Iron:* the Confucians opposed the state's competing with the people in the marketplace; Sang and the Legalists supported such policies to enrich and strengthen the state, especially in its border defenses.

Intellectual and religious currents were tolerated and blossomed from the beginning of the Han, unlike the repressive Qin. **Wudi officially merged Confucian moral precepts with the Legalist state structure.** He used Confucians as officials, and Confucianism became the basis for education at the National University. Daoism also became prevalent in various mystical strains. All three traditions often mixed together as well as with belief in the **Five Elements** (wood, metal, fire, water, earth) theory concerning the makeup of the cosmos and correspondences with nature, the seasons, and the life cycle. **Dong Zhongshu,** who exerted an influence over Wudi, is alleged to have provided a synthesis of these strains of thought in his *Chunqiu fanlu (The Radiant Dew of the Spring and Autumn Annals),* although his authorship of this text is now questioned. He merged Confucianism and Legalism to argue that human nature was innately good but must continually be nourished through practice, and the ruler was heaven's terrestrial mandated agent who guided men in this direction.

Although many books were destroyed under the Qin, some manuscripts survived; others were reconstructed from memory; and yet others were discovered hidden. There emerged contending versions of the "same" classical works. Texts in Qin script were dubbed **"new text"** *(jinwen);* the discovered ones from earlier, **"old text"** *(quwen).* Major debates ensued over their relative authenticity, lasting into the early 20th century. China's first major dictionary was compiled in 100 C.E. by **Xu Shen,** the *Shuowen jiezi (Analysis of Characters as an Explanation of Writing);* it was both a distinguished scholarly achievement and served a standardizing role for the Chinese language. The 1st century witnessed the first use of "footnotes"—interlineal commentaries on all Five Classics. **Ma Rong** (79–166) invented the device of double-column commentary (138–140) and wrote commentaries on all Five Classics, the first scholar to do so. Another famous commentator was **Zheng Xuan (127–200)** who worked hard to explicate the difficulties of ancient works. Another classic, the *Xiaojing (The Classic of Filial Piety)*, joined the list of revered texts from the early Han, becoming very influential especially in the education of youngsters. **Wang Chong (27–c. 100)** mixed Daoism with Xunzi's fierce rationalism to produce a kind of philosophical fatalism that the world was governed by chance. Religious Daoism or Neo-Daoism began in the Later Han but took off in the subsequent Six Dynasties period; it mixed Daoist proclivities about the cosmos and the self with Confucian beliefs in social duties, but later it became associated with escapism.

There was a strong Daoist influence in the rise of **alchemy** from Qin into Han times. There is a record from 133 B.C.E. of an effort to turn cinnabar into gold. Many elixirs were produced and became important in Chinese religion and science. Other Daoist strains stressed body exercises, breathing techniques, and the like as ways to achieve immortality. Protest movements like the Yellow Turbans owed much to Daoist beliefs. **Gunpowder** also emerged from the work of Daoist alchemists in the Han period, though it was then only used for elixirs; not until the 10th century was it mixed with carbon to make explosives. Closely related to the rise of Daoist alchemy were technological developments, such as the invention of the **compass;** traditionally attributed to the Yellow Emperor of mythology, it first appeared in records the 3rd century B.C.E. It was initially used to determine propitious burial of the dead, and the earliest mention of a compass being used in navigation dates to 1119.

Buddhism first came to China in the Later Han. By the 2nd century, there were both Daoist and Buddhist altars in the imperial palace, with Buddhist communities around China by the end of the Han. From the Later Han, the translation of Buddhist texts into China became a major enterprise; the first of the famous translators was a Parthian with the Chinese name **An Shigao** who came to Luoyang in 148 and stayed for two decades. Both Theravada and Mahayana texts were in China.

In the area of **literature and the arts,** the standardization of the Chinese script led to the emergence of a national intellectual class for government and scholarship, for even if there were many spoken dialects, there was only one written language after Qin. **Paper was invented in the 1st century C.E.** and soon became a more frequently used medium for writing than silk or wood strips. In the writing of **historical works,** the great work of the Former Han, *Shiji (Records of the Grand Historian)*, which was begun by **Sima Tan (d. 110 B.C.E.)** and was primarily the work of his son, SIMA QIAN (145–87 B.C.E.), set standards for literary as well as historical writing. In the Later Han, another family of historians was famed for composing the *Han Shu (History of the Former Han)*: begun by **Ban Biao (3–54)**, primarily the work of his son **BAN GU (32–92)** and completed by his daughter, **Ban Zhao (45–114?)**. Ban Zhao, one of the great women intellectuals and scholars of Han times, also authored *Admonitions for Women* which was read for many centuries thereafter. It became both a primer on correct behavior for women in subsequent centuries and a target for attack in the 20th century for perpetuating a perceived repression position for women. There were new poetic and prose styles in the Han, among them: *fu* (a kind of prose poem), *shi* (a poem with lines of 5 or 7 characters), and *yuefu* (a free-flowing *shi*). **Sima Xiangru (179–113 B.C.E.)**, a famous poet, was brought to the capital by Wudi and there composed court poems.

In the field of **art,** the Han produced glazed stoneware pottery. Early Buddhist influences can be seen in sculpture as well as in painting. Han painting also dealt realistically with everyday themes of life and work. Figure painting emerged as a fine art. From the late Han, calligraphy as an art form developed from cursive script.

In **mathematics,** a treatise from 120 B.C.E. dealt with number theory (concepts of negative numbers, fractions, and rules for measurement). In **astronomy,** the sundial was introduced during Han, and the first observations of sunspots were made (28 B.C.E.). The first Chinese maps also date from this era.

220–589. SIX DYNASTIES OR PERIOD OF DISUNION, named for the

succession of six dynasties, made their capital at Nanjing. After the Yellow Turbans were quelled, Cao Cao tried to reunify China but failed; his major defeat came at the **Battle of Red Cliff** (208) in Hubei. He succeeded in regaining control over the north, but his enemies got control over the south.

220–264. The THREE KINGDOMS PERIOD began when Cao Cao's son, **Cao Pi,** founded the **Wei dynasty** (220) at Luoyang, and the realm was divided into three states, each claiming imperial status. Eunuchs were excluded from government, and the families of empresses were excluded from the future exercise of regency (222); thus, the inner court was cut off from state affairs.

221–263. The Shu-Han dynasty was founded by **Liu Bei** (161–223), a major rival of Cao Cao ever since 194, with its capital in Chengdu and control over Sichuan and the southwest. Liu was supported by Zhang Fei (d. 221) and Guan Yu (d. 219, subsequently deified as the God of War), both of whom rebelled against Cao, their former ally. **Zhuge Liang** (181–234), a brilliant military tactician, served as chief minister under Liu. Sichuan underwent rapid development.

222–280. The Wu dynasty was founded by **Sun Quan** (182–252) in the lower Yangzi Valley, with its capital at Nanjing.

264. Shu-Han was taken over by Wei.

265. The Sima family (military leaders) ousted the Cao family and changed the Wei to the **Jin or Western Jin dynasty** under **Sima Yan** (236–90, r. 265–89).

280. Jin conquered Wu.

280–316. Jin, gaining nominal control over a unified realm, divided the country among the imperial relatives, which was followed by numerous usurpations. Jin established a censorate.

304. A Xiongnu leader established the state of Han in Shanxi, later changing the dynastic name to Zhao.

311. The Jin capital at Luoyang was destroyed and the emperor murdered by a Xiongnu chieftain claiming the throne.

316. After regrouping in Chang'an, the Jin was again attacked and wiped out by the Xiongnu there.

317–589. Southern and Northern dynasties period began, China being divided north and south for over 250 years.

317–420. The **Eastern Jin** was established in Nanjing after remnants of the Western Jin escaped there. They attempted to recapture the north, seizing control of Sichuan in 347.

351. Fu Jian (338–85), a Tibetan general, conquered part of the north and established the Sinicized state of **Former Qin** at Chang'an.

383. The **Battle of Fei River** in northern Anhui ended in a Jin victory over Fu Jian, but the regime subsequently underwent incessant intrigue and regicide and was succeeded by short-lived, weaker states.

420–479. Liu-Song dynasty.

479–502. Southern Qi dynasty.

502–557. Liang dynasty.

557–589. Chen dynasty. During these years of Chinese dynasties who had been forced south by invasions from the north, much of south China became Sinified, as the northerners brought with them their institutions and religious practices.

301–439. The **Sixteen kingdoms** were a succession of states in the north established by three Chinese and 13 leaders of other northern peoples: four Xiongnu, five Xianbi (a proto-Mongolian tribe), and four from two other related groups. They all sought to use Chinese governing principles to set up regimes of their own.

383. Fu Jian was overthrown by a general who founded the Later Qin.

386–534. The **Northern Wei dynasty,** founded at Datong by the Tuoba, a Turkic people, unified the north. They moved their capital to Luoyang in 495, and they were followed by a string of stable regimes in the north, all of non-Chinese extraction but all much Sinified.

534–550. Eastern Wei dynasty.

534–557. Western Wei dynasty.

550–577. Northern Qi dynasty.

557–581. Northern Zhou dynasty. Many Chinese elites remained in the north and were employed by the invaders in their efforts to build cultivated, sedentary, Chinese-style regimes. Buddhism became very popular among the elite and commoners in both north and south China.

551. The **Ruanruan** regime, having founded an empire in Mongolia in the early 5th century, was toppled, and its rulers escaped to the west where they became the Avars. They were succeeded in Mongolia by the **Tujüe,** a Turkish people, who soon (572) divided into eastern and western branches.

During this long period of political division, there was great mixing among peoples and cultures. Chinese cultural forms spread to the south, while northern people of non-Chinese stock flowed into north China. Regimes in the north became highly Sinified, which in turn led to conflicts with advocates of the older ways among the non-Chinese. Some of these regimes eventually retreated back to the north, and some adapted better to Chinese sedentary lifestyles (e.g., the Northern Wei) and even contributed to future "Chinese" civilization.

BUDDHISM was flourishing in China by the end of the Later Han. It preached redemption from this world of pain and suffering for the common man. The most famous translator of Buddhist sutras was **Kumarajiva** (344–413), son of an Indian and a princess of Kucha, who began translation work in Chang'an in 401. The **Bodhidarma** (said to have died in 528) arrived in China in the early 6th century; he stressed concentration and meditation, becoming the founder of the **Chan (Zen** in Japanese) sect. The desire for direct knowledge of the original texts led at least 82 Chinese pilgrims to travel to India during the period 200–600 (61 in the 5th century alone). **Faxian** traveled (399–413) through countless holy sites of Buddhism in India, Ceylon, and Java; he was the first Chinese pilgrim to go to India and return (by sea), bringing back numerous texts.

Chinese Buddhists increasingly neglected the intangible goals of Indian theology and stressed more practical objectives: **immediate response to prayer** by the protective bodhisattva Guanyin (Avaloki-tesvara), **direct rebirth in the Western Paradise** (Sukhavati) of Amituofuo (Amitabha), and **salvation by Miluofuo,** the Buddha of the future (Maitreya). Daoist thought was reflected in the increasingly influential Chan sect, which taught that the Buddha-nature was in everyone and that enlightenment was to be sought solely through meditation (to the exclusion of prayer), asceticism, and good works. Confucian reaction was evident in the emphasis of the **Tiantai sect,** founded (575) in the mountains of Zhejiang province by Zhiyi (531–597), upon education as necessary to the realization of the Buddha-nature.

Unfavorable Confucian reaction to Indian asceticism, parasitic practices (celibacy, monasticism, and mendicancy) and an unrestrained imaginative metaphysical literature, together with the hostility of the competing Daoist priesthood, led to **brief persecutions** by the Northern Wei (446–452) under Emperor Wu who much favored Daoism over Buddhism and by the Northern Zhou (574–578) which sought to revive the classical Chinese tradition and outlawed both Buddhism and Daoism. Buddhism continued to flourish, nonetheless. **Huiyuan** (334–416) of the Eastern Jin defended monastic life in the face of the criticism that Buddhists failed to honor the emperor. The most famous ruler to patronize Buddhism was **Emperor Wu of the Liang** (b. 464, r. 502–549), who reviled Daoism and donated heavily to Buddhist monasteries.

The first **Tripitaka** *(Three Baskets),* the collected writings of Buddhism in China, were compiled in 581. The first Buddhist hagiography, *Gaoseng zhuan (Biographies of Eminent Monks)* by Huijiao (497–544) of the Liang, was completed in the 6th century.

Neo-Daoism continued from the late Han into the Six Dynasties era. **Wang Bi** (226–249) wrote commentaries on the *Yijing* and *Laozi,* while **Guo Xiang** (d. 312) wrote a commentary on the *Zhuangzi.* Both men praised Confucius as well in an eclectic and metaphysical spirit. The most famous eccentrics of the age were the **Seven Sages of the Bamboo Grove,** led by **Qi Kang** (223–262). They sought to escape all social trappings as a means of preserving true ethical integrity; they engaged in "pure conversation" following an apolitical, unregulated style, and they drank a great deal.

Religious Daoism was a combination of Daoism with many strains of folk religion. Some sought elixirs or magical paradises. Many alchemical texts can be dated to the 3rd century. This trend led to early experimentation in various sciences and to the production of dyes, alloys, even gunpowder. Sexual and exercise regimens were also practiced. The first Daoist hagiography, *Liexian zhuan (Biographies of Var-*

ious Immortals), appeared in the 3rd century. *Baopuzi (Master of Preserving Simplicity),* a Daoist encyclopedia by **Ge Hong** (283–c. 343), was completed in the 4th century.

The Han administration and recommendation system were both adopted by Cao Cao with emendations when he established the **Nine Ranks System** by which local capable men (senior rectifiers) graded potential candidates for bureaucratic appointment. This system was adopted by virtually all of the regimes in the Six Dynasties era. Senior rectifiers hailed from local great families and strengthened the authority of the latter.

The **militia system,** newly created by the Western Wei in the mid-6th century, followed their traditional Xianbi tribal organization. Families with over two sons had to send one to serve in one of the many garrisons. This led to those garrisons becoming self-sufficient, run by farmer-soldiers, and the system was later adopted by the Sui and Tang dynasties.

The turmoil at the end of the Han caused a **population** drop. In 280, the unified Jin registered a population of 16,163,863.

The **rise of great families** from the late Han into the period of division brought into existence immense landed estates. The feudal society of the northern and southern dynasties formed around these families; it was effectively the way society girded itself to cope with tremendous turbulence caused by mass migrations and continual incursions. Later northern dynasties, though, also wanted to recentralize authority, leading ultimately to a curtailment of this "feudalism." The **Tuoba Wei** created land registers to increase the amount of land under cultivation (and raise grain production) and to get a handle on the estates of the great families. In the 480s, they developed the **equal field system** whereby the state "owned" all lands and parceled it out to the populace for their lifetime only, at which time it would then return to the state; they ended the land tax and abolished corvée. The poorest were often resettled in both the north and the south on lands to be reclaimed.

Many new developments transpired in **literature.** The *Shishuo xinyu (New Specimens of Social Talk)* by Liu Yiqing (403–444) was an anthology of Daoist-inspired stories; the most famous tale from it was **"Peach Blossom Spring"** by **Tao Yuanming** (Tao Qian, 365–426), a story about travels to a hidden utopia. Poetry witnessed the rise of parallel prose; *lüshi* (regulated verse) became very popular in the south. Major works of literary criticism also appeared: *Wen fu (Prose Poems on Literature)* by Lu Ji (261–303), *Wenxin diaolong (The Literary Mind and the Carving of Dragons)* by Liu Xie (465–531?), and *Wenxuan (Anthology of Literature),* edited by Xiao Tong (501–531), emperor of the Liang.

In **sculpture,** the Northern Wei began to cut cave temples at the Yungang grottoes in northern Shanxi near Datong; after Luoyang became the Northern Wei capital in 495, new caves were cut at nearby Longmen as well. The various Buddhas, bodhisattvas, arhats, and militant guardians of the law reflect Indian iconography given form by Greek artisans in Gandhara, as well as Iranian influence. The great **calligrapher Wang Xizhi** (321–379) was a master of the grass script. In **painting, Gu Kaizhi** (c. 344–c. 406), China's first great painter and a Daoist recluse, perfected the technical refinement of episodic figure painting. Xie He of the early 6th century became a critic of painting styles.

581–618. The **SUI DYNASTY** was founded at Chang'an by Yang Jian (541–604), who had married into the Northern Zhou court of the Tuoba, become its chief minister (580), and had his daughter marry the Northern Zhou emperor; when his grandson acceded to the throne, he then seized it for himself as Wendi (r. 581–604). As he still only controlled north China, in 587 he defeated the Later Liang, and in 588–589 the Chen.

584. Reconstruction was begun on the canal system to tie the capital at Chang'an with the Yellow River.

589. REUNIFICATION OF THE EMPIRE under the Sui ensued.

(To p. 148)

6. KOREA, TO 540 C.E.

Korea is a mountainous peninsula 100–150 miles wide and about 400 miles long, extending southward from Manchuria toward the western tip of Japan. High mountains and the frigid Sea of Japan have inhibited the development of the east coast, but the milder climate and more suitable terrain of the west coast facing China and the south coast opposite Japan have made these regions the natural centers of Korean history. The **Yalu River** in the north forms a natural border with China.

Since prehistoric times, the people seem to have been closely related racially, linguistically, and culturally to the ancient peoples of Manchuria and Siberia as well as to Japan, but post-Neolithic civilization came in large measure from China. The oldest **Paleolithic** (c. 50,000–40,000 B.C.E.) remains from dig sites reveal that the people were cave dwellers and built homes, using fire for food and warmth. They were hunters and gatherers and fishermen and used stone tools. The earliest **Neolithic** remains (c. 4000 B.C.E.) indicate that the people had pottery and polished stone implements. The Korean Peninsula (c. 3000 B.C.E.) had numerous settlements. Its pottery was gray in color with "comb pattern" markings on the outside, similar to pottery in the Russian Maritime Province, in the Amur and Sungari River basins of Manchuria, and in Mongolia. Another pottery culture emerged with painted designs, from Manchuria (c. 1800 B.C.E.).

People lived near waterways and later lived inland in pit dwellings. They hunted and ate fish they caught. Later there was some agriculture, too. There may have been a settled, community life in small villages. Society was organized by clans, each with a clan totem (an animal), headed by a chief; and each clan community was autonomous in its own terrain. Extra-clan bonds were formed through marriage and contiguous territory. They had animistic religious beliefs; nature's objects were revered, some even deified. Most important was the Sun, which figured prominently in Korean myths of human births from eggs following exposure to it.

Bronze was first used with subsequent regional variations (c. 9th–8th cent.–4th cent. B.C.E.). Dolmen burial, bronze daggers, and mirrors have been excavated from the Korean bronze age. People lived on higher ground than in the Neolithic age. Rice agriculture was practiced alongside fishing and hunting. Bronze was employed as weaponry and helped in the conquest of Neolithic communities. Walled-town states emerged as Bronze Age culture developed, and some community chiefs became more powerful than others, the embryos of Korean statelets.

In the 4th century B.C.E., six small states by river basins became sufficiently prominent that they were known even in China. The most prominent among them was **Old Chosŏn** in the basins of the Liao and Taedong Rivers (a major Bronze Age site) in northwest Korea. Rulers of Old Chosŏn combined political and religious affairs, claiming descent from a sun deity. Old Chosŏn later merged with other walled states into a "kingdom," designating its leader a "king," a clear Chinese borrowing. The use of **iron** came to northern Korea from Manchuria and was employed for plows and other farming tools, leading to the domestication of animals and increased agricultural production. Iron was also used for weaponry and horse-drawn vehicles, largely for the elite. People lived in pit dwellings. The influence of Chinese metal culture is evident from numerous Chinese coins unearthed at dig sites.

c. 300 B.C.E. The Chinese state of Yan invaded and conquered Old Chosŏn. It was subsequently taken over by the Qin.

206 B.C.E. Old Chosŏn conquered by Liu Bang, rebellion followed.

194–180 B.C.E. Power was taken back by **Wiman,** a Chinese refugee forced to flee to Korea during the tumult of the time. Wiman established the state of **Chosŏn** (or **Wiman Chosŏn**) which was highly Sinified but not a Chinese colony.

109 B.C.E. As Chosŏn continued to conquer other Korean statelets, the Han dynasty under Wudi, beginning to fear a Chosŏn-Xiongnu alliance, launched an attack.

108 B.C.E. The Chosŏn capital at present-day **P'yŏngyang** fell, and the Han established three commanderies on former Chosŏn terrain: Luolang (Nangnang), Zhenpan (Chinbŏn), and Lintun (Imdun).

107 B.C.E. A fourth commandery at Xuantu (Hyŏndo) was established. Zhenpan and Lintun were dissolved in 82 B.C.E. and linked, respectively, with Luolang and Xuantu. Luolang, near P'yŏngyang, became effectively an outpost of Han civilization with Chinese civil and mil-

itary officials and Chinese colonists. Other Korean states also acquired Chinese culture artifacts through Luolang.

Some of the other more important states along the Korean Peninsula follow. **Puyŏ** (Chinese: Fuyu), in the Sungari River basin of Manchuria, was first mentioned in the 4th century B.C.E. and then often from the 1st century C.E. It was seen as a threat to Wang Man's Xin dynasty. By 49 C.E. the Puyŏ ruler was calling himself "king," implying control over a confederated kingdom. Puyŏ sent emissaries to China with whom it was on good terms. It was later conquered by **Koguryŏ.** Koguryŏ is traditionally said to have been founded by Chumong in 37 B.C.E., south of Puyŏ. It was in the region of the Xuantu Commandery, but in 75 B.C.E. the latter was moved farther to the west into Manchuria due to local resistance and Koguryŏ's emergence as a confederated kingdom. It was led by a warrior aristocracy frequently at odds with the Chinese, and it thus acquired more through warfare than productive work, unlike Puyŏ. It began expanding in the early 1st century C.E. and fought against Wang Mang (12 C.E.); under King T'aejo (53–146?) it continued to spread south. Later in the 1st century it attacked also to the north. The **Chin** state was in the southern part of the peninsula, and it first appeared in records in the 2nd century B.C.E. It attempted contacts with Han China but was cut off from doing so by Wiman Chosŏn. Many Chinese refugees with knowledge of metalwork escaped to Chin. The use of iron in the south was important to social and cultural development, for example, in the greater use of rice agriculture. Chin was eventually subdivided into three statelets: Mahan, Chinhan, and Pyŏnhan (known collectively as Samhan or the "three Hans").

In **society** at the time, agriculture was most important, supplemented by the raising of livestock and the domestication of animals. Koguryŏ retained much hunting. The village communities lived off farming and paid heavy taxes but were forbidden from participation in the military. The elite lived in walled towns apart from these peasant communities. The confederated kingdoms developed from the merging of these walled-town states. Kingship was hereditary from at least the late 2nd to early 3rd century C.E. in Puyŏ and Koguryŏ. Aristocratic relatives controlled the political and economic affairs of the states; the richer ones had large retinues of household slaves. Through this process, the confederated kingdoms became centralized aristocratic states.

There was a separation over time between **religion** and politics. The chief of ritual practice emerged with powers in his own quarters; shamanism continued to be practiced; there were various seasonal rituals; and festivals were open to all classes of populace. Royal burials were extravagant, and the numerous burial objects imply that ancestor worship was strong.

c. 210 C.E. The **Gongson** family of southern Manchuria gained control over Luolang.

c. 238. The **Wei dynasty** (one of the Three Kingdoms in China) captured Luolang.

244. Wei attacked Koguryŏ and took its capital; when it attacked again the next year, the Koguryŏ king fled.

313–668. THE THREE KINGDOMS PERIOD began after Koguryŏ under King Mich'ŏn destroyed the Luolang Commandery (313), ending four centuries of Chinese control, and took the Taedong River area to its south, before confronting the rising state of **Paekche** in the southwest. The third state, **Silla,** was in the southeast.

342. The Xianbei state of **Yan** attacked Koguryŏ from the north, invaded the capital, took thousands of hostages, and burned down the imperial palace.

346–375. The **reign of King Kŭn Ch'ogo** witnessed the state of Paekche, having arisen in the Han River basin, become a centralized aristocratic state with hereditary kingship.

c. 360–390. This was the period of greatest Japanese influence in Korea through activities in the states of Silla and Paekche.

365–402. During the **reign of King Naemul**, Silla, having emerged from a walled-town statelet in the Chinhan area, became a confederated kingdom of considerable size.

369. Paekche destroys Mahan.

371. Paekche attacked north against Koguryŏ, reaching as far as

P'yŏngyang and killing **King Kogugwŏn,** forcing Koguryŏ to reorganize under King Kosurim (r. 371–384). Paekche also sought ties with the Eastern Jin dynasty in China and the Wa in Japan.

372. Buddhism was adopted in Koguryŏ.

373. Koguryŏ established the **National Confucian Academy.** Koguryŏ's administrative code was promulgated, and efforts were begun to rebuild state institutions after attacks from both north and south.

384. The **Paekche king adopted Buddhism.**

391–413. In the **reign of King Kwanggaet'o,** Koguryŏ's expansion drive progressed through military conquest. Lands were gained north of the Yalu River in Manchuria, and Paekche was attacked in the south. Better relations were achieved with Chinese states to the north; meanwhile, Paekche attained better ties with southern Chinese states and with Wa, the former to keep Koguryŏ at bay and the latter to attack Silla.

400. War erupted between Silla and the small, southernmost state of **Kaya,** which had had maritime contacts with the Chinese commanderies and with Wa. Silla obtained help from King Kwanggaet'o of Koguryŏ.

413–490. The **reign of King Changsu** brought Koguryŏ to the height of its power and glory. He kept ties with dynastic houses in both China's north and south and manipulated them to his own advantage. He moved the capital to P'yŏngyang (427), which became a political, economic, and social center of "national" life. The Paekche capital at Hansŏng (near modern Kwangju) was taken and the Paekche king caught and killed (475), forcing Paekche to move its capital to Ungjin.

433. Silla allied with Paekche to ward off Koguryŏ. Under King Chabi (r. 458–479), Silla became independent of Koguryŏ pressures, and the strong ties to Paekche were consolidated through marriage.

500–514. Under the **reign of King Chijŭng,** Silla experienced advances in agricultural technology, rice production, and irrigation.

514–540. King Pŏphŭng's reign saw Silla became a fully centralized autocracy. In 520 he issued an administrative code with Chinese-style bureaucratic titles, and he instituted the **"bone-rank" (kolp'um)** system.

535. Silla officially adopted Buddhism by this time. The last of the Three Korean Kingdoms to do so, Silla now began to develop rapidly at the expense of Japanese influence on the peninsula. *(To p. 155)*

7. JAPAN, TO 527 C.E.

a. GEOGRAPHY

Japan proper consists of a group of islands running eastward from south of the Korean Peninsula for about 700 miles and then turning abruptly to the north for about the same distance, approaching the Asian mainland once more off the coast of the Russian Maritime Province. It is the most geographically isolated of the principal four East Asian countries. Although, like England, Japan is an island country off the coast of a continent, Japan's closest point to the mainland at the Straits of Tsushima is 115 miles, while the English Channel is only 21 miles. The cold Sea of Japan enclosed by this island chain gives the inner side of the archipelago a cold, damp climate, but because of the current from the Pacific Ocean off the southwest coast, that part of Japan enjoys a warm, temperate climate.

The four main islands of Japan are: **Honshū,** the largest; **Hokkaidō,** the second largest and northernmost; **Kyūshū,** at the southwestern extremity; and **Shikoku,** east of Kyūshū. Among the many lesser islands, Tsushima and Iki are the most significant, for they lie in the straits between Japan and Korea. The three main plains are: **Kinai** (500 sq. mi.) at Ōsaka Bay, with Kyoto and Nara forming part of this area; the plain (600 sq. mi.) at **Ise Bay;** and the **Kantō** plain (5,000 sq. mi.) by Tokyo Bay. The Inland Sea, as an artery of communications, and northern and western Kyūshū, which face the Asian mainland, are also important regions.

The rivers are short and shallow. Mountains cover almost the entire area and are especially high in central Honshū. Many are volcanic, and eruptions and earthquakes are frequent. The climate is generally temperate throughout the country, and rain is plentiful. Rice has been the principal crop since antiquity.

b. ETHNOLOGY

The origin of the Japanese people is still debated. Archaeology and physical anthropology indicate a close connection with the Koreans and Tungusic peoples of northeastern Asia. Linguistic evidence, also hotly debated, tends to support this. There may have been a land bridge connecting Japan with Korea in high antiquity, which would help explain the connections. The Japanese are a mixed Mongoloid race, similar to Chinese and Koreans, perhaps with some Southeast Asian contributions as well; the Ainu (a Caucasoidlike people) originally inhabited the northeastern half of Japan and possibly contributed to the racial mix of Japanese today.

c. RELIGION

The early religion of Japan was a simple worship of the manifold manifestations of the powers of nature combined with a system of ritualistic observances, notable among which was an insistence on physical and ritual purity. The deities tended to become anthropomorphic and often merge with memories of past heroes. The Japanese were also affected by attempts to explain the origins of mankind and society in mythical terms. This eventually led to an organized mythology centering around the **Sun Goddess (Amaterasu Ōmikami)** and her descendants, the imperial family. After the introduction of Buddhism, this combination of nature worship, ritualistic observances, and ancestor-honoring mythology was given the name of **Shintō.**

d. EARLY CIVILIZATION

Archaeological evidence indicates that in the Palaeolithic era the Japanese were hunters and gatherers and used stone implements. The **Jōmon** ("cord script") era (c. 10,500–300 B.C.E.), with various subdivisions, acquired its name from the designs on unearthed pottery datable to 10,000 B.C.E. The Jōmon people hunted, fished, and ate vegetables. They lived in sunken pit dwellings and perhaps in villages. Rice only began to be planted in Kyūshū late in the Jōmon era. Archaeologists have uncovered Jōmon sites from Hokkaidō all the way south to the Ryūkyū chain. Jōmon pot designs indicate magical religious beliefs and a variety of cults. Unearthed earrings and ornaments are similar to those discovered in Korea.

e. JAPANESE HISTORICAL MYTHOLOGY

The first verifiable historical accounts of Japan occur in the Chinese dynastic histories of the 3rd century C.E. and picture western Japan, if not all Japan, as divided among a large number of small political units, among which feminine rule may not have been uncommon. Some of these statelets had direct relations with the Chinese colonies in Korea, and embassies from Japanese states to the Chinese capital are recorded from 57 to 266. However, Japanese mythology commences with a creation myth in which the brother-sister pair of deities, Izanagi and Izanami, descend to Earth, create the islands of Japan, and give birth to subsequent gods with various powers. These include Amatera-su and Susano-ō (the storm god). The latter two in turn copulate to produce more gods. Ninigi (grandson of the Sun Goddess) comes to Earth and settles in Kyūshū, whence he also brings the **three sacred imperial regalia:** a bronze mirror (symbol of the sun), an iron sword, and a jeweled necklace. His grandson subsequently conquers as far north as the Kinki plain; there he creates the **Yamato state** in 660 B.C.E., taking the throne as **Emperor Jimmu.** The mythology hints at a successful battle for supremacy of the imperial clan with another clan in **Izumo** on the Sea of Japan. The Izumo clan apparently had a distinctive culture and rather close ties with Korea.

c. 3rd cent. B.C.E.–250 C.E. Yayoi era. Yayoi replaced Jōmon, beginning in Kyūshū and moving toward the Kantō plain where it arrived by the end of the 1st century B.C.E. Yayoi had more refined pottery, settled agriculture (with rice cultivation using sophisticated irrigation techniques), and use of bronze and iron implements. Bronze was employed mainly for symbolic items, such as mirrors, bells, and elegantly thin (ornamental) weapons. The technology to make these items probably came from China and Korea. The discovery of Former Han coins in Yayoi dig sites indicates contact with the mainland. Yayoi pottery was similar in certain ways to Korean pottery, but it also continued Jōmon styles. By the late Yayoi period, a new society altogether had come into existence. Rice paddy cultivation spread from Kyūshū east, and there it needed more sophisticated irrigation methods because of the higher terrain. This emphasis on rice production probably affected social organization, bringing about more intensive farming, increasing wealth, population growth, and geographic expansion.

c. 239 C.E. With the accession of the tenth ruler of Yamato, **Sujin,** Japanese records began to contain material of probable historical accuracy.

c. 250–552. Kofun (tumulus) era. This was an extension of Yayoi culture, as Yayoi people began building huge tombs, traditionally considered to be for "emperors." The largest and most elaborate tomb (120 ft. high) was for **Nintoku** (trad. r. 395–427) near present-day Ōsaka. The tombs were often in a keyhole shape, some with moats. Buddhism later gradually eroded the tomb culture, which was eventually abandoned. Close ties between the state of **Kaya** (in Japanese, **Mimana**) in southeastern Korea and Kofun peoples of southwestern Japan continued until **Silla** conquered Kaya in 562.

Clay tomb figurines, known as *haniwa,* of human beings, houses, and animals were placed outside the tombs. Some figures of warriors on horseback with bronze or iron weapons indicate that this kind of warfare was engaged in. These are similar to Korean figurines of the time. The figurines depict daily life, including some female shamans. According to Chinese sources, the first queen, **Pimiko** (or Himiko, mid-3rd century), ruled the **state of Yamatai** with magic and was buried in a large tomb. There is still no conclusive evidence, however, for the location of Yamatai.

c. 360. Queen Jingū, ruling in the name of her deceased husband and later in the name of her son, is traditionally believed to have led and won military victories over Korea. There probably were Japanese campaigns on the peninsula at this time, which is corroborated by Korean records. A Korean inscription of 391 indicates the presence of Japanese armies. From this time considerable Japanese influence in the Korean state of Kaya can be dated, but recent archaeological research indicates that Japan was probably not receiving tribute from Kaya. Japanese influence in the state of **Paekche** also was growing. With the emerging

strength of Silla, Japanese clout on the Korean Peninsula was on the wane. Via these Korean contacts, Japan opened her doors to continental culture and Chinese civilization. This also enabled **direct contacts with China, initiated in 413.**

Society in the Kofun era was organized around a social elite in *uji* lineages (tribal in structure), each of whom claimed common ancestry and worshipped a deity *(kami)* which fostered *uji* solidarity. *Uji* were led by a hereditary chief *(uji no kami)* who claimed direct descent from the *kami* and ruled as both priest and secular head. The chief and his immediate family often bore one of seven hereditary titles *(kabone),* which in time came to be grouped hierarchically. Beneath the *uji* were commoners or *be,* agricultural tillers who lived in villages and were organized by occupations (e.g., weavers, fishers, cloth weavers). The *uji* used the *be,* the economic fundament of the *uji* system. At the bottom of the social order were domestic servants and slaves. These *uji* communities may correspond to the large number of political groupings mentioned in the early Chinese sources about 3rd-century Japan. The Yamato state emerged from this structure through conquest and the like (c. 5th cent., although perhaps later), either in Kyūshū or in the Kinki area.

Over the course of time, a ranking order developed among *uji,* with the most powerful one claiming its *kami* to be descendant directly from the Sun Goddess. This is thought to be the origin of the **imperial clan,** at first little more than hegemon among the various *uji.* Its chief was the "emperor," and its rule over the country very loose. The clans with the two most important hereditary titles, *omi* and *muraji,* were controlled through the *ōomi* (great *omi*) and *ōmuraji* (great *muraji*).

The **importation of continental culture** came hand in hand with a large influx of Korean refugees to Japan and seriously shook the *uji* system. About the end of the 4th century, scribes able to read and write Chinese came to Japan from the Korean state of Paekche. This development indicates the official **adoption of Chinese writing,** though not the first knowledge of it in Japan. Although writing spread slowly, it was used early on for historical records. In imitation of China, there developed a greater centralization of power in the hands of the imperial *uji* and its ministers. Imperial lands were gradually extended, and imperial authority grew apace, eventually leading to a thorough political and economic reorganization of Japan on the China model.

527? A serious revolt in Kyūshū prevented the crossing of an army to Korea to aid Kaya. Dissension among the Japanese and treachery among some officers on the peninsula reduced Japanese prestige there and opened the way for Silla's subsequent conquest of Kaya.

(To p. 157)

D. CLASSICAL GREECE AND THE HELLENISTIC WORLD

1. THE BRONZE AGE, 3000–1200 B.C.E.

a. GEOGRAPHY

Greece (ancient **Hellas**) is the extension of the mountain ranges of the Balkan Peninsula, with the **Ionian Sea** to the west and the **Aegean Sea** to the east. In antiquity, **northern Greece** comprised **Epirus, Amphilochia,** and **Acarnania** in the west, and **Macedonia,** the **Chalcidice** (whose three peninsulas jutted into the Aegean Sea), and **Thessaly** in the east. Central Greece began at the **Thermopylae Pass** and contained **Aetolia, Locris,** and **Phocis** in the west; **Boeotia** in the center; and **Attica** to the east, with the large island of **Euboea** lying off its eastern coast. After the narrow **Isthmus of Corinth** lay the **Peloponnese** or "Island of Pelops." It had six main regions: the **Argolis,** just south of the Isthmus, **Achaea** along the Gulf of Corinth in the north, **Elis** in the west, **Messene** in the southwest, **Laconia** (or **Lacedaimon**) along the eastern coast, and **Arcadia** in its mountainous center. Off the west coast of Greece lay the **Ionian Islands: Corcyra** (Corfu), **Cephalonia,** and **Zacynthos.** The Aegean Sea was dotted with islands: in the north

Scyros, Lemnos, and **Imbros** (between the Hellespont and Euboea), and **Thasos** and **Samothrace** off the Thracian coast; a string of islands along the coast of Asia Minor, of which the most important were **Lesbos, Chios, Samos,** and **Rhodes;** and the **Cyclades,** stretching southeast from Attica and Euboea and including **Melos, Delos, Paros, Naxos,** and **Thera.** Some fifty miles southeast of the Peloponnese lay **Crete,** the largest of the Aegean islands and its southern boundary.

The climate of Greece is temperate. Rainfall sometimes exceeds forty inches per year in the west but is only about sixteen inches in the east, making drought a constant menace. It rarely freezes, and in the summer the midday heat can exceed 100° F. Only 18 percent of the land surface is arable, and over large areas of the country, the soil is thin and rocky, making the cultivation of grain difficult, though olives and grapes ripen well in the rainless summers. Ancient Greece was more heavily wooded and more fertile than today, as the country has suffered from severe deforestation and erosion of the topsoil. The mountainous terrain in Greece promoted the development of numerous small city-states. There were some large cities, but most Greeks lived in towns and big villages, walking out to their fields, rather than staying in small isolated hamlets. Since many areas had to import grain, seaborne commerce developed at an early stage. But the civilization of ancient Greece at no time depended primarily on manufacture or trade and was always basically agrarian.

b. THE MINOAN CIVILIZATION

c. 3000–2200. EARLY MINOAN. Around 2700 the Bronze Age began in Greece, apparently connected with an immigration from Asia Minor. Pottery was still hand-shaped, and settlement size was small. In the mid-third millennium a rapid rise in culture occurred; towns and cities emerged, as well as the first palaces. **There was contact with Egypt,** and the **votive double axes,** characteristic of later Minoan religion, appeared. An indigenous **Hieroglyphic Script** survives on seals and pottery, but it has not yet been deciphered. This earliest civilization in Crete is called **Minoan** after the legendary King Minos of Knossos.

c. 2200–1700. MIDDLE MINOAN I and II: The Rise of Crete. The great palaces at **Knossos, Phaistos,** and **Mallia** were constructed during this period. These stone palaces, built asymmetrically around a large open court, contained large living quarters, storerooms for goods and products, and toilets superior to any in Europe before modern times. A road system connected Knossos with the plain of Phaestus. Wheel-thrown pottery was perfected, and fine examples were made as thin as an eggshell. A new script called **Linear A** replaced the Hieroglyphic Script, but except for the numeral system and a few pictographic signs, it cannot be read. Conclusions about Minoan culture, particularly government and religion, are necessarily conjectures based on archaeology and later Greek legends. The king was evidently the chief figure in religious worship, and the palace, a seat of religious cults. What appears to be a **Mother Goddess,** associated with snakes, is widely represented. To judge from wall paintings, the Minoans were devoted to sports, including hazardous bull jumping. Scenes of war are rare, and the towns were at all times unwalled. The Minoan palaces were almost all destroyed toward the end of the period, but whether the destruction occurred through war or natural causes (such as an earthquake) is unknown.

c. 1700–1450. MIDDLE MINOAN III–LATE MINOAN I: The "Thalassocracy" of Minos. The art of Minoan Crete reached a high point in this period, and the earliest wall frescoes appear at this time. In the 18th and 17th centuries, Crete had extensive trade relations with Ugarit in Syria and Byblos in Phoenicia. After 1600, this trade declined, but Minoan influence strengthened over the Cyclades, and there was close contact with Egypt. To what extent these changing trade patterns reflect political events is unknown, but legend has Crete's **King Minos** founding a sea empire **(thalassocracy).** Both public and private building reflects great wealth. At the end of this period there was another widespread destruction throughout Crete.

c. 1450–1125. Late Minoan III: Mycenaean Crete. Knossos was the only Cretan palace to be rebuilt, and it was now ruled by Greek-speaking Mycenaeans. Remains in graves and pottery indicate considerable numbers of Greeks moved to Crete. Clay tablets were inscribed with a new type of script, obviously derived from Linear A and known as **Linear B.** In 1952, **Michael Ventris** proved that the Linear B texts were written in Greek. They revealed a highly bureaucratic state centered in the palace of Knossos. A rapid decline in Mycenaean Crete came at the same time as that on the mainland.

c. MAINLAND GREECE: THE EARLY AND MIDDLE HELLADIC PERIODS

c. 2800–2500. Early Helladic I. Around 2800, Greece, like Crete, seems to have been invaded from northwest Asia Minor. The beginning of the Bronze Age corresponds roughly with this invasion. Probably the immigrants were the **Pre-Hellenic** population of Greece who left the non-Indo-European place names in Greece and elsewhere ending in -*ssos* (e.g., Knossos and Parnassos), and in -*inth* (Corinth). New villages sprang up throughout Greece, and there is evidence of trade with the Aegean Islands and especially Crete. Northern Greece and Thessaly were not as advanced in material culture as the southern mainland.

c. 2500–2200. Early Helladic II. Houses in this period were larger and some contained large storage facilities for grain. At Lerna there are remains of what may have been a palace **(House of Tiles),** indicating some sort of central authority. Large settlements at Zygouries and Tiryns, with gold and silver jewelry buried in tombs, suggest a rising prosperity.

c. 2200–1900. Early Helladic III. Signs of massive destruction are present at almost all Early Helladic period III sites. A new material culture was introduced, characterized by **Minyan Ware** (also called Orchomenos ware), a fine, wheel-made pottery. Whether the break in material culture represents the invasion of **Greek-speakers** into the region is debated. Scholars date the intrusion of the Greeks from as early as 2200 to as late as 1500 B.C.E., though most agree that the Greeks seem to have settled for some time in Thessaly before moving into the rest of the peninsula. In classical times, Greek was divided into three dialect groups: **Aeolian, Ionian,** and **Dorian.** Originally thought to predate the Greek invasion, some scholars believe the dialect division occurred after the Greeks took over the peninsula.

c. 1900–1600. Middle Helladic. A rapid rise in wealth and sophistication is associated with a palace-based civilization, which developed under Minoan influence. Kings and other royal persons were buried in shaft graves within a sacred precinct. One such grave at Mycenae, called **Circle B,** contained gold and silver objects on a small scale. In this period, Mycenaean culture was centered in the eastern Peloponnese and central Greece.

d. THE LATE HELLADIC PERIOD: THE MYCENAEAN AGE

c. 1600–1500. Late Helladic I: The Rise of Mycenaean culture. The shaft-grave culture continued but became wealthier. The shaft graves in **Circle A** (found earlier but dating later than Circle B) contained a remarkable 80 pounds of gold objects. Mycenaean architecture, called **Cyclopean,** is characterized by use of enormous stones. The rectangular **megaron** was now the typical private building, consisting of a portico *(aithousa),* vestibule *(prodomos),* and main room *(domos).* The largest and most important settlements were **Mycenae** and **Tiryns.** Major centers existed at **Orchomenos** and **Thebes** in Boeotia. Lake Copais, which covered a large area of western Boeotia, was drained during the Mycenaean period, providing fertile land. The fortress at Gla was built to protect the region. **Athens** was an important city and Cyclopean fortifications were built on the Acropolis. **Pylos** was one of the few early Mycenaean sites in western Greece.

c. 1500–1400. Late Helladic II: The "Tholos-Tomb" Dynasty. Around 1500 the Mycenaean burial style changed from the shaft grave to circular rock-lined chambers cut out of hillsides: so-called **tholoi** or "beehive" tombs. After c. 1450, the Mycenaeans conquered Crete and established themselves at Knossos. Evidence of Mycenaean presence is found in the Cyclades, Rhodes, Sicily, and Italy, although where political control ended and trade began is unknown. The prosperity of Mycenaean Greece was due largely to an expansion of trade: Egypt, Babylonia, Assyria, and the Hittite Empire were all ruled by wealthy palace-based governments, which fostered international exchange.

c. 1400–1200. Late Helladic III: The Height of the Mycenaean Age. After 1400, the Mycenaean culture spread throughout Greece, eventually penetrating virtually the entire mainland. The fine pottery found even in nonroyal tombs suggests a general prosperity, and the most impressive Mycenaean architecture dates to the 14th century. Around 1350, the citadel at **Mycenae** was enlarged, and an immense 23-foot-thick wall was constructed of Cyclopean blocks, which included the famous **Lion Gate.** The royal palace at the summit of the acropolis contained a throne room, living apartments, and a shrine. Its walls were covered with painted frescoes showing military scenes. Similar large palaces from this period were found at **Tiryns** and **Pylos.** The largest beehive tombs date to after 1300: the so-called "Treasuries" of Atreus at Mycenae and Minyas at Orchomenos. (The buildings have no connection to these mythical characters.) **Linear B** tablets have been found at Pylos, Mycenae, and Thebes on the mainland, as well as at Knossos in Crete. While limited to accounts and inventories, they give important information on Mycenaean language, government, economy, and religion. The king, or **wanax,** exercised supreme authority, followed by the *lawagetas*, or Leader of the People (or Army). There were a series of lower officials, including the *basileus*, later the Greek word for king. A special class of priests existed (unlike in the Classical period), as well as a palace economy with a complex division of labor, with numerous slaves. The names of later Greek gods, such as Zeus, Hera, Poseidon, Hermes, and Athena, were already present. After 1300 Mycenaean trade with Egypt and Syria declined, although the reasons for this are unclear.

c. 1200–1100. Late Helladic C: The Decline of Mycenae. Around 1230 most of the large Mycenaean cities, with the exception of Athens and Mycenae itself, were destroyed. Texts from Pylos, written just before the city's destruction, discuss military dispositions against an apparent invasion. Around the same time, the export of Mycenaean pottery to Syria and Egypt ceased completely. A number of factors probably brought Mycenaean culture to an end, but a major one was probably the movement of the **Sea Peoples,** which affected the Middle East at the same time (p. 33).

e. THE GREEKS IN ASIA MINOR

c. 1500–1200. The Ahhiyawa. Hittite records mention the **Ahhiyawa,** who lived in, or raided, western Asia Minor. Some scholars have connected the Ahhiyawa with the Achaeans, Homer's name for the Greeks. Attacks on Cyprus by Attarissyas the Ahhiyawan, reported by the Hittites, may refer to the activities of Atreus, the father of Agamemnon, referred to in Greek mythology.

c. 1200. The Trojan War. Troy, located where the Aegean meets the Hellespont, was inhabited after 2000 by people who shared cultural characteristics with the population on the Greek mainland. There are nine levels of habitation, from the Early Bronze Age to Roman times, numbered I to IX. Around 1300 Troy VI was destroyed by an earthquake and replaced by Troy VIIa, generally identified with the city of the Trojan War celebrated in Greek mythology. Troy VIIa was destroyed by fire c. 1200.

2. THE DARK AGES, 1200–800 B.C.E.

a. ECONOMY, TECHNOLOGY, SOCIETY, AND CULTURE

The Greek **Dark Ages** were characterized by a gradual, though severe, decline in material culture. Mycenaean pottery styles were gradually replaced by proto-Geometric ware, cremation supplanted burial, and the appearance of **long pins** and **spectacle-fibula** suggest a new style of dress. International trade, monumental building, and the size of the Greek population declined considerably from Mycenaean times. There is no evidence for writing, and cities dramatically shrank in size. The new technology introduced in the Dark Ages was mainly military: iron weapons and tools appeared, and the slashing sword and throwing spear were introduced. In the 11th or 10th century, cavalry replaced the chariots of the Bronze Age. The later Greeks saw this period as a **Heroic Age,** and much of our information about Greek society and culture in the Dark Ages comes from legends preserved in later literature. The exploits of these heroes formed three "cycles": The **Theban Cycle,** supposedly occurring two generations before the Trojan War and concerning **Oedipus** and his family; the **Cycle of Heracles** and his sons, the **Heraclidae;** and, the **Trojan Cycle,** the war of the Achaeans against Troy, led by **Agamemnon, Achilles,** and **Odysseus.** These legends are preserved in Attic drama of the fifth century B.C.E. and in the epic poems called the *Iliad* and the *Odyssey.* The epics were ascribed to the blind poet, **Homer,** who probably lived sometime between 850 and 650 B.C.E. Both works may have been composed by the same individual, but it is more likely that the *Iliad* predates the *Odyssey* by about a century. The poems contain some reliable traditions dating back to the Mycenaean Age: the use of chariots and bronze weapons, large royal palaces, and the **Catalog of Ships** (*Iliad* 2.484 ff), which reflects the importance of Mycenaean, not Dark Age, states. Other elements clearly belong to the 10th and 9th centuries: the use of the dipylon or "figure 8" shield, the ritual gift of tripods, and the cremation of the dead. In both epics, the Mycenaean world and the Dark Ages are blended together, and it is difficult to distinguish the date of various elements of the poems.

In the Dark Ages, Greek states were considerably smaller and less wealthy than in Mycenaean times, though the basic unit is already the walled *polis* or city-state. Social organization was tribal: Ionians, for example, were grouped into four tribes. Within the tribes there were "brotherhoods" (*phratriai*) composed of members sufficiently related to each other to certify legitimate birth and citizenship. The landless day-laborers (*thetes*) were at the bottom of the social ladder, below even slaves. Most of the people (*demos*) were free peasants, who might be convened in the assembly place (*agora*) to listen to their superiors but expressed their wishes only by silence or applause. There was no voting and it was not normal for a commoner to speak in the assembly. **An aristocratic warrior class,** based on birth, wealth, and military prowess, formed clans (*gene*), which maintained relations with each other through arranged marriages and guest-friendship (*xenia*), involving the ritual exchange of gifts. The leaders of the aristocratic clans

met in a council (*boule*) and advised the king, now called a **basileus** instead of **wanax.** Royal powers were not absolute but depended on the consent of the nobles and clan leaders. Religion was family-based and centered around the *hestia*, or hearth. Zeus was the king of the gods, but the other gods sat in council, gave advice, and even sometimes opposed Zeus. The gods had local associations: Hera with Argos, Sparta, and Mycenae; Athena with Athens and Troy; Aphrodite with Paphos in Cyprus; and Ares with Thrace.

b. THE DORIAN INVASION

In the 12th century, the power vacuum created by the decline of Mycenaean civilization was filled by Greeks speaking the **Dorian** dialect, who invaded the peninsula from the north. Greek tradition characterized this movement as the "return" of the sons of Heracles (**Heraclidae**): Hyllus, Dymas, and Pamphylas, who were the eponymous founders of the three Dorian tribes. The Dorians originally came from southern Macedonia, though the Greeks derived their name from the city of **Doris** in central Greece. It may be that the Dorians settled there for some time before moving into the **Peloponnese.** The Argolis, Lacedaemon, and Messenia were conquered, and the Achaeans and Arcadians pushed into corners of the peninsula. Other Dorian groups attacked the Aegean Islands, and conquered Thera, Melos, and the central portion of Crete. A few cities in Asia Minor (principally, Halicarnassus and Cnidos) were founded or cofounded by Dorians. The Dorian invasion corresponded with the start of the **Iron Age** in Greece, but despite the introduction of this superior metal, culture as a whole declined in Greece as a result of the Dorian invasion.

c. THE AEOLIAN AND IONIAN MIGRATIONS AND THE GREEK RENAISSANCE

The speakers of the Aeolian and Ionian dialects were pushed out of their original territories by the Dorian invaders. The Aeolians settled on the northwest coast of Asia Minor and on the islands of Tenedos and Lesbos. This **Aeolian migration** seems to have started around 1130 and to have lasted until 1000 or even later. Athens resisted the Dorians, though in the 11th and 10th centuries there were changes in Athenian burial customs, dress, and pottery style, which suggests the arrival of new peoples. These were probably Ionian and perhaps Mycenaean refugees fleeing the Dorians. Athens also formed a base for an **Ionian migration** to the east. The Ionians invaded the western coast of Asia Minor, which was subsequently called **Ionia,** taking over the existing cities of Colophon, Miletus, Smyrna, Myus, Priene, Ephesus, Phocaea, and others. The Cyclades were also settled by Ionians in this period. The spread of **proto-Geometric** pottery from Athens to all over the Aegean world in the 10th century is probably connected to this Ionian migration. The Ionians shared common religious festivals, particularly the **Panionium** and Delian festival of Apollo.

900–800 B.C.E. The Greek Renaissance. After 900, eastern ("orientaliz-

MACEDONIA

EPIRUS

Olympus

THESSALY

CORCYRA

Aegean Sea

SCYROS

CEPHALONIA

Thermopylae (480)

AETOLIA

EUBOEA

BOEOTIA

Thebes

ATTICA

Athens

Piraeus

ANDROS

ACHAEA

ELIS

ARCADIA

Corinth

AEGINA

Olympia

Argos

ARGOLIS

ZACYNTHOS

C Y C L A D E S

PAROS

Myrtoum Sea

MESSENIA

Messene

Sparta

LACONIA

MELOS

I o n i a n   S e a

CYTHERA

GREEK
CITY STATES

0 10 20 30 40 50
MILES

M e d i t e r r a n e a n   S e a

Sacred Way

ATHENS

Acropolis

SALAMIS

Long Walls

Gulf of Saronica

Piraeus

N

Mt. Hymettus

ing") influence resulted in the development of the **proto-Corinthian** and **proto-Attic** pottery styles. The stiffness of geometric design gave way to lively representations of humans and animals: color reappeared; ornament, often symmetrical, was vigorous. A whole new set of vase shapes was invented. Spread by the growing trade with distant places, then by colonies, proto-Corinthian became the luxury pottery of the Mediterranean world. Grave sites at Athens indicate a remarkably high rate of population increase in the 9th century.

3. THE ARCHAIC PERIOD, 800–510 B.C.E.

a. ECONOMY, TECHNOLOGY, SOCIETY, AND CULTURE

The Greek diet was simple: bread, cheese, vegetables, olive oil, wine, and occasionally fish or pork. Beef was seldom eaten, and sheep and goats were kept mainly for hides, wool, and milk. Most farms were small, and slave labor was apparently rarely used in agriculture in the Archaic period. By 800 the **classical *polis*** was beginning to emerge, the city-state with its own central palace, territory, government, and loyal citizens (along with many noncitizen inhabitants). Many cities, including Athens, were dependent on the **importation of grain**, particularly from the Black Sea region. The main centers for **manufacture** were Athens, famous for its painted vases; Corinth; Sicyon; Argos and Chalcis, noted for metal-work; and Miletus and Samos, which made furniture and textiles. **Mining** was extensive: marble came from Mt. Pentelicus and Paros; silver, from Mt. Laurium and Mt. Pangaeus; gold, from Mt. Pangaeus and Thasos; iron, from Laconia; and copper, from Cyprus. Rough terrain and poor roads made overland travel difficult, so most **commerce** was by sea. The introduction of **coined money** from Lydia in the 7th century facilitated trade and capital investment but also increased debt. The two prominent standards of currency were the **Euboean** and the **Aeginetan**. By c. 750 B.C.E. the Greeks had borrowed the **Phoenician alphabet**, adapted certain letters to represent vowels, and added others for sounds found only in Greek. Marble temples appeared, and the three architectural orders—**Doric, Ionic,** and **Aeolic**—developed. **Sculpture** began representing the human body in the nude. Marble statues were generally painted in lifelike colors. Early Greek painting is known mainly from decorated pottery: red-figured vases replaced black-figured c. 500 B.C.E.

In the early Archaic period, **aristocratic oligarchies** generally replaced Dark Age monarchies, except in Sparta and Macedonia. Later, ambitious individuals overthrew the constituted governments of many cities and established themselves as **tyrants. Beginning c. 760 B.C.E., Greek cities started founding colonies,** which eventually occupied much of the coastline of both the Mediterranean and Black Seas. Colonists, led by a founder, or **oikistes,** generally adopted the religious cults and constitution of the "mother city" (**metropolis**) but were politically independent. In the 7th century, **hoplite warfare** developed. Hoplites were citizen soldiers who provided their own equipment: a round bronze shield *(hoplon)*, a bronze helmet with cheek and nose guards, and a nine-foot spear. They fought in a **phalanx,** shoulder-to-shoulder in line, facing the enemy with a wall of shields and spears and marching in step to the music of flutes. **Athletics** was an important element of Greek culture. There were major international festivals which involved athletic contest, such as the **Pythian Games** at Delphi and the **Olympian Games,** starting (traditionally) in 776 and held every four years.

The Boeotian poet **Hesiod** (c. 700) wrote the **Theogony,** on the genealogy of the gods, and the **Works and Days,** giving advice on proper living. Other early poets included the Ionian **Archilochus** (c. 700), the Aeolians **Alcaeus** and **Sappho** (c. 600), and the Dorians **Stesichorus** (630–555) and **Arion** (c. 600). **Lyric poetry** was exemplified by **Alcman** (c. 654–611), **Anacreon** (born c. 570), **Simonides** (c. 556–468), **Pindar** (518–442), and **Bacchylides** (c. 480). Tragic drama grew out of cultic songs, originally performed by a chorus at religious festivals. The poet **Thespis** first introduced a speaking actor into a tragedy in 534 B.C.E. Greek philosophy began with **Thales** (c. 600), who was said, probably falsely, to have predicted a solar eclipse in 585 B.C.E. **Anaximenes** (c. 600) and **Anaximander** (c. 610–540) and other early philosophers started to seek knowledge for its own sake and to develop rational explanations for natural phenomena. The so-called **logographoi** wrote local histories, the best example being **Hecataeus** of Miletus (c. 500).

The normal age for **marriage** in Greece was 30 for men and 15–16 for women. Most marriages were arranged. **Women took little part in public life and, in some cases, had no more legal rights than slaves.** Most citizen women spent their lives secluded in women's quarters. Spartan women were the exception and received the same physical training as men. At least one woman poet wrote in the Archaic period: **Sappho of Lesbos.**

b. ASIA MINOR AND THE AEGEAN ISLANDS

c. 800–680. Rise of the Ionian cities. The Ionian cities of Asia Minor were the wealthiest and most advanced Greek city-states in Archaic times and served as conduits for Near Eastern technology and culture entering Greece. The Ionian cities, particularly Miletus and Phocaea, were also leaders in the colonization movement.

757. Miletus colonized **Cyzicus** on the southern shore of the Propontus.

680–652. Beginnings of Lydian Conflict. King Gyges turned Lydia into the leading power in Asia Minor. He frequently attacked the Ionian cities but was unable to conquer them.

675. The Milesians send a colony to **Abydos** on the Hellespont.

630. The southern Aegean island of Thera colonized **Cyrene** in North Africa.

610. With permission of the Pharaoh **Psammetichus I,** Miletus founded a trading post in the Nile Delta, which developed into the Greek city of **Naucratis** (p. 70).

609–560. Alyattes of Lydia conquered Smyrna, but Miletus and Clazomenae continued to resist. Ionian culture reached its height, particularly in **philosophy: Thales, Anaximenes,** and **Anaximander** were all active at Miletus.

600. Phocaea settled **Massalia** (Marseilles) on the southern coast of Gaul.

560–546. The Lydian king **Croesus** conquered Ionia, though Miletus maintained its privileged position. Tyrants ruled most of the cities and paid tribute to Lydia.

546–499. Persian rule. Cyrus defeated Croesus in 546. The Persian general Harpagus subdued Ionia and installed pro-Persian tyrants. Miletus continued to enjoy a favored status. The Ionian cities were placed together with Lydia and Mysia in a single satrapy and ruled from **Sardis.**

c. SPARTA AND THE PELOPONNESE

c. 900–700. The Rise of Sparta. In the 9th century, four or five Laconian villages joined to form the city of **Sparta,** with two royal dynasties, the **Agiads** and the **Eurypontids,** reigning jointly. Between 800 and 730, Sparta conquered the rest of Laconia. Around the same time, the Spartans reorganized their constitution, introducing lifelong military training, a rigid oligarchic government, and a code of absolute obedience and austerity. At the age of seven, boys were taken from their parents for military training. Men of military age lived away from their wives in barracks and ate at common messes *(syssitia)*. Five tribes replaced the three Dorian ones, each providing a regiment *(lochos)* for the army. A council (**Gerousia**) composed of 28 elders and the two kings proposed legislation, which was then approved by the assembly (**Apella**), made up of adult male citizens (**spartiates**). The chief magistrates (**ephors**), eventually five in number, had wide powers. The non-Spartan Laconians, called **Perioikoi,** tithed to the Spartans and were drafted into the army but had no vote in the assembly. The introduction of this constitution was later ascribed to **Lycurgus,** though some scholars doubt his existence.

c. 735–715. The First Messenian War. Sparta, led by **King Theopompus** (c. 720–675), defeated Messenia and divided it into allotments *(klaroi)*, rent which supported the individual Spartiates, leaving them free to train for war. The Spartans turned the Messenians into serfs *(helots)* who worked the land for them.

733. Corinth, ruled by an oligarchy under the **Bacchiadae** clan, founded two colonies: one at **Syracuse** in Sicily and another on the island of Corcyra (modern Corfu) in northwestern Greece.

728. The Megarians colonized **Megara Hyblaea** in Sicily.

720. Achaea and Troezen jointly founded a colony at **Sybaris** in southern Italy, which became proverbial for its wealth and opulence.

c. 710. Achaea settled the colony of **Croton** on the "toe" of Italy.

706. Sparta founded its only colony, **Taras** (Tarentum), in southern Italy (p. 62).

c. 680. King **Pheidon of Argos** defeated Sparta and Tegea in the **Battle of Hysiae** (669). He later overcame Epidaurus and Athens, and Argos became the leading Greek power. Pheidon may have introduced coinage into mainland Greece, perhaps with a mint at Aegina.

676. Megara colonized **Chalcedon** on the Asiatic side of the Hellespont. It was called "the city of the blind," because the settlers missed a better site at Byzantium on the European shore.

660. Megara founded a colony at **Byzantium**.

657. The Cypselid Tyranny in Corinth. Cypselus (657–625) overthrew the Bacchiad oligarchy and made himself tyrant of Corinth.

c. 650–630. The Second Messenian War. Messenia revolted against the Spartans. Allied to the Arcadians and Argos, Messenia won the **Battle of Senyclarus.** But in a 19-year war, Sparta finally defeated the Messenians and reintroduced helotry.

625. Cypselus's son **Periander** (625–585) succeeded him and brought Corinth to its political and cultural zenith. He had wide international dealings—his nephew **Psammetichus** was named after the pharaoh of Egypt.

600. Corinth founded the colony of **Potidaea** in the northern Aegean in order to foster trade with Macedonia.

585. Psammetichus (585–582) became tyrant of Corinth but was soon murdered. An oligarchic government was reestablished.

c. 575–555. The Tegean War. Sparta defeated Tegea after a long and difficult war (c. 575–555). Tegea became a subject ally, nominally independent, but bound to follow Spartan foreign policy and provide it with troops.

c. 555. Sparta extended its alliance system, the **Peloponnesian League,** which eventually included all the states in the peninsula except Achaea and Argos. Allies contributed two-thirds of their military forces in war, always under Spartan leadership, though each member had a vote in foreign-policy decisions. **King Anaxandridas** (560–520) led a campaign which overthrew the tyrant of Sicyon. In Sparta, **Cheilon** and the other ephors dominated Spartan politics.

c. 544. The Battle of the 300 Champions. Sparta and Argos fought a war over control of the Thyrean plain. Each side picked 300 "champions" for a fight to the death to decide the issue. When neither side accepted the result, the two armies fought a pitched battle, which the Spartans won. Argos retained its independence but lost its regional power.

c. 524–510. Pursuing their antityrannical policy, the Spartans supported an unsuccessful attempt to overthrow **Polycrates,** the tyrant of Samos in 524. They succeeded in deposing tyrannies in Naxos (522) and Athens (510).

c. 519–490. The Reign of Cleomenes I. The Agiad king **Cleomenes I** reasserted royal power in Sparta and brought the Peloponnesian League to its height. When the expulsion of the Peisistratid tyrants from Athens resulted not in a pro-Spartan oligarchy but in democratic reforms (p. 64), Cleomenes led an expedition into Attica. The invasion failed due to the opposition of the Eurypontid king **Demaratus** (c. 515–491) and the defection of Corinth.

d. ATHENS

c. 800–680. Athens gradually unified Attica by conquest and by **synoecism,** the process of merging with smaller towns. The Athenians were divided into four tribes (phylai) made up of phratries. Each phratry was divided into two groups: the clansmen (gennetai), made up of the aristocratic eupatridae, and the guildsmen (orgeones), who practiced trade and manufacture. Where poor farmers and serfs (hektemoroi) were enrolled is unclear. For administrative purposes, each tribe was divided into 12 naucrariai, each providing one ship for the navy. The army was provided by two of three classes: the knights (**hippeis**), wealthy aristocrats who made up the cavalry, and the hoplite class (**zeugitai**) who provided their own arms and made up the infantry. The **thetes,** who

had no property, did no military service. The **Medonidae** ruled as kings, but during the 8th and 7th centuries, the aristocrats gradually usurped royal power. The king's military functions were absorbed by the war archon (**polemarch**) and his civil duties were absorbed by a civil archon (archon eponymos) after whom the year was named. The kingship retained only religious significance.

683. Athens abolished the monarchy completely. The king's religious duties were now performed by a king archon (archon basileus). Six thesmothetai were created to be judges and interpreters of law, and these officials along with the civil archon, the king archon and the polemarch were known as the **Nine Archons.** They were chosen each year from among the aristocracy by the **Areopagus,** the council of ruling aristocrats, which ran the state. The important priesthoods were hereditary in aristocratic families. The **Ecclesia,** or assembly of citizens, had little power.

623. Cylon attempted to establish a **tyranny** in Athens, but the people did not support him. Cylon himself escaped, but many of his followers were massacred by Megacles and the aristocratic Alcmaeonid clan while in a religious sanctuary. This impious slaughter gave rise to the so-called **"Curse of the Alcmaeonidae."**

628–620. According to tradition, **Draco,** one of the thesmothetai, issued Athens' first written laws. The "Draconian" penalties were most severe—death in most cases.

c. 600. Athens seized **Sigeum** from Mytilene. The resulting war was arbitrated around 590 by the tyrant **Periander** of Corinth in Athens' favor.

594–591. THE REFORMS OF SOLON. The introduction of **coined money,** and high rates of interest, led to increased indebtedness. Debt slavery in turn brought civil unrest. To solve the crisis, **Solon** was made sole archon in 595, with special legislative powers. In 592, he was appointed "reformer of the constitution." His **Seisachtheia** ("shaking-off-of-burdens") canceled all debts on land, banned debt slavery, and freed all debt slaves. Those who had been sold abroad were redeemed at state expense. Solon replaced Draco's laws, except those on homicide, with a milder code. A popular court, the **heliaea,** was created, to which the citizens could appeal the decisions of the magistrates. Solon created a Council (boule) of 400 (100 from each tribe), which proposed laws to the assembly (ecclesia). The assembly could still only accept or reject the council's proposals but now elected all the magistrates. The Areopagus council continued, but in a reduced capacity. Four classes of citizens, based on wealth, were established: (1) the **pentacosiomedimnoi** had annual revenues of 500 bushels (medimnoi) of grain or measures (metretai) of wine or olive oil, (2) the hippeis, with revenues of 300 bushels or measures, (3) the zeugitai, with 200, and (4) the thetes who made up the rest of the citizen body. At some later date, these classes were redefined in terms of money and based on property rather than income. Every member of the first two classes was eligible for the archonships. Since ex-archons automatically joined the Areopagus council, it ceased to be exclusively aristocratic. The first three property classes could run for the lower magistracies, but the fourth class, the lowest and largest, could participate only in the heliaea court and the assembly. Solon's reforms were important but did not solve the underlying class tensions, perhaps because no provision was made to supply freed slaves with land or to relieve the burdens of the serfs (hektemoroi, "sixth-parters"). Unlike other contemporary political leaders, Solon did not try to become a tyrant. After making his reforms, he left Athens for ten years, traveling around the Mediterranean. Factional fighting broke out immediately after Solon's departure between two parties: the rich aristocrats of the plain (pediakoi) led by **Lycurgus,** and the merchants and craftsmen (paralioi) headed by **Megacles** the Alcmaeonid.

c. 565. Peisistratus, a relative of Solon, acquired fame by conquering the island of Salamis from Megara. He organized a new party, the diakrioi, based in the hill country of north Attica, made up of small farmers, shepherds, artisans, and the poor.

561–510. THE TYRANNY OF THE PEISISTRATIDS.

561–527. The Rule of Peisistratus. In 561, Peisistratus made himself tyrant of Athens but shortly thereafter was driven out of the city by Megacles and Lycurgus. In 560/559, allying himself with Megacles, he was restored to power, but was expelled again in 556. Peisistratus spent some years in Thrace, gaining wealth from mines he owned there. In 546, he was again made tyrant with help from Thessaly and from **Lygdamis,** the tyrant of Naxos. Peisistratus exiled his opponents, confiscated their lands, and distributed them to the poor, so that the **hektemoroi** now became landowners. Peisistratus encouraged industry and trade and introduced the popular **cult of Dionysus,** which reduced the power of the aristocrats' hereditary priesthoods. He sent **Miltiades** to establish a tyranny over the Thracian Chersonese, which controlled the passage between Europe and Asia. Peisistratus also "purified" the island of Delos, the center of an Ionian religious league, which extended his political control into the Cyclades. At home, Peisistratus kept the form of the Solonian constitution, while holding all real power.

527. Upon Peisistratus's death, his sons **Hippias** and **Hipparchus** succeeded to the tyranny.

519. Athens defeated Thebes and prevented it from forcing **Plataea** into the Boeotian League.

514. Two aristocrats, **Harmodius** and **Aristogeiton,** attempted to assassinate the two Athenian tyrants. Only Hipparchus was killed, and the sole tyranny of Hippias grew more oppressive. The Alcmaeonidae, apparently part of the plot, fled from Athens.

e. CENTRAL AND NORTHERN GREECE

c. 800. Chalcis and **Eretria,** the two largest cities on **Euboea,** were major powers in the Archaic period, and Euboean coinage, weights, and measures were used throughout the Greek world.

c. 775. Chalcis, Eretria, and the Aeolian city of Cyme jointly settled a colony on the island of **Pithecusae** (Ischia) in the Bay of Naples.

757. These same cities, along with the Pithecusans, established a colony at **Cumae** on the Italian mainland.

c. 730. Eretria settled colonies at **Mende** in the Chalcidice and at **Methone** and **Dicaea** in Macedonia.

c. 720. Chalcidian colonists established **Rhegium** in southern Italy.

c. 710. Chalcis colonized **Torone** in the Chalcidice and subsequently founded some 30 small colonies on the peninsula.

c. 700–500. THE TAGEIA OF THESSALY. Before 700, Thessaly was organized into four **tetrads,** each ruled by a **tetrarch.** In the 7th century, Aleuas of Larissa organized the **Thessalian League** and led it as **tagos,** or general. The *tagos* was an elected office but generally held by a member of the **Aleuadae** clan. A federal assembly levied taxes and troops, and until the 6th century the Thessalian League possessed the strongest army in Greece. The League's loose organization, however, prevented Thessaly from playing a leading political role, though it dominated the **Amphictyony of Anthela,** a religious league which, by 600, included all the city-states of central Greece.

c. 700. Chalcis, supported by Corinth, Samos, and Thessaly, fought the **Lelantine War** against Eretria, Aegina, Miletus, and Megara, over the rich Lelantine plain. Chalcis and its allies were victorious.

c. 640. Perdiccas I of the Argead dynasty conquered the Macedonian plain and established a capital at Aegae (Vergina). Macedon was inhabited by a variety of ethnic groups, including Greeks, Illyrians, and Thracians. Whether the Macedonians themselves spoke a dialect of Greek or a separate language is a hotly debated subject. The royal family and the aristocracy, in any case, became increasingly Hellenized.

c. 590. THE FIRST SACRED WAR. Crisa, in whose territory Delphi lay, started levying tolls on visitors to the shrine of Apollo. The **Amphictyony of Anthela,** under Thessaly's leadership, and with help from Sicyon and Athens, declared war. Crisa was defeated and demolished. The Amphictyony took over the administration of Delphi and moved its headquarters there. Athens and the Peloponnesian Dorians were admitted as members.

c. 550. THE BOEOTIAN LEAGUE. Thebes formed the **Boeotian League** and began subordinating the smaller states in the region. After a long struggle, the city of **Orchomenos** was defeated and forced to join the league.

519. Plataea, on the border with Attica, refused to join the Boeotian League. In the ensuing conflict (519–506) the Boeotians, allied with the Euboeans, were defeated by the Athenians and Plataeans.

c. 512. Darius I invaded the Balkans and the Macedonian king **Amyntas I** became a Persian vassal.

f. SICILY AND MAGNA GRAECIA

c. 800. Before the Greeks arrived, **Sicans, Sicels,** and **Elymi,** along with **Phoenician colonists,** inhabited Sicily. Sicels also lived in south Italy, along with other native peoples such as the **Messapii** and **Apuli.**

c. 775. Pithecusae (Ischia) was settled from Chalcis, Eretria, and Cyme on an island in the Bay of Naples. A very early Greek inscription (c. 730) was found there.

757. Cumae was established by Pithecusan colonists, Chalcidians and Eretrians. Southern Italy came to be known as Greater Greece (**Magna Graecia**).

735. Thucles, the *oikistes* for a group of Chalcidians, established **Naxos,** the first Greek colony in Sicily. Subsequent Greek colonization drove the Phoenicians from most of Sicily. Only three Phoenician cities remained: **Motya, Panormus,** and **Solus,** all on the west coast.

c. 734. Corinth founded **Syracuse,** which grew to be the preeminent city in Sicily.

c. 729. Thucles, leading a party of Naxian colonists, founded **Leontini** in Sicily. Around the same time another group of Naxians, under **Evarchus,** settled **Catana.**

728. The Megarians, failing at colonizing Trotilon and Thapsos, succeeded at **Megara Hyblaea,** 14 miles north of Syracuse.

c. 720. Chalcis settled **Rhegium,** in Italy, just across the strait of Messene from Sicily.

c. 710. The Achaeans established **Croton** on the toe of Italy, which became a leading city in Magna Graecia.

706. Sparta established its sole colony, **Taras** (Tarentum), in southern Italy. The colonists, lead by Phalanthus, were **Partheniae,** children of Spartan men and helot women.

688. Gela on the southern coast of Sicily was founded by Cretans and Rhodians.

651 (or 628). Colonists from Megara Hyblaea established **Selinus.** This was the Sicilian Greek colony that was closest to the Phoenician cities and at times joined the Phoenicians against its fellow Greeks.

580. Gela founded **Acragas** in southwest Sicily, which became larger and wealthier than its metropolis.

c. 580. An attempt by the Spartan **Pentathlus** to colonize western Sicily was defeated by the Elymians and Carthaginians.

c. 570–554. Phalaris, tyrant of Acragas, pursued a policy of extreme repression and ruthless expansion.

c. 550. The Carthaginian **Malchus** campaigned, with some success, against the Sicilian Greeks.

535. In the naval **Battle of Alalia** the Carthaginians and Etruscans defeated Phocaean settlers from Corsica and forced them to abandon their colony. Shortly thereafter **Massalia** defeated Carthage and limited Carthaginian influence in the northwestern Mediterranean.

c. 530. Pythagoras founded his sect of mystical philosophy at Croton. The details of his life and his teachings are obscured by legend, but a belief in reincarnation, numerology, and dietary restrictions were involved. By 510, the Pythagoreans had seized political control of Croton.

510. Internal dissensions in **Sybaris** allowed Croton to defeat it. Sybaris was sacked and a river diverted over its site. The Spartan **Dorieus,** who had allied himself with Croton, tried to colonize western Sicily but was killed by the Segestans and Phoenicians.

4. THE CLASSICAL AGE, 510-323 B.C.E.

a. ECONOMY, TECHNOLOGY, SOCIETY, AND CULTURE

In this period, **crop rotation** was introduced, dramatically increasing agricultural production. Large estates that were worked by slave labor emerged, though small farms owned by free citizens remained the rule. **Slavery became more important in Greek economy.** Slaves were employed mainly in domestic service and mining, but also in manufacture and agriculture. The ruling class in all Greek cities, including democracies, depended on unfree labor both for income and personal services. War and piracy were the main sources of slaves, and slavery was never confined to any particular ethnic group. Slaves were often freed, or **manumitted,** and eventually their descendants merged with the free population. By the 5th century, Athenian **coinage** became the predominant medium of exchange in the Greek world, though after the Peloponnesian War, the Rhodian standard replaced it in Ionia. Temples continued to serve as depositories of money, but c. 500 B.C.E., **private bankers** *(trapezitai)* took over most of the business of exchanging and lending money. **Bottomry loans** *(nautika)* developed, repayable only if a cargo safely reached its destination; often given by groups of investors, such loans spread out risk and encouraged trade. Around the same time, the Athenians developed a new kind of colony, the **cleruchy.** Each settler received an allotment *(kleros)* but retained Athenian citizenship. The **financial system** of most Greek cities was highly developed. Cities generally covered the costs of some sort of police force or night watch, the military (except equipment provided by the hoplites themselves), fortifications, sacrifices and religious festivals, public buildings, salaries for officials and jurors, and pensions for orphans and crippled soldiers. Food and money were also distributed to the population under certain circumstances. **Direct taxes** were unusual, and paid mainly by resident aliens *(metics)*, freed slaves, and those employed in certain low-class crafts and trades. Most state income was provided by **indirect taxes,** excise duties, and assessments, such as court fees and fines, gate tolls, auction taxes, sales taxes, harbor dues, fees for fishing rights and pasturage, and duties for using public scales and temple precincts. Many cities had income from **state property,** such as mines, quarries, and state-owned land. Hegemonic states received **tribute** from allies and subject states. Compulsory contributions by wealthy citizens, called **liturgies,** helped with certain large expenditures such as equipping warships. In peacetime, cities were able to amass cash reserves, usually deposited in temples. But during famine or war, regular revenues were not always sufficient to meet expenditures. In such cases, direct property taxes *(eisphora)* were sometimes introduced, state property and political rights were sold, and public loans were raised, often on a compulsory basis. Some cities debased their coinage to raise cash. Public finance in **Sparta** remained simple: it had no regular taxes at all except a small contribution in kind to the kings. Administration and the army were provided by the Spartiates, financially supported by their helots.

The best examples of 5th-century architecture were erected on the **Acropolis** at Athens: the **Parthenon** (447-432), the **Propylaea** (437-432), and the **Erechtheum** (420-408). In the mid-4th century, the center of architecture shifted to Ionia, with masterpieces such as the tomb of Mausolus (**Mausoleum**) in Caria, and the **Temple of Artemis** at Ephesus. By the 5th century the Greek sculpture was representing the body very accurately, reaching its height in the works of **Myron** (c. 480-445) and **Polyclitus** (c. 430) of the Argive School and **Phidias** (c. 490-431). Phidias is best known for his colossal **chryselephantine** (gold and ivory) statue of Athena in the Parthenon and of Zeus at Olympia, but he also designed the architectural sculptures of the Parthenon (**Elgin Marbles).** From 500 to 415, Attic painters of red-figured vases developed line drawing in a series of exquisite styles. **Polygnotus** (c. 490-447) mastered the technique of large-scale painting, and **Agatharchus** of Samos (c. 430) was the first to use perspective on a large scale.

The level of literacy in the classical period is controversial. Probably only a minority of even the citizen body could read and write, but the proportion had clearly increased dramatically from archaic times. The number of teachers and schools grew, though there was no public education in the classical period. The culture remained essentially oral, but written works now became more common. **Aeschylus** (525-456) introduced a second actor into tragic drama, and by the time of **Sophocles** (c. 496-405) there could be up to four. **Euripides** (480-406) developed tragedy to its height. Plots were usually mythological, but sometimes reflected current events, for example, Aeschylus's *Persians.* **Aristophanes** (c. 448-385) was the acknowledged master of the **Old Comedy.** Comic plots were fantastic, often took off on contemporary events, and held important people up to ridicule. The little-known **Middle Comedy** was replaced by **New Comedy,** in which plays became less vulgar and plots more sentimental. Its most outstanding playwright was **Menander** (342-c. 280).

The first true historian in the Western world, **Herodotus** of Halicarnassus (484-425), wrote a lengthy account of the Persian War. **Thucydides** (471-c. 400) perfected the writing of history in his *Peloponnesian War.* **Xenophon** (431-354) continued Thucydides' history from 410 to 362, in addition to writing other prose works. Instruction in rhetoric was given by professional teachers, called **Sophists,** such as **Gorgias** (c. 485-380), who came from Sicily to Athens in 427; **Protagoras** (c. 485-415); **Prodicus** (c. 430); and **Hippias** (c. 400). The best-known Attic orators were **Lysias** (c. 459-380), **Demosthenes** (384-322), and the advocate of Pan-Hellenism, **Isocrates** (436-338).

The philosopher **Heraclitus** of Ephesus (c. 550-480) envisioned a universe in constant flux governed by universal law (**Logos). Parmenides** of Elea (c. 515-445) and the **Eleatic School** argued that what is real is motionless and made the distinction between belief and knowledge. **Empedocles** in Sicily (c. 500-430) developed the idea of the **four elements** (fire, air, water, and earth). **Leucippus** (c. 450) and his student **Democritus** of Abdera (c. 460-370) advanced the **atomic theory:** the universe was made up of indivisible units (**atoms**) whose motion created the sensible world. **Anaxagoras** of Miletus (c. 500-425), the first philosopher to live in Athens, argued that the world was made up of "elements" *(homoeomeries)* organized by the cosmic mind *(nous).* Anaxagoras strongly influenced **Socrates** (469-399), the key figure in Greek philosophy. Socrates emphasized ethics over physics and was known for his morality, personal courage, and relentless pursuit of the truth by means of dialectic inquiry (the **Socratic Method**). His greatest pupil, **Plato** (427-347) founded the **Academy,** the most important philosophical school in Greece. Plato reconciled reason and observation, arguing that while perception is flawed, everything is a reflection of a perfect form (**idea).** True knowledge is obtained by recollecting the ideas our souls knew before they were imprisoned in our bodies. Plato's antidemocratic political ideas are set out in the *Republic* and the *Laws.* Another of Socrates' students, Antisthenes (c. 445-360) inspired **Diogenes** (c. 400-325), the founder of Cynicism, a philosophy which rejected all unnatural conventions. **Aristotle** (384-322) studied under Plato, became the teacher of Alexander the Great, and upon returning to Athens in 335 B.C.E. founded the **Lyceum** or **Peripatetic School.** Aristotle ultimately rejected the idea of forms and felt that flaws in perception could be overcome by careful categorization of reality. In medicine **Hippocrates of Cos** (born c. 460) founded a school combining common sense, natural medicine, and personal hygiene. In the classical period women continued to lead very limited lives. Most women remained under the guardianship of a man, generally their father or husband, their entire life. Women could not inherit, witness in court, or own property. While divorce was theoretically easy to obtain, the woman's case had to be brought by a male third party. Most citizen women remained at home, but poor women worked in the fields and in the cities as washerwomen, woolworkers, vendors (mostly of food or flowers), nurses, and midwives. Women did not participate in the government in any direct way, though **Aspasia,** the mistress of Pericles, wielded considerable political power. Women did play an important role in religion as priests and seers. Many prostitutes were slaves, but the free ones, while they had to register with the state and pay taxes, had control over their own money.

b. THE RISE OF ATHENIAN DEMOCRACY AND THE PERSIAN WARS

510. Enlisting Spartan aid, the Alcmaeonidae returned to Athens. They overthrew Hippias, who fled to Persia and was made the tyrant of Sigeum. A struggle ensued between the aristocrats, led by **Isagoras,** and the common people, headed by the Alcmaeonid **Cleisthenes.** The latter won and a democratic reform of the constitution was instituted.

508. THE REFORMS OF CLEISTHENES. To end regional divisions, Cleisthenes created over 140 townships (demes), which replaced the phratries as the basis of citizenship. Ten tribes (phylai) were created, and Attica divided into three regions: the city of Athens, the coast, and the interior. Several demes comprised a "third" (trittys) and ten trittys formed a region. Each tribe was made up of one trittys from each region, so had members in all parts of Attica. A Council of 500, with 50 men chosen by lot from each of the tribes, replaced the Solonian Council of 400. The army was organized into ten tribal regiments. Some scholars believe that an early form of **ostracism,** a milder form of banishment, was introduced under Cleisthenes.

507. Isagoras invited the Spartans to invade Attica. King Cleomenes expelled Cleisthenes and restored the aristocracy. The Athenian people rose up, however, drove out the Spartans, and restored Cleisthenes.

506. A second Spartan expedition failed. The Athenians crushed the Boeotians and Euboeans and annexed part of the territory of Chalcis. When the Persian king Darius I demanded the restoration of Hippias as tyrant, the Athenians disregarded his ultimatum.

501. The general (strategos) of each of the ten tribal regiments was now elected annually.

499–494. The Ionian cities of Asia Minor revolted against the Persians (p. 40), led by **Aristagoras** of Miletus. In 498, Aristagoras traveled to mainland Greece, soliciting aid. Athens responded with 20 ships and Eretria with five. The rebels captured and burned Sardis, the satrapy's capital, but were defeated in the naval **Battle of Lade** in 494. Persian control of the sea enabled them to take and sack Miletus, which ended the revolt. One of the rebel leaders, **Miltiades** (c. 550–489), the tyrant of Chersonese, fled to Athens and, despite the opposition of the Alcmaeonidae, rose to political prominence.

c. 494. The Spartans under King Cleomenes defeated Argos in the **Battle of Sepeia** and forced it into the Peloponnesian League. Cleomenes tried to punish Aegina for supporting Persia but was blocked by the other king, Demaratus.

493. In Athens, **Themistocles,** leader of the anti-Persian party, was selected as archon. He began fortifying the Piraeus.

492. First Persian Expedition. Darius I sent **Mardonius** to punish Athens and Eretria for aiding the Ionian cities in their revolt. The Persian fleet was destroyed in a storm while rounding the Chalcidice. Mardonius did not advance further, but Thrace and Macedonia remained under Persian domination.

491. Cleomenes deposed Demaratus as Eurypontid king on a charge of illegitimacy, despite the opposition of the ephors, and replaced him with the more compliant **Leotychides II** (491–469).

c. 490. Traditionally, Cleomenes went mad, was imprisoned, and committed suicide. He may in fact have been arrested and executed by the ephors. Cleomenes' half-brother **Leonidas** (c. 490–480) succeeded him as Agiad king.

490. Themistocles was elected general (strategos) at Athens and began agitating for a larger navy.

490. Second Persian Expedition. King Darius sent another Persian force, this time across the Aegean Sea, under **Artaphernes** and **Datis.** Artaphernes besieged Eretria on Euboea, which fell through treachery. Datis, accompanied by the aged former tyrant **Hippias,** landed at **Marathon,** a center of Peisistratid strength.

490. BATTLE OF MARATHON. Miltiades, one of the ten regimental generals (strategoi), persuaded the Athenians to attack. The Athenians completely defeated the Persian army. The Persians embarked on their ships and sailed around Cape Sunium to assault Athens itself, but the Athenians hurried back, and the Persians, finding the city defended, retreated to Asia.

c. 490–480. RISE OF THE SICILIAN TYRANNY. In this decade, tyrants took power in many Sicilian cities. The most important were **Theron** of Acragas (488–471) and **Gelon of Gela,** later of **Syracuse** (485–478). Gelon made Syracuse into the leading city of Sicily by transporting the populations of conquered neighbors there. He differed from most tyrants in favoring the landed aristocracy (gamoroi) at the expense of the people.

489. Miltiades led an Athenian expedition to capture Paros but failed. He was brought to trial for "deceiving the people" and condemned to pay a heavy fine. He died soon after of wounds sustained at Paros.

489–483. Athens waged an indecisive war with Aegina, whom the Athenians blamed for helping the Persians.

c. THE RISE OF THE ATHENIAN EMPIRE

487. REFORM OF THE ATHENIAN CONSTITUTION. A series of reforms made the constitution more democratic. The nine archons were now chosen by lot from some 500 candidates elected by the demes. Subsequently ten preliminary candidates were elected from each tribe. Later these preliminary candidates were also chosen by lot. The military functions of the polemarch were taken over by the ten elected generals (strategoi), who were now assigned to command expeditionary armies. A general-in-chief (strategos autocrator) was sometimes promoted over the others. The anti-Persian party regained power with a noble faction led by **Aristides** and a common wing by **Themistocles.**

487. The first known **ostracism** was conducted, that of **Hipparchus,** a relative of the tyrant, who was suspected of being pro-Persian. At a special assembly, citizens cast potsherds or ostraca with an individual's name written on it as ballots. If 6,000 ballots were submitted against a particular man, he was obliged to leave Athens for a period of ten years, although he retained his property and remained a citizen.

486. Xerxes succeeded to the Persian throne and demanded earth and water (i.e., submission) from the Greek states, most of which refused. The Alcmaeonid leader Megacles was ostracized.

483. A rich new vein of silver was discovered at the state mines at Mt. Laurium. Themistocles convinced the assembly to use the money to build a fleet of 200 **triremes,** a type of warship. **Aristides** was ostracized for his opposition to this measure.

481. The Greek states, led by Sparta and Athens, set up the Hellenic League to resist the coming Persian invasion. Themistocles was elected strategos autocrator at Athens and became its most powerful political figure.

480. Third Persian Expedition. The Persian king Xerxes personally led an expedition which marched into Greece through Thrace and Macedonia. Herodotus says the Persian army had 5 million men (including camp followers): modern estimates range from 100,000–500,000. The Persian fleet included from 600–1200 ships. A Greek army of 7,000 hoplites occupied the pass at Thermopylae, and a fleet of 270 ships stationed itself at the nearby Gulf of Artemisium. Unable to take the pass by direct assault, the Persians took a side path and turned the Greek position. Most of the Greeks withdrew, but King **Leonidas** with 300 Spartans and 700 Thespians refused to retreat, and at the **BATTLE OF THERMOPYLAE** they were surrounded and annihilated. The Persian navy suffered heavy damage from storms, losing half their ships, but they still outnumbered the Greeks. The **Battle of Artemisium** was indecisive, but the Greeks withdrew after Thermopylae was taken. The Boeotians, Phocians, and Locrians went over to the Persians (**medized**). The Greek army retreated to the Peloponnese and built a wall across the Isthmus of Corinth. The fleet moved to the Saronic Gulf between Athens and Salamis. Unable to defend their city, the Athenians fled and the Persians occupied Attica and destroyed Athens. In **THE BATTLE OF SALAMIS,** the Persians attacked the Greek fleet in the narrow strait, losing their advantage of numbers, and were decisively defeated. Xerxes, probably fearful for his supply lines, returned to Asia Minor with a third of his army, leaving another third with Artabazus in Thrace, and the rest in Boeotia under Mardonius.

480. In Sicily, **Terillus,** the tyrant of Himera, appealed to Carthage for help against Theron of Acragas and Gelon of Syracuse. Hamilcar led a Carthaginian army onto the island, but it was decisively defeated by Theron and Gelon at the **Battle of Himera.**

479. The Persians under Mardonius again invaded Attica. The Greek forces, led by the Spartan king **Pausanias,** defeated the Persians at the

BATTLE OF PLATAEA. Mardonius was killed and his camp plundered. The Greeks took Thebes by siege, abolished the oligarchy, and instituted a democracy.

479. The Battle of Mycale. King **Leotychides II** of Sparta led a small Greek fleet to guard the Cyclades against Persia. The Samians and Chians convinced him to attack the Persians, who had drawn their ships up on the beach at Mycale near Samos. In the ensuing battle the Persian fleet was destroyed.

479–478. The Siege of Sestos. The Ionian cities in Asia Minor and several of the island cities (Samos, Lesbos, and Chios) revolted from the Persians. The allied Greek fleet laid siege to Sestos, a Persian stronghold in the Thracian Chersonese. The Spartans returned home in the fall, but the Athenians and Ionians succeeded in reducing Sestos during the winter.

478. Pausanias, leading the allied Greek fleet, reduced Cyprus and Byzantium. Suspected of treasonous negotiations with the Persians, the Spartan ephors recalled him. He was tried for treason, but acquitted, and sent back to Byzantium.

478–477. THE DELIAN LEAGUE. The Spartans sent a new commander, Dorcis, to head the allied fleet. The Ionians refused to recognize Dorcis and made an alliance with the Athenians for the expulsion of Persians from all Greek territory. Each ally was to contribute either a quota of ships or of money, and most of the smaller states chose the later. **Aristides** (called "the Just") assessed the tribute for the league, whose headquarters and treasury were on the island of Delos. A general assembly *(synhedrion)* met there, each ally having one vote, but Athens, the richest and most powerful member, soon dominated the Delian League.

478–466. Hieron I, the brother of Gelon, brought the tyranny in Syracuse, now the most powerful state in Sicily, to its height.

476–475. Cimon, the son of Miltiades, was elected *strategos*, led an expedition to Thrace, captured almost all the Persian forts along the coast, and expelled Pausanias from Byzantium. After a long siege, Cimon took **Eion** from the Persians and then defeated pirates on the island of Scyros. Athenian *cleruchs* were sent to both Eion and Scyros.

c. 475. Carystus, a city on Euboea, was forced to join the Delian League against its will.

474. Hieron of Syracuse, in alliance with Aristodemus, the tyrant of Cumae in southern Italy, defeated the Etruscans in the naval **Battle of Cumae** (474).

472. Thrasydaeus succeeded his father Theron as tyrant of Acragas. A cruel and hated ruler, Thrasydaeus was defeated in a war with Hieron of Syracuse and deposed. Acragas and Himera set up democracies.

471. Cimon secured the **OSTRACISM OF THEMISTOCLES,** who fled to Argos and conducted anti-Spartan activity in the Peloponnese, possibly inspiring the *synoecism* which united Elis.

c. 471–469. Tegea, Argos, and all of Arcadia except Mantinea joined in an anti-Spartan alliance. Argos succeeded in capturing Tiryns and Mycenae (c. 469), but the allies were defeated at the Battles of **Tegea** and **Diplaea,** and Spartan hegemony was restored.

c. 468. Under pressure from Sparta, Athens condemned Themistocles to death *in absentia* and sent officers to arrest him. Themistocles fled from Argos to Corcyra, Epirus, and then Macedonia. Around 464, he arrived in Persian territory, where King Artaxerxes made him governor of Magnesia. He died in 462.

467. When **Naxos** attempted to withdraw from the Delian League, Athens defeated the Naxians and forced them to raze the city's walls and to surrender their navy. After this, Athens frequently interfered in the internal affairs of the "allies," and the Delian League became, in fact if not in name, an **Athenian Empire.** Commercial disputes between citizens of two allied states or between an ally and Athens, as well as all capital criminal cases, were now tried in Athenian courts. If an ally rebelled, part of its lands were confiscated and an Athenian colony **(cleruchy)** was established, which served both a military purpose and a civil one to help relieve unemployment at Athens. If necessary, Athenian garrisons were established under military officers called *phrourarchoi*, though sometimes only civilian "overseers" *(episkopoi)* were sent. Athenian surveyors *(taktai)* reassessed tribute, and the Athenian assembly controlled the use of both the tribute and allied naval contingents. One-sixtieth of the League's tribute was dedicated to the Temple of Athena.

467–466. The Greek colonies of **Rhegium** and **Taras** in southern Italy were defeated by the native Iapyges. A democracy was established in Taras, and the Pythagoreans were expelled from all the Italian Greek cities.

466. Cimon defeated the Persians in a great naval victory at the **Battle of the Eurymedon River** on the south coast of Asia Minor.

466. In Sicily, **Thrasybulus** succeeded his brother Hieron as tyrant of Syracuse but was soon expelled and a democracy set up. The attempt of **Tyndaridas** to establish a tyranny led to the introduction of **petalism,** similar to Athenian ostracism.

465–463. Cimon crushed the revolt of Thasos, which had attempted to leave the Delian League. After his return to Athens, he was charged by **Ephialtes,** the head of the popular party, with taking a bribe from Alexander, the king of Macedon, but he was acquitted.

c. 465–461. The Third Messenian War. A serious earthquake set off a revolt of the Messenian helots. Defeated in battle by the Spartans, the Messenians retreated to Mt. Ithome. Unable to take the stronghold, the Spartans summoned the Hellenic League, including Athens. In 462, Cimon led an Athenian force to the Peloponnese, but the Spartans sent it home. This insult marked the end of the Spartan-Athenian alliance. The fall of Ithome in 461 ended the helots' revolt.

463–454. In the aftermath of a series of conflicts the mercenaries of the deposed Sicilian tyrants were left in possession of **Messana** (formerly Zancle). **Ducetius** united the Sicels and defeated the former mercenaries. He established the federal capital of a Sicel state at Menaenum (c. 454), which was later moved to Palice.

462. Megara, involved in a border war with Corinth, appealed to Sparta for help; rebuffed, the Megarians allied themselves with Athens. Athenian alliances with Thessaly and Argos soon followed.

461. The Athenians, blaming Cimon for the Spartan insult of rejecting their help, ostracized him. Led by Ephialtes, the assembly deprived the Areopagus council of all its powers except jurisdiction in homicide cases. The 6,000-member popular court *(heliaea)* was then divided into several panels, or juries, of 201 or more. Soon after instituting these reforms, Ephialtes was murdered, probably by his political opponents. **Pericles** (c. 500–429) replaced Ephialtes as head of the popular party.

c. 461–457. Using the money collected from the allies' tribute, the Athenians connected Piraeus with Athens by the **Long Walls,** four miles long.

d. THE FIRST PELOPONNESIAN WAR

460. The First Peloponnesian War broke out between the Athenians and Peloponnesians, caused in part by Athens' alliance with Megara and Argos. In the same year, the Athenians sent a fleet of some 200 ships to Egypt to aid its revolt against the Persians. The Athenians defeated a Persian fleet on the Nile and besieged a Persian army in the citadel of Memphis.

c. 459/8. The Athenians were defeated at **Halieis** by the Corinthians and Epidaurians, but their fleet won a victory at **Cecryphaleia.**

458. The Aeginetans joined the Peloponnesian alliance, but their combined fleet was defeated by the Athenians in the **Battle of Aegina.** The Athenians, under the command of Leosthenes, landed on the island of Aegina and besieged the city. The Corinthians invaded Attica, trying to force the Athenians to raise the siege, but were defeated by a reserve force of old men and boys under **Myronides.** A second force of Corinthians was surrounded and annihilated in the Megarid.

457. The Aeginetans surrendered, turned their fleet over to the Athenians, and joined the Delian League. **Sparta** then entered the war, sent an army across the Corinthian Gulf, and restored the Boeotian League under the hegemony of Thebes. The Athenians were defeated at the **Battle of Tanagra,** but the Spartans then returned home, and the Athenians then defeated the Boeotians at the **Battle of Oenophyta.** Athens then enrolled all the Boeotian cities except Thebes in the Delian League; Phocis and Opuntian Locris also joined.

457. Pericles made the *zeugitai* class eligible for the archonship. The *thetes*, though never legally eligible, were soon permitted to hold the office.

456. A Persian force under **Megabyzus** defeated the Athenians at the citadel of Memphis. The Athenians were in turn besieged on the island of Prosopitis in the Nile Valley.

455. The Athenian general **Tolmides** sailed around the Peloponnese, raiding the coast, burning the Spartan naval base at Gytheum, and recruiting Achaea into the Delian League.

454. An Athenian force led by **Pericles** landed in Sicyon and defeated the Sicyonians. Joined by Achaeans, Pericles unsuccessfully tried to take Oeniadea on the Corinthian Gulf, before returning to Athens. After an eighteen-month siege, the Athenians beseiged on Prosipitis in Egypt were defeated, and all but a few killed or captured. A relief expedition of 50 ships was also destroyed by the Persians. Due to this defeat, the treasury of the Delian League was moved to Athens.

453. In Sicily, the towns of **Segesta** and **Halicyae** started a war with **Selinus** and approached Athens for an alliance, which was granted.

451. After three years of inactivity, **Cimon** returned from exile and negotiated a five years' truce with Sparta. Argos, losing Athenian protection, was forced to make a thirty years' peace with Sparta.

451. At Athens, pay was instituted for the *dicasts* or jurors of the popular courts, which made it possible for the poorest citizens to serve. In the same year, Pericles passed a law restricting Athenian citizenship to those having two Athenian parents (repealed in 429, reenacted in 403).

c. 450. Perdiccas II (c. 450–413) became king of Macedon.

450–449. Cimon led a large Athenian force to Cyprus to fight the Persians. The Athenians defeated the Persians in the **Battle of Salamis** (the city in Cyprus, not the island off Attica). The Athenians beseiged the Persians at **Citium,** but Cimon died of disease (449). Lack of supplies forced the Athenians to return home.

450. Syracuse and Acragas defeated the Sicels under Ducetius at the **Battle of Noae.** Ducetius was banished to Corinth, and the Sicel federation fell apart.

449–448. SECOND SACRED WAR. Sparta took Delphi from Phocis and made it independent; Athens took it back and restored it to the Phocians.

448. According to some sources, a **Peace of Callias** (p. 40) was reached between Athens and Persia, in which the Persians gave up the coastline of Asia Minor, and the Athenians agreed not to invade Persian territory. Some scholars consider this the official end of the Persian Wars, although others doubt the existence of a formal treaty.

447. Boeotia revolted from the Delian League, and an inadequate Athenian force was crushed at the **Battle of Coronea.** Oligarchies were set up in all the Boeotian cities, and the Boeotian League was reestablished. The League was organized on a federal principle: the cities had proportional representation both in the federal assembly and among the magistrates *(Boeotarchs)* according to population. Troops were also levied in accordance with population size, and there were a federal treasury and coinage. In the same year, Phocis and Locris also quit the Delian League.

447. The Athenians began construction of the **Parthenon.**

c. 446. Athens received a free gift of grain from Egypt, and the citizenship rolls were revised: 5,000 citizens' names were removed from the lists.

446. Revolt of Euboea. Pericles crossed over to Euboea with an army, but a Peloponnesian invasion of the Megarid, which drove out the Athenian garrison there, forced him to return. The Peloponnesians reached Eleusis but came to terms with the Athenians and withdrew. Pericles then crossed back to Euboea, crushed the revolt, and established a cleruchy in Histaiaea. Negotiations with the Spartans continued.

446/5. Over the winter the Athenians and Spartans concluded a **Thirty Years' Peace.** Megara was returned to the Peloponnesian League, Troezen and Achaea became independent, Aegina was to be a tributary to Athens but autonomous, and disputes were to be settled by arbitration.

445. The failure of the anti-Spartan policy of Pericles led to an attempt to ostracize him, which failed. Instead, the opposition leader **Thucydides, son of Melesias** (not the historian), was ostracized. Pericles continued to hold undisputed control of Athens. He devoted much of Athens' wealth to fostering its culture, particularly in building and in the arts.

c. 445. Syracuse and Acragas fought over the division of territory from the former Sicel federation. Syracuse was victorious and became the recognized leader of Sicily.

443. Nervous over Syracusan power, Rhegium, Leontini, and perhaps Catana and Naxos made alliances with Athens. At the same time, Athens founded a colony at Thurii, upriver from the former Sybaris, using colonists from all over Greece.

441–439. Miletus, involved in a war with Samos, appealed to the Athenians, who replaced the Samian oligarchy with a democracy by force. Samos revolted (440) and threw out the democracy, but after a long siege, the Athenians took the city (439). Athens razed the city's walls and confiscated its fleet. Chios and Lesbos were now the only allies in the Delian League who contributed ships instead of money.

440–439. Ducetius, who had returned to Sicily in 446, restored the Sicel federation, but died soon after. Syracuse forcibly broke up the federation and destroyed its capital **Palice.**

437. A policy of Athenian expansion to the north was begun with the foundation of **Amphipolis** in Thrace, which controlled the mines at Mt. Pangaeus.

c. 437. Pericles took an expedition into the Euxine and established good relations with the rulers of Panticapaeum, who exported grain to Athens. Athenian settlers were sent to various Pontic cities. In the Corinthian Gulf, the Athenian *strategos* Phormio made an alliance with some of the Acarnanians.

e. THE SECOND (GREAT) PELOPONNESIAN WAR

435. Corcyra, in northwestern Greece, objected to Corinth's interference with their joint colony, **Epidamnus.** Corcyra defeated the much more powerful Corinth but, fearing reprisal, called on Athens for help, and the Corinthians backed down. The Athenians then sought to break Corinthian influence over **Potidaea,** a colony of Corinth but a subject of Athens.

432. Potidaea revolted against Athens, with the tacit support of the Peloponnesian League. Athens then retaliated with the **Megarian decree,** barring the Megarians from Athenian harbors and markets. Outraged and fearful of further Athenian action, Megara, Corinth, and Aegina pressured a reluctant Sparta to take action. Over **King Archidamus's** opposition, the ephor Sthenelaïdas convinced the Spartan assembly to declare the Thirty Years' Peace broken.

1. THE ARCHIDAMIAN WAR

432–431. The winter was taken up by fruitless negotiation between the Spartans and Athenians.

431. Fighting began when the Thebans unsuccessfully attacked **Plataea.** The strategy of the Peloponnesians was to march through Attica annually, burning the fields, in order to lure the Athenians into a land battle, as well as to encourage the revolt of the allies from the Delian League. The Athenian strategy in the war, developed by Pericles, was to remain in the city and allow the countryside to be ravaged by the Peloponnesian army. Siege warfare was not sufficiently developed for the Spartans to break down Athens' walls or surmount them with a siege ramp. As long as the Athenians controlled the sea, the Long Walls connecting the city to the port at Piraeus prevented the city from being starved out. Athens hoped to wear down the Peloponnesians by coastal raids and interference with their trade.

430. A **plague** (perhaps smallpox) broke out in Athens. It spread rapidly due to the crowded conditions in the city and about 25 percent of Athens' population died. The plague spread to the army besieging Potidaea, but that city fell toward the end of the year.

429. Pericles died of the plague. Despite the mounting death toll, Athens continued to win victories: **Phormio** defeated two Peloponnesian fleets off Naupactus.

427. The Athenians crushed a revolt in **Lesbos,** and the Spartans had their first success: the **capture of Plataea.**

427–424. A general war broke out in Sicily. Naxos, Catana, Leontini, Rhegium, Camarina, and most of the Sicels opposed Syracuse, Gela, Messana, Himera, Lipara, and Locri. **Gorgias of Leontini** went to Athens and appealed for aid, which was granted. After indecisive fighting, the aristocrat **Hermocrates of Syracuse** persuaded the warring cities to make peace at the **Conference of Gela.**

425. A fleet under **Demosthenes** captured Pylos, on the west coast of the Peloponnese. When reinforcements arrived under **Cleon,** the Athenians defeated the Spartans. Athens captured 120 Spartiates, who were held as hostages to prevent another invasion of Attica. The Spartans sued for peace. Over the objections of **Nicias,** leading the antiwar party, **Cleon** convinced the assembly to reject the Spartan peace overtures.

424. Nicias led an expedition which captured Cythera, an island off the coast of Laconia. The Athenians then sent an army to aid a democratic revolution in Megara, but they were outmaneuvered by the Spartan general **Brasidas.** Megara remained a Peloponnesian ally. Brasidas led a small force overland to Thrace and encouraged the revolt of a number of Athenian allies. The Athenians attempted to invade Boeotia but were defeated at the **Battle of Delium.** Brasidas took the important Athenian colony of **Amphipolis** in Thrace.

423. The Athenians and Spartans made a year's truce, but Brasidas continued operations in Thrace. The Athenians broke off peace negotiations.

422. Cleon led a force to Thrace, and both he and Brasidas were killed at the **Battle of Amphipolis.**

421. With the main prowar figures on both sides dead, the Spartans and Athenians negotiated the **Peace of Nicias.** It was to last 50 years, but the terms of the peace were never carried out.

2. THE ARGIVE WAR

420. The Boeotians refused to sign the Peace of Nicias and left the Peloponnesian League, as did Elis, Mantinea, Corinth, and Argos. These last four made an alliance (called the **Quadruple Alliance**), which Corinth soon left and Athens joined, and went to war with Sparta.

418. The Spartans, led by **King Agis II** (427–399), invaded Argos, decisively defeating the Quadruple Alliance at the **First Battle of Mantinea** and restoring Spartan hegemony.

416. The island of Melos refused to join the Delian League and was besieged by Athens. When the city was taken the Athenians massacred all the men and enslaved the women and children.

416. Selinus, in Sicily, called on Athens for assistance in its war against Segesta. A new Athenian leader, **Alcibiades,** proposed an expedition to Sicily, which the assembly approved over Nicias's objections.

415. THE SICILIAN EXPEDITION was organized under the joint command of Alcibiades, Nicias, and Lamachus. Soon after the Athenians' arrival in Sicily, Alcibiades was ordered to return to Athens and face charges of having mutilated the **Herms** (sacred pillars) and of profaning the **Eleusinian mysteries.** His guilt or innocence is unknown, but Alcibiades fled, eventually going over to the Spartans.

414. The Athenians began their attack on Syracuse, which was defended by Hermocrates. A small Spartan force under Gylippus arrived and prevented an Athenian circumvallation by taking the **heights of Epipolae.**

414. The Spartans invaded Argos, and an Athenian fleet supporting the Argives raided the coast of Laconia.

413. Athenian reinforcements arrived in Sicily under **Demosthenes.** Help for Syracuse came from Sparta, Corinth, and Boeotia. An Athenian assault on the heights of Epipolae failed, and their position became untenable. Nicias delayed too long in retreating, and the entire force, some 50,000 men including both generals, was killed or captured at the **Battle of Assinarus.**

c. 413. Archelaus (c. 413–399) succeeded his father Perdiccas as king of Macedon. He built up Macedonia's military strength, particularly in infantry. Archelaus moved the court to Pella and encouraged Hellenistic culture among the aristocracy, inviting many Greek artists, including Euripides, to Macedon.

3. THE DECELEAN (OR IONIAN) WAR

413. The Sicilian defeat led to the overthrow of the popular party in Athens. A college of ten "deliberators" *(probouloi)* was instituted which replaced many of the former functions of the Areopagus Council. A 5 percent tariff in all the harbors of the Delian League replaced the tribute paid by the allies. Following the advice of Alcibiades, the Spartans seized the fortress of **Decelea** in Attica and kept a garrison there year-round, bringing Athenian agriculture to a virtual standstill.

412. Using the last 1,000 talents of their war reserve, the Athenians rebuilt the fleet they had lost in Sicily, but it lacked training. Alcibiades negotiated the **Treaty of Miletus** between the Spartans and Persians. The Spartans recognized the king's right to subjugate the Ionian

cities in return for money with which to build a Peloponnesian fleet. This fleet was sent to stir up revolts along the Ionian coast and threaten Athens' grain shipments from Egypt and the Black Sea.

411. Alcibiades approached the Athenians, claiming he could obtain Persian support for them if the democracy was overthrown. Political clubs *(hetairiai)* took control of the government and instituted **the oligarchy of the Four Hundred.** The Athenian fleet at Samos refused to recognize the new government and elected its own generals: principally **Thrasybulus** and, remarkably, Alcibiades. When the Peloponnesians attacked Euboea, the oligarchy sent a small fleet which was defeated. When the oligarchs prepared to surrender to Sparta, they were overthrown and the democracy restored.

410. Alcibiades decisively defeated the Spartan fleet at the **Battle of Cyzicus.** The Spartans again offered peace and were again rejected. With more Persian money, the Peloponnesian fleet was rebuilt and put under the command of **Lysander.**

409. An Athenian expedition under Thrasyllus failed to take Ephesus. Sparta recovered Pylos.

408. Both Spartans and Athenians courted the Persians, who decided to back the Spartans decisively. The Athenians recovered Byzantium.

407. The Athenians lost the sea battles of **Notium** (after which Alcibiades left Athens) and **Mytilene.**

406. The Athenians managed to raise another fleet and won the **Battle of Arginusae,** but they put several of their victorious generals to death for not rescuing drowning sailors after the battle.

405. Lysander caught the Athenian fleet unawares and annihilated it in the **Battle of Aegospotamai.** He then sailed across the Aegean, replacing pro-Athenian democracies on the allied islands with oligarchies of Ten (decarchies) under a Spartan overseer *(harmost)*. The Spartans then besieged Athens itself.

405. Dionysius I secured his election as one of the ten generals at Syracuse and then seized power as tyrant. He confiscated land from the oligarchs, distributed it to the poor, and enfranchised the serfs.

404. The Surrender of Athens. After holding out over the winter, Athens surrendered in 404. The Long Walls were dismantled to the sound of Spartan flutes.

f. THE SPARTAN HEGEMONY

404. The Tyranny of the Thirty at Athens. The Athenian oligarchic party, supported by Lysander and the Spartans and led by Theramenes, set up a **Commission of Thirty** which was to make a few immediate reforms and then devise a new constitution. Instead, the commission, with Critias at their head, seized power and ruled as the **Thirty Tyrants.** They executed their colleague Theramenes when he advocated a more moderate course. Finally, 3,000 of the richest citizens were nominally enfranchised but never given any real power. Many citizens were exiled or fled to Argos and Thebes. These cities now feared the excessive power of Sparta. In the autumn Thrasybulus led back some exiles, who occupied Phyle and then the Piraeus.

403. In the beginning of the year, the Athenians deposed the Thirty, who fled to Eleusis, and elected a **Government of Ten.** These, instead of bringing in the democrats from the Piraeus, asked for help from Sparta, which sent Lysander. The anti-Lysander party in Sparta replaced him with King Pausanias, who brought about a settlement. The democracy was restored in Athens, and a general amnesty decreed, with only a few exceptions. The Spartan decarchies in the former Athenian allies were soon abolished.

403–400. Dionysius I of Syracuse conquered Catana (403), Naxos, and Leontini (400) and extended his control over the Sicels.

400. The Persian satrap **Tissaphernes** besieged Cyme, and the Spartans sent Thibron to hire a mercenary army and liberate the Ionians from Persia.

399–397. **Dercyllidas** took over the command of Spartan forces in Asia Minor. He played one satrap, Tissaphernes, against another, Pharnabazus, and conquered nine cities in eight days in the Aeolus. He then, against the orders of the ephors, made a truce with the Persians. The truce held, but Artaxerxes built up his fleet, putting the renegade Athenian Conon in command.

399. THE DEATH OF SOCRATES. Socrates was convicted in the assembly of introducing strange gods and corrupting the youth. He was sentenced to death, but although given an opportunity, refused to flee into exile. Socrates was given poisonous **hemlock** to drink and died.

398–392. Dionysius I of Syracuse fought a war with Carthage but failed to drive the Carthaginians out of Sicily.

396/5. King Agesilaus II (399–360) succeeded Dercyllidas as commander in Asia Minor. He campaigned in Phrygia, beating Tissaphernes' army, but was unable to defeat the Persian fleet. Persia sent **Timocrates of Rhodes** to bribe the leaders of Athens, Thebes, Corinth, and Argos to attack Sparta.

395. Athens made defensive alliances with Boeotia, Corinth, Argos, Megara, and Euboea. The **Corinthian War** (395–387) against Sparta broke out.

394. Agesilaus returned to Greece from Asia Minor with most of his force. The Spartans beat the Greek allies at the **Battles of the Nemea and Coronea**, but the Spartan fleet was annihilated by the Persians, under Conon, at the **Battle of Cnidus.** Persia granted autonomy to the Greek cities of Asia Minor and withdrew its garrisons. The Ionians then revolted from Sparta and established democracies.

393. Conon returned to Athens and began rebuilding the Long Walls. Athens recovered Lemnos, Imbros, Scyros, and Delos, and made alliances with Chios, Mitylene, Rhodes, Cos, and Cnidus.

392. The Persians deposed Conon, who died soon after. A peace conference was held over the winter at Sparta, but the Athenians rejected its terms.

390. The Spartan fleet captured Samos, but an Athenian army under **Iphicrates** defeated a Spartan army at the **Battle of Lechaeum.** Evagoras revolted from the Persians in Cyprus.

390–379. Dionysius I of Syracuse conquered southern Italy (Magna Graecia), crushing the Italiote (Greek) League at the **Battle of the Elleporus** (388) and destroying Rhegium (386).

389/8. The Athenian navy under Thrasybulus recovered Thasos, Samothrace, Tenos, the Chersonese, Byzantium, Chalcedon, and other cities. Garrisons were placed in the more important towns and a 5 percent harbor toll levied.

388. Lacking financial support from Athens, the Athenian fleet plundered Aspendus. The inhabitants broke into the Athenian camp and murdered Thrasybulus.

387. THE KING'S PEACE. The Spartan **Antalcidas** negotiated a general Greek settlement with Persia. All the Greek cities were to be autonomous except those in Asia, which were to belong to Persia.

386. The Spartan navy forced Athens to accept the King's Peace by blockading the Hellespont; Thebes was frightened into accepting. The Boeotian and the Athenian Leagues were temporarily dissolved.

384. After a long siege, Sparta forced Mantinea to dismantle its walls and broke the city up into five villages.

383–c. 381. Dionysius I fought another war with Carthage but suffered a defeat at the **Battle of Cronium.**

382. After an appeal from King Amyntas of Macedonia, Sparta went to war with the Chalcidian League, which was led by the city of **Olynthus.** A Spartan force of 10,000 marched north and while in Thebes seized the citadel (**Cadmea**) and turned it over to the oligarchic party. The democratic party fled to Athens. When the Spartans reached the Chalcidice, they were defeated by the League's army.

381–379. A second Spartan expedition, under King Agesilaus, marched to Olynthus. After a long siege, during which Agesilaus died, the city was captured and the Chalcidian League dissolved (379).

379–378. Theban democratic exiles led by Pelopidas returned from Athens, recovered the **Cadmea** by a stratagem, and established a democracy at Thebes. Two Athenian generals who aided the Thebans were executed by Athens for operating without authority. The Spartans did not intervene but left **Sphodrias** with a garrison at Thespiae. Sphodrias, also operating on his own, raided Attica, but was not punished. In response, Athens allied itself with Thebes against Sparta.

378. King Agesilaus was assigned the campaign against Thebes and Athens and reorganized the Peloponnesian League to support it. He formed ten districts, each of which was responsible for providing either men or money.

377. Athens, Thebes, and other states formed a league against Sparta, which became the basis of a **Second Athenian League** (the first being the Delian League). An allied fleet was rapidly built up. All decisions were to be made jointly by the Athenian assembly (**ecclesia**) and a

council (**synhedrion**) of the allies, excluding Athens; funds were to be derived from contributions levied by the council and handled by Athens. Athens gave up all claims to its former cleruchies and promised not to send any more.

377. Hecatomnus, the virtually independent satrap of Caria (395–377), died and was succeeded by **Mausolus** (377–353) who embarked on an expansionist policy.

376. Chabrias and the allies crushed the Spartan fleet off **Naxos,** giving Athens control of the sea. Thebes restored the Boeotian League on a democratic basis.

g. THE THEBAN HEGEMONY

371. A **general peace settlement** was reached between the allies and Sparta in the summer, but the Theban leader **Epaminondas** withdrew when he was not permitted to sign on behalf of all Boeotia. Sparta immediately sent King Cleombrotus to chastise Thebes, but the Spartan army was crushed by Epaminondas at the **Battle of Leuctra.** This defeat shattered Spartan military prestige and ended its hegemony over Greece. Thebes withdrew from the Athenian League, along with the cities in Acarnania, Euboea, and the Chalcidice.

370. An **Arcadian League** was formed under Theban protection as a counterweight to Sparta, and Mantinea was restored as a city. The government of the Arcadian League consisted of a general assembly (**the Ten Thousand**), made up of all freeborn citizens, with sovereignty in matters of war and peace. A council of *damiurgoi* gave proportional representation to the member cities, and a college of generals *(strategoi)* served as a civil and military executive. There was a standing mercenary army *(eparitoi)*. The Theban army, under Epaminondas, liberated Messenia from Sparta, and the city of **Messene** was built.

369. Athens and Sparta made an alliance on equal terms. The Arcadians founded **Megalopolis** as a federal capital. In the following years, Thebes secured the union of all Thessaly except Pherae under a single ruler *(archon).*

367/6. Dionysius I died in the course of another war with Carthage. He was succeeded by his weak son **Dionysius II,** under the regency of his uncle **Dion** who immediately made peace.

366/5. Dion brought **Plato** to Syracuse in order to educate Dionysius as a "philosopher king." The attempt failed, and both Dion and Plato were driven out of Syracuse.

365. The pro-Spartan party of **Callistratus** in Athens was replaced in power by the party of Timotheus. Peace was made with Thebes on the basis of the *status quo*. Breaking its promise, Athens sent a cleruchy to garrison its ally Samos.

364. The Thebans defeated Alexander, the tyrant of Pherae, in the **Battle of Cynoscephalae** but their commander, Pelopidas, was killed in action.

363. Epaminondas led a Theban army into Thessaly and again defeated Alexander of Pherae. Athens subjected its allies Ceos and Naxos to Athenian jurisdiction.

362. The Arcadian League broke up, and oligarchs took control of many of its cities.

362. In the **Second Battle of Mantinea** the Thebans beat the Spartans, but Epaminondas was killed in the battle. A general peace was made but not accepted by Sparta, which refused to recognize the independence of Messenia.

361. Athens sent a cleruchy to occupy Potidaea.

359. Philip II (359–336) **became king of Macedonia.**

358. The Athenians, involved in fighting the Odrysae in Thrace, made peace with the Macedonians. Macedonia gave up its claim to Amphipolis, and Athens promised to turn over Pydna. Philip thoroughly reorganized the Macedonian army, placing more importance on the **phalanx** of infantry.

357. Dion took over Syracuse by force and established himself as tyrant.

357. Angered by Athens' increasingly domineering attitude toward its league, Chios, Rhodes, and Cos overthrew their democratic governments and together with Byzantium revolted against Athens, beginning the **Social War** ("War of the Allies," 357–353). In midsummer the Athenian fleet was decisively defeated and Chabrias, its commander, killed. The Athenians, under **Chares,** withdrew to the Hellespont and began operations against Byzantium.

357. Philip of Macedon captured Amphipolis but, instead of turning it over to Athens, granted it independence. Over the winter, he also conquered and kept Pydna. Making a treaty with Olynthus against Athens, Philip also took the city of Crenides from the Odrysae and renamed it **Philippi.**

356. The revolting allies ravaged Lemnos and Imbros, which had remained loyal to Athens, and then laid siege to Samos, which was defended by cleruchs. The Athenian fleet under Chares was decisively defeated in the **Battle of Embata.** Persia ordered Athens to leave Asia Minor, threatening war.

356. The **Amphictyonic Council,** at the instigation of Thebes, fined the Phocians for tilling land sacred to Apollo. Phocis refused to pay the fine despite a threat by the Amphictyons to declare war.

355. Caving in to Persian pressure, Athens withdrew from Asia Minor and recognized the independence of its allies there. The war party of Chares and Aristophon was replaced at Athens by a peace party under **Eubulus.** All financial surpluses were put in the **theoric fund** to be used for the public's entertainment.

355. Led by **Philomelus,** the Phocians seized Delphi, initiating the **Third Sacred War** (355–346) and made alliances with Athens and Sparta. When the Amphictyons declared war, Phocis used the sacred money of Delphi to recruit a large mercenary army.

354. The Phocian mercenary army was defeated by the Boeotians at the **Battle of Neon,** and Philomelus was killed. **Onomarchus** succeeded him as the leader of Phocis.

354–347. Dion of Syracuse was assassinated, and two other sons of Dionysius I successively seized power but were unable to stabilize a deteriorating political situation in Sicily (p. 75).

353. The Phocians, led by Onomarchus, seized Thermopylae and Orchomenos and twice defeated Philip of Macedon. Mausolus of Caria annexed Rhodes and Cos.

352. Philip defeated and killed Onomarchus and united Thessaly under his rule. He marched south toward Greece but was stopped at Thermopylae by the Phocians in alliance with the Athenians, Achaeans, and Spartans.

351. Olynthus, suspicious of Philip, appealed to Athens for aid. **Demosthenes** appeared as the leader of the anti-Macedonian party, urging action in his three *Olynthiac Orations.*

349. Athens made an alliance with Olynthus, but an attempt by Demosthenes to divert money from the theoric fund for military purposes failed.

348. Philip induced Euboea to revolt from the Athenian League. Athens, against Demosthenes' advice, divided its effort by sending forces both to Euboea and Olynthus. The Athenian commander **Phocian** was successful in Euboea, but his successor Molossus lost the country. Philip took Olynthus, razed it, and enslaved its citizens. Athens could not secure help from the other Greeks, and even Demosthenes favored peace.

347–345. Dionysius II returned to Syracuse and briefly ruled as tyrant but was replaced in 345, first by **Hicetas,** tyrant of Leontini, and then by **Timoleon,** a Corinthian, who took the city with a small mercenary force. Timoleon did not make himself tyrant but instituted a moderate oligarchy, with the priest *(amphipolos)* of Zeus as chief magistrate and with 600 rich citizens as a council. Timoleon began a campaign to unseat other tyrants in Sicily and southern Italy.

347. Frustrated by continued Phocian resistance, the Thebans and Thessalians called on Philip to intervene on behalf of the Amphictyonic League.

346. Peace of Philocrates. Philocrates, Aeschines, Demosthenes, and seven other Athenian ambassadors were sent to negotiate a peace with Philip. The terms left each side in possession of cities held when the peace was sworn. The Athenian assembly accepted the terms and sent the embassy back to swear the oaths. The ambassadors, however, were delayed on the way, and Philip profited by conquering more of Thrace.

346. Athens first supported Phocis but then signed the **Peace of Philocrates,** which ended the Third Sacred War. Philip then conquered Phocis and had its seats on the Amphictyonic Council transferred to him.

344. Demosthenes traveled through the Peloponnese trying to develop an anti-Philip alliance. At Athens, he delivered his **Second Philippic.**

341–339. The Carthaginians tried to conquer Sicily but were defeated by Timoleon at the **Battle of the Crimissus** (341). The Sicilian tyrants then joined the Carthaginians, but Timoleon made a separate peace with Carthage, establishing a boundary at the Halycus River (339). Turning against the tyrants, Timoleon expelled them and formed a military league against Carthage. Timoleon then retired from public life and lived out his days as a private citizen.

341–339. Athens, at the urging of Demosthenes, made anti-Philip alliances with Euboea and the Peloponnese. The Athenians also sent help to Byzantium, which was fighting Philip.

339. Demosthenes reformed the financial system which supported the navy by replacing the individual liturgy *(trierarchia)* with more equitable and efficient groups of contributors *(symmoriae)*. He also succeeded in devoting surplus state income to military purposes instead of the theoric fund.

339. Philip attempted to convince the Amphictyonic Council to fine Athens for improper dedication of spoils from Persia and Thebes. **Aeschines,** in a brilliant speech, diverted the council's attention by bringing charges against the Locrians of Amphissa.

339–338. The **Fourth Sacred War** was fought against the Locrians of Amphissa. The Amphictyonic Council gave command of the League's forces to Philip, and in response the Athenians made an anti-Macedonian alliance with Thebes. Athens sent a force of 10,000 mercenaries to guard Amphissa.

338. THE BATTLE OF CHAERONEA. Philip annihilated Athens' mercenary force and captured Amphissa. In August, at the **Battle of Chaeronea,** Philip crushed the allied armies of Thebes and Athens. He garrisoned Thebes but let Athens go free. Philip called the **Congress of Corinth,** during which all the Greek states, except Sparta, entered a **Hellenic League** against Persia, under Macedonian hegemony. The league council had proportional representation and was presided over by a chairman, replaced by the Macedonian king in wartime. The autonomy of the members was guaranteed, existing constitutions were not to be altered, and no private property was to be confiscated. There was no tribute required and no more than four garrisons—Thebes, Corinth, Chalcis, and Ambracia. The king had supreme military command, and the Amphictyonic Council served as a court of appeals. Philip announced plans for a campaign against the Persian Empire.

c. 342–338. Under pressure from the Lucanians, invading from central Italy, **Tarentum** called on Sparta for assistance. Sparta sent **King Archidamus III** of Sparta (360–338) with an army and a fleet but he was defeated and killed at the **Battle of Manduria** (338).

337. The **Second Congress of Corinth** declared war on Persia.

336. Philip sent an army of 10,000 under his general Parmenio to Asia Minor. In the spring, Persia underwent two coups d'état—ultimately **Darius III** took the throne. Philip was assassinated during the summer by a disgruntled bodyguard, allegedly at the instigation of Olympias, one of his wives.

h. THE MACEDONIAN EMPIRE

336. ALEXANDER THE GREAT. Alexander III (336–323) succeeded to the Macedonian throne and immediately invaded Illyria and Thrace.

335. Inspired by a rumor that Alexander had died while on campaign, Thebes, Athens, Arcadia, Elis, and Aetolia revolted against Macedonian hegemony. Alexander swiftly moved south, took Thebes, destroyed it, and enslaved its inhabitants. The other revolting states submitted.

334. In the spring, Alexander left Antipater as governor in Greece and crossed the Hellespont with an army of 32,000 infantry and 5,000 cavalry. The army was supported by a navy of 160 ships, mostly made up of Greek allies. Memnon of Rhodes, the commander of Greek forces in the Persian service, advised a tactical retreat, but the satraps insisted on fighting. The Persians were completely defeated by Alexander at the **Battle of Granicus.**

334–330. Alexander I of Epirus (342–330) was called in to assist the Italiote League which was fighting the Lucanians in southern Italy. He won a series of victories and concluded a treaty with Rome. But the Italiote League broke up, and when Alexander was killed in battle (330) the Epirotes left Italy.

334–333. Most of the Greek cities of Ionia revolted against the Persians. Memnon died and Darius withdrew the Greek mercenaries into Syria, where he gathered a large army.

333. Alexander subdued Caria and Cilicia, then advanced into Syria. He again defeated the Persian army, under the personal command of Darius III, at the **Battle of Issus.** After this defeat, Darius offered to give up all of Asia west of the Euphrates and to pay 10,000 talents, but Alexander demanded unconditional surrender. After Issus, all of Phoenicia except Tyre submitted to Alexander.

332. After a difficult siege of seven months, Tyre was captured. The provinces of Galilee, Samaria, and Judah surrendered to Alexander. When he approached Egypt, its satrap turned the richest province of the Persian Empire over to Alexander without a fight.

332–331. During a year-long stay, Alexander founded **Alexandria** on the coast of Egypt and visited the **oracle of Ammon** at the oasis of Siwa in the Western Desert, where he was proclaimed the son of a god.

331. Leaving Egypt during the spring, Alexander marched into Mesopotamia. In October he met and defeated another Persian army under Darius in the **Battle of Gaugamela.** Babylonia and Susa soon surrendered. One of the Persian capitals, Persepolis, was looted and burned, ostensibly in revenge for the destruction of Athens in 480.

331. Sparta under King Agis III (338–331), aided by Persian money and in alliance with Elis, Achaea, and part of Arcadia, defeated a Macedonian force and besieged Megalopolis. Antipater marched into the Peloponnese with a greatly superior force and crushed the Spartans and their allies.

330. In the spring, Alexander pursued Darius through Media. Finally, the Persian king was murdered by the satrap **Bessus.** Alexander subdued the Caspian region and then marched southward. Once Parmenio's son Philotas had been executed for complicity in a plot, Alexander sent messengers who murdered Parmenio in Media: Alexander feared a revolt and Parmenio was too powerful to be discharged.

330. Athens had recouped its strength under the financial administration of **Lycurgus.** Compulsory military training for all youth (epheboi) was established. Demosthenes was acquitted in a trial brought by Aeschines on the legality of the award to Demosthenes of a civic crown.

329–328. Alexander marched into Bactria and Sogdiana, overcoming the Iranians under Spitamenes, but with difficulty.

328. Alexander adopted Persian dress and court etiquette, including proskynesis, or prostration before the king. In a drunken fury, he murdered his friend Cleitus who had reproached him for this. Alexander had 30,000 Persians trained to fight in the Macedonian fashion.

327. Alexander married the Bactrian princess **Roxane.** Invited into India by **"Taxiles"** (King Ambhi of Taxila) against **Porus** (King Parvataka), **Alexander crossed the Indus.**

326. Alexander defeated Porus at the **Battle of the Hydaspes** (Jhelum) and advanced as far as the **Hyphasis** (Beas) River. At this point the Macedonian army refused to march any farther east.

325. Alexander marched to the Indian Ocean via the Hydaspes and Indus. In a campaign against the **Mallians,** Alexander leapt alone from the wall of their city into the midst of the enemy. He was wounded by an arrow but rescued by his troops. In July, **Nearchus** set out with the fleet to return via the coast of the Indian Ocean and Persian Gulf. Alexander returned through the **Gedrosian Desert,** where the army suffered serious losses due to lack of supplies.

325. A Macedonian noble, **Harpalus,** guilty of embezzling massive funds while Alexander fought in India, fled to Athens. He bribed many Athenian politicians, including Demosthenes, in an attempt to secure sanctuary.

324. Alexander's army and navy met in Caramania, and after resting, continued on to Susa. Alexander had left many of the native satraps in office, but most of these were now replaced by Macedonians. His friend Hephaestion was made *hipparch,* or second-in-command. Alexander married **Barsine,** the eldest daughter of Darius, and 80 of his officers took wives from the Persian and Median aristocracy. Alexander made official the unions of soldiers with concubines who had been taken along the route and paid all the debts of his soldiers. He ordered all exiles recalled by the Greek cities and ordered them to recognize him as the **son of Zeus Ammon.** He sent home 10,000 Macedonians considered no longer able to fight and replaced them with Persians and other Iranians. Hephaestion died at Ecbatana and was extravagantly mourned but not replaced as hipparch.

324. Demosthenes was exiled from Athens for taking bribes from Harpalus.

323. Alexander gathered a large army and navy at Babylon, apparently preparing for a campaign against Arabia.

June 13, 323. DEATH OF ALEXANDER THE GREAT. Alexander died of a fever at Babylon without clearly designating a successor. His death is generally considered the dividing point between the Classical and Hellenistic periods.

5. THE HELLENISTIC WORLD, TO 30 B.C.E.

a. ECONOMY, SOCIETY, AND CULTURE

The Hellenistic Age began with a century of large-scale Greco-Macedonian emigration into the territories conquered by Alexander. The consequent spread of Hellenic civilization brought about changes both in the expanded Greek world and among the native populations of Asia and Egypt. The economy of the Hellenistic world, however, continued to be overwhelmingly agricultural. **Colonial settlement was urban in character in Seleucid Asia, but predominantly rural** in Ptolemaic Egypt. Traditional patterns of land tenure predominated in Asia, where large tracts of royal land were worked by peasants tied to it. Much of this land was assigned to prominent individuals, to temple estates, or to cities. The economy of the numerous Seleucid cities, however, followed the **Greek model, with land owned by citizens who worked it with the help of slave labor.** In Egypt, urban settlements were rare. Outside of the three cities of Naucratis, Ptolemais, and Alexandria, all land was theoretically owned by the king, divided into districts (nomes), and administered by both traditional civic officials—nomarch, royal scribe, komarch—and by newly created financial officers—the *dioiketes* in the capital, and the *oikonomos* and his underlings in the nome. In addition, military officials—*strategos, hipparchos,* and *hegemon*—oversaw the nomes. **Royal land** was also assigned to individuals, to temple estates, and especially to smallholder soldiers (*klerouchoi,* later called *katoikoi*) who initially held the land in return for military service, but whose tenure eventually became permanent and hereditary. All land seems to have been worked by native peasants attached to it, chattel slavery being relatively rare in Ptolemaic Egypt. **Ptolemaic policy was to increase agricultural production,** and innovations in farming were largely the result of royal patronage. We are particularly well informed by the mid-third-century archive of Zenon about large-scale reclamation in the Fayyûm, where new crops and techniques were introduced. **But most innovations, in both Egypt and Asia, were directed toward luxury items and, with the exception of new strains of wheat, had little effect on traditional agriculture.** In Seleucid Asia the major challenge for agriculture was to feed the numerous new cities, in Egypt to feed the metropolis of Alexandria and to supply the grain used in Ptolemaic diplomacy. In the Greek homeland, established forms of agriculture continued. **In most areas, free citizens farmed with the help of a slave or two,** while other traditional forms of dependent labor also persisted—helots in Sparta, serfs in Crete. Changes did occur in the pattern of land tenure, with land accumulated by the wealthy at the expense of marginal farmers.

Although **most trade in the Hellenistic Age was local**—between villages and nearby urban centers—Alexander's opening of Achaemenid stores of precious metals, together with the establishment of new cities, caused an increase in trade and an initial boom. The amount of coined money in circulation increased greatly, and a monetary economy spread to many cities of Asia. There was a marked increase in maritime trade, especially in grain and slaves, but chronic piracy was a hindrance. Cities favored by trade or royal munificence became rich and competed in the splendor of their festivals and public buildings. Industry flourished in some cities, but its organization continued on a small scale: a proprietor and a few slaves, with rare exceptions. The new prosperity did not, however, affect most cities of old Greece, where c. 250 a serious economic decline occurred, marked by inflation and debt. Extreme concentration of wealth at Sparta caused military decline, which led to the attempts of Kings Agis (242–241) and Cleomenes (227–222) to redistribute land and cancel debt.

Alexander's conquests had opened up vast areas to **GREEK IMMI-GRATION, which continued on a large scale until about 250.** Kings encouraged potential administrators and especially soldiers to settle in new Seleucid cities and in the Egyptian countryside, where land was granted in exchange for service. The policy had mixed success for the Seleucids, who relied heavily on native forces. Ptolemaic military requirements were met primarily by soldier settlers until the late third century, after which native troops were recruited together with Jews, Galatians, and Mysians. Hellenistic royal armies were large, sometimes comprising 60,000 or even 100,000 men. In the colonial areas some intermarriage occurred between early settlers and native women, but **the Greco-Macedonian colonists rigorously excluded natives from military and civic institutions and all positions of power and wealth.** Although small numbers of native aristocrats became Hellenized, the social pattern for most was set by village life, where native languages, religions, and attitudes prevailed. In Asia the economic and political focus was provided by the estates of native aristocrats or temple priests, in Egypt by royal officials. The exclusionary policy changed in Egypt after the Battle of Raphia (217), where Ptolemy IV employed 20,000 Egyptians in his victory over Antiochus III. Economic and social pressures caused more power to be granted to Egyptian priesthoods, land to be assigned to native soldiers, and Egyptians to be admitted into the administration. In the second century Greeks married Egyptian women and took up native religious practices. **The influence of non-Greeks on Greeks was carried out by the movements of peoples and ideas.** There was a major **diaspora of Jews,** and Egyptian cults of **Sarapis** and **Isis,** as well as **Babylonian astrology,** gained great popularity among Greeks. Both non-Greek and Greek populations continued traditional religious practices. Among the latter, new developments included the elevation of Fortune *(Tyche)* to a major deity and practices associated with Hellenistic monarchs: patron deities, dynastic cults, and ruler cults in which sacrifice was made both for and to living rulers.

Colonization provided an outlet for overpopulation in the Greek homeland for about a century. The depopulation noted by literary sources reflects elite behavior and concerns. **The average family was small—one or two children— and infanticide (especially of females) by exposure was common.** Outside of the royal courts, the position of women remained largely unchanged, the ambiguous evidence of comedy, mimes, and sculpture notwithstanding. **Women remained tied to the domestic sphere** and lived under the control of father, husband, or male agnate. Unmarried free women were rare. **In Egypt some women had greater freedom of movement,** others the right to divorce without the permission of a male relative. A new form of marriage contract to which the wife was party (the traditional contract was between father and husband) also appeared.

Cities came to be dominated by the upper classes—small groups of families or enormously wealthy individuals on whom the cities became increasingly dependent. Monarchy became a dominant form of political organization, while the importance of the city-state declined. The military resources of the individual *polis* were dwarfed by those of the monarchies and of federal leagues, whose protection was sought. Citizenship was no longer as exclusive as it had been. Honorary privileges and even citizenship itself were frequently granted to individual benefactors as well as to entire communities. Municipal administration reached a high level. Public institutions, such as gymnasia, were endowed by wealthy benefactors, often royal, and supervised by public officials. By the late third century foundations were being established to subsidize elementary education for boys and sometimes for girls.

Cultural and intellectual life flourished in various cities. Writers of Middle Comedy—**Eubulis** (c. 405–335), **Alexis** (c. 375–275)—and New Comedy—Diphilus (c. 360–300), Philemon (c. 360–263), and **Menander** (c. 342–289)—kept the dramatic arts alive in Athens, while wide enthusiasm for Athenian-style plays helped make the theater a characteristically Hellenistic building type. Athens remained the center for philosophy. The Academy continued the Platonic tradition with

increased emphasis on skepticism, and the Peripatetics concentrated on scientific and historical studies. The shift away from metaphysics to practical ethics was fostered by two new schools. **Epicurus of Samos** (342–270) founded Epicureanism around a closed community that included slaves and women. Members sought pleasure by attaining a state of imperturbability *(ataraxia)*. Adopting Democritus's atomic theory, and subscribing to the indifference of the gods and the universe, Epicureans denied the afterlife and eschewed emotion and politics. Migrating from Cyprus, **Zeno of Citium** (336–264) founded **STOICISM,** teaching in the Painted Porch *(stoa poikile)*. Stoics believed that the universe was governed by reason *(logos*—God, nature, providence)* and that virtue consisted of understanding and being in harmony with it, everything else being at best indifferent. The capital cities became great centers of intellectual life, with royal patrons competing for the talents of scholars, poets, and scientists. The establishment of the Museum (a research institute) and the Library made Alexandria preeminent. Here scholars such as Zenodotus of Ephesus (c. 325–c. 260), Aristophanes of Byzantium (257–180), and Aristarchus of Samothrace (217–145) collected and edited the "classics" of earlier Greek literature. Here contemporary literature also thrived. "Alexandrianism"—short, highly refined, esoteric poetry—was fashioned by Callimachus (c. 360–240) and Theocritus (c. 300–260? from Syracuse), while Apollonius of Rhodes (c. 295–214) revived the epic.

Alexandria was also the home for scientific research. Herophilus of Chalcedon and **Erasistratos of Ceos** (at Antioch?) made great advances in anatomy, physiology, and pathology. Astronomical measurements were made by **Aristarchus of Samos;** Eratosthenes of Cyrene (275–194) computed Earth's circumference; and **Euclid** (c. 300) systematized mathematics, while in Syracuse the wide-ranging **Archimedes** (287–212) made startling advances in mathematics and physics. With the exception of lifting devices, such as Archimedes' screw, technological discoveries in the Hellenistic Age were primarily curiosities. **General lack of interest and support for the application of technology was overcome only in military science,** where advances in siege-craft and fortification were made by Ctesipius of Alexandria (fl. c. 270) and Archimedes. Competitive and cosmopolitan patronage, both royal and private, also stimulated innovations in art and architecture. Hellenistic architecture is marked by the relaxing of classical canons and the introduction of new building types and construction techniques. Public building saw the proliferation of secular structures (stoas, theatres, council-halls, arsenals), as well as of religious sanctuaries. Wealthier citizens resided in more elaborate private houses built around a colonnaded court *(peristyle)*. Innovations in construction included the vault and the use of architectural drawings. Hellenistic sculpture is distinguished from classical by a wider range and greater complexity of style and subjects. Genre types, royal portraiture, and a baroque style in historical and mythological group scenes were some of the innovations of the period.

b. THE WARS OF THE DIADOCHI

322–315. After **Perdiccas** became regent for Philip III Arrhidaeus, the other generals—Antigonus, Antipater, Craterus, and Ptolemy— formed a coalition against him. Perdiccas's general Eumenes defeated and killed Craterus in Asia Minor, but Perdiccas was himself assassinated while campaigning against Ptolemy in Egypt (320). At Triparadeisus in northern Syria, **Antigonus, Ptolemy,** and **Antipater** agreed that the latter should be regent. Antigonus then defeated and besieged Eumenes in Cappadocia. Antipater died (319) leaving Polyperchon as regent. This was unacceptable to Antigonus, to Ptolemy, and to Antipater's son **Cassander.** After negotiating his release, Eumenes promptly accepted Polyperchon's offer to oppose Antigonus in Asia. Meanwhile Cassander seized Piraeus and left Demetrius of Phaleron in command of Athens (317). He then drove Polyperchon from Macedon, executed Olympias, who had earlier killed Philip Arrhidaeus, and imprisoned Roxana and her son Alexander IV, both of whom he put to death in 310. Antigonus pursued Eumenes into central Iran and, after the indecisive **Battle at Paraetacene,** surprised him as he was wintering in Gabiene and executed him (316). Antigonus then drove **Seleucus**

from Babylon to Egypt, where he sought refuge with Ptolemy and where the two, together with Cassander and **Lysimachus,** who ruled Thrace, formed a coalition against Antigonus.

315–307. Antigonus, after besieging and capturing Tyre (314–313), took Syria from Ptolemy. Fighting went on in the Aegean, the Peloponnese, and Asia Minor (313–312). Demetrius, Antigonus' son, was defeated at Gaza (312), and Seleucus recaptured Babylon (311). Cassander consolidated his position in Macedon. Antigonus sent Demetrius to Athens, whence he expelled Demetrius of Phaleron (307).

306. Demetrius won a great naval victory over Ptolemy at Salamis in Cyprus after which both **ANTIGONUS I MONOPHTHALMOS** ("one-eyed") and **Demetrius I Poliorcetes** ("besieger") took the title of king. Ptolemy assumed the royal title in 304, followed immediately by **Seleucus, Lysimachus,** and **Cassander.** Alexander's empire was thus officially dissolved. Demetrius failed to reduce Rhodes by a year's siege (305–304) but relieved Athens from the **Four Years' War** waged by Cassander (307–304). He then revived the **Hellenic League of Philip II** (302). In 302 Lysimachus, Seleucus, Ptolemy, and Cassander formed an alliance against Antigonus and Demetrius.

301. BATTLE OF IPSUS (in Phrygia). The armies of Lysimachus and Seleucus, but not Ptolemy, defeated and killed the eighty-one-year-old Antigonus. Demetrius escaped and continued hostilities, dominating the Aegean with his fleet. Of Antigonus's possessions, Seleucus received Syria and Lysimachus central Asia Minor. Cassander kept Macedon, and his brother Pleistarchus was allotted Cilicia. Ptolemy seized Coele-Syria from Seleucus.

299. Aided by Seleucus, Demetrius expelled Pleistarchus from Cilicia. Cassander died in 298 and his two young sons, Antipater and Alexander V, ruled jointly in Macedon but soon quarreled.

295–294. Demetrius besieged and recovered Athens. He then killed Alexander V, expelled his brother, and ruled Macedon (294). He conquered northeastern and central Greece except for Aetolia.

288. A coalition was formed against Demetrius, and Lysimachus and **King Pyrrhus** of Epirus drove him from Macedon. Demetrius then attempted to campaign in Asia Minor but was eventually captured by Seleucus in Cilicia (286).

283. Demetrius died in captivity, leaving a son, Antigonus, in Greece.

281. Lysimachus, who ruled Macedon, Thrace, and Asia Minor, was defeated and killed at the Battle of Corupedium in Lydia by Seleucus, who became master of Asia Minor. When he tried to seize Macedon, however, he was treacherously assassinated by the disinherited son of Ptolemy, Ptolemy Ceraunus, who ruled Macedon until he was killed opposing the Celtic invasion in 279.

279. The Celts ravaged Macedon, defeated the Greeks at Thermopylae, and were turned back at Delphi. Celtic rule was then established in Thrace, lasting until 210. In central Asia Minor the Celtic kingdom of Galatia was established.

277–276. Meanwhile Demetrius's son, Antigonus Gonatas, recovered Macedon from the Celts and established the **Antigonid dynasty** which lasted until 168.

c. MACEDON AND GREECE, TO 146 B.C.E.

290. Emergence of the **Aetolian League,** a military federation in western Greece. It had a council with proportional representation and a semiannual assembly. Affairs were handled by a committee of 100 *apokletoi* and a single general *(strategos)* in wartime. The league expanded into Phocis (254) and Boeotia (245) and dominated Greece from sea to sea. It also included Elis and part of Arcadia (245) and made an alliance with Messene, thus separating Sparta from the Achaean League.

280. Formation of the **Achaean League,** consisting of twelve towns in the northern Peloponnese. It had a general (two until 255), a board of ten *demiourgoi*, and a federal council with proportional representation of members. There was also an annual assembly of all free citizens. After 251, **Aratus of Sicyon** dominated its policy, and after 245 he was *strategos* in alternate years. With Ptolemaic backing he opposed Macedonian and Aetolian power, extending Achaean influence in the Peloponnese and taking Corinth from Macedon in 243.

276–239. ANTIGONUS II GONATAS ("knock-kneed"?) was driven from Macedon by Pyrrhus of Epirus (274). Pyrrhus was then called into Greece by Cleonymus, pretender to the Spartan kingship. After Pyr-

rhus was killed in Corinth (272), Antigonus returned to rule Macedon. He established control over Greece by garrisoning the cities of Demetrius in Thrace, Chalcis in Euboea, and Corinth; by supporting pro-Macedonian tyrants in several cities of the Peloponnese; and by making peace with the Aetolian League.

268–262? Ptolemy II of Egypt stirred up Athens and Sparta to wage the **Chremonidean War** (from Chremonides, an Athenian leader) against Antigonus. When Ptolemy failed to give energetic aid, Athens was obliged to surrender after a two-year siege (262). Antigonus garrisoned several strong points of Attica and imposed a moderate oligarchy on Athens.

261 (256?). Antigonus defeated Ptolemy in a naval **battle off Cos** and took the Cyclades, though he had to reconquer them later in the **Battle of Andros** (245).

c. 249. Antigonus's governor of the Peloponnese, Alexander, revolted and held the peninsula until his death (c. 245).

251. Aratus of Sicyon recovered that city from Antigonus's tyrant and then joined the Achaean League, which he soon dominated.

245–235. Sparta had fallen into a serious economic crisis because of the excessive concentration of land and wealth in the hands of a few. Coined money had been introduced by King Areus. The number of full citizens who could contribute to their mess-tables *(syssitia)* had fallen to 700. When **King Agis IV** (244–240) tried to redistribute the land into 4,500 equal lots, the great landowners executed him. **Cleomenes III,** who married Agis's widow, became king (235).

239–229. Demetrius II succeeded his father, Antigonus. He protected Epirus against Aetolia, so that the latter broke with Macedon and made an alliance with Achaea. Demetrius attacked it in the **War of Demetrius** (238–229) but was recalled by invasions from the north (233). Argos expelled the pro-Macedonian tyrant Aristomachus and joined the Achaean League (229), while Athens asserted its independence.

229–221. Antigonus III Doson ("going to give," i.e., always promising) succeeded his cousin Demetrius as guardian of the latter's eight-year-old son, Philip, whom he deposed in 227 to become king himself. He made peace with Aetolia and drove the northern tribes out of Macedon.

228–227. Cleomenes defeated the Achaeans under Aratus. He then seized the power in Sparta, redivided the land, enfranchised 4000 *perioikoi*, and abolished the *ephorate*. With an increased citizen army, he reduced Aratus to appeal to Antigonus (225).

222. Antigonus formed a new Hellenic League and crushed Cleomenes at the **Battle of Sellasia** (222). Cleomenes fled to Egypt. Antigonus abolished the Spartan kingship, restored the ephors, and forced Sparta into his league.

221–178. Philip V, son of Demetrius II, succeeded Antigonus III. At his instigation the Hellenic League assembled at Corinth to declare the Social War.

219–217. The Social War against the Aetolians. The war was engineered by Aratus. Philip and his allies fought the Aetolians and *their* allies, Elis and Sparta. At Sparta an anti-Macedonian faction tried to recall Cleomenes. When he was slain in Egypt, the Spartans nevertheless restored the dual kingship.

217. The **Peace of Naupactus** was negotiated between the discouraged Aetolians and Philip, who wanted freedom to act against Rome and secure Illyria.

215–205. In the **FIRST MACEDONIAN WAR** Philip V of Macedon attempted to help Hannibal and the Carthaginians against Rome, but a Roman fleet in the Adriatic prevented him from crossing to Italy and the Romans secured the support of the Aetolian League and Pergamum (212), as well as of Elis, Mantinea, and Sparta. When the Achaean League under **Philopoemen** (since the murder of Aratus in 213) slew the Spartan regent, Machanidas, at Mantinea (207), Nabis became regent and soon, by deposing young Pelops, king. The Greeks came to terms with Philip in 206, and Rome accepted the settlement by the **Peace of Phoenice** (205).

203–200. Philip, allied with Antiochus III against Egypt (203), began operations in the Aegean, but was defeated by Rhodes, Byzantium, and Attalus of Pergamum in the **Battle of Chios** (201).

200–196. The **SECOND MACEDONIAN WAR** arose from an appeal by Attalus and Rhodes to Rome (201). When Philip refused to keep the peace, many Greek states joined Rome (200–198), and Flamininus defeated Philip at **Cynoscephalae** (197) and proclaimed the freedom of

Greece at the Isthmian Games (196). Flamininus then campaigned against Nabis of Sparta (above), who had carried through agrarian reforms (207–204) and expanded his power in the Peloponnese, especially by acquiring Argos (198). He now lost Argos and much of Laconia and was placed under the supervision of the Achaean League (195). Upon the murder of Nabis (192), Sparta was forced into the Achaean League by Rome, and Messene and Elis soon joined, so that the league controlled all the Peloponnese.

192–189. The **Aetolians declared war on Rome** and secured the support of Antiochus III with a small force. The Achaeans and Philip supported Rome. The Romans drove Antiochus back to Asia in the **Battle of Thermopylae** (191), and the Aetolians were finally made subject allies of Rome by M. Fulvius Nobilior (189).

189–181. Philopoemen humbled Sparta but lost his life in suppressing a revolt in Messenia (183). His successor in the Achaean League, Callicrates, was subservient to Rome and allowed Sparta to revive.

179–167. **Perseus** became king of Macedon on the death of his father Philip V. He had already persuaded Philip to execute his pro-Roman brother Demetrius, and now Eumenes II of Pergamum laid charges against him (III).

171–167. In the **THIRD MACEDONIAN WAR** Perseus was crushed by Aemilius Paullus at **Pydna** (168). He later died in captivity in Italy, and the Antigonids came to an end. Rome made Macedon into four unrelated republics, paying a moderate yearly tribute (167). In Aetolia, 500 anti-Romans were slain. One thousand hostages, including the historian Polybius, were taken from Achaea to Italy.

149–148. The **FOURTH MACEDONIAN WAR** was begun by Andriscus, who pretended to be a son of Perseus. On his defeat, Macedon became a Roman province (148).

146. When the Achaean hostages had returned (151) and Callicrates had died (149), the Achaean League attacked Sparta but was crushed by the Roman general Mummius (146). The Roman Senate ordered Mummius to abolish the leagues, substitute oligarchies for all democracies, destroy Corinth, and place Greece under the supervision of the governor of Macedon. This marked the end of Greek and Macedonian independence, though some Greek states retained autonomy for a long time. *(To p. 81)*

d. THE SELEUCIDS AND PERGAMUM

304–281. SELEUCUS I NICATOR ("conqueror"), after securing Babylon (311–308) and assuming the royal title (304), ceded northwestern India to Chandragupta (Sandrocottus) (303). He failed to reduce Mithridates I of Pontus but gained control of Asia Minor on the defeat of Lysimachus (281).

281–261. ANTIOCHUS I SOTER ("savior") succeeded upon the murder of his father Seleucus. He fought and defeated the Galatians (275, 270?). In the First War of Succession (280–279) and First Syrian War (274–271), he lost Miletus, Phoenicia, Cilicia, Pamphylia, and Lycia to Ptolemy II.

263–241. Eumenes I made himself virtually independent of Antiochus as ruler of **Pergamum,** where his uncle, **Philetaerus,** had ruled as governor, first for Lysimachus and then semi-independently for the Seleucids.

261–246. Antiochus II Theos ("god"), son of Antiochus I, secured the support of Antigonus II and Rhodes against Egypt in the **Second Syrian War** (260–253?). The succeeding peace restored to Antiochus Ionia (including Miletus), Coele-Syria, Cilicia, and Pamphylia (253).

250–230. Diodotus I declared himself independent king of Bactria. In 248–247, Arsaces I founded the **Parthian Kingdom.**

246–226. SELEUCUS II CALLINICUS ("gloriously victorious"), son of Antiochus II by his divorced wife, Laodice I, succeeded. As a result **Berenice II,** daughter of Ptolemy II, whom Antiochus had married in 253, provoked the Syrian War in favor of her infant son.

246–241. Berenice II provoked the **Third Syrian War** ("Laodicean War" or "War of Berenice"). Though she and her son were murdered in Antioch, her brother, Ptolemy III, invaded Asia and Mesopotamia, and ultimately forced Seleucus to surrender the coasts of Syria and southern Asia Minor (241).

241–197. Attalus I Soter ("savior"), who succeeded his father's cousin Eumenes I as ruler of Pergamum, took advantage of Seleucus's diffi-

culties to secure for himself western Asia Minor by crushing the Galatians near Pergamum (230), after which he took the title "king."

240–236. Seleucus attacked **Antiochus Hierax** ("falcon"), whom he in 241 had recognized as ruler of Asia Minor. Hierax secured the aid of Mithridates II of Pontus and the Galatians. The Galatians crushed Seleucus at Ancyra (240–239?).

229–226. Attalus I of Pergamum drove Hierax out of Asia Minor (229–228), after which Seleucus drove him out of Syria (227) to Thrace, where he was killed. Seleucus died and was succeeded by his son (226).

226–223. **Seleucus III Soter** or Ceraunus ("thunderbolt"), son of Seleucus II, was murdered during a war with Attalus I (224–221).

223–187. ANTIOCHUS III, THE GREAT, brother of Seleucus III, regained from Attalus most of the territory lost since 241. He recovered the Mesopotamian provinces from the revolting governor, Molon (221).

221–217. Fourth Syrian War. Antiochus III's initial successes were followed by his defeat at **Raphia** (217), and Antiochus retained only Seleucia, the port of Antioch on the Syrian coast.

212–205. Anabasis of Antiochus III. In a series of victorious campaigns, Antiochus compelled Arsaces III of Parthia to pay tribute, formed an alliance with Euthydemus of Bactria, and made a treaty with the Indian ruler Sophagaesenus (p. 43). Thus he consolidated Seleucid power in the east for a time.

202–200. The Fifth Syrian War resulted from the treaty between Antiochus III and Philip V of Macedon. The war was decided by Antiochus's **victory of Panium** whereby he secured from Egypt most of Coele-Syria and southern Asia Minor (save Cyprus).

197–194. Antiochus then campaigned in Asia Minor and Thrace, causing **Eumenes II Sotor** of Pergamum (197–159) to complain to Rome. Diplomacy failed to resolve Rome's dispute with Antiochus (194–192).

192–189. WAR WITH ROME broke out when Antiochus crossed to Greece to aid the Aetolians and the Romans declared war. The forces of Antiochus were driven from Greece (191) and his fleet was defeated at **Myonnesus** (190). The Roman army entered Asia Minor and defeated Antiochus himself at **Magnesia** (190). In the peace of **Apamea** (188), Antiochus paid a large indemnity, lost his fleet, and surrendered Asia Minor, which was divided between Rhodes and Pergamum. This defeat led to the complete breaking away of Armenia (under Artaxias) and of Bactria.

187–175. Seleucus IV Philopater ("loving his father") succeeded Antiochus III, and during his reign the empire gradually recovered strength. Meanwhile Eumenes II of Pergamum successfully fought against Prusias I of Bithynia (187–183) and Pharnaces I of Pontus (183–179).

175–163. Antiochus IV Epiphanes ("god manifest") succeeded upon the murder of his brother Seleucus. Though friendly to Rome, he was prevented by the Romans from concluding successfully the **Sixth Syrian War** against Egypt (170–168). The Romans also weakened Rhodes by making Delos a free port (167).

168–163. Dissent between Hellenized and observant Jews caused violence in Jerusalem that Antiochus suppressed with force and repression. Led by **Judas Maccabeus,** the Jews began a successful guerrilla war (168). A large Seleucid army forced negotiations and, as a result, the temple fortifications were dismantled and Jewish religious freedom was restored (163).

164–162. Antiochus V Eupator, with Lysias as regent, succeeded his father Antiochus IV, who died campaigning against the Parthians.

162–150. Demetrius I Soter, son of Seleucus IV, returned from Rome and executed Antiochus but was himself defeated and killed in 150 by a pretender, **Alexander Balas** (150–145). In 145 Alexander was defeated by the son of Demetrius I who ruled as Demetrius II Nicator.

145–139. Demetrius II Nicator. Demetrius was challenged by several usurpers. In 142 Demetrius made an alliance with Simon Maccabeus who established an independent Jewish state under the Hasmonean dynasty. His successors—John Hyrcanus (134–104), Judah-Aristobulus (104–103), and Alexander Jannaeus (102–76)—took advantage of the weakness of Seleucid rulers to extend the power of the Jewish state. Meanwhile in 139 Demetrius was captured by Mithridates I of Parthia and was succeeded by his younger brother, Antiochus VII Euergetes Eusebes Soter Sidetes.

139–129. Antiochus VII Euergetes Eusebes Soter Sidetes ("benefactor, pious, savior") did much to restore the Seleucid power. However, after several victories over Phraates II of Parthia, he was finally crushed and killed at Ecbatana (129).

138–133. Attalus III Philometor ("loving his mother") **of Pergamum,** a son of Eumenes II, succeeded his uncle, Attalus II. In his will, he bequeathed his kingdom to Rome. Rome suppressed the pretender Aristonicus and made the kingdom of Pergamum into the province of Asia (129). *(To p. 82)*

129–125. Demetrius II was sent back to Syria by Phraates II in 129 and was slain in 125 by a pretender.

125–96. Antiochus VIII Epiphanes Philometor Callinicus "Grypus" ("hook-nosed"), a younger son of Demetrius II, reigned with Cleopatra until her death (c. 120). The pretender, Alexander Zabinas, was killed in 123. In 117 Antiochus was forced into retirement by a half-brother, **Antiochus IX Philopater, "Cyzicenus"** ("of Cyzicus"), son of Cleopatra and Antiochus VII. They divided the realm in 111 and both reigned until Antiochus VIII was murdered in 96 by his favorite, Heracleon.

95–64. Seleucus VI, son of Antiochus VIII, defeated and killed Antiochus IX (95). The son of the latter, **Antiochus X,** defeated and killed Seleucus VI, but the latter's brother, Demetrius III, seized Damascus. Another son of Antiochus VIII, **Antiochus XI,** was defeated and killed, but his brother, Philip I, continued the war with Antiochus X. The latter was killed in 93 fighting the Parthians in Commagene. Demetrius III and Philip I engaged in civil war until Demetrius was captured by the Parthians in 88. **Antiochus XII,** another son of Antiochus VIII, seized Damascus, which he held until he was killed on an expedition against the Nabataeans in 84. An insurrection expelled Philip I from Antioch, and Tigranes of Armenia seized Syria and held it until he was defeated by Lucullus in 69. **Antiochus XIII,** son of Antiochus X, was installed at Antioch (68) and soon had to fight with Philip II, son of Philip I. The Arabian prince of Emesa slew Antiochus XIII by treachery in 67; Philip was unable to secure his rule. In 64 Pompey made Syria a Roman province (p. 84).

63. In 63 Pompey captured Jerusalem and ended the rivalry over the Hasmonean kingship by making Hyrcanus high priest and ethnarch. His descendants retained these offices until 37, when Rome appointed Herod (the Great) as king of Judaea. *(To p. 84)*

e. PARTHIA

247, 238?–211. Arsaces I founded the **kingdom of Parthia,** including at first only Parthia and Hyrcania, between the Seleucid kingdom in the west and the Bactrian kingdom in the east. Parthian society was hierarchical and dominated by elite orders of priests and nobles. The king's power rested on the support of the leading nobles who supplied soldiers and tribute from their estates. Zoroastrianism was the religion of the Parthians. In 238 Arsaces was expelled by Seleucus II but returned when the latter withdrew to deal with a revolt in Syria.

211–c. 190. Arsaces II withstood the attacks of Antiochus III, the Great, in 209; he was followed by Arsaces III (Priapatius, 190–176) and Arsaces IV (Phraates I, 176–c. 171).

c. 171–138. Mithridates I conquered Babylonia and Media from the Seleucids (c. 147); later he added to his kingdom Elam, Persia, and parts of Bactria, thus founding the Parthian Empire. Ctesiphon-Seleucia became the capital. He captured Demetrius II in 139.

138–128. Phraates II (138–127) defeated Antiochus VII in Media (129), and as a result the Seleucids were permanently excluded from the lands east of the Euphrates; but he died in battle fighting the Tochari (the Scythians or *Sacae* of the Greeks), a tribe driven out of central Asia by the Yuezhi. The kingdom was devastated and Artabanus I (128–124) fell likewise fighting against the Tochari.

124–87. Mithridates II, the Great, defeated the Scythians and also Artavasdes, king of Armenia Major. He stabilized the eastern boundaries of the kingdom.

87–70. Parthia suffered a collapse and was greatly reduced in territory by Tigranes I of Armenia (c. 100–56).

70–57. Phraates III restored order but was not strong enough to resist the Roman advance, led by Lucullus and Pompey.

57–37. Orodes II defeated Crassus at **Carrhae** (53) and regained Mesopotamia. His son, Pacorus, unsuccessfully invaded the Roman province of Syria in 51 and again in 40.

37–20. Phraates IV defeated Antony in 36 but could not prevent him

from conquering Armenia in 34. In 20 he returned the standards of Crassus and Antony to Augustus, while a line of kings (the **Arcasids**) persisted in Armenia. Parthia itself was badly divided for almost two centuries after 77 C.E. Rome conquered further Parthian territory, including Armenia, by 117 C.E. *(To p. 93).*

f. BACTRIA

323–302. After Alexander's death, Greek auxiliaries mutinied and were crushed by **Perdiccas.** Control over Bactria, frequently nominal, passed from Perdiccas (d. 319), to Eumenes (d. 316), to Antigonus, and to Seleucus, who campaigned in the eastern provinces (311–302).

c. 250–210? Diodotus, the satrap of Bactria, made himself independent and conquered Sogdiana. He founded a dynasty that withstood the attacks of the Seleucids.

210? Euthydemus overthrew Diodotus II (c. 210?) and withstood a two-year siege at Bactra by Antiochus III before making an alliance (208–206?). After the defeat of Antiochus at Magnesia (190), Euthydemus and his son Demetrius began to expand into the Indus Valley. But while Demetrius was campaigning in the Punjab, Eucratides made himself king of Bactria (c. 170). **Menander** (c. 155–130) then became king of Bactria and extended his power into India. About 100 the Yuezhi crossed the Oxus River, breaking Bactrian Greek power and confining their territory to the Hindu Kush and the upper Indus and Swat Valleys. They were then overcome by the Sakas and Scytho-Parthians.

g. PTOLEMAIC EGYPT TO THE ROMAN CONQUEST

(From p. 32)

304–283. PTOLEMY I SOTER ("savior"), the son of Lagus (hence the "Lagid" house), had been governor of Egypt since 323 and king since 304. He had seized Coele-Syria in 301 and acquired from Demetrius, Pamphylia and Lycia (296–295) and Caria and the island of Cos (286).

285–246. PTOLEMY II PHILADELPHUS ("loving his sister") was co-regent for two years and revived an old Pharaonic practice by marrying his sister Arsinoe II (276?). He explored the upper Nile and extended his power along the Red Sea and into northern Arabia (278) for commercial purposes.

280–272. In the **First War of Succession** (280–279) and **First Syrian War** (274–271), Ptolemy II secured Miletus, Phoenicia, western Cilicia, Pamphylia, and Lycia. He subsidized Pyrrhus against Antigonus (274) and aided Athens and Sparta in the Chremonidean War (268–262?). He incited Eumenes of Pergamum to revolt from Antiochus (263) and supported the seizure of Ephesus (262–259) by his own son, Ptolemy. These activities brought Antiochus II, Antigonus II, and Rhodes together to wage the Second Syrian War.

260–250. During the **Second Syrian War** (260–253?), Antigonus defeated Ptolemy in the **Battle of Cos** (261 or 256). Though by the resulting peace he lost Cilicia and western Pamphylia (255), he later recovered the Cyclades (250) and also Cyrene (c. 248), which had become independent in 274.

246–221. Ptolemy III Euergetes ("benefactor") supported his sister Berenice II in the **Third Syrian War** (246–241) and acquired the coasts of Syria and southern Asia Minor, as well as some Aegean ports. But he lost the Cyclades to Antigonus through the **Battle of Andros** (246?). This was the height of the Ptolemaic power.

221–203. Ptolemy IV Philopator ("loving his father") was a weak monarch, dominated by his minister, Sosibius. In the **Fourth Syrian War** (221–217) he at first lost much of the Syrian coast to Antiochus III, but the victory of **Raphia** (217) brought the recovery of all, save the port of Seleucia.

203–181. Ptolemy V Epiphanes ("god manifest"), a young boy, succeeded his father. While the Egyptian natives revolted in the Delta (201–200), Antiochus III attacked him in the Fifth Syrian War.

202–195. The Fifth Syrian War (202–200?) saw the defeat of Ptolemy at **Panium** (200). He retained only Cyprus of his Asiatic possessions. When he came of age (195), he succeeded in suppressing the native revolts.

181–145. Ptolemy VI Philometor ("loving his mother") followed Ptolemy V under the regency of his mother Cleopatra I. In consequence of Ptolemy's cowardice during the **Sixth Syrian War** with Antiochus IV (170–168), the people of Alexandria forced him to associate his brother, **Ptolemy VII,** in his rule. Rome prevented Antiochus from completing his victory over Egypt (168). When Ptolemy VI was expelled by his brother (164), the Roman Senate restored him and gave Cyrene and Cyprus to Ptolemy VII, who, however, secured only Cyrene (163). Ptolemy supported Alexander Balas against Demetrius I (153–150) but then switched his support from Alexander to Demetrius II. Ptolemy and Alexander Balas were killed in this war (147–45).

145–116. Ptolemy VII Euergetes II ("benefactor") or Physcon ("fat-bellied") reunited the empire after his brother's death and restored order. At his death, he left Cyrene separately to his son Apion, who willed it to Rome in 96, though it was not actually annexed until 75. Another son, Ptolemy IX, received Cyprus, which was ultimately bequeathed to Rome and annexed in 58.

116–47. Ptolemy VIII Soter II or Lathyrus ("chick-pea"), son of Ptolemy VII, was eventually expelled by his brother **Ptolemy IX Alexander I** (108–88). The people of Alexandria, however, slew Ptolemy IX and restored Ptolemy VIII (88–80). **Ptolemy X Alexander II,** son of Ptolemy IX, succeeded but was at once slain by the people of Alexandria (80), who set up an illegitimate son of Ptolemy VIII, **Ptolemy XI Auletes** ("flute-player") or **Neos** ("new") **Dionysos.** Though expelled in 58, he bribed the "first triumvirate" to send Gabinius to restore him (55). On his death in 51, he left his throne jointly to his children, **Cleopatra VII** and **Ptolemy XII** (51–47). When Ptolemy expelled his sister, Caesar forced her restoration (48) and, since Ptolemy died during the fighting about Alexandria (48–47), Caesar joined with Cleopatra a younger brother, **Ptolemy XIII** (47–44), whom Cleopatra murdered on Caesar's death (44).

47–30. Cleopatra VII sought to restore the Ptolemaic Empire by winning to her support Caesar and later Antony (41). Because of her association with Antony, Octavian declared war on Egypt (32). After their defeat at Actium (31), and Antony's suicide at Alexandria, Cleopatra took her life rather than adorn Octavian's triumph (30). This brought to an end the last of the Hellenistic monarchies.   *(To p. 85)*

h. SICILY

(From p. 69)

316–289. AGATHOCLES made himself tyrant of Syracuse in consequence of a civil war (c. 323–316) in which, as a democratic leader, he had executed and expelled the Syracusan oligarchs, dividing their property among the poor. He established Syracusan suzerainty over eastern Sicily.

311. The exiled oligarchs appealed to Carthage whose general, Hamilcar, defeated Agathocles at the Himera River and besieged Syracuse. In 310 Agathocles slipped across to Africa and attacked Carthage. The siege of Syracuse was lifted, and Agathocles maintained himself in Africa until 307, when his army, under his sons, was annihilated during his absence.

304. Agathocles came to terms with Carthage and the oligarchs and took the title of king. In the meantime, the Tarentines had made peace with the Samnites (c. 320) but were attacked by the Lucanians and eventually called in Agathocles for help.

302. Agathocles arrived in Italy (c. 300), established his power in Bruttium, but was called back to Syracuse, where he died in 289. He bequeathed freedom to the Syracusans, who restored the democracy. A certain group of the Campanian mercenaries of Agathocles, calling themselves Mamertines ("sons of Mars"), seized Messana.

282–275. The Tarentines, angered by Roman occupation of towns in southern Italy, sunk four Roman ships that had violated a treaty by sailing into Tarentine waters. They then drove a Roman garrison from Thurii. When Rome declared war, they called in Pyrrhus (280). After victories over the Romans, Pyrrhus campaigned against the Carthaginians in Sicily (279–276). He returned to Italy, was defeated by the Romans, and departed (275), leaving southern Italy under the Romans and much of Sicily under the Carthaginians.

275–215. Hiero II made himself tyrant of Syracuse, defeated the Mamertines, and took the title of king (270). He joined the Carthaginians in attacking the Roman force which occupied Messana in 264. When he was defeated and besieged in Syracuse, he made peace with Rome (263). At the end of the **First Punic War** (241) (p. 80), Hiero's kingdom encompassed about a quarter of Sicily; most of the rest became Rome's possession. Denied the possibility of expansion by Rome, Hiero pursued a peaceful policy and Sicily prospered for a quarter century. He died in 215 and was succeeded by his grandson Hieronymus.

(To p. 80)

E. ROME

1. THE MONARCHY AND THE EARLY REPUBLIC, 334 [338]–264 B.C.E.

a. GEOGRAPHY AND CLIMATE

[*Note on dates:* Virtually all precise dates for early Rome are antiquarian reconstructions. The conventional (Varronian) dates for Roman events before the late 4th century are high by four years due to the insertion of the fabricated "dictator-years"—333, 324, 309, and 301. In what follows, the conventional dates will appear in square brackets.]

Rome's site on the **Tiber River** lies where the foothills of the Apennines, the mountain chain that dominates central and southern Italy, come down to the central plain. The Tiber, like the other navigable rivers of antiquity, was a vital channel of trade. **Latium,** the region to the east and south of **Rome,** was bounded to the north by Etruria—distinguished by mineral deposits which were heavily exploited from the 8th century B.C.E.—and to the south by **Campania,** with good farmland and harbors. Italy itself was a geographical unit long before it was a political one; it came to include northern Italy only in the 2nd to 1st centuries B.C.E. and never included Sicily or Sardinia. The climate of peninsular Italy in antiquity was not very different from that of today, except that extensive deforestation in some regions has caused a decrease in rainfall.

b. THE PEOPLES OF ITALY

The wide diffusion of Indo-European tongues—Latin, Osco-Umbrian, Venetic, and Messapian—spoken in Italy at the beginning of the historical period, together with the general continuity of prehistoric cultures attested by archaeology, show that the **introduction of Indo-European languages** into Italy was a long and complicated process stretching back to the late Neolithic age. The great cultural units of historical Italy—Etruscan, Latin, Sabellian, and Iapygian in Apulia; Venetic in Venetia—were formed in the 9th and 8th centuries.

During the 7th century B.C.E., the non-Indo-European **ETRUSCANS** became the dominant people of central Italy. Their homeland corresponds roughly to modern Tuscany. The rise of the Etruscans coincided with intensified trade with Greeks in search of metals in the 8th century. Greek imports, increased use of metals, greater division of labor, the adoption of writing (from the Chalcidian alphabet of Cumae), and urbanization were all part of the rapid social and economic transformation in southern and coastal Etruria. Etruscan power, though never unified, was extended through migration, colonization, and conquest. Etruscans founded cities in the Po Valley and in Campania and subjugated various Latin communities, Rome among them. The Etruscan cities were loosely united in a religious league of 12 but were politically independent with independent artistic traditions. The economy was based on agriculture, maritime trade and piracy, and exploitation of minerals. Tomb paintings portray a luxurious upper-class existence, while literary sources tell of a class of peasants tied to the land, comparable to Spartan helots. Etruscan hegemony ended in the 5th century with their expulsion from Latium and the loss of the sea to Greeks, of Campania to the Sabelli, and of the Po Valley to the Gauls. From the 4th through the 1st centuries, Roman conquest, colonization, and co-optation caused Etruscan civilization to decline and finally end. The Etruscans influenced Roman institutions in various ways, and in spite of the fact that many of their gods were different from those of Rome, they had a reputation at Rome for religious expertise. They were also renowned for luxury, because women were relatively free by the standards of classical Greece.

The **LATINS** lived on the western (Tyrrhenian) coastal plain—**Latium**—that stretches from the Tiber in the north to Monte Circeo 65 miles to the south. Northern Latium is enclosed on the east by the foothills of the Apennines; further south, the Lepini Mountains mark the eastern boundary. Traditionally there were 50 small Latin communities which were united by common Latin cults and by the common Latin rights of intermarriage, contractual dealing, and intermigration. By the 7th century, contacts with Etruscans and Greeks had influenced the Latins to organize themselves into about a dozen communities resembling Greek *poleis*. Although still tied to each other by intercommunal rights and common cults, these Latin "city-states" became increasingly independent and competitive. By the late 6th century several of them had formed a **political league** centered around Aricia, at the time when Etruscan Rome was pursuing an aggressive policy. Roman preeminence in Latium ended abruptly with the expulsion of Etruscan kings in the late 6th century. Soon after this the **Latin League** was formed, and a military alliance was made with Rome to defend the homeland against invading Aequi and Volsci. A century of war left Latium free of invaders, but Rome was again poised to dominate the other Latins. This was achieved by a Roman victory in the Latin War, 337–334 [343–338].

In the historical period the Apennines were inhabited by Sabellian peoples who spoke a variety of Osco-Umbrian languages and who periodically raided and sometimes conquered the fertile plains around them. In historical times the **Sabines** had moved into Latium where they are said to have exerted a formative influence on early Rome. The territories of the **Umbrians** extended from the highlands east of the Arno and Tiber to the Adriatic coast between Rimini and Ancona. Another Osco-Umbrian-speaking people from the central Apennines were the **Aequi**, who invaded Latium c. 500 B.C.E. The central Apennines were also home to the Umbrian-speaking Marsi. Further east, Oscan speakers—the Paeligni, Vestini, and Marrucini—held sway; to the southeast, along the Adriatic coast, the Oscan-speaking Frentani dominated. Inhabiting the south-central Apennines were the **SAMNITES**, who spoke an Oscan language and by the 4th century were united in a loose but formidable confederation. During the late 5th and early 4th centuries, Oscan-speaking peoples moved into Campania, Lucania, and Bruttium, where they came to be known as Campani, Lucani, and Bruttii, respectively.

GREEK COLONIZATION (p. 62) had a major influence on all the peoples of Italy and Sicily. The first Greek colony was established at Cumae in 750, and Greeks continued founding colonies in Campania, Apulia, and eastern Sicily (**Magna Graecia**) for the following two centuries.

The advent of **CELTIC** peoples into the Alpine regions of Italy occurred during the historical period. Since their movements were nomadic and they mixed with previous inhabitants of regions, it is difficult to date the earlier Celtic presence, but by the 5th century they had begun to displace the Etruscans in the **Po Valley.**

c. ECONOMY, SOCIETY, AND CULTURE

The economy of early Rome was **agrarian,** and most citizens were farmers working privately owned land. Their diet centered on hulled wheat or emmer *(far)* consumed as porridge *(puls)* rather than bread, together with garden vegetables. Cultivation of grapes seems to have begun in central Italy in the 8th century B.C.E., and the olive was introduced in the 6th; both became staples. Meat played a greater role in the diet of ancient Romans than in that of Greeks, and while sheep and larger stock animals were raised by wealthier Romans, the major source of meat in Rome was the ubiquitous pig. That a significant number of Roman farmers were relatively affluent in the mid-sixth century is shown by their organization into a force of hoplite soldiers who provided their own armor. The majority, however, worked plots too small to allow farming above near-subsistence levels, which had to be supplemented with labor on land that was either public or belonged to the wealthy.

The importance of **trade** and **small-scale industry** for the economy of archaic Rome is suggested by its site on the Tiber River at the point of a natural ford (Tiber Island). Commercial activity is confirmed by archaeological evidence. By the mid-sixth century local Roman industry was producing fine pottery and bronze work, as well as public and domestic buildings decorated with high-quality terra-cotta ornaments. From the earliest times, however, **economic well-being at Rome was dependent on military success.** Increases in population during the 7th and 6th centuries, and the overall Roman prosperity during the 6th century was a function of expansion under Etruscan rule. Conversely, 5th-century military setbacks coincide with economic decline, which continued until the end of the century when conquered land was distributed to poor Romans. The pattern recurs in the 4th century, with decades of economic dislocation and social unrest following the Gallic sack of Rome in 386 [390], ending with Roman victories midcentury. Great victories over the Samnites, Etruscans, and Greeks in the late 4th and early 3rd centuries placed the economy of Rome on a higher level. Large numbers of Romans were granted land both in the greatly enlarged Roman territory *(ager Romanus)* and in the **Latin colonies** established in more distant parts of Italy. War captives increased the numbers of rural and urban slaves, and, to meet the needs of the city's swelling population, aqueducts, the *Aqua Appia* in 310 [312] and the *Aqua Anio Vetus* in 272, were constructed. The technology for Rome's first aqueducts was probably modeled on earlier drainage tunnels. Public buildings paid for by war booty, especially temples, were erected at an unprecedented rate. Pottery made in Rome began to be exported in quantity, and Roman artisans produced sculpture in terra cotta, stone, and bronze. In the early 3rd century state-issued coinage was introduced. The Etruscans had introduced **technological advances** to archaic Rome in the form of drainage projects, both urban and rural, and impressive public buildings. The conquest of **Veii** in 392 [396] gave Rome access to a superior building material, *Grotta Oscura* tufa. Rome's monumental stone wall, begun in 374 [378], was constructed principally of this stone, which remained the city's chief building material for almost two centuries. By the end of the 4th century the first of Rome's major roads had been built, the *Via Appia* to Capua 310 [312].

From early times the Roman family was governed by the principle of *patria potestas.* This was the power held by the oldest surviving male ascendant *(paterfamilias)* over the property, conduct, and survival of his agnatic descendants—sons, unmarried daughters, grandchildren by sons, married daughters in *sine manu* relationships, and daughters-in-law if married with *manus*, plus slaves (these together constituted the *familia*). All these remained under the power of the *paterfamilias* until his death, at which time each son became a *paterfamilias* and head of his own *familia,*while daughters gained limited independence under the supervision of a male guardian *(tutor)* and slaves together with other property were passed on through inheritance. Inherited property, including land, was equally divided among heirs. From at least the mid-fifth century, there were two forms of marriage at Rome; under one, the wife passed into the *manus* (authority) of the head of her husband's family, while under the other she did not.

Beyond the *familia,* the larger social unit was the **gens** (clan), whose development is reflected in early onomastic practices. The gens consisted of those who shared a *nomen* (family name), who were sometimes thought to descend from a common clan ancestor. Men had personal names *(praenomina)*, women did not. The division of large clans into subgroups came to be denoted by a third name, the *cognomen*, which was certainly in use by the 4th century. Sometime during the regal period a group of *gentes*, called **patricians**, secured for themselves certain political and religious privileges to the exclusion of other **plebeian** *gentes*. Various theories try to explain the basis for the distinction—native vs. immigrant; patron vs. client; cavalry vs. infantry—but none is entirely convincing. A characteristic feature of Roman life was **patronage** *(clientela)*. This extralegal relationship that occurred at a variety of social levels involved mutual obligations between a free Roman citizen of inferior status *(cliens)* and a more powerful citizen *(patronus)*. Its origin, stability, extension through society, and political function are obscure and debated, but its importance is undeniable. **Slavery** is mentioned in the mid-fifth century Twelve Tables but must have been practiced on a relatively small scale in the Archaic period. At that time the need for labor on the estates of wealthy Romans would have been met by citizens who had fallen into **debt-bondage**, *nexum*, which is also mentioned in the Twelve Tables. Enslavement of defeated enemies was the principal source of slaves, and the military successes of the 4th century increased the supply greatly. It is not coincidental that debt-bondage was formally abolished at the beginning of a major war in 323 [326]. The institution of a tax on manumissions in 353 [357] attests to a substantial number of slaves. A Roman slave on being manumitted was called a **freedman** *(libertinus)* and became a citizen.

The cultural life of archaic Rome was heavily affected by **Etruscan** and **Greek** influences, the latter either direct or mediated through the Etruscans. The presence in 6th-century Rome of the Italic (Etruscan) temple and the Latin alphabet (adapted from the Etruscan, which in turn was adapted from Greek) reflects Etruscan variations on Greek forms. Direct Greek influence is attested in the 6th century by a votive inscription to the Greek gods Castor and Pollux at the pan-Latin sanctuary at Lavinium, by the syncretization in Rome of native and Greek deities, and by early 5th-century Roman temples dedicated to Greek deities. Political revolution, foreign invasion, and internal unrest brought on a century of decline that ended with the cultural advances produced by late 4th-century military successes and prosperity. Rome was once again open to foreign, particularly Greek, influences, which can be seen in the renewed production of pottery and bronze work. The "publication" of the civil law by **Cn. Flavius** in 303 [304] shows that writing, though still limited to relatively small numbers of citizens, had gained a new importance. The capture of cities of Magna Graecia in the early 3rd century brought substantial numbers of Greek slaves to Rome. The Tarentine **Livius Andronicus** worked as a teacher and poet, but other captive Greeks were employed in a variety of occupations throughout the city. The process of "Hellenization," therefore, was taking place in the streets as well as the salons of Rome long before the 2nd-century conquest of Greece.

d. THE REGAL PERIOD

The history of early Rome rests on a highly dubious literary tradition, based mostly on oral tradition, and a sketchy archaeological record. The latter suggests that Rome's first residents were herdsmen living in seasonal settlements on Rome's various hills (**Palatine, Esquiline, Quirinal**) and using the low-lying areas for burials (both inhumation and cremation). The chronology is disputed, but permanent settlements on these hills seem to have been established by the 10th century B.C.E. The early importance of the Tiber ford as the crossroads of the two principal trade routes of central Italy is suggested by the presence of 8th-century Greek geometric pottery in the adjacent area—the later Forum Boarium. By the early 7th century settlements began to move down from the hills to the eastern fringes of the **Roman Forum.** Around 625, the central area of the Roman Forum was drained and paved. During the second half of the 6th century, an enormous Etruscan-style temple (with three rooms or *cellae*) was built on the Capitoline hill; in the *Forum Boarium* remains of a large temple have been found with an Etruscan inscription nearby.

Roman tradition said that **Romulus** founded **Rome,** and antiquarians later fixed the date at 753. Tradition also said that early Rome was ruled by seven kings—**Romulus, Numa Pompilius, Tullius Hostilius, Ancus Marcius, Tarquinius Priscus, Servius Tullus,** and **Tarquinius Superbus.** The latter was supposed to have been expelled in 505 [509]. The last three rulers represent a foreign, Etruscan dynasty responsible for major building projects, among them the construction of a great drainage sewer *(cloaca maxima)* and the temple of Jupiter Optimus Maximus on the Capitol. The tradition also says that the **political organization** of regal Rome was originally based on three tribes and 30 *curiae* (wards), and that the kingship was elective not hereditary. The king was advised by a **senate** of 100 elders *(patres)*. The penultimate king, **Servius Tullius,** reputed to be of Latin servile descent, is credited with a reorganization of the army (hoplite reform) that divided citizens into five classes and 193 centuries determined by wealth.

e. THE EARLY REPUBLIC

The Republic was founded in 505 [509], according to tradition, when the last king, **Tarquinius Superbus,** was expelled by a revolt of native Roman aristocrats led by **L. Junius Brutus.** The dominant tradition states that the Republic was led from the beginning by two annual, eponymous officials called **consuls,** but some scholars think that until 363 [367] they were known as praetors (the latter then became the second tier of officials). The consuls exercised *imperium*, which gave them absolute power (including over life and death and in war), while in the city they exercised the power of *coercitio*, a sort of summary police power. The consuls were elected by the *comitia centuriata*, a plutocratically organized assembly of the male citizens, but their imperium continued to be conferred by the *comitia curiata (lex curiata)*. Assisting the consuls were two financial officials called *quaestors* who were originally appointed by the chief officials and after 443 [447] were elected. Two plebeian quaestors seem to have been added in 418 [421] to administer the state treasury *(aerarium)* in Rome. In either 439 [443] or 431 [435], the job of counting Roman citizens was transferred from the consuls to two censors, nonmilitary but prestigious officials. Every four years the censors, holding office for a maximum of 18 months, made up the citizen lists for tax and military purposes (the census), enrolled senators *(lectio senatus)* and cavalrymen *(recognitio equitum)*, and examined public morals *(regimen morum)*. A third magistrate with imperium, the *praetor urbanus*, was created in 363 [367] to relieve the consuls of some judicial responsibilities. In a time of crisis the senate could establish unity of command by instructing the consuls to appoint a **dictator,** who appointed his own assistant as a master of the cavalry *(magister equitum)*. The dictator had *imperium* and absolute power in all fields but had to resign when his task was completed, and in no case could he remain in office for more than six months. All magistrates with *imperium*, and also the censors, were elected by the military assembly, *comitia centuriata*. Other officials were elected by the *comitia tributa*, which passed the great majority of laws *(leges)*.

Religious power was closely intertwined with political power. The relationship between the Roman people and the divine, which had once been controlled by the king and by priests of specific deities, was taken over under the Republic by three boards or colleges of religious officials who were experts in, and managers of, the various methods of communication between the community and the gods. The three priestly colleges were (1) the augurs (originally three? in number, raised to nine by 300), who were expert advisers in determining whether the gods approved courses of action; (2) the *decemviri sacris faciundis*, a committee of ten (earlier, fewer in number), who supervised the Sibylline Books and the few other oracular documents recognized at Rome; and (3) the *pontifices* (priests, originally three?, raised to nine by 300), who exercised a general supervision over the religious life of the Romans. Members of these colleges were selected by co-optation and were originally limited to patricians. Plebeians were admitted to the college of *decemviri sacris faciundis* in 364 [367], of priests and augurs in 300. But members of the three colleges were always drawn from the best senatorial families, be they patrician or plebeian, and individual augurs, *decemviri*, and priests pursued full political and military careers like other Roman aristocrats.

The internal political history of the early Republic centers on the STRUGGLE OF THE ORDERS—the campaign by **plebeians** to break the political and religious monopoly of the **patricians** and to relieve the economic distress of poor citizens. In the early 5th century, the plebeians organized their own assembly, the *concilium plebis*, whose resolutions, called *plebiscita*, were binding only on plebeians. The plebs elected their own officials, *tribuni plebis* (plebeian tribunes), and two *aediles plebis* (plebeian aediles), who handled fines imposed by the tribunes or the *concilium*. The plebeian tribunes at first numbered either two, four, or five but by sometime in the 5th century had reached their canonical number of ten. They were elected by and presided over the *concilium plebis* and, in order to carry out their mandate to defend the lives and property of plebeians against patrician magistrates, they exercised a veto (*intercessio*) over laws, elections, and the acts of magistrates. The plebeians swore an oath binding themselves to avenge any injury done to the tribunes and making their persons inviolate.

505 [509]. L. Junius Brutus and L. Tarquinius Collatinus were supposedly the first pair of consuls.

504 [508]. A very early treaty between Carthage and the new Republic, confirming Rome's dominant position in Latium, was later attributed to this year. Tradition said that shortly after Tarquinius's explusion, **Lars Porsenna**, the king of Etruscan Clusium, attacked Rome; he may well have captured it. Later he was apparently defeated by the Latins at the Battle of Aricia (504).

495 [499] or 492 [496]. On this antiquarian date the dictator A. Postumius defeated the Latins in the **Battle of Lake Regillus.**

491 [495] or 489 [493]. On this antiquarian date Sp. Cassius supposedly negotiated the treaty named after him (*foedus Cassianum*) with the Latin League, establishing a defensive alliance to combat the invasion of Latium by the **Aequi** and **Volsci.** Rome and the Latin League agreed to conduct joint annual campaigns with command alternating between Roman and Latin generals, to distribute booty equally, and to establish joint colonies on reconquered territories.

490–489 [494–493]. The antiquarian date the office of plebeian tribune and the plebeian assembly were created. These events were supposed to have happened when the plebeians, oppressed by debt, moved to the Sacred Mount to return only after patrician concessions.

473 [477]. On this antiquarian date the Fabian *gens*, fighting as a unit on behalf of Rome against the Etruscan city of Veii, was annihilated on the **Cremera** (a tributary of the Tiber).

454 [458]. On this antiquarian date **L. Quinctius Cincinnatus** was called from his farm to become dictator and then defeated the Aequi.

c. 447 [451]. **Agitation of the plebs** for the codification of law led to the creation of **ten patrician decemviri** in the place of consuls and tribunes. The first decemviri published ten tables of laws that proved insufficient, so new decemviri created in 446 [450] added two more tables. The **TWELVE TABLES** set out the basic rules for civil law, confirming the privileges of patricians. This was the last codification of Roman law until the 3rd century C.E. Shortly after the writing of the Twelve Tables there was a plebeian protest, supposedly in 445 [449].

445 [449]. **The Second Secession** of the plebs supposedly occurred, followed by the election of tribunes and then of patrician consuls L. Valerius and M. Horatius. The latter passed a series of **Valerio-Horatian** laws, whose provisions are obscure, though important. They perhaps established *provocatio*, the right of appeal of magisterial decisions, and affirmed the inviolability of the tribunes and also the aediles.

441 [445]. On this antiquarian date, the **lex Canuleia** took effect, which allowed marriage between patricians and plebeians, with children inheriting the father's status.

440 [444]. Two patrician **censors** were created. Either as a compromise in the face of plebeian agitation that the consulship be opened to plebeians, or as a measure to meet increased military commands, **military tribunes with consular power,** who might be plebeians, were created. These alternated irregularly with consuls until 363 [367].

427 [431]. The dictator A. Postumius Tubertus decisively defeated the Aequi at the Algidus Pass.

392 [396]. The seige of **Veii**, during which pay for the Roman army was allegedly introduced, was ended when the dictator **M. Furius Camillus** captured and destroyed the city. Veian territory was annexed and Roman territory doubled.

386 [390]. Rome was sacked by the Gauls under Brennus, who defeated the Roman army on the Allia on July 18.

363 [367]. **Licinio-Sextian Laws.** After ten years of agitation, the tribunes C. Licinius and L. Sextius passed a reform package which probably included: (1) some sort of debt relief; (2) a limit of 500 *iugera* (one *iugerum* = five-eighths of an acre) as the amount of *ager publicus* (public land) that any citizen could hold, and (3) abolition of the office of consular tribunes and restoration of the consulship now opened to plebeians. The office of *praetor urbanus* was created. Two patrician *curule aediles* were created with functions much like that of the plebeian aediles.

363–345 [367–349]. Four wars were fought with Gauls who raided central Italy, during which T. Manlius Torquatus in 357 [361] and M. Valerius Corvus in 345 [349] defeated Gallic champions in single combat.

358–341 [362–345]. Wars were fought with the **Hernici** and some Latin cities. The latter were forced into the Latin League 354 [358]. The *foedus Cassianum* was renewed.

344 [348]. The second treaty between Rome and Carthage, which some consider to be the first, was struck (p. 37).

339–337 [343–341]. **The First Samnite War** was started by a request for aid by Campanians against the Samnites. After minor Roman victories, the war ended in a draw.

337–334 [341–338]. **The Latin War** began with the revolt of Latin cities against Roman domination of the league. In 336 [340] the consul P. Decius Mus sacrificed himself to the gods to ensure a victory (*devotio*). Roman victory was secured at the **Battle of Trifanum.**

f. THE CONQUEST OF ITALY

334 [338]. **The Latin League was dissolved,** and its former members forfeited an independent foreign policy, being bound to Rome by the various methods discussed below.

323 [326] or 310 [313]. The **lex Poetelia** abolished *nexum* (debt-bondage).

323–303 [326–304]. **THE SECOND SAMNITE WAR** began when Rome violated a treaty by establishing a Latin colony across the Liris River at Fregellae. The war was fought principally in Samnium. After initial successes from 323–320 [326–322], a Roman army was trapped at the **Caudine Forks** in 319 [321], and Rome was forced to negotiate an unfavorable peace. Rome resumed hostilities in 314 [316], suffered a defeat at Lautulae 313 [315], but soon reversed its fortunes. In 304 [305] the Samnites were decisively defeated and forced to sign a peace in 303 [304], giving sole hegemony of Campania to Rome.

310 [312]. **Appius Claudius** (later Caecus, "the blind") as censor distributed freedmen among the rural tribes (in 302 [304] freedmen were confined once again to the four urban tribes).

298–290. The **THIRD SAMNITE WAR** was the final effort by the Samnites—aided by the Etruscans, Umbrians, and Gauls—to halt Roman domination. In 295 a large force of Samnites and Gauls was defeated at Sentinum, where a second Decius Mus was reputed to have secured a Roman victory by a *devotio*—that is, by seeking death in battle in exchange for divine assurance of Roman victory. The Gauls scattered, the Etruscans sued for peace in 294, and the Samnites finally surrendered in 290. Samnite land was taken, and Latin colonies were established on it. In 290 the Sabines were given Latin rights.

287. After a period of violence and the Third Secession of the plebs to the Janiculum, the dictator Q. Hortensius passed the **lex Hortensia.** It made *plebiscita* passed by the *concilium plebis* binding on all Romans. This marked the legal end to the Struggle of the Orders and the formation of a **joint patrician-plebeian nobility.**

284–283. The Romans defeated a Gallic army at Lake Vadimon in Etruria and then annexed the land of the Senones (the *ager Gallicus*) along the Adriatic.

282–272. **WAR WITH PYRRHUS** arose from Roman occupation of Thurii, a Greek city of Magna Graecia. The Tarentines sunk four Roman ships that had violated a treaty by sailing into Tarentine waters and expelled a Roman garrison from Thurii. Rome declared war, and the Tarentines called in **King Pyrrhus** of Epirus. In 280, Pyrrhus suffered heavy casualties but won a "Pyrrhic victory" over the Romans at **Heraclea** in Lucania. The Bruttii, Lucani, and Samnites joined Pyrrhus, but the

Roman senate, rallied by the blind ex-censor Ap. Claudius, rejected the peace offer of Cineas, Pyrrhus's ambassador. In 279 Pyrrhus won a hard-fought victory at **Ausculum.**

279–276. Pyrrhus campaigned in Sicily (p. 75) and returned to Italy to be defeated by Rome at Beneventum in 275. He went back to Greece, leaving his general, Milo, to surrender Tarentum to the Romans in 272. Rome garrisoned Tarentum and other Italiot Greek cities; reduced the Bruttii, Lucani, and Samnites; and took Rhegium from the Mamertines in 270. Minor rebellions in Etruria occurred until 264.

Rome's aggressive foreign policy had won it domination of all Italy south of the Po Valley. In its relationships with other communities, Rome denied them an independent foreign policy but customarily permitted local autonomy. Italian communities outside the *ager Romanus* (Roman territory immediately around Rome), fell into the following main categories:

(1) *Municipia* or *praefecturae.* These were states, such as Capua and Cumae, whose governments managed their own internal affairs, subject to the supervision of a Roman official called *praefectus Capuam Cumas.* Their aristocrats were full Roman citizens, while others were *cives sine suffragio* (Roman citizens without the vote).

(2) *Old Latin states.* States such as Tibur and Praeneste, defeated in the Latin War, retained autonomous governments by the treaty of 338. They passed their own laws, managed their internal affairs, and retained the Latin rights of *ius migrationis,* by which citizens could move to Rome and become Roman citizens. They were obliged to provide soldiers for Rome, but not tribute.

(3) *Colonies of Roman citizens.* These were established for defensive purposes, usually on land taken from conquered peoples, and comprised about 300 Roman citizens. They did not have independent local governments. Eight of these had been founded by 264, all coastal.

(4) *Latin colonies.* These were established as military outposts on conquered land and usually had 2,500–4,000 settlers drawn from Rome or Latin communities. The colonists had the status of Latins, and their governments, modeled on that of Rome, passed their own laws and managed their internal affairs. They were obliged to provide soldiers for Rome, but not tribute.

(5) *Civitates foederatae, socii* (allied states). The great majority of Italic states fell into this category. Most had been defeated by Rome and had suffered confiscation of land which became *ager publicus* of Rome. Their governments passed their own laws and managed internal affairs, subject to interference from Rome. They had to contribute troops to Rome, but did not pay tribute.

2. THE REPUBLIC, 264–70 B.C.E.

a. GEOGRAPHY AND CLIMATE

During this period Rome acquired a Mediterranean empire that comprised the following areas:

(1) Sicily's eastern end is mountainous and dominated by Etna. Farther west, a central plateau recedes into a coastal plain toward the south. There were fine harbors at Syracuse on the east, at Panormus on the north, and at Drepana on the west. Sicily's major rivers were navigable in antiquity, and its mountains were heavily forested. Excellent volcanic soil produced an extraordinary yield and a variety of crops; by the mid-third century, Sicily was the major exporter of grain in the Mediterranean. The hills of the interior contained good summer grazing land and made Sicily a major exporter of wool, as well as the home of outstanding horses and livestock. Sicily's climate follows the Mediterranean pattern and, except for a longer summer's drought lasting four months, is like that of peninsular Italy. Before the Romans, eastern Sicily was held by the **Greeks;** Phoenicians inhabited the west; and Sicels lived in isolated communities in the interior.

(2) Located in the Po Valley, **Cisalpine Gaul** had a continental climate with summers that were cooler, and winters that were harsher, but not as wet as those of peninsular Italy. Although rainfall was well distributed over the seasons, melting snow caused frequent flooding and permanent swamps, especially in the east. The region was covered with dense forests that provided timber as well as a home to large herds of pigs. Forest clearing and drainage made Cisalpine Gaul into an enormously fertile land, producing prodigious yields of grain and, in the southern regions, abundant wine harvests. Good grazing land provided a wide variety of fine wools. Once drained, the flat plain facilitated road building and overland trade, while navigation on the Po River was possible as far as Turin. The Po Valley was inhabited by three principal Celtic tribes: the **Boii** in the south, the **Cenomani** in the center, and the **Insubres** in the north. To the east in Venetia lived the Veneti, and to the west in the Apennines lived the Ligurians, both non-Celtic peoples.

(3) The **Spanish peninsula** comprises an elevated central plateau whose climate is continental and whose sparse rainfall makes it suitable for pasturage rather than agriculture. On the north and south are high mountains, forested in antiquity—the Pyrenees and Sierra Nevada, respectively. Lower interior mountains border fertile river valleys—Baetis (Guadalquivir) and Ebro—that lead down to fertile coastal plains. Spanish agriculture was noted for its cereals, wines, and especially olive oil, while flax was a specialty of the Ebro Valley. Spain's mountains were particularly abundant in minerals—copper, iron, and, in the Sierra Morena, prodigious amounts of silver. There were good harbors on the southern coast at Gades and Carthago Nova. **Celtiberians** inhabited the north-central plateau, to the west were **Lusitanians,** and throughout the rest of the peninsula lived some 20 other independent peoples. (For the other area of the empire—the Balkan Peninsula, Asia Minor, Syria, and North Africa—see p. 94.)

b. ECONOMY, SOCIETY, AND CULTURE

In 225, Roman citizens living in all parts of Italy numbered about 280,000; the free population was between 3,000,000 and 3,500,000; and slaves brought the total population to over 5 million. Foreign wars of the 3rd century brought significant numbers of slaves to Italy, and during the 2nd century the number of war captives vastly increased. Between 225 B.C.E. and 14 C.E., the population of Italy seems to have increased by 50 percent, slaves accounting for most of the increase. The economy of Italy was consequently transformed by the **slave labor,** which was fundamental to the creation of *latifundia*—large, scattered estates devoted in part to the production of grapes and olives. The upper classes invested wealth newly acquired from conquests in these estates. To facilitate such investments, **small citizen farmers,** many of whom were also burdened by extended military service, were pressured to **leave their land** and emigrate to Rome. The consequent **economic dislocation** led to chronic social and political problems. The devastation during the Hannibalic War of large stretches of Italian land, particularly in the south, also contributed to the growth of *latifundia,* as well as that of large-scale sheep farming. Much of this land was confiscated by Rome and rented as *ager publicus* to wealthy citizens. To meet the needs of a city swelled by immigrants and slaves, as well as those of Rome's armies, **grain was imported** on a large scale, primarily from Sicily. Sometime before the mid-third century, wheat *(triticum)* had displaced emmer *(far),* allowing bread to replace porridge as the staple of the diet, although Greeks continued to refer to Romans as "porridge eaters." Public bakeries were said to have been introduced in Rome c. 170. After the disruptions of the Pyrrhic and First Punic wars, **trade** revived. Grain, metals, slaves, and wines were imported into Italy, and beginning with the second half of the 3rd century, wines of Latium, Campania, and Etruria began to be exported to the Adriatic, and later, to southern France. The 2nd-century conquests of Spain and Cisalpine Gaul, and then of the Aegean, opened up markets which were fully exploited by Roman and Italian businessmen who brought wealth to the towns of Italy, as well as to the capital. The earliest Roman money was minted in bronze, beginning in the 4th century. The first silver coinage was produced c. 300, and what would become the standard silver coin—the *denarius*—was first issued in 211. Like all ancient states, Rome produced coinage to facilitate the collection of taxes and state payments, not to encourage trade. **A technological revolution** occurred when the traditional method of building in stone was replaced by stronger, more flexible, and cheaper **concrete** construction, with the discovery of *pozzolana* mortar made from volcanic stone. Cement's first use was purely functional, that is, the building of the warehouse—the *Porticus Aemilia*, in Rome's new dockyards (193). By the century's end cement was being fully exploited in the construction of vaulted and terraced sanctuaries, such as that at Praenestae, and in high-rise urban tenements.

The **Roman family** had become nuclear and smaller by the 2nd century, and most **marriages** seem to have been *sine manu* (without authority). **Restrictions on women** were legislated—the **lex Voconia** (169) limited the amount a woman could inherit by will. But by the 1st century these and other restrictions could be circumvented by various legal dodges, and a woman who was *sui iuris* (independent) could acquire considerable freedom—to transfer property and to divorce—through a legal device which permitted her to select her own guardian. Educated Greeks began working as teachers in the early 3rd century, and Rome's first **elementary school** opened in 234. By the mid- to late 2nd century most upper-class Romans knew some Greek; literacy in Latin existed among the elite, and, to a lesser degree, among skilled craftsmen. With the ending of the Struggle of the Orders, a **new nobility** of office-holding families, both patricians and plebeians, grew up. A man without office-holding ancestors was called a **novus homo,** or "new man," and required the help of a nobleman to obtain high office.

A major **social change** that occurred during the 3rd and 2nd centuries was the growing **disparity of wealth,** owing to the unequal distribution of riches acquired from foreign conquests. The traditional aristocratic practice of spending on public building was augmented by private spending and public largess. Viewed as *luxuria,* such conduct raised opposition expressed in the form of censorial reprimands, **sumptuary laws** (in 215, 181, 161, and 115), and numerous speeches. This prompted the wealthy to seek the pleasures of a Hellenic private life in **suburban villas** or, beginning in the 170s, in villas in **Greek Campania.**

From the 3rd century on, the major **cultural phenomena** were **Hellenism** and, beginning in the mid-second century, the articulation of a Roman culture that attempted to define itself, first in literature then in art, in opposition to Hellenism. **Latin literature** began formally in 240 with the translation of a Greek play by **Livius Andronicus,** a Greek freedman who had been captured at Tarentum in 272 and who also translated Homer's *Odyssey.* Before Livius, Latin poetry consisted of hymns and drinking songs. Greek culture continued to exercise its influence as seen in the Latin epic on the First Punic War, *Bellum Punicum,* by **Cn. Naevius** (c. 270–200), who also composed dramas. Enormously popular Latin comedies modeled on Greek originals were written by **T. Maccius Plautus** (?–184). **Q. Ennius** wrote in many genres and produced the national epic, the *Annales,* in a Greek meter (dactylic hexameter). The comic tradition was carried on by the highly regarded **P. Terentius Afer** (194–159), **Caecilis Statius** (fl. 179), and **L. Afranius** (c. 160–120). Tragedies were written by **M. Pacuvius** (220–131), a nephew of Ennius who was also a noted painter, and by **L. Accius** (170–87). It was **C. Lucilius** who invented the Roman genre of satire. Rome's earliest historians, **Q. Fabius Pictor, L. Alimentus, A. Postumius Albinus,** and **C. Acilius,** composed in Greek. The first to write a history in Latin was the "new man" from Tusculum, **M. Porcius Cato** (234–149), whose *Origines* was about Rome and Italy. Cato also wrote a treatise on agriculture and numerous influential speeches. He was a critic of Greek culture. In 173 and 161, Greek philosophers were banished from Rome. Noted Roman orators included **C. Sempronius Gracchus** (154–121), **M. Antonius** (c. 140–87), and **L. Licinius Crassus** (140–91). **Q. Mucius Scaevola** (c. 140–82) wrote to organize Roman civil law by Greek logical categories. Beginning with the 3rd century, **Roman art** celebrated victory, its principal manifestations being representations of battles or triumphant generals and the decoration of Rome with **art plundered** from major Hellenistic capitals—Syracuse and Tarentum, and later, Corinth and Carthage. By the mid-second century, Rome's wealth was attracting artists from all over the Greek world. The result was that **eclecticism** became a fundamental element of Roman art. It was in **portrait sculpture** that Roman art sought to define itself against Greek models by stressing hard-headed maturity, warts and all (realism), over beauty and youth. **Architecture** remained conservative in the 3rd century, continuing to produce tra-

ditional Italic temples, along with aqueducts—the *Anio Vetus* (272), and roads—the *Via Aurelia* (241) and the *Via Flaminia* (c. 220). The **basilica,** a building type with multiple civic functions, was introduced to Rome in the early 2nd century. The first stone bridge, the *Pons Aemilia,* was begun in 179; in 144 a large new aqueduct, the *Aqua Marcia,* was constructed, followed by the *Aqua Tepula* (125). In religious architecture, distinctively **Greek influences** began to appear both in plan and building material (e.g., the round temple in the *Forum Boarium,* c. 146 or 125, which in form resembles a Greek *tholos* and which was built with imported Attic Pentalic marble). **Private architecture** was marked by the addition of the Greek **peristyle** garden to the Italic atrium house and by the construction of large luxury villas outside of Rome. Romans followed the Greek fashion of decorating their houses with painting. The **First or "Masonry" Style** imitated marble architectural decoration in single-dimensional painted walls.

c. THE PUNIC WARS

264–241. The **FIRST PUNIC WAR** arose from the Roman decision to accept the appeal of the **Mamertines**—Campanian mercenaries in Messana—to aid them against King Hiero of Syracuse and the Carthaginians (p. 75). In 264 Ap. Claudius Pulcher defeated the Carthaginians and Hiero and besieged Syracuse; Hiero shifted his alliance to Rome.

262. After sacking Agrigentum, the Romans decided to expel the Carthaginians entirely from Sicily.

260. The Romans under C. Duilius won the **naval victory of Mylae.**

256. A Roman army under M. Atilius Regulus landed in Africa. Carthage rejected Regulus's stringent terms and continued resistance under the Spartan mercenary Xanthippus.

255. Xanthippus captured Regulus and part of his army.

254. Rome seized **Panormus** and, in 250, began an unsuccessful nine-year siege of **Lilybaeum.**

244. The Romans failed to dislodge the Carthaginian general **Hamilcar Barca** from the promontory of Eryx.

241. At the **Aegates Islands** C. Lutatius Catulus destroyed the Carthaginian fleet. Carthage eventually negotiated peace on the condition of the surrender of Sicily and a payment of 3,200 talents over ten years. At Rome the final two **voting tribes** were created, making a total of 35 in the tribal assembly. Sometime between 241 and 217, the *comitia centuriata* was reorganized to make it partially correspond to the tribal system. The reform was democratic to the extent that it reduced the number of voting units (centuries) of the wealthiest first class from 80 to 70, to produce a multiple of the 35 tribes of the more egalitarian tribal assembly, and that it transferred the right of first vote from the elite equestrian centuries to those of the first class.

237 (238?). Carthage, weakened in the recent **Mercenary War** (241–238), was blackmailed by the threat of war into surrendering **Sardinia** to Rome and paying an additional 1,200 talents.

237–228. Hamilcar Barca established a Carthaginian dominion in southern and southeastern Spain.

229–228. The First Illyrian War. To suppress Illyrian pirates, Rome sent a large army and fleet, defeated Queen Teuta, and established "friendship" with the Greek cities of Illyria.

227. Sicily (excluding Hiero's Syracusan kingdom in the east), and Sardinia and Corsica together, became Rome's first two **provinces,** administered by two new praetors.

226. Rome struck a treaty with Carthage, making the **Ebro River** the northern extent of Carthaginian dominion in Spain.

225–222. A large Gallic army moved from the Po Valley into Etruria. The Romans destroyed it at Telamon, then proceeded to expel the Gauls from the Po Valley.

220. Two colonies, Cremona and Placentia, were founded in the Po Valley, and the *Via Flaminia* was built from Rome to Ariminum.

219. The Second Illyrian War. Rome defeated Demetrius of Pharos and Queen Teuta's successor, Scerdilaidas.

218. A *plebiscitum Claudianum* forbade senators and their sons to own a ship of more than 300 *amphoras.*

218–201. The **SECOND PUNIC WAR** arose from Rome's jealousy of Carthaginian expansion in Spain. Some time either before or after the Ebro Treaty (226), Rome had made an alliance with Saguntum, one hundred miles south of the Ebro. **Hannibal,** the twenty-five-year-old son of Hamilcar who assumed command in 221, refused to be bullied by Roman threats and sacked Saguntum in 219. Rome declared war the next year.

218. Hannibal marched his army through southern France, across the Alps, and into the Po Valley. The consul **P. Cornelius Scipio** was defeated by Hannibal at the **Ticinus,** a branch of the Po River. Hannibal then defeated the other consul at the **Battle of the Trebia.** The Gauls of the Po Valley rallied to Hannibal.

217. Hannibal crossed the Apennines and ambushed and annihilated the army of the consul C. Flaminius at **Lake Trasimene.**

216. The consuls L. Aemilius Paullus and C. Terentius Varro lost an army of 86,000 to Hannibal at **Cannae,** in Apulia. Capua deserted to Hannibal, along with the Samnites, Lucanians, and other peoples of southern Italy. The Romans refused Hannibal's terms and sent out an army under M. Claudius Marcellus. Carthage made alliances with Philip V of Macedon and Hieronymus, grandson of Hiero of Syracuse, who had died in 217. Hannibal wintered at Capua.

215. **Marcellus** defeated Hannibal at **Nola** and forced him into Apulia.

218–211. Publius Scipio had rejoined his brother Gnaeus in Spain. They kept Hasdrubal (Hannibal's brother) busy and stirred up Syphax, king of western Numidia, against Carthage.

215–205. By using a few troops for the **First Macedonian War,** the Romans prevented Philip from helping Hannibal. In 211 they organized a Greek alliance, under the lead of the Aetolians **(Treaty of Naupactus).** In 206, Rome was forced to make the **Peace of Phoenice.**

214–210. Marcellus saved Sicily and the war by **capturing Syracuse** in 211, despite the ingenious defensive machinery devised by Archimedes. Hieronymus (p. 75) having been killed, his kingdom was incorporated into the Roman province, giving Rome control of all Sicily.

212. Hannibal seized Tarentum. Both Scipios were slain in Spain.

211. Capua surrendered to Rome and was deprived of all self-government.

210. P. Cornelius Scipio, son of the late general, was sent to Spain with proconsular powers, though only 25 years old.

209. Scipio captured New Carthage in Spain. Marcellus checked Hannibal and Fabius captured Tarentum. In the following year, Hasdrubal evaded Scipio and reached the Po Valley.

208. Marcellus was killed in an ambush.

207. In the **Battle of the Metaurus River** M. Livius Salinator defeated and slew Hasdrubal. Hannibal withdrew to Bruttium.

206. Scipio drove the Carthaginians out of Spain and made a secret treaty with their ally Massinissa of Numidia. He returned to Italy and was elected consul for 205.

204. Scipio invaded Africa and defeated the Carthaginians (203). Carthage was forced to recall Hannibal, who attempted in vain to negotiate.

202. In the **Battle of Zama,** Scipio annihilated the Carthaginian army, though Hannibal escaped.

201. Carthage accepted **Rome's terms:** surrender of Spain and all other Mediterranean islands, transfer of Numidia to Massinissa, payment of 200 talents a year for 50 years, destruction of all except 10 warships, and promise not to make war without Rome's permission. Scipio, now entitled *Africanus,* celebrated a splendid triumph. The unfaithful Italian allies were forced to cede land and were deprived of some autonomy.

d. CONQUEST OF THE MEDITERRANEAN

201–190. Annual campaigns were conducted in **Cisalpine Gaul** against the Cenomani, Insubres, and Boii until 190.

200–197. The **SECOND MACEDONIAN WAR.** Encouraged by Pergamum, Rhodes, and Athens, the senate resolved to make war on **Philip V** of Macedon and frightened an unwilling *comitia centuriata* into declaring war by visions of a renewed invasion of Italy. **T. Quinctius Flamininus,** supported by both the Aetolian and Achaean Leagues, finally (197) defeated Philip at **Cynoscephalae** in Thessaly and forced him to make peace (196) on the following terms: surrender of all cities in Greece; payment of 1,000 talents in 10 years; reduction of his navy to five ships; promise not to declare war without permission of Rome.

At the ensuing Isthmian Games, Flamininus proclaimed the **independence of the Greek cities.**

197–180. Regulation of the *cursus honorum* (succession of offices). After 197, candidates for the consulship had to have held the praetorship. In 180, the *lex Villia annalis* established minimum ages for magistracies.

197–155. Roman armies invaded **Liguria** almost yearly until 172. The region was not conquered until 155.

197–175. Two provinces were created in 197—Nearer Spain *(Hispania Citerior)* in the Ebro Valley, and Farther Spain *(Hispania Ulterior)* in the Baetis Valley. The Romans began war with the Celtiberians in 195, and with the Lusitanians in 193, and campaigned until victory in 175.

192–189. THE SYRIAN WAR (p. 73). Failed negotiations with Rome over Greece and Asia led Antiochus III, invited by the Aetolians, to invade Greece, but M. Acilius Glabrio routed his forces at Thermopylae (191).

190. The Roman army, under **L. Cornelius Scipio** (later *Asiaticus*) and his brother Scipio Africanus, crossed the Hellespont and defeated Antiochus in the **Battle of Magnesia.** By the **Treaty of Apamea** (189), Antiochus was obliged to surrender all European and Asiatic possessions north of the Taurus Mountains, and pay 15,000 talents in 12 years. Rome divided the Anatolian territory of Antiochus between Pergamum and Rhodes and aided Eumenes II of Pergamum against the Galatians (189). In Greece, Rome subjected the Aetolians but left the other cities free.

171–167. The **THIRD MACEDONIAN WAR.** Uneasy over the dealing in Greece of Philip's successor Perseus, and encouraged by Pergamum, Rome declared war. After several unsuccessful campaigns, the Romans placed L. Aemilius Paullus in command.

168. Battle of Pydna. Paullus defeated Perseus and brought him back to Rome in a triumphal procession. So great was the booty and tribute that Roman citizens were thereafter relieved of direct taxation. Macedonia was broken up into four wholly distinct confederacies. Illyria was reduced to three tributary confederacies, and Epirus was devastated. From the Achaean cities 1,000 of the chief citizens were taken as hostages and kept in Italy for 16 years. Rome likewise dictated to Eumenes of Pergamum, to Rhodes, and to Antiochus IV, who was prevented by the ambassador C. Popilius Laenas from making war on the Ptolemies of Egypt.

154–133. A major rebellion broke out in Spain. The Celtiberians were brought to terms in 151; the Lusitanians, under Viriathus, fought on until 139. The city of Numantia was taken by **P. Cornelius Scipio Aemilianus** in 133.

149. The tribune L. Calpurnius Piso enacted a *lex Calpurnia* which set up a permanent commission of senators to hear the suits of provincials to recover from governors money unjustly collected *(quaestio de rebus repetundis).* Decisions were motivated not by justice but by class selfishness.

149–146. The **THIRD PUNIC WAR** arose from alarm and hatred among conservative Romans over Carthage's economic revival. Carthage had completed its 50 years of indemnity payment in 152. The occasion was an attack by Carthage (150) on Rome's ally, Massinissa. The Carthaginians offered submission but refused to vacate their city. With almost no resources they withstood a siege until **Scipio Aemilianus** captured and **destroyed Carthage** (146). The Romans organized a small area around Carthage as the province of Africa but left the rest to the sons of Massinissa (d. 149).

149–148. THE FOURTH MACEDONIAN WAR. A pretended son of Perseus, Andriscus, provoked the war but was defeated by Q. Caecilius Metellus. In 146 Macedonia became a Roman province.

146. Against Roman orders, the **Achaeans made war on Sparta.** They were defeated by Metellus and L. Mummius. The latter sacked Corinth, sent its art treasures to Rome, sold its inhabitants into slavery, and burned the city (at the order of the Roman senate). The remaining Greek cities retained a certain measure of autonomy under the governor of Macedonia, though they paid tribute. Not until later (127) did they become organized as the Province of Achaea.

135–132. The **First Servile War** broke out when the ill-treated slaves of the large Sicilian estates revolted under the Syrian Eunus, who called himself King Antiochus. Eunus held Henna and Tauromenium against Roman armies but was finally captured and his supporters brutally executed.

By 133 Rome possessed nine overseas provinces. The methods employed by the Romans to organize their Italian conquests proved inadequate for these territories. Rome determined to **administer provinces** by maintaining an army in the conquered territory and placing it under the command of a magistrate with *imperium* (a consul or praetor), who also exercised a supervisory judicial function. Thus the word *provincia*, which traditionally signified a magistrate's sphere of military responsibility, came to have the territorial denotation of **"province."** The inhabitants of overseas provinces were required to pay **annual tribute** to Rome, but not ordinarily to send soldiers to fight in Rome's wars. Since the staff of a provincial magistrate was small, interference with local communities was limited to maintaining order and ensuring the collection of tribute. The growing number of provinces, together with Rome's other increasing military commitments, created the need for more magistrates capable of commanding armies. **Additional praetors** were elected—two in 227 for Sicily and Sardinia-Corsica, and two in 197 for the two Spanish provinces—raising the **total to six** a year, but the more economical solution of **prolonging provincial commands** was adopted. It was within the discretion of the senate to extend or "prorogue" the *imperium* of magistrates, making them **proconsuls** or **propraetors.** Empire also increased administrative needs. Field armies had to be equipped, roads built and maintained, and tribute collected. Rome had a very scant civil service because such tasks were contracted out through bidding conducted every five years by the censors to companies of private businessmen (**publicani**). As the Empire grew, such contracts became lucrative and attracted members of Rome's wealthy nonpolitical class—the *equites* or knights. The system led to corruption and abuse of provincials by both senatorial governors and the *publicani,* and eventually created serious conflicts of interest between equestrians and the senatorial class responsible for governing. A further effect of transmarine provinces was the necessity for a **standing provincial army.** Citizen soldiers stationed in provinces were not only prohibited from returning to their farms for harvest or for winter—that had been impractical for some time—but could be kept in overseas service for up to six consecutive years, with serious economic and social consequences.

e. DOMESTIC STRIFE

Foreign conquests engendered domestic changes and problems. Among them were: (1) the growth of large estates and slave labor in Italian agriculture; (2) the flight of citizen farmers from the land; (3) consequent shortages of military manpower, since military service was based on a property qualification that could no longer be met; (4) the danger of slave revolt; (5) increased aristocratic competition for high office, and the growing rift between the interests of senators and *equites;* (6) a swelling poor urban population; (7) and, behind it all, the desire of the Italian allied states to have Roman citizenship. During the 2nd century, these problems were manifested in various ways; they came to a head with the tribunate of Tiberius Gracchus in 133.

133. Ti. Sempronius Gracchus as plebeian tribune proposed an **agrarian law** that limited holding of public land to 500 *iugera* (312 acres) per person, with an additional 250 *iugera* for each son, thereby threatening the wealthy and certain Italian cities. The measure was vetoed by another tribune, but Tiberius had him deposed, and the bill passed. A commission of three began to confiscate land held in violation of the law and to **distribute lots** of 30 *iugera* to **landless Romans.** To finance his program, Tiberius proposed that Attalus's bequest of Pergamum be used, intruding on a senatorial prerogative in foreign affairs. Violating custom, Tiberius stood for a second tribunate. During the voting, Tiberius and 300 followers were murdered by conservative senators.

129. The kingdom of Pergamum was organized into the **province of Asia.**

123–122. The **Tribunates of C. Sempronius Gracchus.** Gaius Gracchus proposed a more extensive program aimed to win wider support against conservative opposition. He reaffirmed his brother's **agrarian law** and legislated for founding **colonies** at Tarentum, Capua, and Carthage. For the urban poor he passed a **grain bill** that subsidized prices. He transferred membership on **extortion juries** from senators to equestrians, giving the latter power over senatorial governors. He also won equestrian support by giving the right of collecting the **taxes of the province of Asia** to Roman *publicani.* He proposed that **Roman citi-**zenship be given to Latin communities and that Latin rights be given to the Italian allies. Conservative senators divided Gaius's support by playing to the plebeian unwillingness to share the citizenship. Gaius was defeated in his bid for a third tribunate.

121. When conservatives attempted to annul Gaius's colony bill, riots ensued. The senate passed the *senatus consultum ultimum*—**SCU**—which permitted the consuls to execute without trial any citizen deemed to be a danger to the Republic. Gaius and 3,000 of his supporters were then attacked and killed in the city. The Gracchan crisis caused a divide in subsequent Roman politics between **optimates,** conservatives who opposed the Gracchan approach, and **populares** who supported it.

125–118. Roman armies campaigned in Transalpine Gaul in 125–124. The **province of Gallia Narbonensis** was created in 121(?), and the colony of **Narbo** founded in 118.

111–105. The **Jugurthine War** resulted when the kingdom of Numidia was usurped by **Jugurtha,** who eventually had to fight Q. Caecilius Metellus (Numidicus). The latter won victories but failed to end the war.

107. Gaius Marius, a new man, while Metellus's legate and against senatorial opposition, won the consulship and the Jugurthine command. Refused funds for an army, Marius enlisted **volunteers** without the requisite **property qualification.** The Roman legion was reformed, the **cohort** replacing the **maniple** as the tactical unit.

107–105. Marius ended the Jugurthine War and triumphed in Rome.

105. German tribes—**Cimbri** and **Teutones**—had been defeating Roman armies in the north since 113. In 105 they wiped out two consular armies at Arausio (Orange).

104–100. Marius was elected consul for five consecutive years to combat the German threat.

102. Marius followed the Teutoni to **Aquae Sextiae** *(Aix en Provence)* and annihilated them.

101. Marius defeated the Cimbri at **Vercellae** in northern Italy and was hailed as savior of Italy.

100. Marius employed the *popularis* tribune, **L. Appuleius Saturninus,** to secure a land bill for his veterans. When electoral violence broke out, the senate passed the **SCU** against Saturninus and his followers, who were arrested by Marius and killed by a mob.

91. The tribune **M. Livius Drusus** proposed a comprehensive program that included a grain bill, a colony bill, mixed senatorial-equestrian juries, and, most important, Roman citizenship for the now desperate and bellicose Italian allies. United opposition voided Livius's laws, Livius himself was assassinated, and the Italians prepared for a war of secession against Rome.

f. WAR AND POLITICS, TO 70 B.C.E.

91–87. THE SOCIAL WAR (War of the Allies). Italian allied states formed their own republic, **Italia,** and declared war on Rome. Latin communities, together with Etruscans and Umbrians, remained loyal.

90. The *lex Iulia* extended **Roman citizenship to all Italians,** thus undermining Italian solidarity. The new citizens, however, were enrolled in only eight tribes, severely limiting their voting power.

89–88. Roman victories effectively ended the war, though it dragged into 87. Before it was over, 50,000 had died on each side and Italy was devastated.

88–84. First Mithridatic War. Taking advantage of the Social War and Greek hatred of Rome, **Mithridates VI Eupator** of Pontus invaded Bithynia and the province of Asia. **L. Cornelius Sulla,** a successful optimate general in the Social War and consul in 88, received the command against Mithridates.

88–82. CIVIL WAR broke out in Rome when a *popularis* tribune, **P. Sulpicius Rufus,** passed laws distributing new Italian citizens through the 35 tribes and transferring the Mithridatic command to Marius. Sulla **marched his army on Rome,** killed his opponents (Sulpicius among them—Marius escaped), passed conservative laws, and then left to fight in the east as proconsul of 87.

87–84. The *popularis* consul of 87, **L. Cornelius Cinna,** went to war with his optimate colleague and captured Rome with the support of Marius, who then began slaughtering his optimate enemies. Cinna and Marius became consuls for 86, but Marius soon died. Cinna's attempts to negotiate with Sulla were fruitless, and he died in a mutiny in 84. Meanwhile, Sulla had defeated Mithridates' generals in Greece (86–85) and driven Mithridates from Asia; then, eager to return to Italy, he made peace (85). Sulla demanded the enormous sum of 20,000 talents from the cities of Asia.

83–81. The Second Mithridatic War resulted from a Roman invasion of Cappadocia. Peace was made on the terms of 84.

83–82. Sulla landed at Brundisium, attracting talented young commanders—**M. Licinius Crassus** and **Cn. Pompeius** (Pompey). He routed his opponents in the field and in Rome "proscribed" his enemies by listing those whose lives and property were forfeited; over 2,000 died. Eighty thousand **Sullan veterans** were settled in 20 **military colonies** founded on confiscated Italian land.

82–79. Sulla was appointed **dictator for restoring the Republic.** He passed a legislative program that included: (1) increasing the senate from 300 to 600 by adding new equestrian members; (2) severely limiting the powers of plebeian tribunes and forbidding tribunes to hold further office; (3) regulating the provincial system by increasing praetors to eight, quaestors to 20, and forbidding governors to lead armies outside their provinces; (4) establishing seven additional permanent courts, in which juries were exclusively senatorial. Sulla retired in 79

and died the following year. He had tried to ensure senatorial rule and optimate supremacy against the challenges of tribunes and generals like himself.

78–77. M. Aemilius Lepidus, consul of 78, sought to undo Sulla's reform. He raised an army but was defeated in 77 by his optimate colleague, Q. Lutatius Catulus, and Pompey.

82–72. The Marian leader **Q. Sertorius** held optimate generals at bay in Spain. Pompey arrived in 77, but was not victorious until Sertorius's assassination in 72.

73–71. The Third Servile War was raised in Campania by the gladiator **Spartacus.** After many victories, he was finally defeated by **M. Licinius Crassus.**

70. Crassus and Pompey, both leading armies, united against the senate and had themselves made consuls for 70; Pompey had held no previous elective office. They abandoned the optimate cause by restoring the powers of the tribunes, reconstructing the jury panels (as one-third senators, one-third equestrians, and one-third of the next wealthiest class—*tribuni aerarii*), and reinstituting censors, who enrolled great numbers of new Italian citizens. **M. Tullius Cicero** became Rome's leading orator by successfully prosecuting C. Verres, the corrupt governor of Sicily.

3. CIVIL WAR AND RENEWAL, 70 B.C.E.–14 C.E.

a. ECONOMY, SOCIETY, AND CULTURE

In 70 B.C.E., Rome's empire comprised most of the lands bounding the Mediterranean. By 14 B.C.E., it had been extended to include, in the west, large areas of **continental Europe** (France, the low countries, and the lands bordering the Rhine and Danube Rivers), and, in the east, substantial parts of **Anatolia,** plus **Syria, Judaea,** and **Egypt.** Although the **economy** continued to be characterized by **small-scale industry,** and by **agriculture and trade** that were predominantly **local,** a substantial **Mediterranean-wide commerce** was conducted between cities united by river and maritime communications, a common material culture, and a common coinage. The potential benefits were hampered by the frequently rapacious treatment of provincial resources, by piracy, and, above all, by war. Some 200,000 Italian men were killed in the wars of 90–81; those of 49–31 claimed perhaps another 100,000. Italian agriculture was devastated by pillaging and the large-scale reallotment of land. The result was debt, lawlessness, social unrest, and economic disarray. During all this time the provincial economies were being ruthlessly exploited by Roman armies. The great achievement of the **emperor Augustus** was to end war within the Empire.

The growing complexity of economic life made the traditional system of Roman **civil law** untenable. By recognizing the praetor's *formulae,* the *lex Aebutia* (c. 150?) officially liberated the *ius civile* from the constraints of the highly formalistic and narrow rules of the legal procedure called the *legis actio* system, which had been established in the Twelve Tables. Under the new **formulary system,** the praetor "interpreted" as actionable circumstances not strictly covered by the traditional "actions," thereby greatly extending the protection of the law. The **praetor's edict** defined what formulae would be employed. These edicts were passed on to succeeding praetors, creating a body of "tralatician" law, which became the chief authority for civil law. The edicts, and the innovative interpretations they embodied, were not, however, the work of the praetors themselves, but of legal scholars *(jurisconsults)* who advised the praetors. **Criminal law** evolved from the Twelve Tables' regulation of private vengeance to a more active concern for public safety and order. Criminal actions were initiated by either magistrates or private citizens, and trials traditionally were conducted before one of the popular assemblies. Around 200, the senate entrusted certain cases to special courts, *quaestiones extraordinariae,* composed of senators and presided over by a consul or praetor. Sulla's legislation defined other types of crimes and established permanent courts to adjudicate them. Under Augustus, these permanent courts continued, but emphasis began to shift to a more expedient procedure, the *cognitio extraordinaria,* wherein a magistrate appointed by the emperor, the *praefectus urbi,* conducted trials and rendered decisions without the aid of a jury.

The late Republic was a time of great **social upheaval. Slaves continued to flood into Italy.** The slave population of Italy in 14 C.E. has been estimated at around 3 million out of a free population of about 7,500,000. Hundreds of thousands of Italian peasants were conscripted into armies to wage civil wars. For those who survived, land had to be found, and the resultant confiscations produced great numbers of dispossessed, many of whom immigrated to Rome where living conditions were worsening. Debt and violence brought about social discontent in both city and countryside, which led to the call for revolution by such men as Catiline. The **composition** of the governing **aristocracy changed.** A generation after receiving the Roman citizenship, Italian aristocrats began entering the Roman senate in numbers. The process was accelerated by civil wars, which killed off many of the old Roman nobility and provided opportunity for advancement to the capable and unscrupulous. Competition for office led aristocrats to finance ever more **spectacular public entertainment**—dramas, mimes, public banquets, and gladiatorial contests. Augustus's attempts to curb public aristocratic display were successful, but his programs to put an end to private *luxuria* failed utterly. By the late Republic, women had acquired the ability to divorce independently and to force the consent of a male guardian (tutor). Augustus **curbed the relaxing of traditional restrictions on upper-class women but released women from guardians if they had three children (four for freed women).** The numbers and influence of freedmen grew significantly; some of them gained great wealth and considerable indirect power. The primary avenue of social mobility for the Roman citizens remained the army, the vast majority of whose members came from the peasantry.

If the 1st century B.C.E. was a period of political turmoil, it was also a time of extraordinary **cultural activity.** Elite education included pursuing advanced studies in the Greek east. **Latin literature** entered its golden age. **Cicero's** (106–43) works in oratory and philosophy transformed the language. **Julius Caesar's** (100–44) masterly **commentaries** on the Gallic and Civil wars combined rapid narrative with political propaganda. **C. Sallustius Crispus** (Sallust, c. 86–c. 35) wrote two classic historical monographs—the *Catilinarian Conspiracy* and the *Jugurthine War,* as well as a major history (lost). Latin biography was composed by **Cornelius Nepos** (c. 99– c. 24), while the polymath **M. Terentius Varro** (116–27) wrote on a wide variety of subjects, including etymology, antiquities, farming, and satire; most of his work is lost. Latin poetry displayed tremendous vigor and range. **T. Lucretius Carus** (c. 94–55) penned an epic, *De Rerum Natura* (On the Nature of Things), elucidating the philosophical doctrines of Epicurus, while **C. Valerius Catullus** (87–54?) used Alexandrian models to produce an elegant and personal poetry. The vigor of late republican Latin carried over into the Age of Augustus, where it was harnessed by the patronage of the imperial court, most effectively by **C. Maecenas,** friend and adviser of Augustus. **P. Vergilius Maro** (Vergil, 70–19) wrote the pastoral *Eclogues*, then the didactic poem, *Georgics*, and finally Rome's national epic, the *Aeneid*. **Q. Horatius Flaccus** (Horace, 65–8) mastered a wide range of genres (satire, ode, and epode), while the composition of Catullan love elegies was continued by **Sextus Propertius** (c. 50–15) and **Albius Tibullus** (c. 55–19). **P. Ovidius Naso** (Ovid, 43 B.C.E.–17 C.E.) wrote elegies and a distinctively light didactic and epic poetry. **T. Livius** (Livy, 64 B.C.E.–12 C.E.) capped the annalistic tradition by writing a monumental history of Rome from its origin. In **public architecture** military dynasts of the late Republic drove less wealthy aristocrats from the field of competition and transformed the political centers of the Republic to reflect their glory. Julius Caesar and then Augustus recast the **Roman Forum** with the new Curia Iulia, the Basilica Iulia, the temple of Divus Iulius, the Portico of Gaius and Lucius, and the triumphal arches of Augustus. In addition, Caesar and Augustus built completely new fora—the Forum Iulium and the Forum of Augustus—dedicated to their personal achievements. Rome's other political center, the **Campus Martius,** was altered, first by Pompey with the erection of Rome's first stone theater in 55, then by Caesar who remodeled the *Saepta* (voting stalls). In the late Republic, works of **Greek art** continued to accumulate in Rome and Italy as a result of being brought there as war booty and of being purchased or stolen to satisfy the elite obsession with "collecting." Old masterworks were joined with copies of Greek originals to decorate private villas. Meanwhile, in public art, Roman military leaders increasingly disregarded traditional republican constraints and were portrayed in the manner of Hellenistic kings—as nudes or in equestrian statues. In wall painting the **Second Style** (60–20) created the illusion of depth, both in architectural features and in framed tableaux using theatrical and other decorative conventions from Hellenistic art. The Augustan court created a center of patronage which affected architecture and art, no less than literature. A self-consciously new architectural style—**Roman Corinthian**—was introduced, which intentionally distanced itself from its Greek predecessors (Ionic and Doric). Augustus and Agrippa changed the Campus Martius from a voting center into an area for public amenities and entertainment by building theaters, an amphitheater, a public bath, temples, and museums. The Augustan program of rebuilding and renewal made greater use of travertine and introduced Italian Carrara marble. In sculpture, official portrait types moved away from the realism of the Republic to **ideal types** (the Prima Porta Augustus). In private art, the extravagance of developed Second Style wall painting was succeeded by the **Third Style** (20 B.C.E.–20 C.E.), which abandoned the illusion of depth and emphasized the solidity of the wall. Architectural decoration in this style was intricate and fanciful rather than grand.

b. MILITARY DYNASTS AND CIVIL WARS

The years 70 to 31 witnessed the **collapse of the Roman Republic** and its replacement by military dictatorships. After Sulla, the inability of the senatorial oligarchy to find generals led to the creation of extended **special commands,** and to the **new imperialism** of Lucullus, Pompey, and Caesar.

102–67. The menace of **Mediterranean piracy** had prompted sporadic Roman responses with commands in 102, 78, 74, and 68. In 67 the *lex Gabinia* conferred an **extraordinary three-year command on Pompey.** In three months Pompey cleared the sea of pirates and pacified their homeland of Cilicia.

74–64. The Third Mithridatic War. Mithridates' opposition to the Roman annexation of Bithynia led him to attack the Roman province of Asia. The consul of 74, **L. Licinius Lucullus,** drove Mithridates out of Asia and Bithynia, and in 73 he invaded Pontus without permission of the senate. In 69 Lucullus, again on his own initiative, invaded Armenia and defeated Tigranes I, the son-in-law of Mithridates, who had been expanding into Cappadocia, Cilicia, Phoenicia, and Syria. But Lucullus's armies mutinied in 68 and 67, he failed to capture Mithridates, and he had antagonized the *publicani* by reducing the debt of Asian cities.

66–63. The *lex Manila,* spoken for by Cicero, transferred **command of the Mithridatic War to Pompey.** Pompey defeated Mithridates, then Tigranes, pursuing the former to the Crimea where he committed suicide in 63. Pompey proceeded to march through the former Seleucid domains and **reorganize the east** (65–63), with Roman provinces in Asia, Cilicia, Bithynia-Pontus, and Syria, and with client kingdoms in Pontus, Cappadocia, Galatia, Lycia, and Judaea (p. 74). His settlement vastly **increased** both the **revenues of the Roman state** (from 50 million to 135 million denarii) and his own **personal wealth.**

64–63. Conspiracy of Catiline. The oppressed and discontented classes at Rome—debtors, veterans, ruined nobles, and those proscribed by Sulla—found a leader in the aristocrat **L. Sergius Catilina,** who proposed a program of debt cancellation *(novae tabulae).* Disgruntled over setbacks and defeats in the consular elections of 66 and 64, Catilina turned to armed revolt. **As consul in 63,** Cicero uncovered the conspiracy and in a series of speeches **(the Catilinarians)** convinced the senate to pass the SCU. Catilina's associates were arrested and executed without trial. Catilina himself died bravely in battle.

62–61. Pompey returned to Italy, disbanded his army, and triumphed. But the optimate senate, led by **M. Porcius Cato,** refused to ratify his eastern settlement and blocked a land bill for his veterans.

60. The First Triumvirate. The frustrated military hero **Pompey** then formed a political alliance with **M. Licinius Crassus,** who had the support of the *publicani,* and the patrician **C. Julius Caesar,** a *popularis* politician and favorite of the people.

59. Caesar, as consul, employed Pompey's veterans to overcome violently optimate opposition. He passed a land bill and ratification of his eastern settlement for Pompey, had an unfavorable tax contract remitted for Crassus's *publicani,* and secured for himself, by the *lex Vatinia,* the provinces of Cisalpine Gaul and Illyricum for five years. Later the province of Gallia Narbonensis was added.

58–51. THE CONQUEST OF GAUL. Using Narbonensis as a base, Caesar subjugated Gaul in a series of annual campaigns. In 55 he invaded Britain (p. 180) but soon withdrew; in 54 he made a demonstration across the Rhine. **Vercingetorix** led a serious national revolt in 52 but was defeated by Caesar, who suppressed the rebellion by 51. With his Gallic victories, Caesar equaled or surpassed the military reputation and personal wealth of Pompey.

58–57. In Rome the tribune **P. Clodius** pursued a *popularis* program (e.g., free grain), thwarting optimate opposition with gangs of thugs organized under the guise of legitimate *collegia* (clubs). His opponents retaliated by having the optimate tribune T. Annius Milo organize his own band of thugs. In 57 a shortage of grain prompted the senate to grant a **special command to Pompey** for supervision of the grain supply—*cura annonae.*

56. Worried by growing dissension between Pompey and Crassus, Caesar called for a meeting at **Luca** on the southern border of Cisalpine Gaul, where reconciliation and future plans were arranged between the three.

55. Pursuant to the arrangement, **Pompey and Crassus were consuls** and carried the following measures by force. Caesar's command was extended for another five years, and Crassus and Pompey were given matching **five-year proconsular commands**—Crassus in Syria, Pompey in the two Spanish provinces. Crassus departed for his province, while Pompey, contrary to custom, remained near Rome and governed Spain through *legati.*

54–53. In Rome, optimates opposed the agents of the triumvirate. Violence ensued and Rome moved toward anarchy. Crassus's invasion of Parthia ended in disaster when he and his army were wiped out at **Carrhae** (53).

52. Milo's gang murdered Clodius and rioting broke out in Rome. Elections could not be held, and the senate appointed **Pompey sole consul** for 52. Pompey began to move away from Caesar by marrying the daughter of the optimate, Metellus Scipio, whom he had elected as his consular colleague.

51–50. Caesar, as long as he held office, was immune to optimate attempts to prosecute him for illegal acts as consul in 59. Caesar's attempts to extend his command and canvass in absence as proconsul in 49 (so he could proceed directly to the consulship in 48) were thwarted by the optimates, who were encouraged by Pompey's growing support.

49. Negotiations with Caesar broke down, and the senate passed the SCU, declaring Caesar a public enemy unless he disbanded his army. Caesar initiated **CIVIL WAR** by leading his army over the **Rubicon**

River, the boundary between Cisalpine Gaul and Italy. Caesar's swift march forced Pompey and the optimates to abandon Italy for Greece, leaving Caesar between Pompeian forces in the east and in Spain. Caesar averted the danger with a lightning-fast **campaign in Spain,** defeating Pompey's commanders and securing the two provinces.

48. Caesar landed in Greece and defeated Pompey at **Pharsalus** in Thessaly. Pompey fled to Egypt where he was murdered. Caesar arrived in Alexandria where, after defeating a native army (48–47), he made **Cleopatra** ruler of Egypt (p. 75).

47. In Asia Minor, Caesar defeated Pharnaces, a son of Mithridates, at **Zela** (veni, vidi, vici).

46. After returning to Rome, Caesar crossed to Africa and defeated the Pompeians, led by Pompey's son Sextus, at **Thapsus.** M. Cato committed suicide at Utica (hence he was called Uticensis). After four simultaneous triumphs in Rome, Caesar went to Spain where Sextus Pompey had joined his brother Gnaeus.

45. Caesar defeated the Pompeians at **Munda,** ending armed opposition. **Caesar's Reforms.** Caesar restored the rights of those proscribed by Sulla; **reformed the calendar** according to the nearly correct basis of 356¼ days per year; provided moderate debt relief; reduced the numbers of those receiving free grain; raised the pay of the army; transferred the collection of Asian taxes from publicani to state officials; raised the numbers of praetors to 16, aediles to 6, and quaestors to 40; increased the size of the senate to 900 (?) by enrolling Italians as well as Roman citizens from Spain and Narbonensis; granted Roman citizenship to all Cisalpine Gaul; and founded some 20 extra-Italian colonies for veterans and the poor. **Caesar's constitutional position** was eventually that of a monarch. He held the consulship in 48, 46, 45 (alone), and 44. He was dictator in 48 and 47 and in 46 was made praefectus morum and dictator for ten years; in 44, dictator for life.

44. The Assassination of Caesar. Once in power, Caesar faced a dilemma. The Roman aristocratic tradition of competition, patronage, and exclusivity had led to two generations of violence and war and had to be curbed. But to govern, Caesar also needed the administrative experience of the senatorial class. He knew his autocratic behavior offended, so he attempted to win over senatorial sentiment with his friendship, money, and clemency—to no avail. A broadly based senatorial conspiracy, which included some of Caesar's old comrades and friends and was led by **C. Cassius Longinus** and **M. Junius Brutus,** murdered the dictator at a meeting of the senate on the Ides (15) of March. The conspirators had no plan, and the situation soon passed to men who controlled troops—**M. Aemilius Lepidus,** Caesar's magister equitum, and **M. Antonius** (Antony), Caesar's co-consul. But Antony's attempt to gain power without bloodshed, by compromising with the conspirators, was foiled by the appearance of Caesar's eighteen-year-old great nephew, heir, and adopted son, **Gaius Julius Caesar Octavianus.** Octavian publicly attacked Antony for treating with Caesar's killers and privately negotiated with optimate senators. Supported by **Cicero** and others, who hoped to use him against Antony, Octavian illegally raised an army among Caesar's veterans in Campania. Meanwhile, **Brutus and Cassius** had left Italy to **raise an army in the east.** When Antony marched north to claim his province of Cisalpine Gaul, Cicero attacked him in a series of speeches **(the Philippics).**

43. The consuls Hirtius and Pansa proceeded against Antony, and the senate gave **Octavian a special propraetorian command.** Antony was bested at **Mutina** and forced to retire north, but the consuls were killed, leaving Octavian in command. The nineteen-year-old Octavian then demanded the vacant consulship. When refused, he **marched his army on Rome,** where he forced a special election. As consul, Octavian abandoned his optimate friends, passed laws calling for the arrest of Caesar's assassins, and began to negotiate with Antony, who had joined Lepidus in northern Italy.

43, Nov. The Second Triumvirate. A lex Titia made Antony, Lepidus, and Octavian a commission of three to reform the state for five years. In essence, they were three dictators who would control elections, legislation, and armies. The triumvirs instituted widespread **proscriptions** inspired by political enmity and the need for money. Three hundred senators, including **Cicero,** and 2,000 equestrians were executed.

42. Lepidus remained in the west, while Antony and Octavian crossed to Thrace and defeated the armies of Cassius and Brutus at **Philippi.**

Antony was the hero of a battle in which some 40,000 Romans died. The victors divided the Empire, giving Africa to Lepidus; Gaul, the east, and the prospect of a glorious Parthian war to Antony; Spain, Sicily, and the problem of settling 50,000 veterans in Italy to Octavian.

41–40. Octavian's policy of confiscation led to a war against Antony's wife, Fulvia, and brother, Lucius Antonius, which Octavian won by reducing them at **Perugia** in 40.

40. War was averted by the **Pact of Brundisium,** where the recently widowed Antony agreed to marry Octavian's sister, Octavia.

39. Sextus Pompey, who since Munda had waged a naval war against the Caesarians, gained control of Sicily, Sardinia, and the Peloponnese; by cutting off Rome's grain supply, he forced the triumvirs to recognize his power by the **Treaty of Misenum.** Octavian divorced his second wife, Scribonia, and married **Livia,** previously the wife of Tiberius Claudius Nero.

37. Growing tensions between Octavian and Antony were resolved by the **Treaty of Tarentum.** The triumvirate was renewed for another five years.

36. At **Naulochus** in Sicily, Octavian's fleet under his general **M. Vipsanius Agrippa** defeated Sextus Pompey, who fled to Greece, where he was executed. **Lepidus,** now odd man out, attempted to take Sicily but was deserted by his army. Octavian deprived him of his triumviral powers but spared his life. Octavian campaigned in Illyricum (35–34).

36. Antony suffered a **major defeat** in his **invasion of Parthia,** losing 22,000 men in his retreat through Armenia. On his return, he rejected the aid of Octavia in favor of that of **Cleopatra,** with whom he openly consorted.

34. Antony conducted a victorious campaign in Armenia and by the **donations of Alexandria** distributed various eastern Roman territories to his children by Cleopatra.

32. The Second Triumvirate expired without renewal, and Octavian drove the Antonian consuls and 300 senators to Antony. Octavian stirred up anti-Egyptian sentiment in Italy and had the cities of Italy and the west take an **oath of allegiance** to him as dux (military leader).

31. Octavian was elected consul and declared war against Cleopatra. The opposing forces meet in western Greece; in a naval battle at **ACTIUM,** Antony and Cleopatra were defeated and retreated to Egypt.

30. Octavian pursued them to Egypt, where first Antony, then Cleopatra, committed suicide, marking an end to opposition to Octavian, as well the end of the Ptolemaic dynasty (p. 75).

c. AUGUSTUS AND THE PRINCIPATE

The Roman Republic had fallen, a victim of its own success. The post-Sullan nobility had proved incapable of governing a Mediterranean empire, while some, such as Caesar, succumbed to the temptation of personal power. In addition, the **enfranchisement of millions of Italians** had overwhelmed a political system designed for a citizen body of about 300,000. Finally, the **development of a professional army** necessary for an overseas empire had presented the new problem of who was going to pay for it. Because the governing classes had been unwilling to foot the bill, the loyalty of landless soldiers had shifted from the government to generals who promised land after service. The force that used soldiers to acquire that land helped to bring the Republic down. Augustus solved these problems by effectively **putting an end to free elections and aristocratic competition; by opening up the government to equestrians and Italians;** by continuing the policy, initiated by Caesar, of **extending the Roman citizenship beyond Italy to the provinces;** and by **securing the loyalty of the armies by taxing the upper classes** and using the proceeds to finance a regular program of payment for veterans.

30–29. On returning from Egypt, Octavian's first task was to control the military. He reduced the legions from about 60 to 29, and between the years 30 and 29 settled some 57,000 veterans in colonies. He eventually established a system of **28 legions** (about 150,000 men), wherein legionaries received regular pay and retired after 20 years with land or a monetary bonus. Complementing this was an equal number of noncitizen **auxiliary soldiers** who, after 25 years, received Roman citizenship on retirement.

27. The Senate bestowed on Octavian the title **Augustus,** chosen by himself. Augustus then gave up all extraordinary powers, ostensibly **re-**

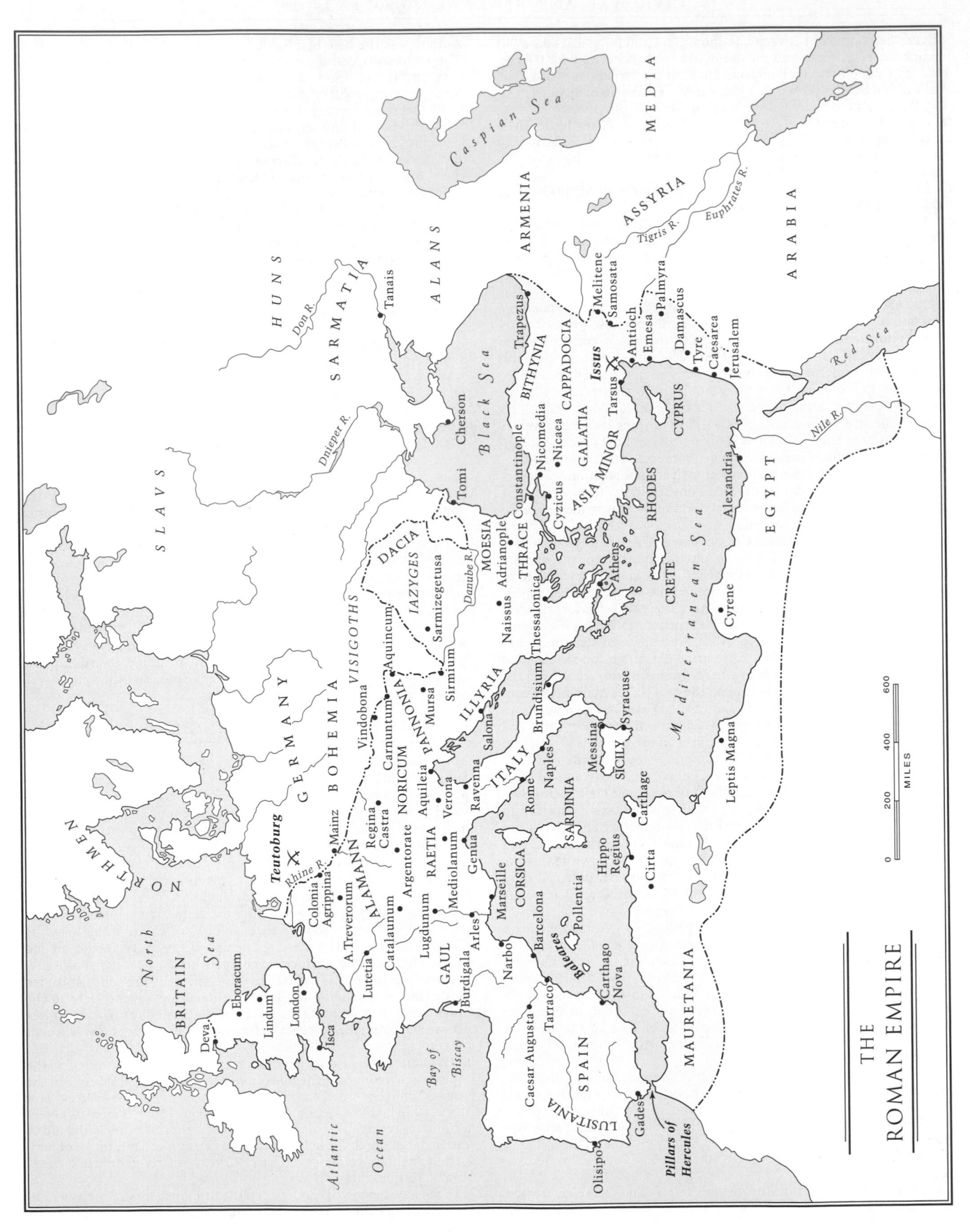

THE
ROMAN EMPIRE

MEDIA

ASSYRIA

ARABIA

Caspian Sea

Tigris R.

Euphrates R.

ARMENIA

Melitene
Samosata
Palmyra
Antioch
Emesa
Damascus
Tyre
Caesarea
Jerusalem

Red Sea

Nile R.

Trapezus
BITHYNIA
CAPPADOCIA
Issus
Tarsus

Nicomedia
Nicaea
GALATIA
ASIA MINOR
Cyzicus
CYPRUS

Cherson

Black Sea

Tomi
Constantinople
THRACE
Adrianople
Athens
RHODES
Alexandria

EGYPT

HUNS

SARMATIA

ALANS

Don R.
Tanais

Dnieper R.

SLAVS

MOESIA
Naissus
Thessalonica
DACIA
IAZYGES
Sarmizegetusa
Danube R.

CRETE

Mediterranean Sea

Cyrene

Leptis Magna

VISIGOTHS
Vindobona
Aquincum
Carnuntum
PANNONIA
Mursa
Sirmium
ILLYRIA
Salona

GERMANY
BOHEMIA

NORTHMEN

BRITAIN

North Sea

Atlantic Ocean

Bay of Biscay

Teutoburg
Rhine R.
Colonia
Agrippina
Mainz
A.Treverorum
ALAMANN
Regina
Castra
NORICUM
Argentorate
Aquileia
Verona
RAETIA
Ravenna
Mediolanum
Genúa
Vindobona

Lutetia
Lugdunum
Catalaunum
Arles
GAUL
Burdigala
Narbo

Eboracum
Lindum
London
Isca
Deva

Baleares

Marseille
Barcelona
Pollentia
CORSICA
SARDINIA
Hippo Regius
Cirta

ITALY
Rome
Naples
Brundisium
Salona
Ravenna

Messina
SICILY
Syracuse
Carthage

MAURETANIA

Caesar Augusta
Tarraco
SPAIN
LUSITANIA
Carthago Nova
Gades
Olisipo
Pillars of Hercules

0   200   400   600
MILES

storing the Republic by returning it to the "senate and people." But he was careful to retain exclusive control of the army by **dividing the provinces between the senate and himself.** "Senatorial provinces" were those that required few troops and were governed by regular senatorial proconsuls serving for one year. Augustus retained for himself as "imperial provinces" all those provinces where large armies were stationed. These he governed by carefully chosen legates—*legati Augusti pro praetore*—who tended to have longer terms of office. All provincial governors were salaried. Augustus also excluded independently minded senators from power by employing **equestrians** in military positions and administrators—prefects or procurators. The most important of these equestrian positions were the *praefectus annonae*, who was in charge of Rome's grain supply; the *praefectus vigilum*, who oversaw the city's fire brigade; the *praefectus Aegypti*, who governed Egypt as Augustus's private holding; and the *praefectus praetorio*, who controlled the **praetorian guard**—nine cohorts scattered over Italy. Augustus's vast private wealth was organized into an imperial treasury—the *fiscus*—distinct from the senatorial treasure—the *aerarium*.

23. From 31, Augustus had held the consulship every year; then in 23 Augustus resigned the consulship and arranged a **new settlement** whereby he received *tribunicia potestas*—the power of a tribune—giving him the authority to initiate and veto legislation and convene the senate. He and all subsequent emperors would number their reigns by tribunician years. He retained control of the military by a grant of **imperium maius,** a "command greater" than that of other magistrates. To control elections, Augustus exercised the right to nominate and commend candidates of his choice. Thus, without holding office, and merely as first man (*princeps*), Augustus controlled the Roman state.

20. A **diplomatic settlement** of Rome's eastern frontier was struck with **Parthia,** whereby Rome recovered the standards lost by Crassus and Antony, while a compromise candidate governed Armenia, the strategic high road between Parthia and Roman Syria. Augustus otherwise followed a policy of **military expansion.**

19. Agrippa subdued **northwest Spain.** Gaul had been organized into three provinces, and beginning in 12, Roman armies extended Roman territory **across the Rhine** (abandoned after a disaster in 9 C.E.). Augustus's armies also fought along the **Danube,** creating four provinces:

Raetia was formed by 16, **Noricum** in 16, **Pannonia** in 13, and **Moesia** by 6 C.E.

18. Augustus used his tribunician power to pass the *lex Iulia de maritandis ordinibus*, which regulated marriages between the various social orders, and the *lex Iulia de adulteriis coercendis* (18?), which made adultery a crime. This was the beginning of Augustus's **program of social improvement,** which he continued with legislation restricting the manumission of slaves—the *lex Fufia Caninia* of 2 C.E. and the *lex Aelia Sentia* of 4 C.E.—and a law, the *lex Papia Poppaea* (9 C.E.), to encourage marriages.

12. **Agrippa died** in Pannonia. Since 18 he had shared *tribunicia potestas* and since 21 had been married to Augustus's daughter, **Julia,** the union producing two sons, **Gaius** (b. 20) and **Lucius** (b. 17), whom Augustus adopted as his sons. In 11, Julia was married to **Tiberius Claudius Nero** (Tiberius), the son, along with **Nero Claudius Drusus** (Drusus), of **Livia** by her first husband.

12–9. Drusus led Roman armies **across the Rhine** to the Elbe, while Tiberius campaigned in Pannonia. Drusus died in 9 and was replaced by Tiberius, who campaigned in Germany until 7.

6. Tiberius, after receiving *tribunicia potestas* for five years, suddenly renounced public life and **retired to Rhodes.**

2 B.C.E.–4 C.E. Augustus's daughter, **Julia,** was banished for adultery in 2. In 2 C.E., Augustus's grandson Lucius died in Spain. In 4 C.E. his other grandson, Gaius, died in the east. Left with no heirs, **Augustus adopted his stepson, Tiberius,** who had returned to Rome in 2 C.E.

4–6. Tiberius campaigned in Germany, until he was called to suppress a serious **revolt in Pannonia** in 6.

6. Augustus created the *aerarium militare*, a special treasury to provide bonuses for retiring soldiers, which was financed by a sales tax and an inheritance tax.

8. After arresting her husband for conspiring against him, Augustus **banished his granddaughter, Julia,** for adultery.

9. The legate **P. Quinctilius Varus** with a Roman army of 20,000 was annihilated by the Germans under Arminius in the **Teutoburg Forest.** The Romans withdrew west of the Rhine.

14. AUGUSTUS DIED at Nola. Tiberius, who held both *tribunicia potestas* and *imperium maius*, succeeded.

4. THE ROMAN EMPIRE, 14–284 C.E.

a. GEOGRAPHY AND CLIMATE

During this period Rome organized the provinces of Gallia Transalpina, Britannia, Raetia, Noricum, Pannonia, Moesia, Dacia, Mauretania, Cyrenaica, Egypt, Thrace, Syria, Judaea, Mesopotamia, Bithynia et Pontus, Galatia, Cilicia, and Lycia et Pamphylia. **The Roman world therefore encompassed an enormous area centering around the Mediterranean but extending, significantly in places, into continental Europe, Asia, and Africa.** It can be conveniently divided into several climatic and geographic zones. Provinces circling the Mediterranean enjoyed mild rainy winters and summers which were moderate on the northern coasts and warmer and drier on the southern. Agricultural productivity depended on exploiting the winter rains and working soil which, except for volcanic regions, was comparatively light. In lands such as Greece, where rocky soil is common, the typically Mediterranean combination of olive trees and grapevines predominated. These crops were combined with intensive cultivation of cereals in the more fertile areas of North Africa (modern Tunisia) and Sicily, and to a lesser degree in Italy, in the valleys of Anatolia, and southwestern Spain. The land of Egypt was uniquely fertile, since it depended not on rainfall, but on the regular flooding of the Nile. In most Mediterranean countries, however, rivers that were navigable year-round were uncommon; cities therefore tended to cluster along the coasts or in nearby valleys and plains. The climate of northern European provinces was characterized by seasons that were more extreme and by rainfall that was more evenly distributed than in Mediterranean countries. Agricultural development was impeded by various factors. The soil was fertile but heavy and consequently more difficult to work. In addition, a climate that was generally more humid resulted in wide belts of heavy forests, many of which were also swampy. Highlands made for excellent pasturage, while mountains were frequently rich in minerals of various kinds. Navigable rivers were the principal avenues of communication and trade, and it was on these that cities were founded. Few cities of the Roman Empire had populations of more than 20,000 persons. Larger ones, like Pergamum, reached 100,000, while a few, such as Alexandria and Antioch, approached 500,000. **The city of Rome was unique in having about one million inhabitants. The population of the Roman Empire is estimated to have been between fifty and sixty million persons in 14 C.E.** The southern boundaries of the Roman world were **desert country.** Here irrigation extended agriculture and urban life into regions where pasturage and nomadic life prevailed.

The Romans had a clear idea of the **frontiers** *(limes)* of their empire and had armies to guard them. But these borders were very permeable, and the function of soldiers was as much to monitor the movements of persons and goods across the frontier as it was to defend them. The Roman world, in fact, extended beyond the borders of Roman provinces to trans-Danubian areas where overland commerce was constant, as well to the Indian Ocean, where long-distance, seasonal maritime trade was conducted. The true boundaries of the Roman world were not marked by frontiers. Roman civilization was urban, and it was delimited by deserts and mountains both outside and inside its imperial borders.

The ancient Roman view was of a spherical world, the inhabited region of which (the *oikoumene*) was surrounded by oceans, and this world centered around the Mediterranean. It was bordered on the west by the Atlantic Ocean and on the east by the mouth of the Ganges River. The southern extent of the African continent and the northern expanses of the land masses of Europe and Asia were vastly underestimated.

b. ECONOMY, SOCIETY, AND CULTURE

With the *Principate* came a long period of civic peace *(pax Romana)*, which greatly benefited the **economy of the Roman Empire.** Older areas devastated by war, such as Italy and Asia, returned to their former prosperity, while recently conquered regions underwent population increases, urbanization, and intensified agricultural cultivation. **Increased agricultural productivity** was a response to the consumer needs of growing and newly founded cities and of the provincial armies, though in some respects Roman technology, as opposed to engineering, lagged behind eastern and southern Asia. The wheeled plow was introduced in Gaul, in order to till the heavier earth. Other innovations included an improved scythe and a mechanical reaper. From the 1st through the 3rd centuries, **the overall trend in the agrarian labor force was a change from slavery to tenancy.** How this occurred is very unclear, but it was certainly a long and slow process; slaves were still regularly employed in agriculture in the 2nd and 3rd centuries. The major source of slaves, foreign conquest, did slow down, but the wars of Claudius, Vespasian, and Trajan brought in large numbers of slaves, while other sources—the exposure of unwanted infants, as well as slave breeding—continued to provide slaves in substantial numbers. Few figures are available, but in the mid-2nd century slaves totaled 40,000, or one-third of the adult population of the Asian city of Pergamum. In Roman Egypt, the slave population was lower, making up less than one-tenth. **The proliferation of cities** was a major development of the imperial period. Most of the newly founded cities were in the western empire, especially in south and central Gaul, in the lowlands of Spain, and in the fertile valleys and coasts of North Africa. Many cities relied on local production for their food. When intensified cultivation made regions productive, however, their surpluses were sent to large cities which required imports. The grain of North Africa and Egypt surpassed that of Sicily as Rome's major source, while olive oil from Spain and wine from many regions were imported into the capital. Industry remained small-scale, but trade of the local, interprovincial, and extraprovincial types was very significant by a scale of preindustrial societies. Produce, large amounts of timber, metals, and textiles were carried primarily by a sophisticated system of water transport but also by much used overland routes.

The Roman government was committed to founding cities as centers of civic and judicial administration, and of tax collecting. Archaeology testifies to the great number of cities that prospered during the high empire, although food shortages and financial and administrative difficulties were chronic problems which required outside assistance and which came increasingly from Rome. Cities were largely autonomous and governed by local elites, who resided in the cities and drew rents from their rural properties. Annual magistrates *(duoviri, archontes, strategoi, grammateis)* drawn from the body of municipal senators *(decuriones, bouleutai)* were responsible for maintaining law and order and ensuring municipal as well as imperial taxes. They also supported the cities' essential services and amenities through largess, giving their money and services in exchange for public recognition and status. Much of the space in a Roman city was taken up by public buildings and the large houses and gardens of the rich. For the nonelite, urban living conditions were crowded and, by modern standards, unsanitary, so life was lived outdoors during daylight hours. Most private dwellings were not connected to the public sewers, and few had running water. Although public baths were inexpensive and often sumptuous, they were also unhygienic, since the water was infrequently changed.

A major trend in the imperial period was the **extension of Roman citizenship.** Under Julius Caesar and the triumvirs, whole regions—Cisalpine Gaul, Sicily, along with Romanized provincial cities in the west—had received citizenship, while in more recently conquered areas, and in the Greek-speaking east, citizenship had been rewarded to prominent individuals. The establishment of Roman citizen colonies around the Empire, which had been greatly favored by Caesar and Augustus, slackened during the first century but was continued under Trajan and Hadrian. Citizenship status—either Roman or Latin—was granted to communities and whole regions. Latin status was granted to the Alpine provinces by Claudius and Nero, and to all of Spain by Vespanian. Roman citizenship was also extended by the auxiliary units of the army, where after 25 years of service noncitizen provincial soldiers received the citizenship for themselves and, until c. 140, their families. By the early 3rd century, every province of the Empire had large numbers of Roman citizens. In 212 the distinction between citizen and noncitizen was eliminated by the *constitutio Antoniniana*, which granted Roman citizenship to virtually all free male inhabitants of the Empire. As Roman citizenship became more common, its privileges diminished, and two legal statuses developed. One status included Roman citizens of the upper classes—senators, equestrians, and local magistrates, who were called *honestiores*. Everyone else, Roman citizen or not, fell into the class of *humiliores* and were subject to harsh punishments—crucifixion, burning, the arena, chained labor—which had previously been associated with servile punishments. Another function of the spread of Roman citizenship was the opening up of the equestrian order and, later, the senatorial order to **upper-class provincials.** The number of easterners in imperial equestrian service began to rise from about 100 C.E. In the Roman senate, old Roman noble families died out and were replaced by Italians. Wishing to exploit their wealth and energy, emperors then began to appoint wealthy provincials to the senate. Finally, emperors were chosen from provincial families. Trajan and Hadrian were descendants of old families of Roman settlers in Spain; Septimius Severus came from North Africa. The upwardly mobile freedman class was of great importance to the urban society and economy of the Empire. Beginning with Augustus, the energies and wealth of freedmen were officially recognized and channeled into government service. In Rome, freedmen became ward leaders *(magistri vici)*, while in the municipalities of Italy and the west, they served the imperial cult as honorary officials *(seviri Augustales)*. Women remained subordinate. Their legal status changed little, but a **significant reform came when Claudius abolished guardianship** *(tutela)* for adult women of free birth. And for a time, starting with Augustus, the husband lost the right to kill an adulterous wife. In the upper classes women received a literary education. Outside of the elite, many worked—most as fieldworkers, with others in a wide variety of urban occupations. Almost all women married. In the upper classes, women on average had their first child at 15. Family size was limited through infanticide, by exposure to the elements; by effective, if dangerous, forms of artificial birth control; and by equally dangerous abortions. Life expectancy for males at birth was between 20 and 30 years.

In law the formulary system was replaced by juristic interpretation and various forms of imperial intervention. After the praetor's edict was codified under Hadrian, the pronouncements of the emperor *(constitutiones principis)*, in the form of edicts, decrees, and rescripts, became the principal source of law. By the 2nd century C.E. **the culture of the upper classes of the Roman Empire had become truly Greco-Roman.** The ruling classes of Greek cities learned Latin in order to participate in the Roman imperial government, while in Rome and Italy, the upper classes had been Hellenized since the late Republic. Roman elite education was centered on rhetoric and included the study of both Greek and Latin literature. Romans also took up the various schools of Greek philosophy—Platonism, Epicureanism, and Stoicism—the latter becoming dominant during the imperial period and counting among its chief exponents the senator **Seneca** (c. 1–65), the slave **Epictetus** (c. 55–c. 135), and the emperor **Marcus Aurelius** (122–180). A **moderate rise in literacy** is indicated by, among other things, the great increase in inscriptions, the production of Greek papyrus texts, and the expansion of the Roman Empire into less advanced areas. While Greek and Latin became international languages, vernacular languages continued to be spoken by many populations in many parts of the Empire.

Latin literature entered its so-called Silver Age, characterized by its penchant for rhetoric. The Roman satirical tradition was continued by **A. Persius Flaccus** (34–62) and mastered by **D. Iunius Iuvenalis** (Juvenal, c. 55–138). Prose satire was cultivated in the picaresque novel *Satyricon* by **Petronius Arbiter** (d. 66), probably Nero's friend. Under Tiberius, **Valerius Maximus** composed *Facta et dicta memorabilia*, nine books of historical examples of virtues and vices. Spain was home to a noted literary family which flourished in Rome. **Lucius Annaeus Seneca,** the rhetorician (c. 55 B.C.E.–c. 40 C.E.), wrote *declamationes* (set speeches). His son, **L. Annaeus Seneca** (c. 1–65), wrote **Stoic philosophical treatises** as well as tragedies; this man's nephew, **M. An-**

naeus Lucanus (Lucan, 39–65), composed the historical epic *Pharsalia*. **M. Valerius Martialis** (Martial, c. 40–104) of Spain wrote satirical epigrams in Rome, as did the noted teacher of rhetoric and author of *Institutio Oratoria*, **M. Fabius Quintilianus** (c. 35–c. 100). The provinces were also the birthplace of the historian **Cornelius Tacitus** (c. 56–118?), author of *Dialogus de oratoribus*, the biography *Agricola*, the ethnological *Germania* and his historical works, the *Historiae* and *Annales*. In science, **Galen** of Pergamum (c. 130–200) furthered the Greek scientific tradition with prolific writings on medicine. **Ptolemy** (c. 85–165) wrote on astronomy, furthering the Hellenistic belief in an Earth-centered universe. **C. Plinius Caecilius Secundus** (Pliny, c. 61–c. 113) was a noted political and literary figure, who composed elegant *Epistulae*; his prolific uncle, **C. Plinius Secundus** (c. 23–79) wrote, among other works, the encyclopedic but uncritical *Historia Naturalis*. Another prolific author was **C. Suetonius Tranquillus** (c. 69–121?), whose biographies, *De Vita Caesarum*, extended from Caesar through Domitian. Under Hadrian and the Antonines began a revival of interest in pre-Ciceronian Latin, and a school of florid Latin writers emerged. Its exponents were the orator and writer **M. Cornelius Fronto** (c. 100–c. 166), whose correspondence with his student Marcus Aurelius survives, and the author of *Metamorphoses*, **L. Apuleius** (c. 124–170?), both from North Africa. **Aulus Gellius** (c. 130–c. 180) wrote the literary miscellany, *Noctes Atticae (Attic nights)*, and the emperor **Marcus Aurelius** penned his stoical *Meditations* in Greek.

In early imperial architecture, concrete vaulting was increasingly exploited to create novel spatial effects (the *Domus Aurea*). **Brick** became the preferred facing material for concrete construction during Tiberius's reign. By the Flavian period, a new type of vaulting (the groin vault) was introduced (the Colosseum). In the 2nd century, the old canons were being rethought to create a new sumptuousness. Novelties included the broken pediment (first seen in Trajanic Rome) and the aedicular facades (the library of Celsus at Ephesus). In the **city of Rome**, architectural sophistication and daring reached its zenith under Hadrian in the 150-foot-wide concrete dome of the **Pantheon** and the large and radical Temple of Venus and Roma, whose top-heavy proportions evoked older temple types and marked a deliberate break with the Augustan Corinthian canon. Afterwards, creative experimentation in architecture increasingly shifted from the capital to the provinces (e.g., Leptis Magna in North Africa, Baalbek in Syria, and Ephesus in Asia Minor). In Roman state art, historical relief came into prominence. In Augustan reliefs the emperor had been consistently portrayed as first among equals in a realistic context *(Ara Pacis)*, but in the course of the 1st century new conventions (such as the juxtaposition of real and allegorical figures, divinizing attributes, and apotheosis) made their way into the representations of rulers in state art (e.g., the Flavian Arch of Titus and Cancellaria reliefs). In the early 2nd century, emperors began to be portrayed showing imperial virtues in increasingly varied and elaborate, but essentially realistic, contexts in both peace and war. In portrait sculpture the realistic-looking portraiture of the late Republic continued to be employed. Imperial portraits of the Julio-Claudian dynasty adapted various ages and physiognomies to the ageless Augustan model. Under the Flavians a literal element was introduced into imperial portraiture. Portraits of Hadrian broke from tradition by showing the emperor wearing a beard, which reflected military fashion, philosophical phil-Hellenism, or both. A trend was introduced in the 3rd century by Caracella, whose portrait types sported the close-cropped hair and beard, and became the canonical style of the 3rd-century soldier emperors. In **Roman painting**, the **Fourth Style**, introduced about 62, combined Third Style panel painting motifs with Second Style representations of architecture in depth.

c. THE JULIO-CLAUDIANS

14–37. **TIBERIUS Claudius Nero** (b. 42 B.C.E.) became emperor, when the senate conferred on him the powers and titles of Augustus. He transferred the elections from the assemblies to the senate. Already the passage of laws in the assemblies had become a formality.

14–16. The **revolt of the Pannonian legions** was suppressed by Tiberius's son, the younger Drusus. The son of Tiberius's brother Drusus, who is known by his father's title, **Germanicus,** and whom Augustus had forced Tiberius to adopt as a possible successor, suppressed the German mutiny and campaigned in Germany with some successes. He defeated Arminius, and recovered the eagles of Varus's legions. He was, however, recalled, probably not because Tiberius begrudged his victories, but because he found them too costly.

17. On the death of their kings, Cappadocia and Commagene became a province.

17–19. **Germanicus,** sent to install a king in Armenia, conducted himself in a high-handed manner both in Syria and in Egypt. When he died in Syria, however, the enemies of Tiberius rallied about his wife Agrippina.

21. **A revolt against Rome broke out in Gaul** among the Treveri, led by Julius Florus, and the Aedui, led by Julius Sacrovir. Although suppressed, it showed that anti-Roman feeling was still strong in Gaul.

23–31. Tiberius fell increasingly under the influence of the ambitious equestrian prefect of the guard **L. Aelius Sejanus** who quartered the praetorian cohorts in one camp in Rome. He encouraged the gathering of information against those hostile to Tiberius by informers *(delatores)* and the prosecution of the accused under the law of treason *(lex de maiestate imminuta)*. When such trials involved senators or important equestrians, they were heard by the senate, which came increasingly to act as a court under the presidency of the emperor or the consuls. In 23, Sejanus probably poisoned Tiberius's son Drusus, in order to plot his own succession.

26. Tiberius retired from an increasingly hostile Rome and eventually settled on **Capreae** (Capri).

29. **Livia,** accused of attempting to dominate the Empire after Augustus's death, died. Sejanus secured the exile of **Agrippina,** wife of Germanicus (she died in 33), and the arrest of his two eldest sons, Nero (d. 31) and a third Drusus (d. 33).

31. The plots of Sejanus finally came to the notice of Tiberius, who engineered his arrest and execution. Tiberius remained in seclusion in Capreae.

36. **Artabanus, king of Parthia,** made peace with Rome.

37. **Tiberius,** dying at Misenum (Mar. 16), indicated as his successors his young grandson, **Tiberius Gemellus,** and the twenty-four-year-old surviving son of Germanicus, **Gaius Caesar,** nicknamed *Caligula* ("Bootsy"). Gaius soon put Gemellus to death.

37–41. **Gaius CALIGULA** (b. 12), emperor. Greeted with enthusiasm, Gaius's reign turned into a tyranny, marked by extravagant spending and the execution of senators. Though the follies ascribed to him may be exaggerated, his conduct was irrational, and he may have been unbalanced. Behind his behavior may have lain the desire for an absolute monarchy. He had his sister and himself worshiped as gods and attempted to erect a statue of himself in the temple of Jerusalem.

39. Caligula's **campaign into Germany** was stopped by a conspiracy led by Cn. Cornelius Lentulus Gaetulicus.

40. A campaign against Britain was aborted before it began.

41, Jan. 24. **Caligula was assassinated** by conspirators of senators, palace ministers, and the praetorian guard, the latter led by the tribune Cassius Chaerea. The attempt of the senate to make their own candidate emperor, or to restore the Republic, was frustrated by the praetorian guard who supported Caligula's scholarly uncle **Claudius** and imposed him on the senate as emperor. Claudius's political position was consequently weak, forcing him to bolster it through marriage and political alliances.

41–54. **Tiberius CLAUDIUS Drusus** (b. 10 B.C.E.) ruled for nearly 14 years and was responsible for a number of significant changes. He **extended the Empire** through conquest and annexation, adding the two **Mauretanian provinces** (Tingitana and Caesariensis) (41–43), **Britain** (43) (p. 180), **Lycia** (43), **Thrace** (46), and **Noricum** (46). Claudius eventually made **Judaea** a procuratorial province (44). Under Claudius the role of **imperial freedmen** in the imperial administration grew, and such men as Narcissus, Polybius, Pallas, and Callistus became wealthy and powerful, much to the chagrin of the senate. Claudius recruited wealthy nobles from Transalpine Gaul into the senate (48) and transferred supervision of the state treasury *(aerarium)* from two praetors to quaestors appointed by the emperor. Pilloried by ancient sources for being the dupe of his wives and servants, Claudius's behavior should be attributed to his chronic political weakness. Threatened by real and potential conspiracies, Claudius tried and executed many senators.

42. The governor of Dalmatia, L. Arruntius Camillus Scribonianus

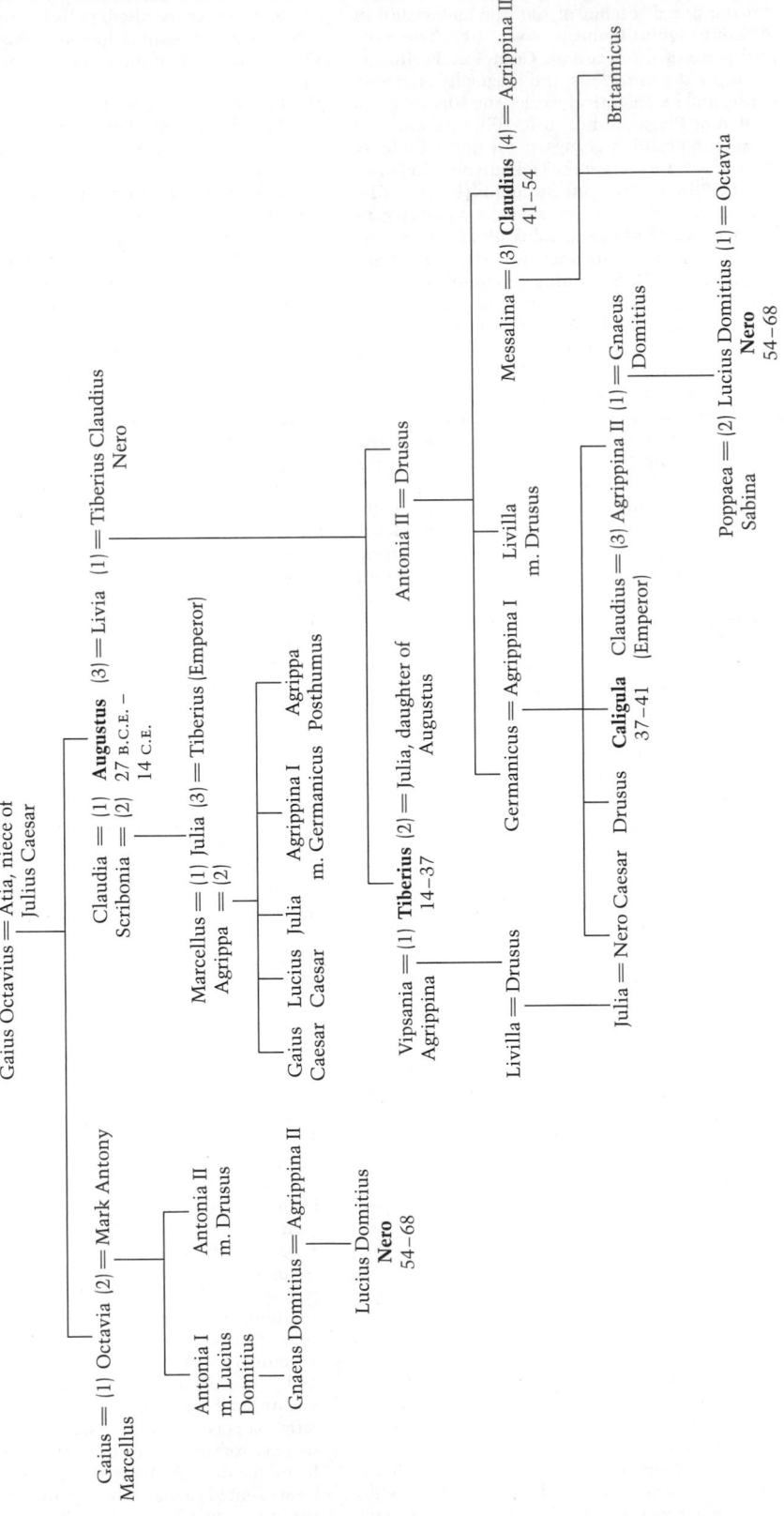

THE JULIAN-CLAUDIAN HOUSE

raised **rebellion** in his province, accompanied by a senatorial conspiracy in Rome. The army remained loyal to the Julio-Claudian dynasty, and the threat to Claudius ended quickly. Trials and executions of senators followed.

43. To establish a military reputation for Claudius, Britain was invaded. By 49, the Romans had reached Lincoln and Chester and south Wales. Claudius himself visited the island. The British leader **Caractacus** was finally captured in 51.

47. Claudius revived the censorship and celebrated secular games *(ludi saeculares)*.

48. On the execution of his wife, Messalina, Claudius was permitted by a special senatorial enactment to marry his niece Agrippina. In 50 he adopted her son, Lucius Domitius Ahenobarbus, who took the name **Nero** and ousted from the succession Claudius's son by Messalina, Britannicus (b. 41 or 42 and inheriting his name from his father's British triumph). In 53 Nero married Claudius's daughter by Messalina, Octavia.

54. Claudius died (Oct. 13), probably from poison administered in a dish of mushrooms by Agrippina. When Agrippina secured the recognition by the praetorian guard of **Claudius Nero Caesar** as successor, the senate then conferred on him the imperial powers.

54–69. Claudius **NERO** Caesar came to power when he was sixteen and began his rule well under the guidance of the praetorian prefect **Sextus Afranius Burrus** and the orator-philosopher **L. Annaeus Seneca,** who with Agrippina kept the phil-Hellenic young emperor's avidity for poetry, music, painting, sculpture, and horseracing, as well as his hooliganism, under restraint. The discharge of Pallas and the murder of Britannicus were political acts, but **Nero** soon chafed and deserted his wife Octavia, first for the freedwoman Acte and then for Poppaea Sabina, the wife of his friend Otho. Tiring of her interference, Nero then murdered his mother Agrippina in 59. After the death of Burrus in 62, Seneca was dismissed, Octavia was divorced, then murdered, and Nero married Poppaea. Restraint had come to an end, and Nero began to rule as an autocrat. His court became a center of literary and artistic patronage; he wooed and won popular favor with lavish spending and displays. Nero's conduct and his executions of senators alienated the upper classes, but it was his neglect of the military that brought his rule to an end. He was the first emperor never to have visited the armies and the last of the Julio-Claudian dynasty.

55–63. The general **Cn. Domitius Corbulo** was sent to settle the Parthian problem. Corbulo successfully invaded Armenia and took Artaxata (58) and Tigranocerta (59). In 61, however, Nero replaced him with Paetus, who was thoroughly defeated at **Rhandeia** (62). In 63, therefore, Corbulo's solution, peace without conquest, was accepted by Nero. The Parthian Tiridates came to Rome in 66 to receive his crown.

61. While Suetonius Paulinus, governor of Britain since 59, was engaged in the subjugation of the Druidical center, the queen of the Iceni, **Boudicca,** led a serious revolt. Paulinus succeeded in defeating and killing Boudicca.

64. A fire destroyed a great part of Rome. When unjustly suspected of having set the fire himself, Nero found convenient culprits in the new and despised sect of the **Christians,** who were put to death with refined tortures. Nero passed preventive regulations and built an enormous (over 200 acres) villa-garden in the center of Rome, the **Domus Aurea.**

65. A widespread conspiracy was organized to put **C. Calpurnius Piso** into the principate. It was discovered, and many senators, including Seneca, his nephew Lucan the poet, Faenius Rufus (successor to Burrus as praetorian prefect), and Petronius (the writer and friend of Nero), were executed or forced to commit suicide.

66–70. REVOLT IN JUDAEA. When the governor of Syria failed to suppress it, **Vespasian** was sent as special legate with three legions (67). He slowly reduced the country, took prisoner the pro-Roman Jewish historian **Josephus,** and laid siege to Jerusalem (69). **The Jewish council *(sanhedrin)* and high priesthood were abolished,** and direct Roman rule was installed.

67. Nero undertook an artistic tour in Greece, in the course of which he executed Corbulo and two ex-legates of Germany.

68. On Nero's return to Italy, he heard that **C. Julius Vindex,** legate of Gallia Lugdunensis, had revolted. Though the revolt was put down by the legate of upper Germany, L. Verginius Rufus, who refused to be saluted as emperor *(imperator)* by his troops, the two legions in His-

pania Tarraconensis, had already (Mar.) saluted as emperor their 72-year-old legate, **Servius Sulpicius Galba.** When the praetorian guard, under the prefect Nymphidius Sabinus, recognized Galba, the senate declared Nero a public enemy. He committed suicide in a villa outside Rome, and the Julio-Claudian line came to an end.

d. EARLY CHRISTIANITY

By the 1st century B.C.E., **JUDAISM** had been diffused in the Roman Empire, with **Jews** residing mainly in Palestine and in the cities of the east. Palestine itself, however, was by no means wholly Jewish; it had a substantial population of non-Jewish Semites as well as Greeks. The area was consequently home to an amalgam of beliefs, and to religious contention. The god of the Jews was Yahweh; his worship was centered around the cult of his temple in Jerusalem, which was run by a hereditary high priesthood, and around his law, which was preserved in Hebrew scriptures. By the 1st century, however, observant Jews were divided into three principal sects, each of which regarded the others as ritually unclean: upper-class **Saducees,** who were devoted to ritual sacrifice at the temple; **Pharisees,** whose worship was organized around the synagogue and the rabbi, rather than the temple and the priesthood; and a number of ascetic sects, the most important being the **Essenes,** whose strict observance of the law led them to live in isolated monastic communities. **The kingdom of Judaea was annexed by Rome in 6 C.E.** and placed under a procurator; the other areas of Palestine—Galilee, Samaria, Peraea, Idumaea, and Batanaea—were ruled intermittently by vassals (the descendants of **Herod the Great,** king of Judaea 37–4 B.C.E.); all of Palestine became a Roman province in 44 C.E. But foreign rule engendered the belief in a national liberator called the **Messiah,** who would restore political freedom; in some versions the liberation would be accompanied by an apocalyptic reckoning. **CHRISTIANITY** originated as a Jewish sect. Its founder, **JESUS,** was a Jew born in Palestine, somewhere within eight or ten years of 1 C.E.; he grew up in Galilee. When he was about 30, he was baptized by John the Baptist. He then formed his own group and began his public career as a teacher and miracle man, practicing principally in Galilee. Jesus's historical teachings are obscure, but included some form of freedom from the Jewish law, the promise of salvation after death, immediate salvation for the chosen, and the claim that he was the son of the Jewish god. On visiting Jerusalem, Jesus gained notoriety by attacking the temple priesthood. He was arrested, then tried and convicted, probably for sedition, by the Roman prefect Pontius Pilate (26–36 C.E.), and was crucified. After his death, his followers began to preach in Jerusalem that Jesus had been resurrected and that he was the Messiah (Christ). The early Christian community comprised poor Jews and Greeks and was led by **Peter,** who seemed to have espoused a doctrine of freedom from Jewish law, which quickly led to violent reactions by observant Jews. **Paul of Tarsus,** a devoted Pharisee, at first persecuted Christians but was later converted. Against the opposition of some Christian leaders, Paul went on missions (48–51 and 52–55) to convert non-Jews, founding Christian communities in Asia Minor and Greece. Paul's brand of Christianity taught freedom from Jewish law for gentiles and salvation with baptism. In Jerusalem, persecution of Christians ended when leadership passed from Peter to James, the brother of Jesus, who was a strict observer of the Jewish law and on good terms with the Pharisees. But James was executed by the Saducees in 62; after the destruction of the temple by the Romans in 70, a reconstituted Pharisee leadership excluded Christians from their worship. The center of Christianity then passed from Jewish Jerusalem to gentile Christian communities around the Empire.

e. THE HIGH EMPIRE

1. CIVIL WAR AND A NEW SETTLEMENT

68–69. Servius Sulpicius **GALBA** (b. 5 or 3 B.C.E.). The senate's acquiescence to the army's proclamation of Galba as emperor in 68 had exposed what Tacitus called the great secret of the empire—"that emperors could be made elsewhere than at Rome." The power of the praetorian guard in choosing an emperor had already been demonstrated. In 69, **the year of the emperors** (Galba, Otho, Vitellius, and Vespasian), the provincial armies asserted their powers in a civil war, which ended with the victory of Vespasian, and the establishment of the **Flavian dynasty.**

69, Jan. 1. The eight legions on the **Rhine** refused allegiance to Galba, and on Jan. 3 the four in lower Germany saluted as emperor their legate **Aulus Vitellius** (b. 15). He was also accepted by the four legions of upper Germany. Galba had reached Rome, where he adopted as his successor the aristocrat L. Piso Licinianus.

Thereupon, **M. Salvius Otho** (b. 32), the friend of Nero, secured the support of the praetorians and had Galba and Piso murdered (Jan. 15). The helpless senate then recognized him.

Meanwhile, the troops of Vitellius approached Italy in two divisions under Valens and Caecina. They met in the plain of the Po Valley and defeated the forces of Otho (Apr. 19) in the **First Battle of Bedriacum** (near Cremona), whereupon **Otho,** to avert further bloodshed, committed suicide. The senate immediately recognized Vitellius, who presently reached Rome himself.

In the meantime (July 1) the prefect of Egypt, Tiberius Julius Alexander, proclaimed as emperor **Vespasian,** legate in Judaea. Mucianus, legate of Syria, lent his support. Antonius Primus, commander of the seventh legion in Pannonia, rallied all the Danubian legions to Vespasian and moved rapidly into northern Italy. There he defeated the forces of Vitellius in the **Second Battle of Bedriacum** and sacked Cremona (late Oct.). When Antonius approached Rome, Vespasian's brother seized the Capitol, which was burnt in the ensuing struggle. The Vitellians fought bitterly in the city streets, but Vitellius was finally slain (Dec. 20). The senate immediately recognized Vespasian. After his proclamation as emperor, Vespasian left his son, **Titus,** to complete the siege of Jerusalem. **In 70 Titus sacked the city, destroyed the temple,** and installed a garrison. He celebrated a triumph in 71, which is commemorated on the Arch of Titus in Rome.

69–79. Titus Flavius VESPASIANUS (b. 9) was the son of a tax collector from the Italian municipality of Reate. The Augustan system had survived the idiosyncrasies of its rulers because the administration of the Empire had been separated from the politics of the palace and senate at Rome. But the civil war of 69 had shown the need to control the Empire and its armies more closely, and so the extravagance and self-indulgence of the Julio-Claudians were replaced by the hands-on work ethic of the Flavians. Vespasian oversaw a careful and frugal administration of the Empire, in which the frontiers and finances were reorganized and the armies and upper classes monitored. Respectful to the senate, Vespasian nevertheless insisted on establishing dynastic succession, and he and his son Titus were consular colleagues in every year of his reign except 73 and 78. To reorganize the senate, Vespasian felt compelled to revive the censorship with Titus in 73, instead of tacitly assuming the right of enrollment (*adlectio*) exercised by his predecessors. In 74 he granted Latin rights to all of Spain.

69–71. The revolt of some Batavian auxiliaries under their native commander, Julius Civilis, won the support of some of the legions of Germany. This inflamed the Gallic Treveri under Julius Classicus and Julius Tutor and the Lingones under Julius Sabinus. Petillius Cerealis crushed the revolt piecemeal. Thereafter auxiliaries were not employed in the country of their origin, and the corps soon came to be composed of recruits of different nationalities. By this time the praetorian guards alone were recruited in Italy; the legions drew from Roman settlers in the provinces or Romanized provincials, to whom citizenship was often granted to secure their enlistment. Thus the army had become less Italian, more provincial.

70–75. Vespasian consolidated the eastern frontier against Armenia and Parthia.

71. Titus, though a senator, was made praetorian prefect, a post hitherto equestrian. He also received both proconsular imperium and tribunician power. He ruthlessly suppressed senatorial opposition to his father.

71–84. Further Conquest in Britain. Under the Flavian commander Petillius Cerealis (71–74), Sextus Iulius Frontinus (74–78), and Cn. Julius Agricola (78–84), Roman conquest advanced into Wales and Scotland (p. 180).

73–74. Vespasian began the conquest of the territory east of the upper Rhine and south of the Main, the later *agri decumates* (or *decumathes*; the meaning is uncertain). He furthermore reorganized the defenses of the upper and lower Danube.

73. At about this time Vespasian banished Helvidius Priscus, son-in-law of Thrasea and his successor as leader of the Stoic opposition to the Empire. He also banished the professors of philosophy, perhaps because their doctrines encouraged disloyalty.

79–81. TITUS Flavius Vespasianus, who was co-ruler with his father, succeeded on the death of Vespasian (June 23). His hostility toward the senate ceased, and he won popularity by his largess.

79. An **eruption of Mt. Vesuvius,** on the Bay of Naples, buried the cities **Pompeii** and **Herculaneum.** In 80 a severe fire occurred in Rome. During this year, Titus dedicated magnificently the Colosseum (*amphitheatrum Flavianum*) and some elaborate public baths (*thermae Titianae*).

81–96. Titus Flavius DOMITIANUS (b. 51) succeeded on the premature death of Titus. Twelve years younger than Titus, and not as close to their father, Domitian had developed strong opinions on the nature of imperial power. He ruled as an autocrat, but unlike Caligula and Nero, who had exercised their power on trivial matters, Domitian took personal interest in the Empire's administration. Power was centralized, the senate ignored. Money was lavishly spent, not on private luxury, but on public displays of the majesty of an emperor who was addressed as lord and god. The result was a well-run empire, but disastrous relations with the senate, culminating in conspiracies and executions.

83. Domitian crossed the Rhine at Mainz to **campaign against the Chatti.** His victory allowed him to begin the construction of a series of forts connected by a road and later by an earth rampart surmounted by a wooden palisade, which served to prevent the infiltration of barbarians into Roman territory and as a base for offensive or defensive operations.

84. Through his election as consul for ten years and censor for life, Domitian openly subordinated the republican aspect of the state to the monarchical. By increasing the pay of the troops by one-third, he secured their loyalty.

85–89. Moesia was invaded by the Dacians who were recently organized into a powerful kingdom by **Decebalus.** The Roman campaign, led by Domitian, ended in defeat in 86. A second Dacian War in 88 was successful, but final victory was precluded by the revolt of the legate of upper Germany, L. Antonius Saturninus (in 89), and by the rebellion of the Quadi, Marcomanni, and Iazyges, client peoples north of the Danube. Domitian made peace with the Dacians.

89. After Saturninus's revolt was put down, Domitian ceased the quartering of more than one legion in one camp and proceeded bitterly against his senatorial opponents.

92. Using Dacia as a base of operations, Domitian waged war against the Marcomanni, Quadi, and Iazyges. The war was unfinished at Domitian's death in 96.

93–96. Returning to Rome, Domitian initiated a series of treason trials in the senate, whose members where forced to condemn their colleagues.

96. Assassination of Domitian. The execution of Domitian's cousin Flavius Clemens caused general insecurity, and the forty-five-year-old Domitian was killed in a palace plot, ending the Flavian dynasty.

2. CONQUEST AND CONSOLIDATION

The conspirators, together with the praetorian prefects and certain senators, had arranged for **M. Cocceius Nerva,** an elderly senator from an old Roman noble family, to become emperor. Since Nerva and his three successors had no sons of their own, the principle of adoption prevailed in the succession, and what the senatorial tradition called the reign of the **five good emperors**—Nerva, Trajan, Hadrian, Antoninus Pius, and Marcus Aurelius—began.

96–98. Marcus Cocceius NERVA (b. 35) became emperor. Although favorable to the senate, Nerva had no military experience. The liability became apparent in 97 when the praetorian guard forced Nerva to execute Domitian's assassins. Nerva avoided a crisis by adopting the legate of upper Germany, Trajan, as his co-ruler and successor. Trajan remained in Germany until the death of Nerva on Jan. 27, 98.

98–117. Marcus Ulpius TRAIANUS (Trajan, b. 53), the descendant of an old Roman colonial family in Spain, was the first emperor born in the provinces. Trajan cultivated good relations with the senate but ruled independently of it. Continuing a policy of Nerva's, Trajan instituted a government program (*alimenta*) to support orphans in Italy.

101–107. In two hard-fought Dacian Wars (101–102 and 105–107), Trajan defeated Decebalus and annexed Dacia as a Roman province. Dacian gold financed building programs in Rome, including Trajan's Forum, with its sculptured column commemorating the war.

110, 111? Pliny the Younger went as a legate to reorganize the finances of the province of Bithynia. *Curatores* (overseers) were sent to supervise the troubled finances of various cities around the Empire. In Italy, the imperial *fiscus* advanced loans to municipalities to provide grain or money to poor children *(alimentarii)*.

113–117. Parthian War. Trajan declared war on Parthia. Victories enabled Trajan to create the provinces of Armenia (114), Mesopotamia (116), and Assyria (117). He was, however, recalled from the Persian Gulf by a widespread **revolt of the Jews** and of the newly conquered areas. Both revolts were suppressed with great severity. In 117 Trajan was repulsed from the desert town of Hatra. He died at Selinus in Cilicia (June 22 or July 9) after having adopted on his deathbed (some suspected his wife Plotina of having invented the adoption) his ward and cousin, **Hadrian,** at the time legate of Syria. Trajan's conquests, though spectacular, were of no permanent value.

117–138. Publius Aelius HADRIANUS (b. 75), emperor. He was recognized as emperor by the senate on Aug. 11. Almost immediately he abandoned the new provinces across the Euphrates. Under him the appointment of equestrians rather than freedmen to the important posts in the imperial secretariat became regular. He spent most of his reign (121–126, 128–134) traveling through the provinces, where he erected many buildings. He especially favored the Greek cities, notably Athens. In Britain he built (122–127) 80 miles of road, ditches, and stone-wall from the Tyne to the Solway. In Numidia he completed the extensive permanent camp of the Third Augustan Legion at Lambaesis.

In the collection of taxes, the companies of *publicani* had given way to individual collectors *(conductores)* under municipal supervision. Like his predecessors, Hadrian lightened or remitted certain taxes.

131. The **Praetor's Edict** was definitively codified by the jurist Salvius Julianus under Hadrian's orders. Since no praetor could thereafter alter it, the extension of legal procedure by praetorian *formulae* ended. Senatorial decrees became only a confirmation of the imperial speech *(oratio principis)* that initiated them. The only source of law was now the **edicts of the emperor.**

132–135. The **Jews of Judaea revolted** upon the founding of a Roman colony (Aelia Capitolina) in Jerusalem and the dedication of a temple to Jupiter Capitolinus on the site of their temple. Their leaders were the rabbi **Akiba** and **Simon Bar Kozebah.** The suppression of the revolt all but depopulated Judaea and thereafter Jews could enter Jerusalem but once a year. This furthered the dispersion, or **Diaspora,** of Jews to other regions. Centers of Jewish learning continued in Babylon, where the great edition of the **Talmud** was prepared in the late 5th century.

138. Upon the death of his first choice for successor, **L. Ceionius Commodus,** Hadrian adopted (Feb. 25) the competent Titus Aurelius Fulvius Boionius Arrius **Antoninus,** who received the imperial powers and took the name Imperator Titus Aelius Caesar Antoninus. He, in his turn, had to adopt the young son of Commodus, L. Aelius Aurelius Commodus (later Lucius Aurelius Verus) and M. Annius Verus, henceforth called Marcus Aurelius Verus Antoninus. Hadrian died on July 10.

138–161. Titus Aurelius ANTONINUS PIUS (b. 86), who spent his reign in Rome, became emperor. For his filial piety in securing the deification of Hadrian from a hostile senate, he received the title *Pius.*

139–143. Quintus Lollius Urbicus, legate of Britain, suppressed a revolt of the Brigantes in Yorkshire and, along the temporary line of forts built by Agricola from the Forth to the Clyde, constructed a turf wall north of Hadrian's. This, however, was soon abandoned.

145. Marcus Aurelius, who had married Faustina, daughter of Antoninus, received the imperial powers.

155. A brief **war with Vologesus of Parthia** ended in an inconclusive peace.

161–180. MARCUS AURELIUS Antoninus (b. 121) became emperor on the death of Antoninus (Mar. 7). Loyal to the wishes of Hadrian, he shared the imperial powers in full equality with **Lucius Aurelius Verus** (b. 130).

162–166. Verus was sent by Marcus to command in the east against Parthia. Though Verus dissipated at Antioch, his generals sacked Artaxata, Seleucia, and Ctesiphon and put a Roman puppet on the throne of Armenia.

166–167. The troops of Verus brought from the east a plague, which seriously weakened the frontier armies. The claims that the plague depopulated the entire Empire are later Christian exaggerations.

167–174. The Marcomannic War was a major revolt of the client peoples (the Chatti, Marcomanni, Quadi, Hermunduri, Iazyges, and Roxolani) along the upper Rhine and Danube. Marcus and Lucius raised two Italian legions and proceeded to the north. In 169, Lucius died of an illness, and Marcus suffered a major defeat. Pannonia was overrun; Raetia, Noricum, and Moesia were invaded; and, in Italy, **Aquileia was besieged.** Not until 172 did the tide turn, and the enemy began to be brought to terms, one by one.

175. C. Avidius Cassius, a distinguished general and legate of Syria, revolted but was quickly suppressed.

177. Marcus's fifteen-year-old son, Commodus, became Augustus, co-ruler with his father.

178–180. Planning to create two new provinces, Marcomannia and Sarmatia, Marcus, accompanied by Commodus, went north and resumed the Marcomannic War. Marcus died at Vindobona (Vienna) on Mar. 17, 180.

180–192. Marcus Aurelius COMMODUS Antoninus (b. 161) inherited his father's war and the economic problems it was causing. He quickly made peace with the Marcomanni and Quadi and returned to Rome. A foreign policy of diplomacy and containment, instituted by the praetorian prefect Tigidius Perennis (182–185), brought fifteen years of peace to the northern frontier. It did not sit well with Marcus's old advisers, however. In 182 a conspiracy involving Commodus's sister and many senators was uncovered. Trials, executions, and confiscations followed. Consumed by other interests, the young emperor spent lavishly and left governing to his ministers. In 186 Rome's grain supply was secured by the creation of a fleet, the *classis Africana.* But Commodus consistently failed to support his praetorian prefects. When attacked by his enemies, Perennis was abandoned by Commodus and executed. The same fate befell his corrupt successor, M. Aurelius Cleander (186–189). During the last years of his reign, Commodus became increasingly despotic. He identified himself with Hercules and spent time and money on games and the hunt, in which he participated. A palace conspiracy engineered Commodus's death. On Dec. 31, 192, he was strangled by his wrestling companion.

f. THE THIRD CENTURY

1. CIVIL WAR AND THE SEVERANS

Augustus had created a system whereby a large empire was defended by a limited use of force, and at a relatively small cost to the upper classes. **Soldiers, numbering about 300,000, were disposed judiciously along the frontiers and were moved to meet changing threats.** A second element in the defense of the frontiers was **client states**—peoples living just outside the Empire whom the Romans controlled through diplomacy and money. These states helped protect the borders and provided soldiers for units of the Roman army. It was the movements of peoples from northern and eastern Europe beginning in the latter 2nd century which upset the balance. The **Marcomannic War,** which was a revolt of the client peoples along the Rhine and Danube, signaled the end of diplomacy as an effective and inexpensive method of defending the northern borders. The only alternative was more soldiers, but this entailed greater expense. As a "good emperor," Marcus Aurelius was unwilling to tax the wealthy. The result was a drawn-out war which seriously strained the Empire's resources. Subsequent emperors felt less compunction about expropriating the wealth of the upper classes to pay for the armies. The civil war which followed the murder of Commodus exacerbated the trend, and its ultimate victor, Septimius Severus, ruthlessly exposed the military basis of imperial power and made the upper classes pay for it. The political reality of the 3rd century is summarized in the dying Septimius's advice to his sons—"Enrich the soldiers, despise everyone else."

193. Publius Helvetius PERTINAX, a sixty-six-year-old senator, who had risen from obscurity as an officer under Marcus Aurelius, was chosen emperor by the senate. His strict and frugal rule led to his murder (Mar. 23) by the praetorian guard, who then auctioned off the Empire to **M. Didius Julianus,** who promised to pay them the highest donative. The provincial armies reacted by nominating their own candidates; the British legions proclaiming the legate **D. Clodius Albinus;** the Syrian army, **C. Pescennius Niger;** and the Pannonian legions, **L. Septimius Severus.** Severus marched to Rome, where the senate deposed and executed Julianus.

193–211. Lucius SEPTIMIUS SEVERUS (b. 146, at Leptis in Africa), emperor. He dissolved the existing praetorian cohorts, composed of recruits from Italy, and enrolled new ones from legionary veterans. He kept Albinus quiet by recognizing him as Caesar (i.e., heir). He then defeated Niger in **Battles at Cyzicus** and **Nicaea** and at **Issus** (the Cilician Gates) and put him to death near Antioch (194). Albinus, who now claimed full equality, was defeated and slain (197, Feb. 19) at Lugdunum (Lyons), which was also sacked and which never recovered its prosperity. Severus executed the supporters of Albinus in Gaul and Italy.

Severus created three new legions, one of which was quartered near the Alban Lake in Italy, hitherto free from the presence of legionary troops. He appointed equestrians to command these legions, contrary to the Augustan rule, and also put the new province of Mesopotamia under an equestrian. He thus initiated the replacement of senators by equestrians in military posts which culminated under Gallienus. Military marriages were recognized, auxiliaries were settled on public land in return for military service, and the legionary pay was raised. Severus gave the jurisdiction over Rome and the area within 100 miles to the prefect of the city and over the rest of Italy to the praetorian prefect, who also exercised jurisdiction on appeal from the provinces. The emperor began the subdivision of provinces into smaller units, which culminated under Diocletian, and extended the organization of municipalities as the basis of tax collecting even to Egypt, which shows how valueless municipal status had become. He created a new treasury in addition to the *fiscus* (the original imperial treasury) and the *patrimonium Caesaris* (originally the ruler's private property, then crown property), namely the *res privata*, his personal funds, which were swelled by confiscations. He reduced the state senatorial treasury (*aerarium*) to a municipal treasury of Rome. He depreciated the silver content of the *denarius* to below 60 percent. Extensive and magnificent building programs were carried out in Rome, Africa, and Syria.

197–199. In a successful **Parthian war** Severus advanced as far as Ctesiphon and reconstituted the province of Mesopotamia under an equestrian governor with two legions.

205–211. A recurrence of **troubles in Britain** required the presence of Septimius himself to fight the Caledonians. He definitely withdrew from the wall of Antoninus to that of Hadrian, which he rebuilt. He died at Eboracum (York) on Feb. 4, 211.

211–217. CARACALLA (properly Caracallus), so named from a Gallic cloak which he wore, began to rule. He was the oldest son of Septimius and had been associated with him as Augustus (198). To strengthen the bond between the Severi and the Antonines he had changed his name from Septimius Bassianus to Marcus Aurelius (Severus) Antoninus (197). Upon his accession, he murdered his colleague (since 209) and younger brother, P. (originally L.) Septimius (Antoninus) Geta (b. 189), along with the jurist Papinian and many others. He increased the pay of the troops. To meet the consequent deficit he issued a new coin, the **antoninianus,** with a face value of two *denarii* but a weight of only one and two-thirds. He erected at Rome the vast **Baths of Caracalla** (*thermae Antoninianae*).

212. The **EDICT OF CARACALLA** (*constitutio Antoniniana*) extended Roman citizenship to all free inhabitants of the Empire save a limited group, perhaps including the Egyptians. Citizenship now meant so little that this step was a natural culmination of the leveling down of distinctions that had been continuous throughout the Empire. Caracalla's motive has been much disputed; he probably hoped to extend to all inhabitants the inheritance tax paid by Roman citizens.

213–217. Caracalla successfully defended the northern frontier against the Alamanni in southern Germany and the Goths on the lower Danube (214), and in the east he annexed Armenia (216). But as he was preparing an invasion of Parthia, he was murdered by a group of his officers (217, Apr. 8).

217–218. Marcus Opellius (Severus) MACRINUS (b. 164?), emperor. He was a Mauretanian who had risen from the ranks to be praetorian pre-

fect and was the first equestrian emperor. He surrendered Caracalla's eastern gains and sought to reduce the pay of the troops, who set up as a rival (218, May 16) at Emesa in Syria Bassianus, a grandnephew of Julia Domna, the Syrian wife of Septimius. Macrinus was assassinated on June 8, 218.

218–222. The young Bassianus, surnamed **ELAGABALUS** (Heliogabalus, b. c. 205), came to power. He derived his cognomen from the Emesa god, whose priest he was. To legitimize his rule, he changed his name from (Varius) Avitus to Marcus Aurelius Antoninus and claimed to be a son of Caracalla. While Elagabalus surrendered himself to license and introduced the worship of his god to Rome, the Empire was really ruled by his forceful mother, **Julia Maesa.** She obliged him to adopt his cousin (Gessius) Bassianus (Alexianus?), son of her sister, Julia Mamaea. The praetorians murdered Elagabalus (222, March 11).

222–235. Marcus Aurelius SEVERUS ALEXANDER (b. c. 208), emperor. He was the adopted son of Elagabalus and was dominated by his mother, Mamaea. She established a regency committee of senators and used the advice of the jurists Paulus and Ulpian.

223, 226?–235. The **New Persian (Sassanian) Empire** was founded by **Ardashir,** a Persian who overthrew the Parthian Arsacid, Artabanus V. In 230, Ardashir attacked the Roman provinces of Mesopotamia and Syria. He was repulsed by Alexander in 232. On Alexander's death in 235, Ardashir invaded Mesopotamia.

234–235. Alexander was forced to buy peace from the Alamanni on the Rhine. His disgruntled troops murdered him (235, March), ending the Severan dynasty.

2. FOREIGN INVASION AND INTERNAL DISARRAY

The military problems caused by the emergence of an aggressive Persian (Sassanian) kingdom on Rome's eastern borders (p. 100) and the continuing pressure of northern tribes on the Danube and Rhine frontiers increased during the rest of the 3rd century. In the mid-third century a coalition of German tribes on the middle and lower Rhine, the **Franks,** began invading Gaul and Spain (p. 95). The **Goths** started to raid Asia Minor and the Balkans c. 238 and later split into the **Visigoths,** who entered the Empire along the central Danube in the 4th century, and the **Ostrogoths,** who acquired an empire in the Ukraine and later entered Italy under Theodoric the Great. The **Vandals** first appeared on the central Danube c. 270. In the early 4th century they overran Gaul and Spain and in 428 invaded Africa. The nomadic **Huns** drove the Ostrogoths from the Ukraine c. 370 and in the 5th century advanced into central Europe and the Empire.

On the death of Severus Alexander, the **internal stability of the Empire** evaporated, and no emperor was able to secure the loyalty of the armies for long. Of those who ruled from 235 to 284, one died in battle, one was captured by the enemy, and one died of plague—all others either died in civil wars or were assassinated. The power of the armies and the predominantly military function of the imperial government dictated that 3rd-century emperors would be military men drawn primarily from the martial Danubian provinces. The combination of foreign wars and internal disorder caused an economic crisis. The imperial government was bankrupt, the currency was debased until it was worthless, and inflation was rampant. **Trade declined and taxes were paid in kind.** Agriculture was in disarray. In the war-torn border provinces, land went out of cultivation. The resultant demands placed on peasants in more peaceful areas became intolerable, causing many to flee the land or revolt. The threat of war caused cities, including Rome, to be fortified with large walls. Pressure to meet the **ever-increasing imperial taxes** and to maintain the civic institutions of their own communities drove the urban elite into ruin and led to the decline of cities. **Population declined** as a result of epidemics and economic decline. The extent of depopulation is disputed, however, and varied greatly by region.

235–238. Gaius Julius Verus MAXIMINUS "Thrax," a Thracian peasant noted for his great size and strength, who had risen from the ranks under Septimius, was proclaimed emperor by the Rhine legions after the murder of Alexander. Maximinus beat back the threats of Sarmatians, Dacians, and Goths but was opposed by the senate. In Africa, the legions proclaimed as emperors the 80-year-old proconsul **M. Antonius Gordianus** and his son **Gordianus II** (238). Both perished in a war with the prefect of Mauretania who supported Maximinus. In Rome the senate raised from their own numbers **M. Clodius Pupienus** and **D. Caelius Calvinus Balbinus.** Maximinus was slain by his own troops while besieging Aquileia (June 238). The praetorian guard murdered Pupienus and Balbinus, and forced the senate to recognize the thirteen-year-old grandson of Gordianus, Gordianus III, as emperor.

238–244. Marcus Antonius GORDIANUS III (b. 225) was dominated by the praetorian prefect **C. Furius Timesitheus,** whose daughter he married (241). Timesitheus drove the Persian king Shapur (Sapor) out of Carrhae (242–243) but died of disease. The new praetorian prefect made himself co-Augustus, then murdered Gordianus (early in 244).

244–249. Marcus Julius PHILIPPUS "the Arab" bought peace with the Persians, won victories in Germany and Dacia, and, at Rome, celebrated the *ludi saeculares* for Rome's thousandth birthday (248). He was killed at Verona (249) in battle against his commander in Dacia, Decius.

249–251. Gaius Messius Quintus Traianus DECIUS (b. 200?) instituted the first general **persecution of the Christians** and perhaps of all who would not sacrifice to the emperor. The entire Roman field army was wiped out, and Decius was slain (the first emperor killed in battle) by the Goths in 251.

251–253. Gaius Vibius Trebonianus GALLUS (b. c. 207) was proclaimed emperor by the army of Moesia. In his reign began a 15-year plague. When he marched against his successor in Moesia, the Moor M. Aemilius Aemilianus, his own troops slew him (before Oct. 253).

253. Marcus Aemilius Aemilianus, emperor, was proclaimed emperor, then murdered, by his own troops.

253–260. Publius Licinius VALERIANUS (b. c. 193), commander in Raetia, became emperor, with his son Gallienus as co-Augustus; they divided the Empire, east and west. Gallienus fought unsuccessfully against the Franks, who crossed the Rhine in 256; the Alamanni, who reached Milan; and the Goths. As the frontiers ceased to hold, cities within the Empire began to build walls. In the east, Valerian campaigned against Shapur (256–259) but was captured and died in captivity.

259–268. Publius Licinius Egnatius GALLIENUS (b. 218) continued to reign alone, though pretenders appeared throughout the Empire and the period has been called that of the **"thirty tyrants"** (nine are attested). He completed the substitution of equestrians for senators as legionary commanders and as governors.

The **Goths,** who had broken through to the Black Sea, harried Asia and the Aegean area from ships.

258–267. Odenathus, ruler of Palmyra in the Syrian desert, kept the Persians out of Asia (260). His queen and successor, **Zenobia,** declared her independence (267).

259–268. Postumus set himself up as emperor in Gaul. **Gallienus** was murdered by his own troops before Mediolanum (Milan), where he was besieging the pretender **Aureolus** (before Sept., 268). Aureolus in his turn was slain by Claudius II.

268–270. Marcus Aurelius CLAUDIUS II "Gothicus" (b. ?) was the first of a series of capable Illyrian emperors who prepared the way for Diocletian. He repelled a Gothic invasion of the Balkans (269, whence his title) at **Naissus** (Nisch) and settled numbers of Goths in the vacant lands of the Danubian provinces. Upon his death from plague, his brother Quintillus was proclaimed as emperor.

270. Marcus Aurelius Claudius QUINTILLUS deserted by his troops, he committed suicide and was succeeded by an associate of Claudius Gothicus.

270–275. Lucius Domitius AURELIANUS (Aurelian, b. c. 214?) was rightly entitled "restorer of the world" (*restitutor orbis*). He abandoned trans-Danubian Dacia and settled its Roman inhabitants in a new Dacia carved out of Moesia. He repulsed the Alamanni from Italy (271) and built the existing walls of Rome (271–276).

271–272. Aurelian and his associate Probus defeated and captured Zenobia and, upon a second revolt, sacked Palmyra (273).

273 or 274. Aurelian recovered Gaul from the successor of Postumus, Tetricus, in a **Battle at Châlons.** Both Zenobia and Tetricus adorned his magnificent triumph in Rome (274). He was murdered by some officers while preparing to invade Persia (275).

275–276. Marcus Claudius TACITUS, an elderly senator, was appointed emperor against his will by the senate. Though he defeated the Goths and Alans, who had invaded Asia Minor, the troops slew him.

276. Marcus Annius FLORIANUS, brother of Tacitus, was slain soon after assuming the purple.

276–282. Marcus Aurelius PROBUS (b. 232), an Illyrian, was saluted by the eastern armies (276). He repelled from Gaul the Franks and Alamanni and other peoples, who had inflicted great devastation. He also strengthened the Danube frontier, quieted Asia Minor, and suppressed pretenders in Gaul. When the praetorian prefect Carus was proclaimed emperor by the troops in Raetia, Probus was murdered in Pannonia.

282–283. Marcus Aurelius CARUS, an Illyrian (?) and praetorian prefect to Aurelian, succeeded and campaigned successfully against the Persian monarch Bahram (Varahran). He perished in 283, and his son Marcus Aurelius Numerius **Numerianus,** co-Augustus with him, was murdered (284, autumn). A second son, M. Aurelius **Carinus** (emperor, 283–285), tried to hold the west against **Diocletian,** an officer whom the eastern army had elected emperor, but he was slain by his own troops during the battle at the river Margus in Moravia (285, summer?).

g. THE RISE OF CHRISTIANITY

The principal characteristic of **early Christianity** was its **plurality.** A wide variety of **divergent and competing doctrines**—gnostic, libertine, observant—were practiced, all claiming the authority of Jesus Christ. The "orthodox" church—it was only after the Roman government had given its support to one sect that the terms "orthodox" and "heretical" became official—eventually accepted **four Gospels**—Mark (c. 64–70), Matthew (c. 80–90), Luke (c. 70–90), and John (c. 95–115)—the book of **Acts,** fifteen **Pauline letters** (only six are certainly by Paul), and a few other works as canonical. Other, "heretical" texts were burned. The success of the form of Christianity that would eventually prevail was a function of its superior organization. Paul had formed his communities (c. 48–60) with overseers (bishops), and ministers (deacons), and had stressed obedience. In the writings of the **Apostolic Fathers**—the martyred bishops Clement of Rome (d. 96), Ignatius of Antioch (d. 98–117), and Polycarp of Smyrna (d. 155)—we find churches organized around the three-fold ministry of bishops, presbyters (councils of elders), and deacons; these writings also put the same emphasis on discipline and authority. By the mid-second century, this disciplined Christian sect began to attract educated converts—Justin Martyr (d. 160?), Athenagoras (fl. 176–177), Irenaeus (fl. 177), Tertullian (c. 160–240), and Minucius Felix (fl. 200–240), and the bishops Theophilus of Antioch (d. 180), Melito of Sardis (fl. 175), Clement of Alexandria (fl. 190–203), and Origen (c. 185–254)—who wrote Apologies defending the Christian faith against calumnies and official persecutions. In Rome, Christians were executed under Nero, Domitian, and Marcus Aurelius; in the provinces **persecutions of Christians** were equally sporadic. Whether Christianity was illegal per se or whether Christians were persecuted for alleged criminal behavior is problematic. Well-organized Christian communities provided its members with benefits both social—burial; care for orphans, the sick, and the poor—and psychological—institutional identity and protections from demons. Their successes in urban centers around the Empire left these Christian churches poised to assume more important social roles when the civic institutions of the Roman Empire were shaken by the crisis of the 3rd century.

5. THE LATER EMPIRE, 284–527 C.E.

a. ECONOMY, SOCIETY, AND CULTURE

The **economy** of the Empire continued to be troubled. **Land went out of cultivation** because of war, the flight or revolt of hard-pressed peasants, and an overall decline in population. In an effort to maintain agricultural production, the **settling of barbarians inside the Empire,** which had become regular in the 3rd century, assumed a grand scale in the 4th century. **The number of slaves continued to decline,** but slavery by no means disappeared. In agriculture, the labor of slaves tended to be replaced by that of *coloni* (tenant-farmers), whose status was originally free but fell over time to that of being tied to the land. By 400, the legal codes refer to *coloni* as *servi terrae* (slaves of the land). The **power of landowners grew** correspondingly, and those in the west became independent of the imperial government, even raising private armies. In the east, where the imperial presence in Constantinople assured a strong central administration, wealthy landholders were less independent. Another reflection of the decreasing need for slaves is the dramatic decline in freedmen, both in and outside of the imperial service. In the late Empire, freedmen were replaced by freeborn bureaucrats, as the imperial bureaucracy, together with the army, became the principal avenue of social mobility. The economic focus, and increasingly the cultural focus, of the Empire shifted from cities to large estates, particularly in the west. **Municipal office** had lost most of its authority and independence to imperial officials, and from the time of Diocletian and Constantine it was a **hereditary duty.** Laws forbidding municipal aristocrats to escape the ruinous burdens of office were regularly circumvented or ignored, and many of the **urban elite retreated to their countryside estates,** which had always been their sources of wealth. In the east, however, where the institution of the city-state had a longer tradition, and where proximity to Constantinople and imperial armies afforded protection, cities remained prosperous until the 6th century. Not all areas of the Empire were equally affected by economic decline. The Danubian provinces and large parts of Gaul suffered from foreign invasion (p. 94), but Sicily enjoyed continuing prosperity, and Africa remained prosperous until it was taken by the Vandals (429–39) (p. 168). The eastern provinces, which were less affected by foreign invasion, remained relatively prosperous. **Interprovincial trade** in grain and other articles of mass consumption revived under Diocletian and lasted, though at a reduced rate, through the 4th century. It was the **invasions of the 5th century** that brought about irreversible decline.

Trade was to a great degree subordinated to **imperial needs.** By the end of the 3rd century, members of *collegia*, who had originally been partners in independent business associations, were legally tied to their occupations. By the 4th century all trades and occupations were organized into hereditary **collegia,** which were bound to provide services for the state. Compensation was paid at a fixed rate, which became lower over time, and was accompanied by increased regulations. The economic troubles of the 3rd century had led to a **severe debasement of the coinage,** but although the monetary element of the economy was severely curtailed, it never disappeared. Diocletian's attempt to reestablish the currency with the issuing of the new gold *aureus* and silver *argenteus* failed, and bronze and silver coins continued to decline in value; silver coins ceased to be minted altogether by the 5th century. Stability was established by Constantine's new gold coin—the *solidus*—which remained the standard coinage of the Eastern Empire until 1070.

The **emperor** was now the **sole source of Roman law.** But the extension of the Roman citizenship to virtually all free inhabitants of the Empire had affected the practice of law in the provinces, which became a mixture of debased Roman law and local practice. An example of this "vulgar law" is the *lex Romana Visigothorum* issued in 506 by Alaric II, king of the Visigoths (p. 168). Classical Roman law was continued in the east by the law schools of Beirut and Constantinople. The problem of codifying the enormous body of earlier law was met by the publication of the *codex Theodosianus* in 438, which continued to be used in the west. The greatest work of legal compilation was carried out under **Justinian** (p. 183) by the jurist Tribonian and encompassed the publication (between 530 and 534) of the *Digest* (or *Pandects*), the *Institutes*, the *Codex Justinianus*, and the *Novellae Constitutiones* (the *Novels*), which together make up the *Corpus Iuris Civilis*, as it was later called.

As a function of urbanism, **literacy,** together with schools and the production of books, underwent a general if uneven decline beginning in the mid-third century. A cultural disjuncture grew up among the governing classes between administrators who continued to be highly educated and less-literate military men. It was for the latter that the numerous epitomes of the lengthier works of classical literature were now produced. The rise of Christianity affected a change in the pattern of literacy but did not cause an overall increase. For while literacy was important for church leaders, most Christians heard rather than read holy scripture. Christians were in the forefront of the **replacement of the book scroll by the codex.** The majority of non-Christian texts began to be affected by the change only in the 4th and 5th centuries.

The relative peace established by Diocletian and Constantine led to a revival of literature, but with a number of significant changes. As the Empire had been administratively divided between east and west, so too was its culture. Knowledge of Greek became rarer in the west, and Latin literature no longer drew so heavily on Greek models. The focus of Latin literature moved away from Rome, as centers of literary patronage shifted to other imperial capitals. To varying degrees authors began to use the classical tradition in writing about Christian themes. Latin poetry was continued by Decimus Magnus **Ausonius** (310–394), who became tutor to young Gratian and composed a great number of poems in a variety of genres. Claudius **Claudianus** (Claudian, c. 370–404) was born in Alexandria and became court poet at Milan, where he wrote panegyric and historical and mythological epics. Aurelius **Prudentius** Clemens (348–405), born in Spain, wrote lyric poems on Christian themes. Gaius Sollius Apollinaris **Sidonius** (c. 431–486), who eventually became a bishop, was from a Gallic family of distinguished imperial officials. Dividing his life and his work between politics and leisured retirement, he wrote light poems (*nugae*), verse panegyrics, and letters, which give a vivid description of Romans and barbarians in fifth-century Gaul. Latin biography was continued in the form of the 4th-century collection of imperial lives (Hadrian to Numerianus) called the *Historia Augusta*. **Ammianus Marcellinus** (c. 330–395), an army officer from Syria, wrote the last great history in Latin (*Res Gestae*), which treated the years 96–378 (only the parts covering 353–378 survive). The letters and speeches of Quintus Aurelius **Symmachus** portray the life of a distinguished Roman senator who revived and fought for classical literature and traditional culture. The antiquarian **Macrobius** Ambrosius Theodosius (fl. 430) preserved a vast amount of earlier learning in his *Saturnalia*, while **Martianus Capella** (fl. 420) wrote *The Marriage of Mercury and Philosophy*, an allegorical potpourri of classical learning.

Concrete and brick **architecture** reached truly **grandiose proportions.** In Rome, Diocletian surpassed the great *thermae* of Caracalla, with his own enormous **bath complex,** while Maxentius began, and Constantine completed, the equally enormous **Basilica Nova** on the Via Sacra. Imperial complexes which combined **palaces** and circuses, and sometimes mausolea, were built in or near most imperial capitals—Rome, Milan, Thessalonica, Antioch, and Trier, while Diocletian built a grand palace at Salona (Split) on the Dalmatian coast. With Constantine's conversion to Christianity, imperial largess went to building **great churches.** Public and private buildings were decorated with varieties of imported marbles, wall paintings, and mosaic work (e.g., Santa Costanza in Rome). The sculptural programs of late Roman imperial monuments witness not a degeneration of technique, but an expansion of the repertoire of styles to include the traditional and new (the arches of Diocletian and Constantine in Rome). In official portraiture, the tetrarchs continued to be presented in the style of third-century military emperors (the Venice Tetrarchs). After 312 Constantine, wishing to distance himself from his predecessors, adopted a new image which was civilian and youthful. After 324 the diadem and the upward gaze were added, evoking both contemporary religiosity and the image of Hellenistic kingship.

b. DIOCLETIAN AND THE HOUSE OF CONSTANTINE

The **advent of Diocletian** saw a thoroughgoing administrative reform of the Empire. Since it is difficult to distinguish which innovations were due to Diocletian and which to Constantine, a general summary will be given here. **Senatorial governors of provinces** had been first relegated to solely civic functions, then **virtually eliminated in favor of equestrians** by Diocletian. At Rome, the power of the senate and of magistrates waned when the emperor and his court moved to cities closer to the theaters of war. The **function of the Roman senate was limited** to governing the city of Rome. Meetings, presided over by the urban prefect, were often unattended, most senators preferring to remain on their estates. But the prestige of the Roman senate was sufficiently high in the 4th century for Constantine to established a **sec-**

ond senate at his new capital of **Constantinople.** Over the course of the 3rd century, the duties of most traditional Roman magistracies had been either eliminated or absorbed by equestrian officials appointed by the emperor. **The consulship survived as a largely honorary office.** In the 3rd century its prestige declined, but it was revived in the 4th, when Constantine established two annual consuls in Constantinople to match the pair in Rome. Thereafter, in the west the consulship became the prerogative of a narrow circle of aristocratic Roman families, while in the east the office tended to be monopolized by emperors, or used by them to reward both military and civic service. The emperor was chosen by the army and ruled absolutely. Beginning with Diocletian, **the pomp and ceremony of the Persian court was adopted.** The emperor was lord (*dominus*), and everything surrounding him sacred (*sacrum*). He wore a diadem, purple and gold robes, and jeweled slippers. Subjects prostrated themselves in his presence. The imperial court (*comitatus*) comprised great numbers of officials which included a large domestic staff headed by a eunuch, various offices (*officia*), and a *magister memoriae* (master of records), all supervised to one degree or another by the *magister officiorum*. In addition, there was the imperial guard (*scholae*), from which 40 men were selected to be the emperor's bodyguard (called *candidati* after their white uniforms). Also present at court was the officer training corps (*protectores*), in which promising officers served for a few years before being posted to high office. At court, protocol ruled.

The Empire was divided for administrative purposes into two spheres, eastern and western. Instituted by Diocletian, the division was in effect sporadically during the 4th century and became permanent with Arcadius and Honorius (395). Under Diocletian's tetrarchic system, there were two co-ruling senior emperors (*Augusti*), one in the east, the other in the west. Each Augustus chose an assistant and successor (*Caesar*). Imperial edicts were issued in the names of all four. There were four praetorian prefects who served under each of the four rulers and administered the four prefectures—Gaul, Italy, Illyricum, and the east. Each prefecture was divided into several dioceses under *vicarii* (vicars). In 312 Constantine disbanded the praetorian guard; and the prefects, together with their subordinate vicars, lost all military functions which were transferred to a *magister militum*. The dioceses were subdivided into provinces, which had themselves been divided so that their number doubled. Provinces were under the supervision of equestrian governors called *praesides*. Italy assumed the status of a province, its districts supervised by senatorial *correctores*.

In the late Empire, the **military** was wholly **separated from the civilian administration,** with the army bureaucracy usurping many administrative functions. The imperial armies of the high Empire had been tied to the defense of particular provinces. The system had proved inadequate during the third-century invasions, and so two distinct types of armies had developed. In the provinces, stationed along the borders, were the **frontier armies** made up of resident soldiers (*limitanei*) and commanded by a *dux*. A larger, better trained, and more mobile field army (*comitatenses*) was under the command of masters of infantry and cavalry (*magistri peditum, equitum*). Auxiliary troops were mostly foreign soldiers commanded by their own leaders, some of whom became very influential. Under Constantine a large part of the field army stayed with the emperor. Another contingent was permanently stationed on the eastern frontier under a *magister equitum et peditum per Orientem*, while the west was defended by another field army stationed in Gaul and commanded by a *magister equitum et peditum per Galliam*. Smaller units of the field army, stationed in Illyricum and Thrace, were commanded by officers called *comites rei militaris*. The size of all these units is controversial. Diocletian seems to have increased the numbers of legions of the frontier army from about 40 to 60. Under Constantine the field army might have reached 200,000 men. The Roman armies of the 4th century have been estimated at between 500,000 and 730,000 men.

Diocletian attempted to create a **more efficient tax system.** He established a regular system of requisitioning food and transport, and his taxes were based both on the *iugum* (a unit of land) and the *caput* (a unit of labor) and included Italy. Annual estimates were made for the imperial costs for the army, administration, and city of Rome, and a budget was produced to which taxes were adjusted. To facilitate the reform, a new census was conducted. Diocletian's attempt to control inflation by fixing prices and maximum wages in his **Edict on Prices**

(301) resulted in goods being withdrawn from market and in violence, while prices continued to rise.

284–305. Gaius Aurelius Valerius DIOCLETIANUS (Diocletian, b. 245, saluted as emperor Nov. 284).

285. Upon the defeat of Carinus, Diocletian chose as his colleague the Illyrian, M. Aurelius Valerius **Maximianus** (Maximian), who was given the title of **Caesar.**

286. After suppressing the peasant revolt of the **Baucaudae** in Gaul, Maximian was raised to the position of **Augustus.** Diocletian took up residence at Nicomedia in Bithynia, while Maximian lived mostly at Mediolanum (Milan). Diocletian assumed the title Jovius, and Maximian assumed that of Herculius.

288–292. Diocletian and Maximian waged constant war to hold the Empire together. Maximian was unable to oust M. Aurelius Mausaeus Carasius, who had seized the province of Britain and declared himself Augustus.

293, Mar 1. Creation of the Tetrarchy. Diocletian chose as his subordinate Caesar, **C. Galcrius** Valcrius Maximianus (b. c. 250). Galerius became Diocletian's son-in-law and governed most of the Balkan provinces; Diocletian governed the rest of the east. Maximian chose as his Caesar, Flavius Valerius **Constantius,** who divorced his wife **Helena** to marry Maximian's daughter. Constantius governed Gaul whence he drove Carasius to Britain, where he was killed and superseded by **Allectus.**

296. Constantius crossed to Britain, defeated and killed Allectus, and restored Britain to the Empire. Egypt revolted under Aurelius Achilleus, and L. Domitius **Domitianus** was proclaimed emperor. Diocletian put down the revolt in the winter of 296–7.

297. Narseh (Narses), the king of Persia, expelled the pro-Roman king of Armenia (p. 101). Galerius invaded Persia and was defeated but returned in the following year to crush the Persians. Narseh ceded Mesopotamia and other territories east of the Tigris to Rome.

298. Constantius returned to Gaul and defeated the Alamanni.

301. Diocletian's **Edict on Prices.**

303, Feb. 23. Galerius persuaded Diocletian to declare a **general persecution of the Christians,** which, however, Constantius did not fully enforce in his prefecture. The persecution was stopped in the entire west in 306 but raged in the east until 313.

305, May 1. Diocletian and Maximian abdicated voluntarily; Galerius and Constantius became Augusti; Diocletian and Galerius selected as Caesars **Flavius Valerius Severus** under Constantius, receiving the prefecture of Italy, and for Galerius his own nephew Galerius Valerius **Maximinus Daia,** who received Syria and Egypt. The hereditary claims of Maximian's son Maxentius and Constantius's son Constantine were neglected.

306–337. Flavius Valerius CONSTANTINUS I THE GREAT (b. 288? of Constantius and Helena) fled from Galerius to his father in Britain. On the death of the latter (July), Constantine was saluted as emperor by the troops but made an agreement with Galerius by which he became Caesar and Severus became Augustus. In Rome the praetorians and the people proclaimed **Maxentius** *princeps* (Oct. 28); he called his father Maximian to be Augustus and temporarily took the title of Caesar. When the emperor Severus came with an army, it deserted and he surrendered to Maximian and was later executed by Maxentius. In fear of Galerius, Maximian went to Constantine in Gaul; Constantine recognized him as senior Augustus and married his daughter, Fausta. Galerius attempted an invasion of Italy (307), but disloyalty in his army forced its abandonment. Maxentius took the title of Augustus (308), and Maximian fled to Constantine; for four years Maxentius ruled in Italy. Galerius induced Diocletian to preside over a conference at Carnuntum, where it was decided that Maximian should abdicate. Valerius Licinianus **Licinius** was to be Augustus in the west, and Constantine was to return to the rank of Caesar. Constantine refused and Galerius gave him and Daia the rank of *filius Augusti;* both were still unsatisfied and were finally given the rank of Augustus (310). Maximian attempted to revolt, but Constantine killed him. When Galerius died of disease (311, May), Daia seized Asia Minor, leaving the Balkans to Licinius. Constantine made an alliance with Licinius.

312. Constantine invaded Italy from Gaul and, after winning a battle over Maxentius's general at Verona, defeated and killed Maxentius himself near Rome at the **Milvian Bridge** (Saxa Rubra) (Oct. 28). Sometime later he became a Christian. At a meeting with Licinius in Milan (early 313?) equal rights were proclaimed for all religions by the **Edict of Milan.**

313. Daia crossed to Europe, but was defeated by Licinius near Adrianople and fled to Tarsus, where he died soon after. Licinius now held the entire east and Constantine the west.

316. After a brief war, in which Licinius was defeated at **Cibalae,** a peace was made giving Constantine all of the Balkans except Thrace.

324. Relations between the two were strained, and war finally broke out. Licinius was first defeated at **Adrianople** (July 3) and again defeated at Chrysopolis in Anatolia (Sept. 18). He surrendered and was executed in the next year.

324–337. CONSTANTINE REUNITED THE EMPIRE under his sole rule.

330, May 11. Constantine dedicated as his capital **CONSTANTINOPLE,** which he had spent four years in building on the site of Byzantium, commanding the strategic center of the east, the Bosphorus.

337, May 22. Constantine died at Nicomedia. He had executed Crispus, his son by his first wife, in 326. His remaining sons succeeded: Constantinus II (b. 317) received the prefectures of Italy and Gaul; Constantius II (b. 317) took the east, and Constans (b. 323?) got Illyricum and part of Africa. The nephews of Constantine, Dalmatius and Annibalianus, were killed by the army.

337–363. THE HOUSE OF CONSTANTINE. While Constantius carried on an indecisive war against the Persians (p. 101), Constantinus attacked Constans but was slain at Aquileia (340). Constans was killed by the pretender **Magnus Magnentius** (350, Jan.).

351, Sept. 28. Constantius defeated Magnentius at Mursa. The latter slew himself at Lugdunum (353), and the Empire was once more united.

351, Mar. 15. Constantius chose his cousin Gallus as Caesar, but had him executed in 354.

355, Nov. 6. Constantius chose as Caesar the half brother of Gallus, **Julian,** who had been educated by non-Christian teachers. Julian was sent to Gaul where he won great victories over the Alamanni and Franks.

360. Julian was proclaimed emperor by his army and marched against Constantius, who died before Julian reached the east (361).

361–363. Flavius JULIANUS, "the Apostate," (b. 332) attempted to organize a non-Christian, polytheistic church (p. 99). He defeated the Persians but died on his way back from an attack on Ctesiphon (363, July 26). With him ended the line of Constantine.

c. FROM THE DEATH OF JULIAN TO THE DEATH OF VALENTINIAN III

363–364. Flavius JOVIANUS (b. c. 331) was elected emperor by Julian's soldiers. He surrendered Mesopotamia to the Persians and died soon after (364, Feb. 17).

364–375. Flavius VALENTINIANUS I (Valentinian, b. 321) was the next choice of the army. He ably defended the west against the barbarians and made his brother **Valens** co-Augustus in the east (364, Mar. 28).

367. Valentinian made his son, **Gratian,** co-emperor in the west.

374. Valentinian died on an expedition against the Quadi and Sarmatians (Nov. 17).

375–383. Flavius GRATIANUS (Gratian, b. 359) named his young half brother **Valentinian II** (b. 371) co-Augustus in the west.

376. The **Visigoths** (West Goths) crossed the Danube and wiped out Valens and his army at **Adrianople** (378, Aug. 9). The Goths continued to ravage the Balkan region.

379, Jan. 19. Gratian appointed as co-Augustus for the east, **Theodosius,** son of Valentinian's *magister equitum.*

379–395. Flavius THEODOSIUS "THE GREAT" (b. 346). He came to terms with the Goths by settling them as military allies *(federates)* in the Balkans.

383. The British legions proclaimed **Magnus Maximus,** who seized Gaul. Gratian was slain at Lugdunum (Aug. 25). Theodosius recognized Maximus.

387. When Maximus drove Valentinian II from Italy, Theodosius captured and executed Maximus at Aquileia (388, July 28).

392, May 15. The Frankish *magister militum* **Arbogast** murdered Valentinian II at Vienne and set up as emperor the non-Christian rhetorician **Eugenius.**

394, Sept. 6. Theodosius defeated and slew Eugenius and Arbogast at the Frigidus, just east of Aquileia. The Empire was reunited for a brief time.

395, Jan. 17. Theodosius died at Milan. The Empire was divided between his elder son **Arcadius** (made Augustus in the east in 383) and the younger son **Honorius** (made Augustus in the west in 393).

395–408. Flavius ARCADIUS (b. 377) became emperor of the east. The praetorian prefect Rufinus managed to check the inroads of the Visigoths in the Balkans until his murder by the troops at the instigation of Stilicho, but thereafter the eunuch Eutropius failed to prevent the invasions of the Visigoths or of the Huns, who overran Asia.

395–423. Flavius HONORIUS (b. 384), emperor of the west fell under the influence of the Vandal **Stilicho** who, as master of the troops *(magister militum),* commanded all the forces and married his daughter Maria to Honorius (398).

396–397. Stilicho drove the Visigoths, led by Alaric, out of Greece.

402, Apr. 6. Stilicho defeated Alaric again at Pollentia and Verona (403).

406, Aug. 23. Stilicho at Florence broke up a miscellaneous force of barbarians which Radagaisus had led into Italy.

At about this time Gaul was overrun by Vandals, Alans, Suevi, and Burgundians.

407. EVACUATION OF BRITAIN by the Romans. Constantine, whom the troops in Britain had proclaimed emperor, crossed to Gaul with his forces, and it is probable that Roman troops were never sent back.

408, Aug. 22. Murder of Stilicho, at Honorius's order.

408–450. THEODOSIUS II (b. 401) on the death of his father Arcadius, became emperor of the east. He was a weak ruler dominated by his sister Pulcheria.

409. Alaric again invaded Italy and set up a usurper, **Attalus** (prefect of Rome, the last non-Christian "emperor"). Alaric soon deposed him again. The **Vandals** occupied Spain.

410, Aug. 24. ALARIC SACKED ROME (p. 168). He died soon after in southern Italy. His brother-in-law Athaulf led the Visigoths into Gaul (412) and thence began the conquest of Spain from the Vandals (415). There **Wallia** (416–419), successor of Athaulf, established the first recognized barbarian kingdom in southwest Gaul (419).

411. Constantine was besieged by Honorius's commander Constantius and taken near Arles.

423–425. Johannes usurped the purple on the death of Honorius at Ravenna (which he had made the capital in place of Milan).

425. Forces sent from the east by Theodosius II captured Johannes and put him to death.

425–455. VALENTINIAN III (b. 419) became child-emperor of the west. He was the son of Honorius's half sister Galla Placidia, who exercised power, and the general Constantius, who had been made Augustus in 421 but had died almost at once. Valentinian was recognized by Theodosius II and married his daughter Eudoxia (437).

429. The general **Bonifatius** tried to set himself up as independent in Africa, with the aid of the Vandals. But the Vandals seized Africa for themselves after a two-year siege of Hippo Regius (430–431) during which the bishop **St. Augustine** died (430, Aug. 28).

430. Aëtius, master of the troops, disposed of his rivals, Felix and Bonifatius (recalled from Africa in 432). He then devoted himself to clearing Gaul of barbarians, which he did by a resounding victory over the Visigoths (436) and by suppressing an uprising of the peasants and slaves *(Bagaudae,* 437).

435. The **Vandal kingdom in Africa** was recognized. The Vandals took Carthage in 439.

438. Publication of the **Theodosian Code.**

450–457. MARCIAN, an able general, became emperor when Theodosius II died and Marcian married Theodosius's sister, Pulcheria. He allowed the Ostrogoths to settle as military allies *(federates)* in Pannonia.

450. Attila, leader of the Huns, after ravaging the Eastern Empire (441–3 and 447) led his people into Gaul. Galla Placidia, the empress, died.

451, June. Aëtius defeated the Huns in the **Battle of Châlons** (actually the *campi Catalauni* near Troyes).

452. Attila invaded Italy but turned back (p. 167). Attila died in 453 and his hordes broke up.

454, Sept. 21. Valentinian rewarded Aëtius by murdering him with his own hand.

455, Mar. 16. Valentinian was murdered by two of Aëtius's guards, marking the end of the house of Theodosius.

d. CHRISTIANS AND PAGANS

Christian churches flourished in the third-century crisis that affected the civic institutions of the Empire (p. 95). The extent of Christian belief at the end of the century is controversial, however. While some Christians held positions in the government and army, and some were well-to-do, the great majority were uneducated, poor city-dwellers. Nevertheless, Christians were sufficiently conspicuous for them to be perceived as a threat and to be officially and systematically persecuted by Decius in 250, by Valerian in 257–260, and, finally, from 303 to 311 by Diocletian and Galerius. The persecutions, which entailed the burning of sacred books, the destruction and confiscation of church property, the loss of high status *(honestiores)* for Christians, and the arrest of the clergy, failed to curtail the growth of Christian communities.

Constantine, whose mother, Helena, was a Christian, and who described himself as a Christian after 312, is the pivotal figure in Christianity's rise. As emperor he ended all persecution and restored church property, and in 313 with his **Edict of Milan,** he granted toleration and legal recognition to Christian churches. He also enforced the legitimacy of the particular Christian sect he supported by actively suppressing other "heretical" sects (e.g., the Donatists) and by insisting on compromise in doctrinal disputes within the "orthodox" church. The bitter controversy between **Arius** of Alexandria, who held that Christ was of a different substance—*heterousios*—than god, and Bishop Alexander (to be succeeded by **Athenaeus**), who held that they were of the same substance, was settled by the emperor at the **Council of Nicea** in 325, where the doctrine that Christ was consubstantial—*homoousios*—was sanctioned. (The dispute raged on until the reign of Theodosius I.) The conversion of Constantine did not, however, make Christianity the religion of the Roman state. Under Constantine and his successors, the Empire remained officially multireligious, and traditional polytheism continued to be openly practiced. But Constantine did turn the tide by shifting imperial largess away from the traditional Roman cults to Christian churches (the bishops of large cities became enormously wealthy due to imperial largess), by granting exemption and immunities to Christian clergy, and by favoring Christians in the army and administration. The gradual **conversion of the upper classes to Christianity** was accomplished, not by force or persuasion, but by the patronage and example of the imperial family. Constantine's sons, especially Constantius, were fervent Arians, and under them the cults of traditional Roman religion suffered from lack of government support, confiscation of land, and official indifference to organized Christian attacks, as well as from the actual closings of temples. The tide was briefly reversed by **Julian** (361–363), who attempted to restore the traditional religion by granting toleration to polytheists, by shifting imperial funding back to the old cults, by revoking privileges for the Christian clergy, by forbidding Christians to teach Greek and Latin literature, and by passively condoning attacks on Christian churches. The official revival of polytheism ended with Julian's premature death. That Julian's successors as emperor were all Christians shows how far the faith had penetrated the army. Yet Julian's reform was not entirely in vain, since it was almost 30 years before the vehement intolerance of Constantius was again official policy. On becoming emperor, Jovian issued an edict of general toleration, which was renewed by Valentinian and Valens, under whose reigns non-Christian temple lands were confiscated, although the temples remained open.

It was the growing numbers of powerful men who were entering the higher orders of the Church that effected a change. In 374, **Aurelius Ambrosius** (Ambrose, c. 339–397), the son of a praetorian prefect and himself consul of Aemilia, was elected bishop of Milan. In this position he exerted great influence, first over the emperor Gratian (who revoked the edict of toleration, dropped the title *pontifex maximus*, confiscated the revenues of the Vestal Virgins and other priesthoods in Rome, and removed the Altar of Victory from the senate house), then over Val-

entinian II (whose denial in 384 of **Symmachus's** request to restore the Altar of Victory was due to Ambrose), and finally over Theodosius. The aim of Ambrose and men like him to create a Christian state in which traditional Roman polytheism, Judaism, and Christian heresies (especially Arianism) would not be tolerated was accomplished during the reign of Theodosius. Christian letters were continued in Greek by such men as **Eusebius of Caesarea** (260–340), who among other things established the tradition of Christian chronography, and by the theologian **Gregory of Nazianzus** (329–89). Latin Christian writing was dominated by North Africans such as **Arnobius** (fl. 295) and **Lactatius** (c. 240–320). The preeminent figures of the late 4th century were **Jerome** (Hieronymus, 348–430), who composed a major revision of the Latin Bible (the Vulgate), and **Augustine** (354–430), whose Neo-platonic thinking revolutionized Christian theology in the west (p. 166).

The subsequent religious history of the Christian Roman Empire is essentially that of doctrinal disputes. Under Theodosius II (408–450), **Nestorius,** the bishop of Constantinople, who argued for a sharp distinction between the divine and human nature of Christ, was condemned at the **Council of Ephesus** in 431. During the 5th and 6th centuries, the eastern Church was torn by the Monophysite heresy, whose doctrine was that Christ had a single nature. Although the doctrine was condemned at the **Council of Chalcedon** in 451, the eastern emperors on the whole were Monophysite. As imperial authority weakened in the west, the bishop of Rome became powerful and wielded political as well as religious power. A major development was **monasticism** which had a long tradition in the east (Antony in Egypt, c. 285). The work of **Martin of Tours** (362) (p. 166) spread monasticism in the west, culminating in the rule of **St. Benedict** *(regula Sancti Benedicti),* who founded his monastery at **Monte Cassino** in 529. The rule was adopted by **Cassiodorus** (480–575), secretary of Theodoric, who founded a monastery at Beneventum in 540. The closing of the philosophical schools in Athens by Justinian, the execution of **Boethius,** and the founding of the Benedictine monastery mark the transition from the classical to the medieval world.　*(To p. 165)*

e. THE LATER FIFTH CENTURY

455–472. A succession of puppet rulers in the west. In 455 Eudoxia, widow of Valentinian, set up **Petronius Maximus** at Rome. On his murder, in the same year, she called the Vandals from Africa.

455, June 2–16. Gaiseric and the Vandals sacked Rome.

456. Avitus advanced from southern Gaul to Rome but was deposed by his able general, the Suevian **Ricimer.** Ricimer retained power by securing the consent of the eastern emperors to his nominees, who were **Majorianus** (457–461), **Severus** (461–465), and, after a two-year interregnum, **Anthemius** (467–472) and **Olybrius** (472). When in 472 both Ricimer and Olybrius died, the eastern emperor, Leo I, appointed **Glycerius** (473) and **Julius Nepos** (473–475).

457–474. LEO I (b. ?), a Thracian (?), succeeded Marcian as emperor of the east. To offset his master of the troops, the Alan Aspar, he married his daughter Ariadne to Zeno, an Isaurian from the mountains of southern Asia Minor (467) and made Zeno's son, Leo, his colleague (473).

474. Leo II succeeded on the death of Leo I. His father, Zeno, made himself his colleague. Leo died the same year.

474–491. ZENO (b. 426) disposed of the pretender Basiliscus, brother-in-law of Leo I (475).

475. The master of the troops, **Orestes,** removed Nepos in favor of his own son, whose name combined those of the founder of Rome and of the Empire.

475–476. ROMULUS AUGUSTUS (nicknamed *Augustulus*).

476, Sept. 4. After defeating and killing Orestes at Pavia, the Herulian **Odovacar** *(Odoacer)* deposed Romulus Augustulus, the last emperor of the west, at Ravenna. **Traditional end of the Roman Empire.**
　(To p. 165)

The eastern emperor **Zeno** apparently recognized Odovacar as "patrician" (*patricius* had become the title of honor for barbarian commanders). Nepos retained titular claim as emperor until his death in 480, and after that date the Empire was theoretically reunited under the eastern emperors, but actually Odovacar ruled as an independent king in Italy.

481. On the death of Theodoric, the son of Strabo, Zeno recognized his rival as patrician and master of the troops. His people were established in Moesia as *foederati*.

488. Theodoric, ostensibly as **Zeno's** agent, invaded Italy.

493, Feb. 27. After a three-year siege of Ravenna, Odovacar surrendered. He was soon after murdered by Theodoric. Italy was united under Theodoric the Great (b. c. 455) as the kingdom of the Ostrogoths.

491–518. ANASTASIUS I (b. 431), emperor of the east, married Zeno's widow and removed the Isaurians from power, thus causing a serious revolt in Isauria (suppressed only in 497). The inroads of the Slavic Getae forced him to protect Constantinople by a wall.

502–506. The emperor waged a long war with the Persians.

514–518. Anastasius fought the pretender Vitalian, commander of the Bulgarian *foederati*. The emperor died on July 1, 518.

518–527. JUSTINUS I (b. 450?), a humble Illyrian who had risen to be commander of the imperial bodyguard, took as his colleague his able nephew Justinian (527) and died the same year.

527–565. JUSTINIAN. (For his reign see Byzantine Empire, p. 183.)

F. THE NEO-PERSIAN EMPIRE OF THE SASSANIANS, 223– 651 C.E.

(From p. 40)

a. ECONOMY, SOCIETY, AND CULTURE

The economy of the Sassanian Empire was based on agriculture, and the great majority of its inhabitants were peasants. While most farming was done by free peasants, chattel slavery was employed in royal mines, in building, in the crafts, and in agriculture, particularly on temple estates. Sassanian rulers, especially **Shapur I** (240–270) and **Khusrau I** (531–579), undertook a great increase in irrigation and land under cultivation. Much of the empire's agricultural wealth was centered in Mesopotamia, especially in the south region of Asuristan, where extensive irrigation produced an abundance of wheat and barley. To the southeast and across the Tigris was **Khuzistan,** which also produced great harvests of wheat and barley, sesame and rice. The district of **Meshan** (modern Kuwait) was famous for its palm dates; it also controlled access to the Persian Gulf and trade with India. Commerce was predominantly local, but a lucrative international caravan trade followed the **royal road,** extending north to Merv, Samarkand, and then on the **silk road** to China. Syrian glass, dyed fabrics, and metals were exchanged for silk, which served a diplomatic as well as an economic function. The primary form of taxation under the Sassanians was a land tax and, for religious minorities, a poll tax. The reforms of Khusrau I made the land tax, which began to be calculated in monetary terms, more efficient and extended the poll tax to all inhabitants between the ages of 20 and 50.

Sassanian society was divided into the traditional Iranian estates: priest *(magian)*, noble *(azatan)*, and farmer *(ram)*; the last estate also included traders, craftsmen, and bureaucrats. The basic social unit was the extended family of three or four patrilineal generations. Members shared religious and secular obligations and rights, as well as joint family property. Beyond the agnatic family, the larger social group was the clan *(naf, toxum,* or *gohr)* which comprised several dozen families whose heads shared a common ancestor and within which endogamous marriage was the rule. A wife and her property entered into the family of her husband, he becoming her guardian. The exercise of full legal rights required membership in a recognized urban or rural community, which in turn was determined by membership in one of the clans which formed the community. Free persons who were not members of a community—aliens, illegitimate children, freed slaves— were semidependent and had restricted rights.

The Sassanian period saw an increase in **centralization.** The semi-independent kingdoms characteristic of the Parthian era gave way to a unified state administration. Independent city-states that flourished under the Parthians were replaced by "royal cities," that is, military centers governed by state-appointed officials called *shahrabs*. Rural districts were under the jurisdiction of the city administration. In the late Sassanian period, the kingdom was divided into four large divisions headed by a military and civil authority. The numerous religions tolerated by the Parthians were replaced by the single state religion, **Zoroastrianism,** whose administration of temple lands throughout the empire by officials called *magupats* paralleled that of the civil and military administration.

In Sassanian Persia, state and religion were twin sisters. By the mid-fourth century, thanks to the efforts of the priest **Kartir, Zoroastrianism** had become the official state religion, whose priesthood sometimes challenged the authority of the king. The ruler, the king of kings, was chosen by God and crowned by the chief priest *(mobadan-mobad)*. All power and law devolved from the king, who ruled with the support of the priesthood and the nobility that monopolized high administrative and court positions. The court of the Sassanian king was famous for its elaborate protocol and hierarchy of officials in which the priests played an important role. Despite the intolerance of Zoroastrianism, a number of influential religious movements sprang up during the Sassanian period. **Mani** (216–277), the founder of **Manichaeism,** was born in Babylonia of an Arsacid priestly family. He gained the support of the upper levels of Iranian society and become a companion of Shapur I. His doctrine became especially strong in Parthia and central Asia. Mani eventually fell afoul of the powerful Zoroastrian priest, Kartir, and in 277 he was imprisoned and died. Manichaeism spread from Spain to China. Another new religion was **Mazdakism.** The gnostic-socialist offshoot of Zorastrianism caused major social unrest during the reign of Kavad I (488–531), who initially supported it as a counterbalance to the power of the nobles and the priesthood. Its leader, Mazdak, son of Bamdad, preached a radical doctrine of redistribution of wealth and women which threatened the privileges and power of the upper classes. Mazdak was executed at the end of Kavad's reign, and the sect was persecuted and went underground. The official attitude toward previously established religions varied. The large Jewish population of Mesopotamia suffered sporadic persecution at the hands of Zoroastrian magi. Because of its connection with Rome, Christianity aroused the political as well as the religious opposition of the Sassanian state and church and was frequently persecuted.

b. ARDASHIR I TO SHAPUR II

223, 226?–243. Ardashir I *(Artaxerxes, Artashatr)*, founder of the Sassanian dynasty. The son of Papak, a vassal king of the Parthians ruling in Persis (Fars), Ardashir revolted against Artabanus, the last king of the Arsacid dynasty of Parthia, defeating and killing him at **Hormuz** (Hormizdagan, c. 224). Ardashir ruled over the territories of the Parthian empire, received the submissions of the kings of the Kushans and of Turan (Pakistan and Baluchistan, respectively) in the east, and gained control of Merv in the northeast.

230–243. War with Rome. Ardashir besieged Nisibis in Roman Mesopotamia and raided Syria (230). In 232 his forces were repulsed by Alexander Serverus, after whose murder in 235 Ardashir took Nisibis, Carrhae, and the strategic city of Hatra.

243–270, 273? Shapur I *(Sapor)* had been co-ruler with his father, Ardashir, since 240. After conquering the peoples along the coast of the Caspian Sea, he had to defend his kingdom against Rome.

242–244. SHAPUR I'S FIRST WAR WITH ROME. The Roman emperor Gordian recaptured Carrhae and Nisibis and then defeated the Persians near Resaina. But Gordian was murdered, and his successor, Philip, losing a battle near Ctesiphon, was forced to sue for peace and pay a ransom. Having deprived Armenia of Roman support, Shapur engineered the assassination of its Arsacid king, Chosroes (c. 252). When the Armenian prince Tiridates was received by the Romans, Shapur attacked and began the second Roman war.

253, 256?–260. SECOND ROMAN WAR. A Roman army was defeated at Barbalissa, Syria was invaded, and Antioch was taken (256). When the Romans counterattacked, Shapur defeated and captured the emperor Valerian near Edessa (258, 259?); Valerian remained a captive until his death (265–66). Syria and Asia Minor were invaded by Persian forces, but no attempt was made to retain the conquered territories.

260–267. Palmyra. Roman territory was defended by Odenathus, the ruler of Palmyra, who chased the Persians back across the Euphrates and defeated Shapur (260). Soon after (262–267) he reconquered Mesopotamia, failed to take Ctesiphon, and was given the title of *imperator* by Gallienus. In 267 he was murdered and was succeeded by his widow, Zenobia.

Shapur devoted his remaining years to consolidating his power. He installed his sons as kings in Armenia, Mesene (southern Mesopotamia), Gilan (on the Caspian coast), and Sakas (in eastern Iran). In the north his kingdom extended to Iberia (Georgia); in the east to the borders of Sogdiana and central Asia. He built dams and a new city, Bishapur, in Persis. He also took an interest in the teachings of Mani, the founder of Manichaeism. Shapur was succeeded by his son, Hormizd I.

270, 273?–293. Hormizd I (*Hormisdas*, 270–271), son of Shapur, was killed in battle against the Sogdians and was followed by his brother, **Bahram I** (*Varahan*, 271–274). During his reign Aurelian defeated Zenobia of Palmyra and reestablished Roman rule in the east. Conservative Zoroastrian priests brought about the execution of Mani. Bahram was succeeded by his son, **Bahram II** (274–293). An eastern campaign against the Sakae was brought to an end by the Roman invasion of Persia under the emperor Carus, who conquered Mesopotamia and took Ctesiphon. The mysterious death of Carus ended the war (283). The new Roman emperor Diocletian installed **Tiridates III** in Armenia (c. 288). **Bahram III,** son of Bahram II, reigned for a few months and was deposed by his uncle, Narseh.

293–302. Narseh (*Narses*) worsted his brother and rival, Hormizd, and drove Tiridates from Armenia (296).

297. WAR WITH ROME. A Roman army under Galerius (p. 97) was defeated near Carrhae and Narseh recaptured Mesopotamia (297). The following year, Galerius returned and crushed the Persians. Narseh surrendered to Rome Mesopotamia and other territories east of the Tigris, the western part of Media was ceded to Armenia, and Iberia became a Roman protectorate. The Romans and Persians then remained at peace for forty years. During the reign of Narseh, the king of Armenia was converted to Christianity.

302–309. Hormizd II, son of Narseh, was remembered as a just ruler. On the death of Hormizd his natural heir, Hormizd III, was set aside by the nobility, who elected his posthumous son, the child Shapur II.

c. SHAPUR II TO THE REFORMS OF KHUSRAU I

309–379. SHAPUR II, the Great.

337–350. FIRST WAR WITH ROME (p. 98). Shapur invaded Mesopotamia, won some victories, but failed in three attempts to take Nisibis. In 350 he had to break off the war and go east to counter an invasion of the Chionites (Huns), whom he defeated and forced into an alliance (357). Beginning in 339 Christians began to be persecuted. Jews and Manichaeans also suffered.

359–361. SECOND WAR WITH ROME. Syria was invaded, and Amida was taken after a heroic defense (359). Singara and Bezabde were captured (360). Constantius attempted in vain to recapture Bezabde and died in the following year. His successor, Julian, invaded Persia, forced the passage of the Tigris, defeated the Persians north of Ctesiphon but retreated before investing that city, and was mortally wounded in a battle near Samarra (363). His successor, Jovian, made a treaty with Shapur in which Rome restored all the Mesopotamian territories ceded by Narseh, as well as Nisibis and Singara. Shapur was also given a free hand in Armenia, which he invaded and devastated in 365. He later made it and Iberia vassal states (378).

371–376. THIRD WAR WITH ROME. There were no decisive results,

and an obscure peace followed. Persian power was at its zenith at the death of Shapur II. His immediate successors, **Ardashir II** (379–383) and **Shapur III** (383–388), were weak, however. Shapur concluded a peace with Rome (384) whereby Armenia was partitioned between Rome and Persia. **Bahram IV** (388–399), probably the son of Shapur III, succeeded. He placed his brother on the throne of Armenia. Bahram was killed in a mutiny and was succeeded by his son, Yazdgird I.

399–420. Yazdgird I, the Wicked, was so called because of his conflict with the Zoroastrian priesthood. The persecution of Christians and Jews ended for a time. Under the patronage of Yazdgird, Sassanian Christians held the **Council of Seleucia** and adopted the anti-Arian creed of the Council of Nicaea. Near the end of Yazdgird's reign, toleration ceased when Christians began burning down Zoroastrian fire temples. In 409 Yazdgird struck a treaty with Rome and his rule was peaceful. He was succeeded by his son Bahram V.

420–438. Bahram V, known as the "wild ass," was supported by the Arabs against his cousin, Khusrau, the choice of the nobles. He continued persecution of the Christians and declared war on Rome (421) when the Christians crossed the border seeking Roman protection. Bahram was defeated (422) and agreed to permit Persian Christians to seek refuge in the Roman empire and to halt persecution. The eastern Christian church declared itself independent at the **Council of Dadiso** (424). Persian Armenia was reduced to a satrapy (428). Bahram campaigned against the Hephthalites (of Turkish stock?), driving them out of Persia across the Oxus. Bahram was succeeded by his son Yazdgird II.

438–457. Yazdgird II declared war on Rome and concluded peace in the same year (440). He then campaigned successfully against the Hephthalites (443–451). Urged on by his minister, **Mihr-Narseh,** and the clergy, Yazdgird sought to impose Zoroastrianism on Armenia and Iberia (449). Strong Armenian opposition was crushed at the Battle of Avarair (451). Yazdgird's last years were spent fighting on the northern borders against the Hephthalites. He died in 457 without a decisive victory. His younger son, Hormizd, seized the throne.

459–484. Peroz, the elder son of Yazdgird, defeated the usurper Hormizd with the help of the Hephthalites. His reign was marked by a severe famine and the renewed enmity of the Hephthalites who in 469? captured Peroz and forced him to give his son as hostage and to pay tribute. National resistance in Iberia and Armenia led to a revolt led by Vahan (481–483). Persian forces were withdrawn from Armenia to aid Peroz's campaign against the Hephthalites in which he was killed in 484. He was succeeded by his brother Balash.

484–488. Balash, Peroz's brother, was selected by the nobles. The Persians agreed to pay tribute to the Hephthalites. After Vahan had aided Balash in civil war, the king permitted Armenians to practice Christianity and ended Zoroastrian practice in the province. With royal approval, **Bar-Sauma** established **Nestorianism** (two natures of Christ) as the sole doctrine of the Persian Christian Church (484–489). Balash was assassinated and succeeded by the son of Peroz, Kavad.

488–496. Kavad (*Kabades*, first reign), son of Peroz, lived with the Hephthalites as a hostage and was supported by them. Kavad supported the religiosocialist movement of **Mazdak,** son of Bamdad. Mazdak seems to have been a Zoroastrian priest whose gnostic and egalitarian doctrine gained support among the common people but hostility from the nobles and the traditional priesthood. A conspiracy was formed against Kavad; he was arrested and replaced by his brother, **Zamasp,** who ruled from 496–498. Kavad escaped to the Hephthalmites, who accompanied him back to Persia where Zamasp resigned.

498–531. Kavad (second reign) returned to power and withdrew official support for increasingly radical reforms demanded by Mazdak.

502–506. FIRST WAR WITH ROME (Byzantium). The Byzantine emperor's failure to support Kavad led to an indecisive war in which the Persians took Amida. Peace was made, and Amida and other Persian conquests were ceded (506).

506–523. The nobility and the Zoroastrian priesthood continued to oppose the Mazdakites, who were massacred late in the reign (523). The Arab kingdom of the Kinda occupied parts of Mesopotamia (506–528), and unrest in Iberia led to the introduction of a Persian garrison.

527–531. SECOND WAR WITH ROME (Byzantium). Hostilities began in the Caucasus with Persian victories in Iberia and Mesopotamia (527–528) (p. 185). Belisarius defeated Persia at the **Battle of Daras** (528) but was himself defeated at the Battle of Callinicum (531). The war ended with the death of Kavad. Khusrau, the crown prince, engineered the execution of Mazdak and his followers as heretics (531) and then succeeded his father, Kavad.

531–579. KHUSRAU *(Chosroes)* **I ANUSHIRVAN** ("of the immortal soul"). After putting down a revolt and concluding formal peace with Byzantium, Khusrau undertook a series of great reforms. A fixed land tax and a head tax were instituted, which improved efficiency and equity while increasing state revenues. Irrigation and communications were improved, and new agriculture was encouraged. The army was restructured, with the state supplying equipment and salaries to the poorer nobles, the *dehkan* (knights). The empire was divided into four great administrative districts under a military governor *(spahbad)*. Toleration was granted to Christians, and learning was patronized. When the Athenian Academy was closed in 529, philosophers found refuge with Khusrau.

540–562. WAR WITH ROME (Byzantium). Disturbed by the policy of Justinian, Khusrau invaded Syria and sacked Antioch (540) (p. 185). A treaty was struck but denounced when Khusrau extorted money from Byzantine cities. The Persians campaigned successfully in Lazica (ancient Colchis, southwest of Iberia), making it a province (541). Khusrau's unsuccessful siege of Edessa (544) led to a five-year truce which was broken when the Byzantines invaded and eventually retook Lazica (549–555). A fifty-year peace was concluded with the Byzantines in 561 in which Lazica was recognized as Roman in exchange for an annual payment in gold to the Sassanians.

557. Allied with the Turks of Transoxiana, Khusrau finally brought an end to Hephthalite power.

572–579. WAR WITH ROME (Byzantium) (p. 185). The attempt to impose Zoroastrianism on the Armenians caused a revolt that encouraged the emperor Justin II to break the peace. Syria was ravaged by the Persians, and peace was negotiated with the co-emperor Tiberius (574); after renewed hostilities in Armenia, an uneasy truce was struck when Khusrau died (579) and was succeeded by his son, Hormizd IV.

d. HORMIZD IV TO THE MUSLIM CONQUEST

579–90. Hormizd IV. War with Rome (Byzantium) continued. The Persians were defeated by Maurice at Constantia (581). In 589 the Romans took Martyropolis, while the Romans won an important victory near Nisibis. The war continued indecisively, weakening both sides.

589. Persia was invaded by Arabs. The advance of the Turks constituted a real danger, but they were defeated by the Persian general **Bahram.** Bahram was ordered to invade Lazica but was met and defeated by the Romans on the Araxes. Superseded and insulted by the king, he rebelled. Hormizd was deposed and murdered; he was succeeded by his son, Khusrau.

590–628. KHUSRAU II PARVIZ ("the victorious"). Challenged by Bahram, Khusrau sought help from Constantinople; Bahram then seized the throne and ruled as **Bahram VI** (590–591). Khusrau was restored with the help of the emperor Maurice. Bahram fled to the Turks, where he was assassinated. Under Khusrau the Sassanian empire reached its greatest extent but then suffered a precipitous decline. Khusrau initially tolerated Christianity and in the disputes between Nestorians and Monophysites favored the latter. At the end of his reign, persecution was resumed.

603–606. The assassination of Maurice and his sons by **Phocas** (602) gave Khusrau the opportunity to declare war against Constantinople. After defeating the forces of Phocas, Khusrau's armies invaded Armenia and Syria and ravaged Cappadocia; many cities were captured, including Dara (603), Amida, and Resaina (606). In 604 a Sassanian army had been defeated by the Arabs at the **Battle of Dhu Qar.**

610–619. After Phocas was overthrown, Khusrau continued the war against his successor, **Heraclius** (p. 185). The leading cities of Armenia and Cappadocia were taken (610–611), and Persian armies captured Antioch, Damascus, and Tarsus (613). Jerusalem was occupied and the "true cross" taken to Ctesiphon (614). Anatolia was invaded, Chalcedon taken (615), and Constantinople endangered (616). In 619 Alexandria was taken, and Egypt came under Persian rule. Khusrau had restored the Achaemenid empire.

622–627. Heraclius counterattacked by invading Armenia, flanking and decisively defeating the Persians, who then evacuated Asia Minor. Heraclius again invaded Armenia, defeated the Persians, and ravaged Azerbaijan (623–624). Persian forces invaded Anatolia and took Chalcedon but were prevented from aiding the Avars in their abortive siege of Constantinople (626). In 627 Heraclius swept down into Mesopotamia and defeated a Persian army near Nineveh. Khusrau fled, a revolt ensued, and Khusrau was murdered and succeeded by his son Shiroe, who ruled as Kavad II.

628–629. Kavad II made peace with Heraclius, agreeing to evacuate Egypt, Palestine, Syria, Asia Minor, and western Mesopotamia and to restore prisoners and the true cross. Kavad died of the plague. The general **Shahrbaraz** *(Sarbaros)* usurped the throne and killed the infant son of Kavad, Ardashir III (628–629), but was himself murdered (629). Khusrau's daughter **Borandukht** (630–631) ruled for a year. On her death there was anarchy that seriously undermined the central authority of the monarchy (631–632).

632–651. Yazdgird III, the grandson of Khusrau, ascended the throne in 632 but did not receive the support of the Persian nobility in the face of the invasion to follow.

636–651. Arab invasion of Persia (p. 109). The Persian army under the general Rustam was defeated at Qadisiyya, near Hira (636). In 637 the armies of Islam occupied Ctesiphon. Yazdgir's appeal for Chinese aid went unanswered (638). The Arab army swept over the Iranian plateau and wiped out the imperial Sassanian army at Nihavand (642). Yazdgird fled to Merv, where he was murdered while hiding in a mill (651). Sassanian rule had ended, and the Persian provinces were incorporated into the caliphate. *(To p. 107)*

III. THE POSTCLASSICAL PERIOD, 500–1500

A. GLOBAL AND COMPARATIVE DIMENSIONS

1. PERIODIZATION, 500–1000

During the postclassical period, following the decline of the great classical empires of Asia and the Mediterranean, three major developments stand out in world history and the history of many individual societies: **the expansion of civilization to new areas**—in Asia, Africa, and Europe, this involved contact with and outreach from the older centers (China, India, the Middle East and North Africa, and Byzantium); **the spread of major world religions,** including the development of Islam, the most successful single religion during this period; and **the intensification of international contacts in the Eastern Hemisphere.** These themes were all established in the **first part of the postclassical period, 500–1000.** Changes in the Islamic world, the rise of new empires spreading from central Asia, new patterns of international contact (involving new policies in China and in Europe), and solidification of the major religions mark the **second phase of the postclassical period, 1000–1500.** In European history this period coincides with the Middle Ages (p. 165), and the resultant label "medieval" was formerly applied to world history more generally during the postclassical era.

The regional civilizations of the Eastern Hemisphere were transformed in this period. The Eastern Hemisphere ecumene continued to expand through trade, the spread of religions, migrations of peoples, and conquests. In the Western Hemisphere, Mesoamerican and Andean civilizations emerged in a context of complex, nonurbanized societies.

a. TRANSFORMATION OF REGIONAL CIVILIZATIONS

The major traditions of classical empires ended either through defeat and collapse or transformation.

220–960. CHINESE IMPERIAL EXPERIENCE. The end of the **Han Empire** in 220 created an era of warfare among small rival states. This "period of the Six Dynasties" lasted until the reestablishment of imperial unity by the **SUI DYNASTY** (589–618) and the **TANG DYNASTY** (618–907) (p. 148). The new imperial system was more clearly based on the bureaucratic skills of the **scholar-gentry class,** with the aristocracy and military playing a less central role than in the classical system. This postclassical style of empire was confirmed by its continuation in the **SONG DYNASTY** in 960, following a time of instability after the fall of the Tang.

476–973. POST-ROMAN WESTERN EUROPE. When Roman rule collapsed in western Europe, a number of states were established by groups that had migrated into the region. The **Franks** (p. 169), in the area of modern France and Germany, established a kingdom whose leader, Charles the Great, or **CHARLEMAGNE** (r. 768–814), was crowned **Holy Roman Emperor** by the pope in 800. The **Carolingian Empire** disintegrated, and the later efforts by a German king, **OTTO THE GREAT** (r. 936–73), also failed to reestablish regional imperial unity. The major sources of unity were the **ROMAN CATHOLIC CHURCH** and the teachings of **Latin Christianity.**

527–1025. EASTERN ROMAN EMPIRE AND BYZANTIUM (p. 183). Imperial rule continued in the eastern Roman Empire under the emperors in Constantinople. **JUSTINIAN** (r. 527–65) reconquered most of the Mediterranean areas of the Roman Empire (p. 185), but was unable to recreate broader Roman unity. The postclassical eastern Roman Empire gradually became a powerful **Greek imperial monarchy** known as the **BYZANTINE EMPIRE,** identified with the **ORTHODOX CHRISTIAN CHURCH.** Despite losses to invaders from central Eurasia in the north and to **Muslims,** it remained a major regional empire. The **MACEDONIAN DYNASTY** (867–1055) led a resurgence, but following the death of **Basil II** (1025), internal divisions and territorial losses reduced the empire to a minor state around Constantinople.

535–977. POST-GUPTA INDIA. The most successful effort to restore regional imperial unity in India was made by **HARSHA** (r. 606–47) (p. 132). However, his empire collapsed at his death, and no later state assumed a dominant position until the end of the 10th century, when **Muslim military dynasties** from the northwest continued the Muslim conquest of India. **Hindu culture** provided the foundation for regional civilizational unity without political integration.

651–945. EMERGENCE OF THE ISLAMIC MIDDLE EAST. The rise of **ISLAM** (p. 104) in the 7th century brought an end to the classical imperial systems of the Middle East. Islam was a continuation of **ethical monotheism** and is recorded as the revelation to the prophet **MUHAMMAD** (570–632). Muhammad's successors as leader of the Muslim community, called **caliphs,** conquered most of the Middle Eastern provinces of the Byzantine Empire in 634–43 and brought an end to the Sassanid Empire in 637. Civil wars brought the **UMAYYAD CALIPHATE** (661–750) and then the **ABBASID CALIPHATE** (750–1258) to power in an empire that initially continued classical Sassanid and eastern Roman structures. However, the Islamic world became a postclassical society unified by the faith and institutions of Islam. By the mid-10th century, the caliphate imperial structure was replaced by a new style of state based on commanders called **sultans** (p. 116), who initially gained titles and legitimacy by supporting the then-powerless caliphs.

b. COMPARISONS

In all regional civilizations, new structures emerged that were significantly different from the classical imperial societies. In China, India, and the western Roman Empire, imperial traditions were interrupted, and only in China was a restoration possible. However, in China the restored empire emerged in a postclassical form dominated by the scholar-gentry. In eastern Rome and the Middle East, there was continuity of imperial unity, but the basic nature of the imperial community was transformed. In all regional civilizations, the basis of identity shifted from imperial unity to community identified by religion or cultural worldview.

c. INTERREGIONAL RELATIONSHIPS

MIGRATIONS. In the Far Western region of the Eastern Hemisphere, the invasions of the **Huns** in the 4th century were followed by Germanic migrations and the arrival of additional peoples from the central Asian steppes, such as the **Avars** and **Bulgars** in the 6th and 7th centuries. Later invasions and migrations from **Scandinavia** laid the foundations for new states from the Volga River to England and Greenland.

On the frontiers of China, tribal federations continued to rise and fall, exhibiting increasing skill in managing large states. Some, like the **Khitans** (p. 149), who ruled much of Mongolia and Manchuria from 907 to 1123, integrated Chinese and nomadic elements. In central Asia, the **Uighars** became important in interregional trade and cross-cultural contacts.

Turkish peoples began to migrate into the Middle East during the Abbasid Caliphate; they became the dominant political and military force in a new-style Muslim society which was emerging by the 11th century.

TRADE. Commercial relations along the great **Silk Road** of Eurasia continued despite the rise and fall of imperial states. By 1000, Muslim traders, Indian merchants, and Chinese products and technologies were important elements in a growing hemispheric network. Maritime trade in the **Indian Ocean basin** and growing **trans-Saharan** trade in Africa, both dominated by Muslim merchants, opened vast regions to closer involvement in hemispheric networks.

d. CONTINUED SPREAD OF RELIGIONS

The communities identified by the major religions expanded far beyond the boundaries of the classical regional civilizations.

BUDDHISM became firmly established in both the mainland and island societies of Southeast Asia, receiving support from rulers in **Srivijaya** on Sumatra, a major maritime power from the 7th to the 13th century. Central Asian societies, like that of the **Uighars,** also saw an increasing Buddhist influence. During the **SUI** and **TANG DYNASTIES** in China, Buddhism became a significant part of the broad synthesis of popular Chinese religion, enabling Buddhism to survive periods of official opposition (p. 150). In **JAPAN,** the emerging centralized monarchy in the 6th and 7th centuries supported Buddhism, which became an important part of Japanese life.

CHINESE WORLDVIEW as a combination of cultural patterns, political concepts, and religion spread significantly in the postclassical era. Chinese interactions with central Asian societies continued, and peoples like the Khitans created effective political systems combining Chinese and local traditions. In **JAPAN** during the **Taika period** (645–710) (p. 158), major efforts were made to shape the developing centralized monarchy into one governed by a **Confucian**-style emperor. Aristocratic and warrior families and Buddhist leaders were able to limit the impact of Confucian political models, but the Chinese worldview in political, literary, and religious terms became a major component of Japanese society in the postclassical era. **KOREA** was unified as a centralized monarchy by the **Silla dynasty** (668–935) following Confucian models, and Korean society and culture became strongly **Sinified. VIETNAM** had been conquered by the **Han Empire** and later by the **Tang.** The **LE DYNASTY** (r. 980–1009) (p. 164) brought independence, but the state was influenced by Chinese models, which provided a basis for expansion. Chinese commercial involvement in the whole Southeast Asian region as well as in central Asia in the postclassical era meant that Chinese influences on culture and worldview were very strong in a vast part of Asia.

CHRISTIANITY spread significantly in the postclassical era. **CATHOLIC CHRISTIANITY** emerged as the major unifying force in western Europe after competition with other forms of Christianity, overcoming **Arian Christianity** among the Franks and **Celtic Christianity** in the British Isles in the 6th and 7th centuries. Spreading north and east, Catholic Christianity was adopted by rulers of **Bohemia** (9th century) and, in the 10th and 11th centuries, rulers in **Denmark, Norway, Sweden, Poland,** and **Hungary. ORTHODOX CHRISTIANITY** spread beyond the borders of the **Byzantine Empire,** with rulers of the **Bulgars** and early **Serbs** converting in the 9th and 10th centuries. The conversion of King **VLADIMIR I** (r. 980–1015) of Kiev (p. 224) brought Russia into the Orthodox Christian world. **NESTORIAN CHRISTIANITY** (p. 154) spread through a diaspora of traders and missionaries in central Asia and as far as China. It was an intellectual force in the ruling courts but did not succeed in winning mass support, and it lost many followers in the Middle East to **Islam** after the 7th century.

ISLAM was the major new religious force in the postclassical era. Although the Muslim community was identified in many ways with the **Umayyad** and **Abbasid** empires, social institutions of learned scholars, or **ulama,** and pious devotional teachers, as well as widely traveling Muslim merchants, provided vehicles for the expansion of Islam beyond the military boundaries of the Muslim Empires. By 1000, the majority of the populations throughout the Middle East were Muslims, having been converted by a long process of social and religious transformation (p. 107). Muslims represented diaspora communities of teachers, preachers, and merchants throughout Central, South, and Southeast Asia, as well as in many parts of Africa.

ABSORBED WORLDVIEWS. Some of the major classical worldviews ceased to have a separate existence by 1000 C.E., although they were still influential, as their major themes were absorbed into other religious traditions. **HELLENISM** disappeared as an independent worldview, but its concepts strongly influenced the development of **Judaism, Christianity,** and **Islam. ZOROASTRIANISM** all but disappeared following the end of the **Sassanid Empire,** but many of its major themes influenced Jewish, Christian, and Islamic thought. **MANICHAEISM** declined after the fall of the classical empires (p. 149) but had some missionary success in central Asia and China, being declared the state religion for a time in the 8th century by the **Uighars.** Even though it disappeared as a separate religion, its concepts of conflict between good and evil shaped later thought, especially in Europe and the Middle East, and occasionally provided the foundations for counterestablishment religions.

1000. RELIGIOUS CONTEXT. The great **classical empires** had been replaced as the dominant features of the major societies in the Eastern Hemisphere by major interregional **religious communities.** In the Far West, there were the two emerging Christian worlds of **Catholic** and **Orthodox Christianity;** the **Islamic world** extended from Spain to central Asia and south into Africa; in central and eastern Asia, **Buddhism,** either by itself or in conjunction with the **Confucian-based Chinese** worldview dominated the societies from Japan to Southeast Asia. **Hinduism** established itself as the culturally dominant force within the broad complexity of South Asian society.

e. THE GLOBAL PICTURE

The **EASTERN HEMISPHERE ECUMENE** expanded with continuing interaction between the great civilizations and the complex noncitied societies. The distinction between the two types of societies and also among the civilizations became less clear as religions, trade, and the movements of people widened to create networks that included all but the most isolated societies of the Asian far north and African far south. The way was opened for expansion on a hemispheric and a global scale.

Entirely separate from the Eastern Hemisphere ecumene, **WESTERN HEMISPHERE** societies developed major temple-palace civilizations in the Mexican highlands around **Teotihuacán,** in the **MAYAN** areas of the Yucatán Peninsula, and in the Andes around great cities like **Tihuanaco.** These civilizations did not establish persistent dynamism or continuity over time, however, as they experienced significant eras of decline, followed by the emergence of new societies. By the year 1000, great "classical" periods in both Mesoamerica and the Andes had come to an end, and networks of smaller complex states existed.

COMPLEX NONURBANIZED SOCIETIES continued to develop in North America, building on the traditions of earlier mound builders. **HOPEWELL CULTURE** created large new centers in the Mississippi Valley (p. 18), like **Cahokia,** and in the southwestern desert areas, large settlements were built by such peoples as the **ANASAZI.** In the **PACIFIC OCEAN BASIN,** this was an era of movement for the **POLYNESIAN** peoples (p. 386) who settled many of the islands and possibly facilitated interregional exchange of plants.

LARGE INTERREGIONAL NETWORKS in the Eastern Hemisphere and new contacts within the Western Hemisphere and in oceanic regions were developing by 1000, changing the picture of scattered but interacting separate societies and opening the way for the creation of even larger basic networks.

2. THE HIGH POSTCLASSICAL PERIOD, 1000–1500

The emerging networks involved different types of interactions, ranging from the exchange of scientific ideas and commercial goods to religious conversions and military conquests. These laid the foundations for more global integration by 1500. **Improvements in navigation** facilitated some expansions. They included the **magnetic compass,** in use on Chinese ships by 1100 and on Arab ships soon after; and development of more **accurate maps** by the Arabs.

a. MAJOR INTERREGIONAL EXPANSIONS

INTERREGIONAL EURASIAN EMPIRES. Central Asian peoples created a series of great conquest empires. The **SELJUK SULTANATE** emerged as a part of the migrations of Turkish peoples into the Middle East. Seljuks conquered the eastern provinces of the **Abbasid Caliphate** in the 11th century, proclaiming themselves the protectors of the caliphs and **Sunni Islam,** and following their victory over the **Byzantine Empire** at Manzikert in 1071 (p. 229), they took control of Anatolia. Although the extended Seljuk Sultanate lasted only from 1037 to 1092, Turkish soldiers became the ruling elite in many Muslim lands.

The **MONGOL EMPIRE** was the largest of the central Asian empires. It began with the conquests of **Chinggis Khan** (c. 1170–1227) (p. 153), and by the time of his grandsons' rule, it had become a network of large states. One grandson, **KHUBILAI KHAN** (r. 1260–94), established the **Yuan dynasty,** which controlled China until 1368, although expeditions to conquer **Japan** (1274 and 1280), Vietnam, and Java failed. A second grandson, **HULEGU** (r. 1256–65), established the **ILKHAN EMPIRE** (1256–1335) in the Middle East (p. 120) and brought an end to the **Abbasid Caliphate** with the conquest of Baghdad in 1258. Mongol expansion was stopped in Syria in 1260 by **MAMLUKS** from Egypt. The central Asian territories were under the control of **Djagatai** (d. 1241) and were the basis for later Mongol-Turkish states. In the Far West, most Russian states, including **Kiev** and **Moscow,** came under the control of the khans of the **GOLDEN HORDE,** whose descendants ruled parts of Russia until the 18th century. Invasions of Poland and Hungary brought devastation but no permanent occupation. The fact that Mongols did not rule the Ukraine and the Baltic regions encouraged those areas to distinguish themselves from Russia. The khans of the Golden Horde converted to **Islam** in 1257, and the Ilkhan ruler **Ghazan Khan** became Muslim in 1295. For almost two centuries, Mongol rulers provided a vast domain within which trade flourished and ideas and technologies were exchanged across much of Asia and Europe. However, Mongol leaders were unable to create effectively centralized control, and the Mongol world gradually disintegrated.

TIMUR-I LANG (r. 1360–1405) (pp. 136, 155) created the last great central Asian conquest empire, which controlled most of the territories of the **Ilkhans** and Djagatai's successors. However, the empire collapsed with his death.

1000–1400. EARLY EUROPEAN EXPANSIONS. The postclassical states in Europe attempted a number of interregional expansion efforts. (Irish monks had discovered Iceland in 790, and **Erik the Red** discovered Greenland in 981.) **SCANDINAVIANS** made some of the earliest efforts to expand, across the North Atlantic. Permanent settlements were established in Iceland, and by the 11th century communities were established for a time in Greenland and some people had traveled even farther west.

1000. Leif Ericsson driven off course to Newfoundland (which he called Vinland).

1003–6. Thorfinn Karlsefni, with three ships, explored parts of the North American coast. Contacts definitely continued until 1189, perhaps until 1347, by which point Greenland's settlements were in decline (p. 183).

TEUTONIC KNIGHTS, a Christian military order, provided leadership for an eastward expansion of warriors and farmers, changing the character of northeast Europe.

THE RECONQUISTA (reconquest) (p. 218) of the Iberian Peninsula by Christians from the Muslims increased in intensity by the 11th century, and continued until the final Muslim defeat in 1492.

THE CRUSADES (1095–1291) were the efforts led by the Catholic Church to take the Middle East (p. 233)—especially the Holy Land and Jerusalem—from Muslims. Although western European knights ruled Jerusalem for almost a century, after a number of formally proclaimed Crusades, Crusader control in the Holy Land came to an end in the 13th century. The Crusades had an important impact in that they intensified commercial and cultural contacts, but they did not reflect any distinctive European power.

Isolated efforts to explore the Atlantic were launched from Portugal,

Spain, and Italy. 1270: the Portuguese began to explore the west coast of Africa. 1291: the Vivaldo brothers from Genoa sailed into the Atlantic seeking a western route to "the Indies"; did not return. 1340–41: the Portuguese rediscovered the **Canary Islands** (assigned to Spain after conflicts, by **Treaty of Alcaçovas,** 1480). 1351: Genoese sailors may have reached the Azores. 1360s: regular expeditions from Barcelona were made along the northwest African coast. Technological limits prevented further activity until after 1430. Other contacts with Africa: papal representatives sent to Ethiopia, 1316; Ethiopian delegations visited Venice, beginning in 1402, to discuss alliance against Muslims.

1368–1500. CHINESE EXPANSION. The Yuan (Mongol) dynasty was defeated by an antiforeign revolution that established the **MING DYNASTY** (1368–1644). Early Ming rulers worked to reestablish Chinese dominance in the areas of long-standing Chinese interests and influence, such as Korea, Vietnam, Tibet, and central Asia. In addition, in 1405–33, Ming rulers sponsored a series of major commercial expeditions led by **CHENG HO (Zheng He)** (p. 155). Great Chinese fleets sailed as far as East Africa and the Middle East, establishing the potential for regular, Chinese-dominated trade throughout the Indian Ocean. However, the emperor ordered the halt of the expeditions by 1433. Nonofficial Chinese merchant activity continued in Southeast Asia, where Chinese commercial communities became an important force.

1000–1500. ISLAMIC EXPANSION continued throughout the Eastern Hemisphere. **Turkish peoples and sultanates** were important vehicles for this expansion. Although the **Seljuk sultans** were defeated, other sultanates were established, creating a belt of states controlled by mercenary military establishments identified with Islam. The **OTTOMAN SULTANATE** (p. 123), established in the thirteenth century, gained control over most of northern Africa, the eastern Arab world, Anatolia, and much of the Balkan Peninsula by the early 16th century. The Muslim Mongol rulers in Russia and Persia confirmed the military-style Muslim state in those regions, and the **DELHI SULTANATE** (1206–1526) (p. 134) was the major Muslim state in India. Non-Turkish sultanates developed as combinations of Muslim and local monarchical traditions throughout Southeast Asia.

WEST AFRICAN MUSLIM STATES followed the pattern of combining Islamic and local traditions. Islamic expansion in the region was confirmed by a sequence of major states, beginning with the conversion of the rulers of **Ghana** in the 10th century (p. 141), followed by **MALI** in the 13th century. The next state in the sequence was the **SONGHAY EMPIRE** (emerging in the 14th century and ending in 1591), whose leaders took the title of *askia,* or military commander.

EXPANSION THROUGH MISSIONARIES AND TRADERS. The major means by which Islam expanded beyond the ruling elites in societies outside of the Middle East was through the activities of **merchants,** who carried their faith abroad, along with their products. From the South China Sea and the India Ocean basin to sub-Saharan Africa, merchants were often the first contact between local peoples and Islam. An important means for combining local and Islamic traditions was the development of **SUFISM,** the Islamic form of mystical piety (p. 117). Sufism provided the basis for **brotherhoods** that combined popular piety with organizations for social cohesion. Sufi teachers were the major missionary force in the Islamic frontier areas. Great commercial cities on the East African coast, in central Asia, and on the islands of Southeast Asia became special centers for the popular expansion of Islam.

The Islamic world more than doubled in size between the 10th-century decline of the Abbasid Caliphate and the early 16th century. This was largely the result of the activities of Sufis, Muslim merchants, and sultans.

1400–1550. LATER EUROPEAN EXPANSIONS. By 1439 **Portugal controlled the Azores** and granted land to colonists; Spain soon did the same in the Madeiras and (1480) the Canaries (previously, the islands were inhabited by hunter-gatherers). Both countries imported European plants, weapons, and diseases, set up **sugar plantations** for exports to Europe, and brought in **slaves from northwestern Africa** as workers, foreshadowing later developments in the Americas.

Western European states began larger efforts at expansion in the 15th century. The new national monarchies of **PORTUGAL** and **SPAIN** played leading roles in supporting maritime expeditions for commercial and crusading purposes. **Developing European naval technologies,** utilizing rigid hulls and multiple masts with adjustable sails, made transoceanic travel possible in the Atlantic. Such ships were also able to carry cannons to give them extra firepower. Contacts with Asia gave Europeans knowledge of the **compass** and explosive powder. Motivation for expansions included fear of the new Ottoman Empire and the resultant desire to find independent trade routes, and an unfavorable balance of trade with Asia.

PORTUGAL began a major program of oceanic exploration and trade under the leadership of **PRINCE HENRY THE NAVIGATOR** (1394–1460).

Portuguese Exploration

1418–19	Exploration of Madeira Islands.
1427–31	Definitive discovery of Azores by Diogo de Sevilla.
1433	After ten-year effort, Portuguese ships rounded Cape Bojador; increased slave raiding.
1444	Nuño Tristam reached Senegal River.
1445	Dinís Dias rounded Cape Verde; increased trade, Portugal–West Africa.
1455–57	Alvise da Cadamosto, Venetian serving Prince Henry, explored Senegal and Gambia Rivers, discovered Cape Verde Islands.
1470–71	João de Santarem and Pedro Escolar reached Mina on Gold Coast, set up Portugese trading station (fort, 1482).
1472	Expeditions passed equator; Fernando Po discovered island that bears his name.
1482–84	Diogo Cão reached Congo River.
1487	Portuguese King John sent overland expedition (Pedro da Covilhā) to India and east coast of Africa.

Portuguese ships gradually moved along the African coast, with **Bartolomeu Dias** reaching the Cape of Good Hope in 1487 and **VASCO DA GAMA** sailing around Africa and entering the Indian Ocean in 1497. **PEDRO CABRAL** touched Brazil en route to India (1500); **regular Portuguese trade** to India began. Da Gama attempted to close the Red Sea to Arab trade (1501). Almeida defeated Muslim Indian Ocean fleet (1509). Within the next half century, Portuguese commercial and military bases were established throughout the Indian Ocean basin and in the South China Sea, in **Goa** (1510; governorship of **Alfonso de Albuquerque**), in **Malacca** (1511), and in **Macao** by 1557. **Jorge Alvarez** first reached China in 1513. In 1542 **Antonio de Mota** first reached Japan, after being blown off course.

SPAIN began building a major global empire after emerging as a national monarchy through the union of Aragon and Castile, beginning in 1469, and the completion of the **Reconquista** in 1492. In that year, **QUEEN ISABELLA** provided support for the expedition of **Christopher Columbus** (p. 277), who hoped to find a westward route to eastern Asia. He landed in the islands of the Western Hemisphere, and his trips were followed by other expeditions that established Spanish control in Mesoamerican and South American areas outside of those claimed by Portugal. Spanish expeditions conquered and effectively brought an end to the regional civilizations of the Western Hemisphere. **Hernando Cortés** destroyed the **AZTEC EMPIRE** of Mexico in 1518–21, and **Francisco Pizarro** conquered the **INCA EMPIRE** in Peru in 1531–36.

Further European expeditions opened the way for travel between the Atlantic and Pacific Oceans, with **Vasco Núñez de Balboa** sighting the ocean to be called the Pacific in 1513 and **Ferdinand Magellan** organizing the fleet supported by Spain that in 1519–22 was the first to sail around the world (p. 278).

b. INTERREGIONAL EXCHANGES

COMMERCIAL AND MATERIAL. Expansion efforts involved increasing interregional exchanges of goods. Traveling merchants were often a major vehicle for creating broad interregional networks.

Trade routes in the great overland and oceanic networks increased in importance. The **Silk Road** of central Eurasia flourished in the era of Mongol power, but gradually declined in importance as other routes developed and security became less reliable following the breakup of the Mongol Empire. **Indian Ocean trade** increased, first under the lead-

ership of local groups from southern Arabia, India, and Southeast Asia, and then outside groups, such as the **Chinese,** became involved. A trade network was established linking East African commercial city-states with the Middle East, India, and emerging commercial centers like **Malacca** in Southeast Asia. At the beginning of the 16th century, the **Portuguese** were able to dominate this system and link it directly, rather than through Mediterranean intermediaries, with Europe. Products exchanged continued to include **spices** from Southeast Asia and other expensive goods, but bulk goods, like sugar and textiles, were increasingly involved. **Trans-Saharan** trade continued to flourish between the Mediterranean lands and central Africa, but this was increasingly superseded by the coastal trade that developed with the emergence of the city-states of East Africa and especially with **Portuguese** expansion in the 15th century. The **SLAVE TRADE** came to be a major element in this commercial network as trade in the Atlantic developed.

BUBONIC PLAGUE, or **Black Death,** spread interregionally along trade routes through the exchange of bulk goods like grains. It began in the 1320s in the Gobi Desert, from which it spread to China. It began moving west in 1339; hit the Middle East and North Africa in 1347–48; reached Sicily in 1347, France in 1348, and western Russia in 1351. Major population losses occurred in China, India, the Middle East, and Europe.

1000–1500. TECHNOLOGICAL AND SCIENTIFIC EXCHANGES. New technologies were exchanged relatively rapidly as they developed in the major societies. The **MAGNETIC COMPASS** was developed in China and was adopted as a navigational tool by western Europeans. This and other developments in navigation transformed the nature of oceanic travel. **GUNPOWDER** was originally developed in China around 1000, but it had limited use there until **Mongols** began to use "bombs" in sieges and the **Ming** military developed some form of cannon. Other states developed artillery and hand-carried weapons to give them military firepower. Cannons helped to defeat castle-based nobility and, by 1500, the more successful centralized states were **"gunpowder empires"** (p. 279). These included the Ottoman and emerging Russian Empires as well as the European monarchies.

c. THE RELIGIOUS CONTEXT

The interregional religious communities developed comprehensive articulations that became the standard for religious establishments in the regional civilizations. **NEO-CONFUCIANISM** in China, especially as presented in the writings of **Zhu Xi** (1130–1200) (p. 152), provided a comprehensive statement of the Confucian tradition that became basic for the scholar-gentry-dominated state. **CHRISTIAN SCHOLASTICISM** in western Europe was the product of a similar comprehensive definition by teachers like **Thomas Aquinas** (1225–74) (p. 204), whose writings became fundamental for **Catholic Christianity. JUDAISM** received an influential and comprehensive presentation by **Maimonides,** or Moses ben Maimon (1135–1204). In **ISLAM,** a broad standard synthesis also emerged but was not as identified with a single person. In **SUNNI ISLAM,** four standard law schools developed, and **Sufism** was integrated into the broader canon by **al-Ghazali** (d. 1111) (p. 119). In **HINDUISM,** teachers like **Sankara** (c. 800) and **Ramanuja** (1017–1137) created a comprehensive philosophical framework for the immense diversity of Hindu thought and practice. In this way, the major religious traditions experienced an important standardization and rearticulation of basic worldviews with roots in the earlier **Axial Age** (p. 22).

d. THE GLOBAL PICTURE

Great interregional networks of trade, conquests, and exchanges of ideas blurred the boundaries between the major societies in the Eastern Hemisphere, and oceanic travel opened the way for a fully global network. In this emerging global network, as Europeans began to cross the Atlantic, the older temple-palace civilizations of the Western Hemisphere were destroyed. Although the nomadic peoples of central Eurasia played a significant role in hemispheric interactions, by 1500 they had become peripheral peoples with little ability to influence major developments. The emerging great powers were the monarchical states of western Europe and the bureaucratic gunpowder empires in the rest of the Eastern Hemisphere. *(To p. 279)*

B. THE MIDDLE EAST AND NORTH AFRICA, 500–1500

1. THE RISE AND EXPANSION OF ISLAM, 610–945

(From p. 102)

a. OVERVIEW

In the early 7th century, Arab Muslim armies spread out from the Arabian Peninsula into the surrounding lands and, in a wave of expansion that lasted about a hundred years, conquered almost the entire Middle East and North Africa. The **Sassanian Empire** based in Iran and Iraq ceased to exist, while the **Byzantine Empire** to the west lost large territories around the Mediterranean basin, including Syria, Egypt, and North Africa (p. 185). The political map of the region was completely redrawn as a **new Islamic empire** established its dominion over lands stretching from Spain to central Asia. The conquerors were initially a small minority ruling a non-Muslim society, but they set in motion changes that in time reshaped the overall identity and fortunes of the region.

The Arabs brought with them their newly founded faith of **Islam.** While they did not force conversion on the conquered population—mostly Christians, Jews, and Zoroastrians—the Muslims made the adoption of the new faith socially and economically advantageous. By the mid-10th century a sizable part of the population had converted, and while the region was not yet predominantly Muslim, **mass conversion** was well advanced, to be completed in the following three centuries or so.

The **Arabic language,** which until the conquests was confined to Arabia, spread in the region together with Islam. In the lands from Iraq to Morocco the populations became essentially Arabic-speaking; other languages, such as **Greek, Aramaic, and Coptic,** steadily disappeared from common use, surviving mostly in liturgy and religious writings. In Iran, the **Persian language** held out against this process of Arabicization, but not without adopting the Arabic script and a vast vocabulary of Arabic words.

The **Islamic religion** that arrived in the Middle East in the 7th century was rudimentary in form, consisting mostly of basic rituals, the divine revelation of the Qur'an, and the directives of the Prophet Muhammad. The period up to the mid-10th century marked the **formative stage** in which Islam elaborated its structures and established its **distinctive institutions.** Islamic law, theology, tradition, and mysticism took shape, to be developed to full maturity in the succeeding three or four centuries. A class of **Muslim religious leaders and scholars,** the *ulama,* emerged as the custodians and interpreters of the faith for the growing community. Their writings defined the terms of speculative thought and communal debate on the nature of Islam and its place in society.

During this formative phase, Islam, and **Arab-Islamic civilization** in general, were very much influenced by the Middle Eastern milieu in which they evolved. Greek philosophy and medicine, Iranian concepts of state, Byzantine administrative practice, Christian asceticism, Jewish and Zoroastrian codes of ritual purity, local architecture, cuisine, and popular lore—these and other elements of the **regional heritage** carried over into the Islamic period. Arab-Islamic civilization evolved as a synthesis of elements of different origins brought together in an original unity.

The **structure of politics** also underwent great changes. The Islamic empire was initially a unitary state ruled by a **caliph** and dominated by a **small Arab elite** that excluded non-Arab converts to Islam from an equal share in the benefits of power. By the mid-10th century the Abbasid Caliphate had been broken up into many virtually independent political entities. Struggles over succession gave rise to opposition and separatist movements, and to the greatest sectarian divide within Islam: that between **Sunnis** and **Shi'ites.** The Arabs lost their monopoly on power as the system was opened to all Muslims regardless of origin. The Abbasid caliphs became figureheads with little political authority, and the creation of an imperial **slave army** composed of imported Turks—an innovation of the period that remained a feature of Middle Eastern regimes until modern times—further transformed the political landscape, introducing a new power group that came to dominate the region's politics.

But while government became fragmented, the region evolved into a **thriving commonwealth.** A **single trading system** now linked the basins of the Mediterranean and the Indian Ocean. People, goods, and ideas moved freely within this vast sphere of interaction, relying on transport by water and caravans (**wheeled transport** having essentially disappeared in the region around the time of the Arab conquest, not to return until the 19th century). **Large cities,** foremost among them Baghdad, emerged as luxurious centers of culture, power, manufacturing, and consumption. In the agricultural countryside, where most of the population continued to live, a **"green revolution"** took place. **New crops,** including rice, sugarcane, cotton, oranges, and lemons, entered the region from China and India, and these, together with **new techniques** and investments in **irrigation,** improved both yields and diets. The **population** of the Middle East and North Africa may have experienced an **overall expansion** during the period, reaching a relatively high level of some 25 to 30 million in the 10th century.

b. MUHAMMAD AND THE RISE OF ISLAM

On the eve of the rise of Islam, **Arabia** was a tribal, desert environment with no single political organization or faith. The majority of its inhabitants were **pastoral nomads** organized by tribe and clan, who fought with one another for access to precious resources such as water, herds, and land. Some Arabs were sedentary and farmed at oases, such as Yathrib, while at **Mecca** many of the inhabitants drew their livelihood from trade caravans between Yemen and Syria.

Around 100 B.C.E., the northern Arabs developed a new saddle that allowed them to gain greater **control over the camels** they rode. This breakthrough gave them the ability to use the camel for military purposes, which allowed them to control trade in Arabia and earn enough money from the transport and protection of goods to buy metal weapons. Although confined to a largely nomadic environment, many Arabs, especially those in the caravan trade, had **contact with the two major empires** to the north: the Byzantine Empire centered at Constantinople (324–1453) and the Zoroastrian Sassanian Empire (224–651), with its capital at Ctesiphon in Iraq. Both empires employed **Arab mercenaries** to protect their borders with Arabia. The Byzantines used the tribe of Ghassan, which converted to Christianity, while the Sassanians paid the Lakhmids, at al-Hira, for their military services.

Before the advent of Islam, most Arabs worshipped a variety of male and female deities. Only a minority, who were neither Christians nor Jews, were monotheists *(hanif)*. Despite the vagaries of frequent feuds and raids *(ghazwa)*, Arab tribes from surrounding areas journeyed to Mecca during truce months to worship at the **polytheist shrine of the Ka'ba.** The **tribe of Quraysh** in Mecca enjoyed special prestige as keepers of the Ka'ba, as well as political and economic prominence built on fortunes drawn from trade.

610. FOUNDATION OF THE FAITH OF ISLAM. The founder of Islam was **Muhammad ibn Abdallah,** a member of the tribe of Quraysh and the clan of Hashim who was born in Mecca around the year 570. Orphaned at an early age, Muhammad found employment in the caravan company of a rich widow named **Khadija,** whom he later married. According to Islamic tradition, in 610 he received his first divine revelation. He was ordered to recite the words that the angel Gabriel conveyed to him in Arabic from Allah, the supreme and sole deity of the new faith of Islam. The **revelations** continued throughout his lifetime and formed the Qur'an ("recitation"), regarded by all Muslims as their divinely dictated scripture. As the Prophet of Allah, Muhammad's task, according to Muslims, was to deliver the final and perfect message from God to all humanity. Previous communications had been misunderstood or corrupted by the Jews and Christians. As the bearer of the true message, Muhammad was considered the "Seal of the Prophets," the last in a line of monotheistic messengers from Adam to Jesus.

The name of the religion, **Islam,** means submission to Allah, to be demonstrated by the **five pillars of the faith** defining the duties incumbent on all Muslims: *salat* (ritual prayer), *zakat* (almsgiving), *hajj* (the pilgrimage to Mecca), *sawm* (the fast during the month of Ramadan, when the Qur'an was first revealed), and the *shahada*, the recitation of faith that states, "There is no god but Allah, and Muhammad is His messenger."

The **Qur'an** consists of 114 chapters *(suras)* organized, after the first short opening chapter (the *fatiha*), from longest to shortest. Each chapter is divided into verses *(ayas)*, the longest chapter containing 286. The text covers a multitude of themes, from descriptions of paradise and hell to social codes in matters of marriage and inheritance. The Qur'an was **not set down in writing** by the Prophet himself during his lifetime. He may have dictated parts of it to a secretary, but much of it remained scattered in written fragments and in the memory of men, not unusual in a society that favored oral tradition. The text was **collected and organized** in its definitive form around 644, some 12 years after the Prophet's death.

During Muhammad's lifetime and for many years to follow, the new faith remained rough and unformed. It took several centuries for Muslims to develop Islam's rich theological and legal traditions, including its elaborate code of laws (the *shari'a*).

613. Muhammad began preaching Islam publicly in Mecca. His early themes involved warnings about the end of the world and the Day of Judgment. Initially the Prophet met little opposition, because he was perceived as merely a poet or a soothsayer *(kahin)*, but when he became insistent that there was only one god and that the Ka'ba must be reserved for Allah alone, **the response of the Meccans grew harsh,** even violent. They understood that Islam threatened their own beliefs, their prestige as the keepers of the sacred shrine, and the prominence of Mecca as a site for pilgrimage and trade. The earliest converts to Islam *(Muslims)* were members of Muhammad's family, young men from weak Meccan clans, and outsiders, often of slave origin.

According to the Qur'an and later Islamic tradition, Muhammad made his famous **night journey and ascension to heaven** *(mi'raj)* during this period. The Prophet began his journey from Mecca or, according to many other traditions, from Jerusalem, on the winged mule named Buraq. He met the prophets who had preceded him, and in the highest level of heaven he appeared before the throne of Allah.

615. Emigration of a small group of Muslims to Ethiopia, in search of a new site in which to practice their faith peacefully.

619. Death of Abu Talib, Muhammad's uncle and chief protector in Mecca. Without Abu Talib's influence, life for Muhammad and his followers, a persecuted minority, became increasingly difficult.

Death of **Khadija bint Khuwaylid,** the first wife of Muhammad and the first convert to Islam. She supported Muhammad economically and stood by him when, as a prophet, he was reviled by the Meccans. Muhammad had remained in a monogamous union with Khadija, with whom he had many children. The only child to survive the Prophet was his daughter **Fatima** (d. 633), whose sons would play a major role in later Islamic history. None of Muhammad's sons by Khadija lived through infancy.

622, Sept. The *hijra*, or emigration, of Muhammad and his followers from Mecca to Medina. Forced to flee the threatening environment of Mecca, Muhammad was asked to arbitrate a bloody dispute between the rival Aws and Khazraj tribes at the oasis town of Yathrib, known thereafter simply as **Medina,** meaning "the city" (of the Prophet). He soon emerged as the local leader, establishing **the first Islamic theocratic community** *(umma)*, with himself as both Prophet and political leader.

The Islamic polity at Medina included those Meccan Muslims who had followed the Prophet to Medina *(muhajirun)* and Medinan converts to Islam *(ansar)*. Inhabitants of Medina who did not accept Muhammad as their spiritual leader acknowledged his political supremacy. These groups included three Medinan Jewish tribes (Banu Qaynuqa', Banu al-Nadir, and Banu Qurayza) as well as non-Muslim Arabs. In an **effort to win the support of the Jews,** Muhammad initially incorporated Jewish observances, such as the fast of Yom Kippur, into Islamic ritual, and designated Jerusalem as the Muslim direction of prayer. The Jews, however, rejected Islam and opposed the Prophet's mission on religious grounds.

The *hijra* became the first year of **the Islamic calendar,** a lunar calendar of 354 days—twelve months of either 29 or 30 days. The Islamic calendar is not adjusted periodically to correspond with the seasons, and over time, religious holidays fall in all seasons of the solar year.

624. The Battle of Badr. The victory of a small Muslim force over more numerous troops protecting a Meccan caravan resulted in the strengthening of Muhammad's political and economic position. Many of those Medinans who doubted him *(munafiqun)* were silenced, and **the Jewish tribe of Banu Qaynuqa' was exiled.**

625, March. The Battle of Uhud. Meccan forces marched to the outskirts of Medina to take revenge for those slain at Badr, but the confrontation was inconclusive. The Jewish tribes avowed neutrality, but Muhammad accused the most wealthy of them, the **Banu al-Nadir,** of aiding the Meccans and expelled them from Medina.

627, March. Battle of the Trench *(al-Khandaq).* About 10,000 Meccan troops unsuccessfully besieged Medina. Muhammad and his 3,000 supporters dug a trench to prevent an attack on the city. The failure of the Meccans demonstrated that the Muslims of Medina had become a power to be reckoned with in western Arabia. After the battle, the Muslims accused the remaining Jewish tribe, the **Banu Qurayza,** of treason. The men were executed and the women and children sold into slavery. The Prophet now ruled a unified Medina and sought further influence among the tribes of western and northern Arabia.

628. Treaty of Hudaybiyya. The Meccans agreed to peace with Muhammad for ten years.

629. The Meccans vacated their city for three days to allow the Muslims to worship at the Ka'ba. All Muslims now focused on **Mecca as the direction of prayer** *(qibla).*

630, Jan. Meccan capitulation to Muhammad. The Muslims entered Mecca, cleared the Ka'ba of idols, and established the city as their religious center. Three weeks later the unified Muslim and Meccan forces defeated a confederation of beduin tribes from the nearby city of Ta'if, at the Battle of Hunayn. Muhammad's prestige was confirmed and the support of the Meccans cemented.

630–32. Subjugation of the tribes of the Arabian Peninsula. During the last two years of his life, Muhammad expanded his political influence, receiving tribal delegations *(wufud)* from throughout Arabia. Although many of those tribes paid the alms tax *(sadaqa)* to Medina, not all of them accepted Muhammad as either a political leader or a prophet.

632. Farewell pilgrimage. Muhammad journeyed from Medina to Mecca on the *hajj*, the journey since enjoined for all believers.

632, June 8. Death of the Prophet Muhammad. After a short illness the Prophet died in the house of his favorite wife, A'isha. At the time of his death, the Muslim community retained the collective power of a "supertribe," one forged in faith with an infinite potential for expansion.

It is believed by most Muslims that the Prophet made **no provisions for political succession** at the time of his death. A committee *(shura)* of prominent Muslims met to decide who should be the Prophet's political successor [khalifa, or caliph], since no one could follow Muhammad as Prophet. The issues of political succession and authority proved difficult to define and quickly became points of contention within the Islamic community.

632–61. RASHIDUN CALIPHS. The Rashidun ("rightly guided") caliphs is what the majority of Muslims call **the first four successors to the Prophet Muhammad.** Each was among the earliest of the Meccan members of the Quraysh to convert to Islam and was regarded by the Prophet as one of his close companions *(sahaba).* The Rashidun caliphs were all tied to Muhammad through marriage, since each of them had either married a daughter of the Prophet or given his daughter to him in marriage. They maintained the unity of the Prophet's community, oversaw the conquest of the Middle East, and established basic Islamic political and socioeconomic institutions.

632–34. ABU BAKR, THE FIRST CALIPH. Abu Bakr was one of the first Meccans to convert to Islam and was the Prophet's father-in-law. His daughter was the Prophet's favorite wife. On his accession he was faced with **rebellion by many Arab tribes** that had previously accepted

Muhammad's authority. In a series of campaigns known as the Ridda, or wars of apostasy, he succeeded in reconsolidating Arabia under Islamic authority. At his death (Aug. 23, 634), he had also begun the conquest of Syria, the first phase of the Islamic expansion in the Middle East.

632–750. THE ARAB CONQUESTS. In a remarkable wave of conquests, Arab and Muslim troops occupied territories extending from Spain to India. The **Sassanian Empire** (p. 100) was brought to an end, and the **Byzantines** lost most of their possessions in the Middle East and North Africa. The conquered populations came under Muslim rule, although it took several centuries of **conversion to Islam** to change their religious identity. The majority of the inhabitants of the conquered Byzantine territory in Syria and Egypt remained Christian for centuries, just as the majority of those who lived in territories once controlled by the Sassanians in Iraq and Iran retained their Zoroastrian creed.

The conquests began as an attempt to bring all the Arab tribes of the Middle East under the control of the Islamic polity established at Medina. Their scope expanded with each success. The first expeditions against Syria were organized in Medina under the able direction of the Meccan Quraysh, an elite with great organizational and tactical skills. It is estimated that about 24,000 men were engaged in the conquest of Syria, with fewer still occupied in the later conquest of Iraq. Many of these recruits were prompted not by the new faith of Islam, but by the **lure of booty and government stipends** (*'ata*).

The **tactics of the Arab armies** included surprise and laying siege to the garrisons of opponents ill-prepared for the new invaders. Arab military success was enhanced by the relative **weakness of their two major imperial opponents** in the Middle East: the Byzantines and Sassanians. Throughout the 6th and 7th centuries these two great powers had fought each other in a series of wars that had left both economically and strategically vulnerable to surprise attacks from the south. Both powers had also persecuted their Monophysite and Nestorian Christian citizens as heretics, thus undermining the support of their people.

634–40. Conquest of Palestine and Syria. After defeating the Byzantines at Ajnadayn in southern Palestine (634), the Arabs advanced into Palestine and Syria. **Damascus** surrendered in 637, and **Jerusalem** surrendered shortly after.

634–44. UMAR IBN AL-KHATTAB, THE SECOND CALIPH. Umar directed the first phase of the Islamic conquests in Egypt, Syria, and Mesopotamia. To keep Arab troops separate from newly conquered populations, he ordered the creation **of garrison settlements** (*amsar*), which became the foundation of several **new Islamic cities**, such as Kufa and Basra in Iraq and Fustat in Egypt. Muslims entitled to salaries from the state were recorded on a list (*diwan*), with the earlier converts enjoying higher pay. Umar established the **system of Islamic taxation** by which Jews and Christians, as "People of the Book" (*Ahl al-kitab*), paid a special poll tax (*jizya*) and a land tax (*kharaj*), as a form of tribute in return for being allowed to practice their faith.

637–38. Conquest of Iraq. In the battle of Qadisiyya (637), the Muslims vanquished the Persian army in Iraq. Shortly thereafter they occupied the Sassanian imperial capital of Ctesiphon and conquered Iraq as far north as Mosul.

639–42. Conquest of Egypt. The general Amr ibn al-As invaded Egypt and destroyed the Byzantine army at Heliopolis in 641. The capital of Alexandria surrendered in Sept. 642. The Muslims established the garrison city of **Fustat** (now part of Cairo) as their capital.

642–44. The defeat of the Sassanian counterattack at the Battle of Nihavand (642) began the **Muslim conquest of the cities of western Iran,** including Isfahan, Hamadan, Rayy, and Qazvin.

643. The North African city of **Tripoli conquered** by the Muslims.

644–56. UTHMAN IBN AFFAN, THE THIRD CALIPH. Umar died of wounds inflicted by a Persian slave, an assassination not motivated by political intent. Before his death, he appointed a committee to determine his successor. The choice, Uthman ibn Affan, attempted to **centralize the administration** of the newly conquered territories. He demanded that provincial governors (*emirs*) send tax and conquest revenue back to Medina for distribution, a policy that met with much resistance. He continued the conquest of the Iranian plateau and ordered the creation of a **definitive written version of the Qur'an.**

651. Death of the last Sassanian shah, Yazdgird III, and **final demise of the Zoroastrian Empire.**

651–54. The eastern Iranian province of **Khurasan subdued by Muslim forces,** following the conquest of the capital, Nishapur, in 651.

655. Battle of the Masts. The Muslim navy defeated the Byzantines off the Lycian coast.

656. The third caliph, Uthman, was murdered in his home in Medina by rebellious Muslim forces from Egypt, whose grievances as early converts concerned the erosion of their pay and prestige. Uthman's appointment of members of his own clan of Umayya to top administrative positions had weakened his support among them as well as among troops in Iraq and the Quraysh in Medina.

656–61. ALI IBN ABI TALIB, THE FOURTH CALIPH. As the first cousin of the Prophet Muhammad, Ali was also his closest male relative. His marriage to the Prophet's daughter Fatima further enhanced his prestige in the Islamic community, as he was the father of the Prophet's grandsons Hasan and Husayn. He attempted to stress the equality of all Muslims and the role of the caliph as a spiritual leader (*imam*).

Ali's was a tumultuous reign, throughout which raged the **FIRST CIVIL WAR** (*fitna*). The political strife begun with the murder of Uthman developed into a full-fledged, **bloody struggle over succession** and Muslim self-definition that ended Ali's rule and gave birth to the new Arab-Islamic dynasty of the **Umayyads** and to two major religio-political factions, the **Shi'ites** and the **Kharijis.**

656, Dec. Battle of the Camel. The first military confrontation in the civil war took place outside the town of Basra in Iraq. There Ali's forces defeated a triad of leaders—the Prophet's widow **A'isha** and two of his male companions, **al-Zubayr** and **Talha**—who challenged Ali on the grounds that he had failed to punish those who had killed Uthman. The triad also represented the interests of the Quraysh, who were threatened by Ali's identification with the Medinan converts (*ansar*). Al-Zubayr and Talha were killed in the confrontation, and A'isha retired from politics after her defeat.

657. The battle and arbitration of Siffin. In the second phase of the civil war, Ali was challenged by **Mu'awiya ibn Abi Sufyan,** the governor of Syria, who sought to avenge the murder of his relative, the third caliph Uthman (both were of the Umayya clan). When a battle began at Siffin on the upper Euphrates, the Syrian troops of Mu'awiya demanded arbitration of the dispute, brandishing pages of the Qur'an. Ali agreed to negotiate, but the dispute over Uthman's murder soon evolved into a tacit **struggle for the leadership** of the Islamic community. The negotiators agreed that a new caliph should be selected by committee, and by 659, at the arbitration of Adhruh, Mu'awiya had openly asserted his claim to the caliphate.

The immediate result of the arbitration was that a small number of Ali's supporters deserted him. Those who had walked out, known as the Kharijis, believed that only Allah could arbitrate the dispute and that Ali and his followers had ceased to be true Muslims. The Kharijis advocated an **egalitarian form of Islam** in which leaders would be chosen without regard to descent or any other form of inherited social priority. They established their own enclaves along the Persian Gulf, raided settled communities, and found new adherents in Oman and North Africa. The defection of the Kharijis signaled the start of a decline in Ali's support.

658. Ali defeated a force of the Kharijis at the battle of Nahrawan.

661. THE MURDER OF ALI by a member of the Kharijis, marking the end of the first civil war and of the reign of the Rashidun caliphs. Ali's son, Hasan, renounced his claim to the caliphate. **Mu'awiya** asserted his right to rule the Islamic community, a contention based largely on the might vested in his crack military forces. He moved rapidly to consolidate his rule and **founded the Umayyad dynasty.**

The supporters of Ali did not abandon his political cause even after his death. They formed a party (*shi'a*) from which evolved the sect of Muslims known as the **Shi'a or shi'ites.** They maintained that only Ali's male descendants had the right to head the Islamic community as both religious and political leaders. The evolution of these Shi'ite religio-political doctrines eventually defined the first three Rashidun caliphs as usurpers. The notion that true Islamic political authority could be wielded only by Muhammad's family as embodied by Ali's line led to **active Shi'ite opposition** to other forms of Islamic leadership throughout the 7th, 8th, and 9th centuries. The majority of Muslims who did not accept Shi'ite assumptions came to be known as **Sunni**

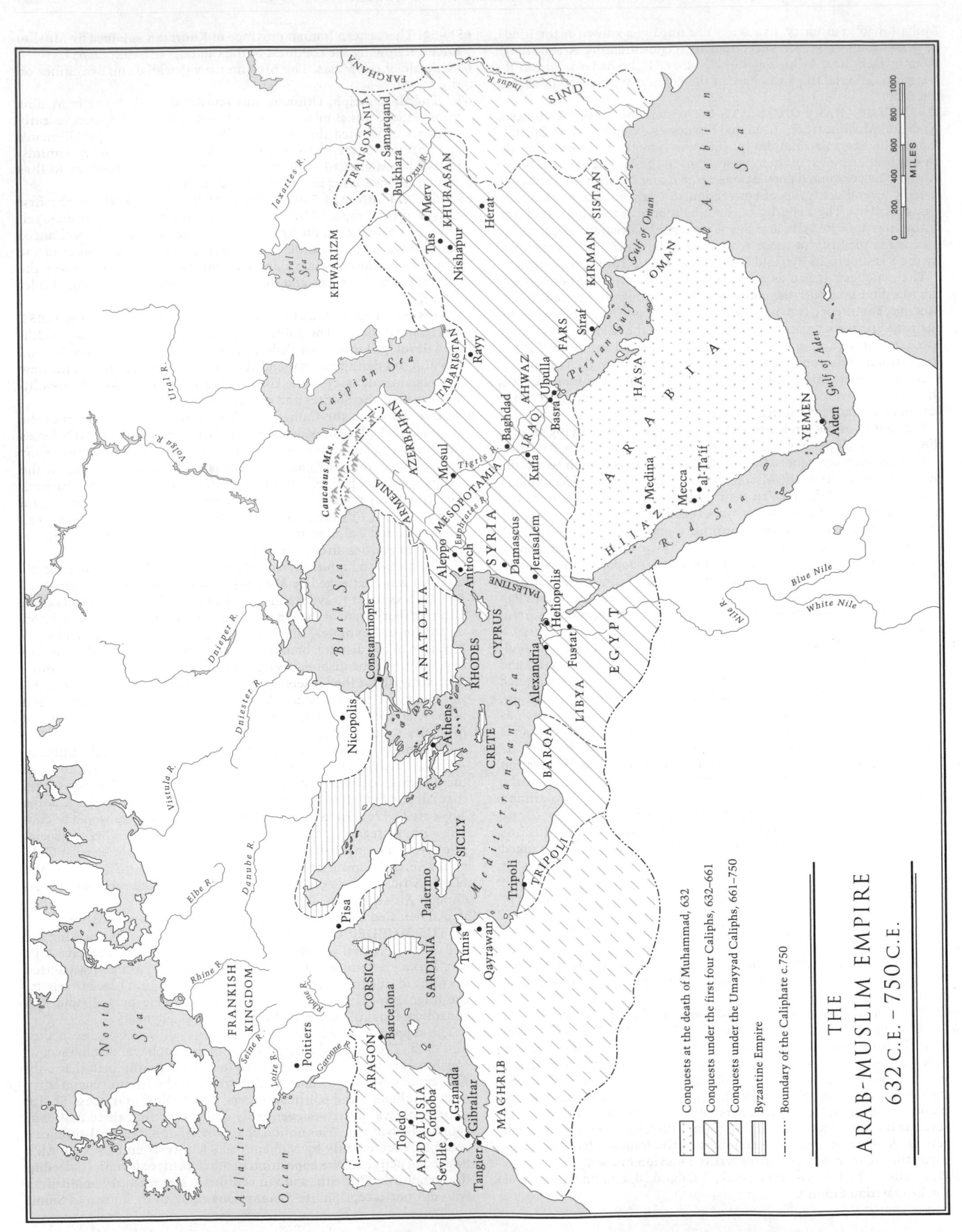

THE
ARAB-MUSLIM EMPIRE
632 C.E. – 750 C.E.

	Conquests at the death of Muhammad, 632
	Conquests under the first four Caliphs, 632–661
	Conquests under the Umayyad Caliphs, 661–750
	Byzantine Empire
-----	Boundary of the Caliphate c.750

MUHAMMAD AND THE DESCENT OF THE CALIPHAL DYNASTIES

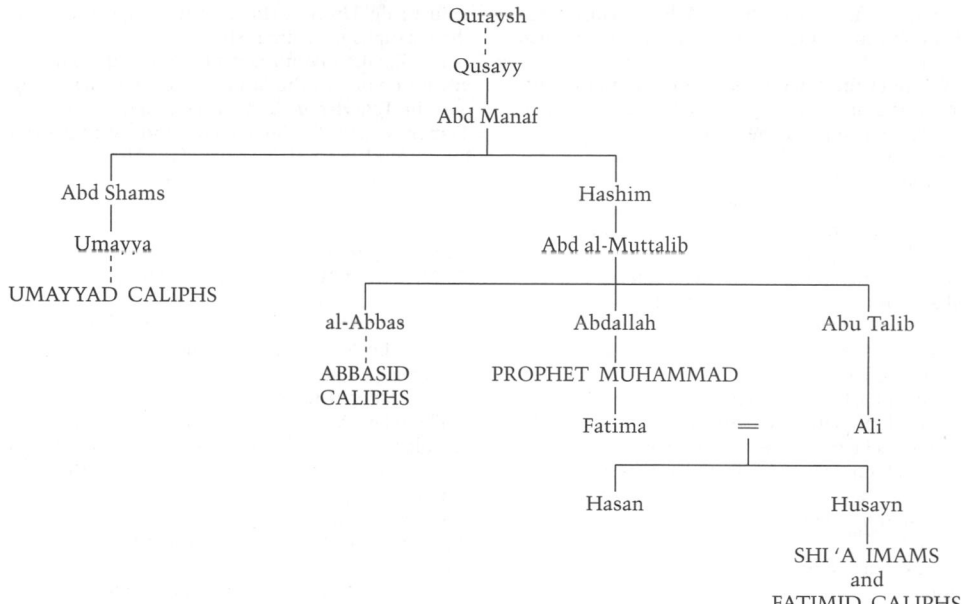

Muslims. As the "people of the [Prophet's] example and community" *(ahl al-sunna wa al-jama'a)*, Sunni Muslims retrospectively defined political authority—in light of the first civil war and their later collective experience—as whatever form of authority functioned effectively to protect the faith of Islam and the Muslim community. The division between the Sunni Muslim majority and the Shi'ite Muslim minority persists to the present day.

c. THE UMAYYAD CALIPHATE

For a complete list of the Umayyad caliphs, see Appendix III.

661–80. MU'AWIYA I, THE FOUNDER OF THE UMAYYAD DYNASTY. Mu'awiya established the first Arab-Islamic dynasty, with its **capital at Damascus.** He rested his state on the support of the **Arab tribes,** gathering around him a circle of tribal chieftains with whom he consulted regularly. While he ruled as a caliph, opponents defined his regime as a form of kingship *(mulk)*, an un-Islamic departure from the precedent of the Rashidun caliphs.

Mu'awiya founded a **decentralized state** in which local governors, particularly in the most troublesome province of Iraq, were given free rein to collect taxes and punish rebels. The day-to-day administration of each province continued to be **run by Byzantine and Sassanid bureaucrats** who maintained pre-Islamic governmental divisions *(diwans)* and conducted official business in Greek and Pahlavi.

667. Islamic forces crossed the Oxus River into central Asia, the northeastern boundary of the Islamic expansion.

669. First Muslim attack on **Constantinople.**

670. The garrison city of **Qayrawan** in Tunisia was founded. It served as the base for the further expansion of Islam westward across North Africa.

671. Ziyad ibn Abihi, governor of Kufa, sent 50,000 troops to the Iranian oasis of Merv as part of a policy to **resettle Arabs** in the area. These soldiers eventually intermarried with the indigenous Zoroastrian-Iranian population, and their descendants played a major role in the 8th-century Abbasid revolution that overthrew the Umayyad dynasty.

672. The isle of **Rhodes** was taken by the Umayyads.

674. Arab forces captured **Crete.**

674–80. A series of unsuccessful campaigns against **Constantinople** (p. 186) as well as raids against **Armenia.**

680, Oct. 10. Death of Husayn, the son of Ali, grandson of the Prophet Muhammad and third leader (imam) of the Shi'ite Muslims. After Mu'awiya's death, Husayn had attempted to wrest political control from the Umayyad government. On his way to Kufa in search of military support he and his followers were surrounded by Umayyad troops at Karbala and then killed after being deprived of water for days. The suffering and death of the Prophet Muhammad's grandson came eventually to be **commemorated by the Shi'ite community** as a martyrdom, in a yearly ritual of **communal mourning** (the *ashura*) held on the tenth day of the Islamic month of Muharram.

683. Umayyad forces reached **Tangier** and the Atlantic Ocean.

683–92. SECOND CIVIL WAR. The Umayyads put down several serious challenges to their rule, restoring their effective hold on power after almost a decade of rebellions. The most lengthy threat came from **Abdallah ibn al-Zubayr,** whose father, al-Zubayr, had risen against the fourth caliph, Ali, in 656. Ibn al-Zubayr demanded that the caliph be selected from among the tribe of Quraysh, not just the Umayyad clan. He claimed the office and raised a **revolt in Arabia and Iraq** that lasted till 692, when Umayyad forces killed him in Mecca.

Another challenge to the Umayyads came from the **Qays tribal confederation** based in northern Syria and Iraq. It threw its support behind Ibn al-Zubayr, but the **rival tribal confederation of Kalb** (based in southern Syria and Palestine) backed the Umayyads, and in a bloody battle in **Marj Rahit** (July 684) they defeated the Qaysis. The feud between the northern and southern tribal groups continued to fester, weakening the Umayyad base of political and military support.

In 685–87 the Umayyads also faced the revolt organized in Kufa by **al-Mukhtar** on behalf of **Muhammad ibn al-Hanafiyya,** a son of Ali by a concubine. The uprising tapped the support of the *mawali*, or non-Arab converts to Islam, who were emerging as an important social group with grievances against the regime for being treated as second class Muslims and having to pay the taxes demanded of non-Muslims, despite their conversion. Al-Mukhtar proclaimed Ibn al-Hanafiyya as the Mahdi, the messianic redeemer who would come at the end of time to institute a reign of justice. (This was the first appearance of this idea, which became common in Islam, particularly in its Shi'ite forms.) The uprising was crushed in 687.

684–85. MARWAN I. Elected after a major conference among the Arab tribes, Marwan represented the first ruler of the **Marwanid branch** of the Umayyad clan. (The first three Umayyad rulers had been descendants of the **Sufyanid branch** of the family.)

685–705. ABD AL-MALIK. He ended the second civil war, initiated the centralization of the Umayyad Empire, and insisted that **all administrative business be conducted in Arabic,** which slowly became the tongue of the majority in the Middle East. Abd al-Malik also instituted the *barid,* a postal and spy system designed to keep the ruler informed about events in the provinces.

692. Completion of the **Dome of the Rock mosque in Jerusalem.** Built on the Temple Mount, on the orders of Abd al-Malik, it features an octagonal plan and is today considered the earliest outstanding example of Islamic architecture.

c. 697. Umayyad coinage reformed by Abd al-Malik, who instituted a standard Umayyad currency that did not rely on the imitation of either Byzantine or Sassanid issues. The new coins of gold (dinar) and silver (dirham) were standardized in weight. For the first time all the issues were devoid of pictorial representation and bore Arabic inscriptions.

700–701. Revolt of Ibn al-Ash'ath, an Arab tribal leader in Iraq. He found support among many of Kufa's inhabitants, including non-Arab converts to Islam, but was defeated by the governor of Iraq, al-Hajjaj.

706–9. Bukhara captured by the Umayyads.

711. Invasion of Spain (al-Andalus) by the Muslims under the command of the Berber **Tariq ibn Ziyad** (p. 179). The peninsula was subdued by 716. Raids across the Pyrenees began in the next year and culminated at **Poitiers** in 732, where Arab forces were defeated by Charles Martel (p. 179). The battle retrospectively retained far greater significance in European annals than in Islamic accounts, where it is described only as a skirmish.

711–13. Conquest of Transoxania and the Sind. Arab armies reached the port of Daybul on the Indus River by 713 (p. 132). These forays did not result in settlement but did achieve the exaction of tribute from local authorities.

715. Completion of the **Great Mosque of Damascus,** built by the caliph al-Walid (705–15) on the site of the church of St. John, which was largely destroyed.

717–20. UMAR II, known for his piety, ended former policies of military expansion. Umar attempted to ameliorate the **status of the *mawali*** (non-Arab Muslims) by reducing their tax burden. This policy did not provide a permanent solution to grievances of the *mawali,* although Umar remained the only Umayyad ruler to advocate a more egalitarian policy toward them.

720. Rebellion of Yazid ibn al-Muhallab in Iraq. A deposed appointee of the brutal governor al-Hajjaj, he declared a holy war against Umayyad rule and was killed in battle.

728. Death of al-Hasan al-Basri. A scholar and mystic, he attracted a wide following near Basra, where he preached asceticism. At this early stage, **Muslim mystics** signaled their rejection of the luxurious material world of Umayyad urban centers by wearing wool *(suf),* the cloth from which the Sufi movement of Islamic mysticism later took its name.

Death of **Wasil ibn Ata,** religious scholar and founder of the school of theology known as the **Mu'tazila.** In debates over the authority of the caliph, the Mu'tazila took a middle position between those who argued that the caliph had to stay within the limits set by the Qur'an and tradition, and those who allowed him freedom of interpretation to meet the changing needs of society. The Mu'tazila also assumed neutrality in disputes over the moral positions of Ali and his enemies. Their doctrines would become the focus of intense controversy about a hundred years later.

c. 730. Death of **al-Farazdaq** (Tammam ibn Ghalib), a poet born in Arabia who made his fortune and name at the Umayyad court in Damascus. He had a special flair for panegyrics and was paid to write many for famous officials.

737–38. Campaigns against the Khazars, Turks from southern Russia, who invaded the Caucasus and threatened Arab possessions in Armenia, Azerbaijan, and northern Iraq. The Umayyads defeated the Khazars and conducted raids as far as their capital on the lower Volga.

740–42. Berber revolt in North Africa, provoked by unjust treatment and Khariji propaganda. The uprising forced the retreat of Arab-Umayyad forces, but was quelled by fresh reinforcements from Damascus, although the Umayyad link to Spain was severed.

740. Death of **Zayd ibn Ali,** the fifth Shi'ite imam, after an unsuccessful revolt at Kufa in which he claimed the caliphate as the grandson of Ali's son Husayn. After Zayd's death, his followers were known as **Zaydi Shi'ites, or Fivers.** They argued that any descendant of Ali and the Prophet's daughter Fatima had the right to military support against unjust rule. Unlike other Shi'ite groups, they would not condemn the three caliphs preceding Ali.

The Zaydis maintained a base in Kufa and sponsored many unsuccessful revolts in the 8th and 9th centuries. They found many adherents in **Tabaristan** (Iran), where they converted local tribes, and in **Yemen,** where the Zaydi community survives to the present day.

744–50. MARWAN II. The last of the Umayyad rulers, he came to power after a brief civil war. Marwan moved the capital to Harran in northeast Syria, to be near his most loyal troops. A seasoned warrior, he was known for his strength and endurance. Much of his reign was spent attempting to hold the Umayyad Caliphate together.

747–50. THE ABBASID REVOLUTION. In June 747 an anti-Umayyad rebellion erupted that toppled the dynasty in the span of three years of bloody warfare and, more important, brought a **major transformation of the Islamic polity.** The system of rule based on **Arab caste supremacy,** upheld by the Umayyads, was shattered and replaced by a more **cosmopolitan conception of Islam.**

The rebels began their struggle in northeastern Iran, where they assembled armies and popular support. They steadily took over the territories of Iran, Iraq, and Syria, occupied the Umayyad capital of Damascus (Apr. 750), and killed off the Umayyad ruling house. Marwan II suffered a major defeat at the **Battle of the Great Zab** near Mosul (Jan. 750) and fled to Egypt, where he was captured and killed (Aug. 750).

In Nov. 749, as the Umayyad regime disintegrated, the rebels proclaimed **a new caliph, Abu al-Abbas al-Saffah** of the Arab family of al-Abbas. With him began the dynastic line of the **Abbasids,** who held the caliphate in Baghdad until 1258. The Abbasids claimed the caliphate as blood relatives of the Prophet Muhammad through his uncle al-Abbas. They had begun subversive activities against the Umayyads some 30 years before the open revolt, building an organized underground network of agents and propagandists who cultivated disaffected people, especially in the area of **Khurasan.** Their most famous agent was **Abu Muslim,** an Iranian convert to Islam who declared the opening of the revolt. The multitudes who rallied behind the Abbasids were driven by various grievances and aspiration for change. Among them were the **non-Arab converts** to Islam (the *mawali*), who were attracted by the Abbasid promise of egalitarian treatment for all Muslims. **Shi'ite groups,** too, gave important support to the revolution, in the expectation of seeing an Alid candidate installed, but they would be bitterly disappointed by the outcome.

The Abbasid Revolution marked a great watershed in Middle Eastern history. It swept away the Arab monopoly on power and ushered in **a new order** in which all Muslims, regardless of origin, could participate in the political, social, and cultural life of the empire.

d. THE ABBASID CALIPHATE AND ITS BREAKUP

For a complete list of the Abbasid caliphs, see Appendix III.

749–54. ABU AL-ABBAS AL-SAFFAH, FOUNDER OF THE ABBASID DYNASTY. The first Abbasid ruler, a descendant of the Prophet's uncle al-Abbas, was proclaimed caliph publicly in the mosque in Kufa on Nov. 28, 749, just months before the forces of the Abbasid Revolution brought a final end to Umayyad rule. His regnal title, al-Saffah, "the Shedder of Blood," announced his promise to avenge the Shi'ites and Abbasids killed by the Umayyads. He set up the **initial Abbasid capital at Kufa.**

751. Abbasid forces triumphed over the **Chinese** at the **Battle of Talas** in central Asia (p. 149). Chinese papermakers were captured after this largely symbolic victory. **Paper manufacture** then spread westward throughout the Islamic world, and factories were founded in Baghdad (c. 800), Egypt (c. 900), Morocco (c. 1100), and Spain (c. 1150). The advent of readily available paper increased the rate of **manuscript production** throughout the Islamic world.

754–75. AL-MANSUR consolidated Abbasid authority, turned the troops of Khurasan—the mainstay of his support—into a professional army, and created a highly **centralized bureaucracy** that employed many *mawali*. The opening of this new avenue of social mobility was one aspect of the general **improvement in the status of non-Arab converts** to Islam. The new policy speeded up the process of **conversion,** especially in Iran, where the estimated Muslim population increased from 8 percent in 750 to some 80 percent in 950. Some tensions remained between Arabs and Iranians, and they prompted a court-centered literary movement called the Shu'ubiyya, which championed the Persian language and Iranian cultural values above those of the Arabs. The pre-Islamic Iranian ideas promoted by the Shu'ubiyya shaped Arabic literature, Abbasid court ceremony, and notions of kingship and social hierarchy.

755. Abu Muslim, the former leader of the Abbasid Revolution in Khurasan, was killed by order of the caliph, who feared his power in the province.

755–56. Revolt of Sunpadh (Sinbad) in Khurasan. Sunpadh was a Zoroastrian who preached that Abu Muslim had not died, but would return again in the company of the Islamic Mahdi, or redeemer, to institute a reign of justice. He fomented rebellion in the cities of Nishapur, Rayy, and Qum.

c. 757. Death of Ibn al-Muqaffa, a Zoroastrian convert to Islam who became a secretary in the Abbasid administration and translated many works from Pahlavi (Middle Persian) into Arabic, including the famous fables *Kalila wa Dimna.*

757–960. THE MIDRARID DYNASTY. Centered in Sijilmasa in Morocco, the dynasty was founded by **Midrar** (Sam'un ibn Yazlan), a Khariji Muslim and Zanata Berber from Meknes, after a revolt against the Abbasid governor of Qayrawan. The Midrarid state signaled that the egalitarian message of **Kharijism** continued to appeal to Berber groups who resented Arab elitism and discrimination. The **capital of Sijilmasa** was founded during the reign of Abu Mansur al-Yasa (790–823), who consolidated the dynasty's territory. He married one of his sons to the neighboring Rustamid dynasty to ensure peaceful relations. Sijilmasa became a major point on the **gold trade route** with Sudan and attracted refugees from Muslim Spain (c. 818) as well as Jews interested in commercial opportunities. The Midrarids sided with the Umayyads of Spain, along with other Zanata Berber groups, but were vanquished by Fatimid forces in the 10th century.

758. Muslim armies destroyed parts of the Chinese city of **Canton.**

761–909. THE RUSTAMID DYNASTY. The second **Khariji** state in North Africa was founded by an Iranian Muslim named **Ibn Rustam,** who had come to North Africa to serve as the Abbasid governor of Qayrawan (758–61). He won Zanata Berber military backing and founded his own theocratic state, where he took the title of imam and ruled as both a spiritual and a political authority. The Rustamid state was significant as a center of Khariji scholarship and was a focus of allegiance for other Khariji communities scattered throughout North Africa. The **capital of Tahert** attracted many Khariji Muslims from Iraq and flourished as a northern point on the trans-Saharan trade route. The Rustamids failed to organize an effective army and lost Tahert to the Fatimids in 909. The survivors escaped to the southern oasis of Wargala. Kharijism has survived to the present day in the oasis of Mzab, on the island of Jerba, and in Jabal Nafusa.

762. FOUNDATION OF BAGHDAD, the new Abbasid capital, by al-Mansur. This first truly Islamic imperial city, situated 18 miles north of the Sassanian capital of Ctesiphon, was designed on a circular plan and was known as the City of Peace (Madinat al-Salam). Canals were dug to make the site accessible to both the Tigris and Euphrates rivers. Riverine access to Baghdad **attracted traders** from as far away as China, India, and northern Europe. By the 9th century, the city's population had reached more than 300,000.

762. Unsuccessful revolt of the Shi'ite **Muhammad ibn Abdallah,** known as the **Pure Soul** (al-Nafs al-Zakiyya), in Medina. His brother Ibrahim led an uprising in Iraq in Feb. 763 that briefly captured Basra and Wasit but was soon thereafter quashed by Abbasid troops.

765. Death of the sixth Shi'ite imam **Ja'far al-Sadiq,** a renowned scholar and theologian who transformed **Shi'ism** from a mainly political movement into a spiritual one. Ja'far asserted that the Shi'ite imams possessed special knowledge received from Ali regarding religious doctrine and were infallible as sources of spiritual wisdom. Ja'far named his eldest **son, Isma'il,** as his successor, but Isma'il predeceased his father (d. 760). The majority of Shi'ites believe that Ja'far then conferred the title

of imam on his third son, Musa. They chose to follow Musa's descendants as far as the twelfth imam, and became known as **Twelver, or Imami Shi'ites.** Some, however, recognized Isma'il as the seventh imam, and came to be known as Sevener, or **Isma'ili Shi'ites.** These two branches of Shi'ism varied on matters of doctrine and politics but shared a belief in the **return of the imam** as a messiah.

767. Death of **Abu Hanifa,** a leading authority on Islamic law (the *shari'a*) and founder of the **Hanafi law school,** one of the four major Sunni legal interpretations. His school spread from Iraq to western Iran and central Asia, and later became the officially preferred legal interpretation followed by the Ottoman Empire.

Islamic law evolved during the 8th and 9th centuries from key roots of jurisprudence *(usul al-fiqh)* that included the Qur'an, the example of the Prophet *(sunna),* analogy *(qiyas),* and the consensus of the scholarly community *(ijma').* The *shari'a* became a code that dictated most aspects of Muslim life, including prayer, marriage, divorce, inheritance, business, and other civil and criminal legal issues.

768. Death of **Muhammad ibn Ishaq,** author of the earliest biography of the Prophet Muhammad. His work survived in a later recension by Ibn Hisham (d. 833).

775–85. AL-MAHDI. He created a centralized bureaucracy with divisions *(diwans)* dedicated to tax collection, correspondence, and the military. The need to coordinate these ministries created the position of chief minister *(wazir),* which enjoyed great influence. Al-Mahdi tried to pacify Shi'ite hostilities with special gifts and status, but his efforts were unsuccessful.

776–89. Rebellion of the heretic **al-Muqanna,** "the Veiled Prophet," in Khurasan. His movement attracted much peasant support by calling on the memory of Abu Muslim. His socioeconomic program stressed the communality of all property and women, and echoed the 6th-century Iranian heretic Mazdak.

786–809. HARUN AL-RASHID, the most famous of all the Abbasid rulers, initially allowed his mother and his prime minister, Yahya of the **Barmak family,** to run affairs of state. He increased central control of the collection of agricultural taxes *(kharaj),* the main source of Abbasid revenue, and led several campaigns against the Byzantines in Anatolia. His reign was the last during which the Abbasids governed an empire unifed from Tunisia to central Asia.

789. Death of **al-Khayzuran,** influential wife of the caliph al-Mahdi and mother of the caliphs al-Hadi and Harun al-Rashid. She began her life as a concubine but later became the ruler's favorite legal wife and dominated the harem *(harim),* the exclusively female area within the palace. The precedent for the **seclusion of women** was attributed to injunctions first placed on the Prophet's wives in the Qur'an. The harem became a fixture of Islamic urban life.

789–926. THE IDRISID DYNASTY. The **first Shi'ite state** was also the first attempt to unify much of Morocco. **Idris ibn Abdallah** (d. 791), a descendant of the Prophet Muhammad through Ali, relied on Awraba Berbers for military support. He was recognized as a spiritual and political leader who possessed divine powers *(baraka),* which he transmitted to his descendants. In 790 Idris captured Tlemcen from the Khariji Zanata Berbers. His son Idris II founded **Fez** sometime before 808; it soon grew into the chief city of northern Morocco and an important center of religious study. After the death of Idris II (828), the state was divided into a series of principalities governed by family members in western Algeria and Morocco. The Idrisid presence increased the diffusion of Islamic beliefs among the indigenous population during the 9th century. The Fatimids put an end to the dynasty in Morocco.

795. Death of **Malik ibn Anas,** a prominent jurist and founder of the **Maliki school of Islamic law,** which flourished in Spain, Egypt, and North Africa. His work *al-Muwatta (The Beaten Path)* was the earliest collection of the Prophet's word and deed *(sunna)* as preserved in writing *(hadith),* and was also the first book of law. In the 8th century, scholars collected these **oral sources of prophetic precedent** and then wrote and codified them in the 9th century. *Hadith* served to extend and clarify the Prophet's example on a wide range of critical issues relevant to Islamic law and not contained in the Qur'an.

797. Harun al-Rashid received emissaries from the Emperor **Charlemagne** (p. 174), a fact noted in Latin annals but not in Arabic ones. The European-inspired diplomacy resumed in 807, but did not lead to further contacts. Charlemagne may have hoped to negotiate better Christian access to holy sites in Jerusalem.

800–909. THE AGHLABID DYNASTY, founded by **Ibrahim ibn Aghlab,** an Abbasid governor of the province of Ifriqiya (present Tunisia and the northeast corner of Algeria). In 800 the Abbasids allowed Ibn Aghlab the right to pass on his position as governor (emir) to his male offspring. The Aghlabids sent tribute to Baghdad and recognized the caliph's authority, but effectively ruled as an independent dynasty until 909. After 800, the Abbasids lost control of all territories west of Egypt.

Ziyadat Allah I (d. 838), one of the most effective rulers, channeled military energies and the religious zeal of Maliki legal scholars into a plan for Mediterranean conquest. He assembled an extensive corsair fleet, which made the Aghlabids a serious naval power and enabled them to invade **Sicily** (827) and raid **Sardinia, Corsica,** and southern Italy.

The Aghlabids attempted to create an African slave military, but their efforts to defend themselves against the Fatimids failed, and the Fatimids ended their dynasty in 909.

801. Death of **Rabi'a al-Adawiyya,** a female mystic (Sufi) and saint who lived a celibate and ascetic life outside of Basra. She is credited with the doctrine of divine love (mahabba) and many miracles.

803. Fall of the Barmakid family. The caliph Harun al-Rashid ended the family's role as chief administrators when the Barmakids became too powerful. One of them was killed and the rest imprisoned. Their demise underscored the vulnerability of those who served the caliph at the highest levels.

809. The **first public hospital** in the Islamic world was founded in Baghdad. Similar institutions, usually supported by endowed property, appeared in other major cities and served as teaching centers for medical students.

c. 815. Death of **Abu Nuwas** (al-Hasan ibn Hani), a renowned lyric poet who cut a colorful and raucous figure at the court of Harun al-Rashid.

816–38. The **revolt of Babak** in Azerbaijan. This heretical movement, called the Khurramiyya, attracted peasants and villagers. Followers waged the longest dissident uprising in Abbasid history. Babak espoused the doctrines of Mazdak (d. 528) in regard to shared property and women, and also advocated transmigration of souls (tanasukh), a doctrine unacceptable in Islam.

818. Death of the eighth Shi'ite imam, **Ali al-Rida.** The caliph al-Ma'mun appointed the imam his heir (Mar. 817), to placate Shi'ite Muslims in his realm, but Ali died before the caliph did. Since the imam was 20 years older than al-Ma'mun, the appointment was largely symbolic.

820. Death of **Muhammad al-Shafi'i** (b. 767), founder of the Shafi'i law school. He systematized Islamic law and is considered the greatest legal scholar of the formative period of the *shari'a.* The **Shafi'i school** predominates in lower Egypt, Malaysia, Indonesia, and East Africa to this day.

821–73. THE TAHIRID DYNASTY. Situated in Khurasan, this semi-independent dynasty was founded by the general **Tahir ibn al-Husayn** (d. 822), who gained the governorship of the province as a reward for his services to the caliph al-Ma'mun. The Tahirids rendered tribute to the caliph in Baghdad and acknowledged him on the coins they minted. They held court at **Nishapur** and encouraged the opening of trade routes to central Asia. They were defeated by the Saffarid regime in 873.

823. Death of **Muhammad al-Waqidi,** a historian whose work, the *Kitab al-maghazi,* ranks among the earliest accounts of the conquests directed by the Prophet Muhammad.

827. Invasion of Sicily by the Aghlabids. The island was captured from the Byzantines in a series of campaigns lasting about half a century, in the course of which Muslim forces even attacked Rome (846). Sicily remained under Islamic control until the Norman conquest (completed 1091) (p. 213).

827–48. The *mihna* (ordeal, or inquisition) imposed by the caliph al-Ma'mun. All judges, scholars, and theologians had to take an oath, a test of faith that was also a test of political loyalty to the caliph and his preference for the **theology of the Mu'tazili school.** Most Muslims believed the Qur'an was uncreated and coeternal with Allah, but the Mu'tazili believed this contravened their central notion of the unity of God. In attempting to dictate theology, the caliph also sought to ensure the loyalty of his subjects and the uniformity of their political and doctrinal thought. Such tyranical interference was **opposed by the ulama,** some of whom refused to accept Mu'tazili doctrine and faced torture, imprisonment, and death.

The *mihna* was an attempt by al-Ma'mun to enlarge the scope of the caliphate into the religious sphere. His inquisition lasted beyond his death, but was ultimately abandoned in 848 by the caliph al-Mutawakkil. The failure of the Islamic inquisition meant the **triumph of the ulama** as a body of jurists, educators, scholars, and theologians who served as the sole interpreters of the Islamic faith. After the *mihna,* no Abbasid caliph would ever again attempt to impose religious doctrine.

830. House of Wisdom (Bayt al-Hikma) founded in Baghdad by al-Ma'mun for the **translation of Greek and Syriac works** into Arabic. The translations included the works of Aristotle, Plato, Galen, and Hippocrates. Texts from Sanskrit translated into Arabic also included manuals that described plants and medicinal herbs.

833–42. AL-MU'TASIM. In an attempt to strengthen his political position, al-Mu'tasim introduced an innovation that took root and reshaped the structure of Middle Eastern regimes. He created a **slave army** designed to be loyal to him alone, to serve as a trustworthy counterweight to ambitious opponents in Baghdad. The recruits consisted of **central Asian Turks,** who were captured as youths and converted to Islam, trained for a life in the military, and paid for their services. The slave soldier (called *ghulam* and, from the 11th century, *mamluk*) became a member of a new military elite that steadily took control of Abbasid politics. Subsequent Middle Eastern regimes, including the Ottoman and the Safavid empires, adopted the institution of the slave army.

835. The capital of **Samarra,** 62 miles north of Baghdad, was founded by the caliph al-Mu'tasim to house his new Turkish guard.

838. The Byzantine city of Amorion was sacked by Abbasid troops.

845. Death of **Muhammad ibn Sa'd** (b. 784), author of the earliest extant collection of biographies of distinguished Muslims (*Kitab al-tabaqat al-kabir*). His work contains more than 4,000 individual entries, with 600 devoted to women. **Biographical dictionaries** formed a distinct literary genre in the region, providing over the centuries a detailed treasury of information on noteworthy men and women.

847–61. AL-MUTAWAKKIL. He ended the *mihna,* persecuted Shi'ite Muslims, and harshly enforced disused codes designating special clothing and other tokens of social inequality for Jews and Christians.

c. 847. Death of **Muhammad al-Khwarizmi,** a mathematician whose writings discussed the use of **Arabic numerals**—actually of Indian origin—in arithmetic calculations. The system of Indian reckoning by means of nine figures and a zero was first transmitted to Europe through a Latin translation of his work.

c. 850. Yunus, a great-grandson of the Barghawata Berber and self-proclaimed prophet Salih, attempted to create a state south of Casablanca with a new religion that modified Islam and promoted a Qur'an written in the Berber language. The state, whose origins lay in the 8th-century Khariji Berber revolts, subsisted on booty obtained from raiding and did not survive the 9th century.

c. 850. The *Kitab al-hiyal (Book of Ingenious Devices),* an illustrated manual of mechanics, was written by three brothers, known as the **Banu Musa,** for the caliph al-Ma'mun. The work was inspired by the Alexandrian school of engineering founded by Hero and Philo, but proved more sophisticated in its designs.

855. Death of **Ahmad ibn Hanbal** (b. 780), the revered religious scholar who had refused to accept the Mu'tazili doctrine promoted by the caliph during the *mihna,* for which he was subsequently tortured and imprisoned. He compiled a major work of *hadith* (the *Musnad*), and was the founder of the **Hanbali school of law,** which predominates today in Saudi Arabia.

861–70. The dominance of the **Turkish military force** at Samarra made virtual captives of a series of Abbasid caliphs. Coups, mutinies, and murders were easily provoked by the rulers' inability to pay the salaries of the army on time. Effective political power rested in the hands of the Turkish military, not the caliph.

862–63. The **Great Mosque of Qayrawan** in Tunisia built by the Aghlabid dynasty.

865. RISE OF THE SAFFARID DYNASTY. Ya'qub al-Saffar, who began as leader of a band of vigilantes *(ayyarun)*, established his control over Sistan in eastern Iran. From this base he went on to build a large state that at its height included Khurasan (taken from the Tahirids in 873), parts of northern India, and western Iran. His brother and successor, Amr, lost Khurasan to the Samanids in 900, although Sistan remained in Saffarid possession for much of the 10th century. The dynasty represented a genuinely independent local force that advertised its **Persian identity** and even claimed descent from the Sassanian royal family.

c. 868. Death of **Amr al-Jahiz**, a famed master of *adab*, or belles lettres. He wrote on a wide range of subjects, including philology and history. His masterpiece was *The Book of Animals*, a voluminous treasury of proverbs, jokes, and anecdotal material.

868–905. THE TULUNIDS. The dynasty ruled Egypt and Syria as semi-independent governors. Its founder, **Ahmad ibn Tulun** (d. 884), was the son of a Turkish military slave. He started out as a deputy-governor of Egypt and then, using the Abbasid slave-military model, created his own army of Turkish cavalry and African infantry. Although he did not seek total independence from the Abbasids, he exercised a great measure of **autonomous power** in the province of Egypt, which began under him to assume a greater political importance in regional affairs. The local economy prospered, with much of the revenue staying in the province. The Abbasids did not acquiesce to Tulunid autonomy, and in 905, after several attempts, restored their direct rule over Egypt.

868. Malta captured by the Aghlabids.

869–83. The Zanj rebellion. The Zanj, slaves of East African origin employed to reclaim salinated farmlands, rose in a great rebellion that laid waste to much of lower Iraq and put a strain on Abbasid resources. Their charismatic leader claimed descent from the Shi'ite imam Ali and led his troops to sack Basra and establish a city in the marshlands. **Agricultural slaves** were never again used on such a massive scale. After the Zanj rebellion, slavery persisted in urban and village settings in the Islamic world, for the Qur'an allowed slavery but enjoined the kind treatment of slaves and defined their manumission as a blessing. **Slaves** labored in domestic, mercantile, and military situations.

c. 870. Death of **Ya'qub al-Kindi**, considered the first Islamic philosopher. A native of Kufa, he benefited directly from the translation of **Greek philosophical works** into Arabic and analyzed all of Aristotle's work in 260 treatises. His most famous work, *On First Philosophy*, attempted to place Greek assumptions about creation and matter within an acceptable Islamic framework. He also wrote one of the earliest treatises on **musical theory**.

870. Death of **Muhammad al-Bukhari** (b. 810), who collected one of the most famous of the reliable Sunni compilations of *hadith*. By the 10th century, Sunni religious authorities recognized al-Bukhari's compendium as one of six canonical collections.

877. Ahmad ibn Tulun occupied **Syria**. He began construction of the mosque that remains in modern Cairo.

892. Death of **Ahmad al-Baladhuri**, the author of an important biographical dictionary *(Ansab al-ashraf)* and a history of the Muslim conquests *(Futuh al-buldan)*.

892–902. AL-MU'TADID. The son of the regent al-Muwaffaq displayed talent in pulling together the military, which remained loyal to him and became critical to implementing his policies of state reconsolidation. He moved the capital from Samarra to Baghdad.

897. A Zaydi Shi'ite state was established in northern **Yemen** by the imam Husayn al-Rassi. The main Zaydi religious center remained there into the 20th century.

c. 897. The Qarmati (Qaramita) movement of Isma'ili, or Sevener, Shi'ite Muslims began a series of rebellions against the Abbasid Empire. The founder, **Hamdan Qarmat**, believed that after the seventh imam, Isma'il (d. 760), no religio-political leader remained on earth, and that anyone who claimed to be the Mahdi, or redeemer, was not the true leader of the community—a belief that caused the Qarmatis' violent opposition to the Isma'ili Fatimid regime founded in Egypt by a Muslim who claimed descent from the seventh imam. The Qarmati movement combined **esoteric religious doctrine** with a program that advocated social justice and **violence** against other Islamic governments. The message spread in the late 9th century among the peasantry of Iraq and nomadic Arab tribes of Syria and Bahrain. Qarmati armies besieged Damascus (903), sacked Basra (923), threatened Baghdad (c.

928), and extracted payment for the peaceful continuance of the annual Muslim pilgrimage to Mecca.

900. The Samanids occupied Khurasan, adding the province to their Transoxanian territories. They held the area until 999, when Mahmud of Ghazna annexed it. The dynasty was of **Persian origin** and encouraged Persian literary activity, which flourished.

905. The Abbasids regained Egypt in a military campaign that ended Tulunid rule. **Syria** was also captured (903).

908–32. AL-MUQTADIR. Raised to the Abbasid throne at the age of 13 because he could be easily manipulated, he lived for pleasure. The hard work of restoration achieved by his three predecessors was reversed. The economy declined due to the **breakdown of the irrigation system** on which agriculture in Iraq was dependent.

909–1171. THE FATIMID DYNASTY. Ubayd Allah, the founder of the Isma'ili Shi'ite dynasty, declared himself caliph in Qayrawan in 910, with the support of the Kutama Berbers. He claimed descent from the son of the seventh imam, Isma'il (d. 760). Isma'ili Shi'ism did not become the faith of the region. The Fatimids first invaded Morocco (917) and tried unsuccessfully for the next 40 years to consolidate control there. In 969 they conquered Egypt and later, Syria.

910. Death of **Abu al-Qasim al-Junayd**, master of the Baghdad school of mysticism. The development of **Sufism** during this period moved away from earlier forms of asceticism after splitting in the 9th century into two branches, the sober *(sahw)* and the drunken *(sukr)*. Al-Junayd became the first to formalize the sober school of Sufism, which advocated the integration of the divine into the soul in this world. He opposed the drunken, or ecstatic, approach of mystics like **Bayazid al-Bistami** (d. 874), who suggested that they had achieved personal union with the divine.

913. Death of the geographer **Ibn Khuradadhbih**, who had served in the Abbasid administration as the director of the royal post and spy service. His *Book of Routes and Kingdoms* remains the earliest Islamic work of geography.

922. Death of **Husayn al-Hallaj**. The mystic was executed in Baghdad after a trial for heresy in which his opponents accused him of claiming divinity. Political disapproval of his contacts with Isma'ili Shi'ite groups probably was most responsible for his execution in the Sunni Abbasid capital. His poetry and **mystical thought** inspired many Sufis after his death.

923. Death of **Muhammad al-Tabari**, known for his monumental chronicle, *The History of the Prophets and Kings*, as well as for his Qur'anic exegesis.

c. 925. Death of **Muhammad al-Razi**, a famous philosopher and physician who first diagnosed the difference between smallpox and measles. His medical observations were informed by the study of classical authors but also relied on empirical observation. He wrote a 12-volume **medical encyclopedia** and developed the discipline of pharmacology. Al-Razi's medical observations synthesized Greek and Arab knowledge about **birth control**, which was generally considered permissible in Islam. His compendium listed 50 **contraceptive methods** for women.

927–1090. THE ZIYARID DYNASTY. The founder of the dynasty, **Mardawij ibn Ziyar**, was a native of Daylam who established an independent **Sunni regime in northern Iran.** He claimed descent from pre-Islamic Iranian royalty and asserted his independence in 930, when he conquered the cities of Rayy, Qazvin, Zanjan, and Qum. In the following year he took Hamadan and Isfahan. By 932 he had consolidated control of the provinces of Tabaristan and Gurgan. Under pressure, he entered the service of the Samanid dynasty (933) and planned to overthrow the Abbasid caliph in Baghdad, but was murdered by his Turkish slave troops (935). The dynasty struggled on through the 10th century, caught between Buyids and Samanids, and maintained a presence in northern Iran into the 11th century.

929. Death of **Muhammad al-Battani**, a mathematician famed for his accurate calculations of planetary movements.

929–90. THE HAMDANIDS OF MOSUL. The Hamdanids were an Arab family of Twelver Shi'ite Muslims descended from the Arab tribe of Taghlib. They served the Abbasids as governors of northern Iraq, and in 929 the Hamdanid **Nasir al-Dawla al-Hasan** (d. 969) began to establish his independent rule at Mosul. He paid tribute to the Abbasids only when forced. He drew support from his brother Sayf al-Dawla, who established a Hamdanid regime in Aleppo in 945. Nasir al-Dawla's sons fought among themselves, and Hamdanid control of Mosul ended when the Uqaylids took the city.

930. The **Qarmatis sacked Mecca** and carried off the black stone from the Ka'ba. It was not returned until 951.

934–40. AL-RADI. The caliph, manipulated by the military and the prime minister, had little control over territory beyond the city of Baghdad. Real power became vested in the new position of the supreme commander *(amir al-umara)*, which was seized by the military governor Ibn Ra'iq. The Abbasid government was bankrupt.

934. Ali ibn Buya took control of the region of Fars in western Iran, the first step in the building of the **Buyid (Buwayhid) family's empire.** An able military man from Daylam in northern Iran, he began as a mercenary for the local potentate Mardawij ibn Ziyar before assembling his own army. His brothers, **Hasan and Ahmad,** participated in what became a **familial venture of expansion** in which Hasan took central Iran and Ahmad occupied Iraq and Baghdad.

935. Death of **Ali al-Ash'ari,** the founder of Sunni theology *(kalam)* and author of a number of works on Islam. *Kalam* emerged with the **Mu'tazili school,** which attempted to apply rationalist argument, inspired by Greek philosophy, to theological problems. Al-Ash'ari started as a Mu'tazili theologian, but rejected this path as un-Islamic. He used **Greek dialectic** to establish his theological school and so, although asserting sure limits to logic in the discussion of the divine, established a place for speculative inquiry within the faith.

940. Death of **Muhammad al-Kulayni,** a Shi'ite theologian and the author of the first major collection of Shi'ite *hadith,* titled *Usul al-Kafi (Foundations of the Compendium).*

945, Dec. BUYID OCCUPATION OF BAGHDAD. Ahmad ibn Buya, whose brothers, Ali and Hasan, controlled much of western and central Iran, entered Baghdad with his forces and was recognized by the caliph as *amir al-umara* (supreme commander) with the honorific title of **Mu'izz al-Dawla.** With the loss of its capital, the Abbasid Caliphate, which had already disintegrated into a number of independent provincial regimes, ceased to exist as a meaningful political entity. The Abbasid dynasty remained in place until 1258, but most of its caliphs were mere figureheads. The Buyid takeover marked the end of an era in Middle Eastern political history.

2. THE MUSLIM MIDDLE EAST AND NORTH AFRICA, c. 945–1500

a. OVERVIEW

Between the breakup of the Abbasid Empire in the 10th century and the restoration of an imperial hegemony under the Ottomans in the 16th century, the Middle East and North Africa lost any semblance of political unity. **Dozens of dynasties** ruling over parts of the region came and went, and the boundaries of states shifted endlessly. A broad political division emerged, however, among several territorial units: Iran and Iraq, Egypt and Syria, and North Africa. To these was added the area of **Anatolia** (Asia Minor), which first came under Muslim rule during this period; after being tied initially to the political destinies of Iran and Iraq, it developed into a distinct political entity that became linked, under the expanding Ottoman state, with the newly conquered Balkan lands.

The Muslim advance into Anatolia and Europe brought a final end to the **Byzantine Empire,** for eight centuries a neighbor and adversary of the Muslim states in the eastern Mediterranean. In the western Mediterranean, however, Muslim states were on the defensive as the Christians reconquered all of **Spain** and established military outposts on the **North African coast.**

The end of the Abbasid imperial order reduced the **caliphate in Baghdad** to little more than a symbolic presence; real power was vested in the institution of the **sultanate** and a new type of regime characteristic of the postimperial era. The bureaucratic, landowning, and merchant elites that had dominated the region gave way to **slave soldiers and tribal warriors.** Slave armies, composed most commonly of Turks, became the mainstay of dynasties everywhere; in Mamluk Egypt and Syria (1250–1517) the Turkish and Circassian slave soldiers even became the rulers in place of a dynastic order. From the 11th century, large-scale **migration of central Asian Turkish nomads** into the region overran large territories and brought to power Turkish tribal chieftains. In North Africa, **Berber tribal warriors** defeated Arab-dominated regimes and established new dynasties.

In the midst of this political upheaval, the Middle East endured two major non-Muslim military invasions, by the **Crusaders** and the **Mongols.** The onslaught from the east was by far the more consequential for the region and caused unparalleled devastation. The Crusader presence, on the other hand, was more in the nature of a prolonged nuisance; it loomed large only in European annals. In the long term, neither invasion was able to reverse the Muslim hold on the region.

The long-term **social and economic effects** of these movements of tribes and armies across the region were felt most acutely in Iran, Iraq, and Anatolia. The influx of Turkish nomads made large tracts of agricultural land the **domain of pastoralists.** It also brought into the region a **new ethnic element,** one that became a formidable presence not only within the political elites. The economic fortune of the lands farther west, especially Egypt and Syria, was generally better, although

the **Black Death** (p. 106) and the recurrent plague epidemics that followed it caused massive dislocations everywhere. The **population** appears to have suffered an **overall decline** during the period.

Despite the unsettled conditions and political fragmentation, this was a period of remarkable **cultural achievement.** A unity built on a universal religion and civilization took the place of political unity. The mass **conversion to Islam** was completed, and the population became almost solidly Muslim. And the faith itself reached maturity as an elaborate system of belief: **Islamic law** developed into a comprehensive code, with four recognized schools of interpretation; the *madrasa* came into being as the institution of advanced religious learning; **Sufism** developed organized orders and became integrated into Islamic thought and worship (p. 117); the **Sunni-Shi'ite sectarian divide** became clearly defined; and a large body of distinguished writing gave definitive form to Islamic tradition and learning.

Impressive creativity also marked **secular fields of study,** ranging from astronomy and algebra to philosophy and history. The period produced some of the region's most celebrated Arabic, Persian, and Turkish **literary works,** and some of its finest **architectural and artistic creations.** While religious opinion had its quarrels with **philosophy,** Islam in general did not seriously oppose or stifle work in the physical and natural sciences, which remained productive into the 15th century.

In the sphere of high culture, as in politics and economics, men were dominant. The period reinforced an inherited social order based on the **superior rights and power of men.** Islamic law, more readily enforced in the cities, did provide **women** with rights to property, inheritance, and matrimonial support, and these helped them acquire leverage within their families. But in many respects the legal norms and social practice worked in men's favor. In both the city and the countryside, needy **women worked outdoors,** in menial and lowly professions. The **female seclusion** associated with Islamic society was an ideal achieved only in the better-off classes. Women's veiling, part of a code of female modesty and sexual segregation, was commonplace, particularly in the cities.

b. IRAN, IRAQ, AND ANATOLIA

945–1055. THE BUYIDS (BUWAYHIDS). The fall of Baghdad, as well as parts of Iraq and Iran, to the three conquering Buyid brothers established a new regime in the region. While maintaining the Abbasid caliphs as titular heads of state, the Buyids created a confederation of **several principalities** ruled by members of their family (based primarily in Baghdad, Shiraz, and Rayy). They revived some of the **Persian monarchical traditions,** including the Sassanian title of *shahanshah* (king of kings), held by the leading family member. Their ability to rule effectively in Baghdad was undermined in part by the poor state of the **Iraqi economy,** which could not adequately support their army (made up of Daylamites and Turkish slaves). After the death of their greatest ruler, Adud al-Dawla, in 983, the Buyids suffered from succession struggles, factionalism, and the loss of outlying territories. Rayy fell to the Ghaznavids in 1029, and the Seljuks brought an end to Buyid rule in Baghdad in 1055 and in Shiraz in 1062.

The Buyids had Shi'ite leanings, and it was during their period of rule that the **Sunni-Shi'ite divide** in Islam became fully established and Shi'ism developed its distinct sectarian character. Buyid officials intermittently patronized the Shi'ites in Baghdad and encouraged their developing into an armed political group that fought it out with Sunni groups. At the same time, Shi'ite scholars put Shi'ite *hadith*, law, and theology into written form, and new, typically **Shi'ite communal rituals** became established, notably the annual public mourning for the death of Husayn at Karbala (the *ashura*), the public cursing of the first two caliphs, and pilgrimages to the tombs of Ali's family. Largely in response to this Shi'ite sectarianism and its challenges, the **Sunnis** developed a conception of themselves as a distinct Muslim community. The Abbasid **caliph al-Qadir** (991–1031) took the lead in asserting an explicitly Sunni position, one that upheld the legitimacy of all four of the first caliphs.

950. Death of **Abu Nasr Muhammad al-Farabi** (b. c. 870), one of the greatest Middle Eastern scholars and philosophers. He wrote extensively on logic, ethics, politics, grammar, mathematics, and music. Drawing on Aristotelian and Platonic thought, he gave primacy to **philosophy** as the path to divine truth, presenting religion as an approximation of the truth more suitable to the masses. His *Kitab al-musiqi al-kabir (Grand Book of Music)* remains one of the most comprehensive and systematic treatises on the **theory of Middle Eastern music.** It discusses the science of sound, intervals, tetrachords, instruments, and compositions, and outlines a lute fretting that incorporated two newly introduced neutral or microtonal intervals in addition to the basic diatonic arrangement of Pythagorean intervals.

950–1080. Ascendancy of Kurdish dynasties. Several Kurdish dynasties established states in the second half of the 10th century: the **Shaddadids** (c. 950) and the **Rawwadids** (later 10th century) in Azerbaijan, the **Hasanuyids** (c. 960) and **Annazids** (c. 990) in the central Zagros region, and the **Marwanids** (982) in southeastern Anatolia. Their regimes were set up in mountainous regions, relied on the military power of Kurdish tribesmen rather than slave soldiers, and worked with rudimentary administrative systems. Their rise reflected the general flourishing of **local autonomy** brought about by the breakup of the Abbasid Caliphate.

950–1100. Emergence of the Muslim religious college (madrasa). The *madrasa* had its origins probably in 10th-century Khurasan, from which it spread steadily throughout the region to become the standard Muslim institution of advanced religious and legal training. **Subjects** commonly taught in the *madrasas* included Islamic law, *hadith*, Qur'anic commentary, Arabic grammar, and theology. **Students** worked individually with teachers to acquire mastery of particular texts along with written certification of their authority to teach those texts to others. The colleges were set up as private **acts of charity** and were supported by endowed property *(waqf),* which paid the salaries of the staff and stipends for students.

950–1250. DEVELOPMENT OF ISLAMIC LAW. The four major schools *(madhhabs)* of Islamic law—the Hanafi, Shafi'i, Maliki, and Hanbali—were established during the period as the only recognized interpretations; over time, a variety of other schools that had emerged disappeared from the scene. The differences among the four schools revolved around matters of detail rather than grand issues of principle.

Legal scholarship mushroomed as jurists codified rules and case materials, issued standardized legal manuals and collections of legal opinions *(fatawa),* and even created legal devices *(hiyal)* for getting around certain restrictive principles without violating the letter of the law. Islamic law, the *shari'a,* was regarded as immutable and, according to most jurists, no longer open to independent interpretation by scholars. In practice, however, judges and jurisconsults accommodated legal principles to custom and circumstance, and a great degree of **flexibility in the interpretation** and application of the law prevailed.

One of the striking developments of the period was the **fierce factional rivalry** among the schools of law. In the 11th and 12th centuries the schools evolved from scholarly groups committed to a shared legal

doctrine into sectarian movements that cultivated mass followings and stirred popular passions. In Baghdad and eastern Iran there were struggles, including bloody street battles, between adherents of different schools competing for influence and patronage. This factionalism subsided after the 12th century, and affiliation with the legal schools ceased to be a source of intense contention.

950–1300. THE DEVELOPMENT OF SUFI ORDERS AND THOUGHT. From numerous loose associations of mystics led by independent masters, the Sufi movement matured during the period into a number of formally organized religious orders or brotherhoods *(tariqat).* Each order defined its own particular **doctrines,** modes of **worship,** and **initiation rites,** which it attributed to an originating master, after whom the order was usually named. The major orders, such as the Qadiriyya, Rifa'iyya, and Suhrawardiyya, grew beyond their local origins and became regional, establishing **chapters** whose members were all considered disciples of a common spiritual ancestor.

The Sufi orders varied widely in their practices and general outlook: some tended toward a **sober** pietistic and ascetic view consistent with the scripturalist conception of Islam; others promoted **ecstatic** practices, magical beliefs, and the veneration of saints. But everywhere, Sufi lodges *(khanaqas)* became centers of prayer, instruction, and pilgrimage, and **worship at the tombs of saints** developed into a central feature of popular Islam.

Alongside the institutional development of Sufism came also the steady integration of its initially separate ways of thought and practice with mainstream Islamic belief and worship. Treating Sufism as a science, writers worked out a systematic body of thought that **integrated Sufism with law and theology** and helped to legitimize it as an acceptable path to Muslim spiritual fulfillment. Most noteworthy was the work of the great theologian **al-Ghazali** (d. 1111), who developed a definitive conception of Islam that brought together law and Sufism as compatible and complementary aspects of the faith.

967. The death in Baghdad of **Abu al-Faraj Ali al-Isfahani** (b. 897), the poet and socialite famous for his monumental *Kitab al-aghani (Book of Songs).* The work compiled an immense corpus of songs, anecdotal material, and popular lore; it forms an unequalled treasure of information on the culture, musical life, and social history of early Islamic society.

977–97. SEBUKTIGIN, FOUNDER OF THE GHAZNAVID DYNASTY. A Turkish slave general in the service of the Samanids, Sebuktigin established a state with its capital at **Ghazna,** south of Kabul in Afghanistan (then on the remote fringes of the Islamic world). He actually built on the base prepared by his commander, **Alptigin,** who had set up an autonomous city-state in Ghazna in 961. The Ghaznavid regime was rather decentralized, relying on the services of **slave soldiers** paid by way of grants of tax revenue from land (known as *iqta').* The regime proclaimed its allegiance to the Abbasid Caliphate and cultivated Islamic learning and Persian literature. The dynasty lasted until 1186, and at its height (under Sebuktigin's son Mahmud, 998–1030) it ruled Afghanistan, Khurasan, Khwarazm, and northern India.

990–1096. Uqaylid rule in Mosul. The Buyids took the region of Mosul from the Hamdanids in 979, but in 990 the Uqayli Arab tribe established itself there, after a short-lived attempt by the Hamdanids to restore their rule. The Uqaylid dynasty, which held Mosul until 1096, is usually said to have been Shi'ite, although the evidence of its religious leanings appears inconclusive.

995. Death of **Ibn al-Nadim,** a librarian whose *Fihrist (Catalogue)* was an annotated bibliography of all the works of Arabic literature available at the time, including many now lost.

Death of **Abu Ali al-Tanukhi,** a judge in Buyid service and author of a book of anecdotes *(Nishwar al-muhadara)* that throws light on the social life of his time.

c. 998. Ali ibn Mazyad, leader of the Arab tribe of Banu Asad, established a virtually independent **Mazyadid state** in the **Kufa** area south of Baghdad. Backed by a powerful tribal army, the Mazyadids enjoyed great influence in the area for a century and a half. They acquired titles and subsidies from the Buyids in return for military services. Their most lasting achievement was the founding of the city of **Hilla,** which became their capital.

998–1030. MAHMUD OF GHAZNA. The Ghaznavid state based in Afghanistan reached the height of its power under Mahmud, who ranked among the great Middle Eastern leaders of his time. He distinguished himself with his extensive **military conquests,** his **patronage** of literary talents (including Firdawsi), and his fervent **championship of Sunnism** in an age of Shi'ite victories. He annexed **Khurasan** from the Samanids in 999, took the region of **Rayy** in western Iran from the Buyids in 1029, and occupied parts of northern India. But within ten years of his death the Ghaznavids lost his Iranian acquisitions to the Seljuks.

1008. Death of **Badi' al-Zaman al-Hamadhani,** a master of Arabic prose who established the literary genre known as *maqamat,* dramatic anecdotes narrated in elaborate rhymed prose. **Abu Muhammad al-Qasim al-Hariri** (d. 1122), a writer from Basra, raised this form to new heights in his *maqamat,* although his excessive concern with displaying his verbal tricks drove Arabic prose to a certain formalistic extreme.

c. 1020. Death of **Firdawsi,** among the preeminent poets of Iran. His monumental historical epic, *Shah-nama (Book of Kings),* narrates (in some 60,000 double lines) the **legendary history of Iran,** describing the exploits of the hero Rustam as well as court histories of the Sassanians. Exquisitely **illuminated manuscripts** of the work were produced over the centuries.

1030. Death of **Abu Ali Miskawayh,** author of *Tajarib al-umam (The Experiences of the Nations),* one of the greatest histories of the region. He served in the Buyid administration, and a strong sense of good government and official responsibility colors his accounts and interpretations of events.

1036–51. RISE OF SELJUK POWER IN IRAN. Chagri Beg and his brother **Tughril Beg,** chieftains of the Seljuk family, invaded Khurasan at the head of armies of Turkoman nomads. They defeated the Ghaznavids in the **Battle of Dandanqan** (1040) and won control of **Khurasan** before moving west to take the regions of Rayy (1042) and Isfahan (1051).

THE SELJUKS were a leading family of the **Oghuz Turks** from central Asia, a nomadic tribal people who converted to Islam around the end of the 10th century. The Seljuks moved to Transoxania and became involved as mercenaries in the struggles among Muslim dynasties in the region before crossing the Oxus River into Ghaznavid territories in Khurasan around 1025. Their campaigns of conquest formed part of the great **migration of nomadic Turks** into the Middle East in the 11th century, a period when whole tribes of Turkoman pastoralists in search of booty and grazing land swept through the region, overrunning settled areas on their trek westward. The Seljuks rode this human wave to create **a new Islamic empire.**

1037. Death of **Abu Ali al-Husayn ibn Sina** (Avicenna), the great physician, scientist, and philosopher. Born to a Persian official in 980, he studied **science and medicine** and produced numerous scholarly works that contributed to all natural sciences. His monumental study of medical science, *al-Qanun fi al-tibb (Canon of Medicine),* became a standard reference work. He also gave a new vitality to **philosophic thought,** incorporating mystical approaches to the reconciliation of Greek theosophy with the scriptural tradition.

c. 1050. Death of **Muhammad al-Biruni** (b. 973), considered among the most learned scholars of the Islamic world. He wrote more than 100 books, including works on natural science, mathematics, and astronomy, and a remarkable **description of India.**

1055, Dec. SELJUK OCCUPATION OF BAGHDAD, AND THE SELJUK SULTANATE. Tughril Beg entered the Abbasid capital, put an **end to Buyid power,** and was recognized by the caliph as **sultan.** By the time of his death in 1063 he had established Seljuk rule throughout Iran and Iraq. Under his successors **Alp Arslan** (1063–72) and **Malikshah** (1072–92), the Seljuks extended their domination into parts of Syria and Anatolia, establishing an empire that stretched from the Oxus River to the Mediterranean. But after Malikshah's death, and especially after the rule of his son **Muhammad I** (1105–18), the empire ceased to exist as a unified state. Members of the Seljuk family divided the provinces among themselves, founding **independent dynasties** in various parts of Iran, Iraq, Syria, and Anatolia. These were largely **short-lived provincial regimes** that disappeared before the 13th-century Mongol invasion or in its wake.

The Seljuks tried to establish a unified empire by adopting a **central administration** along Persian lines and creating **slave armies** that would reduce their dependence on the unruly Turkoman nomads who

had conquered the empire. But several of their tribal practices worked to disperse political power and fragment the state. They viewed the **right to rule** as belonging to various members of the family rather than to a single person, and recognized the **right of tribes** to receive whole areas for grazing and habitation, along with a great degree of autonomy. They also resorted to the institution of the *atabeg,* a Turkish commander appointed to serve as tutor to a minor Seljuk prince and to govern in his name. In time, some *atabegs* won control of their wards' provinces and established their own principalities and dynasties. The most notable was founded by Zangi, who governed Mosul and Aleppo (1127–46).

Another distinct feature of the Seljuk regime was payment of soldiers with *iqta',* which granted them the right to collect taxes from the population of assigned lands and keep them in lieu of salary. Due to abuse and the decline of central authority, these grants became **hereditary,** and the tax-collecting rights were turned by the assignees into private property and became the basis of **autonomous political power.** The institution of the *iqta'* predated the Seljuks, but became under them a central feature of Middle Eastern government.

The Seljuks set in motion the process by which Iran acquired its **large Turkish population.** The greatest influx of Turks into the region appears to have taken place later on, as a result of the Mongol invasions.

1058. Death of **Ali al-Mawardi** (b. c. 974), an important Sunni jurist and political theorist whose work *al-Ahkam al-sultaniyya (The Principles of Government)* was a comprehensive blueprint for the functioning of an Islamic government. His concern was to make a case for the relevance of the caliphate at a time when its actual powers were stripped by the sultanates.

1063–92. Nizam al-Mulk (b. 1018) served as chief minister for the Seljuk sultans Alp Arslan and Malikshah. An able statesman, he centralized the empire along Persian bureaucratic lines. His treatise *Siyasat-nama (The Book of Government)* remains one of the most notable examples of the "mirrors for princes" literature. It defined the rules of good government and gave the sultan practical **advice on statecraft.** He was assassinated by the Nizari Isma'ilis (the Assassins).

1067. The **Madrasa al-Nizamiyya,** an important Shafi'i religious college, was founded in Baghdad by the Seljuk chief minister Nizam al-Mulk. He established *madrasas* in other major cities as well, as part of a state policy of **patronizing religious institutions** and calming the fierce factional rivalries that raged at the time among the Shafi'i, Hanafi, and Hanbali schools of law.

1071, Aug. 26. BATTLE OF MANZIKERT. The armies of the Seljuk sultan Alp Arslan defeated the Byzantine forces on the Muslim-Byzantine frontier near Lake Van and captured the Byzantine emperor. The battle resulted in the collapse of the Byzantine frontier defenses and the **opening of Anatolia to Turkish invasion** and settlement. In the following two centuries, Turkoman tribesmen and war bands occupied most of Anatolia, setting in motion the transformation of this Christian land into a Muslim, Turkish-speaking territory.

1071–1177. The Danishmendids of Anatolia. Malik Danishmend, whose origins and exploits remain obscure, founded a principality based in the north and center of Anatolia. It was a rival of the neighboring Seljuk Sultanate of Rum, which finally absorbed its territories.

1075–1307. THE SELJUK SULTANATE OF RUM. A Seljuk prince named **Suleyman ibn Kutalmish** (d. 1086) launched a campaign of conquests in Anatolia and founded an extensive state that formed one of the leading powers in the region. Its capital, initially in Iznik (Nicaea), was established at Konya (Iconium) in 1097. The Seljuks built up an impressive **sedentary Islamic state** in the newly conquered lands: they maintained a standing army and developed bureaucracy, promoted agriculture and trade, and lent support to the creation of Sunni religious institutions. They attained the zenith of their power and prosperity in the period from 1200 to 1243, after which they became a **Mongol protectorate.** The sultanate faded out of history after the death of its last ruler, Mas'ud III, in 1307.

1082. Death of **Kai Kavus ibn Iskandar,** a ruler in northern Iran and author of the *Qabus-nama,* an important book of **advice to rulers.** The work offers the wisdom of an old king to his favorite son, teaching him how to be a statesman and a gentleman.

1084. Suleyman, ruler of the Seljuk Sultanate of Rum, captured **Antioch,**

which had been under Byzantine rule since 969. The city fell to the Crusaders 15 years later.

c. 1088. Death of **Nasir-i Khusraw** (b. 1004), an Isma'ili theologian and poet from Balkh. He wrote a **travel account** of his journeys west in 1045–52, noting the prosperity of Egypt and Syria, among others, in comparison with the eastern parts of the Middle East.

1090–1256. The Isma'ili (Assassin) stronghold in Alamut. An independent Isma'ili Shi'ite sect known as the **Nizaris** (or Assassins) maintained a base in the inaccessible fortress of Alamut in the Alborz Mountains south of the Caspian Sea. It was established by **Hasan-i Sabbah** (d. 1124), a Fatimid agent in Iran who took up the cause of Nizar, a Fatimid defeated in a struggle for succession to the caliphate in Egypt. The Nizaris saw themselves as representatives of the rightful Isma'ili imams and enemies of the Fatimids in Cairo. Despite their limited territorial power, they **spread terror** in the region by resorting to suicide missions of assassination directed against leaders (among them, Nizam al-Mulk). The **Mongols** destroyed the Nizari base in Alamut in 1256, but the Nizari sect has survived to this day, with the Aga Khan as its head.

1097–98. Muslim confrontation with the First Crusade in Anatolia (p. 233). Moving from Constantinople into Anatolia, the Crusader forces captured **Iznik** from the Seljuks (June 1097) and then inflicted two more defeats on the Turks: at **Dorylaeum** (Eskishehir) in July 1097 and at **Heraclea** (Ereghli) in Aug. 1097. **Edessa** (Urfa) was taken and established as the first Crusader state in 1098, followed shortly thereafter by the creation of a Crusader principality at **Antioch.**

1111. Death of **Abu Hamid Muhammad AL-GHAZALI** (b. 1058), the most celebrated Sunni theologian of all time. He wrote widely on Islam and its relationship to the sciences, philosophy, and mysticism. His monumental work, *Ihya' 'ulum al-din (Revivification of the Religious Sciences)*, developed his conception of an ideal Islam that **integrated the shari'a and Sufism** as two essential parts representing the outer and inner life of Muslims. Tormented by inner conflicts about his faith and his worldly activities, he gave up his professorship at the prestigious Nizamiyya religious college in Baghdad and spent some ten years (1095–1106) wandering and in seclusion, resolving his spiritual dilemmas.

Ghazali added his authoritative voice to the Islamic **debate over contraception,** offering the most thorough statement permitting birth control, and specifically withdrawal, on medical and economic grounds. The majority of Muslim jurists allowed the **practice of withdrawal,** but required the **woman's permission** in order to protect her rights to children and to complete sexual fulfillment. Women's use of contraceptives, such as tampons and suppositories, was regarded as legal and, by most jurists, as the woman's prerogative, not requiring the husband's permission.

1127–1222. THE ZANGIDS OF MOSUL. Imad al-Din Zangi, the *atabeg* (tutor) of a Seljuk prince, established himself in Mosul in 1127 and in Aleppo the following year. He reconquered **Edessa** (Urfa) from the Crusaders in 1144. His dynasty held out in Mosul until 1222, although it was a dependent of the Ayyubids after 1187.

1130. Death of **Umar Khayyam,** the Persian poet and scientist. While his *Ruba'iyyat (Quatrains)* has won him fame, his scientific achievements were no less considerable. He wrote works on **algebra** that advanced equations from the quadratic to the cubic stage, and participated in revising the old **Persian solar calendar.**

1137–75. Shams al-Din Eldiguz, the *atabeg* of the Seljuk sultan of Baghdad, established an independent dynastic state in **Azerbaijan** and northwestern Iran that lasted until 1225.

1148. The Seljuks of Rum defeated both the German army of the **Second Crusade** at Dorylaeum (Eskishehir) and the French forces at Laodicaea (Denizli).

1150–1215. Ascendancy of the Ghurids in Afghanistan. A dynasty based in the inaccessible mountains of central Afghanistan, the Ghurids were rivals of their Ghaznavid neighbors. They brought an end to Ghaznavid rule in **Ghazna** after destroying the city in 1150, and in 1187 expanded to take the Ghaznavid lands in the Punjab, thus ending the Ghaznavid state. Their expansion was halted, however, by the **Khwarazm-shahs,** who conquered the Ghurids' Afghan possessions by 1215 and forced them to withdraw to their lands in northern India.

1157–1220. ASCENDANCY OF THE KHWARAZM-SHAHS in Iran and Afghanistan. With the death of **Sanjar,** the supreme sultan of the Seljuks (1118–57), Seljuk power in Iran collapsed. The Khwarazm-shahs, who were descendants of the Turkish general appointed by the Seljuks to govern Khwarazm, stepped in and steadily extended their control to **eastern and central Iran,** in addition to conquering much of **Afghanistan** from the Ghurids and occupying Transoxania. Their empire reached its height in the period from 1200 to 1220, after which it was overrun by the **Mongols.**

1166. Death of **Abd al-Qadir al-Jilani** (b. 1078), founder of the **Qadiriyya Sufi order.** Beginning as a local chapter centered around his tomb in Baghdad, the order spread throughout the Arab world and sub-Saharan Africa, and now forms the oldest of the still-surviving Sufi orders in the region.

1176, Sept. BATTLE OF MYRIOKEPHALON. The army of the Seljuks of Rum ambushed and defeated the Byzantine army advancing on the Seljuk capital of Konya. The decisive encounter ended any possibility of a Byzantine reconquest of lost Anatolian territories.

1180–1225. Reign of the **Abbasid caliph al-Nasir,** the last great figure of the Abbasid family. He revived the temporal power of the caliphate and established himself as the leading authority in Iraq in the wake of the Seljuks' declining control. He built his position partly by giving state support to the *futuwwa* brotherhoods, which organized craftsmen and urban dwellers around an ideology of manly virtue and social justice.

1182. Death of **Ahmad al-Rifa'i** (b. c. 1106), founder of the **Rifa'iyya Sufi order.** The order, which is still widespread in Egypt and Syria, involves practices of self-mortification as part of its initiation rites and devotional exercises.

1209. Death of **Nizami,** perhaps the greatest romantic poet to write in Persian. His verses are so filled with learning and allusion that they defy direct translation. His five masterpieces, known as the *Khamsa (Quintet),* have been superbly illustrated by miniaturist painters over the centuries.

Death of **Fakhr al-Din al-Razi** (b. 1149), a prominent theologian whose work integrated philosophy and logic into Islamic theological doctrines.

1220–23. THE FIRST MONGOL INVASION OF IRAN (p. 152). Leading a punitive expedition against the Khwarazm-shahs, Chinggis Khan invaded Transoxania and Khurasan. In a massive **campaign of terror** in eastern Iran, the Mongols razed cities and exterminated their populations. After this brutal assault, the main Mongol army withdrew from Iran, although the northern parts of the country remained under Mongol viceroys. The empire of the Khwarazm-shahs was brought to an end. The last ruler of the dynasty, Jalal al-Din, led a futile movement of resistance against the Mongols before his murder in 1231.

1221. Death of **Farid al-Din Attar** (b. 1142), a highly accomplished Sufi poet from Khurasan. His works dwell on the stages of the soul's progressive journey from this world to the next.

1229. Death of **Yaqut** (Ya'qub al-Hamawi), a Baghdadi scholar who authored a monumental geographical lexicon (*Mu'jam al-buldan*). The work is a mine of information, incorporating material from geographers whose original work has been lost.

1233. Death of **Ali ibn al-Athir** (b. 1160), a scholar of Mosul whose monumental history, *al-Kamil fi al-ta'rikh,* ranks among the greatest Middle Eastern chronicles.

1234. Death of **Umar al-Suhrawardi** (b. 1145), founder of the **Suhrawardiyya Sufi order** in Baghdad. The order was carried to India by Baha' al-Din al-Multani.

1240. The Seljuks of Rum suppressed the revolt led by the messianic figure **Baba Ishak** (Baba Resul) in central Anatolia. Many of the rebels fled for refuge in the frontier regions of western Anatolia, where they spread their syncretic religious beliefs and practices.

1242–43. THE MONGOL INVASION OF ANATOLIA. Mongol forces routed the Seljuk army at the **Battle of Köse Dagh** (June 1243) and reduced the Seljuk Sultanate of Rum to a vassal state. The Mongol advance changed political and social conditions dramatically in Anatolia. As the authority of the central state represented by the Seljuks weakened, a host of **Turkoman principalities** began to arise, waging frontier warfare against the Byzantines. They drew on the large waves of **Muslim refugees** who fled the Mongol advance and sought new fortunes in Anatolia.

1256–58. MONGOL CONQUEST OF IRAN AND IRAQ. A large Mongol army led by **Hulegu,** brother of the Mongol Great Khan Möngke, invaded Iran, destroyed the strongholds of the Nizari Isma'ilis in Alamut and other locations, and subdued much of Iran and Iraq.

1258, Feb. FALL OF BAGHDAD AND END OF THE ABBASID CALIPHATE. The Mongols subjected Baghdad to plundering and widespread massacres. The caliph al-Musta'sim was put to death, and with him ended the more than 500 years of the **Abbasid Caliphate.** A new era in Middle Eastern history began, with a **non-Muslim empire** dominating region's eastern lands.

c. THE MONGOL EMPIRE AND ITS SUCCESSORS

1258–60. Mongol forces brought territories in **Iraq and Anatolia** under Hulegu's rule, but failed to hold on to **Syria,** where they suffered defeat by the Mamluks (p. 129).

c. 1260. The **principality of Karaman** in the foothills of the Taurus Mountains was founded by the Turkoman leader Karaman ibn Musa. It emerged as a formidable power in **central Anatolia** and a rival to the Ottomans until its annexation by them in 1468.

1261. Menteshe Bey, a Turkoman leader, launched the conquest of Byzantine ports and lands in western Anatolia, establishing the **principality of Menteshe** in the area. It survived until its absorption by the Ottomans in 1390.

1265–1335. THE ILKHANID STATE AFTER HULEGU. Hulegu succeeded in creating an extensive Middle Eastern empire that included Iran, Iraq, and much of Anatolia. His descendants, who held the title of *ilkhan* (viceroy), ruled the empire as a unified state until 1335, after which it **disintegrated** into rival provincial regimes. The capital was set up initially at **Maragha** in Azerbaijan, but it was moved by Ilkhan Abaqa (1265–82) to **Tabriz,** and then by Oljeitu (1304–16) southeast to **Sultaniyya.**

The **Ilkhanids** relied on the existing **Iranian bureaucracy** to handle their administrative and financial affairs. Iranian Muslims served commonly as their chief ministers, the most famous of whom was **Rashid al-Din** (1247–1318). At least in the first three decades after Hulegu, their main aim was to extract as much revenue as possible from the population, which suffered **enormous tax demands.** During that period the Mongols were **pagan or Buddhist** in their religious inclinations, and freed their non-Muslim subjects from their previous social restrictions and tax burdens. The rule of **Ghazan** (1295–1304), who converted to Islam, marked an important shift in Ilkhanid policies, both fiscal and religious.

The Mongol period was of cataclysmic consequences for the region. In addition to the **unparalleled massacre and destruction**—described by Muslim chroniclers as a holocaust—the Mongol invasions caused **lasting demographic and economic changes.** Large numbers of Turks settled permanently in Iran, establishing a formidable Turkish presence in the country, especially in the northwestern region of Azerbaijan. The nomadic influx also turned extensive lands from agricultural to pastoral use and brought a long-term shift in the area's economic balance.

1273. Death of **Jalal al-Din Rumi,** perhaps the greatest of the Persian mystical poets. Born in Balkh in 1207, he fled west from the advancing Mongol hordes and finally settled in **Konya.** His large collection of impassioned lyrical works (among them the celebrated *Mathnavi*) explores the spiritual paths to the identification of the human self with the divine being, blending mystical sentiment with amorous feelings. He became the patron saint of the **Mevlevi Sufi order,** whose ceremonies incorporated music and whirling dances in special dress (from which came their common description as "whirling dervishes"). The order spread from its headquarters in Konya to other cities, and won adherents among the Ottoman elite and the patronage of Ottoman sultans.

1274. Death of **Nasir al-Din Tusi,** a prominent Shi'ite theologian famous for his work in **astronomy.** He was high in the counsels of Hulegu, who built for him an **observatory in Maragha** that produced important findings. **Qutb al-Din Shirazi** (d. 1131), another distinguished astronomer, collaborated with Tusi in his scientific research.

c. 1283. The **principality of Germiyan** was founded in western Anatolia, with its capital in Kutahya. It was one of the leading Turkoman prin-

cipalities on the Byzantine frontier, and was annexed by the Ottomans in 1389–90.

1291. Anti-Jewish riots in Iraq and Iran. The chief minister of the state, the Jewish scholar and physician Sa'd al-Dawla, was murdered along with his Jewish associates, and a widespread purge removed numerous Jewish officials who had entered the service of the Mongol administration. This marked the end of three decades of unusual opportunity and freedom enjoyed by the Jews during the non-Muslim phase of Ilkhanid rule.

1292. Death of **Sa'di,** among the giants of Persian prose and lyric poetry. His *Gulistan,* a volume of practical wisdom and wit, ranks among the finest works of Persian classical literature.

1294. The Ilkhanids introduced **paper money** in an attempt to deal with the bankruptcy of the treasury. The paper certificates, which followed Chinese models, brought all business to a standstill and had to be withdrawn.

Death of **Safi al-Din al-Urmawi** (b. 1216), an accomplished Baghdadi musician and author of an important treatise on musical theory *(al-Adwar).* His detailed analysis of melodic modes and scale intervals had a profound influence on later writers and on the musical systems of Iran and Turkey.

1295–1304. RULE OF THE ILKHAN GHAZAN. Breaking away from the pagan or Buddhist affiliations of his predecessors, Ghazan **embraced Islam** and instituted it as the religion of the state. Buddhist temples were destroyed and the traditional restrictions on Christians and Jews restored. The conversion of the Mongols contributed to their gradual **assimilation** into local society. With the aid of his able minister Rashid al-Din, Ghazan also attempted to correct the damage caused by decades of Mongol misgovernment and exploitation of the population. He instituted **reforms** to regulate taxation, improve security in the countryside, encourage recultivation, and correct disorder in the military and administration. It is not clear to what degree his program was actually implemented, although the new official orientation probably improved efficiency and the overall treatment of the population.

c. 1297. Death of **Haji Bektash,** a Sufi leader who was widely revered in Seljuk Anatolia, where he preached a version of Islam that combined Sunni, Shi'ite, and Christian practices and beliefs. From his teachings evolved the influential **Bektashi Sufi order,** which gained strong support among the Turkoman tribesmen and later became the adopted order of the Janissary corps in the Ottoman Empire.

1307. Founding of the city of **Sultaniyya** in Azerbaijan, to which the Ilkhanid ruler Oljeitu moved his capital from Tabriz. The magnificent mausoleum built for him in the city survives to this day.

1308. The Turkoman leader **Mehmed Bey,** son of Aydin, conquered Birge (Pyrgion) and made it the capital of a principality in western Anatolia that extended as far as Izmir (Smyrna). The **principality of Aydin** survived until its annexation by the Ottomans in 1389–90.

1313. Saruhan Bey conquered Manisa (Magnesia), which formed the base of the Turkoman **principality of Saruhan** in western Anatolia. The principality fell to the Ottomans in 1389–90.

1314. Konya, former capital of the Seljuk Sultanate of Rum, was captured by the principality of Karaman and made its capital. The Karamanids increasingly represented themselves as the heirs of the sultans of Rum.

1318. Execution of **Rashid al-Din** (b. 1247), the Ilkhanid minister. A Jewish convert to Islam and a physician by training, he emerged as a central power in the Ilkhanid state, especially under Ghazan. He wrote an important general **history** that includes primary material on the Ilkhanid state as well as a treatment of Europe, India, and Judaism.

1321. Death of **Yunus Emre** (b. c. 1250), the most celebrated of the early Turkish poets of Anatolia. His verses, which used colloquial Turkish to express his mystic devotion, achieved unmatched force and lyricism and are sung to this day.

1334. Death of **Shaykh Safi al-Din** (b. 1252), founder of the **Safavid movement** that ultimately brought the Safavid dynasty to power in Iran (p. 123). In 1301 he became the head of a Sufi organization in **Ardabil** and developed a body of devoted followers who attributed to him miraculous deeds. (He was a Sunni, which embarrassed his Shi'ite descendants when they came to power, and led them to portray him as a Shi'ite.) Under the leadership of his descendants the order grew, expanding its headquarters in Ardabil and acquiring extensive property

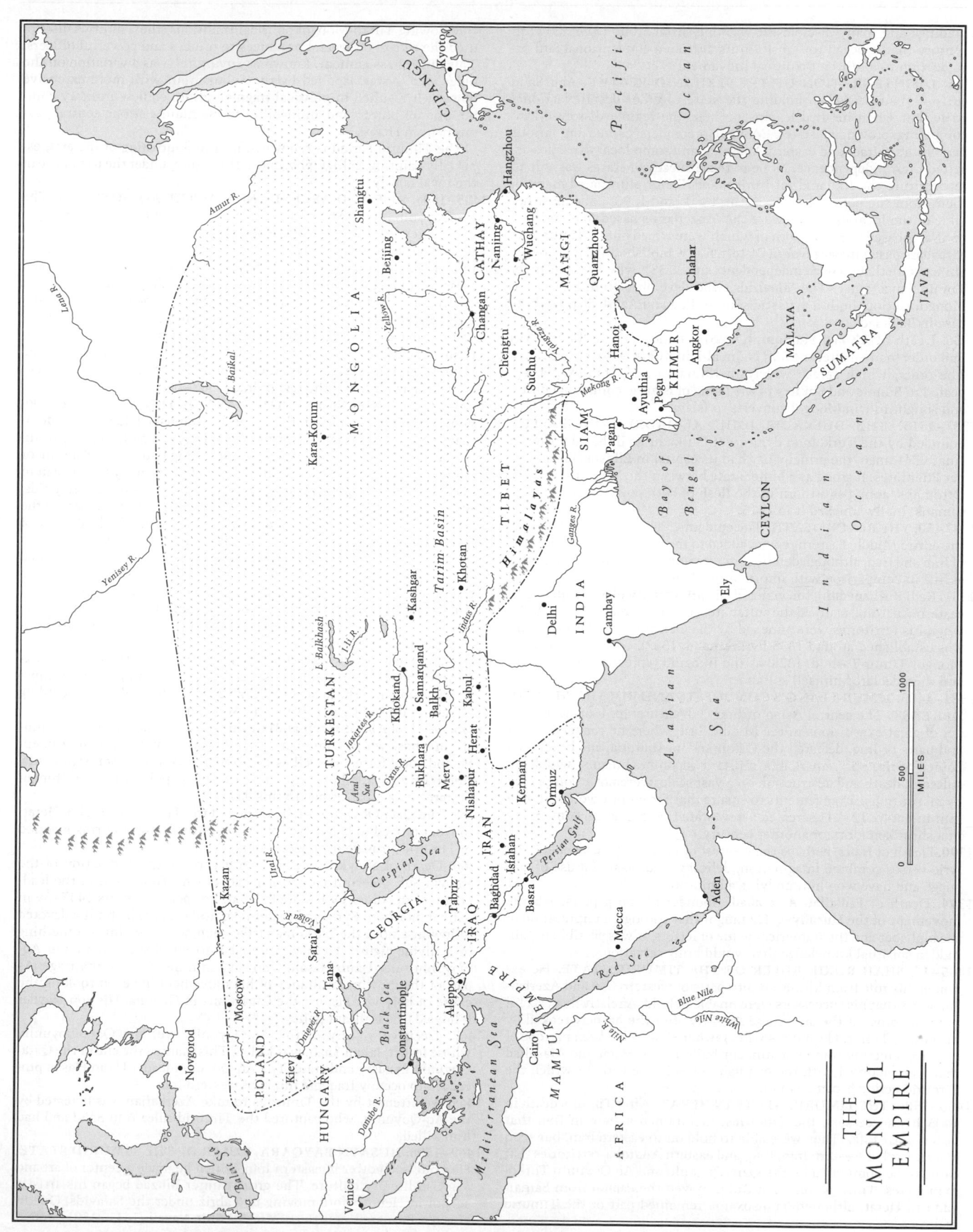

THE
MONGOL
EMPIRE

Kyoto

CIPANGU

Pacific

Ocean

Amur R.

Shangtu

MONGOLIA

Beijing

Yellow R.

Shangtu

CATHAY

Nanjing

Hangzhou

Wuchang

MANGI

Changan

Quanzhou

Chahar

Chengtu

Yangtze R.

Suchu

Hanoi

KHMER

Angkor

MALAYA

JAVA

Kara-Korum

TIBET

SIAM

Pegu

Ayuthia

Pagan

Mekong R.

SUMATRA

L. Baikal

Himalayas

Ganges R.

Bay

of

Bengal

CEYLON

Indian

Lena R.

Tarim Basin

Kashgar

Khotan

Indus R.

Ely

Ocean

Yenisey R.

TURKESTAN

L. Balkhash

I.LI.R.

Khokand

Samarqand

Delhi

INDIA

Cambay

Jaxartes R.

Balkh

Kabul

Bukhara

Merv

Herat

Arabian

Oxus R.

Nishapur

Kerman

Sea

Aral
Sea

IRAN

Ormuz

1000

Utal R.

Caspian Sea

Tabriz

Isfahan

Persian Gulf

500

Kazan

Volga R.

Baghdad

Basra

MILES

Aden

IRAQ

GEORGIA

Moscow

Sarai

Mecca

Tana

Black Sea

Aleppo

Red Sea

Blue Nile

POLAND

Kiev

Constantinople

EMPIRE

Cairo

White Nile

Novgorod

Dnieper R.

MAMLUK

Nile R.

HUNGARY

Mediterranean Sea

AFRICA

Danube R.

Baltic Sea

Venice

holdings and many disciples. It was only from around the mid-15th century that it began to transform itself from a conventional Sufi organization to a militant political movement.

1335. DISINTEGRATION OF THE ILKHANID REGIME. Abu Sa'id (1316–35) succeeded in holding the state together despite factional strife, but when he died leaving no heir, the regime dissolved into competing provincial states. Mongol pretenders carved up various parts of Iran, Iraq, and eastern Anatolia, and some local dynasties asserted their independence. None of these successor states was able to reconstitute the Ilkhanid territories, and Timur eliminated many of them from the political scene in the 1380s and 1390s. The most notable of the local dynasties were the **Muzaffarids** based in Shiraz and the **Karts** based in Herat, both of which were wiped out by Timur. The **Sarbadars** based in Sabzavar in eastern Iran established a revolutionary Shi'ite state that enjoyed independence until 1381, when it came under Timur's suzerainty. The **Jalayirids,** who developed from a powerful Mongol faction, built a dynastic state in Iraq and Azerbaijan, with its base in Baghdad.

1336. Death of **Ahmad Simnani** (b. 1261), founder of the **Kubrawiyya Sufi order** (named after the Sufi **Najm al-Din Kubra,** who died in 1221). The order, which spread widely in Khurasan and Transoxania, appealed to Sunnis and Shi'ites in the name of Islamic communal unity, and sought to win Mongol converts to Islam.

1337–1515. THE DULKADIR (DHU AL-QADR) PRINCIPALITY. Founded by the Turkoman dynasty of Dulkadir as Ilkhanid power in Anatolia waned, the principality had its capital in **Elbistan** on the upper Euphrates. It stood as a **buffer state** between the Mamluks and the Ottomans, acting as a thorn in the flesh of both powers until the Ottomans finally annexed it in 1515.

1347–50. THE BLACK DEATH. The epidemic, which wreaked havoc in the entire Middle Eastern region, added to the troubled economic state of Iran and Iraq, although details about its impact in those lands remain scarce in comparison with information about Egypt.

1381. Kadi Burhaneddin, the vizier of the **principality of Eretna** in northeastern Anatolia, usurped the sultanate. He ruled forcefully until 1398, when his territories were annexed by the Ottomans. The principality was established around 1335 by **Eretna** (d. 1352), who succeeded the Mongol Timur-Tash (d. 1328) as the Ilkhanid representative in Rum, and then declared himself sultan.

1381–1405. TIMUR-I LANG'S CONQUESTS AND RULE IN THE MIDDLE EAST. The central Asian military adventurer (p. 136) led a number of great expeditions in the Middle East, where he conquered **Iran** and parts of **Iraq,** defeated the Ottomans in **Anatolia,** and briefly occupied **Syria.** His remarkable military accomplishments, which resulted in death and destruction on a vast scale, were not accompanied by institutional arrangements to ensure that the empire would survive him intact (p. 125). He created a **new state** that his descendants ruled in a shrunken form for another century.

1390. Death of **Hafiz,** perhaps the greatest of Persian classical poets. His lyric verses combine imagination, delicacy, and masterful use of language and have won him undying admiration.

1394. Death of **Fadlallah Astarabadi,** founder of the populist Islamic movement of the **Hurufiyya.** He taught that through interpretation of the alphabet and the numerical value of letters, it was possible to gain hidden spiritual knowledge that would bring salvation.

1405–47. SHAH RUKH, RULER OF THE TIMURID STATE. He extended his rule from Khurasan into parts of western Iran and Azerbaijan, areas that his successors were unable to retain. A relatively peaceful ruler, he brought the area some **stability** after the havoc wreaked by his father, Timur. He and his wife, **Jawhar Shad,** were keen patrons of the arts, erecting some magnificent buildings in Herat and Mashhad that were adorned with the exquisite mosaic tilework for which the Timurid period became famous.

1405–1506. THE TIMURID STATE IN HERAT. After Timur's death in 1405 his successors, the **Timurids,** maintained a state in Iran that lasted until 1506. They were able to hold on to eastern Iran, but soon lost control of western Iran, Iraq, and eastern Anatolia, territories that came to be dominated by the Qara-Qoyunlu and Aq-Qoyunlu Turkoman states. Timur's son Shah Rukh moved the capital from Samarqand to **Herat,** although Transoxania remained part of the Timurid realm.

Following Turko-Mongol political traditions, the Timurids distributed the rule of cities and provinces to princes and powerful officers. This kind of assignment, known as *suyurghal,* was a variation on the older *iqta'* system applied by the Seljuks, but with more extensive powers. It resulted in **political fragmentation,** endless military competition for power, and an inability to maintain a strong central government in Herat.

The Timurid period is renowned for the **flourishing of the arts,** especially painting, calligraphy, and architecture, under the patronage of the royal family.

1405–1508. RISE AND ASCENDANCY OF THE AQ-QOYUNLU. The Aq-Qoyunlu (White Sheep) Turkoman confederation emerged as a political force in the area of **Diyarbakr** during the 14th century, but began to expand its territory only from the early 15th century. During the rule of **Qara Uthman** (1403–35), the Aq-Qoyunlu acquired additional areas, including the cities of Erzurum and Mardin, which gave them control of important trade routes. Their state reached its height under **Uzun Hasan** (1452–78), who defeated the Qara-Qoyunlu (Black Sheep) and occupied Iraq, Azerbaijan, and western Iran. After his death, intermittent wars over succession plagued the Aq-Qoyunlu. Their end came when the **Safavids** took their capital Tabriz (1501) and then Diyarbakr, Baghdad, and the rest of Iraq (1507–08).

1410–67. ASCENDANCY OF THE QARA-QOYUNLU. The Qara-Qoyunlu Turkoman confederation steadily established itself as the dominant power in Azerbaijan, western Iran, Iraq, and parts of eastern Anatolia. The origins of the Qara-Qoyunlu ruling family, the Baharlu, or Barani, remain obscure, but from the mid-14th century they began to play an important political role as clients and allies of the **Jalayirids,** who dominated Iraq and Azerbaijan. Their territorial center was in the area of Lake Van in **eastern Anatolia.** In 1410, under the leadership of Qara Yusuf, they defeated the **Jalayirids** and brought their rule to an end. They then took Baghdad, Iraq, and Azerbaijan. Their state reached the peak of its power under **Jahan Shah,** who ruled as sultan from the capital of Tabriz until his defeat in 1467 by the rival Turkoman confederation of the Aq-Qoyunlu. Jahan Shah issued coins bearing Shi'ite as well as Sunni inscriptions, but he may not have been a Shi'ite himself, as has often been assumed.

1420–34. Shah Rukh mounted three campaigns against the Qara-Qoyunlu in western Iran that succeeded in containing their attempts at expansion into the area. Shah Rukh also maintained a long-standing alliance with their chief rivals, the Aq-Qoyunlu.

1435. Death of **Abd al-Qadir al-Maraghi,** an Azerbaijani scholar and musician whose works contain a comprehensive inventory of instrumental and vocal forms, as well as an extensive catalogue of instruments. Compositions attributed to him became popular in the Ottoman Empire and are performed to this day.

1458. The Qara-Qoyunlu briefly occupied the Timurid capital of **Herat,** in what proved to be an overextension of their power during a period of Timurid struggle over succession.

1460. Death of **Shaykh Junayd,** who began the transformation of the Safavid Sufi order into a political movement. Forced out of the leadership of the order by his uncle Ja'far, he spent the years 1447–59 in exile in northern Syria and eastern Anatolia. There he built a devoted following among the **Turkoman tribesmen,** who saw him as something of a divine figure. He also entered into an alliance with the Aq-Qoyunlu ruler **Uzun Hasan,** who gave him his sister in marriage. As part of the growing militancy of his movement, he even took on the cause of **holy war** against the Christians in Georgia. His son Haydar followed this militant policy.

1467. Decisive victory of the Aq-Qoyunlu over the Qara-Qoyunlu, whose leader, Jahan Shah, was killed. This marked the **end of the Qara-Qoyunlu dynasty** and state. The Aq-Qoyunlu leader Uzun Hasan proceeded to occupy Iraq and much of western Iran.

1469. An attempt by the Timurids to take **Azerbaijan** was defeated by the Aq-Qoyunlu, who captured the Timurid ruler Abu Sa'id and had him killed.

1469–1506. HUSAYN BAYQARA, RULER OF THE TIMURID STATE. He exercised power in eastern Iran, which he made a center of art and Turkish literary culture. The great painter **Bihzad** began his artistic school in Herat before moving to Tabriz under the Safavids. One of Husayn Bayqara's courtiers, **Mir Ali Shir Nava'i** (1441–1501), translated Persian literature into **Chaghatay Turkish,** which he is credited with transforming into a literary language.

With Husayn Bayqara's death, Timurid rule in Iran effectively ended. The **Uzbeks,** led by Muhammad Shaybani, occupied his capital, Herat (1507), and then took all of Khurasan (1508). In 1510 the **Safavids** conquered those lands from the Uzbeks.

1473, Aug. 11. Battle of Bashkent in eastern Anatolia, in which the Aq-Qoyunlu suffered a decisive defeat by the **Ottomans.** Uzun Hasan wanted to contain the Ottoman expansion in Anatolia and made an alliance with Venice, which was engaged in a long war with the Ottomans. The defeat proved a severe blow to his prestige.

1488. Death of Haydar, the head of the Safavid order. Following in the footsteps of his father, Junayd, Haydar had continued using the religious authority of the Safavid family to build popular support. Safavid propagandists went out from the headquarters of the movement in Ardabil to spread their **message of revolution.** The Safavid recruits were known as **Qizilbash** (Redheads), after their distinctive headgear, said to have been introduced by Haydar.

Haydar was married to a daughter of the Aq-Qoyunlu ruler Uzun Hasan, but had a falling out with Uzun Hasan's successor Ya'qub (1481–90), who probably saw the political danger posed by the Safavids and, in alliance with the ruler of Shirvan, had Haydar killed. There followed a **crackdown on the movement** by the Aq-Qoyunlu, but the factionalism and decline of the latter helped the Safavids survive politically and build momentum toward the eventual takeover of authority in Iran by Haydar's son Isma'il.

1494. Isma'il, the 7-year-old son of Haydar, became the head of the Safavid order. He fled from Ardabil to Gilan to escape the Aq-Qoyunlu assault on his movement, finding asylum with a local Shi'ite ruler. During his five years of exile, he developed his **heterodox ideas** regarding his divine leadership and messianic mission, and made plans for the **overthrow of the Aq-Qoyunlu state.** In 1499 he reemerged in public, assembled a large army in eastern Anatolia, and began his march to power.

1501. THE SAFAVID VICTORY. Isma'il defeated a large Aq-Qoyunlu army in Azerbaijan and **occupied Tabriz,** where he proclaimed himself **shah** and Shi'ism the religion of the new state. His accession ushered in a revolutionary change in the political and religious landscape of the region. The **Aq-Qoyunlu** were soon eliminated, and a **Shi'ite empire** incorporating Iran, Iraq, and parts of eastern Anatolia came into being, poised as a rival to the other leading Middle Eastern state, the Sunni Ottoman Empire.   *(To p. 359)*

d. THE OTTOMAN EMPIRE

The story of the Ottoman Empire has its beginning around the turn of the 14th century, in a corner of **northwestern Anatolia** where a group of Muslim Turkish tribesmen led by their chieftain, **Osman,** started to expand beyond their small principality on the Byzantine frontier. Their territorial base eventually grew into a great world empire that was named after Osman and was ruled by his descendants in unbroken succession throughout its nearly six and a half centuries of history.

When the Ottomans emerged on the scene as a political force, Anatolia was divided into a number of **principalities** *(beyliks)* ruled largely by Turkoman chieftains and families. The population was a mix of Muslims and native Christians, many of whom were converting to Islam. This situation was the outcome of a long process, beginning in the 11th century, by which Muslims, primarily western (Oghuz) Turks originating in central Asia, steadily broke through the Byzantine defenses and conquered Anatolia. New waves of Turkish and Muslim refugees fleeing from the Mongols entered Anatolia in the 13th century.

Information on the **early Ottomans** remains very patchy, and **legends** woven around their origins and exploits further complicate the task of reconstructing their formative years. Ottoman chroniclers portrayed them as Muslim *ghazis,* or **holy warriors,** driven to conquest and expansion by their religious zeal for the struggle against the infidel. This view, which modern scholarship has often perpetuated, appears to have been very much an **idealization** created by later writers and servants of the royal house. In reality the early Ottomans, like other Turkish nomads in the milieu of western Anatolia, conquered

land and engaged in predation to meet the **economic needs** of their pastoral society rather than as part of a strictly religious campaign. They expanded at the expense of fellow Muslims, did not force conversion on the conquered Christian peoples, and maintained friendly ties with the Byzantine population, even using Christians in their armies.

The early Ottomans were **nomadic pastoralists** with an elected chieftain and an armed force made up of bands of tribesmen on horseback. But as the territory under their rule expanded and the tasks of governing and fighting became more complicated, their tribal organization was transformed into a **settled state.** In the course of the 14th century, they developed a standing army and a bureaucracy, shifted from pastoral life to agriculture, and transformed their chieftains into sultans who ruled as despotic monarchs. The result was a complex imperial system fashioned from a blend of Islamic, Turko-Mongol, and Byzantine institutions.

1. FROM FRONTIER PRINCIPALITY TO REGIONAL POWER

c. 1280–c. 1324. OSMAN I, FOUNDER OF THE OTTOMAN DYNASTY. Although the chronology of his activities before 1302 cannot be established accurately, Osman appears to have been **elected chieftain** by his tribesmen sometime around 1280, and to have led their seasonal migrations and predatory raids from their pasture areas around Dorylaeum (Eskishehir) in **northwestern Anatolia.** He took advantage of the weakness of the Byzantines by launching attacks against their frontier settlements. His territorial base expanded steadily, especially in the fertile plains of Bithynia, and many native Christians became subject to his authority and even entered his service.

1302, July 27. Battle of Bapheus, outside Nicomedia, in which Osman defeated a Byzantine force and strengthened his standing as a recognized local leader. In the following years his forces were able to capture small forts in the area, although the larger cities, too heavily fortified for the light arms of the Ottomans, held out for a while.

c. 1324–62. ORHAN, Osman's son, continued the policy of **territorial expansion,** conquering virtually all of northwestern Anatolia and establishing a **foothold in Europe.** Cities and agricultural populations came under his family's control, and the frontier principality developed more fully into a **settled state** as well as a formidable player in the region's affairs. The **title of sultan** first appeared on coins minted by Orhan.

1326, Apr. 6. Fall of Bursa to the Ottomans, after a lengthy siege. Orhan made the city his capital.

1327, May 13. Ottoman conquest of **Lopadion (Ulubad).**

1329, June 10. Battle of Pelekanon, in which Orhan defeated a Byzantine expedition personally commanded by the emperor Andronicus III. The Byzantines abandoned further efforts to organize resistance to the Ottomans in Anatolia or to supply the remaining Byzantine cities there.

1331, Mar. 2. Ottoman conquest of **Nicaea (Iznik).** The first Ottoman *medrese,* or Muslim religious college, was created in the city that year, using a converted church building.

1337. Ottoman conquest of **Nicomedia (Izmit).**

1345. The Ottomans absorbed the neighboring Turkoman principality of **Karasi,** which brought them to the southern shores of the Dardanelles. They first **crossed into Europe** that year at the request of John Cantacuzenos, a claimant to the Byzantine throne who solicited their military assistance in his struggle for power. Orhan helped him take the towns along the Black Sea, and to cement the political alliance was given Cantacuzenos's daughter Theodora in marriage. From that point on, Ottoman troops moved back and forth across the straits.

1354. Ottoman conquest of **Gallipoli,** after the establishment of a bridgehead on the peninsula (in Tzympe) in 1352. From this European base, troops led by Orhan's sons Suleyman and Murad began to launch raids northward into **Thrace** and to expand the area of Ottoman occupation. The Ottomans lost Gallipoli in 1366, but in 1376 the Byzantine emperor ceded it to the sultan by way of tribute.

1362–89. SULTAN MURAD I. Under Orhan's son, the Ottomans extended their control into Thrace, Macedonia, Bulgaria, and Serbia, establishing the core of their **empire in Europe.** At this stage of expansion, their hold in these territories (which were known as Rumeli or

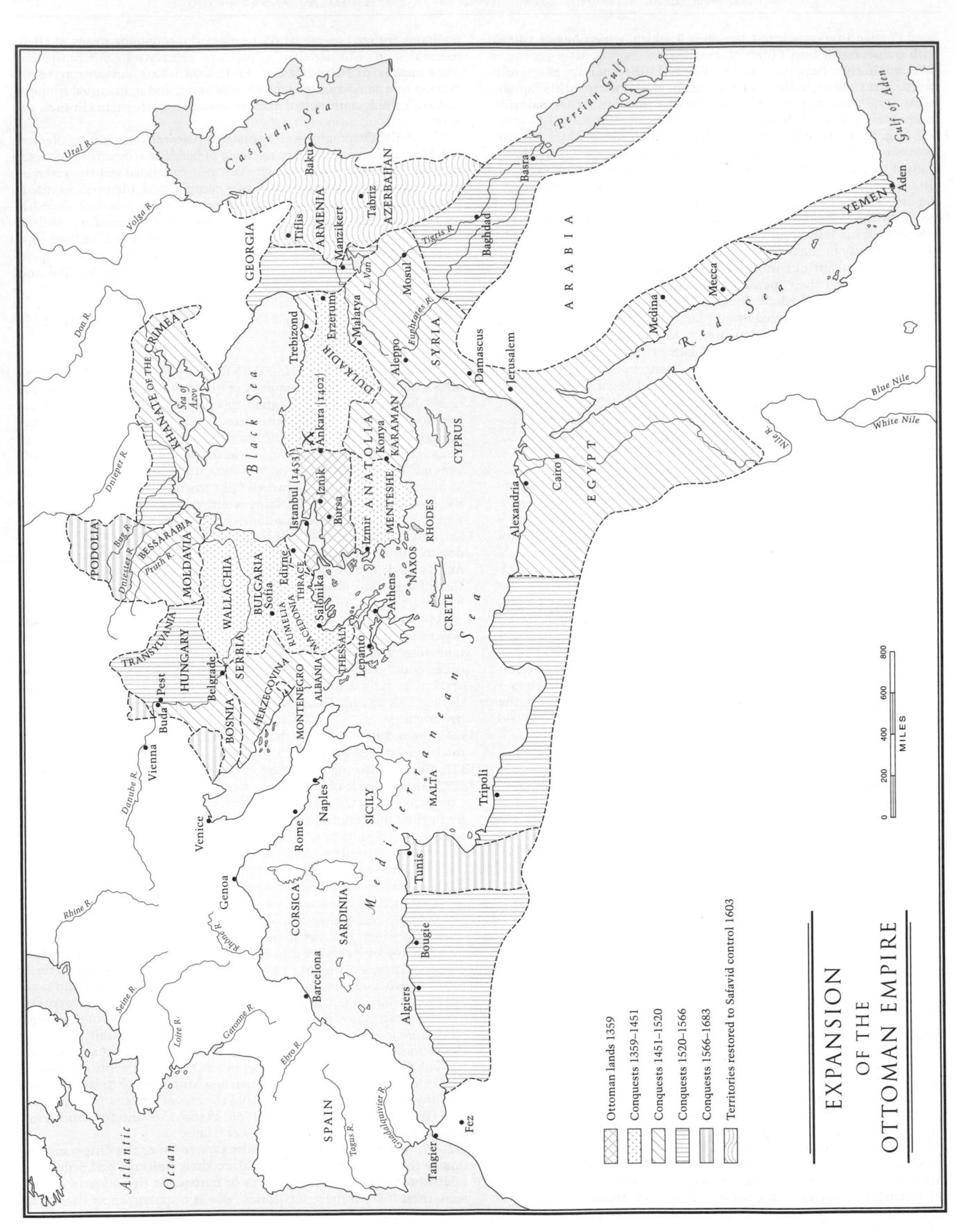

EXPANSION
OF THE
OTTOMAN EMPIRE

Ottoman lands 1359
Conquests 1359–1451
Conquests 1451–1520
Conquests 1520–1566
Conquests 1566–1683
Territories restored to Safavid control 1603

MILES
0   200   400   600   800

Atlantic Ocean

Mediterranean Sea

Black Sea

Caspian Sea

Red Sea

Persian Gulf

Gulf of Aden

SPAIN
FEZ
TANGIER
ALGIERS
BOUGIE
TUNIS
SARDINIA
CORSICA
SICILY
MALTA
TRIPOLI
NAPLES
ROME
GENOA
VENICE
VIENNA
BUDA
PEST
HUNGARY
TRANSYLVANIA
BOSNIA
HERZEGOVINA
MONTENEGRO
ALBANIA
SERBIA
BELGRADE
WALLACHIA
MOLDAVIA
BESSARABIA
PODOLIA
KHANATE OF THE CRIMEA
Sea of Azov
BULGARIA
Sofia
MACEDONIA
RUMELIA
THESSALY
Salónika
Lepanto
Athens
NAXOS
CRETE
RHODES
CYPRUS
THRACE
Edirne
Istanbul (1453)
Iznik
Bursa
Izmir
MENTESHE
ANATOLIA
KARAMAN
Konya
DULKADIR
Ankara (1402)
Trebizond
Erzerum
Malatya
L. Van
Manzikert
ARMENIA
Tabriz
AZERBAIJAN
Baku
Tiflis
GEORGIA
Aleppo
SYRIA
Damascus
Jerusalem
Mosul
Baghdad
Basra
ARABIA
Mecca
Medina
Aden
YEMEN
EGYPT
Cairo
Alexandria

Utal R.
Volga R.
Don R.
Dnieper R.
Dniester R.
Bug R.
Prut R.
Danube R.
Rhine R.
Seine R.
Loire R.
Garonne R.
Rhône R.
Ebro R.
Tagus R.
Guadalquivir R.
Tigris R.
Euphrates R.
Nile R.
Blue Nile
White Nile

Barcelona

Rumelia) was based in good part on suzerainty over **tributary vassals** rather than direct rule. Turkish populations were encouraged or forced to settle in the conquered lands, and fiefs (called *timars*) were granted to the army commanders, entitling them to the taxes on the land in return for military service and the administration of the population in their areas. Murad created the **JANISSARIES** (in Turkish, *Yenicheri*, or "New Force"), an infantry corps drawn from **slaves** originally captured in warfare. These troops developed into the principal fighting force of the Ottoman Empire.

1363–66. Ottoman conquests in **southern Bulgaria and Thrace.** Adrianople (Edirne), the capital of Thrace, was captured and soon became the seat of government and the main base for further conquest in Europe.

1375–80. Ottoman annexation of parts of the Anatolian principalities of **Germiyan** and **Hamideli.**

1385. Ottoman conquest of **Sofia.**

1386. Ottoman conquest of **Nish** in southern Serbia.

1387. Ottoman conquest of the port of **Salonika** (Thessaloníki).

1389, June 15. BATTLE OF KOSOVO (p. 273). The Ottomans defeated a large combined Serbian and Bosnian force in what was their first victory against a major European allied army. The success established their presence as the leading power in the Balkans south of the Danube. **Murad** was killed in the battle, but his son **Bayezid,** present on the scene, immediately assumed leadership.

1389–1402. SULTAN BAYEZID I, the energetic new ruler (known as Yildirim, or the Thunderbolt), inherited a fragile empire. The news of his father's death prompted the subjugated principalities in Anatolia as well as the Balkan vassals to assert themselves against Ottoman control, and Bayezid responded with a series of campaigns that brought much of **Anatolia** and the **Balkans** under **direct Ottoman rule.**

Although his efforts at empire building were dealt a serious setback by the onslaught of **Timur-I Lang** from the east (p. 122), Bayezid left an important mark on Ottoman state institutions. Most noteworthy was his promotion on a large scale of the practice (known as the *devshirme*) of **levying Christian children** to fill positions in the palace, administration, and the Janissary corps. These recruits, who were educated, converted to Islam, and then employed in official positions, provided the sultan with an elite group of loyal servants as well as a useful counterweight to the political power of the Turkish notables. Under Bayezid's successors, the recruitment of slaves for official service grew into one of the distinctive institutions of the Ottoman state.

1389–90. Ottoman conquest of the Turkoman principalities of **Saruhan, Aydin, Menteshe, Hamideli,** and **Germiyan,** and the eastern territories of **Karaman.** Most of western and central Anatolia thus became Ottoman.

1391. The Ottomans captured **Skopje** in Macedonia and annexed the **Jandarid principality** based in Kastamonu.

1392. Ottoman annexation of most of **Bulgaria,** which had been a vassal state.

1393–95. Ottoman conquest of parts of **Albania.**

1394. The Ottomans conquered **Thessaly** and imposed a blockade on **Constantinople** that lasted until 1402.

1395. The Ottomans occupied the **Dobruja** and invaded Wallachia and Hungary.

1396. The Crusade of Nicopolis. A large allied army drawn from many countries in Europe and led by King Sigismund of Hungary advanced against the Ottomans, along the Danube. The Ottomans defeated these Crusaders near Nicopolis (Sept. 25) in a major victory that consolidated their hold in the Balkans (p. 246).

1397–99. Ottoman occupation of **Karaman** (1397), the state of **Kadi Burhaneddin** based in Sivas (1398), and the areas of **Elbistan and Malatya** west of the Euphrates (1399); Ottoman control was thus extended over most of Anatolia.

2. DEFEAT, RECOVERY, AND IMPERIAL EXPANSION

1402. TIMUR'S INVASION AND OTTOMAN NEAR-COLLAPSE. The central Asian conqueror Timur advanced into Anatolia with a large force, occupying Ottoman lands and restoring the old **Turkoman principalities.** Bayezid moved against him, and in the **battle of Ankara** (July 28) his army was completely defeated and he himself was taken prisoner. He died in captivity (Mar. 9, 1403), by suicide according to some accounts.

1402–13. THE INTERREGNUM. The decade following the defeat at Ankara was a period of **power struggles** for the Ottomans, with a real danger of dismemberment and collapse facing the empire. Bayezid's extensive acquisitions in Anatolia were lost to the **revived principalities,** and three of his sons recognized **Timur's suzerainty** and were installed as local rulers: Isa in Bursa, Mehmed in Amasya, and Suleyman in Edirne. When Timur died in 1405, the three princes and their brother Musa (who had been in captivity with his father) entered into a struggle for sole control of the state. Their battles with each other, and their shifting alliances with domestic groups and neighboring rulers in Anatolia and Europe, continued until 1413, when **Mehmed** emerged victorious.

1413–21. SULTAN MEHMED I. After his triumph over his brothers, Mehmed set about restoring Ottoman strength. He succeeded in holding the Ottoman domain together during a crucial period in which the weakened empire had to deal with challenges from several directions: the restored Anatolian principalities, European neighbors, and domestic rebels.

1413. Death of **Tajuddin Ibrahim Ahmedi** (b. 1334), among the greatest of the early Anatolian poets. He composed the famous *Iskendername,* a life of Alexander the Great in verse, dedicated as a panegyric to Bayezid I's son Suleyman.

1414–15. Ottoman recapture of **Izmir** and territories previously recovered by the principality of Karaman.

1415–16. Confrontation with Venice (p. 259), provoked by raids of pirates based in the Aegean islands. The Ottoman fleet, still in its early stages of development, was completely routed near Gallipoli (May 29, 1416). The peace concluded in 1419 recognized Ottoman and Venetian interests in Albania.

1415–17. Ottoman capture of the areas of Kroya and Avlonya in **Albania,** restoring the Ottoman hold in the area that had been lost during the interregnum.

1416. The revolts of Mustafa and Bedreddin. A man claiming to be the son of Bayezid I, and known in Ottoman tradition as the **False Mustafa,** organized an uprising against the sultan, with the backing of the rulers of Byzantium and Wallachia as well as some Ottoman notables. His forces were defeated, and he fled to refuge with the Byzantine emperor. (He was killed by the Ottomans in 1422, after he launched another revolt.) At the same time, a popular religious scholar and mystic named **Sheik Bedreddin** raised major revolts in the European provinces as well as in Anatolia, also drawing on the support of external enemies and masses of discontented subjects. It took a large-scale military expedition to suppress his rebellions, and he himself was put to death.

1421–44, 1446–51. SULTAN MURAD II. After his father's efforts to hold the empire together, Murad began the process of **restoring Ottoman imperial expansion.** Although generally cautious in his foreign policy, he responded forcefully to challenges from the Anatolian principalities and his European neighbors, and extended Ottoman power in Europe and Asia. Domestically Murad restored the **recruitment of slaves** and their training for government service (the *devshirme*), promoting the slaves as a counterweight to the political power of the Turkish notables. Slave recruits became the basis of the Janissary infantry.

1423–30. War with Venice. Ottoman ambitions in Macedonia and Albania, and especially Murad's interest in recovering the port of Salonika, which the Byzantines transferred to Venice in 1423, precipitated the first major war between the two powers (p. 259). The Ottomans besieged **Salonika** and captured it (Mar. 1430). In the **Peace of Lapseki** (July 1430) Venice confirmed Ottoman control of Salonika while Murad recognized the Venetian possessions in Greece and Albania.

1425–26. The Ottomans annexed the Turkoman principalities of **Aydin, Menteshe,** and **Teke,** thus regaining control of western Anatolia and its Aegean coastline.

1428. The Ottomans absorbed the principality of **Germiyan** in southwestern Anatolia.

1432–33. Rebellion in southern Albania. After the Ottomans occupied the area of Janina and sought to impose their direct rule, the Albanians rose in a major revolt, with secret Venetian help, under the leadership of **George Skanderbeg** (Castriotes). He continued the resistance for many years.

1438–44. Campaigns in Europe. Murad led a military expedition against Transylvania and Hungary (p. 272) that ravaged those areas (1438). He then conquered **Serbia**, made the ruler of **Bosnia** an Ottoman tributary (1439), and laid an unsuccessful siege to **Belgrade** (1440). A counter-offensive led by the governor of Transylvania, **John Hunyadi**, inflicted defeats on the Ottoman armies in Hungary in 1441–42, and then, with allied European support, captured most of southern Serbia as well as Sofia in an advance on the Ottoman capital (1443). Fear of a renewed European attack after the winter prompted Murad to sign a ten-year **truce with Hungary** at Adrianople (June 12, 1444), according to which the kingdom of Serbia was restored (p. 273) and Ottoman suzerainty in Bulgaria and Wallachia recognized.

1444, Aug. Murad concluded a peace treaty with the principality of **Karaman,** his main adversary in the east.

1444–46. SULTAN MEHMED II (FIRST REIGN). Having secured the Ottoman frontiers in both Europe and Anatolia, Murad renounced the throne in favor of his 12-year-old son, Mehmed, and retired to Bursa (Aug. 1444). Mehmed failed to win the support of leading notables and the Janissaries, who engineered his father's return to the throne (May 1446).

1444, Nov. 10. The Battle of Varna. A Crusader army organized by Hungary, Venice, and the pope launched a new offensive against the Ottomans, despite the peace recently signed at Adrianople. Murad, called out of retirement, met the European force near Varna and defeated it.

1448, Oct. 17–19. The second Battle of Kosovo, in which Murad crushed another Crusader army led by Hunyadi and thus dashed European hopes of pushing the Ottomans out of the Balkans.

1451–81. SULTAN MEHMED II (SECOND REIGN). Upon his accession (Feb. 18, 1451) Mehmed inherited a revived empire that he proceeded to expand and reorganize with extraordinary vigor. He is best known for his extensive **conquests in Europe and Anatolia,** for which he became known as the Conqueror *(Fatih).* His drive to build a **centralized state** with himself as absolute ruler prompted him to reduce the power of the leading Turkish families (partly by confiscation of their landed property) and to promote members of his slave *(devshirme)* elite to positions of power, including the office of grand vizier. Mehmed was the first Ottoman ruler known to **codify state legislation,** which he had compiled in two major codes *(kanunnames)* that dealt with the rules governing state organization, penal law, and the relations of the state with the subjects. Despite his impressive feats domestically and abroad, however, his period of rule was accompanied by **economic problems and discontent,** due to the periodic debasement of the currency, the increases in taxes, the confiscations of property, and other unpopular measures used to raise revenue.

1453, May 29. CONQUEST OF CONSTANTINOPLE. The heavily fortified Byzantine capital, long coveted by the Ottomans, fell to Mehmed's troops after a **siege** lasting 54 days. Constantine, the last Byzantine emperor, died in the fighting, and his seat of power became the new Ottoman capital, now called **Istanbul.** The city was in a neglected state, with its population reduced to some 50,000 people, and the Ottomans launched a major **official drive to repopulate and rebuild it.** Thousands of new residents were encouraged or forced to resettle in the capital, and the **infrastructure**—roads, bridges, walls, markets, and water supply—was restored and expanded. By order of the sultan, high government officials founded hundreds of schools, mosques, water fountains, and other **public facilities** endowed with substantial private property to pay for their long-term upkeep. The city soon emerged as the largest and most glamorous urban center in the Middle East. Its population reached some 400,000 before the 19th century, about 45 percent of it Christians and Jews.

1454, Jan. Sultan Mehmed reinstalled the **Greek Orthodox Church** with all its traditional privileges, while banning all Latin Catholic organizations from his domain.

1454–59. Conquest of Serbia. In several major campaigns, the Ottomans occupied the southern part of Serbia (1454–55), mounted an unsuccessful siege of Belgrade (1456), and then annexed the rest of the country with the exception of Belgrade (1459).

1458–60. Conquest of the Morea. Conflicts between the two Byzantine rulers of the Morea, and their failure to continue the payments of tribute to the sultan, led to Ottoman military intervention and the annexation of the peninsula, including **Athens.**

1461. The Ottomans conquered the **Jandarid principality** in Kastamonu

and the last Byzantine possession around **Trebizond (Trabzon),** thus gaining virtual control of the Black Sea coastline of Anatolia.

1463. Ottoman conquest of **Bosnia.**

1463–70. Construction of the **Mosque of Mehmed the Conqueror** in Istanbul.

1463–79. The long war with Venice (p. 259). Ottoman expansion into Greece and Bosnia made Venice apprehensive about the future of its outposts on the Aegean and Adriatic coasts, and led it to initiate a war to roll back Ottoman advances. In 1463 the **Venetians** seized much of the Morea while their Hungarian allies retook Bosnia, but an **Ottoman counteroffensive** reversed these early successes (1464). Mehmed proceeded to occupy parts of Albania (1466–68) and then the island of Negroponte (Euboea), the main Venetian naval base in the Aegean (July 1470). **Uzun Hasan,** leader of the Aq-Qoyunlu Turkoman state based in Tabriz, allied with Venice and marched with a large army into central Anatolia, but was defeated decisively by the Ottomans (Aug. 11, 1473) and withdrew from the war. In 1477–78 the Ottomans expanded their control over virtually all of **Albania** and took southern Montenegro, leaving the Venetians outflanked and ready for a settlement. The **peace treaty** (signed Jan. 25, 1479) recognized Ottoman rule in Albania as well as Ottoman conquests of the Aegean islands, and restored Venetian commercial privileges in the Ottoman Empire in return for an annual tribute of 10,000 ducats.

1465. Completion of the main part of the **Topkapi Palace** in Istanbul. Known as the New Palace (Yeni Saray), it replaced the Old Palace (Eski Saray) built in the city center in 1455, and remained the official imperial residence until the 19th century. Continuous construction and renovation work made the palace (spread over grounds some 700,000 square meters in area) a mirror of four centuries of Ottoman architectural and decorative styles.

1468. Ottoman conquest of the **principality of Karaman** in central Anatolia. The area remained for many years the source of periodic Turkoman revolts around pretenders to the throne of Karaman.

1475. The Ottomans established formal suzerainty over the **Crimea.**

1479. The Italian artist **Gentile Bellini** visited Istanbul and painted his famous portrait of Mehmed II (now in the National Gallery in London).

1480, May–Aug. The Ottoman **siege of Rhodes,** the only major Aegean island not under Ottoman control. The Knights of St. John organized an effective defense, forcing the Ottoman forces to withdraw with heavy losses.

Aug. 11. An Ottoman force occupied **Otranto** in southern Italy, but a year later lost this bridgehead into what could have become a new area of Ottoman expansion in the wake of Sultan Mehmed's sudden death (May 3, 1481) and the subsequent power struggle in Istanbul.

c. 1481. Death of the historian **Ashikpashazade** (b. c. 1392), whose chronicle *Tevarih-i Al-i Osman (Histories of the House of Osman)* ranks among the most valuable sources of early Ottoman history.

1481–1512. SULTAN BAYEZID II. His reign brought a needed respite from the almost relentless campaigns of his father, Mehmed, and marked a **period of consolidation** before the conquests were resumed in full force by his successors. Bayezid ended some of his father's unpopular modes of raising revenue, restoring the private and *vakif* (endowed) property he had confiscated. He organized an orderly system of administration and public finance that increased revenues and contributed to economic growth. Although he owed his accession to the backing of the Janissaries, he gradually freed himself of their powerful influence. In the last ten years of his life he devoted himself mainly to religion and the encouragement of learning.

1481–82. Civil war. Following Bayezid's accession, his younger brother **Jem** declared himself sultan of Anatolia and assembled an army to defend his claim to the Asian provinces of the empire. Bayezid rejected the proposed division and decisively defeated Jem's forces near Yenishehir (June 20, 1481). After another failed military effort one year later, Jem went into **exile in Europe,** where he was a political instrument in the hands of various Catholic rulers, and a potential threat to his brother, until his death in Naples in 1495.

1483. The Ottomans completed the absorption of **Herzegovina** into the empire.

1484. Capture of **Kilia** and **Akkerman** in Moldavia, which gave the Ottomans mastery of the **Black Sea** as well as control of the important trade in these two commercial centers.

1485–91. War with the Mamluks. Competition over influence in the buffer principality of **Dulkadir** led to the first Ottoman-Mamluk war. The intermittent campaigns, fought in southern Anatolia, were inconclusive, and the Ottomans failed in their attempts to take the Cilician towns of Adana and Tarsus. The **peace** signed in May 1491 left the boundaries approximately as they had been before the war.

1492. Beginning of the mass **migration of Spanish Jews** into the empire. Following the edicts of expulsion against the Jews of Spain (1492) and Portugal (1496), as many as 200,000 Jews from the Iberian Peninsula settled in Ottoman territories, setting up large **Sephardic communities** in Istanbul, Izmir, Salonika, and other cities in Anatolia, the Balkans, and in Arab lands that were later absorbed into the empire. With their valuable commercial and professional skills, they were **welcomed** by the Ottoman authorities, and they enjoyed a period of prosperity and cultural efflorescence during the 16th century.

1493. The first Hebrew printing press in Istanbul was established by two Jewish exiles from Spain, Samuel ibn Nahmias and his brother David. Other Jewish presses soon followed in various cities, notably Salonika. A **Muslim ban on printing** in Arabic and Turkish remained in effect until the 18th century and kept the new technology from spreading to the Muslim population earlier.

1499–1502. War with Venice. Using their newly expanded fleet, the Ottomans captured **Lepanto,** the major Venetian ports in the **Morea,** and **Durazzo** in Albania. Their gains, recognized in the peace signed in Dec. 1502, established their presence as a major naval and commercial power in the eastern Mediterranean.

1501. The writer **Idris Bitlisi** (d. 1520) wrote his monumental chronicle, *Hesht Bihisht,* at the order of Bayezid II. It recorded the history of the first eight sultans, providing much firsthand information on events in Iran and eastern Anatolia.

1505. Completion of the **Mosque of Bayezid II** in Istanbul, the first Ottoman monument in which the influence of the basilica of **Hagia Sophia** was clearly evident.

1509, Aug. 22. A great **earthquake in Istanbul,** with several weeks of aftershocks that caused immense devastation and loss of life. The city was subject to many earthquakes, suffering 66 shocks between 1711 and 1894.

1511. The pro-Safavid insurrection of Shah Kulu succeeded in capturing most of central and southeastern Anatolia and winning the support of disaffected Turkomans and Ottoman troops sent to suppress it. A force commanded by the grand vizier finally defeated the rebels and killed their leader. The revolt followed a decade of rising **tensions in Ottoman-Safavid relations,** as the new regime in Iran suppressed its Sunni subjects and sent out preachers into Ottoman Anatolia to spread the Shi'ite message and stir up opposition to Ottoman rule among the Turkoman tribesmen.

1512, Apr. 24. Forced abdication of Bayezid. This followed a prolonged power struggle in which his son **Selim** intrigued against him and eventually triumphed over his brothers, with the support of the Janissaries.

(To p. 350)

e. EGYPT AND SYRIA

935–69. The **IKHSHIDID DYNASTY** in Egypt and southern Syria. The first of this line was **Muhammad ibn Tughj,** later known as the **Ikhshid** (r. 935–46); he arrived in Fustat in 935 as the new Abbasid governor. His outstanding accomplishments were the **defense of Egypt** against Fatimid raids and the **reorganization of the government.** Under the Ikhshidids, Egypt continued its reemergence, begun during the Tulunid period, as a political and economic center. Ties with the caliphal government in Baghdad were slowly loosening, allowing the Egyptian administration to retain more of the country's revenue, build a large army, and assume a **more independent role** in regional affairs. After the Hamdanid takeover of Aleppo in 945, the Ikhshidids retained a hold on the areas of Damascus and Palestine.

945–67. Reign of **SAYF AL-DAWLA,** emir of Aleppo and founder of the Syrian branch of the **HAMDANID DYNASTY.** At the time of his ascent to power, the city had nominally been under the rule of the Ikhshidids, based in Egypt. Formerly the commander of Hamdanid forces in Iraq, he was able to seize Aleppo for himself, thanks to support from the **Banu Kilab,** a local beduin tribe. The emirate of Aleppo, which

embraced most of central and northern Syria, including Homs, functioned as a **buffer state** between the Ikhshidids, the Byzantine Empire, and the Iraqi states. During the final years of Sayf al-Dawla's reign, the Byzantines put increasing pressure on his state and occupied its northern and western provinces. The **conflict with Byzantium** conferred on Sayf al-Dawla a reputation as a Muslim crusader, a noble image that court poets such as al-Mutanabbi and Abu al-Firas helped to perpetuate.

965. Death of **Abu al-Tayyib AL-MUTANABBI** (b. 915), the most honored poet of medieval Arabic literature. He was most renowned for his panegyrics and masterful manipulation of language. He spent a good part of his career at the court of the Syrian ruler Sayf al-Dawla, whose exploits he immortalized in his poetry.

969–1171. The **FATIMID DYNASTY** in Egypt. The Fatimids, who had already established an empire in North Africa, moved their base of operations to Egypt, which they invaded in 969. The dynasty was the chief exponent of a radical religious movement, the **Isma'ili sect** of Shi'ite Islam. The Fatimids denied the legitimacy of the Abbasid caliphate and sought to install themselves as the spiritual and temporal leaders of the Islamic world. But their **bid to overthrow Abbasid power** ended in failure, despite the **extensive proselytizing** that their Isma'ili missionaries conducted throughout the Islamic world. Their spiritual authority remained circumscribed even in Egypt, where Shi'ite Islam was confined largely to the ruling elites.

At its greatest extent, the Fatimid Empire embraced Egypt, North Africa, the Hijaz, and much of Syria. But North Africa gradually slipped away, and control of the remaining provinces was always infirm. On the whole, the Fatimid period was remembered as a time of **general prosperity.** Agriculture flourished, and Fatimid commercial policy succeeded in diverting the lucrative **spice trade** from the Persian Gulf to the Red Sea.

During the 11th century, various **military cliques** progressively usurped the caliphs' powers and reduced them to mere figureheads. By the middle of the 12th century, the Fatimid government had become so decrepit that it functioned as little more than a pawn in the power struggle that was then taking place in Syria.

969. The **FOUNDING OF CAIRO** under orders from the Fatimid conquerers of Egypt. The new city replaced adjacent **Fustat** (three miles south of Cairo) as the capital, a rank it has held into modern times. But during most of the Fatimid era, Fustat remained the center of commerce, industry, and population.

969. **Byzantine capture of Antioch** and the coastal lands of northern Syria (p. 188), which remained in Christian hands until 1084. The **Hamdanid emirate of Aleppo** shrank to the city and its hinterland and became, in effect, a **Byzantine satellite** during the late 10th century. Riven by internal rivalries, the Hamdanids of Syria grew ever weaker until their line finally ended in 1016.

971. Opening of **AL-AZHAR** Mosque. It operated originally as a center for **Shi'ite propaganda.** After the fall of the Fatimids (1171), it was transformed into the **premier Sunni religious college** in the **Muslim world.**

978. Fatimid victory in Palestine over Turkish and **Qaramita** forces, which had seized control of southern Syria after the fall of the Ikhshidids. As a result the **Fatimids were able,** at least for a short time, **to gain control of southern Syria,** and the Qaramita were permanently cleared from Syria and its commercial routes. Equally significant was the **introduction of Turkish slave recruits** (mamluks or *ghilman*) into the Fatimid military and administration. The government in Egypt relied increasingly on slaves to serve as officials and troops. The Turkish presence among the elites, together with an influx of Iraqi bureaucrats and soldiers, served as a counterweight to North African contingents, which had formerly been dominant in the Fatimid state.

996–1021. Rule of the **Fatimid caliph al-Hakim,** who vanished at the end of his reign. Al-Hakim is remembered for his **eccentric** and cruel behavior, repudiation of orthodox Islam, and persecution of non-Muslim subjects. His most devoted followers declared him to be an incarnation of God. After his mysterious disappearance (he was probably murdered), his followers formed their own **sect of Islam** and became known as the **DRUZE.** One of the chief missionaries of the radical doctrines was **Hamza ibn Ahmad,** who established the Druze in Syria, where they live to this day.

1023–79. The **MIRDASID DYNASTY** in Aleppo. The Mirdasids were a prominent family from among the **Banu Kilab,** the most powerful tribe in the northern Syrian Desert. Backed by their fellow tribesmen and Fatimid allies, the Mirdasids overcame the successors of the Hamdanid dynasty (the general Lu'lu' and his Turkish troops), who had received unavailing support from the Byzantines. The state that the Mirdasids carved out for themselves occupied a territory not much larger than Aleppo and its extended hinterland. The Mirdasid regime owed its survival largely to **skillful diplomacy,** balancing Fatimid and Byzantine interests on the international scene and tribal and urban factions locally. For the people of Aleppo, the reign of the Mirdasids was remembered as a **period of general prosperity.** The Mirdasids were ousted from Aleppo only after the rise of the Seljuk Turks, who disrupted the fragile diplomatic equilibrium that had been maintained in Syria for more than half a century.

1057. Death of **Abu al-'Ala' al-Ma'arri,** one of the most famous poets of medieval Arabic literature. He was noted for his ornate imagery, mastery of rhetoric, and highly refined verse. In tone, his poetry displayed an open irreverence and contempt for orthodox religion.

1064. Entry into Syria of the first Turkoman tribes. One of their chiefs, named **Atsiz,** conquered Palestine (1071) and then southern Syria, including Damascus (1076).

The **migration of the Turkomans** during the late 11th century **upset the tribal balance** within the Syrian Desert and reduced the traditionally extensive role of Arab tribes in Syrian politics and commerce. For the next two centuries, the Turkomans operated as the paramount tribal power in Syria.

c. 1065. Establishment of the office of *ra'is al-yahud,* an officially recognized **Jewish leader for all of Egypt.** From the late 12th to the early 15th century, the position was in the hands of Maimonides' descendants.

1079-95. Reign of the Seljuk chieftain Tutush, whose kingdom eventually covered most of Syria. He conquered southern Syria (1079) from the Turkoman chieftan Atsiz and reduced the Fatimid presence to a thin strip of coastline in Palestine. **After Tutush's death,** his state fell apart while his sons contested the succession. The resulting **political disorganization** of Syria coincided with the arrival of the Crusaders (p. 233), rendering unified Muslim resistance impossible.

1095-1128. Seljuk rule over the Syrian interior. Even after the arrival of the Crusaders (1099), a succession of petty dynasties, related to the Seljuk house, retained control of the major towns east of the Frankish states. **Muslim political authority remained fragmented** until the rise of the Ayyubids in the mid-12th century.

1099-1291. The CRUSADER STATES in coastal Syria. The **First Crusade** (p. 233), a response to Byzantine pleas for assistance, took Jerusalem (1099) and established a loose feudal federation known as the **Latin Kingdom of Jerusalem.** Even at their peak, the petty states constituting the Latin Kingdom—**based on the cities of Jerusalem, Antioch, and Tripoli**—covered only a sliver of territory along the Syrian coastline. The exception was the County of Edessa, which survived for a time (1098-1144) in southeastern Anatolia. The other Frankish states, their territory gradually diminishing, held out longer: Jerusalem fell in 1187, Antioch in 1268, and Tripoli in 1289 (the last Crusader fortress, Acre, was overrun in 1291).

During their fitful lifetimes, the **Crusader kingdoms** became fully **integrated into the local political system,** concluding alliances with Muslim states and engaging in intrigues among themselves. As an **alien ruling elite,** the Latin governments **depended on later Crusades**— in 1148, 1188, 1202, 1217, 1228, and 1249—for fresh infusions of reinforcements to prolong their occupation. Viewed over the long term, their impact on the Middle East was negligible. Their **modest successes** owed more to the temporary fragmentation of Muslim power than to their own military and political capacities. The Crusaders figured much less prominently in Middle Eastern literature than in European annals.

1100-1200. The founding of specialized Sunni Muslim religious schools *(madrasas)* in the cities of Egypt and Syria, partly in **response to Shi'ite propaganda** emanating from Fatimid Egypt. Sunni political figures took a leading role in encouraging and underwriting these establishments.

1100-1280. The NIZARI ISMA'ILIS (ASSASSINS) in Syria. They were an extreme Shi'ite sect renowned for their hostility to the Sunni political establishment. Their **agents conducted assassinations** of prominent political figures throughout the Muslim world. The sect operated briefly out of Aleppo, until 1113, before its expulsion to Damascus, where it settled under official protection. In 1128 its members fled to northern coastal Syria and established forts in the rugged highlands.

1128. Capture of Aleppo by the ruler of Mosul, **IMAD AL-DIN ZANGI.** He constructed a powerful state arching from northern Mesopotamia into northern Syria (as far south as Homs). In the north, he conquered the Frankish kingdom of Edessa (1144), the first Crusader state to be eliminated.

1128-54. The BURID DYNASTY in Damascus. The Burids were the last of the petty Turkoman rulers in Syria. By the middle of the 12th century their position had weakened irretrievably. Particularly after the Second Crusade's rash and **unsuccessful siege of Damascus** (1148), their capital became the **focal point of the military struggle** involving Nur al-Din and the Frankish states.

1146-74. Reign of **NUR AL-DIN,** one of the two sons of Zangi. He became the **principal Muslim political figure in Syria** and a fervent enemy of the Frankish kingdoms. He originally inherited the western portion of Zangi's kingdom, based in Aleppo. In 1154 he **unified the Syrian interior** by seizing Damascus. He later rounded out his empire by acquiring Egypt under Abbasid suzerainty (1171).

1164-68. Syrian struggle over Egypt. The forces of Nur al-Din came to the defense of the Fatimids, repelling successive Frankish raids and taking over the Egyptian administration. After the death of Nur al-Din's lieutenant, Shirkuh, **SALAH AL-DIN AL-AYYUBI (SALADIN)** became chief minister of the Fatimid government (1169).

1171. Death of the last Fatimid caliph, ending Shi'ite rule of Egypt. Formal sovereignty over Egypt reverted to the **Abbasids** in Baghdad, but **Nur al-Din** received the right to administer the territory. In reality, **Egypt quickly became an independent base of power for Saladin.**

1174-93. SALADIN, FOUNDER OF THE AYYUBID DYNASTY. Though the Muslim sources have memorialized him as a holy warrior and a champion of the faith, his great accomplishment was the **reunification of Nur al-Din's domain,** which had been distributed to his relatives and lieutenants at his death. In several campaigns (1174-85) Saladin asserted his authority over Damascus, Aleppo, and Mosul. Once he had consolidated his position in the interior, he turned his attention to the **Crusader kingdoms,** which he nearly eliminated.

1191. Execution of **SHIHAB AL-DIN AL-SUHRAWARDI,** a Muslim philosopher and theologian, in Aleppo, on charges of heresy. His main contribution to Islamic thought was to help turn **philosophy** away from a strictly rational method and toward a more **mystical investigation of the universe.** Over the following centuries, **Sufism** owed an incalculable debt to his theories.

1193-1249. The AYYUBID DYNASTY, the successors of Saladin, in Egypt and Syria. Like the kingdom of Nur al-Din earlier in the century, Saladin's lands were parceled out among his family and closest aides. **Three of his descendants**—al-Adil Sayf al-Din (1200-1218), al-Kamil Muhammad (1218-38), and al-Salih Ayyub (1240-49)—were **able to reimpose unity** on his former domain and check the ambitions of their rivals and relatives. Yet power remained broadly diffused within the state, and local princes retained a large degree of autonomy and influence, particularly in Syria.

1204. Death of **MOSES MAIMONIDES** (b. 1135), the greatest scholar and philosopher of medieval Judaism. During his lifetime he was court physician to Saladin and leader of the Jewish community in Egypt. His philosophical work *(Guide of the Perplexed)* represented an ambitious attempt to **clarify the basic doctrines of Judaism** and to define the differences that set it apart from Islam and Christianity. His daring **synthesis of Jewish scripture and Aristotelian philosophy** outraged most contemporary Jewish theologians, who preferred a more literal and conservative interpretation of the sources.

1218-21. Crusaders landed in Egypt and briefly occupied Damietta before being driven out.

1240. Death of **IBN AL-'ARABI** (b. 1165), one of the giants of Sufism and the Islamic philosophical tradition. He was an extremely productive author whose work made a **lasting impression** on the orthodox orders of **Sufism.** The central idea of his writings was the fundamental unity of all existence. Born in Spain, he emigrated to Damascus, where he lived until his death.

1244. Invasion of Syria by the Khwarazmians, bands of freebooters and unemployed soldiers. They had once served the Khwarazm-shahs of central Asia, until the Mongols overran their kingdom in 1220. **Wandering westward** ahead of the Mongol advance, they settled in Anatolia before **entering Syria and sacking Jerusalem** (1244). **Ayyubid forces** finally defeated and scattered them in 1246.

1250–1517. THE MAMLUK EMPIRE. The mamluks were the Turkish and Circassian military slaves who formed the mainstay of the late Ayyubid army. Turkish slaves had served in Middle Eastern armies for more than three centuries, but none had dared to dispense with dynastic facades and hold power in their own right. The **Mamluks maintained legitimacy** at first through Ayyubid puppets and then, after 1261, through the presence of an **Abbasid caliph**, descended from a refugee of the caliphal family following the sack of Baghdad by the Mongols.

The Mamluks organized themselves into **military households** in which young slaves, usually purchased from the lands north of the Caspian Sea and, later, from the Caucasus, were trained as soldiers, brought up as Muslims, and eventually set free. Militarily, they fought as cavalry and gained a wide reputation for their bravery and ferocity. Their **political system** functioned effectively, but was hardly a model of stability. Most sultans were sooner or later murdered in the constant factional disputes that plagued the empire. The administration operated essentially as a **spoils system**, in which provinces, as well as political and fiscal posts, were distributed among the leaders of the reigning Mamluk coalitions. **Mamluk solidarity** was reinforced by their cultural isolation within the society. Unlike the general population, they spoke Turkish far better than Arabic, and they were largely unfamiliar with local customs.

The Mamluks could not have ruled for so long without the cooperation of the **local Arabic-speaking notables.** Drawn from a small circle of leading families, these men occupied high places in the administrative and fiscal hierarchy, monopolized the upper reaches of the religious establishment, and served as mediators between the Mamluks and the society at large.

1250–1382. The **Bahriyya Sultanate** of the Mamluk Empire. During this period, the Mamluk Empire became the leading Muslim state in the world. One of its major accomplishments was the **integrating of the Syrian provinces** more fully into the imperial political system.

As the Mamluks came to rely increasingly on the Caucasus as their chief recruiting grounds, **ethnic tensions** between Turkish and Circassian Mamluks steadily mounted. The most notable sultans from this line were **al-Zahir Baybars** (1260–77), **al-Mansur Kalavun** (1279–90), and **al-Nasir Muhammad** (1293–94, 1299–1309, and 1310–41).

1260. THE MONGOL INVASION OF SYRIA (p. 120). Mongol forces took Aleppo and Damascus and penetrated deep into Palestine. A Mamluk army confronted and defeated them at the **Battle of Ayn Jalut** (Sept. 3). The victory **preserved the Mamluk Empire** and set a limit on Mongol expansion in the Middle East. Nevertheless, a state of enmity continued between the Mamluks and the Ilkhans until a peace agreement was reached in 1323. The **Mongols launched several invasions** of Syria, notably in 1281 and 1299.

1261. Coronation in Cairo of the fugitive Abbasid prince al-Mustansir as caliph and nominal head of state. The Mamluk state, in which the sultans retained all real power, thereby asserted itself as the **premier Muslim state in the world.** The status of the state was further enhanced when, soon afterward, the sharif of Mecca transferred his allegiance to Cairo. In consequence the Mamluks became the **guardians of the Holy Cities** of the Hijaz, a tremendous boon to their prestige and honor.

1276. Mamluk expedition to Nubia (p. 146). Over the next century, the Mamluks tried to incorporate Nubia as a province within the empire by manipulating the Nubian political system and installing puppet rulers on the throne. Although the sultans were able to gain suzerainty over the kingdom, their control was always indirect at best, and it grew feebler in the course of the 14th century.

1291. Capture of Acre, the last Frankish stronghold in Syria. With the **elimination of the Crusaders,** the Mamluk Empire now held all of Egypt and Syria under its direct authority.

1328. Death of **AHMAD IBN TAYMIYYA** (b. 1263), one of the most renowned scholars of medieval Islam. He stirred up controversy among his contemporaries by demanding a **more rigorous interpretation of Muslim religious sources** (the Qur'an and *hadith*) and by publicly denouncing many practices associated with popular religion and Sufi rit-

ual. His thinking made a deep imprint on the puritanical Wahhabi movement in 18th-century Arabia and on Muslim reformers, such as Rashid Rida, in modern times.

1347–49. THE BLACK DEATH (p. 122). In Egypt and Syria, about one-third of the population was wiped out by the plague. The decimation was particularly severe among the Mamluk households and may have been a factor in the political decline that later overtook the Mamluk Empire. During this pandemic and the succeeding ones in the 14th and 15th centuries, the **Muslim religious establishment** set an **enduring precedent** by adopting an attitude of pious resignation as the only proper response to outbreaks of the plague. Since nothing could be done to treat the victims, religious thinkers argued that it was better to carry on with everyday activities than to submit to paralyzing quarantines or to desert the cities and disrupt settled life.

1382–1517. The **Circassian (also Burji) households** of Mamluk rulers. Almost all the emirs of this period were Circassian in origin. They faced the difficult task of maintaining the power of the empire against an accelerating economic decline and slackening fiscal receipts. The most formidable rulers of these years were **Barkuk** (1382–99), **al-Ashraf Barsbay** (1422–38), **Qayitbey** (1468–96), and **al-Ashraf Kansawh al-Ghawri** (1501–16).

1400–1401. Invasion of Syria by TIMUR-I LANG (Tamerlane), the central Asian conqueror (p. 122). His army sacked both Aleppo and Damascus and wreaked great devastation. Thousands of artisans and religious scholars were deported to Samarkand, the Timurid capital in central Asia, leaving the urban economy of Syria in a shambles.

1426. Punitive expedition to Cyprus. A Mamluk force raided the island, still in Christian possession, and captured its Frankish king, who had been sponsoring piratical attacks on Muslim shipping in the eastern Mediterranean. The king was released on condition that he recognize the Mamluk sultan as his overlord and pay an annual tribute.

1429. Establishment of the Mamluk monopoly on the pepper trade. The decree was symptomatic of Mamluk economic policy throughout the 15th century. In response to falling revenues, the state resorted to **monopolies on lucrative commodities** such as sugar, perfumes, and spices. The **debasement of the currency** was another drastic measure that the government proved all too ready to adopt.

1442. Death of **Ahmad al-Maqrizi,** one of the outstanding writers of the Mamluk period. He was a leading religious scholar and wrote extensively as a chronicler. Perhaps his best-known work is a massive and meticulous description of 15th-century Cairo.

1470. Death of **Yusuf ibn Taghribirdi,** one of the major chroniclers of 15th-century Egypt. He was descended from a prominent family of religious officials and, through his connections, gained an intimate knowledge of contemporary political affairs.

1516. OTTOMAN CONQUEST OF SYRIA. Ottoman forces annihilated the Mamluk army at the **Battle of Marj Dabiq** (Aug.), north of Aleppo. They quickly occupied the rest of Syria, which was incorporated into the Ottoman Empire.

In the Ottoman-Mamluk conflict, the **Mamluks** were severely hampered by their sneering **disdain for firearms,** which they refused to carry, regarding them as effeminate innovations. Unlike the Ottomans, they never fully made the transition to the gunpowder age and unwisely relegated their guns and cannons to inferior units. Consequently they paid a staggering price in battle, despite their celebrated valor and martial élan.

1517. OTTOMAN CONQUEST OF EGYPT, which became an Ottoman province. The **Mamluk state ceased to exist.** Egypt and Syria remained part of the Ottoman Empire until the 20th century. *(To p. 350)*

f. NORTH AFRICA

943–47. The **great revolt of Abu Yazid,** a Khariji leader who assembled a **large tribal coalition against Fatimid rule.** The movement nearly toppled the Fatimids before it was finally suppressed. The difficulties of the Fatimids in restoring their authority revealed the shallow base of the regime in North Africa. In 972 they relocated their capital to Egypt and gradually relinquished their North African possessions to the Zirids, who originally operated as their governors.

951. The **Fatimids** persuaded the **Qarmatis** (Qaramitas) to return to Mecca the **Black Stone of the Ka'ba,** which they had earlier stolen. The success of Fatimid diplomacy raised their prestige throughout the Islamic world.

958–60. The **Fatimids** temporarily secured Morocco against **Umayyad** influence. Their victory on the western front allowed them later to resume their dynastic ambition of conquering Egypt. Earlier raids had been turned back (913–15, 920, and 935).

972–1148. The **ZIRID DYNASTY,** which ruled Tunisia and eastern Algeria. The Zirids were originally appointed as governors of the North African provinces within the Fatimid Empire. They gradually **broke away from the Fatimids,** who adhered to Shi'ite Islam, and restored Sunni doctrine as the official religion of the state. Their public **conversion to Sunnism** occurred sometime during the 1040s (probably 1044). A simultaneous development was the growing predominance of the **Maliki school** of Islamic law and the rapid spread of **Sufism** among all sections of the population.

973. The **Umayyad invasion of Morocco** from Spain decisively ended the Umayyad-Fatimid struggle over the country that had begun in the first decade of the 10th century. The Umayyad forces succeeded in establishing indirect control through local allies, until they were overcome by the **Almoravids** in the late 11th century. Among local factions, the most powerful was the **Zanata** tribe, operating primarily in the northeast.

981. Death of **Ibn al-Tabban** (b. 923), a renowned scholar and polymath. Among the fields treated in his writings were Islamic law, philology, medicine, astronomy, and mathematics.

1012. Death of **al-Qabisi** (b. 935), a noted Muslim theologian and mystic who advocated a highly ascetic version of Islam.

1015–1152. The **HAMMADID DYNASTY,** which governed much of central and eastern Algeria. The dynasty was founded by a revolt of the Banu Hammad (1015) under the leadership of the Zirid governor of eastern Algeria.

1016–17. Widespread rioting in Tunisia by Sunni agitators demonstrating against the position of **Shi'ite Islam** as the official religion of the state. The clashes developed out of social tensions pitting the Shi'ite ruling elites against the largely Sunni urban populations.

1051–57. Invasion of Tunisia and Algeria by the Banu Hilal and Banu Sulaym, warlike Arab tribes that had migrated to Egypt in the 8th century. They were encouraged by the **Fatimid** rulers of Egypt to move to the dynasty's former North African provinces, which were "granted" to them. As they moved westward, the **Banu Sulaym** stopped early and settled in Cyrenaica. The **Banu Hilal** pushed on to Tunisia and eastern Algeria, where they seized most of Zirid and Hammadid territory during the 1050s.

For Tunisia, one of the principal consequences of the tribal invasion was the **spread of the Arabic language** to large parts of the countryside, where, unlike in the towns, Berber had formerly predominated. At the same time, the tribes' constant raids sent the region's **economic and urban life into decline.** The most notable casualty was the city of **Qayrawan,** which was sacked in 1057 and thereafter lost its cultural and commercial preeminence.

1056–1147. Reign of the **ALMORAVIDS.** The Almoravid movement (al-Murabitun) sprang up among **Saharan tribal groups** in the mid-11th century. It was inspired by the teachings of a religious *sheik* (leader), **IBN YASIN,** who introduced orthodox Islam among the tribes and strictly imposed Islamic law. Under the later rule of **Ibn Tashfin** (r. 1061–1106), this religious ideology became the justification for a campaign of conquest that subjugated Morocco, Algeria, and Spain by the end of the 11th century. The Almoravid capital was located at the Moroccan city of **Marrakesh,** founded around 1070. Among the lasting achievements of the Almoravids were the **introduction of the Maliki school of Islamic law** to the Maghrib and the importation and sponsorship of **Andalusian art and culture.** They also made possible the political unification of Morocco, which had formerly been fragmented into petty tribal domains.

1087. Norman devastation of the city of Mahdiyya, which had been founded as the Fatimid capital around 912.

1130–1236. The **ALMOHAD** (al-Muwahhidun) **DYNASTY** ruled Morocco. In successive stages, it established its authority in Algeria (from 1151), Tunisia and Tripolitania (from 1160), and Spain (all of the Muslim territories by 1172). The founder of the dynasty was the religious firebrand **MUHAMMAD IBN TUMART** (1080–1130). He antagonized the Almoravid government in North Africa by calling for the **purifi-**

cation of the faith and the rejection of the Maliki school of law and its religious teachings. After fleeing to the mountains of Morocco, he allied himself with **Abu Hafs Umar,** a leader within the Hintata tribal confederation. Under Ibn Tumart's successor, **Abd al-Mu'min,** the Almohads gradually absorbed the Almoravid dominions until they finally took Marrakesh itself in 1147. The greatest ruler of the dynasty was **ABU YA'QUB** (r. 1163–84), a renowned patron of religious learning and the arts. Among the scholars he sponsored were **Ibn Rushd** (Averroes) and **Abu Bakr ibn Tufayl** (Abbubacer).

1135–53. Norman raids and conquests in the coastal area between Cape Bon and Tripoli.

1146. Death of **Ali ibn Hirzihim,** a Moroccan Sufi who openly criticized the strict orthodoxy of the Almoravid dynasty. He was largely responsible for the propagation of **al-Ghazali's** works in northwest Africa.

1197. Death of **Abu Maydan al-Andalusi,** a Muslim scholar from Spain who settled in North Africa. He founded a scholarly tradition that combined the study of Islamic law and *hadith* with the practice of Sufism. His tomb later became a famous destination for pilgrimages.

1228–1574. The **HAFSID DYNASTY,** which ruled Tunisia and eastern Algeria. The dynasty was founded by the Almohad governors of Tunis, who broke away when the caliph Abd al-Ma'mun renounced (1228) the religious doctrines of Ibn Tumart, the original leader of the Almohad movement.

1230. The chief of a Berber tribe, the Banu Abd al-Wad, was appointed governor of Tlemcen, paving the way for the future **ZAYYANID DYNASTY.** His successors gradually carved out a sizable state for themselves in western Algeria, keeping their **capital at Tlemcen.** The extent of Zayyanid territory fluctuated greatly throughout the dynasty's history. The Zayyanids experienced **two peaks:** during the late 13th and the early 16th century, they held most of Algeria, including large sections of the coast. But throughout their history, they were **vulnerable to attacks** from their Marinid and Hafsid neighbors, as well as to tribal unrest inside their own dominions. The dynasty was finally extinguished in the mid-16th century by a combination of **Spanish encroachment** along the coast and the intervention of the **Ottoman Empire,** the latter ostensibly taking up the Muslim cause against Christian aggression.

1245–75. Overthrow of the Almohad dynasty by the MARINIDS, a coalition of Berber tribes. **Fez** was captured in 1248 and became the Marinid capital; expanded and partly rebuilt, it thrived as a center of religion and commerce. Marrakesh, the Almohad capital, finally submitted in 1269. Throughout Marinid history (1275–1465), the dynasty rested on **Berber military strength.** Its authority covered the plains of central and northern Morocco, but the mountainous regions remained beyond its reach. The system of **government was essentially tribal.** Tribes closest to the ruling family received government offices and, in the provinces, enjoyed a degree of autonomy within their territories.

1258. The death of **ALI AL-SHADHILI,** one of the most famous Sufis of medieval Islam. After his death, his followers formed the **Shadhiliyya Sufi order,** which quickly spread throughout the Middle East and North Africa.

1270. The **Eighth Crusade,** led by Louis IX of France, landed at Carthage. After besieging Tunis for more than a month, the Crusaders agreed to withdraw.

1277–1317. Power struggle in Tunisia. On the death of the Hafsid ruler al-Mustansir (r. 1249–77), tribal factions rose up to contest the throne. The **Hafsid Sultanate** temporarily split up into petty tribal domains and city-states. This period marked the zenith of **outside interference** in Hafsid affairs, especially from the Christian kingdom of Aragon, which exploited tribal divisions to wrest commercial and political concessions from the nominal Hafsid rulers.

1317–46. Reign of the sultan **ABU BAKR,** who **restored Hafsid authority** throughout Tunisia. The Hafsid state nevertheless remained vulnerable, depending on a delicate balance of internal forces to sustain its power. The **chief bulwarks of the sultanate** were **tribal leaders,** who retained great prestige through their connection with the extinct Almohad dynasty; **Andalusian refugees** who, from the mid-13th century, increasingly filled key positions in the bureaucracy; and **local tribal forces and (in the south) urban notables,** who entered into alliances with the central government without entirely ceding their power. One of the most momentous developments during this period was the formation of a **pirate fleet** in Hafsid ports, particularly Mahdiyya and Bijaya. Over the next four centuries, piracy became a considerable source of revenue for North African states.

1335–58. Unsuccessful attempts by the Marinid sultans **Abu al-Hasan** (r. 1331–48) and **Abu Inan** (r. 1348–58) to conquer Algeria and (after 1347) Tunisia. The campaigns were probably motivated by a desire to capture the **trans-Saharan gold trade,** the principal outlets of which had shifted away from Morocco and toward the eastern lands of the Maghrib.

1347–70. Breakdown of Hafsid authority in the Tunisian countryside. The central government was disrupted first by the **Marinid invasions** (1347–58) and then by the **assertion of tribal power** (1358–70) after the Marinid withdrawal.

1370–94. Reign of the sultan **ABU AL-ABBAS,** who revived Hafsid authority in Tunisia and eastern Algeria. Abu al-Abbas consolidated the Hafsid hold on the cities (particularly in the south) and played off tribal factions against one another in the countryside. At about this time, Tunisia began to experience a **shift in economic focus** from the interior to the coast. Commercial activity in the ports assumed a new and lasting importance for the region. As part of this trend, **TUNIS** emerged for the first time as the paramount city in government, commerce, and religion—a position it maintained into the Ottoman and modern periods.

1377. Death of **MUHAMMAD IBN BATTUTA** (b. 1304), one of the most adventurous travelers in the world and author of one of history's greatest travel accounts (the *Rihla*). From his native town of Tangier, he journeyed to nearly all parts of the medieval Muslim world: North Africa, Syria, Arabia, Iraq, Iran, Yemen, East Africa, the Persian Gulf, Anatolia, the Caucasus, southern Russia, India, the Maldive Islands, China, Spain, and Saharan Africa.

1401. Death of **MUHAMMAD IBN ARAFA AL-WARGHAMI** (b. 1316), the most influential legal scholar of 14th-century Tunisia. His chief contributions were his role in **reviving the Maliki school of legal thought** and in recognizing the validity of **customary law** *(urf)* when it did not contradict Islamic law. His long career coincided with the rise of Tunis as Tunisia's new religious center, eclipsing Qayrawan.

1406. Death of **ABD AL-RAHMAN IBN KHALDUN** (b. 1333), perhaps the greatest social theorist in medieval Islamic history. He spent most of his life in North Africa, and moved to Cairo in his later years. His most enduring work, the *Muqaddima (Prolegomena to History)*, discusses the sources of power, the causes of political decay, and the necessary preconditions for a just government.

1415–1505. European foothold in the Maghrib. The shifting balance of power between Iberia and the Maghrib was first signaled by the **Portuguese** capture of the cities of Ceuta (1415) (p. 250) and Tangiers (1471). **Spain** joined the offensive by taking Melilla (1497) and Qassasa and Marsa al-Kabir (1505), as a prelude to further expansion along the Moroccan and Algerian seaboard during the early 16th century. Across the Maghrib, hostility toward non-Muslims mounted as Muslim states demonstrated their inability to expel the Christian invaders. The conflict over territory quickly assumed the character of a holy war.

1435–88. The reign of the Hafsid sultan **ABU AMR UTHMAN.** Under his long and prosperous rule, the Hafsid state emerged as the preeminent power in North Africa. The **Zayyanids** in western Algeria became little more than vassals, and even the **Wattasids** of Morocco submitted to formal Hafsid suzerainty. After Uthman's death, Hafsid authority again crumbled, due to feuding within the ruling family.

1465. Death of **MUHAMMAD AL-JAZULI,** the Sufi leader who reorganized Moroccan Sufism. Under the impetus of his reforms, independent Sufi lodges were affiliated with larger preexisting orders *(tariqat)*. The consolidation of the Sufi network coincided with the **intrusion of Portuguese power** and the **rise of Sufi** *sheiks* as leaders of tribal factions responsible for providing defense and repelling the infidels. By the late 15th century, Spanish and Portuguese activity had ignited intense **anti-Christian feelings.** A spirit of intolerance overcame relations between Muslims and non-Muslims across the Maghrib, mirroring the religious hatreds that consumed 15th-century Spain.

1472–1549. The **WATTASID DYNASTY** in Morocco. The Wattasids consisted originally of tribal groups loyal to the **Marinid dynasty.** They had held effective power since 1428 as regents to the Marinid sultans, whom they eventually replaced.

1492. Massive influx of Jews to North Africa, following their expulsion from Spain (p. 249). The Sephardic Jews possessed a greater cultural and commercial sophistication than their North African counterparts, whom they regarded with condescension, and the leading families from Spain soon took command of the reinvigorated Jewish community. Despite rising religious tensions, North African Jews enjoyed a **large degree of toleration.** Prominent newcomers even found positions in government, serving in some cases as diplomatic envoys or commercial agents.

1504. Death of **MUHAMMAD AL-MAGHILI,** a renowned theologian from Tlemcen. Reflecting the anxiety and alarm provoked by European encroachment, he **sanctioned the persecution** not merely of Christians and Jews, but also of Muslims who deviated from orthodox practices.

(To pp. 349, 364)

C. SOUTH AND SOUTHEAST ASIA, 500–1500

1. SOUTH ASIA, 500–1199

(From p. 43)

Through invasions, immigration, and related changes, South Asia was increasingly drawn in this period into what would be characterized by the end date as an Islamicate world system. As representatives of Islam (soldiers as well as merchants and Sufi mystics) spread across the known world, the global community shared for the first time a set of understandings about legal premises, state structures, and the model of the ideal ruler, as well as the accepted attributes of a cultured person and the resulting criteria for poetic and artistic production. Of course the interaction of these Islamicate understandings with local cultures led to a range of variations on the Islamicate theme.

At the same time, regional cultures within the South Asian subcontinent were beginning to emerge (primarily around linguistic bases). At least five distinctive regional cultures eventually emerged: Punjab in the northwest, home to both settled agriculture and pastoralists; the agriculturalist Gangetic Plain; deltaic Bengal in the east; the Dec-can plateau in the middle, encompassing several cultural zones; and Dravidian South India.

a. NORTH INDIA

(From p. 44)

The **White Huns** or Hephthalites, a branch of the Mongol Juan-juan who dominated central Asia (407–553), had occupied Bactria (425) and, after defeat by Sassanid Bahram Gor (428), Gandhara. Victory over Sassanid Peroz (484) freed them for raids from the Punjab into Hindustan.

c. 500–502. Toramana ruled as far as Eran.

502–c. 528. Mihirakula from Sialkot controlled Gwalior and Kashmir. Bhanugupta probably expelled him from Eran (510). Yasodharman of Mandasor (?) boasts (533) of victory over him. Although the Huns in central Asia were crushed by Turks and Sassanians (553–67), their chiefs kept rank in the Punjab and Rajputana till the 11th century.

From the decline of the Guptas until the rise of Harsha, the area was characterized by a confused political scene and the large-scale **displacement of peoples.** The dramatic movement of populations (especially from the Punjab and Rajasthan, where the impact of the Huns was felt most acutely) and the resulting new ethnic combinations of people did much to underscore the confusion and insecurity of the period.

606–47. HARSHA, fourth king of Thanesar, north of Delhi (new era Oct. 606), succeeded his brother-in-law as king of Kanauj (royal title 612), and quickly conquered an empire across northern India, to which he left no heir. Although Harsha aspired to a closely integrated empire following the Mauryan model, all he managed to achieve was a large kingdom in the north only loosely connected through feudal ties. Decisions of policy as well as pragmatic practice were made locally. Because commercial activities did not provide as large an income to the state as they had earlier, revenue came mainly from the land (in the form of a variety of taxes). Autonomous guilds continued to serve as the major institutions organizing manufacture and trade, with textiles being the most important industry (meeting both internal and foreign demand). The Buddhist church, or *sangha,* was now rich enough to act as banker, lending money on interest and renting out land, as well as performing mercantile functions.

Harsha received an embassy (643) from Emperor T'ang T'ai-tsung. A poet and dramatist, he patronized men of letters. He is well known through **Bana's** poetic romance *Harshacharita,* and by the *Hsi vü chi (Record of Western Lands)* of his guest, the pilgrim **Hsüan-tsang,** whose exact observations in India (630–43) have given priceless guidance to modern archaeology.

Tantrism meanwhile sought to secure for its adepts in magic arts, through esoteric texts (tantra) and charms, rapid attainment of Buddhahood or at least supernatural powers. Partial syncretism with Saivism led to a cult of Vairochana and various new divinities, largely terrible or erotic. Spells *(dharanis)* appear early (Chinese trans. 4th century), but the *Panchakrama* is in part the work of Sakyamitra (c. 850). Tantrism seems to have flourished chiefly along the northern borderland. Buddhism, however, progressively disappeared from India from the 9th century, lingering in Bengal and Bihar until the Muslim conquest (1202). It was largely absorbed by Hinduism.

647. A second Chinese embassy, under Wang Hsüan-tse, having been attacked by a usurper on a local throne (Tirhut, north of Patna?), secured 7,000 troops from Amsuvarman, king of Nepal, and 1,200 from his son-in-law, Srong-tsan-sgampo, king of Tibet; captured the malefactor; and haled him to Ch'ang-an (648).

c. 730–c. 740. YASOVARMAN, king of Kanauj, an author, patronized the Prakrit poet **Vakpatiraja** and **Bhavabhuti,** a Sanskrit dramatist ranked by Indian criticism next to **Kalidasa.**

c. 725–1197. The Pala Buddhist kings ruled Bengal (till c. 1125) and Magadha. Leading rulers: Dharmapala (c. 770–c. 883), and Devapala (c. 881–c. 883), who endowed a monastery founded at Nalanda by Balaputradeva, king of Sumatra.

c. 1125–c. 1225? Senas from the Carnatic gradually advanced from North Orissa into Bengal.

c. 1169–c. 1199. Lakshmanasena patronized Jayadeva, whose *Gitagovinda,* mystic call to love of Krishna, is considered a Sanskrit masterpiece. Tightening of caste restrictions was accompanied in some areas by the origin of **kulinism:** the prohibition of marriage of any girl below her own caste, which led to female infanticide; and the rise in caste by marriage to a man of higher caste, which led to polygamy of high-caste husbands to collect dowries.

b. DECCAN AND WESTERN INDIA

Western India, thanks to the many impregnable fortresses in Rajputana, was usually divided among local dynasties from the time of the Gupta power to the advent of the Muslims.

c. 490–766. A dynasty of Maitrakas, foreigners of the Rajput type, usually independent at Valabhi in Surashtra, created a Buddhist scholastic center that rivaled Nalanda. Their gifts reveal that Buddhist images were honored with *puja* of the kind devoted to Hindu gods.

c. 550–861. The **GURJARA** horde of central Asiatic nomads established a dynasty of 12 kings at Mandor in central Rajputana. Two retired to Jain contemplation, and a third to self-starvation.

712–66. Arab raids from Sind (p. 112) devastated Gujarat and Broach (724–43) and finally shattered the Maitraka dynasty (766).

c. 740–1036. The **GURJARA-PRATIHARA DYNASTY,** by uniting much of northern India, excluded the Muslims till the end of the 10th century. Prominent early rulers were Nagabhata I (c. 740–60), who defeated the Arabs; Vatsaraja (c. 775–800); and Nagabhata II (c. 800–36), conqueror of Kanauj.

746–c. 974. The Chapas (or Chapotkatas), a Gurjara clan, founded Anahillapura (or Anandapura, 746), the principal city of western India until the 15th century.

831–1310. A **Dravidian dynasty of Chandellas** (in present Bundelkhand) built numerous Vaishnava temples, notably at Khajuraho, under Yasovarman (c. 930–54) and Dhanga (954–1002).

c. 840–c. 890. Mihira, or Bhoja, devoted to Vishnu and the Sun, ruled from the Sutlej to the Narmada, but failed to subdue Kashmir.

c. 950–c. 1200. The **Paramaras of Dhara,** near Indore, were known for two rulers: Munja (974–c. 994) who invaded the Deccan, and Bhoja (c. 1018–60), author of books on astronomy, poetics, and architecture, and founder of a Sanskrit college.

c. 974–c. 1240. The **Chalukya** or Solanki Rajput clan, led by Mularaja (known dates 974–95), ruled from Anahillapura over Surashtra and Mt. Abu.

977–1186. The **Ghaznavid (Yamini) dynasty** ruled at Ghazni and Lahore. It was founded by **Subaktagin** (977–97), a Turkish slave converted to Islam, who extended his rule from the Oxus to the Indus and broke the power of a Deccan confederacy that included King Jaipal of Bhatinda, the Gurjara-Prathihara king of Kanauj, and the Chandella king Dhanga.

998–1030. MAHMUD OF GHAZNI made 17 plundering raids into the Punjab (defeat of Jaipal, 1001) to Kangra (1009), Mathura and Kanauj (1018–19), Gwalior (1022), and Somnath (1024–26). Vast destruction, pillage of immensely rich Hindu temples, and wholesale massacre resulted only in enrichment of Ghazni and annexation of the Punjab. Ghazni, heir to the rich artistic heritage of the Samanids of northeastern Persia, was now one of the most brilliant capitals of the Islamic world. **Alberuni** (973–1048) of Khiva, the leading scientist of his time, followed Mahmud to the Punjab, learned Sanskrit, and wrote the invaluable *Tahkik-i Hind (Inquiry into India).*

c. SOUTH INDIA

(From p. 45)

In this period in the south, a series of cultural reconfigurations led to greater integration between Aryan and Dravidian cultural systems. The Pallava period, for instance, saw a greater assimilation by the elite of Aryan ideals, while popular culture reasserted Tamil ideas and values—and the tension between these developments helped to shape a distinct and new Tamil culture. Geopolitically, the conflict between the two geographical regions of the Deccan and Tamilnad (the fertile plain south of Madras) marked the early centuries of this period. The area between the Godavari and Krishna deltas often served as the focus of the political contests. Three major kingdoms were involved in the conflict: the Chalukyas of Badami, the Pallavas of Kanchipuram, and the Pandyas of Madurai.

The pattern of warring states, with no single polity able to establish hegemony over the others, continued through much of this period. The ascendancy, around 900, of the Cholas also marked the crystallization of Tamil culture, as expressed in social institutions, religion, and the fine arts. Chola cultural production, in fact, came to be defined as "classical" and influenced models of kingship, cultural patronage, community formation, and religious views not only throughout the south, but also in the Deccan. Chola culture also spread to Southeast Asia in this period, as South India intervened actively in the commerce with that region.

Despite a somewhat elaborate administrative structure connecting the king to the realm, villages had significant degrees of autonomy under the Cholas. Village sociopolitical structure distinguished sharply between those who paid land taxes and the landless laborers who worked the fields, with the latter being in positions of agrestic slavery. Wealthier members of rural society found strong motivations to invest their wealth in irrigation and land-clearing activities, or to patronize temple complexes. Until the end of this period, when Chola expansion of trade fostered the growth of cities and the need for a monetary economy to move agricultural surplus to the cities, villages had relatively little connection to the larger society. Chola political power extended well past the year 1000 (p. 137).

c. 300–800. The Pallava warrior dynasty ruled from its base at **Kanchi** (near Madras) and exercised hegemony over the Deccan while disputing throughout this period with the Chalukyas and others.

c. 500–753. The first Chalukya dynasty in Maharashtra advanced from Aihole on the upper Kistna to nearby Vatapi (or Badami, c. 550) and to Banavasi (566–97) at the expense of the Kadambas. Construction of the earliest temples at Aihole was followed by that of Mahakutesvara (c. 525) and completion of the cave-temple to Vishnu at Vatapi (578).

c. 575. The Pallava **Simhavishnu** seized the Chola basin of the Kaveri, which his family held until after 812.

c. 600–625. The Pallava **Mahendravarman I**, converted from Jainism to Saivism, destroyed a Jain temple, but dug the first (Saivite) cave-temples in the south (at Trichinopoly, Chingleput, etc.). From his reign date **Buddhist monasteries** (in part excavated) and *stupas* on the Samkaram Hills (near Vizagapatam).

609–42. The Chalukya **Pulakesin II** placed his brother on the throne of Vengi, where he ruled as viceroy (611–32), repulsed an attack by Harsha of Kanauj (c. 620), sent an embassy to Khosroes II of Persia (625), and enthroned a son, who headed a branch dynasty in Gujarat and Surat (c. 640–740). Hsüan-tsang (641) describes the prosperity of the country just before the Pallavas pillaged the capital (642), a disaster that was avenged by pillage of the Pallava capital, Kanchi, by Vikramaditya (c. 674).

611–c. 1078. The **Eastern Chalukyas** of Vengi (independent after 629–32), were continually at war with Kalinga to the north, the Rashtrakutas to the west, and the Pandyas to the south.

c. 625–c. 645. The Pallava **Narasimhavarman** defeated Chalukya Pulakesin II (c. 642) and took Vatapi. He defeated also his southern neighbors and enthroned Manavalla in Ceylon (?). He improved the port of Mamallapuram, near Kanchi, and cut there the first of five *raths*, monolithic sanctuaries in the form of cars, the earliest monuments of the Dravidian style; also the cliffside relief depicting the descent of the River Ganges from Heaven.

c. 675–c. 705. The Pallava **Narasimhavarman II** built in stone and brick the Shore temple at Mamalla, and the central shrine of the Kailasa temple at Kanchi, completed by his son.

c. 700. Conversion of King Srimaravarman to Saivism by Tirujnana Sambandhar, the first of 63 *nayanmars*, or Tamil saints, led the king to impale 8,000 Jains at Madura in a single day, since celebrated by the Saivas. Another saint, Manikka Vasagar (9th century), wrote poems of his own religious experience which correspond to our Psalms. The Tamil Vaishnavas, too, had their saints, 12 *alvars*, who also expressed emotional religion and whose works were collected c. 1000–1050.

733–46. The Chalukya **Vikramaditya II** thrice took Kanchi, and distributed presents to the temples. He imported Tamil artists, and his queen commissioned Gunda, "the best southern architect," to build the temple of Virupaksha. The **frescoes of Ajanta caves** I and II are believed to date from this period. So too the Saiva and Vaishnava sculptures of the Das Avatara cave-temple at Ellora.

c. 735–c. 800. Nandivarman II, a collateral kinsman 12 years of age, accepted the Pallava throne offered him by the ministers and elders, who defended him against rival claimants.

753–973. The **Rashtrakuta dynasty** of Canarese kings, already enthroned in North Berar (631) and in Gujarat (c. 700), was elevated to empire by Dantidurga, who soon overthrew the Chalukyas.

758–72. Rashtrakuta **Krishnaraja I** cut from the cliff and decorated with Saiva sculpture the Kailasa (*natha*) temple at Ellora to rival that of Kanchi. To the same Canarese dynasty, if not to the same reign, belong the equally classic Saiva sculptures of the **cave-temples at Elephanta**

(an island in Bombay harbor). The successors of Krishnaraja were Govinda II (779) and Dhruva (783), who defeated the Pallava Nandivarman II and the Gurjara Vatsaraja.

774–13th century. The **Eastern Gangas** ruled Kalinga, waging constant war with the Chalukyas of Vengi and the princes of Orissa.

c. 788–c. 850. Samkara of Malabar revitalized the Vedanta, creating an unobtrusively new but consistent synthesis of tradition. His doctrine became accepted as orthodox Brahmanism. He taught a rigorous monism (*advaita*). For those engrossed in worldly phenomena (*maya*), he recognized that a simpler kind of knowledge was necessary; and for them he was a practical apostle of Saivism. Although he denounced Buddhism, he imitated its moral teaching. He founded four scholastic monasteries (*maths*), which still survive at Sringeri (Mysore), Puri (Orissa), Badrinath (the Himalaya), and Dwaraka (western Kathiawar). **Ramanuja** (c. 1055–1137) of Kanchi (Conjeeveran, near Madras) also interpreted the Vedanta. For him, souls are distinct from Brahman, whose representatives they are, and from the material world with which they are entangled. It is through piety toward Vishnu and his saving grace that they may recover their divine nature.

c. 790. The Chalukya **Vikramaditya II** was defeated by the Rashtrakuta Dhruva (779–94).

794–813. Rashtrakuta **Govinda II** seized Malwa with Chitor from the Gurjaras, and enthroned his brother as head of a second Rashtrakuta dynasty in Gujarat (till c. 900). He took from the Pallava (c. 800) tribute and territory as far as the Tungabhadra.

c. 812–44. Pallava **Nandivarman III** helped Govinda III to crown Sivamara II as Ganga king of Mysore. At the same time (c. 812) Pandya **Varaguna I** imposed suzerainty on the Pallavas.

817–77. Rashtrakuta **Amoghavarsha I** moved the capital from Nasik to Malkhed, the better to carry on war against the Vengi. He abdicated and died in saintly Jain fashion. The last of his line found death in Jain starvation (982).

c. 825–1312. The **Yadavas**, early suzerains of a score of petty vassal kings, occupied in turn three capitals: (modern) Chandor and Sinnar (1069), both near Nasik, and the fortress of Devagiri (c. 1111), renamed Daulatabad (1327). They fell heir to the northern possessions of the Chalukyas of Kalyani.

843–1249. The **Silaharas**, another petty dynasty, under Chalukya or Rashtrakuta suzerainty, provided 45 kings in three different areas along the west coast north of Goa. The Parsis (Parsees), refugees in Kathiawar, had probably already reached Thana near Bombay during the 8th century.

844–88. Gunaga **Vijayaditya III** fought successfully against western and northern enemies, and by the defeat of the Pallava Aparajita and the Pandya Varaguna II helped the rising Chola to supersede both. His association of two brothers as kings-consort led ultimately to succession struggles that placed eight kings on the throne in ten years (918–27).

c. 844–70. Pallava **Nripatungavarman** recovered Tanjore and obtained the submission of Varaguna II (862) and of Ganga Prithivipati I.

c. 870–88. Pallava **Aparajitavarman**, with Ganga Prithivipati I, crushed Varaguna II but was himself defeated and killed by the Chola Aditya I. Numerous Pallava chiefs continued to rule locally. Perungina, in the Tamil south, claimed imperial titles for at least 31 years.

888–1267. The **Chola dynasty of Tamil kings** from Tanjore, under **Aditya I** (870–c. 906), with the aid of the Chalukyas of Vengi, replaced the Pallavas at Kanchi. The Chola territory extended along the east coast from Telugu to the Pandya lands.

927–34. A royal inscription is the earliest extant specimen of Telugu literature. It records the erection of a Saiva temple and sectarian hostel.

973–c. 1190. The Chalukyas of Kalyani (near Bombay) were restored to power by Taila II (or Tailapa), who spent his reign fighting the Cholas and Paramaras.

985–1014. Chola **Rajaraja I** acquired hegemony over the Deccan.

994. Conquest of the Cheras and Pandyas justified the title "Thrice-crowned Chola," marking the first historical union of the southern peninsula.

999. The conquest of Vengi drove a usurper from the East Chalukyan throne and was extended (1000) to Kalinga.

2. SOUTHEAST ASIA, 500–900

(From p. 46)

In Southeast Asia, the years 500–900 are referred to as the classical period. The Indic concept of mandalas, or circles of kings, continued to be the primary form of state organization, developing into more widespread centers of power than had existed in the region earlier. In large part because of the importance of trade, one should envision Southeast Asia as an area united by bodies of water—the sea surrounding (and, to some extent, connecting) the mainland and the archipelago, as well as the rivers flowing south from the Himalaya into mainland Southeast Asia. Government, religion, and art were closely intertwined; common aspects for both mainland and peninsular Southeast Asia related in part to Indian literary models.

a. THE MALAY ARCHIPELAGO AND PENINSULA

Early Indian commercial settlements in **Sumatra** and **Java,** at first Brahman in religion and later influenced by Buddhism, became the center of organized states. Through trading networks, the more influential mandalas (such as **Srivijaya**) fostered Malay acculturation across a network of Malay-speaking centers dotted throughout the Riau-

Lingga Archipelago to the southern part of the Malay Peninsula. Toward the end of the **7th century, Srivijaya** (a trade-based empire; Malay rulers exercised influence in Sumatra and the Malay Peninsula, 600–1000) became the dominant state of Sumatra and built up a commercial empire.

b. MAINLAND SOUTHEAST ASIA

(From p. 46)

Dvaravati settlements in central Thailand (6th–11th centuries). During the early centuries C.E., the Khmer peoples of the Menam Valley came under the influence of Indian civilization, and about the 6th century there was organized, in the region of Lopburi, the kingdom of Dvaravati, which was Buddhist rather than Brahman in religion, and from which, during the **8th century,** migrants to the upper Menam Valley established the independent and predominantly Buddhist kingdom of **Haripunjaya** (p. 139), with its capital near the present Chiang Mai.

3. SOUTH ASIA, 1000–1500

State forms began to be elaborated in this period, both in the north and the south, under the influence of models and values imported from other parts of the Islamicate world and renegotiated in the subcontinent as they met with emerging regional cultural systems. Though scholars and commentators have used shorthand labels that identify these kingdoms as Hindu or Muslim, they became increasingly distinctive as Indian or South Asian in ways that are independent of particular religious practices or values.

Throughout much of this period, the dominant pattern continued to be that of smaller kingdoms vying for dominance in a region, although the **Delhi Sultanate** did manage to expand its rather loose hold over significant parts of the subcontinent before it was superseded by the Mughals. In the Deccan, particularly, a range of differing regional cultures met and interacted, including the Telugu kingly culture from the south, the Maharashtrian military culture from the west, and Muslim notions of ruler and state brought through Islamicate ties. In this politico-cultural melting pot, much influence from Islamicate states helped to shape, especially, the emerging empire of Vijayanagara.

(To p. 367)

a. NORTH INDIA AND DECCAN

1093–1143. The Chalukya ruler, **Jayasimha Siddharaja,** a patron of letters, although himself a Saiva, organized disputations on philosophy and religion, and favored a Jain monk, **Hemachandra,** who converted and dominated **Kumarapala.**

1143–72. As a good Jain, **Kumarapala** decreed respect for life *(ahimsa);* prohibited alcohol, dice, and animal fights; and rescinded a law for confiscation of property of widows without sons. He also built (c. 1169) a new edifice about the Saiva temple of Somanatha, which had been reconstructed by **Bhimadeva I** (1022–62) after destruction by the Moslems.

1151–1206. The Shansabani Persian princes of Ghur (Ghor), having burned Ghazni (1151), drove the Yamini to the Punjab and deposed them there (1186).

1172–76. Ajayapala, a Saiva reactionary, ordered the massacre of Jains and the sacking of their temples, until he was assassinated. Jain rule was restored under a mayor of the palace whose descendants displaced the dynasty (c. 1240).

Two Jain temples at Mt. Abu are the work of a governor, **Vimala Saha** (1031), and a minister, **Tejpala** (1230). Built of white marble with a profusion of ornamented colonnades, brackets, and elaborately

carved ceilings, they represent the most elegant version of the northern or Indo-Aryan architectural style.

Kashmir, already (c. 100) an important home of the Sarvastivadin Buddhist sect, remained a center for Buddhist studies (till the 10th century; degenerate before the Muslim conquest, 1340) and the study of Sanskrit literature (until today). Its history from c. 700 is rather fully known through the *Rajatarangini,* the only extant document by **Kalhana** (c. 1100), the sole early Indian historian, who consulted literary sources and inscriptions but accepted tradition without criticism.

1175–1206. Muhammad of Ghur, Mu'izz-ud-Din, undertook conquest of Hindustan by capture of Multan and Uch. He ruled from Ghazni as governor for his elder brother, **Ghiyas-ud-Din Muhammad,** whom he succeeded as ruler of Ghur (1203).

1192. A battle at Tararori (14 miles from Thanesar) decisively crushed a new Hindu confederacy led by the Chauhan king of Ajmer and Delhi. Cumbersome traditional tactics, disunited command, and caste restrictions handicapped the Hindu armies in conflict with the mounted archers from the northwest. Victory led to **occupation of Delhi** (1193) and to conquest of Bihar, where the organized Buddhist community was extinguished (c. 1197), Bengal (c. 1199), and the Chandella state in Bundelkhand. Muhammad appointed **Kutb-ud-din Aibak,** a slave from Turkestan, viceroy of his Indian conquests, and left him full discretion (1192, confirmed 1195).

1206–66. A dynasty of slave kings, the first of six to rule at Delhi (until 1526), was founded by Aibak (killed playing polo, 1210).

The numerically weak early Muslim rulers in India were forced to employ Indian troops and civilian agents, welcome allegiance of Indian landholders, and afford their native subjects much the same limited protection (including tacit religious toleration) and justice to which they were accustomed. This led to active efforts to create a polity regarded as legitimate both in the Islamicate world and in the eyes of local elites. Rebels, both Hindu and Muslim, were slaughtered with ruthless barbarity.

1211–36. Shams-ud-din Iltutmish, the ablest slave and son-in-law of Aibak, succeeded to his lands in the Ganges Valley only, but recovered the upper Punjab (1217), Bengal (1225), the lower Punjab with Sind (1228), and Gwalior after a long siege (Feb.–Dec. 1232). He advanced to sack Ujjain (1234).

1229. Iltutmish was invested as sultan of India by the Abbasid caliph of Baghdad.

Islamic architects brought to India a developed tradition of a spacious, light, and airy prayer chamber covered by arch, vault, and dome,

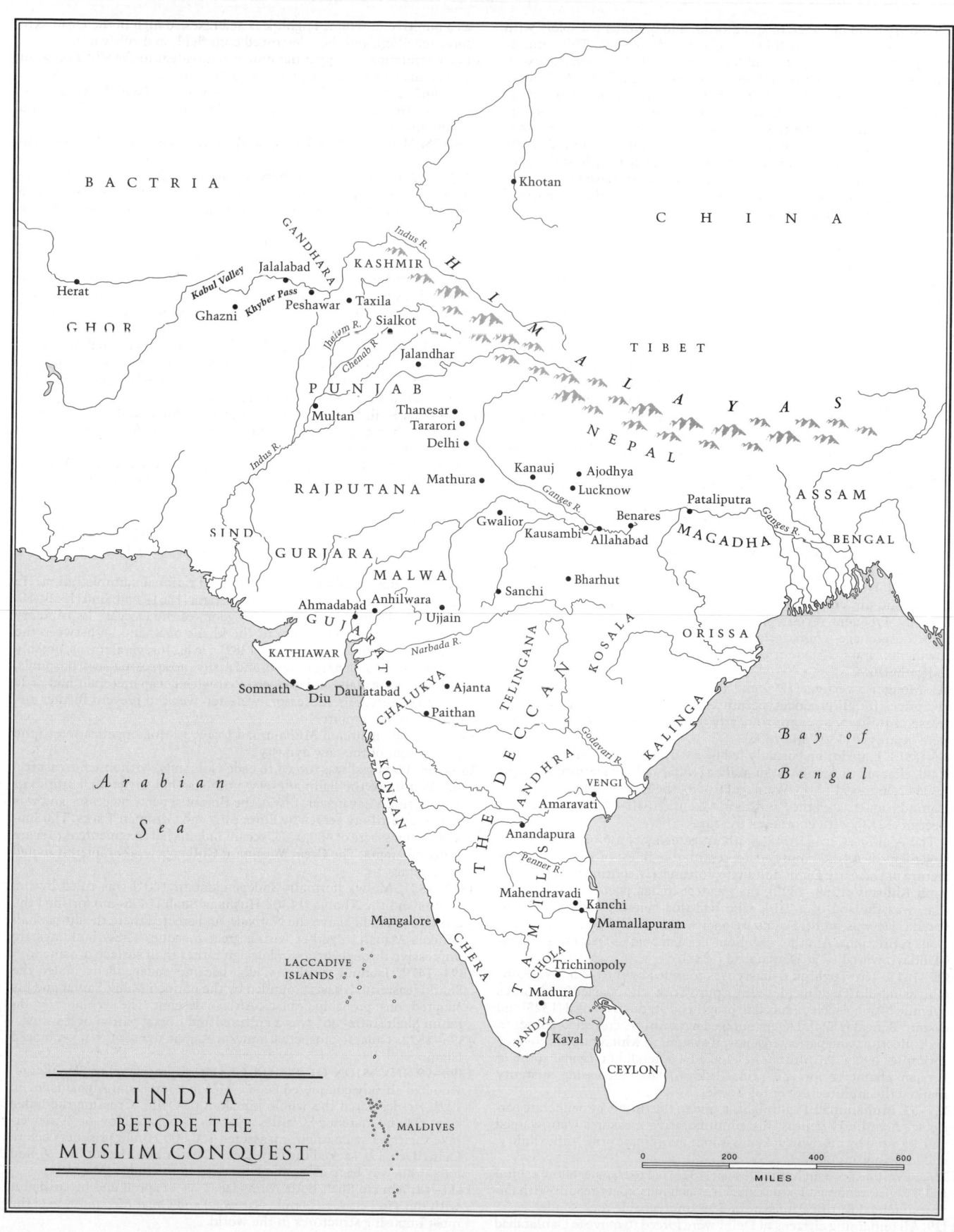

BACTRIA

GHOR

Herat

CHINA

Khotan

GANDHARA

Jalalabad

KASHMIR

Indus R.

H I M A L A Y A S

TIBET

Khyber Pass

Ghazni

Peshawar

Kabul Valley

Taxila

Jhelum R.

Sialkot

Chenab R.

Jalandhar

NEPAL

ASSAM

PUNJAB

Multan

Thanesar

Tararori

Delhi

Kanauj

Ajodhya

Lucknow

Pataliputra

Ganges R.

BENGAL

Indus R.

RAJPUTANA

Mathura

MAGADHA

Benares

Ganges R.

SIND

Gwalior

Kausambi

Allahabad

GURJARA

MALWA

Bharhut

ORISSA

Ahmadabad

Anhilwara

Sanchi

GUJARAT

Ujjain

KOSALA

KATHIAWAR

Narbada R.

KALINGA

Somnath

Diu

Daulatabad

Ajanta

CHALUKYA

Paithan

TELINGANA

THE DECCAN

ANDHRA

Godavari R.

Bay of
Bengal

Arabian

Sea

VENGI

Amaravati

KONKAN

Anandapura

Penner R.

Mahendravadi

Kanchi

Mangalore

Mamallapuram

LACCADIVE
ISLANDS

CHERA

TAMILS

CHOLA

Trichinopoly

Madura

PANDYA

Kayal

CEYLON

INDIA
BEFORE THE
MUSLIM CONQUEST

MALDIVES

0   200   400   600

MILES

erected with aid of concrete and mortar, and ornamented solely with color and flat linear, usually conventional, decoration. This formula was applied with recognition of local structural styles and the excellence of Indian ornamental design. Aibak built at Delhi (1193–96) with the spoils of 27 temples a mosque of "Hindu" appearance to which he added (1198) an Islamic screen of arches framed with Indian carving. He began (before 1206) a tower for call to prayer, which was finished (1231–32) and named Kutb Minar to honor a Muslim saint (d. 1235) by Iltutmish, who also enlarged the mosque in strictly Islamic style. In the new architectural style that emerged, the emphasis shifted from mosques to tombs of rulers and of Sufi saints. The shift underscored the importance of local rulers (rather than an internationalized Islam) and of the new force of devotionalism (which expressed a value common to those called Hindus and Muslims).

Upon the death of Iltutmish, actual power passed to a group of 40 Turks who divided all offices save that of sultan and controlled the succession.

1266–90. A new dynasty at Delhi was founded by **Balban** (d. 1287), a slave purchased by Iltutmish (1233) who was made chamberlain (1242) and became father-in-law and lieutenant (1249–52 and 1255–66) of King Mahmud (1246–66). As king, aided by an effective army and corps of royal news writers, Balban repressed the 40 nobles, ended highway robbery in the south and east, and suppressed rebellion in Bengal. His son repelled the Mongols established in Ghazni (since 1221) but was killed by them (1285).

The **tomb of Balban** is the first structure in India built with true arches instead of Hindu corbeling.

1290–1320. The **Khalji dynasty of Delhi** was founded by **Firuz** of the Khalji tribe of Turks, long resident among the Afghans. He is known for releasing in Bengal 1000 Thugs (robber-murderers in honor of Siva's consort Kali) captured in Delhi.

1296–1316. Ala-ud-din, Firuz's nephew and murderer, bought allegiance with booty secured by a surprise attack on Devagiri in Maharashtra (1294–95). He consolidated the empire.

1297. Ala-ud-din conquered and despoiled Gujarat with its rich port, Cambay. Frequent revolts prompted a program of repression that included espionage; confiscation of wealth (especially of Hindus), endowments, and tax-exempt lands; and prohibition of liquor and all social gatherings.

1303. Mongol invasions (1299 and 1303) led to decrees that, by fixing low prices for all products, permitted reduction of army pay and increase of military strength to nearly 500,000 cavalry. Mongol armies were destroyed (1304 and 1306).

1305–1313. Expeditions, usually led by a eunuch, Kafur, entitled Malik Naib, effected the **conquest of Malwa** (1305) and the Deccan: Devagiri (1306–7, annexed 1313), Warangal (1308), the Hoysala capital at Dvarasamudra and that of the Pandyas at Madura (1310–11), and the central Deccan (1313), with enormous treasure.

The Alai Darwaza (1311), southern gateway of a proposed vast enlargement of Aibak's mosque, represents the finest ornamental architecture of the early Delhi Sultanate, fortunately continued in Gujarat. **Amir Khusrav** (1253–1325), the greatest Indian poet to write in Persian, was the son of a Turk who had fled before Chinggis Khan to Patiala. He was prolific as court poet to Ala-ud-din and later in religious retirement. Another excellent Persian poet of Delhi was **Hasan-i-Dihlavi,** who died at Daulatabad (1338).

1320–1413. The **Tughluk dynasty** was founded by the old but vigorous **Ghiyas-ud-din Tughluk** (d. 1325), a pure Turk who boasted 29 victories over the Mongols. He reduced to provincial status Warangal (1323) and eastern Bengal (1324). He encouraged agriculture, corrected abuses in tax collection, and perfected a postal system in which runners covered 200 miles a day. At Multan he erected a splendid octagonal tomb of Persian character for the saint Rukn-i-Alam. Increasing austerity marked the architecture of his house.

1325–51. Muhammad Tughluk hastened to the throne by deliberate parricide. A military genius, his administrative measures were warped and defeated by his own lack of wisdom, inordinate pride, inflexibility, and ferocious cruelty.

1327. Revolt of a cousin in the Deccan (1326) led to transfer of the capital to Devagiri, renamed Daulatabad. It was handsomely rebuilt with European feudal fortifications around an impregnable rock citadel.

1329. All remaining citizens of Delhi were forced to move to Daulatabad as a punitive measure. Tughluk raised taxes so high in the Doab as to force rebellion, and then destroyed both fields and cultivators.

1330. Circulation of copper fiat money equivalent to the silver *tanga* of 140 grains failed because of easy counterfeiting.

1334. Ibn Battuta, a Moorish traveler, was welcomed with fantastic gifts, as were other foreigners who might help in world conquest. He left on a mission to China (1342).

1334–78. Madura revolted under a Muslim dynasty, ended by Vijayanagar.

1337–38. An army of 100,000 horses, sent through Kangra into the Himalaya to conquer Tibet and China, was destroyed by rains, disease, and hill men; and with it, the resources needed to avert the **loss of Bengal** (1338) to the house of Balban, independent until 1539. Muslim architects used at Gaur, its capital, local brick and terra cotta to build the bold Dakhil Gateway (1459–74?).

1340. Tughluk sought recognition (received 1344) from the caliph in Egypt. He vainly tried to restore prosperity by redistricting and by appointing undertakers to supervise fixed crop rotation and to maintain a mounted militia.

1344–45. Increased penal severity culminated when Tughluk began wholesale extermination of his centurions, revenue collectors who usually failed to meet his quotas. Rebellion begun by them in Gujarat led to permanent loss of the whole south.

1346–1589. Shah Mirza (1346–49) founded a Muslim dynasty in Kashmir. He substituted the usual land tax of one-sixth for the extortionate rates of southern kings.

1347–1527. The **Bahmani dynasty,** founded by rebels against Muhammad Tughluk, who elected **Bahman Shah** (1347–48), at first ruled four provinces: Gulbarga, Daulatabad, Berar, and Bidar. The capital at Gulbarga and many other fortresses were built or strengthened with European science, to serve against Gujarat, Malwa, and Khandesh in the northwest, the Gonds, Orissa, and Telingana in the northeast; and Vijayanagar in the south.

1351–88. Firuz Tughluk (b. 1305) restored rational administration. He exacted tribute from Orissa (1360), Kangra (1361), and Sind (1363). He refused to disturb the Bahmani kingdom of the Deccan, its tributary Warangal, or the rebels from it, the khans of Khandesh between the Tapti and Narbada (independent 1382). He built several towns, notably Jaunpur north of Benares (1359), and many mosques, palaces, hospitals, baths, tanks, canals, and bridges—but with cheap materials and little artistic quality. His successors were too weak to prevent further dissolution of the empire.

1358–75. The Bahmani **Muhammad I** gave lasting organization to the government of the new dynasty.

1363–64. Warangal was forced to cede Golconda, with much treasure.

1367. Victory of the Bahmani over immense but ineffectual armies of neighboring Vijayanagar. It was the first of several successes and was won with artillery served by Europeans and Ottoman Turks. The subsequent massacre of 400,000 Deccani Indians led to agreement to spare noncombatants. The **Great Mosque at Gulbarga** was completely roofed with domes.

1392–1531. Malwa (formally independent in 1401) was ruled by the Ghuris and the Khaljis (1436). **Hushang Shah** (1405–35) fortified the capital at Mandu above the Narbada, and erected there the durbar hall Hindola Mahall, together with a great mosque. These buildings are impressive through structural design rather than surface ornament.

1394–1479. Jaunpur, with Awadh, became independent under the Sharki (eastern) dynasty, founded by the eunuch Malik Sarvar and his adopted sons, probably of black African descent. The second ruler, **Ibrahim Shah** (1402–36), was a cultured and liberal patron of learning.

1396–1572. Gujarat prospered under a Rajput dynasty that embraced Islam.

1398–99. INVASION OF TIMUR-I LANG (Tamerlane) of Samarkand, who had already conquered Persia, Mesopotamia, and Afghanistan (p. 122). He desolated the whole kingdom of Delhi. Crossing the Indus (Sept. 24), he marched 80 miles a day for two days (Nov. 6–7) to overtake fugitives at Bhatnair, massacred 100,000 Hindu prisoners before Delhi (Dec. 12), sacked the city (Dec. 17), stormed Meerut (Jan. 9), and fought his way back along the Himalaya to the Indus (Mar. 19).

1411–42. Ahmad Shah built Ahmadabad as a capital and beautified it with the Tin Darwaza (Triple Gateway) and Great Mosque, one of the most imposing structures in the world.

1414–1526. The **KINGDOM OF DELHI,** reduced to the Jumna Valley, with tenuous control over the Punjab, was ruled by the Sayyids, who laid nebulous claim to Arab descent from the Prophet, but could collect their revenues only by force. Later the Afghan **Buhlul Lodi** (1451–89) founded the Lodi dynasty.

1420–70. Zain-ul-Abidin, learned and tolerant, recalled the exiles, permitted Brahman rites, employed convicts on public works, and exacted communal responsibility for order.

1422–36. Ahmad Shah enrolled 3,000 foreign mounted archers, who, like the Turks, Arabs, Mongols, and Persians, when employed as ministers, earned by superior qualities and disdain the envy and hostility (massacre 1446) of the native Deccanis, Africans, and Muwallads, half-breed offspring of the latter.

1429. Bidar, rebuilt under Persian decorative influence, became capital of the Bahmani kingdom.

1458–1511. Mahmud I, called Begarha (Two Forts) because of his conquest of Girnar (with Kathiawar, 1469–70) and Champanir (near Baroda, 1483–84), when 700 Hindu Rajputs preferred ritual death *(jauhar)* to Islam. He built magnificently and in exquisite taste the Great Mosque at Champanir, the palace at Sarkhej, the step well at Adalaj, and the pierced stone window screens of Sidi Sayyid's mosque. The tiny Rani Sipari mosque at Ahmadabad (1514) displays harmonious perfection of the ornamental style.

1463–82. Muhammad III conquered the Konkan and Telingana to both coasts. He died at 28 of drink, the curse of nearly all his house, and of remorse at having slain (while drunk) his best minister, Mahmud Gavan, the builder of the large quadrangular college at Bidar.

1490. Ahmadnagar (1490–1633), Bijapur (1490–1686), and Berar (1490–1574) became in fact independent of Mahmud (1482–1518), the incompetent prisoner of his minister, Kasim Barid, whose dynasty mounted the throne of Bidar in 1527 (till 1619).   *(To p. 367)*

b. BENGAL

From an area marked by strong adherence to Buddhism and Brahman-dominated Hinduism, Bengal began to change in this period into a culture marked by Islam-oriented devotional life. This reflected political, social, and economic changes that occurred at different rates. Monumental royal temples remain as witness to the fully elaborated style of medieval Hindu kingship that had emerged in deltaic Bengal, as do the Buddhist *stupas.* The conquest of Bengal by Muhammad of Ghazni in 1199 initiated the first political changes, as a Muslim elite was imported to serve as soldiers and administrators in the new territory.

Buddhism and Islam, both being institutionalized, proselytizing religions, attracted many of the same followers. This competition prompted attacks on Buddhist monasteries by the Muslim elite as it moved in, with a resulting exodus of Buddhists from eastern India into Southeast Asia. Indeed, Islam found its greatest support in areas previously dominated by Buddhism. Moreover, beginning in the 14th century, the vacuum left by the exodus of Buddhists began to be filled with a new form of popular devotionalism, bhakti, which also left room for Sufism as a related phenomenon.

Even with Persianized Turks as rulers, however, the population of the area remained Buddhist or Brahman-ordered for a long time. Ultimately, as Sufi saints came to dominate popular religion in a world filled with saintly figures, Bengali cosmologies first used Islamicate terms interchangeably with local (Hindu) ones, and then began to prefer the Islamic concepts. But this slow, shifting form of conversion did not show concrete results (for example, in the choices of names for children) until well after the end of the period.

c. SOUTH INDIA

1001–4. A successful **invasion of Ceylon** permitted assignment of Singhalese revenues to the Saiva great pagoda of Rajarajesvara, which Rajaraja I built at Tanjore, the masterpiece of baroque Dravidian architecture. He also endowed a Buddhist monastery built at Negapatam by a king of Srivijaya (Sumatra).

1014–42. Rule of Rajendra Choladeva, who had helped his father since 1002.

1014–17. A second invasion of Ceylon secured the regalia and treasure of the Pandya kings, so that a son of the Chola could be consecrated king of Pandya.

1024. An **invasion of Bengal** enabled the Chola to assume a new title and establish a new capital near Trichinopoly.

c. 1030. By use of sea power, the Chola exacted tribute from Pegu, Malaiyur (Malay Peninsula), and the empire of Srivijaya.

1040–68. Chalukya **Somesvara I** founded Kalyani, the capital until c. 1156. He drowned himself in Jain rites in the Tungabhadra, a sacred river of the south.

1042–52. Rule of Chola **Rajadhiraja I,** who had aided his father since 1018. He was killed in battle at Koppam against Somesvara I of Kalyani.

1062–70. Chola **Virarajendra** defeated the Chalukyas and gave his daughter to Vikramaditya VI. He founded a vedic college and a hospital. His two sons fell into conflict and extinguished their line by assassination (1074).

1073–1327. The **Hoysalas,** at first a petty dynasty, ruled at Dvarasamudra (Halebid) in Mysore.

1074–1267. The **Chalukya-Chola dynasty,** founded by Rajendra, son and grandson of Chola princesses, king of Vengi (b. 1070), who took the vacant throne of Kanchi (1074) and thenceforth ruled Vengi through a viceroy. His authority was recognized by the Ganga king of Kalinga.

1075–1125. Vikramaditya VI of Kalyani began a new era in place of the Saka era, but with small success. He built temples to Vishnu, but made gifts also to two Buddhist monasteries that must have been among the last in the south to withstand Hindu reaction and absorption. **Bilhana of Kashmir,** in return for hospitality, a blue parasol, and an elephant, wrote the *Vikramankacharita* in praise of his host.

1076–1147. Anantavarman Codaganga extended his authority from the Ganges to the Godavari, and built at Puri (south of Cuttack) the temple of Jagannath (Vishnu) which, at first open to all Hindu castes, is now barred to 15. The great Sun temple, in form of a solar car, known as the **Black Pagoda,** at Konarak, may be earlier than its attribution to Ganga Narasimha (1238–64).

1111–41. Bittideva, independent, fought successfully against Chola, Pandya, and Chera. As viceroy before accession, he was converted from Jainism to Vishnu by Ramanuja, at that time a refugee from Saiva persecution by the Cholas. He began construction at Belur and Halebid of temples in a distinctively ornate Hoysala style, especially featuring a high, richly carved plinth of stellate plan.

c. 1150–1323. The **Kakatiyas** reigned in the east at Kakati or Warangal between the Godavari and the Kistna. They held an important kingdom under **Ganapati** (1197–1259) and his daughter (1259–88), whom Marco Polo knew.

c. 1156–83. A revolt against the Chalukya ruler **Taila III** (known dates 1150–55) led to usurpation by a general who was soon assassinated by Basava, who was in turn compelled to commit suicide. Basava created and organized the Lingayat sect of fanatic, anti-Brahman worshipers of Siva under a phallic emblem. The movement at the outset appeared in the form of a religious and social (equalitarian) war.

1183. Taila's son **Somesvara IV** regained Kalyani, but was unable to resist the Hoysalas (last date 1189).

1292–1342. The Hoysala ruler **Viraballala III** inherited an empire comprising most of southern India.

1327. After the sack of Halebid by **Mohammed Tughluk,** Viraballala moved his capital to Tiruvannamalai (South Arcot).

c. 1335–1565. Vijayanagar (present Hampi), founded by two brothers from the region of Warangal, fought steadily against the neighboring states of sultans north of Kistna and Tungabhadra. Vijayanagar became an important center for Brahman studies and for Dravidian nationalism and art. **Madhava** wrote at Sringeri (c. 1380) the *Sarva darsana samgraha,* which remains the classic summary of the various Brahman philosophical points of view.

A practice encouraged by the Vijayanagara Empire, and continued under the Nayaka kingdoms that succeeded it (p. 368), opened up temple patronage to a variety of actors not included within the twice-born castes previously privileged by normative texts. In particular, **Shudras** (from whose ranks came the Nayaka kings), **merchants,** and **women** began to endow temples and to present gifts (often not of land but of animals and other commodities easier to purchase) that conveyed the greater freedom and wealth to which they gained access in these periods.

1498. Vasco da Gama, having rounded the Cape of Good Hope, reached Malabar. The Portuguese, after constructing forts at Cochin (1506) and Socotra (1507), soon diverted the spice trade from the Red Sea route.

(To p. 367)

d. CEYLON

846. The capital of Ceylon (modern Sri Lanka) was moved south to Polonnaruva to escape Tamil invasions.

1001–17. The **two great invasions** (1001–4 and 1014–17) by Chola Rajaraja and his son Rajendra.

1065–1120. Vijayabahu ruled prosperously despite further incursions (1046, 1055).

1164–97. Parakramabahu I repelled the Tamils (1168), invaded Madura, and united the two rival monasteries.

1225–60. Parakramabahu II repelled two attacks (c. 1236 and c. 1256) by a king of Tambralinga (Ligor on the Straits of Malacca), with Pandya help.

1284. The king sent a relic of the Buddha to Khubilai Khan. *(To p. 367)*

4. SOUTHEAST ASIA, c. 900–1557

In this period developed distinct civilizations that can be divided into three main patterns: those based on Theravada Buddhism (p. 43) (the present-day countries of Myanmar, Thailand, Laos, and Cambodia); those shaped by Sinitic influences (Vietnam); and those influenced by mercantile connections to the Islamicate world (Malaya). Theravada Buddhism probably came not from India but from Ceylon in the 11th century. Buddhist concepts were interpolated into Hindu concepts of kingship. The Hindu concept of *devaraja*, or the divine connection between the king and god, played a crucial role in forming the notions of power and state during this period. With this delineation came a transition from what scholars have called "early kingdoms" to "imperial kingdoms" and a changing "ritual policy," important for the functioning and distribution of temples.

Srivijaya and other kingdoms of central Java as well as the kingdoms of the mainland relied on alliances, often via marriage, and on relationships that were mutually beneficial. Once again, the flexibility of Southeast Asian conceptualizations of polities meant that the ruler's power did not need to be based on rooted infrastructures such as landholding, bureaucracy, or highly institutionalized state organizations. Local units continued to have separate identities. A ruler's power was based on "ritual sovereignty": the king was endowed with sacred powers, and he reinforced the aura of divine majesty through his patronage of temple complexes, patronage of monks and priests possessing the sacred Indian learning, and support for sacred monuments, elaborate rituals, and state ceremonies. The ruler's creation of ceremonial centers—centers of religion, art, and learning—was the source of his ability to attract and maintain alliances. They were demonstrations of his connections to higher gods and higher learning, and of his spiritual superiority.

Scholarly debate among historians of Southeast Asia recently has centered on the issue of how a "state" is defined. One school of thought has emphasized the standard of a unified, bureaucratized polity that is consistent with traditional Western understanding of an "advanced civilization." However, in view of the nature of state organization in Southeast Asia, it seems clear that an institutionally weak yet integrated society could still be considered a major civilization. This is demonstrated by the fact that the Indic concept of mandalas, or circles of kings, continued as the dominant model of state organization in the region during this period. Each kingdom—such as Angkor, Ayudhya, Majapahit—formed concentric circles of influence radiating out from a center representing the ruler (whose authority generally became weaker the further from the center an area was located), and moving toward more distant or geographically remote territories. This model was often unstable politically and represented a form of "state" with a vaguely defined geographical area and no fixed boundaries, which could expand and contract depending on interactions with other competitive state centers. Smaller centers would switch allegiances as they looked for security. *Negeri*, a Malay-Indonesian word for state, was particularly applicable to riverine or coastal principalities in the Malayo-Muslim world; derived from the Sanskrit term for "kingdom" or "capital," *negeri* continued to be used to define the state during this period in Southeast Asia.

Java (or Mataram) provides one example of the concentric-circles model of power relationships. *Kraton* was the word used for the sacral palace-city of the Javanese kings that formed the center of their kingdom. *Negara agung* was used to describe the second administrative circle in the kingdom of Mataram; it consisted of the core area immediately outside the palace-city. *Manca negara* was the term used for the third administrative circle of Mataram, which consisted of most of Java outside the palace city and the core administrative area. *(To p. 372)*

a. THE MALAY ARCHIPELAGO AND PENINSULA

The prominence of the kingdom of **Srivijaya,** crucial to the development of Malay society and the founding of **Malacca,** continued during this period. Along with developments in wet-rice cultivation in agrarian societies in the Indic mode came the spread of Islam, especially in Java (14th–18th centuries) and initially in trading ports along the north coast. (Trading ports served as part of the great network of shipping in the archipelago, moving spices to the archipelago and rice to Malacca after 1400. This network, in turn, was connected to an international system of commerce reaching from the Moluccas to the Mediterranean, linking Southeast Asia to the expanding world of European trade and conquest. Through this period, however, the general linkage was to the larger Islamicate world.)

At the end of the 7th century, **Srivijaya** became the dominant state of Sumatra and built up a commercial empire. Srivijaya, at its height (c. 1180), controlled the Straits of Malacca and of Sunda, all of Sumatra and the Malay Peninsula, and the western half of Java; its authority was recognized as far away as Ceylon and Formosa, and in many colonies throughout the East Indies. The **Sailendra dynasty,** rulers of Srivijaya, were ardent patrons of Buddhism, as is shown in the great Borobudur victory monument in central Java. The consolidation of petty Javanese states, begun after the middle of the 9th century, led to the rise of **Singosari** in eastern Java, which under Kartanagara (who ruled 1268–92) challenged and finally destroyed the power of Srivijaya.

1293. A Mongol expedition, sent to avenge insult offered by Kartanagara, was forced out of Java by a new kingdom, **Madjapahit,** which during the 14th century built up a commercial empire with authority extending over Borneo, Sumatra, and parts of the Philippines and of the Malay Peninsula, and profited by an extensive trade with China, Indo-China, and India.

1389. Death of Hayam Wuruk, after which the power of Madjapahit disintegrated.

1405–7. The first Chinese expedition under Zheng He (p. 155) established tributary relations between many Malay states and the Ming Empire; the authority of Madjapahit rapidly gave way to that of the Muslim Arabs. During the 15th century Muslim commercial operations, based chiefly on Malacca, were extended to the whole archipelago, and some 20 states accepted Islam as the state religion.

(To p. 372)

b. MAINLAND SOUTHEAST ASIA

This period witnessed the strengthening of administrative centralization, the augmentation of the political and coercive authority of the state, and the dissemination of a normative value system (from Theravada Buddhism) that began to supplant local custom.

Similarly, the movement of Tai peoples, a gradual infiltration along the rivers and streams, culminated by the 11th century in the introduction of an alternative social structure (neither Indic nor Sinitic but similar to that of the Mongols), based on territorial units. Interaction with other polities led to political dominance by the Tais, especially from the 13th century onward.

1. ANGKOR
(From p. 46)

Based on limited information, the **economy** of Angkor (present-day Cambodia) seems to have been focused on wet-rice agriculture rather than on coastal trade. The king's authority appears to have been expressed through a well-developed hierarchy that included priests and religious sanctions. In addition, **temples** played a prominent role as custodians over land and peasants.

889–900. Rule of **Yasovarman I,** first king to reside at the actual site of Angkor. He built numerous monasteries that variously worshipped the three chief deities of Angkor: **Siva, Vishnu,** and **Buddha.** These cults all favored royal power and all received patronage from Angkorian kings.

940s. Rajendravarman is remembered for his conquests and his architectural achievements.

1006. Suryavarman I (d. 1050) extended his authority to the north and west. **Udayadityavarman II** is credited with the construction of the Baphuon, one of the great Saivite temples at Angkor, and also the Western Baray, the large artificial lake of a Vaisnavite temple.

1113. Suryavarman II (d. 1150) was famous for his military conquests. During his reign, the most famous of all Angkorian edifices, the **Angkor Wat,** was built for him as his personal funerary temple. (Angkor Wat represents the splendor of Khmer architecture and reflected the status of the god-kings of Angkor, as succeeding rulers added to its vastness.) Angkor Wat was devoted to Vishnu; this may reveal an awareness of and sensitivity to the larger Sanskritic world, since this sect was prominent at the time in India and Java. Suryavarman II also conducted diplomatic relations with China.

1177. Cham raid resulted in the sacking of Angkor. (The series of Cham raids probably reflected Angkor's weakness due to internal problems over succession.)

1180s. Jayavarman VII (reign ended c. 1220), successfully expelled the Cham and established his authority. He favored Mahayana Buddhism and built many impressive buildings, including the **Bayon,** a Mahayana Buddhist temple in the center of the Angkor Thom wall enclosure.

1190s. Jayavarman VII sent expeditions into Champa, which came under Angkorian rule for almost 20 years.

1220. Khmer lost their dominance over the Cham.

By the **late 14th century, Tai military pressures** made defense of Angkor difficult. In addition to this pressure, the Khmer kings were led to abandon Angkor for sites in the vicinity of modern Phnom Penh by a shift in their state's focus from wet-rice agriculture to revitalized maritime trade which, at this time, benefited from China's commercial initiatives.

By the **1430s,** Angkor was finally abandoned. Rather than a dramatic collapse, it was more like a Khmer reorientation. It represented not only an economic shift but also a shift in religious culture, from priestly to monastic. In addition, the cult of personality of the Angkorian rulers had not led Khmers to invest in any particular cultural or political heritage.

(To p. 376)

2. BURMA (PAGAN)
(From p. 46)

1044. Anawrata (d. 1077) seized royal power at Pagan and by his patronage of Hinayana Buddhism and conquests, both north and south, made it the political, religious, and cultural center of Burma; the Burmese written language was developed and Buddhist scriptures translated;

architectural monuments followed the inspiration of Ceylon and southern India.

1057. Conquest of **Thaton, Mon kingdom,** which was in maritime contact with Ceylon and the Indian subcontinent and was a center for Buddhism as well as overseas trade. Mon had a strong cultural influence at Pagan. Able rulers succeeded Anawrata.

1060s–1070s. Anawrata initiated communication and exchanges with Vijayabahu I, Ceylon's ruler (1055–1110), including the sharing of Pali Buddhist texts and monks.

1084–1112. Rule of **Kyanzittha,** best known for his synthesis of various cultural developments and the process of assimilation of different ethnic groups that took place during his reign. He created a distinctive Burman style.

1106. A Burmese embassy at the Sung capital in China was received as from a fully sovereign state.

1287. Following the rejection of Mongol demands for tribute (1271 and later), Burmese raids into Yünnan, and the death of Narathihapate (who ruled 1254–87), **Mongol forces looted Pagan** and destroyed its power. The invasion of Shan tribes, forced southward by the Mongols, led to the division of Burma into a number of petty states, chief among them being Toungoo (established 1280), Pegu in southern Burma, and Ava in the middle and lower Irrawaddy Valley (established as capital 1365).

(To p. 374)

3. SIAM

Early in the 11th century, **Dvaravati** (p. 134) was annexed to Cambodia; **Haripunjaya** retained its independence. In the 13th century, Haripunjaya was overrun by a migration of Tai, or Shan, peoples from the north.

1281. Tai leader Mangrai (1239–1317) conquered the kingdom of Haripunjaya at Lamphun. For two decades he fought Mongols who were threatening Tais from the north. He is known as the founder of the kingdom of **Lan Na,** centered at Chiengmai, with cultural contributions influenced by Buddhist thought.

1279–98. Ramkamhaeng ruled over the kingdom of **Sukothai,** which he extended from Vientiane in the east to Pegu in the west. Most important contributions were in areas of literature, sculpture, and religion; these developments strongly influenced Tai cultural attainments as well.

1350. Migration of Tai, or Shan, accelerated by the Mongol conquest of the Tai state of **Nan-chao** (in modern Yünnan and southern Szechwan) in 1253, led eventually to the suppression of the Khmer kingdoms and the setting up of the Tai kingdom of Siam, with its capital at Ayuthia, founded by Rama Tiboti. The early Siamese state was from the first under the influence of both Hinayana Buddhism and Chinese political institutions. The location of the Siamese state at a center of maritime commerce gave it a distinct advantage in its power struggle with Angkor. The ability to adopt the Angkorian-style administrative skills of the Mons and Khmers, the martial skills of the Tais, and the wealth and commercial skills of the local Chinese merchant communities was its legacy to the Tais' cultural development. Toward the end of the 13th century, a form of writing had been invented for the Siamese language.

1350–1460. Siamese **invasion of Cambodia** finally led to the abandonment of Angkor (1431) and collapse of the Khmer Empire.

1371. A Siamese embassy at Nanking inaugurated tributary relations with the newly founded Ming dynasty.

1376–1557. Intermittent friction between Siam and the Tai state of Chiengmai in the northern Menam Valley ended with the destruction of Chiengmai by the Burmese.

During the 14th and 15th centuries, strong Siamese influence was exerted over the disunited states of Burma and the northern part of the Malay Peninsula.

(To p. 375)

D. AFRICA, 500–1500

1. HISTORICAL TRENDS, 500–1000

This period was a formative one, during which processes of change and adaptation originating in local and regional African conditions accelerated in response to new forces emanating from outside the subcontinental region. Change occurred unevenly in sub-Saharan Africa. On the cultural level, the most important processes include the **migration of Bantu speakers** throughout the central and southern half of the continent; the **widespread diffusion of iron technology,** which accelerated the Bantu migrations; the **domestication of new cultigens,** especially varieties of banana; and the **development of communities** that mixed agriculture and cattle raising. On the political level, this period witnessed the burgeoning of polities and the **articulation of complex political organizations.** Associated with the development of polities was social stratification based on wealth and access to political and religious power. On the religious level, **Islam expanded militarily** up the Nile, into the region between the fourth and fifth cataracts, throughout North Africa, and into the Sahara. Most of the expansion of Islam in sub-Saharan Africa, however, followed the **quietest path,** associated with Muslim merchants. Throughout the *sahel* (an Arabic term for shore) along the desert's edge and on the East African coast, Muslim communities established mutually beneficial relations with communities and political leaders practicing traditional or animist religions. These Muslim communities often developed in **diasporas,** dispersed communities settled along trade routes. **Long-distance trade** across the Sahara, up the Red Sea, and across the Indian Ocean linked Africa with the peoples of the Mediterranean, the Near East, and the Indian subcontinent. Long-distance trade was built on local and regional trade and stimulated both. Merchants imported exotic goods, which often entered **complex circuits of prestige and patronage** and contributed to social stratification and political centralization. The emergence of the East African **Swahili communities** represents a variant of this process.

Developing a **chronology** for these changes has been difficult, due in part to the paucity of archeological investigations for this period and to the absence of written documentary evidence. With very few exceptions, sub-Saharan African societies did not develop written language. As Islam spread throughout the continent, writing was widely diffused, often taking the form of vernacular uses of Arabic script, called *ajami.* Wider diffusion of writing took place at a later time and was largely limited to clerics and bureaucracies. To be without writing was not, however, to be without history. Instead, African societies produced **oral traditions** to recount the past. Historians of Africa make extensive use of oral traditions, although these traditions cover relatively short time spans and, like all historical sources, are characterized by certain distortions, especially: bias toward political events, continuous potential for revisionism, telescoping of events to occur within particular reigns, and artificial lengthening of reigns of certain rulers. Historians have developed sophisticated methodologies to control for these potential problems, and they make use of corroborating evidence from archeology, dendochronology, genetic mapping, historical linguistics, and related disciplines. Historical linguistics, in particular, has provided a method for measuring change in language, called glottochronology. Although many historians are dubious about the assumptions of a constant rate of language change, historical linguistics has yielded important evidence for cultural change, especially for the period anterior to the historical reach of oral traditions. The net result is a general chronology that illuminates relative, sequential change.

Three historical trends during this period warrant special attention: **the spread of the Bantu, the rise of complex polities in the West African** *sahel,* **and the emergence of the Indian Ocean Swahili communities.**

The **Bantu languages** are part of the larger Niger-Congo language family. Numbering some 300 languages, Bantu predominates in the central and southern half of the continent. What is remarkable about Bantu languages is their **relatively close linguistic structure,** which suggests to historians a fairly recent and rapid expansion. Based on

historical linguistic evidence, scholars generally agree that in the late Stone Age the early Bantu speakers developed a sophisticated food-producing and fishing complex in the forested region of what is now southern Nigeria and northern Cameroon. Armed with these skills, early Bantu speakers pursued two routes, eastward and southward. Already well dispersed, they probably acquired iron technology around 500 C.E. On their route eastward, the Bantu speakers skirted the northern forest edge toward the interlacustrine region of East Africa. Along the way, they adapted livestock keeping to their agricultural skills. As cattle-keeping farmers, they were able to sustain much higher population growth, attracting both the hunter-gatherers and the livestock nomads of the region for trade. The southward-moving group penetrated the equatorial forest. Iron implements and food-producing skills permitted them to colonize this region more effectively than the autochthonous inhabitants.

The two groups rejoined in the eastern and southern edge of the forest, where the southward-traveling Bantu groups acquired livestock. Sustained increases in human and livestock populations contributed to the **emergence of "big-men" and chiefdoms.** By 1000, Bantu-speaking communities were forming polities in the more densely populated regions of eastern and central Africa, and they were expanding rapidly into southern Africa. Loans of cattle and livestock-based bridewealth payments were common means of building large followings and tying communities together. Cattle-keeping Bantu farmers predominated in central and southern Africa, and they shared economic, cultural, and political traditions. Many non-Bantu-speaking people adapted Bantu languages to participate in these dynamic communities; others moved to less hospitable regions and retained their hunting and gathering traditions.

Roughly contemporary with the spread of the Bantu speakers, from the middle of the first millennium B.C.E. to the middle of the first millennium of the current era, **West Africans** along the *sahel* and savanna developed an **urban tradition.** This urban tradition seems to have its roots in the fortified villages found along the desert's edge, which may have been the result of episodic periods of conflict in the ordinarily symbiotic relations between desert nomads and settled agriculturalists. Whatever its particular origin, the urban tradition spread along the West African *sahel* and savanna to Lake Chad, and supported communities as small as several hundred to some as large as several thousand. These urban communities were largely agricultural with significant occupational specialization, including artisanal castes, religious specialists, and, increasingly, military and political leaders.

By around 500 C.E., clearly identifiable but **small-scale polities had emerged.** They set the stage for the development of larger **empires** around 800, such as that of Ghana and Kanem. These empires were superimposed above the smaller polities and held together through powerful armies and tribute collecting. Despite their capacity to survive for many centuries, these West African empires were fragile polities, rarely able to transform daily life in their smaller, outlying communities. Nonetheless, the empires fostered military and political specialists and encouraged trade. Carried by merchants, **Islam** found a fertile foothold in these urban settings.

Islam, commerce, and an urban tradition were also emerging along the **East African coast** at this time. Although East Africa had been a central part of the **developing world of the Indian Ocean** since at least the 2nd century B.C.E., the emergence of a distinctive urban, cosmopolitan, and **Muslim African culture** occurred from about the 9th century. This was the beginning of the **Swahili culture,** which was to dominate the East African coast until the end of the 19th century.

East Africa's place in the Indian Ocean system was partly due to the **monsoon winds,** which blow consistently from the northeast from November to March (facilitating navigation from the Persian Gulf and the Indian subcontinent) and from the southwest from April to August (facilitating the return voyage). Ivory, gold, incense, building materials, and slaves were part of this Indian Ocean trading system, although the intensity of the maritime commerce increased as the Abbasid capital shifted from Syria to Iraq and as the Persian Gulf increased in importance. Already by the 9th century, **large numbers of slaves** were draining the swamps of southern Iraq and planting sugarcane. These slaves, referred to as **Zenj,** the term for East Africa, were involved in the **896 slave revolt,** which lasted for 14 years before the Abbasids suppressed it.

Visiting Ibadi, Omani, and Indian merchants found good anchorage on the archipelago of offshore islands along the Kenyan and Somali coast. There they entered into relations with Bantu speakers who controlled the commodities the merchants wanted. To accommodate this commerce, permanent settlements were created on these islands, although the pace of urban development increased in the 9th century. The **process of interaction** between these foreign merchants and local Africans over the course of many centuries led to the **development of Swahili,** both as a cosmopolitan, urban culture and as the language of that culture. Swahili is a Bantu language with many Arabic loanwords. The development of Swahili demonstrates the processes of social and cultural synthesis that were also occurring in other regions of sub-Saharan Africa. *(To p. 143)*

2. REGIONS, 500–1000

a. SUDANIC WEST AND CENTRAL AFRICA

c. 1st century C.E. Camels were introduced into the Sahara from the lower Nile Valley during the late 1st and early 2nd centuries. These animals thrived in the sandy, arid conditions of the Sahara—they could carry heavy loads, travel vast distances, and go without water for prolonged periods. Their increasing use from the 2nd and 3rd centuries onward strengthened nomadic societies by facilitating travel and improving military capabilities. The use of camels significantly expanded the scale of **TRANS-SAHARAN TRADE.**

500–800. Alternating **symbiosis and conflict between nomadic and settled agricultural communities led to the consolidation of states** along the desert edge. Especially during periods of drought, nomads from the Sahara raided the sedentary societies of the *sahel.* Nomadic incursions encouraged the **Soninke** to adopt a more complex sociopolitical organization. **They formed the kingdom of GHANA between the 6th and 9th centuries.** The kingdom's rulers asserted control over key trans-Saharan trade routes. Soninke merchants traded gold and slaves for desert salt and imported goods from the north. The presence of Muslim merchants residing at Kumbi-Saleh, Ghana's capital, is attested to by evidence of two separate parts of the capital: one for the ruler and his court and the other for Muslims.

Other West African kingdoms arising in this period included **Gao** and **Kanem.** By the mid-11th century, Ghana had become the largest and most powerful kingdom in the western Sudan. The kingdom of **Songhay,** referred to as Kawkaw (Gao) in the Muslim travelers' accounts, was contemporary with Ghana, although it emerged to a position of power only in the 14th century (p. 143).

700–800. Ibadi traders from North Africa were the first to **introduce Islam** into the Sudan in this period. Their success in gaining Sudanese converts greatly stimulated trans-Saharan trading networks. Although Islam flourished along trade routes and in urban trading enclaves, the peoples of the Sudanic hinterland initially remained wedded to traditional beliefs. Many Muslim merchants also practiced **syncretic forms** of Islam.

Oases attracted settlers and became important centers of the growing trans-Saharan trade. Inhabitants of oases became experts in constructing wells. They grew such produce as dates, figs, grapes, lemons, raisins, and wheat, and engaged in trade with traveling merchants. Caravan routes passing through Saharan oases solidified **trading relations between North Africa and the Sudan** and led to the **political consolidation of nomadic groups.** The principal trans-Saharan trade routes extended north-south. Traders from the Sudan, south of the Sahara, exchanged slaves and gold for Saharan salt and North African horses. **Long-distance trade across the Sahara stimulated regional and local commerce** in a wide variety of commodities.

Founding of Islamic military and commercial centers. Berbers in the Sahara began converting to Islam during the first half of the 8th century. By the latter half of the 8th century, Muslims formed the Amal Wah state around four Libyan oases.

c. 800–900. First established in the 2nd century in the **inland Niger Delta** region, the settlement at Jenne-Jeno developed into an important urban center by the 9th century. Its position as a major center of regional and long-distance trade lasted several centuries. Foodstuffs traded in Jenne-Jeno included fish, rice, and millet.

872. Kingdom of Kanem is mentioned in Arabic chronicles. Nomads herding sheep, cattle, camels, and horses initially founded the kingdom of Kanem in the Lake Chad region. Kanem was the first and largest state to be established between the Nile and the Niger River in this era. By the 10th century, urban centers had arisen and a royal palace had been built.

900–1100. Nomadic Berber pastoralists of the western Sahara, the **Sanhadja,** gained power and influence in the western Sahara by establishing control over many trans-Saharan caravan routes and commercial centers. Sanhadja chiefs collected dues from traders, dispatched guides on trade routes, and exerted authority over a confederation of ethnic groups.

The **Almoravids,** also desert nomads, conducted a series of successful holy wars in northwestern Africa. By the late 11th century they had established a powerful Islamic empire stretching from present Spain and Morocco to Mauritania. The Almoravid **conquest of West Africa** was led by **Abdallah ibn Yasin.**

1000–1100. The rulers of Kanem and Ghana converted to Islam. Consolidation of the kingdom of **Takrur** along the Senegal River Valley (p. 144). According to Muslim travelers' accounts, Takrur was the most Islamized kingdom of the western Sudan. Even more than that of West African merchants, the Islam practiced by West African rulers at this time was syncretic. Few rulers were able completely to shed traditional religions, since their political positions had religious roots. Nonetheless, the conversion of West African leaders greatly hastened the spread of Islam into the entire region.

1076. The Almoravids pillaged **Kumbi-Saleh,** the capital of Ghana, which led to the gradual **disintegration of the Ghanaian Empire** (p. 143).

c. 1179–80. King of Mali converted to Islam by an Ibadi traveler from North Africa.

1100–1200. Decline of Almoravid Empire. *(To p. 144)*

b. FOREST WEST AFRICA

5th–1st centuries B.C.E. Rise of Nok culture. The Nok culture in southeastern Nigeria was one of the earliest and most influential of the West African Iron Age societies. Besides developing **ironworking technology,** the Nok culture possessed a unique artistic tradition that it spread widely in the West African forest region.

The 1st century C.E. and onward saw a **transition to more extensive use of iron.** The spread of ironworking technology led to an agricultural revolution. Iron hoes and other tools enabled farmers to produce surplus crops, which supported the growth of urban centers and royal courts. **Expanded agricultural productivity** also encouraged a greater division of labor in the rural areas. Besides greatly aiding subsistence efforts, the Iron Age led to the development of new, more effective weapons.

3rd century B.C.E. onward. By adopting **improved agricultural techniques,** including new stone axes and hoes, residents of the West African forest region began to enhance greatly their agricultural capabilities. The new tools facilitated the clearance of vegetation and the preparation of soil for planting, especially of root crops such as yams.

1st century C.E. Forest region of Nigeria became settled by populations practicing root crop and oil palm cultivation.

600–1100. The **Akan** region of present Ghana became an important center of ironworking. Iron tools greatly facilitated **clearing of the forest.** Inhabitants of the region became increasingly urbanized, formed states, and engaged in long-distance trade.

600–1200. Gradual process of village settlement and intensification of agriculture in the Yoruba area of Nigeria. Archeological evidence suggests emergence of religious specialists. Forest clearing and population concentration led to the **formation of polities.** By the 10th century, development of distinctive, naturalistic terra-cotta sculpture of the **Ife tradition.**

700–1100. Archaeological excavations in southeastern Nigeria suggest that a rich and complex civilization existed. Artifacts unearthed at shrines and burial grounds at **Igbo-Ukwe**—mostly ironware and pottery—attest to the society's **multilayered social organization.** Using Iron Age technology to harness agricultural wealth, inhabitants of Igbo-Ukwe became urbanized, participated in long-distance trade, and instituted new social and political hierarchies. Atop the society, generally characterized by the absence of rulers, were wealthy individuals. The civilization at Igbo-Ukwe marked a high point of Iron Age development in the region.

900–980. Beginning of **state formation among iron-using Edo of Benin.** King lists indicate that the first Benin ruler *(ogiso)* emerged c. 950. Early use of bronze in casting suggests **complex long-distance trade routes** feeding this region.

900–1100. Increasing root and tree agriculture led to increased population growth and permitted trade across the ecological frontier with the settled cereal farmers of the grasslands. **Kola nuts,** sea salt, and dried fish were traded northward for livestock, desert salt, and cloth.

(To p. 145)

c. NORTHEAST AFRICA (HORN)

African states existed in this region considerably earlier than the beginning of this period. In **Nubia** (northern part of present **Sudan**), for instance, **Kush** became independent from Egyptian rule around 750 B.C.E.; later politics were centered further south at **Meroë,** which was situated in a more fertile region. The history of Meroë was marked by long-term stability, centralized kingship, and a distinctive (although Egyptian-derived) artistic and architectural tradition. After a period of decline, it was for a time conquered by Axum (350 C.E.).

500 C.E. Nubia was predominantly Christian, and remained so until Muslim rulers came to power in the 14th century.

651–52. As part of the **Arab conquest of North Africa,** Arab armies attacked **Nubia.** A nonaggression treaty (the *bakt*) was concluded in 651, resulting in five centuries of freedom from attack, with continued trade and cultural contact with Egypt.

697. Peaceful *bakt* conditions allowed Nubia to achieve political unity from this year, as well as religious unity (under the **Monophysite Egyptian Church**) and economic prosperity.

800–1000. Nubia flourished from the end of the 8th to the 12th century.

956. A militarily powerful **Nubia attacked Aswan** (Egypt).

962. Nubia occupied much of upper Egypt.

969. The Nubian king refused payment of the tribute required by the *bakt* and refused to convert to Islam.

The area of present-day **Ethiopia** also had states that long predated this period. The kingdom of **Axum** came into being in the 2nd century C.E. and enjoyed wealth based on trade in the Red Sea and Mediterranean areas. It was predominantly Christian from the 3rd century.

300–600. States in what became Ethiopia flourished with **Indian Ocean trade** from the 4th to the 6th century.

600–800. Ethiopia began to decline in the 7th century, disappearing in the 8th century. Axum came into conflict with the early Muslims in southern Ethiopia (including **Shoa** and **Ifat**) and on the Red Sea coast in this period.

(To p. 146)

d. EAST AFRICA

500–600. The **interior** was not yet greatly involved with the coastal commerce. The most important changes in the interior in this period concerned the introduction of the **banana** and the development of highland agriculture based on it, and the spread of **iron technology.**

The dominant groups (in terms of language) were the **Cushites,** who had entered the region between 3000 and 2000 B.C.E., and the **Bantu,** who had spread through the area in the first centuries C.E. Nilotes, Khoisan, and central Sudanic groups were also present. Cushites were cattle keepers and grain cultivators, while Bantu peoples practiced forest agriculture based on the yam, and therefore were concentrated in the wetter regions. During this period they began to adopt cattle and grain agriculture from their neighbors in the eastern part of the region. By the 7th century, **Bantu dialects were diverging,** indicating an end to the great sweep of migration and expansion by separate groups within more limited areas.

500–1000. The **interlacustrine** region saw a buildup of population along the western and southwestern shores of Lake Victoria, leading to expansion to the northwest and north, settling the protopopulations of later communities such as the Ganda, Soga, Nkore, and Bunyoro. **Iron tools** slowly expanded in the interior, supplanting the earlier stone technology. Bantu groups made iron tools from the beginning of the Christian era. Such tools were also acquired in coastal trade by Cushites.

The processes leading to **the development of Swahili culture** on the coast accelerated in this period. Most important were the expansion of trade, the emergence of **urban centers** on the coast, and the beginnings of **Islamic influence.** The **monsoon winds** of the northern Indian Ocean region and the **equatorial current,** flowing south along the coast from Somalia, facilitated development of **maritime trade linking India, Persia, southern Arabia, and the East Africa coast** from the era of the Greek and Roman Empires.

650–800. Maritime trade was greatly stimulated by the growth of the Arab Islamic Empire beginning in the 7th century. The East African coast began to export new goods, and coastal towns grew and fell on the strength of the trade. **Islam came with small numbers of immigrant merchants** from Arabia and Persia from the 8th century, most of whom settled on offshore islands. Islam was slowly adopted by coastal Africans involved in trade but did not become dominant until the 12th century. However, the influence of the immigrant traders led to the absorption of a large number of **Arabic loanwords** into the developing indigenous language, **Swahili, in the Bantu group,** and to the use of Arabic script for writing Swahili.

800–1000. Many coastal urban centers emerged during the 9th and 10th centuries, but most did not become prominent until the 11th century.

850–1000. A new type of agriculture emerged toward the end of this period, practiced on the highland slopes of the Pare Mountains by the proto-Chagga (a blend of Nilotes, Cushites, and Bantu) and based on **intensive cultivation of bananas,** probably introduced by Indonesian traders. Bananas also spread in this period from the south to the interlacustrine region and to Mt. Elgon. *(To p. 146)*

e. WEST CENTRAL AFRICA

500–1000. This was a period marked by a change from hunting and gathering to food production and a transition from Stone Age to **Iron Age technology,** as well as a rapid expansion of Bantu languages and an increase in population. Bantu speakers were present on the north margins of the **Congo forest,** from where they began to spread throughout the region. On the northern edge, Bantu speakers were raising cereals and livestock, while those in the forest practiced fishing and forest agriculture. Cereal agriculture and cattle keeping were made more efficient by the coming of Iron Age technology, which facilitated Bantu expansion into the east and southeast, displacing the hunters who preceded them by pushing them into more remote and less hospitable regions. The spread of Iron Age Bantu speakers was also associated with a **rapid expansion of population** and by the establishment of **local and regional trade links** involving salt, iron, and copper.

700–800. By the 8th century, a relatively advanced metalworking culture had developed in the **Katanga (Shaba)** region of southeastern Congo. The culture grew up as a result of important deposits of minerals in the region, especially copper and iron, and it may have been an important center of independent invention of metallurgy. In any case, the wealth developed from exploitation of **mineral resources encouraged the emergence of differentiated "big men"** among the **proto-Luba and proto-Lunda cultures.**

1000. Bantu expansion was complete. Bantu ascendancy had been established by Iron Age farmers who were adaptable to a variety of environments. Cattle-keeping farmers augmented the **economic diversity** among expanding Bantu communities.   *(To p. 147)*

f. SOUTHERN AFRICA

500. By this time, several **Iron Age farming populations** had long been present in southern Africa.

600–700. The **Leopard's Kopje** culture (**proto-Shona**) were farmers who also kept cattle and lived in semipermanent villages in southwestern present-day Zimbabwe and northern Transvaal. Also by this century, there is evidence of the **southern African Bantu cattle culture,** in which men, ancestors, and cattle played pivotal roles. Archaeological evidence shows the presence of central cattle byres containing storage pots and burial remains.

700–1000. **Zhizo** people on the eastern fringe of the Kalahari desert practiced Bantu cattle culture.

1000. Bantu speakers evolved the Zimbabwe culture at **Great Zimbabwe** and other centers. Autochthonous inhabitants were pushed into less hospitable areas.   *(To p. 147)*

g. MADAGASCAR

500. Early in the first millennium, **Austronesian seafarers** brought people, language, and culture to the island that was already part of an **inter-regional Indian Ocean trade network** for timber, gum, and aromatics. Very little is known about the early history of this region, although it was the site of important ethnic, agronomic, and cultural exchanges with Indian Ocean neighbors.

650–1000. The period saw a development of trade with the Muslim world and a conversion of some to Islam.   *(To p. 148)*

3. HISTORICAL TRENDS, 1000–1500

(From p. 141)

Between 1000 and 1500, processes of political, economic, and cultural change moved along the same trajectories as in the earlier period, but at an accelerated pace. This is a period still beyond the reach of all but the most mythical of traditions. Oral traditions, especially those dealing with the origins of kingdoms, often portray the complex processes that led to the formation of larger kingdoms in terms of the heroic actions of the kingdom's founder. Rather than seeing these oral traditions as discrete historical experiences, historians interpret such "foundation traditions" as **symbolic templates** for examining the general historical processes of transforming small-scale polities into larger kingdoms. Using corroborative historical sources—including archeology, king lists, and written records, including *tarikhs*, or chronicles—historians date the founding of many African kingdoms to this period.

In interpreting the history of this period, Africanists have found it difficult to separate political, economic, and cultural change. Instead, they understand change as mutually reinforcing processes that led to the gradual formation of larger polities, which in turn stimulated increased commercial activities and accelerated cultural change and experimentation. Although the central historical experience on the political level during this period was the **gradual process of forming larger states out of clusters of smaller polities,** large states or empires remained inherently unstable and prone to periodic dissolution. Oral traditions dealing with this period, as well as the available written records, are biased toward the more stable and enduring polities and their political histories. In contrast, we know relatively little about **acephalous societies,** although the archaeological excavations at Igbo-Ukwu in southeastern Nigeria demonstrate that complex political organizations may have existed even in societies without rulers. These excavations also point to important patterns of cultural change and social differentiation based on wealth.

In the West African savanna, this period witnessed the flowering of the **medieval West African empires.** Ancient **Ghana** (p. 141), to be distinguished from the modern nation of Ghana, was formed around the 9th century and reached its apogee at the beginning of the 11th century. The Morocco-based **Almoravids** sacked Kumbi-Saleh, the *sahel* capital of Ghana, in 1086, which ushered in the gradual decline of the first West African Empire. The sack of Kumbi-Saleh led to a dispersion of Soninke chiefs, princes, and merchants that stimulated state formation elsewhere in the region.

Mali, located in the Mande zone farther south, congealed around a series of micropolities and transformed them into a larger state. The founding of Mali is told in the **epic of Sundiata.** Using armies of conquest, Mali succeeded Ghana in forming a huge territorial empire, which stretched from Senegambia in the west to the Niger Bend in the east, and from the desert's edge in the north to the forest in the south. Mali's rulers converted to Islam, and **Mansa Musa made the pilgrimage** to Mecca in 1325. He was accompanied by such a large entourage and carried so much gold that Arab and European geographers began to include Mali on their world maps.

By the beginning of the 15th century, Mali was in decline and the Niger Bend state of **Songhay** was ascendant. By the time of Sonni Ali (r. 1464–92), Songhay had transformed itself from a small riverain polity into a great empire. Due to the existence of two important *tarikhs* originally written at this time, historians know that Songhay's core military divisions consisted of tightly organized cavalry, infantry, and river-based naval units; territory was governed by appointed military leaders; and bureaucracies managed diplomacy and the massive slave plantations that supplied the court and the standing army with food and materials.

The same processes of change represented in the formation and decline of the West African empires played out on a smaller scale throughout much of sub-Saharan Africa during this period, but the details are less available to historians. In the West African forest zone, **Yoruba and Edo kingdoms** emerged out of compact village communities. In the **interlacustrine** region of East Africa, five or six larger kingdoms developed out of a cluster of some 200 micropolities. Similar patterns yielded the kingdoms of the **BaKongo, Luba,** and **Lunda** of the savannas to the south of the equatorial forest, and they occurred in central Africa, where the **Mwene Mutapa Empire** transformed smaller Shona chieftancies into a larger territorial unit. In all cases, political consolidation was linked with military exploits, commerce, and culture change.

Political power in precolonial Africa was often expressed in terms of **control over people and resources.** The formation of larger polities in sub-Saharan Africa invariably involved competition. Military force was one, but only one, means of achieving control over people and resources. Alternatively, emergent rulers solidified their control over followers through **patronage,** often loaning cattle or distributing women to followers. **Redistribution of wealth,** especially of exotic trade goods, also bound followers to rulers.

Military force was a prime means of maintaining control over people and resources. **Warfare became a central expression of political and economic power,** although communities without formal state organizations also engaged in raiding and warfare. Warfare yielded booty, especially livestock and slaves. **Slaves** were important elements of most premodern societies, especially in societies where land was abundant in relation to the number of people to cultivate it. Since slaves could easily run away, they did not have much value at the point of capture; slaves' value increased the farther away they were transported. Thus **warfare was inextricably linked to long-distance trade.**

This period witnessed the development of important long-distance trade systems that linked sub-Saharan Africa with the Indian Ocean and with North Africa and the Middle East. Slaves, as a by-product of the consolidation of African polities, fed the growing demand for soldiers, for loyal government officials, for concubines, and for agricultural labor in the Muslim empires of North Africa and the Middle East. The trans-Saharan, Nile Valley, and Red Sea slave trades carried approximately 1 million slaves each century, from the 9th to the late 19th century.

Long-distance traders were also interested in **African gold**—which became the principal gold supply for the commercial world of the Mediterranean—as well as in exotic feathers, skins, and incense. Because long-distance trade deals primarily in low-weight, high-value items, it tends to cater to wealthy consumers. African consumers in the intercontinental market were interested in exotic luxuries, such as glass beads, fine ceramics, luxury textiles, paper, and books (especially copies of the Qur'an), as well as mineral salt, horses, and weapons.

Long-distance traders needed to resolve several important technical impediments to **cross-cultural trade,** including the lack of a common language, adjudication in disputes, and reliable market information. To solve these problems, traders developed a network of linked yet dispersed communities known as **diasporas.** Long-distance trade depended on—and stimulated—local and regional trade. Trade was ubiquitous throughout sub-Saharan Africa, stimulated by specialized economic activities. Economic specialization grew out of adaptation to specialized environments, such as through herding or fishing, and out of specialized knowledge, such as smelting, weaving, or ceramics. Long-distance trade was one form of specialized economic activity, which flowed from the demand for commodities not locally available. The list of imported luxuries illuminates the **close links between long-distance trade, political change, and cultural change.** Most of the goods imported by long-distance traders catered to wealthy consumers and served military or patronage needs. Control over trade was a central part of maintaining political power, and it created needs that required continued participation in long-distance trade.

The traders best able to resolve the technical impediments to cross-cultural trade were those who shared a sense of belonging to supra-national communities. In sub-Saharan Africa, most long-distance trad-ers who plied the intercontinental trade routes were Muslims. In their diaspora settlements, Muslim merchants settled with clerics and created Muslim communities. African rulers, particularly those involved in the trans-Saharan, Red Sea, and Indian Ocean trades, saw in Islam a means of participating in a different moral and political community. The **conversion of African rulers to Islam** is indicative of the complex cultural changes that swept the continent during this period. Conversion must also be understood as part of a political calculus, in which some African rulers sought to consolidate their own power at the expense of traditional religious authorities. These were some of the reasons that, in 1492 or 1493, Muhammad Rumfa, ruler of the Hausa city-state of Kano, invited the Saharan cleric al-Maghili to instruct him in the arts of Islamic statecraft.

Although the historical evidence on social change is not very reliable for this period, some trends that became clearer over the period 1500–1800 certainly had their roots in this period. Increasing **social differentiation** by wealth and rank occurred simultaneously with increased trade and political consolidation. There were **no sumptuary laws** to distinguish noble from commoner, although such distinctions must have been fairly obvious. Nobles and the wealthy simply had more possessions than common folk: more wives, more children, more grain, more cattle, more slaves and dependents, bigger houses, and so on. **Warrior aristocracies** also emerged during this period to serve the political needs of larger polities and to provide slaves for the intercontinental trade. Increased trade between African groups and increased warfare heightened a sense of ethnic separateness, and led to the articulation of bounded ethnic identities. These trends became more pronounced in the period 1500–1800, which coincided with Africa's increased participation in the international slave trade.   (*To p. 388*)

4. REGIONS, 1000-1500

(*From p. 143*)

a. SUDANIC WEST AND CENTRAL AFRICA

1076. Almoravid destruction of the empire of Ghana and the spread of Islam in the political center of the emerging states of Takrur, Songhay, Soso, and Kanem-Borno. The empire of **Ghana** had reached its zenith by the late 11th century. In 1076 the **Almoravids** conquered Ghana and forcibly converted its people to Islam. The conquest of Ghana led to the gradual decline of Ghana's power, which encouraged the rise of regional polities and the wider diffusion of Islam. Even before the conquest of Ghana, the king of **Takrur** had converted to Islam. By the 12th century, the Takrur state controlled the Senegal River and reaped profits by controlling the trade from nearby gold and salt mines. Takrur's influence spread throughout the Senegal River basin. The rulers of **Songhay** converted to Islam around 1010. In the 12th century, the Songhay kingdom occupied the Niger Bend region. **Timbuktu** emerged as an important entrepôt on the southern edge of the desert. **Soso,** another state to emerge in Ghana's wake, arose in the late 12th and early 13th centuries. It developed a rich tradition in ironworking. The powerful **Kanem** kingdom (p. 141) dominated the Lake Chad region by the 12th century. The only major political entity between the Nile Valley and the Niger Bend, Kanem served as the southern terminus of a major caravan route between Lake Chad and the Mediterranean. In the 12th century, the peoples of Kanem began to migrate to **Borno,** west of Lake Chad, to a region better suited to agriculture and sitting astride important trade routes down the **Benue River Valley** toward the coast.

1. MALI

c. 1235. Sundiata Keita, military leader of Mali, defeated Sumanguru (r. c. 1200–1235), king of Soso, at the battle of **Kirina.** The battle ended decades of warfare and strengthened Sundiata's claim to rule over the **Malinke.** Sundiata united the various Malinke clans and chiefdoms in the surrounding territories into the powerful **Mali empire,** the successor of Ghana. The rise of Mali permitted a more thorough political and military organization of the empire and set the stage for the future expansion of Islam.

1325–54. Voyages of **Ibn Battuta.** Ibn Battuta's records provide precious details on sub-Saharan Africa. In 1328 (or 1330), he journeyed by sea to East Africa, and in 1353–55 he journeyed across the Sahara to the western Sudan before returning home.

1325. Mansa Musa ruled Mali from 1307 to 1332; at the time of his pilgrimage to **Mecca** in 1325, he was the most powerful king in the Sudan. His huge entourage, including thousands of porters, servants, and praise singers, left a deep impression on the territories through which it passed on the way to Mecca—especially Egypt. Mansa Musa was received in **Cairo** with great honor, and he distributed large amounts of **gold** among his Egyptian hosts. Following his return to Mali, Mansa Musa encouraged the building of mosques and the development of Islamic learning. His pilgrimage to Mecca strongly boosted Mali's international prestige. Egypt, Portugal, Italy, and societies of the Maghrib began vying to do business with this wealthy Sudanese empire, and knowledge of Mali became a central part of the emerging geography of the world. European efforts to tap into the **West African gold trade** contributed to Portuguese exploration of the West African coast.

c. 1382. Death of **Mansa Musa II ushered in a succession crisis in Malian Empire** between descendants of Sundiata and Sundiata's younger brother, Mande Bory. Led to a weakening of the empire.

2. KANEM-BORNO

c. 1075. Hummay, most likely a Berber, **introduced Islam** to the Kanem kingdom after seizing power c. 1075. The **Sefuwa dynasty,** which Hummay founded, continued to rule Kanem-Borno until the mid-19th century.

1465–97. Ali Ghadjideni, known as Ali Gaji, established Islamic rule over Borno, putting an end to a century-long dynastic conflict. The new state would henceforth be ruled by a powerful clique of Muslim rulers. Ali Gaji was succeeded by his son **Idris ben Ali,** called Katatarambe (r. 1497–1519), who consolidated his father's gains and strengthened the power of the Sefuwa dynasty.

3. HAUSALAND

900–1100 onward. The beginning of **state formation** in Hausaland. Walled Hausa cities gradually became centers of political power, exerting influence over the surrounding countryside.

1200–1600. Rise of the **seven city-states** of Hausaland. City-states such as Kano, Katsina, Zazzau, Gobir, and Kebbi emerged with strong centralized governments. These city-states became important commercial centers. Some states developed strong military capabilities and undertook campaigns both within and beyond the borders of Hausaland.

1300–1400. Soninke merchants of the Malian Empire pushed the commercial frontier eastward, linking **Hausaland** of the central Sudan to the commercial centers in the *sahel* and the gold sources in the south. These merchants, the *Wangara*, engaged in trade and promoted Islam. Long-distance merchants promoted trade and Islam through settlements along trade routes. The Wangara and other Muslim African traders built **COMMERCIAL DIASPORAS** to facilitate trade across cultural boundaries.

c. 1300–1400. Islam was initially introduced in Hausaland by foreigners, including the Fulani, Kanuri, and Wangarawa. At first the Hausa rulers remained wedded to their traditional beliefs, but by the 15th century, many Hausa rulers converted to Islam. By the mid-15th century, the Hausa ruling class had become increasingly Islamized, sparking a **flowering of Muslim learning** and piety in the Hausa city-states. The masses were slower to convert to Islam and largely maintained their traditional beliefs. The spread of Islam among Hausaland's ruling elites and merchants led to increased political centralization, the growth of literacy, and the expansion of the region's cultural world. The region's importance was due to a prosperous agricultural and herding economy, the development of important export-oriented craft industries, and a dense population.

1492. Commissioned by **Muhammad Rumfa**, ruler of Kano, **al-Maghili wrote the *Obligations of Princes*,** designed to guide Hausa rulers in proper **Muslim administration.** Conversion of Hausa rulers to Islam had accelerated in the 15th century, in response to increased commerce and the immigration of cattle-keeping **Fulani,** which helped to diversify the economy. Several Hausa rulers sought a more thoroughgoing Islamization of society, in part to secure their power over rival Hausa earth priests. Over the next century, mosques and schools were built, but the majority of the Hausa peasantry remained animists.

4. SONGHAY

1464–92. Under ruler **Sunni Ali Ber,** Songhay forces conquered extensive territory along the Niger River. **Control over the river routes** became a central part of the Songhay's challenge to Mali's hegemony. Sunni Ali Ber conquered Timbuktu, Jenne, the inner delta of the Niger, and other areas along the Niger waterway to the east. Although he came under Muslim influence, like other West African rulers Sunni Ali Ber did not completely abandon his traditional beliefs. In the late 15th and early 16th centuries, he commanded a large, well-organized army comprised of a flotilla, foot soldiers, and an elite cavalry corps. He and his successors presided over a **hierarchical bureaucracy of ministers and advisers.** Governors ruled outlying areas. Government departments within the Songhay state included the military, home affairs, agriculture, and the treasury. The highly centralized administrative system in place in Songhay enabled economic development to take place in an atmosphere of relative security. The government collected revenue from farmers, herdsmen, fishermen, merchants, and those defeated in war.

1492–1528. Sunni Ali Ber's successor, **Askiya Muhammad I,** was a devout Muslim. He went on a **pilgrimage to Mecca** in 1496–97 and established closer ties between the Songhay state and Muslim clerics. Askiya Muhammad applied Islamic models of the state and worked to extend Islam in the region.

1500–1600. Toward the end of the 14th century, Mali's far-flung provinces had already begun to assert their independence. In the early 16th

century, forces from the Songhay kingdom launched an increasing number of attacks against Mali and claimed **control over the gold trade.**

Conquests by the military ruler **Askiya Muhammad** consolidated the territory controlled by the Songhay Empire. Songhay became deeply involved in the **trans-Saharan trade** and developed a flourishing market economy. The urban centers that arose to facilitate trade became centers of Islamic culture. Askiya Muhammad **promoted Islamic learning and piety.**

c. 1545. Songhay forces entered the Malian capital, hastening Mali's decline. By 1600, Mali had become a small regional polity.

5. TIMBUKTU

c. 1100. Establishment of Timbuktu.

1300–1400. Timbuktu gained Islamic and commercial significance. The Malian ruler Mansa Musa encouraged the development of Timbuktu as a **center of Islamic learning.** The city became a principal terminus of the trans-Saharan caravan trade.

1400–1600. Timbuktu emerged as the **religious and scholarly center of West Africa.** Following its conquest by Songhay (c. 1468), Timbuktu entered a golden age of Islamic learning and culture. Mosques and schools dotted the city's growing landscape. Scholars founded an Islamic university to teach such subjects as theology, grammar, rhetoric, logic, astrology, astronomy, history, and geography. By the 16th century, Timbuktu was considered West Africa's major Islamic metropolis and experienced the peak of its commercial prosperity.

1433. Timbuktu, Walata, Nama, Gao, and other desert-edge cities captured by militarily ascendant **Tuareg.**

6. OTHER REGIONS IN WEST AFRICA

1200–1300. Founding of the **Wolof Empire in Senegal by Ndiadiane N'Diaye.**

1400–1500. Located in the interior of the Niger Bend region, the **Mossi** developed a centralized political system and a powerful military. Their forces raided the middle Niger region between the 1430s and 1480s in an attempt to fill the political vacuum left after the decline of Mali. In 1483, Sunni Ali Ber of Songhay defeated the Mossi and drove them away from the middle Niger.

1434. Cape Bojador was the first Portuguese landing point on Africa's northwest coast (p. 106). The Portuguese arrival there served as a prelude to further voyages along the West African coast. Between 1441 and 1483 the Portuguese would land on what became known as the Malaguetta, Ivory, Gold, and Slave coasts. In 1483 they reached as far south as the **Kongo kingdom.**

1455. A Portuguese explorer, **Alvise da Cadamosto,** established contact with the **Wolof** on the coast south of the Senegal River, and with the Malinke states on the Gambia River. His visit marked the beginning of sub-Saharan Africa's participation in the **international commercial system based in the Atlantic.** The Portuguese traded textiles, cooperware, cowries, and horses for gold, ivory, slaves, and locally made cotton cloth.

(To p. 390)

b. FOREST WEST AFRICA

(From p. 142)

c. 1000–1100. The first **Yoruba kingdom** to develop a highly centralized state, **Ife** achieved renown for its patronage of skilled craftsmen. Ife kings especially encouraged the production of cooper and brass ornaments. As the 11th century progressed, the hierarchy of courtly officials serving under the monarchy expanded.

1200–1300. The city of Benin flourished as a regional center of politics and commerce.

c. 1300–1400. The powerful kingdom of **Benin** entered a new phase of growth and consolidation, according to the oral traditions surrounding **Prince Oranyon.**

1400–1500. During the rule of **Ewuare,** the power of the Benin monarchy grew considerably, far outstripping that of Ife at its height. He ushered in **a political revolution that led to the emergence of a bureaucracy** to support the ruler's power against the hereditary chiefs. Benin city walls were built, and Benin expanded militarily and commercially throughout the Niger Delta region. At the time of the Portuguese contact, Benin was the **most powerful forest kingdom.** The artisanal caste of bronze casters was under the direct patronage of the *oba*, the ruler of Benin, and produced very impressive bronze works.

c. 1400–1500. The Upper Guinea coast—between present-day Senegal and Sierra Leone—witnessed the development of several kingdoms prior to the arrival of the Portuguese, including the **Niumi, Badibu, Niani,** and **Wuli.** Part of the stimulus to state formation in the region was the expansion of Malian authority. One of **Sundiata's** generals established the **Kaabu** state there, providing the kingdom of Mali with a western outpost.

1462. Seeking a local base near Africa, the Portuguese established their headquarters on **São Tiago, one of the Cape Verde Islands** close to the African mainland. Following Portuguese occupation, herding, cotton cultivation, and weaving became the mainstays of the Cape Verde economy. Slaves from Senegambia and Upper Guinea were imported soon after Europeans settled on the islands.

1472. With the help of African slave labor, the Portuguese established sugarcane plantations on **São Tomé Island** in the Bight of Benin. Exclusively using African slaves to cultivate sugar, São Tomé became the **harbinger of the slave system of the Atlantic economy.**

1481. Portuguese constructed the **fort of Elmina** on the Gold Coast. Elmina was the first Portuguese settlement on the African mainland. From this strategic site, the Portuguese began to engage in trade with the indigenous peoples, often acting as middlemen between two African societies. The Portuguese traded **African slaves for locally mined gold.** Slaves helped to clear the forests and provided new power to the emerging African rulers of the Gold Coast.   *(To p. 391)*

c. NORTHEAST AFRICA (HORN)

(From p. 142)

The defining characteristics of this period were the expansion of **Arab** peoples and the **growth of Islam** as a result of migration; pastoralism; and the **establishment of trade networks of Muslim merchants.**

1000–1170. Nubia, dominated by the central state of **Mukurra,** reached the height of its power as a Christian kingdom during the *bakt* (in force since 651).

1150–1270. Although Islam had also begun to expand in the Horn of Africa region in the new millennium, especially in the trading centers along the Red Sea Coast, there was a **revival of Christian central power** under the **Zagwe dynasty,** based in Ethiopia's northern highlands.

1171–1250. Good relations between Nubia and Egypt, existing while the latter was under **Fatimid** rule and the *bakt* continued to be observed, gave way to hostility under the **Ayyubid dynasty** in Egypt. Nubia began to decline during the Egyptian dynasty of the Ayyubids. Egyptian campaigns against **rebellious Arab groups** encouraged the latter to move into Nubian territory.

1250–1500. Nubian decline intensified under the Egyptian **Mamluks** (1250–1517), a result of direct Egyptian pressure as well as the immigration of Arabic nomadic pastoralists. **Nubia eventually fell to the Mamluk Empire.**

1270–85. Succession problems in Ethiopia led to the Zagwe dynasty's overthrow at the hands of **Yekunno-Amlak** (1270–85), who established the **Solomonic dynasty,** claiming legitimate succession from ancient Ethiopian kings who had claimed descent from King Solomon of the Old Testament.

1272. When the Mamluk sultan **Baybars** (1260–77) demanded resumption of the *bakt,* Nubian king **Dawud** responded by taking the Egyptian Red Sea port of 'Aydhab.

1275–1325. The weakening of the Nubian state encouraged depredation by migrating Arab groups, which in turn resulted in further Egyptian incursions in the late 13th and early 14th centuries.

1276. Baybars mounted a punitive expedition (p. 129) and installed Dawud's cousin Shakanda as king. As a result Nubia became a vassal state contributing slaves, state revenue, and revenue from a poll tax on non-Muslims.

1300–1500. The **fall of Christian power in Nubia** left Ethiopia the only Christian state in the region. **Arabization and Islamization** of the population—including the royal family (encouraged by the indigenous matrilineal descent pattern)—continued, along with decentralization of power. Nubian decline led to a much wider dispersion of Arab groups toward southern pastures, carrying them west as far as Lake Chad.

1314–44. Amda-Siyon, grandson of the founder of the Solomonic dynasty in Ethiopia, gained the throne in 1314 and ruled until 1344. Under his rule the state established military dominance over its Muslim neighbors and conquered extensive new territories. **Ifat,** the most important Muslim neighbor, became a tributary. **Lack of Muslim unity** contributed to Amda-Siyon's successes. The new regions were not ruled directly, but by local rulers under the authority of the Christian emperor, who reigned from a mobile capital. **Tribute and control over trade** in slaves, ivory, and gold made the Solomonic state wealthy. The establishment of new monasteries in the interior spearheaded the **spread of Christianity and learning.**

1315. Nubia's failure to pay tribute resulted in the naming of a Muslim nephew of King Dawud to the Nubian throne.

1317. The **cathedral at Dunkula** in Nubia was converted into a mosque.

1434–68. Zera-Yakob centralized the Solomonic Empire and established a fixed capital. He reorganized the church, encouraging its evangelical and teaching role, and he suppressed traditional beliefs. He also strengthened the empire militarily within its borders and repelled the attacks of neighboring **Adal.** With the end of his rule, the **Christian Empire began to wane.**   *(To p. 392)*

d. EAST AFRICA

(From p. 142)

The monsoon wind patterns that facilitated the rise of East African Indian Ocean trade (p. 140) led to the development of coastal fishing and farming communities into large African towns with trading, religious, and ultimately political ties to Arabia, Persia, and India. These contacts are exemplified by Arab geographer **al-Idrisi's** description of the known world (1154), which divided the Swahili coast into the **land of Zanj,** in the north, and the **land of Sofala,** in the south.

1000–1500. The **Swahili civilization,** which grew out of coastal communities of Bantu speakers, and augmented by peoples from the interior and immigrants from Arabia, Persia, and India, reached its height in this period. Wealth from trading activities led to the development of several important trading towns along the coast, from **Mogadishu** in the north through **Lamu** and **Zanzibar** to **Kilwa** in the south. These towns imported Arabic pottery and Chinese porcelain and, for the interior trade, Indian cloth. They exported tropical woods and ivory, shells, slaves, iron, and, from Kilwa, gold from the mines of Zimbabwe.

In the **interlacustrine zone,** trade between specialized agriculturalists and pastoralists led to the **formation of new polities** late in the period.

1100. Bantu-speaking groups (who had emerged from the western forests) were still few in number and were concentrated in the areas of higher rainfall (at least 1000 mm annually). The Bantu speakers therefore continued to be root agriculturalists. The drier plains and highlands were dominated by cattle-raising and grain-growing **Nilotic** and southern **Cushitic** groups. Some hunter-gatherer groups were interspersed throughout the region. Bantu movements into the drier areas resulted in their adoption of cattle raising and grain cultivation. They also adopted some cultural patterns. For example, Bantu groups affected by contact with southern Cushites and southern Nilotes on the east side of Lake Victoria adopted male and female circumcision and discontinued chieftaincy. **Intensive banana and grain cultivation** grew out of a merger of Bantu and Cushitic traditions on the slopes of **Mt. Kilimanjaro.** The Bantu's adaptability, therefore, encouraged their expansion. The western interior, however, continued to be dominated by southern Nilotic groups. In **eastern Uganda,** the migration of Bantu speakers (known in tradition as the founder Kintu and his followers) from Mt. Elgon and northeastern Lake Victoria led to the **formation of several small states** from 1100.

1100–1200. A new dynasty identifying itself as **Shirazi** (from Shiraz, Persia) came to power in the coastal town of **Kilwa** in the 12th century.

The culture of the immigrants from Persia and Arabia was important in East African religion and politics, though the immigrants were not numerous and intermarried with Africans. The ruling classes in the towns were probably of mixed Afro-Arab descent, while commoners and slaves were Africans. Recent immigrants from Arabia and Persia formed a separate group. Islam, adopted first by the merchants and then by other elites and urbanites along the coast, began to spread in the 12th century. The **Swahili language was put into written form using Arabic script** in the early part of this period.

1300–1500. The rise of the **gold trade** led to Kilwa's eclipse of Mogadishu, Lamu, and Zanzibar after the 13th century. **Cowrie shells and locally minted coins** were used as currency in this trade. New wealth led to construction in coral in the towns, in a distinctive **Swahili style of architecture.** One of the most outstanding examples is the **Great Mosque of Kilwa,** reconstructed in the first half of the 15th century. **Swahili civilization reached its peak** in the 13th through the 15th centuries, before being overshadowed by the arrival of Portuguese power in the early 16th century. Less is known about the **East African interior,** because of the absence of written sources, but important developments can be discerned from archaeology and linguistics and in some cases from oral traditions. The history that emerges is one of the movements of various populations, identified by language groups, and changes in material culture due to contact with other people and the entry into new ecological zones.

Larger kingdoms, based on the interaction between pastoralists and cultivators, began to emerge in the interlacustrine region. These kingdoms succeeded smaller states organized by Bantu cultivators in the region from around 900. Thus, the **Bito dynasty** in the **Bunyoro kingdom** (southwestern Uganda), founded by **Luo or Hima** pastoralists in about 1400, succeeded the **Chwezi dynasty** of Bantu cultivators. A new **larger kingdom succeeded smaller Bantu states in Rwanda** in the same period, incorporating both pastoralist and agriculturalist elements under **Tutsi domination** from about 1400.

r. 1344–74. Another tradition based on migrations from the west following the Chwezi collapse names **Kimera** (1344–74) as founder of a **new dynasty in Buganda,** which was to become an important state in the succeeding era.
(To p. 393)

e. WEST CENTRAL AFRICA

(From p. 143)

1000. Despite an expansion of population in the preceding half millennium, the region was still **sparsely populated** compared with West Africa and the interlacustrine region. **Sanga,** on the Lualaba River in the **Katanga** (Shaba) region of present-day Zaire, had by this time a **rich metalworking tradition** in an area that attracted Iron Age populations, due to a good supply of fish and game and good rainfall for agriculture. These populations worked **copper mines** on the upper Lualaba River, to the southeast. The presence of salt and minerals also **favored the development of trade**—with standardized copper ingots as currency—and towns, which facilitated **political centralization.** This area was the core region for the development of the political culture that evolved into the **Luba and Lunda Empires.**

1250. The transition to later Iron Age culture in **Lunda** led to a centralization of power by territorial chiefdoms, in competition with lineage-based authority.

1350. The **Kongo kingdom** developed out of a prosperous farming community near the mouth of the **Congo River.** This location, with access to both forest and grassland economies, stimulated growth and trade. Kings at the settlement of **Mbanza Kongo centralized power** based on a **hierarchical system of tribute and trade.** The kingdom slowly expanded south of the river, conquering other chiefdoms.

1400. Lunda arrived at political stability based on the alliance of a central chief of real or putative foreign origin and the old lineages. A system of "perpetual kingship" developed, in which the new officeholder "becomes" his predecessor, ensuring continuation of alliances based on kinship, marriage, and alliance.

1400–1500. In **Angola,** this period saw the **emergence of many small kingdoms or chiefdoms** among the **Ndongo** peoples of the Luanda plateau. These small kingdoms coalesced around two types of **cults:** the *malunga,* associated with rainmaking, and the *ngola,* associated with

iron. The *ngola* kings began to consolidate political and spiritual authority as well as control of trade and important resources, such as salt.

1483. Portuguese arrived in Kongo with commercial, religious, and strategic interests. They found a distinct class of aristocrats at the urban center and slaves who performed agricultural labor to support the elite class. The king appointed provincial governors, often his relatives. The king was chosen by a group of electors, and his power was to some degree limited by a council. The capital was the focus of **regional trade networks** involving iron, pottery, salt, copper, and ivory. **Imported European trade goods, along with teachers, priests, craftsmen, and Christianity created a distinctive court culture and had far-reaching effects** on the development of Kongo.

1500. Sometime before this date, the **Luba state** emerged, fusing several clans under one chief. By this time, Kongo was becoming a conquest state and a trading empire, with a separate aristocracy and middle class. Increasing commerce linked the forest zone to the interlacustrine region in the east and the emerging state systems to the west.
(To p. 393)

f. SOUTHERN AFRICA

(From p. 143)

1. NORTH OF THE LIMPOPO

1000. By this date, the **Zambezi** and **Limpopo** basins were widely settled by Iron Age peoples, who farmed sorghum and millet and kept cattle and small livestock. Pockets of Stone Age hunter-gatherers remained in the savanna. Hunter-gatherers, ancestors of modern **San** groups, occupied the **Kalahari** to the southwest.

1000–1200. New cultures, including the **Leopard's Kopje** tradition in modern Zimbabwe, supplanted the early Iron Age cultures of this region. The new developments may have been influenced by the immigration of pastoralists in the 9th or 10th century. By the 12th century, Leopard's Kopje people were engaged in gold mining. The mining and trading economy led to the **accumulation of wealth** by a privileged class and **political centralization.** Other new farming-based societies, sparked by immigration or technological innovation, emerged in this region in the 12th century among **Shona** speakers. Later Iron Age peoples settled at what became **Great Zimbabwe** in the 10th or 11th century. Trading states linked to the trade of the East African coast appeared in coastal Mozambique.

1100–1300. From the 12th century, gold mining increased in the Leopard's Kopje area. In the 12th century, significant changes took place in **Great Zimbabwe,** through which Leopard's Kopje exports were traded to the coast. These changes included the building of stone walls and the import of glass beads and other luxury goods, indicating new trade and wealth. A **powerful state structure** emerged there by 1300. Its domain included much of central and southern Mashonaland. Both Zimbabwe and Leopard's Kopje developed **extensive trading networks and political centralization.** Long-distance trade led to the accumulation of considerable wealth by the rulers at Great Zimbabwe. This in turn led to **greater population densities,** which in the long run probably resulted in overgrazing and loss of fertility of the land.

1300–1400. Great Zimbabwe's trade continued to flourish through the 14th century. By this century, imports at Great Zimbabwe included glass beads as well as ceramics from Persia, Syria, and China.

1400–1500. The **gold trade** from Sofala to Kilwa, on which Great Zimbabwe's wealth depended, reached its height in this century and then went into a steep decline, influencing the rapid decline of Great Zimbabwe as a political and trading center. The site was abandoned at the end of the 15th century, perhaps as a result of environmental degradation. The decline of Great Zimbabwe coincided with the **emergence of the Rozwi Empire** under a ruler known as **Mwene Mutapa** (Master Pillager). About 1490 the southern part split off, leaving Mutapa with domain over a region south of the Zambezi stretching to the Indian Ocean. This northward shift of power was related to new gold production from 1450 on the Zambezi tributaries.

2. SOUTH OF THE LIMPOPO

1000–1500. In this period in modern South Africa and Botswana, the **Khoikhoi** peoples became pastoralists and metal forgers and spread over an extensive area of relatively arid southern Africa, from northern Botswana to the Cape; they were also significant in Natal and Transkei. **Cattle** also took on increased importance for **Bantu speakers,** who spread throughout the well-watered eastern half of the region, parallel to the spread of later Iron Age culture. Bantu speakers consisted of two major groups, the **Sotho-Tswana** and the **Nguni,** whose major cultural traditions took shape in this era.

1100–1350. North of the **Drakensberg (Ukhahlamba) Mountains,** there were dramatic changes from this date; there was a greatly increased **cultural and economic role for cattle and expansion in the size of settlements.** A pastoral and agricultural economy evolved, and cattle were used for **bridewealth** *(lobola),* to compensate the bride's kin for her loss to them. These changes may have been associated with a shift in population from Botswana to the western Transvaal, which had a more favorable environment for large-scale cattle raising.

1200–1500. Nguni Bantu speakers spread throughout the southeastern coastal region. The language group was heavily influenced by Khoikhoi, especially in the southwest, and the population groups were also significantly mixed. Khoikhoi were gradually absorbed into the Bantu-speaking populations in Natal and Transkei. Nguni speakers in this region practiced semipastoralism, and Khoikhoi influence was notable in matters concerning cattle keeping.

1488. Bartolemeu Dias of Portugal "discovered" the Cape of Good Hope (p. 106) and made contact with the Khoikhoi.

1497. Vasco da Gama made contact with the Khoikhoi at Mossel Bay.

(To p. 394)

g. MADAGASCAR

(From p. 143)

1000. Indonesian immigrants had been settled on the island since the previous century.

1100–1500. Arab Muslim influence became important as a result of immigrants involved with trade to the Arab and Swahili worlds.

1200–1500. A new wave of **Indonesian immigration** to the east coast or northwest brought irrigated cultivation of rice, bananas, yams, and cocoa. Immigrants encountered earlier mix of Indonesian settlers and Africans, whom they called **Vazimba.** The two groups initially cooperated but eventually come into conflict, which led to the founding of **Merina state** on the interior plateau, toward the end of the period. The new immigrants (including Muslims) brought **institutions of royalty,** which had not existed previously on the island, but the developing political institutions reflected the contributions of Asians, Africans, and Muslims.

1300. Muslim settlers arrived in the **Comoro Islands** from the east coast of Africa, and later settled in northwestern and northeastern Madagascar.

1400–1500. By this time, **Muslim settlements comparable to the Swahili coastal towns** had been established on the northwestern and (later in the century) northeastern coasts, for trading with the Swahili and Arab worlds. The settlements exported rice and soapstone carvings in exchange for imported pearls, cloth, and Chinese ceramics.

(To p. 395)

E. EAST ASIA, TO 1527

1. CHINA, 589–960

(From p. 53)

a. PERIODIZATION AND EVENTS

The period from 589 to 960 covers the short Sui dynasty, the Tang—one of the longest Chinese dynasties—a period of splendorous growth in every way, and a half century of disunion. Most historians of China, regardless of their subspeciality, would agree that a breaking point of great significance occurred at the end of the Tang and the beginning of the next imperial dynasty, the Song; others place it more generally over the course of the 10th century. This period has been forcefully argued as marking the beginning of Chinese modernity, the end of aristocracy and the commencement of meritocratic government, the shift from slavery to feudalism, the rise of centralized autocracy, and a host of other important transitions. Irrespective of ideological bent, though, virtually all historians recognize an all-important shift.

589. With the Sui dynasty, efforts began immediately to link the Yellow River with the Yangzi River. A reintegration of north and south China began.

602–5. Liu Fang suppressed a rebellion in An-nam, repelled the Cham, and sacked their capital at Indrapura.

604–18. The **reign of Yangdi** (569–618) was tyrannical and egocentric; he was alleged to have killed his father. He moved the capital to Luoyang, began rebuilding the Great Wall (607–8), and completed the **Grand Canal** (605) to link Luoyang to the Yangzi River, which later was linked further to Beijing (608) and Hangzhou (610), as well as undertaking other fiscally draining public works projects.

606. The **National University** was enlarged and the **doctoral, or *jinshi*, degree** was first awarded. The first Japanese embassy was received from **Empress Suiko.**

607–8. Sui armies under Pei Ju attacked west into Xinjiang but were defeated.

612, 613, 614. Three huge assaults on Koguryŏ, a state on the Korean peninsula, by massive Sui armies proved economically and militarily debilitating. They destroyed the Sui economy and incurred popular ire, leading to domestic upheaval.

615. Sui forces were defeated by the Turks, prompting Yangdi to send **Gen. Li Yuan** (566–635) to combat the Turks, while he retired to the south, where he was murdered (618).

The recentralization policies set in motion by the Northern Zhou were continued by the Sui, and this aided the reunification of the empire and helped break the back of the great families. The Sui central government took control of all appointments to the regular bureaucracy and used extensive examinations. The Sui also adopted the Western Wei's militia system. The Sui census of 606 gave a national population of 46,019,956, a great rise from earlier. The Sui also continued the Tuoba Wei's equal-field system for land distribution and taxation. Like the Qin, the Sui unified the country rapidly after centuries of disunion, but moved too quickly and too forcefully to try to secure its achievement; both were extremely short-lived.

618–907. The **TANG DYNASTY,** founded by Li Yuan (r. 618–26, as Taizu) and his son **LI SHIMIN** (600–49). The Tang was a truly brilliant age in Chinese history, and Tang institutions became models for the other countries of East Asia. **The Tang's principal capital was placed at Chang'an,** which became the largest city in the world and attracted visitors from many different lands, and an eastern capital was set up at Luoyang. The basic institutional foundation on which the Tang built—centralized authority, the civil service examination system, and the like—had been laid by the Sui. Li Shimin had pushed his father to depose Yangdi of the Sui and seize the throne. When the Tang came into existence, rebellions were still going on throughout the empire. Li Shimin fought them for seven years, and by 624 north China had been reconquered. The south was brought into line more through ameliorative, less harsh measures.

624. Li Shimin ambushed and eliminated his two elder brothers, had himself named crown prince, and two years later compelled his father to step down.

626–49. During his reign, **Taizong** (Li Shimin) continued to amass military victories, defeating the Turks in Mongolia (630), who made him their Great Khan, and the Tibetans in two campaigns (639–40, 647–48). His two assaults on Korea (640s) both failed. He was equally famous as a civil ruler. Primarily of a Confucian bent, he tolerated both Daoism and Buddhism, and even received a Nestorian Christian (p. 101) visitor by the name of A-luo-ben in the capital (635). He subsequently gave the Nestorians freedom of movement and sanctioned the construction of their church in Chang'an (638).

641. A Chinese princess was married to the king of Tibet, Srong-tsan-sgam-po, and helped convert Tibet to Buddhism.

649–83. Taizong's son, **Gaozong** (b. 628), fell in love with one of his father's many concubines, **WU ZETIAN** (624–705), and she became his empress, the **EMPRESS WU.** Gaozong made her effective regent (660) as his reign began to decline.

683. Empress Wu put two of her sons in succession on the throne as puppet rulers.

690–705. Empress Wu took the throne herself, the only woman in Chinese history ever to rule in her own name as emperor, and changed the dynastic name to **Zhou.** Contrary to a long tradition of Chinese criticism, she ruled capably in domestic and foreign affairs alike.

712–56. The **reign of XUANZONG** (b. 685) was a period of brilliant artistic and literary efflorescence. He came to the throne a capable ruler, cleaned up the court and the civil administration, and abolished capital punishment. He was a great patron of the arts. He founded the **Hanlin Academy** (725) to further the cause of scholarship, and he established schools in every prefecture and district in the empire (738). Later in his reign he foundered, allowing many nefarious sorts into his entourage and relinquishing control over his border armies to local generals, often non-Chinese. He all but ignored government. His bountiful love for the beautiful **Yang Guifei** (719–56) is remembered in poetry of this age. One general by the name of **AN LUSHAN** (705–57), a man of mixed non-Chinese origin with control over the strongest armies in the north, was adopted by her.

732. Manichaeism, the dualistic religion originally from Persia that posited an ongoing battle between equal forces of good and evil, was condemned as perverse doctrine, but it was permitted to Persians and Tokharians, who had introduced it (694, 719) and who were favored for their competence in astronomy and astrology.

738. The title of king was conferred on a Tai ruler who united six principalities as **Nanzhao** (730). After two disastrous attempts at conquest (750, 754), the Tang made peace (789–94), leaving the Nanzhao kings with full autonomy. In the 9th century, their forces were repelled from Chengdu (829, 874) and from Hanoi (863).

747. Gao Xianzhi (d. 755) led an army against Tibet. In another attack (750), Gao's forces crossed the Pamirs and the Hindukush before meeting defeat (751) at the Talas River near Samarkand, at the hands of the Arabs and western Turks (p. 112).

755–63. The Rebellion of An Lu-shan erupted following An's gaining control over three regional commanderies. The city of Luoyang was invaded and later (762–63) sacked, forcing Xuanzong and his entire court to flee to Sichuan (756–57). Yang Guifei was murdered by the royal guard en route, and Xuanzong abdicated in exile in favor of his son. In a surprise attack (763), the Tibetans sacked Chang'an. An Lu-shan was himself slain (757) by his own son, who was in turn slain by General **Shi Siming,** an ally rebel. There were widescale rebellions throughout the regional commanderies.

By the time the An Lu-shan Rebellion was finally quelled, the Tang militia and the equal-field land system (p. 150) were in ruins. To crush the rebels, the Tang court had hired Uighur armies, who had toppled the eastern Turks (744), and the Tang rebuilt itself relying heavily on Uighur support. From the early 9th century, eunuchs and other cliques at court effectively seized control of authority. Emperors Xianzong (r. 805–20) and Jingzong (r. 824–26) were both murdered by eunuchs, while Muzong (r. 820–24) and most emperors thereafter were installed by eunuchs.

840–46. The overthrow of the Uighur Empire by the Kirghiz and the Karluk led to the migration of many tribes from the Orkhon to the Tarim Basin, where they carved out a second Uighur Empire in which the Turkish language prevailed.

841–45. Under the **reign of Wuzong,** a man of Daoist predilections, Buddhists (along with Manicheans, Mazdeans, and Nestorians) were persecuted.

875–84. The **Rebellion of Huang Chao** (d. 884) began in Henan. When the rebels attacked Guangzhou (879), they murdered many thousands of Muslims, Christians, Manicheans (p. 100), and Jews. They occupied Chang'an (881), forcing the court to flee to Sichuan. Turkish armies helped the Tang crush the rebels.

903. Zhu Wen (852–914), a former ally of Huang Chao, took control over Chang'an, installed a boy emperor on the throne in Luoyang (904), and then seized the throne in his own name (907), ruling until his death seven years later.

907–60. The **FIVE DYNASTIES PERIOD** witnessed a succession of five short-lived states assuming imperial authority but scarcely ruling beyond the reach of the Yellow River Basin. These were basically military regimes with barely enough time to consolidate power.

907–23. Later Liang, founded by Zhu Wen, was based in Kaifeng.

923–34. Later Tang.

936–47. Later Jin.

947–51. Later Han.

951–60. Later Zhou.

There were as well ten successive regimes in central and south China. At the same time, the **Khitan** (in Chinese, Qitan) Empire formed to the northeast (905), and Yelü Abaoji (872–926) declared himself emperor (916). The Khitans were a Mongolian people living in southern Manchuria. When they aided the establishment of the Later Jin in Kaifeng, the Jin paid the Khitan tribute, though when the second Jin emperor refused to do so, the Khitans destroyed their erstwhile allies and took Kaifeng and northern China (946–47). They established their capital at Yanjing (present-day Beijing, 938), but later withdrew from northern China due the daunting task of ruling there. In 916 the Khitan established the **Liao dynasty,** which lasted until 1125.

b. POLITICAL, SOCIAL, AND CULTURAL PATTERNS

The **Tang government** built on the Sui foundations of recentralized administrative control. In addition to the armed forces and the censorate, **the administration was split into three parts: the Department of State Affairs, the Secretariat, and the Chancellery.** At the beginning of the dynasty, the highest officials of these three agencies met daily with the emperor to hammer out decisions of state. Prior to his accession to the throne, Li Shimin headed the Department of State Affairs. Imperial edicts had to go through both the Secretariat and the Chancellery, which thus served as a check on the autocratic control of the sovereign. The Department of State Affairs had six ministries under its aegis: personnel, revenues, rites, war, justice, and public works. The entire administrative organization of state was laid out in the *Tang liudian (Six Canons of the Tang)*, which was written under Xuanzong.

In 711 all prefectures in the empire were placed into one of 10 circuits, later (733) expanded to 15, and later yet to 20. These circuits in the Xuanzong reign of the mid-Tang were headed by regional commanders who held both civil and military authority. After the Rebellion of An Lu-shan, they became virtual satrapies, the bases for the Five Dynasties era that followed the Tang.

Personnel tapped for bureaucratic appointments came from a much wider group in the Tang than before; far more men (only men) sat for the **civil service examinations,** and only a small percentage passed them. As the examination system became the regularized route to government service, the importance of education, necessary to pass the exams, skyrocketed. This in turn caused the spread of education. **There were two national universities in the Tang period,** one in Chang'an and one in Luoyang. The student populations were dominated by the aristocracy and sons of officials; the education offered was geared to taking the examinations at the various levels. The two most important examinations tested one's literary skills and one's knowledge of the classics of antiquity. A standard appointment lasted for three years, after which time one reapplied to the Ministry of Personnel. While on duty, all officials were evaluated annually by higher officials. There were nine bureaucratic ranks attached to the level and importance of a position, and movement up the ladder depended on receiving good reports, the availability of openings, and good family background. The Tang system mixed aristocracy with meritocracy; the great families retained their prestige, but rising egalitarianism was creating more access to government for others. The Tang legal codes became the models for all of East Asia.

The **Tang militia system** also carried on from that of the Sui, but the Tang had professional career soldiers who tilled their own fields, a revered group in Tang times. There were 600 garrisons throughout the empire, mostly near Chang'an, Luoyang, and along the northern border. There was also a standing army, stationed in the capital, which served as an imperial bodyguard. It provided the base of the Tang fighting force into the 8th century. By 749 the militia system had effectively become defunct in the capital region, although it remained in force along the border areas; even it needed conscription, though, to keep troop strength up. Later in the dynasty, the state was compelled to rely on mercenaries hired in the regional commanderies, a background cause of both the Rebellion of An Lu-shan and the subsequent decentralization of power.

In **population,** the census of 753 (on the eve of the Rebellion of An Lu-shan) recorded a figure of 52,880,488. Eleven years later, the census of 764 (after the rebellion) gave a figure of 16,900,000. Although this figure is certainly too low, it does indicate a clear decline in population. Two-thirds of the population still lived in northern China until after the rebellion; from that point on, the population of the Yangzi Delta reached parity with the north. In the early 8th century, the 26 largest prefectures all had more than 500,000 people. Chang'an prefecture had 2 million, and Luoyang was in excess of 1 million. Chang'an in the mid-Tang was both the largest and the most cosmopolitan city in the world. There were 30 square miles within the city walls, divided into countless wards for specific uses, and boasting hundreds of temples.

Either in the late Tang or during the Five Dynasties period, the practice of **foot binding** began to spread. Young girls would be guided, usually by their mothers, to wrap their feet extremely tightly with pieces of cloth. These would then restrict the growth of the foot and keep it stylishly small and dainty, albeit at cost of great pain for the young women. The practice eventually spread to various social classes, although certain ethnic groups (such as the Hakka people) never practiced the custom.

The **equal-field land system** was in full force early in the Tang. Under this system, all families were allocated land by the state, and in return they paid a tripartite tax: a grain payment for land rent, a corvée labor assessment or payment in its stead, and payment of a set amount of cloth. This system held up through the middle of the Tang, despite inequities and favoritism, and helped the peasantry's state of affairs. Buddhist temples and monasteries acquired land without taxation. The tax reforms of 780 instituted by the official Yang Yan (727–81) aimed at saving the declining equal-field system. This created a new structure known as the **double-tax system** (paid in summer and fall): half was a household tax payable in cash, indicating the rise of monetary economy; and half was a land tax payable in grain. These measures brought stability to the national taxation system, although they did favor those with land. In fiscal administration, Liu Yan (715–80) rebuilt and oversaw the state's monopoly on salt, which brought the state considerable revenue before the double-tax reforms.

The variety of **religions** present in the Tang period was remarkable. It was an era of great development, particularly for **Buddhism.** After 16 years spent in India, the famed pilgrim XUANZANG (c. 596–664) returned to China in 645 with a large quantity of original Indian texts. He chronicled his travels and later headed a commission that translated 75 books in 1335 volumes, creating a system of consistent tran-

scription from Sanskrit. He introduced the scholastic doctrine of Vasubandhu, that the visual universe is only a mental image. The **Pure Land sect** of Buddhism enjoyed popular favor for the next 70 years. Based on texts translated earlier, it taught direct salvation through faith in Amitabha and the repeated invocation of his name. The **Chan sect** was developed by **Huineng** (638–713), the sixth patriarch. It continued to acquire followers, especially as disorder grew in the later years of the dynasty, offering refuge through introspective contemplation.

As early as 607, the Sui had ordered all Buddhist sects to pay homage to the throne and had tried to regulate entry into the Buddhist and Daoist clergy. These practices were continued by the Tang, and Buddhism flourished through the Tang until the persecution of 841–45. Earlier, the great poet and prose writer **Han Yu** (786–824) had vilified Buddhism as a foreign, non-Chinese religion, as part of an effort to revive Confucianism. The persecutions of the 840s destroyed 4600 monasteries and 40,000 temples and shrines; 260,500 monks and nuns and 150,000 lay servants were returned to the tax rolls; and huge amounts of land were likewise returned to the tax registers. The attacks were not so much inspired by anti-Buddhist sentiments as they were an effort to regain state control in that sector, and they reveal that even at a time when there was an allegedly weak center, the state had the capacity to carry out such a repression.

Daoism also prospered in the Tang. It was, in many ways, reorganized on the Buddhist model, gaining imperial patronage. It was argued that since Laozi was said to have been surnamed Li and so was the Tang imperial house, he must have been the ancestor of the Tang emperors. A large compendium of Daoist writings, the **Daozang,** was prepared along Buddhist lines.

In **historical scholarship, Liu Zhiji** (661–721) composed the *Shitong (Generalities on History),* the world's first work explicitly in the field of historiography. **Du You** (735–812) devoted 36 years (766–801) to the compilation of the *Tongdian (Comprehensive Canon),* a historical encyclopedia with 200 sections, covering a panoply of topics from high antiquity through the year 755. In literature, **fiction** began to develop, especially toward the end of the Tang, in the form of the *chuanji* (strange tales), short stories that appeared in numerous anthologies. They were composed in the literary language, and only later appeared in the colloquial. Han Yu urged a return to a simple "ancient style," and he spawned a movement that produced much *chuanji* writing. The Tang was the golden age for Chinese poetry. The **Quan Tang shi** (*Complete Tang Poems*) includes 48,900 poems written by 2300 authors, mostly officials or candidates (and hence intellectuals). Regulated verse, prose poems, songs, and other forms flourished. During the Xuanzong reign lived three of the greatest poets: **Wang Wei** (699–759), **Li Bo** (701–62), and **Du Fu** (712–70). In the 9th century, in addition to Han Yu, **Bo Juyi** (772–846) was a high official and a brilliant poet and essayist.

In the field of art, **Wu Daoyuan** (c. 700–60) painted murals in temples and monasteries and was also a fine figure painter. **Li Sixun** (651–716) and the poet Wang Wei created two of the first and most influential landscape styles. Tang-period pottery was resplendent with new colors in soft lead glazes, applied with new technical versatility. The first true porcelain with high-fired feldspathic glaze probably dates from about this time.

Yixing (c. 725), a Buddhist astronomer, invented the first known clock escapement. The Buddhists also enlarged the seal and produced wood blocks for **printing on paper,** although the oldest extant datable text is from 8th-century Korea. During the Five Dynasties era, **a complete, 130-volume set of the classics was first printed** (932–53), with commentaries, from wood blocks—a cheap substitute for stone engraving. The volumes were printed in the Later Tang capital of Luoyang by **Feng Dao** (882–954), who had seen the process in Sichuan. The text used was that of the stone inscription of 836–41.

2. CHINA, 960–1521

a. PERIODIZATION AND EVENTS

The period from 960 through 1521 covers two great Chinese dynasties, the Song and the first part of the Ming, and the first complete conquest of China by the Mongols.

960–1279. The **SONG DYNASTY** marked a shift away from the earlier aristocratic traditions toward a more open, meritocratic state and society. Reflections of this development can be found in scholarship, literature, thought, and art. Some have identified the Song with the advent of modernity or early modernity; others have seen it as a Chinese counterpart to the European Renaissance; still others have seen fit not to name it as such. It was an age marked by humanism and a turning inward, an age of less cosmopolitanism than in the Tang, an age that saw Confucianism eclipse Buddhism and Daoism. The Song was the only major dynasty in Chinese history not to be overthrown by rebellion from within. The first half of the dynasty is usually distinguished as the **Northern Song** (960–1127), when the capital was at Kaifeng, then called Bianjing or Bianliang.

960–76. The **reign of Zhao Kuangyin** (b. 927), or (Song) Taizu, who founded the Song dynasty, brought a measure of order and unity to the empire. Zhao had been a general in the Later Zhou state, the last of the Five Dynasties. Zhao and the Song were immediately beset by problems on the Song state's borders: from the Khitan Liao to the northeast; the Tangut kingdom of **Xixia**, a confederation of Tibetan tribes in the northwest; and separatist kingdoms in the south. Through expansion of the civil service examination system, Zhao began a process of increasing civil control over the military and of ensuring that all civil officials were beholden to the center. This also served to centralize the authority of the imperial institution.

963–75. Through continued campaigns against various regimes in the south, the Song brought those peoples under Chinese control. Exceptions were An-nam, which secured its independence, and the Nanzhao kingdom and Wuyue, which were not attacked.

976–97. The **reign of Taizong** (b. 939) completed the program of reunifying the empire (979), except for the 16 northern prefectures that were seized earlier by the Khitan and held despite several attacks against them (979, 986).

1004. An invasion by the Khitan reached the Yellow River area near Kaifeng. The invaders were appeased with an annual tribute payment in silver and silk, which was increased in 1042.

1006. Granaries for emergency relief were established in every prefecture.

1040–44. War was begun by the Xixia, but there was no discernible victor. To gain peace, the Song agreed to pay an annual tribute of silver and silk. Subsequent efforts (1069, 1081–82) by the Chinese failed to halt continued trouble from the Xixia.

By the year 1100, the **population** of China probably neared 100 million, having surpassed the Tang's highest figure of 60 million some time in the middle of the 11th century. The introduction of new seeds from Southeast Asia and advances in technology for both industry and agriculture helped fuel this growth. The **cities** of Song China became complex urban networks, and **commerce** flourished as it had never before. The spread of printing served to bring literacy and education to a much wider segment of the populace than had earlier been the case, and the old Chinese aristocracy effectively lost all hold on Chinese politics, education, and government. The military, from the Taizu and Taizong reigns forward, was permanently placed at a social level beneath civil positions.

1043–44. Fan Zhongyan (989–1052) proposed a ten-point program of reform. Abuses through the course of the prosperous 11th century, especially in the countryside, brought rural misery and the depletion of the central treasury. Fan sought to bring better men into government and to concentrate on local government.

1069–73. WANG ANSHI (1021–86) attempted to implement a program of radical reforms, his famous **New Laws** (Xinfa) with the full confidence of **Emperor Shenzong** (r. 1068–85) and in the face of the bitter opposition of more conservative statesmen. These reforms included the following. Through a **financial bureau** (1069), he cut the budget by

40 percent and raised salaries, in an effort to make honesty feasible for ordinary officials. To avoid excessive transport costs and to control prices, he empowered the chief transport officer to accept taxes in cash or kind, to sell from the granaries, and to buy from the cheapest markets. To protect poor farmers further against usurers and monopolists, loans of cash or grain were offered in the spring against crop estimates to be repaid in the fall with an interest of 2 percent monthly (moderate for China at the time). Ambitious officials forced these loans on merchants and others who did not want them. Objections to both the principles and the administration of these measures, which were accompanied by a considerable centralization of power and credit in state hands and by disregard for precedent, led to numerous resignations and the transfer of many of the best officials, whose help might have made them successful. **Conscript militia** were organized (1070) and trained for police purposes and national defense. The standing army of well over a million less-than-efficient men was gradually cut in half. By 1076 the militia, volunteer guards, and border bowmen numbered more than 7 million men. **Cash assessments** graded in proportion to property were substituted (1071) for compulsory public services, such as corvée. The exemption for officials, clergy, and small families was reduced by half. **State banking** and barter offices were opened (1072), first at the capital and later in every prefecture, with the object of controlling prices for popular benefit. Among those most fervently opposed to Wang were the brilliant writer **Ouyang Xiu** (1007–72), the great historian **Sima Guang** (1019–86), and the most famous poet of the day, **Su Shi, or Su Dongpo** (1037–1101).

1074–85. Wang's reform program was continued, despite claims of excessive cash levies and other abuses, until the death of Shenzong.

1086–93. During the **Yuanyou reign**, the hostile empress dowager recalled Sima Guang, Su Shi, and others to court to rescind the entire Wang reform package. The anti-Wang group became known as the Yuanyou clique.

1100–25. During the **reign of Emperor Huizong** (1082–1135), anti-Wang forces were dismissed. **Cai Jing** (1047–1126), his prime minister, proscribed (1102) the work of 98 of the Yuanyou partisans.

1114. **Jurchen tribes,** forerunners of the Manchus who would later conquer China, defeated the Khitans in Manchuria.

1115. Wangyan Aguda (1068–1123), the Jurchen leader, declared himself emperor of the **JIN DYNASTY.** Having long received Jurchen tribute, the Song assumed amicable ties with them, sending allied armies (1118) to attack the Khitans from the south. A Song-Jurchen treaty of 1122 led to a joint attack on the Khitans. The Liao dynasty was finally destroyed in 1125, when the Jurchens took Beijing. They returned the 16 Chinese prefectures held for many years by the Khitans.

1125. The Jurchens attacked the Song and were at the door of Kaifeng. Huizong abdicated in favor of his son. The capital finally surrendered, and the Song were forced to send tribute. When they failed to keep the provisions of the treaty, the Jurchens invaded Kaifeng again, took Huizong and his son captive along with the entire court, and moved their own capital to Beijing.

1127–1279. The **SOUTHERN SONG DYNASTY** effectively began when a younger prince, **Gaozong** (1107–87, r. 1127–62), was placed on an itinerant throne in Nanjing and later Hangzhou. Only from 1130, when Chinese forces began to defeat the Jurchens, did the Southern Song acquire some sense of security; the capital was firmly established in Hangzhou in 1138. A peace treaty with the Jin was signed in 1142, with the Chinese accepting vassal status to the Jin, relinquishing everything north of the Jinling Mountains and the Huai River to the Jurchens, and paying annual tribute. Debates continued throughout the Southern Song about the feasibility of reconquering the north, dating from the somewhat earlier discord between General Yue Fei (1103–41) and Prime Minister Qin Gui (1090–1155).

b. POLITICAL, SOCIAL, AND CULTURAL PATTERNS

The Tang-Song transition in Chinese **government** was marked by two seemingly contradictory trends, rising absolutism in the imperial institution and growing, institutionalized meritocracy through regularization of the civil service examination system. In earlier eras, the emperor had ruled on behalf of a collegial body of aristocrats, among whom his family might not even have been the highest ranking. With the disappearance of the aristocracy, the Song needed able men to staff its bureaucracy, and it turned to the male population at large. Thus status in the civil service became a function of knowledge, acquired through long hours of rigorous study of the Confucian canon. Concomitant with the centralizing trend in imperial authority was the trend to consolidate as much power as possible in fewer and fewer hands directly answerable to the emperor.

In **military affairs,** the Song seems to have learned an important lesson from the experience of the Tang and earlier states. Centralization of authority in all military matters served to eliminate regional military power. Civil authority came to gain control over the military. With this trend came a sharp decline in the prestige of military careers.

Local society in the Song, below the level of centrally appointed local officials, remained largely in the hands of local leaders. All the normal functions of government—taxation, jurisprudence, social order, and the like—were the responsibility of local elites. Even as the population grew, though, the number of local political units—counties and prefectures—remained roughly the same; they were simply much more heavily populated. In addition there was rapid **commercialization** and **urbanization** as Song cities grew and new ones came into existence. After the Jurchens conquered the north, the Southern Song's population was roughly 60 million. Approximately 2 million people lived within the walls of the Southern Song capital of Hangzhou, which **Marco Polo** (1254–1324) visited and described shortly after the fall of the Song.

Printing, invented earlier, developed rapidly in the Song into a vibrant industry. The entire Buddhist canon, or **Tripitaka** *(Three Baskets)*, was printed (972–83), a collection of 1521 texts on 130,000 pages, and it was reprinted many times thereafter.

Chinese **agriculture** from the late Tang through the Northern Song underwent a major transformation. As a larger percentage of the population moved into the south, the production of rice rapidly grew in importance. It required new kinds of irrigation techniques and intensive labor. Introduced from Champa in Southeast Asia was a strain of rice that ripened more quickly and thus enabled Chinese farmers to plant a second crop after their rice was harvested. In some areas, three crops could be grown and harvested in one season.

The **world of thought** in the Song period witnessed the decline of Buddhism and the rise of Neo-Confucianism. This occurred in tandem with the wide extension and regularization of the examination system, the education that was necessary to pass the exams, and the explosion in printing. Following the model of the Buddhist *Tripitaka*, the *Daozang*, a Daoist *Tripitaka*, was published (1019). The major Buddhist sects that remained vital after the Song were the Pure Land and Chan sects, the latter splitting into a number of subdivisions of its own.

Neo-Confucianism, although datable to trends in the late Tang, took off as a movement in the Northern Song. It was an attempt to go back to the original sources of Chinese tradition, before the coming of Buddhism, to create a Chinese tradition with answers to the metaphysical and cosmic questions that until then only Buddhism and Daoism had been able to answer. It reinterpreted many of the texts thought to date from the Zhou period in new ways that could present secular counterparts to a range of ideas to which Buddhism appealed. It was closely tied to state service through its great stress on education and on making officials as sagacious as possible.

The principal figures in what became known as the Cheng-Zhu school of Neo-Confucianism were: **Zhou Dunyi** (1017–73), who worked extensively on explicating the "Supreme Ultimate" (from the *Yijing*), describing a "diagram" of it that linked man to nature and the cosmos; **Shao Yong** (1011–77) who studied the *Yijing* as well; **Zhang Zai** (1020–77), who is often seen as an early materialist because of his belief in the omnipresence in the universe of *qi* (ether, or material stuff); and the Cheng brothers, **Cheng Hao** (1032–85), who worked further in the field of metaphysics, and **Cheng Yi** (1033–1108), who was principally responsible for identifying four texts—*Mencius, The Great Learning, The Doctrine of the Mean,* and *The Analects of Confucius*—

as the most essential and which became the basis of Neo-Confucian education thereafter. The final synthesis of the Cheng-Zhu system (also known as *lixue*, or the learning of principle) was the work of **ZHU XI** (1130–1200). Zhu was a great polymath who wrote on education, philosophy, the family, and the state, and commentaries on all the classics. The **Four Books** identified by Cheng Yi were later almost always published with Zhu's interlinear commentaries. Although Zhu was not overly successful in his lifetime and his work was subject to imperial ban shortly before his death, his posthumous influence would be unmatched from his time forward. His major work, **Jinsi lu** *(Reflections on Things at Hand)*, was compiled in 1175–76 and was intended as a guide to Cheng-Zhu doctrines and the classics.

The principal opponent of the Cheng-Zhu school in the Song period was **Lu Jiuyuan** (1139–93), who argued that human nature was a function of one's mind or heart. Hence, the school he spawned was known as *xinxue*, or learning of the mind-and-heart. Zhu Xi had not denied the mind as much as Lu Jiuyuan did deny the importance of principle. Lu's school was developed much further by more influential and prolific scholars during the Ming dynasty.

Historical scholarship similarly made great advances in the Song era. The "rediscovery" of the ancient classical texts required extensive explanations and commentaries of those works. **Ouyang Xiu** (1007–72) was a prominent statesman and an advocate of composition in the ancient style of writing; he prepared the *New History of the Tang Dynasty* and was famed for his prose style. **Sima Guang** (1019–86), well known for his political opposition to Wang Anshi, spent 19 years compiling his comprehensive history of China from 404 B.C.E. into the first reign of the Song dynasty, the **Zizhi tongjian** *(Comprehensive Mirror for Aid in Government)*, which was presented to the emperor in 1084. Other forms of historical writing also prospered in the Southern Song, among them local histories and gazetteers. Several major encyclopedias were also completed in the Song, including *Wenxian tongkao,* by Ma Duanlin (c. 1250–1325); *Taiping yulan* (983); *Cefu yuangui* (1013); and *Yuhai,* by Wang Yinglin (1223–96).

Poetry was produced in great quantity by Song writers, but not of a quality as great as that of the Tang. There were exceptions, like the poems of the great Su Shi, who was also a master **calligrapher.** Another exceptional poet was **Lu You** (1125–1209), an author of patriotic poetry.

Painting developed dramatically in the Song. Emperor Huizong, himself an able painter, was an active patron of the arts. He founded the Imperial Academy of Painting. The Northern Song was a golden age for **landscape painting,** with compositions of immense size and great detail rendered in monochrome and color on long rolls or broad panels of silk. **Guo Xi** (1020–90?) not only painted landscapes but also wrote on the theory of painting. **Mi Fei,** or **Mi Fu** (1051–1107), scarcely used lines in his work, building mountains and forests from graded accumulations of ink; he was also a master calligrapher, as was **Huang Tingjian** (1045–1105). All considered themselves "amateur" or "literati" painters rather than specialized artists. In the Southern Song, painters most often reproduced the misty landscapes of the Hangzhou area. **Ma Yuan** (1190–1224), **Xia Gui** (c. 1180–1230), and their school placed special emphasis on economy of line and the representation of mists and clouds. Religious painters continued to produce work as well; **Chen Rong** (c. 1235–55) ranks as China's greatest painter of dragons.

During the Song period, **ceramics** became objects of both art and everyday use in the household. Local areas became known for their pottery, usually in conjunction with state-sponsored kilns. Song ceramicists mastered the technique of high-fired glazes.

Although tea was cited as early as the 3rd century as a substitute for wine, **tea drinking** became prominent in the Northern Song.

Exactly when the **principle of magnetic polarity,** known to the Chinese at least from the 1st century C.E., was first employed in the invention of the mariner's compass with the floating needle has not been firmly established. However, Chinese ships were outfitted with them in the Song period. The compass is mentioned by Chinese writers in the 12th century. The volume of **maritime commerce** swelled greatly as Arabs in the 9th and 10th centuries entered into competition with Persians at Guangzhou (Canton) and Quanzhou, and later at Hangzhou as well.

c. THE MONGOL PERIOD

1190s. THE MONGOLS in central Asia formed a new empire under **Temujin** (1167–1227), who rapidly expanded the empire by use of strategy and his military machine, employing discipline, extraordinary mobility (especially on horseback), espionage, terror, and superior siege material.

1194. The **Yellow River** shifted direction and flowed south of the Shandong Peninsula until 1853.

1206. Temujin was proclaimed CHINGGIS KHAN "ruler of the world") at the Mongolian capital of Karakorum.

1210. The Mongols under Chinggis Khan first attacked the northern border of the Jin, seizing Beijing in 1215 and the Xixia state two years later. The Jin were driven south to the Yellow River (1211–22).

1215. Yelü Chucai (1189–1243), Sinified descendant of the royal Khitan house, became an adviser to Chinggis. He allegedly convinced his lord that it might not be a wise idea to depopulate northern China and make it into a grazing land for the migrating herds; instead he taught the Mongols how to collect agricultural taxes by time-tested Chinese methods.

1219–21. Mongol armies conquered the Turkish empire of Khwarazm (p. 119).

1227. The Xixia was finally destroyed with a massacre at Ningxia. At the end of his life, Chinggis divided his massive empire into four khanates and bequeathed them to his immediate descendants: the Kipchak khanate (Golden Horde) to **Batu** (1207–55); the Chaghadai khanate (the former Kara-Khitai empire) to Chaghadai (d. 1242); the Great Khan to Ögödei (1186–1241); and the Persian khanate (the Ilkhanids) to Tului (1192–1232).

1232. Using the same policy ill-advisedly used with the Jurchens against the Liao, the Song allied with the Mongols to defeat the Jin. Kaifeng was taken. Within two years, the Jin were overwhelmed, but in 1235 the Mongols began to attack the Song, taking Sichuan in 1236–38.

1241. After stunning Mongol military successes in Russia in the late 1230s, two Mongol armies entered central Europe and the Balkans and were poised on attacks to Western Christendom. Mongol horsemen were outside the walls of Vienna when news arrived that the Great Khan had died. As per Mongol custom, the armies withdrew to Karakorum so that the generals could participate in the election of a new Great Khan, Chinggis's son Ögödei.

1251–59. After discord and several short-reigning Great Khans, **Möngke** (1208–59) was elected by the Mongolian diet. His brother **Khubilai** (1214–94) led armies on attacks to the south and west, defeating Nanzhao (1252–53). Khubilai's forces laid siege to the city of Wuhan (1259), but again news of the death of the Great Khan forced the Mongols to withdraw to Karakorum.

1254. Möngke, the son of a Nestorian woman and Tului, told William of Rubruck (c. 1220–c. 1293), envoy of Louis IX of France, that religions were like the fingers of one hand.

1260. After having unilaterally moved the capital to Shangdu (Coleridge's Xanadu) during the squabbling over the succession, Khubilai (r. 1260–94) was elected Great Khan.

1260–1368. The **YUAN DYNASTY** was effectively founded for Mongol rule in China when Khubilai became Great Khan. The dynastic name was adopted in 1271.

1267. Khubilai transferred the winter capital to Yanjing, where he constructed Khanbalig, modern Beijing. He had an astronomical observa-

THE SUCCESSORS OF CHINGGIS KHAN (1227–1336)

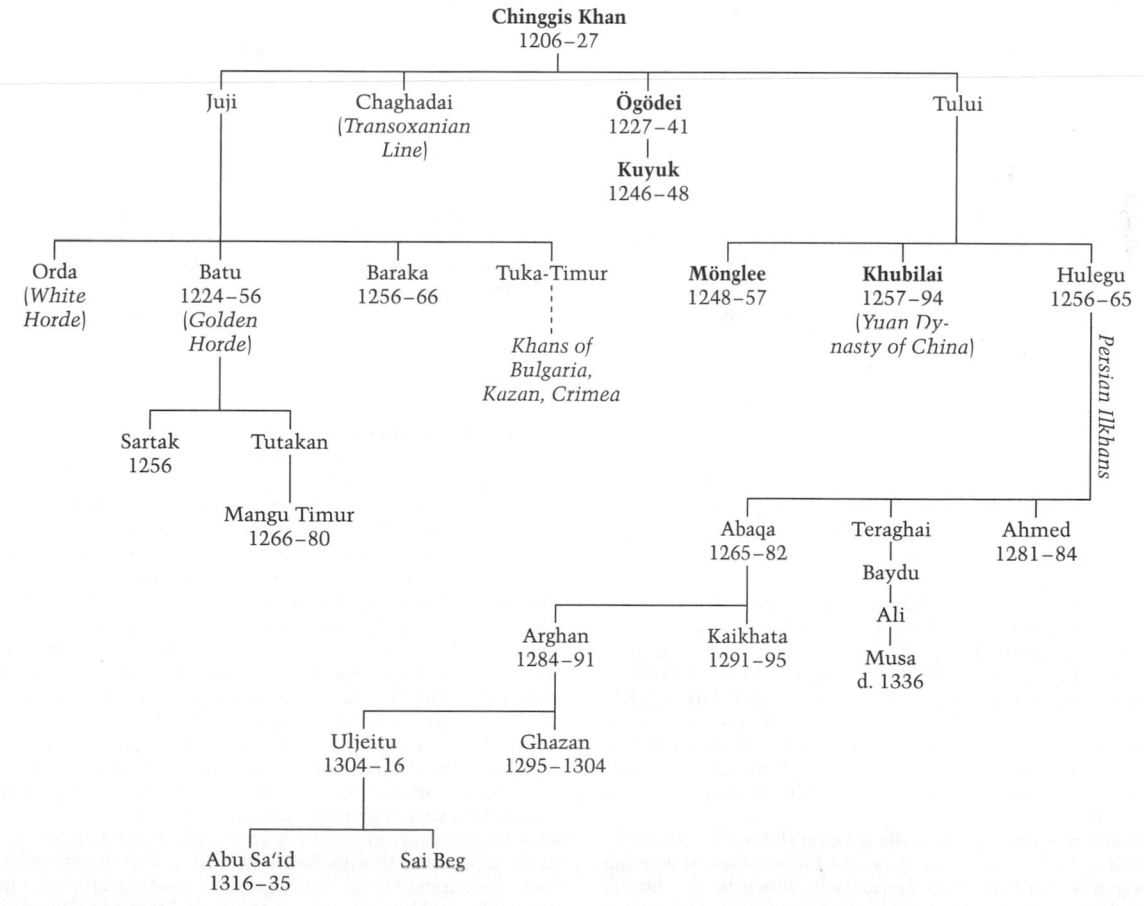

tory (1279) built on the city wall, wherein were installed bronze instruments cast by Guo Shoujing (1231–1316).

1273. After four and a half years of desperate and brilliant fighting, the last two strongholds of the Song against the Mongols, Xiangyang and Fancheng—both walled cities in modern Hubei Province—fell. Explosives were used by both sides as weaponry in the fighting, perhaps for the first time in history. Hangzhou was captured in 1276, Guangzhou the following year. The Song fleet carrying the last pretender to the throne was destroyed in 1279.

1274, 1281. Disastrous Mongol attacks on Japan both ended in defeat for Khubilai. Naval forces set off from Korea and the lower Yangzi Delta—numbering all told in excess of 150,000 men and 4500 vessels. They were repulsed by well-prepared Japanese defenders and by the ill effects of a typhoon (the "divine wind," or *kamikaze*, of popular Japanese belief), which destroyed their ships.

1282–83. An army sent by sea from South China against Champa seized the capital but was forced to withdraw because of local conditions. There were further assaults on Southeast Asia: An-nam and Champa (1285, 1287–88), Burma (1287), and Java (1292–93).

1315. Despite misgivings, the civil service examinations were reinstated, but with built-in safeguards discriminating in favor of Mongols and their non-Han supporters and against the Han Chinese.

The Mongol **military system** was based on a stadial structure of units—in garrisons spread around the country—that was much more centralized than the tribal divisions of the Khitans and Jurchens. The elite imperial bodyguard, or *kesig,* was staffed by Mongols of noble blood and served at the capital.

Unlike any Chinese experience before or since, the Yuan dynasty was but one part of a much larger Mongol Empire. In China, the empire adopted many of the trappings of Chinese state and society. Khubilai's court was patterned after those of his Chinese predecessors, and he and his successors adopted Chinese-style reign titles. The Yuan **government** followed the Jurchens' example of consolidating the central government's bureaus into one big department. It retained the censorate but used primarily Mongols, and it built up a powerful, independent military-affairs bureau. There was a four-tiered system for bureaucratic preference: Mongols came first, followed by non-Chinese ethnicities, northern Chinese, and finally southern Chinese. The same quotas applied to examination candidates, and since some 75 percent of the population was southern Chinese, the Chinese were greatly disfavored.

The **population** of China was hit hard by the Mongol invasions and wars. The depopulation of the north and migrations to the south were so great that during the Yuan, at least 75 percent of the Chinese population lived in the south.

Agriculture remained central to the national **economy** during the Yuan. The introduction of sorghum helped revitalize and repopulate northern China. The Mongols seized land for their own use—such as in support of their armed forces—and often forced Chinese peasants into servitude on that land. Imperial inspectors annually examined crops and the food supply with a view to purchasing when stocks were ample, for storage against famine. The Grand Canal was rebuilt (1289–92) from the former Song capital at Hangzhou, a bustling metropolis in Yuan times, to the Huai River, and it was extended farther north to the outskirts of Beijing. Imperial roads were improved, and postal relays of 200,000 horses were established. Charitable relief was organized (1260) for scholars, orphans, and the sick, for whom hospitals were provided (1271).

Paper money, first used in the Tang and carried on in Song and Jin times, was continued under the Mongols. When the issuance of paper currency was suggested to Ögödei (1236), Yelü Chucai secured limitation to a value of 100,000 ounces of silver. Khubilai's Muslim financier kept annual issues at an average of 511,400 ounces (1260–69). His successor increased distributions (1276–82) to 10 million ounces each year. After the murder of that financier, inflation ensued until a Uighur replacement reduced the rate of printing to 5 million ounces (1290–91). All printing was discontinued in 1311, as the dynasty's fortunes were on the wane.

In **thought and religion,** the Mongols were on the whole extremely tolerant, and a wide host of religious groups built houses of worship in Yuan-era cities. Chinggis was particularly drawn to the Daoist monk Changchun (1148–1227). Other Great Khans favored **Nestorian**

Christianity (p. 101). The patriarch of Baghdad created an archbishopric of Beijing (1275), and churches were built elsewhere in Chinese cities. **Mar Yabalaha,** a pilgrim who traveled from Beijing to Jerusalem, was elected patriarch (1281), and he sent his companion Rabban Sauna to Rome and France. He negotiated with Pope Nicholas IV an entente between the Nestorian and Roman churches. **John of Montecorvino** (1246?–1328) was the first of several Roman missionaries to China. He is said to have baptized 5,000 converts and was named by the pope archbishop of Beijing (1307). Khubilai, for his part, favored Tibetan Lamaist Buddhism; **'Phags-pa** (1238–80), the man who devised a script for the Mongolian language, was appointed Khubilai's imperial mentor and governor of Tibet, and later became a close confidante of the Great Khan. In the 1250s, Möngke Khan opened a series of debates at court between Buddhists and Daoists, with Confucians in attendance. In the end, Daoism lost out, and it even suffered some repression under Khubilai, but it was never stamped out. The Cheng-Zhu school of Neo-Confucianism became very popular through the private academies throughout China during the Yuan.

Marco Polo (p. 218), the Venetian merchant who traveled widely in China (his "Cathay," from Khitai) between 1275 and 1292 in the service of Khubilai, has been the source of Western fascination from his own day forward. His *Description of the World* was immediately translated into other languages of Europe, and it became an instant success. He left rich portraits of Hangzhou (Quinsai), Quanzhou (Zayton), and elsewhere in the Mongol Empire; in his time, Quanzhou was the busiest deep-sea port in the world.

In the realm of **science,** the itineraries of Zhao Rugua (1225) imply in the precision of their bearings the use of a compass needle mounted on a dry pivot. Meteorology developed to the extent that by the 14th century the correlation between climatic changes and the sunspot cycle was known.

During the Mongol period, **new genres of literature** appeared. Yuan drama, or *zaju,* developed in north China, combining music and acting, drawing on stories of older vintages. Vernacular fiction, perhaps begun at the end of the Song, developed further in the Yuan. It took several centuries for these genres to gain respectability.

Zhao Mengfu (1254–1322) was considered one of the great masters of **calligraphy** in his day; he was as highly praised for his **paintings** of horses and other livestock that were prominent in the Mongol economy. **Qian Xuan** (1235–c. 1290) was perhaps the finest painter of flowers and insects. Yuan-period painters drew inspiration from the Northern Song artist Guo Xi, turning to a sharper, more expressionistic view of nature. Yuan **porcelain** reveals in its arabesques and its technique of writing in cobalt blue directly on clear white paste the debt of Chinese potters to Persian models. From these also is derived the Byzantine form of cloisonné.

d. THE EARLY MING

The **MING DYNASTY** was founded by **ZHU YUANZHANG** (b. 1328, r. 1368–98), who reigned as Taizu, the second time a peasant had risen all the way to emperor. Owing to poverty, Taizu had become a Buddhist monk, but later he turned to rebellion against the Mongols, leading a huge band of followers in south China to conquer the north, the first time the country was reunited through conquest from the south (the only other time was by the Chinese Communists). He first took Nanjing (1356) and set up a government there, and then he expanded to force the Mongols out of Beijing (1368), Manchuria (1387), and Xinjiang (1388), as well as through western and southwestern China. He kept Nanjing as his capital. He changed the practice of reign titles, so that there would be only one per reign, his being **Hongwu.** He furthered the two earlier trends toward the centralization of power and the opening of the avenues of access to bureaucratic advancement. The early Ming launched expansion drives on the borders and overseas, while working to minimize contacts between Chinese and foreigners; these restrictions abated by the mid-15th century.

1402–24. After a short second reign, Taizu's son **Chengzu,** or **Yongle** (b. 1360), seized the throne. He proceeded to have Beijing rebuilt and to have the Grand Canal refurbished to handle traffic in supplies and foodstuffs, and he then ordered the capital moved to Beijing (1421). He began the process of building up the Grand Secretariat. Yongle led a series of military missions into Mongolia (1410, 1414, 1422–24); he sent expeditions south against Dai Viet and annexed it (1406); and he tried to quell the coastal raiders known as "Japanese pirates," forcing Japan to accept tributary status.

1405. The death of **Timur I-Lang** (known in the West as Tamerlane, b. 1336) (p. 105) brought to an end an imminent military threat to the Ming from the east. Having risen to power in 1369, Timur had taken over the Chaghadai khanate, conquered the Kipchak khanate, and, with his capital in Samarkand, was in the process of rebuilding the Mongolian Empire.

1405–33. Zheng He (1371–1433), the eunuch Muslim admiral, was sent on a **series of seven naval expeditions to the Indian Ocean,** going as far as the east coast of Africa and bringing a number of regimes en route into vassalage status with respect to the Ming. The expeditions were discontinued for reasons still not well understood, although they never were seen in the same light as later European explorations to other continents. The voyages were extremely expensive, and the goods obtained in trade were ultimately not that dearly desired back in China.

1449. Emperor Yingzong (b. 1427, r. 1435–49, 1457–64) was captured in battle by the chief of the Oirat, a new Mongol confederation of four tribes. He was released the next year and recovered the throne seven years later.

1520–21. The Portuguese, who under Albuquerque (1453–1515) had seized Malacca (1511), sent Thomé Pires to Beijing. The Portuguese established a permanent settlement at Macao (1557).

1521. Death of the Chengde emperor Wu-tsung (r. 1506–21). The Jiajing emperor (r. 1522–66) assumed the throne the following year.

(To p. 376)

3. KOREA, 540–918

(From p. 55)

This period began with Korea divided into three contending kingdoms at war with one another: Silla, Paekche, and Koguryŏ. When the Sui dynasty reunified China (589), it attempted to incorporate Korea militarily into the new empire, but was unsuccessful. The Silla state eventually reunited the kingdoms into a single state on the Korean Peninsula (668), and this lasted for two and a half centuries before breaking up again. The major Sinitic schools of thought and religion continued to penetrate Korean society and culture, and many Koreans actually traveled to China to study with great teachers at the source, returning home to sponsor new schools, reform programs, doctrines, and the like.

540–76. During the **reign of King Chinhŭng,** Silla's expansion progressed. Silla launched an attack, together with Paekche (551), and took the entire Han River Basin area. The Paekche king Sŏng (r. 523–54) moved the capital from Ungjin to Sabi and then attacked Silla, thus ending an alliance of 121 years. Silla won, thus opening a window for sea contact with southern China across the Yellow Sea.

562. The small Kaya kingdom at the southern tip of the Korean Peninsula was finished off by Silla.

589. The Sui reunified China and confronted the Tujue from the northern steppe (p. 148). Koguryŏ allied with the Tujue against the Sui; Paekche, Koguryŏ's erstwhile ally, linked up with the Wa state in Japan; Silla joined forces with the Sui.

598. Koguryŏ attacked across the Liao River. Wendi of the Sui responded militarily but was beaten back.

612. Yangdi of the Sui sent a huge force of more than one million against Koguryŏ, but was defeated and suffered many casualties.

618. The Sui fell after several more attempts to conquer Koguryŏ, which then prepared for Tang invasions.

Chinese political institutions, Buddhism, Confucianism, and the Chinese writing system were imported to all three of the principal Korean kingdoms, in spite of changing conditions of war and peace with various Chinese states.

The **Three Kingdoms period** was an age of **strong, centralized aristocracy** in all three states. The best known was Silla's "bone-rank" system, which implied a hereditary bloodline; it had a detailed differentiation of social strata, with stratified privileges. Bureaucratic administrations were also uniformly structured around the aristocracies in all three kingdoms. The highest aristocrats controlled politics, often in collegial bodies such as Silla's Council of Nobles. Although the states were each subdivided into administrative units (districts), centralized authority remained in the capitals. The military was also organized under each state's king.

Gradually the idea emerged that the king owned all the **land,** even though aristocrats held immense landed estates; others were given land for meritorious deeds. The states theoretically had control over the farming populace, which paid **taxes** and performed **corvée labor.**

In **culture,** the Three Kingdoms witnessed a wide usage of Chinese writing, with various adaptations attempting to accommodate the Korean language, which is radically different in structure from Chinese.

The first **historical compilations** in, respectively, Koguryŏ, Paekche, and Silla were: *Sinjip (New Compilation)* by Yi Mun-jin (600); *Sŏgi (Documentary Records)* by Kohŭng (mid-4th century); and *Kuksa (History of the Nation)* by Kŏch'ilbu (545). None of these is now extant, but they were said to have later been used by **Kim Pu-sik** (1075–1171) in his magnum opus, ***Samguk sagi** (History of the Three Kingdoms).* All three states pushed Confucianism as a way to preserve the aristocratic orders.

Buddhism was adopted in all three states as a part of the Chinese cultural package. It was probably seen by the elite as supportive of the aristocratic state structure. High monks acquired political clout as royal advisers.

640s. Paekche attacked Silla (early 640s), and Silla sought out Chinese help. Two Tang expeditions against Koguryŏ (645–47) ended in defeat for the Chinese.

654. King Muyŏl (r. 654–61) seized the throne, commencing a trend toward a more autocratic Silla royal institution, at the expense of the aristocracy.

660. Tang armies attacked Paekche, took the capital at Sabi, forced the surrender of King Ŭija (r. 641–60), and destroyed the state of Paekche.

667. Tang and Silla joined forces to attack Koguryŏ, already weakened by war and internecine dissension. Koguryŏ was defeated the following year.

668–918. Unified Silla reunited the Korean Peninsula. The Tang wanted to retain control over the terrain of the former Koguryŏ and set up commanderies there, some headed by Koreans. Silla became apprehensive about Tang objectives. Silla took Sabi from the Chinese (671), and with it control over Paekche. After 676 the Tang dynasty accepted Silla as master over the peninsula, though much of the Manchurian territory under former Koguryŏ control did not fall into the hands of Unified Silla. The capital was placed at Kyŏngju, where the Silla aristocracy settled.

681–91. During the **reign of King Sinmun,** the governmental and military administrations were reorganized, further curtailing the prerogatives of the aristocracy and strengthening the king. A new local-government system was implemented. After the announcement of five "secondary capitals" (685), aristocrats from conquered states were transferred to them. From 687, the aristocracy was allowed to extract only grain from farmers on lands allocated to them, a measure further tightening central state control. Aristocrats still managed to amass great fortunes and often large numbers of slaves. The army was brought under the direct command of the throne, and garrisons were established at various locales.

698–926. Former Koguryŏ terrain in Manchuria came under the control of the state of **Parhae** (or **Bohai** in Chinese), founded by a former Koguryŏ general who first proclaimed a state of Chin, renamed Parhae in 713. It was made up of Koguryŏ remnants and several Tungusic peoples (largely Malgal) living in central Manchuria (the present Heilongjiang Province in China). Parhae was on tense terms with the Tang to the west and with Silla to the south. In 733 Silla and the Tang allied against

Parhae, which sought ties with the Tujue to the north and with Japan. Parhae managed to spread into northeastern Manchuria under King Mu (r. 719–37) and continued to expand into the mid-9th century. Its government was modeled after the Tang, with three chancelleries and six ministries. Its capital was placed at Sanggyŏng and patterned after Chang'an. To encourage the introduction of Chinese culture, Parhae sent students to Tang China; some took and passed the civil service examinations there. Parhae was conquered (926) by the Khitan, the Mongolian people who were soon to establish their own state, the Liao dynasty. Parhae was the last state of Korean origin to control Manchuria.

885. Ch'oe Ch'i-wŏn (b. 858) returned from China 21 years after he had left Silla. He had passed the Chinese civil service examinations, taken offices, written memorials, and earned a name for himself. On returning, he called for a similar process in Korea, but all of his reform proposals were rejected.

889. The government instituted a forced tax levy in the countryside, but the peasantry was already being taxed by castle lords, a newly emerging force of regionally powerful families who were sapping the center's hold on local villages and tax revenues. The result was great social destabilization.

891. The first of many rebellions. Between the late 9th and early 10th centuries, Unified Silla was broken up by rebellions into a brief **Later Three Kingdoms** period.

An ally of the Tang dynasty, Unified Silla imported much of China's administrative practice, as well as its culture, through books and art. Korean students and monks studied in Tang China and brought back Buddhism, Confucianism, and other aspects of Chinese culture.

Buddhism became extremely important in Unified Silla. Many monks traveled to study at holy places in China. The monk Hyech'o (b. 704) also went on to India and wrote an account of his travels. Several new sects came to Korea; especially popular was Hwaŏm (Huayan in Chinese), brought to Korea by the monk **Ŭisang** (625–702), who had studied under the great Zhiyi in China. **Wŏnhyo** (617–86), a popular religious teacher, taught an eclectic Buddhist synthesis and was opposed to sectarianism. The Pure Land sect, with its less intellectual bent and its stress on devotion leading to rebirth in the Western Paradise, was the most popular sect among commoners. Late in Unified Silla, Sŏn Buddhism (Zen in Japanese) became popular, especially among local gentry families.

Confucianism also flourished. A **National Confucian College** was founded (682), and portraits of Confucius and his disciples were brought from China and placed there (717). Around 750 it was renamed the National Confucian University, and its entire curriculum centered around Chinese texts. Entrance was limited to the higher aristocratic ranks. An examination system was begun (788) for bureaucratic appointments, indicating the beginning of an effort to prize learning, not just bone-rank, and this worked in tandem with the throne's attempt to sap aristocratic privileges. Late in the era, Confucianism was invoked as the doctrine for political reform by many, like Ch'oe Ch'i-wŏn, who had been to China.

Woodblock printing was developed especially for the production and dissemination of Buddhist scriptures and Confucian texts. A copy of a sutra (dated 751) found at Muyŏng-t'ap (Pagoda That Casts No Shadow) is the oldest printed work in the world.

Various **poetic forms** continued to develop in Unified Silla, often stressing Buddhist themes. The Pulguk Temple, a major complex of Buddhist art, was built (751) in Kyŏngju at the order of the chief minister; he also ordered construction that year of Sŏkkuram, manmade stone Buddhist grottoes like those in China.

Unified Silla traded extensively with both Tang China and Japan. Over time, Korean settlements cropped up in Shandong and Jiangsu, with Silla offices instituted to run the affairs of local Koreans. When the Japanese monk Ennin (794–864) traveled to China, he found some 250 natives of Silla living at a temple in Shandong (839, 845).

The years of war leading to unification under Silla had brought misery and poverty to the commoners, many of whom had to become slaves to aristocratic houses or government bureaus. A village system with headmen was set up and used for census and taxation purposes as well as for local administration. In the late 9th century, the **population** of Kyŏngju was given as 178,936 households and 35 immense aristocratic mansions.

4. KOREA, 918–1392

a. MAJOR EVENTS

918–1392. The **KORYŎ STATE** was founded by **Wang Kŏn** (b. 877, r. 918–43), who through military and civil capacities had become king of Later Koguryŏ (Later Three Kingdoms era). He renamed it Koryŏ.

934–36. Koryŏ began the process of reunification of the Later Three Kingdoms by defeating Later Paekche. Silla surrendered in 935. Wang Kŏn became **King T'aejo.** He treated the former Silla aristocrats well, and many of them became Koryŏ bureaucrats, even as he set out to dismantle the bone-rank system. He established good relations with the castle lords in the local areas.

942. King T'aejo responded to peaceful overtures from the Khitans by snubbing them, as he considered them barbarians.

949–75. During the **reign of King Kwangjong,** order was revived in the face of the rebellions following T'aejo's death. Kwangjong began a military push toward the Yalu River, in the Khitans' direction.

958. Kwangjong implemented a **civil service examination** to bring Confucian-minded men into civil office and to build a new bureaucratic apparatus.

981–97. During **Sŏngjong's reign,** efforts continued to create a new aristocratic order with aristocrats drawn from many different great families, not just high-born royal clans. They came to control the politics and government under Koryŏ, with its capital at Kaesŏng. Measures were adopted to guarantee that social status would be hereditary, though there were many cases of social mobility in civil and military realms.

983–1076. Koryŏ governmental administration took shape, with three principal agencies and six boards modeled after those of Tang China.

992. A **National University** was established in the capital under Sŏngjong, who was particularly attentive to spreading education among the larger populace.

993. The Khitans crossed the Yalu and invaded Koryŏ (993), but were talked into withdrawing by an adept Koryŏ diplomat. A second invasion early in the 11th century led to the occupation of Kaesŏng, but the Khitans again withdrew when their supply lines grew dangerously stretched. The third and final Khitan attack (1018) was vigorously repulsed at the great loss of Khitan life.

1087. Printing of the **Koryŏ Tripitaka,** an edition of the Buddhist canon printed from wood blocks, was completed. It was begun early in the century in supplication to forestall the Khitan attacks.

1107. The Jurchens presented the next threat to Koryŏ, but the latter carried out a preemptive strike. As the Jurchens pressed south, conquering the Khitans (1125) and the Northern Song, great pressure was brought to bear on Koryŏ. Koryŏ leaders decided to accept Jurchen demands for Koryŏ to recognize Jurchen suzerainty over their land, thus avoiding military conflict. Unlike the Khitans and the Jurchen, Koryŏ looked up to Song China and wanted amicable relations. As it was pressured by Khitan and Jurchen forces in turn, Song looked to Koryŏ for military support, but Koryŏ refused.

1126. The first of a series of coups, this one inspired by Yi Cha-gyŏm, erupted among the aristocrats.

1170. A coup by military officers deposed Ŭijong (r. 1164–70), unleashing a quarter-century of chaos at the center.

1172. The first of many popular uprisings erupted, lasting into the early 13th century and indicating that all was not well at the foundations of the Koryŏ social order.

1196. Ch'oe Ch'ung-hŏn (1149–1219) restored order in the central government through both civil and military dictatorship. Over the next 16 years, he deposed two kings and put four on the Koryŏ throne, all power remaining solidly in his family's hands. He also fought to end independent Buddhist military authority, and succeeded.

1231. The Mongols invaded Koryŏ and met tough fighting. The next year the Koryŏ court was moved off the coast to Kanghwa Island, because it was known that the Mongols feared waterborne assaults. Mongol armies continued their attacks for three decades, and the Koryŏ court remained in hiding. When the Mongols eventually conquered the Jurchens, they looked to Koryŏ as a point from which to launch attacks on the Southern Song and Japan.

1234. Cast-metal type, a form of movable type, was first mentioned in the printing of a Buddhist work. This was probably the earliest use of movable type in the world.

1258. In a move calculated to overturn the powerful Ch'oe clan, civil officials came to a peaceful agreement with the Mongols and real power was returned to the king.

1270. The capital was eventually returned to Kaesŏng. Through subsequent intermarriage, Koryŏ kings became merely a branch of the Mongol imperial family, their &ldquoènts" in Korea; Koryŏ crown princes characteristically lived in Beijing, effectively as hostages. Koryŏ kings adopted Mongol customs, dress, and names.

1274, 1281. The **two Mongol attempts to conquer Japan** were both launched with the forced assistance of Koryŏ, and both failed. Koryŏ had to build the ships and provide supplies for the armies.

1351–74. During the **reign of King Kongmin**, with the Mongols in retreat and their aristocratic supporters discredited, reforms were begun to regularize a scholar-official class of appointees to the bureaucracy, selected on the basis of examinations to test scholarly knowledge.

1368. Cotton seeds were transported to Korea from the Mongol Empire in China, and cotton was subsequently grown for the production of cloth in Korea.

With the accession of the Ming dynasty in China, King Kongmin quickly moved to establish amicable contacts.

1388. Shortly after the withdrawal of the Mongols and Koryŏ's support of the Ming, the latter moved to establish a commandery on Koryŏ soil. Korean armies set out to attack, but one commander, **Yi Sŏnggye** (1339–98), refused to go along and took control of the government himself. The next year he placed a Koryŏ king on the throne and began wide-ranging land reform, supported by the rising scholar-official class. Land reform entailed a thorough cadastral survey (1390); all land registers were abolished, and all lands reverted to the state. Two years later, Koryŏ fell, to be replaced when Yi Sŏnggye assumed the throne of the **Yi dynasty.**

b. POLITICAL, SOCIAL, AND CULTURAL PATTERNS

In **military** matters, Koryŏ achieved power through military conquest of the other Later Three Kingdoms and was confronted with problems from the Khitans soon after taking power. However, the rise of aristocratic rule was premised on the superiority of civil to military affairs, and thus military men were given lower social and economic status in Koryŏ. Denigration of the military grew severe under King Ŭijong. Military officers rebelled (1170), deposed Ŭijong, placed a puppet king on the throne, and wiped out numerous civil officials. Bloody infighting ensued.

Land was granted by quality and allocated (998) in accordance with an official's bureaucratic rank, thus providing said official's salary. When the official died, his land reverted to the state, following the theory that all land belonged to the king. The state managed the land and collected rents. Higher officials earned special stipends of land in addition. In fact, there was private land as well. During the 13th century, large portions of land were given to the Mongols. With the reforms at the end of Koryŏ, and the reversion of all private and public lands to state control, the powerful families found their economic underpinnings demolished.

The Koryŏ **taxation system** was tripartite in structure, again much like Tang China. The peasants who worked the land paid a rent based on a percentage of crop yield, they paid a tribute tax in cloth, and all able-bodied men were obliged to serve in corvée labor annually. Below the peasantry was a slave class, some state-owned and some in private hands. To relieve the harsh lives of the farming population and prevent large-scale vacating of lands and roving bands of landless peasants, the state instituted a number of measures, such as "ever-normal granaries" (as in China).

The Koryŏ **civil service examinations** were theoretically open to all men, with several exceptions, but in fact only the elite sat for them. There were two types of examinations, one on composition and one on the Chinese classics; the latter tended to be more important. Since, unlike earlier, access to government office was opened to a wide number of elite families, the civil service examinations became the means of controlling entrance into the bureaucracy.

Confucianism, in the political mold it had taken in China as working together with the Legalist state, proved desirable to Koryŏ aristocrats and thus developed rapidly in the Koryŏ era. Private academies, the primary avenue for the education of aristocrats, flourished. **Ch'oe Ch'ung** (984–1068), known as the Confucius of Korea, ran one such academy. At the same time, state schools went into decline. Under Yejong (r. 1103–22) and Injong (r. 1122–46), efforts were made to stem this tide. Confucianism stressed moral cultivation and social order. The rise of the scholar-official class in late Koryŏ went hand in glove with the rising popularity of Neo-Confucianism, especially with its stress on moral character as the foundation of the state.

Buddhism was not repudiated but was supplemented by Confucianism's worldly rationalism. The Ch'ŏnt'ae (Tiantai in Chinese) sect became very popular. Tax-exempt Buddhist monasteries became exceedingly wealthy, and monks armed themselves to defend their wealth. The Chogye sect of Sŏn Buddhism, a tradition native to Korea, developed following the Ch'oe coup; it taught that sudden enlightenment must be followed by gradual cultivation of the mind.

In **painting,** little remains from the Koryŏ period, though here Chinese models seem not to have been dominant. In the late Koryŏ, a trend similar to one in Song China emerged: that of the literati (nonprofessional) painter. Calligraphy also flourished. Koryŏ **celadon** ware showed Song influence, but it is considered even better than its Chinese models.

Several major works of **historical scholarship** date from this era, including ***Samguk sagi*** (*History of the Three Kingdoms*) by **Kim Pu-sik** (1075–1151), a thoroughly Confucian work written in the Chinese annalistic style; and ***Samguk yusa*** (*Memorabilia of the Three Kingdoms*) by the Buddhist monk **Iryŏn** (1206–89), which traced Korean history back to the legendary Tan'gun. *(To p. 380)*

5. JAPAN, 552–1185

(From p. 56)

552. It is traditionally believed that in this year **Buddhism** was introduced to Yamato Japan from Paekche. Although there were probably Buddhist converts already in Japan at the time, at this point Buddhism began to play a major role in Japanese history and to stimulate the continued influx of mainland culture by way of Paekche. Supported by the powerful **Soga clan** and strengthened by the recent arrival of Buddhist monks from Korea, Buddhism made headway at court, but a temporary proscription of it was enacted by the Nakatomi and Mononobe clans, political rivals of the Soga. It was soon restored and embraced by Emperor Yōmei (r. 587–88) shortly before his death.

562. Silla drove Japan out of Kaya, ending Japan's long influence over a portion of the Korean Peninsula.

587. The Soga crushed their rivals in a short civil war, thereby establishing their political supremacy and the right of Buddhism to an unhampered development in Japan.

592. Soga Umako (d. 626), having decided not to occupy the throne himself and enthroning children of Soga women instead, had one of them, Emperor Suchun (r. 588–92), assassinated.

593–628. Soga Umako placed his niece **Empress Suiko** on the Yamato throne, the first officially recognized empress. Suiko was served as regent by **Crown Prince Shōtoku** (574–624), who worked vigorously to import continental civilization to Japan. Under his aegis, the foundations for a Chinese-style state and Buddhist religion were laid that would last for several centuries. During this period, such famous Buddhist temples as Shitennōji (593), Hōkōji (or Asukadera, 588–96) and Hōryūuji (607?) were built.

603. A "cap ranks" *(kan'i)* system of bureaucratic rankings at court was adopted by Shōtoku that closely followed comparable systems from 6th-century Koguryŏ and Paekche.

604. Prince Shōtoku issued his **Seventeen-Article Constitution** (or Seventeen Injunctions), a list of moral injunctions imbued with the spirit of Confucian ethics and mainland theories of centralized political rule. They also bore clear Buddhist influences, indicating an awareness of Buddhism's philosophical and ethical importance. In this same year, the court adopted the Chinese-style calendar.

607. Ono no Imoko, the first official envoy from the Yamato government, was dispatched to the Sui court, and relations with China were thus established. Another embassy followed in 608, a third in 614, and there were many more over the course of the next three centuries, with the subsequent Tang dynasty. Since Japanese students, scholars, and monks accompanied the envoys to China—during the Tang, the embassies tended to be extremely large—and sometimes remained there for prolonged periods of study, these embassies were a very important factor in the importation of Chinese civilization to Japan.

630. The first embassy to the Tang.

643. Prince Yamashiro no Ōe, heir of Prince Shōtoku, was forced to commit suicide by Soga no Iruka (d. 645), son of Emishi (d. 645), the kingmaker of the period. This was the culmination of a power struggle, following the death of Shōtoku in 622, between the Soga and Nakatomi clans.

645. The **Downfall of the Soga** in a coup led by Nakatomi no Kamatari (614–69) and the future Emperor Tenchi (r. 668–71); the Nakatomi were henceforth given the surname **Fujiwara.** The coup was supported by the Sinophilic elements at court who encouraged continued reforms along mainland models and continued ties with China and Korea. There were five missions between 653 and 669 alone.

646–784. A period of imitation of continental civilization commenced with the **Taika Reforms,** an edict outlining general principles of national reorganization promulgated in 646, but only over the course of several decades were the reforms put into practice. The major features of the new system included: (1) nationalization of the land, (2) adoption of the Tang land distribution and tax systems, (3) reorganization of local government and other measures designed to increase the authority of the central government and maximize tax revenues, and (4) reorganization of the central government. The principles and many of the details of the reforms were borrowed directly from China, but in Japan, dominated as it was by a hereditary aristocracy, **it proved extremely difficult to carry them out fully,** and from the start they were **modified in practice.**

Although land was nationalized in theory, in actuality the **large hereditary estates of clan chiefs** were returned to them as salary for their official position and rank. The land was to be periodically divided among the tillers as determined by census, and **uniform taxes** were to be levied on all alike: a land tax paid in rice, corvée (often commuted at a fixed rate into a textile tax), and an excise levied on produce rather than rice. Closely patterned after the Chinese model, this system worked poorly in Japan. Powerful families and institutions frequently deprived the public domain of tax-yielding lands, and the peasants, impoverished by taxes, were often anxious to transfer themselves and their land from the taxpaying public domain to the care of privately owned manors. As a result, the history of economic development over the next few centuries was largely the story of **land returning to private control** and the emergence of **large tax-free estates** owned by the court nobility and great religious institutions.

Improved means of communication aided the **centralization of government and tax collection,** but while provincial governmental officials were to be the central appointees, in practice **lower leaders retained their supremacy by occupying the local posts.** It soon became the accepted custom for high provincial officials to remain at the capital and to delegate their powers to underlings in the provinces. An essential and permanent feature of the reforms was the **reorganization and elaboration of the central government.** A department of religion and a great council of state were established as two parallel organs. Below the latter were eight ministries, with many smaller bureaus below them. This organization proved to be too ponderous, however. Moreover, with the collapse of economic supports resulting from the growth of tax-free estates, this elaborate organism was effectively starved. In adopting the Chinese form of government, the Japanese

made one significant change: **the official hierarchy of Japan remained a hereditary aristocracy.** With rare exceptions, there was little opportunity for the able or learned to rise very high. In the period from 701 to 777, **seven more missions** were sent to China.

During this period, the **classic era of Japanese culture,** poetry and prose in Chinese were composed, and native Japanese poetry enjoyed an early flowering. In the preceding century, Japanese artists had been imitating continental styles, and now the art of Tang China found fertile soil in Japan, which produced many of the greatest extant examples of East Asian architecture, sculpture, painting, and applied arts of that time.

663. The Japanese withdrew from Korea after the defeat of a Japanese force, sent to the aid of Paekche, by a combined army from China and Silla (662). Thus ended the first period of Japanese continental expansion. The fall of Paekche (663) and of Koguryŏ (668) (p. 155) left Silla supreme on the peninsula and resulted in a great migration of Korean refugees into Japan.

670. The first Japanese census was taken through a system of household registers.

697. The **Empress Jitō** (r. 686–97) abdicated in favor of her grandson, **Monmu** (r. 697–707), in the first instance in Japan of the accession of a minor and the second of the abdication of a ruler; both practices would soon become the rule.

702. The **Taihō Code,** a new civil and penal legal code, was promulgated, probably the first complete codification of the laws embodied in the reforms that began in 646. These laws, together with their revision of 718, the **Yōrō Code** (not enforced until 757), have come down to us only through later legal commentaries, *Ryō no gige* (833) and *Ryō no shūge* (920). A supplementary code, *Engi shiki (Procedures of the Engi Era),* was completed in 928.

710–84. The **Nara Period** began with the establishment of the capital at **Heijō** (or Nara), the first permanent capital of Japan, which was laid out on the model of Chang'an, the Tang capital, except that it had no city walls. The Nara period ended with the move of the capital to Nagaoka.

712. The *Kojiki (Record of Ancient Matters),* Japan's oldest book, recorded the history of the imperial line from its mythical origins; it was written in Chinese characters (used to a large extent phonetically to represent Japanese words).

720. The *Nihon shoki* (or *Nihongi, Chronicles of Japan),* a more detailed history of Japan, was compiled. It was continued to 887 by five other official histories, which together constituted the *Rikkokushi (Six National Histories).*

724–49. Emperor Shōmu's reign, and the years when he dominated the court as a retired emperor (749–56), marked the height of Nara culture.

737. The deaths of the four grandsons of Kamatari delayed for several decades the complete domination of the imperial court by the Fujiwara clan.

741. Government temples were ordered erected in each province.

752. The dedication of the **Great Buddha** at Nara marked the completion of Shōmu's most cherished project. The 53-foot bronze figure of the Buddha Rushana (in Sanskrit, Vaitocana) and the large hall built to house it were massive undertakings for the Japanese court, evidence of the great Buddhist fervor of the time. Many of the objects used in the dedication service, together with Shōmu's personal belongings, form the basis of the collection of 8th-century furniture and art preserved at the imperial treasury in Nara (Shōsōin, begun in 756).

Shortly before the erection of the Great Buddha, the famous monk **Gyōki** (668–749) was said to have propagated the concept that Buddhism and Shinto were two aspects of the same faith. Such beliefs served as justification for the growing amalgamation of the two religions, which was to lead by the 12th century to the development of Dual Shinto, in which Shinto gods were considered to be manifestations of Buddhist deities.

754. The Chinese Buddhist monk **Ganjin** (in Chinese, Jianzhen, 688–763), after five unsuccessful attempts to reach Japan, finally arrived in Nara, where he set up the first ordination platform and firmly established the **Ritsu sect** (in Sanskrit, Vinaya), which stressed discipline over doctrine. This sect and five others formed the **Nara sects,** the oldest sectarian division of Japanese Buddhism. The other five were: **Sanron** (Madhyamika), said to have been introduced in 625; **Hossō** (Dharmalaksana), brought from China by Dōshō (629–700); **Kegon**

(Avatamsaka), which was largely responsible for the cult of Rushana, the universal and omnipresent Buddha; **Kusha** (Abhidharmakosa); and **Jōjitsu** (Satyasiddhi). The last two may not have existed as independent religious bodies in Japan.

759. The *Manyōshū (Collection of 10,000 Leaves)*, an anthology of more than 4,500 poems composed largely by court nobility between 687 and 759, was compiled shortly after this date, followed in later centuries by similar works. In 751 the *Kaifusō (Fond Recollections of Poetry)*, an anthology of 120 poems, had been completed, and was similarly followed by like works.

764. A clash for power between **Fujiwara no Nakamaro** (706–64), the leading statesman during Junnin's reign (758–64), and Dōkyō (d. 772), the favorite monk of retired Empress Kōken (r. 749–58), led to the death of Nakamaro, the exile of Junnin and his subsequent assassination, and the reascension to the throne of Kōken as Empress Shōtoku (r. 764–70).

764–70. Dōkyō was all-powerful during Shōtoku's reign and even aspired to the throne himself. Strong opposition and the empress's death led to his downfall. For almost nine centuries thereafter, no woman occupied the throne.

718–806. The reign of the energetic **Kanmu** witnessed the conquest of much of northern Honshū in a prolonged border struggle with the Ainu. After several initial failures, the natives of this region, both Ainu and Japanese frontiersmen, were brought under central control by Sakanoue Tamuramaro (d. 811). His campaigns concluded centuries of slow advance into Ainu territory.

794. Kanmu moved the capital from Nagaoka to **Heian,** the modern Kyoto, where it remained until 1868. Among the reasons (still unclear) for his abandoning of Nara for Nagaoka in 784 were possibly the desire to make a new political and economic start, the desire to escape the influence of the powerful Nara monasteries; and the superior location of Nagaoka (and, later, Kyoto), which had better water access to the sea. The reasons for the sudden removal of the capital ten years later from Nagaoka to Kyoto, a few miles further inland, are still more obscure, but it may have been connected with Kanmu's fear that the first site had incurred the curse of certain deities. The establishing of the capital at Kyoto marked the beginning of the Heian period.

794–1185. The **Heian period** encompassed nearly four centuries marked by few violent upheavals, in which the transition from an era of imitating of China to the subsequent feudalism of the Kamakura period was evident. The centuries were characterized by an increasingly rarefied court society, ever more divorced from political and economic realities; the gradual decline and collapse of the economic and political systems borrowed from China; the growth of tax-free manors; the slow emergence of a new military class in the provinces; the full glory and subsequent decline of the Fujiwara family; the appearance and development of the Buddhist sects that would dominate much of Japanese religious history; a firmer understanding of the imported Chinese civilization and a greater ability to synthesize it with native traditions and beliefs, or to modify it to fit the distinctive needs of Japan; a resultant growing cultural independence from China; and the reappearance of more distinctly Japanese art and literature.

800–816. New offices appeared in the central government that were to affect profoundly the whole administration. These included the *kageyushi* (audit board, 790), which in time usurped the prerogatives of the original audit and revenue offices; the *kurōdo-dokoro* (bureau of archivists, 810), which gradually attained control of palace affairs and became the organ for issuing imperial decrees; and the *kebiishi chō* (police commission, 816), which in time became the primary law enforcement organ of the state and eventually created, outside the official codes, its own code of customary law.

805. The **Tendai sect** of Buddhism was founded by **Saichō** (Dengyō Daishi, 767–822), and the following year (806) the **Shingon sect** was founded by **Kūkai** (Kōbō Daishi, 774–835). These were the two leading sects of Heian Buddhism. Both monks accompanied the eleventh embassy to Tang China in 804. Saichō returned the next year to found his sect, named after Mt. Tiantai in China. The syncretic, inclusive nature of the philosophy of Tendai appealed to many Japanese, and its central monastery, Enryakuji, founded by Saichō on Mt. Hiei, overlooking Kyoto, became the center from which sprang most of the later significant movements in Japanese Buddhism. Kūkai returned from China in 806, bringing with him the Shingon or Tantric sect, a late esoteric

and mystical form of Indian Buddhism. Because of his charismatic personality and the powerful appeal of Shingon to popular beliefs at the time, the new sect won considerable support among the populace, and the Kongōbuji monastery on Mt. Kōya, which Kūkai founded (816), became one of the great centers of Buddhism. Tendai and Shingon seem to have appealed to more native strains that did the Nara sects, and the Shingon sect in particular furthered the union of Buddhism and Shinto.

838. The twelfth and **final embassy to the Tang** was dispatched. When in 894 Sugawara no Michizane (845–903) was appointed to be the next envoy, he persuaded the court to discontinue the practice on the grounds that China was in chaos and was no longer able to teach Japan. Although some unofficial intercourse continued between the two countries, this brought to an end three centuries of the greatest cultural borrowing from China and marked the beginning of a period in which distinctive Japanese traits increasingly asserted themselves in all phases of Japanese life.

858. The complete **domination of the Fujiwara clan** over the imperial family was achieved by Yoshifusa (804–72) when he became de facto regent of the child-emperor Seiwa (r. 858–76). In 866, after Seiwa had attained his majority, Yoshifusa assumed the title of regent (*sesshō*), becoming the first nonimperial regent. Seiwa was the first male adult emperor to have a regent. The typical inner-family control that the Fujiwara exercised over the emperors can be seen in the relationship that existed between Seiwa and Yoshifusa, for the latter was both the grandfather and father-in-law of the young ruler. It was the policy of the Fujiwara to have a young imperial grandson of the head of the clan occupy the throne and to have him abdicate early in favor of another child.

866–1160. The **Fujiwara period** was one characterized by the domination of the Fujiwara family.

880. Fujiwara Mototsune (836–91) became the first *kanpaku* (regent for an emperor who was no longer a minor), a post thereafter customarily held by the head of the clan when an adult emperor was on the throne, while the post of *sesshō* came to be reserved for the clan head in the time of a minor emperor.

889. The branch of the warrior **Taira clan** (or Heike), which was to rule Japan for part of the 12th century, was founded when a great-grandson of Kanmu was given this surname. The clan was established in 825 by another imperial prince. In 814 the rival military **clan of Minamoto** (or Genji) was founded by other members of the imperial clan, and in 961 the princely progenitor of the later Minamoto rulers received this surname. The descendants of such imperial princes, reduced to the ranks of commoners, often went to the provinces to seek their fortunes, and there some of them merged with the rising class of warriors that was soon to dominate the land.

891. Emperor Uda (r. 887–97, d. 931), who was not the son of a Fujiwara mother, made a determined effort to rule independently without Fujiwara influence and refused to appoint a new *kanpaku* after Mototsune's death. To further this end, he used the brilliant scholar **Sugawara no Michizane** as his confidential minister, but after Uda's abdication, Fujiwara Tokihira (871–909) managed to have Michizane removed to a provincial post, where he soon died. He was posthumously awarded many honors and deified, because it was believed that his vengeful spirit had caused certain calamities. Throughout his official career, Tokihira strove valiantly but in vain to stem the tide of governmental corruption and disintegration.

905. The *Kokinshū (Collection of Ancient and Modern Times)*, an anthology of more than 1,000 poems, was compiled by imperial order in a revival of interest in Japanese poetry. For more than a century, almost all literary effort and scholarship had been devoted to prose and poetry in Chinese, but **Ki no Tsurayuki** (869–946) wrote the preface to the *Kokinshū* in Japanese and followed it in 935 with a travel account, *Tosa nikki (Tosa Diary)*, also in Japanese. Within but a century, Japanese prose would rise to great heights of literary achievement. An important contributing factor to the **revival of Japanese literature** at this time was the fact that in the preceding century a simple syllabary for writing Japanese phonetically had been devised from the more complicated Chinese characters.

930. The offices of *sesshō* and *kanpaku* were revived after a lapse of four decades when **Fujiwara Tadahira** (880–949) became *sesshō* in 930 and *kanpaku* in 941.

935–41. Civil strife in the provinces broke out on an unprecedented scale, giving witness to the rise of a provincial military class. From 936 until his death in 941, former provincial official Fujiwara no Sumitomo controlled the Inland Sea as a pirate captain, while in eastern Japan an imperial scion, Taira no Masakado, after waging war on his relatives and neighbors, declared himself emperor (940) but was soon killed.

967–1068. Although **Emperor Murakami** (r. 947–67) did not appoint a successor to Tadahira in 949, after the former's demise, the successive heads of the Fujiwara clan occupied the posts of *sesshō* and *kanpaku* almost uninterruptedly for a full century. This was the heyday of the Fujiwara clan and the core of the Fujiwara period. Court life was ostentatious and extravagant. At the same time, petty jealousies and intrigues began to disrupt the Fujiwara; members of the provincial warrior class began to appear on the capital stage as petty military officers and came to be used by court nobles in their disputes; manors continued to grow apace, further limiting government resources; and the general collapse of the central government continued unabated.

985. The *Ōjō yōshū* (*Essentials of Salvation*), written by the monk **Genshin** (942–1017), gave literary expression to new religious currents that were emerging. A belief had sprung up that the age of *mappō* (the latter days of the Buddhist law), a period of degeneracy to come 2,000 years after the Buddha's death, had already commenced. There was a growing belief in the **Pure Land** (Jōdo), the Paradise of Amida (in Sanskrit, Amitābha), and in salvation through his benign intervention in favor of the believer and not only through one's own efforts, as earlier Buddhists had taught. Emphasis was increasingly placed on *nenbutsu*, the repetition of Amida's name or a simple Amidist formula. **Kūya** (903–72), an itinerant monk, was the first to articulate this new religious movement, and Genshin gave it sound literary formulation. The movement continued to develop, and in the 12th and 13th centuries it produced important new Buddhists sects.

995–1027. The rule of Fujiwara Michinaga (966–1027) over clan and state saw the zenith of clan power and some of the most brilliant decades of artistic and literary achievement of the epoch. Although he was never officially *kanpaku* and was *sesshō* for only a short period prior to his official retirement in 1017, he was perhaps the most powerful leader the Fujiwara produced. At this time, the classic prose of Japan reached its height in *Genji monogatari* (*The Tale of Genji*) by **Murasaki Shikibu** (978–c. 1016), a court lady, and in *Makura no sōshi* (*Pillow Book*), a shorter miscellany by another court lady, **Sei Shōnagon. Jōchō** (d. 1057), a famous Buddhist sculptor, was active, and Michinaga's successor, Yorimichi (992–1074; *sesshō* 1017–20, *kanpaku* 1020–68), built the Byōdōin, the outstanding architectural work remaining from the age.

1039. Armed Enryakuji monks invaded Kyoto to force their will on the government, but were driven off by Taira troops at Yorimichi's command. Such descents on the capital, known as "forceful appeals," were common during the 11th and later centuries and occasionally led to actual fighting. The turbulence of the monks, who fought fiercely among themselves as well as with the court, made it necessary for the court to appeal to the Taira and Minamoto for military aid, and the warrior clans consequently became more influential at court.

1051–62. In the **Earlier Nine Years War**, Minamoto Yoriyoshi, on imperial command, destroyed the **Abe,** a powerful military clan from northern Japan. He thus established the prestige of his branch of the Minamoto clan in eastern and northern Japan. Yoriyoshi's ancestors had already started the military renown of the house, and its status at court as "the claws and teeth of the Fujiwara" greatly increased its power.

1068–72. Emperor Gosanjō, not born of a Fujiwara mother, ruled directly without interference from the Fujiwara. Although the latter continued to occupy the posts of *sesshō* and *kanpaku*, they never again

gained full control of the government. Gosanjō established a records office *(kirokujo)* to examine title deeds of manors in an effort to check their growth, but in this attempt he was blocked by Fujiwara opposition.

1083–87. In the **Later Three Years War,** Minamoto Yoshiie (1039–1106) destroyed the Kiyowara family of northern Japan, thereby increasing Minamoto prestige in that region.

1086–1129. Emperor Shirakawa (r.1072–86) continued to rule as a retired emperor after his abdication, and, after 1096, as a priestly retired emperor. He built up a complete governmental organization of his own (*insei,* camera government), which was continued during much of the next two and a half centuries by other retired emperors and priestly retired emperors; however, after 1156 they lost control of the government to the warrior clans.

1129–56. Emperor Toba (r. 1107–23) ruled after Shirakawa's death as a priestly retired emperor.

1156. Civil war *(Hōgen no ran)* broke out between the reigning emperor, **Goshirakawa** (r. 1155–58), and the retired emperor, Sutoku (r. 1123–42). Both were supported by prominent members of the Fujiwara, Minamoto, and Taira clans. Goshirakawa's partisans, who included Minamoto no Yoshitomo (1123–60) and Taira no Kiyomori (1118–81), were victorious. Sutoku was exiled, and many of his supporters were executed, but this war brought no lasting peace.

1159–60. A second civil war *(Heiji no ran)* broke out, in which Minamoto no Yoshitomo and an adventurous young Fujiwara noble, Nobuyori (1133–60), gained temporary control of the capital in a successful coup, but they were soon crushed by the Taira.

1160–81. Taira no Kiyomori was left in control of the nation. The two civil wars of 1156 and 1159–60 had not been struggles for power between the court and the military clans, but the result was to make a single victorious warrior, backed by his personal troops, the dominant figure in Japanese politics. Goshirakawa, as retired emperor (1158–92), had some influence in the government, but in 1167 Kiyomori had himself appointed prime minister and gave important posts in the central and provincial governments to his clansmen. He married his daughters into both the imperial and Fujiwara families. In 1180 his infant grandson, Antoku, was put on the throne. Thus he attained the same hold over the imperial family that the Fujiwara had once had.

1175. The **Pure Land** (Jōdo) sect of Buddhism was founded by Hōnen Shōnin (1133–1212). It was the first of the Amidist sects, and this event marked the beginning of a great new sectarian movement.

1179. The **death of Shigemori** (b. 1138), Kiyomori's eldest son and perhaps the wisest of the Taira, removed a stabilizing check on Kiyomori, whose desire for more power was leading him to excesses that alienated the sympathies of the imperial family, the court nobility, and the Buddhist monasteries. The rapid adoption by Kiyomori and his family of the customs and mentality of court nobles also estranged many of the provincial supports of the clan.

1180. An abortive uprising against the Taira, led by an imperial prince and Minamoto Yorimasa (1106–80) together with certain monasteries, started a general uprising of the remnants of the Minamoto clan under the leadership of Yoshitomo's son, Yoritomo (1147–99), backed by Taira and other clansmen of eastern Japan.

1183. The Taira were driven out of Kyoto by Yoshinaka (1154–84), a cousin of Yoritomo. A long campaign in the Inland Sea region followed.

1185. The fighting culminated in the **Battle of Dan no ura,** at the western outlet of the Inland Sea, where Yoritomo's younger brother, Yoshitsune (1159–89), annihilated the Taira. The child-emperor, Antoku, whom the fleeing Taira had taken with them, died in the battle. The elimination of the Taira left Yoritomo, as head of the Minamoto, virtual ruler of the nation and marked the beginning of the first period of feudal rule in Japan.

6. JAPAN, 1185–1493

a. GENERAL CHARACTERISTICS

1185–1333. The Kamakura period. The outstanding feature of this era was the clear division between the now powerless civil and religious

government of the imperial court at Kyoto and the military government *(bakufu)* of the Minamoto established at Kamakura, near the clan estates in eastern Japan and away from the enervating influence of the court nobility. The transition from civil to feudal military rule had begun with the Taira and was not completed until centuries later, but it was in the Kamakura period that the most significant changes occurred, and the political and economic institutions of the next several centuries began to take shape.

1. FEUDALISM

The usurpation of the powers of the imperial court was largely unconscious and developed out of the economic and political conditions of the late Heian era. Primary factors in this evolution were: first, the wars of the 11th century, which had hastened the transfer of the prerogatives of ownership of the great aristocratic manors to military men who resided on them as bailiffs or wardens and who often had feudal ties with the warrior clans. The actual ownership of the estates usually remained unchanged, but ownership was robbed of most of its meaning by a complicated series of feudal rights *(shiki)*, which ranged from rights to cultivate the land to rights to the income from it. A second factor in the evolution of feudalism was the breakdown of the old centralized government and the need for self-defense. **Feudal military groups had grown up in the provinces** as a result, with their own "house laws" governing the conduct and relations of the members of that group. Moreover, a **feudal code of ethics had been developed that emphasized personal loyalty to a feudal lord rather than to a political ideal.** A third factor was Minamoto prestige, which had for a long time induced landed warriors to commend themselves and their lands to the Minamoto for protection. The victory over the Taira greatly increased Minamoto feudal authority, both through new additions of this sort and through the confiscation of the vast Taira lands. The single Minamoto feudal union had consequently grown so large that it now controlled the nation, and its *bakufu*, not the impotent Kyoto administration, was the real government of the land.

2. FOREIGN RELATIONS

For four and a half centuries, few Japanese monks had gone abroad, and foreign trade had been in the hands of the Koreans and Chinese, but in the Kamakura period the Japanese once more began to take part in foreign commerce. At the same time, Japanese pirates began to raid and plunder the coasts of Korea and China; in time they became a serious nuisance and occasionally even a menace to both countries.

3. ART

Kyoto, though it remained the scene of a colorful court life, was forced to share honors with Kamakura as a center of art and culture. Many Kyoto scholars moved to Kamakura to aid the civil administration of the *bakufu*, and the warrior class brought a new creative energy to art and literature, which were approaching sterility in the late Heian period. Significant artistic trends included a final great flowering of sculpture before its gradual demise in later centuries; the introduction from China of two new architectural styles known as the Chinese and the Indian styles, which came to blend with the traditional Japanese style; and the perfection of the narrative picture scroll *(emakimono)*.

4. LITERATURE

Significant literary trends included the increasing use of Japanese in preference to Chinese; the revival of native poetry in the *Shinkokinshū (New Kokinshū)*, an imperial anthology of 1205; and the popularity of historical military tales written in rhythmical prose. Among the most famous works were *Heike monogatari (Tale of the Heike)* by Kamo no Chōmei (1153–1216) and *Tsurezuregusa (Essays in Idleness)* by Yoshida Kenkō (1283–1350).

5. RELIGION

The Kamakura period was one of great religious and intellectual ferment. It witnessed the birth and development of new sects growing out of the popular movements of the late Heian. It saw the introduction of the **Zen** (in Sanskrit, Dhyana) sect from China and the growth of a military cult that glorified the sword, Spartan endurance, and loy-

alty. From these two elements was born the combination of the aesthetic and mystical penchants of the Zen monk with the qualities of the Kamakura warrior.

b. MAJOR EVENTS

1185–99. Minamoto no Yoritomo, as the effective military dictator, organized the new *bakufu* with the aid of Kyoto scholars like Ōe Hiromoto (1148–1225). He had already created, in 1180, the Samuraidokoro (Board of Retainers) to perform police duties and to control affairs of the warrior class. In 1184 he had established an administrative board, renamed the Mandokoro in 1191. In 1184 the Monchūjo (Board of Inquiry) had also been established as a final court of appeal. Impartial administration of justice characterized the rule of the Kamakura *bakufu* and was one of the chief reasons for its long duration.

In 1185 Yoritomo appointed military constables *(shugo)* in some provinces and placed military stewards *(jitō)* in many of the large manors. A few such appointments had been made in preceding years, but now he expanded this system to strengthen his influence in regions in which he had hitherto had no direct control. The constables were special military governors in charge of the direct vassals of the Minamoto. The stewards, representing Yoritomo on estates not otherwise under his control, levied taxes on the estates for military purposes. Thus the fiscal immunity of the estates was violated, and Kamakura retainers were scattered in key posts throughout the country. The constables and stewards rapidly grew in importance in the economic and political life of the provinces, and in time developed into the feudal lords of later centuries.

1189. Yoshitsune was killed on the orders of Yoritomo, who apparently was jealous of the fame the former had won as the brilliant general responsible for the greatest victories over the Taira. Yoritomo similarly disposed of other prominent members of the family, including his cousin Yoshinaka (1184), who as a warrior ranked next only to Yoshitsune; his uncle Yukiie (1186), who was one of the prime movers in the Minamoto uprising; and his brother Noriyori (1193), who was also one of the clan's great generals. His cruel treatment of his own relatives contributed to the early extinction of the family.

1189. Yoritomo crushed the powerful Fujiwara family of northern Japan on the grounds that they had killed Yoshitsune, albeit on his own orders. The northern Fujiwara in the course of the previous century had become a great military power and had made their capital, Hiraizumi, a major center of culture. Their elimination removed a serious menace to Minamoto supremacy.

1191. Eisai (1141–1215) propagated the Rinzai branch of the Zen sect after his return from a second study trip to China. The Zen sect enjoyed the official patronage of the Kamakura *bakufu* and the special favor of the warrior class in general.

1192. Yoritomo had himself appointed *Seii taishōgun* ("barbarian-subduing great general"), or shogun for short. Though not the first to bear this title, he was the first of the long line of military rulers called shoguns.

1199–1219. Transition from Minamoto to Hōjō rule. Yoritomo was succeeded as the head of the Minamoto by his eldest son, Yoriie (1182–1204), who was not appointed shogun until 1202; instead his mother, Masako (1157–1225), ruled with the aid of a council headed by her father, **Hōjō Tokimasa** (1138–1215). The latter, though a member of the Taira clan, from the start had cast his lot with Yoritomo and had exercised great influence in the Kamakura councils before Yoritomo's death. The Hōjō, though loyal to the military government, unscrupulously did away with Yoritomo's descendants and crushed their rivals among other Minamoto vassals.

1203. Yoriie was exiled and his younger brother, Sanetomo (1192–1219), was made shogun by Tokimasa. The following year Yoriie was murdered.

1205. Tokimasa was eliminated from government by Masako. His son, Yoshitoki (1163–1224), then became regent *(shikken)* of the shogun, a post held by successive Hōjō leaders, who were the real rulers.

1219. The Minamoto line came to an end when Sanetomo was assassinated, probably with Hōjō connivance, by his nephew, who was in turn executed.

1219–1333. The period of **rule by the Hōjō as regents** for weak shoguns of Fujiwara and imperial stock was characterized by administrative efficiency.

1221. An uprising under the leadership of retired emperor **Gotoba** (r. 1184–98) was the gravest menace the Hōjō faced, but it was quickly crushed. Two prominent Hōjō leaders were left in Kyoto as joint civil and military governors of the capital region. The estates confiscated from the defeated partisans of Gotoba gave the Kamakura much needed land with which to reward its followers, and the abortive uprising gave the Hōjō a chance to extend the system of constables, stewards, and military taxes to regions hitherto unaffected by it.

1224. Shinran Shōnin (1173–1262), a disciple of Genkū, founded the **True Pure Land** sect of Buddhism, as an offshoot of the Pure Land sect of his master. The True Pure Land sect introduced such innovations as marriage for the clergy. It became the most popular of all Japanese Buddhist sects, with Zen its only close rival.

1224–52. Fujiwara nobles served as figurehead shoguns.

1229. Dōgen (1200–1253) introduced the Sōtō branch of Zen after his return from study in China.

1232. The **Jōei Formulary**, a legal code based primarily on custom rather than on earlier, Sinicized law codes, was adopted for all those directly under Kamakura feudal rule. A military code, among its provisions were property rights for women.

1252–1333. Imperial princes served as figurehead shoguns.

1253. Nichiren (1222–82) founded the Lotus (Hokke) sect, popularly known as Nichiren Buddhism. In it the Lotus Sutra was venerated, much as the Amidist sects venerated Amida. A fiery religious and political reformer, Nichiren was an ardent nationalist, and his writings illustrate the gradual emergence of a national consciousness at the time. Imbued with the turbulent nature of its founder, the sect had a stormy career.

1274. First Mongol invasion (p. 154). The Mongols, having conquered Korea and most of China, repeatedly sent embassies (1268–73) enjoining Japan to submit, but the Kamakura government, under the bold leadership of regent Hōjō Tokimune (1251–84), refused. In 1274 the Mongols dispatched an expeditionary fleet from Korea. The islands of Tsushima and Iki were taken, a landing was made in Hakata (Hakozaki) Bay in northern Kyūshū, and an inconclusive encounter, in which superior weapons and military organization gave the Mongols the advantage, was fought with local warriors. That same night, the invaders set sail back to Korea because of their insecure position and the threat of a storm.

1281. Second Mongol invasion. Mongol envoys sent to Japan in 1275 and 1280 were summarily executed, and the *bakufu* hastily prepared defensive works in western Japan. In 1281 the Mongols sent a huge force in two large fleets, one Korean and one Chinese, and again, after capturing Tsushima and Iki, landed in northern Kyūshū. Although the invaders numbered some 150,000, the Japanese checked their advance on land with walls they had prepared for this emergency, and they defeated them at sea through the great mobility of their smaller craft in close quarters. After almost two months of fighting a great storm defeated a large portion of the invading armada, and the remainder departed with serious losses. The Mongols continued plans for another invasion of Japan until the death of Khubilai (1294), and the Japanese continued their defense preparations for a still longer time.

The Mongol invasions no doubt spurred on Japan's nascent national consciousness and also contributed greatly to the final collapse of the Kamakura *bakufu*. Military preparations against the Mongols seriously taxed the nation's resources, and after the two invasions the *bakufu*, lacking land confiscated from the enemy, was without its usual means of rewarding its vassals for their efforts. This state of affairs helped to undermine the loyalty of the warrior retainers for the *bakufu*. At the same time, the monasteries were becoming increasingly restive, the ruling nobility was again beginning to intrigue with disaffected warriors against the Hōjō, and the Hōjō themselves had lost their earlier reputation for frugality and justice.

The Hōjō, during the final decades of their rule, began to resort to **Acts of Grace** (Tokusei), canceling certain indebtedness in an effort to save the lands of their vassals from mortgages, but such clearly biased measures antagonized certain powerful interests and failed adequately to protect the Kamakura vassals.

1331–33. The **Imperial Restoration** of **Godaigo** (r. 1318–39) and the fall

of the Hōjō. The energetic emperor Godaigo, after bringing to an end (1322) the domination of the court by retired emperors, organized an abortive plot to overthrow the Hōjō as early as 1324. In 1331 open warfare broke out between Godaigo (supported by his able sons), some of the large monasteries in the capital region, and various local nobles and warriors, such as **Kitabatake Chikafusa** (1293–1354) and **Kusunoki Masashige** (1294–1336), two outstanding patriotic heroes of medieval Japan. The following year the emperor was captured and exiled to Oki Island, but in 1333 he escaped. Most of western Japan declared for the imperial cause. **Ashikaga Takauji** (1305–58), one of the two chief generals dispatched by the Hōjō from eastern Japan, deserted to support Godaigo, and the sudden capture of Kamakura by another prominent Hōjō vassal, Nitta Yoshisada (1301–38), brought the Kamakura *bakufu* to an end.

1333–36. Godaigo, in a short period of personal rule, failed to face economic and political realities and attempted to revive the civil imperial rule of the 8th century. However, he did make his able son Morinaga (1308–35) shogun, and he appointed his leading generals as military governors of large sections of the land.

1335. Because of his dissatisfaction with his share of the spoils in northeastern Japan, **Takauji** revolted against the throne, defeating the Nitta, Kitabatake, and other loyal families.

1336. Takauji drove Godaigo from Kyoto and set up a new emperor from a branch of the imperial family that had been jealously contending for the throne with Godaigo's branch for several decades. Takauji thereby became the virtual dictator of the central government, although he was not appointed shogun until 1338, when he captured Kyoto.

1336–1568. The Ashikaga (or Muromachi) period. The Ashikaga shogunate continued the outward forms of the military rule of the Minamoto and Hōjō, but during most of the first and last centuries of the period, open warfare disrupted the nation, and at best the Ashikaga exercised limited control over the great feudatories who made their appearance at this time. The age was characterized by quickly shifting alliances and political instability, which at times amounted to anarchy. There was a general redistribution of feudal and economic rights, and the Kyoto nobility, which now lost most of its few remaining lands and provincial sources of income, was reduced to penury. The complicated feudal relations of the Kamakura era broke down into a simpler, more compact system in which virtually independent lords, often the former provincial constables, ruled large territories that were in turn subdivided into smaller units administered by their direct vassals. The collapse of clan unity and an organized feudal system necessitated stronger solidarity within the smaller family and feudal units. The division of patrimonies among heirs was abandoned, and women were reduced to subordinate status. Lords exercised closer, paternalistic supervision over their vassals, and the latter in turn served their lords with greater personal loyalty.

The **overseas trade** and **pirate enterprises** of the Japanese increased in the Ashikaga period; the central government once more established official relations with China; and another important period of borrowing from abroad commenced. Foreign trade stimulated the growth of towns and provincial ports, such as Sakai (part of modern Ōsaka), Hyōgo (modern Kōbe), and Hakata (part of modern Fukuoka). Despite political disruption and incessant warfare, phenomenal economic development took place. Nascent industries grew and expanded, and trade guilds (za), usually operating under the patronage of a religious institution, appeared and flourished. However, the unrestricted rise of various levies and customs barriers proved a serious curb to the development of trade.

Kyoto was once more the undisputed political and cultural capital, and there the warrior class and the court nobility tended to fuse. Constant warfare made the period in some respects an intellectual valley, but political disunity helped to diffuse learning throughout the land. Zen monks dominated the intellectual and artistic life of the nation, and through their intimate contacts with China, where many had lived and studied, they expanded Japan's intellectual and artistic horizons. Although this was a great age for Zen, other sects, particularly the Amidist sects, flourished and sometimes developed powerful military organizations. Although still a thoroughly Buddhist age, intellectual life began to free itself from the bonds of Buddhism. Song Neo-Confucian philosophy was introduced from China, and stirrings of new life appeared in Shinto, where for the first time systemic, syncretic philosophies were developed.

Despite the violent internecine strife of the early and late Ashikaga era, in the middle decades literature and art flourished, ruled by Zen standards of restraint and refinement. The literature of the **Five Mountains,** as the Zen school in Kyoto was known, revived poetic composition in Chinese, and the great lyric drama called *nō* (in English, Noh) appeared. The Song style of painting, often in monochrome and usually of landscapes, reached its zenith with such masters as **Shūbun** (d. c. 1460) and **Sesshū** (1420–1506), and the two greatest Japanese schools of painting, the **Tosa** and **Kano,** flourished. The independent architectural styles of the Kamakura era were blended to form a composite style. Arts such as landscape gardening, flower arranging, and the tea ceremony grew up. Under Zen's influence there developed a refined simplicity of taste and a harmony with nature that has had a lasting impact on Japanese art.

1336–92. Civil wars of the Yoshino period. When Takauji drove Godaigo out of Kyoto and set up a rival emperor, Godaigo and his partisans, Kitabatake, Kusunoki, and others, withdrew to the mountainous Yoshino region south of Nara, where Godaigo and three imperial successors maintained for almost 60 years a rival court, called the **Southern Court** because of its location. During this period, known as the Yoshino period, or the **Period of the Northern and Southern Courts,** civil war convulsed Japan.

1339. In support of the legitimacy of the Southern Court, **Kitabatake Chikafusa** wrote the *Jinnō shōtōki (Chronicle of the Direct Descent of the Gods),* a history of Japan imbued with extreme nationalistic and patriotic sentiments. It was an important landmark in the growth of national consciousness and the imperial cult.

1392. The reunion of the two courts. Although at times the Yoshino warriors even captured Kyoto, gradually the hopes of the Southern Court waned. Eventually peace was made in 1392, and Gokameyama (r. 1383–92) of the southern line abdicated in favor of **Gokomatsu** (r. 1382–1412) of the northern line, with the understanding that the throne would thereafter alternate between members of the two branches of the imperial family, as it had for several reigns preceding that of Godaigo. However, the northern line never yielded the throne to its rivals, despite futile uprisings on their behalf. Official history regards those of the southern line as the legitimate rulers during the Yoshino period.

1395–1408. Rule of Ashikaga Yoshimitsu as retired shogun. Yoshimitsu, the third Ashikaga shogun (b. 1358; r. 1369–95)—acter crushing his principal opponents, uniting the two imperial courts, and bringing Ashikaga power to its apogee—passed on the title of shogun to his son and retired as a monk to his Kitayama estate on the outskirts of Kyoto. The **Golden Pavilion** (Kinkakuji) he erected there is the outstanding remaining architectural work of the day, and his coterie of artists formed the center of the artistic movements of the most creative epoch of Ashikaga rule. There, **Kan'ami** (1333–84) and his son, **Zeami** (1363–

1443), perfected the highly refined *nō* drama from earlier dramatic and terpsichorean performances. The luxurious but artistically creative life of the Kitayama estate was continued by Yoshimitsu's successors for several decades after his death.

1449–90. Rule of Ashikaga Yoshimasa (b. 1436; r. 1449–74) as shogun and retired shogun. This was the second great creative period of Ashikaga art. In his Higashiyama estate on the edge of Kyoto, Yoshimasa built the **Silver Pavilion** (Ginkakuji), which as an architectural work ranks second only to the Golden Pavilion, and there he and a brilliant group of artists and aesthetes, presided over by Nōami (1397–1476), enjoyed a life of luxury and artistic elegance.

At the same time, the complete collapse of what little authority Ashikaga had exercised over the nation became apparent, and there was great social unrest, resulting in numerous popular uprisings. Under popular pressure, Yoshimasa, like other Ashikaga shoguns, repeatedly issued Acts of Grace, which, unlike those of the Kamakura period, were sweeping debt cancellations for the benefit of the whole debtor class.

1465. The monks of Enryakuji destroyed the Honganji, the central monastery of the True Pure Land sect in Kyoto. Such affrays between the great monasteries were common at this time. Rennyō (1415–99), the eighth hereditary head of the sect, fled to the region north of Kyoto, where his teachings met with great success and his numerous followers built up a military organization to defend their interests.

1467–77. The **Ōnin War,** ostensibly a contest over succession in the Ashikaga *bakufu* and other great military families, was actually a reshuffling of domains and power among the feudal lords, who divided into two camps under the leadership of two great lords of western Japan, **Yamana Mochitoyo** (Sōzen, 1404–73) and his son-in-law, **Hosokawa Katsumoto** (1430?–73), long the shogunal deputy of the *bakufu* (1453–64, 1468–73). Kyoto was soon laid waste, but both leaders died in 1473, and exhaustion eventually brought peace in 1477. However, local struggles went unabated. In fact, the Ōnin War was but the prelude to more than a century of almost uninterrupted warfare. This period, known as the **Warring States period,** witnessed a continuing shift of fiefs and power, the elimination of many of the old feudal families, and the emergence of a new group of territorial lords, now known as *daimyō.*

1488. The True Pure Land sect followers north of Kyoto defeated and killed a local lord. This is considered the first of the *Ikkō ikki,* or uprisings of the Ikkō sect, another name for the True Pure Land sect. Such uprisings became increasingly common and acted as a medium for manifestations of popular discontent.

1493. Hosokawa Masamoto (1466–1507) drove the shogun Yoshitane (r. 1490–94, 1508–21) out of Kyoto and set up a puppet shogun (1494), acts which were repeated by his adopted son, Takakuni (1484–1531), in 1521. Yoshitane's successors suffered similar indignities as the prestige of the Ashikaga dwindled further.   *(To p. 381)*

7. VIETNAM

a. ORIGINS TO 1009

Vietnam's history is intimately tied, for better or for worse, to its long relationship with China. The impact of Chinese cultural and political forms is difficult to overestimate, as is the impact of wars begun by its powerful neighbor to the north. Although the borders of what is now called Vietnam and the country's name have changed many times, a continuous history can be delineated.

In the early to mid-2nd millennium B.C.E., it appears that bronze implements began to be used. The **Dông-son archeological site** has unearthed particularly fine items in bronze. Legend recounts a Van Lang kingdom, supposedly a strictly hierarchical, feudal regime, that held sway from 2879 until 258 B.C.E. It was thereupon replaced by the Au Lac kingdom, which ruled in the south. In 214 B.C.E. the newly unified Qin empire of China sent a military expedition south to conquer northern Vietnam. The ruler there, fearing devastation, submitted to the Qin, and the north was divided into three commandaries,

much like Korea was under the Han. With the decline of the Qin, the governor of one commandery in 208 B.C.E. conquered Au Lac and renamed the new entity under him Nam Viêt. During the Han dynasty, Nam Viêt became part of the Chinese tributary system. This relationship continued through the end of the 2nd century B.C.E., but in 111 B.C.E. Chinese troops attacked and captured Nam Viêt on the order of Emperor Wu of the Han. The country was renamed Giao-chi (Jiaozhi in Chinese) and was incorporated into the Han empire. There it remained for more than a millennium.

The Han did not draw Giao-chi (Vietnam) closely into its orbit, seeing it primarily as providing access to trade routes and luxury goods from the south. Local notables were given jurisdiction in the counties and prefectures under the control of Han governors. The population census of 2 C.E. recorded more than 1 million residents in northern Vietnam. There is also evidence that farmers were already double-cropping before the Han conquest, and this too may indicate that a well-organized, centralized form of government was in place earlier.

During the Wang Mang era (9–23 C.E.), a noteworthy number of elite Han families fled to Vietnam, strengthening the Chinese official stratum already there. They pushed for a more concerted program of patriarchal control of the economy, rather than the bilateral kin patterns favored in Vietnam and elsewhere in Southeast Asia. In 43, the **Trung sisters** led an unsuccessful rebellion against Han rule.

From this point, Dông-son culture began to disappear, as Chinese-style centralized bureaucracy and tax-assessed landholdings replaced native systems. The newly emergent elite was a Han-Viêt mix, due to cultural interpenetration as well as intermarriage. With the decline and collapse of the Later Han, Chinese influence in Vietnam waned. During the centuries of disunion in China, Vietnam fell under the domination of a succession of smaller states to the north. In the 540s and 550s, a number of rebellions against the Chinese erupted, and fighting continued for some time. By the end of the 6th century, Vietnam had been defeated and returned to the Chinese sphere.

When China was reunified under the Sui and Tang dynasties, Vietnam fell again under Chinese control. The Tang set up the Protectorate of An-nam (literally, the "pacified south") in the northern part of the country in the 7th and 8th centuries, typical of Chinese regional control structures at the time. When the central control of the Tang waned in the 9th century, control in the extremities waned as well and gave rise to instability. During the Tang, the political center of what was then Vietnam became Hanoi.

939. After a defeat of the army of the Southern Han, **Ngô Quyên** (898–944) declared himself king, although infighting continued for the entire three decades of his and his descendants' rule.

968. Dinh Bô Ling (c. 925–79) established a stable regime, with himself as king, from Hoa-lu, near the southern rim of the Red River plain. The country was renamed Dai Viêt. He sent his son (972) to China to establish contacts, and he was recognized as the king of Giao-châu, while his son became commander in chief of the An-nam Protectorate. Both were assassinated in 979.

980. Lê Hoan (950–1005) continued rule from Hoa-lu after defeating a Song expeditionary force from China, but he and his descendants, being thoroughly military men, were unable to establish the foundations of long-term political stability. What is sometimes called the Early Lê dynasty ended in 1009, when it was replaced by the **Ly dynasty.**

As Thang-long (Hanoi) became the political center of the country during Tang hegemony, Chinese-style agricultural organizations and taxation systems came to Vietnam, in part aimed at breaking up the older, entrenched great families. Thang-long was the first urban center south of the Red River, and these new systems opened up rich new farmlands that were placed in the hands of free peasants trained militarily to defend their lands against the older elites. By the end of the 8th century, the Tang's double-tax reform had fostered the emergence of a new great landlord class. Vietnam was seen by its northern master as a source of revenue and luxury items.

Buddhism probably came to Vietnam between the 4th and 5th centuries C.E., perhaps as early as the 2nd century. A number of famous Buddhist travelers passed through Vietnam en route to or from China, and by the early years of the Tang, Vietnamese monks were among those travelers. In the 7th century, **Vân-Ky** brought home Chinese-language Buddhist texts from China. The most popular and influential Chinese sect in Vietnam was the Chan (in Vietnamese, **Thiên**). An Indian traveler in China in the 6th century had proceeded to Vietnam and launched the first Thiên sect. Another took root during the Tang; by the late 10th century, the fourth patriarch of the sect was a teacher at the Lê Palace.

While the **status of women** in pre-China-dominated Vietnam may have been better than it became, women were never the legal or social equals of men of their same class. Nonetheless, the relatively more important roles women played throughout Vietnamese society mark a significant distinction with respect to China.

b. 1009–1527, INDEPENDENCE AND ITS DEFENSE

These five centuries mark the first vibrant era of Vietnamese independence. They include rule by three major dynasties, wars with China, and three gruesome but ultimately unsuccessful invasions by Mongol armies. Despite conflicts with the rulers of China, Sinitic culture continued to make inroads into Vietnam, just as classical Chinese remained the language of the elite throughout these years.

1009–1225. The **Ly dynasty** came to power when **Ly Công Uan** (or Ly Thai-tô, 974–1028), commander of the palace guard, seized the throne. Raised by Buddhist monks and supported by the Buddhist establishment, he worked to create a close relationship with the clergy. He was also much influenced by traditional Chinese notions of kingship. He frequently remitted taxes in an effort to create better ruler-populace relations. The country became known as Dai Viêt.

1010. Ly moved the capital to **Thang-long** (present Hanoi).

1028–54. During the **reign of Ly Phât Ma** (or Ly Thai-tông, b. 1000), an apparently brilliant leader, Ly rule was regularized. He had six reign titles in 26 years. Through his constructive interaction with officials, they came to understand the relative importance of bureaucracy and the throne in institutional development. The Buddhist clergy entered an ever closer relationship with government, and Phât Ma became a patriarch of a Thiên sect himself.

1042. A new legal code was enacted in an effort to make the law more fair and put it in tune with the times.

1044. A naval expedition by sea was led by Phât Ma himself to Champa. Champa was defeated, and the war booty enabled the king to remit taxes.

1054–72. The **reign of Ly Nhat Ton** (or Ly Thanh-tông, b. 1023) continued the policies and institutional arrangements put in place by his father. He began to adopt many of the ritual trappings of a Chinese-style emperor, which worried the Song court to the north.

1069. Nhat Ton repeated his father's expedition to Champa, this time sparing the life of the Champa king.

1072. At the time of Nhat Ton's death and the accession of **Ly Can Duc** (1066–1127), **Wang Anshi** was in the midst of implementing his New Laws in China (p. 151). Among them was a vigorous response to border encroachments by China's neighbors, and Ly attempts at such provoked him. Vietnamese troops attacked (1075), defeating Song naval forces and sacking several sites.

1075–77. The **first examinations** for recruitment to bureaucratic office were implemented but were abandoned soon thereafter. A national college was allegedly founded (1076) for the best scholars of the land.

1076–77. The Song sent a military force south but reached no conclusive victory; after several years of talks, borders were determined.

1127. Ly Can Duc's death without an heir left the succession problematic. Maternal clansmen of the crown placed "kings" on the throne, but they tended to be little more than nominal rulers. Civil wars wracked the country for much of the 12th century.

Buddhism became an essential component of traditional Vietnamese kingship, as the throne and the clergy developed an intricate, symbiotic relationship. Confucianism, too, made inroads into elite society. Scholars wrote commentaries on the Chinese classics, and those texts became the basis for the state examinations. Native Vietnamese "deities" also became associated with the throne.

1225–1400. The **Trân dynasty** came to power in the decay and strife at the end of the Ly. The last queen of Ly was from the Trân family. Thereafter, the Trân took queens only from its own family. Collegial rule among senior Trân men, with royal abdication on the death of a predecessor, became the rule. Trân family members were given local prerogatives in political and economic control that enabled them to gain control through hegemony over the Red River plain. As with the Ly, the royal family was made up of pious Buddhists.

1230s. The Trân inaugurated an **examination system** to recruit civil servants into government service. The curriculum was Chinese classical lore. This fostered the slow emergence of a Confucian literati among scholar-officials, much as earlier in China, in tandem with the centralizing policies of the throne. Military service became compulsory for every able-bodied man; and this had a salutary effect on the fighting prowess of the Vietnamese army.

1257–58. The **Mongols** tried to surround the Southern Song by entering northern Dai Viêt, but they were repelled. After the defeat of the Song in 1279, the Mongols sent an emissary to Thang-long, as was their practice, to secure a Vietnamese surrender or tell them they would face Khubilai's wrath. Fighting ensued.

1272. The first comprehensive history of Vietnam, in 30 volumes, was published.

1284. Mongol armies swept into Dai Viêt, took Thang-long, and won a number of early victories. The Vietnamese counterattack trapped Mongol forces in the inclement heat and humidity, cut them off from troop support, and finally routed them.

1287–88. Immense land and seaborne Mongol forces descended on Dai Viêt. Far outnumbered, Vietnamese forces resorted to guerrilla tactics, cut off Mongol armies from their supply lines, and soundly defeated them.

1340s. A series of domestic rebellions erupted as the Trân central leadership declined sharply through the 14th century.

1390s. After two decades of regional wars, particularly with Champa, a modicum of stability was attained by **Hô Quy Ly** (1336–1407), leader of a powerful family. During these years the great Buddhist aristocracy was also in ruins.

1400. Hô Quy Ly seized the throne for himself, but his kingship was not widely accepted.

Probably during the 13th century, the Vietnamese developed their own written script, based on the Chinese ideographic language. Called **chu nôm** or **nôm**, its fortunes as a literary language waxed and waned over the centuries.

1406. In the disorder that ensued, Emperor Yongle in China, under the Ming dynasty, sent armies to Dai Viêt, occupied the country, and tried to transform it into a province of the Chinese Empire (p. 154). However, this plan soon foundered, and it was abandoned shortly after the death of Yongle in 1424.

1418. Lê Loi (1385–1433), a rich landlord, led Vietnamese forces in the first of a series of battles against the Chinese armies. The Ming forces were finally defeated in 1428.

1428–1527. Lê Loi founded the **Lê dynasty.** Lê Loi (or Le Thai-tô) himself reigned for only five years, followed by several short reigns dominated by regents. To placate China, Dai Viêt sent a tributary mission once every three years to the Ming court. Lê Loi started to rebuild the educational system with a national university and an examination system. There was as well an effort to redistribute land according to the equal-field system of China, in part to prevent the reemergence of great landed clans.

1460–97. During the celebrated **reign of Le Thanh-tông** (b. 1442), a wide range of reform measures in the realms of law, landholding, and government set the form of bureaucratic rule for all subsequent, precolonial rule. He continued the land distribution policies of Lê Loi. To enlarge the amount of arable land in Dai Viêt, Cham terrain was annexed in 1471. Eventually a decisive victory was sustained over Champa, giving Dai Viêt further access to the south. This was also an age of great cultural achievements and scholarship.

The Ming invasion had destroyed much of the aristocratic Buddhist tradition established in Ly and Trân times. The new elite was now comprised of military clans and scholar-officials, as in China, of the Neo-Confucian sort. Le Thanh-tông strongly supported Confucianization in Dai Viêt. The chaos that followed the reign of Le Thanh-tông threw Vietnam into a succession of civil and regional wars that continued for many years. *(To p. 385)*

F. EUROPE, 461–1500

In Europe, particularly western Europe, the postclassical period is commonly called the **Middle Ages** (Lat., *Medii Aevi*), originally a pejorative term coined by the 14th-century Florentine poet Francesco Petrarch (p. 255) to describe what he considered a period of cultural stagnation (c. 400–1300) between two eras of cultural brilliance, the ancient Roman and his own. Scholars often divide the Middle Ages into three time periods: an early phase, c. 500–1000; the central or High Middle Ages c. 1000–1300; and a later period, c. 1300–1500, when medieval patterns of culture began to decline.

1. WESTERN EUROPE IN THE EARLY MIDDLE AGES, 461–1000

(From p. 100)

The general characteristics that made the early Middle Ages are the **collapse of the centralized state** (the Roman Empire), which had provided much of western Europe with a government of law and social order, and the assumption of power by local strongmen. The **decay of the ancient city-state** as a physical and social unit and as a way of life meant that the isolated **rural estate** became the typical form of social and economic organization; some cities survived as ecclesiastical or political centers, but not as economic or cultural ones. The **decline of long-distance trade** forced the individual to depend for all of his or her needs on locally produced goods. **Disease,** especially periodic outbreaks of bubonic plague, chronic **domestic violence,** and **assaults from outside Europe** made for drastic **population decline.** The slow, steady, but very imperfect **conversion of peoples to Christianity** led to a **shift of basic loyalty from the state to religion;** Europeans came to define themselves and their world in religious terms, and they gave a spiritual loyalty to Rome that was slowly transformed into a supranational authority independent of any secular power.

The ancient Roman world had been a Mediterranean-based civilization whose "center of gravity" lay in the East. The subsequent consolidation of the Byzantine Empire, the expansion of Islam through the Mediterranean, and the rise of Frankish power meant that no single culture would unite the former Roman world. When the term **Europa** was first used around 1500, it referred to the areas over which the Frankish ruler Charlemagne had nominally held jurisdiction, a territory far smaller than that which the word "Europe" implies today.

a. CONDITIONS OF LIFE

In the 3rd, 4th, and 5th centuries, the Germanic invasions led to the decline of city-states throughout the Mediterranean world; free tenant farmers abandoned their small farms, and the land was acquired by large landowners. Large, economically self-sufficient **villas** or **manors** became the dominant form of social organization, and agriculture the major occupation. Political instability and invasions (p. 167) also reduced long-distance trade. Most commerce was local. Existence for most people was rural, isolated, and limited by the borders of the province.

Free farmers, weak and defenseless before barbarian invaders, brigands, and greedy officials, sought protection from powerful local landowners. In return for support and protection, small landholders surrendered their lands to, and became the dependents of, the strong. The weak became bound to the soil, working their patron's lands; they lost their freedom, could not move, and became serfs. This trend toward **serfdom** continued to the 11th century.

Communication was difficult; roads and harbors were unused and in disrepair until about the 8th century. Building was stagnant; the art of brick-laying appears to have been lost; few stone buildings were erected in northern Europe. Metalworking was still important, although stamping was unskilled, and hence coins were crude. Precious metals were worked with enamel decorations, while silver and bronze could be cast. Unlike the light Mediterranean soils, those of northern

Europe could not be pulverized for farming purposes; these heavy soils had to be sliced, broken up. This was impossible until the introduction of the iron, wheeled plowshare, with moldboard. The basic farm tools evolved during this period: rake, spade, fork, pick, balanced sickle, scythe. Development of the horse collar was very important, for an efficient draft animal relieved the small workforce. With an effective harness and stirrup (the latter depicted in a drawing c. 900), and tandem rather than fan-hitched teams of horses or oxen, men were freed of even more work. Another important source of power was water: the Roman water mill (in use 536) spread throughout Europe.

b. THE EARLY CHURCH

For a complete list of the Roman popes, see Appendix IV.

Christianity emerged in the cities of the eastern part of the Roman Empire. The earliest Christians, because they refused to honor the Roman pagan gods, were considered atheists, and thus were subject to civil penalties, sporadic persecutions, the contempt of the Roman social establishment. The first Christians, Jesus' followers, were Jews. An urban religion, Christianity initially spread to the Gentiles through the preachings of St. Paul (p. 95), and it subsequently attracted converts from all social classes: senators, knights, merchants, the poor, servants. The series of decrees issued by Constantine I (p. 99) between 312 and 330 formally tolerated Christianity, gave Christians the right to build churches, to accommodate property, to establish courts with jurisdiction over clergy; these decrees were known as the Peace of Constantine and marked the beginning of the institutional Church. Emperor Theodosius (391–94) outlawed the pagan religions and made Christianity the **official religion** of the empire. Since a profession of faith advanced one's public career, the number of followers increased, but piety was weakened.

In the 2nd century, the **Church** (Gr., *ecclesia*; the Christian community) consisted of widely scattered, loosely knit groups, united by their faith in New Testament teachings and sometimes divided by doctrinal disagreements. Baptism and participation in the Eucharist became the basic signs **(sacraments)** of the Christians. **Ecumenical** (general, theoretically universal) **councils** such as **Nicaea** (325), **Constantinople I** (381), **Ephesus** (431), and **Chalcedon** (451) tried to resolve conflicts and to define doctrine. These councils were called by the emperor and presided over by him in person or by legate. Local problems were dealt with in synods.

Christian communities of the apostolic age made no distinction between clergy and laity, but by 100 C.E. *episkopoi* (supervisors) and *presbyteroi* (elders) sat apart at religious ceremonies from the *laikoi* (the people). *Episkopoi*, or **bishops** from the 4th century onward, often descended from the Roman senatorial aristocracy or provincial officials and were elected directly by Christians of local communities on the basis of spiritual charisma and reputation for piety. They served as overseers, responsible for distribution of goods to the poor, for preaching, for maintenance of gospel standards. Each town had its bishop, and his church (cathedral) possessed his throne or chair (Lat., *cathedra*), the symbol of his authority. Christians considered bishops to be successors of the apostles: just as Jesus had consecrated his apostles by laying hands on them and sending them out to teach what he had taught them, so the apostles consecrated their successors and they, further successors. This **apostolic succession** gave the bishops organizational authority and doctrinal security. **Papa** was a title applied to all bishops until c. 425; it did not take on its present meaning until the 7th century.

The emergence of Roman primacy. As Christian communities developed organizations, they adopted the diocesan (territorial unit) system of the Roman Empire. Just as the eastern part of the Mediterranean world contained the population and commercial centers of the Roman Empire and, after the establishment of Constantinople, the political capital, so the East held the **patriarchal** or **metropolitan** sees of Jerusalem, Antioch, Alexandria, and Constantinople, which had provincial, not just diocesan, jurisdiction; Rome was the only western metropolitan see.

In the first four centuries C.E., authority in the Church rested in: (1) the emperor, who continued to take the title *pontifex maximus* and to exercise a prominent role in religious affairs. Thus, Constantine I considered himself the equal of the apostles and called and controlled the Council of Nicaea (p. 99); (2) the universal or ecumenical council, whose canons (decisions) held an authority second only to Scripture; (3) the Roman papacy, whose influence grew very gradually. As the seat of the empire and the site of the martyrdoms of the apostles Peter and Paul, Rome held a primacy of respect and honor throughout the Church. Moreover, according to the gospel tradition (Matt. 16:16–18, Luke 22:31–32, John 21:16–17) Jesus had assigned Peter a position of leadership among the apostles. Peter led (as bishop) the Christian community in Rome, and, in turn, transmitted "the power of the keys of the kingdom of heaven" to his successors. Popes Innocent I (401–17) and Celestine I (422–32) used this **Petrine theory** to extend the rights of Rome. The bishops of Rome slowly acquired the rights to resolve disputes in other dioceses, to define doctrine, and to exercise administration and discipline throughout the Church. Under **Pope Leo I** (440–61) the weakness of the imperial power forced the bishop of Rome to assume defensive, financial, civil, and political responsibilities for the city, because the imperial government was unable to do so. Leo I claimed to possess the *plenitudo postestasis* (fullness of power or jurisdiction) over the entire Church. This impetus to universal Roman authority, however, could not be sustained by Leo's immediate successors.

c. 340. MONASTICISM originated in Egypt and Syria as an ascetic (disciplined) reaction to the moral corruption of the late antique city-state, and was introduced into the West by Athanasius (d. 373). Monastic individuals withdrew (Lat. *anchoreo*, to withdraw) from urban society to seek God alone, through prayer in the desert (Gr., *eremos*), hence Eastern monks were called "men of the desert." Many women were also attracted to monasticism. Hermits led a solitary life. In his *Life of St. Anthony*, Athanasius described the first (Egyptian) monk (c. 251?–350), now considered the **father of Christian monasticism.** Although monks (and nuns) led isolated lives and the monastic movement represented the antithesis of the ancient ideal of an urbane social existence, monks were soon recognized as holy people and sought out as spiritual guides. In the first half of the 4th century **Pachomius** (c. 290–346) established **cenobitic** (communal, in contrast to eremitic) monasteries for men and for women in Upper Egypt. **Basil of Caesarea** (330–79), a leading Greek theologian, attacked the eremitic life, because of the impossibility of material self-sufficiency, the excessive concern with the self, and the lack of opportunity for the exercise of charity; he espoused cenobitism, which eventually became the common form of monasticism in the West. The Egyptian monastic experience came to the West through *The Institutes* (c. 417–18) and *The Conferences* (426–29) of the monk **Cassian** (c. 360–c. 435), based on his eyewitness accounts and conversations with the Desert Fathers. **Martin of Tours** founded (c. 362) a cenobitic community of monks near Poitiers.

The Latin Fathers of the Church (Lat., *Patres Ecclesiae*), was a term first used in the late 4th century by the Greek writers and Sts. Basil and Gregory of Nazianzos to refer to Sts. Ambrose, Jerome, and Augustine. **Jerome** (c. 342–420), a Dalmatian, was devoted to pagan learning despite his keen ascetic convictions. The first great Western exponent of monasticism. One of the greatest scholars of the Latin Church, his translation of the Bible into Latin (the Vulgate) is still authoritative in the Roman Church today. This excellent version exerted stylistic and theological influence throughout the Middle Ages. **Ambrose** (c. 339–97) of Trier, a Roman provincial governor, was elected (374) bishop of Milan before he was baptized (p. 99). His *Duties of the Clergy* (based largely on Cicero, *de Officiis*) was for centuries the standard work on ethics, and is probably the chief single source of the Stoic tradition in early Western thought. He made Milan almost the equal of Rome in prestige, and forced the Emperor Theodosius to do penance, maintaining that in ecclesiastical matters a bishop was superior to an emperor. **Augustine** (354–430) of Hippo was the greatest of the Western Fathers. Converted to Christianity after ventures into Neo-Platonism and Manichaeism, he was founder of Western theology, the link between the classical tradition and the medieval schoolmen. Through him a great stream of Platonic and Neo-Platonic thought came into the Church. For a thousand years all thought was influenced by Augustine, and theology betrays his influence to this day. He gave wide currency to the doctrines of original sin, predestination, and salvation through divine grace, and his influence was felt by Calvin and Luther. His *City of God* presents a dualism of the heavenly city (those who live according to the spirit; those who live according to the flesh) and the earthly city (Rome), and was written to prove that the misfortunes of Rome (e.g., the sack of 410) were not due to Christianity; all history is the account of God acting in time. The *Confessions* set the fashion in spiritual autobiography.

The Latin Fathers debated matters of **sexuality and marriage.** In the ancient world, many thinkers, both Gentile and Jewish, held that sexual relations between man and woman hindered the soul's rise to higher things, but Jesus' apostles believed marriage was no sin and that celibacy was a grace not given to all. In the 2nd century, Christian writers advanced the revolutionary ethic that husbands should be as faithful to their wives as wives were expected to be to their husbands; that marriage was a free partnership of equals, with ideals of mutual respect and affection. Early Christians condemned infant exposure, abortion, and capital punishment—all widely practiced in the ancient world. With this benign attitude, however, there gradually emerged a strong current of negativism toward the body, of hostility toward sexuality. The Fathers took for granted the superiority of celibacy (total abstinence from all sexual activity) over marriage. Thus, Jerome denigrated marriage; Augustine held marriage to be "a cure for concupiscence," with procreation the only truly moral use of, or justification for, sexuality. As in the ancient world, marriage remained a private arrangement, not the concern of civil authorities. Recent historians have disputed the early Christian attitude toward homosexuality. Some scholars argue that early Christian thinkers had a tolerant and positive position on male love and eroticism as being natural; other modern writers claim the Fathers condemned same-sex love and activity. The debate continues.

401–17. Innocent I asserted that the pope was custodian of the apostolic tradition and claimed universal jurisdiction for the Roman Church.

440–61. Leo the Great, the first great pope, a highly cultivated Roman, a vigorous foe of the Manichaean heresy. He procured an edict from Emperor Valentinian III (445) declaring that papal decisions have the force of law. Leo was probably the first pope to enunciate the theory of the mystical unity of Peter and his successors, and to attribute all their doings and sayings to Peter. The tradition of Leo's miraculous arrest of Attila's advance and his efforts to stop Gaiseric's attack (455) won the papacy tremendous prestige in later days.   *(To pp. 169, 171)*

c. INVADERS OF THE WEST

Origins of the invaders. The Germanic peoples were established in Scandinavia (Denmark) and between the Elbe and Oder as early as the 2nd millennium B.C.E. Eastward lay the Balts (Letts), and the west of the Elbe were the Celts.

Expansion. The western Germans (Teutons) displaced (c. 1000 B.C.E.) the Celts, moving up the Elbe and Rhine (the Main reached c. 200 B.C.E.). South Germany was occupied (c. 100 B.C.E.); Gaul threatened (cf. Caesar's *Commentaries*). These invaders were a pastoral, agricultural folk, tending to settle down. By the time of Tacitus's (c. 55–c. 117 C.E.) *Germania* they were wholly agricultural. Later new tribal names and a new kind of federated organization appeared. The eastern Germans (Scandinavians) crossed the Baltic (c. 600–300 B.C.E.) and pushed up the Vistula to the Carpathians. The northern Germans remained in Scandinavia.

The Greeks and Romans invented the concept of "barbarian," applying it to all peoples (except the Persians) living outside Greco-Roman civilization—peoples who did not share urban Mediterranean culture, who did not speak Greek or Latin. To the Romans, such peoples had no history and encountered history only when they entered the civilized Roman world. Barbarian peoples as they entered the Roman orbit had many **changing ethnic identities;** all viewed the Roman empire as the source of great wealth.

GERMANIC SOCIETIES. The basic unit was the tribe (folk), united by blood kinship and guided by unwritten customary law passed down through the generations by word of mouth. Thinking in social not political terms, the Germans had no notion of the state. Basic institutions were the kings and the war bands. The **kings, or chieftains,** were elected from male members of the strongest or physically toughest family. They led religious sacrifices to the gods. Kingship was strengthened during period of migrations; tribes that did not migrate did not develop kingships. The **comitatus, or war band,** the bravest young men of the tribe, was bound by loyalty to the king, fought beside him in battle, and was not supposed to leave the field without him—to do so brought social disgrace.

The role and status of **women** has yet to be thoroughly explored. Society was patriarchal: within each household the male head had authority over his wives (polygamy was practiced by the wealthy), children, and slaves (captured in war). Women were viewed as property; marriageable daughters were sold to the highest bidder; and their subsequent status depended on their production of children, especially sons. In settled communities, women performed the heavy work of raising, grinding, preserving cereal crops; making beer and ale; weaving and spinning; caring for the children, and other domestic tasks.

Progress of migrations. The eastern Germans (Bastarnac, Burgundians, Gepids, Goths, Heruls, Rugians, Sciri) moved toward the Black Sea; they arrived there by 214 C.E. The division of Visigoth (West Goth) and Ostrogoth (East Goth) probably arose after their arrival at the Black Sea.

1. THE HUNS

The **Huns,** nomadic Mongols of the Ural-Altaic group, probably under pressure from the Zhu-Zhu Empire in Asia, swept into Europe in the 4th century and halted for some fifty years in the valley of the Danube and Theiss.

445–53. Height of the Hun power under Attila. Honoria, sister of Valentinian III, to escape an unwelcome marriage, sent her ring to Attila and asked for aid. Attila claimed this to be an offer of marriage. About the same time, Gaiseric the Vandal was intriguing to induce Attila to attack the Visigoths. By a clever pretense of friendliness to both sides, Attila kept the Romans and Goths apart, and set out westward with a great force (451). Metz was taken and the Belgic provinces ravaged. To meet Attila, the Roman Aëtius mustered a force of Salian Franks, Ripuarians, Burgundians, Celts, and Visigoths under Theodoric I, as well as his own Gallo-Romans. Attila apparently declined battle near Orleans and turned back.

451. Aëtius overtook him at an unknown spot near Troyes, and a drawn battle was fought. Attila continued his withdrawal. Still claiming Honoria, Attila turned into Italy, razed Aquileia, ravaged the countryside (foundation of Venice), and opened the road to Rome. Pope Leo, one of a commission of three sent by the emperor, appeared before Attila. Attila retreated after plague had broken out in his force, food supplies had run low, and reinforcements arrived from the east for the Roman army. Attila's death (453) was followed by a revolt of his German vassals and the defeat of the Huns on the Nedao (in Pannonia). The remnant of the Huns settled on the lower Danube; the Gepids set up a kingdom in Dacia; the Ostrogoths settled in Pannonia.

2. THE VISIGOTHS

After their defeat by the Huns, the Visigoths (perhaps 80,000 in number) sought refuge in the Roman Empire.

376. Emperor **Valens** ordered them disarmed and allowed to cross the Danube to settle in Lower Moesia. Faced with the unprecedented problem of these refugees, the Roman government bungled the administration, failed to disarm the Goths, and ultimately had to fight a two-year war with them.

378. The Visigoths, under **Fritigern,** defeated and killed **Valens** near Adrianople, thereby making the first decisive break in the Rhine-Danube frontier.

Fritigern, hoping to carve a Visigothic empire out of the Roman provinces, ravaged Thrace for two years but could not take Adrianople. After his death (379), Emperor **Theodosius** arranged a pacification of the Visigoths as part of a general policy of assimilation. He won over the chieftain **Alaric,** of the royal house of Balthas, who hoped for a career in the Roman service. Alaric, disappointed in his hopes at the death of Theodosius, was elected king by the Visigoths, and ravaged Thrace to the gates of Constantinople. Arcadius, emperor of the east (395–408), was helpless until the arrival of Stilicho, *magister utriusque militiae* (field marshal of both services) in the east.

Stilicho, son of a Vandal father and a Roman mother and married to Theodosius' sister, was guardian of Theodosius' sons, Arcadius and Honorius. He faced Alaric in Thessaly and the Peloponnesus, avoiding battle apparently on orders from Honorius. Alaric was made *magister militum* in Illyricum, and Stilicho, out of favor in Constantinople, was declared a public enemy.

401. Alaric began a thrust into Italy, probably because of the triumph of an anti-German faction in Constantinople, and ravaged Venetia. Simultaneously Radagaisus (an Ostrogoth) began an invasion of Raetia and Italy. Stilicho, firmly against any Germanic invasion of the west, repulsed Radagaisus.

402. Pollentia (in Liguria, south of present-day Turin), site of a drawn battle between Stilicho and Alaric, was a strategic defeat for Alaric. Alaric's next advance was stopped, probably through an understanding with Stilicho. Halted again (403) at Verona, the Visigoths withdrew to Epirus.

406. The **Rhine frontier,** denuded of troops for the defense of Italy, was crossed by a great wave of migrants, chiefly eastern Germans: Vandals, Sueves, and Alans (non-German). The usurper **Constantine** having crossed from Britain to Gaul, Alaric in Noricum was paid a huge sum of gold by the senate as a sort of retainer for his services against Constantine. Stilicho, his popularity undermined by these events and by the hostility of Constantinople, was beheaded (408). Stilicho was the archetypal barbarian army general exercising power in the name of a weak emperor. There is no evidence of treason by Stilicho. His execution was followed by a general massacre of the families of the barbarian auxiliaries in Italy, and some 30,000 of them went over to Alaric in Noricum.

410. Alaric took Rome after alternate sieges and negotiations. He sacked it, then moved south toward Africa, the granary of Italy. Turned back by the loss of his fleet, Alaric died and was buried in the bed of the Busento River. His brother-in-law Ataulf was elected to succeed him. Ataulf, originally bent on the destruction of the very name of Rome, now bent his energies to the fusion of Visigothic vigor and Roman tradition.

412. Ataulf led the Visigoths north, ravaged Etruria, crossed the Alps, ravaged Gaul, and married (against her brother Honorius's will) Galla Placidia (414) after the Roman ritual. He was forced into Spain (415), where he was murdered. **Wallia** (414–c. 418), after the brief reign of Sigeric, succeeded him.

Ulfilas (311–81), a Gothic bishop of Arian convictions, invented the Gothic alphabet for his translation of the Bible. This translation, the first literary monument of the German invaders, had enormous influence and recalls the wide extent of the **Arian heresy,** which won every important Germanic invader except the Franks, a development with the greatest political consequences, since the lands where the Germans settled were peopled by orthodox Roman Catholics.

Spain had already been overrun by a horde of Vandals, Sueves, and Alans (409), and the Roman blockade made food hard to get. Wallia planned to cross to the African granary but lost his ships; he was forced to make terms with Honorius and restore Galla Placidia to her brother. He agreed to clear Spain of other barbarians. Succeeding in this, he received the grant of *Aquitania Secunda* (i.e., the land between the Loire and the Garonne) with Toulouse as a capital.

419–507. Thus began the **Kingdom of Toulouse.** The Visigoths received two-thirds of the land, the remainder being left to the Roman proprietors. A Gothic kingdom was created within the Roman state. Honorius, hoping to counteract alien influences, revived a Roman custom of holding provincial councils, decreeing an annual meeting of the leading officials and the chief landowners for discussion of common problems. The most important rulers of Toulouse were **Theodoric I,** (419–51), who fell in the **battle of Châlons,** and **Euric,** (466–84), whose reign marked the apogee of the kingdom. He continued the pressure of the Visigoths on Gaul and Spain, and by 481 extended his domain from the Pyrenees to the Loire and eastward to the Rhône, securing Provence from Odovacar (481). Euric first codified Visigothic law, but the *Breviary of Alaric* (506), a codification of Roman law for Visigothic use, had tremendous influence among the Visigoths and among many other barbarian peoples. Under Visigothic rule the administration in general remained Roman, and the language of government continued to be a Latin vernacular. The Gallo-Roman population and clergy were hostile to the Visigoths as Arians, and this hostility opened the way

for the **Frankish conquest** (507), which reduced the Visigothic power to its Spanish domains.

507–711. The **Visigothic Kingdom of Spain** dragged out a miserable existence until the arrival of the Muslims (p. 179).

554. Belisarius's invasion of Spain, part of Justinian's reconstruction of the Roman Empire (p. 183), was a brilliant campaign, but it reduced only the southeast corner of Spain, later regained by the Visigoths, who also reduced the Sueves in the north.

3. THE VANDALS

406. The **Vandals** crossed the Rhine near the Main, followed the Moselle and Aisne (sacking Reims, Amiens, Arras, Tournai), then turned southward into Aquitaine, and crossed the Pyrenees into Spain (409).

429–534. The Vandal Kingdom in Africa. The Vandals and Alani had been established in southern Spain under Gunderic. His brother **Gaiseric** received an appeal from Bonifatius, the Roman governor of Africa, following which the Vandals (perhaps 80,000 in number) crossed into Africa (429).

430. The **first siege of Hippo** in North Africa failed, but Bonifatius, now reconciled to the regency of Galla Placidia, was annihilated, and the city fell (431). **St. Augustine,** bishop of Hippo, died during the siege. The creation of a great Vandal power in Africa, supported as it soon was by a powerful navy, distracted the attention of the Roman government from the new barbarian kingdoms of the west and had a decisive effect of a negative kind.

In Africa the Vandals spared nothing, and the treaty made with the Romans was no restraint. After the arrival of a fleet from Constantinople, a second treaty was made. Eudocia, daughter of Valentinian, was betrothed to Gaiseric's son, Huneric, and the Vandals received most of the Roman territory except the region about Carthage.

455. Gaiseric attacked Rome, on the invitation (according to tradition) of Valentinian's widow, Eudoxia. He took it easily, and for two weeks pillaged the city.

In Africa the Vandals were hated as Arians, and they had to deal with serious **Berber revolts.**

533–48. Power was held by the Vandals until the **Vandalic Wars of Justinian.** Belisarius quickly defeated the Carthaginian power of the Vandals; the ensuing Berber revolt was not put down until 548.

4. THE BURGUNDIANS

411–532. The **Burgundians,** arriving from the Oder-Vistula region, moved along the Main athwart the Rhine, entered Gaul under King Gundicar, and finally settled as federates of the Roman Empire in upper Burgundy (i.e., the lands including Lyons, Vienne, Besançon, Geneva, Autun, Mâcon). King **Gundibald** (d. 516) codified Burgundian law in the *Lex Gundobada.* The Burgundians were finally conquered by the sons of Clovis (c. 532), but the Burgundian state remained separate under Frankish control with Merovingian princes until 613. After 613 it was a province of the Frankish Empire.

d. THE OSTROGOTHS IN ITALY

On the breakup of the Hunnic Empire (after Nedao, 454), the Ostrogoths settled in Pannonia (their first settlement inside the Roman frontier) as federates of the empire. Under the Huns, the emergence of a single ruler had been impossible. Thiudareiks ("ruler of the people"), corrupted into Theodoric, had been educated as a hostage at Constantinople, was elected (471), and soon became leader of his people on a march into the Balkan Peninsula, where he forced the Emperor Leo to grant him lands in Macedonia. His ambition for imperial appointment was realized when he was made *magister militum praesentalis* (483), and *consul* (484). He quarreled with the emperor and marched on Constantinople. To get rid of him, the emperor commissioned him (informally) to expel Odovacar from Italy. Arriving in Italy (489) the Ostrogoths triumphed over Odovacar, but did not reduce Ravenna until 493. Theodoric killed Odovacar with his own hands and had his troops massacred.

489–526. Theodoric the Great. In general Theodoric continued Odovacar's policy, substituting Ostrogoths for Odovacar's Germans, and assigning one-third of the Roman estates (as Odovacar had probably done) to his own people. Theodoric's rule was officially recognized (497) by Constantinople. Together with the emperors he named the consuls in the west, but never named an Ostrogoth. Theodoric was the only member of his people who was a Roman citizen; constitutionally the others were alien soldiers in the service of the empire. No Roman was in military command, no Ostrogoth in the civil service. Imperial legislation and coinage continued. The so-called *Edictum Theodorici* was a codification of Theodoric's administrative decrees rather than a body of legislation, as none of Theodoric's "laws" were anything more than clarifications of imperial legislation. Theodoric's secretary was the learned Italian **Cassiodorus,** and the dual state was paralleled by a dual religious system. Theodoric was tolerant of the orthodox Catholics and a protector of the Jews. His chief aim was to civilize his people under the Roman environment and to keep peace.

Theodoric's cooperation with the other Germanic peoples was close, and he cemented his associations with marriage alliances (one daughter married Alaric II, the Visigoth, another Sigismund the Burgundian, and he himself married Clovis's sister). He intervened to protect the Alamanni from Clovis and tried to save the Visigoths. Provence was acquired from Burgundy and annexed to Italy. He was regent and protector of his grandson Amalaric after Alaric II's death, and virtually ruled the Visigothic Kingdom until his death (526).

To the Italians, Ostrogothic rule was alien and heretical, and they resented it. The end of Theodoric's reign was marked by growing ill feelings and suspicion. **Boethius,** the Roman philosopher and commentator on Aristotle, author of *De consolatione philosophiae* and an official of Theodoric's government, and his father-in-law, the brilliant and polished Roman **Symmachus,** were both executed (c. 524) on a charge of treasonable conspiracy.

535–54. Reconquest of Italy by the Emperor. Justinian, as part of his grandiose reconstitution of the Roman Empire, dispatched **Belisarius** and later **Narses,** who reduced the stubborn Ostrogoths and drove them over the Alps to an unknown end.

After the expulsion of the Ostrogoths, the **Exarchate of Ravenna** was established under Emperor Maurice (582–602). The exarch had military and civil powers and received full imperial honors. He exercised imperial control over the Church, including the bishopric of Rome. War and pestilence had completely ruined northern Italy; Rome, in ruins, had sunk from her imperial position to that of a provincial town.

Ravenna was the capital of the West (c. 402–76) and was the home of Theodoric's brilliant court. The architecture of the city offers a unique series of examples of Roman and Romano-Byzantine buildings begun under the emperors and continued by Theodoric. Theodoric's fame survives in the Middle High German epic *Nibelungelied* (c. 1200).

Ruined by invasion, its aqueducts cut, **Rome** was reduced in population from a half million to perhaps 50,000. Its aristocracy had fled, and medieval decay had replaced pagan grandeur. The city was not revived until the Renaissance.

Progress of the papacy. Gelasius (492–96) was the first pope to proclaim the independence of the papacy from both emperor and Church council in matters of faith. He asserted that two powers rule the world, the *sacerdotium* and the *imperium*. The *sacerdotium*, since it is the instrument of human salvation, was declared superior to the *imperium*.

The barbarian invasions had isolated Italy, accentuated the break with the empire, and left the pope as the sole representative of ancient unity and Roman hegemony. At the same time, the Ostrogoths (half romanized as they were) did not destroy the culture, but encouraged the Church to transmit the Greco-Roman tradition (linguistic, social, cultural, administrative, and religious) in the West.

529. Having originated in the East in the 2nd century, **monasticism,** female as well as male, rapidly expanded in the West in the 5th and 6th centuries, but it had no structure, and had ascetic extremes on the one hand, laxness on the other. In 529 Benedict of Nursia, scandalized by conditions in Rome, withdrew to Monte Cassino between Rome and Naples, established a colony, and gave it a **Rule,** or constitution. The ***Rule of St. Benedict*** represents the accumulated spiritual wisdom of earlier centuries of monastic experience, drawing as it does on the writings of Cassian (p. 166), the practice of monastic life in southern Europe, and (especially) *The Rule of the Master*, a long, detailed, ex-

hortatory document. By classical standards, Benedict was not well educated: his *Rule* contains not one reference to an ancient Greek or Latin author. But it displays a deep knowledge of Scripture, the writings of the Church fathers, and the Egyptian monastic tradition. Modern scholars stress the major influence of the wisdom literature of the Old Testament—the Book of Proverbs, the Psalms, Sirach, and Wisdom. Benedict's *Rule* contains both theoretical principles for the monastic life and practical, everyday directives. He legislated for a community of laypersons governed benevolently by an abbot (father)—a community whose purpose was the glorification of God and the salvation of the individual. After a year's novitiate, or probation, the monk professed three vows: stability (in the monastery), the reformation of his life, and obedience. Benedictine life meant a routine lived in a spirit of silence, dedicated to prayer and work and characterized by moderation and flexibility in all things.

Benedict planned the **monastery as a self-sufficient socioeconomic unit,** "so constructed that within it all the necessities, such as water, mill, and garden are contained and the various crafts are practiced. Then there will be no need for the monks to roam outside, because that is not at all good for their souls" (ch. 66). Having stated that "idleness is the enemy of the soul; therefore, the brethren should be occupied at stated times in manual labor, and at other fixed times in sacred reading" (ch. 48), the *Rule* prescribes that all monks in good health should spend part of the day in manual labor. Anticipating the entrance of persons of all social classes, Benedict advised the abbot, "Let him make no distinction of persons . . . Let not the one of noble birth be put before him who was formerly a slave" (ch. 2). He expected that many recruits would be oblates, children offered to the monastery by their parents to be brought up and eventually professed (vowed) there (ch. 59), a system that lasted well into the 19th century; thus monasticism fulfilled an important social function in a world in which career opportunities were severely limited. Each monastery was autonomous; strictly speaking, there was and is no Benedictine order. Gradually replacing other forms of monastic life in the West, and drawing both men and women, Benedictine monasticism served as the chief instrument for the reform of the Frankish Church and for the conversion and civilization of England and Germany. It was the sole form of corporate and organized religious life between the 6th and 11th century.

541–42. Probably more destructive of population than the Germanic invasions and the wars connected with Justinian's reconquest was the plague. In 541–42 the **bubonic plague** (identified only in 1894 by bacteriologists, who labeled the bacillus that causes the disease *Pasteurella pestis* after one scientist's teacher, Louis Pasteur) swept into Italy, southern France, the Rhine Valley, and the Iberian Peninsula, killing 20 percent of the population. Reappearing in cycles (558–61, 580–82, 588–91, 599–600), though each time with reduced intensity, it swept as far north as Sweden and as far west as Ireland. Scholars estimate that by 700 southern Europe and the Rhine Valley had lost between 50 and 60 percent of their populations. Consequences of the plague were a sharp rise in the price of labor, reduced trade, and an intensification of religious belief (that disease, suffering, and death are God's punishment for sin).

554. Justinian's Pragmatic Sanction restored the Italian lands taken by the Ostrogoths and made a pro forma restoration of government, but agricultural lands had been depopulated and had reverted into wilderness, and the rural proprietors were sinking into serfdom. Town decline was similar. The Roman Senate ceased to function after 603, and the local curiae disappeared at about the same time.

Duces were appointed, probably over each *civitas*, as part of the imperial administration, but they gradually became great landowners, and their military functions dominated their civil duties. A fusion of the ducal title and landownership ensued, and a new class of hereditary military proprietors emerged beside the clergy and the old nobles. The details of this process are, of course, hard to determine, because evidence is scant.

e. THE FRANKISH KINGDOM

The **Franks** first appeared as settlers on the lower Rhine in two divisions, the **Salians** (dwellers by the sea, *sal*) and the **Ripuarians** (dwellers

THE MEROVINGIAN KINGS

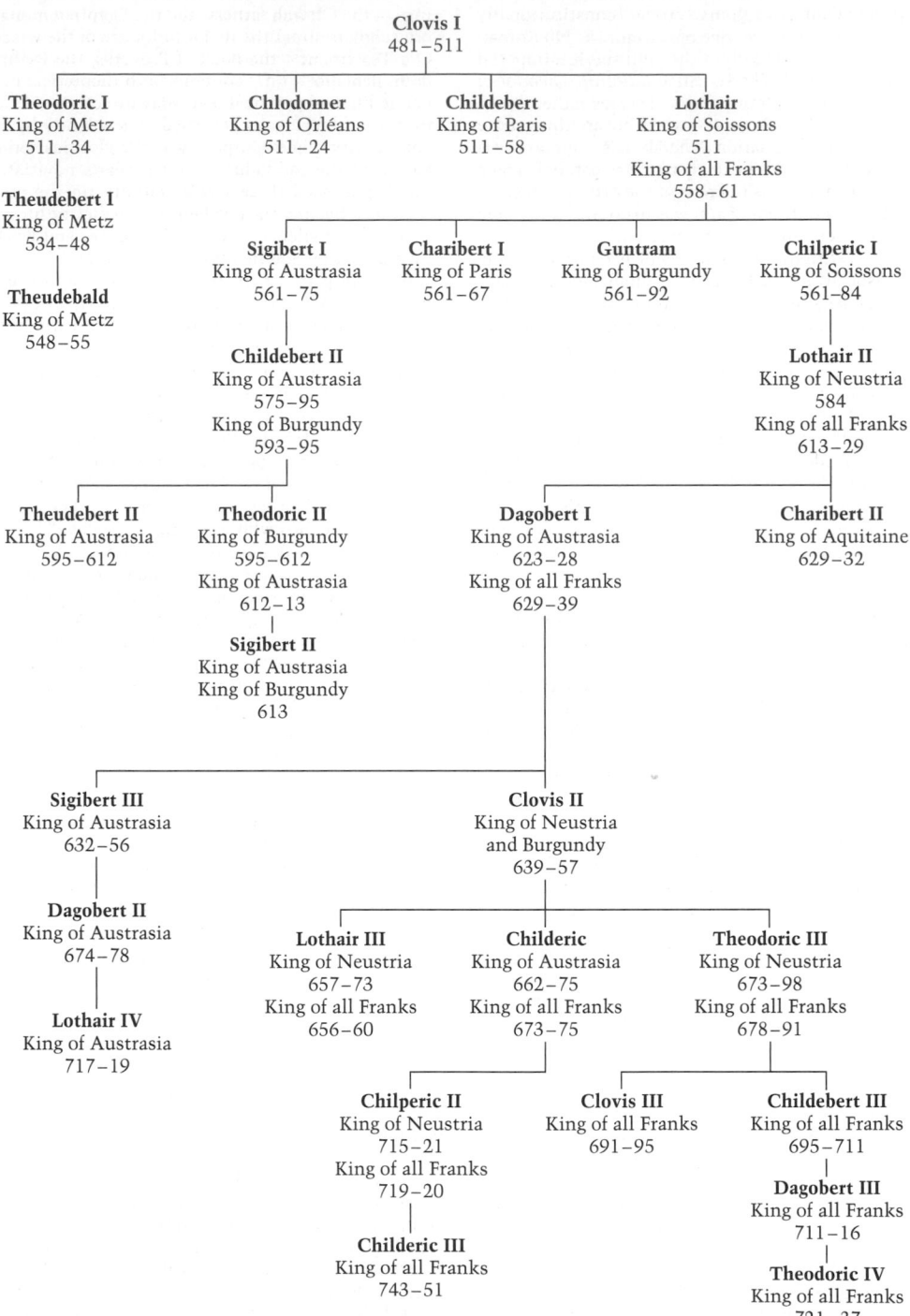

Clovis I
481–511

Theodoric I
King of Metz
511–34

Chlodomer
King of Orléans
511–24

Childebert
King of Paris
511–58

Lothair
King of Soissons
511
King of all Franks
558–61

Theudebert I
King of Metz
534–48

Theudebald
King of Metz
548–55

Sigibert I
King of Austrasia
561–75

Charibert I
King of Paris
561–67

Guntram
King of Burgundy
561–92

Chilperic I
King of Soissons
561–84

Childebert II
King of Austrasia
575–95
King of Burgundy
593–95

Lothair II
King of Neustria
584
King of all Franks
613–29

Theudebert II
King of Austrasia
595–612

Theodoric II
King of Burgundy
595–612
King of Austrasia
612–13

Dagobert I
King of Austrasia
623–28
King of all Franks
629–39

Charibert II
King of Aquitaine
629–32

Sigibert II
King of Austrasia
King of Burgundy
613

Sigibert III
King of Austrasia
632–56

Clovis II
King of Neustria
and Burgundy
639–57

Dagobert II
King of Austrasia
674–78

Lothair III
King of Neustria
657–73
King of all Franks
656–60

Childeric
King of Austrasia
662–75
King of all Franks
673–75

Theodoric III
King of Neustria
673–98
King of all Franks
678–91

Lothair IV
King of Austrasia
717–19

Chilperic II
King of Neustria
715–21
King of all Franks
719–20

Clovis III
King of all Franks
691–95

Childebert III
King of all Franks
695–711

Childeric III
King of all Franks
743–51

Dagobert III
King of all Franks
711–16

Theodoric IV
King of all Franks
721–37

by the riverbank, *ripa*). By the end of the 4th century the Salians were established in the area between the Meuse and the Scheldt as federates of the Roman Empire; the Ripuarians, in the tract between the Rhine and Meuse. They formed no permanent confederations, and, unlike the other Germanic peoples, did not migrate as a nation, but expanded.

431–751. The Salian Franks under the Merovingians. The dynasty descended from the semilegendary Merowech, first noted c. 430. **King Childeric** (d. 481) fought as a federate of the empire at Orleans when

Aëtius defeated the Visigoths, and he later defeated the Saxons on the Loire. His tomb was found (1653) at Tournai, the "capital" of the Salians.

481–511. Clovis (Chlodovech), son of Childeric, in the service of Julius Nepos and Zeno. He defeated the Gallo-Roman general Syagrius at Soissons (486), expanding Salian power to the Loire. Friendly relations existed between Clovis and Bishop Remigius, who later baptized him. Sigebert, the Ripuarian, defeated an Alamannic invasion at Tolbiac

(496) with Salian support. Clovis, in the same year, defeated the Alamanni (Strasburg?) and later, after election as king of the Ripuarians, emerged as master of the Franks on both sides of the Rhine.

496. The traditional date of the **conversion of Clovis** to Roman Catholicism is 496. He had previously married a Burgundian, Clotilda, who was of the Roman communion. The Burgundians in general were Arians, and Clovis's choice may have been deliberate. In any case his conversion won him papal support and opened the way to wide conquests from the heretic (i.e., Arian) German peoples. Burgundy was conquered (after 500); the Visigoths defeated at Vouillé (507); and their whole kingdom north of the Pyrenees (except Septimania and Provence) was soon subjugated. These conquests were supported by the Gallo-Roman clergy as a religious war. Clovis founded the Church of the Holy Apostles (Ste. Geneviève) at Paris, and shortly moved his "capital" from Soissons to Paris. He was made an honorary consul by Emperor Anastasius, a proceeding that brought the Franks technically into the empire.

Frankish Administration. The old Roman **civitas**, city and surrounding territory, served as the basis of Merovingian and (later) Carolingian administration. **Comites,** later called counts, royal officials of Gallo-Roman descent, presided over the civitas, collected taxes, heard lawsuits, enforced justice, and raised troops. Clovis and his descendants issued **capitulares,** legislative and administrative orders divided by chapters, that tried to reduce violence; these showed the strong influence of Roman law.

511–628. Divisions of the Frankish lands after the death of Clovis: (1) His four sons established four capitals—Metz, Orleans, Paris, Soissons. Expansion eastward continued along the upper Elbe; Burgundy was added, and the territory of the Ostrogoths north of the Alps. After a period of ruthless conflict, only **Lothair** (Chlothar) survived, and for a brief time (558–61) the Frankish lands were under one head again. (2) Lothair's division of his lands among his four sons led to a great feud from which three kingdoms emerged: **Austrasia** (capital Metz) lying to the east (Auster) and mostly Teutonic; **Neustria** (the "new land," as the name implies; capital Soissons), Gallo-Roman in blood; and **Burgundy,** which had no king of its own but joined Neustria under a common ruler. The prince of Neustria exterminated the rival house in Austrasia, but the local chieftains preserved the kingdom's identity. Under **Lothair II** all three kingdoms were united again (613) under one ruler.

629–39. Dagobert (Lothair's son), the last strong ruler of the Merovingian house, made wide dynastic alliances and found wise advisers in **Bishop Arnulf** and **Pepin of Landen.** His firm rule led to a revolt. Under the *rois fainéants* (lazy, "do-nothing kings," who were rulers in name only) following Dagobert, the **mayors of the palace** emerged from a menial position to take a dominant role in the government both in Austrasia and Neustria.

Merovingian government retained the Roman *civitas* as a unit of administration and set a count (*comes* or *graf*) over it. The source of law was not the king but local custom, administered by the *graf* with the aid of local landowners. Military leaders of large districts were the duces, who were over several counts. Land grants were made in lieu of pay to officials.

Gregory, bishop of Tours (c. 540–94), a Frank, wrote in Latin the *Historia Francorum,* the best single source on the history of the Merovingian period.

Decline of royal power under the last Merovingians and **feudal decentralization. Feudalism** implies a kind of politically decentralized society in which public power—to raise an army, to hold courts that administer some form of law or justice, to coin money, and to negotiate with outside powers—passes into private hands. Feudal decentralization was characterized by the breakdown of the old class and Germanic tribal organizations without an effective system to replace it, which led to the personal and economic dependence on private individuals; by the increasing concentration of land in the hands of a few (i.e., a landed "aristocracy" of which the mayors of the palace were representative; and perhaps by the increasing importance of the possession of a horse and the ability to fight on horseback. (This was due in part to the arrival of the stirrup, an Asian invention, that attached rider to horse, enabling him to use the force of his galloping animal to strike and cripple his enemy.) However, although Charles Martel used some cavalry in his wars against the Muslims, the **infantry** was **the typical**

and decisive unit in all Carolingian warfare, and so the stirrup's importance has been downplayed. Warriors who attached themselves to strong "lords" were at first supported in the lord's own household; they were later rewarded, sometimes with land, sometimes with cash, with which they maintained themselves. In the lord's household, the wife frequently had responsibility for the dispersal of cash and goods.

Emergence of the Carolingians in Austrasia. The son of Arnulf married the daughter of **Count Pepin I** (of Landen, d. 640), mayor of the palace, founding the line later called Carolingian.

687. Pepin II (of Heristal), grandson of Pepin I, gained supremacy in Austrasia and Neustria by his victory at Tertry. The kingdom was on the verge of dissolution (ducal separatism), and Pepin began an effort to reduce the landed aristocracy from which he himself had sprung.

714–41. Charles Martel (i.e., the Hammer), Pepin's son, an ally of the Lombards.

716–54. Missionary activities of **St. Boniface** (Winfrid, Wynfrith), Apostle of Germany. With the support of Charles Martel and Pope Gregory II, Boniface worked to establish a centralized and episcopal church in Germany under Carolingian supervision. He founded dioceses, made Mainz a metropolitan see, established several monasteries, including Fulda, and encouraged the observance of the *Rule of St. Benedict* in all houses of men and women.

733. Martel's **victory at Tours** arrested the advance of the Muslims in the west, and was followed by their final retreat over the Pyrenees (759).

Pepin's **conquest of the Frisians** was continued, five wars were waged against the Saxons, and powerful decentralizing forces (notably in Burgundy and Alamannia) were broken down.

739. Pope Gregory III, threatened by the Lombards, sent an embassy to Martel, and offered the title of consul in return for protection. Charles, an ally of the Lombard king, ignored the appeal. At the end of his life, Martel, like a true sovereign, divided the Merovingian lands between his sons, Austrasia and the German duchies going to Carloman, Neustria and Burgundy to Pepin. Carloman and Pepin ruled together, 741–47; Pepin ruled alone, 747–68. (To p. 173)

f. THE LOMBARDS AND THE POPES

(From p. 167)
For a complete list of the Roman popes, see Appendix IV.

Under Emperor Augustus, the Lombards were still established on the lower Elbe (Bardengau) and were defeated (5 C.E.) by the Romans. Their history for the next 400 years is confused. They were members of the Hunnic Empire and were probably Arians. They were given land by Justinian in Noricum and Pannonia, and they aided (553) the imperial attacks on the Ostrogoths. The Lombards took part in Belisarius's conquest, and soon they began to move south toward Italy.

568. The Lombard conquest of Italy. Italy, worn out by the Gothic wars, famine, and disease, offered little resistance. Constantinople was indifferent, and the conquest was easy. The Lombards, always few in number, had associated other peoples (including Saxons and some Slavs) in their invasion, but even then they were not numerous enough to occupy the whole peninsula. Rome and Naples were never held, and Ravenna only briefly. The coast was not really mastered. The Lombards did not enter into a compact with the empire, and Italian feeling against them was bitter. Pavia became the capital (Italy, until 774, always had two and usually three capitals: Rome, the papal capital; Ravenna, the Byzantine capital; and Pavia, the Lombardian capital after 573), and the peninsula was a mosaic of Byzantine, papal, and Lombardian jurisdictions.

Lombard occupation (virtually military rule at first) covered inland Liguria, inland Tuscany, inland Venetia, the duchy of Spoleto and the duchy of Benevento. **Imperial Italy** comprised Venice and the land from north of Ravenna to the south of Ancona, and included the duchy of Rome and the duchy of Naples, as well as the toe and heel of Italy. *Hospitalitas* was revived, and one third of the produce of the land (not one third of the land) was given to the Lombards. Lombards also took the lands of the dead and the exiled.

The Lombards took Roman titles and names, and in the end ac-

THE HOUSE OF PEPIN (640-814)

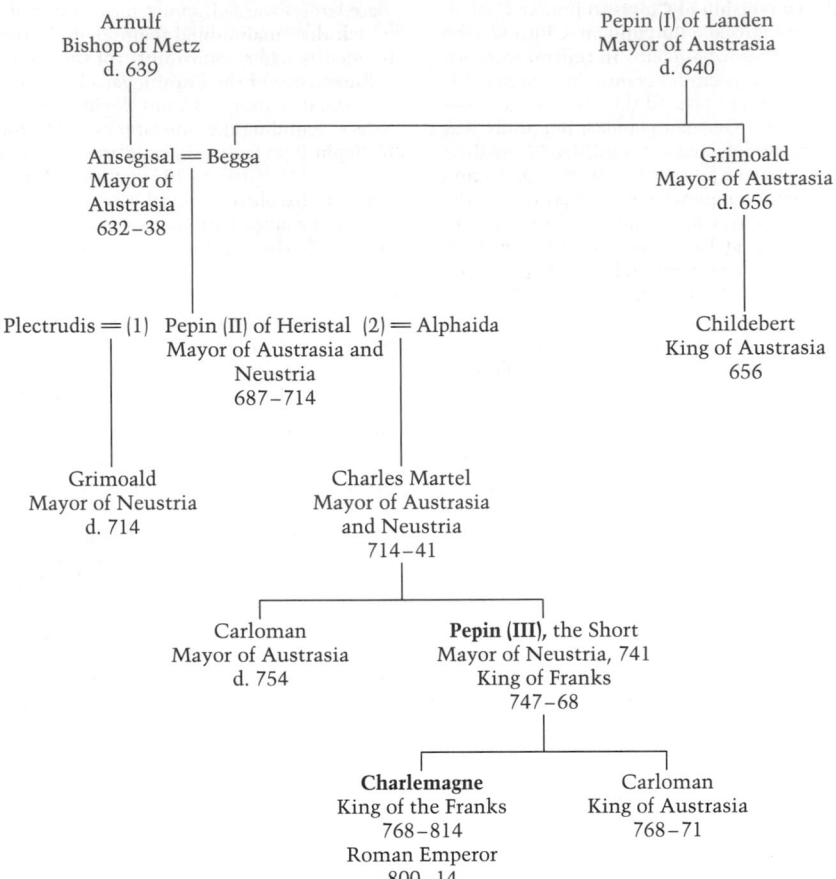

cepted Roman Catholicism. Legally there was a dual system of private law, and in Lombard territories there was a dual episcopal system (i.e., Arian and Roman).

573–84. A period of anarchy and private war under a loose federation of dukes (some 36 in number). Roman Catholic opposition and papal negotiations with the Franks alarmed the Lombards, and led to the election of **King Authari** in 584.

584–90. King Authari was endowed with half the baronial lands as royal domain. The dukedoms were gradually absorbed (the marches, like Fruili, Trent, Turin, survived longest).

Authari's widow, Theodolinda, a devoted Roman Catholic, bidden to choose a husband who should also be king, selected a Thuringian.

590–604. Gregory the Great. His family was a rich senatorial house, and Gregory was prefect of Rome (573). He founded (c. 574) six monasteries in Sicily and one at Rome (St. Andrews) into which he immediately retired as a monk. Embassy to Constantinople (c. 579–86). Elected pope (590) against his will, he began a vigorous administration. Discipline within his patriarchate was rigorous (stress on celibacy, close watch on elections, insistence on exclusive clerical jurisdiction over clerical offenders). Church revenue was divided into four shares, for the bishop, the clergy, the poor, and church buildings. His administration of the wide estates of the Church was honest, and the revenue was expanded to meet the tremendous demands on Rome for charity. The pope continued the old imperial grain doles in Rome and elsewhere, aqueducts were repaired, urban administration, especially in Rome, was reformed.

Outside his immediate patriarchal jurisdiction, Gregory expanded the influence and prestige of the pope, maintaining that the pope was by divine designation head of all churches. Appeals to Rome were heard even against the patriarch of Constantinople, whose claim to

the title of universal bishop was denied. Without secular authority, Gregory assumed the powers of a temporal prince, counterbalancing the prestige of Constantinople. Gregory was the real leader against the Lombards, appointing governors of cities, directing the generals in war, and receiving from Constantinople pay for the army.

The first monk to become pope, Gregory made a close alliance between the Benedictines and the papacy (at the expense of the bishops). The monks were given charters and protected from the bishops, the Benedictine Rule was imposed, and a great missionary campaign was begun with monastic aid: the mission to Britain (596) under **Augustine of Canterbury** and the conversion of England provided a base from which the Frankish Church was later reformed and the German people converted; and campaigns were waged against paganism in Gaul, Italy, and Sicily, and against heresy in Africa and Sicily.

Gregory was the last of the four great Latin Fathers, and first of the medieval prelates, a link between the classical Greco-Roman tradition and the medieval Romano-German one. Not a great scholar, he was a great popularizer, and he spread the doctrines of Augustine of Hippo throughout the West. At the same time he gave wide currency through his *Dialogues* to the popular (often originally pagan) ideas of angels, demons, devils, relic worship, miracles, the doctrine of purgatory, and the use of allegory. His *Book of Pastoral Care* remained for centuries an essential in the education of the clergy. There was a school of music at Rome, but how much Gregory had to do with it, and how much with the introduction of the Gregorian chant, is uncertain. Gregory introduced the papal style, *Servus Servorum Dei*.

590–615. Duke Agilulf of Turin was friendly to the Roman Church and was the true founder of the Lombard state. Gregory the Great blocked an Italian conspiracy against the Lombards. **Rothari** (636–52) became a Roman Catholic. He collected Lombard customary law in Latin and began the consolidation of Lombard power. Eventually Roman law triumphed and Lombard law survived only in the schools (e.g., Pavia).

The Italian bishops since 476 had been the leaders of the peaceful civilians in the cities, the protectors of the oppressed, and the dispensers of charity. Under the Lombards, a system of **episcopal immunities** emerged that made the bishops virtually local temporal sovereigns and enabled them to preserve the local spirit of municipal independence and organization (e.g., consuls, guilds). The urban population was free, and the town walls (often built by the bishops) were refuges. Milan resumed her greatness and almost equaled Rome. These developments prepared the way for the assertion of Italian town independence against Roman clerical and German feudal encroachments. **Paul the Deacon** (c. 720–c. 800), the first important medieval historian, wrote the *Historia gentis Langobardorum*. **Martianus Capella** (fl. c. 600), encyclopedist, formulated the seven arts (grammar, logic, rhetoric, geometry, astronomy, arithmetic, music), which were to guide education down to the Renaissance.

Continued alienation of Italy from the East. Arrest (653), by the exarch, of Pope Martin I (649–55), who died in exile in the East. The **Council of Constantinople** (692) reasserted the equality of the patriarchates of Constantinople and Rome.

Emperor Leo III the Isaurican (717–41) attempted to bring Italy back to obedience: heavy taxation to reduce the great landowners angered Pope Gregory II (the largest landowner in Italy) and Leo's iconoclastic decree (726) aroused all Italy. Gregory III excommunicated all Iconoclasts (731). Gregory's defeat and final humiliation weakened the pope and opened the way for the final Lombard advance.

712–44. Destruction of the Lombard Kingdom. Liutprand, king of the Lombards **(712–44),** extended his rule over the duchies of Benevento and Spoleto. Ravenna was taken temporarily. During the Iconoclastic controversy, Liutprand's sincere efforts at rapprochement with the papacy met a brief success.

749–56. Aistulf continued Liutprand's policy of consolidation. The pope, alarmed at Lombard progress, had already (741) made overtures to Charles Martel. Martel, busy with the Muslims, remained faithful to his alliance with the Lombards, but Aistulf's continued advance brought a visit (753) from Pope Stephen II. Stephen had already begun negotiations with Pepin III, king of the Franks, and the mutual needs of the rising papacy and the upstart Carolingian dynasty drew them into alliance.

754, 756. Pepin, in two expeditions, forced Aistulf to abandon the Pentapolis and Ravenna (bringing the Lombards virtually to their holdings of 681). Legally the lands involved in the **Donation of Pepin** (756) belonged to the Eastern Empire. The Donation was a tacit recognition of implicit claims of the popes to be the heirs of the empire in Italy. Most important from the papal point of view was the fact that the Church had won a powerful military ally outside Italy. Henceforth the Carolingians maintained a protectorate over the papacy in Italy.

774. Charlemagne, heir to the traditions of Pepin, having repudiated the daughter of the Lombard king, Desiderius, appeared in Italy to protect the pope. After a nine-month siege, Pavia was taken, Spoleto and Benevento were conquered, and Charlemagne (Charles the Great) absorbed the Lombard Kingdom into the rising Frankish Empire and assumed the crown of the Lombards. On a visit to Rome (774), Charlemagne confirmed the Donation of Pepin but made it plain that he was sovereign even in the papal lands. At no time did Charlemagne allow the pope any but a primacy in honor (in this respect, following the strict Byzantine tradition). The Donation of Pepin was the **foundation of the Papal States** and the true beginning of the temporal power of the papacy. Henceforth there was neither a Lombard menace nor the overlordship of the exarch to interfere with the rising papal monarchy. In this sense the fall of the Lombard Kingdom was decisive in papal history. It was equally decisive in Italian history, for the papal victory over the Lombards terminated the last effective effort to establish unity and a centralized government until the end of the 19th century. For the Carolingian monarchy, the episode was equally significant.

Under the successors of Charlemagne, the emperors continued to participate in the papal elections and did what they could to protect Italy against the attacks of the Muslims from Africa.

827–31. The Muslims conquered Sicily.

837. Muslims attacked Naples, pillaged Ancona (839), and captured Bari (840).

846. In the **battle of Licosa,** Duke Sergius of Naples defeated the Muslims at sea.

847–48. Construction of the **Leonine Wall** by Pope Leo IV (847–55) to defend St. Peter's from the Muslims.

Pope Nicholas I (858–67), one of the few great popes between Gregory I and Gregory VII. He forced Lothair II of Lorraine to take back his first wife, Theutberga, whom he had divorced, and deposed the archbishops of Trier and Cologne for endorsing the divorce; affirmed the right of suffragan bishops to appeal directly to Rome over their metropolitan in a case involving the powerful **Hincmar,** archbishop of Reims; encouraged **Sts. Cyril and Methodius** in their missionary work among the Slavs (p. 187); and, in the bitter controversy over the patriarchate of Constantinople, supported Ignatius and excommunicated **Photius** (863). Nicholas first propounded the theory that no bishop may be elected or deposed without papal approval.

867–. **Decline of the papacy,** after the pontificate of Nicholas and the death of Louis II. As the popes had no powerful protectors outside Italy until 961, they fell increasingly under the dominance of the Roman and Italian aristocracy. The lapse of the imperial power left room for the insinuation of a new **doctrine of papal autonomy,** well formulated in the *Forged Decretals.* Outside Italy the relaxation of papal control and the decline of papal prestige, accompanied by the rise of dominant local feudal lords, accentuated the power of the bishops and made the unity of the Western Church a mere shadow until the papacy, having learned to cope with feudalism in the second half of the 11th century, once again made its influence felt in the Church.

875–77. Emperor **Charles the Bald** continued to support the papacy against the invader and came to Rome (875) to be crowned, having forced Charles the Fat to retreat and having induced his brother Carloman to sign a truce and withdraw. He was then elected king of Italy by the local magnates.

888. Berengar of Friuli was crowned king of Italy at Pavia.

891. Guido of Spoleto was consecrated emperor, with his son Lambert as co-emperor and co-king.

892–98. Lambert. Arnulf embarked on a second expedition, took Rome, and was formally crowned (896).   *(To p. 212)*

g. THE EMPIRE OF CHARLEMAGNE AND ITS DISINTEGRATION

(From p. 171)

747–68. Pepin the Short, who attempted to conciliate the Church by granting and restoring lands to it.

752. Pepin was elected king by the Frankish magnates. Both the house of Pepin and the papacy (in the process of securing independence from the emperor at Constantinople) needed each other's support. The immediate need of the popes was for protection against the expanding Lombard monarchy. **Aistulf,** king of the Lombards, had taken Ravenna (751), the seat of the exarch, besieged Rome, and exacted tribute.

754. Pope Stephen II arrived in Gaul, anointed Pepin, and by conferring the title *Patricius Romanorum* (which could legally come only from Constantinople), designated him in a sense regent and protector of Italy. The result was to give some authority to Pepin's new title as king of the Franks.

754. Pepin marched into Italy, defeated the Lombards, and required them to hand over the exarchate and Pentapolis to the pope. The Lombards failed to do so.

756. Pepin returned and, after defeating the Lombards again, made his famous Donation. The **Donation of Pepin** established the Franks, a distant, non-Italian power, as the allies and defenders of the papacy.

759. Pepin conquered Septimania, disciplined Aquitaine, and so brought effective Frankish rule to the Pyrenees. On his death his lands were given to his sons, Charles receiving Austrasia, Neustria, and northern Aquitaine; Carloman, southern Aquitaine, Burgundy, Provence, Septimania. The brothers ruled together, 768–71; Charles alone, 771–814.

771–814. Charles the Great (Charlemagne), a reign of the first magnitude in European history. Charles was well over six feet tall, a superb swimmer, with an athletic frame, large expressive eyes, and a merry disposition. He understood Greek, spoke Latin, but did not learn to write. He preferred the Frankish dress. In general he continued the Frankish policies: (1) expansion of Frankish rule to include all the Germans was completed (omitting only Scandinavia and Britain); (2) a close understanding with the papacy; (3) support of Church reform (which settled the foundations of medieval Christian unity).

Already overlord of the Lombards, Charles married King Desiderius's daughter but soon repudiated her.

773–74. Charlemagne conquered Lombard Italy and became king of the Lombards, whose kingdom was absorbed into the Frankish Empire. Charlemagne also established his rule in Venetia, Istria, Dalmatia, and Corsica.

778. At **Roncesvalles** near Pamplona, on a pass in the western Pyrenees, the Basques destroyed the rear guard of Charlemagne's army as it was returning to France. The battle inspired the late 11th-century poem *The Song of Roland*, the most famous of the *chansons de geste*, or medieval epics. The poem celebrates Roland as the perfect chivalric knight and Charlemagne as the ideal Christian king. The poem was popular in French, Spanish, and Italian literature of the later Middle Ages; the values expressed are those of the 11th, not the 8th century.

787–88. Bavaria was incorporated; its duke, Tassilo, first made a vassal and then deposed.

785. Saxony, after a costly and bitter struggle of 30 years that involved 18 campaigns, was conquered, and Christianity was forcibly introduced despite stubborn pagan resistance. Foundation of the bishopric of Bremen (781).

795–96. The Avars (on the lower Danube) were reduced.

Establishment of marks (after c. 782) to hold the conquests: Dane Mark, the Altmark (against the Wends), Thuringian Mark, Bohemian Mark, Ostmark (against the Avars), Friulian Mark (on the Italian border), and the Spanish Mark. These marks were also centers of colonization and germanization.

Reform of the Church along Roman lines had, for Charlemagne, three purposes: (1) the establishment of peace throughout the empire by means of a uniform Roman ritual (replacing the Gallican) that would win divine favor; (2) development of an educated clergy capable of effective pastoral and missionary work; (3) the creation of a body of literate clerics who could serve as instruments of his administration. The **Capitulary** (a royal-administrative order divided into *capitula*, or articles) **of Herstal** (779) advanced these goals by providing secular assistance to local clergy and assisting in the expansion of a **parish system** with regular services into rural areas throughout the empire. Charlemagne presided at synods, settled dogmatic questions, established schools for the education of the clergy, made ecclesiastical appointments, and, above all, insisted that all clerics—bishops, abbots, parish priests—properly discharge their religious duties; thus, he subordinated the institutional Church to the king as the divinely appointed head of Christendom. The Church was strengthened and tied closely to the monarchy.

800. Imperial Coronation of Charlemagne. The political and religious turmoil in the Byzantine Empire, especially during the iconoclastic controversy (p. 186); Charlemagne's behavior as leader of the West in his relations with the Abbasid Caliphate of Baghdad (p. 113) and with the patriarch of Jerusalem; the removal of the Byzantine emperor's name from papal documents during the reign of Pope Adrian (771–95); and the difficulties Pope Leo III (795–816) experienced with both the emperor at Constantinople and the Roman nobility, leading to the pope's increasing dependence on Charles—these developments form the background to the imperial coronation.

According to Charlemagne's biographer, **Einhard**, on Christmas Day 800, at the beginning of Mass, the pope crowned Charles emperor, the Romans acclaimed him as emperor, and the pope performed the (Byzantine) *proskynesis* (obeisance) due an emperor. Eventually the Frankish chancery adopted the description "the most serene, august, pacific great emperor crowned by God governing the Roman Empire, who is, by the mercy of God, King of the Franks and the Lombards" as an integral part of Charles's title. For **Alcuin and the political theorists** at Charles's court, the image implied a return to the model of the biblical King David and to the images of Theodoric and Constantine, not to the image of the Byzantine emperor. While the imperial style conferred dignity and some political advantage in Italy, and the imperial motto

Renovatio romani imperii (Renewal of the Roman Empire) suggested a revival of the Roman Empire in the West, still, for the aristocratic families in the rest of the Carolingian world, the title was meaningless—his Frankish supporters considered him a Frankish king. The Greeks regarded Charlemagne as a usurper and the papal coronation as an act of rebellion; that event marked a decisive break between Rome and Constantinople.

GOVERNMENT. (1) **In the Frankish kingdom:** centralization continued; taxation in the Roman sense (which survived only under local and private auspices) was replaced by services in return for land grants (the economic basis of Carolingian society). Such services included labor on public works among the lower ranks, the provision of food for the court and public officials on duty, and judicial and military obligations (primarily among the upper ranks). Charlemagne's continuous campaigns reduced the small farmers, accentuating the tendency to serfdom. Charlemagne tried to offset this tendency by allowing groups of poorer farmers to cooperate in sending a single soldier, and by excusing the poorest from ordinary field service. Systematization of the army and of military service was also begun. Commendation and immunity continued, and the basis of later feudal development was firmly established.

Administration. Modern scholarship stresses that Carolingian political power and effective administration rested on the cooperation of the Frankish aristocracy, the dominant social class. The great comital landlords held real power at the local level. Their loyalty to the monarchy was acquired and maintained by grants of land and war booty. Aristocratic families gradually improved their economic position, and countships often became hereditary in one family, "though not usually in patrilinear succession." With the help of the aristocracy, Pepin III and Charlemagne were able to wage wars of expansion and to suppress rebellion. To limit local abuses, the *missi dominici* (usually a bishop and count) were introduced (802) as officers on circuit in a given district. The *missi* held their own courts, had power to remove a count for cause, and were charged with the supervision of financial, judicial, and clerical administration. They formed an essential link between the local and central governments. Under the counts were viscounts and vicars (*centenarii*). Margraves (*Mark Grafen*) were set over the marks, with extended powers to meet the needs of their position. Local administration of justice was reformed by the introduction of *scabini*, local landowners appointed by the counts to sit as permanent judiciary officers.

Education and learning. To advance his religious and educational reforms, Charlemagne drew scholars from across Europe: Alcuin of York (England); Peter of Pisa, and Paul the Deacon of Aquileia (Italy); Theodulf of Orleans and Einhard of Fulda to his court at Aachen, where Alcuin set up the **Palace School**, which became a center for the study of liberal arts and the copying of manuscripts. (Other scriptoria were at the monasteries of Corbie, St. Denis, St. Wandrille, St. Martin of Tours, Metz, Verona, Lucca.) Scholars at these centers expanded literacy, developed the Carolingian minuscule script (so called because it has lowercase letters; the Romans had only capitals), and copied and preserved classical, patristic, and early medieval texts. Using minuscule meant that a sheet of vellum (lambskin or calfskin) could contain more letters, which illustrates how a small technological change had broad cultural consequences. Though the scriptoria showed little creativity, many manuscripts were preserved and the foundation was laid for later study.

814–87. The disintegration of the Carolingian Empire. Such efficiency as the Carolingian government possessed under Charlemagne derived from his personality rather than from permanent institutions. The empire's vast size, the poor communication among the parts, the great ethnic diversity, and the lack of adequate administrative machinery (bureaucracy) sped disintegration. Local administration was carried on by unpaid officials whose compensation was a share of the revenue. Local offices tended to become hereditary. The tentative partitions of the empire in Charlemagne's lifetime followed Frankish tradition. Only one son, Louis the Pious, survived, and the empire was passed on to him undivided. The decisive stage in the partition of the empire came under Louis and his heirs.

814–40. Louis the Pious (emperor), educated at the Palace School, crowned in his father's lifetime. Sincerely religious, a reformer of his

THE CAROLINGIAN DYNASTY (768–987)

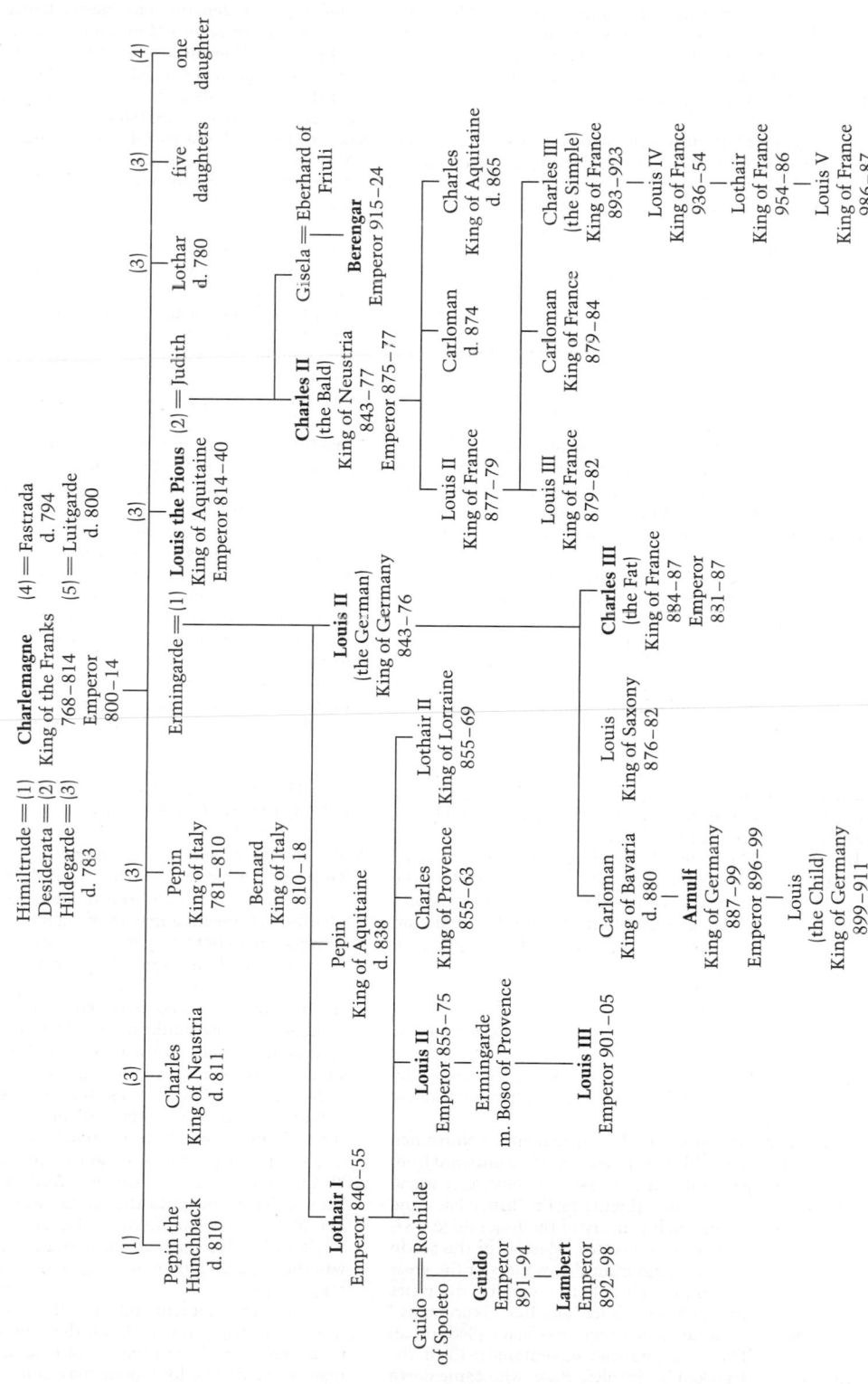

court, the Frankish Church, and the monasteries, he allowed himself to be crowned again by the pope (816). The influence of his ecclesiastical adviser Benedict of Aniane on an ideology of political Augustinianism—to the detriment of traditional Frankish principles—increased tension with the aristocracy. Louis was ineffectual as a soldier and ruler. He and his heirs concentrated on a long struggle (leading to civil war) over territorial questions, to the neglect of government, foreign policy, and defense—a program that hastened the breakup of the empire.

817–38. A significant series of **partitions** involved Louis's sons: Lothair (d. 855), Louis the German (d. 876), Pepin (d. 838), and their half-brother, Charles the Bald (d. 877).

The division of 817: Aquitaine and parts of Septimania and Burgundy went to Pepin, as subking; Bavaria and the marches to the east were assigned to Louis the German as subking, undivided; Francia, German and Gallic, and most of Burgundy were retained by Louis and his eldest son, Lothair. Italy went to a third subking.

The division of 838: Charles the Bald was assigned Neustria, and to this was added Aquitaine on the death of Pepin. Charles's holding, which had no name, approximated (accidentally) medieval France and was mainly Romance in speech.

840–55. Lothair I (emperor). On the death of Louis the Pious, the three heirs contained their struggle, and after the indecisive **battle of Fontenay** (841), Carolingian prestige sank to a new depth. Charles the Bald and Louis the German formed an alliance against Lothair (who was supported by the clergy in the interests of unity) in the bilingual (Teutonic and Romance) **Oaths of Strassburg** (842), sworn by the rulers and their armies, each in their own vernacular. They then forced a family compact on Lothair at Verdun.

843. The **Treaty of Verdun** divided the administration and control of the Carolingian Empire as follows: (1) **Lothair** kept the (empty) title of emperor and was king of Italy and of an amorphous territory (the "middle kingdom") which was bounded roughly by the Scheldt, the upper Meuse, the Saône, and the Rhône on the west, and by the Rhine and Frisia on the east (i.e., the territory of Provence, Burgundy, and what was later called Lotharingia); (2) **Louis the German,** as king of the (East) Franks, ruled a realm essentially Teutonic in blood, speech, and geography, extending from the Rhine (except Frisia) to the eastern frontier of the empire; (3) **Charles the Bald,** as king of the (West) Franks, received a realm (loosely called Carolingia for a time) made up of West Francia and Aquitaine, Gascony, Septimania, etc.; mainly Romance in speech; approximating medieval France in general outline.

855–75. Louis II (emperor). At Lothair I's death, his lands were divided as follows among his sons: Louis II received Italy; Charles (d. 863), the newly formed kingdom of Provence (centered around the city of Arles); and Lothair II, the inchoate aggregate (from Frisia to the Alps and from the Rhine to Scheldt) which began to be called *Lotharii regnum* or *Lotharingia* (modern Lorraine).

875–77. Charles the Bald, emperor.

877–81. Anarchy and interregnum in the empire.

879. The **kingdom of Burgundy** (Cisjuran Burgundy) was established by Boso of Provence.

888. The **kingdom of Juran Burgundy** (Besançon, Basel, Lausanne, Geneva, etc.) was erected by Rudolf I. It passed to the empire by bequest in the time of Conrad II.

c. 787–925. The 9th-century invasions. In the north: Bands of Northmen (also called Norsemen, Danes, Vikings; p. 183), pushed outward from Scandinavia. The Swedes penetrated into Russia, the Norwegians and Danes moved into the northern islands (including the British Isles) and south to the Continent. Within a half century of the first raid (c. 787) on England, the British Isles had been flooded. Masters of the sea in the west, the Northmen pushed inland from the mouths of the great rivers (the Rhine, Scheldt, Somme, Seine, Loire), sacking the cities (Utrecht, Paris, Nantes, Bordeaux, Hamburg, Seville). "Normandy" was invaded (841), and a simultaneous attack was made (845) on all three Frankish kingdoms. The Mediterranean was entered (843). In the east, Constantinople was attacked by Swedes *(Rus)*, who came down from Russia. A great attack on Paris (885) was heroically met by Count Odo (Eudes), son of Robert the Strong. Raids pushed farther into France and the Mediterranean in the course of the 9th century.

In the east: Bulgarian expansion produced a great Bulgar state between the Frankish and Byzantine Empires. The Bulgars were converted to the Greek communion (870). Hungarians (Magyars), closely followed by Pechenegs, crossed the Carpathians and the lower Danube, pushing into Venetia, Lombardy, Bavaria, Thuringia, Saxony, the Rhineland, Lorraine, and Burgundy (925).

In the Mediterranean: Muslim domination of Sicily, Corsica, Sardinia, and the Balearic Islands made the Mediterranean virtually a Muslim lake. Raids were almost continuous, Rome was attacked (846) and later Monte Cassino (883).

852–86. Political and social consequences. The pressures of Muslim, Magyar, and Viking invasions, combined with the civil wars among Charlemagne's descendants who could do little to halt those invasions, accelerated the disintegration of the Carolingian Empire and hastened the development of what modern students call **feudalism** and **manorialism.** As regional aristocracies assumed responsibility for defense and the protection of the weak, aristocratic authority accordingly increased. Strong men governed virtually independent territories in which weak and distant kings could not interfere. "Political power became a private, heritable property for great lords and counts," in the apt words of Joseph R. Strayer. Feudalism concerned the rights, powers, and lifestyle of the military elite; manorialism involved the services and obligations of the peasant classes. Since the economic power of the military elite rested on estates worked by peasants, feudalism and manorialism were inextricably linked. During the great invasions, peasants needed protection, and lords demanded something in return for their protection. Thus, free peasants surrendered themselves and their land to the lords' jurisdiction. The land was given back to them, but the peasants were then tied to the land by various kinds of payments and services. Local custom determined what those services were, but everywhere in the old Carolingian world peasants became part of the lord's permanent labor force and were obliged to turn over to him a portion of their annual harvest—usually in produce, sometimes in cash. In entering a relationship with a feudal lord, free farmers lost status and became servile, or serfs. They were subject to the lord's jurisdiction and were bound to the land and could not leave it without his permission. The unstable conditions created by the Viking assaults on Europe led to a great loss of personal freedom.

h. THE WEST FRANKS UNDER THE CAROLINGIAN KINGS

840–77. Charles the Bald (emperor, 875–77). His kingdom under the **Treaty of Verdun** was roughly equivalent to modern France, with additions in the north and south and a restricted frontier on the east. Charles was effective master of Laon, but his sway over Neustria was nominal, his control sporadically maintained by war and intrigue. Charles granted three great fiefs as a buffer for his frontiers: the county of Flanders to his son-in-law, Baldwin Iron-Arm (862); Neustria to Robert the Strong as "duke between Seine and Loire"; the French duchy of Burgundy to Richard, count of Autun. Brittany (Amorica) was semi-independent under its own dukes and counts in the 9th century and continued so virtually to the end of the Middle Ages. Aquitaine, joined to Neustria for Charles (838), soon emerged as a duchy and was consistently hostile. The duchy of Gascony was joined to Aquitaine in 1052. From Neustria were carved the counties of Anjou (870) and Champagne. Septimania remained refractory.

870. Carloman, Charles's son, emerged from monastic retirement and led a series of intrigues that ended when he was blinded and fled to his uncle, Louis the German. He died in 874. Charles was further weakened by his intrigues in Lorraine and Italy, and by his efforts to win the imperial crown, leaving France open to invasion, anarchy, and brigandage.

The crown, impotent and virtually bankrupt, commanded no respect from magnates or prelates, and the **Capitulary of Mersen** (847) shows clear evidence of the progress of essentially feudal ideas: every free man is to choose a lord; none may quit his lord; each must follow his lord in battle. It must be noted that this was purely a military measure. France was already divided into *comtés* under counts theoretically removable by the king.

875. Expedition of Charles to Italy and imperial coronation.

877. The **Capitulary of Kiersy** made honors hereditary, but lands were still granted only for life.

877–79. Louis II (the Stammerer), son of Charles the Bald, maintained himself with difficulty, despite the support of the Church.

884–87. Charles the Fat, son of Louis the German, already king of the East Franks (879) and emperor (876–87), was chosen king of the West Franks instead of Charles the Simple, the five-year-old brother of Louis and Carloman. Charles the Fat, having failed (886) to aid the gallant Odo (Eudes) against the Northmen, was deposed (887).

887–98. Odo (Eudes), count of Paris, marquis of Neustria (son of Count Robert the Strong), was elected king of the West Franks by one faction of magnates, to avoid a minority on the deposition (887) of Charles the Fat. Another faction chose Charles III, the Simple, son of Louis II (Carolingian).

893–923. Despite five years of civil war, **Charles III** ruled from Laon, the last Carolingian with any real authority in France. Charles, unable to expel the Northmen from the mouth of the Seine, granted (911) **Rollo** (Hrolf the Ganger, d. 931), a large part of what was later Normandy, for which Rollo did homage.

    Formation of Normandy. Rollo was baptized (912) under the name **Robert**, acquired middle Normandy (the Bessin, 924) and the western part of the duchy (Cotentin and Avranche, 933). Fresh settlers from Scandinavia were recruited for the colony for the best part of a century, and it was able to retain a strong local individuality. Yet soon after 1000, the duchy was French in both speech and law. Between this period and the accession of Duke William I (the Conqueror), Norman history is fragmentary.

923–87. The French kingship. Robert, count of Paris, duke between the Seine and Loire, won the West Frankish crown with the aid of his sons-in-law, Herbert, count of Vermandois, and Rudolf, duke of Burgundy, but was killed (923), leaving a son (later Hugh the Great) too young to rule.

929–36. Rudolf followed Robert as the foe of Charles the Simple, and ruled with no opposition after Charles's death. **Hugh the Great,** master of Burgundy and Neustria, declined the crown, preferring to rule through the young Carolingian heir,

936–54. Louis IV, a son of Charles the Simple. Hugh's title, duke of the French, seems to have implied governmental functions as much as territorial sovereignty, and he held most of the northern barons under his suzerainty.

954–86. Lothair succeeded his father, Louis IV. On the death of Hugh the Great, his son Hugh, known as Capet, succeeded him (956).

978. Lothair's effort to gain Lorraine led to an invasion by Emperoro Otto II to the walls of Paris. Hugh Capet, in alliance with Emperor Otto III and aided by Gerbert of Reims, reduced Lothair's rule at Laon to a nullity.

986–87. Lothair's son **Louis V** was the last Carolingian ruler.

987. Election of Hugh Capet, engineered by Adalbero, bishop of Reims, and by Gerbert. Hugh was crowned at Noyon with the support of the duke of Normandy and the count of Anjou. His title was recognized by Emperor Otto III in exchange for Hugh's claims to Lorraine. The emergence of the new house of Capet was not the victory of a race, a nationality, or a principle, but the triumph of a family, already distinguished, over a decadent rival.   (To p. 197)

i. GERMANY UNDER THE CAROLINGIAN AND SAXON EMPERORS

843–76. Louis the German. Increasing Slavic and Norse pressure (general Norse attack on Carolingian lands, 845). Louis had three sons: Carloman (d. 880), Louis (d. 882), and Charles the Fat. Carloman was assigned Bavaria and the East Mark; Louis, Saxony and Franconia; Charles, Alamannia. Contest with Charles the Bald for Lorraine. By the **Treaty of Mersen** (870) Louis added a strip of land west of the Rhine.

876–87. Charles the Fat. He blocked Charles the Bald's advance toward the Rhine. Emergence of the kingdom of Cisjuran Burgundy (i.e., Dauphiné, Provence, part of Languedoc) under Boso (879). Expedition to Italy and coronation by John VIII (881). Negotiations (882) with the

Northmen, now permanently established in Flanders. While Charles was in Italy settling a papal election, a great Norse invasion burst on France. **Deposition of Charles** by the Franconian, Saxon, Bavarian, Thuringian, and Swabian magnates at Tribur (887).

887–99. Arnulf (illegitimate son of Carloman, grandson of Louis the German). A certain supremacy was conceded to Arnulf by the various rulers of Germany and Italy who rendered homage to him. Victory over the Norse on the Dyle (Löwen, 891); resistance to the Slavic (Moravian) advance (893), with Magyar aid. Magyar raids after 900. Arnulf went to Italy (894), was crowned king (896), and received homage from most of the magnates. On appeal from Formosus (895), he took Rome and was crowned emperor (896).

899–911. Louis the Child (born 893), last of the Carolingians, elected king by the magnates at Forchheim (900). Increasing Norse, Slavic, and Magyar pressure and devastation.

    The **weakening of the royal power** as the East Frankish kingdom of the Carolingians declined, and the survival of tribal consciousness left the way open for the emergence of the stem (Ger., *Stamm*, tribe) duchies. These duchies preserved the traditions of ancient tribal culture, and their independent development under semiroyal dukes (beginning in the 9th century) contributed to the disruption of German unity. These stem duchies were: **Franconia** (the Conradiners ultimately drove the Babenbergers into the East Mark, later Austria); **Lorraine** (not strictly a stem duchy but with a tradition of unity); **Swabia** (the early ducal history is obscure); **Bavaria** (under the Arnulfings; repulse of the Magyars, acquisition of the mark of Carinthia); **Saxony** (under the Liudolfingers; repulse of the Danes and Wends, addition of Thuringia); **Frisia** (no tribal duke appeared).

911. End of the East Frankish line of the Carolingians with the death of Louis the Child (911); the German magnates, to avoid accepting a ruler of the West Frankish (French) line, elected Conrad, duke of Franconia.

911–18. Conrad I. Magyar raids and ducal rebellions in Saxony, Bavaria, and Swabia met vigorous but futile resistance from Conrad. Lorraine passed (911) temporarily under the suzerainty of the West Frankish ruler, Charles the Simple. Conrad nominated his strongest foe, Henry, duke of Saxony, as his successor, and he was elected.

919–1024. The Saxon (or Ottonian) House.

919–36. King Henry I (called the Fowler, supposedly because the messengers announcing his election found him hawking). Tolerant of the dukes, he forced recognition of his authority; cool to the Church, he avoided ecclesiastical coronation.

920–21. Reduction of the duke of Bavaria; alliance with Charles the Simple.

923–25. Lorraine restored to the German Kingdom and unified into the **duchy of Lorraine,** a center of spiritual and intellectual ferment. Henry's daughter married the duke of Lorraine (928).

924–33. Truce (and tribute) **with the Magyars;** fortification of the Elbe and Weser Valleys (Saxony and Thuringia); palisading of towns, villas, monasteries; establishment of garrisons (which later often became towns like Naumburg, Quedlinburg).

928. Saxon expedition across the frozen Havel River **against the Wends:** Branibor (Brandenburg) stormed; the Wends driven up the Elbe; creation of the marks of Branibor, Meissen, and (later) Lusatia as guardians of the middle Elbe.

933. Henry ended the Magyar truce with his **victory at Riade** on the Unstrut River, the first great defeat of the Magyars. Occupation of the land between the Schlei and the Eider (Charlemagne's Dane Mark), and erection of the mark of Schleswig, guardian of the Elbe mouth; the Danish king was made tributary and forced to receive Christian missionaries. Henry had prepared the way for his son, whose election was a formality, the succession becoming virtually hereditary.

936–73. King Otto I (the Great). Otto was crowned and anointed at Aachen, Charlemagne's capital; his coronation banquet revived the Carolingian coronation banquet (of Roman origin), at which the duke of Franconia served ceremonially as steward, the duke of Swabia as cup bearer, the duke of Lorraine as chamberlain, and the duke of Bavaria as marshal.

    Otto vigorously **asserted royal authority** (a three-year war reduced the dukes of Bavaria, Franconia, Lorraine, and Saxony). He followed the policy of keeping the great duchies (except Saxony) in his own hands or those of his family.

THE SAXON AND SALIAN EMPERORS (919-1125)

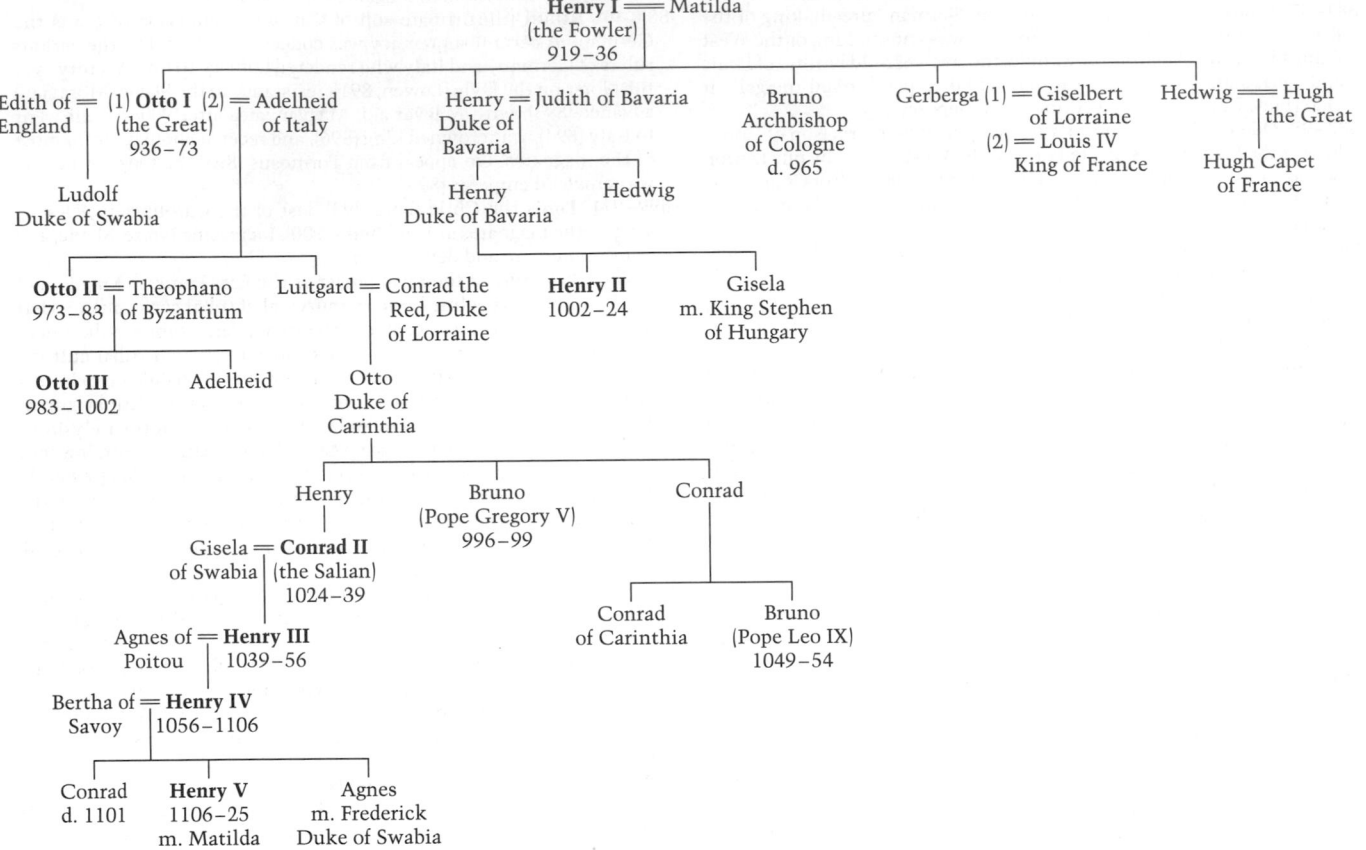

951-52. Otto's first expedition to Italy to keep the passes through the mountains open. Marriage to Adelheid and assumption of the crown of Italy; the pope refused him imperial coronation; Berengar of Ivrea, forced into vassalage, ceded the marks of Verona, Friuli, Istria (the keys to the passes) to Otto's brother Henry, duke of Bavaria.

953. Revolt of Otto's son (Ludolf, duke of Swabia), his son-in-law Conrad (duke of Lorraine), and others (suppressed, 955).

955. Battle of Lechfeld, a plain near Augsburg in southwest Germany, drained by the Lech River. Otto, with an army recruited from all the duchies, ended the Magyar menace with a great victory. Defeat of the Wends on the Recknitz River. Reestablishment and colonization with Bavarians of Charlemagne's East Mark (Austria).

968. The bishoprics established among the Slavs (e.g., Brandenburg, Merseburg, Meissen, Zeitz) were consolidated under the new **archbishopric of Magdeburg.** German bishoprics were everywhere filled with bishops loyal to the monarchy, marking the alliance of the king and the Church against aristocratic lay opposition.

961-64. Otto's second expedition to Italy on the appeal of Pope John XII for protection. Assumption of the crown of Italy at Pavia.

962. Imperial coronation by the pope: Revival of the Roman Empire in the West. Otto put a temporary end to feudal anarchy in Rome, deposed one pope and nominated another, and compelled the pope to recognize the emperor's right to approve or reject papal elections.

966-72. Otto's third expedition to Italy: deposition of one pope, restoration of another; nomination of a new pope; punishment of the Romans. Imperial coronation (967) of the future Otto II and assertion of suzerainty over Capua and Benevento (967).

Otto, with the able assistance of his brother Bruno, archbishop of Cologne, began a cultural revival (the so-called **Ottonian Renaissance**)

in the manner of Charlemagne; late in life, he learned to read, but not to speak, Latin; Bruno knew Greek. The cosmopolitan court literary circle included Irish and English monks and learned Greeks and Italians, notably **Liutprand of Cremona**(*History of the Deeds of Otto,* a major source on the reign, and *Narrative of an Embassy to Constantinople,* basic for studying East-West relations). Great literary activity of the monasteries: **Widukind of Corvey** (*Res Gestae Saxonicae*); **Roswitha,** the nun of Gandersheim, author of the*Carmen de Gestis Ottonis* and of learned Latin comedies in a bowdlerized Terentine style, celebrating saintly virginity; the vernacular *Heliand* (9th century), a Christian epic; **Ekkekard of St. Gall's** *Waltherius,* inspired by German legends.

973-83. Otto II. The revolt of Henry the Wrangler, duke of Bavaria, in alliance with Boleslav of Bohemia and others, required five years to put down; Henry was banished (978). Repulsion of a Danish incursion.

978. Lothair, king of the West Franks, invaded Lorraine but was forced to abandon his claims by Otto's invasion of France (980).

981-82. Otto's campaign in southern Italy, to expel the Saracens and reduce the Byzantine power, ended in defeat.

983-1002. Otto III (an infant of three years). Rule of his brilliant mother, Theophano (983-91), his grandmother Adelheid, and Archbishop Willigis of Mainz (991-96). Under Theophano's influence, his education was in the Byzantine tradition; his tutor was **Gerbert of Aurillac,** one of the most learned men of his day, whose brilliance won him the nickname *Stupor Mundi* (Wonder of the World). Henry the Wrangler proclaimed himself king, but was forced to submit.

996. Otto's first expedition to Italy ended Crescentius II's sway in Rome; Otto designated his cousin Bruno as pope (Gregory V).

998. Returning to Rome on his **second expedition to Italy,** Otto deposed the Crescentine pope, John XVI, and decapitated Crescentius. Otto made Gerbert of Aurillac pope, as Sylvester II. Sylvester shared Otto's devotion to the Carolingian tradition of an intimate union and cooperation between pope and emperor. Otto's antiquarianism led him to a plan of reform through universal imperial overlordship independent of the German crown. He settled down at Rome and began a restoration of the splendors of the city: palace on the Aventine, Byzantine court and Byzantine titles, futile revival of ancient formulas (seals inscribed *Renovatio imperii romani,* etc.); rapid alienation of the Roman populace. He left no heir and was buried on his own orders beside Charlemagne at Aachen.

1002–24. Henry II (son of Henry the Wrangler, cousin of Otto, great-grandson of Henry the Fowler) emerged from the contest for the throne, and was crowned emperor at Rome (1014). Devout (canonized with his wife, St. Kunigunde) but a political realist and firm with the Church, he concentrated his attention on Germany. Against episcopal objections, he founded (1007) the bishopric of Bamberg, endowed it richly as an outpost of German culture against Slavdom; the cathedral, one of the glories of German architecture, contains his tomb. Vigorous (Gorzian) monastic reform with many confiscations.

1003–17. A long, unsuccessful struggle with Boleslav Chrobry (992–1025) of Poland, duke of Bohemia, who had acquired Lusatia and Silesia.

1006–7. Unrest in Burgundy and **revolt of Baldwin of Flanders** (suppressed, 1007).

In practice Henry had no choice but to allow the great fiefs to become hereditary. He relied heavily on the clergy to supply advisers and administrators, and looked to the Church also for military and financial support, but he dominated the Church in Germany through his control of the episcopal appointments. Extensive secularization and reform of the monasteries of the Church resulted.   *(To p. 205)*

j. SPAIN

1. THE VISIGOTHIC KINGDOM
For a complete list of the caliphs, see Appendix III.

In the time of **Euric** (466–84) the Visigothic rule extended from the Loire to Gibraltar and from the Bay of Biscay to the Rhône. The capital was Toulouse.

507. Clovis's victory in the **Battle of Vouillé** obliged the Visigoths to withdraw over the Pyrenees, retaining only Septimania north of the mountains. The new capital was Toledo.

The Visigoths in Spain were a small minority and were rapidly romanized. The conversion of King Reccared (587) from Arianism to Roman orthodoxy brought an end to their religious separateness and accelerated the process of romanization. The **Synod of Toledo** (633) assumed the right of nobles and clergy to confirm elections to the crown. After 600 the Jews were forced to accept baptism, for which reason they later on welcomed the Muslim invasion. Visigothic speech gradually disappeared, and the current vernacular was of Latin origin. Roman organization and tradition survived to a marked degree. **Isidore of Seville** (c. 560–636), a bishop, theologian, historian, man of letters, and scientist, produced in his *Etymologiae* a general reference work that remained a standard manual for 500 years and was a medium for transmitting much ancient knowledge to the medieval world.

2. MUSLIM SPAIN

711–15. The Muslim conquest (p. 112). In 711 a mixed force of Arabs and Berbers, led by the Berber **Tariq** (whence Gibraltar, *Gebel al-Tariq*) crossed from Africa. Roderick, the last Visigothic king, was completely defeated in the **battle on the Guadalete** (Rio Barbate), whereupon his kingdom collapsed. The Muslims took Córdoba and the capital, Toledo. Tariq was followed (712) by his master, **Musa,** who took Medina Sidonia, Seville, Merida, and Saragossa. The Muslims soon reached the Pyrenees (719), having driven the remnants of the Christians into the mountains of the north and west.

732. At the **battle of Tours** the Muslims, having crossed into France, were defeated by Charles Martel and the Franks. (In Muslim annals, a minor skirmish.) By 759 they had been expelled from France.

756–1031. The Umayyad dynasty of Córdoba.

756–88. Abd al-Rahman I, grandson of the Umayyad caliph of Damascus who, when the triumphant Abbasids (p. 112) ordered all princes of the Umayyad family killed, escaped (after many romantic adventures) to Spain, defeated the emir (Arabic title for governor of Córdoba), assumed the title, and founded an independent Muslim kingdom. Jews and Christians (*dhimmis,* or protected people, because they were people of the Book, the Old Testament Scriptures) were tolerated and well treated, but had to pay a special tax. Abd al-Rahman began construction of the great **Mosque of Córdoba,** considered by some architectural historians to be the most spectacular Islamic building in the world. Charlemagne's support for Muslim dissidents stimulated agitation against al-Rahman.

777. Invasion of Spain by Charlemagne, checked by the heroic defense of Saragossa. Annihilation of his rear guard by Basques at Roncesvalles (p. 174). Wars with the Franks continued throughout the rest of the century, with Charlemagne ultimately conquering northeastern Spain as far as the Ebro River (capture of Barcelona, 801).

822–53. Abd ar-Rahman II, son of Al-Hakam. During his reign, Alfonso II of Leon invaded Aragon. He was defeated and his kingdom destroyed. The Franks too were driven back in Catalonia. The Normans first appeared on the coasts. In 837 a revolt of Christians and Jews in Toledo was suppressed, but Christian fanatics continued to be active, especially in Córdoba.

852–86. Muhammad I. He put down another Christian uprising in Córdoba, and carried on extensive operations against the Christian states of Leon, Galicia, and Navarre (Pampeluna taken 861).

912–61. Abd ar-Rahman III. The ablest and most gifted of the Umayyads of Spain, he assumed the titles of caliph and Amir al-Mu'minin in 929, thus asserting supremacy in Islam against the Abbasid caliphs of Baghdad. Abd ar-Rahman's reign was marked by the pacification of the country, completion of governmental organization (centralization), and naval activity. In agricultural development, the Muslims introduced the cultivation of rice, sugarcane, oranges, lemons, grapefruits, eggplants, carrots, and, after the 11th century, cotton; these crops, together with new methods of field irrigation and crop rotation, led to "a green revolution" in Spain.

Córdoba, with a population of possibly 500,000 people, 1,600 mosques, 900 public baths, 80,455 shops, and a library with 400,000 volumes (the Swiss abbey of St. Gall at the same time had but 600 books) was so great a cultural and intellectual center that the Saxon nun Roswitha of Gandersheim described the city as "the ornament of the world." Córdobans invented the process of manufacturing crystal and pioneered the making of paper (huge paper mills) using a technique learned from the Chinese. They brought the Indian game of chess to western Europe, and they made significant advances in chemistry, medicine and surgery, mathematics, and philosophy.

The old Visigothic aristocracy, by this time almost extinguished, was replaced by a rich middle class. Christians and Jews continued to enjoy whole toleration.

Abd ar-Rahman continued the wars with Leon and Navarre, which extended over most of his long reign. By the **Peace of 955** with Ordono III of Leon, the independence of Leon and Navarre was recognized and the Muslim frontier withdrawn to the Ebro; on the other hand, Leon and Navarre recognized the suzerainty of the caliph and paid tribute. This peace was soon broken by Ordono's brother Sancho (957) who, after his defeat, was expelled by his subjects but restored by the caliph (959).

961–76. Al-Hakam al Mustansir continued the wars against Castile, Leon, and Navarre and forced their rulers to sue for peace (962–70). At the same time, he waged successful war against the Fatimid dynasty in Morocco, which was brought to an end (973) and replaced by the Umayyad power.

976–1009. Hisham II al Muayyad, whose reign marked the decline of the Umayyad dynasty. Power was seized by Muhammad ibn Abi'-Amir, with the title of Hajib al-Mansur (or Alamansor) the Victorious Chamberlain; he was a brilliant reforming minister (army and administration). He carried on successful campaigns against Leon, Navarre, Catalonia, and Mauretania, and temporarily checked the religious and racial separatism that later on brought about the collapse of the Umayyad Caliphate. On his death in 1002 he was succeeded by his son,

Abdulmalik al-Muzaffar (the Victorious), who several times defeated the Christians and was followed by his brother, Abd ar-Rahman, named Sanchol. The latter obliged Hisham and proclaimed him his heir, whereupon a revolt took place in Córdoba under the leadership of Muhammad, a member of the royal family. Hisham was compelled to abdicate in favor of Muhammad II al-Mahdi (1009–10), and Sanchol was executed. In the meantime the Berbers nominated Sulaiman al-Mustain as caliph (1009–10, 1013–16). Civil war ensued, reducing Spain to a score of petty kingships *(taifas)* and making easier the Christian reconquest.

1027–31. Hisham III, the last Umayyad caliph.

3. CHRISTIAN SPAIN, CASTILE AND LEON

718–37. Pelayo, with the Visigothic leaders who escaped Tarik, created the kingdom of Asturias in northwestern Spain, south of the Bay of Biscay. Pelayo's victory over the Moors at Covadonga (718?–725) marks, according to 13th-century clerical propagandists of royal and aristocratic elites, the start of the *reconquista* (reconquest), a sacred patriotic effort to wrest power from the Muslims and restore Christian rule in Spain. Asturias, a remote and barren land, did not interest the Muslims.

739–57. Alfonso I assigned to the Church a generous share of the lands conquered from the Muslims and used the clergy as a counterweight to the aristocracy.

791–842. Alfonso II reestablished Visigothic styles of administration in Asturias.

899. Miraculous discovery of the bones of **St. James the Greater** and erection of the first church of Santiago de Campostella, which became the center of the Spanish national cult and one of the most influential shrines in Europe.

910–14. Garcia, king of Leon, began a rapid expansion of his domain to the east (construction of numerous castles, hence the name Castile).

c. 930–70. Count Fernán González, count of Burgos (later, Castile), marked the rise of the counts of Burgos. By intrigue and alliance with the Muslims, he expanded his domain at the expense of Leon, and made the country of Castile autonomous and hereditary. His progress was arrested by Sancho the Fat of Leon (d. 966), who was in alliance with Abd ar-Rahman III.

1001–35. Sancho the Great of Navarre effected a close union of Castile and Navarre and began the conquest of Leon.

1035–65. Ferdinand (Fernando) I, of Castile, completed the work by conquering Leon (1037) and assuming the title of king of Leon.

(To p. 218)

k. THE BRITISH ISLES

1. ENGLAND

Prehistoric Britain. The prehistoric inhabitants of Britain (called Celts on the basis of their language) were apparently a fusion of Mediterranean, Alpine, and Nordic strains that included a dark Iberian and a light-haired stock. Archaeological evidence points to contacts with the Iberian Peninsula (2500 B.C.E.) and Egypt (1300 B.C.E.)

1200–600 B.C.E. The true **Celts** are represented by two stocks: Goidels (Gaels), surviving in northern Ireland and high Scotland, and Cymri and Brythons (Britons), still represented in Wales. The Brythons were close kin to the Gauls, particularly the Belgi. Their religion was dominated by a powerful, organized, priestly caste, the druids of Gaul and Britain, who monopolized religion, education, and justice.

55 B.C.E.–c. 450 C.E. Roman occupation began with Julius Caesar's conquests in Gaul and Britain (57–50 B.C.E.); Emperor Claudius's personal expedition and conquest (43 C.E.) were decisive in the romanization of Britain. Construction of the great network of Roman roads began (eventually five systems, four centering on London). Bath emerged as a center of Romano-British fashion.

78–142. Roman conquests in the north began under Agricola (p. 92); results north of the Clyde-Forth line were not decisive. Emperor Hadrian completed the conquest of Britain in person; construction of **Hadrian's Wall** (123) from Solway Firth to Tyne mouth. Firth-Clyde rampart (c. 142).

208. Emperor Septimius Severus arrived (208), invaded Caledonia (Scotland), restored Roman military supremacy in the north, and fixed Hadrian's Wall as the final frontier of Roman conquest.

300–350. Height of villa construction in the plain of Britain. Chief towns: Verulamium (St. Albans), Colchester, Lincoln, Gloucester, York. Sheep raising was widespread, and the skill of the artisans and clothworkers of Britain was already famous on the Continent in the 4th century. The island south of the wall was considerably romanized. Recent archaeological investigations suggest that Christianity had made progress.

410–42. Withdrawal of the Roman legions and the end of the Roman administration coincided with an intensification of Nordic pressure and the influx of **Jutes, Angles, and Saxons,** which permanently altered the racial base of the island. By c. 615 the Angles and Jutes had reached the Irish Channel and were masters of what is virtually modern England. A Celtic recrudescence appeared in the highlands of the west and northwest. The history of Britain for two centuries (c. 350–597) is obscure.

Seven Anglo-Saxon kingdoms, the Heptarchy, emerged after the Teutonic conquest: Essex, Wessex, Sussex (Saxon, as the names suggest); Kent (Jutes); East Anglia, Mercia, Northumbria (Angles).

560–616. The supremacy of **Ethelbert of Kent** in the Heptarchy.

597. Ethelbert's supremacy coincided with the arrival of **Augustine the Monk** (p. 172) and the conversion of Kent to Christianity. The Frankish princess Bertha, Ethelbert's wife, who was already Christian, probably exercised a strong influence on him; she was archetypical of the role of women in evangelization. The hegemony in the Heptarchy passed eventually to **Edwin of Northumbria** (who had also been converted).

633. Oswald of Northumbria called Aidan from Iona, a monastery on an island off the west coast of Scotland. His mission began the great influence of Celtic Christianity, which for a time threatened to replace the Roman Church.

c. 628–89. Benet Biscop, a strong supporter of Benedictine monasticism. He founded the monastery of Wearmouth in Northumbria and on five trips to Italy collected books, manuscripts, and paintings that formed the intellectual milieu for the work of **Bede.**

616–80. Abbess Hilda of Whitby, a woman of great piety and administrative ability, ruled a **double monastery** (housing both men and women in two adjoining establishments), shared in the work of Christian evangelization, and hosted the 664 **Synod of Whitby** at which representatives of the Celtic Church in northern England agreed to the Roman date of Easter and certain disciplinary practices, and thus brought Britain back into the Roman and Continental religious and intellectual orbit.

669–90. Theodore of Tarsus. A Greek, as archbishop of Canterbury he introduced a Roman parochial system and a centralized episcopal (diocesan) organization that became the model for a unified kingdom. "National" synods brought representatives of rival kingdoms together for the first time. Theodore's episcopate promoted a Greco-Roman cultural tradition that, together with the efforts of Benet Biscop, flowered in the monk **Bede (673–735) of Jarrow.** Bede considered his 25 commentaries on Scripture his most important work; modern scholars praise his *Ecclesiastical History of the English Nation* (731) as his most significant book. A master of chronology, Bede introduced the system of dating events from the Incarnation (A.D., or *anno domini*, in the year of our Lord) that, encouraged by Charlemagne's use, facilitated accurate record keeping and comparison of time spans. (The practice of dating events before Christ's birth (B.C.) in reverse sequence developed in Europe only in the 18th century.) As the works of Bede represent the finest in Anglo-Saxon religious scholarship, so the late 8th-century epic poem *Beowulf*, by a monk or a court poet, exemplifies the finest secular literature. The monk **Alcuin of York** carried Northumbrian learning to Charlemagne's court.

787. The first recorded **raid of the Danes** in England was followed by the Danish inundation of Ireland.

802–39. In the pause before the great wave of Viking advance, Wessex under **Egbert**, who had been in Charlemagne's service, emerged supreme (conquering Mercia), exercised a vague suzerainty over Northumbria, and received the homage of all the English kinglets.

856–75. Full tide of the **first Viking assault.** Wessex was the spearhead of resistance.

THE ANGLO-SAXON KINGS OF ENGLAND (802–1066)

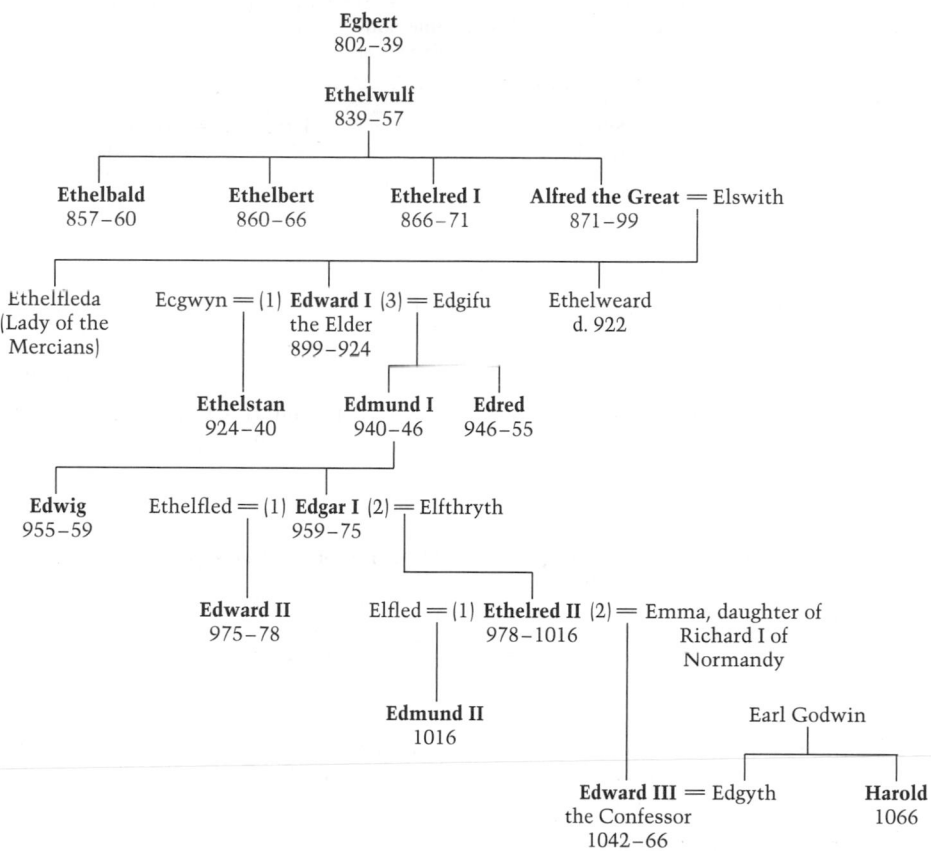

871–99. ALFRED THE GREAT purchased peace until he could organize his forces and build up a navy. Almost overwhelmed by the winter invasion of 878, he finally defeated the Danes and forced the **peace of Wedmore,** whereby Guthrun the Dane became a Christian and divided England with Alfred. The Danelaw, north of the Thames-Lea line, went to Guthrun; the south, together with London, went to Alfred.

878–900. The Danes were masters of the northeast, and under Danish pressure **Scotland** began to unify.

Alfred proceeded to organize the defense of his kingdom. London was walled and garrisoned, with burghers charged with its defense. Earth forts *(burhs)* of the Viking type were thrown up and garrisoned. The *fyrd* (army of foot soldiers) and the fleet were reorganized, the army increased, the thegns (thanes) began to be used as a mounted infantry. All citizens of the requisite wealth were forced into thegnhood—to join the military class attached to the royal household. A Danish reaction (892–96) was firmly suppressed.

Alfred was a **patron of learning.** Foreign scholars and learned refugees were welcomed at court. Alfred translated Bede's *Historia,* Orosius, and Boethius's *Consolatio* into the vernacular. To provide trained administrators, Alfred established schools for the sons of thegns and nobles. The *Anglo-Saxon Chronicle* was started.

924–40. Ethelstan, Alfred's grandson. The descendants of Alfred were the first true kings of England; his great-grandson **Edgar** (959–75) was recognized as such. Archbishop Dunstan, Edgar's chief counselor, was a great ecclesiastical reformer (simony and morals) of the Church and the people. He followed a policy of fusion and conciliation toward the Danes, and Oda, a full-blooded Dane, became (942) archbishop of Canterbury. The absorption of the Danelaw by Wessex left the Celtic fringe in Scotland and Wales independent under a vague kind of vassalage to the king.

As the Danelaw was absorbed, the shire (county) system was extended to it, with the old Danish boroughs as a nucleus. The old tribal and clan organization was superseded by a system of quasi-feudal form in which each man had a lord who was responsible for him at law. Great earldoms were beginning to emerge.

Shire and hundred courts administered local custom with the freeman suitors under the king's representative-ealdorman, shire-reeve, or hundred-reeve. From the days of Edgar, the feudal element tended to encroach on royal authority, especially in the hundred courts. The old monasticism had been destroyed by the invasions, and the Church in England fell into corruption and decadence, only reformed by the influence of Cluny and Fleury and the Norman conquest.

991. An ebb in Viking raids was followed by a fresh onset during the reign of **Ethelred the Unready** (978–1016), led by Sven I (Forked Beard), king of Denmark. Danegeld had been sporadically collected under Alfred; now it was regularly levied and used as tribute to buy off the invaders. This tax, and the invasions, led to a rapid decline of the freeholders to a servile status. Under Canute, the Danegeld was transformed into a regular tax for defense. Collection of the Danegeld, originally in the hands of the towns, fell increasingly to the lord of the manor, and it was only a step from holding him for the tax to making him lord of the land from which the tax came.

1016–35. King Canute (Cnut), elected by the witan, a heterogeneous body of prelates, magnates, and officials without precise status. Canute ruled on the model of Charlemagne, over a northern empire that included Denmark, Norway, and England. His reign was marked by conciliation and fusion. The Church was under Anglo-Saxon clergy. Canute maintained a good navy, and his standing army included the famous housecarls, who soon had an Anglo-Saxon contingent. Four great earldoms, Wessex, East Anglia, Mercia, Northumbria, and seven

THE DANISH KINGS OF ENGLAND (1013–66)

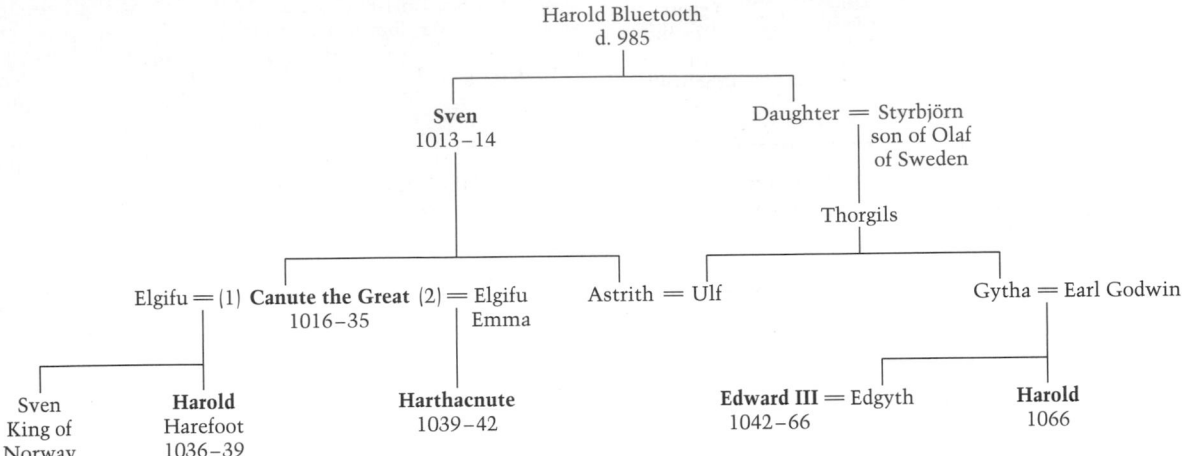

lesser earldoms can be distinguished in this period. The greatest of the earls was **Godwin of Wessex.** Canute's sons were incompetent, and his line ended (1042).

Godwin was chiefly responsible for the election of the successor to Canute's line, Edward, son of Emma and Ethelred, who married (1045) Godwin's daughter.

1042–66. Edward the Confessor, of the line of Alfred, was under Godwin's domination. Brought up at the Norman court, speaking French, he tried to Normanize the English court. Godwin's influence led to the deposition of the Norman archbishop of Canterbury and the selection of the Saxon Stigand by the witan. Godwin's son **Harold** succeeded him (1053) as earl of Wessex and dominated Edward as his father had. Another son of Godwin, Tostig, became earl of Northumbria. Harold (c. 1064) was driven ashore on the Channel, fell into the hands of William, duke of Normandy, a cousin of Edward the Confessor, and was forced to take an oath to help William attain the crown of England, which William declared Edward had promised him.

1066. Tostig, exiled after a Northumbrian revolt (1065), returned with **Harald Haardraade** to attack Northumbria. The Confessor died in January (1066) and William at once began vigorous preparations for the conquest of England.

1066. On Edward's death **Harold was chosen king** by the witan and was guarding the coasts of England against William when Tostig and Haardraade appeared in the north. After a brilliant dash northward, Harold defeated them at **Stamford Bridge** in September, at the very moment that the Norman invaders arrived in the Channel. Rushing southward after his victory, Harold confronted the Normans, who had already landed, with a reduced, wearied, and shaken force, and was beaten and killed in the **Battle of Hastings,** or Senlac *(Oct. 14).*   *(To p. 192)*

2. SCOTLAND

A wave of Neolithic peoples from the Mediterranean was followed by Celts, Goidels, Brythons, Saxons in the 6th century B.C.E., and then by Picts. The Romans arrived at the end of the 1st century C.E., but made no permanent impression.

450–600. Four **political nuclei: Picts** (Pentland Firth to the central plain); **Dalriada** (Argyllshire and the islands of Jura and Islay); **"Welsh" refugees** in Strathclyde; **Ida of Bernicia's realm** (from the Tweed to the Firth of Forth).

c. 565. Columba arrived from Iona and converted the king of the Picts to the Celtic Church, giving Scotland her first cultural contact with the Roman world.

685. The English power was broken on the southern frontier, and Scotland began her independent evolution. Under **Kenneth I** (d. 858) began the first Scottish union.

794. Arrival of the Norse. Iona burned (802); a series of devastations followed.

921. Edward, son of Alfred the Great, was acknowledged lord of Scotland. Ethelstan enforced the bond in arms (934), and a Scottish effort to revolt was crushed (937).

1005–34. Under **Malcolm II,** Lothian was added to the Scottish crown.

1034–40. Strathclyde completed (1034) the union of the four nuclei under **Duncan,** but without a homogeneous racial or political basis. The isles and the north were under Scandinavian dominance, and England aimed to make Scotland her vassal.   *(To p. 197)*

3. IRELAND

Neolithic inhabitants, followed by Celts and Goidels (c. 600–500 B.C.E.). The "fifths" (Ulster, Leinster, Connaught, East and West Munster) may date from the Goidel arrival. Belgic and other Brythonic migrations (300–150 B.C.E.) probably in the southeast. Supremacy of the Brythonic **kingdom of Tara** in the 4th century C.E. The **Picts** pushed into Antrim and Down. There is an enormous body of legend dealing with the early origins.

431. Traditional date for the arrival of **Bishop Palladius** and his mission.

432. PATRICK, a pupil of Germanus of Auxerre, especially trained for this mission, arrived to continue Palladius's work. He founded churches in Meath, Ulster, Connaught, and probably established the bishopric of Armagh. Chieftains were converted, but much paganism survived. Patrick began the education of the priesthood. Patrick's ecclesiastical organization was probably close to that of Britain and Gaul, but with the withdrawal of the Roman legions from the latter countries the Roman connection was cut, and there was a recrudescence of paganism. The diocesan organization of Patrick apparently slipped back into the native system.

Chieftains, on their conversion, made donations of land to the Church, and at first the ecclesiastical offices seem to have remained in the hands of the sept, with the *coarb* (inheritor) as bishop or abbot. The cenobitic organization of the 5th century was that of a sept, whose chief was a Christian. Later there was a rigorous form that separated the sexes. As the earlier diocesan organization declined, the number of bishops rose to fantastic figures. There was a great exodus of Irish scholars and monks to Europe during the 8th and 9th centuries.

c. 500–800. The **Golden Age of Irish monastic scholarship** occurred in the 6th to the 9th centuries. A great school founded by **Eudo,** prince of Oriel (c. 450–540), at Aranmore drew scholars from all Europe. Establishment of the monastery of **Clonard** (c. 520) under Welsh inspiration. Here there were said to be 3000 students living in separate, wattled huts and receiving open-air instruction. From Clonard went forth the so-called **Twelve Apostles of Ireland,** founding schools all over Ireland and later the Continent.

Columba founded Iona (563), the Mother Church of Scotland, whence Aidan, the apostle of England, founded Lindisfarne (635) for the conversion of Northumbria. The *Book of Kells* and the flowering of Gaelic vernacular poetry date from this period.

590. Columban of Leinster, from Bangor, began his mission to Europe, founding Luxeuil and a great series of other foundations (e.g., Gall, Würzburg, Salzburg, Tarantum, Bobbio). The 8th century saw a great wave of missions from the Rhine-Meuse area inland to the Rhône-Alps line. Irish and English missionaries to the Continent carried **penitentials,** manuals for the instruction of priests, containing a list of sins and recommended penances; penitentials played a large role in the conversion of pagan peoples. This powerful advance of Celtic Christianity at one time seemed destined to win northern Europe from Rome. The chief formal differences from Rome were in tonsure, the date of Easter, the consecration of bishops. In the 7th century the Irish Church conformed to Roman usage, but the bond with Rome was not close.

Before the coming of the Norse there were no cities, no stone bridges in Ireland, and no foreign trade of importance.

795. The first Norse attack. Dublin (840), Waterford, and Limerick founded as centers of Norse trade with the Continent. The Scandinavians remained chiefly in the ports.

1002–14. Brian of Munster established his supremacy. A period of road and fort building. At Clontarf (1014) Brian defeated the Norse, ending the domination of Dublin, though the Norse remained in their cities. Brian fell in the battle and anarchy followed—the struggle of the O'Brians of Munster, the O'Neils of Ulster, the O'Connors of Connaught—which ended in an appeal to King Henry II of England by Dermond (or Dermot) MacMurrough.

1152. The **Synod of Kells** established the diocesan system of Ireland, recognized the primacy of Armagh and the archbishoprics of Cashel, Tuam, Dublin. Tithes were voted.

1167–71. The Norman Conquest. Henry II, on his accession, had the idea of conquering Ireland. John of Salisbury records that on his request, as Henry's envoy (1155), Pope Adrian IV sent Henry a letter granting him lordship of Ireland and a ring as the symbol of his investiture.

1167. On the appeal of Dermond MacMurrough, Henry issued a letter allowing Dermond to raise troops in England for his cause. Dermond came to terms with Richard of Clare, a Norman, earl of Pembroke, and with other Normans, most of whom were related to one another. A series of expeditions to Ireland brought to the island a group of Norman families (e.g., Fitzmaurices, Carews, Gerards, Davids, Barries), who began to establish a powerful colony. This greatly alarmed Henry.

1171. HENRY II, with papal sanction, landed in Ireland to assert his supremacy and to reconcile the natives. The **Synod of Cashel,** at which Henry was not present, acknowledged his sovereignty.   *(To p. 197)*

1. SCANDINAVIA

Origins. References in Pytheas, Pomponius Mela, Pliny the Elder, Tacitus, Ptolemy, Procopius, Jordanes. Archaeological remains indicate Roman connections in the 3rd century after Christ, but there is no evidence for close Continental relations until the Viking period.

Viking period. Scandinavia developed in isolation during the barbarian migrations until the 2nd century C.E. The Viking expansion from Scandinavia itself prolonged the period of migrations in Europe for 400 years. The traditional participation of Scandinavia was as follows: **Norwegians** (westward): raids in Scotland, Ireland, Iceland, Greenland, east coast of North America, perhaps as far south as present-day Connecticut (Hrolf the Ganger, or "Rollo"); **Danes** (the middle passage): British Isles, France, the Low Countries; **Swedes** (eastward): across Slavdom to Byzantium (foundation of Novgorod, 862, Kiev c. 900). There never was a mass migration, and probably all shared in the various movements to some degree. **Causes:** scholars speculate that polygamy may have created population pressures for emigrations; that the practice of primogeniture forced younger sons to seek their fortunes abroad; that mercantile expansion, especially among the Frisians (people in area of modern Holland) whetted the Viking appetite for trade, and that the Viking culture encouraged the desire for adventure and plunder abroad. **Means:** shallow longboats, equipped with sails, oars, a rudder at the stern and capable of carrying 40 to 60 men, proved easily maneuverable on both rough northern waters and inland rivers, and were versatile—used for raiding and commerce.

Norwegian Colonization. Ireland: the Norwegian conquest began c. 823, and centers were established at Dublin (the kingdom endured until 1014), Waterford, and Limerick. Exodus of learned monks to Europe **(Scotus Erigena?).** Attacks by the Picts and Danes. The subsequent colonization of the Scottish Islands drew Norwegians from Ireland and accelerated the celticization of the colonists who remained there. **The Islands:** Hebrides, Man, Faroes, Orkneys, Shetlands. **Iceland:** reached by Irish monks c. 790; discovered by the Northmen (Norsemen) in 874 and colonized almost at once; establishment of a New Norway, with a high culture. **Greenland:** visited by Eric the Red of Iceland (981) and colonized at once; expeditions from Greenland to the North American continent (p. 105). The Norse settlements in Greenland continued until the 15th century.

Civilization. Large coin hoards indicate the profits of raids and trade with the British Isles, Mediterranean, Byzantium, and Muslim Asia. Export of furs, slaves, arms (to eastern Europe), and mercenary services to rulers (e.g., bodyguards of Ethelred, Canute, Slavic princes, Byzantine emperors). Trade eastward was cut off by the Huns and Avars (5th and 6th century) but resumed after Rurik's expedition (862) reopened Russia.

Runes (from a Scandinavian root meaning to inscribe) were already ancient in the Viking period, and probably are modified Roman letters. The *Eddas,* dramatic lays (prose and verse) of the Norwegian aristocracy (especially in Iceland) dealing with gods and heroes (many in the German tradition, e.g., Sigurd and the Nibelungs), are the highest literary production of pagan Scandinavia.

Scandinavian society rested on wealth from raids and commerce and consisted of a landed aristocracy with farmer tenants who had the right and obligation to attend local courts. The only general assembly was the Allthing of Iceland (established 930), the oldest continuous parliamentary body in existence.

Mythology and religion. The Norwegians had a more complicated mythology than any other Teutonic people: giants, elves, dwarfs, serpents, succeeded by the triumph of **Odin,** his wife, **Friga,** and his son, **Thor.**

Conversion to Christianity. The first Christians (probably captives) appeared in the 6th century. The first Christian missionary was the Anglo-Saxon **Willibord** (c. 700), who accomplished little. A Carolingian mission (c. 820) was welcomed by King Bjorn of Sweden. A few years later (c. 831) the archbishopric of Hamburg was established and became at once the center for missionary work in the north.

(To p. 210)

2. EASTERN EUROPE, 500–1025

a. THE BYZANTINE EMPIRE

(From p. 100)
For a complete list of the Byzantine emperors, see Appendix II.

The **Eastern Roman Empire,** or Byzantine Empire, was a polyglot, multiethnic, polysectarian state, at the head of which was the **emperor** (*basileus, autokrator*), whose autonomous monarchical power rested on Hellenistic political philosophy and Christian political theory.

527–65. Justinian. Justinian was a man of autocratic character and grandiose conceptions. He was strongly influenced by his wife, **Theodora** (d. 548), a woman of humble origin but of iron will and unusual political judgment. Justinian's whole policy was directed toward the revival of a universal Christian Roman Empire. The entire reign was filled with wars in the east and the west, punctuated by constant incursions of the barbarians from the north.

Justinian and the Church. Peace had been made with Rome in 519 and Pope John I had visited Constantinople in 525. Justinian made a great effort to maintain the unity of the western and eastern churches, but this led him into trouble with the **Monophysites** of Syria and

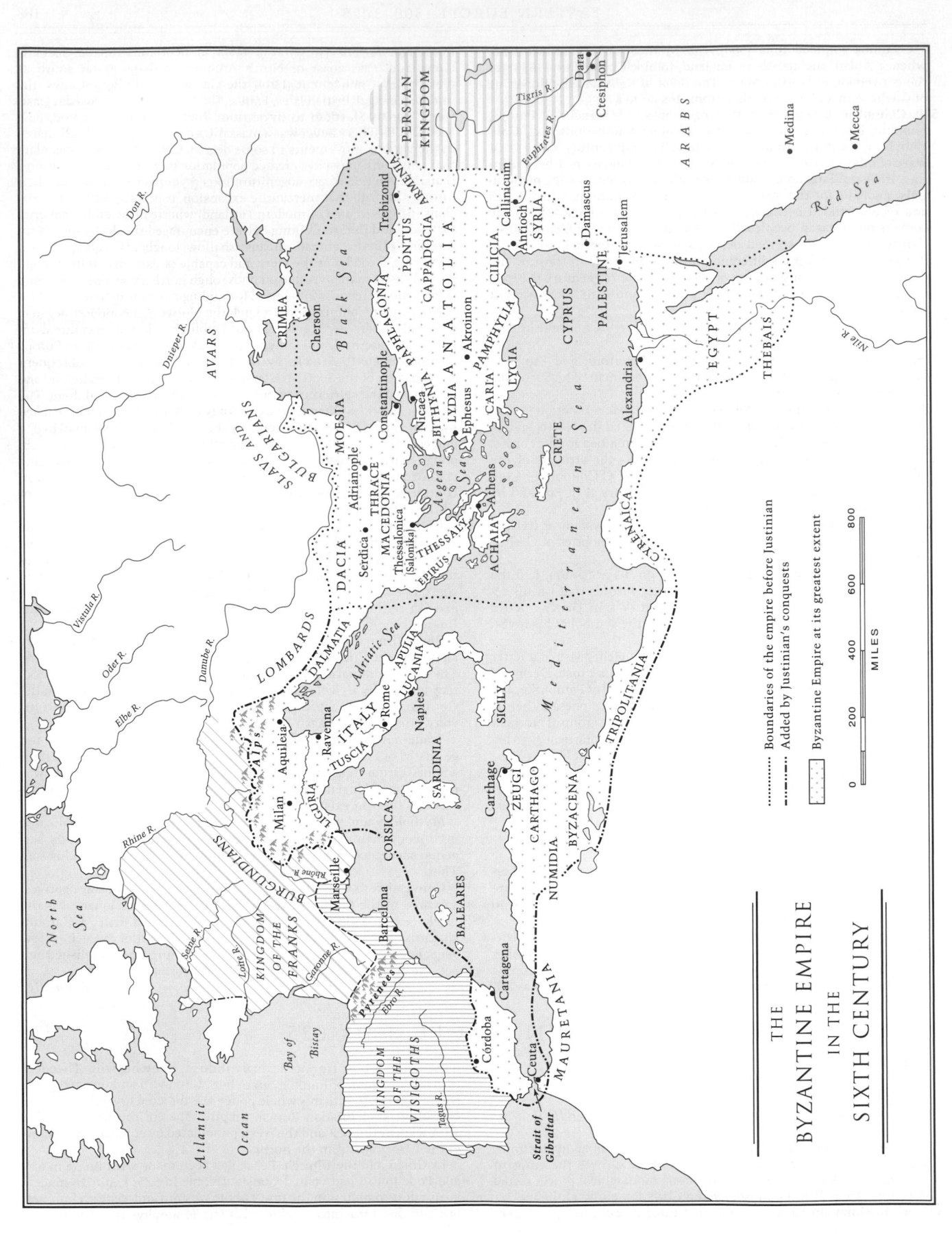

THE
BYZANTINE EMPIRE
IN THE
SIXTH CENTURY

Boundaries of the empire before Justinian
Added by Justinian's conquests
Byzantine Empire at its greatest extent

0   200   400   600   800
MILES

PERSIAN KINGDOM

Tigris R.
Dara
Ctesiphon
Euphrates R.

ARABS

Medina
Mecca

Red Sea

ARMENIA
Trebizond
PONTUS
PAPHLAGONIA
CAPPADOCIA
Callinicum
Antioch
SYRIA
Damascus
Jerusalem
PALESTINE

Don R.

Dnieper R.

AVARS

CRIMEA
Cherson

Black Sea

ANATOLIA
Nicaea
BITHYNIA
LYDIA
Akroinon
Ephesus
CARIA
PAMPHYLIA
LYCIA
CILICIA
CYPRUS

EGYPT
Alexandria
THEBAIS
Nile R.

Constantinople

Vistula R.

SLAVS AND BULGARIANS

MOESIA
Adrianople
THRACE
Serdica
MACEDONIA
DACIA
Thessalonica
(Salonika)
THESSALY
EPIRUS
ACHAIA
Athens

Aegean Sea

CRETE

Mediterranean Sea

CYRENAICA

Oder R.

Elbe R.

Danube R.

LOMBARDS
DALMATIA

Adriatic Sea

Rhine R.

BURGUNDIANS

KINGDOM
OF THE
FRANKS

Seine R.
Loire R.
Garonne R.
Rhône R.

Marseille
Barcelona
Pyrenees
Ebro R.

KINGDOM
OF THE
VISIGOTHS

Tagus R.

Córdoba
Cartagena
Ceuta
MAURETANIA

Strait of Gibraltar

North
Sea

Atlantic
Ocean

Bay of
Biscay

ALPS
Milan
Aquileia
Ravenna
TUSCIA
LIGURIA
ITALY
Rome
APULIA
LUCANIA
Naples

SARDINIA

CORSICA

SICILY

BALEARES

Carthage
ZEUGI
CARTHAGO
NUMIDIA
BYZACENA
TRIPOLITANIA

Egypt. He attempted to reconcile them also, but with indifferent success. The cleavage between Latin and Greek Christianity became ever more marked. Justinian suppressed all heresies and paganism (closing of the Neo-Platonic Academy at Athens, 529). Extensive missionary work was carried on among the pagans and in Ethiopia. For the rest, the emperor, with a great taste for dogma, set himself up as the master of the Church and arrogated to himself the right to make binding pronouncements in even purely theological matters.

Administration. The emperor abolished the sale of offices, improved salaries, united the civil and military powers of provincial authorities. To hold back invaders, he built hundreds of forts along the frontiers and established a regular system of frontier forces (limitanei). Financially the empire suffered greatly from the extensive military operations and from the great building activities of the court.

Law reform. To clarify the law, Justinian appointed a commission headed by the jurist **Tribonian.** This commission collected and ordered all the constitutions promulgated since the time of Hadrian and published them as the *Codex Justinianus* (529). There followed the collection of opinions of the jurists, the *Digest, or Pandects* (533), and a general textbook of the law, the *Institutes.* Justinian's own legislation was collected in the *Novellae* (565). By this great work of codification Justinian assured for the Roman Law an immense prestige and far-reaching influence, but at the same time diminished its chances of further development.

Building activity. The period was one of unexampled construction, ranging from whole towns to public baths, palaces, bridges, roads, and forts, as well as countless churches and cloisters. It was a period of much free experimentation and originality in architecture, resulting in unusual variety of types, all of them, however, marked by grandeur and splendor. The **Church of St. Sophia** (constructed between 532 and 537 by Anthemois of Tralles and Isidoros of Miletus) is the greatest of the many monuments of Justinian's reign.

Literature. An age of revival. The *Anekdota* (Secret History) of **Procopius;** the historians **Agathias** and **John of Ephesus.** Renascence of Greek classical poetry; creation of religious poetry by **Romanos.**

527–31. The **first Persian War** of Justinian (p. 101). His commander, **Belisarius,** won a victory at Dara (530), but was then defeated at **Callinicum.** The conflict ended with the **Perpetual Peace** of 532, designed to free the imperial armies for operations in the west.

532. The **Nika Insurrection** (so called from the cry of the popular parties, *nika* meaning victory). This was the last great uprising of the circus parties. Much of Constantinople was destroyed by fire. Justinian was deterred from flight only through the arguments of Theodora. Ultimately Belisarius and the forces put down the insurrection with much cruelty (30,000 slain). Therewith autocracy was reaffirmed. People started to regard the emperor as God's regent on earth, and church and state became one. Not only land ownership but also lucrative economic activities, like the silk industry, were state monopolies (Byzantium succeeded in importing silkworms directly from China and developed a silk industry of its own). Another precedent to be followed by most Byzantine emperors until the 13th century was Justinian's ambition to restore the previous Roman Empire with the entire Mediterranean under its control.

533–34. The Vandal usurper Gelimer was defeated, and the **whole of North Africa** was reincorporated into the empire.

535–54. After a series of devastating wars against the Ostrogoths, **all of Italy** was brought under imperial rule.

540. The **Huns, Bulgars** (p. 190), and other barbarian tribes crossed the Danube and raided the Balkan area as far south as the Isthmus of Corinth.

540–62. The great **Persian War against Khusru I** (Chosroes) (p. 101). The Persians invaded Syria and took Antioch. A truce was concluded in 545, but hostilities were soon resumed in the Transcaucasus region. By the 50-year **Peace of 562,** Justinian agreed to pay tribute, but Lazistan was retained for the empire.

542–46. Constantinople and the empire were affected by the first main cycle of bubonic plague, which struck the Mediterranean world throughout the 6th century and recurred periodically perhaps for the next 200–300 years. The 542–46 epidemic possibly caused the death of as many as 300,000 people in Constantinople alone. By the end of the 6th century, Byzantium saw its manpower severely debilitated.

554. The **conquest of southeastern Spain** by the imperial armies. Cordoba became the capital of the province.

559. The **Huns and Slavs,** having advanced to the very gates of Constantinople, were driven off by Belisarius.

565–78. Justin II, nephew of Justinian, who seized the throne with the aid of Tiberius, commander of the guard. Justin was a careful, economical ruler; he continued the policies of his predecessor but attempted to concentrate attention on the economic plight of the empire and the growing danger from the barbarians. In 574 he became insane, after which the empire was ruled by Tiberius, in conjunction with the Empress Sophia.

568–71. The **Lombard invasion of Italy** led to the loss of most of the imperial possessions in the north and center, though Ravenna, Rome, and Naples were retained.

572–91. War with Persia, growing out of an insurrection in Armenia, which was supported by the emperor. The Persians took Dara (573) and devastated Syria. In 575, Khusru ravaged the country as far as Cappadocia, but was finally driven back by the imperial commander Maurikios.

578–82. Tiberius, emperor. His reign was marked by a great inundation of the Slavs, who advanced into Thrace and Greece and settled in large numbers, thus changing profoundly the ethnographic composition of the Balkan populations.

582–602. Maurice (Maurikios), emperor. Like Justin, he pursued a policy of retrenchment, which only made him unpopular in the capital.

583. The **Avars,** an Altaic people grown to be a formidable power, took the forts along the Danube.

589–91. Last phase of the Persian War. Khusru I had died in 579. In 589 a military revolt led to the deposition of Khusru II, who fled to Constantinople. The emperor, espousing his cause, led a great army to the east (591) and restored him to the throne. In return the emperor received Dara and the larger part of Armenia.

591. The Avars raided to the very gates of Constantinople.

593. The imperial armies, under the general **Priscus,** proceeded against the Avars. The latter were defeated in 601 at **Viminacium** (now Kostolac, in Serbia), after which Priscus pushed on to the Tisza River.

602. A **mutiny of the troops on the Danube,** led by Phocas, resulted in a march to the capital, the outbreak of popular insurrection in the city, and the flight of the emperor.

602–10. Phocas, emperor. He was an untutored soldier, cruel and utterly incompetent. Maurice was captured and executed with his sons and all his supporters.

606–8. Resumption of the Persian War (p. 102). The Persians again captured Dara and overran Syria and Mesopotamia (608), advancing through Anatolia as far as Chalcedon.

610. Conspiracy against Phocas, led by Priscus and supported by the exarch of Africa. The latter sent an army by land that conquered Egypt, while a fleet from Carthage arrived at Constantinople. The mob thereupon rose, slew Phocas, and proclaimed Heraclius, the son of the exarch, as emperor.

610–41. Heraclius I, founder of a new dynasty in whose reign **Greek definitively replaced Latin** as the empire's official language. Heraclius found the empire in a perilous state, threatened from the north by the Avars and from the east by the Persians. But he showed himself to be an able organizer, general, and statesman, and found in the patriarch Sergius a courageous supporter.

611–22. The Persian advance. The Persians took Antioch, Apameia, Emesa, Kaisareia, Damascus (613), and Jerusalem (614), which was sacked, the inhabitants and the Holy Cross being transferred to Ctesiphon. In 615 the Persians were at Chalcedon. In 619 they conquered Egypt.

616. The imperial possessions in Spain were lost to the Visigoths.

619. The **Avars appeared at Constantinople,** which was threatened on the Asiatic side by the Persians. Heraclius was deterred from flight to Africa only by the influence of the patriarch.

622–30. Defeat of the Persians. Heraclius, with a newly organized army and supported by a tremendous outburst of religious enthusiasm, took the offensive against the Persians and carried on three brilliant campaigns in the Transcaucasian region, refusing to allow himself to be distracted by the constant attacks of the Avars in the Balkans. The death of Khusru (628) and dynastic disorders in Persia made possible the conclusion of a victorious peace. All the Persian conquests were returned, and the Holy Cross was restored to Jerusalem, but the war also fatally weakened the Byzantine Empire, and facilitated the expansion of both the Slavs from the north and the Arabs from the southeast.

626. The Avars and Slavs attacked Constantinople by land and sea, but were unable to storm the walls. This marked the height of the Avar power.

632–41. Beginning of Arab expansion (p. 108). They took Bostra (634) and Damascus (635); by the **Battle of Yarmuk** (636) gained all Syria; forced the surrender of Jerusalem (637); overran Mesopotamia (639); and conquered Egypt (640–42) (p. 109).

635. Alliance between the emperor and Kubrat, or Kurt, king of the Bulgars, intended to break the power of the Avars.

641–68. CONSTANS II (Constantinus), grandson of Heraclius, emperor. He was an energetic and able ruler, who did his utmost to check the Arab advance. With this object in view, he reorganized the provincial administration by establishing *themes (themata)* under *strategoi*, military governors with wide powers and authority over civil officials. This system greatly strengthened administrative control and was the basis of the imperial organization for centuries.

643. The Arabs took Alexandria, last outpost of the Greeks in Egypt.

647–48. Arab invasion of North Africa.

648. The Arabs, having assembled a fleet, took Cyprus.

653. The Arab advance continued. Armenia was conquered (653) and Rhodes plundered (654). In 655 the Arab fleet defeated an imperial armada under the emperor's own command off the Lycian coast. But in 659 a truce was concluded with the Arab commander in Syria.

663–68. Transfer of the court to Italy. Constans was intent on blocking the Arab conquest of Sicily and Italy and had dreams of restoring Rome as the basis of the imperial power. But he failed to make any conquests in Italy at the expense of the Lombards, and in his absence the Arabs annually invaded and devastated Anatolia.

668. Constans was murdered in the course of a mutiny at Syracuse.

668–85. Constantine IV (Pogonatus), the son of Constans, a harsh character, but an able soldier. He had been in charge of affairs and had come to Sicily to put down the revolt that had resulted in his father's death. On his return to Constantinople, the troops obliged him to accept his brothers Heraclius and Tiberius as corulers, but after 680 Constantine was sole emperor. His reign witnessed the high point of the Arab attack, accompanied, as usual, by repeated incursions of the Slavs in the Balkans.

673–78. The **Arab attacks on Constantinople.** After a siege by land and sea (Apr.–Sept. 673), the assailants blockaded the city and attacked it every year for five years. The city was saved by the strength of its walls and by the newly invented **Greek fire,** which raised havoc with the Arab fleet. The exact composition and means of propulsion of Greek fire, invented by the architect and mathematician **Kallinikos,** are still uncertain. According to most scholars, it apparently consisted of crude oil mixed with resin and sulfur, which was propelled by a pump through a bronze tube and was ignited either as it left the tube or by firing flaming projectiles after it.

675–81. Repeated assaults of the Slavs on Salonika. The city held out, but the settlement of Thrace, Macedonia, and Greece by Slavic tribes continued.

677. The Byzantines destroyed the Arab fleet at **Syllaeum** and secured a favorable 30-year peace (678).

680–81. Appearance of the **Bulgarian menace.** The Bulgars, a people of mixed Ural-Altaic and Indo-European origin, had pressed westward through the lands of today's southern Russia and Ukraine. Threatened by another Altaic people, the Khazars, the Bulgars eventually crossed the Danube. The emperor failed to defeat them and had to cede all the lands to the north of the Balkan Mountains, with the exception of some Black Sea ports. The Bulgars submitted the Slavs to systematic deportation to the north of the Danube. Some Slavic tribes fled as far to the south as the Peloponnesus.

680–81. The **sixth ecumenical council** at Constantinople condemned the monothelite heresy and returned to orthodoxy. Since the loss of Syria and Egypt, there was no longer any need for favoring the monophysite view. The return to orthodoxy was a victory for the papal stand and was probably intended to strengthen the Byzantine hold on Italy. In actual fact the patriarch of Constantinople (now that the patriarchs

of Antioch, Jerusalem, and Alexandria were under Muslim power) became more influential in the east, and the primacy of the Roman pope was hardly more than nominal.

685–95. Justinian II, the son of Constantine and the last of the Heraclian dynasty. He ascended the throne when only 16 and soon showed himself to be harsh and cruel, though energetic and ambitious like most members of his family.

689. The emperor defeated the Slavs in Thrace and transferred a considerable number of them to Anatolia.

692. The Byzantine forces were severely defeated by the Arabs in the **Battle of Sevastopol** in the Crimea.

695. A revolt against the emperor, led by Leontius and supported by the clergy and people, initiated a period of 20 years of anarchy. Justinian was deposed and exiled to the Crimea (Cherson).

695–98. Leontius, emperor. His reign was marked by the domination of the army.

697–98. The Arabs finally took **Carthage,** ending Byzantine rule in North Africa.

698–705. Tiberius II, made emperor by another revolt in the army. The reign was distinguished by an insurrection against Byzantine rule in Armenia and by constant Arab raids in eastern Anatolia.

705–11. Justinian II, who returned to the throne with the aid of the Bulgarian king. He took an insane revenge on all his enemies and instituted a reign of terror.

711. The emperor failed to suppress a serious **revolt in the Crimea** supported by the Khazars. The insurgent troops, under Philippicus, marched on Constantinople and finally defeated and killed Justinian in the engagement in northern Anatolia.

715–17. Theodosius III, an obscure official put on the throne by the army. He was helpless in the face of the Arabs, who in 716 advanced as far as Pergamon. The invaders were finally repulsed by the *strategos* of the Anatolian *theme,* Leo, who forced the abdication of the emperor and was enthusiastically proclaimed by the clergy and populace of the capital.

717–41. LEO III (the Isaurican), founder of the **Isaurican dynasty,** an eminent general and a great organizer. Leo used drastic measures to suppress revolts in the army and reestablished discipline by issuing new regulations. The finances were restored by heavy, systematic taxation. An **agrarian code** confirmed the village communities as collective owners of land, collectively responsible to the state. In the *Ecloga* (739) the empire was given a simplified law code, distinguished by the Christian charity of its provisions. Leo completed the **theme organization,** dividing the original units and making seven *themes* in Asia and four in Europe.

717–18. Second great siege of Constantinople by the Arabs. The siege lasted just a year and ended in failure, due to the energetic conduct of the defense and to the assistance of the Bulgars.

726. Beginning of the great **iconoclastic controversy.** Leo found the empire generally demoralized and prey to superstition and miracle-mongering. Like many devout persons (especially in the Anatolian regions), he disapproved of the widespread image worshiping, which he proceeded to forbid. Behind these measures there undoubtedly lay the desire to check the alarming **spread of monasticism,** which withdrew thousands of men from active economic life and concentrated great wealth in the cloisters, which were free from taxation. The first measures led at once to a revolt in Greece (727), whence a fleet set out for Constantinople with an "anti-emperor." This was destroyed by the Greek fire of the imperial fleet. The pope at Rome (Gregory II) likewise declared against the emperor's iconoclasm, and the population of the exarchate of Ravenna rose in revolt and made an alliance with the Lombards. With the aid of Venice, a few crucial stations were held by the imperial forces. A fleet from the east failed to restore Byzantine authority (731). In revenge the emperor in 733 withdrew Calabria, Sicily, and Illyria from the jurisdiction of the pope and placed them under the Constantinople patriarch.

739. The Byzantine forces won an important victory over the Muslim invaders of Anatolia in the **battle of Akroinon.**

741–75. CONSTANTINE V (Kopronymos, or "dung-named," for supposedly having defecated while being baptized; the name reflects clerical hostility to his zealous support of iconoclasm), the son of Leo and for years associated with him in the government. Constantine was autocratic, uncompromising, and violent, but withal able and energetic as well as sincere. A revolt of his brother-in-law, Artavasdos, was supported by the idolaters and by part of the army. It took fully two years to suppress it.

745. The emperor, taking the offensive against the Arabs, carried the war into Syria.

746. Constantine destroyed an Arab armada and reconquered Cyprus. The empire suffered from the greatest **plague epidemic** since the time of Justinian.

751–52. The emperor led a successful campaign against the Arabs in Armenia. The Arabs were weakened by the fall of the Umayyad Caliphate and the removal of the capital from Damascus to Baghdad (p. 112).

751. The Lombards conquered the exarchate of Ravenna. The pope thereupon called in the Franks and was given the former Byzantine territory by Pepin (**Donation of Pepin,** 756) (p. 173).

753. The **Church Council of Hieria** approved of the emperor's iconoclastic policy. Therewith began the violent phase of the controversy. The monks offered vigorous resistance, but the emperor was unbending. The monks were imprisoned, exiled, and some even executed; monasteries were closed and their properties confiscated; images were destroyed or whitewashed.

755–64. Nine successive **campaigns against the Bulgars.** The emperor won important victories at Marcellae (759) and Anchialus (763), and forced the Bulgars to conclude peace (764).

758. The Slavs were defeated in Thrace, and a large number of them settled in Asia.

772. Renewal of the **war with the Bulgars,** marked by further victories for the emperor.

775–80. Leo IV, the son of Constantine.

778–79. Victory over the Muslims at **Germanikeia** (778), and their expulsion from Anatolia.

780–97. Constantine VI ascended the throne as a child, wholly under the influence of his ambitious, unscrupulous, and scheming mother, **Irene,** and her favorites. Irene, anxious to secure support for her personal power, devoted herself almost exclusively to the religious question. The Muslims, who again advanced to the Bosporus (782), were bought off with heavy tribute (783). On the other hand, the general Staurakios carried on a successful campaign against the Slavs in Macedonia and Greece (783).

787. The **Council of Nicaea** abandoned iconoclasm and permitted the veneration of images. Tremendous victory for the monkish party, which soon advanced far-reaching claims to complete freedom for the Church in religious matters.

790. The army, opposed to the monks, mutinied and put Constantine in power. Irene was forced into retirement. The emperor set out on campaigns against the Arabs and Bulgars, but met with mixed success.

792. Constantine recalled his mother and made her coruler. She took vile advantage of him and, after his divorce and a remarriage arranged by her (795), put herself at the head of a party of the monks in opposing iconoclasm. A rising of the army put her in control, and she had her son blinded (797).

797–802. Irene, the first empress. Though supported by able generals (Staurakios and Aëtios), she preferred to buy peace with the Arabs (798) and to devote herself to domestic intrigue.

800. Resurrection of the empire in the west, through the coronation of Charlemagne (p. 174). The Eastern Empire refused to recognize the claim.

802–11. Nicephorus, who was put on the throne by a group of conspiring officials of the government. Irene, deposed, died in 803. Nicephorus was a firm ruler who carried through a number of much-needed financial reforms.

803. The emperor made **peace with Charlemagne,** the Eastern Empire retaining southern Italy, Venice, and Dalmatia.

809. Banishment of the monks of Studion, who, under **Theodoros of Studion,** took the lead in advancing claims to church freedom. They went so far as to appeal to the Roman pope and offer to recognize his primacy.

809–13. War with Krum, the powerful king of the Bulgars. The emperor was defeated and killed in a great battle (811).

811–13. Michael I (Rhangabé), emperor. He proved himself quite incom-

petent, being unable to check the advance of Krum to Constantinople or the success of the party of monks in domestic affairs.

813–20. Leo V (the Armenian), called to the throne by the army. Though personally not much moved by the religious controversy, he could not avoid taking up the challenge of the monks.

814–15. The emperor won a great victory over the Bulgars at **Burtudizus** (today, Babaeski in Turkey's European part), Krum having died (814). The Bulgars were obliged to accept a 30-year peace.

815. The **Council of St. Sophia** marked the return to iconoclasm and the beginning of the second period of active and violent persecution of the monks.

820–29. Michael II (Phrygian dynasty), succeeded to the throne after the murder of Leo by conspirators.

822–24. Insurrection of the general **Thomas** in Anatolia. This was supported by the lower classes and encouraged by the Arabs. Thomas attempted twice to take Constantinople, but was ultimately defeated and executed in Thrace.

826. Crete was seized by Muslim freebooters from Spain, and until 961 it remained the headquarters of pirates who ravaged the eastern Mediterranean.

827–78. Conquest of Sicily by Muslims from North Africa.

829–42. THEOPHILUS, emperor. He was an arrogant, theologizing fanatic who promulgated a new edict against idolaters (832) and pushed persecution to the limit.

837–38. War against the Arabs. The Byzantine armies, after invading the caliphate, were repulsed. After a long siege, Amorion, one of the key positions on the frontier, was taken by the Muslims (838).

842–67. Michael III, for whom his mother Theodora was regent. Advised by her brother **Bardas,** she decided to end the religious controversy.

843. Image worship was restored. This was a great victory for the opposition party, but only in the matter of doctrine. Politically the power of the emperor over the Church remained unimpaired, if not strengthened.

856. Theodora was obliged to retire, but her brother Bardas, an able but unprincipled politician, remained the real ruler of the empire by exploiting to the full the weaknesses of the emperor.

860. First appearance of the Russians (Varangians) at Constantinople.

863–85. Missionary activity of **Cyril and Methodius** of Thessalonica among the Slavs of Moravia and Bohemia. They invented the glagolitic alphabet—from which the Cyrillic derives (p. 190)—which came to be used in various Slavonic languages and was later restricted to liturgical books; hence Cyril and Methodius are regarded as founders of Slavonic literature.

865. Boris of Bulgaria (852–89) allowed himself to be baptized. Although Michael III acted as godfather, the Bulgarian ruler was for a time undecided between the claims of Rome and Constantinople to religious jurisdiction in Bulgaria.

866. Bardas was murdered by Michael's favorite, Basil.

867. Michael himself was deposed and done away with at Basil's order.

867. Schism with Rome. The great patriarch **Photius** had replaced **Ignatius** in 858, whereupon the latter had appealed to the pope for an inquiry. Photius came to represent the Greek national feeling in opposition to Rome. He took a strong stand toward the papal claims, and the **Council of Constantinople** (867) anathematized the pope, accused the papacy of doctrinal aberrations, rejected the idea of Rome's primacy.

867–86. Basil I, founder of the Macedonian dynasty (he was really of Armenian extraction, though born in Macedonia). His reign initiated what was probably the most glorious period of Byzantine history, a period of brilliant military success, material prosperity, and cultural development. Basil I's ambition was to restore the empire both internally and externally. He rebuilt the army and, especially, the navy and did much to revise the legal system: the *Procheiros Nomos* (879), a compilation of the most important parts of the Justinian code; the *Epanagoge* (886), a manual of customary law.

Basil I's reign was also marked by the gradual emergence of a system comparable to western European feudalism: in return for their service to the state, high-ranking officials were given land with peasants to till the fields. This practice led to the appearance of powerful provincial magnates, called *dynatoi.* However, there was no contract between lord and vassal: the emperor could dispossess the *dynatoi* at any time.

869. The eighth ecumenical synod. Photius was banished (867) and Ignatius recalled. The latter made peace with Rome on papal terms, but conflict and friction continued.

871–79. Campaigns in the east. Border warfare with the Arabs was chronic, but the campaign against the Paulicians (Christian purists hostile to the empire) was a new departure. The imperial armies advanced to the upper Euphrates and took Samosata (873). In 878–79 victorious campaigns were carried through in Cappadocia and Cilicia. By land, the Byzantine forces were gradually taking the offensive against the Muslims, wracked by internal dissension.

875. The Byzantine forces seized **Bari** in southern Italy. Some years later (880) they took Tarentum and then (885) Calabria, establishing two new *themes* in southern Italy, which became a refuge for Greeks driven from Sicily by the completion of the Muslim conquest (Syracuse taken in 878; Taormina taken in 902).

877. Photius was restored as patriarch, and the break with Rome was renewed.

880–81. A number of naval **victories over the Muslim pirates** of the eastern Mediterranean marked the beginning of a long campaign.

886–912. Leo VI (the Wise), a somewhat pedantic philosopher, but nevertheless a determined ruler with a high sense of his office and obligations. He deposed Photius at once and put the Ignatians back in power. The result was a renewal of the **union with Rome** (900), which, however, could hardly have been more than external. The reign of Leo was also marked by further legislative work. The *Basilika* (887–93) provided a series of 60 new law books, consisting largely of a compilation of decrees since the time of Justinian.

894–96. War with the Bulgarians, who now entered the period of greatness under **Tsar Symeon** (893–927). The emperor encouraged the Hungarians to attack by way of diversion, and most of Symeon's reign was taken up with continued campaigns against this enemy. Symeon was educated at Constantinople and was deeply impressed by Greek culture, which he introduced in Bulgaria.

904. The Saracen corsair **Leo of Tripoli** stormed Thessalonica, plundered it, and carried off some 20,000 of the inhabitants.

907. The **Russians,** under their prince, Oleg, appeared again at Constantinople and secured rights of trade.

912–13. Alexander II, the brother of Leo, emperor for less than a year.

912–59. Constantine VII (Porphyrogenetos) ascended the throne as a child, with a regency composed of his mother, Zoë, the patriarch Nikolas, and John Eladas. Constantine was a learned man of artistic tastes. He never really governed, leaving the actual conduct of affairs to strong men who were associated with him.

913–27. The Bulgarian threat. Symeon styled himself emperor (tsar) of the Romans and undoubtedly hoped to possess himself of the imperial crown. In 913 he appeared at Constantinople; in 914 he took Adrianople, only to lose it again. But in 917 he defeated a Byzantine army at Anchialus. The war ended only after Symeon's death in 927.

915. A Byzantine victory over the Arabs at **Garigliano** assured the empire of its possessions in south Italy.

920–44. Romanus Lecapenus, coemperor with Constantine. He was the emperor's father-in-law, an able but ruthless Armenian whose whole policy was designed to strengthen his own control and establish that of his family.

920–42. Brilliant campaigns of the Byzantine general **John Kurkuas** in the east. He took the modern Erzerum (928) and Melitene (934) and extended the imperial power to the Euphrates and Tigris.

920. Official reunion with Rome.

924. The piratical fleets of **Leo of Tripoli** were completely defeated off **Lemnos.** Nevertheless, the Muslims continued activity in the Mediterranean.

927. The empire suffered from a **great famine,** which probably explains the stringent legislation of the government to prevent the purchase of small holdings by the great landed magnates.

941. A great armada of Russians, under **Prince Igor,** was signally defeated by the Greeks.

944. Emperor Romanus was seized and imprisoned (d. 948) by the very sons whose interests he had attempted to serve. Emperor Constantine became officially the sole ruler, but governed with the aid of the great

general **Bardas Phocas,** and under the influence of Empress Helena and her favorite, Basil.

957. Visit to Constantinople and baptism of **Princess Olga** of Russia.

961. Reconquest of Crete from the Muslim pirates. A great armada was sent out under Nicephorus Phocas. Candia was stormed, the Muslims expelled from the island or converted to Christianity.

962. Otto I, Roman emperor in the west, claimed suzerainty over the Lombards in southern Italy, initiating a period of friction with Constantinople, which was only temporarily broken by the marriage of Otto II and the Byzantine princess Theophano (972).

963–1025. Basil II, an infant at the death of his father. The principle of legitimacy was carefully respected, but before Basil II really assumed power, the empire was governed by two great generals associated with him.

963–69. Nicephorus II Phocas, who had carried on a successful campaign in the east. He seized control and married the widowed Empress Theophano. Never popular, especially with the clergy, Nicephorus, by his victories in the field, helped to raise the empire to its greatest glory.

964–68. Victorious campaign in the east. Adana was taken (964) and then Tarsus (965). Cyprus was reconquered, and in 968 northern Syria was invaded. **Aleppo** and even **Antioch** fell into the hands of the Greeks.

966–69. The Bulgarian campaign, carried through with the aid of Sviatoslav and the Russians. The latter, with their fleets, were so successful on the Danube that the Greeks made peace with the Bulgars.

969. Nicephorus Phocas was overthrown by a conspiracy of officers led by his own nephew, **John Tzimisces.**

Sviatoslav, the Russian, crossed the Balkan Mountains and took Philippopolis. John Tzimisces marched against him, defeated him near Adrianople, and, with the aid of the Byzantine fleet on the Danube, forced him to evacuate Bulgaria (972). John thereupon annexed eastern Bulgaria as far as the Danube to the empire. The patriarchate of Preslav was abolished.

969–76. John I Tzimisces, an Armenian by birth and one of the greatest of Byzantine generals.

971. A great insurrection, led by Bardas Phocas, was put down only with difficulty.

972–76. Continuation of the campaigns in the east. John took Edessa and Nezib (974), Damascus and Beirut (976), and advanced to the very gates of Jerusalem, where he was halted by the Muslim forces from Egypt.

976. Sudden death of John Tzimisces, at the early age of 51.

976. Basil II (Bulgaroktonos, Slayer of the Bulgarians) now became sole emperor. He was only 20 years old, but was serious and energetic, cynical and cruel. Until 989 he was much influenced by Basil the Eunuch, the illegitimate son of Romanus Lecapenus. The reign of Basil began with another great upheaval, led by **Bardas Skleros,** who marched his armies from the east through Anatolia and to Constantinople. Basil appealed to Bardas Phocas, defeated leader of the earlier rising, to save the situation, which he did by defeating Skleros at Pankalia (979).

976–1014. Tsar Samuel of Bulgaria. He built up another great Bulgarian Empire, with its capital at Ochrid, extending from the Adriatic to the Black Sea and from the Danube to the Peloponnesus. In 981 he defeated Basil near Sofia.

987. Rising of Bardas Phocas and Bardas Skleros against Basil and the imperial authority. The great magnates overran Anatolia. In 988 they threatened Constantinople, but the movement collapsed with the defeat of Phocas at Abydos (989) and his subsequent death. Skleros then submitted.

989. Conversion of Prince Vladimir of Russia, at Cherson. This initiated the general conversion of the Russians to eastern Christianity and the close connection between Kiev and Constantinople.

992. Extensive trade privileges in the empire were granted to **Venice,** by this time quite independent of imperial control, but in close cooperation with Constantinople in the Adriatic.

995. Victorious campaigns of the emperor in the east. Aleppo and Homs were taken and Syria incorporated with the empire.

996. Land legislation of Basil II. Many of the great estates were confiscated and divided among the peasants, and provision was made to prevent the emergence of powerful landed magnates.

THE MACEDONIAN EMPERORS (867–1056)

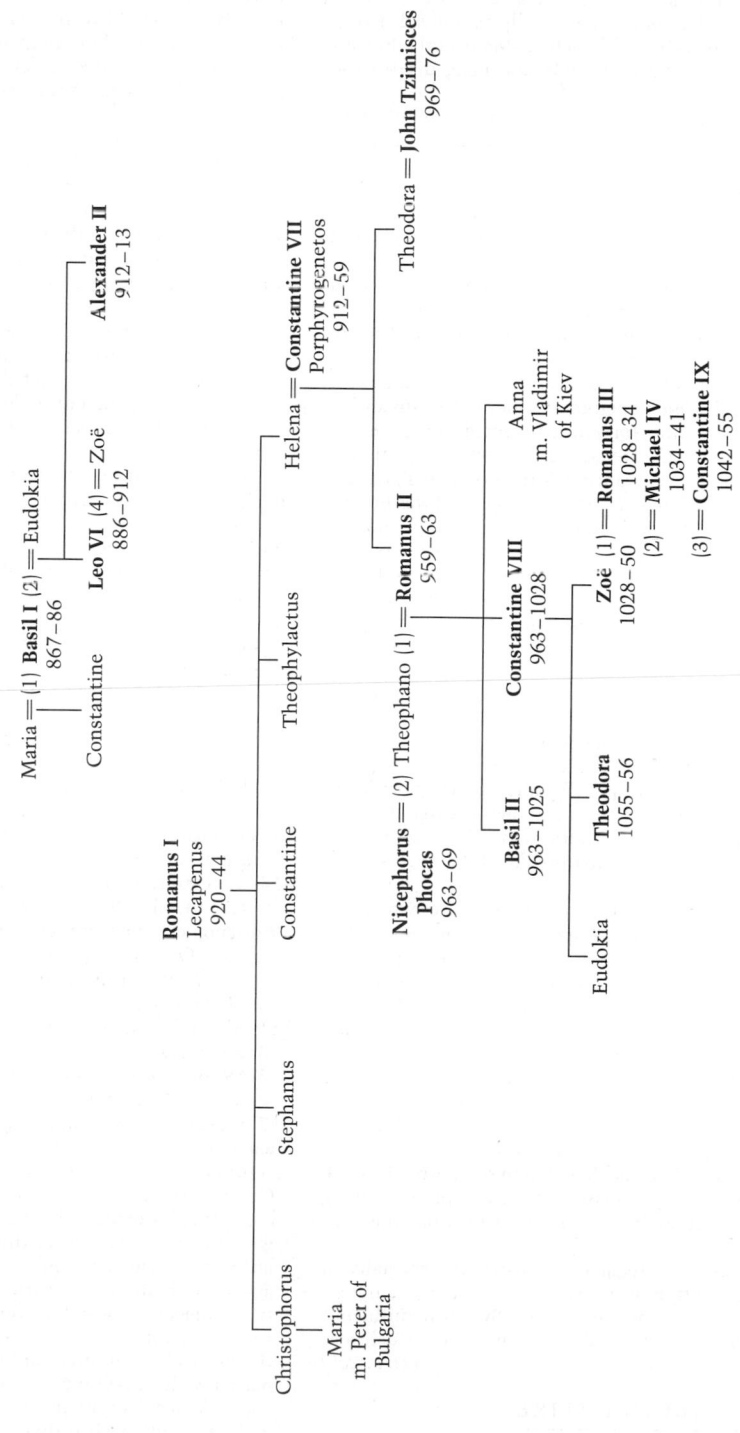

996-1014. The great Bulgarian campaigns. In 996 Basil defeated Samuel on the Spercheios River and reconquered Greece. In 1002 he overran Macedonia. Samuel recovered, however, reconquered Macedonia, and sacked Adrianople (1003). In 1007 Basil subdued Macedonia again and after years of indecisive conflict annihilated the Bulgarian army at **Belasitsa** (1014). He sent several thousand blinded soldiers back to Samuel, who died of the shock. The Bulgarians finally submitted (1018), but were left an autocephalous church at Ochrid. Many of the Bulgarian noble families settled in Constantinople and merged with the Greek and Armenian aristocracy.

1018. The Byzantine forces won a great victory over the combined Lombards and Normans at **Cannae**, thus assuring continuance of the Greek domination in southern Italy.

1020. The **king of Armenia**, long in alliance with the Greeks against the Arabs, turned over his kingdom to Basil to escape the new threat from the Seljuk Turks. The empire thereby became firmly established in Transcaucasia and along the Euphrates.

Byzantine culture reached its apogee in the late 10th and early 11th centuries. The empire extended from Italy to Mesopotamia, and its influence radiated much farther. Constantinople was indeed the economic and artistic center of the Mediterranean world.

Government. The emperor was an absolute ruler, regarded almost as sacred. Under the Macedonian emperors, the idea of legitimacy became firmly established. The imperial court reflected the emperor's power and splendor. There was an extensive and elaborate ceremonial (cf. the *Book of Ceremonies* of Constantine Porphyrogenetos); the administration was highly centralized in Constantinople and was unique for its efficiency; the treasury was full and continued to draw income from taxes, customs, and monopolies; the army and navy were both at the peak of their development, with excellent organization and leadership; the provinces were governed by the *strategoi*; there were by this time 30 *themes* (18 in Asia and 12 in Europe), but throughout this period there was a steady growth in the number and power of the provincial magnates *(dynatoi)*, feudal barons who acquired more and more of the small holdings and exercised an ever greater influence, even challenging the emperor himself. All the legislation of the Macedonian emperors failed to check this development.

The **Church** was closely connected with the throne, but during this period it too became more and more wealthy and gradually produced a clerical aristocracy. The union with Rome, when it existed, was a purely formal thing. The Greek patriarchate in practice resented the Roman claim to primacy, and the popular dislike of the Latins made any real cooperation impossible.

Economic life. This was closely controlled by the state, which derived much of its income from the customs and monopolies. Yet it was a period of great commercial development, Constantinople serving as the entrepôt between east and west. It was also a great center of the industry in luxuries (organization of trades in rigid guilds, etc.).

Learning. The university of Constantinople (opened c. 850) had quickly become a center of philosophical and humanistic study, in which the emperors took a direct interest. In the 11th century there appeared the greatest of the Byzantine scholars, **Psellus**, reviver of the Platonic philosophy and universal genius. In the field of literature there was a conscious return to the great Greek models of the early Byzantine period, historians **Constantine Porphyrogenetos, Leo the Deacon**, and others. The great popular epic *Digenis Akritas*, describing the heroic life of the frontier soldiers *(Akritai)*, dates from the 10th century.

Art. The period was one of extensive construction, especially in Constantinople; full exploitation of the St. Sophia type in church architecture; mosaics; ikons; gold and silver work. Byzantine influence in this period permeated the entire Mediterranean world, Muslim as well as Christian.   *(To p. 229)*

b. THE FIRST BULGARIAN EMPIRE

584-642. Rule of **Kubrat**, or **Kurt**, of the Dulo tribe, approximately one century after Bulgarian settlement in the Balkans (p. 186). His dominion extended from the Don to the Caucasus. In 619 he visited Constantinople to secure aid against the Avars, at which time he became converted to Christianity, though this step seems to have had no consequences for his people.

643-701. Isperikh (Asperuch), the son of Kurt. The old Great Bulgaria was disrupted by the attacks of Avars and Khazars, and various tribes of Bulgars moved westward into Pannonia and even into Italy. Those under Isperikh crossed the Danube (650-70) and established a capital at Pliska. In 680 they defeated a Byzantine army and occupied the territory between the Danube and the Balkan Mountains. At the same time they still held Wallachia, Moldova, and Bessarabia.

701-18. Tervel, to whom Emperor Justinian II paid a subsidy or tribute, but only after the imperial forces had been defeated at Anchialus (708) and after Tervel had advanced to the very gates of Constantinople (712).

718-24. Ruler unknown.

724-39. Sevar, during whose reign the peace with the empire was maintained. The Dulo dynasty came to an end with Sevar, whose death was followed by an obscure intertribal struggle.

739-56. Kormisosh, of the Ukil tribe. Until the very end of his reign he maintained peace with the empire, until further domestic disorders gave the signal for Byzantine attacks (from 755 on).

756-61. Vinekh, who was killed in the course of an uprising.

c. 760. 208,000 Slavs fled from Bulgaria, asked Byzantium for asylum, and were allowed to settle in Asia Minor.

761-64. Telets, of the Ugain tribe. He was defeated at Anchialus by the Byzantines (763) and put to death by the Bulgarians.

764. Sabin, of the family of Kormisosh. He was deposed and fled to Constantinople.

764? Pagan, or **Boyan**, who finally concluded peace with the emperor.

766. Umor, who was deposed by **Toktu**. Toktu was captured and killed by the Greeks.

773-77? Telerig, whose family is unknown. The Greeks renewed their attacks, which were on the whole successful.

777-802. Kardam, whose reign marked the turning of the tide. He took advantage of the confusion in the empire to defeat the Greeks at **Marcellae** (792) and to rebuild the foundations of the state.

803-14. Krum, one of the greatest Bulgarian rulers. He appears to have been of the Dulo tribe's Panonian branch. He rose to power as a result of his victories over the Avars. For four years (809-13) he carried on war with the Byzantine Empire. The Greeks sacked Pliska (809, 811), but Krum defeated and killed the emperor in a battle in the mountains (811). In 812 he took the important fortress of Mesembria, and in 813 won another victory at Versinicia. In the same year he appeared at Constantinople. The city was too strong for him, and he retired, devastating Thrace and taking Adrianople.

814-31. Omurtag, the son of Krum. After a defeat by the Greeks (814), he concluded a 30-year peace with them, returning Mesembria and Adrianople. Construction of palaces in Pliska; founding of the city of Preslav. Omurtag left many stone inscriptions, written mostly in Greek. During the peace in the east, the Bulgars began systematic raids into Croatia and Pannonia (827-29).

831-52. Malamir, the son of Omortag. Gradual expansion into upper Macedonia and Serbia (839).

852-89. Boris I. He continued the campaigns in the west, but suffered severe defeats by the Serbs (860).

865. Boris's reign was important chiefly for his **conversion to Christianity.** Boris was induced to take the step under pressure from Constantinople, where the government was eager to frustrate a possible German-Roman advance. Boris had all his subjects baptized, which constituted a drastic change of their whole way of life. The Bulgars were forced, among other things, to reshape entirely their family relationships. The high-ranking state officials had to abandon polygamy and were thenceforth entitled to no more than three divorces. Traditional objects of worship were now proclaimed evil. The traditional tribal structures, kept together by a network of marital links between the chieftains' children and the children of the king, were to be replaced with a system of government along the Byzantine model. As a consequence, Christianization led to a revolt and the execution of 52 leaders, together with their families. At the same time, Boris spared no efforts to put the Church under his control and hesitated between Constantinople and Rome. Apparently intending to replace the Greek and Latin clergy with a clergy personally devoted to him, he encouraged the introduction of the Slavonic liturgy among the Slavs of Bulgaria by the disciples of Cyril and Methodius. To that effect, **Kliment of Okhrid** may have invented the **Cyrillic alphabet**, based on Greek characters and Bulgarian runes. In 889 Boris voluntarily retired to a monastery.

889–93. Rasate (known also as Vladimir), the son of Boris, who was soon exposed to a violent heathen reaction.

893. Boris reemerged from retirement, put down the revolt, deposed and blinded his son, and made the Slavonic liturgy general in its application. The capital was moved to Preslav. Boris then returned to his monastery, where he died (907).

893–927. Symeon I, another son of Boris, the first Bulgarian ruler to assume the title tsar. Symeon had been educated at Constantinople, as a monk. He was deeply imbued with Greek culture, but under his reign Slavic definitively replaced Greek as the official and Church language. Its impact on Bulgarian was as strong as that of Latin and French on English. Many books were translated from Greek into Slavic and would be later used by the Serbs and the Eastern Slavs, who thus adopted the Cyrillic alphabet. Bulgaria played a crucial role in the spread of Eastern Orthodoxy from Byzantium to a number of eastern European peoples.

894–96. Symeon's reign was filled with **wars against the Byzantine Empire,** which originally grew out of disputes regarding trade rights and ultimately developed into a contest for possession of the imperial throne. The war began in 894, with the defeat of a Greek army. The emperor thereupon induced the Magyars, located on the Pruth River, to attack the Bulgarians in Bessarabia (895). By trickery, Symeon induced the Greeks to withdraw and then defeated the Magyars, after which he returned and fell on the Greeks at Bulgarophygon. Peace was made in 896, the emperor paying tribute.

In the meantime the **Magyars,** driven westward by the Patzinaks (Pechenegs), advanced into Transylvania and Pannonia, which were lost to the Bulgars.

913. Symeon, taking advantage of the dynastic troubles in the empire, advanced to Constantinople, but withdrew with many presents and the promise that the young emperor, Constantine Porphyrogenitus, should marry one of his daughters. Symeon evidently hoped to attain the crown for himself, but was frustrated by the seizure of power by Zoë. He thereupon made war (914), raiding into Macedonia, Thessaly, and Albania. But the Patzinaks, instigated by the Greeks, invaded and occupied Wallachia (917), while Symeon defeated the Greeks near **Anchialus** (917). In 918 Symeon defeated the Serbs, who had also been aroused by the empress.

919–24. Symeon four times advanced to the Hellespont and Constantinople, but was unable to take the city because of his lack of a fleet. In 924 he had an interview with Emperor Romanus Lecapenus and finally made peace.

925. Symeon proclaimed himself **emperor of the Romans and the Bulgars.** The Greek emperor protested, but the pope recognized the title.

926. Symeon set up Leontius of Preslav as a patriarch.

926. Conquest and devastation of Serbia.

927–69. Peter, the son of Symeon, a pious, well-intentioned, but weak ruler, who married the granddaughter of Romanus Lecapenus. Peace with Constantinople was maintained, the Greek emperor recognizing the Bulgar ruler as emperor and acknowledging the Bulgarian patriarchate. Bulgaria was, during this period, occupied by the constant threat from the Magyars (raids in 934, 943, 958, 962) and the Patzinaks (great raid of 944). Internally the period seems to have been one of unrest and religious ferment (founding of monasteries; St. John of Rila; beginning of the **Bogomil heresy,** c. 950, a dualistic creed possibly inspired by the Paulicians settled in the Thracian region by the Byzantine emperors).

967. Invasion of Bulgaria by Sviatoslav and the Russians. Tsar Peter roused the Patzinaks, who attacked Kiev in 968 and forced Sviatoslav to withdraw.

969–72. Boris II. The reign was filled with the second invasion of Sviatoslav, who took Preslav and captured Boris and his family (969). The Greeks, in alarm, sent an army against him and defeated him at **Arcadiopolis** (970). In 971 Emperor John Tzimisces attacked the Russians by land and sea. He took Preslav and destroyed it, besieged Sviatoslav at Dristra on the Danube, and finally forced him to evacuate Bulgaria. Boris was obliged to abdicate, and the patriarchate was abolished.

976–1014. Samuel, son of a governor of one of the western districts, which had been unaffected by the Russian invasion, set himself up as ruler. He soon expanded his domain to Sofia, and reestablished the patriarchate (ultimately fixed at Okhrid, which was the center of the new state).

986–89. Samuel took Larissa after several annual raids into Thessaly. In the east he extended his power to the Black Sea.

996–1014. the **campaigns of Basil II** (Bulgaroktonos, Slayer of the Bulgarians) against Samuel. Basil proceeded to reduce one stronghold after another. Samuel avoided open battle as much as possible, but throughout suffered from the defection of his leaders, who were bribed with attractive offers from the emperor. The crowning defeat of the Bulgarians at Belasitsa (1014) and the sight of his 15,000 blinded warriors brought on Samuel's death.

1014–16. Gabriel Radomir (or Romanus), the son of Samuel. He tried to make peace, but was murdered by his cousin

1016–18. John Vladislav, who continued the war but was killed in a battle near Dyrrhacium. He left only young sons. The Bulgar leaders thereupon decided to submit. Bulgaria was incorporated into the Byzantine Empire (*themes* of Bulgaria and Paristrium); the patriarchate was abolished, but the archbishop of Okhrid retained practical autonomy. The Bulgarian aristocracy settled in Constantinople and merged with the leading Greek families. *(To p. 228)*

3. WESTERN EUROPE AND THE AGE OF THE CATHEDRALS, 1000–1300

a. OVERVIEW

This period witnessed great **agricultural expansion,** which made possible considerable **population growth,** which in turn contributed to the **rise and growth of towns.** A general **commercial revival,** especially of long-distance trade, brought Europeans, at least indirectly, into contact with many parts of the eastern Mediterranean, East Africa, East and Southeast Asia. Agricultural and commercial revivals allowed for **upward social mobility.** The period also saw remarkable intellectual creativity, with results including the uniquely European educational institution, **the university;** stunning **architectural** and **artistic vitality; technological change,** especially in the tremendous spurt in the **use of energy,** as in water and windmills, and the discovery of new iron-casting techniques; and **spiritual piety.** Perhaps the best indication of all this change is the **medieval cathedral,** a symbol of local civic pride, wealth, architectural imagination, and deep religious feeling. In this rich and creative era, the Roman papacy led the way in the development of administrative techniques; England, in the formation of political institutions, including the law; and France, in the evolution of sophisticated cultural influences.

SOCIAL INTOLERANCE. Xenophobia (especially against Muslims) resulted from the long crusading tradition; the general systematization of civil and ecclesiastical law stressing social and religious conformity led to increasing hostility against those perceived as social outsiders, aliens. This **new intolerance** manifested itself first in the **expulsion of the Jews** (from England in 1290, France in 1306), then in **legislation against homosexuals,** enacted in Norway (1250), Castile (1250), Siena (1262), Bologna (1265), England (1275), France (1283), Florence (c. 1340); adults convicted were sentenced to death by burning. These laws remained on the books until the 1960s.

Estimates of Population Growth, c. 1000–1300	
Italy (including Sicily)	from 5 million to 10 million
British Isles	2 million to 5 million
France	7 million to 16 million
Iberia	7 million to 9 million
Germany and Scandinavia	4 million to 11.5 million

DEVELOPMENTS IN TECHNOLOGY. The great availability of slave labor in the ancient and early medieval worlds had retarded the development of **water mills.** The 10th and 11th centuries, however, witnessed a spectacular increase in the number of water mills; for example, the Robec River near Rouen in Normandy had 2 mills in the 10th century, 4 in the 11th century, 10 in the 13th century, and 12 in the 14th century. The *Domesday Book* (p. 192) recorded 5,624 water mills in England in 1086; many manors had at least one mill for grinding grain, fulling (the process of scouring, cleaning, and thickening cloth), stone cutting, and wood cutting. The **windmill** (documented from the 12th century) was more complex than that used in the East, due to the more variable winds of Europe. Cistercian monks often took the lead in establishing **mines:** iron (Furness in Lancashire, Igny in Champagne), coal (Newbattle in Scotland, Grünhain in Bohemia), salt (Wachock near Kraków in Poland, Aussee in Austria), and silver (Grünhain, Altzelle in Saxony). **Communications** improved partly because bridge and road building was considered a social duty and partly because of the more effective use of animal power. Communication by sea was improved by the **Lateen sail,** in use in Italy in the 11th century, and by the **sternpost rudder compass** and the **astrolabe,** about which Europeans learned from the Muslims.

Along with the increase in the construction of stone bridges came an increase in the number of **stone buildings;** between 1180 and 1270 in France alone, 80 cathedrals, 500 abbey churches, and tens of thousands of parish churches were constructed in stone; more stone was quarried for churches in medieval France than had been extracted for the Great Pyramid in ancient Egypt, which alone had consumed 40.5 million cubic feet of stone. All these churches displayed a new architectural style, which 15th-century critics called **gothic.** Europeans' greater knowledge of architectural techniques—the distribution of weight, arches—derived from Arabic contacts and sources.

The **textile industry** developed, making use of wool, linen, cotton, and silk. The spinning wheel dates from the 13th century and is the first example of belt-driven power transmission. **Soap** was also invented and produced on a large scale by the 12th century.

The most important development was in the discovery of **iron-casting techniques;** tools and weapons could be more efficiently produced. **Gunpowder,** although known in Europe in the 13th century, did not become revolutionary until the 14th century, when it was first used to propel missiles.

DEVELOPMENTS IN POPULAR CULTURE. As in earlier centuries, **women** worked alongside men in all agricultural work, such as grain cultivation and viticulture, and in the preparation of wool and dyes in the textile industry; they dominated the production of ale and beer; they supplemented household income with poultry farming and the manufacture of cheese. Through a practical apprenticeship, women learned **midwifery,** and, until around 1400, women attended all births; beginning in the 13th century, midwives sometimes found it necessary to deliver the child by **cesarian section,** but in the 14th century doctors' guilds and medical schools restricted the performance of cesarians to licensed surgeons, while denying women entrance to medical schools. By the late 14th century, women were engaged in every urban commercial activity as helpmates to husbands and independently; in many manufacturing trades (e.g., in the Parisian silk and woolen industries), women predominated. In the 15th century many **craft guilds** (such as at Cologne) greatly restricted or entirely excluded female members.

In the 12th century, the **cult of the saints** (persons considered outstanding in holiness) gained great popularity: resting on the customary relationship of mutual fidelity and aid, the pious offered prayers and gifts in return for support and healing. **Initiative** in creating a saint belonged to ordinary believers, in spite of papal efforts at centralization. Social structures in different parts of Europe had **different models of holiness:** Italy and Mediterranean lands chose **popolani** (non-nobles), whereas in France, Germany, and England, primarily persons of noble status tended to be selected as saints.

At the center of the new (12th-century) **sacramental system** stood the **Eucharist** of the Mass, which Christians believed after priestly consecration became the living body and blood of Christ and a most important channel of grace. **Beginning in the 11th century,** because of her special relationship to Christ, there was a huge outpouring of **devotion to the Virgin Mary,** as a powerful intercessor with Christ. Prayers, hymns, ceremonies were created to honor her; many churches, including all Cistercian monasteries, were dedicated to her.

b. THE BRITISH ISLES

(From p. 182)

1. ENGLAND

1066–87. William I (the Conqueror), a man of medium height, corpulent, choleric, but majestic in person and a great soldier, governor, centralizer, legislator, innovator.

1066–72. Speedy submission or reduction of the south and east. The Confessor's bequest, acceptance by the witan, and coronation "legalized" William's title. Reduction of the southwest (1068). Reduction of the rest of England (1067–70): a series of local risings leniently dealt with; construction by forced native labor of garrison castles (Norman mounds). Great **rising of the north** (Edwin and Morca's second) with Danish aid (1069) put down by William in person. The "harrying of the north" (1069–70), a devastation (often depopulation) of a strip from York to Durham (the consequences survived to modern times), ended Scandinavian opposition in England.

Norman fusion, conciliation, innovation: (1) **Feudalization** on centralized Norman lines (on the ruins of the nascent Saxon feudalism) followed military reduction and confiscation of the rebel lands (1066–70). Theoretically every bit of land in England belonged to the crown; in practice only the great estates changed hands and were assigned to William's followers on Norman tenures. The king retained about one-sixth of the land; less than half of the land went to Normans on feudal tenures. Except on the border, few compact holdings survived; the earldoms, reduced in size, became chiefly honorific. Some 170 great tenants-in-chief and numerous lesser tenants emerged. A direct oath (the *Oath of Salisbury*) of primary vassalage to the crown was exacted from all vassals, making them directly responsible to the crown (1086). Construction of castles (except on the borders) subject to royal license; coinage a royal monopoly; private war prohibited. (2) The **Anglo-Saxon shires** (34) and hundreds continued for local administration and local justice (bishops no longer sat in the shire courts and the earls were reduced) under the sheriffs (usually of baronial rank), retained from Anglo-Saxon days, but subject to removal by the king. The sheriffs were an essential link between the (native) local machinery and the central (Norman) government. Communities were held responsible for local good order; sporadic visitations of royal commissioners. Anglo-Saxon laws little altered. (3) Early grant of a charter to London guaranteeing local customs. (4) **Innovations of the centralizing monarch:** a royal council, the **great council,** meeting infrequently (three stated meetings annually), replaced the Anglo-Saxon witan and was of almost the same personnel: tenants-in-chief; the chancellor (introduced from Normandy by Edward the Confessor); a new official, the justiciar (in charge of justice and finance, and William's viceroy during his absences); the heads of the royal household staff. This same body, meeting frequently and including only such tenants-in-chief as happened to be on hand, constituted the **small council,** a body that tended to absorb more and more of the actual administration.

The **Church** retained its lands (perhaps a fourth of the land in England). Pope Alexander II had blessed William's conquest, and William introduced the (much-needed) Cluniac reforms (p. 212). Archbishop Stigand and most of the bishops and great abbots were deprived or died, and were replaced by zealous Norman reformers; **Lanfranc** (an Italian lawyer, a former prior of Bec), as archbishop of Canterbury, carried through a wide reform: celibacy enforced, chapters reorganized, new discipline in the schools, numerous new monastic foundations. By royal decree, episcopal jurisdiction was separated from lay jurisdiction, and the bishops were given their own courts, a decisive step in the evolution of the canon law of the Church and the common law as separate jurisdictions. William refused an oath of fealty to Pope Gregory VII for his English conquests and (despite the papal decree of 1075) retained control of the appointment of bishops and important abbots, from whom he drew his chief administrators (thereby making the Church, in effect, pay for the administration of the state). No papal bull or brief, no papal legate might be received without royal approval, and no tenant-in-chief or royal officer could be excommunicated without royal permission. The king retained a right of veto on all decrees

ENGLAND: THE NORMAN AND PLANTAGENET KINGS (1066–1377)

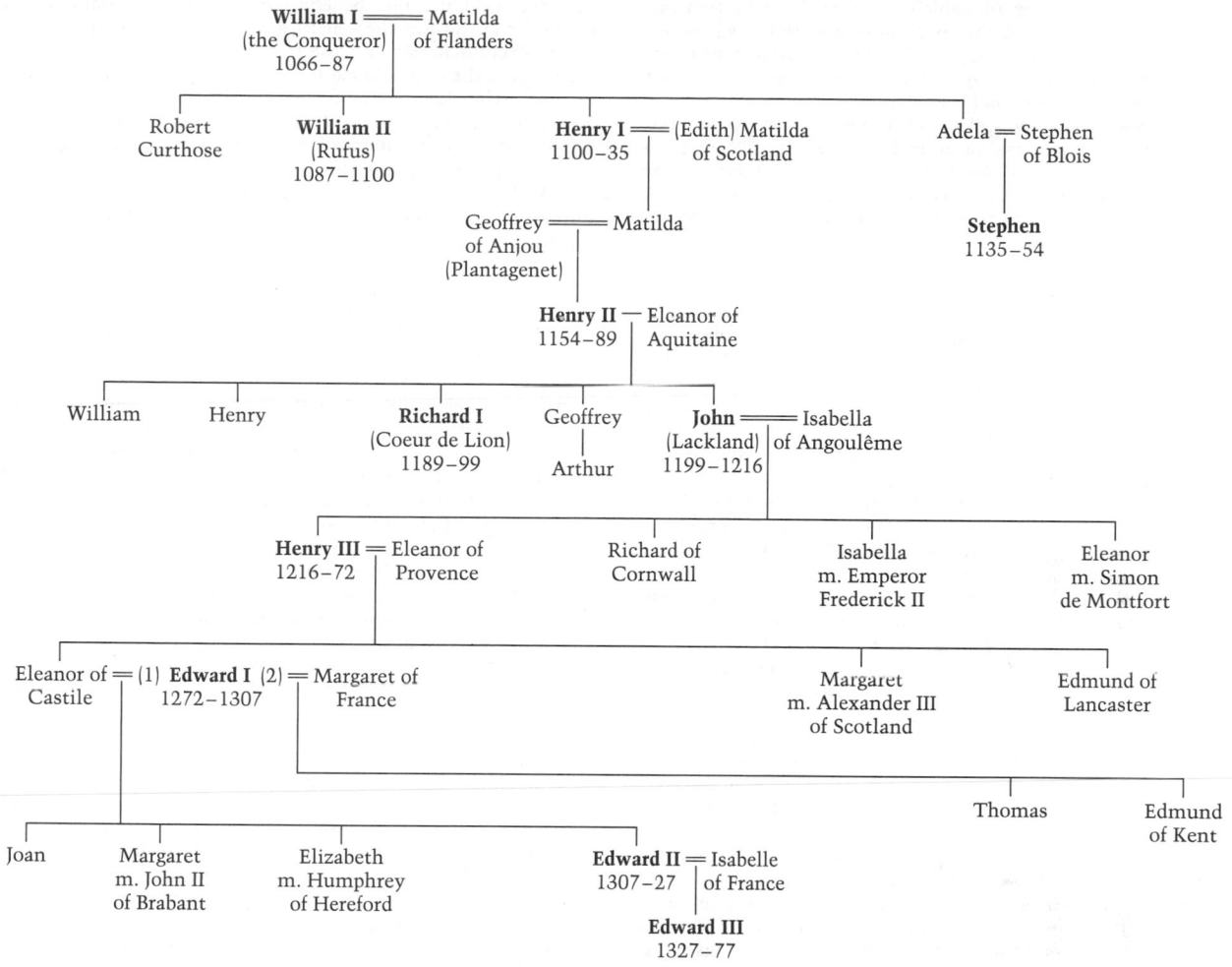

of local synods. The great prelates were required to attend the great council, even to do military service.

1086. The great **Domesday survey.** Royal commissions on circuit collected on oath (sworn inquest) from peoples of the counties and vills full information as to size, resources, and present and past ownership of every hide of land. The results, arranged by counties in the *Domesday Book*, gave a unique record as a basis for taxation and administration. Recent research on the *Domesday Book* allows tentative and **approximate population** estimates for England in 1086: slaves, 9 percent (in some western counties, such as Cornwall, 20 percent); serfs, 85 percent; burghers and townspeople, 3.5 percent; clerics (priests, monks, nuns), .5 percent; knights and nobles, 1 percent.

Royal finance: (1) nonfeudal revenues: Danegeld, shire farms, judicial fines; (2) the usual feudal revenues: relief (inheritance tax on great fiefs), scutage (paid in lieu of performance of knight's service).

Military resources of the crown: (1) (nonfeudal) the old Anglo-Saxon *fyrd* (including *ship fyrd*) was retained (i.e., a national nonfeudal militia, loyal to the crown, was used, as against the Norman rebellion of 1075); (2) (feudal) about five thousand knights' fees owing service on the usual feudal terms. The prosperity of England under Norman rule was great, and an era of extensive building (largely churches, cathedrals, and monasteries) began under the Conqueror and continued even through the anarchy of Stephen and Matilda.

1087–1100. William II (Rufus), a passionate, greedy ruffian, second son of the Conqueror, designated by his father on his deathbed (Robert, the eldest, received Normandy; Henry, cash). A Norman revolt (1088) was put down, largely with English aid, and William was firmly settled on the throne. Justice was venal and expensive, the administration cruel and unpopular, taxation heavy, the Church exploited. On Lanfranc's death (1089), William kept the revenues of the see of Canterbury without appointing a successor until he thought himself dying, when he named (1093) Anselm (an Italian, abbot of Bec, a most learned man, and a devoted churchman), who clashed with William over the recognition of rival popes; Anselm maintained church law to be above civil law and went into voluntary exile (1097). William, deeply hated, was assassinated (?) in the New Forest.

1100–35. Henry I (Beauclerc, Lion of Justice), an educated, licentious, prudent ruler, a good judge of men, won the crown by a dash to the royal treasury at Winchester and a quick appeal to the barons by his so-called *Coronation Charter*, a promise of reform by a return to the good ways of the Conqueror (a promise often broken). Anarchy in Normandy under Robert's slack rule, an invitation from the revolting Norman barons, and the victory of **Tinchebray** (1106) gave Henry Normandy (Robert remained a prisoner until his death). **Anselm,** faithful to the reforming program of the revived papacy, on his recall from exile refused homage for the archiepiscopal estates (i.e., he refused to recognize lay investiture) and refused to consecrate the bishops who had rendered such homage. Henry temporized until firmly on the throne, then seized the fiefs and exiled Anselm. Adela, Henry's sister, suggested the **Compromise of 1107,** which terminated the struggle by establishing clerical homage for fiefs held of the king, while the king allowed clerical investiture with the spiritual symbols. The crown continued to designate candidates for the great prelacies.

This reign was marked by a notable expansion, specialization, and differentiation of function in the royal administration (e.g., the exchequer, influenced by accounting methods from Lorraine, or Laon). Extension of the jurisdiction of royal courts: growing use of royal writs, detailing of members of the small council as judges on circuit (hitherto a sporadic, now a regular practice), who not merely did justice but took over increasingly the business formerly done by the sheriffs (e.g., assessment and negotiation of aids and other levies), and brought the curia regis into closer contact with shire and hundred courts.

Prosperity was general, and trade in London attracted Norman immigrants. The **Cistercians** arrived (1128) and began an extensive program of sheep farming, mill and road building, agricultural improvement, and stock breeding. Henry began the sale of charters to towns on royal domain.

Influence of the conquest on English culture. In **architecture:** wide introduction of the Norman (Romanesque) style (St. John's Chapel in the Tower of London, end of the 11th century; Durham Cathedral, c. 1096–1133). In **literature:** Anglo-Saxon, the speech of the conquered, almost ceased to have a literary history, rapidly lost its formality of inflections and terminations, and became flexible and simple, if inelegant. Norman French, the tongue of the court, the aristocracy, the schools, the lawyers and judges, drew its inspiration from the Continent until the loss of Normandy (1204). The Normans then began to learn English, and Anglo-Saxon was enriched with a second vocabulary of Norman words, ideas, and refinements.

Anglo-Norman culture. In **historical writing: Geoffrey of Monmouth,** *History of the Kings of Britain* (written in Latin, before 1147), created the tale of Arthur for Europe; **Walter Map** (c. 1140–c. 1200), author of Goliardic verse, welded the Grail story into the Arthurian cycle, giving it a moral and religious slant; **Wace** (c. 1124–c. 1174), *Roman de Brut* and *Roman de Rou;* **Marie de France;** all three were at the court of Henry II. In **science: Adelard of Bath,** a student of Arabic science, in the service of Henry II, observed and experimented (e.g., studying the comparative speed of sound and light), translated Al-Khwarizmi's astronomical tables into Latin (1126) and introduced Al-Khwarizmi's trigonometric tables to the West; **Robert of Chester** translated Al-Khwarizmi's algebra into Latin (1145); **Alexander Neckham** (1157–1217), encyclopedist, wrote on botany and on the magnet. In **philosophy: John of Salisbury** (d. 1180), pupil of Abelard, the best classical, humanistic scholar of his day, attached to the court of Henry II and later bishop of Chartres, wrote the *Policraticus.* **Beginnings of Oxford University** (c. 1167) on the model of Paris, a center of national culture.

1135–54. Stephen. Henry's son drowned on the *White Ship* (1120), and Henry had had his daughter **Matilda** (widow of the emperor Henry V) accepted as his heir and married to Geoffrey of Anjou, as protector. Stephen of Blois (son of Henry's sister Adela) asserted and maintained his claim to the throne at the price of a dynastic war (till 1153) with Matilda, the climax of feudal anarchy, and the ruin of English prosperity. Archbishop Theobald finally negotiated a compromise (1153) whereby Matilda's son Henry should succeed to the crown on Stephen's death. The reign was remarkable for a tremendous growth of ecclesiastical influence.

1154–1399. The house of Plantagenet (Angevin).

1154–89. Henry II. Master of a hybrid "empire" (England, Normandy, Anjou, Maine and Touraine by inheritance; Poitou, Aquitaine and Gascony by marriage with Eleanor of Aquitaine [1152]; Brittany [acquired 1169], and Wales, Ireland, and Scotland [on a loose bond]) without unity save in the person of the ruler. **Dynastic marriages:** daughter Eleanor to the king of Castile, Joan to the king of Sicily, Matilda to Henry the Lion. King Henry was a man of education, exhaustless energy, experience as an administrator; a realist; violent of temper.

Restoration of England to the good order of Henry I: dismissal of mercenaries, razing of unlicensed castles (1000?), reconquest of Northumberland and Cumberland from the Scots, resumption of crown lands and offices alienated under Stephen. Reconstitution of the exchequer and great council. After 1155 Henry felt free to leave England, and spent less than half his reign in the realm.

1155–72. Struggle to reduce clerical encroachment on the royal courts. Under Stephen, anarchy and the theories of Roman law had favored the expansion of clerical courts, extending to all who were literate, even accused murderers, benefit of clergy—that is, trial in the ecclesiastical court, where the penalties were far milder than in the king's court. **Thomas Becket** (a close friend of Henry's at the time of his elevation to the chancellorship, 1155) resigned as chancellor when he became archbishop of Canterbury (1162), and clashed at once with Henry over the criminous clerks. The *Constitutions of Clarendon* (1164), largely a restatement of old customs (including the Conqueror's), provided (inter alia) for the indictment of clerics in royal courts, their trial in ecclesiastical courts, and their degradation, followed by their sentencing and punishment in royal courts. Becket claimed this amounted to double jeopardy, that "not even God judges twice for the same thing." Henry argued that too many criminals were escaping justice. The *Constitutions* also extended royal jurisdiction (at the expense of clerical), and asserted royal rights of control in episcopal elections. Becket yielded, was dispensed from his oath by the pope, violated the *Constitutions,* and fled to France. Reconciled (1170) with Henry, Becket returned, excommunicated certain bishops friendly to Henry, and was murdered in the cathedral of Canterbury by four knights of Henry's court, spurred by Henry's outbreak of fury against Becket, but not by Henry's orders. Henry escaped excommunication by promising to abide by the papal judgment, and was reconciled with the papacy (1172) after swearing an oath denying all share in the crime. Henry retained the right of presentation and virtual control over episcopal elections.

Judicial reforms: (1) Increasing concentration of judicial business in the small council. (2) Designation (1178) of five professional judges from the small council as a **permanent central court;** extension of the transfer of judicial business to royal courts by the increase and specialization of royal writs (the fees a valuable source of revenue); formalization and regularization (c. 1166) of the itinerant justices (justices *in eyre*), the great source of the **common law** (a law universal in the realm). One of the judges, **Glanvil,** wrote the *Treatise on the Laws and Customs of the Kingdom of England,* the first serious book on the common law, which revealed the formal influence of Roman law but was English in substance. The itinerant judges were charged with cases dealing with crimes like murder, robbery, forgery, and arson, and with financial business as well as judicial. (3) **Expansion of the sworn inquest** (probably of Roman origin, introduced into England by the Conqueror): statements by neighbors (freeholders) under oath in the shire courts, in the form of a **jury** (12 members) of presentment in criminal cases (Assize of Clarendon, 1166) later called the accusing, indicting, or **grand jury,** but guilt in criminal cases determined by ordeal by battle or hot iron or cold water, which were appeals to the supernatural; local juries used to determine rightful possession of land in civil cases.

Reorganization of the exchequer. Nigel, bishop of Ely (nephew of the original organizer, Roger of Salisbury), restored the exchequer to the general form of Henry I. **Innovations in the raising of revenue:** (1) **tallage,** levied by local negotiations (i.e., by the itinerant justices) with boroughs and tenants: (2) **hidage (carucage)** replaced the Danegeld; (3) **scutage,** levied by Henry I on the clergy, now extended to knights' fees in lieu of military service (due to Henry's need of nonfeudal levies across the channel); (4) **personal property taxes** (the first, 1166), Saladin tithe (1188), assessed by neighborhood juries. *The Dialogue of the Exchequer* was written by one of the officials of the exchequer.

Extension of trade. German merchants were well established in London by 1157; there was a large Italian business in wool; and there was extensive development of domestic trade.

Foreign affairs. The **Norman penetration of Wales** since the conquest bred a sporadic national resistance; Henry, with three expeditions, reduced Wales to nominal homage to the English crown. **Ireland,** despite a brilliant native culture, was in political chaos under rival tribal kinglets and was economically exhausted. Pope Adrian IV, hoping that Henry would reform the Church in Ireland, "gave" Ireland (1154) to Henry. Richard of Clare's (Strongbow) expedition (1169–70) established a harsh rule; Henry landed (1171), temporarily reduced the rigors of the baronial administration, and reformed the Irish Church (Synod of Cashel, 1172). **John Lackland** (Henry's son) was appointed lord of Ireland (1177), arrived (1185), and was soon recalled for incompetence.

Intrigues and revolts (beginning 1173) of Henry's sons, supported by their mother, Eleanor, King Louis VII, and later Philip II of France, as well as by disgruntled local barons.

The ruling class continued to speak French during this reign, but the establishment of primogeniture as applied to land inheritance ensured that younger sons would mingle with the nonaristocratic sections of society and accelerate the fusion of Norman and native elements. Manor houses began to appear in increasing numbers as domestic peace continued. Numerous Cistercian houses spread new agricultural methods and especially improved wool raising.

1189–99. Richard I (Coeur de Lion). Neither legislator, administrator, nor statesman, but the greatest of knights errant, an absentee ruler who spent less than a year of his reign in England, he visited his realm only twice, to raise money for Continental ventures. Taxation was heavy. The government remained in the hands of ministers largely trained by Henry II, but there appeared a tendency toward a common antipathy of barons and people toward the crown. Richard (having taken the Cross, 1188) went on the Third Crusade with Frederick Barbarossa and Philip II, his most dangerous foe. On his return trip Richard was captured by Duke Leopold of Austria and turned over to Emperor Henry VI, who held him for a staggering ransom. John and Philip bid for the prisoner, but Richard finally bought his freedom (1194) with a ransom raised partly through taxation in England. The crusade gave Englishmen their first taste of Eastern adventure, but drew few except the adventurous portion of the baronage. The domestic reflection was a series of anti-Semitic outbreaks. John Lackland (despite his known character) was given charge of several counties; his plot against Richard was put down by **Hubert Walter** with the support of London. Hubert Walter, archbishop of Canterbury and justiciar (1194–98), ruled England well, maintained the king's peace, and began a clear reliance on the support of the middle class in town and shire. Charters were granted towns (London received the right to elect its mayor)—and the knights of the shire were called on to assume a share of county business as a balance to the sheriffs. Knights (elected by the local gentry) served as coroners and chose the local juries, a departure looking to the day when local election and amateur justices of the peace would be the basis of government. The first known merchant guild established in 1193.

1194–99. Richard's Continental struggle against Philip II, in which Richard more than held his own. Château Gaillard, a new departure in castle architecture based on Eastern lessons, was built by Richard on the Seine as an outpost against Philip.

1199–1216. JOHN (Lackland, Softsword), weak-willed and treacherous, but crippled from the start by inflation and baronial opposition to further taxation. Crowned with the support of the Norman barons against his nephew Arthur's claims (by primogeniture), he became Arthur's guardian.

1202–4. John's first contest with Philip (to protect his French possessions): struggle over Brittany, Maine, Anjou (temporary acceptance of John's title by Philip, 1200). John's marriage to Isabella of Angoulême (who had been betrothed to his vassal Hugh of Lusignan) led Hugh to appeal to Philip II as their common overlord. John ignored Philip's summons to judgment (1202); his French fiefs were declared forfeit, and Philip began a war with rapid successes. The death of Arthur (1203), possibly by John's own hand, ruined John's cause, and Philip, already master of Anjou, Brittany, and Maine, took Normandy (1204) and soon Touraine. John's vassals in southern France (preferring an absent Angevin to an encroaching Capetian) resisted Philip's advance south of the Loire. John's loss of the lands north of the Loire reduced the power and prestige of the English crown, cut off the Norman baronage in England from their French connections, and turned the barons' interests back to the island, with decisive constitutional and social consequences.

1205–13. John's struggle with Pope Innocent III. After a double election to the see of Canterbury, Innocent rejected both elections (including John's nominee) and named (1207) **Stephen Langton**, a noted scholar and theologian. John refused to accept Langton, confiscated the estates of the see, expelled the monks of Canterbury; Innocent laid an interdict on England (1208). John confiscated the property of the English clergy who obeyed Innocent's ban, without arousing serious public opposition. Innocent excommunicated John (1208), but John, holding

as hostages the children of some of the barons, weathered the storm. Innocent deposed John (1213) and authorized Philip II to execute the sentence. John, aware of treason and mounting hostility, promised indemnity to the clergy, did homage to the pope for England and Ireland, agreed to an annual tribute, and was freed of the ban.

1213–14. Final contest with Philip II (to regain the lands north of the Loire): John's great coalition (including his nephew, Emperor Otto IV, and the Count of Flanders) against Philip; most of the English baronage held aloof. Crushing defeat of the coalition at **Bouvines** in Flanders (1214) ended all hope of regaining the lands north of the Loire (formal renunciation of English claims, 1259).

1215. Magna Carta. The first politico-constitutional struggle in English history: this struggle resulted from an effort of the feudal barons, supported by Archbishop Langton (notwithstanding papal support of John) and public opinion, to enforce their rights under their feudal contract with the king; it did not aim to destroy the monarchy or the royal administration. Preliminary demands of the barons (1213); John's concessions to the Church and negotiations with Pope Innocent; civil war. London opposed John (despite his liberal charter to the city). John accepted the **great charter** at Runnymede. Magna Carta was essentially a feudal document, exacted by feudal barons from their lord but with national implications in its reforms. Concessions to the barons: reform in the exaction of scutage, aid, and relief, in the administration of wardship and in the demands for feudal service; writ of summons to the great council to be sent individually to the great magnates, collectively proclaimed by the sheriffs to the lesser nobles (i.e., knights). Concessions to the agricultural and commercial classes: mesne tenants granted the privileges of tenants-in-chief; uniform weights and measures; affirmation of the ancient liberties of London and other towns; limitation on royal seizure of private property; reform of the forest law; reform of the courts. Two chapters reflect the anti-Semitism of the age; one chapter that forbids women to accuse in criminal cases, except in cases involving death of a husband, attests to the low social status of women. Concessions to the Church (in addition to John's charter of 1214): promise of freedom and free elections.

The **most significant provisions of the great charter:** (1) chapter 12: no scutage or aid (except for the traditional feudal three) to be levied without the consent of the great council; (2) chapter 14: definition of the great council and its powers; (3) chapter 39: "No freeman shall be arrested and imprisoned, or dispossessed, or outlawed, or banished, or in any way molested; nor will we set forth against him, nor send against him, unless by the lawful judgment of his peers and by the law of the land." (Often taken as the origin of the idea of due process by law.) Even these clauses were feudal and specific in background, but centuries of experience transformed them into a generalized formula of constitutional procedure, making them the basis of the modern English constitution. At the time, their chief significance lay in the assertion of the supremacy of law over the king. Provisions were made for the enforcement of the charter by the barons, even by force of arms, but in practice such enforcement was impossible. The charter was repeatedly reissued by succeeding rulers. The pope, as John's feudal suzerain, declared the great charter void. Civil war followed; a Francophile section of the barons called Louis, son of Philip II, to the throne (1216). John opportunely died; his young son Henry, with the support of the Anglophile barons, succeeded him.

1216–72. Henry III (a boy of nine). Guardianship (1216–19) of **William Marshal,** earl of Pembroke; an able, patriotic regime: two reissues (1216, 1217) of the (modified) great charter; elimination of French influence and interference; opposition to papal encroachments, reduction of feudal castles. William Marshal had designated the pope as Henry's guardian, and the government passed on his death (1219) to the papal legate Pandulph, the justiciar Hubert de Burgh, and Peter des Roches, tutor to Henry. Arrival of the **Dominicans** (1220) and the **Franciscans** (1224). Henry's personal rule (1227–58) was marked by a major constitutional crisis.

Birth of national consciousness. After a futile but expensive effort (1229) to recover Aquitaine, Henry, always devoted to the papacy, gave free reign to papal exactions. At the same time, the increase of papal provisions filled the English Church with alien (usually absentee Italian) appointees, to the exclusion of natives. A bitter antipapal outbreak (perhaps supported by de Burgh) drove de Burgh from office; des Roches succeeded him (1232–34), filling the civil offices with fellow Poitevins. Henry's French marriage increased the alien influx, and public opinion grew bitter. The papal collector was driven out (1244), and the great council refused (1242) a grant for Henry's effort to recover Poitou, which failed. Henry's acceptance of the crown of Sicily from the pope for his second son Edmund (1254), and his permission to his brother, Richard of Cornwall, to seek election as emperor (1257), both costly ventures, added to public ill feelings. Finally, in a period of great economic distress, Richard asked the great council for one-third of the revenue of England for the pope. This grant was refused, and the barons set out to reform the government, with public approval (1258). A committee of 24, representing king and barons equally, brought in a proposal.

1258. The **Provisions of Oxford,** a baronial effort to restore the charter, with strong clerical and middle-class support; creation of a council with a veto over the king's decisions. All officials, including the king and his son, took an oath of loyalty to the Provisions.

1260–64. The **knights,** alienated by the baronial oligarchy, appealed to Edward (Henry's eldest son). Gradually there emerged a group of progressive reformers (younger barons, many of the clergy and knights, townsmen, notably of London and Oxford); the more conservative barons turned to the king. Henry obtained papal release from his oaths (1261) and replaced the council of 15 with his own appointees; chaos was followed by civil war (1263). Papal exactions continued. Louis IX (asked to arbitrate the Provisions of Oxford), in the **Mise of Amiens** (1264), decided in favor of the king. This decision was rejected by London and the commercial towns, and civil war soon broke out.

1264. Simon de Montfort (son of Simon of the Albigensian crusade), Henry's brother-in-law, of French blood and education, emerged as leader of the reforming group. This group manifested traces of democratic ideas. Simon's victory at **Lewes** (1265), capture of Henry, and exaction of the **Mise of Lewes** (a return to the reforms of 1258).

In the course of this reign, the great council came to be called **Parliament** (c. 1240) and at various times knights of the shire were summoned to share in its deliberations. Parliament was still more concerned with administration and justice than with "legislation"; its membership, control of finance, and specific functions were by no means precisely defined. The summoning of the knights in effect merely transformed the negotiation of shire business into a collective negotiation by the same men who managed it locally.

1265. De Montfort's Parliament: two knights from each shire, and two burgesses from each borough were summoned, probably the first summons to townsmen in parliamentary history.

1265. Edward, now leader of the baronial, conservative opposition, defeated de Montfort at **Evesham** (death of de Montfort).

Henry's return to power was a formality, as Edward was the real ruler, and Edward and the barons were aware of the need of reform. Edward, on a crusade with Louis IX when Henry died, was proclaimed king while still absent, spent a year in Gascony on the way back, and was not crowned until 1274.

1272–1307. Edward I (Longshanks; the English Justinian), an able ruler and a great legislator, fit to rank with Frederick II, Louis IX, and Alfonso the Wise. He observed his motto, *Pactum serva* (Keep troth), but tempered it with realism. The first truly English king, he surrounded himself with able ministers and lawyers. The reign was marked by a frequent consultation of the knights and townsmen, not always in Parliament.

1276–84. Reduction of Wales. Wales during the reign of Henry III had experienced a revival of "national" sentiment (bardic poetry and tribal union under the Llewelyns around Snowdon in the north). **Llewelyn,** prince of Wales, had joined de Montfort's opposition, refused homage (1276), and, with his brother David, renewed war with the English (1282). Edward marched into Wales, killed Llewelyn, and executed David (1283), asserting the full dominion of the English crown. In these wars Edward became aware of the efficiency of the Welsh longbow. Edward's fourth son, Edward (later Edward II), was born at Carnarvon (1284), and with him began the customary title **Prince of Wales,** bestowed on the heir to the English throne. Local government was organized in Wales, and the **Statute of Wales** settled the legal status of the newly disciplined Welsh.

1293–1303. France. Ill feeling between sailors from the Cinque Ports (Sandwich, Dover, Rommey, Hythe, and Hastings, and [later] Rye and Winchelsea) and the French culminated in a victory for an Anglo-Gascon fleet (1293) and Edward's summons to the court of his French overlord, King Philip IV. Under a pro forma compromise (1294), Edward turned over his Gascon fortresses to Philip, who refused to return them, and declared Gascony forfeited. Futile expeditions of Edward (1294, 1296, and 1297, in alliance with the count of Flanders) against Philip. Philip, busy with his contest against Boniface VIII and other matters, returned Gascony to Edward (1303).

SOCIAL CHANGE. The steady reclamation of waste and forest land and the growth of towns and commercial activity, especially the wool trade, brought relative **economic prosperity** and promoted upward **social mobility.** Many serfs secured their freedom either by purchasing it from the lord with cash savings, or by flight to a town in which, after a year, they were legally free.

The Jews, who were an important source for loans, were treated fairly decently by the English crown in the 12th century. By the late 13th century, however, the crown relied on Italian banking houses—such as the Bardi and the Peruzzi—for cash, and the Jewish bankers were reduced to making small personal loans at high interest that were difficult to collect. Growing anti-Semitism throughout the century, combined with mercantile and aristocratic pressure, led Edward I in 1290 to **expel the Jews.** Thereafter, Italians, Germans, and Flemings dominated banking and foreign trade, though English merchants controlled about 35 percent of the wool trade. Edward established the English wool staple at Antwerp.

LEGAL DEVELOPMENTS. The Fourth Lateran Council's proscription against clerical participation in trial by ordeal (p. 215) effectively abolished it. Uncertain what to do, English judges experimented with several methods of trying a case. Gradually the judges settled on the practice of selecting from the freemen in court a second (petty) jury of 12 to answer the question of guilt or innocence. By the end of the 13th century, trial by jury was almost universal throughout the land; men's distrust of women's ability to reason, however, postponed women's right to serve on juries until 1928.

The Parliament of 1275 granted the king (hitherto permission had not been asked) an increase of the export duty on wool and leather, to meet the rising cost of government.

Distraint of knighthood. Various enactments (beginning in 1278) to ensure that all men with a given income (e.g., £20 a year from land) should assume the duties of knighthood. Probably primarily an effort to raise money, the acts also ensured a militia under royal control.

Statute of Gloucester (1278), providing for *quo warranto* inquests into the right of feudal magnates to hold public (i.e., not manorial) courts. **Statute of Mortmain** (1279) forbade gifts of land to the clergy without consent of the overlord (the usual policy elsewhere in Europe). Such consent was often given; the statute was frequently evaded. Second **Statute of Westminster** (*De donis conditionalibus,* 1285) perpetuated feudal entail (conditional grants of lands) and led to the later law of trusts. It also reorganized the militia and provided for care of the roads. Third **Statute of Westminster** (*quia emptores,* 1290) forbade new sub-infeudations of land. Land could be freely transferred, but the new vassal must hold direct of the king or from a tenant-in-chief.

Judicial developments. Under Edward, the differentiation of the great common law courts is clear: (1) **Court of King's Bench** (concerned with criminal and crown cases); (2) **Court of Exchequer** (dealing with royal finance); (3) **Court of Common Pleas** (handling cases between subjects). The **King's Council** (small council) still remained supreme as a court by virtue of its residual and appellate jurisdiction, and the councilors were expected to take the councilor's oath to the king. Edward began the practice of referring residual cases that did not readily come within the jurisdiction of the common law courts to the chancellor, with a committee of assessors from the council. This chancellor's court tended to absorb the judicial business of the council and finally emerged as a court of equity. The **Year Books**—unofficial, verbatim reports in French (the language of the courts) of legal proceedings, a record unique for completeness in the period—began in this reign. Coherence and continuity of tradition among the lawyers was greatly facilitated by the establishment of the **Inns of Court** under the three Edwards. There the lawyers assembled their libraries, lodged, and studied, transmitting with increasing strength the living force of the common law, to the virtual exclusion of Roman law.

1295. The Model Parliament, called "model" because representatives of the shires (knights) *and* towns (burgesses), as well as aristocracy and clergy, were summoned (not known if all actually attended). The writs of summons included (probably by accident) the famous phrase, *"quod omnes tangit ab omnibus approbetur"* (let that which toucheth all be approved by all). The clergy did not long continue to attend Parliament, preferring their own assembly (Convocation), and left only the great prelates, who sat rather as feudal than ecclesiastical persons.

1296. The **clash with Pope Boniface VIII. Winchelsea,** archbishop of Canterbury, in accordance with the bull *Clericis laicos,* led the clergy in refusing a grant to the crown. Edward, with the general support of public opinion, withdrew the protection of the royal courts and thus promptly brought the clergy to an evasion of the bull through "presents" to the crown; the lands of recalcitrant clergy were confiscated, and the pope soon backed down.

1297. The **Confirmation of Charters** *(Confirmatio cartarum),* a document almost as important as the Magna Carta, extorted by a coalition of the barons (angered by taxation and the Gascon expedition) and the middle classes (irritated by mounting taxes) under the leadership of Archbishop Winchelsea. In effect, the Confirmation included Magna Carta (and other charters), with the added provision that no nonfeudal levy could be laid by the crown without a parliamentary grant. Edward left the actual granting of this concession to his son Edward as regent, and Pope Clement V later dispensed Edward from the promise in exchange for the right to collect (for the first time) annates in England.

1303. The *carta mercatoria* granted the merchants full freedom of trade and safe conduct, in return for a new schedule of customs dues.

1305. The petition from the barons and commonalty of the Parliament of Carlisle to end papal encroachments, notably in provisions and annates. Edward enforced the petition except in the matter of annates.

The reign is remarkable for frequent consultation of the middle class (in Parliament and out), for the encouragement of petition to Parliament (now one of its chief functions), and for frequent meetings of Parliament.

English culture. Architecture: Early English Gothic (under French influence). Canterbury Cathedral, begun 1175; Lincoln, 1185–1200; Salisbury, 1220–58. Decorated Gothic: Choir of Lincoln, 1255–80; York, west front, 1261–1324.

Painting and minor arts: St. Albans at the opening of the 13th century was the greatest artistic center in Europe (manuscript painting by Matthew Paris). The court of Henry III was a mecca for European craftsmen, especially from France.

Literature: Orm's *Ormulum* (early 13th century), a translation into English of portions of the Gospels; the *Ancren Rewle,* rules for the ascetic life, tinged with the cult of the Virgin (c. 1200); political songs and satires of the Barons' War, etc. (*Song of the Battle of Lewes; the Husbandman's Complaint*). **Matthew Paris** (c. 1200–59), a friend of Henry III, monk of St. Albans, in his compilation, the *Historia Maior,* covered the history of the world, but in the portion dealing with the years 1235–59 he produced a work of original research in which he glorified England and things English.

Foundation of Cambridge University (1209). The foundation of University College (1249), Balliol (1261), Merton (1264) began the collegiate system of Oxford.

The English Franciscans at Oxford. Robert Grosseteste (d. 1253), bishop of Lincoln: insisted on the study of the sources (the Fathers and the Bible); knew Greek and Hebrew, a precursor of the Christian humanists; student of philosophy, mathematics, astronomy, physics, teacher of Roger Bacon. **Roger Bacon** (d. 1292), greatest medieval exponent of observation and experiment. Foresaw the application of medieval power to transport, including flying; "formula" for gunpowder; author of the *Opus Maius* and *Opus Minus.*

Opponents of the Thomist rationalists. Duns Scotus (c. 1270–1308) and **William of Occam** (c. 1300–1349).   *(To p. 239)*

2. SCOTLAND
(From p. 182)

1034–1286. Racial and political turmoil.

1034–40. Duncan I, followed by his murderer, the usurper Macbeth.

1040–57. Macbeth's rule was followed by Duncan's son and avenger, Malcolm.

1057–93. MALCOLM CANMORE. Malcolm was forced to do homage, by William the Conqueror (1072) and by William Rufus (1091), and Anglo-Norman penetration began. Malcolm's wife, (St.) Margaret (sister of Edgar Aetheling, grandniece of Edward the Confessor), was a masterful and remarkable woman whose Anglicizing influence on Scottish culture and the native Church was profound. Notable among her three sons were David I and Alexander III.

1124–53. DAVID I continued the so-called bloodless Norman conquest, and the new Anglo-Norman aristocracy (Baliols, Bruces, Lindsays, Fitz Alans—that is, Stewarts) became the bulwark of the crown.

1153–1286. The next four reigns were notable for the consolidation of Scotland, and for signs of impending collision with the English monarchy. William the Lion, captured in a raid by the English, accepted (1174) the feudal lordship of the English crown and did ceremonial allegiance at York (1175). Richard I weakened England's position, John tried to restore it.

1249–86. ALEXANDER III did homage (1278) to the English king for his English lands, "reserving" his Scottish fealty. All of Alexander's issue were dead by 1284, leaving only his granddaughter Margaret. Margaret's death (1290) made impossible the personal union of England and Scotland (by Margaret's marriage to Edward I's heir). Thirteen claimants to the Scottish crown were narrowed down to **Robert Bruce** and **John Baliol.** Edward I of England, called on to arbitrate, awarded the crown to Baliol (1292), but when Baliol ignored a summons to attend Edward and instead embarked on an alliance with France (1295), the English invaded the country and, after some years of warfare, reduced it in 1304.   *(To p. 243)*

3. IRELAND
(From p. 183)

The period following the **expedition of Henry II** (1171) was marked by a steadily developing conflict between the feudalization of the incoming Anglo-Normans and the old tribal organization of the Irish. In its later phases this struggle bred centuries of discord and bloodshed. Henry's authority was precariously maintained by a viceroy who had orders to be fair to the natives, a policy that estranged the Norman elements.

1185. Henry's son, John Lackland, returned to England after a short and inglorious rule as lord of Ireland, but his authority was maintained by his representative, **William Marshal,** earl of Pembroke, who married the daughter of Richard of Clare.

1213. John abandoned Ireland, along with England, to Pope Innocent III.

1216–72. Under Henry III the power and possessions of the Anglo-Norman colony expanded rapidly: bridges and castles were built, towns modestly prospered, and guilds were formed.

English colonists practiced an extreme form of ethnic discrimination in Ireland: entire population divided between free and unfree, with native Irish on basis of blood declared unfree. Legal structures on English model with county courts, itinerant judges, and the common law set up, but Irish denied access to them; in civil dispute English defendant need not respond to Irish plaintiff; Irish could not make a will; in criminal cases, murder of an Irish person not considered a felony.

1216. Irish denied access to all higher ecclesiastical offices.

1366. Statute of Kilkenny, to protect racial purity of English, forbade marriage between English and Irish, required that Irish use the English language, and again denied Irish access to church offices (bishoprics).

1272–1307. Edward I's revolutionary legislation in England was extended to Ireland, which continued to prosper, at least in the Anglo-Norman sections. But the cleavage between conquerors and oppressed became very marked.

(To p. 244)

c. FRANCE

(From p. 177)

987–1328. Direct line of the Capetian house (the dynasty continued until 1792).

987–96. HUGH (called *Capet,* for the cloak he wore as abbot of St. Martin de Tours). At Hugh's accession, the kingship was at its nadir; such power as Hugh had was feudal; the royal title meant little more than

KINGS OF SCOTLAND (1034–1390)

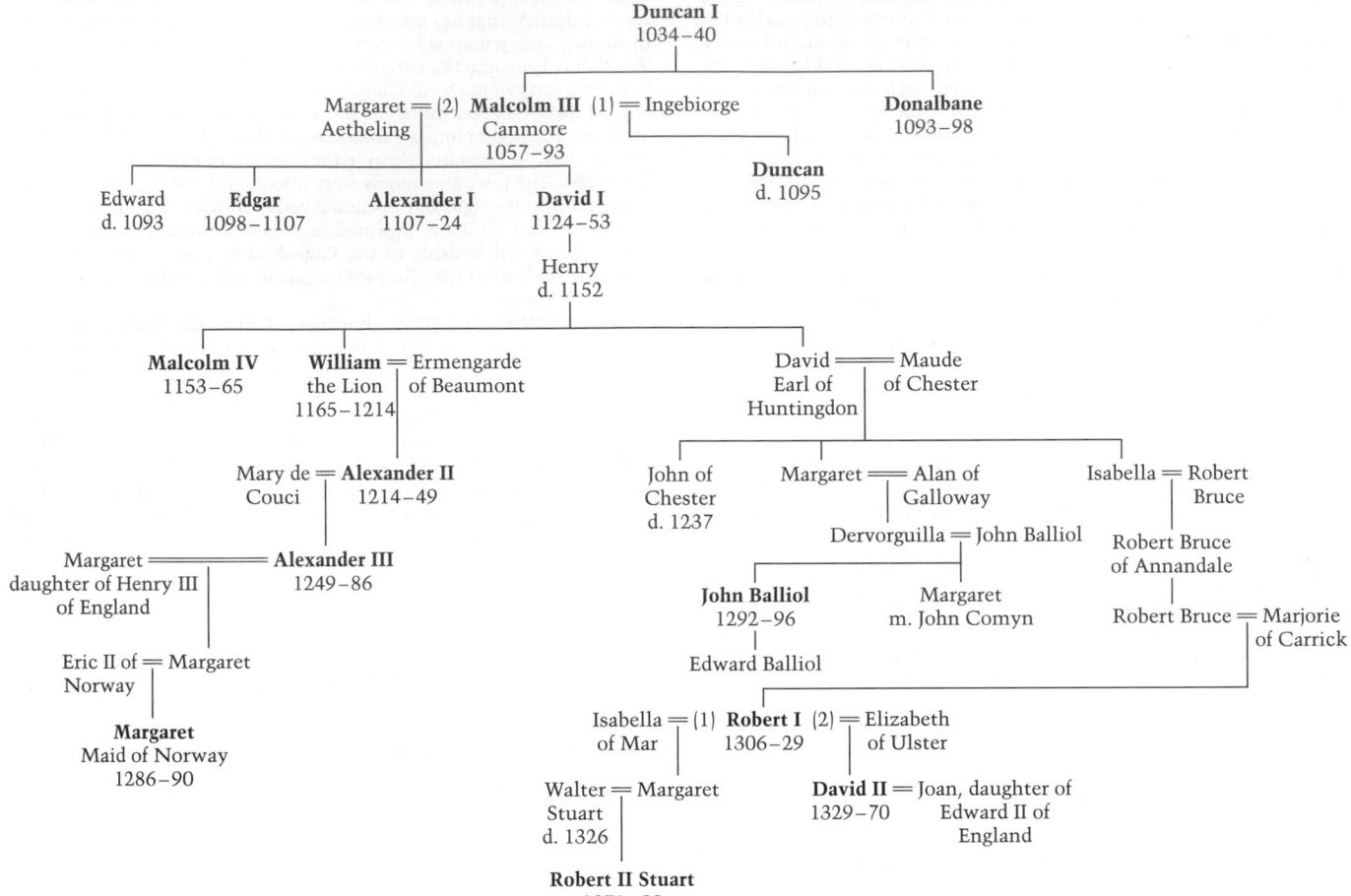

hegemony over a feudal patchwork, an ill-defined area called France, and the prestige of ancient monarchical tradition sanctified by ecclesiastical consecration. Hugh's own feudal domain consisted of the Île de France (extending from Laon to Orleans, with its center at Paris) and a few scattered holdings. The great barons of the so-called royal fiefs recognized Hugh as their suzerain, but never did homage nor rendered service. Hugh's special interest was to maintain his control over his chief resources, the archbishopric of Reims and the great bishoprics (Sens, Tours, Bourges) and abbeys of the Île de France, and to wean northeastern France away from the Carolingian and imperial interest. Despite clerical pressure, he avoided submission to imperial suzerainty, a policy that facilitated the demarcation between France and Germany. In defiance of pope and emperor, he forced his own candidate into the archbishopric of Reims. Hugh crowned his son shortly after his own coronation and began a practice (cooptation) that the early Capetians continued (until Philip II no longer felt it necessary), thus ensuring the succession and weakening the principle (dear to the feudality) of elective kingship.

996–1031. ROBERT II (the Pious), an active, well-educated, polished, amiable ruler, a good soldier, supported by the duke of Normandy in constant wars against his neighbors, and by the monasteries of Burgundy in attacks on the dukes of Burgundy. The duchy of Burgundy escheated to the crown and was given to Robert, a younger son. Robert the Pious, like his father, supported the Cluniac reformers. Minor territorial additions signify the revival of royal power.

1031–60. HENRY I, an active, brave, indefatigable ruler whose reign nevertheless marked the lowest ebb of the Capetian fortunes. The rebellion of his brother Robert, supported by Eudes, count of Chartres

and Troyes, was put down with the aid of the duke of Normandy, and Robert was pacified by the grant of the duchy of Burgundy (which continued in his family until 1361). Henry supported the duke of Normandy (1047), but led a coalition against him two years later and was defeated. The *prévôts* were introduced to administer justice and taxation in the royal lands. The kingdom of Burgundy passed (1032) to the empire.

1035–66. Rise and expansion of Normandy. William I became duke (1035) and until 1047 faced a series of baronial revolts. With the aid of his feudal suzerain, King Henry of France, William defeated his revolting barons (1047) and razed their castles. The union of Normandy and Maine was completed (1063) against powerful opposition from the counts of Anjou. William's alliance with Henry was broken (1053), and Henry ravaged the heart of Normandy (1058). Normandy was becoming a developed feudal state under firm ducal control: military service, assessed in knights' fees, was attached to specific pieces of land; no castles could be built or maintained without ducal license; private warfare and blood feud were strictly limited. Coinage was a ducal monopoly. The legal jurisdiction of the duke was wide, local government was under the duke's representatives (the *vicomtes*), who commanded the local forces, guarded the castles, did justice, collected the revenue (a large part of which was cash). The Church had been revivified with the duke supreme, naming bishops, most of the abbots, and sitting in provincial synods.

Norman **relations with England** had grown closer, and this tendency culminated (1002) in the marriage of Duke Robert's sister Emma with King Ethelred. The son of this marriage, Edward the Confessor, educated largely at the Norman court, came to the throne of England

(1042) and died without heirs (1066). The witan at once elected Harold, Earl Godwin's son. **William I** of Normandy, with a volunteer force (perhaps 5,000–6,000) collected from Normandy and the Continent, defeated Harold in the **Battle of Hastings** (Oct. 14) and was crowned king of England on Christmas Day (pp. 182, 192). The Bayeux Tapestry (actually a long 230-foot-by-20-inch strip of embroidery), made in the south of England before 1082, gives a narrative in picture and text of events surrounding the Norman Conquest; it is a primary historical source for the period.

1060–1108. PHILIP I, enormously fat but active and vigorous; excommunicated and unpopular with the clergy as the result of an adulterous marriage (1092) and because of his hostility to clerical reform. He defeated (1079) Duke William of Normandy (the Conqueror) and steadily supported **Robert Curthose**, William's son, against Anglo-Norman pressure. His reign was characterized by systematic expansion of the resources of his house and regular annexations to its domains in the face of stubborn feudal resistance.

The growth of feudalism tended to diminish anarchy and to improve the general security of life, and ultimately led to decisive economic recovery in western Europe, a trend toward urban economy, and the emergence of a bourgeoisie that was beginning to accumulate capital. This development was a determining factor in the economic, social, and monarchical evolution of the 13th century. The **Peace of God** and the **Truce of God** (p. 212) were promoted by the Church with Capetian support but had limited effect.

1108–1328. A period in which the Capetians reduced the great feudatories north of the Loire and began the transformation of the vague ecclesiastical, judicial, and military rights derived from Carolingian tradition into royal powers.

1108–37. LOUIS VI (the Fat). A brave soldier of tremendous physique, intelligent, affable; liked by the peasantry, commercial class, and clergy; the first popular Capetian. Consolidation of his Norman frontier (wars with Henry I of England: 1109–12; 1116–20), and steady reduction of his lesser vassals as far as the Loire. His charters to colonizers *(hôtes)* of waste lands, and frequent if inconsistent support of the communes, especially on the lands of the Church and the baronage, began the long alliance of the Capetians with bourgeois interests; Louis's charter of Lorris, widely copied in town charters, was a significant sign of the great **urban development** setting in all over Europe in this period. As protector of the Church, Louis gained a foothold in the lands of his vassals. Careers at court were opened to talented clergy and bourgeois. Louis's compromise with the Church over feudal patronage and investiture initiated the king of France's effective role as **eldest son of the Church.** He was the first Capetian to intervene effectively outside his own feudal lands. He defeated the alliance of Henry I of England with the Emperor Henry V, and stopped a German invasion (1124). The marriage (1137) of his son Louis to Eleanor, heiress of William X of Aquitaine (i.e., Guienne *[Aquitania Secunda]* and Gascony), marked the Capetian effort to balance the Anglo-Norman menace in the north with additions of territory south of the Loire. The Anglo-Norman danger had appeared in aggravated form when, in 1129, Geoffrey became count of Anjou, Maine, and Touraine. He had married Matilda (daughter of Henry I of England) in 1128 and proceeded (1135) to conquer Normandy.

Development of royal administration under the early Capetians. The court of the king, usually known as the *curia regis,* consisting as it did of magnates, royal vassals, and court officials (mainly chosen from the baronage), was essentially feudal in spirit and tradition. Meeting on royal summons and relatively frequently, its early duties were undifferentiated, its functions judicial, advisory, legislative. The royal administration was in control of the great officers of the crown, whose aim was to concentrate power in their own hands, a process that culminated in a virtual monopoly of such power by the **Garlande family** early in the 12th century. Louis VI, after a struggle (1128–30), terminated their dominance, and thenceforth the Capetians relied increasingly on lesser and more docile nobles, clerics, and bourgeois men of affairs. These career men were devoted to the crown rather than to feudal ambitions, and their presence in the *curia regis* began the differentiation of its functions and its subjection to royal rather than feudal influences. Most notable of these careerists was **Suger,** Louis's old tutor, a cleric of peasant origin, who became abbot of St. Denis (1122). An able statesman, his influence was decisive in the reigns of Louis

and his son Louis VII. Suger began (c. 1136) the new abbey church of St. Denis, the first edifice Gothic in design.

1100–1400. Rise of towns. The economic revival of western Europe was paralleled by a resumption of town life and development throughout the west, which was most notable in France, where the movement reached its apogee in the 12th century, before the consistent advance of the Capetian monarchy began to retard its progress. Types of town development were by no means uniform, but important general categories can be distinguished. (1) The **commune** proper, a collective person endowed with legal rights and powers (e.g., financial, judicial), able to hold property. As a feudal person, the commune could have vassals, render and exact homage, establish courts for its tenants, and even declare war and make treaties. Symbols of its independence were the belfry, town hall, and seal. Typical communes of northern France and Flanders were the *communes jurées* (e.g., Beauvais, St. Quentin [chartered before 1080], Rouen [chartered 1145], and Amiens [chartered in the 12th century]); in southern France the corresponding communes were called *consulates,* which enjoyed even greater rights than in the north, especially in Roussillon, Provence, Languedoc, Gascony, and Guienne. In the south the nobles took an active part in the formation of consulates and shared in their government. (2) *Villes de bourgeoisie* (or *communes surveillées*) had elements of communal powers in varying degrees, but lacked full political independence (i.e., they were privileged but unfree). They were found all over France, but especially in the center, and were the prevailing type in the royal domain. Citizens enjoyed specific privileges, but the crown retained judicial and other powers in varying degrees. (3) *Villes neuves* (characteristic of the commercial north) and *bastides* (typical of the south, and usually strongholds) were small rural creations of kings or feudal lords, given a charter from the first that established their status. (4) **Peasant associations** and village federations (influential in the north), which sought to define and guarantee the rights of their citizens. Governmentally, town development seems to have been hardly the result of conscious effort to introduce a new political dispensation. It was, rather, an attempt to establish and define the rights of nonfeudal groups, and aimed at economic prosperity and personal security. The movement constantly enjoyed royal support, but royal policy toward it was governed by immediate political or financial considerations, and the crown always strove to reduce or control town independence in the interest of its own power. Ultimately monarchy triumphed, but not before the bourgeois groups and the serfs had gained substantial advantages.

1137–80. LOUIS VII (the Young). Pious and therefore popular with the clergy. He remained under the influence of Suger until the latter's death in 1151. A papal interdict on the royal lands, resulting from Louis's insistence on his feudal rights, led to intervention by Bernard of Clairvaux.

1147. Louis inspired the **Second Crusade** (p. 233). He induced the German king, Conrad III, and Bernard of Clairvaux to join him, and, leaving the kingdom in the hands of Suger, he set out for the east. He returned (1149) beaten, humiliated, and estranged from his wife, Eleanor, who had accompanied him. The marriage was annulled (1152), probably due to lack of a male heir. This step cost the Capetians the territories of Poitou, Guienne, and Gascony, for Eleanor at once married Henry, duke of Normandy, who in 1151 had succeeded his father as count of Anjou, Maine, and Touraine. The acquisition of Eleanor's domains made Henry master of more than half of France and put him in a position to bring pressure on the holdings of the king of France both from the north and the south. When Henry in 1154 became king of England, the so-called Angevin Empire extended roughly from the Tweed to the Pyrenees.

1165–70. Louis supported **Thomas Becket** (p. 194) against Henry II of England and was saved from Henry's wrath only through the mediation of the pope, Alexander III, a refugee in France against whom the Emperor Frederick had raised an antipope. It was in Louis's interest to support the anti-imperial party, because of the emperor's pressure upon Burgundy.

The appointment of nonfeudal experts to the *curia regis* continued, and their influence on the administration began to be decisive. Grants of town charters also continued. The period was, moreover, one of marked cultural development. The guild of masters (germ of the University of Paris) was recognized (c. 1170), and a number of eminent scholars appeared on the scene: **St. Bernard of Clairvaux** (1091–1153),

FRANCE: THE CAPETIAN KINGS (987–1328)

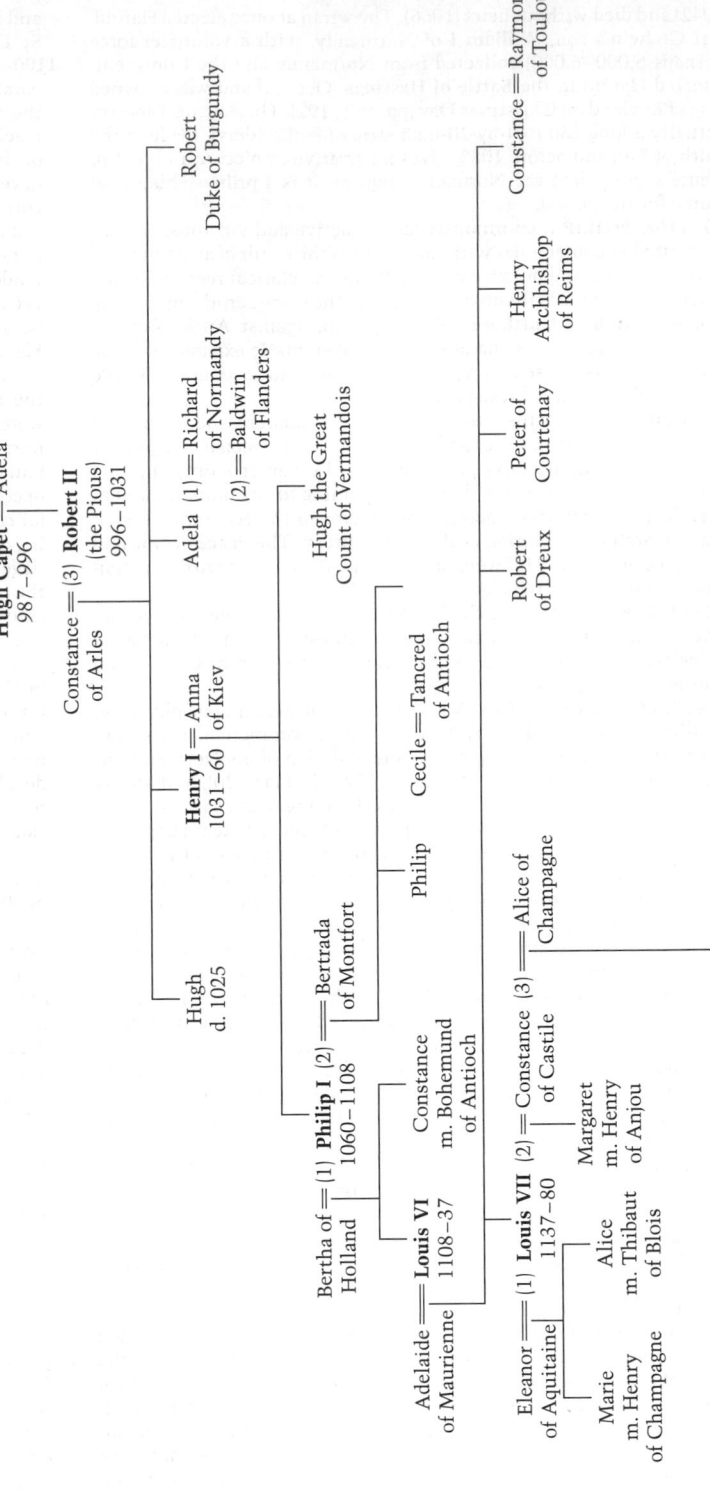

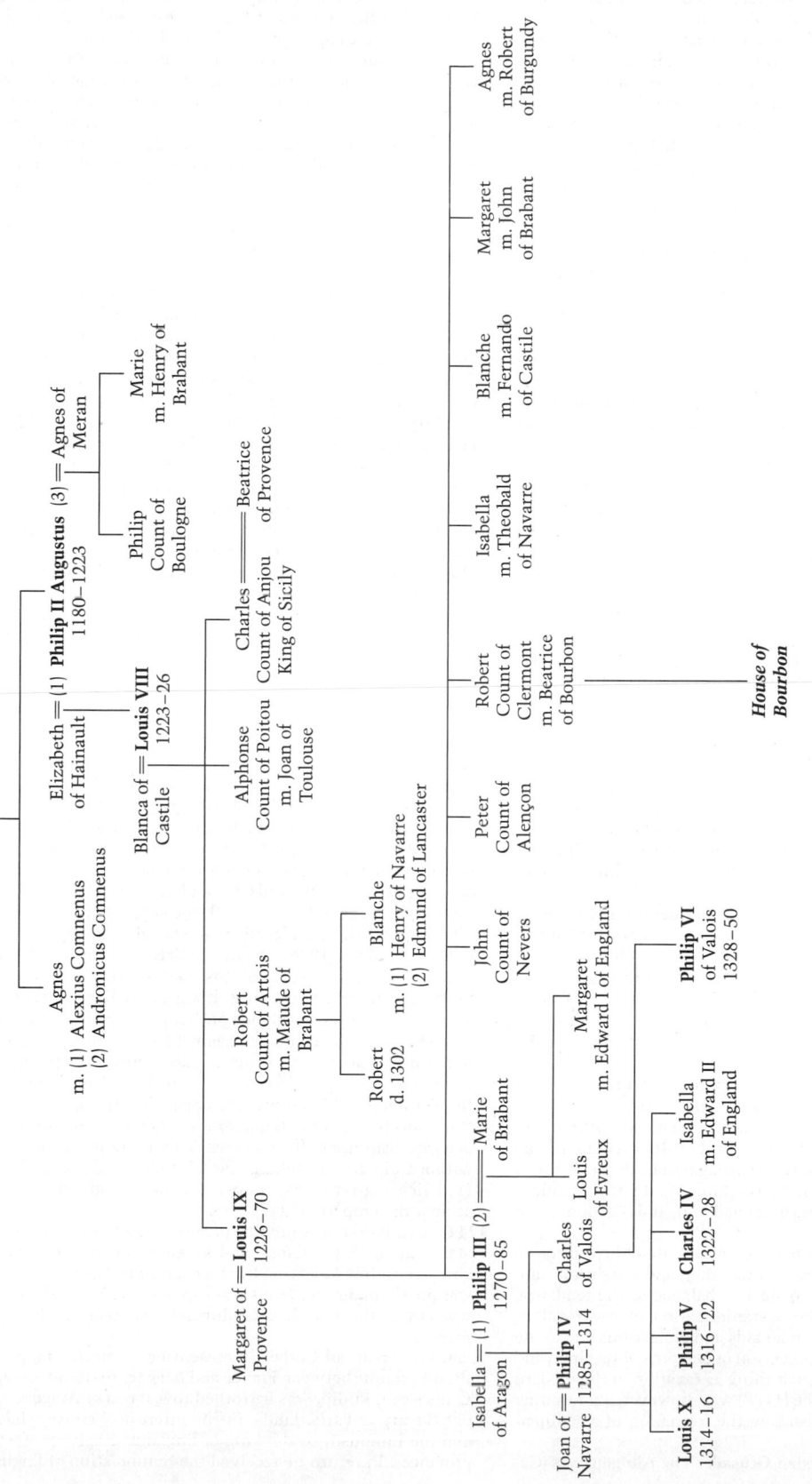

Margaret of = **Louis IX**
Provence   1226–70

Agnes
m. (1) Alexius Comnenus
(2) Andronicus Comnenus

Elizabeth = (1) **Philip II Augustus** (3) = Agnes of
of Hainault   1180–1223   Meran

Blanca of = **Louis VIII**
Castile   1223–26

Philip
Count of
Boulogne

Marie
m. Henry of
Brabant

Alphonse
Count of Poitou
m. Joan of
Toulouse

Charles ——— Beatrice
Count of Anjou   of Provence
King of Sicily

Robert
Count of Artois
m. Maude of
Brabant

Robert
d. 1302

Blanche
m. (1) Henry of Navarre
(2) Edmund of Lancaster

John
Count of Nevers

Peter
Count of Alençon

Robert
Count of
Clermont
m. Beatrice
of Bourbon

Isabella
m. Theobald
of Navarre

Blanche
m. Fernando
of Castile

Margaret
m. John
of Brabant

Agnes
m. Robert
of Burgundy

Isabella = (1) **Philip III** (2) ——— Marie
of Aragon   1270–85   of Brabant

Charles
of Valois

Louis
of Evreux

Margaret
m. Edward I of England

Philip VI
of Valois
1328–50

Joan of = **Philip IV**
Navarre   1285–1314

Louis X
1314–16

Philip V
1316–22

Charles IV
1322–28

Isabella
m. Edward II
of England

*House of
Bourbon*

member of the Cistercian order, a great preacher, fervent reformer, and dominant spiritual figure of the West; **Roscellinus** (d. c. 1121), champion of nominalism; **Anselm** (d. 1109), abbot of Bec, later archbishop of Canterbury, champion of realism; **Peter Abélard** (d. 1142), eminent master at Paris (after about 1115), supporter of conceptualism, a middle ground in the great controversy over universals. Abélard's *sic et non* presented without solution the conflicting theological arguments on 158 important problems. **John of Salisbury** (d. 1180), bishop of Chartres, favored the humanistic rather than the dialectical approach to knowledge. Before the rise of the University of Paris, Chartres was the cultural center where Ptolemaic astronomy and Aristotelian logic were taught. **Thierry of Chartres** put forward a rational explanation of the creation, within the Mosaic framework, as well as a cosmology based on the Aristotelian pattern. **Peter Lombard,** bishop of Paris (1159), in his *Sententiae,* offered a cautious solution of theological and philosophical problems that became a standard text of the Paris schools. In literature the period produced the epics of poets like Chrétien de Troyes, and the troubadour lyrics.

1180–1223. Philip II (Augustus), so called because he greatly expanded the royal domain) began his rule at 14 and had no time for education (he knew no Latin). A calculating realist, perhaps the outstanding figure of his time, he was the consolidator of the monarchy and the founder of the organized state. As the "maker of Paris," he paved the streets, walled the city, and began the building of the Louvre.

1180. A six-year alliance with King Henry II of England enabled Philip to defeat Philip of Artois and the counts of Champagne, to crush a baronial league against him, and to gain recognition for his title to Artois and Vermandois. Philip intrigued with the sons of Henry, welcomed the rebellious Richard (1187), and, joining him, defeated Henry (1189), who died the same year.

1182. Philip expelled the Jews from France, but in 1198, convinced that they were a useful source of revenue (taxes on usury), he rescinded the order. Many Christian businesspeople, who also practiced usury and resented Jewish competition, fanned the flames of anti-Semitism.

1191. Philip, under pressure of public opinion, joined King Richard on the **Third Crusade;** eclipsed by Richard, he quarreled with him, returned to France, and intrigued against John during his (Richard's) captivity (1192–94).

1194–99. Richard, in a pitiless war of vengeance, built Château Gaillard on the Seine and restored the Angevin power in northern France.

1198. Excommunicated by Pope Innocent III for his divorce of Ingeborg of Denmark, Philip was forced by public opinion to a reconciliation, but sharply refused Innocent's offer of mediation with John, who succeeded Richard (1199).

1202–4. The final duel with John for, and the conquest of, the Angevin lands north of the Loire. On King John's refusal to stand trial as Philip's vassal on charges by Philip's vassal, Hugh of Lusignan, Philip declared John's French fiefs forfeited (1203) and supported John's nephew, Arthur of Brittany. The murder of Arthur (1203) cost John his French support, Château Gaillard was lost (1204), Normandy and Poitou followed, and Philip emerged master of the Angevin lands north of the Loire.

New royal officials, the *baillis* (*sénéchaux* in the south), paid professionals (often Roman lawyers), superseded the now feudalized *prévôts* as the chief local administrators (financial, judicial, military) on the Capetian lands (c. 1190). In the course of the 13th century, *baillis* began to be assigned to regular districts (*baillages*), but they continued to be responsible for and removable by the king. As the royal domain expanded, royal administration was extended to it, and the foundation laid for a professional system.

Philip played the barons off against each other, used his position as protector of the Church to weaken them further, and sought the support of the towns and rich bourgeoisie as a balance to the feudality. Part of this process involved the systematization of the royal finances—the regular exaction of feudal aids and obligations due to the crown, as well as the systematic collection of customs, tolls, fines, and fees, though as yet there was no such thing as taxation in the modern sense. The levy of the Saladin tithe (1188) was, however, a forerunner of true taxation. Philip's reign also saw the formation of a semipermanent royal army.

1208–13. The Albigensian-Waldensian Crusade. The Albigensians (Catharists of Albi) and the Waldensians (followers of Peter Waldo) originally represented a reaction of the lower classes against clerical corruption, but the movement was soon espoused by the nobles, who saw in it a chance to appropriate Church lands. Innocent III, after a vain appeal to Philip, proclaimed a crusade against these heretics. Philip took no direct part in the action, but allowed his northern vassals to begin the penetration of the south and thus prepare the way for the advance of the Capetian power. **Simon de Montfort** (the elder), a baron of the Île de France, emerged as the leader of the crusaders. His **victory at Muret** (1213) sealed the fate of the brilliant Provençal culture, the leading southern barons, and the heretics. After a long chapter of horrors, the conquest was finally completed in a campaign by Louis VIII (1226). In the reign of Louis IX, the county of Toulouse passed under Capetian administration and the royal domain was extended to the Mediterranean.

c. 1210–c. 1289. Period of rising anti-Semitism, marked by the periodic seizure of Jewish goods and special (additional) taxes; in 1244, 24 cartloads of the Talmud were publicly burned in Paris.

1213–14. The great **anti-Capetian alliance** (John of England, Emperor Otto IV, the counts of Boulogne and Flanders, and most of the feudality of Flanders, Belgium, and Lorraine).

1214, July 27. Battle of Bouvines. Philip, in alliance with Emperor Frederick II, defeated the alliance near Tournai and thereby established the French monarchy in the first rank of the European powers, at the same time ruining John of England, assuring Frederick II of the imperial crown, and bringing Flanders under French influence. Militarily speaking, the battle was a triumph of Philip's professional cavalry and bourgeois militia over the older infantry.

1223–26. LOUIS VIII. The first Capetian king not crowned in his father's lifetime.

1224. Temporary conquest of the lands between the Loire and the Garonne; the English soon regained all but Poitou, the Limousin, and Périgord (1225).

1226. Renewal of the Albigensian Crusade and Louis's **conquest of the south.** Louis began the dangerous practice of bestowing great fiefs as appanages on the princes of the blood, a practice later had almost fatal consequences to the monarchy (the case of Burgundy).

1226–70. LOUIS IX (St. Louis, canonized 1297). The most chivalrous man of his age and the ideal medieval king. Handsome and lofty in character, Louis's careful education prepared him for a unique reign in which ethics dominated policy. His reputation for justice won him national support and made him the arbiter of Europe. His reign considered the golden age of medieval France.

1226–34. Minority of Louis IX and regency of his able and devout mother, Blanche of Castile. With the support of the Church, the royal officials, and the people, Blanche was able to suppress a number of feudal rebellions (1226–31). By the **Treaty of Paris** (1129), Raymond of Toulouse surrendered, and his heiress was betrothed to Louis's brother, Alphonse. Louis himself was married to Margaret of Provence, and thus began the severance of that province from the empire.

1233. As part of the campaign against heresy, Pope Gregory IX granted independent authority to investigate heresy to the **Dominicans,** requiring the bishops to cooperate with them. Louis later supported the **Inquisition** (p. 249), despite episcopal objections.

1241. Louis induced the Emperor Frederick II to release the prelates and delegates captured off Genoa while en route to a synod at Rome, but, without directly attacking the Church, he associated himself with Frederick's grievances against the pope and refused to intervene against the emperor (1247).

1242. Submission of Aquitaine (disputed) and Toulouse (1243).

1244. Louis took the Cross, and sailed on his first crusade (1248). His aim was to free Palestine by the capture of Egypt, but the expedition was poorly managed, Louis was captured (1250), and most of his army was put to the sword. Louis himself was ransomed and returned to France.

1258. The **Treaty of Corbeil,** representing a peaceful adjustment of conflicting claims between France and Aragon, to the advantage of France. Louis's son, Philip, was betrothed to Isabella of Aragon.

1259. Treaty of Paris. Louis, in the interest of amity, yielded Périgord and the Limousin to the king of England, despite protests from both provinces. In return he received the renunciation of English claims to

ENGLAND

North Sea

London ●
Winchester ● Canterbury
Hastings ●
Exeter ● Calais

Bruges ●
Ypres ● Ghent
Liège ●
FLANDERS

ARTOIS ✕ *Bouvines 1214*
Arras ●

HOLY

English Channel

VERMANDOIS
Amiens ●

Rouen ● PICARDY Laon ●
Bayeux ● Caen ● Soissons ● Reims ●

ROMAN

NORMANDY *Seine R.* CHAMPAGNE

Paris ⊙
BRITTANY Chartres ● ÎLE-DE-FRANCE (Royal Domain) Troyes ●
MAINE Sens ●

BLOIS Orléans ●

Angers ● *Loire R.*
Nantes ● BURGUNDY EMPIRE
ANJOU Tours ●
TOURAINE Bourges ●

Bay

POITOU BOURBON Cluny ●
Poitiers ●

of

Clermont ●
Biscay Lyons ●

AQUITAINE

Crown lands in 1180
Added by Philip Augustus, 1180–1223 Bordeaux ●
Added 1223–1270
Added 1270–1314 *Garonne R.*
Royal fiefs

Avignon ●
TOULOUSE
GASCONY Montpellier ● PROVENCE
Toulouse ● Marseilles ●
Carcassonne ●

Mediterranean Sea

THE GROWTH OF
THE KINGDOM OF
FRANCE
LANGUEDOC
SPAIN

0   50   100
MILES

Normandy, Maine, Poitou. Henceforth Guienne became distinct from Aquitaine. This pacific gesture displeased opinion in both countries and weakened the French position in the south.

1265. Louis permitted his brother, Charles of Anjou, to accept the crown of Sicily, a step that later involved France in Italian problems.

1270. Louis's Second Crusade. Probably influenced by Charles of Anjou, who cherished far-reaching Mediterranean ambitions, Louis set out for Tunis. He died of pestilence without accomplishing anything.

Louis's reign was marked by rigorous insistence on inherent royal rights even at the expense of the Church, and despite episcopal protests. Royal justice was notably efficient and was constantly expanded. The right of appeal from feudal to royal courts was clearly established. The old *curia regis* had already become somewhat differentiated: a *chambre des comptes* and a *parlement* (high court) were already recognizable. Louis introduced the *enquêteurs*, itinerant investigators, to supervise the *baillis* and *sénéchaux*, but he made few other administrative innovations. Many of his diplomats, *baillis*, and other officials were chosen from the royal household, notably from the so-called *chevaliers du roi*, and from the clergy. Assemblies of royal vassals, irregularly held, gave such sanction as there was to royal policy. Louis was the first king to issue **ordonnances** (laws) for the whole realm on his sole authority. By *ordonnance* he outlawed private warfare, the carrying of arms, and trial by battle as part of the royal judicial process, and extended the royal coinage to the whole realm. By 1270 the communal movement was already in decline, and the crown profited by enforcing a more rigorous control over the towns. Only one new charter (to the port of Aigues Mortes) was granted during the reign. The bourgeois oligarchy of the towns was on increasingly bad terms with the working class, often reducing the town finances to chaos. Louis took advantage of this state of affairs to introduce a town audit (1262). The country at large was prosperous, but the financing of the two crusades and of the grandiose schemes of Charles of Anjou led to complaints that royal taxation was leading to bankruptcy, and formed a bad precedent for Philip IV.

A brilliant **cultural advance** accompanied the general material and political progress of the time of Philip II and Louis IX. Perfection of the **French Gothic** style: Cathedral of Chartres (c. 1194, Romanesque and Gothic); Amiens (c. 1200); Reims (1210); Louis IX's *Sainte Chapelle*; progress of naturalism in Gothic sculpture. **University of Paris:** foundation charter (1200); regulations of Innocent III (1215); endowment of Robert de Sorbon (hence, Sorbonne) in 1257. Advance of **vernacular literature:** Villehardouin's (d. c. 1218) *Conquête de Constantinople* (the first vernacular historical writing); **Chrétien de Troyes** and the Arthurian romances; Goliardic verse (with pagan touch); *fabliaux* (risqué, semirealistic bourgeois tales); *Aucassin et Nicolette* (a *chante fable* marked by irony and realism); **Jean de Meun's** (d. 1305) completion of William of Lorris's *Roman de la Rose* (a satire on the follies of all classes, especially women and clergy); **Jean de Joinville's** *Histoire du roi Saint Louis* (1309), the first vernacular classic of lay biography. Paris was the center of **13th-century philosophy:** harmonization of the Greek philosophy, especially Aristotle (newly recovered during the Renaissance of the 12th century in Latin translations), with Christian orthodoxy; **Vincent of Beauvais's** (d. 1264) *Speculum Maius* (a compendium of contemporary knowledge); **Albertus Magnus** (a German, d. 1280), chief of the great Dominican teachers in Paris; **Thomas Aquinas** (an Italian, d. 1274), the pupil of Albertus Magnus. Thomas Aquinas's *Summa Theologiae* reconciled reason and religion, completed the integration of classical learning and Christian theology, and remains to this day the basis of Catholic theological teaching. Also at Paris was **Jordanus Nemorarius** (d. 1237), a German, who wrote arithmetical and geometrical treatises and worked in physics.

1270-85. PHILIP III (the Bold, so called because contemporaries considered him rash and hasty in judgment); His father's officials dominated his government. The death of Philip's uncle, Alphonse of Poitiers, brought Languedoc under royal sway and established the royal power firmly in southern France (1272). The walls of Carcassonne and Aigues Mortes were built, the latter place giving access to the Mediterranean. Unsuccessful candidacy (1273) of Charles of Anjou for the imperial crown. Crusade (1282) against the king of Aragon, Philip acting as papal champion against the successful rival of the house of Anjou in Sicily.

1281-85. The pontificate of Martin IV brought to an end an anti-French period of papal policy; papal support of Charles of Anjou's ambitious dreams of Byzantine conquest until the **Sicilian Vespers** (p. 253). There followed another period of papal opposition to French ambitions.

1285-1314. Philip the Fair, so called because of his good looks; reserved, sarcastic, cautious, pious in a formal and ritualistic sense, very conscious of his royal dignity; a "constitutional king" in that he believed himself bound by the law and precedent. He personally "controlled and directed the ordinary operations of government," with the goal of building a sovereign state in which no territory or authority was exempt from the king's jurisdiction. Non-noble laymen lawyers, trained at Bologna and Montpellier, predominated in the expanding state bureaucracy, but nobles, most of them clergy, held the highest offices. *Enquêteurs*, working in pairs and with almost viceregal powers, investigated the conduct of local officials, such as the *baillis* and seneschals *(sénéchaux)*; royal finances, organized in the Chambre de Comptes, superseded the feudal; appeals to the Parlement, the highest court that enforced and interpreted the law, were encouraged.

1286. Edward I of England did homage for Guienne.

1288-90. In conflicts with the cathedral chapter of Chartres and with the bishop of Poitiers, Philip pressed for and won from the Church the principle that no territory in the realm is exempt from royal jurisdiction, that all who hold judicial rights over temporal matters hold them from the king; clerical privileges were guaranteed by the king, not by the pope. The principle embodied in this victory, that the king of France was final and supreme judge in all temporal affairs in the realm, provided the royal justification for the later, more serious conflict with Pope Boniface VIII.

1293. Philip treacherously confiscated Gascony, which had been temporarily surrendered by Edward as a pledge, after a Gascon-Norman sea fight.

1294-98. War with Edward I over Guienne. Philip announced a war levy on the clergy and followed a protest with a violent anti-papal pamphlet campaign. To finance the war, Philip debased the coinage. He first made an **alliance with the Scots** (1295) and excluded English ships from all ports. In 1297 Edward invaded northern France, in alliance with the count of Flanders, but the war was brought to a close by a truce negotiated by Pope Boniface VIII.

1296-1303. Philip's **conflict with Pope Boniface VIII.** The bull *Clericis laicos* (1296) forbade secular rulers to levy taxes on the clergy without papal consent (p. 215). Philip retorted by forbidding the export of precious metals (a serious threat to the papal finances) and by waging a vigorous propaganda campaign. Boniface, engaged in a feud with the Colonna in Rome and absorbed in Sicilian affairs, gave way and practically annulled the bull (1297).

1297, Aug. 11. Boniface attempted to seal the peace by his canonization of Philip's grandfather Louis IX. Boniface hoped this act would inaugurate a new period of French-papal cooperation, but the quarrel resumed after the papal jubilee of 1300.

1301, Oct. The arrest, probably on the *enquêteurs'* charge of treason, of Bernard Saisset, bishop of Pamiers, and royal seizure of his lands.

1301, Dec. Boniface published the bull *Ausculta fili* (Listen, my son), condemning Philip's administration of his kingdom, rescinding the agreement giving Philip the right to tax the clergy, implying papal sovereignty over France, and summoning all French bishops to a council in Rome. The bull implicitly denied a principle that Philip had long stressed: that all persons, including clergy, are subject to his jurisdiction. Philip responded by summoning the first well-authenticated (April 10, 1302) **Estates General** of the clergy, nobility, and representatives of the towns, to win national support for his struggle with the pope. The barons and representatives of the towns wholeheartedly supported the king; the clergy, caught between two masters, asked the pope to revoke the summons to a council. Boniface retaliated with the bull (Nov. 18, 1302) *Unam sanctam* (one holy catholic and apostolic church) that bases papal jurisdiction over laymen on the pope's right to correct sin; the letter could also be interpreted to mean that the Roman curia had final jurisdiction over the temporal affairs of kings (p. 215). Boniface multiplied threats in trying to get Philip to yield.

1302, June. A French council, using trumped-up charges, accused Boniface of illegally gaining the papacy, of simony, heresy, and sexual perversion, and called for a general church council to depose him. Boniface prepared another bull (to be published Sept. 8, 1303), declaring Philip automatically excommunicated for preventing the French bishops from going to Rome, and stated that Philip had lost all authority and claim to his subjects' fidelity.

To prevent publication of the papal letter, Guillaume de Nogaret, Philip's influential councillor, and Sciarra Colonna, one of Boniface's bitterest enemies, forced their way into the Gaetani palace (Sept. 7, 1303) at Anagni (central Italy) and arrested Boniface. This event marks the culmination of Philip's struggle with the pope. Local townspeople released the pope after three days. He was taken back to Rome but died a broken man about a month after this humiliation. Boniface's successor, **Benedict XI** (1303–4), desperate to gain French friendship, dismissed all blame for the attack at Anagni, restored privileges revoked by Boniface VIII, and renewed the royal right to tax the clergy.

1302, May 18. Angered by heavy taxes imposed by French army of occupation, Flemish workers at Bruges rebelled and drove out the French garrison. Although not a great victory, this **Matin of Bruges** reflected Flemish artisan class's deep resentment at French domination. July 11. Flemish infantry crushed aristocratic French cavalry at **Courtrai (Battle of the Spurs)**, killing all leaders of the French army and some of Philip's councillors.

1306. Convinced that he had a special duty to achieve unity and purity of faith in France, in response to anti-Semitic popular opinion, and anxious to pay off the debts of the war with England, Philip ordered the arrest of the Jews of France (about 10,000), seized their property, and gave them the choice of conversion or exile. Most chose exile in Flanders, in the Rhenish towns, across the Rhône, or in Spain.

1307. The new efficiency of the French government was demonstrated by the suppression of the Order of the **Knights Templar**, a large, wealthy, and influential religious order that served as Philip's bankers. On Oct. 13, 1307, almost every Templar in France was simultaneously arrested and the order's property seized, in a police action a modern dictatorship might envy. Using false charges (heresy and homosexuality), Philip waged a propaganda campaign, applied horrible tortures, and pressured Pope Clement V to suppress the order.

1312. The Order of the Templars was formally abolished by the **Synod of Vienne**. Its property was transferred to the Hospitalers (except in Spain and in France, where it passed to the crown). Philip made the Temple treasury a section of the royal finance administration.

New economic and social alignments. The rapid expansion of France, and especially the wars of Philip III and Philip VI against England and Flanders, raised an acute financial problem. Philip IV tried every device to raise money (feudal *aides*, war levies to replace military service, tallage of towns, special levies on clergy and nobles, "loans" and "gifts," the *maltôte* or sales tax, debasement of the coinage, attacks on the Jews and Templars), but without finding an adequate solution. It was this situation primarily that explains the emergence of the **Estates General.** Levies on the nobles and clergy had long been arranged in meetings of representatives of these two orders; by negotiations between the towns and the royal agents, the burghers had been brought to contribute. Provincial estates had been called frequently during the 13th century. The convocation of the Estates General meant the substitution of national for provincial or local negotiation, but implied no principle of consent or control over royal taxation. The royal revenue was increased perhaps tenfold between the time of Louis IX and the time of Philip IV, but this meant overtaxation of all classes, harmful effects on economic life, and estrangement of public opinion. Antitax leagues were organized, and local assemblies drew up lists of grievances. Philip was obliged to call the Estates General again in 1314, but as the bourgeoisie and the nobility distrusted each other, no effective measures were taken and no permanent constitutional development took place.

Characteristic of the period was **Pierre Dubois's** *De Recuperatione Sanctae Terrae* (c. 1306), ostensibly an appeal to Philip to undertake a crusade to recover the Holy Land from the Saracens, in reality an extensive program of reform in the interests of stronger national monarchy. Dubois envisaged the formation of a European league to enforce peace through common military action and economic boycott, with disputes between parties to be settled by judicial methods. He called also for a system of universal education and for the secularization of Church property.

(To p. 244)

d. GERMANY

(From p. 179)

1024–1125. The Franconian (or Salian) **house.** Dawn of the great imperial age.

1024–39. Conrad II (the Salian). He continued the general policy of Henry: personally interested only in the churches of Limburg and Speyer, he was firm in his dealings with the Church in general and relied on the lesser nobles to balance the clergy and magnates. The *ministeriales*, laymen of servile origin, were used to replace the clergy in many administrative posts; regalian rights were retained and exploited. Dukedoms were not regranted as they fell vacant, but were assigned to Conrad's son Henry, who, on his accession to the crown, held all but the duchies of Lorraine and Saxony. By encouraging the making of fiefs heritable, Conrad weakened the dukes and got the support of the lesser nobles but ensured the ultimate feudalization of Germany. Conrad's brilliant imperial coronation (1027), in Rome, was witnessed by two kings, Canute the Great and Rudolf III of Burgundy. Burgundy, willed to Conrad by Rudolf III and guardian of one road to Italy, was reincorporated (1033) in the empire on the death of Rudolf. Failure of an expedition (1030) against Stephen of Hungary; successful disciplinary expedition (1031) against the Poles; recovery of Lusatia; payment of homage by the Poles.

1039–56. Henry III (the Black). Imperial authority at its height. A period of great town prosperity, due to development of trade. His wife, Agnes of Poitou, was an ardent devotee of Cluny; Henry, an honest reformer, abandoned simony and purified the court along Cluniac lines, but retained a firm hold on the Church. Strongest of the German emperors, he asserted his mastery in parts of Poland, Bohemia, and Hungary; Saxony was the only duchy to keep a trace of its original independence; resumption of the dangerous practice of granting duchies outside the royal house made Germany a feudal volcano; use of the *ministeriales* in administration, but retention of the bishops as principal advisers and administrators. Henry's reforms alienated the bishops, the magnates, and the nobles.

1043. Henry proclaimed the **Day of Indulgence,** forgiving all his foes and exhorting his subjects to do likewise; Břetislav of Bohemia forced (1041) to do homage; pagan reaction in Hungary put down (1044); final peace in Hungary (1052), which became a fief of the German crown. Homage of Denmark, repudiated soon after.

1046. Synods of Sutri and Rome. Deposition, at Henry's instigation, of three rival popes, and election of his nominee, Clement II, the first of a series (Clement, Leo IX, and Nicholas II) of reforming German popes; reaffirmation of the imperial right of nomination to the papacy.

1047. Godfrey the Bearded, duke of Upper Lorraine, joined Baldwin of Flanders in a revolt at first supported by Henry of France (1047); he married (1054) Beatrice, widow of Boniface, marquis of Tuscany, one of the most powerful Italian supporters of the popes.

1050–1400. While France and England witnessed the slow beginnings of centralized national states through royal efforts to check or reduce powers of independent feudal barons, Germany experienced the development of **territorial lordships.** German emperors consciously supported princely territorial power and legal jurisdictions.

1056–1106. Henry IV. (Age six at his accession; nine-year regency of his pious mother, Agnes.) During the regency, lay and clerical magnates appropriated royal resources and sovereign rights with impunity, and dealt a serious blow to the monarchy.

1062. Anno, archbishop of Cologne, kidnaped the young king and, with **Adalbert,** archbishop of Hamburg-Bremen, governed in his name; they divided the monasteries (one of the chief resources of the crown) between themselves.

1066. The **Diet of Tribur,** thanks to the reaction of the clergy and nobles against Adalbert, freed Henry from Adalbert, and his personal government began.

Henry was a remarkable but undisciplined man, intelligent, resolute, headstrong, with the odds against him from the start; under papal pressure he was reconciled (1069) with his wife, Bertha, reformed his personal life, and began a vigorous rule. His policy was a return to the Ottonian habit of using the Church as a major source of revenue; simony was open, and the reforming party appealed to Rome against Henry. Henry began the recapture, reorganization, and consolidation of royal lands and revenues, especially in Saxony, and probably planned to consolidate the monarchy in the Capetian manner, around a compact core of royal domain in the Harz-Goslar region.

1073. A great **conspiracy of the leading princes** led to a rising of virtually all of Saxony. Henry came to terms with the pope, played one faction off against the other, won the South German baronage, and finally defeated the rebels (1075).

1074. Charter of Worms, the first imperial charter issued directly to citizens without episcopal intervention.

1075–1122. The struggle over lay investiture. The German bishops, alarmed at Gregory VII's reform policy (p. 213), opposed his confirmation as pope, but Henry, in the midst of the Saxon revolt, sanctioned it, and apparently promised reforms in Germany. The sudden abolition of lay investiture would have reduced the emperor's power in Germany and would have made government impossible. With the end of the Saxon revolt, Henry's interest in reform vanished.

1077. A faction of the nobles elected an antiking, **Rudolf of Swabia,** with the approval of Gregory's legates, but without papal confirmation.

1077–80. Civil war ensued, but Henry, loyally supported by the towns, gained strength steadily; Rudolf of Swabia was defeated and killed (1080); Gregory excommunicated and deposed Henry, but a synod of German and North Italian prelates then deposed Gregory, naming as his successor Guibert of Ravenna, a reforming bishop and former friend of Gregory (1080).

1083. Henry, at the end of a series of expeditions to Italy (1081–82), besieged Rome; after futile efforts at reconciliation, he gained entrance to the city, and Gregory called in his Norman allies. Henry, crowned at Rome by his antipope, invaded Apulia; **Robert Guiscard** expelled him from Rome and sacked (1084) the city. The horrors of the Norman sacking made it impossible for Gregory to remain in Rome, and he departed with his allies, dying as their "guest" in Salerno (1085).

1093–1106. Gregory's successors, champions of reform, supported the revolts of Henry's sons in Germany and Italy: **Conrad** (1093), and the future **Henry V** (1104). Henry was elected king, but his father retained the loyalty of the towns to the end. Henry V shamefully entrapped and imprisoned his father, who abdicated, escaped, and was regaining ground when he died.

1106–25. HENRY V (married to Matilda, daughter of Henry I of England, in 1114). A brutal, resourceful, treacherous ruler, Henry continued his father's policies. Skillfully pretending to be dependent on the princes, he continued lay investiture, opposed papal interference in Germany, and retained the support of the lay and clerical princes; in the meantime, relying on the towns and *ministeriales*, he built up the nucleus of a strong power. Wars against Hungary, Poland, and Bohemia (1108–10).

1110–11. Imposing **expedition to Italy** to secure the imperial crown, universally supported in Germany. In Italy the Lombard towns (except Milan) and even the Countess Matilda yielded to Henry. Pope Paschal II (1099–1118) offered to renounce all feudal and secular holdings of the Church (except those of the see of Rome) in return for the concession of free elections and the abandonment of lay investiture, a papal humiliation more than equal to the imperial mortification at Canossa.

1114–15. A series of revolts (in Lorraine, along the lower Rhine, in Westphalia, and soon in East Saxony and Thuringia). Henry was saved by the loyalty of the South Germans.

1115. Matilda, countess of Tuscany, who had originally made over all her vast holdings to the papacy, retaining them as fiefs with free right of disposition, willed these lands to Henry on her death, and Henry arrived in Italy to claim them (1116–18).

Both pope and emperor were weary of the investiture controversy, Europe was preoccupied with the Crusades (p. 233), and the time was ripe for compromise. The first important compromise negotiated by the pope was with Henry I of England (1107) and provided that the king should not invest with the spiritual symbols (the ring and the staff), but that he was to be present or represented at all elections. After due homage, the king should then invest with the symbols of temporal authority. In France a similar compromise was reached in practice with Philip I (c. 1108).

1122. At the **Synod of Worms,** under the presidency of a papal legate,

the **Concordat of Worms** was drawn up in two documents of three brief sentences each that provided that: (1) elections in Germany were to be in the presence of the emperor or his representative, without simony or violence; in the event of disagreement, the emperor was to decide; the emperor was to invest with the temporalities before the spiritual investiture; (2) in Italy and Burgundy, consecration was to follow within six months of election; the emperor to invest with the regalia after homage. This concordat ended the investiture struggle, but not the rivalry of pope and emperor. In Germany the nobles were the real victors.

1125. Henry left no direct heir, and at the bitterly fought election of 1125, the archbishops of Mainz and Cologne, foes of the anticlerical Salian line, cleverly prevented, with papal aid, the election of the nearest heir, Frederick of Swabia, of the house of Hohenstaufen, on the grounds that the hereditary principle was dangerous. Lothair of Supplinburg, duke of Saxony, was chosen, opening the great struggle of Welf and Waiblinger (Hohenstaufen) in Germany (**Guelf** and **Ghibelline** in Italy).

1125–37. Lothair II. Elected with the support of the clergy, he remained loyal to the Church, was the first German king to ask for papal approval of his election, and did not exercise his rights under the Concordat of Worms for some years. Bitter civil war against the Hohenstaufens (1125–35); vigorous policy of German expansion among the Wends and Scandinavians; renewal of Wendish conversions (1127).

1133. Influenced by Bernard of Clairvaux, Lothair decided in favor of Pope Innocent II (against Anacletus II) and went to Italy to settle the papal schism; he was crowned, had the Concordat of Worms confirmed, and received the lands of Matilda as fiefs.

1135. The **"year of pacification"** in Germany—general peace proclaimed. Lothair apparently planned to create a vast dynastic holding for his son-in-law, the Welf Henry the Proud, to include Bavaria, Swabia, Saxony, the allodial lands and fiefs of Matilda of Tuscany, and to secure for him the imperial crown. Lothair died suddenly on his return from an expedition against King Roger II of Sicily, and in the election (1138) the clergy, led by Adalbert of Trier, had the Waiblinger Conrad of Hohenstaufen chosen. Conrad almost at once put Henry the Proud under the ban, gave Saxony to Albert the Bear, Bavaria to Leopold of Austria, his half-brother, and reopened the civil war.

1138–1268. The house of Hohenstaufen (from Staufen, their Swabian castle). The first German dynasty to be conscious of the full historical implications of the imperial tradition and the significance of Roman law for imperial pretensions. Their consequent devotion to a policy of centralization and to the aggrandizement of the lay imperial power in the face of the new spiritual supremacy and political aspirations of the papacy precipitated a second great struggle between the popes and the emperors, centered in Italy but turning on a sharp conflict between rival spiritual and political concepts.

1138–52. Conrad III, a gallant, knightly, attractive, popular hero, but no statesman. The Welf **Henry the Lion** (son and successor of Henry the Proud) acknowledged Conrad's title, but regained Saxony by force and was granted it by the peace (1142); the struggle of Welf and Waiblinger reduced Germany to chaos, and Conrad left on the Second Crusade. On his return, Conrad found Germany in worse confusion.

The most significant development of the reign was the renewal of **expansion against the Slavs and Scandinavians** (chiefly on the initiative of Albert the Bear and Henry the Lion): a regularly authorized German crusade against the Slavs (1147); colonization of eastern Holstein; foundation of Lübeck (1143); conversion of Brandenburg and Pomerania; Albert the Bear began to style himself as the margrave of Brandenburg; Henry the Lion began the creation of a principality east of the Elbe. Conrad took no share in these developments; he was the only king since Henry the Fowler not to attain the imperial title. On Conrad's death, anarchy was so prevalent in Germany that even the magnates favored a strong ruler, and Conrad's candidate, Frederick, duke of Swabia, was unanimously elected.

1152–90. Frederick I (Barbarossa, or Red Beard), a handsome man, the embodiment of the ideal medieval German king. A close student of history and surrounded with Roman legists, he regarded himself as heir to the tradition of Constantine, Justinian, and Charlemagne (whom he had canonized by his antipope) and aimed at restoring the glories of the Roman Empire. He began the style "Holy Roman Empire."

THE WELF AND HOHENSTAUFEN FAMILIES

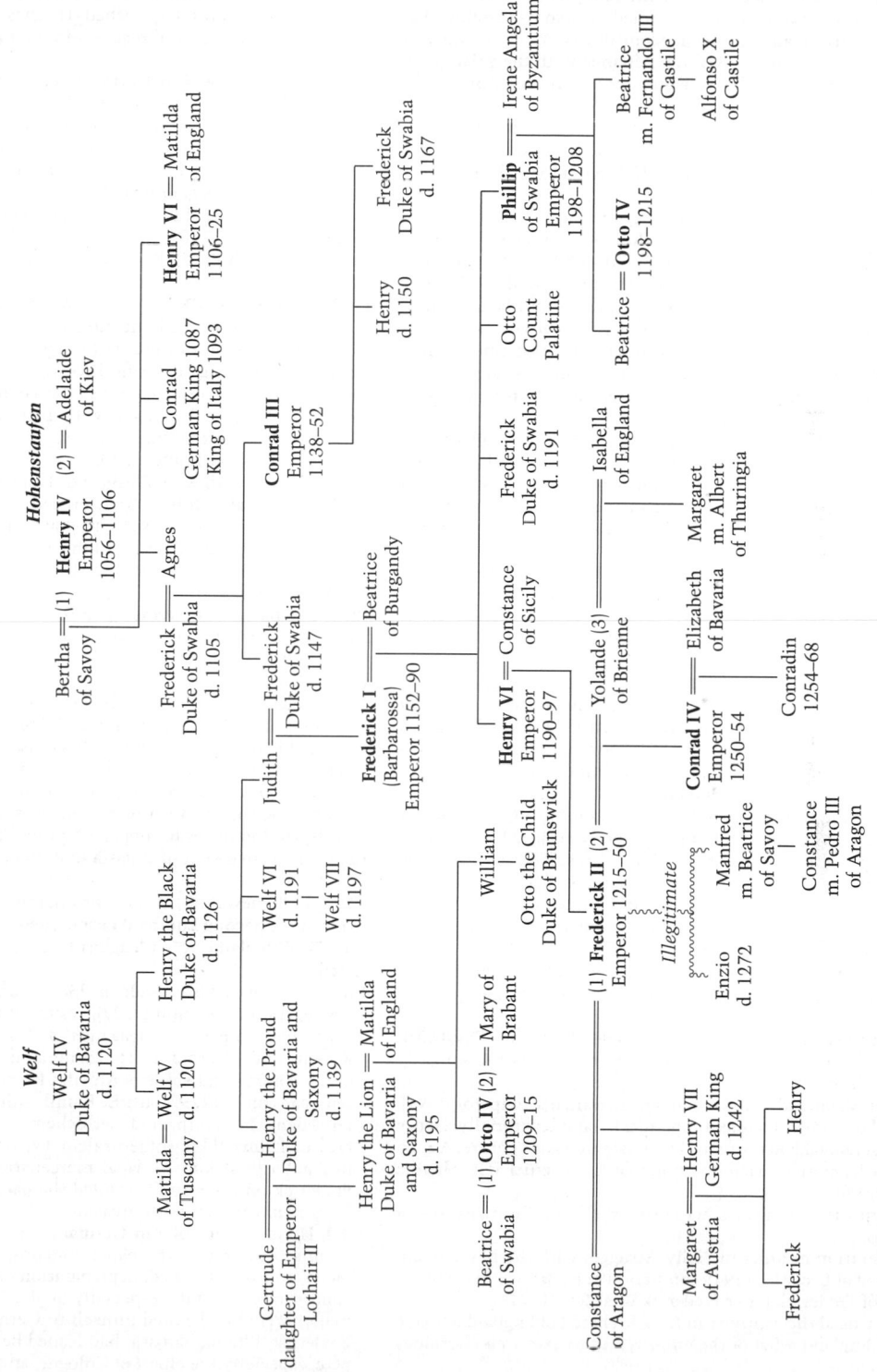

Policy of consolidation and expansion of royal lands. Burgundian lands regained by marriage (1156) with Beatrice, heiress of the county of Burgundy; purchase of lands from the Welfs in Swabia and Italy; exploitation of regalian rights.

Conciliation of the magnates. Henry the Lion, recognized as virtually independent beyond the Elbe; confirmed in Saxony; regranted Bavaria (1156). **Austria made an independent duchy** (1156), granted to Henry of Austria in return for Bavaria. **Alliance with the episcopate:** free exercise of rights under the Concordat of Worms; reforming bishops replaced with hard-headed appointees of the old school, loyal to the crown. Administration delegated to the *ministeriales.* Successful maintenance of public order; Frederick won the title *pacificus.*

Expeditions to Italy (p. 214, seq.): 1154–55, 1158–62, 1163–64, 1166–68, 1174–77, 1184–86.

1156–80. Henry the Lion's "principality" beyond the Elbe: military progress against the Slavs and colonization (Hollanders, Danes, Flemings); Bremen taken from the archbishop (1156), Lübeck from Adolf of Holstein (1158); commercial relations with Denmark, Sweden, Norway; alliance with Waldemar II of Denmark; reduction of Slavic pirates; colonization of Mecklenburg, extension of Christianity; war with Albert the Bear; refusal of aid to Frederick in Italy (1176); confiscation of Henry's holdings, and exile (1180); dismemberment of Saxony.

1156. Diet of Regensburg. Emergence of the **prince electors** as a substantive body in the German state.

1157. Diet of Besançon. Emissaries from Rome, France, England, the Spanish princes, Apulia, Tuscany, Venice, and the Lombard towns did honor to Frederick. Frederick saved the life of the papal legate Cardinal Roland, whose statement of papal claims enraged the German nobles (translation of *beneficia* as "fiefs"). Boleslav, king of Poland, granted the style of "king" (1157).

1176. Legnano. Decisive defeat of Frederick by the Lombard League, the first major defeat of feudal cavalry by infantry, herald of the new role of the bourgeoisie.

1183. Final Peace of Constance between Frederick, the pope, and the Lombard towns: restoration of all imperial confiscations during the papal schism confirmed, recognition of general imperial suzerainty in Italy; the Lombard towns virtually autonomous city-states under a loose administration by imperial legates and vicars. Frederick retained the Matildan lands without a specific definition of their status. Henceforth there was no shadow of unity in the empire, as Germany and Italy followed a divergent development.

1186. Marriage of the future Henry VI to Constance (daughter of Roger II of Sicily), heiress of King William II; possibly arranged in the hope of permanent peace with the empire. The net results of the marriage were the transfer of the center of gravity in the struggle between the popes and the emperors to Sicily, the continued destruction of German unity, and the ruin of the house of Hohenstaufen. The pope refused imperial coronation to Henry.

1186. Triple coronation at Milan. Frederick as king of Burgundy; Henry as Caesar (a deliberate revival of the title), and Constance as queen of the Germans.

1189. Frederick took the Cross, and until his death, led the Third Crusade (p. 233) in the traditional role of the emperor as the knightly champion of Christendom.

1190–97. Henry VI (already Caesar and regent, crowned emperor, 1191). The medieval empire at its maximum, ideally and territorially. Henry was not robust and lacked the usual Hohenstaufen good nature. A good soldier, learned, practical, a shrewd diplomat, stern, cruel, but of heroic and original mind.

1190–95. Intermittent struggles with the Welfs in Germany under Henry the Lion.

1191–94. Restoration of order in Sicily. Struggle with the Norman antiking, Tancred of Lecce (d. 1194); coronation of Henry as king of Sicily (1194); birth of Frederick (later Frederick II) at Jesi (1194).

1192–94. Henry used the captivity of King Richard I of England to make the crown of England a fief of the empire, and to extort an enormous ransom.

Henry's plans to unite the German and Sicilian crowns, and to crown Frederick without election, thereby establishing the heredity of the German crown, were blocked by powerful German and papal opposition. Frederick was elected king of the Romans (1196). Plans (tra-

ditional with the Norman kings of Sicily) for the foundations of a Mediterranean empire on the ruins of the Byzantine Empire as the basis for a universal dominion; dynastic marriage with the Greek imperial house; active preparations for a crusade; advance in central Italy and conciliation of northern Italy. Sicilian outbreak against the German administration brutally crushed. Henry's sudden death was followed by a bitter anti-imperial reaction in Italy and by 14 years of civil war in Germany.

1197–1212. Civil war in Germany, chaos in the empire. Rival kings: Henry's brother, the Waiblinger **Philip of Swabia** (supported by King Philip II of France) and the Welf **Otto of Brunswick,** son of Henry the Lion (supported by King Richard I of England). The German nobles played one side off against the other. Chaos in Sicily, where Pope Innocent III acted as guardian of Frederick (after 1198). Otto's title validated by Innocent (1201); assassination of Philip (1208); imperial coronation of Otto (1209); papal break with Otto (1210) and support of Frederick (with Philip II); Frederick's second election (1211) and dash to Germany.

1212–50. FREDERICK II (Stupor Mundi), amiable, charming, pitiless, arrogant; the most brilliant ruler and one of the most learned men of his day; a legislator of the first order, able soldier, diplomat, skeptic, one of the leading scientific investigators of his time; an astrologer with the mind of a Renaissance rationalist; Sicilian by taste and training, half Norman by blood, with little of the German about him. Crowned king of the Romans, 1212; king of the Germans, at Aachen, 1215; emperor, at Rome, 1220.

1212. Alliance with King Philip II of France.

1213. The **Golden Bull of Eger:** Frederick, who had already sworn an oath to keep his two crowns separate and to support the pope, abandoned the German Church to Innocent (conceding the free election of bishops, the right of appeal to Rome) and undertook to support the pope against heretics.

1214. The **Battle of Bouvines** (p. 202): Frederick and Philip II completed the defeat of Otto and the Welfs. On the death of Innocent III (1216), Frederick's personal rule may be said to have begun.

1216–27. Frederick on tolerable terms with Pope Honorius III, his old tutor: election (1220) of Frederick's son Henry as king of the Romans (a violation of Frederick's promise); Frederick allowed to retain Sicily during his lifetime; renewal of his crusading oath. Granting of generous privileges (1220) to the clergy: exemption of the Church from taxation and of clerics from lay jurisdiction, making clerical princes virtually independent territorial princes; support of the bishops against the towns; promises to suppress heresy. Crusade postponed until 1225.

1226. The **conversion of Prussia** undertaken by the Teutonic Order (p. 210).

1226–32. Renewal of the ancient imperial claims in Lombardy, formation of the **Second Lombard League,** and appearance of the **First League of the Rhineland;** town leagues in central Italy; Pope Gregory alienated.

1227–29. Frederick's crusade (p. 236): return of Frederick due to illness; first excommunication (1227); resumption of crusade (1228); violent papal and imperial propaganda and recrimination; the Teutonic Knights under Hermann of Salza remained faithful to Frederick. Aware of the commercial value of Muslim friendship, Frederick negotiated a ten-year truce (1229) with El-Kamil, sultan of Egypt, which restored Jerusalem, Nazareth, and Bethlehem to Christian hands. Frederick crowned himself king of Jerusalem. Papal war (1228–29) of devastation in Apulia (first known papal mercenaries, the **soldiers of the keys**); Frederick on his return expelled the papal forces and threatened the *Patrimonium Petri* with invasion.

1230. Hollow **Peace of San Germano** with Pope Gregory IX: Frederick promised to protect the papal domains, confirmed papal rights over Sicily, and was absolved. In preparation for the next struggle, Frederick concentrated on Italy, especially Sicily. Frederick's son Henry, on his majority (1228), devoted himself to Germany and favored the towns. Frederick, like Barbarossa, had leaned heavily on the German episcopate, especially Engelbert of Cologne, and had increased the independence of the lay princes and *ministeriales;* administrative offices tended to become hereditary, and after Engelbert's death (1225), the administration had become less efficient. Settlement of the Teutonic Knights in Prussia: union (1237) with the Livonian Brothers of the Sword and eastward expansion: foundation of Thorn (1231), Kulm (1232), and Marienwerder (1233).

1231. Privilege of Worms. Hoping for German support for his Italian policy, Frederick extended to the lay princes his generous grants of 1220 to the clergy, giving them control over local justice, minting rights, roads, streams, and so on. Territorial sovereignty of both lay and clerical princes strengthened. The **Decree of Ravenna** (1232) allowed expansion of the power of the princes at the expense of the towns. Henry objected, revolted (1234), and tried to win the German and Italian towns to his side.

1231. Completion of the **reorganization of Sicily:** clean sweep of private titles and royal privileges in the Norman manner; resumption of royal domain; destruction of private garrisons and feudal castles; ban on private war; criminal jurisdiction transferred from feudal to royal courts; towns deprived of magistrates and put under royal officers; clergy taxed and excluded from civil office; heavy influence of Muslim bureaucratic techniques, such as *diwan*, or financial office. Sicily reduced to order (1221–25): feudal revolts put down, towns brought to heel; large Saracen garrison-colonies (loyal to Frederick and indifferent to papal threats) established at Lucera and Nocera. Recognizing in Sicily the true source of his strength in money and men, Frederick aimed to unify Sicily and Italy into a kingdom of the empire. Local risings (1228–30 and 1232) in Apulia and Sicily; unrest (1234) in southern Italy.

1231. Constitutions of Melfi, officially *Lex Augustalis.* Based on **Roman jurisprudence,** not customary law, the Constitutions attempted to subordinate churchmen, nobility, and towns to royal control: feudal and ecclesiastical courts subordinated to royal courts; royal judges to visit all parts of the kingdom annually, and "supreme court" at Capua to hear appeals from lesser courts; careful financial organization. The Constitutions represent the first systematic legal code in western Europe.

The University of Naples (the first European university on a royal charter) founded (1224) to train state officials, and given a monopoly on higher education; Salerno revived as a school of medicine.

Advanced economic policy in Sicily based on Muslim practice: abolition of internal tolls; mercantilistic regulation, state monopolies. Replacement of feudal dues by fixed payments; direct taxation in crises, efficient customs collection, and internal prosperity.

1235–37. Frederick's last visit to Germany. Deposition, arrest, and imprisonment of Henry, who committed suicide in prison (1242) and was succeeded by his brother Conrad (1237); conciliation and peace with the Welfs strengthened Frederick in Germany. Great reform **Diet of Mainz** (the German Melfi, 1235); issue of the model *Landfrieden,* ordinances for the reestablishment of peace. Frederick was unable to stem the steady progress of towns (resulting from expanding commerce) in Germany or Italy.

1237. At **Cortenuova,** Frederick smashed the Second Lombard League and humiliated Milan.

1239. Pope Gregory's **second excommunication of Frederick,** followed by battle of pamphlets and preaching: Frederick painted as a heretic, rake, anti-Christ. He retorted with a demand for reform of the Church and an appeal to the princes of Europe, proposing a league of monarchs against the papacy.

Beginning of the amalgamation of northern and central Italy with the imperial administration on Sicilian lines: a system of general vicariates under imperial vicars, each city with an imperial *podestà* (generally Apulians, and often relatives of Frederick).

1241. Gregory's call for a **synod at Rome** to depose Frederick. Frederick ravaged papal territory, almost took Rome, and his fleet captured a large delegation of prelates off Genoa on their way to the synod; annexation of papal Tuscany to the empire. Gregory's death (1241), Celestine IV (1241). During the two-year interregnum in the papacy, Frederick intrigued for a friendly pope.

1243. Frederick welcomed the **election of Innocent IV,** who turned out to be the architect of his ruin.

1244. Frederick's invasion of the Campagna and vain efforts at reconciliation with the pope; Innocent's flight to Lyons and call for a synod.

1245. The Synod of Lyons. Appeal to the Germans to revolt and elect a new king; deposition of Frederick; Louis IX's efforts at conciliation and Frederick's offers rebuffed by the pope: Innocent unleashed the Franciscans and Dominicans in a war of propaganda and proclaimed a crusade against Frederick. Henry Raspe, duke of Thuringia (d. 1247), was set up (1246) as an antiking in Germany.

1247–56. Henry Raspe was followed by **William of Holland,** who was supported by a newly formed **league of Rhenish towns.** Innocent's ruthless but vain campaign against Frederick's episcopal allies in Germany; bitter warfare in northern Italy with extreme cruelty on both sides; Italian conspiracy to assassinate Frederick (probably with Innocent's knowledge) put down in cold blood.

1248. The **defeat of Frederick** after a long siege of Parma did not destroy his hold on northern Italy.

1250. Sudden **death of Frederick;** burial in the cathedral at Palmero, where his sarcophagus remains.

1250–68. Relentless persecution of the Hohenstaufens by the popes.

1250–54. Conrad IV, king of Germany, and king of Sicily by the will of his father, Frederick; Manfred, his illegitimate half-brother, regent of Sicily; Pope Innocent IV's offer (1253) of the Sicilian crown under papal suzerainty to Edmund (son of Henry III of England); renewal of Conrad's excommunication and proclamation of a crusade against him; papal invasion of the kingdom (i.e., southern Italy and Sicily).

1254–73. The great interregnum, an epilogue to the medieval struggle of the popes and the emperors, marks the end of the medieval Holy Roman Empire and the failure of imperial efforts to establish German unity; it preceded the complete triumph of particularism, which dominated German life into the 19th century.

1255–61. Manfred regained southern Italy (1255) and Sicily (1256), was crowned king of Sicily (1258) and, after the Sienese (Ghibelline) victory over Florence at Montaperto (1260), almost dominated Italy; Alexander IV's peace offers were rejected by Manfred (1261).

1257. Double election in Germany of two foreigners: **Richard of Cornwall** (brother of Henry III of England, brother-in-law of Frederick II), and **Alfonso X** of Castile.

1266. Charles of Anjou (brother of Louis IX of France), accepting Urban IV's offer (1262) of the Sicilian crown under papal suzerainty, invaded southern Italy in accordance with papal plans and with his own ambitions to create a Mediterranean empire. He defeated Manfred, who fell in the battle (**Benevento,** 1266), ending any hope of a native ruler for Italy.

1268. Conradin (Conrad IV's son, age 15), called from Germany by the Italian Ghibellines, was defeated at **Tagliacozzo,** betrayed to Charles of Anjou, and beheaded at Naples with at least the tacit approval of Pope Clement IV. The European public was shocked and Henry III of England and Louis IX of France were aroused. The heir of the house of Hohenstaufen was Constance, daughter of Manfred, whose husband, Pedro III of Aragon, was destined to become the first Aragonese king of Sicily (1282–85) (p. 249).

The imperial title remained (1268–1806) an appendage of the German monarchy, but as the Germans were little interested in the title, the way to the imperial throne was opened to ambitious foreigners.

The princes of Germany, busy consolidating their own power, were not eager to elect a king.

SIGNIFICANT ELEMENTS IN 13TH-CENTURY GERMANY. Great tenants-in-chief: Four ancient princely houses: the **Ascanians** (Brandenburg and eastern Saxony with the ducal title), the **Welfs** (Brunswick), the **Wittelsbachs** (Upper Bavaria, the County Palatine of the Rhine, Lower Bavaria), and the **Wettins** (Saxony after the 15th century). **Ottokar,** king of the Slavic kingdom of Bohemia (1253–78), with claims to Austria, Styria, Carinthia, Carniola.

Great ecclesiastical tenants-in-chief, especially in the Rhineland (notably the archbishops of **Mainz, Trier,** and **Köln**).

Three minor houses about to emerge into importance: **Luxemburgs, Habsburgs,** and **Hohenzollerns.**

Lesser tenants-in-chief (the so-called *Ritterschaft*), who regarded the central power as their defense against the great princes.

Imperial cities (*Reichsstädte*), growing richer and more powerful and disposed to support the crown against the princes. Tendency of the cities to organize as leagues.

The informal (until the 14th century) constitution of the **German monarchy:** Election of the king (originally by tribal chieftains) devolved on the tenants-in-chief, then on a group of them; election to be followed by ratification by the others. In the 13th century, the group election became the final election and was confined to a body of **seven electors** (of varying personnel).

The ancient feudal Reichstag (*curia regis*) became (in the 13th century) the **German Diet** (comparable to Parliament or the Estates General) divided into two houses: princes and electors. Its functions remained vague and amorphous. Towns were admitted in 1489.

The great ecclesiastical states of the Rhineland and their feudal satellites reached the zenith of their power in the 13th century, and strove to maintain their position in the face of the rising lay states to the east (Saxony, Brandenburg, Austria, and Bohemia) by electing to the monarchy feeble princes who could pay well for election and would remain amenable. The lay states became dynastic principalities primarily concerned with their own fortunes and anticlerical in policy.

Theophilus the Presbyter (fl. second half of 11th century) described the techniques of building a cathedral, including the making of stained glass.

Epic poetry flourished in the Middle High German period, in national epics such as the *Nibelungenlied* (c. 1160) and *Gudrun* (c. 1210–20); court epics, the romance of chivalry, as sung by **Hartmann von Aue, Wolfram von Eschenbach** (c. 1200), **Gottfried von Strassburg** *(Tristan)*, and **Conrad von Würzburg** (1220–87). The art of the *Minnesang* reached its peak with **Walther von der Vogelweide** (c. 1165–1230) and **Neidhart von Reuenthal** (c. 1215–40). *(To p. 259)*

1. THE TEUTONIC KNIGHTS

1190–91. Crusading origin. Merchants of Lübeck and Bremen founded a hospital at Acre that soon became attached to the German Church of Mary the Virgin in Jerusalem.

1198. The brethren of this hospital were raised to a military order of knighthood (Order of the Knights of the Hospital of St. Mary of the Teutons in Jerusalem) by the Germans gathered for Henry VI's crusade. Thenceforth membership in the order was open only to Germans, and knighthood only to nobles. Pope Innocent III gave them the rule of the Templars. Headquarters were successively at Acre (1191–1291), Venice, and (after 1309) Marienburg, clear evidence of the new orientation of the Knights. Intense rivalry existed between the order and the Templars and Hospitalers in the Holy Land, until the failure of the crusades turned them to other fields of action. The robes of the Teutonic Knights were white with a black cross.

Reconstitution of the order and **transfer to the eastern frontier** of Germany. The eastward advance (*Drang nach Osten*) of the Germans, begun under Charlemagne and never wholly ceased, and colonization with Netherlandish farmers and German merchants, coupled with Cistercian efforts during the days of Adolf of Holstein, Albert the Bear (self-styled margrave of Brandenburg), and Henry the Lion of Saxony established the Germans firmly in Mecklenburg and Brandenburg. Lübeck (founded 1143) early became an important commercial center. The foundation of Riga (1201), as a crusading and missionary center, the establishment of the Livonian **Brothers of the Sword**, and an influx of Westphalian nobles and peasant immigrants ensured the continued advance of Germanization and the progress of Christianity (largely under Cistercian auspices) in Livonia. The defeat of the Danes at Bornhöved (1227) by the combined princes of North Germany cost them Holstein, Lübeck, Mecklenberg, and Pomerania, leaving only Estonia to Denmark. The Poles had already begun the conversion of the Prussians and East Pomeranians.

1210–39. Under **HERMANN VON SALZA**, the first great grand master, the order, at the invitation of Andrew of Hungary, was established (1211–24) in Transylvania as a bulwark against the Comans (Cumani), until their progress alarmed the Hungarian monarch.

Hermann was a friend of Emperor Frederick II, and was the real founder of the greatness and prosperity of the still relatively poor and insignificant order.

1226. By the **Golden Bull of Rimini**, Frederick laid down the organization of the order (on Sicilian lines) and prepared the Knights for a new career as pioneers of Germanization and as Christian missionaries on the eastern frontier. Frederick repeatedly made them generous gifts, used them for his own crusade, and employed individual knights on

important missions. The grand master was given the status of a prince of the empire.

Organization of the order. Districts, each under a commander; a general chapter, acting as advisers to the grand master; five chief officers; the grand master elected for life by the Knights. The order was nominally under the pope and the emperor, but in the days of its might, only strong popes exerted any influence.

1229. The call of Prussia. (The name "Prussia" is probably derived from a native word Prusiaskai, not from Bo-Russia.) An appeal (1225–26) from Conrad of Masovia, duke of Poland, for aid, coinciding with Frederick's reorganization, was accepted by Hermann von Salza, and the Knights embarked on a unique crusade comparable only with that in the Iberian Peninsula, as champions of Christianity and Germanism. Conrad gave them Kulmerland (1230), and promised them whatever they conquered from the Prussians. Frederick confirmed their rights.

1234. The Knights transferred all their holdings to the pope, receiving them back as fiefs of the Church, and thus had no other lord than the distant papacy.

1237. Union with the Livonian Brothers of the Sword was followed by notable progress in Livonia and plans for the conversion of the Russians from the Greek Church to the Roman, which led to a serious defeat for the order. Courland was also gained, and Memel was founded (1252) to hold the conquests. Eventually the southern Baltic coast from the Elbe to Finland was opened by the order to the missions of the Church and the trade and colonies of the Germans.

A **great era of town foundations** (some 80 in all) opened under the order, including Thorn (castle, 1231), Kulm (castle, 1232), Marienwerder (1233), Elbing (castle, 1237), Memel (1252), Königsberg (1254).

1242–53. A **Prussian revolt** was put down, and the conquest of Prussia continued with aid from Ottokar of Bohemia, Rudolf of Habsburg, Otto of Brandenburg.

1260. The **Battle of Durben,** a disastrous defeat of the order by the Lithuanians, was followed by another Prussian revolt that had national aspects and was put down with Polish aid. The suppression was marked by deliberate extermination, and the virtually complete Germanization of Prussia ensued. Castle Brandenburg was built (1266) and the reduction of Prussia completed (1285).

The order allowed great freedom to the towns (especially after 1233); no tolls were collected, only customs dues. The large commercial towns joined the Hanseatic League (p. 265). The Knights were also generous (after 1236) in charters to German (and Polish) nobles, the peasants were treated well, and mass migrations into territories of the Knights became common.

1263. The pope granted the order permission to trade, but not for profit, a concession later expanded into full commercial freedom. As a result the order, founded as a semimonastic crusading society, eventually became a military and commercial corporation of great wealth and selfish aims and a serious competitor of the very towns it had founded. The Teutonic Knights escaped the fate of the Templars, though they were temporarily on the defensive.

A magnificent court was kept at the headquarters in Marienburg, and under Grand Master Winrich (1351–82) the order was the school of northern chivalry, just as later it became a great cultural influence through the foundation of schools everywhere in its domain and the maintenance of its houses as centers of learning. *(To p. 265)*

e. SCANDINAVIA

(From p. 183)

1. DENMARK

c. 950–85. Harald II (Bluetooth), whose reign saw a steady advance of Christianity and expansion of Danish power over Schleswig, the Oder mouth, and Norway.

985–1014. The kingship was of little importance until the reign of **Sven I** (Forked Beard). He defeated the Norwegians, Swedes, and Wends and conquered England (1013).

1014–35. Canute II, the Great (Knut), Sven's son, was king of Denmark,

Norway (1028), and England (1016–35), the first "northern empire." Canute's conversion meant the conversion of his people. He imported priests, architects, and artisans from his English realm, and new influences spread from Denmark to Norway and Sweden. On his death, Norway broke away; England passed to Edward the Confessor. By the late 12th century, Arhurs and Copenhagen were sizable trading centers, exporting great amounts of fish, especially herring.

1157–82. Under **Waldemar I, the Great,** the founder of the **Waldemarian dynasty,** a great expansion eastward took place at the expense of the Wends; Copenhagen was established as the capital.

1182–1202. Canute VI made conquests in (Slavonic) Mecklenburg and Pomerania.

1202–41. Waldemar II (the Conqueror) led crusading expeditions into Livonia and Estonia (Reval founded), and penetrated the Gulf of Finland, making the southern Baltic a Danish lake (the second "northern empire"). This empire collapsed in 1223, and the advance was in fact more in the nature of a crusade than a permanent imperial expansion. The monarchy was now dominant, the nobles largely feudalized, the clergy (with royal grants) powerful, the bourgeoisie vigorous (fisheries and cattle raising), the yeoman class strong and independent.

1241–50. Eric IV (Plowpenny), whose reign was taken up with civil war against his brothers Christopher and Abel.

1250–52. ABEL was supported by his brother-in-law, the count of Holstein, and also by the Swedes and the city of Lübeck.

1252–59. Christopher I. His effort to tax the Church opened a struggle that lasted nearly a century.

1259–86. Eric V (Glipping). He was forced by the nobility to sign a charter, the **Danish Magna Carta** (1282), recognizing the national assembly and initiating the subordination of the king to the law. He continued the contest with the clergy, fought against dynastic rivals, planned expansion in Mecklenburg and Pomerania, and lost Scania and North Halland to Sweden.

1286–1319. Eric VI (Menved), during whose reign the conflict between the crown and the Church came to a head. By a compromise (1303), the rights of the Church were guaranteed, but the king's right to levy military service on Church lands was upheld.   (To p. 266)

2. SWEDEN

The origins of the Swedish kingship are obscure, but the kingdom may be dated back to the **union of Gothia and Svealand** (prior to 836). The conversion of the country to Christianity took place in the 9th century.

993–1024. Olaf Skutkonung was the first Christian ruler. His wars with St. Olaf of Norway led to some conquests, which were soon lost, and the pagan population expelled his son. The century following his death was marked by wars between the Goths and the Swedes and by religious conflicts.

1134–50. Sverker. Amalgamation of the Swedes and Goths, with alternation of rulers from the two peoples (an arrangement that continued for a century). The monarchy gradually became established on a firm basis, and the progress of Christianity was marked by the foundation of many bishoprics (including Uppsala, 1163). The first monasteries also belong to this period.

1150–60. Eric IX (the Saint), whose reign was a short golden age. He led a crusade into Finland, the first real expansion of Sweden. The line of St. Eric ended with Eric XI.

1223–50. Eric XI (Laespe). His reign was dominated by his brother-in-law, Jarl (Earl) **Birger Magnusson,** the greatest statesman of medieval Sweden, who controlled the government from 1248 to 1266 and had his son Waldemar elected king in 1250, thus founding the **Folkung line.**

1250–75. Waldemar. As regent, Jarl Birger abolished judicial ordeal by fire, ended serfdom by choice, encouraged commerce, favored the settlement of German artisans, checked the power of the baronage. He attempted to introduce some form of setting up his other sons in quasi-independent duchies.

1279–90. Magnus Ladulos, who had dethroned and imprisoned his brother Waldemar. Magnus continued his father's feudal innovations, extended the powers of the clergy, and set up a hereditary nobility.

Town charters became numerous as the burghers became prosperous through trade and mining.

1290–1319. BIRGER (son of Magnus). His rule was chaotic, due to civil war with his brothers, whom Birger ultimately captured and executed. This led to a popular uprising and the expulsion of Birger, who was followed by his 3-year-old nephew.   (To p. 266)

3. NORWAY

Norway was a region with little natural unity; in the earlier medieval period it was ruled by numerous petty kings.

872–930. Harold I (Haarfager) began the unification of the country by deposing many of the chieftains (traditionally including Hrolf of Rollo). It was in this period that the Norsemen (Northmen) supposedly made their conquests in Iceland; in the Faroes, Shetlands, Orkneys, Hebrides; and in Scotland and Ireland.

935–61. HAAKON I (the Good), who attempted, prematurely, to convert the country to Christianity.

995–1000. Olaf I, Trygvesson, who, with the aid of English clergy, converted Norway, Iceland, and Greenland. He was defeated by the kings of Denmark and Sweden, who supported the Norwegian nobility. There followed a period of noble disruption.

1016–28. Olaf II (St. Olaf) reunited the country and established Christianity on a firm footing.

1046–66. Harald III, Haardraade, who was defeated by King Harold of England in the **Battle of Stamford Bridge** (p. 181). There followed another period of confusion, marked by constant wars of succession and by a struggle against the growing power of the clergy. Nevertheless the expansion of trade brought increasing prosperity.

1184–1202. Sverre. He was able to maintain a strong monarchy in the face of aristocratic and clerical opposition, thanks to support from the small landowners. Nevertheless Norway continued to be troubled with dynastic conflict.

1223–63. Haakon IV, a strong king who temporarily restored order, conquered Iceland, but was defeated in a war with Scotland.

1280–99. Erik II (the Priest Hater), whose reign was marked by a war with the Hansa towns, in which he suffered a reverse. As a result he was obliged to grant the towns full privileges in Norway and to join the Hanseatic League.

1299–1319. Haakon V, who marked the final decline of the royal power.

The crown in Scandinavia depended on its vassals for soldiers and for administration. The introduction of cavalry (first recorded in Denmark, 1134) accentuated this feudal tendency, and a new nobility emerged. This nobility was a professional military class always ready for war, exempt from taxes; it quickly became a governing class receiving local offices and lands as a reward for military services. From Denmark this new society spread to Norway and Sweden. Thenceforth the nobles added a further complication to dynastic wars, causing a series of crises and restricting the normal evolution of royal power.

German capital and German merchants began to penetrate Scandinavia, achieving by the second half of the 13th century a dominating position. The growth of the Hanseatic League delayed the progress of the native bourgeoisie, but commerce led to the active growth of towns and town life. Population was increasing rapidly, lands were cleared, the arts were advancing in distinction and perfection under the patronage of wealthy kings and prosperous prelates.

The **heroic age of the Icelandic** *skalds* (court poets) in the 10th and 11th centuries brought the art to an involved perfection and a concentration on war, which ultimately killed it. Meanwhile the kings, interested in politics as well as war (notably Sverre of Norway, 1185), began to patronize the Norwegian storytellers, particularly the Icelanders, and the **sagas** emerged. The greatest master of the new form was an Icelander, **Snorri Sturleson** (1179–1241), an active political figure in both Iceland and Norway. Snorri's *Edda Snorra Sturlusonar (Younger Edda)* in prose and verse, containing the rules of versification, the old myths, and a collection of ancient Icelandic poems, is unique. History was written by **Saxo Grammaticus** (c. 1208), whose *Historia Danica* is the chief source for the Hamlet story. Both Snorri and Saxo were preoccupied with the ideals of national unity, strong royal power, and resistance to baronial particularism.   (To p. 266)

f. THE PAPACY AND ITALY

(From p. 173)
For a complete list of the Roman popes, see Appendix IV.

The papacy, frequently in immoral hands and the political football of Roman families until c. 1048, initially exercised no broad religious influence; the Italian Peninsula was without effective political leadership.

888–924. Berengar I, last of the phantom "emperors" (vacancy in the empire, 924–62), was the grandson of Louis the Pious. **Raids of Saracens** (c. 889) and **Magyars** (c. 898) into Lombardy; a Saracen stronghold at Freinet controlled the Alpine passes; Saracen settlements in southern Italy, and the **Muslim conquest (827) of Sicily;** Italian urban life had become almost extinct; the invasions were checked not by the shadowy monarchs, but by the rise of feudal defenders.

914–63. The nadir of the papacy (the "pornocracy"): the landed aristocracy of Rome, under the leadership of the senator Theophylact, his wife, Theodora, and his daughter Marozia (mistress of Pope Sergius III and mother of Sergius's son John, later Pope John XI), dominated the curia.

928. Marozia, having imprisoned Pope John XI, took control of Rome.

932–54. Alberic II, Marozia's son, assumed power. The *Patrimonium Petri* was a plaything of the **Crescentii** (Marozia's family), who maintained an intermittent supremacy in Rome during the 10th century. The papacy was without political power or spiritual prestige, and the western Church for all practical purposes became a loose organism under its bishops, who gave "national churches" such coherence as they had, and acknowledged a vague kind of allegiance to Rome.

950–61. Berengar II. He imprisoned his widow, Adelheid, who appealed (according to tradition) to Otto the Great.

951–52. Otto the Great's first expedition to Italy.

961–64. Otto's second expedition to Italy, in answer to the appeal of the profligate pope, John XII, for protection against Berengar.

962. Otto's coronation at Pavia as king of Italy and his coronation by the pope as Roman emperor, marked the **revival of the Roman Empire.** Otto confirmed his predecessors' grants in the *Patrimonium Petri* (probably with additions), but carefully reserved the imperial right to sanction papal elections and treated the pope like a German bishop (i.e., subject to the state). Otto also exacted a promise from the Romans not to elect a pope without imperial consent. He established a precedent by calling a synod at Rome that deposed (963) Pope John XII for various crimes, and selected a (lay) successor, Leo VIII (963–64). This synod opened a period of about a hundred years when the papacy was dominated by the German emperors and by the counts of Tusculum, vassals of the emperors, who had the title of *patricius* in Rome. In the same period, the bishops in the west lost the position they had won in the 9th century and became increasingly dependent on the kings and feudal nobility, and increasingly secular in outlook. The homage of Pandolf I for Capua and Benevento (967) and his investiture with the duchy of Spoleto mark the beginning of the long imperial effort to include southern Italy in the empire.

964. Pope Leo VIII was expelled by the Romans shortly after his election, and **Benedict V** was elected (964) by the Romans without imperial consent.

966–72. Otto's third expedition to Italy. Otto held a synod that deposed Benedict. **Pope John XIII** (elected with imperial cooperation) was soon expelled by the Romans, and Otto, after a terrible vengeance on Rome, restored him. Imperial coronation of the future Otto II (967) by John XIII.

980–83. Otto II's expedition to Italy. Otto crushed Crescentius I, duke of the Romans, restored Pope Benedict VII (981), and was utterly defeated in his effort to expel the Saracens from southern Italy by a Greco-Muslim alliance (982). Otto dominated **Pope John XIV** (983–84).

983. Great Diet of Verona. Remarkable unity of the Italian and German magnates; resolve on a holy war against the Muslims; election of the future Otto III as successor to his father. Venice, already profiting by its Muslim trade, refused ships and defied the emperor.

996. Otto III, on his first expedition to Italy, deposed the *patricius* Crescentius II and (at the request of the Roman people) nominated as pope

his cousin Bruno, **Gregory V** (996–99), the first German pope, an ardent Cluniac. As the successor of Pope Gregory, Otto named **Gerbert of Aurillac.**

999–1003. Sylvester II (Gerbert of Aurillac), the first French pope, a man of humble origin but one of the most learned men of his day (Arabic, mathematics, and science). An intriguer and diplomat who cooperated with Otto in his mystic renewal of the empire; he was a moderate reformer, asserting that simony was the worst evil of the Church.

1012–46. The Tusculan popes were either the relatives or the creatures of the counts of Tusculum. The emperors, preoccupied with German affairs, made only rare visits to Italy. Yet the period witnessed the beginnings of efforts, originating in France and Germany, for the reform of Church and society:

(1) Local synods decreed clerical celibacy (e.g., Augsburg, 952; Poitiers, 1000; Seligenstadt, 1023; Bourges, 1031), attacked simony.

(2) William the Pious, duke of Aquitaine, founded (909) the **abbey of Cluny** near Mâcon in Burgundy, completely free of feudal and secular control, directly subordinate to Sts. Peter and Paul, as represented by the pope. The strict observance of the *Rule of St. Benedict,* the emphasis placed on the execution of the liturgy, the pious reputations of the first abbots and the long lives of the 11th-century abbots who stressed sound economic management, and the monastery's strong position on clerical celibacy and the suppression of simony (the sale of Church offices) made Cluny a cynosure of good monastic living in a disorderly world. Thus, wealthy laypeople placed monasteries under Cluny's jurisdiction for reform, and hundreds of priories in France and Spain came under Cluny's centralizing influence. A second reforming monastic impulse, springing from **Gorze** (founded 933) in Lotharingia (modern Lorraine) exercised an influence in Germany and central Europe.

(3) **Synods in Aquitaine and Burgundy** (where monarchical opposition to feudal anarchy was weak) pronounced (c. 989) anathema on ravagers of the Church and despoilers of the poor, initiating a long series of clerical efforts throughout Europe to force feudal self-regulation, referred to as the **Peace of God.** These decrees, repeatedly renewed and extended, were supplemented (after c. 1040) by the **Truce of God,** an effort to limit fighting to certain days and seasons of the year.

(4) An effort to restore the central authority of the Church by reference to past decrees, of which the most notable were the so-called **Isidorean** (or **Forged**) **Decretals,** attributed to Isidorus Mercator and produced (c. 850) by a Frankish cleric. A combination of authentic and forged papal decrees, they aimed to establish the authority and power of the bishops and the position of the pope as supreme lawgiver and judge, and to make him supreme over councils.

(5) A burst of monastic piety was reflected in the foundation of new ascetic orders (e.g., **Vallumbrosan Order,** founded c. 1036 by St. John Gualbert in Tuscany; **Carthusian Order,** founded c. 1084 by **St. Bruno** at the Grande Chartreuse in the Dauphine Alps near Grenoble) and in outstanding individual reformers, such as **Peter Damian** (d. 1092), scholar, papal diplomat, preacher against the worldliness and simoniacal practices of the clergy; **Lanfranc** of Pavia (d. 1089), lawyer, monkscholar, abbot of **Bec** in Normandy, archbishop of Canterbury, adviser to William the Conqueror; and **Anselm** of Aosta (d. 1109), monk of Bec, scholar, archbishop of Canterbury.

Italy at the opening of the 11th century. Sicily was in the hands of the Saracens; Apulia and Calabria under the feeble rule of Constantinople; Gaeta, Naples, Amalfi, were city-republics; Benevento, Capua, and Salerno the capitals of Lombard principalities. Norman pilgrims arriving (1016) at the shrine of St. Michael on Monte Gargano began the penetration of the south by Norman soldiers of fortune in the service of rival states: the first permanent Norman establishment was at Aversa (c. 1029); the sons of the Norman Tancred of Hauteville (including Robert Guiscard) appeared (after c. 1035), and their steady advance at the expense of the Greeks led Benevento to appeal for papal protection (1051). Anarchy prevailed in the north.

1027. Conrad II, in Italy for his coronation, restored order in the north, reducing the Lombard nobles.

1037. On a second expedition, Conrad disciplined Archbishop Aribert of Milan, restored order in the south; his *constitutio de feudis* made Italian fiefs hereditary.

1046. The synods of Sutri and of Rome, under pressure from the reforming emperor Henry III, deposed three rival popes and made Suitgar, bishop of Bamberg, pope as Clement II (1046–47). Henry pacified southern Italy, reaffirmed the imperial right of nomination to the papacy, and left Italy in sound order.

1047. The **Synod of Rome** issued stern decrees against simony and clerical marriage.

1049–85. Gradual resumption of papal leadership in the Church and of spiritual influence in the west.

1049–54. LEO IX (Bruno of Toul, a kinsman of Henry III) began the restoration of the spiritual primacy of the Holy See. He insisted on his own canonical election to the papal throne, reorganized the chancery on the imperial model, reformed the Church by personal or legatine visitation, giving reform reality in the west.

1052. Henry III granted the duchy of Benevento to the papacy.

1054. The long doctrinal **controversy with the Greek Orthodox Church** ended with the final schism between the eastern (Orthodox) and western (Roman) Church (p. 229).

1055–57. VICTOR II. Elected at the urging of Hildebrand (later Gregory VII), who dominated this pontificate and the following one and who made the papacy the leader in reform. Beatrice, mother of Matilda, and widow of Count Boniface of Tuscany, married (1054) Godfrey the Bearded, duke of Upper Lorraine, Henry's most dangerous foe in Germany, as Boniface had been in Italy. Henry arrested Beatrice and her daughter Matilda, Boniface's heiress; Godfrey fled; Matilda remained all her life a powerful ally of the papacy and kept middle Italy loyal to the popes.

1057–58. STEPHEN IX (brother of Godfrey the Bearded), a zealous Cluniac. The **Pataria** (c. 1056), a popular movement, gained wide currency in the Milan region for its demands for clerical celibacy, the end of simony, and apostolic simplicity among the clergy. It came into sharp conflict with the bishop and clergy. Peter Damian, sent by the pope, maintained the papal position (1059) and brought the archbishop to terms; there was a later outbreak of the Pataria.

1058–61. Nicholas II.

1059. At the **Synod of the Lateran,** Pope Nicholas II promulgated a decree that fixed the right of electing the pope in a **college of cardinals,** composed of bishops of dioceses in the vicinity of Rome (who were to have the initiative in the election), and certain priests and deacons of Rome; all held the title of cardinal, which implied superior rank and association with the pope in the government of the Church. Cardinals served as the pope's chief advisers and administrative assistants (legates, arbitrators, judges). The cardinals met as a group, in **consistory,** to express their opinions on a wide variety of theological and political matters. Popes rarely acted on important matters without seeking the cardinals' advice, and from this practice of consultation developed the cardinals' claim to share in the governance of the Church. The papal decree of 1059 also marked the increasing expansion of the **papal curia** (court or administrative bureaucracy) as it began to handle legal appeals from all over Europe.

1059. Under Hildebrand's influence, an alliance was made with the Norman Richard of Aversa, and Nicholas, after exacting an oath, later invested Robert Guiscard with the duchy of Apulia and Calabria and promised him Sicily if he could conquer it, thereby establishing papal suzerainty over southern Italy, the first great expansion of temporal suzerainty by the popes. The **Synod of Melfi** condemned (1059) the marriage of clergy.

1061–73. ALEXANDER II. His election without consultation of Henry IV created serious tension; the **Synod of Basel** declared the election invalid, and chose an antipope. Alexander, on friendly terms with William the Conqueror, blessed the Norman conquest of England.

1071. Robert Guiscard (d. 1085) captured Bari, ending the Greek power in Italy.

1072–91. Guiscard's capture of Palermo (1072) began the **Norman conquest of Sicily.** Roger I (d. 1101) succeeded Guiscard as lord of southern Italy (except Capua, Amalfi, and papal Benevento).

1073–85. GREGORY VII (Hildebrand). Short, corpulent, with glittering eyes, the son of an Italian peasant educated at Rome, possibly under Cluniac influence. Inspired by Gregory the Great, Gregory VI, and the study of the Decretals, he was neither an original thinker nor a scholar, but was intensely practical and of lofty moral stature. After a brilliant career in the curia he was acclaimed pope by the Romans before his election. German bishops protested the election, and Gregory postponed his consecration, awaiting Henry's decision in a sincere effort to live up to his ideal of perfect cooperation between pope and emperor in the interest of peace, reform, and the universal monarchy of the papacy. His program was summed up by his *Dictatus*, an informal memorandum that asserted: (1) the Roman Church has never erred, can never err; (2) the pope is supreme judge and may be judged by none, and there is no appeal from him; (3) no synod may be called a general one without his order; (4) he may depose, transfer, reinstate bishops; (5) he alone is entitled to the homage of all princes; (6) he alone may depose an emperor.

1075–1122. The investiture struggle.

1075, Feb. At the Synod of Rome, Gregory published decrees against simony (the sale of Church offices), clerical marriage, and (for the first time) **lay investiture**—the investment by laymen of bishops and abbots with the religious symbols of their office (the crozier or staff, representing pastoral authority; the ring, indicating permanent union with the diocese), the penalty being deposition for the cleric and excommunication for the layman. Since public opinion generally favored his moral reforms, Gregory believed the people would support his political reform, the abolition of lay investiture. Henry IV in Germany, William I in England, and Philip I in France at once protested.

The 11th-century rulers depended on the literacy and administrative ability of churchmen for a variety of diplomatic, financial, political, and clerical tasks; royal government, given the lack of educated laymen, could not function without clerics. Kings, therefore, selected them, invested them, and usually required that they perform feudal homage before investiture. Gregory's decrees raised a revolutionary question: did kings have ultimate or final jurisdiction over all subjects, including the clergy? Tradition strongly favored the ruler. Gregory's assertion undermined royal and imperial power and sought to make papal authority supreme. A bitter exchange of letters followed.

1076, Jan. Synod of Worms. The German bishops, appointed and invested by the emperor, accused Gregory of immorality, misuse of his powers, and usurping his office, and withdrew their allegiance from him. Gregory responded by excommunicating them and deposing the emperor. The lay nobility, delighted with the bind in which the emperor had been put, because it advanced their feudal independence, supported the pope.

1077, Jan. Dangerously threatened, Henry sought and received papal absolution at **Canossa,** Countess Matilda's castle in Tuscany, where Gregory was visiting. (Legend holds that Gregory kept Henry waiting three days in the snow.) Older scholarship described the incident as marking the peak of medieval papal power: the emperor had bowed before the pope. Recent research sees Henry as the temporary victor, since getting the ban of excommunication lifted meant that he regained the kingship and authority over his subjects. Canossa settled nothing, and the conflict continued.

Henry's second deposition (1080) was without serious effect. After a series of invasions (1081–84), Henry entered Rome and was crowned by his antipope, only to be expelled by Gregory's Norman ally, Robert Guiscard, with a motley army that included Saracens; the atrocity of the Norman sacking made it impossible for Gregory to remain, and he died a virtual exile, almost a prisoner of his allies at Salerno, leaving Henry and his antipope master of Rome for the time.

Gregory was on excellent terms with William the Conqueror, but William, true to the Norman conception of strong monarchy, ignored Gregory's pressure to make England a fief of the papacy and forbade the circulation of papal bulls in England without his permission. Gregory asserted papal suzerainty over Hungary, Spain, Sardinia, and Corsica. After a vacancy of a year, **Victor III** (1086–87), an aged, unwilling pontiff, was elected pope but was soon driven from Rome by Henry's partisans.

1088–99. URBAN II. A Frenchman of noble blood, long intimate with Gregory; handsome, eloquent, learned; he continued Gregory's policy of maintaining the complete independence of the papacy and vigorous opposition to the emperors. Urban arranged the marriage of Countess Matilda and the son of the (Welf) duke of Bavaria (1089).

Henry invaded northern Italy successfully, but Matilda held out in the hills; Urban, profiting by the anarchy in Germany, urged Henry's son Conrad to a revolt (1093), which was taken up by half of Lombardy. Urban received the appeal of the Byzantine emperor for help against the Turks at the **Synod of Clermont** (1095), excommunicated King Philip I of France for adultery, and proclaimed the **First Crusade** (p. 233), directing his appeal to the nobles and peoples rather than the monarchs, most of whom were hostile to the papacy. On a visit to southern Italy, Urban made Roger of Sicily his legate (1098), thus exempting him from the visits of an ordinary legate. The First Crusade was the first great victory for the reformed papacy; the papal dominance of the military effort to defend Christendom is significant of the new prestige of the papacy and the decline of the emperors.

1099–1118. PASCHAL II renewed the excommunication of Henry IV; intrigued with Henry, his son. Anselm waged the investiture battle in England (1103–7), ending in a compromise (1107), followed almost at once by the lapse of lay investiture in France (formerly one of the worst offenders). Paschal's humiliating renunciation (1111) of papal fiefs and secular revenues, his repudiation by his clergy, and his arrest by Henry V made a much more profound impression in Europe than Canossa. Paschal recalled (1112) his concessions.

1115. The **Countess Matilda,** having made a donation (1086 and 1102) of her allodial lands (the second great addition to papal holdings) to the papacy (subject to free testamentary disposition), willed them at her death (1115) to Henry V, who came and occupied the Matildine lands (1117), which were destined to be a bone of contention between the popes and emperors for a century.

1119–24. CALIXTUS II, a Burgundian, related to half the rulers of Europe and a skilled diplomat, arranged the **Concordat of Worms** (1122), which closed the investiture controversy with a compromise. Bishops were to be chosen according to canon (Church) law, by the clergy in the presence of the emperor or his delegate; the emperor surrendered the right of investing with the ring and staff. Since lay rulers were permitted to be present at ecclesiastical elections and to accept or refuse feudal homage from the new prelates, they retained an effective veto over Church appointments. The papacy won the technical victory. The **Synod of Reims** (1119) renewed the decrees against simony, clerical marriage, and lay investiture, as well as the excommunication of Henry V.

1130–38. Papal schism. Precipitated by the corrupt election of the (Cluniac) Cardinal Pierleone (son of a rich converted Jewish banker of Rome), as **Anacletus II** (1130–38), and the hostility of the rival houses of Corsi and Frangipani. The rival pope, **Innocent II** (1130–43), supported by Bernard of Clairvaux and most of Europe, was given military support by Lothair in return for confirmation of his rights under the concordat of 1122, imperial coronation, and investiture with the Matildine lands. Anacletus confirmed Roger II's title as king in return for his support.

1139. The **Second Lateran Council** (the tenth general council in the west) was attended by a thousand bishops. It marked the end of the schism.

1140–60. Great acceleration of appeals to Rome (disputes over Church property, ecclesiastical elections and, above all, issues of marriage and annulment) and development of system of local judges delegate who heard, with papal authority, cases in their own countries. Through Church courts, the popes pressed goals of reform.

The papal curia, or administrative bureaucracy, represents the first well-organized institution of monarchical authority in medieval Europe. The first half of the 12th century witnessed the steady expansion of the papal curia, which contained secretarial (the chancery), financial, and legal agencies. The publication in 1140 of the monk **Gratian's** *Decretum (Concordance of Discordant Canons)* provided a standard reference book for all ecclesiastical tribunals.

1143. The **Commune of Rome** established in opposition to the non-Roman pope; it defied three feeble popes (Celestine II, Lucius II, Eugene III). **Arnold of Brescia,** pupil of Abelard, emerged as the eloquent leader, with bitter denunciations of clerical wealth and papal bloodshed and burning appeals for a return to apostolic poverty and simplicity. Temporary restoration of the ancient Roman state, appeal to the emperor's protection. **Bernard of Clairvaux** agreed with Arnold's indictment (cf. *De Consideratione,* addressed to Pope Eugenius), but saw salvation for the Church in purification from within, not in diminution of its powers, and opposed Arnold as he had Abelard.

1154–59. Adrian IV (Nicholas Breakspear, the only English pope). Son of a poor man, learned, kindly, of high character, he had risen by his own merits; Roman anarchy ended by a stern interdict. Arnold expelled; alliance with **Frederick Barbarossa** against William, king of Sicily; altercation with Frederick over his haughty refusal of ceremonial service to the pope. The bitter hostility of the Romans to pope and emperor forced a surreptitious coronation and hurried departure from Rome.

1155. Frederick executed Arnold as a heretic, but abandoned Adrian to the Normans and forced him into an independent Italian policy (i.e., alliance with an anti-Norman league of southern barons and with Constantinople) which brought William of Sicily to his knees as the pope's vassal. Adrian accepted the Roman Commune and returned to Rome.

1158–62. Frederick's second expedition to Italy: the **League of Pavia** (Brescia, Cremona, Parma, Piacenza) supported Frederick; Milan and its league were reduced to submission. The great **Diet of Roncaglia:** Frederick, using Roman law to justify an extreme assertion of imperial rights and a brusque resumption of imperial regalia, substituted an imperial *podestà* for the consuls in the Lombard cities, drove Milan into open revolt (1159–62), and turned the towns to alliance with the pope. Renewal of the papal alliance with Byzantium; formation of an alliance of Lombard towns under papal auspices.

1159–81. ALEXANDER III (imperialist antipopes: Victor IV, Paschal III, Calixtus III). Frederick, citing precedents from Constantine, Charlemagne, and Otto the Great, held a synod at Pavia to adjudicate the claims of Alexander III and Victor IV. Alexander ignored the synod; Victor was recognized. Alexander, after an exile in France, returned and excommunicated Frederick (1165). Renewal of the town leagues (1164); Milan rebuilt; expulsion of imperial *podestàs.*

Marriage defined. In the popular mind (and in spite of centuries of Church preaching) the traditional idea persisted, especially among the masses of country people, that marriage was a private matter, with no special formula or public official involved and no public registration required. What constituted valid marriage? After hesitating between Gratian's view (that marriage was initiated by the consent of the parties and rendered indissoluble by sexual intercourse) and Peter Lombard's definition (that present consent alone established the bond), Alexander III adopted Lombard's position: the contract of indissoluble marriage was established by the words of consent. Couples urged to have parental approval, to have a public announcement made (the banns), and to have their union blessed by the parish priest at the Church, but a marriage was still valid without these. The result was frequent appeals to ecclesiastical courts to enforce a promise, not to dissolve.

1166–68. Frederick's **fourth expedition to Italy:** Alexander's flight to the Normans; Frederick's capture of Rome. Renewal of the Lombard League (1168): promises of mutual aid; organization for federal administration; erection of Alessandria, a great fortress city (named for the pope), to guard the passes (1168); Italy virtually independent.

1174–77. Frederick's **fifth expedition to Italy:** vain siege of Alessandria, complete **defeat at Legnano** (1176); preliminary peace of Venice (1177, the centenary of Canossa).

1179. The **Third Lateran Council** decreed a two-thirds vote of the conclave to be necessary for a valid papal election.

1183. Peace of Constance: imperial suzerainty in Italy recognized, resumption by the Lombard towns of all regalia they had ever enjoyed, including the right to maintain an army, to fortify, to keep the league or expand it, full judicial jurisdiction, control of their own coinage, abolition of the imperial *podestàs.* The only relic of imperial control was the reservation of the emperor's right to confirm elected consuls, the right of appeal to the imperial court, and the retention of the *fodrum* as a contribution to military needs. The Lombard towns were autonomous for all practical purposes, under a very loose system of imperial legates and vicars.

1184. Frederick's **sixth expedition to Italy:** utilizing the split in the Lombard League (after 1181) and local feuds in Tuscany and Bologna, Frederick created a strong imperial party in middle Italy and by a liberal charter (1185) even won over Milan.

1198–1216. INNOCENT III. A tough-minded Italian patrician chosen by the cardinals to restore the political power of the papacy. Animated by a historical mysticism, he looked on Christendom as a single community in which he aimed to combine moral unity with a world-state under papal guidance. He deduced the papal powers from the **Petrine Theory,** the **Old Testament,** the **Donation of Constantine,** and from the duty of the pope to ensure justice, maintain peace, prevent and punish sin, and aid the unfortunate. With a clear grasp of essentials, he never lost sight of this concept, but his frequent opportunism injured his moral grandeur. Insistence, not on moral or theological but on historical grounds (i.e., the Translation of the Empire), on the right (claimed by Gregory VII) to pass on imperial elections. A brilliant administrator, he first brought the papal chancery into systematic organization (division into four sections under experts; careful, systematized treatment of documents) and made a great collection of canons and decretals. This pontificate was the zenith of the medieval papacy.

Restoration of the Papal States (Spoleto, Ancona, Romagna regained); many towns succeeded in escaping and keeping their local autonomy. Tuscany: an anti-imperial league under papal auspices; towns like Florence, Lucca, and Siena retained their appropriations of the Matildine lands (a partial foundation of their later power); the rest of the Matildine lands were regained by the Church. Innocent used his position first as protector, then as guardian of Frederick II, in an attempt to alienate Sicily from the Hohenstaufens.

1208–29. The **Albigensian Crusade** (p. 202), directed against the spreading heresy of southern France, drenched that region with blood and exterminated one of the most advanced local cultures in Europe, under revolting circumstances of feudal cynicism. Simon de Montfort nullified Innocent's efforts to divert the crusaders' ardor to Spain against the Muslims.

Vindication of the political claims of the papacy. (1) Asserting his right to pass on imperial elections, Innocent rejected the Hohenstaufen claimant (Philip of Swabia) to the imperial crown, ignored the undoubted rights of Frederick, crowned and supported Otto (in return for promises of obedience to papal authority), and then procured (in alliance with King Philip II) the election of Frederick II. (2) By excommunicating Philip II (1198), Innocent forced him to a formal recognition of his wife, Ingeborg, but was coldly rebuffed when he intervened in Philip's struggle with the Angevins. (3) Maintaining the rights of his nominee to the See of Canterbury (Langton), Innocent forced King John of England (interdict, 1208) to cede England to the Holy See and receive it back as a fief (1213). (4) Innocent received the homage of the following states as papal vassals: Aragon, Bulgaria, Denmark, Hungary, Poland, Portugal, Serbia; he brought the Roman Church to its closest approximation to an ideal Christian universal commonwealth.

The struggle against urban heresy. The Church, long organized to deal with a predominantly rural society, was increasingly out of touch with the rising bourgeoisie and urban proletariat as town life revived and expanded; the anticlericalism of the cities had become a major problem. The Italian **Francis of Assisi** and the Spaniard **Dominic** organized the spontaneous response within the Church to this crisis: Francis (d. 1226), a converted gilded youth, as the joyous "troubadour of religion," began preaching the beauties of humility, poverty, simplicity, and devotion; of the brotherhood of man, of man and the animals, of man and nature. His cheerful vernacular hymns won tremendous success in the towns of Italy. Founded as a brotherhood, whence the name **Friars Minor** (Minorities, Gray Friars, also Cordeliers), the **Franciscans** won cautious support from Innocent but did not win formal ratification as a corporation until 1223. The second of the mendicant orders (or begging orders, from their initial refusal to own property, hence their dependence on the people for sustenance), the **Dominican,** born of Dominic's campaign against the Albigensian heresy, was sanctioned by Innocent (1215). Organized as a preaching order, the Dominicans (Friars Preachers, Black Friars, or Jacobins in Paris) patterned their constitution on the Franciscan. Members of these two mendicant orders were not monastic, rural monks, but town-dwellers devoted to preaching and charity. Franciscan and Dominicans **recruited** friars from the burgher class, small property owners, shopkeepers. The Franciscans accepted the uneducated; Dominicans (in Germany) preferred university graduates. The conduct of the Inquisition (an ecclesiastical court for the investigation of heresy) was entrusted to them (1233), and their direct influence on education (especially that of the Dominicans) was enormous.

1215. The **Fourth Lateran Council** was the climax of Innocent's pontif-

icate (attended by 400 bishops, 800 abbots and priors, and the representatives of the monarchs of Christendom) and its decrees were of tremendous significance: (1) the Church was pronounced one and universal; (2) the sacraments were decreed a channel of grace, and the chief sacrament, the Eucharist; (3) the dogma of transubstantiation was proclaimed; (4) annual confession, penance, and communion were enjoined; (5) careful rules were made as to episcopal elections and the qualifications of the clergy; (6) injunctions for the maintenance of education in each cathedral and for theological instruction were formulated; (7) the Albigensian and Catharist heresies were condemned; (8) trial by ordeal and by battle were forbidden; (9) the veneration of relics was regulated; and (10) rules of monastic life were made more rigorous. Finally, another crusade was proclaimed.

1227–41. GREGORY IX, a relative of Innocent III, aged and fiery, he never relaxed his relentless pressure on Frederick. **Canonization of Francis of Assisi** (1228) and **Dominic** (1234).

Leonardo of Pisa (Fibonacci) (c. 1170–1240), the mathematician, who wrote the first rigorous, systematic demonstration of Hindu mathematics. He also wrote treatises on geometry and algebra, including quadratic and cubic equations.

1243–54. INNOCENT IV, a canon lawyer. Supposedly friendly to Frederick, he continued the uncompromising attack on the emperor, and encompassed the final ruin of the Hohenstaufen.

1271–76. GREGORY X (Visconti), a high-minded pope with three aims: to pacify Italy, to check Charles of Anjou and the rising power of France, and to pacify Germany. At the **Synod of Lyons** (1274), he provided for the seclusion of papal conclaves to avoid corruption. His successors were occupied with Italian affairs (the war of Naples and Sicily, baronial anarchy in Rome, etc.), and the advancement of their own houses. The rivalries of the great houses were so close that two years were required to elect Nicholas's successor **Celestine V** (1294), an ascetic hermit dragged unwilling to the Holy See, a puppet of Charles of Anjou who never saw Rome. Induced by the cardinals, he resigned ("the great refusal," Dante, *Inf.* III, 60) and was kept a prisoner by his successor, Boniface VIII (Gaetani).

1294–1303. BONIFACE VIII (Gaetani). Surpassed all his colleagues in the Sacred College as canon lawyer (in 1298 he promulgated a revision of the Code, the *Sext*), as diplomat, and as administrator, but with a violent temper and prone to dangerous remarks (e.g., "I'd rather be a dog than a Frenchman," which, since the most miserable Frenchman had a soul and a dog did not, later opened him to a charge of heresy—denying the immortality of the soul). A fierce defender of papal authority over secular powers, in the tradition of Gregory VII and Innocent III, Boniface failed to understand the growth of national sentiment in the later 13th century. Addicted to low company, he was not as vicious as contemporary propaganda painted him. Handsome and vain, on occasion he substituted imperial dress and regalia for papal vestments ("I am pope, I am Caesar"). An intelligent patron of architecture and art: Giotto in Rome.

1295. Bent on regaining Sicily for the papacy, Boniface continued the support of the Angevin claimant, Charles II of Naples, arranged the **Peace of 1295,** by which James of Aragon exchanged Sicily for the investiture of Sardinia and Corsica and the extinction of French claims in Aragon.

1296. The **bull** *Clericis laicos,* designed to stop the war between France and England by depriving the belligerents of their main financial resources, forbade the payment of taxes by the clergy to lay rulers without papal consent (a vain attempt to maintain a medieval custom in the face of rising national states). Philip IV of France answered with an embargo on the export of bullion; Edward I of England with the outlawing of the clergy; both were supported by public opinion expressed in their national assemblies (pp. 196, 204). Boniface backed down.

1297. Angered by the Colonna and their insistence on the validity of Celestine V's election, their appeal to a general council, and their support of the Aragonese in Sicily, the pope began a veritable crusade that exiled the Colonna.

Recognition of the rights of Robert (second son of Charles II) in Naples. Beginning of the formation of a Gaetani state as a threat to the barons.

1300. The **Great Jubilee,** zenith of the pontificate, one of the magnificent pageants of the medieval papacy, managed with tremendous pomp by Boniface; huge donations (raked over public tables by papal "croupiers"); the proceeds intended by Boniface for the second Gaetani state, to be formed in Tuscany, and for the subjection of Sicily.

1302–3. Boniface's defeat and humiliation by the national states.

The **bull** *Unam sanctam* (1302) was long believed to be the most extreme assertion of papal power. Modern scholarship considers it to be a pastiche of earlier canonical and theological arguments with little that was new; still, it marked the last papal claim to superiority over lay rulers. Philip IV dispatched his aggressive councillor Nogaret to bring the pope to French soil for trial by a general council called by Philip.

1303, Sept. 8. Nogaret and Sciarra Colonna (p. 204) penetrated to the papal apartment at **Anagni,** found Boniface in bed, threatened him with death, tried to force his resignation, took him prisoner. Faced with a public reaction, Nogaret and Colonna fled, and Boniface died shortly thereafter of humiliation. The events of Anagni marked the culmination of the conflict between the papacy and the French monarchy. Recently triumphant over the German Empire, the papacy was defeated by a strong centralized monarchy backed by national sentiment; the defeat vindicated the royal claim to criminal jurisdiction over the clergy, and to the right to tax it.

1303–4. Benedict XI. A learned Dominican from a poor family, he had no connection with the quarreling Colonna family, and he had been absent from Rome during most of Boniface's disputes with Philip the Fair. He saw himself as a peacemaker (p. 205). Because of the disorders in Rome related to the Colonna family, Benedict withdrew to Perugia, and soon died. A long conclave (July 1304–June 1305) followed his death, and the cardinals, without French pressure, compromised on Bertrand de Gôt, archbishop of Bordeaux, who took the name Clement V.

1305–14. Clement V. Convinced that the Church needed the support of the French monarchy, Clement continued the work begun by Benedict, revoking the acts of Boniface VIII that had annoyed Philip of France. Clement chose 12 new cardinals, 9 of them French. But angered by Philip's attack on the Templars (p. 205) and his insistent pressure, Clement removed the papal court to Avignon, a territory in the Venaissin in southeastern France that was outside Philip's jurisdiction. Thus began the Avignon papacy.   *(To p. 251)*

1. THE NORMAN KINGDOM IN SOUTH ITALY AND SICILY

1103–54. The Norman count **Roger II of Sicily** succeeded the Norman duke William of Apulia (1111–27) and assumed the title of king of Sicily, Apulia, and Capua with the approval of the antipope Anacletus II. Excommunicated by Pope Innocent II (1139) for his alliance with Anacletus, he defeated Innocent (1140), took him prisoner, and forced recognition of his title. By skillful diplomacy he prevented a joint invasion of Sicily by the Greek and Roman emperors. Planning a Mediterranean commercial empire, Roger established an extensive North African holding (at its maximum, 1153).

1154–66. William I, continuing Roger's policy, defeated (1156) the Byzantine allies of Pope Adrian IV and compelled Adrian to recognize his title in Sicily, Apulia, Naples, Amalfi, and Salerno. He supported Pope Alexander III against Frederick I.

1166–89. William II continued this policy, but as he planned a Mediterranean empire and wished a free hand, he welcomed the marriage (1186) of Constance (Roger II's daughter), his heiress, to the future emperor Henry VI. He himself married Joan, sister of King Richard I of England, and intended to lead the Third Crusade as part of his imperial plans.

1190–94. On William's death, **Tancred of Lecce** (son of Roger, duke of Apulia, the brother of Constance) led a vigorous native resistance to the emperor Henry VI (king, 1194–97), with the support of the pope and Richard I. Henry reduced Sicily, southern Italy, and part of Tuscany, with the aid of Pisa and Genoa; retained the Matildine lands in central Italy; organized an imperial administration of his holdings; and planned a great empire with Italy as its base. Purely Norman rule ended with Tancred.

The Norman kingship in southern Italy and Sicily was theocratic,

on Byzantine lines; the administration was an efficient, departmentalized bureaucracy. Tremendous prosperity and efficient taxation made the Sicilian monarchs perhaps the richest in Europe. Dealing with a cosmopolitan kingdom containing Italian, Greek, and Arabic elements, and needing settlers, the Norman rulers practiced a tolerant eclecticism that provided for wide racial divergences in law, religion, and culture.

Roger II's cosmopolitan court and generous patronage of the learned produced a brilliant circle that included the Arab geographer **Edrisi, Eugenius,** the translator of Ptolemy's *Optics,* and **Henry Aristippus,** translator of Plato's *Phaedo* and Book IV of Aristotle's *Meterologica.*

2. THE DEVELOPMENT OF ITALIAN TOWNS

No continuous tradition of medieval and classical town government in Italy can be traced. The post-Carolingian anarchy left defense in local hands, and rural refuges and town walls were the work of local cooperation. The bishops in Lombardy, traditional guardians of their peoples, with large episcopal and comital powers delegated from the monarchs, played a decisive role in communal organization for defense (e.g., Bergamo, 904). The first cases of true urban autonomy were in Amalfi, Benevento, and Naples (1000–34), a development cut short by the advent of the Normans.

The great urban evolution took place in the north, and particularly in Lombardy, where **communes,** sworn associations of free men seeking complete political and economic independence from local lords, appeared (probably) in the later 10th century. The emperors, busy in Germany or preoccupied with the popes, made wide grants of regalian rights over local coinage, tolls, customs dues, police powers, and justice (diplomas of Henry I, Lothair II, and Conrad II); there were also considerable delegations of local episcopal powers. Full-fledged communes appeared in the 11th and 12th centuries (e.g., Asti, 1093; Pavia, 1105; Florence, 1138; and Rome itself, by papal charter, 1188). Expansion in the great maritime and commercial republics was rapid (e.g., Pisa's new walls, 1081; Florence's second wall, 1172–74; Venetian expansion in the Adriatic after the capture of Bari from the Saracens, 1002).

As a result of revolt and negotiation, the towns of Lombardy were largely self-governing communes by the opening of the 12th century, and the consulate or its equivalent was in full activity by the end of the century. Typical town organization: an assembly (legislation, declaration of war and peace, etc.); the consuls, the core of the magistracy, usually 4 to 20 in number, serving a one-year term, and chosen from the leading families; the town council and minor magistrates.

Gradual merger of northern Italian feudal nobility and the commercial aristocracy: nobles attracted by opportunities of long-distance trade, the rising value of urban real estate, the new public offices available in the communes, and the possibilities of advantageous marriages with rich commercial families; marriage vows often sealed business contracts between rural nobility and wealthy merchant families. A new social class, an **urban nobility,** appeared.

The development of the merchant and craft guilds led to vigorous class warfare as the rising bourgeoisie asserted itself and brought, in the podestate (the *podestà*), a kind of local dictator during the last quarter of the 12th century.

3. THE RISE OF VENICE

Fugitives from the Huns found refuge among the fishing villages of the lagoons; the permanent establishment of Venice seems to date from the Lombard invasion (568). Venetian aid to Belisarius began the formal connection between Venice and Constantinople and a (largely) theoretical connection with the Eastern Roman Empire. The *tribuni maiores* (a central governing committee of the islands) dated from c. 568.

687. Election of the first doge. A salt monopoly and salt-fish trade were the sources of the first prosperity of Venice. Two great parties: pro-Byzantine aristocrats favoring a hereditary doge; democrats friendly to the Roman Church and (later) the Franks. Venice offered asylum to the exarch of Ravenna fleeing from Liutprand, and gained trading rights with Ravenna. When Charlemagne ordered the pope to expel

THE HOUSE OF TANCRED (1057–1287)

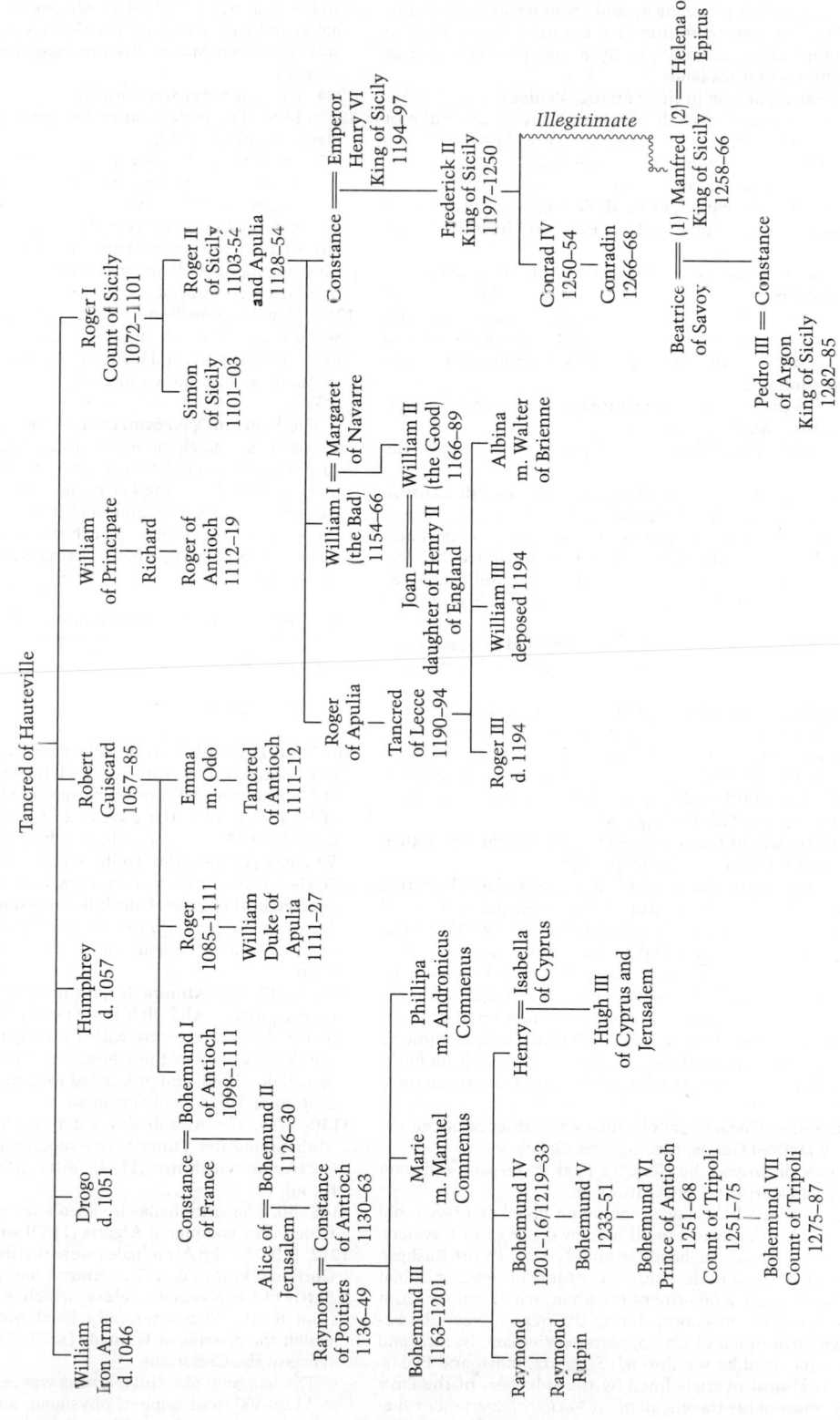

the Venetians from the Pentapolis and threatened the settlement in the lagoons, Venice turned again to Constantinople.

810. In a treaty, Charlemagne and the Byzantine emperor Nicephorus recognized Venice as Byzantine territory and acknowledged her mainland trading rights. This agreement marks the start of Venice's rise to commercial preponderance, initially as a Byzantine province, later as a Byzantine ally protecting sea lanes.

1000. After a 200-year expansion in the Adriatic, Venice completely reduced the Dalmatian pirates, and the doge took the title of duke of Dalmatia. Venice was mistress of the sea route to the Holy Land (commemorated in the wedding of the doge and the sea).

1032. Establishment of a council and senate.

1043. The construction of the **church of St. Mark** begun; one of the most notable and influential examples of Byzantine architecture in the West.

1095. The first three crusades established Venetian trading rights in a number of Levantine ports (e.g., Sidon, 1102; Tyre, 1123) and founded the power of a wealthy ruling class. A war with the Eastern Empire (financed by the first known government bonds) was unsuccessful, and led to the institution of a deliberative assembly of 480 members (the germ of the **great council**).

1171. Appointment of the doge was transferred to this council, a complete triumph for the commercial aristocracy.

1198. A coronation oath (in varying terms) began to be exacted of the doge.

1204. The Frankish capture of Constantinople in the **Fourth Crusade** proved a tremendous economic bonanza for Venice (p. 236), which gained the Cyclades, Sporades, Propontis, the Black Sea coasts, Thessalian littoral, and control of the Morea. Venice administered this vast empire on a kind of feudal tenure, portioning it out to families charged with defense of the seaways. Venice had also gained a further foothold in Syrian ports.

From this period dates a great epoch of building and increasing oligarchic pressure, as the government began to become a closed corporation of leading families.

1253–99. The **struggle with Genoa** for the Black Sea and Levantine trade. The feud of Genoa and Venice was ancient, and trouble began at Acre (1253). The first war with Genoa ended in the complete defeat (1258) of the Genoese. By the later 12th century, Venice served as an international entrepôt for world trade, selling silk brought from China across central Asia via the **Silk Road** (p. 24).

1255–66. Venetian traders in the Black Sea region, **Nicolo and Maffeo Polo** traveled to central Asia and China (p. 154).

The pursuit of trading possibilities had always stimulated Venetian enterprise. Since before the 1st century C.E., Asian merchants had traded on the Silk Road in central Asia (westward through Mongolia, south or north around the Takla Makan Desert to Songdiana, then westward to Transoxiana, from which this regular long-distance trade entered the Roman Empire). These merchants exchanged Chinese silks and lacquerware for Western woolen and linen textiles, glass, coral, and precious stones. With the rise of Islam, Persians came to control the western parts of the trade, traveling northward from Baghdad to the Black Sea coast, from which Jewish merchants carried trade west to Europe.

1261. The Greeks seized Constantinople during the absence of the Venetian fleet; they favored Genoa, turning over Galata to her.

1264. The Venetians destroyed the Genoese fleet at **Trepani** and soon returned to their old status in Constantinople.

1271–95. Second journey of the Polos, including Nicolo's 17-year-old son **Marco** (1254–1324?), greatest of all medieval European travelers. They took the route Mosul-Baghdad-Ormuz-Kerman-Pamir-Kashgar, then across the Gobi Desert to the court of the Mongol emperor Kublai Khan. Marco Polo became a favorite of the khan, who employed him on several administrative missions; during the next 15 years he became acquainted with much of China, parts of Vietnam, Burma, and India. The Polos returned by sea through Sumatra, India, and Persia. Although he was almost overwhelmed by the splendors of the East, Marco Polo's account of his travels, *Book of Various Experiences*, dictated in 1297 while a prisoner of Genoa, proved basically accurate, promoted the study of scientific geography, and provided virtually the only source of solid European information about East Asia before the 17th century. Christopher Columbus and others relied heavily on it.

1289–99. The **advance of the Mamluks** (p. 129; capture of Tripoli, 1289; of Acre, 1291) led Venice to a treaty with this new power in the eastern Mediterranean. Genoa met this with an effort to close the Dardanelles, and won a victory (1294) at Alexandretta; Venice forced the Dardanelles and sacked Galata. The Genoese defeated the Venetians at **Curzola** (1299), but Matteo Visconti negotiated an honorable peace (1299) for them.

1284. The **first ducat** was coined.

1290–1300. The perfection of the great galleys. Establishment of the **Flanders galleys** (1317).

1297. The **great council** was restricted in membership to those who had been members within the preceding four years. A commission added other names and then the council was closed to new members (except by heredity). In effect this excluded a large section of the citizens from any share of the government, in favor of a narrow, hereditary, commercial oligarchy. Popular reaction led to a revolt (1300), the leaders of which were hanged.

1310. Tiepolo's rebellion, the only serious uprising in Venetian history, was crushed. This seems to have been a patrician protest against the extreme oligarchy, and led to the creation of an emergency committee of public safety, the **council of ten,** which soon became permanent (1335).

The **Venetian government** thus consisted of: the great council (i.e., the patrician caste); the senate (a deliberative and legislative body dealing with foreign affairs, peace, war, finances, trade); the council of ten (a secret, rapidly acting body concerned with morals, conspiracy, European affairs, finance, and the war department, which could override the senate); the *collegio* or cabinet (the administrative branch); the doge and his council, which, sitting with the ten, made the council of seventeen. *(To p. 259)*

g. THE IBERIAN PENINSULA

(From p. 180)

1. MUSLIM SPAIN

1037–86. The Muluk al-Tawa'if (Party Kings). These were petty dynasties founded on the ruins of the Umayyad caliphate: the Hammudids of Malaga (from 1016 onward) and of Algeciras (1039–); the Abbadids of Sevilla (1031–); the Zayrids of Granada (1012–); the Jahwarids of Córdoba (1031–); the Dhul-Nunids of Toledo (1035–); the Amirids of Valencia (1021–); the Tojibids and Hudids of Saragossa (1019– and 1031–). Most of these dynasties were absorbed by the most distinguished of them, the **Abbadids,** who summoned the Almoravids from Africa to aid them against Alfonso VI of Castile. This lack of Muslim unity encouraged expansion of northern Christian kingdoms southward.

1056–1147. The **Almoravids,** a Puritanical Berber sect founded by the Berber prophet **Abdullah ibn Tashfin.** They conquered Morocco and part of Algeria and were called into Spain by the Abbadids to help in the defense against the Christians. They defeated Alfonso of Castile at **Zallaka** (1086) and proceeded to annex Moorish Spain, with the exception of Toledo and Saragossa.

1130–1269. The **Almohades,** a dynasty founded by the Berber prophet **Muhammad ibn Tumart.** His successor, Abdul-Mu'min, annihilated the Almoravid army (1144), after which Morocco was conquered (1146).

1145–50. The Almohades invaded and conquered Moorish Spain, after which they conquered Algeria (1152) and Tunis (1158).

1212, July 16. The Almohades were finally defeated by an alliance of the Christian kings Peter II of Aragon and Alfonso VIII of Castile, in the **Battle of Las Navas de Tolosa,** which was followed by their expulsion from Spain. Thereafter only local Muslim dynasties remained, of which the **Nasrids of Granada** (1232–1492) alone offered much resistance to the Christians.

The height of **Muslim learning** was reached by **Averroës** (ibn-Rushd, c. 1126–98), philosopher, physician, and commentator on Plato and Aristotle, master of the Christian schoolmen.

In the 10th through the 15th century, Christian kingdoms in the north, propelled by demographic pressure, land hunger, nobles' demands for estates, advances in military technology, and the appetites of transhumant sheep, pushed southward. In the 14th century, clerical propagandists labeled this movement the **Reconquista (Reconquest):** a sacred crusading struggle to wrest the country from alien Muslim hands and to restore Christian control. This religious myth subsequently became part of Spanish political history and the Spanish "national" psychology.

1238. The Nasrid rulers began reconstructing an old fortress, **the Alhambra** in Granada, a monumental and magnificent complex of buildings combining fortress, palace, and small city. Completed in the 14th century, these buildings and gardens survive as the finest example of Muslim culture in Europe.

2. CASTILE

1072–1109. ALFONSO VI, of Castile. He captured Toledo from the Moors (1085) and made his son-in-law, Henry of Burgundy, count of Portugal (1093).

1086. The Muslims, alarmed by Alfonso's progress, called from Africa the great **Yusuf ibn Tashfin** (d. 1106), leader of the newly dominant sect of puritanical berbers, the Almoravids. Ibn Yusuf landed at Algeciras (1086) and, with the support of Sevilla (Seville), began a successful counterthrust against the Christians (defeat of Alfonso at **Zallaka,** 1086). Yusuf, recalled by the African situation, did not at once exploit his advantage, but on his return to Spain his energetic reforms strengthened the Muslims and brought them into an integral relationship (c. 1091) with his great African empire, which was centered in Morocco. This empire quickly disintegrated on Yusuf's death.

Alfonso resumed the Christian Reconquest with the aid of **Rodrigo (Ruy) Diaz** (c. 1043–95) of Vivar, the **Cid** (Cid as applied by the Muslims means lord or master). Alfonso's style of "emperor" represented personal prestige and a vague hegemony rather than political reality.

The **Cid,** a Castilian originally in the service of Sancho II of Castile, later passed into that of Alfonso VI; he was exiled (1081); returned to Castilian service (1087–88); went over to the Muslim king of Saragossa after his second exile. Eventually he became ruler of Valencia. The Cid served both sides; he was cruel, selfish, and proud. Despite these characteristics, the legendary figure of the man became the great national hero of Spain. After his death (1099), Valencia was soon abandoned to the Almoravids.

In the course of the 11th century, French influence began to penetrate the peninsula. The Cluniacs, already (1033) strong in Catalonia, Castile, and Aragon, reinforced French influence and stimulated clerical reform and the Reconquest. A literary reflection of this is to be found in the *Cantar de mio Cid* (c. 1140).

1126–57. Alfonso VII, crowned "emperor" (1135) on the basis of military ascendancy and an intense feeling of equality with rival monarchs, especially the Holy Roman emperors. The weakening of the Almoravids by luxury, and the rise of rivals (the Almohades) in Africa (c. 1125), made possible a resumption of the Reconquest (1144–47) with wide raids into Andalusia. The Almohades, summoned from Africa (1146), completed (1172) the second **restoration of Muslim unity,** and made Muslim Spain a province of their African empire, reducing the Arab influence. Alfonso's death was followed by a minority and an eight-year dynastic crisis from which his son Alfonso VIII finally emerged as master.

1158–1214. Alfonso VIII. After a series of successful attacks on the Muslims, Alfonso was overwhelmingly defeated (**Alarcos,** 1195) by the Almohades, then at the zenith of their power. Leon and Navarre promptly invaded Castile, but Alfonso triumphed over them and, with the aid of Pope Innocent III and the clergy, began the preparation of a unified general assault on the Muslims that led to the greatest victory of the Reconquest, **Las Navas de Tolosa** (1212), soon followed by the decline of the Almohade power in Spain and Africa and by Christian dissension.

1179. Portugal's independence and royal title were recognized by Pope Alexander III.

1217–52. FERDINAND III ended the dynastic war in Castile and attacked the Moors in the Guadalquivir Valley, taking Córdoba (1236) and Sevilla (1248). On the appeal of the Almohade emperor, he sent aid to him, gaining in return a line of African fortresses and permission

to establish a Christian church at Marrakah. His plans for an invasion of Africa were cut short by his death. After the capture of Jaen (1246), the emir was allowed to establish himself at Granada, the last Moorish stronghold, as Ferdinand's vassal.

The long history of guerrilla warfare in Castile disorganized tillage, made the people averse to agriculture, led to a concentration of population in the towns, and accounts for the poverty of Castilian agriculture, the tremendous influence of municipalities in medieval Castile, the development of a race of soldiers, and the isolation of Spanish thought from general European currents. In general the Moors were not disliked, and intermarriages were not unusual until the 13th century.

The war of Christian Reconquest gave birth to three great native military orders, modeled partly on Moorish societies for border defense and partly on the international crusading orders, notably the Templars, already established in the Peninsula. Some members took the regular monkish vows, others did not. Two Cistercian monks assumed (1158) the defense of Calatrava (when the Templars gave it up), and the **Order of Calatrava** that grew up was confirmed by the pope (1164). The **Order of Santiago** (established 1171) was the largest and richest, the **Order of Alcántara** (founded c. 1156), an offshoot of Calatrava, was the most clerical in type.

In the period following 1252, fear of the Muslim was no longer a dominant force in Iberian politics, and the nobles turned from assaults on the Moors to attacks on the monarchy. The struggle between crown and baronage (which found a parallel all through Europe) was notable in Spain for the depth of governmental degradation that it produced.

1252–84. The new elements in the situation were clearly indicated in the reign of **Alfonso X** (the Wise), a versatile and learned ruler who presided over a court of poets, scholars, musicians, and artists; promoted Castilian as a literary language; supported the compilation and translation of Arabic scientific works, including the *Alfonsine Tables,* which tabulated the movements of the planets, and the *Siete Partidas,* which codified Spanish legal knowledge; and supported schools at Sevilla, Murcia, and Salamanca. Jewish and Muslim knowledge inspired at his court flowed into northern Europe. He built the Castilian navy, continued Christian efforts against the Moors, and captured Cadiz (1262).

As a politician, however, Alfonso was not so "wise." His claim to the German throne (his mother, Beatrice, was a daughter of Philip of Swabia; p. 207) and his campaign for election as Holy Roman emperor proved ruinously expensive and ultimately humiliating: he won election by a faction of the German princes in 1257, but the pope vetoed the selection. Concessions forced on him by a very rebellious nobility gravely weakened the monarchy. Domestic discontent, combined with rivalry over the succession, led to revolt and his deposition.

3. BARCELONA AND CATALONIA

The **Spanish Mark** had been established as a result of the conquest of Catalonia by Charlemagne (785–811). The county of Barcelona (erected 817) under the Frankish crown became independent, perhaps as early as the 9th century. By the beginning of the 12th century, the counts of Barcelona had large holdings north of the Pyrenees (notably in Provence), to which they added for a brief period Majorca and Iviza (1114–15) and, permanently, Tarragona.

1137. The **union of Catalonia and Aragon,** begun by Ramón Berenguer IV of Catalonia, was epochal, for it created a powerful state with access to the sea. Catalonian territories included Cerdagne and a large part of Provence, with the later addition of Roussillon (1172), Montpellier (1204, under French suzerainty), Foix, Nîmes, Béziers (1162–96).

Ramón Berenguer IV continued pressure against the Moors: Tortosa fell (1148), and Lerida and Fraga (1149); he encouraged Christian immigration and the establishment of monasteries (e.g., the Cistercian abbey of **Poblet,** c. 1150). His experts produced the *Usages of Barcelona,* a legal code that stressed his regalian rights over justice, the peace, and the coinage.

Social change. The period from 1150 to 1213 witnessed considerable agricultural development, population expansion, and the growth of peasant freedom. In towns such as Tarragona, Lerida, and especially

SPANISH RULERS (970–1285)

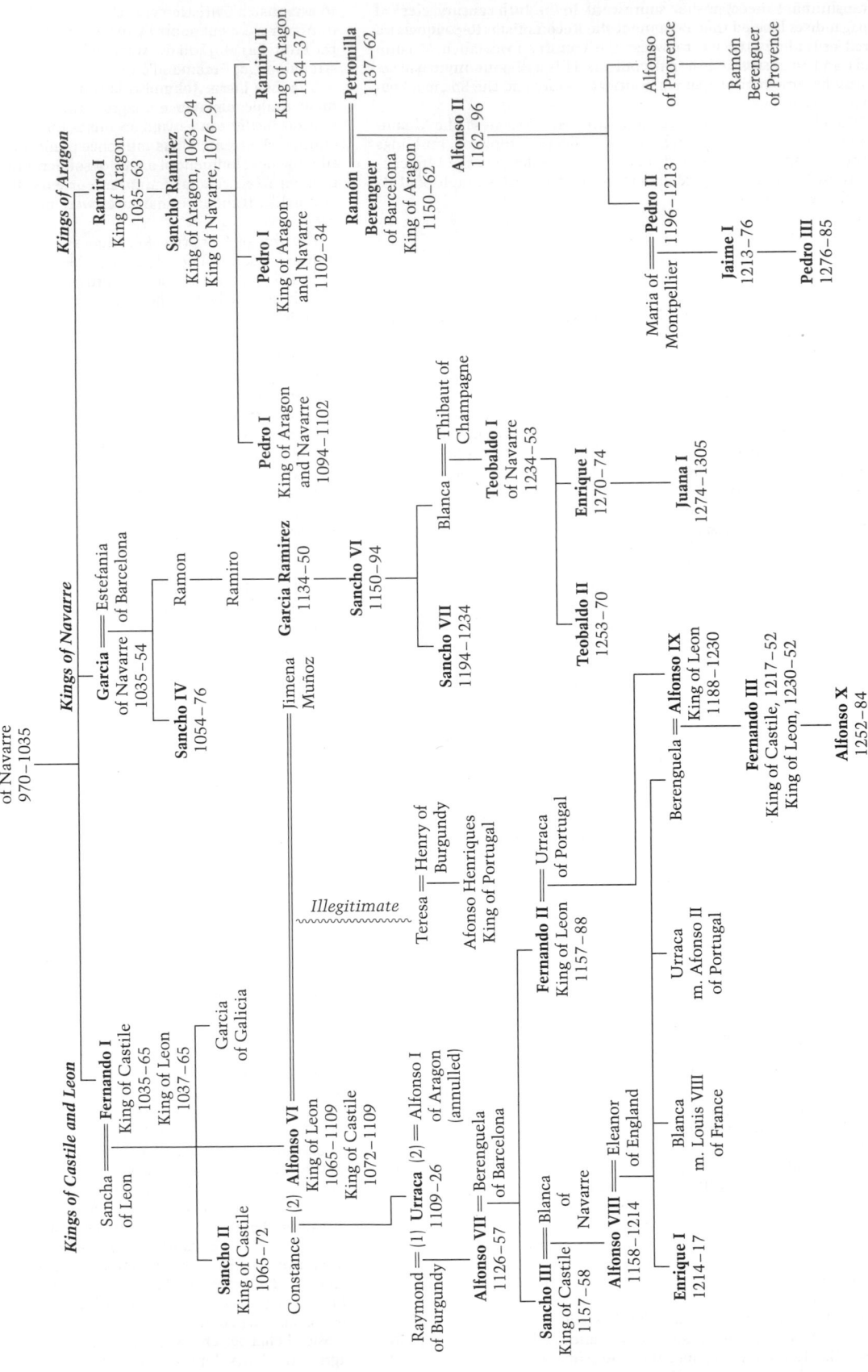

Barcelona, entrepreneurs, often funded by Jewish capital and involved in the trade of Moorish slaves, emerged as a class of "proto-patricians," businesspeople whose local power rested on their wealth. Both commercial and agrarian prosperity depended on the continuation of Muslim industry and technology. The towns gained independence from feudal and ecclesiastical authorities.

4. NAVARRE

Navarre gained its independence from Carolingian rule in the 9th century and fell heir to the Carolingian rights in Aragon, which was absorbed by Navarre in the 10th century. **Sancho the Great** (970–1035) secured the succession of Castile, conquered most of Leon, and temporarily united the Iberian kingdoms. By his will, Aragon passed to his son Ramiro and the union came to an end. On the death of **Alfonso the Warrior** (1104–34), Navarre returned to its old ruling house until it passed under French control (1234) for two centuries.

5. ARAGON

Aragon, beginning as a county on the river Arago under Carolingian control, emerged from Carolingian domination in the middle of the 9th century, passed under the control of Navarre, and then became independent under Ramiro (d. 1069). The period from 1069 to 1134 is marked by confusion, intrigue, some progress against the Moors, and the annexation of Navarre (1076).

1102–34. ALFONSO I (the Battler) advanced to the Ebro, captured Saragossa (1118), and made raids to the Mediterranean, his victories defined the medieval realm of Aragon, and he ranks among the greatest kings of the Reconquest. On Alfonso's death, Aragon chose his brother, **Ramiro,** a monk who emerged from retirement long enough to marry and produce a daughter, Petronilla, whom he betrothed to Ramón Berenguer IV (1131–62), count of Barcelona. He then returned (1137) to his monastery, leaving Petronilla under the guardianship of Ramón. On his marriage to Petronilla in 1150, Ramón became king of Aragon. The resulting **union of Catalonia and Aragon** was a decisive event in Spanish history.

After the union, the Aragonese kings, preoccupied with Spanish affairs, let Provence drift, and on the death of Alfonso II (1162–96) it passed to his son Alfonso, nominally under the suzerainty of his brother **Peter (Pedro) II** (1196–1213), but in fact lost for good. Alfonso tried to keep his Provençal holdings clear of the Albigensian heresy, but Raymond, count of Toulouse, a supporter of the heresy, sought to win Peter II to his views. Peter went to Rome (1204) for a papal coronation, declared himself a vassal of the Holy See, and bore an honorable part at Las Navas de Tolosa, but he was forced by the horrors of the Albigensian Crusade and the legitimate appeals of his vassals to oppose Simon de Montfort at Muret, where he fell.

1213. The **Battle of Muret** marked the end of Aragonese interests north of the Pyrenees.

1258. With the **Treaty of Corbeil,** the king of France renounced his claims to Barcelona, Urgel, Cerdagne, Roussillon. Aragon was ceded, including Carcassonne, Foix, Béziers, Nîmes, Narbonne, Toulouse. All rights in Provence passed to Margaret, wife of Louis IX; a marriage was arranged between Louis's son Philip and Isabella, daughter of James I of Aragon.

1213–76. JAMES (Jaime) I (the Conqueror). After the weakness and anarchy of his minority, James, one of the greatest soldiers of the Middle Ages, conquered Valencia in an intermittent campaign (1233–45), took the kingdom of Murcia for Castile (1266), and freed the Aragonese frontier of the Muslim menace. James also attempted to establish his overlordship in Tlemcen and Bugia in North Africa, and to secure a hold in Tunis. Against the will of his Aragonese nobles, but with the support of his Catalonian and French vassals, James conquered the Balearic Islands (1229–35), thus beginning the creation of an Aragonese Mediterranean empire.

Spanish culture in the Middle Ages was greatly enriched by Muslim and Jewish influences. The Muslim tradition of scholarship continued, and the translations from Arabic to Latin made Spain the avenue by which the knowledge of antiquity came to the West. **Gerard of Cremona** translated the works of Ptolemy, Euclid, Galen, and the Hippocratic corpus. Toledo, which had been a center of learning for the Arabic world, became a center for the translation of Arabic and Greek works into Latin. **John of Sevilla** (fl. 1135–53), also at Toledo, translated Arabic texts on mathematics, astronomy, and philosophy into Latin and the vernacular. Abraham bar-Hiyya (d. 1136) **(Sarasorda)** was one of the earliest to introduce Muslim mathematics to the West. Moses ben Maimon **(Maimonides)** (1135–1204), born in Córdoba, became one of the most influential thinkers of the West; he also translated medical and astronomical texts from Arabic. **Ibn-Rushd** (1126–98), born in Córdoba, was known as "the commentator," through whom the West relearned the works of Aristotle.

Ramón Lull (1232–1315) was the greatest Catalonian intellectual figure of the Middle Ages, a vernacular poet, novelist, missionary, mystic, educator, reformer, logician, scientist, and traveler.

Architecture. (1) **Pre-Romanesque** architecture revealed traces of Visigothic, Carolingian, Persian, Byzantine, and Muslim traditions. (2) **Romanesque** architecture showed particularly the influence of Auvergne and Languedoc (second church of Santiago de Compostella). (3) The **Gothic** was marked by strong elements of the Burgundian style, brought by the Cluniacs. The full tide of the Gothic was probably introduced by the Cistercians (cathedrals of Toledo, c. 1230; Burgos, 1226; Leon, c. 1230). Catalan Gothic shows German influences (cathedrals of Barcelona, 1298; Gerona, 1312). The later Spanish Gothic revealed French, German, and Flemish currents (cathedral of Sevilla, begun 1401; west towers of Burgos cathedral, 1442). (4) **Moorish** architecture had a development of its own: the great mosque of Córdoba (completed 1118), the Alcazar in Sevilla (c. 1181), and the Alhambra (mostly 14th century).

Foundation of the first universities: Valencia (1209); Salamanca (1242).   (To p. 249)

6. PORTUGAL

1055–. Reconquest from the Muslims of much of present Portugal by **Ferdinand the Great** of Leon and Castile. Ferdinand organized the territory as a county, with Coimbra as the capital.

1093–1112. Henry of Burgundy, a descendant of King Robert of France, came to Spain with other knight-adventurers to fight against the Moors. In return, the king of Castile granted him the county of Portugal and gave him the hand of his (illegitimate) daughter, Teresa. Henry himself was a typical crusader, restless and enterprising, whose main hope appears to have been to establish a dynasty in Castile.

1112–85. AFONSO HENRIQUES, the founder of the Portuguese monarchy and of the Burgundian dynasty. Afonso was only three years old at the death of his father. His mother, Teresa, ruled as regent, but soon became involved in a struggle with Galicia and Castile. Being defeated, she agreed to accept Castilian domination.

1128. Afonso assumed authority and repudiated the agreement.

1139. Afonso, one of the most famous knights of his age, began a long series of struggles against the Moors by defeating them in the **battle of Ourique.**

1143. Afonso was **proclaimed king** by the *cortes*. The pope arranged the **Treaty of Zamora** between Portugal and Castile, the latter recognizing Portuguese independence, while Portugal accepted the suzerainty of the pope.

1147. The Portuguese took Lisbon and established a frontier on the Tagus.

1169. Further conflicts with Castile led to Afonso's attack on Badajoz. He was defeated and captured, but was soon released.

1185–1211. SANCHO I, the son of Afonso Henriques. His reign was noteworthy for the development of towns and for the establishment of military orders of knighthood. Sancho did much to settle colonists on the lands that were won back in the prolonged wars against the Moors.

1211–23. AFONSO II. Beginning of the king's conflict with the clergy, which led to interference by the pope and to restlessness among the nobility.

PORTUGAL: THE BURGUNDIAN HOUSE (1112–1325)

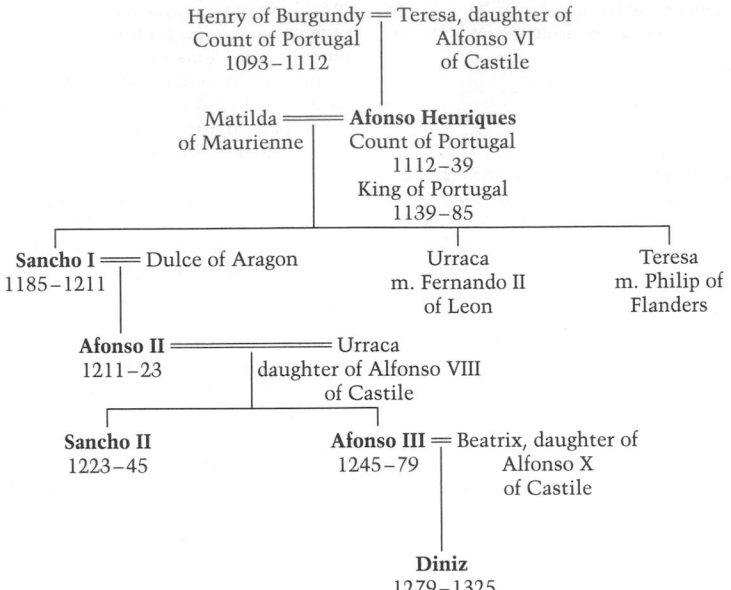

Henry of Burgundy = Teresa, daughter of
Count of Portugal   Alfonso VI
1093–1112   of Castile

Matilda ===== **Afonso Henriques**
of Maurienne   Count of Portugal
                1112–39
                King of Portugal
                1139–85

Sancho I === Dulce of Aragon   Urraca   Teresa
1185–1211   m. Fernando II   m. Philip of
                                    of Leon   Flanders

Afonso II ================ Urraca
1211–23   daughter of Alfonso VIII
                   of Castile

Sancho II   **Afonso III** = Beatrix, daughter of
1223–45   1245–79   Alfonso X
                                of Castile

Diniz
1279–1325

1223–1245. SANCHO II. His trouble with the clergy and nobility led ultimately to his deposition by the pope.

1245–79. AFONSO III, the brother of Sancho II and count of Boulogne; offered the crown by the pope. His title being weak, Afonso was much dependent on the *cortes* (1254) in which the commoners were for the first time represented. **War with Castile** was ended by a peace in 1253.

(To p. 250)

4. EASTERN EUROPE, 1000–1300

a. THE SLAVS

The Slavs, an eastern branch of the Indo-European family, were known to the Roman and Greek writers of the 1st and 2nd centuries C.E., under the name of **Venedi,** as inhabiting the region beyond the Vistula. The majority of modern scholars agree that the "original home" of the Slavs was the territory to the southeast of the Vistula and to the northeast of the Carpathian Mountains, in the upper basins of the Western Bug, the Pripet, and the Dniester. In the course of the early centuries of our era, the Slavs expanded in all directions, and by the 6th century, when they were known to Gothic and Byzantine writers as **Sclaveni,** they were apparently already separated into three main divisions: (1) the western Slavs (the present-day Poles, Czechs, Slovaks, and Moravians); (2) the southern Slavs (the Bulgarians, Serbs, Croats, and Slovenes); (3) the eastern Slavs (the Russians, subsequently subdivided into the Great Russians, the Little Russians or the Ukrainians, and the Belorussians, Russian for "White Russians").

The Slavs emerged as a distinct people after mingling with the Goths and Huns. Those not affected by the invasions of the Goths and Huns constituted another branch of Indo-European people, namely the **Balts** (Lithuanians, Latvians, and the early Prussians). These peoples inhabited the southeastern coast of the Baltic Sea, between the present Klaipéda (Memel) and Estonia.

b. BOHEMIA AND MORAVIA

c. 623–58. The earliest recorded attempt at the construction of a Slavic kingdom was that made by **Samo,** who appears to have been a Frankish tradesman traveling in central Europe. Probably taking advantage of the defeat of the Avars by the Greeks in 626, he managed to unite the Czechs and some of the Wends, and succeeded in repulsing not only the Avars, but also the Franks under King Dagobert (631). But on the death of Samo, the union of the tribes disintegrated.

833–36. Mojmir, founder of the Moravian state, maintained himself against pressure from the East Franks.

846–69. Rastislav, prince of Moravia, made an alliance (862) with **Michael III,** the Byzantine emperor, to counteract the close relationship between the East Franks and the Bulgarians.

863. Conversion of the Moravians by Cyril (Constantine, 826–69) and **Methodius** (815–85), two monks from Salonika (Thessalonica) sent at Rastislav's request (p. 187). Beginning of Slavic church language and liturgy. **Glagolitic alphabet.**

869. Rastislav captured and blinded by Carloman.

870–94. Sviatopluk, a Moravian prince, succeeded in uniting under his authority Moravia, Bohemia, and present-day Slovakia, and managed to maintain his position as against the Germans. During his reign, the western Slavs were converted to Christianity by Cyril and Methodius, but in the last years of the century, the German clergy redoubled its efforts and won Bohemia and Moravia for the Latin Church, thus establishing the ecclesiastical dependence of the western Slavs on Rome.

906. The **kingdom of Moravia** was dissolved as the result of a great defeat by the Hungarians.

c. 907–29. St. Wenceslaus (in Czech, Vaclav), duke of the Premysl house from c. 922. Educated by his grandmother, **St. Ludmilla,** a devout Christian. He worked for the cultural improvement of his people, and seeking broader Christian contacts, maintained friendly relations with the German king Henry I (the Fowler) (p. 177). This policy, combined with a pagan reaction against a determined Christian king, led to Wenceslaus's murder by his brother Boleslav I. Prague soon became the center of a Wenceslaus cult; by 1100 he was recognized as Bohemia's patron saint, and his crown has served as the symbol of Czech independence.

929–67. BOLESLAV I. He seems to have carried on constant warfare against the encroaching Germans, until forced (950) to accept German suzerainty. To the east he conquered Moravia, part of Slovakia, part of Silesia, and even Kraków. Furthermore, he appears to have established a fairly strong royal power over the old tribal chiefs.

967–99. BOLESLAV II. He apparently continued the policies of his father and saw to the final victory of the Christian faith (foundation of the bishopric of Prague, 973). Missionaries from Bohemia took an active part in the conversion of Hungary and Poland.

The entire 11th and 12th centuries were filled with chronic dynastic conflicts between members of the Premysl family and the various claimants appealing to Poland and more particularly to the German emperors for support. The result was the gradual integration of Bohemia with Germany, and the extension of feudalism to the Czech lands.

999–1000. Boleslav the Brave of Poland took advantage of the anarchy in Bohemia to conquer Silesia, Moravia, and Kraków. In 1003 he became duke of Bohemia, but he was driven out in the next year by a German army.

1031. The reacquisition of Moravia, which thenceforth remained connected with Bohemia.

1034–55. BŘETISLAV I (the Restorer), who overran Silesia, took Kraków (1039), and for a time ruled Poland, which had entered into a period of disruption.

1041. Emperior **Henry III,** alarmed by the expansion of the Bohemian power, invaded the country and advanced to Prague. Břetislav agreed to give up his Polish conquests and pay tribute to the emperor.

1061–92. VRATISLAV II, who, throughout his reign, loyally supported the German emperor, Henry IV, in his struggle with the papacy and took part in the Italian campaigns. He was rewarded by Henry with a crown (1086), but only for his own person.

1140–73. VLADISLAV II. Like his predecessors, he supported the German emperors in the main, and he was rewarded (1158) by Frederick Barbarossa with a hereditary crown for his aid against the Italian cities.

1173–97. Another period of dynastic conflict, during which there were some ten rulers.

1198–1230. OTTOKAR I. He took full advantage of the struggles for the succession that began to wrack the German Empire. Siding now with one party, now with another, he made the Bohemian king (an imperial elector since the early 12th century) one of the decisive powers in German affairs. On the other hand, a long-drawn conflict with the clergy (1214–21) led to the almost complete independence of the Church.

1212. The **Golden Bull** of Frederick II recognized the right of the Bohemian nobility to elect its own ruler.

1230–53. WENCESLAS (VACLAV) I. His reign was marked by an acceleration of German immigration that was encouraged by the ruler, possibly to counteract the growing power of the nobility. Germans began to open up large forested tracts and to build cities, which were given practical autonomy under German (Magdeburg) law.

1247–50. Rising of the nobility against the king, possibly in protest against the favor shown the Germans.

1251. The Austrian estates, after the death of the last Babenberg duke, elected Ottokar, son of Wenceslas, as duke.

1253–78. OTTOKAR II (the Great) whose reign marked the widest expansion of Bohemian power and was characterized by great prosperity (opening of the famous silver mines, which made Bohemia one of the wealthiest countries in the later Middle Ages).

1255. Ottokar carried on a successful campaign in support of the Teutonic Knights against the heathen Prussians.

1260. After defeating the Hungarians, Ottokar took from them the province of Styria.

1269. Ottokar, taking advantage of the interregnum in the German Empire, extended his power over Carinthia, Carniola, and Istria.

1273. Election of **Rudolf of Habsburg** as king of Germany. Ottokar refused to recognize him. The Diet of Regensburg (1274) therefore declared all Ottokar's acquisitions void. The king, supported by the Hungarians and by some of the Bohemian nobility, attacked Ottokar, who agreed to give up all but Bohemia and Moravia, and to recognize Rudolf's suzerainty even over these.

1278. New war between Rudolf and Ottokar. Ottokar was decisively defeated on the **Marchfeld** (Aug. 26) and killed.

1278–1305. Rule of **Wenceslas (Vaclav) II,** a boy of seven, for whom Otto of Brandenburg at first acted as regent.

1300. Wenceslas was elected and crowned king of Poland.

1301. His son, Wenceslas, was elected king of Hungary (ruled to 1304).

1305–6. Wenceslas (Vaclav) III. He gave up the claim to Hungary and was murdered while en route to Poland to suppress a revolt of the nobles. **End of the Premyslid line.**   (To p. 263)

c. POLAND

The Polish kingdom emerged in the 10th century, the result of the unification of some six tribes under the **Polani,** who were ruled by the members of the semimythical **family of Piast.** From the outset the Poles were obliged to fight against the encroachment of the Germans from the west, the Prussians from the north, the Bohemians from the south, and the Hungarians, also from the south.

c. 960–92. MIESZKO I, of the house of Piast, the first ruler for whom written evidence survives. He conquered the territory between the Oder and the Warthe Rivers, but was defeated by Markgraf Gero and obliged to recognize German suzerainty (973).

966. Mieszko was converted to Christianity by Bohemian missionaries, probably for political reasons, to deprive the Germans of any further excuse for aggression. The acceptance of Latin Christianity meant the connection of Poland, like Bohemia and Hungary, with Roman-European culture.

992–1025. BOLESLAV I (Chrobry, the Brave). He ascended the throne at 25 and was the real organizer of the Polish state. An energetic but at times treacherous and cruel ruler, he built up an efficient military machine, laid the basis for an administrative system (**comites = castellani = Burggrafen,** with civil and military powers), organized the Church (establishment of Benedictine monasteries). Politically his aim appears to have been the union of all western Slavs under his rule. He conquered eastern Pomerania and gained access to the Baltic (992–94), added Silesia, Moravia, and Kraków to his domain (999), and induced Otto III to erect an independent archbishopric of Gnesen (1000). On the death of Otto, he took advantage of the confusion in Germany to occupy Lusatia and Meissen, and in 1003 made himself duke of Bohemia. The new emperor, Henry II, carried on long wars against Boleslav and ultimately forced the abandonment of Bohemia and Lusatia (1005). But in the **Treaty of Bautzen** (1018), Boleslav was given Lusatia as an imperial fief, and just before his death he was able to make himself king of Poland (1025).

1025–34. MIESZKO II, whose reign marked the culmination of feudal separatism. The Poles, like the other Slavs, divided their domain among the various sons of a deceased king, thus creating endless dynastic conflict and ample opportunity for intervention by neighboring rulers. During Mieszko's reign, most of the territorial gains of Boleslav were lost: St. Stephen of Hungary conquered Slovakia (1027); Břetislav of Bohemia took Moravia (1031); Yaroslav of Russia acquired Ruthenia (1031); Canute of Denmark took Pomerania (1031). In 1032 the Emperor Conrad actually divided Poland between Mieszko and two of his relatives.

1034–40. A period of violent dynastic struggle and general insurrection, including a pagan reaction (burning of monasteries, massacre of the clergy) and a peasant uprising against the landlords. Meanwhile Břetislav of Bohemia seized Silesia (1038).

1038–58. CASIMIR I (the Restorer), who succeeded, with the aid of the Emperor Henry III, in reconquering his domain, reestablishing Christianity, and restoring order. Silesia was recovered (1054). In return Casimir was obliged to give up the royal title (becoming merely a **grand duke**) and to make numerous concessions to the nobility and clergy, thus initiating a baneful practice.

1058–79. BOLESLAV II (the Bold), one of the great medieval Polish rulers. In the great struggle between the emperor and the pope, he consistently supported the latter, as a counterweight to German influence. At the same time, he did his utmost to throw off the pressure of the nobility. In his countless campaigns, he reconquered upper Slovakia (1061–63) and marched as far as Kiev to put his relative on the Russian throne (1069). In 1076 he reassumed the royal crown, with the pope's approval. But his entire policy estranged the nobility, which ultimately drove him from his throne.

1079–1102. Vladislav I (Ladislas), an indolent and unwarlike ruler, brother of Boleslav. He resigned the royal title and attempted to secure peace by supporting the Emperor Henry IV, as well as by courting the nobility and clergy.

1102–38. BOLESLAV III (Wry-mouth), who acquired the throne after a violent struggle with his brother Zbigniew. He was one of the greatest Polish kings; he defeated the Pomeranians (**battle of Naklo,** 1109) and, by the incorporation of Pomerania (1119–23), reestablished access to the sea. At the same time, he defeated the Emperor Henry V (1109, **battle of Hundsfeld,** near Breslau, now Wrocław) and checked the German advance, but his campaigns in Hungary (1132–35) had no permanent results.

Boleslav completed the organization of the state, in which the great landlords (*nobiles*, or magnates) and gentry (*milites*, knights, or *szlachta*) had become well-defined social classes, the peasantry having steadily lost ground in the periods of confusion. The Church was reorganized under the archbishop of Gnesen, by the papal legate Walo. To avoid dispute, Boleslav fixed the royal succession by seniority. Poland was divided into **five principalities** (Silesia, Great Poland, Masovia, Sandomir, Kraków) for his sons; Kraków was established as the capital, and was to go, with the title of grand duke, to the eldest member of the house of Piast. In actual fact, this arrangement by no means eliminated the dynastic competition but introduced a long period of disruption, during which the nobility and clergy waxed ever more powerful and the ducal or royal power became insignificant. Only the weakness of the neighboring states saved Poland from destruction.

1146–73. Boleslav IV, an ineffectual ruler, during whose reign the Germans, under Albert the Bear and Henry the Lion, supported by Waldemar of Denmark, drove back the Poles from the entire territory along the Baltic and west of the Vistula (1147). Emperor Frederick Barbarossa intervened and forced the submission of Boleslav (1157).

1173–77. Mieszko III, a brutal and despotic prince who antagonized the nobility and was soon driven out by them.

1177–94. CASIMIR II (the Just) was elected by the practical magnates, who extorted privileges from him. In the **Assembly of Lenczyca** (1180) the clergy was also given far-reaching concessions. Casimir attempted to preclude further strife by making the principality of Kraków hereditary in his own line.

1194–1227. Leszek I (the White), whose reign was punctuated by constant wars against Mieszko III, who attempted to regain the throne (d. 1202), and against the latter's son Vladislav Laskonogi (1202–6). The period was one of complete feudal anarchy, with the nobility and clergy controlling the situation.

1227–79. Boleslav V, whose unhappy reign was marked by complete disruption and by constant aggression from neighboring states.

1228. Arrival of the **Teutonic Knights,** called to Prussia by Duke Conrad of Masovia (p. 210). Within the next 50 years, they conquered Prussia and erected a most formidable barrier to Polish access to the sea.

1240. Beginning of great Mongol expansion westward.

1241, April 9. Mongols smashed combined Polish and German forces at Legnica (Leignitz) in southwestern Poland (now Silesia). Although the Mongol leader Batu withdrew for consultation after the death of the Great Khan, enabling the Poles to stave off complete domination, the country was devastated. One result was that large numbers of German settlers were called in, some of whom cleared forest land and colonized new areas in Silesia and Posen (Poznań), others of whom settled in the towns, while the aristocratic parliament (the Sejm) became an ever more powerful institution. In all cases, large concessions in the direction of autonomy were made (Magdeburg law). The German influence meant greater and more efficient exploitation of the soil, development of trade, cultural advance.

1288–90. Further dynastic and feudal warfare with the brief reign of Henry Probus.

1290–96. Przemyslav II. He was crowned king with the consent of the pope (1295) but was murdered soon afterward.

1300–1305. Wenceslas I, king of Bohemia, elected by the nobility but challenged by claimants of the Piast family. He soon resigned the position and returned home.   (To p. 268)

d. KIEVAN RUSSIA

The **eastern Slavs** settled on the territory of present-day European Russia from the 5th to the 8th century A.D. In the 8th century some of the eastern Slavs were under the protectorate of the **Khazars,** an Altaic people who established a strong and prosperous state along the lower Volga. After the end of the 8th century, the northern part of Russia began to be penetrated by the Scandinavian Vikings, called in the old Russian chronicles **Varangians** or **Rus** (hence the name of **Russia**). In the course of the 9th century, the Varangians constantly moved southward along the main waterway leading from the Baltic to the Black Sea, gradually establishing domination over the Slav communities. According to tradition, the Scandinavian chieftain **Rurik** ruled in Novgorod in the 860s. Later he was recognized as the founder of the Russian princely dynasty.

860. The first recorded appearance of the Russians (Varangians) at Constantinople. This was a raid not unlike those of the Norsemen on Britain and France in the same period.

879–912. Prince Oleg, who transferred his residence to Kiev on the Dnieper River. Kiev remained the capital of **Kievan Russia,** a loose federation of territories, until 1169. Oleg also united the eastern Slavs, freed them from Khazar control, and signed a commercial treaty with the Byzantine Empire.

907. The Russians again appeared at Constantinople and extracted trade privileges from the Byzantine emperor. Trade became a leading occupation of the Russian princes, who, with their followers (*druzhina*), protected the merchant ships. On the other hand, private property appears to have been less developed among the eastern Slavs than in the West.

945. Further trade agreements with the Greek Empire testify to ever closer economic connections and no doubt to an increasing cultural contact.

957. The Russian princess **Olga** visited Constantinople and was converted to the Christian faith. This was, however, a personal conversion and may in fact have been Olga's second.

964–72. SVIATOSLAV, the son of Olga. He was the first of the great conquering princes. In 965 he defeated the Khazars on the lower Volga and proceeded to establish a Russian state in place of the Khazar Empire. Called to the Balkans to aid the Greek emperor against the powerful Bulgars, he carried on a successful campaign (967) and decided to establish himself on the lower Danube. At this time his power extended from Novgorod in the north to the Danube in the southwest and to the lower Volga in the southeast. He was forced to abandon Bulgaria in order to resist the **Patzinaks** (Pechenegs), who had entered southern Russia from the east and were threatening Kiev. Having repulsed them (968), Sviatoslav returned to Bulgaria, but he was no more welcome to the Greeks than were the Bulgars. In 971 he was defeated and driven out by the Emperor John Tzimisces (p. 191). Sviatoslav was defeated and killed by the Patzinaks on his way back to Kiev (972).

972–80. With Sviatoslav's death began a dynastic struggle between his sons.

980–1015. The battle ended with the victory of **Vladimir the Saint,** in whose reign (c. 990) the Russians were converted en masse to Christianity in the Orthodox (Byzantine) form. The Russian church was organized on the Greek pattern and was considered to be under the canonical authority of the patriarch of Constantinople. From this time on, the cultural relations between Constantinople and Kiev were very close.

1015–19. Dynastic conflict between the sons of Vladimir.

1019–54. YAROSLAV (the Wise), the greatest ruler of Russia in the Kievan period. He was successful in the struggle with his brother Sviatopolk, but was obliged to leave to another brother, Mstislav, that part of the principality that lay east of the Dnieper River, until Mstislav's death in 1036. Yaroslav was then supreme ruler of all Russia. Extensive building activity at Kiev (Cathedral of St. Sophia). Religious activity (Metropolitan Hilarion and the Monastery of the Caves). Promotion of education. Revision of the **Russian Law** (the earliest known Russian law code), under Byzantine influence. Dynastic alliances with western states (Yaroslav's daughter, Anna, married Henry I of France).

The period following the death of Yaroslav the Great was one of disintegration and decline. Technically the primacy of Kiev continued

GRAND PRINCES OF KIEV (862–1212)

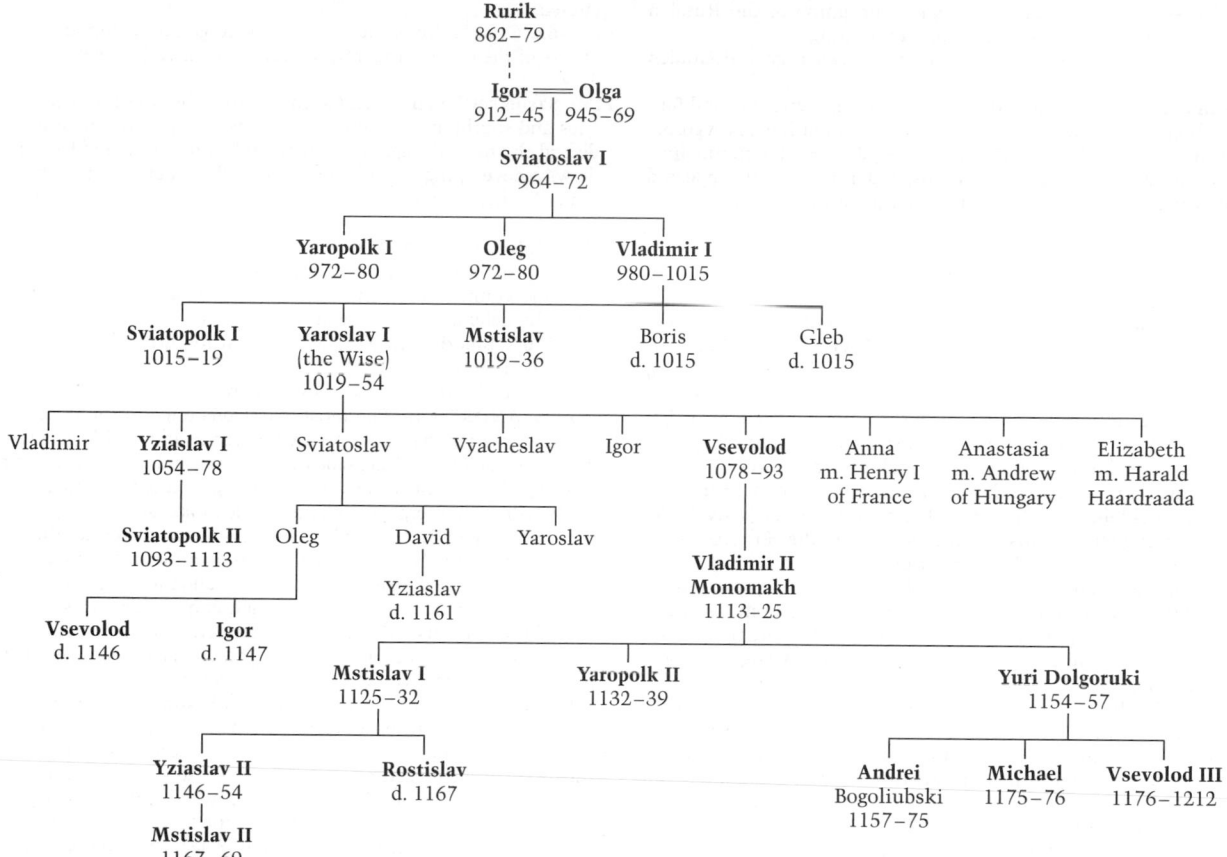

and the power remained concentrated in the family of Yaroslav. Actually, however, Kiev continued to decline in importance, and authority came to be divided between members of the princely family according to a system of seniority and rotation, which led of necessity to much dynastic rivalry and countless combinations, sometimes with Poles and Hungarians.

At the same time the Kievan state was subjected to ever greater pressure from the nomads (Patzinaks and Cumans) moving into southern Russia from the east. The period also witnessed a shifting of the older trade routes, due to the decline of the Baghdad Caliphate and the conquest of Constantinople (1204) by the Latin crusaders.

Emergence of new political centers: Galicia and Volynia in the southwest, principalities characterized by a strongly aristocratic form of government; Novgorod the Great, in the north, controlling territory to the east to the Urals. In Novgorod the assembly of freemen (**Vieche**) reached its fullest development; Suzdal-Vladimir in central Russia, the precursor of the grand duchy of Moscow. In this region the princely power was dominant, and private property was the least developed.

1113–25. VLADIMIR MONOMAKH, prince of Kiev. His reign marked the last period of brilliance at Kiev.

1147. First mention of **Moscow** in one of the chronicles.

1157–74. ANDREI BOGOLIUBSKI, prince of Suzdal. He repressed the rising power of the nobles (boyars), united a large block of territory, and established his capital at Vladimir.

1169. Andrei conquered Kiev, which became part of the Vladimir principality. But the new state underwent a marked decline on the death of the ruler.

1199–1205. Zenith of the Galician principality under Prince Roman.

1201. Foundation of Riga, which became the center of German missionary enterprise and commercial expansion.

1202. Foundation of the German Order of Swordbearers by Bishop Albert of Livonia (Latvia).

1219. Conquest of Estonia by Waldemar II of Denmark.

1223. Battle of the Kalka River, near the Sea of Azov. The Mongols (Tatars), under Subutai, invaded southern Russia from the Transcaucasus region and completely defeated a coalition of Russian princes and Cuman leaders.

1226. The **Teutonic Knights** (p. 210) were commissioned to conquer and convert Prussia. They united with the Swordbearers in 1237.

1236–63. ALEXANDER NEVSKI, prince first of Novgorod and after 1252, of Vladimir.

1237–40. The **Mongol conquest,** under the leadership of Batu (p. 153). The great armies of the invaders swept over southern and central Russia and into Europe, coming within 60 miles of Novgorod. They took Kiev (1240) and ultimately established themselves (1242) at Sarai on the lower Volga. The **Khanate of the Golden Horde** for two centuries thereafter acted as suzerain of all Russia, levying tribute and taking military contingents, but for the rest leaving the princes in control, respecting the Russian Church, and interfering little. Moreover, the most western parts of Russia had a substantially different fate. The principalities of **Galicia** and **Volynia** gradually replaced Mongol suzerainty with that of Lithuania. The rulers of these lands became members of the Lithuanian *seimas* (assembly of nobles). This was the beginning of the **Ukrainians** and the **Belorussians** as peoples distinct from the Great Russians.

1240. Alexander Nevski defeated the Swedes under Birger Jarl on the Neva River and thus broke the force of the Swedish advance.

1242. Alexander defeated the Teutonic Knights in a **battle on Lake Peipus.**

1252. As prince of Vladimir, Alexander Nevski did his utmost to prevent insurrections against Tatar rule and built up a system of protection based on submission and conciliation.

1253. Daniel of Volynia attempted to organize a crusade against the Tatars. To secure papal aid, he accepted the union of the Russian Church with Rome, but his efforts came to nothing.

1263. Death of Alexander Nevski on his way back from the Golden Horde.

Russian culture in this period was under strong Byzantine and Bulgarian influence. Noteworthy churches were built at Kiev, Novgorod, and Cernigov in the 11th and 12th centuries, decorated with fine frescoes. Church literature was voluminous, and, further, there appeared the first chronicles and epics of struggles against the nomads.

(To p. 270)

e. HUNGARY

896. The Hungarians, or Magyars, organized in a number of tribes, occupied the valley of the middle Danube and Theiss (Tisza). Under **Arpad** (d. 907) they had come from southern Russia by way of Moldova, driven on by the Patzinaks (Pechenegs) and other Asian peoples. The Hungarians were themselves nomads of the Finno-Ugrian family. For more than half a century after their occupation of Hungary, they continued their raids, both toward the east and toward the west.

906. The Hungarians destroyed the rising Slavic kingdom of Moravia.

955. Battle of Lechfeld (p. 178), in which Emperor Otto I decisively defeated the raiding Hungarians. From this time on, the Hungarians began to settle down and establish a frontier.

972–97. Geza, the organizer of the princely power. He began to reduce the tribal leaders and invited Christian missionaries from Germany (Pilgrim of Passau, 974; **St. Adalbert of Prague**, 993). Christianization had already begun from the east, and was furthered by large numbers of war prisoners.

997–1038. St. Stephen (I), greatest ruler of the Arpad dynasty. He suppressed eastern Christianity by force and crusaded against paganism, which was still favored by the tribal chiefs. Stephen allied with the west, married a Bavarian princess, called in Roman churchmen and monks, and endowed them with huge tracts of land. With the help of the clergy, he broke the power of the tribal chieftains, took over their land as royal domain, administered through counts *(föispán)* placed over counties *(vármegyék).* The counts and high churchmen formed a royal council. Every encouragement was given to agriculture and trade, and a methodical system of frontier defense was built up (large belt of swamps and forests, wholly uninhabited and protected by regular frontier guards; as time went on this frontier was gradually extended).

1001. Stephen was crowned with a crown sent by the pope. He was canonized in 1083.

1002. Stephen defeated an anti-Christian insurrection in Transylvania.

1030. Attacks of the Germans under Conrad II.

1038–77. A period of dynastic struggles over the succession, every member of the Arpad family claiming a share of the power and sometimes calling in the Germans for support.

1038–46. Peter Urseolo, son of Stephen's sister and the doge of Venice, succeeded to the throne.

1046. Peter was overthrown in the course of a great **pagan rising** of the tribal chiefs, who massacred the Christians and destroyed the churches. This was the last serious revolt.

1047–60. Andrew I, who managed to restore the royal power.

1049–52. The three campaigns of Emperor Henry III against the Hungarians. Andrew managed to hold his own, and in 1058 the emperor recognized Hungary's independence from the empire.

1061–63. Bela I, brother of Andrew and popular hero of the campaigns against the Germans.

1074–77. Geza I.

1077–95. ST. LADISLAS (László) I (canonized 1192), the first great king after St. Stephen. He supported the pope in his conflicts with the emperor, and at home restored order and prosperity.

1095–1116. Coloman (Kalman) I. Another strong ruler.

1097–1102. Coloman conquered Dalmatia from the Venetian Republic. Thus practically the whole of Croatia was incorporated into Hungary and came to be governed for the king by a *ban* (viceroy). Nevertheless, the Croat landed magnates preserved their local assembly, while the Adriatic port of Dubrovnik (Ragusa) gradually emerged as an independent city-republic with strong commercial positions in southeastern Europe.

1116–31. Stephen II, in whose reign the dynastic struggles were resumed.

1141–62. Geza II. Intestine conflicts were greatly complicated by the efforts of the Greek emperor, Manual I, to extend his sway over Hungary.

1150. Saxon settlement (i.e., Germans from the Moselle region) in the Zips and southern Transylvania regions. They were called in to help defend the frontiers against Poland and Byzantium, and had much to do with developing agriculture, trade, and townbuilding. In this period many Pechenegs and Szeklers were also established for frontier protection.

1173–96. BELA III, who had been educated at Constantinople. He married the sister of Philip Augustus of France and established a close dynastic connection with France. Bela was a strong ruler who successfully defended Dalmatia against Venice.

1196–1204. Emeric (Imre) I, whose position was challenged by his brother Andrew.

1204–5. Ladislas III, dethroned by Andrew.

1205–35. ANDREW II. The most disastrous reign in the Arpad period. Andrew was renowned for his extravagance and for his generosity to his foreign favorites. A crusade to the Holy Land (1217) cost him much money, which he raised by alienating huge tracts of the royal domain, facilitating the emergence of large landed magnates, or oligarchs.

1222. The **Golden Bull,** forced on Andrew by the lesser nobility or gentry, led by Andrew's own son, Bela. This document became the charter of feudal privilege. It exempted the gentry and the clergy from taxation, granted them freedom to dispose of their domains as they saw fit, guaranteed them against arbitrary imprisonment and confiscation, and assured them an annual assembly to present grievances. No lands or offices were to be given to foreigners or Jews.

1224. The privileges of the Transylvanian Saxons were set down. They were given practical self-government, directly under the king.

1235–70. BELA IV. A strong ruler who tried desperately to make good the losses of the preceding reign. The magnates, in reply, attempted to set up a rival ruler, and Bela in turn allowed some 40,000 families of Cumans, who were driven westward by the Mongol invasions, to settle in the Theiss (Tisza) region in the hope of securing support against the magnates.

1241. The **great Mongol invasion,** which took the country by surprise, in the midst of its own dissensions. Bela's army was overwhelmingly defeated at Muhi on the Theiss, and he was obliged to flee to the Adriatic. The Mongols followed him, but suddenly gave up their conquests when news arrived of the death of the Great Khan. Nevertheless, the Mongol invasion left the country devastated. For defense purposes, the nobility was allowed to build castles, and these soon became bases for feudal warfare and for campaigns against the king himself.

1246. Bela defeated Frederick of Austria, the last of the Babenbergs, who had taken advantage of the Mongol invasion to appropriate some of the western provinces.

1265–70. Wars of Bela against Ottokar II of Bohemia.

1270–72. Stephen V, a weak ruler.

1272–90. Ladislas (László) IV. His efforts to curb the feudal aristocracy were of little avail, but in alliance with Rudolf of Habsburg he succeeded in breaking the power of Ottokar in the **battle of Dürnkrut** (1278).

1290–1301. Andrew III, last of the native dynasty. He continued the struggle against the domination of the feudal aristocracy, but with little success. (To p. 272)

f. SERBIA

650. Approximate date of the completion of the Slav occupation of the Balkan area. Part of the Slav people extended as far west as Carniola and Carinthia, but these (the Slovenes) were conquered by the Franks in the early 9th century and were thenceforth part of the German Empire.

818. The **Croats,** who had also been conquered by the Franks, revolted but were again subdued.

924. Tomislav became king of Croatia, accepting his crown from the pope. He ruled over latter-day Croatia and over the territory as far

THE ARPAD DYNASTY OF HUNGARY (907–1301) AND
THE PREMYSLID KINGS OF BOHEMIA (1198–1378)

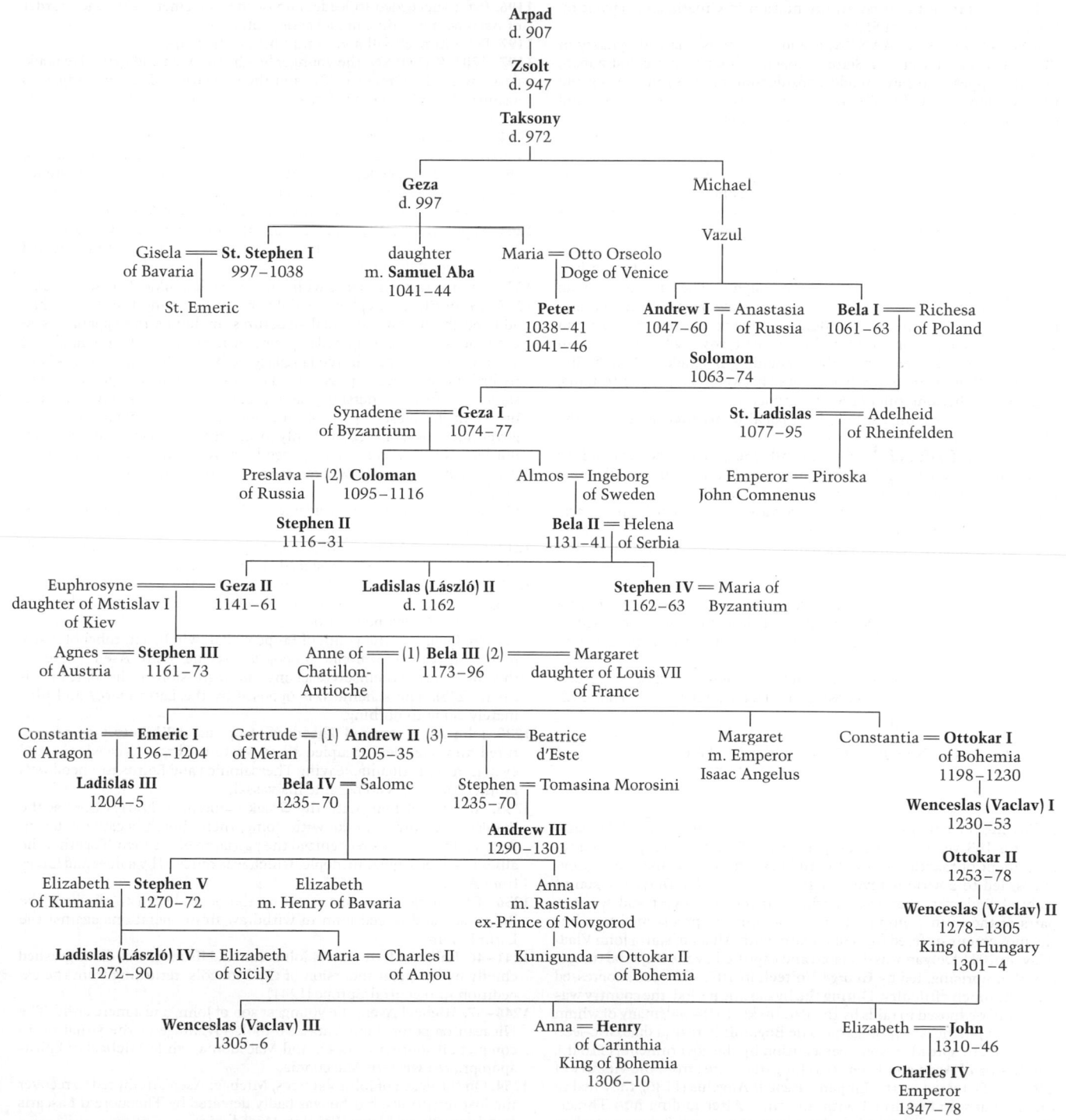

south as Montenegro, though the coastal towns were mostly under Byzantine control.

960. Death of Cheslav, who had made the first effort to unite the Serbs. The Serbs, inhabiting a mountainous area, were divided into tribes and clans, under headmen or *zupans*. The grand zupan held an honorary preeminence. Technically the territory was under Byzantine suzer-

ainty, which, when the Eastern Empire was strong, was effectively exercised. By the end of the 10th century the inhabitants of present Serbia and eastern Bosnia had for the most part accepted Eastern Christianity, while western Bosnia and Croatia leaned toward Roman Catholicism. However, both socially and culturally, the Serbs seemed to be one of the most westernized Eastern Orthodox peoples.

1077. Mikhail of Serbia was crowned by a papal legate.

1081–1101. Bodin established a Serbian state in Zeta (i.e., Montenegro).

1102. Croatia was joined with Hungary in a dynastic union, after the defeat of the last ruler, Petar, by King Ladislas. This involved the definitive victory of the western orientation in Croatia and separation from the other southern Slavs.

1168–96. STEPHEN NEMANYA, founder of the Nemanyid dynasty in the Raska (i.e., Rascia, or Serbia proper). Though only grand zupan, Stephen appears to have made considerable progress in uniting the various clans. He definitely adopted the Eastern Orthodox faith and persecuted the **Bogomils,** who were forced across the frontier into Bosnia, which at that time was ruled by a strong prince, Kulin (d. 1204). The death of Manuel I Comnenus (1180) and the subsequent decline of the Eastern Empire gave Stephen an opportunity to establish his independence from Constantinople and to conquer extensive territories to the south. In 1196 he retired to a monastery on Mt. Athos that had been founded by his son, **St. Sava.** Stephen died in 1200.

1196–1223. STEPHEN NEMANYA II, the son of the preceding. The beginning of his reign was marked by a struggle with his elder brother, Vukan, to whom Montenegro had been assigned. The Hungarians, who became an ever greater menace to Serbia, supported Vukan, and Stephen was forced to flee to the Bulgarian court. He returned with an army of Cumans supplied by **Kaloyan** (see below), who appropriated for himself most of eastern Serbia, including Belgrade and Nish. Stephen's brother St. Sava finally mediated between the two contestants, and Stephen became ruler of Serbia proper.

1217. Stephen was crowned king by a papal legate (hence Stephen the First-Crowned).

1219. St. Sava, fearful of the Roman influence, visited Nicaea and induced the Greek patriarch to recognize him as archbishop of all Serbia and as head of an autocephalous (independent) church.

1222. Stephen was recrowned by St. Sava with a crown from Nicaea, thus reestablishing the Eastern orientation.

1234–42. Vladislav. He married a daughter of Tsar John Asen II of Bulgaria, and during this period much of eastern Serbia was under Bulgarian domination.

1242–76. Urosh I, brother of the preceding two rulers. He married a daughter of the deposed Latin emperor, Baldwin II, and established an alliance with Charles of Anjou, heir of the Latin claims to Constantinople.

1254. The Hungarians, who already held part of northern Serbia, established their suzerainty over Bosnia and Herzegovina.   *(To p. 272)*

g. THE SECOND BULGARIAN EMPIRE

(From p. 191)

Following the collapse of the First Bulgarian Empire in 1018, Bulgaria was, for 168 years, an integral part of the Byzantine Empire. The replacement of taxation in kind with taxation in cash, and other grievances, led to a serious revolt in 1040, led by **Peter Delyan,** a son of Gabriel Radomir, that was confined to the northwest and western parts of the former empire. Delyan had himself proclaimed tsar, but the movement suffered from his rivalry with Alusian, son of John Vladislav. In 1041 Delyan was defeated and captured by the imperial troops. Another uprising, led by **George Voitech** in 1072–73, was suppressed without much difficulty. During the Byzantine period, the country was constantly exposed to raids by the Patzinaks (1048–54), many of whom settled in northeastern Bulgaria. The **Bogomil heresy** (a dualistic sect) continued to spread, despite persecution by the government (1110 ff.).

1185. Rising of Asen and Peter, two Bulgarian lords from the vicinity of Tirnovo. Defeated by the Emperor Isaac II Angelus (1186), they fled to the Cumans and returned with an army. After raiding into Thrace, they accepted a truce that left them in possession of Bulgaria north of the Balkan Mountains.

1189. Asen attempted to effect an alliance with Frederick Barbarossa and the leaders of the Third Crusade, against the Greeks. This came to nothing, but the Bulgarians resumed their raids into Thrace and Macedonia. An imperial army under Isaac Angelus was completely defeated in a **battle near Berrhoe.**

1196. Peter succeeded to leadership of the movement after the murder of Asen by boyar (i.e., noble) conspirators.

1197. Peter himself fell a victim to his boyar rivals.

1197–1207. KALOJAN, the younger brother of Asen and Peter. He made peace with the Greeks (1201) and then engaged (1202) in campaigns against the Serbs (taking of Nish) and the Hungarians, whom he drove back over the Danube.

1204. The **collapse of the Byzantine Empire** gave Kalojan an excellent opportunity to reaffirm his dominion. By recognizing the primacy of the pope, he succeeded in securing the appointment of a primate for Bulgaria and in getting himself crowned king by the papal legate. At the same time, he took over the whole of western Macedonia.

1205. Supported by the Cumans and the local Greeks, Kalojan completely defeated the Frankish crusaders near Adrianople and captured the Emperor Baldwin I.

1207. Kalojan was murdered while besieging Salonika (Thessalonica).

1207–18. Boril, the nephew of Kalojan. By this time the Bulgars had adopted the Byzantine social structures, including the **appanage system:** the tsar was considered supreme owner of the state, the land, and even the official and Church language; only members of the tsar's family had the privilege of possessing large estates as **appanage,** where the same system of ownership was reproduced on a local level. Hence, unlike in the West, separatism did not lead to the emergence of self-governing cities, but resulted only in an overall weakening of the state. Boril's position was not recognized by most of the other members of Asens family, some of whom attempted to set up independent principalities.

1208. Boril was completely defeated by the Franks and ultimately (1213) was obliged to make peace.

1217. Ivan (John) **Asen,** son of Asen, supported by Galicia, began a revolt in northern Bulgaria. He besieged and took Tirnovo.

1218–41. JOHN ASEN II, whose reign marked the apogee of the Second Bulgarian Empire. John was a mild and generous ruler, much beloved even by the Greek population.

1228–30. Owing to the youth of Emperor Baldwin II, a number of Frank nobles at Constantinople proposed making John Asen emperor, thereby securing themselves against the aggression of Theodore of Epirus (p. 238). The scheme was opposed by the Latin clergy and ultimately came to nothing.

1230. John Asen defeated Theodore of Epirus at **Klokotnitsa** and captured him. He then occupied all of western Thrace, Macedonia, and even northern Albania, leaving Thessalonica and Epirus to Theodore's brother Manuel, who became his vassal.

1235. Alliance of John with the Greek emperor of Nicaea against the Franks. The Bulgars broke with Rome, their church became independent, and the Greeks recognized the patriarch of Tirnovo. Together the allies besieged Constantinople, which was relieved by a fleet and forces from Achaia.

1236. The Hungarians, instigated by the pope, began to threaten the Bulgarians and forced John to withdraw from operations against the Latin Empire.

1241–46. Kaliman I, the son of John Asen II. His reign was distinguished chiefly by the great incursion of the Mongols, returning from the expedition into central Europe (1241).

1246–57. Michael Asen, the youngest son of John, and a mere child. The Nicaean emperor, John Vatatzes, took advantage of the situation to conquer all southern Thrace and Macedonia, while Michael of Epirus appropriated western Macedonia.

1254. On the death of John Vatatzes, Michael Asen attempted to recover the lost territories, but he was badly defeated by Theodore II Lascaris at **Adrianople** and later (1255) in Macedonia.

1256. Kaliman II, who, with support of the boyars, drove out Michael Asen, only to be deposed and expelled in his turn.   *(To p. 272)*

5. CHRISTIAN STATES IN THE EASTERN MEDITERRANEAN, 1000–1300

a. THE BYZANTINE EMPIRE

(From p. 190)
For a complete list of the Byzantine emperors, see Appendix II.

The period of the later Macedonian emperors (to 1055) and the succeeding century was marked by barbarian invasions in the Balkans, advances of the Normans on the remaining Byzantine possessions in Italy, pressure from the Seljuk Turks on the eastern frontier, popular hostility to mercantile privileges granted to Pisan and Venetian businessmen, and political disputes between the clerical bureaucratic nobility in the capital and the military baronage in the countryside.

1025–28. CONSTANTINE VIII, the younger brother of Basil II.

1027. The **Patzinaks,** who had invaded the Balkans, were finally driven back over the Danube by General Constantine Diogenes.

1028–50. ZOË, empress. She was the third daughter of Constantine and, though 48 years old at her accession, married three times, associating her husbands: Romanos, Michael, and Constantine IX *seriatum* in the imperial office.

1028–34. ROMANUS III (Argyropolus), an official 60 years old, first husband of Zoë. He made great efforts to gain popularity by catering to the populace, the nobility, and especially the Church. The patriarchate was permitted to persecute the Monophysites of Syria, thousands of whom fled to Muslim territory. The hatred engendered by this policy helps to explain the Seljuk advance in subsequent years.

1030. Romanus suffered a severe defeat in a campaign against the Muslim emirs who attacked Syria.

1031. The situation was saved by the victories of **Georgios Maniakes,** greatest imperial general of the period.

1032. A combined Byzantine-Ragusan fleet defeated the Saracen pirates in the Adriatic.

1034–41. MICHAEL IV (the Paphlagonian), second husband of Zoë. He was a man of lowly origin who promptly established his brothers (mostly men of energy and ability) in high office.

1034–35. The Byzantine fleets, manned by the Norseman Harald Haardraade and Scandinavian mercenaries, repeatedly defeated the Saracen pirates off the Anatolian coast and ravaged the coasts of North Africa.

1038. Maniakes and Haardraade, with Scandinavian and Italian mercenaries and with the support of the Byzantine fleets, stormed Messina and defeated the Sicilian Saracens, first at **Rametta** (1038), then at **Dragina** (1040).

1040. Revolt of the Bulgarians under Peter Delyan, a descendant of Tsar Samuel. The revolt was directed against the harsh fiscal policy of the government. The Bulgars attacked Salonika (Thessalonica), but the city held out. Ultimately the movement collapsed as a result of dissension among the leaders. Bulgaria was then incorporated in the empire and the autocephalous church of Ochrid became the prey of the patriarchal hierarchy.

1042–55. CONSTANTINE IX (Monomachus), the third husband of Zoë, a scholarly person wholly out of sympathy with the army and with the military aristocracy. He systematically neglected the frontier defenses and the forces.

1042. Maniakes totally defeated the Normans, who had begun their attack on southern Italy in the **Battle of Monopoli** (near Naples).

1043. Revolt of Maniakes, representing the disaffection of the military classes. Maniakes landed at Durazzo and prepared to march on the capital, but he was accidentally killed on the way.

1046. The Byzantine forces occupied Ani and took over the government of Armenia, which became another field for clerical exploitation.

1048. The imperial generals defeated the advancing Seljuk armies at **Stragna.**

1050. Death of Zoë. Her husband Constantine continued to reign alone.

1051. Expulsion of the Patzinaks from Bulgaria, after years of ravaging and unsuccessful Byzantine campaigns.

1042–56. THEODORA, empress, the elder sister of Zoë. An intelligent, vigorous, and popular ruler, but already advanced in age.

1054. Final schism between Rome and Constantinople. The long-standing friction between the papacy and the Eastern patriarch had come to a head with the conquest of parts of southern Italy by the Normans, who were supported by the papacy. The patriarch Michael Kerularios disputed the claim of Pope Leo IX to jurisdiction in southern Italy. Negotiations were opened, but each side assumed an uncompromising attitude, and the rift became unbridgeable.

1057–59. Isaac I Comnenus, proclaimed by the insurgents. He was an able and energetic army man who promptly abolished a host of sinecures, undertook the reform of the finances. Isaac, already advanced in years, soon found his work too arduous and abdicated.

1059–67. CONSTANTINE X (Dukas), a high official of the finance department, ascended the throne after Isaac's abdication. Constantine introduced a period of domination by the civil officials, church, and scholars, during which the army was viewed with suspicion, neglected, and driven to hostile acts.

1060. The Normans took Rheggio, completing the conquest of Calabria.

1064. The Seljuks, under Alp Arslan, took Ani and ravaged Armenia.

1068–71. Romanus IV Diogenes, who, on Constantine's death, married the widowed empress, Eudoxia. Romanus was an ambitious soldier who did his best to check the advance of the enemy in the east and the west.

1068. The Normans took Otranto and then Bari (1071), the last Byzantine outpost. This marked the **end of the Byzantine rule in Italy.**

1068–69. Romanus succeeded in repulsing the Seljuks, though they repeatedly raided through the whole of eastern Anatolia.

1071. BATTLE OF MANZIKERT (north of Lake Van). Romanus had concentrated huge forces for a decisive battle, and he rejected all offers of a settlement. In the course of a hard-fought battle he was deserted by Andronicus Dukas and other Byzantine magnates. Romanus was defeated and captured, but then was released by the Seljuks. He attempted to regain the Byzantine throne, but was defeated by his opponents and blinded. He died soon afterward.

1071–78. MICHAEL VII (Parapinakes), a son of Constantine X. His elevation meant another victory for the bureaucratic group. Michael made the great scholar **Michael Psellus** his chief adviser and devoted himself to the pursuit of learning. The military system was again allowed to fall into neglect.

1074. The emperor concluded a **treaty with the Seljuks** in order to secure their aid against his uncle, who had set himself up as a pretender. The Seljuks defeated the pretender, but took advantage of the situation to spread themselves over a large part of Anatolia.

1078–81. NICEPHORUS III (Botaniates), emperor after Michael's abdication. His accession was met by a number of insurrections in various parts of the army, but these were suppressed by General Alexius Comnenus.

1081. Revolt of Alexius Comnenus himself. He seized Constantinople with a force of mercenaries, who thereupon plundered the capital. The victory of Comnenus meant the final success of the military aristocracy and the beginning of a new period of military achievement.

1081–1118. Alexius I Comnenus, an able general, vigorous administrator, conscientious ruler, and shrewd diplomat. Having to rely on the great feudal families, he attempted to win their support with lavish grants of honors and ranks. At the same time, he tried to use the high clergy to counterbalance the influence of the nobility. He reformed the judicial and financial systems and systematically used his financial resources to buy off the enemies he could not conquer.

1081–85. The war against the Normans under **Robert Guiscard.** The latter landed in Epirus with a large force and besieged Durazzo (Dyracchium). Alexius bought the support of the Venetians with extensive trade privileges (1082), but Guiscard defeated the emperor in the **Battle of Pharsalus,** after which he took Durazzo. The war was continued by Robert's son, Bohemund, who again defeated Alexius and in 1083 conquered all Macedonia as far as the Vardar. But the advance was broken by the resistance of Larissa, by the guerrilla tactics of the natives (who hated the heretical Latins), and by the Seljuk cavalry employed by the emperor. In 1085 the combined Byzantine and Venetian fleets defeated the Normans near Corfu. The death of Robert Guiscard at the same time led to dissension among his sons and the abandonment of the Balkan project.

SELJUK SULTANS (1055–1194)

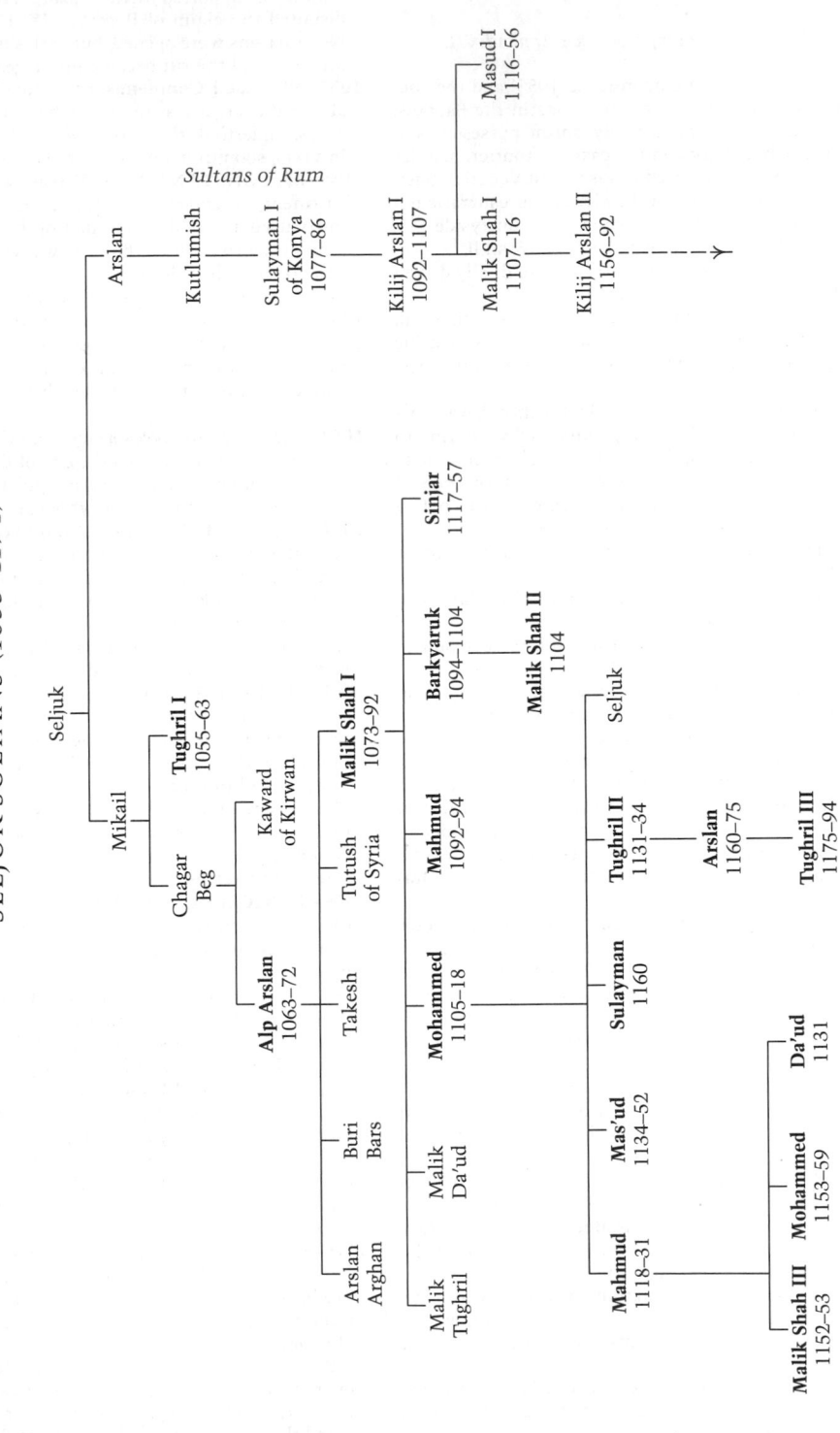

1083–1153/54. Anna Comnenus, eldest daughter of Alexius I, a patron of scholarship, and, with the production of the *Alexiad*, an able scholar in her own right. The *Alexiad*, a long panegyric on her father's reign, is a major historical source for the period.

1086–91. Revolt of the Bogomils in Thrace and Bulgaria. The heretics were supported by the Patzinaks and Cumans and were able to defeat Alexius and a large army (**battle of Drystra**, or Dorostolon, 1087). The Cumans then ravaged the entire eastern Balkan region as far as Constantinople until Alexius bought them off, took them into imperial service, and used them (1091) to annihilate the Patzinaks (**Battle of Leburnion**).

1092. Death of Malik Shah, ruler of the Seljuk Empire of Iconium; this paved the way for the partial reconquest of Anatolia.

1094. Constantine Diogenes, a pretender to the throne, crossed the Danube with an army of Cumans and besieged Adrianople, but was then defeated in the battle of **Taurocomon.**

1096–97. The First Crusade (p. 233). The Crusaders, of whom Bohemund was one of the leaders, were looked on with great suspicion in the east, where there was little interest in a movement organized by the heretical Latin pope. But Alexius was unable to stop the Crusaders and therefore devoted himself to managing the movement. He induced them to promise to do homage to the empire for all territory reconquered from the infidel. The crusading **victories at Nicaea** and **Dorylaeum** (1097) enabled Alexius to recover the entire western coast of Anatolia.

1098–1108. Second war with the Normans. The Crusaders, having regained Antioch (lost to the Turks only in 1085), turned it over to Bohemund, who refused to recognize Alexius's suzerainty. War broke out. Bohemund returned to Italy and raised a huge army, with which he appeared in Epirus (1104). He failed in his siege of Durazzo, and Alexius wisely avoided open battle. Ultimately (1108) Bohemund agreed to make peace, recognizing Byzantine suzerainty over Antioch.

1110–17. War against the Seljuks, who again advanced to the Bosporus. In 1116 Alexius won a resounding victory at **Philomelion,** which induced the Turks to make peace at **Akroinon** (1117); they abandoned the entire coastal area of Anatolia (north, west, and south) and all of Anatolia west of a line from Sinope through Ancyra (Ankara) and Philomelion.

1111. Trade privileges granted to the Pisans. This was part of the emperor's effort to draw the Pisans away from the Normans and at the same time to counterbalance the extensive trade position of the Venetians.

1118–43. JOHN II COMNENUS, a ruler of high moral integrity; mild, brave, and sincere. He devoted his attention chiefly to the east, with the object of recovering the old frontier of the Euphrates and of subjecting the Latin states of Syria to the empire.

1120–21. In a successful campaign against the Seljuks, John recovered southwestern Anatolia. He was diverted from further conquests by continued incursions of the Patzinaks in the Balkans.

1122. The Patzinaks were completely defeated and thenceforth did not threaten the empire.

1122–26. War with Venice, resulting from John's refusal to renew the extensive trading privileges, which the Venetians had been exploiting to the full. The Venetian fleets ravaged the islands of the Aegean, occupied Corfu and Cephalonia, and ultimately (1126) forced John to renew the privileges.

1124. Intervention of the emperor on behalf of Bela II in Hungary, initiating a policy that continued throughout the century. The objective of the Comneni was to prevent the Hungarians from establishing control over the Slavic regions of Dalmatia, Croatia, and Serbia. Through the **Peace of 1126** the emperor secured Branicova, a vital bridgehead on the Danube.

1134–37. Conquest of Cilician (Little) Armenia, which was allied with the Latin kingdom of Antioch. John forced Raymond of Antioch to do homage for his domain.

1143–80. Manuel I Comnenus, the son of John, an adroit statesman and ambitious soldier, and the greatest and most splendid of the Comneni. During his reign Constantinople came to be accepted as the capital of the Western world and the center of culture. Its brilliant art was imitated in the East and in the West. Manuel married a Latin princess (Maria of Antioch) and throughout his career cherished the hope of resurrecting a universal empire. Hence his association with and employment of Latin nobles, who intermarried with the Greek aristocracy; his constant toying with the idea of reunion with Rome; his designs on Italian territory; and his antagonism toward the Hohenstaufen emperors. All this tended to arouse much hostility among the Greeks (accentuated by the high-handed activities of the Italian traders), to cost the empire inordinate sums of money, and to involve repeated conflict with the Normans. The emperor's preoccupation in the west at the same time forced him to neglect the east, where the Seljuk sultanate of Iconium (Rum) was able to effect a marked recovery.

1147–58. War with Roger of Sicily. The Norman fleets ravaged Euboea and Attica, took and plundered Thebes and Corinth, carried away large numbers of the silk workers, who were established at Palermo. The emperor, having neglected the Byzantine fleet, was obliged to buy the aid of Venice with extensive trading rights (1148). The Venetians helped to reconquer Corfu (1149) and paved the way for the Byzantine conquest of Ancona (1151). But efforts to extend the Greek power in Italy met with failure (1154), and Manuel in the end had to agree to an inconclusive peace (1158).

1147–49. The Second Crusade (p. 233). The Crusaders almost came to blows with the Greeks at Constantinople; Manuel, by diplomacy, prevented a clash. The Greeks did nothing to prevent the defeat of the Crusaders in Anatolia.

1152–54. Successful war against the Hungarians, who attempted to make good their claims to Serbia and Bosnia. Peace was made in 1156, with the Hungarians recognizing the emperor's suzerainty.

1155. Trade privileges granted to Genoa, the emperor hoping thereby to counteract the domination of the Venetians.

1158–59. An expedition against Raymond of Antioch forced the latter to renew his homage.

1161. Kilidj Asrlan IV, sultan of Rum, made peace with the empire, recognizing the emperor's primacy.

1165–68. War with the Hungarians. The imperial forces took Dalmatia and in the final peace (1168) received also part of Croatia. The following years Manuel interfered actively in Hungarian dynastic affairs. Bela III was practically his vassal.

1170–77. War with Venice, the natural result of the Byzantine acquisitions in Dalmatia and Italy. The emperor arrested all Venetian traders in Constantinople and confiscated their goods, but with a neglected fleet he was able to do little. The Venetians conquered Ragusa (1171) and Chios (1171), though they failed in an attack on Ancona (1173). In 1175 the Venetians made an alliance with the Normans against the empire and thereby forced Manuel to yield. Through the **Peace of 1176,** the trade privileges were renewed and the emperor paid a heavy indemnity.

1176–77. War against the Seljuks. The Byzantines were defeated at **Myriocephalon** (1176), but in the next year Manuel defeated the enemy in Bithynia, while John Vatatzes drove the Seljuks out of the Meander Valley.

1180–83. Alexius II Comnenus, the son of Manuel, who ruled under the regency of his mother, Maria of Antioch. The regent relied almost entirely on Latins in her service.

1182. Revolt of the populace of Constantinople against the Latins, officials, and traders, who were brutally cut down in a great massacre. The mob forced the proclamation of **Andronicus I Comnenus.**

1183–85. Andronicus, an uncle of the boy-emperor. He ruled first as co-emperor but in 1183 had Alexius strangled and became sole ruler. Through persecution, confiscations, and executions, Andronicus cleaned the court circle; got rid of the hated Latins; abolished the sale of offices, sinecures, etc.; reformed the judiciary; lightened the taxes. All this was a policy directed against the powerful official and landed aristocracy and, had it been carried through, might have led to a thoroughgoing reform of the empire.

1185. The Norman attack. The Normans took Durazzo, sent an army and a navy against Salonika, which they stormed, and massacred the Greeks. This attack led to a revolt of the Greek nobility against Andronicus, who was deposed, tortured, and executed.

1185. Victory of the Byzantine general Alexius Branas over the Normans at Demetritsa. By 1191 the Normans were driven out of the Balkans and even out of Durazzo and Corfu.

1185–88. The great insurrection in Bulgaria, led by Peter and Asen. This

THE COMNENI AND ANGELI (1057–1204)

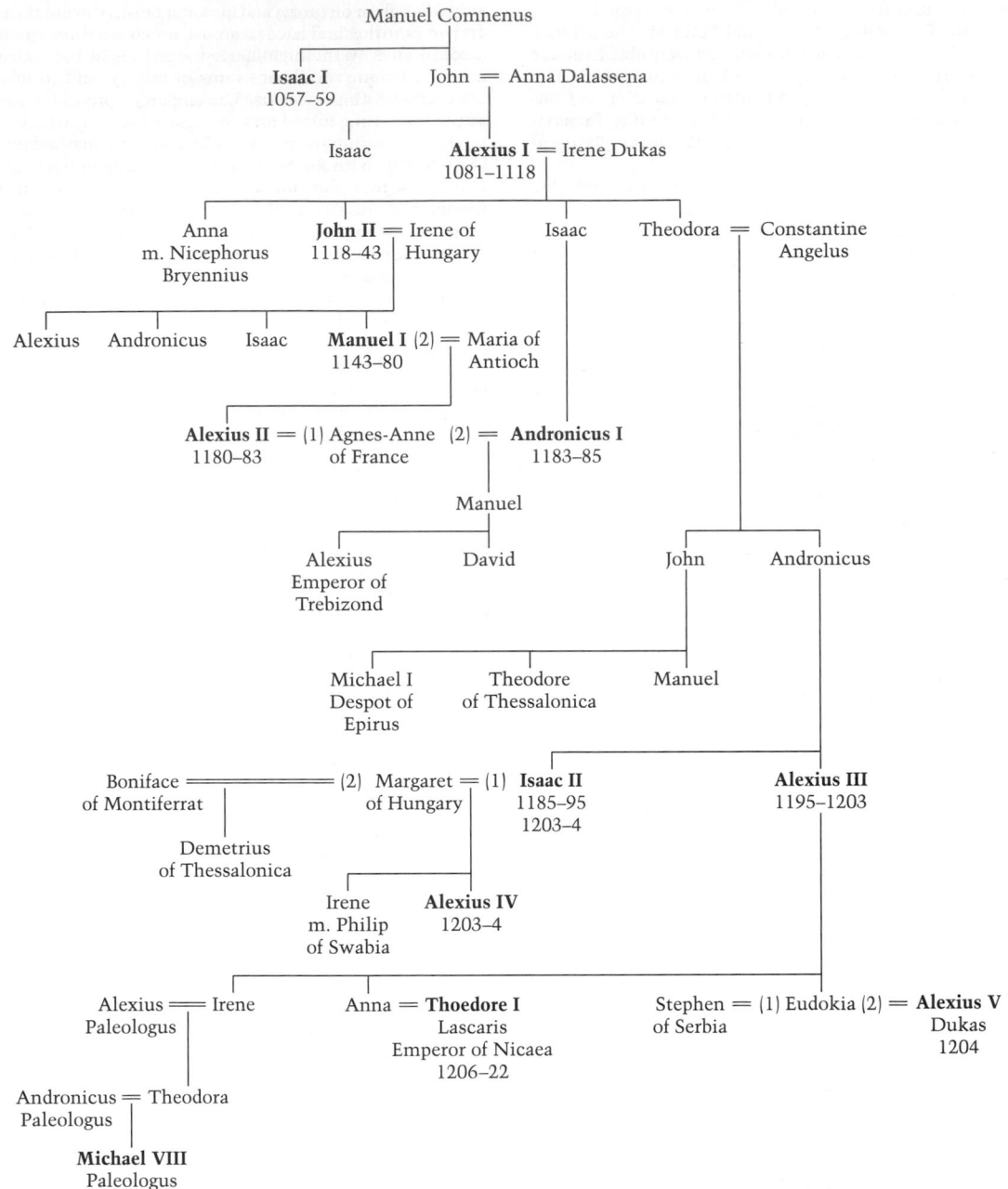

was due primarily to the extortion of the imperial fiscal agents. The revolt was supported by the Cumans and resulted in the devastation of much of the Balkan region and the annihilation of much of the Greek population. Though at times successful, the Greek commanders were unable to suppress the movement, which resulted in the formation of a new Bulgarian state north of the Balkan Mountains (1188).

1185–95. ISAAC ANGELUS, leader of the insurgents. His accession meant a return of the old negligence and corruption. Within a brief time, the entire empire began to disintegrate. In the provinces, the powerful families (i.e., Sguros in Greece; Gabras at Trebizond) began to set up as independent potentates.

1187. Fall of Jerusalem. Isaac, in fear of another crusade, allied himself with Saladin.

1189. The Third Crusade (p. 233). Frederick Barbarossa was welcomed in Bulgaria by Asen, who offered him an army for use against the empire. But Frederick avoided friction, and Isaac did not oppose the crossing of the Crusaders into Anatolia. The death of Saladin (1193) relieved the danger from the east.

1190–94. Continuation of the war in Bulgaria. The Byzantine forces were defeated at Berrhoe (1190) and at Arcadiopolis (1194).

1195–1203. ALEXIUS III, the brother of Isaac, whom he deposed and blinded.

1196. The Western emperor, Henry VI, heir to the Norman domains, demanded Durazzo and Thessalonica. Alexius settled for a huge monetary payment, and Henry's death (1197) removed the immediate threat from that quarter.

1201. Peace with the Bulgars, who were allowed to retain most of the eastern Balkan area, under the younger brother of the Asens, Joannitsa (Kaloyan, 1197–1207).

1202–4. The Fourth Crusade (p. 236). The Crusaders took Durazzo (1203) and arrived at Constantinople (June 1203). The emperor thereupon fled to Adrianople (July). His deposed brother, Isaac, was set upon the throne with his son, the accomplice of the Crusaders.

1203–4. ALEXIUS IV. He was wholly under the control of the Crusaders and was forced to pay a heavy tribute.

1204, Jan. 25. Popular discontent led to a revolution and the proclamation of **Alexius V** (Dukas). Alexius IV was killed. The new ruler refused to make payments to the Crusaders and demanded their withdrawal.

April 12. The Crusaders stormed the city, which was given over to a merciless sack. The emperor succeeded in escaping. *(To p. 237)*

b. THE CRUSADES

Definition. In the 11th and 12th centuries, the Crusades were military expeditions sponsored by the papacy, charged with recovering Christian holy places in the Middle East from the Muslim Arabs and Seljuk Turks (p. 128). In the 13th century, crusading impulses were often directed against groups within Europe perceived as being social or political enemies, such as the Albigensian heretics (p. 202). By the 15th and 16th centuries, crusading had become an old European tradition. Thus explorers and adventurers, such as Christopher Columbus and Hernán Cortés (pp. 277, 399), in South and North America, Africa, and Asia, explained their goals in religious and crusading terms—they were for the conversion of the Muslims, Indians, or Asian and African peoples.

The **origins** of the medieval Crusades lie in the Christian tradition of penitential **pilgrimages** to the sites of Jesus' life and death in Palestine, dating to that of Helena, Constantine's mother (4th century); the long tradition of Christian wars of **reconquest** against the Muslims in Spain beginning in the 8th century and encouraged by the popes Alexander II and Gregory VII in the 11th century; the hostilities created by Muslim attacks on southern Europe in the 9th and 10th centuries. In 1071, Turkish soldiers, financed by Muslims, defeated a Greek army at **Manzikert** in Armenia; in 1076 the Turks captured Jerusalem, although they subsequently showed no special animosity against Christians. The Byzantine emperor appealed to the West at the Synod of Piacenza (March 1095) for help against Muslim-Turkish expansion.

1095, Nov. Council of Clermont. Pope Urban, a Cluniac and a Frenchman, speaking to Frenchmen, recited the glorious deeds of the French and tales of Muslim atrocities, made open allusions to the chances for profit and advancement, attacked feudal violence at home, and brought the audience to a state of wild enthusiasm; he himself distributed crosses. Urban's propaganda journeys and the preaching of **Peter the Hermit** and others stirred the West, but had the greatest effect in France and Lorraine, the area most under Cluniac influence. The great rulers were all at odds with the papacy or busy at home; the rest of Europe was indifferent. The Crusades began as they continued, largely under French auspices.

The **motives** that inspired Europeans to embark on the Crusades varied with the time, the place, and the individual, but on the first expeditions, to the religious goal of the recapture of the holy places and their restoration to Christian jurisdiction, the reunion of the Greek and Roman churches, and the spiritual advantages of the popes' crusading indulgence, the following secular or material objects should be added. **Political:** to acquire land, fiefs, power in the Middle East; for a ruler, to rid his country or territory of troublesome and rebellious knights. **Social:** to seek adventure, excitement, the novelty of travel in an exotic world; to gain the respect, prestige, and status that Crusaders earned. **Economic:** to gain the loot and booty taken by victorious armies; for European townspeople and bankers, the opportunity to profit from the sale of armor, equipment, horseshoes, fodder; for innkeepers along the crusading routes and prostitutes who accompanied or followed crusading armies, business and profit.

1096–99. The First Crusade. Best recorded and most successful of the Crusades. Five popular, aimless mass migrations (1096) that emptied whole villages; two (perhaps 7000 under Peter the Hermit and perhaps 5000 under Walter the Penniless) reached Asia Minor and were annihilated. The Norman-French baronage flocked to the Cross and converged in three divisions on Constantinople: the Lorrainers under **Godfrey of Bouillon** and his brother Baldwin, via Hungary; the Provençals under **Count Raymond of Toulouse** and the papal legate, Adhemar of Puy, via Illyria; the Normans under **Bohemund of Otranto** (the most effective leader) via Durazzo by sea and land. Perhaps they were 30,000 in all.

The **Muslim opposition:** the Seljuks had merely garrisoned Syria and were not popular with the native population. Muslim unity in Asia Minor ended with the death of Malik Shah (1092), and Syria was divided politically, racially, and theologically (Sunni[s] versus Shi'ite; the Fatimid capture of Jerusalem [1098] from the Sunnis).

1096, Spring. Violent crusader assaults on Jewish communities led to terrible massacres in Speyer, Mainz, Cologne, and other Rhineland cities.

1097. Nicaea (İznik) (p. 119), the Seljuk capital in Asia Minor, taken by the combined Greek and crusading force; defeat of the Muslim field army at Dorylaeum; excursion of Baldwin and Tancred, and rivalry in Cilicia; Bohemund established himself in the Antioch area. Siege and capture (by treachery) of Antioch (1097–98); countersiege of the Christians in Antioch by the emir of Mosul; election of Bohemund as leader. Baldwin's conquest of Edessa (1097); Christian divisions: rivalry of Norman and Provençal.

1099. March to Jerusalem (Genoese convoy and food supply); siege, capture, and horrors of the sack. The death of the papal legate left the organization of the government of Jerusalem to feudal laymen. **Godfrey of Bouillon,** elected king, assumed the title of Defender of the Holy Sepulcher (for pious reasons). The main body of the Crusaders soon streamed back home. The Norman effort to dominate the government through their patriarch Dagobert led to his deposition by the anti-Norman party, and Jerusalem became a feudal kingdom. The government (as revealed by the *Assizes of Jerusalem,* the most complete feudal code extant) was narrowly feudal, with the king a feudal suzerain, not a sovereign, the tenants-in-chief dominant. Besides the feudal organization there were burgher and ecclesiastical organizations, with their own courts.

Continued divisions among the Muslims and the weakness of the Greeks favored the progress of the Latin states: the **kingdom of Jerusalem,** in close commercial alliance with the Italian towns (Genoa, Pisa, and, later, Venice), profited by the commerce through its ports and extended south to tap the Red Sea trade. The other states: the **county of Edessa** (established by Baldwin), the **principality of Antioch** (established by Bohemund), and the **county of Tripoli** (set up by Raymond of Toulouse) were fiefs of Jerusalem (divided into four great baronies and into lesser fiefs).

Muslim unification in Syria was completed by the Atabegs of Mosul and signalized by the capture of Edessa (1144). Mosul soon mastered Egypt; Saladin emerged supreme in Egypt (1171), quickly reduced Damascus and Aleppo, and brought Syria and Egypt under a single efficient rule.

1147–49. The Second Crusade. Bernard of Clairvaux, persuaded by Pope Eugenius III, preached (1145) the Second Crusade. Conrad III and King Louis VII of France took the Cross. To avoid conflicts, the two monarchs went by separate routes; there never was coherent direction or unity of command. The Norman Roger of Sicily took advantage of the Second Crusade to seize the Greek islands and to attack Athens, Thebes, and Corinth. Nothing of importance was achieved by the Second Crusade, and the movement was discredited throughout Europe.

1184. Saladin's steady advance led to a great appeal to the West; King Philip II of France and Henry II of England declined the crown of Jerusalem but levied a **Saladin tithe** (1188) to finance a Crusade. Christian attack on a caravan (said to be escorting Saladin's sister) provoked Saladin's holy war (1187–89): **capture of Jerusalem** (1187) without a sack and reduction of the Latin states to the cities of Antioch, Tyre, Tripoli, and a small area around each. Crusader control of Jerusalem, without heavy European support, was doomed from the start.

1189–92. The Third Crusade. Precipitated by the fall of Jerusalem, the Third Crusade was a completely lay and royal affair, despite the efforts of the papacy to regain control. It was supported partly by the Saladin

KINGS OF JERUSALEM (1099–1489)

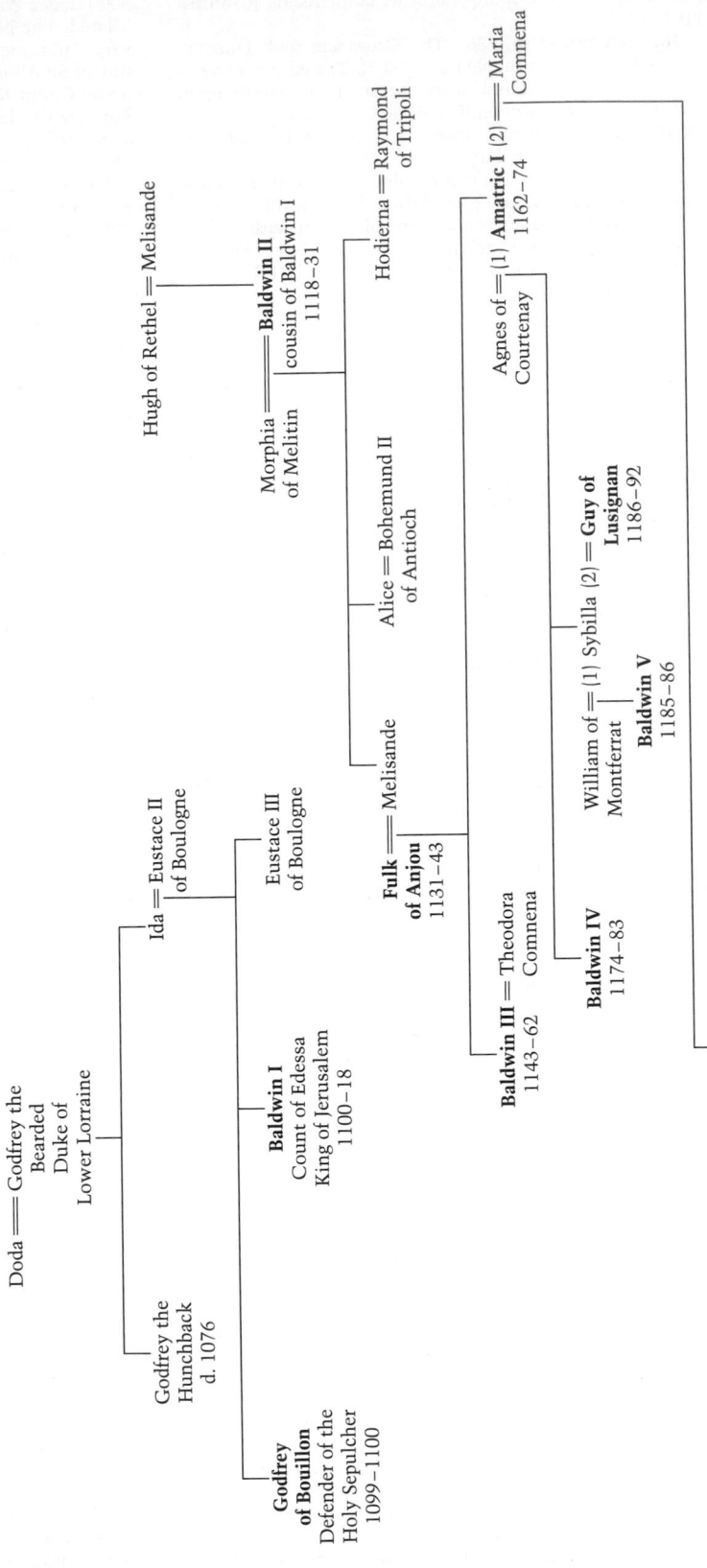

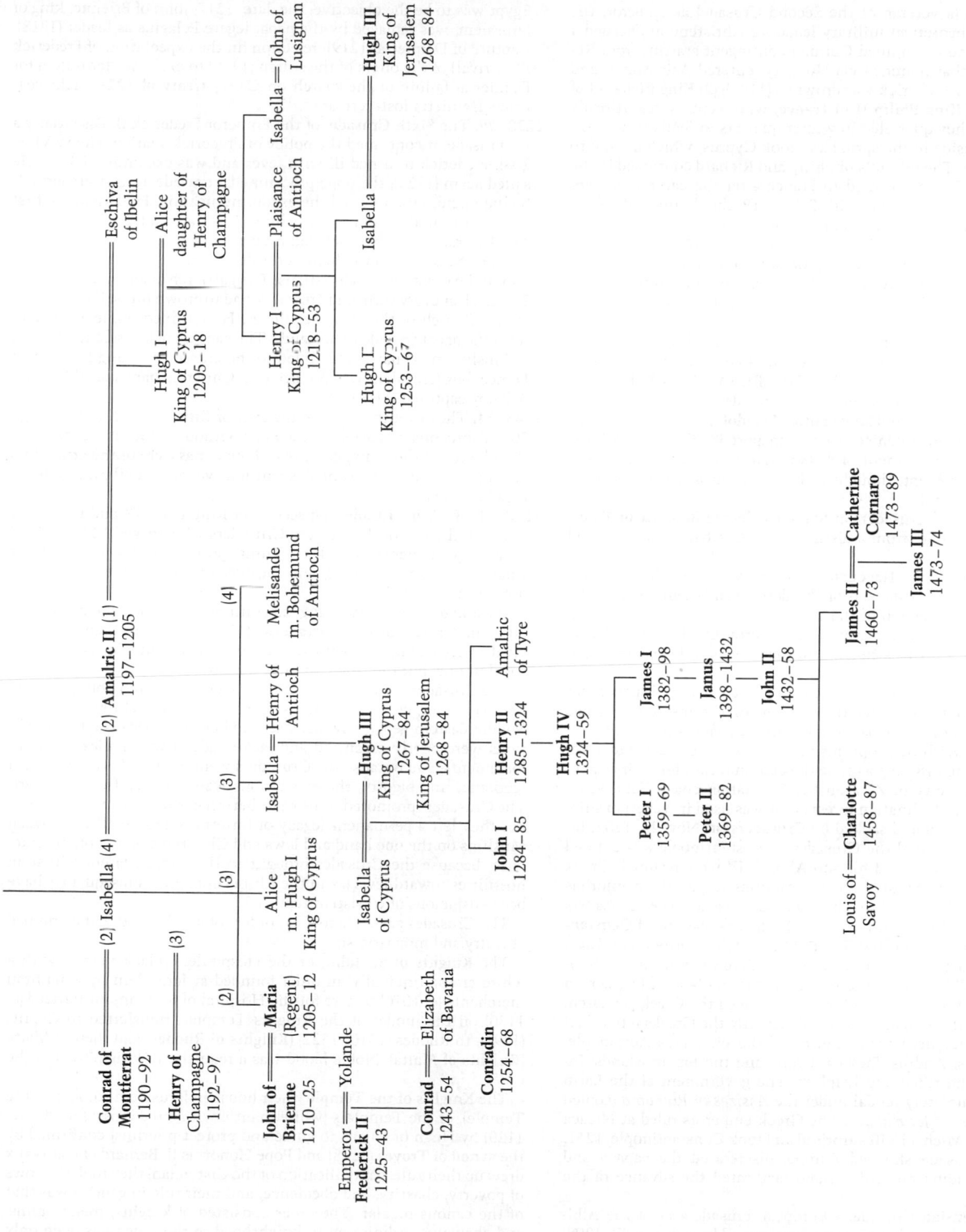

tithe, and was led by the three greatest monarchs of the day: (1) **Frederick Barbarossa** (a veteran of the Second Crusade) as emperor, the traditional and theoretical military leader of Christendom, headed a well-organized and disciplined German contingent starting from Regensburg (1189) that marched via Hungary, entered Asia Minor, and disintegrated after Frederick was drowned (1190); (2) **King Richard I of England;** and (3) **King Philip II of France,** who went by sea. Already political rivals, they quarreled in winter quarters in Sicily (1190–91); Richard turned aside in the spring and took Cyprus, which he sold to Guy de Lusignan. The quarrels of Philip and Richard continued in the Holy Land, and Philip returned to France after the capture of Acre (1191). Richard's negotiations with Saladin (Richard proposed a marriage of his sister Joan to Saladin's brother, who was to be invested with Jerusalem) resulted (1192) in a three-year truce allowing the Christians a coastal strip between Jaffa and Acre and access to Jerusalem. Captivity of Richard (1192–94) and heavy ransom to the Emperor Henry VI. The Third Crusade ended the golden age of the Crusades.

1199, Aug. 15. Pope Innocent III (p. 214), determined to regain papal direction of the Crusades and to reunite the Greek and Latin churches, proclaimed a new crusade, the **FOURTH CRUSADE (1202–4).**

1201, Lent. Crusade envoys, including Geoffroy de Villehardouin (major chronicler of the events) and **Doge Enrico Dandolo,** reached agreement in the **Treaty of Venice:** Venice was to transport 33,500 men and 4,500 horses, in return for payment of 85,000 marks. The fleet was to sail June 29, 1202, for Egypt, thought to be a strategically better site for recovery of Holy Land.

    June. Assembly of Crusaders at Soissons elected **Boniface of Montferrat,** a famous soldier from a distinguished Lombard family, to lead the crusade.

    Christmas. Meeting at **Hagenau** in Germany of King Philip of Swabia, Boniface, and Alexius, son of the dethroned Byzantine emperor Isaac II Angelus. Diversion of the crusade to Constantinople to reinstate the deposed emperor was almost certainly discussed; Irene, Philip's wife and Alexius's sister, said that she would support her father's cause.

1202, Summer. The Crusaders trickled into Venice, only to discover that they had grossly overestimated the numbers to be transported; Venice had fulfilled her side of the bargain, but the Crusaders could not raise the agreed sum. With their options very limited, they agreed to a Venetian proposal (p. 218) to postpone the debt in return for their attacking the Christian city of Zara on the Dalmatian coast (Zara was a source of oak from Dalmatian forests that was used in Venetian shipbuilding). Zara taken and sacked by Crusaders on Nov. 24, 1202. Innocent excommunicated the Crusaders. Constantinople was entered (1203); Isaac II Angelus and his son Alexius IV were restored; Greek opinion was furious about the new exactions to pay the clamorous Crusaders, and Alexius V soon succeeded Isaac. The Crusaders stormed and took Constantinople (1204), the first **capture of Constantinople** in history, and sacked it with unparalleled horrors. The Latin Empire of the East (Romania) replaced the Greek Empire at Constantinople from 1204 to 1261; the first emperor, Baldwin of Flanders; a Latin patriarch, the Venetian Morosini, replaced the Greek patriarch, and technically the schism was ended; actually the Greeks refused all union. Venice acquired three-eighths of the city, plus Adrianople, Gallipoli, Naxos, Andros, Euboea, Crete, and the Ionian islands. Innocent III was horrified and helpless. The government of the Latin Empire was completely feudal under the *Assizes of Romania* (copied from the *Assizes of Jerusalem*). The Greek emperors ruled at Nicaea (1204–61) until Michael VIII surprised and took Constantinople, 1261. The Fourth Crusade shocked Europe, discredited the papacy and the whole crusading movement, and facilitated the advance of the Turks.

1208. The **Albigensian Crusade,** a European crusade against the Albigensian heretics in southern France, proclaimed by Innocent III (1208) (see p. 202).

1212. The so-called **Children's Crusade,** preached by the lad Stephen of Vendôme and by Nicholas of Cologne in Germany. Stephen's contingent reached Marseilles and was sold into slavery. Nicholas's company was turned back. The whole episode is supposed to have been the origin of the story of the Pied Piper.

1218–21. The Fifth Crusade. Innocent III, unwilling to let the crusading idea lapse, preached the Fifth Crusade at the Fourth Lateran Council. Egypt was to be the objective; the date, 1217; John of Brienne, king of Jerusalem, was replaced by the papal legate Pelagius as leader (1218). Capture of Damietta (1219); rejection (in the expectation of Frederick II's arrival) of the offers of the sultan (1219) to exchange Jerusalem for Damietta; failure of the march on Cairo; **treaty of 1221:** eight-year truce; Damietta lost; retreat.

1228–29. The **Sixth Crusade,** of the Emperor Frederick II. Essentially a lay crusade, it continued the policy of Frederick's father, Henry VI (p. 208). Frederick returned ill with fever and was excommunicated. He sailed again (1228); the pope proclaimed a crusade against Frederick's Sicilian lands and renewed the excommunication. Frederick, the first Crusader to understand the Muslims, negotiated a treaty (1229) with Malik al-Kamil, nephew of Saladin, sultan of Egypt; peace for ten years, grant of Nazareth, Bethlehem, Jerusalem, and a corridor from Jerusalem to the coast for the Christians. The patriarch of Jerusalem opposed Frederick at every turn, and Frederick had to crown himself king (1229) in the Church of the Holy Sepulcher. He returned home at once to repel the papal crusade in his lands. The capture of Jerusalem by a rush of Muslim mercenaries (1244) led to the crusades of King Louis IX of France, but Jerusalem was not again in Christian hands until General Allenby captured it (1917).

1248–54. The **Seventh Crusade,** the first of King Louis IX of France (p. 204). Poorly organized; Damietta taken without a blow; march to Cairo (1249); rout of the army; capture of Louis; massacre of the army; loss of Damietta. Louis, ransomed, spent four years on a pilgrimage to Jerusalem (1251–54).

1270. The **Eighth Crusade,** the second of King Louis IX and Edward of England (the last of the western Crusaders who arrived 1271, and did nothing permanent). Attack on Tunis, possibly at the insistence of Charles of Anjou; death of Louis; the expedition continued by Charles; nothing accomplished.

    Local and specific crusading expeditions were subsequently undertaken under various circumstances at different times; there was a revival of crusading zeal with the fall of Constantinople (1453) under papal urging, but the true Crusades were over.

    The Crusades testify to the Europeans' enormous religious piety and zeal. However, because the Crusaders had a very slight knowledge of Middle Eastern geography, defenses, and culture; because the expeditions were poorly organized and lacked adequate supplies and reinforcements; and because the Crusades went equipped primarily with ignorance and bigotry, the expeditions were doomed from the start. The Crusaders promoted some trade between Muslims and Europeans, but they left a permanent legacy of bitterness and hostility between Muslims on the one hand and Jews and Christians on the other. Likewise, because the Crusades brought to the surface latent Christian hostilities toward Jews (as in the Rhineland), Jews subsequently have been suspicious of Christian zeal.

    The Crusades gave rise to great orders of knighthood that combined chivalry and monasticism.

    The **Knights of St. John,** or the Hospitalers (black mantle with a white cross), originally an order founded at Jerusalem by Amalfitan merchants (c. 1070) to care for the Hospital of St. John; militarized (c. 1130) on the model of the Knights Templar; transferred to Cyprus (1291); to Rhodes (1310–1522) **(Knights of Rhodes)** and then to Malta **(Knights of Malta).** Noble blood was a requisite to knighthood in the order.

    The **Knights of the Temple** (their house in Jerusalem stood near the Temple), or the Templars (white mantle with a red cross) founded (c. 1120) by Hugh of Pajens to guide and protect pilgrims; confirmed by the **synod of Troyes** (1128) and Pope Honorius II. Bernard of Clairvaux drew up their rule, a modification of the Cistercian; they took the vows of poverty, chastity, and obedience, and their rule in general was that of the canons regular. The order consisted of knights, men-at-arms, and chaplains. Admission to knighthood in the order was open only to those of noble blood. Organization: by commanderies, under a grand master.

    Famous orders of chivalry of royal foundation: the **Order of the Garter** (English), founded c. 1344; the **Order of the Star** (French), founded 1351, replaced by the **Order of St. Michael** (1469–1830); and the **Order of the Golden Fleece** (Burgundian), founded 1429, became Habsburg 1477.

c. LATIN AND GREEK STATES IN THE MIDDLE EAST

(From p. 233)

Division of the Eastern Empire after the fall of Constantinople: A council, composed equally of Crusaders and Venetians, decided to award the imperial crown to **Count Baldwin of Flanders**, while a Venetian (Pier Morosini) was made patriarch of Constantinople. **Boniface of Montferrat** was made king of Salonika (Thessalonica) and the remaining parts of the empire were assigned to various barons as vassals of the emperor. In Anatolia the Crusaders were never able to establish themselves except in a part of Bithynia near the Bosporus. In Europe they were constantly exposed to the attacks of the Bulgarians. The kingdom of Thessalonica at first extended over part of Thrace, Macedonia, and Thessaly, but to the west the Greek **Michael Angelus Comnenus** set himself up as despot of Epirus and soon began to expand his dominion eastward. Attica and the Peloponnesus were conquered by crusading barons in a short time, and these territories were organized on a feudal basis as the **lordship of Athens** (Otto de la Roche, 1205–25; Guy I, 1225–63; John I, 1263–80), and the **principality of Achaea** (conquered by Guillaume de Champlitte and Geoffroy de Villehardouin in 1205). Achaea was in turn divided into 12 feudal baronies, an example of the French feudal pattern. Under the Villehardouin family (Geoffroy I, 1209–18; Geoffroy II, 1218–46; Guillaume, 1246–78) it was well governed and popular with the Greco-Slavic population, which was considerately treated.

The **Venetians** took as their share of the empire most of the islands and other important strategic or commercial posts. They kept for themselves part of Constantinople, Gallipoli, Euboea, Crete, the southwestern tip of the Peloponnesus (Coron and Modon), Durazzo, and other posts on the Epiran coast, as well as the islands of the Ionian and Aegean Seas. For the most part these possessions were granted as fiefs to the leading Venetian families (e.g., triarchies of Euboea, duchy of the Archipelago).

1204–5. BALDWIN I, Latin emperor.

1204–14. Michael Angelus Comnenus, despot of Epirus.

1204. Theodore Lascaris, son-in-law of Alexius III, with some of the Byzantine leaders, established himself in Bithynia; Alexius and David Comnenus organized a state on the north coast of Anatolia, with David at Sinope and Alexius at Trebizond, thus founding the **empire of Trebizond,** which lasted until Ottoman conquest in 1461.

1204–22. Theodore I (Lascaris) became founder of the Nicaean Empire. In 1204 he made an alliance with the (Turkish) sultan of Rum to resist the advance of the Crusaders into Anatolia, but was defeated by the latter under Peter of Bracheuil.

1205. The **Bulgars,** under Kaloyan, defeated Emperor Baldwin and Doge Dandolo in a **battle near Adrianople.** Baldwin was captured and died in captivity. The Bulgars then overran much of Thrace and Macedonia, exterminating a large part of the Greek population.

1205–16. HENRY I, Latin emperor, the brother of Baldwin, and the ablest of the Latin emperors.

1207. Kaloyan and the Bulgarians besieged Thessalonica, but in vain. Kaloyan died suddenly, probably murdered.

1207. Theodore Lascaris, allied with the Seljuks of Rum, defeated David Comnenus and drove him back to Sinope. Theodore then concluded a truce with Emperor Henry, in order to oppose the advance of Alexius of Trebizond, who was now allied with the Seljuks.

1209. Theodore repulsed a second attempt by Peter of Bracheuil and the Crusaders to conquer Bithynia.

1211. Theodore Lascaris defeated Alexius of Trebizond and the sultan of Rum, both of whom were captured. As a result, a large part of the Anatolian coast was added to the Empire of Nicaea.

1212. Henry I defeated Theodore at Luparcos and began the invasion of Anatolia. Theodore made peace, abandoning to the Latin Empire part of Mysia and Bithynia.

LATIN EMPERORS OF CONSTANTINOPLE (1204–1373)

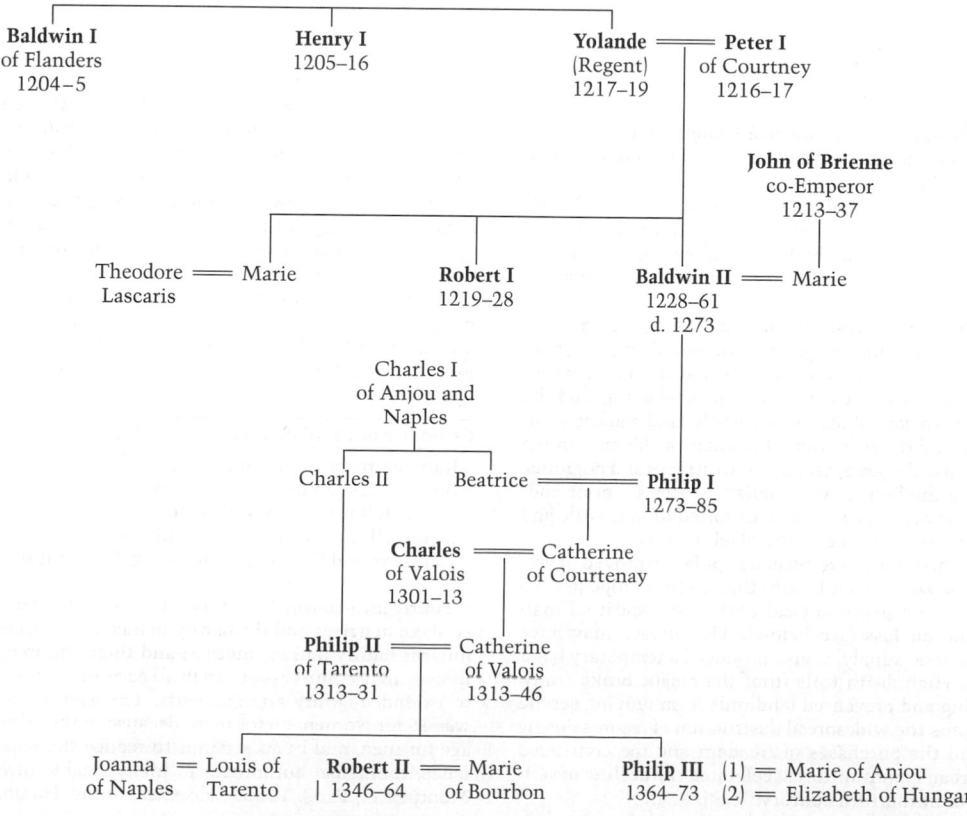

1214–30. Theodore Dukas Angelus, nephew of Michael, became despot of Epirus. He began the work of expansion at the expense of the Latins and Bulgars, taking Durazzo and Corfu from the Venetians (1214).

1219–28. Robert of Courtenay, Latin emperor. His domain was reduced to Constantinople, and he spent most of his time soliciting aid in the West.

1222. Theodore Dukas of Epirus captured Thessalonica and extinguished the kingdom. He then had himself proclaimed Emperor of the West, and before long extended his conquests to the vicinity of Philippopolis and Adrianople.

1222–54. JOHN III (Dukas Vatatzes), emperor at Nicaea. He proved himself a great ruler as well as an able general. During his reign agriculture was encouraged, trade and industry developed, and finances reformed. The Nicaean Empire enjoyed a period of real prosperity and power.

1224. John Vatatzes defeated the Franks at Poimanenon. In succession he took the islands near the Anatolian coast (Samos, Chios, Lemnos) and subjected Rhodes. An army was even sent across the straits to capture Adrianople.

1224. Theodore of Epirus defeated an army of the Latin emperor at Serres and then drove the invading Nicaean army away from Adrianople.

1228. On the death of Robert of Courtenay, it was proposed that a regency be established under the Bulgarian ruler, John Asen II (1218–41), but this suggestion was frustrated by the Latin clergy.

1228–61. BALDWIN II, Latin emperor. He was the eleven-year-old nephew of Robert of Courtenay. The reign was a helpless one, during which the emperor was reduced to peddling the Constantinople relics through Europe.

1229–37. Regency of John of Brienne, former king of Jerusalem, for the boy-emperor. John became co-emperor in 1231.

1230. Theodore of Epirus was defeated and captured by the Bulgarian Tsar John Asen, eldest son of Asen I at battle of Klokotnica. He then expanded his territories from Adrianople in the east to Dyrrachion in the west, and styled himself tsar of the Bulgarians and the Greeks. Thessalonica and Thessaly passed to

MANUEL. (1230–36), the brother of Theodore, and

JOHN. (1236–44), the son of Theodore Dukas of Epirus, who became despot of Thessaly and Emperor of the West.

1236–71. MICHAEL II, despot of Epirus.

1242. John Vatatzes, in company with Theodore, who had been liberated by the Bulgarians, set out with an army and besieged Thessalonica. He failed to take the city, owing to his lack of seapower, but John, the despot of Thessaly, was obliged to give up the title Emperor of the West and to recognize the suzerainty of the Nicaean emperor.

1243. The **Mongol invasion** of Anatolia, after the defeat of the Seljuks in the **Battle of Kösedağ.** The Mongols reached Ancyra (Ankara). John Vatatzes established friendly relations with them and succeeded to much of the Seljuk territory in central Anatolia.

1246. Second expedition of John Vatatzes to the Balkans. He conquered northern Macedonia and finally took Thessalonica, deposing Demetrius Angelus, despot since 1244.

1254. Michael II, of Epirus, recognized Nicaean suzerainty after a defeat by the forces of John Vatatzes.

1254–58. THEODORE II (Lascaris), Greek emperor at Nicaea.

1255. Theodore defeated the Bulgarian armies of Michael Asen, grandson of John Asen, in northern Macedonia.

1258–61. JOHN IV (Lascaris), emperor. He was a mere child, and his accession caused a military uprising, led by Michael Paleologus, who became regent and then (1259) co-emperor.

1259–82. MICHAEL VIII (Paleologus), who was first co-emperor with the boy John, whom in 1261 he had imprisoned and blinded. Michael was an able and energetic general, whose great objective was to reestablish the Greek power at Constantinople.

1261. Reconquest of Constantinople. Michael made an alliance with the Bulgarians and concluded the **Treaty of Nymphaion** with Genoa, promising the Genoese all the privileges hitherto enjoyed by the Venetians. On July 25 a Greek army under **Alexius Stragopulos,** taking advantage of the absence of the Venetian fleet, crossed the Bosporus and retook Constantinople without much difficulty. Baldwin II fled (d. 1273). End of the Latin Empire. (To p. 273)

6. WESTERN EUROPE, 1300–1500

(From p. 222)

a. OVERVIEW

The period began with significant **ecological changes:** the end of the optimal hydrological and thermal conditions that had produced large harvests between c. 1000 and 1250. Bad weather led to poor harvests, while sheep murrain (disease) in England reduced the size of flocks and the volume of wool exported, severely hurting Flemish and Italian weavers. The result was **general agricultural and commercial weakness,** economic distress for which weak and **incompetent governments** had no solution.

Social consequences: Poor harvests and famine led to great increase in number of vagabonds or homeless people; the abandonment of entire villages (as in parts of the Low Countries and on the Scottish-English border); great increase in the mortgaging, subleasing, and the sale of land, which in turn contributed to a volatile land market; postponement of marriage and the reduction of population; blame thrown on creditors, the rich, and the Jews, which led to attacks and pogroms. Government remedies: the French and English crowns set price controls and forbade the export of grain. Grain exported from Castile and the Baltic seized by pirates and sold on the black market.

A weak, undernourished, and overcrowded population proved ill prepared for the **bubonic plague** (Black Death) that swept Europe periodically (1347–1450), causing psychological pessimism, spiritual malaise, and **huge population loss** (see below). The disease may have adjusted population to food supply; it also produced a temporary labor storage and inflation. High death tolls from the plague broke continuity in record keeping and prevented landlords from proving servile status; those factors plus the widespread destruction of records during **peasant uprisings,** and the purchases of freedom and the continued flight from rural to urban communities accelerated the **decline of serfdom,** which had begun in the 13th century.

The Christian Church, centered first at Avignon, not Rome, and then divided by **schism,** provided little spiritual consolation and few strong moral examples; **papal prestige declined.** The series of conflicts known as the **Hundred Years' War** (1337–1453), in which England and France became deadlocked, involved the **Burgundian struggle** for control of the French crown, **aristocratic resurgence, civil war,** peasant and urban revolts in both countries. The long wars promoted the development of **national consciousness,** as reflected in the growth of **vernacular languages.**

Meanwhile, the steady accumulation of wealth in the Italian cities made possible a great cultural efflorescence, which the 16th-century art historian Vasari (1511–74) first labeled **the Renaissance** (It., *renascita*). In the 15th century this movement spread to France, England, Germany, and Spain.

Estimates of population decline c. 1300–1500:

Italy fell from 10 million to 7.5 million
British Isles fell from 5 million to 3 million
France fell from 17.5 million to 12.5 million
Iberia fell from 9 million to 7 million
Germany and Scandinavia fell from 11.5 million to 7 million.

Fourteenth-century records, the earliest available for structural study of **marriage and the family** in medieval Europe, indicate that the **nuclear family** (father, mother, and their children) was becoming an increasingly common pattern in all parts of western Europe, as opposed to extended-family arrangements. The average age at first marriage was 16 for women, 26 for men. Because of the relatively late marriage age for men, and in an attempt to reduce the potential for male violence, municipal authorities in many sizable towns (e.g., Toulouse, Montpellier, Paris, Venice, Florence, Rome, Hamburg, London, Sandwich) established brothels for the regulation of **female prostitution.** These cities had large numbers of unmarried young men and transient merchants, and a culture resting on a cash exchange. Medieval prostitution was an urban phenomenon and a social issue. (Research on male prostitution continues.) *(To p. 273)*

b. THE BRITISH ISLES

(From p. 197)

1. ENGLAND

1307–27. EDWARD II. Married to Isabelle, daughter of Philip IV of France. A weak ruler and the tool of ambitious favorites, Edward was dominated first by the Gascon Piers Gaveston (d. 1312), probably his lover. The Scottish war was continued in desultory fashion. The baronage, angered by Gaveston, followed the leadership of Edward's nephew, Thomas, duke of Lancaster, an ambitious, incompetent person. They forced Edward to accept a committee of reform, the 21 **Lords Ordainers** (1310), whose reform ordinances, suggestive of the Provisions of Oxford, were confirmed by parliament (1311). The ordinances required a baronial consent to royal appointments, to a declaration of war, and to the departure of the king from the realm, this consent to be given through parliament. Gaveston was captured and slain (1312).

1313–14. The Scottish War. By 1313 only the castle of Stirling remained in the hands of the English. Edward set out (1314) to relieve the castle, but at **Bannockburn** (1314) he was overwhelmingly defeated, and Scottish independence was won.

In Gascony the French kings began a policy of egging Edward's vassals on to resistance, a process that culminated in the French conquest of Gascony and its retention by the French with the consent (1327) of the regents who ruled after Edward's abdication.

1314–22. Supremacy of Lancaster, who offered no resistance to the Scottish raids nor to the civil disorders that broke out in England. In 1322 Edward defeated him at Boroughbridge, beheaded him, and had the ordinances of 1311 repealed at the parliament of York.

1322–26. Rule of the Despensers, father and son: Scottish truce (1323); decline of the popularity of the Despensers; alienation of Queen Isabelle. Isabelle went to France (1325), arranged the marriage of her son, the future Edward III, to Philippa of Hainault, and returned (1326) with Mortimer and foreign troops. Supported by the barons, Isabelle gained London, the Despensers were hanged, and the **parliament of Westminster** (1327), dominated by Isabelle and by Edward's enemies, forced an abdication that was tantamount to deposition. Edward was brutally murdered in prison eight months later.

Burgesses and knights sat in the parliaments of 1311, 1322, and 1327.

1327–77. EDWARD III (age 15 at his accession). Council of regency and rule (1327–30) under Mortimer, Isabelle's paramour; Bruce's invasion of England forced the acknowledgment of Scottish independence (1328). Edward led the baronial opposition to Mortimer (hanged, 1330) and opened his personal rule (1330).

1338. Outbreak of the **Hundred Years' War.** Edward did homage (1329) for his French lands and renewed the homage (1331). French support of Scottish aggression continued, and Edward, profiting by civil war in Scotland, supported Baliol; after a series of expeditions, he avenged Bannockburn at **Halidon Hill** (1333). French intrigues to alienate Aquitaine continued. The economic interdependence, due to the wool trade, of England and the Flemish cities made an English alliance with them likely. Philip continued his advance into the English lands south of the Loire (1337), and open hostilities broke out (1338). Edward ravaged northern and eastern France without a decisive battle. Urged on by the Flemings, Edward proclaimed himself king of France (in right of his mother, Isabelle), and enabled the Flanders towns under Jan van Arteveldt to support him without violating their oaths.

1340. The **naval victory of Sluys** transferred the mastery of the Channel from France to England (until 1372). Intermittent truces (1340–45) were followed by Edward's invasion of France.

1346, Aug. 26. Great victory at **CRÉCY,** near Ponthieu in northern France, where English longbowmen, supported by dismounted horsemen, routed the undisciplined cavalry and mercenary crossbowmen of France. This tactical innovation, the result of English experiences in Wales and Scotland, began the joint participation of the yeomanry and the aristocracy in war, and gave the English a unique military power and new social orientation.

1346. The invasion of Philip's Scottish allies was halted at **Neville's Cross,** and the king of Scotland captured.

1347. Calais was taken after a long siege in which artillery was used, and it remained an English military and commercial outpost in France until 1558.

1347–55. A **series of truces** with France was ended by the expedition of Edward's son, **the Black Prince** (so called because of the color of his armor), to Bordeaux, followed by ruthless plundering raids using Bordeaux as a base, which enriched the English and alienated the populace.

1356, Sept. 19. Battle of Poitiers. The Black Prince, using the tactics of Crécy, defeated King John, capturing him, his son, and the king of Bohemia, as well as the flower of French chivalry.

1359–60. Edward's last expedition to France penetrated to the walls of Paris; the south had been so devastated that the English could hardly find food.

1360. Peace of Bretigny, ending the first period of the war (p. 244); the war was resumed in 1369.

After the hideous **sack of Limoges** (1370), the Black Prince returned to England (1371) and was replaced (1372–74) by his brother, **John of Gaunt,** the duke of Lancaster and an incompetent soldier, who lost town after town until only Calais, Cherbourg, Brest, Bayonne, and Bordeaux remained in English hands (1375).

Edward's personal rule and domestic developments in England. Edward, a majestic, affable man, opened his reign with generous concessions to the baronage and a courteous welcome to the complaints of the middle class. He grew steadily in popularity. He was fond of war and the war was popular; the nation backed him.

Growth of Parliament. Medieval people believed, in the words of historian Charles Howard McIlwain, that "to kings belong government, to subjects property." Since ecclesiastical organizations, local communites, and private individuals provided all social services, "good" governments did not tax, except in the case of a just war. The necessities of war financing over the long span of the Hundred Years' War had, in retrospect, profound consequences for the development of the English Parliament. First, it met frequently. Edward III's need for money to pay for the war forced him to call not only the great barons and bishops but also knights of the shires and burgesses from the towns. He called them 27 times between 1337 and his death in 1377; in Edward's 50-year reign, Parliament met 37 times. It was becoming a habit. Second, the knights and burgesses soon realized that they held the purse strings: the Second Statute of 14 Edward III (1341), sometimes called the Statute *de Tallagio non Concedendo* ("no taxation without representation") required that all nonfeudal levies receive parliamentary approval. In return for a grant, Parliament increasingly asked for royal redress of grievances. These requests were framed as petitions (or *billa*, from which derives the modern **bill**) which, when supported by the lords and approved by the king, became **statutes**—laws enacted by the legislative branch. Most petitions or bills in the 14th and 15th centuries supported the interests of individuals, corporations (such as a university or guild), or local communities; they had no broad "national" significance. Third, by 1340 the knights and burgesses were meeting apart from the magnates, frequently in the monks' Chapter House at Westminster Abbey. In the late 15th century, the term Commons' House, or **House of Commons,** came into use; the phrase **House of Lords** appeared first in the reign of Henry VIII. In the 14th century, the Commons developed its organization, with a **speaker** to preside over debates and to represent the Commons' interests before the House of Lords and the king, and clerks began to keep records of discussions. The first speaker for whom evidence survives was Peter de la Mare (1376). In the 15th century, Parliament met frequently and for longer sessions (than in the 14th century), but it was still more of an occasional gathering than an institution. Only at the time of Parliament were petitions presented, kings deposed (e.g., Richard II), new rulers legalized (e.g., Henry IV), and popular support sought. But Parliament remained the king's servant; it met for an **ad hoc purpose** and when it had fulfilled the king's wishes, it was dismissed. It was not a continuing body. Actual power remained in the hands of the king and his council.

Development of **justices of the peace.** The conservators of the peace established under Henry III to keep the peace had no judicial powers; the statute of 1327 allowed them to receive indictments for trial before the itinerant judges. In 1332 their jurisdiction was made to include felonies and trespass. Established as police judges in each county (1360), they were also charged with price and labor regulation. By 1485 they had absorbed most of the functions of the sheriffs. Chosen from the local gentry, under royal commission, they constituted an amateur body of administrators who carried on local government in England until well into the 19th century.

1348–49. The ravages of the **Black Death** probably reduced the population by one-third. (Some scholars argue that food poisoning, especially from cereals—the bulk of most people's diet—infected with toxins, had weakened people's immune systems and thus contributed to the occurrence of the disease.) The population loss, coupled with the tremendous war prosperity, dislocated the wage and price structure and produced economic chaos. The **Statute of Laborers** (1351) attempted to fix wages and prices and to compel able-bodied unemployed to accept work when offered. The labor shortage accelerated the transition (already begun) from servile to free tenures and fluid labor; the statute in practice destroyed English social unity without markedly arresting servile emancipation or diminishing the crisis.

War prosperity affected everybody and led to a general surge of luxury (e.g., the new and generous proportions of contemporary Perpendicular Gothic architecture). Landowners, confronted with a labor shortage, began to enclose land for sheep raising, and the accumulation of capital and landholdings founded great fortunes, which soon altered the political and social position of the baronage. The yeomanry, exhilarated by their joint military achievement with the aristocracy and their share of war plunder, lost their traditional passivity, and a new ferment began among the lower sections of society.

Growth of national and anticlerical (antipapal) **feeling.** Hostility to the francophile papacy at Avignon: **statute of Provisors** (1351), an effort to stem the influx of alien clergy under papal provisions (widely ignored); **statute of Praemunire** (1353), forbidding appeals to courts (i.e., Avignon) outside England (widely ignored).

The vernacular. English became, by statute (1362), the language of pleading and judgment in the courts (legal French retained in documents). English began to be taught in the schools (1375). Parliament was opened (1399) with a speech in English.

c. 1362. Growth of social tension. William Langland's *Piers Plowman*, a vernacular indictment of governmental and ecclesiastical corruption and an appeal (unique in Europe) on behalf of the poor peasant. Langland, a poor country priest, typical of the section of the church directly in contact with public opinion, was the voice of the old-fashioned godly England, bewildered and angered by a new epoch. Preaching of scriptural equalitarianism by various itinerant preachers (e.g., John Ball); growing bitterness against landlords and lawyers.

c. 1376. JOHN WICLIF, an Oxford don and chaplain of Edward, already employed (1374) by the government in negotiations with the papacy over provisions, published his *Civil Dominion,* asserting that, as Christians hold all things of God under a contract to be virtuous, sin violates this contract and destroys title to goods and offices. Wiclif insisted that his doctrine was a philosophical and theological theory, not a political concept, but extremists ignored this point. A precursor of the Reformation, Wiclif advocated a propertyless Church, emphasizing its purely spiritual function; attacked the clergy; and insisted on the direct access of the individual to God (e.g., reduction of the importance of the sacraments, notably auricular confession) and the right of individual judgment. He also was responsible (with Purvey and Nicholas of Hereford) for the first complete, vernacular **English Bible.** He wrote pamphlets, both in Latin and English, and carried on a wide agitation through his poor priests for his doctrines **(Lollardy),** until it was said every fourth man was a Lollard.

1369–77. Edward's great prestige had rested on a successful foreign war; once England ceased to be victorious in the French war (after 1369), Edward's ascendancy declined and baronial influence increased.

1371. William of Wykeham, bishop of Winchester, requested that Parliament grant supply (revenue) for the war and provoked great anticlerical opposition: Parliament petitioned the king that, since most high royal officials were ecclesiastics and thus could not be held accountable in secular courts such as Parliament, only laymen should

be appointed. John of Gaunt supported this anticlerical feeling and the social unrest that accompanied it.

1376. The Black Prince led the Good Parliament (the best reported assembly thus far) in a series of reforms: the Commons refused supply until given an audit of accounts; two notorious war profiteers, Latimer and Lyons, were **impeached**—that is, accused of serious crimes with the full Parliament sitting as a court of law. This was the first impeachment of officials by Parliament in English history.

1377. After the death of the Black Prince (1376), John of Gaunt's packed Parliament undid the reforms and passed a general poll tax.

Art, Literature, and Science. Perpendicular Gothic: Gloucester, transepts and choir (1331–35); cloisters (1351–1412). Minor arts: *Louterell Psalter* (opening of the 14th century), illuminations. English influence on craftsmen of the Rhineland, Paris, Lorraine.

Historical writing: Higden's *Polychronicon* (before 1363), a brilliant universal history in Latin; Walsingham of St. Albans's (end of the 14th century) *Chronicle,* in Latin, rivaling Froissart in brilliance of description.

Geoffrey Chaucer (c. 1340–1400), the son of a London burgher, a layman, a diplomat, active at court, later a member of Parliament, combined observation with learning. Representative of the new cosmopolitanism of English society, he was under Italian and French influences and probably knew Petrarch. Translator of Boethius's *Consolatio;* creator of English versification; recaster of the English vocabulary by adding Continental grace to the ruder Anglo-Saxon word treasury. The influence of Wiclif, Oxford, Cambridge, the court, and, above all, Chaucer fixed Midland English as the language of the English people. The *Canterbury Tales* offer a witty, sympathetic, sophisticated, realistic picture of contemporary society (omitting the aristocracy).

Foundation of Winchester College (St. Mary's College) **and New College, Oxford,** by William of Wykeham (1393). **Merton College,** Oxford, became a center for scientific investigations, especially in mechanics. **Robert Grosseteste, Roger Bacon, Richard Swineshead,** and **Thomas of Bradwardine** began a tradition of logical analysis and experiment that remained influential until the Renaissance.

1377–99. RICHARD II (son of the Black Prince, age 10 at his accession).

1377–89. Richard's minority. Marriage to Anne of Bohemia (1382); rule by the council under the domination of John of Gaunt. Activity of Parliament: insistence by the Commons on the nomination of 12 new councillors. Renewal of war in France (1383): loss of the Flanders trade, complaints at the cost by Parliament. Poll taxes (1370 and 1380); sporadic violence, growing tension in the agricultural and urban classes.

1381. Peasants' Revolt. Efforts by the landlords to revert to the old servile tenures culminated in a peasant rising, the burning of manors, the destruction of records of tenures and of game parks, the assassination of landlords and lawyers, and a march (100,000[?] men) from the south and east of England on London, led by **Jack Straw, Wat Tyler,** and others (release of John Ball from prison). London admitted the marchers; lawyers and officials were murdered, their houses sacked, the Savoy (John of Gaunt's palace) burned. Significant **demands:** commutation of servile dues, disendowment of the Church, abolition of game laws. The Tower was seized, Archbishop Sudbury (mover, as chancellor, of the poll taxes) murdered. Richard met the rebels (Mile End), issued charters of manumission, and started most of them home. After the murder of Wat Tyler, Richard cleverly took command of the remnant (possibly 30,000), deluded them with false promises, and dispersed them. Cruel reaction ensued: Richard and Parliament annulled the charters; terrible repression followed, and a deliberate effort was made to restore villeinage. This proved impossible, and serfdom continued to disappear.

1381. Passage of the first **Navigation Act,** followed by clear signs of growing national monopoly of commerce.

1382. Wiclif, who had alienated his upper-class supporters by a denial of transubstantiation, was discredited by the Peasants' Revolt and condemned by the Church; he withdrew to Lutterworth (1382–84), where he continued to foster Lollardy until he died (1384). His body, by order of the Council of Constance, was dug up and burned (1428).

Archbishop Courtenay purged Oxford of Lollardy, thus separating the movement from the cultured classes. Parliament refused to allow persecution of the Lollards. The position of the English Church was not wholly due to its own corruption nor to the paralysis of the Avignonese Captivity, but was partly a result of the increase of secular influences on learning and society.

1389–97. Richard's personal rule. Truce with France (1389), peace negotiations, marriage to Isabelle, infant daughter of Charles VI (1396). Richard was on good terms with Parliament; England prosperous and quiet.

1397–99. Richard's attempt at absolutism. Richard, furious at a parliamentary demand for financial accounting, had the mover (Haxey) condemned for treason (not executed). In the next Parliament (Commons packed for Richard; Lords friendly) three of the lords appellant were convicted and executed for treason, Richard was voted an income for life (1398), and the powers of Parliament were delegated to a committee friendly to Richard. Heavy taxation led to the **conspiracy of Henry of Bolingbroke** (exiled son of John of Gaunt).

1399. Bolingbroke landed while Richard was in Ireland. Richard returned, and having alienated all important groups, was forced to abdicate. He was thrown into the Tower and later died (was murdered?) in prison (1400). Parliament accepted the abdication and, returning to the ancient custom of election, made Henry king. Henry's title by heredity was faulty; his claim was based on usurpation, legalized by Parliament, and backed by public opinion.

1399–1461. The House of Lancaster.

1399–1413. HENRY IV. The reign, in view of Henry's title to the throne, was dependent on Parliament. To retain the support of the Church, Henry opposed the demand (1404) of the Commons that Church property be confiscated and applied to poor relief.

1413–22. HENRY V, whose military achievements brought England to the first rank in Europe. Bent on the revival of the Church, he led a strong attack on Lollardy: **Sir John Oldcastle** (Lord Cobham), the leading Lollard, was excommunicated by Archbishop Arundel but escaped; a Lollard plot against the king's life was discovered; Henry attacked (1414) and captured a Lollard group, most of whom were hanged; anti-Lollard legislation allowed seizure of their books; Oldcastle, the last influential Lollard, executed (1417). Henceforth Lollardy was a lower-class movement driven underground until the Reformation.

1415. Henry, in alliance with Burgundy, reasserted his claims to the throne of France. Relying on the anarchy in France and hoping through military successes to unite the English behind the house of Lancaster, he advanced into France.

1415, Oct. 25. Battle of Agincourt, near Arras in Flanders.

1420. Henry's great victory over vastly superior forces opened the way to the **Treaty of Troyes** (p. 246).

1422–61. Henry VI (age nine months on his accession) acclaimed king of France; his uncle, the duke of Gloucester, regent (under the council) in England; another uncle, the duke of Bedford, regent in France.

1428–29. English failure at Orléans; coronation of Charles VII at Reims (1429).

1431. The English burned **Joan of Arc** (p. 246) at Rouen and crowned Henry VI king of France in Paris. Steady advance of Charles VII; unpopularity of the war in England; parliamentary resistance to grants; loss of the Burgundian alliance (1435) and of Paris (1436).

1436–37. Richard, duke of York (heir to throne), regent in France. He was replaced, after a few successes, by the earl of Warwick (1437–39) but later returned to France (1440–43). Continued rivalry of Beaufort and Gloucester.

1442. French conquest of Gascony except Bordeaux and Bayonne.

1448–51. The French reconquest of Maine (1448), Normandy (1450), and Bordeaux and Bayonne (1451) left only Calais in English hands at the end of the Hundred Years' War.

Domestic disorders. Henry, declared of age (1437), was unfit to rule; the council continued in power, and factions and favorites encouraged the rise of disorder. The nobles, enriched by the war and the new progress in sheep farming with enclosures, maintained increasing numbers of private armed retainers (livery and maintenance) with which they fought one another, terrorized their neighbors, paralyzed the courts, and dominated the government.

1450. Cade's rebellion: a revolt of perhaps 30,000 men of Kent and Sussex, including many respectable small landowners, who marched on London to demand reform in government and the restoration of the duke of York to power. Admitted to London, the marchers were finally

crushed after they resorted to violence. **Richard of York** was regent during Henry's periods of insanity (1453–54; 1455–56), but on his recovery (1454) Somerset returned to power.

1455–85. The Wars of the Roses. A dreary civil war between the houses of Lancaster and York (the Yorkists wearing a white rose, the Lancastrians [later] a red rose). The nation as such took little part. **Battle of St. Albans** (1455): Somerset defeated and killed. **Battle of Northampton** (1460): the Yorkists defeated the royal army and took Henry prisoner. York asserted his hereditary claim to the throne, and the lords decided that he should succeed Henry on his death (excluding Henry's son, Edward). Richard's son Edward (age 19) defeated the Lancastrians at **Mortimer's Cross** (1461), but was defeated at the **second battle of St. Albans** (1461). London admitted Edward to the town, and after his victory at Towton, acclaimed him king (1461).

Under the Lancastrians, Parliament forced a reversal of the Haxey judgment (1399), asserting a right to freedom of speech in debate. Opposition to packing began to develop, and a statute was passed defining the franchise for elections (1430); this statute was in force until the great reform bill of 1832.

Under Henry VI the aristocratic council ruled and dominated Parliament; finally the chaos of the Wars of the Roses saw the temporary eclipse of ordered government.

1461–85. The House of York.

1461–83. EDWARD IV. Parliament declared the three Lancastrian kings usurpers and Henry VI, his wife, son, and chief adherents, traitors. Edward closed the session with a speech of thanks to the Commons, the first time an English king had addressed that body. The mass of Englishmen now wanted a monarch to keep order and to allow them to attend to trade, industry, and agriculture. Civil war continued intermittently, and Henry VI was finally captured (1465) and put in the Tower. Edward's marriage to the commoner Elizabeth Woodville, and the beginnings of the creation of a new nobility, angered the older nobles. Edward now increasingly unpopular (1469–70).

1471. Edward's victory at Barnet (1471), where Warwick was killed. Henry VI died (in all probability, was murdered) in the Tower.

After the death of Henry VI, Edward faced no serious internal threat. Parliament denied him adequate support for war against Louis XI, and, in any case, when Edward invaded France in 1475, he was bought off without fighting. Thereafter he concentrated on domestic affairs: he reorganized revenues from crown lands (greatly expanded by the addition of the Yorkist estates); began the practice of taking **benevolences,** theoretically free gifts but actually forced; supported the wool trade and benefited from the increased customs duties. His resulting wealth, combined with a peaceful foreign policy, made him independent of Parliament. These policies served as precedents for later Tudor government.

1483. Edward V, age 12, the elder son of Edward IV and the tool of the competing ambitions of his paternal uncle, Richard, duke of Gloucester, and his maternal uncle Earl Rivers. Gloucester arrested Rivers, confined Edward and his younger brother in the Tower of London, had the boys declared illegitimate, and assumed the throne as Richard III. The children disappeared, probably murdered. According to a theory promoted by the Tudors after 1485, they were smothered in their sleep on Richard's orders. Their death provoked great public indignation. (In 1674, archaeologists unearthed in the Tower skeletons of two boys age 12 or 13 and 10, the ages of the princes in 1483.)

1483–85. Richard III. He aborted a rebellion conceived by Morton, bishop of Ely, and led by the duke of Buckingham; the latter was beheaded. Richard and Henry, earl of Richmond, both sought to marry Edward IV's daughter, Elizabeth of York, now heiress to the throne. As she was Richard's niece, the relationship scandalized even Richard's followers.

1485. The landing at Milford Haven of Henry, earl of Richmond, a remote descendant of Edward III, led to widespread defections among Richard's supporters. Henry defeated Richard (Aug. 22) on **Bosworth Field** (Leicestershire), where Richard fell. The crown of England was supposedly found on a rosebush. The battle marks the end of the Wars of the Roses and the beginning of the **House of Tudor,** by virtue of victory in battle and later act of Parliament.

Cultural movements. The Italian humanist Poggio Bracciolini's visit (1418–23) to England. *The Paston Letters* (1422–1509), a remarkable

THE HOUSES OF LANCASTER AND YORK (1377–1485)

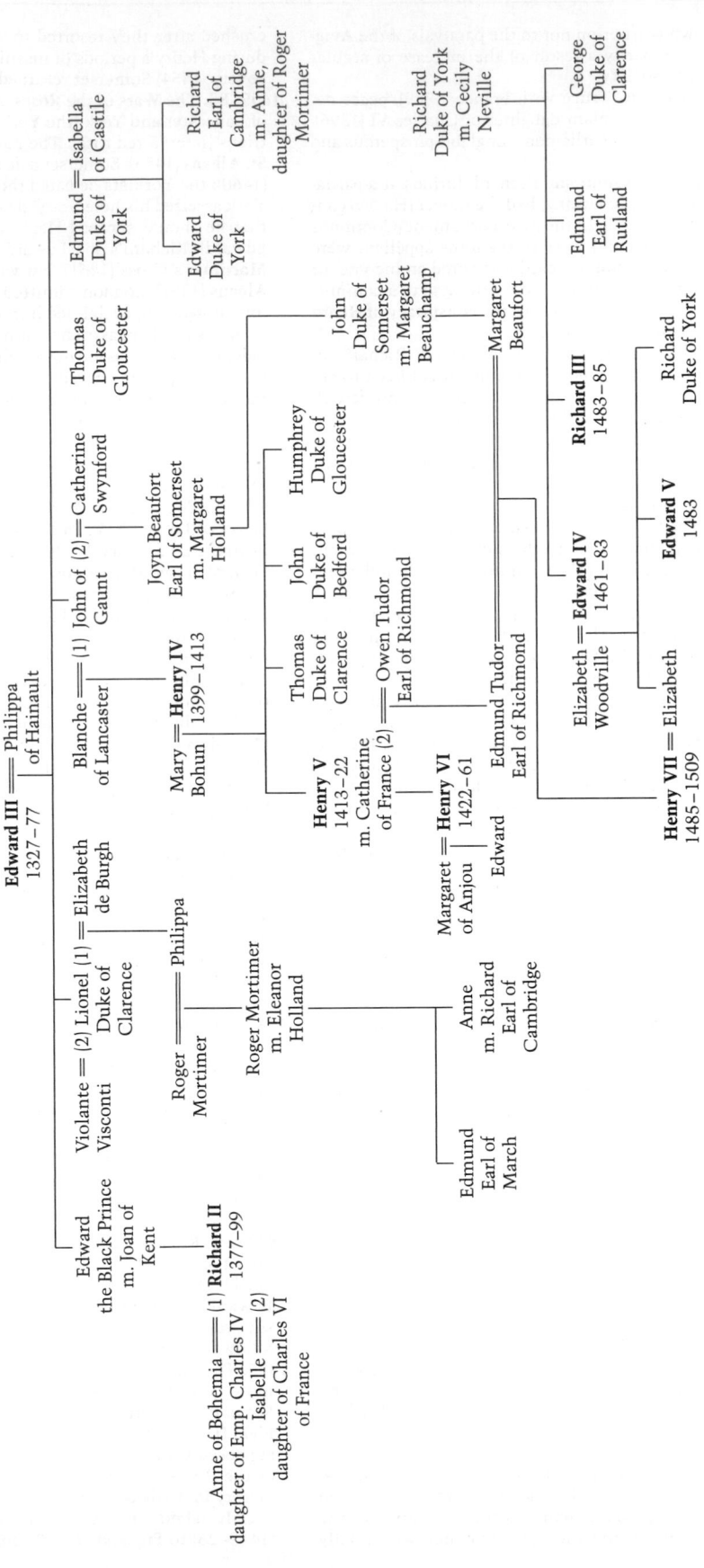

THE HOUSE OF STUART (1370–1625)

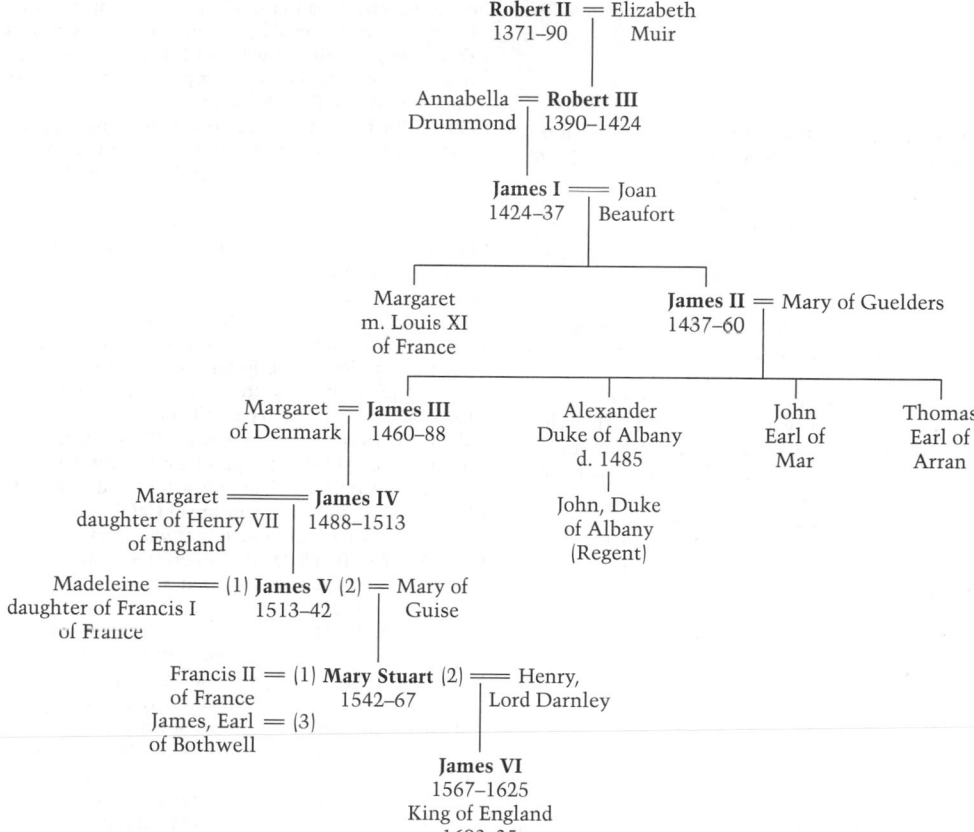

collection of the correspondence (in the vernacular) of a middle-class English family. **Eton College founded** by Henry VI.

Humphrey, duke of Gloucester (d. 1447), influential patron of classical learning and Italian humanism, was the donor of 279 classical manuscripts to Oxford, the nucleus of the university library. **Sir John Fortescue** (d. c. 1476), chief justice of the king's bench, wrote *On the Governance of the Kingdom of England* and *De Laudibus Legum Angliae*, contrasting the "political" (i.e., constitutional) spirit of the English common law with the absolutism of the Roman law, and comparing the French monarchy unfavorably with the English.

Caxton's printing press set up at Westminster (1476) under the patronage of Edward IV. Malory's *Morte Arthure* printed (1485), the first book in poetic prose in the English language. *(To p. 284)*

2. SCOTLAND
(From p. 197)

1305. The conquest of Scotland by Edward I of England saved the country from civil war. Edward's plan of union seemed possible for a brief period, until the emergence of Bruce's great-grandson, Robert, who turned against the English and maintained himself until the incompetence of Edward II gave him a chance to extend the opposition to the English.

1311–13. Bruce began a great advance into England and besieged Stirling (1314).

1314, June 24. Battle of Bannockburn. Bruce completely defeated the English and established himself on the throne.

1323. A truce of five years with England was followed by the **Treaty of Northampton,** which recognized Robert Bruce's title and provided for the marriage of his son David to Joan, daughter of Edward II.

1329–70. DAVID II, son of Robert, king. His minority was followed by an incompetent rule.

1332. Edward Baliol, with English support, was crowned, and Bruce fled to France. After Baliol's recall to England, Bruce returned and was defeated.

1346. Bruce was captured at the **Battle of Neville's Cross** in an effort to aid France by invading England. He was not ransomed until 1357.

Edward Baliol's futile reign gave the Scottish parliament its chance; the burghs had sent representatives to the parliament of 1326, but the practice was not a regular one until 1424. On at least two occasions the parliamentary majority went home (1367, 1369) and left the session to commissions, thus establishing the **Lords of Articles,** who assumed deliberative functions and soon became tools of the crown. Nevertheless, parliament managed to gain some control over royal acts, and kept its hand on the declaration of war and peace and the coinage. The lower clergy began sending representatives to parliament (e.g., 1367, 1369, 1370).

1356. Edward Baliol handed over his crown to Edward III.

1371. The **Stuart line** was established on the Scottish throne by the accession of **ROBERT II,** grandson of Robert Bruce (1371–90).

The family maintained itself for three centuries, despite a succession of futilities and minorities. The rival **house of Douglas** was finally extinguished (1488).

1406–37. JAMES I. After imprisonment (since 1405) in England, James began a vigorous reform, reduction of violence, restoration of the judicial process, and new legislation that ended anarchy and disciplined the Church. The country lairds were given representation in parliament as a support to the crown (1428). James was assassinated, 1437. St. Andrew's University founded.

1437–60. JAMES II. From James I to Charles I (1625), every sovereign was a minor on his accession. The reduction of the earls of Douglas (1452), followed by confiscation of their lands, enriched the crown. Rosburgh was taken from the English, leaving only Berwick in alien hands.

1460–88. JAMES III, a feeble figure, was kidnapped (1466) by Lord Boyd, who ruled as governor (by vote of parliament). The Orkneys and Shetlands were acquired from Norway (1472). France kept Scotland in contact with the Continent.   *(To p. 284)*

3. IRELAND
(From p. 197)

1315. Edward Bruce, brother of Robert Bruce of Scotland, landed in Ireland and, with the aid of native chieftains, had himself crowned (1316). But he was able to maintain himself only until 1318.

The Anglo-Norman colony began to weaken from internal quarrels while Edward III was preoccupied with the Hundred Years' War. The chieftains thereupon seized the opportunity to encroach on the position of the outsiders. From this period dates the gradual ebb of English influence. The Black Death (1348–49).

1366. The statute of Kilkenny attempted to prevent intermarriage and protect (English) racial purity by forbidding marriage between native Irish and English; Irish denied access to church benefices.

1398. Expedition of Richard II to reduce Ireland, but without results. Under Henry V misery in Ireland reached a new peak and perhaps half of the English colony returned home. The danger in this situation is mentioned in the *Libel of English Policie* (c. 1436). Fear that Ireland might pass into other hands was widespread.

1449. Richard of York arrived as viceroy and ingratiated himself equally with colonists and natives. He departed to England in 1450, but on his return made Ireland virtually independent, with the approval of the Irish parliament. English rule was repudiated and a separate coinage was established. Richard continued this policy until his death, but then Edward IV resumed a harsh policy. Under Richard III the strongest figure in Ireland was **Kildare,** leader of the Yorkists.   *(To p. 284)*

c. FRANCE

(From p. 205)

1314–16. LOUIS X (the Quarrelsome). The real ruler was Louis's uncle, Charles of Valois. A reaction against the monarchy forced concessions from the king.

1316. Louis was succeeded by his posthumous son, John I, who lived only a few days. Louis's daughter by his first wife, Jeanne, was also an infant. A great national council awarded the crown to Louis's brother.

1316–22. PHILIP V (the Tall). There were frequent meetings of assemblies that included burghers. Philip, in an enormous number of royal ordinances, gave definitive form to the Capetian government. He left no male heir.

1322–28. CHARLES IV (the Fair), the last Capetian of the direct line, succeeded his brother Philip, to the exclusion of Edward III of England, grandson of Philip IV. This established the principle, later called the **Salic Law,** that the throne could pass only through males. On Charles's death, an assembly of barons declared that "no woman nor her son could succeed to the monarchy."

1328–50. PHILIP VI (nephew of Philip IV, son of Charles of Valois), the nearest male heir. Jeanne, daughter of Louis X, became queen of Navarre. Brittany, Flanders, Guienne, and Burgundy remained outside the royal sway. The papacy was under French influence; rulers of the Capetian house of Anjou were seated on the thrones of Naples, Provence, and Hungary; Dauphiné, the first important imperial fief added to French territory, was purchased (1336). The king had become less accessible; the kingdom, regarded as a possession rather than an obligation, was left to the administration of the royal bureaucracy.

1338–1453. The Hundred Years' War. English commercial dominance in Flanders precipitated a political crisis. The communes made the count of Flanders, Louis of Nevers, prisoner (1325–26); Philip marched to his relief, massacred the burghers on the field of Cassel (1328), and established French administration in Flanders. Edward III retorted with an embargo on wool exports from England (1336); the weavers of Ghent, under the wealthy Jan van Arteveldt, became virtual masters of the country and made a commercial treaty with England (1338). On van Arteveldt's insistence, Edward declared himself king of France; the

Flemings recognized him as their sovereign, and made a political alliance with him (1340).

1338. Philip declared Edward's French fiefs forfeited and invested Guienne. Edward was made vicar of the empire, and his title as king of France was recognized by the emperor. Thus began the **Hundred Years' War,** really a series of wars with continuous common objectives: the retention of their French "empire" by the English, the liberation of their soil by the French.

1340. Philip, by dismissing two squadrons of Levantine mercenary ships, lost his mastery of the Channel until 1372 and was overwhelmingly defeated by Edward at the **naval battle of Sluys** (June 24) on Scheldt estuary on (modern) Belgian border. This opened the Channel to the English and gave them free access to northern France.

1341–64. A dynastic contest in Brittany, in which both Edward and Philip intervened.

1341. First collection of the *gabelle* (salt tax) in France; increasing war levies and mounting dissatisfaction.

1346. Edward's invasion of Normandy and overwhelming **victory at Crécy,** Aug. 26 (10,000 English defeated some 20,000 French) (p. 239). The French military system was outmoded, the people unaccustomed to arms, and the cavalry inefficient. Blind King John of Bohemia was slain. **Artillery** came into use (1335–45). Continued war levies led to open refusal (1346) of a grant by the estates of Langue d'Oïl, and a demand for reforms. The king attempted some reforms.

1347. Edward's siege and **capture of Calais** gave the English an economic and military base in France that was held until 1558.

1348–50. The **Black Death** penetrated northern Europe, gradually reducing the population by about a third and contributing to the crisis of 1357–58 in France.

1350–64. JOHN II (the Good Fellow), a "good knight and a mediocre king," a spendthrift who repeatedly debased the currency.

1355. English **renewal of the war** in a triple advance: into Brittany; from the Channel; and from Bordeaux, by the Black Prince. Virtual collapse of French finance. The estates of Languedoc and Langue d'Oïl (the latter under the leadership of **Etienne Marcel,** the richest man in Paris, provost of the merchants), forced the king (ordinance of 1355) to agree to consult the provincial estates before making new levies of money, a policy already in practice, and to accept supervision of the collection and expenditure of these levies by a commission from the estates. John cleverly induced the estates to adjourn, debased the coinage in the interest of his treasury, and organized his opposition to the estates.

1356. The **Black Prince** (the English "model of chivalry") defeated John, the last "chivalrous" king of France, at **Poitiers** (Sept. 19) (p. 239). Royal authority in France was reduced to a shadow; civil chaos reigned. Charles, the 18-year-old son of John, became regent.

1357. Climax of the power of the **Estates General:** The Estates General again had to be called, and it passed the **Great Ordinance,** which provided for supervision of the levy and expenditure of taxes by a standing committee of the estates, regular and frequent meetings of the estates, poor relief, and many other reforms, but did not attempt to reduce the traditional powers of the monarchy. The estates had met frequently, were divided, and had no real coherence or skill in government. They were discredited by Marcel's alliance with Charles the Bad of Navarre (a son of Jeanne, daughter of Louis X), who had a better claim to the throne than Edward III. The regent Charles fled from Paris and created a powerful coalition against the estates and Charles the Bad.

1358. The **Jacquerie,** a violent peasant reaction against war taxes, the weight of the ransoms of the captives at Poitiers, and the pillage of the free companies (demobilized soldiers), led to a merciless reaction by the nobles. Marcel, already distrusted, was further discredited by intrigues with the revolted peasantry and with the English. Charles, after the murder of Marcel (1358), returned to the capital, repressed disorder with a firm hand, and refused to approve John's preliminary peace (1359), which virtually restored the old Angevin lands in France to Edward.

1360. The **Peace of Bretigny** (Calais), virtually a truce of mutual exhaustion: Edward practically abandoned his claims to the French crown; Charles yielded southwestern France (Guienne), Calais, Ponthieu, and the territory immediately about them, and promised an enormous ransom for John. King John was released on partial payment of the ransom, but returned after the flight of a hostage to die in his

THE FRENCH SUCCESSION (1328)

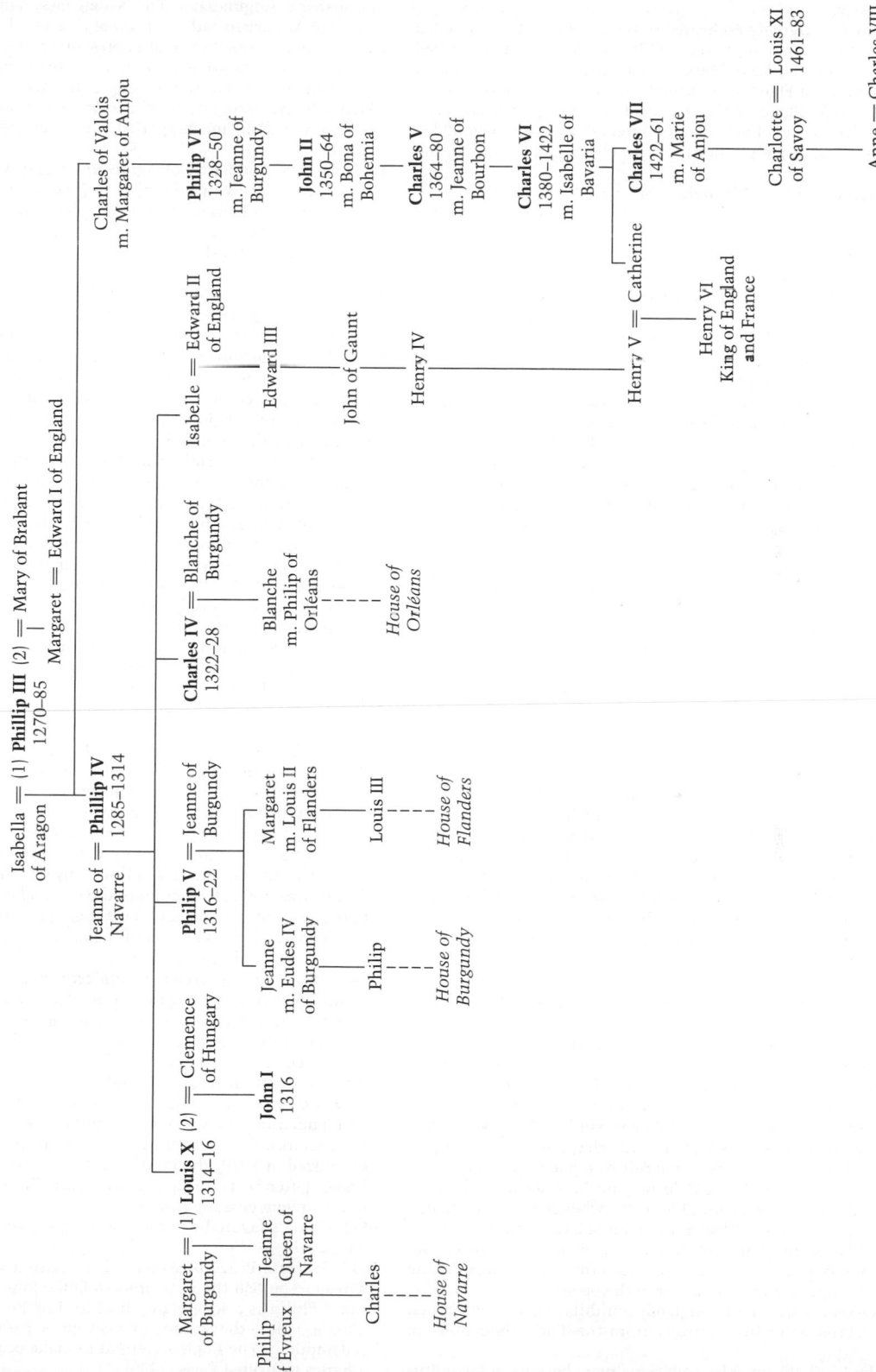

luxurious and welcome captivity in England. The southern provinces protested their return to English rule, clear signs of national sentiment born of adversity.

1361. The **duchy of Burgundy** escheated to the crown, and John handed it to his son Philip as an appanage (1363). Charles negotiated (1369) the marriage of Duke Philip to Margaret, daughter and heiress of Louis de Male, last count of Flanders, to keep Flanders out of English hands. As Margaret brought Flanders, the county of Burgundy, Artois, Nevers, and Rethel under control of the dukes of Burgundy, this marriage added a new danger on the east and north to the Plantagenet threat in the west.

1364–80. CHARLES V (the Wise), neither strong of body, handsome, nor chivalrous; a pious, refined, realistic statesman of "modern" cast. He saved France and made it plain that national well-being depended on the monarchy rather than on the Estates General.

The reign opened with bad harvests, plague, and pillage by the free companies. The Breton **Bertrand Du Guesclin,** the first great soldier on the French side in the Hundred Years' War, was sent with some 30,000 men to support Henry of Trastamara against Pedro the Cruel of Castile, who had become an ally of the Black Prince.

Charles managed to dominate the new financial machinery set up by the Estates General, continued the war levies (e.g., hearth tax, *gabelle*, sales taxes) and utilized the peace for general reform and reconstruction: castles were rebuilt, and royal control of them strengthened; permanent companies of professional cavalry and infantry were established; artillery was organized and supported by pioneers and sappers; a military staff and hierarchy of command was established in the army (1374); the navy was reorganized, and French sea power restored. New walls were built around Paris.

The grant from the estate of Langue d'Oïl (1360) for John's ransom had been for a term of six years; the grant of a hearth tax (1363) was without a time limit. Following these precedents, Charles was able (1369) to induce the estates to agree to the general principle that old grants of funds need not be renewed by the estates unless their terms were to be changed. This freed the king from control by the estates unless new taxes were needed, and it meant that the estates no longer had a vital function. The financial control established by the estates (1357) was transferred to the royal *chambre de comptes* in Paris.

1369. The appeal of the count of Armagnac to Charles against the Black Prince and the Black Prince's refusal to appear at Charles's court served as an excuse for the **resumption of the war.** The reconquest of Poitou and Brittany (1370–72) was followed by the death of the Black Prince (1376); the French fleet, supported by the Castilian, regained control (La Rochelle, 1372) of the Channel, and blocked English transport in the north. By 1380 the English held only Bordeaux, Bayonne, Brest, Calais, Cherbourg, Valais, and their immediately surrounding territory. France was cleared of the enemy, but it was in ruins.

1380–1422. CHARLES VI. A minority reign accompanied by the disruptive rivalry of the king's uncles (the dukes of Anjou, Berri, and Burgundy, the "Princes of the Lilies"), who exploited France for their own ends. This was followed by the intermittent insanity of the king, and paralysis in the government.

General **economic distress,** popular unrest, and general revolts, usually against taxes. Flanders, on the death of the count (1384), passed to Burgundy; its pacification was completed in 1385. The hearth tax was renewed, and taxation remained heavy.

1388. The death (1384) of the duke of Anjou had left the duke of Burgundy in a position of great power, and Charles, angered at Philip of Burgundy's policies, began his personal rule by replacing the duke with his own brother Louis, duke of Orléans, and by restoring (1389) his father's old advisers, men of humble birth (whence their nickname, the Marmousets). Louis of Orléans was a refined, talented spendthrift, unpopular in Paris, and Philip of Burgundy (supported by Queen Isabelle) was able to pose as a reformer and lead the opposition, bringing the rivalry of Burgundy and Orléans into the open.

1396. Twenty-year truce with England; annihilation of the French knights on a crusade to free Hungary from the Turks (Nicopolis, p. 125).

1404. John (the Fearless), an able, ambitious man, became **duke of Burgundy.** After the sudden transfer of Isabelle's support to Louis of Orléans, John's orders led to the assassination of Louis, duke of Orléans

(1407). John became the hero of Paris, but caused the emergence of two great factions in France and began the civil war of the **Armagnacs** against the Burgundians. The Armagnacs, named for their head, the count of Armagnac (father-in-law of Charles, the new duke of Orléans), were strong among the great nobles, drew their power from the south and southeast, and were a reactionary, anti-English war party. The Burgundians, supported by the people, the University of Paris, and the Wittelsbachs, were strong in the north and northeast, favored peace, were pro-English, and supported Pope Clement VII and his papal successors.

1415, Oct. 25. The Battle of Agincourt. Henry V, with 10,000 men, defeated three times that number of French; the duke of Orléans was taken prisoner; **Normandy was reconquered** by the English, undoing for the time the work of Philip Augustus; the dauphin (later Charles VII) fled to the south of France (1418); the Burgundians returned to power, and there was a massacre of Armagnacs in Paris (1418).

1419. Rouen fell; the Burgundians, alarmed at the English advance, began negotiating with the Armagnacs; John of Burgundy was assassinated at a conference with the dauphin at the bridge of Montereau, and the Burgundians returned to the English alliance.

1420. Charles, under Burgundian influence, and supported by his wife, Isabelle, accepted the **Treaty of Troyes** (which repudiated the dauphin as illegitimate), adopted Henry V of England as his heir and immediate regent (with the approval of the University of Paris and the Estates General, 1421). Charles's daughter, Catherine, was married to Henry V and, also under the treaty, the English were allowed to retain all their conquests as far as the Loire. King Henry V drove the forces of the dauphin across the Loire and began the steady conquest of France that continued uninterrupted until his death (1422). The dauphin remained at Bourges (whence his nickname, the Roi de Bourges).

1422–61. CHARLES VII (the Roi de Bourges, not crowned until 1429). Physically weak, bowed, and lethargic from misfortune; the puppet of unscrupulous advisers until the advent of a better group. **Regency of the duke of Bedford** (1422–28) for the infant Henry VI of England, who was recognized as king of France in the north, supported by the Burgundians, and crowned in Paris (1436).

1424. Bedford's decisive **victory at Verneuil** was followed by the defeat of the Armagnacs and the Scots at Verneuil.

1428. The English began the **siege of Orléans. Jeanne d'Arc** (Joan of Arc, the Maid of Orléans), born in 1412 at Domrémy, was from a comfortable village family, illiterate, but a good seamstress. A devout mystic, she began to have visions at the age of 13.

1429. Jeanne presented herself to the king at Chinon, and was allowed to lead an army (with the empty title of *chef de guerre*) to relieve Orléans. The relief of the city, followed by **Charles's coronation** (1429) at Reims, was the turning point of the war and marked a decisive change in the spirit of the king and the nation. Jealous ministers (e.g., La Trémoille) of Charles soon undermined Jeanne's position, despite the progress of the royal cause.

1430. Jeanne was captured at Compiègne by the Burgundians, ransomed by the English. Without intervention by Charles in her behalf, she was tried for witchcraft. Joan's wearing of men's clothes appeared not only aberrant but indicative of contact with the devil.

1431. An ecclesiastical court condemned her as a heretic: her claim of direct inspiration from God and the saints, thereby denying the authority of church officials, constituted heresy. After her confession and its repudiation, she was burned by the English at Rouen. Death came from suffocation, not burning. A new trial (1456) rehabilitated her; canonized in 1920, she is today revered as the second patron saint of France (after St. Louis) and as the symbol of the vitality and strength of the French peasant classes.

1432. Charles favored the **council of Basel,** which was pro-French and antipapal.

1435. Separate **Peace of Arras,** reconciliation with Burgundy: Charles agreed to punish the murderers of Duke John of Burgundy and recognized Philip as a sovereign prince for life. Burgundy was to recognize Charles's title; the Somme towns were to pass to Burgundy (subject to redemption). The English refused to make peace on acceptable terms. **Charles recovered Paris** (1436).

1437–39. Famine, pestilence, anarchy, but steady progress against the English.

1438, July 7. Pragmatic Sanction of Bourges. The French clergy asserted, under direction of Charles VII and while the Council of Basle was sitting, that a general council of the church was superior to the pope; that French clergy had the right to administer its temporal property independent of the papacy, and denied papal right of nomination to church offices. A general statement of the autonomy of the French church and of its independence for the papacy.

1440. The Praguerie, part of a series of coalitions of great nobles against the king, with support from the dauphin (later Louis XI), was put down; the dauphin was ordered to the Dauphiné, where he continued his intrigues.

1444. Louis the dauphin made a treaty of **alliance with the Swiss cantons.** The alliance was strengthened (1452), and an alliance was made with the towns of Trier, Cologne, et al. (1452), and with Saxony, as part of a developing anti-Burgundian policy. Intermittent support for the house of Anjou in Naples and the house of Orléans in Milan. Under **Jacques Coeur,** the merchant prince of Montpellier, royal finances were reformed, control of the public revenue by the king was established, and French commercial penetration of the Middle East was furthered (c. 1447).

1445–46. Army reforms: establishment of the first permanent royal army by the creation of 20 companies of élite cavalry (200 *lances* to a company, six men to a *lance*) under captains chosen by the king; a paid force, the backbone of the army.

1449–61. Expulsion of the English (p. 241): Normandy and Guienne regained; Talbot slain (1453).

1461–83. LOUIS XI (the Spider), of simple, bourgeois habits, superficial piety, and a feeble, ungainly body, the architect of French reconstruction. He was well educated, a brilliant diplomat, a relentless statesman, an endless traveler throughout his kingdom. He perfected the governmental system begun under Charles V (revived by Charles VII), and established the basic structure of the country until 1789. The recognized right of the king to the *taille, aides,* and *gabelle* taxes made a good revenue available for defense and diplomacy. Louis improved and perfected the standing army with added emphasis on the artillery but seldom waged war. Feudal anarchy and brigandage were stopped; a wise economic policy restored prosperity despite grinding taxes.

1461. Louis's first step in the reconstruction of the kingdom was a rapprochement with the papacy by the formal **revocation of the Pragmatic Sanction of Bourges.** Little of the royal power was sacrificed, and the national Church remained under the firm control of the crown.

1462. Acquisition of Cerdagne and Roussillon; redemption of the Somme towns (1463) revealing the resumption of national expansion.

1465. League of the Public Weal, a conspiracy against Louis by the dukes of Alençon, Burgundy, Berri, Bourbon, Lorraine.

1465. Louis's defeat by the league at Montlhéry. Louis split the league by diplomacy.

Louis's greatest rival was **Duke Philip the Good** of Burgundy. Philip was head of the first union of the Low Countries since the days of Charlemagne, a curious approximation of the ancient Lotharingia that included: the duchy and county of Burgundy, Flanders, Artois, Brabant, Luxemburg, Holland, Zealand, Friesland, Hainault. The dukes lacked only Alsace and Lorraine and the royal title.

1467. The accession of **Charles the Bold** as duke of Burgundy opened the final duel with Burgundy.

1468. Anglo-Burgundian alliance; marriage of Charles the Bold to Margaret of York.

1474. Louis formed the **Union of Constance** (a coalition of the foes of Burgundy, under French subsidies), which opened the war on Charles.

1475. Edward IV, an ally of Charles, invaded France; Louis met him at Piquigny and bought him off.

1476. Charles's conquest of Lorraine and war on the Swiss cantons: defeat of Charles at **Grandson** and **Morat.**

1477, Jan. 5. Defeat and death of Charles at Nancy (triumph of the Swiss pikemen over cavalry); end of the Burgundian menace. Louis united the duchy of Burgundy with the crown and occupied the county of Burgundy (Franche Comté). Flanders stood by the daughter of Charles, Mary of Burgundy, and was lost to France forever. Mary hurriedly married the Habsburg archduke Maximilian, the "heir" to the empire.

1480. On the **extinction of the house of Anjou,** Anjou, Bar, Maine, and

Provence fell to the French crown. Bar completed Louis's mastery on the eastern frontier.

The most significant internal fact of the reign was the development of a clear basis for royal power. Only one meeting of the Estates General was held (1469), and on that occasion the Estates asked the king to rule without them in future. Legislation was thenceforth by royal decree, a situation that facilitated Louis's thoroughgoing reform of the government and administration.

Cultural Developments. Jean Froissart (1337–1410) wrote his *Chroniques,* a colorful history of his times. **Philippe de Commines** (1447–1511), a Fleming who left the service of Charles the Bold for that of Louis, produced in his *Mémoires* a fine piece of critical history. **François Villon** (1430–70) was a lyric poet of the first rank. **Christine de Pisan** (1363?–1434?), whose writings include *Livre de la mutacion de fortune,* a major historical work; a biography of King Charles V; *The City of Ladies,* which lists the great women of history and their contributions; the *Book of Three Virtues,* which gives prudent advice on household management for women of all classes; and many letters and an autobiography.

Jan (d. 1441) **and Hubert van Eyck** (d. 1426), Flemish painters in the service of the court of Burgundy, perfected oil technique, religious painting, and portraiture, raising the painter's art to the highest stage of proficiency and perfection.

The Burgundian school of music flourished under the patronage of Charles the Bold: **Gilles Binchois** (d. 1470); **Guillaume Dufay** (d. 1474).

The only professional engineering document of the Middle Ages is the notebook of **Villard de Honnecourt** (fl. late 14th century), a French architect who worked in Cambrai, Laon, Reims, Meaux, and Chartres, as well as in Hungary. His notebook contains architectural plans, practical geometry, descriptions of machines. **Jean Buridan** (d. 1358) used the concept of impetus as an explanation for motion and acceleration. **Nicole Oresme,** College of Navarre, used geometrical diagrams to display the variation of physical quantities under various conditions.

(To p. 291)

d. THE IBERIAN PENINSULA

(From p. 222)

Parliamentary institutions. As elsewhere in Western Europe (p. 239), parliamentary assemblies developed in the Iberian Peninsula during the 13th to 15th centuries. In addition to the nobles and higher ecclesiastics of their courts, Spanish kings summoned representatives of those towns that were centers of trade, industry, and administration. The *cortes* (Sp. vernacular for king's court, the plural implying size and importance) emerged in Leon (1188), Aragon (1214), Catalonia (1225?), Castile-Leon (1250), and Portugal (1254). Because ordinary (feudal) revenues failed to meet the rising needs of the crown, kings had to secure consent for extraordinary levies. The initiative for summoning assemblies belonged to the king alone. As the clergy and nobles were usually exempt from taxation, the burden fell chiefly on the townspeople; the townspeople, however, often attached conditions to their grants: a royal promise of redress of grievances; a restriction to a fixed number of years; a promise that the levy would not prejudice town liberties (special privileges previously granted). Although approval of taxation was the *cortes'* most important function, they also played a role in matters of the succession (e.g., Isabella of Castile in 1474) and foreign policy. Neither Navarre nor the lands in southern Spain under Muslim control developed the *cortes,* nor did the Iberian Peninsula again experiment with one "national" assembly—because it was a collection of separate kingdoms. The disorders of the late 15th century and the trend toward absolutism in the 16th century weakened the influence of the *cortes.*

1. CASTILE

The successors of Alfonso X were not conspicuous for capacity. Frequent minorities and constant dynastic contests weakened the authority of the crown still further.

1312–50. Most outstanding of the Castilian rulers in this period was **ALFONSO XI,** who decisively defeated the joint attack of the Spanish

THE HOUSE OF CASTILE (1252–1504)

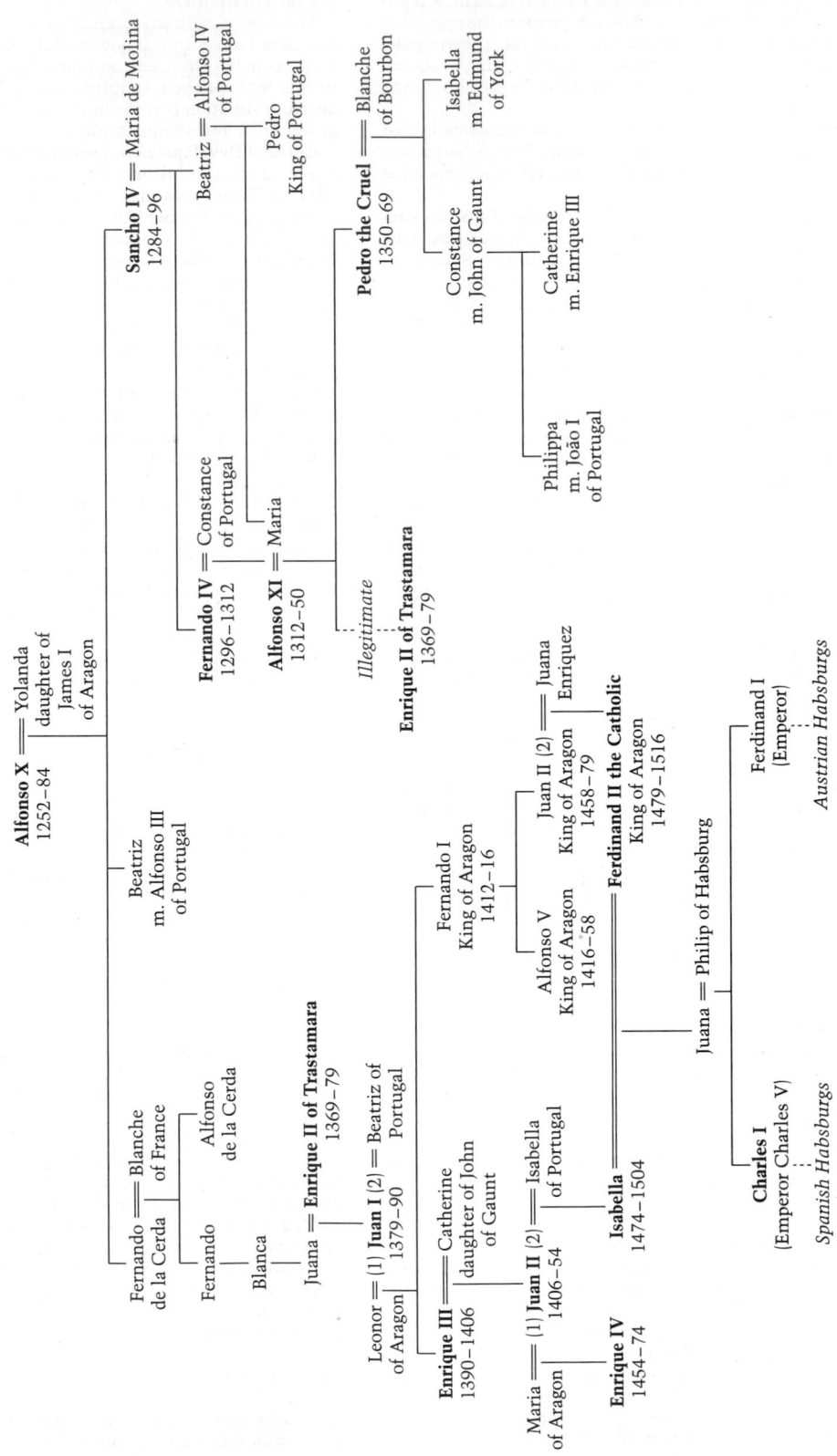

Alfonso X 1252–84 == Yolanda daughter of James I of Aragon

Fernando == Blanche de la Cerda of France

Alfonso de la Cerda

Fernando

Blanca

Juana == **Enrique II of Trastamara** 1369–79

Leonor == (1) **Juan I** (2) == Beatriz of Aragon 1379–90 of Portugal

Enrique III 1390–1406 == Catherine daughter of John of Gaunt

Maria == (1) **Juan II** (2) == Isabella of Aragon 1406–54 of Portugal

Enrique IV 1454–74

Isabella 1474–1504

Beatriz m. Alfonso III of Portugal

Sancho IV 1284–96 == Maria de Molina

Fernando IV 1296–1312 == Constance of Portugal

Beatriz == Alfonso IV of Portugal

Pedro King of Portugal

Alfonso XI 1312–50 == Maria

Illegitimate

Enrique II of Trastamara 1369–79

Pedro the Cruel 1350–69 == Blanche of Bourbon

Constance m. John of Gaunt

Catherine m. Enrique III

Isabella m. Edmund of York

Philippa m. João I of Portugal

Fernando I King of Aragon 1412–16

Alfonso V King of Aragon 1416–58

Juan II (2) == Juana King of Aragon Enriquez 1458–79

Ferdinand II the Catholic King of Aragon 1479–1516

Juana == Philip of Habsburg

Charles I (Emperor Charles V)

Spanish Habsburgs

Ferdinand I (Emperor)

Austrian Habsburgs

and Moroccan Muslims. His **victory at Rio Salado** (Oct. 30, 1340) ended the African menace forever and was the chief battle in the whole history of the Reconquest.

Throughout the **Hundred Years' War,** Castile supported France but attempted to avoid hostility with England as much as possible.

1350–69. PETER (Pedro, the Cruel). His reign was in fact little more than a 19-year dynastic conflict with his half-brother, the bastard **Henry of Trastamara.** Ultimately Henry defeated and killed Peter (1369).

1369–79. Henry (Enrique) II (Trastamara), who renewed the alliance with France. The Castilian fleet, through its victory over the English in the **Battle of La Rochelle** (1372), restored command of the Channel to the French. Peace between Castile on the one side and Portugal and Aragon on the other concluded at **Almazan** (1374).

1375. Rapprochement of Castile and Aragon, through the marriage of Henry's son, John, to Eleanor, daughter of Peter IV of Aragon.

Castilian leadership in the reconquest of Muslim Spain led to a degree of local and municipal self-government between the middle of the 12th and the middle of the 14th centuries. The *cortes* apparently originated from councils of nobles dating from Visigothic days. The Castilian rulers freely granted *fueros* (charters of self-government) to towns in the early stages of the Reconquest, and elements of local liberty appeared in municipal government in this period.

Urban groups, the *hermandades* (brotherhoods), sworn to defend the laws of the realm and the lives and property of their members, were clearly developed in the 13th century (e.g., Sancho's, 1282, directed against his father, Alfonso X) and usually supported the kings in periods of crisis (minorities, succession struggles, baronial assaults). The decline of the *hermandades* is associated with the municipal decline and the appearance of the royal *corregidores* (mayors) in the towns (14th century), but it is not clear whether the crown hastened the decay of the towns and the brotherhoods or sought to stave it off.

Despite all this support, the battle of the kings with the aristocracy, firmly entrenched during the early stages of the Reconquest, was a losing one. The nobles were exempt from taxes and from many laws; in general the same was true of the clergy, and some of the great bishops were virtual sovereigns.

The Jewish population of medieval Spain (p. 219) had generally prospered under first Muslim and then Christian rule. Christian kings welcomed Jews, because they represented capital investment, banking, and commercial expertise.

1391–1420. The nobility's attempt to reimpose serfdom, oppressive taxation, and general working-class frustration over poor socioeconomic conditions led to **widespread Christian attacks on the Jews** (e.g., in Barcelona and Sevilla), some spontaneous, others incited by churchmen, such as the Dominican **St. Vincent Ferrer.** Many wealthy Jews—courtiers, businessmen, scholars, rabbis—lost interest in traditional (Talmudic) Judaism, and perhaps 100,000 Jews **converted to Christianity (c. 1425–50).** The vast majority of these *conversos* were, within a generation or so, little different in religious practice and commitment from the rest of the population.

1469. Marriage of Isabella, half-sister and heiress of Henry IV, to **Ferdinand,** heir of the king of Aragon.

1474. ISABELLA succeeded to the Castilian throne. Isabella's succession was challenged by the daughter of Henry IV, supported by Afonso V of Portugal. But the *cortes* of Segovia (1475) recognized Isabella and Ferdinand and the latter defeated the Portuguese in 1476 (**Battle of Toro**).

1479. FERDINAND (FERNANDO) succeeded to the rule of Aragon, Catalonia, Valencia. A form of dyarchical government was set up for the united Castilian and Aragonese crowns. Rule of the **Catholic kings** (Ferdinand and Isabella). Restoration of the royal power in Castile: by revising the town charters, the towns were made centers of resistance to feudal aggression; formation of the **Santa Hermandad,** a union of Castilian towns in the interest of royal authority and order. The great feudal magnates were deprived of many of their possessions and rights, and a royal administration was gradually established. The *Libro de Montalvo* (1485), an early codification of Spanish law.

Christian resentment of the important economic and ecclesiastical positions attained by former Jews (p. 294) led to the spread of two ideas: that leadership in Iberian society required **"purity of blood,"** and that many new Christians were crypto-Jews (**Marranos**), secretly practicing

their old religion. On **Nov. 1, 1478,** at the request of King Ferdinand (who himself had a Jewish grandmother), Pope Sixtus approved the establishment of the **Inquisition** in Spain. It became an instrument for centralizing royal power against the nobility, of whom the converted Jewish elite was a sizable minority (perhaps one third). Converted (from Judaism) bishops played a prominent role in the early work of the Inquisition.

1492, Jan. Granada fell to a Christian army, marking the end of the reconquest of Spain from the Muslims. On March 31, 1492, Ferdinand and Isabella issued an edict from Granada giving the Jews until July 31 to choose between accepting baptism or leaving the country. About 40,000, perhaps half the practicing Jews, left the country for Portugal, Venice, Rome, or Ottoman Turkey.

Art and literature. Castilian painting showed the influence of the school of Giotto (after c. 1380), and in the 15th century painting came under Flemish inspiration (visit of Jan van Eyck, 1428–29). In general, literature and learning followed the same foreign tendencies as architecture and painting: French influence came in early, followed later by Italian and English (notably Dante, Petrarch, Boccaccio, Gower). Introduction of printing at Valencia (c. 1474) and in Castile (c. 1475).

2. ARAGON

1276–85. PETER (PEDRO) III, who was married to Constance, daughter of Manfred and heir of the Hohenstaufen. In 1282 he sailed on a long-planned expedition for the **conquest of Sicily** (which he disguised as an African crusade). He landed at Collo, was called to the throne, defeated Charles of Anjou, and became Peter I of Sicily (1282–85), refusing to do homage to the pope for his island kingdom. This expansion of the Aragonese kingdom gave Aragon for a time predominance in the western Mediterranean, but it estranged the Aragonese aristocracy, as well as the towns. The nobility therefore formed the **Union for Liberty** and, in the *cortes* of 1283, extorted from Peter a **General Privilege,** which defined the rights and duties of the nobles, affirmed the principle of due process of law, and provided for annual meetings of the *cortes.*

1285–91. ALFONSO III was obliged to make a sweeping regrant of the Privileges of Union (1287), the so-called **Magna Carta of Aragon.**

1291–1327. JAMES II (king of Sicily, 1285–95). He exchanged the investiture of Sardinia and Corsica for that of Sicily (1295), which thereupon passed to his brother Frederick, who established the separate Sicilian dynasty. James began the expulsion of the Genoese and Pisans from Sardinia (1323–24), a process not finally completed until 1421. For a period Aragon held the duchy of Athens (first indirectly through Sicily, 1311–77, then directly, to 1388), thanks to the activity of the **Grand Catalan Company** (p. 274).

1327–36. ALFONSO IV.

1336–87. PETER (PEDRO) IV. He was virtually a prisoner of the revived union of the nobility and had to confirm their privileges. But after a victory over the union (at **Epila,** 1348), he broke up the coalition and gradually restricted the power of the aristocracy in Aragon and Valencia. The clergy and the towns had far less power than in Castile, while the rural workers and serfs suffered a much harder lot.

1377. On the death of Frederick II of Sicily, Peter IV, as the husband of Frederick's sister, sent his son Martin as viceroy to Sicily.

1387–95. John (Juan) king.

1395–1410. Martin king. He reunited Aragon and Sicily (1409). On his death, the native dynasty came to an end after a period of dynastic struggle.

1412–16. Ferdinand (Fernando) I, of Castile, a grandson of Peter IV, succeeded to the throne.

1416–58. ALFONSO V (the Magnanimous). His attention was engrossed by the desire to conquer Naples. After long diplomatic intrigues and occasional combats, he succeeded (1435) in being recognized as king by the pope in 1442. Alfonso, a lover of Italy and a passionate devotee of the Renaissance, shifted the center of gravity of the Aragonese empire and subordinated the interest of Aragon to that of Naples. Aragon was ruled by his brother John, as viceroy. On the death of Alfonso, Naples passed to his son Ferrante (1458–94).

1458–79. John (Juan) II king.

THE HOUSE OF ARAGON (1276–1516)

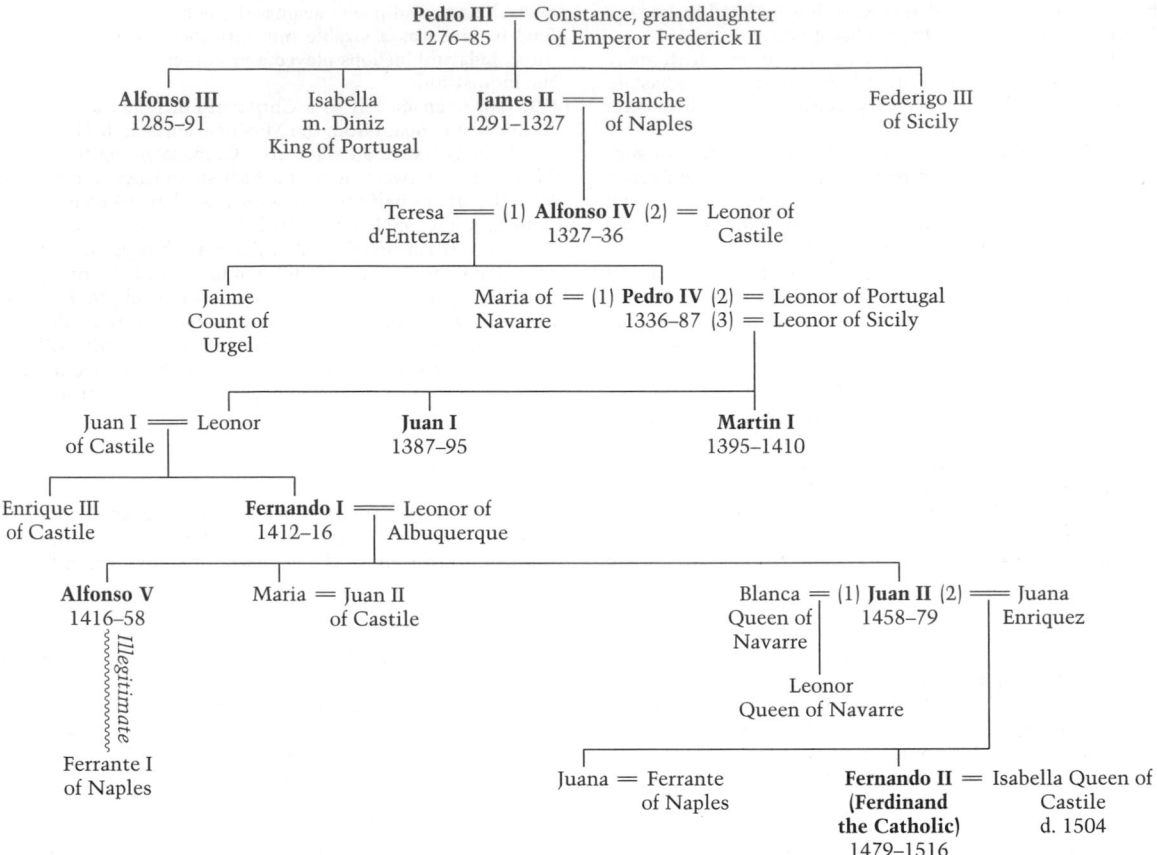

1479–1516. FERDINAND (FERNANDO) II king. **Union of Aragon with Castile.**   *(To p. 294)*

3. PORTUGAL
(From p. 222)

1279–1325. DINIZ (the Worker), the best-known and best-loved king of medieval Portugal. An ardent poet, he did much to raise the cultural level of the court. His interest in agriculture and his constant effort toward economic development (commercial treaty with England, 1294) resulted in greater prosperity. Beginning of **Portuguese naval activity** (under Venetian and Genoese guidance). Foundation (1290) of the University of Lisbon, which was soon (1308) moved to Coimbra.

1325–57. AFONSO IV (the Brave), whose reign was scarred by dynastic troubles. The **murder of Inez de Castro** (1355), the mistress and later the wife of Afonso's son Peter, at the behest of Afonso. This episode, the subject of much literature, led to the revolt of Peter.

1340. The Portuguese, in alliance with Castile, defeated the Moors in the **battle of Salado.**

1357–67. PETER (PEDRO) I (the Severe), a harsh and hasty, though just, ruler who continued his predecessor's efforts in behalf of the general welfare.

1367–83. FERDINAND (FERNÃO) I (the Handsome), a weak ruler whose love for Leonora Telles led him to repudiate his betrothal to a Castilian princess and so bring on a war with Castile.

1383. Regency of Queen Leonora on behalf of Ferdinand's daughter, Beatrice, who was married to John I of Castile. This arrangement led to strong opposition among the Portuguese, who detested both the regent and her lover, and resented all control from outside.

1385–1433. JOHN (JOÃO) I, an illegitimate son of Peter I, established the **Avis dynasty** after leading a successful revolt and driving the regent

out of the country. He was proclaimed king by the *cortes* of Coimbra, but his position was at once challenged by the Castilians, who twice invaded Portugal and besieged Lisbon.

1385, Aug. 14. The **Battle of Aljubarrota,** in which the Portuguese defeated the Castilians. A decisive date in the history of the country, this battle established the **independence of Portugal.** With the Avis dynasty, Portugal entered on the greatest period of her history. The king himself was an able and enlightened ruler, who enjoyed the aid of five outstanding sons, of whom **Henry the Navigator** (1394–1460) became the greatest figure in the history of the epoch-making discoveries of the 15th century (p. 105).

1386, May 9. The **Treaty of Windsor,** by which England and Portugal became permanently allied. King John married Philippa, the daughter of John of Gaunt. The dynasty thereby became part English.

1411. Peace was finally concluded with Castile.

1415, Aug. 24. The Portuguese took **Ceuta** from the Moors (p. 131), thus initiating a policy of expansion on the African continent.

1433–38. Edward (Duarte) I, a learned and intelligent prince, eldest son of John. His short reign was marked by a terrific epidemic of the plague and by the **disaster at Tangier.**

1437. In the disaster at Tangier, the Portuguese were overwhelmingly defeated. They were obliged to promise to return Ceuta, and to leave in Moorish hands the youngest brother of the king, **Ferdinand** (the Constant Prince), who died in captivity after five years of suffering. Ceuta was not returned.

1438–81. AFONSO V (the African), an attractive and chivalrous ruler, but lacking the hard-headed realism of his predecessors. The reign began with the regency of the king's mother, Eleonora, a Spanish princess, who again was confronted with Portuguese opposition to a Spanish connection. The nobility revolted, the regent fled, and the king's uncle, Peter, was made regent. His able and enlightened rule came to

KINGS OF PORTUGAL (1248–1521)

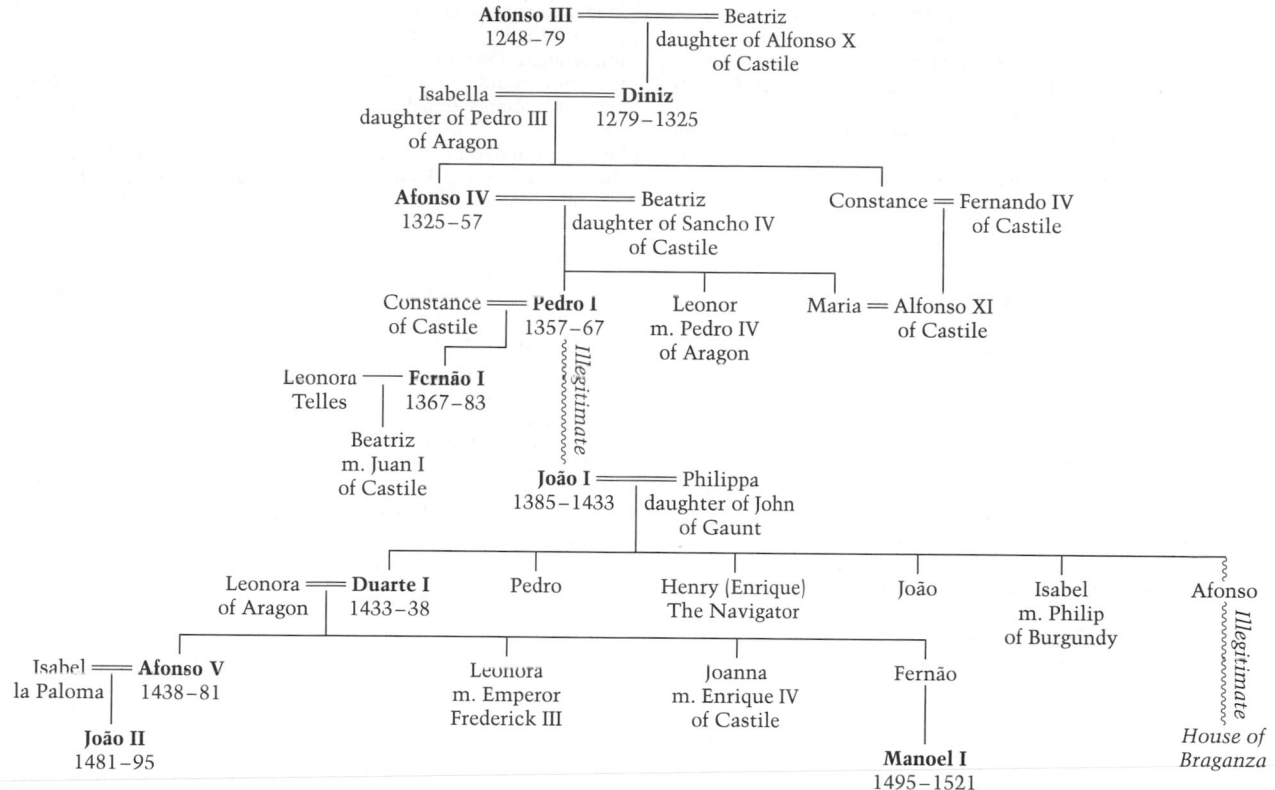

an end when the king, having reached his majority, allowed himself to be persuaded by favorites to make war on Peter. The latter and his son were defeated and killed in the **Battle of Alfarrobeira** (1449).

1446. The *Ordenaçoes Affonsinas,* the first great law code of the Portuguese, representing an amalgam of Roman, Visigothic, and customary law.

1463. Campaigns against the kingdom of Fez. The Portuguese captured Casablanca.

1471. The Portuguese captured Tangiers.

1476. Battle of Toro. Defeat of the Portuguese by the Castilians, after Afonso, who had married a sister of Isabella, attempted to dispute the latter's succession to the throne.

1481–95. JOHN (JOÃO) II, an energetic prince who at once undertook to restrict the property and power of the nobility, which had become very great during the preceding reign. This led to a revolt of the nobles, led by **Ferdinand of Braganza** and supported by the Catholic kings of Castile and Aragon. The revolt was suppressed in 1483; Braganza and many of his followers were executed. The royal power thenceforth was more firmly established than ever before. *(To p. 296)*

e. THE PAPACY AND ITALY

(From p. 216)

1. THE PAPACY
For a complete list of the Roman popes, see Appendix IV.

1308. Clement V (1304–14), who had been residing in France, made the decision to settle at Avignon, in southeast France on the Rhône River. Although technically not in French territory—it belonged to the Angevin princes of Naples—French influence was very strong. The actual move of the papal court occurred the following year.

1309–78. The Avignonese papacy. The seven popes of Avignon, all French (as were 113 of the 134 cardinals appointed during this period), removed themselves from Rome, the spiritual center of the West, and devoted their attentions to the reform of the papal bureaucracy and to the construction of the beautiful Gothic papal palace rather than to the spiritual problems of the Church and the political difficulties of Rome and Italy. The term "Babylonian captivity," sometimes used for the same period, represents a conflation of the ideas of the 14th-century Florentine poet Francesco Petrarch and the 16th-century German reformer Martin Luther. Petrarch's career in the service of Clement VI provoked Italian resentment of the French dominance at the papal curia and hostility toward the fiscal and moral vices of the city and court. His sense of exile led him to quote the beginning of Psalm 137: "By the rivers of Babylon we sat down and wept," the Rhône being the river of the new Babylon. Martin Luther used the term Babylonian captivity to refer to the entire period of medieval Christianity, when (he believed) the doctrine of salvation by works predominated. The term became a Protestant image implying fiscal and moral corruption and should be avoided by those who do not want to imply a Protestant continuation of medieval Christianity.

1310–13. Expedition of the Emperor Henry VII to Italy (p. 261). Henry asserted his independence of the spiritual power and claimed control of Italy. Clement V and Philip IV (opposed to him as a rival of the Angevins) combined against him.

1316–34. JOHN XXII, who supported the Angevins in Naples. His attempt to decide the validity of Emperor Louis IV's title led to a long struggle (1323–47). Louis was supported by the German people, who resented the Avignonese papacy, and by the Franciscans. John was unable to return to Italy because of the continued anarchy.

1342–52. CLEMENT VI's pontificate was marked by a revolution.

1347. Revolution of Cola di Rienzi at Rome. With the support of the populace, Cola overthrew the rule of the patricians, set himself up as tribune of the people, and summoned an Italian national parliament. Expelled by his opponents (1348), he returned in 1352 and was appointed senator by the pope (1354), but was in the same year slain by his baronial opponents. The lords of the Papal States resumed control and were, for all intents and purposes, independent of papal authority. Cola is considered a forerunner of Italian nationalism.

1352–62. INNOCENT VI. He sent the Spanish cardinal Albornoz to Italy, and the latter succeeded in reducing the powerful barons to obedience, thus making possible an eventual return of the pope.

Reform of the Curia during the Avignon period. General work of centralization and departmentalization: (1) the *camera apostolica;* (2) the chancery; (3) justice; (4) the penitentiary (dispensations). The loss of Italian revenues forced the popes to be more exacting in the levying of their spiritual income; thus the centralization of the papal curia put many clerical appointments under direct papal control through an extension of the papal rights of provision (appointment to benefices). The new efficiency in the levying and collection of taxes, combined with the appointment of Italians to offices in northern Europe, increased resentment, especially in England and the German Empire after the outbreak of the Hundred Years' War. Significant items of the budget of John XXII: war, 63.7 percent; upkeep and entertainment, 12.7 percent; alms, 7.16 percent; stables, 0.4 percent; art, 0.33 percent; library, 0.17 percent.

Vying with the growing magnificence of the monarchies of Europe, the Avignonese popes and cardinals became known for their pomp and luxury, and these tendencies spread to the episcopate, despite the thundering of the Franciscans and the decrees of local synods. The insubordination of outraged reformers, like the Bohemian preachers and **Wiclif,** soon penetrated to the masses.

Virtually every pope (notably Clement V and John XXII) made serious and honest efforts to combat these alarming developments, but the general anarchy in Europe made success impossible. There was a notable **expansion of missions to East Asia:** China (an archbishop and ten suffragans, 1312; 50 Franciscan houses, 1314; missions to Persia). Rome, the ancient spiritual center of the West, was reduced to an anarchic, poverty-stricken, provincial city, and clamored for the return of the popes.

1376, June 18. Visit of **Catherine of Siena** (1347–80) to Avignon. Caterina Beninsara, who cultivated piety and claimed from childhood to have received visions, joined the Dominican Third Order in 1363 and, with a group of followers, traveled through Italy preaching reform and ministering in hospitals and leper houses. Her reputation as a mystic and a miracle worker propelled her into a public role: anxious to see the papacy returned to Rome, she went to Avignon to urge Gregory IX to return; public opinion credited her influence as having been decisive. Catherine later supported Urban VI against the Avignonese antipope, and she died in Urban's service. Her 350 letters and mystical compositions, dictated because of her own illiteracy, survive. Canonized (1461) by the Sienese Pope Pius II, she is revered as one of the patron saints of Italy.

1370–78. GREGORY XI visited Rome and died before he could leave. The conclave, under threat of personal violence from the Roman mob, yielded to demands for an Italian pope.

1378–89. URBAN VI was elected. His worthy goals of reform were soon vitiated by his tactless and ill-tempered manner.

1378–1417. This led to the **GREAT SCHISM,** in which the papacy was divided and dishonored. Thirteen cardinals met at Anagni.

1378–94. They elected **CLEMENT VII,** thus dividing western Christendom into obediences:

The Roman Line	The Avignonese Line
Urban VI	**Clement VII**
(1378–89)	(1378–94)
Boniface IX	**Benedict XIII**
(1389–1404)	(1394–1423)
Innocent VII	
(1404–6)	
Gregory XII	
(1406–15)	

Allegiance to the rivals was determined partly by political considerations, but often was settled after careful study of the claims of each and consultation with the clergy (e.g., King Charles V of France, John of Castile); England's decision was based largely on hostility to France; Scotland's on its hostility to England; in Naples and Sicily the rulers and their subjects took opposite positions.

Emergence of the conciliar movement. The basic ideas were inherent in the works of such writers as **Marsiglio of Padua;** specific arguments that a general council is superior to a pope, can be called by a king, and is competent to judge a pope or call a new conclave, were advanced in 1379 (**Henry of Langenstein**) and from then on grew in importance. Two Roman popes were elected with the understanding that they would resign if Benedict XIII would also do so. The two colleges of cardinals joined in a call for a general council to meet at Pisa, 1409.

1409. The **Council of Pisa,** attended by 500 prelates and delegates from the states of Europe. Two parties: (1) a moderate majority with the sole aim of ending the schism; (2) radical reformers (including d'Ailly and Gerson from Paris), who were compelled to accept postponement of reform until a council supposed to meet in 1412. After hearing specific charges against both popes, the council deposed both. The conclave chose **Alexander V** (d. 1410). Neither the Roman nor the Avignonese pope resigned, and the schism became a triple one.

1410–15. JOHN XXIII, expelled from Rome by Ladislas of Naples, was forced by the Emperor Sigismund to issue a call for the **Council of Constance** (1414) in return for protection. This marked the passing of the initiative in reform from the king of France to the Roman emperor, a return in theory to the days of the Ottos.

1414–17. The **Council of Constance:** one of the greatest assemblies of medieval history; three aims: (1) **restoration of unity to the Church;** (2) **reform in head and members;** (3) **extirpation of heresy,** particularly the Hussite heresy (p. 263). Following university practice, voting was by nations, and the numbers of the Italian prelates did no good to Pope John. John, seeing a chance to divide the council and the emperor, allowed the imprisonment of Hus (in violation of the imperial safe conduct).

Hus, heard three times by the whole council (and cleverly induced to expand his doctrine that sin vitiates a clerical office to include civil office as well), lost Sigismund's support, was condemned, and was executed (1415) as was his companion, Jerome of Prague (1416).

John XXIII, having agreed to resign if his rivals did so, fled the council and was brought back, tried, and deposed (1415); **Gregory XII** resigned (1415); Sigismund, unable to induce Benedict XIII to resign, won away his supporters and isolated him. Reform was again postponed, but two decrees are significant: *Sacrosancta* (1415), asserting that a council is superior to a pope; and *Frequens* (1417), providing for stated meetings of general councils.

The conclave elected Cardinal Colonna as Martin V. Christendom ignored the obstinate Benedict, and the schism was over. The schism badly weakened the prestige of the papacy and the ordinary Christian's respect for papal authority; it also exposed the need for general ecclesiastical reform.

1417–31. Martin V, a Roman of Romans, dissolved the Council of Constance. In response to the decree *Frequens,* which required the summoning of regular general councils of the Church, he convened the Council of Pavia-Siena (1424–25), but he refused to attend and encouraged divisions among the representatives. Its failure led to new calls for a council, and Martin was forced to summon the assembly at Basel, but died before it met. **Recovery of the Papal States:** most of the cities were under their own lords, who bore pro forma titles as papal vicars but were in fact independent. Concentration on Italian political problems at the expense of the universal spiritual interests of Christendom.

1431–47. EUGENE IV, a Venetian who favored summoning the **council of Basel.**

1431–49. The **Council of Basel,** dominated by strong antipapal feeling. Dissolved by Eugene because of negotiations with the Hussites, the council ignored the order and decreed (with the support of the princes) that no general council could be dissolved without its consent; it continued in session and summoned Eugene and the cardinals to attend. Eugene ignored the summons but was forced (1433) to accept the council. Temporary compromise with the Hussites registered in the *Compactata.* **Reforms voted:** abolition of commendations, reservations, appeals to Rome, annates, etc.; provision for regular provincial and diocesan synods; confirmation of the right of chapter elections; appeal from a general council to a pope pronounced heresy. Already divided over these reforms, the council split over reunion with the Greek church. Eugene and his cardinals ignored a second summons, were pronounced contumacious; Eugene dissolved the council and called another to meet at Ferrara; his supporters left Basel. The rump council continued to meet, deposed Eugene (1439), and elected Amadeus of Savoy.

1439–49. FELIX V (Amadeus of Savoy). Moved to Laussanne, the council continued with dwindling numbers and prestige.

1438–45. The **Council of Ferrara-Florence** (under the presidency of Eugene). After months of futile discussion (over the *filioque* question, unleavened bread at the sacrament, purgatory, and papal supremacy), the Greeks were forced to accept the Roman formula for union (1439) and the schism between East and West, dating from 1054, was technically healed. As the Greeks at home repudiated the union, it was of no effect. Isidore of Kiev and Bessarion remained as cardinals of the Roman Church. The long residence of Greek scholars in Florence contributed to the development of Italian humanistic studies.

1438. Pragmatic Sanction of Bourges. An announcement made by the French clergy under the aegis of Charles VII was the first assertion by a local church of the right to organize itself. It affirmed the supremacy of a general council (as opposed to the papacy) over the Church, and gave the crown control over Church appointments (thereby preparing for the efficient extortion of ecclesiastical revenues by the monarchy) and over papal letters and judicial appeals.

1439. The **diet of Mainz** accepted the **Pragmatic Sanction of Mainz,** abolishing annates and papal provisions, and providing for diocesan and provincial synods.

Enea Silvio de'Piccolomini, sent to win Germany back for the papacy, came to an agreement with Emperor Frederick III on such cynical terms that the German princes flocked to Felix V, but a provisional concordat, embodying the Pragmatic of 1439, enabled Enea Silvio to detach the princes one by one.

1448. Concordat of Vienna (p. 261) abandoned most of the restrictions on papal patronage.

1449. Dissolution of the Council of Basel: abdication of Felix V (who became a cardinal). Papal celebration of the triumph over the conciliar movement in the **Jubilee of 1450.** Postponement of moderate reform led to the radical Reformation of the 16th century.

1447–55. NICHOLAS V, former librarian of Cosimo de' Medici, scholar, humanist, collector of manuscripts, founder of the **Vatican Library.** Rome temporarily a center of humanism. Nicholas's circle included: **Poggio Bracciolini, Alberti,** and **Lorenzo Valla** (a scientific humanist and critic who had just demolished the *Donation of Constantine* as a forgery). Plans for a new St. Peter's.

1453, May 31. The **Ottoman (Turkish) capture of Constantinople** (pp. 126, 261) ended the Greek Empire in the East; generated grave fears of Turkish expansion throughout Europe; halted the flow of white slaves from the Caucasus, southern Russia and the Balkans into Europe and stimulated the centuries-old trans-Saharan traffic in black slaves; and, because of Ottoman control of the trade routes in the eastern Mediterranean, directed (by the late 15th century) Europeans' attention westward, to the Atlantic.

1458–64. PIUS II (Aeneas Sylvius Piccolomini). A flamboyant youth, in later life austere; most brilliant and versatile of the literary popes; a humanist, lover of nature, eloquent essayist, orator, and Latin stylist. A short, bent man with smiling eyes and a fringe of white hair; seldom free of pain; a tireless worker, always accessible. Advocate of papal supremacy, obstinate foe of conciliar reform. When his appeals for a crusade against the Ottoman Turks were ignored by a preoccupied Europe, he gallantly took the Cross himself to shame the princes of Christendom, but died at Ancona. His family was large and poor, and he was a nepotist.

1464–71. PAUL II, a Venetian, rich, kindly, handsome, a collector of jewels and carvings, founder of the Corso horse races. A strong centralizer, supporter of the Hungarian crusade. The Turkish victory at **Negroponte,** the main Venetian naval base in the Aegean (1470), gave the Turks mastery of the eastern Mediterranean waters.

1471–84. SIXTUS IV (della Rovere) aimed to consolidate the Papal States and reduce the power of the cardinals; methodical nepotist (three nephews, the Riarios, one of them later Pope Julius II).

1475. Rapprochement with Ferrante of Naples; alienation of the Medici, who were replaced as papal bankers by the Pazzi. The Riarios organized with Sixtus's knowledge, if not approval, the **Pazzi conspiracy** (assassination of Giuliano de' Medici, 1478). This destroyed the alliance of Florence, Naples, and Milan to maintain the Italian balance of power and led to a war involving most of Italy; the war was terminated by the capture of Otranto (1480) and by the diplomacy of Lorenzo de' Medici. Sixtus's coalition with Venice led to the Ferrarese War (1482–84). Sixtus and Julius II were the great beautifiers of Rome: **Sistine Chapel** (c. 1473); paving and widening of streets and squares; patronage of **Ghirlandaio, Botticelli, Perugino, Pinturicchio,** et al.

1484–92. INNOCENT VIII, a kindly, handsome Genoese, the first pope to recognize his children and to dine publicly with ladies. Anxious to stop the Turkish threat, he secured the promise of the Sultan Beyazid II (1490) to leave Europe, provided Innocent kept the sultan's brother and rival Djem, who had pretensions to the sultanate, confined. A baronial revolt (1485–87) in Naples (supported by Innocent and, secretly, by Venice) led to a revival of the Angevin claims to Naples. Florence and Milan, fearing French intervention in Italy, opposed the war, and peace and amnesty were arranged. Ferrante's cynical violation of the amnesty led the exiles (on Ludovico Sforza's advice) to call in King Charles VIII of France. Sforza struck an alliance with Charles to protect Milan and opened the road into Italy to this alien invader (1494).

Girolamo Savonarola (1452–98), a Dominican, prior of San Marco in Florence (1491), eloquent reforming preacher, and precursor of the Reformation, was already denouncing the new paganism of the Renaissance, the corruption of the state and the papacy, and foretelling the ruin of Italy (p. 258).   *(To p. 298)*

2. SICILY AND NAPLES
(From p. 216)

1268 85. CHARLES I (Angevin) king of Naples and of Sicily (1268–82). His grandiose scheme for the creation of a Mediterranean empire in succession to the Byzantine (a revival of the Latin Empire under French auspices), financed by new and heavy taxation, provoked the bloody **Sicilian Vespers (1282),** a revolt against the rule of Charles that began at the hour of Vespers on Easter Monday, near a church outside Palermo; perhaps 2,000 French men, women, and children were killed. The Sicilians expelled the French, offered the crown to Peter III of Aragon, and hostilities between the Angevins in Naples and Aragonese on the island of Sicily continued for almost a century, to the destruction of good order and the Sicilian economy, and the impoverishment of the Sicilian people.

1282–. Sicily under Aragonese rule: Peter (1282–85); **James** (1285–95). James exchanged the investiture of Sardinia and Corsica for that of Sicily, and Sicily passed to his brother, **Frederick** (1295–1337). Frederick brought to a close the war with Naples (**Peace of Caltabeleotta, 1302),** marrying the daughter of Charles I and accepting the stipulation that the Sicilian crown should pass to the Angevins on his death. This agreement was not fulfilled, with the result that the struggle continued until, in 1373, Joanna of Naples abandoned Sicily to the Aragonese in return for tribute. Sicily was ruled as a viceroyalty until the reunion with Aragon in 1409.

1309–43. Robert (Angevin) of Naples. He was the leader of the Italian Guelfs and, having been appointed imperial vicar on the death of Emperor Henry VII, planned to create an Italian kingdom. He patronized the artists Giotto and Simone Martine, and the humanists Petrarch and Dionigi di San Sepolcro.

1382–86. Charles III, a grandnephew of Robert.

1386–1414. Ladislas, son of Charles III, finally succeeded in establishing some measure of order in the kingdom and began a vigorous campaign of expansion in central Italy. In 1409 he bought the States of the Church from Pope Gregory XII, but his designs were blocked by Florence and Siena.

1414–35. JOANNA (GIOVANNA) II, sister of Ladislas. The amazing intrigues of this amorous widow kept Italian diplomacy in turmoil, and culminated in a struggle between **René,** the Angevin claimant (supported by the pope), and **Alfonso V of Aragon** (supported by Filippo Maria Visconti). This conflict ended in the triumph of Alfonso, who secured Naples in 1435 and was recognized as king by the pope in 1442.

1435–58. Alfonso (the Magnanimous, so called because of his generous patronage of the arts). Convinced that Aragonese control of the west-

ern Mediterranean would be dependent on his gaining a foothold on mainland Italy, he waged a long but successful war to secure Naples, which he entered in 1443. Naples became the center of his Mediterranean empire. He centralized the administration, reformed taxation, and arranged a series of dynastic marriages. Alfonso supported public instruction, strengthened the University of Naples, patronized Lorenzo Valla, and made Naples one of the great centers of Renaissance culture. He divided his empire at his death, leaving Aragon and Sicily to his brother John, Naples to his illegitimate son.

1458–94. FERRANTE (FERDINAND I). Educated by Lorenzo Valla, he continued his father's support for art and learning, and he tried to develop a more just tax structure. But baronial opposition troubled his entire reign. In 1458, he defeated a baronial coalition with the aid of Francesco Sforza and Cosimo de' Medici. In 1485 he granted rebelling barons an unequivocal amnesty, and after their surrender he massacred them, which gave him the reputation of being notoriously unscrupulous. Innocent (1492) guaranteed the succession in Naples. Alexander VI stood by the bargain and opposed Charles VIII's demand for investiture.

The **claims of the Valois kings** to Naples. Based on (1) the marriage of Margaret (daughter of Charles II of Naples) and Charles of Valois, the parents of King Philip VI; and (2) the claims of the so-called second house of Anjou founded by Duke Louis I (d. 1384) of Anjou, count of Provence. Louis was grandson of Philip VI and grandfather of (1) Maria, wife of Charles VII of France, mother of Louis XI; and (2) Duke Louis III (d. 1434) and his brother René of Lorraine (d. 1480).

(To. p. 299)

3. FLORENCE

Early history. The **margraviate of Tuscany,** set up by the Carolingians, extended from the Po to the Roman state under the Margrave Boniface (d. 1052), whose daughter, the great **Countess Matilda** (1052–1115), was probably the strongest papal supporter in Italy. Associated with her in the government was a council of *boni homines*, whose administration during her frequent absences, and after her death, laid the foundation for the emergence of the commune. Florence, already a commercial center, opposed the Ghibelline hill barons, who preyed on her commerce. The burghers continued Guelf in sympathy; trade and financial connections with France made them Francophiles and friendly to Charles of Anjou. Under Matilda the **guild organization** emerged, which came to form the basis of the city government. Control of the government was concentrated in the hands of the great guilds (one of which included the bankers). Consuls appeared after 1138. The populace was divided into two great groups, the *grandi* (nobles) and the *arti* (guilds). Consuls were chosen by the grandi.

On the breakup of the margraviate following Matilda's death, Florence began her advance, and by 1176 was master of the dioceses of Florence and Fiesole. The institution of the *podestà* (magistrates) after 1202 was favored by the feudal elements and the lesser guilds. Intermittent rivalry of the noble houses continued. Wars were fought with Pisa, Lucca, Pistoia, Siena. Under the *podestà*, the commune developed a strong organization paralleled by the growth of the *popolo* (populace) under its *capitano* (chief).

The great struggle of **Guelf and Ghibelline** was reflected in Florentine civil strife. After a Guelf regime, Frederick of Antioch (son of Frederick II) as imperial vicar instituted the first mass expulsion in Florentine history by driving out the Guelfs (1249).

1252. The first **gold florin** *(fiorino)* was coined, and soon became the standard gold coin in Europe.

1260. Siena, with the aid of Manfred and the Florentine Ghibellines, inflicted a great defeat on the Florentine Guelfs **(Montaperti),** beginning a Ghibelline dominance that lasted until Manfred's death (1266). This was followed by a reaction, and the expulsion of the Ghibellines. Under the Ghibelline regime the *popolo* lost all share in the government.

In the reaction following the Ghibelline regime, Ghibelline property was confiscated to support persecution of the Ghibellines. Under Charles of Anjou, the formulas of the old constitution were restored; the party struggle continued. The Sicilian Vespers (1282) weakened Charles, strengthened the commune, and the Florentine "republic"

became in effect a commercial oligarchy in the hands of the greater guilds.

1282. According to the **Law of 1282,** nobles could participate in the government only by joining a guild. The last traces of serfdom were abolished (1289), and the number of guilds increased to 21 (7 greater, 14 lesser).

1293. The **ordinance of 1293** excluded from the guilds anyone not actively practicing his profession, and thus in effect removed the nobles from all share in the government.

Two factions arose: the **Blacks** (Neri), extreme Guelfs led by Corso Donati; and the **Whites** (Bianchi), moderate Guelfs (and later Ghibellines) under Vieri Cerchi. The Neri favored repeal of the ordinance of 1293.

Emperor Henry VII was unable to capture Florence.

1320–23. Castruccio Castracani, lord of Lucca, humiliated the city in the field. Growing financial troubles, partly the result of Edward III's repudiation of his debts to the Florentine bankers, culminated in the failures of the Peruzzi (1343) and Bardi (1344), and damaged Florentine banking prestige. The government was discredited, and civil war ensued. **Walter of Brienne** (duke of Athens) was called in, reformed the government, began a usurpation, and was expelled (1343). The restored commune was under the domination of the businessmen, who had three objectives: access to the sea (hence hostility to Pisa), expansion in Tuscany (to dominate the trade roads), and support of the popes (to retain papal banking business). Social conflict continued and grew as the oligarchy gained power and the Guelfs opposed the increasing industrial proletariat. The lesser guilds were pushed into the background, the unguilded were worse off. The first social revolt came in 1345.

1347–48. Famine, followed by the **Black Death,** reduced the population seriously.

1351. The commutation of military service for cash marked the decline of the citizen militia and the golden age of the *condottieri* (mercenary captains). War with Milan resulted (1351) from Giovanni Visconti's attempt to reduce Florence and master Tuscany.

1375–78. Papal efforts to annex Tuscany led Florence into a temporary alliance with Milan.

1378. Continued pressure by Guelf extremists to exclude the lesser guilds led to a series of violent explosions. **Salvestro de' Medici,** gonfalonier, ended the **admonitions,** which were the basis of the Guelf terrorism, and a violent **revolt of the *ciompi*** (the poorest workmen) broke out. The *ciompi* made temporary gains, but Salvestro was exiled, and by 1382 the oligarchy was back in the saddle and even the admonitions were revived.

Florentine culture: Precursors of the Renaissance. Dante (1265–1321): *Vita Nuova*, which celebrates in the Tuscan vernacular his love for Beatrice Portinari; the *Commedia* (the adjective *Divina* was added in the 16th century), a vernacular poem of 100 cantos, more than 14,000 lines, recounting the poet's journey through hell, purgatory, and heaven, constituting a brilliant synthesis of medieval culture and establishing Tuscan as the literary language of Italy; the *De Monarchia*, a treatise on the need for kingly dominion over secular affairs, centered at Rome; and *De Vulgari Eloquentia*, a defense of the vernacular, written in Latin. **Petrarch** (1304–74), of Florentine origin, greatest of Italian lyricists, brilliant Latinist, the first great humanist; interested in every aspect of humanity; a lover of nature; a universal mind. **Boccaccio** (1313–75), friend of Petrarch, knew both Greek and Latin, the first modern student of Tacitus, collector of classical manuscripts, first lecturer on Dante (1373); wrote the *Decameron*, a collection of 100 fictional stories that completely ignore medieval spiritual ideas and exalt bourgeois enterprise and sophistication; founder of Italian prose. **Giotto** (1276–1337), architect (employed on the cathedral), sculptor, painter, revealed Renaissance tendencies. **Villani** (d. 1348), author of *Chronicon Universale*, which has clear bourgeois elements. **Chrysoloras** (called from Constantinople), the first public lecturer on Greek in the West c. 1350–1415; he had many famous humanists as pupils.

1382–1432. A half century of oligarchic domination in Florentine politics, in many ways the **zenith of Florentine power.** Constitutional reform (1382) broadened popular participation in government, but little was done for the *ciompi*, and sporadic revolts continued as the Guelfs slowly regained power.

THE HOUSE OF ANJOU (1266–1435)

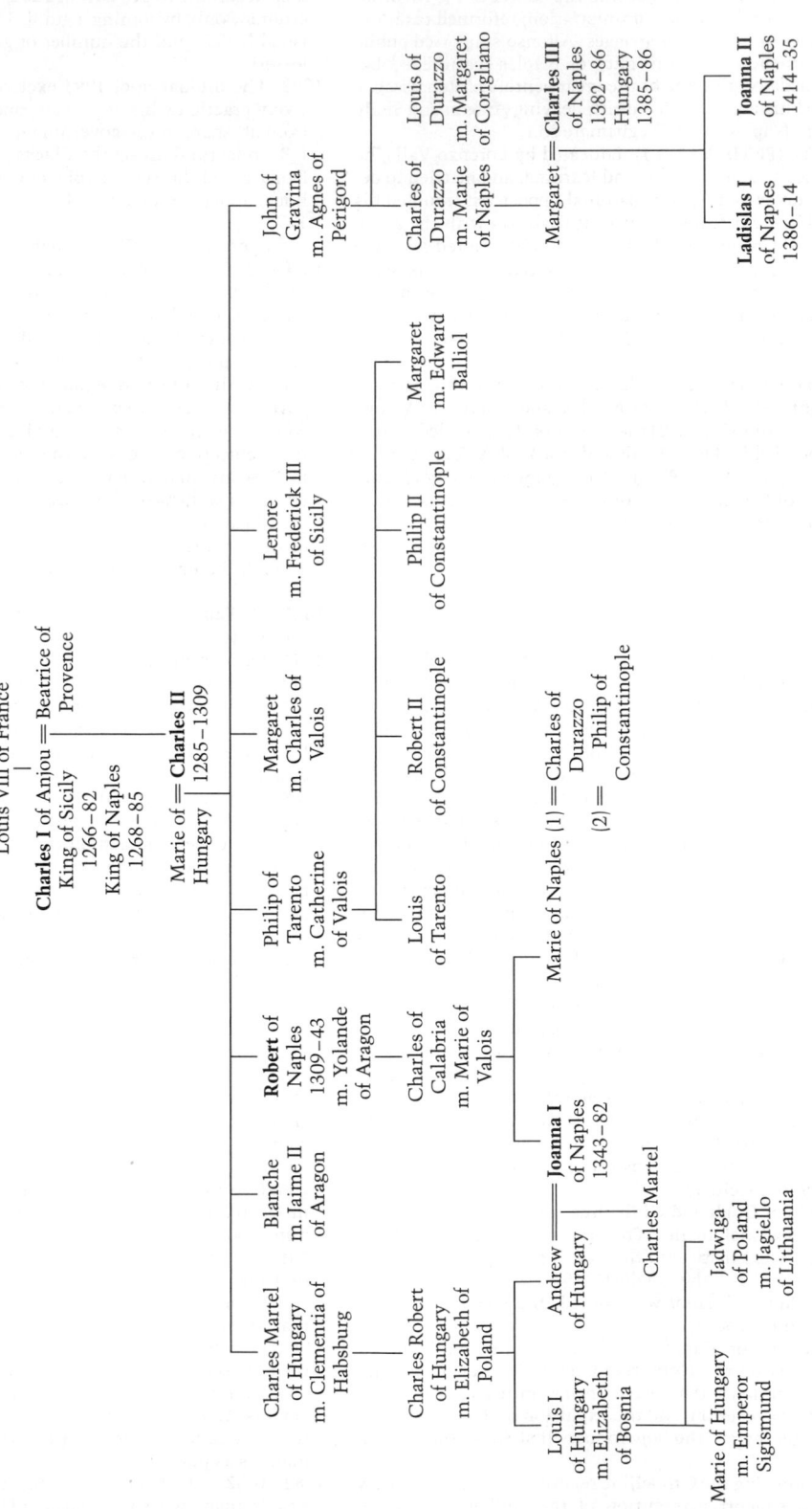

THE MEDICI FAMILY (1434–1737)

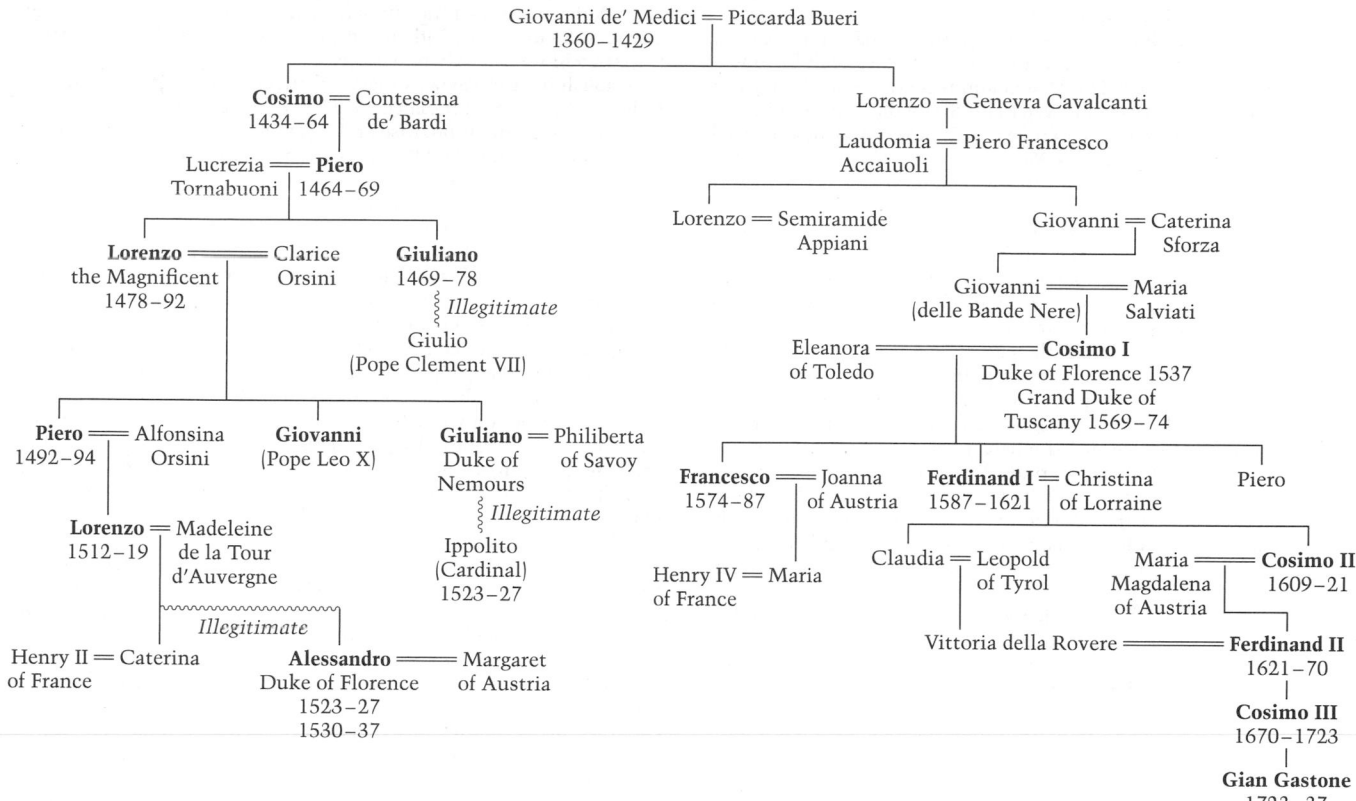

1393. Maso degli Albizzi's long control of the government began with the exile or disenfranchisement of the Alberti and their supporters. Capitalism had destroyed the guild organization as a vital political force, and Albizzi ruled for the advantage of his own house and the Arte della Lana (wool guild) with which he was associated. Democratic elements in the state had vanished.

1405. Pisa was bought and reduced to obedience (1406), giving Florence direct access to the sea. Filippo Maria Visconti's drive into Tuscany led Florence to declare war. The peace party was led by **Giovanni de' Medici**, a wool dealer and international banker, probably Italy's richest man. Several defeats of Florence were accompanied by a decline of Florentine credit and a number of serious bankruptcies. Alliance with Venice and defeat of the Visconti, who accepted peace on onerous terms (1429); Venice monopolized the gains of the war.

1424–94. Judicial records confirm the complaints of the Franciscan preacher **Bernardo of Siena** (1380–1444) that **homosexual activity** was widespread among all social classes in Renaissance Tuscany. For many individuals, homosexual relations were only one aspect of what we call bisexuality, and the activity (anal relations) involved mainly adult men (active) and adolescent boys (passive). Male (ecclesiastical) ignorance of female psychology and biology, and the great reluctance even to mention or name lesbianism, means that very little evidence of such activity survives.

1427. Taxation reform, the *catàsto*, an income tax intended to be of general and democratic incidence.

1433. The fiasco of the war on Lucca (1429–33) led to Cosimo (son of Giovanni) de' Medici's imprisonment as a scapegoat, and his sentence to ten year exile. The next election to the signory (governing body) favored the Medici, and Cosimo was recalled (1434). Medici dominance in Florence began, opening three centuries of close identity between the fortunes of the family and those of Florence. Cosimo, without holding office himself, determined who should hold office.

1434–64. COSIMO (Pater Patriae). His power rested on his great business and financial skills, which brought enormous wealth, and his shrewd political genius.

1434–94. Domination of the Medici.

1440. Florence and Venice in alliance defeated Filippo Maria Visconti at **Anghiari**. The *catàsto* was replaced by a progressive income tax designed to lighten the burdens of the poor (i.e., the Medici adherents). Cosimo supported Francesco Sforza's contest for the duchy of Milan and aided him in his war with Venice. For commercial reasons he favored France, but backed Ferrante of Naples against the Angevin claims. He was thus the real creator of the **triple alliance** of Florence, Milan, and Naples in the interest of the Italian equilibrium and security.

In the **14th and 15th centuries,** Italians invented a basic **principle of modern diplomacy** and the machinery by which that principle functioned. Whenever one state appeared to gain a predominant position within the peninsula, other Italian states combined to establish a **balance of power** against the major threat. A pattern of shifting alliances resulted. In addition, permanent embassies with **resident ambassadors,** in capitals where political relations and commercial interests needed monitoring, became regular features of diplomatic relations among states.

1464–69. Piero the Gouty, son of Cosimo, a semi-invalid who was opposed by Luca Pitti.

1469–78. Lorenzo and Giuliano de' Medici.

1478–92. Lorenzo de' Medici (the Magnificent). Lorenzo continued the general policy of Cosimo. He enjoyed the power and prestige of a prince, though he had neither the title nor the office. His marriage to Clarice Orsini was the first princely marriage of the Medici.

1471. Lorenzo's effort to conciliate Pope Sixtus IV netted him a confirmation of the Medici banking privileges and an appointment as receiver of the papal revenues.

1474. Pope Sixtus and Ferrante of Naples were asked to join the alliance of Florence, Venice, and Milan (concluded in 1474), but Ferrante, feeling isolated, and Sixtus, angered at Lorenzo's opposition to his nephews, the Riarios, drew together. Italy became divided into two camps. The Pazzi family, rivals of the Medici, were given the lucrative position of receiver of the papal revenues.

1478. The Pazzi conspiracy. The Riarios plotted to have Lorenzo and Giuliano assassinated in the cathedral at Easter Mass. Giuliano was killed, Lorenzo wounded. The Medici almost exterminated the Pazzi and hounded the fugitives all over Italy. Sixtus laid an interdict on Florence and excommunicated Lorenzo; Alfonso of Calabria invaded Tuscany. Ferrante engineered a Milanese revolt; the Turks diverted Venice at Scutari; plague broke out. Desperate, Lorenzo visited Ferrante (the cruelest and most cynical despot in Italy), and through his charm and the threat of a revival of Angevin claims, arranged (1480) a peace. Florence suffered considerable losses, but Lorenzo was a popular hero and succeeded in establishing the council of seventy, a completely Medici organ, the instrument of *de facto* despotism, but a source of real stability in government.

The princely court. In the 15th century, political power and elite culture were centered in the princely courts of despots and oligarchs such as the Medici. "A court was the space and personnel around a prince as he made laws, received ambassadors, made appointments, took his meals and proceeded through the streets," in the words of Lauro Martines. At his court, a prince flaunted his patronage of learning and the arts through lavish gifts to writers, artists, philosophers. The princely court gave the ruler the opportunity to display his wealth, in ceremonies such as baptisms, marriages, funerals, and triumphal entries into the city. Ritual and pageantry were used to display wealth and power.

Lorenzo's brilliant **foreign policy** was costly; he had neglected the family business and apparently used some of the state money for Medici purposes; he also debased the coinage. Florentine prosperity, under the pressure of rivals, heavy taxation, and business depression, declined. Nonetheless, Lorenzo, the leading statesman of his day, brought a 12-year calm to Italy, resuming the Medici alliance with Naples and Milan to balance the papacy and Venice, and to keep a united front against alien invasion. Florence, on good terms with Charles VIII, regained most of her Tuscan losses. **Savonarola,** prior of San Marco (1491), had begun his denunciations of Florentine corruption and his attacks on Lorenzo (p. 253).

1492. PIERO succeeded Lorenzo on his death. Son of an Orsini mother, married to an Orsini, he supported Naples, angered Milan, and threw Ludovico Sforza into alliance with the Neapolitan exiles, who summoned Charles VIII.

1494. Charles's invasion began the age-long subjugation of Italy to alien invaders, who dominated Italy until 1859. Piero, alarmed at public opinion, fled the city.

1498. Florentine rejection of Savonarola's moral crusade, together with papal anger at his preachings against Alexander VI, led to Savonarola's fall: accused of heresy, he was hanged and burned.

Florence, center of the Italian Renaissance. For more than a century the Medici were the greatest patrons of the Renaissance and led the rich bourgeoisie of Florence in fostering a brilliant development of culture. **Cosimo** was an enthusiastic patron of manuscript collectors, copyists, and humanists; he established the **library of San Marco** and the **Medici library.** The council of Ferrara-Florence sat in Florence (1439) and brought a number of learned Greeks to the city who stimulated Platonic studies. Under Cosimo's auspices, **Ficino** was trained to make his great translation of Plato and the **Platonic Academy** was founded. **Lorenzo,** a graceful poet (carnival songs), ardent champion of the vernacular, lover of the countryside, and generous patron, drew about him a brilliant circle. He continued the support of Ficino. Florentine leaders in the arts during the Renaissance: (1) **painting: Masaccio** (1401–28?), **Botticelli** (1444–1510), **Leonardo da Vinci** (1452–1519), sculptor and polymath; (2) **architecture: Brunelleschi** (1377–1446); **Alberti** (1405–71); (3) **sculpture: Donatello** (c. 1386–1466), **Ghiberti** (1378–1455), **Verrocchio** (1435–88), **Michelangelo** (1475–1564), also painter, poet, architect; (4) **history and political theory: Machiavelli** (1469–1527), **Guicciardini** (1485–1540); (5) **romantic poetry: Pulci** (1432–c. 1487).

(To p. 299)

4. MILAN

Early history. An ancient center of the agriculture of the Lombard plain, Milan was self-sufficient in food, the master of important passes (Brenner, Splügen, St. Gothard) in the Alps, and was for a long time surpassed in wealth only by Venice.

Establishment of Pavia as the Lombard capital (569). Emergence of Milan as the center of Italian opposition in the Lombard plain to alien and heretical domination. Rise of the archbishop as defender of native liberty and orthodoxy laid the basis for the evolution of archiepiscopal temporal power (military, administrative, judicial), exercised through his viscounts. The end of Lombard domination (774), followed by Carolingian destruction of the great Lombard fiefs, strengthened the episcopal power still further.

The spirit of municipal independence emerged from intense rivalries for the archiepiscopal see and the necessities of defense; Milan became an island of safety and justice in the Lombard plain, a populous, self-sufficient, city-state. Under **Archbishop Heribert** (1018–45) the *carroccio* (arc of municipal patriotism) was set up; expansion in the Lombard plain began (reduction of Lodi, Como, Pavia). A moat was dug after the destruction wrought by Emperor Frederick I (1162); the city was rebuilt by its allies, Bergamo, Brescia, Mantua, and Verona. (For the Lombard League and the wars with Frederick, see p. 214.) Rapid growth, extension of the walls (after 1183). Chief industry: armor manufacturing and the wool trade; later, silk manufacture; irrigation made the plain productive.

Government: (1) *parlamento (consiglio grande)* (membership successively reduced to 2,000, 1,500, 800); (2) *credenza,* a committee of 12 for urgent and secret business; (3) consuls (the executive) elected for a year, responsible to the assembly.

Bitter warfare between populace and nobles led to the rise of two great families, the Della Torre (lords of the tower, or castle) and the Visconti (i.e., the viscounts).

1237–77. Rule of the (Guelf) **Della Torre.** Martino implemented the *catàsto,* a tax of democratic and uniform incidence. The title *signore,* lord of Milan, established (1259); defeat and capture of the (Ghibelline) Visconti and their adherents. Milan established her power over Bergamo, Lodi, Como, and Vercelli.

1277–1447. Rule of the **VISCONTI.** Established by Archbishop Otto Visconti. Establishment (1312) of the Visconti supremacy (Matteo designated imperial vicar). Ruthless Visconti rule and expansion over northern Italy (including Genoa). Stefano's sons Bernabò, Galeazzo, Matteo divided the domains but ruled jointly until Matteo was assassinated (1355) by his brothers. Intolerably harsh joint rule of Bernabò (1354–85) at Milan and Galeazzo (1354–78) at Pavia; ostentatious patronage of learning and art.

1378–1402. Gian Galeazzo succeeded his father Galeazzo and did away with Bernabò (1385), thereafter ruling alone (1385–1402). Gian Galeazzo married Isabelle, daughter of King John of France; one of his daughters, Valentina, married Louis of Orléans (the source of Louis XII's claims to Milan). Gian Galeazzo began the creation of a northern Italian kingdom: mastery of Verona, Vicenza, Padua (1386–88); Tuscan advance blocked by Florence (1390–92) and by the rebellion of Padua. Made hereditary duke (1395) by Emperor Wenceslas, the first such title among Italian regional rulers, he added Pisa and Siena (1399), Assisi and Perugia (1400) to his domains, and routed (1401) Elector Rupert III (in Florentine pay). The Certósa (Charterhouse) and Duomo (Cathedral) were begun. Gian Galeazzo's death (1402) saved Florence and opened a period of anarchy in Milan under his sons Gian Maria (1402–12) and Filippo Maria (1402–47), which undid much of their father's work.

1402–47. FILIPPO MARIA, after the assassination (1412) of Gian Maria, regained Gian Galeazzo's lands (even Genoa). Venice joined Florence against Filippo and took Bergamo, Brescia (1425).

1447–50. Filippo, last of the Visconti, was followed by the **republic** and the supremacy of Francesco Sforza, son-in-law of Filippo, who fought his way to mastery, defeating Venice and conquering the Lombard plain.

1450. Francesco Sforza was invested with the ducal title by popular acclaim.

1450–1500. Rule of the **SFORZA.** Francesco, eager for peace, came to terms with Cosimo de' Medici and Naples (the so-called triple alliance for the Italian balance of power). Louis XI was on intimate terms with Francesco and made him his political model. Francesco completed the Certósa and the Duomo with Florentine architects under Renaissance influence and began the Castello (Castle). Patron of the humanist **Filelfo**, Francesco gave his son Galeazzo and his daughter Ippolita a humanist education; Ippolita was famous for her Latin style. His court was full of humanists and learned Greeks.

1466–76. Galeazzo Maria Sforza was assassinated after a cruel but able rule.

1476–79. Galeazzo's son, **GIAN GALEAZZO,** husband of Isabella of Naples, under the regency of his mother, supported Florence against Naples after the Pazzi conspiracy (1478). Gian Galeazzo's uncle Ludovico usurped the duchy (1479).

1479–1500. LUDOVICO (called "il Moro," perhaps because he was dark). The 19th-century Swiss historian Jakob Burckhardt called him "the perfect type of the despot." Alarmed at his isolation after the death (1492) of Lorenzo de' Medici, Ludovico supported the appeals of Neapolitan refugees to Charles VIII of France, whose expedition (1494) began the destruction of Italian autonomy. In Charles's train came Louis of Orléans, who, as Louis XII (1498–1515), added claims to Milan to his other Italian claims, took Milan (1499), and captured Ludovico (1500), who ended his days (1508) as a prisoner of Louis.

Ludovico's generous patronage marked the **golden age of the Renaissance in Milan.** Ludovico, an artist, man of letters, economist, and experimenter, beautified the city, improved irrigation, bettered agriculture. He was the patron of Bramante and Leonardo.   *(To p. 299)*

5. VENICE
(From p. 218)

In the early 14th century, Venice dominated the trade of the Adriatic and possessed many colonies throughout the Middle East. Her position in the eastern trade was challenged primarily by her ancient enemy, Genoa, at that time at the height of her power.

1353–55. War between Venice and Genoa. The Venetians were defeated at **Sapienza** (1354) and suffered the loss of their fleet. Peace was mediated by Milan.

1378–81. The **war of Chioggia,** between Venice and Genoa. This grew out of the grant, by John V Paleologus, of the island of Tenedos, key to the Dardanelles. Luciano Doria, the Genoese admiral, defeated the Venetians at **Pola,** seized Chioggia, and blockaded Venice. The Venetians, under **Vittorio Pisano,** blocked the channel and starved out the fleet of Pietro Doria, forcing its surrender. From this blow Genoa never recovered. Thenceforth Venice was mistress of the Levantine trade, which made an outlet for her goods over the Alpine passes more urgent than ever.

1388. Treaty of the Venetians with the Ottoman Turks, the first effort to assure trade privileges despite the rise of the Turkish power.

1405. Venice seized Padua, Bassano, Vicenza, and Verona after the breakup of the Visconti domains (1402) and the defeat of the Carrara family.

1416. First war of Venice against the Ottoman Turks (p. 125), the result of Turkish activity in the Aegean. The **Doge Loredano** won a resounding victory at the Dardanelles and forced the sultan to conclude peace.

1425–30. Second war against the Turks. The Turkish fleets ravaged the Aegean stations of the Venetians and took Salonika (Thessalonica) (1430).

1426–29. The Venetians were obliged to make peace, in view of the **war with Filippo Maria of Milan,** by which the Venetians established a permanent hold over Verona and Vicenza and gained Brescia (1426), Bergamo (1428), and Crema (1429).

1453. Participation of the Venetians in the **defense of Constantinople** against Mehmed II (p. 126). After the capture of Constantinople, Mehmed proceeded to the conquest of Greece and Albania, thus isolating and endangering the Venetian stations.

1454. Treaty of Lodi. Scholars use this term to refer to (1) the peace agreement between Venice and Milan signed at Lodi, in Lombardy near Milan (April 9), and (2) the mutual nonaggression pact signed at Venice (Aug. 30) between Venice, Milan, and Florence, and later by Naples and the papacy, binding the five major Italian powers for 25 years. This treaty stabilized the balance of power (see p. 257) in the peninsula until 1494.

1463–79. The great **war against the Turks** (p. 126). Negroponte was lost (1470). The Turks throughout maintained the upper hand and at times raided to the very outskirts of Venice. In the **Treaty of Constantinople** (1479), the Venetians gave up Scutari and other Albanian stations, as well as Negroponte and Lemnos. Thenceforth the Venetians paid an annual tribute for permission to trade in the Black Sea.

1482–84. War with Ferrara, as a result of which Venice acquired Rovigo. This marked the limit of Venetian expansion on the mainland. The frontiers remained substantially unaltered until the days of Napoleon.

1489. Acquisition of Cyprus (partly by gift, partly by extortion) from Catherine Cornaro, widow of James of Lusignan.

VENETIAN CULTURE IN THE QUATTROCENTO. The second half of the 15th century witnessed the restoration by **Gentile Bellini** (1429–1507) of the massive mural paintings in the Great Council Hall of the ducal palace (where the patricians gathered every Sunday afternoon to conduct affairs of state), the beginnings of the great narrative paintings in the *scuola* (**lay confraternities** formed for purposes of mutual aid and devotion), and the completion of the tympanum relief on the Scuola di San Marco by the architectural sculptor **Bartolomeo Buon** (1374–c. 1465). Nevertheless, Venetians' preoccupation with commercial enterprises and wars with the Ottoman Turks; with massive shipbuilding at the Arsenale, which employed perhaps 16,000 workers and at one time produced one galley a day for 100 days; and with the replacement of wooden bridges with stone ones over the canals delayed the full flowering of Venetian Renaissance art until the 16th century.

The printing press apparently appealed to the practical Venetian nature, and the senate decreed (1469) that the art of printing should be fostered. Much of the finest early printing issued from the Venetian presses of the 15th and 16th centuries.   *(To p. 299)*

f. THE HOLY ROMAN EMPIRE

(From p. 210)

1273. The election fell to **Rudolf of Habsburg** (b. 1218), who ranked as a prince and wished to restore and retain in his family the duchy of Swabia. The Habsburgs or Hapsburgs (from *Habichts-Burg,* or Hawk-Castle; 10th century) of the district of Brugg (junction of the Aar and Reuss) had steadily expanded their lands in the Breisgau, Alsace, and Switzerland, emerging as one of the leading families of Swabia.

1273–91. RUDOLF I. Indifferent to the Roman tradition, he concentrated on the advancement of his dynasty, and founded the power of the Habsburgs on territorial expansion of the family holdings and dynastic marriages. Edicts for the abolition of private war and support of local peace compacts *(Landfrieden).*

1276–78. Struggle with Ottokar, king of Bohemia, over the usurped imperial fiefs of Austria, Styria, Carinthia, Carniola. Rudolf expelled Ottokar from Austria by force (1276), but allowed him to retain Bohemia and Moravia (after homage) as a buffer against Slavdom. Ottokar was ultimately defeated and killed (Aug. 26, 1278, **Battle of the Marchfeld**); investiture of Rudolf's sons with the imperial fiefs of Austria, Styria, and Carniola (1282) established the Habsburgs on the Danube.

Rudolf yielded the last remnants of Frederick II's great imperial fabric: confirmation of papal rights in Italy and Angevin rights in southern Italy (1275); renunciation of all imperial claims to the Papal States and Sicily (1279).

1291. Alarmed at the rapid rise of the Habsburgs to first rank, the electors passed over Rudolf's son, choosing instead **Adolf of Nassau,** in return for substantial considerations.

1291. Revolt of the three Forest Cantons, Uri, Schwyz, and Unterwalden, and formation of a (Swiss) confederacy (p. 264).

1292–98. ADOLF, a strong imperialist. He supported the towns and lesser nobles and entered into alliance with Edward I of England against Philip IV; the alliance came to nothing, as the German princes were indifferent. The princes, alarmed at Adolf's advance in Meissen and Thuringia, deposed him (1298), electing Rudolf's rejected son.

1298–1308. ALBERT (ALBRECHT) I, son of Rudolf. Firm reduction of

THE VISCONTI AND SFORZA FAMILIES (1310–1535)

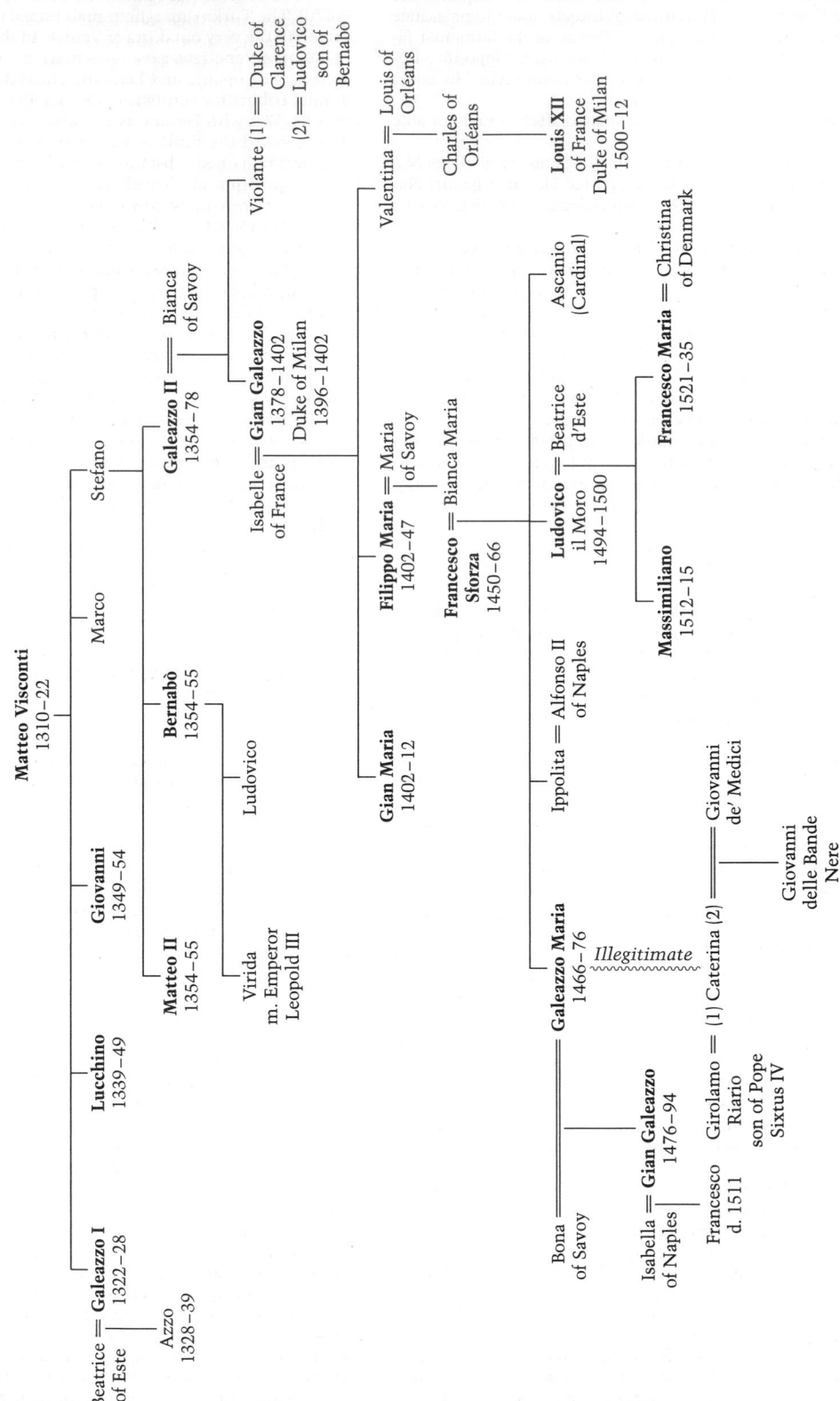

the ecclesiastical electoral princes (aid of the French and the towns); double dynastic marriage with the Capetians; acquisition of the crown of Bohemia (on the extinction of the Premyslids, 1306); Albert supported the Angevin Carobert's acquisition of Hungary; the Rhineland was filled with Francophile clerical appointees of the pope, and the election of 1308 was dominated by French influence. Charles of Valois procured the election of Henry of Luxemburg.

1308–13. HENRY VII (Luxemburg), a Francophile and bent on restoring the empire. The marriage of his son John to the sister of King Wenceslas of Bohemia brought the throne of Bohemia to the house of Luxemburg (1311–1489).

1310–13. Expedition to Italy at the urging of Pope Clement V and the Ghibellines; order restored and Milan, Cremona, Rome reduced; imperial coronation (1312); alliance of the pope and King Philip IV of France to save Naples from Henry.

1314–47. LOUIS IV (Wittelsbach). A Habsburg antiking, **Frederick the Handsome,** and civil war (until 1325). Bitter papal opposition (1323–47, refusal of confirmation of Louis's title to the empire); Louis, backed by the German people, against the Avignonese pope. Violent war of propaganda: **Marsiglio of Padua** (*Defensor Pacis,* 1324) and **William of Occam,** defending the imperial position, gave wide currency to conciliar ideas; **Dante's** *De Monarchia.*

1327–30. Louis's futile expedition to Italy and "lay" coronation (1328); his demand for a general council welcomed by the Italian Ghibellines. Effort to give the German monarchy a formal constitution.

1338. The **diet of Frankfurt:** declaration (the *Licet juris*) that the electors are competent to choose an emperor (i.e., papal intervention is not necessary); in effect the Holy Roman Empire was divorced entirely from the papacy.

1346. Louis was deposed, but fought against his successor, Charles (son of King John of Bohemia, who had been elected after an open alliance with the pope).

1347–78. CHARLES IV (Luxemburg). Concentration on the advancement of his dynasty (in Silesia, the Palatinate, Lusatia, Brandenburg) and on the progress of Bohemia. Prague became one of the chief cities of the empire (the university founded, 1348). The **Black Death** (1348–49) took an especially heavy toll in Germany; the Flagellants; anti-Semitic massacres. Promulgation of the Swabian League and numerous *Landfrieden* (imperial proclamations of public peace) reduced private warfare. Dauphiné and Arles continued to drift into the French orbit.

1356. The **Golden Bull** issued by Charles IV (in force until 1806) transformed the empire from a monarchy into an aristocratic federation, to avoid the evils of disputed elections. Seven **electors,** each a virtual sovereign: the archbishops of Mainz, Trier, and Cologne, the count palatine of the Rhine, the duke of Saxony, the margrave of Brandenburg, the king of Bohemia. Secular electorates to be indivisible and pass by primogeniture. Elections to be by majority vote and without delays. The electors to exercise supervision over the empire, a new function. The crown to remain in the house of Luxemburg.

Charles openly regarded the empire as an anachronism, but valued the emperor's right to nominate to vacant fiefs.

1364. Treaty of Brünn with the Habsburgs, whereby either house (Luxemburg or Habsburg) was to succeed to the lands of the other upon its extinction.

Internal anarchy; climax of localism; the only islands of order and prosperity were the walled towns; the only basis for order were the town leagues (e.g., revival of the **Rhine League** [1354]; the **Swabian League**); bitter warfare of classes; and princely opposition to the towns. Charles's vain appeal to the princes of Europe to resist France and end the Avignonese Captivity.

Apogee of the **Hanseatic League** (p. 265).

1378–1400. WENCESLAS (Wenzel, son of Charles IV, king of Bohemia, 1378–1419). Formation of the **Knights' League** (League of the Lion) followed by a series of political quarrels between the knights and lords on one side and the towns on the other, ending in the town war (1387–89) and the defeat of the towns, but not their ruin. Rising Bohemian nationalism: revolts, 1387–96.

1400. Deposition of Wenceslas for drunkenness and incompetence. He refused to accept the decision, and the result was that at the end of the confused period (1400–10) there were **three rival rulers** (Sigismund, Jobst, and Wenceslas), to correspond to the three rival popes.

1410–37. SIGISMUND (Luxemburg; king of Bohemia, 1419–37; king of Hungary by marriage). His main concern was to end the Papal Schism, and he succeeded the king of France as protagonist of conciliar reform by forcing (anti) Pope John XXIII to call the **Council of Constance** (p. 252). Establishment of the **house of Wettin** in Saxony (1423); the **Hohenzollerns (Frederick)** in Brandenburg (1415). Sigismund's failure at Constance not only alienated Bohemia but also ended any hope of German unification.

1410. Utter **defeat of the Teutonic Knights** by the Polish-Lithuanian army at **Tannenberg,** beginning of the decline of the Teutonic Knights.

1411. Peace of Thorn, halting of the Slavic advance.

1420–31. Hussite Wars reflect strong Bohemian national feeling (p. 263).

1433. Called to the **Council of Basel** (p. 252), the Hussites finally accepted the *Compactata* (which embodied the **Four Articles**), but the Church alienated them, and they began a final break. Bohemian nationality asserted itself increasingly in the 15th century, and Bohemia never returned to the German orbit.

Sigismund struggled against the Ottoman Turkish advance (1426–27) and was crowned at Rome (1433). In the election of 1438, Frederick of Brandenburg (candidate of the political reformers in Germany) withdrew, making the choice of Albert of Habsburg (Sigismund's son-in-law) unanimous. Albert also succeeded Sigismund on the thrones of Hungary and Bohemia.

1438–(1740) 1806. Henceforth the imperial crown in practice became hereditary in **the House of Habsburg.**

1438–39. ALBERT II.

1439. The **Pragmatic Sanction of Mainz** (abolition of annates, papal reservations, and provisions), a preliminary agreement between the papacy and the emperor, left the German Church under imperial and princely control.

1440–93. FREDERICK III. The last emperor crowned (1452) at Rome by the pope; a handsome amateur astrologer, botanist, minerologist.

Ladislas Posthumus (d. 1457), ward of Frederick, became duke of Austria (1440), was acknowledged king of Hungary (1445) and elected king of Bohemia (1452) with a council of regency. **George Podiebrad** (champion of the *Compactata*) emerged (1452) from the Bohemian civil war (Catholics vs. Utraquists) as regent of Bohemia, and later king (1458–71) (p. 264).

1448. The Concordat of Vienna, a cynical compromise whereby Pope Nicholas V confirmed the emperor's right to nominate to the highest ecclesiastical offices in Habsburg lands, but the papacy was entitled to annates.

1453. The **capture of Constantinople** (p. 126) brought the Ottoman Turks to the frontier of Germany.

1454. Traditional date for the **invention of printing** from movable metal type. This invention is usually attributed to **Johann Gutenberg** (?1400–1468) of Mainz, printer of the **Bible** (1456), the first important book printed from movable type. Printing had been in the process of development for many years and was probably perfected not only by Gutenberg, but also by others like Peter Schoeffer and Johann Fust of Mainz.

Schools sprang up, especially in South Germany, to teach the art of *Meistergesang* (musical and poetic guilds) in accordance with very strict and complicated rules.

1456. The Hungarian national leader **John Hunyadi** (without imperial support) repulsed the Ottoman Turks from Belgrade.

1458. Election of Hunyadi's son **Matthias Corvinus,** king of Hungary (to 1490) and George Podiebrad, king of Bohemia (to 1471), the climax of national spirit in Bohemia and Hungary.

1462. Pius II's **annulment of the *Compactata*** and the excommunication and deposition (1466) of Podiebrad reopened the Bohemian religious wars. **Ladislas** (elected 1468) succeeded on Podiebrad's death as king of Bohemia (1471–1516), becoming king of Hungary in 1490.

1473. Frederick, faced with the threat of (French) Burgundian expansion in the empire, avoided giving Charles the Bold, duke of Burgundy, the royal title and married his son Maximilian to Charles's daughter Mary (1477), bringing the Habsburg fortunes to their zenith, and giving reality to his own monogram: **A.E.I.O.U.** (*Austriae est imperare orbi universo,* or *Alles Erdreich ist Oesterreich unterthan.*)

1485. Expelled from Vienna by Matthias Corvinus, Frederick became a cheery imperial mendicant.

THE HOUSE OF HABSBURG (1273–1519)

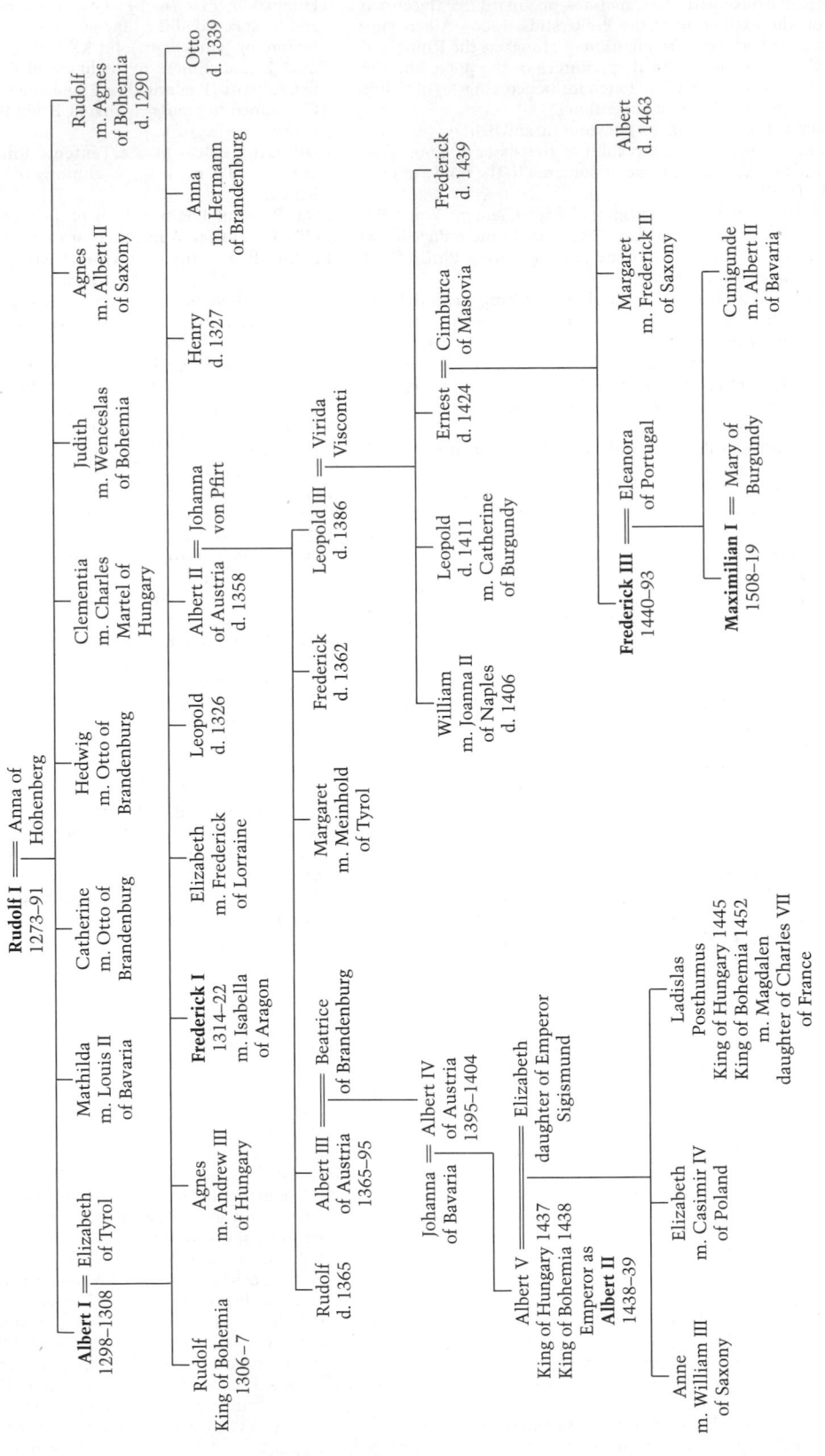

LUXEMBURG RULERS (1308–1437)

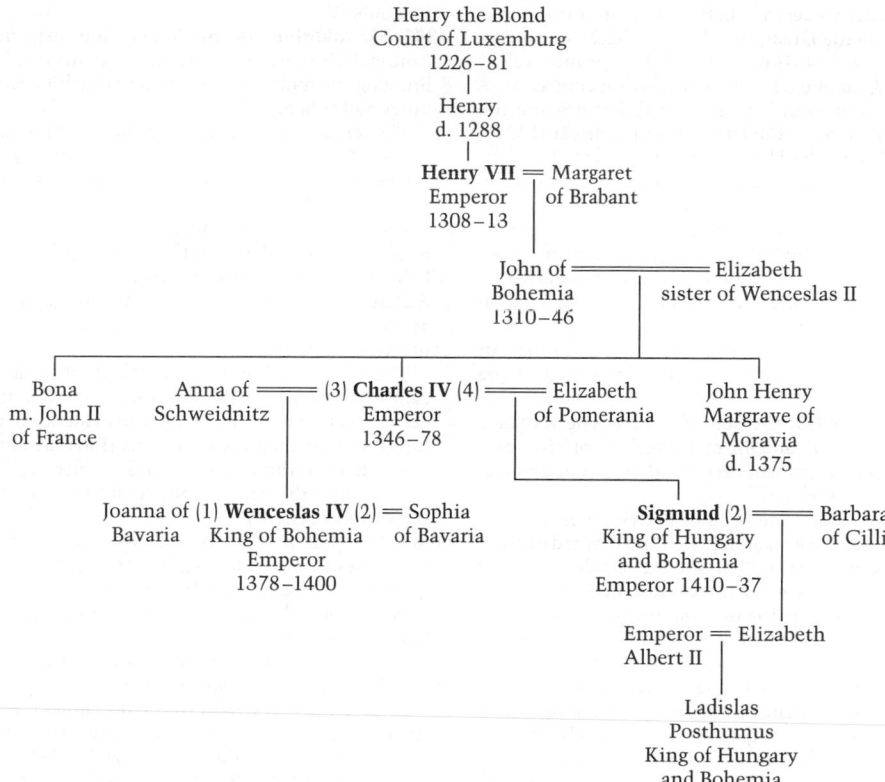

Henry the Blond
Count of Luxemburg
1226–81

Henry
d. 1288

Henry VII = Margaret
Emperor   of Brabant
1308–13

John of ============ Elizabeth
Bohemia   sister of Wenceslas II
1310–46

Bona   Anna of = (3) **Charles IV** (4) === Elizabeth   John Henry
m. John II   Schweidnitz   Emperor   of Pomerania   Margrave of
of France   1346–78   Moravia
                                                              d. 1375

Joanna of (1) **Wenceslas IV** (2) = Sophia   **Sigmund** (2) ===== Barbara
Bavaria   King of Bohemia   of Bavaria   King of Hungary   of Cilli
          Emperor   and Bohemia
          1378–1400   Emperor 1410–37

                                            Emperor = Elizabeth
                                            Albert II

                                            Ladislas
                                            Posthumus
                                            King of Hungary
                                            and Bohemia

1486. Maximilian, elected king of the Romans, became the real ruler of Germany.

(To p. 300)

1. BOHEMIA
(From p. 223)

1306. The **Premyslid dynasty** came to an end with the death of Wenceslas (Vaclav) III. There followed an interregnum, during which the Bohemians were driven out of Poland.

1310–46. The interregnum ended with the election of **JOHN OF LUXEMBURG,** son of Emperor Henry VII. The circumstances of his accession forced John to issue a charter guaranteeing the rights and privileges of the nobility and clergy. The "national" Diet, theretofore called only on special occasions, became a regular institution. During this reign Bohemian overlordship over Upper Lusatia and Silesia was established.

John supported the Teutonic Knights against the Lithuanians and participated in three campaigns (1328, 1337, 1346). For a time (1331–33) he ruled western Lombardy, as well as the Tyrol (1336–41). John was killed in the **battle of Crécy,** where he fought on the side of the French.

1346–78. CHARLES I (Charles IV as German Emperor), the son of John of Luxemburg. His reign is regarded as the golden age of Bohemian history. A series of charters issued in 1348 established an order of dynastic succession and determined Bohemia's place in the Holy Roman Empire. Moravia, Silesia, and Upper Lusatia were to be indissolubly connected with the Bohemian crown. By the **Golden Bull** (1356, see p. 261), the king of Bohemia was given first place among the empire's secular electors. At the same time, Bohemia's internal independence was guaranteed. Acquisition of Lower Lusatia (1370) and Brandenburg (1373). Charles ruled as a constitutional king and spared no effort to promote material well-being and cultural progress. A new code of laws, the *Maiestas Carolina,* was published. Prague was rebuilt and beautified. The **University of Prague** founded (1348), the first university in central Europe.

1349. Germany and Bohemia were affected by the second cycle of the plague epidemics (the **Black Death**). The clergy as a whole, and the monastic communities within the towns in particular, provided the highest percentage of victims. This necessitated hasty recruiting of new priests, whose moral integrity was often questionable. The abuses that followed and the continuing terror of the Black Death led to frenzies of religious excess, as well as to the emergence of lay piety movements and heresy.

1378–1419. WENCESLAS (Vaclav) IV, son of Charles. Gradual weakening of the connection with the German Empire. Loss of Brandenburg (1411). Continued conflicts with the barons. This was hastened by the development (since the end of the 14th century) of a national-religious movement that culminated in **Hussitism. JOHN HUS** (1369–1415), a professor at the University of Prague and a popular preacher in the vernacular, was perhaps influenced by the teaching of Wiclif and the Lollards in England. He attacked the sale of indulgences, demanded reforms in the Church, challenged the primacy of the pope, and emphasized the supreme authority of the Scriptures. He also supported the native element in the university in the struggle that ended in the exodus of the alien Germans (1409), becoming rector of the university. Excommunicated by the pope and eager for vindication, he went to the **Council of Constance** (1415) under a safe-conduct from the emperor. His arrest in violation of this guaranty, and his trial and burning (July 6), identified religious reform with Bohemian nationalism.

1420–33. These events also split the empire in the **Hussite Wars.** Refusal to recognize Sigismund as king. The reformers divided into two groups. (1) The moderate **Calixtines,** with the university as a center, favored separation of religious and political reform and formulated their program in the **Four Articles of Prague** (1420): full liberty of preaching; sacramental Communion of both kinds, bread *and* wine (Ultraquism), for the laity; exclusion of the clergy from temporal activity and their subjection to civil penalties for crime. (2) The radical **Taborites,** under extreme Waldensian, Catharist, and Wiclifite influences, with a program of democracy and apostolic communism. The papal proclamation of a **Bohemian Crusade** (not opposed by the Emperor Sigismund) united the nation behind **John Ziska,** a brilliant soldier, who led the Hussites in a series of victories (1420–22). Ziska's "modernization" of tactics: improved mobile artillery, use of baggage wagons for mobile cover. Ziska's death (1424) did not affect the movement. Under a priest, **Procop the Great,** the Hussites defeated one crusade after another (1426, 1427, 1431) and carried the war into neighboring regions of Germany, on one occasion (1432) advancing as far as the Baltic. Then civil war broke out between the Calixtines and the Taborites (led by Procop the Great), the latter suffering defeat (1434).

1431–36. The Council of Basel. The Hussites finally accepted a compromise, the *Compactata* (1436), recognizing them as true sons of the Church and conceding to them the cup in the Communion.

1436. Sigismund was finally accepted as king by all parties. He attempted a Catholic reaction, but died in 1437. Disputes continued between the Catholics and the Hussites, complicated by factional struggles between Hussite moderates and radicals and by social tension between nobility, townsmen, and peasantry.

1437–39. Albert of Austria (son-in-law of Sigismund) elected king. An opposition group chose Ladislas, king of Poland. Albert died in the course of a civil war.

1439–57. LADISLAS POSTHUMUS, the son of Albert. The Emperor Frederick III acted as his guardian, and for many years kept him from Bohemia. In the midst of continued factional conflict, a young nobleman, **George Podiebrad,** rose to power.

1448. George seized Prague and became head of the Hussites. He was recognized as administrator of the kingdom (1452) and devoted himself to the task of reconciling Catholics and Hussites. The radical wing of the latter was completely suppressed by the **capture of Tabor** (1452). George ultimately succeeded in bringing the young king to Prague, but Ladislas died before he could accomplish much on behalf of the Catholics.

1458–71. GEORGE PODIEBRAD elected king. Policy of conciliation: vigorous persecution of the **Bohemian Brotherhood,** a puritanical sect with outspokenly democratic leanings dating from the teaching of **Peter of Chelchich** (d. 1460) and, like the Taborites, rejecting all subordination to Rome. George, an avowed Hussite of the moderate school, was technically a heretic and soon found himself in conflict with the pope.

1462. The pope denounced the agreements of Basel and deposed George (1465). Thereupon the Catholic nobility of Bohemia elected **Matthias of Hungary** as king. George defeated him in a series of engagements, but the issue was undecided when George died. *(To p. 309)*

2. THE SWISS CONFEDERATION

Lake Lucerne and the original **Forest Cantons** belonged to the duchy of Swabia, and the expansion of powerful Swabian families during the Great Interregnum led the Forest Cantons to a determined effort to replace feudal allegiances to various nobles with a single direct allegiance to the emperor. Most powerful of the Swabian families was the rising **house of Habsburg** (whose original lands expanded in the 13th century into the Aargau, Breisgau, and Alsace). **Rudolf I** (b. 1218) of Habsburg sought to restore the duchy of Swabia under his house.

The **Forest Cantons of Uri** (already acknowledged independent of any but a loose imperial allegiance in 1231), **Schwyz,** and **Unterwalden** emerged as champions of local independence and masters of the St. Gothard Pass into Italy. Rudolf, during the Interregnum, expanded his suzerainty, but as emperor he was too busy to assert it.

1291. First (known) **League of the Three Forest Cantons** (sometimes called the Everlasting League), an undertaking for mutual defense, a kind of constitution, but not an independent federal league, as the cantons did not claim independence. Emperor Adolf confirmed the status of Uri and Schwyz, Henry VII that of Unterwalden, and thenceforth the three Forest Cantons were thought of as a unit. The Swiss sent Henry VII 300 soldiers for his Italian expedition, the first recorded use of Swiss troops outside their own borders. The legend of the Swiss patriot **William Tell,** whom Austrian officials forced to shoot an apple off his small son's head, derives from this period.

1315, Nov. 15. Battle of Morgarten. Leopold of Austria, in an effort to crush the Swiss and punish them for support of Louis IV against the Habsburg Frederick the Handsome, was thoroughly beaten at Morgarten, a battle that began the brilliant career of the Swiss infantry in Europe. Renewal and strengthening of the league and its confirmation by Louis IV.

1332–53. Additions to the Forest Cantons: canton of Lucerne (1332); canton of Zurich (1351); canton of Glarus (1352); canton of Bern (1353), bringing the number to seven, half of which were peasant cantons, the other half urban.

The terror that accompanied the spread of the Black Death to Swiss lands led to charges of witchcraft and to pogroms against those perceived as social outcasts, such as the Jews, who were accused of poisoning the wells.

1386, July 9. Battle of Sempach. The confederation, supported by the Swabian League, defeated the Habsburg Leopold III of Swabia.

1394. Twenty-year truce between the confederation and the duke of Austria. Austria abandoned claims on Zug and Glarus. The confederation became solely dependent on the empire, which amounted to practical independence.

The confederation was controlled by a **federal Diet** (1393), but the cantons retained the widest possible autonomy. Throughout the succeeding period there was but little evidence of union. The various cantons followed their own interests (Lucerne and Schwyz looked to the north; Bern to the west; Uri to the south) and wrangled among themselves. Only the threat from Austria invariably united them against the common enemy.

1403. The canton of Uri began expansion southward, to get control of the passes to the Milanese. In 1410 the whole Val Antigorio was conquered, with Domodossola. The Swiss were driven out by the duke of Savoy in 1413, but in 1416 they regained mastery of the country.

1415. Conquest in the north of the Aargau, from Frederick of Austria, at the behest of his rival, the Emperor Sigismund.

1436–50. Civil war between Zurich and some of the neighboring cantons over the succession to the domains of the count of Toggenburg. Zurich allied itself with Emperor Frederick III (1442) but was defeated by Schwyz (1443); Zurich besieged (1444). Frederick called in the French, but after a defeat near Basel, the French withdrew. The emperor made the **Peace at Constance** (June 12, 1446) and in 1450, peace was made within the confederation. The general effect of the war was to strengthen the confederacy.

1460. Conquest of the Thurgau from Austria gave the confederation a frontier on Lake Constance.

1474–77. The great war against **Charles the Bold of Burgundy,** whose designs on Alsace were regarded as a menace to the confederation. The Swiss allied themselves with the South German cities. This combination was joined by the emperor. Louis XI of France also joined, but in 1475 both the emperor and the king withdrew again. Great victories of the Swiss at **Grandson** (March 2, 1476), **Morat** or Murten (June 22, 1476), and **Nancy** (Jan. 5, 1477) sealed the fate of Charles's plans and established the great military reputation of the Swiss, who were thenceforth sought far and wide as mercenaries.

1478. War with Milan. Victory of the Swiss at **Giornico** (Dec. 28). Alliance with the pope, who was allowed to engage Swiss forces.

1481. Solothurn and Fribourg were admitted to the confederation after a long dispute among the members. The **Diet of Stans** drew up a covenant by which federal relations were regulated until 1798. Thenceforth the urban cantons were in a majority.

1499. War with the emperor over disputed territories in the east. The emperor was supported by the South German cities, while the Swiss enjoyed the support, especially financial, of the French. The Swiss won a series of victories and forced the emperor to conclude the **Treaty of Basel** (Sept. 22), which granted the confederation independence of the empire in fact, if not formally (this came only in 1648). With the inclusion of **Basel** and **Schaffhausen** (1501) and later **Appenzell** (1513), the confederation rounded out its northern frontier.

The Swiss at the end of the 15th century enjoyed immense military prestige, but within the confederation there was much social unrest, especially among the peasants, and a good deal of demoralization in the towns. **Hans Waldmann,** *bürgermeister* of Zurich (1483–89), was only the most outstanding of the typically ruthless, mercenary, cynical figures who dominated the scene, reminding one of the contemporaneous Italian despots. *(To p. 305)*

3. THE HANSEATIC LEAGUE

Associations (Hansas, from Old Fr. *Hanse*; Med. Lat. *Hansa*; meaning a group, company, or association) of North German towns date from the 13th century and were an important aspect of the great town development of Germany in that period.

c. 1000. German traders were established on the island of Gothland and in London.

c. 1150–c. 1250. Revival of the German river trade, notably along the Rhine, centering in the towns of Cologne, Dortmund, Soest, and Münster. At the same time, the German expansion toward the Slavic east extended the sphere of German trade along the Baltic coasts. In the later 12th century the German settlement on Gothland **(Wisby)** became autonomous and established an offshoot at **Novgorod** (St. Peter's Yard), which became the focus of the important Russian trade.

1226. Lübeck (founded 1143) secured an imperial charter from Frederick II. Hamburg followed in 1266–67.

1237. Wisby secured trading rights in England, and soon afterward in Flanders.

1241. Lübeck and Hamburg formed an alliance to protect the Baltic trade routes.

1256. The **Wendish towns** (Lübeck, Stralsund, Wismar, Rostock, Greifswald, and later Lüneburg), held their first recorded meeting. Lübeck began to emerge as the dominant North German town, a position it retained throughout the history of the Hanseatic League. Most of the commercial towns followed the **Code of Lübeck,** which was an early source of unity between them. By the end of the century, the Wendish towns had taken the leadership from the Gothland merchants.

1282. The **Germans in London** formed a corporation and established their own guildhall and steelyard. Other German yards were opened at York, Bristol, Yarmouth, Lynn, and Boston. The London trade was dominated by Cologne, but the yards at Lynn and Boston were under the control of Lübeck and Hamburg.

The Hanseatic League. No date can be fixed for its organization, which was evidently the result of the lack of a strong central German government able to guarantee security for trade. Its formation was no doubt facilitated by the medieval affinity for cooperative action and for monopoly. The Hanseatic League was first mentioned in a document in 1344. The exclusion of Germans abroad (1366) from the privileges of the Hansa indicates a growing sense of unity, but league members spoke of the association merely as a *firma confederatio* for trade, and throughout its history it remained a loose aggregation. This looseness of organization allowed its members a maximum of independence and was not modified until the league was put on the defensive in the 15th century. The league never had a true treasury or officials in a strict sense; its only common seal was that of Lübeck. Assemblies of the members *(Hansetage)* were summoned by Lübeck at irregular intervals, except in time of crisis. The objectives of the league were mutual security, extortion of trading privileges, and maintenance of trade monopoly wherever possible. The chief weapons against foreigners or recalcitrant members were the economic boycott and (rarely) war. Primarily concerned with the North European trade, the Hansa towns dealt chiefly in raw materials (timber, pitch, tar, turpentine, iron, copper), livestock (horses, hawks, etc.), salt fish (cod and especially herring), leather, hides, wool, grain, beer, amber, drugs, and some textiles. The four chief *kontors* (trading stations) were Wisby, Bergen, London, and Bruges.

1340–75. WALDEMAR IV of Denmark, who took up the struggle against the powerful Hansa towns. He threatened the Hanseatic monopoly of the herring trade with his seizure of Scandinavia and, in 1361, cut the Russian-Baltic trade route with his capture of Wisby. In 1362 he defeated the German fleets at **Helsingborg.** By the **Peace of Wordingborg** (1365) the Hansa was deprived of many of its privileges in Denmark.

1367. The **Confederation of Cologne,** effected by a meeting of representatives of 77 towns, organized common finance and naval preparations for the struggle. Reconstruction of Scandinavian alliances to meet the threat from Waldemar.

1370. After a series of victories, the German towns extorted from the Danish Reichsrat the **Peace of Stralsund,** which gave the league four castles in Scandinavia (dominating the sound), control of two thirds of the Scandinavian revenues for 15 years, and the right to veto the succession to the Danish throne unless their monopoly was renewed by the candidate. The treaty marked the **apogee of Hanseatic power** and virtually established control over the Baltic trade and over Scandinavian politics.

Flanders. The Germans in Bruges received a special grant of privileges in 1252, which allowed them their own ordinances and officials. Bruges was the most ardent champion of Hanseatic unity, and, with Lübeck, was the chief source of such cohesion as the league attained. A boycott in 1360 brought the town into complete submission to the league.

England. The Hansa towns, by maintaining friendly relations with the crown, were able to ignore the growing national hostility to alien traders (directed at first mainly against the Italians) and to avoid granting reciprocal privileges to the English in return for their own exclusive rights (notably those claimed under Edward I's *Carta Mercatoria* of 1303). A source of Hanseatic influence derived from loans to the crown, especially during the Hundred Years' War. The English themselves began to penetrate into the Baltic (c. 1360), and growing public resentment against the league led to increased customs dues, but Richard II in 1377 renewed the privileges of the league, thus firmly establishing the Hanseatic power in England. The sound was opened to the English in 1451, and the league, profiting by the Wars of the Roses, secured full title to the steelyard in London (1474) and the renewal of rights in Boston and Lynn.

Decline of the league. Externally the league was weakened by the disorders of the Hundred Years' War; by the rise of Burgundy and the new orientation thereby given to Dutch trade (e.g., Brill wrested the monopoly of the herring trade from the league); and by the great discoveries and the opening of new trade routes. But above all, the monopolistic policies of the league aroused ever sharper opposition in the countries where the league operated. **Internally** the league continued to suffer from lack of organization. In the 15th century, the league was further weakened by the struggle within the member towns between the democratic guildsmen and the patrician oligarchy. The league threatened the expulsion of "democratic" towns. The German princes (notably the Hohenzollerns of Brandenburg) gradually reduced the freedom of various powerful members of the league, and rivalries broke out within the league itself (Cologne and the Westphalian towns stood together, as did Danzig and the Prussian towns, especially after 1467). The South German towns opened direct trade relations of their own with Flanders, Breslau (Wrocław), Prague, and other centers, and began to establish their own fairs. Leipzig, for example, replaced Lübeck as the center of the fur trade.

1629. The assembly entrusted the guardianship of the common welfare to Lübeck, Hamburg, and Bremen.

1669. The last assembly (attended by six towns) was held. The league by this time was the merest shadow of its former self, but its *kontors* survived in Bergen until 1775, in London until 1852, and in Augsburg until 1863.

4. THE TEUTONIC KNIGHTS
(From p. 210)

The 14th century marked the apogee of the power of the **Teutonic Order** in eastern Europe. The Knights began the penetration of Poland, where Germans settled some 650 districts and where the middle class in the towns became German in speech and law, much to the alarm of the rulers and nobles. In the same period, the Knights advanced into Lithuania, a huge region extending from the Baltic to the Black Sea, the last pagan area in Europe. German colonization and town building first opened and civilized this region.

1326–33. The **first Polish war,** marking a sharp reaction to German penetration and putting the order for the first time on the defensive. With the aid of John of Bohemia, Louis of Hungary, Albert of Austria, Louis of Brandenburg, and others, the order emerged triumphant, and the Poles were obliged to conclude a truce.

1343. Peace of Kalisz. The Poles, despite papal support of their claims to Pomerelia, were obliged to recognize the order's possession of the territory, in return for a promise of aid against the Lithuanians. Poland was thus cut off from the Baltic.

1343–45. The **Estonian Revolt,** one of the worst working-class uprisings of the Middle Ages. Estonia was taken by the order from the Danes in 1346.

1386. Union of Poland and Lithuania, creating a strong barrier to the further advance of the Germans and, indeed, sealing the ultimate fate of the Knights.

1410, July 15. Defeat of the Knights in the **battle of Tannenberg** by a huge army of Poles and Lithuanians (p. 268).

1411. Poland, unable to exploit the victory, concluded the **first Peace of Thorn,** which cost the Knights only Samogitia and an indemnity.

1454. The **Prussian Revolt,** a great uprising against the oppressive rule of the order, in which the Prussian nobility and towns took part. The movement was supported by the Poles, and Casimir of Poland declared war on the order.

1466. Second Peace of Thorn: Prussia was divided: (1) **West Prussia** (including Danzig, Kulm, Marienwerder, Thorn, and Ermeland) went to Poland, thus cutting East Prussia off from the rest of Germany and securing for Poland access to the sea; (2) **East Prussia** was retained by the order, with Königsberg as the capital. East Prussia, Brandenburg, and Memel (today Klaipeda in Lithuania) were all to be held as Polish fiefs. The order was opened to Polish members. This peace marked the definitive end of the German advance until the partitions of Poland.

The **decline of the Teutonic Order** continued (growing commercialization, exclusiveness, lack of new blood, loss of discipline, Slavic pressure), despite efforts at reform.

1525. East Prussia was finally secularized by the grand master, Albrecht (Hohenzollern) of Brandenburg, and became a fief of the Hohenzollerns under the Polish crown.

The order itself survived in Germany until 1809 and was later revived in 1840 under Habsburg auspices, with its original functions (e.g., ambulance service in war).

g. SCANDINAVIA

1. DENMARK
(From p. 211)

The active and on the whole successful reign of **Eric Menved** (1286–1319) was followed in Denmark by a period of weakness and decline, marked by the ascendancy of the nobility and the constant advance of German influence.

1320–32. CHRISTOPHER II, elected king after a capitulation, the first in Danish history, limiting the royal power in the interest of the nobility and clergy. The towns of the Hanseatic League, having acquired a monopoly of trade in Denmark, soon became dominant in Danish politics.

1332–40. A period of complete anarchy. Christopher was driven from the throne by Gerhard, count of Holstein, who parceled out the territories of the crown, established German nobles in all the important fortresses, and gave the German traders full rein. Gerhard was murdered in 1340.

1340–75. WALDEMAR IV, the youngest son of Christopher and one of the greatest Danish kings. At home he did his utmost to break the German influence and to restrict the power of the nobility and the clergy. The Church was subordinated to the royal power and the nobles and towns obliged to perform their military obligations. Abroad, Waldemar devoted himself to the reconquest of the territories lost by his father. In wars with Sweden, Holstein, and Schleswig he regained Zeeland (1346), most of Fünen and Jutland (1348), and Scandinavia (1360). His seizure of Gothland (1361) brought him into direct conflict with the powerful Hansa towns, which were supported by Sweden.

1361–63. First war against the Hansa. Copenhagen was sacked, but Waldemar defeated the Hansa fleets at **Helsingborg** (1362) and forced the Hansa to accept peace (1363), which greatly curtailed their privileges.

1368. A revolt against heavy taxation led to Waldemar's flight. His return (1370) was purchased by tremendous concessions.

1368–70. Meanwhile the **second war with the Hansa** had broken out. The German towns were supported by Sweden, Norway, Holstein, Mecklenburg, and even by some of the Danish nobles.

1370. Waldemar, badly defeated, was obliged to accept the **Peace of Stralsund,** renewing the privileges of the German Hansa, turning over the larger part of the revenues of four places, and accepting interference in the royal succession. This treaty marked the **ascendency of the Hansa** in the Baltic.

1376–87. Olaf, grandson of Waldemar, who, until his death, ruled with his mother, Margaret, as regent.

1387–1412. MARGARET, mother of Olaf, was queen, ruling, at the same time, Norway and Sweden and thus uniting Scandinavia.
(To p. 305)

2. SWEDEN
(From p. 211)

1319–65. MAGNUS II (Smek), age three at his accession and, until 1333, ruler under the regency of his mother. He was a weak and ineffectual ruler, but through his mother succeeded (1319) to the Norwegian crown and, during the troubled period in Denmark, managed to acquire, temporarily, Scandinavia, Halland, and Bleking (given up again in 1360, to Waldemar IV). His long minority and his reliance on unworthy favorites led to a striking weakening of the royal power and an equally striking rise of the aristocratic party (first Riksdag, including burghers, 1359).

1363–88. Magnus was ultimately deposed and was succeeded by **Albert of Mecklenburg,** from the outset merely a tool of the nobility.

1387–1412. The magnates eventually deposed him and defeated him, calling to the throne **MARGARET,** the regent of Denmark.
(To p. 266)

3. NORWAY
(From p. 211)

1319–43. Magnus VII, who was also king of Sweden.

1343–80. In 1343 he turned over Norway to his son. **Haakon VI,** who was married (1363) to Margaret of Denmark.

1380–87. Olaf, the son of Haakon and Margaret, already king of Denmark, succeeded to the throne. His death ended the Norwegian line.

1387–1412. MARGARET, mother of Olaf, was elected to the throne, thus introducing into Norway the system of election already in practice in Denmark and Sweden. *(To p. 305)*

4. THE UNION OF KALMAR

1387–1412. Margaret of Denmark, ruler of all three Scandinavian kingdoms. She had her grandnephew, Eric of Pomerania, elected king of all three countries but retained effective power herself.

1397. Coronation of Eric. Margaret presented a draft for the union of the three kingdoms. Vague and incomplete, the plan provided for a single king, established rules of succession, and set up a system of common defense. It was never ratified by the councils of the three kingdoms, but as long as Margaret lived, it worked relatively well. The union left the internal government of each kingdom much as it was. Margaret, an able despot, repressed the nobles, maintained order, and began the recovery of the Danish royal domain. In general the Danes profited by the union, and Danes and Germans were gradually insinuated into power in Sweden and Norway. Effective government of Scandinavia was centered in Denmark.

1412–39. ERIC, Margaret's successor, proved himself less able. His efforts to regain control in Schleswig led to a long contest with the dukes of Holstein, who, in alliance with the Hansa towns, finally conquered Schleswig completely (1432). At the same time, much unrest developed among the peasantry (especially in Sweden, where **Engelbrecht Engelbrechtson** emerged as a leader of the lower classes).

1434. Engelbrecht marched through eastern and southern Sweden, seizing castles and driving out bailiffs, until the **Diet of 1435** recognized his demands, electing him regent. This Diet included representatives of all four orders, and for four hundred years it continued to be an important institution.

1439–48. Eric finally took flight, and the Danish council called in **CHRISTOPHER** (of Bavaria), nephew of Eric, who again ruled all three countries (elected in Sweden, 1440; in Norway, 1442). His reign marked the **nadir of the monarchy,** for Christopher was entirely dependent on the Hansa towns and was obliged to renew all their privileges, despite protests from the Danish burghers.

1448–81. CHRISTIAN I (of Oldenburg) was elected by the Danish coun-

SCANDINAVIAN RULERS (1263–1533)

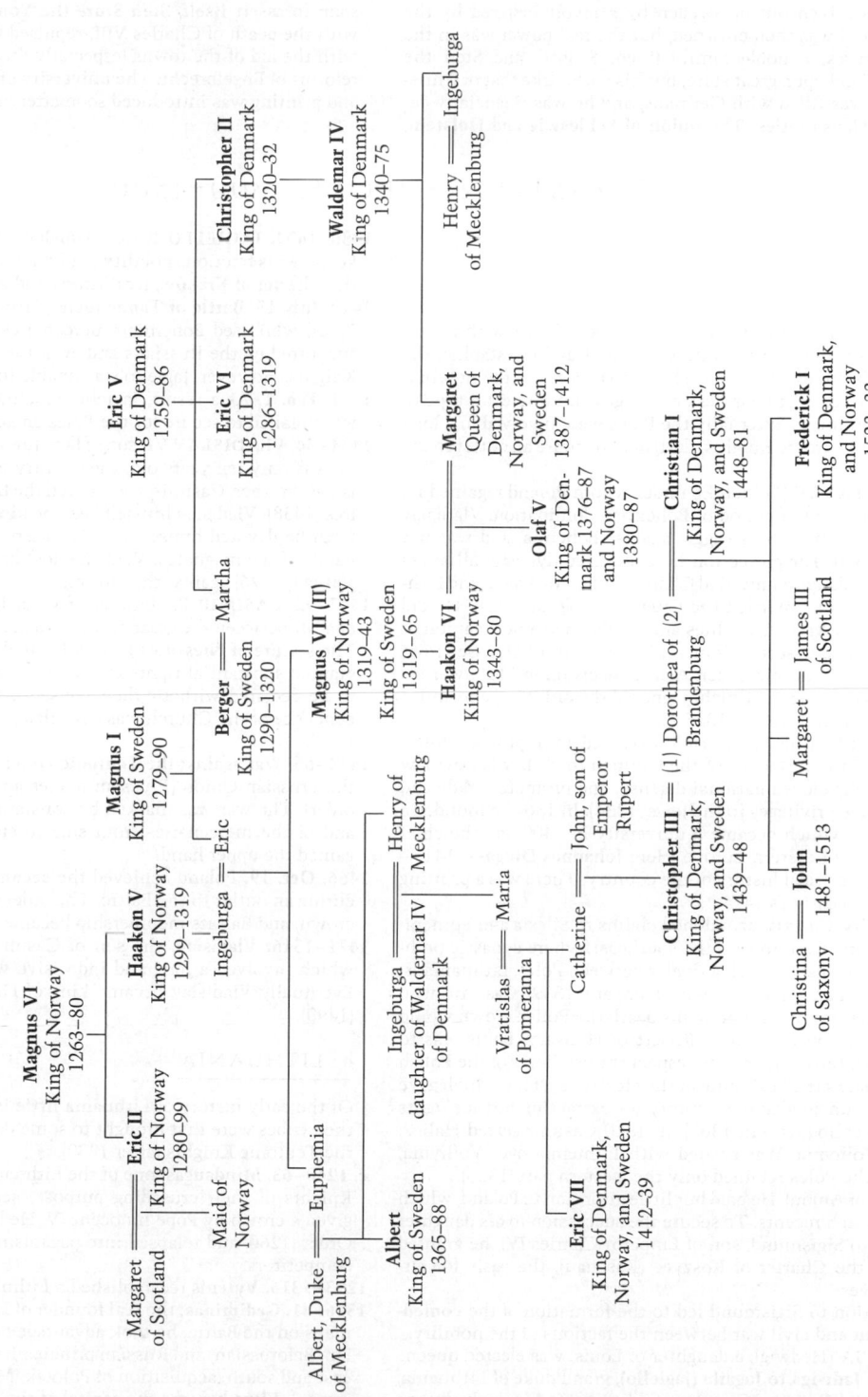

cil under a capitulation that left all real power in the hands of that body. He had to accept a similar engagement on assuming the crown of Norway. The Swedish nobility, on the other hand, elected **Knut Knutsson** as king, with the title of **Charles VIII** (1449–57). Charles tried to secure the throne of Norway, but was ousted by Christian.

1457. Charles was driven out of Sweden by a revolt inspired by the Church. Christian I was then crowned, but the real power was in the hands of the **Stures,** a noble family (Sten, Svante, and Sten the Younger). Christian kept a great state, but his court, like that of Christopher and Eric, was filled with Germans, and he was financially dependent on the Hansa cities. The **union of Schleswig and Holstein,** each autonomous under the crown of Denmark, was arranged in 1460. Christian founded the **university of Copenhagen** (1479).

Sweden in the later 15th century. The crown was a plaything of the nobles, while the clergy supported the king of Denmark. Rising commerce and industry were, however, creating a burgher class that was soon to assert itself. **Sten Sture the Younger,** who came into power with the death of Charles VIII, repulsed Christian of Denmark (1471) with the aid of the towns (especially Stockholm) and returned to the reforms of Engelbrecht. The **university of Uppsala** was founded (1477), and **printing** was introduced soon afterward.   (To p. 305)

7. EASTERN EUROPE, 1300–1500

a. POLAND

(From p. 224)

The history of Poland in this period is concerned chiefly with the efforts of the kings to reunite the various duchies and to establish the royal power. This policy was opposed, with success, by the nobility, which managed to extract countless privileges and to erect a type of oligarchical government. Externally the Poles were involved in a long struggle with the Teutonic Knights, designed to secure an outlet to the Baltic.

1305–33. VLADISLAV IV (Lokietek), under whom Poland regained its independence after a brief period of Bohemian domination. Vladislav was obliged to continue the struggle against Bohemia, and was not crowned until 1320. For protection he concluded dynastic alliances with Hungary (his daughter married Charles Robert of Anjou) and Lithuania (his son Casimir married the daughter of Gediminas). He did much to reunite the various duchies and established a new capital at Kraków. But he failed to secure Pomerania, which in 1309 passed from Brandenburg to the Teutonic Order. A papal decision in 1321 awarded the region to Poland, but the Knights ignored the order and continued their raids into Polish territory (1326–33).

1333–70. CASIMIR III (the Great). He introduced an improved administration, reduced the influence of the German town law (a new law code published), developed national defense, and promoted trade and industry (extensive privileges to the Jews, 1334). In 1364 he founded a school at Kraków, which became a university in 1400 and the chief intellectual center of eastern Europe. Here **Johannes Dlugosz** (1415–80) wrote the first critical history of the country. There was a printing press in Kraków as early as 1474.

In **foreign affairs,** Casimir abandoned claims to Silesia and Pomerania, turning his attention toward the southeast, where dynastic problems in the Ukraine called forth a rivalry between Poles, Lithuanians, and Hungarians. In an agreement with Hungary (1339), Casimir, who had no direct heir, promised that on his death the Polish crown would pass to Louis, the son of Charles Robert of Hungary. Louis was to reconquer the lost territories and to respect the privileges of the Polish nobility. This marks the beginning of the elective system, which gave the magnates an unequaled opportunity for extracting further rights (first real diet—colloquia—in 1367). In 1340 Casimir seized Halicz, Lemberg, and Volhynia. War ensued with Lithuania over Volhynia, and ultimately the Poles retained only the western part (1366).

1370–82. LOUIS (of Anjou). He paid but little attention to Poland, which he governed through regents. To secure the succession to his daughter Maria (married to Sigismund, son of Emperor Charles IV), he granted to the nobility the **Charter of Koszyce** (Kaschau), the basis for far-reaching privileges.

1382–84. Opposition to Sigismund led to the formation of the **confederation of Radom** and civil war between the factions of the nobility.

1384–99. JADWIGA (Hedwig), a daughter of Louis, was elected queen.

1386. Marriage of Jadwiga to Jogaila (Jagiello), grand duke of Lithuania, who promised to become a Christian and to unite his duchy (three times the size of Poland) with the Polish crown. As a matter of fact, though the marriage prepared the way for union, he was obliged to recognize his cousin Vytautas (Witold) as grand duke of Lithuania, and the connection continued to be tenuous.

1386–1434. JAGIELLO (title **Vladislav V**). He had great difficulty in keeping his fractious nobility in order and in 1433 was obliged to grant the **Charter of Kraków,** reaffirming and extending their privileges.

1410, July 15. Battle of Tannenberg (Grünwald), a great victory for the Poles, who used Bohemian mercenaries under John Ziska and were supported by the Russians and even the Tatars, against the Teutonic Knights. However, Jagiello was unable to keep his vassals in order.

1411, Feb. 1. As a result, Jagiello concluded the **first Peace of Thorn,** which failed to secure for the Poles an access to the Baltic.

1434–44. VLADISLAV VI, son of Jagiello, succeeded to the throne. Since he was only ten years old, the country was ruled by a regency. Vladislav's brother, Casimir, was offered the Bohemian throne by the Hussites (1438); Vladislav himself became **king of Hungary** (1440). Thenceforth he devoted himself to Hungarian affairs, leaving Poland in the hands of the magnates. Vladislav lost his life in 1444 at the **Battle of Varna** (p. 126) against the Ottomans.

1447–92. CASIMIR IV, brother of Vladislav. He was able to make use of a rift between the great nobles (magnates) and the gentry *(szlachta).* The **statute of Nieszawa** greatly limited the power of the former and granted substantial rights to the latter (no laws to be passed, no war to be declared without their consent). At the same time, the independence of the Church was curtailed (bishops to be appointed by the king).

1454–66. War against the Teutonic Order. The Poles took advantage of the Prussian Union (Prussian nobles and towns in opposition to the order). The war was marked by constant shifting of the feudal forces and of the mercenaries from side to side, but the Poles ultimately gained the upper hand.

1466, Oct. 19. Poland achieved the **second Peace of Thorn,** finally securing an outlet to the Baltic. The order became a vassal of the Polish crown, and half its membership became Polish.

1471–1516. Vladislav, the son of Casimir, became king of Bohemia, which involved a long and indecisive war with Hungary (1471–78). Eventually Vladislav became king of Hungary as Ladislas (László) II (1490).   (To p. 308)

b. LITHUANIA

Of the early history of Lithuania little is known. The numerous heathen tribes were first brought to some degree of unity by the threat of the Teutonic Knights (after 1230).

c. 1240–63. Mindaugas, one of the Lithuanian chieftains, to deprive the Knights of their crusading purpose, accepted Christianity and was given a crown by Pope Innocent IV. He later broke with the Teutonic Order (1260) and relapsed into paganism. He was killed by one of his competitors.

1293–1316. Vytenis reestablished a Lithuanian state.

1316–41. Gediminas, the real founder of Lithuania. Blocked by the Germans on the Baltic, he took advantage of the weakness of the Ukrainian, Belorussian, and Russian principalities to extend his control to the east and south (acquisition of Polotsk, Minsk, and the middle Dnieper region). **Vilna** became the capital of the new state.

1341–77. Algirdas, the son of Gediminas, was the ablest of the dynasty. Defeated by the Knights (1360), he too turned eastward. Siding with Tver in the dynastic conflicts of Russia, he advanced several times to the very outskirts of Moscow. During his reign the domain of Lithu-

EASTERN
EUROPE
C. 1430

0 100 200 300 400
MILES

LAPLAND

NORWAY

SWEDEN

DENMARK

Baltic Sea

NORVGOROD

GRAND DUCHY
OF
MOSCOW

Oslo

Stockholm

Reval

Novgorod

Kazan

ROSTOV.

SUZDAL

Nishni-
Novgorod

Pskov

TEUTONIC
ORDER

PSKOV

TVER

Moscow

Riga

Vitebsk

Smolensk

Tula

Ryazan

Hamburg

Danzig

EAST PRUSSIA

Vilna

Minsk

RYAZAN

Volga R.

Bremen

Berlin

Poznań

Warsaw

LITHUANIA

GOLDEN HORDE

*SMALL
STATES*

Breslau

BOHEMIAN
CROWN
LANDS

POLAND

Kiev

Dnieper R.

Sarai

Frankfurt

Prague

Cracow

Lemberg

Stuttgart

Munich

AUSTRIA

Kassa

Astrakhan

Vienna

Pozsony

Debrecen

MOLDAVIA

TYROL

Graz

Buda

STYRIA

HUNGARY

VENICE

Pécs

Brassó

Venice

Belgrade

WALLACHIA

Black Sea

GEORGIA

FLORENCE

BOSNIA

SERBIA

Nish

Nicopolis

PAPAL
STATES

Sofia

Rome

NAPLES

OTTOMAN

Edirne

Constantinople

TREBIZOND

*LOCAL
RULERS*

Naples

Bari

*LOCAL
RULERS*

Salonika

EMPIRE

Angora

AK KOYUNLU

SICILY

BYZANTINE
EMPIRE

Izmir

KARAMAN

DULKADIR

*LOCAL
RULERS*

Mosul

RAMAZAN

Tigris R.

BYZANTINE
EMPIRE

DUCHY OF
ATHENS

MAMLUK
EMPIRE

Euphrates R.

RULERS OF HUNGARY, POLAND, AND LITHUANIA (1205–1492)

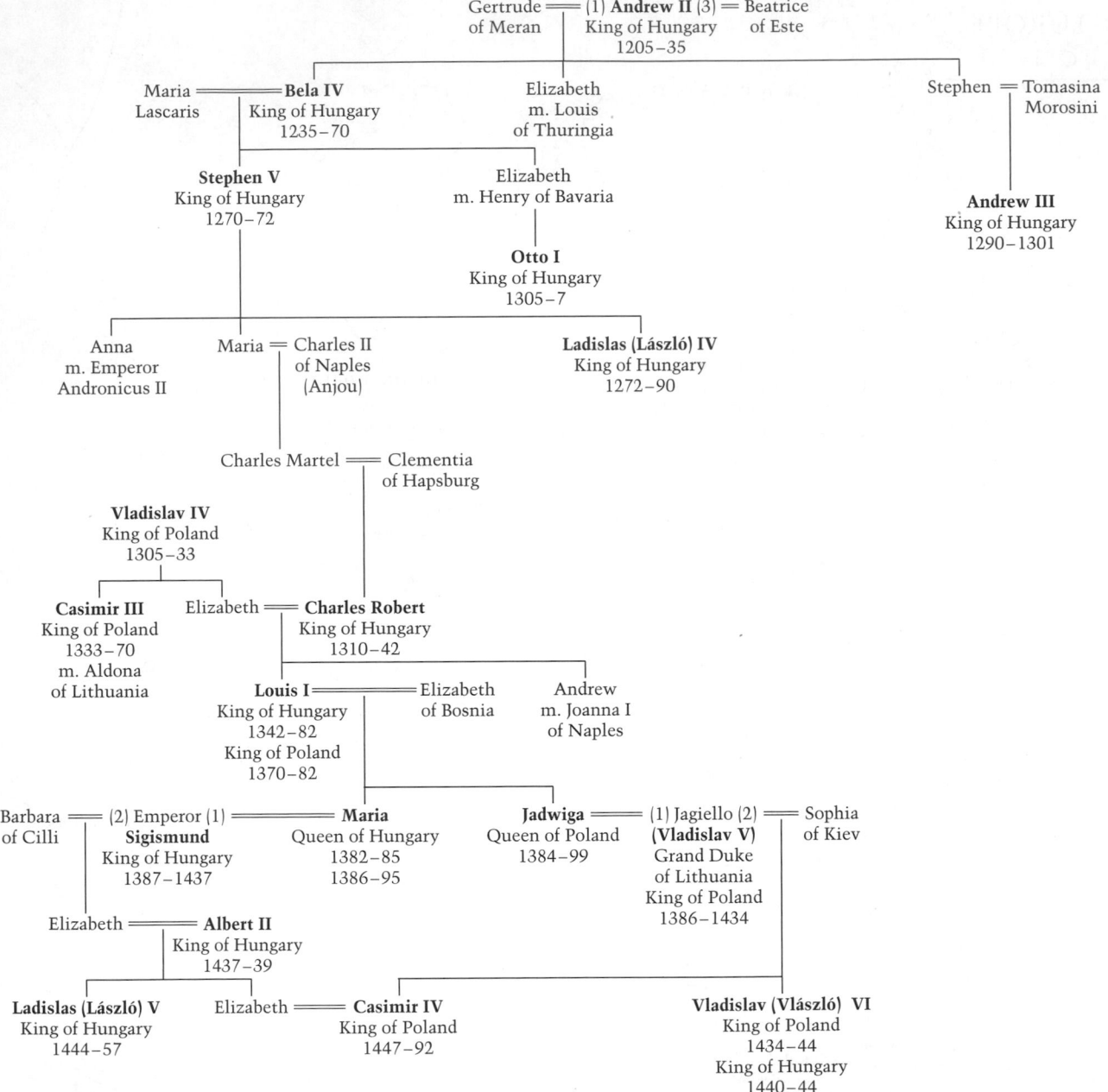

ania was extended as far as the Black Sea, where Algirdas defeated the Tatars (1368).

1350. The **bubonic plague** (Black Death) swept through the Baltic region.

1377–1434. JOGAILA (Jagiello), the son of Algirdas, married Jadwiga of Poland (1386) and established the **first union of Lithuania and Poland** under one king. As a result, Lithuania was converted to Roman Catholicism. However, the Polish and the Lithuanian aristocratic assemblies were preserved as separate bodies, while pagan traditions proved to be much stronger among the Lithuanians than among most of their neighbors. At the same time, Lithuanian society was somewhat less male-dominated: when she married, the woman did not lose all relations with her family, and she enjoyed the protection both of her own family and of her husband's; only the husband could ask for divorce but, on the other hand, one third of his property was to serve as a guarantee of his own fidelity.

1398. Jagiello was obliged to recognize his cousin, **Vytautas** (Witold) as grand duke of Lithuania. Vytautas hoped to reestablish the independence of the country from Poland, but his failure in a crusade against the Tatars greatly weakened him.

1447. Casimir IV of Poland, having been grand duke of Lithuania before his accession, once again united the grand duchy and the Polish kingdom.
(To p. 308)

c. RUSSIA

(From p. 226)

The period following the death of **Alexander Nevski** (1263) was marked by the continued and repeated disruption of the Russian lands, due to the complicated and unfortunate system of succession in the princely family. Russia was under the **suzerainty of the Tatars** (Mongols), who played off one candidate against another, thus increasing the confusion and perpetuating the weakness of the country. The gradual **rise of Moscow** to prominence among the Russian principalities resulted, among other things, from a skillful policy of colonization and of loyalty to the Tatars. The Tatars often responded by supporting the Muscovite rulers against their neighbors, while nobles and peasants from the other Russian principalities were attracted by the abundance of land in a sparsely populated region. The princes of Moscow provided the nobles with land and peasants in exchange for military and administrative services, but the bulk of the peasants remained on state land (land owned directly by the prince). Moreover, the peasants were organized in village communes, and they redistributed their holdings periodically among themselves, while the nobles, unlike their counterparts in western Europe, did not have alodial estates into which to consolidate their tenures. Thus the princes of Moscow were able to restrict ever more successfully the influence of the nobility, despite some violent reactions to that policy.

1328-40. IVAN I KALITA (Moneybag), grand prince of Moscow. His was the first of a series of noteworthy reigns. Extremely cautious and parsimonious, Ivan bought immunity from Tatar interference and was ultimately entrusted by the Tatars with the collection of tribute from the other princes.

1340-53. Simeon I continued the policy of his predecessor and was placed, by the Tatar overlord, above all the other princes.

1350. The second cycle of plague epidemics spread to Russia.

1359-89. DMITRI DONSKOI (of the Don), who ascended to the princely throne at the age of nine. His reign was filled with a struggle against **Michael of Tver,** his chief rival, who was supported by Algirdas of Lithuania. At the same time, he began the conflict with the Tatars, whose power was fading but who also enjoyed the support of Lithuania.

1380, Sept. 8. The Battle of Kulikovo. Dmitri completely defeated the Tatar armies before the Lithuanians arrived. The victory was in no sense decisive, for the Tatars on several occasions thereafter advanced to the very gates of Moscow. But Kulikovo broke the prestige of the Tatar arms.

1389-1425. Basil I (Vasili). He annexed Nizhni-Novgorod and continued the struggle with the Tatars and the Lithuanians, without forcing a decision.

1425-62. Basil II, whose reign was distinguished by a relapse into anarchy. A long civil war with his rivals, Yuri and Shemyaka, was followed by Tatar invasion (1451, the Tatars beaten back from Moscow). Nevertheless the Moscow principality managed to maintain itself. In 1439 Basil refused to accept the union of the eastern and western churches, arranged for at the council of Florence. Thenceforth the Russian metropolitan, who had moved to Moscow in the time of Ivan Kalita, became more and more the head of an independent Russian Church.

1462-1505. IVAN III (the Great). Through a cautious but persistent policy, he annexed most of the rival principalities and, after a series of wars, subjected Novgorod, where the patrician elements tended to side with Lithuania. In 1471 Novgorod was obliged to renounce the alliance of Lithuania and to pay tribute. After a second war, in 1478, **Novgorod's independence was ended** and the troublesome upper classes were deported to central Russia. In 1494 Ivan drove out the German merchants and closed the Hanseatic trading station. Thus he acquired the huge territory of Novgorod, extending eastward to the Urals. The **annexation of Tver** (1485) put an end to the most formidable rival of Moscow.

1472. Marriage of Ivan with Zoë (Sophia), niece of the last Greek emperor of Constantinople. This was arranged by the pope, in the hope of bringing the Russians into the Roman Church, but all efforts in that direction failed. It also served to introduce into Moscow the Byzantine conception of the autocrat (Ivan took the title of tsar—i.e., caesar) and the practice of Byzantine court ceremonial.

1480. Ivan threw off the Tatar yoke after a last Tatar advance on Moscow. Ivan avoided open warfare but took advantage of the Tatars' disunion. Mengli Girai, the khan of the Crimea, joined him against the Lithuanians.

1475-95. Rebuilding of the **Kremlin** (Russian for "citadel"), including

GRAND PRINCES OF MOSCOW (1176-1505)

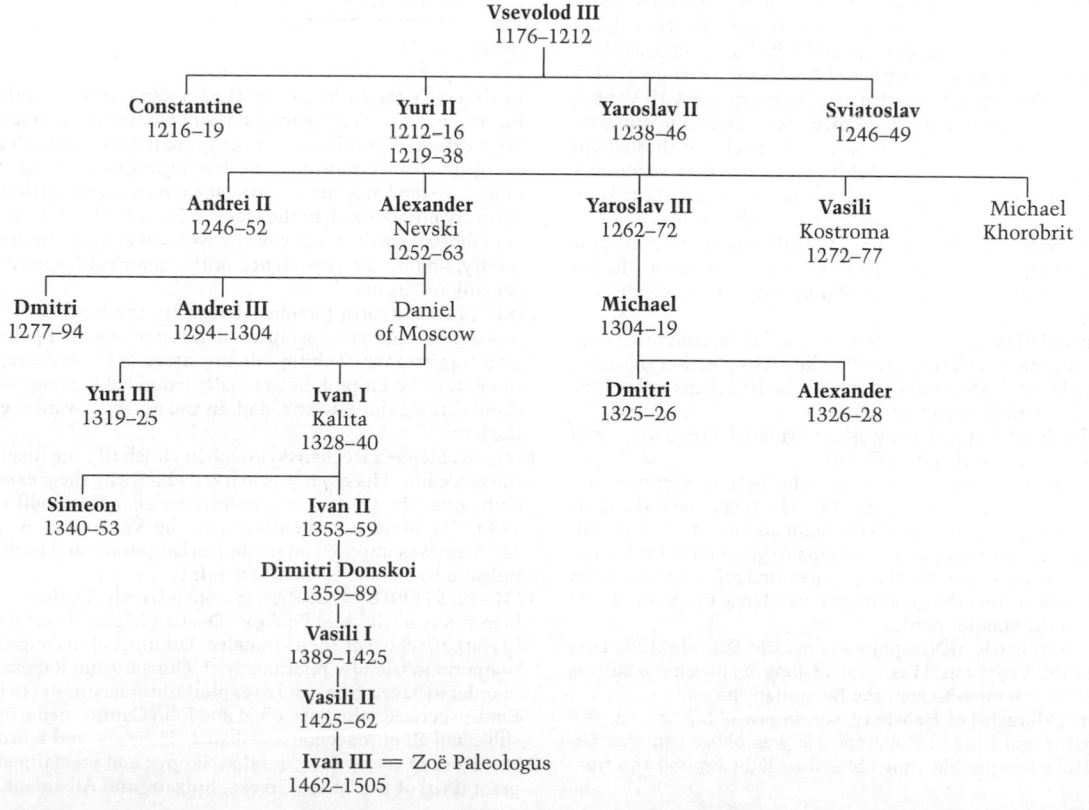

the present wall, 7,200 feet (2,195 meters) long, and the **Uspenski** (Assumption) **Cathedral,** which was the work of the Italian architect **Aristotele Fioravanti.** The Kremlin was to be the residence of Russia's monarchs until the 18th century. The **Granovitaya Palace** (Hall of Facets), also built in the 15th century, served as an audience chamber.

1492. Invasion of Lithuania, made possible by dynastic troubles in Lithuania and Poland. A **second invasion** (1501) led to the conclusion of peace in 1503, which brought Russia many of the border territories of Belarus and Ukraine. Resumption of active diplomatic relations with western countries. The art of icon painting reached its apogee in the 15th century with Master **Andrew Rublyor** (1370–1430). *(To p. 306)*

d. HUNGARY

(From p. 226)

At the beginning of the 14th century, Hungary was already an essentially feudal country, in which the great magnates and the bishops, richly endowed with land, ruled as virtually independent potentates ("little kings"), while the lower nobility, organized in the *Comitats* (provincial governments), had, to a large degree, control of the administration. The nobility, freed of taxation, was responsible for defense, but acted only as it saw fit.

1301–8. The **extinction of the Arpad dynasty** led to a period of conflict, during which Czech, German, and Italian parties each attempted to put their candidates on the throne. **Wenceslas (Vaclav),** son of the king of Bohemia, 13 years old, was first elevated, but could not maintain himself, nor could **Otto of Bavaria.**

1310–42. CHARLES I (Charles Robert of Anjou), a grandson of Maria, the daughter of Stephen V, was elected and founded the brilliant and successful **Anjou line.** Charles established his capital at Visegrad and introduced Italian chivalry and Western influences. After 15 years of effort, he succeeded in subduing the "little kings," of whom **Matthias of Csak** and **Ladislas of Transylvania** were the most powerful. Recognizing the hopelessness of suppressing the nobility entirely, he regulated its position and obliged it to furnish specified contingents to the army. Regulation of taxation (first direct tax); encouragement of towns and trade.

1342–82. LOUIS (Lajos the Great), the son of Charles, a patron of learning who established a brilliant court at Buda. He attempted to solidify the position of his house in Naples and embarked on a successful expedition to Italy to avenge the murder of his brother Andrew (1347). In conjunction with Genoa, he carried on a long struggle with Venice, which ended in the **Peace of 1381:** Venice ceded Dalmatia and paid tribute. In the east the Hungarian power made itself felt throughout the Balkans: Serbia, Wallachia, and Moldova recognized the suzerainty of Louis; foundation of the border districts *(banats)* south of the Danube and the Sava, as protection against the Turkish advance.

1370. Louis became king of Poland but paid little attention to his new obligations. In Hungary he continued the work of his father: the *jus aviticum* (1351) restricted the freedom of the great magnates to dispose of their property.

1382–85. Maria of Anjou, queen. She was married to Sigismund of Luxemburg, who became guardian of the kingdom. His position was challenged by Charles of Durazzo and Naples, who had many adherents, especially in southern Hungary and Croatia.

1385–86. Charles II (of Naples). He was assassinated after a very brief reign, which led to a new revolt in Croatia.

1387–1437. SIGISMUND (of Luxemburg), who became German emperor in 1410 and king of Bohemia in 1436. His reign marked a great decline in the royal power, due to his constant absence from the country and his practice of selling royal domains to get money for his far-reaching schemes elsewhere. In general Sigismund relied on the towns and lesser nobility against the great magnates. Hence the grant of ever greater rights to the smaller nobles.

1396. The disastrous **battle of Nicopolis** against the Turks (p. 125). Loss of Dalmatia to the Venetians. Hussite invasions of Hungary, resulting from Sigismund's attempts to gain the Bohemian throne.

1437–39. Albert (Albrecht) of Habsburg, son-in-law of Sigismund, also German emperor and king of Bohemia. He was obliged to sign far-reaching capitulations (nobles not obliged to fight beyond the frontiers).

1437. First victory of John Hunyadi over the Turks. Hunyadi was a powerful frontier lord and patriot.

1440–44. Vladislav (Vlászló) I (Vladislav VI of Poland), a weak ruler whose reign was distinguished chiefly by the continued victories of Hunyadi (1443). Crusade against the Ottomans (p. 125).

1444, Nov. 10. Disaster at Varna and death of Vladislav.

1444–57. Ladislas (László) V, the son of Albert of Habsburg, also king of Bohemia. He was only four years old at his accession, and Hunyadi was therefore appointed governor of the kingdom until 1552.

1456. Crusade against the Ottomans preached by the Italian Franciscan John of Capistrano and led by Hunyadi. The Turks were turned back from the siege of Belgrade, but Hunyadi died in the same year.

1458–90. MATTHIAS CORVINUS (the Just), the son of John Hunyadi and one of the greatest of the Hungarian kings. He was only 15 at his election, but soon distinguished himself as a soldier, statesman, and patron of art and learning. He reestablished the power of the crown, once again broke the power of the oligarchs, and drew on the support of the lesser nobility. Development of a central administration; regulation and increase of the taxes. The **Bibliotheca Corvina,** consisting of more than 10,000 manuscripts and books, many beautifully illuminated by Italian artists. Matthias the patron of Renaissance learning. Famous law code (1486). University of Buda (c. 1475) refounded 1635. Development of Magyar literature. Creation of a standing army (Black Troop), composed first of Bohemian, Moravian, and Silesian mercenaries. This gave Matthias one of the most effective fighting forces in the Europe of his day. **Matthias's aims:** to secure the Bohemian throne and ultimately the empire and then to direct a united central Europe against the Ottomans. Long struggles against **George Podiebrad** of Bohemia ended with George's death in 1471, after Matthias had been proclaimed king of Bohemia (1470). Equally prolonged struggle against Emperor Frederick III, who had been elected king of Hungary by a faction of nobles in 1439. Matthias, disposing of much greater funds and forces than Frederick, conquered not only Silesia and Moravia, but also lower Austria. His capital established at Vienna (1485). Matthias died at 47, leaving Hungary the dominant state in central Europe and a decisive factor in European diplomacy.

(To p. 309)

e. THE SERBIAN STATES

(From p. 228)

By the end of the 13th century, the Serbian states, like others of eastern Europe, had evolved a strong lay and clerical aristocracy, which, to a large extent, controlled even the more outstanding rulers. In view of the general uncertainty of the law regarding succession and inheritance, the tendency toward dynastic conflict and territorial disruption was very pronounced. In the western Balkans the situation was further complicated by the rivalry of the western and eastern forms of Christianity, and by the persistence of the heretical Bogomil teaching, especially in Bosnia.

1281–1321. Milyutin (Stephen Urosh II), the brother of Dragutin. He was a pious and yet dissolute ruler, but above all a political and religious opportunist. Taking full advantage of the growing weakness of the Byzantine Empire, he gradually extended his possessions in Macedonia, along the Adriatic, and, in the north, toward the Danube and the Save.

1321–31. Stephen Dechanski (Stephen Urosh III), the illegitimate son of the preceding. His reign was marked chiefly by the great victory of the Serbs over the Greeks and Bulgarians near **Küstendil** (Velbŭzhd) in 1330. The Serbs now held most of the Vardar Valley. A nephew of Milyutin was imposed on the Bulgarian throne, and from 1330 to 1331 Bulgaria was under Serbian suzerainty.

1331–55. STEPHEN DUSHAN (Stephen Urosh IV), the ablest of the Serbian rulers in the Middle Ages. Dushan began his career by deposing his father, who was then strangled. For most of his reign he attempted to maintain friendly relations with Hungary and Ragusa (Dubrovnik), in order to have a free hand to exploit the dynastic war in the Byzantine Empire between the Palaeologi and John Cantacuzene. By 1344 he had subjected all of Macedonia, Albania, Thessaly, and Epirus.

1346. Dushan set up his capital at Skopye and proclaimed himself emperor (tsar) of the Serbs, Greeks, Bulgars, and Albanians. At the same time, he set up a Serbian patriarchate at Peć (Ipek), for which he was anathematized by the Greek patriarch. Dushan established a court wholly Byzantine in character. In the years 1349–54 he drew up a law code (Zabonnik).

1353. Dushan defeated Louis of Hungary, who had been urged by the pope to lead a Catholic crusade. The Serbs acquired Belgrade.

1355. Dushan died at the age of 46, en route to Constantinople. Thus perished his hope of succeeding to the imperial throne and consolidating the Balkans in the face of the growing power of the Ottoman Turks (p. 274).

1355–71. Stephen Urosh V, a weak ruler who was faced from the outset by the disruptive ambitions of his uncle Simeon and other powerful magnates. He was the last of the Nemanyid house.

1358. Hungary obtained most of Dalmatia, after defeating Venice. Ragusa (Dubrovnik) became a Hungarian protectorate.

1371. Battle of the Maritza River, in which the Turks, having settled in Thrace, defeated a combination of Serbian lords.

1371. Zeta (Montenegro) became a separate principality under the Balsha family (until 1421).

1375. The Greek patriarch finally recognized the patriarchate of Peć.

1376. TVRTKO I, lord of Bosnia from 1353 to 1391, proclaimed himself king of Serbia and Bosnia, taking over parts of western Serbia and controlling most of the Adriatic coast, excepting Zara and Ragusa. Tvrtko was the greatest of the Bosnian rulers and made his state for a time the strongest Slavic state in the Balkans.

1389 (traditionally June 15). **Battle of Kossovo** (p. 125), a decisive date in all Balkan history. **Prince Lazar** of the Hrebelanovich family, at the head of a coalition of Serbs, Bosnians, Albanians, and Wallachians, attempted to stop the advance of the Ottomans under **Murad I** (p. 123). Murad was killed by a Serb who posed as a traitor, but his son Bayezid won a victory. Lazar was captured and killed, due to the reputed desertion of Vuk Branković. Thenceforth Serbia was a vassal state of the Ottomans.

1389–1427. STEPHEN LAZAREVIĆ, the son of Lazar I. He was a literary person and an able statesman. During the early years of his reign he loyally supported the Turks, being present with his forces at the **battles of Nicopolis** (1396) and **Angora** (1402). In return the Turks recognized him as despot of Serbia, and supported him against Hungary and other enemies.

1391. Death of Tvrtko I of Bosnia; gradual disintegration of the Bosnian Kingdom.

1392. Venice acquired Durazzo, beginning the process of establishment on the Dalmatian and Albanian coasts. Scutari was acquired in 1396, and when, in 1420, Venice secured **Cattaro,** it possessed practically all the fortified coast towns.

1393. Hungary recovered Croatia and Dalmatia from the Bosnian Kingdom. Hungarian campaigns against Bosnia itself continued for years, until the native elements in 1416 called in the Turks.

1427–56. GEORGE BRANKOVIĆ, the nephew of Stephen Lazarević, despot of Serbia. He built himself a new capital at Semendria (Smederevo) on the Danube and attempted, with Hungarian support, to hold his own against the Turks. This policy led to an Ottoman invasion (1439) and conquest of the country; the Hungarians, however, saved Belgrade. But in 1444 Branković, with the aid of **John Hunyadi** (p. 126), recovered his possessions, and the Serbian state was recognized in the **Treaty of Szegedin.** Thereafter Branković deserted Hunyadi and tried to maintain himself through close relations with the Turks.

1456–58. Lazar III, the son of George Branković.

1458–59. On his death Lazar left his kingdom to **Stephen Tomašević,** the heir to the Bosnian throne. Stephen, as a Roman Catholic, was much disliked by the Serbs, who consequently offered less resistance to the Ottoman Turks.

The evidence for issues involving **WOMEN, SEXUALITY, and MARRIAGE** in eastern Europe and Russia before the 17th century derives from ecclesiastical law codes, saints' lives, penitential literature, and other religious records; as such, the sources reflect ecclesiastical theory, not social practice. Information about actual social conduct is extremely scarce.

Eastern Orthodox societies seem to have been more male-dominated than the Roman Catholic world, and the status of women was decidedly inferior to that of men. Women, according to Eve Levin, "did not appear freely in public, did not participate openly in the institutions

of political power, and did not choose their own husbands"; the few women who ruled as queens represent great exceptions.

The Orthodox Church in Slavic countries regulated sexual behavior through private confession and the ecclesiastical courts. All sexual activity was considered sinful, because it caused ritual impurity, although the Greek Church Fathers had agreed that procreation was in conformity to God's will. Bulgarians, Serbs, and Russians accepted the sexual standards of the Byzantine Church, but they treated homosexuality and lesbianism more leniently than adultery, since adultery had a more disruptive effect on the institution of the family. In the Byzantine state, civil authorities punished serious sexual offenses with mutilation, but in the Slavic world religious officials imposed religious penances.

Marriages were private arrangements made by parents; they often involved property transactions and, especially among the upper social strata, political alliances; the Church gave its sanction to these social needs. Some written sources, such as love letters and Bulgarian, Serbian, and Russian love songs, suggest that there was room for romantic love and some freedom of choice, particularly among the common people. Ecclesiastical laws placed so many restrictions on sexual contact that husband and wife could, in theory, have relations on fewer than 50 days in the year. The only practical alternative for women who did not wish to marry was the convent; widows were also encouraged to take religious vows, though second marriages were not prohibited.

1459–99. The Ottoman Turks conquered Serbia (1459), Bosnia (1463), Herzegovina (1483), and Zeta (Montenegro; 1499) and incorporated these territories into the Ottoman Empire.   *(To p. 350)*

f. THE BYZANTINE EMPIRE

(From p. 238)

After the recapture of Constantinople by the Greeks in 1261, the **empire of the Paleologi** was still a relatively small domain, consisting of the former Nicaean Empire, the city of Constantinople and its immediate surroundings, the coastal part of Thrace, Salonika (Thessalonica), and southern Macedonia with the islands of Imbros, Samothrace, Lesbos, and Rhodes. The northeastern part of Anatolia was still held by the Greek **empire of Trebizond,** which, in the course of the 13th century, had managed to hold a balance between the Seljuk Turks and the Mongols and had become the great entrepôt of the eastern trade coming to the Black Sea by way of Persia and Armenia. The city and the court reached their highest prosperity and brilliance under the Emperor **Alexius II** (1297–1330), whose reign was followed by a period of dynastic and factional struggle. The reign of **John Alexius III** (1350–90) marked a second period of splendor, but the 15th century was one of decline. The empire of Trebizond ended with the Ottoman conquest in 1461 (last ruler, **David,** 1458–61).

The European territories of the earlier empire were divided between the Greek despotate of Epirus and the Greek duchy of Neopatras (Thessaly, Locris), the Latin duchy of Athens, the Latin principality of Achaea, and the Venetian duchy of the Archipelago.

1259–82. MICHAEL VIII (Paleologus). He was the ablest of the Paleologi, a man who devoted himself to the restoration of Byzantine authority throughout the Balkan area, persisting despite many setbacks.

1261. Michael established a foothold in the southeastern part of the Peloponnese (Morea). **Mistra** (Misithra) became the capital of a flourishing principality and one of the great centers of late-Byzantine culture.

1262. Michael II of Epirus was forced to recognize the suzerainty of the Constantinople emperor. In a series of campaigns, much of the despotate was regained for the empire (Janina taken, 1265).

1264–65. Constant raids of the Bulgars into Thrace led to a formidable campaign against them and the reconquest of part of Macedonia.

1266. Charles of Anjou became king of Sicily. He made an alliance with Baldwin II, the last Latin emperor, and, through the marriage of his son with the heiress of the Villehardouins, extended his authority over Achaea. He soon became the most formidable opponent of the Greeks, for by the **Treaty of Viterbo** (1267), he took over the claims of Baldwin II.

1271. Death of Michael II of Epirus. Charles of Anjou had already taken Corfu (1267) and now undertook the conquest of the Epiran coast, the essential base for any advance on Thessalonica and Constantinople.

Durazzo was taken in 1272. **John Angelus,** driven out of Epirus, set up as lord of Neopatras (to 1295). **Nicephorus I** was the titular ruler of a much-reduced Epiran state (to 1296). Charles of Anjou proclaimed himself king of Albania and entered into alliance with the Serbs, who had begun the construction of a large state by advancing down the Vardar Valley.

1274. The Council of Lyons. Michael, to escape from the Angevin danger, accepted the Roman creed and the primacy of the pope, thus effecting the **reunion with Rome.** This purely political move met with vigorous resistance on the part of the Orthodox Greeks.

1274. Campaigns of Michael against the Angevins in Epirus had varying success.

1278. The death of William of Villehardouin, prince of Achaea, gave the Greeks an opportunity to expand their holding in the southeastern part.

1281. Michael VIII won a great victory over the Angevins at **Berat.** Thereupon Charles made an alliance with the papacy and with Venice, with which the Serbs and Bulgars were associated. Michael, in reply, effected a rapprochement with Peter of Aragon.

1282. The Sicilian Vespers (p. 253) served to relieve the pressure on the Greek Empire.

1282–1328. ANDRONICUS II, the son of Michael, a learned, pious, but weak ruler whose first move was to give up the hated union with Rome and conciliate the Orthodox clergy.

1285. Venice deserted the Angevin alliance and made a ten-year peace with the Greeks.

1295–1320. MICHAEL IX, son of Andronicus, co-emperor with his father.

1296. The Serbs, continuing their advance, conquered western Macedonia and northern Albania. Andronicus was obliged to recognize these losses (1298).

1302. Peace between the Angevins and the Aragonese. Andronicus, once again exposed to Angevin ambition, engaged **Roger de Flor,** commander of a body of mercenaries called the Catalan Grand Company, to fight against the Italians. They raised havoc at Constantinople, where 3,000 Italians are said to have been killed in the disorders.

1302, July 27. At **Bapheus** in Bithynia (northwest Asia Minor) the Ottoman Turks inflicted a severe defeat on the Greeks under George Mouzalon; fatal weakening of the Byzantine position, with Bithynia soon overrun by the Ottomans.

1304. The Catalans repulsed an attack of the Turks on Philadelphia, but then turned and attacked Constantinople (1305–7), without being able to take it.

1305. Murder of Roger de Flor. The Catalan Company became a veritable scourge, roaming through Thrace and Macedonia and laying waste to the country.

1311. The Catalans, having advanced into Greece, took the duchy of Athens, where they set up a dynasty of their own.

1321–28. Civil war between the emperor and his grandson Andronicus. In the course of the struggle much of the empire was devastated.

1325. Andronicus was obliged to accept his grandson as co-emperor.

1328–41. ANDRONICUS III, the grandson of Andronicus II, who forced the emperor's abdication (d. 1332). Andronicus III was a frivolous and irresponsible ruler, unequal to the great problems presented by the rise of the Ottoman and Serb powers.

1329. The Greeks managed to take the important island of Chios from the Genoese.

1330. The Serbs defeated the Bulgars in a decisive battle and put an end to the Bulgar power.

1334–35. Andronicus conquered Thessaly and part of Epirus from the despot John II Orsini.

1336. The Greeks reconquered Lesbos.

1340. Stefan Uroš IV Dušan, Serbian ruler, having conquered the Albanian coastal territory (as far as Valona) from the Angevins, drove the Greeks out of the interior and took Janina. His conquest intensified the political and cultural hellenization of Serbia.

1341–76. JOHN V, the son of Andronicus III, ascended the throne as a child, under the regency of his mother, Anna of Savoy.

1341–47. Civil war in the empire. John Cantacuzene, supported by the aristocratic elements, set himself up as a rival emperor. John V was supported by the popular elements. In the ensuing war, much of

Thrace and Macedonia was ravaged. The war was the undoing of the empire, since both sides freely called in Serbs or Ottoman Turks to support them.

1341–51. The **HESYCHAST CONTROVERSY** in the Greek Church added to the confusion. Hesychasm (literally, to be quiet) is a term used for the method of monastic prayer and contemplation designed to achieve union with God through interior quietude. Although hesychasm is commonly and misleadingly used to describe various currents of 14th-century spirituality, it became a social and political phenomenon when it was drawn into the civil wars of the period. The hesychasts supported and were victorious with Cantacuzene against John V, supported by the secular clergy. The dispute led to a great popular **rising in Thessalonica** where extremists tried to set up an independent state (1342–47).

1343. The Venetians, taking advantage of the civil war, seized Smyrna.

1346. Stefan Dušan was crowned emperor of the Serbs and the Greeks, and made preparations to seize Constantinople and replace the Greek dynasty.

1347. Cantacuzene managed to take Constantinople, through treachery.

1347–54. JOHN VI (Cantacuzene), sole emperor. He made his son Manuel despot of the Morea (1348). The Serbs held all of Macedonia.

1351. Stefan Dušan besieged Thessalonica.

1353. The **Ottoman Turks,** called in by Cantacuzene, defeated the Serbs.

1354. The Ottoman Turks established themselves at Gallipoli, thus continuing their career of expansion (p. 123).

1354. John V took Constantinople and forced the abdication of Cantacuzene (d. 1383). At the same time Dušan, having taken Adrianople, advanced on the capital. His sudden death (1355) led to the disintegration of the Serbian Empire and to the removal of a great threat to the Greeks. On the other hand, it left the Christians an easier prey to the advancing Ottomans.

1365. The Ottomans, having overrun Thrace, took Adrianople, which became their capital.

1366. John V, who had been captured by Tsar Shishman of Bulgaria, was liberated by his cousin, Amadeus of Savoy.

1369. John V appeared before the pope at Avignon and agreed to union of the churches, in order to secure the aid of the west against the Turks.

1376–79. ANDRONICUS IV, the son of John V, dethroned his father with the aid of the Genoese.

1379–91. John V, supported by the Ottomans, recovered his throne.

1386. The Venetians recovered Corfu, which they held until 1797.

1388. The Venetians purchased Argos and Nauplia.

1389. Battle of Kosovo Polje (Kossovo), in a valley in southern Serbia between Pristina and the Laba River, waged between Serbian and Ottoman forces (p. 273). The Byzantine, Ottoman, and Serbian historical sources sharply conflict, though modern scholars believe that the battle was a draw. In any case, Serbia became an Ottoman vassal state and the Balkan Peninsula was opened to further Ottoman expansion.

1390. John VII, a grandson of John V, deposed the latter, but after a few months the old emperor was restored by his second son, Manuel.

1391–1425. MANUEL II, an able ruler in a hopeless position. By this time the empire had been reduced to the city of Constantinople, the city of Thessalonica, and the province of Morea. The Ottomans held Thrace and Macedonia.

1391–95. The Ottomans, under Bayezid I, blockaded Constantinople, and only the Christian crusade that ended in the disastrous **battle of Nicopolis** (1396) gave the Greeks some respite (p. 125).

1397. Bayezid attacked Constantinople, which was valiantly defended by Marshal Boucicaut. This time the advance of the Tatars under Timur-I Lang distracted the Turks. The defeat and capture of Bayezid in the **battle of Ankara** (p. 125) (1402) led to a period of confusion and dynastic war among the Ottomans.

1422. The Ottomans again attacked Constantinople, because of Manuel's support of the Turkish pretender Mustapha, against Murad II.

1423. The Venetians bought the city of Salonika.

1425–48. JOHN VIII, the son of Manuel, whose position was, from the outset, desperate.

1428. Constantine and Thomas Paleologus, brothers of the emperor, conquered Frankish Morea, with the exception of the Venetian ports.

1430. The Ottomans took Salonika from the Venetians.

1439. The Council of Florence. John VIII, having traveled to Italy, once

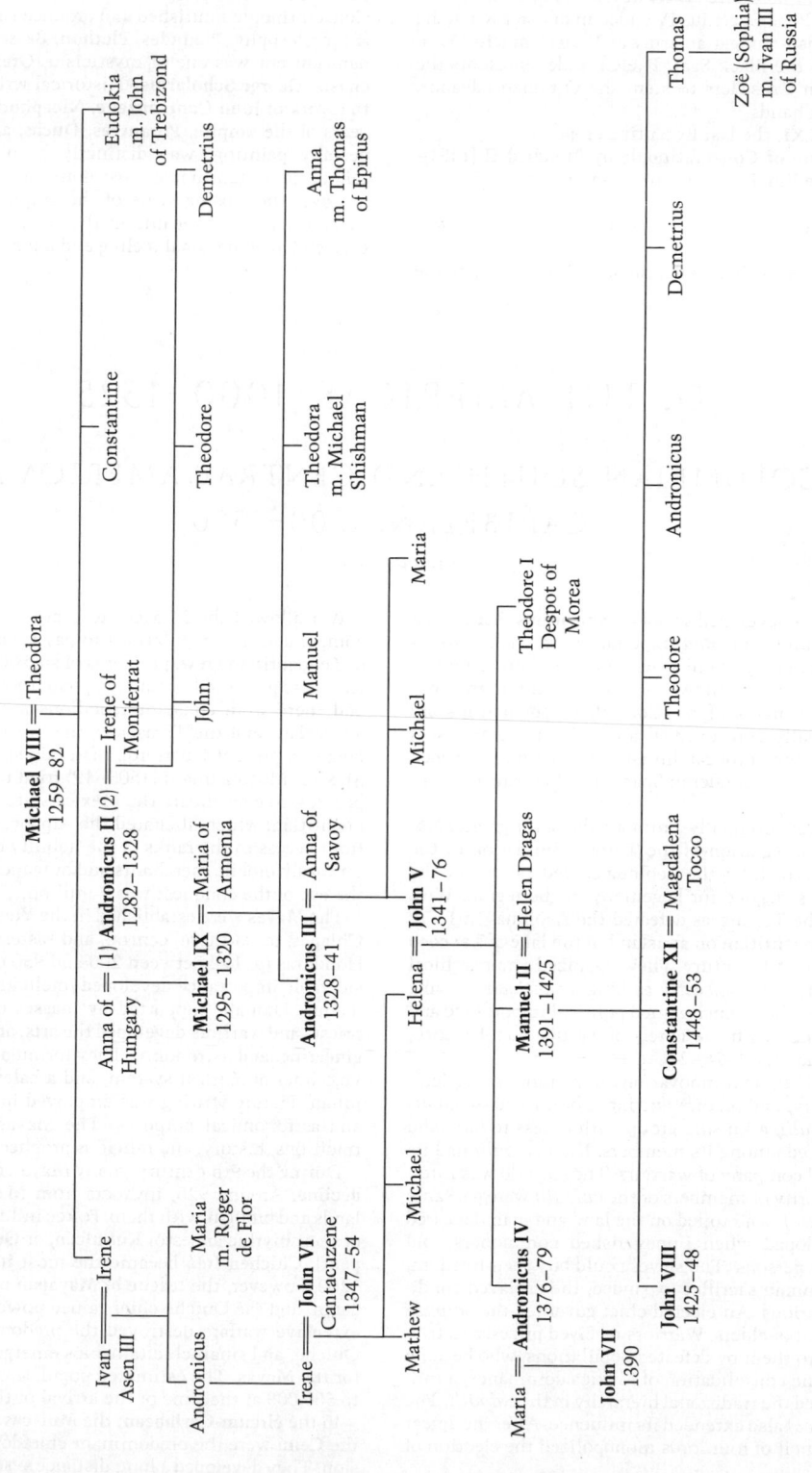

THE PALEOLOGUS FAMILY (1260–1453)

again accepted the union with Rome and the papal primacy. As on earlier occasions, this step raised a storm of opposition among the Greeks and to some extent facilitated the Turkish conquests.

A crusade preached by Pope Eugenius IV ended in disaster when the Ottomans defeated a Polish-Hungarian army at **Varna** (ancient Odessos, on the west coast of the Black Sea). The Crusade represents the final attempt by Western Crusaders to stem the Ottoman advance. Corinth fell into Turkish hands.

1448–53. CONSTANTINE XI, the last Byzantine emperor.

1453. The siege and capture of Constantinople by **Mehmed II (1451–81). End of the Byzantine Empire** after a thousand years of existence (p. 253).

1460. Conquest of the Morea by the Turks. End of the rule of the Paleologi in Greece.

1461. Conquest of the empire of Trebizond, the last Greek state, by the Turks.

Byzantine culture in the time of the Paleologi. The territorial and political decline of the empire was accompanied by an extraordinary cultural revival, analogous to the Renaissance in Italy. The schools of Constantinople flourished and produced a group of outstanding scholars (philosophy: **Planudes, Plethon, Bessarion**). In theology the dominant current was one of mysticism (**Gregory Palamas** and the hesychasts; **George Scholarius**). Historical writing reached a high plane in the work of **John Cantacuzene, Nicephorus Gregoras,** and, in the last years of the empire, **Phrantzes, Ducas, and Chalcocondylas.** Art, especially painting, was distinctly humanized, and three different schools (Constantinople, Macedonia, and Crete) cast a flood of splendor over the closing years of the empire. **Mistra,** the capital of the Morean province, became in the early 15th century the center of a revived Greek national feeling and a home of scholars and artists.

G. THE AMERICAS, 1000–1525

1. PRE-COLUMBIAN SOUTH AND CENTRAL AMERICA AND THE CARIBBEAN, 1200–1530

(From p. 20)

The aborigines of America developed social organizations that ranged from stateless tribes to kingdoms and imperial states. Many groups remained simple hunters and gatherers, while others built complex agricultural systems. Iron was unknown, as was the utilitarian application of the wheel. Estimates of pre-Columbian populations are highly debatable. Especially controversial are estimates that assess population at the time of the European invasion, since they have been used politically to justify or to condemn Spanish and Portuguese conquest.

The **Mexica (Aztecs)** were originally a minor tribe of the greater Nahua group. After the disintegration of the Toltec domination of the valley of Mexico (about 1200 C.E.), the Acolhua confederation and the Tepaneca confederation struggled for hegemony in the region. With help from the Mexica, the Tepanecas defeated the Acolhuas in 1370. The Mexica founded **Tenochtitlán** on an island in the lake of **Texcoco** during the first half of the 14th century. They organized a monarchical system, with a prince of Toltec ancestry as king, or *tlatoani*. Owing to their military prowess, the Mexica gained political importance and formed the **Triple Alliance** with the chiefs of Tacuba and Texcoco, which defeated the Tepanecas (1426–28).

The Mexica promoted regional innovations in astronomy, agriculture, architecture, jewelry, and picture writing. Their basic **social organization** was the *calpulli*, a kinship group with access to land and resources to be distributed among its members. Each *calpulli* had its own school, temple, and company of warriors. The *calpulli* was internally stratified: the majority of members of the *calpulli* were peasants and workers *(macehualtin)*, who toiled on the land and manufactured products. Slavery developed when impoverished commoners sold themselves to wealthier persons. The slaves could buy their freedom, but as the practice of human sacrifice expanded, the enslaved condition became more precarious. An elected chief governed the *calpulli* with the help of a council of elders. Warriors received prizes, and tributes were paid directly to them by defeated populations, who became serfs *(mayeque)*. With the consolidation of Mexica dominance, a military aristocracy displaced the traditional hierarchy in the *calpulli*. The merchant class *(popochca)* also extended its influence. After the defeat of the Tepanecas, a council of four lords monopolized the election of the king.

Mexica religion was **polytheistic.** With the increasing role of war and warriors in society, the state promoted the cult of **Huitzilopochtli, a war god.** His worship led to the practice of human sacrifice and ritual cannibalism on an unprecedented scale for the area.

War allowed the Mexicas to capture victims for sacrifices, and to compel defeated populations to pay them tribute. As the population of Tenochtitlán grew, problems of supply and famine developed. Mexica rulers pressured conquered populations to provide more resources, and there were constant rebellions against Mexica exactions. The Tlaxcalans and the Tarascans, the inhabitants of Oaxaca and Yopitzingo (in present Guerrero), maintained their independence from the Mexica. Moctezuma II (1503–19) tried to conquer these independent peoples, to consolidate the Mexica state. He centralized power in Tenochtitlán, which alienated the support of Texcoco. His attempts to limit access to the ranks of the nobility caused dissatisfaction among upwardly mobile merchants and bureaucrats. Estimated population at the eve of the conquest was 9 million.

The **Mayas** were established in the Yucatán Peninsula, Tabasco, and Chiapas; in northern, central, and eastern Guatemala; and in western Honduras (p. 19). Between 200 and 950 C.E., **religious centers** of considerable importance developed (including Tikal, Copán, Nakum, Palenque, Uxmal). Supported by masses of agriculturalists, a class of priests and warriors developed the **arts, architecture, mathematics, engineering, and astronomy.** They formulated the conception of zero, a vigesimal numerical system, and a calendar more accurate than the Julian. Picture writing was employed in codices formed for religious and astronomical purposes. The Mayas preserved orally a body of traditions, history, and religious prophecies.

During the 9th century, many Mayan centers went into **irreversible decline.** Around 925, invaders from Mexico took control of Mayan lands and brought with them Toltec influence. They promoted the cult of their mythic ancestor **Kukulcán,** or **Quetzalcoatl** (the feathered serpent). **Chichén Itzá** became the most important center of power. In 1200, however, the **league of Mayapán** became hegemonic in the Yucatán, and the Quiché chief gained power in Guatemala. About 1450, extensive warfare destroyed the predominance of Mayapán and the Quiché, and small chieftainships emerged as the main political units for the Mayas. The estimated population in the Yucatán was 400,000 to 500,000 at the time of the arrival of the Spaniards.

In the **circum-Caribbean,** the **Muiscas (Chibchas),** the **Taironas,** and the **Cenú** were the predominant chiefdoms before the European invasion. They developed a long-distance system for the exchange of sumptuary goods of religious character, such as emeralds, gold jewelry, fine textiles, and fine seashells, as well as war slaves. The populations were mostly of agriculturalists organized into kinship groups, who paid tribute and worked their lords' lands. Estimated population of this area was 3 million. In the **Caribbean islands,** the indigenous population was about 750,000, with most of the people living on the island known as Española (Santo Domingo). There were three ethnic groups in the islands: the **Ciboney** or Guanahuatebey, the **Taino Arawak,** and the **Carib.** The Ciboney were the oldest settlers, having migrated in several waves from the mainland (1000 B.C.E.–1000 C.E.). They were hunters and gatherers, organized in independent nomadic clans. The Arawak migration (1100–1450) displaced and absorbed the Ciboney. The Arawak formed chiefdoms based on agriculture. The Caribs formed a highly mobile society, being the last migrant group to enter the Caribbean. By 1500 they dominated all of the eastern Caribbean islands. They settled in places that facilitated both agriculture and fishing. Land was communally held by the extended family. The head of the family supervised productive activities, settled internal disputes, and served in military groups of the most experienced warriors in raids against surrounding populations, to seize women for the local young men. Warfare was a central activity of Carib males, and ritual cannibalism was practiced. Caribs believed in the existence of spirits, and shamans were in charge of religious activities.

The **Incas,** with their capital in Cusco, extended their control over the area from Ecuador to central Chile along the coast and inland to the eastern slopes of the Andes, including the Bolivian Plateau (p. 20). Expansion was particularly rapid from the 14th century onward. Inca myths claimed that, previously, Andean peoples had lived in a primitive state, but that the Inca institutions were based on those developed earlier in the area.

In the Andes, the fundamental **social unit** was the *ayllu,* a kinship group with a common ancestor. Women were organized matrilineally and men patrilineally, with marriage being endogamous. The chief of the *ayllu* was called the *kuraka.* The *ayllu* had access to land, and the *ayllu* families cultivated assigned plots and had reciprocal duties in community activities. Leadership in war was provided by elected chiefs, called *sinchis.*

Frequent skirmishes among tribes in the Cusco area helped to consolidate warrior leadership among the Incas, eventually producing a **monarchial system.** Oral tradition preserved a list of 13 kings (Incas), but imperial expansion only began with **Pachacútec,** the ninth Inca king (1438–71). In 1438, the **Chancas** put Cusco under siege, but the Incas under Pachacútec defeated them completely. After Pachacútec, Túpac Inca (1471–93) and Huayna Cápac (1493–1525) continued rapid **military expansion.** Plebeians who distinguished themselves as warriors could obtain positions in the administration and a secondary nobility.

The Incas subjected different ethnic groups, recognizing their original chiefs (*kurakas*) and making them responsible for the fulfillment of labor corvées on Inca lands. The royal *ayllus,* called *panacas,* inherited all the properties of the dead sovereign, to preserve the cult of his mummy. To secure manpower to cultivate lands of the nobility as well as the Inca and state lands, a class of perpetual **serfs** (*yanas*) was formed. The Incas displaced original populations to establish loyal settlers (*mitmaqkuna*) who would deter rebellions and expand cultivation of maize for the state. Rebellions against state exactions were constant. **Huayna Cápac** subdued uprisings in Ecuador, and Túpac Inca Yupanqui suppressed them on the Titicaca Plateau. Inca expansion confronted insurmountable obstacles in the eastern tropical lowlands and in the southern area dominated by the Araucanians (Mapuche).

Inca religion included a heaven god, the cult of the ancestors (especially the deceased Inca kings), and *huacas* (objects and places considered sacred). The Inca state emphasized the solar aspect of the heaven god, as the Incas claimed to be children of the sun (**Inti**).

After the death of Huayna Cápac, his sons **Atahuallpa** and **Huáscar** warred over the kingdom. Atahuallpa, son of a secondary wife, gained the nobility's support, and a civil war began (1529–30). In 1532 the war ended with the defeat of Huáscar, but by that time the Spaniards had already destroyed the Inca domination of Peru. Population at this time was estimated at 9 million.

The area of the Río de la Plata was occupied by several tribes who combined hunting and gathering with agriculture. In the lower Paraná resided the **Charrúas** and the **Caingang.** The more numerous of the **Guaycuru** inhabited the Chaco, and were divided into the **Abipón, Mocovi, Toba, Mbayá,** and **Caduveo** tribes. The **Guaraní** expanded in the Paraná basin and practiced slash-and-burn agriculture. In Patagonia and Tierra del Fuego, the **Ona** and the **Tehuelche** lived as hunters of guanacos and rhea. In the area of the Beagle Channel and on the islands, **Alacaluf, Yahgan,** and **Chono** tribes were migrant fishermen. In the south of Chile, the **Mapuche, Araucanian,** and **Huilliche** groups subsisted on llama husbandry and agriculture that combined rotating-field and slash-and-burn methods.

Brazil was inhabited by groups from four linguistic families: **Tupi-Guaraní, Gê, Carib,** and **Arawak.** The Tupi-Guaraní were established along the Atlantic coast, from the mouth of the Amazon River to south of present São Paulo. They were divided into many tribes and frequently engaged in war. Tupi, Arawak, and Carib tribes populated the Amazon basin. The Gê tribes lived in central Brazil. All of Brazil's native populations were organized in seminomadic communities. Hunting and gathering were important activities, complementing slash-and-burn agriculture. The estimated population in the Amazon basin was 5 million; for the rest of Brazil, 6.8 million.

2. PRE-COLUMBIAN EXPLORATIONS BY EUROPEANS, 1000–1189

1000. Leif Ericson, returning from Norway to Greenland, was driven onto the North American coast. Settlements near L'Anse aux Meadows, at the northern tip of Newfoundland, show evidence of Norse presence and might be the Wineland (Vinland) mentioned by Ericson.

1003. Thorfinn Karlsefni set out from Greenland with three ships, to settle Wineland. He and his party spent three winters on the North American continent. The localities he visited have not been determined.

The last mentioned visit to Wineland was in 1189, although it is possible Norsemen came at least as far as southern Labrador for ship timber as late as 1347. After that date, the Greenland colonies declined, though the West Colony (in southeast Greenland) continued to exist until at least the mid-15th century.

It is possible, though there is no evidence, that Breton, Gascon, or Basque fishermen regularly visited Labrador in this period. Many theories have been advanced to demonstrate a European presence before Columbus, but most rest on hypotheses and clever deductions. After the translation of Ptolemy's *Geography* into Latin (1410), the idea that the earth was spherical (never entirely lost during the Middle Ages) spread rapidly in scientific circles and revived the goal of reaching Asia by sailing west.

3. THE VOYAGES OF COLUMBUS, 1492–1504

1451, between Aug. 26 and Oct. 31. CRISTOFORO COLOMBO (Christopher Columbus; in Spanish, Cristóbal Colón) was born near Genoa, the son of a weaver. Almost nothing definite is known of his youth. He seems to have gone to Portugal in 1476 and to have been in England in 1477. In 1480 he married the daughter of Bartholomew Perestrello, hereditary captain of Porto Santo, near Madeira. He was familiar with the idea then popular of seeking to reach India or China by navigating westward.

1483 or 1484. Columbus appealed to King John II of Portugal to finance a voyage to the West, but experts at the court rejected his project as unfeasible.

1486. Columbus, through the mediation of some Franciscan monks, was able to submit his project to the king and queen of Spain, **Ferdinand of Aragon and Isabella of Castile.** His religious fervor and personal magnetism impressed the queen, but experts rejected his project again.

In the following years, Columbus met the three Pinzón brothers, wealthy traders and expert navigators.

1492. Columbus, again in the court, induced Queen Isabella to finance his expedition. His objective was to find a route to the Indies, rather than to discover a new world. The queen named him admiral and governor of the territories to be discovered, and gave him letters to the Great Khan.

1492–93. The first voyage (Aug. 3–March 15). Columbus left Palos, Spain, with three caravels, *La Pinta, La Niña,* and the *Santa María.* Martín Pinzón and Juan de la Cosa commanded two of them. They left the Canaries (Sept. 6) and reached land in the Bahamas (Oct. 12), naming it **San Salvador.** Columbus then discovered Cuba, which he thought was the territory of the Great Khan, and Santo Domingo (Española). He established a post, Navidad, on Santo Domingo, and set out on the return voyage (Jan. 4, 1493), touching the Azores (Feb. 15), landing at Lisbon (March 4), and finally reaching Palos (March 15). Columbus announced that he had discovered the route to the Indies, news of which quickly spread throughout Europe and caused much excitement.

1493, May 4. The line of demarcation. At the insistence of the Spanish rulers, who feared counterclaims by Portugal, Pope Alexander VI granted them the exclusive right to and possession of all lands to the south and west toward India not held by Christian princes on Christmas Day 1492, beyond a line drawn 100 leagues west of the Azores and the Cape Verde Islands.

1493–95. Second voyage of Columbus (Sept. 25, 1493 to June 11, 1495). He left with 17 caravels and 1,500 men to establish Spanish settlements. On this voyage he discovered Dominica, Puerto Rico, Jamaica, and other islands of the Antilles; explored the southern coast of Cuba; and circumnavigated Española, where he founded the town of Isabella. There he left in charge his brother Bartholomeo, who in 1496 transferred the settlement to the southern coast (Santo Domingo).

1494, June 7. Treaty of Tordesillas, between Spain and Portugal. The line of demarcation was moved 270 leagues farther west, Portugal to have exclusive rights to all lands to the east of the line, and Spain to have rights to the west.

1498–1500. Third voyage of Columbus (May 30, 1498, to Nov. 15, 1500). Discovery of Trinidad Island (July 31, 1498) and South America (Aug. 1), near the mouth of the Orinoco. Columbus explored the coast westward as far as Margarita Island. He then went to Española, where a revolt broke out against him. The Spanish government sent a judge, **Francisco de Bobadilla,** who imprisoned Columbus and his brother and sent them to Spain. Columbus was released and treated with distinction, but the queen never restored him to his former authority and monopolistic grants. Bobadilla established direct royal control in the territories.

1502–1504. Fourth voyage of Columbus (May 11, 1502, to Nov. 7, 1504). He reached the coast of Honduras and passed south to Panama, returning after having suffered a shipwreck in Jamaica.

1506, May 21. Columbus died in relative obscurity in Spain, at Valladolid. He believed to the end of his days that he had discovered outlying parts of Asia, despite the conviction of other experts since 1493 that a new world had been discovered.

4. POST-COLUMBIAN DISCOVERIES, 1497–1522

1497, May 2–Aug. 6. Voyage of John Cabot. Cabot was a wealthy Italian merchant who settled in England about 1495. He organized an expedition that reached land (June 24) on northern Newfoundland. Cabot was convinced he had discovered the country of the Great Khan. He intended a second voyage but failed.

1499–1500. Voyage of Alonso de Ojeda and Amerigo Vespucci in the service of Spain (May 1499–June 1500). They landed in what would be French Guiana, discovered the mouth of the Amazon, and proceeded as far as Cape St. Roque, after which they turned north and west along the coast as far as the Magdalena River.

  Voyage of Vicente Yáñez Pinzón (Sept. 1499–Dec. 1500). He made a landfall near Cape St. Roque (Jan. 1500) and thence followed the coast northwest. At about the same time, the Spaniard **Diego de Lepe** explored the Brazilian coast from Cape St. Roque to about 10 degrees S.L.

1500, Apr. 21. The Portuguese commander **PEDRO CABRAL,** sailing to India from the Cape Verde Islands with 13 caravels, landed in **BRAZIL.** The expedition stayed only ten days, but took official possession of the country, which Cabral named **Terra da Vera Cruz.**

1500–2. Rodrigo de Bastidas traced the coast from Panama to Port Manzanilla.

1501–2. Second voyage of Amerigo Vespucci (May 1501–Sept. 1502), this time in the service of Portugal. He voyaged south along the Brazilian coast to about 32 degrees S.L. Vespucci published an account of this voyage in which he expressed the conviction that what had been found was a "New World." On this basis, the German geographer, **Martin Waldseemüller,** proposed that this New World be called **AMERICA** (1507). The name was first applied to South America, and the use of it spread slowly until its general adoption.

1508. Vicente Pinzón followed the mainland from the Bay of Honduras to beyond the easternmost point of Brazil.

1512. Juan Ponce de León, the governor of Puerto Rico, discovered Florida.

1513, Sept. 25. Vasco Núñez de Balboa crossed the Isthmus of Panama and discovered the **Pacific Ocean.**

1515–16. Juan Díaz de Solís, chief pilot of Spain, searching for a strait to the Pacific, explored the coast of South America from the area of Rio de Janeiro to Río de la Plata, where he was slain by the indigenous inhabitants.

1517. Francisco Hernández de Córdoba discovered the Yucatán Peninsula.

1518. Juan de Grijalva followed the coast north from the Yucatán to the Panuco River.

1519. Álvarez Pineda completed exploration of the Gulf of Mexico by following the coast from Florida to Vera Cruz and back. **Francisco de Gordillo** advanced up the Atlantic coast to South Carolina (1521), and **Pedro de Quexos** traveled as far as 40 degrees N.L. (1525).

1519–22. Circumnavigation of the globe by Ferdinand Magellan (Fernão de Magalhães, c. 1480–1521). The crown of Spain sent Magellan to find a strait to the Moluccas. He sailed on Sept. 20, 1519, reached the Brazilian coast near Pernambuco, explored the estuary of the Río de la Plata, passed through the strait that bears his name, and entered the Pacific Ocean. After following the coast to about 40 degrees S.L. he turned northwest and then west, and eventually, after sighting only two tiny atolls, reached Guam (March 6) and the Philippines (March 15, 1521). At Mactan, near Cebu, Filipinos killed him (April 27). His ship *Victoria,* under **Juan Sebastián del Cano,** continued westward and reached Spain (Sept. 6, 1522), thus completing the first circumnavigation of the globe.

1524–25. Esteban Gómez, sailing from Spain, followed the North American coast from Nova Scotia in the north to Florida in the south.

(To pp. 396, 399)

IV. THE EARLY MODERN PERIOD, 1500–1800

A. GLOBAL AND COMPARATIVE DIMENSIONS

(From p. 106)

During the early modern period, the context of human affairs was changing dramatically. Within the globalization of life, three major changes were of special significance. 1. **The development of new-style empires and large state systems that came to dominate global political and military affairs.** 2. The internal transformation of the major societies, but especially the transformation of society in western Europe.

3. **The emergence of networks of interaction that were global in their scope.** These developments reoriented the global balance of societal power. In 1500 there were four predominant traditions of civilization in the Eastern Hemisphere in a position of relative parity, but by 1800, one of these societies, the West, was in a position to assume political and military control over the whole world.

1. NEW-STYLE EMPIRES AND STATES, 1500–1700

a. GUNPOWDER EMPIRES

These empires established strong centralized control through employing the military potential of gunpowder (naval and land-based siege cannon were particularly important). The major states of the Western Hemisphere were destroyed by European gunpowder empires while throughout the Eastern Hemisphere, regional empires developed on the basis of military power and new centralized administrations.

1453–1699. OTTOMAN EMPIRE. The Ottoman conquest of Constantinople in 1453 brought an end to the Byzantine Empire. The Ottomans emerged as one of the strongest empires in the world, employing artillery to support their cavalry and then creating the **Janissary Corps,** an infantry using firearms. The new and expensive military was supported by the development of an effective bureaucracy. This centralized gunpowder empire rapidly expanded, conquering most of the Arab Middle East and the Balkan Peninsula. Ottoman forces laid siege to Vienna in 1529 and 1683 but did not capture this central European capital. However, in both eastern Europe and the Middle East the Ottomans remained essentially dominant until the war ending with the **Treaty of Karlowitz** (1699) (p. 339).

1492–1700. THE IBERIAN EMPIRES. Large maritime empires were created by the emerging monarchies on the Iberian Peninsula. European ship design enabled ships to carry cannons, giving them a military advantage over other ships in the 15th and 16th centuries. The **PORTUGUESE EMPIRE** expanded rapidly in the Indian Ocean basin but its largest stations in **Goa, Malacca,** and **Macao** were soon integrated into the local trade networks. Territories in **Brazil** and **southern Africa** were the only major territorial units within the Portuguese empire by the end of the 16th century. This overseas empire remained intact despite the problems of homeland, which included a forced union with **Spain** between 1580 and 1640. However, by the 17th century, the Portuguese empire had ceased to be a major world power.

The **SPANISH EMPIRE** expanded rapidly in the Western Hemisphere and gained control of all of Central and South America except Brazil (p. 396). Despite setbacks in Europe, Spain's overseas empire remained intact as the largest in the Western Hemisphere until the early 19th century. In the European context, Spain was joined with the Netherlands and Austria in the **HABSBURG EMPIRE** of **Charles V** (1519–58) (pp. 294, 300). This empire, though vast and powerful, lacked an effective central administration and geographic core, and soon divided. The **Spanish Habsburgs,** especially during the reign of **Philip II** (1556–98), were a major power on the European continent but were weakened by a long series of wars with France; the **Treaty of the Pyrenees** (1659) marked the end of Spanish dominance. The last Habsburg king of Spain died in 1700, and the long disintegration of the Spanish Empire was hastened by the **War of the Spanish Succession** (1701–14) (p. 316).

1526–1707. MUGHAL EMPIRE. India was conquered by the Mughals, Muslim invaders from central Asia led by **Babur** (1483–30), a military adventurer. Small Mughal armies defeated huge Indian armies through effective use of firearms. Artillery enabled Mughal rulers to control local notables, and after the conquest of all of India, significant administrative reorganization during the reign of **AKBAR** (1556–1605) established a major centralized gunpowder empire. Dynastic disputes and attempts to impose a standard form of Islam along with drastic limitations on the practice of **Hinduism** led to growing conflict, and, following the death of **Aurangzeb** (r. 1658–1707), Mughal power rapidly declined, though the empire technically lasted into the following century.

1501–1722. SAFAVID EMPIRE. In the instability following the disintegration of the empire of Timur-I Lang (p. 105), various tribal and religious groups competed for power. The **Safavids,** under the leadership of **SHAH ISMAIL** (r. 1502–24), conquered most of present-day Iran and established a state whose official religion was **Shi'ite Islam.** The early state had a traditional military structure, but **SHAH ABBAS I** (r. 1587–1629) created a gunpowder-based military force that enabled him to further centralize control. However, internal conflicts arose between the imperial and traditional military forces, and under the weak leadership of Shah Abbas's successors, the Safavid state disintegrated by 1722 and was replaced by the rule of a warrior-adventurer, **Nadir Shah** (r. 1736–47), who was a successful conqueror but was unable to establish an effective centralized state (p. 363).

1462–1725. RUSSIAN EMPIRE. In central Eurasia, the huge Russian Empire began to emerge in the 15th century under the leadership of the Grand Duke of Moscow, **Ivan III** (r. 1462–1505), who created an effective artillery and a centralized absolutism that enabled him and his successors to conquer the other Russian city-states and, by the end of the 16th century, free them from the old Mongol domination. By the early 18th century, the military power and centralized absolutism of the Russian Empire brought the superiority of nomadic cavalry to an end and the Eurasian steppes into the ecumene. The modernizing efforts of **PETER THE GREAT** (r. 1689–1725) brought Russian power to near parity with its European and Ottoman neighbors and superiority over the central Asian Muslim and Chinese states to the east.

b. OTHER EMERGING STATES

In addition to the great empires that were based on centralized administration and gunpowder weaponry, other types of states developed. These ranged from empires that continued more traditional approaches of ruling to new centralized national monarchies with potential for significant expansive power. All were departures from the standard postclassical systems.

1644–1722. QING DYNASTY IN CHINA. Manchus in areas northeast of China established an effective state, in the later years of the **Ming dynasty**, which combined nomadic war skills with Chinese administrative ideas. In 1644, the Manchus took control of Beijing and established the **Qing dynasty**, which ruled China until 1911. During the first century of Qing rule, when it gained control of Tibet, Xinjiang, and Outer Mongolia, the Chinese Empire became larger than it had ever been except in the greatest days of the T'ang dynasty. The Qing maintained the **examination system** and the structure of the **scholar-gentry bureaucracy.** The Manchu military was well organized but was not primarily a gunpowder-based force. However, the Qing use of artillery in crushing a major Mongol force led by **Galdan** in 1696 marked the end of serious nomadic military threats on the inner Asian frontiers. Similarly, the **Treaty of Nerchinsk** (1689) (p. 379) between Russia and China essentially divided central Asia, reflecting the end of independent nomad power as a force in world history. The reign of **KANGXI** (1661–1722) (p. 378) marked the high point of Qing power.

1543–1853. JAPANESE CENTRALIZED STATE. Japan emerged from an era of political turmoil with the careers of three prominent military leaders who defeated local military nobles and reestablished strong central control. Firearms, introduced into Japan in 1542 or 1543, played an important role in the unification process through the power that they gave to these three commanders. **Nobunaga** (1534–82), the first, gained control of central Honshu Island, and his successor, **TOYOTOMI HIDEYOSHI** (1537–98), destroyed the power of the last resisting local lords and tried to establish a mainland empire by invading Korea in 1592 and 1597. Although these efforts failed, Japanese unification was continued following Hideyoshi's death when a former vassal, **TOKUGAWA IEYASU** (1542–1616), defeated rival commanders in 1600. He established the **TOKUGAWA SHOGUNATE** (p. 382), which initiated a period of almost two and a half centuries of internal stability. Important keys to this era of peace were a policy of relatively rigid isolation (enforceable because of Japan's island location, strict limitations on foreign religions, and the maintenance of the old **Samurai** warrior-gentleman domination, which involved the imposition of strict controls on guns and a return to more traditional weaponry. The coming of the American ships commanded by **Matthew Perry** in 1853 brought a formal end to this long era.

c. EUROPEAN NATIONAL MONARCHIES

At the beginning of the early modern era, political leaders and systems in Europe responded in many ways. Some established strong institutions of centralized control and administration, frequently with the aid of gunpowder weaponry. This process strengthened the monarchy as the most visible central institution and opened the way for expansion. Other states were unable to establish effective central control and gradually became minor elements on the continental and global scene. The turning point in many areas was the **ending of wars of religious division and national consolidation** by the second half of the 17th century.

FRANCE emerged from the One Hundred Years' War of the 15th century with an independent monarchy and substantial territory. After a period of internal and external wars, the development of a strong centralized monarchy made France the foremost continental power in Europe and a global imperial power. By creating a highly effective gunpowder-based army and a centralized bureaucracy, France represented the culmination of the age of the gunpowder empires. During the reign of **LOUIS XIV** (r. 1643–1715), the transition to centralized national monarchy and the modern state had begun (p. 326).

ENGLAND, under the **TUDORS,** developed a centralized monarchy with an increasingly professional administration. After the subsequent civil war, the monarchy was restored in 1660; it was not absolute in the same sense as the emerging French monarchy, but the absolute power of the central government, combining the monarchy and parliament, was established. The Puritan **New Model Army** laid the foundations for a permanent standing army for the central government. By 1700 an administratively and militarily centralized state emerged in England.

SWEDEN emerged as a unified monarchy under the **House of Vasa** in the 16th century. A centralized administration helped the monarchs reduce the power of the aristocracy. Under **GUSTAVUS II ADOLPHUS** (1611–32), Sweden became a major power and its army was in the forefront of the development of disciplined musket warfare. Sweden unsuccessfully tried to establish a North American trading colony in **Delaware** (1638–55). A long series of wars and costly efforts to create a northern European empire reduced Sweden's influence and power. By the end of the **Great Northern War** (1700–1721) (p. 316), aristocratic and parliamentary forces had placed limits on the powers of the monarchy internally, and the rise of Russia and Prussia effectively ended Swedish expansion. The Swedish experience showed that an efficient central administration and a strong gunpowder military could provide the basis for significant power but did not inevitably result in the creation of a large empire or long-term great-power status.

d. THE NEW CONTEXT OF THE 18TH CENTURY

Outside Europe, the older pattern of the rise and decline of major states continued, with the predominant gunpowder states entering periods of reduced effectiveness. However, in Europe, the development of the centralized monarchies opened the way for growing power at the beginning of the great socioeconomic transformations of early modernization.

1700–1800. NON-EUROPEAN EMPIRES. The **OTTOMAN EMPIRE** continued to be a major power but lost a series of wars and considerable territory, especially to Russia and Habsburg Austria. The administrative system and the military became increasingly ineffective as corruption and internal rivalries grew. Local governors in Egypt, North Africa, and the Balkans grew more independent, and attempts at administrative and military reform had little effect. Finally, a more comprehensive reform effort strongly influenced by European models as undertaken by **SELIM III** (1789–1807), but he was overthrown by conservative opponents of reform (p. 359). The **MUGHAL EMPIRE** experienced succession conflicts and the growing power of provincial governors (p. 368). Mughal authority was seriously threatened by a revival of Hindu forces under the **Marathas** and the **Rajputs** and the emergence of the **SIKHS** as a new militant religious community (p. 368). However, the expansion of European powers brought the Mughal Empire to an end. Portuguese influence declined and was replaced by the growing power of the **EAST INDIA COMPANIES** (p. 371) of the British, French, and Dutch. In a series of conflicts, the British ultimately defeated the Dutch (1759) and the French (1763). The **English East India Company** gained full control of Bengal and Bihar by 1764 but ruled in the name of the Mughal emperor. By the early 19th century, the British controlled nearly all of India. The formal end of the Mughal Empire followed a major revolt in many areas of northern India in 1857–58. The last Mughal was deposed, and in 1858 **THE GOVERNMENT OF INDIA ACT** (p. 555) by the British Parliament created direct rule by the monarch of England, ending government by the **East India Company** and the **Mughals.** Other major non-European empires also declined during the 18th century. The collapse of the **Safavid** state in Iran brought a period of warfare and disunity to Iran. By the end of the 18th century, the **Qing dynasty** in China exhibited the characteristics of decline. The strength of the military was reduced; the bureaucracy became increasingly corrupt and inefficient. Large-scale revolts, like that of the **White Lotus Society** (1796–1804), emphasized the growing weakness of the empire (p. 561).

EMERGING GREAT POWERS. Some states in Europe made an important transition during the 18th century to new centralized systems that could draw strength from the growing commercialization of society and the beginnings of industrialization. As a result, by the end of the century, **France, Great Britain,** and **Prussia,** along with the **Russian Empire,** displaced **Spain, Habsburg Austria,** and **Portugal** as major powers in European and global affairs. The **Dutch Republic** became a preeminent commercial power with large overseas possessions but was not a significant military presence.

ROYAL ABSOLUTISM was the primary force in developing strong central governments in some of the emerging powers. **FRANCE** was earliest, with the effective absolutism of **LOUIS XIV** (r. 1643–1715), but his successors were less effective and French monarchical absolutism came to an end with the **FRENCH REVOLUTION**, beginning in 1789 (p. 431). During the reign of **Frederick II, the Great** (1740–86),

Prussian royal absolutism and great-power status were confirmed. **RUSSIA** modernization, centralization, and expansion in both Europe and Asia were strengthened by **CATHERINE THE GREAT** (r. 1762–96) as Russia became a major intercontinental power, with some overseas expansion into North America and northern Pacific islands. The **AUSTRIAN HABSBURGS** gained territories at the expense of weaker neighbors like Poland and the Ottoman Empire, but were less successful than Prussia and Russia in improving the effectiveness of their royal absolutism. The reforms and policies of **Maria Theresa** (r. 1740–80) and **Joseph II** (r. 1780–90) were not sufficient to create administrative unity among the scattered Habsburg domains. In **SPAIN** and **PORTUGAL** reform efforts by leaders like the **Marquis de Pombal** in Portugal failed to revive effective state power. In **POLAND** the state simply ceased to exist as nobles limited the ability of monarchs to institute reforms and Russia, Prussia, and Austria took control of all of Poland in three partitions (1772, 1793, 1795) (p. 346).

PARLIAMENTARY STATES. The centralized parliamentary state in **ENGLAND** provided the effective support for expansion. English colonial settlements in **North America** and the expansion of the **East India Company** in India created a global empire during the 18th century. After its successful revolt against Habsburg control at the beginning of the 17th century, the **DUTCH REPUBLIC** emerged as a significant commercial power. The Dutch created an overseas empire with holdings in North and South America, South Africa, and the Indian Ocean basin, especially in southeast Asia; its wealth made it an important political force in Europe. By the middle of the 18th century, it had become a minor European power and its commercial preeminence was lost to Britain, although the Dutch still maintained a small but important overseas empire.

"WORLD WARS" OF THE 18TH CENTURY. Many of the conflicts among the European powers involved clashes beyond the European continent. They were primarily European wars fought on a global scale, with two chief lines of conflict: the struggle for continental domination in Europe and the battle for control of overseas colonies and naval access to them. In the continental struggle, **France, Prussia,** and **Russia** became the great powers, and in global maritime empires, **Great Britain** was the major force. The European names of the most important global wars in creating this power structure are the **War of the Spanish Succession** (1701–14) (p. 316), which began the reduction of French power in North America; the **War of the Austrian Succession** (1740–48) (p. 317); and the **Seven Years' War** (1756–63), which resulted in France's loss of most of its overseas empire in India and North America; finally, there were the wars of the era of the **French Revolution** and **Napoleon** (p. 431), which were fought in North America, Asia, and Africa as well as in Europe.

2. TRANSFORMATIONS OF MAJOR WORLD SOCIETIES, 1500–1800

The major world societies experienced significant social transformations in the early modern era. The most comprehensive changes took place in the **West,** where the city-centered but agricultural societies typical of premodern civilizations were transformed by 1800 into early **industrial societies.** Important changes also altered the nature of other major world societies in this era. Two important lines of internal change involved (1) the **commercialization of societies** and (2) reorientations of worldviews in what frequently took the form of **religious reformations.**

a. COMMERCIALIZATION

Commercialization involved changing structures of regional and national economies as well as the growing globalization of commercial networks and their increasing domination by western European organizations and states. The growth of global trade in the 16th century was part of a transformation involving increasing importance of markets and specialized production of agricultural and manufactured goods. This commercialization of economic life had significant effects on all of society.

EUROPEAN TRANSFORMATION. Western Europe experienced a **Commercial Revolution** that had a major impact during the 16th century. Growing global contacts increased demand for a variety of goods in Europe. The development of new overseas colonies in the 16th and 17th centuries provided both new products and new markets. The influx of gold and silver from the Spanish possessions in the Western Hemisphere increased the monetarization of European national economies and provided the basis for growing demand and price inflation. The development of more effective methods of managing trade and investment heightened the impact and extent of commercialization. Emerging institutions like **national banks** and **chartered companies** provided the means for expanding commercial activities. What was in effect an **AGRICULTURAL REVOLUTION** took place by the 17th and 18th centuries. New products like potatoes and maize from the Western Hemisphere and new farming techniques and technologies transformed old peasant agriculture, providing more food for expanding cities and growing numbers of workers who were peasants displaced by new farming methods. Processed products like refined sugar and manufactured textiles became important for the general population. Agricultural developments in this way further strengthened the commercialization of societies. The **INDUSTRIAL REVOLUTION,** especially in Great Britain and France, transformed the means, methods, and concepts of production and gave immense economic power to those societies that industrialized in this early modern era. By 1800 much of western Europe no longer comprised basically agricultural societies with growing commercialization. Instead, the profound transformation to industrial societies had begun.

WESTERN HEMISPHERE. European colonies in the Western Hemisphere effectively eliminated the independent indigenous societies. Local populations decreased disastrously during the 16th century, and European immigrants and African slaves became important elements in the emerging societies. In the north, **French** and **British** settlement colonies were integrated into the larger commercial networks through trade in furs, forest products, naval stores, and similar goods. In the **Spanish** Caribbean and South American colonies and in **Portuguese** Brazil, highly commercialized plantation economies producing sugar and other popular export products made these regions an important market for African slaves and a significant element in the emerging global trade system. The Americas provided vital raw materials but the terms of trade were established by European commercial companies, which dominated shipping and provided manufactured and luxury goods. By the 18th century, many of these colonies were nearing the ability to assert independence from the imperial center. The first to succeed were 13 of the British North American colonies in the **American Revolution** (1776–83). In 1794, **Haiti** gained its independence, and most of the rest of **Central** and **South America** followed in a series of revolutions in the early 19th century. These revolutions did not, however, represent the emergence of industrial societies, except in the new United States to a degree. Instead, both colonies and independent states in the Western Hemisphere (including the U.S. South) remained commercialized agricultural societies tied to the European economies.

ISLAMIC SOCIETIES experienced significant changes that also represented the increasing commercialization of economic life. In the **Ottoman Empire,** a growing monetarization of the economy occurred contemporaneously with a significant movement of peoples from rural to urban areas. Development of urban manufacturing and the increased production of cash crops like cotton changed urban and rural social institutions. During the same period, the diversion of Asian trade away from Muslim intermediaries, first as Portuguese and then as Dutch and British commercial activities expanded in the Indian Ocean, proved deleterious to Ottoman merchants, as did the price inflation resulting from the influx of American silver. The Ottoman government and ruling elite tended not to be directly involved in commercial and manufacturing activities, and these areas gradually came under the control of non-Muslim Ottoman subjects and European commercial interests. Special exemptions, or **capitulations,** for European merchants from Ottoman law began to be granted with an agreement with France in 1536; these extraterritorial rights meant that outsiders gained increasing control of Ottoman commercial life by the end of the 18th century. In the **Safavid Empire,** the changes were similar but less significant. The Safavid ruler, Shah Abbas I (r. 1587–1629), encouraged the manufacture of luxury textiles, and Safavid shahs worked first with Portuguese and Dutch and later with British commercial interests to integrate Iran into the broader patterns of world trade. However, the Iranian economy was less commercialized, and after the fall of the Safavids in the early 18th century, instability and wars led to economic disorganization and increasing control of large-scale economic activity by Europeans. The military power of the **Mughal Empire** did not deter the expansion of Portuguese and then French and British commercial interests. The great East India Companies gradually took increasing control of Indian economic life. This process involved a significant commercialization of the society, as new agricultural products were developed for world markets and a broad, controlled internal market economy emerged. All of these changes took place in the context of the military and political developments that led to British domination of India by the end of the 18th century.

CHINA experienced significant changes but was the most successfully conservative of the major urban-agrarian societies. The establishment of the **Qing dynasty** in 1644 provided a strong central power that could afford to pay relatively little attention to developments elsewhere. Yet the stability of the early Qing period opened the way for expanded production of important export products like tea, silk, and porcelain. China also benefited from the influx of American silver into the world markets. In addition to the commercial growth and prosperity of the merchant classes, there was a significant growth in population and in large cities as new agricultural products increased food supplies. However, this prosperity tended to occur outside the areas of state control, and by the end of the 18th century the cultural conservatism of the Qing period had laid the foundation for the loss of control of both politics and the economy to European powers.

AFRICAN SOCIETIES also experienced significant transformations in the early modern era. Until the age of European expansion beginning in the 15th century, the primary interaction of African societies with other parts of the world had been with the Islamic world, along a frontier across the continent that, by the 15th century, extended from the Atlantic to the Indian Oceans just south of the Sahara and along the east African coast. East Africa, in the longer span of world history, had also participated in the broad cultural and economic exchanges of the Indian Ocean basin. **European expansion changed the orientation of movement of peoples and goods from the old north-south axis to movement toward the coastal regions.** This had already been an important direction of movement in east Africa under the influence of Muslim merchants, but it represented a dramatic transformation for much of the rest of Africa.

The most important dimension of the commercialization of African economies was the development of the large-scale **SLAVE TRADE,** especially in the Atlantic region. The growth of the colonial plantation economies created a vast market that was filled by slaves from Africa. In the process African societies, especially along the Atlantic coasts, were transformed by political reorganization and depopulation. The importation of **firearms** gave impetus to the establishment of more centralized west African states, like the kingdoms of **Asante** and **Dahomey** (p. 391). Commercialization of societies had profound effects in different African regions by changing the nature of political systems and the orientation of trade.

COMPARISONS. In the early modern era, many societies experienced important economic transformations. In western European societies these changes led to increased strength and expansion. In other parts of the world, the results were very different. Local economies in the Western Hemisphere were destroyed by European expansion, and the new commercialized colonial economies retained a dependence on Europe despite the achievement of political independence. In the major urban societies of the Eastern Hemisphere, local economies experienced a significant reorientation by the end of the 18th century, also coming under the European influence. By 1800 the leading world economies, earlier a network of interacting but autonomous urban-centered, agrarian economies, had become a vast global network of commercialized societies dominated by the economic power of west-

ern European societies. In this transformation, western Europe had emerged as an assembly of independent industrial societies while the rest of the world entered the era of industrial society in a dependent condition.

b. WORLDVIEW REFORMATIONS

In the major regional civilizations in the Eastern Hemisphere, the comprehensive religious syntheses that developed in the postclassical era were challenged in a number of ways. In general terms, there were efforts to articulate the basic themes of the traditions of world religions in new ways, sometimes resulting in **reformations** and sometimes in the creation of new religions and, more dramatically, in the emergence of altogether new worldviews by the end of the 18th century in western Europe.

EUROPEAN TRANSFORMATION. In western Europe, the changes involved significant challenges to the postclassical synthesis. In the **Renaissance** of the 15th and 16th centuries, there was a rebirth of interest in and respect for classical Greek and Roman thought. The foremost challenge to the comprehensive synthesis of the **Christian scholasticism** of **Catholic Christianity** emerged with the **PROTESTANT REFORMATION** of the 16th and 17th centuries. In this, the authority of the Roman Church to define doctrine and practice was challenged in a variety of ways by Protestant leaders like **Martin Luther** and **John Calvin.** Nevertheless, all of these challenges remained within the framework of **Western Christianity** and accepted the authority of the Bible. By the 17th century, the beginnings of the **SCIENTIFIC REVOLUTION** marked the start of a wholly new style of cosmology and worldview that came to characterize the modern approach. This approach did not necessarily reject traditional religious beliefs but tended to see them as only indirectly relevant to understanding the natural world. In the 18th century, the beginnings of modern **secularism** sought to separate religion from other areas of life, especially the political. By the end of the 18th century, foundations were created for modern worldviews and cosmologies which transformed rather than simply reformed the religious traditions of western Europe.

NON-EUROPEAN WORLDVIEWS also experienced a variety of reformations. In the **ISLAMIC WORLD,** the establishment of **Shi'ite Islam** as the religion of the Safavid Empire brought renewed prominence to Shi'ism and a new era of Sunni-Shi'ite conflicts in the wars between the Ottoman and Safavid states. In the world of **Sunni Islam,** challenges to the postclassical synthesis assumed a number of forms by the 18th century. The tolerant missionary approaches of Sufi teachers in various regions allowed for inclusion of pre-Islamic elements in the practices of newly converted societies. By the 18th century, activist reform movements in a number of regions sought to bring local practices in line with stricter interpretations of the Islamic tradition. In West Africa a series of puritanical movements and holy wars began with the jihad of **Karamoko Alifa** (d. 1751) in the Futa Jallon region of modern Guinea and culminated with the holy war of **Usuman dan Fodio** (1754–1817) (p. 391) in the area of modern Nigeria. **Abd al-Ra'uf al-Sinkili** (d. after 1693) expressed a similar reforming spirit in Aceh in Sumatra. **Muhammad ibn Abd al-Wahhab** (1703–92) (p. 364) established a major puritanical reform tradition in Arabia which remains the foundation for the fundamentalist Saudi state today. In India a comprehensive examination of Islamic thought and practice in light of the decline of Muslim power was undertaken by **Shah Wali Allah al-Dihlawi** (1702–62), whose ideas provide the basis for much of modern Islamic thinking in south Asia. Within the central parts of the Ottoman Empire were a variety of reformers who were more politically oriented. In general terms, important aspects of the postclassical synthesis were rearticulated in Islamic reformations, but the overall structure of faith and practice remained intact at the end of the 18th century.

HINDUISM developed in a number of directions as a result of internal developments and in response to the challenges of Muslim rule. One such response constituted an attempt at reformulations that could combine Islamic and Hindu elements. For instance, **Nanak** (1469–1539) (p. 368) created a body of devotional literature that became the starting point for **SIKHISM,** a new religion that emerged during the 16th century. The Mughal emperor **Akbar** (1556–1605) tried unsuccessfully to establish a syncretistic court religion that could bring together the different religions of India. Within mainstream Hinduism, reform further developed in the traditions of popular devotional piety, including the special worship of **Rama** that emerged after the composition of the *Ramcaritmanas*, a retelling in the Hindi language of the story of the ancient hero Rama by the poet **Tulsi Das,** around 1575.

NEO-CONFUCIAN SYNTHESIS in China remained dominant throughout the later Ming and the Qing dynasties. Confucianism also gained new influence in China. The writings of Zhu Xi remained au-

thoritative and officially sanctioned, but the thought of **Wang Yangming** (1472–1529) provided an idealist alternative Confucian tradition that strongly influenced reformers in the 19th and 20th centuries in both China and Japan.

COMPARISONS. While all of the prominent worldview traditions underwent some significant reformulation of basic positions, it was only in western Europe that, in addition to renaissance and reformation experiences, there was a major transformation of worldview. Here modern worldviews emerged as the dominant perspective by the end of the 18th century, rather than as reformed postclassical traditions.

3. GLOBAL INTERACTION NETWORKS

In the early modern era a number of global patterns of interaction developed. These emerging networks, which created a worldwide context for human activity, involved (1) the more consciously organized commercial activities, (2) the exchange of new products, and (3) the spread of diseases.

a. THE EMERGING WORLD ECONOMY

The commercialization of societies opened the way for the commercialization of global interactions. In the 16th century, local and regional networks of commercial exchange continued to be of great importance. The Mediterranean and Indian Ocean basins remained important zones of interaction, and the growth of the European-controlled oceanic trade created new regional networks in both the Atlantic Ocean and the Pacific Ocean. These large zones became increasingly interconnected and integrated with the older continental overland routes of Asia and the emerging continental systems of Russia and Europe and in the Western Hemisphere. By the end of the 18th century, maritime trade represented a European-controlled global commercial network in which products from nearly every part of the world were exchanged.

b. THE EXCHANGE OF NEW PRODUCTS

An important part of the growing global integration of the early modern era was the exchange of many new goods and products both interregionally and globally (called the "Columbian exchange"). Agricultural goods from the Western Hemisphere had a profound impact on societies throughout the Eastern Hemisphere. The introduction of **maize** and **potatoes** aided in the rapid growth of population in China,

Africa, and western Europe, and **tobacco** changed lifestyles around the globe. In the Western Hemisphere the introduction of new domesticated animals like **horses** and **cattle** transformed indigenous societies in many areas even before their conquest by Europeans. A special case of product exchange that had a major impact on global economies was the rapid increase in the available quantities of precious metals used for money, especially **SILVER** from the Spanish colonies in the Western Hemisphere. In some areas of Europe the growing money supply increased demand and encouraged productivity, thereby strengthening the economy. This was an important part of the economic growth in **England, France,** and **Holland** and may have played a role in the decline of **Spain.** It had a negative impact in those areas where the power of ruling elites was associated more with ownership or control of land. Outside western Europe, the influx of American silver appears to have bolstered commercial elements and to have aided the growing European economic dominance.

c. THE SPREAD OF DISEASES

A tragic dimension of early modern global interactions was the exchange of diseases. Populations in the Western Hemisphere lacked established immunities to diseases that were common in the Eastern Hemisphere. As a result, epidemics of **SMALLPOX, measles,** and other diseases killed whole populations in some regions and more than half of the total population of the hemisphere. In global terms, the increasing levels of contact and population movements created a more uniform level of contact with diseases and immunity. Great plagues like the Black Death of postclassical times became less common, and by the end of the 18th century, pandemic diseases had less ability to destroy entire populations. *(To p. 418)*

B. EARLY MODERN EUROPE, 1479–1815

The early modern period in Europe can be said to begin around 1648. Between 1500 and 1648 dominant trends reflected intense religious conflict and colonial expansion. After 1648 the emphasis shifted to the activities of national monarchies and their mutual wars as well as the rise of science. Popular unrest receded somewhat, but profound changes in beliefs and in economic activities took shape beneath the surface.

Many trends in eastern Europe differed from those in the West. Eastern Europe saw a tightening of serfdom, rather than the rise of wage labor and the growth of commercial cities. Soon after 1648, however, eastern Europe began to share in many of the intellectual and political trends of the West, and a more European-wide diplomatic framework emerged.

1. EUROPE, 1479–1675

(From p. 240)

a. OVERVIEW

The **reformation** of the Christian Church, launched in 1517 by the Augustinian friar **Martin Luther** (1483–1546), had profound political, social, and economic as well as religious consequences that redounded throughout the entire period. Religious beliefs became conflated with national sentiment and political ambitions, with economic goals and

perceived social injustices; and religious schism, civil and international wars, and domestic revolts ensued. The Roman Catholic Church responded to calls for reform with the establishment of new religious orders (notably the Society of Jesus, or **Jesuits**); with the **Holy Office,** which investigated heresy; and with the **Council of Trent** (1545–63), which defined doctrine (notably on the issue of **marriage**) for the next four centuries.

Meantime, the centuries-old European **expansion accelerated.** Overseas expansion broadened the geographical horizons of Europeans and brought them into confrontations with ancient civilizations in the Americas, Africa, and Asia. These conflicts led first to conquest, then to exploitations, and eventually to economic changes in both Europe and overseas territories. For example, gold and silver from Mexico and Peru which began to flow into Europe in 1503 caused a continent-wide inflation between 1550 and 1565 (though the peak period of Spanish bullion imports was 1580–1620). American **potatoes, tomatoes,** and **maize** (Indian corn) began to revolutionize Europeans' diet. By 1575 Europe participated in the first truly **global economy,** paying for Asian silks, spices, and porcelain, Persian carpets, and Ottoman Turkish kilims with South American silver.

Furniture and house decor testified to rising bourgeois wealth, to economic and cultural change: chairs; cupboards, dressers, and sideboards that supported gold, silver, and pewterware and held supplies of table and bed linens, laces, and brocades; canopied four-poster beds; and mirrors and paintings. Ceramic tile floors were common by the 17th century, as were, in wealthy homes, oak parquet floors often covered by Ottoman Turkish or Persian rugs. Such luxuries were depicted in the paintings of Ghirlandaio, Jan van Eyck, Holbein, and the Venetians Carpaccio and Crivelli, reflecting the close commercial ties between Venice and the Ottoman world. In the 16th century, transparent glass **windowpanes** spread so rapidly that by the 1560s prosperous peasant homes had them, although in eastern Europe, even the grandest houses continued to cover windows with oiled paper. The indoor **water closet** (toilet), invented by the Englishman **Sir John Harrington** in 1596, was a luxury everywhere before the 18th century. By the mid-17th century, the houses of wealthy Dutch merchants displayed a conspicuous consumption.

The **expansion of the Ottoman Turks** into southeastern Europe provoked great fears and preoccupied Europeans far more than did "discoveries" and developments in Asia and the Americas.

The 17th century opened with **agricultural and commercial crises** that had serious social and political consequences. Colder, wetter weather meant shorter farming seasons, which in turn meant smaller harvests, food shortages, and widespread starvation. The output of textiles also declined. The **Thirty Years' War** (1618–48) in Germany, which at some point involved most of the states of Europe, proved the greatest economic disaster for Germany before the 20th century. The **widespread use of gunpowder** increased the costs and destructiveness of war while reducing its glamour. To finance the larger armies that warfare required, governments resorted to heavier taxation mainly on overburdened peasantry, sparking revolts. To free themselves from the restrictions of competing institutions (such as the churches) or social groups (such as the nobilities), governments claimed to possess **sovereignty,** the right to make law for all people, a monopoly over the instruments of justice (the courts), and the use of force (police and state armies). In the process two patterns of government began to emerge in the early 17th century: **absolutism and constitutionalism.**

Peasant and urban workers' revolts erupted frequently between 1550 and 1650, cresting around 1648, because of bad harvests that led to widespread starvation, extraordinary royal and seigneurial taxation, and rampant pillaging by soldiers during the Thirty Years' War. A new class structure was taking shape with a growing group of **landless wage laborers** at the bottom, and this process mobilized many groups in its early phases. Radical outbursts in London, Lyons, Bordeaux, Naples, Salerno, Palermo, Granada, Cordoba (where women led the rebellion), Salzburg, parts of the Swiss cantons, Lithuania, and Moscow often had an egalitarian flavor and, in urban centers, reflected the **growth of class consciousness** among wage laborers. These revolts, in the towns in western Europe and in the countryside in eastern Europe, constituted the most widespread movements of social protest before 1848.

CULTURAL CHANGES. Although **skepticism, sexism, and racism** originated in ancient times, during the age of religious wars these attitudes took on distinctively modern forms. New religious conflicts spurred **changes in popular beliefs,** while **segments of the European elite** (including Catholic as well as Protestant leaders) tried to discipline many traditional values and behaviors.

Skepticism, which is based on the doubt that certainty, especially religious certainty, is ever attainable, rejected dogmatism and increased secularism. The French essayist **Michel de Montaigne** (1533–92) is perhaps the best representative of early modern skepticism, which was ultimately linked to, though modified by, the **rise of science.**

Witchcraft was an integral part of the mental climate of the age. Educated as well as illiterate people (the French political philosopher Jean Bodin [1530–96] and the English jurist Sir Edward Coke [1552–1634] are just two examples of the former) believed in the existence of witches. They were popularly described as old women (but sometimes children and young women) who convened for sabbath (midnight assemblies), worshiped, engaged in sexual orgies, and made pacts with the devil (thus renouncing Christian baptism), in return for which they acquired powers to control natural forces such as storms, destroy crops, harm cattle, or incapacitate human genitals. Almost all witches seemed to come from the lower levels of society and were female: the poor, the aged, the senile, and those least able to defend themselves. In the period **1470–1700,** 5,417 women were executed (by burning or hanging) in the Swiss Confederation; in 1559–1736, 1,000 women were executed in England; and in 1561–1670, 3,229 women were executed in southeastern Germany. Some possible explanations for these persecutions: pervasive misogyny; treatment of the poor as scapegoats in times of economic and social distress, when outbursts of hysteria toward witches most often occurred; identification of these women with heresy; a desire to control, or to have the appearance of controlling, the scientifically inexplicable and uncontrollable; and a means of eliminating the social nonconformist.

Racism. Europeans carried to the Americas **racial stereotypes** derived from Christian theological speculation and from Muslim theories: that the color white represented light and godliness and that black stood for the hostile forces of the underworld; that sub-Saharan Africans' morals were heathen, their languages barbarous; that Blacks possessed an especially potent sexuality; and, according to the Muslim traveler Ibn Khaldun, that Blacks readily accepted slavery "owing to their low degree of humanity and their proximity to the animal stage." Such absurd hypotheses provided justification for and rationalization of slavery.

Estimates of Population Growth, 1500–1648

France:	12 to 15 million
Spain:	6.5 to 7.5 million rise (in addition to heavy emigration to the Americas)
Holy Roman Empire:	steady at 8 million (the Thirty Years' War took about 8 million lives)
Italy:	10 to 12 million
Low Countries:	2.5 to 3.5 million rise
British Isles:	5 to 7.5 million rise
Scandinavia:	2 to 2.5 million rise

(To p. 312)

b. ENGLAND, SCOTLAND, AND IRELAND

(From p. 243)

1485–1603. HOUSE OF TUDOR.

1485–1509. HENRY VII. Henry's first act was to imprison the **earl of Warwick,** son of the duke of Clarence. His first parliament (1485) confirmed the crown to him and his heirs. Though the traditional medieval checks on the power of the crown were maintained in theory, in practice Henry went a long way toward developing royal power—establishment of the administrative court later called the **Star Chamber** (1487), suppression of recalcitrant nobles and livery and maintenance (private armies clothed and supported by nobles and representing a resurgence of feudalism) (p. 192), development of an efficient if arbitrary royal financial system.

1494. STATUTE OF DROGHEDA (Poyning's law): (1) No Irish parliament should be held without the consent of the king of England. (2) No bill could be brought forward in an Irish parliament without his consent. (3) All recent laws enacted in the English parliament should hold in Ireland.

1496. Percy Warbeck, a Fleming, and James IV of Scotland invaded England. In 1497 a formidable insurrection broke out in Cornwall on occasion of an imposition of a tax by parliament. It was suppressed by the defeat at **Blackheath** (June 22, 1497), and the leaders executed (Flammock). **Peace with Scotland** (Sept. 1497). Warbeck was soon taken and imprisoned in the Tower.

1496. *Intercursus magnus*, commercial treaty with Netherlands, granted mutual privileges to English and Flemings and provided fixed duties. Support of the wool trade; taxes on that trade augmented Henry's treasury and made him financially independent of parliament.

1501. Marriage of Henry's eldest son, Arthur, and Catherine of Aragon of Spain.

1502. Marriage of Henry's eldest daughter, Margaret, with James IV, king of Scotland.

1509–47. HENRY VIII. He was six times married: (1) **Catherine of Aragon,** widow of his brother Arthur, mother of Mary the Catholic (married on June 3, 1509, divorced on March 30, 1533). (2) **Anne Boleyn,** mother of Elizabeth I (married on Jan. 25, 1533, beheaded on May 19, 1536). (3) **Jane Seymour** (married on May 20, 1536, died after the birth of her son Edward VI, on October 24, 1537). (4) **Anne of Cleves** (married on Jan. 6, 1540, divorced on June 24, 1540). (5) **Catherine Howard** (married on Aug. 8, 1540, beheaded on Feb. 12, 1542). (6) **Catherine Parr** (married on July 10, 1543, outlived the king).

1511. Henry a member of the **Holy League** (pp. 291, 294). Having laid claim to the French crown, he sent troops to Spain, which were unsuccessful (1512). In 1513 the king went to France in person and with Emperor Maximilian won on Aug. 17, the bloodless victory of **Guinegate,** the battle of the Spurs.

1513, Sept. 9. Battle of Flodden Field. Defeat and death of James IV of Scotland, who was allied with France.

1514, Aug. Peace with France and with Scotland.

1515. Thomas Wolsey (1475?–1530), the king's favorite, cardinal and chancellor, papal legate.

1520, June 7. Meeting of Henry VIII and Francis I of France near Calais (Field of the Cloth of Gold).

1521. Henry wrote the *Assertion of the Seven Sacraments* in reply to Luther, and received the title Defender of the Faith from Pope Leo X.

After the **battle of Pavia** (p. 294), the relations between Henry and the emperor, were strained by Charles V's refusal to support Henry's plan to divide France, and then by England's covert support for the League of Cognac.

1527. Henry, desiring to marry Anne Boleyn and claiming that Catherine's failure to produce a male heir was God's punishment for his marriage to his brother's widow (Lev. 18:16, 20:21), appealed to Rome for a divorce. Papal delays and Wolsey's hesitations enraged Henry, who blamed Wolsey and deprived him of the great seal (1529). Henry then appointed **Sir Thomas More** as Lord Chancellor.

Religious Background. Although the Lollard movement (p. 240), which stressed Bible study and attacked clerical wealth, attracted working-class people in southern England and the Midlands, the number of followers was always small. Recent scholarship has shown that traditional Catholicism exerted an extremely strong hold on the loyalty of the people. The teachings of Christianity were graphically represented in the liturgy, constantly reiterated in sermons, enacted in plays, and carved and printed on the walls and windows of parish churches. That is to say, no substantial gulf existed between the religion of the clergy, the educated elite, and the broad mass of the English people. The Reformation in England was an act of state. When Henry VIII's marital difficulties became inextricably tied to domestic and then to international politics, religious schism resulted.

1529–36. The Reformation Parliament was summoned to reform the Church, to give the appearance of broad national support for the king's divorce, and thus to pressure Pope Clement to grant the divorce. Though there is no evidence of direct royal intervention in elections, ties to the court constituted the most important factor in the elections of the knights of the shires.

1533, Jan. 25. Anne Boleyn's pregnancy and the prospect of an heir compelled Henry to hurry; he and Anne secretly married.

1533, Feb. Parliament passed the **Act in Restraint of Appeals,** which declared that the king possessed full and **sovereign power to yield justice** to his subjects on any matter without the restraint of any foreign prince (the pope) or any domestic group (the clergy). This act, intended to halt Catherine's appeal to Rome and to pressure the papacy to grant

the annulment (divorce), made it possible for an English court to resolve the matter and, by giving the king control of justice, marked a decisive moment in the development of a national state. Nevertheless, Henry sought, and Pope Clement approved in **March 1533,** the bulls appointing **Thomas Cranmer** (1489–1556) archbishop of Canterbury; the customary payment of 10,000 marks was remitted to Rome.

May 23, 1533. Cranmer held a secret court that declared Henry's marriage to Catherine null and void.

May 28, 1533. Cranmer pronounced Henry's secret marriage to Anne valid.

June 1, 1533. Anne Boleyn crowned **queen** of England.

1534. ACT OF SUPREMACY, appointing the king and his successors Protector and only Supreme Head of the Church and Clergy of England. This may be taken as the decisive moment of the **English Reformation.** The break with Rome had political and personal origins; at first there were no real differences in dogma and liturgy. Refusal to take the oath of supremacy was made high treason, under which vote Sir Thomas More was condemned and beheaded (1535).

Thomas Cromwell (1485?–1540), a former servant of Wolsey and his successor in the favor of the king, now viceregent in matters relating to the Church in England, issued a commission for the inspection of monasteries.

1536–1539. Dissolution of the monasteries on the basis of rigged evidence, the smaller ones in 1536, the larger ones in 1539, ended a millennium of monastic cultural influence on English life. The lands sold, eventually bringing into being a powerful gentry class.

1536. Publication of **Tyndale's translation of the Bible,** by Coverdale, under authority from the king.

1536. Suppression of the Catholic rebellion of the Yorkshireman **Robert Aske,** aided by **Reginald Pole,** son of Margaret, countess of Salisbury.

1539. STATUTE OF THE SIX ARTICLES, defining heresy; denial of any of these positions constituted heresy: (1) transubstantiation; (2) communion in one kind by laymen; (3) celibacy of the priesthood; (4) inviolability of vows of chastity; (5) necessity of private masses; (6) necessity of auricular confession. These were all traditional Roman Catholic Doctrines.

1540. Execution of Cromwell on a charge of treason. Cromwell had fallen under Henry's displeasure by his advocacy of the king's marriage with **Anne of Cleves,** with whom the king was ill pleased.

1542. IRELAND MADE A KINGDOM.

1544. Parliament recognized **Mary** and **Elizabeth** as heirs to the crown in the event of the death of Edward without issue.

Henry VIII died on Jan. 28, 1547, leaving a will, wherein the crown was left to the heirs of his sister, **Mary, duchess of Suffolk,** in the event of failure of issue by all of his children.

1547–53. EDWARD VI, ten years of age; his uncle, earl of Hertford, was appointed lord protector and **duke of Somerset** and assumed the government. **Repeal of the Six Articles** (1547). Introduction of Protestant doctrines (1549). Establishment of uniformity of service by act of parliament; introduction of Edward VI's *Book of Common Prayer* (1549) (second, 1552).

1550. Fall of the protector, Somerset, who was superseded by Lord Warwick, afterward **duke of Northumberland.** Execution of Somerset (1552).

1553. July 6. Death of Edward VI.

1553–58. MARY, who had been brought up a Catholic. Restoration of Catholic bishops. **Stephen Gardiner,** bishop of Winchester, author of the Six Articles, lord chancellor.

1553. Marriage treaty between Mary and **Philip of Spain,** son of Charles V, afterward Philip II. This transaction being unpopular, an insurrection broke out, headed by Sir Thomas Carew, the duke of Suffolk, and Sir Thomas Wyatt. The rebellion was suppressed.

1554, July 25. Marriage of Mary and Philip.

1555. Return to Catholicism and persecution of the Protestants (**Bonner,** bishop of London). Oct. 16, **Ridley** and **Latimer;** March 21, 1556, **Cranmer** burned at the stake. About 300 are said to have been burned during this persecution. **Cardinal Pole,** archbishop of Canterbury and papal legate (1556).

1557. England drawn into the Spanish war with France. Defeat of the French at the **battle of St. Quentin** (Aug. 10, 1557).

1558, Jan. 7. Loss of Calais, which was captured by the duke of Guise.

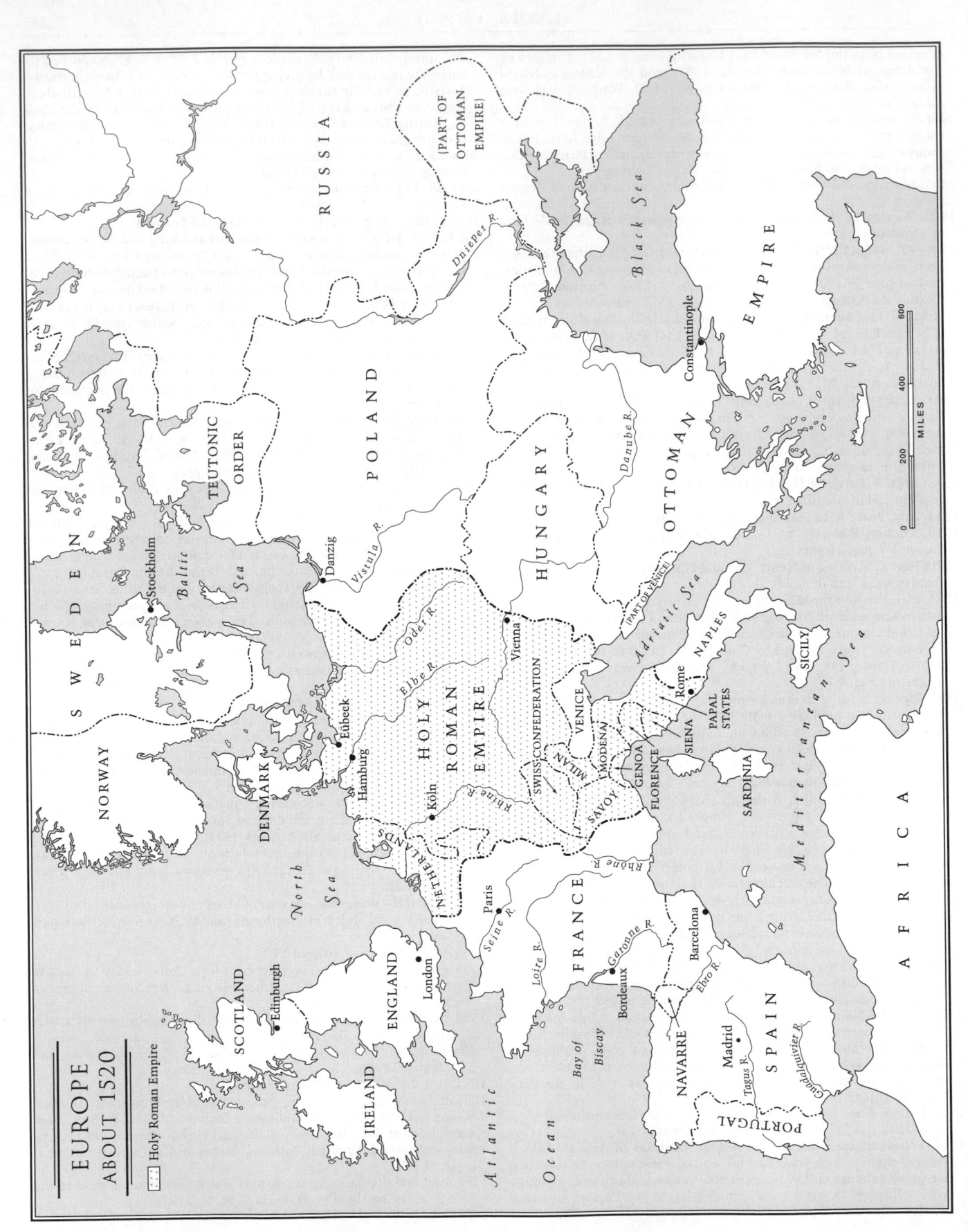

EUROPE
ABOUT 1520

Holy Roman Empire

RUSSIA

(PART OF OTTOMAN EMPIRE)

Dnieper R.

Black Sea

EMPIRE

Constantinople

600

400

200

0

MILES

SWEDEN

Stockholm

Baltic Sea

TEUTONIC
ORDER

Danzig

Vistula R.

POLAND

HUNGARY

Danube R.

OTTOMAN

NORWAY

DENMARK

North Sea

Lübeck

Hamburg

Elbe R.

Oder R.

HOLY
ROMAN
EMPIRE

Köln

Rhine R.

NETHERLANDS

Vienna

SWISS CONFEDERATION

MILAN

MODENA

SAVOY

GENOA

FLORENCE

VENICE

(PART OF VENICE)

Adriatic Sea

SIENA

Rome

PAPAL
STATES

NAPLES

SICILY

SARDINIA

Mediterranean Sea

AFRICA

SCOTLAND

Edinburgh

ENGLAND

London

IRELAND

Atlantic

Ocean

Paris

Seine R.

Loire R.

FRANCE

Garonne R.

Bordeaux

Bay of Biscay

Rhône R.

Barcelona

Ebro R.

NAVARRE

Madrid

SPAIN

Tagus R.

Guadalquivier R.

PORTUGAL

1558–1603. ELIZABETH I, brought up a Protestant. **Sir William Cecil** (Baron Burleigh, 1571) secretary of state. **Sir Nicholas Bacon** lord privy seal. Repeal of the Catholic legislation of Mary; reenactment of the laws of Henry VIII relating to the Church; **act of Supremacy, act of Uniformity.** Revision of the prayer book.

1559, April 3. Treaty of Cateau-Cambrésis with France. Calais to be ceded to England in eight years.

On the accession of Francis II, king of France, Mary Stuart, his wife, assumed the title Queen of England and Scotland. Conformity exacted in Scotland. Adoption of a **Confession of Faith** by the Scotch estates. Mary returned to Scotland (1561) after Francis II died and was at once involved in conflict with the Calvinists **(John Knox).**

1563. Adoption of the **Thirty-Nine Articles.** Completion of the **establishment of the Anglican church** (Church of England, Episcopal church). A compromise church, largely Protestant in dogma (though many of the thirty-nine articles are ambiguous), but with a hierarchical organization similar to the Catholic and a liturgy reminiscent of the Roman Catholic. Numerous **dissenters** or **nonconformists: Puritans—** even then a broad, inexact term, covering various groups that wished to "purify" the Church; to substitute a simple early-Christian ritual for the existing ritual, to make the Church more "Protestant"; **Separatists,** Puritans who left the Anglican church entirely to organize their own churches; **Presbyterians,** Puritans who sought to substitute organization by presbyters and synods for organization by bishops within the Anglican church: **Brownists,** extreme leftist Puritans religiously, the nucleus of the later **Independents** or **Congregationalists;** Brownists and Catholics alone of the Elizabethan religious groups could not be brought under the queen's policy of toleration within the Anglican church. Elizabeth therefore did not "tolerate" and did "persecute" Catholics, Brownists, and, of course, Unitarians (who denied the doctrine of the Trinity).

1564. Peace of Troyes with France. English claims to Calais renounced for 222,000 crowns.

In Scotland Mary married her cousin Henry Stuart, **Lord Darnley,** who caused her favorite, David Rizzio, to be murdered (1566) and was himself murdered (Feb. 10, 1567) by Earl Bothwell. The exact part played by Mary in these intrigues is still debated by historians. **Marriage of Mary and Bothwell** (May 15, 1567). The nobles under Earl Moray, Mary's natural brother, revolted, defeated Mary at **Carbury Hill,** near Edinburgh, and imprisoned her at Lochleven Castle. **Abdication of Mary** in favor of her son, by Darnley, **James VI** (July 24, 1567). **Moray** (Murray), regent. In May 1568 Mary escaped from captivity; defeated at **Langside** on May 13, she took refuge in England, where, after some delay, she was placed in confinement (1568).

1577. Alliance of Elizabeth and the Netherlands.

1583–84. Plots against the queen; execution of the **earl of Arundel** for corresponding with Mary.

1585. Troops sent to the aid of the Dutch Republic under the **earl of Leicester. Victory of Zutphen** (Sept. 22, 1586).

1586. Expedition of **Sir Francis Drake** to the West Indies, sack of Santo Domingo and Cartagena; rescue of the Virginia colony.

1586. Conspiracy of **Savage, Ballard, Babington,** and others, discovered by the secretary of state, **Sir Francis Walsingham;** execution of the conspirators. The government involved Mary, queen of Scots, in the plot. She was tried at Fotheringay Castle (Oct.) and convicted on the presentation of letters that she alleged to be forged. She was convicted on Oct. 25 and executed on Feb. 8, 1587.

1587. WAR WITH SPAIN. Construction of an English fleet of war against the Spanish Armada (p. 295).

1597. Rebellion of the Irish under **Hugh O'Neill, earl of Tyrone;** Lord Mountjoy quickly subjugated the country (1601). Capture of Tyrone, flight of the **earl of Desmond.**

1600. Charter of the East India Company created a **joint stock venture,** the 219 members each to receive a percentage of the profits proportional to the amount each invested; the crown to participate in election of governor and company officials; company officials exempted from the charter; the company exempted from restrictions on bullion export. First voyages were to the Spice Islands.

1601. Elizabethan Poor Law, preceded by various measures regulating apprenticeship (1563), vagrancy, and so on. This famous law charged the parishes with providing for the needy. The measure implicitly recognized the problem of poverty and the large numbers of displaced persons created by noble enclosure of former common lands and new state authority in English society.

1603–49 (1714). THE HOUSE OF STUART. Personal Union of England and Scotland.

1603–25. JAMES I (as king of Scotland **James VI**), son of Mary Stuart. The Scots had brought him up in the Protestant faith. He was learned and initially popular but was devoted to the theory of the divine right of kingship. In this century the after-effects of the Reformation made themselves felt in England as on the Continent, and in both places resulted in war. Inflation, the debt inherited from Elizabeth, an expensive foreign policy (wars), and their own extravagances forced James I and Charles I to seek financial support from parliament. The sale of monastic lands in the late 16th century, general agricultural improvements and the reclamation of wasteland, and investment in lucrative financial ventures had brought about a social revolution: **the growth of a rich and articulate upper middle class** that wanted to discuss royal expenditure, religious reform, and foreign policy. In effect, this class wanted **sovereignty,** and it was learning to use the power of the purse to get it. In their repeated clashes, kings and parliamentarians both appealed to medieval precedents, which tended to support the crown. In the 1640s, advanced democratic ideas, coupled usually with extreme religious doctrines, appealed in minority groups **(Levelers, Fifth Monarchy Men).**

1603, March 24. James I was proclaimed king; he entered London on May 7 and was crowned on July 25. Presentation of the **millenary petition** immediately after James's arrival in London, signed by 1,000 ministers, asking for the reform of abuses.

1604, Jan. Hampton Court Conference, between the bishops and the Puritans, James presiding. The Puritans failed to secure any relaxation of the rules of the Church. James issued a proclamation enforcing the **act of Uniformity** and another banishing Jesuits and seminary priests. Friction between the king and parliament over a disputed election in Bucks.

1604, March 19–1611, Feb. 9. First parliament of James I. The king's scheme of a real union of England and Scotland unfavorably received. Appointment of a commission to investigate the matter.

Convocation (ecclesiastical court and legislature, at first established [Edward I] as an instrument for ecclesiastical taxation; afterward convened by archbishops for the settlement of church questions; since Henry VIII, convened only by writ from the king, and sitting and enacting canons only by permission of the king) adopted some new canons which bore so hard upon the Puritans that 300 clergymen left their livings rather than conform.

1604. Peace with Spain. James proclaimed King of Great Britain, France, and Ireland (Oct. 24). Punishment of many recusants (under the recusancy laws of Elizabeth, whereby refusing to attend services of the Church of England and celebrating or assisting at the Roman Catholic Mass were severely punished).

1605, Nov. 5. GUNPOWDER PLOT, originating in 1604 with **Robert Catesby,** a Catholic, after the edict banishing Roman Catholic priests. Preparations for blowing up the Houses of Parliament with 36 barrels of gunpowder. Disclosure of the plot led to arrest of **Guy Fawkes** in the vaults on Nov. 4, the day before the meeting of parliament. Trial and execution of the conspirators.

1606. Plague in London. **Episcopacy restored in Scotland.** James urged the union anew but in vain.

Impositions. The grant of customs duties made at the beginning of every reign (tonnage and poundage, established by Edward III) proving insufficient to meet James's expenditure, he had recourse to impositions without parliamentary grant, which Mary and Elizabeth had used only to a small extent. Trial of Bates for refusing to pay an imposition on currants. The court of exchequer decided in favor of the king.

1611. Plantation of Ulster, which was forfeited to the crown by the rebellion of Tyrone.

1611. Completion of the **translation of the Bible,** which was authorized by the king and had occupied 47 ministers since 1604.

1614, April 5–June 7. Second parliament of James I. Three hundred new members, among whom were **John Pym** (Somersetshire), **Thomas Wentworth** (Yorkshire), **John Eliot** (St. Germains). The whole session was spent in quarreling with the king over the impositions, and parliament was dissolved without making an enactment, whence it is called the Addled Parliament.

1615. Rise of George Villiers in the king's favor; Viscount Villiers, earl, marquis, **duke of Buckingham.**

1621, Jan. 30–1622, Feb. 8. Third parliament of James I. The parliament granted a supply for the prosecution of the war in the Palatinate (p. 303), in which James was halfhearted, and then took up the subject of grievances. **Impeachment of Francis Bacon** (1561–1626), famous essayist and writer on scientific method, lord chancellor since 1618. Bacon admitted that he had received presents from parties in suits but denied that they had affected his judgment. He was fined £40,000 (which was remitted) and declared incapable of holding office in the future. Petition of the commons against popery and the Spanish marriage. The angry rebuke of the king for meddling in affairs of state drew from the parliament.

1621, Dec. 18. The GREAT PROTESTATION: "That the liberties, franchises, privileges, and jurisdictions of parliament are the ancient and undoubted birthright and inheritance of the subjects of England, and that the arduous and urgent affairs concerning the king, state, and defense of the realm . . . are proper subjects and matter of council and debate in parliament." The king tore the page containing the protestation from the journal of the commons, dissolved parliament (Feb. 8, 1622), and imprisoned **Southampton, Coke, Pym,** and **Selden.**

1623. Charles, prince of Wales, and the **duke of Buckingham** went to Spain and negotiated a marriage treaty, the provisions of which were so favorable to the Catholics as to excite great dissatisfaction in England.

1624, Feb. 12–1625, March 27. Fourth parliament of James I. The Spanish marriage was broken off, but even the anger of Buckingham could not drive the parliament into a declaration of war with Spain. Supplies voted for defense. Mansfeld raised 1,200 men in England who reached Holland, but nearly all perished there from lack of proper provisions. This was, in fact, a breach with Spain. Marriage treaty with France for the marriage of Prince Charles with **Henriette Marie,** sister of Louis XIII.

1625–49. CHARLES I.

1625, May 11. Marriage of Charles I and Henriette Marie. Ships sent to Louis XIII secretly engaged not to fight against the Huguenots.

1625. First parliament of Charles I. (Assembled on June 18; adjourned to Oxford on July 11; dissolved on Aug. 12.) Grant of tonnage and poundage for one year only, and of £140,000 for the war with Spain.

1626, Feb. 6–June 15. Second parliament of Charles I. Charles had hoped for a more pliable parliament, as he had appointed several of the leaders of the first parliament sheriffs and so kept them out of the second. But this parliament, under the lead of **Sir John Eliot,** was more intractable than the last. **Charges against Buckingham,** on which that lord was impeached (May). Imprisonment of Sir John Eliot and Sir Dudley Digges, who were set at liberty only upon the refusal of parliament to proceed to business without them.

1626–30. War against France. Inglorious expedition of Buckingham to the relief of Rochelle (1627).

Exaction of a **forced loan** to raise money for the French war.

1628, Mar. 17–1629, Mar. 10. Third parliament of Charles I. (May): Passage of the **PETITION OF RIGHT:** (1) Prohibition of benevolences and all forms of taxation without consent of parliament. (2) Soldiers should not be billeted in private houses. (3) No commission should be given to military officers to execute martial law in time of peace. (4) No one should be imprisoned unless upon a specified charge. Assent of the king (June 7). Grant of five subsidies.

Charles having, after the first year of his reign, continued to levy tonnage and poundage, the commons drew up a remonstrance against that practice. **Prorogation of parliament** (June 26). Seizure of goods of merchants who refused to pay tonnage and poundage.

Assassination of Buckingham (Aug. 23) by Felton, a disgruntled naval officer.

1629, Jan. New session of parliament. The Commons at once took up the question of **tonnage and poundage.** Turbulent scene in the House of Commons; the speaker held in the chair while the **resolutions of Eliot** were read: Whoever introduced innovations in religion, or opinions disagreeing with those of the true Church; whoever advised the levy of tonnage and poundage without grant of parliament; whoever voluntarily paid such duties, was an enemy of the kingdom.

1629. Eliot and eight other members were arrested (March 5); Eliot died in the Tower in Nov. 1632 and the others made submission. **Parliament dissolved** (March 10). For 11 years (1629–40) Charles governed without a parliament, raising money by hand-to-mouth expedients, reviving old taxes and old feudal privileges of the crown and selling monopolies. These were rarely wholly illegal but seemed to parliamentarians contrary to the spirit of the constitution. **Charles's advisers: William Laud** (1573–1645), bishop of London, 1628, archbishop of Canterbury, 1633; **Thomas Wentworth** (1593–1641), earl of Strafford and lord lieutenant of Ireland, 1639. Both were extremists. Strafford's policy embittered Ireland. **Peace was made with France** (April 1630) **and with Spain** (Nov. 1630). Conformity was enforced.

1634. The tax that focused hatred on Charles was **ship-money,** by which a writ issued in 1635 extended to the whole country a tax hitherto levied only on seaboard towns. **John Hampden,** a Buckinghamshire country gentleman, defying the tax, was tried, 1637–38, and lost his case in court but won it with the public.

1637. An attempt to read the English liturgy in Edinburgh, ordered by Charles, produced a **riot at St. Giles's** (June 23). This was followed by the organization of the Scottish Presbyterians to resist episcopacy. On Feb. 28, 1638, was signed the **Solemn League and Covenant** (whence Covenanters) for the defense of the reformed religion. In November a general assembly at Glasgow abolished episcopacy, settled liturgy and canons, and gave final form to the **Scottish Kirk.**

1639. The First Bishops' War. The Scots seized Edinburgh Castle and raised an army. Charles marched to meet them near Berwick but concluded with them, without battle, the **pacification of Dunse** (June 18).

1640. Charles, in trouble in Scotland and financially distressed in England, now called his **fourth parliament,** the Short Parliament at Westminster (April 13–May 5). This parliament, refusing to vote money until grievances were settled, was immediately dissolved. By the **treaty of Ripon** (Oct. 26) Charles agreed to pay the Scottish army £850 a day until a permanent settlement could be made. These obligations made the calling of a parliament inevitable.

1640. The **LONG PARLIAMENT, the fifth parliament of Charles I** (Nov. 3, 1640–March 16, 1660). First session until Sept. 8, 1641.

The fact that the Scottish army was not to be disbanded until paid gave the commons an unusual hold over Charles. On Nov. 11, **Strafford was impeached,** followed by **Laud,** and both were sent to the Tower. At the trial of Strafford, impeachment being uncertain, a bill of attainder was introduced which passed both commons and lords in April. Strafford was executed on May 12. Meanwhile, parliament passed the revolutionary **Triennial Act,** requiring the summoning of parliament every three years even without the initiative of the crown (May 15, 1641). This was followed in May by a bill to prevent the dissolution or proroguing of the present parliament without its own consent, which Charles reluctantly signed, along with Strafford's attainder. The culmination of radicalism was the introduction of a bill for the abolition of bishops. This was the **Root and Branch Bill,** on which the moderate Puritans split with the more radical Presbyterians.

1641. In August a **treaty of pacification with Scotland** was made, and Scottish and English armies were paid with the proceeds of a special poll tax granted by parliament. Charles took refuge with the Scots. On the proroguing of parliament in September, each house appointed a committee to sit in the vacation (**Pym,** chairman of the commons' committee). Charles attempted to conciliate the moderate parliamentarians by giving office to their leader, Lucius Cary, Lord Falkland.

1641, Oct. 21. Parliament assembled and heard the news of the **massacre of Protestants in Ulster** (30,000 killed). Still unwilling to entrust Charles with an army, it presented him with the **Grand Remonstrance** (Dec. 1) passed in the Commons in November by 11 votes, a summary of all the grievances of his reign.

1642, Jan. 3. The commons put before the king bills excluding bishops from the lords and giving command of the militia to parliament. From York he refused to sign the latter (March), and there he was joined by 32 peers and 65 members of the commons. He also had the great seal. The parliament at Westminster now was obliged to pass ordinances that were not submitted to the king and did not appear under the great seal.

July. Parliament appointed a **committee of public safety** and put Essex in charge of an army of 20,000 foot and 4,000 cavalry. When on

Aug. 22 Charles raised the royal standard at Nottingham, the military phase of the **Great Rebellion** began.

1642–46. THE CIVIL WAR. Roughly, northern and west-central England stood by the king; East Anglia, London, and the south with parliament. Socially, the gentry, the Anglican clergy, and the peasantry were royalist; the middle classes, the great merchants, and many great nobles were parliamentarians. But neither Roundhead (parliamentarian, Puritan) nor Cavalier (royalist) describes completely an economic or social class. Armies were small. Until Cromwell's Ironsides the royalist cavalry was superior. The war was relatively free from excesses.

1642. After the drawn **Battle of Edgehill** (Oct. 23), the king marched on London but turned back at Brentford when confronted by Essex (Nov. 12). The eastern counties raised a force entrusted to **Oliver Cromwell** (1599–1658), which as the Ironsides finally became the best troops in the war. **First Battle of Newbury** (Sept. 20).

Sept. 25. The **SOLEMN LEAGUE AND COVENANT,** signed by 25 peers and 288 members of the commons, agreeing to make the religions of England, Ireland, and Scotland as nearly uniform as possible and to reform religion "according to the word of God, and the examples of the best reformed churches." All civil and military officials were required to sign the covenant (nearly 2,000 clergymen refused and lost their living). The Scots now consented to help the English parliamentarians; a Scottish army crossed the Tweed (Jan. 1644). Charles rashly enlisted Irish Catholic insurgents with whom he concluded peace, (p. 324) thus alienating many Englishmen.

July 2. BATTLE OF MARSTON MOOR. Prince Rupert, after defeating the Scots, was decisively beaten by Cromwell and his Ironsides. This was the crucial battle of the war and gave the north to parliament. York surrendered (July 16); Newcastle (Oct. 16).

In Scotland, **Montrose,** after slipping into the country in disguise (Aug. 1644), raised highland clans for Charles and gained several victories over the Covenanters. At one time he held most of Scotland, but his armies melted away when the parliament sent General Leslie into Scotland after Naseby, and at **Philiphaugh** (Sept. 13, 1645) the Stuart partisans were decisively beaten. Montrose fled to the Continent.

1645, Jan. Laud, tried in March 1644, was attainted and executed. England was fast moving toward extreme Protestantism. With Cromwell, the **Independents** rose to leadership. **Presbyterianism,** with some reservations for the Independents, became the established Church. The **Self-Denying Ordinance** (April 3) having excluded members of either house from military command, Fairfax superseded Essex as captain-general, and Cromwell, with the ordinance suspended in his case, became lieutenant-general. The army was reformed into the New Model on the lines of the Ironsides.

1645, June 14. BATTLE OF NASEBY, decisive defeat of the king, ruin of his cause. Charles surrendered himself to the Scots (May 5).

1647, Jan. 30. The **Scots surrendered Charles to parliament** in return for their back pay (£400,000). He was brought to Holmby House in Northamptonshire. **Army and parliament in open conflict.** Parliament reappointed Fairfax commander in chief, reenacted the self-denying ordinance, and voted the disbandment of all soldiers not needed for garrisons or for service in Ireland. This the army refused to accept, claiming full payment for arrears in salary. A detachment headed by Cornet Joyce seized Charles at Holmby House (June 4) and carried him prisoner to the army, thus forestalling an agreement between king and Presbyterians.

Proposals were presented to the king by the army: that worship be free for all; that parliament control army and navy for ten years and appoint officers of state; that parliament serve for three years (**triennial parliaments**). The king rejected them and moved to take refuge with the Presbyterian members of parliament; but the army entered London (Aug. 6) and forced parliament to take back the members who had fled to the army. Charles removed to Hampton Court, where he rejected a modified form of the previous proposals and fled to the Isle of Wight, where he was detained by the governor of Carisbrooke Castle (Nov. 11).

1648, Jan. 15. Parliament renounced allegiance to the king and voted to have no more communication with him.

1648. SECOND CIVIL WAR. At once a war between Scotland and England, a war between the royalists and the Roundheads, and a war between the Presbyterians and the Independents.

March. At a meeting of army officers at Windsor it was decided to bring the king to trial. Parliament, having reassembled with 306 members (and the Presbyterians again in control), repealed the noncommunication resolution and attempted to reopen negotiations with the king (July).

Aug. 17–20. Battle of Preston. Under the duke of Hamilton, a Scottish army invaded England but was beaten by Cromwell. This ended the second civil war. Parliament having again attempted to treat with the king, **Colonel Thomas Pride,** by order of the council of affairs, forcibly excluded 96 Presbyterian members from the parliament (Pride's Purge, Dec. 6, 7), which is henceforth known as the Rump Parliament (some 60 members).

Dec. 13. The **Rump** repealed the vote to continue negotiations with Charles and voted that Charles be brought to trial. Appointment of a high court of justice of 135 members to try the king was rejected by the lords (1649, Jan. 2), whereupon the commons resolved that the legislative power resided solely with the commons (Jan. 4; passed Jan. 6 without concurrence of the lords).

1649, Jan. 20. The army council drew up a temporary **Instrument of Government.** Charles was tried before the high court (67 members present, Bradshaw presiding), whose jurisdiction he simply denied (Jan. 20–27). **The king was sentenced to death and beheaded at Whitehall** (Jan. 30).   (To p. 319)

CULTURAL DEVELOPMENTS. Inigo Jones (1573–1652) built Lincoln's Inn Chapel, the Banqueting Hall at Whitehall, the Queen's House at Greenwich.

University of Glasgow (1452); University of Aberdeen (1494); St. Paul's School, London (1510); Rugby (1567); Harrow (1571); Trinity College, Dublin (1591).

Prose: Archbishop Cranmer, *Book of Common Prayer;* **Thomas More** (1478–1535), *Utopia,* 1516; **Roger Ascham** (1515–68), *The Schoolmaster;* **Raphael Holinshed** (d. 1580), *Chronicles of England, Scotland, and Ireland;* **Richard Hakluyt** (1552–1616), *Principall Navigations, Voyages and Discoveries of the English Nation,* 1589; **Richard Hooker** (1554–1600), *Laws of Ecclesiastical Polity;* **Sir Philip Sidney** (1554–86), poet and critic, *Defense of Poesie;* **Sir Walter Raleigh** (1552–1618), *The History of the World;* **John Lyly** (1554–1606), *Euphues; The Anatomy of Wit;* the essayist **Francis Bacon** (1561–1626), *Essays, New Atlantis,* 1621; **Robert Burton** (1577–1640), *Anatomy of Melancholy;* the political philosophers **Thomas Hobbes** (1588–1679), *Leviathan,* 1651, and **James Harrington** (1611–77), *Oceana,* 1656; **Izaak Walton** (1593–1683), *The Compleat Angler,* 1653; **Sir Thomas Browne** (1605–82), *Religio Medici.*

Poets: Edmund Spenser (c. 1552–99). *Faerie Queene;* **Sir Walter Raleigh; Sir Philip Sidney; Ben Jonson** (1573–1637); **John Donne** (1573–1631).

Composers: Thomas Tallis (c. 1505–85); **William Byrd** (1540–1623); **Orlando Gibbons** (1583–1625).

Miracle plays ceased after the Reformation, but dramas in a popular vein were produced. **Christopher Marlowe's** use of blank verse in his morality plays (*Dr. Faustus,* 1588; *The Jew of Malta,* 1589) established its use in the English theater.

William Shakespeare (1564–1616) was the greatest dramatist of the Elizabethan or any other age. The power of his dramas derives from his extraordinary development of individual characters, his forceful and precise vocabulary, and the universal and enduring appeal of his plots to other ages and other cultures. Many of his plays, especially the tragedies, relied on history for their stories (*Julius Caesar, Henry IV, Henry V, Henry VI*); the greatest tragedies are probably *Hamlet, King Lear, Othello,* and *Macbeth;* among the comedies are *A Midsummer Night's Dream, As You Like It,* and *Twelfth Night.* Shakespeare also wrote some of the best sonnets in the English language, using a rhyme scheme of his own devising; also lyrics, incorporated in the narrative poems *Venus and Adonis* and *The Rape of Lucrece* and often in the plays.

Shakespeare established the drama as a respected literary medium. The collaborators **Francis Beaumont** (1579–1625) and **John Fletcher** (1584–1616) dared to poke fun at their society (*The Knight of the Burning Pestle,* 1607).

John Milton (1608–74), the blind poet of the Puritan Revolution, composed sonnets and lyric poems (*L'Allegro, Il Penseroso, Lycidas*) in his youth; published his three major poems after the Restoration (*Paradise Lost,* 1667; *Paradise Regained,* 1671; *Samson Agonistes,*

1671); and a *History of Britain to the Conquest* (1670). During the 20 years of political unrest he wrote prose tracts in support of liberty—in religion, education, and the press (*Areopagitica*, 1644).

c. THE NETHERLANDS

The provinces of the **Low Countries** (so called because much of the land lies below sea level), originally inhabited by Batavians and other Germanic tribes, had formed a part of the empire of Charlemagne and, after the **treaty of Mersen** (870), belonged in large part to Germany, forming a dependency of the kingdom of Lotharingia. The decline of the ducal power favored the growth of powerful counties and duchies, such as Brabant, Flanders, Gelders, Holland, Zeeland, Hainault, and the bishopric of Utrecht. After 1384 the provinces were brought under the control of the dukes of Burgundy in the following manner: **Philip II** (the Bold), fourth son of **John II** of France, became the duke of Burgundy in 1363. He acquired Flanders and Artois (1384) through marriage with Margaret, heiress of Count Louis II. Their son was **John the Fearless,** duke of Burgundy (1404–19), who was succeeded by his son, **Philip the Good** (1419–67). Philip acquired Namur by purchase (1425). Brabant and Limburg came to him by bequest (Joanna, daughter of John III, duke of Brabant, left them to her great-nephew, Antoine, brother of John the Fearless). In 1433 he acquired Holland, Hainault, and Zeeland by cession from Jacqueline, countess of Holland; and in 1443, Luxemburg, by cession from Elizabeth of Luxemburg. He also added Antwerp and Mechlin. His son, **Charles the Bold** (duke of Burgundy 1467–77), acquired Gelderland and Zutphen by bequest from Duke Arnold (1472).

Mary, the daughter and heiress of Charles the Bold, married **Maximilian,** archduke of Austria and later emperor (p. 261). Their son, **Philip the Handsome** (duke of Burgundy), married **Joanna,** the daughter of Ferdinand of Aragon and Isabella of Castile, and thus the Netherland provinces passed ultimately into the hands of Philip's son, **Charles I** (Charles V as emperor).

1548. Charles annexed the 17 provinces (Brabant, Limburg, Luxemburg, Gelderland, Flanders, Artois, Hainault, Holland, Zeeland, Namur, Zutphen, East Friesland, West Friesland, Mechlin, Utrecht, Overyssel, Groningen) to the Burgundian circle of the empire.

1556. Abdication of Charles. The Netherlands, like Spain, passed to his son.

1556–98. PHILIP II.

1567–1648. REVOLT OF THE NETHERLANDS. The provinces had long enjoyed ancient and important privileges. The estates (*staaten, états*) granted taxes and troops. The Spanish garrison, the penal edicts against heretics, the dread of the introduction of the Spanish Inquisition, all these factors led (during the rule [1559–67] of **Margaret of Parma,** the natural sister of Philip II, and her adviser, **Cardinal Granvelle**) to the formation of a **league of nobles** (Compromise of Breda), headed by Philip Marnix of St. Aldegonde.

Religious background: the 13th-century tradition of the **Beguines,** communities of women who led lives of prayer and meditation; the 14th-century **Brethren of the Common Life,** groups of pious laypeople who living in stark simplicity provided relief to the poor, taught the young, and emphasized the centrality of scripture in the Christian life—these groups found in most large cities of the Low Countries; great mobility of merchants who traveled widely and brought back **Lutheran and Calvinist ideas;** the high level of literacy in an urban commercial society with many able to read Luther's and Calvin's writings. **Calvinism took firm root in the northern provinces,** commonly called Holland (the southern provinces, now Belgium, remained Catholic).

To finance the government, Margaret raised taxes, thus uniting opposition to the government's fiscal policies with its official repression of Calvinism.

1566, Aug. A year of high grain prices. Fanatical Calvinists of the poorest classes incited by popular preaching embarked on a wave of iconoclastic destruction of artwork, libraries, and churches in Antwerp; disorders spread to Ghent and Brussels. These disturbances initially opposed by Lamoral, Count of **Egmont** (1522–68), and **William of Nassau,** prince of Orange (1533–84), later called **William the Silent** because of his reputation for diplomatic tact, and other members of the great nobility who, however, lost control of the movement. Revolt, sparked by

religious and economic protests and by sectional discontents, won support by uniting the elite classes' appeal to constitutionalism (royal attacks on aristocratic liberties) with the general population's antipathy to Spanish outsiders.

1567. Philip sent to the Netherlands the duke of Alva (1508–82) with an army of 20,000. Creation of a tribunal at Brussels to investigate rebellion and heresy, subsequently called the Council of Blood because 18,000 executed, including the Catholic Egmont, Hoorn, and other prominent figures. Estates of those who failed to appear before the tribunal, including those of William of Orange, confiscated; additional arbitrary taxes levied. These measures led (1568) to open rebellion against Spanish rule.

1572–76. The northern provinces under leadership of William of Orange expelled the Spanish garrisons, but in 1576 the Spanish capture of Antwerp, Maestricht, and Ghent led to the **PACIFICATION OF GHENT,** a treaty among all the provinces by which they united, without regard to national or religious differences, to drive out the Spaniards. The new governor, **Don John of Austria,** was unable to quiet the country, despite disputes between the various parties.

1578–92. Don John died in 1578 and was succeeded by **Alexander Farnese (duke of Parma),** a shrewd statesman and an excellent general. Parma ultimately subdued the southern provinces, on the promise that their old political freedom should be restored. The seven northern provinces (Holland, Zeeland, Utrecht, Gelderland, Groningen, Friesland, Overyssel) thereupon concluded the **UNION OF UTRECHT** (1579), followed by a proclamation of **independence from Spain** (1581). The office of **stadholder,** chief executive officer of a Dutch province that later formed union, the United Provinces, and usually a member of the House of Orange, was settled on William of Orange. After his murder at Delft (July 10, 1584), he was succeeded by his son.

1584. Maurice of Nassau, son of William of Orange, was only 17 years old when he assumed stadholdership. Parma continued his victorious campaigns and managed to capture Antwerp. Thereupon the English came to the aid of the insurgents.

1588. Philip II, hoping to put an end to the Anglo-Dutch combination, organized the **Armada,** which was defeated by the English and destroyed in a terrible storm (p. 288).

1609. The **Twelve Years' Truce** put an end to sporadic and inconclusive fighting and essentially established the independence of the northern provinces. After its expiration the war was resumed by the Spaniards. The Hollanders, who had grown rich and powerful at sea in the course of the struggle, were well able to hold their own, and finally

1648. The **TREATY OF WESTPHALIA** (p. 304) recognized the independence of the Republic of the United Provinces. The **Dutch Republic** was a confederation, a weak union of strong provinces, in each of which an oligarchy of wealthy merchants, the regents, handled nearly all matters in the local Estates. A "national" body, the **States General** (the legislative assembly of representatives of the orders or classes of society) appointed the stadholder for each province. The States General also handled foreign affairs, but major decisions had to be referred back to provincial Estates for approval.

Political power and economic strength rested on great commercial prosperity: the fishing industry (herring), shipbuilding, a vast merchant marine; the Bank of Amsterdam the best source of cheap credit and commercial intelligence in Europe. (To. p. 325)

1602. The Dutch East India Company (Oost Indische Compagnie), chartered by regents of the States General, was granted a monopoly on Dutch trade east of the Cape of Good Hope, west of the Strait of Magellan. The company subdued local rulers; drove Portuguese and British traders from the Spice Islands (Moluccas), Malaya, and Ceylon (p. 373); and controlled this rich trade, primarily in nutmeg and cloves. In the 1630s a phenomenally high return (35 percent) paid to investors.

1621. The Dutch West India Company chartered by the States General with a monopoly on trade in African and North American waters.

1626. This led to establishment of Fort Amsterdam on southern tip of Manhattan island, after **1664** New York (p. 411).

1652. Jan van Riebeeck founded a fueling station for the Dutch East India Company (p. 395) at the Cape of Good Hope. In middle decades of the 17th century, prodigious wealth enabled the Dutch to enjoy the highest standard of living in Europe in a cosmopolitan society unique for its spirit of religious toleration.

CULTURAL DEVELOPMENTS. Josquin Des Près (c. 1445–1521)

composed sacred songs in the polyphonic style of the Flemish school, which dominated 16th-century Renaissance music: for example, the madrigals of **Adrian Willaert** (1480–1563); the sacred and secular songs of the greatest Flemish composer, **Orlando di Lasso** (1532–94). The religious tradition in painting carried over from the **Van Eycks, Hans Memling** (c. 1433–95), and **Hieronymus Bosch** (1460–1516) to the engravings of **Lucas Van Leyden** (1494–1533) and the paintings of **Quentin Massays** (c. 1466–1530). **Pieter Breughel** (1525–69) painted both religious and everyday subjects, with the addition of humorous, earthy touches.

The golden age of painting occurred in the first half of the 17th century, especially with the portraits and religious paintings of **Peter Paul Rubens** (1577–1640); the portraits of **Anthony Van Dyck** (1599–1641), court painter to Charles I of England, and **Franz Hals** (1580–1666); the landscapes of **Meyndaert Hobbema** (1638–1709) and **Jacob Ruysdael** (1628–82); the genre works of **Jan Vermeer** (1632–75) and Jan Steen (1625–79); and culminating in the work of **Rembrandt van Rijn** (1606–69): his numerous paintings of himself and of Saskia (1633–41), *The Anatomy Lesson* (1632), *The Night Watch* (1642), his etchings, and his religious paintings.

Hugo Grotius (1583–1645) laid the bases of international law in his *Mare liberum* (1609) and *De jure belli ac pacis* (1625).   *(To p. 325)*

d. FRANCE

(From p. 247)

1483–98. CHARLES VIII. Death of the duke of Brittany (1488) called forth a coalition of the empire, Spain and England to preserve the independence of the duchy, but this proved futile. Charles married Anne, the heiress, in 1491 and concluded the **Treaties of Senlis** (with the emperor) and **Étaples** (with England). Spain was bought off by the cession of Roussillon and Cerdagne.

1495–96. Charles's expedition to Italy to claim the inheritance of Naples (through his father from Charles, duke of Maine and Provence; see genealogical table). Charles marched victoriously through Italy and conquered Naples (bringing the venereal disease **syphilis,** which rapidly spread across Europe), but he was soon obliged to withdraw in the face of the **Holy League** (Emperor Maximilian, Pope Alexander VI, Spain, Venice, Milan, and England), formed to protect Italy from foreign domination. Expedition led to the introduction of Renaissance culture into France and marked beginning of Habsburg (Spanish)–Valois (French) conflict (1494–1559) over Italy.

1498–1589. HOUSES OF ORLÉANS AND ANGOULÊME. Branch lines of the house of Valois (since 1328), whose relation to the main line is shown on page 292.

1498–1515. LOUIS XII obtained a divorce from Jeanne, daughter of Louis XI, and married **Anne of Brittany,** widow of Charles VIII, in order to keep this duchy for the crown; as grandson of Valentina Visconti he laid claim to Milan and drove out Ludovico Moro, who was imprisoned when he tried to return (1500).

1501. Louis, in alliance with Ferdinand the Catholic, king of Aragon, conquered the kingdom of Naples. The Spaniards and French soon falling out, the latter were defeated by the Spanish general Gonzalvo de Córdoba on the Garigliano (1503). Louis XII gave up his claims to Naples.

1508. League of Cambrai (p. 300). In 1511 the pope, Ferdinand the Catholic, and Venice renewed the **Holy League,** with the object of driving the French out of Italy. The latter, under the young **Gaston de Foix,** duke of Nemours, nephew of Louis XII, were at first successful in the war, taking Brescia (1512) by storm and defeating the united Spanish and papal armies at **Ravenna,** with the aid of 5,000 German mercenaries, in the same year; they were, however, compelled by the Swiss to evacuate Milan. In 1513 the French formed a new alliance with Venice but were defeated by the Swiss at **Novara** and withdrew from Italy. **Henry VIII of England,** who had joined the Holy League in 1512, and the **Emperor Maximilian,** who had joined in 1513, invaded France.

1513, Aug. 17. They defeated the French at **Guinegate,** called the Battle of the Spurs from the hasty flight of the French.

France concluded peace with the pope, with Spain (1511), with the emperor, and with Henry VIII (1514). Anne of Brittany having died,

Louis took as his third wife Mary, the sister of Henry VIII. He died soon after the marriage (1515).

1515–47. Louis was succeeded by his cousin and son-in-law, the count of Angoulême, **FRANCIS I.**

1515, Sept. 13–14. Francis reconquered Milan by the brilliant **victory of Marignano** over the Swiss. Peace and alliance between France and Switzerland. **Treaty of Geneva** (Nov. 7, 1515); **Treaty of Fribourg** (Nov. 29, 1516). The latter *(la paix perpétuelle)* endured until the French Revolution.

1516. Increase of the royal power by the **concordat of Bologna** with the pope, which rescinded the Pragmatic Sanction of 1438 and placed the choice of bishops and abbots in the hands of the king; the pope on the other hand received the annates, or the first year's revenue of every ecclesiastical domain where the king's right of presentation was exercised. Francis in return abandoned the principle of the council of Basel that the pope was subordinate to an ecumenical council.

Francis invited the Florentine artists Leonardo da Vinci, Andrea del Sarto, and Benvenuto Cellini and the architect Rosso to grace and decorate his court; established lectureships that formed the basis of the Collège de France; and supported the navigator **Jacques Cartier** (1491–1557), who established French interests in North America.

1536. The humanist and theologian **John Calvin** (1509–64) published the *Institutes of the Christian Religion* (definitive edition 1559), a systematic theology for Protestantism; because of its social and economic implications and Calvin's remarkable facility with language (French) the work won a wide readership and many converts, especially in urban centers such as Paris, Lyons, and Grenoble. Members of the **Reformed Church,** as Calvinists were called, became the dynamic force in international Protestantism.

1539. Royal ordinance (issued by Council) placed all of France under the jurisdiction of the royal courts with French the language of the courts; this law had a strongly centralizing effect.

1547–59. HENRY II, son of Francis. Growing power of the **house of Guise** (Francis, duke of Guise, and **Charles,** cardinal of Lorraine). Persecution of the Protestants in France; assistance to German Protestants with goal of keeping Germany divided and weak.

1547. Final union of Brittany with the French crown.

1548. Massive peasant revolt in Aquitaine, where they refused to pay the *Gabelle,* tax on salt.

1552–59. Intermittent War with Spain. The French were defeated by the Spaniards, who were supported by the English, in the **Battle of St. Quentin** (1557) and by Egmont at **Gravelines** (1558).

1558. Calais, the last English possession in France, was captured by the duke of Guise.

1559, April 3. PEACE OF CATEAU-CAMBRESIS, which ended the Habsburg-Valois wars. Henry II, who died of a wound received in a tournament, succeeded by his son.

1559–60. FRANCIS II, the first husband of Mary Stuart of Scotland, who was a niece of the Guises. Measures against the Protestants *(chambres ardentes).* The king's mother, **Catherine de' Medici** (1519–89), struggled for power and influence against the Bourbon princes: **Anthony** (king of Navarre) and **Louis de Condé,** who were descended from Louis IX. The **Guises,** at first rivals of the queen-mother and then in alliance with her, conducted the affairs of state and surpassed in influence their opponents, the Catholic constable, **Montmorency,** and his nephews, the three Châtillon brothers: **Gaspard, Admiral de Coligny; François d'Andelot,** and **Cardinal Châtillon,** later leaders of the Huguenots. Death of Francis II.

1560–74. CHARLES IX (ten years old), the brother of Francis. He was wholly under the influence of his mother. Weak monarchy and civil war characterized the latter part of the century.

1562–98. THE RELIGIOUS WARS. Persecution compelled the **Huguenots** (as the French Protestants were called—derivation uncertain) to take up arms. At the same time they formed a political party. Taking advantage of monarchial weakness, between two-fifths and one-half of the nobility at one time or another adopted the reformed religion as a cloak for political independence; the struggles thus constituted a civil, as well as a religious, war. Many new capitalists and artisans also turned Protestant. Save in the southwest, very few peasants became Protestants. Paris and the northeast remained Catholic throughout.

1569. TEMPORARY PEACE after Protestant losses at battles of Dreux (1562), Jarnac (1569), Moncontour (1569).

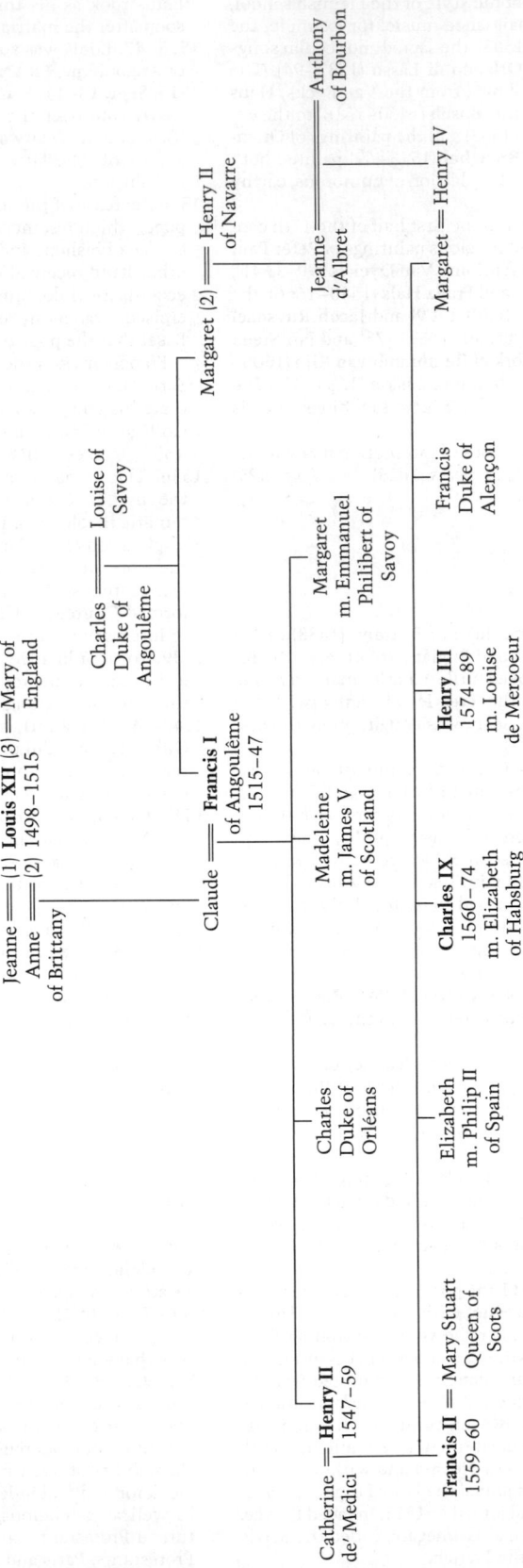

THE LAST VALOIS KINGS (1498–1589)

Jeanne ══ (1) **Louis XII** (3) ══ Mary of
Anne ══ (2) 1498–1515   England
of Brittany

Charles ══ Louise of
Duke of   Savoy
Angoulême

Margaret (2) ══ Henry II
                of Navarre

Anthony
of Bourbon

Jeanne ══ Margaret ══ Henry IV
d'Albret

Claude ══ **Francis I**
            of Angoulême
            1515–47

Charles
Duke of
Orléans

Madeleine
m. James V
of Scotland

Margaret
m. Emmanuel
Philibert of
Savoy

Francis
Duke of Alençon

Catherine ══ **Henry II**
de' Medici   1547–59

Elizabeth
m. Philip II
of Spain

Charles IX
1560–74
m. Elizabeth
of Habsburg

Henry III
1574–89
m. Louise
de Mercoeur

Francis II ══ Mary Stuart
1559–60   Queen of
               Scots

1572, Aug. 23–24. MASSACRE OF ST. BARTHOLOMEW. Murder of Coligny and general massacre of Protestants in Paris and in the provinces, on the occasion of the marriage of **Henry of Bourbon,** king of Navarre, and the sister of Charles IX, **Margaret of Valois.** Henry of Navarre saved his life by a pretended conversion to Catholicism. The massacre led to

1572–73. Renewal of war. La Rochelle, a Protestant stronghold, besieged by Henry, brother of Charles IX, made a brave defense. The election of the duke of Anjou to the crown of Poland brought about a compromise. **Edict of Boulogne** (July 8, 1573) ended the war favorably for the Huguenots.

Charles IX died on May 30, 1574. His brother, who fled from Poland, became king.

1574–89. HENRY III.

1574–76. Another renewal of war, during which **Henry of Navarre** reassumed the Protestant faith, was concluded by conditions more favorable to the Huguenots than those of any previous peace. **Peace of Chastenoy** (Paix de Monsieur, after the duke of Alençon) on May 6, 1576. Hence dissatisfaction among the Catholics. Origin of the French **Holy League** (1576), which, in alliance with Philip II of Spain, purposed the annihilation of the reformed party and the elevation of the Guises to the throne. The king, fearing the league, proclaimed himself its head and forbade the exercise of the Protestant religion throughout France. The Protestants and moderate Catholics had joined forces in 1575 by the **confederation of Milhaud.**

1584. The death of Francis, duke of Alençon, the younger brother of the king, rendered the extinction of the house of Valois certain. As it was the intention of the Holy League to exclude from the throne Henry of Navarre, who belonged to the reformed religion, and to give the crown to the latter's uncle, the **cardinal of Bourbon,** and as the league meantime had induced the king to revoke the concessions granted to the Huguenots, broke out a war.

1585–89. War of the Three Henrys (Henry III of Valois, Henry of Navarre, Henry of Guise). The Catholic party triumphed in spite of the **victory of Coutras** (Oct. 20, 1587), gained by Henry of Navarre. Formation of the **League of Sixteen** at Paris, which purposed the deposition of the weak king. Guise entered Paris, was received with acclamation (King of Paris); the timid resistance of the king was broken by a popular insurrection (Day of the Barricades, May 12, 1588). Henry III fled to Blois, where he summoned the Estates General of the kingdom. Finding no support among them against the Holy League, he caused Henry, duke of Guise, and his brother, Louis the Cardinal, to be murdered (Dec. 23, 1588). At this news, a revolt of the Catholic party broke out, headed by the brother of the murdered men, the **duke of Mayenne.** Henry III fled to Henry of Navarre in the Huguenot camp, where he was murdered at St. Cloud, a suburb of Paris, by the monk **Jacques Clément** (July 31). The wars destroyed agriculture in many parts of France, and commerce severely weakened. France experienced **thirteen general famines** in the 16th century.

1589–1792. HOUSE OF BOURBON, descended from Louis IX's younger son Robert, count of Clermont, husband of Beatrice of Bourbon.

1589–1610. HENRY IV. The Catholic Party refused to recognize Henry and made the old cardinal of Bourbon king under the name **Charles X** (1590). Victory of Henry IV over the duke of Mayenne at **Arques** (1589).

1590, March 14. In the **Battle of Ivry,** crucial battle of these wars, Henry IV was also victorious. Henry's ultimate success was made possible by the *politiques,* often moderate Catholics, but above all patriots who believed no religious creed was worth the chronic disorder and destruction, and who maintained that only a strong French monarchy could prevent complete collapse. The political philosopher **Jean Bodin** (1530?–96) in *Six Books of the Commonweal* (1576) held that religious toleration and the establishment of a sovereign monarchy were essential to the restoration of public order; Bodin is a prominent theoretician of the modern national state. Henry abjured the reformed religion at St. Denis (1593) and was crowned at Chartres (1594). Brissac having thereupon surrendered Paris to him, the power of the Holy League was broken. Not, however, until Henry, after public penance by his ambassadors at Rome, had been freed from the papal ban was he generally recognized (by Mayenne too).

1598, April 13. The civil wars of religion were ended by the **EDICT OF NANTES,** which gave the Huguenots equal political rights with the Catholics but not complete freedom of religious worship. The edict granted the exercise of the reformed religion to nobles having the right of criminal jurisdiction *(seigneurs hauts justiciers)* and to the citizens of a certain number of cities and towns, but prohibited it in all episcopal and archiepiscopal cities, at the court of the king, and in Paris, as well as within a circle of 20 miles around the capital. Public offices were opened to the Huguenots and **mixed chambers** were established in four *parlements* (Paris, Toulouse, Grenoble, Bordeaux). The Huguenots obtained some fortified towns and were recognized, to a certain extent, as an armed political party. **Treaty of Vervins** (May 2, 1598) with Spain; restoration of all conquests to France.

Adoption of measures looking to the improvement of the finances and the general prosperity, which had gone to decay, especially by Rosny, afterward **duke of Sully** (1560–1641). Grand Design, attributed to Henry IV by Sully in his *Mémoires,* for the ensurance of perpetual peace through organization of a Christian Republic with the Holy Roman Emperor as first magistrate and a general council of Europe to discuss affairs of common interest and if possible settle disputes. Intended primarily to limit the Habsburg power, this plan is interesting as one of many projects for organizing Europe and ending war. In the midst of great preparations for war, **Henry was assassinated** at Paris (May 14, 1610) by the fanatic **François Ravaillac.**

1610–43. LOUIS XIII, his son, nine years old. Regency of his mother, **Marie de' Medici** (1573–1642). Sully removed from office; the Italian **Concini** placed in control of affairs. Louis XIII, declared of age in 1614, was in fact all his life under the guidance of others. **Summons of the estates-general,** 1614, being the last before the Revolution of 1789. Arrest and murder of Concini; the queen-mother banished to Blois (1617). The king under the influence of his favorite, the duke of Luynes. By the mediation of Armand-Jean du Plessis (1585–1642), **cardinal-duke of Richelieu,** a treaty was concluded between Luynes and the queen-mother (1619). New **civil war.** Contest of the crown with the nobility and the Huguenots. After the death of Luynes (1621), Marie de' Medici and her favorite, Richelieu, obtained control of affairs.

1624–42. Administration of Richelieu, whose influence over the king was henceforward unbroken. Numerous conspiracies against him instigated by Gaston of Orléans, the king's brother.

1625. Revolt of the Huguenots under the dukes of Rohan and Soubise.

1627–28. Siege of La Rochelle under the personal supervision of Richelieu. Despite the dispatch of three fleets from England to the aid of the Huguenots, the city surrendered on Oct. 28, 1628, after a heroic resistance of 14 months. Defeat of the duke of Rohan and complete subjugation of the Huguenots, who thereafter were no longer an armed political party but only a tolerated sect.

War in Italy with Spain; subjugation of Savoy, Richelieu at the head of the army.

1631. Treaty of Cherasco. France renounced all conquests in Italy, but by a secret treaty with Victor Amadeus, duke of Savoy, Pignerol was surrendered to France.

1631–48. FRENCH PARTICIPATION IN THE THIRTY YEARS' WAR (pp. 304–305).

Richelieu's fundamental goal was the establishment of a strong monarchy through the subordination of its historic enemy, the nobility; the reduction of the parliaments and the Huguenots; and the strengthening of the state bureaucracy *(intendants).* Although he wrote, "Finances are the sinews of the state," 17th-century France remained "a collection of local economies and local societies dominated by local elites," and Richelieu's power to tax was severely limited. His foreign policy was more successful. He restored French influence in Italy, the Netherlands, and Germany and established it in Sweden. His work laid the foundation for the power of Louis XIV and became the traditional basis of French foreign policy.   *(To p. 326)*

CULTURAL DEVELOPMENTS. The literature of the French Renaissance bore the stamp of Italy. **François Rabelais** (1494–1553), a former friar, satirized the foibles of his society in *Pantagruel* (1532) and *Gargantua* (1534). His books also bear testimony to the importance the Renaissance placed on humanistic education. The poets **Pierre de Ronsard** (1524–85) and **Joachim du Bellay** (1522–60) were the leaders of **La Pléiade,** a group of young poets who urged the use of the French language in literature, at the same time reverting to a classical style. **Michel Eyquem de Montaigne** (1533–92) introduced a question-and-answer technique in his *Essais* (1580–88); his influence on the philosophy, style, and form of later writers such as Rousseau and the essayist Charles Lamb was marked.

In the 16th century several of the chateaux in the Loire Valley were built. The sculptors **Michel Colombe** (1430–1512), **Jean Goujon** (1515–60), and **Germain Pillon** (1535–90) were active; and **François Clouet** (1516–72) painted royal portraits.

e. THE IBERIAN PENINSULA

(From p. 251)

1. SPAIN

1479–1516. REIGN OF FERDINAND of Aragon and his wife, **ISABELLA,** queen of Castile (1474–1504). During this period much progress was made, notably in Castile, toward the suppression of the fractious aristocracy and the regulation of the Church. Aragon, on the other hand, retained most of its privileges. Ferdinand devoted his efforts to the conclusion of profitable marriage alliances and to the furtherance of his designs in Italy, which brought him into conflict with France and other Italian powers.

In the 14th century, economic dislocation, the search for scapegoats during visits of the Black Death, and anti-Jewish preaching contributed to growing anti-semitism in Spain. In 1331, a mob attacked the Jewish community of Gerona in Catalonia; in 1335, royal troops massacred Jews in Toledo; in 1391, mobs sacked and burned the Jewish community in Seville, and from Seville, anti-semitic pogroms swept Valencia, Majorica, Barcelona, Burgos, Madrid, and Segovia. Those forced to convert were called "New Christians."

In the 15th century, New Christians held high positions in the administration of Castile, including the royal secretaryship; controlled the royal treasury; composed one-third of the royal council; were archbishops, bishops, and abbots; included some of the leading merchants; intermarried with the nobility; and held prominent positions in law and medicine. They numbered perhaps 200,000 in a total population of 7.5 million. New Christians, also called *conversos,* insisted their faith was identical *to* that of other Christians. Detractors stressed not belief, but blood, developing the racial theory that New Christians were the same as their ancestors, Jews. This theory emerged at the same time as Spanish nationalism. Courting public opinion, on **Sept. 28, 1480,** Ferdinand and Isabella (with papal permission) established the Inquisition, ecclesiastical tribunals to judge "heretical depravity . . . to search out and punish converts from Judaism who had transgressed against Christianity by secretly adhering to Jewish beliefs and performing Jewish rites." The inquisition became an important instrument of Spanish royal policy. The Most Catholic kings, as they were called, had the able assistance of **Francisco Jiménez de Cisneros** (1436–1517), an austere Franciscan and (1507) cardinal: he directed the **forcible conversion** of the **Muslims of Granada;** pressed **monastic reform** and education of the clergy; served as **regent of Castile** (1506–7); and financed and led an **expedition to Africa** (1510–11), resulting in the capture of Oran.

The centuries-long *reconquista* (reconquest), the term given the Crusades led by the northern kingdoms to expel the Muslims from the Iberian peninsula by 14th-century clerical propagandists, ended **Jan. 2, 1492** with the **conquest of Granada.**

1492, March 11. Ferdinand and Isabella **expelled the Jews** from Spain, giving them four months to leave. Many went to Istanbul and other parts of the Ottoman Turkish empire.

1494. Foundation of the Consulado for foreign trade at Burgos. This chamber and the Casa de Contratación at Seville (1503) undertook to regulate Spanish trade and had much to do with the commercial expansion of the 16th century.

1500. By the **Treaty of Granada,** France and Spain again engaged to cooperate in Italian affairs, but friction over Naples soon led to hostilities. Victories of the great Spanish commander **Gonzalvo de Córdoba** (especially at **Garigliano,** 1503). Aragon retained Naples.

1503. The first gold from Mexico arrived at the Port of San Lucar at Seville. Beginning of Spanish emigration to the Americas.

1504. The **death of Isabella** made **Joanna** (wife of Philip, archduke of Austria) legal heiress to Castile. Ferdinand, who had long planned the union of Castile and Aragon, in Joanna's absence secured from the Cortes authority to carry on the government in his daughter's behalf. In 1506 Philip and Joanna came to claim their inheritance. **Treaty of Villafavila** between Philip and Ferdinand, the former securing the regency. Philip's death in the same year and the **insanity of Joanna** (kept in confinement for 49 years, d. 1555) allowed Ferdinand to resume control.

1509–11. African campaigns, organized, financed, and led by **Cardinal Jiménez de Cisneros** (1436–1517), aided by **Pedro Navarro.** Cisneros was one of the ablest statesmen of his time who, having reformed the Spanish church, now devoted himself to the crusade. The Spanish forces took Oran, Bougie, and Tripoli and forced the Muslim rulers to pay tribute.

1511. The **Holy League** (the pope, Ferdinand, and Venice) against France and the Empire. **Victory of the league at Novara** (1513). At the same time (1512) the Spaniards conquered **Navarre,** which was annexed to the Castilian crown, though it retained its own government (1515).

1516. The death of Ferdinand led to the **regency of Cardinal Cisneros,** who vigorously repressed incipient disturbances by the nobles. The crowns now passed to the son of Philip and Joanna, Charles of Ghent, who became

1516–56. CHARLES I of Spain, founder of the Spanish **Habsburg dynasty.** Charles, who had been educated in Flanders, arrived (1517) with a large Flemish following, which regarded the Spaniards with disdain. Dissatisfaction of the Spaniards with Charles's election to the imperial throne (1519) led to widespread opposition to his leaving the country and using Spanish money and men for imperial purposes.

1520–21. UPRISING OF THE *COMUNEROS*. A group of cities (led by Toledo and by the Toledan **Juan de Padilla**) took issue with the government and organized a **Holy League** (Santa Junta) at Avila (July 1520). Though this was originally as much an aristocratic as a bourgeois movement, radical tendencies soon appeared and the noble elements withdrew. After the **defeat of the *comuneros* at Villalar** (April 23, 1521), the leaders were executed and government authority reestablished.

1521–29. War between France and Spain, the result of French support of the *comuneros* and French designs on Navarre. The French took Pampeluna and Fontarabia, but Charles, supported by the pope, Florence, and Mantua, expelled the French from Milan (1522). In 1524 the Spanish commanders, the **Constable de Bourbon** and the **Marqués de Pescara,** invaded Provence and advanced to Marseilles. Francis I was decisively defeated and captured at the **Battle of Pavia** (Feb. 24, 1525) and in captivity at Madrid was obliged to sign the **Treaty of Madrid,** by which he abandoned his Italian claims and ceded Burgundy. On his release he violated his promises and the war was resumed. By the **Treaty of Cambrai** (1529), Charles was obliged to renounce Burgundy, while Francis once more abandoned his claims to Naples.

1535. The expedition of Charles to Tunis, part of a great duel between Spain and the Ottoman Turks.

1535–38. Another war with France, arising from the succession to Milan (p. 297), led to another invasion of Provence (1536) and to the inconclusive **Treaty of Nice** (1538).

1545. Discovery of silver mines at Potosi in (what was then) Peru (p. 403).

1546. Discovery of silver at Zacatecas in Mexico; the quinto, or one-fifth of all mines' production, belonged to the Spanish crown.

1551–59. The last war between Charles and the French kings, ending in the **Treaty of Cateau-Cambrésis** (April 3, 1559) (p. 295).

Charles I (Charles V as emperor) gave Spain efficient government, continuing the work of Ferdinand and Isabella. On the other hand, his imperial position resulted in the involvement of Spain in all general European problems and in the expenditure of much blood and money, the latter drain not so noticeable at the time because of the great influx of gold from the New World.

On the abdication of Charles I, Spain and the colonies, as well as the Netherlands, Franche-Comté, Naples, and Milan passed to his son

1556–98. PHILIP II (b. at Valladolid in 1527), the most Spanish of the Habsburg rulers and a monarch who spent most of his reign in Spain. He was grave, serious yet affable, and conscientious to a fault in his bureaucratic duties. Philip's most serious defect was a certain rigidity: tenaciously clinging to an idea. His policy centered on the determination to defend the faith and to stamp out Protestantism, and further to stand by the Habsburg interests, outside as well as inside Spain. This involved constant intervention in general European affairs and costly wars. During this period the Spanish infantry (largely volunteer and with a considerable noble element) reached the pinnacle of its prestige.

Philip married four times: **Mary of Portugal,** mother of Don Carlos; **Mary the Catholic,** queen of England; **Elizabeth of Valois; Anne of Austria,** daughter of Maximilian II.

1556–59. Continuance of the **war with France.** Victories of the Spaniards under the **duke of Alva,** at **St. Quentin** (Aug. 10, 1557) and at **Gravelines** (July 13, 1558), led to the **Treaty of Cateau-Cambrésis** (April 3, 1559), which reaffirmed the Spanish possession of Franche-Comté and the Italian states. The capital was definitively established at **Madrid.** In 1563 the construction of the Escorial Palace was begun.

1560–1600. Acceleration of emigration to the Americas: about 240,000 men and women, many of whom were *conversos,* Spaniards of Jewish ancestry; some, such as at least one brother of St. Teresa of Avila, returned to Spain having made fortunes.

1567. Beginning of the Netherlands' prolonged struggle for independence (p. 290).

1567–1616. The identification of religious heresy with sexual deviance led to the execution by burning of 71 men convicted of *pecado nefando,* anal intercourse with other men, at Sevilla.

1569–71. Revolt of the Moriscos (converted Muslims suspected of secretly retaining their original faith). The rising was put down with great severity and ultimately (1609) the Moriscos were expelled from Spain.

1571. Discovery of mercury mines in Peru and the development of new silver refining process led to flood of silver into Spain (p. 403). Philip used this wealth to finance his military ventures; anticipated galleons of silver served as basis for credit extended by Genoese bankers.

1571, Oct. 7. Battle of Lepanto. The naval fleet of the Holy League (Spain, Venice, and the papacy) under Don John of Austria met the Ottoman navy in a bay at the mouth of the Gulf of Patras off Lepanto in western Greece (p. 352). The Ottoman fleet was hardly prepared; most of its sailors had been sent home for winter and the remaining officers were involved in political quarrels. Superior European numbers and command prevailed and the Ottoman fleet was routed. While Europe celebrated a great victory, the battle was not decisive: the Ottomans quickly rebuilt their navy with larger vessels, and their ability to ravage the coasts of Sicily and Italy in 1573 and to seize Tunis in 1574 showed that they retained control of the western as well as the eastern Mediterranean. The spell of complete Ottoman supremacy, however, had been broken, and the Christian galleys gained a huge crop of prisoners to man the oars.

1580. Philip succeeded to the **Portuguese throne** (p. 296).

1587. Sir Francis Drake destroyed the Spanish fleet at Cadiz. England had for some time been incurring the displeasure of Philip; the succession of Elizabeth and the progress of Protestantism, the aid given the Dutch rebels, and the piratical raids on the Spanish treasure ships all were factors. The **execution of Mary Stuart** (1587) brought matters to a crisis.

1588, Aug. 8. Philip sent against England the Spanish fleet, "la felicissima armada" (the most fortunate armada") as it was ironically called. Comprising 130 vessels and perhaps 30,000 men, it sailed from Lisbon harbor and met 150 smaller, more maneuverable English ships in the Channel, where the English attacked (Aug. 8). (p. 290). Storms, spoiled food and rank water, inadequate ammunition, and, to a lesser extent, English fire ships that caused the Spanish to scatter combined to give England the victory. The Spanish soon rebuilt their navy and the war continued.

The battle proved that Philip II could not reimpose Catholicism on western Europe by force.

1589–98. War with France, arising from Philip's intervention against Henry IV. The Spaniards played an important role in this last phase of the religious wars in France but failed to attain their objectives. The war ended with the **Treaty of Vervins** (p. 293).

1599–1600. Devastating plague hit Castile, causing labor shortage, rapid rise in wages, psychological depression, and increased illegal emigration to the Indies.

1598–1621. PHILIP III, the son of Philip II by his last marriage. A melancholy, retiring, and deeply religious man, the king devoted himself

to the interests of the Church (9,000 monasteries in this period and one-third of the population in the church service). Philip left the government to his favorite *(privado),* the **duke of Lerma.** Formation of elaborate court ceremonial to emphasize the sacred character of the king; vast court nobility; growth of huge estates. Philip II had financed imperialist ventures in Europe by borrowing on future imports of silver, which in 1570s and 1580s created false sense of endless wealth. Decline in silver imports forced the crown to repudiate state debts, which undermined confidence in government; population decline caused by war, plague, and emigration led to marked decline in agriculture, trade, and industry. Increasing sense that the costs of empire outweighed its presumed or real benefits.

1618. Beginning of the Thirty Years' War (p. 303), into which Spain was drawn by Habsburg interests and religious considerations.

1621–65. PHILIP IV, an amiable prince, not interested in politics and therefore quite content to leave the conduct of affairs to his *privado,* the **Count-Duke Olivares** (1587–1645; count of Olivares, duke of Sanlúcar), an able and patriotic administrator who, until his fall in 1643, made valiant efforts to modernize the governmental system by means of greater centralization and increase of the royal power.

1622. The occupation of the **Valtelline Pass** (between Milan and the Austrian lands) by the Spanish led to war with France, which, in a sense, was merely one aspect of the Thirty Years' War. France, under the able leadership of Richelieu, gradually established its ascendancy over Spain.

1640–59. The great **REVOLT IN CATALONIA,** a direct result of the policy of Olivares. The king's failure to summon the Catalan Cortes, the imposition of new taxes, the demands for aid for the foreign wars, the quartering of troops in the country, and in general the centralizing tendencies of the count-duke precipitated the conflict. The movement was supported by France, which even recognized a **Catalan republic.** After the struggle had gone on for 12 years, Barcelona was obliged to submit (Oct. 1652). In the final settlement (1659) the Catalans retained most of their former rights and privileges.

1643, May 19. The Battle of Rocroi in Picardy. Defeat of the Spanish infantry is generally taken as marking the end of supremacy.

1648. The peace of Westphalia (p. 304). This did not apply to the war between France and Spain, which continued for another 11 years.

1658, June 14. Battle of the Dunes; decisive defeat of the Spaniards.

1659, Nov. 7. TREATY OF THE PYRENEES (signed on the Isle of Pheasants, in the Bidassoa River). Spain was obliged to cede to France the frontier fortresses in Flanders and Artois as well as Roussillon and Cerdagne. Louis XIV married Maria Teresa, daughter of Philip IV.

(To p. 329)

CULTURAL DEVELOPMENTS. Culturally speaking, the entire 16th century and the first half of the 17th century comprised Spain's golden age, a period of humanism: **Luis Vives** (1492–1540), for a time professor at Oxford; **Elio Antonio de Nebrija** (or Lebrija), the leading humanist (1444–1532); **Juan del Encina** (c. 1469–1529), popular dramatist; poets **Garcilaso de la Vega** (1503–36) and **Juan Boscán Almogáver** (d. 1542); **Luis Ponce de León** (b. 1528), theologian, poet, and one of those who made Castillian a great literary language. To this period belong the first printings of the chivalrous romance *Amadis de Gaul* (1508) and the first realistic novel, *Celestina* (c. 1499). **Religious leadership** in the cause of Roman Catholicism: **Arias Montano** (1527–98) one of the outstanding scholars at the **Council of Trent; Francisco Suarez** (1548–1617), a Jesuit, a neoscholastic and an outstanding jurist *(De Legibus ac Deo Legislatore,* 1612); while **Francisco de Vitoria** (1486–1546) wrote extensively on the government of the colonies and became a pioneer of international law *(De Indis et de iure belli relectiones,* 1532). In political theory **Juan Marquez** (1564–1621), *El Gobernador cristiano* (1612), and **Diego Saavedra Fajardo** (1584–1648), *Idea de un Principe politico cristiano* (1640). At the same time the Spaniards took the lead in the work of the Catholic Reformation. **Ignatius of Loyola** (Iñigo Lopez de Recalde, 1491–1556) with five associates founded the **Society of Jesus, Jesuits,** which was officially approved by Pope Paul III in 1540. The first Jesuits, recruited primarily from the wealthy merchant and professional classes, saw the Reformation as a pastoral problem, its causes and cures related less to doctrinal issues than to the spiritual condition of the persons concerned. Although the Reformation played no role in the future they planned for themselves, the highly centralized Jesuits became major agents in the Catholic Reformation through missionary activity (eastern Europe, India, China, Japan, the Americas), preaching, and superb teaching. **Sta. Teresa de Jesús** (1515–82) undertook the reorganization of the Carmelite nunneries and, in her autobiography and her *Castillo interior*, made outstanding contributions to mystical literature, as did **San Juan de la Cruz** (1542–91), her disciple, who effected similar reforms of the monasteries.

The period was one of equal greatness in the realm of literature and art. **Juan de Mariana** (1536–1624) wrote a popular history of Spain and an important work on political theory, *De Rege et Regis Institutione* (1599), while **Bartolomé de Las Casas** (1474–1566), **Fernandez de Oviedo,** and **Lopez de Gómara** distinguished themselves in treatments of the New World. **Felix Lope de Vega** (1562–1635), who produced more than 2,000 plays, poems, and stories, was one of the great literary figures of all time and a founder of the modern drama; **Tirso de Molina** (c. 1571–1648) and **Pedro Calderón** (1600–1681) continued the drama on a high plane; **Miguel de Cervantes Saavedra** (1547–1616) in his *Don Quijote* (1605) produced an incomparable picture of the Spain of his day and at the same time one of the world's most popular masterpieces. In the same year, **Mateo Alemán** (1547–1610) published the second part of *Guzmán de Alfarache*, a picaresque novel with a moral for each adventure.

In the field of art the Italian influence was very strong, though the **Escorial** (begun in 1563 and built by **Juan de Herrera**) had a severe style of its own. But the achievements of painting overshadowed those of the other arts. **El Greco** (1541–1614; really a Greek [Kyriakos Theotokopoulos] from Crete, trained in Italy) came to Spain in 1575 and lived at Toledo until his death in 1614. One of the greatest painters of the Renaissance, he was the first of a number of world-famous artists: **José Ribera**, called Spagnaletto (1588–1652); **Francisco de Zurbarán** (1598–1664); **Bartolomé Murillo** (1617–82); **Juan de Valdés Leal** (1630–91); and above all the incomparable **Diego Rodríguez de Silva y Velásquez** (1599–1660). In music **Tomás Luis de Vittoria** was a worthy contemporary of Palestrina.

2. PORTUGAL
(From p. 251)

1495–1521. MANOEL I (the Great, the Fortunate), brother-in-law of John II. His reign and that of his successor mark the apogee of Portuguese power and empire, following the great discoveries (**Vasco da Gama's** voyage to India, 1497–98; **Pedro Alvares Cabral's** discovery of Brazil, 1500; **Magellan's** circumnavigation of the globe, 1519–22 (p. 278). The new empire was at first ruled by men of ability and courage (**Francisco de Almeida**, first viceroy of the Indies, 1505; **Afonso de Albuquerque**, viceroy, 1507–11) and brought in large returns. Lisbon displaced Venice as the entrepôt for Asian goods and became a center of wealth and luxury. Colonial trade was a royal monopoly, and the court became a mecca for concession seekers.

1497. To facilitate a marriage alliance with the Spanish crown, Manuel ordered the **EXPULSION OF THE JEWS.** He wanted to eliminate Judaism, while retaining the Jews for their wealth and business acumen. On March 19 during the Passover holiday he ordered that all Jewish children age 4 to 14 be separated from their parents and baptized. As Jews naturally would not leave without their children, all tolerated forced baptism. The decree of expulsion did not have to be carried out, because now all Portuguese Jews were conversos, baptized Christians.

1490–1550. Steady **importation of black slaves** (between 300 and 2,000 annually from 1490 to 1530 entered the port of Lisbon); they supplemented the labor force, especially in agriculture, the manufacture of olive oil, as domestic servants in aristocratic and religious households, as seamen. By 1550 blacks constituted 10 percent of the populations of Lisbon and Evora, 3 percent of total Portuguese population.

On the **Madeira, Cape Verde, and Azores islands,** the Portuguese, following a pattern of economic organization long used by the Genoese in Sicily and Majorca, used black slave labor in the production of **sugar** in **plantation societies** that served in effect as laboratories for later plantation economies in Brazil, the Caribbean, and North America. Thus, an "American" form of slavery existed before the "discovery" of America.

1500, April 22. Pedro Alvares Cabral sighted the coast of **Brazil** and claimed it for the Portuguese crown (p. 278).

1521–57. JOHN (João) III (the Pious), during whose reign the **Inquisition** (pp. 249, 402) was established in Portugal (1536).

1557–78. SEBASTIAN I, the grandson of John, succeeded. Regency of his mother, Joanna of Austria, a daughter of Charles V, until 1562, followed by the regency of **Cardinal Henry** (Enrique), brother of John III and grand inquisitor. Sebastian himself was educated by the Jesuits and was consumed with the idea of a crusade against the infidel, which he undertook despite the contrary advice of Philip II of Spain and of the pope.

1578, Aug. 4. The **BATTLE OF AL KASR AL-KABIR** (Alcazar-Qivir), in which the Portuguese and their mercenary troops were completely defeated by the Moors. Sebastian, the king of Fez, and the Moorish pretender all lost their lives (battle of the three kings).

1578–80. CARDINAL HENRY, king.

1580. Death of **Luis de Camões** (b. 1524), greatest of Portuguese poets (*The Lusiads*, published 1572), whose work served as a profound commentary on Portuguese national life and imperial enterprise.

1580. A **regency of five** was established to govern the country on the death of Cardinal Henry. There were no less than seven claimants to the throne, of whom the most powerful was **Philip II of Spain** (son of Isabella, the daughter of Manoel I) and the most popular was **Antonio,** the prior of Crato (illegitimate son of Luis, the brother of John III). Philip's candidacy was supported by the high clergy and by part of the nobility. Antonio enjoyed the support of the townsmen and of the peasants and was backed by France.

Aug. 25. The Spaniards, under the duke of Alva, invaded Portugal and defeated their opponents in the **Battle of Alcántara,** near Lisbon.

1580–98. PHILIP I (Philip II of Spain), who was accepted by the Cortes. Philip promised to respect the rights of the country and to rule only through Portuguese. He himself generally observed this obligation, but under his successors it was often ignored. First Portugal itself, then the Portuguese Empire was turned over to Spanish officials. The result was growing discontent in Portugal and increasing weakness abroad. After the defeat of the Spanish armada (1588; p. 295), the British and the Dutch began to attack the Portuguese possessions, many of which were conquered before 1640.

1598. Dutch trade with Lisbon was prohibited. This marked the beginning of Dutch enterprise in the east and of the gradual conquest of Portuguese possessions.

1640, Dec. 1. REVOLT OF THE PORTUGUESE, inspired and organized by **João Ribeiro,** a professor at the University of Coimbra, and supported by the nobility and clergy. The insurgents, all disillusioned with Spanish rule, took advantage of the revolt in Catalonia. Like the Catalonians they were supported by France, which was at war with Spain. The Spanish government, unable to devote much attention to Portugal, could not prevent the **election of John of Braganza** to the throne.
(To p. 331)

f. ITALY

(From p. 259)

1. THE ITALIAN WARS

The period from about 1450 to 1550 marked not only the apogee of the Renaissance but also the intellectual and artistic primacy of Italy. In the field of history and political science, **Francesco Guicciardini** (1483–1540; *Istoria d' Italia* published only in 1561) and **Niccolò Machiavelli** (1469–1527; *Il Principe*, 1513) were outstanding. In art history, *Lives of the most excellent painters, sculptors, and architects* (1550, rev. ed. 1568), by **Giorgio Vasari** (1511–74), stands as the first and most influential of all critical histories of art. The satirist **Pietro Aretino** (1492–1556) used the shock of sex in **pornography** as a vehicle to criticize: his *Sonnetti lussuriosi* (1527) and *Ragionamenti* (1534–36), sonnets accompanying 16 engravings of as many sexual positions, attacked princely court life, humanist education, and false clerical piety, while **Baldassare Castiglione** (*Il Cortegiano*, 1528) produced a famous handbook of the courtier. **Ludovico Ariosto** (1474–1533; *Orlando Furioso*, 1516) was one of the greatest epic poets of all time. In the field of music **Giovanni da Palestrina** (1525–94; at St. Peter's after 1551) and **Orlando di Lasso** were men of the first rank. Architects and painters of eminence are too numerous to be listed, and it will suffice to recall names like **Leonardo da Vinci** (1452–1519); **Raffael Santi** (1483–1520; *Sistine Madonna*, 1516); **Michelangelo Buonarroti** (1475–1564; Sistine Chapel paintings, 1508–12, 1534–41; dome of St. Peter's, 1547); **Andrea del Sarto** (1486–1531); **Giorgione da Castelfranco** (1477–1510); **Titian** (Tiziano Vecelli, 1477–1576); **Gentile Bellini** (1429–1507); **Tintoretto** (Jacopo Robusti, 1518–94); **Paolo Veronese** (1528–88); **Sofonisba Anguissola** (c. 1530–1625) of Cremona, who produced superb family portraits and was the first woman artist to achieve international renown; **Andrea Mantegna, Allegri da Correggio, Benvenuto Cellini,** and the extraordinary and formidable woman artist **Artemisa Gentileschi** (1593–c. 1652), whose *Judith and Holofernes* reflects her bloodthirsty themes.

Politically, however, Italy was divided and soon became the "cockpit" of Europe, the victim of the rivalries of the rising monarchies, which coveted the wealth of the peninsula. There were, at the time, five major Italian states: **Venice,** the strongest of all, deriving its wealth and influence from the extensive eastern trade, from its possessions in the Adriatic, Ionian, and Aegean Seas, and from domination of the neighboring mainland; **Milan,** ruled by Ludovico Sforza and commanding the rich valley of the Po; **Florence,** long one of the most progressive of Italian communities, having attained to great splendor under Lorenzo the Magnificent; the **Papal States,** carved from the central part of the peninsula and in process of expansion under the political popes of the late 15th century; the **kingdom of Naples,** deeply involved in the Middle East, ruled by a branch of the Aragonese house. These states maintained a precarious balance among themselves but were almost all so imperialistic that they were constantly endeavoring to victimize one another and ultimately reached the point of calling in the foreigner, with the result that Italy became the prey of French, German, and Spanish ambitions.

1492. Formation of a secret alliance between Florence and Naples for the spoliation of Milan. This led to Ludovico Sforza's appeal to Charles VIII of France to make good the Anjou claims on Naples.

1494–95. THE FRENCH INVASION OF ITALY. Charles arrived in September and met with no real resistance. Florence submitted but then drove out **Piero de' Medici** (Nov.) and abandoned the French connection. Thereupon Charles attacked and took Florence, which was obliged to give up Pisa and other towns. Charles advanced on Rome (Jan. 1495) and thence into Naples. Alfonso fled to Sicily, leaving Naples to his son Ferrante, who was driven out by a revolt. The French entered Naples (Feb. 22, 1495), but their very success led to the formation of a coalition directed against them: Milan, Venice, Emperor Maximilian, Pope Alexander VI, and Ferdinand of Aragon leagued together against Charles, forcing his retreat to the north. The Spaniards (Gonzalvo de Córdoba) soon reconquered Naples.

1499, Feb. Venice agreed to support the claims of Louis XII of France to Milan in return for a promise of Cremona. The French thereupon invaded Italy a second time (Aug.) and forced **Ludovico Sforza** to flee from Milan to Germany. Milan surrendered (Sept. 14). The next year Sforza returned with an army of German mercenaries and obliged the French to evacuate. Before long the German forces began to disintegrate and the French returned to Milan. Sforza was captured and died (1508) in a French prison. Milan thus became French.

1500, Nov. 11. By the **Treaty of Granada,** Ferdinand of Aragon agreed to support Louis's claim to Naples, which was to be divided between France and Spain. In 1501 (June) the French army, marching south, entered Rome, whereupon the pope declared Federigo of Naples deposed and invested Louis and Ferdinand with the kingdom. The French took Capua (July), while the Spanish fleet seized Taranto (March 1502). So much having been gained, the two allies fell to quarreling over the division of the spoils, and war resulted (July). The Spaniards at first suffered reverses but in 1503 defeated a French fleet and won a decisive victory at **Cerignola** (April 28). They took Naples (May 13), and after another victory at **Garigliano** (Dec. 28), forced the French to surrender at **Gaeta** (Jan. 1, 1504). This completed the Spanish conquest of Naples, which, with Sicily, gave them control of southern Italy, as the French had control of Milan in the north.

1508, Dec. 10. The **LEAGUE OF CAMBRAI,** organized to despoil Venice of its possessions on the mainland and in Apulia. Emperor Maximilian promised Louis XII the investiture of Milan in return for support. Ferdinand of Aragon and Pope Julius II joined the coalition. The French attacked and defeated the Venetians at **Agnadello** (May 14, 1509). Sur-

render of Verona, Vicenza, and Padua, which were handed over to Maximilian. But the Venetians soon rallied and retook Padua (July 17), which was besieged in vain by Maximilian. Vicenza too rose against the emperor and recalled the Venetians. After a French victory at **Ravenna** (Easter, 1512), even the emperor and the Swiss cantons joined the coalition against the French, who were driven out of Milan (May). In a **congress of the league at Mantua** (Aug.), the Spaniards forced the Florentines to take back the Medici and join the league. Milan was given to Maximilian Sforza (son of Ludovico). The war continued until the French were badly defeated at **Novara** (June 6, 1513), after which the pope, Ferdinand, and Henry of England all made peace.

1515. The new French king, **Francis I,** as deeply interested in Italy as his two predecessors and quite as adventurous, concluded an alliance with Henry VIII and Venice against the emperor Maximilian, the pope, Ferdinand, Milan, Florence, and the Swiss. The French won a great victory at **Marignano** (Sept. 13), by which they recovered Milan. Thereupon the pope came to terms, surrendered Parma and Piacenza, and in return secured the **Concordat of Bologna** (p. 291). After the death of Ferdinand (Jan. 1516), his successor, Charles I (later Emperor Charles V), confronted with problems in Spain and Germany and eager to secure European cooperation against the advance of the Ottoman Turks, concluded with Francis the **Treaty of Noyon** (Aug. 13, 1516), by which the French retained Milan but gave up their claims to Naples. Maximilian returned Brescia and Verona to Venice in consideration of a money payment.

1522–23. First of the **Habsburg-Valois Wars,** (p. 294) for many of which Italy became a battlefield. The pope and England supported Charles V against Francis. Having been driven out of Milan, Parma, and Piacenza, the French were defeated at **Bicocca** (April 27, 1522) and retained only the citadel of Milan. In May they were even driven from Genoa, their all-important sea base. But in Oct. 1524 the French invaded Italy with a large army and retook Milan (Oct. 29). The pope changed sides and joined the French.

1525, Feb. 24. The **BATTLE OF PAVIA,** the most important engagement of the long Italian wars. The Spanish commanders, **Constable de Bourbon** (prominent French noble and opponent of Francis) and **Marquís de Pescara,** completely defeated the French. Francis himself was captured and sent to Madrid. There he concluded the **Treaty of Madrid** (Jan. 14, 1526) (p. 294).

1526, May 22. The **LEAGUE OF COGNAC,** a coalition of Francis I, the pope, Sforza, Venice, and Florence against Charles and the Spaniards. The league was the natural result of the too great success of the Spaniards in Italy, and the objective was to restore the status quo of 1522. But the Spaniards forced Sforza out of Milan (July 24) and before long attacked Rome (Sept. 21).

1527, May 6. The pope was helpless and could not prevent the **SACK OF ROME** by the Spanish and German mercenaries of Charles. The sack was horrible even when judged by the customs of the day.

May 17. Florence rose against the Medici, who were again driven out and replaced by a republic (under **Niccolò Capponi**). **Genoa also revolted,** under **Andrea Doria.** The French were expelled and a republican constitution established. The French, however, having overrun Lombardy (Oct.), began to march south. Meanwhile the pope, who had fled to Orvieto (Dec.), made his peace with Charles (**Treaty of Barcelona,** June 29, 1529—the Papal States to be restored and the Medici returned to Florence).

1529, Aug. 3. The war was ended by the **Treaty of Cambrai** (p. 300).

1535. The **death of Francesco Sforza** opened the question of the Milanese succession. Charles V claimed it as suzerain, but the French invaded Italy and took Turin (April 1536). After an invasion of Provence by the imperialists, the **truce of Nice** was concluded for ten years (June 18, 1538). It reaffirmed the Treaty of Cambrai, but the French remained in occupation of two-thirds of Piedmont and the emperor retained the rest.

1542–44. The **war between Francis I and Charles V,** though fought in the Netherlands and Roussillon, had repercussions in Italy. The **Treaty of Crespy** (Sept. 18, 1544) involved abandonment of French claims to Naples.

1556. Alliance of Pope Paul IV and Henry II of France to get Naples. The French, under the **duke of Guise,** invaded Italy but were obliged to withdraw after their defeat at **St. Quentin** (1557). This practically ended the French struggle for Italy. The **Treaty of Cateau-Cambrésis**

(April 3, 1559) involved the abandonment of French possessions, except Turin, Saluzzo, and Pignerol.

2. THE PAPACY
(From p. 253)

For a complete list of the Roman popes, see Appendix IV.

The Florentine political theorist Niccolò Machiavelli's remark captures the moral disorder in the leadership of the Church in the earlier part of this period: "We Italians are irreligious and corrupt above others, because the Church and her representatives set us the worst example." Most of the popes were typical products of the Renaissance, patronizing the arts, living in splendor and luxury, using their position either to aggrandize their families or to strengthen the temporal position of the Church. Of spiritual leadership there was little, yet politically and culturally the period was of the utmost importance.

1492–1503. ALEXANDER VI (Rodrigo Lanzol y Borgia), a stately, energetic, ruthless, and immoral man, whose life was a scandal. The main objective of his policy was to establish the rule of his family in central Italy. He broke the power of the great Roman families (Orsini, Colonna), and, through his son, **Cesare Borgia** (1475–1507), a former cardinal and the hero of Machiavelli's *Prince*, undertook the conquest of the Romagna. Cesare reduced most of the principalities (1499–1501) and became duke of the Romagna. In 1501 the Borgias joined France in the attack on Naples, and the French aided Cesare in putting down a revolt of his captains at Sinigaglia (Dec. 1502). But the death of the pope and the hostility of the new pontiff, Julius II, frustrated Cesare's schemes. Forced to disgorge his conquests, he turned to Spain for aid. In 1506 he was arrested at Naples and sent to Spain, where he died (1507).

1503–13. JULIUS II (Guillano della Rovere, nephew of Sixtus IV). Although a flourishing pluralist, having accumulated eight bishoprics and one archbishopric (Avignon), Julius was also a skilled diplomat, a financial genius, a brilliant administrator, and an enlightened patron of the arts (employing Michelangelo and Raphael): he ranks as one of the greatest of the popes. Participating himself in the military campaigns, he recovered territories taken by Cesare Borgia and was responsible for reconstituting the Papal State into the form it kept for the next four centuries. Although his interest in Church reform was only occasional, he summoned the **Fifth Lateran Council** (1512–17), in which one serious set of proposals condemned the Renaissance popes for their absorption in politics and bureaucracy; and recommended reform of the Roman Curia; translation of the Bible into the vernacular for the laity; centralization of several religious orders (such as the Benedictines, for whom each house was and still is autonomous); the restriction of admission to holy orders to educated and morally suitable candidates; a thorough revision of the *Code of Canon Law*; and the dispatch of missions to the recently "discovered" continents of America. This reform program was to preoccupy the Church for the next century.

1513–21. Leo X (Giovanni de' Medici, son of Lorenzo the Magnificent. He was a noteworthy patron of the arts and an easy going churchman whose first remark after his election, according to the Venetian ambassador, was "Now that God has given us the papacy, let us enjoy it." Leo continued the Fifth Lateran council called by Julius II, but it yielded no practical results. He also continued Julius's construction of the new St. Peter's, financing it with the sale of indulgences, which in turn provoked Martin Luther's attack on the Church. His pontificate marks the **beginning of the Reformation** (p. 300). Preoccupied with the interests of his family and insulated from currents outside the papal court and Rome, Leo was insensitive to the wider religious problems of his day.

1522–23. ADRIAN VI (of Utrecht), the last non-Italian pope until 1978. Adrian was, at the time of his election, regent of Spain for Charles V. An upright and austere man, he attempted to purge the papacy of abuses and tried to reconcile Charles V and Francis I in order to unite Christendom in a crusade against the Ottoman Turks. His efforts brought him great unpopularity in Italy and conflict, even with Charles V, and he died before accomplishing much.

1523–34. CLEMENT VII (Giulio de' Medici), a hard-working but indecisive pontiff. He failed entirely to cope with the religious revolt in Germany, and failed also to maintain a safe position in the conflict between the French and the Spaniards for domination of Italy. Hence the terrible **sack of Rome** (May 6, 1527; p. 297), which may be said to have brought to a close the greatness of Rome in the Renaissance.

In the papal conclave following Clement's death, Cardinal Alexander Farnese promised two German cardinals that if elected, he would summon a council. He was elected and ruled as **Paul III** (1534–49). A Roman aristocrat, humanist, and astrologer who immediately appointed his teenage grandsons cardinals, Paul nevertheless recognized the urgent need for reform. Accordingly, he named several devout scholars as cardinals (including Gian Pietro Caraffa, later Pope Paul IV); appointed a **reform commission** (1536); on Sept. 27, 1540, officially recognized the **Society of Jesus (Jesuits)**; established the **Roman Inquisition** (July 21, 1542); and, finally, overcame political and curial opposition and summoned (1544) the **Council of Trent** (1545–63) to reform the Church and secure reconciliation with Protestants. Lutherans and Calvinists were invited to attend; because they insisted that Scripture alone serve as the basis for deliberations (and as the basis for authority in the Church), Protestants declined to attend, while Catholics held that Scripture *and* tradition act as the basis for discussions. International developments and the threat of plague in Trent interrupted the work of the council, which thus falls into three periods: 1545–47, 1551–52, and 1562–63. The ten years' delay (1534–44) in opening allowed for careful preparation of all issues facing the Church.

Tridentine (from Tridentum, Lat., Trent) **decrees** attacked old abuses (clerical absenteeism, pluralism, simony) by strengthening and centralizing ecclesiastical discipline: bishops were required to reside in their dioceses; pluralism and simony were suppressed. The *Catechism of the Council of Trent*, also called the *Roman Catechism* (1566), lucidly described the doctrinal beliefs of Roman Catholics. Two decrees had especially important social consequences: (1) Since the time of the Roman empire, many couples had exchanged marriage vows privately, without witnesses, forming what were called clandestine (secret) unions. This practice led to denials by one party and disputes in the ecclesiastical courts, which had jurisdiction over marriage, because, since the 12th century, it had been one of the sacraments. The decree **Tametsi** (Nov. 11, 1563) stipulated that for a marriage to be valid, consent (the essence of marriage; p. 314) must be made publicly before witnesses, one of whom must be the parish priest. Trent thereby abolished clandestine marriages in all Catholic countries (consensual and clandestine marriages remained a serious problem for the civil and church courts in England until the **Hardwicke Act** of 1753 abolished them). (2) To raise the pitiful educational level of the clergy, "whose intellectual bankruptcy was . . . common," the council in the decree of July 1563 stipulated that every diocese must set up a **seminary**, with a preferential option given to sons of the poor. Seminaries provided advanced theological training for candidates for ordination; equally, they served as centers for spiritual formation, inspiring students with an "ecclesiastical spirit," a moral attitude that brings a Christian viewpoint to all things. In the 17th century, seminary professors sought to discern whether candidates had religious **vocations** (a new idea, since, from the time of the early Church, parents had determined sons' religious careers), the criteria being purity of life, detachment from the broader secular culture, a steady inclination toward the priesthood, and the capability to carry out clerical functions. Between 1566 and 1650, steady ecclesiastical pressure to enforce the Tridentine goals radically transformed the intellectual and spiritual qualities of the Catholic clergy.

1555–59. PAUL IV (Gian Pietro Caraffa), a sincere and vigorous reformer and one of the chief inspirers of the **Catholic Reformation.** The powers and activities of the Inquisition were extended and the **first index of forbidden books** was drawn up (1559). As a Neapolitan, the pope detested the Spanish rule and was soon in conflict with the Habsburgs. He allied himself with France but was defeated by the duke of Alba.

1559–65. PIUS IV (Giovanni Medici, not related to the famous Florentine family), an amiable pontiff who followed the guidance of his high-minded and able nephew, **Carlo Borromeo**, archbishop of Milan. He made peace with the Habsburgs and concluded the Council of Trent (Professio Fidei Tridentina, 1564). In 1565 Pius officially recognized the **Ursuline Order** formed by **Angela Merici** of Brescia (1474–1540), the first women's religious order to concentrate entirely on teaching young girls. (The idea of an order of **unenclosed** and mobile religious women shocked the Roman authorities, who long delayed official approval.) The Ursulines rapidly spread throughout Europe and the New World, carrying the ideals of the Catholic Reformation.

1566–72. ST. PIUS V (Antonio Michele Ghislieri). Pius was an exceedingly devout and ascetic priest whose attitude was reflected in the financing of the naval crusade against the Ottoman Turks which culminated in the **Battle of Lepanto** (Oct. 7, 1571; p. 295).

1572–85. GREGORY XIII (Ugo Buoncampagni), who continued the policy of his predecessor and did much to encourage the Jesuit colleges and mission to Japan. He is remembered chiefly for his **reform of the calendar** (1582), which involved the dropping of ten days, and, for the future, the striking out of leap year at the close of each century excepting every fourth century. This reform was not accepted by Protestant countries until much later (in Russia not until 1918).

1585–90. SIXTUS V (Felice Peretti), one of the great popes of the Catholic Reformation period who, after suppressing the powerful nobility of the Papal States and purging the territory of bandits, reorganized the government, reestablished the finances on a sound basis, and encouraged industry (silk culture). In the same way he fixed the size of the college of cardinals at 70, and established 15 congregations or commissions of cardinals to deal with particular aspects of church affairs. New edition of the Vulgate Bible. Beautification of Rome, which now took on its characteristic baroque appearance (construction of the Vatican Palace and Library, the Lateran Palace, the Santa Scala; completion of the dome of St. Peter's according to Michelangelo's plans).

1592–1605. CLEMENT VIII (Ippolito Aldobrandini), distinguished for his deep piety. He pushed the Tridentine measures for the reform of the clergy; greatly assisted the charitable institutions of Rome; and absolved Henry IV of France after his abjuration of Calvinism (p. 293), when the two became close friends. He appointed as cardinals his confessors **St. Philip Neri** (1515–95), founder of the **Congregation of the Oratory**, a community of diocesan priests, and **Caesar Baronius** (1538–1607), an exceptionally able church historian respected even by Protestants.

1605–21. PAUL V (Camillo Borghese), whose reign was distinguished by the Jesuit Cardinal **Robert Bellarmine** (1542–1621), scholar, humanitarian, and theologian whose book *On the Power of the Supreme Pontiff in Temporal Affairs* (1610) may have encouraged Paul to press papal prerogatives in Venice; the ensuing conflict ended in a Venetian victory. Paul also quarreled with France over Gallicanism and with James I of England over oaths of allegiance. He supported the Habsburgs in the Thirty Years' War (p. 303).

1623–44. URBAN VIII (Maffeo Barberini). He secured Urbino by reversion (1631), thus completing the dominions of the Papal States. In the Thirty Years' War he attempted to maintain a neutrality that brought him much criticism from the imperialist side. His main concern appears to have been for the States of the Church, which he carefully fortified. *(To p. 332)*

3. VENICE
(From p. 259)

The discovery of the new route to the Indies struck at the old traditional trade through the Levant and at once began to undermine the prosperity of Venice. At the same time the steady advance of the Ottoman Turks left the Venetians the choice between active opposition and accommodation. In general the latter policy was followed, but nevertheless Venice became involved in a number of disastrous conflicts, which cost it most of its outposts in the east. The assault upon the possessions of Venice in Italy (**League of Cambrai**; p. 300) proved less successful than the powers had expected, but thenceforth Venice was obliged to remain on the defensive and to observe a neutral attitude as between France and Spain and later between France and Austria.

1570. The **Ottoman Turks attacked Cyprus,** the largest and most important base of Venetian power in the east. In the ensuing war, the allied Spaniards and Venetians, supported by the papal fleet, won the

1571, Oct. 7. Battle of Lepanto (p. 352). The Venetians made peace.

1573. Venice abandoned Cyprus and agreed to pay a heavy indemnity.

Thenceforth only Candia (Crete), Paros, and the Ionian Islands remained in Venetian hands. *(To p. 334)*

4. OTHER ITALIAN STATES
(From p. 259)

After the Treaty of Cateau-Cambrésis (1559; p. 291), all the Italian states, with the possible exception of Venice, were more or less directly under Spanish influence. By the end of the 16th century Italy was losing the intellectual and cultural primacy that it had held during the Renaissance.

MILAN declined rapidly in economic and political importance after 1525. The death of the last Sforza (**Francesco II**) in 1535 brought Milan under direct Spanish rule. Having failed to respond to the challenges of foreign competition and international industry, the **cities of Lombardy** atrophied economically and politically; but rural agriculture, which laid increased emphasis on technological improvements (fodder crops) and commercial production, thrived. Hence, political power shifted from the urban patriciates to the rural nobility. The countryside became the cradle of modern Lombard (and Italian) industry.

GENOA had been, in the later 15th century, a bone of contention between France and Milan. Torn by internal struggles of rival families (**Adorno** and **Fregoso**), it had lost its great commercial power and was important chiefly as a base of operations for France. In 1528 (Sept. 9), however, the great Genoese admiral **Andrea Doria,** having left the French service, seized the town and reestablished the republic, with a pronouncedly aristocratic constitution. Efforts of the French to recapture it failed. In a conspiracy (1542) Andrea Doria was forced to flee but returned as doge and the constitution was restored. On Andrea Doria's death (1560) he was succeeded by **Gian Andrea Doria.** The **loss of Chios** to the Ottomans (1566) marked the end of Genoese power in the east.

SAVOY was an independent state whose rulers also governed Piedmont. Lying astride the Alps and commanding the passes from France into Italy, the state was one of considerable importance, but the feudal organization resulted in such weakness that the dukes were long unable to pursue an independent policy. In the early 16th century Savoy was decidedly under French influence, and when in 1536 the duke departed from the traditional policy, his dominions were overrun and for the larger part occupied by the French. **Emmanuel Philibert** (1553–80) was the first really outstanding ruler. By following the Spanish lead he secured his dominions again in 1559, and in the course of his reign acquired Asti and other territories by negotiation. He made much progress in breaking the power of the nobility and in organizing a central government and an effective army. His successor, **Charles Emmanuel I** (1580–1630), squandered much of his father's achievement, waging war and neglecting the economic development of the country. **Victor Amadeus I** (1630–37) was a wise and just ruler, but his short reign was followed by a civil war, and when finally **Charles Emmanuel II** (1638–75) ascended the throne, his mother **Christina** (daughter of Henry IV of France) dominated the situation as regent.

MANTUA played a fleeting role on the international stage in the years 1627–31, when the death of **Vincenzo II** (Gonzaga) without heirs provoked the **War of the Mantuan Succession.** The best claim was that of **Charles of Nevers,** of the French branch of the Gonzaga line, but the emperor, at Spain's suggestion, sequestered the territory in order to keep the French out. The invasion of Germany by Gustavus Adolphus finally turned the scales in France's favor and by the **Treaty of Cherasco** (April 26, 1631), Nevers was invested with the duchy.

FLORENCE, like Milan, sank in importance during the 16th century. The Medici, restored in 1512, were expelled for a second time in 1527, when the republic was reestablished. But in 1530 Charles V appointed **Alessandro de' Medici** hereditary ruler. **Cosimo de' Medici** became duke in 1537 and ruled until 1574. During this period Siena was incorporated with Florence (1555), and Florence became the **grand duchy of Tuscany** (1569). Elite descendants of great Renaissance merchant families retained control of the government and laid the foundations of a modern state bureaucracy.

NAPLES, conquered by the Spaniards in 1504, became an appendage of the Spanish crown and was, throughout this period, the headquarters of Spanish power in Italy. Though unpopular, the Spaniards were not threatened in their position except by the **revolt of Masaniello** (Tommaso Aniello, a fisherman) in July 1647. The **medieval pattern of feudal landholding** continued: aristocratic families in the 17th century exercised judicial and economic rights over peasants working their lands and bent their efforts toward retaining familial lands. With the rise in grain prices, richer peasants, who could afford more land, got richer; poor, indebted peasants unable to pay rents sank in status.

(To p. 334)

g. THE GERMAN EMPIRE

(From p. 263)

1. OVERVIEW, to 1618

1493–1519. MAXIMILIAN I, who first took the title Roman Emperor elect.

1495. Diet of Worms. Constitutional reform. Attempted modernization of the medieval empire. Perpetual public peace. Imperial chamber *(Reichskammergericht)*, first at Frankfurt, then at Speier, finally at Wetzlar (1689). At the **Diet of Köln** (1512) the reorganization of the empire was carried further: establishment of ten circles for the better maintenance of public peace *(Landfriedenskreise):* (1) Austria; (2) Bavaria; (3) Swabia; (4) Franconia; (5) Upper Rhine; (6) Lower Rhine; (7) Burgundy (ceded to the Spanish line of the Habsburgs, 1556); (8) Westphalia; (9) Lower Saxony; (10) Upper Saxony. In all there were 240 states in the empire, exclusive of the imperial knights. Bohemia and the neighboring states (Moravia, Silesia, Lusatia) with Prussia and Switzerland (which was already completely independent) were not included in the circles. Establishment of the **Aulic Council,** a court more under the control of the emperor than the imperial chamber, and to which a large part of the work of the latter was gradually diverted.

1508. The **League of Cambrai,** among Maximilian, Louis XII, Pope Julius II, and Ferdinand the Catholic (p. 297).

1511. Pope Julius II, Venice, and Ferdinand of Spain formed the **Holy League** aimed at France; in 1513 Maximilian joined.

The genealogical table shows the **claim of the Habsburgs to Spain** and division of the house into Spanish and German lines. Through these marriages the central European lands of the Habsburgs, the Burgundian lands in what are now France and Belgium, and the united lands of the crowns of Castile and Aragon (Spain, Naples, and the Americas) all came by birth to **Charles I of Spain** (eldest son of Philip and Joanna). He acquired the empire and his better known title **Charles V** by election in 1519.

1517. BEGINNING OF THE PROTESTANT REFORMATION. Background: Wiclifite, Hussite, and other preceding rebellions against the Roman church; Babylonian Captivity and the Great Schism, which weakened the prestige of Rome; corruption and worldliness of Church officials during the Renaissance; development of critical scholarship, as represented by **Desiderius Erasmus** of Rotterdam, whose editions of the Church Fathers and whose Greek text of the New Testament (1516) revealed the scriptural weakness of ecclesiastical writings; rise of national feeling and dislike of foreigners, especially in Germany and England; growth of a middle class and a capitalist economy, which felt Roman Catholicism as a restraint (economic interpretation of the Reformation in modern writings of Max Weber and R. H. Tawney); resentment by civic authorities, as at Zurich, of clerical privileges and exemption from taxation; establishment of endowed preacherships by pious townspeople (such as Stuttgart, Eisenach, Jena) to raise intellectual level of sermons; great landed wealth of the Church available for confiscation by ambitious and unscrupulous princes.

Martin Luther (1483–1546), born at Eisleben, the son of a miner; friar in the Augustine convent at Erfurt; priest (1507); professor at Wittenberg (1508); visit to Rome (1511).

1517, Oct. 31. Luther nailed on the door of the castle church at Wittenberg his **95 theses** (in Latin) against the misuse of absolution or indulgences (especially by the Dominican friar **Johann Tetzel**); translated into German, the theses soon circulated widely.

1518. Summoned to Augsburg by Cardinal de Vio of Gaëta (Cajetanus),

Luther refused to abjure but appealed to the pope. Mediation of the papal chamberlain, Karl von Miltitz.

1519. Discussion at Leipzig between **Andreas Bodenstein** (called Karlstadt) and **Johann Eck.** The latter secured a papal bull against 41 articles in Luther's writings. Luther burned the papal bull and the canon law (1520). Thereupon he was excommunicated.

The German electors chose as emperor the grandson of Maximilian, King Charles I of Spain, who as emperor became

1519–56. CHARLES V. He came to Germany for the first time in 1520 to preside at the **Diet of Worms** (1521). There Luther defended his doctrines, coming under a safe conduct. The ban of the empire having been pronounced against him, he was taken under the protection of Frederick the Wise, elector of Saxony. The **Edict of Worms** prohibited all new doctrines. Luther's **translation of the Bible.**

1521. Hieronymus, envoy of the king of Hungary, pled for Western support against the advancing Ottoman Turks (p. 351). Charles preoccupied with imperial matters and the Lutheran revolt.

Aug. 28. The Ottoman Turkish sultan Suleyman the Magnificent conquered Belgrade, gateway to Hungary and Habsburg lands along the Danube.

1521–26. First war of Charles V against Francis I of France (p. 297). Invasion of Italy by the French under Bonnivert (1523–24). Imperial forces thereupon invaded southern France. Francis I crossed the Mt. Cenis Pass and recaptured Milan.

1523. Development of the Reformation. Luther returned to Wittenberg and introduced public worship, with the liturgy in German and communion in both kinds in Electoral Saxony and in Hesse. The spread of the Reformation was favored by the emperor's deep involvement in the war with France.

1522. The Knights' War, led by Franz von Sickingen and Ulrich von Hutten (the humanist knight), who hoped to improve the position of the imperial knights by strengthening the authority of the emperor at the expense of the princes. Without Luther's knowledge, they wanted to use the Lutheran movement for their political purposes. Sickingen's attack on the archiepiscopal city of Trier failed; he was besieged in his castle at Landstuhl and mortally wounded. Hutten fled to Switzerland. Luther published the **Larger Catechism** (1529), brief sermons on articles of faith, and the **Shorter Catechism,** concise explanations of doctrine in question-and-answer form. The printing press rapidly spread his teaching. Luther's remarkable gift for language a major reason for his fame; hymns such as the stirring "A Mighty Fortress Is Our God" (1530).

1524–25. The **PEASANTS' WAR,** in Swabia and Franconia. The peasants took the occasion of the disorders attendant on Luther's revolt (inspiration of his passionate attacks on the constituted authorities) to rise against the social and economic inequalities of German feudalism. They incorporated their demands in the revolutionary **Twelve Articles.** Luther totally condemned this attack on legal authority. The peasants were defeated at Königshofen and perhaps 60,000 executed.

1524. Ferdinand of Austria, younger brother of Charles V, to whom the emperor had entrusted the government of Germany in 1522, formed an alliance with the two dukes of Bavaria and the bishop of southern Germany in the hope of checking the religious changes.

1525. The **BATTLE OF PAVIA** (p. 297).

1526, Aug. 29. Battle of Mohács (plain on the Danube in southern Hungary). The janissaries and artillery of the Ottoman Turks smashed the Hungarian army, killing King Louis II and many of the nobility. A week later Suleiman reached Buda, and two-thirds of Hungary came into the hands of the Ottoman Turks.

1527–29. Second war between Charles V and Francis I, who had declared that the conditions of the peace of Madrid were extorted by force and hence void. **Alliance of Cognac** between Francis, the pope, Venice, and Francesco Sforza, against the emperor. The imperial army, unpaid and mutinous, took Rome by storm under the Constable de Bourbon, who fell in the assault; the pope besieged in the Castle of St. Angelo (1527; p. 297). The French general **Lautrec** invaded Naples, but the revolt of Genoa (Doria), whose independence Charles V promised to recognize, and the epidemic of plague, of which Lautrec himself died, compelled the French to raise the siege of the capital and retire to France.

1529. Diet of Speyer. Charles's envoys insisted that the Edict of Worms be enforced, that Lutheran estates allow Catholics to attend the Mass,

THE HOUSE OF HABSBURG (1493–1780)

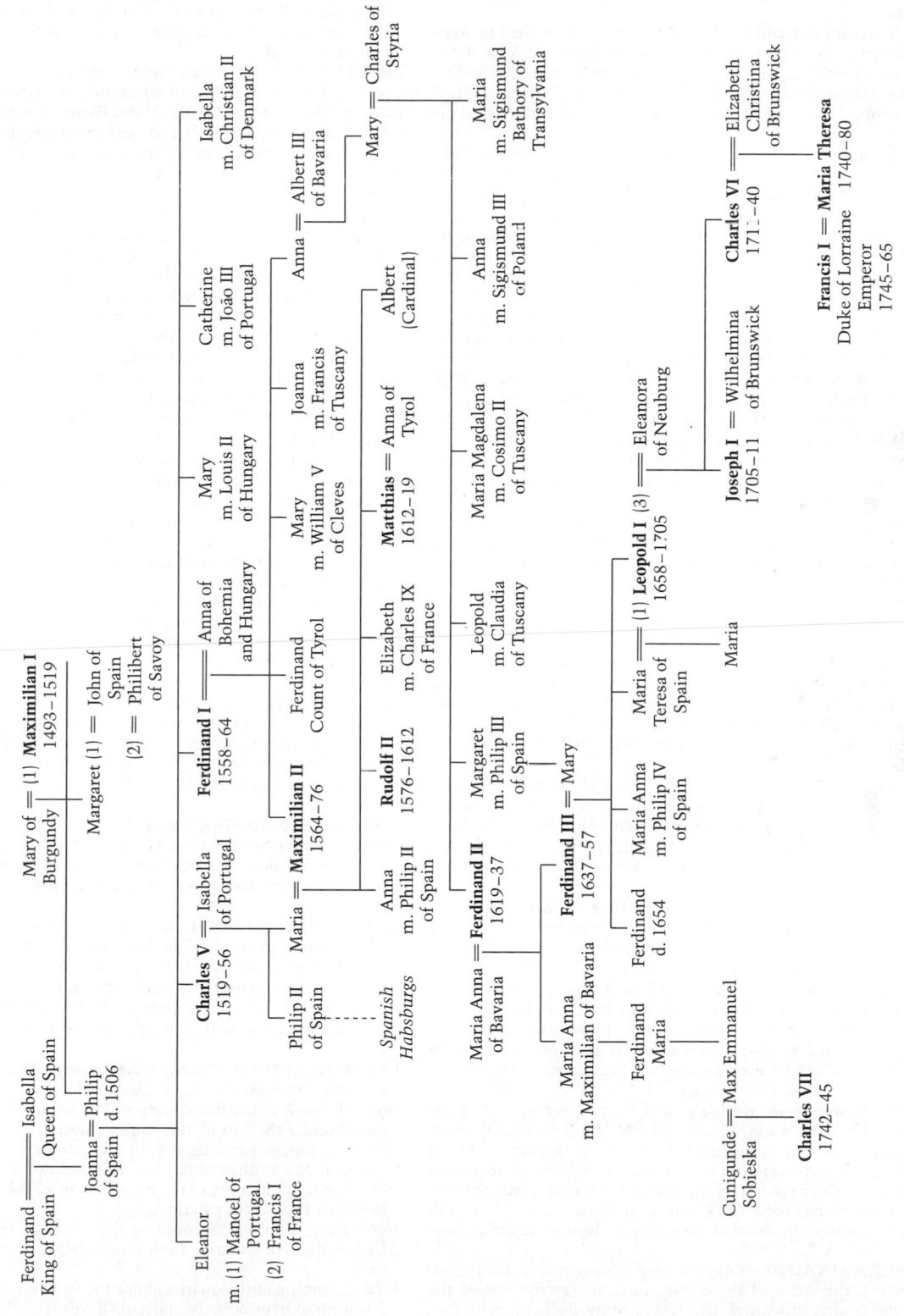

and that Zwinglianism (p. 305) and Anabaptism be suppressed. Lutherans protested that they could not be compelled to act against conscience; hence, they and all who left the Catholic Church were called **Protestants.**

1529, Aug. 3. Treaty of Cambrai (Paix des dames), negotiated by Margaret of Austria, Charles's aunt, and Louise of Savoy, duchess of Angoulême, mother of Francis. Francis paid two million crowns and renounced his claims upon Italy, Flanders, and Artois; Charles promised not to press his claims upon Burgundy for the present and released the French princes.

1530. Diet of Augsburg, with the emperor presiding. Lutheran doctrine, drafted by Luther's associate Philip **Melanchthon,** was officially formulated in the **Confession of Augsburg: justification** (salvation) by faith, a free and arbitrary gift of God, not by good works; **authority** in the Church exists in Scripture alone (*sola scriptura*), meaning the rejection of ecclesiastical tradition and of the papacy as source of authority; the *church* equivalent to the community of believers, thus rejecting identification of church with the clergy. These principles became the basic tenets of all Protestant groups. Although Charles had summoned the diet to achieve religious reconciliation and win unified opposition to the Ottoman threat, the assembly confirmed the schism.

1530, Feb. Charles crowned Holy Roman Emperor at Bologna by Pope Clement VII, in the last papal coronation of a German emperor.

1531, Feb. 6. Schmalkaldic League, agreed upon in 1530, between the majority of Protestant princes and imperial cities.

Charles caused his brother, Ferdinand, to be elected king of Rome and crowned at Aachen. The elector of Saxony protested against this proceeding in the name of the evangelicals.

1532. In consequence of the new danger that threatened from the Ottoman Turks, Ferdinand concluded the **religious peace of Nürnberg.** The Augsburg edict was revoked, and free exercise of their religion was granted the Protestants until the meeting of a new council to be called within a year.

1534–35. Anabaptists (literally, "to baptize again") held that only adults could make a free choice about baptism and that the church was a voluntary association of those (few) who experienced an inner light. Thus they favored **separation of church and state; religious toleration; pacifism; admission of women to ministry.** Münster, the scene of an experimental Anabaptist community, attracted many followers, but the movement was crushed and its leader, **John of Leiden,** (1509–36) beheaded.

1536–38. Third war of Charles against Francis I of France. The latter, having renewed his claims to Milan after the death of Francesco Sforza II without issue, Charles invaded Provence anew but fruitlessly. Francis made an inroad into Savoy and Piedmont and sought the alliance of **Suleiman,** who thereupon pressed his advance on Hungary and sent his fleets to ravage the coasts of Italy.

1538, June 18. The war was ended by the **Truce of Nice,** which was concluded on the basis of possession and for ten years.

1541. JOHN CALVIN (p. 291) introduced the Reformation into Geneva. Calvinist churches had a strict moral code, and, unlike Lutheran, maintained independence of the Church from the lay authority. In Geneva, in Scotland (**John Knox,** 1505–72), briefly in England, and even in the New World (at Boston), the Calvinists erected theocratic states. In France and Hungary they became an important minority. In Holland and parts of Germany they were soon the dominant Protestant group.

1542–44. Fourth war between Charles and Francis, occasioned by the investiture of Charles's son, Philip, with Milan. Two secret agents whom Francis had sent to Suleiman having been captured in Milan and put to death served Francis as a pretext. Francis in **alliance with Suleiman** and the duke of Cleve. The allied Turkish and French fleets bombarded and plundered Nice. Charles, in alliance with Henry VIII of England, defeated the duke of Cleves and advanced as far as Soissons.

1546–47. SCHMALKALDIC WAR. Charles V sought to crush the independence of the states of the empire in Germany and restore the unity of the Church, to which he was urged by the pope, who concluded an alliance with him and promised money and troops. The leaders of the League of Schmalkalden—John Frederick, elector of Saxony, and Philip, landgrave of Hesse—placed under the ban. Irresolute conduct of the war by the allies in upper Germany. They could not be

induced to make a decisive attack and finally retired, each to his own land. Charles V first reduced the members of the league in southern Germany, then went to Saxony and defeated the elector of Saxony and the German Protestant princes in the **Battle of Mühlberg** (April 24, 1547). However, Charles could not exploit his victory, because the princes reunited.

1551–52. War with Ottoman Turks over Hungary, leading ultimately to peace (1562) and Habsburg renunciation of Transylvania (p. 351).

1552–56. War between **Charles V** and **Henry II,** who, as the ally of Maurice, had seized Metz, Toul, and Verdun. Charles besieged Metz, which was successfully defended by Francis of Guise. The **Truce of Vaucelles** left France, provisionally, in possession of the cities that had been occupied.

1555, Sept. 25. PEACE OF AUGSBURG granted legal (imperial) recognition to the Confession of Augsburg (1530). The basic principle of the diet, *cuius regio ejus religio* (freely, the prince determines the religion of the territory), meant that the territorial princes and free cities gained freedom of worship, the right to introduce the Lutheran faith (*jus reformandi*), and equal rights with Catholic states. No agreement reached on the **ecclesiastical reservation** that Catholic bishops and abbots who became Lutheran should lose their offices and incomes, but this provision had been inserted by imperial decree. No provision made for the reformed (Calvinist) faith.

SOCIAL TRENDS. Protestantism held considerable **appeal for women:** Luther's belief that routine domestic work had merit in God's sight; Luther and Calvin's stress on the **home** as special **domain of women** meant that the home, in contrast to the place of business, became the setting for peace, reconciliation, love; Protestants established **schools** where **girls,** as well as boys, became literate in the Bible and the catechism; reformers' emphasis on marriage as the cure for concupiscence meant that priests' concubines could become legal and honorable wives.

The **Lutheran clergy** derived from the lower to middle burger class and after the 16th century tended to be self-perpetuating; **Calvinist clergy** were from the educated upper bourgeoisie; **Catholic diocesan priests** of Reformation Europe descended from middling groups of the towns, from the peasantry in rural areas.

1556. ABDICATION OF CHARLES V at Brussels (effective 1558).

The crown of Spain, with the colonies, Naples, Milan, Franche-Comté, and the Netherlands, went to his son **Philip;** the imperial office and the Habsburg lands to his brother **Ferdinand I.** Charles lived in the monastery of Yuste as a private individual, not as a monk, and died there in 1558.

1558–64. FERDINAND I, husband of Anna, sister of Louis II, king of Bohemia and Hungary, after whose death he was elected king of these countries by their estates. Constant warfare over the latter country, which he was obliged to abandon, in great part, to the Ottoman Turks (p. 351).

1564–76. MAXIMILIAN II, son of Ferdinand, was of a mild disposition and favorably inclined to the Protestants, whom he left undisturbed in the free exercise of their religion. War with John Zápolya, prince of Transylvania, and the Ottoman Turks. Sultan **Suleyman I** died in camp before Szigeth, which was defended by the heroic Nicholas Zrinyi. By the **truce with Selim II** (1566, p. 352) each party retained its possessions.

1576–1612. RUDOLF II, son of the emperor Maximilian II, a learned astrologer and astronomer but incapable of governing. New quarrels over the ecclesiastical reservation. The imperial city of Donauwörth, placed under the ban by the emperor because a mob had disturbed a Catholic procession, was, despite the prohibition of the emperor, retained by Maximilian of Bavaria, who had executed the ban (1607).

1608. These troubles led to the formation of a **Protestant Union** (leader, **Frederick IV,** elector palatine).

1609. The Union was opposed by the **Catholic League** (leader, **Maximilian,** duke of Bavaria). Both princes were of the house of Wittelsbach.

1609. Beginning of the quarrel about the **succession of Cleves-Jülich** on the death of John William, duke of Cleves. The elector of Brandenburg and the prince of Neuburg were the principal claimants.

Rudolf, toward the close of his life, was forced by Matthias to abdicate the government of Bohemia.

1612–19. MATTHIAS, being childless, and having obtained the renunciation of his brothers, secured for his cousin Ferdinand, duke of Styria, Carinthia, and Carniola, who had been educated by the Jesuits in strict Catholicism, the succession in Bohemia and Hungary, notwithstanding the objections of the Protestant states.

CULTURAL DEVELOPMENTS. The greatest of the *Meistersinger* was **Hans Sachs** (1494–1576), composer also of numerous *Fastnachtspiele*, the popular plays that emerged as drama became more secular. Satire appeared in prose and poetry, in fable and in *Schwank*, or comic anecdote (**Sebastian Brant,** *Narrenschiff*, 1494); in the writings of **Thomas Murner** (1475–1537) and **Johann Fischart** (c. 1550–c. 1591); most particularly in the writings of the humanist scholar and great Reformation author **Desiderius Erasmus** (b. Rotterdam c. 1466, d. 1536). His *Encomium Moriae (Praise of Folly,* 1509) satirized the foibles of individuals and of institutions, especially Monasticism; his *Colloqui* likewise contain criticisms of contemporary usage. The *Volkslied* remained a popular vehicle for lyric poetry, having gradually expanded to a polyphonic *Lied* in style.

The drama was further popularized by touring English players late in the 16th century. *Dr. Faustus,* first published anonymously in 1587 as a "chap-book," was immediately popular and translated into English.

Pre-Reformation artists continued to be concerned with church decoration: the sculptors **Tilman Riemenschneider** (1468–1531) and the two **Peter Vischers;** the artist **Matthias Grünewald** (1460–1527; *Isenheimer Altar*). The influence of the Reformation and a trend toward secularism are evident in the works of **Albrecht Dürer** (1471–1528), whose careful studies and theoretical treatises exerted tremendous influence on the development of techniques in the graphic arts. The paintings of **Lucas Cranach** (1472–1553) and **Hans Holbein the Younger** (1497–1543), court painter to Henry VIII of England, reflect a growing secularism in art.

2. THE THIRTY YEARS' WAR

The **Thirty Years' War** is generally divided into four periods, which were properly as many different wars. The first two, the Bohemian and the Danish, had a predominantly religious character; they developed from a revolt in Bohemia into a general conflict of Catholic Europe with Protestant Europe. The third and fourth conflicts, the Swedish and the French-Swedish, were primarily political struggles, wars directed against the power of the Habsburg house and wars of conquest by Sweden and France, fought on German soil.

a. The Bohemian Period, 1618–25

Origin of the war: Closing of a (Protestant) Utraquist church in the territory of the abbot of Braunau and destruction of another in a city of the archbishop of Prague. The irritation of the Bohemian Protestants was increased by the transference of the administration to ten governors, seven of whom were Catholics. Meeting of the defensors and revolt in Prague, headed by **Count Matthias von Thurn.**

1618, May 23. Defenestration of Prague. The governors, Martinitz and Slawata, were thrown from a window in the palace of Prague. They fell 50 feet into a ditch but escaped with their lives. The rebels then appointed 30 directors. The Protestant Union sent Count Peter Ernst Mansfeld to their aid, and from Silesia and Lusatia came troops under Margrave John George of Jägerndorf. The imperial forces were defeated by Mansfeld and Thurn.

1619–37. FERDINAND II. Thurn marched upon Vienna. The Austrian Estates, for the most part Protestant, threatened to join the Bohemians and made rough demands upon Ferdinand, who, by his courage and the arrival of a few troops, was rescued from a dangerous situation. Thurn, who arrived before Vienna shortly afterward, was soon obliged to retire. Ferdinand went to Frankfurt, where he was elected emperor by the other six electors.

Meanwhile, in 1618, the Bohemian Estates deposed Ferdinand from the throne of Bohemia and gave the crown to Frederick V, son-in-law of James I of England and elector palatine. He became head of the Protestant Union and of the German Calvinists, but because he survived as king of Bohemia only through the winter of 1619–20, he is often known as the **Winter King.**

Thurn, for the second time before Vienna, allied with **Bethlen Gabor** (i.e., Gabriel Bethlen), prince of Transylvania (Nov. 1619). Cold, want, and the inroad of an imperial partisan in Hungary caused a retreat.

Ferdinand leagued himself with (1) **Maximilian,** duke of Bavaria, head of the Catholic League, who helped him subdue the Austrian estates; (2) Spain (Spinola invaded the County Palatine; **Treaty of Ulm,** July 3, 1620; neutrality of the Protestant Union secured); and (3) the Lutheran elector of Saxony, who resubjugated Lusatia and Silesia. Maximilian of Bavaria, with the army of the league commanded by **Tilly** (Jan Tserkales, baron von Tilly, in Brabant, 1559–1632), marched to Bohemia and joined the imperial general Buquoy. They were victorious in the **BATTLE OF THE WHITE MOUNTAIN** (Nov. 8, 1620), over the troops of Frederick V, under the command of **Christian of Anhalt.** Frederick was put under the ban and his lands confiscated; he himself fled to Holland. Subjugation of the Bohemians, destruction of the royal charter, execution of the leading rebels, extirpation of Protestantism in Bohemia. Afterward, violent counter-reformation in Austria, and, with less violence, in Silesia.

Dissolution of the Protestant Union and transfer of the seat of war to the Palatinate, which was conquered in execution of the imperial ban by Maximilian's general, Tilly, aided by Spanish troops under Spinola.

b. The Danish Period, 1625–29

Christian IV, king of Denmark and duke of Holstein, was the head of the Lower Saxon circle of the empire and leader of the Protestants.

Albert (Albrecht) von Wallenstein (1583–1634), born in Bohemia of an Utraquist family but educated in the Catholic faith, made duke of Friedland in 1624 and became the commander of an imperial army recruited by himself and provisioned by a system of robbery.

1626. Wallenstein defeated Mansfeld at the **Bridge of Dessau** and pursued him through Silesia to Hungary, where Mansfeld joined Bethlen Gabor. Death of Mansfeld and of Christian of Brunswick (1626).

Aug. Tilly defeated Christian IV at **Lutter am Barenberge,** in Brunswick.

1627. Tilly and Wallenstein conquered Holstein. Wallenstein alone subdued Schleswig and Jutland, drove the dukes of Mecklenburg from their country, and forced the duke of Pomerania into submission.

1628. Wallenstein besieged **Stralsund.** Heroic defense of the citizens for ten weeks obliged Wallenstein to raise the siege.

1629, March 29. EDICT OF RESTITUTION: (1) Agreeably to the ecclesiastical reservation, all ecclesiastical estates that had been confiscated since the convention of Passau (1552) should be restored. (2) Only the adherents of the Augsburg Confession were to have free exercise of religion; all other "sects" were to be broken up. Beginning of a merciless execution of the edict by Wallenstein's troops and those of the league.

1629, May 22. TREATY OF LÜBECK, between the emperor and Christian IV. The latter received his lands back but promised not to interfere in German affairs and abandoned his allies.

1630. Electoral Assembly at Regensburg. The party of Bavaria and the league was hostile to Wallenstein and took up a position of determined opposition to the too powerful general. An excuse was found in the well-grounded complaints of all states of the empire, particularly the Catholics, about the terrible extortion and cruelty practiced by Wallenstein's army. The emperor consented to decree the dismissal of the general and a large part of the army.

c. The Swedish Period, 1630–35

1630, July. GUSTAVUS II ADOLPHUS (1594–1632), king of Sweden, landed on the coast of Pomerania.

Object and grounds of his interference: protection of the oppressed Protestants; restoration of the dukes of Mecklenburg, his relatives; rejection of his mediation at the **Treaty of Lübeck;** anxiety in regard to the maritime plans of the emperor.

Political position of Sweden: Finland, Ingermannland, Estonia, Livonia belonged to the kingdom of Gustavus; Courland was under Swedish influence; the acquisition of Prussia and Pomerania would have made the Baltic almost a Swedish sea. Gustavus concluded a subsidy treaty with France (**Richelieu**); drove the imperial forces from Pomerania and captured Frankfurt-on-the-Oder.

1631, May 20. Capture of Magdeburg by Tilly. The storm was conducted by Count Gottfried Pappenheim. Terrible massacre and sack of the city by the unbridled soldiers of Tilly, who did what he could to check the outrages. Leipzig occupied by Tilly. The imperial army and that of the Swedes and Saxons, each about 40,000 strong, were face to face.

1631, Sept. 17. BATTLE OF LEIPZIG or BREITENFELD. The Saxons were at first put to rout by Tilly, but after a bloody fight Gustavus Adolphus won a brilliant victory.

The Saxons entered Bohemia. Gustavus crossed Thuringia and Franconia to the Rhine and occupied Mainz.

At the urgent request of Ferdinand, Wallenstein collected an army, over which he received unrestricted command. He recaptured Prague and drove the Saxons from Bohemia. Their eagerness for the war and the Swedish alliance was already chilled.

1632. Gustavus met Tilly at Rain, confluence of the Lenz and Danube rivers: Tilly mortally wounded.

1632, Nov. 16. BATTLE OF LÜTZEN. Death of Gustavus Adolphus. Pappenheim, recalled in haste, took part in the battle with his cavalry, after three o'clock; he was mortally wounded. The victory of the Swedes was completed by **Bernhard von Saxe-Weimar.**

Bernhard, Gustavus Horn, and Johann Baner took command of the Swedish forces. The conduct of foreign affairs was assumed by the Swedish chancellor, **Axel Oxenstierna** (1583–1654). **League of Heilbronn** between the circles of Swabia, Franconia, Upper and Lower Rhine, on the one part, and Sweden on the other.

1633, Feb. After Wallenstein had tried and punished with death many of his officers in Prague and had filled their places with new recruits, he marched to Silesia; fought with the Saxon, Brandenburg, and Swedish troops; and negotiated frequently with Arnim. Negotiations with Oxenstierna.

Nov. Regensburg captured by Bernhard von Saxe-Weimar. Wallenstein found himself unable to go to the assistance of the elector of Bavaria, as the emperor urged, and went into winter quarters in Bohemia.

Growing **estrangement between Wallenstein and the imperial court.** The Spanish party and the league wished him removed from his command. Wallenstein conducted secret negotiations with the Saxons, the Swedes, the French. He intended to create, with the help of the army, an independent position for himself, whence he could, with the aid of the two north German electors, liberate the emperor from the control of the Spanish party, and, if necessary, compel him to make peace and reorganize the internal affairs of the empire.

Feb. 18. Proclamation formally deposing Wallenstein. On Feb. 24 Wallenstein went to Eger, where he was to be met by Bernhard von Saxe-Weimar and Arnim.

Feb. 25. The **assassination of Wallenstein** by Captain Devereux occurred in Eger at the instigation of the Irish general Butler after his intimate friends had been treacherously massacred. The emperor had not commanded the murder, nor had he definitely desired it; but he had given rein to the party who he knew wished "to bring in Wallenstein, alive or dead," and, after the deed was done, he rewarded the murderers with honor and riches.

1634. Victory of the imperialists under Ferdinand, the emperor's son, and the Bavarians (Johann von Werth) over the Swedes at **Battle of Nördlingen.**

Widespread agricultural destruction and commercial ruin, strong feeling against the pillaging of foreign troops, and almost universal desire for peace led to

1635, May 30. PEACE OF PRAGUE, which modified the Edict of Restitution, promoted reconciliation between Protestants and Catholics, and planned a united campaign against Swedish troops. Lutherans, but **not** Calvinists, Ultraquists, or Anabaptists, were granted religious freedom. Most princes and free cities accepted the peace.

d. The Swedish-French Period, 1635–48

The policy of Sweden was determined by **Oxenstierna;** that of France by **Richelieu** and later by **Mazarin.** France fought at first in the person of Bernhard von Saxe-Weimar only, with whom subsidy treaties had been concluded and who was trying to conquer for himself a new state in Alsace in place of the duchy of Franconia, which he had lost by the **Battle of Nördlingen. Capture of Breisach** (1638). After the death of Bernhard von Saxe-Weimar (1639), France took control of his army.

1636. Victory of the Swedes under Baner at **Wittstock** over the imperialists and the Saxons. Death of Ferdinand II (1637).

1637–57. FERDINAND III, his son, was desirous of peace. **Count Lennart Torstenson** became commander in chief of the Swedes.

1640. Death of George William. Frederick William, elector of Brandenburg (the **Great Elector,** 1640–88).

1641. Discussion of the preliminaries of peace in Hamburg. A congress agreed upon.

1642. Second Battle of Leipzig (Breitenfeld). Torstenson defeated the imperialists under Piccolomini. He then threatened the hereditary states of the emperor. These Swedish successes aroused the envy of Christian IV of Denmark.

1643–45. Thence began a **war between Denmark and Sweden.**

1643. Opening of negotiations for peace in Osnabrück; 1644 in Münster: Protestants met in Osnabrück, Catholics in Münster, with the papal nuncio Chigi as mediator.

Marshal Turenne and the 21-year-old prince of Bourbon, duke of Enghien, afterward **prince of Condé,** appointed commanders in chief of the French troops.

1643, Sept. Torstenson hastened by forced marches to the north, conquered Holstein and Schleswig, and invaded Jutland.

1644. The French forced the Bavarians under Mercy to retreat. Condé captured Mannheim, Speier, and Philippsburg. Turenne took Worms, Oppenheim, Mainz, and Landau.

Meanwhile an imperial army, under Count Matthias Gallas, had been sent to the aid of the Danes, who were hard pressed, both by land and by sea, by the Swedish admiral Gustavus Wrangel.

1645, March. Brilliant victory of Torstenson over the imperialists at **Jankau** in Bohemia, whereupon, in union with the prince of Transylvania, George Rákóczi, he conquered the whole of Moravia and advanced hard upon Vienna.

May. Turenne defeated by Werth at **Mergentheim** in Franconia.

Aug. Turenne, at the head of the French and Hessians, defeated the Bavarians at **Allersheim.**

Peace between Sweden and Denmark at **Brömsebro.**

1646. Wrangel left Bohemia, united to his own force the Swedish troops under Königsmark in Westphalia, and joined Turenne at Giessen. Swedes and French invaded Bavaria and forced the elector Maximilian to conclude the **Truce of Ulm** (1647) and to renounce his alliance with the emperor. After Turenne had been recalled, owing to envy in regard to the Swedish successes, and Wrangel had gone to Bohemia, Maximilian broke the truce and joined the imperialists again.

1648. Second invasion of Bavaria by the French and Swedes; terrible ravages. A flood on the Inn prevented the further advance of the allies, who returned to the Upper Palatinate.

Disastrous condition of Germany. Irreparable losses of men and wealth; destruction of towns and trade. Reduction of population; increase of poverty.

1648, Oct. 24. TREATIES OF WESTPHALIA, signed at Münster and Osnabruck. Negotiations from 1643 to 1648. Imperial ambassadors, Count Maximilian Trautmanssdorf and Dr. Volmar. French, Count d'Avaux and Count Servien. Swedish, Count Oxenstierna, son of the chancellor, and Baron Salvius. France and Sweden, against the will of the emperor, secured the participation of the states of the empire in the negotiations.

Political consequences: The German states (about 250) were recognized as sovereign; thus the **Holy Roman Empire** as an effective political institution ended and the influence of the Habsburgs declined. **France,** emerging as the dominant European power, acquired sovereignty over the bishoprics of Metz, Toul, and Verdun; control of Alsace, though title left ambiguous and Strasbourg retained membership in the empire; and the city of Breisach. **Sweden gained West Pomerania,** including Stettin and the island of Rügen; the archbishopric (but not the city) of Bremen; the bishopric of Veden; Wismar; the island of Pöl; and a large financial indemnity. The **Swiss Confederation** and the **Netherlands** were explicitly recognized as independent states. Territorial compensation also went to Brandenburg and Mecklenburg. **Religious consequences:** Territorial rulers continued to determine the religion of their subjects, but **Calvinism** was officially **recognized** and rulers could allow full toleration; peoples were allowed to emigrate to states of their own confessions. Protestant and Catholic states were to be in complete equality in imperial affairs, future disputes to be resolved by compromise. **ECONOMIC and SOCIAL CONSEQUENCES:** The wars took 8 million lives and population remained at 8 million, where it was in 1618. Although armies were small (by 20th-century standards), they caused terrible destruction agriculturally and commercially. The diversity of growth and decline within the empire before 1618 makes generalizations about the wars' effects dangerous. Certainly, "the Thirty Years' War started a general decline that had not previously existed; at worst, it replaced prosperity with disaster," according to T. K. Rabb.

The Treaties of Westphalia were guaranteed by France and Sweden.
(To pp. 314, 336)

SOCIAL AND CULTURAL DEVELOPMENTS. Literary output during the Thirty Years' War was sparse: hymns of **Paul Gerhardt** (1607–76); mystical poems of **Angelus Silesius** (1624–77), who was indebted to **Jakob Böhme** (1575–1624); poems and plays of another Silesian, **Andreas Gryphius** (1616–64), especially his satiric comedy *Horribilicribrifax* (c. 1650); and the great German prose classic of the century, *Simplicissimus* (1669), a vivid picture of contemporary life and manners by **Hans Jakob von Grimmelshausen** (c. 1625–76). Another Silesian, **Martin Opitz** (1597–1639), won recognition as purifier of the language by his insistence on proper form in *Das Buch von der deutschen Poeterey* (1624).

Music in the period was chiefly for church use: **Heinrich Schütz** (1585–1672) composed vocal and instrumental music in various forms; his influence was apparent on Buxtehude and J. S. Bach.

3. THE SWISS CONFEDERATION
(From p. 264)

The confederation, at the beginning of the 16th century, was still a loose union of practically independent cantons, each sending two representatives to a federal diet. There were, after 1513, thirteen cantons, of which six (Schwyz, Uri, Zug, Unterwalden, Glarus, and Appenzell) were rural and seven (Lucerne, Zürich, Bern, Solothurn, Fribourg, Basel, and Schaffhausen) were urban. The Aargau, Thurgau, Ticino, and parts of Vaud were governed by the confederation or one or more of its members. Franche-Comté was under Swiss protectorate. In addition various states allied with the confederation (St. Gall, Upper Valais, Neuchâtel, Rothweil, Mülhausen, Geneva).

Swiss military prestige had reached its zenith in the latter part of the 15th century. Swiss mercenaries took an important part in the Italian expedition of Charles VIII and continued to form a crucial part of the French and Italian armies.

1510. The Swiss joined in the **Holy League** against France. In partnership with the Venetians they restored the Sforza to the Milanese duchy (1512), taking for themselves Locarno, Lugano, and Ossola. Great victory of the Swiss over the French in the **Battle of Novara** (June 6, 1513).

1515, Sept. 13–14. In the **Battle of Marignano** (p. 291) the French won a decisive victory over the Swiss and Venetians. This led to the conclusion of peace (Nov. 12, 1515): the Swiss retained most of the Alpine passes and received a French subsidy in return for the right of the French to enlist mercenaries.

1519, Jan. 1. Beginning of the **REFORMATION IN SWITZERLAND,** under the leadership of **Ulrich Zwingli** (b. 1484; educated at Basel and Bern; priest at Glarus, 1506; priest at Einsiedeln, 1516; preacher at Zürich, 1518). Zwingli denounced indulgences and other abuses in the Church and made a great impression in Zürich. In 1521 he denounced the hiring of mercenaries and in 1522 condemned fasts and celibacy (he himself married in 1524). The town, following his teaching, abolished confession (1524) and closed the monasteries. Zwingli acted independently of Luther, from whom he was separated chiefly by difference of opinion on transubstantiation.

1524. Five cantons (Lucerne, Uri, Schwyz, Unterwalden, and Zug) banded together against Zürich and the Reformation movement.

1528. Bern and Basel accepted the Reformation and were followed by three others. Fribourg and Solothurn remained Catholic and sided with the original five (rural) cantons.

1531. War of the Catholic cantons against Zürich. The Zürichers were defeated in the **Battle of Kappel** (Oct. 11) and Zwingli was killed. Thus the division of the confederation was complete; the weakness resulting therefrom made impossible all effective action in the ensuing century.

1536. Geneva (allied with Bern) adopted the Reformation, largely through the efforts of William Farel. In the same year **John Calvin** (p. 302) arrived in the city. His teaching made a deep impression but also

aroused much opposition. In 1538 he was banished and retired to Strassbourg.

1536. Bern subdued Vaud, Chablais, Lausanne, and other territories of the duke of Savoy, thus laying the basis for a long-drawn duel between the two powers.

1541–64. CALVIN, recalled to Geneva, organized the town as a theocratic state (City of God). A consistory of twelve laymen and six clericals controlled the council and the government. Drastic suppression of everything at variance with Calvinist doctrine.

1553. Execution of the Spanish theologian Servetus, who had refugeed in Geneva, for denying the Trinity.

1555. Ruthless suppression of an anti-Calvinist uprising. Geneva a center for Protestant refugees from England and France and a radiating point for Calvinist doctrine. But the Protestant cantons of Switzerland remained predominantly Zwinglian.

1564. Bern was obliged, under pressure from the Spanish power in Italy, to retrocede Gex and Chablais to Savoy. The Savoyards, supported by Spain and by the Catholic cantons, began a prolonged offensive against Geneva and Bern, which drove the Protestant cantons into the French fold.

1577. Opening of a seminary at Lucerne, marking the most active phase of the **Counter-Reformation,** directed chiefly by Cardinal Carlo Borromeo of Milan.

1584. Alliance of Bern, Geneva, and Zürich against Savoy and the Catholic cantons, followed by an alliance of the latter with Spain (1587).

1602. Savoyard attack on Geneva. This was frustrated, but one important result was the renewal of the alliance between the whole confederation and France (the Catholic cantons, however, retained also their alliance with Spain).

1620–39. Struggle for control of the **Valtelline Pass,** the most important link in the communications between Habsburg Austria and the Spanish Habsburg possessions in Italy. The pass was controlled by the **Grisons League** but in 1620 was seized by the Spaniards, who enjoyed the support of the Catholic faction (under **Rudolf Planta**). Thereupon Bern and Zürich sent aid to the Protestant faction, led by the pastor **George Jenatsch** (1596–1639). The Protestants were at first successful but in 1621 were expelled by the Austrians, Spain taking control of the pass. In 1625 it was seized by a Swiss force in French pay. Governorship of the duke de Rohan. But in 1637 Jenatsch, having turned Catholic in the interest of patriotism, secured Austrian aid and once more drove out the foreigner. By **treaty with Spain** (Sept. 3, 1639) the passes were left open to the use of Spanish troops. The war had been conducted by both sides with the utmost cruelty, typical of the Thirty Years' War. In that great struggle the Swiss Confederation remained officially neutral, being paralyzed by the division between Catholic and Protestant cantons.

1648. Nevertheless, by the **Treaties of Westphalia,** the confederation, owing to the efforts and diplomacy of **John Rudolf Wettstein,** burgomaster of Basel, was able to secure a European recognition of its independence of the German Empire.
(To p. 335)

h. SCANDINAVIA

(From p. 268)

1. DENMARK AND NORWAY

During this period the union of the three Scandinavian kingdoms became dissolved.

1513–23. The attempt of the Danish king, **CHRISTIAN II,** to assert Danish supremacy in Sweden by invading it and executing the leaders of the national Swedish party (the **massacre of Stockholm,** 1520) led to a national revolt (1520) headed by **Gustavus Ericksson Vasa,** a young Swedish nobleman.

1523. The Danes were defeated, and Gustavus Vasa became first administrator of the kingdom, then king (see below, Sweden).

In his domestic policy Christian II, in alliance with the middle classes, tried to strengthen royal authority at the expense of the nobility and the Church. This caused a rebellion, led by the nobles and the bishops.

1523–33. They invited the duke of Holstein to rule over Denmark as **FREDERICK I.** A civil war followed in which the middle classes sided with Christian II. Christian was defeated and deposed in 1532. After the death of Frederick in 1533, civil war broke out anew (the **Counts' War**).

1534–59. Order was restored with the accession of Frederick's son **CHRISTIAN III.** During his reign, Protestantism triumphed in Denmark. Church property was secularized and a national (Lutheran) church was established. Simultaneously there was a great strengthening of royal power. Christian III intervened in the religious struggle in Germany, siding with the Protestant princes against the emperor.

1559–88. Frederick II.

1588–1648. CHRISTIAN IV. At the same time, rivalry with Sweden in the Baltic caused the **War of Kalmar** (1611–13), with indecisive results, and Denmark's participation in the **Thirty Years' War** (1625–29) (p. 303).

1643–45. A second war, in which the Swedes were victorious. Denmark lost some territory on the farther side of the Sound. Upon the death of Christian IV, an aristocratic reaction brought about a temporary weakening of the royal power.

Norway during this period remained under Danish domination: all the important posts in the administration were occupied by the Danes, and the Danish language was predominant. However, Norway benefited from the activity of some of the Danish kings. Christian IV improved administration, developed national resources, founded **Christiania** (Oslo). Under the influence of Denmark, Norway also became Protestant (Lutheran). *(To p. 342)*

2. SWEDEN

1523–1654. The **HOUSE OF VASA,** under whom Sweden became the strongest power in the Baltic.

1523–60. GUSTAVUS I. War with Lübeck, concluded by the **Treaty of 1537,** put an end to the trade monopoly of the Hanseatic League in the Baltic region. In the internal life of Sweden, the most important event was the progress of the **Reformation. Olaus Petri** successfully preached Lutheran doctrine and translated the New Testament into Swedish (1526).

1527. By the decision of the **riksdag (parliament) of Västeras,** bishops were made entirely dependent on the king; payment of the Peter's pence to the pope was discontinued; church estates were partially secularized.

1529. The ordinances of the **Synod of Örebro** modified the church service in the Protestant sense.

1560–68. As the Swedish crown was made hereditary, Gustavus Vasa was succeeded by his son **ERIC XIV.** Under him Baltic expansion continued and Sweden came into the possession of Reval (1561) and the adjoining territory. Toward the end of his life Eric became insane and finally was deposed. Under his brother **John III** and John's son **Sigismund** (king of Poland since 1587), Sweden participated in the **Livonian War** (p. 309), in which it acquired all of Estonia with Narva, by the **Treaty of Teusina** (1595).

1593. Sigismund's attempt to restore Catholicism was met by the reaffirmation of the Protestant faith, based on the **Confession of Augsburg,** at the **Convention of Uppsala,** while his absolutist tendencies provoked.

1599. A rebellion ended in Sigismund's deposition. He was succeeded by the youngest son of Gustavus Vasa.

1604–11. CHARLES IX (in virtual control of the government since 1599), under whom Sweden intervened in Russia during the **Time of Troubles** (p. 309).

1611–32. Under his son and successor, **GUSTAVUS II ADOLPHUS,** war with Russia was ended by the **Treaty of Stolbovo** (1617), in which Sweden acquired eastern Carelia and Ingria, cutting Russia off from the Baltic Sea.

1621–29. A war with Poland, the result of dynastic competition, in the course of which Sweden occupied all of Livonia. (For Swedish participation in the **Thirty Years' War,** see p. 303).

The **domestic policy** of Gustavus Adolphus was one of conciliation. A royal charter (1611) gave the council and the estates a voice in all questions of legislation and a power of veto in matters of war and peace. Administration and courts were modernized, education promoted, commerce and industry sponsored, foreign immigration invited. The king's chief collaborator was his chancellor, **Axel Oxenstierna** (1583–1654).

1632–54. Oxenstierna became the ruler of Sweden under Gustavus Adolphus's daughter, **CHRISTINA.** (For Swedish acquisitions under the **Treaties of Westphalia,** p. 304). *(To p. 340)*

i. RUSSIA

(From p. 272)

In Russia, the early 16th to the mid-17th century was a time of conflict between the crown and the powerful landed nobility, which was eventually destroyed. This was accompanied by a decline in the influence of the townsmen and a gradual relapsing of the peasantry into **serfdom.** The latter problem was closely connected with defense and territorial expansion. Since 1454 the grand dukes of Moscow had granted nonhereditary military fiefs *(pomestye)* to secure a supply of fighting men for use in the struggle against the Tatars. The corollary was a steady debasement in the position of the peasants, who consequently tended to run off to newly conquered territories in the southeast. Depopulation in the center resulted in ever more drastic measures to hold the cultivator on the land. At the same time there grew up on the borders the Cossack colonies, independent communities of peasant soldiers that were to play a great role in this period.

1505–33. BASIL III, the son of Ivan the Great and Sophia. The reign was a fairly quiet one, during which the work of consolidation was continued by the reduction of Pskov (1510), Smolensk (1514), and Riazan (1517).

1533–84. IVAN IV (the Terrible), the son of Basil. He ascended the throne at the age of three. The regency was in the hands of his mother, **Helen Glinski** (of Lithuanian family), until 1538, and then fell into the hands of powerful noble (boyar) families, notably the **Shuiskys** and **Belskys.**

1547. Ivan assumed power and had himself crowned tsar, the first Russian ruler to assume the title formally. At the same time he established a "chosen council," composed of personally selected advisers, which he hoped to make a counterweight to the power of the **council of boyars** (duma). This was followed in 1549 with the convocation of the first national assembly, or *zemski sobor*, including merchants and lesser nobles and meant to broaden the support of the crown. In these early years Ivan made considerable progress in breaking down the power of the provincial governors and establishing a measure of local government.

1552–56. The **conquest of Kazan and Astrakhan** from the Tatars gave Russia control of the entire course of the Volga and opened the way for expansion to the east and southeast. Already in the last years of Ivan's reign (1581–83), Russian traders (the Stroganov family) established themselves east of the Urals, and Cossack pioneers, under **Yermak,** began the conquest of Siberia.

1553. The British, under Richard Chancellor, reached Moscow by way of the White Sea and Archangel. They were given trade rights in 1555 and formed an important link in Russian communications with the west.

1557–82. The **LIVONIAN WAR,** arising from the disputed succession to the Baltic territories ruled by the Teutonic Knights. Ivan appreciated to the full the importance of an outlet to the Baltic, and seized Narva and Dorpat. In 1563 he conquered part of Livonia, which had been taken over by the Poles.

1564. Conflict of Ivan with the powerful boyars, led by **Prince Andrei Kurbski.** Ivan eventually withdrew from Moscow and issued an appeal to the people, who, through the metropolitan, urged him to return. He took a terrible revenge on his opponents and began a reign of terror marked by the execution or exile of many boyars, as well as violent rages, in one of which he killed his son and heir, alternating with deep repentance. At the same time Ivan set aside about half of the realm as his personal domain *(oprichnina)*, in which he established a new administration and a separate royal army. Printing introduced into Russia during Ivan's reign.

1570. Ivan ravaged Novgorod and massacred many of the inhabitants, whom he suspected of sympathy for the Poles.

1571. The **Crimean Tatars** attacked and sacked Moscow.

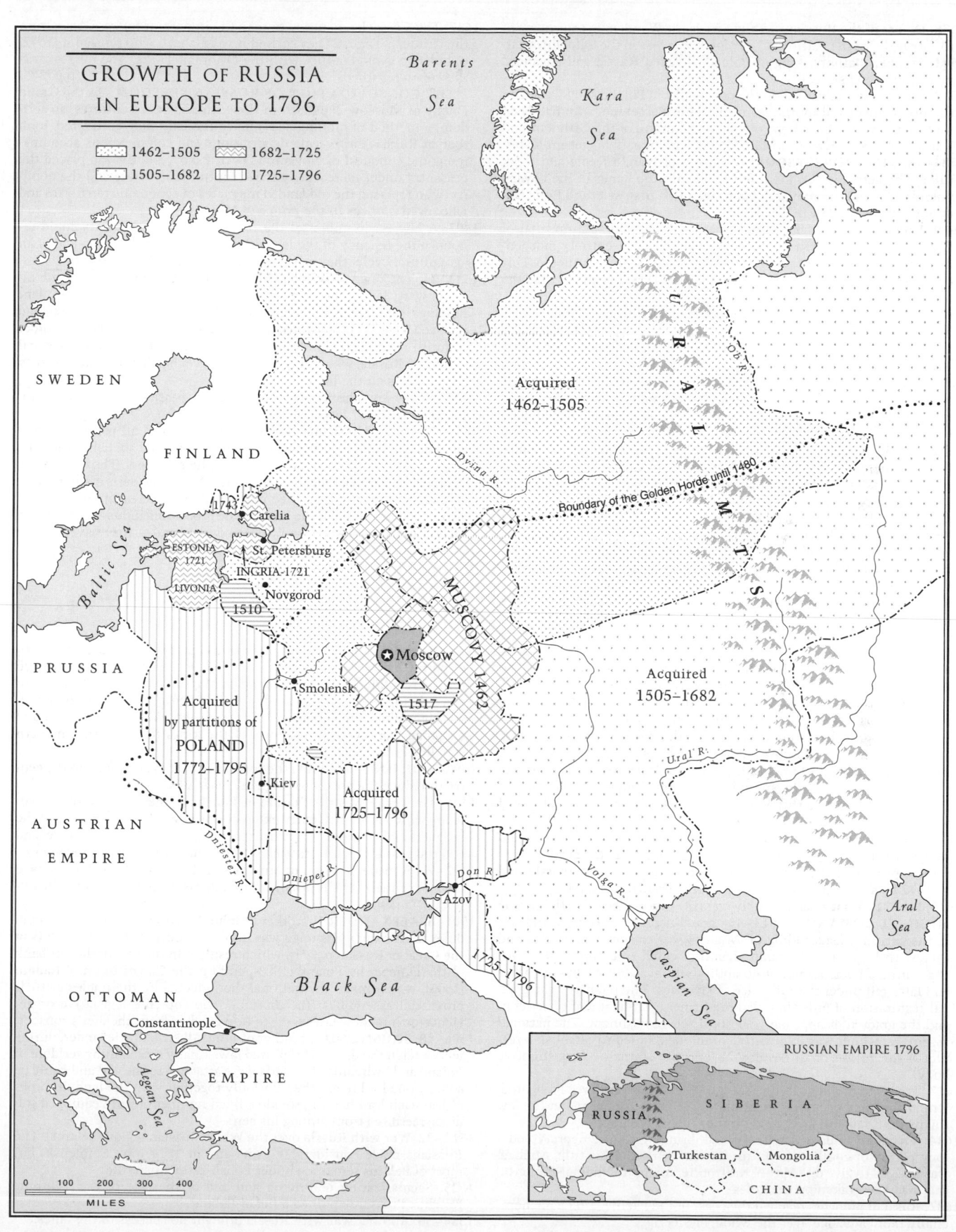

GROWTH OF RUSSIA IN EUROPE TO 1796

- 1462–1505
- 1505–1682
- 1682–1725
- 1725–1796

Barents Sea

Kara Sea

SWEDEN

FINLAND

Acquired 1462–1505

U R A L   M T S

Ob R.

Dvina R.

Boundary of the Golden Horde until 1480

1743

Carelia

ESTONIA 1721

↑ St. Petersburg

INGRIA-1721

LIVONIA

1510

Novgorod

Baltic Sea

MUSCOVY 1462

⊛ Moscow

PRUSSIA

Smolensk

1517

Acquired 1505–1682

Acquired by partitions of POLAND 1772–1795

Kiev

Acquired 1725–1796

Ural R.

AUSTRIAN EMPIRE

Dniester R.

Dnieper R.

Don R.

Azov

Volga R.

1725–1796

Caspian Sea

Aral Sea

OTTOMAN

Black Sea

Constantinople

Aegean Sea

EMPIRE

0 100 200 300 400
MILES

RUSSIAN EMPIRE 1796

RUSSIA   S I B E R I A

Turkestan   Mongolia

CHINA

1578. Defeat of the Russians by the Swedes at Wenden, in the course of the struggle for the Baltic lands. Polotsk was lost in the following year.

1581. Stephen Bathory, king of Poland, invaded Russia and advanced victoriously to Pskov.

1582. Peace between Russia on the one hand and Poland and Sweden on the other, mediated by the Jesuit **Antonio Possevino,** who had been sent by the pope in the hope of effecting a union of the Orthodox and Roman churches. Ivan was obliged to accept most of his recent losses.

1584–98. THEODORE (FEDOR) I, the son of Ivan, a feeble and weak ruler. The actual government fell again into the hands of the boyars, notably Nikita Romanov (related to Ivan IV's first wife) and **Boris Godunov,** brother-in-law of Theodore.

1589. Establishment of the Russian patriarchate separate from that of Constantinople. The Russian church thus became entirely independent and even claimed to be more orthodox than Constantinople. This corresponded to a more ascetic approach to marriage and sex than the respective Byzantine standards.

1598–1605. BORIS GODUNOV, who was elected to the throne by the boyars, since Theodore had died without issue. The new tsar acted against the jealousy of other boyar families with intrigue and persecution.

1604–13. The **TIME OF TROUBLES,** which began with the appearance of a **false Dmitri,** that is, a pretender who claimed to be the supposedly murdered son of Ivan IV. Dmitri was an able and forceful person who soon found extensive support among the Poles and the Cossacks. The death of Boris at this crucial time initiated a period of utmost confusion, during which boyar families struggled for supremacy while their position was challenged by the poorer classes (led by the Cossacks) and while foreigners (Poles and Swedes) took full advantage of the situation to further their own interests.

1605. Theodore (Fedor) II, the son of Boris, succeeded to the throne. He was soon deposed and murdered by the boyars, many of whom accepted Dmitri, who advanced to Moscow and established himself on the throne.

1606. Basil Shuisky and a faction of the boyars succeeded in driving out the pretender and murdering him. Shuisky thereupon became tsar. But new pretenders soon appeared, and the situation became desperate when the Cossacks and peasants in the south and east rose in revolt.

1608. Dmitri defeated Basil and advanced to Tushino, outside Moscow. Basil ceded Carelia to the Swedes in return for aid.

1609. Sigismund of Poland advanced to Smolensk and made extensive promises to the Russian boyars in the hope of acquiring the crown.

1610. Skopin-Shuisky, nephew of Basil, with a Swedish force under De La Gardie, relieved Moscow, but the Poles continued their advance. The Russians then deposed Basil, and a boyar faction offered the throne to Wladyslaw, son of Sigismund. The latter, jealous of his son and anxious to secure the throne himself, evaded the offer and advanced to Moscow.

1611. The turn of the tide was marked by the death of the pretender and by a powerful reaction against the Poles, especially in the northern and eastern provinces. A national militia was formed under **Pozharsky** and in **1612** this militia relieved Moscow and drove out the Poles.

1613, Feb. 21. A national assembly *(zemski sobor)* elected to the throne **MICHAEL ROMANOV** (1613–45), grand-nephew of Ivan IV and son of the patriotic leader **Philaret.** Michael was crowned on July 11 and therewith began the **Romanov dynasty,** which ruled until 1917. Michael himself was a man of no ability who was guided by his father and later fell under the influence of favorites. The reign saw the gradual restoration of order but also the firmer establishment of serfdom and the gradual disappearance of local self-government. The national assembly, which was frequently summoned, failed to establish a regular organization or to develop beyond the status of a consultative body.

1617. Treaty of Stolbovo, with Sweden. The Swedes restored Novgorod, which they had occupied, but Russia was obliged to abandon the few towns that had still been held on the Gulf of Finland.

1634. Treaty of Polianov, with Poland, bringing to a temporary end a long period of conflict. In return for recognition of his title, Michael was obliged to give up many of the frontier towns (including Smolensk) that had been taken by the Poles.

1637. Russian pioneers reached the coast of the Pacific, after a phenomenally rapid advance over the whole of Siberia.

1637. The **Cossacks** managed to take the important fortress **Azov** from the Crimean Tatars. They offered it to Michael, who refused it (1642) in order to avoid conflict with the Ottoman Turks. The fortress was thereupon returned. (To p. 346)

THE CONSOLIDATION OF RUSSIAN SERFDOM. As the Grand Duchy of Moscow expanded in the 15th and 16th centuries, so **serfdom,** a method of binding peasants to the land they cultivated, took root in Russia. Large-scale deportations and colonizations accompanying the conquest of Novgorod, Tver, Pskov, and Ryazan placed the peasantry under increasingly strict control of the state and the nobility, who replaced the old landed magnates of conquered territories and who owed services to the prince of Moscow.

1497. A law made universal the requirement that peasants could renounce the tenancy of the lands they cultivated only at the end of an agricultural cycle, that is, the week of St. Yuri's Day (Nov. 26).

1533–84. The reign of Ivan the Terrible (p. 306), and especially the Livonia wars, led to the ruin of many great estates: large independent holdings were destroyed together with their village communes and replaced with smaller estates whose holders needed serf labor in order to fulfill their service obligations. Many peasants fled to the central regions of Russia, which responded with ever harsher measures to keep the peasants on the land.

1590. A new law confirmed restrictions on peasants' movements imposed by the 1497 law.

1649. The great **Ulozhenie** (law code) summarized all previous provisions about serfdom, imposed new restrictions, and abolished the time limit for the return of runaway serfs to their masters. Thus serfs were deprived of their last legal escape route. Moreover, serfs could now be sold apart from the land they cultivated, and increasing numbers of them were exploited in the mining and processing industries. No basic distinction existed between Russian serfdom and chattel slavery as the latter was practiced in the Western Hemisphere.

j. POLAND-LITHUANIA

(From p. 270)

The history of Poland in this period was marked by a constant growth of power by the lesser nobility, so that Poland became transformed into a republic of the gentry *(szlachta) (Rzeczpospolita)* with an elected king as the titular head. The *Rzeczpospolita* had to fight constantly against the expansion of two powers, Muscovite Russia and Ottoman Turkey, but all efforts of the kings to establish a modern standing army failed.

1492–1501. JOHN ALBERT, the son of Casimir IV, relied upon the gentry to reduce the power of the great magnates.

1496. The result was the **Statute of Piotrkow** (the Magna Carta of Poland), which gave the gentry extensive privileges at the expense of the burghers and peasants. The burghers were restricted from buying land and the peasants were practically deprived of freedom of movement.

1497–98. A futile **invasion of Moldova,** which was intended to secure a throne for the king's brother, led to a devastating invasion by the Ottoman Turks.

1501–6. ALEXANDER I, brother of John Albert and, since 1492, grand duke of Lithuania. His reign was important only for the **war with Ivan the Great** of Russia (p. 271), which resulted in the loss of the left bank of the Dnieper by Poland (1503), and for the **Constitution of Radom** (1505), which made the national diet, elected by the nobles at their provincial assemblies (the *dietines*), the supreme legislative organ. Henceforth no new laws were to be passed without the diet's consent.

1506–48. SIGISMUND I, brother of John Albert and Alexander, during whose reign the diet (1511) passed laws finally establishing **serfdom** in Poland and Lithuania. The **serfs** were attached to the soil and could be sold by one lord to another, but only together with the land. In times of war each lord had to provide a fixed number of fully equipped soldiers, recruited from among his serfs.

1512–22. War with Russia over the White Russian region (Belarus). The Russians made considerable gains and in 1514 took Smolensk, but most of Belarus remained under Polish-Lithuanian rule.

1525. Secularization of Prussia and end of the rule of the Teutonic Knights. Prussia remained a fief of Poland.

1534–36. Another war with Russia brought no success to the Poles.

1548–72. SIGISMUND II (Aug.). His reign was distinguished by the wide spread of the **Protestant Reformation,** which had taken root in 1518 and had gained ground, especially in the Baltic lands and in the towns, despite many edicts penalizing the adherents, who were known as **Dissidents.** Demands for a national church, marriage of the clergy, communion in both kinds, Slavonic liturgy, and so on. **Calvinism** and **Antitrinitarianism** also established themselves. After the **Council of Trent** (p. 298) the crown, backed by the recently formed Polish-Lithuanian chapter of the Jesuit Order (1565), succeeded in checking the movement and in restoring the supremacy of Roman Catholicism.

1557–71. The **Livonian War,** arising from a disputed succession and from the conflicting claims of Poland, Russia, Sweden, and Denmark. The Russians invaded the country (1557) and the Swedes took Estonia, while the Danes acquired part of Courland. In 1561 the Poles took over Livonia, but Ivan the Terrible of Russia conquered part of it in 1563.

1569, July 1. The **UNION OF LUBLIN,** which, despite opposition on the part of Lithuania, merged that country with the Polish kingdom. The two nations were to have a common sovereign and a common diet, though Lithuania was to retain a separate administration and army.

With the death of Sigismund II the **Jagellon dynasty** came to an end and the Polish crown, already elective in theory, became so in fact.

1573–74. HENRY OF VALOIS was elected king on condition of signing the Pacta Conventa, formally recognizing the right of the nobility to elect kings and strictly limiting the royal power. The diet was to meet at least once every two years. Henry paid richly for his election and for the alliance of Poland with France, but, on the death of his brother, Charles IX, he slipped away and returned to France. There followed a period of confusion, during which the Habsburgs made great efforts to secure the crown.

1575–86. The Poles ultimately elected **STEPHEN BATHORY,** husband of Anna, the last Jagellon. Stephen was a strong ruler but was unable to make much progress against the powerful nobility. His great success was in foreign affairs and war. With a new army of peasant infantry, raised on the royal estates, he was able, in the last phase of the Livonian War (1579–82), to retake Polotsk and put an end to the steady encroachment of Russia upon Belarus.

1587–1632. SIGISMUND III (Vasa), son of King John of Sweden. He had been educated by the Jesuits and threw his entire influence on the side of the Counter-Reformation. He involved Poland in endless wars with Sweden because of his claims to the Swedish throne.

1595–96. Attempts to reunite the Eastern Orthodox church in Poland with Rome foundered on Jesuit opposition. However, part of the Orthodox formed the so-called **Uniate Church,** retaining Eastern rites but recognizing papal authority. The result was the **confederation of Vilna** (1599), an alliance between the Orthodox and the Dissidents against the Roman church.

1609–18. Polish intervention in Russia during the **Time of Troubles** (p. 308). An attempt to put Sigismund's son, Wladyslaw, on the Russian throne ended in the expulsion of the Poles from Moscow.

1629. The **Treaty of Altmark,** a truce in the long conflict with Sweden, signaled the defeat of the Poles and confirmed the loss of Livonia.

1632–48. WLADYSLAW, the son of Sigismund. He was elected without opposition and pursued a policy diametrically opposed to that of his father. But his efforts to restrict the powers of the Jesuits were in vain.

1632–34. War with Russia, which was ended by the **Treaty of Polianov** (1634): Wladyslaw renounced his claims to the Russian throne but regained the Smolensk region for Poland. *(To p. 343)*

CULTURAL DEVELOPMENTS. Literature: *Aesop's Fables* were paraphrased and a life written by **Bernard of Lublin** (c. 1515). The spread of Renaissance culture and of the Reformation culminated in a golden age of prose and poetry: poets **Nicholas Rej of Naglowice** (1505–69) and **Jan Kochanowski** (1530–84). Prose writers **Lucas Gornicki** and **Peter Skarga** (1536–1612). Foremost poet of the 17th century: **Waclaw Potocki** (1625–96).

k. BOHEMIA

(From p. 264)

1471–1516. LADISLAS II, son of the king of Poland, first ruler of the **Jagiello family,** a boy of 16 at his accession. Ladislas continued the persecution of the Bohemian Brotherhood but made no progress

toward unifying the country. As king of Hungary also, he spent most of his time at Pressburg (today Bratislava, the capital of Slovakia), leaving open the way for the domination of Bohemia by powerful nobles. During the entire later 15th century the aristocracy extended its possessions and power at the expense of the crown and Church. The towns declined in power and the peasantry sank back into serfdom or a status close to it. Great influx of German peasants in the west and north and in the towns.

1516–26. LOUIS, son of Ladislas, who ascended the throne of Bohemia and Hungary at the age of ten. Conditions continued as under Ladislas, further complicated by the spread and persecution of Lutheranism.

1526. Louis was defeated and killed by the Ottoman Turks at the **Battle of Mohács. Ferdinand,** brother of Emperor Charles V and brother-in-law of Louis, was elected king, beginning a long period of Habsburg rule.

1547. The Bohemian crown was proclaimed hereditary in the house of Habsburg. Constant growth of the royal prerogative at the expense of the diet and town government.

1618. Defenestration of Prague and beginning of the Thirty Years' War (p. 303). Ferdinand II was declared deposed and the Protestant Frederick of the Palatinate was elected king (the Winter King).

1620, Nov. 8. BATTLE OF THE WHITE MOUNTAIN; defeat of Frederick and the Bohemians. Bohemia was virtually deprived of independence, and a wholesale confiscation of the lands of the native nobility took place.

1627. A **new constitution** confirmed the hereditary rule of the Habsburgs and strengthened royal power. The incorporation of Bohemia with the Habsburg empire was completed in the 18th century with the extension of the imperial administration under Joseph I (1705–11) and with the **Pragmatic Sanction of 1720** (p. 339). *(To p. 346)*

l. HUNGARY

(From p. 272)

1490–1516. LADISLAS II, king of Bohemia, was elected king of Hungary by the nobles. To secure recognition from the Habsburgs, he gave up the conquests of Matthias and arranged dynastic marriages with the Habsburgs (his infant son Louis was married to Mary, granddaughter of Maximilian; his own daughter, Anne, was married to Maximilian's grandson Ferdinand). This policy led to the formation of a national party among the Hungarian nobility, headed by Stephen Zápolya (Szapolyai), the *vajdu* (prince) of Transylvania. The nobles refused Ladislas all effective financial support, so he was unable to maintain an army and was soon at the mercy of the nobles.

1514. A great **revolt of the peasants,** led by George Dózsa, was directed against the ruthless exploitation by the aristocrats. It was suppressed in a sea of blood by John Zápolya, leader of the nobility.

1514. The **Tripartitum,** a constitution worked out by Stephen Verböczy, was passed by the diet. It established the equality of all nobles and at the same time fixed the system of serfdom on the peasantry.

1516–26. LOUIS II, the son of Ladislas, succeeded his father at the age of ten. His reign was marked chiefly by the spread of **Protestantism.** The movement first took root in the German areas and in the towns and was vigorously opposed by the nobles. In 1523 it was declared punishable by death and confiscation of property, but despite all edicts it took firm hold of the country.

1521. The Ottomans took Belgrade, beginning their victorious advance into Hungary.

1526, Aug. 29–30. BATTLE OF MOHÁCS. Defeat and death of Louis when the Ottomans completely overwhelmed his disorganized army of 20,000.

1526–28. The death of Louis was followed by a hot contest over the succession. Part of the nobility, hoping for German aid against the Ottomans, elected **Ferdinand of Habsburg,** brother of Emperor Charles V. The national party, on the other hand, elected **John Zápolya** king. After a civil war lasting two years, Zápolya was defeated. He appealed to the Ottomans, who supported him vigorously. By the **Peace of Nagyvarad** the two kings recognized each other, each ruling part of the territory. Zápolya became a vassal of the Ottomans but Ferdinand continued the war against them, which was interrupted only by occasional truces (p. 351).

1540. Death of John Zápolya. The Ottomans recognized his infant son, **John II** (Sigismund) **Zápolya** (1540–71). This led to a new clash with Ferdinand, who began the invasion of eastern Hungary. The Ottomans again invaded and took Buda. They now took over the entire central part of Hungary (the great plain), which was organized in four *pashaliks* (border districts). There was no settlement by the Ottoman Turks, but the territory was granted in military fiefs and subjected to heavy taxation. Religious tolerance of the Ottoman Turks. Transylvania, under Zápolya, was a vassal state of the Ottoman Turks but was left almost entirely free. Under **Cardinal Martinuzzi** it was organized as a state (three nations: Magyars, Szeklers, and Germans, meeting in a Landtag, elected the king and passed laws). The Transylvanians (even the nobility) soon accepted **Calvinism**, so that during the later 16th century the larger part of Hungary was either Lutheran or Calvinist. In 1560 religious toleration was established in Transylvania. The **Habsburgs**, on the other hand, held only a narrow strip of western and northern Hungary, and even for this they long paid tribute to the Ottoman Turks. The Habsburgs employed Italian and Spanish mercenaries to defend their possessions, and these ravaged the country as much as Ottoman territory. Ferdinand and his successors governed from Vienna or Prague and with little reference to the traditional rights of the Hungarian nobility. This led to growing friction and later to serious conflict.

1581–1602. Sigismund Bathory, prince of Transylvania. His efforts to unite with the Habsburgs for a grand assault on the weakening Ottoman power met with vigorous opposition on the part of the Transylvanian nobility.

1604. Beginning of the Counter-Reformation, under Habsburg auspices. This resulted in a revolt of the Hungarians, supported by the Transylvanians.

1604–6. STEPHEN BOCSKAY became prince of Transylvania and, after defeating the Habsburgs, secured the **Treaty of Vienna,** by which Protestantism was given equal status with Catholicism. Nevertheless, the Counter-Reformation made great strides, especially among the nobility, owing to the efforts of Cardinal Pazmany and the Jesuits.

1613–29. BETHLEN GABOR (Gabriel Bethlen), prince of Transylvania. He made his state the center of Hungarian culture and national feeling. On the outbreak of the **Thirty Years' War,** he openly sided with the enemies of the Habsburgs and made Transylvania a vital factor in European politics.

1630–48. GEORGE RÁKÓCZI I, another eminent prince of Transylvania. He continued the policy of his predecessor and managed to guide the country through the storms of the European crisis. At the same time he took full advantage of the growing weakness of the Ottoman Turks, making Transylvania virtually an independent state, which played a part of some importance in international affairs.

Literary efforts of the 16th and early 17th centuries centered on Scripture translations, along with the poetry of **Valentine Balassa, John Rimay,** and **Nicholas Zrinyi** (1620–64).

2. SCIENCE AND LEARNING, 1450–1700

a. SCIENCE

1469. Publication of Pliny's *Historia naturalis*, the first scientific book to be printed.

1500. Hieronymus Brunschwig (1450–c. 1512) published *Das Buch der rechten kunst zu distillieren;* its bold woodcuts were the first illustrations to depict chemical apparatus and operations.

1527–41. Philippus Paracelsus [Theophrastus von Hohenheim] (1493–1541) crusaded for the use of chemicals in the treatment of disease. He introduced the system of salt, sulphur, and mercury as the three prime "elements," from which all things are made.

1537. Niccolò Tartaglia (?1500–1557), in *Nova scientia*, discussed the motion of heavy bodies and the shape of the trajectory of projectiles.

1540. Posthumous publication of *De la pirotechnica*, a handbook of metallurgy containing information about smelting and ore reduction compiled by **Vannoccio Biringuccio** (1480–1539).

1542. Leonhart Fuchs (1501–66) used the botanical work of his contemporaries, **Otto Brunsfels** (1488–1534), **Jerome Bock** (1498–1554), and **Conrad Gesner** (1516–65), to prepare a great herbal, describing some 400 plants, illustrated by realistic woodcuts.

1543. The Polish astronomer **NICOLAUS COPERNICUS** [Niklas Kopernik] (1473–1543) published *De revolutionibus orbium coelestium*, which asserted that the planets, including the earth, circle around a stationary sun. Modern astronomy rests on his work.

1543. ANDREAS VESALIUS (1514–64) produced *De fabrica corporis humani*, an illustrated, systematic study of the human body. This work is a union of Renaissance artistic endeavor and a revived interest in the empirical study of **human anatomy.**

1545. Geronimo Cardano (1501–76) published the solution of the **cubic equation** in *Ars Magna;* this first major advance in mathematics in the European Renaissance provoked a bitter dispute with Niccolò Tartaglia, who claimed to have discovered it. Cardano described a tactile system similar to Braille for teaching the blind and believed the deaf could be taught by signs.

1545–73. Ambroise Paré (1510–90) encouraged a **pragmatic approach to surgery.** He promoted the dressing of gunshot wounds rather than the traditional practice of cauterizing them with boiling oil.

1546. Georgius Agricola [Georg Bauer] (1494–1555) applied observation rather than mere speculation to the study of rocks, publishing *De natura fossilium*, an early handbook of mineralogy, and *De re metallica* (1556), which dealt with mining and metallurgy.

1546. Girolamo Fracastoro (?1483–1553) developed the theory that **contagion** (infectious disease) is caused by a living agent transmitted from person to person.

1551–87. The Swiss Naturalist **Conrad Gesner** (1516–65) amassed in the first great Renaissance encyclopedia, *Historia animalium*, ancient and contemporary knowledge of the animal kingdom.

1572. The Danish astronomer **TYCHO BRAHE** (1546–1601) observed a bright new star, a *supernova*, and determined that it was beyond the moon, thereby destroying the prevailing Aristotelian notion that no change occurred in celestial regions. Through systematic observation, using instruments designed by himself, Brahe accumulated very accurate data on planetary and lunar positions and produced the **first modern star catalog.**

1583. The Italian botanist **Andrea Cesalpino** (1519–1603) compiled the first modern **classification of plants** based on a comparative study of forms; he also described as a theory the circulation of the blood.

1585. Simon Stevin (1548–1620) published *La disme*, introducing decimal fractions into arithmetic. A year later he published treatises on **statics and hydrostatics.** The work on statics gave a mathematical proof of the law of the lever, elegantly proved the law of the inclined plane, and showed that two unequal weights fall through the same distance in the same time.

1591. François Viète [Vieta] (1540–1603) introduced **literal notation** in algebra, that is, the systematic use of letters to represent both coefficients and unknown quantities in algebraic equations.

c. 1600. Dutch lens-grinders in Middleburg are thought to have constructed the **first refracting telescope** and the **compound microscope.**

1600. William Gilbert (1540–1603) provided in *De magnete* a methodical experimental study of the **electric and magnetic properties of bodies** and established that the earth itself is a magnet.

1603. Foundation of the **Accademia dei Lincei,** one of the earliest learned societies, at Rome.

1609. The German astronomer **JOHANNES KEPLER** (1571–1630), much influenced by Copernicus and later Tycho Brahe's assistant, announced in *Astronomia nova* his first two **laws of planetary motion:** planets move in ellipses with the sun in one focus; the radius vector from the sun to a planet sweeps out equal areas in equal times. In *Harmonices mundi* (1619) he added his third law: the squares of the periods of revolution of all planets are proportional to the cubes of their mean distances from the sun.

1610. GALILEO GALILEI (1564–1642), in *Sidereus nuncius*, revealed the results of the first telescopic observations of celestial phenomena. He used these observations to destroy the Aristotelian-Ptolemaic cosmology and to argue for the plausibility of the Copernican system.

1614. John Napier (1550–1617) introduced **logarithms** as a computational tool.

1627. Kepler, on the basis of Tycho Brahe's observations and his own theories, compiled the Rudolphine Tables, which made possible the calculation of future planetary positions and other astronomical events; the tables were standard for over a century.

1628. WILLIAM HARVEY (1578–1657), in his classic *Exercitatio anatomica de motu cordis et sanguinis in animalibus,* blended reason, comparative observation, and experimentation to demonstrate the **circulation of the blood.**

1632. Galileo fashioned in *Dialogo sopra i due massimi sistemi del mondo Tolemaico e Copernicano* a brilliant polemical masterpiece, which clearly showed the superiority of the Copernican system over the Ptolemaic system of the world. This work led to **Galileo's trial and recantation** before the Roman Inquisition of the Catholic church.

1637. RENÉ DESCARTES (1596–1650) published *Discours de la méthode,* an introduction to his philosophy, which served as a preface to his works on dioptrics, meteorology, and geometry. In the same year he published *La géometrie,* setting forth an **analytic geometry,** that is, representation of geometric figures by algebraic equations and algebraic equations by geometric figures. **Pierre de Fermat** (?1608–65) simultaneously and independently developed an analytic geometry. Both Descartes and Fermat applied analytic geometry to the finding of tangents to curves; Fermat also devised a general method for finding maxima and minima.

1638. Galileo in *Discorsi e demonstrazione matematiche intorno a due nuove scienze* established the basic principles of a mathematical description of falling bodies and projectile motion.

1642–71. Blaise Pascal (1623–62) constructed the first **adding machine** that could perform the operation of carrying. Some 30 years later, **Gottfried Wilhelm Leibniz** (1646–1716) invented a more complex calculating machine that would multiply rapidly by repeated additions.

1644. Descartes in his *Principia philosophiae* provided mechanistic explanations in terms of matter and motion for a wide variety of physical, chemical, and biological phenomena and presented his **vortex theory of planetary motion.**

1648. Jan Baptista van Helmont (1577–1644), in his posthumously published collected works, *Ortus medicinae,* assigned the name "gas" to the "wild spirits" that were produced in various chemical processes and argued that acid fermentation, not "innate heat," was the operative agent of digestion.

1654. Correspondence between Pascal and Fermat on mathematical treatment of games of chance resulted in the beginning of **probability theory.**

1655. John Wallis (1616–1703) published *Arithmetica infinitorum,* which studied infinite series and infinite products, solved problems of quadratures, and found tangents by use of infinitesimals.

1655. The natural philosopher **Margaret Cavendish,** duchess of Newcastle (1623–73), published *The Philosophical and Physical Opinions,* in 1666 *Observations upon Experimental Philosophy,* and four other works. She was the only woman to attend a meeting of the Royal Society, in 1667, when she listened to Boyle.

1657. The foundation of the **Accademia del Cimento** of Florence, the first organized scientific academy and a center for the new experimental science that stemmed from the work of Galileo.

1659. Christiaan Huygens (1629–95) revealed, in *Systema Saturnium,* that Saturn is surrounded by a thin, flat ring.

1660–74. ROBERT BOYLE (1627–91) described his first **pneumatic pump,** an improvement on that invented by **Otto von Guericke** (1602–86), in *New Experiments Physicomechanical, Touching the Spring of the Air.* In the second edition (1662) Boyle noted the relation between pressure and volume now called **Boyle's law.** With this pump Boyle showed that animals die from a lack of air, not from the accumulation of noxious vapors. So began an era in respiration studies that included the elucidation of lung structure (1661) by **Marcello Malpighi** (1628–94), the proof that fresh air is necessary for respiration (1667) by **Robert Hooke** (1635–1703), the observation that blood changes color when in contact with air (1667–69) by **Richard Lower** (1631–91), and the demonstration that the volume of air is reduced in respiration (1674) by **John Mayow** (1640–79).

1661. Boyle published his *Sceptical Chymist,* which contained a vigorous criticism of the Aristotelian theory of elements and the Paracelsian theory of principles.

1662. Charles II of England chartered the **Royal Society of London,** an independent organization that became the major center of English scientific activity during the 17th and 18th centuries.

1662. Jeremiah Horrocks (1619–41) predicted and was the first man to observe (1639) a **transit of Venus** across the disk of the sun. His work was posthumously published in *Venus in sole visa* (1662).

1664. Publication of Descartes's posthumous work *L'homme,* expounding a mechanistic interpretation of the animal body. **Giovanni Borelli** (1608–79), in *De motu animalium* (1680), linked Galilean mechanics to Cartesian mechanistic biology.

1664–68. Isaac Barrow (1630–77), the teacher of **Isaac Newton,** showed, in his mathematical lectures at Cambridge University, that the method of finding tangents and the method of finding areas were inverse processes.

1665. The Royal Society of London published the first issue of its *Philosophical Transactions* (March 1665), the first scientific journal in the English-speaking world.

1665. Robert Hooke published *Micrographia,* containing descriptions of his microscopic observations. He first used the word *cells* to describe the lacework of rigid walls seen in cork. The observations of Hooke and other classical microscopists—**Marcello Malpighi, Nehemiah Grew** (1641–1712), **Jan Swammerdam** (1637–80), **Antony van Leeuwenhoek** (1632–1723)—revealed the complex minute structure of living matter and the existence of microorganisms.

1666. Louis XIV of France founded the **Académie Royale des Sciences,** a government-controlled and -financed organization dedicated to experimental science. The activity of the Académie was regularly recorded in the *Journal des Savants,* one of the earliest scientific periodicals. Women were not allowed to be members of the Académie Royale, nor of the English Royal Society.

1669. Erasmus Bartholin (1625–98) published his observations on double refraction in crystals of Iceland spar.

1669. ISAAC NEWTON (1642–1727) announced his **calculus,** in *De analysi per aequationes numero terminorum infinitas,* which circulated in manuscript but was first published in 1711. He further developed the calculus in *Methodus fluxionum et serierum infinitarum* (1671, published 1736), using as fundamental notions "fluxions" (time derivatives) and "fluents" (inverse of fluxions), fluents being interpreted as areas.

1669. Johann Joachim Becher (1635–82) asserted that all bodies are composed of air, water, and three earths: *terra lapida, terra mercurialis,* and *terra pinguis.* In combustion the "fatty earth" *(terra pinguis)* burns away, and in calcination it is driven off by the action of fire. This was a forerunner of the phlogiston theory (1723), which claimed, before the discovery of oxygen, that a nonexistent chemical called phlogiston was released during combustion.

1671–73. Jean Richer (1630–96), on a scientific expedition to Cayenne (latitude 5°N), found that the **intensity of gravity** was less near the equator than in higher latitudes.

1672. Newton presented to the Royal Society a **reflecting telescope** that he constructed on principles learned in his optical studies. Newton also published his "New Theory about Light and Colors," showing notably that white light is composed of the various spectral colors, each of which has a different index of refraction.

1673. Christiaan Huygens announced in *Horologium oscillatorium* the invention and theory of the **pendulum clock.** This work included theorems on centrifugal force in circular motion.

1675. Olaus Roemer (1644–1710), by studying the eclipses of Jupiter's moons, determined that light is transmitted with a finite though very great speed.

1676. Thomas Sydenham (1624–89) rejected the view that the diseased state is an exception to natural law. He emphasized the importance of clinical observation, experience, and common sense in therapy.

1678. Robert Hooke provided an account of the law of elastic force, *ut tensio, sic vis* (stress is proportional to strain), which is now known by his name.

1679. Edmé Mariotte (?1620–84) announced his discovery of the constant **relation between the pressure and volume** of an enclosed quantity of air (discovered independently of Robert Boyle).

1684. LEIBNIZ first published his **differential calculus,** based on work done independently of Newton during the period 1673–76. Leibniz based his calculus on the finding of differentials, which he understood as infinitesimal differences, and defined the integral as an infinite sum of infinitesimals; the operations of summing and of finding the differences were mutually inverse.

1686–1704. John Ray (1627–1705) in the three volumes of *Historia generalis plantarum* provided an able account of the structure, physiology, and distribution of plants and laid the foundations of modern **systematic classification.**

1687. NEWTON in his *Philosophiae naturalis principia mathematica* founded mechanics, both celestial and terrestrial, on his three axioms, or **laws of motion.** He demonstrated that the sun attracts the planets and the earth attracts the moon with a force inversely proportional to the square of the distance between them. In his **principle of universal gravitation** he states that any two bodies attract each other with a force proportional to the product of their masses and inversely proportional to the square of the distance between them.

1688. Francesco Redi (1621–97) challenged the ancient belief in spontaneous generation and began a two-century-long debate on the subject by his controlled experimentation on the production of maggots.

1690. Christiaan Huygens developed in his *Traité de la lumière* a mechanistic theory that presents light as a propagation of impulses in a subtle ether. He used this theory to explain reflection, refraction, and double refraction.

1696. Guillaume de L'Hôpital (1661–1704) published the first textbook of the **infinitesimal calculus,** *Analyse des infiniment petits,* based on the lectures of his teacher, **Johann Bernoulli** (1667–1748).

1697. Bernoulli showed that the curve of quickest descent is the cycloid, thereby solving the first problem of the **calculus of variations.**

(To p. 314)

b. INVENTIONS AND TECHNOLOGY

c. 1455. Printing with movable type, perhaps based on the Chinese method of block printing that reached Europe c. 1250, introduced through the combined efforts of Johann Guttenberg, Johann Fust, and Peter Schoffer, all experimenting at Mainz. Consequences: Though felt only gradually over the next 200 years, printing transformed the public and private lives of Europeans. Governments used it to announce wars, battles, peace, to persuade; propaganda made possible, showing differences between opposing groups, such as crown and nobility, Protestants and Catholics, church and state; the literacy of laypeople stimulated. Although most early books and pamphlets dealt with religious subjects, printers also responded with medical, practical, household, travel manuals; pornography as well as piety assumed new forms. Since printed materials were read aloud to the illiterate, the bridge between written and oral cultures grew. The development of printing with movable type accompanied an increased use of wood-block illustrations.

1485. Publication of **Leon Battista Alberti's** (1404–72) *De re aedificora* exemplified the extended interests of Renaissance architects and artists in the realm of applied science. A more famous example is **Leonardo da Vinci** (1452–1519), who studied human and animal anatomy and speculated on hydraulics, mechanics, air travel, and on military and engineering devices. Structural theory did not advance until the work of **Galileo Galilei** *(Dialogues Concerning Two New Sciences,* 1638), **Christopher Wren,** and **Robert Hooke.** The revival of interest in classical architecture, sparked by the rediscovery of the works of Vitruvius, led architects to develop new techniques, flat ceiling, and the dome. Some architects of the period were **Filippo Brunelleschi** (?1377–1446), **François Mansard** (1598–1666), **Claude Perrault** (1613–88), **François Blondel** (1617–86), **Inigo Jones** (1573–1652), and **Christopher Wren** (1632–1723).

c. 1500. The Portuguese developed the **caravel,** a small, light three-masted (square, lateen, or both) ship that when fitted with cannon could dominate larger vessels and carry more cargo; caravels enabled the Portuguese to take the lead in exploration and expansion. By 1700 the four-masted galleon had evolved.

c. 1510. First of the handbooks on metallurgy appeared, *Probierbergbüchlein* on assaying, *Bergbüchlein* on mining. In 1540 **Vannocio Biringuccio's** (1480–1539) *Pyrotechnica* published, the first practical, comprehensive metallurgy text by a professional metallurgist. Included were descriptions of alloying and cannon-molding processes. In 1556 *De re metallica* of Agricola (Georg Bauer), a physician in the mining area of Saxony, appeared. It covered all aspects of mining from the survey of the site through the equipment and methods of mining to assaying, descriptions of glass-making and blast furnaces, and the treatment of iron, copper, and glass. Agricola was concerned with miners' health and described the diseases to which they are prone.

1520. Wheel lock invented, probably in Italy, one of the steps to a single-handed pistol. By 1525 **rifling** of the gun barrel was a known technique; by 1650 lead shot was molded by means of a split mold; and by 1697 iron cannon were cast directly from the blast furnace. The widespread use of cannon and gunpowder, especially during the Thirty Years' War, increased the costs and destructiveness of war and reduced its glamour.

(To p. 314)

3. EUROPE, 1648–1814

(From p. 284)

a. ECONOMIC AND SOCIAL CHANGES

THE LEGACY OF THE THIRTY YEARS' WAR: This war left two legacies—massive **destruction of land and population** and the **end of Catholic supremacy** in Europe. Armies moved back and forth across Europe, destroying crops and routing people from their homes. Estimates indicate that European population declined by as much as 30 percent in some areas. The war also resulted in major dislocation and migration throughout Europe. Even countries largely untouched by armies suffered loss of trade. **The Baltic grain trade was devastated.** The **Peace of Westphalia** not only ended the war and established territorial boundaries, it codified the principle that the prince would choose the religion (Calvinism, Lutheranism, or Catholicism) of his territory. This principle weakened the Holy Roman Empire because it recognized princely sovereignty. It also furthered **the gradual decline of the Catholic Church** in the 17th and 18th centuries.

THE GENERAL CRISIS OF THE 17TH CENTURY has sparked intense debate among historians. The term "crisis," originally used in the medical sense, refers to an economic and political turning point.

Historians cite the **shift of economic growth in Europe** from the Mediterranean (especially Spain and Italy) toward western Europe (particularly England and France) in demonstrating this turning point. They also recognize the **repeated challenges to political authority.** The 17th century witnessed numerous revolutions (England, the Fronde, the Dutch Republic, etc.) and revolts. **Peasant revolts** regarding taxes spread throughout the 17th century. These revolts focused either on new taxes or on extensions of old ones but were characterized by a desire to return to the status quo.

DEMOGRAPHY (see also individual countries): **Population grew very slowly or remained stagnant before 1730.** It was hampered by **high infant mortality.** Among infants, girls fared better than boys, and adult males characteristically had higher mortality rates than adult females. However, women had higher mortality rates during their childbearing years because childbirth was often deadly. **Relatively low birth rates** also contributed to a lack of population growth. European men and women typically married quite late and had only small families. They generally lived in a nuclear family, often leaving older family members without any recourse but charity and poor assistance from the state.

The lack of support for the elderly may have been a byproduct of the **European marriage pattern;** families suffered greater poverty when they had several children too small to contribute to the family economy in the household. This arrangement also decreased the mother's economic contribution. As a result of late ages at marriage, families often experienced such **life-cycle poverty** at the same time as their elderly parents needed assistance. Problems of life-cycle poverty were exacerbated by the problems of disease that persisted between 1650 and 1730. **Several waves of plague** spread through Europe along trading routes and via armies. Europe also suffered from famine, typhus, and smallpox. After 1730, these problems decreased and population began to grow rapidly, encouraged by the development of proto-industrialization, which led to earlier marriages. However, growth rates varied dramatically from country to country.

The decline of mortality and rise in fertility were partially the result of the **AGRICULTURAL REVOLUTION.** Characterized less by major technological breakthroughs than by **changes in farming technique,** the Agricultural Revolution increased productivity without a corresponding increase in the labor needed to produce food beginning in the late 17th century. This increase came from the **introduction of the nitrogen-fixing crops, which reduced fallow lands, enclosure, and drainage of wetlands.** In the process, some western European landholders consolidated their property, removing tenants and peasants. These peasants eventually worked as day laborers or went to the cities in search of work. Their availability also encouraged the development of protoindustrialization.

PROTOINDUSTRIALIZATION: Partially in an effort to bypass the regulations of guilds, merchants extending the **putting-out system,** in which they supplied cottiers and other poor families in the countryside with the necessary tools and supplies, such as a loom and thread, to complete a given step in a production process. The merchant then deducted charges for those supplies from the overall piece rate and paid the family the difference. This process enabled families living on marginal land to supplement their produce not only with work on neighboring farms but also with nonagricultural work. **The process fit into the family economy** but furthered the creation of a family wage rather than a subsistence economy. It also helped lead to a **decline in the age at first marriage** because it gave couples another means of income. These couples no longer had to secure sufficient land for their livelihood. Likewise, it encouraged **increased family size,** as more children meant more hands available for cottage production. However, unlike the artisan who owned his means of production, these families worked for a middleman who owned both the materials and the equipment. This distinction led many historians to argue that the putting-out system was **a precursor to the factory system.** The process had **three consequences** for industrialization. It increased the size of the labor force by increasing population growth. It created a group of families dependent on cash payment for their labor rather than the sale of their goods. It enabled merchants to amass capital in a system that had greater elasticity than the factory system—protoindustrialization required smaller outlays, and fluctuations in demand could be met by depressing the piece rates. However, protoindustrialization could also lead to **deindustrialization** after 1800. In areas where the putting-out process was not followed by industrial development, emigration drew workers into industrialized areas, resulting in a decline in population and productivity in nonindustrialized areas.

COMMERCIAL SHIFTS: The crisis of the 17th century shifted economic prospects throughout Europe. The **countries bordering the Mediterranean, especially Italy and Spain, declined economically and their position within Europe was taken by Holland and, subsequently, England.** This change was partially owing to **shifts from trade** exclusively with the east to trade with both the east and the Americas. Such trade favored England because of its position on the Atlantic. These shifts also resulted from **changes in investment and the necessity for capital expansion.** Northwest Europeans created banks and other institutions capable of financing expanding trade networks and the putting-out system. Southern Europeans continued to invest in property and land, seldom having a large amount of ready capital available for new ventures. Northwestern Europe also benefited from the **eastern European grain trade.** Eastern European lords **increased serfdom** in an effort to provide the necessary labor for grain production. This enabled eastern

Europe to provide large quantities of cheap grain to the west, fueling western population growth and urbanization. Population growth was also affected by the **introduction of products from the Americas,** notably the **potato and sugar.** The potato gradually spread throughout western Europe and, because it grew well in poor soil, became one of the major foodstuffs for many poorer Europeans. The increases in trade, development of cheap sources of grain and foodstuffs, and population growth ultimately led to the **Industrial Revolution** of the late 18th and the 19th centuries (p. 441).

b. INTELLECTUAL DEVELOPMENTS

(From p. 312)

The **18th-Century Enlightenment** dominated western thought, a product of the **Scientific Revolution** with its emphasis on inductive reasoning and rationality. Though most intense in France, enlightenment thought affected most parts of Europe to some degree. Enlightenment thinkers **critiqued existing government, society, and economic development.** In all aspects, they emphasized reason and frequently embraced notions of the **perfectability of people and progress.** Some, notably **Malthus** (p. 324) and **Burke,** rejected some notions, while in Germany some reaction against Enlightenment universality occurred in the form of cultural nationalism. In political thought, Enlightenment thinkers built upon **John Locke** (p. 322), arguing for a **government that rested on a contract among individuals,** in some cases including women, and those established laws which were reasonable. These ideas threatened the basis for absolutism but also encouraged notions of enlightened absolutism in which the monarch claimed to rule for the good of all based on reason. They also gave rise to a **radical enlightenment** whose thinkers demanded equality for men, and sometimes women, in political and economic terms. The Enlightenment thinkers were particularly influential in shaping economic policies. Many monarchs followed the dictates of **mercantilism** in the late 17th and early 18th centuries. Mercantilists argued that the world contained a fixed-size market and that each country had to secure as large a portion of this market as possible, through tariffs and colonization. Mercantilism was gradually replaced by laissez faire capitalism. The **Physiocrats** stressed agricultural bases for wealth but also discouraged government intervention as counter to natural economic law. However, **Adam Smith** provided the most advanced formulation of this law. He argued that division of labor in an unregulated market would secure high profits and maximum prosperity for all concerned because it would be controlled by the invisible hand of commerce, that is, regulated by supply and demand. The Enlightenment interest in science and human society set the basis for formal study not only in economics, but also in political science and psychology. Among the **major thinkers of the Enlightenment** were (see also individual countries):

Political: Montesquieu, *L'Esprit des lois* (1748); William **Blackstone,** *Commentaries on the Laws of England* (1765–69); Johann Gottfried Herder, *Ideen zur Philosophie der Geschichte der Menschheit* (1784-91); Jeremy **Bentham,** *Introduction to the Principles of Morals and Legislation* (1789); Edmund **Burke,** *Reflections on the Revolution in France* (1790); Thomas **Paine,** *The Rights of Man;* Mary **Wollstonecraft,** *Vindication of the Rights of Women* (1792); William **Godwin,** *Enquiry concerning Political Justice* (1793).

Social and Religious: Bishop George **Berkeley,** *Treatise Concerning the Principles of Human Knowledge* (1710); David **Hume,** *Treatise on Human Nature and Philosophical Essays* (1739); Emanuel **Swedenborg,** *De Nova Hierosolyma* (basis for the Church of the New Jerusalem—1758); Johann P. **Süssmilch,** *Die göttliche Ordnung in den Veränerungen des menschlichen Geschlechts aus der Geburt, dem Tode, und der Fortpflanzung desselben erwiesen,* pioneering statistical and demographic work (1761); Cesare **Beccaria,** *Tratto dei delitti e delle pene* (1764); Thomas **Malthus,** *Essay on the Principle of Population* (1798); Friedrich **Schleiermacher,** *Reden über die Religion* (1799).

General Philosophical and Historical: Pierre **Bayle,** *Dictionnaire historique et critique* (1697); Giambattista **Vico,** *Principi di una scienza nuova intorno alla commune natura delle nazione* (1725); **Voltaire,** *Lettres anglaises ou philosophiques* (1734); Denis **Diderot** and Jean d'Alembert, ed. *L'Encyclopédie* (1751–72); Jean Jacques **Rousseau,** *Le* *contrat social* and *Émile* (1762); Edward **Gibbon**, *The History of the Decline and Fall of the Roman Empire* (1776–88); Immanuel **Kant**, *Die Kritik der reinen Vernunft* (1781); Marie-Jean **Condorcet**, *Tableau historique des progrès de l'esprit humain* (1795).

Economic: Richard **Cantillon**, *Essai sur la nature du commerce en général* (1755); François **Quesnay**, *Tableau économique* (1758); Pierre Dupont **de Nemours**, *La physiocratie* (1768); A. R. J. **Turgot**, *Réflexions sur la formation des richesses* (1766); Adam **Smith**, *An Inquiry into the Nature and Causes of the Wealth of Nations* (1776).   *(To p. 442)*

c. CULTURE AND POPULAR CULTURE

Recurrent interest in classical styles of art and architecture characterized much European culture in the later 17th and through the 18th century. The 17th century saw the perfecting of the **Baroque style** (characterized by freedom of form, motion, and feeling combined with ornamentation) and its use in the great palaces, statuery, and gardens of the absolute monarchs. In literature and drama, **French classicism** held considerable sway. The Enlightenment also encouraged a new interest in the essay.

In the 18th century, a countercurrent of **sentimental literature** began to gain ground, as the novel was introduced. This would lead to more formal **Romanticism** by the 1790s, as in the emotionally charged work of German writers like Johann Wolfgang **Goethe** (1749–1832).

Significant changes in popular culture also occurred from the 17th century onward in western Europe. Protestant and then Catholic writers encouraged **new attention to family relationships.** An emphasis on the importance of **love in marriage** developed in various social groups, resulting in growing tolerance by the 1730s for young people who sought to avoid marriages arranged against their will. New interest in children, encouraged by Enlightenment interest in education, led to a **reduction in the swaddling of infants** in western Europe and, in the wealthier classes, a growing interest in providing educational toys and books. From about 1780 onward, particularly in the lower classes, sexual habits began to change, involving an **increase in non-marital sexual activity,** which did not lead to marriage between partners and, thus, produced a rise in illegitimate births.

Spurred by shifts in government policy, popular beliefs in magic and witchcraft either declined or found less opportunity for public expression. **Popularization of science** and the Enlightenment encouraged interest in new forms of thought, particularly among urban groups. Literacy increased. New institutions, like insurance companies, fire houses, and lost-and-found departments, signaled a growing belief that planning could reduce risks. Traditional practitioners like cunning

men, previously used to seek lost items, declined, though in medicine popular healers continued to be valued.

With commercial expansion, a **new consumer spirit** spread. Popular use of purchased goods like sugar, coffee, and tea expanded. Interest in manufactured, stylish clothing increased.

Popular culture was also colored by new, enthusiastic religious beliefs, like **Pietism** in Germany (p. 337) and **Methodism** in England (p. 323).   *(To p. 443)*

d. SCIENCE AND TECHNOLOGY

(From p. 312)

SCIENCE: The Enlightenment continued the scientific methods used during the Scientific Revolution, emphasizing inductive reasoning and careful analysis. Efforts to catalogue and study plants and animals closely, including dissections, continued, and many of today's scientific principles emanated from this period. **Leading scientific thinkers of the period included** (see also individual countries): Gottfried Wilhelm **Leibniz** (1646–1716); Isaac **Newton** (1642–1727); Edmund **Halley** (1656–1742); Gabriel D. **Fahrenheit** (1686–1736); Etienne F. **Geoffroy** (1672–1731); Leonhard **Euler** (*Mechanica sive motus analytice exposita*, 1736); Johann **Lehmann** (d. 1767); Carl **Linnaeus** (1707–78); Albrecht **von Haller** (1708–77); Giovanni **Morgagni** (1682–1771); John **Hunter** (1728–93); Joseph **Priestley** (1733–1804); Antoine **Lavoisier** (1743–94); Edward **Jenner** (1749-1823); Joseph Louis **Proust** (1754–1826).   *(To p. 443)*

TECHNOLOGY AND NEW TECHNIQUES: Technology during this period concentrated on the development of steam engines, machinery, and improved techniques in engineering, construction, and farming. These were designed as part of the process of protoindustrialization but ultimately contributed to the Industrial Revolution (p. 441) because they provided means of producing goods more quickly and efficiently and offered alternatives to animal and human power, especially coal and water power. **Leading figures in such development** were:

Thomas **Newcomen,** whose steam engine pumped water from mines (1712); roadmakers P. M. J. **Trésaguet** (1716–94) and John L. **McAdam** (invented macadamized roads, 1756–1836); Jethro **Tull,** *New Horse Hoeing Husbandry* (1732); John **Kay** invented the flying shuttle (1733); Robert **Bakewell** introduced selective breeding (1725–95); Arthur **Young** publicized new advances in agriculture; Benjamin **Huntsman's** (1704–76) steel processing and Henry **Cort's** (1740–1800) puddling process; Josiah **Wedgewood,** who established his Etruria bone china works (1769); James **Hargreaves** invented the spinning jenny (1764); James **Watt's** steam engine, a great improvement over Newcomen's (1776).

4. EUROPEAN DIPLOMACY AND WARS, 1648–1795

(From p. 304)

Overview After the **Treaties of Westphalia** (p. 304), European warfare and foreign policy shifted from a concentration on religious differences to focus on issues of trade and territorial acquisition. Declining powers, such as Spain, Poland, and Sweden, attempted to maintain at least regional independence from rising powers such as Prussia, France, and Russia. The struggle to maintain a balance of power as dynastic lines died out or were removed—notably in Spain and Poland—also caused tension. The scale of war and diplomacy increased.

1652–54. First Anglo-Dutch War resulting from the Navigation Acts (p. 320).

1655–60. The First Northern War, with Sweden against Poland (p. 340), concluded by the **Treaty of Oliva** and **Treaty of Copenhagen.** Russia, Denmark, and the empire had joined against Sweden after initial Polish defeat. The **Treaty of Kardis (1661)** between Sweden and Russia reestablished the status quo ante bellum.

1656–59. War between England and Spain. War began after the English captured Jamaica (May). Spanish treasure ships captured off **Cádiz** (Sept. 9, 1956) and Blake victorious (**Santa Cruz,** April 20, 1657). **Dunkirk** (1658) besieged by the English and French. The Spanish were

beaten (**Battle of Dunes,** June 14, 1658). Dunkirk surrendered and the English retained it in Peace of the Pyrenees.

1659. Treaty of the Pyrenees settled the War between France and Spain begun during the Thirty Years' War: (1) **France** received part of Roussillon, Conflans, Cerdagne, and several towns in Artios and Flanders, Hainault, and Luxemburg; (2) the **Duke of Lorraine,** the ally of Spain, was partially reinstated (France received Bar, Clermont, etc., and right of passage for troops); the Prince of Condé entirely reinstated; (3) marriage between **Louis XIV and the infanta Maria Teresa,** Philip IV of Spain's eldest daughter. Maria Teresa renounced her claim to that throne if Spain paid the entirety of her 500,000-crown dowry. Because such a payment seemed unlikely, Louis XIV entertained notions of controlling the Spanish throne.

1661, June 23. Treaty between England and Portugal. Charles II and the infanta Catherine of Braganza to wed. England received Tangier, Bombay, and 2 million crowns.

1665–67. Second Anglo-Dutch War. England defeated the Dutch fleet off **Lowestoft** (June) but the Dutch blocked the **Thames** (Oct.).

1666, Jan. Following foiled efforts to mediate between England and Holland, France allied itself with Holland. English navy defeated at **the Four Days Fight** but successful at **North Foreland.** Robert Holmes set 250 Dutch merchant ships ablaze (**Holmes' Bonfire,** Aug.).

1667. England and Holland began peace talks (May). **Medway Disaster** (June) and English defeat of French off **Martinique** (June 20).

July 31. Peace of Breda. England agreed to the Dutch interpretation of the Navigation Acts and confirmed control of "the New Netherlands" (p. 411).

1667–68. War of Devolution. This began a series of wars of conquest by Louis XIV. French strength and ambition provided the main issues in European diplomacy for the ensuing 50 years.

Cause: After Philip IV of Spain's death, Louis XIV laid claim to the Spanish royal family's personal estates in the Netherlands on behalf of his wife. He based this claim on Spain's failure to pay his wife's entire dowry (invalidating her renunciation of her inheritance) and the local **droit de dévolution,** a principle in private law which gave the survivor (widow or widower) usufruct of the property but vested its ownership in the children. Under this law, daughters of the first marriage inherited before sons of a second marriage.

1667. Turenne invaded **Flanders,** where he met with little resistance. Flanders received no support from the Holy Roman Emperor because the Rhineland states refused to assist him.

1668, Jan. Louis XIV and the emperor signed a partition treaty.

Jan. 23. Sweden, Holland, and England signed the Triple Alliance.

May 2. Treaty of Aix-la-Chapelle: Louis XIV restored Franche-Comté (the fortresses having been dismantled) to Spain, in return for 12 fortified towns on the border of the Spanish Netherlands (Lille, Tournay, Oudenarde, etc.) The question of succession was deferred.

1670. Secret Treaty of Dover between Charles II of England and Louis XIV. Louis XIV sought to undermine the Triple Alliance and so followed this treaty with another.

1672. Treaty between Sweden and France and subsidy treaties with Cologne and Münster.

1672–78. French War against the Dutch.

1672. Passage of the Rhine. Louis XIV, Turenne, and Condé led 100,000 men in an easy conquest of southern Holland. The province of Holland and the city of Amsterdam were saved by opening the sluices.

March 17. England declared war on the Dutch (**Third Anglo-Dutch War, 1672–74**).

May 28. Anglo-French forces defeated at **Battle of Sole Bay.**

June. French take Utrecht. De Witt Brothers fell and William of Orange became stadholder.

1673. Failure of the Cologne Peace Conference and naval setbacks for French and English stopped allied plans to invade Holland.

Aug. Dutch allied with the emperor, Spain, and Lorraine.

1673. Frederick William of Prussia concluded the separate peace of Vossem, in which he retained his possessions in Cleves, except Wesel and Rees.

1674. Declaration of war by the empire.

1674. Continuation of French-Dutch war. Louis conquered **Franche-Comté in person;** Condé fought against Orange (drawn battle of **Senef**) in the Netherlands. Turenne on the upper Rhine fought brilliantly (first ravaging of the Palatinate) against Montecuccoli, the imperial general, and the elector of Brandenburg. The latter, recalled because Swedish allies of Louis XIV had entered his lands, defeated the Swedes in the **Battle of Fehrbellin (June 28, 1675).**

July 27. Turenne fell at Sasbach, in Baden. The French retreated across the Rhine.

1676. French naval successes in the Mediterranean against the Dutch and Spanish.

1678. Surprise and **capture of Ghent and Ypres** by the French. Negotiations with each combatant had been in progress for some time.

1678–79. Negotiations resulted in the **Treaties of Nimwegen (Nijmwegen, Nimeguen).** Holland and France (Aug. 10, 1678); Spain and France (Sept. 17, 1678); the emperor, with France and Sweden (Feb. 6, 1679); Holland with Sweden (Oct. 12, 1679). At Fontainebleau, France and Denmark (Sept. 2, 1679). At Lund, Denmark and Sweden (Sept. 26, 1679).

(1) **Holland** received its whole territory back provided it remained neutral. (2) **France received from Spain** Franche-Comté, Valenciennes, Cambray, the Cambrésis, Aire, Poperingen, St. Omer, Ypres, Condé,

Bouchain, Maubeuge, and so on; **Spain received from France** Charleroi, Binche, Oudenarde, Ath, Courtray, Limburg, Ghent, and Waes, among others; and in Catalonia, Puycerda. (3) **The emperor ceded to France** Freiburg in the Breisgau; France gave up the right of garrison in Phillippsburg; the Duke of Lorraine was to be restored to his duchy but refused to accept the conditions pertaining to that restoration.

1679, June 29. Peace of St. Germain-en-Laye forced on the elector of Prussia by France. The elector surrendered most of his conquests in Pomerania to Sweden in exchange for the reversion of East Friesland, which became Prussian in 1744, and a small indemnification.

1683. Invasions of the Spanish Netherlands by France, occupation of **Luxemburg,** and **seizure of Trier (1684).** Lorraine permanently occupied by France.

1684. A temporary truce concluded at Regensburg (Ratisbon) between Louis, the emperor, and the empire.

1686, July 9. Formation of the League of Augsburg under the direction of William of Orange and signed by the emperor, Sweden, Spain, Bavaria, Saxony, and the Palatinate. The English Revolution of 1688 added England to France's foes.

1688–97. WAR OF THE LEAGUE OF AUGSBURG. Causes: The elector of the Palatinate, Charles, died in 1685, leaving no male heirs to his throne. Louis XIV claimed a portion of the Palatinate because his sister-in-law (wife of the duke of Orléans) was Charles's sister. Louis XIV also supported Von Fürstenberg, bishop of Strasbourg, for election of the archbishopric of Cologne rather than Prince of Clement of Bavaria (1688).

1689, May 12. The Grand Alliance, including the powers of the League of Augsburg, England, and Holland (Savoy had joined the league in 1687). The principal scene of war was the Netherlands.

1690, June 30. French victorious at the **Battle of Fleurus,** followed by French successes in Piedmont, Savoy, and at Staffarda.

1692, May 19. French fleet under Tourville defeated at **La Hogue** by Dutch and English ships.

Aug. 3. Battle of Steinkirk (Steenkerken). Victory of General Luxembourg over William III of England.

1693, June. Battle of Lagos. British fleet defeated by the French under Tourville.

July 29. Battle of Neerwinden. Victory of Luxembourg over William III, who in spite of his many defeats still kept the field.

In Italy, Marshal Catinat defeated the duke of Savoy at **Marsaglia.**

1695. Death of Luxembourg, who was succeeded by Villeroy.

Sept. William III recaptured Namur.

1696. Separate peace with Savoy at Turin. All conquests restored to the duke (Pignerol and Casale). His daughter married Louis's grandson, the duke of Burgundy. Savoy promised to remain neutral.

1697, Sept. 20. Treaty of Ryswick among France, England, Spain, and Holland. (1) Confirmed separate peace with **Savoy.** (2) Restored all conquests among **France, England, and Holland;** William III acknowledged as king of England and Anne as his successor, Louis promising not to help his enemies. (3) Chief fortresses in the **Spanish Netherlands** to be garrisoned with Dutch troops as a barrier between France and Holland. (4) France restored all conquests and all but 82 places that had been "reunited" since the Treaty of Nimwegen to **Spain** (p. 329). (5) Holland restored Pondichéry in India to the **French East India Company** and received commercial privileges in return.

Oct. 30. Treaty between France and the emperor ratified the treaty of Ryswick. (1) **France** ceded all the "reunions" except Alsace. (2) **Strasbourg** ceded to France. (3) **France** ceded Freiburg and Breisack to the emperor and Phillipsburg to the empire. (4) **Zweibrücken restored** to the king of Sweden, as Count Palatine of the Rhine. (5) **Lorraine restored** to Duke Leopold (excepting Saarlouis). (6) **The claims of Cardinal Fürsternburg** to the archbishopric of Cologne were disavowed. (7) **The Rhine** was made free.

1698, Oct. 11. First Treaty of Partition to determine succession in Spain (p. 330). **Joseph Ferdinand,** electoral prince of Bavaria, named as primary heir. He would receive Spain, Indies, and the Netherlands. **The Dauphin** would receive Naples, Sicily, seaports in Tuscany, and the province of Guipozcoa. **Archduke Charles** would receive the Duchy of Milan.

This treaty angered **Charles II** of Spain because he had not been consulted. In order to preserve the unity of the monarchy, he made the

prince elector of Bavaria, then seven years old, sole heir to the whole inheritance, a settlement to which the naval powers agreed.

1699, Feb. 6. Sudden death of the prince elector and more maneuvering by the French led to the **Second Treaty of Partition (March 13, 1700).** Spain and the Indies to **Archduke Charles;** Naples and Sicily and the Duchy of Lorraine to **the Dauphin;** Milan to the **duke of Lorraine** in exchange. **The two branches of the house of the Habsburgs were always to remain separate.** Charles II signed a new will, making Louis's grandson, **Philip of Anjou,** heir.

1700–1721. The GREAT NORTHERN WAR (p. 340). Tsar Peter was at first no match for the Swedish king, Charles XII, who defeated him at **Narva (Nov. 30, 1700).** But Charles spent the next years campaigning in Poland, thus giving Peter an opportunity to reorganize this army on European lines and to construct a fleet in the Baltic.

1709, July 8. The BATTLE OF POLTAVA. Charles XII, allied with Mazeppa, the Cossack hetman, began to march on Moscow but then turned south. At Poltava, Peter won a resounding victory that broke the power of Charles and marked the emergence of Russia as the dominant northern power.

1701–14. WAR OF THE SPANISH SUCCESSION.

Cause: Charles II, King of Spain, was childless and Europe preoccupied with finding an appropriate heir who would maintain the balance of power. **England and Holland** did not want the crown to fall to the French or Austrian monarchs; both **Leopold I and Louis XIV established claims** on behalf of members of their families: (1) **Louis XIV** at once as son of the elder daughter of Philip III and husband of the elder daughter of Philip IV. The solemn renunciations of both princesses were declared null and void by the parlement of Paris. (2) **Leopold I,** the representative of the German Habsburg line, as son of the younger daughter of Philip III and husband of the younger daughter of Philip IV. Both princesses had expressly reserved their right of inheritance. Leopold claimed on behalf of his second son, Charles. (3) The **electoral prince of Bavaria,** as great-grandson of Philip IV and grandson of the younger sister of the present possessor Charles II.

1701, Sept. 7. Grand Alliance of the naval powers with Emperor Leopold I to secure the Spanish possessions in the Netherlands and in Italy for the Austrian house. **France** allied itself with the dukes of **Savoy and Mantua,** the electors of **Bavaria and Cologne.** The other states of the empire, especially Prussia, joined the emperor. Portugal afterward joined the Grand Alliance and in 1703 Savoy did likewise, deserting France. Allied victory at **Carpi** and **Chiara.**

1702. Drawn battle at Luzzara gave France the advantage in Italy until 1706.

1703. The Bavarians invaded Tyrol but were repulsed. Eugene went to **Germany** along the Rhine. Marlborough invaded the **Spanish Netherlands.** Archduke Charles landed in Spain and invaded **Catalonia,** where he established himself as Charles III.

1704. The English captured **Gibraltar.**

Aug. 13. Battle of Höchstädt and Blenheim (Blindheim). Bavarians and French (Tallard) defeated by Eugene and Marlborough.

1706. Charles (Habsburg) conquered Madrid but held it for a short time only.

May 23. Victory of Marlborough at Ramillies over Villeroy. Submission of Brussels, Antwerp, Ghent, Ostend, etc.

Sept. 7. Victory of Eugene at Turin. Submission of all Lombardy. **Charles III (Habsburg) proclaimed at Milan.** The French excluded from Italy.

1708, July 11. Victory of Marlborough and Eugene at **Oudenarde** over Vendôme and the duke of Burgundy. **Siege and surrender of Lille.**

Negotiations for peace broke down when the Allies demanded that Louis XIV drive his grandson from Spain with French weapons.

1709, Sept. 11. Battle of Malplaquet. French defeat and the bloodiest battle of the war. In Spain, Philip, with the aid of Vendôme, had the advantage over Charles. The Spanish people favored Philip. **Renewal of the negotiations at Gertruydenburg.** Louis offered to pay subsidized troops against his grandson. The allies demanded he send his armies against Philip. Renewal of the war.

1710. French victories over the British (**Brihuega**) and the empire (**Villa Viciosa,** in Spain).

1710–11. War with the Ottoman Empire, owing to pressure from the Swedish Charles XII (a refugee in Turkey) and France. The Russians were surrounded by the Ottoman forces on the Pruth River and Peter had to buy himself off. By the **Treaty of the Pruth (July 21, 1711),** he was obliged to return Azov to the Ottomans.

1711. Death of the emperor Joseph, whereby Charles VI became heir to all the Austrian possessions, so that the Habsburgs would have been restored had the Spanish inheritance also devolved upon him. These events completely altered all political relations in favor of Louis XIV, as the other powers feared a Habsburg hold over Spain as well as Austria.

1712. Victory of the French at **Denain;** recapture of **Douai, Le Quesnoy, and Bouchain.** Opening of the **Congress at Utrecht.** Dissensions among the allies caused the conclusion of separate treaties of peace under the name of

1713, April 11. TREATY OF UTRECHT, which ended Louis XIV's wars.

(1) **Britain:** Recognition of the Protestant succession in England; confirmation of the permanent separation of the crowns of France and Spain. France ceded to Britain Newfoundland, Nova Scotia (Acadia), and the Hudson Bay territory but retained Quebec; Spain ceded to Britain Gibraltar, the island of Minorca, and the *asiento.*

(2) **Holland:** Surrender of the Spanish Netherlands to the Republic of Holland, to be turned over to the Austrians after a barrier treaty agreed to regarding fortresses along the French border from Furnes to Namur, garrisoned by the Dutch. Lille restored to France. Demolition of the fortifications of Dunkirk.

(3) **Savoy** received the island of Sicily as a kingdom and an advantageous change of boundary in upper Italy and renounced its claims upon Spain, reserving, however, its right of inheritance in case the house of Bourbon should become extinct.

(4) **Prussia** received recognition of the royal title (p. 337) and possession of Neuchâtel and the upper quarter of Guelders. Prussia's claim upon the principality of Orange, on the Rhône, was transferred to France.

(5) **Portugal** obtained a correction of boundaries in South America (p. 406).

Philip V (founder of the Spanish branch of the Bourbons) (p. 330) was recognized as king of Spain and the colonies.

1713. The emperor and the empire continued the war, but, after defeats at Landau and Freiburg, concluded peace with France in his own name at **Rastatt** and in that of the empire at **Baden** (in Switzerland).

1714 March–Sept.. Treaty of Rastatt and Baden. Austria took possession of the Spanish Netherlands, after the barrier for Holland had been agreed upon, and retained Naples, Sardinia, and Milan. The electors of Bavaria and Cologne, who had been placed under the ban of the empire, were reinstated in their lands and dignities. Landau was left in the hands of France. No peace between Spain and the emperor, who did not recognize the Bourbons in Spain.

After Utrecht, with French strength reduced, major 18th-century diplomacy revolved around **Anglo-French rivalry** in Europe and colonial areas and **Austrian-Prussian rivalry** in Central Europe. Russian, Spain, Holland, Sweden, and some smaller German states fit variously into the resulting alliances and wars.

1718, Aug. 2. Quadruple Alliance for the maintenance of the Treaty of Utrecht, among France, Britain, and the emperor, and (1719) the Republic of Holland. After a short war and the fall of Alberoni, who went to Rome, the agreements of the **Quadruple Alliance were executed in 1720:** (1) **Spain** evacuated Sicily and Sardinia and made a renunciation of the appanages forever, in return for which the emperor recognized the Spanish Bourbons; (2) **Savoy** was obliged to exchange Sicily for Sardinia. After this time the dukes of Savoy called themselves kings of Sardinia.

The **emperor Charles VI was without male offspring** (p. 339). His principal endeavor throughout his reign was to secure the various lands that were united under the scepter of Austria against division after his death. Hence he established an order of succession under the name of the **Pragmatic Sanction,** which decreed that (1) the lands belonging to the Austrian empire should be indivisible; (2) in case male heirs should fail, the lands should devolve upon Charles's daughters, the eldest of whom was **Maria Theresa,** and their heirs according to the law of primogeniture; (3) in case of the extinction of this line the daughters of Joseph I and their descendants were to inherit.

Securing the assent of the various powers to the **Pragmatic Sanction** was the object of numerous diplomatic negotiations. **The Hungarian Diet accepted it in 1723** (p. 339). A special agreement between **Austria and Spain (1725)** in regard to this measure produced the **alliance of Herrenhausen** in opposition, in the same year, between **Britain, France, and Prussia.** Prussia soon withdrew from the alliance and joined Austria by the **Treaty of Wusterhausen.** The alliance between Austria and Spain was also of short duration.

1720–21. Conclusion of Northern War by Treaties of Stockholm (prewar boundaries among Sweden, Saxony, Poland restored; cession of Swedish territory to Hanover and Prussia; Denmark yields conquests in return for Swedish payment) and

1721, Aug. 30. Treaty of Nystadt between Russia and Sweden. Russia acquired Livonia, Estonia, Ingermanland, part of Karelia, and a number of Baltic islands. Thus Peter had achieved his great purpose of **acquiring a window on the Baltic** which would open up connections with the west.

1733–35. WAR OF THE POLISH SUCCESSION, after the death of Augustus II.

Cause: Most of the Polish nobles, under the influence of France, elected **Stanislas Leszczynski,** who had become the father-in-law of Louis XV, king for a second time. Russia and Austria induced a minority to choose **Augustus III, Elector of Saxony** (son of Augustus II) and supported the election by the presence of troops in Poland; France, Spain, and Sardinia took up arms for Stanislas.

War was initially concentrated in Italy, though Russia invaded Poland (p. 344). Milan, Naples, and Sicily were conquered, and the Austrians lost everything except Milan. **Lorraine** occupied by the French. **Kehl** captured. **Preliminaries of peace (1735),** and, after long negotiations,

1738, Nov. 18. TREATY OF VIENNA ratified. (1) Stanislas Leszczynski renounced the Polish throne, receiving as compensation the Duchies of Lorraine and Bar, which at his death were to devolve to France. Stanislas died in 1766. (2) **The duke of Lorraine,** Francis Stephen, received an indemnification in Tuscany, whose ducal throne had become vacant by the extinction of the family of Medici, 1737. (3) **Austria** ceded Naples and Sicily, the island of Elba, and the *stati degli Presidi* to Spain as a secundogeniture for Don Carlos so that these lands could never be united with the crown of Spain. It received in exchange Parma and Piacenza, which Don Carlos had inherited in 1731 upon the death of the last Farnese, his great uncle. (4) **France** guaranteed the Pragmatic Sanction.

1739–48. WAR BETWEEN BRITAIN AND SPAIN (War of Jenkins' Ear). Cause: English trading in the Spanish empire and Spain's efforts to stop it. English captured **Porto Bello in Darien (Nov. 22, 1739)** and unsuccessfully attacked **Cartagena (1740).** Voyage of the **English Commodore Anson to Chile and Peru** and around the world (Sept. 1740–June 1744).

1740–48. WAR OF AUSTRIAN SUCCESSION: Cause: Charles Albert, elector of Bavaria, Philip V, king of Spain, and Augustus III of Saxony all claimed the Austrian throne. **Charles Albert** cited Ferdinand I's will, which stated that succession should fall to descendants of his eldest daughter, Anna, should legitimate heirs to the Habsburg throne become extinct. A descendant of Anna, Charles Albert interpreted this will to mean male heirs of the Habsburgs. **Philip V** cited a treaty between Charles V and his brother, Ferdinand. **Augustus III** claimed the throne by virtue of marriage to Joseph I's eldest daughter. Prussia accepted the succession but claimed the right to annex Silesia. Frederick II offered to support Austria in exchange for this right.

Course of War: 1740–42. First Silesian War. As a result of a dispute over Prussian claims to Silesian territories, Frederick occupied Silesia and captured Glogau. Prussia victorious at **Mollwitz** (April 10, 1741), then Czaslau and **Chotusitz** (May 17, 1742).

1741. Secret alliance of Nymphenburg against Austria concluded by France, Bavaria, and Spain, afterward joined by Saxony and lastly by Prussia. The allied French (Belle-Isle) and Bavarian army **invaded Austria and Bohemia.** Prague taken in alliance with the Saxons. **Charles Albert** proclaimed archduke in Linz, while **Frederick II received** homage in Silesia. **Charles Albert was elected emperor in Frankfurt (Charles VII).**

1742, June–July. To rid herself of a dangerous enemy, Maria Theresa signed the **Treaty of Breslau and Berlin between Austria and Prussia.**

Prussia received Silesia and the country of Glatz, with the Oppa forming the boundary between Austrian and Prussian territories. In exchange, Frederick withdrew from the alliance against Maria Theresa and assumed the Silesian debt to English and Dutch creditors (1.7 million rix dollars).

1744–45. SECOND SILESIAN WAR. Austrian successes and treaties with Sardinia and Saxony (1743) made the king of Prussia anxious. He concluded a second alliance with Charles VII and France and forced his way through Saxony with 80,000 men, invading Bohemia. He took Prague but, deserted by the French, was soon driven back into Saxony (1744).

1745, Jan. Alliance among Austria, Saxony, Britain, and Holland against Prussia. The French and Bavarians took Munich. Charles VII died (Jan. 1745).

April. Charles's son Maximilian Joseph concluded the **Separate Treaty of Füssen, with Austria.** (1) Austria restored all conquests to Bavaria. (2) The elector of Bavaria surrendered his pretensions to Austria and promised Francis Stephen, the husband of Maria Theresa, his vote at the imperial election.

The French under Marshall Maurice of Saxony (Maréchal de Saxe, son of Augustus II and the Countess Aurora of Königsmark) defeated the Pragmatic army in the **Battle of Fontenoy (Irish Brigade) on May 11** and began the conquest of the Austrian Netherlands.

June 4. Battle of Hohenfriedberg. Austrians and Saxons defeated by Frederick the Great.

Sept. 30. Battle of Soor, Austrians defeated.

Dec. 25. Treaty of Dresden concluded between Prussia and Austria (Saxony). (1) Ratification of the Treaty of Breslau and Berlin in regard to the possession of Silesia. (2) Frederick II recognized Francis I as emperor. (3) Saxony paid Prussia one million rix dollars.

The Russian empress, Elizabeth, allied herself with Austria and sent an army to the Rhine.

1748, Oct. 18. This resulted in a congress and the **Treaty of Aix-la-Chapelle.** (1) Reciprocal restoration of all conquests (p. 413). (2) Cessions of Parma, Piacenz, and Guastalla to the Spanish infanta. **The following guaranties were given:** Silesia should belong to Prussia; the Pragmatic Sanction should be sustained in Austria; the house of Hanover should retain the succession in its German states and in Great Britain.

1756–63. Third Silesian or SEVEN YEARS' WAR.

Cause: Before the Treaty of Aix-la-Chapelle, **Maria Theresa** had concluded a defensive alliance with Frederick's personal enemy, **Elizabeth, tsarina of Russia in May 1746.** Secret articles of this treaty provided for the **reunion of Silesia with Austria under certain specified conditions.** In Sept. 1750, **George II of Great Britain,** moved by anxiety for his principality of Hanover, signed the main treaty, the secret articles being excepted. **Saxony** (minister, Count Brühl) signed the treaty unconditionally. Count (prince in 1764) **Wenzel von Kaunitz** (until 1753 Austrian ambassador in France, then chancellor of the empire in Vienna) succeeded in promoting a reconciliation between the cabinets of Versailles and Vienna and **securing the Marquise de Pompadour in favor of an Austrian alliance. Formation of a party inimical to the Prussian alliance at the French court.**

Maria Theresa and Kaunitz induced Britain to conclude a new subsidy treaty with Russia in 1755. In June of the same year, however, hostilities broke out between Britain and France in North America without any declaration of war. Dreading a French attack upon Hanover, **George II concluded, in Jan. 1756, a treaty of neutrality with Frederick at Westminster,** which caused a rupture between Britain and Russia. Kaunitz made skillful use of the indignation at Versailles over the Treaty of Westminster. **In May 1756,** conclusion of a **defensive alliance between France and Austria.** In June 1756 war broke out between France and Britain in Europe.

Frederick, well-informed concerning the alliances of the powers and knowing that Russia and France were not in condition to take the offensive against him in 1756, **decided to take his enemies by surprise.**

1756, Aug. He invaded Saxony with 67,000 men and took **Dresden.** On Oct. 1, he defeated the Austrians at **Lobostiz.** The Saxons surrendered at **Pirna (Oct. 15).**

1757, Jan. 10. War was declared on Frederick in the name of the empire. Hanover, Hesse, Brunswick, and Gotha, however, continued in alliance with Prussia. Conclusion of an agreement between **Austria and**

THE HOUSE OF HANOVER (1714–1837)

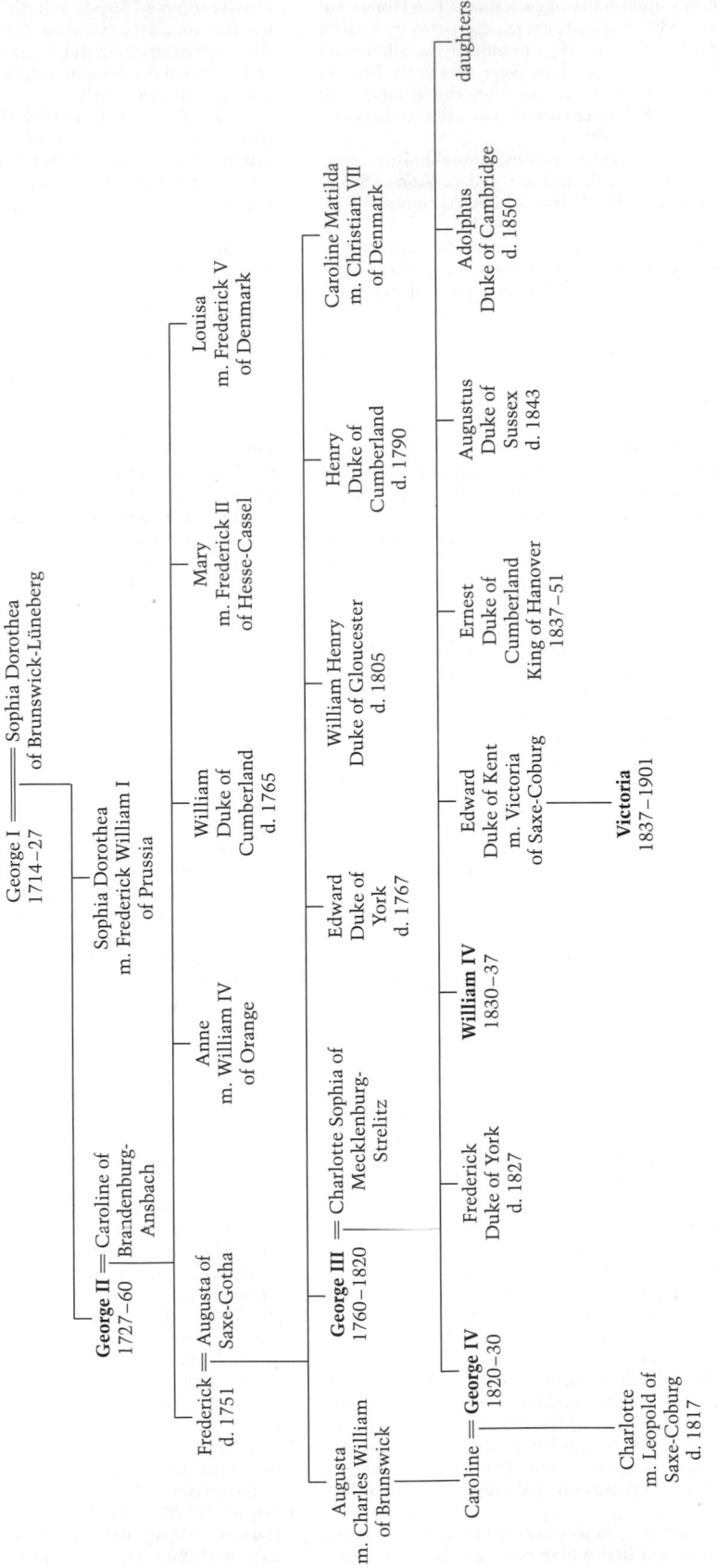

Russia (Jan.) concerning the partition of the Prussian monarchy. Offensive treaty between **Austria and France (May 1).**

1757, May 6. Frederick invaded Bohemia in four columns and won a **victory over the Austrians at Prague.** Frederick besieged Prague and attacked the army of Count Daun, who attempted to relieve the city.

June 18. Frederick was defeated in the **Battle of Kolin,** as a result of which he had to evacuate Bohemia.

July 26. Victory of the French over the British at Hastenbeck, which led to the capitulation of the British army at Kloster-Zeven (Sept. 8). The French occupied Hanover, though the treaty was rejected by the British government.

July 30. Battle of Grossjägerndorf, in which the Russians, under Apraxin, defeated the Prussians, under Lehwald. The Russians then withdrew from East Prussia. The **Swedes began to occupy Pomerania,** promised them in return for participation in the war.

Nov. 5. BATTLE OF ROSSBACH. The French had joined the imperial army to liberate Saxony. Frederick surprised them on the march and completely overwhelmed them.

Dec. 5. Battle of Leuthen. Frederick defeated the Austrians.

1758. Frederick campaigned in Moravia but failed to take Olmütz.

June 23. In the west, Ferdinand of Brunswick drove the French back over the Rhine and defeated them in the **Battle of Crefeld.**

Aug. 25. Battle of Zorndorf. Prussian victory over Russian army.

Oct. 14. Battle of Hochkirch. The Austrians had invaded the Lusatia and Frederick had hurried to the relief of his brother Henry. Baun defeated the Prussians at Hochkirch but was unable to drive Frederick out of Saxony and Silesia.

1759. The French resumed the offensive in the west and defeated Ferdinand of Brunswick at **Bergen, near Frankfurt (April 13).** The Russians once again advanced into Germany and defeated the Prussians at **Kay (July 23).** Ferdinand defeated the French at **Minden (Aug. 1).** Frederick was unable to prevent their union with the Austrians and suffered a major reverse in the **BATTLE OF KUNERSDORF (Aug. 12).** The Austrians thereupon captured Dresden on Nov. 20.

1760, June 23. The Prussians, under Fouqué, were defeated and captured by the Austrians in the battle of **Landshut,** but on **Aug. 15, Frederick's victory** over Laudon in the Battle of Liegnitz (Pfaffendorf) enabled him to prevent the union of the Austrians and Russians.

Oct. 9–12. The Russians, under Tottleben, nevertheless **surprised and burned Berlin.**

Nov. 3. Victory of Frederick over Daun at Torgau.

1761. On Oct. 1, the Austrians took **Schweidnitz.** The Russians occupied Kolberg (Dec. 16). Frederick, deprived of the British subsidies by the accession of George III (p. 318), was in great distress.

1762, Jan. 5. Frederick's position was saved by the death of Elizabeth of Russia. Her successor, Peter II, was an admirer of Frederick and very soon concluded the **Truce of Stargard (March 16),** which was followed by the **Treaty of St. Petersburg (May 5, 1762).** Russia restored all conquests and both parties renounced all hostile alliances.

May 22. The defection of Russia brought with it also the **Treaty of Hamburg** between Sweden and Prussia, which restored the status quo ante bellum. The alliance between Prussia and Russia was soon broken off by the deposition of Peter III (July 9). His successor, Catherine II, recalled her troops from Frederick's army; nevertheless their inactivity upon the field contributed to the **victory of Frederick at Burkersdorf** (July 21) over the Austrians.

Oct. 29. Battle of Freiburg. Austrians and imperial forces defeated. The preliminaries of the Treaty of Fontainebleau between England and France assured French withdrawal from Germany and prepared the

1763, Feb. 10. TREATY OF PARIS among Great Britain, France, and Spain. (1) France ceded to Britain: in North America, Canada and Cape Breton Island; the Mississippi was recognized as the boundary between Louisiana and the British colonies; in the West Indies, Grenada; in Africa, the French possessions on the Senegal. Britain restored to France Goree in Africa and Pondichéry and Chandernagor in India. (2) Spain ceded to Britain Florida, as indemnification for which France had already ceded Louisiana to Spain; Spain received from Britain all conquests in Cuba including Havana (p. 413).

Feb. 15. TREATY OF HUBERT(U)SBURG between Austria and Prussia: (1) **Ratification of the treaties of Breslau and Berlin,** and of Dresden, that is, Prussia retained Silesia. (2) Prussia promised its vote for the archduke Joseph at the election of the king of Rome. Saxony (restoration to the status quo) and the empire were included in the peace.

1772, Aug. 5. THE FIRST PARTITION OF POLAND (p. 344). Frederick the Great engineered the partition of Poland to quell Russian and Austrian antagonisms. **Russia acquired White Russia** and all territory to the Dvina and Dnieper, about 1.8 million inhabitants (mostly Eastern Orthodox); **Austria took Red Russia, Galicia, and western Podolia,** with Lemberg and part of Kraków (2.7 inhabitants); **Prussia took Polish Prussia,** except Danzig and Thorn (416,000 inhabitants). Poland lost about one-third of its territory and about half of its inhabitants.

1776–83. Britain and France at war in the American colonies, France siding with the colonists against Britain.

1778–79. War of Bavarian Succession opposed Prussia and Austria over choices of New Bavarian Royal House; resolved in 1779 Treaty of Teschen.

1793, Jan. 23. SECOND PARTITION OF POLAND. Russia took most of Lithuania and most of the western Ukraine, including Podolia (3 million inhabitants); **Prussia took Danzig and Thorn as well as Great Poland** (1.1 million inhabitants). Russia forced Poland to accept a **treaty of alliance giving Russian troops free entry in Poland** and Russia control of Polish foreign policy.

1795, Oct. 24. THIRD PARTITION OF POLAND. Russia took what remained of **Lithuania and the Ukraine** (1.2 million inhabitants); **Prussia secured Mazovia with Warsaw** (1 million inhabitants), while **Austria obtained the remainder of the Kraków region** (1 million inhabitants). Courland was incorporated with Russia.   *(To p. 431)*

5. NATIONAL PATTERNS, 1648–1815

a. ENGLAND, SCOTLAND, AND IRELAND

(From p. 289)

1. ENGLAND AND SCOTLAND

Monarchs: The Commonwealth (1649–60). Charles II (1660–85). James II (1685–88). William and Mary (1689–95). William (1695–1702). Anne (1702–14). George I (1714–27). George II (1727–60). George III (1760–1820).

DEMOGRAPHY: Population remained largely unchanged between 1650 and 1730 but doubled in the latter half of the 18th century, mostly because of increased birth rates, as infant mortality did not begin to decline until the early 19th century.

1648. Typhus epidemic struck Britain.

1649–60. THE COMMONWEALTH. Power in the new model army and Oliver Cromwell. Legislative power theoretically in the Rump, executive power in a council of state of 41. House of Lords and title and office of the king abolished.

Economy: Bad harvests (1647–50) and civil war led to an increase in food prices and in rents. Lands seized during the civil war were redistributed, which facilitated improvement of lands after 1668.

Society: Non-Anglican congregations and radical movements flourished in the 1650s. Some congregations gave increased roles to women, who were allowed to teach, preach, and prophesy. As a result of these increased roles and women's growing independence during the civil wars, women's status improved after 1648.

1648, Sept. 11. Levellers' petition repudiated the notion of economic equality through redistribution of property. This notion was espoused by the **Diggers, or True Levellers,** who combined the Levellers' demands for democracy presented in the **Putney Debates** with the Leveller definition of a free Englishman as someone who could freely dispose of his labor, property, or person.

1649. Diggers began cultivating St. George's Hill. Led by Gerrard Win-stanley, they called for wasteland to be given to the poor for cultivation.

Feb. 5. Scots proclaimed Charles II in Edinburgh. Cromwell suppressed rebellion in Ireland, which raised the Irish question to a new height.

1650. Adultery became a capital offense. Local acts began to regulate drinking and government tried to enact legislation to regulate morals, for example, drunkenness and dancing.

1650. Montrose came again to Scotland, was beaten at **Corbiesdale (April 27)**, captured and executed at **Edinburgh (May 21).**

June 23. Charles II landed in Scotland, took the oath, and was proclaimed king (June 24). Despite Scottish defeat at **Dunbar (Sept. 3)**, Charles II crowned at Scone and marched into England.

1651–60. All court proceedings written in English rather than in French and Latin. This movement symbolized efforts to throw off the "**Norman yoke" associated with William the Conqueror.**

1651, Aug. 2. Cromwell took the Perth and then completely defeated the royal army at Worcester (Sept. 3).

Oct. 9. Navigation Act (in conjunction with one passed Oct. 1650) forbade import of goods except in English vessels or in vessels of the producing country.

1652. War with the Dutch, primarily naval, resulted from Navigation Act. The English won off the **Downs** (May). War declared. English defeated Tromp off **Portland, Feb. 18, 1653,** and off **North Foreland** (June 2–3), and **Texel** (July 31).

1653, April 20. Cromwell expelled the Rump Parliament and called a nominated parliament of 140 members, the **Barebones' Parliament** (July 4). The Cromwellians in Parliament resigned their powers to Cromwell (Dec. 12).

1653, Dec. 16–1658, Sept. 3. CROMWELL LORD PROTECTOR of the Commonwealth of England, Scotland, and Ireland. The **Instrument of Government,** a written constitution. The executive (lord protector) had a cooperative council of 21; a standing army of 30,000; triennial parliaments of 460 members; once summoned, parliament could not be dissolved within five months. The protector and council could issue ordinances between sessions, but parliament alone could grant supplies and levy taxes.

1654, Sept. 3. The new Parliament quarreled with Cromwell. Cromwell ordered an exclusion of members (Sept. 12). Parliament made the office of protector elective and was dissolved (Jan. 22, 1655).

1655, March–May. The rising of Penruddock at Salisbury suppressed and Penruddock executed. England divided into 12 military districts; each district's force supported by 10 percent tax on royalist estates. Press censored. Anglican clergy forbidden to teach or preach. Catholic priests ordered out of the kingdom.

Oct. Pacification of Pinerolo, with France: the duke of Savoy stopped the persecution of Vaudois and Charles II was to be expelled from France.

1656–59. War with Spain (p. 314).

1657, March–May. Humble Petition and Advice, which established a second house and reduced the power of the council of state and protector. It proclaimed toleration of all Trinitarian Christians except Episcopalians and Catholics.

May 8. Cromwell rejected title of king.

1658, Sept. 3–1659, May 25. Richard Cromwell, lord protector. New Parliament involved in a dispute with the army and Richard dissolved Parliament (April 22). **Rump Parliament** formed under Lenthall (speaker) and Richard induced to resign as lord protector. The army expelled the Rump and appointed a military committee of safety (Oct.). Reaction against the military restored the Rump (Dec. 26).

1660, Feb. 3. General George Monck and his army went to London. Monck **reestablished the Long Parliament,** including members of Parliament excluded by Pride's Purge (Feb. 21).

April–Dec. 29. The **Convention Parliament** reconstituted from the Long Parliament.

1660–85. CHARLES II. As a result of the Declaration of Breda and Act of Indemnity and Oblivion, **abolition of rights** of knight service, worship, and purveyance in consideration of a yearly income of £1.2 million. **Restoration of the bishops** to their sees and to the House of Lords. **Acts of indemnity** for all political offenses committed between Jan. 1, 1637, and June 24, 1660. All acts of Long Parliament assented to by Charles I declared in force. **Army disbanded** except 5,000 men. Cromwellian settlement of Ireland reaffirmed.

1660. Royalist Parliament in Scotland abolished the covenant and repealed all parliamentary enactments for the preceding 28 years.

1660. Navigation Act stipulated that nothing could be imported from Africa, Asia, or America except in English or Irish ships.

1661, May 8–1679, Jan. 24. Cavalier Parliament, overwhelmingly royalist. Revival of games and more luxurious fashions and enactment of the **Clarendon Code** included the **Corporation Act, Act of Uniformity, Conventicle Act, and Five-Mile Act.**

1661. Corporation Act obligated magistrates to take the sacrament according to the Church of England, abjure the covenant, and take an oath declaring it illegal to bear arms against the king.

1661, Dec. Under **Vasasor Powell** and Thomas Venner, the **Fifth Monarchists** led a series of risings against the government in anticipation of the arrival of Jesus Christ to claim the throne.

1662–95. Licensing Acts censored many works of religion, science, and government by requiring prior approval for publication from the appropriate authority (secretary of state, archbishop of Canterbury, and so on). These acts were temporarily lifted in 1679, resulting in an increase in the number of publications before the acts resumed.

1662. Act of Settlement passed in wake of demobilization partially to help local authorities cope with numerous disbanded soldiers throughout the country. It empowered justices to return any person who might become a recipient of poor relief to his or her place of settlement— determined by birthplace, apprenticeship, property ownership, or, for women, husband's place of settlement.

May 19. Act of Uniformity required clergymen, college fellows, and schoolmasters to accept everything in the *Book of Common Prayer.*

May 20. Charles married Catherine of Braganza, daughter of John IV of Portugal. Dunkirk was sold to France for £400,000.

1664, July. Conventicle Act forbade nonconformist and dissenters' meetings of more than five people except in private households.

1665, Oct. Five-Mile Act required all who had not subscribed to the Act of Uniformity to take an oath of nonresistance, swearing never to attempt any change in church or state or to come within five miles of any incorporated town or place where they had been ministers. Strict enforcement of this law proved impossible.

1665–66. Two great domestic disasters: the **great plague in London** (1665) and the **great London fire** (Sept. 1666), burning 450 acres. St. Paul's destroyed and rebuilt by Christopher Wren. The fire led to a building trades boom in London.

1665–67. Second Dutch War (p. 314) ended with the **Treaties of Breda** signed among Holland, France, Denmark, and England.

1666. Act stipulated that the **dead were to be buried in English woolens** rather than from foreign textiles.

1666. Newton discovered the principle of gravity.

1667. Clarendon forced to resign, impeached, and exiled. Chief officers of the state began to be considered a council, forerunner of the cabinet system. The **Cabal** (Clifford, Arlington, Buckingham, Ashley, Lauderdale) rose to power. Powers divided between court supporters (royalists) and country supporters (parliamentarians), anticipating the Tories and Whigs, respectively.

1667. John Milton's *Paradise Lost* **published.**

1668, Jan. 23. Sir William Temple and John De Witt negotiated the **Triple Alliance** (England, Holland, and Sweden) as a check on Louis XIV. Charles II secretly signed the **Treaty of Dover** with Louis XIV, after which James immediately professed his Catholicism (p. 315).

1671. Tax farming abolished. As a result, the civil service was expanded; new sources of employment for younger sons of wealthy elites created.

1672, March. Charles issued a **Declaration of Indulgence** on behalf of nonconformist Protestants and Catholics but Parliament forced him to withdraw it (1673).

March–1674, Feb. 9. WAR WITH HOLLAND concluded by the **Treaty of Westminster.**

1673. Test Act. All persons holding office were compelled to take oaths of allegiance and of supremacy, to adjure transubstantiation, and to take the sacrament of the Church of England. After 1689, English passed bills of indemnity for individual magistrates who had not conformed.

1677, Nov. 4. Mary, daughter of the duke of York, **married William of Orange.**

1678, Sept. Popish Plot. Titus Oates alleged that Don John of Austria

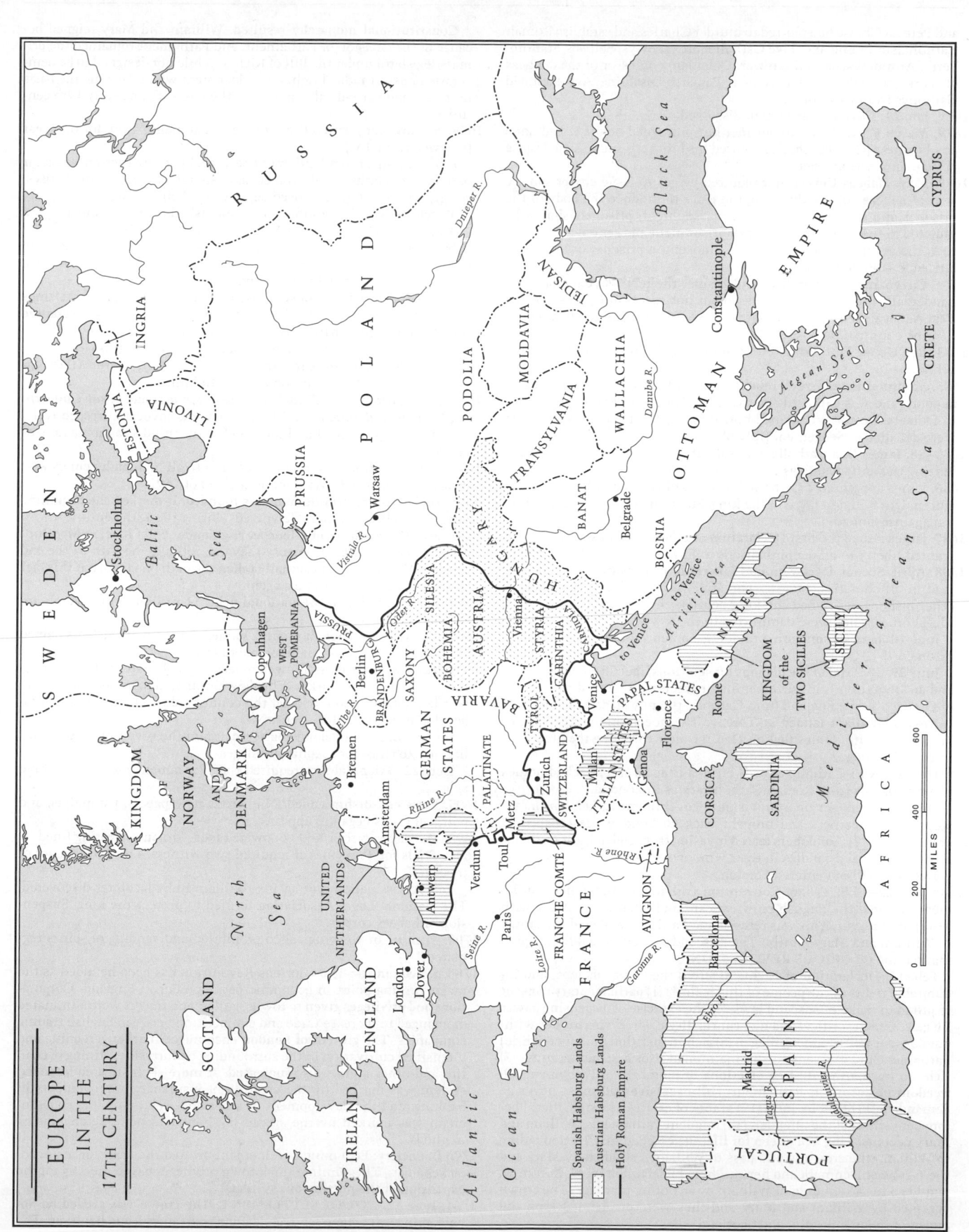

EUROPE
IN THE
17TH CENTURY

SCOTLAND

IRELAND

ENGLAND
London
Dover

UNITED
NETHERLANDS
Amsterdam
Antwerp

KINGDOM
OF
NORWAY
AND
DENMARK
Copenhagen
Bremen

SWEDEN
Stockholm

RUSSIA

INGRIA

ESTONIA
LIVONIA

PRUSSIA
Warsaw

POLAND

PODOLIA

MOLDAVIA

TRANSYLVANIA

WALLACHIA

BANAT

Belgrade

BOSNIA

OTTOMAN
EMPIRE

Constantinople

Black Sea

CYPRUS

CRETE

Aegean Sea

Adriatic Sea

to Venice
to Venice

WEST
POMERANIA
Berlin
BRANDENBURG
Elbe R.
SAXONY
Oder R.
SILESIA
BOHEMIA
AUSTRIA
Vienna
STYRIA
CARINTHIA
CARNIOLA
TYROL
BAVARIA
Venice
PAPAL STATES
Rome
KINGDOM
of the
TWO SICILIES
SICILY

GERMAN
STATES
PALATINATE
Rhine R.
Zurich
SWITZERLAND
Milan
ITALIAN STATES
Florence
Genoa

HUNGARY

PRUSSIA

Vistula R.

Dnieper R.

Danube R.

Baltic Sea

North
Sea

Atlantic
Ocean

Paris
Seine R.
Loire R.
FRANCHE COMTÉ
Metz
Toul
Verdun
Rhône R.
AVIGNON
Garonne R.

FRANCE

Barcelona
Ebro R.

SPAIN
Madrid
Tagus R.
Guadalquivir R.

PORTUGAL

CORSICA

SARDINIA

Mediterranean Sea

AFRICA

Spanish Habsburg Lands
Austrian Habsburg Lands
Holy Roman Empire

MILES
0   200   400   600

and Père La Chaise had plotted to murder Charles and establish Roman Catholicism in England. Five Catholic lords (Powys, Bellasis, Stafford, Petre, Arundel) sent to the tower. Coleman, confessor of the duchess of York, convicted and executed. **Papists' Disabling Act** excluded Catholics from Parliament.

1679, Jan. 24. Cavalier Parliament dissolved.

1679, March 6. New Parliament met but prorogued before it had done any business (Oct. 7). Charles secured his brother's succession despite parliamentary resistance.

1679, May. Habeas Corpus Act required judges to issue any prisoner a writ of habeas corpus, directing the jailer to produce the body of the prisoner and show cause for his imprisonment; **prisoners should be indicted in the first term of their imprisonment** and sentenced no later than the second term. Once found innocent, a prisoner could not be retried for the same crime.

1679. Covenanters rose in Scotland against the repressive measures of Lauderdale. Presbyterians repressed but not successfully. Passage of a **Test Act** against Presbyterians (1681). Argyle tried and condemned; he fled the country (Dec. 1681).

1683. Rye House Plot. Whig plot to seize king led to the arrest of many Whigs.

1685. Monmouth and Argyll rebelled. Argyll landed in Scotland, lacked support, and was captured and executed (June 30). Monmouth landed in Dorsetshire and proclaimed himself king, but he and his followers were defeated at **Sedgemoor (July 6).**

1685–88. James II, a Catholic who sought to test his authority by challenging the antipapal laws.

1686. James appointed a Catholic, Sir Edward Hales, to office. In a test suit, judges found in favor of the king. Such cases rapidly roused opinion against James.

1687. James issued the **first Declaration of Liberty of Conscience,** which granted liberty to all denominations in England and Scotland.

1688, April. Second Declaration of Liberty of Conscience (ordered to be read in all churches, May 4). The archbishop of Canterbury and six other bishops petitioned the king because they believed this was an illegal order. They were committed to the tower.

June 10. James's son born, providing a potential Catholic heir to the throne.

June 29, 30. Trial of the bishops for seditious libel. Bishops acquitted and an invitation from seven eminent leaders dispatched to William of Orange to save England from Catholic tyranny (accepted Sept. 30).

Nov. 5. William landed at Torbay. The queen and prince sent to France (Dec. 10). **James fled on Dec. 11** after throwing the great seal into the Thames.

Dec. 11. Anti-Catholic crowds burned chapels and attacked homes of ambassadors from Roman Catholic states in London.

Dec. 12. Peers set up a **provisional government in London.** James stopped at Sheerness and brought back to London. He escaped to France (Dec. 22). **Londoners feared invasion from Ireland,** armed themselves, and placed candles in their windows.

Dec. 19. William entered London.

1689, Jan. 22–1690, Feb. 6. Convention Parliament summoned. Parliament declared the English crown vacant and offered it to Mary with William as regent. This was refused and Parliament offered the crown to William and Mary jointly. Their ascendancy and the Bill of Rights marked the **GLORIOUS REVOLUTION.**

Feb. 13. Declaration of Rights asserted the "true, ancient, and indubitable rights of the people of this realm": (1) **parliamentary consent** required to make or suspend laws; (2) **the exercise of dispensing power illegal;** (3) **ecclesiastical and like courts illegal;** (4) **levying money** without consent of Parliament illegal; (5) right to **petition** the sovereign; (6) Parliament must assent to the maintenance of a standing army; (7) right to keep arms; (8) **free elections** of members of Parliament; (9) **freedom of debate** in Parliament; (10) **excessive bail** must never be demanded; (11) **trial by jury;** (12) grants of estates as forfeit illegal before conviction of the offender; (13) **frequent Parliaments. William and Mary declared king and queen for life,** the chief administration falling to William; the crown would pass to William's children by Mary and then Anne of Denmark and her children. In default of these, the crown would go to the children of William by any other marriage. The crown accepted by **William and Mary** and they were proclaimed king and queen of Ireland, Britain, and Scotland.

Constitutional monarchy resulted. William and Mary reigned because of the decision of Parliament, and Parliament remained the primary legislator under the Bill of Rights. While not designed to be democratic or assert radical rights, the document would become the basis for many popular radical demands in the late 18th and early 19th centuries.

1689. Mutiny Act granted the monarchs a standing army for one year (renewed annually.)

Feb. 22. Convention Parliament became, by its own action, a regular parliament. Oaths of allegiance and supremacy taken by houses, clergy, with those who refused deprived of their benefices.

March 14. Scottish committee reestablished Presbyterianism.

May 7. WAR BROKE OUT WITH FRANCE (p. 315).

May 24. Toleration Act exempted dissenters who had taken the oaths of allegiance and supremacy from penalties for nonattendance at the services of the Church of England.

In Scotland, **Claverhouse (Viscount Dundee)** supported James among the Highlanders. He defeated General Mackay at **Killiecrankie (July 27)** but died in battle. The revolt gradually dwindled.

Dec. 16. Declaration or Rights enacted as **Bill of Rights.**

1690, May 20. Act of Grace indemnified all supporters of James II except those in treasonable correspondence with him.

1690. John Locke's *Two Treatises on Government* and *Essay Concerning Human Understanding.* These two works advocated, respectively, government by contract and the belief in the mind as a tabula rasa, or blank slate, at birth.

1691, Aug. Government offered indemnity to all highlander chiefs who declared allegiance to William by the end of 1691.

1691. Society for reforming manners founded. It marked the beginning of moves to become more "civilized" during the 18th century.

1692, Feb. 13. Massacre of Glencoe. Highlander chief MacIan MacDonald and clan massacred because they did not take the oath by the end of 1691. MacDonald had actually taken the oath on Jan. 6, but this fact was suppressed by William's agent.

1693, Jan. Beginning of the national debt. £1 million borrowed on annuities at 10 percent.

1693. Recoinage of English money. Values of money fixed. This helped create a monetary system favorable to trade.

1694. Rural working class allowed to legally participate in the manufacture of woolens for market. This law eliminated town monopolies on textile production and opened the countryside up for protoindustrial development in the 18th century.

July 27. Bank of England chartered. It lent the government £1.2 million in exchange for specific privileges.

Dec. 22. Triennial Act required that Parliament meet every three years.

1695. Press censorship ended. Numerous newspapers, pamphlets, and political tracts began to appear.

1695. Marriages, births, and widowers taxed. Profane swearing fined.

1696. Trials for Treason Act required two witnesses to prove an act of treason.

Feb. Assassination plot against William III by Jacobites discovered. The **National Loyal Association** formed to protect the king. **Suspension of habeas corpus.**

1700. Printing or weaving calico prohibited and vending of spirits regulated.

1700 ff. Economics: The Glorious Revolution has been heralded as the major turning point in economic development in England. **Corporations and privileges** given to towns, guilds, and traders were eliminated or changed to increase trade and competition between English trading companies. The **growth of London** encouraged market gardening and intensified cultivation in the surrounding countryside. **Mining** of coal, tin, and other metals also increased. A **more sophisticated financial system** was marked by the creation of insurance, improvements in banking, and the development of a national debt. Growing consumerism was marked by the spread of shops and new merchandising methods.

1700 ff. Society: Economic development created the basis for major social changes. The elimination of town privileges paved the way for the **expansion of the putting-out system.**

1701, June 12. ACT OF SETTLEMENT. The crown was settled on Sophia, princess of Hanover, granddaughter of James I, and her issue. The sovereigns of Great Britain were to be Protestant and not leave the kingdom without consent of Parliament. **The country should not be involved in war for the defense of the foreign possessions of the sovereigns. No foreigner** should receive a grant from the crown or hold office, civil or military; ministers should be responsible for the acts of their sovereigns. **Judges** should hold office for life unless guilty of misconduct.

1702, May 4. War declared on France (the War of the Spanish Succession; p. 316).

1703, Nov. Establishment of Queen Anne's Bounty, a grant of the first fruits and tithes that Henry VIII had confiscated for the crown, in trust for increasing the incomes of small benefices.

Dec. 27. Treaty between England and Portugal (Methuen-Alegrete Treaty). England admitted Portuguese wines at duties one-third less than those paid by French wines, while Portugal agreed to import all its woolens from England.

1706. First life insurance office opened.

1707, May 1. UNION OF ENGLAND AND SCOTLAND under the name of Great Britain. This measure was necessary because Scotland was omitted from the Act of Succession. It established one Parliament with Scottish representation (16 in Lords, 45 in Commons) and stopped the creation of any more Scottish peers. Scottish law, legal administration, and the Church remained unchanged; the **Adoption of the Union Jack** (Crosses of St. George and St. Andrew) as national flag.

1708, March. James Edward (the Old Pretender, son of James II, d. 1701) landed in Scotland, but the French fleet assisting him was beaten and he returned to France.

1710–20. South Sea Bubble. Speculation on stock in the South Sea Company led to panic when the stock crashed and speculators lost large amounts of money.

1711. Occasional Conformity Bill stopped dissenters from technically satisfying the Test Act by taking communion once in an Anglican Church and attending a nonconformist "chapel" regularly.

1711. Qualification Act established a landed property qualification on all members of Parliament in an effort to exclude merchants, financiers, and industrialists (repealed 1866 but never rigorously enforced).

1711. Stamp duty on newspapers introduced.

1713, April 11. Treaty of Utrecht (p. 316).

1714. Schism Act stopped dissenters from running schools or tutoring privately.

Sept. 18. George I landed in England. He favored a Whig ministry. Lord Townshend, secretary of state.

1715, Sept.–1716, Feb. Jacobite rising in Scotland. Battles of **Sheriffmuir** and **Preston.** Arrival of the Pretender (James III) from France (Dec. 1715). The duke of Argyll (John Campbell) dispersed the Jacobite troops without a battle and the Pretender fled (Feb. 1716). Impeachment of Jacobite leaders, **execution of Dernwentwater and Kenmure** (Feb. 24).

June. Riot Act passed as a result of Jacobite risings. The act enabled a magistrate to order any crowd (12 or more persons) to disperse by reading a proclamation **(reading the riot act).** This reading created great problems in implementation.

1716. Bank of England debt to be paid as a result of **Sinking Fund Act.**

1716. Septennial Act, partly as a reaction to Jacobite risings, prolonged Parliament's life to seven years.

1717. First Freemasons' Lodge in England founded.

1718. Quadruple alliance among Britain, France, the Holy Roman Empire, and Holland (p. 316).

1718. Wool export forbidden.

1719, Jan. Repeal of the Occasional Conformity Act and the Schism Act.

1719. Treaty of Stockholm. Sweden ceded Bremen and Verdun to George I (as elector of Hanover) for 1 million rix dollars.

1720. Bubble Act prohibited the development of joint-stock companies without a royal charter or act of Parliament. This act was the direct result of the influence in Parliament of the South Sea Company, which sought to eliminate rivals.

Feb. Spain joined the Quadruple Alliance, making peace with Great Britain (p. 316).

1720. Marine insurance first established.

1721–42. Administration of Sir Robert Walpole. Cabinet system and the party system now took the form they held until 1832.

1722. Last execution of a witch in Scotland.

1722. Knatchbull's Act enabled parishes to build **workhouses** for able-bodied paupers and form poor law unions. However, outdoor relief generally proved cheaper.

1725, Sept. 3. Treaty of Hanover among Britain, France, and Prussia.

1727, May 19. Bishop of London stated that holding Christians as slaves did not contradict Christian doctrine.

1729, Nov. 9. Treaty of Seville with Spain; restoration of conquests; *asiento* confirmed.

1731, March 16. Treaty of Vienna with the empire. The Ostend East India Company dissolved.

1733, March 14. Walpole introduced an excise bill. Led to many demonstrations against new excise, including a procession of sheriffs and merchants (April 11) with a petition against the taxes.

1735, June 29. Witchcraft laws repealed.

1736. Spitalfields weavers rioted to protest introduction of Irish weavers. The riot was put down by the military.

1737. Worcester nailers marched to Birmingham in protest to pursue a dispute with iron merchants.

1738, May 24. John Wesley, founder of Methodism, converted. His conversion led Methodists to emphasize personal experience and training over corporate expressions of belief.

1739, Jan. Methodists met at conference that marked beginning of move to formalize Methodism.

1739–48. WAR WITH SPAIN (War of Jenkins' Ear) (p. 317). The name is colorfully derived from the fate of Captain Robert Jenkins, who lost his ear in a fracas with Spaniards. He produced the preserved ear in the House of Commons during the war.

1740–48. WAR OF AUSTRIAN SUCCESSION (p. 317).

1740s. Hospitals founded, including the first lying-in hospital, which sparked great controversy.

1742, April 13. Handel's *Messiah* performed for the first time, in Dublin.

1745. London College of Surgeons established.

1745–46. SECOND JACOBITE REBELLION. The Young Pretender, Charles Edward, landed in Scotland (July 25) and proclaimed his father as James VIII of Scotland and III of England. **The Jacobites won some victories** but were beaten decisively at **Culloden** (April 16, 1746). The Pretender escaped to France. This was the last Stuart effort to reclaim the throne.

1750 ff. Enclosure increased substantially. Because rights on all common lands were guaranteed by common law, individual owners could not enclose their lands without parliamentary consent. **Wasteland and commons were extensively enclosed** during the second half of the 18th century. While the actual land in agricultural production during this period remained the same, **enclosure marked a significant increase in pasturage.**

1751. Ruth Osborne, a **suspected witch,** was tried by the swimming test and died as a result. Thomas Colley, a chimney sweep who participated in the test, was tried and sentenced for Osborne's murder.

1752, Sept. 3. Gregorian Calendar introduced (Jan.) with a loss of 11 days (between Sept. 3 and Sept. 14).

1753. Irregular Marriages Act prohibited marriages without proper licenses.

1753. Jewish Naturalization Bill.

1755. Samuel Johnson's dictionary first published.

1756–63. WAR BETWEEN BRITAIN AND FRANCE (Seven Years' War) originated in boundary disputes in North America (p. 413).

1761, Oct. 5. Pitt, insisting that war be declared against Spain, resigned. Lord Bute, adviser to the king.

1763, Feb. 10. TREATY OF PARIS (p. 319).

1763–64. Issue 45 of the *North Briton* (April 23, 1763), by **John Wilkes,** attacked the ministerial policies the king expressed in his speech proroguing Parliament. Wilkes was arrested but claimed immunity as a member of Parliament. He was removed from Parliament and fled to France. **The attempt to try Wilkes led to riots in London supporting** him. He espoused radical political ideas and, after being returned to his seat in 1774, introduced **a bill for sweeping parliamentary reform, including a significant broadening of the franchise.**

1760s. Bread and Corn Riots. Lower classes protested the increased cost of foodstuffs. These riots also expressed lower-class discontent over the **gradual destruction of the "moral economy,"** in which local elites had a moral obligation to provide adequate provisions for the lower orders. **These riots followed a distinct pattern.** The merchant was generally offered a fair price for his bread or corn, and if he refused to accept it, rioters seized the goods, distributed them, and left the "fair" price in exchange.

1769. First Sunday school established by Hannah Ball. Sunday schools were initially a nondenominational product of Methodism as well as an effort to increase education among the lower classes.

1772. Cotton machinery exportation prohibited. This law attempted to protect English manufacturers.

    June 22. Slavery in Britain eliminated by Court of King's High Bench.

1772. Royal Marriage Act required princes and princesses to gain the sovereign's consent to their marriages.

1776. Adam Smith's *Wealth of Nations* established the **science of political economy**, which argued that individuals, acting in self-interest, would be able to benefit through a free market.

1780, May 10, June 2–9. No popery riots (Gordon riots) erupted after Parliament rejected Gordon's proposal to repeal indulgences for Catholics.

1782. Gilbert's Act allowed for the **creation of parish unions and more efficient poor law management.** It also introduced the **plural voting system** and **eliminated indoor relief** for able-bodied paupers.

1787, May. First transport left for Botany Bay, Australia (p. 387).

    Repeal of Tonnage and Poundage. These taxes were replaced by other means of taxing shipments.

    Oct. 12. George III insane. A regency established 1789.

1788. Court of Common Pleas declared **gleaning as trespass.** This marked the continued destruction of customary rights of the poor.

1791. Corresponding Society founded in London. These societies provided the basis for spreading radical ideas during the late 18th and early 19th centuries.

1792. Joanna Southcott organized a millenarian sect, claiming she would bear a son, Shiloh of Gen. 49:10. She convinced several doctors she was pregnant prior to her death, and her followers continued to await the arrival of a spiritual rather than temporal son.

    May 21. Growing agitation for parliamentary reform led to a proclamation against seditious writings.

1793, Feb. 1. French Republic declared war on Great Britain (p. 433).

    Jan. 4. Alien Act enabled government to remove Irish to Ireland.

1793. Friendly Societies' Act outlawed trade unions other than friendly societies. This law proved difficult to implement in practice.

1795. Speenhamland System: Named after the location of a meeting of Berkshire justices who developed the system, it sought to alleviate some of the hardship caused by poor harvests by subsidizing wages with poor relief funds. The subsidies were based on the price of bread and the size of the family. Critics claimed the system served only to drive down the wages actually paid by farmers and to create permanent poverty.

1798. Malthus's *Essay on the Principle of Population* published. Malthus argued that population tends to increase geometrically, while food production only increases arithmetically, thus creating acute shortages. Shortages cause famine and disease, which act as checks on population growth. Humans could also control population through **preventive checks** such as abstinence. Poor relief, however, only worsened the situation by increasing the demands on the food supply.

1799. Act outlawed corresponding societies.

1800. Combination Acts outlawed any combination in restraint of trade. While technically applicable to both masters and workers, these laws really attempted to stop the growth of trade unions.

1801. The Health and Morals of Apprentices Act forbade the hiring out of pauper children for work in the cotton mills until they were nine years of age, restricted their working day to 12 hours, and prohibited their employment at night.

1801. Pitt resigned and Henry Addington headed the cabinet. Addington, under Pitt's advice, concluded peace with France (March 27, 1802).

1803, May 18. War against France was renewed (p. 437).

1810. Primitive Methodists organized, with an emphasis on prophecy and enthusiasm. While Methodism became progressively more middle class as it sought financial support, the Primitive Methodists relied on "mechanik" (nonprofessional) preachers and free-will offerings.

1811, Feb. 5. George the IV became prince regent on account of George III's insanity.

(To p. 446)

2. IRELAND
(From p. 289)

1648–49. Outbreaks of dysentery and smallpox as well as plague (which reached Galway 1649). Problems with disease continued over next few years.

1649, Jan. 17. Treaty between Ormond and the Confederacy assured Ormond that Irish Catholics would not be molested and resulted in Ormond joining royalist forces after Charles I was executed (Jan. 30).

    March 30. Parliament approved **Cromwell as commander in chief** of the forces in Ireland.

    June 22. Cromwell made governor general of Ireland.

    Aug. 15. Cromwell arrived in Dublin and proceeded to take **Drogheda** (Sept. 11) and **Wexford** (Oct. 11). He massacred the troops and townspeople in both cases.

    Dec. 4. In the wake of Cromwell's success, Irish bishops met and **appealed for Catholic unity.** The lord lieutenant of Ireland responded with a declaration for the "undeceiving of deluded and seduced people."

1650. Rump Parliament applied **revenues of the archbishop of Dublin and St. Patrick's** to educational purposes.

1652, Aug. 12. Act of Settlement required all Catholics to give up at least a portion of their lands.

1652–55. Orders of Transportation issued against two classes of people: **vagabonds and paupers, and those considered dangerous to the state.** Policies also exiled priests throughout Ireland. Priests who refused exile were transported to Barbados.

1653, March 2. The Rump Parliament voted that 30 members in the new House of Commons would represent Ireland. **The Irish House of Commons eliminated.**

    April 27. Capitulation of Philip O'Reilly at Cloghoughton completed Cromwell's conquest of Ireland.

    July 2. Cromwell decided on clearance of lands under Act of Settlement (confirmed by Parliament, Sept. 26) and began the process of settling forfeiting proprietors in Clare and Connacht. **Some landowners were to be compensated with land elsewhere,** and some loyal Cromwellian subjects were to receive land. This led to massive confusion and **created large classes of Protestant landowners and Catholic tenants.**

1657, June 26. Act for the Attainder of the Rebels in Ireland declared resettlement over, although it had been inefficient and incomplete.

1660, May 14. Charles II proclaimed in Dublin.

1660. Navigation Act established England and Ireland as an economic unit and allowed Ireland to ship directly to the colonies.

1662. Act of Settlement declared that the crown received all lands confiscated under Cromwell. However, innocents were excluded from such confiscation and could return to their lands immediately.

1663, July 27. Act confined direct exports from Ireland to the colonies to provisions, horses, and servants.

1665, Dec. 23. Act of Explanation clarified the Act of Settlement of 1661. These two acts placed **two-thirds of the land in Ireland in Protestant hands.**

1666, June 18. An act strengthened the Act of Uniformity by requiring use of the *Book of Common Prayer* and Episcopal orders in the Church of Ireland.

1670. General Synod of Irish Bishops in Dublin discussed organizational problems of the Church following Cromwell. This discussion led to decreased centralization.

1671. Importation of certain goods prohibited. This act lapsed 1681 but was reimposed in 1685. Smuggling constant under these regulations.

1678. In the wake of the Popish plot, the **Papists' Disabling Act** passed. This act excluded Roman Catholics from Parliament and became a rallying point for Irish reformers in the late 18th and early 19th centuries.

1689, Feb. 22. William III called on Ireland to surrender. He offered them security of property and religious toleration but Ireland continued to support James II.

    March 12. James landed in Ireland.

    April 18–July 31. Siege of Londonderry, a Protestant town, by royalist forces. The Williamite ships finally broke the boom on the Foyle River and relieved the city.

May 7–July 18. James II called an Irish Parliament, which declared that the English Parliament could not legislate for Ireland.

June 22. Irish Parliament passed a bill that repealed the land settlement under Charles II.

1690, July 1. Battle of the Boyne. William successful and James fled.

1691, Oct. 3. Treaty of Limerick allowed the Irish army to go to France; Catholics were promised religious privileges they enjoyed under Charles II.

Dec. 24. Catholics barred from public positions.

1695, Sept. 7. Catholics forbidden to teach or send their children abroad for an education, keep arms, or own a horse valued at over £5.

1696, April 27. Irish linen allowed into England without any duty.

1697, April 5. Export of Irish woolens regulated. This marked the beginning of an effort to ban Irish woolen import and protect the English woolen trade.

Sept. 25. Banishment Act. All Catholic clergy required to leave Ireland by May 1, 1698.

1701. Archbishop Marsh's library in Dublin built—the **first Irish public library.**

1704. Dublin Workhouse Act provided for construction of a workhouse in Dublin.

1709. First Irish Banking Act.

1711, Aug. 16. The Trinity College Medical School building completed.

Oct. 10. Linen Board met for the first time. This board sought to encourage linen production in Ireland by setting up a system of cottage industry.

1716. Parliament passed a bill designed to **make the Shannon** navigable by improving drainage.

1720, April 7. Declaratory Act established British Parliament's supremacy and made the English House of Lords rather than the Irish the final court of appeal.

1726–28. A series of harvest failures caused partially by a potato shortage. While the potato crop did not fail, growing dependence on it made it more difficult for the Irish to endure other crop failures until they began planting enough potatoes to survive the winter.

1726, Oct. 28. Jonathan Swift's *Gulliver's Travels* published.

1728. Catholics specifically deprived of the franchise.

1730. George Rye's Irish manual on agriculture appeared—the first such manual in Ireland. It indicated a growing interest in agriculture, also evident in the creation of the **Dublin Society for Improving Husbandry and Manufacture** (1731).

1739. Duties on Irish woolen exports to Great Britain lifted.

1740s. A series of hard winters, aggravated in some cases by diseases such as typhus, led to bread riots and general hardship.

1740, May 31–June 2. Bread riots in Dublin, in protest of dearth. Another hard winter and famine followed the next year.

1758, March 3. Bounties on grain and flour imports into Dublin issued. Exports of salted beef, pork, and butter to Great Britain allowed.

1759, Dec. 3. Rioting in Dublin after the Irish heard rumors of the possibility of an Act of Union with Britain. Discontent over the possibility of union led to a series of protests by whiteboys, oakboys, steelboys, and so on.

1763, Sept. 10. First issue of *Freeman's Journal*, an Irish radical paper, published.

1766, June–Aug. More rioting regarding food shortages, which were partly the result of droughts in the preceding year.

1769. The Belfast barracks attacked by Steelboys, a Presbyterian peasant movement.

1772. Dublin Foundling Hospital and Workhouse Act established overseers to care for abandoned children. Parliament also enacted legislation to badge beggars and establish workhouses.

1778. Catholic Relief Act allowed Catholics to sign 999-year leases and use normal inheritance proceedings. This act partially rectified the land legislation of the 17th century.

1782. Catholic Relief Acts allowed Catholics to acquire land and teach school.

1782. Protestant dissenter Relief Act recognized the legality of Presbyterian marriages.

1783. National Volunteer Convention proposed parliamentary reforms which the House of Commons rejected. The Volunteers provided a strong impetus for resisting the Act of Union.

1787. Tumultuous Rising Act sought to quell riots. It was patterned after the English Riot Act.

1791, July 14. Demonstrations throughout Ireland in commemoration of the fall of the Bastille. The Irish sought support for their own independence from the French revolutionaries, which greatly concerned the British.

1792, Jan. 4. The first issue of the *Northern Star*, published by the United Irishmen of Belfast. This organization supported efforts to gain independence from Britain.

1793, Aug. 16. Convention Act prohibited assemblies for the purpose of petitioning the king. It marked the beginning of efforts to quell the activities of the United Irishmen and Volunteers.

1798. Martial Law imposed in an effort to quell insurrection.

Aug. 22. French force landed at Killala and had success at Castlebar. It surrendered at **Bullinamuck** on Sept. 8.

1800, Aug. 1. The Act of Union passed, forming the **UNITED KINGDOM** and a single legislature for Britain and Ireland. It took effect on Jan. 1, 1801.

1803, July 23. Robert Emmet, who proclaimed an independent Irish government, led an uprising and was subsequently executed, on Sept. 20.

1805–6. Unrest in County Mayo, over the Church of England tithes and Roman Catholic dues, led by the **Threshers,** whose name referred to their threats to "comb" the flesh on the opponents.

1813, July 12. Sectarian riots in Belfast.   *(To p. 450)*

b. THE DUTCH REPUBLIC

(From p. 290)

1647–50. WILLIAM II succeeded his father, Frederick Henry, in the stadholdership. Able, ambitious, and restless, William disapproved of the **Treaty of Münster (1648),** which recognized the independence of the provinces, and would have preferred to continue the war. He soon became involved in conflict with the states-general and, by arresting some of the leaders of Holland and attacking Amsterdam itself (1650), forced the submission of the state-rights group.

1650, Nov. 6. William died. His son was born posthumously.

1651. The Estates held a constituent assembly but only agreed to stop the possibility of recreating the office of captain-general.

1652–54. The FIRST ANGLO-DUTCH WAR, the direct outgrowth of the English Navigation Act (1651) (p. 314).

1652. Dutch South Africa founded (p. 395).

1653. John De Witt became pensionary of Holland and thereby controlled the general policy. An able statesman and adroit diplomat, he easily maintained Dutch prestige and greatness.

1657–60. The Dutch prevented the entrance of the Baltic from falling into exclusively Swedish control by supporting the Danish in the Swedish-Danish War (p. 342).

1657–61. War with Portugal, over conflicting interests in Brazil.

1660. Dutch states-general rescinded the exclusion of the House of Orange from the stadholdership following the restoration in England.

1662. The Dutch allied themselves with the French to provide against the danger of attack by the British.

1664. The British seized New Amsterdam (New York) and appropriated various Dutch stations on the African coast.

1665–67. SECOND ANGLO-DUTCH WAR. France and Denmark supported the Dutch (p. 314).

1667. The Eternal Edict abolished the stadholdership. It would be reinstated and made hereditary after 1748.

1668, Jan. 23. Triple Alliance of England, Holland, and Sweden (p. 315).

1669. Beginning of a number of government policies **restricting emigration** (continued reforms until 1750).

1672–78. WAR WITH FRANCE AND ENGLAND. The French were able to overrun much of the Netherlands (p. 315). **John De Witt was murdered in a riot** (Aug. 27, 1672).

1672–1702. WILLIAM III (son of William II), stadholder. The British abandoned the war (1674) and the Dutch came off without losses.

1688–97. WAR OF THE LEAGUE OF AUGSBURG against Louis XIV. William led the coalition (p. 315).

1702, March 8. The death of William III, without children, brought to an end the direct line of the house of Orange, which, however, was continued by the related house of Naussau.

1701–14. The WAR OF THE SPANISH SUCCESSION (p. 316).

1715, Nov. 15. The Barrier Treaty. Holland received key territories on the French frontier from the empire as protection against attack from France.

1743. The Dutch Republic joined Britain in the alliance with Maria Theresa against Prussia and France. The French conquests in the Austrian Netherlands constituted a direct danger to the republic.

1747. The Revolution of 1747 restored the stadholderate to William IV.

1748–51. WILLIAM IV of Orange Naussau (grandson of William III's cousin) proclaimed stadholder, a dignity that now became hereditary.

1751. On the death of William IV, his widow, Anne, acted as regent for the three-year-old heir.

1766–95. WILLIAM V assumed the position of stadholder.

1780–84. The Dutch went to war with Britain over the question of the right to search ships at sea.

1785. Beginning of the serious conflict between William and the states-general, owing to the emergence of the Patriot Party (representing the French influence). William ultimately had to call in Prussian troops (1787) to restore his authority.

1793. France declared war on the Dutch Republic as well as on Britain (friction over the opening of the Scheldt by the French in 1792) (p. 433).

1794–95. The French captured the Dutch fleet while it was frozen in the ice in the Texel. William V fled to England.

1795–1806. The BATAVIAN REPUBLIC, modeled on France and governed by the Patriots. In the interval the British, still at war with France, seized the Dutch colonies.

1795. Treaty with France normalized relations between the two countries, enabling the new states-general to concentrate on other issues.

1796. A National Assembly elected by the Batavian people. A first constitution was rejected and a second National Assembly called (1797).

1798, Jan. The French army staged a coup, purging the Assembly of moderates. The radicals were driven out and the moderates returned.

1806–10. LOUIS, the brother of Napoleon, king of Holland (p. 437). His policy, aimed at the good of his adopted kingdom, brought him into conflict with Napoleon.

1810. The KINGDOM OF HOLLAND was incorporated with France as an integral part of the empire. *(To p. 450)*

c. FRANCE

(From p. 294)

Monarchs: Louis XIV (1643–1715), Louis XV (1715–74), Louis XVI (1774–92).

Demography: Between 1700 and 1789, French population increased from approximately 19 million to 25 million. Population growth was more rapid in the latter half of the 18th century than in the first half but lagged behind British population growth.

Economics: Colbert subscribed to **mercantilism,** arguing that France could improve its economic position only at the cost of another country. Colbert pursued protectionist policies and introduced considerable regulation of urban trades. The sale of offices and the way in which the French national debt was financed discouraged venturesome investment by the *rentier* class of established capitalists. Despite such constraints, reassessments of French industrial development demonstrate the French economic growth per capita matched that of Britain after 1750.

Women: Women were very influential in shaping ideas at court and among the philosophes. The **Enlightenment thinkers** in France often gathered in **salons** run by wealthy women (e.g., Mme. Geoffrin, Mlle. de Lespinasse, Mme. de Tencin, Mme. du Deffand), which gave upperclass women increasing access to philosophical and political ideas. The court society created by Louis XIV at Versailles also provided women with the opportunity to participate in political discussions. Individual women gained influence over Louis XV.

1643–1715. LOUIS XIV ascended the throne at age five. His mother, **Anne of Austria** (daughter of Philip III of Spain), acted as guardian. The government, even after Louis reached his majority, was conducted by **Cardinal Mazarin.**

1648. Treaty of Westphalia gave Metz, Toul, Verdun, Dreisach, and Pinerolo to France (p. 304).

1648–49. Unrest in provinces, especially regarding tax increases. Mazarin responded by lowering taxes.

1648–53. THE FRONDE, revolt against the regency named after the catapult children used to hurl clods at passing coaches. This was the last attempt of the nobility to oppose the court by armed resistance. It had two phases: a parlementary revolt and a revolt of the princes.

Jan. 15. A *lit de justice*—a sitting of representatives to enforce an edict—created new offices and raised taxes. Contrary to French traditions, the Parlement examined the edict before passing it under pressure from Anne.

April 7. Parlement presented oral remonstrances to the edict and called upon the queen to relieve the people of heavy taxes.

April 29. Droit annuel granted provided that three of the four courts (the Parlement excepted) refused wages for four years. These courts appealed to the Parlement for assistance. **Parlement passed an act of union and called all four courts to an assembly** (May 13) despite Anne's objections. Anne arrested deputies and judges responsible for continued deputations between courts.

June 8. Queen's attorneys forbade the meeting of the assembly but capitulated when Parlement refused to disband. Anne asked that the meeting be immediate and quick.

July 4. Parlement assumed legislative powers in the struggle, contravening tradition, and amended a government declaration that future taxes would be cleared by Parlement before enacting. Parlement declared all taxes not cleared null and all back taxes uncollectable.

Oct. 24. Parlement registered a declaration of government which was a product of compromise at a convention. Wages were restored but some offices removed and tax farming regulated. However, the government began to negotiate further amendments to this declaration.

1649, Jan. 5. Following such amendments, **king, family, and ministers fled to St. Germain** and troops concentrated around Paris. The Parlement took action to maintain supply lines in and out of city. **Ineffective siege** ensued and government ordered elections of estate general. The Parisian blockage sought to bring Parlement into line.

March 4. Treaty of Rueil between Parlement and the government. Parlement went to St. Germain until a *lit de justice* declared the treaty.

1649. King and regent returned to Paris. Serious provincial unrest but also beginning of **revolt of princes.** The prince of Condé opposed the first minister and gained control of the government. His friends earned the right to sit with the king and queen, but other nobles demanded that right be revoked.

1650, Jan. 18. Condé and the duke of Longueville arrested and second phase of Fronde began.

Jan. 19. War broke out between princes in the provinces and the regency. Normandy was rapidly subdued (March 5).

Jan. 21. The party of the Fronde arrested during the first phase acquitted. This completed the separation of interests of the nobility and Parlement.

1651, Feb. 6. Mazarin quit Paris and the princes were released (Feb. 11). The government met demand for estates general by promising one would be convened Oct. 1.

March 16. The court moved to Dijon as the effort to quell rebellion in Burgundy began. **Bellegarde surrendered (April 11).**

April 20. Mme. de Lonqueville and Turenne sought an alliance with Spain. However, the war proved inconclusive.

Oct. 2. Parlement was forbidden to consider general affairs, which thus destroyed gains made by the Parlement.

1651. Tontine system of life insurance created by Lorenzo Tonti in Paris. This system paid a sum of money to the last surviving contributor.

1652. Louis XIV confirmed the Edict of Nantes, which gave French Protestants, particularly the Huguenots, freedom of worship.

1653, Feb. 3. Mazarin returned to power. The Fronde had ended with little gained.

1656. Hôpital Général opened in Paris.

1659. Treaty of the Pyrenees settled war between Spain and France.

1661. Death of Mazarin. Louis XIV (1661–1715) declared he would be his own first minister and **created an ABSOLUTE MONARCHY** (*"L'état c'est moi"*). Louis gained control of the French military. He

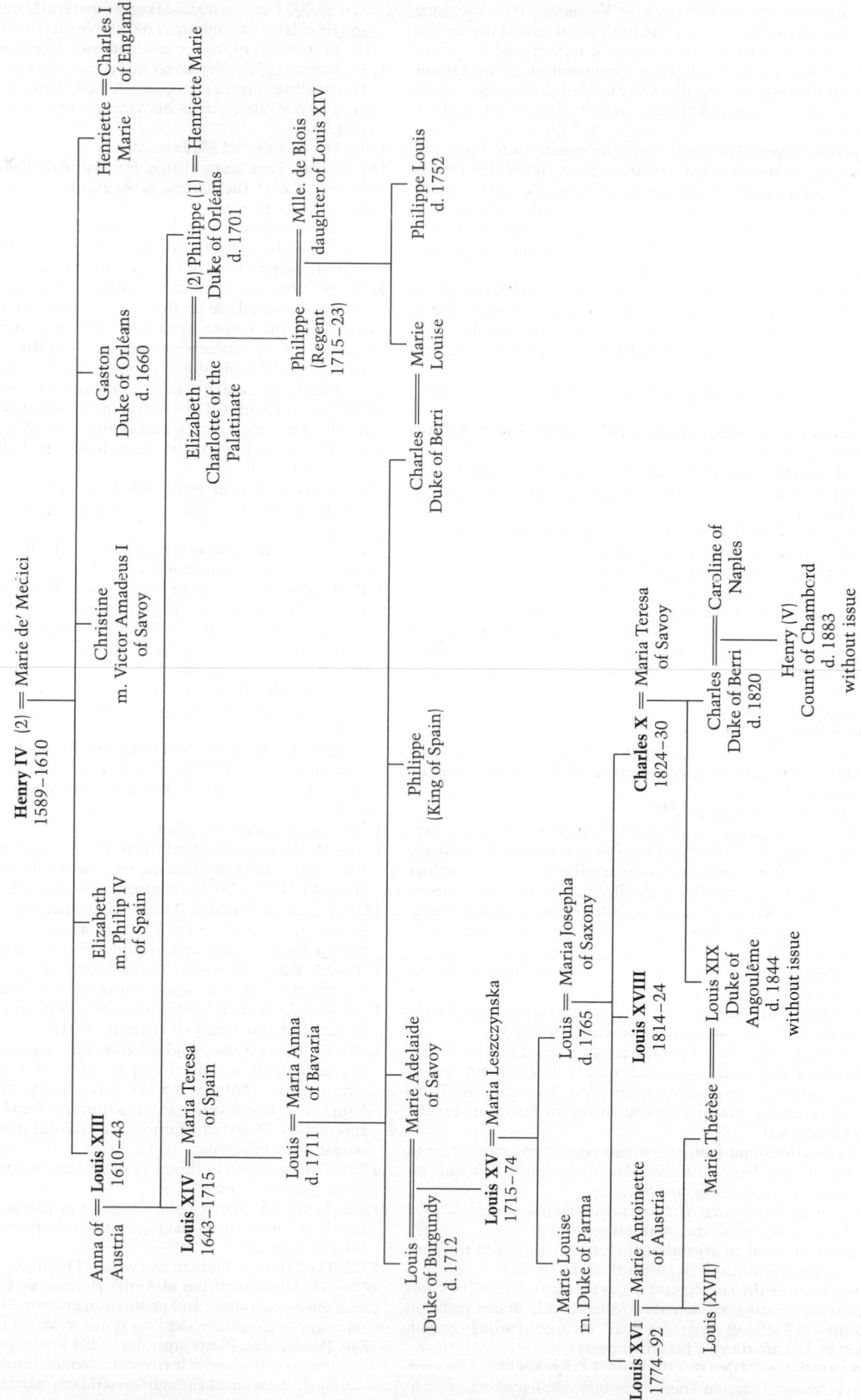

THE FRENCH BOURBONS (1589–1883)

Henry IV (2) = Marie de' Medici
1589–1610

Anna of = **Louis XIII**
Austria   1610–43

Elizabeth
m. Philip IV
of Spain

Christine
m. Victor Amadeus I
of Savoy

Gaston
Duke of Orléans
d. 1660

Henriette = Charles I
Marie   of England

Louis XIV = Maria Teresa
1643–1715   of Spain

Elizabeth
Charlotte of the
Palatinate

= (2) Philippe (1) = Henriette Marie
Duke of Orléans
d. 1701

Philippe = Mlle. de Blois
(Regent   daughter of Louis XIV
1715–23)

Philippe Louis
d. 1752

Louis = Maria Anna
d. 1711   of Bavaria

Philippe
(King of Spain)

Charles = Marie
Duke of Berri   Louise

Louis = Marie Adelaide
Duke of Burgundy   of Savoy
d. 1712

Louis XV = Maria Leszczynska
1715–74

Louis = Maria Josepha
d. 1765   of Saxony

Charles X = Maria Teresa
1824–30   of Savoy

Charles = Caroline of
Duke of Berri   Naples
d. 1820

Henry (V)
Count of Chambord
d. 1883
without issue

Marie Louise
m. Duke of Parma

Louis XVI = Marie Antoinette
1774–92   of Austria

Marie Thérèse = Louis XIX
Duke of
Angoulême
d. 1844
without issue

Louis XVIII
1814–24

Louis [XVII]

also focused high society on the **court at Versailles,** impoverishing nobles by encouraging them to emulate him. He extended the French bureaucracy and thus enlarged the number of nobles holding offices who owed their loyalty solely to the king. **Three customary limitations on the crown continued:** the king must be a Catholic; no woman could occupy the throne (Salic law); the king could not alienate his lands by appanage system.

1662. Jean-Baptiste Colbert (1619–83) controller general until his death. Colbert subscribed to **mercantilistic policies.** He believed that French trade could be advanced only at the expense of another country's trade. Colbert responded to hardships within France by **reducing the *taille* and shifting some of the tax burden away from the peasantry.** He also regulated tax farming closely. Such policies resulted in increased revenues for the crown between 1662 and 1672.

1663–67. Series of institutions directed at furthering academic and scientific knowledge founded: Academy of Inscriptions and Belle Lettres (1663), Academy of Sciences (1666), Royal Observatory (1667).

1666, Jan. France allied itself with Holland during Second Anglo-Dutch War (p. 314).

1667. Tariff doubled the duty on cloth, part of the mercantilist protectionist system.

    July 31. Peace of Breda ended Second Anglo-Dutch War with restoration of territories (p. 315).

1667–68. War of Devolution (p. 315) over the claims to the Spanish royal family's personal estates. Louis XIV claimed these estates as part of his wife's inheritance.

1668, May 2. Treaty of Aix-la-Chapelle (p. 315) deferred the question of succession and settled the lands in question.

1669. "Peace of Church" allowed **Jansenism** to spread (p. 333). Named after Cornelius Jansen (1583–1638), the Jansenists adhered to doctrines similar to Calvinism. They believed all but the few touched by the grace of God were damned. Jansenism centered on Port Royal and its convent. They were declared heretical by the pope in 1653, but with the assistance of Blaise Pascal, the pope agreed to allow Jansenists to continue within the Church (1669).

1670. Secret Treaty of Dover with Charles II of England (p. 320).

1672–78. War against the Dutch.

1672. The Plague, spreading through Europe, struck Lyon; 60,000 died.

1673, Feb. Edict of **Louis XIV stopped Parlement of Paris** from objecting to unregistered royal edicts.

1678–79. Treaties of Nimwegen (p. 315).

1678. Le Tellier tightened state control of army, improved direct payment of troops. Under le Tellier and his son and successor, **Louvois,** France established better inspection and discipline of troops (**Martinet** served as first inspector-general), standardized uniforms and regimental organization, and began to introduce **military pensions** and hospitals. **Provision of supplies** also improved. Other countries paralleled or imitated these reforms.

    Sept. 17. Religious liberty of Lutherans in French territory confirmed by Peace of Nimwegen.

1679. The "man in the iron mask" became a prisoner in the Bastille. He died on Nov. 19, 1707, and his identity is still debated.

1680s. Beginning of popular use of **potato;** fried potato stands in Paris.

1680–83. Chambers of Reunion—French courts determining French claims to various towns—met at Metz, Breisach, Besançon, and Tournay. Louis XIV's troops annexed several towns to France under the direction of these courts.

1680s. Price fluctuations and famine sparked revolts and discontent in the late 17th and early 18th centuries. Growing popular demands for government support against high food prices.

1681. France annexed Strasbourg. The Lanquedoc Canal completed. The latter linked the Atlantic and the Mediterranean.

1682. Louis XIV convoked an assembly of clergy that decided the pope had no right to involve himself in political affairs (p. 333).

1682. Versailles became the French seat of government. Louis XIV spent large amounts in creating a court that reflected his desire to be an absolute monarch. He then created a court society in which attendance at court by the aristocracy became necessary.

1685, Oct. 18. REVOCATION OF THE EDICT OF NANTES. The exercise of the reformed religion in France was forbidden; children were to be educated in the Catholic faith. Emigration was prohibited, but more than 50,000 families (called **Huguenots**) emigrated to Holland, England (Spitalfields), Brandenburg, English North America, and South Africa. The **Protestants of Alsace retained their freedom of worship.**

1685. Slavery in French plantations encouraged the establishment of the slave-trading Guinea Company. A Code Noir required that plantation owners treat their slaves humanely, but it was often ignored in the colonies.

1686. France annexed **Madagascar.**

1687. Bishop Fénelon published his *Traité de l'éducation des Filles.*

1688–97. War of the League of Augsburg concluded by the Treaty of Ryswick (see p. 315).

1694. Pierre le Pesant called on France to switch from the mercantilism established by Colbert to a system of free enterprise as a means of righting the problems of famine and poverty plaguing France.

1695. Fénelon wrote a letter to Mme. de Maintenon, who had Louis XIV's ear, **complaining that Louis's wars and protectionism were destroying the French economy.** He joined many in arguing for free trade and more progressive taxation. The **first graduated tax** was introduced—the **capitation**—partly as a result of such complaints.

1697. Charles Perrault published his Mother Goose rhymes for children.

1700, Nov. 1. Charles II of Spain died. Louis XIV followed Charles's will and duke of Anjou proclaimed Philip V (p. 330).

1701–14. War of the Spanish Succession concluded with the Treaty of Utrecht (p. 316).

1701. *Conseil de commerce* called. Deputies from commercial towns criticized protectionism as favoring agriculture rather than manufacturing.

1702–4. Cévennes peasants rebelled but rebellion put down by military. Guerrilla activity continued until 1711.

1709. Food riots throughout France sparked by a terrible winter, famine, and a decline in agricultural production.

1713. Jansenist nuns at Port Royal dispersed as the result of the papal encyclical *Unigenitus* (p. 333). Louis XIV supported the Jesuits against the Jansenists and declared the encyclical valid in France. This contravened Gallican law, which prohibited the French government from accepting such encyclicals without the unanimous consent of the clergy.

    April 11. Treaty of Utrecht ended period of Louis XIV's wars. War continued to be a significant factor in French diplomacy, and the cost of war created financial difficulties for the government in the 18th century.

1715, Sept. 1. Louis XIV died.

1715–74. He was succeeded by his five-year-old great-grandson, **LOUIS XV.** Philip, duke of Orléans, became regent during the minority of Louis XV (1715–23), thus setting aside the will of Louis XIV.

1716. John Law founded Banque Générale, which became the Banque Royale. He gained the right to coin money from the government and financed government debts through his Mississippi scheme.

1718–20. War with Spain. By the Treaty of the Hague (Feb. 17, 1720), the emperor received Sicily, and Savoy received Sardinia in exchange.

1718, Aug. 2. Quadruple Alliance with Britain, the emperor, and Holland to maintain the Treaty of Utrecht (p. 316).

1718–20. Law's Mississippi scheme. John Law encouraged investment in Louisiana through his Company of the West. Supported by the government, the company's stock rose rapidly, but when gold was not found in Louisiana, the stock plummeted and proved disastrous for speculators. Despite its failure, the plan did increase shipping and colonization in Louisiana.

1720. The last major outbreak of the **plague** in Europe struck Marseilles. More than 50,000 died.

1725. Louis XV married the daughter of the deposed king of Poland, Stanislas Leszczynski, having broken off a projected marriage with the Infanta of Spain.

1725. Food riots in Paris in the wake of famine.

1726–43. Administration of André-Hercule de Fleury, the king's tutor, marked by economic and population growth. Fleury fixed the value of currency and reestablished tax farming which Law had abandoned.

1730. Abbé de St. Pierre introduced his *Projet pour perfectionner l'education des filles,* which advocated education for both boys and girls, although it assumed that girls would not need to be trained for public office.

1730. Law allowed a convicted seducer of an unwed, pregnant woman to choose to marry her rather than suffer the death penalty. In reality, conviction and punishment of the seducer were rare.

1731. France forbade barbers to practice surgery, although the practice continued elsewhere in Europe. Jean-Sorieus Petit established the **French Royal Surgery.**

1739. Corvée (forced labor) **employed for maintenance of roads.** This increased the quality of French roads and transportation in the 18th century.

1740. Famine struck France again. Peasants forced to eat ferns and roots.

1744. Bouquel's *Supériorité de l'homme sur la femme* argued that men were superior to women but in 1749 Dinouart argued, in *Le Triomphe du sexe*, that women were the equals of men.

1749. A 5 percent tax on all incomes introduced, but the clergy were exempted after they protested. The Parlement objected to their exclusion but the king overruled that objection.

1750. Louis XV began storing grain surpluses to be used in case of famine. Rather than relieve concern, this practice led to increases in prices and continued shortages.

1750ff. Aristocratic Reaction. Population pressure on aristocratic families, along with weaker monarchy, encouraged aristocratic pretensions. Few middle-class people allowed to obtain noble titles. Aristocrats' sons had a growing monopoly on top offices within the French church.

1751. Diderot's encyclopedia banned for containing radical ideas. Despite a temporary relaxation of censorship in the early 18th century, the government continued to censor objectionable works of the Enlightenment.

1756. Louis XV issued edicts that limited parlementary power and outlawed the judicial strike. Louis and the Parlement were engaged in a struggle for control, with Louis trying to continue as an absolute monarch.

May. A defensive alliance between France and Austria followed by war between France and Britain (p. 317).

1758. François Quesnay published *Tableau economique*, which argued that agriculture was the only basis of wealth and provided a method of distributing the fruits of that wealth among the industrious and idle classes. Quesnay was Mirabeau's mentor.

1760s. The decline in the merchant marine and navy led to an increased number of pirates.

1761. Illegitimacy: The practice of subjecting unwed pregnant women to **physical examinations** whenever the authorities chose banned. By this practice, local authorities could demand that a woman subject herself to an examination at any time. While designed to assure the pregnancy was not interfered with, this law was also used to force single women to have such examinations even if they were not known to be pregnant. The practice continued after 1761 in some parts of France despite the ban.

1762. Jean Jacques Rousseau's *Social Contract* and *Émile* published. The former argued for government based on a contract between all members of society which would guarantee harmony within that society. The latter argued for a flexible, responsive system of education, though stipulating that women's education must be relative to men's education and to women's role in society.

1764. Jesuits expelled from France, a move to discipline the Church.

1765. France abolished free trade within the country on grain.

1770–89. Prices on grain increased and a financial crisis resulted in bankruptcies.

1771. Coup Maupéou. As new chief minister, René de Maupéou, **asserted the claim of Louis XV as absolute monarch.** The government improved the roads into Brittany for use by the military. The Breton Parlement objected but Louis XV issued statement of absolutism and, under direction of Maupéou, abolished the Parlements in Paris and the provinces and replaced them with lower, more easily controlled courts—an unpopular reform.

1774. In the wake of famine, Turgot **lifted ban on free trade of grain** but the rivers in France froze, making it impossible to move grain.

1775. Flour War. Violent food riots in Paris and surrounding region. Increased male participation reflected economic problems of wage laborers and roused new government concern.

1776–83. American Revolution (p. 416). France supported the colonists.

1787. French government allowed grain producers to sell directly to consumers and export grain. As a result, granaries were emptied and prices rose.
(To p. 431)

d. THE IBERIAN PENINSULA

1. SPAIN
(From p. 295)

Demography: Subsistence crises and high infant mortality led to very slow population growth in Spain in the last half of the 17th century. Spain experienced rapid growth in the first half of the 18th century, then slower growth again after 1750.

Economy and Society: The Spanish economy was characterized by diversity in agriculture but dominated by textiles in manufacturing. In most of Spain, **land was owned by nobles and clergy** who continued to use traditional farming methods. In some areas, dominated by sheep and pasturage, enclosure came late. In other areas, such as Andalucia, landowners controlled huge estates—*latafundia*—creating a large rural proletariat of day laborers. In most cases, Spanish agriculture lagged behind that of much of western Europe. **Industry also developed slowly,** hampered by lack of investment, strong guilds, and poor transport. Spain characteristically concentrated on foreign trade, which suffered with decline of Spanish colonies. In this setting, society remained split into peasants and nobles throughout much of the countryside, while guilds dominated the cities.

Culture: The French Enlightenment had only limited impact in Spain because the Spanish Inquisition tried to suppress it. Nonetheless, some Spanish intellectuals did try to spread Enlightenment ideas. They were led by **Benito Jerónimo Feijóo,** whose *Teatro Crítico Universal* (1726–39) began the compilation of information on a wide variety of works, which he continued with other, later works. **Luis Cañuelo's** *El Censor* provided Spain with an organ of social criticism, while **Pedro Rodríguez** theorized on government.

Monarchs: Charles II (1665–1700), Philip V (1700–1746), Ferdinand VI (1746–59), Charles III (1759–88), Charles IV (1788–1808).

1648. The Peace of Westphalia marked the beginning of decline for the Spanish Empire. Spain continued at war with France.

1652, Oct. The Catalan revolt begun in 1640 finally ended when the citizen army in Barcelona surrendered to **Don Juan** of Austria, the king's illegitimate son.

1658. The French besieged Dunkirk; the Spanish were unable to relieve it.

1656–59. War with England (p. 314).

1659. The Treaty of the Pyrenees (1659) ended the war with France.

1660. In an effort to stop inflation, the **government introduced a new copper coinage** but prices continued to rise.

1660. Crown took control of municipalities, destroying their autonomy.

1665–1700. CHARLES II, the four-year-old son of Philip IV and the last of the Spanish Habsburgs. Until 1676 his mother, **Mariana of Austria,** headed the council of regency. She appointed her personal confessor, **John Everard Nithard,** inquisitor general, but he was uniformly disliked.

1665. The Cortes lost its right to approve grants for the crown but retained its right to recognize a new monarch.

1667–68. The War of Devolution (p. 315).

1668, Feb. 13. Spain granted Portugal its independence (p. 331).

Distressed by Father Nithard's policies in foreign affairs, **Don Juan** refused to command the Spanish army. When one of his friends was executed for plotting to assassinate Father Nithard, Don Juan fled to Catalonia.

1669. Don Juan threatened Madrid with 500 soldiers, forcing Father Nithard to flee the city. Don Juan then demanded rational justice, tax decreases, and budget cutting. Don Juan was temporarily appeased but returned in

1677 with 12,000 men and **took control of the government.** Charles II had just reached his majority but, suffering physical and mental disabilities, was unfit to rule. Don Juan therefore dominated the government. However, food shortages, his preoccupation with intrigues launched by Mariana, and continued Spanish decline undermined his popularity.

1674. Spain joined the coalition against France and lost territory by the **Treaty of Nimwegen** (Sept. 17, 1678; p. 315).

1679. Board of Commerce and Money established to approve all guild regulations, centralizing and strengthening the guilds.

1680. Last mass execution of accused heretics under Inquisition (120 people, in Madrid).

1683. The Junta de comercia established. It was unsuccessful until reorganized under the Bourbons (1705).

1684. Treaty of Ratisbon (Regensburg) (p. 315). Spain lost Luxemburg to France after France invaded Catalonia, attacked Genoa, and laid siege to Gerona.

1686. Government devaluation because of persistent hardship, in combination with good harvests that followed, led to some financial stability.

1689. Temporary halt to ordinations in Spain because of the large number of young single men already in the priesthood.

1690. Spain joined the League of Augsburg against Louis XIV and lost Haiti by the Treaty of **Ryswick** (1697; p. 315).

1697. Royal Society of Medicine of Seville founded.

1698, Oct. 11, and March 13, 1700. First and Second partition treaties between England, Holland, and France regarding the successions to Spain and the Spanish empire (p. 315).

1699. Famine resulted in **bread riots in Madrid.** The king, though gravely ill, rose to address the people and promised them aid.

1700, Oct. Charles named **Philip of Anjou,** grandson of Louis XIV of France and great-grandson of Philip IV, heir to his dominions. The king, long ill, died on Nov. 1.

1701–14. WAR OF THE SPANISH SUCCESSION (p. 316).

1703. The powers of the Grand Alliance against France proclaimed Archduke Charles of Austria king of Spain.

1703. Philip V introduced new weapons in an effort to mimic the French army.

1704. Walloon Guards created, reorganizing the royal guard.

1705. Charles landed in Catalonia and took Barcelona. Catalonia and Valencia, ever strongholds of anti-French sentiment, accepted Charles and supported him.

1706, June. The Portuguese invaded Spain and occupied Madrid but were driven out by Philip in October (p. 331).

1707. Catalonia, Aragon, and Valencia lost their constitutions, viceroys, and Cortes.

1710. Charles took Madrid. Philip and the French won victories at Brihuega and Villa Viciosa (Dec. 10), and Charles was obliged to abandon Madrid again.

1713, April 11. The Treaty of Utrecht (p. 316). **Philip was recognized as king of Spain** by Britain and Holland on condition that the French and Spanish crowns should never be united. **Bourbon reforms:** the new **Bourbon dynasty** pushed with mixed success over the next decades for reforms that would reduce feudalism, improve the army and firearms as well as finances, and encourage industry and trade (new roads, agricultural improvements, etc.).

May. The Salic Law was introduced in Spain to govern the succession to the throne.

July. The Catalans declared war in protest of the loss of their autonomy. Relying on guerrilla warfare, they resisted Spanish troops until Sept. 1714, when they surrendered to prevent the burning of Barcelona.

1714. Philip V's Royal Library first opened to the public; founded 1712. However, women were generally not admitted to the library.

1714. Royal Spanish Academy founded.

1714, March–Sept. Treaty of Rastatt (p. 316), ending the war with Austria. Spain gave up its possessions in Flanders (henceforth the Austrian Netherlands), Luxemburg, and Italy.

Sept. 11. Barcelona finally capitulated to Berwick. The provinces were put under Castilian law and the use of the Catalan language was forbidden in the courts.

1714. Philip married Elizabeth Farnese of Parma after the death of his first wife, Maria Louisa of Savoy. With the aid of her adviser, **Abbé (later Cardinal) Giulio Alberoni,** she devoted herself to the problem of supplanting the Austrian power in Italy and providing the Italian thrones for her children. Philip, on the other hand, appeared to have hoped for many years to succeed to the French throne and did his

utmost to undermine the position of the French regent, the duke of Orléans.

1717. Philip secretly sent an expeditionary force that seized **Sardinia** and **Sicily** (Nov.).

1718, Aug. 2. Conclusion of the Quadruple Alliance (Britain, France, Holland, and Austria) to counteract the attempts of Philip to overturn the peace settlements (p. 316).

1720, Feb. 17. The Treaty of the Hague, by which Philip abandoned his Italian claims in return for an Austrian promise of the succession to Parma, Piacenza, and Tuscany for Charles, the eldest son of Philip and Elizabeth Farnese.

1721, June. Spain joined the alliance of Britain and France. Louis, son of Philip by his first wife, married Louise Elizabeth of Orléans (1722), while Louis XV of France was betrothed to a daughter of Philip and Elizabeth, who was then only five years old.

1724. Abdication of Philip. He was succeeded by his son, **Louis I,** who, however, died in the same year. **Philip then resumed the crown.**

1725. The duke of Bourbon, chief minister of **Louis XV of France, canceled the engagement of the king to Elizabeth.** Philip then allied himself with Austria (work of the adventurer **Baron de Ripperdá**) by the Treaty of Vienna (April 30, 1725).

1727–29. War with Britain and France. By the **Treaty of Seville (1729),** Britain and France agreed to the Spanish successions in the Italian duchies.

1727. Abolition of juros, sinecures issued by the government in recognition of advances on capital. These had been under scrutiny because of their high costs.

1733. First *pacte de famille* between France and Spain. Spain thereupon joined France in the **War of the Polish Succession against Austria (1733–35).**

1735. Academy of History founded.

1739–48. Anglo-Spanish War (p. 317).

1740–48. War of the Austrian Succession (p. 317). Spain took part in the war as the ally of France against Austria.

1749. The marquis of Ensenada, minister of Finance, introduced a **tax plan** that consolidated all Spanish taxes. His plan was never implemented, because Spanish officials would not follow it. These sorts of difficulties hampered any major reforms in the first half of the 18th century.

1754. Concordat with the Vatican. Thereby the Spanish church became practically independent of Rome and was placed under the control of the government.

1754. Ferdinand VI made all Viscayans nobles. This demonstrated the gradual erosion of privilege in Spanish society.

1756–63. The Seven Years' War (p. 317). Spain at first remained neutral, though Spanish troops recovered **Minorca (1756).**

1759–88. CHARLES III, son of Elizabeth Farnese and hitherto king of the Two Sicilies, which he now passed on to his son Ferdinand. **Charles adopted a policy of vigorous reform** in an attempt to strengthen the monarchy along absolutist lines. He built an extensive road system outward from Madrid and founded a hospital, an observatory, and the Prado, a natural history museum.

1761, Aug. 15. Second *pacte de famille* with France, against Britain. In this generally defensive arrangement the Bourbon states of Italy were included.

1762. Spain joined in the war against Britain. The British seized Cuba and the Philippines. By the **Treaty of Paris (Feb. 10, 1763),** Spain recovered these possessions but lost Minorca and Florida. In return for the loss of Florida, France ceded Louisiana to Spain.

1765. Charles III established free trade in grain and prohibited any monopolies or guilds from restricting such trade. While designed to provide better trade, this law and the subsequent poor harvest resulted in hoarding.

1766. Riots and hoarding throughout Spain.

1767. Jesuits secretly expelled from Spain.

1769. Charles began nominating the directors to all universities and submitted them to inspection.

1771. Charles created a **new order of nobility** open to the bourgeoisie.

1773. Mutiny in Barcelona after a system of selecting one of every five men by lot to serve in the army (the *quinta*) was introduced. It was suspected immediately.

1779, June. Spain joined France in the War of American Independence against Britain (p. 319).

1780. Education reorganized. Only members of the teaching guild allowed to teach in Spain. This measure demonstrated the growing interest in education through the end of the 18th century.

1783. Declaration indicating that **labor did not demean either the family or person** who performed it.

1785. The title *hidalgo* restricted to those who earned it through their merits.

1785. Archive of the Indies founded in Seville.

1790. King began awarding prizes in manufacturing and exporting.

1793. Godoy presented with a memorial by disciples of the **Pestalozzi method of education** (p. 336). (Pestalozzi was a Swiss educator.) Godoy had established the Royal Pestalozzi Institute, but the memorial did little to further the cause.

March 7. FRANCE DECLARED WAR ON SPAIN (p. 433). Spain allied itself with Great Britain (March 13) and invaded Roussillon and Navarre. The French took the offensive, invading Catalonia and Guipúzcoa (1794–95).

1796, Aug. 19. Treaty of San Ildefonso. Spain joined France in the war against Britain. Defeat of the Franco-Spanish fleet at Cape St. Vincent (Feb. 14, 1797).

1800, Oct. Second Treaty of San Ildefonso. By agreement of Jan. 20, 1801, Spain promised to detach Portugal from Britain, by force if necessary.

1802, March. Treaty of Amiens, between Great Britain, France, and Spain (p. 437).

1805, Jan. 4. Spain entered the War of the Third Coalition on the side of France. Defeat of the Franco-Spanish fleet at Trafalgar (Oct. 21, 1805).

1807, March 17. Popular uprising against Godoy at Aranjuez. Charles thereupon abdicated (March 19), but Murat, who arrived soon afterward at Madrid, induced the king to retract his abdication and persuaded both Charles and Ferdinand to meet Napoleon.

1808, May. The Bayonne Conference. Napoleon told Ferdinand to abdicate the throne he had just assumed. Then Charles was forced to abdicate in Napoleon's favor (May 10). Both princes were given estates in France and handsome pensions.

June 7. JOSEPH, Napoleon's brother, became king of Spain (p. 437). Joseph attempted to improve government and social welfare, introducing a cabinet system of government and increasing government centralization. He also increased government control of medical facilities, improved innoculation facilities, and founded or improved hospitals. Before this, welfare had rested largely in the hands of the church and the family. **Inquisition abolished** (restored 1814, abolished again 1820). *(To p. 456)*

2. PORTUGAL
(From p. 296)

Monarchs: John IV (1640–56), Afonso VI (1656–83), Peter II (1683–1706), John V (1706–50), Joseph I (1750–77), Maria I (1777–1816).

The Thirty Years' War, Spain's economic problems, and revolts in the Netherlands and Catalonia enabled Portugal to gain its independence (p. 329) even though it lacked a strong modern army. King John faced financial difficulties and problems of recognition. **France and England** recognized him immediately, but the **papacy** refused to recognize Portuguese independence, so when peace was finally reached, the vast majority of Portuguese dioceses had no prelate. John fought the wars of independence with money borrowed from Jews within Portugal and so **granted "new Christians" some privileges.**

DEMOGRAPHY. Population remained steady during the second half of the 17th century but increased dramatically after about 1730.

ECONOMY. The Portuguese government depended on Brazil for most of its income, so colonial trade remained key to the economy. Portugal also relied heavily on **two major agricultural products, wine and olive oil**—demand for both of which increased following 1648. This reliance meant a **decline in grain production** and grain scarcity in Portugal. In industry, **Portugal regulated manufactures, adhering to mercantilist policies.** However, manufacturing fared poorly because Portuguese products could not compete with superior-quality imports. As a result, **Portugal sustained a permanent trade deficit** between 1648 and 1814.

CULTURE. The Portuguese Enlightenment was largely the creation of Portuguese who had resided abroad and who brought back foreign ideas upon their return to Portugal. **Marquis de Pombal** dominated political theory, along with **Luis da Cunha's** *Political Testament.* **Father Luís António** in education with his *True Method of Study* (1746). **Gomes Freire** supported the French Revolution in his late-18th-century writings. In literature and the arts, **Antonio José da Silva (1705–39), Manuel Bocage (1765–1805), Filinto Elísio (1734–1819), Cruz e Silva (1731–99), Correia Garção (1724–72).**

1649–59. Immunity granted to the property of new Christians sentenced by the Inquisition.

1654. The Dutch were finally driven from Brazil, where they had established themselves during the Spanish period.

1656–67. AFONSO VI, whose mother, **Luisa María de Guzmán,** served as regent during the first period of his reign. Hostilities with Spain reopened. The Spaniards defeated at **Elvas (Jan. 14, 1659)** and the **Battle of Ameixal** (June 8, 1663).

1662. Charles II of England married Catherine, the daughter of John IV.

1662. A palace coup placed Afonso on the throne, eliminating Queen-Mother Luisa's regency and resulting in appointment of **Count of Castelo Melhor** as prime minister.

1665. The battle of Montes Claros effectively ended the war with Spain.

1667. Castelo Melhor signed an alliance with France because he believed England was not negotiating for the best possible peace with Spain.

1667. Peter (Pedro), the brother of Afonso, **led a second coup,** forced Castelo Melhor's dismissal, and imprisoned the king. He set himself up as regent and **exiled Afonso to the Azores** (d. 1683).

1668. Peter married Afonso's wife, Mlle. d'Aumale, after exposing his brother's impotence.

Feb. 13. Conclusion of peace with Spain (Treaty of Lisbon). Spain recognized Portuguese independence.

1668. Olive trees were replanted in areas devastated by the war, helping restore the economy.

1669–92. Economic crisis hit Portugal.

1675. "Discourse on the Introduction of the Arts in the Realm," by Duarter Ribeiro de Macedo. This work became the leading economic doctrine. Ribeiro de Macedo was an ambassador to France, heavily influenced by Colbert. His work stressed industry and the search for new sources of revenue. The government followed such policies. It **established a number of industries** (glass factories in Lisbon, textiles in Estremoz, etc.) and enacted a series of laws (1677–98) **prohibiting the use of foreign goods** such as hats, cloths, and ribbons. However, owing to the poor quality of Portuguese products, the laws were unenforceable and the policy failed.

1683–1706. PETER II ruled as king after the death of Afonso.

1685–86. Introduction of new methods of minting coins which prevented clipping of coins and, along with debasement, temporarily stabilized Portugal's currency.

1697–98. The Cortes met for the last time.

1703, Dec. 27. Methuen-Alegrete agreement. British wool and woolens admitted into Portugal duty-free and Portuguese wine admitted into England at a greatly reduced rate. The agreement led to great gains in the Portuguese trade for the British, at French and Spanish expense (p. 323).

1704. Invasions of Portugal by a French-Spanish force, as a result of Portuguese participation in the War of the Spanish Succession. The British and the Portuguese succeeded in driving out the enemy.

1706. Anglo-Portuguese invasion of Spain and brief occupation of Madrid (June).

1706–50. John V, the son of Peter II, during whose reign the court was patterned after Versailles (construction of the Mafra palace).

1707, April 25. Battle of Almanza. Defeat of the Anglo-Portuguese army by the French forces under Marshal Berwick.

1712–28. Rafael Bluteau completed the first comprehensive Portuguese dictionary. This achievement underscored the development of a Portuguese culture distinct from Spanish influence following independence.

1720. John V established the **Royal Academy of History.**

1736. Government moved toward a **cabinet government** rather than one controlled by nobles. Three secretaries were given wider power and became the effective cabinet, the Junta dos Três Estados (suppressed 1813).

1750–77. JOSEPH I. Government run by the **Marquis de Pombal** (Sebastião José de Carvalho e Mello, who became Marquis de Pombal only in 1770). He devoted himself to breaking the power of the privileged nobility and the Church. He reformed the finances and the army, encouraged industry and trade (establishment of trade companies with monopolistic powers), tried to revive agriculture (silk raising), and did much to develop primary and technical education.

1755, Nov. 1. The GREAT EARTHQUAKE AT LISBON, which was accompanied by fire and by flood of the Tagus. Tens of thousands lost their lives in the disaster. Lisbon destroyed, with many of its treasures. The city was rebuilt under Pombal's energetic direction.

1757. Riot at Porto of small producers and trades, protesting attempted control of the wine market by Company for the Agriculture of the Alto Douro Wines. The company continued its policies despite the riots.

1758, Sept. Conspiracy of the Tavoras. A group of nobles against the king and Pombal. The leaders, among them members of the highest aristocracy, were tortured and executed.

1759, Sept. 3. Expulsion of the Jesuits resulted. They were deported to the Papal States.

1759. Jesuit manuals and methods forbidden for use in teaching children. Classes in Latin, Greek, Hebrew, and rhetoric established for children throughout Portugal.

1760. The office of General Intendant of the Court and Kingdom Police established and police system reformed.

1761. A Royal Treasury (Real Erário) established to supervise public funds and provide greater efficiency.

1761. Royal College of the Nobles established.

1761. Slavery abolished in Portugal (but not its colonies).

1765. The government ordered vineyards in areas suitable for grain production uprooted and replaced with wheat and other crops. The move was an attempt to decrease Portuguese need to import grain, but it was unsuccessful.

1768. The distinction made by the Inquisition between **old and new Christians abolished.**

1768. Censorship transferred from the Church to the state. A royal printing press established. Such reforms were paid for through a tax on wine, brandy, and vinegar.

1769. The Law of the Good Reason limited valid laws to only those which rested on "good reason." This was a triumph for Enlightenment thinking.

1769. Pombal turned the Inquisition into a royal court rather than an independent institution.

1770. Trade declared a noble and necessary profession and traders given the right to establish entailed estates.

1774. Insanity of Joseph I and regency of his wife, Maria Anna. She began gradually to reduce the power of Pombal.

1774. Pombal decreed the **free circulation of goods** throughout Portugal.

1774. New regulation eliminated the inquisitors' use of the **death penalty and public autos-da-fé.**

1777–1816. MARIA I, the daughter of Joseph I, queen. She married her uncle Peter, who assumed the title of king as Peter III but who died in 1786. Under Maria, the nobility began to recover its position. **Pombal was exiled** (d. 1782) but his reform policies continued.

1779. Establishment of the Royal Academy of Science.

1780. Police prerogatives enlarged.

1780. The Casa Pia established in Lisbon for the care and education of poor orphans.

1790. All vestiges of feudal justice abolished. The administration of justice rationalized and centralized.

1792. Insanity of Maria and regency of her son John, who, with the ardent support of the clergy, undertook a drastic repression of all revolutionary agitation and thought.

1796. Royal Public Library established.

1801, Feb.–Sept. War of the Oranges with Spain, resulting from dealings between Spain and France. After a Spanish invasion the Portuguese made peace. By the **Treaty of Madrid** (Sept. 29), Portugal paid a heavy indemnity and renounced the treaties with Britain.

1807, July. Napoleon sent Portugal a directive on how to implement the **continental system** (p. 438). Portugal was hesitant to break off ties with England but was under continued pressure from Napoleon.

Aug. French and Spanish envoys gave Portugal an ultimatum: Declare war on England by Sept. 1 or be invaded.

1807. Royal Guard of Police established.

Oct. 27. Treaty of Fontainebleau between France and Spain, envisaging the partition of Portugal.

Nov. 30. Lisbon was taken by a French army under Junot, assisted by the Spanish. The Portuguese royal family fled to Brazil. Popular resistance began throughout the city (p. 438).

1808, June. Prince-Regent John proclaimed in north. Widespread development of juntas and resistance movements.

July. English troops arrived in Portugal.

1809. Second French Invasion, but French were gradually driven back and the **Vienna Congress** (p. 440) **restored Portugal's independence.**

(To p. 456)

e. ITALY AND THE PAPACY

(From p. 299)

1. OVERVIEW

Economy and Society: The **general crisis of the 17th century** weakened the basis of Italian economic development. **Population growth** stagnated as a result of plague and famine. Trade with the east suffered from the war with the Ottoman empire and the decline of the **Mediterranean spice trade.** Holland and England, situated on the western European coast, developed seaborne trade routes that took advantage of both eastern and western trade opportunities and contributed to the decline of the Italian economy. **Italian production** also declined dramatically. Investment in Italy had been concentrated in luxury goods and buildings rather than trade and capital development. In some parts of Italy, **investment in land** led to **agricultural changes,** increased the number of acres in production, and encouraged a shift from crops such as millet to rye or wheat.

In the **18th century, Italy experienced a gradual recovery.** It switched crops and lifted trade barriers. **Population increased,** especially in the countryside. Reforms in education, gradual decline of the power of the papacy, and introduction of some manufacturing innovations all spurred this recovery.

Italian towns continued to be controlled by small, often hereditary oligarchies while the countryside remained dominated by large landowners. The Italian nobility sometimes proved capable of significant innovation. **Peasants protested taxation and overbearing policies,** which led to an 18th-century age of reform fueled by Enlightenment thinking.

CULTURE: In music Italy was outstanding. **Niccolò Amati (1596–1684)** and **Antonio Stradivari (1644–1737);** in opera, **Claudio Monteverdi (1567–1643)** and **Giovanni Pergolesi (1710–36), Domenico Cimarosa (1749–1801),** and **Giovanni Paisiello (1741–1816). Girolamo Frescobaldi (1583–1643),** composer of organ music; **Arcangelo Corelli (1653–1713),** eminent violinist and composer of sonatas and concerti grossi; **Alessandro Scarlatti (1659–1725),** of operas; and **Antonio Vivaldi (c. 1678–1741),** of chamber music. Two great schools of music at Venice and Naples.

Lorenzo Bernini (1598–1680), architect and sculptor, was one of the leading artists of the Baroque period, which preceded the Rococco of the 18th century and the classical revival represented by **Antonio Canova (1757–1822).** Bernini designed and built the **Vatican Palace** and **St. Peter's Square,** while **Francesco Borromini (1599–1667)** reconstructed St. John Lateran and built other Roman churches.

In painting, **Giambattista Tiepolo (1696–1770)** for a time brought Venice a final burst of glory.

The Academy of Arcadia (1692) started a widespread vogue of the conventional and artificial in literature, which was counterbalanced by the comedies of **Carlo Goldoni (1707–93)** and the serious patriotic dramas of **Vittorio Alfieri (1749–1803).** A return to classicism was apparent in the dramas of Goldoni and in the work of Alfierie and poetry of **Gaicomo Leopardi (1798–1837).**

Italy was preeminent also in the fields of social and physical science. **Pietro Giannone (1676–1748)** created a profound stir with his anticlerical *Historia civile del regno di Napoli* (1723); **Antonio Genovesi (1713–69)** was an outstanding physiocrat; **Giambattista Vico (1668–1744),** with his *Scienza nuova* (1725), laid the basis of the modern philosophy of history; while **Cesare Beccaria (1738–94)** in his *Dei de-*

litti e delle pene (1764) founded the modern science of penology. In the natural sciences **Lazzaro Spallanzani (1729–99)** made fundamental contributions to the study of digestion, while **Luigi Galvani (1737–98)** and **Alessandro Volta (1745–1827)** were in the front rank among the pioneers of electricity.

Politics: Italy remained divided between 1648 and 1815, different regions coming under the control of various monarchies in Europe. However, regions dominated by the Bourbons and the Habsburgs experienced an **age of reform fueled by Enlightenment thinking** during the 18th century. *(To p. 458)*

2. THE PAPACY
(From p. 299)

By attempting to remain neutral in the great conflicts between **the Bourbons and the Habsburgs**, the popes sacrificed the support of both. Furthermore, the Church divided on the question of **Jansenism** (from Cornelius Jansenius, bishop of Ypres), which emphasized inner regeneration rather than external reorganization of the Church, as represented by the Jesuits.

1644–55. Innocent X (Giambattista Pamfili), a pope who was entirely under the control of his sister-in-law, Olympia Maidalchini. The **pope denounced the Treaty of Westphalia** because of the abolition of bishoprics and concessions to Protestants, but the protest had no effect.

1653, May 31. The bull *Cum occasione impressionis libri* condemned five propositions in the work of Jansenius, thus initiating the Jansenist controversy (p. 328).

1655–67. Alexander VII (Fabio Chigi).

1667–69. Clement IX (Giulio Rospigliosi), elected by French influence.

1670–76. Clement X (Cardinal Altieri), regarded as pro-Spanish. He disapproved of the French alliance with the Ottoman Empire and did what he could to support the war of the Habsburgs with the enemy.

1676–89. Innocent XI (Benedetto Odescalchi), one of the outstanding popes of the period. He undertook a much-needed **financial reorganization of the papacy,** refused to practice nepotism, enforced regulations to improve the morality of the clergy. At the same time he financed the Austrians in their campaigns against the Ottoman empire.

1682. Church assembly at St. Germain called by Louis XIV (p. 328). It adopted four articles: (1) sovereigns are not subject to the pope in temporal matters; (2) a general council is superior to a pope; (3) the power of the pope is subject to the regulations of a council and a pope cannot decide contrary to the rules of the Gallican church; (4) decisions of the papacy are not irrevocable.

In reply to these articles **the pope refused to invest as bishops** any French clerics who had taken part in the assembly. Ultimately, 35 French bishoprics were vacant. Further friction developed. **The pope protested against the suppression and expulsion of the Huguenots** and actually approved the expedition of William III to England, as part of an anti-French policy.

1689–91. Alexander VIII (Pietro Ottoboni).

1691–1700. Innocent XII (Antonio Pignatelli).

1692. The bull *Romanum decet pontificem* limited the number of offices that could be held by relatives of the pope, thus putting an end to nepotism in its worst form. Innocent also checked the sale of offices.

1697. The pope made peace with France, winning a substantial victory. Louis XIV abrogated the four articles of 1682, probably in order to win support in the matter of the Spanish succession.

1700–1721. Clement XI (Gian Francesco Albani), who attempted to maintain neutrality in the Bourbon-Habsburg struggle. The Austrians therefore ignored papal claims. During the war they occupied Parma and Piacenza, marched through the Papal States, and conquered Naples. In **1709 the pope was obliged to recognize Charles as king of Spain.** But Clement's pontificate was noteworthy chiefly for the renewed condemnation of Jansenism, which had made extraordinary progress in France (p. 328).

1713, Sept. 8. The bull *Unigenitus* again condemned Jansenism, causing religious discontent in France, where the movement had made great progress.

1721–24. Innocent XIII (Michelangelo dei Conti).

1724–30. Benedict XIII (Pietro Francesco Orsini).

1730–40. Clement XII (Lorenzo Corsini).

1740–58. Benedict XIV (Prospero Lambertini). He was much influenced by the Enlightenment in Europe and encouraged agriculture and trade. He sought a compromise with the absolute rulers, whose efforts to establish national churches had weakened the papacy. **Conclusion of concordats with Naples (1741) and Spain (1753)** were important steps in this direction, though they cost the papacy far-reaching concessions.

1758–69. Clement XIII (Carlo Rezzonico), a pope elected through the efforts of the Jesuits. The Jesuits had become unpopular as a result of Jansenist attacks and because of their interference in politics, their engagement in commercial and industrial enterprise, and so on.

1769–74. Clement XIV (Lorenzo Gaganelli) was unable to resist the pressure of the Bourbon governments. The Society of Jesus was ordered dissolved (1773).

1775–99. Pius VI tried to deter Emperor Joseph II from his anticlerical policy (p. 339) but was soon confronted with the radical anticlericalism of the French Revolution. The French armies invaded papal territory (1796) and, after a short truce, intervened in Rome to set up the **revolutionary Roman Republic** (1798). The pope was taken off to southern France (Valence), where he died in the next year.

(To p. 458)

3. SAVOY (SARDINIA)
(From p. 299)

1638–75. CHARLES EMMANUEL II, who came of age in 1648, submitted to the domination of his mother until her death in 1663. His reign was scarred by the **massacres of the Waldenses** (1655), which stirred the indignation of Europe.

1675–1730. VICTOR AMADEUS II. His mother, Jeanne de Nemours, acted as regent until 1684. She continued the Francophile orientation of Savoyard policy.

1685. Further persecution of the heretics, at the behest of Louis XIV.

1690. The duke joined the League of Augsburg against the French (p. 315). But in 1696, hoping to make better terms with Louis, he reversed himself and received Pinerolo in return.

1697. The Perequazione, a new tax system, introduced. Lands surveyed and valued in an effort to properly assess them.

1701–14. War of the Spanish Succession (p. 316). Victor Amadeus allowed **the French to occupy Milan and Mantua** but joined the Grand Alliance in 1703. As a result the French, under Vendôme, overran Savoy in 1704, but the Austrians, under Prince Eugene of Savoy, relieved the situation in 1705. The French again invaded (1706) and **besieged Turin** until they were driven out by Prince Eugene. **Occupation of Milan by the Austrians and Savoyards.** This practically ended the war in Italy.

1713. By the Treaty of Utrecht (p. 316), Victor Amadeus was awarded Sicily as his share of the Spanish spoils. At the same time he assumed the royal title.

1716ff. Poor relief reforms introduced. Public begging and private assistance forbidden; over the next several years, hospices and confraternities were established in cities. These sought to train children for trades and put able-bodied paupers to work.

1717. A Council of State and General Council of Finance established.

1717. A Spanish raid on Sicily resulted in war and a new peace settlement.

1720. By terms of the settlement, **Victor Amadeus gave up Sicily to Austria** and received in exchange the island of Sardinia (p. 316). Henceforth he was king of Sardinia.

1722. New nobles created—titles given primarily to Victor Amadeus's reformers.

1729. The Constitutions sought to provide a clear, organized body of law. It also established a **Collegio della Provincie** that gave an education to poor but talented students.

1730–73. CHARLES EMMANUEL III.

1731. Edict supported the reforms made under Victor Amadeus II, putting the tax system for which he surveyed into effect.

1742–47. Savoy sided with Austria in the **War of the Austrian Succession** (p. 317) and received the part of the Ducy of Milan west of the Ticino.

1762. A provision limited the mortmain and restricted endowments to the Church.

1764–65. Famine in Italy. Grain banks established to assist the peasants.

1771. Government began abolishing the remnants of feudalism.

1773–96. VICTOR AMADEUS III. In 1792, he joined Austria in the war against France. His territories were soon overrun by the French.

1796. Napoleon's appearance in Italy. The armies of the king were quickly defeated. By the armistice of **Cherasco** (April 28), the king was obliged to abandon the Austrian alliance. Napoleon's defeat of the Austrians led to a fundamental remaking of the whole Italian situation (p. 335).

4. NAPLES
(From p. 300)

The Spanish rule continued in Naples until the **War of the Spanish Succession:**

1707. The Austrians occupied Naples.

1713. By the **Treaty of Utrecht** (p. 316) Spain ceded Sardinia and Naples to Austria while Sicily passed to Savoy. In 1720 Austria exchanged Sardinia for Sicily.

1734–35. Feudal obligations and offices revamped to assure a more stable financial base. A census of offices taken. These reforms helped stabilize government finances.

1735. Austria ceded Naples and Sicily to the **Spanish Bourbons** on condition that they should never be united with Spain as one crown.

1735–59. CHARLES III (son of Philip V of Spain), king of Naples and Sicily.

1739. The Supreme Magistrature for Trade established. It was widely resisted because it replaced officials and guilds that had often restricted trade.

1740. Edict granted Jews certain freedoms within the kingdom.

1740. A revision of the land register begun.

1740. Treaty of peace and trade signed with the Ottoman Empire.

1741, June 2. A concordat with the papacy regulated papal involvement in legal matters.

1746. Abolition of the Tribunal of the Holy Office in Naples.

1746. The Supreme Magistracy of Commerce disbanded.

1759–1825. FERDINAND I. Ferdinand was only nine years old and continued under the influence of **Tanucci** until the latter's fall in 1771. By that time his wife, **Maria Carolina** (daughter of Maria Theresa), already dominated him.

1762. Clergy with benefices required to give a third of their income to the poor.

1764–65. Famine throughout the south of Italy. It hit Naples particularly hard and demonstrated the gap between southern agriculture and the rest of Europe. This famine prompted many efforts at reform, although the government showed limited enthusiasm.

1765. The Communal Council reformed so that 15 professional men sat as well as nobles.

1777. Confiscation of Jesuit property, including the College of San Salvatore, paved the way to reform.

5. LOMBARDY
(From p. 299)

Lombardy, under the control of the Habsburgs, was one of the **most modern agricultural regions in Europe.** The 18th century saw the continued development of agriculture in Lombardy but no corresponding shifts in social structure. **Land continued to be held by the Church and large estate holders.** Maria Theresa and Joseph II sought to **reform tax collection and bureaucracy** to reflect agricultural developments.

1718. The land register started but, because of opposition from the nobility, it was never completed.

1748–55. A commission (Junta) completed the land register, which provided the Habsburgs with a means of determining taxes on the basis of land.

1750. Pompeo Neri, a professor and chairman of the Junta, published his *Relazione*, an account of the principles to be applied to the new land register. He argued for the abolition of all taxes except the land tax as well as the elimination of privileges.

1753. Bank of Santa Teresa set up to guarantee the state's debt to its tax farmers.

1760, Jan. 1. New fiscal law, based on land register, in effect. Taxes now passed on assessment of land and the principle of equal taxation for all landowners established.

1765. A special Junta established to deal with the problem of getting **tax support from the clergy.** It limited the role the Church could play in government.

1765. The Tax Farm reformed to give the government more control and a share of the profits.

1765. A new council, **Supremo Consiglio di Economia,** established to break the power of the Milanese oligarchy.

1767. Pavia University reformed and new curriculum introduced.

1768, Dec. 30. Censorship removed from the hands of the Inquisition and invested in Giunta agli studi, a special commission authorized by the state.

1769. Prisons in religious houses closed; religious services reformed.

1770. Right of sanctuary abolished.

1770. Tax farming put to an end; instead of taxes collected by private agents (farmers) on commission, collection now under the jurisdiction of the public treasury.

1771. Maria Theresa completed a coach pass through the Alps.

1776. Paderno canal completed; Milan now connected to Adda.

1778. La Scala opened.

6. TUSCANY
(From p. 299)

Tuscany fell into Habsburg hands only after the extinction of the Medici line in 1737. The Medicis continued to use the aristocratic Comune created in the 16th century. As a result of this and Medici policies generally, money was heavily invested in land because land brought prestige. However, such investments did not provide the large yields that trade and banking would have provided.

1733. Monsignor Cerati became director of University of Pisa. Cerati provided an intellectual basis for many of the reforms introduced in the 18th century. Most important, he called for new economic policies eliminating trade restrictions and tariffs.

1737–45. Francis of Lorraine, Grand Duke of Tuscany.

1738. Francis refused to publish the papal bull condemning freemasonry and introduced a law limiting the right to bear arms. The latter **disarmed the Inquisitor's agents.**

1739. Government dismissed all the consuls of the city's guilds and appointed officials to carry out its reforms. The tax system and fiscal system completely revamped.

1740, Dec. Tuscan finances contracted to a private French company. This new tax farm replaced the numerous private collectors in an effort to rationalize tax collection.

1743, May 28. Censorship of books and presses transferred from the Church to the state.

1747–90. Leopold I. The administration was remade, serfdom abolished, trade and industry encouraged.

1747. Gabriele Verri **redrafted the Milanese legal code** to improve its clarity and structure.

1747. Edict restricted the *fidecommesso* (property settlement) to nobility and allowed land inheritances to be passed down in this manner for only four generations.

1750. Law required that all titles held before the 18th century be verified. While this was designed to limit the nobility to those considered worthy (i.e., without demeaning professions, etc.), it met with opposition from the nobility.

1751. A law of mortmain set limits on donations of land and moveable goods to the Church. Above those limits, the Regency Council had to approve the transfer.

7. OTHER STATES
(From p. 300)

Venice continued to fall into ever deeper decline. In international affairs, it became increasingly cautious and neutral.

1645–69. The Candian War, during the earlier part of which the Venetians won resounding naval victories at the Dardanelles. The war ultimately centered on the **siege of Candia (Crete) (1658–69).** France came to the aid of Venice and the Venetians themselves put up a tough defense, but by the peace settlement they lost Candia to the Ottomans.

1684. Venice joined with Austria and Poland in the war against the Ottomans (p. 337).

1718. By the Treaty of Passarowitz, the Venetians lost the Morea. Venice retained only the Ionian islands and the Dalmatian coast.

Milan remained under Spanish rule until by **the Treaty of Utrecht (1713)** it passed to Austria. Mantua was incorporated with the duchy of Milan (p. 316).

Parma and Piaceza changed hands several times during the 18th century.

1731. On the extinction of the Farnese family, the duchies were given to Charles, the son of Philip V of Spain and his second wife, Elizabeth Farnese. In 1733 (**War of the Polish Succession**) Charles conquered Naples and Sicily, and these territories were awarded him in the peace settlement. In return he abandoned **Parma and Piacenza to Austria** (p. 317).

1748. As a result of the War of the Austrian Succession (p. 317), Maria Theresa ceded Parma and Piacenza to **Philip,** the younger brother of Charles of Naples. Philip ruled until 1765 and was succeeded by his son Ferdinand.

The **Genoese Republic** remained independent, though constantly exposed to encroachment by Savoy, France, and Austria.

1730. Revolt of Corsica against Genoese rule.

After a long and variable struggle, during which a German adventurer, Baron Neuhof of Westphalia, appeared for a time as **King Theodore I** (1736), the Genoese called upon the French for assistance. The French subjugated the island, which the Genoese ceded to them (1768).

8. ITALY DURING THE FRENCH REVOLUTION

1790. Filippo Buonarroti, a student and later a radical leader, moved to Corsica and started the *Giornale patriottico di Corsica (Patriotic Journal of Corsica).*

1794–95. A series of attempted revolutions organized in Piedmont, Bologna, Palermo, and Sardinia.

1796–97. Napoleon's military campaigns in Italy met with tremendous success (p. 434).

1796, Oct.–1797, March. A series of conferences in Italy to write the constitution of a Cispadane (south of the Po) Republic. The Cispadane Republic was merged into the Cisalpine Republic (1797: Milan, Modena, Ferrara, Bologna, Romagna).

1797, June. Genoa formed its own republic.

1798. Roman Republic formed, although it remained primarily a French protectorate. It recognized Jewish equality.

1799. Piedmont annexed to France.

1799, Jan. Neapolitan Republic formed. It lasted just five months. Austrian and Russian troops entered Italy and the republics met with resistance throughout the countryside.

1800. The Battle of Marengo (p. 435) enabled Napoleon to begin retaking Italy.

1802. Lyons. The Italian Republic declared. It would become the Italian Kingdom when the empire was established.

1805. After the Italian legislators requested decreases in taxes, **Napoleon dissolved the legislature,** never calling it again.

1806, Aug. 2. Feudalism abolished and state sovereignty asserted.

1814, April 20. The Italian Kingdom's finance minister, Prina, assassinated. This marked the growing agitation for independence that followed news of Napoleon's retreat from Russia. (To p. 458)

f. THE SWISS CONFEDERATION

(From p. 305)

The Legacy of the Thirty Years' War: Despite the involvement of Swiss mercenaries, Swiss **neutrality** during the Thirty Years' War made Switzerland a center for refugees who, along with soldiers, brought the **bubonic plague** and other diseases into the country. Swiss neutrality also demanded a strong Swiss army, which the Swiss paid for partly through **the Defensionale of Wyl (1647).** This defensionale strengthened bonds among cantons. The Peace of Westphalia recognized Swiss independence.

DEMOGRAPHY: Population remained static during the latter half of the 17th century but grew in the 18th century, climbing from about 1.2 million to 1.7 million.

ECONOMICS: As with most of western Europe, **mercantilist** thought heavily influenced Swiss industry and agriculture (p. 326). Switzerland sought foreign markets for its products and increased independence from foreign imports. It developed two leading sectors of industry, in the east and west respectively, between 1648 and 1815. **Textiles** developed largely free from guild regulation and under the influence of French immigrants. **Clock making** remained regulated by guilds but advanced because of the reputation of Swiss clock makers. **Trade** also benefited from knowledge of foreign trade gained by Swiss mercenaries. **Agriculture** made slow progress during much of this period, but the latter half of the 18th century saw a **back-to-the-land movement** encouraging the foundation of agricultural societies and some improvements in agricultural techniques. Animal husbandry was encouraged by **mercantilism,** which sought to decrease Swiss wool imports. However, Swiss terrain made farming difficult and Switzerland continued to import agricultural products.

SOCIETY: Swiss society reflected the diversity of Swiss cantons—divided by religion and geography. **Protestants** generally occupied the plain and **Catholics** the mountainous regions. **Peasant** life reflected long-standing methods of farming; small family holdings, commons, and continued emphasis on milk production. **Cities,** on the other hand, generally had strong **guilds** regulating production and often dependent on the surrounding countryside for agricultural products. While never legally abolished, trials and persecutions for **witchcraft** came to an end between 1648 and 1815 (Vaud, 1680; Zürich, 1714; Glarus, 1782).

GOVERNMENT: The Swiss cantons established **a loose federalist government,** assuring each canton a large measure of independence. Each canton chose its form of government—ranging from old styles of open-air meetings in forest cantons to elaborate patriarchies and even absolutism. The **Swiss diet** had 13 seats; the Protestants held 6 of these but demanded recognition because of their economic and military strength.

1653. Lucerne. Peasants, led by Nicholas Leuenberg, revolted (Jan.) and demanded relief from taxes and more recognition of tenant rights. **Leuenberg amassed an army of 16,000** but was defeated by federal forces at **Wohlenschwil** and surrendered on June 8; the terms of their surrender were renounced.

1655. Proposals for the establishment of a more centralized state, put forward by Zürich, were defeated by the Catholic cantons.

1655. The Catholic canton of Schwyz threatened the **Protestants** within its borders with suppression. Some fled to Zürich but the remainder were **persecuted** and, in three cases, turned over to the Inquisition in Milan. **Zürich** demanded that Schwyz restore Protestant land and possessions. Schwyz refused and demanded the return of Protestant refugees.

1656. This conflict escalated into the **FIRST VILLMERGEN WAR.** Bern and Zürich declared war against five Catholic cantons. The Protestants were defeated at **Villmergen (Jan. 24),** reaffirming each canton's right to determine religious activity. However, Protestant and Catholic conflicts continued.

1663. Renewal of the alliance with France, enabling Louis XIV to draw mercenaries from the cantons despite opposition from Zürich and some of the Protestant cantons.

1663–1776. During more than a century there was no meeting of the federal diet, indicating the almost complete collapse of the federal connection.

1678. Franche-Comté (Treaty of Nimwegen) (p. 315), hitherto under federal protection, was annexed to France.

1693. The Protestant cantons agreed to supply soldiers to the Dutch and later to the English. The Catholic cantons responded, agreeing to supply men to the Spaniards.

1707. Efforts to extend the franchise in Geneva to include more men were put down.

1707. A popular insurrection in Geneva, led by Peter Fatio, was suppressed with the aid of the Bern and Zürich oligarchies.

1708. The house of Hohenzollern succeeded to the principality of Neuchâtel. Louis XIV was prevented by the war (p. 316) from pressing the claims of the prince of Conti.

1712. Escalating tensions between Catholics and Protestants led to the **SECOND VILLMERGEN WAR. Cause:** A highway was designed that connected Schwyz with the Austrian border, separating Zürich and Protestant Glarus. The **abbot of St. Gallen, Leodegar Bürgisser,** demanded labor service for the road from the inhabitants of **Wattwil,** but they refused because they were exempt from compulsory labor services. Zürich and Bern supported them, and the Bernese won a decisive victory at **Villmergen (July 25)**, firmly establishing Protestant dominance.

1712, Aug. 11. The Peace of Aarau ended the Second Villmergen War, increasing Zürich's and Bern's control and establishing tribunals equally representing both religious groups to settle disputes.

1715, May 9. The Trücklibund. A secret agreement, named after the locked box it was placed in, signed by the Catholic cantons giving France exclusive rights to recruit military personnel in their territories.

1723. Revolt of Abraham Davel. Davel seized upon growing discontent with the government in Bern and demanded self-government for the Vaud. He saw such independence as the first step in religious transformation. When Bern rejected his demand, he asked the city council of Lausanne to rule the region independently. The city council refused and condemned Davel to death.

1725. Renewal of the treaty with France, but this time with the abstention of the Protestant cantons.

1734, 1737. Uprisings in Geneva led to some constitutional revision; uprisings continued throughout the 18th century.

With the middle of the century there came a **distinct economic improvement** in Switzerland, marked by the expansion of industry. This brought with it a falling off of the mercenary system but also a **rise of the middle class and an intellectual renaissance: Zürich** (with **Johannes J. Bodmer,** 1698–1783, **Albrecht von Haller,** 1708–77, and **Johannes C. Lavater,** 1741–1801) became an important center of German literature and thought; **Geneva** (with **Rousseau,** 1712–78, **Voltaire,** resident in the vicinity after 1755, etc.) became a refuge for advanced thinkers of the French school. The **Helvetic Society** (founded 1762) was an exuberant organization devoted to the new ideas. The educational reformer Johann **Heinrich Pestalozzi** (1746–1827) was strongly influenced by Lavater. After publication of *How Gertrude Teaches Her Children* (1801), Pestalozzi's influence became international.

1776. The whole confederation once more allied itself with France, but Swiss mercenaries in French service fell to under 10,000.

1789–92. The Swiss seriously considered intervention against the French but determined to remain neutral, pursuing repressive policy at home (crushing of unrest in the Vaud by the Bern government).

1792, Dec. 5. A revolutionary coup at Geneva put the government in the hands of the popular party. Thenceforth the developments in France were faithfully mirrored in Geneva.

1793. The French Republic annexed the bishopric (not the town) of Basel.

1797–98. Last diet of the old confederation renewed the oath to the confederation in an effort to maintain Swiss unity and autonomy. However, the diet merely demonstrated the weakness of the Swiss confederation.

1797, Oct. Napoleon annexed the Valtelline and Chiavenna to the Cisalpine Republic (p. 434).

Dec. Revolutionists seized the town of Basel.

1798, Jan. 23. The French declared the Vaud free from Bernese rule and organized it as a **Lemanic Republic.**

Feb. 9. France decreed the establishment of a Helvetic Republic. The move was inspired by the Helvetic Committee in Paris, a revolutionary group headed by **Frédéric-César de La Harpe,** (1754–1838), a Vaudois whose great aim was the liberation of his homeland from the hated Bernese aristocracy, and by **Peter Ochs** of Basel, who drafted the Helvetic constitution and submitted it to the directory. The new republic was to be organized along French lines; with the exception of the areas annexed to France, all **Swiss territory was organized into 23 cantons,** with a **centralized government** consisting of an elected chamber of deputies (eight members from each canton), a senate (four from each canton), and a directory of five. The new constitution guaranteed **freedom of the press, association, petition, and conscience.** It also **made manorial dues salable.** This violated promises made to the peasantry, who anticipated the end of manorial dues. Under pressure, the government did eliminate some of the dues but undermined the Swiss tax base in doing so.

Bern declared war and the Bernese defeated the French army under Brune at **Laupen (March 5).** But another Bernese force was vanquished

on the same day by Schauenberg. Bern surrendered and was sacked. Indemnity of 17 million francs.

April. Five Forest (Catholic) cantons revolted. They won some successes, accepting the Helvetic constitution on condition that the French should not interfere or occupy their territory.

April 26. Geneva was annexed to France.

1799. Bad harvests and ravaged land (the result of French occupation) caused hardship and rises in prices. Unemployment also rose.

1803. Napoleon reestablished the original 13 cantons and added 6 new ones in the **Act of Mediation.** This act eliminated the special privileges of birth in certain cantons and established 6 director cantons to oversee the entire republic. It also **suppressed the press,** increasing censorship. The central government drained the marshes in Glarus, providing more fertile land for agriculture.

1813. Diet convened at Zürich following the Battle of Leipzig declared **Swiss armed neutrality** in the war with Napoleon.

Helvetic Republic Culture: Influenced by the Enlightenment but pressing toward Romanticism, Swiss culture included a strong strain of nationalism. Johannes von Müller's *History of the Swiss Confederation* encouraged study of the Swiss past. Patriotic poetry flourished (e.g., **Rudolf Wyss's** hymn "Rufst Du, mein Vaterland," which had become the national anthem, and **Gottlieb Jakob Kuhn's** "Ha an em Ort es Blüemli gseh"). *(To p. 459)*

g. THE HOLY ROMAN EMPIRE

(From p. 303)

HOLY ROMAN EMPERORS: Ferdinand III (1637–57), Leopold I (1657–1705), Joseph I (1705–11), Charles VI (1711–40), Charles VII (of Bavaria, 1742–45), Francis I (1745–65), Joseph II (1765–90), Leopold II (1790–92).

The territorial states of the Holy Roman Empire gained strength and independence during the 17th and 18th centuries. While each state determined its internal policies, the empire was dominated by two powers, Austria-Hungary in the east and Prussia in the west. The Imperial Diet continued to meet and make decisions regarding trade and foreign policy.

Economy and Society: After the Thirty Years' War, Germany suffered agricultural upheaval. There was a shortage of agricultural labor, and agricultural prices declined because urban populations had been decimated by the war. This decline encouraged the continued transformation of *Grundherrschaft* to *Gutsherrschaft,* eliminating the free peasantry east of the Elbe. The Junkers' continued strength encouraged this policy. The guild recess of 1731 marked the decline of guilds in Germany and the development of the **Verlagssystem** (contract or wage labor) west of the Elbe. The Verlagssystem was fueled by population increases in the 18th century.

1650ff. Development of *Ritterakademien* to teach manners and other niceties to sons of the nobility.

1661. Münster and Erfurt lost their status as **free imperial cities.** Magdeburg came under the control of the great elector (1666) and admitted a garrison. Surrounding territories eliminated the autonomy of many free imperial cities. Imperial control declined.

1655–60. First Northern War (p. 314).

1659. Grimmelshausen's *Simplicissimus.*

1661–64. War against the Ottoman Empire (p. 356).

1667. Samuel Pufendorf's (1632–94) *De statute imperii Germanici* appeared and would become a standard text in Germany and Sweden. In it and *De jure Naturae et Gentium,* Pufendorf argued for a strong German state, but unlike Hobbes in England, he believed that the ruler had an obligation to assure the well-being of his subjects.

1667–68. War of Devolution against France (p. 315).

1674. The Dutch War. Holy Roman Empire sided with Dutch against Louis XIV aggression.

1681. The *Reichskriegsverfaßung* (imperial military declaration) passed in the Imperial Diet. This established military organization on the basis of the circles of empire. It established a peacetime force of 40,000 men.

1688–97. War of the League of Augsburg, against Louis XIV (p. 315).

1692–1701. German princes elevated in rank: Hanover an electorate;

Augustus II, Elector of Saxony, became king of Poland and adopted the Catholic faith.

1701–14. War of the Spanish Succession (p. 316).

1712. Hamburg's constitution revised as a result of a struggle against the city's elites. Popular protest in the 17th century led to a constitution that expanded representation and preserved social mobility.

1731. An imperial law eliminated journeymen's associations and guilds' judicial power, placing the guilds under government control.

1736–39. Unsuccessful war with the Ottoman Empire.

1785, July. League of the German Princes among Prussia, Electoral Saxony, and Hanover, which was afterward joined by Brunswick, Mainz, Hesse-Cassel, Baden, Mecklenburg, Anhalt, and the Thuringian lands, directed against Joseph II's reform schemes (p. 339).

1790–92. LEOPOLD II, emperor. He restored the old constitution and the old privileges. A conference at Reichenbach prevented a war with Prussia, which (Jan. 31, 1790) had concluded a treaty with the Ottomans in order to procure more favorable conditions for the latter from Austria and Russia.

(To p. 460)

1. THE HOHENZOLLERN DYNASTY

Prussian Rulers: Frederick William the Great Elector (1640–88), Frederick I (1688–1713, crowned king of Prussia 1701), Frederick William I, elector and king (1713–40), Frederick II the Great of Prussia (1740–86).

Rise of Brandenburg-Prussia dominated the period. Prussia became a military and political power within Europe, demonstrating its strength in many European wars. It also practiced mercantilism and religious toleration.

Pietism: Pietists emphasized personal commitment, Bible reading, and spiritualism over liturgical rituals and deeds. Frederick William I undermined Lutheran strength in Brandenburg-Prussia by sponsoring Pietism as a state religion and adopting policies of religious toleration. The latter encouraged Huguenots to emigrate from France (p. 328).

1653. Recess of Brandenburg Estates. Frederick William recognized serfdom where it existed, rights of lords, and the continued right of the estates to participate in foreign policy (a right generally conceded by the estates to the elector in practice). In exchange, the recess granted Frederick William taxes that enabled him to maintain a standing army. Prussian electors built upon this base, using European wars to demand more funds for the army.

1666. Succession in Cleve-Jülich settled. Brandenburg ultimately received Cleve, Mark, and Revensberg.

1667. Taxes reorganized. Towns now subjected to an excise tax and rural areas to a direct tax. The taxes technically set out to eliminate hardship in the cities but also provided the elector with a more flexible tax base.

1682. The African Company founded in Prussia. Frederick William was the first shareholder. He also established military forts in Guinea (1684).

1686. Frederick William renounced his claims to the Silesian duchies in return for the cession of Schwiebus.

1701, Jan. 18. FREDERICK III, elector of Brandenburg (1688–1713), with the consent of the emperor assumed the title of **king in Prussia** and crowned himself in Königsberg.

1713–40. FREDERICK WILLIAM I laid the foundation of the future power of Prussia. Maintenance of a standing army of 83,000 men, with a population of 2.5 million inhabitants.

1713. Table of Ranks revised. It established military ranks that gave precedence to military officers over civilian officers.

1718. Export of raw wool prohibited in Brandenburg-Prussia.

1722. Creation of **General Directory** to supervise royal fiscal, judicial, and military policies throughout the kingdom.

1723. Frederick William I created a state administrative apparatus that combined the General War Commissary and General Finance Directory.

1730ff. Rapid population growth (doubled by 1800).

1733. Canton system for organizing peasants established.

1740–86. Reign of Frederick the Great marked by wars, economic initiative, and promotion of Enlightenment ideas (upgrading of Prussian Academy, etc.).

1740–42. First Silesian War concluded by the Treaty of Breslau and Berlin between Austria and Prussia (p. 317).

1744–45. SECOND SILESIAN WAR. East Friesland, upon the extinction of the reigning house, fell to Prussia (p. 317).

1747–53. Oder valley drained, increasing the farmland in that region. **Frederick the Great** also promoted use of the potato and improved conditions of serfs on royal lands. Promotion of **immigration** to Prussia to foster economic growth (300,000 newcomers).

1748. The **Codex Fredericianus Marchicus** simplified judicial procedure and made judges salaried officials of the state.

1756–63. Third Silesian (Seven Years') War. (p. 317).

1766. Introduction of the Regie, a French system of collecting revenues. It greatly increased revenues but also caused resistance to such foreign influence.

1792, Feb. Austria and Prussia entered a defensive alliance against France.

1794. The *Allgemeines Landrecht* published. This recodification of Prussian law determined the rights of citizens on the basis of their standing within society.

1806. The Städtordnung promulgated. This developed modern government systems within towns and brought towns more completely under control of the monarchy.

1807. Baron Stein took control of the government. He and his successor, **Hardenberg,** continued the process of rationalizing government procedure and eliminating legal privileges for certain classes. However, they met continued resistance from the Junkers. These policies were partly the product of the **ongoing struggle to maintain Prussian autonomy under Napoleon** (p. 438). Frederick William sought to encourage nationalism and popular support by reforming the state in keeping with the German Enlightenment.

1807. Edict abolished serfdom by 1810.

1811. Edict established the principles for transmuting peasants to free-holders. Under the edict, any peasant wishing to change status had to relinquish either a third or a half of his holdings (depending on his previous status). **This law would be superseded by the Edict of 1816.**

(To p. 460)

2. THE HABSBURG MONARCHY
(From pp. 305, 310)

Monarchs: Ferdinand III (1637–57), Leopold I (1657–1705), Joseph I (1705–11), Charles VI (1711–40), Maria Theresa (1740–80), Joseph II (coregent 1765–80, emperor 1780–90), Leopold II (emperor, 1790–92).

The Habsburgs faced serious difficulties in uniting and maintaining the Austro-Hungarian portions of the empire. Its diverse nationalities and threats of Prussia in the west and the Ottoman Empire in the east created difficulties for the monarchs. In addition, succession created several contenders for the throne.

1655–60. The First Northern War (see 314).

1658. John Amos Comenius's *Orbis Sensualism Pictus,* the first children's picture book, appeared.

1663–64. Ottoman war. Despite imperial successes at **St. Gotthard (1664), Großwardein** and **Neuhäusel** in Hungary ceded to the Ottomans (1664, at Vasvár). These terms were partly the result of the empire's need to make a hasty peace because of unrest in Transylvania and Hungary.

1669–79. Jews expelled from Vienna by Leopold under the pretense of lack of loyalty to the crown. Despite this, Jewish businessmen helped finance imperial warfare in the early 18th century but then became scapegoats when government economic policies ended in failure and bankruptcy.

1671. The Austrian order of police distinguished among five classes of individuals and established regulations regarding what they might eat and wear.

1675. A German university founded at Czernowitz in Austria. Such universities reinforced the German domination of government.

1683, July 14–Sept. 12. Siege of Vienna by Ottomans (p. 356) lifted by combined imperial and Polish forces. The siege gave Austrian troops the rationale for invading Hungary (**Second Ottoman War,** 1683–88). **Buda** taken (1687) and a decisive victory won at **Nágy-Harkány** near Mohács. Ottoman forces driven across Danube (1697).

THE HOUSE OF HOHENZOLLERN (1701–1918)

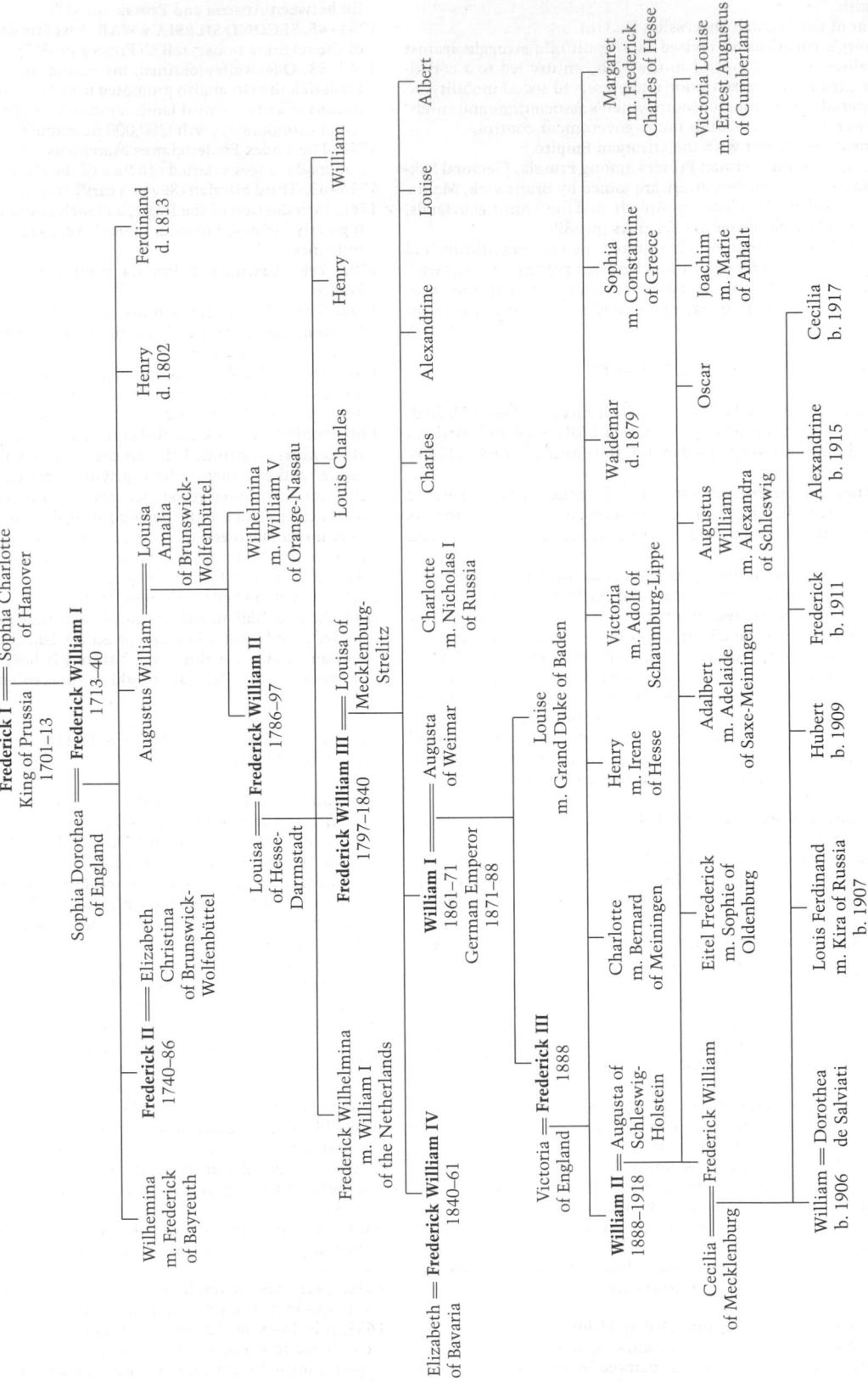

1684. Wilhelm von Hörnigk's *Österreich über alles, wenn es nur will.* The book combined patriotism and mercantilism in arguing for economic and national development. However, proponents of mercantilism in Austria failed to recognize limitations placed on them by religious and economic government policies. While Prussia and many other western states developed by encouraging immigration of religious minorities, Austria continued a policy generally excluding religious minorities.

1687–88. Diet of Pressburg (Pozsony). Hungarian Diet recognized the male line of Habsburgs as their monarchs. Transylvania was to remain separate from the Habsburg lands.

1690. The sultan recognized Count Thököly as prince of Transylvania, which challenged the emperor.

1691. Following imperial forces' advances into Ottoman-held eastern territories, the emperor passed the **Diplomum Leopolinum,** guaranteeing religious freedom to Magyars, Szekels, and Saxons within Transylvania. A Transylvanian court chancery established in Vienna and Transylvania ruled as territory separate from the crown lands.

1699, Jan. 26. Treaty of Karlowitz (p. 356) with the Ottomans. The Habsburgs secured all of Hungary except the Banat of Temesvar. The territories acquired by the Habsburgs were awarded in large part to German commanders and settled with Serbs and Germans.

1703–11. Revolt of the Hungarians under Francis II Rákóczi, who called upon Hungarians to free themselves from Habsburg domination. Hungarian and Transylvania insurgents deposed the emperor as king of Hungary at the assembly at Ónod (1707). This assembly was the result not only of Rákóczi's declaration but also of peasant revolts, which were closely tied to nationalist causes.

1711, May 1. Peace of Szatmár. Charles VI settled the controversy with Hungary and Transylvania by reaffirming Hungarian rights guaranteed at Pressburg and by the Diplomum Leopoldinum, and by issuing a general amnesty. Rákóczi refused the terms, dying in Turkey (1735).

1712–23. Charles VI's Pragmatic Sanction (p. 316) fixing Habsburg succession was gradually passed by most of the lands concerned. It assured Maria Theresa's ascension even though the male line of Habsburgs had died out. However, her claim to the throne was still challenged at Charles's death.

1719–22. Austrian Ostende Trade Company founded for trade with the East and West Indies and Africa. The company was recognized by Spain, but it failed to provide the necessary impetus for Austrian colonial development outside eastern Europe.

1740–80. Maria Theresa.

1740. Maria Theresa transferred control of schools from church to state, a major step in her efforts to reform government in Austria and Hungary and strengthen the monarchy.

1740–48. War of the Austrian Succession concluded by the **Treaty of Aix-la-Chapelle (p. 317).**

   Economic Reforms under Maria Theresa and Joseph II: Influenced by physiocrat doctrine, the Austrian monarchs sought to assure exports through protectionism but also recognized the importance of skilled labor within Austria and Hungary. Internal customs abolished and the guilds were modified so that they no longer remained compulsory in some industries. Such policies resulted in growth in Austria and Bohemia but Hungary remained primarily agricultural with the exception of some mining regions.

1745. Maria Theresa donated a library to the University of Innsbruck.

1749, Feb. 7. State reserved the right to appoint professors at the University of Vienna.

1756–63. Seven Years' War. Austrian alliance against Prussia (p. 317).

1763. Maria Theresa established several schools and expelled the Jesuits in a continued effort to strengthen the state.

1770, Sept. 24. Hungary declared that school organization would always be an affair of state.

1776. Hungarians granted **religious toleration.** Feudal service and torture as punishment abolished.

1778–79. WAR OF THE BAVARIAN SUCCESSION. Cause: With Maximilian Joseph's death (1777), the Bavarian house was extinct and Charles Theodore, elector palatine, legally inherited the Bavarian throne. Charles Theodore was persuaded to recognize Austrian claims to parts of Bavaria and the Upper Palatinate. Austria occupied Lower Bavaria. Frederick II convinced Charles Augustus Christian, duke of the palatinate of Zweibrücken, to contest Austrian claims. Saxony and Prussia invaded Bohemia, following inconclusive warfare.

1779, May 13. TREATY OF TESCHEN. (1) Austria retained the part of the Lower Bavaria between the Inn, Salzach, and Danube and agreed to the future union of Ansbach and Baireuth with the Prussian monarchy. (2) Saxony obtained rights of sovereignty and 9 million rix dollars.

1780–90. JOSEPH II, pursuing a policy of **Josephism** characterized by massive reforms in the hands of a centralized state designed to further economic and secular development that was begun under Maria Theresa.

1780. Abbeys suppressed by Joseph II.

1781, Oct. 13. Edict of Tolerance. A new organization prescribed for those abbeys still in existence. Connections between the abbeys and Rome were weakened and schools established, using church properties. Internal organization of Church altered and worship changed.

1781. Disputes between Joseph and the Dutch. Joseph demanded that the Scheldt, which had been closed by the Treaty of Westphalia, should be opened. French mediation brought about the Treaty of Versailles (1785). Joseph withdrew his demands in consideration of 10 million florins.

1783. Austrian Marriage Law allowed marriages to be civilly contracted and legalized divorce.

1784. Protestants allowed to hold church services in churches in Hungary.

1784. Joseph II decreed that officials in Hungary must use German rather than Latin. While primarily a practical matter, it increased discontent over the growing German influence in Hungary.

1785. Joseph II's plan of an exchange of territory, according to which Charles Theodore was to cede the whole of Bavaria to Austria and accept in exchange the Austrian Netherlands (Belgium), except Luxemburg and Namur, as the kingdom of Burgundy. France maintained an attitude of indifference. Russia supported the project and endeavored by persuasion and threats to induce the heir of Bavaria, the count palatine of Zweibrücken, to consent to the plan. The latter sought help from Frederick the Great, who succeeded in forming the League of the German Princes.

1787. Code of Criminal Law did away with capital punishment, replacing it with life imprisonment at hard labor.

1791. A compromise declared **Hungary a separate country** subject to the same succession as other Habsburg lands.

1794. Jacobins discovered in Austria-Hungary. Many arrested, imprisoned, and executed.

1795. Government began to curtail service exemptions in the military.

1797, Oct. 17. Peace of Campo Formio ended conflict between Austria and France (p. 434). Despite its inability to maintain hostilities, Austria continued to oppose France.

1801. Government centralization began with the creation of a Conference Ministry.

1804. Francis II assumed title emperor of Austria and then **abdicated (Aug. 6, 1806)** as Holy Roman Emperor and thus ended the Holy Roman Empire.

1808–9. Austria created a national militia.

1811. The codification of law begun under Joseph II promulgated.

1813. Separate Ministry of Finance appointed. (To p. 462)

h. SCANDINAVIA

(From p. 306)

DEMOGRAPHY: With the exception of Iceland, Scandinavian population grew in the 17th and 18th centuries, particularly after 1721 (end of the Great Northern War). Icelandic population remained steady, punctuated by the oscillations of natural disaster and famine. **Denmark's population** increased most rapidly in the 18th century; population in 1600 was about 700,000, in 1700 about 800,000, and in 1800, one million. **Finland's population** did not increase substantially until after the Great Northern War (p. 316), but then growth seemed to be closely tied to the availability of land (by 1750 about 420,000 and by 1800 about 833,000). Norway also experienced slow growth before 1750 and more rapid growth after 1750, spurred by declining death rates and increasing birth rates.

Culture: Scandinavian cultural development included scientific, political, and literary advances during the 17th and 18th centuries. **Linnaeus (1707–78),** a Swedish botanist, published his *Systemae Naturae* (1735). **Anders Celsius (1701–44)** invented the centigrade thermometer, although his version set the boiling point at zero degrees and freezing at 100 degrees. Two Swedish political theorists followed Lockean notions of politics: **Johan Henrik Kellgren** and **Nils von Rosenstern.** Scandinavian satirists included **Olof Dalin** and **Holberg. Hedvig Charlotta Nordenflycht** and **Gustaf Philip Cruetz** were writers and leading members of the **Tankebyggarorden,** a literary society in Stockholm modeled after similar French societies.

1. SWEDEN AND FINLAND
(From p. 306)

Monarchs: Christiana (1632–54), Charles X (1654–60), Charles XI (1660–97), Charles XII (1697–1718), Ulrika Eleanora (1718–20; she turned the throne over to her husband), Frederick I (1720–51), Adolphus Frederick (1751–71), Gustavus III (1771–92), Gustavus IV Adolphus (1792-1809).

Sweden controlled Finland but was challenged by Russia in the 18th century, finally relinquishing control in 1809.

Legacy of the Thirty Years' War: Sweden emerged as the dominant power in the Baltic region, but its power gradually declined over the next century and a half. Sweden gained control of **Pomerania (Treaty of Westphalia)** and sought control of **Poland.** Its territorial aggressions resulted in several wars and required huge military expenditures.

Agriculture remained unchanged during the 17th century. Peasants still used the strip system; barley was the primary crop, and crops frequently failed. Finnish settlers in northern and western Sweden still used the slash-and-burn technique; land was burned, cultivated, exhausted, and abandoned.

Economy: Swedes pursued mercantilistic policies and exported iron, copper, and timber. They encouraged **immigration** to provide the necessary labor force for such production, especially in mining regions and the Umeå Lappmark in the north, and created several colonial interests, including an **African Company (1649-1717) and West India companies.**

Society: Lutheran pastors had great sway within Swedish society and spread Lutheran teachings everywhere Swedish armies conquered. At the end of the century, the Swedish church received a new hymnal and began a new translation of the Bible. **Towns** became more important in the 17th century; their guilds maintained strict control of their crafts. The government tried to keep its Swedish workforce and encourage foreign workers to immigrate, regulating when and where workers might go within the country.

1648ff. Sweden expanded its colonial influence by establishing several colonial **tar companies.**

1650. The riksdag's protests regarding noble control of former crown lands stifled. These protests demonstrated growing impatience with state debts incurred in the wake of such benevolence.

1654. Queen Christina, the daughter of Gustavus Adolphus, abdicated the throne in favor of her cousin, **Charles Gustavus of Pfalz-Zweibrücken.**

1654–60. He became **CHARLES X GUSTAVUS.** His reign concentrated on military developments because of his attack on Poland.

1655–60. This attempt to gain new Baltic territory, the **First Northern War,** was concluded by the **Treaty of Oliva** and the **Treaty of Copenhagen (1660;** p. 314).

1655. Riksdag began the process of **"reduction,"** eliminating noble control of and benefits from crown lands, by ordering reductions on mines, forts, and other property.

1658, Feb. 26. Treaty of Roskilde between Sweden and Denmark. Sweden received the provinces of Skåne, Halland, Blekinge, Bohuslän, Trondheim (Norway), and the island of Bornholm.

Charles XI began to develop an **absolutist monarchy.**

1660s. Education emphasized by the establishment of several schools, especially a medical school (1663) and Lund University (1668).

1668. National Bank of Sweden founded after an abortive attempt earlier in the century.

1680. Under the pressure of the king, the estates passed a law by the

terms of which all earldoms, baronies, and other large fiefs should revert to the crown. The riksdag also affirmed the king's right to reclaim grants to the nobles without the riksdag's intervention. This weakened the nobility and forced many to sell their lands, which increased the percentages of land held by free farmers and office-holding nobility.

1686. Charles XI promulgated a church ordinance that placed the Lutheran church under the king's jurisdiction and established Lutheran doctrine.

1691–93, 1695–97. A series of crop failures resulted in famine and hardship.

1697. A technical school founded.

1700–1721. GREAT NORTHERN WAR (p. 316), caused by the common opposition of Russia, Poland, and Denmark to the Swedish supremacy in the Baltic region. Heavy population losses (Finland 16 percent and Sweden 10 percent).

1708–9, 1717–20. Crop failures, the first worsened by the spread of the **plague.**

1719–22. THE AGE OF FREEDOM ushered in by the constitution established under Queen Ulrika Eleanora.

18th-century Economics and Society: Writings on **agricultural reforms** appeared in the 1720s, sparked by mercantilism. These writings encouraged improved methods and the end to farming in strips, but progress was slow. **Industry** also received increasing attention. Swedes concentrated on iron and shipbuilding. Sweden signed a series of **trade agreements** with other countries and introduced tariffs and controls on imports.

1718–20. ULRIKA ELEANORA, who, after Charles XII was shot (Dec. 11, 1715) on a military expedition to Norway, was accepted on condition that the riksdag should be allowed to draw up a constitution. The **new constitution** provided for **joint rule of the monarch and the council** when the riksdag was not in session. While the riksdag was sitting, the principal decisions were to be made by a secret committee comprising members of the three higher estates (nobility, clergy, and burghers). The peasants were, however, to be heard in matters of taxation. The riksdag was chosen by **separate elections for each estate** in which certain "qualified" women (mainly propertied widows) among the burghers and farmers could vote. The constitution also recognized the **bureaucratic elements** within the state and determined that Sweden would **be ruled by four separate estates** rather than a body representing the Swedish people as a whole.

1720–51. FREDERICK I (of Hesse-Cassel), Ulrika Eleanora's husband, to whom she turned over the government. **Count Arvid Horn,** as minister, sought better relations with Great Britain and Russia and weakened connections with France. Ruling class divided between "Caps" and "Hats," the former backing Horn and favoring cautious foreign policy.

1720–21. Conclusion of the Northern War by the Treaties of Stockholm and Nystadt (p. 316).

1723. The farmers' estate received a constitutional provision that forbade officers or members of another estate from holding a seat in the farmers' estate.

1724. Swedish administration prohibiting imports of non-Swedish goods carried on foreign ships **(Produktplakatet).**

1731. Swedish East India Company founded (Ostindiska Kompaniet). It engaged in extensive trade and smuggling.

1734. Swedish law was codified and the national and city laws combined (the *landslag* and *stadslag*).

1738. Horne was overthrown by **Count Gyllenborg and the Hats,** who favored mercantilism and pro-French policies, coming from the western part of the country and Stockholm. The Hats remained in power until 1766.

1738 ff. The Hats pursued more ambitious **mercantilist policies** than the Caps had. The former set up a **Manufacturing Office** (1739), increased tariffs, and gave industries certain privileges.

1741. Ulrika Eleonora died childless, thus forcing the issue of succession. Russia and Denmark both made demands for successors favorable to their respective interests.

1741–43. War against Russia, provoked by the Hats. Sweden ceded to Russia more territory in Finland **(Treaty of Åbo,** Aug. 7, 1743; p. 317).

1742. The four estates elected Duke Charles Peter Ulrik crown prince, but the duke became Czarina Elizabeth's heir at the same time.

1743, June. Economic hardship and the questions of succession caused a **peasant uprising.** A group of peasants marched on Stockholm, terrifying residents, until they were dispersed by cannon fire.

1747. The Ironmasters' Association founded.

1751–71. ADOLPHUS FREDERICK of Oldenburg-Holstein-Gottorp, king, introduced a collateral line. Adolphus requested veto power from the estates.

1756. In the struggle over veto power, the farmers objected to buying and selling of bureaucratic offices. The king refused to sign legislation and the **queen, Louisa Ulrika, planned a coup to overthrow the estates.** The coup was discovered and put down; eight instigators were executed.

1766. The Caps passed the Freedom of Press Act, advanced by Anders Chydenius, which became part of the constitution. Following such legislation, the riksdag debates were published.

1767. Peter Momma's *Dagliot Allenhanda* became Sweden's first daily newspaper and supported the Caps.

1768, Dec. The king "abdicated" for a few days in protest of the riksdag's refusal to call a special session. The Caps were forced to call an election, which returned the Hats. Both Hats and Caps were receiving bribes from foreign countries to implement favorable policies.

1772, Aug. 9. A military coup ended the power of the council, giving Gustavus III full authority over the administration. The riksdag lost its initiative in legislation. **Gustavus tried to be an "enlightened despot."**

1770s. Torture abolished; illegitimate children's status improved; and judges and officers reviewed—many removed from office.

1774. Press law revised. The right to publish riksdag debates and discuss affairs with foreign powers removed. The law also lost its constitutional status.

1777, Jan. 1. The paper currency (circulating since 1745) replaced with silver-based coinage—the **riksdaler.**

1781. Religious freedom extended to foreigners but not to the Swedes. Non-Lutheran Christians did receive some degree of toleration.

1782. Jews were allowed to build synagogues but still faced restrictions with regard to purchase of land, residence, and so on.

1788–90. War with Russia. Gustavus invaded Russian Finland and achieved several victories but was attacked by the Danes and in the end was obliged to conclude the **Treaty of Wereloe,** which left Finland and Karelia in Russian hands.

1789, Feb. By the Act of Unity and Security, Gustavus, taking advantage of his victory over the Danes, eliminated the council and established **a new secret committee that represented all four estates.** He established a **bureaucracy of professionals** rather than nobles. He also made concessions to the lower estates—granting farmers the right to hold their land in absolute ownership and restoring tax-favored *(frälse)* land to them. He thus **eliminated most vestiges of feudalism** and further weakened the nobility.

1792, March. Gustavus III was murdered by Jacob Johan Ankarström, a Swedish aristocrat, as part of a political plot. Forty conspirators were sentenced to death.

1792–1809. Gustavus IV Adolphus took control, after a regency, on Nov. 1, 1796, but he faced serious internal difficulties heightened by the French Revolution.

1803. Enclosure acts consolidated farms in the Skåne. Patterned after British acts, enclosure was extended throughout most of Sweden in 1807.

1808. Sweden lost Finland to Russia.

1809, March. Georg Adlersparre arrested Gustav IV, who abdicated on March 29. Gustav left Sweden (Dec. 24, 1809). Gustav's uncle, Duke Charles, accepted the regency again.

1809, May 1. A riksdag called which established a constitutional committee.

1809. The committee drafted the **constitution,** which reaffirmed the **king's sovereignty** but only within its constitutional limits. It established a **balance of powers,** giving the riksdag and king vetoes over legislation. The king had both executive and legislative power; the riksdag only legislative. The constitution also established an **independent high court** that included the king (granting him two votes, which he never used). The constitution did not resolve the difficulties created by a system of four estates.

The riksdag also **lifted bans on private distilling and created an income tax** to replace older taxes on windows, cards, and so on.

1809, June 6. Duke Charles accepted the crown after approval of the riksdag (June 5). However, he had no heirs. Prince **Christian August of Norway** was chosen as heir, but he died on May 28, 1810.

1810, Aug. 21. General Bernedotte (p. 438) **elected as crown prince** and successor to the throne. Bernedotte arrived in Sweden and converted to Lutheranism, changing his name to Charles Johan. Charles Johan easily assumed effective control of the government because Charles XIII was in poor health. Charles Johan showed concern over the Swedish consumption of alcohol and encouraged agricultural reforms.

1814, Jan. 14. The Treaty of Kiel. Sweden received Norway from Denmark in exchange for Pomerania and payment of Norway's share of the Danish national debt. Denmark retained Iceland, Greenland, and the Faroes.   *(To p. 463)*

Finland

Economy and Society: Finland suffered horribly from war and famine during the **Great Northern War.** Russian occupation and Swedish policies of extracting grain and shipping it west exacerbated problems of declining population. However, after the **Great Wrath,** Finland experienced a gradual increase in population as well as economic improvements. Finnish culture and language developed during the 18th century, and Russian control proved relatively benign after the Great Wrath.

1648. Per Brahe returned to Finland as governor-general (he first served from 1637 to 1640). Brahe encouraged the use of the Finnish language, convincing Charles XI to learn Finnish and beginning the translation of the Bible into Finnish, and promoted the notion of a Greater Finland. He retired in 1654.

1696–97. Finland suffered a terrible famine and hard winter, worsened by Swedish policies. The Swedes shipped grain out of Finland and, in 1697, sent tax collectors into Finland to collect taxes and rents for the king.

1714, Feb. The Finnish army, under General K. G. Armfelt, defeated by the Russian army at **Napue** (Isokyrö). The Russians crushed organized Finnish resistance and marked the beginning of

1714–21. The Great Wrath. Russian occupation of Finland.

1721, Aug. 30. The occupation was ended by the **Treaty of Uusikaupunki (Nystadt)** (p. 317). However, the treaty also marked the beginning of Swedish military decline.

1742. Tsarina Elizabeth sent an envoy **offering Finland measured autonomy** as a duchy under Russian control. This offer sparked nationalist sentiment throughout Finland.

1743. Peace of Turku gave Russia control of all Finnish lands east of the Kymi River.

1766–78. Henrik Gabriel Porthan, a professor at the University of Turku after 1777, published his five-volume history of Finland, *Dissertatio de poesi Fennica.* Porthan cited Finnish folk culture and heritage as expressions of national character.

1770s. First appearance of a Finnish-language newspaper. The diet also accepted Finnish for use in deliberations, and it appeared on bank notes.

1788–90. War with Russia. A group of officers near Anjala sent secret correspondence to **Catherine the Great** in an effort to end the war between Sweden and Russia. Gustavus heard of their actions and demanded an oath of loyalty. The officers responded with the **Covenant of Anjala,** accusing him of fighting an unwanted war of aggression and indicating that they would fight against him if Catherine refused their plea.

1807. Treaty of Tilset between Napoleon and Tsar Alexander I gave Alexander a free hand in the Baltic. Alexander declared war on the British (Nov. 1807) and advanced through Finland, hoping to take the Baltic before the thaw would allow the British navy into the Baltic Sea.

1808. Finnish forces defeated by advancing Russians at **Sveabor,** but the Finns won a victory at **Lapua** (July 14).

1809, March 29. The Finnish diet ratified Finland's annexation to Russia (proclaimed in 1808), but with guarantees of internal autonomy. The **Finnish diet** became an entirely Finnish institution rather than combining with another diet (as with the Swedish)—four estates elected by restricted suffrage.

1812. Alexander returned territories annexed to Russia in 1721 and 1743.
1812. Helsinki became the Finnish capital. *(To p. 465)*

2. DENMARK, NORWAY, AND ICELAND
(From p. 306)

Monarchs: Frederick III (1648–70), Christian V (1670–99), Frederick IV (1699–1730), Christian V (1730–46), Frederick V (1746–66), Christian VII (1766–1808).

Denmark remained in control of Norway and Iceland between 1648 and 1814.

Denmark

Economics and Society: After years of warfare, Denmark suffered from plagues, famine, and hardship during the second half of the 17th century. **Agricultural development** continued to be based on manorialism, and peasants remained tied to the land until the late 18th century. **Economic development** was always hampered by Denmark's difficulties in financing the government, worsened by the development of a court society in the 18th century. This **court society** contributed to the growth of Copenhagen, but other **Danish cities** also experienced growth with the increase in trade and industry in the 18th century. The long period of peace after the Great Northern War stimulated further economic development.

1648. Frederick III compelled to accept the **hândfœstning** (charter), which required that candidates for seats in the council be selected by nobles from the province which held that seat. However, Frederick sought to limit control of the council from the start.

1648. Nobles exempted from excise duty on beer and spirits imposed on commoners.

1655–60. War with Sweden. Denmark entered the war after Sweden invaded Poland. Charles of Sweden advanced across the frozen Belts to Zealand. **Denmark sued for peace (1658)** and surrendered central Norway and Bohuslän. However, Charles marched on **Copenhagen** but sustained heavy losses and failed to gain his objective (Feb. 1659). He began another campaign in 1660 but died unexpectedly.

1660. Charles's son's regents sued for peace and a **treaty was signed at Copenhagen restoring territory to Denmark.**

1660, Sept. Estates summoned to discuss the acute economic situation caused by war and ensuing devastation. The two commons' estates protested noble tax privileges and demanded tax equality.

1660. Lower estates barred the gates of Copenhagen and called out the militia to force the nobles to agree to a hereditary monarchy and declare the *hândfœstning* invalid.

1661. Signatures collected from the Danes on a document granting **absolute authority** to the monarch.

1661. Anders Arrebo's *Hexaëmeron* published posthumously. Arrebo has been heralded as the Father of Danish Poetry.

1665. The Royal Law (Kongelov) promulgated. It became the only absolutist constitution in Europe. The king was required to remain Lutheran, maintain his territories intact, and assure the full force of his laws within the bureaucracy.

1671. The noble ranks of baron and count instituted. These ranks were more dependent on the crown. They received tax privileges and estates, undermining measures of equality won in 1660–61.

1683. A new law code introduced which eliminated local autonomy and abolished juries. It established the principle of **equality before the law** and reduced the use of torture but maintained death penalties on infanticide, blasphemy, and bigamy.

1688. Establishment of a College of Commerce wedded to mercantilism.

1688. A new land survey completed to provide the basis for more equitable taxation.

1691. The Treaty of Armed Neutrality with Sweden. This treaty sought to protect Danish and Swedish ships that were being attacked and taken over by English and Dutch warships.

1692. Christian von Plessen, an immigrant from Mecklenburg, took over the treasury and revamped the tax system.

1699. Denmark entered alliances with Russia and Saxony.

1700–1721. The Great Northern War (p. 316). Denmark at first remained neutral but entered the war following Peter's defeat of Charles in the **Ukraine (1709).** Denmark forced the abolition of Sweden's privileges regarding the Sound Tolls and gained the Slesvig lands.

The Great Northern War exacted a tremendous toll on Danish society. It worsened agricultural hardships existing in the late 17th century.

1721. Hans Egede, a Norwegian priest, established **Godthâb, the first European settlement in Greenland** since the Vikings. He received the support of the king in his missionary work among the Inuit of Greenland.

1730. Frederick promulgated a Sabbath ordinance that penalized anyone who did not attend church or who indulged in worldly pleasures on Sunday.

1732. A new Asiatic Company set up.

1733. The great palace of Christiansborg begun on site of the destroyed Castle of Copenhagen.

1733. After abolishing the militia in 1730, **Christian reestablished military service;** one man between 18 and 36 would be selected by each landlord per approximately 100 acres of estate. This man would serve eight years.

1733. Denmark purchased St. Croix from France.

1736. Compulsory confirmation introduced. Such confirmation required a certain degree of reading knowledge.

1739. An ordinance established the principle of schools to teach peasant children throughout Denmark.

1746–66. Frederick V. Frederick's chief minister from 1751 to 1770, **Johan Hartvig Ernst Bernstorff,** directed foreign policy and economics. Bernstorff encouraged new agricultural techniques that increased agricultural production.

1746. Age limits on military service extended to 9 and 40 years.

1754. The Royal Academy of Art founded.

1766–1808. CHRISTIAN VII. Christian retained many of his father's advisers but was challenged by an emerging court party. **Johann Friedrick Struensee** took control of the government after becoming the royal physician. Struensee eliminated the privy council; replaced the German chancery with a foreign ministry; reorganized the administration; abolished torture; and established freedom of the press. He also stopped parents from incarcerating their children and reduced taxation (without reducing government expenditures).

1771, July. Struensee became royal secretary; his policies angered industrialists, who lost government subsidies, the court, and many elements of the middle class.

1771. The Royal Guards ordered to disband. They mutinied.

1772, Jan. 17. Struensee arrested and later beheaded. Replaced by reactionary aristocrats headed by **Prince Frederick** and **Ove Høegh-Guldberg.** This group emphasized the importance of "Danish" government, eschewing foreigners.

1776. Law forbade employment of foreigners in royal service.

1780. Denmark joined the League of Armed Neutrality, formed by Catherine II (p. 348) of Russia, to protect its ships.

1784, April. Christian's son, Frederik, convinced his father to grant him **legal control of the state.**

1784. Count Andreas Peter Bernstorff came to power. He began by regulating relations between the landlords and their peasant tenants. The council also made significant reforms in tariffs and introduced a **system of poor relief** and other social reforms between 1784 and 1797 (Bernstorff's death).

1786. Bernstorff and the council created the Great Land Commission. Tenants received the right to gain compensation for **improvements** and landlords forbidden to use degrading **punishments** against their tenants. The *stavnsbând* abolished (completed in stages between 1788 and 1800), leaving the peasants free but still obligated to labor services. The *stavnsbând* had tied peasants to their parish, unless permitted by their landlord to leave.

1789. Universal free education proposed.

1792. A measure assured the **end of Dutch slave trade** by 1803.

1798. Jews granted the right to marry Christians and enter secondary school.

1800. A League of Armed Neutrality signed with Russia, Prussia, and Sweden in response to British naval activity.

1807, Aug. 16. Denmark declared war against the British, who landed north of Copenhagen and attacked, burning large portions of the city and forcing Frederik to surrender. **Frederik's decision to join France** proved disastrous. The Danish economy suffered from the **continental system** (p. 438) and British blockades. Taxes increased, as did inflation.

1814. The School Law established compulsory education for children between 7 and 14, the age of confirmation.

1813. Danish banks replaced by a single state bank capable of issuing notes.

1814, Jan. Treaty of Kiel. Denmark gave Sweden Norway in exchange for Swedish Pomerania but retained Iceland, Greenland, and the Faroes.

Norway

1648, Aug. Frederik received the oath of allegiance at a combined meeting of the four estates in Christiania, the nobles refusing to recognize him as monarch. Frederik guaranteed rights of cities and increased noble privileges.

1664. Ulrik Frederik Gyldenløve sent to Norway as stadholder. Gyldenløve was sympathetic to Norwegian difficulties and introduced significant reforms, including tax cuts and curtailment of abuse by officials.

1688. Christian V's Norwegian Law sought to codify laws of Norway. It established the principle of equality before the law and protected some personal liberties.

1699–1730. Frederik IV began his reign by touring Norway. He set up a permanent **Commission of Akershus** to handle government business and decrease the work referred to Copenhagen.

1733. In an effort to conserve Norwegian forests, the **lumber industry was severely regulated.** As a result, the industry was concentrated in the hands of a few wealthy individuals.

1735. Norway began registering vital statistics.

1739. A School Law sought to establish state schools.

1740s. Development of manufactures: Factories, ironworks, and flour mills established. Mining flourished, but Norway still lagged behind Danish industry with its larger firms and circumscribed government assistance.

1741. The Conventicle Act prohibited any religious meetings not authorized by the state church: a response to radical Pietism within Norwegian cities.

1750. The crofters, settlers who often paid for their rent in labor, **received legal recognition.** The government required that farmers issue them a lease.

1765, March 1. The Stril War. Several hundred men assembled in Bergen to **protest the introduction of a poll tax.**

1765, April 18. When the king failed to reply promptly to their petition, a crowd attacked the governor's residence. The governor refunded the tax and the Danish government instigated an investigation. Poll tax removed (1772).

1769. First Norwegian census taken. The Norwegian population was approximately 700,000.

1786. The Lofthus Rising. Christian Jensen Lofthus went to Copenhagen as spokesman for the farmers to appeal for justice. Lofthus voiced discontent over government tax policies and bureaucracy. After he left, he was arrested.

1809. The Society for Norway's Welfare founded to work for Norway's economic and educational progress and possible independence.

1811. Royal Frederik's University established in Oslo.

1814, Jan. Treaty of Kiel transferred control of Norway to Sweden.

(To p. 463)

Iceland

Economy and Society: Icelandic economics were dictated by a **Danish trade monopoly** that severely hampered economic growth. This along with a series of natural disasters **decreased population** (from 50,444 to 34,000 between 1703 and 1708).

Landowners exacted heavy payments from their peasants in both goods and labor. Peasants were required to row the landowners' fishing boats and assist in bringing the fish to market.

1649. King Frederik III sent a royal letter to Iceland assuring Icelanders that their traditions and laws would be respected under his reign.

1662, July 28. Representatives assembled at Kopavog and **took an oath of loyalty to King Frederik III** after assurances that their laws would be respected.

1662, July 31. A new Danish company chartered to control Icelandic trade. Severe punishments were exacted on those who violated this monopoly by purchasing goods from other foreign vessels. Iceland was also **divided into four commercial districts,** and trade between districts was forbidden.

1684. A new administrative office created in Iceland to conduct official business and oversee judicial activities regarding the Church. **New price schedules for imports and exports** raised prices on Icelandic imports and lowered them on exports.

1690. Clemens Bjarnason sentenced to death for witchcraft but pardoned. His sentence was the last for such a crime in Iceland.

1699. King Frederik IV's ascension led the Althing (Icelandic parliament) to prepare a **memorial requesting relief from economic hardship.** This memorial resulted in

1702. A better price schedule and lighter punishments for buying goods from non-Danish vessels.

1707. Smallpox epidemic killed about a third of the population.

1752. Frederik V granted Skuli Magnussaon, an Icelandic official, a royal rescript for the latter's plan to improve trade and industry in Iceland. Magnussaon made some advances despite continued opposition of Danish interests in the Icelandic trade.

1770. A commission sent by the king reported conditions in Iceland and made several recommendations for change. Cabbage and potato crops encouraged.

1776. Improvements to roads and mails undertaken by government as well as awards to farmers willing to resettle devastated farmlands.

1786. Commerce with Iceland free to all Danes and Norwegians.

1787. Iceland divided into three amts and Icelandic affairs controlled from Copenhagen. The Allthing lost its legislative power and was dissolved in 1800.

The **Napoleonic Wars** hurt Iceland because the continental system blocked trade with England. They also gave Iceland a taste of freedom.

1809, June 26. Jørgen Jørgensen posted a proclamation in Reykjavik declaring Iceland free and indicating that a national Icelandic government would be established. Icelandic officials backed by English naval power voided this on Aug. 22.

Cultural Development: Despite its lack of a university, Iceland enjoyed considerable cultural activity during the late 17th and 18th centuries. **Thormod Torfœus** wrote many historical works, including *Historia Rerum Norwegicarum.* Icelanders were heavily influenced by the *Aufklärung* movement and Danish culture, the upper classes taking Danish dress after 1780. **Magnus Stephensen** played a major role in this dissemination, establishing the first Icelandic monthly and a society for general enlightenment (1794). *(To p. 463)*

i. POLAND

(From p. 309)

Monarchs: John Casimir (1648–68), Michael Wisnowiecki (1669–73), John Sobieski (1674–96), Augustus II (1696–1704), Stanislas Leszchzynski (1704–9), Augustus II (1709–33), Augustus III (1734–1763), Stanislas Poniatowski (1764–1795).

The Legacy of the Thirty Years' War: Poland had not suffered as greatly from the war as other central European powers. It remained neutral after the **Treaty of Stummdorf (1635).** Poland still had a weak government, owing to a lack of bureaucracy and a relatively weak army without a stable financial base. It also had few merchants, traders, or other members of a middle class.

ECONOMY AND SOCIETY: The Polish economy underwent steady decline between 1648 and 1795. The **Vistula grain trade** collapsed as a result of warfare. The Polish economy rested on this trade, exporting more than it imported. It had **few large cities** and these remained organized by burghers and guilds. Some of these cities made limited progress in the 18th century. However, the wars that ravaged Poland took a heavy toll on its cities, which were frequently captured or sieged. The **nobility** dominated Polish society but, unlike the nobility of many Western countries, did not necessarily secure economic wealth. Nobles with little or no land retained their position long into the 18th century because nobility rested largely on political and social obligations. Each noble held an **absolute veto** over any actions in the **Sejm** (parliament) and a **vote in electing the monarch.** Nobility also continued the tradition of dividing their land among all their children, male and female, which split many larger estates into increasingly smaller pieces. **Peasants** constituted the largest part of the population, especially if the many "peasants" with the rights of burghers are taken into account. Polish society was divided by **nationality;** Ukrainians initiated an uprising in 1647 and 1648. It was also divided by **religion**—Catholics, Orthodox, and Lutherans as well as Jews and Muslims.

1647–48. Bogdan Khmelnitsky launched his Cossack uprising against Poland. Initially he sought only to address his grievances to the king in person. John Casimir's ascension changed the situation, as did the killings of rebelling Ukrainian peasants by government officials.

1651, June 28–30. Khmelnitsky defeated by King John at Berestczko.

1652. The Liberum Veto (absolute veto of any member of the Polish Sejm) used by Jan Sicínski in a motion to prolong the Sejm. This use stopped the proceedings and paralyzed the Sejm.

1654. The Treaty of Peryslavl with Russia. Khmelnitsky swore an oath of allegiance to the tsar in exchange for assurances that the Ukraine would receive a large amount of autonomy, a promise the tsar ignored. The Ukrainian situation thus became incorporated into wider struggles for Polish territory.

1655–60. War between Sweden and Poland (p. 314). Invasion of the Swedes. Poland lost its remaining Baltic territories (**Treaty of Oliva, May 3, 1660**).

1655. Swedes took Warsaw. They then demanded Kraków surrender. The king fled to the Silesian borders; the Polish paid homage to Charles Gustavus.

Dec. 26. Siege lifted at monastery of Czestochowa, where the prior had organized a small force of soldiers to protect the **Black Madonna.** King John swore that the Virgin would be venerated (the Cult of Our Lady) and that he would free the serfs following restoration of Poland.

1656, June 30. Warsaw liberated. It was retaken by Swedes a few weeks later.

1660s. Two Masters of the Mint, **Boratini and Tymff,** each tried to stabilize the country's finances by minting coins. Their schemes led to debasement and economic hardship.

1661–67. John Casimir faced a revolt of the nobility. Jerzy Lubomirski, marshal of the crown, led a mutiny subdued by crown forces at the Silesian border. Lubomirski chose to be exiled to Breslau.

1667, Jan. 20. Treaty of Andrussavo, ending the conflict with Russia. Russia received eastern Ukraine and Smolensk.

1668. John Casimir abdicated and, following a period of upheaval, the Poles finally elected a national candidate in 1669, **King Michael.**

1670, July. Michael married Archduchess Eleonora of Habsburg.

1670. Prussians raided Warsaw to recapture Kalkstein, a fugitive from Königsberg.

1672–76. Second Ottoman War. The Ottomans took **Podolia** (p. 356) and captured the fortress of Kamieniec Podolsk.

Oct. Treaty with Ottoman Empire. Turkey received all remaining Polish districts of the Ukraine and tribute of 22,000 gold ducats per year.

1673. The order of the Marian Fathers, followed by the **Sacramentalist Sisters (1683),** founded in veneration of the Virgin. These Polish orders demonstrated the strength of Polish Catholicism.

Nov. 10. King Michael died.

1674. John III Sobieski elected king.

After a victory over the Ottomans at **Lemberg (1675),** John Sobieski concluded with them the **Treaty of Zuravno (Oct. 1676),** by which the Ottomans retained only part of the Ukraine.

1676. John Sobieski began a major reorganization of the Polish military. It was hampered by inefficiency in collecting taxes and Sobieski's reliance on noble financial support rather than a strong bureaucratic state.

1683, March 31. John Sobieski made an alliance with Austria in order to present a united front to the Turkish advance on Vienna.

Sept. 12. Polish troops arrived and assisted in lifting the siege of Vienna (p. 337). Sobieski then pursued the Ottomans and committed himself to a holy war. This war was costly and severely weakened Poland, leaving it subject to disorder and partitioning.

1690s. Unpaid troops became vigilantes throughout Poland. The country faced economic hardship.

1697–1733. AUGUSTUS II (elector of Saxony), king of Poland. He attempted to strengthen the royal power but without much success.

1699, Jan. 26. Treaty of Karlowitz, ending the long war against the Ottoman Empire. The Poles regained Podolia and the Ottoman part of the Ukraine.

1699. Preobrazhenskiy Treaty. Poland and Russia became allies.

1699. Nobility ordered **phrases distinguishing the greater and lesser nobility struck from the Sejm's records** because they undermined the principle of equality.

1700–1725. Burning witches at the stake reached an apex. Poland had initially burned very few of those convicted but, over the course of the 17th century, those numbers had increased **until about half of convictions resulted in burning between 1700 and 1725.**

1700–1721. The Great Northern War, which was fought largely on Polish soil (p. 316).

By the **Treaty of Altranstädt** with Sweden (1706), Augustus gave up his claims. The Holy Roman Empire, Brandenburg, England, and Holland all recognized Stanislas. But after the defeat of Charles at Poltava (1709), Augustus returned and drove out his rival.

1715, Nov. The General Confederation of Tornogród. The Polish nobility swore to expel the Saxon king and began a war against him. The king withdrew his troops at the tsar's suggestion while the confederation limited its revenues and the size of the republic's army. The **tsar then guaranteed the agreements with a written constitution.**

1717. The Silent Sejm. The Sejm, sworn to accept the agreement of the confederation without debate, signed the constitution guaranteeing Russian supremacy and limited military power.

1718. Edict of limitation against all Protestants allowed them to practice their religion freely but forbade them to use it to any personal or political advantage.

1724, July 16–17. The Tumult of Thorn. The Procession of Our Lady was interrupted by Lutheran and Jesuit altercations, which led to a full-scale riot (July 17). Thorn had a larger Lutheran population than Catholic but, at the insistence of the Jesuits, the **citizens were charged with sedition. The Burgomaster was beheaded.**

1733–35. WAR OF THE POLISH SUCCESSION (p. 317). The Poles, supported by France, elected **Stanislas Leszchzynski,** who had become the father-in-law of Louis XV. The Russians and Austrians insisted on the election of **Augustus of Saxony,** son of Augustus II. A huge Russian army invaded the country and drove out Stanislas, who withdrew to Danzig. France, supported by Spain and Sardinia, declared war on the empire. French expedition to the Baltic to relieve Danzig (besieged by the Russians from Oct. 1733 onward).

1734, June 2. Capitulation of Danzig; Stanislas fled to Prussia. The war was ended by the **Treaty of Vienna (Oct. 5, 1735, ratified 1738),** which assured the victory of the Russian-Austrian policy in Poland.

1734–63. AUGUSTUS III, king. He spent a little time in Poland and did little to prevent Russian encroachment, especially during the Seven Years' War. Growing agitation for reform in Poland after 1740; two parties, led by the Potocki and Czartoryski families. The former looked to France for support and aimed at the establishment of an aristocratic constitution; the latter, relying on Russian support, envisaged strengthening of the royal power, abolition of the liberum veto, and so on. However, most reforms were private rather than public.

1740. The Collegium Nobilium founded by the educator Stanislaw Konarski.

1740s. Michal Ogiński built canals.

1748. Public library opened in Lunéville. The library was plundered by the Russians in 1795 and sent to St. Petersburg.

1760ff. Andrzej Zamoysky abolished serfdom on his estates.

1764. The Sejm created a Commission of Finance to develop a modern customs system. Prussia responded by creating a fortress at Marienwerder to terrorize Polish trade.

1766–68. Eastern Orthodox Catholics and Protestants granted equal rights with Roman Catholics at the insistence of Russia and Prussia. This raised a storm of protest in Poland and led (1768) to the formation of the **Confederation of Bar,** an anti-Russian association that soon enjoyed the active support of France.

1772, Aug. 5. THE FIRST PARTITION OF POLAND. Poland lost about a third of its territory and about half of its inhabitants (p. 319).

1773. The Polish Diet, forced to accept the partition, began to effect reforms (council of state, divided into five ministries, to govern when the diet was not in session).

1775. Land possession made a requirement for all new nobles. Before

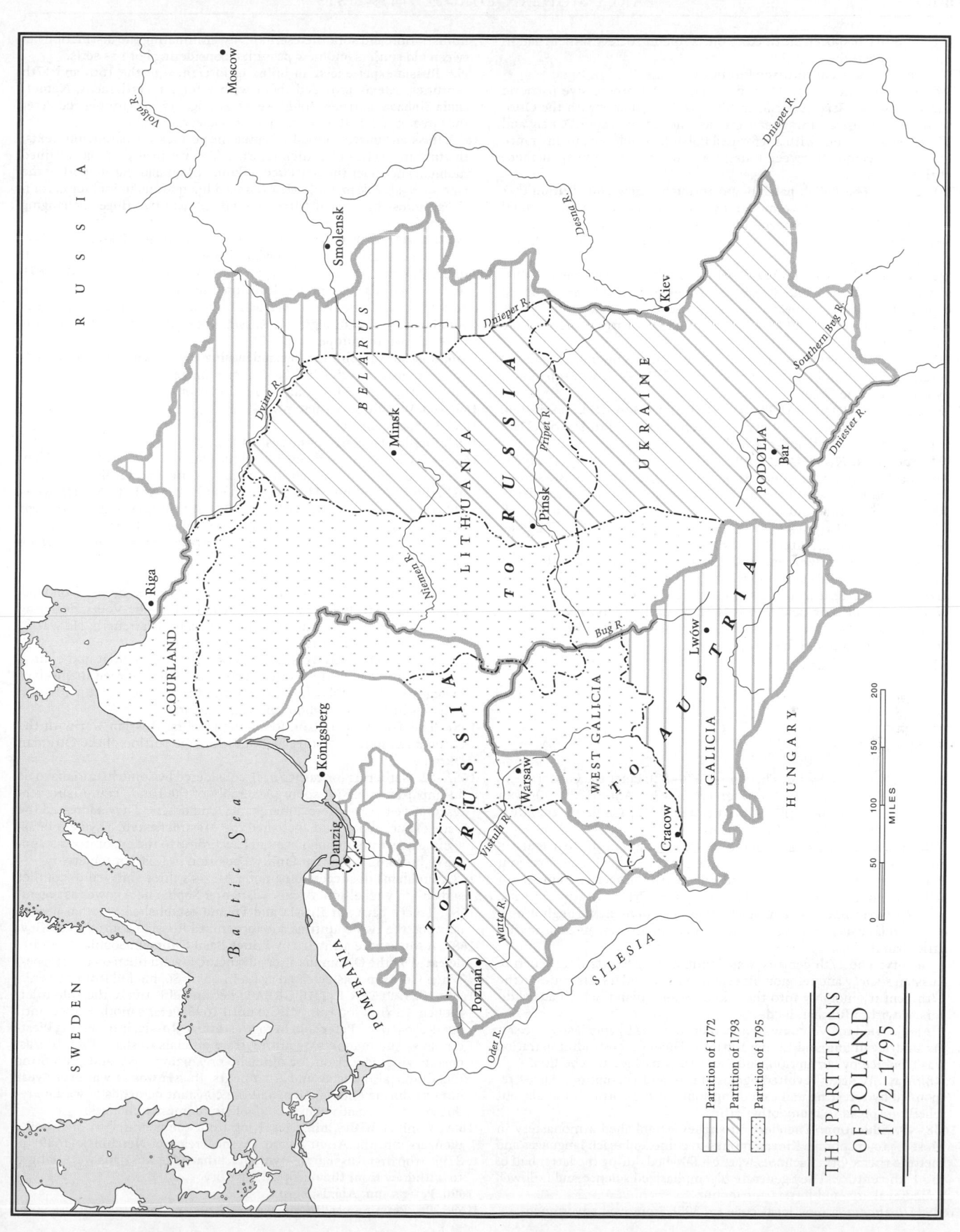

RUSSIA

Moscow

Volga R.

Smolensk

Dnieper R.

Desna R.

B E L A R U S

Minsk

Dvina R.

Kiev

U K R A I N E

Southern Bug R.

L I T H U A N I A   T O   R U S S I A

Dnieper R.

Pinsk

Pripet R.

Niemen R.

PODOLIA

Bar

Dniester R.

Riga

COURLAND

Königsberg

Bug R.

Lwów

Bug R.

WEST GALICIA

Danzig

Warsaw

Vistula R.

G A L I C I A   T O   A U S T R I A

Cracow

GALICIA

HUNGARY

T O   P R U S S I A

Baltic Sea

POMERANIA

Warta R.

Poznań

Oder R.

SILESIA

SWEDEN

200

150

100

50

0

MILES

Partition of 1772

Partition of 1793

Partition of 1795

THE PARTITIONS
OF POLAND
1772–1795

this, nobility had been ascribed to one's role in society rather than to economic position.

1776. Royal decree ended witch hunts.

1788–92. The Four Years' Diet, dominated by a progressive patriotic party, while Prussia, Austria, and Russia were at war with the Ottomans. The Prussian minister Hertzberg hoped to secure Danzig and Thorn by agreement with a reformed Poland. Developments in France led to an agreement between Prussia and Austria and to postponement of the scheme.

1791, May 3. The Polish patriots put through a new constitution that (1) converted the elective monarchy into a hereditary monarchy; (2) conferred the executive power upon the king and council of state; (3) vested the legislative power in a diet of two chambers; (4) abolished the liberum veto.

1792, May 14. Prussia and Austria accepted this change, but the Russians organized the **Confederation of Targowicz,** in defense of the old constitution. Russian invasion was followed by similar action on the part of the Prussians and finally led to the 1793 bargain between the two powers.

1792. Virtuti Militari, a military order founded to honor distinguished veterans of the Russian-Polish conflict of 1791–92. It was suppressed by Catherine the Great.

1793, Jan. 23. SECOND PARTITION OF POLAND (p. 319). Russia took most of Lithuania and most of the western Ukraine; Prussia took Danzig and Thorn as well as Great Poland.

1794, March 24. NATIONAL UPRISING in Poland, led by Thaddeus Kosciuszko. After an unequal struggle against the forces of Russia and Prussia, the Poles were defeated (capture of Kosciuszko, surrender of Warsaw to Suvorov), and Austria joined Russia and Prussia on Oct. 24, 1795 in the **THIRD PARTITION OF POLAND** (p. 319), ending independent Poland until after World War I.

The **Age of Enlightenment** produced much satirical writing; **Ignatius Krasicki** (1735–1801), poet, novelist, author of satires and fables. New dramatists emerged when the first public theater was established in Warsaw; **Francis Zoblocki (1754–1821)** and **Julian Ursyn Niemciwicz (1757–1841),** also translator of English poems, author of novels, memoirs, and a collection of historical songs *(Spiewy historyczne).*

(To p. 512)

j. RUSSIA

(From p. 308)

Rulers: Alexis (1645–76), Theodore (1676–82), Peter the Great (1682–1725), Catherine I (1725–27), Peter II (1727–30), Anne (1730–40), Ivan VI (1740–41), Elizabeth (1741–61), Peter III (1762), Catherine the Great (1762–96), Paul (1796–1801).

Economy: The Russian economy rested on agriculture, particularly upon grain production. Estates relied on increasingly intense serfdom to provide the necessary labor and trade with Europe. The number of artisans and merchants expanded during the 17th and 18th centuries, and **the government encouraged some development through a new commercial code.** However, the Russian economy remained primarily agricultural.

Society: The 17th century was dominated by efforts to restructure Russian society and religion. Russia also expanded its territories in the 17th century, notably into the Ukraine and Poland, which added diversity within Russian lands.

Alexis tried to overcome financial difficulties by increasing the salt tax and legalizing and taxing tobacco. However, his administration was troubled by corruption, and increased taxes led to rebellion.

1648, May. Moscow revolted against taxes and corruption. Alexis responded by arresting and executing some of the corrupt officials, but rebellion spread to many other cities.

1648–49. Education: Theodore Rtishchev established a monastery in Moscow to encourage Kievan monks to come and teach languages and rhetoric there. Other schools were established during the latter half of the 17th century. They generally deemphasized science and followed a medieval arts-and-letters curriculum.

1649. *Ulozhenie,* a new legal code (p. 308), improved government ad-

ministration and solidified serfdom by eliminating the distinction between old settlers and new peasants, considering both as serfs.

1652. Russia experienced an **influx of foreigners** in the 16th and 17th centuries. Alexis provided them with a foreign settlement, **Nemetskaia Sloboda,** northeast of Moscow. Foreigners later influenced Peter the Great's efforts to reform Russian society and culture.

1653. Russian church council accepted the verification of religious texts, the first in a series of church reforms. The verification project gained momentum under the **patriarch Nikon.** Nikon had the support of the tsar until a break in 1658. He expanded his reforms to include certain rituals (crossing oneself with three rather than two fingers, changing the spelling of Jesus, etc.).

1654–67. War with Poland for the possession of the Ukraine (p. 344) after the cossack Hetman, **Bogdan Khmelnitsky,** had placed himself under Russian protection. By the Treaty of Andrusovo (Jan. 20, 1667), Russia obtained the Smolensk region and the eastern Ukraine, with Kiev. The outcome of the war was of great importance, because the Russian gains first brought the Russians in contact with the Ottomans in southeastern Europe.

1656. Russian government began debasing the currency by adding copper to silver coins. Such debasement reflected Russian financial collapse in the 17th century and led to inflation.

1656–60. War with Sweden (p. 314).

1662. Copper coin riot.

1664. Russian post office established.

1666–67. Church council considered the changes made by Nikon. They defrocked Nikon for his efforts to gain political power but supported his religious reforms. This acceptance led to a **SPLIT IN THE RUSSIAN ORTHODOX CHURCH;** the **OLD BELIEVERS** refused to accept the reforms although they included no changes in belief. In later decades Old Believers colonized various territories acquired in Russian expansion.

1667. New commercial code established.

1670–71. A great peasant revolt in the southeast, led by the Don Cossacks, under **Stephen Razin.** Razin advanced up the Volga, declaring freedom from landlords and officials and gaining strength. He was finally **defeated at Simbirsk** by the tsar's troops.

1672–91. The Old Believers saw Nikon as the Antichrist and church reform as the end of the world. More than **20,000 burned themselves** in huge fires. The Old Believers would continue to be a force in Russian religious history throughout the 18th century.

1681. The Treaty of Radzin, following the first Russian war with the Ottoman Empire (p. 356), gave Russia a large portion of the Ottoman Ukraine.

1681–82. Gathering (or gatherings), considered by some historians to be an important *zemskii sobor* (Assembly of the Land), comprising representative boyars, clergy, merchants, and others. They addressed the issue of succession and abolished **the Mestnichestvo,** a system of assigning government appointments according to the appointee's standing in his family and that family's position in Russian society.

1682. Problems of succession among Alexis's three sons led to conflict and an army rebellion. Alexis's daughter Sophia held power as regent.

1686. Treaty between Russia and Poland established "eternal peace" between the two countries and recognized Russian control over Kiev.

1687. A Muscovite army led by **Prince Basil Golitsyn,** Sophia's favorite, **defeated by the Ottomans** after advancing toward them on the steppes. When Golitsyn was defeated again in 1689, Sophia fell from power.

1689–1725. PETER I (THE GREAT) became effectively the sole ruler, though Alexis's son Ivan V lived until 1696. Peter's mother ruled until her death (1694). **Peter sought to Westernize Russia,** introducing Western dress and manners, requiring state officials to shave their beards, encouraging education for officials, organizing navy and promoting metallurgical industry and armaments. Russia was at war every year but one during Peter's reign, and the constant demands of warfare reduced the time and money available for domestic changes.

1689. Conflict with China, resulting from the penetration of Russian pioneers into the Amur region. By the **Treaty of Nerchinsk (1689)** (p. 379)—the first Russian treaty with China—the Russians were obliged to withdraw from the occupied territory.

1690. Peter's son, Alexis, born.

1695–96. Peter's expeditions against Azov (p. 356), the fortress com-

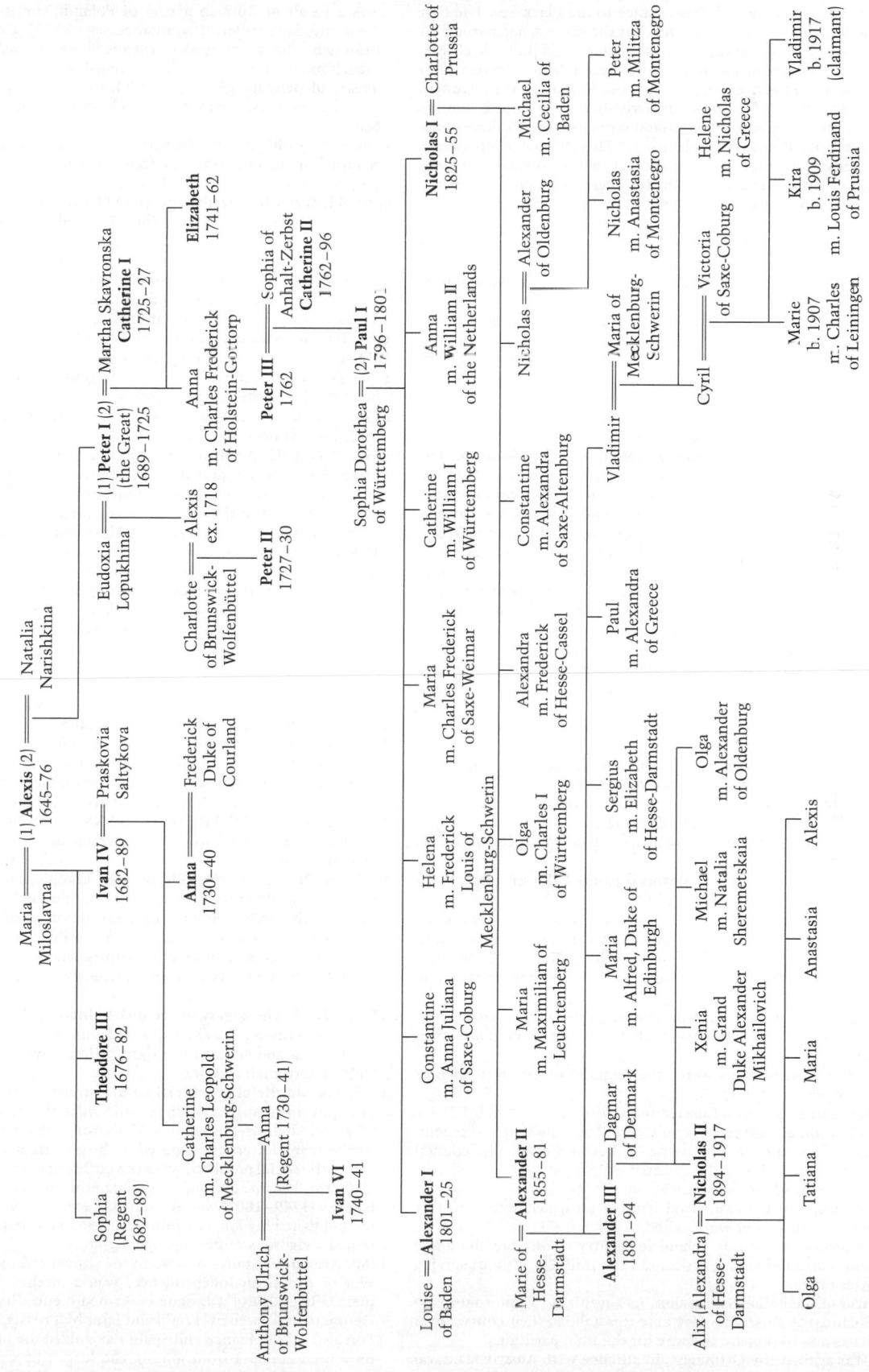

RUSSIAN TSARS (1645–1917)

manding the Sea of Azov and the entrance to the Black Sea. The first expedition, by land, was unsuccessful, but the second, supported by a naval force, resulted in the capture of the stronghold (July 28, 1696).

1697–98. Peter's European journey, which he undertook incognito to secure allies in western Europe for a crusade against the Ottoman Empire. Peter was the first Russian sovereign to go abroad, and his travels in France, England, and Holland strengthened his determination to Westernize Russia (but selectively). He returned to Moscow to suppress a **revolt of the** *streltsy* (soldiers of the Moscow garrison, among whom there were many Old Believers). He concluded peace with the Ottomans but Russia retained Azov (1700).

1698. Peter forced his first wife, **Endoxia Lopukhina,** to become a nun.

1699. Peter began a series of **municipal reforms** by reorganizing towns for better tax collection.

1700–1721. THE GREAT NORTHERN WAR between Sweden and Russia (p. 316).

1701. School of Mathematics and Navigation founded as one of Peter the Great's efforts to introduce cultural reforms patterned on Western models. Peter advocated compulsory education for nobles, Western dress, and Western institutions of learning.

1703. Capital moved to newly founded city of St. Petersburg.

1710–11. War with Ottomans (p. 357).

1711. Alexis married to a German princess.

1711–21. Reorganization and centralization of the administration. The old council of the boyars replaced by a **Governing Senate (1711),** consisting of nine members appointed by the tsar. New government bureaus were set up (1717) under the name of **colleges.** The nobility was made to serve the state **(establishment of a hierarchy of offices)** and Peter encouraged trade, industry, and education; government promoted metallurgy, armaments manufacture, and so on. In order to subordinate the Church to state control, Peter **abolished the patriarchate** and in its place established (1721) **a synod composed of bishops** but presided over by a layman (the Holy Synod).

1712. Peter the Great married to Catherine.

1714. Russian officials sent to the Ukraine. Peter attempted to unify Russian territories by emulating English examples in Scotland and Wales.

1714. A law of inheritance established the principle of primogeniture (repealed 1731).

1715. Alexis's son, Peter, born. Alexis had become the center of growing opposition to Peter I. Peter demanded that Alexis support his reforms or renounce the throne. Alexis fled to Austria (1716) but returned in 1718 and died in prison as a result of torture.

1718. Introduction of the poll tax. A census was taken to determine this tax (1718–22).

1719. Administrative and judicial powers separated (the separation gradually broke down, disappearing in 1727).

1721. Spiritual Reglament. The Holy Synod replaced the system of patriarchs. It consisted of 10 (then 12) clerics with the Ober-Procurator, a layman, appointed to oversee the synod. The Church had been without a patriarch since the death of Hadrian in 1700 because the tsar had left the position vacant.

Aug. 30. Treaty of Nystadt and **major Russian gains** in the Baltic (p. 317).

1722. Table of Ranks created. It established an order for civil and military positions.

1722. Law of Succession empowered the reigning sovereign to appoint his own successor.

1724. Russian tariff protected Russian industry.

1726, Feb. Creation of Supreme Secret Council. It consisted of six members to advise the tsarina. Following Catherine's death, the council limited Anne's control over the country.

1726. Opening of Academy of Science.

1727. The Menshikov and Dolgoruki families struggled over control of the throne and the former were exiled.

1731. Anne opened a military school for gentry in St. Petersburg and allowed graduates to become officers in the military without serving in the lower ranks.

1733–35. War of the Polish Succession. As a result of the internal weakness of Poland, the Russians were able to establish their control over Polish affairs and to prepare the way for the final partitions.

1736–39. War against the Ottomans, in alliance with Austria. The war was a result of Russian action in Poland. The Russians recaptured Azov and, after suffering some reverses in 1737, Count Burkhard von Münnich, the army leader, advanced victoriously into Moldavia. French mediation deprived Russia of gains it might have made. By the **Treaty of Belgrade (Sept. 18, 1739),** the Russians retained Azov but agreed to raze the fortifications and not to build a fleet on the Black Sea.

1736. Service obligations of gentry to the state limited to 25 years. Serfs required to obtain permission from their lords to seek temporary employment elsewhere.

1741–43. War with Sweden, provoked by the pro-French party in Sweden (p. 340). The Swedes, by the **Treaty of Åbö (Aug. 7, 1743),** were obliged to cede to Russia further territory in Finland.

1746. Acquisition of serfs limited to members of the gentry.

June 2. By treaty with Austria, Russia finally joined in the War of the Austrian Succession (1740–48) (p. 317), in which, however, the Russians played an insignificant role.

1755. First Russian university founded at Moscow.

1756–63. Seven Years' War (p. 317).

1756. The senate determined that **only gentry of proven heritage could be entered into the gentry registers.**

1758. Anyone owning serfs who was not a member of the gentry was forced to sell his serfs.

1762. PETER III. As an intense admirer of Frederick the Great, he effected Russia's withdrawal from the war, thereby causing much resentment among the officers and the aristocracy (despite his proclaiming the freedom of the nobility from obligatory state service). After a six-month reign, **Peter was deposed by a military revolution led by the Orlov brothers.** A few days later he was killed while in captivity. Peter was succeeded by his wife, Catherine II.

March 1. Gentry requirements of **service to the state abolished.**

1762–96. CATHERINE II (the Great), an exceptionally astute and energetic ruler, who furthered the work begun by Peter the Great. In domestic affairs, Catherine was influenced by the teachings of the French Enlightenment (especially Voltaire) and tried to establish a benevolent despotism. On the other hand, she was obliged to cultivate the goodwill of the nobility, to which she owed her power.

1762–63. Catherine secularized church lands.

1766. Catherine called a legislative commission (met 1767–68). This commission reflected Catherine's commitment to Enlightenment thought. It comprised 564 deputies, the vast majority elected, but was unable to agree on any changes and divided along class lines.

1768–72. WAR WITH THE OTTOMANS (p. 358), as a result of Russian advances into Poland (p. 344), in which the Russians won unprecedented victories.

1773–75. PUGACHEV'S REBELLION. Emelian Pugachev declared he was Emperor Peter III, having escaped Catherine's plot to kill him. He declared the serfs free and the elimination of officials and officers. Helped by the war with the Ottomans, Pugachev was initially successful in gaining support and territory. However, he was defeated in 1774, fled to the Urals, and was handed over to the government by his own forces.

1774, July 21. The Treaty of Kuchuk Kainarji ended the war against the Ottoman Empire. Russia acquired Kinburn, Yenikale, and Kertch in the Crimea and secured the right of free navigation for commercial ships in Ottoman waters.

1775. The statute of provincial administration completely reorganized local government in an effort to minimize the possibilities of another rebellion such as Pugachev's. Catherine's encouragement of education, art, and letters contributed to the growth of a liberal public opinion on the social problem. After the outbreak of the French Revolution, Catherine became decidedly hostile to this movement. **Alexander Radishchev (1749–1802)** was arrested and exiled to Siberia (1790) for having published his *Journey from St. Petersburg to Moscow,* which contained a vigorous protest against serfdom.

1780. Armed neutrality at sea, an idea advanced by Russia during the War of American Independence, was a method of protecting commerce. The idea of a League of Armed Neutrality was supported by Denmark and Sweden (1780), and later by Prussia, Austria (1782), and Portugal (1783); France and Spain recognized the principle, but Britain prevented Holland from joining the league by declaring war on the

Dutch. The league demanded **(1) free passage of neutral ships** from port to port and along the coasts of combatants; **(2) freedom of enemy goods in neutral ships** *(le pavillon couvre la marchandise)*, except for contraband; **(3) definition of blockade** (nominal "paper" blockade not sufficient; a blockade, to be legal, must be effective).

1780. Visit of Emperor Joseph II to Catherine and conclusion (1781) of an Austro-Russian treaty. Catherine's **Greek scheme** for the disruption of the Ottoman Empire and division of the Balkans between Russia and Austria.

1783. In keeping with her Near Eastern plans, Catherine carried through the **Annexation of the Crimea,** on the plea of restoring order. The Ottoman leaders were with difficulty dissuaded by Britain and Austria from declaring war on Russia.

1785. Charter of the nobility, recognizing their corporate rights. A similar charter was issued for the towns but not for the peasantry.

1788–90. War with Sweden and the Swedish invasion of Finland. Under Prussian pressure, the Austrians finally backed out of the Ottoman

war and Russia concluded the **Treaty of Jassy (Jan. 9, 1792),** by which it secured Oczakov and the boundary of the Dniester River.

1793, Jan. 23. The second partition of Poland (p. 319), between Russia and Prussia. Catherine, though hostile to the French Revolution, took care not to become involved. Instead, she furthered her own design in Poland, and by the **third partition of Poland (Oct. 24, 1795)** helped to extinguish the kingdom (p. 319).

1796–1801. PAUL I was the first Russian ruler who tried to put **certain limits to the spread of serfdom** (1797, manifesto limiting the peasants' work for the landlord to three days a week).

1797. Paul repealed the law of succession of Peter the Great and decreed that succession should be by genealogical seniority.

1799–1801. Russia participated in the **War of the Second Coalition** against France (see p. 434).

1801, March 24. Paul was assassinated in the course of a palace revolution and was succeeded by his son, **Alexander I.** *(To p. 508)*

C. THE MIDDLE EAST AND NORTH AFRICA, 1500–1800

(From p. 131)

1. OVERVIEW

In the 16th century, **a simpler political map** took shape in the region with the integration of the Middle Eastern and North African lands into **three states:** the Ottoman Empire, Safavid Iran, and Morocco. **The Ottomans,** based until then in Anatolia and southeastern Europe, absorbed nearly all of the Arabic-speaking lands with the exception of Morocco and parts of the Arabian peninsula. Theirs became the dominant regional power, although **Iran** emerged as a formidable foe and bloody conflicts between the two countries erupted periodically.

Several major developments altered the political scene in the 17th and 18th centuries: **the Ottoman Empire became decentralized** as Istanbul's hold on the provinces weakened and autonomous authorities sprang up almost everywhere; **the Safavid regime collapsed,** giving way to several decades of internal fragmentation and turmoil; and two new Middle Eastern countries were born: **Afghanistan and the Saudi state** in Arabia.

Alongside the shifts in the internal power relations came changes in the **region's position vis-à-vis Europe.** While Middle Easterners remained virtually untouched by European culture, they now fought and traded with Europeans on a more extensive basis than before and on increasingly unfavorable terms. **Military conflict** with European countries raged along a wide front extending from the Black Sea area and the Balkans to the western Mediterranean. The region's armies were able to hold their own until the second half of the 18th century, when disastrous defeats by Russia and the easy fall of Egypt to Napoleon brought home to the Ottoman leaders the recognition that **global power had shifted definitely in favor of Europe.** This alarming sense prompted their 19th-century drive to modernize.

The region's **place in global trade** also weakened. European merchants and governments grew increasingly strong in the Indian Ocean and the Mediterranean through the use of new trade routes, the control of shipping, and the acquisition of colonies with cheap labor. With these assets they were able to **circumvent the Middle East** in their import of Eastern pepper and spices, **to compete successfully** with Middle Eastern products such as coffee and sugar, and to sell in the region some finished goods such as textiles in return largely for local raw materials. A **colonial pattern of exchange** (raw materials for finished goods) was beginning to develop in the early modern period, although it remained of limited economic importance for the Middle East before the 19th century because the bulk of the region's trade was still internal or directed toward Asia and Africa rather than Europe.

Like Europe, the Middle East experienced **a marked demographic expansion** during the 16th century. But population levels did not continue to rise in the following two centuries, when **plague epidemics** hit the region with greater frequency and added to the already high mortality rates. With about 28 million people in 1800, the society was still **primarily rural,** some 80 to 85 percent living in village or tribal communities and the rest in towns.

Economic conditions in this diverse region varied from place to place and fluctuated over time. But throughout, **agriculture** remained the predominant sector and **industry** continued to be based on small-scale artisanal production. Between them they supplied the population with its needs in food, raw materials, and manufactured goods at a level that maintained the **region's self-sufficiency.** Among the important institutional developments of the period was the emergence of **the guild system** in its full-fledged form and its leading role in regulating the urban economies.

Religion remained a central focus of identity as well as the ideological underpinning for a variety of social and political movements. The period saw the establishment of **Shi'ism as the state religion of Iran,** with the forced conversion of its largely Sunni population under Safavid pressure. **New Sufi orders** emerged throughout the region and often became vehicles of protest against the establishment. In Arabia, the Muslim puritanical movement of the **Wahhabis** rose to challenge Sufi practices and Ottoman authority and succeeded in establishing its own brand of Islamic state under the Saudi dynasty. Among the Christian minorities, **Catholicism spread** as a result of European missionary work, causing bitter schisms and a lasting **split of the Greek, Armenian, and other Eastern churches** into rival Orthodox and Catholic branches.

Religion also remained the core of **formal education and higher learning** throughout the period. Both continued to be the preserve of a relative few, especially as an Islamic **ban on printing** set limits on the diffusion of knowledge and literacy. But the largely **oral culture** that thrived at the mass level produced a rich corpus of skills, stories, plays, music, pastimes, and popular wisdom. Among the remarkable innovations of this oral culture was the **introduction of the coffeehouse** and its rapid emergence as the region's central institution of public socializing and entertainment. *(To p. 525)*

2. THE MIDDLE EAST, 1501-1808

a. THE OTTOMAN EMPIRE

(From p. 127)

1. THE RISE TO WORLD EMPIRE

1512–20. SULTAN SELIM I. In his first year as ruler Selim faced down a challenge to his throne by his brothers and nephews; he extinguished their **rebellion in Anatolia** and had them eliminated. His ruthlessness and harsh temper made him known as "the Grim" *(Yavuz).* His **conquest of Syria and Egypt** began the empire's absorption of the Arab lands of the Middle East and North Africa, which established the **Ottomans as heirs to the great Islamic imperial states.**

1514. First war with Safavid Iran. Ottoman expansion and Sunni-Shi'ite religious antagonism brought the Ottomans and Safavids into rivalry for control of eastern Anatolia. Selim led a large army against Iran, and in the decisive **Battle of Chaldiran** in Azerbaijan (Aug. 23), his forces defeated Shah Isma'il's army and temporarily occupied the Safavid capital of Tabriz. The victory opened the way for **Ottoman expansion in eastern Anatolia and northern Iraq.**

1515–16. Annexation of Diyarbakr, the principality of **Dulkadir,** and the greater part of **northern Iraq,** including Mosul.

1516. THE CONQUEST OF SYRIA, following the defeat of the Mamluk army in Marj Dabiq near Aleppo (Aug. 24). The Syrian lands as far as the frontier town of Gaza fell to the Ottomans. **Aleppo and Damascus** became the administrative capitals of two newly constituted provinces.

1517. THE CONQUEST OF EGYPT, following the decisive defeat of the Mamluk army at al-Raydaniyya (Jan. 22) and at Giza (April 2). Egypt was organized as a single province with its capital in Cairo. **The Holy Cities of Mecca and Medina** were also absorbed into the empire after the Hashemite emir of Mecca pledged submission to the sultan (July). The Mamluk state thus ceased to exist, but many of the defeated **Mamluk officers and administrators entered Ottoman service.** They continued to purchase new slaves, mostly Circassians, and gradually regained control of the government machinery of Egypt.

1520–66. SULTAN SULEYMAN I (THE MAGNIFICENT). With the death of Selim I (Sept. 1520), his only son, Suleyman, inherited a powerful empire, which rose under him to the peak of its grandeur. Suleyman **added new territories in Europe, Asia, and Africa,** leading his army in person on numerous campaigns. He **systematized the institutions of law and administration,** for which he came to be known by his own people as the Lawgiver *(Kanuni).* In his reign began the rise to **power of the imperial harem,** as high-ranking women of the dynasty (especially the mother of the reigning sultan and his favorite concubines) acquired an unusual degree of political influence and public promi-

OTTOMAN SULTANS (1451–1648)

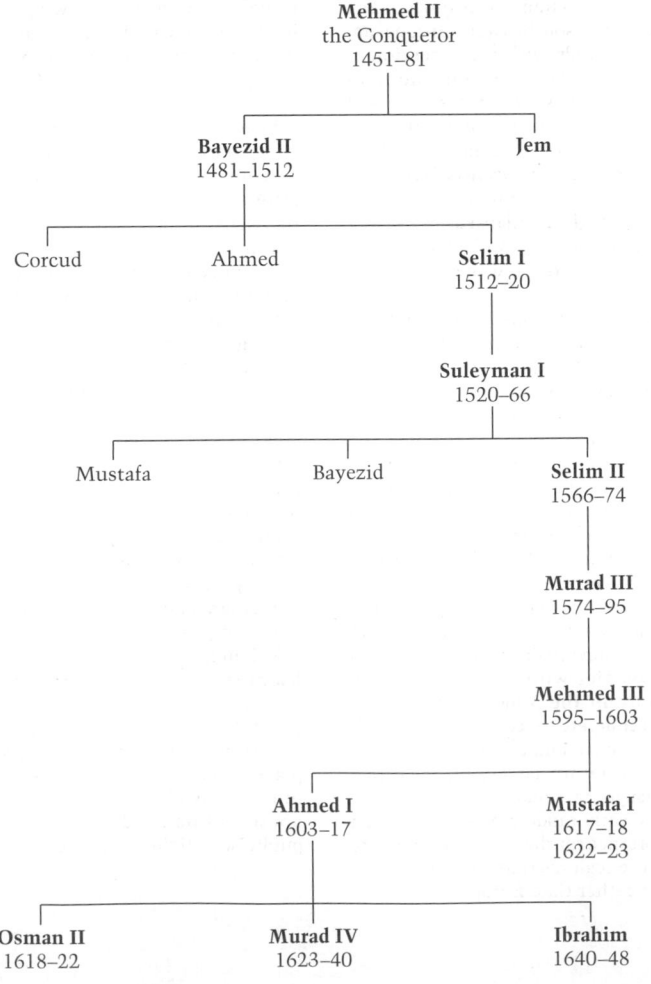

nence. This power, which continued until the mid-17th century, has led to references to the period as **"the sultanate of the women."**

Although Suleyman is the most celebrated of Ottoman sultans, various **problems associated with Ottoman decline** began to emerge during his reign: rural overpopulation, unemployment, inflation, and heavy taxation. These fueled discontent and popular revolts.

1520–21. Anti-Ottoman revolt in Damascus, led by **Janbardi al-Ghazali,** the Mamluk notable appointed by the Ottomans in 1516 to govern the newly conquered province. An Ottoman force defeated his troops in Damascus and killed him (Feb. 1521), ending his bid for independent rule. The governorship of Damascus was henceforth given to Ottoman officials.

1521. The Ottomans captured **Belgrade** (Aug.) and completed the **conquest of Serbia.**

1522, Dec. 20. The **conquest of Rhodes,** after some five months of siege. With the elimination of this center of Christian piracy, the Ottomans secured the maritime routes in the eastern Mediterranean.

1523. Death of **Ahi Ahmed Chelebi** (b. 1436), chief physician of the empire during the reign of Bayezid I and in Suleyman's early years. He built small **hospitals** in the villages he owned, founded the first Ottoman **medical school,** and wrote a work on kidney and bladder stones.

1523–24. Anti-Ottoman revolt in Egypt. The governor Ahmed Pasha declared himself sultan of Egypt, but his power collapsed within a few months and he was killed by local opponents. An expedition headed by the grand vezir Ibrahim Pasha suppressed the disloyal elements in Egypt and reorganized the administration of the province.

c. 1524. Death of **Muhammad ibn Iyas** (b. 1448), an Egyptian historian of Mamluk descent. He wrote an important chronicle *(Bada'i' al-zuhur)* providing a firsthand description of the Ottoman conquest of the Mamluk state.

1526. Suleyman's first Hungarian campaign. The Ottoman army invaded Hungary and defeated the Habsburg forces in the **Battle of Mohács** (Aug. 29) (p. 309). Buda and Pest fell ten days later. The Ottomans withdrew after the Transylvanian notable John Zapolya recognized Ottoman suzerainty.

1526–27. Large-scale insurrections in Anatolia, fed largely by the resistance of Turkomans to the imposition of direct state control and taxation. Renewed **Safavid propaganda fanned this discontent.** The most serious revolt was led by Kalender Chelebi, whose supporters defeated an initial Ottoman expedition before being crushed (June 1527).

1528–29. Suleyman's second Hungarian campaign. After the Habsburgs took Hungary from Zapolya (1527), Suleyman reoccupied the country and reinstated Zapolya as king. He then mounted the **FIRST OTTOMAN SIEGE OF VIENNA** (Sept. 27–Oct. 15, 1529) but failed to take the city. His forces withdrew to Istanbul, leaving the Habsburgs to continue ruling the northern and western border areas of Hungary.

1532. Suleyman's third Hungarian campaign. Following a new Habsburg siege of Buda, Suleyman led a massive force to deal with the threat and penetrate central Europe. The campaign succeeded in conducting raids in Austria but without forcing the main Habsburg army into battle. The two sides agreed to a **peace** (June 22, 1533), by which the **Habsburgs abandoned their claims to Hungary** except for the border areas they had originally occupied and agreed to **pay an annual tribute to the sultan.**

1534. Death of **Ahmed Kemalpashazade** (b. 1469), one the greatest Ottoman historians and scholars. His chronicle, *Tarih-i Al-i Osman (History of the House of Osman),* provides one of the most important sources on his period.

1534. Ottoman conquest of Baghdad and most of Iraq from the Safavids.

1536, Feb. 18. An Ottoman-French commercial treaty granting French subjects extraterritorial privileges in the empire.

1537–40. War with Venice. The Ottoman fleet under Hayruddin Barbarossa imposed Ottoman suzerainty on most of the **islands of the Aegean** (1537) and raided other Venetian islands in the area. An allied European fleet was defeated near Preveza in the Adriatic (Sept. 1538) and failed to break Ottoman control of the Aegean and Ionian seas. Venice made peace (Oct. 20, 1540), surrendering its last possessions in the Morea and acknowledging Hayruddin's Aegean conquests.

1538. Annexation of southern Bessarabia between the Pruth and the Dniester, following a campaign led by Sultan Suleyman against the rebellious vassal prince of Moldavia.

1538. Occupation of Aden, accomplished by a naval expedition on the way to India. The Ottomans lost Aden temporarily to the Portuguese but recaptured it in Feb. 1548.

1539. Occupation of southern Yemen. Ottoman control spread inland steadily, culminating in the **capture of San'a** in 1547 and the establishment of a regular Ottoman administration in the country, with coastal Zabid and inland San'a organized into separate provinces. **The native Zaydis held out** in the mountainous interior and continued to resist Ottoman rule.

1540–41. Administrative and legal reforms. Under the direction of the grand vezir Lutfi Pasha, the laws *(kanuns)* governing the administration of the various provinces were codified. A **new general code of laws** *(Kanunname)* was drawn up, providing specific **penalties for serious crimes** as well as regulations for the financial administration of the **military fiefs** *(timars).* This work was continued in the following few years by Ebussuud Efendi, the *sheik ul-islam* (chief jurisconsult of the empire).

1541. Suleyman's fourth Hungarian campaign. The Habsburgs invaded Hungary following Zapolya's death (1540) but were defeated by the Ottoman army led by Suleyman. **Hungary was now annexed to the empire** and subsequently organized as the province of Buda.

1543. Suleyman's fifth Hungarian campaign. The Habsburgs attempted to reverse the Ottoman successes by attacking Buda. An expedition led by Suleyman captured most of the remaining Habsburg forts in Hungary and Slovenia. In a **peace agreement** (June 1547), the Habsburgs recognized all the Ottoman conquests and promised to pay tribute for their few holdings in northern and western Hungary.

1544. Construction of the **Khusrawiyya mosque in Aleppo,** the earliest monument built in this city in the Ottoman imperial style (by the great **Ottoman architect Sinan).**

1546. Capture of Basra from the Arab chief Rashid ibn Mughamis and establishment of direct Ottoman rule over it. The area of southern Iraq, subsequently organized as a province, proved chronically difficult for the Ottomans to control because of its distance from the center and the considerable power of the Arab tribes there.

1546. Death of **Shams al-Din Muhammad Ibn Tulun,** a Damascene scholar and author of important works on local history, including chronicles covering the transition from Mamluk to Ottoman rule.

1548–49. Suleyman's second Iranian campaign. The Ottomans occupied Tabriz and Azerbaijan again but withdrew. Their only territorial gains from two years of warfare were **Van,** which was organized as a province, and some forts in Georgia.

1550. Ottoman occupation of **Qatif** on the Persian Gulf.

1550–57. Construction of the Suleymaniye, the most beautiful mosque in Istanbul, designed by the **architect Sinan.** Sultan Suleyman and his wife, Roxelana, were buried in the cemetery behind the mosque, in tombs built by Sinan.

1551–52. Ottoman expeditions to subdue **Shahrizor** in the Kurdish mountains of northern Iraq. After heavy fighting an agreement was reached with the local chieftains, who confirmed their allegiance to the sultan.

1551–62. Renewed war with the Habsburgs. In 1551 the Habsburgs occupied Transylvania, an Ottoman vassal principality. An Ottoman military expedition **took Temesvar** (July 1552) **and most of Transylvania** and organized southern Transylvania as the province of Temesvar. The war continued intermittently for another decade in sieges on the frontier and naval clashes in the Mediterranean. The **peace agreement** signed on June 1, 1562, essentially restored the settlement of 1547. The Habsburgs renounced their claims to Transylvania.

1552. Ottoman occupation of the **region of Hasa** (al-Ahsa) in eastern Arabia, which was organized as an Ottoman province.

1553. Sultan Suleyman put to death his son Mustafa, governor of Amasya, for building political support for a possible uprising. This removed from the scene the ablest of the princes.

1553–55. Suleyman's third Iranian campaign. His forces ravaged parts of Iran but failed to force a showdown with the shah's army, which withdrew into the mountains of Luristan. In the **peace agreement signed at Amasya** (May 29, 1555), the shah recognized the existing boundaries and promised to end his propaganda and raids into Ottoman territory.

1554. Death of **Piri Reis** (b. 1465), the greatest Ottoman admiral and naval hero of the 16th century. In 1521 he wrote a major geographical compendium, *Kitab-i Bahriye (Book of the Sea),* which compiled knowledge on the seas and navigation as well as his own maritime experience. He also produced (in 1513) a **map of the known world** in two parts, of which the western portion only has survived.

1554. The Portuguese defeated an Ottoman fleet off Hormuz, frustrating Ottoman attempts to gain control of the Persian Gulf. The gulf remained largely closed to Ottoman shipping thereafter.

1554–66. Construction in Damascus of the religious college (madrasa) and Sufi lodge (takiyya) of Sultan Suleyman, built in the Ottoman imperial style by the **great architect Sinan.**

1555. A major revolt against the sultan, led by a man claiming to be the dead prince **Mustafa,** who had supposedly escaped execution. This Mustafa gathered around him discontented holders of timars (military fiefs), peasants, and members of the religious establishment unhappy with the dominance of the devshirme (slave) class in Istanbul. The rebels **captured most of Macedonia and Thrace** and distributed to the masses wealth seized from government officials. Suleyman's son Bayezid suppressed the revolt and executed its leader.

c. 1555. The introduction of coffee and **coffeehouses** to Istanbul, reportedly by two merchants from Syria. The innovations, which gained **great popularity** throughout the region, stirred **debates among religious scholars,** some of whom condemned them as sources of indolence and spiritual laxity.

1556. Death of **Mehmed Fuzuli,** one of the greatest 16th-century poets. Working in Baghdad under the Safavids and later the Ottomans, he wrote verses in Persian and Turkish that dwelt on mystic love, the unity of divine creation, and the tragic martyrdom of the Shi'ite heroes Hasan and Husayn. His *Leyla and Mejnun,* a poem on platonic love built on a classic theme, is considered his masterpiece.

1557. The Ottomans captured the **ports of Suakin and Massawa** on the African shores of the Red Sea, which allowed them to revive for a time the old international trade routes through Egypt. Shortly thereafter they occupied a strip of the hinterland, which became a **new province known as Habesh (Abyssinia),** governed from Massawa.

1559. Suleyman's son Selim defeated his brother Bayezid in a battle over the succession, fought near Konya. **Selim was appointed heir to the sultan,** and Bayezid, who had fled to Iran, was executed there at Suleyman's request.

1561. Death of **Ahmed Tashkopruluzade** (b. 1495), the greatest scholar of Suleyman's reign. His works, written mostly in Arabic, included an encyclopedic compendium of the state of knowledge at his time (Miftah al-sa'ada) and a biographical dictionary (Shaqa'iq al-nu'maniyya) covering some 600 learned men of the previous century, which was updated by later scholars.

1563. Death of **Lutfi Pasha** (b. 1488), one of the ablest and most cultured Ottoman grand vezirs. He is famous for his administrative reforms and for his treatise *Asafname,* in which he offered guidance on good governance and analyzed the sources of administrative disorder in the empire.

1565. Ottoman siege of Malta (May 20–Sept. 11).

1566, April. The Ottoman navy captured the **isle of Chios** from the Genoese.

1566. Suleyman's last Hungarian campaign. Following increasing border tensions with the Habsburgs, Suleyman left Istanbul in May at the head of an army. His forces **captured Szigetvar** and the strategic fort of Gyula, but he himself fell ill and **died in the midst of the campaign** (Sept. 7) (p. 302).

1566–74. SULTAN SELIM II. Suleyman's only surviving son, often known as Selim the Sot for his love of drinking, was not an active ruler. He retired to the pleasures of the harem while **his able grand vezir, Mehmed Sokullu, ran the state,** with growing input from the palace women. Selim **kept the princes in the harem** rather than placing them, as was customary until then, in military and administrative posts that would gain them the experience needed to rule. His practice, followed by subsequent sultans, weakened the quality of the rulers.

1567. Anti-Ottoman revolt in Yemen led by the Zaydi imam, who captured almost the whole country except Zabid (1567). Sultan Selim II unified the two provinces in Yemen under one governor (April 1568) and sent an expedition that by 1570 **regained the lost territories.** The Zaydis retained their control in the mountains.

1567. An Armenian press was established in Istanbul by Apkar of Sivas, a priest who had studied typography in Venice.

1567. Death of **Moshe Hamon,** member of a notable Jewish family of Spanish origin who served as **physician to Selim I and Suleyman I** and enjoyed considerable influence in the Jewish community and in the Ottoman court. His **son Joseph** (d. 1577) and other members of the Hamon family also gained prominence during the 16th century.

1568, Feb. 17. Peace agreement with the Habsburgs, after a year of hostilities on the frontier. The peace was renewed periodically (Oct. 3, 1573; Jan. 1, 1577; Nov. 29, 1590).

1569, Oct. 18. A new capitulations agreement with France, which helped establish French commercial and political preeminence in the region. It allowed free passage for French ships into Ottoman waters and required vessels from other western European countries to fly the French flag in order to enjoy the same privileges. The capitulations were renewed several times (July 1581, Feb. 1597, May 1604, June 1673, and May 1740).

1569–74. Construction of the **Selimiye mosque in Edirne,** the greatest monument designed by the **architect Sinan.**

c. 1570. Death of **Pir Sultan Abdal,** one of the most renowned of the Anatolian ashiks (minstrels). A Shi'ite (Alevi), he participated in pro-Safavid agitation around Sivas and was executed by the Ottoman authorities. His verses express protest as well as the themes of love and natural beauty, and are **still sung today.**

1570–71. The conquest of Cyprus. Famagusta, the last major stronghold of the Venetians on the island, fell after a siege lasting about a year (Aug. 1571). Venice recognized the conquest in a peace signed on March 7, 1573.

1571, Oct. 7. The Battle of Lepanto (p. 295), between the Ottoman fleet (230 galleys) and an allied European armada of more than 200 vessels under the command of Don John of Austria. **The Ottoman fleet was almost totally destroyed** in this naval battle, the greatest ever fought on the Mediterranean.

Lepanto proved less decisive than it first appeared. While Europe celebrated the victory, the **Ottomans speedily rebuilt their fleet** and soon restored their naval supremacy in the eastern Mediterranean. Their new navy was able to ravage the coasts of Sicily and southern Italy in 1573 and to capture Tunis from the Spaniards a year later.

1572. Death of **Rabbi Isaac Luria** (b. 1534), the most famous student of **Jewish mysticism, the cabala.** He spent his last years in Safed, in Palestine, teaching his esoteric doctrines, which were published and amplified by his disciple and successor **Hayim Vital** (1542–1620). Their ideas spread throughout the Jewish world, especially among those expelled from Spain.

1572. Death of **Nigari,** or Reis Haydar (b. c. 1492), a naval officer famous for his artistic talent. He left fine color portraits of Suleyman the Magnificent, Selim II, and the admiral Barbarossa.

1574. Death of **Ebussuud Efendi** (b. 1490), one of the greatest Ottoman legal scholars. He served as *sheik ul-islam* (chief jurisconsult of the empire) for 29 years and issued **thousands of legal opinions** interpreting the law and reconciling Islamic codes with state legislation.

1574–95. SULTAN MURAD III. Selim's eldest son, who took over after his father's death in late 1574, was the last of the sultans to possess some field experience before assuming the throne. The **influence of palace women,** especially Murad's mother, became pervasive, and after the execution of Mehmed Sokullu in 1579 grand vezirs changed almost annually, according to shifts in court politics. Murad captured substantial territories from Iran, but they were lost just ten years after his death.

1575. Death in Safed of **Rabbi Joseph Karo** (b. 1488), one of the greatest of Jewish legal scholars. His work *Shulhan Arukh* (printed in 1550–59), in which he codified the laws and precepts of Judaism in a clear and simple manner, remains the most authoritative handbook of Jewish law to this day.

1576–90. War with Iran. The Ottomans initiated the war in the hope of conquering the Caucasus and Azerbaijan permanently. The campaigns dragged on for years but the Ottomans were able to capture new territories, bringing under their direct rule **Azerbaijan and the Caucasus** as far as the Caspian. In the **peace treaty** concluding the war (March 21, 1590), Iran confirmed all these conquests and pledged to end all Shi'ite propaganda in Ottoman territory and the persecution of Sunnis in Iran.

1577. A Hebrew press was established in Safed by Eliezer and Abraham

Ashkenazi. It remained in operation for a decade and was the first press of any kind east of Istanbul and west of China.

1579. Death of **Don Joseph Nasi,** a wealthy Jewish businessman (born as a Marrano in Portugal) who moved to Istanbul from Europe in 1554 and gained much influence by financing the rise to power of Selim II. He represented the sultan in diplomatic missions and was **appointed duke of Naxos.** He worked closely with his aunt **Doña Gracia Mendes** (1510-68), an enterprising Jewish woman who settled in Istanbul in 1553 and gained considerable economic power and political influence. They donated generously to Jewish causes and in the 1560s invested in the **rebuilding of Tiberias,** in Palestine, as part of a project to revive the town as a center for Jewish learning.

1580, Jan. Destruction of the astronomical observatory in Istanbul by the sultan's order, following objections by religious leaders to the scientific activity there.

June. Treaty of commerce between the Ottoman Empire and England, the first capitulatory agreement between the two governments (ratified in Istanbul, May 3, 1583). England acquired privileges formerly limited to France and Venice. The Ottomans broadened English extraterritorial rights by successive renewals and expansions (in 1603, 1606, 1624, 1641, 1662, and 1675).

1581, Sept. 11. Royal charter creating the Levant Company, which inaugurated English trade with the Ottoman Empire on a sustained basis. The company operated as **a monopoly** and survived as the organizational framework of English trade in the Middle East until its dissolution by an act of Parliament in 1825.

1586. The first revolt of the military in Egypt; the troops put the governor under house arrest. It was followed by a series of revolts by the soldiery in 1589, 1598, 1601, 1604, and 1609, all of which were suppressed.

1588. Death of **Mimar Sinan** (b. 1489), the greatest of Ottoman architects. After an early career in the military he devoted his artistic and technical genius to architecture, **designing some 360 monuments** (mosques, bathhouses, soup kitchens, and mausoleums). The Selimiye mosque in Edirne is his masterpiece. He introduced **innovations of style and design** and inaugurated an Ottoman classical tradition that lived long after him.

1590-1635. Rule of Fakhr al-Din II of the Ma'nid family in Mount Lebanon. He was one of the most ambitious provincial leaders of his time and worked to establish a dynastic hegemony over Mount Lebanon and the neighboring territories. His success rested on a strong professional army of mercenaries, religious tolerance, and the promotion of trade and agriculture.

1593-1606. War with the Habsburgs. Growing tensions on the Hungarian border and a serious defeat of an Ottoman force at Sissek on the Kulpa River (June 20, 1593) led the grand vezir to declare war. In addition to Habsburg advances toward the Danube, the Ottomans faced, from 1595, **rebellions by the vassal principalities of Wallachia, Moldavia, and Transylvania.** An Ottoman offensive led by the new sultan Mehmed III captured the fortress of Erlau and routed the Habsburgs in Mezö Keresztés (Oct. 26, 1596), but because of political problems at home the Ottoman army lost momentum and suffered setbacks. In 1604-5 the Ottomans succeeded in **recapturing Pest and Gran and restoring the Danubian principalities** to obedience. The tremendous costs of the war and the new threats from Iran prompted them to accept peace offers. In the **Treaty of Szitvatorok** (Nov. 11, 1606), the prewar boundaries were confirmed, and for the first time the sultan accepted the Habsburg emperor as his equal and ended his payments of tribute for northern Hungary.

2. DECENTRALIZATION AND EXTERNAL CHALLENGES

1595-1603. SULTAN MEHMED III. Upon his accession following his father's death, he had his 19 brothers strangled. He **ended the traditional practice of sending princes to governorships,** confining them instead to special quarters in the harem known as the *kafes* (the cage). Future sultans thus lacked the training and experience of their predecessors. The period was dominated by the exhausting war with the Habsburgs (1593-1606) and a series of great revolts in Anatolia.

c. 1596. Afrasiyab, a notable from Basra, acquired the governorship of the province, establishing a **dynasty that ruled Basra** as a virtually autonomous area until 1668.

1596-1602. Jelali revolts. Kara Yaziji, an Ottoman soldier, began to organize around him an army of dissident and unemployed soldiers and emerged as the best-known early leader of those rebel groups of the period known collectively as **Jelalis.** From 1599 the government sent expeditions against his forces, but with limited success. He died in 1602, but various Jelali rebel groups under different leaders continued their violent protest against the authorities for much of the decade. They engaged in **large-scale brigandage** and threw Anatolia into a state of increasing lawlessness and civil disorder.

1597-1602. A large-scale revolt of the Zaydi imam Qasim in Yemen, put down by the Ottomans.

1599. Death of **Saduddin Efendi** (b. 1536), Ottoman religious scholar and author of an important chronicle, *Taj ul-tevarih (The Crown of Histories),* providing a detailed history of the Ottoman dynasty from its origins to 1520.

1599. Death of **Mustafa Âli** (b. 1541), an Ottoman official and historian who wrote a universal history *(Kunh ul-ahbar)* as well as a description of Cairo and a book of counsel for sultans (1581) in which he reflected on the causes of Ottoman decline.

1600. Death of **Baki** (b. 1526), the most brilliant classical Ottoman poet of the period. He rose from a humble background to become the palace poet and a close companion of Sultan Suleyman I. His elegy on the sultan's death is considered his finest work.

Death of **Mustafa Selaniki,** an official scribe who composed an important chronicle *(Tarih-i Selaniki)* covering the years 1563-99, in which he gives a first hand account of the deterioration of Ottoman administration.

1603. Anti-Ottoman rebellion in Baghdad. Muhammad al-Tawil, a Janissary officer, seized power and defeated an Ottoman force sent against him. He was assassinated in 1607, and a year later the Ottomans reasserted their rule in the city.

1603-17. SULTAN AHMED I. Mehmed III's eldest surviving son, aged 13, inherited an empire besieged from without by the Habsburgs and Safavids and from within by the Jelali rebels. He gradually brought peace on all fronts. A deeply religious man, he attempted to enforce the observance of religious duties and to **crack down on the consumption of wine.**

1603-12. War with Iran. In a series of campaigns in 1603-1607, Shah Abbas I recaptured Azerbaijan and the Caucasus from the Ottomans. After some unsuccessful attempts to reverse this setback, the Ottomans signed a **peace treaty** (Nov. 20, 1612) in which they surrendered their conquests of 1590 and accepted the boundaries fixed in 1555. Boundary disputes and raids upset the peace for a time, but a new agreement (Sept. 26, 1618) confirmed the Treaty of 1612.

1606-7. The rebellion of Ali Pasha Janbulat of Aleppo, member of a powerful Kurdish clan in northern Syria, originally to protest the execution by Ottoman officials of his uncle Husayn Pasha Janbulat. He soon moved to establish a state in northern Syria, but an Ottoman force sent against him demolished his army (Oct. 1607).

1608-9. Suppression of the Jelali rebels. Brigandage in parts of Anatolia mounted from 1603, leading to the mass flight of peasants to the security of walled cities and the mountains. In 1608, after various failed attempts to defeat and appease the rebels, an Ottoman army crushed the forces of the paramount **Jelali leader, Kalenderoğlu Mehmed.** In the following months, other rebel leaders were eliminated and the great Jelali revolts extinguished.

1608. Fakhr al-Din II of Mount Lebanon signed a commercial treaty with the grand duchy of Tuscany.

1609. A serious revolt by the soldiery in Egypt, which turned into a separatist movement, was crushed by loyal Ottoman forces.

1609-16. The construction in Istanbul of the **monumental mosque of Ahmed I,** known also as the **Blue Mosque** because of the dominant tone of the tilework in its interior.

1610. The construction in Cairo of the **mosque of Malika Safiya,** which reproduced the Ottoman imperial style more purely than any other local mosque.

The first printing press established in Lebanon (in Dayr Qazhaya). It printed the Book of Psalms in Syriac characters.

1612. A treaty of commerce between the Ottoman Empire and the Neth-

erlands, granting Dutch nationals capitulatory privileges in the Ottoman Empire.

1613. An Ottoman army moved against **Fakhr al-Din II of Lebanon** for his encroachment on territories in the province of Damascus (Ajlun and Hawran). Fakhr al-Din fled to Italy but **returned to power in 1618** after obtaining an amnesty from Istanbul.

1617–18. SULTAN MUSTAFA I (FIRST REIGN). After the death of Ahmed I, court politics secured the throne for his brother Mustafa. He proved incompetent and was deposed on grounds of insanity (Feb. 22, 1618) after three months, in favor of Ahmed I's son Osman.

1618–22. SULTAN OSMAN II. Although only 13, Osman proved to be an active ruler with ambitious plans for restoring the power of the sultanate. He restricted the privileges of the ulama and considered replacing the Janissaries with a new army recruited from the Anatolian population. The Janissaries revolted, killed him, and restored Mustafa I (May 1622). This was **the first assassination of a sultan,** and it set a precedent in Ottoman politics.

1622–23. SULTAN MUSTAFA I (SECOND REIGN). Istanbul degenerated into lawlessness and revolts broke out in Anatolia as the new sultan stood helpless to handle the crisis. He was finally deposed in favor of Ahmed I's son Murad (Sept. 10, 1623).

1623–40. SULTAN MURAD IV. To a state beset by serious political and financial problems, Murad was able to bring some stability and rejuvenation. After 1632 he asserted himself against the various power groups and worked ruthlessly to subordinate them to his will.

1623. Fakhr al-Din II of Lebanon obtained possession of Safed, Nablus, and Ajlun, defeating an attempt by the governor of Damascus to dislodge him.

Ottoman siege of Baghdad, to crush the rebellion of Bakr Subashi, a Janissary officer who built a large following among the local troops and became the most powerful man in the city. Bakr turned for aid to the Safavid ruler **Shah Abbas I,** who took the opportunity to **occupy Baghdad** (Jan. 1624) and parts of Iraq. The Ottomans recaptured the area in 1638.

1627. A Greek press was founded in Istanbul by Nicodemus Metaxas, with printing equipment imported from England.

1631. Mustafa Kochi Bey, close adviser to Murad IV, presented to the sultan his perceptive treatise *(Risale)* on the state and prospects of reforming the Ottoman Empire. He recommended resolute action by the sultan to eliminate corruption and factional politics and restore the financial strength of the state.

1633, Sept. 2. A great fire in Istanbul burned large parts of the city. With its densely built wooden houses, the capital suffered an unusually high number of fires that often caused immense damage (109 major fires between 1633 and 1839). The disaster of 1633 prompted **a crusade by Sultan Murad to restore public morality** by prohibiting the use of coffee and tobacco and ordering the **closing of all coffeehouses.** The effects of this effort were short-lived.

1635. End of Ottoman rule in Yemen. The province was lost to the Zaydis, who had launched a successful war against the Ottoman forces beginning around 1626.

1635. End of Fakhr al-Din's rule in Lebanon, after his defeat by an Ottoman army sent against him. He was put to death in Istanbul. Other rulers of the **Ma'nid family** retained control of the Shuf Mountain until the extinction of their line in 1697.

1635. Death of **Nef'i** (b. 1582), the dominant Ottoman poet of the 17th century. He was patronized by Sultan Murad IV, for whom he wrote poems of praise. His **satirical poems** criticizing important figures and corrupt practices led to his downfall and execution.

1635. Death of **Kadizade Mehmed Efendi,** a conservative member of the Ottoman ulama who led a **fundamentalist movement** calling for the enforcement of a strict interpretation of Islam and the ending of illegitimate religious innovations, including the Sufi mystical orders. His followers, known as the **Kadizadelis, gained political influence** and sought by violence and bribery to enforce their vision until the grand vezir **Mehmed Koprulu confiscated their properties and banished their leaders in 1656.**

1638, Dec. 25. The Ottoman reconquest of Baghdad from the Safavids, after previous attempts to take the city (in 1625 and 1630) had failed. A **peace treaty** between the Ottoman Empire and Iran (signed May 17, 1639) confirmed Baghdad as an Ottoman possession and established a rough boundary between the two states which endured with little change for more than 200 years.

1640–48. SULTAN IBRAHIM. The death of Murad IV (Feb. 1640) brought to the throne his brother Ibrahim, whose personal indulgences and crazes, including his passion for women and furs, made him known as **Ibrahim the Mad.** The treasury was depleted, bribery and extortion became rampant in all levels of the administration, and the currency was debased. His **disastrous reign** came to an end with his execution in Aug. 1648, under pressure from the Janissaries.

1645–69. The Ottoman capture of Crete. After occupying part of the island from Venice, the Ottomans in 1647 laid siege to the capital, **Candia,** which finally surrendered in Sept. 1669. The **peace agreement** allowed Venice to retain three fortified posts on the island.

1648–54. Venetian blockade of the Dardanelles, which interrupted the shipment of supplies to Crete and the importation of grains to the capital from Egypt and Syria.

1648–87. SULTAN MEHMED IV. Ibrahim's son came to power while still a boy, and his first eight years as sultan were marked by political disorder in the capital and provinces, domination by military officers, and a financial crisis. In 1656, after a major revolt in Istanbul and a new Venetian naval blockade, he appointed as grand vezir a **ruthless reformer, Mehmed Koprulu,** who inaugurated a **new era of political stability.**

1649, April 28. Louis XIV of France issued a proclamation declaring **French protection of the Maronite community in Lebanon** and instructing French representatives in the region to look after Maronite interests.

1651, Sept. 2. Execution of **Kosem Sultan** (b. 1585), wife of Sultan Ahmed I and mother of three succeeding sultans. For some 35 years she was one of the most powerful figures in the palace and had a hand in numerous decisions and changes of personnel at the top.

1654. The grand vezir's office, which had been steadily expanding its executive functions, was moved to its own buildings outside the palace.

1656, April. Death of **Ridwan Bey al-Faqari,** a Circassian Mamluk grandee who dominated the political scene in Egypt for 25 years. He held key offices and was the **leader of the Faqariyya political faction,** rival of the **Qasimiyya faction** (Egyptian politics were polarized into these two parties).

June 26. Venetian destruction of the Ottoman fleet at the mouth of the Dardanelles, in the worst Ottoman naval defeat since Lepanto (p. 352). A new Venetian blockade of the Dardanelles, which caused food prices in Istanbul to soar, was ended a year later.

1656–61. Mehmed Koprulu's term as grand vezir. Born in Albania (in 1575), Koprulu entered government service and held numerous positions that gained him an intimate familiarity with the workings of Ottoman government. Despite his advanced years, he approached his new post with brutal vigor. He cracked down on the Kadizade movement of conservative ulama, executed rebellious soldiers and officials, purged the court, balanced the state budget, and broke the Venetian blockade of the Dardanelles. When he died (Oct. 31, 1661), his son succeeded him, establishing the rule of a **dynasty of grand vezirs that dominated the state until the end of the century.**

1657. Death of **Katip Chelebi,** known also as Haji Halifa (b. 1609), perhaps the greatest Ottoman secular intellectual and the most learned man of his time. He possessed a versatile and unconventional mind and was one of the first Ottoman writers to show **interest in Western knowledge.** His masterwork, reflecting his consummate love of books, was *Keshf ul-zunun,* a bibliography of more than 1,500 books in Turkish, Arabic, and Persian, with biographies of their authors. He also wrote works on geography and history and a treatise on the causes and remedies of the chronic imperial debt.

1658–59. The revolt of Abaza Hasan Pasha, governor of Aleppo, who assembled a large army of soldiers and peasants and declared his rule in Anatolia. A force organized by Mehmed Koprulu crushed the rebellion and had Abaza Hasan killed (Feb. 1659).

1659. The Ottoman government sent **a new force of Janissaries to Damascus** to neutralize the existing Janissary force (made up largely of local recruits), which had supported Abaza Hasan Pasha's revolt. Two units came to exist side by side: **the old Janissaries,** designated as *yerliyya* (local), and **the new force,** known as *kapi kul* (imperial). The

OTTOMAN SULTANS (1640–1922)

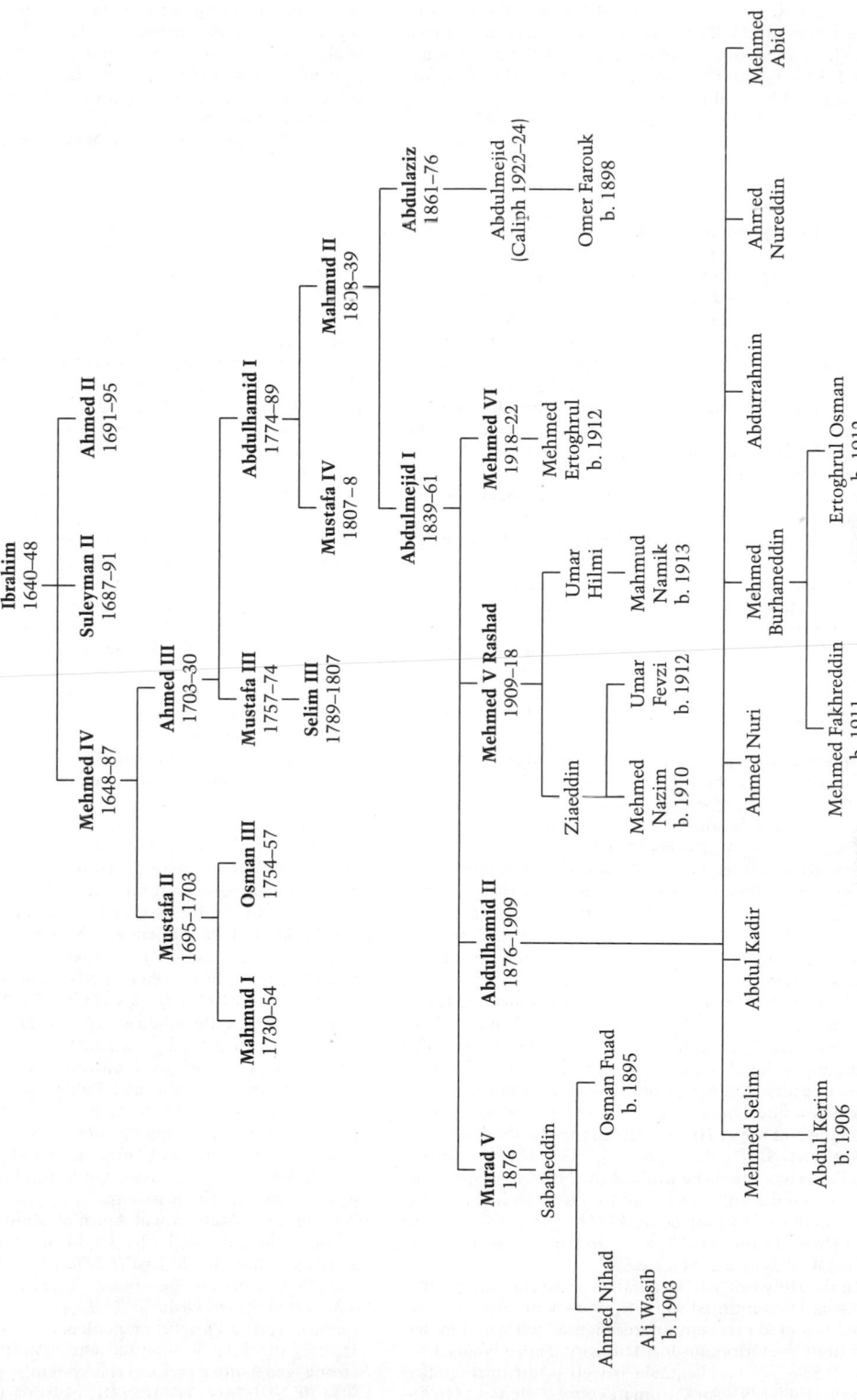

politics of Damascus were dominated henceforth by the **factional conflict between the two contingents.**

1660. Construction of the Egyptian Market (Misir Charshi) in Istanbul.

1661–76. Kopruluzade Fazil Ahmed Pasha (b. 1635), son of Mehmed Koprulu, served as grand vezir. He continued his father's efforts to maintain a tight administration and, as a learned man, patronized scholars and established the **Koprulu library,** which has since become one of Istanbul's most important historical collections. However, foreign campaigns occupied most of his term.

1663–64. War with Austria. The Ottomans launched a campaign to restore their authority in Transylvania following Habsburg efforts to intervene there. After some successes and setbacks, the two sides signed a **peace at Vasvar** (Aug. 10, 1664), by which the Ottoman territories were restored.

1665–66. The messianic movement of Sabbatai Sevi (Shabbatai Tzvi). Sevi, an ascetic Jew from Izmir who had been propagating his mystical ideas among Jewish communities in the region for some years, was **proclaimed the Jewish messiah** during a visit to Gaza (May 31, 1665). He defied or replaced many of the rules of rabbinic Judaism and called on Jews to join him in **preparations for the promised day of judgment,** which he claimed would arrive on June 18, 1666. Masses of excited Jews became his followers even as many rabbis condemned the movement as heresy. Because of the turmoil he was creating, **Sevi was arrested in Istanbul** by the Ottoman authorities (Feb. 1666), **and he agreed to convert to Islam** instead of facing execution (Sept. 1666). His surprising conversion crushed his followers' hopes for redemption, although some continued to believe in Sevi's eventual return as the messiah even after his death (Sept. 1676).

1668. An Ottoman force captured Basra and overthrew the dynastic rule of the **Afrasiyabs.**

1670. Loss of Hasa in eastern Arabia. The region, occupied by the Ottomans in 1552, was retaken by the Banu Khalid Arabs.

1672–76. War with Poland (p. 344). Rivalry over control of the Ukraine, which the Poles occupied in 1671, led to Ottoman military intervention and the **capture of most of Podolia** in the southwestern Ukraine. By the **treaty signed at Zorawno** (Oct. 27, 1676), Podolia came under direct Ottoman rule and the rest of the Ukraine under the sultan's suzerainty.

1675, Sept. Final treaty of capitulations between the Ottoman Empire and England, which included the original treaty of 1580 and subsequent additions to it. The treaty was terminated on Aug. 6, 1924.

1676–83. Kara Mustafa Pasha, brother-in-law of his predecessor, Kopruluzade Fazil Ahmed Pasha, served as grand vezir.

1677–81. First war with Russia (p. 346). Problems with maintaining the sultan's suzerainty in the Ukraine, encouraged by the Russians, led to several unsuccessful Ottoman campaigns against Russian forces that occupied the area between the Dnieper and the Bug. In the **Treaty of Radzyn (Bahchesaray),** signed in 1681, the Ottomans abandoned claims to the **Ukrainian territory** beyond the Dnieper.

1682. Death of **Evliya Chelebi** (b. 1611), famous for his massive travelogue *Seyahatname.* In the course of his service as an Ottoman soldier and official, he spent a good part of his life traveling in all parts of the empire and recording in detail his impressions of people and places. His accounts are a treasury of information, although in some instances he appears to have described journeys that he never made himself.

1682. Ottoman conquest of upper Hungary from the Habsburgs.

1683, July–Sept. SECOND SIEGE OF VIENNA (p. 337). A large army led by Kara Mustafa Pasha assaulted the walls of the Habsburg capital but met with a staunch defense and was **forced to retreat** after the arrival of Polish reinforcements led by John Sobieski. The Ottoman army was defeated at Gran (Nov. 1) and withdrew in disarray. Blamed for the debacle, Kara Mustafa was executed (Dec.).

1683–99. War with the Holy League. An alliance of the Habsburgs, Venice, Poland, and Russia confronted the Ottomans with offensives on several fronts and inflicted on them **unprecedented territorial losses.** On the Austrian front the Ottomans lost Hungary, Transylvania, Croatia and Slovenia (1684–87), and Belgrade as well as territories in Serbia and Macedonia (1688–89). An Ottoman counteroffensive (1690–91) recovered Belgrade and restored the Danube defense line but failed to recapture Hungary. The Ottoman army successfully defended Temesvar (1695–97) but was then virtually destroyed at Zenta (Sept. 11, 1697), leading the sultan to make peace overtures.

1685–87. The Venetians captured the Dalmatian coast, the Morea, and Athens.

1687–91. SULTAN SULEYMAN II. Sultan Mehmed was deposed (Nov. 8, 1687) for failing to handle the crisis that developed in the wake of the disastrous European war. The new ruler, Sultan Ibrahim's second son, faced **mass discontent** over the burden of new taxes, debasements of the coinage, arrears in the payment of soldiers' salaries, soaring of food prices, and the widespread famine of 1687. Bands of rebellious troops terrorized the capital for several months until Suleyman led a crackdown on them.

1689, Oct. 25. Kopruluzade Fazil Mustafa Pasha, younger brother of Fazil Ahmed Pasha, was appointed grand vezir. He worked vigorously to bring discipline to the army and reform state finances, but was killed on the battlefield in Aug. 1691.

1691–95. SULTAN AHMED II. After Suleyman's death, Sultan Ibrahim's third son assumed the throne. He proved incapable of directing the affairs of state or pursuing the reforms set in motion by Fazil Mustafa Pasha. He also took an intransigent position with the European enemies, keeping the costly war going.

1694. Capture of **Basra** by the Muntafiq Arabs, who had been steadily extending their power in southern Iraq at the expense of Ottoman authority. It was retaken by the Ottomans in 1701.

1695–1703. SULTAN MUSTAFA II. With the death of Ahmed (Feb. 6, 1695), Mehmed IV's son Mustafa took over. Serious defeats prompted him to end the long European war, while domestically his able grand vezir, Amjazade Huseyin Pasha, tried to improve conditions.

1695. Reorganization of the tax farming system, with the introduction of tax farms available for a life term (known as *malikane*) instead of the one-year term of the traditional *iltizam.* By providing individuals with the right to collect taxes on a continuous basis and allowing them to transfer this right to their heirs, the state hoped **to curb the exploitation of the peasantry by reckless tax farmers** concerned only with short-term profits. The new system **strengthened the power base of notable (ayan) families in the provinces,** who accumulated large hereditary holdings.

1696. The Russians took Azov (p. 346), establishing a strong foothold for their subsequent campaign to change the Black Sea from an Ottoman to a Russian lake.

1697–1702. Amjazade Huseyin Pasha (1644–1702) served as grand vezir. The son of Mehmed Koprulu's eldest brother, he was the fourth member of the Koprulu family to hold the office. He took steps to modernize the Ottoman navy and cut the size of the Janissary corps. He also reduced taxes, offered tax incentives to peasants to resume cultivation, and restored the value of the coinage. His attempts to reform the government and palace administration led to opposition from vested interests and to his resignation (Sept. 1702).

1697. Bashir I of the Shihab clan was elected by the sheiks of Mount Lebanon as emir of the territories of the **Ma'nids,** whose last ruler, Bashir's uncle Ahmad Ma'n, died childless.

1699, Jan. 26. TREATY OF KARLOWITZ (p. 339). The agreement basically confirmed the conditions on the ground at the end of the 1683–99 war: **Austria** gained all of Hungary (except the Banat of Temesvar), Transylvania, Croatia, and Slovenia; **Venice** kept the Morea and its conquests in Dalmatia; and **Poland** obtained Podolia and western Ukraine. In a separate treaty (signed in Istanbul on June 13, 1700), **Russia** retained Azov and its conquests along the Dniester. The treaty marked the beginning of Ottoman withdrawal from Europe. The empire shifted to the defensive while **the initiative passed to the Europeans, primarily the Russians.**

1699. Death of **Muhammad Amin al-Muhibbi** (b. 1651), a Damascene scholar who compiled a biographical dictionary of 17th-century personages in the Middle East (*Khulasat al-athar*) and a massive anthology of contemporary poetry (*Nafhat al-rayhana*).

1703. Sari Mehmed Pasha (d. 1717), chief of the Ottoman treasury (*defterdar*), wrote an important book of advice on governance (*Nesayih ul-vuzera*), in which he analyzed administrative corruption and called for strong leadership to reform the system.

1703–30. SULTAN AHMED III. Mustafa II abdicated in favor of his brother Ahmed (Aug. 22, 1703), following a **widespread rebellion** against his rule begun by Janissaries in Istanbul and soon joined by thousands of soldiers, tradesmen, and ulama. The new sultan was a cultivated man whose time of rule came to be known as **the Tulip**

Period *(Lale devri)* for the passionate obsession with tulips that took hold among the upper classes. A distinct **spirit of extravagance and cultural vibrance** marked the period, especially under the grand vezir Damad Ibrahim Pasha (1718–30).

1704. Hasan Pasha, an able Ottoman official, was appointed governor of Baghdad, establishing **a quasi-hereditary dynasty** of **pashas that ruled central Iraq** (and, for most of the time, Basra) until 1831. His rule (1704–24) and that of his son Ahmad Pasha (1724–34, 1736–47) relied on the service of personal slaves *(mamluks)*, mostly Georgians, who filled key military and administrative positions. After Ahmad Pasha, who had no son, Mamluks succeeded to the governorship despite periodic attempts by Istanbul to dislodge them.

1704. Death of **Istifan al-Duwayhi** (b. 1603), a Maronite patriarch who was the first important historian to emerge among Arabic-speaking Christians in Lebanon. His main chronicle *(Ta'rikh al-azmina)* was a history of the Maronite community and of Lebanon's emergence as a territorial unit.

1706. The first Arabic printing press in the Arab world was established in Aleppo by local Christians; it published several religious works and then continued operation in Lebanon.

1708. The office of **commander of the annual Damascus pilgrimage** to Mecca *(emir al-hajj)* was vested in the governor of Damascus instead of a separate official. The arrangement, which lasted until the end of Ottoman rule in Damascus in 1918, enhanced the power and prestige of the governor.

1710–11. War with Russia. Seeking to advance in the Black Sea area and raise a Balkan revolt against the sultan, Peter the Great provoked a confrontation with the Ottomans. His army crossed the Pruth into Moldavia (July 1711) but was soon surrounded by the Ottoman army and sued for peace. The **agreement signed at the Pruth** (July 21, 1711) provided the basis for the definitive peace treaty concluded in June 1713. The Russians agreed to return all the conquered lands and evacuate **Azov.** The collusion with Russia by the native **princes of Moldavia and Wallachia** prompted the Ottoman government to replace them with its own **appointees from among the Greek Phanariote families of Istanbul.** This new regime lasted until 1822.

1711. A civil war in Egypt, which raged for some two months and involved nearly all military and ruling groups. In its aftermath, the **Mamluk beys emerged as the dominant political force,** while the Ottoman governors became figureheads. The factional struggle between beys of the **Faqariyya and Qasimiyya factions** dominated the subsequent history of Egypt in the 18th century.

1711. The battle of Ayn Dara in Lebanon, in which Amir Haydar Shihab defeated the chieftain of the Shuf region and consolidated the **hegemony of the Shihab family.**

1711. Death of **Buhurizade Mustafa Itri** (b. c. 1640), a gifted musician who composed sacred and secular pieces (of which only 27 have been found). He belonged to the Mevlevi order and was employed in the sultan's court.

1712. Death of **Yusuf Nabi** (b. 1642), an Ottoman scholar and masterly poet who was highly learned in Arabic and Persian literature. In a small book of counsel *(Hayriye)* written in verse for his son, he provided a vivid commentary on the ways of his time.

1714–18. War with Venice and Austria. The Ottomans declared war on Venice (Dec. 1714) to regain the Morea. They **took the Morea** (summer 1715), but their attempts to recover Hungary from the Habsburgs brought them disastrous defeats, including the **loss of Temesvar** (Oct. 1716) **and Belgrade** (Aug. 1717). By the **Treaty of Passarowitz** (July 21, 1718), the Ottomans lost the Banat of Temesvar, western Wallachia (Little Wallachia), and northern Serbia, including Belgrade, but retained the Morea. Their losses indicated again the shift in military power in favor of Europe.

1716. Death of **Mustafa Naima** (b. 1655), the first and possibly greatest of the official Ottoman court chroniclers. His history *(Razvat al-Huseyin),* covering the period 1591–1659, was remarkable for going beyond the traditional chronicling of events and presenting interpretation as well as reflections on the causes of Ottoman decline.

1718–30. Damad Ibrahim Pasha served as grand vezir, presiding over the innovative changes of the Tulip Period. He began sending **Ottoman ambassadors to European capitals** for the first time, to secure information about developments in Europe. Sketches brought from France became models for a new pleasure palace he built for the sultan.

Named Saadabad, the palace was surrounded by pavilions, statues, fountains, and gardens. The upper classes imitated this new style in **a wave of extravagant construction** and imported European furniture and artwork. Damad Ibrahim also encouraged scholarship and the introduction of printing.

1723. Death of **Demetrius Cantemir** (b. 1673), a Moldavian prince and scholar who acquired knowledge of Turkish, Arabic, and Persian during a period of exile in Istanbul after 1711. He wrote a history of the Ottoman Empire as well as a **treatise on Turkish music** that included a notated collection of 353 instrumental pieces. This collection remains one of only two extant records of the premodern repertoire of the Middle East (the other being that of Ali Ufki, 1610–1675).

1723–25. The Ottomans occupied Georgia, Azerbaijan, and Shirvan following the chaos in Iran caused by the Afghan invasion. The Russians also advanced into the Caucasus, and to avert war with the Ottomans, **an Ottoman-Russian treaty** (June 24, 1724) partitioned Iran's northwestern provinces between the two powers.

1725. Beginning of **rule of the Azm family in Damascus** with the appointment of Isma'il Pasha al-Azm as governor of the province. Between 1725 and 1783, members of the family held power in Damascus for a **total of 47 years,** in addition to periodic appointments in the provinces of Sidon, Tripoli, and Aleppo. The Azms, whose origins are not known with certainty, belonged to a notable family from the region of Ma'arra, south of Aleppo.

1726. Beginning of **rule of the Jalilis in Mosul** with the appointment of Isma'il ibn Abd al-Jalil, member of a local notable family, as governor of the province. Between 1726 and 1834, members of the Jalili family held the office **a total of 78 years,** forming a dynasty of sorts in the area. Periodic attempts by the central government to replace them or reduce their power proved unsuccessful.

1727. Relaxation of the official ban on printing in Turkish, giving permission for the establishment of a **Turkish press** and the printing of books on subjects other than religion. **Ibrahim Muteferrika** (1674–1745), a Hungarian convert to Islam, directed the press, which published 17 books by the time of his death, when it was closed down. The press was reopened only in 1784.

1730. Death of **Ahmed Nedim** (b. 1681), a distinguished court poet whose exuberant verses reflected the passion for pleasure characteristic of the Tulip Period. His poems on love and the joys of living were spontaneous in spirit and free of the strict formal styles of classical poetry. No court poet after him matched his talent and originality.

1730–36. Ottoman loss of conquests in Iran. An Iranian offensive routed the Ottoman army near Tabriz and led the Ottomans to agree (Jan. 1732) to Iranian control of Azerbaijan and western Iran. Hostilities soon resumed, and the Iranians laid siege to Baghdad (1733), then captured Shirvan, Daghistan, Georgia, and Armenia. In the **peace treaty** ending the conflict (Sept. 1736), the Ottomans abandoned their conquests in Iran.

1730. The Patrona Halil revolt. Patrona Halil, an Albanian Janissary, stirred a public protest in Istanbul against the surrender of territory captured from Iran, but it soon mushroomed into a **large-scale revolt against the grand vezir and his associates. The sultan executed Damad Ibrahim and then abdicated** in favor of Mustafa II's son Mahmud (Oct. 1). Patrona Halil and his men went on a rampage, destroying the palaces of the wealthy and killing many before being executed by the authorities.

1730–54. SULTAN MAHMUD I. War with Iran and European powers occupied a good part of Mahmud's reign. Domestically, he took an active interest in reforming the army and suppressing banditry in Anatolia. He also **upgraded Istanbul's water supply system.** More than 60 fountains of public drinking water were built by him and others in the capital, and the example was followed in some provincial towns.

1731. Death of **Abd al-Ghani al-Nabulusi** (b. 1641), a prolific Damascene scholar and mystic whose creative mind was engaged in a wide range of subjects. His dozens of works (most of them still unpublished) include religious commentaries, poetry, a study of farming, and several descriptions of journeys he made to shrines in the region, including Mecca.

1732. Comte de Bonneval (1675–1747), a French military expert and convert to Islam, undertook the **modernization of the Ottoman bombardier corps.** He opened a military engineering school (1734) and created a trained unit of bombardiers. **Janissary opposition** to his reforms limited their effects, and after his death his unit was broken up and the school closed (1750).

1732. Death of **Levni,** the last great Ottoman painter. The 137 miniatures illustrating his *Surname (Book of Festivals)* reflected his acute sense of observation, use of soft colors, and interest in portraying women.

1736. **Concordat of the Maronite Church with the Vatican,** in which the Maronite Church accepted the pope's authority while having its hierarchy, liturgy, canon law, and customs recognized.

1736–39. War with Austria and Russia. A Russian offensive in the Crimea took Azov (July 1736), and the Habsburgs invaded southern Serbia (1737). The Ottomans pushed back the Austrians. By the **Treaty of Belgrade** (Sept. 18, 1739), **Russia retained Azov** on the condition of demilitarizing the area. The Austrians gave up **northern Serbia and Belgrade** as well as western Wallachia, thus surrendering many of their gains at Passarowitz (1718).

1743–46. War with Iran. Nadir Shah laid siege to **Mosul,** which held out heroically (1743). His offensive in **Kurdistan** was also beaten back, but he made advances in the **Caucasus.** The war dragged on inconclusively until an **agreement** was reached (Sept. 4, 1746) whereby the boundaries established in the Treaty of 1639 were restored.

1746. Zahir al-Umar gained control of Acre, which he fortified and turned into the capital of his sheikdom and the most important economic and political center in Palestine. Zahir was a powerful tax farmer from the Arab Zaydani clan who began building a power base in the Galilee in the 1730s. He successfully withstood expeditions against his previous stronghold of Tiberias by the governor of Damascus (in 1737, 1742, and 1743).

1748–56. Construction of the **Nur-u Osmaniye mosque in Istanbul,** the last great work of Ottoman religious architecture. It assimilated **European stylistic influences** into the classical Ottoman tradition.

1750. Construction of the Sultan Mahmud fountain in Cairo, which introduced **a new type of public fountain** *(sabil)* with a round shape and original decorative elements (probably copied from Istanbul). The design became a popular model for other fountains built in the following 50 years.

1754–57. SULTAN OSMAN III. The second son of Mustafa II was an inept man who left little mark on Ottoman affairs. His edicts restricting the public activities of women and enforcing the distinct clothing of non-Muslims won him no popularity with the public.

1755, Sept. An immense **fire in Istanbul,** followed by another in July 1756.

1757, Oct. A disastrous **attack by beduins on the annual Damascus pilgrimage caravan** to Mecca, in which thousands of pilgrims were killed or left to die in the desert. This was the worst of the 19 serious attacks on the caravan since 1700.

1757–74. SULTAN MUSTAFA III. The accession of Mehmed III's son Mustafa (Oct. 30) inaugurated some internal improvements directed by his able grand vezir, Ragib Pasha. But during the second part of his rule he brought to an end the **longest continuous period of peace in Ottoman history (1747–68)** with a disastrous war against Russia.

1757–63. Mehmed Ragib Pasha (1699–1763) served as grand vezir. A learned man and capable administrator, he succeeded in keeping the empire out of foreign entanglements. Like previous reformers, he worked against great odds to fight government corruption and reform state finances.

1759. A major earthquake in southern Syria and Palestine, causing massive damage.

1768. Death of **Yusuf al-Sim'ani** (Joseph Assemani), a Maronite Christian from Lebanon known for his learning in Syriac and Arabic manuscripts. He became librarian at the Vatican Library.

1768–74. War with Russia. Russian advances in Poland and designs on the Crimea prompted the Ottomans to declare war, for which their forces proved ill-prepared. The Russians occupied Moldavia and Wallachia (1769–70), incited a short-lived revolt in the Morea (1770), **destroyed the Ottoman fleet** in the port of Cheshme, near Chios (July 6, 1770), and took the Crimea (1771). After their army was routed in Bulgaria (1774), the Ottomans sued for peace. The **Treaty of Kuchuk Kaynarja** (July 21, 1774) gave Russia the territory between the Dnieper and the Bug as well as Azov, but returned Moldavia and Wallachia to the Ottomans and **recognized the Crimea as independent.** The Russians gained the right to build an Orthodox church in Istanbul and

protect the Orthodox in Istanbul, provisions that they subsequently used to **claim Russian protection over all Orthodox Christians in the empire.** During the war the Austrians had seized the northwestern part of Moldavia (the Bukovina), which the Ottomans ceded to them (May 7, 1775).

1768–73. Ali Bey al-Kabir established virtually independent rule in Egypt. He was a Mamluk of Circassian origin who was purchased in Cairo in 1743 and gradually rose in influence, winning the top office of *sheik al-balad* in 1760. In 1768 he deposed the Ottoman governor and assumed the post of acting governor. He **stopped the annual tribute to Istanbul** and in an unprecedented usurpation of the Ottoman sultan's privileges had his name struck on local coins in 1769 (alongside the sultan's emblem). In 1770 he gained control of the Hijaz and a year later temporarily occupied Syria, thereby **reconstituting the Mamluk state** that had disappeared in 1517. But he lost power in 1772, and died on May 8, 1773.

1771. Ali Bey of Egypt, in alliance with Zahir al-Umar of Galilee, overthrew Ottoman authority throughout Palestine and captured Damascus. But the Egyptian commander Muhammad Bey Abu al-Dhahab abruptly withdrew and returned with his forces to Egypt, while Zahir continued his revolt against the sultan.

1774–89. SULTAN ABDULHAMID I. Beginning his rule in the shadow of the humiliation by Russia, Mustafa III's brother was driven by a desire to rebuild the military. He was the first sultan to **import large numbers of foreign military advisers** to help modernize the army and navy. His period saw a marked **erosion of central authority** in the provinces and a growing assertiveness of local rulers all over the empire. With rare exceptions, the sultan tried manipulation and patronage rather than force to maintain his authority in the provinces.

1774. Baron François de Tott (1730–93), a Hungarian soldier who had entered the service of France, established a **new rapid-fire artillery corps** for the sultan.

1774. Rebuilding and modernization of the Ottoman navy begun by the grand admiral Gazi Hasan Pasha. French naval engineers and artisans directed the construction of new ships to replace the fleet destroyed at Cheshme (1770).

1775. End of the rule of Zahir al-Umar. He was removed from power in Acre by an Egyptian force acting on behalf of the Ottoman government. Soon after he was killed, and his territories reverted to the provinces of Damascus and Sidon. **Ahmad Pasha al-Jazzar** ("the Butcher"), a ruthless power figure of Bosnian origin, was appointed governor of Sidon to restore Ottoman authority there. He made **Acre the base of a powerful dominion** extending over Palestine and southern Syria.

1775. A revolt in Aleppo led by the Janissaries, who expelled the governor Ali Pasha from the city. This was the first in a string of such revolts during the next 30 years (1784, 1787, 1791, and 1804). Aleppo remained the only Arab province in which the governors were outsiders rotated annually by Istanbul, but after 1775 **central authority in the city declined** as the Janissaries and the *ashraf* (lineal descendants of the prophet Muhammad) steadily took control. By the early 1790s the two political factions dominated the city, manipulated food supplies, and taxed the population. The competition between them, sometimes violent, became the central feature of local politics.

1776, April. Occupation of **Basra** by Iran after a long siege. The city was evacuated in 1779 owing to internal instability in Iran.

1780–1802. Governorship of **Sulayman Pasha** ("the Great"), a member of the Mamluk caste of Baghdad. His lengthy tenure in office marked the zenith of the Mamluk regime of Baghdad.

1780. Death of **Zubeyde Fitnat Hanim,** the best-known Ottoman poetess of the 18th century. Born into an upper-class religious family, she took part in literary competitions with other women poets and composed verses in a natural and vivid style.

1783. Russia annexed the Crimea. The Ottomans were dismayed by this first loss of territory inhabited by Muslims but accepted the reality in an agreement with Russia (Jan. 1784).

1784. Reopening of the Turkish printing press that was closed down in the 1740s.

1786. Reassertion of Ottoman control over Egypt. A large naval expedition commanded by Gazi Hasan Pasha was sent to reestablish direct control over Egypt, where the leading Mamluk power figures, Ibrahim Bey and Murad Bey, **had become practically independent.** Between 1779 and 1785 their arrears in payments to Istanbul had risen to 103 million paras. The defiant Mamluks fled to Upper Egypt. Hasan Pasha placed loyal beys in control and departed in October 1787, but by July 1791 the duumvirate of Ibrahim and Murad was back in power and, two years later, again ceased the transfer of tribute to Istanbul.

1787–92. War with Russia and Austria. The Ottomans declared war on Russia (Aug. 1787) in the hope of recovering the Crimea and containing Russian expansion. The **Austrians** entered the war (Feb. 1788), but after taking land in Bosnia, Serbia, and Moldavia they agreed to a separate peace (signed at Sistova on Aug. 4, 1791) by which they surrendered their conquests in return for the right to protect the sultan's Christian subjects. The **Russians** routed the Ottoman army and took Moldavia and Wallachia. By the **Treaty of Jassy** (Jan. 9, 1792), the Ottomans acknowledged the Russian annexation of the Crimea and Georgia and accepted the Dniester as the new boundary between the two empires, while the Russians agreed to evacuate the principalities.

1788–1840. Rule of Bashir II of the Shihab family as emir of Mount Lebanon. He emerged as one of the dominant Middle Eastern leaders of the period.

1788. Ali Pasha of Janina began his rise to power **in central Albania.** In the following three decades he built an impressive autonomous base extending from northern Albania to the Gulf of Corinth, with a pretentious court and direct diplomatic relations with European powers. An Ottoman force eliminated him in 1822.

1789–1807. SULTAN SELIM III. The death of Abdulhamid brought to the throne his nephew Selim, who recognized the urgent need to reform the empire. Insubordination in the provinces had reached new heights, while on the battlefield the Ottoman military showed itself to be no match for the European armies. Once peace was reached with Russia in 1792, Selim **launched a reform program** focused largely on **reorganizing the military.** The Janissaries, ulama, and others with vested interest in the existing system sabotaged the reforms and finally undid them and their author. Despite his failure and the limited scope of his effort, Selim was **an important transitional figure** who opened the way for the vigorous modernization pursued by his successors. He was also a patron of music and an accomplished composer.

1791. Death of **Muhammad Khalil al-Muradi** (b. 1760), a Damascene scholar who compiled biographies of distinguished Muslims of the 18th century (Silk al-durar).

1792–1807. SELIM'S "NEW ORDER" AND OTHER REFORMS. Military reorganization was Selim's main focus. He tried, with limited success, to upgrade the Janissary troops and the cavalry, and he greatly improved the artillery corps and the navy. He also **established an entirely new corps,** the Nizam-i Jedid (New Order), which at the end of 1806 had 24,000 men armed with new weapons and trained and commanded by European officers. Selim's **administrative reforms** primarily involved the reorganization of the scribal service according to higher standards of honesty and efficiency. In the area of **diplomacy** Selim made genuine innovations by **stationing Ottoman ambassadors permanently in European capitals** for the first time. All these changes proved too piecemeal and narrow to address the underlying weaknesses in the Ottoman system.

1798–1801. THE FRENCH OCCUPATION OF EGYPT (p. 434). As part of a French global strategy in the war against Britain, a large expedition led by Bonaparte landed in Alexandria (July 1, 1798) and, after defeating the Mamluk army in the **Battle of the Pyramids** (July 21), occupied Cairo and proceeded to consolidate its control of the Nile Delta. **The adventure encountered several setbacks.** The British fleet destroyed the French ships off Abukir (Aug. 1), isolating the troops from France. **The sultan declared war on France** (Sept. 11) and signed a triple alliance with Russia and Britain (Jan. 1799). Napoleon's **attempt to take Syria failed** after Acre held out, and plague decimated the French troops, forcing them to retreat to Egypt (Feb.–May 1799). The French defeated an Ottoman force at Abukir (July 1799) and then at Heliopolis (March 20, 1800), but a joint Ottoman-British force finally obtained **French surrender and evacuation** (Sept. 1801).

The short-lived occupation left the **power of the Mamluks much weakened** and various groups in the Egyptian population exposed for the first time to European modes of warfare, administration, taxation, and scientific inquiry. In Middle Eastern historiography the episode is often taken as **the symbolic beginning of the modern era.**

1799. Death of **Galip Dede** (b. 1757), the last of the great traditional poets of the Ottoman Empire. A mystic who headed the Mevlevi lodge of

Galata, he displayed a religious intellectualism and a literary virtuosity that won him the patronage of Sultan Selim III. His masterpiece was a long allegorical poem, Husn ve ashk (Beauty and Love).

1799. Osman Pasvanoğlu (1758–1807) rose in Vidin as a powerful autonomous notable, spreading his **rule over much of northwestern Bulgaria** and into Serbia and Wallachia. He refused to pay taxes to Istanbul and was among the chief opponents of Selim III's reforms.

1799. Ibrahim Pasha Qattar Aghasi became the first native of Aleppo to win appointment to the governorship of the province in the 18th century. His son Muhammad succeeded him in 1804, but the attempt to create a dynastic line was aborted almost immediately when he was attacked and defeated by the rebellious Janissaries and ashraf.

1802, June 25. The Treaty of Amiens with France, ending the war over Egypt. It provided for peace and friendship between the two countries as well as mutual assistance in case of war. All prewar treaties and capitulations were renewed.

1803. Fall of Mecca to the Wahhabis, followed by the fall of **Medina in 1804.** The loss of the two Holy Cities of Islam and the suspension of the annual pilgrimage posed **a challenge to Ottoman authority** and to the sultan's role as guardian of the Holy Cities. An Egyptian expedition on behalf of the sultan recovered the two cities in 1812–13.

1804, April. Death of Ahmad Pasha al-Jazzar, the ruthless governor of Sidon. The news was greeted with open joy by the population.

1804. The Serbian uprising (p. 518). Misrule and excesses by the Janissary garrison in Belgrade sparked an insurrection led by a local chief, George Petrovich, or **Karageorge** (c. 1768–1817). Directed initially against the Janissaries, it developed into a **full-scale revolt against Ottoman rule.** With Russian aid the rebels established their own authority until they were **suppressed by the Ottomans in 1813.** Karageorge fled to Habsburg territory.

1805, June. The Janissaries in Aleppo won virtual domination of the city and its resources after defeating the forces of the governor and the ashraf (lineal descendants of the prophet Muhammad). An Ottoman force dislodged them in 1813.

1806–12. War with Russia. The Russian invasion of Moldavia and Wallachia in Nov. 1806, brought on by fears of growing French influence in the empire, precipitated a war that dragged on for six years. **The Russians made substantial territorial gains** in the Balkans and Caucasus, but the French invasion of Russia prompted them to settle with the Ottomans in the **Treaty of Bucharest** (May 28, 1812). They returned to Ottoman control the two principalities as well as their gains in the Caucasus and north of the Black Sea, but retained Bessarabia.

1807–9. War with Britain. The British went to war against the Ottomans in support of their Russian allies, but their **operations were limited** to a show of naval force off Istanbul (Feb. 1807) and an abortive attempt to reinstall the Mamluks in Egypt (March–Sept. 1807). In the **peace treaty of the Dardanelles** (Jan. 5, 1809), Britain had its capitulatory rights reaffirmed and became the first European power to acknowledge the **right of the Ottomans to close the straits to foreign warships** in time of peace (a principle that received general European recognition in the London convention of July 13, 1841).

1807, May 29. The fall of Selim III. A revolt in Istanbul led by Janissaries, ulama, and various conservatives long opposed to the sultan forced his abdication in favor of his cousin Mustafa.

1807–8. SULTAN MUSTAFA IV. As a puppet of the conservative power figures behind the reaction, Mustafa IV **decreed the end of Selim's reforms** and the restoration of the preexisting arrangements. The New Order troops were hunted down and killed. Some of Selim's supporters took refuge at Ruschuk in Bulgaria with the local governor, **Bayrakdar Mustafa Pasha,** who emerged as the **leader of the movement to restore Selim III.** In July 1808 Bayrakdar entered Istanbul with his army and crushed the groups in control. In the turmoil, **Selim III was assassinated** and Bayrakdar placed his cousin Mahmud on the throne (July 28, 1808). (To p. 525)

b. IRAN

(From p. 123)

1501–24. SHAH ISMA'IL, FOUNDER OF THE SAFAVID DYNASTY. In 1501 Isma'il occupied Tabriz and proclaimed himself shah. Within a decade he conquered the territories constituting present-day Iran as well as Iraq and parts of eastern Anatolia. His ascension to power culminated a long struggle by the **Safavid movement**, which had built a mass following in northwestern Iran and eastern Anatolia, especially among the Turkoman tribesmen. These followers of the Safavids, known as the **Qizilbash ("Redheads")** because of their distinctive red headgear, felt a devotion to Isma'il both as a temporal leader and as head of the Safavid religious order. Isma'il, who claimed descent from the founder of the movement, the Sufi leader Sheik Safi al-Din (1252–1334), **embraced Shi'ism**, although some of his beliefs—in his own divine qualities, messianic mission, and infallibility—reflected the **religious syncretisms** of the contemporary Safavid milieu.

Isma'il's advent to power signaled the **end of Sunni Islam in Iran**. He imposed Shi'ism as the state religion, forcing conversion upon the largely Sunni population of the country. Initially he had to import Shi'ite religious authorities from Lebanon, Iraq, and Bahrain, so few were their numbers in Iran. By the 18th century, the great majority of the population had become Shi'ites, and Shi'ite theologians dominated the religious establishment.

The Safavid dynasty founded by Isma'il held effective power in Iran until 1722, although nominal Safavid rulers remained on the scene as political pawns for many years after. The regime rested in good part on the **support of the Qizilbash**, who helped bring it to power. Tribal chiefs were granted **governorships** of provinces and high positions in the central government. The Qizilbash also controlled **military forces** that helped them maintain their influence. A second element in the ruling elite was the **Persian bureaucracy**, which was essential to the machinery of government. Although there were rivalries between the two elements, in the course of time they formed marital and political alliances that cut across group lines.

1501. Muhammad Baha' al-Dawla, an Iranian physician and scholar, published *The Quintessence of Experience*, a work based on his clinical medical experience, which contained the first known description of whooping cough as well as accounts of chicken pox and German measles. His manuscript also detailed the earliest description of syphilis in the East.

1504. Death of **Sayfi of Bukhara,** an artisan and poet who wrote more than a hundred odes, each dedicated to practitioners of different crafts. This form of poetry, called *shahr-ashub* ("city disturbing"), combined Sufi mystical terminology with details about specific crafts. The verses reveal technical, religious, and social aspects of the many **guilds** *(asnaf)* that flourished throughout Iran. Often these poems were written in a jargon understood only by guild members.

1505. Death of **Mulla Husayn Kashefi,** the author of *Rawzat al-shuhada'* *(The Garden of Martyrs),* the earliest text for the public recitation and remembrance of the martyrdom of the third Shi'ite imam Husayn (d. 680). The **commemoration of Husayn's death** during the Muslim month of Muharram became part of an annual public mourning ritual that reached its full dramatic potential in the later Safavid period in the form of the *ta'ziyeh,* or **passion play,** a distinctly Iranian Shi'ite form of popular religious remembrance.

1507. The Portuguese capture of the island of Hormuz in the Persian Gulf. It became a naval base and trade outpost. The shah, who had no navy, reluctantly accepted this European presence, which lasted until 1622, when the Portuguese were **evicted with British help.**

1507. The Safavids extended their control into the region of **Diyarbakr** in eastern Anatolia.

1508. The Safavids took **Baghdad and Iraq.**

1510. Capture of Khurasan. Shah Isma'il absorbed the large province into his state after defeating the Uzbeks and killing their leader, Muhammad Shaybani, in a battle near Merv. The **Uzbeks** remained a formidable adversary of the Safavids throughout the century.

1514, Aug. 23. Battle of Chaldiran, in which Shah Isma'il's army suffered a crushing defeat by the Ottomans, who acted in retaliation for Safavid support of Turkoman revolts in Anatolia. The **Ottoman victory** resulted from superior numbers as well as the use of field artillery and guns, not employed by the Safavid army on this occasion. The battle opened the way for the Ottoman conquest of Diyarbakr, Erzinjan, and other parts of eastern Anatolia as well as northern Iraq.

1522. Shah Isma'il brought the famous **Timurid painter Bihzad** from Herat to Tabriz and appointed him director of the royal library. Bihzad's successors formed a **brilliant artistic school** that produced some of the finest Persian manuscript illustrations.

1524–76. SHAH TAHMASP I. The eldest son of Isma'il ascended the throne at the age of ten, and for the first ten years of his reign, real power was held by a number of leaders of competing Qizilbash factions, whose feuding caused much political instability. In 1533 Tahmasp asserted his authority. One of his legacies was the **introduction of converted slaves into court and the military.** They were drawn from thousands of Georgian, Circassian, and Armenian prisoners captured in campaigns fought in the Caucasus in the 1540s and 1550s. **Female slaves** entered the royal harem, becoming mothers of princes and a force in court politics and dynastic quarrels. Some of the male slaves began to acquire positions of influence, reaching, under Shah Abbas, high offices that challenged the supremacy of the Qizilbash.

1524–37. War with the Uzbeks, who launched as many as five major invasions of Khurasan with the intent of retaking the area. The Safavids succeeded in repelling the invaders.

c. 1537. The exquisite miniatures illustrating the Houghton version of the **Iranian national epic** known as the *Shah-nama (Book of Kings)* were painted at the request of Shah Tahmasp. The work was presented by the Safavid ruler to the Ottoman sultan Selim II in 1568.

1545. Safavid **capture of Qandahar** from the Mughal Empire.

1548. The Safavid capital was moved to **Qazvin,** following the temporary capture of Tabriz by the Ottomans. Despite periodic wars between them, Iran and the Ottoman Empire maintained an **extensive trade,** especially in the highly prized **Iranian silk.** Until the early decades of the 18th century, large quantities of silk were shipped from Iran to commercial centers such as Aleppo and Bursa and from there distributed in the region and reexported to Marseilles, London, and Venice.

1576–77. SHAH ISMA'IL II. This son of Tahmasp was brought to power by a Qizilbash faction interested in a prince whose mother was Turkoman rather than Circassian or Georgian. His short reign was marked by brutality and a pro-Sunni policy. He was poisoned in Nov. 1577 with the connivance of his sister Pari Khan Khanum.

1578–87. SULTAN MUHAMMAD SHAH. The only surviving brother of Isma'il II, Sultan Muhammad (Muhammad Khudabanda before his accession) proved a **weak leader.** He was dominated initially by his wife Mahd-i Ulya, and after her assassination in 1579 the Qizilbash took control. There was much **factional feuding** in the country until a revolt by Qizilbash leaders finally removed him from power and installed his son Abbas as shah.

1578–90. War with the Ottomans, who took advantage of Iran's political turmoil to launch a major invasion of the country. The **Safavids lost extensive territories,** including most of Azerbaijan (with Tabriz) and Georgia.

1587. Death of **Muhtasham of Kashan,** a poet famed for his panegyrics of the 12 imams. His elegies in the service of the faith *(marasi)* were praised by Shah Tahmasp, who had once rebuked him for dabbling in secular verse. Many important **Safavid poets left Iran** for the more supportive and less strictly religious environment of the Mughal court of India. Not all poets wrote in Persian during the 16th century. Many like **Habib** (d. 1514), the poet laureate of Shah Isma'il, wrote in the Azeri Turkish dialect spoken by the Safavids and their Qizilbash entourage.

1588–1629. SHAH ABBAS I. The reign of Abbas marked the apogee of the Safavid state. Abbas drove the Ottomans and Uzbeks out of the vast territories they had conquered after 1576 and checked the Qizilbash factional strife that was threatening to fragment the country. He introduced **bold reforms** in the military, administrative, and fiscal structures that helped **centralize state authority** to a degree not achieved by his predecessors. One of his innovations, however, weakened the Safavid state in the long run: fear of revolts by his sons led him to abandon the traditional practice of employing the princes to govern provinces, leaving them instead in **confinement in the harem.** The new practice, followed also by his successors, resulted in ill-educated shahs of lower caliber. Shah Abbas also founded a carpet factory in Isfahan. Royal patronage and the influence of court designers assured that **Persian carpets** reached their zenith in elegance during the Safavid period.

1588. INTRODUCTION OF A SLAVE ARMY. Abbas began right away to build a new corps based on Georgian and Circassian **slaves** *(ghulam,* or *qullar).* They formed the core of a **standing army** intended to reduce the shah's dependence on the Qizilbash chiefs for levies of fighting men in times of need. To finance the new army, Abbas **converted large**

THE SAFAVID DYNASTY

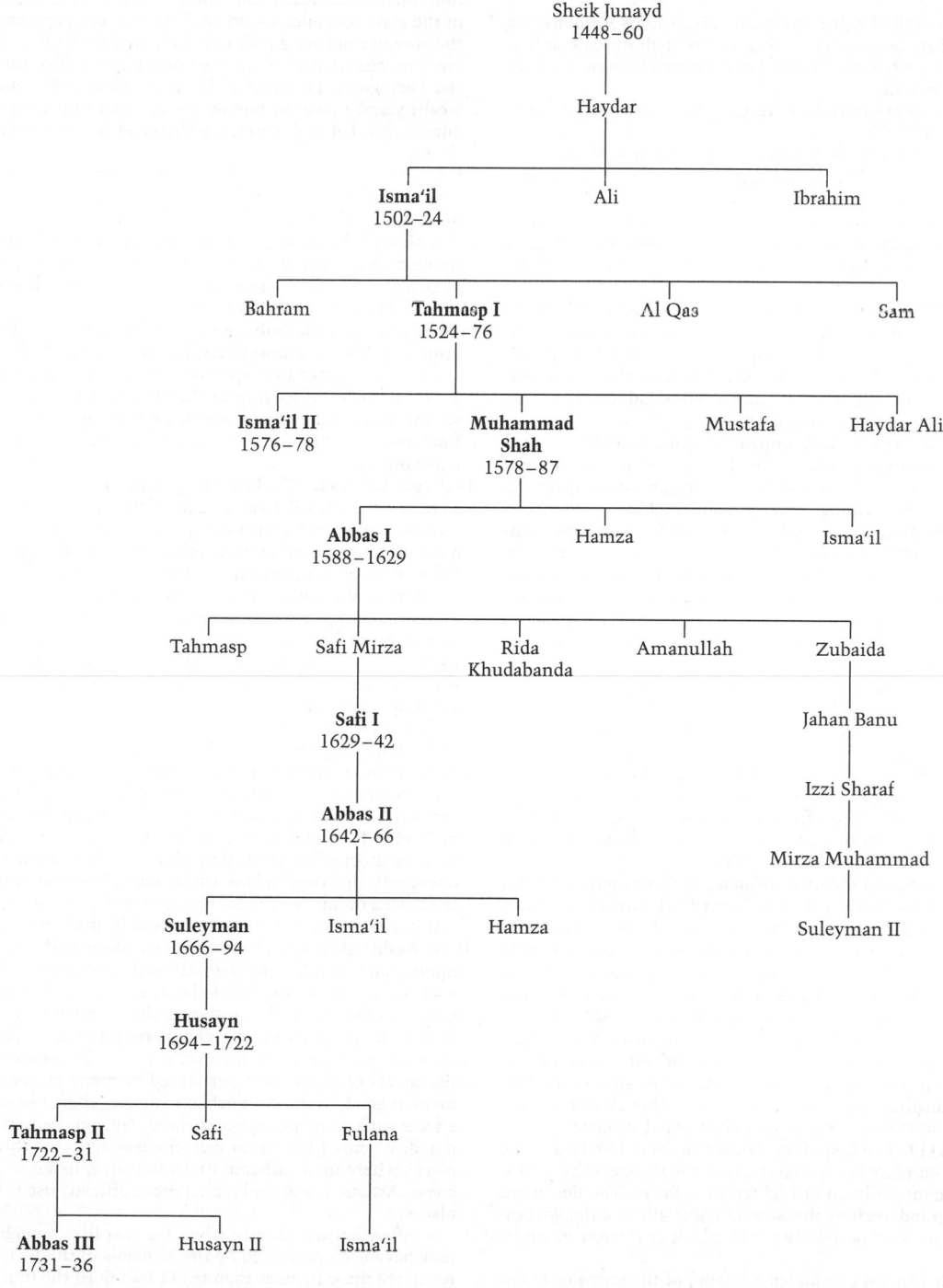

tracts of land traditionally granted to tribal chiefs as assignments (ma-malik) into crown lands (khassa) that he taxed directly. This strengthened his authority in the provinces at the expense of the Qizilbash, although the rapacious practices of the shah's tax collectors tended to undermine the prosperity of agriculture. Under Abbas, *ghulams* rose to high positions, such as provincial governors, which also weakened the influence of the Qizilbash.

1591. Loss of Qandahar to the Mughals. It was recovered by the Safavids in 1622.

1598. The Safavids defeated the Uzbeks and **recovered Herat** and territories in Khurasan, including **Mashhad,** lost several years earlier. The shah rebuilt the **shrine of the eighth Shi'ite imam** Ali al-Rida in Mashhad, which was damaged by the Uzbeks. The shrine became a major center for Shi'ite pilgrimage.

1598. Shah Abbas moved the Safavid capital to **Isfahan,** a city more centrally situated than Qazvin. Imperial town planning made it a **magnificent urban center,** laid out with a great public square, the Maydan, and a host of new buildings, including a royal mosque. The beauty of the city prompted the saying *Isfahan nisf-i jahan*, or "Isfahan is half the world." The new capital also served as a **major commercial center.** The authorities moved to it thousands of Armenian merchant families from the city of Julfa.

1598. Arrival in Iran of the English merchant adventurers **Anthony and Robert Sherley.** Anthony returned to England as Shah Abbas's ambassador the following year, while his brother remained for some years in the shah's service in Iran.

1603–7. Safavid offensive against the Ottomans recovered the territories lost in the war of 1578–90.

1604. The Mughal emperor Akbar's envoy Amir Masum al-Bhakkari arrived in Iran to offer Shah Abbas gifts and assurances of friendship after a period of border disputes over Afghanistan.

1617. Merchants of the English East India Company established trading houses in Shiraz and Isfahan. After the fall of the Portuguese base at Hormuz in 1622, **Bandar Abbas** became the center of the East India Company's trade.

1621. Death of **Sheik Baha'i,** the most powerful Shi'ite cleric under Shah Abbas. His written works included treatises on mathematics, medicine, logic, astronomy, poetry, and jurisprudence. He also helped construct the great mosque and other architectural sites in the new capital of Isfahan. After his time the study of mathematics and science as part of the Shi'ite religious curriculum ended.

Nov. 17. The Dutch East India Company (founded in 1602) received **trade capitulations** from Shah Abbas. The Dutch soon gained supremacy in the European trade with Iran, outdistancing British competitors. They established a spice trading center at **Bandar Abbas.**

1623. Death of **Mulla Muhammad Amin Astarabadi,** founder of the **Akhbari school of Shi'ism.** His position emphasized the primacy of *akhbar*, the words and deeds of the prophet Muhammad and the 12 imams, over the interpretation of individual *mujtahids*, the most eminent authorities of Shi'ite law and theology. He argued that no independent judgments could be made by religious authorities in the absence of the hidden twelfth imam.

1623–24. A **Safavid offensive in Iraq** established control over Kurdish territories, Baghdad and the Shi'ite Holy Cities of Karbala and Najaf.

1628. First French religious mission established in Iran. The Capuchins were quickly followed by the Jesuits, Carmelites, and Dominicans. The missions' activities focused on the Christians of Iran.

c. 1629. Completion of *The History of Shah Abbas the Great*, by Iskandar Beg Munshi (d. 1632). The chronicle records the reigns of the Safavid rulers Isma'il, Tahmasp I, and Abbas I and is considered one of the greatest works of Islamic historiography.

1629. Death of **Hasan Sharaf al-Din of Isfahan,** the court physician and close companion of Shah Abbas I. Safavid **medical practice** depended on medieval precedent for the treatment of most illnesses. The standard reference work remained the *Canon* of Ibn Sina (d. 1037), but **new clinical works** *(majarrabat)* were written during the Safavid period. In the 17th century a unique work called *The Treasury of Surgery* was written by the army surgeon known as **Hakim Muhammad** and dedicated to Shah Safi I. It included a detailed list of the instruments available to surgeons, including a special device for the removal of bullets; outlined various forms of anesthesia; and advocated surgery for cancerous tumors. **Hospitals** existed in Isfahan and other cities but were unpopular, since most people preferred to be treated at home.

1629–42. SHAH SAFI I. The first of the Safavid shahs to be raised in the harem, Shah Safi murdered potential rivals to the throne on his accession as well as many influential high court officers. The **dominant influence of the grand vezir** at the Safavid court allowed the government to be run smoothly despite the shah's lack of interest in affairs of state.

1630. Abd al-Fattah Fumani completed a history of the province of Gilan, where most of the production of silk cocoons was concentrated. He recounted political events from 1517 to 1629 in the treatise, with many details about local resistance to the silk monopoly imposed by Shah Abbas I. **Silk** was the most lucrative export of the Safavid Empire. The **royal monopoly** was later revoked by Shah Safi I when growers in Rasht revolted against the low prices paid for the commodity.

1631. Death of **Mir Damad,** founder of the **School of Isfahan,** the principal center of Shi'ite scholarship, which flourished under the patronage of Shah Abbas I. Mir Damad was both a philosopher and a theologian whose interest in the works of Aristotle, Ibn Sina (Avicenna; d.

1037), and Suhrawardi (d. 1191) restated their importance in Shi'ite theosophy.

1632. Execution of **Imam Quli Khan** by Shah Safi I. Of Georgian extraction, Imam Quli Khan had followed his father in rising to high office in the state bureaucracy. In 1613, he had been appointed governor of the province of Fars, a position that gave him great authority in southern Iran. His dealings with the English had helped rid the Safavids of the Portuguese presence at Hormuz. Shah Safi's execution of this wealthy and powerful bureaucrat allowed him to absorb vast lands once controlled by Imam Quli Khan and strengthened his central authority.

1634. The appointment of **Mirza Taqi,** known as Saru Taqi, as grand vezir, or prime minister. Until his murder in 1645 he remained the most powerful figure in the Safavid government.

1639, May 17. Peace treaty with the Ottomans, which established the Ottoman-Safavid frontier and put an end to more than a hundred years of sporadic conflict. The shah accepted the **final loss of Baghdad,** recaptured by the Ottomans in 1638.

1640. Death of **Mulla Sadra,** a pupil of Mir Damad and one of the most important Shi'ite philosophers. In his work *The Four Journeys*, he described the first of four spiritual voyages as a process in which the seeker detaches himself from the physical world. After achieving the second and third goals of sainthood and union with the divine, the final journey would be the return of the enlightened one to earth, to guide others.

1642–66. ABBAS II. The last fully competent period of rule by a Safavid shah. Shah Abbas II took an active role in government matters. He increased the central authority of the state by **increasing crown lands** and often intervened in provincial affairs on the side of the peasants, but with peace on the frontiers **the army declined in size and quality.** He clung to the notion that the Safavid ruler was sacred and infallible, and disputed openly with members of the Shi'ite religious establishment who had begun to articulate the idea that in the absence of the hidden twelfth imam, true temporal authority rightly belonged to the mujtahid, who merited emulation by the faithful.

1648. Capture of the Afghan city of Qandahar from the Mughals, who had seized it some ten years earlier. From this time, the city remained in the Iranian sphere.

c. 1662. Death of **Baba'i ben Lutf,** a Jewish poet and historian who wrote the *Kitab-i anusi (The Book of a Forced Convert)*. In 5,300 verses written in the Persian language, using Hebrew script, he detailed the **status of Iranian Jews** and, in particular, their persecution and forced conversion under Shah Abbas II in 1656–62. He and other Jews of Kashan outwardly practiced Islam while secretly maintaining their Jewish faith. This unique work also provides details about the socioeconomic status and organizations of the Jews of Isfahan and Kashan.

1664. Kashif al-Din, a pharmacologist, dedicated a treatise on coffee *(qahva)* and tea *(chay)* to Shah Abbas II. During the 17th century many poems and essays were devoted to the merits and morality of **drinking coffee.** Coffee reached Iran during the 16th century. It was probably brought by pilgrims and merchants returning from Arabia, where the beverage had been consumed since the 15th century. Experiments on the effects of coffee were performed by many physicians in Iran who found it good for the stomach and for the relief of headaches. Harmful effects such as palpitations, melancholy, and hemorrhoids were also noted. Within a few years **coffeehouses** appeared throughout Iran as places where men gathered to drink coffee, listen to music, and play chess. Artists, poets, and government officials used them as meeting places.

It is not known exactly when **tea** was first brought to Iran, but it may have been promoted by the Mongols in the 13th century. Coffee remained more popular than tea in Iran until the first half of the 19th century.

1666–94. SHAH SULEYMAN (SAFI II). Renamed because the first year and a half of his reign was so disastrous, Shah Suleyman was neither an able nor a vigorous ruler. Shortly after his accession, food prices soared and famine and disease spread throughout the country. Although pressing problems faced the Safavid shah, he increasingly **retreated into the harem** and set up a separate council of eunuchs. The shah's indifference left his grand vezir to cope with affairs of state. Shah Suleyman did, however, support the work of the three greatest painters in late-17th-century Iran.

c. 1682. The English East India Company established trade with Mashhad and Kirman for the purchase of **Iranian imitations of Chinese blue and white porcelain.** Shah Abbas I had encouraged the initial production of this ware.

1694. Muhammad Baqir Majlisi (d. 1699), the most influential member of the Shi'ite religious establishment, was appointed to the new office of *mulla bashi* (head mulla). Majlisi wrote the Shi'ite compendium *Bihar al-anwar (The Seas of Light)*, an encyclopedic work dedicated to the preservation of the prophet Muhammad's words and deeds. He devoted himself to the propagation of a legalistic form of Shi'ism and to the **eradication of Sufism and Sunni Islam** in Iran. Under his guidance specifically Shi'ite popular rituals, such as mourning for the martyred third Shi'ite imam Husayn (d. 680), were encouraged, as were **pilgrimages** to the tombs of holy Shi'ite personages. Majlisi's policies also included the **persecution of non-Muslims** in Iran, including Zoroastrians, Jews, and Christians. Unchecked by the Safavid regime, Majlisi and the **Shi'ite clergy emerged with increased strength** and independence from the ruling government in the 17th and 18th centuries.

1694–1722. SHAH SULTAN HUSAYN. The reign of Shah Sultan Husayn effectively ended Safavid rule in Iran. Indifferent to affairs of state, Shah Sultan Husayn was the most pious of the Safavids and came under the influence of the Shi'ite religious establishment. At their insistence, he issued decrees forbidding the consumption of alcohol and banning Sufism in Isfahan.

1708, Sept. 7. Treaty with France, granting trading privileges to French merchants as well as protection to the French religious missions in Iran. Trade between the two countries, which had been very limited, did not flourish.

1709. Mir Vays, leader of the Ghilzay Afghans, **seized Qandahar.** He ruled the area until 1715, followed by his son Mahmud, who built a powerful base from which he invaded Iran and overthrew the Safavids in 1722.

1722. THE AFGHAN INVASION. An Afghan army led by **Mahmud,** a leader of the Ghilzay Afghans, defeated the Safavid army at Gulnabad near Isfahan. In Oct. 1722 **Isfahan fell** after a siege of six months. Sultan Husayn surrendered and abdicated in favor of Mahmud, declaring him his successor as shah of Iran. **Safavid rule in Iran collapsed,** but the Afghans succeeded in capturing only part of the country (central and southern Iran, the province of Sistan, and western Khurasan), and their takeover lasted only until 1730.

1722–23. Russian and Ottoman incursions. Taking advantage of the overthrow of the Safavids, the **Russians** seized territories around the Caspian Sea while the **Ottomans** captured parts of western Iran as far as Hamadan. In June 1724 the two powers agreed on a peaceful partitioning of Iran's northwestern provinces.

1726. Completion of *Tadhkirat al-Muluk,* a manual of Safavid administration that detailed the **power of the vezir** as chief minister and the influence of the harem over rulers. The work also described the more than 50 **royal guilds** that produced articles for the rulers, such as clothing, books for the royal library, and weaponry for the army. Expensive silk textiles and carpets for export to Europe and India were also produced for the shah, who received the profits from this trade.

1726–36. RECONQUEST OF IRAN BY NADIR KHAN. An able general from the Turkoman tribe of Afshar, **Nadir Khan** (Nadir Quli) assembled an army in northern Iran and began the reconsolidation of the country under his control. He became the **de facto ruler of Iran,** although he acknowledged Tahmasp II, the son of Sultan Husayn, as Safavid shah until 1732, then Tahmasp's infant son Abbas III until 1736, at which time he declared himself shah. Nadir expelled the Afghans by 1730; reconquered the northwestern provinces of Iran from the Ottomans in 1730; and had the lands occupied by the Russians restored in 1735.

1736–47. NADIR SHAH. After years of building his power under the nominal rule of puppet Safavid princes, Nadir proclaimed himself shah. He **transferred the capital to Mashhad** in eastern Iran and continued his spectacular career of **military conquest** beyond Iran's frontiers, although his extensive empire disintegrated after his assassination in 1747. To finance his numerous campaigns he made **enormous tax demands** that added to the economic hardships of the population.

Nadir made an unsuccessful **attempt to return Iran to the Sunni fold** by proposing the integration of Shi'ism into Sunnism as the fifth of the already extant four Sunni schools of law (to be called the Ja'fari school). The scheme, which may have been political in purpose, failed to win support.

1736. Capture of **Herat** by Nadir Shah.

1736–44. Iranian occupation of **Oman.**

1738. Nadir Shah occupied **Qandahar, Ghazna, Kabul, and Peshawar.**

1739. Nadir Shah **invaded India** and sacked the Mughal capital of Delhi.

1740. Nadir Shah attacked the Uzbeks, **invaded Bukhara and Khiva,** and annexed the lands up to the Oxus River.

1750–96. SHAHRUKH SHAH. After Nadir Shah's assassination in 1747, his family proved unable to maintain the **Afshar dynasty** as rulers of Iran. One of them, the blind Shahrukh, continued to hold **Mashhad and the province of Khurasan,** ruling under the suzerainty of the Afghan Durrani dynasty that occupied eastern Iran. Most of the rest of the country fell to Karim Khan Zand.

1751–79. KARIM KHAN ZAND. A soldier in Nadir Shah's army and a member of the Persian Zand tribe, Karim Khan established himself as **ruler in western Iran,** making **Shiraz** his capital. He took the title of *wakil* (deputy or representative) rather than shah and reversed Nadir Shah's anti-Shi'ite policy. **His dynasty proved short-lived:** after his death in 1779 Zand princes continued to rule, but only until 1794. Conditions became increasingly turbulent, and the **Qajar leader Agha Khan** steadily took control of the country.

1763, July 2. Agreement with the English East India Company, allowing its agents to establish a commercial base in the **port of Bushire,** after the company's trading outpost in Bandar Abbas was destroyed by the French (1759). Bushire served as a headquarters of British commercial and political activity in the Persian Gulf region into the 20th century.

1792. Death of **Vahid Bihbahani,** the religious scholar responsible for the final Usuli victory over the Akhbari position in Shi'ism. Bihbahani's treatises defined the **Usuli Shi'ite system** of jurisprudence and established the authority of mujtahids, as supreme religious authorities, to issue opinions in all matters of faith and law. It became obligatory for all Shi'ite believers to obey these men and the precedents they set. This approach **established the structure of religious authority in Iran** current in the 19th and 20th centuries.

1794. Agha Muhammad Khan, the Qajar leader, had **the last Zand ruler,** Lutf Ali Khan, put to death. In 1796 he dealt similarly with **Shahrukh,** the Afshar ruler of Khurasan.

1796. Agha Muhammad Khan crowned himself shah, establishing the rule of the **Qajar dynasty.**
(To p. 534)

c. AFGHANISTAN

(From p. 137)

In the 16th and 17th centuries, the Mughal Empire of India and the Safavid Empire of Iran held between them the area that would emerge in the 18th century as Afghanistan. The **province of Herat** remained with Iran, while **Kabul** was administered by the Mughals. The contested **province of Qandahar** moved between the two empires during this period but by 1700 became part of the Iranian sphere. Unlike Shi'ite Iran, the populace of Afghanistan remained Sunni Muslim.

c. 1700. The Afghan tribes of Ghilzay situated in Qandahar became essentially independent of Safavid rule, as did their enemies, **the Abdali tribe located in Herat.**

1709–22. Consolidation of Ghilzay control of Qandahar. Mir Vays, leader of the Ghilzay Afghans, fell out with the Safavids and defeated their attempts to assert control over Qandahar, which he held until his death in 1715. His son Mahmud, who succeeded him, consolidated his command of the area.

1722. THE AFGHAN INVASION OF IRAN. Led by Mahmud, **the Ghilzays defeated the Safavid army** and entered Isfahan after a six-month siege (Oct. 1722). The Safavid shah Sultan Husayn abdicated after declaring the Afghan victor Mahmud his successor. **The Ghilzay Afghan dynasty ruled much of Iran and Afghanistan** under Mahmud (1722–25) and his successor Ashraf (1725–30). But **Nadir Shah,** the Safavid general, mounted a campaign that **expelled the Afghans from Iran** and made him master of the country.

1737–38. OCCUPATION OF AFGHANISTAN BY NADIR SHAH. The ruler of Iran captured Herat, Qandahar, Ghazna, and Kabul. **The power of the Ghilzay was broken** in this campaign. Nadir favored the Abdalis and enlisted large numbers in his army for his invasion of India in 1739. His army comprised largely Sunni Afghan troops, since his own Sunni beliefs had alienated his Shi'ite Iranian soldiers. **His reign consolidated all of Afghanistan,** a situation that ended with his death in 1747.

1747–73. AHMAD SHAH DURRANI, FOUNDER OF THE SADOZAY DYNASTY. Following the death of Nadir Shah, Ahmad Shah, the Afghan commander of his bodyguard and a member of the Abdali tribe, proclaimed himself the ruler in Qandahar. He adopted the title *Durr-i Duran* ("Pearl of Pearls"), and after that the Abdalis were known as **the Durranis.** He invaded India several times and extended Afghan control from the eastern borders of Iran to Lahore, Kashmir, and Delhi.

1773–93. TIMUR SHAH. The son of Ahmad Shah inherited an extensive empire. He faced many revolts in his Indian possessions as well as internal difficulties in controlling the Durranis. In 1776 he **moved the capital from Qandahar to Kabul.**

1793–1800. ZAMAN SHAH. The fifth son of Timur ruled the Durrani Empire with the help of the chief of the Afghan tribe of Barakzay. His attempt to invade India alarmed the British, who induced the Iranian Qajar ruler Fath Ali Shah to support Zaman Shah's brother Mahmud in his struggle for power. With British help Mahmud advanced on Kabul, captured and blinded his brother, and assumed power.

(To p. 537)

d. ARABIA

(From p. 116)

The Arabian peninsula, the birthplace of Muhammad and Islam, became of marginal importance in Middle Eastern history not long after the Arabs began their conquests in the 7th century. Various Middle Eastern states extended their formal authority to the coastal region of the Hijaz, site of Mecca and Medina, and intermittently to Yemen, but seldom to the interior of the peninsula. The Ottomans established a hold in Yemen and eastern Arabia in the 16th century, but by the 18th century their authority was confined to **the Hijaz, where the Hashemite emirs enjoyed autonomy** while acknowledging Ottoman suzerainty. Throughout the peninsula powerful family and tribal elites ruled over **essentially sovereign emirates.** Several of the dynastic regimes established in the 18th century—in Saudi Arabia, Kuwait, Oman, and Bahrain—have survived to this day.

1745. BIRTH OF THE FIRST SAUDI-WAHHABI STATE. Muhammad ibn Sa'ud (d. 1765), chief of a tribal emirate based in Dar'iyya in the central Arabian region of Najd, forged an alliance with **MUHAMMAD IBN ABD AL-WAHHAB** (1703–92), a theologian preaching a message of **puritanical reform of Islam.** Ibn Abd al-Wahhab criticized the laxities of Muslim observance. He sought to do away with all misguided innovations in Islam, such as the veneration of saints and Sufi rituals, and to return the faith to its fundamental scriptural principles. In the next 60 years Ibn Sa'ud and his successors **extended their domination and the Wahhabi ideas over most of Arabia.** The first Saudi state was finally destroyed in 1818.

1748–75. Abbas al-Mahdi ruled as imam of Yemen.

1749. Ahmad ibn Sa'id became ruler of Oman, beginning the rule of the **BU SA'ID DYNASTY,** which remains in power today.

1752. Sabah ibn Jabir of the Banu Utub Arabs became ruler of Kuwait, beginning the rule of the **SABAH DYNASTY,** which still holds power today.

1762–1812. Abdallah ibn Sabah ruled as sheik of Kuwait.

1765–1803. Abd al-Aziz ruled as Saudi emir after the death of his father Muhammad ibn Sa'ud, who had unified most of Najd under his rule. He continued the **expansion of Saudi control** in the peninsula.

1773. The Wahhabis annexed Riyadh.

1775–1809. Ali al-Mansur ruled as imam of Yemen.

1782. Ahmad ibn Khalifa of the Banu Utub Arabs became the ruler of Bahrain, establishing the rule of the **AL-KHALIFA DYNASTY,** which still holds power today.

1783. Death of Ahmad, ruler of Oman; he was succeeded by his son Sa'id.

1787. The Wahhabis took Hail and gained control of the region of **Jabal Shammar** in central Arabia.

1793. Sultan ibn Ahmad, by a compact with his brother the imam of Oman, became the recognized ruler of Muscat (until 1804).

1795. The Wahhabis conquered the region of Hasa on the Persian Gulf, completing their control of central and eastern Arabia. For the next 15 years they directed their **raids and expansion toward the Hijaz, Iraq, Syria,** and the principalities of the Persian Gulf.

1796–1825. Salman ibn Ahmad ruled as sheik of Kuwait.

1798. The ruler of Muscat leased from Iran the port of Bandar Abbas and the islands of Qishm and Hormuz for an annual payment of 6,000 tomans.

1799–1800. Wahhabi raids into Iraq.   *(To p. 539)*

3. NORTH AFRICA, 1504–1799

(From p. 131)

a. MOROCCO

1505–24. MUHAMMAD AL-BURTUGHALI. The sultan of the Banu Wattas (Wattasids) **reigned at Fez** but retained no authority over the rest of the country. The remainder of Morocco was ruled by local tribal authorities and Sufi orders.

1505. Portuguese occupation of Tangier and Agadir. A series of Portuguese garrison forts on the Atlantic coast called presidios was established during this period, while in the Mediterranean, Spanish forces threatened the Moroccan littoral. These **Christian invasions** prompted a renewed religious and martial vigor among the Muslim inhabitants of Morocco. Local tribesmen who claimed descent from the prophet Muhammad combined with Sufi leaders to eject both Europeans and the reigning Wattasid dynasty during the 16th century.

1508. Death of **Ahmad al-Wansharisi** of Fez, one of the best-known jurists in North Africa. His multivolume work *al-Mi'yar* compiled a large corpus of his *fatawa* (legal opinions), which shed light on social conditions as well as legal thought.

1509–17. MUHAMMAD AL-QA'IM, FOUNDER OF THE SA'DI DYNASTY. Originally from Sus, the **Sa'di family** took a strong position in support of jihad (holy war) against the Portuguese, a position that put them in immediate **opposition to the Wattasid policy** of appeasement and collaboration. The Sa'dis claimed descent from Muhammad and were called **sharifs.** The founder of their dynasty identified with

the Sufi **al-Jazuli** (d. 1465), whose order had militantly opposed the European presence in Morocco. He began to build a territorial base in southern Morocco, which his sons **Ahmad al-A'raj** and **Muhammad al-Sheik** expanded after his death. By 1530 they held between them the **southern half of Morocco.**

1513. Death of **Ibn Abi Abdallah Ghazi,** a theologian and jurist from Meknes. He served as the official preacher of Meknes and wrote a three-volume history of the city.

1526. Hasan ibn Muhammad al-Wazzani, known in the West as **Leo Africanus,** translated from the Arabic his description of Africa, which furnished the Christian world with most of its geographical knowledge about North and West Africa. Born in Granada before its capture by the Spanish, al-Wazzani relocated to Fez. He was captured by European privateers off the North African coast and **converted to Christianity.** His learning and travel experience brought him to the attention of the pope, who became his patron.

1536. The Wattasids of Fez, alarmed at the Sa'di control of southern Morocco, declared war. In a truce negotiated by the religious leaders, they accepted **the autonomy of Sa'di Marrakesh.**

1541. Muhammad al-Sheik, Sa'di ruler of southern Morocco, captured the Portuguese fortress of **Santa Cruz (Agadir).** The victory strengthened Muhammad's political position over his brother Ahmad al-A'raj, the heir-designate of the Sa'di dynasty.

1545–57. MUHAMMAD AL-SHEIK (AL-MAHDI). The Sa'di ruler was proclaimed sultan in Marrakesh in 1545. In Jan. 1549 he **occupied Fez,** ejected the Wattasids, and became sultan of Morocco. The Sa'dis defended their territory from both Christian and Muslim incursions, most notably by the Portuguese and by the Ottomans based in Algeria. Under them Morocco remained the only North African state to evade Ottoman occupation.

c. 1550. The Portuguese evacuated their remaining forts on the Moroccan coast.

1553–54. The Wattasids, with Ottoman support, **captured the city of Fez.** The Ottomans supported the Wattasid claimant Bu Hassun in the hope of gaining control over the city of Fez, but the Sa'di ruler Muhammad al-Sheik retook it in Sept. 1554.

1557–74. ABDALLAH AL-GHALIB. The assassination of his predecessor, Muhammad al-Sheik, plunged the regime into a precarious position. Al-Ghalib successfully courted al-Samlali, the leader of the Jazuli order, in order to win his support for the dynasty. The Sufi leader appealed to all Moroccans, whether Arab or Berber, to accept Sa'di rule. The ruler allowed the Sufi leaders almost complete authority within their *zawiyas*, or lodges. In return, the Sa'di ruler was elevated to a Sufi spiritual authority within the Jazuliyya order second only to its leader.

c. 1560. The Dila (Dila'iyya), an important Sufi order, was founded in the Middle Atlas Mountains. The order was founded by a *marabout* (the name given in North Africa to a Muslim saint) who had the power to grant *baraka* (divine blessing) and perform *karamat* (miracles). **Maraboutism** played an active part in social and religious life throughout Morocco, where the reigning sultan would court the support of these holy men and their followers. Nearly every city in Morocco had a patron *marabout* whose tomb became a place of popular pilgrimage and veneration. The Dila'iyya rose to prominence during the decline of the Sa'di dynasty in the 17th century. Mawlay Rashid defeated them in 1668 and destroyed their lodge. The order was later revived but took no further part in political affairs.

1576–78. ABD AL-MALIK. In an effort to win Ottoman support and oust his nephew Muhammad al-Mutawakkil (r. 1574–76), Abd al-Malik took part in the final Ottoman reconquest of Tunis in 1574. The Ottoman army intervened to put him on the Sa'di throne, in return for which he agreed to recognize the Ottoman sultan as the caliph. However, Abd al-Malik would not comply with the Ottoman suggestion that Morocco participate in holy war activities against Christian states in the Mediterranean. A shrewd negotiator in foreign affairs, Abd al-Malik also understood the power of propaganda. He commissioned a Christian missionary to write a book in Spanish praising his virtues, for which he duly obtained the Inquisitor's license for publication in Spain.

1578, Aug. 4. Battle of the Three Kings (Alcazar). King Sebastian of Portugal allied himself with the ousted al-Mutawakkil against the Sa'di ruler Abd al-Malik. The invading army was routed at Wadi al-Makhazin but all three leaders were killed. In the Islamic world, the conflict became renowned as the battle that **saved Morocco's independence.**

1578–1603. AHMAD AL-MANSUR (AL-DHAHABI). The caliph determined Sa'di foreign policy to ensure that Morocco would be politically dependent on neither the Ottomans nor the Christians. Al-Mansur established **trade relations with the English,** who exchanged cloth for Moroccan sugar, and built Morocco's first professional standing army.

1585. The British Barbary Company received a monopoly on trade with Morocco, which expired 12 years later.

1591. Ahmad al-Mansur undertook a massive **military campaign against the Songhay Empire,** whose territory encompassed present-day Mali and Nigeria. The expedition, unanimously opposed by the ulama, opened up **sources of gold and slaves.**

1603–64. DISINTEGRATION OF MOROCCAN POLITICAL UNITY. Following the death of al-Mansur, the Sa'di dynasty's authority declined. His sons' struggle for power resulted in the creation of a **Sa'di dynasty in Fez** (1610–41) and a **rival one in Marrakesh** (which lasted until 1659). Autonomous authorities emerged in various parts of the country, most prominent among them the **Dila'iyya Sufi order,** which captured Meknes and Fez. The **Alawis,** a family of *sharifs* (lineal descendants of Muhammad), established a power base in Tafilelt, from

which they expanded to gain control of the country and reunify it beginning in the 1660s.

1608. A community of Moriscos (Muslims expelled from Spain) who originally had been highwaymen at Hornacho near Merida resettled in Rabat. They founded an **autonomous city-state devoted to piracy.** The last wave of Morisco expulsions from Spain between 1609 and 1614 resulted in settlements in Tetuan and Tangier. In Fez, Moriscos contributed to craft guilds involved in the leather, silk, and ceramic trades.

1613. Death of **Abu al-Abbas Mahalli,** a prominent *marabout*. After a pilgrimage to Mecca, he declared himself the *mahdi* (rightly guided one) who had come to restore orthodox Islam to Morocco. He formed an army supported by the Ottoman ruler of Algiers, defeated the Sa'di Sultan Zaydan (r. 1603–18), and **occupied Marrakesh.** He was killed in 1613 by rival *marabouts*.

1621. Death of **Abd al-Aziz al-Fishtali,** the secretary of state for correspondence of the Sa'dis, poet laureate and historiographer to the ruler Ahmad al-Mansur.

1662. Britain inherited from Portugal part of the Moroccan port of Tangier.

1664–72. MAWLAY AL-RASHID, FOUNDER OF THE ALAWI DYNASTY. He began the reunification of Morocco and the rule of a family that remains in power to this day. In 1666 he took **Fez as his capital.**

1672–1727. MAWLAY ISMA'IL. A powerful ruler, he succeeded in reunifying Morocco with the help of a **professional army** drawn largely from black slaves taken from the Sudan. Mawlay Isma'il came close to asserting central authority throughout almost all of Morocco. In order to do this he also destroyed the power of the Sufi brotherhoods. **Piracy** provided the state with major sources of income in the form of a piracy tax levied on goods and captives. The port of Salé formed the privateering center of Morocco. **Meknes became a new capital** built largely by Christian slave labor. Once a provincial town, it was improved and restructured with new mosques and a palace with a garden city reserved for the use of high government officials.

1682, Jan. 29. Treaty of peace and commerce with France. The agreement was not effectively executed because of continued piratical warfare. Mawlay Isma'il made **piracy a state monopoly** and Moroccan corsairs harried shipping in the Atlantic and the entrance to the Mediterranean. French pirates turned over their Muslim captives to their government for impressment as galley slaves in the French navy. **French-Moroccan relations deteriorated** steadily and were finally broken in 1718, not to be resumed until 1767.

1684. Mawlay Isma'il expelled the British from Tangier.

1691. Death of **Hasan al-Yusi** (b. 1631), one of the most learned religious scholars of 17th-century Morocco. He addressed an epistle to Mawlay Isma'il denouncing the repression of the population.

1694. Death of **Muhammad al-Arbi,** a historian and genealogist who wrote *al-Durr al-sani*, a study of the sharifian families of Fez. The work is considered a major source for Moroccan history.

1704. The British captured Gibraltar. Opposed by the government of Spain, they received supplies from Morocco. Gibraltar became a point of sale for English goods to Morocco.

1707. Death of **Muhammad al-Wazir Ghassani,** a statesman and diplomat who served Mawlay Isma'il. He undertook a diplomatic mission to Spain to ransom Moroccan corsairs and find Arabic manuscripts abandoned after the final Muslim expulsion from 1609 to 1614. He wrote about the mission and detailed life at the Spanish court.

1721, Jan. 23. Treaty of peace and commerce with Britain, providing British shipping with protection from Moroccan pirates and official extortion.

1735–45. Period of civil war, with power contested by various usurpers and pretenders to the Alawi caliphate. **Sultan Abdallah** (r. 1729–57) was deposed five times.

c. 1743. Death of **Muhammad al-Ifrani,** a historian and biographer whose famed chronicle of the Sa'di dynasty, *Nuzhat al-hadi*, remains the most important historical work for the period from 1511 to 1670.

1757–90. SULTAN MUHAMMAD III. The dynasty recovered from internal dissension under the direction of Sultan Muhammad III. His governmental innovation consisted of a marked emphasis on **decentralization of state authority.** Since taxes had previously been collected in order to support a large standing salaried army, Muhammad III sought to recruit a smaller army from local conscripts. He reformed the currency, attempted to gain state revenue from **trade,** and dispensed with taxes on agriculture. His foreign policy rested on the **development of trade and friendship treaties with the European powers.**

After the reign of Mawlay Isma'il, successive rulers did not exercise authority over all of Morocco. Parts of the country demonstrated allegiance by the payment of taxes and the provision of troops, and were known as the *bilad al-makhzan* ("government lands"). On the other hand, in the *bilad al-siba* ("the lands of no authority"), government control remained tenuous. The size of the two spheres was fluid, varying with the strength of the ruler and his administration.

1765. Muhammad III established the **port city of Mogador (Essaouira)** to serve as an outlet for the Atlantic trade with European countries, which provided the main source of state revenue until the early 20th century.

1769. The Portuguese were evicted from **Mazagan,** their last post in Morocco.

1786, June 28. Treaty with the United States, granting the latter diplomatic representation at the consular level, commerce on a most-favored-nation basis, capitulatory privileges, and above all, assurances against Moroccan piracy. American vessels had been **vulnerable to pirates** since the assertion of independence from Britain, which had negotiated protection for ships carrying its flag. The treaty was renewed on Sept. 18, 1836, for an additional 50 years.

1790–92. SULTAN AL-YAZID. The brief rule of Sultan Muhammad's son threw Morocco into **political instability** as two of his brothers revolted against him. He was killed in combat with one of them, and his brother **Sulayman,** who was proclaimed sultan, faced some four years of warfare against three pretenders before he established control of the country. *(To p. 545)*

b. ALGERIA, TUNISIA, AND LIBYA

(From p. 131)

In the 16th century the North African countries, with the exception of Morocco, were **absorbed into the Ottoman Empire.** The provincial administrations set up in Algiers, Tripoli, and Tunis soon developed an **autonomous character,** with local regimes run largely by the military. They were not, however, entirely independent of Ottoman authority: they continued to acknowledge **Ottoman suzerainty,** to draw on **Turkish recruits** for their armies, and to seek Ottoman diplomatic support and mediation in local disputes.

1504. The corsairs Aruj and **Khayr al-Din Barbarossa** accepted the patronage of the Hafsid ruler of Tunisia. They made the island of Jerba their base of Mediterranean operations for their jihad, or holy war, against Christian ships. The **corsairs,** as pirate captains, belonged to a highly valued and organized profession in Muslim North Africa. They banded together into guilds, or *ta'ifas,* for their mutual benefit. Most of them were Europeans who had converted to Islam. They played a **prominent role in the governments of Algiers, Tunis, and Tripoli,** the three ports that came under Ottoman control in the 16th century.

1509. The Algerian port of **Oran** taken by the Spanish.

1510. Tripoli and Bougie captured by the Spanish. Spanish victories prompted the inhabitants of Algiers to call upon Muslim corsairs to assist with their defense. The Spanish controlled all of the Algerian littoral through a series of coastal garrisons (presidios). They did not occupy Algiers but constructed a fort called the Peñon on an islet overlooking the harbor. They remained isolated in their coastal enclaves, dependent on naval support.

1515–16. Aruj and Khayr al-Din Barbarossa installed at Algiers at the request of the city's inhabitants.

1518. ESTABLISHMENT OF OTTOMAN RULE IN ALGIERS. Besieged by the Spanish, Khayr al-Din Barbarossa placed himself under the direct authority of the Ottoman sultan Selim I, who appointed him *beylerbey* (provincial governor) and sent him as military reinforcement a unit of Janissary musket-bearing infantry. In 1529, after a protracted struggle with the Spanish, he won full control of Algiers and began conquering the interior of Algeria. Garrisons brought the countryside into the sphere of Ottoman control, and provincial taxes were collected in yearly military expeditions *(mahallas).* But already by the late 16th century, real power rested with local Janissary commanders, not the Ottoman governor.

ALGIERS became the prosperous center of an economy based primarily on **privateering,** or state-sponsored piracy. Corsair wealth funded the development of an imposing city, with tall protective walls, a citadel (completed in 1590), gracious homes, fine public buildings, and various urban amenities. The **population** grew from some 20,000 to about 100,000 by the 17th century and included a mix of Turks, corsairs, native Algerians *(baldis),* Berbers, and Jews. Thousands of **Christian captives** taken on raids were held in prisons called *bagnios.* They were sold, ransomed, or used as slaves.

1528. The Knights of St. John, an order founded by the Habsburg emperor Charles V, established a garrison at Tripoli.

1533. Khayr al-Din Barbarossa was appointed admiral of the Ottoman fleet and took direction of Ottoman naval operations in the western Mediterranean.

1534. First Ottoman conquest of **Tunis** by Khayr al-Din Barbarossa. He was pushed out by Spanish forces, which established a garrison in the port. Al-Hasan, the Hafsid ruler of Tunis, became a vassal of Emperor Charles V.

1543. Tlemcen captured by the Habsburgs.

1551. ESTABLISHMENT OF OTTOMAN RULE IN TRIPOLI. The Ottoman fleet dislodged the Hospitallers of St. John from Tripoli. The corsair captain **Draghut (Turghut)** was appointed Ottoman governor of the province of Tripoli and began bringing the interior under Ottoman rule. The province remained under direct Ottoman control, through governors appointed by Istanbul, until 1629.

1569. Second Ottoman conquest of **Tunis.** The city was recaptured by the Europeans after their naval victory at Lepanto in 1571.

1574. ESTABLISHMENT OF OTTOMAN RULE IN TUNIS. The Ottomans captured Tunis for the third and final time, putting an **end to the Hafsid dynasty** and the Spanish presence. They established direct control of the province but this changed in 1591, when a group of local **Janissaries revolted,** formed a council (divan), and elected a leader (dey) to share power with the governor. The authority of the **dey** was based in urban areas, while a **bey** appointed by him handled the administration of the countryside and the collection of taxes there. The beys, who commanded a military force, soon emerged as a rival center of power to the military elite in Tunis.

1577. Ottoman conquest of **Fezzan,** the southern province of Libya.

1580. French consul established in Algiers. The British also had a representative admitted in 1584.

1609–1711. Regime of the deys in Tripoli. The Janissaries revolted in 1609 and proclaimed one of their junior officers the governing authority, with the title of dey. Although the Ottomans continued to send pashas to Tripoli, their presence became symbolic. The deys, selected by the Janissaries or the corsairs, were the real power.

1609–14. Immigration of the Moriscos, Muslims who were only nominally Christian, from Spain. About 100,000 Morisco refugees arrived in Tunisia and Algeria. They were slowly absorbed into their new North African environment. In various localities they founded their own suburbs and villages and introduced **innovations in irrigation.** In Tunis they started the **felt cap (shashiyya) industry** and retained their own representative for tax collection.

1612–31. MURAD BEY, FOUNDER OF THE MURADID DYNASTY IN TUNISIA. This Corsican renegade distinguished himself as bey, or governor of the Tunisian countryside, and was awarded by the Ottoman sultan the title of pasha and the right to pass the office on to his descendants. With this official recognition as well as the control of force and of the revenue from taxation, Murad Bey and his successors emerged as **the real center of power in Tunisia,** overshadowing the deys based in the capital. The Muradid dynasty, which lasted until 1702, provided Tunisia with relative peace and prosperity.

1622–83. English and French conflicts with Algiers. Foreign relations between Algiers and European powers were strained in the 17th century by the Algerian capture of ships and Christian prisoners. England, Holland, and France were **frequently at war** with the regime and, in an effort to enforce or promote a treaty, the terms of which were quickly broken, often blockaded or shelled the port. Ineffectual negotiations thus resulted in **English bombardments** in 1622, 1655, and 1672. The French, moved by a similar antagonism and an unrealized desire to launch a crusade, bombarded Algiers in 1661, 1665, 1682, and 1683.

1630. French consul appointed in Tripoli. He was forced to leave in 1632 after an ineffectual protest concerning corsair raids. Despite this diplomatic rupture, French merchants continued to arrive in Tripoli and often performed diplomatic duties.

1632–49. Muhammad Sakizli, a corsair leader in Tripoli, seized power and gained the support of the Turkish militia. A skilled administrator, he established a program of taxation that ensured peace in the countryside. His foreign policy **expanded privateering** to include raids aimed at coastal towns throughout the Christian Mediterranean.

1659. French consul and merchant residence *(funduq)* established in Tunis. The site became the center of French commercial life in North Africa and housed all European merchants except the English and Dutch. In contrast with Algiers and Tripoli, **trade with Europe,** particularly France, developed as an important part of the local economy during the 17th century. Sicilians, Maltese, Neapolitans, and Calabrians also established informal commercial relations.

1659–1711. Restructuring of the Algerian regime. The Janissaries, who held effective power in Algiers from the late 16th century, revolted against the Ottoman governor in 1659 and appointed their agha, or commanding officer, as the governing authority. The aghas ruled with the aid of the **Janissary council** (divan) until 1671, when the **corsair captains** replaced the rule of the agha with that of a dey elected by them, and from 1689, by the Janissaries. Governors continued to be sent from Istanbul until 1711, when the dey was able to obtain from the Ottomans the office and title of governor. This system of government, based on a **military oligarchy,** lasted until the French occupation in 1830. The deys acknowledged Ottoman suzerainty but **the Algerian state was quasi-independent.**

1660. Construction of the al-Jadid Mosque (or Mosque of the Fishery) in Algiers, on the initiative of the military leaders. It bore **Ottoman architectural features.**

1682, April 10. Treaty of peace and commerce between Britain and Algiers. It dealt primarily with protections for piracy and the rights of British subjects in Algiers, and was renewed and enlarged several times (in 1686, 1700, 1703, 1716, 1729, 1762, and 1800).

1696. Construction of the Sidi Mehrez Mosque in Tunis by the ruler Murad II (1659–75). The building, dedicated to the patron saint of Tunis, strongly reflected the influences of **Ottoman imperial architecture.**

1702. END OF THE MURADID DYNASTY IN TUNISIA. The last bey, Murad III, was assassinated following a plot by the military officer **Ibrahim al-Sharif,** who immediately assumed the offices of both dey and bey. Algerian forces invaded Tunisia and captured him but were finally repulsed by **Husayn ibn Ali,** a cavalry officer in Muradid service who seized power.

1705–35. HUSAYN IBN ALI, FOUNDER OF THE HUSAYNID DYNASTY IN TUNISIA. After securing for himself the title of bey he arranged for the position to become **hereditary** in his family, which held the office until the abolition of the monarchy in 1957. His rule brought calm to the country, in which he built wells, bridges, markets, and mosques.

1708. Algerian forces took Oran, held by the Spanish since 1509. The Spanish reconquered it in 1732 but finally surrendered it in 1792.

1711–45. AHMAD QARAMANLI, FOUNDER OF THE QARAMANLI DYNASTY IN TRIPOLI. A local officer and son of a Turkish corsair, he seized power and was recognized by the Ottomans as governor.

Under his dynasty, which ruled until 1835, the provinces of Tripolitania and Cyrenaica were united. He sponsored corsair ventures but maintained treaties of peace and commerce with both Britain and France. He restored the fortifications of Tripoli and constructed there a mosque and religious college that bear his name.

1716, July 19. Treaty of peace and capitulations between Britain and Tripoli. Britain accredited a resident consul at Tripoli as early as 1658 and had concluded five treaties with Tripoli between 1658 and 1694, dealing largely with the regulation of piracy.

1735–56. Rule of Ali Pasha in Tunisia. With the help of Algerian troops he deposed his uncle Husayn ibn Ali, whom he executed in 1740, and ruled until 1756, when Husayn's son Muhammad recaptured the throne and restored Husaynid rule.

1751, Oct. 19. Treaty of peace and commerce between Britain and Tunis. It laid down in detail provisions for the avoidance of piracy, enlarging on the first durable treaty between the two countries concluded in 1662 and expanded in 1716. A **British consul** was appointed to Tunis in 1638.

1759–82. Ali Bey ruled in Tunis. He had the *sultani* **gold coins debased** and reduced in size in response to increased competition with multinational currencies in the Mediterranean.

1766–91. Muhammad ibn Uthman Dey ruled in Algiers. One of the most capable deys, he tried to establish greater central authority in Algeria, but provincial appointees in Constantine and Oran asserted their independence with the help of local tribal leaders.

Algerian privateering declined sharply during the period. The size of the corsair fleet fell to ten ships, and the human and material spoils dwindled. In 1788 the number of captives held in Algiers stood at about 1,000, down from a high of 25,000 in the 17th century. With the **lucrative revenue from piracy drying up,** taxes had to be raised, causing popular discontent.

1768–70. French-Tunisian war. When Ali Bey of Tunis refused a French demand to release the Corsican ships and passengers seized by his corsairs, France declared war and bombarded the ports of La Goulette, Bizerte, and Sousse. The bey agreed to a **treaty of peace** (signed Sept. 13, 1770) and restored to the (French) Royal Company of Africa **coral fishery rights** off the Tunisian coast.

1782. The Tijaniyya Sufi order founded in Algeria by **Ahmad al-Tijani** (d. 1815). The brotherhood, which spread throughout North Africa, rejected popular rituals such as pilgrimages to tombs and the celebration of the prophet Muhammad's birthday. Its more **ascetic doctrine** stressed instead the importance of the founder as the sole effective intercessor between this world and the next.

1793. Death of **Abd al-Rahman al-Ghushtuli,** founder of the **Rahmaniyya Sufi order** in Algeria. Another important Sufi order founded around the same time was the **Darqawiyya,** established in Morocco by **Abu Hamid al-Darqawi.** The order came to play an important part in the politics of early 19th-century Algeria.

1799, March 26. Treaty between the United States and Tunis, granting American ships a measure of protection from corsair attacks in return for costly presents. Similar treaties were concluded with **Algiers** (Sept. 5, 1795) and **Tripoli** (Nov. 4, 1796, and Jan. 3, 1797).

(To pp. 547, 548, 550)

D. SOUTH AND SOUTHEAST ASIA, 1500–1800

1. INDIA, 1500–1800

(From p. 138)

Early modern India continued to be marked by the pattern of alternation between larger, inclusive (imperial) states and smaller states or kingdoms based on regional power bases and linguistic/cultural formations. New in this period was a **dramatic increase in urbanization** and a greater **commercialization of agriculture and trade**—results of the expanded imperial system, which fostered integration of localities into larger economic networks both within the subcontinent and between South Asia and other imperial centers. Very little speculation has been put forward regarding demographic changes before the 19th century; the regions of greatest population density when censuses began to be taken are presumed to be the same as those during this earlier period as well (with the rice-growing areas of the eastern Gangetic Basin and the east coast having the highest population). The increasing size and number of urban centers established in the early modern period have been presumed to foster as well as absorb the population increases in the subcontinent.

Initially in the north and ultimately over much of the South Asian subcontinent, the **Mughal Empire** emerged in this period to tie India to the larger Islamic world. Beyond economic integration with this larger system, the Mughals encouraged further integration through the opportunities offered to military and administrative elite migrating from Persia and the Arabic areas of the Middle East. Still, faced with the necessity of creating a shared political culture that would tie the immigrant ruling class to indigenous power structures, the Mughals fashioned a new **Indo-Persian cultural system** that created a shared elite culture focused on the emperor. Particular values—including Indian notions of good rule, Indian aesthetics, and hierarchical conceptualizations of the relationship between community and state—became incorporated within the ruling ethos.

At the same time in the south, the **Vijayanagara Empire** consolidated around a state ideology fashioned from Hindu theories of kingship and new claims to power by soldier-merchant groups. The elaboration of this state made clear the similarities of economic and political processes faced by both the empires. Key to success were the administrative and ideological ties established between the state and its constituent communities; the nature of these ties indicated that while one empire is called Islamic and the other Hindu, the Mughal and Vijayanagara rulers built their respective politico-cultural systems on the basis of many similar cultural assumptions that may be seen as typically South Asian in nature.

Toward the end of this period, the imperial systems in both the north and the south began to break apart. Across the subcontinent **successor states** arose, solidifying political and cultural coherence around regional identities expressed in local vernacular languages and literary works. The political and economic opportunities presented to local elite claimants enabled them to direct **cultural patronage** to solidify these regional cultures and identities. The ferment provided by the new political formations, and the contestations that naturally accompanied new claims to power, provided a period of great flux and creative reinvention of political forms and legitimations.

Into this flux moved a **variety of European actors,** brought to the subcontinent by their interest in trade and their new organization at home as commercial monopolies (the **East India Companies** of the English, the Dutch, and the French). These monopolistic enterprises facilitated the financing of ambitious pursuit of trade overseas. Still "bit" players in the unfolding drama, Europeans tried to ally themselves with different Indian princes absorbed by their internecine warfare, hoping to capitalize on the victories won by their allies.

By 1500. THE VIJAYANAGARA EMPIRE developed, in its second half, into what is known as the **nayaka** state-system, in which administrative and political relations differed significantly from what had gone before. While the Vijayanagara rulers continued to hold ultimate power over a broad belt of territory, they shared authority locally with a number of military chiefs, or nayakas. Originally part of the great Telugu migrations southward into the Tamil country in the 15th and 16th centuries, **Balija merchant-warriors** who claimed these nayaka positions rose to political and cultural power and supported an ethos that emphasized nonascriptive, heroic criteria in legitimizing political power. The Balijas were proud of their Sudra status, in a world previously dominated by a classical Sanskritic varna scheme that insisted that kings had to be Kshatriya (two castes higher than Sudras). The new egalitarian ethos made it easier for claimants from a variety of communities to succeed to political control.

1500s. Kaikkolas (weavers) and **kanmalas** (smiths) increased in power during the 15th and 16th centuries: set privileges were granted to them by nayakas and their subordinate local magnates. Indeed, the diversity of artisan and merchant communities in this period shows the increased importance of these professions in the emerging socioeconomic structure.

1500. Spread of the **Sikh** faith in Bengal. Founded by Nānak (1469–1538), who merged Hinduism with Muslim egalitarianism. Later turned militant under persecution by the Mughals.

1504. Yusuf Adil Shah of Bijapur, having annexed Gulbarga, established the Shi'ite form of Islam under state patronage, despite protest from many Sunnis.

1509. The Portuguese, under **Francisco de Almeida,** at Diu destroyed an Egyptian-Indian fleet that had, in the previous year, defeated a Portuguese squadron at Chaul.

1510. The **Portuguese acquired Goa** as headquarters, in place of Cochin.

1512. Golconda became independent (till 1687).

1526–37. Bahadur, the last active sultan of the "sultanate state" period, with the aid of Khandesh captured Mandu and annexed Malwa (1531), after which he captured Chitor (1534).

To 1550s. In the heyday of the Vijayanagara Empire, the center retained full control of the nayaka chiefs, receiving a third of the revenues collected in the territories assigned to the chiefs. The nayakas had only limited lordship over territory and had to maintain from their income armed forces for the king.

1526–1761 (1857). The **MUGHAL EMPIRE** in India was founded by **Babar** (1483–1530), descendant of Timur-I Lang in the fifth generation, who had seized Kabul (1504) and Lahore (1524) as compensation for loss of Ferghana and Samarkand. Decisive victory at **Panipat** over Ibrahim Shah Lodi gave him Delhi and Agra, which he defended in the **Battle of Khanua (1527)** against Rana Sanga of Chitor, chief of a Rajput confederacy.

1529. Victory on the Gogra, where it meets the Ganges, completed conquest of the kingdom of Delhi to the frontier of Bengal.

Babar's acts, problems, and personality appeared in his Turki *Memoirs,* or *Baburnama.*

1530–56. Humayun drove Bahadur Shah of Gujarat to flight before Chitor and captured Mandu and Champanir (1535) but lost both through a year of inaction. The same fault and treachery of his brothers lost the empire to the nayakas.

1530s–1730s. The nayakas established rule at **Madurai,** longest-lived of the nayaka "little kingdoms." Also established were two other prominent nayaka centers at **Tanjuvur** (defeated by the 1670s) and the territory controlled by the **Senji Nayakas** (defeated by the 1630s, this territory passed first to Bijapur and then to the Mughals). Marked economic change in these territories caused by introduction of new crops, expanded sphere of manufacturing production, and creation of important marketing centers. Revenues collected by the states on agriculture and trade permitted them to **build towns and large temple complexes** and to develop a new kingly ethos of consumption that altered the philosophical and ideological definitions of kingship, especially in terms of the relationship of the king to the communities of his realm.

1535. The Portuguese secured by treaty Bassein and were allowed to fortify Diu, which they defended against an Ottoman fleet and a Gujarati army (1538).

1539–55. Sur dynasty of the Afghan **Sher Shah** (1539–45), who had consolidated his power in Bihar and had driven Humayun to seek refuge in Persia, whence he returned precariously to Delhi and Agra (1555). In north India, Sher Shah began administrative experiments that later served as the basis for the Mughal system of governance.

1546. Efforts to expel the Portuguese failed miserably.

1556–1605. AKBAR (b. 1542, personal rule 1562) restored and consolidated the empire throughout northern India.

1556. Guided by **Bairam Khan,** his guardian (till 1560), he crushed the Afghans at Panipat.

1559. Constantine de Braganza seized Daman.

1561. Conquest of Malwa was effected by the harem party (dominant 1560–62).

1562. Akbar's marriage to a Rajput princess of Amber (mother of Jahangir) and abolition of the *jizya* tax on non-Muslims (1564) marked a new policy of impartiality and conciliation of subjects. Marriage alliances and taxation policies served as aspects of new cultural system focused on elite loyalty to the emperor who, in turn, reinforced connections to the populace through patronage of various cultural activities.

1565. A coalition of Ahmadnagar, Bijapur Bidar, and Golconda decisively defeated **Vijayanagar** at Talikota and led to the execution of the rajah. In 1574 Ahmadnagar annexed Berar, which had hindered the allied campaign.

1568. Chitor was taken by Akbar and about 30,000 Rajputs massacred.

1571. A new Mughal capital city at Fatehpur Sikri, near Agra, was founded and magnificently built but abandoned on Akbar's death. Architecture became a key strategy in affirming the connection between Mughal rulers and the country; Akbar and his regional governors mounted an aggressive building campaign across expanded territories.

1572–73. Conquest of Gujarat gave Akbar access to the sea, new ideas, and revenues. To defend his conquest he rode 450 miles in 11 days with 3,000 horsemen.

Reorganization of administration was begun by (1) resumption to the crown of all lands, hitherto held by officials as temporary assignments but now to be administered and revenues collected directly; (2) establishment of the **Mansabdari system,** a unified state service of officers arranged in a hierarchy of military (cavalry) rank but performing civil (mainly financial) as well as military functions if required; (3) substitution of a single tax of one-third produce of the land for the traditional levy of one-sixth plus numerous cesses that were now declared abolished; (4) the branding of all horses maintained for government service, to prevent usual fraud.

1576. Bengal was definitely conquered from the Afghans.

1577. Khandesh was induced to submit as first step toward reconquest of the Deccan, actually accomplished only by Aurangzib (1659–1707).

1578. Public debates on religion held at the Mughal court and presided over by Akbar, and instituted for Muslims only in 1575, were thrown open to Hindus, Jains, Zoroastrians, Sabaeans, and Christians. Akbar showed new respect for animal life (Jain *ahimsa*) and Zoroastrian reverence for the sun, and invited to court from Goa the Portuguese Jesuits Antonio Monserrate and Rodolfo Acquaviva (1579; arr. 1580). These, like later missions (1590, 1595), failed despite a friendly reception.

1582. In spite of revolt that followed a claim to infallibility under Muslim law (1579), the emperor decreed a new Divine Faith much influenced by Sufi practice. The limited support he won for it collapsed at his death. Cultural patronage—including support for translation and illustration of Hindu epics—formed a central strategy in the development of a unique Indo-Persian cultural system.

1589–91. Jamal Khan, minister of Ahmadnagar, an adherent of the Mahdavi heresy that anticipated the advent of the Mahdi (world savior) in A.H. 1000, persecuted both Sunnis and Shi'ites.

1601–4. Prince Salim, later Jahangir, rebelled but was restored to favor.

1603. John Mildenhall, representative of the English East India Company (London Company, founded Dec. 31, 1600), arrived at Agra but secured no concession until 1608.

1605–27. JAHANGIR maintained his father's empire in northern India but allowed much political power to pass to his wife, Nur Jahan (1611). His personal interest in painting, however, led to expansion of Mughal cultural patronage, an important aspect in continuing political legitimacy.

1609–11. William Hawkins failed to secure a treaty for James I, as did **Sir Thomas Roe** (1615–19), but the English won trading rights at Surat after defeating a Portuguese fleet (1612).

1616. Bubonic plague, clearly identified for the first time, became epidemic.

1628–57. SHAH JAHAN (d. 1666) was greatly interested in artistic patronage but destroyed Ahmadnagar (1632) and defeated Golconda (1635) and Bijapur (1636). His active patronage of cultural production extended Akbar's cultural system.

1632–53. The **Taj Mahal** was built as tomb for Shah Jahan's wife, Mumtaz Mahal, for whom he had already built the splendid palace Khass Mahal on the fort at Agra.

1639. The site of **Madras** was granted to an Englishman.

1647. Aurangzib campaigned unsuccessfully in Badakhshan and Balkh as part of constant program for expansion carried on by the Mughals.

1649–53. Aurangzib failed to wrest Kandahar from the Persians.

1653–57. Again governing the Deccan, Aurangzib campaigned ambitiously and arrested the revival of Bijapur but failed to check the Maratha raider Sivaji.

1658. Dutch (East India Company) expelled Portuguese (1638–58) from Ceylon.

1658. Aurangzib rebelled, following the illness of Shah Jahan and competition for the succession among his four sons.

1658–1707. Having imprisoned Shah Jahan, **AURANGZIB** became emperor. The Mughal dominion was undermined, in part, by Aurangzib's continued effort to expand his dominions, lack of sufficient good land to award to new mansabdars, and a renewed emphasis on Islamic definitions of good rule, all of which led to reversals in Mughal cultural system and, thus, to a decline in political stability.

1659–80. Sivaji reduced Bijapur (1659) and sacked Surat (1664 and 1670); the English factory escaped harm. In 1667 he won the title of rajah from Aurangzib and began to levy land taxes in Mughal territory (Khandesh, 1670); he successfully organized Maratha government on Hindu principles with the guidance of the poets Ramdas and Tukaram and was enthroned as an independent ruler (1674). Marathas thus became most formidable force in the Deccan and laid claim to the mantle of Vijayanagara, which now stood as model of "Hindu" kingship.

1666. Chittagong was annexed for Aurangzib by the Bengal governor.

1669. In an attempt to placate restive immigrants from other parts of the Islamicate world who served as his most important military and administrative elite, Aurangzib adopted policies that led to **prohibition of the Hindu religion** and destruction of Hindu temples, with great loss to Indian art and the *jizya* reimposed on non-Muslims (1679). These actions appeared to abrogate the cultural system integrating Mughal rule with local elites. The period was marked by Jat rebellions (1669, 1681, 1688–1707), Hindu uprisings, and troubles with Afghan tribes and with the now militant and theocratic Sikhs (1675–78).

1679. Marwar was annexed in war against the Rajputs; hostilities continued nearly 30 years.

1681. Prince Akbar revolted unsuccessfully against his father's misgovernment and died in exile.

1681–1707. Assuming personal command in the Deccan, Aurangzib subjugated Bijapur (1686) and Golconda (1687) but failed to check the **Marathas.**

1685–88. Aurangzib seized Surat (1685), intending to expel the English, whose unwise attempt to seize Chittagong lost them all their claims in Bengal (1688); their naval superiority menaced Mughal trade, however, and they were encouraged to return to Bengal (**Calcutta founded, 1690).**

Following the decline of the Portuguese power in India, that of the English had been increased by the acquisition of **Bombay** (1661) and the absorption of Dutch ambitions chiefly in the Spice Islands. Foundation of the French Compagnie des Indes Orientales (1664) under strict government control, along with numerous settlements (Pondichéry, 1674), now opened the way for acute Anglo-French rivalry (p. 315).

1689. Capture of Sivaji's successor, **Sambhaji,** failed to crush the Marathas, and indecisive warfare continued until 1707.

The intellectual curiosity and luxurious tastes of the Mughal rulers, except Aurangzib, fostered brilliant cultural progress. Histories, annals, and memoirs, chiefly in Persian, a dictionary supported by Jahangir, and the unsurpassed poems of **Tulsi Das** (1532–1623) formed important literary contributions. Slavish imitation of Persian painting was modified by Hindu and even European influences; a height of keen observation and delicate rendering was attained under Shah Jahan. Under him also the building of palaces, mausoleums, and mosques in Indo-Persian style attained an exquisite elegance.

1707. Following Aurangzib's death the empire rapidly disintegrated; various provincial governors became virtually independent (1772 ff.). As these regional rulers competed for control over territory, they sought alliances with Europeans to gain additional armies and military prowess. Political control devolved to the regional courts of successor states. In the cities, rule devolved to various self-regulating communities of merchants and to displaced Mughal courtiers, who took up cultural patronage and began to remake cultural systems in the interests of localities. This creative ferment was viewed as anarchy and decline by European observers.

c. 1708. The **Sikhs,** who had been founded in the 15th century as a strictly religious order, proclaiming Muslim and Hindu fellowship and monotheism and opposing caste restrictions and priestcraft (except for the secular and religious authority vested in the guru Hargovind, 1606), became a thoroughly militant order under the last guru, **Govind Singh** (1666–1708); they menaced Mughal rights in the Deccan but their strength was broken by Bahadur Shah (1707–12).

1717. The **English East India Company,** through gifts and medical service, secured from the Mughal emperor exemption from customs duties and other concessions.

THE MUGHAL EMPERORS (1526–1858)

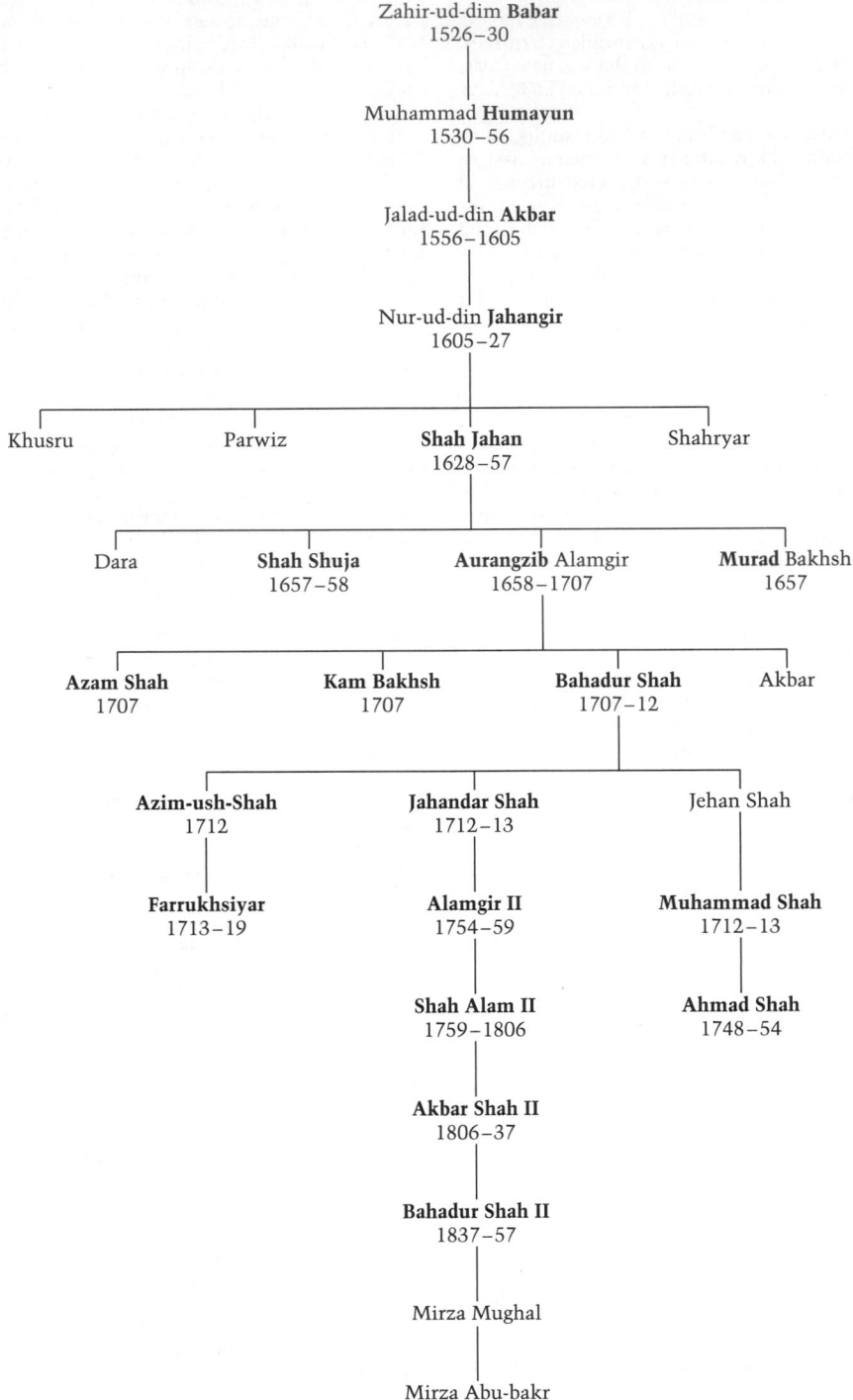

Zahir-ud-dim **Babar**
1526–30

Muhammad **Humayun**
1530–56

Jalad-ud-din **Akbar**
1556–1605

Nur-ud-din **Jahangir**
1605–27

Khusru — Parwiz — **Shah Jahan**
1628–57 — Shahryar

Dara — **Shah Shuja**
1657–58 — **Aurangzib** Alamgir
1658–1707 — **Murad** Bakhsh
1657

Azam Shah
1707 — **Kam Bakhsh**
1707 — **Bahadur Shah**
1707–12 — Akbar

Azim-ush-Shah
1712 — **Jahandar Shah**
1712–13 — Jehan Shah

Farrukhsiyar
1713–19 — **Alamgir II**
1754–59 — **Muhammad Shah**
1712–13

Shah Alam II
1759–1806 — **Ahmad Shah**
1748–54

Akbar Shah II
1806–37

Bahadur Shah II
1837–57

Mirza Mughal

Mirza Abu-bakr

The reorganized Maratha government gradually became preeminent in India, exacting taxes from the whole Deccan except Hyderabad, which became essentially independent of Delhi (1724) under its governor, the **Nizam-ul-Mulk** (d. 1748). The governors of Avadh (Oudh) (1724) and Bengal (1740) also became independent but maintained the fiction of allegiance to the Mughal emperor.

1739. A pillaging invasion of Persians under **Nadir Shah** checked the Maratha expansion northward, defeated imperial troops, and withdrew, retaining possession of Afghanistan and the wealth of Delhi.

1746–48. Following the outbreak of the **War of the Austrian Succession** in Europe, the French, strengthened by their participation in Indian intrigue under the guidance of **Joseph Dupleix**, captured Madras (1746) and defeated the protesting nawab of the Carnatic. The **Treaty of Aix-la-Chapelle** (1748) restored Madras to Britain.

1748–54. Anglo-French rivalry continued, each side supporting candidates for the positions of nizam of the Deccan and nawab of the Carnatic. French domination, at its height in 1751 when **Bussy** virtually ruled the Deccan and Dupleix the Carnatic, was checked by **Robert Clive's** (1727–74) brilliant seizure of Arcot (Sept. 12, 1751). The recall of Dupleix (1754) left English prestige firmly established.

Early 1700s. As the Successor States attempted to solidify their authority through cultural patronage and military supremacy, distinct painting and architectural styles emerged, especially in the Deccan, Bengal, among Rajput princes, and at Awadh. Merchants and courtiers also sponsored expanding performance genres, from street theater to processions and including dance, poetry, and music. Local political competition often was expressed through artistic competition.

1756. The nawab **(Siraj-ud-Daulah)** of the Bengal region captured Calcutta (June 20) and imprisoned unescaped residents in a small storeroom in the fort (later called the Black Hole), where over a hundred perished from suffocation, wounds, and the heat.

1757. British forces under **Watson** and Clive retook Calcutta and, being again at war with France, seized Chandernagor (March 23). Clive formed a conspiracy with Hindu bankers and the nawab's general, **Mir Jafar,** which enabled his forces to rout those remaining loyal to the nawab at **Plassey** (June 23). Mir Jafar, having executed Siraj-ud-Daulah, was installed as nawab under what was in effect an English protectorate of Bengal.

1758–60. As part of a general expansion of influence, Maratha cultural patronage reached far into north India. Significant urban centers, such as the pilgrimage city of Banaras, were almost completely rebuilt by Maratha patrons, who also supported vast numbers of mendicants, intellectuals, and widows. Maratha occupation of the Punjab (1758) and renewed northern activity (1760) excited allied opposition of the Rohilla Afghans and **Ahmad Shah Abdali** (the Durani Afghan chief, who had invaded the Punjab almost annually between 1748 and 1759).

1761, Jan. 14. The Marathas were crushingly defeated by this coalition in the **Battle of Panipat.** Subsequent mutiny caused Ahmad Shah's withdrawal, leaving India in dissension.

British supremacy over other European contenders in India's foreign relations was assured by their defeat of the Dutch (1759) and capture of **Pondichéry** from the French, who by the **Treaty of Paris** (1763) (p. 319) retained only Pondichéry, Chandernagor, and other scattered stations, with limited numbers of troops. The Compagnie des Indes Orientales was dissolved in 1769.

1764, Oct. 22. Victory at Baksar over forces of the deposed nawab of Bengal, the nawab of Avadh, and the titular Mughal emperor gave the British uncontested control in Bengal and Bihar, awarded in the form of the diwani of Bengal (1756–67). Clive administered Bengal affairs for the company through collection of the land revenue in Bengal, Bihar, and part of Orissa, taking over the actual collection of revenue in 1771. Irresponsible administration in the face of famine as company servants lined their own pockets led to the reduction of official perquisites for those whose rapacity since 1757 Clive had encouraged by his own example.

The militarism of the Mughals and the predatory policy of the Marathas led to an emphasis on warfare and piracy as sources of prestige and wealth and a gradual devolution of state responsibility for industry, education, and cultural progress. Such activity took place, instead, on a local and regional level, notably by the Delhi Muslim reformer **Shah Wali-Ullah** (1703–60) and the Bengali poet **Bharatchandra** (1717–60). General economic chaos ensued, with Europeans profiting greatly from gifts, forced sales, and usury. One exception was Indore (1765–95) under the rule of the pious **Ahalya Bai.**

During dissension in the Maratha confederacy, **Haidar Ali** (1721–82) gained power, usurped the throne of Mysore (1761), and claimed the authority previously held by other Muslim rulers in the Deccan.

1769. He compelled the British at Madras, who became involved in war against him (1767), to sign a treaty of mutual assistance.

1769–70. Disastrous famine in Bengal wiped out an estimated third of the population.

1772–85. As governor of Bengal, **Warren Hastings** (1732–1818) initiated reforms, including simplification of the revenue system and improved coinage, government control of salt and opium manufacture, reduction of dacoity (robbery), and study of Muslim and Hindu law (Calcutta Madrasa, 1781). He was styled governor-general, with certain supervisory powers over the other two company presidencies (Bombay and Madras) under the Regulating Act.

1773. The **REGULATING ACT,** by which Parliament also established a supreme court for British subjects in the company's territories, limited the rights of the company's directors, and prohibited officers' private trade and receipt of presents. Hastings's high-handed measures kept the company solvent and relatively secure in a turbulent period but incurred the censure of jealous colleagues, notably Philip Francis, and led to his impeachment (after his retirement in 1785) with a trial (1788–95) resulting in acquittal.

1775–82. First Anglo-Maratha War, the result of the Bombay government's alliance with the would-be Maratha peshwa, **Raghoba.** Hastings sent an expedition across the peninsula from Calcutta to Surat (1778, arrived 1779) and broke the coalition between the Marathas, Haidar Ali, and the nizam. The **Treaty of Salbai** (1782) obtained for Bombay 20 years' peace with the Marathas and the cession of Salsette and Elephanta.

1778. France and Britain being again at war, Hastings took Pondichéry and Mahé.

1780–84. Provoked by this action, Haidar Ali, with French help, attacked the British in the Carnatic but was defeated at **Porto Novo** (1781) and died (1782); the **Second Anglo-Mysore War,** continued by his son, **Tipu Sultan,** was terminated when French aid was withdrawn.

1784. PITT'S INDIA ACT, in an endeavor to check territorial expansion, forbade interference by the East India Company in native affairs or declaration of war except in case of aggression and made the company's directors answerable to a board of control appointed by the crown.

1786–93. Lord Cornwallis (after a 20-month interregnum of Sir John MacPherson) became governor-general and commander in chief, with power to overrule his council. Under injunctions to preserve peace, he made administrative reforms: company officers given adequate fixed salaries and their private trade eliminated; separation of administrative from commercial branches of service.

1790–92. Tipu attacked Travancore, opening the **Third Anglo-Mysore War;** Cornwallis allied himself with the peshwa and the nizam, and Tipu was defeated and forced to cede half his territory, paying a large indemnity (March 19, 1792).

1791. The Sanskrit College was established at Benares by Jonathan Duncan.

1793. Cornwallis's Code inaugurated substantial reforms. The Permanent Settlement stabilized the revenue system by fixing the assessment in Bengal, Bihar, and Orissa (and Benares Province, 1795) with collection through zamindars (large landlords) (zamindari system), but failed to check the latter's exploitation of the peasantry; it also effected ruthless sale of zamindar rights in case of default and closed the way to later reassessments, thereby eventually causing great financial loss to the government. The **judicial system** was reshaped on the British model but with a paucity of courts. **Indians were excluded from all higher posts.** Zamindars were left only revenue duties, their magisterial and police functions being transferred to European district judges and Indian police *(darogas).*

In the Madras presidency a careful survey along the lines of local practice led to a system of direct levy (periodically reassessed) from the ryot (peasant), later extended to Bombay presidency (ryotwari system); in the Northwest and Central Provinces, somewhat later, a third type of revenue settlement, the mahalwari system, was introduced, collecting revenue through villages or estates.

Meanwhile the principal Maratha leader, **Mahadaji Sindhia** (d. 1794), assumed protection of the emperor, reclaimed Delhi, and extended his power in northern India.

1793. Sir John Shore, governor-general.

1796. Ceylon conquered from the Dutch and administered jointly by the East India Company and the crown until 1802, the latter assuming full responsibility thereafter. *(To p. 552)*

2. SOUTHEAST ASIA, 1500-1800

(From p. 138)

Southeast Asia played a pivotal role in the changes that mark the early modern world. It was a maritime region, already to a large extent **organized around long-distance trade** and located in the midst of crucial trade routes. It encountered and interpreted in distinctive local ways the consolidation of the **Islamicate world** accomplished during the previous, postclassical period, and the following shift from that world system to one shaped by European expansion through trade and technology. Consequently, this part of Asia suffered most quickly and directly the impact of European intrusion; by 1650 Europeans had gained control of most of the vital ports and products through which the region had been connected to an expanding world economy.

Four major kinds of change marked these three centuries in Southeast Asia. The first was the **rise of a number of new states,** fostered in part by external factors—new military techniques, the presence of Islamic models of state organization, and the expansion of commerce, which helped dynamic new leaders to emerge. Internal factors also facilitated these new state configurations, particularly the capacity of origin myths and political theories to be reinterpreted in defining commonalities and identities that fit new circumstances. The second change also related to ideology: between about **1400 and 1700, three universalist faiths** based on sacred scripture became firmly entrenched in the region. An Islamic arc in the south; a Confucian orthodoxy in Vietnam and a Theravada Buddhist region in the rest of mainland Southeast Asia; and a Christian presence in the Philippines (p. 388) were consolidated in the early modern period and are still the important configurations today. In the midst of the commercial and political changes altering the region, a preference emerged for textually based belief systems with sources of authority beyond the localities.

The third major change related to a **dramatic expansion of commercial activity** in the region. This activity predated the appearance of Europeans, relating instead to the linkages forged as the Islamicate world system emerged. In the 15th century, significant activity by Chinese and Indian merchants had increased the circulation of silver and other metals in the area and initiated a demand for Indian cloth in exchange for spices grown for export. Before 1650, tons of pepper, cloves, and nutmegs were carried by Muslim traders (of various nationalities) across the Indian Ocean to markets in Egypt and Beirut. There Italian merchants bought and shipped them back to Europe. At the peak of early-17th-century commercial activity, the Chinese, Japanese, Spanish, Portuguese, and Indians all competed for the region's produce. During the second half of the century, however, many of these players withdrew and a small number came to dominate international markets in the region, most particularly the Dutch East India Company. These external changes around the dividing line of 1650 may also be seen as the point at which promising capitalist economic developments atrophied in the face of massive European domination.

Accompanying important economic changes were technological and scientific **innovations,** particularly in **military techniques**—the fourth major change. The increasing presence of firearms marked the opening of this period and influenced other military practices, including naval technologies and land-based fortifications for establishing permanent, defensible enclaves. Foreign traders proved especially adept in this new technology and, over the 16th century, were often impressed into the service of the most ambitious claimants to royal power in the region. In areas now known as Burma and Thailand, **new states were established** with the capacity to exercise unprecedented power. Relatively centralized powers also emerged in Java and Aceh, and in Makassar and Ayutthaya (Siam) in the early 17th century. Similarly, new naval techniques proved crucial for Aceh and Maluku.

Before 1750, the region had a low population density except in concentrated areas of Java (the northern coastal plain and the Mataram area), south Sulawesi, and Bali. Periods of strong rule and security would foster dramatic population growth in, for example, Aceh in 1550-1640, Makassar in 1600-1660, and areas of Java after 1650. By contrast, devastating contractions of numbers may be attributed to the practice, during warfare, of large-scale forced relocation of captured populations. For example, the Malayan population was dramatically depopulated by the conquests of Sultan Iskander Muda of Aceh from 1618 to 1624.

(To p. 522)

a. THE MALAY PENINSULA AND ARCHIPELAGO

(From p. 138)

1511-1722. JOHOR Sultanate (Malay). The power structure in Johor reflected many features that originated in the Malacca kingdom. Johor continued the Malacca tradition of a maritime state dependent upon the rivers and the sea; Johor built, as well, on Malaccan perceptions of a state, perceiving in the presence of a ruler with an illustrious and impeccable lineage the distinction between a "state" such as the Kingdom of Johor and any number of the small, individual **kampung** under the leadership of a minor chieftain which existed along the rivers, estuaries, and coasts of the Malay world. Court literature, such as the **Sejarah Melayu** (a work begun in the 15th century in Malacca containing later interpolations, including the early history of Johor) expounded the ideal of the ruler responsible solely to God.

The importance of the ministers' role, in efficiently handling mundane affairs of state, is shown by rivalries between **Bendahara** and **Laksamana** families in the 16th and early 17th centuries. The **Orang Kaya, or Council of Nobles,** consisted of these most powerful families, who formed individual centers of power within the kingdom. They performed services for the ruler, including assembling their men and leading them as a group in battle when the kingdom was at war, and acted as an intermediary between their people and ruler. They also played an essential role in international trade under a system of patronage to traders (offering protection and providing capital to traders in return for commission and share of profits).

Orang Laut, a broad term referring to **seafaring peoples in the Malay world,** in reality referred to numerous tribes and status groups inhabiting the islands and estuaries in the **Riau-Lingga Archipelagos, the Pulau Tujuh Islands, the Batam Archipelago, and the coasts and off-shore islands of eastern Sumatra and southern Malay Peninsula.** They gathered sea products for the China trade; performed special services for the ruler at weddings, funerals, or on a hunt; provided transport for envoys and royal missives; and manned ships to act as ruler's naval fleet and to patrol the waters.

Early 1530s. Sultan Alauddin Riayat Syah, successor to the last ruler of Malacca (Sultan Mahmud Syah, who died between November 1527 and July 1528), moved his residence to the Johor River and became the first ruler of the Malacca dynasty to establish a permanent settlement in Johor.

1564 and 1613. Ruler of Johor was **taken prisoner** during the repeated destruction of Johor capitals in 16th and 17th centuries by Portuguese and Acehnese. Both times the conquerors made a point of setting on the throne another ruler from the same royal family in order to fulfill expectations about how a kingdom could be perpetuated.

1641. Capture of Malacca by the Dutch, who thenceforth dominated the East Indies. The Dutch extended free passes to all Johor Orang Kaya to trade in areas restricted to other kingdoms; this enabled these traders to fly the flag of their patrons while conducting a lucrative trade under Dutch protection.

Johor had lost some of the areas that traditionally had been dependencies of Malacca, but it still controlled extensive areas, including Johor; Selangor; areas on the Kelang, Linggi, Siak, Kampar, Muar, and Batu Pahat Rivers; and the islands of Ungaran, Karimum, the Riau-Lingga Archipelagos, and Singapore.

1673. Resilience of kingdom shown when Dutch takeover of Johor Lama counterattacked by Johor's Orang Laut–manned fleet.

1691. Having successfully challenged power of **Laksamana** family by gaining control of young ruler and through the ruler using the royal drums and reedpipes (*nobat* and *nafiri*) as symbols to legitimize authority, **Bendahara Tun Habib Abdul Majid** nevertheless refused to sign any written agreements with Dutch until ruler reached his majority.

1699. Assassination of Sultan Mahmud Syah, last male ruler of Malacca dynasty in Johor, significantly undermined traditional values, especially the sacredness of the ruler; the depth and extent of loyalty accorded to him; and the special nature of his position within society. Many **Orang** Kaya, including **Bendahara** family, implicated in assassination, which served to undermine subjects' loyalty to succeeding Bendahara dynasty. **Orang Laut** had a strong reaction against assassination, refusing to recognize the new Bendahara dynasty, which subsequently was forced to rely on apparent and visible manifestations of power and on close, personal ties with powerful individuals within kingdom, a significant change from the traditional concept of power.

1709. Bendahara ruler **moved capital to Riau** to meet an invading Siamese force; about a quarter of entire population moved to assist Siamese against Bendahara ruler because of questionable legitimacy of new ruler.

1718. Raja Kecil, Minangkabau adventurer, claimed to be son of the last male heir of the Malacca dynasty, gaining mass support among Malay subjects and among almost all Orang Laut in Johor.

1722. Sultan Sulaiman Syah, new Bendahara ruler of Johor, regained throne with help of **Buginese,** warriors and seamen from southwest Sulawesi. Buginese regained control of coronation regalia, possession of which was key to ruler's legitimization.

Raja Kecil, accompanied by some of his loyal Orang Laut groups, such as the Orang Suku Bentan and the Orang Suku Bulang, established a **new kingdom in Siak** following his expulsion from Johor.

Major shift in power relationships in Johor resulted when the Buginese became an effective power bloc: replaced the Orang Laut role (in trading, patrolling, and military functions) and the Orang Kaya role (in the principal decision-making functions).

The ongoing tensions between Bugis and Malay ministers and officials is described in the **Tuhfat al-Nafis,** a Malay history primarily of the kingdom of Johor-Riau-Lingga (but also in other areas, e.g., West-Kalimanta, Siak, Kedah, and Terengganu) covering the early 18th century until 1864.

b. KEDAH

Like Perak, Kedah was a Muslim state with a political structure and culture based on the model of the Malacca Empire, having a Muslim sultan at the center of power who was assisted by ministers drawn from powerful local families.

Unlike other Malay states such as **Perak, Salalngor, Pahang,** and **Negeri Sembilan,** which by 1896 had surrendered most control to the British, Kedah **maintained internal independence** and strong cohesion within the ruling class. Relatively limited economic resources precluded the formation of a large body of aristocrats; consequently, members of the ruling family were appointed to most political posts. Dependent more on rice crop than on trade, Kedah was also spared the disruption of the large-scale Chinese immigration that occurred in southern Malay states.

1713, 1722, and 1770. Civil wars in these years involved jostling within the Kedah royal family for control; Bugis served as mercenaries for various factions.

c. 1741-1778. Muhammed Jiwa Abidin Syah (d. 1778). Provided stability and increased trade and rice crops.

c. ACEH

Rise of Aceh clearly demonstrates impact of Islam and trade in contestation with Europeans. Portuguese efforts to intervene in Pasai and Pidie, and takeover of Melaka across the straits, drove elements interested in Islam, commerce, or local patriotism to unite in support of **Sultan Ali Mughayat Syah.**

1520s. Sultan worked to unite the north Sumatran coast into a new and explicitly anti-Portuguese kingdom; ideological identity and authority of Aceh competed directly with Portuguese Melaka as center of Islamic spice route. (Similarly, **Banten** in western Java emerged as an Islamic kingdom in competition with the Hindu port of Sunda Kelapa, ruled by a Portuguese ally.)

1534-38. Ottoman expansion (first to Egypt, Syria, and the Hejaz in 1516-17, then to Iraq in 1534-35) provided new military defense of Muslim spice-trading route in the Indian Ocean. First Ottoman fleet to combat the Portuguese in the Indian Ocean was launched by the governor of Egypt in 1537-38; this failed.

1560s. Establishment of **direct commercial and diplomatic** relations between Ottomans and Aceh; this led to concept of pan-Islamic counter-crusade against the Portuguese in Southeast Asia (e.g., 1566 petition for assistance, sent from sultan of Aceh to Ottoman sultan).

1560-1580s. High point for Islamic military success in Southeast Asia and for Muslim-Christian polarization in the region.

Early 1600s. Evidence that **Shari'a courts** in use in Aceh, to apply Islamic law in enforcing precepts relating to prayer, fasting, and religious orthodoxy and to deal with civil matters of debt, marriage, divorce, and inheritance as well as criminal matters of theft, drunkenness, and so on. Introduction of the **kadi** (law officer, an important figure in urban governance) dates from the 1580s. A number of Islamic leaders, from various parts of the archipelago, centered in Aceh during the 17th century, writing voluminously on religious topics both in Arabic and Malay. The last great mystic was 'Abd al-Ra'uf of Singkel, born around 1615. After studying in the Middle East, he returned to Aceh, served the sultan as secretary, and wrote widely on law and religion. His fame as a religious reformer spread widely, before and after his death sometime following 1693. *(To p. 559)*

d. MALAYSIA, 1509-1790

Sultanate of Melaka served as a model for the Malay world but was not original. Funan, Champa, and Srivijaya in earlier periods had created a similar economic structure based on trade rather than agriculture. The Islamicate nature of the cultural system and the cosmopolitan character of society also had precedents in the area, but taken together these characteristics came to be perceived as the proper aspects of a Malay state. Cosmopolitanism of the state was legendary; the state served as the meeting place of two kinds of solidarities: one based on the traders' mother country identity (including religious solidarity), the other on identification with the local ruler and local law.

1500s. Nature of trade in this mercantile state involved the whole ruling class as well as the sultan himself. Networks for long-distance trade intersected at Melaka, connecting Indian Ocean, Red Sea, and Persian Gulf tradeways. But in Melaka this trade connected to a **market economy** (where merchants conducted trade on their own behalf), not just the administered trade that characterized earlier empires (where trade was conducted on behalf of the sovereign); prices were fixed by supply and demand; and one could choose to become a merchant without having to secure a royal appointment to do so. Results included a vigorous monetary economy based on mass trade (rather than trade in luxury goods).

The territorial base for the sultanate's realm composed three concentric circles. At the center were territories ruled directly by the sultan; in the middle were territories administered by appointees of the sultan; at the periphery were tributary, vassal, and allied kingdoms (some ruled by the sultan's kinsmen). Especially where the sultan's hold was weakest, the ruler would offer shares in commercial profits—a practice that provided the sultans with almost a third of the capital required to finance trading expeditions, and this reinforced the economic solidarity between the sultanate and its dependencies.

1509-10. Competing alliances of merchants in Melaka took different stances toward the Portuguese: one group (including Chinese, some Tamils, and a few Javanese) inclined to accept them, anticipating new markets and an increase in demand for the commodities they conveyed. The other party (led by Gujaratis and supported by the local elite) saw them as competition and a threat to the moral solidarity between the sultanate and its dependency seaports. The second group prevailed in the short run and seized all the Portuguese they could in 1509, thus delaying advent of the European influence for two years.

1511. The Portuguese, under **Albuquerque, captured Malacca,** center of the spice trade. By this time, the crown was more interested in spice trade than establishing a land-bound empire. The Portuguese then sent envoys to open trade relations with native states and set up fortified posts to protect the trade.

1515. Portuguese governor ordered **cadastral survey**, which counted not land for taxation but irregular occupation of plots abandoned during 1511 uprising; this shows that the sultanate's economic basis depended on sea, not land.

1560s. First **Malay mosque** built under Sultan Muzaffar (d. 1564).

1580s. Dutch began to work in secret with Jambi to corner the pepper production in Sumatra.

1594. The Lisbon spice market was closed to Dutch and English traders, thus providing an incentive for direct trade with the Far East. The English and Dutch **East India Companies** (1600, 1602) presently destroyed the Portuguese forts in Malaysia.

1596. The Dutch set up a factory at **Palembang** (Sumatra).

1602. The English established themselves at **Bantam** (northwest Java).

1605. The Dutch seized Amboina, then settled in western Timor (1613).

1615. British and Dutch gained access to the **pepper trade** in Jambi (Sumatra). Competition included Chinese, Malays, Makassarese, and Javanese as well as the three European trading monopolies.

1619. Batavia became the headquarters of the Dutch East India Company, which worked trade to the limit.

1620s–50s. No further shipments of Southeast Asian pepper and spice were permitted along the old Muslim route to the Red Sea, owing to increasing dominance of European traders. **Dutch blockade** excluded Gujarati ships from Aceh for several years in 1650s, and this led to collapse of direct Acehnese shipping by the 1690s. (Disruption of shipping routes also led to much more difficult pilgrimage routing for Muslims going from Southeast Asia to main pilgrimage sites in Middle East.)

1623. Massacre of the English by the Dutch at **Amboina.** The English forced to abandon trade in Siam, Japan, and the East Indies.

1639. Expulsion of the Portuguese from Japan.

1641. Capture of Malacca by the Dutch, who thenceforth dominated the East Indies.

1650s. Possible at this point to identify a **community of Muslim scholars,** working to translate Islamic concepts into vernacular texts. Within 50 years Islamic writing in Malay reached its greatest heights in the work of Hamzah Fansuri, Syamsu'd-din as-Samatrani, Nuru'd-din ar-Raniri, and Abdur-rauf as-Singkili. Javanese Islamic texts date from the same period.

1666. The Dutch took Celebes from the Portuguese.

1670s. Internal contestation in Sumatra, especially around control of trade asserted by Jambi over upstream pepper cultivators in the interior. Complete rupture prevented by prestige of Jambi's ruler, **the Pangeran** (r. 1630–79).

1677. Conflicts erupted between Jambi and Johor as well as Pelambang, in the process fully rupturing the fragile connections between upriver and downriver economic alliances in Jambi.

1685. The British set up a **factory at Bengkulen** (Sumatra).

During the 18th century the Dutch continued to hold the upper hand. Growing ruthlessness and corruption of the company. In order to control the trade, the company had to widen its control over northern Java.

1769. The **British East India Company** opened stations in northern Borneo, but the settlements (especially **Balambangan,** 1773) had to be given up under pressure from the natives (1775).

1781. The British conquered all the Dutch settlements on the west coast of **Sumatra,** Holland having joined the armed neutrality against Britain.

1783. By the **Treaty of Paris,** the British returned the Dutch colonies but secured the right to trade throughout the Dutch island possessions.

1786. The British East India Company secured a grant of Penang (permanent cession 1790), which made a fourth Indian presidency (1805) but proved useless as a naval and commercial base.   (To p. 560)

e. MALUKU (EASTERN INDONESIA), 1500–17TH CENTURY

In this period, emphasis on an origin myth underscored unities that were island-wide, area-wide, and region-wide. Ceremonies recognizing the origin myth connected five kingdoms, with Ternate depicted as the center.

1500s. Islam had been introduced over the turn of the century, but conversion touched only sultans and their own kin-based settlements.

1550s. Ternate and **Tidore** became the two most important centers in North Maluku, incorporating nearby areas. Expansion due to rapid increase in demand for cloves, which provided rulers with Indian cloth and iron implements, items that were highly valued.

1535–70. Under **Sultan Hairun** in North Maluku, rulers of area began to become much more identifiable by European concepts of kings; Sultan Hairun took on imagery of European rulers; consequently Portuguese treated him as the leader of the Malukan world, which reinforced the authority and power exercised by this kingdom over the other polities of eastern Indonesia.

1570. Portuguese killed Sultan Hairun; the Ternaten court mobilized resources of sufficient power to oust the Portuguese from Ternate; avenging his father's death gave the new sultan grounds for a campaign to make Ternate the single center in the Malukan world. He subdued Bacan and Tidore, then sent a conquering fleet to Banggai, Tobunku, Butung, and Salayar. Though some parts remained restive, the origin myth helped to underscore shared culture and the political claims of Ternate.

1570–83. Rule of **Sultan Babullah** witnessed the culmination of a centralizing process that reinforced the power of this ruler in North Maluku. Before this period the sultan was still a kin-based leader; afterward, he could act without the consensus of the elders of many settlements.

By 1600s. Islam had spread to fellow rulers of Ternate and gradually to the rest of population. Since Muslim traders preferred to work in ports where they could find a mosque and where they could assume the protection of a Muslim ruler, the spread of Islam also brought important economic benefits to the sultan.   (To p. 560)

3. MAINLAND SOUTHEAST ASIA, 1500–1800

a. BURMA

(From p. 139)

Heritage of ethnic fragmentation complicated rivalry between developing religious and political centers. While the prestige of **Mon** capital at **Pegu** was on the rise following the revival of Mon strength in the 15th century (including a renewed patronage of Buddhism), the center of Burman power, Ava, steadily declined as it found itself the target of repeated raids by various Shan tribal groups. The early 16th century witnessed downward **Shan** pressure, reflecting the development of a greater cohesiveness and a hierarchical society among the Shan tribal groups leading to a process of expansion into more desirable lowland areas.

Result was an **increasing cultural homogeneity** achieved in this period, beginning with policies of first Toungoo kings in the 16th century and continued in 17th and 18th, especially through integration of Shans and Mons into a Burman-dominated polity. **Maritime trade** played a reduced role when the capital was moved inland, but monetization of the economy continued throughout the 18th century.

1519. Following the arrival during the 15th century of a few European travelers (Nicolo di Conti, c. 1435), the Portuguese by treaty secured trading privileges at Martaban, and an increasing portion of the foreign trade was conducted by Europeans.

By 1527. Ava was under **Shan** control, with the killing of the Burmese king and the installation of a Shan prince on the throne. This led to the flight of Burman refugees southward to Toungoo, which was situated on the Sittang River.

r. 1531–50. Tabinshwehti founded new Burman dynasty originating at Toungoo. His goal was to establish a centralized state in the Irrawaddy basin.

Late 1530s. He made successful attacks on the Mon capital of Pegu.

By 1539. He captured Pegu.

1542. **Tabinshwehti crowned king** of Lower Burma.

1546. He extended his power northward to Pagan and assumed the title King of All Burma. With Portuguese mercenaries he attacked unsuccessfully both Arakan to the west and Siam to the east. (The Portuguese had secured trading privileges in Martaban in 1519, and Europeans were increasing their involvement in foreign trade.)

Late 1540s. Tabinshwehti launched attacks on Martaban.

r. 1551–81. **Bayinnaung,** successor to Tabinshwehti. Acted as a **model Buddhist king:** building and repairing pagodas and monasteries, ordaining and feeding monks, and distributing copies of the **Tipitaka** (the Buddhist scriptures). By bringing **Mon** princesses into the palace and taking Mon chiefs as brothers, Bayinnaung sought to resolve the longstanding Burman-Mon rivalry. In the tradition of great Burmese kings, he exchanged missions with China, Bengal, Sri Lanka, and Portuguese Goa, reflecting his vision of a Burmese role in a wide diplomatic world. Bayinnaung himself launched ships on commercial voyages. He promoted commerce by appointing officials to supervise merchant shipping, by standardizing weights and measures, and by collecting and collating laws and judicial decisions. His was an exceptional rule because he was able to extend his overlordship over such a great distance from Pegu, his capital, into areas like Lan Sang, which had never before been under Burmese control.

By late 1550s. Bayinnaung's overlordship accepted by most Shan states.

1555. He took Ava.

1558. Bayinnaung **defeated the Thai kingdom** of Chiengmai in northern Siam, which 11 years earlier had resisted armies of Ayutthaya.

1569, August. Ayutthaya fell to Bayinnaung.

By 1574. **Vientiane,** one of two centers in Lan Sang (encompassing much of modern Laos), was in Burman hands.

After Bayinnaung's rule, Burmese power fragmented, since the state was unable to maintain large-scale military expeditions from the capital at Pegu; considerable loss of manpower as villagers fled to escape military service. Regional towns asserted their independence from capital. In addition, relationships between different ethnic groups that Bayinnaung had so carefully built up quickly disintegrated with his death.

r. 1581–99. **Nandabayan** successor to Bayinnaung. In a disastrous effort to retain overextended empire established by his predecessor, the great wealth of Pegu and its ports in the Bay of Bengal was dissipated in ruinous campaigns. The Mons of Pegu, along with the Javanese of the pasisir (Java's northern coast), had been two of the most dynamic actors in the region's maritime commerce.

1593. **Defeat of major Burmese** offensive by Ayutthaya signaled its freedom from Burmese control.

1594. **Alliance between Mons and Ayutthaya** threw back Pegu's forces, and Naresan, the Ayutthayan king, succeeded in taking the entire southeast coast, even threatening Pegu itself.

1599. Pegu finally **fell** before an alliance of Toungoo and Arakan. Both armies took home all that was movable of the remaining population and wealth of the coastal region.

By 1600. Burma once again divided into a number of petty states, as in the early 16th century.

1619. The **Dutch and English East India Companies** opened factories. They did not flourish and were closed later in the century.

Between 1599 and 1635. Truncated version of empire restored, with the capital removed from the maritime region to Ava, a relatively remote center 400 miles up the Irrawaddy from the center of foreign trade.

Beginning in **1600 and continuing to 1830,** a second dramatic **expansion of agriculture** ensued in Upper Burma, including a large portion of rice fields (representing at least a 50 percent growth in total cultivated acreage over figure for 1350). In Lower Burma, too, cultivation expanded. New crops were grown on this increased acreage, including tea and cotton and longer-maturing strains of rice. Better systems of irrigation and drainage were introduced. The **growth in population** and productivity that resulted from this agricultural expansion led, as well, to greater domestic commerce (i.e., demand for salt, dried fish and fish paste, iron goods, pottery, cheap textiles, etc.) and interregional exchange. These developments led, in turn, to greater monetization and economic specialization. All of these internal changes reinforced the administrative centralization characteristic of the period.

Between 1660 and 1715. At least 11 attempts to usurp the throne at Ava.

1727. **Chiengmai rebelled** against Ava control.

1739. The **Shan state of Kengtung rebelled** as well. Between 1727 and 1743, governors of Martaban, Tavoy, Syriam, Toungoo, and Prome were killed or driven out by local rebels.

1740. Leaders of **Pegu rebelled** and declared their independence.

1752. **Ava fell** after two months of siege by a southern army that included representatives of several ethnic groups and was led by a prince of Shan descent. The king fled and the Toungoo dynasty ended.

1753. **Alaungpaya,** founder of the Konbaung dynasty, reunited Burma with assistance from the English East India Company and in opposition to the French. His second successor destroyed Ayutthaya (1767) and subdued Siam for a time, retaining the Tenasserim coast in Burmese possession. *(To p. 556)*

b. SIAM (AYUTTHAYA)

(From p. 139)

Administrative centralization of Siam attributed to efforts of **King Trailokanat** (r. 1448–88); but most of institutionalized form of government probably resulted from reign of King Naresuen the Great (r. 1590–1605). Under this king, Siam regained its independence from Burma and emerged as most powerful kingdom in mainland Southeast Asia.

Development of **overseas trade** can be dated as early as 1368. By the early modern period, Siam was a major source for sappanwood and pepper in the Chinese trading network.

Siamese **adopted Hinduism** along with **Theravada Buddhism.** Hindu concept of divine kingship, and accompanying rituals, provided important sources of legitimation. But in Siamese society, the claim to divinity operated without the internal checks characteristic of India, for Brahmans had little influence at the court. This may explain the pronounced aspect of absolutism in Siam. Yet Buddhism was dominant in the cultural system that emerged in the early modern period, particularly in providing signs of legitimation (and delegitimation in the face of popular unrest) for rulers. **Royal interaction with sangha** (groups of monks) provided especially important occasions for public statements of rulers' support of Buddhist precepts; nevertheless, Thai rulers closely controlled the sangha through cultural patronage (their support ranged from sponsorship of architecture and sculpture to public processions).

1538. As a measure of impact of military technology, King **Phrachai** (r. 1534–46) retained 120 Portuguese to instruct Siamese soldiers in musketry.

1550. **New fortification style** was introduced around the Siamese capital. King Maha Thammarcha (r. 1569–90) also purchased large supplies of foreign cannon. Consequently, by the time Naresuen the Great launched campaign to consolidate Siam, the Siamese royal army was well equipped and trained in the use of firearms.

1569. First **fall of Ayutthaya** to invading Burmese army.

By 1579. China created the **Siamese Language Department** at the Official Translation Office, perhaps a measure of the importance of Siam as a trading partner.

1590. **King Naresuen the Great** regained independence and utilized political, economic, and military forces to transform fragmented kingdom into relatively centralized state.

Portuguese trading stations were established in the 16th century, and around the beginning of the 17th century large numbers of Japanese were active in Siam in war and trade.

1602. A Dutch trading post was established at Patani, where the English soon followed, until their withdrawal from Siam in 1623.

r. 1656–88. King Narai most energetic in pursuit of trade with foreigners. His curiosity about Persian and French cultures made his court known for its openness.

1664. By a commercial treaty, the Dutch gained a monopoly of Siamese foreign trade, which was, however, thwarted by French intrigue; a French embassy and military expedition (1685) in turn failed to secure the acceptance of Christianity and French influence and led to

1688. A popular revolt that began a period of prolonged civil war. Prompted in part by reaction against Narai's openness, it became anti-

European. European trade languished, but Chinese and Muslim trade continued at a high level to take up the slack.

1690s. By this time a dramatic **decline in trade** with Muslims and Europeans could be measured, although the Chinese trade helped to fill the gap.

1767. A **Burmese invasion** destroyed Ayuthia and compelled temporary acceptance of Burmese rule until

1782. Rama I founded a new Siamese dynasty, with its capital at Bangkok. Even in period of political anarchy, great cultural activity emerged. Connecting cultural patronage to political control, Rama issued royal decrees aimed at controlling the sangha and addressing the need to harness the manpower represented by idle monks.

(To p. 557)

c. CAMBODIA

(From p. 139)

Endemic instability characterized this period in Cambodia. By mid-15th century, the Thai-oriented administration of **Angkor** region was overthrown by forces loyal to **Phnom Penh,** but by end of the 15th century, conflict developed among the new rulers.

A **Khmer** revival in early 17th century was followed by a Thai overlordship of Cambodia in the 18th century. From the 17th century, the traditional regions of dissidence could rely on Vietnamese support, setting in motion a whipsaw between Vietnam and Siam, with Cambodia in between. As the importance of foreign powers in Cambodian internal affairs increased, the pattern of increasing intrusion of the Vietnamese into Cambodian life was symbolized by Vietnamese activities that resulted in the sealing off of Cambodia from maritime access to the outside world. This occurred at the time that other Southeast Asian countries, especially Siam, were becoming more involved in the outside world.

Significant social changes occurred during this period: the decline in the importance of a brahmanical priestly class (which had effectively linked landholdings, control of slaves, religious practices, education, and the throne) and the increasingly widespread influence of the Thai on Cambodian life (including the transformation of the Khmer language, i.e., the replacement of Angkorean syntax with Thai syntax). The shift of the capital from the rice-growing hinterlands of northwestern Cambodia to the trade-oriented riverbanks in the vicinity of **Phnom Penh** took place during this period. Another important element at this time was the inability of the king to deliver protection and stability, which undermined his position in the eyes of his subjects.

1560–90. Cambodian troops took advantage of Thai weakness (exacerbated by **1569** Burmese sacking of **Ayudhya**) to raid Thai territories.

1594. Defeat of **Lovek (Khmer)** by **Ayudhya.**

1620s. Territorial expansionist activities by the **Nguyen** overlords of Vietnam cut off Cambodia from maritime access to the outside world and resulted in the loss of thousands of ethnic **Khmer** to Vietnamese rather than Cambodian control.

1750s and early 1760s. Relative calm with respect to invasions from Siam and Vietnam, but internal chaos from a series of coups and countercoups by rivals in the royal family.

1767. A Thai prince and supporters fled to Cambodia when **Ayudhya** fell to Burmese army.

1768. Taksin, new ruler in Siam, invaded Cambodia to defeat potential Thai rival who was trying to set up a competing Thai kingdom.

1770s. Continued Thai pressure on Cambodia while Vietnamese powers were distracted by internal threats (the **Nguyen** dealing with a populist rebellion led by the **Tay Son** brothers).

1772. Thai burned down **Phnom Penh.**

1778. Thai invasion of Cambodia.

1779. Thai placed their own protégé, seven-year-old Cambodian prince **Eng,** on throne under Thai guardianship.

1790. Boy prince **Eng** was taken to Bangkok to be anointed; returned to Cambodia in **1794.**   (To p. 559)

E. EAST ASIA, c. 1500–c. 1800

1. OVERVIEW

The early modern period in East Asia involved deliberate **isolation** from many larger world patterns, though Vietnam was open to significant contact with other civilizations. **Consolidation of many established patterns in China and Korea contrasted with important new political and cultural developments in Japan.**

2. CHINA, 1522–1796

a. THE REMAINDER OF THE MING DYNASTY

(From p. 155)

1522–67. The period began with the completion of Ming political forms, sketched earlier (see p. 154). During the later Ming, **cultural developments and population growth** seized center stage. During the **Jiajing reign** of Shizong (b. 1507), Ming armies fought off the attacks of Altan Khan, prince of the Ordos, and "Japanese pirates," many of them not originally from Japan, but so designated in contemporary sources.

1572–1629. The **Wanli reign** of Shenzong (b. 1563) was famed for its cultural achievements as well as for corruption, in-fighting, and the power of eunuchs at court.

1592, 1597–98. Japanese invasions of Korea, sent by Hideyoshi (1536–98), necessitated Chinese military assistance and were eventually repelled, though not without considerable loss of life and great expense.

In **government,** Ming continued the trend begun in Song, and exacerbated in Yuan, of centralizing autocratic power. Taizu abolished the position of prime minister (1380), eliminating the last impediment to complete autocracy; he also began the practice of flogging ministers at court. The rise of a new administrative body, the Grand Secretariat, dated from the early 15th century. The tradition of remonstrating officials remained alive; especially famous in this regard was Hai Rui (1514–87), who risked life and limb in confronting his master. The Ming **military** built on the Yuan garrison model and the native militia system.

In **local government,** Ming instituted the *lijia* system for local tax collection and surveillance. Ming effectively created provincial-level government, and it would subsequently remain as such. Local governance became increasingly difficult, for as population grew steadily, the number of counties and prefectures did not keep pace, thus allowing the number of residents within a given magistrate's jurisdiction to mushroom. China's **population** returned to 100 million probably in the early 15th century and soared to perhaps as high as 200 million a century later. China's major cities of Song and Yuan did not continue to grow, but middle-level market towns sprouted around the country.

From the start of the Ming, efforts were made to repopulate northern China, sparsely populated under the Yuan, with migrant farmers so as to develop the **economy** there. Land taxes were graduated according to the arable quality of the land, and thus the far richer south paid an overwhelming percentage of the state's tax revenues. Under Grand Secretary **Zhang Juzheng** (1525–82), the rationalizing **"single whip" laws** simplified tax collection nationwide. The only major state monopoly was on salt, though by late Ming the government empowered a group of salt merchants with distribution responsibilities; they later became fabulously wealthy.

In addition, new crops from the Americas were introduced to China via the Philippines, effectively contributing to the capacity of agriculture to support a larger population.

In **education,** Taizu ordered the creation of a nationwide system, with schools in every county and prefecture, as a means of nurturing future officials for the state. He reinstituted civil service examinations at the provincial and national levels (1370–71). Private academies, which prospered especially in the 16th century, also provided talented men for recruitment to state service. By the end of Ming, there were far more men who had passed the examinations than positions for them, a cause of social disorder. Stipends were kept purposefully low. The continued spread of **printing** resulted in greater access to the state bureaucracy and a seeping down of Chinese cultural traditions to local society.

Ming **intellectual life** was initially dominated by followers of the Cheng-Zhu school of Neo-Confucianism, such as Xue Xuan (1392–1464). The *Xingli daquan (Great Collection on Nature and Principle),* a digest of moral philosophy from the writings of 120 scholars of the Cheng-Zhu school, was published under imperial authority in 1416. Signs of a divergence from orthodox Cheng-Zhu teachings were evident in the naturalism and quiescence of Chen Baisha (1428–1500), a popular teacher from southern China. **WANG YANGMING (Wang Shouren, 1472–1529)** was the greatest thinker of his age and an eminent official as well. Although perceived as attacking the Cheng-Zhu school, he saw himself as developing from it a style of Neo-Confucianism that asserted the importance of extending the individual's "intuitive knowledge." Influenced by Buddhist practice, he stressed meditation as the nurturing praxis for the mind to come to moral judgment, the "unity of knowledge and action," and the innate capacity of every man to attain sagehood. Wang's disciples, however, went their own ways. Irreverent iconoclasm eventually cost one of them, **Li Zhi** (1527–1602), his life. Wang's teachings were popular elsewhere in East Asia, especially in Japan.

Less vital than they had been earlier, Buddhism and Daoism remained eclipsed through the Ming. A number of thinkers, such as **Lin Zhao'en** (1517–98), taught the "unity of the three teachings" (namely, Confucianism, Buddhism, and Daoism).

In **scholarship** there was a growing trend toward compiling massive encyclopedias and compendia. One such project was supervised by the Hanlin Academy in Beijing: *Yongle dadian (The Yongle Encyclopedia),* into which entire works were transcribed—an imposing work of 12,000 manuscript volumes, completed in 1407. Following Tang, Song, and Yuan precedents, numerous dynastic legal and administrative codes were compiled.

Contacts between Chinese elites (and the late Ming court) and the **Jesuits** produced a short-lived but curious bond. One such project was supervised by the **Matteo Ricci** (1552–1610) won toleration for the Jesuits by adopting Chinese ways; he lived in Beijing and served the court by, among other things, preparing a map of the world. **Adam Schall von Bell** (1591–1666) went to Beijing (1662), where he was charged (1630) with reforming the dynastic calendar; he cast astronomical instruments based on the latest Western technology, which was much appreciated by the Ming court. In addition to works of religious content, the Jesuits published works on mathematics and other sciences, providing an important conduit for Western knowledge to penetrate China. The first major Western work on Chinese history was by the Augustinian monk Juan Gonzalez de Mendoza, *Historia de las cosas mas notables, ritos y costumbres del gran reyno de la China* (1585).

The Ming is considered the literary apex for **vernacular fiction.** Such long novels, often lifeworks, included *Xiyou ji (Journey to the West, also known as Monkey),* by Wu Cheng'en (1506?–82?); *Shuihu zhuan (Water Margin, also known as All Men Are Brothers),* traditionally attributed to Luo Guanzhong (1330?–1400?); *Sanguo zhi yanyi (Ro-*

mance of the Three Kingdoms), also attributed to Luo Guanzhong; and *Jin ping mei (Golden Lotus),* a 16th-century novel whose author is unknown. During the Ming, **vernacular drama** continued to be popular. **Tang Xianzu** (1550–1616) wrote what is considered the greatest drama of the era, *Peony Pavilion.*

In **art,** Ming painting styles generally followed those of the Song. Emperor **Xuanzong** (b. 1399, r. 1425–35) was a fine painter in the southern Song fashion. **Dong Qichang** (1555–1636) was one of the great calligraphers and painters of the late Ming; he was an art critic as well. **Pottery** in the early Ming achieved bold effects by application of "three color" glazes. The **Jingdezhen** imperial kiln gained renown for its production of such pottery. In the late Ming, decoration in overglaze enamels, often in combination with underglaze blue, was used to startling effect, especially in urban areas.

By 1500 a rotary disc cutter was being used to cut jade, highly valued in China since the 13th century B.C.E. By 1593 a **modern form of the abacus** was in use.

b. THE QING DYNASTY

Peasant rebellion and ethnic strife erupted at the end of the Ming dynasty, and an impoverished central government was no longer able to meet these challenges. A rebel band under the command of **Li Zicheng** (1605?–1645) finally captured the capital at Beijing, and the last Ming emperor committed suicide. Several decades earlier, in eastern Manchuria, **NURHACHI (1559–1626, Taizu)** had organized militarily (1615) under eight banners a group of Tungusic tribes. Later, Mongol and Han Chinese living in northeastern China were incorporated into each of their own eight banners. In 1616 Nurhachi, who had had considerable contact with the Ming, took the title of emperor of the Hou Jin (or Later Jin) dynasty, following on the ethnic descent of his own people from the Jurchens of the 12th and 13th centuries, and took the clan name of Aisin Gioro. Only later (1634) did his people adopt the name **MANCHUS** (probably from the bodhisattva of learning, Manjusri). In 1618 his armies defeated the Ming and seized part of Liaodong, where he began to set up a government with local Han Chinese assistance. In the year before his death (1625), Nurhachi moved the capital to Shenyang (Manchu name, Mukden) and began to build a civil administration patterned closely on the Chinese model. There in 1636 the Manchus, under Nurhachi's son **Abahai** (1592–1643), proclaimed the **Qing Dynasty,** having already quelled the other northeastern peoples and attacked south of the Great Wall on several occasions. When Li Zicheng's forces took Beijing in 1644, a Ming general, **Wu Sangui** (1612–78), in collaboration with Manchu prince regent **Dorgon** (1612–50), allowed the Manchus to cross the Shanhai Pass into China unhindered rather than surrender to the rebels.

1644–1911. The **Qing dynasty** commenced when Manchu forces entered Beijing, attacked the rebel forces of Li Zicheng, and defeated them.

Whereas earlier conquerers had discriminated against the subject Han populace, the Manchus worked to establish good relations with the Chinese under their rule. The Qing carried over the Ming **governmental structure** in large part, save the addition of the Grand Council. There was Manchu-Chinese parity in the leadership of each of the six ministries. Local self-governance was handled through the *lijia* system taken over from Ming, with tax-collecting duties added to its functions in Qing. Through a community compact system, the laws and Confucian values were directly imparted to local people in periodic lectures.

The **population** surged to more than 300 million by 1750, as high as 400 million by 1850; changes in local administration did not keep pace. Sparsely populated areas such as Yunnan and Guizhou began to receive larger numbers of Han Chinese.

The **recruitment system into government service**—the civil service examination system—was carried over from Ming. These were highly competitive exams, held at three stages (local, provincial, and national or metropolitan). Once a person was appointed to a post, he usually held it for three years. With the rapid population increase of the 18th century and the lack of concomitant expansion of government, many

THE MANCHU (QING) DYNASTY (1644–1796)

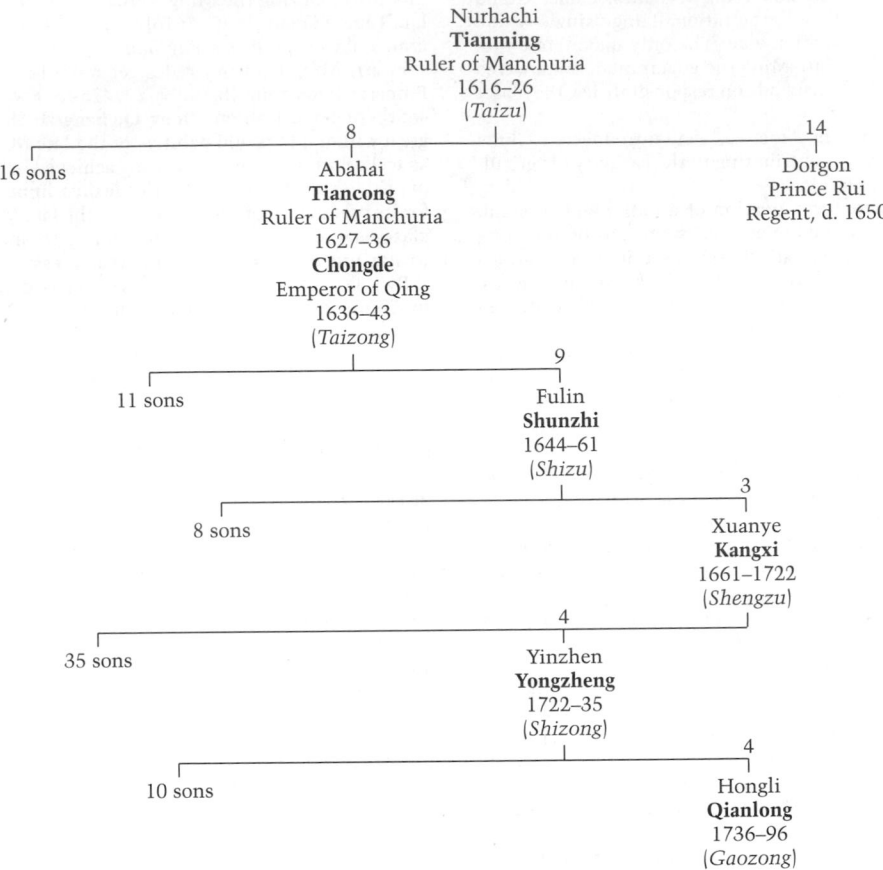

Nurhachi
Tianming
Ruler of Manchuria
1616–26
(*Taizu*)

8   14

16 sons   Abahai
Tiancong
Ruler of Manchuria
1627–36
Chongde
Emperor of Qing
1636–43
(*Taizong*)

Dorgon
Prince Rui
Regent, d. 1650

9

11 sons   Fulin
Shunzhi
1644–61
(*Shizu*)

3

8 sons   Xuanye
Kangxi
1661–1722
(*Shengzu*)

4

35 sons   Yinzhen
Yongzheng
1722–35
(*Shizong*)

4

10 sons   Hongli
Qianlong
1736–96
(*Gaozong*)

Names in lightface type are personal names, taboo after a ruler
ascended the throne. **Names in boldface type** are reign titles, adopted
for reckoning time but often applied by Westerners to the emperor
himself. Dates are reign dates. *Names in italic type are dynastic titles,*
or temple names, conferred posthumously to refer to the ruler.

graduates, unable to find employment, became professional scholars
and teachers.

Military garrisons of the eight Manchu banners were distributed
among strategic provincial cities, though Han Chinese were appointed
in the provinces to the command of Chinese auxiliary troops. Four
Chinese were sent as governors to hold the south and southwest during
the Shunzhi reign at the beginning of the dynasty.

In **agriculture,** the development of faster-ripening strains of rice—
30-day growing cycles were achieved in Qing times—made possible
larger yields, which in turn meant more crops and the ability to sustain
more people from the same amount of land.

1644–61. During the **Shunzhi reign** of Emperor Shizong (nephew of Dorgon), the Manchus, together with Han Chinese armies, consolidated
Qing control, defeating various itinerant Ming pretenders and loyalist
bands in the south by 1659. Conquest was accompanied by the imposition of the Manchu-style shaven head with the queue for men.
Foot-binding, at first forbidden (1638, 1645, 1662), was ultimately permitted to Chinese only (1668).

1645–83. A Taiwan-based pirate band, claiming continued allegiance to
the Ming, was begun by Zheng Zhilong (1604–61, executed in Beijing),
and he was succeeded by his son, **Zheng Chenggong** (1624–62), known
to Westerners as Koxinga from a rendering of his Chinese title, Lord
of the Imperial Surname. They raided the southeast China coast, seiz-

ing Xiamen (Amoy, 1653) and Chongming Island (1656), attacking as
far as Nanjing (1657), and finally expelling the Dutch from Taiwan
after a prolonged battle (1661–62). In 1663–64, Balthasar Bort with a
Dutch fleet helped a Qing army drive Koxinga's son, **Zheng Jing** (1642–
81), from the Fujian coast back to Taiwan. Ultimately, the Qing sent
an armada to put an end to the Zhengs' attacks on its coast, when
Zheng Keshuang (1670–1707), Zheng Jing's son and the last of the
Zhengs to control Taiwan, surrendered to the Qing. Taiwan was then
brought under Chinese imperial administration as an appendage of Fujian province.

1673–81. The Rebellion of the Three Feudatories erupted when Wu Sangui and two other former Han collaborators with the Manchus, having
been awarded healthy satrapies in the south for their efforts in bringing
Manchu rule to China, revolted against the Qing. After eight years of
fighting, the rebels were quelled with the help of other Han generals.

1661–1722. The **KANGXI REIGN** of Emperor Shengzu (b. 1654, personal
rule began in form 1667, in fact 1669) opened an extraordinary period
of cultural achievement, possibly surpassing the best of earlier dynasties. His was the longest reign in Chinese history. Kangxi acquired
many of the habits and capacities of the well-educated Han elite. He
was initially tolerant of Jesuit missionaries and very interested in the
technology they introduced from the West, but later grew weary of
their doctrinal squabbles. He was a patron of the arts and of learning,

sponsoring major scholarly enterprises. He also made six personal tours of his empire to observe local conditions firsthand.

1670. A Portuguese embassy under Manoel de Saldanha, like that of Bento Pereyra de Faria (1678–79), won only confirmation of the status of Macao. The subsequent missions of A. M. de Souza y Menezas (1726) and F.-X. Assis Pacheco y Sampayo (1742) achieved no more.

1675. A revolt in Chahar was quickly suppressed.

1688. Galdan (1632?–97), chief of the Olöt (Eleuth, western Mongol) Dzungars, attacked Mongolia from Central Asia. Kangxi personally led the defense of the Khalka states of central Mongolia (1690). After several assaults, Galdan's forces were finally crushed (1696) near Urga, and Galdan took poison the following year. Qing military colonies were established in the region.

1689. The **Treaty of Nerchinsk** with Russia was China's first treaty with a European nation. Earlier, the Russian Poyarkhov explored the Amur River region (1643–46), and Khabarov built a fort at Albazin (p. 346). Qing forces attacked Fort Albazin (1685–86), territory the Manchus considered their own. The treaty stipulated Russian abandonment of Albazin and of military pressure for commercial contacts and continued peace. L. V. Izmailov established a trading agent and Russian Orthodox church in Beijing (1720–21).

1717. The Olöt **seizure of Lhasa** under the direction of Galdan's nephew, Tsewang Rabdan (1697–1727), was learned of too late in Beijing to save a relief column from annihilation (1718). Well-prepared armies from Gansu and Sichuan drove the Mongols out of Tibet (1720), enthroned a popular Dalai Lama, and established imperial garrisons there.

1721. A revolt in Taiwan led by Zhu Yigui was suppressed.

1722–35. During the **YONGZHENG REIGN** of Emperor Shizong, peace was the rule at home, although battles with the Mongols and tribesmen to the west continued to an inconclusive end.

1727. The **Kiakhta Treaty,** fixing the Russian border, was concluded with Sava Vladislavich after a mission to Beijing (1726–27).

1729. Following large-scale operations against the Dzungars, the Grand Council was established and gradually usurped the executive functions of the Grand Secretariat. In 1735 the Qing acquired control over the eastern part of Turkestan.

1736–96. The long **reign of the Qianlong emperor** was an era of energetic cultural and scholarly endeavors. It witnessed a large population growth, vigorous foreign relations, and an explosion of market networks and urban ways of life. Newly acquired sources of wealth enabled Qianlong to impose Manchu imperial control further into central Asia. Corruption (led by Heshen, 1750–99) in the highest echelons of the bureaucracy during the last 20 years of the reign set off revolts. This failing became typical of the last Qianlong years.

1751. After several bruising campaigns against recalcitrant tribes in Tibet, Qing forces invaded and **conquered Tibet.** Thereafter, the Manchus dominated the Dalai Lama succession.

1755. Amursana, grandson of Tsewang Rabdan, was enthroned by Qing forces as prince of the Dzungars, but the Dzungars revolted. Suppression of the revolt, following a smallpox epidemic, depopulated the Ili Valley. The Dzungars who were not annihilated later dispersed. Mongol power was thus finally eliminated from the region and all of Turkestan fell to Qing control (1759).

1757–1842. Restrictions on foreign maritime trade to Guangzhou were maintained despite efforts of the British interpeter Flint at Tianjin (1759), Captain Skottowe at Guangzhou (1761), and the earl of Macartney at Rehe (Jehol) and Beijing (1793).

1765–69. The **invasion of Burma** failed to reach the capital at Ava but secured recognition of suzerainty, as did a later invasion of Vietnam (1788).

1784. The United States entered the Guangzhou trade.

1786–87. A rebellion in Taiwan was suppressed.

1792. The **invasion of Nepal** by Qing forces from Tibet was provoked by an attack on Tashilunpo, the seat of the Panchen Lama. It resulted in the defeat of the Gurkas and their recognition of Qing suzerainty.

1795–97. A revolt by Hmong tribesmen in Hunan and Guizhou was suppressed.

1796. The Qianlong emperor abdicated but continued to direct affairs until his death three years later.

The Jesuits continued to enjoy imperial toleration and favor in return for scientific services. **Adam Schall von Bell** (1591–1666) prepared the dynastic calendar (1630–64), indispensable to agriculture, until he was imprisoned on representations of jealous Muslim astronomers. **Ferdinand Verbiest** (1623–88) arrived in China in 1659 and was put in charge of the almanac (1669). He installed a new set of astronomic instruments in the imperial observatory (1674) and promulgated a perpetual calendar (1678). Fontaney cured the emperor with quinine (1693). Regis and eight others prepared the first maps of China based on astronomic observation, triangulation, and measurement (1708–18). The Jesuit acceptance of Chinese rituals toward heaven, Confucius, and their ancestors was bitterly condemned by the Dominican and Franciscan orders, culminating in the **Rites Controversy** in the 17th and 18th centuries. In 1742 the pope decreed that no Chinese convert could continue such Chinese rites as ancestor worship.

From the early years of the 19th century, **Protestant missionaries** began their effort to convert the Chinese masses, though with extremely limited success.

In **literature,** Qing writers continued to produce large quantities of poetry and prose. Especially noteworthy were the great vernacular novels *Rulin waishi* (*Unofficial History of the Confucians,* or *The Scholars*) by Wu Jingzi (1701–54) and *Honglou meng* (*Dream of the Red Chamber;* also known as *Shitou ji,* or *Story of the Stone*) by Cao Xueqin (1724?–64). Both provide intimate details of elite family life.

The Qing period, not noted for major developments or innovations in **painting,** largely remained within molds set in Song, Yuan, and Ming times. A brilliant epoch in the history of the imperial kilns of Jingdezhen followed the appointment of **Cang Yingxuan** as superintendent (1682). The techniques of enameling on the biscuit, of composite monochrome glazing, of application of underglaze blue in powder form, and of decoration overglaze in transparent *famille verte* enamels were perfected. Later, under Tang Ying (1736–49), the imperial craftsmen developed the elaborate *famille rose* palette of opaque overglaze enamels, which is distinguished by mixed colors and replacement of ferric oxide red by carmine derived from gold.

Scholarly writings continued to grow in quantity and erudition. The earlier trend of writing local gazetteers reached a crescendo in Qing times. Among the state-sponsored encyclopedic projects was the massive *Gujin tushu jicheng* (*Compendium of Books Past and Present,* 1725), in 10,000 volumes, covering a wide variety of subjects. The best critical edition of the 24 dynastic *Standard Histories* was issued by imperial authority (1739–46). The greatest effort to bring together all known writings was the colossal *Siku quanshu* (*Complete Works of the Four Treasuries*) project (1772–81). It embraced 3,462 works in 36,300 volumes. Seven copies were eventually distributed. A *General Catalog* in 92 volumes (1789) contained notices on these and an additional 6,734 works not included in the library. Qianlong exploited the occasion of this compilation for another end as well, to expurgate from Chinese literature all derogatory references to the Manchus and their northern predecessors. Works were thus doctored and nearly 2,500 were destroyed (1774–82), many of them from the late Ming and early Qing years. Manchu emperors in the 17th and 18th centuries, being great patrons of Confucianism and scholarship, provided funds for many other projects as well. Among the many collections to be issued as a result of Kangxi's order were *Ming History* (53 scholars appointed, 1679); *Complete Tang Poetry* (1707); *Peiwen yunfu,* a thesaurus of literary phrases (1716); and the *Kangxi Dictionary* (1716).

Individual scholars and private groups or teams also produced formidable works in the Qing years. A number of prominent Han Chinese intellectuals from the Ming-Qing transition era refused to sit for the Manchu civil service examinations, devoting their lives instead to scholarship. These included **Huang Zongxi** (1610–95), author of *Mingyi daifang lu* (*A Plan for the Prince*), a sharp critique of autocratic government, and *Ming Ru xue an* (*Case Studies of Ming Confucians*); **Gu Yanwu** (1613–81), author of *Ri zhi lu* (*Record of Knowledge Acquired Daily*); and **Wang Fuzhi** (1619–92), sharply anti-Manchu author of *Du Tongjian lun* (*On Reading the "Zizhi tongjian"*) and *Song lun* (*On Reading the History of the Song Dynasty*).

The Cheng-Zhu school of **Neo-Confucianism** remained state orthodoxy for the civil service examinations in Qing, and the widespread nonconformity of thought in the late Ming came under serious attack by early Qing thinkers, some even blaming it for the decline and collapse of the dynasty. The fall of Ming led many intellectuals into deep introspection.

The principal intellectual movement of the 17th and especially the 18th century was the *kaozheng* (textual critical) movement. It represented an effort to establish through rigorous methods the authenticity of the classical cannon; it represented as well a turn away from the more speculative thinking of Song and Ming times. The *kaozheng* movement was also known as the Han Learning movement, because it harked back to Han-period styles of textual scholarly research. In addition to Gu Yanwu, one of the founders of the movement, important *kaozheng* scholars would include **Xu Qianxue** (1631–94), who brought together 480 volumes of the best of classical commentaries in his *Tongzhi tang jingjie (Exegeses of the Classics from the Tongzhi*

Hall); **Mei Wending** (1633–1721), a famous mathematician; **Yan Ruoju** (1636–1704), a scholar of the *Great Learning, Mencius,* and especially the *Book of History,* the old text version of which he showed to be spurious; **Cui Shu** (1740–1816), who independently came to similar conclusions about the old text *Book of History;* **Dai Zhen** (1724–77), a great philosopher in his own right and a philologist who wrote a penetrating study of the language of the *Mencius;* and **Duan Yucai** (1735–1815), **Wang Mingsheng** (1722–97), **Qian Daxin** (1728–1804), and many others. **Bi Yuan** (1730–97) compiled a supplement to the general history of China by Sima Guang of the Song. **Zhang Xuecheng** (1738–1801) wrote philosophically about history in his great *Wenshi tongyi (Comprehensive Explanation of Literature and History);* he argued that "the Six Classics are all history."   (To p. 561)

3. KOREA, 1392–1800

(From p. 157)

1392–1910. The **YI DYNASTY** (or **CHOSŎN**) lasted longer than any other in Korean history. **YI SŎNGGYE (KING T'AEJO, r. 1392–98)** built the dynasty through a combination of military might and the backing of the literati. The rising sociopolitical importance of this literati class marked the entire period. Yi Sŏnggye began with a policy of deference toward the Ming dynasty in China, both to keep the peace with China and to prop up his legitimacy at home. Embassies were sent to Beijing at regular intervals each year. "Japanese pirates" continued to harass the Korean coast from the island of Tsushima.

The hereditary literati class was known as the **yangban,** or "two orders," because its members combined the civil and military functions of state control. During the Yi period, far more families acquired *yangban* status than under the Koryŏ aristocracy. The increased number of potential officials meant that the examination system loomed ever more important as a means of selecting the best. Likewise, *yangban* monopolized the civil service exams and hence access to office. There was a National Confucian Academy in the capital at Seoul. Examinations were held every three years, but they also could be taken at many irregular times. In the latter half of the 15th century, Neo-Confucian literati began to gain attention in the central government. These were *yangban* scholars of a moralistic bent, unlike the primarily scholar-official group of *yangban* who had been influential until then. The conflict between the two groups led to a series of four "literati purges" from 1498 to 1545.

The highest Yi **governmental body** was originally the State Council. Under it were the Six Ministries, which, as government became increasingly bureaucratized, grew in importance. In addition, the Royal Secretariat was responsible for handling documents of state that passed to and from the throne.

Land allocations in the Yi period followed guidelines established by T'aejo. Current and former officials received lands commensurate with their rank. **King Sejo** (b. 1417, r. 1455–68) revised this law (1466) to eliminate former officials from allocations. This system was later changed (1556) to a straight salary system. Improvements in agricultural techniques led to greater productivity for the peasantry. As early as 1430, a farmer's manual for Korea was published, *Straight Talk on Agricultural Matters.* Peasants were legally forbidden from abandoning the land they worked. Most were self-sufficient tenant farmers. They were responsible for a **land tax,** a tribute tax, and military and corvee duties, much like the system in Tang China. There was also a slave population. Over time, the landed estates of *yangban* families grew larger, especially after the state ceased allocating lands to them. This reduced the tax revenues coming into the central government and brought further misery to the peasantry. Changes were effected in the various taxes and duties, and Ever Normal Granaries were established throughout the country. By the middle of the 16th century, these dislocations had caused many peasants to leave their land and led to the rise of rebel forces. The Japanese invasions not only decimated the land, they also destroyed many land registers. Taxable lands in the early 17th century were reduced to a third of the figure prior to the invasions.

A monetary **economy** developed rather late in Korea. Paper (1401)

and coin (1423, 1464) currency were issued but did not circulate widely at the time. Cloth was still the mainstay of transactions. During the 17th and 18th centuries, rural markets cropped up in ever larger numbers, with more than 1,000 by the end of this period. Commercial growth spurred the development of merchant organizations.

1400–1418. During the **reign of King T'aejong** (1367–1422), efforts to reconstitute an aristocracy were severely crushed as a Chinese bureaucratic structure was regularized. He had already abolished all private armies, a holdover from the late Koryŏ era, in an effort to centralize military control of the state.

1418–50. The **reign of King Sejong** continued this trend with the establishment of the Hall of Worthies, at which the finest scholars studied ancient Chinese texts and institutions.

1442. A gauge for measuring rainfall was invented, roughly two centuries before a similar invention emerged in the West.

1446. On orders of the king, a group of scholars devised an ingenious alphabet for the Korean language, **han'gŭl.** This invention was not received happily by many *yangban,* because it made learning to read much easier and broke their control over learning solely in the more difficult literary Chinese language. Sejong persevered, founding an Office for Publication in Han'gŭl. **King Sejo** later set up a similar office to translate Buddhist sutras into Korean.

1451. The state-sponsored *Koryŏ sa (History of Koryŏ)* was finished.

1457. The military structure was completely reorganized.

1469–94. During the **reign of King Sŏngjong,** rural-based Neo-Confucian scholars began to rise to center stage, rather than remaining influential as a group locally. They were principally influenced by the works of Zhu Xi (1130–1200) from Song-period China.

1471. After a number of earlier efforts, a national code of laws was promulgated. It effectively standardized the new *yangban* governing structure.

1495. *Tongguk t'onggam (Comprehensive Mirror of the Eastern Kingdom [Korea])* was issued, the first full history of Korea, covering from Tan'gun through the fall of Koryŏ.

1498. The first **literati purge,** during the reign of King Yŏnsan'gun (r. 1494–1506, b. 1476), in which the older *yangban* elite sought to get rid of many of the Neo-Confucians. A second purge occurred in 1504.

1506–44. The **reign of Chungjong** returned to a more stable period. He favored the Neo-Confucians and patronized the scholar Cho Kwang-jo (1482–1519), who taught basic Confucian values of rule by moral exemplar. He enacted the "village compact" system, as in China. He also saw to it that certain basic texts be translated into Korean. He was ousted and executed during factional strife that set off the third literati purge (1519).

1545. The last of the literati purges again hit the Neo-Confucian elite hard, though as before, their base in rural society remained intact.

1567–1608. During the **reign of King Sŏnjo** (b. 1552), the Neo-Confucian literati came to dominate central governmental affairs. Private Confucian academies through which Neo-Confucian elites fortified local control began to appear throughout the land; by the end of Sŏnjo's reign, there were more than 100. Beginning in 1575, factional strife within this newly risen elite began to rip it apart, and the private academies joined in the political fray.

1592. The first Japanese invasion (p. 382), sent by Toyotomi Hideyoshi, was met by irresoluteness and poor planning. The king and his minions fled Seoul, further infuriating the populace. The Japanese armies laid waste the land. Almost single-handedly, Admiral **Yi Sun-sin** (1545–98) rebuilt the Korean navy, created his celebrated "turtle ships" (with protective canopies to ward off enemy fire), and eventually defeated the Japanese navy. His victories cut off supply lines to the Japanese army, ensuring Japan's defeat.

1597–98. The second Japanese invasion was met by a better-prepared Korea and by Chinese reinforcements. When Hideyoshi died in 1598, Japanese forces withdrew.

1606. The newly formed Tokugawa shogunate in Japan commenced amicable ties with Korea.

1608–23. The reign of King Kwanghaegun (1571–1641) restored domestic and diplomatic peace to the peninsula.

1610. The culmination of nearly two centuries of writings on Korean medicine, *Tongŭi pogam (Exemplar of Korean Medicine)*, was completed. Many of its remedies were developed as a result of the famine and destruction caused by the Japanese invasions.

1623–49. The reign of King Injo (b. 1595), brought to the throne by one faction (the "Westerners") of the Neo-Confucians, moved Korea toward an openly pro-Ming and anti-Manchu stance.

1627. The Manchus invaded Korea. When Emperor Taizong of the Qing demanded that Korea accept vassal status to the Manchus, Injo refused and the Manchus invaded again (1636). Korea became a vassal state.

1708. A Uniform Land Tax Law, enacted in the 17th century, was promulgated nationwide. Also in the early 17th century, new methods of improving the rice yield enabled farmers to double-crop. This enriched some, but at the expense of others. The former were able to acquire land and rent it to poorer peasants, thus creating a new class of non-*yangban* landlords.

1785. The Rites Controversy brought to a head the issue of Catholicism, as was the case in China and Vietnam, and King Chŏngjo (b. 1752, r. 1776–1880) banned the religion as heterodox.

Buddhism declined as Neo-Confucianism soared to supremacy with the rise of the *yangban*. T'aejo forbade the building of new temples, and in 1406 T'aejong suppressed all but 242 temples nationwide and confiscated all their lands and slaves. Further acts of repression followed in the 16th century. In the early 17th century, Korean scholars became interested in **Catholicism.** Texts, not missionaries, circulated, and it was seen as a religion that could help correct the social and political ills of Chosŏn.

The greatest **Neo-Confucian** thinker of the Yi period, **Yi T'oegye** (Yi Hwang, 1501–70), developed basic ideas laid out by Zhu Xi on the primacy of principle to material force. He also dealt with issues of moral self-cultivation. Other major figures of this school included Yu Sŏng-nyong (1542–1607), Kim Sŏng-il (1538–93), and Chŏng Ku (1543–1620). The most famous advocate of the primacy of material force was **Yi Yulgok** (Yi I, 1536–84); he also formulated proposals on the reform of government and the economy. The most important Korean supporter of the Wang Yangming school was **Chŏng Che-du** (1649–1736). Under **King Sukchong** (r. 1674–1720), the "Westerners" faction divided into bitterly squabbling Old and Young Doctrine cliques. Neo-Confucianism had ousted its original *foes* of the older *yangban* elite only to divide into warring factions. Many retired from the infighting to pursue teaching careers at local private academies. General intellectual antipathy for the "Westerners," principally by those prevented from having a voice in Yi social or political life, began to take form as a school of **"practical learning"** *(sirhak)*, at once a scholarly and reformist political movement. The social rupture in the *yangban* order over the 17th and 18th centuries also caused practically oriented scholars to focus attention on their own society and those who had allowed it to decay. *Sirhak* scholars turned to many different kinds of institutional learning, the first being agricultural conditions and land systems. One important name in this institutional approach was **Yu Hyŏng-wŏn** (1622–73), who examined many aspects of Yi-dynasty institutions. He was followed by Yi Ik (1681–1763). Another *sirhak*-oriented school argued for the enrichment of the country through the promotion of commerce. The great stylist **Pak Chi-wŏn** (1737–1805) accompanied an official Korean emissary to Beijing in 1780 and wrote a diary in which he lamented how poor Korea was by comparison with China. There were many similar accounts of travelers to China who were vitriolic in their condemnation of the unproductive *yangban* style of life.

Painting in Korea, as in China at the time, was seen as an avocation, not a full-time profession, by the *yangban* class. Kang Hŭi-an (1419–64) and An Kyŏn—the former a *yangban* aristocrat and the latter a government painter—were two early masters in the ink-and-brush style. In the 17th century, a trend toward realism appeared in landscape painting, as in the work of Chŏng Sŏn (1676–1759). Genre painting also became popular in the 18th century.

In **literature**, Sŏ Kŏ-jŏng compiled his *Tongmun sŏn (Anthology of Korean Literature)* in 1478, bringing together Korean writings over the ages in Chinese. From the middle years of Chosŏn, new poetic styles (*kasa* and *sijo*) emerged for composition in Korean. Some *sirhak* scholars, such as Pak Chi-wŏn, turned to writing fiction in literary Chinese. However, the most important new development in literature as a whole was the use of *han'gŭl*, the Korean alphabet. There were authors from non-*yangban* classes as well. *(To p. 566)*

4. JAPAN, 1542–1793

(From p. 163)

1542 or 1543. Portuguese aboard a Chinese vessel landed near the island of Tanegashima, off the southern coast of Kyūshū. They introduced the musket, which soon modified Japanese warfare. Other Portuguese ships followed and entered into trading relations with the lords of western Japan.

1549–51. Francis Xavier (1506–52), the famous Jesuit missionary, introduced Christianity into Japan, proselytizing among the feudal domains of the west and also in Kyoto, but with little success. On the whole he was well received, and in some cases the feudal lords even encouraged conversions in the hope of attracting Portuguese trade. But the doctrinal intolerance of the missionaries soon earned them the bitter enmity of the Buddhist clergy and led to proscriptions of the new religion in certain fiefs. Xavier left behind two Jesuits and the Japanese converts who formed the nucleus of the new church.

1568. ODA NOBUNAGA (1534–82) seized Kyoto and set up a puppet shogun, Ashikaga Yoshiaki (1537–97, r. 1568–73). Lord of the provinces of Owari, Mino, and Mikawa east of Kyoto, Nobunaga had acted in response to a secret appeal from the emperor. This daring blow gave him all but total control of central Japan.

1568–1600. The process of political disintegration had already run its course by the **period of national unification,** or **Azuchi-Momoyama period,** and in these few decades, through the efforts of three great leaders, the nation was again united as the periphery was gradually subjugated by the military hegemons of the capital region. This was unquestionably one of the most dynamic epochs of Japanese history. "Japanese pirates" were at their height and were active even in Thai and Philippine waters. Korea was invaded on two separate occasions. **Closer contacts with the Asian mainland and with Europeans resulted in an influx of new intellectual and artistic currents.** Buddhism was in decline and its monasteries were being deprived of their military power, but militant Christianity was at its peak in Japan, and lay learning was revived after the years of warfare. New skills and new products from the West profoundly affected the economy of the land, and in those years of relative peace Japan's wealth and productivity expanded rapidly. The private-customs barriers that had hampered trade were abolished, and the old monopolistic guilds *(za)* for the most part came to an end.

The artistic and intellectual spirit of the period contrasted sharply with what it had been in the Ashikaga era. It was a more exuberant, expansive age. Earlier Zen-inspired stress on refinement and simplicity gave way to shows of great pomp and to ostentatiousness. Architecture, for example, demonstrated a love of gorgeous design and majestic size. Castles and palaces rather than monasteries were the typical structures of the day.

1570. Nagasaki was opened to foreign trade by the local lord, Ōmura (sometimes dated 1567 or 1568). This small fishing village soon became Japan's greatest port for foreign commerce.

1571. Nobunaga destroyed the Enryakuji on Mount Hiei, thus eliminating the most powerful of all the monasteries as a military force. In these same years he also waged usually successful wars against other Buddhist groups, especially the militant cliques of the True Pure Land sect (Ikkō sect), as in the siege of their central monastery, Ishiyama honganji, in Osaka (1570–80). Nobunaga's violent opposition to Buddhism as an organized political force finally broke the temporal power of the monasteries.

1576. Nobunaga set to work on the **Azuchi castle** on the shores of Lake Biwa. This was the first great castle of Japan and heralded the beginning of several decades of widespread castle building. Azuchi was destroyed at the time of Nobunaga's death.

1577–82. TOYOTOMI HIDEYOSHI (1536–98), Nobunaga's brilliant, lowborn general, conquered much of western Japan from the Mōri family in the name of Nobunaga.

1578. The death of **Uesugi Kenshin** (1530–78), together with the earlier demise of his great enemy, **Takeda Shingen** (1521–73), removed two formidable rivals of Nobunaga in eastern Japan.

1578. The conversion of **Ōtomo Sōrin** (Yoshishige, 1530–87), a powerful lord of Kyūshū, to Christianity gave the foreign religion a greater foothold on that island, where it had become quite strong since the conversion of some lesser lords of the western littoral, such as Ōmura (1562) and Arima (1576). The Christians, who were for the most part confined to the fiefs with Christian lords, were estimated at 150,000 in 1582.

1582. Nobunaga was killed by a discontented general, Akechi Mitsuhide (1526–82). Hideyoshi returned from his western campaigns and destroyed Mitsuhide. A contest for power with the remaining members of the Oda family, supported by **TOKUGAWA IEYASU (1542–1616)**, one of Nobunaga's vassal lords in eastern Japan, brought about the elimination of the Oda, and an understanding was reached with Ieyasu.

1584. This resulted in Hideyoshi's hegemony over central Japan. In the preceding year he had already commenced the construction of the great Ōsaka Castle as his home base.

1585. Hideyoshi was appointed regent (kanpaku) and two years later became prime minister (dajō daijin) as well.

1585–86. A greater stratification of classes was brought about by legislation: (1) warriors (samurai), (2) farmers, (3) artisans, and (4) merchants.

1587. The subjugation of the Shimazu family of southern Kyūshū completed Hideyoshi's conquest of western Japan.

1587. Hideyoshi issued a decree banishing the Portuguese missionaries from Japan but failed to enforce it for ten years. His motive for this sudden opposition to Christianity was probably apprehension at the growing political and military strength of the Christians.

1588. The peasantry was disarmed in Hideyoshi's **sword hunt**, it thereafter becoming illegal for anyone other than warriors to carry weapons.

1590. The capture of the stronghold of the Hōjō family at Odaware induced all eastern and northern Japan to accept Hideyoshi's rule and completed the unification of the land. At this time Hideyoshi's prominent vassal, Tokugawa Ieyasu, moved his administrative and military base to Edo (present-day Tokyo), a strategic spot for the domination of the great Kantō plain of eastern Japan.

1592. The **first invasion of Korea** by the armies of Hideyoshi was possibly motivated by fear of the excess of experienced warriors in Japan, although the overly ambitious Hideyoshi was indeed planning the conquest of China. When Korea refused to grant the Japanese transit up the peninsula and into China, they invaded (p. 381). Under the leadership of **Katō Kiyomasa** (1562–1611) and **Konishi Yukinaga** (1556?–1600), the expeditionary force of some 200,000 overran almost the whole of Korea but was forced by a large Chinese army and a capable Korean navy to withdraw to the southern coast.

1597. The second Korean campaign was launched but with even less success. After Hideyoshi's death (1598), all the surviving Japanese soldiers returned to Japan. The lasting political results of the Korean venture were negligible, but a rapid development and expansion of the ceramic industry in Japan was brought about by the many Korean potters who were kidnapped back to Japan by the retreating captains.

1597. Hideyoshi, irritated by the bickering between the Portuguese Jesuits and the Spanish Franciscans (who came to Japan in 1593) and suspecting that Christian proselytizing was merely an opening wedge for the subsequent conquest of Japan by Europeans, executed 3 Jesuits, 6 Franciscans, and 17 Japanese Christians. The remaining missionaries were ordered to leave, but only a small number did so. Hideyoshi did not press the persecution further, because he did not wish to drive away the Portuguese traders, who were then especially welcome, since direct commercial intercourse with China had been stopped.

1598. Hideyoshi's death was soon followed by a struggle for power among his former vassals.

1600. The power struggle culminated in the **Battle of Sekigahara,** where Tokugawa Ieyasu defeated a coalition of his rivals. This victory made Ieyasu in effect the ruler of the whole land, although he was not appointed shogun until 1603.

1600–1867. The **TOKUGAWA** (or **EDO**) **PERIOD.** Ieyasu established the military capital at Edo (Tokyo), which grew phenomenally to become the economic and cultural as well as political capital of the nation. Given the fate of the Oda and Toyotomi families, Ieyasu made the perpetuation of the rule of his family his major objective. The feudal lords, or daimyos, were divided into three groups: shinpan, fudai, and tozama. The shinpan daimyos were all the related and collateral branches of the larger Tokugawa house; fudai were the vassals and allies of Ieyasu before the Battle of Sekigahara, and they now occupied the central provinces; and tozama were those who submitted only after Sekigahara and were located in more remote regions, usually excluded from the central government. The lords of all domains were compelled to spend at least half of each year in residence at Edo, whence came the name of the system of "alternate attendance."

The **administrative hierarchy,** which grew out of the Tokugawa family organization, comprised, in order of rank, a shogun; at times, and especially between 1638 and 1684, one or more great counselors (tairō); four or five senior counselors (toshiyori or rōjū) as a council of state; a group of junior counselors (wakadoshiyori), who controlled the direct petty vassals of Edo; a class of officials known as metsuke, who served as inspectors or intelligence officers; and a large group of civil administrators called bugyō. The laws lacked coherent organization but were based on certain fundamental moral precepts, primarily the principle of loyalty. Criminal codes were severe. There was a stringent stratification of classes. Daimyos were to a large extent autonomous rulers in their own domains, but Edo kept a watchful eye on them, and the feudatories had a strong tendency to adopt the laws and organization of Edo.

The peace and prosperity of the early Tokugawa period brought a gradual rise in the standard of living and an increase in population and national wealth. With the **growth of industry and commerce,** a powerful merchant class gradually grew up in the larger cities, and a slow transition from a rice economy to a money economy commenced. This transition, together with the rise in living standards and the increase in population, tended to make production inadequate and brought about great economic ills during much of the period.

Political conservatism and **seclusion** made the Tokugawa period outwardly stagnant, but it was a time of great intellectual development. Buddhism was ostensibly in decline, and Christianity was early stamped out. There was a great **revival of lay learning,** and the old feudal code of conduct received definitive formulation under the name of *bushidō.* **Neo-Confucian philosophy** enjoyed a protracted period of unparalleled growth and popularity; philosophers and teachers of ethics abounded; interest in Japanese antiquity resumed; Shinto developed new life both as a nativist philosophy and as a popular religion; and the newly risen merchant class contributed greatly to the intellectual and cultural growth of the country.

Literature and art in the Tokugawa period were comparatively free from Chinese influence and were less aristocratic and more popular than in earlier periods because of the influence of the merchant class.

THE TOKUGAWA SHOGUNS (1603–1867)

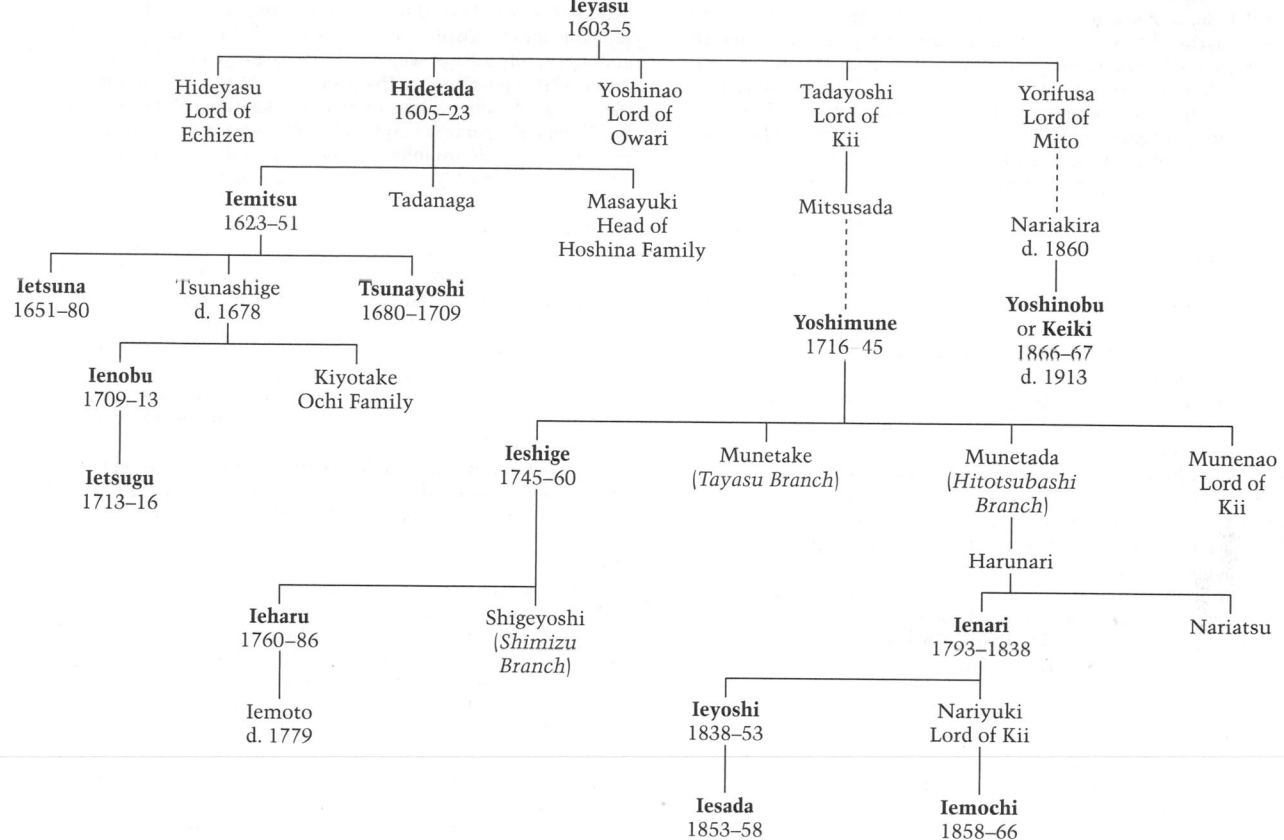

A new poetic form, the *haiku*, which consists of 17 syllables as opposed to the classical *tanka* form of 31 syllables, was popular at this time. The novel enjoyed a great second flowering. The refined *nō* drama slowly gave way to more realistic, more lively, and decidedly less restrained forms, *kabuki* and *bunraku* (puppet) plays, which both developed from long poetic recitations called *jōruri*. Applied arts reached great heights of technical excellence. Painting remained largely traditional, but there were able masters of design and an important new school of realism. One of the most interesting developments in painting was the *ukiyo-e* (paintings of the floating world), a school of woodblock artists who chose for their subject matter not Chinese scenes and historical events but the people, street scenes, and landscapes of contemporary Japan. The style, introduced in the 17th century, found prolific expression in the prints of woodblock masters of the 18th and 19th centuries.

c. 1602. Spanish traders arrived in eastern Japan. Ieyasu befriended Spanish missionaries, hoping thereby to persuade the traders to deal directly with eastern Japan. Although a formal treaty was negotiated with the acting Spanish governor of the Philippines in 1610, few traders actually ever came.

1605–23. Hidetada as shogun (d. 1632). This was the formative period of Edo government, first under the direction of the retired shogun Ieyasu (d. 1616) and then under that of his somewhat less capable son, Hidetada.

1607. Hayashi Razan (1583–1657), a former Zen monk turned Neo-Confucian scholar, was appointed attendant scholar to Ieyasu. This marked the beginning of a Tokugawa policy of using **Neo-Confucianism** as a stabilizing force in politics and society. Razan, who founded the Edo Confucian temple in 1623 and whose descendants continued to run the school throughout the Edo period, represented the orthodox

Song Neo-Confucian school of Zhu Xi (1130–1200). Other schools of Neo-Confucian philosophy included those of **Wang Yangming** (1472–1529) of Ming China (represented by **Nakae Tōju** [1608–48] and **Kumazawa Banzan** [1619–91]) and the **Ancient Learning school,** a movement that returned to pre–Song Confucian commentators and the original texts of the late Zhou period (represented by **Itō Jinsai** [1627–1705] and **Ogyū Sorai** [1666–1728]). The Japanese Neo-Confucians made numerous contributions in various fields of learning, and some attacked the pressing economic problems of the day.

1609. The **Dutch** established a trading post at Hirado in western Japan after an invitation from Ieyasu in 1605. This invitation had been obtained by Will Adams (d. 1620), the English pilot of a Dutch vessel wrecked in Japan in 1600. Adams was forced to remain in Japan by Ieyasu, who made of him an honored adviser.

1612. A **persecution of Christianity** commenced after a series of anti-Christian edicts beginning in 1606. Ieyasu's mounting fears of the political menace from Christianity and his realization that trade with Europe could be maintained without the presence of Catholic missionaries as decoys had led him to gradually abandon his at first friendly attitude toward the missionaries.

1613. Date Masamune (1565–1636), a prominent daimyo of northern Japan, dispatched emissaries to Spain and to the pope.

1614–15. The Siege of Ōsaka Castle. Hideyori (1593–1615), the son and heir of Hideyoshi, and the former's mother, **Yodogimi** (1577–1615), had remained in the Ōsaka Castle after the Battle of Sekigahara, constituting a dangerous rallying point for disaffected elements, according to Ieyasu's way of thinking. Their ultimate destruction was deemed necessary by Ieyasu. In 1614, using a trumped-up charge as a pretext, he laid siege to the castle, and after a short truce captured and destroyed it and its inhabitants the next year.

1615. The *Buke shohatto*, a collection of general maxims for the warrior class, was promulgated.

1616. Ieyasu died.

1617. Hidetada, aroused by the mutual recriminations of the various European nationalities and religious groups in Japan, intensified the persecution of Christians (estimated at 300,000), and for the first time since 1597, European missionaries were executed. Jesuits, Franciscans, and native believers were executed in increasing numbers in the following years (particularly 1622–24). This marked the height of the Christian persecution. Catholic missionaries still continued to arrive, but eventually all were killed or forced to leave or to apostatize.

1623–51. Iemitsu as shogun. This was the period of consolidation of Tokugawa rule. As a means of achieving this goal, the **suppression of Christianity** was carried to a successful end, and a policy of national seclusion was adopted.

1623. The English voluntarily left Hirado, because their trade with Japan had not proved profitable.

1624. The Spaniards were driven from Japan, and intercourse with the Philippines was stopped.

1636. Japanese were forbidden to go abroad, and those abroad were not, as a rule, allowed to return. **Two years later the building of large ships was also proscribed.**

1637–38. The Shimabara Rebellion. The peasants of the peninsula of Shimabara and the island of Amakusa, near Nagasaki (on the island of Kyūshū), which had been a well-Christianized region for decades, rose in desperation over economic and religious oppression. Some 37,000 of them defended themselves in the dilapidated Hara Castle on the coast of Shimabara for almost three months against vastly superior forces, aided by a Dutch vessel, until food and musket ammunition, on which they depended, failed them. They were killed almost to a person in the fall of the castle, and with this slaughter Christianity was essentially stamped out.

1638. The Portuguese traders were expelled because of suspicions concerning their complicity in the Shimabara Rebellion. When they sent emissaries in 1640 to reopen trade, almost the entire party was summarily executed. This left the Dutch at Hirado and Chinese traders at Nagasaki as Japan's sole means of contact with the outside world.

1641. The Dutch traders were moved from Hirado to the islet of Deshima in Nagasaki harbor, where they were kept under close surveillance and on a short leash. They were responsible for providing periodic reports to the authorities on events in Europe.

1651–80. Ietsuna as shogun.

1651–52. Two successive abortive coups at Edo were the last rebellions the Tokugawa had to face until the 19th century.

1657. Tokugawa Mitsukuni (1628–1700), lord of Mito, commenced the compilation of the *Dai Nihon shi (History of Great Japan)* on the model of the Chinese dynastic histories. Among the many scholars who aided him was the Chinese émigré **Zhu Shunsui** (1640–1701). The original task was not officially completed until 1720, and supplementary work was continued until 1906. The school of Japanese historians that grew up around this enterprise placed great emphasis on the centrality of the imperial institution to their nation's history and thus became one of the important facets in the imperial restoration movement later.

1657. A great fire destroyed much of Edo and the Edo castle buildings.

1680–1709. Tsunayoshi as shogun. Sakai Tadakiyo (1600–82), great counselor at the time of Ietsuna's death, proposed to have an imperial prince succeed the heirless Ietsuna, but on the insistence of Hotta Masatoshi (1634?–84), Ietsuna's brother, Tsunayoshi, was made shogun, and soon Masatoshi succeeded Tadakiyo as great counselor. The early years of this period were characterized by vigorous administrative measures.

1684. The **assassination of Hotta Masatoshi** left Tsunayoshi with less able counselors who allowed him to ruin Edo finances and bring great hardships on the people by edicts inspired by Buddhism. These edicts prohibited the killing of any living creature and extended special protection and privileges to dogs. Hence Tsunayoshi's subsequent moniker, "the dog shogun."

1688–1704. The **Genroku period** is regarded as the apogee of the vigorous culture of the merchant class of the Tokugawa period. Already the samurai class was becoming mired in debt to the merchants, into whose hands the wealth of the nation was beginning to pass. Consequently this was a time of ebullient and unsuppressed self-expression on the part of the merchant class. The extravagant life in the cities centered on the *bunraku* and *kabuki* theaters and the licensed quarters, the famous Yoshiwara in the case of Edo. Among the great writers and artists of the age were **Matsuo Bashō** (1644–94), who made the *haiku* a great poetic form; **Ihara Saikaku** (1642–93), the author of many risqué novels about courtesans; **Chikamatsu Monzaemon** (1653–1725), Japan's greatest playwright, who wrote about love and loyalty; and **Hishikawa Moronobu** (d. 1694), generally considered the founder and a master of *ukiyo-e*. Repressive measures in time tempered the Genroku spirit.

1703. The **Chūshingura** (also called the Forty-seven Rōnin) **Incident** occurred. Kira Yoshinaka was killed by a group of former retainers of Asano Naganori, *daimyō* of Akō, whose execution in 1701 they felt to be Yoshinaka's fault. The deed shocked the nation, for, although they had clearly broken the law, the group claimed that they were simply following Confucian ethics in avenging their lord's death. They were eventually ordered to commit suicide.

1703. A great earthquake and fire at Edo were followed in the next five years by several other natural catastrophes, including the last eruption of Mount Fuji (1707).

1709–13. Ienobu as shogun. With the aid of the orthodox Confucian scholar **Arai Hakuseki** (1657–1725), this able and vigorous ruler carried out a series of much-needed economic reforms.

1713–16. The infant **Ietsugu** as shogun.

1715. The quantity of copper allowed to be exported by the Dutch was greatly reduced. Copper was the mainstay of the Dutch trade, but its export by the Dutch and the Chinese was a drain on Japan's resources. This reduction was followed later by even greater decreases, and the number of Dutch vessels calling at Deshima declined to two per year.

1716–45. Yoshimune as shogun (d. 1751). Since Hidetada's line had come to an end, the new shogun was chosen from the Tokugawa house of Kii, which, with the houses of Owari and Mito, had been named by Ieyasu the three Tokugawa cadet branches *(gosanke)* from which shoguns were to be selected. Perhaps next to Ieyasu the ablest and wisest of all Tokugawa rulers, Yoshimune attempted to revive the feudal regimentation and military virtues of Ieyasu's day and to carry through economic reforms. He also encouraged scholarship in all fields, and the Neo-Confucian scholar **Muro Kyūsō** (1658–1734) was one of his chief advisers. Despite this able leadership, **economic and social ills began to become acute in Yoshimune's time.** Peasants were losing ownership of their land, and the farm population began to decline because of infanticide and migration to towns and cities. The samurai were deeply indebted to merchants. These economic conditions led to a mingling of the classes, which began to efface the old rigid barriers.

1720. Yoshimune removed the ban on the study of Western subjects and on the importation of European books, exclusive of those on religion. This move made possible the development of a small but vigorous group of **students of Dutch**—the principal language in which books coming to Japan were written—and of Western sciences, particularly medicine. A manuscript Dutch-Japanese dictionary was produced in 1745, and in 1774 **Sugita Genpaku** (1733–1817) translated a text on anatomy. This early start in Western scientific methods produced results in cartography and military science, which later proved of great value.

1732–33. A great famine in western Japan was met with positive measures of relief by Yoshimune.

1742. The criminal law of the land was codified for the benefit of judges and administrators. This codification remained the basis of criminal law for the rest of the Tokugawa period.

1758. Takenouchi Shikibu (1712–67), a scholar favoring an imperial restoration, and his noble disciples in Kyoto were punished by Edo.

1760–86. Ieharu as shogun. Though an able man, Ieharu was dominated by **Tanuma Okitsugu** (1719–88), who unsuccessfully attempted a number of reforms, and Tokugawa rule continued its downward course. During this period, peasant uprisings became frequent and serious, and they continued to be so until the fall of the regime. Although begun in the 17th century, there flourished in this period a National Learning (or Nativist) movement that sought a response within Japan's own cultural roots to the overwhelming presence of Neo-Confucianism from China and Korea. Since it found many of those roots in Shinto, the movement is also referred to as the Shinto revival, or Neo-Shintoism. Perhaps its greatest advocate was **Motoori Norinaga** (1730–1801), who wrote a penetrating study of the Kojiki and effectively revived serious consideration of *The Tale of Genji*.

1783. A great eruption of Mount Asama and a famine in the north came as a double climax to a series of disasters.

1787. Rice riots exploded in Edo.

1787–93. Matsudaira Sadanobu (1759–1829) as head of the government for the child shogun, **Ienari,** carried through the Kansei Reforms. Strict sumptuary laws were enacted; restrictions were imposed on commercial activity; financial retrenchment at the center was pursued; and efforts were made to bolster the sagging prestige of the samurai class. At this time, imperial opposition to Edo became apparent in Kyoto and the *bakufu* became aware of the rapidly expanding European powers.

(To p. 569)

5. VIETNAM, 1527–1802

(From p. 165)

The **Lê dynasty** ceased controlling the country in 1527, though the Lê nominally continued to reign until 1787. Several smaller states and contending Vietnamese parties arose, and the country was divided in half for much of the period under consideration. The 17th and 18th centuries also witnessed the arrival of ever larger numbers of missionaries and travelers from the newly expanding West. The period ended in a great rebellion and eventually the founding of an apparently secure regime, only to fall victim later to foreign powers.

1527. After eight kings were successively placed on the Lê throne (1505–27), and six of them assassinated, **Mac Dang Dung,** the head of one powerful family (the Mac), seized the throne and established the **Mac dynasty.** Other powerful families were unhappy, and all turned to China to act as mediator. China proposed a division of the land, with Mac ruling in the north and Lê, with its supporters, ruling in the south. During these years, the **Nguyên,** one of the most powerful families, was establishing a firm base in south central Vietnam, with a capital at **Huê.** This compromise lasted only a short time. In the civil wars that followed, the **Trinh,** another powerful house, actively supported the Lê in name, with a base at the capital in **Thang-long.** Throughout the period the population of Thang-long exceeded 100,000. Both Nguyên and Trinh cloaked their effort in the mantle of the Lê and sought to destroy the Mac.

1592. The Mac were effectively eliminated as a force. Trinh and Nguyên continued their standoff, with the former still installing puppet Lê kings and running all affairs of government. From 1599 Trinh family leaders took over the title of prince, which was then passed on hereditarily. The Nguyên were not amused.

The Trinh in the north tried to run an efficient government by periodically examining officials, though with limited results. The legal codes were made less stringent and tax laws were made fairer. The examination system was rebuilt, with public schools preparing students for them at various levels of the society. In the south, the Nguyên ran an administration similar to that of the north, though after war later broke out with the Trinh, Nguyên began to fashion a regime more appropriate to the south. Its examination system was geared to train men in three areas—administration, taxation matters, and ceremonial issues—a more practically oriented variant of the traditional Chinese model. Both used Confucianism to strengthen state control, as both sought control over all of Vietnam; the more Confucian a state one built, the more worthy of control over the entire land it appeared. Vietnamese Confucian scholars participated in reform efforts in the hope of stabilizing a bureaucracy that could control the military.

1624. With the arrival of **Alexandre de Rhodes** (1591–1660) and several other Jesuits, Catholic missionary work began in earnest, although Catholics had been in the country in the 16th century. In 1627, Alexandre was sent north into Trinh territory to found a mission. When it closed down (1630), there were nearly 7,000 Vietnamese converts; ten years later there were said to be 39,000 Christians in Nguyên territory and 82,000 in Trinh lands. Alexandre lived in Vietnam for many years and learned the language extremely well; he compiled an early Latin-Vietnamese-Portuguese dictionary and is considered the pioneer in romanizing the Vietnamese language. This romanization system, *quôc ngu*, enabled missionaries to acquire Vietnamese more rapidly. By 1700 there were 45 Vietnamese Catholic priests.

1627. Nguyên-Trinh warfare erupted, lasting for several decades and involving huge campaigns (1648, 1661, 1672) by Trinh forces before a tentative peace agreement was reached in the late 1670s. The Nguyên continued to gain control over the Meking Delta region.

Domestic troubles were complicated by the arrival of European trading vessels in significant numbers from the early 17th century, first from Portugal and soon thereafter from Holland. Relations with the West were initially less problematic than elsewhere in East Asia. From the early 17th century, though, Chinese traders outnumbered other foreigners in Vietnam; many Chinese families stayed for generations and established extensive trading networks throughout the region. English and French ships had arrived by mid-century. At first, the Trinh favored the Dutch while the Nguyen favored the Portuguese, but this changed over time. By century's end, the French were the most active in Vietnam. Catholic missionaries (Dominicans) had arrived in Vietnam by the middle of the 16th century, and Jesuits followed by the early 17th. Both Nguyên and Trinh tried to use Catholic monks, especially the Jesuits, to acquire Western scientific information, although the clear success of the missionizing effort also made both regimes rather apprehensive.

1711. Despite efforts to centralize control over its villages, the Trinh had no choice but to allow village leaders to allot public lands within their ken. Eventually, local elites were avoiding taxation, adding to the onus on the poorer or less resourceful. By 1713, only a third of the populace was being taxed.

1730. The Trinh appointed officials to get peasants who had left their lands to return home; by 1740, it was estimated that a third of all villages under Trinh control had been deserted. Decline of social and public order meant that less land was under proper cultivation and less food was being produced. Famines ensued and rebellions brewed. Similar corruption and decay of the economic infrastructure characterized Nguyên lands. This striking decline of social norms led to serious rethinking of traditional Vietnamese identity, including sharp words from women writers, such as Hô Xuân Huong. Local rebellions became endemic, often coalescing around Buddhist temples, with monks arming their followers. Confucianism, closely associated with the discredited state, was openly abused. A crisis ensued.

1771–1802. The **Tây-son Rebellion,** led by three brothers surnamed Nguyên from the village of Tây-son in south central Vietnam, erupted and quickly gained wide popular support. It first toppled the Nguyên regime in the south in 1778 and then moved on the Trinh in the north. The country was reunited. At first, an effort was made to prop up the Lê house, but that was eventually abandoned in 1787. Chinese armies invaded in 1788 in an attempt to seize Hanoi for the Trinh but were defeated by the brilliant general **Nguyên Huê** (1752–92), who proceeded to place himself on the throne.

1788–92. The **reign of Quang-trung** saw an effort to rebuild the economy through agrarian reforms and the establishment of communal population registers to return the wandering populace to the land. Tribute relations with China began again. The civil service examinations were reinstated, but in addition to competence in literary Chinese, successful candidates also had to demonstrate competence in works written in the demotic *nôm*.

In an effort to stimulate commerce and trade, a unified currency was instituted during the 31 years of Tây-son rule. Industry was also encouraged. Initial results were positive but proved short-lived. There were no strong rulers after the death of Quang-trung. As in other Southeast Asian societies and unlike elsewhere in East Asia, **Vietnamese women played a considerable role in commerce and trade,** including traveling aboard trading vessels internationally.

1788. Rebellious forces under **Nguyên Anh** (1762–1820) took Saigon with French help. Successive victories ended with the capture of Huê

(1801). He took the throne as **Gia-long** (r. 1802–20) of the **Nguyên dynasty.**

One of the great works of Vietnamese literature, *The Tale of Kiêu,* was written by Nguyên Du (1765–1820) at the end of the 18th century. A long poem or novel written in verse form, it combined Chinese characters and Vietnamese *nôm* ideographs.   *(To p. 574)*

F. THE PACIFIC REGION, 1513–1798

The term "Pacific" is used here to refer to the "island Pacific," not the Pacific Rim or the Pacific Basin. The latter two terms are generally used to describe the larger continental masses and nations that surround the Pacific Ocean, the Americas in the east and Asia and Australia in the west.

1. THE PACIFIC ISLANDS IN PRE-EUROPEAN TIMES

The **Pacific Ocean** is the largest single feature of the globe, covering a third of the earth's surface. It contains some 25,000 islands totaling 1.6 million square kilometers scattered across about 88 million square kilometers of water. The region, which exhibits considerable physical and cultural diversity, is conveniently divided into **Melanesia** (islands of Solomons, Vanuatu, New Caledonia, Papua New Guinea, and parts of Fiji), **Micronesia** (small islands north of the equator), and **Polynesia** (many islands in the triangle stretching from Hawaii through New Zealand to Easter Island). The region contains several distinct types of island formations. Many of the Melanesian islands in the east are large continental masses with tall, densely forested mountains, deep valleys, large rivers, and swampy coastal areas. Many of the Polynesian islands are volcanic, with corrugated mountain ranges divided by deep valleys. The central and northern parts of the Pacific have low-lying coral islands surrounded by reef and sometimes just a meter or two above water. The physical geography of the islands helps shape their climate. Thus, the larger continental islands have warm temperatures, high humidity, and heavy rainfall. The atolls, with much smaller land masses, are more vulnerable to the elements.

The Pacific was the last major habitable area to be settled by humans (p. 18). There was once much disagreement among scholars about how and by what route the Pacific Islands were settled, but recent archaeological, linguistic, and botanical research has resolved the controversy. It is now accepted that the ancestral homeland of Pacific Island peoples was in Southeast Asia, which was settled some 2 million years ago. From there, small numbers of people, probably in several waves, settled the then joint landmass of Australia and Papua New Guinea, perhaps 35,000 to 40,000 years ago. About 4,000 years ago, they branched out from the New Guinea mainland and reached island Melanesia, settling New Caledonia and New Hebrides (Vanuatu). By about 3,500 years ago, Fiji was settled. Five hundred years later, Tonga and Samoa were settled. In Samoa, from where no further migration seems to have taken place for the next 2,000 years, the basic institutions of Polynesian culture took shape. The Marquesas Islands were settled around 300 C.E., Hawaii and Tahiti around 600 C.E., and New Zealand 750 C.E.

The manner in which the islands were settled once aroused much debate. Andrew Sharp, a New Zealand scholar, argued that the Polynesians lacked the navigational technology and skill to embark on purposeful voyages of settlement across vast expanses of empty seas. Some of the islands were undoubtedly settled accidentally. However, combining oral and documentary evidence with practical seamanship, David Lewis has shown that ancient Polynesians had the knowledge and the skill to make a three-way voyage, to discover an island, return home, and then return to the new island to settle it. For the Polynesians, Lewis argued, the empty ocean was full of telltale signs (cloud formations, swell patterns, drift objects, patterns of bird flights), and they read these just as Western navigators read their charts. Purposeful voyages thus probably served as a major vehicle for the initial colonization of the islands.

Cultural diversity characterized the traditional Pacific, though most Polynesian islands exhibit linguistic and cultural similarities that are due, in part, to frequent trading and social contacts. The greatest diversity is found in the larger continental islands of Melanesia, where over a thousand languages are known to exist, most spoken by just a few thousand people. Ancestor worship, initiation ceremonies, warfare, and other such practices were an integral part of the traditional Melanesian world, as was subsistence agriculture. Melanesian societies were generally small in scale and egalitarian in ethos. Leadership was exercised by "big men" who achieved positions of power and authority through personal ability, ambition, adept manipulation of kinship and social networks, and the accumulation and strategic distribution of wealth. The position of big men was generally not heritable, though sons of big men, if they were able, had an advantage over other competitors.

Polynesian societies, on the other hand, were larger in scale and more hierarchically organized. Lineage defined and structured the social system. The lineage that could trace its roots back through several generations to a common founding ancestor, real or fictitious, claimed, and was accorded, a higher social standing and seniority. Its head was often the leading or paramount chief of the entire clan. Chiefs, variously known throughout Polynesia as ariki or *ali'i*, were thought to possess mana—moral power and authority—and had well-defined rights and obligations in relation to their people. They commanded respect and deference, exercised control over the production and distribution of the primary resources, and often received the first fruits of the land as symbolic tribute.

The chiefs exercised greater power in some Polynesian societies than in others. In Tonga, Tahiti, and Hawaii, for example, their rule extended over large areas and thousands of people. Here, chiefs formed an exclusive and powerful class and married within that group. In Marquesas and New Zealand, the system of stratification was less developed. Micronesian societies exhibited traits found both in Melanesia and Polynesia. The smaller atolls in the Carolines, for example, were basically egalitarian in character, while high islands such as Pohnpei and the Marshall Islands had a highly developed system of chieftainships.

The population of the Pacific Islands at the time of European contact cannot be estimated with any accuracy. Some estimates place the population of Melanesia at 3.5 million, of which 3 million were found in New Guinea and 500,000 in the smaller islands of Melanesia. In Polynesia, the population numbered around half a million, though recent work suggests a much higher figure. In Hawaii, according to most conventional figures, the population at contact was around 250,000, but some recent researchers have put the figure at 700,000 to 800,000. The Micronesian islands probably had 100,000 to 150,000 people. People in the larger islands practiced some form of subsistence agriculture, while those in the smaller islands and atolls of the central and northern Pacific depended on the exploitation of marine resources.

2. EUROPEAN EXPLORATION, 1513–1800

The first Europeans entered the Pacific Ocean in 1520. Between then and 1779, when Captain Cook died in Hawaii, hundreds of European explorers traversed the Pacific. In the 16th and 17th centuries, the main reason for the exploration was the search for the **Terra Australis Incognita,** which was believed to contain fabulous wealth. Later, scientific discovery and the search for alternative trade routes were important factors. The 16th century of European exploration was dominated by the Spanish and the Portuguese, the 17th century by the Dutch, and the 18th century by the English and the French. By the time of Cook's death, the islands had been charted and added to the world's rapidly growing corpus of geographical knowledge. The romance of the islands had entered European folklore, and the stage was set for more intensive European movement into the islands. Some of the main dates of European discovery are listed below.

1513, Sept. 25. Vasco Núñez de Balboa became the first European to sight the Pacific Ocean, from the isthmus of Panama, and named it the Great South Sea.

1520, Nov. 28. Ferdinand Magellan (Fernao de Magalhaes) entered the Pacific and reached the Philippine Islands in 98 days, making no major discoveries en route. He was killed on Cebu.

1564–65. First Spanish colony on Philippines. Good route discovered, Philippines to Mexico.

1567. Alvaro de Mendana (Spanish) set sail from Callao and early in 1568 sighted one of the islands of Tuvalu and Ontong Java before reaching the Solomon Archipelago.

1577–80. Francis Drake became the first English circumnavigator when he crossed the Pacific to the East Indies.

1595. Mendana left Callao in April on his second voyage to colonize the Solomon Islands. In May, he discovered a group he named **Las Marquesas de Mendoza** (Marquesas). He died in the Santa Cruz group in the Solomons on October 18, 1595.

1605–6. Pedro Fernández de Quirós, one of Mendana's captains, set sail again from Callao in December 1605 in search of new lands and unknown southern continents **(Terra Australis Incognita).** In April 1606, he sighted **La Australia del Espiritu Santo** (now Espiritu Santo) in the New Hebrides.

1642–44. Abel Janzoon Tasman (Dutch) sighted Tasmania, which he named **Anthony Van Dieman's Land.** He also explored **New Zealand**

and parts of Tonga, Fiji, New Ireland, and New Britain. He proved that Australia was not part of a great Antarctic continent.

1722. Jacob Roggeveen (Dutch), sailing east to west, entered the Pacific in March, discovered Easter Island and Samoa.

1766–67. Captains Wallis and **Carteret** entered the Pacific in search of the southern continent and discovered **Tahiti** and the Pitcairn Islands, respectively.

1768. Louis Antoine de Bougainville entered the Pacific in January and visited **Tahiti;** subsequently, he went to **Samoa** and **Espiritu Santo.** His journal contributed greatly to the cult of the **noble savage** in France and Europe generally.

1768–71. The first voyage of **Captain James Cook** to observe the transit of Venus from Tahiti. He then sailed around the North and South Islands of **New Zealand** and along the eastern coast of Australia.

1772–74. Cook's second voyage to find the **Terra Australis,** which his voyage proved did not exist.

1776–79. Cook's third voyage in search of a passage from Hudson Bay to the Pacific. He was killed at **Kealakekua Bay** (Hawaii) in February 1779. The surviving sailors returned to England via the East Indies and the **Cape of Good Hope.**

1785–88. Jean-François de La Pérouse (French) entered the Pacific with his two ships, **Astrolabe** and **Boussole,** and explored Samoa, where his crew encountered hostility. Both the ships were wrecked at Vanikoro (Solomons), and La Pérouse's own fate remains unknown.

1788, Jan. 18. The first shipload of British convicts was landed at **Botany Bay,** Australia, and the foundation of **Sydney (Port Jackson).** Britain claimed Australia east of 135° east longitude.

1789. Mutiny on the **HMS Bounty** (April 28) under the command of Lieutenant **William Bligh,** who had been sent to Tahiti to procure breadfruit for transportation to the West Indies. Mutineers from the ship settled on **Pitcairn Island,** which was annexed by Britain in 1838.

1791–93. Captain George Vancouver discovered the **Chatham Islands** and sailed to Hawaii, where he became embroiled in the islands' internal political affairs.

1792–93. Bruni d'Entrecasteaux (French) visited many Pacific Islands in search of La Pérouse and examined New Caledonia closely.

(To p. 576)

3. THE PHILIPPINES, 1500–1800

The earliest historical sources on the Philippines show that the archipelago had trade and diplomatic relations with East and Southeast Asia from at least the 11th century C.E. Medieval Chinese accounts of the Philippines show a **plurality of ethnic groups** living in **decentralized societies** and trading in forest and ocean products. Ethnolinguistic diversity in the archipelago was considerable, and modes of living ranged from swidden agriculture to fishing and wet rice cultivation.

Spanish sources from the 16th century depict societies made up of local communities *(barangay)* under the leadership of hereditary chieftains *(datu)* who sprang from a noble class. Philippine society at this time can be broadly divided into those who had the right to bring lawsuits and change their political allegiance and those who did not. Within each stratum there was considerable variation in status. Leadership in warfare, particularly marine raiding, was a key constituent of political authority. *Datus* acted as judges in lawsuits, exercised control over communal property, and received a portion of the harvest as tribute as well as military support from the nobles who owed them fealty. The unfree classes included people who had fallen into bondage through debt, those who inherited the status of bondage, and chattel slaves. Movement between the free and unfree classes was possible in some areas of the archipelago, but in others social status was fixed and unchallengeable. Most parts of the archipelago had oral cultures, although an indigenous script apparently based on Indian models was used for Tagalog in the 16th century. By the 15th century, entrepôt ports were present in Cebu, Butuan, and Manila. Internal trading networks were highly developed within the archipelago, especially in the

Visayas, with rice, raw materials, manufactured goods, and slaves exchanged over a wide area. Commerce and raiding tended to be combined in a distinctive political and economic matrix, which was based on the seafaring expertise of the region's inhabitants.

In the 1400s, **Muslim trading states** were established in the southern Philippines and in parts of Luzon, a development connected with the spread of Islam throughout island Southeast Asia at this time (p. 138). These states were often alliances of *datus,* who cooperated for military and economic advantage under the authority of a sultan. The rights and powers of sultans varied from state to state, depending in large measure on the charisma of individual leaders and their ability to inspire loyalty, although the more commercially developed polities had relatively stable ruling classes. *Sharif* status (claimed descent from the family of the prophet Muhammad) was a component in political leadership.

Strategic position and naval strength, together with commerce, made the sultanate of **Sulu** an important economic and political power. The other major Islamic kingdoms were **Buayan** and **Magindanao** on Mindanao, which rose to prominence in the 16th century.

1521. Ferdinand Magellan became the first European to reach the Philippines. He was killed in a conflict with local people under the leadership of **Lapulapu** on April 27.

1543. The expedition of **Ruy de Villalobos,** sent by Charles I of Spain, was driven off by local resistance. The name **Felipinas** was given to the areas around Leyte and was later applied to the whole of the archipelago.

1565. Establishment of a permanent Spanish presence in the archipelago under the command of **Miguel de Legazpi.**

1571. Manila became the center of Spanish power. Much of the area of the modern Philippines was nominally under Spanish control by 1576, although their actual authority was severely restricted in many areas, and Mindanao and Sulu remained completely independent. Spanish expansion was fueled by a desire to take control of the trade routes from Malacca and Eastern Indonesia and those to China, all of which had their terminus in Manila.

Socially, the Spanish colony was a mix of indigenous people **(indios),** Spaniards, a small but influential population of Chinese, and **mestizos** (those of mixed descent). In later times mestizos and creoles from the Spanish colonies in Latin America also came to the Philippines. Ethnic segregation was practiced, causing political tension. **Socioeconomic inequalities** were considerable. At village level, the Spanish sought to co-opt local leaders by increasing their privileges, in return for which the leaders took responsibility for collecting taxes and organizing labor service.

A **governor-general** was the supreme political authority in the colony. He was officially subordinate to the **Council of the Indies** in Spain. The **Royal Audencia** (est. 1584) acted as the supreme court and was intended to check abuses of power by the colonial government. Provincial governors were virtually independent of Manila.

Under the **Galleon trade** system set up in the late 16th century, only China and Mexico could trade in Manila, isolating the Spanish Philippines from commercial contacts with the rest of the Pacific region.

Augustinian friars accompanied Legazpi (1565) and were followed later by the Franciscans, Jesuits, Dominicans, and Recollects. The friars became a powerful political and economic force, exercising considerable influence on the colonial government. Following a decision in the 1580s, the church did all its proselytizing in vernacular languages, making priests vital intermediaries between the colonial government and the people. In the first few centuries of Spanish rule, there was close cooperation between the church and the colonial administration, partly because the papacy gave the Spanish crown complete authority over the missionary enterprise in the Philippines. Printing and education were by-products of the friars' missionary work. A Spanish-Tagalog Christian tract was the first book printed in the Philippines (1596), and in 1611 the Dominicans founded the University of Santo Thomas.

Revolts among the indigenous people broke out sporadically after the establishment of Spanish rule, ranging from indio attempts to regain sovereignty, such as the abortive revolt of **Magat Salamat** and **Augustin de Legazpi** in 1587, to expressions of economic discontent (e.g., the rebellion of **Magalat** in 1596) to religious movements, like the revolt in the **Kagayan Valley** in the 1620s.

From the late 16th century, Sulu, Magindanao, Buayan, and the Spanish competed for dominance of the southern Philippine region. Under the powerful sultan **Quadarat,** Magindanao had become the most important commercial, military, and political force in the region by the mid-17th century.

1635. The Spaniards established a fort at **Zamboanga** on Mindanao to provide a base for expansion in the southern Philippines. Magindanao and Sulu subsequently fought a number of wars with Spain, punctuated by peace treaties and trade agreements.

1663. Zamboanga fort abandoned. Spain played no part in the southern Philippines for the rest of the 17th century. In this period the **Muslim states** consolidated their internal power and traded with the Dutch.

1717. Attempts by Governor **Fernando Manuel de Bustamente** to reform government finances.

1718. The Spanish reestablished the Zamboanga fort, reopening hostilities with the Muslims.

1719. Clerical opposition to Bustamente's reforms led to his murder by friars.

1734. Volume of galleon trade increased through pressure from the Manila business community.

1744. Outbreak of the rebellion of **Dagohoy** the result of religious and political discontents. The rebellion lasted for several decades.

Political competition in the southern Philippines continued in the mid-18th century. The sultanate of **Cotabato** dominated Mindanao. In 1751 a major war broke out between Spain and Sulu. Sulu forces carried out extensive raids in the Visayas and Luzon, which caused serious problems for the Spanish, whose financial resources were strained by the unremitting warfare.

1751. Royal decree permitting provincial governors to engage in trade gave them **a commercial monopoly.**

1755. Non-Christian Chinese were expelled from the Philippines as part of an attempt by the Spanish government to increase its control over the revenue from the Galleon trade; the **Chinese mestizos** became a significant economic force in their place.

1762. Manila captured by Britain as a result of the Seven Years' War. A series of indio **uprisings** occurred throughout the archipelago, the most serious being that of **Diego Silang** in Ilocos.

1764. The British returned control of the Philippines to Spain. The returning colonial government faced serious economic problems, which were connected with the general decline in the Spanish empire.

1765. In response to financial problems, Governor **Francisco Leandro de Viana** proposed military and fiscal reforms along with increased trade, expansion of plantations, and immigration from Spain.

1768. The British East India Company established a trading post and garrison in Sulu, initiating a period of regional commercial and political dominance by Sulu which lasted until the mid-19th century. Piracy and slave trading were crucial to Sulu's power. In the latter half of the 18th century, Muslim raids disrupted the Spanish areas of the Philippines, significantly reducing the population.

1774. Royal decree that parishes run by friars be turned over to secular priests. **The government appointed indio and mestizo priests to weaken the friars' power.** This was symbolic of the increasing divergence between the interests of the Church and the state in this period. By the late 18th century the Church had become the major landholding and moneylending body in the colony. Peasant indebtedness increased markedly and popular resentment of the Church grew as a result.

1775. British military forces expelled from Sulu.

1776. Spain halted the replacement of Spanish clerics by mestizo and indio priests.

1781. Jose Basco y Vargos established a **tobacco monopoly** that produced substantial revenue for Spain but exploited the producers, resulting in uprisings.

1785. Establishment of the **Royal Philippine Company,** which was required to invest 4 percent of its earnings in the development of the Philippine economy in return for extensive international trading rights. Most of the company's profit came from Latin American trade, and its ships seldom visited the Philippines after 1789. *(To p. 577)*

G. AFRICA, 1500–1800

1. OVERVIEW

(From p. 144)

The arrival of Europeans and Africa's consequent participation in the new South Atlantic system were the primary events in African history during this period. The supply of slaves entering the South Atlantic system first affected West Africa, oscillated between West and West Central Africa in the 17th through the 19th century, and drew slaves from Central and East Africa in the 18th and 19th centuries. Historians have **vigorously debated the impact of European contact on Africa and the impact of the transatlantic slave trade on African development.** The debate focuses on whether the transatlantic slave trade built on long-established patterns or involved profoundly different political and economic forces leading to new patterns of economic dependence.

The **volume of slave exports** from Africa is also highly contested, although most historians agree on some broad estimates and on the fact that the trans-Saharan and Red Sea slave trades predated and then continued alongside the transatlantic slave trade. The exact numbers of slave exports will never be known for certain, but historians generally agree that **roughly 9.5 million slaves were exported along the trans-Saharan and Red Sea trade routes over 11 centuries, and roughly 9.5 million slaves were imported into the Americas over four centuries.** The similarity of these two figures masks considerable differences, however. The transatlantic slave trade estimates imports. When **mortality of the Middle Passage** is factored in (approximately 25 percent, although it was higher earlier in the trade and lower later), the exports from Africa rise to around 12 million slaves. More important, the volume of slave exports across the Sahara and up the Red Sea was relatively stable over 11 centuries, while **more than 70 percent of slave exports across the Atlantic occurred during the 150 years** from 1700 to 1850, when the trade was most active. The magnitude of the transatlantic slave trade, therefore, was much higher and its impact more concentrated than the longer-lasting trans-Saharan and Red Sea trades.

The acquisition of slaves was not foremost in the mind of the first Portuguese navigator as he sailed in 1434 to Cape Bojador, in present-day Mauritania—and successfully returned. **Portuguese overseas exploration** of sub-Saharan Africa was motivated by a series of linked objectives. It grew out of the political and economic transformation in Europe, particularly the consolidation of royal power in Portugal and the realignment of economic forces favoring trade over agriculture there. It was linked to the developing sense of European cultural, religious, and political superiority over non-Europeans, fueled by the Christian-Muslim wars and the Reconquista of the Iberian Peninsula. It was part of a general geopolitical strategy to outflank what the Portuguese understood as a monolithic Muslim world: to assist the besieged Christian monarch of the East, Prester John (there was indeed a besieged Christian ruler of Abyssinia) and to bypass Muslim and Jewish merchants' control over the **trans-Saharan gold trade,** which supplied 70 percent of the Mediterranean demand for gold before the discovery of the New World. The Portuguese were also interested in the commerce of exotic spices, textiles, and luxury goods and found themselves excluded from the established trade routes of the Mediterranean. The trade in slaves dominates the history of this period, but it is important to bear in mind that the Portuguese and other European merchants were interested in trade in a wide variety of goods as well as in forming political alliances.

It is also important to remember that **Europeans were not yet able to impose their will on Africans.** Indeed, Europeans did not have significant military superiority over Africans until the widespread use of the repeating rifle in Africa in the 1870s. Moreover, when Europeans actually sought to impose their will on Africans—as the Portuguese did in Angola and in Mozambique—they quickly found that they had to **adopt African political and military tactics in order to survive.** And finally, Europeans suffered extremely high mortality in tropical Africa, which undercut any sustained effort to colonize and control African territory directly, except for the more temperate regions of South Africa and isolated offshore islands of West Africa, the Bight of Benin, and the East African coast.

Because force did not work, the success of European commerce in Africa depended upon **Africans' willingness to participate.** This raises two important questions, which lie at the heart of historians' efforts to interpret the impact of the slave trade on Africa: Why did Africans willingly exchange such vast numbers of young men and women of the most productive and reproductive ages? Why did Africans become the laborers of choice in the New World plantation economies?

The second question must be answered first. Since the 12th century, there had been a renaissance in the Mediterranean Basin of large-scale agricultural units associated with **sugar production.** Sugar was a demanding crop, requiring strict, regimented labor. Slaves were widely used on these new sugar estates, and they were drawn from a variety

of sources, including religious wars, the slave trade from the Black Sea, and sub-Saharan Africa. With the fall of Constantinople in 1452, the Black Sea sources of slaves for the expanding sugar frontier of the Mediterranean dried up, leaving the African slave trade the largest single source. Moreover, **Africans had the misfortune of being part of two great disease environments:** the Old World temperate and the Old World tropical. Africans therefore had childhood immunities to a host of nasty illnesses, which provided them with a statistically lower rate of mortality than European bonded labor or Amerindians and which made them simply a better investment—particularly when sugar plantations spread to the New World in the late 16th century.

The question of why Africans sold so many slaves also points to the intersection of a variety of processes. Captives had long been a by-product of conflicts between groups in Africa. The volume of slaves increased as smaller polities fused into larger ones. The transatlantic slave trade favored the participation of larger enterprises, like states, as opposed to individual raiders or kidnappers. When states organized large military campaigns, these wars yielded more slaves. The demand for slaves unquestionably **encouraged the military expression of political power** and led to the development of **warrior aristocracies** throughout the regions of the continent engaged in the slave trade. While rulers might go to war for political reasons, warriors did so for the booty. Increased warfare and the pace of political consolidation sharpened perceived differences between groups, helped to crystallize **ethnic identities,** and heightened political instability, which in turn fueled more wars. Warfare and enslavement directed the investment of capital into horses and firearms (the means of destruction), into defensive walls, and into consumer goods at the expense of investment in the means of production, like agriculture, crafts, and mining.

Slaves were exchanged for an assortment of European and reexported goods from the Orient, especially Indian cloth. Cheap baubles and shoddy manufactures were included in this assortment, but so were firearms, metal utensils, hardware, fine cloth, iron bars, and cowrie shells, which served as a currency in much of West Africa. Moreover, the **barter terms of trade** (the composition of the assortment of goods exchanged for a slave "unit") consistently moved in favor of African sellers, who demanded and received a larger volume and greater variety of goods over the course of the slave trade. Especially where kings controlled the slave trade (in Benin, the kingdom of the Kongo, and Dahomey, for example) many of these goods flowed outward from the political center through patronage systems. Rulers' efforts to control the slave trade were also expressed in the development of bureaucracies designed to regulate external commerce.

Rulers were not always successful in regulating the slave trade or in controlling its potentially dangerous consequences. The kingdom of the Kongo was a well-established polity in the interior, south of the Zaire River, when the Portuguese first arrived there in 1481. It was held together by military power, kinship, and the judicious redistribution of scarce goods. The BaKongo king, Alfonso I, initially welcomed the Portuguese, who came as traders and as missionaries. Alfonso sought to monopolize the new traders and to insert their new goods into the system of redistribution that tied outlying governors to the political center. He encouraged his son to convert to Catholicism and to be consecrated as bishop. He encouraged the court nobility to convert and invited the Portuguese missionaries and craftsmen to settle in the capital. As Portuguese demand for slaves increased, outlying governors became more interested in dealing directly with the newcomers. Eventually, the redistributive system collapsed and the Kongo kingdom plunged into civil war. In this period of chaos, a noblewoman, **Beatrice Kimpa Vita,** who was a Catholic, led a millenarian movement that married Christianity and local BaKongo beliefs in an effort to create a new sense of community, to Africanize Church teachings, and to expel Portuguese missionaries. The Portuguese and their BaKongo allies executed her as a heretic in 1706. The Kongo kingdom never regained its former prominence.

African participation in the slave trade had contradictory consequences for Africa. On the one hand, it led to **political consolidation.** On the other, because it fostered warfare, it created conditions for **political dissolution.** Similarly, the slave trade favored commerce, since many imported goods found their way into internal circuits of trade. Yet the export of millions of human beings reduced the size of the domestic African market. Warfare also discouraged long-term investment in agriculture, mining, and industry. Three aspects of the many contradictory consequences merit further discussion.

First, Africa's participation in the South Atlantic system clearly led to the **export of many millions of young, productive men and women.** However, it also led to the importation into Africa of **New World cultigens,** including maize, sweet potato, and cassava, which have become staples throughout much of tropical Africa. These New World crops yielded higher caloric returns than indigenous crops per unit of labor, and, according to some historical demographers, arrested population decline during the slave trade era. On a continent where land-to-labor ratios have historically been high, economic development might have been quite different if these cultigens had been imported and people not exported.

Second, although the proportion of male to female slaves exported from Africa to the New World changed over time and by region, historians estimate that **60 to 70 percent of those entering the transatlantic slave trade were males.** Since warfare, kidnapping, and other forms of enslavement netted more females than males (because more males were likely to have been killed while resisting or defending or because they were more intransigent), what happened to those female slaves not exported overseas? The answer is that female slaves were retained in Africa because they were more valued than male slaves. The retention of female slaves in Africa hints at subtle changes in gender roles and contributed to both **polygyny** (many wives) and **patriarchy** (male power).

Finally, just as in the case of Beatrice Kimpa Vita, the slave trade contributed to new forms of resistance against established political rule. In West Africa, many ordinary Africans increasingly turned to Islam as a means of providing a model for a **new and different community.** Beginning around 1660 with Nasir al-Din, a more **militant Islam** emerged as a reaction against the old, established political order. Although the early jihads, or holy wars, actually contributed to the slave trade by producing captives, by the late 18th century Hausa peasants and Fulani herders swelled the forces of Usuman dan Fodio's militant Islamic movement. Many joined to protest the enslavement of Muslims by nominally Muslim Hausa aristocracy. Paradoxically, the success of this jihad led to the creation of the Sokoto Caliphate, one of the most powerful and dynamic polities in West Africa, which maintained itself through annual military campaigns. These campaigns yielded a steady supply of slaves to feed the demand for agricultural labor in the caliphate. *(To p. 586)*

2. REGIONS

a. SUDANIC WEST AND CENTRAL AFRICA

(From p. 145)

17th century. The nomadic **Moors** of the western Sahara dominated the region. Two main groups constituted Moorish society in this era, the **Hassani** and the **Zawaya.** The Hassani, the military clans, ruled the Sahara north of Senegal and achieved political dominance over rival Moors, thanks to their military strength. The Zawaya, essentially clerical and commercial clans, occupied the southwestern Sahara and contributed the bulk of Islamic scholars and clerics. Most of the region's commerce was in the hands of the Zawaya.

1591. A **Moroccan army under Djudar Pasha defeated the Songhay army.** Djudar Pasha's invasion of Songhay was triggered by the Moroccan desire to spread Islam and to gain direct access to Sudanese gold and slaves. Equipped with firearms, Djudar Pasha's invading force of 3,000 to 4,000 troops scored an easy victory over a Songhay cavalry equipped with lances and an infantry equipped with lances and bows and arrows. This was the **first recorded use of muskets in sub-Saharan Africa.** Songhay's defeat signaled the end of the last great Sudanese Empire. The decline of Songhay ushered in a period of intense but **localized political consolidation and economic development.**

1599. In an effort to revive the Mali Empire's power, **Mansa Mahmud** attacked Jenne but was repulsed by Moroccan forces dispatched from Timbuktu. Mansa Mahmud's defeat marked the end of Mali's influence in the Middle Niger region; henceforth the kingdom disintegrated.

1618 onward. The bulk of the Moroccan army returned, leaving garrisons in the important towns of the Middle Niger region and in Timbuktu. Decades after the Moroccan occupation of Timbuktu, descendants of the conquering troops began to assert their autonomy. These descendants, known as the **Arma,** exerted influence only in the regions neighboring their garrisons. The Arma became the overlords of Timbuktu, a position they would hold until the early 19th century. The Arma, however, faced **constant revolts from Timbuktu's inhabitants and from the nomadic tribes of the western desert.** Arma authorities regularly suppressed uprisings led by local Muslim scholars.

c. 1537. The formation of the kingdom of **Kaabu,** which arose as a consequence of Mali's westward expansion. Malinke traders had migrated west to obtain gold and salt, paving the way for Kaabu to become the western seat of the Mali government. By the 16th century, Kaabu was the dominant power in the Senegambian region.

c. 1500–1620. Hausa city-states gained strength in this era, largely because of their strong armies. Ruling aristocracies controlled these states' political, administrative, and military personnel. Underpinning the Hausa city-states' economies were productive peasants and lucrative trade routes. One major route linked Hausaland with the Volta Basin; another led to the Sahara. In the trans-Saharan trade, the Hausa exchanged slaves, cloth, gold dust, and kola nuts for horses, camels, and salt. From the 16th to the early 18th century, **Hausa states fought among themselves for supremacy.** As Hausa states gained strength, bitter rivalries developed. Military conflicts between Kano and Katsina erupted throughout the 16th century, as both states struggled for control over eastern Hausaland. In the 18th century, the city-state of Gobir clashed with Kebbi, Kano, and Katsina.

17th century. The Mossi were one of several kingdoms to emerge in the political vacuum created by the fall of Songhay. Its development was hastened by the 17th-century expansion of **Yatenga,** a Mossi state that gained new territory by conquest. Mossi officials superimposed their own political structures throughout much of the Volta Basin, incorporating many non-Mossi peoples into their empire.

c. 1730. The **Kano aristocracy** had developed formidable military capabilities and become the most powerful state in Hausaland. In the 17th and 18th centuries, new forms of **political and military offices** emerged in Hausaland. City-state bureaucracies greatly expanded, and officials established specialized government departments to oversee protocol, internal and external affairs, regional governments, and the treasury. Military rulers played an especially important role in city-states. In order to maintain security vis-à-vis their neighbors, these rulers made their forces more efficient and tightened their chains of command. Significant **expansion of central Sudan's economy, by means of slave labor,** occurred during the 17th and 18th centuries. Slavery and the slave trade underpinned the central Sudanese economy in this era. Besides contributing to land cultivation and pastoralism, slaves helped maintain the region's system of transport, trade, craft production, and communications. Their labor as caravan workers was particularly crucial to the trans-Saharan trade. Slaves also worked as soldiers and civil servants.

18th century. Height of kingdom of **Salum,** western Senegal, and development of a military aristocracy. The kingdom of Salum's strategic location on the Salum River near the Senegambian coast enabled it to profit from the nearby salt deposits and the European slave trade. The Salum kingdom's **ruling warrior aristocracy** came to power through its control of the coastal slave trade. The kingdom eventually expanded toward the Gambia.

c. 1710. Biton Kulubali and his largely slave army restructured Bambara society through force and founded the **Segu Bambara kingdom,** with its capital at Segu. The Bambara state of Segu expanded in the delta region of the Middle Niger, near trade routes and commercial centers. Biton Kulubali steadily gained young followers, who swelled the ranks of his slave army. Following Biton's death in about 1755, the state was racked by civil war. It was rebuilt by Ngolo Jara in about 1767 and remained an important regional center until 1860.

18th and early 19th centuries. Despite perennial warfare, warrior states of West Africa encouraged **economic development.** Ruling warlords ensured the territorial integrity of Segu Bambara. Warriors raided other territories for captives and used their human booty in agriculture and the military. The resulting slave-based economy revolved around farming, fishing, and trade. The **Massassi of Kaarta** became another warrior state and, like the Bambara of Segu, benefited from slave raiding and conquest.

c. 1564–96. Borno's influence and power expanded under **Idris ben Ali, referred to as Alawoma.** Under Alawoma, a metropolitan core emerged and was controlled by a standing army and bureaucracy. This period witnessed significant population increase. Alawoma made the pilgrimage to Mecca around 1571 and instituted **diplomatic ties with the Ottomans and the Sa'adi dynasty of Morocco.**

c. 1611–55. 'Abd al-Karim ben Jame founded the state of Wadai, which fell within the political, cultural, and commercial sphere of Borno.

c. 1616–39. Umar ben Idris ruled during the peak of the Borno Empire. He oversaw the establishment of semiautonomous vassals and set up buffer states along Borno's desert borders. At this time trade expanded with Egypt and other states along the Mediterranean and with the non-Muslim communities to the south and southwest. Contact with the Mediterranean led to the **introduction of new crops** into Borno, including maize, tomatoes, and paw paw. From the south and southwest flowed slaves, many of whom entered the **trans-Saharan slave trade.** Umar ben Idris instituted **religious and political reforms,** making the Borno Caliphate a prosperous Islamic state.

1621. The island of **Gorée,** off the Senegambian coast, became a staging area for Dutch trade in 1594–95. By 1621, the Dutch had transformed Gorée into the major European trading post for the transatlantic slave trade. Portugal took control of the island in 1629, followed by England in 1667 and France in 1677.

c. 1660. Increasing European presence and the **intensification of the overseas slave trade contributed to the rise of Islamic militancy** in Senegambia and the western desert. **Nasir al-Din,** a Moorish cleric, sought to impose a Muslim "theocracy" in the region to counteract the new influences. Around 1660, Nasir al-Din launched a **jihad.** His followers, mostly Berbers from present-day southern Mauritania, sought to gain Islamic converts and take control of the slave trade. Nasir al-Din's jihad represented the **growth of Islam from a religion of the ruling and commercial elite to a popular religious and political movement.**

1674. In the course of pursuing his jihad, Nasir al-Din died in battle. His death led to the movement's decline. Thus the first popular resistance against the overseas slave trade and against the African rulers who participated in it had failed.

1690. Influenced by the earlier example of Nasir al-Din, **Maalik Sy** waged a holy war of his own in the Senegambian region. He and his followers successfully founded the theocratic state of **Bundu,** located on the trade route between the Niger Bend and the Gambia. Maalik Sy's success was due largely to the strong military organization he commanded.

1725. Maalik Sy's influence spread and contributed to the Muslim revolution in **Futa Jallon.** The holy war in Futa Jallon was, like its predecessors in the region, partly a reaction to the upheavals brought about by the overseas slave trade and by tensions within African societies. The leaders of the jihad had come from the Senegal Valley and gained experience from Nasir al-Din's short-lived marabout movement. Their holy war against the Jallonke aristocracies became one of the most successful Muslim revolutions in 18th-century Senegambia. The newly founded **Islamic kingdom of Futa Jallon would preserve its character until the beginning of colonial rule.**

1727. Karamaxo Alfa led the Muslim revolution in **Futa Jallon,** on the borders of Senegambia. His efforts culminated in the establishment of a powerful Muslim theocracy in the region. After his death in 1751, religious and political wars in Futa Jallon and surrounding regions continued.

1742–92. Borno under **Ali ibn Dunama** entered a sustained period of decline. Increasing slave raids and aggressive nomadic attacks led to abandonment of desert-edge regions of the state. Rebellions in outlying districts encouraged movement of populations and herds to more se-

cure locations, including the migration westward to the Central Sudan. **Internal dissent in court between Sefuwa dynasty and clerics.** Crisis peaked around 1805 as Fulani nomads of Borno launched jihad against state.

1754, Dec. 15. Birth of **'Uthman ben Muhammad ben Salih,** known as **Shehu Usuman dan Fodio,** in Maratta, kingdom of Gobir. In 1804 he led a jihad against the nominally Muslim Hausa kings of the central Sudan and against the kingdom of Borno. Usuman dan Fodio ultimately established the powerful **Sokoto Caliphate,** the most powerful Muslim state in West Africa (p. 589).

1776. **Suleyman Baal,** leader of the clerical party in the emerging civil war among the **Futanke** of the Senegal River Valley, won military victories in the middle Senegal River Valley, paving the way for the new Islamic state of Futa Toro. His successor, **Abd al-Qadir,** greatly strengthened the new regime. He promoted religious education and the construction of mosques and extended Islamic authority by waging wars of conquest. Abd al-Qadir's jihad of 1776 entrenched the Islamic character of state and society in the region. *(To p. 589)*

b. FOREST WEST AFRICA

(From p. 146)

15th century onward. The first state to provide Europeans with a significant supply of slaves from the forests of eastern Nigeria, **Benin** owed its rapid development to its centralized kingship and its location along major West African trade routes. Benin's rulers extended their authority through military force and consequently maintained a monarchy that lasted through the 19th century. By the beginning of the 16th century, Benin had two hierarchies of power, centered on palace chiefs and town chiefs. The state earned revenue from its monopoly over certain commodities, taxation, and judicial fines. Benin was the most important African state the Portuguese came in contact with up to 1486.

1562. John Hawkins initiated the **British slave trade** by taking a load of 300 slaves from Sierra Leone.

c. 1575. The **Fon kingdom of Dahomey** arose amid the unstable conditions and rivalries spawned by the Atlantic slave trade. Located in the southern portion of present-day Benin, Dahomey developed into a highly centralized state. By absorbing other polities in its midst, it became a major power by 1700.

1598. Dutch established trading stations along the Guinea coast.

c. 1606. **Dutch, Flemish, and Portuguese** traders active in Sierra Leone.

1612. French effort to operate a factory on the Gambia River failed.

1618. British established post at Bathurst, mouth of the Gambia River.

1621. Dutch founded trading stations on Gorée Island and at Arguin.

1626. The **French** established themselves at Saint-Louis at the mouth of the Senegal River.

c. 1630–70. The first **Asante towns** began attracting immigrants in the early 17th century. Each developed its own political structure but shared certain common traits, including matrilineal descent. **State building progressed steadily,** spurred by the abundant human and natural resources of the region, aided by the **use of slave labor.** The Akan occupied and colonized the densely populated region between the eastern Ivory Coast and the Volta River, also noted for having the most productive gold deposits in the region. In addition to the trade in gold northward to the grasslands and to the Mediterranean via the trans-Saharan trade, the arrival of Europeans stimulated increased production of gold for trade along the coast. Africans purchased as slaves or captured in wars of conquest were used within Akan society as farm laborers, miners, and porters.

In the late 17th century, Asante began to battle neighboring states for supremacy; by the early 18th century, Asante had become the strongest of the Akan centralized states. Its empire was based on military exploits and conquest.

17th century. Small states along the Gold Coast emerged, stimulated by the state building of the Asante to the north and by the commercial opportunities offered by the Europeans. The growth of this trade led to the formation of several small states along the Gold Coast, including **Adansi, Denkyira, Assin, and Akwamu.**

1635. Catholic mission established at Rufisque.

1637. Dutch took Elmina from the Portuguese and built numerous forts along the Gold Coast.

1637. Five **French Capuchin** missionaries established themselves along the Gold Coast.

1638. French reoccupied posts at Saint-Louis and built one at Rufisque.

1652. Swedes established trading posts along the Gold Coast.

1657. Danes drove Swedes from their Gold Coast stations.

1659. Town of Saint-Louis on the Senegal River founded.

1662. British built Cape Coast fort.

1663. First **British** trading station on Sierra Leone founded.

1672. The Royal Africa Company founded.

1673. The French Senegal Company founded.

1678. French captured Dutch posts along the Senegalese coast.

1679. Second French Senegal Company founded.

1681-83. Capuchin Fr. Celestin established a school for chiefs and notables at Whydah.

1683. Prussians built the fort of Grossfriedrichsburg on the Gold Coast.

1685-88. Dominican missions established at Kommenda, Whydah, and Benin.

Mid-17th century. Outlying provinces of the **Benin Empire,** such as Warri and other coastal towns, began to break away in order to trade directly with Europeans. As late as 1691, Benin cavalry could still impose tribute from coastal and riverine polities, but they could no longer regulate their internal affairs.

　　Slave trade expanded in this region in the 18th century. Benin's power waxed and waned through 18th and 19th centuries but remained intact until its capture and plunder by British in 1897.

18th century. City-states along the Bight of Biafra emerged in response to political and economic conditions brought about by European demand for slaves and other commodities. The Atlantic slave trade played a key role in encouraging the evolution of coastal city-states. By the 18th century, organized political units in the Bight of Biafra controlled the trade with Europeans, especially the trade in slaves.

17th-18th centuries. The period witnessed further **concentration of bureaucracy and central power in Yoruba states. Oyo became the most powerful state among the Yoruba communities of southwestern Nigeria.** Its military, staffed partly by slaves, included cavalry and archery divisions. Oyo's military supremacy rested on cavalry, but horses had to be imported from the drier Sahel regions to the north. Trade, therefore, was a central part of state organization. Other Yoruba states included Igana, Ikoyi, Ede, and Iwo. Like Oyo, these states employed messengers and envoys, tax collectors, and provincial governors. Political officeholders supervised their states' major economic enterprises. Rivalries among Yoruba states led to wars, which fed the Atlantic slave trade.

1696-97. Third and fourth French Senegal Companies founded. André Brue named director.

1697-1724. The French, under **André Brue,** explored the Senegal region and built posts along the coast from Arguin to Sierra Leone.

1698. Royal Africa Company monopoly of West African trade abolished.

1714. Jesuit mission established in Sierra Leone.

1717. Dutch purchased Brandenburger forts on the Gold Coast.

1724-27. Dahomey ruler Agaja embarked on conquest of smaller and older polities in area of Abomey, greatly increasing the power of the state.

1730. Oyo attacked Dahomey in punitive action against Dahomey's aggressiveness toward Oyo's western flank. Dahomey was forced into nominal tribute role to Oyo.

c. 1730. First reported harvest of **peanuts** in the Gambia.

1731-42. Opoku Ware, the Asantehene, emerged as the ruler and consolidated Asante state.

1732-34. Following Oyo campaign against Dahomey, smaller polities sought to free themselves from Dahomey and rebelled against it. Dahomey troops carried out severe reprisals, asserting Dahomey's regional hegemony and **feeding the slave trade.**

1737. War between **Asante and Wassaw.**

1747. Asante expansionism toward the coast; Asante overran Accra and besieged Christianbourg Castle.

1749-53. Michel **Andanson** explored the Senegambian coast.

1751-56. Thomas **Thomson,** Anglican chaplain to Cape Coast Castle, evangelized among the Fante.

1756-83. Dutch encouraged cotton production at Axim and Shama.

1763. Catholic mission established at Gorée.

1763-79. British seized Senegambia and administered it as a crown colony.

1765-1816. Philip Quaqua, first African Anglican deacon of the Gold Coast.

c. 1770. Asante seized Gomba and enforced tribute until 1874.

c. 1776. Yoruba introduced Islam into Dahomey.

1787. Freetown in Sierra Leone was founded to aid the repatriation of freed slaves from Britain and British colonies.

　　May 9. Britain's **resettlement of more than 400 ex-slaves** to Sierra Leone marked the first repatriation of freed slaves back to Africa. British abolitionists hoped the newly settled community of ex-slaves would spread Christianity, support the abolition of the slave trade, and become integrated into the Atlantic economy.

1788. Sir Joseph Banks founded the **African Association** for the furtherance of exploration and the development of trade.

1789. Smallpox epidemic broke out at Cape Coast Castle. Slaves awaiting shipment were compulsorily vaccinated.

c. 1789. Catholicism introduced at Warri.

1789-91. Daniel Houghton explored Bambuk from the Gambia.

1792. Denmark prohibited the slave trade.

1794. French National Assembly freed all slaves without compensation (p. 433).

1795. London Missionary Society (Anglican) founded.

1795-97. Mungo Park's first mission to the interior. Park reached Segu on the Niger River and discovered that the river flowed eastward.

1796. Wesleyan missionaries began work in Sierra Leone.

1796. Glasgow Missionary Society (Presbyterian) founded.

1799. Church Missionary Society (Anglican) founded. *(To p. 590)*

c. NORTHEAST AFRICA (HORN)

(From p. 146)

1500. Christian empire in Ethiopia reached its peak, having no significant rivals in the region. Emperor granted land or tributary or service rights to deserving individuals in **feudal system** based on grants of territory in exchange for loyalty, but feudal aristocratic class did not develop at this stage. **Galla** peoples, Cushitic-speaking pastoralists, began migration into Ethiopia from the south.

1500-1650. Growth in trade in Horn of Africa.

1504. Funj, cattle-keeping nomads moving north along the Blue Nile, established sultanate after defeating Nubians. Abdallabi emerged as ruling clan and **Sennar** became their seat of government around 1616. The **Funj-Abdallabi sultanate** encouraged spread of Islam by scholars who introduced **Sufi mysticism.**

1520-26. Portuguese mission under **Rodrigo de Lima** to Ethiopia. **Francesco Alvares** acted as chaplain, with objectives to establish **Christian alliance with Ethiopia** (following earlier mission in 1487). Alvares provided first detailed reports on the strength of the Ethiopian empire and church.

1529-43. Ahmad ibn Ibrahim al-Ghazi led jihad in Ethiopia growing out of wars between Ethiopia and the neighboring Islamic trading states. Ethiopia came to the brink of defeat, but the jihad lost momentum after the death of Ahmad in 1543.

1541-43. Soldiers from the **Portuguese fleet in Massawa fought with Ethiopian army against Muslim forces.** Muslim forces were decisively defeated and Ethiopia began to regain some lost territory, but empire remained weak until Restoration.

1555-1633. Portuguese Jesuit missions to Ethiopia. Conversion of two successive rulers. Remarkable influence and work of **Pedro Paez** (d. 1622). Conversion, however, led to repeated intrigues and wars against the Portuguese.

1640. Portuguese expelled from Ethiopia and Catholic missions prohibited.

1559. Galla, adopting horses, made renewed push toward Ethiopian plateau in wake of Muslim invasion.

1572-75. Ethiopian emperor Serse-Dingil (d. 1597) took over feudal armies under direct royal control and **defeated Ottoman attempt to conquer Ethiopia.**

1607-32. Emperor Susenyos of Ethiopia **incorporated Galla** into Ethiopian army and settled loyal Galla in strategic provinces. In 1622 he sided with the pro-Jesuit factions at the court and **proclaimed himself Catholic,** but he was unable to carry the court or country against the tradition of the Ethiopian church.

1632. Ethiopian empire and church restored, but policy of southern expansion was abandoned and emperor struggled to retain power at center.

1636. Castle built at **Gondar as fixed imperial residence,** marking end of religious wars and end of the empire's expansionism.

1640–1874. Fur sultanate at Darfur, which had arisen in western savannah of Bilad al-Sudan at the **crossroads of several trade routes,** flourished under **Kayra dynasty** (based on wealth from long-distance trade) and pursued expansionist policy. Darfur completed the line of Islamic states across the Sudan, **opening a pilgrimage route to Mecca.**

1667–82. Emperor Yohannes of Ethiopia required acceptance of Orthodox faith by Catholics, who were in any case few in number. Muslim merchants were allowed to retain their religion but were required to live in separate communities.

1675–1700. Rapid development in Red Sea trade as a result of **growth of Omani maritime power and new European imports of coffee.**

1700–1800. Acceleration of Islamization in Darfur; rulers encouraged foreign Muslim scholars to settle there. **Noble class arose in Ethiopia** with decline of imperial central power.

1702. Franciscan Fr. Joseph visited Ethiopian court. Seven young Ethiopians went to Rome for instruction.

1704. Major **earthquake** destroyed buildings at Gondar.

c. 1716. Three **Capuchin missionaries** reached Gondar but were stoned to death.

c. 1750. Three **Franciscans** reached Gondar but were forced to return to Europe.

1762. Sheik Muhammad Abu Likaylik deposed Funj sultan and effectively established new dynasty, known as Hamadj, with Funj royal family as puppet rulers.

1768–73. James Bruce explored Ethiopia, traveling from Massawa to Gondar. He returned by way of the Nile River and reported that the Ethiopian Empire was in decline.

1800. Most of Horn was under control of Galla peoples, among whom Islam was spreading. *(To p. 592)*

d. EAST AFRICA

(From p. 147)

1. SWAHILI COAST

1500. Most of **Swahili coast at an economic and cultural peak,** though Kilwa was in decline on eve of Portuguese arrival. All the towns by this stage were Muslim, speaking an early form of Swahili, while hinterland peoples remained animist.

1591. Mombassa fell to Portuguese in alliance with Malindi. **Sheik Ahmad of Malindi** was made sheik of Mombassa.

1592–96. Portuguese built a factory on Zanzibar and established Fort Jesus and put in place a garrison of 100 men at Mombassa to secure a foothold on the Swahili coast. Elsewhere, their presence was minimal, involving only the collection of tribute.

1652–1729. Omani Arabs struggled with Portuguese for control of the Swahili coast. Omani raid led ruling dynasty in Zanzibar to proclaim its independence from Portuguese.

1696–98. Omani Arabs besieged Fort Jesus, leading to surrender by the Portuguese in 1698.

1729. Portuguese were finally driven out of Mombassa and other Swahili towns by local forces.

1741. Rise of Bas'idi dynasty in Oman set stage for rise of Zanzibar under Omani rule in 19th century.

2. INTERLACUSTRINE EAST AFRICA

1500–1580. Consolidation of **successor states to Bachwezi Empire,** beginning in about 1400. The most important of these was the **Bito kingdom of Bunyoro,** whose ruling dynasty was of Nilotic origin.

1500–1600. Rwanda faced by crisis, including two invasions from Bunyoro, leading to succession dispute and the establishment of a new dynasty in about 1600 by **Ruganzu Ndori.**

1520. Bunyoro armies defeated Buganda and Nkore but fled from latter during an eclipse of the sun.

1523–50. Bunyoro established buffer states in south to protect it against BaHima.

1588–1621. The Great Lakes region hit by a series of **droughts and ensuing devastating famines.** The time was remembered in northern Ugandan traditions as the period of Nyarubanga ("sent by God"). The droughts and famines led to **political upheaval and mass migrations.**

1600. Bunyoro was dominant state in subregion.

1600–1700. Rwanda expansionism under dynasty established by Ruganzu Ndori was stopped by new dynasty in Burundi in about 1700.

1600–1800. Rise of Buganda under centralized power of Ganda rulers and military expansion. Conquered areas were incorporated under appointed chiefs. **Bunyoro's power declined** as a result of succession disputes and rebellions by tributaries. By end of the period Bunyoro was still the strongest state but was one among many strong states in the region, including Buganda, a former tributary. **Anti-royalist Ryangombe movement developed in Rwanda as a cult of suffering,** but was co-opted by ruling dynasty.

1644–74. Buganda strengthened central rule under **Kabaka Tebandeke** through latter's reduction of power of religious officers.

1650–1750. Crisis in Bunyoro, leading to decline, based on the opening of kingship candidacy to all sons of the king, which resulted in a series of succession disputes and disintegration.

1674–1704. Buganda began territorial expansion under Mwanda. Mwanda appointed commoners to the bureaucracy and these outstripped the importance of territorial Bataka chiefs.

1700–1800. After temporary setback at hands of Burundi, **Rwanda resumed military expansion.** Rwanda at end of period was dominant in its subregion, as Buganda was in its subregion. Rwanda and other states in the region **consolidated royal power through clientship, military expansion, regional trade in salt, iron hoes, and copper, and the development of new religious cults centered on the monarchy.**

1733–60. Bunyoro centralization through the appointment of royal princes by **King Isansa** in the southern provinces led to their succession, while persecution of the Paluo led to their emigration.

1734–94. Buganda continued its territorial expansion.

1750. Bugandan **king Semakokiro** purged the royal princes to prevent succession disputes.

1800. Buganda was securely supreme over Bunyoro. *(To p. 593)*

e. WEST CENTRAL AFRICA

(From p. 147)

1500–1600. Kongo kingdom dominated subregion south of lower Congo (Zaire) River as far as Luanda (modern-day Angola). From 1500 **Kongo was becoming a conquest state and trading empire and was sharply influenced by the arrival of the Portuguese.** It was ruled from a central capital by a monarchy and a class of urban nobles who presided over villagers and slaves. The political structure was centralized; officeholders, including provincial governors, were appointed by the king.

1500–1700. Social and cultural change in Kongo. Trade in north African cloth and European goods, along with the presence of Portuguese teachers and priests, helped to create a **distinct court culture and enhanced royal power. Diminishing importance of matrilineality and of the village.** Increasing exploitation of villagers led to rebellion and to **Kimpasi cult, aimed at the elimination of suffering. Decline in the status of rural free women.** Among nobles, growth in patrilineal descent patterns. **Rapid expansion of the slave trade led to increased militarization of society and presence of two classes of slaves, those who were considered exportable and those who could not be sold.**

Rund state, which was to become the wider Lunda Empire, emerged between Kasai and Bushimai Rivers in southern present-day Zaire. **Luba Empire** had come into existence somewhat earlier in Shaba between Bushimai and Lualaba Rivers. Luba had a royal ideology based on **sacred kingship and rule by a secret association, the Bambudye,** who promoted state ideology and control. Population clusters in subregion of poor soils and a long dry season were linked by trade in raffia cloth, palm oil, fish, copper, and salt. Copper crosses were used as standardized currency by 1500 but declined in size by 1600 and disappeared after 1700.

1506–43. Reign of **Alfonso I,** who became king after succession dispute. He was a **convert to Christianity under the influence of Portuguese missionaries,** and his rule was pivotal in opening up to Portuguese influence. Increased Portuguese influence **engendered internal crisis.** Alfonso made the Catholic Church the official religion and his **son Henrique was consecrated as a bishop in Rome** and directed the Christianization of the country in 1518–36. Revenue from the trade in slaves, ivory, and raffia cloth was used to attract Portuguese craftsmen, traders, and missionaries. The **growing wealth and Christianization of the nobility widened the gap between nobles and commoners** during Alfonso's rule. The nobility became literate Christians, and the royalty was strengthened by a slave guard. The Portuguese played an important role in the capital and in succession disputes in the kingdom. **The social structure changed from three strata (nobles, villagers, and slaves) to two (nobles and laborers/peasants). A tension emerged and grew between the nobility of Mbanza Kongo, the capital, and governors of outlying regions.** In Angola, the Portuguese placed themselves above the other strata and there emerged a group of **Afro-Portuguese mulatto traders** of mixed culture and language.

1514. Slave trade developed in Kongo from this date, under a **royal monopoly.** Increased demand for slaves encouraged outlying governors to deal directly with Portuguese traders, leading to political and military conflicts.

1526. Kongo king Alfonso made a failed effort to abolish the slave trade.

1548–83. Introduction of maize cultivation in Kongo. Other **NEW WORLD PLANTS,** including tobacco and manioc, along with pigs, were introduced in Kongo at about this time.

1560. Smallpox epidemic in Kongo. Along with the slave trade, new **DISEASES** had a significant effect on population.

1567. Kongo routed by nomadic Jaga warriors from the east during disarray following war with **Tio kingdom.**

1571–73. Kongo kingdom regained with help of Portuguese troops, but Kongo's regional dominance was lost as **Portuguese traders shifted focus to Loango,** north of the Congo River.

1575. Portuguese established colony of Angola as a slaving territory.

1576. Paulo Dias founded **Luanda** in Angola colony and began to trade in slaves.

1576–1671. From Luanda, **Portugal conquered Ndongo** in a century-long war. Portugal was aided by **alliance with nomadic Jaga warriors,** 1612–21.

1600–1650. By this date **Loango had become an important commercial power,** trading with Europeans, especially Dutch, in ivory, hides, red dyewood, and raffia but relatively few slaves. Political change in Loango led to emergence of a **bureaucracy. Lunda began to grow as a centralized empire,** possibly aided by the growth of international trade as a supplement to preexisting regional trade.

1612. Around 10,000 **slaves shipped annually from Angola.** Slave exports from West Central Africa remained more or less at 10,000 per year until 1720, when annual exports rose to 40,000 per year in the 1780s and 1790s.

1622. Angolan colony and its Jaga warrior mercenaries attacked southern provinces of Kongo to raid for slaves, **undermining Portuguese influence** and thus the monarchy, in Kongo. From this time the **central authority in Kongo was weakened.**

1624–63. Nzinga, queen of the Mbundu, revived the slave trade with Europeans.

1641–48. Dutch captured Luanda and occupied much of Angola in order to increase slave supply.

1641–1700. Italian Capuchin missionaries in Kongo began campaign to spread Christianity beyond nobles; **they baptized large portions of the population.** There was a much more limited spread of Christianity in Angola. Throughout West Central Africa, there was a **gradual evolution of a syncretic religion, combining animist and Christian ideas in the 16th and 17th centuries.**

1648–1730. Brazilians dominated Angolan slave trade.

1650. Portuguese recovery of Angola completed.

1659–1893. About 642,000 slaves shipped from Luanda and Benguela to Brazil.

c. 1629. First reported efforts to grow **maize, manioc, sweet potatoes, pawpaw, coconuts, guavas,** and **peanuts** on small farms near Luanda.

1650. From this time, **New World crops,** especially the **drought-resistant manioc (cassava),** transformed agriculture in Kongo-Angola region, in-

creasing yields and leading to better nutrition and supporting increased population growth. Manioc required careful processing; as a primary staple, manioc can lead to malnutrition.

1650–1800. Loango became one of the most important slave-exporting regions, trading more than 10,000 slaves each year, as a result of new Dutch demand and increased Portuguese demand. Traders and trading officials grew more powerful than nobility.

1666–78. War with Angola and **civil war over succession and over central power destroyed Kongo kingdom.** Capital was destroyed and political system collapsed into collection of small principalities.

1700. From this time, **large matrilineal clans grew up around the newly emerging rural nobles** in Kongo.

1700–1800. Angola remained overwhelmingly dependent on the **slave trade. Slave trade relied on cooperation between Portuguese, Brazilians, and Africans.** By 1800, slave trade yielded 88 percent of the colony's revenue.

1704–6. Social collapse in Kongo led to the emergence of prophetess Dona Beatrice Kimpa Vita preaching an AFRICANIZED CHRISTIANITY called Antonianism (as she claimed to speak for St. Anthony). In 1706 she was burned as a heretic.

1760. Jesuits expelled from Angola and Mozambique.

1800. Lunda Empire emerged from Rund kingdom, having a political organization based on the assumption of the personality of predecessors in office in perpetual kingship. Alliances were maintained through fictions of continuing kin and marriage relationships. The loosely organized empire began to expand toward the south and southeast. Northward and westward expansion had proceeded in conjunction with the Angolan slave trade from 1670s. This enabled nobility to import European cloth and other luxury goods. The **state developed bureaucracy to control trade.** Growing trade in captured and convicted slaves was placed under royal control.

1800. By this date, **Luba and Lunda Empires** covered the entire savannah east of the Kwango River with a common cultural system. Lunda militarism and slave raiding led to widescale destruction. *(To p. 594)*

f. SOUTHERN AFRICA

(From p. 148)

1. NORTH OF THE LIMPOPO

1500–1700. Expansion of **Maravi state system in Chewa-speaking area of the Shire Valley.** The state was centered at Manthimba on the southwest side of Lake Malawi. It integrated pre-Maravi inhabitants through ritual and appointments, and expanded, around 1575, by settlement of lineage heads in adjacent territories.

1514. By this date, **Swahili traders had established bazaars** for regional trade in the **Mutapa Empire.**

1531. Swahili traders were ousted from Sena and Tete but remained in Zambezi region as agents for Portuguese.

1550. Portuguese began trading along the Zambezi River.

1575–1684. Portuguese transformed Swahili bazaars in lower Zambezi into *feiras,* central areas for Afro-Portuguese commerce, on land granted by local chiefs. The most celebrated *feira* was **Dambarane.**

1500–1800. NEW CROPS from Europe and Asia and the Americas entered southern Zambezi, including rice, yams, various fruit trees, groundnuts, cowpeas, and maize. New crops contributed to population increase.

1600–1700. Chewa-Maravi peoples became most important group in subregion north of Zambezi River; the **Portuguese were forced to cooperate with them** in the Zambezi Valley.

1624. Jesuit missions established along the Zambezi River.

1645. Portuguese began to export slaves from Mozambique to Brazil.

1677. Two thousand Portuguese colonialists arrived in Mozambique.

1684–95. Rozvi state broke away from Karanga section of **Mutapa Empire.** Ruler **Changamire Dombo I** created **Rozvi Empire,** which controlled considerable part of modern Zimbabwe, from a core area in modern Matabeleland.

1693–95. Portuguese were expelled from Shona area by Rozvi emperor **Dombo Changamire** and withdrew from *feiras,* though some were reestablished in the next century.

1700–1800. Portuguese colonialists set up **prazo estates,** granted by the crown, along the Zambezi River, in effect establishing African-style chiefdoms. In the century, prazos dominated the lower Zambezi. Prazos exploited local agricultural labor and used **Chikunda slave armies. Prazeros developed gold and ivory trade** with trading states north of the Zambezi. There was rapid gold production around 1740–80, but **Portuguese lost control over ivory trade to Yao.** There was a decline in trade between the Rozvi Empire and Portugal despite their continued alliance, owing to a gold rush north of the Zambezi by individual adventurers, a decline in overall gold production, and a turn to ivory hunting by both Portuguese and Africans.

　　Rozvi Empire operated through distribution of land to newly appointed chiefs and collection of tribute. **Mwari oracle cult** developed and was manipulated by rulers for political ends. MAIZE was introduced in Zimbabwe region and became a staple of Shona-speakers, along with millet and sorghum.

1750. Maravi state system began to decline as a result of succession disputes by several paramount chiefdoms within it.

1750–1850. Yao came to fore as dominant traders of ivory from Zambezi interior to coast.

1752. Administration of Mozambique separated from that of Gao.

1777. Dominicans expelled from Mozambique.

1780. Portuguese, having lost control of ivory trade in Zambezi, turned to **slave trade.** The slave trade was then joined by **Yao and Bisa.** From 1770, the **Kilwa market** was dominated by the slave trade.

c. 1780–1800. Ten thousand slaves annually exported from Mozambique to South America.

2. SOUTH OF THE LIMPOPO

1500–1650. Arid western half of southern Africa was dominated by **Khoi herdsmen** and by **San hunters** who in lean times became clients of the Khoi. San lived in small nomadic bands while Khoi lived in larger, seminomadic, and differentiated groups. At the Cape, **Khoi traded cattle to occasional European ships.** At the east-west divide, marked by grazing land that was marginal for agriculture, there were economic relationships between Khoi herders and **Bantu cattle-keeping farmers.** The latter (**Nguni** along the coast and **Sotho/Tswana** in the interior) lived in late-iron-age mixed farming communities based on grain and livestock. These communities were formed into **chiefdoms** but were not highly centralized; the **basic unit was the homestead,** linked to the chiefdom through a patrilineage and a clan.

1652. Dutch East India Company established a settlement at Cape Town as refreshment station for ships in trade between Europe and Asia, under command of **Jan van Riebeeck.** Meat was procured from the Khoi and vegetables grown in the company garden. Since Khoi labor was not forthcoming, the company **imported slaves from Asia and other parts of Africa** (especially Madagascar). The settlement slowly expanded as **Europeans engaged in extensive pastoralism and hunting** with Khoi and slave laborers. **Burghers** freed from company service at Cape Town came into **conflict with Khoi on Cape Peninsula,** leading to series of wars between the company and Khoi.

　　Bantu speakers in present-day South Africa also began to adopt MAIZE, which has higher yields but is less drought-resistant than sorghum. The century was generally dry in South Africa and concluded with a **serious drought and famine.** Preceding the drought, however, there was considerable **population growth** based on the early adoption of maize in the northern **Nguni** areas and a **proliferation of chiefdoms. Sotho-Tswana** peoples began to form **large chiefdoms** in southern and western **Transvaal** and in **Botswana,** living in large central settlements and ruled by a chief with religious and political authority advised by a council.

　　Cape Town became an entrepôt for an extensive pastoralist economy. Its population increased from **slave importations and immigration;** by 1800 there were 20,000 free burghers and 25,000 slaves. The colony's expansion pushed the Khoisan from the western interior.

1666. First **Calvinist church** erected at Cape Town.

1667. Indians and Malaysians began to arrive at the Cape.

c. 1685. First **wines** successfully grown at the Cape.

1688. Two hundred **Huguenot refugees from France** arrived at the Cape and strengthened Dutch settlement.

1707. At least one Dutch settler began to call himself an **Afrikaner.**

1713. Smallpox epidemic in Cape killed large numbers of Khoi and was

followed by cattle disease that led to loss of herds. Impoverished Khoi became clients of cattle-keeping Africans and Afrikaners.

c. 1730. Dutch began **trekking** into the interior of the Cape.

1730–80. Independent mixed-race communities of Kora, Griqua, and Nama cattle-raiding and trading pastoralists thrived north of Cape Town along the Orange River beyond the white frontier. The **trading frontier** east of Cape Town for ivory and cattle became the frontier of white settlement, leading to **conflict with Xhosa** semipastoralists over grazing land and to series of **frontier wars** at end of century.

1736–42. George Schmidt, first Protestant missionary at the Cape, began evangelization among the Khoi.

1755. Smallpox epidemic at the Cape.

1775–82. Series of succession disputes following the death of **Xhosa ruler Phalo** and his sons.

c. 1776. First direct contacts between **Dutch and Xhosa on the Zeekse River.**

1779–81. First **frontier war** of a hundred-year series of wars between colonists of Cape and Xhosa on eastern frontier at **Fish River.**

1789. Xhosa crossed the Fish River.

1795. Whites rebelled against company rule on eastern frontier of South Africa. **British captured Cape Town** and put down rebellion.

1799. Khoi revolt on eastern frontier, supported by Khoi soldiers in British service. At this time there were 14,000 Khoi in the colony, cast in the role of intermediary between the settlement and Bantu farmers, but the rebellion ended this role in the east.

1800. Emergence in southeast coast among northern **Nguni**–speakers of **larger chiefdoms that would become the Zulu state** early in the next century, perhaps sparked by conflict over the ivory trade at Delagoa Bay or conflict over drought-stricken grazing land. (To p. 595)

g. MADAGASCAR

(From p. 148)

1500. Four **Swahili-speaking trading communities** had been established in the north, exporting **rice and slaves** to East Africa and Arabia.

1550. End of immigration of main components of Malagasy population. **Aristocratic Zafikasimambo** emerged among the **Antemoro,** recent immigrants, in the east at Matitana. This **priestly caste** monopolized the privilege of slaughtering domestic animals, reduced freedoms accorded common people, and centralized power to create the first strong **Antemoro kingdom.** The **Portuguese** became the most active **slave buyers** in the northwest trading communities. They also traded for cattle, ambergris, and raffia cloth.

1600. Many small independent chiefdoms were scattered across the island.

1600–1700. There was **increasing contact with Europeans;** the focus of the slave trade shifted from East Africa and Arabia to the Cape of Good Hope and the New World. However, the Portuguese took fewer slaves than the Africans and Arabs did. The **Comoro Islands** became the collection point for Madagascar's trade to East Africa and Arabia. The **Dutch and English** also began trading in Madagascar.

1600–1800. English were the most active traders of slaves to the New World from the island.

1643–74. French established fort in the southeast.

1645. English Puritans established short-lived colony at St. Augustine Bay.

1647–74. Carmelite mission started in Madagascar. **Lazerites and Capuchins** also participated.

1690. Tsimanatona established **Iboina state** with **Sakalava warriors.**

1700. By this time much of the west was under the **Sakalava Empire** and there were kingdoms in the highlands and in the south.

1721. French annexed Mauritius, renaming it Île de France.

1733–44. Sugar industry established on Île de France and Bourbon.

1752. The **Sakalava kingdom** of Iboina reached height under **Andrianinevenarivo.**

1767–1808. Iboina began decline under **Queen Ravahiny,** partly under pressure of **Muslim claims** to the throne.

1778–1800. Andrianampoinimerina reunited Merina kingdom. He centralized power, fortified the borders with settlers, acquired firearms, and pursued aggressive diplomacy. Under his rule, Merina ceased to pay tribute to Sakalava. (To p. 598)

H. LATIN AMERICA, 1500–1800

1. THE SPANISH CONQUEST

(From p. 278)

The conquest and colonization of Spanish America progressed outward from the earliest colony in Santo Domingo. By 1600, the territory from New Mexico and Florida in the north to Chile and the Río de la Plata in the south was, with the exception of Brazil, under the rule of the Crown of Castile.

At the time that Spaniards engaged in the exploration, conquest, and colonization of America, Spain was a multiethnic society in the process of centralization and unification under the Crown of Castile (p. 294). The crucial element for unity was the imposition of the Christian faith on the entire population. The Catholic kings consequently expelled Jews and Muslims unwilling to become Christians. In the expansion of Christian control, the kings distributed land and people taken from the Muslim rulers. Using the same method in America, **the crown took advantage of the conquerors' individual initiatives while remaining the source of political legitimacy and organization in the New World settlements.**

The triumph of the Spaniards over incredible numerical odds was due to their ability to exploit the fissures of local societies and to adapt their military training to new conditions. Spaniards allied with discontented native lords and learned to use native weaponry. Interpreters and translators provided them with better knowledge of the societies they intended to dominate. **Through warfare and slavery, the**

Spanish conquest took a heavy toll on native lives. The cruelty of the conquerors gave rise to the **Black Legend,** popularized by Protestant European states in their wars against Spain. Besides the horrors intentionally provoked, contact with the conquerors caused **native inhabitants to suffer epidemics of diseases to which they had not developed immunological defenses.** Also, the introduction of European cattle destroyed the ecological system on which Indian agriculture was based. The conquerors quickly subdued those societies where centralized states had been established; in other areas, their advance was slower and suffered repeated setbacks.

The crown acted swiftly to prevent conquerors from becoming a new feudal aristocracy. It reserved for itself the power to issue authorizations *(capitulaciones)* for the exploration, conquest, and settlement of new territories. It issued laws prohibiting Indian slavery. Christianizing campaigns also strengthened royal control over conquered territories, since the Church was directly subordinated to the crown. In their eagerness to convert natives to Christianity, members of religious orders carefully studied native societies to improve their methods of uprooting native religions. The crown prohibited non-Castilians from immigrating to the New World, but many foreigners could obtain legal permission to travel and settle there. Soon, the original conquerors gave way to a colonial bureaucracy.

2. THE CARIBBEAN AND THE ISTHMUS, 1499–1531

Santo Domingo, called **Española,** became the first seat of Spanish government in the Indies. The Indian population rapidly diminished as a result of warfare, overwork, enslavement, and disease.

1499. Discovery of gold mines in Santo Domingo.

1501. The crown authorized the African **slave trade** under its monopoly, giving permission to Flemish, German, Dutch, Genoan, and Portuguese merchants to engage in it.

1502. Nicolás de Ovando assumed governorship of Santo Domingo. He brought 1,500 families to populate the island.

1503. Ovando carried out a ruthless campaign to control the Indian population. He distributed Indians in *encomiendas* (p. 402), to work essentially as slaves in gold mines for the Spaniards. The conquerors founded 15 towns on the island.

1508–11. Juan Ponce de León conquered **Puerto Rico,** founded **San Juan,** and discovered gold. **Juan de Esquivel** settled **Jamaica.** Conquerors organized enslavement expeditions to the nearby islands. First sugar mills established on Española.

1511. Establishment of the *audiencia* of Santo Domingo (royal tribunal and government), the first in America.

1511–15. Diego Velázquez conquered **Cuba.** Colonizers founded **Baracoa** (1512), **Bayamo** (1513), **Trinidad** (1514), **Puerto Príncipe** (1514), **Havana** (1514), and **Santiago de Cuba** (1515). They quickly defeated Indians and subjected them to such exploitation that it led to their extermination within a few years. Havana was relocated to the north coast (1519).

1509–13. Alonso de Ojeda, with royal authorization, founded a colony on the east coast of the Isthmus of Panama. **Diego de Nicuesa** founded **Nombre de Díos** on the Isthmus. Ojeda's settlers later united with those of Nicuesa, under the governorship of **Vasco Núñez de Balboa** (1474–1519). Balboa claimed discovery of the **Pacific Ocean** (South Sea) and declared it a possession of the Crown of Castile (1513).

1513–14. A jurisdiction independent of Española, **Castilla del Oro** (Darien), was created in the region of the Isthmus. **Pedro Arias de Ávila** (1442–1531) was named royal governor and brought some 1,500 colonists from Spain.

1514–19. Ávila dispatched expeditions by land and sea to adjacent areas. He founded **Panama** as the seat of government, refounded Nombre de Díos, and cleared a route across the Isthmus. Balboa continued explorations on the Pacific coast. He clashed with Governor Ávila, who ordered his execution.

1522–23. Under independent authority, **Gil González Dávila** and **Andrés Niño** led a combined land and sea expedition westward from the Isthmus. Dávila conquered the area around the Gulf of Nicoya and Lake Nicaragua, and Niño sailed to Fonseca Bay. Governor Ávila then dispatched **Francisco Hernández de Córdoba** to conquer **Nicaragua.**

1523–31. Dávila secured license to continue exploration and conquest and returned to Central America by way of Honduras. Hernández de Córdoba entered Nicaragua and founded **León** and **Granada** (1523). Following a conflict with Dávila, Hernández de Córdoba rebelled against Governor Ávila and was executed (1526). Ávila became governor of Nicaragua and dispatched an expedition along the San Juan River to the sea, sacking and enslaving the Indian population.

3. VENEZUELA AND NUEVA GRANADA, 1521–1549

1521. Bartolomé de las Casas (1474–1566), who fought against exploitative excesses by conquerors, failed in his attempt to found a peaceful settlement for Indians at Cumaná.

1531–35. Diego de Ordaz explored the region of the Orinoco but left no permanent settlement. In the western areas, ongoing colonization was established at an early date.

1527. Juan de Ampíes (or **Ampúes**), commissioned by the *audiencia* de

Santo Domingo, founded Santa Ana de Coro. Emperor Charles V granted this territory to the **Welsers,** a great Augsburg banking family to which he was heavily indebted.

1529. The Welsers sent out colonists and established an administration. **Ambrosio Alfinger** became the first governor of **Venezuela.** Dreams of **El Dorado** prompted explorations through the valley of the Orinoco and into the Andes. The rule of the Welsers was extremely harsh for

TEXAS

Rio Grande

Zacatecas

Guadalajara

Tlaxcala
Mexico
Campeche
Veracruz
Oaxaca
YUCATÁN
Tehuántepec
GUATEMALA
Guatemala
HONDURAS

Atlantic

Ocean

Havana

CUBA

Santiago

ESPAÑOLA

PUERTO
RICO

Santa Marta

Nombre
de Dios

Porto Bello

Cartagena, 1533

Darién

Panama,
1519

Bogotá, 1538

Cali

Popayán

Cumaná

Trinidad

Caracas, 1567
VENEZUELA

Orinoco R.

GUIANAS

Viceroyalty of
NEW GRANADA

COSTA RICA

Vi c e r o y a l t y   o f   N E W   S P A I N

Galápagos
Islands

EQUATOR

Quito, 1587

Guayaquil
Tumbes

Amazon R.

Amazon R.

Belém
(Para)

São Luis
do Maranhão

Natal

Paraiba

Cajamarca

B R A Z I L

Recife
(Pernambuco),
1536

Lima,
1535

Cuzco

*L.
Titicaca*

São Francisco R.

Salvador
(Bahia), 1549

Charcas,
1538

MINAS GERAIS

Porto Seguro,
1537

P a c i f i c

O c e a n

Potosí

Paraná R.

São Paulo

Asunción

Rio de Janeiro
Santos, 1532

V i c e r o y a l t y   o f   P E R U

Córdoba

Mendoza

Valparaiso
Santiago

CG of Chile

BANDA
ORIENTAL

Rio Grande do Sul, 1736

Buenos
Aires,
1580

Montevideo, 1723

Río de la Plata

V i c e r o y a l t y   o f   L A   P L A T A

Atlantic

Ocean

Strait of Magellan

Cape Horn

COLONIAL
LATIN AMERICA
1500–1750

0   250   500   750   1000

MILES

the Indians. This brutality, along with protests in Spain against grant-ing land to foreigners, moved the crown to revoke their concession (1546–56). Spanish leaders undertook the conquest of Venezuela. An Indian confederation opposed their advance for ten years, but smallpox epidemics greatly diminished the natives' resistance. **Diego de Losada** founded **Caracas** in 1567.

1525. Rodrigo de Bastidas founded **Santa Marta,** the first permanent set-tlement in what was to become **Nueva Granada. Pedro de Heredia,** acting directly under royal authority, founded **Cartagena** in 1533.

1535–36. Sebastián de Belalcázar, Pizarro's lieutenant, coming from Quito, founded **Cali** and **Popayán.**

1536–38. Gonzalo Jiménez de Quesada (1495–1576), under commission from the government of Santa Marta, moved up the Magdalena River, reached the plateau of Bogotá, defeated and sacked Chibcha chiefdoms, and founded **Santa Fe de Bogotá** (1538).

1539. Advancing toward the Bogotá plateau, Belalcázar met **Nikolaus Federmann,** an agent of the Welsers. Federmann, Belalcázar, and Jiménez de Quesada disputed over jurisdiction. The crown resolved the controversy, confirming Belalcázar in the governorship of Popayán.

1549. The *audiencia* of Nueva Granada was created. It included Santa Marta, Cartagena, Popayán, and Santa Fe de Bogotá, the latter town becoming the seat of government for this large area.

4. PERU AND THE WEST COAST, 1522–1581

1522. Continuing exploration southward from Panama, **Pascual de An-dagoya** (c. 1495–1548) advanced into **Biru (Peru),** where he learned of the rich and powerful **Inca Empire.** His ill health forced him to aban-don plans of conquest.

1524–28. Francisco Pizarro (1470–1541), under Ávila's authority and in association with **Diego de Almagro** (1475–1538) and **Hernando de Luque,** a priest, undertook the conquest of Peru. An initial expedition reached the San Juan River and a second the Gulf of Guayaquil and Tumbes, where they encountered more evidence of the Inca Empire.

1528–29. Pizarro went to Spain and concluded a capitulation with the crown by which he obtained the right of discovery and conquest of Peru for a distance of 200 leagues south of the Gulf of Guayaquil and the office of adelantado, governor and captain-general. Almagro was assigned command of the fortress of Tumbes, and Luque was named its bishop.

1531. Returning to Panama, accompanied by his brothers Gonzalo (c. 1505–48) and Hernando and a small group of recruits, Pizarro orga-nized a military expedition and sailed for the conquest. He consoli-dated his position at Tumbes and founded **San Miguel de Piura,** then gathered more recruits and moved into the interior. He reached **Ca-jamarca,** where the Inca **Atahualpa** had camped with his retinue.

1532, Nov. 16. Pizarro seized Atahualpa by surprise. While prisoner, Ata-hualpa ordered the assassination of his rival, his half-brother Huáscar.

1533. Despite Atahualpa's having paid an enormous ransom in gold and silver, Pizarro ordered his execution. Pizarro, with the help of Almagro, advanced toward **Cusco,** the Inca capital. **Manco,** brother of Huáscar, viewed the Spaniards as allies and they installed him as Inca. Pizarro distributed lands and *encomiendas* among his troops.

1534. Sebastián de Belalcázar (1495–1550) defeated Atahualpa's lieuten-ants and established control in the region of Quito. **Pedro de Alvarado,** governor of Guatemala, came with an expedition of 500 men to seize Quito. He abandoned his claims in exchange for monetary compen-sation.

1535, Jan. 18. Pizarro, having left Cusco, founded **Lima,** which became the capital of the later viceroyalty of Peru. Almagro led Spanish troops and Inca warriors to conquer Chile. In Cusco, Pizarro's brothers at-tacked Manco to obtain more riches. Manco rebelled and conducted a lengthy but unsuccessful siege of Cusco (1535–36). The Inca leader retreated to **Vilcabamba,** a region that became his kingdom.

1537–41. Civil war between Pizarro and Almagro. Having failed in his attempt to conquer Chile, Almagro clashed with Pizarro regarding ju-risdiction over the city of Cusco. Almagro occupied the city but was defeated and executed. Spaniards gained control over the region sur-rounding Lake Titicaca (1538) and founded the city of **La Plata** (today's Sucre) in 1539. Settlements at **Chachapoyas** (1538) and **León de Huá-nuco** (1539) were built on the northeastern frontier.

1541. Partisans of Almagro assassinated Pizarro and set up **Diego de Almagro the Younger,** Almagro's mestizo son, as governor. **Cristóbal**

Vaca de Castro, the royal judge, deposed him. Almagro died in battle in **Chupas** (1542).

1539. Gonzalo Pizarro, as governor of Quito, led an expedition across the Andes and reached the upper Amazon.

1540–41. Pedro de Valdivia (c. 1498–1553), with a contingent of Span-iards and Peruvian Indians, penetrated the fertile central valley of Chile and founded **Santiago** (1541). **Mapuche (Araucanian)** Indians strongly resisted the invaders.

1542. Creation of viceroyalty and *audiencia* of Peru.

1544. First viceroy of Peru, **Blasco Núñez de Vela,** proclaimed the **New Laws,** with provision for eventual abolition of the *encomiendas.* The conquerors rebelled and, led by Gonzalo Pizarro, deposed the viceroy and made Pizarro governor. **Sayri Túpac** became Inca in Vilcabamba, after exiled Almagro partisans assassinated Manco.

1546. Gonzalo Pizarro defeated and executed the viceroy.

1546–50. The crown appointed **Pedro de la Gasca** as its representative and endowed him with unlimited powers to deal with the rebels. La Gasca adopted a conciliatory policy and won over many from the rebel party. Valdivia came from Chile to support La Gasca, who restored royal authority after defeating Pizarro in the **Battle of Xaquixaguana** (1548). Gonzalo Pizarro was executed. La Gasca redistributed enco-miendas, but some conquerors remained discontented.

1549. Valdivia returned to Chile and expanded Spanish control to the south. **Concepción** founded (1550).

1550–51. Antonio de Mendoza was named viceroy of Peru but died after a short period in office. The *audiencia* exercised interim authority, crushing a revolt led by **Francisco Girón.**

1553. Valdivia died in battle against Mapuche Indians who, led by **Lau-taro,** stopped the Spanish advance.

1557–61. Andrés Hurtado de Mendoza assumed the position of viceroy of Peru. **García Hurtado de Mendoza,** his son, resumed conquest of Chile. **Lautaro** died in battle. Spaniards reached Cuyo and founded **Mendoza** (1561). Spaniards were allowed to enslave rebel Indians.

1561. Sayri Túpac died in Cusco, where he had moved after accepting offer by the Spaniards. **Titu Cusi** became Inca and agreed to let priests enter Vilcabamba to preach to the Indians. He died in 1571. **Túpac Amaru** succeeded him as Inca and decided to avoid further contact with the Spaniards.

1569–81. Viceroy **Francisco de Toledo** organized the administration of the viceroyalty. He instituted the *corregimientos* (governance dis-tricts); the tribute system for the Indian population; the *mita,* or sys-tem of forced Indian labor for, mines; haciendas; and public works. He concentrated natives in towns to facilitate tax collection and Chris-tianization. Toledo performed a general *visita,* which produced exten-sive economic and demographic data for the viceroyalty. He also or-ganized a military expedition against Vilcabamba, captured the Inca, and executed him.

5. THE RÍO DE LA PLATA

1526–32. Sebastián Cabot, in the service of a group of merchants of Sevilla, set out with an expedition to reach the Moluccas but was di-verted into the **Río de la Plata** while searching for a passage to the east. The expedition passed up the Paraná and Paraguay Rivers and founded

a short-lived settlement, which Indians, having suffered punitive ex-peditions, destroyed.

1535. Pedro de Mendoza established permanent colonization of the area.

1536. Mendoza founded **Buenos Aires** (Santa María de Buenos Aires) on the estuary of the Río de la Plata. The Indian population became increasingly hostile. **Juan de Ayola** and **Domingo de Irala** led explorations up the Paraná and Paraguay.

1537. Abandoning Buenos Aires, **Juan Salazar de Espinoza** led colonists up to the Paraná and Paraguay and founded **Asunción.** Spaniards established strong ties with Guaraní Indians, adopting many of their customs. Mendoza died on his way to Spain, and colonists elected Irala as governor.

1542–44. The crown named **Alvar Núñez Cabeza de Vaca** to replace Mendoza. He reached Asunción with more colonists and encountered opposition from Irala, who again became governor and was confirmed by the crown.

1563. Establishment of governorship of **Tucumán,** under jurisdiction of the *audiencia* of Charcas.

1573. Juan de Garay, with colonists from Asunción, founded Santa Fe. Spaniards from the northwest settled at Córdoba.

1580. Garay led an expedition from Asunción and **refounded Buenos Aires.**

6. NEW SPAIN, 1518–1574

(From p. 278)

a. THE CONQUEST OF MEXICO

1518–19. Continuing the explorations of Hernández de Córdova and Grijalva, Diego Velázquez and **HERNÁN CORTÉS** (1485–1547) organized a military expedition. Cortés assumed the leadership, and despite the orders of Velázquez followed the coast of Yucatán, subjugated Tabasco, and reached San Juan de Ulúa. As a token of goodwill, Tabasco natives gave Cortés several women, among them **Malitzin (Doña Marina** or **Malinche),** a Mexica woman living in servitude, who became his common-law wife. She had a crucial role as interpreter and Spanish representative in the conquest. Cortés renounced the authority of Velázquez and, acting as a direct agent of the crown, founded **Villa Rica de la Vera Cruz,** where he left a garrison. The soldiers elected Cortés as chief magistrate and sent representatives to the crown for confirmation.

Cortés gained support from the **Totonac,** who were subjects of the Mexica. He sent envoys to **Moctezuma,** ruler of the Mexica (Aztecs), who, uneasy about prophecies indicating the end of his rule, avoided confrontation with the Spaniards. Cortés defeated **Tlaxcala** armies and, knowing their enmity toward the Mexicas, formed an alliance with them. Cortés entered **Tenochtitlán** (Nov. 8, 1519) after defeating resistance at Cholula. Moctezuma received him cordially. Cortés, upon learning of a Mexica attack against Spaniards at Vera Cruz, imprisoned Moctezuma and forced him to accept the sovereignty of Charles V.

1520. Meanwhile Velázquez, named *adelantado*, sent an expedition under **Pánfilo de Narváez** to reduce Cortés to obedience. Cortés placed **Pedro de Alvarado** (1485–1541) in command at Tenochtitlán, went to the coast, and won most of Narváez's forces to his side, whereupon he returned to the city. Alvarado's ruthless attack against Mexica warriors during religious celebrations prompted them to revolt against the Spaniards and Moctezuma. Cortés was forced to evacuate Tenochtitlán with heavy losses (June 30). Moctezuma died or was killed during the evacuation. **Cuautehmóc,** his nephew, assumed command of the Mexica and organized war against the invaders. At **Otumba,** Cortés defeated the Mexica army (July 7) and reached Tlaxcala, where he had allies and reorganized his forces. Having received reinforcements, Cortés established his base at Texcoco and undertook the invasion of Tenochtitlán by land and water.

1521, May 26–Aug. 13. With the help of native allies, enemies of the Mexica, Cortés captured Tenochtitlán and imprisoned Cuauhtemóc. Spaniards razed the Mexica capital and established **Mexico City,** which became the seat of government of the future viceroyalty of New Spain. The crown named Cortés governor and captain general of New Spain (Oct. 15, 1522). He distributed Indians in *encomiendas* to the conquerors.

1524. Cortés received 12 Franciscan missionaries, known as the **Twelve Apostles,** who organized massive Christianization of native peoples.

b. EXPANSION TO THE SOUTH

1522–24. Cristóbal de Olid subdued Colima and part of Jalisco. Spaniards settled in Michoacán, territory of the Tarascans, who allied with Cortés. Alvarado subdued Tehuantepec.

1523–25. Alvarado conquered the Quiché and Cakchiquel and founded **Guatemala City** (1524). He extended the conquest into **Salvador** and became governor of the general district of Guatemala. Expeditions from New Spain subdued Chiapas (1523–28).

1524–26. Cortés sent Olid to conquer and settle **Honduras.** Olid rejected Cortés's authority but failed, and Cortés's lieutenant killed him. Cortés led an expedition to Honduras to establish his authority and founded **Trujillo** (1524), thereupon returning to Mexico.

1526–36. Internecine strife in Honduras prevailed. Alvarado as governor founded **San Pedro** and dispatched an expedition to found Gracias a Dios, but he departed for Spain without definitively gaining control of the area (1536).

1527–35. *Adelantado* **Francisco Montejo** failed in his attempt to conquer **Yucatán.** After eight years of effort, he was appointed governor of Honduras. He subdued Tabasco (1529–40).

1537–44. Governor Montejo conclusively subjugated Higueras, in Honduras, and founded **Comayagua** (1537). Alvarado returned and again became governor.

1542–44. Establishment of the *audiencia* **of Confines,** with jurisdiction over Chiapas, Yucatán (from 1549 to 1560), and Guatemala.

1544. Gaspar and Melchor Pacheco finally conquered and colonized the area. Founding of **Valladolid** and **Salamanca de Bacalar.** The area of Petén remained unconquered until the close of the 17th century.

1546. Led by their native priests, Maya revolted against *encomiendas* in eastern Yucatán.

c. EXPANSION TO THE NORTH AND THE PACIFIC COAST

1522–27. Cortés subdued the region of the Pánuco River and founded a town. Indian revolt suppressed by Cortés's lieutenant (1523). The Pánuco district became subject to the crown, with **Nuño de Guzmán** as governor (1527).

1529–31. Guzmán, as first president of the *audiencia* of New Spain, conquered Chichimeca areas to the north and west of Mexico City, including Jalisco and Sinaloa. **Guadalajara** founded (c. 1530). This area was called **Nueva Galicia,** of which **Compostela** became the capital (1531).

1531–50. In the interior, Spanish expansion was slower. Spanish subdued **Querétaro** in 1531. **Francisco de Urdiñola** founded San Luis de Potosí in 1550.

1532–33. In search of a strait and of new lands, Cortés dispatched an expedition that reached northern Sinaloa and Baja California.

1535. Cortés attempted to found a colony in Baja California but failed. **Francisco de Ulloa** reached the head of the **Gulf of California** (1539). Alarcón, cooperating by sea with Coronado's expedition to New Mexico, reached the same district and traveled up the **Colorado River** (1540).

1539. Viceroy Mendoza sent the Franciscan **Fray Marcos de Niza** northward to investigate reports by Cabeza de Vaca about the legendary Seven Cities of Cíbola. He reached the Zuñi pueblos of New Mexico and returned with exaggerated reports.

1540–42. Francisco Vázquez de Coronado, governor of Nueva Galicia, led an expedition overland to the new lands, while **Hernando de Alarcón** went on by sea along the Pacific coast. Coronado reached the Zuñis, and his lieutenants reached the Moqui pueblos and the **Grand Canyon** of the Colorado. Coronado traversed northern Texas, Oklahoma, and eastern Kansas before his return.

1541. Natives of Nueva Galicia rose in revolt against abuses committed by Nuño de Guzmán. Viceroy Antonio de Mendoza subdued them.

1542–43. As part of his project for South Sea discovery, Viceroy Mendoza sent **Juan Rodríguez de Cabrillo** to search for a northern strait. Cabrillo and, after his death, the pilot **Bartolomé Ferrelo** explored the Pacific coast as far as **Oregon.**

1546. Discovery of rich silver mines in **Zacatecas.**

1548. An *audiencia* was created to govern Nueva Galicia, Guadalajara becoming the political and ecclesiastical capital.

1562–70. Francisco de Ibarra, governor and captain-general, conquered Nueva Vizcaya and founded Durango.

1598–1608. Under royal patent, **Juan de Oñate** secured the submission of New Mexico and sent out expeditions that explored the region from Kansas to the Gulf of California. **Santa Fe** founded in 1610.

1602. The conquest of the Philippines, the development of trade, and the need for protection against English, French, and Dutch incursions aroused interest in exploring the Pacific coast. **Sebastián Vizcaíno** reached the area of San Francisco.

1680. Pueblo Indians revolted, driving Spaniards out of New Mexico. Spanish reconquest led by **Diego Vargas Zapata y Luján** occurred in 1696.

1720–22. Marquis de Aguayo, governor of Coahuila, organized permanent Spanish settlements in Texas to counter French encroachment.

1769–86. Minister Gálvez promoted occupation of Alta California with a system of military forts (presidios) and Franciscan-led missions. San Diego (1769), Monterrey (1770), Los Angeles (1781), and San Francisco (1776) founded.

1774–76. Spanish explorers, sent north along the coast to counter British and Russian activity, discovered the mouth of the **Columbia River.**

1776. Minister Gálvez organized Nueva Vizcaya, Sinaloa, Sonora, the Californias, New Mexico, and Texas into the Provincias Internas, under the governorship of a commandant-general directly responsible to the crown.

1789–95. Attempts to colonize the region north of California. Settlements on Vancouver Island and at Cape Flattery failed to become permanent.

d. THE GULF COAST, FLORIDA, AND THE CAROLINAS

1521. Juan Ponce de León, under royal patent, failed to colonize Florida.

1526. Lucas Vázquez de Ayllón established the colony **San Miguel de Guadalupe** in the Carolinas, but it was abandoned on his death.

1528. Pánfilo de Narváez landed in Florida with colonists from Spain. After exploration he tried to reach the Pánuco River, but his expedition was shipwrecked on the coast of Texas. Most of the colonists died of hunger, disease, or at the hands of the Indians.

1536. Alvar Núñez Cabeza de Vaca and three companions, after six years of captivity, escaped and traversed Texas and northern Mexico, reaching Culiacán.

1539–43. Hernando de Soto (1499–1542) obtained a patent for the colonization of the Gulf coast. His expedition landed in Florida, traversed Arkansas and Oklahoma, and discovered the **Mississippi River** (1541). De Soto died (1542) and his companions continued to the area of the Pánuco.

1559–61. Viceroy Velasco dispatched an expedition under **Tristán de Luna** to colonize the region of the Carolinas (Santa Elena). Luna established a garrison at Pensacola, moved inland, and founded a settlement, whose inhabitants later moved to Pensacola. **Ángel Villafañe** replaced Luna as governor and tried to colonize the Carolinas but failed. The garrison at Pensacola was abandoned.

1562. Jean Ribaut failed to establish a French Huguenot settlement at Port Royal in South Carolina. **Laudonnière** founded Fort Caroline, on the St. John River (1564). As a result of these activities, Philip II ordered the expulsion of the French from Florida.

1565. Pedro Menéndez de Avilés, as *adelantado* of Florida, founded **St. Augustine,** captured Fort Caroline, and slew the garrison, securing Spanish control of the peninsula of Florida.

1565–74. Menéndez de Avilés built presidios and posts across a wide area. He supported the establishment of missions by **Jesuits** and later by **Franciscans,** as far north as Virginia.

7. FOREIGN ENCROACHMENTS AND TERRITORIAL CHANGES, 1580–1800

England, France, and the Netherlands engaged in war against Spain and sought to dispute Spain's preeminence in the New World by attacking shipping and setting up colonies in territories controlled by Spain and Portugal (p. 405).

16th century. French corsairs early on attacked the Spanish fleet off the coast of Europe and at the Azores and Canaries and soon extended their activities into the Caribbean, attacking towns and trade. Portuguese repelled French attempts to establish themselves in Brazil. English privateers, with tacit approval of the British crown, became active in the Atlantic, Caribbean, and Pacific. **Francis Drake** raided the Pacific coast during his voyage around the world (1577–80). After the outbreak of war between Spain and England, the English made privateering an official activity. Many towns were held for ransom or sacked, among them Nombre de Dios, Cartagena, Santo Domingo, and Valparaíso. Coincident with the struggle for independence in the Netherlands, Dutch freebooters became active.

17th century. England, France, and the Netherlands started settlements in the Guianas. England colonized Bermuda and the Bahamas. A Dutch armada captured a treasure convoy from New Spain (1628). An English expedition captured Jamaica and established a colony (1655). Slaves and their Spanish masters fled to the bush. Slaves formed runaway (Maroon) communities and attacked English settlements. In the 18th century, the British and Maroons engaged in wars. English, French, and Dutch buccaneering in the Caribbean played an important role in disrupting Spanish-American commerce.

18th century. Constant wars in Europe and control of the sea by Great Britain made it difficult for the Spanish crown to maintain a trade monopoly. British, French, and Dutch merchants developed extensive illicit commerce. Wars against Spain had as one objective the obtaining of trade concessions, in which the slave trade was a very important element.

1701–13. After the **War of the Spanish Succession** (p. 316), Great Britain obtained the *asiento*, or monopoly of slave trade with the Spanish possessions, by the **Treaty of Utrecht** (1713) (p. 316).

1728. Montevideo was founded to counter Portuguese **Colonia** (founded in 1680), where British and Portuguese carried on illicit trade with the province of the Río de la Plata.

1741. A British expedition failed to capture Cartagena, which had been heavily fortified as a bulwark of colonial defense.

1750. The **Treaty of Madrid** stipulated that Portugal give Colonia to Spain in return for seven Jesuit reductions (settlements for Christianized Indians) on the east bank of the Uruguay. The Guaraní of the reductions rebelled against the transfer, unleashing the **War of the Seven Reductions** (1752–56), which ended with Portuguese repression. Portuguese retained Colonia and the treaty was void.

1762. When Spain entered the **Seven Years' War** (p. 317) as an ally of France, British expeditions captured Havana and Manila (1762). Spanish forces captured Colonia and occupied Rio Grande do Sul in Brazil. By the **Treaty of Paris** (1763) (p. 319), Spain ceded Florida to Great Britain in exchange for Havana and Manila, and returned Colonia and Rio Grande do Sul to Portugal. France ceded Louisiana to Spain, although French colonists opposed establishment of Spanish authority.

1771. Dispute between Spain and Great Britain over possession of the **Falkland-Malvinas Islands.**

1774. Spain established a garrison in the Falklands to defend the Strait of Magellan.

1776–77. Spain invaded Colonia and other Portuguese territories. Creation of the **Viceroyalty of Río de la Plata** helped to solidify Spanish control in that area.

1777. The **Treaty of San Ildefonso** assigned Colonia and disputed Paraguayan territory to Spain.

1779–83. Spain intervened in **American War of Independence** (p. 416).

Spanish forces captured Mobile and Pensacola, overran Bahamas, and blocked British attempts to control the Mississippi. By the **Treaty of Versailles** (1783), Spain recovered Florida and relinquished the Bahamas.

1795. By the **Treaty of Basel** Spain relinquished the eastern two-thirds of Española to France.

1797. Trinidad was occupied by British and ceded to them by the **Treaty of Amiens** (1802).

1800. France under the consulate forced Spain to return Louisiana.

1801. Portuguese occupied mission territories in Paraguay, but subsequent accords gave Spain Colonia and Uruguay, while Portugal secured Rio Grande do Sul.

1803. Pressure from the U.S. moved France to sell Louisiana and Spain to sell Florida to the U.S.

8. THE SPANISH COLONIAL SYSTEM, 1550–1800

a. POPULATION DEVELOPMENT

The **native population** of the Americas declined drastically owing to the effects of war and epidemics. Unchecked proliferation of European livestock at the expense of Indian agriculture destroyed ecological equilibrium. In the **Caribbean,** depopulation was aggravated by the enslavement of natives to work in gold placers. Devastating epidemics spread throughout the islands (1519, 1530), reducing the population from an estimated 500,000 at the eve of the conquest to 22,000 in 1570. Yellow fever became endemic in the tropical lowlands and coasts of the Caribbean and circum-Caribbean.

On the eve of the conquest, Indian population in **central Mexico** was estimated at 11 million. Severely affected by recurrent epidemics of European diseases (1519–24, 1529, 1545–46, 1558, 1576–79, 1588), the Indian population had no opportunity to recover, and by 1597 had plunged to 2.5 million. In **Peru,** the Indian population was an estimated 6 million at the beginning of the conquest. Affected by military mobilization, by the resettlement policy in new towns, and by deadly epidemics (1545–46, 1558, 1576, 1588), Indians were reduced to 1.3 million by 1590. Their decline was especially dramatic in the coastal areas.

By 1650 the Indian population had reached its nadir in New Spain (Mexico) with 1.5 million. **Recovery began at the end of the 17th century,** when Indians numbered about 2 million. By the end of the 18th century, the Indian population had increased to 3.7 million. In Peru, the native population dropped to 1.5 million in 1570. Its recovery, at the beginning of the 18th century, did not follow a uniform trend. The portion of the population identified as Indian continually declined throughout the Spanish domains. Many Indians sought to be counted as **mestizos** to avoid tribute payment.

Early on, **African slaves** were brought to the New World. The rapid decline of the Indian population in the Caribbean led to increased slave trade. By 1570 the Caribbean had 56,000 inhabitants of African origin, easily surpassing the Indian and white population. Most of the slaves were captured in Senegambia, Guinea, and the mouth of the Congo River. During the 16th century, 75,000 slaves were introduced in Spanish-American domains. Between 1600 and 1650, slave traders sold 125,000 slaves in the region. The uneven distribution of the sexes and the harsh conditions of slavery made reproduction and the formation of slave families difficult. Nevertheless, slaves formed unions with native women, which increased the size of the mixed population. Children of these unions were born free, since the child's status derived from the mother. Between 1651 and 1760, slave traders shipped some 344,000 slaves to Spanish dominions. Between 1761 and 1810, in response to the booming plantation economy, 300,000 slaves were imported, mainly into Cuba and Puerto Rico. However, by that time most of the black population in Spanish domains was free.

Much of the **Spanish population** was concentrated in urban settlements. The crown created the Casa de Contratación to control emigration to the Indies. Heretics, Moors, Jews, and their descendants were excluded from traveling to Spanish domains. **Most Spanish emigrants came from the territories subject to the Castilian crown, especially Andalusia and Castile,** although a few non-Spanish subjects of the Spanish king also migrated. Women were scarce at the beginning, but as the crown promoted family emigration, their numbers increased to a quarter of the total emigration. Some 240,000 Europeans came to America during the 16th century. Between 1601 and 1650, European emigrants totaled about 194,000. For the 18th century, estimates of Spanish emigration indicate a minimum of 53,000 individuals, coming mainly from northern areas of Spain—the Basque country and Catalonia.

Predominantly male migration at the beginning of colonization promoted unions between Spanish men and native women, which led to the growth of the **mestizo population.** Some were incorporated into the Spanish group, but illegitimate births were common among the mixed population. The mestizo rate of growth quickly surpassed that of the Indian population.

Mortality rates began to fall around the end of the 18th century. In 1803, **Francisco Javier de Balmis** (1753–1819), a Spanish physician, carried out a general campaign of vaccination against smallpox, helping to improve health conditions in the colonies. At the close of the colonial period, the estimated population of the Spanish colonies was 3,276,000 whites, 5,328,000 mestizos, 7,530,000 Indians, and 776,000 blacks. (New Spain, 1,230,000 whites, 1,860,000 mestizos, 3,700,000 Indians; Guatemala, 280,000 whites, 420,000 mestizos, 880,000 Indians; Peru and Chile, 465,000 whites, 853,000 mestizos, 1,030,000 Indians; Colombia and Venezuela, 642,000 whites, 1,256,000 mestizos, 720,000 Indians; Río de la Plata, 320,000 whites, 742,000 mestizos, 1,200,000 Indians; Cuba and Puerto Rico, 339,000 whites, 197,000 mixed, 389,000 blacks). The black population in all colonies, excluding Cuba and Puerto Rico, numbered 387,000.

b. ADMINISTRATION

The Crown of Castile incorporated the new territories into its domains. Early on, Queen Isabella withdrew the authority granted Columbus and the first conquerors and established direct royal control. The structure of colonial government was fully formed by the third quarter of the 16th century.

After appointment to supervise preparations for the second voyage of Columbus (1493), **Juan Rodríguez de Fonseca** effectively became minister of the Indies and laid the foundations for the expansion of the colonial bureaucracy. The development of trade between the new lands and the metropolis led to the establishment of the Casa de la Contratación at Sevilla to control colonial commerce, emigration, and maritime enterprise (1503). Rodríguez de Fonseca presided over the newly founded **Council of the Indies** (Consejo de Indias), which was designed to administer the colonies and which exercised supreme authority over the Indies and the Casa de Contratación. The legislation for the Indies promulgated by the crown and the Council of the Indies was codified in the *Recopilación de Leyes . . . de las Indias* (1680). At the beginning of the 17th century, the crown created a Junta de Guerra y Armadas de las Indias to administer the armed forces and the dispatch of fleets to the Indies, and a Cámara de Indias to control ecclesiastical affairs and appointments, as adjuncts to the Council of Indies. With the advent of the Bourbon dynasty (1700), the Council of the Indies declined in importance. In 1714, the office of Minister of the Indies was created with the establishment of a Secretaría de Guerra, Marina e Indias (1714). This secretariat underwent numerous changes, and before the close of the century, a separate **Secretariat of the Indies** was formed.

Direct royal government in the Indies was instituted with the appointment of **Francisco de Bobadilla** as judge and governor of Española and the removal of Columbus (1499–1500). A tribunal of three royal judges was created in Santo Domingo as a check on the governor (1511), and this body evolved into the *audiencia* (governance tribunal) of Santo Domingo, with authority over the Caribbean (1526).

On the mainland, during the first years, conquerors ruled with the titles of *adelantado*, governor or captain-general. The institution of adelantado was important during the conquest. By agreement with the crown, the adelantado undertook the conquest of a specified area at his own expense, and in return the crown assigned him governmental authority and hereditary privileges. The institution helped to bring new lands under Spanish dominion, but the crown revoked individual privileges, since they threatened royal authority. Some conquerors rebelled against royal control, and this contributed to the decision to fortify the royal bureaucracy in the Indies.

The **Viceroyalty of New Spain** was created in **1535,** with its capital at Mexico City, and included the Caribbean, Venezuela, the Philippine Islands, and all territories north of Panama. The New Laws created the **Viceroyalty of Peru** in **1542,** with an *audiencia* at Lima, and included all Spanish territories in South America except Venezuela. *Audiencias,* each with its specific area, were created in Guatemala (1542); Nueva Galicia (1548); Nueva Granada (1549); Charcas, or Upper Peru (1556); Quito (1563); and the Philippine Islands (1583–93). American-born Spaniards (**creoles**) gained access to government through direct royal appointment and through purchase of public offices.

The viceroys as direct representatives of the sovereign possessed wide civil and military authority. They were presidents of the *audiencias* of their capitals. The *audiencias*, comprising a president, *oidores* (judges), a *fiscal* (crown prosecutor), and lesser officials, exercised supreme authority within their districts, and the *audiencias* not directly under viceroys exercised governmental authority. The viceregal *audiencia* acted as an advisory council to the viceroy and in this function exercised legislative power. The *audiencias* dealt with judicial affairs and appeals going directly before the Council of the Indies, and they had authority to correspond directly with the crown. The status of *audiencias* varied according to the rank of the presiding officer, that is, viceroy, president and captain-general, or president. The presidents of the *audiencias* of Santo Domingo, Guatemala, and Nueva Granada had military authority and became presidents and captains-general. As such they were practically independent from the viceroys. Guadalajara, Quito, and Charcas remained as presidencies. In the absence of the viceroy or president and captain-general, the *audiencia* assumed the powers of government. Major administrative areas were divided into *gobiernos, corregimientos,* and *alcaldías mayores,* with the *gobiernos,* in general, the most important and frequently consisting of more than one province.

In accord with medieval Castilian traditions, the municipalities at first enjoyed a large measure of self-government under their *cabildos* (town councils), composed of *regidores* (councilmen) and *alcaldes* (mayors), the former elected by the householders and the latter by the councilmen. Before the close of the 16th century, the election of councilmen gave way to royal appointment, hereditary tenure, and purchase of positions. *Cabildos abiertos* (open town meetings) of all householders were at times held to discuss important matters. The municipal government exercised executive, legislative, and judicial authority within its district, although frequently under the control of royal officials.

The Spanish organized the Indian population in towns, called *reducciones* in Peru and **congregaciones** in Mexico, with municipal governments following the Castilian model. In many cases, traditional chiefs (*kurakas* or *caciques*) managed to preserve their authority in the new structure, occupying positions as mayors and councilmen. Indian mayors were responsible for the allocation of services and labor required from Indians by local entrepreneurs and public projects. Local Spanish officials had jurisdiction over the native towns in their districts. They supervised the fulfillment of compulsory labor for mining and public works. Protectors of the Indians were created for general and local districts to guard the interests of the native population. The *repartimiento-encomienda,* which developed early on, was an institution of great political, social, and economic importance. In the earlier period this institution involved the assignment of specified towns to conquerors and colonists. Indians from the *encomienda* gave tribute, labor, and service to the *encomendero,* who was obligated to provide them with protection and indoctrination in Christianity. The *encomenderos'* increasing control over the Indian population moved the crown to regulate the system. Fixed quotas of tribute were established, and royal officials (*corregidores*) took charge of the distribution of Indian labor and services. With the publication of the **New Laws** (1542–43), the crown assumed control of the many towns and *encomiendas.* Before the end of the century, the *encomienda* was essentially reduced to the right to enjoy the revenues from specified towns. It was abolished formally at the end of the 18th century.

Fiscal administration was directly under the crown through the Casa de Contratación and accountants called *contadores, factores, tesoreros,* and *veedores* in the New World jurisdictions. With the establishment of the intendants, those officials assumed administration of fiscal affairs. The Castilian institutions of the *residencia, visita,* and *pesquisa,* set up to assess the performance of officials and the situation of the regions, were implemented in the colonies. The principal sources of **crown revenues** were the *quinto,* or one-fifth of the products of the subsoil (gold, silver, precious stones); the *almojarifazgo* (customs imposts); the *alcabala* (sales tax); the tributes of the natives; the *media anata* (emoluments) of civil and ecclesiastical offices; and the sale of the *Cruzada* (papal bulls sold by the crown to subsidize ecclesiastical expenses).

The **Bourbon kings** implemented sweeping administrative **reforms** (p. 330) to improve the economic efficiency of their dominions. Thus they elevated Nueva Granada, Panama, Venezuela, and Quito into the **Viceroyalty of Nueva Granada (1717–39).** They ordered inspections to obtain data to undertake further reform in Cuba and Louisiana (**1763**), New Spain (**1765**), and Peru (**1777**). From 1713 on, the Bourbon kings began to name mostly Spaniards to the *audiencias,* which caused creoles to protest. **José de Gálvez,** who acted as **minister of the Indies,** was the main architect of the change. The **Viceroyalty of Río de la Plata** (1776) and the captaincies-general of Venezuela (1773), Cuba (1777), and Chile (1778) were created. *Audiencias* were established in Buenos Aires (1783), Caracas (1786), and Cusco (1789). Under Philip VI, a system of intendants was established throughout the Indies (**1769–90**), which reduced the viceroys' powers. At the end of the colonial era, the crown established tribute obligations for mestizos and other people of color previously exempted.

c. THE CHURCH AND THE MISSIONS

Pope Alexander VI in the bull *Inter caeterea* (May 4, 1493) assigned dominion over the Indies and exclusive authority to convert the natives to the Spanish crown. His bull *Eximiae devotionis* (Nov. 16, 1501) granted the kings the titles and the first fruits of the Church in the Indies. Julius II in the bull *Universalis ecclesiae* (July 28, 1508) conceded them universal patronage. The crown exercised the patronage of the Indies (*real patronato de Indias*) through the Council of the Indies and later through that body and the Cámara de Indias.

The **religious orders** early obtained broad powers in the colonies. Mainly the **Franciscans**—but also the **Dominicans** and the **Augustinians**—carried out a massive campaign to Christianize the natives, especially in New Spain. The organization of the Church with bishops from the secular clergy diminished the influence of these orders and enhanced the power of the crown. The orders, however, remained important in extending Spanish control in outlying areas. Dominicans and Franciscans were active in Guatemala. **Capuchins** established themselves in the area of the lower Orinoco. Toward the end of the 17th century, **Jesuits** undertook the establishment of missions in Pimería Alta (Arizona) and in Lower California. In the south, they expanded into the territory of Araucanía (Chile) and developed an important **mission system** in Paraguay. Jesuits obtained complete authority to convert and organize the Guaraní east of Asunción. Portuguese slave raids forced the Jesuits to move their missions to the south. The Jesuits established a complete governmental organization under the rule of a father superior, and Indians received some military training to defend themselves from enslavement. Commercial agriculture of yerba mate helped to support the missions. The expulsion of the Jesuits (1767) led to the decline of the missions.

The Church enjoyed the ecclesiastical exemption *(fuero),* operating its own courts with jurisdiction over all cases involving the clergy and spiritual affairs. The Church also had extensive wealth. By the close of the colonial period, the **Church probably controlled half of the productive real estate of the Indies.** During the Habsburg dynasty (1516–1700), the power of archbishops could rival that of high civil authorities, and quarrels over jurisdiction were frequent. At the end of the colonial period there were seven archbishoprics and some 35 dioceses.

The **Spanish Inquisition,** operating under the Council of the Inquisition, was introduced and tribunals were established in Mexico City (1569), Lima (1571), and Cartagena (1610). These tribunals were in charge of repressing people who practiced religions other than Catholicism (Protestants, Jews, Moors) as well as those who used sorcery and witchcraft, uttered blasphemies, lived in bigamy, or practiced sodomy. In the 17th century the Inquisition brought to trial New Christians accused of practicing the Jewish religion. It condemned a few to execution and many to exile and prison. Indians were exempted from the Inquisition, but the bishops judged their religious infractions, generally understood as regression to idolatry. Campaigns against idolatrous practices were especially important in Peru (1610–60), where Jesuits encouraged the formation of a special tribunal to deal with such cases. Slaves were subjected to the Inquisition, generally accused of witchcraft against their masters and of blasphemy.

d. ECONOMIC CONDITIONS

The crown fostered gold and silver mining in its colonies. Rich silver deposits were first discovered in Peru, where **POTOSÍ became the most important mining center from 1540 to 1585.** During the early years of silver extraction, wage labor predominated, but with the organization of the **mita** (forced labor) in 1574 by **Viceroy Toledo,** workers were recruited on a compulsory basis. Indian communities also had to provide a fixed allocation of workers to **Huancavelica** to extract mercury, an essential element for silver amalgamation. Forced recruitment mainly affected provinces in the southern highlands. After 1590, Peruvian silver production decreased, partly owing to irregular mercury production. Only at the beginning of the 18th century did Peruvian silver mining show signs of recovery, encouraged by improvements in mercury production in Huancavelica. From the 1770s on, the steady supply of mercury propelled a silver boom in Peru.

Between 1590 and 1630, Mexico's mines became the most productive, with important mines in the districts of **Zacatecas, Guanajuato, Pachuca, Taxco,** and **San Luis de Potosí.** Mestizo and Indian workers went to the mines as free laborers attracted by higher wages, though eventually many became trapped in their place of employment by debts, and a system of debt peonage developed. From 1640 to 1680, mining production contracted, recovering in the last decades of the 17th century with the return to smelting techniques to offset mercury shortages. In the 18th century, silver production increased decisively, owing to the steady influx of mercury from the Almadén and Idrija mines in Spain.

Agricultural and pastoral landholdings developed. In New Spain, Spanish-creole sectors and religious corporations increased their **estates** (haciendas) during the second half of the 16th century in vast areas, especially in the Bajío region. As a result, white landowners controlled Indian crops such as maize and *pulque* (alcoholic drink made from *maguey*), which led to profiteering and price speculation highly beneficial to the elite. In Peru, great landowners made more limited advances, and middle-size haciendas predominated. Throughout the Spanish domains—especially in the Caribbean and coastal areas—sugar plantations and mills evolved on the basis of **slave labor,** while haciendas used forced Indian labor (*mita* in Peru and *repartimiento* in New Spain) and resorted to debt peonage to retain workers. Between 1590 and 1620, the crown ordered legalization of illegal occupation of land through a procedure called *composiciones de tierras,* which allowed the consolidation of haciendas.

Mestizo and Indian peasants also participated in the commercial economy, producing foodstuffs for the market and working in haciendas, mines, and transport as wage laborers. **Indian villages** were the main source of temporary and low-cost labor for all Spanish-creole enterprises.

During the 16th century, silk production developed in Mexico, Puebla, and Oaxaca for the internal market and export to Peru, but it was soon replaced by Chinese silk in the Peruvian market. Cochineal and indigo were important export commodities in Yucatán and Guatemala. In Peru, New Spain, and Nueva Granada, **textile factories** (*obrajes*) produced cheap textiles for the internal market. Muleteers' con-

voys provided **transport** connecting the diverse economic areas of the viceroyalties.

Overseas trade was under direct crown control, and Seville, seat of the Casa de Contratación, had the monopoly of the American trade during the 16th century. An influential merchant class developed in Sevilla with connections to the designated trading ports in the colonies: **Vera Cruz, Cartagena,** and **Porto Bello,** which alone were allowed to trade directly with Spain. They imposed restrictions on intercolonial trade and limited trade with the **Philippines** for the colonies. Naval warfare and attacks by corsairs led to the creation of a system of **convoyed fleets** for the protection of gold and silver shipments, one each year for New Spain and one for Peru (1543–61). For the return trip, the fleets united at Havana and sailed together for Spain. **Market fairs** were held annually at Porto Bello and Jalapa (Mexico). Peru had the greatest trade volume and value between 1540 and 1585, but New Spain surpassed them between 1590 and 1620. After 1620, transatlantic trade suffered a contraction owing to the decline of mineral production. Recovery began about 1660 in Mexico. In the 1670s, because of peace treaties, privateering subsided. A new **contraband trade** developed that was mutually advantageous to Spanish merchants and to British, Dutch, Portuguese, and French smugglers trading manufactures and slaves.

Wholesalers dominated merchant guilds (**Tribunal del Consulado)** organized in the main capitals of the Spanish colonies (Mexico, 1592; Lima, 1613). Big merchants based in the colonies carried out a vigorous intercolonial trade despite restrictions. Chinese textiles reached **Acapulco** via the Philippines and were reexported to Peru in exchange for silver, mercury, and wines. In Central America, **Santiago de Guatemala** became a significant commercial entrepôt, exporting cacao, cochineal, indigo, and livestock to New Spain in exchange for silver, Mexican textiles, Chinese silk, and mules. **Venezuela** and **Guayaquil** exported cacao to New Spain in return for silver. Havana and Guayaquil became the most important shipbuilding centers, followed by Realejo, Maracaibo, and Cartagena. After 1640, trade with Asia decreased and interregional commerce lost vigor.

Under the Bourbon dynasty new policies, known as the **Bourbon Reforms** (p. 402), were introduced. The Treaty of Utrecht (1713) (p. 316) granted Great Britain the monopoly of the slave trade with the colonies and the right to send one vessel each year to Porto Bello to trade. The Casa de la Contratación was transferred to Cádiz in 1717. Monopolistic **chartered companies** were established in Honduras (1714), Caracas (1728), Havana (1740), and Santo Domingo (1757). In 1763, Charles III abolished the system of fleets and authorized eight other Spanish ports, besides Seville and Cádiz, to trade with the Indies. He also permitted intercolonial trade between New Spain and Peru and between Guatemala and Nueva Granada (1764–82), but internal custom houses were established and state monopolies of certain goods reinforced. The Casa de Contratación was abolished in 1790. Under the Bourbons, areas previously marginal in the colonial system were transformed into dynamic economies (Buenos Aires, Venezuela, Chile), while Peru and Upper Peru declined.

e. SOCIAL AND CULTURAL EVOLUTION

The upper crust of society was composed of the high colonial officers, both civil and ecclesiastical, and wealthy Spanish and creole merchants. Mine owners, despite their economic importance, rarely achieved a high social standing. **Creoles,** descendants of Spaniards but born in American domains, resented the preference for Peninsulars in appointments to higher and lesser office, but both groups belonged to the **República de Españoles** (Commonwealth of the Spanish) and were connected through kinship, marriage, and business. **Several universities were open to colonial male students: the Royal University of Mexico** (1551), **San Marcos de Lima** (1551), **St. Thomas de Aquinas** in Santo Domingo (1558). Women could follow religious careers, but professing required a costly dowry only the wealthy could afford. Nuns belonged to the elite and were far more highly regarded than married women. Very few Indian or mestizo women reached the status of nun. Lower-class women worked as retailers, street vendors, servants. Marriage was under the jurisdiction of the Church. Divorce was allowed, but wives had to show proof of continuous mistreatment and cruelty to qualify. Authorities created special houses *(casas de recogidas)* to shelter fallen women and virtuous women without means of support.

The population of the viceregal capitals and other cities included a high level of slaves, who worked as domestic servants and in artisanal trades to support their masters. Urban Indians lived in segregated neighborhoods near the downtown areas of Lima and Mexico City.

Several individuals attained distinction through their religious piety and cultural pursuits. The first Spanish-American saints belong to this era: **St. Rosa de Lima** (1586–1617), **St. Mariana de Jesús** (1618–45), **St. Felipe de Jesús** (1572–97), martyr of the conversion of Japan, **St. Martín de Porres** (1579–1639), a mulatto. The Church became the main patron of the arts and architecture. The famous Gothic cathedral of Santo Domingo (1514–40) was planned by **Alonso Rodríguez**. **Francisco Becerra**, a Spanish architect working in Lima, Quito, and Cusco, planned the cathedral of Puebla (1576–1626), which was inaugurated in 1649 by Bishop **Juan de Palafox**. Becerra also began to build the cathedral of Lima in 1569. The cathedral of Mexico was initiated in 1573, according to **Claudio de Arciniega's** design. Although consecrated in 1667, it was completed only in 1813 by Valencian sculptor **Manuel Tolsá**. The cathedral of Cusco was consecrated in 1654. **Local schools of painting** developed in Mexico, Quito, Cusco, and Lima. Many Spanish-American authors gained widespread recognition, among them **Inca Garcilaso de la Vega** (1539–1616), **Juan Ruiz de Alarcón** (1580–1639), **Sor Juana Inés de la Cruz** (1651–95), and **Pedro de Peralta y Barnuevo** (1663–1700).

Despite the importance of cities as political and cultural centers, rural areas were predominant. Indians constituted the **República de Indios** (Commonwealth of Indians) and were supposed to live separated from Spaniards to avoid abuse. The Indian *kurakas*, or *caciques*, formed the upper crust of the population. Many Indians chose to dissociate themselves from Indian communities to avoid forced labor and tribute and migrated to other rural or urban areas, becoming *forasteros*. **The Mestizo population, distributed in urban and rural areas, became peasants, squatters, wage laborers, servants, and artisans and were exempted from tribute.** Spanish authorities and rural parish priests frequently owned haciendas and textile mills in Indian towns, compelling Indians to labor for them. Clerics often denounced Indian religious practices as pagan or idolatrous. Despite campaigns of repression, native beliefs survived and mixed with Christian beliefs.

In plantation areas, slaves frequently rebelled against their bondage, fleeing to liberated zones where they created free settlements. Colonial authorities tried to prevent the spread of **marronage**, sending raids against maroon villages or making treaties with them. Some slaves managed to obtain freedom by manumission or by self-purchase, becoming free people of color. Free and slave blacks re-created their African religious beliefs and influenced popular culture, especially in the Caribbean, circum-Caribbean, and coastal areas of Mexico and the Pacific.

The Bourbon campaign to reform colonial government by prohibiting office purchases adversely affected the position of upper-class creoles, who saw themselves displaced in favor of Peninsular bureaucrats. The institution of intendant diminished the power of the viceroys but did not increase the influence of elite creoles.

f. INSURRECTIONS

During the 18th century, social groups and regions affected by the redefinition of colonial exactions on their labor force and resources, and by centralization under the Bourbon reforms, organized insurrectionary movements to resist or modify the terms of colonial control. In most cases these movements legitimized themselves as defending the traditional colonial system against the reforms; elsewhere, as in Paraguay, the renewal of old grievances fueled rebellion against Spanish authorities. Total confrontation with the colonial system, as in the cases of Chiapas and central Peru, was a rare occurrence. Class alliances were fragile, and this contributed to the failure of these movements to break the hold of the colonial state.

1712, June–Nov. Maya Rebellion in Chiapas. Maya villagers faced increased fiscal and labor demands and forced sales, and their authorities lost ground to Spanish officials and curates in the struggle over control of villages and religious brotherhoods. In the village of Cancuc, **María de la Candelaria,** a young Maya woman, claimed to have seen the Virgin Mary, prompting a circle of notable Maya to organize a shrine to worship the Virgin. Maya pilgrims converged on the new sacred place, but curates disputed the authenticity of the miracle and labeled it idolatrous. Confrontation escalated and Maya from 21 towns gathered at Cancuc to pay allegiance to the Virgin Mary, openly renounced God and the king, and took up arms. They captured the village church, killed friars, plundered mestizo and Spanish estates, and massacred white and mestizo children in Ocosingo. Rebel leader **Sebastián Gómez de la Gloria** ordained priests and organized an independent religion of the Virgin Mary. Ethnic solidarity crumbled when Maya allies disputed concentration of power in the Cancuc leadership. Spanish authorities sent an army from Guatemala City and subdued the rebels. Almost 100 rebels were sentenced to death and many suffered physical punishment, forced labor, and exile. In the aftermath of the rebellion, measures limiting the labor draft and Indian services were adopted.

1721–35. The *Comuneros* of Paraguay. Colonists in Paraguay resented the Jesuit missions where Indians could avoid the colonists' labor demands. Dissatisfied with Governor Diego de los Reyes y Balmaceda's pro-Jesuit policy, the local elite sought his dismissal. The Audiencia of Charcas sent **José de Antequera y Castro** to make inquiries in Asunción. Antequera made himself governor of Paraguay and, with the support of the colonists, expelled Governor Reyes and later the Jesuits. The viceroy of Peru, Marqués de Castellfuerte, ordered military action against the colonists, forcing them to readmit the Jesuits. Antequera left for Lima, where he tried to defend himself against charges of treason. In Asunción, **Fernando Mompó de Zayas** proclaimed the right of the people to elect their own representatives. His propaganda attracted poor colonists, traditionally excluded from political life in the city, who called themselves *comuneros* and elected a **Junta Gubernativa** to run the province. Antequera was executed in Lima. A new governor, Manuel Agustín Ruyloba, arrived and tried to eject *comuneros* from the city and its institutions, but he was assassinated when *comuneros* marched on Asunción to expel the Jesuits once again. *Comuneros* dominated the countryside, occupying estates and confiscating wealthy landowners' properties. As a result, the upper classes felt increasingly alienated from the movement. The viceroy of Peru ordered the governor of Buenos Aires to invade Paraguay and squelch the insurrection. Asunción landowners joined the occupying forces and defeated the rebels. Three *comunero* leaders were executed, while others suffered exile, physical punishment, and prison.

1742. Juan Santos Atahualpa, who proclaimed himself descendant of the Incas, led tropical lowland communities opposed to the presence of Franciscan missions as well as some Indian and mestizo peasants from the highlands in a campaign to oust colonists and friars from the eastern lowlands of central Peru. Several viceroys sent military expeditions in 1742, 1743, 1746, and 1759, and all failed against the guerrilla force organized by the rebels. The Spaniards established a system of forts to prevent an expansion of the movement into the highlands, which could have jeopardized mining production. In the neighboring districts, Indians were exempted from the *mita* (forced labor) in order to remove a grievance that could generate support for the jungle rebels. The rebels attempted to set up a permanent base in the highlands in 1752 but failed on account of weak local backing. Juan Santos Atahualpa kept control of the lowland area, however, and was never captured.

1780–82. The Great Rebellion of Túpac Amaru and the Kataris. New fiscal and commercial policies created broad sources of tension in the viceroyalty of Peru. Peasants felt particularly aggrieved by forced sales of goods *(repartimiento de mercancías)*. **José Gabriel Condorcanqui,** *kuraka* of Tinta, Surimana, and Tungasuca, took the name **Túpac Amaru II** and led a rebellion against the abusive administration of certain local authorities. He ordered the execution of Corregidor Antonio de Arriaga in Nov. 1780. The revolt initially earned some support from the creole upper class in Cusco, who resented the recent policies, but the rank and file of the rebel army were Indian peasants who attacked landed property without regard to the owners' birthplaces. Creole sympathy, already limited, quickly evaporated. Túpac Amaru attempted to march against Cusco, whose defense was organized by local militias and Indian regiments led by *kurakas* loyal to the crown. A civil war broke out in the Indian ranks between loyalists and rebels.

Túpac Amaru, his wife, Micaela Bastidas, and his family were imprisoned after his defeat at the hands of loyalist *kuraka* **Mateo Pumacahua.** Diego Cristóbal and Mariano Túpac Amaru took over as leaders of the rebellion, while Túpac Amaru and his family were executed in Cusco. In **Chayanta,** *kuraka* **Tomás Katari** denounced those who usurped his position and led a movement to reduce tributes. Local Spanish authorities imprisoned him, and when an Indian multitude attempted his rescue, his captors killed him, unleashing a full-scale rebellion. During the same period, a nonnoble Aymara Indian, **Julián Apaza,** taking the name **Túpac Katari,** gathered an Indian army to lay siege to La Paz, which was temporarily broken by royal troops. Andrés Túpac Amaru joined Túpac Katari in a renewed siege of La Paz, but promises of amnesty and internal dissension gradually dispersed their followers. Local elites, wary of the rebels' anti-creole sentiment, supported the repressive forces. The joint efforts of the colonial army, loyal *kurakas,* and creoles managed to crush the uprising. Rebel leaders were imprisoned and executed, and the properties of rebel *kurakas* were confiscated. These measures ruined the Indian nobility and severely reduced their hold on the Indian population, favoring Indian authorities directly named by the colonial state.

1781. *Comuneros* of Nueva Granada. The reorganization of state monopolies for rum, anisette, and tobacco to increase royal revenues adversely affected farmers in Socorro, a town of predominantly white and mestizo cultivators. Under the leadership of two creoles, **Juan Francisco de Berbeo** and **José Antonio Galán,** they refused to pay taxes and expelled the Spanish authorities. The rebels marched to Bogotá and negotiated a treaty that rescinded the new fiscal program and gave creoles greater access to office. However, former rebel allies split after the agreement, which redressed the grievances of only one faction. Indians and landless workers wanted either to protect their holdings or to secure access to land, and slaves expected to gain their freedom. José Antonio Galán emerged as a leader of this more radical group, while the creole *comunero* leadership collaborated with the colonial authorities to capture him and defeat his followers. Galán was executed and many of his followers imprisoned. *(To p. 622)*

9. PORTUGUESE AMERICA, 1500–1815

In the era of colonial expansion, Portugal's main orientation was to maintain and exploit trade posts in Africa and India, where slave trade and commerce in exotic goods produced high profits. Attention shifted to Brazil only because of French and Dutch attempts to gain territories there.

Although no **Black Legend** has been popularized about Portuguese colonization, the extermination and enslavement of the native population equaled the exploits of Spanish conquerors. Native peoples in Brazil were organized mainly in tribes with no centralized structures and were engaged in constant warfare. The Portuguese intervened in these conflicts to escalate them as a means of obtaining Indian slaves. Indian enslavement continued practically unchecked throughout the colonial period, and a demographic catastrophe of unknown dimensions occurred, aggravated by warfare and disease.

1500–1521. Under **Manuel the Fortunate** (1495–1521), Portuguese merchants established some trading posts, bartering tools and metal artifacts for Brazil wood gathered by natives.

1521–30. **John III** (1521–57) undertook systematic colonization to counter French activities in Portuguese possessions. The king promoted private investment in colonization.

1530–32. Martin Affonso de Souza as captain-major of a colonizing expedition founded São Vicente and introduced sugarcane cultivation.

1532–36. The crown established the *donatários,* a system of feudal hereditary captaincies with nearly sovereign authority, but they did little to advance colonization. A more centralized administration with a governor-general at its head was established. Sugarcane cultivation expanded and Indian enslavement assumed wider proportions. Although African slaves were also used, their price was high in comparison to that of Indian slaves.

1549. Thomé de Souza, the first governor-general, founded **São Salvador** (Bahia) as seat of the government and established a colony. **São Paulo** was founded shortly after midcentury.

Jesuits undertook the conversion of the natives and established mission villages in Bahia.

1551. The bishopric of Bahia, subordinate to the archbishop of Lisbon, was erected.

1555. With the intention of creating an "Antarctic France," **Nicolás Durand de Villegagnon** founded a colony on the Bay of Rio de Janeiro.

1565–67. Mem de Sá (1558–72) led Portuguese to destroy the French colony and founded the city of **Rio de Janeiro.** He promoted enslavement of unfriendly Indians.

1570. The crown issued decrees against enslavement of Indians, which colonists disregarded. Expansion of sugar mills led to an increase in the African slave trade and to further Indian enslavement, affecting even Indian cultures allied with the Portuguese.

1587. Dutch privateers attacked Recife. Attacks repeated in 1595, 1604, 1616, and 1623.

1594. French attacked Paraíba. Portuguese built a fort, which became the city of **Natal.**

1612. French colonists founded a town in the island of **São Luis de Maranhão** and sought alliance with Indian groups.

1615. Portuguese expelled French from Maranhão and founded **Belém** near the mouth of the Amazon River. The crown created the province of Maranhão, directly subordinated to the home government (1621). Maranhão was independent of Brazil until 1777.

1624–25. The Dutch captured Bahia but the Spanish fleet forced them to capitulate (1625).

1629. Slave-raiding parties *(bandeirantes)* penetrated the interior from São Paulo and attacked Spanish Jesuit missions on the upper Paraná (Guaira), forcing their transfer farther south and establishing Portuguese control of the region.

1630. A Dutch armada captured Recife and Olinda. The **Dutch West India Company,** a commercial corporation with investments in colonial commerce and slave trade and in privateering expeditions, named **Prince Maurice of Nassau-Siegen** governor. He extended Dutch control from the São Francisco River to Maranhão and established religious tolerance. Portuguese resisted in the countryside but **Domingo Fernandes Calabar,** a mulatto leader, gave support to the Dutch and they overcame Portuguese resistance. War between Portugal and Holland continued in Asia, where Portugal lost most of its colonies. Many slaves took advantage of the Dutch invasion to flee and form **quilombos** (fortified maroon villages) in remote areas beyond the reach of colonial authorities. **Palmares,** a territory between Alagoas and Pernambuco, was the most important *quilombo,* where a maroon society based on small tenancies and agriculture developed with a population of about 8,000, though some estimates go as high as 20,000.

1638. Departure of Prince Maurice ended policy of religious tolerance. Calvinist pastors preached against Catholics, causing widespread discontent among Portuguese.

1640. Conflicts between the Portuguese Jesuits and the *bandeirantes* erupted as the former attempted to protect the Indians from enslavement. Colonists expelled Jesuits from São Paulo and Rio de Janeiro.

1654. The Portuguese forced the Dutch out of Brazil.

1667. Pernambuco authorities failed to subdue maroon area of Palmares.

1672. Expansion of cattle ranching in central Brazil. New expeditions of extermination against Gê and Tupi tribes depopulated Bahian countryside. Expeditions against the *quilombo* of Palmares intensified.

1680–83. Conflict between Spain and Portugal over control of the left bank of the Rio de la Plata (Banda Oriental). The Portuguese founded **Colonia** and the Spanish, **Montevideo** (1726). The territory changed hands frequently during the remainder of the colonial period.

In 1680 the crown issued a law to distribute lands to Indians, which colonists rejected (1684).

1683–1713. Guerra dos Bárbaros unleashed in Rio Grande do Norte and Ceará. Allied Gê and Tupi Indians rebelled against ruthless exploitation by colonists.

1693. Paulista *bandeirantes* discovered extensive gold deposits in **Minas**

Gerais. An influx of gold seekers followed, among them many newly arrived Portuguese. Stagnation of sugar economy.

1694–95. A military expedition captured Palmares, reenslaving maroon dwellers. Their leader, **Zumbi,** continued resistance until 1695, when he was captured and executed.

1701–13. French attacked Brazilian ports as a result of alliance of Portugal with England in the War of the Succession. They sacked and held for ransom Rio de Janeiro (1711).

1708–9. War of the Emboabas. The Paulista gold prospectors attacked Emboabas (Portuguese newcomers), whom they saw as taking undue advantage of their findings.

1709. Paulistas colonized Mato Grosso and Goiás, areas far west of the Line of Demarcation. The crown created the captaincy of **São Paulo and Minas Gerais** with a captain-general directly responsible to the sovereign. Later it elevated Minas Gerais into a separate jurisdiction (1720) and established the captaincies of Mato Grosso (1744) and Goiás (1748).

1710–11. The War of the Mascates. Disputes between native Brazilians of Olinda, capital of Pernambuco, and the Portuguese of the commercial town of Recife led to armed conflict. Recife obtained municipal privileges and eventually displaced Olinda as the seat of government.

1718. Against ruthless Portuguese expansion, Gê and Tupi Indians, led by **Mandu Ladino,** rebelled in southern Maranhão and Ceará. Portuguese, using Tobajara Indians, subdued the rebellion after seven years. Portuguese advances in the Amazon basin destroyed **Omagua** and **Yurimagua** tribes.

1755. Law of liberties declared Indians free citizens but had little effect in improving treatment of Indians.

1750–77. The Marquês de Pombal (Sebastião José de Carvalho e Melo), as minister to Joseph I, introduced broad colonial reforms. The capital was transferred from Bahia to Rio de Janeiro, and Maranhão was incorporated into Brazil (1777). He declared Indians free citizens (1755) and ordered the expulsion of Jesuits from Portugal and its possessions (1759). Pombal strongly pressed Portuguese territorial claims.

1760. Treaty of Madrid. Although this treaty was voided in 1761, it was important because both Spain and Portugal abandoned the boundaries set by the **Treaty of Tordesillas** (1494).

1777. By the **Treaty of San Ildefonso,** Spain recognized Portuguese claims to extensive areas in the basins of the Amazon and Paraná.

1789. The **Conspiracy of Minas Gerais (Inconfidência Mineira). Joaquim José da Silva Xavier** (Tiradentes) led a failed revolution to make Minas Gerais an independent republic.

1807–8. Invasion of Portugal by Napoleon's army prompted **Prince John,** regent after 1792, to create a regency in Portugal, flee to Brazil, and establish his court at Rio de Janeiro. He declared war on France, dispatched an expedition to French Guiana, and sought to annex the Banda Oriental of the Río de la Plata.

1812. The opposition of the viceroy and the revolutionary junta of Buenos Aires, along with British influence, caused the regent to renounce temporarily intervention in the Río de la Plata.

1815–16. The regent elevated Brazil into a coordinate member of the **United Kingdom of Portugal, Brazil, and the Algarve** (Dec. 16, 1815). He became **John VI** upon the death of Maria I (March 1, 1816).

10. THE PORTUGUESE COLONIAL SYSTEM

Population. At the beginning of Portuguese colonization, a large group of mestiços emerged as a result of intermixture between Portuguese men and Indian women. The heavy influx of African slaves from the mid-16th century on resulted in new racially mixed groups, children of African and Indian parents and of African and white parents. In 1583 the population was estimated at 25,000 whites and mestiços, 18,000 subjugated Indians, and 14,000 slaves. In the mid-17th century, considerable immigration occurred. Population was estimated at 150,000 to 200,000, three-quarters of whom were Indians, blacks, and mestiços or mulattos. In 1818 the population was estimated at 843,000 whites, 1,887,000 blacks, 628,000 mestiços, and 259,400 Indians. The bulk of the population was concentrated in São Paulo, Minas Gerais, Pernambuco, and Bahia. Originally the crown permitted any person of Catholic faith to enter Brazil, but after 1591 aliens were excluded.

Portuguese **colonial administration** was not clearly differentiated from that of the metropolis prior to the union of the crowns of Portugal and Spain. The Mesa da Conciência e Ordens, with ecclesiastical and financial powers, was created in 1532. Upon the establishment of a more centralized government in Brazil, a commissioner of finances and a chief justice were appointed for the colony (1548). Corregidores, with judicial and military functions, were in charge of local administration. Municipal organization was patterned on that of Portugal. The fundamental code was the Ordenanças Manuelinas (1521).

During the period of the union of the thrones of Spain and Portugal (1581–1640), Spanish administrative forms were introduced. The Casa da Índia was established (1591). The inspector of finance was created (1604), a supreme court was established in Bahia (1609), and the title of viceroy was introduced (1640). Under Philip III (1598–1621), the Ordenanças Philipinas, which permitted greater local autonomy, superseded the Ordenanças Manuelinas.

By the close of the 18th century, the structure of royal government was fully formed. The **Overseas Council** (Conselho de Ultramar), created in 1642, exercised general religious and military authority over Brazil. Pará, Maranhão, Pernambuco, Bahia, São Paulo, Minas Gerais, Goiás, Mato Grosso, and Rio de Janeiro were captaincies-general, provinces of the first rank, under captains-general usually appointed by the crown. The viceroy, who was also captain-general of Rio de Janeiro, possessed legal authority over the captains-general in certain matters, but the latter frequently received instructions from the crown, with which they could correspond directly. A tendency toward local auton-

omy existed. Two superior judicial districts existed, with high courts at Bahia and Rio de Janeiro (founded in 1757), respectively. Appeals from these courts went directly to Lisbon. The municipalities, with their councils (senados de câmara), enjoyed a certain degree of self-government.

Economy. Restrictions were placed upon industry and agriculture that competed with Portuguese enterprises, and a government monopoly, which produced important crown revenues, existed for the exploitation of Brazil wood, mining of diamonds, and other activities. Customs duties were levied and a royal fifth (quinto) was collected on all gold mined. The mining of gold and diamonds and the production of sugar, cotton, and hides were the chief industries. Slavery, first Indian, then predominantly African, was the main form of labor in Brazil. Portugal controlled Angola and Portuguese traders supplied slaves to the Brazilian planters.

Commerce was a Portuguese monopoly until 1808 and trade was restricted to Lisbon and Oporto and carried out through convoyed fleets. In 1649 a monopolistic **Commercial Company of Brazil** was organized. In 1682, the also monopolistic **Maranhão Company** was formed. Both companies aroused opposition and were abolished in the first decades of the 18th century. During the Pombaline period, two more monopolistic companies were formed, but both were abolished after his fall. Pombal abolished the system of convoyed fleets.

The Church. The papal bull of Julius III conceded to the crown the right to nominate bishops, collect tithes, dispense church revenues, and receive appeals from ecclesiastical tribunals. The bishopric of Bahia was erected in 1551. In 1676 Innocent XI created the **archbishopric of Brazil,** with Bahia as the metropolitan seat, at the same time erecting the bishoprics of Rio de Janeiro and Pernambuco. The **Jesuits,** until their expulsion by the crown (1759), played an important role through conversion of the natives, extension of the Portuguese influence, and establishment of schools and colleges (1554). They had frequent clashes with the colonists, who abhorred the Jesuit campaign against Indian slavery. Jesuits, however, did not oppose African slavery and owned many slave plantations in Brazil. The **Inquisition of Lisbon** was in charge of religious infractions, but no tribunal was established in Brazil, all the cases being reviewed by visitadores (inspectors).

Society and culture. Sugar mill owners (**senhores de engenho**) and sugarcane growers occupied the highest social and economic positions, along with high royal officers and Portuguese merchants. Marriage and kinship ties solidified their social position. This elite minority sent its children to Portugal for higher education since, in Brazil, there was no university-level instruction during the colonial period. Jesuits controlled most of the institutions of secondary education, with ten colleges and four seminaries. The most distinguished Brazilian-born scholar was the Jesuit **Antônio Vieira** (1608–97), a constant defender of the Indians, whose sermons achieved fame throughout the Iberian dominions. There was a significant population of New Christians (Jews recently converted to Christianity or their children) engaged in commerce, artisanal trades, and sugarcane growing, but Jewish collaboration with Dutch invaders weakened the New Christians' position and inquisitorial inspections frequently harassed them. Wealth from the gold rush and sugar commerce allowed the development of highly elaborate religious architecture and arts in the main cities. The most

distinguished artist of this era was the mulatto architect and sculptor **Antônio Francisco Lisboa** (c. 1730–1814), called **Aleijadinho.**

The rural sector of society was predominant. Indians and African slaves occupied the lowest social position. Often, slaves fled to remote areas to form maroon communities. Slaveholders hired professional slave-catchers *(capitães de mato)* to recapture their slaves. Slaves could also obtain freedom by self-purchase or by manumission. People of mixed background (called mulatos, mamelucos, caboclos), although free, were subjected to discriminatory laws and customs. They lived as squatters, sharecroppers, artisans, wage laborers. Black slaves introduced customs and beliefs from different African societies, which played a major role in the formation of popular religiosity and culture in Brazil. *(To p. 622)*

I. NORTH AMERICA, 1500–1789

1. OVERVIEW

For nearly 300 years before the founding of the American republic, North America had experienced a series of socioeconomic, cultural, and political transformations. In relatively rapid succession, European exploration, settlement, and colonial expansion culminated in an era of reform, revolution, and the birth of the United States and, later, the Dominion of Canada. The exploration and settlement of North America had roots in the transformation of European society from a relatively stable world of feudal agriculture to the dynamic world of commerical capitalism. During the early 16th century, European monarchs gave trading rights to commercial capitalists, encouraged their involvement in international trade, and facilitated European expansion overseas. Although Spain "discovered" the New World and soon controlled vast stretches of land in the Caribbean and South America, the Netherlands, France, and England later gained increasing access to North America.

European expansion and settlement in North America ushered in a new set of social and cultural interactions among diverse peoples from Africa, America, and Europe. While these interactions were salutary

for Europeans, especially elite white men, they were quite destructive, even devastating, for the indigenous peoples (p. 18) and for Africans. Under the onslaught of European weaponry, diseases, and declining access to arable land, the **Native American population in New England, for example, declined from nearly 120,000 in 1570 to about 12,000 in 1670** and continued to drop in subsequent decades. For their part, although the first Africans to arrive in North America occupied a status much like that of European indentured servants, they soon experienced treatment that foreshadowed their transition to a status of slaves for life. Thus, when the new nation embarked upon its political career with the Declaration of Independence in 1776, it did so with huge gaps between its democratic promise and its reality as an elite, slaveholding, white male republic. Progress toward government by, for, and of the people would take years to achieve in North America. While Canada would remain within the British colonial empire, its future was profoundly shaped by developments in the new republic south of the border.

2. EXPLORATION AND SETTLEMENT, 1500–1719

a. THE FRENCH IN NORTH AMERICA

1508. Fishing expedition of Thomas Aubert of Dieppe resulted in first recorded case of Amerindian taken to France for official display.

1524. Giovanni de Verrazano, sent out by Francis I, probably explored the coast from Cape Fear to Newfoundland.

1534–41. Voyages of **Jacques Cartier.** On the first voyage he sighted the Labrador coast, passed through the Straits of Belle Isle, and explored the Gulf of St. Lawrence. He returned to France with **Taignoagny** and **Domagaya,** the sons of **Donnacona,** the chief or "lord of Canada." With Taignoagny and Domagaya serving as guides, on his second trip (1535–36) Cartier sailed up the St. Lawrence, stopped at the site of Quebec, and proceeded to the La Chine Rapids and the site of Montreal. Several members of this voyage contracted scurvy and died, but others recovered when they took an Indian cure for the disease. On the third trip (1541), unsuccessful attempts were made to establish a settlement at Quebec, and therewith the French efforts to colonize the St. Lawrence Valley came to an end until the 17th century.

In the southeast and the southwest, the presence of the Spaniards hampered the activities of the French.

1542. Cartier departed for France and left Roberval in charge. Most of the 200 members of his party were released convicts, primarily men, from the French jail.

1562. Admiral Coligny, as part of his plan to attack Spain, sent **Jean**

Ribaut to establish a colony in Florida. A colony on Port Royal Sound failed, but in 1564 Ribaut and **Rene de Laudonniere** established **Fort Caroline** on St. John's River.

1598. Marquis de La Roche attempted to found a colony on Sable Island. The survivors were rescued five years later.

1600. Pontgrave, Chauvin, and **De Monts,** with a grant of the fur-trade monopoly, made another unsuccessful attempt to colonize, this time at **Tadoussac** on the lower St. Lawrence.

1603. Pontgrave, accompanied by **Samuel de Champlain,** explored the St. Lawrence as far as La Chine Rapids. Champlain also explored the Acadian coast. Champlain followed the New England coast as far as Cape Cod and returned to France in 1607.

1608, July 3. Champlain, acting as lieutenant for De Monts, founded the settlement of **Quebec.** In the following year, accompanied by a party of **Algonquin and Huron Indians,** he ascended the Richelieu River to the lake that now bears his name.

1610. Poutrincourt reestablished Port Royal.

1612–15. Etienne Brule (c. 1592–1633) lived among the Hurons near Georgian Bay, learned their language and customs, and played a critical role in pushing the fur trade deep into the Canadian interior. Brule figured prominently among a group of Frenchmen called *"coureur de bois,"* that is, "runner of the woods" or "bushloper."

1613. Champlain explored the **Ottawa River** to about 100 miles above the present city of Ottawa. In 1615 he went up the river to Lake Nip-

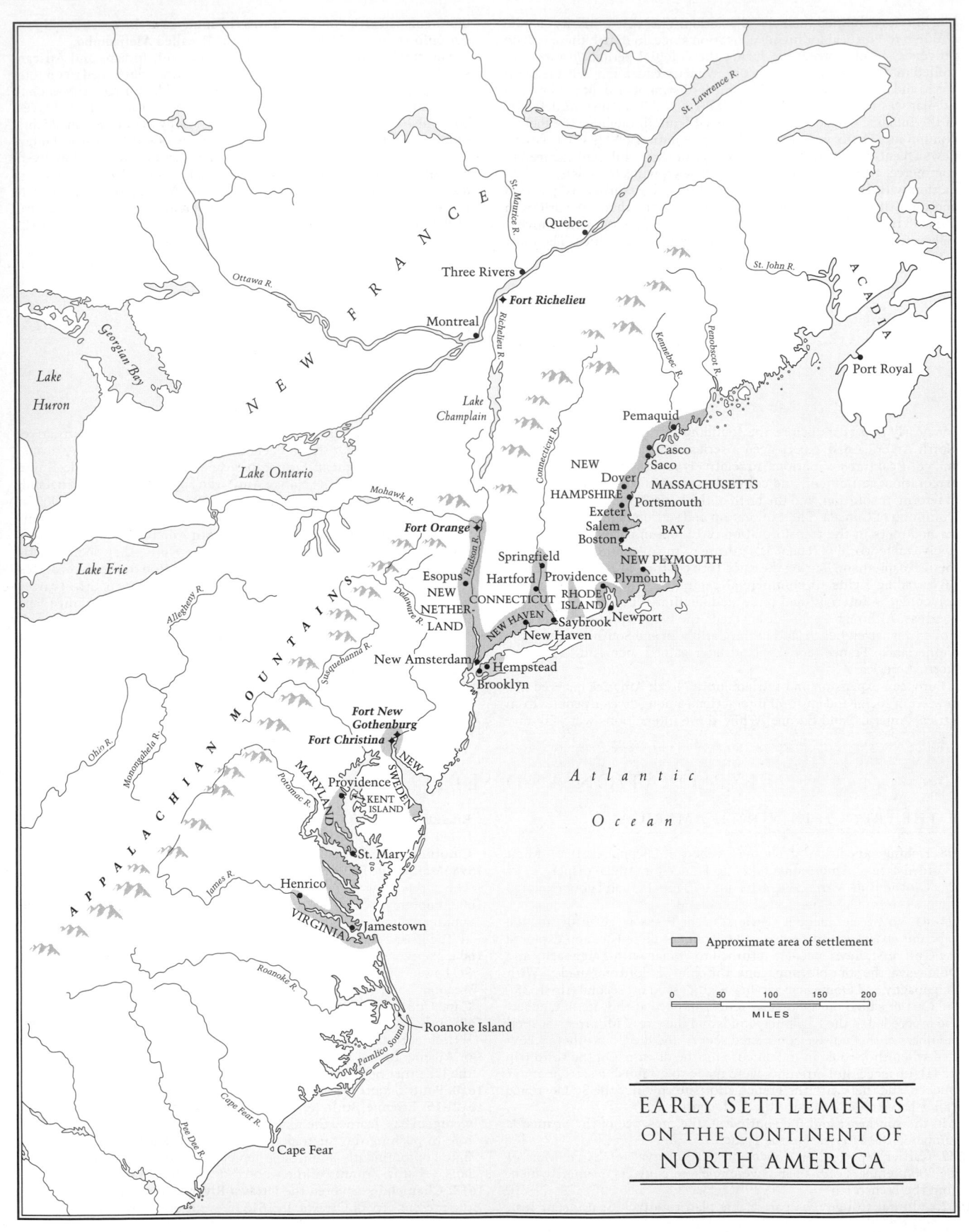

St. Lawrence R.

Quebec

NEW FRANCE

St. Maurice R.

Three Rivers

ACADIA

St. John R.

Fort Richelieu

Montreal

Richelieu R.

Port Royal

Ottawa R.

Kennebec R.

Penobscot R.

Georgian Bay

Lake Huron

Lake
Champlain

Pemaquid

Lake Ontario

Casco

Saco

NEW

Dover

MASSACHUSETTS

Mohawk R.

Connecticut R.

HAMPSHIRE

Portsmouth

Exeter

Fort Orange

Salem

BAY

Lake Erie

Hudson R.

Boston

Allegany R.

Springfield

NEW PLYMOUTH

Delaware R.

Esopus

Hartford

Providence

Plymouth

APPALACHIAN MOUNTAINS

NEW

CONNECTICUT

RHODE

NETHER-

ISLAND

LAND

NEW HAVEN

Saybrook

Newport

Susquehanna R.

New Haven

New Amsterdam

Hempstead

Brooklyn

Fort New
Gothenburg

Fort Christina

NEW

Atlantic

Ohio R.

SWEDEN

Monongahela R.

MARYLAND

Providence

Ocean

Potomac R.

KENT
ISLAND

St. Mary's

James R.

Henrico

VIRGINIA

Jamestown

Roanoke R.

Roanoke Island

Pamlico Sound

Cape Fear R.

Pee Dee R.

Cape Fear

☐ Approximate area of settlement

0   50   100   150   200
MILES

EARLY SETTLEMENTS
ON THE CONTINENT OF
NORTH AMERICA

issing and thence to Georgian Bay, being the first white man to blaze the fur trader's route into the interior.

1615. Four **Recollet friars** arrived at Quebec, marking the beginning of French missionary activity. In 1625 five **Jesuits** arrived, beginning the work of that order.

1627. Richelieu organized the **Company of the Hundred Associates** to colonize New France. The company was given all lands between Florida and the Arctic Circle, with a monopoly of trade except in cod and whale fisheries.

1628. Acadia and Quebec captured by the English but restored in 1632.

1634. Champlain, hearing of a great waterway in the west and believing it might be a passage to China, sent **Jean Nicolet** on an exploring expedition. Nicolet reached Sault Ste. Marie, explored the south shore of the upper peninsula of Michigan, and reached the southern extremity of Green Bay.

1642. Paul de Maisonneuve founded Montreal.

1658–59. Radisson and Groseillers traded and explored in the country at the western end of Lake Superior.

1665. Father Allouez established the La Pointe Mission near the west end of Lake Superior.

1673. Father JACQUES MARQUETTE and **LOUIS JOLIET**, a trader, followed the Fox and Wisconsin Rivers to the Mississippi, which they descended to the confluence of the Arkansas.

1679–83. Explorations of Robert de La Salle, along the shores of Lake Michigan and in the Illinois country. He erected **Fort Crèvecoeur** near present Peoria (1679) and sent Hennepin to explore the upper Mississippi while he himself returned to Fort Frontenac. In 1682 La Salle reached the mouth of the Mississippi and took possession of the whole valley in the name of the king of France.

1683–89. Attempts of **La Salle** to establish a French colony at the mouth of the Mississippi in order to control the fur trade and provide a base for attack upon Spain in America. La Salle conducted four expeditions to the northeast in the hope of finding the Mississippi. **On the fourth of these (1687), he was murdered by his companions.** His colony was completely wiped out by an Indian attack (1689).

1699–1702. To check the Spanish advance, control the Gulf coast, and forestall possible English occupation of the lower Mississippi, French forces under **Pierre D'Iberville** established posts at Biloxi and started the French colony in **Louisiana** (1699). The post was moved to Mobile Bay in 1702 and named St. Louis. **Mobile** was founded in 1710 and **New Orleans** in 1718.

1699. A **Sulpician mission** was set up at **Cahokia** in the **Illinois** country. In 1700 Jesuits moved down the Illinois River to Kaskaskia.

1701. Detroit founded by Antoine de Cadillac, to control the entrance from Lake Erie to Lake Huron and to control the trade from Illinois to the coast. Crozat surrendered his patent (1717) and Louisiana was in the same year taken over by the **Compagnie d'Occident,** which became the **Compagnie des Indes Orientales** (1719).   *(To p. 412)*

b. THE ENGLISH IN NORTH AMERICA

1. EXPLORATION

Following the voyages of the **Cabots** (p. 278), the English showed little interest in the New World until the second half of the 16th century.

1562. John Hawkins, having taken a cargo of slaves in Africa, disposed of them in Espanola. The Spaniards made efforts to stop a second slave-trading voyage (1564–65), and on his third voyage (1567–68) Hawkins was driven by a storm into the harbor of Vera Cruz, where his fleet was largely destroyed.

1572–80. Francis Drake, nephew of Hawkins, carried out reprisals on Spanish commerce. Sailing in 1577, he became **the first Englishman to circumnavigate the globe.**

1576–78. After unsuccessful efforts by explorers of the **Muscovy Company** to find a northeast passage to China, English efforts were concentrated on the search for a northwest passage. **Martin Frobisher** sailed from England in June 1576, explored the Labrador coast, crossed Hudson Strait, coasted along Baffin Land, and entered the inlet known as **Frobisher Bay.** In 1577–78 he made a second voyage (p. 428).

1568. Sir Humphrey Gilbert took possession of Newfoundland in the name of Elizabeth but lost his life on the return voyage.

2. VIRGINIA

1584. Sir Walter Raleigh, under patent, sent out Philip Amadas and Arthur Barlow to establish a colony. They landed on Roanoke Island and named the country **Virginia.** Supply ships were sent out in 1586 but they found the colony deserted, the colonists having been taken back to England by Drake.

1587. Another party of colonists was sent out, under Governor **John White.** Upon his return in 1591, White found only ruins of the colony.

1602–6. A number of voyages were made to America, the most important having been that of **George Weymouth** in 1604. Weymouth visited the New England coast, and his favorable report did much to stimulate the desire to establish further colonies.

1606, April. A group of London men was given a charter to organize the **London Company,** with the object of colonizing the region between 34° and 41° north latitude. Another group, composed of Plymouth, Bristol, and Exeter men, was chartered as the **Plymouth Company,** to operate between 38° and 45° north latitude. The London Company at once sent out (Dec. 1606) three ships with 120 colonists, under command of Captain **Christopher Newport.**

1607, May. FOUNDING OF JAMESTOWN COLONY at the mouth of the James River. The colony was held together largely through the efforts of Captain **John Smith. Of 120 Englishmen who founded the colony, only 35 survived by year's end.** Over the next decade, between half and two-thirds of all newcomers died within a year of settlement.

1609. The London Company was enlarged and given a new charter that vested the government in a council with power to appoint its own officers.

1610. Divine, Moral, and Martial Laws enacted. Prescribed military-like discipline for workers and imposed the death sentence for "slander" against the company.

1610–11. The **Virginia Company** had sent 1,200 indentured servants to Jamestown but fewer than half remained.

1610, May. Captain Newport arrived with 400 more colonists and with **Lord Delaware,** the new governor. Delaware left again in 1611 but remained governor until his death in 1619. **Sir Thomas Dale** was left in command of the colony and ruled with an iron hand.

1612. Beginning of the **cultivation of tobacco,** which was to play a vital part in the economic and social life of the colony.

1612. Third charter of the London Company. The Bermuda Islands were included in its jurisdiction.

1618. Sir Edwin Sandys became the dominant figure in the colony. He assigned 50 acres of land to every person who would transport one more settler to the colony.

1619. John Rolfe reported the arrival of 20 or more Africans in Jamestown. The captain of a Dutch man-of-war exchanged its human cargo for food.

1619. Sir Thomas Yeardley arrived as governor, bringing instructions for each plantation to elect two burgesses to a general assembly. The assembly met at Jamestown on July 30 and was the **first representative assembly** in America.

1621. Sir Francis Wyatt, the governor, brought over new regulations providing for government through a governor, council of state, and assembly, the assembly consisting of two burgesses, or representatives, elected from every plantation and town.

1622. Powhatan's brother **Opechanough** formed an alliance with other Chesapeake Indians and attacked English settlements, killing 347 settlers, about a third of the white population. Settlers retaliated by destroying Indian food supplies.

1624. Revocation of the charter. This step was taken as a result of dissension within the company and because the king disapproved of popular government and the raising of tobacco and desired to please the Spanish, who had protested against the founding of the colony. Virginia became a royal colony, with a governor and council appointed by the crown.

1640. Population increased to 8,000. Adoption of **Indian agricultural technology (corn),** which Indian women controlled, played a major role in the colony's survival.

3. NEW ENGLAND

a. Massachusetts

1606. Granting of the charter to the **Plymouth Company.** In this year two unsuccessful attempts were made to found colonies. In 1607 settlers were landed at the mouth of the **Kennebec River,** but the enterprise was abandoned the next spring.

1614. Captain John Smith, of the Virginia settlement, explored the coast of New England and mapped it. He was made Admiral of New England by the Plymouth Company (1615) and made an abortive effort to start a colony.

1620, Nov. 13. The Council for New England. The Plymouth Company having failed to found a colony, Gorges and others secured the incorporation of the council, which was given jurisdiction between 40° and 48° north latitude.

1620, Nov. ARRIVAL OF THE PILGRIMS at Cape Cod. The **Pilgrims were a group of separatists** who had migrated from Scrooby to Amsterdam and thence to Leyden in Holland. In 1617 they decided to seek a new home in order to preserve their English identity. They obtained a patent from the London Company and **John Carver** was made their governor. They left England in the *Mayflower* and reached Cape Cod, which they found to be outside the jurisdiction of the London Company. They therefore drew up the **Mayflower Compact,** by which they formed themselves into a body politic and agreed to enact laws for the welfare of the colony. The basis of government, then, was the will of the colonists rather than that of the crown. **Plymouth** was selected as the site of the settlement.

1621. William Bradford became governor on the death of Carver.

1623. Settlements at Portsmouth and Dover (New Hampshire) and at **Casco Bay** and **Saco Bay** (Maine) were made under the auspices of the Council for New England. A group of Dorchester merchants settled on Cape Ann (1624).

1628, Sept. John Endicott and some 50 colonists arrived at Salem, acting under a patent obtained by Rev. **John White** of Dorchester from the Council for New England.

1629, March. ROYAL CHARTER issued confirming the grant to Endicott and his associates. The new corporation was known as the **Governor and Company of Massachusetts Bay** in New England.

June 27. Five ships, with some 400 settlers, arrived at Salem. **John Winthrop** and other prominent men meeting at Cambridge (England) agreed to emigrate to Massachusetts Bay, provided the charter and government might be legally transferred to America. The company decided to make the transfer and Winthrop was named governor.

1630. Seventeen ships brought about 1,000 persons to the colony. By the end of the year, settlements had been made at Dorchester, Boston, Watertown, Roxbury, Mystic, and Lynn. The first **general court** of the colony was held at Boston (Oct. 19). From then on no person was to be admitted as a freeman of the corporation unless a member of some church within the colony. In 1634 **a representative system was introduced into the general court,** because the growth of the colony prevented attendance of all freemen.

1630–42. The **Great Migration** to Massachusetts Bay Colony. During these years some 16,000 settlers arrived from England.

1633. Closely associated with the arrival of Europeans, **smallpox epidemic** killed hundreds of Indians.

1635. Council for New England gave up its charter and the king demanded also the charter of the Massachusetts Bay Colony, because of Archbishop Laud's dislike of the Puritan Commonwealth. The king was unsuccessful.

1637. Puritans attacked **Pequot** village, massacred nearly 500 men, women, and children, and sold many of the survivors into slavery.

1637–39. The **Harvard College** founded.

b. Connecticut and Rhode Island

1631. The **earl of Warwick,** to whom the Council for New England had granted much of the Connecticut River Valley, transferred his rights to William Fiennes, **Lord Saye and Sele.**

1633. The **Dutch,** who had explored the coast, erected a fort on the river near the present **Hartford.**

1635. Rev. **John Davenport** and **Theophilus Eaton** founded a theocratic colony at **New Haven.**

1636, June. ROGER WILLIAMS SETTLED AT PROVIDENCE, where he organized a government democratic in character, with separation of church and state.

1638. Anne Hutchinson held weekly prayer meetings in her home, attacked members of the clergy for underestimating the role of faith in salvation, and stressed the importance of direct communication with God. Considerations of **gender** and theology impelled officials to banish her from the colony. She took refuge on the island of Aquidneck, later called **Rhode Island,** where she and a small group of associates founded the settlement of **Portsmouth.** The following year another settlement was made at **Newport.**

1639. Hartford, Windsor, and Wethersfield drew up **Fundamental Orders,** which provided that the governor and assistants, with four representatives from each town, should constitute the general court. These three settlements were commonly referred to as **Connecticut.**

Meanwhile, **Roger Williams** had arrived at Boston, from England (1631). After spending some time at Salem, he repaired to Plymouth, where he concluded that the land rightfully belonged to the Indians and that the king had no right to grant it. He returned to Salem, where he argued that the Church and the state should be separated. He denied the right of the magistrate to control the churches and objected to enforced oaths, since they obliged wicked men to perform a religious act, thereby destroying the freedom of the soul. In Oct. 1635 he was banished from Salem.

4. MARYLAND

1632. George Calvert (later Lord Baltimore)—a proprietor of holdings in Newfoundland—asked for a grant in Virginia, which was made in 1632, despite opposition from the Virginians.

April. The charter of the new colony was drawn up in the name of **Cecilius Calvert,** George Calvert having died. The province was named **Maryland,** and Calvert, as proprietor, was given the right to collect taxes, make grants of land, create manors, appoint ministers, and found churches according to the laws of England. As the charter did not forbid the establishment of other churches than the Protestant, Baltimore (Calvert) made use of it to help his coreligionists, the Catholics.

1633, Oct. Baltimore dispatched to Maryland two vessels with some 20 gentlemen, mostly Catholics, and about 200 laborers, chiefly Protestants. Arriving at the mouth of the Potomac (March 1634), they founded the settlement of **St. Mary's.**

1638. Lord Baltimore accepted the demands of colonists for the right to initiate legislation.

5. ISLAND SETTLEMENTS

1609. The **Somers Islands Company** was formed (1612) for the colonization of **Bermuda.** The island had 600 settlers in 1614 and between 2,000 and 3,000 in 1625. It became an important producer of tobacco.

1625. St. Christopher was settled, and **Sir William Courten** established the first colony on **Barbados. Nevis** was occupied by the British in 1628, and settlements were made on **Antigua and Montserrat** in 1632. By 1640 the island possessions of England had a population of 20,000, devoted chiefly to the cultivation of sugar, which soon supplanted tobacco as the leading crop.

c. DUTCH AND SWEDISH SETTLEMENTS

1602. The **United East India Company** was chartered by the states-general of Holland.

1609. The company employed **Henry Hudson,** an Englishman, to search for the northwest passage. He sighted land at Newfoundland, explored the New England coast, rounded Cape Cod, proceeded south to Virginia, probably entered Chesapeake Bay, entered Delaware Bay, and exploree the **Hudson River** to Albany. Friendly relations with Iroquois Indians.

1612. Dutch merchants sent **Christianson and Block** to Manhattan Island to engage in fur trade. A post was established in 1613.

1614. Fort Nassau, later Fort Orange, built near present Albany. Exploration by Adrian Block of Long Island Sound, Connecticut coast, Narragansett Bay, and Cape Cod. As a result the **New Netherland Company** was formed and given monopoly of trade between the 40th and 45th parallels. Fur trade carried on and the coast explored.

1621. The **Dutch West India Company** was chartered and given a monopoly of trade in Africa and America.

1626. Peter Minuit became director-general of the company. He purchased **Manhattan Island** from the Indians for $24 and founded the settlement of New Amsterdam. Meanwhile the attention of **Gustavus Adolphus** of Sweden was called to the Delaware country. In 1637, the

New Sweden Company was organized, chiefly as a result of the encouragement of two Dutchmen, Samuel Blommaert and Minuit.

1629. Under the urging of **Killiaen Van Rensslaer,** a wealthy Amsterdam jeweler, the Dutch government established the patroon system, which provided huge estates to wealthy Dutchmen in exchange for settling 50 tenants on the land within a four-year period.

1638. Two Swedish vessels arrived on the Delaware and **Fort Christina** was established. This intrusion of the Swedes angered **Peter Stuyvesant** of New Netherland, who urged the West India Company to occupy New Sweden, which was done in 1655.

3. COLONIAL HISTORY, 1641–1737

a. NEW ENGLAND

1641. The **Body of Liberties,** a code of 100 laws, was established by the general court of the Massachusetts Bay Colony.

1643, May 19. The **New England Confederation** was formed by Connecticut (Hartford, Windsor, and Wethersfield), New Haven, Plymouth, and Massachusetts Bay for purposes of defense.

1646. In Massachusetts, **John Eliot** began his missionary work among the Indians, translating the Bible into Massachusetts dialect, 1661–63.

1647. Christian and civil authorities intensified attacks on persons claiming to possess supernatural powers as healers and prophets. Over the next decade and a half, **Massachusetts and Connecticut officials hanged 14 people, mainly women, for witchcraft.**

1662. Charter of Rhode Island and Providence Plantations, kept throughout the colonial period and the constitution of the state until 1842.

1662. Puritan ministers initiated the **"halfway covenant."** This policy allowed children of all baptized Puritans to become active members of the church and helped to concentrate power in the hands of certain established families.

1664. Union of Connecticut and New Haven, because of the latter's fear of annexation to New York.

1675–76. KING PHILIP'S WAR in New England. Displaced by European settlements and ravaged by disease, the population of **New England's Native Americans dropped drastically, from 120,000 in 1570 to 12,000 in 1670.** Metacom (called **Philip** by the Europeans), son of **Massasoit,** chief of the **Wampanoags,** believed only armed resistance could stop the European advance. In 1675, Metacom formed a military league comprising most of the Indians from Maine to Connecticut. Full-scale war ensued. Bitter fighting continued into 1676. **Chief Canonchet of the Narragansetts** was shot (April 1676).

1680. New Hampshire was separated from Massachusetts by royal charter.

1684. ANNULMENT OF THE MASSACHUSETTS CHARTER. The independent course of Massachusetts had long irritated the crown. In 1679 **Edward Randolph** arrived in Boston as collector of the customs, bearing instructions for the colony to relinquish jurisdiction over New Hampshire, which authorities transformed into a royal colony. Friction continued, as did Randolph's complaints against the colony, until legal action in 1684 annulled the charter.

1686. DOMINION OF NEW ENGLAND formed through consolidation of the New England colonies. **Sir Edmund Andros** was made governor. Andros arrived in Boston (Dec. 20) and assumed the government of Plymouth and Rhode Island. In 1687 he assumed the government of Connecticut and demanded the charter, which Captain William Wadsworth concealed in a hollow tree, the famous **Charter Oak.**

1688. The **Glorious Revolution** in England led to a **Bill of Rights** that ensured the traditional powers of Parliament, ended the **divine right** of kings to govern, and forced James II into exile.

1689. Upon news of the flight of **James II** from England, the people of Boston rose in revolt, imprisoned **Andros,** and restored charter government. Similar action was taken in Rhode Island and Connecticut.

1691. New charter for Massachusetts, which included Plymouth, Maine, Nova Scotia, and all land north to the St. Lawrence. **The electoral franchise was extended and religious liberty secured to all except Catholics. Sir William Phips was made governor.**

1692. Salem witchcraft trials. A group of poor Puritans sought to avenge themselves against wealthier church members by bringing charges of

witchcraft against their families. **About 174 men and women were arrested and about 22 "witches" were executed.**

1700. Under the conquest of Europeans, the **Indian** population and culture continued to decline on the eastern seaboard.

1701. Founding of Yale College, New Haven, Connecticut.

1702–13. Boston **artisans and laborers** staged bread riots to prevent the export of grain during Queen Anne's War.

1710. After this date, Boston merchants began purchasing **enslaved Africans** in increasingly large numbers. The number of slaves in other northern cities also began a comparable rise.

1728. Death of **Cotton Mather** (b. 1663), prolific author of Puritan tracts. More liberal were the writings of a later divine, **Jonathan Edwards** (1703–58).

1730s–40s. The Great Awakening. Starting in the mid- to late 1730s, an evangelical religious revival shook the colonies, particularly in the Northeast. The Awakening challenged and weakened the authority of the clergy and the Church and undermined denominational boundaries.

b. NEW YORK, NEW JERSEY, AND PENNSYLVANIA

1664. Grant of New Netherland, from the Connecticut to the Delaware, to the king's brother, **James, duke of York.** The grant included the eastern part of Maine and islands south and west of Cape Cod. The region between the Hudson and the Delaware was granted by the duke of York to **Lord Berkeley** and **Sir George Carteret.**

1664, Aug. 27. SURRENDER OF NEW AMSTERDAM to the English. Name of the colony changed to **New York.** On Sept. 24 surrender of Fort Orange, whose name was changed to **Albany.**

1676. Line of demarcation between East and West New Jersey. **Settlement of Quakers** in West New Jersey (1677–81).

1681, March 4. CHARTER OF PENNSYLVANIA signed, granting to **William Penn** the region between the 40th and 43rd parallels, extending 5° west from the Delaware River. These limits brought the colony into conflict with New York on the north and Maryland on the south. The dispute with Maryland was finally adjusted when in 1767 two surveyors, **Mason and Dixon,** ran the present boundary between the two states. The form of government of the colony was to be determined by the proprietor. The **first body of colonists, primarily Quakers, arrived in 1681** and a frame of government was provided for the governance of the colony. The government guaranteed political liberty and religious freedom.

1682–83. Penn arrived in the colony and **Philadelphia** was laid out (1682). Penn entered into a treaty with the Indians (1783) which had the effect of keeping the colony free from Indian wars.

1688. A group of Germantown Quakers issued the first notable antislavery document in British America.

1702. New Jersey reunited as a royal province.

1715–50. SETTLEMENT OF THE PIEDMONT, partly by newcomers and old settlers, who crossed the fall line into the areas, and partly by German, Swiss, and Scotch-Irish entering at the port of Philadelphia and pushing southward through the valleys, especially the Shenandoah. **German immigration,** which began with the founding of **Germantown, Pennsylvania (1683),** increased greatly after 1710.

1720–26. William Burnet, governor of New York, began efforts to counteract French attempts to hem in the English colonies in the west. He prohibited trade between the Iroquois and the French. In 1722 he established a trading post at Oswego and carried on negotiations at Albany with the Six Nations. A **treaty with the Senecas, Cayugas, and Onondagas (1726)** added their lands to those of the Mohawks and Oneidas, which were already under English protection. The intensification of the fur trade heightened **intra-Indian rivalry,** enabling Europeans to extend their control farther west and deeper into the interior of Indian lands.

1732. Benjamin Franklin (1706–90), journalist as well as statesman, published *Poor Richard's Almanac.*

1735. Trial in New York of **John Peter Zenger,** printer of a paper, for libel. The court contended that it should decide the libelous nature of the statements made and that the jury should determine the fact of publication. **Zenger's lawyer, Andrew Hamilton, argued that the jury must decide whether or not the publication was libelous.** He won his suit, thereby materially safeguarding the freedom of the press.

1750. Under the impetus of expanding colonial trade networks, both New York and Philadelphia increased from no more than 5,000 people at the turn of the century to 13,000. **Artisans** made up about 50 percent of these urban centers, while **slaves and white indentured servants** constituted about 20 to 30 percent. A small fraction of the urban population, about 150 merchants in Philadelphia, accounted for about 70 percent of the city's trade.

c. VIRGINIA, DELAWARE, AND MARYLAND

1640–1710. Lure of America and dreams of becoming landholders drew settlers, many as indentured servants, to the colonies. During the 17th century, 75 to 85 percent of the people who came to the Chesapeake area came as **indentured servants.** Since life expectancy remained precarious until the 1640s, **landowners often willed property to their wife rather than to their oldest son.**

1647. Margaret Brent, a single woman and large landholder, **acted as attorney for Lord Baltimore;** she saved the colony from mutinous soldiers and from a Protestant revolt against the Catholic government.

1652. Parliament assumed control of Maryland and suspended the governor.

1659. Virginia proclaimed Charles II king of England, Scotland, and Ireland and restored the royal governor, **Sir William Berkeley.**

1660. Virginia sanctioned slavery in colonial law. Laws on slavery soon proliferated. Among other things such laws stipulated that the **child's status as free or slave followed the condition of the mother and declared that baptism did not make a person free.** After Bacon's Rebellion (1676), such laws became more restrictive. Slave statutes banned interracial marriage, punished white women who bore black children, and **seized the property of free blacks and stripped them of their rights.** Courts later declared that a master could not be charged for murder if a slave died of injuries received during punishment for insubordination.

1661. Charles Calvert became governor of Maryland. In 1675, upon the death of his father, Cecilius Calvert, the second Lord Baltimore, Charles succeeded as proprietor and third Lord Baltimore.

1676. Bacon's Rebellion in Virginia. Led by **Nathaniel Bacon,** this revolt set discontented freemen against the colony's elite. Those in rebellion believed **Governor Berkeley's** policy toward the Indians was too lax. **The rebels wanted the Indians killed or removed and an end to rule by the wealthy.** Bacon led his followers on an unauthorized attack of a village of friendly Indians. **Soon middling and poor farmers, indentured servants, and even slaves joined the rebel army.** Jamestown was burned, but the rebellion collapsed with the death of Bacon. After the rebellion, the elite tried to ensure that the **interracial alliance** found in Bacon's rebellion would not recur. In particular, elites made a conscious decision to enact laws that would create a free white society and an enslaved black one.

1693. College of William and Mary founded in Virginia.

1750. By midcentury, **as life expectancy increased** and stable families emerged, **landholders increasingly left their property to older sons instead of wives.**

1756. Blacks made up about 40 percent of Virginia's population of over 293,400 and about 30 percent of Maryland's 140,000.

d. THE SOUTHERN COLONIES

1663. Grant of Carolina by the king to eight proprietors, including the earl of Clarendon. The grant included land between 31° and 36° north latitude.

1667. Grant of the Bahamas to the Carolina proprietors.

1669. Adoption of the Fundamental Constitutions, drawn up for Carolina by **John Locke,** which provided for an archaic feudal regime totally unsuited to the needs of a frontier colony.

1708. In Carolina, for the first time in any colony, blacks outnumbered whites.

1715. Defeat of the Yamassees and allied Indian tribes in Carolina. They were driven into Spanish Florida.

1719–29. REORGANIZATION OF THE CAROLINAS. Popular discontent and disputes over the disposition of **Yamassee land** led the Board of Trade to replace the proprietors and establish royal governments in both North and South Carolina.

1722. Slaves had increased to nearly 65 percent of South Carolina's population of 18,350. **African slaves made the cultivation of rice in the colony profitable by introducing the "mortar and pestle" technique for removing rice grains from husks.** In the **Stono Rebellion (1739),** some 20 miles west of Charleston, slaves launched a full-scale effort to gain their freedom. Before the uprising was put down, 30 whites and 44 blacks had lost their lives.

1733. FOUNDING OF GEORGIA, the last of the 13 English colonies on the continent. **James Oglethorpe** became interested in the settlement of the region. An advocate of a strong policy against the Spanish and a humanitarian interested in improving the condition of imprisoned debtors, he conceived the idea of a **buffer colony between the English and the rival French and Spanish settlements.** In 1732 he secured a charter granting to him and his associates the region between the Savannah and the Altamaha Rivers from sea to sea.

1735. Slavery in Georgia was banned. However, in 1749, after rice culture spread to the colony, the ban was rescinded.

1750. The population of **Charles Town,** the region's major urban center, rose to nearly 10,000, representing an increase of more than 500 percent between 1700 and 1740.

4. WARS OF ENGLAND WITH FRANCE AND SPAIN, 1651–1763

1651–73. The British Navigation Laws. These applied mercantilist doctrine to colonial trade. The **Act of 1651,** designed to strike a blow at Dutch shipping, required that colonial products be shipped to England in ships of Great Britain or the plantations. This law was reenacted in 1660, with the additional provision that certain enumerated articles of colonial production could be shipped only to England. The **Staple Act** of 1663 required that articles of European production destined for the colonies must be shipped first to England. The **Act of 1673** imposed intercolonial duties on sugar, tobacco, and other products.

1670. The **Hudson's Bay Company** incorporated and given a monopoly of the trade in Hudson's Bay Basin.

1689–97. KING WILLIAM'S WAR, with France. This was the American phase of the general war against Louis XIV known as the **War of the** League of Augsburg (see p. 315). The French were aided by the Indians of Canada and Maine, while the Iroquois supported the English.

1696–98. A **Board of Commissioners for Trade and Plantations** was organized (1696) and a navigation act of the same year was designed to prevent further evasion of earlier regulations. Since the war with France had interrupted the usual trade, the New Englanders had taken up manufacturing. The **Woolens Act** (1698) forbade the colonists to ship wool or woolen products from one colony to another.

1702–13. QUEEN ANNE'S WAR, the American phase of the War of the Spanish Succession (p. 316). In 1702 the English plundered and burned **St. Augustine in Florida,** while in 1704 the French and Indians surprised Deerfield in the Connecticut Valley. In 1707 the English organized an **expedition against Acadia.** Acadia became the British province of **Nova Scotia** (1710) and the name of **Port Royal** was changed to **Annapolis Royal.** By the **Treaty of Utrecht** (1713), Great Britain secured recognition of its claims in the Hudson's Bay country and the possession of **Newfoundland and Acadia.** The claim of the British to the Iroquois country was also admitted, and **St. Christopher** was ceded to Britain. The French were excluded from fishing on the Acadian coast but were allowed to retain **Cape Breton Island. The** *asiento* **(license) gave the English the exclusive right for 30 years of bringing African slaves into the Spanish possessions.**

1733. The Molasses Act. In response to pleas from the West Indian planters, Parliament enacted the Molasses Act, which placed prohibitive duties on sugar and molasses imported into the colonies from other than British possessions. In 1732 Parliament had stopped the importation of hats from the colonies and had restricted their manufacture.

1739. WAR BETWEEN SPAIN AND ENGLAND (War of Jenkins' Ear, p. 317). Dissatisfied with the provisions of the Treaty of Utrecht with respect to trade with Spanish possessions, British merchants had resorted to extensive smuggling, which, in turn, had led to the seizure of British ships and the rough treatment of British sailors by the Spaniards. The loss of Jenkins' ear was merely one of many similar episodes.

1743–48. KING GEORGE'S WAR, the American phase of the **War of the Austrian Succession** in Europe (p. 317). The outstanding event in the war in America was the **capture of Louisburg** (1745). In the interior, an abortive attempt of the northern colonies to conquer Canada spurred the French and Indians to attack the frontier as far south as New York (1746–48).

1748. The **Treaty of Aix-la-Chapelle** (p. 317), based upon European rather than colonial considerations, restored all the conquests of the war. In America the treaty was merely a truce, for Nova Scotia, the Ohio Valley, and the Cherokee country continued to be areas of conflict. In order to strengthen the British hold on Nova Scotia, Lord Halifax sent out 2,500 settlers in 1749 and founded the town of **Halifax.** In the Ohio Valley, traders from Virginia and Pennsylvania pushed westward as far as the Indian villages on the Mississippi. Virginia frontiersmen made a settlement at **Draper's Meadow** on the Greenbrier River in 1748.

1749. The **Ohio Company,** organized by a group of Virginians and a number of prominent Englishmen. The company obtained a grant of 500,000 acres on the upper Ohio and sent out **Christopher Gist** (1750) to explore the region as far as the falls of the Ohio.

1753. Marquis Duquesne sent an expedition of 1,500 men to occupy the Ohio country. In the same year Governor Robert Dinwiddie of Virginia sent out **George Washington,** a young surveyor, to demand the withdrawal of the French. He proceeded to Fort Le Boeuf but was told that Dinwiddie's letter would be forwarded to Duquesne. It was quite clear that the French would not leave peacefully.

1754. Virginia troops dispatched to the Ohio, with Washington second in command. The French had, in the meantime, built **Fort Duquesne** at the forks of the Ohio. Washington pushed on to Great Meadows, where he constructed **Fort Necessity.** He was attacked by the French and forced to surrender.

1754, June 19. The Albany Convention. The advance of the French had shown the need for a common plan of defense. Representatives of New York, Pennsylvania, Maryland, and the New England states met with the Six Nations (the Five Nations of the Iroquois confederacy and the Tuscaroras). Upon the suggestion of **Benjamin Franklin,** the convention drew up a plan of union which was, however, rejected by the colonies. The plan called for union under a president appointed by the crown, with a grand council of delegates elected by the colonial assemblies, this body to have legislative power subject to approval by the president and the crown.

1755. British authorities in Nova Scotia **relocated some 6,000 French Acadians** to British colonies from Massachusetts to South Carolina **when they failed to swear an oath of allegiance to the British crown.** Immigrants from Britain, Germany, and Switzerland had staged a rebellion against British policies in 1753 and set the stage for attacks on the Acadians.

1755–63. The **FRENCH AND INDIAN WAR,** the American phase of the **Seven Years' War** in Europe (p. 317). In 1755 the governors of Virginia, North Carolina, Pennsylvania, Maryland, New York, and Massachusetts met in conference at Alexandria (Virginia) with **General Edward Braddock,** the British commander. They planned a fourfold attack on the French. In 1756 war was formally declared between France and Great Britain.

For the year 1759 the English planned four campaigns: against Niagara, against settlement on Lake Erie, against Ticonderoga and Crown Point, and against Quebec. The **Battle of the Plains of Abraham** (Quebec) was fought on Sept. 13, and both **Major General James Wolfe and Commander Marquis de Montcalm** were killed. Quebec surrendered to the British **on Sept. 18. On Sept. 8, 1760, Montreal surrendered and all Canada passed into the hands of the British.** In 1762 **Admiral George Rodney** forced the surrender of **Martinique, Grenada, St. Lucia, St. Vincent, and the other French West Indies.**

1763, Feb. 10. The **TREATY OF PARIS** (p. 319), among Great Britain, France, Spain, and Portugal. France ceded to Britain all claim to Acadia, Canada, Cape Breton, and all of Louisiana situated east of the Mississippi except the island of Orleans. France retained certain fishing rights on the Newfoundland Banks and was given the islands of St. Pierre and Miquelon. Britain restored to France the islands of Guadeloupe, Martinique, Belle Isle, Maria Galante, and St. Lucia. Britain restored Havana to Spain, in return for which Spain ceded Florida to Britain. France, by a previous treaty (Nov. 3, 1762), had ceded to Spain all French territory west of the Mississippi and the island of Orleans as compensation for the loss of Florida to Britain.

1763. The Rebellion of Pontiac. This was an aftermath of the war. Indians north of the Ohio, fearing eviction by the British, embittered by the arrogance and dishonesty of British traders, and disappointed by the economy of General Amherst in the matter of presents, were ready to revolt against British occupation of the posts recently held by the French. **Pontiac, chief of the Ottawas, organized a rising of the Algonquins, Iroquis, and Indians on the lower Mississippi.** In a simultaneous attack, all but three of the northwestern posts fell in May. By 1765, however, the British forces were in possession of the last of the French posts in the west.

1763, Oct. 7. Proclamation of 1763, issued by George III. It created four distinct provinces from the recent conquests: Quebec, East Florida, West Florida, and Grenada. It also temporarily closed to white settlement all lands west of the Appalachian Mountains and north of the streams flowing into the Atlantic Ocean. Fur trade in this Indian reserve was opened to licensed subjects. In 1764 **Lord Hillsborough** drew up a plan for the management of the Indians and the fur trade. It continued the **northern and southern departments for Indian affairs** (created in 1755) and provided that in the north all trade must be conducted at regularly established posts and in the south at the Indian towns.

5. REFORM, RESISTANCE, AND REVOLUTION, 1763–1789

1763–75. Expansion beyond the mountains. About 200,000 Indians lived in the region west of the Appalachian Mountains and stood as a barrier to the swift occupation by European settlers. Nonetheless, European settlers increasingly moved into the region. The **Watauga settlement** in eastern Tennessee was made in 1769 and was augmented by the arrival of Virginians and North Carolinians under **James Robertson** and **John Sevier** (1770–71). **Richard Henderson,** of North Carolina, together with his associates organized the **Transylvania Company,** purchased land from the Cherokees, and established the Transylvania settlement in Kentucky in 1775. **Daniel Boone** was Henderson's agent and cleared the wilderness road to Kentucky. The **settlement of Kentucky** (1775–77) was facilitated by the peace forced on the Indians as a result of **Lord Dunmore's War** (1774).

1763–75. The Preliminaries of the American Revolution. By 1761 the British government was thoroughly aroused by the systematic evasion of the **Molasses Act** of 1733 through colonial smuggling and by the illicit trade that the colonies had carried on with the enemy during the War of the Austrian Succession and the Seven Years' War. British officials felt that the trade prolonged French resistance. To prevent smuggling, the British resorted to **writs of assistance**, general search warrants that made possible the search of all premises where smuggled goods might be found. This aroused the opposition of merchants, who alleged that the writs were illegal. In 1761, when Boston customs officers applied for the writs, the merchants contested their use. **James Otis** argued cogently against their legality before the Massachusetts Supreme Court. Although the court decided they were legal, the argument of Otis did much to shape public opinion.

1763–65. George Grenville in power in England. The acquisition of the vast territory from France in America necessitated increased revenues for defense and Indian administration. The ministry decided to enforce the navigation laws, tax the colonies directly, and use that revenue to maintain an army in North America. Powers of the admiralty courts were enlarged, and colonial governors were instructed to enforce the trade law. **The decision to station a peacetime army of about 10,000 soldiers in North America generated resentment from above and below. Colonial elites feared the army would undermine their "liberty," while workers feared competition from soldiers for low-wage work in the port cities.**

1764. Decreeing of the **Sugar Act,** with the avowed purpose of raising revenue in the colonies and reforming the old colonial system, both economically and administratively.

The **Colonial Currency Act** prevented colonies from paying their debts in England in depreciated currency and forbade issues of unsound money. This edict created a shortage of money in the colonies at a time when the Sugar Act injured the West Indian trade of the colonies, which had previously supplied the necessary specie.

1765. Disregarding colonial protests against the two previous measures, Grenville pushed through Parliament the **Stamp Act,** providing for stamps on commercial and legal documents, pamphlets, newspapers, almanacs, playing cards, and dice.

The **Quartering Act** was passed, providing that in the event of insufficiency of barracks in the colonies, British troops might be quartered in public hostelries.

May 29. Patrick Henry introduced into the Virginia House of Burgesses a series of resolutions boldly challenging the position of the British government.

June. The Massachusetts general court sent an invitation to colonial assemblies to send delegates to meet in New York and consider the Stamp Act. Meanwhile **the arrival of the stamp officers led to riots in various cities,** including Boston, where the house of Lieutenant Governor Thomas Hutchinson was sacked.

Oct. 7. Stamp Act Congress at New York. Twenty-eight delegates from nine colonies drew up memorials to the king and Parliament and adopted a **Declaration of Rights and Liberties** (Oct. 19). **Americans rallied to the cry "Liberty, Property, and No Stamps" and forced most stamp distributors to resign by November. A multiclass alliance of merchants, intellectuals, and workers also organized the Sons of Liberty to coordinate resistance to the measure.**

1766, March. Repeal of the Stamp Act, followed by the **Declaratory Act** (March 18), declaring that the king, by and with consent of Parliament, had authority to make laws to bind the colonies in all respects.

1767. Suspension of the New York Assembly because of its refusal fully to comply with the Quartering Act.

The **Townshend Acts** imposed duties on glass, lead, painters' colors, tea, and paper imported into the colonies. Out of these revenues, fixed salaries were to be paid to royal officials in the colonies. A Boston town meeting adopted a **nonimportation agreement.** Poor and working-class people in the port cities were especially receptive to the notion of an economic boycott.

1768. The Massachusetts general court drew up a petition to the king, sent letters to the ministry, and dispatched a circular letter to the other colonies.

October. British troops arrived in Boston and the town refused to provide quarters.

1769. By spring, colonial merchants in the port cities had agreed to an economic boycott of British goods. **The Daughters of Liberty joined the Sons of Liberty and helped ensure the success of the consumer boycott.**

1770, March 5. The Boston Massacre. Popular hatred of the British troops in the city led to a brawl in which several citizens were killed or wounded. Preston, the commanding officer, was acquitted, being defended by John Adams and Josiah Quincy.

An **act repealing duties** on paper, glass, and painters' colors but retaining duties on teas. This gesture produced a conservative reaction in the colonies, in which the merchants worked for conciliation. The truce was broken by the arbitrary acts of crown officials; by the announcement that salaries of governors and judges in Massachusetts were to be paid by the crown, thus rendering them independent of the assembly's control of the purse; and by the **Gaspée Affair (June 10),** in which a revenue boat, whose commander's conduct had enraged public opinion in Rhode Island, was burned by a mob in Narragansett Bay.

1772, Nov. 2–1773, Jan. Formation of 80 town **committees of correspondence** in Massachusetts under the leadership of **Samuel Adams.**

1773, March 12. The Virginia House of Burgesses appointed a **Provincial Committee of Correspondence** to keep in touch with sister colonies. By February 1774 all the colonies except Pennsylvania had appointed such committees.

To provide relief for the East India Company, the government allowed it a drawback of the tea duty in England, but the full duty was to be paid in the colonies. There was a protest to the landing of the tea in Charleston, Philadelphia, and New York.

Dec. 16. In Boston, protest took the form of the **Boston Tea Party,** in which citizens, disguised as Indians, boarded the ships and dumped the tea into the harbor.

1774. The resistance to the landing of the tea provoked the ministry to the adoption of a punitive policy. The so-called **Coercive Acts** were passed, including the **Boston Port Act,** closing the port after June 1; the **Massachusetts Government Act,** depriving the people of most of their chartered rights, and greatly enlarging the governor's powers; the **Administration of Justice Act,** providing that persons accused of a capital crime in aiding the government should be tried in England or a colony other than that in which the crime was committed; the **Quartering Act;** and the **Quebec Act,** extending the boundary of that province to the Ohio River, cutting athwart the claims of Massachusetts, New York, Connecticut, and Virginia. County conventions in Massachusetts protested against the acts (Aug.–Sept.). The **Suffolk Convention** resolved that they should be "rejected as the attempts of a wicked administration to enslave America" **(the Suffolk Resolves).**

May 27. The Virginia House of Burgesses adopted resolutions calling for a congress of the colonies. Copies sent to other assemblies.

Sept. 5. The **FIRST CONTINENTAL CONGRESS** assembled at Philadelphia. All colonies except Georgia represented. Members divided into radicals led by **Samuel Adams** and conservatives led by **Joseph Galloway** of Pennsylvania. The radicals obtained approval of the Suffolk Resolves and defeated Galloway's proposed plan of union, designed to effect an adjustment of difficulties. **Declaration of Rights and Grievances** drawn up.

October. The delegates adopted the Continental Association, providing for nonimportation of English goods after Dec. 1. If redress had not been obtained by Sept. 11, 1775, nonexportation was to go into effect.

1775, Feb 1. Lord Chatham presented to Parliament a plan of conciliation based on mutual concessions, but it was rejected.

Feb. 20. Lord North made an unsuccessful effort toward conciliation.

1775–83. WAR OF INDEPENDENCE.

1775, April 19. Battles of Lexington and Concord. British troops detailed to destroy stores at Concord became embroiled with provincials at Lexington. Proceeding to Concord, the troops destroyed stores but after the fight at the bridge were forced to retreat, first to Lexington, then to Boston.

May 10–12. Ticonderoga captured by **Ethan Allen** and **Crown Point** captured by **Seth Warner.**

May 10. The Second Continental Congress assembled at Philadelphia.

May 31. Troops in the vicinity of Boston were adopted as the **Continental Army.**

June 15. George Washington (1732–99) appointed commander in chief of the forces. The **Continental Army recruited most of its members from the ranks of young poor, working-class white men; slaves; free blacks; and some women,** who served as cooks, nurses, laun-

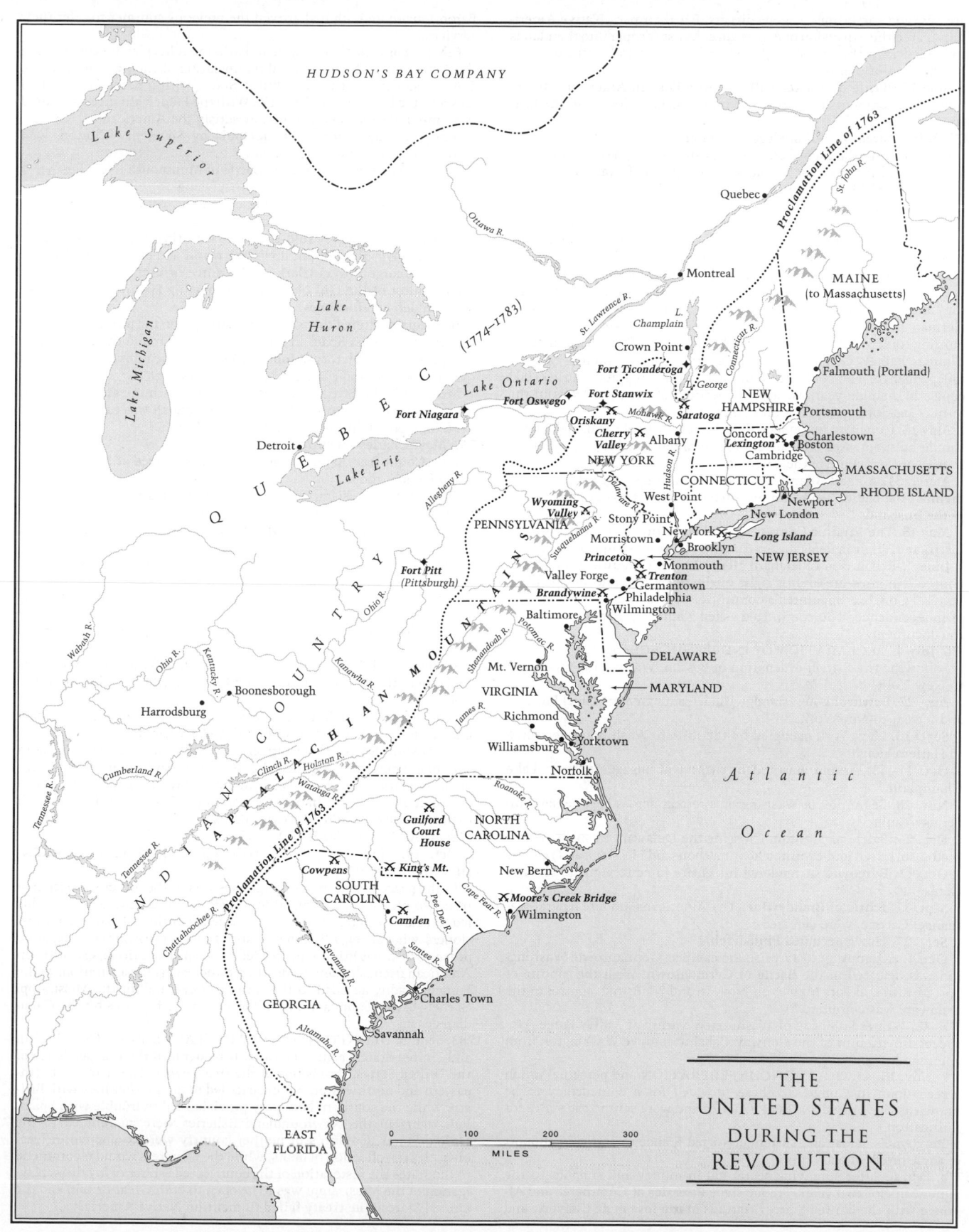

HUDSON'S BAY COMPANY

Lake Superior

Lake Michigan

Lake Huron

Ottawa R.

Quebec

Proclamation Line of 1763

St. John R.

MAINE
(to Massachusetts)

Montreal

St. Lawrence R.

L. Champlain

Crown Point

Falmouth (Portland)

Q U E B E C

(1774–1783)

Lake Ontario

Fort Ticonderoga

L. George

NEW
HAMPSHIRE

Portsmouth

Fort Oswego

Fort Stanwix

Detroit

Lake Erie

Fort Niagara

Mohawk R.

Oriskany

Saratoga

**Cherry
Valley**

Albany

Concord
Lexington
Cambridge

Charlestown
Boston

Connecticut R.

Allegheny R.

NEW YORK

MASSACHUSETTS

CONNECTICUT

RHODE ISLAND

**Wyoming
Valley**

West Point

Delaware R.

Hudson R.

Newport

New London

PENNSYLVANIA

Susquehanna R.

Stony Point

Morristown

Long Island

Fort Pitt
(Pittsburgh)

Princeton
Trenton

New York

Brooklyn

NEW JERSEY

Ohio R.

Valley Forge

Monmouth
Germantown
Philadelphia

Brandywine

Wilmington

Wabash R.

A P P A L A C H I A N   M O U N T A I N S

Baltimore

Potomac R.

DELAWARE

Kanawha R.

Mt. Vernon

MARYLAND

Kentucky R.

Boonesborough

Shenandoah R.

VIRGINIA

Harrodsburg

James R.

Richmond

I N D I A N   C O U N T R Y

Clinch R.

Holston R.

Williamsburg

Yorktown

Cumberland R.

Watauga R.

Norfolk

A t l a n t i c

Roanoke R.

Tennessee R.

Proclamation Line of 1763

**Guilford
Court
House**

NORTH
CAROLINA

O c e a n

Tennessee R.

King's Mt.

New Bern

Cowpens

Pee Dee R.

Cape Fear R.

Moore's Creek Bridge

Chattahoochee R.

SOUTH
CAROLINA

Camden

Santee R.

Wilmington

Savannah R.

GEORGIA

Charles Town

Altamaha R.

Savannah

EAST
FLORIDA

0   100   200   300
MILES

THE
UNITED STATES
DURING THE
REVOLUTION

dresses, and sometimes as gravediggers. For their part, **Native Americans** feared the expansion of American colonists deeper into their lands and sided with the British, although the Oneidas and Tuscaroras did aid the revolutionaries.

June 17. Battle of Bunker Hill, opposite Boston. Americans driven from entrenchments but only after inflicting great losses on the British.

1775, July–March, 17, 1776. Siege of Boston.

1775. The colonies launched an unsuccessful campaign to capture Canada after failing to enlist Canadians' aid against Britain. One force, under **Richard Montgomery,** proceeded by Lake Champlain to Montreal, while another force, under **Benedict Arnold,** advanced by the Kennebec with a view to meeting Montgomery at **Quebeck.** Montgomery was killed before Quebec (Dec. 21). Arnold carried on the unsuccessful siege for the remainder of the winter.

1776, March 4. Occupation of **Dorchester Heights** by Washington.

March 17. Evacuation of Boston by the British forces. Meanwhile the unyielding attitude of the British government, the hiring of German mercenaries, the events on the Canadian frontier, and the burning of Norfolk inflamed public opinion. The appearance of **Thomas Paine's** *Common Sense* crystallized that opinion in favor of independence. The book went through 25 printings and sold 100,000 copies in a single year. Most of the writing of the period was in the form of patriotic pamphlets and essays.

May 15. Congress announced that the authority of the British crown should be suppressed and power of government established under authority of the people of the colonies.

March 31. Abigail Adams wrote to John Adams urging him to "remember the Ladies" and "not put such unlimited power into the hand of the husbands."

May 15. The **Virginia Convention,** called to form a new government, instructed Virginia delegates in Congress to propose independence.

June 7. Resolution of **Richard Henry Lee** in Congress "That these United Colonies are and of right ought to be free and independent States." Congress appointed a committee of five to draft a declaration of independence. The committee asked **Thomas Jefferson** to prepare the document.

1776, July 4. DECLARATION OF INDEPENDENCE adopted.

Following the British evacuation of Boston, Washington proceeded to New York.

Aug. 27. Battle of Long Island, with defeat of General Israel Putnam and retreat to New York.

Sept. 15. New York occupied by the British; Washington retreated to Harlem Heights.

Oct. 11–13. Arnold defeated in two naval engagements on **Lake Champlain.**

Nov. 28. Beginning of Washington's retreat across New Jersey into Pennsylvania.

Dec. 26. Battle of Trenton. Crossing the Delaware by night, Washington surprised and captured about a thousand Hessians at Trenton.

Oct. 17. Burgoyne surrendered his entire force to General Horatio Gates.

Sept. 11. Battle of Brandywine. The Americans, under General Nathanael Greene, were defeated.

Sept. 27. Howe occupied Philadelphia.

Oct. 4. Attempting to surprise the camp at Germantown, Washington was defeated in the **Battle of Germantown.** With the capture of Fort Mifflin and Fort Mercer on Nov. 16 and 20, British control of the Delaware was complete.

1777–78. Winter suffering of Washington's army at **Valley Forge.** Unsuccessful attempt of the **Conway Cabal** to remove Washington from command.

1777, Nov. 15. ARTICLES OF CONFEDERATION and perpetual union agreed upon in Congress. These provided for a confederacy to be known as **the United States of America** and were sent to the states for ratification.

Burgoyne's defeat and surrender stirred France to action in support of the United States.

1778, Feb. 6. After supplying secret aid in money and supplies to the Americans for two years, France signed **treaties of Commerce and Alliance** with the United States. **Marquis Marie Joseph de Lafayette** and

Baron **Johann de Kalb** had arrived the previous summer to offer their services.

Feb. 17. Lord North presented to Parliament his plan for conciliating the Americans, which included renunciation of the right of taxation. Commissioners sent to the United States with a peace offer, which was rejected by Congress (June 17). With the French alliance an assured fact, only independence would now satisfy the Americans.

June 18. Evacuation of Philadelphia by Sir Henry Clinton, who started to march across New Jersey.

June 28. Washington won the **Battle of Monmouth** (New Jersey).

July 4. Wyoming massacre in Pennsylvania.

Nov. 11. Massacre of Cherry Valley in New York.

1779–80. With lack of rations and pay several months in arrears, **Pennsylvania and New Jersey soldiers staged a mutiny** in efforts to improve conditions. Washington put down the revolt and executed its leaders.

1779, Feb. George Rogers Clark, with a force of Virginians, completed the conquest of the Old Northwest, capturing Hamilton, the British commander, at **Vincennes.**

June. Spain entered the war against Britain, on the promise of France that it would assist Spain in recovering Gibraltar and the Floridas.

Sept. 23. Naval victory of **John Paul Jones** of the *Bonhomme Richard* over the *Serapis* and the *Countess of Scarborough.*

Meanwhile the British had decided to try, with the aid of loyalists, to overrun the Southern states. In 1778 **Savannah** was captured and in 1780 Sir Henry Clinton laid siege to Charleston.

1780, May. Charleston surrendered.

July. Count Jean Baptiste de Rochambeau arrived at Newport with 6,000 French troops.

Despite brave resistance of Thomas Sumter and Francis Marion, South Carolina was overrun by the British.

Aug. 16. In the **Battle of Camden,** Gates was defeated by General Charles Cornwallis.

Aug. 18. Sumter's force was defeated by Tarleton, and Marion retreated to North Carolina.

Sept. 23. A plot of **Benedict Arnold** to surrender West Point to Sir Henry Clinton was revealed through capture of the British agent **Major John André.** Arnold escaped, but on **Oct. 2, 1781,** André was hanged as a spy.

Women in Philadelphia proposed to create a **national women's organization** to coordinate their fund-raising efforts to support the troops.

Sept. 8. Battle of Eutaw; defeat of American general Nathanael Greene, followed by retreat of British to Charleston.

Meanwhile British forces under Cornwallis were concentrating in Virginia, where they fortified themselves at **Yorktown.** While Cornwallis remained inactive, Washington, Lafayette, and Rochambeau closed in on him at Williamsburg, and Count François de Grasse, with the French fleet, entered Chesapeake Bay.

Sept. 30–Oct. 19. Siege of Yorktown.

Oct. 19. Finding himself bottled up, **CORNWALLIS SURRENDERED** with 7,000 men.

In the peace negotiations, Vergennes was in the difficult position of trying to please both of his allies, Spain and the United States. This led to delay, which aroused the impatience of the American commissioners, who, disregarding their instructions not to negotiate a separate peace with Great Britain, proceeded to do so. The British, eager to win American friendship and trade, thereby defeating the aspirations of the French, readily acceded to the American demand for the Mississippi as the western boundary and full rights in the fisheries off the Canadian coast.

1783, Sept. 3. DEFINITIVE TREATY OF PEACE between Great Britain and United States, signed at **Paris.** It **recognized the independence of the United States.** Provisions of the treaty with respect to the northeastern and northwestern boundaries led to later difficulties with Britain, while the southern boundary provision led to trouble with Spain. Full rights in the Newfoundland fisheries were guaranteed to the United States. Creditors of neither country were to encounter legal obstacles to collection of debts, while the Congress would recommend to the states the restoration of the confiscated estates of loyalists. Navigation of the Mississippi was to be open to both Great Britain and the United States. **The treaty failed to mention Native Americans.**

1783–87. THE CRITICAL PERIOD OF AMERICAN HISTORY. The **Articles of Confederation** had gone into effect in 1781, and with the achievement of independence in 1783 the young nation found itself in a difficult economic situation, treated as a foreign people by Britain as well as by other European countries and denied participation of their ships in the trade of the British West Indies, so important in their economy before the revolution. Far-reaching economic dislocations resulted, producing a deep depression in 1784–85, from which the country began to recover in 1787. The Articles of Confederation received the blame and were widely believed to be inadequate. The economic situation was aggravated by paper money experiments of the states and by the inability of Congress to raise an adequate revenue. **This period also witnessed the settlement of loyalists from the United States in Canada.** Thousands of these established themselves in **New Brunswick (separated from Nova Scotia, Aug. 16, 1784) and in Upper Canada. The British government assigned lands to them (100 acres to each head of a family and 50 acres to each member) and spent some $30 million in equipping them.** The immigration gave Canada a more English composition and aroused sentiment of the English settlers against the Quebec Act.

1783. Newburgh Conspiracy. Alexander Hamilton and Robert Morris failed to get Washington's support for a military takeover of the government.

1787. The **NORTHWEST ORDINANCE** enacted, providing for the government of the Northwest. The region was to be divided into not less than three and not more than five districts, which, after passing through a territorial or colonial stage, should be admitted to statehood. This **principle of coordinancy,** or ultimate statehood, became the basic and distinguishing feature of the American colonial system of the 19th century. Slavery and involuntary servitude were prohibited in the area **and land was provided for public education.**

1787. Shays Rebellion. Under the leadership of **Daniel Shays,** discontented and indebted farmers in western Massachusetts blocked courts from executing foreclosures on farms and broke into local jails and released debtors before **Governor James Bowdoin** placed 4,000 troops in the field and ended the revolt.

1787, May. The CONSTITUTIONAL CONVENTION assembled at Philadelphia. The inability of Congress to raise revenue, the outbreaks of disorder, and the obstructions to commerce resulted in an increasing desire for a more perfect government. Commissioners from Virginia and Maryland met at **Mount Vernon** in 1785 to consider the possibility of a uniform commercial code. This conference made clear the need for wider cooperation, so Virginia invited all the states to send delegates to a convention at **Annapolis** (1786). This convention was attended by delegates from only five states, who proposed a convention to meet at Philadelphia in May 1787. Congress officially called such a convention to convene on May 5. All states except Rhode Island were represented.

1787, Sept. 17. After four months of labor, the **Constitution was signed** by the delegates present. The document was sent to the states for ratification, with the provision that it should become operative upon the acceptance of nine states.

1788, June. Ratification by New Hampshire, the ninth state, placed the Constitution in operation. In several states the anti-Federalists exacted promises of amendments in return for unconditional ratification. **The Constitution represented a series of compromises:** states could not issue their own currency; slaves were counted as three-fifths of a person toward Southern representation in Congress; Congress could not enact export duties on cash staples produced by the South, and it could not legislate against the international slave trade for 20 years. *(To p. 599)*

V. THE MODERN PERIOD, 1789–1914

A. GLOBAL AND COMPARATIVE DIMENSIONS

(From p. 283)

Global relationships changed significantly during the 19th century. Western European states and world-views came to dominate and frequently to control directly most of the rest of the world. In this way, the transformation of western European societies in the previous centuries extended to much of the rest of the world. The new patterns of global relationships can be seen in two very broad areas: (1) the West's power over the rest of the world in military, economic, and political spheres, and to some extent the cultural spheres as well, and (2) the intensification of international and interstate relationships in diplomatic and political terms by the beginning of the 20th century.

1. EUROPEAN GLOBAL DOMINATION, 1800–1914

The changing relationships involved in the growing global dominance of Western societies can be seen in three important developments: (1) Western imperialist expansion, (2) the spread of industrialism, and (3) the development of modern state systems in all of the major regions of the globe.

a. DEVELOPMENTS IN MAJOR EMPIRES

During the 19th century, major European empires expanded (especially the British, French, and Russian empires, along with the new United States) while older empires, both European and non-European, experienced significant losses.

1800–70. BRITISH EMPIRE. Following the conflicts of the Napoleonic era, the British Empire emerged as the strongest global imperial force, with different manifestations. **SETTLEMENT COLONIES** were consolidated in **Canada, Australia, and New Zealand,** and they received increasing rights of self-rule within the British imperial system. These rights were defined for Canada following a major rebellion in 1837 by the **Union Act (1840)** and the **British North America Act (1867),** for Australia by the **Australia Colonies Government Act (1850),** and for New Zealand by the Constitution of 1852. As they emerged as virtually independent commonwealths in the 20th century, they, along with the United States, were basically parts of the extended European world. **INDIRECT CONTROL** through commercial and naval domination was the basis for British imperial authority in many parts of the world. The **Ottoman Empire** was protected by British policies from Russian, Austrian, and French expansion as well as from internal challengers like **Muhammad Ali** in Egypt (p. 543) (who had revolted and invaded Syria in 1831), and British commercial interests expanded in the region. Britain similarly became the dominant force within **Iran,** ruled in the 19th century by the **Qajar dynasty.** British domination of foreign trade in **China** was confirmed by British victory in the **First British War** of 1841–42 (often called the **Opium War**) (p. 561) and the **Treaty of Nanking** (1842). British naval power similarly ensured British domination in coastal regions of the Indian Ocean and **Africa. DIRECT IMPERIAL RULE** emerged as an important style of domination in **INDIA** by the middle of the 19th century, when control by the **East India Company** was formally replaced by making India a Crown colony. Direct imperial rule was, however, only one of many different forms of British world power in the 19th century.

1800–70. FRENCH EMPIRE. France had lost much of its global empire in the world wars of the 18th century and the final defeats in the Napoleonic era. In the first half of the 19th century, France reemerged as a major global force, both through its growing economic power and its military forces. It was Britain's major rival for influence in the **Mediterranean** region and had expanding commercial and cultural influences in the Middle East. France also developed settlements, trade stations, and military posts in **Senegal** and elsewhere along the coasts of West Africa and Central Africa. In the **Indian Ocean** basin and Asia, France gradually expanded in control in Madagascar and other island areas and, by 1874, gained full control of **Indochina.** Direct French rule in North Africa began in 1830 with the French invasion of **Algeria,** where European settlement was encouraged.

1800–70. OTHER OVERSEAS EMPIRES. The other major European overseas empires remained relatively stable or declined. The **DUTCH** consolidated their control in the islands of Southeast Asia, where they developed a system of direct colonial rule by the end of the century. The **Portuguese Empire in Africa** expanded inland from coastal trading settlements, especially after the formal suppression of the slave trade in 1836 transformed the nature of commerce in Angola and Mozambique. The commercial ports of Goa in India and Macao in China remained under Portuguese control, but **Brazil** was lost in the Latin American wars of independence. These wars also brought an end to most of the **SPANISH EMPIRE** in the Americas, and Spain was only a minor global force by the middle of the century.

b. INTENSIFIED IMPERIAL COMPETITION

Late in the 19th century, the expanding empires engaged in major competitions for influence and control throughout the world. This global struggle was part of the partition and disintegration of some older major empires, like those of the Ottomans and the Chinese. In **AFRICA** the competition resulted in the direct European military occupation and control of virtually the entire continent by 1914. In North Africa, **Egypt** was occupied by Great Britain (1882), French protectorates were proclaimed in **Tunisia** (1881) and **Morocco** (1912), and Italy claimed control of **Libya** (1911) (p. 551). In Africa by 1914, older European empires maintained small but expanded enclaves, the **Spanish** in Morocco, **Río de Oro,** and Río Muni, and the **Portuguese** in Guinea, **Angola,** and **Mozambique.** The **BRITISH** and the **FRENCH** empires gained the largest share, with a number of French colonies established in West Africa and Equatorial Africa as well as Madagascar, and British control established in **Nigeria,** southern and eastern Africa, and, through a nominally joint control with Egypt, in **Sudan.** By the end of the 19th century, **new Western imperial powers** also had important colonies in Africa. The **German Empire** won control of Togo and Cameroons in West Africa and established colonial control in **Tanganyika** and **Southwest Africa.** Italy gained control over Eritrea and much of **Somaliland** in East Africa, and **King Leopold of Belgium** took control of the Congo River basin with the creation of the **CONGO FREE STATE** in 1885 (p. 474). In addition, **Liberia** was created in 1822 as a colony for freed slaves returning from the United States, and although it was nominally independent, it remained an economic colony of the United States. By 1914, Ethiopia was the only noncolonial area, and it would be conquered and briefly controlled by Italy in the 1930s.

1800–1914. EMERGING AMERICAN EMPIRE. In the Western Hemisphere, the new United States began major continental expansion. Vast territories were gained by treaty and purchase arrangements with European powers and subsequent military conquest of indigenous peoples in those areas. This was the method of acquisition of the **Louisiana territories** from France (1803), **Florida** from Spain (1810–19), **Oregon** from Great Britain (1846), and **Alaska** from Russia (1867), whereas **Texas, California,** and the rest of the southwestern region were gained as a result of the U.S. victory in a war with **Mexico** (1846–48). This expansion was temporarily interrupted by the **American Civil War** (1861–65), but in the second half of the 19th century, the United States began important overseas expansion. Some of this involved extension of the American economic and political sphere of influence, as in the beginning of relations with **Japan** initiated by **Matthew Perry** in 1854, and growing American interests in China. The growing domination by the United States of many independent states in **Latin America** led to temporary military occupations in support of U.S. economic interests in many places, like **Nicaragua** (1912). The U.S. also gained direct control of overseas territories, including **Hawaii** (1898) and the Virgin Islands (1917), and, as a result of the **SPANISH-AMERICAN WAR (1898)**, the U.S. established control in the **Philippines, Puerto Rico,** and Guam. By the end of World War I, the United States had emerged as one of the major global empires as well as a powerful economic force.

c. MAJOR LAND-BASED EMPIRES

During the 19th century, several European land-based empires emerged as great powers, while large empires in Asia lost territories and influence. However, all of these empires came to an end during **World War I,** either emerging in significantly different forms or disappearing as political entities.

RUSSIAN EMPIRE. In the final years of the Napoleonic era, Russia began a major era of expansion, winning control of areas in the **Caucasus** in a war with **Persia** (1804–13) and of **Finland** in a war with Sweden (1808–9), as well as building forts in **Alaska** in North America. Expansion in Europe was limited, but the establishment of independent states in former Ottoman territories, especially **Serbia (1817)** (p. 518) and **Bulgaria (1878)** represented expansion of Russian influence. Complete control in the Caucasus was gained with the conquests of **Daghistan** (1859), **Circassia** (1864), and **Kars** (1878) (p. 510). The largest expansions were in the east (p. 509), with the conquests and annexations of **Kazakhistan** by 1854, **Uzbekistan** (1856–76), and **Turkmenistan** (1868–85). Expansion in the Pacific northeastern territories was completed with the ceding by **China** of territories north of the Amur River in the **Treaties of Aigun (1858)** and **Peking (1860)** (p. 510). By World War I, the Russian Empire was the largest in the world, but during that war the tsarist system of rule was overthrown in the **Russian Revolution of 1917.** Baltic and eastern European areas were lost, but imperial control of all of the Asian territories was maintained, although in a form called the Union of Soviet Socialist Republics (USSR).

PRUSSIAN EMPIRE. The steady expansion of Prussia during the 19th century is a major dynamic of European history, but Prussia did not emerge as a major global power until after the **UNIFICATION OF GERMANY** under Prussia led by **Otto von Bismarck** and the **Hohenzollern** dynasty and the formal establishment of the **German Empire** under **William I** in 1871. The new empire actively sought territorial expansion and spheres of influence. By 1914, Germany had gained control in Africa of **Togo** and **Cameroons**(1884), Tanganyika (1885), and Southwest Africa (1890); had won concessions in China and economic influence in the Middle East; and was one of the major global naval powers. Its defeat in World War I brought an end to this empire, and it was replaced by a purely European state of considerably reduced size.

AUSTRO-HUNGARIAN EMPIRE. During the 19th century, the Habsburg Empire did not expand significantly, although its influence grew in southeastern Europe as **Ottoman** power declined, and it gained control of **Bosnia** in 1878. The Habsburg rulers faced serious internal challenges within their multinational empire, and the imperial system was reorganized as a **dual monarchy** of Austria and Hungary. Although this did not resolve the challenges posed by growing nationalist movements, it allowed the empire to survive major defeats by France and Prussia, and revolutionary threats, especially in 1848. It was not until

the defeat in World War I that the empire disappeared and was replaced by a cluster of small, nationally defined states.

DECLINING ASIAN EMPIRES. The older major land-based Asian empires experienced serious losses during the 19th century. The **Mughal Empire** in India came to a formal end with the establishment of direct British colonial rule in 1858.

The **OTTOMAN EMPIRE** undertook major modernizing structural reforms throughout the century, beginning with the attempt to establish a "New System" by **Selim III** at the end of the 18th century, and reaching a culmination in the regime established by the **Young Turk Revolution** in 1908 (p. 533). Despite significant changes, the Ottoman Empire experienced a steady loss of territories to major European states and to nationalist movements supported by various European powers. Nationalist revolts led to the establishment of independent **Serbia** (1817) and **Greece** (1830), and international agreements in 1878, 1908, and 1913 resulted in the loss of all of the rest of the Ottoman territories in the Balkans except for a small area along the Sea of Marmara. European conquests between 1830 and 1912 took all Ottoman territories in North Africa, along with Cyprus (Britain, 1878). The Ottomans joined the losing alliance in World War I, and the empire formally came to an end with the peace settlement, which split the new Republic of Turkey from the Arab territories (p. 753).

The **CHINESE EMPIRE** experienced a steady loss of control within its domain as the European powers and the United States established spheres of influence. The empire lost control of **Taiwan** (1874) and **Korea** (1885) to Japan and territories in the Pacific northeast to Russia in 1858–60. The Chinese defeat in the **SINO-JAPANESE WAR (1894–95)** showed the weakness of the empire in the face of foreign power. The empire also experienced a series of major revolts, which weakened its internal power as well. The **Boxer Revolt** (1899–1901) showed strong opposition to foreign influence and reform efforts, but it was crushed by a combined military force of foreign troops. The empire came to a formal end with the **CHINESE REVOLUTION (1911–13),** which forced the abdication of the emperor and the establishment of the **Chinese Republic.**

d. SPREAD OF MODERN INDUSTRIALISM

The transformation of societies as a result of the **INDUSTRIAL REVOLUTION** began in **England** in the 18th century. The industrialization of society spread from Great Britain to most of western Europe in the first half of the 19th century and then to the rest of Europe and, in differing ways, to much of the rest of the world by 1914. Industrialization developed along with increasing **urbanization,** growing commercial ties, and improvements in means of transportation and communication.

The **IRON AND STEEL INDUSTRY** was a key to the process of industrialization and reflects its spread and development in the 19th century. Although ironworking originated in ancient times, 18th century improvements in production processes of cast iron and wrought iron made iron a more important product for growing modern industries, and it became a key to modern industrialization. In 1820, world output of **pig iron** was about 1 million tons, whereas in 1910, it was almost 65 million tons. The industry was transformed by new production processes that created steel for many different uses. The **BESSEMER PROCESS** (1856) for steel production, developed by Henry Bessemer, was a key step in this process, followed by the development of **open hearth furnaces** by William and Frederick Siemens (1864–68) in Britain and the construction of the first furnaces for continuous steel production by Benjamin Talbot in Pennsylvania (1899). The modern iron and steel industry primarily developed in **Great Britain,** and the British industry dominated the world markets for many years, with British output of pig iron exceeding all of the rest of the world's until 1871. However, as global industrialization occurred, British production of pig iron was surpassed by the **United States** in 1890, **Germany** in 1904, and the **Soviet Union** in 1931. The great coal and iron ore resources of the **United States** allowed the American iron and steel industry to become the world's largest by the early 20th century. However, important steel industries had also begun to emerge by that time in **Japan** and **China,** and in India under the leadership of the **TATA FAMILY.**

TRANSPORTATION and **COMMUNICATION** developments were important aspects of the global processes of industrialization. **RAILROADS** made bulk transportation cheaper and easier, and railroad construction played an important role in industrialization. The first railroads were built in **Great Britain** in the first quarter of the 19th century, and the first railroad was built in **France** in 1828. By 1850, rail networks had been established across western Europe and in the eastern United States. The first railroads were built in **India** in the 1850s, and in **China** and **Japan** in the 1870s. Great transcontinental projects were developed late in the 19th century, beginning with the completion in 1869 of the **Union Pacific–Central Pacific line** crossing the United States, and in 1885 with the **Canadian Pacific Line** extending across the Rocky Mountains to the Pacific in Canada. Construction of the **TRANS-SIBERIAN RAILROAD** began in 1891, and the line from Moscow to Vladivostok was completed in 1916, making it the longest rail line in the world. Other major continental rail schemes were planned but only partially completed. The **Berlin–Baghdad Railroad** was an important scheme for the expansion of German economic influence in the Ottoman Empire, and much of it had been constructed by 1914. British imperial aspirations in Africa were expressed in the 1889 slogan **"Cape-to-Cairo,"** which suggested that a band of colonial possessions be linked by a great railroad system.

CANALS were also important in the transportation systems of emerging industrial societies; in fact, the construction of two major canals transformed the patterns of global maritime movements. The **SUEZ CANAL,** linking the Mediterranean Sea and the Red Sea (and ultimately the Indian Ocean) was completed in 1869 and reduced the need for west-east shipping to go around the African continent. It changed military and commercial shipping patterns and made Egypt a major global strategic location. The **PANAMA CANAL** was opened in 1914 and transformed strategic and commercial shipping in the Western Hemisphere. It joined the Atlantic and Pacific shipping routes in Central America, eliminating the need to go around South America (or through the Arctic regions).

URBANIZATION accompanied the industrialization of societies, and the proportion of populations living in cities grew as societies were transformed. At the end of the 18th century, throughout the world the overwhelming majority of all populations lived outside of cities. In **Great Britain,** the proportion of the population living in urban areas was 25 percent in 1831, became more than 50 percent in 1851, and had reached 77 percent by 1901. In **Prussia,** and then **Germany,** the transition period was longer, beginning with 26 percent in 1816 and becoming more than 50 percent in 1900, whereas **France's** population was still slightly below 50 percent urban at the end of the 19th century. In the later industrial powers, populations of both **Japan** and **the United States** became more than half urban around 1920, whereas **Russia's** population remained more rural, only 13 percent urban in 1900.

e. DEVELOPMENT OF MODERN POLITICAL SYSTEMS

During the 19th century, outside Europe's colonies, states and political systems were increasingly organized along the lines of nation-states with constitutions rather than as dynastic sovereign monarchies. The limitation of monarchical power through instituting **constitutional monarchies** was an important part of this process. Another important development was the establishment of **republics,** with recognition of the need for consent or participation by the people, as an alternative to monarchies. The development of **nationalist consciousness,** the demand for and writing of **constitutions** as definitions of new state systems, and the creation of **republics** were interacting parts of the transformation of the political context in the Western world, and the spread of these ideals throughout the world in the 19th century represented important aspects of the expansion of the West.

1789–1917. REVOLUTIONARY TRANSFORMATIONS. The 19th century was marked by major efforts to transform political systems and societies. **THE FRENCH REVOLUTION** (p. 432), beginning in 1789, was a major starting point, bringing an end to the old dynastic political system in France and inspiring revolutions elsewhere. Throughout the century, major episodes of revolution, often beginning in France, influenced the development of political systems, inducing even conserv-

ative forces to establish constitutional regimes that either established republics or set limits on the powers of monarchs. **REVOLUTIONS OF 1830 AND 1848** (p. 465) were especially important times of political change. Major system-defining revolutions and constitutional reforms transformed the nature of the **Austro-Hungarian Empire** in 1848–49 and 1867 and the **Russian Empire** in 1864, 1905–6, and finally in 1917. Outside of Europe, such changes took place in the **Ottoman Empire** in 1839, 1876, and 1908; in **Japan** in 1868 and 1889; and in **China** in 1911.

1776–1914. NATIONAL INDEPENDENCE MOVEMENTS. Many of the states of the modern world were created as a result of revolutions and movements of national liberation opposing control by large multinational states. These movements exhibited an awareness of identity as a **nation** rather than simply being revolts against rule by foreigners. The **AMERICAN REVOLUTION (1776–83)** (p. 414) ended British control in thirteen North American colonies and resulted in the creation of the **United States.** The new nation consciously identified its political system as a **republic,** in contrast to the British monarchy, and defined its political system after achieving independence in a **constitution** written by a representative constituent assembly. The American experience was an important beginning for the combination of nationalism and constitutionalism, and it contrasted with other late-18th-century revolts against foreign rule, which reflected essential premodern styles. The revolt of **Tupac Amarú** in Peru (1780–82) (p. 404) was a revolt (by Native American forces, in contrast to later revolts in South America) against forced labor and Spanish rule. Similarly, the independence of **Egypt** from **Ottoman** rule proclaimed by **Ali Bey al-Kabir** (r. 1768–73) was an act of a military commander rather than a nationalist. However, by the early 19th century, a growing proportion of major revolts represented combinations of nationalism and constitutionalism.

LATIN AMERICAN WARS OF INDEPENDENCE (p. 622) combined efforts to define independent political life in republican constitutions with growing nationalist sensitivities. In **MEXICO,** a peasant revolt led by **Miguel Hidalgo y Costilla** and, after his death in 1811, by **José Maria Morelos,** led to a declaration of independence in 1813 and promulgation of a constitution in 1814. Attempts to establish an imperial or constitutional monarchy in 1822–23 under **Agustin de Iturbide and Archduke Maximilian of Austria,** with the aid of French troops in 1863–67, were unsuccessful. Mexico was ruled by a series of presidents who sometimes assumed dictatorial powers under a succession of republican constitutions. The war with the United States in the 1840s and French intervention in the 1860s helped to strengthen Mexican nationalist sentiments. The climax of these developments was the **Mexican Revolution,** which began in 1911 and overthrew a presidential dictator. The revolutionary **constitution of 1917** provided a nationalist and socially radical foundation for 20th-century Mexican politics. Similar combinations of nationalism, constitutionalism, and republicanism provided the basis for the rest of the countries in Latin America that gained their independence from Spain and Portugal in the 19th century. By World War I, all independent countries in the Western Hemisphere were constitutional republics with varying degrees of nationalist identity.

EUROPEAN NATIONAL LIBERATION MOVEMENTS. In the multinational states of Europe, many movements of national liberation developed. Some were successful in creating independent states, and most of these state systems were defined by modern constitutions, but they were more frequently constructed as constitutional monarchies than as republics. A major factor in the break with the earlier dynastic state systems was the disruption caused by the **French Revolution** and **NAPOLEON's** conquests. In the conquered territories, Napoleon created new political systems, which, even if they did not last, overturned political institutions and traditions. In addition, local responses to the French conquerors gave strong impetus to the development of nationalist sentiments. Resistance to the French invasion of **SPAIN** strengthened a sense of national identity. Leaders of the resistance convened a **Cortes,** or assembly, in 1810 in Cádiz, and promulgated the **Constitution of 1812,** which affirmed the right of the people to determine the laws within a constitutionally limited monarchy. Although it was never fully implemented, its radical idealism meant that constitutionalism would be a major issue throughout modern Spanish history, and it influenced the drafting of constitutions elsewhere, especially in

Latin America. During the 19th century, a sequence of constitutions and conflicts defined the evolution of the Spanish political system, which remained basically a constitutional monarchy, with a brief republican period (1873–74) (p. 495). Napoleon's conquests in **ITALY** resulted in the establishment of short-lived republics in a number of areas. After the defeat of Napoleon, the **kingdom of Sardinia** played a leading role in developing the constitutional political system of the emerging unified Italy. The **unification of Italy** was completed as a constitutional monarchy in 1870. **PRUSSIA** provided a similar basis for the unification of Germany in 1871, with the important development of a constitutional monarchy with strong powers reserved for the emperor. The conservative German constitution provided a model for conservative constitutionalists elsewhere and had some influence in the articulation of the **Meiji Constitution of 1889** in Japan. **BELGIUM** provided another important nationalist, constitutional experience. In the Napoleonic peace settlement, Belgium was included in the kingdom of the Netherlands, but a nationalist revolt in 1830 led to Belgium's independence and the establishment of a constitutional monarchy whose structure influenced constitutionalists in the Middle East later in the century. **OTTOMAN** territories in the Balkans also experienced nationalist revolts. **Serbia** began a successful revolt in 1804 and gradually expanded its territories and independence throughout the century, becoming an internationally recognized constitutional monarchy in 1882. **Greece** had a successful war for independence (1821–29) and emerged as a constitutional monarchy as well.

GLOBAL CONSTITUTIONAL MOVEMENTS. In major states outside of Europe, there were significant efforts to create constitutional regimes. In the **OTTOMAN EMPIRE**, constitutionalists succeeded in getting the promulgation of a constitution in 1876, although it was quickly suspended by the sultan, **Abdul Hamid II**, and was not fully put into force until the **Young Turk Revolution 1908.** In **PERSIA**, nationalists and liberals combined to force the shah to promulgate a constitution in 1906. In **JAPAN**, the Meiji Constitution of 1889 defined the political framework for the modernization efforts of the Japanese Empire. In **CHINA**, reform efforts were weak, and it was only with the revolution of 1911 and the establishment of the Chinese Republic that China promulgated a constitution.

Constitutions, revolutions, and republics throughout the globe by the time of World War I showed the spread of European political models in the 19th century.

f. CULTURAL PATTERNS

European cultural influence spread less rapidly than its diplomatic, economic, and political influence. **Christian missions** fanned out to Asia and Africa in the late 19th century, from both western Europe and the United States. Only small minorities of Asians converted, but in some Pacific islands the impact was greater. A larger minority of Africans began to be attracted to Christianity by 1900.

The **influence of European secular culture** was in many ways greater. **European nationalism** helped shape nationalist movements in Latin America, in the Arab lands and Turkey, and in India. **European sports,** like English soccer football, began to spread widely around 1900, as did new cultural technologies such as filmmaking. **European science** gained attention from intellectuals in various parts of Asia and Latin America, although Europe and the United States essentially shared innovation in science and technology (p. 424). **Contacts with other parts of the world also affected European culture;** visual artists, particularly, gained inspiration from African and East Asian artistic traditions.

2. INTENSIFICATIONS OF GLOBAL INTERNATIONAL AND ECONOMIC RELATIONS, 1860–1914

The period was characterized by the domination of global international relations by European powers. By the same token, **world diplomacy took on new meaning,** as clashes in various parts of the world led to negotiations and alliances, sometimes including non-European powers as well. **International conferences,** dominated by the European great powers, periodically tried to resolve disputes in the Balkans, Africa, the Middle East, and elsewhere; **conference diplomacy** on a world scale was another important diplomatic innovation. European negotiations also formulated some new **international agreements** concerning the conduct of war, international law, and global facilities such as postal service. Finally, the intensification of global relations also included **growing international commerce,** dominated by Europe and the United States but with growing impact on local economies almost everywhere.

a. INTERNATIONAL AGREEMENTS

During the second half of the 19th century, not only governments but also private organizations formed a growing number of international arrangements. Most of these centered on pacts among European countries, but North America and to some extent other areas were drawn in.

1851. International commercial exhibit at London's new Crystal Palace, the first of a regular series of international exhibitions stretching into the 20th century. Major subsequent world's fairs, to 1914: Paris, 1855; Philadelphia, 1876; Sydney, 1879–80; New Orleans, 1884; Antwerp, 1885; Paris, 1889; Chicago, 1893; Budapest, 1896; Brussels, 1897; Paris, 1900; St. Louis, 1904.

The International Statistical Congress began meeting to standardize statistical practices of the European governments.

1863. An informal committee met to prepare rights for neutral parties to aid the wounded during wars. The **RED CROSS** was created as a voluntary, noncombatant organization to assist the wounded. The International Committee of the Red Cross was established in Geneva.

The 1864 **GENEVA CONVENTION** was drafted to establish rules for the treatment of prisoners of war.

1864. Karl Marx organized the **International Workingman's Association** in London. It collapsed amid internal divisions in 1876.

1865. International Telegraphic Union.

1873. International Meteorological Organization.

1874. Universal Postal Union set up regulations for international postal delivery.

1889. The **Second International,** a loose federation of unions and socialist parties from Europe and North America, was formed in Paris.

1896. The first modern **Olympic Games** were held in Athens, reviving the classical Greek Olympic tradition on a potentially worldwide basis. It was held every four years until World War I, with participation from Europe, North America, and British Dominions.

1899 and 1907. Hague Conferences set up Permanent Court of Arbitration (p. 423).

1904. Fédération Internationale de Football Associations—an international body to coordinate soccer (association) football.

1913. National amateur athletic organizations created the International Amateur Athletic Federation (IAAF), involving Europe, North America, and the British Dominions.

b. THE REDEFINITION OF THE WORLD ECONOMY

Throughout most of the 19th century, the **amount and importance of international trade** increased steadily. The lead of Great Britain and then other parts of western Europe and the United States in industrialization heightened the **economic imbalance** in international trade. Western nations dominated complex manufacturing, shipping, and the great commercial companies; many other areas traded at considerable disadvantage. Western insistence on opening all regions to their trade led to the Opium War with China and the intimidation of Japan.

During the first half of the 19th century, British industrial (particularly textile) exports flooded markets in parts of Europe, Latin America, and India. The result was **massive deindustrialization of traditional textile producers.** Tens of thousands of women weavers and spinners were displaced in Latin America. Hundreds of thousands lost work in India.

Western entrepreneurs and skilled workers set up some **pilot factories** in different parts of the world. In 1843 British textile machinery was imported to Russia. Westerners also set up steamship services on rivers (1820, Volga River) and railroads (1838, Cuba, Havana to Guines; 1851, Russia, St. Petersburg to Moscow) in Russia, Latin America, and elsewhere. These developments did not lead to more general industrialization.

Western industrialization also spurred the **production of commercial crops** and products in other parts of the world. Brazil expanded sugar and coffee production, importing steam engines for processing (1815, first steam-driven sugar mill in Brazil). Nomadic herders in eastern Turkey were pressed by British and French agents to increase production of raw wool. Economic reforms in Egypt included rapid expansion of cotton production, encouraged by Britain. The spread of cotton plantations and ginning in the American South was part of this process.

New shipping technology developed around the mid-19th century. The first transatlantic steamer (the *Savannah*, 1818) sailed from Liverpool to Boston but ran out of coal, finishing by sail; the first full Atlantic steam crossing was achieved by the British-built Dutch *Curaçao*, 1827. In 1840, regular transatlantic steamship service began with the **Cunard line** (founded by Samuel Cunard, 1787–1865) and its four steamships. In 1848, 10 million tons of goods were handled by oceanic sailing ships, and only 750,000 tons in steamships. Expansion from 1850 was rapid, with many Western nations establishing steamship lines. The Suez Canal, and later, the Panama Canal, furthered this trend.

Underwater telegraph cables connected England and Europe, 1851; England and the United States, 1866; England and India, 1870; England and Australia, 1871. Communication time was cut from several weeks to literally minutes. In 1891, the first underwater long-distance telephone cable linked England and France.

Growing international economic links triggered the first **modern economic depression,** in 1856–57. Induced by several bank failures in the United States, rather than by bad harvests (the traditional cause), the brief but sharp slump spread throughout western Europe. Depressions in the mid-1870s and thereafter had international ramifications, particularly among the industrial nations.

After 1870 the global impact of the industrial West increased. A growing number of areas and a growing portion of the economies of these areas were pressed to provide low-cost exports, while importing from Europe and the United States more advanced equipment (including rail lines and rolling stock) and certain luxury goods (such as French fashions). In Latin America, the expansion of coffee production, cultivation of hemp and manufacture of rope in the Yucatán (Mexico), the growth of Peruvian guano output for fertilizer, the spread of foreign-owned copper mines in Chile, and the development (often foreign owned) of tropical fruit production in Central America are all examples of this expansion. Established sectors like sugar and tobacco also grew. More land and more workers were involved in this commercial export sector. On the other side of this equation, by 1910, 57 percent of Mexican imports involved Western-made equipment. Western appetites for Middle Eastern rugs caused the expansion of this traditional industry in the Ottoman Empire, involving thousands of new workers. By the 1890s some factories were established to make cheap carpets, with a mixture of Western and Ottoman ownership. The expansion of Japanese silk production, with low-paid women workers, fit Japan into the export economy while providing earnings to purchase equipment. By the 1890s Africa was beginning to be drawn into the network, with expansion of mines in South Africa and the Belgian Congo. But the main impact on African agriculture came after 1914.

Western companies also began to set up **manufacturing branches in various parts of the world.** Some French textile firms had branch operations in Rhode Island and Latin America by the 1830s. Again, the pattern expanded after 1870. **Singer sewing machine company,** of the United States, set up factories in many countries, including Russia. German electrical and chemical producers, American agricultural equipment producers, and other companies did the same. Operations of this sort, going beyond trade to actual manufacture, constituted the **origins of the modern multinational corporation.**

c. INTERNATIONAL DIPLOMACY

European conflicts over spheres of influence in Asia, Africa, and the Middle East and efforts by non-European states to maintain at least some degree of independence were the central ingredients in international relations between 1870 and 1914.

1869. OPENING OF THE SUEZ CANAL reoriented imperial strategic thinking and gave added importance to the Ottoman Empire in international diplomacy.

1871. Conference of London redefined Russian rights in the Black Sea.

1875–78. Insurrections in Bosnia and Bulgaria (p. 530) led to Ottoman intervention and diplomatic tensions involving Russia and Austria. Negotiations between these two powers were supplemented by international conferences. In Dec. 1876, the **Constantinople Conference** featured British efforts to negotiate a Balkan settlement, but the Ottoman leaders rejected all proposals. Russia declared war on the Ottomans in 1877, which roused British opposition (eager to protect the region from any great-power dominance that might threaten its route to India) and German attempts to prevent a more general conflagration. This led to Bismarck's arranging of the **Berlin Congress** (June 13–July 13, 1878) (p. 531), the **first great international settlement conference in the new imperialist age.** The conference rearranged control of the Balkans, granted Russia territory in Central Asia, gave France the green light to take over Tunisia, and granted Cyprus to Britain. Most European powers gained, in sum, at the expense of the Ottoman Empire.

1882, July 11. Bombardment of Alexandria, Egypt, by the British fleet.

Sept. 13. Defeat of the **Egyptians** by the British in the **Battle of Tel-el-Kebir. British occupation of Egypt** (p. 544).

1883, Feb.–April. Establishment of the Germans, under Lüeritz, at Angra Pequeña (**Southwest Africa**), marking the **beginning of GERMAN COLONIALISM** (growing agitation from 1875 onward—**German Colonial Society,** 1882) and Bismarck's conversion to imperialism. There followed two years of **tension between Britain and Germany,** the dispute extending to both East Africa and West Africa. Bismarck established a loose **entente with the French** (Jules Ferry), especially on the question of Egypt (financial conference at London, June–Aug. 1884), thereby to oblige the British to accept Germany as a colonial power.

Nov. Battle of El Obeid. Gen. William Hicks and an Egyptian force were defeated by the **Mahdi,** messianic leader of a movement directed against Egyptian rule in Sudan.

1884, Feb. 26. British agreement with Portugal, recognizing the latter's rights to territory at the mouth of the Congo. France and Germany protested so strongly that the British abandoned the treaty (June 26).

Nov. 15–1885, Feb. 26. The **BERLIN CONFERENCE ON AFRICAN AFFAIRS** (p. 591), arranged by Bismarck and Ferry. Fourteen nations, including the United States, agreed to work against slavery and the slave trade and recognized the Congo Free State under King Leopold of Belgium with some protections for freedom of trade in the Congo River basin.

1887. Two **Mediterranean Agreements** (p. 474), among Britain, Italy, Austria, and Spain, brokered by Germany, supported British policy in Egypt and affirmed the need to protect the Ottoman Empire from Russian or French expansion.

1894, Aug. 1. Outbreak of the **SINO-JAPANESE WAR** over control of Korea.

Aug.–Sept. Armenian massacres (p. 532). Armenian nationalists, inspired by the example of Russian Pan-Slavs and terrorists, organized secret revolutionary groups (leader **Avetis Nazarbek**), which, operating from Geneva, Tiflis, Paris, and other places, followed a policy of provoking troubles in Armenia in the hope of calling forth reprisals by the Ottomans and thus bringing about European intervention. Beginning in 1890, there were constant disturbances, culminating in the Armenian rising of August 1894 in the vicinity of **Sassun.** This was put down with ferocity by the Kurdish irregular cavalry. The result was a great outcry in Europe, particularly in Britain, where humanitarians called on the Liberal government to intervene. Ultimately, the sultan appointed a **commission of investigation,** which was joined by British,

French, and Russian delegates. Russia, threatened in its own territory by the prospect of an Armenian state, was averse to any action. The commission produced a fairly innocuous program of reform (April 1895).

Oct. 6. Britain invited Germany, France, Russia, and the United States to join in **intervention in East Asia,** the Chinese having been defeated by the Japanese. The intervention failed to take place because of the unwillingness of the United States and Germany to participate.

1895, April 17. TREATY OF SHIMONOSEKI between China and Japan ended their war with substantial territorial losses for the Chinese.

April 23. Russia, Germany, and France protested to Japan and forced some adjustment to the terms of the Sino-Japanese treaty (p. 573).

Oct. Armenian massacres in Constantinople followed a large Armenian demonstration. Massacres continued throughout Anatolia, and European powers considered intervention, but no formal action was taken, other than the announcement by the sultan of a program of reform for Armenia.

1896, March 1. Battle of Adua (p. 592). Major Ethiopian victory over the Italians.

March 12. British decision to begin the **reconquest of Sudan** by an advance on Dongola. The Italian defeat in Ethiopia meant the collapse of the British system of protecting the Nile on the east. Possible French advances into the region (**Marchand mission,** 1896) convinced Britain of the need to establish control in Sudan itself.

June 3. Treaty of alliance between Russia and China, signed by **Li Hung-chang** during his attendance at the coronation of the tsar in Moscow.

June 9. Lobanov-Yamagata Agreement between Russia and Japan regarding cooperation in Korea.

Aug. 26. Attack on the Ottoman Bank by Armenian revolutionaries and other attacks in Constantinople led to major **Armenian massacres,** which were stopped by the intervention of the ambassadors of the powers. However, the powers were unable to agree on any course of action. The disorders continued until June 1897, after which the revolutionary movement gradually collapsed.

1897, Nov. 14. Landing of German forces at Jiaozhou Bay (p. 564), and occupation of Qingdao, following the killing of two German missionaries (Nov. 1). The Germans had sought to gain control of a Chinese port since 1895 and decided upon Jiaozhou, despite Russian objections. The Chinese finally agreed to German demands on March 6, 1898, and granted a 99-year lease and permission to build railroads and operate mines in Shandong Province.

Dec. 14. Russian fleet ordered to Lushun. This was the first step in the Russian acquisition of the port.

Dec.–1898, March. Anglo-Russian conflict over loan to China. Russia demanded a monopoly of railroad building in Manchuria and the right to build a railroad from the Trans-Siberian Railroad south to the Yellow Sea. Britain demanded a concession for a railroad from Burma to the Yangzi basin and a promise not to alienate territory in the Yangzi valley.

1898, Jan. 25. British proposals for division of Asia. Salisbury proposed to Russia that all Asia be divided by a line from Alexandretta in Syria to Beijing into a northern (Russian) sphere and a southern (British) sphere. Russia evaded discussions and pressed China for a lease of Dalian and Lushun, raising Anglo-Russian tensions.

March 8. Britain explored possible collaboration with the United States in East Asia but received no encouragement.

March 17. British advances to Japan were unsuccessful because the Japanese were negotiating with Russia regarding Korea.

March 27. China leased Lushun and Dalian **to Russia** for 25 years. Britain gained a lease for Weihaiwei as a counterweight, and tensions were reduced.

March 29. Anglo-German discussions about joint efforts to counter Russian advances in East Asia had no results.

April 10. France gained lease on Zhanjiang for 99 years and other concessions as a part of the effective partition of China.

April 25. The **Nishi-Rosen Agreement** between Japan and Russia recognized Japan's preponderant economic interests in Korea and supported Russian positions in Manchuria.

Aug. 30. Anglo-German agreement regarding the future of **Portuguese colonies.** The need of the Portuguese government for a major loan led to the lease of **Delagoa Bay,** an important access point to

Transvaal, by the British. German participation in the loan involved the assignment of the northern half of **Mozambique** and all but a central strip of **Angola** as the area from which the revenues would serve for the German share of the loan, whereas the rest of Mozambique and Angola were assigned to the British.

Sept. 18. FASHODA CRISIS BETWEEN BRITAIN AND FRANCE began, with the French ultimately renouncing claims along the Nile. A clash between British north-south expansion and French west-east expansion routes in Africa (p. 475).

1899, May 18–July 29. FIRST HAGUE PEACE CONFERENCE, which met at the invitation of the Russian tsar (Aug. 24, 1898). The general idea was regarded with mistrust and dislike by most powers. Twenty-six states were represented. The conference produced conventions for the peaceful settlement of international disputes and the definition of the laws of war (prohibition for five years of the use of projectiles thrown from balloons, prohibition of gas warfare and dumdum bullets, provision of better treatment of war prisoners and wounded, etc.). Nothing was done about disarmament, and compulsory arbitration was rejected, but a **permanent court of arbitration** was provided for.

Sept. 6. OPEN DOOR NOTE of the American secretary of state, **John Hay.** Following the division of China into spheres of influence, the note proposed that Britain, Germany, and Russia not interfere with treaty ports and should not charge higher harbor or railroad dues on foreign goods than they would on their own within their spheres. The interested powers agreed. The note had little immediate importance but set up an ideal policy often referred to later.

Oct. 9. Outbreak of the BOER WAR, following the failure of negotiations between Britain and the Boer republics in South Africa.

Nov. 1. Anglo-German agreement regarding the **Samoan Islands.** Following a period of rivalry among Britain, Germany, and the United States for control of the islands and considerable internal Samoan fighting, the conflicts were resolved by the abolition of the Samoan monarchy and the division of the islands among the three powers.

Nov. 25. Baghdad Railway concession granted to German syndicate. This followed years of economic schemes and negotiations. The Ottomans had given a German company the concession (1888) to build a railroad from the Bosporus to Angora (Ankara), which was completed in 1892. British competition was withdrawn as a result of diplomatic pressure. The German company received additional concessions, and German ascendancy in this area was confirmed by a successful **state visit by Emperor William II** to Constantinople and Palestine. The French cooperated with German interests, and Britain protected their interests in the Persian Gulf region by establishing a special relationship with the **sheik of Kuwait** in 1899. The Germans obtained the preliminary concession for the final stage of the rail project, Konia to **Baghdad,** on Nov. 25, 1899.

1900, Feb. 28, March 3. A combined Russian, German, and French initiative to bring peace in South Africa was suggested by Muraviev, but Germany rejected the suggestion. The continuation of the Boer War provided opportunities for the Russians to advance their interests in **Persia, Afghanistan,** and **Tibet,** and the French in **Morocco.**

March. Russian squadron at Chemulpo, attempting to secure a naval base on the southern coast of Korea.

June 13–Aug. 14. BOXER RISING (p. 565) and **siege of the Beijing legations.** The legations were relieved by an international military force. The events provided the opportunity for 100,000 Russian troops to occupy Manchuria.

Oct. 16. Anglo-German Yangzi Agreement provided for maintenance of the "Open Door" in all Chinese territories. Other powers acceded to it.

Dec. 14. Franco-Italian Agreement, by which Italy gave France a free hand in **Morocco** in return for a free hand in **Tripoli.**

1901, Feb. 8. Russian proposals to China, extending concessions to Russia in exchange for withdrawal of Russian troops from Manchuria. China appealed for support, and strong stands were taken by Japan and Britain.

March 15. Bülow's speech in the Reichstag declared that the Yangzi Agreement did not apply to Manchuria. This brought an end to diplomatic discussions in London for limiting Russian expansion. The Germans would not go beyond a promise of neutrality in a Russo-Japanese or Anglo-Russian war.

July–Oct. Negotiations for an **Anglo-Japanese alliance.** Negotiations hinged on the definition of Japan's interests in Korea and on the question of whether the alliance should be extended to include Siam and India.

1902, Jan. 30. The **ANGLO-JAPANESE ALLIANCE** was concluded for five years and provided for the independence of China and Korea and the recognition of Japan's special interests in Korea; the two powers each agreed to maintain neutrality in the event of wars with third powers and to join with the other in the event of a larger war.

May 31. TREATY OF VEREENIGING brought an end to the South African war, with the Boers accepting British sovereignty along with the promise of representative institutions.

1902–3. The **Venezuela Crisis** arose over claims by foreign nationals because of injuries during revolutionary disturbances. Britain, Germany, and Italy instituted a blockade, and pressure by the United States forced the powers to accept the arbitration of the **International Court of Justice** at The Hague, which ruled in favor of the powers.

1903, May 15. British declaration of interests in the Persian Gulf made by Lord Landsdowne declared that any naval base in the gulf would be viewed as "a very grave menace to British interests."

Aug. Japanese notes to Russia regarding the failure of the Russians to carry out the evacuation of Manchuria were not viewed by Russia as a threat.

1904–5. THE RUSSIAN-JAPANESE WAR began after Russians failed to respond to Japanese notes. Russia suffered major military defeats, both on land and on sea. A major Russian war fleet was destroyed in the **Battle of Tsushima Straits** (May 1905), and the war came to an end with the **TREATY OF PORTSMOUTH** (Sept. 1905). The settlement represented a major advance of Japanese interests in Korea and northern China.

1904, April 8. The **ANGLO-FRENCH ENTENTE** concluded (p. 476).

Sept. 7. In the **British treaty with Tibet,** the Tibetan lama agreed not to cede or lease territory to any foreign power, thus stopping the Russian advance.

Oct. 3. Franco-Spanish treaty regarding Morocco publicly affirmed Moroccan independence but secretly provided for eventual partition.

Dec.–1905, Feb. Mission of Saint-René Taillandier to Fez proposed virtual French protectorate to the sultan.

1905. The **FIRST MOROCCAN CRISIS** involved German opposition to French expansion (p. 476).

1906, Jan. 16–April 7. ALGECIRAS CONFERENCE on Morocco was the result of intense diplomatic discussions among France, Germany, and Britain. France was supported by all the powers, except Austria, which sided with Germany. The conference reaffirmed the independence and integrity of Morocco and economic liberty. Morocco's police were to be under French and Spanish control, and a French-dominated state bank was to be organized.

Dec. 13. Agreement between Britain, France, and Italy regarding **Ethiopia,** affirming its independence but dividing the country into spheres of influence in the event of Ethiopia's collapse.

1907, June 15–Oct. 18. SECOND HAGUE PEACE CONFERENCE, called at the suggestion of U.S. president Theodore Roosevelt. Limitations on armaments again could not be concluded (Germany feared British efforts to limit its fleet), and Germany also resisted proposals for compulsory arbitration of disputes. But the conference enlarged the machinery for voluntary arbitration and concluded conventions regulating action to collect debts, rules of war, and rights and obligations of neutrals.

Aug. 31. THE ANGLO-RUSSIAN ENTENTE dealt with a variety of colonial areas (p. 477).

Persian Revolution and Counterrevolution (1905–9) (p. 537). Commercial classes, modern educated Persians, and religious leaders joined in protest against incompetent monarchs and growing foreign intervention in internal affairs. In July 1906, several thousand revolutionaries took sanctuary, or the **Great Bast,** in the British legation in Tehran. The shah agreed to convoke a national assembly. In Oct. 1906, this assembly met and drew up a liberal **constitution,** which was signed by the shah. The Anglo-Russian Entente (1907) ignored the new constitution, and in 1908, the Russians supported a successful **coup d'état by the shah,** which shut down the assembly and established martial law.

Constitutionalist resistance continued in Tabriz, but in March 1909 a Russian force occupied the city on behalf of the shah. By June 1909, the **Bakhtiari** tribe sided with the constitutional regime, and its armed forces captured Tehran and deposed the shah. Russian support for the conservative monarch had failed.

1908, July. Mulay Hafid defeated his brother, Abdul Aziz, sultan of Morocco, and captured Fez. German support for Mulay Hafid created new diplomatic tensions.

July 24. YOUNG TURK REVOLUTION succeeded in forcing **Abdul Hamid II** to restore the liberal **constitution of 1876.** This resulted in a major setback for German influence in the Ottoman Empire and a period of popular Anglophilia.

Dec. 4. London Naval Conference, attended by ten powers on rules of war (blockade, contraband, convoys, etc.). Its convention was never ratified.

Feb. 8. German-French agreement on Morocco affirmed Moroccan independence, but Germany recognized France's special political interests in return for recognition of German economic interests.

1911, April–May. French advance in Morocco, following antiforeign disturbances. The French entered Fez despite German protests.

June–Nov. SECOND MOROCCAN CRISIS (p. 478) resulted from French advance and German threats.

Convention of Nov. 4 provided German agreement to French position in Morocco in exchange for cession of parts of French Congo to Germany.

Sept.–1912, Oct. TRIPOLITAN WAR (p. 478) between Italy and Turkey. The major powers could not oppose Italian invasion of Tripoli but resisted expansion of the war to the Balkans. The **Treaty of Lausanne** (October 1912) resulted in the end of Ottoman sovereignty in Tripoli, but the Dodecanese Islands, which had been occupied by Italy, were to be restored to the Ottoman Empire.

Nov. Russian invasion of northern Persia followed an ultimatum demanding the dismissal of **W. Morgan Shuster,** an American who had taken charge of Persian governmental finances.

1912, Oct. 18. Outbreak of the FIRST BALKAN WAR (p. 478), followed by **Treaty of London** (May 30, 1913), which brought an end to the First Balkan War; the Ottomans ceded all territory west of a line between Enos and Midia and abandoned all claim to Crete. The victorious allies were obliged by an ultimatum from Britain to accept the settlement agreed to by the great powers. This was followed by the Second Balkan War, which resulted in a series of bilateral settlements (p. 479).

1913, Nov.–Dec. The **Liman von Sanders incident.** Liman had been appointed by the Ottoman government to reorganize the army. He was to have far-reaching powers. The Russians protested the extensive authority of the German mission and received French support. The Germans accepted a change in Liman's command, but the incident increased Russian suspicions of German designs in the Ottoman Empire.

1914, June 28. ASSASSINATION OF THE ARCHDUKE FRANCIS FERDINAND at Sarajevo set in motion the events that led to the outbreak of World War I (p. 479). *(To p. 640)*

3. TECHNOLOGICAL DEVELOPMENTS, 1800–1914

(From p. 314)

Major technological innovations originated in Europe and North America. Although industrialization owed much to new inventions, the early stages (to the 1840s) were fueled more by the **tinkerings of inventors and craftspeople** than by scientists. The late 19th century witnessed the marriage of science and industry that continues to this day. The development of technology, no longer strictly the realm of independent inventors, was guided and financed by companies searching for new products, resulting in the burgeoning chemical and petrochemical industries. At the same time, technology became a part of everyday life, made the world a smaller place, and became a more important force in shaping European and world events.

The major achievements in technology included:

a. ENERGY AND POWER SOURCES

1800. The **galvanic cell,** or Voltaic pile, of **Alessandro Volta** (1745-1827) was the first electric battery (converting chemical energy into electrical energy).

1802. Richard Trevithick (1771-1833) built the first **high-pressure steam engine,** although the American **Oliver Evans** (1755-1819) had patented one in the United States in 1797. Other advances in steam engine technology included the compound engine (adding a high-pressure cylinder to the original Watt engine) by **William McNaught** (1813-81) in 1845.

1806. First gas lighting of cotton mills. Improvements made in production and distribution of gas as heat source (**Bunsen burner,** 1855) and for illumination (**Welsbach gas mantle,** 1885).

1827. Benoit Fourneyron (1802-67) developed the **water turbine.**

1832. The first mechanical generation of electricity by **Hippolyte Pixii.** Major improvements in **electric generators** followed: the improved armature (1856) designed by **Werner von Siemens** (1816-92); and the ring armature (1870) of **Zénobe T. Gramme** (1826-1901), which represented the first practical dynamo.

1854. Abraham Gesner (1797-1864) manufactured kerosene.

1859. William M. J. Rankine (1820-72) published the first comprehensive manual of the steam engine. The steam engine stimulated theoretical studies in thermodynamics by Clapeyron, Clausius, Joule, Lord Kelvin, and Gibbs.

1859. Edwin L. Drake (1819-80) drilled the **first oil well** in Titusville, Pa., opening up the Pennsylvania oil field and starting the large-scale commercial exploitation of petroleum. **First oil pipeline** (two-inch diameter, six miles long) constructed 1865 in Pennsylvania.

1876. Nicholas August Otto (1832-91) built the first practical gas engine, working upon the so-called **Otto cycle,** which is now almost universally employed for all internal combustion engines. Otto's work was based upon previous engines of **Étienne Lenoir** (1822-1900) and **Alphonse Beau de Rochas** (1815-91). The Otto cycle was employed in the gasoline engine patented (1885) by **Gottlieb Daimler** (1834-1900).

1882. The Pearl Street (New York City) electric generating station, a pioneer central power station designed by **Thomas A. Edison** (1847-1931), commenced operations a few months after Edison dynamos had been installed at Holborn Viaduct Station in England.

1884. Charles A. Parsons (1854-1931) patented the **steam turbine.** The steam turbine (1887) of the Swede **Gustav de Laval** (1845-1913) proved successful for engines of smaller power.

1886. Beginning of the first great **hydroelectric installation** at Niagara Falls, N.Y.

1888. Nikola Tesla (1856-1943) invented the **alternating current electric motor:** he also made possible the polyphase transmission of power over long distances and pioneered the invention of radio.

1892. Rudolf Diesel (1858-1913) patented his heavy oil engine, first manufactured successfully in 1897.

b. MATERIALS AND CONSTRUCTION

1800. Pioneer **suspension bridge,** hung by iron chains, built by **James Finley** (c. 1762-1828) in Pennsylvania; wire suspension employed by **Marc Seguin** (1786-1875) in bridge near Lyons (1825). An American, **Ithiel Town** (1784-1844), patented his truss bridge (1820).

1817-25. Building of the **Erie Canal,** the first great American civil engineering work.

1818. The **Institute of Civil Engineers** (London), the first professional engineering society, founded.

Marc Isambard Brunel (1769-1849) patented the cast iron **tunnel shield; Thomas Cochrane** (1830) used this shield to construct foundations on marshy ground.

1824. Joseph Aspdin (1779-1855) patented **Portland cement,** a hydraulic cement (impervious to water) as durable as that employed by the Romans.

1827. Gay-Lussac tower introduced in manufacture of sulfuric acid, largely replacing John Roebuck's lead-chamber process (1746). **Herman Frasch** (1851-1914) developed process (1891) for mining sulfur (by superheated water and pumping to the surface).

1836. Galvanized iron introduced by Sorel in France. Galvanized fencing and barbed wire (c. 1880) helped to fence off large tracts of cattle land in the American West during the latter part of the 19th century.

1839. Charles Goodyear (1800-60) **vulcanized rubber.** Although introduced into Europe in 1615, rubber had not been commercially successful until a solvent for the latex was found (1765); bonding of rubber to cloth to produce raincoats (macintoshes) had been developed (1824) by **Charles Macintosh** (1766-1843).

1855. John A. Roebling (1806-69) completed **wire cable bridge** at Niagara, N.Y.; Roebling utilized this same method for the **Brooklyn Bridge** (completed by his son, W. A. Roebling, in 1883), and it became standard construction technique for all great suspension bridges.

1856. Henry Bessemer (1813-98) perfected the technique (Bessemer process) for converting pig iron into steel by directing an air blast upon the molten metal.

1856. *Mauve,* first of the **aniline** (coal-tar) **dyes,** discovered by **William H. Perkin** (1838-1907). Beginning of the synthetic dye industry, which was to develop greatly in Germany.

1861. Ernest Solvay (1838-1922) patented the Solvay ammonia process for the manufacture of soda.

1863. The **open-hearth process** for the manufacture of steel developed by the Martin brothers in France using the regenerative furnace devised (1856) by **Frederick Siemens** (1826-1904) (also known as the Siemens-Martin process).

1863. Henry Clifton Sorby (1826-1908) of Sheffield discovered the microstructure of steel, marking the beginning of **modern metallurgical science.**

1867. Alfred Nobel (1833-96) manufactured **dynamite.** Guncotton and nitroglycerine, both discovered in 1846, had previously been used for blasting purposes. In 1875 Nobel discovered blasting gelatine, from which arose the gelignite industry. Cordite, another explosive, was patented in 1889 by Frederick Abel and James Dewar.

1868. Robert F. Mushet (1811-91) began the manufacture of **tungsten steel.** Other steel alloys also developed: chromium steel (France, 1877); manganese steel (Robert Hadfield, England, 1882); nickel steel (France, 1888); stainless steel (many inventors, 1911-20).

1872. John W. Hyatt (1837-1920) began commercial production of celluloid, discovered by Alexander Parkes (1855).

1877. Joseph Monier (1823-1906) patented a **reinforced concrete** beam. In the 1890s two other Frenchmen, Edmond Coignet and François Hennibique, used reinforced concrete for pipes, aqueducts, bridges, tunnels; E. L. Ransome employed it extensively in building construction.

1879. Percy Gilchrist (1851-1935) and **Sidney G. Thomas** (1850-85) developed a method for making steel from phosphoric iron ores, thereby doubling in effect the world's potential steel production.

1886. Charles M. Hall (1863-1914) developed the electrolytic method of obtaining aluminum from its oxide (bauxite).

1889. Completion of the **Eiffel Tower;** wrought iron superstructure on reinforced concrete base. Cast iron used for building construction earlier in the century by James Bogardus (1800-74) for office buildings in New York and by Joseph Paxton (1801-65) for Crystal Palace at Great Exhibition of 1851 (also employing wrought iron and glass, and prefabricated units). The first complete steel-frame structure was built in Chicago in 1890; steel made possible skyscrapers, as did the earlier invention (1854) of the elevator by **Elisha G. Otis** (1811-61).

1902. Arthur D. Little (1863-1935) patented rayon, the **first cellulose fiber,** and also artificial silk. Earlier (1884), Louis, count of Chardonnet (1839-1924), had produced an artificial thread that was woven into a silklike material. Cellophane was developed by J. E. Brandenberger (1912) and further developed by W. H. Church and K. E. Prindle (1926).

1909. The first polymer, **Bakelite,** discovered by Leo H. Baekeland (1863-1944). Subsequent development of polymers included neoprene, arising from work of Father Julius A. Nieuwland beginning in 1906; nylon, developed by Wallace H. Carothers and first manufactured in 1938; acrilan; orlon; dynel; and dacron (called terylene by its British inventors, J. R. Whinfield and J. T. Dickson, 1941). Synthetic polymers included elastomers, fibers, plastics. Silicon polymers developed c. 1945.

c. MACHINES AND INDUSTRIAL TECHNIQUES

1800. Eli Whitney (1765-1825) was credited with the introduction of **interchangeable parts** for manufacturing muskets. The work of Simeon North (1765-1852) on uniform parts was, in fact, more decisive. Although it had European precedents, the system of interchangeable parts became known as "the American system" because it was most fully exploited in the United States and became the foundation of the mass production characteristic of American industry at a later date.

1801. Joseph M. Jacquard (1752–1834) invented a loom for figured silk fabrics, later introduced into the making of worsteds. **William Horrocks** (1776–1849) developed the power loom (1813), improved (1822) by **Richard Roberts** (1789–1864). Machine combing of wool (1845) and ring spinning frame (1830) developed; the Brussels power loom invented by Erastus B. Bigelow (1814–79) of Massachusetts for the weaving of carpets (1845); and the loom invented by J. H. Northrop of Massachusetts (1892), which was almost completely automatic.

1810. Friedrich Koenig's (1774–1833) **power-driven press** in use, followed by the flatbed press (1811). Other developments leading to mass production of printed matter, especially newspapers, were the rotary press of Robert Hoe (1846) and the web printing press, allowing for printing on a continuous roll (web) of paper by a rotary press, invented (1865) by William A. Bullock. In 1885 the Linotype of **Ottmar Mergenthaler** (1854–99) replaced Monotype.

1823–43. Charles Babbage (1792–1871) attempted to build calculating machines (following the lead of Thomas de Colmar, who built the first practical calculating machine in 1820); Babbage's machines were never completed, being too advanced for the technology of the time, but his theories formed a basis for later work in this field.

1830. Joseph Whitworth (1803–87) developed the **standard screw gauge** and a machine to measure one-millionth of an inch, for standards. Made possible more precise machine tools for planing, gear cutting, and milling.

1837 ff. Rapid **development of armament,** keeping pace with improvements in metallurgy, machines, and explosives: **Henri J. Paixhans's** (1783–1854) shell-gun, adopted by France, 1837; rifled, breech-loading artillery used by Piedmont, 1845; the French '75, the first quick-firing artillery piece, firing both shrapnel and high explosive, 1898; the cast steel breech-loading Prussian artillery manufactured by the Krupps beginning in 1849. Small arms included the Colt revolver (1835), the Dreyse needle-gun (1841), the Minié bullet (1849), the Winchester repeating rifle (1860), the Gatling machine gun (1861), the French chassepot (1866), and the Maxim gun (1884). The self-propelled torpedo was invented by Robert Whitehead (1823–1905) in 1864; smokeless powder appeared in 1884.

1839. Steam hammer invented by **James Nasmyth** (1808–90). Also developments in drog-forging and die stamping at this time.

1846. Elias Howe (1819–67) invented the lockstitch **sewing machine;** in 1851 **Isaac M. Singer** (1811–75) invented the first practical domestic sewing machine. This became the first major consumer appliance, soon followed by the **carpet sweeper** of M. R. Bissell (1876), and the **vacuum cleaner** (I. W. McGaffey, 1869; J. Thurman, 1899).

1849–54. Exploiting the increasing accuracy of machine tools, **Samuel Colt** (1814–62) and **Elisha Root** (1808–65) developed a practical system for manufacturing interchangeable parts, especially in connection with Colt's revolver.

1855. Development of **turret lathe** by American machine tool makers. First true **universal milling machine** designed (1862) by **Joseph R. Brown** (1810–76). Other machine tool improvements included Mushet's tool steel, increasing the cutting speed (high-speed tool steel, 1898, by Taylor and White), gearbox mechanisms for better control, multiple-spindle lathes (1890), and tungsten carbide tools (1926).

1873. First **use of electricity to drive machinery,** Vienna. Quickly adopted, usually with the motor incorporated into the machine rather than separate.

1877. Elihu Thomson invented a **resistance welder.** N. V. Bernardos of Russia patented carbon-arc welding, although arc welding (most popularly employed process today) did not come into its own until invention of the coated electrode in the 1920s. Oxyacetylene torch (invented in 1900 by Edmund Fouche) and gas welding was the dominant process until recently. Development of inert-gas-shielded arc welding after 1942.

1882 ff. Invention and use of electric appliances for consumer market: electric fan (S. S. Wheeler); flatiron (H. W. Seely, 1882); stove (W. S. Hadaway, 1896); separate attachable plug (H. Hubbell, 1904); sewing machine (Singer Co., 1889); washing machine (Hurling Co., 1907).

1884. Dorr E. Felt (1862–1930) made first accurate **comptometer. Wil-**

liam S. Burroughs (1857–98) developed first successful recording **adding machine** (1888); Brunsviga calculating machine (1892).

1895. Carl Linde established **liquid air** plant. He had previously (1876) introduced the ammonia compressor machine (the first vapor compression machine invented by Jacob Perkins, 1834). Other refrigerating machines were: ammonia absorption machine (Carré, 1860), air refrigerator (Gorrie, 1845; improved by Kirk, 1862), open-cycle air machine (Giffard, 1873, and later by Bell and Coleman).

1895. King C. Gillette (1855–1932) invented **safety razor** with throwaway blades. **J. Schick** invented **electric razor** (1928). Stainless steel throwaway blades invented in Sweden (1962).

1898. M. J. Owens (1859–1923) invented automatic **bottle-making machine.**

1905–10. Electric precipitation equipment, for prevention of atmospheric pollution by industry, developed by Frederick G. Cottrell (1877–1948).

1913. G. Sundback invented a slide fastener **(zipper);** earlier version patented by W. L. Judson (1891).

1914. Conveyor-belt mass production employed in the United States most dramatically in Henry Ford's assembly line for Model T Ford automobile, which became the symbol for American industrial technique.

d. AGRICULTURAL PRODUCTION AND FOOD TECHNOLOGY

1801. Franz K. Achard (1753–1821) built the first **sugar-beet factory** (Silesia). Sugar-beet cultivation and beet-sugar industry developed primarily in France and Germany.

1810. Nicolas Appert (c. 1750–1840) described system for food preservation by canning, using glass jars. Tin cans introduced 1811.

1834. Cyrus H. McCormick (1809–84) patented his **reaper** and began commercial manufacture c. 1840. Obed Hussey (1792–1860) invented a similar reaper simultaneously and independently.

1837. John Deere (1804–86) introduced the **steel plow.** In 1819 Jethro Wood (1774–1834) had developed a cast iron plow; and John Lane had introduced a steel-blade plowshare in 1833. James Oliver's (1823–1908) chilled plow of 1855 was improved by the Marsh brothers (1857). Mechanical power was applied to plowing with the introduction of **cable plowing** (1850); by 1858 John Fowler had introduced the **steam plow.**

1850–80. Improvements in farm implements included the revolving disc harrow (1847), binder (1850), corn planter (1853), two-horse straddle-row cultivator (1856), combine harvester (1860), combine seed drill (1867), and sheaf-binding harvester (1878).

1860. Gail Borden (1801–74) opened the first factory for the production of **evaporated milk.**

1861. After Louis Pasteur's work on microorganisms, **pasteurization** was introduced as a means of preserving beer, wine, and milk.

1865 ff. Development of **mechanical refrigeration** for preservation of food products, especially Thaddeus Lowe's (1832–1913) compression ice machine (1865) and Linde's ammonia compression refrigerator (1873).

1869 ff. Transcontinental railway aided development of **meat-packing industry** in Chicago.

1877. Gustav de Laval (1845–1913) invented the centrifugal **cream separator.**

1880 ff. Application of **chemical fertilizers** increased food production. J. B. Lawes manufactured superphosphates (1842); Chilean sodium nitrate beds exploited from c. 1870 until methods of fixing atmospheric nitrogen were developed after 1900 by Fritz Haber (1868–1934); use of potash as an inorganic fertilizer from Strassfurt deposits.

1889. Angus Campbell tested the first spindle-type **cotton picker;** this type of machine was not fully developed and marketed successfully until the 1940s, competing with the machine devised by John and Mack Rust in 1924 and also commercially produced in the 1940s.

1892. Gasoline tractor came into use for farming. **Caterpillar tractor** developed 1931.

1902. W. Normann patented a process for hardening liquid fats by hydrogenation, making available an ample supply of solid fats for soap and food.

e. TRANSPORTATION AND COMMUNICATION

1802. Richard Trevithick (1771–1833) patented a **steam carriage;** earlier attempts to use steam power for transport purposes had been made by Nicolas Cugnot in France (1769), William Murdock in England (1785), and Oliver Evans in the United States. In 1804 Trevithick designed and built a locomotive to run on rails.

1807. Robert Fulton (1765–1815) sailed the *Clermont* from New York to Albany. This was by no means the first steamboat: the Marquis Claude de Jouffroy d'Abbans (1751–1832) had built a paddle-wheel steamer in France (1783); John Fitch (1743–98) had launched a steamboat on the Delaware (1787), and James Rumsey (1743–92) one on the Potomac (1787); John Stevens (1749–1838) had designed a successful screw propeller steamboat (1802). However, Fulton's boat was the first steamboat to represent a commercial success. By 1819 steam augmented sail on the first transatlantic steamship crossing, achieved by the *Savannah.*

1814. George Stephenson (1781–1848) built his **first locomotive,** and in 1829 his *Rocket,* designed with the aid of his son Robert (1803–59), won a competition with locomotives of other design and thereby set the pattern for future locomotive developments.

1825. Opening of the **Stockton-Darlington Railway,** the first successful railroad system, using a steam engine built by Stephenson. In 1829 the first railroads were opened in the United States (Pennsylvania) and France (Lyons–St. Étienne), both employing English-built locomotives. The first American locomotive was built (1830) by Peter Cooper (1791–1883).

1837. Charles Wheatstone (1802–75) and **William F. Cooke** (1806–79) patented the **telegraph,** which was also independently invented by the American **Samuel F. B. Morse** (1791–1872), whose **telegraphic code** was universally adopted. By 1866, **Cyrus W. Field** (1819–92) succeeded in laying a **transatlantic cable,** after two previous failures and after overcoming tremendous financial and technical difficulties.

1839. Louis J. M. Daguerre (1787–1851) evolved the **daguerreotype photographic process,** based on the work of Joseph Nicéphore Niepce (1765–1833). Although **William H. F. Talbot** (1800–77) produced paper positives (1841), the first fully practical medium for photography was the wet collodion plate process (1851) of Frederick S. Archer (1813–57).

1860. Construction began on the **London underground railway** system, which was electrified in 1905. Construction began on the Paris *métro* in 1898, and on the New York City subway in 1900.

1864. George M. Pullman (1831–97) built the first **sleeping car,** specially constructed for that purpose.

1867. Ernest Michaux invented the **velocipede,** the first bicycle to put cranks and pedals directly on the front wheel; the "safety" bicycle with geared chain drive to the rear wheel was introduced in 1885.

1869. Union Pacific and Central Pacific Railroads met to complete the **first transcontinental line** in America. The **Trans-Siberian Railway** was begun in 1891.

1869. Opening of the Suez Canal, the work of the French engineer **Ferdinand de Lesseps** (1805–94).

1873. The Remington Company began manufacture of the **typewriter** patented by **Christopher L. Sholes** (1819–90); shift-key system, with capital and small letters on same type bar, was introduced in 1878.

1874. Stephen D. Field's (1846–1913) electrically powered **streetcar** began operation in New York City, replacing the horse-driven cars introduced in 1832. The cable streetcar, invented by Andrew S. Hallidie (1836–1900), was put into use in San Francisco (1873). The first streetcars with overhead trolley lines were in use in Germany by 1884 and first installed in the United States at Richmond, Va., in 1888.

1876. Alexander Graham Bell (1847–1922) patented the **telephone.** The first telephone exchange installed in New Haven (1877) and an automatic switching system introduced in 1879. Much previous experimentation had been done on telephones, including that of Philip Reis of Germany (1861), Antonio Meucci of Italy (1857), and Elisha Gray (simultaneously with Bell). The periodic insertion of loading coils (inductors), originated by M. I. Pupin (1899), made possible long-distance transmission of telephone calls.

1878–79. Joseph W. Swan (1828–1914) of England made the first successful carbon filament **electric lamp** in 1878; working independently,

Thomas A. Edison patented his **incandescent bulb** in 1879. Improved vacuum in the lamp bulb was made possible by the high-vacuum mercury pump developed by Hermann Sprengel (1865). At the same time successful experiments in public lighting were carried on with the use of arc lamps, the most successful systems being those of P. Jablochkoff (Paris, 1876) and Charles F. Brush (Cleveland, 1879). The tungsten filament lamp was introduced in 1913.

1885 ff. Karl Benz (1844–1929) produced the prototype of the **automobile** using an internal combustion motor operating on the Otto four-stroke cycle principle; the same year **Gottlieb Daimler** (1834–1900) also patented his **gasoline engine,** trying it first on a motorcycle, then on a four-wheeled vehicle. These may be said to have been the first automobiles, although there had been experiments with battery-powered electric automobiles beginning in 1851, and some previous internal combustion vehicles had been attempted by the Frenchman Étienne Lenoir (1859) and the Austrian Siegfried Marcus (1864). Other automobile pioneers included the Frenchmen Peugeot and Panhard. The first automobile patent in the United States was taken out by George B. Selden (1879), but the Duryea (1895) was the first auto made for sale in the United States. **Henry Ford** (1863–1947) made his first car in 1896 and founded the Ford Motor Co. in 1903. Important in the development of the automobile was the invention (1888) of the **pneumatic tire** by **John B. Dunlop** (1840–1921).

1888. George Eastman (1854–1932) perfected the **hand camera** (Kodak); he had previously invented the first successful roll film (1880). Leo Baekeland perfected (1893) a photographic paper (Velox) sufficiently sensitive to be printed by artificial light. Work of Rudolph Fischer and Siegrist in dye-coupler color processes (1910–14) provided the basis for the development of a commercially practicable color film (Kodachrome) by Leopold Godowsky, Jr., and Leopold Mannes (1935).

1889–90. Thomas Edison improved his first **phonograph** (patented 1878) by substituting wax for the tinfoil-coated cylinders and by adding a loudspeaker to amplify the sounds produced by the diaphragm. Emile Berliner (1851–1929) improved the quality of sound reproduction (1890) by utilizing disk records and better cutting technique.

1895. The first public **motion picture** showing in Paris, by **Louis** (1864–1948) and **Auguste** (1862–1954) **Lumière,** inventors of the **cinématographe.** This followed by a year the opening of Edison's Kinetoscope Parlor (New York City) where the motion picture (peepshow) could be viewed by only one person at a time. Both these successful attempts at motion pictures had been preceded by earlier devices: the "thaumatrope" of J. A. Paris (1826); the magic lantern, devised by A. Kircher (1645) and improved by Pieter van Musschenbroek (1736); the multicamera apparatus of Edward Muybridge (1872); the "photographic gun" of E. J. Marey (1882); the celluloid motion picture film of William Friese-Green (1889). Prototype of the modern **film projector** was the Vitascope (1896), devised by **Charles Francis Jenkins** (1867–1934) and Thomas Armat on the basis of Edison's kinetoscope.

1895. Guglielmo Marconi (1874–1937) invented the **wireless telegraph,** based on the discovery (1887) of radio waves by Heinrich Hertz (1857–94) (existence of these waves had been deduced by James Clerk Maxwell in 1873). Other contributors to wireless development were E. Branly, Thomas Edison, Alexander Popov (who contributed the aerial), Reginald E. Fessenden (improved transmitter, 1901). In 1901 Marconi succeeded in sending a wireless signal across the Atlantic.

1898. Valdemar Poulsen of Denmark invented the **magnetic recording of sound** (1898). F. Pfleumer of Germany replaced steel wire by plastic tape coated with magnetic material (1930s), and Marvin Camras of the United States made further developments in magnetic recording (1940s).

1900. Count **Ferdinand von Zeppelin** launched the first of the **rigid airships** that were to be called by his name.

1903. Orville (1871–1948) and **Wilbur** (1867–1912) **Wright** made the first flight in a **heavier-than-air craft** on Dec. 17 at Kitty Hawk, N.C. This flight was the culmination of a long series of developments: George Cayley's glider (1804) and studies in aerodynamic theory; the glider flights (1895) of Otto Lilienthal and Octave Chanute; Samuel P. Langley's (1834–1906) steam-powered model airplane (1896); Alberto Santos-Dumont's (1873–1932) model airplane with an internal combustion engine (1898); and others.

1904. John Ambrose Fleming (1849–1945) devised the diode thermionic valve (**radio tube**); **Lee de Forest** (1873–1961) invented the Audion (1906), a three-electrode vacuum tube (triode amplifier), thereby providing the basis for the development of **electronics.**

1909–27. The "heroic age" of **aviation** commenced with **Louis Blériot's** (1872–1936) flight (1909) across the English Channel; included the exploits of the aerial aces of World War I, the flight (1919) of John W. Alcock (1892–1919) and Arthur Whitten Brown (1886–1948) across the Atlantic (Newfoundland to Galway), Richard E. Byrd's (1888–1957) flight (1926) across the North Pole; and culminated in **Charles A. Lindbergh's** (1902–74) solo nonstop flight from New York to Paris in *The Spirit of St. Louis* (1927). Many technical improvements were made, including the first engine specifically intended for aircraft by

Glenn Curtiss (1904) and the **gyroscope stabilizer** of Elmer A. Sperry (1913).

1911. Charles F. Kettering (1876–1958), who had previously invented lighting and ignition systems for the automobile, perfected the **electric self-starter.** The first fully **automatic transmission,** perfected by Earl A. Thompson, was introduced commercially in 1939. Harry Vickers and Francis W. Davis began work on hydraulic **power-assisted steering** systems in 1925 and 1926 respectively, and in 1951 power steering was introduced for passenger cars.

1913. Diesel-electric railway engines first used in Sweden. Coming into use in the United States during the late 1930s, they largely replaced steam locomotives. *(To p. 649)*

4. POLAR EXPLORATIONS

a. EARLY EXPLORATIONS

Scandinavian: c. 870: **Ottar,** a Norseman, sailed along the northern Norwegian coast; 875–900: **Iceland** was colonized; 982–85: **Eric the Red** founded colony in Greenland; 1194: **Spitsbergen** discovered.

b. EARLY MODERN EUROPEAN EXPEDITIONS

1553–54. Sir Hugh Willoughby and **Richard Chancellor** travel to Kola Peninsula.

1576. Sir Martin Frobisher sought the Northwest Passage in northern Canada.

1585–87. John Davis sought the Northwest Passage in northern Canada.

1594–97. Three voyages of **Willem Barents** and **Cornelis Nay** in northern Russia, exploring islands and routes in region of Barents Sea.

1607–11. Voyages of **HENRY HUDSON,** searching for Northwest Passage and exploring northern Canada.

1610–48. Russian Cossacks conquered Siberia and explored north coasts and major Arctic rivers.

1670. Hudson's Bay Company was granted royal charter for trade in North America and began explorations of Arctic areas.

1728–41. Voyages of **VITRUS BERING** to explore north Pacific basin and Bering Strait regions.

1732–43. Russian government survey of the whole **Siberian coast.**

1738–39. Pierre Bouvet sighted land south of Capetown in an expedition to prove or disprove the existence of an Antarctic continent.

1772–75. CAPT. JAMES COOK's second voyage of Pacific exploration circumnavigated Antarctica for the first time, farthest southern penetration to that time.

1778. Capt. James Cook's Arctic voyage.

c. 19TH-CENTURY EXPLORATIONS

1806. William Scoresby reached a record north and wrote the influential *Account of the Arctic Regions.*

1818. Twin expedition of **John Ross** and **Edward Parry** to Baffin Bay.

1819–26. John Franklin's land explorations of northern Canada.

1820–23. Baron Wrangel's explorations of Siberia.

1821–23. Edward Parry's second expedition.

1824. Parry's third expedition, seeking a northern sea passage around North America.

1827. Parry set record north, departing from Spitsbergen.

1829–33. John Ross and his nephew, **James Clark Ross,** explored northern Canada, and James Ross located **north magnetic pole** in 1831.

1841–43. JAMES CLARK ROSS explored Antarctic coasts and islands, claiming large areas for Great Britain, and set a record south that lasted for 60 years.

1845–48. The expedition of **SIR JOHN FRANKLIN** completed the **discovery of the full Northwest Passage,** but all members of the expedition perished.

1848–59. Franklin Relief Expeditions finally discovered the fate of the Franklin group and also discovered and mapped significant portions of regions in North America.

1871–74. Discovery of **Franz Joseph Land** by Austrian explorers Julius Payer and Carl Weyprecht.

1876. A new record north was set by **Albert H. Markham** with the expedition of Sir George S. Nares.

1878–79. A. E. Nordenskiöld completed the **Northeast Passage,** across Siberia, for the first time.

1882. Establishment of **INTERNATIONAL POLAR STATIONS** for research, with nine nations participating.

1888. Fridtjof Nansen, with others, made the first crossing of Greenland.

1895. Sixth International Geographical Conference (London) identified Antarctic exploration as the most pressing geographical need of the time.

1893–96. Nansen expedition drifted with the Arctic ice pack and reached a record north.

1898–1900. Carsten Borchgrevink led first party to winter on Antarctic continent and set a record south.

d. 20TH-CENTURY EXPLORATIONS

1902–4. ROBERT F. SCOTT led a major Antarctic expedition, accomplishing significant discoveries and a record south.

1903–6. Roald Amundsen first sailed the complete Northwest Passage.

1907–9. Expeditions by **F. A. Cook** and **Robert E. Peary** each claimed to have reached the **NORTH POLE,** although it is possible that neither actually accomplished this.

1907–9. Ernest Shackleton led an Antarctic expedition that surpassed Scott's records and reached the **south magnetic pole.**

1910–12. ROALD AMUNDSEN discovered the **South Pole,** on which he placed the Norwegian flag in 1911.

1910–13. Scott's last expedition reached the South Pole in 1912, but the whole party died in a blizzard.

1917. Danish–U.S. treaty strengthened Danish claims to **Greenland** by ceding Virgin Islands to the United States in settlement of U.S. claims resulting from Peary's expeditions.

1918–25. Amundsen and **H. Sverdrup** navigated the Northeast Passage and spent an extended period in planned drift over the North Pole.

1924. Greenland became a Danish crown colony following Danish agreements with Norway and Great Britain.

1925. Spitsbergen came under the sovereignty of **Norway.**

1926. Richard Byrd and **Floyd Bennett** were the first to fly over the **North Pole.**

1928–30. First Antarctic flights by **Hubert Wilkins;** he mapped large portions of the continent.

1928–30. Richard E. Byrd led a large expedition equipped with airplanes and established the base Little America.

1935. Foundation of the **CENTRAL ADMINISTRATION OF THE NORTH SEA ROUTE** by the Soviet government, responsible for exploration of all Soviet territory north of 62°.

1937–38. A Soviet polar station for research was established on an ice floe near the North Pole.

1956–57. The American **Amundsen–Scott Station** was set up at the South Pole.

1957–58. The International Geophysical Year devoted major attention to study in the Antarctic, establishing a network of some 60 research stations in the region.

1958. *NAUTILUS,* an American nuclear-powered submarine, navigated under the North Pole.

THE
ARCTIC REGIONS

SIBERIA

Lena R.

120°

Taimyr Peninsula

Nordenskjöld Sea
C. Chelyuskin

Nicholas II Land

Lonely I.

90°

Liakhov
Islands

New
Siberian
Islands

Bennett I.

Henrietta I.
Jeannette I.

150°

East Siberian Sea

Wrangel I.

180°

Herald I.

*Arctic
Ocean*

NORTH POLE

85°

*Kara
Sea*

Novaya

Zemlya

*Yamal
Peninsula*

Vaigach I.

Kolguev I.

60°

N. Dvina R.

Franz Josef
Land

North East
Land

*Barents
Sea*

*Kola
Peninsula*

FINLAND

30°

North Cape

NORWAY

Bear I.

SPITSBERGEN

80°   75°   70°   0°

Arctic Ocean

Jan Mayen I.

ARCTIC CIRCLE

ALASKA

Pt. Barrow

150°

*Beaufort
Sea*

Banks I.

Prince
Patrick I.

Borden I.

Axel
Heiberg I.

GRANT LAND

ELLESMERE I.

Kane Basin

Etah

Peary
Land

*Greenland
Sea*

GREENLAND

ICELAND

30°

MacKenzie R.

120°
W. Long.

*Melville
Sound*

Melville I. Bathhurst
I.

Devon I.

Somerset
I.

Prince of
Wales I.

Victoria
Island

*Boothia
Pen.*

Lancaster Strait

*Baffin
Bay*

Upernivik

King
William
Land

*Melville
Pen.*

Foxe
Basin

BAFFIN ISLAND

Davis Strait

60°

CANADA

*Hudson

Bay*

90°

LABRADOR

PENINSULA

Tia R. *Pur R.*

Ob R.

0   200   400   600   800

MILES

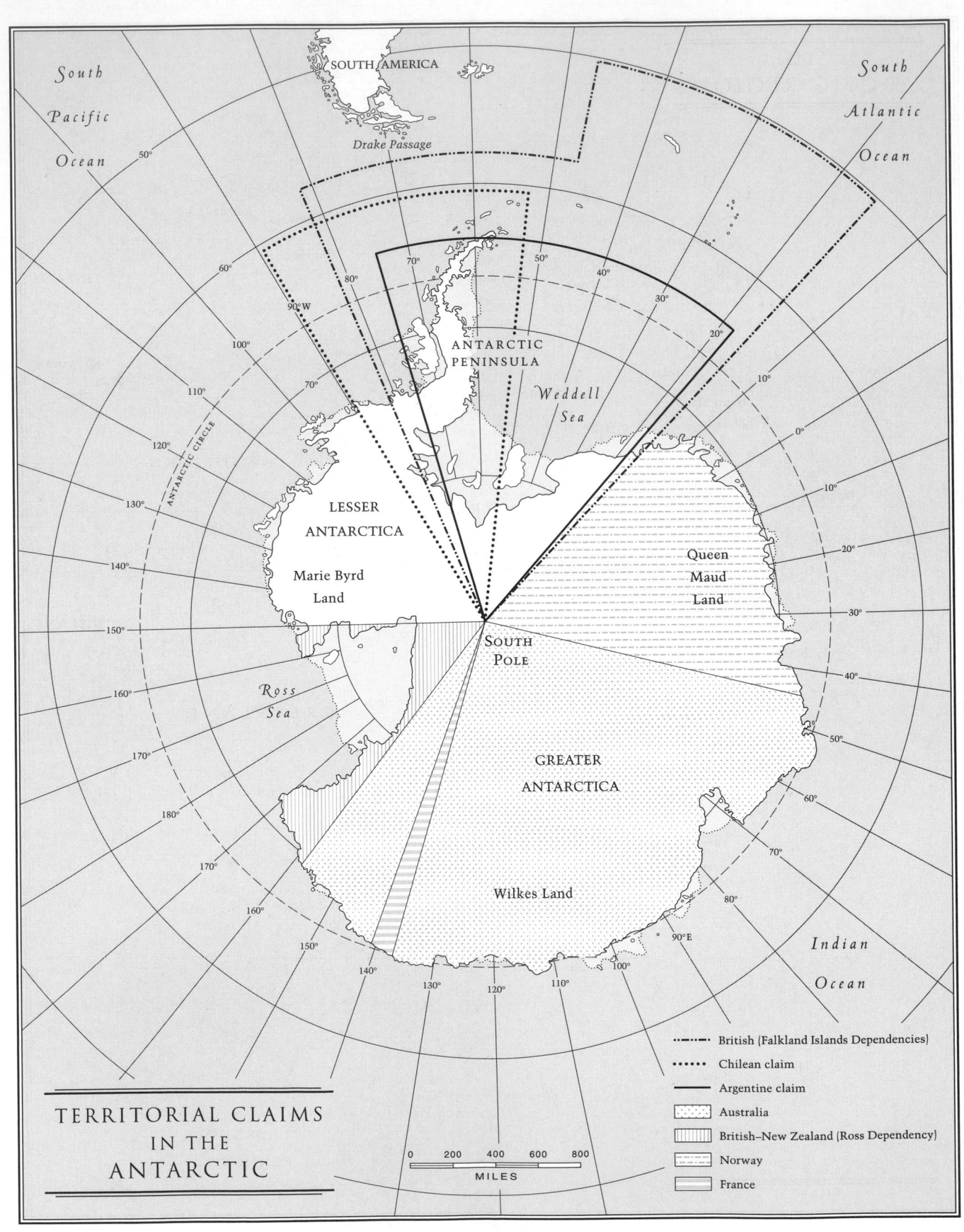

South
Pacific
Ocean

50°

Drake Passage

SOUTH AMERICA

South
Atlantic
Ocean

50°

60°

70°

80°

90° W

100°

ANTARCTIC CIRCLE

110°

120°

130°

140°

150°

160°

170°

180°

170°

160°

150°

140°

130°

120°

110°

100°

90° E

80°

70°

60°

50°

40°

30°

20°

10°

0°

10°

20°

30°

40°

ANTARCTIC
PENINSULA

70°

50°

40°

30°

20°

10°

*Weddell
Sea*

LESSER
ANTARCTICA

Marie Byrd
Land

SOUTH
POLE

Queen
Maud
Land

*Ross
Sea*

GREATER
ANTARCTICA

Wilkes Land

*Indian
Ocean*

TERRITORIAL CLAIMS
IN THE
ANTARCTIC

0   200   400   600   800

MILES

—·—·— British (Falkland Islands Dependencies)

·········· Chilean claim

———— Argentine claim

Australia

British–New Zealand (Ross Dependency)

Norway

France

1959. INTERNATIONAL ANTARCTIC TREATY, signed in Washington by 12 states, agreed to use the Antarctic continent for peaceful purposes only and to suspend territorial claims disputes for 30 years.
1959. *Skate,* an American nuclear-powered submarine, surfaced at the North Pole.

1977. *ARKTIKA,* a Soviet nuclear-powered icebreaker, was the first surface ship to reach the North Pole.
1989. Victoria Murden and **Shirley Metz** were the first women to reach the South Pole overland.

B. THE FRENCH REVOLUTION AND EUROPE, 1789-1914

1. OVERVIEW

Periodization. Basic trends in Europe's modern history began in the 1780s with the first phase of the **Industrial Revolution** in Britain and with the **political and social revolution of 1789** in France. The advent of **World War I in 1914** drew this tumultuous modern period to a close.

During the years **1789-1815,** Europe was dominated by the French Revolution and related reform movements elsewhere, culminating in several revolutionary wars and the Napoleonic Wars. During the next period, **1815-48,** efforts to return to more conservative politics were progressively undermined by the political movements and doctrines tossed up by the French Revolution **(liberalism, radicalism, nationalism, and early socialism)** and by social unrest provoked by increasing commercialization and the **beginning phases of industrialization.** This period culminated in the widespread **revolutions of 1848-49.** These revolutions produced important changes, but their failures also altered European politics, as both conservatives and liberals began to develop new tactics. Between **1850 and 1914, European industrialization advanced,** with a growing array of social and cultural, as well as economic, effects. Debates about constitutional structure began to be re-solved, but pressures for **new government policies to address social issues** increased. **Diplomacy and war** assumed more importance than they had during 1815-48, as governments put their new industrially produced weaponry to use and sought in diplomacy a reduction of political disputes.

Regional as well as purely national differences marked Europe during the 19th century. **Russia and eastern Europe** participated widely in cultural trends and diplomatic engagements, but their political forms and above all their social and economic structures differed markedly from those of western Europe. By 1850, Russia had experienced little significant liberal pressure, while its social structure, predominantly rural, featured divisions between aristocrats and serfs. Russia's early industrialization and growing political turmoil from the 1880s onward thus resembled patterns in western Europe almost a century before, rather than contemporary developments. **The Balkans** formed another region with distinct economic and political issues, while in western Europe, **Spain, southern Italy, and Ireland** participated only partially in many general trends.

2. THE FRENCH REVOLUTION, 1789-1799

(From p. 329)

The period of the French Revolution and French Empire can be divided into several subperiods based on political regime and relationship to the rest of Europe. (1) **Estates General** and **Constituent Assembly,** May 1789-Sept. 1791. Formative period, leading toward constitutional monarchy. (2) **Legislative Assembly,** Oct. 1791-Sept. 1792. New lower-class unrest; beginnings of foreign wars. (3) **National Convention,** Sept. 1792-Oct. 1795. Most radical phase of revolution: end of monarchy, new constitutional measures, and growing impact outside France. (4) **Directory,** Oct. 1795-Nov. 1799. Undid the most radical measures; consolidation efforts. (5) **Consulate,** Dec. 1799-May 1804. Napoleon's coup led to one-man rule though nominally republican forms. New wars. (6) **Empire,** May 1804-June 1815. Napoleon installed new regime, consolidated some revolutionary gains, concentrated on wars. Major period of change in other parts of Europe.

a. CAUSES OF THE REVOLUTION

(1) Intellectual currents of the Enlightenment proposed governments based on contracts or constitutions rather than divine authority. Such ideas were discussed in the salons organized by women in Paris and by the *philosophes* (reform-minded intellectuals) surrounding Diderot's encyclopedia. (2) Economic developments expanded a middle class that, although often involved in the royal bureaucracy, had little access to formal politics. This middle class was concerned with obstructions to economic development and commerce, such as the guild system, internal tariffs, and the lack of common weights and measures and adequate roles for professionals. (3) A social contest had developed between the emerging middle class (especially the bureaucracy) and the old aristocracy. The aristocracy had many privileges, including exemption from many of the taxes levied against the middle classes. After 1750 the aristocracy discouraged middle-class entry and in-creased its own monopoly over upper church offices (the **aristocratic resurgence,** probably a response to population growth, which angered the middle class). At the same time, these aristocratic landowners attempted to collect their full manorial rights from a peasantry already heavily burdened by taxes. Although most peasants were free, many had little land, and surviving manorial dues were galling. (4) A financial crisis within the government resulted from an increasing deficit. This deficit was the result of costly wars of territorial aggression in the 17th and 18th centuries and was worsened by the policy of selling offices, with tax-exempt status, to raise additional revenues. When the king and his advisers tried to levy new taxes through parlement, they were forced to call the Estates General. (5) Revolution was triggered by efforts by the aristocracy to wring concessions from the king (Assembly of Notables, 1787), and bad harvests and unemployment (1787-88) helped stir urban and rural rioters.

b. THE NATIONAL ASSEMBLY

1789, May 5. Estates General met at Versailles with double representation of the third estate (representing the middle class): nobles 300, clergy 300, commons 600. Necker, the king's financial adviser, announced that voting would be by order, not by head, thus eliminating the third estate's advantage. Acting on a motion by **Abbé Sieyès** (author of *What Is the Third Estate?*), the third estate assumed the title of the **National Assembly** (June 17) and invited other orders to join them.

June 20. Tennis Court Oath. The king suspended meetings of the Estates General for three days and closed the hall. Members met at a neighboring tennis court and took an oath not to separate until they had given the realm a constitution.

June 23. The king ordered each estate to meet separately, but deputies refused. Most of the clergy and many of the nobles joined the assembly—prompting the king to order the rumps of the first and second estates to join the assembly (June 27). He dismissed **Necker** (July 11) and concentrated troops near Paris, which led to the attack on the Bastille.

July 14. STORMING OF THE BASTILLE. A mob in Paris attacked the prison although most prisoners had already been removed. Aided by deserters from the French Royal Guard (incorporated into the Parisian National Guard in Aug.), they captured and killed the governor, Jordan de Launay. Louis ordered troops out of Paris, and the Parisian electors formed a commune, with **Lafayette** commanding the National Guard and Bailly elected mayor. **Adoption of tricolor:** blue and red for Paris, and white for France. Necker was recalled (July 17). Beginning of emigration of nobles (*émigrés*).

Rising of the peasants against the manorial lords in Dauphiné, Provence, Burgundy, and throughout France. This *grande peur* (great fear) was not systematically spread from Paris but occurred sporadically as a series of mass movements with numerous centers. Riots, provisional governments, guards in the provincial cities.

Aug. 4. Surrender of feudal rights by representatives of the nobility. The radical nature of this act was undermined by provisions for the gradual elimination of these rights and compensation for the owners (in most cases it was never paid): abolition of titles, prohibition of the sale of offices, dissolution of the guilds, and so on.

Aug. 27. DECLARATION OF THE RIGHTS OF MAN AND CITIZEN, based on English and American precedents, guaranteed to citizens the rights of liberty, equality, security, and property. This provision limited explicit protection to males in every phase of the Revolution and resulted in Marie-Olympe de Gouges's publishing of her **Declaration of the Rights of Women (1791).** These declarations stated that the aim of society was public happiness.

Oct. 5–6. MARCH TO VERSAILLES. Popular riots in Paris, caused by hunger and rumors of an intended reaction against the Revolution, resulted in a march of a band, consisting mostly of women, to Versailles. Lafayette rescued the royal family, but the band forced the king's return to Paris.

The political clubs had existed since early 1789 but were growing in power. The **Jacobins,** enjoying a wide democratic base and led by **Maximilien Robespierre,** became a growing power in the state. The **Cordeliers,** more radical than the Jacobins, were led by **Georges Jacques Danton, Jean Paul Marat, Camille Desmoulins,** and **Jacques Hébert.** The **Feuillants,** moderate monarchists including **Lafayette and Bailly,** had separated from the Jacobins.

As the assembly debated a new constitution for a liberal monarchy (adopted in 1791), it tried to address the fiscal crisis by declaring church lands public property and issuing *assignats* (government notes) on their value. Because *assignats* were frequently overissued, recurrent inflation resulted. On **July 12, 1790, Civil Constitution of the Clergy** placed bishops and priests as well as church income under government control. Fewer than half of all priests declared loyalty to the government, and in 1791 the pope denounced it, setting up a long battle between revolutionaries and much of the Catholic Church.

1790, Sept. 4. Necker resigned, and **Mirabeau,** in an alliance with the court, endeavored to save the monarchy. Mirabeau died on April 2, 1791.

1791, June 14. Le Chapelier Law outlawed all workers' coalitions, including cooperatives and associations. In effect, it attempted to destroy remnants of the guild system still extant. It also demonstrated the commitment of the new government to recognize only one type of property—land—and to further economic individualism. It was extended to agricultural workers and servants on July 20.

June 20–25. The king and his family fled, hoping to reach the northeast frontier and the protection of loyalist troops. They were recognized and stopped at **Varennes,** and then brought back to Paris.

Aug. 27. Declaration of Pillnitz, signed by Frederick William II of Prussia and Leopold II, the emperor (r. 1790–92, succeeded by Francis II), stated that the two rulers would intervene in French affairs only with unanimous consent of the powers, including Great Britain.

Sept. 3. CONSTITUTION OF 1791 was ratified on Sept. 13 by the king, who swore an oath of allegiance to the assembly on Sept. 14. One legislative chamber held the sole right to initiate laws; the king could

delay measures only through veto. Old provinces and provincial parlements were abolished, replaced by 83 **departments** (a move for uniformity and centralization). Abolition of aristocracy confirmed. The constitution distinguished between active (voting) and passive citizens. Only males were considered to be citizens. Passive citizens had to have been born to French parents or born in France. In order to become active citizens, passive citizens had to take a civic oath, be 25 years of age, and pay a tax equivalent to three days' wages. Voters had to be on the rolls of the National Guard and could not be Jewish. The last provision was waived on Sept. 27, 1791. Active citizens chose electors who elected representatives for a two-year term in the legislature. Officers of the departments and districts were selected from the electors, whereas municipal officers and judges were selected from the active citizens. The constitution also required clerics to take a civic oath and dissolved all ecclesiastical orders except those having to do with education and care of the sick.

Sept. 30. The assembly was dissolved after voting that none of its members should be eligible for election to the next assembly.

c. THE LEGISLATIVE ASSEMBLY

1791, Oct. 1–1792, Sept. 21. The legislative assembly, with 745 members, represented primarily the middle class. **Parties:** (1) The Right became weaker almost daily; (2) the Left comprised the majority and consisted of (a) the **Plain,** an unorganized group of moderate republicans and monarchists, which was swayed by (b) the **Girondists,** who advocated the establishment of a form of a federal republic and included the brilliant orators Guadet, Vergniaud, and Brissot; and (c) the **Mountain,** which drew its strength from the Jacobin and Cordelier clubs. Although the divisions between the last two did not attain their clearest form until the Convention, their beginnings were evident in the assembly.

The poor harvest of 1791 and rising grain prices, worsened by distribution problems and increased demands as the result of the war, caused growing unrest and riots in Paris. Abolition of religious orders and elimination of the tithe also led to problems in administering poor relief.

1792, March 20–25. Guillotine accepted as form of execution. First used on April 25, the guillotine symbolized the leveling between classes during the Revolution by eliminating the previous distinction between the execution of elites (beheading) and commoners (hanging). The guillotine was often portrayed as a "feminine" form of execution, and bourgeois males were expected to demonstrate superiority by embracing death without displaying emotion at their executions.

1792–97. WAR OF THE FIRST COALITION. The French interpreted the Declaration of Pillnitz as a bald threat of interference and issued ultimatums against Leopold II and Francis II.

1792, April 20. France declared war against Austria. The French suffered reverses, and allied armies captured Verdun (Sept. 1). The Prussians were finally defeated at the **Battle of Valmy (Sept. 20),** which gave heart to the revolutionary armies.

Aug. 10. Popular demonstrations and the **storming of the Tuileries** led to the **suspension of functions of the monarchy.** The assembly voted to enact all legislation vetoed by the king, who was confined to the Temple (old house of the Knights Templar). The assembly also voted to call a convention elected by universal male suffrage to enact a new constitution. In the meantime, the government was controlled by the Provisional Executive Council (headed by Danton) and the Paris Commune.

Sept. 2–7. September Massacres occurred at Paris as the result of news of the siege of Verdun. Suspects were taken from the prisons and executed by the mob after being tried by hastily improvised tribunals. Similar scenes were enacted at Versailles, Lyons, Rheims, Meaux, and Orléans.

Sept. 9–16. Suspension of **free trade** on grain. Provisions provided for requisitioning for the army and civil authorities. Amnesty was given to individuals arrested for agitation over grain.

Sept. 20. Divorce was legalized, and the state assumed responsibility for recording marriages, births, and deaths, which was formerly done by the church. The **Battle of Valmy** gave a first victory to revolutionary armies over the Prussians.

d. THE NATIONAL CONVENTION: THE REVOLUTION'S MOST RADICAL PHASE

1792, Sept. 21–1795, Aug. 22. THE NATIONAL CONVENTION, longest lived of the revolutionary assemblies. It was elected by male suffrage and composed entirely of republicans (749 members, of whom 486 were new men). **Parties:** The **Plain** had a majority but was dominated by the **Girondists** and then by the **Mountain.** The Girondists now formed the Right, and the Mountain, under Robespierre, Danton, and others, formed the Left.

Sept. 21. Monarchy abolished.

Sept. 22. Republic proclaimed. (First day of Year I of Republican calendar.) On **Sept. 25** the Republic was declared "one and indivisible."

Oct. 2. Committee of General Security was formed, with undefined police powers.

Nov. 6. Allies in retreat following a French victory by Gen. Dumouriez at **Jemappes.**

Nov. 19. The Decree of Fraternity offered French assistance to people who wished to overthrow their governments. Other countries, including England, feared risings. Irish nationalists sought French aid as a result of this declaration.

Dec. 4. Convention declared the death penalty for anyone advocating monarchy.

Dec. 8. Convention repealed suspension on free trade in grain but outlawed grain exports. Nov. and Dec. also saw instances of price fixing and demonstrations among peasants in the Beauce region.

Dec. 10. Louis XVI tried before the Convention. Girondists suggested a referendum to the people (Dec. 27), but on **Jan. 14, 1793,** the Convention decided there would be no referendum and found Louis guilty. Louis sentenced to death by a slim majority (Jan. 20) and executed on **Jan. 21.**

Dec. 16. The death penalty to be administered for threatening the unity and integrity of the Republic.

As a result of a struggle between the Girondists and the Mountain, **all power in the Convention centered in three institutions:** (1) the Committee of General Security; (2) the Paris Commune, reorganized on basis of male suffrage and acting through its committee led by Chaumette and Hébert; and (3) the Committee of Public Safety. The latter was composed of 9 (later 12) members (including Robespierre, Danton, and St. Just) with dictatorial power.

1793–94. THE REIGN OF TERROR. Robespierre gradually came to dominate the whole government. He was never a "dictator" in the modern sense; his power was checked by his colleagues in the Committee of Public Safety, by the opposing Hébertist faction in the Commune and the Convention, and by the commissioners of the Convention sent into the provinces (*représentants en mission*). These commissioners, sent out to suppress counterrevolutionary movements, were often responsible for extreme terrorism in their districts. They collaborated with the local Jacobin clubs and revolutionary committees. Horrors were perpetrated by Tallien at Bordeaux, Lebon at Arras, Carrier at Nantes, and Couthon, Fouché, and Collot d'Herbois at Lyons. Some commissioners, however, were fairly clement and spared their regions (e.g., the younger Robespierre in the east and south, Lakanal in the southwest).

1793. WAR IN THE VENDÉE. Uprising of the peasantry in the west of France. Discontent among the peasantry over the Revolution had been widespread, aggravated by the execution of Louis XVI and the sale of church and émigré lands to the middle class. The Vendée was sparked by the attempt to levy troops because the levy unfairly targeted peasants. The Vendéans succeeded in capturing several towns. They finally suffered a major defeat on **Aug. 13** at the **Battle of Luçon** but continued to fight, suffering defeat at **Cholet** (Oct. 20) and **Le Mans** (Dec. 12). Warfare in the Vendée would continue until finally stopped by Gen. Hoche in March 1796.

At the same time, **federalist revolts** occurred in many departments, protesting the centralization of power. Lyons moderates overthrew the municipal government, and federalists then executed the Jacobin exmayor Chalier **(July 17).** Kellerman laid siege to Lyons **(Aug. 9),** which fell on **Oct. 9.** Meanwhile, Toulon turned its port over to the British **(Aug. 29),** and the French lost their Mediterranean fleet.

Feb. 1. War declared against Great Britain, Holland, and Spain. Sardinia had been at war with France since July 1792, but now Britain,

Holland, Spain, and the empire all joined an alliance against France. Belgium was annexed. The émigrés proclaimed Louis XVI's son (a prisoner in the Temple) **King Louis XVII.**

Feb. Economic problems plagued the Revolution. Sections of Paris demonstrated against price increases (Feb. 3). Consumers protested prices of goods in Paris (Feb. 24–27). Disturbances over prices continued throughout March and April.

March 1. Trade with Britain was forbidden, which pushed foreign trade into a slump throughout the Convention.

Poor relief was a problem because of the disbanding of religious orders responsible for collecting and administering such relief, and shortages due to war and revolution. The Convention passed **two laws of public assistance (March 19 and June 28, 1793).** The first established the basis of a system that provided work for the able-bodied and home relief whenever possible for other needy individuals. The second gave state aid to children, the aged, and unmarried mothers (for the first time in French history). Abandoned children were received in state hospitals until age 12, when they were apprenticed out.

March 29. Freedom of the press restricted.

May 4. Grain price maximum established.

June 24. Constitution of 1793, including universal male suffrage, voted on by the Convention. It was sent to the primary assemblies for ratification but never put in effect.

July 23. Mainz recovered by the Prussians after a three-month siege. The allies also took Condé and Valenciennes. Custine executed by the French for negligence. **British siege of Toulon.** The troops of the Republic were driven back on almost all fronts. As a result, revolts multiplied in the interior, frequently inspired by Girondists who had escaped the purge and fled Paris. Energetic countermeasures were taken by the Committee of Public Safety.

July. Department administrations were authorized to forcibly purchase grain.

Aug. 9. Death penalty was enacted for hoarders of grain.

Aug. 19. Public granaries were established and departments authorized to set prices for firewood and coal.

Aug. 23. Levy of the entire male population capable of bearing arms. (This **levée en masse** established the right of the revolutionary state to universal military conscription.) Fourteen armies were hastily organized and put in the field. Caen, Bordeaux, and Marseilles were conquered by the republicans.

Sept. 29. Establishment of the maximum price for a large number of commodities; wages were also fixed. This system was never fully worked out, and the maximum was frequently violated. It did, however, prevent a catastrophic fall of the *assignats* and ensured the provisioning of the armies. The whole experiment was less a socialistic measure than a way to ration goods during an emergency. These prices were put into effect on Feb. 26, 1794.

Oct. 30. All women's clubs and political societies closed in an effort to control dissension regarding the Terror. Many of these societies had adopted radical democratic, socialist, and feminist positions.

Oct. 31. Girondists were executed. Sixty executions occurred per month, including those of Bailly, Mme. Roland, and Philippe Egalité. Many committed suicide in keeping with the strong stoic tradition and to avoid the state's manipulation of executions to serve its own propaganda purposes.

Dec. The Allied retreat across the Rhine marked the first appearance of **Napoleon Bonaparte,** a young Corsican artillery officer connected with Robespierre and the Jacobins.

Dec. 19. The Bouquier Law on primary schooling established the principle of obligatory primary schooling, to teach reading, writing, arithmetic, and revolutionary civics.

1794. Robespierre consolidated his power. Commune leaders (Hébert, Chaumette, Cloots) were executed on March 24. Dantonists (Desmoulins, Hérault de Sechelles, etc.) were executed on April 6.

Feb. 5. The Convention decreed freedom for all slaves in French colonies (pp. 392, 639).

Feb. 22. A law on primary education provided free education for children between ages 6 and 13. This law was followed by another law (Nov. 17) that declared primary schooling was not compulsory and required that pupils be taught in French. It also included manual labor on the syllabus. This law was not widely implemented.

June 8. Festival of the Supreme Being established, with Robespierre (having abolished the cult of reason) as high priest to provide ceremonies to replace Christianity.

June 10. Law of 22 Prairial bestowed great power on the revolutionary tribunal. Juries were allowed to convict without hearing evidence or argument. Executions increased to 354 per month.

June 26. Battle of Fleurus. French victory led to the evacuation of Belgium by the duke of Coburg. Marked the beginning of the decline of allied opposition to France and the spread of revolutionary laws to adjacent territories.

July 27. A conspiracy by members of the Mountain and more moderate elements led to the **fall of Robespierre.** He, his brother, and St. Just were arrested. Released by friends, they were outlawed, surprised at the Hôtel de Ville, and executed. More than 80 of the party met the same fate over the next few days. The Paris Commune was nearly extinct. The objective was to remove Robespierre, not to end the Terror. Public opinion, however, forced Robespierre's successors to adopt more moderate policies.

Nov. 12. END OF TERROR. Moderates dominated the Convention, and the Paris club of the Jacobins closed. The Girondists who had escaped execution were readmitted to the Convention (Dec. 8).

Dec. 24. Maximum repealed. New issues of *assignats* increased depreciation.

1795, Feb. 25. Law on secondary education. Schools established for secondary education for boys. Scholarships would be provided for poorer children, and teaching would be in French.

March 5. Treaty of Basel between France and Prussia. Prussia, Saxony, Hanover, and Hesse-Cassel withdrew from war, followed by a peace at Basel between Spain and France (June 22).

April 1. Bread riots in Paris marked a growing reaction in the capital and throughout the country. Monarchist agitation revived, and some émigrés returned.

April 7. Adoption of the metric system of standardized weights and measures throughout France, which assisted in trade between regions.

May 20. The White Terror. Further riots and outbreaks included a fierce attack on the Convention. The movement resulted in the extermination of the remnants of the Mountain. Meanwhile, French armies were uniformly successful.

May 23. Women forbidden to attend any political assembly. The decision may have reflected the belief that women, who were believed to be reactive, could not participate in politics and might incite rebellion by emotional actions at meetings. Men, in contrast, were considered capable of rational and constructive behavior.

June 8. Death of the dauphin.

Aug. 22. THE CONSTITUTION OF 1795 (third constitution of the Revolution, also called the Constitution of Year III) was ratified by the assembly. Law of two-thirds determined that two-thirds of the next legislature would be drawn from the ranks of the National Convention.

Oct. 5. The Day of the Sections. Outbreak of sections led by Paris royalists were successfully stopped by Napoleon Bonaparte's "whiff of grapeshot." Cannonade from the Church of St. Roch marked a complete victory for the Convention. The Convention, after voting that relatives of émigrés should not be permitted to hold office, was dissolved.

e. THE DIRECTORY

1795, Aug. 22. The Directory was established by the **Constitution of Year III.** Citizenship was extended to all males of at least 21 years of age who were on the civic lists of a canton and either paid direct taxes or had served in the army. All citizens could vote (no distinction between active and passive citizens). The constitution provided for a bicameral legislature (Council of Five Hundred and Council of the Ancients), with deputies each serving a three-year term, and a five-member executive branch (the Directory) chosen by the legislature. **Freedom of the Press** was confirmed by the constitution, but it could be restricted by the Directory for a year. **Political clubs,** collective petitioning, and popular societies were suppressed (Aug. 23).

The **1795 harvest was poor;** it was preceded and followed by bad winters. Famine conditions existed in many parts of France. Nov. and Dec. saw strikes among Parisian workers, especially in the printing trades. The Directory followed a repressive policy toward workers.

1796, March 18. *Assignats* **replaced with** *mandats territoriaux* in an effort to stabilize the currency. The *mandats* depreciated almost immediately. The government withdrew them and returned to metallic currency in Feb. 1797, but only after decreeing a forced loan on the rich (poorly implemented).

THE WAR OF THE FIRST COALITION proceeded on two fronts. French armies under Jourdan and Moreau separately invaded S. Germany, forcing Baden, Württemberg, and Bavaria to conclude truces (Aug.). Archduke Charles, leading Austrian forces, defeated Jourdan at **Amberg** (Aug.) and **Würzburg** (Sept. 3). In doing so, Charles successfully stopped the attempt to unite the two French armies on German soil and forced Moreau to retreat across the Rhine. The German campaigns were inconclusive.

1796–97. BONAPARTE'S ITALIAN CAMPAIGN. Napoleon Bonaparte split the Austrian and Piedmontese armies—defeating the Austrians at **Millesimo** (April 13) and the Piedmontese at **Mondovi** (April 21). Victor Amadeus was compelled to conclude a separate peace with France. Napoleon then defeated the Austrians at the Battle of Lodi.

1796, May 10. Battle of Lodi. Napoleon entered Milan and conquered all of Lombardy as far as Mantua. Mantua surrendered after being besieged by the French, following Lodi.

1797, Feb. 2. Napoleon advanced toward Rome, but the pope concluded the **Treaty of Tolentino** with him (Feb. 19). Napoleon then crossed the Alps to meet Archduke Charles, but uprisings in Venetia and Tyrol forced him to open negotiations leading to the preliminary peace of Leoben.

April 18. Preliminary peace of Leoben: Austria took over Venetia, and France organized the Cisalpine Republic in northwestern Italy.

Sept. 4. The Fructidor Coup was established by emergency legislation forced through the councils with the support of the military. Paris occupied as the Triumvirs (directors Barras, La-Révellière-Lépeaux, and Reubell) instigated the Directorial Terror, pushing the Revolution left again. Deported members of the opposition included Carnot and Barthélemy.

Sept. The press freedoms were suspended according to the constitution. Right-wing newspapers were closed, and a stamp tax on the press was introduced (Sept. 30 and Oct. 4).

Sept. 30. Bankruptcy of the Two-Thirds repudiated two-thirds of the national debt.

Oct. 17. Treaty of Campo Formio between Austria and France concluded Austria's involvement in the War of the First Coalition. It allowed Austria to annex Venetian territories and secured French support for Austria's efforts to gain control of Salzburg and Bavarian territory around it. Austria ceded Belgium to France and secretly agreed to support French annexation of the left bank of the Rhine from Basel to Andernach.

1797–1801. PAUL I, emperor of Russia.

1797–1840. FREDERICK WILLIAM III, king of Prussia.

1798–99. BONAPARTE'S EGYPTIAN CAMPAIGN (p. 359).

1798. Bonaparte captured **Malta** (June 11) and continued to Egypt where he captured **Alexandria** (July 2). He then took Cairo at the **Battle of the Pyramids** (July 21).

Aug. 1. Battle of the Nile. British admiral Horatio Nelson destroyed the French fleet anchored in the harbor of Abukir. Napoleon was thus cut off from France. The Ottomans, supported by the British, then defeated Napoleon's army at **Abukir (July 25, 1799)** after it returned from an unsuccessful campaign in Syria. Napoleon left Egypt (Aug. 24) for France, leaving Klebér in command. Klebér was assassinated and succeeded by Menou, whom the British defeated at **Alexandria (March 21, 1801).**

May 11. The Coup of 22 Floréal challenged the returns of several elections and thus excluded approximately one-quarter of the candidates.

Sept. 5. Jourdan Law introduced conscription for all able-bodied males, 20 years of age; 200,000 men were then called up.

Dec. 24. Alliance between Russia and Great Britain led to the **Second Coalition.**

1799. WAR OF THE SECOND COALITION (alliance of Britain and Russia joined by Austria, Naples, Portugal, and the Ottoman Empire) proceeded on both the north and the south fronts:

SOUTH (Italian peninsula): Defeating a Neapolitan army commanded by the Austrian general Mack, the French, under Championnet, recaptured **Rome** (Dec. 15) and took the entire kingdom of Naples. The French occupied **Florence** (1799), but a series of defeats followed. The allies entered Milan after the Battle of Cassano.

April 27. Battle of Cassano. Suvorov foiled MacDonald's efforts to unite his army with the French forces in Italy by defeating him at the **Battle of the Trebbia (June 17–19).** Suvorov and Melas then defeated French forces under Joubert at Novi as the latter attempted to advance from Genoa. As a result, the French lost control of the Italian peninsula.

NORTH (Germany and Switzerland): Archduke Charles, commanding an army of Russian and Austrian troops, defeated Jourdan and the army of the upper Rhine at **Stockach** (March 25, 1799). Jourdan re-treated to France and laid down his command. Charles then defeated Masséna, who replaced Jourdan at the **Battle of Zürich (June 4–7).** Korsakov replaced Charles and was defeated and driven out of **Zürich** by Masséna (Sept. 25–30) despite a better tactical position. In the meantime, Suvorov had crossed the Alps to unite with the army under Korsakov but was forced back by French advances. Masséna took Constance and threatened the flank of Archduke Charles, who was preparing the invasion of France from the Rhine. The British and Russian forces that had sought to take the Netherlands failed completely.

Oct. 18. The British surrendered all prisoners taken in Holland in return for unobstructed evacuation.

Oct. 22. Russians withdrew from the coalition.

3. THE NAPOLEONIC PERIOD, 1799–1815

a. THE CONSULATE

1799, Nov. 9 (18 Brumaire). The Coup d'État of Brumaire. Sieyès and Roger-Ducos resigned from the Directory, and Barras then resigned under duress. The Directory could not function with only two members and was disbanded. Sieyès and Roger-Ducos, supported by Napoleon and his brother Lucien Bonaparte (president of the Council of 500), convinced the councils to name Sieyès, Roger-Ducos, and Napoleon as provisional consuls and establish a commission to draft a new constitution.

1. DOMESTIC AFFAIRS: CONSOLIDATION OF SELECTIVE REVOLUTIONARY MEASURES

1799, Nov. 13. Law of Hostages was repealed. Napoleon went to the Temple to personally receive the released hostages.

Nov. 28. Forced loan was replaced by a surtax on existing taxes.

Dec. 25. CONSTITUTION OF YEAR VIII was put into effect. It was passed by a popular vote but implemented before the results of that vote had been announced. The results (3,011,107 in favor and 1,562 opposed) were considered suspicious—the army did not vote, but its ballots were counted, and the navy voted under dubious circumstances. The constitution established a first consul (Napoleon) with a ten-year term, and two other consuls were appointed by the first consul and had only consultative powers. Notables of the communes were elected by universal male suffrage. These notables elected one-tenth of their number as notables of the departments. One-tenth of the latter became notables for France from whom the senate chose the **legislative bodies** (Tribunate and Legislature). The Senate was chosen for life by co-option. The Tribunate discussed laws submitted by government but did not vote, whereas the Legislature voted but did not discuss the laws. The constitution had **no bill of rights** as in earlier revolutionary constitutions. Only inviolability of homes and liberty of the individual were guaranteed.

1800, Feb. 17. Administration centralized. Law of 28 Pluviôse placed the administration of local government in the hands of centrally appointed prefectures and subprefectures. It was followed by a new system, which placed tax collection in the hands of government officials in each district.

1801, July 15. Concordat of 1801 (announced on Easter Sunday, 1802) between the pope and Napoleon reconciled the Consulate and the Catholic Church. Napoleon sought this reconciliation because of the continuing strife in the west of France, where local peasants remained committed to the Catholic Church. The reconciliation was incomplete because many priests in outlying regions (especially in Belgium) formed the Petite Église, which opposed the Concordat, and the Organic Articles that followed it. Christians had been allowed to worship on Sundays since Dec. 30, 1799. Napoleon now **reestablished the Catholic Church** in France under close government supervision. The consul appointed the bishops, who were confirmed by the pope. The bishops chose their own clergy, whom the government paid. The pope continued to control the Papal States, with the exceptions of Ferrara, Bologna, and Romagna.

1802, April 8. Organic Articles for Protestants. Napoleon commissioned Portalis to provide legislation for Protestants similar to the Concordat of 1801. The resulting Organic Articles divided the Calvinist community into congregations of 6,000 souls governed by a pastor and elders chosen from the large taxpayers. Lutheran churches were supervised by directories of which the majority were selected by the consul. The civil government had the right to veto clerical appointments and changes in church doctrine. In 1804, Protestant pastors were salaried by the state. This legislation was favored by Protestants and led to a Calvinist revival in Napoleonic France.

May 1. Napoleon replaced the secondary schools of the Directory with **lycées,** whose purpose was to educate future officials and to emphasize technical and practical skills. The government set aside scholarships for children of government servants and officers. The rewards for service to the state were also reinforced by the **Legion of Honor,** created on May 19. Because Napoleon believed that women should be wives and mothers, women were not admitted to state secondary schools or the universities.

Aug. 2. Napoleon became consul for life, with the right of appointing his successor. A new constitution, approved by plebiscite (3.5 million popular votes), enlarged the powers of the Senate, which was ruled by the consul, and reduced the importance of the other legislative bodies.

1803, April 12. Employers' combinations that acted "unjustly or abusively" to lower wages or hours of work were banned. **Workers' combinations** that challenged established wages or hours were outlawed. This law strengthened the Le Chapelier Law, but the government usually ignored workers' mutual aid societies in prosecuting workers' organizations. Workers were also required to carry a passbook *(livret),* which would be surrendered to an employer during the period of employment. The book had to be validated by employers in order for the worker to be able to find work elsewhere in France. Agricultural laborers and some unskilled workers were exempt, as were most women (with the exception of female silk workers in Lille after 1812).

1804, Feb. Conspiracy against life of Napoleon discovered. Pichegru, implicated in the conspiracy, died mysteriously in prison. Moreau fled to America. Codoudal and the duke of Enghien were executed, the latter without the observation of the ordinary forms of law.

2. FOREIGN AFFAIRS

1800. Renewal of the campaign against Austria. The Austrians took Genoa (June 4) after a horrible famine. Napoleon crossed the St. Bernard Pass in May with 40,000 men to attack the flank of the Austrians. He engaged them and won at the **Battle of Marengo (June 14).** The Austrian general Melas agreed to a truce. Moreau, commanding the French forces of the Rhine, took Munich (July).

Dec. 3. Hohenlinden. The French defeated Archduke John, who had replaced Charles. MacDonald, with the French Army of Italy, began an invasion of Austria from the south (Jan. 1801). The Austrian emperor sought peace.

1801, Feb. 9. Treaty of Lunéville between Austria and France reaffirmed all cessions Austria had made under Campo Formio and gave the French the grand duchy of Tuscany. Princes who lost territory on the left bank of the Rhine were to be indemnified on the right bank according to the *Reichsdeputations-hauptschluss* (Feb. 1803), which eliminated most of the ecclesiastical estates in Germany. French-sponsored Batavian, Helvetian, Cisalpine, and Ligurian republics were rec-

THE HOUSE OF BONAPARTE

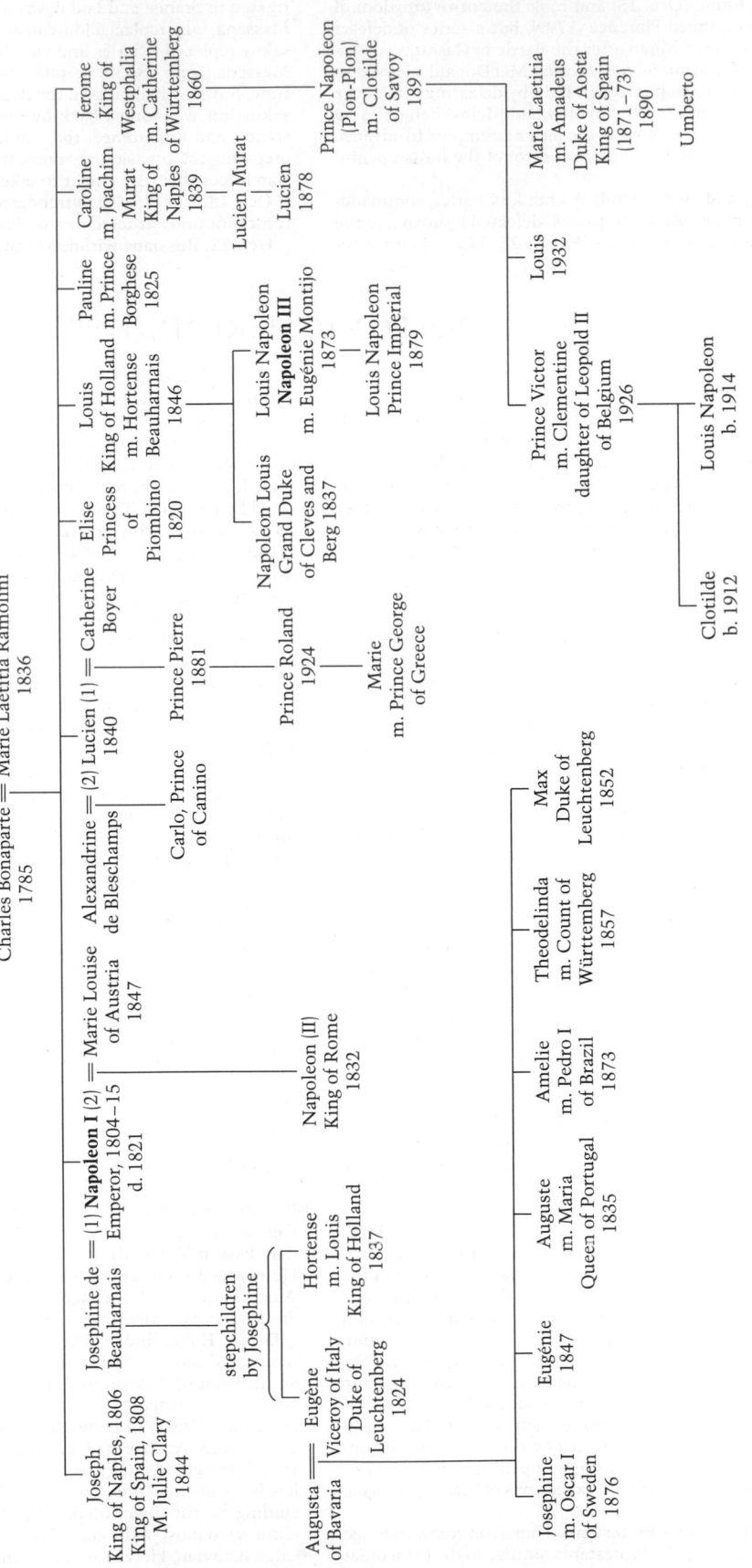

Charles Bonaparte = Marie Laetitia Ramolini
1785   1836

Joseph
King of Naples, 1806
King of Spain, 1808
M. Julie Clary
1844

Josephine de = (1) **Napoleon I** (2) = Marie Louise
Beauharnais   Emperor, 1804–15   of Austria
              d. 1821   1847

Napoleon (II)
King of Rome
1832

stepchildren
by Josephine

Hortense
m. Louis
King of Holland
1837

Eugène
Viceroy of Italy
Duke of
Leuchtenberg
1824

Augusta =
of Bavaria

Josephine
m. Oscar I
of Sweden
1876

Eugénie
1847

Auguste
m. Maria
Queen of Portugal
1835

Amelie
m. Pedro I
of Brazil
1873

Theodelinda
m. Count of
Württemberg
1857

Max
Duke of
Leuchtenberg
1852

Lucien (1) = Catherine
1840   Boyer

Alexandrine = (2)
de Bleschamps

Carlo, Prince
of Canino

Prince Pierre
1881

Prince Roland
1924

Marie
m. Prince George
of Greece

Elise
Princess
of
Piombino
1820

Louis
King of Holland
m. Hortense
Beauharnais
1846

Napoleon Louis
Grand Duke
of Cleves and
Berg 1837

Louis Napoleon
Napoleon III
m. Eugénie Montijo
1873

Louis Napoleon
Prince Imperial
1879

Pauline
m. Prince
Borghese
1825

Caroline
m. Joachim
Murat
King of
Naples
1839

Lucien Murat

Lucien
1878

Jerome
King of
Westphalia
m. Catherine
of Württemberg
1860

Prince Napoleon
(Plon-Plon)
m. Clotilde
of Savoy
1891

Prince Victor
m. Clementine
daughter of Leopold II
of Belgium
1926

Marie Laetitia
m. Amadeus
Duke of Aosta
King of Spain
(1871–73)
1890

Umberto

Louis
1932

Clotilde
b. 1912

Louis Napoleon
b. 1914

Single dates, unless otherwise indicated, are death dates.

ognized. Spain ceded the Louisiana territory to France. This treaty was succeeded by the Treaty of Florence.

March 18. Treaty of Florence between France and Naples. This treaty closed harbors to British and Ottoman vessels. Naples ceded possessions in central Italy and the island of Elba and received French garrisons in several Italian towns.

1802, March 27. Treaty of Amiens between Britain and France: Britain surrendered all conquests to France except Trinidad, which went to Spain, and Ceylon; Ceylon was ceded by the Batavian Republic (the French puppet state in the Low Countries). France recognized the Republic of the Seven Ionian Islands, and Malta was restored to the Knights of Malta. This treaty resulted briefly in the complete pacification of Europe, though war with Britain was resumed in 1803.

1804, March 21. The Civil Code was proclaimed. It strengthened the patriarchal family. Women had no political rights and could not legally be witnesses of births, marriages, or deaths. Divorce, with alimony, was possible only if the wife was under 45 years of age and the marriage had existed for less than 20 years. Causes for divorce did not include adultery on the part of the husband unless he brought his concubine into the home. The code offered no security for tenants—contracts always favored the property owners. The code also allowed for partitioning of estates, thus contravening the tradition of impartible inheritance and, historians have argued, contributing to France's increasingly low birthrates as families sought to pass their land on intact.

b. THE FIRST EMPIRE

1804, May 18. Napoleon I was proclaimed emperor of the French by the Senate and Tribunate; his rule was consecrated at Paris by Pope Pius VII on Dec. 2 and ratified by plebiscite (3,572,329 in favor, 2,569 opposed). The imperial office was made hereditary by male line, with the emperor having the right to adopt the children of his brothers; if without heir, the crown would pass to his brothers. Napoleon immediately established a court and began the development of a new nobility, with many of the privileges of the old, but based on achievement instead of birth. Napoleon really revived the absolute monarchy but made it more modern and efficient. However, Napoleon concentrated his efforts on expanding and consolidating his empire through warfare and foreign policy.

1. DOMESTIC AFFAIRS

Poor relief. No policy of poor relief had existed under the Consulate. The administrators lifted the ban on private and religious charitable foundations.

1805, March 28. The Bureaux de Bienfaisance (bureaus of charity), established under the Directory, were centralized.

1806. Napoleon convened the **Assembly of Jewish Notables,** which redefined traditional Judaism and transformed the Jews into French citizens. Napoleon thus questioned the Jews' loyalty to France on doctrinal issues rather than simply accepting their economic loyalty, as the revolutionaries had done. The assembly led to two laws enacted on May 30, 1806, and March 17, 1808, which proclaimed this loyalty but also deprived northeastern Jews of their economic freedom.

Salt taxes were established, which harked back to the despised gabelle of the ancien régime. Postal rates were raised by 50 percent, and, in 1810, the state reestablished its monopoly on tobacco. The progress of warfare throughout the Napoleonic period placed a heavy financial toll on a government that had not been financially stable when Napoleon replaced the Directory. Until 1810, taxes remained moderate overall because the French relied heavily on indemnities and other monies paid by occupied territories.

Jan. 1. France returned to the Gregorian calendar.

May 10. The principle of the university system was enunciated by law. Napoleon did not actually degree these universities until March 17, 1808. Universities offered higher education, but they also oversaw state schools at the lower level. School inspectors (a maximum of 30) reported on schools at all three levels (primary, secondary, and higher) to the academies. The system never provided a monopoly on teaching for the state, but it did provide the government with stricter control over schools.

Nov. 21. Berlin Decree established the **Continental System,** banning trade between Napoleon-controlled Europe and Britain; designed to weaken Britain's export-based economy.

1808, July 5. Departmental *dépots de mendicité* were established to control begging.

1810. A penal code required all beggars to go to poorhouses.

April 1. Napoleon married the Archduchess Marie Louise, daughter of Francis I of Austria. Metternich, the Austrian foreign minister after 1809, arranged the match. The Church Court of Paris had annulled the marriage between Napoleon and Josephine (Jan. 14, 1810) although Josephine was by law too old to be divorced. Marie Louise bore Napoleon a son on March 20, 1811.

Economic crisis occurred as the result of the heavy cost of war, and sluggish growth in the French economy and the **Continental System.**

Eastern and central European countries could not afford to pay for French exports because they could no longer trade with England. Rise in the cost of textiles, especially cotton, also hurt artisans who could not sell their wares at a price that would pay for their labor and raw materials. **Russia** devalued its currency in Sept. 1810, and **German and Dutch banks failed.** Parisian bankers had invested heavily in the latter, and they were forced to call in their loans. In June, flooding killed large portions of the mulberry leaf crop and thus severely hurt the silk industry.

Unemployment soared; the government estimated that two out of every five workers in Paris were unemployed. France began to recover in the spring of 1811, but storms around Paris and a drought in the south led to a poor harvest. In 1812, Napoleon increased taxes throughout France to help pay for mounting military costs and, particularly, for the cost of the ensuing war with Russia.

Britain also experienced an economic downturn as a result of its inability to market its goods on the Continent. This economic downturn was ameliorated by international trade until the United States, the best alternative, closed its market to Britain in 1807. Poor harvests in 1808 and 1809 worsened Britain's situation. However, Britain strengthened its economy by supporting Napoleon's enemies with subsidies, and France was never able to maintain an absolute blockade. When Russia asserted its independence, the British economic problems were largely over. British textiles boomed as they supplied the forces against Napoleon.

1811, Jan. 19. Napoleon decreed the creation of *tours*—revolving doors at foundling hospitals enabling individuals to place children in the hospitals anonymously. These babies were given to wet nurses and supported by the state until they were 12 years old.

1812, May. The maximum on grain was reinstituted in an effort to ease the suffering on the home front. The maximum was set locally, so prefects undermined its purpose by setting the price above neighboring prefectures in an effort to purchase more grain for their region. In general, brigandage and vagabondage increased as prices rose from 50 percent to 100 percent throughout France.

2. FOREIGN AFFAIRS

1805. THE WAR OF THE THIRD COALITION of Great Britain, Austria, Russia, and Sweden. **Britain** had been at war with France since May 16, 1803. Napoleon planned to invade England from four new French harbors (Ambleteuse, Wimereux, Boulogne, and Étaples), but the resumption of war with Austria in Aug. 1805 forced Napoleon to concentrate his efforts on the Continent.

Oct. 21. Battle of Trafalgar. The British navy, under Nelson, defeated the French and Spanish fleets, thus asserting British control of the seas.

Dec. 2. France defeated **Austria** and **Russia** at the **Battle of Austerlitz** (the Battle of the Three Emperors).

Dec. 26. Austria agreed to a truce that led to the **Treaty of Pressburg** and, combined with a treaty between Prussia and France (Dec. 15), the **territorial destruction of the Holy Roman Empire.** The Austrian emperor, Francis II, had secured the title Francis I, emperor of Austria, and now retained this title alone.

1806. Napoleon replaced the Bourbons as rulers of Naples, where his brother Joseph became king; another brother became king of Holland (which replaced the Batavian Republic).

June 12. The Confederation of the Rhine placed all Germany, except Austria, Prussia, Brunswick, and Hesse, under French protection. As a result of the confederation and subsequent garrisoning of French troops on German soil, **Prussia** entered the war but it met defeat at the **Battles of Jena and Auerstadt (Oct. 14)**.

Oct. 27. Napoleon occupied Berlin, where he issued the Berlin Decree.

Nov. 21. The Berlin Decree ushered in the **CONTINENTAL SYSTEM.** This led to Napoleon's effort to consolidate this system in 1807 by concluding the continuing war with Prussia and with Russia, which had advanced to aid the Prussians. French forces encouraged Polish revolt against Russia; diplomats disengaged the Ottoman Empire from its alliance with Russia and a **war between Russia and the empire** resulted, 1806–12. (The **Treaty of Bucharest** [May 28, 1812] ended this war, with Russia gaining the province of Bessarabia.)

1807, June 14. Napoleon defeated the Russians at the **Battle of Friedland.** Napoleon, Alexander I (Russia), and Frederick William III (Prussia) then concluded the Treaties of Tilsit.

July 7–9. The Treaties of Tilsit. Russia recognized the grand duchy of Warsaw and the Confederation of the Rhine. Alexander agreed to accept French mediation in the war with the Ottoman Empire, and Napoleon accepted Russian mediation for the war with Great Britain. In secret, Russia also agreed to an alliance with France against Britain if the latter refused the peace. **Prussia** lost approximately half its territory and recognized the duchy of Warsaw. It closed its ports to British trade until a peace had been reached. Prussia was also limited to a standing army of not more than 42,000 men and was required to pay indemnities set at 120 millions by the French (raised to 140 millions in 1808).

1807–10. Consolidation of the Continental System. Denmark was summoned to join system (Sept. 1807). The British bombarded Copenhagen and carried off the Danish fleet. Denmark allied itself with France. Portugal was occupied by France after refusing to join the system (Nov. 1807); its royal family fled to Brazil.

1807, Dec. 17. The Milan Decree reiterated the blockade. On paper, Napoleon had now closed the entire European coastline to British trade. **The pope** continued to refuse to join the system.

1809, Feb. 2. The French occupied Rome and incorporated the Papal States into France by declaration on May 17, 1809. Pope Pius VII excommunicated Napoleon, who had him arrested (July 6) and removed to Savona and then to Fontainebleau.

1810. Further consolidation led to France's closing of the North Sea to British trade. Louis, king of Holland, abdicated on July 1, 1810, and **Holland was annexed to France** (July 9). A military takeover in Sweden replaced King Gustavus IV with Charles XIII and restored the power of the aristocracy. The new king concluded the **Treaty of Fredrikshamm** (Sept. 17) with Russia, which received control of Finland as far as the Tornea River and the Aaland Islands. Russia mediated a treaty of Paris between France and Sweden, which included Sweden in the Continental System. A French general, **Bernadotte,** was named Swedish crown prince (later king).

Reforms in Prussia and Austria were spurred by the disasters of 1805–6. Both states sought to modernize and develop greater strength for a further contest with Napoleon. Prussia had already commuted the labor contracts of the peasantry into rent payments between 1799 and 1805. In 1807, the Prussian government, under Baron Karl von Stein, proclaimed that the peasantry would be freed on St. Martin's Day in 1810. City governments were reorganized, and the tax legislation changed to resemble the distribution of the population. Military officers were now to be chosen by education and experience rather than merely by social status, and the principle of universal service was introduced by military planners including **Scharnhorst** and **Clausewitz.** Guilds were abolished as complete freedom of trade was proclaimed. The University of Berlin was established (1810). **Fichte's** *Addresses to the German Nation* helped stimulate profound national feeling. Similar, but less extensive, reforms were introduced in Austria, where Count Johann von Stadion became the leading figure. Archduke Charles reorganized the Austrian army.

1809, April 6. Archduke Charles appealed to the whole German people to embark on a war of liberation and began the invasion of Bavaria. Only Tyrol responded and rose in revolt under **Andreas Hofer.** Napoleon, having hurried back from Spain, engaged the Austrians in Bavaria and drove the archduke across the Danube into Bohemia.

May 13. The French took Vienna, but the Austrians defeated Napoleon at the **Battle of Aspern and Essling** (May 21–22). Napoleon

recrossed the Rhine, joined forces with the Italian viceroy, Eugene, and, after crossing the Rhine again, defeated Charles at the **Battle of Wagram** (July 5–6).

Oct. 14. The Austrians, completely exhausted, agreed to the **Treaty of Schönbrunn (Treaty of Vienna).** Austria lost 32,000 square miles of territory and 3,500,000 inhabitants to Russia, Bavaria, the duchy of Warsaw, and the new Illyrian provinces along the Adriatic coast. The Tyrolese continued the war. In Nov. 1809, Hofer was captured by the French and shot. Tyrol was annexed to the kingdom of Italy. Separate attempts at precipitating a war of liberation were made by Maj. Schill, a Prussian who fell at Stralsund (May 31), and the duke of Brunswick, whose volunteers were evacuated by the British navy after fighting their way across Germany to the North Sea.

1808–14. THE PENINSULAR WAR.

1808, March. Spain was invaded by 100,000 French troops under the pretext of guarding the coasts against the British. Charles IV abdicated in favor of his son Ferdinand, and both then renounced the throne. Napoleon named his brother Joseph as king of Spain, which prompted a popular uprising of the Spaniards that included growing nationalism and used forms of guerrilla warfare. The British landed in Portugal, under **Sir Arthur Wellesley** (later duke of Wellington), and defeated the French under Junot at **Vimeiro** (Aug. 21).

Sept. 18. Napoleon reinforced the alliance between France and Russia at **Erfurt** and then proceeded to Spain.

Dec. 13. Madrid capitulated to Napoleon; he forced the British, advancing from Portugal under Moore, to retreat. Soult succeeded Napoleon in command.

1809, Jan. 16. The British were defeated at the **Battle of Coruña.** The British managed to protect Portugal from further invasion at the **Battle of Talevera** (July 28), but the French overran all of Andalusia, except for Cádiz. In 1810, the British defeated both Masséna and Soult in the north and the south of Spain, respectively. Wellesley, now duke of Wellington, then completely defeated the French under Marshal Marmont at **Salamanca** (July 22).

1812, May 8. A national assembly elected in Cádiz **promulgated a democratic constitution.**

Aug. 12. Joseph and his family abandoned Madrid and fled to Valencia, where they combined forces with Soult and retook Madrid in Nov. Napoleon returned from Russia but, at war with Germany in 1813, he was forced to recall Soult and a large part of the French army. Wellington advanced and cut off Joseph.

1813, June 21. Wellington defeated Jourdan at **Vittoria.** Wellington invaded southern France. Marshal Suchet was driven out of Valencia into Barcelona.

1814, March 12. Wellington crossed the French frontier and captured Bordeaux.

RUSSIAN CAMPAIGN. Napoleon and Alexander were both eager for leadership in Europe. Napoleon's marriage and alliance with the Austrians, as well as fear that Napoleon hoped to restore Poland under the duchy of Warsaw, led Alexander to break with Napoleon. At the same time, Napoleon resented Alexander's unwillingness to honor the Continental System. France amassed a **Grand Army** of about 600,000 men consisting of forces from throughout Europe. Austria supplied 30,000 men, and Prussia, 20,000 (their forces formed the right and left wings of the advancing army, respectively). In the spring of 1812, **Russia** made peace with the Ottomans, the Swedes, and the British.

1812, June 26. Napoleon passed over the Niemen River and **occupied Vilna,** while the Russians, under Barclay de Tolly, retreated without offering battle.

Aug. 17–19. The French destroyed Smolensk.

Sept. 7. Gen. Michael Kutuzov, replacing de Tolly, was defeated at the bloody **Battle of Borodino.** The French lost approximately 30,000, and the Russians left 45,000 dead and wounded behind as they retreated under cover of darkness.

Sept. 14. Napoleon occupied Moscow. By not defending Moscow, Kutuzov saved the Russian army for an attack once French supply lines had been severely taxed. This attack began as Napoleon, hampered by problems of supply, began a retreat from Moscow on Oct. 19.

Nov. 26–28. Napoleon's army virtually disintegrated after the **Crossing of the Berezina** (Nov. 26–28). Ney and Oudinot, with 8,500 men, forced the passage against 25,000 Russians. The Russian winter had set in, and troops suffered from the cold and hunger.

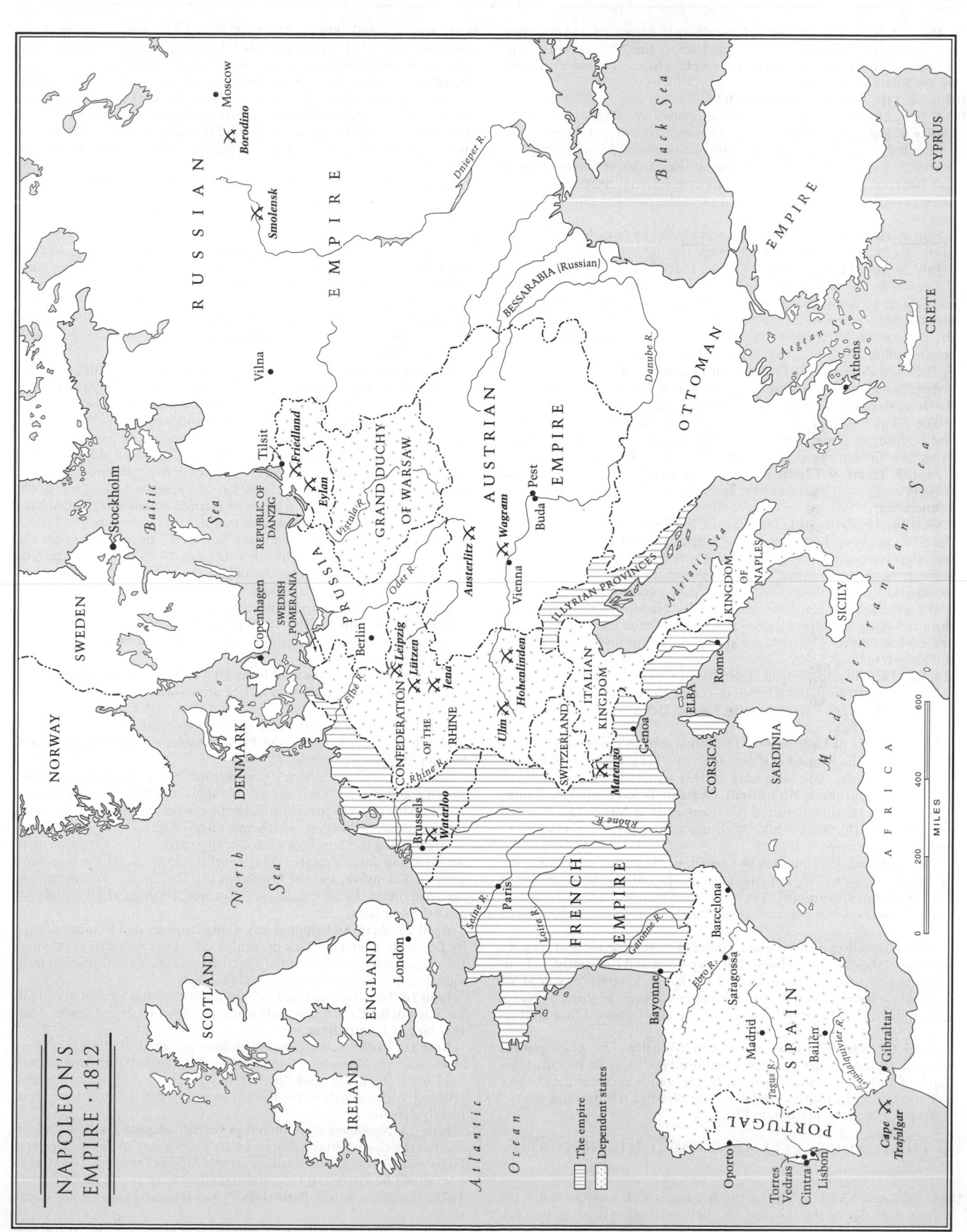

NAPOLEON'S EMPIRE · 1812

The empire
Dependent states

MILES
0   200   400   600

RUSSIAN   EMPIRE

Moscow
Borodino

Smolensk

Black Sea

CYPRUS

Vilna

BESSARABIA (Russian)

Dnieper R.

Danube R.

OTTOMAN   EMPIRE

CRETE

Aegean Sea

Athens

Tilsit
Friedland
Eylau

REPUBLIC OF DANZIG

GRAND DUCHY OF WARSAW

Vistula R.

AUSTRIAN   EMPIRE

Pest
Buda

Wagram

Vienna

Austerlitz

Stockholm

Baltic Sea

PRUSSIA

Oder R.

SWEDEN

Copenhagen

SWEDISH POMERANIA

Berlin
Leipzig
Lützen
Jena

CONFEDERATION OF THE RHINE

Elbe R.

Hohenlinden
Ulm

Rhine R.

ILLYRIAN PROVINCES

Adriatic Sea

KINGDOM OF NAPLES

Rome

ELBA

SICILY

NORWAY

North Sea

DENMARK

SWITZERLAND

ITALIAN KINGDOM

Genoa

Marengo

CORSICA

SARDINIA

Mediterranean Sea

AFRICA

SCOTLAND

IRELAND

ENGLAND

London

Waterloo
Brussels

FRENCH   EMPIRE

Paris

Seine R.

Loire R.

Rhône R.

Garonne R.

Bayonne

Barcelona

Ebro R.

Atlantic Ocean

SPAIN

Madrid

Tagus R.

Saragossa

Bailén

Guadalquivir R.

Gibraltar

PORTUGAL

Oporto

Torres Vedras
Cintra
Lisbon

Cape Trafalgar

Dec. 19. Napoleon arrived in Paris while the remainder of the army (not more than 100,000 men) straggled across the Niemen. He sought to consolidate French support and downplay the terrific losses inflicted by the Russian campaign.

1813–14. THE WARS OF LIBERATION.

1813, Feb. 28. Prussia and Russia established an alliance under the **Treaty of Kalisch** and invited Austria and Britain to join them.

March 27. The Russians and Prussians occupied Dresden, but Napoleon defeated their combined army at the battles of **Lützen (May 2)** and **Bautzen (May 20).** Napoleon, having suffered heavy casualties, agreed to allow Metternich to attempt to mediate peace between the two sides.

June 4. Armistice of Poischwitz was signed by Napoleon (effective until July 26 but later extended to Aug. 10).

July 5–Aug. 11. Congress of Prague: Participants tried to establish the peace, but Napoleon declined all proffered terms. As a result, Austria declared war on France, joining Prussia, Russia, Britain, Spain, and Sweden (under Crown Prince Bernadotte, in return for recognition of the annexation of Norway). The allies adopted a strategy of avoiding battles when Napoleon was present. Britain agreed to subsidies for Prussia and Russia **(June 15 Treaty at Reichenbach).**

Aug. 26–27. Nonetheless, Napoleon defeated Schwarzenberg at the **Battle of Dresden**—his last victory on German soil.

The allies defeated the other French generals as follows: Oudinot and Reynier at **Grossbeeren (Aug. 23)**; MacDonald at the **Katzbach (Aug. 26)**; Vandamme at Kulm (Aug. 30); Ney at **Dennewitz (Sept. 6).**

Sept. 9. Treaty of Teplitz pledged unity among Prussia, Russia, and Austria and, secretly, restoration of Prussia and Austria to their 1805 boundaries.

Oct. 16–19. Battle of Leipzig, or the Battle of the Nations. Finally, the allies converged on Napoleon at Leipzig. They had a complete victory after nine hours; the French army was driven back to the gates of Leipzig. Napoleon crossed the Rhine, and, in Nov., the remaining members of the Confederation of the Rhine joined the allies. On Nov. 9, the allies offered Napoleon peace. When Napoleon failed to accept, the allies (Dec. 1) adopted a resolution to prosecute the war vigorously and invade France. Meanwhile, the Dutch rose in revolt and expelled the French officials (Nov. 15).

1814, Jan. 14. The allies forced Denmark to sign the **Treaty of Kiel** after a short winter campaign. Denmark ceded Norway to Sweden in exchange for Western Pomerania and Rügen. Denmark also made peace with Great Britain.

Feb. 1. Battle of La Rothière. The allied armies defeated Napoleon after crossing the Rhine but then had to divide because of problems of supply. Napoleon took advantage of this situation and defeated the allies at **Champaubert, Montmirail, Château-Thierry, and Vauchamps (Feb. 10–15).** He then defeated the main army at **Nangis and Montereau (Feb. 17–18).** Meanwhile, Wellington had invaded the south of France and captured Bordeaux.

Feb. 5–March 19. Congress of Châtillon. Napoleon was offered the French frontier of 1792, but the negotiations failed. The allies signed the **Treaties of Chaumont** (March 1), which guarded against a separate peace. Napoleon was defeated at the **Battle of Arcis-sur-Aube** (March 20).

March 31. Allies entered Paris. Under French diplomat Talleyrand's influence, the Senate declared that Napoleon and his family had forfeited the throne. Napoleon arrived too late to save the city, and his marshals refused to join him in a foolhardy assault of the city. Napoleon abdicated in favor of his son, but the allies rejected that alternative.

April 11. Napoleon abdicated unconditionally. The allies granted him the island of Elba as a sovereign principality with an annual income of 2 million francs. His wife, Marie Louise, received the duchies of Parma, Piacenza, and Guastalla. Both retained the imperial title.

May 4. Napoleon arrived on Elba.

3. THE PEACE SETTLEMENTS AND THE HUNDRED DAYS

1814–24. Louis XVIII (brother of the late Louis XVI) was restored to the throne partially as the result of the failure of other candidacies. Talleyrand induced Louis and his other advisers to issue a constitution.

1814, May 30. THE FIRST TREATY OF PARIS. France retained the boundaries of 1792, which included Avignon, Venaissin, and parts of the Savoy and German empire, and Belgium. France, in turn, recognized the independence of the Netherlands, the German and Italian states, and Switzerland. Britain restored the French colonies excepting Tobago, St. Lucia, and Mauritius; Britain also retained Malta. France promised to abolish all slave trade, and the allies abandoned all claims to indemnity. The complexities of this treaty led to the Congress of Vienna.

Sept. 15–1815, June 9. THE CONGRESS OF VIENNA. The chief negotiators were Metternich (Austria), Hardenberg and William von Humboldt (Prussia), Castlereagh and Wellington (Great Britain), the tsar for Russia with his advisers, Talleyrand (France), and Cardinal Consalvi (the papacy). The full congress never met officially, and the main decisions were made by the four major allied powers. Talleyrand, in order to gain admission to the inner councils, tried to raise the principle of legitimacy but was only admitted after a dispute over the fate of Poland and Saxony led the allies to the brink of war. The work of the congress was interrupted by Napoleon's return, but the agreement was signed June 9.

Major provisions: (1) Austrian and Prussian monarchies were restored and their territories expanded: Austria received new territories in Italy and the Illyrian Provinces. Prussia received part of the duchy of Warsaw, Danzig, Swedish Pomerania and Rügen, and new parts of Westphalia and Neuchâtel and the greater portion of Saxony. (2) Formation of the kingdom of the Netherlands, comprised of Holland and Belgium. (3) The creation of the Germanic confederation to replace the old Holy Roman Empire. (4) Creation of a kingdom of Poland under the Russian tsar and king. Alexander granted Poland the right to have Polish as the official language and maintain its own army. (5) Britain retained Malta and Heligoland, and assumed a protectorate over the Ionian Islands (Nov. 5–6). Sweden retained Norway. (6) Switzerland was reestablished. (7) Restoration of legitimate dynasties in Spain, Sardinia, and the Papal States, all of which had been governed by members of Napoleon's family during the empire.

1815, March 20–June 22. HUNDRED DAYS. The Bourbon Restoration and the difficulties at the Congress of Vienna encouraged Napoleon to return to France.

March 1. Napoleon escaped from Elba and landed at **Cannes** where the troops sent to oppose him rallied around him. Louis XVIII fled to Ghent.

March 13. Allies issued a ban against Napoleon.

March 20. Napoleon entered **Paris,** established a government, and began rebuilding the army.

March 25. A new alliance was formed between **Austria, Britain, Prussia, and Russia.** Each agreed to supply 180,000 men; all the European nations were invited to join the coalition, and most did (with the exception of Sweden, which was engaged in the conquest of Norway) resulting in a combined force of approximately one million men. An Austrian force defeated Murat, who had declared for Napoleon again at **Tolentino,** and the Bourbon king, Ferdinand, was restored to the Neapolitan throne. Murat was captured, court-martialed, and shot after the war (Oct. 13).

April 23. Acte Additionnel aux Constitutions de l'Empire, drafted by Benjamin Constant, was promulgated. This constitution provided the emperor with only limited executive authority and ensured individual rights, including freedom of the press.

June 16. Napoleon entered Belgium and then forced Blücher to fall back at the **Battle of Ligny,** while the prince of Orange defeated Marshal Ney at **Quatre Bras.**

June 18. Battle of Waterloo. Napoleon attacked Wellington's army after ordering Grouchy to engage the Prussians. Wellington's army held the line all day, and Blücher, having escaped Grouchy's forces, relieved Wellington's army toward evening. The French were completely defeated.

June 22. Napoleon surrendered to British admiral Hotham and abdicated the throne after unsuccessfully attempting to flee to America. Napoleon was exiled, by unanimous resolution of the allies, to **St. Helena,** where he arrived in Oct. and remained until his death on May 5, 1821. The allies retook **Paris (July 7)** and returned Louis XVIII to the throne.

Sept. 26. The Holy Alliance was formed between Alexander I of Russia, Francis I of Austria, and Frederick William III of Prussia, and ultimately accepted by all the European rulers except the British prince regent, the pope, and the sultan of the Ottoman Empire. This document established the premise that European countries would be governed by Christian principles. Although innocuous in its form, it demonstrated an acceptance of more traditional, conservative values by the rulers on the Continent. It clearly spoke against the anticlericalism and territorial aggression of the French Revolution and Napoleonic France. It was later confused in the public mind with the Quadruple Alliance.

Nov. 20. SECOND PEACE OF PARIS. This peace limited France to the boundaries of 1790 (roughly equivalent to those of 1789 with the inclusion of Venaissin and Avignon). France was to pay 700 million francs for the expense of the war and support the garrisoning of 17 allied fortresses on the northern and eastern frontiers for five years.

(To pp. 445, 451)

4. WESTERN AND CENTRAL EUROPE, 1815–1848

a. SOCIAL, CULTURAL, AND ECONOMIC TRENDS

1. ECONOMIC AND SOCIAL CHANGES

THE INDUSTRIAL REVOLUTION. This was one of the most important changes in the history of humanity, altering patterns of life and thought. It meant a shift from an agrarian, handicraft, labor-intensive economy to one dominated by machine manufacture, the factory system, division of labor, a freer flow of capital, and the growth of cities. Yet industrialization did not affect all of Europe at the same time. This process began in the **mid-18th century in England** and gradually spread to the Continent. **Significant industrialization could be found in Belgium and France by the 1820s, and in Germany and Catalonia by the 1830s.**

The long-term origins of industrialization had been building for centuries (p. 313). Chief among newer factors was a **population explosion** during the 18th century. This was due especially to a decline in mortality, the result of a cyclical decline in epidemic diseases, and, above all, the **introduction of new foodstuffs from the Americas**—particularly the **potato.** At the same time, partly due to new foods, **sexual activity** increased; rapid growth occurred in **illegitimate births.** From c. 1780 onward, **premarital sexual intercourse** increased particularly in the growing propertyless classes, both rural and urban, where traditional family and community constraints declined in force. **Sexual expression** became more important, though probably more for men than for women. In all, the nations of western Europe witnessed a population increase from 50 to 100 percent between 1730 and 1800. English population, for example, rose from approximately 5 million in 1700 to over 9 million at the end of the century. The resulting population pressure forced many people off the land and created a labor force for the new cities and factories. Population growth began to decrease slowly in the early 19th century as birth rates began to decline, especially among the middle classes.

The short-term causes of industrialization also included a **number of inventions in key industries, accompanied by changes in finance, which spurred further change.** The first series of inventions resulted mainly from the tinkerings of craftworkers and inventors and required very little capital. **John Kay's** flying shuttle (1733), **James Hargreave's** spinning jenny (1768), **Richard Arkwright's** water frame spinning machine (1769), and **Eli Whitney's** cotton gin (1793) all revolutionized the cotton industry by allowing for increased production and profits, while decreasing the costs of production. Finally, with the substitution of water power and later steam power (developed by **James Watt** in the 1770s) for human energy, these inventions made it more economical to group workers together around large machines than to send out work to individual workers. This spelled the end of the putting-out system and the rise of the **factory system.** This series of changes, especially the invention of the steam engine, spurred similar developments in the iron industry (the production of quality wrought iron by the 1780s) and in transportation (growth of the railroad) and communication (p. 424).

As industrialization developed, investment became more important. In Britain, wealthy merchants and landlords provided most of the investment capital, but banking remained a risky venture. This changed with the laws of **incorporation** and **limited liability** (passed in 1844 in Britain, and in France, Germany, and the United States in the 1860s). Incorporation allowed companies to be treated as individuals before the law, giving them a juridical existence long after the founders had either died or sold their shares. Limited liability protected investors and thereby promoted investment, establishing a system whereby investors were liable for the corporation's debts only in proportion to the number of shares they owned.

Because this first phase of industrialization was gradual, the **social transformation** that accompanied it developed alongside an older social structure. Thus, those who felt the **most severe hardships** from industrialization, at least psychologically, were the **artisans, craftworkers, and rural laborers** who saw the value of their work decline. It was these groups that took the fore in the social and political revolutions that swept Europe in 1848 (p. 465).

Industrialization created two new social groups: the **middle classes** (or bourgeoisie) and the **working classes** (or proletariat). Similarly, each developed in a new setting: the city. Both groups were diverse. The middle classes ranged from shopkeepers to bankers and factory owners, but they shared common beliefs in the virtue of work, thrift, ambition, and caution. The working classes of the first half of the 19th century can be broken down into three categories: **artisans, factory workers, and female domestic servants** (the latter grew in proportion as they became a status symbol in middle-class households). **Industrial cities,** most unplanned, dirty, and unsafe, made conditions difficult for workers, but many devised strategies that made survival possible. For example, in factories, wives and children became economic assets so many factory workers married, or entered conjugal relationships, at a younger age than artisans, and had more children on average. Workers also developed a popular culture that suited their new conditions. At the same time, middle-class leaders began holding their children apart from work and moved their wives from shops to household domesticity. Adult women's economic roles began to decline as their cultural prestige, as mothers and moralizing agents, increased. Overall, however, poor living and working conditions remained the rule, exacerbated in the 1840s (the **hungry forties**), and they contributed to discontent.

Although these developments signified major changes in European life, it is important to remember that up to 1848 Europe remained overwhelmingly rural, and artisans retained an important position in the working classes. Change was more dramatic after 1850, when aspects of the new industrial society that had developed alongside the older agricultural society became more widespread. *(To p. 480)*

Approximate Population, in Thousands, 1700–1846				
	1700	*1750*	*1800*	*1846*
United Kingdom	8,635	10,012	14,997	27,220
France (boundaries of 1819–46)	23,600	24,600	27,800	35,400
Spain	7,250	8,600	10,480	12,650
Portugal	1,739	2,662	3,420	3,940
Italy (boundaries of 1910)	11,500	13,150	16,900	21,200
Belgium	1,610	2,150	2,960	4,350
Holland	1,100	1,460	1,795	2,505
Norway	587	705	1,050	1,325
Sweden	1,640	1,790	2,340	3,340
Denmark	665	745	845	1,400
Prussia (boundaries of 1846)	5,100	6,420	8,880	15,300
Russia (without Finland)	—	—	31,000	—

2. INTELLECTUAL AND RELIGIOUS TRENDS
(From p. 314)

The major trends in thought from 1814 to 1848 can generally be understood as reactions to the Enlightenment and the French Revolution. **Conservatism** arose as a direct, negative response to the changes heralded by revolution and industrialization. Conservatives stressed the value of tradition. They supported religion, the social hierarchy inherited from the early modern period, and the lessons of historical experience. They held that abstract political theory led only to ruin. The major proponents of this philosophy were the English historian of the French Revolution, **Edmund Burke** (1729–97), **Joseph de Maistre** (1754–1821), and **Vicomte Louis de Bonald** (1754–1840). Conservatism was also linked to the rise of **ultramontanism** in the Roman Catholic Church.

Liberals saw much of value in the French Revolution, especially its emphasis on **individual liberty** and the **protection of private property.** For that reason, they opposed the Terror, with its economic and social controls, as a threat to the individual. Liberals sought a rational state, one based on science and natural laws. They thus opposed both the status quo, as supported by the conservatives, and changes that would increase the state's role in society and the economy. Instead, they supported a social structure that rewarded merit. In economics, they emphasized the laws of supply and demand to argue for no restrictions, a system known as **laissez-faire economics.** The foremost proponents of this thought were **Thomas Malthus** (1766–1834), who argued that population and food supply were related in a cyclical association, and **David Ricardo** (1772–1823), who linked wages to labor supply and population. Both scholars posited these conditions as natural, and as such, the state would only worsen conditions if it got involved.

Because liberals saw the Terror as the product of democracy, they feared a widening of suffrage as a danger to individual liberty. Democracy was supported by only a small portion of radical liberals, such as **Jeremy Bentham** (1748–1832).

Two new philosophies also developed from the French Revolution: **socialism** and **nationalism.** Because socialists writing before 1848 sought to combat poverty, oppression, and inequality by creating a new social order based on harmony, they have acquired the label Karl Marx gave them in 1848, **utopian socialists.** Although based on different understandings of how society worked, socialists like **Henri Comte de Saint-Simon** (1760–1825), **Charles Fourier** (1772–1837), and **Robert Owen** (1771–1858) all based their models of the perfect society on idealized traditional notions of community and cooperation.

Nationalism is difficult to define, for it was built on such concepts as the *Volksgeist,* or the soul of the people. This was a concept advanced by the German philosopher **Johann Gottfried Herder** (1744–1803). Nationalism promotes the belief that common language, culture, and traditions create an unbreakable bond among people. Nationalism was most readily grasped by those who lived in politically divided empires, especially Germans and Italians. During the first half of the 19th century, nationalism was frequently linked to liberalism; each sought changes to the status quo, and liberals conflated the struggle for national rights with the extension of individual freedoms. In the latter half of the century, however, this link shattered.

Outside of the realm of politics, supporters of the Enlightenment continued their search for reason through such movements as **positivism.** Positivism, with **Auguste Comte** (1798–1857) as its main proponent, brought a strict empirical approach to the study of society. The scientific method could be used, in this view, to discover a set of laws that governed the operations of society. In this manner, positivists sought a new ideology and new institutions upon which to base society, now that the revolution had destroyed the old regime but left nothing in its place.

Some of the more important publications that marked the development of philosophical, religious, and social thought from 1800 to 1848 included:

1802. The French author **François René de Chateaubriand** (1768–1848) initiated the Catholic revival with his *Génie du christianisme,* stressing the aesthetic rather than the theological aspect of the faith.

1803. The *Traité d'économie politique* of **Jean-Baptiste Say** (1767–1832) was one of the most lucid and influential expositions of economic liberalism. Say followed it in 1828–30 with a much more extensive *Cours complet d'économie politique pratique.*

1806. Johann F. Herbart's (1776–1841) *Allgemeine Pädogogik* was published, a landmark in the development of modern education based on psychology and ethics.

1807. The Hegelian philosophy of the absolute, the dominant philosophy of the early 19th century, was introduced by **George W. F. Hegel** (1770–1831) in his *Phänomenologie des Geistes,* followed by *Wissenschaft der Logik* (1812–16) and *Grundlinien der Philosophie des Rechts* (1821).

1810. The political philosophy of conservatism was further elaborated in the brilliant writings of **Joseph de Maistre** (1754–1821), the *Essai sur le principe générateur des constitutions politiques* (1810) and especially *Du pape* (1819), with its emphasis on the importance of papal authority.

1813. Robert Owen (1771–1858), British industrialist and philanthropist, is generally regarded as the first of the **utopian socialists.** In his *New View of Society* (1813) he argued for cooperation in production and advocated the organization of new social units, many of which (notably **New Harmony,** Indiana, 1825–28) were established in Europe and the United States. Subsequently the French reformer, **Charles Fourier** (1772–1837), proposed the setting up of *phalanstères,* or cooperative communities, in a rural setting; and **Étienne Cabet** (1788–1856) in his *Voyage en Icarie* (1840) pictured an imaginative, highly planned, and regulated community. **Louis Blanc** (1811–82) in his *Organisation du travail* (1839) urged the foundation of state-financed producers' associations, while **Pierre-Joseph Proudhon** (1809–65), the great French polemicist, demanded justice, equality, and anarchy as the only remedies for the corruption of society. In exile in Paris, the self-educated German tailor **Wilhelm Weitling** (1808–71) came under the influence of French socialist ideas. In his *Garantien der Harmonie und Freiheit* (1842), he presented a system not unlike those of Fourier and Cabet. **Johann Karl Rodbertus** (1805–75) was also instrumental in introducing French ideas into Germany.

1815–31. Friedrich Karl von Savigny (1779–1861) in his six-volume *Geschichte des römischen Rechts im Mittelalter* contributed greatly to the development of the historical school of jurisprudence.

1816–26. Karl Ludwig von Haller (1768–1854) published his six-volume *Restauration der Staatswissenschaften,* one of the most comprehensive and one of the last refutations of 18th-century political theory and restatements of the principles of absolutism and paternalism.

1817. The *Principles of Political Economy and Taxation* by the British banker **David Ricardo** (1772–1823) provided a classical formulation of economic doctrine. Ricardo set forth the law of "differential rent" and explained wages as tending to seek the minimum subsistence level. He also analyzed the conflicting interests of social classes, thereby foreshadowing the doctrine of the class struggle. His teaching was enthusiastically adopted by the rising manufacturing class and was further elaborated in England by the utilitarian **James Mill** (1773–1836), **John Ramsay McCulloch** (1789–1864), and **Nassau William Senior** (1790–1864), and in France by **Pellegrino Rossi** (1787–1848), **Charles Dunoyer** (1786–1863), **Michel Chevalier** (1806–79), and **Frédéric Bastiat** (1801–50).

1817–18. Comte Henri de Saint-Simon (1760–1825), eccentric scion of the high French aristocracy, published his four-volume study of industry *(L'industrie, ou discussions politiques, morales et philosophiques)* followed by *Du système industriel* (1821) and *Le catéchisme des industriels* (1823). In these writings he called for a reorganization of society to accord with modern methods of production and to ensure the greatest good for the greatest number. He dreamed of integrating the sciences in a new sociology and forecast modern technocracy. His disciples, **Prosper Enfantin** (1796–1864) and **Saint-Amand Bazard** (1791–1832), not only systematized and expounded his thought but also, on the basis of his later book *Le nouveau christianisme* (1825), organized a Saint-Simonian sect on communist principles. This was soon suppressed by the authorities. Meanwhile Saint-Simon's secretary, **Auguste Comte** (1798–1857), developed his scientific thought and founded the philosophy known as positivism *(Cours de philosophie positive,* six volumes, 1830–42; *Système de politique positive,* four volumes, 1851–54).

1817–21. The Abbé **Félicité de Lamennais** (1782–1854) wrote an eloquent defense of papal and royal authority in his *Essai sur l'indifférence en matière de religion*, but after 1830 he became converted to liberalism. With **Comte Charles de Montalembert** (1810–70) he launched the liberal Catholic movement, which was condemned by the papacy. Eventually Lamennais became identified with the socialist movement. His fervent booklet *Paroles d'un croyant* (1833) was at once translated into many languages and aroused much sympathy for the lower classes.

1819. Arthur Schopenhauer's (1788–1860) *Die Welt als Wille und Vorstellung* formulated a philosophy of pessimism, which, though generally ignored for a generation, became highly influential in the later 19th century.

1819–37. Jakob Grimm's (1785–1863) *Deutsche Grammatik* was a landmark in the development of modern philology. Jakob and his brother Wilhelm (1786–1859) collaborated in collecting folktales, myths, and laws, and in publishing a great dictionary of the German language (volume I, 1854).

1819. The Swiss historian **Simonde de Sismondi** (1773–1842) in his *Nouveaux principes d'économie politique* attacked the laissez-faire doctrines of the liberal school and was one of the first to call for state action on behalf of the helpless working classes.

1821–22. *Der christliche Glaube nach den Grundsätzen der evangelischen Kirche*, one of the great theological treatises of the century, was published by **Friedrich Schleiermacher** (1768–1834). The book emphasized the individual and emotional side of the Protestant religion and contended against dogmatism and rigidity.

1825. Augustin Thierry's (1795–1856) *Histoire de la conquête de l'Angleterre par les Normands* provided a highly colored, romantic narrative history and at the same time pictured the ruling aristocracies as brutal conquerors and exploiters of "the people." The French statesman **François Guizot** (1787–1874), in his brilliant lectures *Histoire de la civilisation en Europe* (1828), likewise stressed the importance of the middle class and the rise of representative institutions.

1825. James Mill's (1773–1836) *Analysis of the Phenomena of the Human Mind* was a basic work of modern psychology.

1826. Beginning of the publication of the *Monumenta Germaniae Historica*, the first of many scholarly collections of historical sources and a landmark in the development of national history.

1833. Establishment of a historical seminar by **Leopold von Ranke** (1795–1886) as a center for advanced training in historical writing. Ranke's emphasis on criticism of sources and the utmost objectivity in presentation marked the beginning of modern professional historical scholarship. His *Die römischen Päpste* (1834–39) was only the first of various historical studies of the 16th and 17th centuries.

1834–40. *La Démocratie en Amérique* by **Alexis de Tocqueville** (1805–59), a most discerning analytical study of democracy, was based largely on personal observation and study.

1835–36. David Friedrich Strauss (1808–74) published *Das Leben Jesu* (two volumes), a critical examination of the sources that led him to question the historicity of Jesus. Strauss's book marked the appearance of the **Young Hegelians,** a group that interpreted the Hegelian philosophy in a radical and critical sense: **Bruno Bauer** (1809–82): *Kritik der evangelischen Synoptiker* (1841); **Ludwig Feuerbach** (1804–72): *Das Wesen des Christentums* (1841); **Max Stirner** (1806–56): *Der einzige und sein Eigentum* (1845).

1841. Friedrich List (1789–1846) in his *Nationales System der politischen Ökonomie* stressed national welfare rather than individual gain and propounded a theory of relativity in economic policy: countries in the early stages of industrialization should protect their industries until free trade should become feasible.

1843–45. In a series of brilliant writings (*Euten-Eller*, 1843; *Begrebet Angst*, 1844; *Stadier paa Livetsvej*, 1845) the Danish philosopher **Søren Kierkegaard** repudiated the Hegelian philosophy and preached a religion of acceptance and suffering on the part of the individual. His teaching presaged the philosophy of existentialism. *(To p. 481)*

3. CULTURE AND POPULAR CULTURE
(From p. 314)

The most important cultural school to emerge from early-19th-century Europe was **romanticism** (1790s–1840s). Built upon earlier cul-

tural developments, romanticism took on new fervor after the French Revolution. Romantics decried the emphasis placed on reason by the *philosophes* and held that human beings were more than just the product of natural laws. Romantics stressed the diversity of individuals, a uniqueness based mainly on their emotions and imaginations. In art and literature, the lone individual was the protagonist, and emotions guided his or her actions. This philosophy inspired poetry, which flourished in this period.

Because of their emphasis on the inner being, most romantics also stressed the place of religion in human society. Finally, romantics also broke the rules of cultural form and technique, valuing free expression above all else. Sometimes this resulted in riots, as in the case of **Victor Hugo's** innovative play *Hernani* (1830), where the first performance degenerated into fist fights. Because of its emphasis on emotion, history, tradition, and "simple" peasant culture, romanticism was more often linked to conservatism and nationalism than to liberalism, but romantics found their way into all of the major schools of political thought.

Romantics also linked with popular culture, helping to further the **sentimental novel** as a staple of middle-class reading. Romantic nationalism expressed in music and art as well as essays, also won wide appeal.

Some of the major proponents of romanticism included Percy Bysshe Shelley (1792–1822), William Wordsworth (1770–1850), John Keats (1795–1821), George Gordon Lord Byron (1788–1824), Samuel Taylor Coleridge (1772–1834), Alphonse de Lamartine (1790–1869), Heinrich Heine (1797–1856), François-René de Chateaubriand (1768–1848), Victor-Marie Hugo (1802–85), A. W. Schlegel (1767–1845), Friedrich Schlegel (1772–1829), John Constable (1776–1837), Joseph Mallord William Turner (1775–1851), Franz Schubert (1797–1828), Robert Schumann (1810–56), and Frédéric Chopin (1810–49).

The drastic changes brought on by industrialization translated into similar change for **popular culture.** With urbanization, workers lost ties to their villages. **Communal traditions and festivals no longer supplied avenues for recreation.** Moreover, employers actively suppressed the transfer of such "frivolous" activities to the city. Yet this suppression came at a time when leisure needs increased. **Industrialization made work more difficult and monotonous.** Individual workers were now expected to work at a steady rhythm—the machine's rhythm. Meanwhile, workers were no longer directly involved in the creation of a product. Division of labor meant that they worked on only one aspect of the product. To counter this monotony, workers sought recreation in the **growing number of bars and cafés.** Dislocated workers also formed **clubs** to ease the separation from their villages and regions. Yet in general, the working class's pursuit of leisure suffered from the inability of the workers themselves to afford many leisure diversions and from employer and government suppression. Only in the latter half of the century did this change.

For the middle classes, with the separation of work and home brought on by industrialization, the **home took on new value.** It became the center of middle-class leisure, becoming, in the words of one historian, a haven in a cruel world. Families were imbued more with emotional, rather than economic, value. Consequently, the middle-class woman's position in society changed. Restricted to the home and family, **women came to represent morality and purity,** untainted by public entanglements, especially in Britain. This became a key element in middle-class culture (**Victorianism** in Britain). Similarly, middle-class **children** became a great expense, as education began to play a larger role in social status. At the same time, they were given new emotional value. This helps to explain why middle-class couples began to have fewer children. These changes affected the working classes only indirectly, as middle-class reformers stressed their view of the family in their push for social reform, especially the **regulation of child and female labor.** *(To p. 483)*

4. SCIENCE AND LEARNING
(From p. 314)

Scientific inquiry continued to proceed along the general lines established during the scientific revolution and the Enlightenment. With the development of **positivism,** the scientific method was used to explain a more diverse field of study, but overall it faced little questioning.

The major benchmarks in scientific inquiry included:

a. Mathematics, Physics, and Astronomy

1799–1825. Pierre Laplace (1749–1827) published his *Traité de mécanique céleste,* in which he aimed at presenting analytically all of the developments in gravitational astronomy since the time of Newton.

1800. The **Royal Institution of Great Britain,** center for the diffusion of technical and scientific knowledge, was founded by the American **Benjamin Thompson (Count Rumford)** (1753–1814).

1801. Giuseppi Piazzi (1746–1826) discovered the first asteroid, Ceres; its orbit was computed by Gauss.

1801. Carl Friedrich Gauss (1777–1855) published *Disquisitiones arithmeticae,* developing the theory of congruences, quadratic forms, and quadratic residues, using methods and concepts basic to the subsequent progress of number theory and algebra.

1802. Thomas Young (1773–1829) demonstrated in his paper "On the Theory of Light and Colours" that the properties of light, including interference phenomena, are satisfactorily explained by considering light as a periodic wave motion in an ether.

1803–4. William Herschel (1738–1822) reported observations on six cases of double stars, and concluded that each was a binary or connected pair of stars in which each member influenced the motion of the other. This was the first observation of changes taking place under gravity beyond the solar system.

1809. Gauss expounded his new "least-squares" method of computing planetary orbits in *Theoria motus corporum coelestium.*

1815–21. Augustin Fresnel (1788–1827), through a series of mathematical and experimental researches on interference, diffraction, polarization, and double refraction, was able to establish the **transverse wave theory of light.**

1817. Joseph von Fraunhofer (1787–1826), following the 1802 observations by **William Wollaston** (1766–1828) that the solar spectrum contains black lines, used an improved spectroscope and charted these lines, naming the principal ones.

1820. Hans Oersted (1777–1851) showed that a magnetic needle placed near a current-carrying wire deviated from its position, and that the direction of deviation depended on the direction of current flow.

1820. André-Marie Ampère (1775–1836) repeated Oersted's experiments (1820) and reported his discovery that two current-carrying wires exercise a reciprocal action upon one another. He later established a mathematical theory of known electrical phenomena and experimentally demonstrated the principles of the electrodynamics of adjacent current-carrying conductors.

1821–59. Michael Faraday (1791–1867) demonstrated electromagnetic rotation (1821) and discovered electromagnetic induction (1831). He independently discovered self-induced currents (1834), found two years earlier by **Joseph Henry** (1797–1878). He propounded the laws of electrochemical decomposition and conduction, and established a general theory of electrolysis. He also introduced the concept of *field* into physics. These and other investigations were collected in his *Experimental Researches in Electricity* (1839–55) and in his *Experimental Researches in Chemistry and Physics* (1859).

1821–23. Augustin-Louis Cauchy (1789–1857) gave the first essentially correct definition of *limit* in *Cours d'analyse* (1821). This work also contained the first systematic study of convergence of series and general tests for it, and the first theory of functions of a complex variable. He defined the derivative and integral in terms of a limit and obtained the fundamental theorem of calculus (1823).

1822. Joseph Fourier (1768–1830) published *Théorie analytique de la chaleur,* giving a mathematical theory of heat conduction. He introduced trigonometric series, *Fourier series* of arbitrary, piecewise, continuous functions, thus extending the notion of function.

1824. Niels Abel (1802–29) proved that the general quintic cannot be solved by radicals.

1824. Nicolas Sadi Carnot (1796–1832) published *Réflexions sur la puissance motrice du feu.* Here he showed that the transformation of heat into motive power depends on the quantity of heat ("caloric") and the temperature difference between the source and sink of heat. He also introduced the reversible cycle of a heat engine—now called the *Carnot cycle.*

1827–29. Niels Abel and **Karl Jacobi** (1804–51) independently founded the theory of elliptic (doubly periodic) functions.

1827. Georg S. Ohm (1789–1854) found that the ratio of electromotive force to the current, in an electric circuit, is a constant *(Ohm's Law)* and called this constant the resistance of the circuit.

1829–32. Nikolai Lobachevskii (1793–1856) and **János Bólyai** (1802–60) independently developed the first **non-Euclidean geometries.**

1831. The foundation of the **British Association for the Advancement of Science,** dedicated to the promotion and professionalization of British science. The B.A.A.S. was based on a German model, **Gesellschaft deutscher Naturforscher,** and served as an example for the **American Association for the Advancement of Science** (1848).

1832. Evariste Galois (1811–32) left posthumous papers showing the use of group theory to give necessary and sufficient conditions for the solution of equations by radicals. He emphasized the importance of the invariant, or normal, subgroup.

1833. Charles Babbage (1792–1871) conceived an "analytical engine" (a large-scale digital calculator). In 1822, he had made a working model of a smaller "difference engine" to calculate tables of functions by finite difference methods.

1833. Gauss, in *Intensitas vis magnetica terrestris,* presented a rigorous mathematical analysis of the earth's magnetic field and proposed a system of absolute units for the measurement of terrestrial magnetism.

1834. Adolphe Quetelet (1796–1874) initiated the **London Statistical Society** and later helped found several other such groups. He applied the theory of probability to the statistics of society, especially in *Sur l'homme* (1835).

1835. Cauchy published the first existence proof for the solution of a differential equation.

1838–39. Friedrich Bessel (1784–1846), **Friedrich Struve** (1793–1864), and **Thomas Henderson** (1798–1844) measured *stellar parallax* for the first time.

1842. Julius von Mayer (1814–78) stated that the total amount of energy in the universe is constant (a form of the **first law of thermodynamics)** and that in natural processes, energy is never lost, but only transformed from one kind to another.

1843–46. John Adams (1819–92) and **Urbain LeVerrier** (1811–77) independently predicted the existence of a new planet and constructed its orbit from a consideration of irregularities in the motion of Uranus. This planet, later named Neptune, was sighted in 1846 by **Johann Galle** (1812–1910)—a great triumph for gravitational astronomy.

1843. James Joule (1818–89) sought the connection between electricity, heat, and mechanical energy in "The Calorific Effects of Magneto-Electricity, and the Mechanical Value of Heat," and determined by four different procedures the mechanical equivalent of heat. In 1847 he enunciated the principle of the **conservation of energy.**

1846. The **Smithsonian Institution** for the increase and diffusion of knowledge was established by the U.S. Congress, utilizing the funds bequeathed by England's **James Smithson** (1765–1829).

1847. Hermann Helmholtz (1821–94) announced the principle of the conservation of energy in *Über die Erhaltung der Kraft.* He discussed the principle in great theoretical detail and elucidated its meaning.

b. Chemistry, Biology, and Geology

1799–1805. Georges Cuvier (1769–1832) founded **comparative anatomy** on functional grounds, maintaining that the parts of the organism are correlated to the functioning whole.

1800–2. Marie-François Bichat (1771–1802) stimulated the separate and systematic study of each anatomical structure and physiological function by his classification of the body into textures, or *tissus,* each with its particular vital property.

1801. Claude Berthollet (1748–1822) opposed the prevailing doctrine of elective affinities with his **law of mass action.**

1802. John Playfair (1748–1819), friend and disciple of **James Hutton** (1726–97), produced *Illustrations of the Huttonian Theory of the Earth,* bringing a clear exposition of uniformitarianism to a wide audience and establishing this philosophy as the basis of modern geology.

1802–4. Jean d'Aubuisson de Voisins (1769–1819) and **Leopold von**

Buch (1774–1853), two of the most illustrious students of **Abraham Werner** (c. 1749–1817), accepted the volcanic origin of basalt, signaling the defeat of Wernerian neptunism.

1804. Nicholas de Saussure (1767–1845) explained the process of photosynthesis in terms of the new chemistry of **Antoine Lavoisier** (1743–94).

1807. Humphry Davy (1778–1829), using the new voltaic battery, isolated the metals potassium and sodium.

1807. Establishment of **U.S. Coast Survey,** the first U.S. scientific agency.

1807. Foundation of the **Geological Society of London,** which served as a center for research and discussion and as a model for similar societies in other countries.

1808. John Dalton (1766–1844) published his *New System of Chemical Philosophy,* which established the **quantitative atomic theory** in chemistry.

1808. Joseph Gay-Lussac (1778–1850) announced his discovery of the law of combining volumes for gases, that is, the ratios of the volumes of reacting gases are small whole numbers.

1809. Jean-Baptiste Lamarck (1744–1829), in *Philosophie zoologique,* gave the most complete explanation of his **theory of evolution.** He argued that through a combination of unconscious striving, the physiological effects of use and disuse, and the influence of the environment, anatomical parts became modified. Furthermore, he believed that by the "inheritance of acquired characteristics," living forms evolved in an ever-ascending scale of perfection.

1809. Lorenz Oken (1779–1815), one of the leaders of the German **Naturphilosophie** movement, published an antimechanist treatise that taught the superiority of intuitively derived concepts, expressed a belief in the archetypal polarities of nature, and championed a search for ideal types and a teleological unity in nature.

1809. Ephraim McDowell (1771–1830) performed a successful ovariotomy, thus showing that surgery of the abdominal cavity was not necessarily fatal.

1811. Amedeo Avogadro (1776–1856) concluded that equal volumes of all gases at the same temperature and pressure contain equal numbers of molecules; in effect, he distinguished between atoms and molecules, but his ideas were neglected until 1858.

1811. Georges Cuvier (1769–1832), the founder of modern vertebrate paleontology, and **Alexandre Brongniart** (1770–1847) brought out their *Essai sur la géographie minéralogique des environs de Paris* with a map, ordering important tertiary strata.

1812. Jöns Berzelius (1779–1848) developed a dualistic electrochemical theory to account for electrolysis and chemical combination.

1815. William Prout (1785–1850) published an anonymous paper in which he advanced the hypothesis that the atoms of all other elements were really aggregates of hydrogen atoms.

1815. William Smith (1769–1839) published his famous **geological map of England and Wales** and established that specific strata can be identified by their fossil content, the principle upon which historical geology is founded. He also worked out the main divisions of the **Secondary,** or **Mesozoic,** strata.

1819. Pierre Dulong (1785–1838) and **Alexis Petit** (1791–1820) formulated the rule that the product of the relative atomic weight and the specific heat of an element is a constant. This made possible the experimental determination of relative atomic weights.

1819. René Laënnec (1781–1826) invented the **stethoscope.**

1822. François Magendie (1783–1855) showed that the sensory and motor functions arise from different spinal roots. He was anticipated in 1811 by the more discursive work of **Charles Bell** (1774–1842).

1824. Justus von Liebig (1803–73) obtained the chair of chemistry at Giessen, where he established the first truly effective laboratory for the teaching of chemistry. He greatly improved methods of organic analysis and, with his students, accurately analyzed a great number of organic compounds.

1826–40. Johannes Müller (1801–58) developed his doctrine of specific nerve energies. He taught some of the most productive men in German physiology.

1828. Friedrich Wöhler (1800–82) announced the **synthesis of urea,** a typical product of animal metabolism. Urea synthesis and subsequent advances in organic synthesis crippled the vitalistic notion that a special force controls life processes.

1828. Karl von Baer (1792–1876) founded modern comparative embryology with the publication of *Über Entwickelungsgeschichte der Thiere.* Here he proclaimed that embryonic development is the history of increasing specificity.

1830–33. Charles Lyell (1797–1875) published his *Principles of Geology,* a powerful synthesis expounding and extending Hutton's uniformitarian theory.

1831–36. Charles Darwin (1809–82), as naturalist aboard HMS *Beagle,* studied South American flora and fauna, and gathered information he was later to use in his theory of evolution.

c. 1831–52. Roderick Murchison (1792–1871) and **Adam Sedgwick** (1785–1873) described the succession of Paleozoic strata in Wales, Murchison defining the *Silurian* system (1839) and Sedgwick defining the *Cambrian* system.

1838–42. The **United States Exploring Expedition,** under the command of Lieut. **Charles Wilkes** (1798–1877), explored the Pacific Ocean, the first example of a U.S. government sponsored scientific maritime venture.

1839. Theodor Schwann (1810–82) extended the 1838 observations on plant cells of **Matthias Schleiden** (1804–81) into the generalization that cells are the common structural and functional unit of all living organisms.

1840. Louis Agassiz (1807–73) elucidated the role of glaciers in geological change and enunciated his **ice age theory.**

1841. Carlo Matteucci (1811–68) demonstrated that a difference of electropotential exists between an excised nerve and damaged muscle. This stimulated **Emil du Bois-Reymond** (1818–96) to work in electrophysiology and to champion the German school of physiologists who wished to reduce physiological phenomena to physical and chemical processes.

1842. Liebig published *Die Thierchemie,* which promoted the analysis of organic compounds and described all physical and mental actions of animals as the result of chemical reactions.

1846. William T. G. Morton (1819–68) gave the first public demonstration of the use of **ether as an anesthetic** in surgery.

1847. Carl Ludwig (1816–95) perfected the **kymograph,** which became an invaluable measuring instrument for physiology.   *(To p. 483)*

b. EUROPEAN DIPLOMACY

(From p. 441)

THE CONGRESS SYSTEM, masterminded by Prince Metternich, rested on the Peace of Paris, the Holy Alliance, and a renewal of the **Quadruple Alliance (Nov. 20, 1815)** between Great Britain, Austria, Prussia, and Russia. Each member agreed to supply 60,000 men should a violation of the Treaty of Paris be attempted. This alliance, signed for a 20-year term, was renewed in 1834. The Quadruple Alliance also established the main tenet of the Congress System—**government by conference.**

1818, Sept. The first congress under this system, **Aix-la-Chapelle,** settled the question of the French indemnity payments and the withdrawal of the allied troops in France. The **Quintuple Alliance,** including the four powers of the Quadruple Alliance and France, was established, and questions of slave trade and the status of Jews were raised. This congress was followed by two more:

1820–21. Congresses at **Troppau and Laibach** were called to consider the revolutions in Spain and Italy (pp. 456, 459). Metternich induced the three eastern powers to accept the **Troppau Protocol,** which directed against revolutions that might upset the peace. England refused to sign the protocol, marking the growing distinction between British laissez-faire liberalism and the German conservatism. This division was stressed further at the Congress of Verona.

1822, Oct. The **Congress of Verona** considered the Spanish and Greek situations. Canning, who replaced Castlereagh after the latter's suicide on the eve of the meeting, refused to cooperate with the conservative powers.

1831, Nov. 15. Treaty ratified the London Protocol of Jan. 21, which recognized Belgian independence and placed Leopold I on the throne (p. 451). It also recognized an independent Greek state, as stipulated in an earlier conference protocol (1829–30) (p. 451). Belgium was also declared neutral in 1831.

1834–39. The Carlist War in Spain (p. 456) threatened to depose Queen Isabella and the constitutionalists. A **Quadruple Alliance** of Britain, France, Spain, and Portugal defeated the Carlists in 1839.

1841, July 13. Convention of the Straits. This convention closed the Straits (the link between the Black Sea and the Mediterranean) to warships, provided that the Ottoman Empire remained at peace. It thus benefited British naval power at the expense of Russian power because the latter lacked access to the Mediterranean from the south.

(To p. 470)

c. THE BRITISH ISLES

(From p. 324)

Monarchs: George III (r. 1760–1820); George IV (r. 1820–30), who served as prince regent from Feb. 5, 1811; William IV (r. 1830–37); and Victoria (r. 1837–1901).

Prime ministers: Tories: Lord Liverpool (1812–27), Canning (1827), Lord Goderich (1827–28), and the duke of Wellington (1828–30); Whigs: Earl Grey (1830–34), Lord Melbourne (1834); Tories: Sir Robert Peel, a liberal Tory, laid out a liberal Tory course in the Tamworth Manifesto (1834–35); Melbourne (1835–41); and Peel (1841–46).

1. ENGLAND, SCOTLAND, AND WALES

Romanticism developed in England during and after the French Revolution and included authors such as Wordsworth (1770–1850), Coleridge (1772–1834), Percy Bysshe (1792–1822) and Mary (1797–1851) Shelley; and painters such as Joseph Turner (1778–1851) and John Constable (1776–1837). Leading novelists included Walter Scott (1771–1832) and Jane Austen (1775–1817).

Economic depression followed the Napoleonic Wars. Government demands for merchandise fell without a compensatory expansion of continental markets. Prices fell and unemployment rose. Military demobilization and industrialization aggravated the latter.

1815. Corn Laws outlawed the import of grain until domestic grain reached the "famine price" of 80 shillings per quarter. This law resulted in higher food prices for the working classes.

1816, March. Abolition of the 10 percent income tax was countered by raising duties on many articles and thus raising prices. **Deflation of currency (May 1821)** may have helped counter these increases to a limited extent.

1817. David Ricardo published his *Principles of Political Economy and Taxation.* Drawing on **Malthus's *Essay on the Principle of Population* (1789)**, which argued that population would increase geometrically while food would only increase arithmetically, Ricardo argued that such population growth could only result in a large supply of labor and keep wages at a subsistence level.

1812–20. Luddism. Northern England was wracked by numerous incidents of machine breakings perpetrated by the apparently fictional **Captain Ludd** and the **Luddites (1812–20).** The Luddites drew their strength from traditional crafts, particularly cropping and framework knitting. Participants disguised themselves and called one another by code names to avoid identification. The government mobilized troops and planted spies within the movement.

The unsatisfactory nature of economic reforms and continuing economic hardship led to **radical activity** on two fronts. Master artisans such as **Francis Place** and reformers such as the factory owner **Robert Owen** sought parliamentary reform and advanced their ideas in radical journals and tracts such as his *New View of Society* (1817), which called upon factory owners to provide for the well-being of workers through moral and practical education in regulated factory towns. **Radicals** also appealed to workers in mass meetings, with speakers such as **Henry Hunt and William Cobbett.**

1816, Dec. 2. At **Spa Fields** one such mass meeting turned into a riot.

1819, Aug. 16. Peterloo Massacre. Local magistrates ordered the cavalry to arrest Hunt as he addressed a crowd at St. Peter's Fields. The cavalry charged the crowd, killing 11. The Tories, under **Lord Liverpool,** extended the act of 1798 against seditious meetings and temporarily suspended the *writ of habeas corpus.*

Dec. The Six Acts following Peterloo ensured speedy trials for misdemeanors, imposed a newspaper stamp tax (and thus required all newspapers to be registered with the government), extended the right of search and seizure, forbade training in the use of arms, and curtailed the right of public meeting. These acts gained passing acceptance after the discovery of the Cato Street conspiracy.

1820, Feb. 23. Cato Street conspiracy, in which 20 extremists plotted to establish a provisional government after blowing up the cabinet as they dined together.

Political reforms. Castlereagh's suicide in 1822 paved the way for moderation. **Robert Peel,** secretary for home affairs, secured the passage of legislation that revised laws stipulating the death penalty for more than 200 offenses. **William Huskisson,** president of the board of trade, lowered import duties on certain items and lifted the secular prohibition on the exportation of wool; these measures foreshadowed the fuller embrace of free trade in the 1840s.

1824, June 21. Joseph Hume, a radical member of Parliament, secured the **repeal of the Combination Acts.** Workers could now organize but still could not strike because the use of violence or threats was forbidden. The Combination Acts had not stopped **organization among skilled workers** who continued to combine under the auspices of **friendly societies.** Following the repeal of the Combination Acts, engineers, mechanics, and printers began to organize in **exclusive skilled unions,** which sought to control that skill within their area. Shorter-lived unions among factory workers also sprang up, like John Doherty's Grand General Union of All the Spinners (1829).

1829, June. The Metropolitan Police Act established a police force in London that patrolled all of London except for the City of London itself.

1828, July 15. Revision of the Corn Laws. Grain could be imported into the country but would be subject to duties fixed on a sliding scale (duties decreased as the price increased).

1830 ff. Cooperative socialism, presented by Robert Owen in publications such as his *New Moral World,* resulted in working and middle-class cooperative societies and workshops. In the mid-1830s, Owen organized the **Equitable Labour Exchange** in London to exchange "labor notes," representing units of labor, for cooperatively produced goods.

1831–32. Cholera epidemic throughout Britain, but particularly bad in large cities.

Impetus for electoral reform. The **radicalism** developing in England grew out of the economic changes that undermined the representative nature of the existing franchise. **Migration into cities** and the **growth of the industrial middle class** resulted in electoral boroughs that did not reflect the distribution of population. In **pocket boroughs,** the patron controlled absolutely the right to return candidates, whereas in **rotten boroughs,** bribery and the use of influence determined the candidate. As a result, the campaign launched by the Whigs during the election following William's ascension focused on the need for electoral reform. The Whigs won the election and began work on the Great Reform Bill.

1832. THE GREAT REFORM BILL. The bill was defeated twice in 1831, once in committee and once by the Lords after it had passed in Commons. The third time, the Lords demanded amendments unacceptable to the Commons; Grey forced the king, who could not form an effective Tory ministry, to create enough new peers to pass the measure. **Provisions:** The bill redistributed 143 seats and eliminated the antiquated forms in the boroughs. It gave the franchise to all householders paying 10 pounds in annual rent. In the counties, the area of enfranchisement was enlarged by retaining the 40-shilling freehold qualification for those owning their own land. It also was the first bill to explicitly exclude women from the franchise. **Results:** The Great Reform Bill helped to shift the balance of power in the Commons to the industrial and commercial elites. It demonstrated that the Lords could be challenged, but it failed to destroy the Lords' authority within the government. Their veto continued to be a powerful weapon for the landholding classes. It also did not eliminate the possibility of influence because it did not provide the secret ballot and offered no means of continued redistricting to keep pace with population growth and migration. Nor did it provide the working classes, who had rallied for the extension of the franchise, with the vote.

1833, Aug. 23. Under the direction of Edward Stanley, Parliament **abolished slavery** in the colonies over a five-year period with compensa-

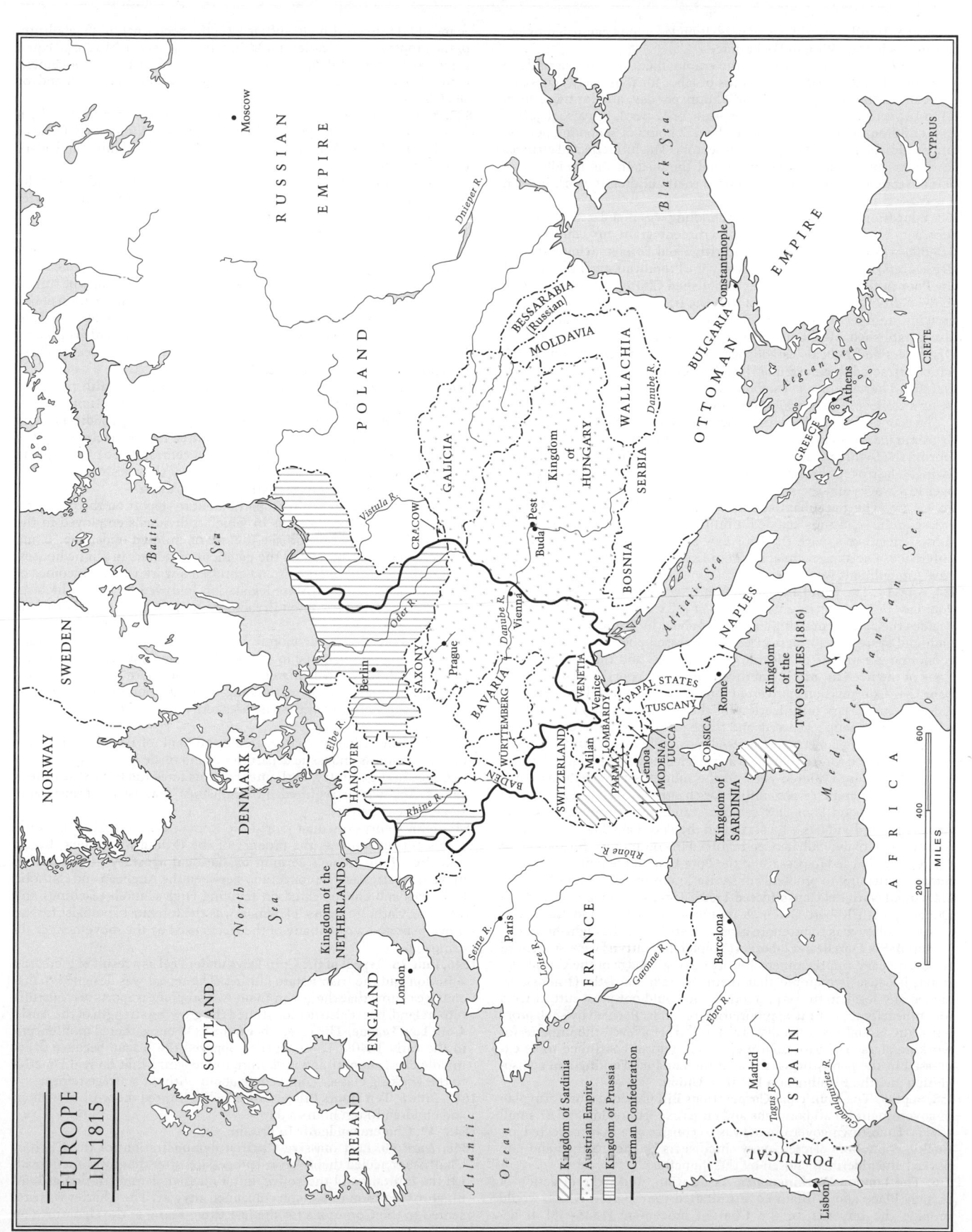

EUROPE
IN 1815

RUSSIAN EMPIRE

Moscow

Dnieper R.

POLAND

BESSARABIA
(Russian)

MOLDAVIA

GALICIA

Vistula R.

CRACOW

Kingdom
of
HUNGARY

Buda
Pest

WALLACHIA

Danube R.

SERBIA

BULGARIA

Constantinople

OTTOMAN EMPIRE

Black Sea

CYPRUS

CRETE

Aegean Sea

Athens

GREECE

BOSNIA

Vienna

Danube R.

Oder R.

SAXONY

Prague

Berlin

Elba R.

BAVARIA

WÜRTTEMBERG

Venetia

Venice

Milan

LOMBARDY

PAPAL STATES

Venice

TUSCANY

Rome

Adriatic Sea

NAPLES

Kingdom of the
TWO SICILIES (1816)

CORSICA

MODENA
LUCCA

PARMA

Genoa

Kingdom of
SARDINIA

SWITZERLAND

BADEN

Rhine R.

HANOVER

Baltic Sea

SWEDEN

NORWAY

DENMARK

North
Sea

SCOTLAND

IRELAND

ENGLAND

London

Kingdom of the
NETHERLANDS

Seine R.

Paris

Loire R.

FRANCE

Garonne R.

Rhône R.

Barcelona

Ebro R.

SPAIN

Madrid

Tagus R.

Guadalquivir R.

PORTUGAL

Lisbon

Atlantic Ocean

Mediterranean Sea

AFRICA

MILES

0   200   400   600

Kingdom of Sardinia

Austrian Empire

Kingdom of Prussia

German Confederation

tions of £20 million to slave owners. It ended a long campaign by abolitionists led by William Wilberforce.

Aug. 29. A factory act forbade the employment of children under 9 years of age and restricted the hours of labor for those between 9 and 13 years to 48 hours per week, or 9 hours per day, and for those from 13 to 18 years of age to 69 hours per week, or 12 per day. It also required that children under 13 years of age have 2 hours of schooling per day and established a system of paid inspectors. The bill reflected changes in the use of children in factories and the disdain the middle class demonstrated for parents who allowed their children to work in such a way.

1833. Educational reform, although schooling was mandated by the factory act, was quite limited. A government **grant for education of £20,000** was divided between the **British and Foreign School Society (Dissenters)** and the **National Society for Promoting the Education of the Poor in the Principles of the Established Church.** No money went to the Catholics despite the fact that the Irish represented a large and growing number of the poorest classes. Working-class organizations also established Mechanics Institutes to educate the working men. Dissenters and radicals established the **University of London (1828),** which attracted those excluded by religious belief from Cambridge and Oxford. The Anglicans established their own London institution (King's College, 1831), which was united with the university in 1836.

The economic hardships resulting from changes in farming, increase in pasturage, and enclosure came to a head in the 1830s and 1840s. During the **Swing riots,** rural laborers, under the direction of **"Captain Swing,"** destroyed threshing machines and burned hayricks in protest over low wages and the necessity of applying for assistance under the Poor Law. **The Speenhamland system,** established in 1795, had increased relief and thus enabled rural landholders to pay wages below subsistence levels, with the Poor Law administration making up the difference. The abuses under the Poor Law system resulted in the Poor Law Amendment Act.

1834, Aug. 14. The Poor Law Amendment Act, supplementing the Great Poor Law of 1601 and its amendments of 1722, 1782, and 1795. **Causes:** Besides the agricultural difficulties and abuse by farmers of the Speenhamland system, reformers cited (1) increased poor rates, and (2) the economic arguments of **Ricardo** and **Malthus,** and the emerging notions of the need for moral improvement of the poor. **Provisions:** (1) A **Poor Law Commission** (converted into a Poor Law Board in 1847) provided the necessary organization for the system; (2) all outdoor relief to able-bodied paupers ceased, and those paupers were to report to the workhouses; (3) paupers were housed separately from their families at workhouses and forced to live on a spartan diet while performing hard labor; (4) bastard children became the mother's responsibility, thus emphasizing female responsibility for chastity as well as eliminating the need to spend Poor Law monies searching for wayward fathers. Among the individuals who served on the Poor Law Board was **Edwin Chadwick.** Chadwick had been involved in compiling information for the reports that led to passage of the Poor Law and remained a tireless reformer, turning to problems of sanitation in the 1840s and 1850s.

1834. Grand National Consolidated Trades Union was organized by John Doherty, with Robert Owen as its president. The Grand National's avowed policy was to promote a general strike for the eight-hour day.

March. Six Dorchester laborers (Tolpuddle Martyrs) were sentenced to seven years' imprisonment for organizing a lodge of the Grand National because it required that members take an oath. Unions also lacked any legal status or protection and could not prosecute officers for embezzlement or misappropriation of funds. Plagued by such problems, the Grand National dissolved in Oct. However, the impetus for working-class, and particularly electoral, reform continued to be expressed in the penny press, through the **London Workingman's Association** and the **Birmingham Political Union.**

1835, Sept. 9. The Municipal Corporations Bill provided a uniform plan of government for all boroughs and cities except London and 67 small towns. Each town government was to consist of a mayor elected annually, councilors elected every three years by the freemen and rate payers, and aldermen chosen by the councilors.

1836. The London Workingman's Association, under the direction of Francis Place and William Lovett, drafted the Charter, which would provide the impetus for the **Chartist movement (1838–48).** It demanded (1) universal male suffrage, (2) the secret ballot, (3) abolition of the property qualification for M.P.'s, (4) payment of M.P.'s, (5) equal electoral districts, and (6) annual Parliaments. The Chartist movement combined diverse local working-class organizations in the demand for the Charter.

1837, Nov. Feargus O'Connor started the national, Chartist *Northern Star* newspaper and advocated the use of physical force in defense of the rights of labor. **William Lovett** differed from O'Connor and advocated moral force.

Female suffrage. Some radicals, such as Thomas Salt, addressed the issue within the working-class press and sought to expand the Charter to include women in the franchise.

1839, Nov. 4. The **Newport Uprising** was the result of rising unemployment and cuts in hours exacerbated by the Chartist activities of John Frost. Welsh miners joined with Frost and other Welsh radicals to march to Newport, take the city, and demand that the mines be turned over to their control. The rising was thwarted by a combination of bad organization and poor weather, which made it impossible to keep to the tightly coordinated time schedule. As a result of the failed uprising, John Frost and several other Chartists were sentenced to death. These sentences were later commuted to life in exile.

1840–42. Chadwick Commission reported on public health problems and overcrowding in the cities, which demanded action from governments in addressing issues such as sewage, housing conditions, and trash removal. This work eventually resulted in the enactment of the **Public Health Bill (1848).** The bill set up a central board of health and allowed communities to set up local boards if they desired.

1840, Feb. 10. Queen Victoria married Prince Albert.

1842. Mining Act carried after a parliamentary report on the mines revealed the terrible conditions in which individuals employed in the mines worked. The bill forbade the use of children under age 10 and all women underground and the payment of miners in public houses. The restrictions on women's and children's work cut the incomes of many miners' families. More legislation followed in 1844, which restricted the work of women in factories and required that dangerous machinery be fenced.

1842. Plug Plot Strikes. Economic hardships coupled with the passage of the Mining Act resulted in a wave of traditional protests in the area of Staffordshire. Crowds marched through northern mill towns, protesting wages and removing the plugs from the boilers in factories to stop employers from using strikebreakers to keep the factories working.

1844. The **Bank Charter Act** separated the Bank of England into commercial business and issue departments and made it the only issuer of currency in the country. Parliament also enacted the **Joint Stock Companies Act,** which required all companies that issued transferable stock to be registered.

1845. John Henry Newman joined the Roman Catholic Church. Newman's conversion was the product of the **Oxford Movement,** begun with **Rev. John Keble's sermon on national apostasy in 1833.** This movement stressed the continuity between the Anglican and Catholic Churches and concentrated on reviving High Church teachings and asserting Catholic rights. Newman was the foremost apologist for the movement and wrote many of the tracts used by the movement in its campaign.

1846, June 26. Repeal of the Corn Laws under Peel as a result of increased agitation and the Irish potato famine. The repeal was designed to discourage claims that the government was stopping imports of foodstuffs into Ireland, but it also demonstrated the growing strength of the **Anti-Corn Law League.** The league began in 1838 but gathered momentum in the early 1840s. The Chartists opposed the league because of its middle-class support and its failure to recognize that no real benefits to the working classes could come about without suffrage reform.

1847, June 8. Ten Hours Bill passed. The bill limited the work of women and children to ten hours a day.

1848–49. Cholera epidemic in Britain.

1848, April 10. Last massive Chartist demonstration for the Charter. Chartists canceled their planned procession after the government readied the military and the police, but a massive demonstration at Kennington Common in London continued anyway. The Charter was presented to the Commons for the last time. Many of the signatures on

THE HOUSE OF SAXE-COBURG-WINDSOR (1837–)

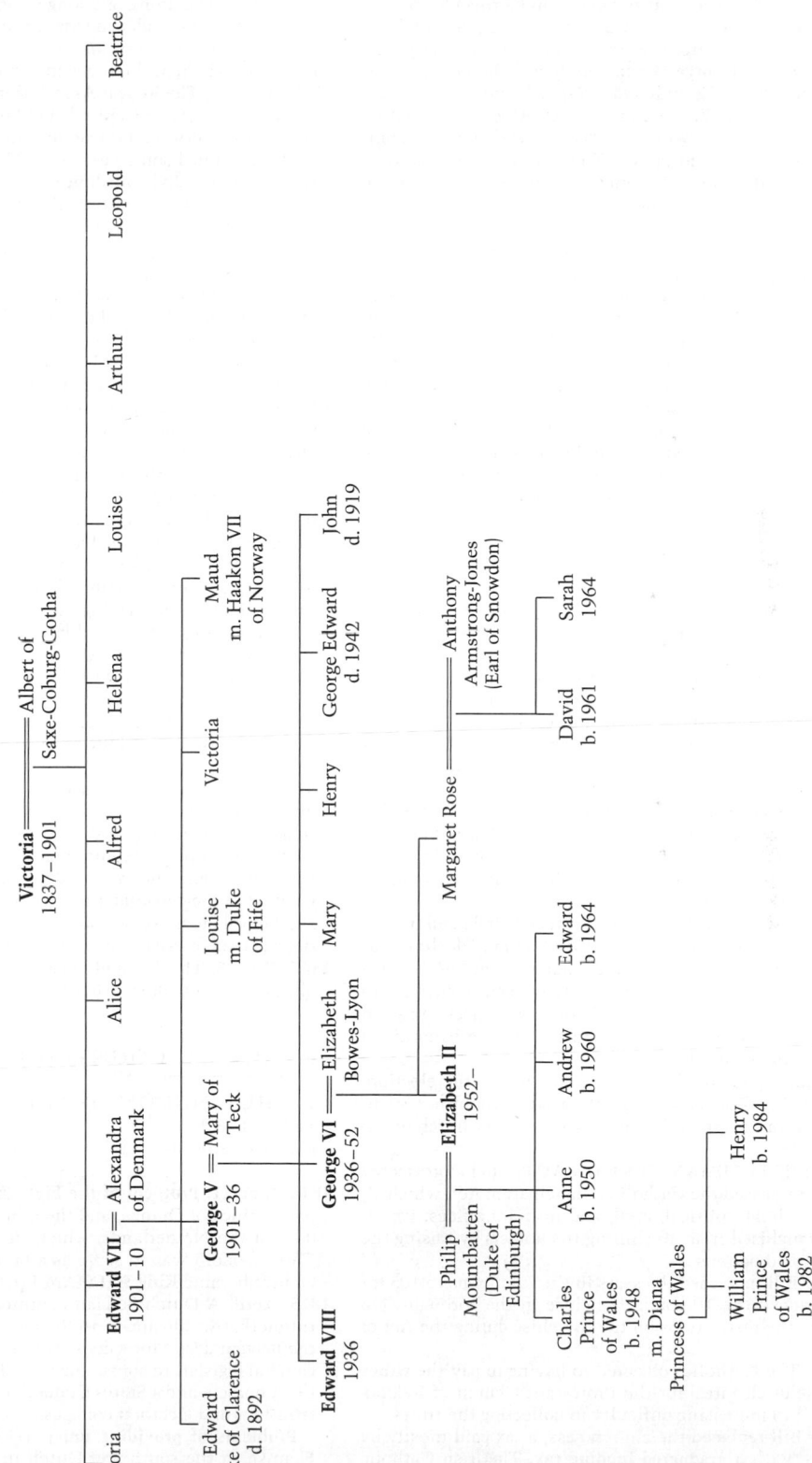

the Charter were found to be spurious, and the Commons refused to grant the Charter.

1848. *The Communist Manifesto* was published in German from London as the platform of the Communist League (meeting in exile). **Ernest Jones** published letters from Marx in his Chartist newspaper, *Notes to the People,* and **George Harney** published the *Manifesto* in English for the first time (1852) in his *Red Republican.*

Victorian culture. Queen Victoria and Prince Albert emulated an idealized middle-class lifestyle, which divided the world into two complementary spheres: private and public. The **public sphere** was controlled by the man and included business and politics. The **private sphere** centered on the home, was the woman's domain, and was pure and holy—a haven away from the vulgarity of the public sphere. Women were expected to develop the necessary skills and virtues to provide the family with a clean, well-decorated, and safe haven. As such, they were not to work outside the home. Men were expected to provide their families with the necessary finances for a proper life by working. In both spheres, proper education, temperance, and respectability were expected to be practiced. This idealized view was probably never realized by the majority of the families in England. Both parents in working-class families often worked in order to survive, and the working class often adapted notions of respectability and self-reliance to their own ends. Middle-class families could live up to the ideal only by drawing upon other family members for support and by relying on servants to maintain their homes in acceptable order. *(To p. 485)*

2. IRELAND
(From p. 325)

1801, Jan. 1. ACT OF UNION dissolved the Irish Parliament. Ireland was now represented by 32 peers in the English House of Lords and 100 members in the English House of Commons. Repealing this act formed the base for most of the subsequent nationalist movements in Ireland, although discontinuation of land ownership by English landlords and emancipation of Catholics were also central.

Catholic emancipation: Daniel O'Connell championed the right of Catholics to participate in government through his Catholic Association.

1823, May 5. Catholic Association formed. The association had to dissolve and reorganize because of the passage of the **Unlawful Societies Act** in 1825, which made the existing association illegal. In 1825, the Lords rejected the Catholic Emancipation Bill, which encouraged growing discontent in Ireland.

1824, April 12. An act established free trade between Britain and Ireland in all manufactured goods. This act, and the economic decline that followed the Napoleonic Wars, devastated what remained of the Irish textile industry in the south, where linens and woolens continued to be manufactured in home-based industry. In the north, mechanization of linen production allowed merchants and textile workers to continue to produce for the English market.

1828, July 5. The county Clare election. O'Connell won the election, but under the **existing Test and Corporation Acts,** could not sit in Parliament without taking an oath of allegiance to the Church of England.

1829, April 13. CATHOLIC EMANCIPATION ACT. After a protracted struggle, Parliament passed the Catholic Emancipation Act, which allowed Catholics to hold political, civil, and military offices. Parliament also disenfranchised Irish 40-shilling freeholders by raising the county franchise to 10 pounds.

1832. Great Reform Bill increased the seats in the Commons to 105 for Ireland and introduced the 10-pound franchise in the boroughs. No attempt to reverse the restrictions on the franchise during the Act of Union was made.

Church reform. The Catholics objected to having to pay the **tithes and church cess** (church rates) for the Protestant Church of Ireland. Popular protest led to increasing difficulty in collecting the tithes.

1833. Irish Church Bill replaced the church cess, a tax paid mostly by Roman Catholics, with a **graduated income tax.** The Irish Catholic Church was also reorganized, and ten bishoprics were abolished. The government responded to agitation surrounding the tithe by commuting **the tithe into a land tax (1838).**

1834, April 22. Repeal of the Union introduced into parliamentary debates by O'Connell, under pressure from Irish radicals. The move marked the beginning of a long struggle for Home Rule and, by more radical Irish, for independence from Britain. The issues frequently helped topple British ministries, as in the fall of the Melbourne cabinet, 1839. The repeal issue gained momentum.

1840, April 15. The Repeal Association founded under O'Connell. This association organized a number of "mass" repeal meetings advocating cooperation between Protestants and Catholics. Repeal and independence had gained some support in Ulster from the dissenting Presbyterians, but the division along confessional lines grew in the latter part of the 19th century. O'Connell's involvement in popular meetings regarding repeal resulted in his **arrest and sentence on conspiracy charges (Feb. 10, 1844)** despite his continued claims of loyalty to the British monarchy. **The judgment was reversed (Sept. 4) by the Lords.**

Administrative reforms. The **Irish Constabulary Act (May 20, 1836)** extended and reorganized the central police force, while the **Irish Poor Law (1838)** established the English system of 1834 in Ireland; the Irish Poor Law was opposed by Irish members of Parliament on grounds that the poor were too numerous to be provided for in workhouses.

1842, Oct. 15. *The Nation,* the official organ of the **Young Ireland Movement,** was first published. The Young Irelanders advocated **defensive physical force** against the government, if necessary, to stop the perceived tyranny of the authorities. The tension between their physical force approach and O'Connell's belief in constitutional activity and moral force led to a **split with the Repeal Association in 1846.** The Young Irelanders included leaders from Protestant and Catholic backgrounds and thus refused to take a stance on religious education or other issues, which, combined with their incidental association with the similarly named Young Italy, resulted in papal opposition.

1845. Potato blight destroyed large portions of potato crops. Peel, concerned about growing scarcity, ordered the importation of Indian corn.

1846–47. IRISH POTATO FAMINE resulted in massive emigration and death. Emigrants flocked to Britain and the United States, but the majority of the poorest cottagers, especially in the west, could not afford passage and died from hunger and disease. The British government did try to provide assistance by **repealing the Corn Laws, establishing soup kitchens, and providing outdoor relief (spring 1847).** But the British unquestionably exacerbated the famine's impact by their **tardy reactions;** ongoing limits on Irish fishing and on potato growing, save on one's own property; requirement that a portion of the potato crop be exported to England; and widespread jailing of beggars. The famine resulted in the **consolidation of land** vacated by emigration and death and helped create strong support for Irish causes from Irish organizations abroad, particularly in the United States.

1847, May 15. The **death of O'Connell** marked the demise of his Catholic Association, despite efforts to maintain it by his sons.

(To p. 489)

d. THE LOW COUNTRIES

1. THE KINGDOM OF THE NETHERLANDS, 1814–1830
(From p. 326)

1814, June 21. Protocol of the Eight Articles, concluded between William, prince of Orange, and the allied powers, created a unified kingdom of the Netherlands, which incorporated Belgium and Holland. This kingdom was to serve as a buffer against France. The prince of Orange became **King WILLIAM I (r. 1815–40)** on March 16, 1815.

1815, April. A Dutch-Belgian commission began to work on a **constitution** that would appeal to the Dutch tradition of republicanism and the Belgian desire for a constitutional monarchy. The result was a bicameral legislature consisting of a Chamber of Notables, appointed by the monarch, and a States General, indirectly elected by urban administrations and electoral colleges.

Problems of providing unity: (1) Different languages, French and Flemish in the south and Dutch in the north, split the country; (2) religious differences caused division between the Calvinist Dutch (William I was a Calvinist) and the Catholic Belgians; (3) economic and social problems differed in their origins. The Dutch economy was based on a declining trading network, which resulted in pauperization in urban areas. The Belgians were beginning to industrialize and thus experienced pauperization in the countryside. Domestic manufacturing in textiles declined. But mines and metallurgical factories had developed around Liège. A British industrialist, **William Cokerill,** employed 2,000 workers in machine building as early as 1812.

1819, Sept. 15. The government decreed that, after a transitional period, Dutch would be the only language used in the law courts.

Economic policies, sometimes considered mercantilist, sought to combine the interests of trade and industry. Belgian goods were to be sent on Dutch ships to the colonies, where they would be traded for products to be sold by Dutch merchants in Europe.

1822. A compromise tariff set the average import duty at 10 percent, and the establishment of the **Société Générale,** a bank for industrial and government credit, furthered heavy industry by providing necessary financing (1822).

Schools were thought to be the ideal place from which to unify the nation. The government concentrated on establishing and controlling primary schools. The primary system succeeded in lowering illiteracy and, because instruction was in Dutch, reinforcing the national language. The rapidly developing bourgeoisie in the south resisted change within the secondary school system because of the emerging humanist and anticlerical attitudes of the government.

1825. A royal decree closed all "Latin schools," including the *petits séminaires* and other church schools. Bishops were also required to admit to the *grands séminaires* only students who had completed their secondary education at a public school. Facing opposition from the south and declining enrollments, the government repealed all legislation regulating secondary education but maintained the primary system in May 1830.

1828, July. The two Belgian parties (the Clericals and Liberals) united after a concordat with the pope gave the king the right to veto elections of bishops and the government introduced a restrictive press law. The two parties called for freedom of press, instruction, and worship, and for ministerial responsibility.

1829–30. A hard winter worsened an economic situation in the south already difficult because overproduction had resulted in rising unemployment and bankruptcies.

1830, Aug. 25. THE BELGIAN REVOLUTION began when workers, spurred on by revolution in France, rioted and attacked the homes of government officials in Belgium. The liberal bourgeoisie, following violent **fighting between workers and troops (Sept. 23–26),** established a provisional government.

Oct. 4. Belgium declared independence.

Oct. 27. The Dutch bombarded Antwerp, which led to a conference of powers in London. These powers ordered an armistice.

Nov. 10. The Belgian National Congress established a constitutional monarchy, **deposing William I.**

Dec. 20. The conference recognized **Belgian independence.**

1831, June 4. The Belgians, after first attempting to make the duke of Nemours (son of Louis-Philippe) king, elected **Prince Leopold of Saxe-Coburg as king.** The London Conference approved the selection and drew up the **Eighteen Articles** regulating the separation. William I broke the armistice and invaded Belgium, defeating a Belgian force before he was forced by the French to withdraw.

1833, May 21. The Dutch were obliged by the British and French to conclude an armistice of indefinite length based on the status quo.

2. THE KINGDOM OF BELGIUM

LEOPOLD I (r. 1831–65) governed with a Clerical-Liberal coalition concerned with industrial growth and guarding against Dutch aggression under the status quo. This fear of attack led to **Unionism,** which emphasized the need for a strong army and allowed linguistic liberty. The latter was possible because French was generally assumed to be the language of choice throughout Belgium.

1834. Belgian railroads built under parliamentary instigation. As a result, 336 kilometers of railroads existed in Belgium by 1840. This endeavor strengthened capital industry in Belgium at a time when international trade was declining and prices were falling in Europe.

However, it favored Wallonia over the western Flemish regions because Wallonia held the raw materials necessary for industrialization.

1835. Bank of Belgium established to help fund capital industry.

1839, April 19. King William recognized Belgian independence and thus superseded the armistice, with only minor territorial readjustments, including part of Luxembourg as a separate grand duchy. The European powers guaranteed Belgian independence and neutrality.

The guarantee of Belgian independence ended the Unionism that had made a coalition government possible in the 1830s. Catholics called for reforms in their interests, while an emerging Belgian left, including Charles Rogier, drew on French utopian socialism. These struggles resulted in demands for reform within the school system and government.

1842. Primary schools, although managed by the government, were required to allow clergy to provide religious instruction.

Paul Devaux had been announcing the need for a government focused on parties rather than Unionism. The latter offered the Catholic majority a guarantee of no organized minority to contend with in the government. For the Liberals, however, it provided no opportunity for their dissenting opinion to be heard. This climate would lead to political reforms during 1847 and 1848, which enabled Belgium to avoid a revolution.

1847. The coalition government was replaced by a party system and ministerial responsibility. **A new electoral law (1848)** slightly lowered property qualifications and doubled the number of voters.

3. THE KINGDOM OF THE NETHERLANDS, 1830–1848

The Dutch accepted William I's status quo policy with regard to Belgium not because they wished to regain control of the country but because they believed the London Conference had challenged Dutch honor. Financing the continued occupation of Limburg and Luxembourg proved costly, and the government looked to the Dutch East Indies for money.

Johannes van den Bosch, the governor-general in Java, established a "culture system" in the colony after 1830. He lowered Javanese taxes in exchange for government control of one-fifth of its soil. Bosch grew coffee, sugar, and indigo on that soil and shipped it back to Amsterdam via the Dutch Trading Company. He thus managed to provide the king with the necessary funding for the status quo campaign by turning profits for the government-controlled trading company.

1840, Oct. 7. Unpopular because of his resistance to reform, William I abdicated in favor of his son, **WILLIAM II (r. 1840–49).**

Economic problems continued to plague the government. William II faced growing pauperization in Holland, which, unlike the economic hardships caused by proletarianization in Belgium, was the result of the continued Dutch commercial decline.

1842. Floris van Hall replaced Van Maanen as minister of justice and exchanged that position for minister of finance in 1843. He managed to **refinance the state debt** at lower interest rates and thus averted the threat of state bankruptcy. However, his actions could not avoid challenges from Liberals that Holland was falling behind because of its failure to industrialize and its conservative banking system.

Between 1839 and 1849, **population in urban areas,** rather than growing, had been slowly declining, and railroad development, with only 17 kilometers constructed in 1840, lagged behind that of Belgium and other industrializing nations. Because of the **economic crisis,** the government received criticism from financiers and Liberals, which would force reforms in 1847 and 1848. *(To p. 491)*

e. FRANCE

(From p. 441)

1. THE RESTORATION MONARCHY

Monarchs: Louis XVIII (r. 1814–24) and Charles X (r. 1824–30).

1814, June 4. The Charter recognized the principles of liberty, equality, property, and freedom of religion, although Catholicism was declared the state religion. The government consisted of a hereditary monarch, a Chamber of Notables nominated by the king, and an elected Cham-

BELGIUM: THE HOUSE OF SAXE-COBURG (1831–)

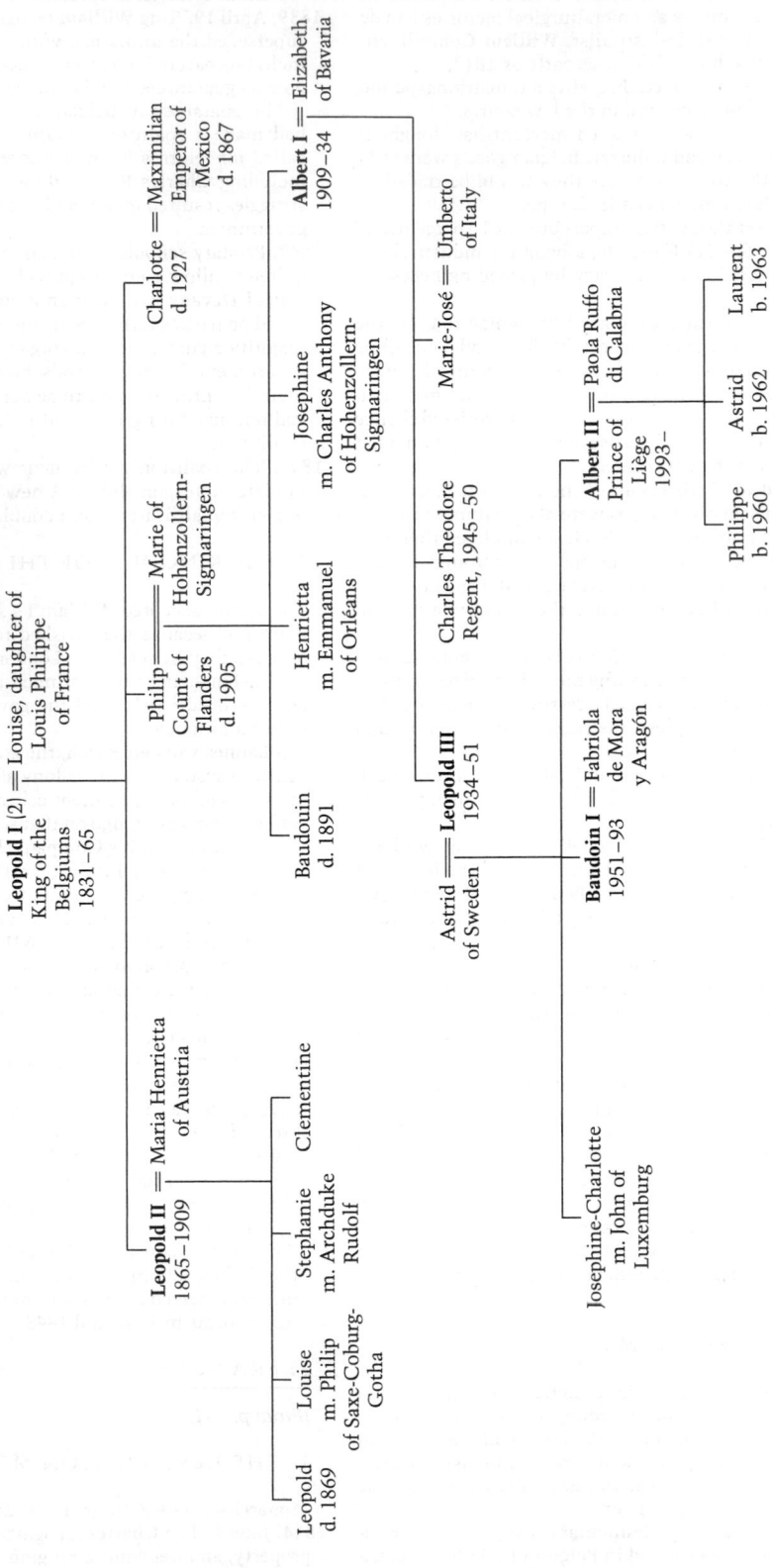

THE HOUSE OF SAXE-COBURG-GOTHA (1800–)

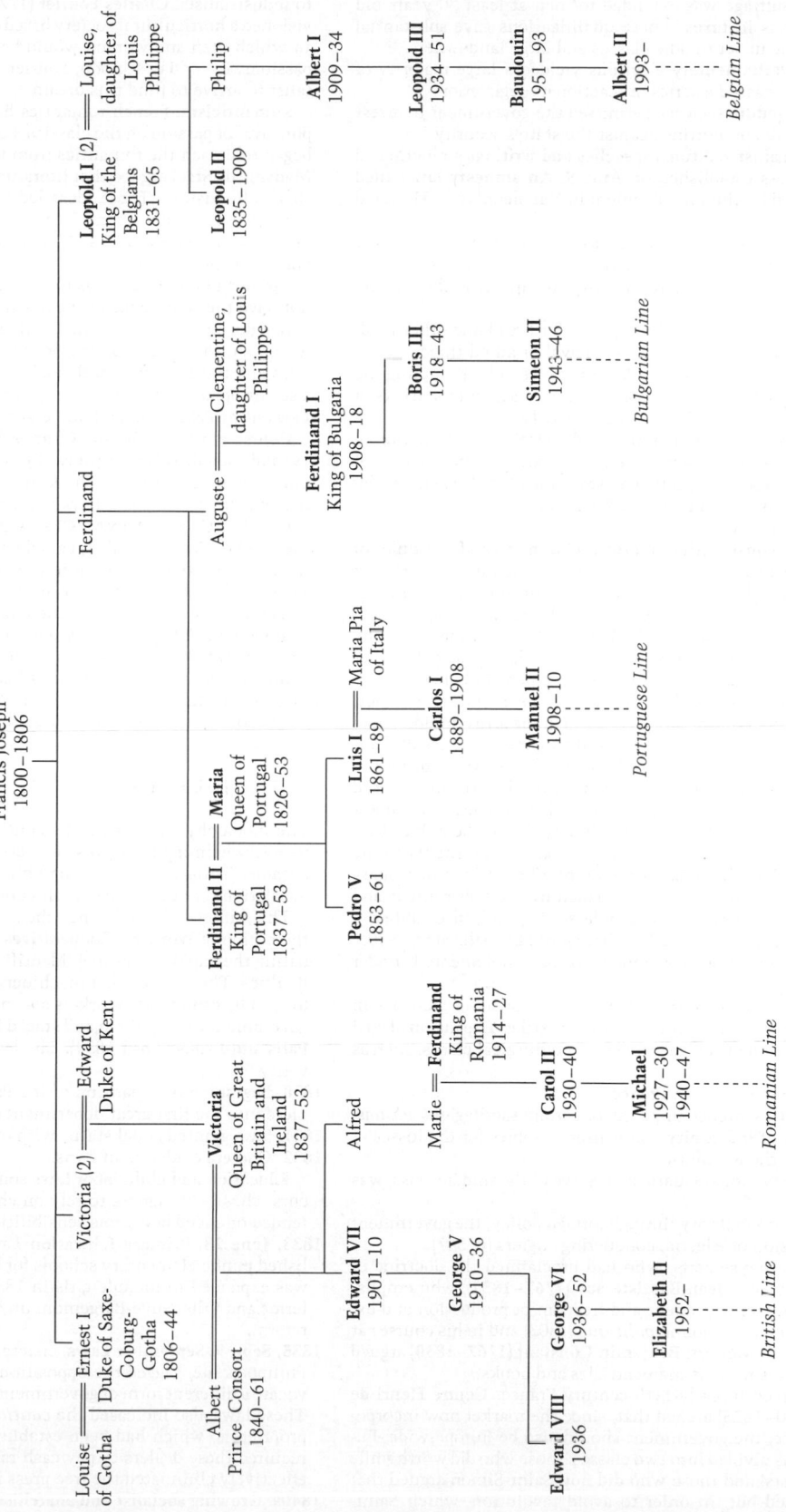

Francis Joseph
1800–1806

Louise ══ Ernest I
of Gotha   Duke of Saxe-
            Coburg-
            Gotha
            1806–44

Victoria (2) ══ Edward
               Duke of Kent

Ferdinand

Leopold I (2) ══ Louise,
King of the   daughter of
Belgians   Louis
1831–65   Philippe

Albert ══ **Victoria**
Prince Consort Queen of Great
1840–61   Britain and
                Ireland
                1837–53

Ferdinand II ══ **Maria**
King of Portugal Queen of Portugal
1837–53   1826–53

Auguste ══ Clementine,
           daughter of Louis
           Philippe

Philip

Edward VII
1901–10

Alfred

Pedro V
1853–61

Luis I ══ Maria Pia
1861–89   of Italy

Ferdinand I
King of Bulgaria
1908–18

Leopold II
1835–1909

Albert I
1909–34

Edward VIII
1936

George V
1910–36

Marie ══ **Ferdinand**
         King of
         Romania
         1914–27

Carlos I
1889–1908

Boris III
1918–43

Leopold III
1934–51

George VI
1936–52

Carol II
1930–40

Manuel II
1908–10

Simeon II
1943–46

Baudouin
1951–93

Elizabeth II
1952–

Michael
1927–30
1940–47

British Line

Romanian Line

Portuguese Line

Bulgarian Line

Albert II
1993–

Belgian Line

ber of Deputies. Suffrage was extended to men at least 30 years old who paid 300 francs in taxes. These qualifications gave substantial voting power to the upper middle classes and large landowners.

1815, Aug 14, 21. Parliamentary elections yielded a large majority of ultraroyalists, who passed a series of reactionary legislation.

Oct. 29. Law of public security permitted the government to arrest individuals suspected of plotting against the state's security.

Nov. 9. A law against seditious speeches and writings strengthened the gag on the press established on Aug. 8. **An amnesty law** exiled individuals arrested for their involvement in Napoleon's One Hundred Days.

1816, Sept. Under pressure from abroad as well as from his minister Richelieu at home, the king dissolved the government and called elections, which returned a moderate majority to support Richelieu and his successors.

1816–17. Grain crisis resulted in high prices for bread and other foodstuffs. The crisis was worsened by the arrival of allied troops in the summer of 1815, who disrupted the growing season by trampling the crops. The food shortage led to riots and demonstrations at markets in the spring of 1816 and again in the spring of 1817.

1818. Payment of the French indemnity, and consequent evacuation of French soil by allied troops, saved the French government the cost of provisioning these troops. Richelieu masterminded these payments by borrowing from banks in London and Amsterdam.

1818. Rights restored to Jews.

1820. Electoral and conservative reforms. The **murder of the duke of Berri,** the presumed last heir of the Bourbon line, reinforced the belief in a threat to monarchy from the liberals within the emerging independent party. The day after the murder (Feb. 13, 1820), a new electoral law was passed (**the Law of the Double Vote**), which increased the weight of voters in the upper tax brackets. This law followed further restriction of press freedoms and suspension of personal liberty.

Secret societies developed throughout France and drew their strength from the noncommissioned officers in the army, middle-class elements who opposed the monarchy, and students. A series of demonstrations in 1820 culminated in the plan of Aug. 19 to bring the military to arms against the government while the students roused Paris to insurrection. This plot was discovered and the leaders, Joubert and Dugied, fled to Italy. They became initiated into the Italian **Carbonari** and, when they returned to France, adapted the rituals to the French situation. The Carbonari staged a number of insurrectionary actions during 1822, but they were crushed by the government and disintegrated under pressure. Nonetheless, they helped establish a groundwork for revolutionary action that would be utilized in 1830.

Conservative legislation continued to be implemented under Charles X.

1820–30. Initial French industrialization. Rapid spread of factories in the north and in Alsace, for cotton and wool textiles. Expansion of coal mining and formation of several modern metallurgical plants, such as Decazeville (1826).

1822–25. Smallpox epidemics in France.

1825, April 15. Death sentence imposed for certain **sacrilegious actions.**

April 27. A law of indemnity compensated nobles for the losses of their lands during the Revolution.

1827, April 29. The National Guard, a preserve of the middle class, was dissolved.

1829–30. Bidding for popularity through foreign policy, the government launched an invasion of Algeria, conquering Algiers (p. 547).

Liberalism. The physiocrats, who had proclaimed the doctrine of laissez faire, influenced **Jean-Baptiste Say (1767–1832),** who emphasized the role of the entrepreneur and freedom of production and exchange in his *Traité d'économie politique* (1803) and in his courses at the École des Arts et Métiers. **Benjamin Constant (1767–1830)** argued for political liberalism in his many articles and books.

Socialism emerged in early-19th-century France. **Comte Henri de Saint-Simon** (1760–1825) argued that, since the market now incorporated all of Europe, the government should also be Europe-wide. European society was divided into two classes: those who did worthwhile labor (industrialists) and those who did not. Saint-Simon argued that the latter governed but, in order to avoid revolution, which Saint-Simon saw as a destructive force, the governments must be turned over

to industrialists. **Charles Fourier (1772–1837),** a utopian socialist, envisioned a horticultural society based on harmony—the phalanstery—in which men and women would be completely free to pursue their passions. Every day at noon, Fourier waited at his lodgings for a capitalist to arrive to fund this dream.

Romanticism. French romantics had built their love of nature and portrayal of passion on the classics, but, in 1824, *The Globe* newspaper began to detach the romantics from the government and the classics. Madame de Staël argued that literature should express society and was shaped by history. These ideas led to a rejection of classicism and a willingness to adopt liberal ideals.

1830. REVOLUTION OF 1830. Causes: (1) The king violated the generally accepted principle of ministerial responsibility by appointing the **prince of Polignac** as his first minister (Aug. 8, 1829). Polignac did not have the confidence of the assembly. (2) A period of relative prosperity during the 1820s ended with a slump between 1827 and 1832, which radicalized demands from the working classes. (3) Secret societies and the growth of both socialism and liberalism developed into a strong opposition to the government. Measures such as the Sacrilege Law and attacks on liberal university professors enhanced the tension.

Course of the revolution. Charles X adjourned the chamber (March 19) and then dissolved it (May 16). New elections returned a majority unfavorable to the king. The king responded by utilizing his constitutional powers to enact laws to pass the July Ordinances.

July 26. JULY ORDINANCES, which censored the press, dissolved the newly elected chamber, called new elections for Sept., and altered the electoral laws so that more weight was given to rural landowners. These ordinances were followed by popular violence in Paris. The working-class insurrection, encouraged by the liberals within the chamber and Adolphe Thiers, a journalist, took the Hôtel de Ville despite heavy fighting on the part of the military. Charles fled to England.

July 31. In order to stem the radical republican edge of the revolution, the liberal deputies declared **Louis-Philippe** king of France, under a new constitution, which limited the king's power, specifically eliminating his right to issue ordinances in protection of the state.

2. THE JULY MONARCHY

The monarchy was marked by continued dissension on the Left and its overwhelming bourgeois character. Workers, particularly artisans, became disillusioned by Louis-Philippe because he failed to provide legislation that guaranteed their continued livelihood.

The printers who published the newspaper *L'Artisan* rallied behind the notion of **Workers' Cooperatives** (Sept. 1830) as a means of eliminating the exploitation they identified as the main cause of their difficulties. They argued that machinery was not evil itself, but was used for evil by capitalists. Workers also protested the unwillingness of the government to help them and staged **insurrections in Lyons (1831) and Paris and Lyons (April 1834).** The latter was put down with great severity.

1830. Beginning of expansion of the Parisian clothing shop Belle Jardinière into the first great department store.

1831. Jews granted equal status with other religious groups.

1832. Cholera epidemic in Paris.

Education and child labor laws sought to protect children from parents whose willingness to rely on child labor or leave children unattended offended bourgeois sensibilities.

1833, June 28. Primary Education Law, introduced by Guizot, established public elementary schools for boys in each commune. This law was expanded to include girls in 1836. Reformers such as Louis Villermé and Villeneuve-Bargemont urged the government toward further reform.

1835, Sept. 9. September Laws, enacted following an attempt on Louis-Philippe's life, gagged the opposition press by making it illegal to advocate a different form of government and by reviving state censorship. These laws also increased the *cautionnement,* or bond by newspaper proprietors, which had been established in Nov. 1830. The new law required these dealers to pay cash rather than post bonds. These acts effectively eliminated the free press in France.

1840s. Growing socialist and anarchist ideology. Louis Blanc (1811–82) published *Organization du travail* (1839). *L'Atelier,* published by **Phi-**

THE HOUSE OF BOURBON-ORLÉANS (1700–)

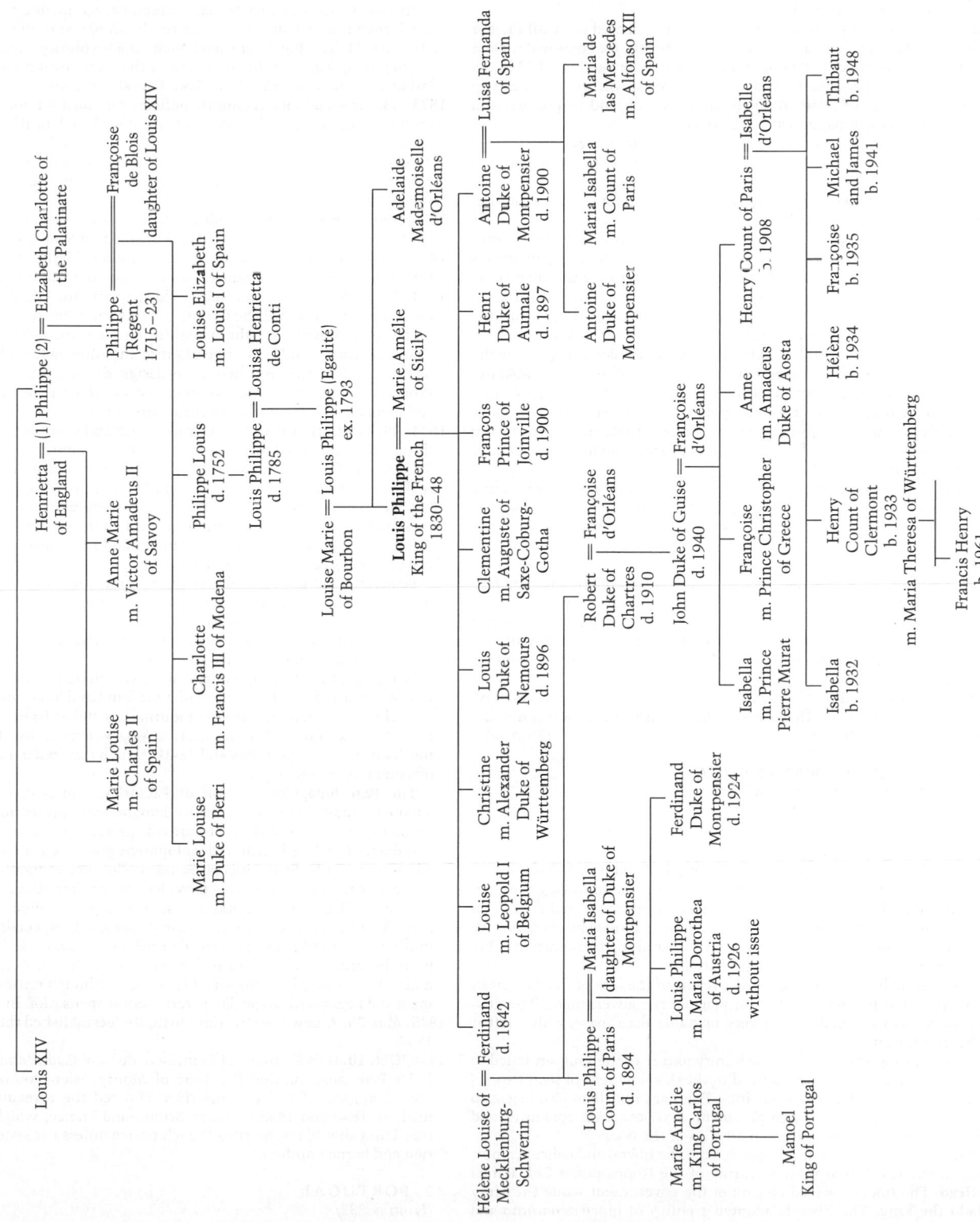

lippe Buchez (1796–1865) between Sept. 1840 and July 1850, advocated a form of Saint-Simonian socialism. **Pierre-Joseph Proudhon (1809–65)** published *Qu'est-ce que la propriété?* (June 1840), which identified property as theft.

1841. After an inquiry (1837), the government enacted the **Child Labor Law of 1841,** which set age 8 as the minimum age for employment and limited the workday to 8 hours for children under age 12 and 12 hours for those between ages 12 and 16. This law proved very difficult to enforce because of falsified documents, lack of paid inspectors, and collusion between parents and employers.

Industrialization. The period of July Monarchy experienced rapid industrial growth (600 steam engines in France in 1830, compared to 4,853 in 1847).

1842. The Railway Act provided government financing for construction and helped the growth of heavy industry.

Family and children became an increasing concern to the government during this period. A growing number of bourgeois organizations sought to encourage correct behavior in the expanding urban working classes. These organizations concentrated on the problems of illegitimate births, child abandonment, and wet-nursing. Many working-class mothers continued to put their babies out to a wet nurse and swaddle their children, although this practice was declining among the middle class. Children, especially illegitimate children, were also frequently abandoned at hospitals and orphanages; special towers *(tours)* often made it easy to do this anonymously. The resulting high infant mortality led the government to close many of these towers during the July Monarchy. Private individuals also began to address the needs of working parents.

1844. F. Marbeau opened the **first *crèche* (nursery) in Paris,** providing care to infants. Other philanthropic individuals opened *salles d'asile* (daycare facilities), which cared for children too young for school but too old for the *crèche.*

1846. The oath required of Jews abolished.

Economic depression, aggravated by the potato blight and crop failures that struck France in 1846–47. The problems of urban development, industrialization, and the declining artisan trades, combined with the hardships caused by this depression, resulted in growing demands for change. This depression helped to precipitate the revolution of 1848.

1847–48. Thiers and others led *banquet campaign* to protest conservative ministries of the 1840s and parliamentary corruption and to demand broader suffrage. *(To p. 465)*

f. THE IBERIAN PENINSULA

1. SPAIN
(From p. 331)

Monarchs: Ferdinand VII (r. 1814–33) and Isabella II (r. 1833–68).

1814–33. Ferdinand VII was restored to the throne following the Peninsular War. He had guaranteed the liberals that he would govern on the basis of the constitution of 1812, but, encouraged by conservative deputies known as the Persians, he repudiated the constitution (May 4) and arrested the liberal leaders (May 10).

Economic hardship occurred as a result of the loss of the American colonies, and postwar depression plagued the government. The government also suffered from a very unstable fiscal base, which left it skirting bankruptcy.

Liberal suppression and the arbitrary nature of the king's rule led to growing dissatisfaction evidenced in the development of secret societies, such as the Masons, and clubs. Popular radicalism also began to develop in response to unemployment, a yellow fever epidemic, and flooding, which increased the hardships of the poor.

1820. The army, confident of support from the liberal and radical camps, began the **revolution** with a mutiny of the troops under **Col. Rafael Riego.** The liberals seized control of the government while the army held the king. The liberals adopted a policy of broad economic and political reforms begun by the Cortes, a bicameral legislature. **They reinstated the constitution of 1812,** decreed the conversion of uncultivated and Crown lands into private property, and incorporated into the state the assets of the monasteries and convents dissolved by the

Cortes. They also banned emigration, believing that economic progress could be achieved only by keeping people in the country. Dissension between liberals and radicals, as well as within the liberal party, weakened the government, which proved unable to withstand the French military intervention after the Congress of Verona (p. 445).

1823, Aug. 31. The Battle of Cádiz ended the revolution and reinstalled Ferdinand as king. Ferdinand revoked the constitution and all legislation enacted under the short-lived liberal government.

1823–33. Financial and economic policies provided for some cautious economic advances. The government introduced tariffs to protect Spanish agriculture and industry in 1825 and established a primitive version of a stock exchange in Madrid. It also staged an industrial exhibition in 1828 and sought to provide enlightened education for its subjects.

1833, June 30. Ferdinand set aside the Salic Law to assure the succession of his infant daughter Isabella. The king died on Sept. 29.

1833–68. Isabella II, represented by her mother, Maria Christina, who turned to the liberals for support and granted the Estatuto Real.

1834, April 10. The **Estatuto Real** divided Spain into 49 administrative provinces and provided the Cortes with financial power, but retained for the government the right of dissolution and control of the ministry. The constitution split the liberals into the Moderados, liberals who had been amnestied and helped to design the constitution, and the Progresistas, liberals whose amnesty occurred after the constitution and demanded a restoration of the charter of 1812.

1834–39. The Carlist War. Don Carlos, Ferdinand's brother, claimed the throne and, supported by the conservatives, the church, and the north, led a revolt. The Carlists were defeated with the help of the **Quadruple Alliance** of Britain, France, Spain, and Portugal (p. 445).

1840, Oct. The Revolt of Gen. Baldomero Espartero forced Maria Christina to abdicate and flee. Espartero controlled the government until he was defeated by a coalition of Moderados and Progresistas (June 1843). **Isabella declared of age at age 13.**

Economic and political liberalism dictated government policy during the war. The government created a ministry of development (Ministerio de Fomento) and sold the uncultivated and Crown lands as had been planned during the Revolution of 1820. The government also declared labor free and abolished the guilds.

Working-class and urban unrest were stimulated by liberal policies in Catalonia and the destruction of guilds. In Barcelona, working-class radicalism centered on a group of journalists and artisans who met in Soler's clock shop. Their frustration was worsened by the textiles mechanization in the 1830s and 1840s, which resulted in periodic layoffs and piecework disputes.

The Barcelona Commission of Factories, which had previously adopted a radical stance, began to demand state protection for their industries but resisted efforts to provide protection for the workers.

Industrial and agricultural development proceeded throughout the 1830s and 1840s. Spain increased its production of foodstuffs, especially wheat and wine. It also provided the industrializing nations of France and Britain with metal ores such as copper, mercury, lead, and iron. As a result, the mining industry expanded, especially after the mining law of 1839. The government helped encourage industry in its ports by prohibiting the importation of ships in 1837. Industry remained hampered by transport difficulties, although railway development did begin with a special government dispensation in 1829.

1845, May 25. A new constitution virtually reestablished the statute of 1834.

1846, Oct. 10. Isabella married Francisco, duke of Cádiz, and her sister, Luisa Fernanda, married the duke of Montpensier (youngest son of Louis-Philippe). The latter marriage violated the **agreements at Eu** made in 1843 and 1845 between Britain and France, which specified that Luisa should not marry a French prince unless her sister had married and borne children. *(To p. 495)*

2. PORTUGAL
(From p. 332)

Economic difficulties. The opening of Portuguese ports to foreign trade resulted in losses of profit aggravated by the decline of the Portuguese Empire, especially Brazil's declaration of independence in 1822 (p.

THE SPANISH BOURBONS (1814–   )

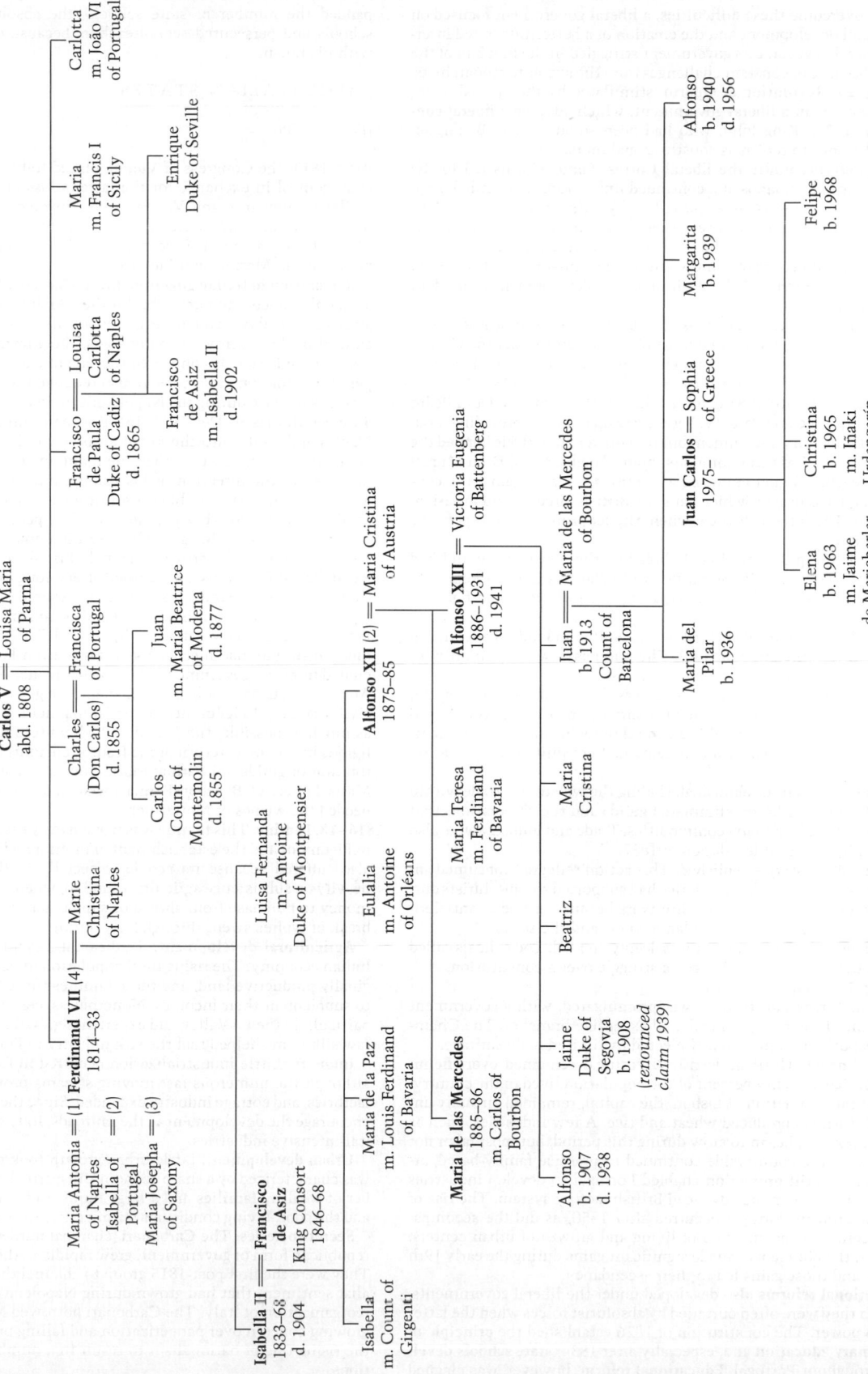

626). To overcome these difficulties, a liberal government focused on agricultural development and the creation of a better-integrated internal market. However, this government struggled in the first half of the century because of constant challenges from the absolute monarchists.

1820, Aug. 29. Revolution at Oporto, stimulated by the Spanish revolution, ushered in a liberal government, which adopted a **liberal constitution (1822)**. King John, who had been sojourning in Brazil, accepted the offer to return as constitutional monarch.

1821–23. Reforms under the liberal Cortes. Land reforms led to the clearing and sale of lands and continued limitations on entailed property. **Religious reforms** were spurred on by a rising wave of anticlericalism throughout Europe. The Cortes eliminated the Inquisition, curtailed the clergy's right to the vote and to representation within the Cortes, and inflicted taxes on the church. Establishment of the **Bank of Lisbon (1821)** marked the beginning of a development of modern industrial organizations.

1823, June 5. John revised the constitution in the interest of absolutism and, in the process, eliminated most of the reforms under the Cortes. His second son, **Dom Miguel,** supported further absolutist policies and, with the support of reactionaries, started a civil war (1823–24).

1826, March 10. Death of King John, who left the throne to Dom Pedro of Brazil, who became Peter IV. Peter drew up a charter providing moderate parliamentary government but remained in Brazil. He handed the throne over to Maria da Gloria, his infant daughter, and Dom Miguel became regent. Miguel launched a reactionary force against the constitutional government, which caused a British force to land in Lisbon (1827–28). The force withdrew when Miguel promised to respect the constitution.

1828, July 4. Coup d'état. Miguel abolished the constitution and had himself proclaimed king. Maria fled to England, and Dom Pedro abdicated the Brazilian throne (1831) to return to Europe and fight for her restoration.

1832–34. The Miguelite Wars (1828–34) resulted in **lands of enemies to Maria's state being auctioned off.** The purchasers were primarily industrialists and bourgeois landowners.

1833, Sept. Maria's restoration. Miguel was finally defeated on May 26, 1834. Portugal suffered continued insurrection between those who supported the constitution of 1822 and those who supported the charter of 1826, but the government remained committed to liberal reforms.

1834. Trade corporations abolished, leading the way to free trade within Portugal. This legislation eliminated guilds and the corporations that controlled the sale of many commodities. Trade and industry were also protected by the tariff legislation of 1837.

May 28. Monasteries abolished. This action reflected continued anticlericalism. The monks and clerics had supported the absolutists during the civil war and the Miguelite Wars because of liberal anticlericalism. The abolition benefited landowners and the state.

Aug. The new Cortes met but was deeply divided. The radicals called a constituent assembly and began a struggle over a constitution.

1837, Aug. 19. Charter restored.

1838, April. A new constitution was promulgated, with a government divided into legislative, judicial, and executive branches. The Chamber of Deputies became directly elected by limited male suffrage.

Social impact. Until midcentury, **Portugal remained overwhelmingly agrarian.** Seventy percent of the population lived in the countryside, and the population of Lisbon, the capital, remained virtually unchanged. Farmers produced wheat and rice. A few industries, such as cork and textiles, began to grow during this period, but most labor not employed in the countryside continued to practice family-based, artisan crafts. **Tariff protection** enabled Portugal to develop industries protected from the more advanced British factory system. The **rise of the proletariat** in Portugal occurred after 1850, as did the accompanying decline in the standard of living and growth of urban centers. However, the bourgeoisie made significant gains during the early 19th century, and those gains led to their ascendancy.

Educational reforms also developed under the liberal governments, although they were often curtailed by absolutist forces when the latter came to power. The constitution of 1826 established the **principle of free primary education** and, especially after 1834, **state schools developed** throughout Portugal. **Educational reform,** however, was plagued by the political instability in Portugal. Just as liberal governments expanded the number of state schools, the absolutists closed down schools and persecuted schoolteachers because of their sympathies with liberalism.
(To p. 496)

g. THE ITALIAN STATES

(From p. 335)

After 1814, the Congress of Vienna placed Italy under effective Austrian control in exchange for the latter's loss of Belgian territory to Holland. Lombardy and Venetia were annexed to Austria, and nine new or revived states were created: kingdom of Sardinia (Piedmont), Modena, Parma, Lucca, Tuscany, Papal States, kingdom of Naples, republic of San Marino, and Monaco.

Restoration in Italian government. (1) **Habsburg Italy** (Lombardy and Venetia): Francis I appointed his brother, Archduke Rainier, as viceroy and established two congregations as consultive bodies to the absolute control of the viceroy. In many ways, the government followed the Napoleonic legacy. It confirmed the sale of church lands and the imperial nomination of bishops. It also retained the majority of the civil servants in place during the Napoleonic period. (2) **The kingdom of the Two Sicilies** (as of Dec. 8, 1816): Ferdinand united the kingdom of Naples and Sicily into the kingdom of Two Sicilies, and he became Ferdinand I of the Two Sicilies. He maintained an absolutist government under the direction of his leading minister, Luigi de' Medici. Medici attempted to combine absolute government with fair taxes and good administration. His policies were hampered by pressure applied by France and Great Britain, which resulted in a decrease in tariffs by 10 percent for goods carried on French, British, and Spanish ships. (3) **Papal States:** Pope Pius VII returned after a long exile and restored the Company of Jesus. Under his secretary, Cardinal Consalvi, he managed to recreate a strong administration and establish a bureaucracy on the French model. Pius was assisted by general Catholic revival and **ultramontanism** but also met with resistance from laymen who were excluded from the government. (4) **Modena:** Francis IV of Modena, under Austrian suasion, abolished Napoleon's legislation and purged the civil service. (5) **Piedmont:** Victor Emmanuel I of Piedmont restored, as much as possible, the previous Piedmontese regime, including religious intolerance, return of the Jesuits, customs barriers, and the restoration of guilds. (6) **Parma:** Maria Louisa of Parma and the infanta Maria Louisa of Bourbon-Parma owed their thrones to Austria and heeded the wishes of Metternich.

1816–18. Famine. This famine was worsened by the restoration of guilds in Piedmont and the establishment of interior and exterior tariffs. Italy also suffered because its people, especially in the south, depended heavily on subsistence agriculture, and so, when crops failed, had little money to purchase from abroad or supplement their harvest. An outbreak of typhus swept through Italy during the famine.

Agricultural development. Traditional agriculture dominated the Italian economy. The rising rural population forced families onto marginally productive land, and these families turned to cottage industry to supplement their incomes. Nonetheless, certain crops and regions, particularly the Po Valley, did experience growth. The development of raw silk farms helped fuel the silk industry in France.

Industry. Little industrialization occurred in Italy until after 1848, although the numerous fast-moving streams provided sites for some factories, and cottage industry expanded. Since the government did not encourage the development of the railroads, Italy did not generate capital-intensive industries.

Urban development. Little urban growth took place. Urban society was characterized by a sharp economic disparity between a small number of wealthy families and a large number of petty traders, artisans, and the poor. Living conditions within cities were bad for the majority.

Secret societies. The Carbonari (charcoal burners), who supported a republican form of government, grew rapidly in the early 19th century. They were the first post-1815 group to channel the liberal and nationalist sentiment that had grown from Napoleon's conquests and the reorganization of Italy. The Carbonari borrowed Masonic rituals. The growing concern over pauperization and falling prices combined with the rising tide of nationalism to result in a number of Italian revolutions.

1818–26. Fall in prices. Prices on agricultural produce fell after the famine as a result of an influx of wheat from Russia, more advanced agricultural techniques abroad, and the freedom of trade created as a result of the end of the Continental System. This fall in agricultural prices led to a rise in pauperism and forced marginal peasants either to emigrate or to supplement their incomes through cottage industry.

1820, July 2. The Neapolitan Revolution. Encouraged by the news from Spain, the Carbonari in the army led a revolt under **Gen. Guglielmo Pepe.** This revolt involved moderate landlords and members of a middle class concerned, among other things, with the lot of the poor. Ferdinand promised a constitution (July 15) but was restored to his former position as a result of Austrian intervention under the Troppau Protocol (p. 445).

July 15–16. Sicilian Revolution. Spurred by the Neapolitan Revolution, economic crisis, and resentment toward conscription and administrative reforms, craftsmen and workers rose in Palermo and demonstrated a violence toward the army not experienced in Naples. The moderates in Naples as well as the newly restored government united in a harsh repression of the Sicilian Revolution.

1821, March 10. Piedmontese Revolution. Spurred on by nationalism but with a sharp division between the moderates and the democrats, the Carbonari engineered a military uprising, hoping that Charles Albert, prince of Carignan, would place himself at the head of a constitutional government. Victor Emmanuel I abdicated in favor of his brother, Charles Felix, with Charles Albert as regent. Charles Albert granted a constitution modeled after the Spanish one, but Charles Felix arrived and ordered Charles Albert to flee. The constitutionalists were then defeated near Novara by a combined force of royalists and Austrians.

Sept. 13. The rising in Naples led to prosecution of the Carbonari in the Papal States, and the pope condemned their principles. Consalvi negotiated a series of concordats.

Repression. Governments followed policies designed to eliminate the threat posed by revolutionary forces. In Lombardy, Carbonari were tried in four mass trials. In Naples, the government purged the army, administration, judiciary, and intellectuals. These purges were accompanied by the concentration of powers in the hands of the princes. This repression led to massive emigration of individuals who might be implicated in the revolutions.

Tariff legislation. Although tariffs had existed before the revolutions, the governments pursued a policy of protective tariffs for agriculture and industry in the 1820s. This policy proved ineffective.

1823–29. POPE LEO XII (Annibale della Genga) continued the policy of Pius VII. He persecuted the Jews, harshly monitored morals, and condemned Protestant Bible societies and all dissenters (1824, 1826). He also extended papal recognition, in return for state protection of the church, by continuing the policy of establishing concordats with various governments.

1829. Smallpox epidemics spread through the cities of Piedmont and Liguria despite the widespread use of vaccinations introduced by the French under Napoleon.

1829–30. POPE PIUS VIII (Francesco Castiglione) continued the reactionary nature of the papacy but managed to influence the British government, which granted the Catholic Emancipation Act.

1831–46. POPE GREGORY XVI was greeted by revolts, which he promptly suppressed.

1831, Feb. Risings in Modena and Parma were inspired by the July Revolution in Paris and connected with a general movement aiming to free all of northern Italy. The risings were weakened by the split between young students and older bourgeois, who accepted defeat. The risings were put down with the help of the Austrians in March.

March. Young Italy was created under the direction of Giuseppe Mazzini. The society sought to provide Italy with a republican constitution as a prelude to a free confederation of all Europe, dominated by a spirit of Christian brotherhood. Mazzini launched his campaign while in exile in Marseilles. The Young Italians planned a rising for 1832, but Piedmontese authorities discovered the plans (March 1832) and arrested those involved. The rising collapsed.

May 21. The ambassadors of the powers **demanded certain reforms in the Papal States,** but the pope contented himself with an amnesty and a few concessions in the administration and the judiciary. Fresh revolts broke out at the end of 1831, but order was restored by Austria.

These revolts led to the occupation of Ancona by the French (March 1832), and foreign troops remained until 1838.

1834, Feb. Another Mazzinian attack on Savoy failed, and Mazzini now extended the scope of his activity by organizing the Young Europe movement, directed from London. It helped stir national sentiments throughout Europe, although they were not always as radical as those in Italy.

1835–37. Cholera epidemics spread through Italian urban centers. Local administrations took action to ensure better drainage and uncontaminated supplies of water, but the conditions in hospitals remained poor.

1843. Publication of **Vincenzo Gioberti's** *On the Moral and Civil Primacy of the Italians* and of **Count Cesare Balbo's** *The Hopes of Italy,* both of which expressed the Italian liberal nationalist position. They called for the unification of the peninsula and constitutional reform, but they distrusted universal male suffrage as presented by Mazzini.

1846, June 16. ELECTION OF POPE PIUS IX (Cardinal Mastai-Ferretti). Pius was liberal in attitude, proclaimed amnesty for political prisoners and refugees, relaxed censorship, and organized an advisory council of laymen. Although he was opposed by reactionaries, the pope's popularity grew throughout Italy.

1846–47. Famine struck Europe again and aggravated the rise of liberalism and radicalism, which would result in revolution. *(To p. 468)*

h. SWITZERLAND

(From p. 336)

1815, March 20, 29. The **Congress of Vienna** laid down the principle of the perpetual neutrality of Switzerland. A constitutional convention drew up a new federal pact, which established a Diet with restricted powers and required the vote of two-thirds of the cantons to ratify any act. Thus, the Swiss cantons maintained their autonomy within the new Swiss government.

The Political Institute, established as a law school in 1806, became a major rallying point for liberals within Zürich. These liberals criticized the government and gained support from newspapers within the city. They advocated a constitutional form of government and drew support from a number of newspapers.

1816–17. Economic hardship hurt Swiss industry because it could not compete, initially, with England. The Swiss, however, benefited from their general policy of free trade, which enabled them to purchase relatively cheap grain from Italy and the Ukraine.

Industry. The Swiss had a long tradition of cottage industry in textiles, which had flourished under the continental blockade. Unable to compete with England, they worked to obtain the necessary technology to mechanize their industry. They were also able to muster the necessary capital because of the strength of their other industry, watchmaking, which provided abundant capital and low interest rates by the early 19th century.

1823. Swiss cantons restricted the press under pressure from the foreign powers.

1828–48. The "Era of Regeneration" was marked by liberal revisions in the constitutions of several cantons.

1830, Nov. 22. Snell's Küsnacht Memorial was accepted at a public meeting in Zürich by acclamation. It reiterated basic liberal freedoms and established an electoral system that gave the countryside two-thirds of the votes and the city one-third. This meeting led the leaders in Zürich to establish the **Constitution of 1831** based on Snell's principles. Zürich also began construction designed to make traffic through the city much easier and to destroy the visual distinction between city and countryside. This new construction helped to fuel a growth in the building industry.

1832, March 17. The Siebener Concordat. The liberal cantons joined together to guarantee their new constitutions. This act was followed by an effort to revise the federal pact in the direction of a stronger central government. The conservative cantons responded by concluding an alliance (League of Sarnen) to maintain the Pact of 1815.

1834, Jan. 20. The struggle over the federal pact became a religious quarrel when the liberal cantons adopted the Articles of Baden, which supported freedom of worship and secular education.

Social change. The development of industry in Switzerland corresponded to a renewed development in agriculture. Textile mills were located not in huge cities, but in smaller communities where abundant labor could be obtained from the surrounding countryside.

1839. Economic hardships developed as the result of the failure of harvests and a crisis within the cotton trade. These hardships seem to have provided the spark for escalation of the clashes between conservatives and liberals and, in Zürich, led to a bloody battle in the streets between peasants supporting the conservatives and the Zürich military and liberals. The conflict brought down the Zürich liberal government.

1845, Dec. 11. THE SONDERBUND. The seven Catholic cantons—Lucerne, Uri, Schwyz, Unterwalden, Zug, Freiburg, and Valais—replied to organized armed bands of the liberal cantons by concluding a league (the Sonderbund) for the purpose of protecting their interests. This league would clash with the liberals in the ensuing struggle for a new constitution in 1847 and 1848.   *(To p. 469)*

i. CENTRAL EUROPE

1. GERMANY
(From p. 337)

1815. The "Metternich System" dominated Germany and Austria during the first half of the century. Metternich and Austria were challenged for control in Germany by Prussia, though this challenge would become especially apparent in the second half of the century. The **Germanic Confederation** created by the Congress of Vienna had as its object the continued internal and external peace of Germany and the independence of the 38 member states. A Diet sat at Frankfurt-on-the-Main, organized into two assemblies and presided over by Austrian representatives. It was a diplomatic Diet, and as such the representatives were instructed by their respective countries.

Prussia, the major hope for liberals and potential counter to conservative Austrian control of central Europe, suffered from financial difficulties and the continued strength of the Junkers (Prussian landowners who controlled large amounts of the eastern territories).

Land reforms. The gradual emancipation of the serfs, which began in Prussia during the Napoleonic era, continued, but it benefited the large landholders (Junkers) far more than it did the serfs.

Agricultural change. The development of a number of societies devoted to agricultural progress and the expansion of the amount of land under cultivation resulted in the production of a larger number of vegetables and other products to balance out grain production. Unlike grain, which required heavy cultivation in the spring and fall but little work during the summer, the vegetables demanded constant attention. As a result, women became engaged in farming year round.

Bourgeois and working women. Bourgeois women's lives focused on their homes and social causes often associated with church. These women employed servants, many of whom were single women, from farm laborers' or poor artisans' families. These poorer women had few choices; although they could attend mandatory schools in Prussia, they had no formalized instruction preparing them for a trade. They worked as servants, farm laborers, and occasionally as factory help, until they married; then they might work in home industries such as clothing production and cigar making.

Economic development began to accelerate in the 1830s and 1840s with the creation of railroads. Major firms in heavy industry and machine building were established by innovative manufacturers like **Alfred Krupp** (factory built in Essen, 1826). The demand for metals transformed the metal-making and coal industries and encouraged their concentration in a few especially rich fields. Despite such development, urbanization and industrialization moved at a slow pace before midcentury.

Artisans continued to maintain some guild practices such as insurance and burial benefits despite the gradual elimination of guilds in much of Germany. Since guild membership was no longer required to produce crafts, many journeymen set up their own shops. Artisans and other members of the working class remained unorganized for the most part because of repressive legislation.

1815-19. The *Burschenschaften.* Universities became the centers of the liberal movements as students organized in liberal societies. One such

society, the Blacks, followed the lead of **Karl Follen** and advocated a unified Germany and liberal government but supported violence, if necessary, to reach these ends.

1816. An edict qualified the right of ownership of land. All those eligible to own land had to have the resources to support a team of animals to work the land. The gradual outcome of land reforms and demographic growth was the continued fragmentation of peasant landholdings and the impoverishment of German agricultural workers who then became involved in cottage industry.

1817, Oct. 18. Wartburg Festival. Students burned papers listing reactionary leaders. Growing concern among conservatives mounted when Karl Sand, an unstable follower of Karl Follen, stabbed to death August von Kotzebue, a reactionary journalist and lecturer. Some liberals supported Sand's actions, but Metternich and Frederick William of Prussia agreed to the Carlsbad Decrees.

1818. Tariff reforms by Prussia abolished internal tariffs but maintained external tariffs. They were followed by the introduction of a class tax (1820), which established different rates of taxes for four classes of individuals. These two acts helped restore the finances of the Prussian government.

1819. Carlsbad Decrees, sanctioned by the Diet of the Germanic Confederation on Sept. 20, established strict censorship, demanded sovereign control of the universities, and organized an inquisition into secret societies.

Prussia also reinforced the legal position of the **Junkers** through a number of governmental reforms in the 1820s, which secured the Junkers' control of local and Prussian elections.

1830. The July Revolution in Paris (p. 454) led to several outbreaks in Germany directed largely against the bureaucracy. Rulers were forced to abdicate in Brunswick, Saxony, and Hesse-Cassel, and new constitutions were adopted in all of these states and in Hanover. In 1832, 25,000 attended the **Hambach Festival** and toasted Lafayette. They demanded a republic and German unity and resolved to adopt both peaceful methods and armed revolt.

1831. A cholera epidemic, spreading west from Russia, struck Germany.

1832. Amalie Sieveking founded the **Women's Association for the Care of the Poor and the Sick.** This organization sent bourgeois women into the homes of workers and lower-middle-class families to instill their own values of cleanliness and virtue on the lower classes. Bourgeois women became especially concerned about the conditions of the poor through such associations and through church organizations such as the Rhenish-Westphalian Association of Deaconesses, which, in 1836, began training Protestant nurses.

June 28. Metternich, disturbed by renewed liberal and radical activity, orchestrated the Germanic Confederation's adoption of the **Six Articles,** which reasserted absolute sovereign authority and the sovereign's obligation to defend that right. In July the Diet also enacted additional repressive measures, including the prohibition of all public meetings and surveillance of suspicious political characters.

1833, April 3. In response to such measures, international dissidents made an unsuccessful attempt to seize Frankfurt and dissolve the Diet. In June, the Diet appointed a central commission to coordinate preventive measures.

1834-44. The German Zollverein, officially established under Prussian tutelage in 1834, created a free trade zone in Western Germany. Prussia initially signed a tariff treaty (1819) with Schwarzburg-Sondershausen and, in 1829, Bavaria and Württemburg joined the union. Smaller states attempted to counter the Zollverein by creating their own tariff unions, but these largely came to nothing. By 1844, the Zollverein included virtually the whole of Germany except German Austria, Hanover, Oldenburg, Mecklenburg, and the three Hanse cities. The continued use of local currencies and the failure to adopt uniform systems of weights and measures undermined the Zollverein's ability to unify Germany. The Zollverein may have had limited economic success by encouraging a wider market and the creation of railways, which stimulated industry.

1837, June 20. The death of William IV of England, who also held the throne in Hanover, resulted in the ascendancy of Ernest Augustus, duke of Cumberland. Ernest Augustus set aside the liberal constitution of Hanover and, backed by Metternich and Prussia, established his own constitution based on the principles of absolute monarchy in 1840.

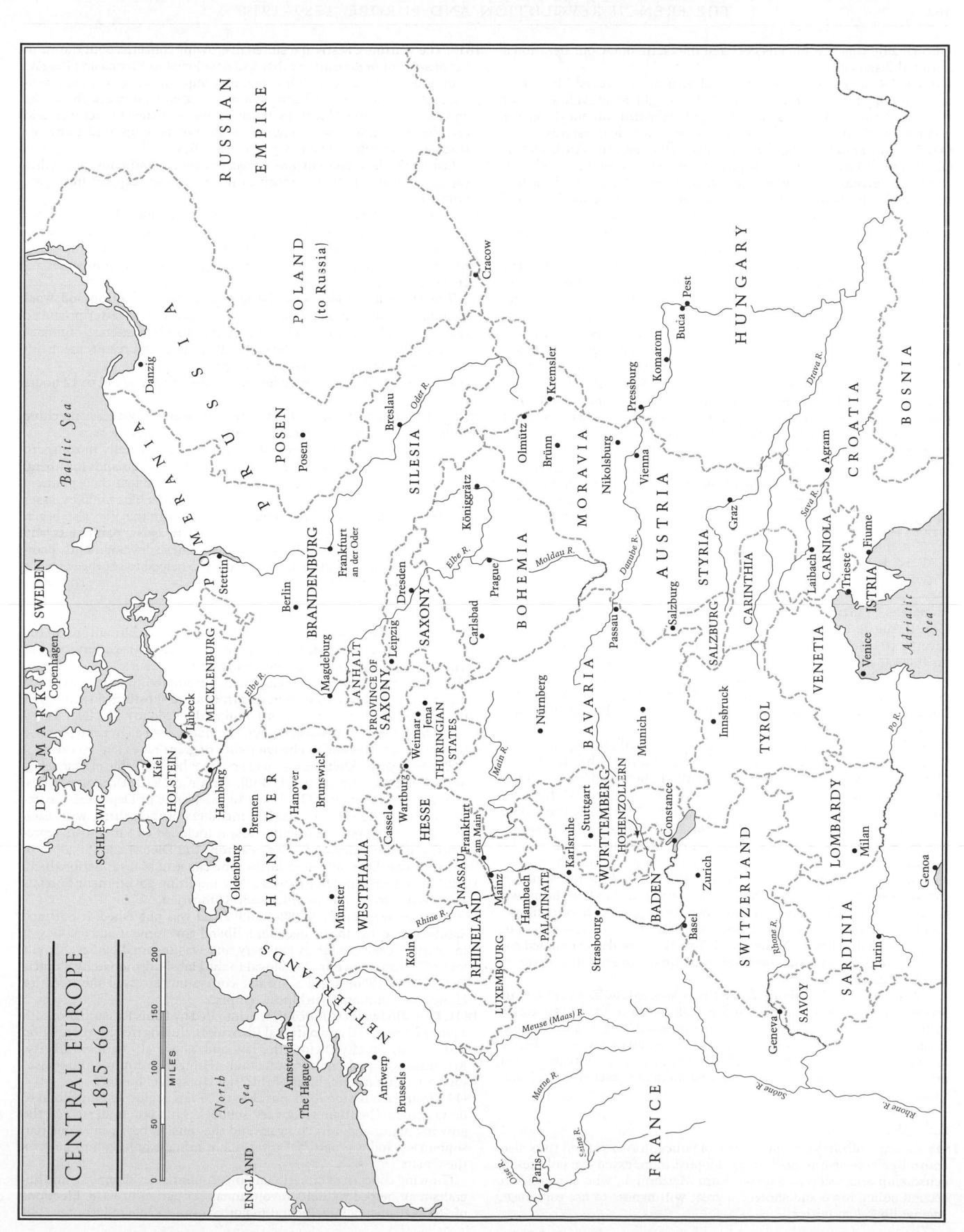

CENTRAL EUROPE
1815–66

MILES
0   50   100   150   200

ENGLAND

North Sea

NETHERLANDS

Amsterdam
The Hague
Antwerp
Brussels

Köln

Meuse (Maas) R.

FRANCE

Paris

Oise R.

Seine R.

Marne R.

Saône R.

Rhône R.

DENMARK

Copenhagen

Baltic Sea

SWEDEN

SCHLESWIG

HOLSTEIN

Kiel

Lübeck

MECKLENBURG

Hamburg

Bremen

Oldenburg

HANOVER

Münster

WESTPHALIA

Hanover

Brunswick

Cassel

HESSE

RHINELAND

LUXEMBOURG

Mainz

Hambach

PALATINATE

Frankfurt
am Main

NASSAU

Strasbourg

Karlsruhe

Stuttgart

WÜRTTEMBERG

HOHENZOLLERN

BADEN

Basel

Constance

Zurich

SWITZERLAND

Geneva

SAVOY

SARDINIA

Turin

Rhone R.

Po R.

Genoa

LOMBARDY

Milan

TYROL

Innsbruck

Munich

BAVARIA

Nürnberg

Passau

Danube R.

Salzburg

SALZBURG

CARINTHIA

STYRIA

Graz

AUSTRIA

Vienna

Nikolsburg

MORAVIA

Brünn

Olmütz

Kremsier

Pressburg

Komorn

Bucsa

Pest

HUNGARY

CROATIA

Agram

BOSNIA

Save R.

Drava R.

CARNIOLA

Laibach

Trieste

Fiume

ISTRIA

Venice

VENETIA

Adriatic Sea

BOHEMIA

Prague

Carlsbad

Königgrätz

Moldau R.

Elbe R.

SAXONY

Dresden

Leipzig

PROVINCE OF
SAXONY

ANHALT

Magdeburg

Wartburg

Weimar

Jena

THURINGIAN
STATES

Main R.

BRANDENBURG

Berlin

Frankfurt
an der Oder

Oder R.

SILESIA

Breslau

POMERANIA

Stettin

Danzig

P R U S S I A

POSEN

Posen

POLAND
(to Russia)

Cracow

RUSSIAN
EMPIRE

Rhine R.

Elbe R.

Outraged by this act, liberals declared the Germanic Confederation a national disgrace.

1840–61. FREDERICK WILLIAM IV of Prussia succeeded his father, who died on June 7, 1840. Although he sought to provide political freedom, he wished to do so not through a constitution but through a restoration of nobility and corporations, and the rule of estates.

1841. *Das Nationale System der politischen Ökonomie* by Friedrich List (1789–1846). List believed that protective tariffs should be used only to protect economic growth until industry could compete in a free market. He also believed the economic future of Europe would be tied directly to the nation and thus advocated the creation of a German nation. List's ideas had only limited influence in Germany during his lifetime. He took his own life in 1846.

1841–42. Frederick William IV gave the provincial Diets established in 1832 the right to elect committees to meet in Berlin and discuss Prussian legislation. At the first meeting of these committees in 1842, the king irritated the delegates by stating that they should not consider themselves a popular assembly. The meeting accomplished little.

1843. The Reform Society of Frankfurt established the basis for **Reformed Judaism** by rejecting the literal interpretation of the Talmud.

1846–47. Economic hardship, which struck most of Europe, did not spare Germany. In Germany it had little to do with industrial overproduction but was the result of potato and wheat failures in 1845 and 1846. The destitution it created was particularly great in the cities and helped to spark the revolutions.

1847, Feb. 13. The king, in financial difficulties, hoped to ease the situation by summoning the **United Landtag** (combined provincial diets) in 1847. This action, combined with economic hardship, contributed to the revolutions of 1848. *(To p. 469)*

2. THE HABSBURG MONARCHY
(From p. 339)

Monarchs. Francis I (r. 1806–35) ruled as Holy Roman Emperor Francis II until Aug. 6, 1806. After 1805, Francis acted as his own minister but gave Metternich wide powers in foreign affairs. He was succeeded by his less capable son, Ferdinand I (1835–48). Ferdinand left Metternich in control of foreign affairs but, under the influence of the court circles, created the state conference *(Staatskonferenz)* composed of Archdukes Ludwig and Francis Charles, Count Franz Anton Kolowrat, and Metternich.

Territories. The Habsburg monarchy controlled (1) the hereditary lands (principally Austria proper and the territories inhabited by the Slovenes to the south); (2) the lands of the Bohemian Crown; (3) the province of Galicia, acquired in the partitions of Poland; (4) the kingdom of Italy—Venetia and Lombardy; and (5) the lands of the crown of St. Stephen—Hungary, Transylvania, and Croatia. The diversity of these lands created several problems for the Habsburg monarchy.

Nationalism. (1) The **Illyrian renaissance** began among the Croats as a literary movement but eventually strengthened the resistance to the Magyars, the dominant ethnic group within the lands of the crown of St. Stephen. (2) The **Czech renaissance** also began as a literary movement but turned, during the 1840s, to demands for the restitution of constitutional rights for Bohemia. (3) The **Magyars** also demanded nationalist reforms, but their demands were linked to economic theories and political control.

Economics. The Habsburg monarchy countered the Zollverein with its own tariff system. It relied on the dualistic nature of its territories to fuel the economies. The west was industrializing and thus could produce materials that could be sold to the agrarian east in exchange for foodstuffs grown in the east. Hungarians, burdened with such food production, often linked liberalism and industrialization to their nationalist demands.

a. Austria

1815. Count Sedlnitzky became chief of police in Austria and thus also controlled censorship. Sedlnitzky adopted more extensive policies of censorship and received support from Metternich, who controlled a second police force and showed a great willingness to use espionage against liberal activities.

1817. The Wartburg Festival resulted in growing concern about the number of student organizations that had developed in Vienna and Prague. Sedlnitzky and Metternich instigated an inquisition against the teaching professions. They utilized espionage networks to track the books checked out of the library by teachers and to listen to lectures, and established a rule that foreigners could not be employed either as teachers or as tutors (even by private families).

Economic development proceeded unevenly. Railroads, and other capital-intensive industry, received little financial support from government.

1829. Austrian Danube Steamship Company was founded. It represented a major effort at providing better communication throughout Austria. It was followed by the creation of the Austrian Lloyd Steamship Company (1836), which navigated on the high seas. Both companies received government support.

The 1830s and 1840s saw the mechanization of cotton and wool spinning in Austria and especially in Moravia. The latter produced textiles for a fashion market and therefore had less interest in manufacturing large amounts of cheap, rough cloths. As a result, mechanization took place in smaller workshops.

1839. Austria reduced the workday for children under age 12 to 12 hours per day.

1842–44. The development of industry led to sporadic waves of **machine breaking** in protest to mechanization and the factory system.

Growing industrialization and urbanization, especially in southern Austria and around Vienna, had created increased demands for liberal reforms. The estates in Vienna, although they had lost their political significance, pressed for legislative and tax reforms. The middle classes and the proletariat, both relatively new classes in the city, also began to demand reforms. Liberalism continued to exist; pamphlets and newspapers were brought in from abroad. These developments, combined with growing nationalist sentiments, helped to set the stage for the revolution of 1848. *(To p. 467)*

b. Hungary

Unlike Austria, Hungary remained almost entirely agricultural in the first half of the 19th century. Landlords increased work-service obligations of their serfs to produce more grain for export.

1825. Francis I, facing a financial crisis, attempted to supplement his income and his army by demanding troops and subsidies directly from the counties in Hungary—thus avoiding the need to call a Diet. However, the counties refused and forced Francis to call a Diet and promise triennial meetings and exclusive rights to grant taxes and recruits.

The Hungarian Diet consisted of an upper house (Table of Magnates) of great nobles (approximately 130), certain ecclesiastical dignitaries, and high officeholders. The lower house (Table of Deputies) was recruited from the roughly 700,000 members of the gentry, with each district electing two representatives; it included two members representing all the cities and delegates from the Diet of the kingdom of Croatia. This Diet helped to further the cause of Magyar nationalism.

1830. The Hungarian Diet passed a law requiring government officials and lawyers to be able to officiate in Hungarian.

1830. István Széchenyi's (1792–1860) *Hitel* **was published.** It outlined Széchenyi's belief in the need for a liberal government and a policy of industrial development in Hungary and was inspired by Széchenyi's love of Hungary; he remained loyal to the Habsburg monarchy. **Francis Deák (1803–1876)** urged a similar course but stressed the need for Hungarian autonomy within the empire.

1841. *Pesti Hirlap (Pest Journal)* was founded by **Louis Kossuth.** Kossuth advocated personal and national liberties including freedom of religion and speech, equality before the law and, above all, national liberty. Kossuth advocated a nation-state under Hungarian control, thus clashing with other nationalities within the Hungarian borders.

1844. Hungarian nationalists put through a law requiring Hungarian to be taught in **Croatian secondary schools.** This law underscored the growing nationalism in Hungary and the tension between Hungarian supremacy and the national interests of other ethnic groups such as the Croats.

Growing concern over nationalism, economic development, and liberalism all helped to fuel a revolutionary situation in 1848. **Elections of 1847** returned a large liberal majority to the Table of Deputies, but the Table of Magnates resisted demands for freedom of the press and of religion, and the abolition of serfdom. (To p. 467)

j. SCANDINAVIA

Regions. Scandinavia consists of the five geographical regions of **Denmark, Norway, Sweden, Finland,** and **Iceland.** Following the Napoleonic Wars, these five regions were controlled by three different governments. **Sweden controlled Norway,** but it had relinquished **Finland to the Russians (1809). Denmark controlled Iceland.** Denmark also controlled **Schleswig-Holstein** despite continued efforts within the latter to gain independence and join the Germanic Confederation.

Economics. All five of the Scandinavian countries remained **largely agricultural** during the first half of the 19th century; however, their products and their means of produce varied. **Finland** concentrated on the production of grains for the European market. **Norway** continued to face difficulties with backward farming methods. At the turn of the century, much of Norwegian land was farmed without crop rotation, and Norway did not represent a major exporter of foodstuffs. However, following the repeal of the British Navigation Acts in 1840, Norway became a major exporter of timber for British industry. **Denmark** managed to maintain steady growth in agriculture. Industry, however, remained limited because it produced primarily for a home market. **Sweden** experienced growth both in agriculture, which it encouraged through government reforms, and in its only major industry, iron production. The latter suffered from a lack of coal and poor transportation.

Scandinavianism. The early part of the 19th century saw both the growth of nationalism and the development of a sense of collective nationalism among the Scandinavian countries. Scandinavianism, or an interest in cooperation among Scandinavian countries, first developed in academia. **Students** from the various universities began to participate in steamship trips together. Whereas the Finnish students suffered suspensions as the result of their activities, Denmark and Sweden were marked by growing cooperation. **In 1828, a Danish steamboat** first entered the Swedish harbor of Malmö and, in **1839, scientists** from throughout Scandinavia met in Gothenburg.
(To p. 506)

1. SWEDEN AND NORWAY
(From pp. 341, 343)

Swedish Monarchs: Charles XIII (r. 1809–18), Charles XIV John (Bernadotte, p. 438) (r. 1818–44), and Oscar I (r. 1844–59).

1814, Jan. 14. Treaty of Kiel. Denmark ceded Norway to Sweden. Sweden sold the island of Guadeloupe to France and thus eliminated its national debt. However, an unfavorable balance of trade resulted in inflation, followed by a reaction and deflation. As a result, agricultural prices first rose and then fell sharply, hurting farmers.

May 17. Norwegian constitution adopted. The constitution established a Storting, or legislative assembly, which met as a body in the Lagting. The Lagting then elected one-third of its members to the Oedlsting, thus dividing the Storting into two houses. The Lagting was elected by men who owned a house or farm, had 300 dollars, or rented a farm for at least five years. The constitution also guaranteed certain rights.

Nov. 4. First regular Norwegian Storting established connection with Sweden through an **Act of Union** (ratified, 1815). The Storting had elected Christian Frederick as king. Christian Frederick abdicated on Oct. 10 after a Swedish invasion and was replaced by the Swedish king on Nov. 4. Under the union, Norway maintained its local and national government.

1824. First commemorative celebration of the birthday of the Norwegian constitution under the direction of the Students' Union.

1830, Dec. 10. Publication of liberal paper *Aftonbladet* by Lars Johan Hierta.

1833. Liberals received growing support partially as a result of the **Institute of Agriculture,** which was founded to train farmers in correct farming methods and to teach agronomy.

1834. Fredrika Bremer published *Presidentens döthar (The President's Daughters).* Bremer argued for women's rights to higher education and freedom to pursue the career of their choice and remain single. Her novels were stylistically exceeded by those of **Emelie Flygare Carlén,** who did not infuse her novels with such ideological intent.

1836. Peter Wieselgren, a pastor, spearheaded the movement that founded the **Swedish Temperance Society** in Skåne. The temperance movement reflected growing concern over the consumption of cheap potato liquor, which was produced throughout Sweden. The temperance movement demanded government action, but such demands went largely unheeded because farmers and distillers mounted their own campaign in an effort to ensure their economic future.

1836. Agitation in Norway against Swedish control led the king to dissolve the Storting. Fearful of revolution, he had to reconvene it within a month. The sense of national independence within Norway also forced the king to grant Norwegian vessels the right to fly the **Norwegian flag** at their own risk (1838). These bids for national control centered on the work of **Jonas Anton Hjelm,** a Norwegian lawyer, who had argued that the Act of Union provided that a Norwegian minister had to be present whenever the Swedish ministers discussed Norwegian affairs. The Swedish king was forced to grant this demand (1837).

1837, Jan. 14. Two Communal Government Acts establishing representative local governments were passed and royally sanctioned in Norway.

1842. An **education law** was passed, which required that a school be set up in every pastorate (or congregation) in Sweden within five years (extended to Norway in 1847). It also raised the teachers' minimum salaries.

1844, March. The death of the king brought new hope to liberals, who expected Oscar I to support their efforts at reform. Among **liberal demands** was the reordering of the **Riksdag,** the Swedish legislative assembly. The Riksdag currently consisted of four orders: nobles, clergy, burghers, and *bönder* (landholding peasants). Liberals wanted to replace it with an elected bicameral legislature, which would eliminate the current distinction of orders. In **Norway,** liberalism was also evident in the passage of a **free trade law (1842)** and the **abolition of feudal nobility.**

1845. Oscar appointed a **special commission** chaired by John Gabriel Richert. The commission formulated a new civil and criminal code and reorganized the judicial system. A commission to consider Riksdag reform was also created (1846). The debates surrounding these reforms continued into the 1850s.

1845. Legal reform assured **women** of more equality before the law. Traditional law had considered women as wards and established the principle that daughters inherited only one-half of what sons did. The new law (1845) gave women legal status as independents at age 25 and eliminated the inequality of inheritance. However, women remained limited to five occupations: selling fancy goods, peddler's wares, or tobacco, and conducting brokerage houses and huckster's stands. Reforms also abolished guilds and established a new system of poor relief. (To p. 506)

2. DENMARK AND ICELAND
(From p. 343)

Monarchs: Frederick VI (r. 1808–39), Christian VIII (r. 1839–48), and Frederick VII (r. 1848–63).

Icelandic trade. The Napoleonic Wars had severely hurt Icelandic trade because of the blockade between Iceland and the Continent as well as continued trade restrictions.

1809, June 26. A proclamation bearing Jørgen Jørgensen's name was posted in Reykjavík. It proclaimed the end of Danish rule in Iceland and requested that all loyal Icelanders remain in their homes. Jørgensen led an armed raid on Danish merchants and declared himself the protector of Iceland (July 12). He was imprisoned, and **Magnus Stephensen** was placed in his stead.

1803–30. Golden age in Danish culture. Writings imbued with the Aladdin theme, which demonstrated that greatness could not be avoided if it was destined, no matter how inadequate the individual. The theme often served as a rationale for nationalistic pride.

1813, Jan. 5. Frederick VI proclaimed bankruptcy of the kingdom of Denmark and replaced the **Kurantbank** with the **Rigsbank.** Paper money was exchanged for new currency, but the inflation continued. In 1818,

THE HOUSE OF BERNADOTTE (1818–   )

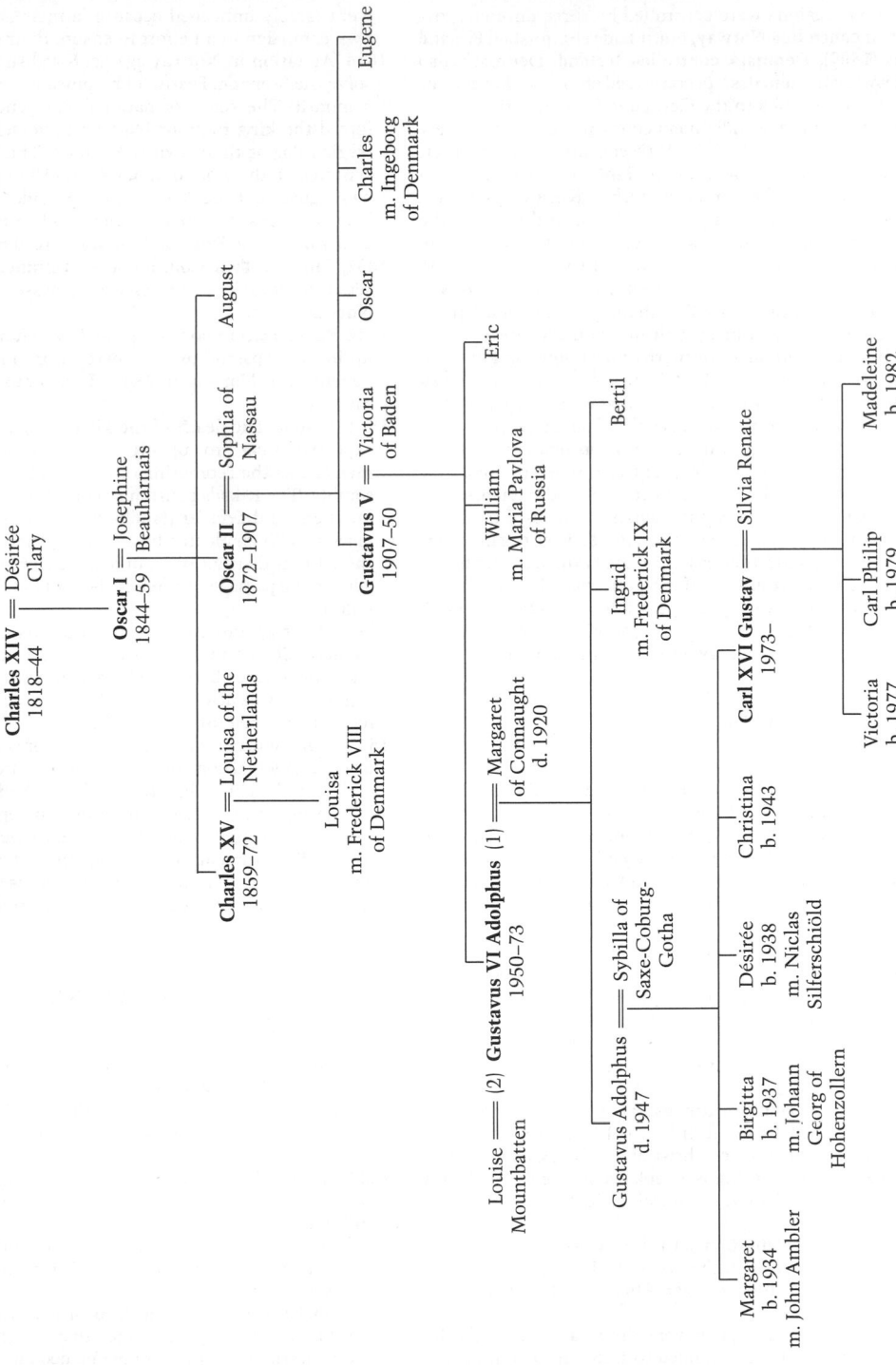

Charles XIV = Désirée
1818–44   Clary

Oscar I = Josephine
1844–59   Beauharnais

Oscar II = Sophia of
1872–1907   Nassau

Charles XV = Louisa of the
1859–72   Netherlands

Louisa
m. Frederick VIII
of Denmark

August

Oscar

Charles
m. Ingeborg
of Denmark

Eugene

Gustavus V = Victoria
1907–50   of Baden

William
m. Maria Pavlova
of Russia

Eric

Louise = (2) **Gustavus VI Adolphus** (1) = Margaret
Mountbatten   1950–73   of Connaught
                                           d. 1920

Ingrid
m. Frederick IX
of Denmark

Bertil

Gustavus Adolphus = Sybilla of
                    Saxe-Coburg-
                    Gotha

Margaret
b. 1934
m. John Ambler

Birgitta
b. 1937
m. Johann
Georg of
Hohenzollern

Désirée
b. 1938
m. Niclas
Silferschiöld

Christina
b. 1943

Carl XVI Gustav = Silvia Renate
1973–

Victoria
b. 1977

Carl Philip
b. 1979

Madeleine
b. 1982

the Rigsbank was replaced by the **National Bank,** which managed to restore the currency to par by 1838.

State bankruptcy and continued inflation led to a large number of bankruptcies and business crises, worsened by the English Corn Laws, which hurt agricultural exports. The government responded by reducing taxes.

1814. Primary education made compulsory.

1815. Stephensen presented a proposal to **establish free trade** between Iceland and Denmark. The Danish government responded by publishing a **proclamation in 1816** that allowed Icelandic ships to deliver their goods directly to foreign ports upon payment of a duty.

1831, Feb. The Danish king ordered legislation for the establishment of four consultive assemblies on independence of Schleswig-Holstein, which would meet in Roskilde, Urbog, Schleswig, and Itzehoe. This action demonstrated not only concessions to liberalism but also the growing strength of the independence movement in Holstein and the pressure exerted by Prussia. For the meetings, the king deliberately chose four cities outside of major population centers and thus somewhat immune to popular pressure.

Scandinavianism. Students meeting in **Copenhagen (1845)** expressed support for a united Scandinavia. Scandinavianism gained strength because of the king's growing recognition that he needed support from Sweden over the Schleswig-Holstein issue. **Christian VIII's son Frederick VII** was the last of the line of Oldenburg and would most likely die without a male heir, which meant that, upon the latter's death, the throne would pass through the female line. Although such a passage was legal under Danish law, Holstein would not accept such a lineage.

1835. Hans Christian Andersen first published his fairy tales. The tales demonstrated an interest in everyday life in Copenhagen and also adopted the popular Alladin motif.

1840. King Christian VIII instructed a commission to consider the establishment of a national assembly for Iceland. The commission favored the founding of an independent assembly (Althing) and recommended that it meet in Reykjavík. The assembly met on March 8, 1843, and consisted of 20 members elected by male property owners and six of the king's appointees.

1841. *Ný félagsrit,* **a paper advocating Icelandic nationalism,** first published. **Jon Sigurdsson,** one of the founders of the paper, became a leading force in Icelandic nationalism.

1843–55. Søren Kierkegaard published his philosophy. His ideas, along with those of **N. F. S. Grundtvig,** led to reforms within a branch of the Danish Lutheran church.

1844. First folk high school established in Rødding under direction of **Christian Kold.** This high school was to educate ordinary people and instill a sense of nationalism through teaching the Danish language.

1846, May. Society of Friends to Farmers (Bondevernnernes Selskab) was formed. This organization demonstrated the developing coalition between farmers and liberals and helped to encourage the king to consider a liberal constitution.

1847. Icelandic Althing met and decided to address a proposal to the king, asking for reforms that would expand suffrage, introduce more direct voting, and require all members to speak in Icelandic.

1848, Jan. 20. Christian VIII died before he could discuss the constitution he had had drafted.

Jan. 28. Frederick VII declared himself in favor of the constitution. The **constitution took effect on June 5, 1849.** It provided freedom of religion and speech as well as other civil liberties and created a bicameral Riksdag consisting of the Folketing and Landsting. Duchies were given equal status. The king retained the right to choose his own ministers and had the veto on all legislation.

March 22. Frederick declared himself a constitutional monarch.

Schleswig-Holstein. The government offered Holstein and Lauenburg a free constitution and right to join the Germanic Confederation, whereas Schleswig would have its own Diet but remain united with Denmark. Schleswig refused, and the Danes became involved in a war against Schleswig and German forces. Danes won the **Battle of Fredericia (July 6, 1849),** and a provisional government was set up in Schleswig. Despite a truce, hostilities resumed, and only in 1851 did the Danes succeed in regaining control of Schleswig.   *(To p. 507)*

3. FINLAND
(From p. 341)

1809, March 29. Annexation of Finland by Russia was formally acknowledged by the Finnish Diet in exchange for guarantees that the Finnish could continue to practice their religion and maintain their traditional rights and privileges. The Finnish Estates took an oath of allegiance to the tsar. Finland was governed by an Imperial Senate and a governor-general appointed by the tsar.

Sept. Sweden made the annexation official by signing a peace treaty transferring Finland from Sweden to Russia.

1812. Finnish capital moved from Turku to Helsinki and thus closer to the Russian capital of St. Petersburg. A German architect, C. L. Engel, designed the main buildings.

1819. The Bank of Finland moved from Turku to Helsinki.

Finnish nationalism centered on the Finnish language, but many of its earliest proponents wrote in Swedish, including J. L. Runeberg, who wrote the Finnish national anthem ("Värtland") in Swedish.

1831. A group of intellectuals, including **Elias Lönnrot,** founded the **Finnish Literature Society.** Lönnrot published their most influential collection of folk tales, *Kalevala,* in 1835. He was able to collect the material for his collection supported by funds collected by the society.

1842. J. V. Snellman returned to Finland after being removed from the Finnish university because of his nationalist and liberal leanings. He founded two newspapers, one in Finnish *(The Farmer's Friend)* and one in Swedish *(Saima).* The latter was closed by government censors in 1846, but Snellman continued to be involved in nationalist issues and, because of the changing climate within the government, **was reinstated as a professor in 1852.**   *(To p. 508)*

5. REVOLUTIONS IN EUROPE, 1848–1852

Causes. Between 1848 and 1852, revolutions rocked most of western and central Europe with exceptions such as the Netherlands, Belgium, and Britain. The immediate cause was the economic hardship of 1846 and 1847. This hardship stemmed from the failure of the potato and wheat crops throughout much of Europe. The consequent rise in food prices drove demand for other products down and thus hurt the emerging industrial sectors as well. In addition, cholera spread through Europe in 1848 and 1849. Early industrialization strengthened the middle classes, who embraced liberalism and nationalism. Industrial developments also threatened the livelihoods of the many craftworkers who became instrumental in the early phases of the revolutions. Industrialization and economic hardships were not sufficient causes, however. Britain and Belgium, the most advanced industrial nations, avoided revolution by adopting liberal forms of government in the years preceding 1848 and expanding the franchise to include many of the industrialists and other members of the middle classes. The third factor, therefore, was a state that continued to resist liberal and nationalist reforms.

Chronology. Unrest actually began in Italy and Switzerland, but historians usually consider the Parisian revolution first, because it sent the widest signals. The revolutions then moved to Austria-Hungary, Italy, and finally north through Germany.

a. FRANCE

(From p. 456)

1847–48. The banquets. A series of political banquets (p. 456) planned by Liberals and Republicans throughout France aimed at gaining support for opposition parties. The government let these banquets proceed until Feb. 22, 1848, when it stopped one scheduled in Paris that was to be preceded by a public procession. Students and workers gathered to march despite the prohibition. The police dispersed the marchers, but the workers and students began erecting barricades throughout Paris. The National Guard joined the cause, and the revolutionaries controlled Paris by Feb. 24. They chose a red banner as their flag—a banner that came to represent the left wing of the Second Republic.

1848, Feb. 23. The king appeased the middle class by replacing conservative prime minister Guizot with Molé, but revolutionaries in Paris continued to mount the barricades.

Feb. 24. Faced with continued activity in Paris, Louis-Philippe replaced Molé with Thiers, abdicated in favor of his grandson the comte de Paris, and fled Paris. The comte's mother, Hélène Louis of Mecklenburg-Shwerin, was dissuaded from showing herself and her children to the people and instead went before the Chamber of Deputies. Many of the rioters had entered the chamber and called for the comte to be dethroned. As a result, a provisional government was chosen and a republic proclaimed. The romantic poet **Alphonse-Louis-Marie de Lamartine** dominated the right wing of the government, and **Louis Blanc,** a socialist, dominated the left wing.

Workers' demands. The economic hardships of the 1840s had left many people without employment. Workers and the socialists demanded that workers be guaranteed the right to work, the right to a minimum wage, and the right to be provided for in the case of illness and old age.

Feb. 25. The government recognized the **right to work,** the right to a living wage, and the right of workers to organize.

Feb. 26. National Workshops were decreed to provide work or relief to all the unemployed.

Feb. 27. Following abortive attempts to overthrow the provisional government and place a Paris commune in its stead, the government attempted to appease demands that they adopt the red flag as an indicator of their commitment to democracy by declaring the **tricolor** of the Revolution of 1789 the national flag and ascribing to the belief in liberty, equality, and fraternity.

Feb. 28. The Luxembourg Commission was established by the provisional government under the direction of Albert (a worker) and Blanc to develop a permanent plan for the organization of labor. The Luxembourg Commission had little authority and suffered from a lack of staffing and funding. It managed to produce a "General Survey of Works," which never received a first reading within the government. The failure of the commission to gain any real attention from the government resulted in the resignation of Albert and Blanc (May 8), who had represented the workers' concerns in the provisional government.

Women. The year 1848 saw the proliferation of women's political newspapers. These newspapers generally connected women's rights with workers' rights by focusing on the many women in France who worked. Both women and workers failed to gain their objectives in a revolution dominated not by democrats and socialists but by liberals.

April 23. The **elections to the national (or constituent) assembly,** which was to give France a new constitution, were a victory for the moderate Republicans (**Lamartine**) with some 500 seats; the left wing (**Louis Blanc**) had fewer than 100; the Legitimists (seeking the return of the Bourbon line) had about 100; the Orléanists (supporters of the fallen dynasty of Louis-Philippe), about 200.

Social legislation. The provisional government had abolished sweated labor (March 2) and reduced workers' hours to 10 per day in Paris and 11 per day in the provinces. It also set up free labor exchanges in town halls and stopped work projects in prisons and barracks because the latter were considered to be in competition with workers.

Perhaps the biggest piece of social legislation was also the most flawed—the **National Workshops** were inundated with the unemployed, who were attracted by the promise of 2 francs per day when they worked and 1½ francs when they did not. They were organized along military lines and put to work two days per week. The strict discipline and hard, often pointless labor, inflicted in the workshops led to worker demonstrations, including a riot on May 15. Not only artisans but also some factory workers participated, marking a change in the social base for urban political protest in France.

June 21. The government abolished the workshops. As a result, many workers in Paris participated in the June Days Rebellion.

June 23–26. THE JUNE DAYS REBELLION. The workers set up barricades while Gen. Louis Cavaignac, in charge of the army, became dictator pro tempore. Cavaignac waited until he had mustered all of his troops in Paris, including reinforcements from the National Guard from outside Paris, to march on the barricades rather than take each

barricade down as it was being erected. Cavaignac's strategy inflicted heavy casualties but also cleared the streets of Paris.

Reaction followed the June Days. The government repealed the limitations on working hours, adopted legislation regulating the press, suppressed secret societies, and dictated rigid control for clubs and political associations.

Nov. 4. The assembly completed the **new constitution** and provided a strong president and a single chamber—both elected directly by universal male suffrage. The constitution also replaced the notion of the right to work with the notion of the right to receive fraternal assistance. It provided such assistance to the elderly, the ill, and the children if their families could not support them. In doing so, it changed "liberty, equality, fraternity" to "liberty, equality, fraternity, and Family, Work, Property, and Public Order."

Dec. 10. Louis-Napoleon was elected president with 5,327,345 votes to 1,879,298 for his opponent. Prince Louis-Napoleon Bonaparte, Napoleon I's nephew, profited by his link with the "Napoleonic Legend" and the perception of the need for a strong man in government. He took the oath as president (Dec. 20) and appointed a ministry dominated by Orléanists, despite the fact that the national assembly was Republican.

1849, Jan. 29. With the troops in Paris, the assembly was obliged to vote for its own dissolution after passing the budget and completing the constitution. The conservative forces—the Legitimists, Orléanists, and Bonapartists—united through a central committee (Union électorale) to win votes under a program designed to save society from the radical elements of 1848 through revival of the influence of the Catholic Church. The Conservatives won a large majority of the seats, but the radical Republicans fared much better than they had anticipated.

June 13. Alexandre Ledru-Rollin engineered a revolt in Paris, which led to a series of arrests, repression of the banquets, and dissolution of the mutual benefit societies.

Oct. 31. Louis-Napoleon dismissed his cabinet over a dispute regarding French support for the restoration of the papal regime in Rome (p. 468). He then summoned Gen. d'Hautpoul as premier and created a cabinet "devoted to his own person," dominated by Eugène Rouher, minister of justice. The president had, in fact, established a thinly veiled dictatorship.

1850. Education reform. The president placed schoolteachers under the control of prefects (Jan. 9).

March 15. The **Falloux Law,** a concession to the Catholic majority, was approved by the president. The law extended the role of the Catholic clergy in education by providing lower standards for Catholic teachers than for state teachers. It gave the clergy a role in school inspection and permitted the substitution of Catholic schools for lay schools in communes and departments.

May 31. A new electoral law required three years of residence in one place for eligibility to vote; residence had to be attested by a tax receipt or employer's affidavit. This affected migratory industrial workers, who tended to be radicals. Clubs and public meetings were forbidden (June 9) and Republican newspapers overwhelmed with lawsuits and fines.

Louis-Napoleon attempted to have the assembly **revise Article 45** of the constitution, which forbade the president to serve two consecutive four-year terms, but the assembly defeated the revision by nearly 100 votes (July 15, 1851). Louis-Napoleon decided to resort to force.

1851, Dec. 2. The coup d'état. Comte Auguste de Morny, the president's half-brother, had a proclamation printed to inform the people of the dissolution of the assembly and the restoration of universal male suffrage and called a plebiscite for a fundamental revision of the constitution. The proclamations were posted while Republican and Royalist journalists and deputies were arrested during the night of Dec. 1–2. A popular rising was organized on Dec. 3, but troops under the direction of **Gen. Jacques de Saint-Arnaud** quelled the rebellion (Dec. 4).

Dec. 21. The **plebiscite** gave the president the right to draw up a new constitution (7,500,000 votes to 640,000) in the midst of continued repression of those who opposed Louis-Napoleon (over 20,000 arrested, amid widespread rioting in favor of a republic).

1852, Jan. 14. The **new constitution** concentrated authority in Louis-Napoleon's hands. He alone could make laws and issue decrees. The constitution also provided a **Council of State** and a **Senate** chosen by the president. Both met in secret, and the former drew up legislation that the latter could reject if it was considered unconstitutional. A **legislative assembly** (Corps législatif) could accept or reject legislation but could not amend it.

Nov. 2. The Senate declared **the empire reestablished.** The empire was subsequently ratified by plebiscite (Nov. 21) and promulgated by decree (Dec. 2).   (To p. 491)

b. HUNGARY

(From p. 463)

1848, Feb. 29. The news of the French revolution reached Pressburg and instilled a **financial panic** among merchants, who recalled the failure of the Bank of Vienna in 1789 and 1830. *Pesti Hirlap* reported that shops were refusing to accept bank notes, and on March 5, a crowd tried to exchange their bank notes for silver at the state bank in Buda.

March 3. Kossuth, in a speech in the Diet, **denounced the Vienna system** and called for a constitution for Hungary that would establish authority in the representatives of the people.

March 15. The youth of Budapest met in Pest to demonstrate in support of **the twelve points** drafted by radicals. The points included a responsible government, freedom of the press, and equality before the law as well as national claims for a Hungarian national bank, a national army, and the formation of a national guard. The twelve points were accepted by the municipal council, which established the Committee of Public Order. Separately, Croats organized a national committee demanding a government autonomous from Hungary.

March. The Pressburg Diet responded to the Hungarian revolutionaries at Pest with moderate reforms. The Diet abolished forced labor but maintained many other manorial rights. Count Batthyány established a government that included both Kossuth and Széchenyi.

Austrian challenge. Austria notified Batthyány that it wanted to maintain control of Hungary's finances. The Committee of Public Order called a meeting and demanded that, if Vienna refused to ratify the March Laws, it would form a provisional government in Pest. Vienna recognized the Hungarian government at once.

The Committee of Public Order mirrored the feelings of the middle classes and peasants. The middle classes had armed themselves in preparation for the continuation of the revolution, and the peasants had freed themselves of manorial obligations without waiting for resolution from Vienna. Vienna, having been defeated in Italy and struggling to maintain control in Bohemia, conceded to Hungarian demands.

Sept. Vienna attempted to regain control of Hungary. The emperor revoked his acceptance of the March Laws. The Vienna government attempted to establish a puppet government under Baron Nicholas Vay. Gen. Count Lamberg, at Pressburg, was given full powers to dissolve the Hungarian Assembly, but he was killed by a popular uprising (Sept. 28) before he could read the act of dissolution.

War between Hungarian nationalists and portions of the Hungarian army under Kossuth, and the Viennese army, started with the escalation of Austrian troops crossing the Drave on Sept. 1.

1849. Jan. Windischgrätz occupied **Budapest,** but then was pushed back by Gen. Görgei and the Hungarian army.

April 13–14. Hungarian independence declared with Kossuth as "governor-president."

June–August. The Russian tsar, whose troops were moving through Cracow, announced that he would send his army into Hungary. Russian and Austrian invasions were joined by risings of Serb and Romanian minorities. Kossuth's claims died under military repression (final surrender, Aug. 13, by **Görgei**), and Vienna executed 13 generals despite promises of leniency.   (To p. 504)

c. AUSTRIA AND BOHEMIA

(From p. 462)

1848, March 11. Prague meeting drew up **Twelve Articles of St. Wenceslas,** demanding Czech-German equality in education and government service.

March 13–14. Students in Vienna marched to the Landhaus to present a petition after hearing Kossuth's speech read aloud. The crowd reached the Hofburg where the Diet sat and, when the guards would allow only the delegates in, began to spread throughout the streets and squares surrounding the Hofburg. Alarmed by their large numbers, the authorities fired on the crowd in an effort to clear the area. Meanwhile, workers had been prevented from entering the city. They burned several factories and looted shops in protest.

March 15. the emperor summoned the Diet to begin consideration of a constitution.

April 8. Czechs obliged Vienna to promise a Bohemian constitutional assembly. Revolutionary movements also took place in Galicia, Moravia, and elsewhere.

April 25. The new government, under Pillersdorf, published a **new constitution.** The new constitution provided for a bicameral legislature with a Senate composed of both life members and members elected by the great landowners and a Chamber of Deputies elected by voters who met a high property qualification, thus limiting the vote so that workers would not be directly represented. Women could not vote.

May 9. A new electoral law, passed in response to demonstrations, enabled the lower middle class and the peasants to vote but excluded workmen who were paid by the day or the week, domestic servants, those receiving public assistance, and all women.

May 14. The government dissolved the Central Committee, formed by students and members of the National Guard during March.

May 15. The Storm Petition (Sturmpetition). Students, workers, and the members of the National Guard marched to the Hofburg and demanded that the government establish universal adult male suffrage, that the army be called up only at the request of the National Guard, and that parliament consist of a single chamber. The government promised to revise the constitution. **The emperor and his family fled to Innsbruck.**

May 26. The government retrenched and ordered the **dissolution of the University Legion,** and the troops ordered the National Guard to stand down. As a result, barricades went up throughout Vienna, and the workers and National Guard came to the students' aid. A committee of safety controlled Vienna during the following months.

June. The **first Pan-Slav Congress** (composed, however, almost entirely of Czech delegates) met at Prague under the presidency of **Francis Palácky,** the eminent Bohemian historian and national leader. It proclaimed the solidarity of the Slavic peoples (as against the Germans), but stressed also the equality of all peoples, and proposed a European congress to deal with outstanding international problems.

June 12. The Princess Windischgrätz, wife of the commander of the forces at Prague, was accidentally shot and killed during a student demonstration. **Prince Alfred Windischgrätz,** who favored strong repressive measures, seized this opportunity to bring up reinforcements.

June 17. Windischgrätz bombarded **Prague,** crushed the Czech revolutionary movement, and established a military dictatorship in Bohemia. This was the first step in the recovery of the governmental power. Slav demands were ignored.

July 8. The Pillersdorf government was replaced. Schwarzer became the minister of public works and reduced the wages paid by public works for women and children. Schwarzer reminded the workers' delegation sent to complain about this action of the bloody June Days in France.

July 22. The constituent assembly *(Reichstag)* met in Vienna. It discarded the constitution previously promulgated by the government and drew up a new document, pronouncedly democratic. Its only act of lasting importance was the **emancipation of the peasants** from manorial burdens (law of Sept. 7).

Aug. 23. Battle of the Prater. Workers' demonstrations clashed with police in Vienna, over the public works issue. The National Guard supported the police and a bloody battle ensued. The workers were put down, and with the armies winning on all fronts, it appeared that the revolution was over. However, the continued struggle in Hungary led to one more attempt by Austrian democrats.

Oct. 6. As a battalion prepared to leave for Hungary, the democrats in Vienna, supported by the National Guard, resumed demonstrations.

Oct. 7. The emperor again left Vienna and threatened reprisals if the democrats did not surrender. The Imperial Army, joined by Bohemian forces, threatened Vienna. The failure of the Hungarian and Viennese troops to communicate resulted in the Hungarian troops falling back.

Oct. 31. Vienna fell and thus destroyed the democratic bid for power.

Dec. 2. Ferdinand abdicated in favor of his nephew, Francis Joseph, and a new government was established by **Prince Felix von Schwarzenberg.** Schwarzenberg expressed a desire to cooperate with the **constitutional assembly.**

1849, March 7. The assembly, having been moved to Kremsier to protect it from public opinion, **approved a constitution** unanimously. The constitution provided for a bicameral Parliament with the lower house elected by universal male suffrage and the upper house composed of delegates from the local diets. The emperor could call for a new assembly or suspend legislation and could choose a minister of state who was responsible to the Parliament. The constitution provided a federalist system and ensured the rights of all the peoples and languages within the Habsburg states.

The government dissolved the constitutional assembly but introduced its own constitution, which did not provide for a federalist system, declared the state indivisible, and limited the franchise to those who held property. The government also ignored this constitution and finally withdrew it in 1851.   *(To p. 504)*

d. ITALY

(From p. 459)

Italy's revolutions, which began to take shape before the Paris rising, proceeded against two interrelated problems: (1) Austrian dominance in northern Italy, and (2) the demand for liberal, political reform. Because Italians viewed the conservative government as linked to Austrian influence, the middle classes found support for the revolution among nobles as well as among the working class. The latter suffered from the devastating harvests of 1846–47 and the increases in prices that accompanied them.

1846, June 15. THE ELECTION OF PIUS IX increased liberal activity because of his liberalism. Liberals organized banquets and demonstrations and demanded the organization of a civic guard, which they saw as the first step toward armed resistance against the Austrians.

Piedmont. Charles Albert, influenced by liberal nobles such as Camillo di Cavour, eased press censorship and revised the police system (1847). He then expanded his army (Jan. 1848) and, on Feb. 13, 1848, yielded to liberal demands—he promised to create a civic guard, gave the government a two-chamber parliament, and lowered the price of salt.

March 4. Constitution (Statute) promulgated, the basis for the later constitution of the kingdom of Italy. The king also appointed Cesare Balbo as prime minister, and Balbo began preparing for war against Austria.

1848, Jan. 12. Palermo. A rising resulted from the economic problems of the lower classes and Neapolitan rule. The liberals declared the fall of the royal house and forced the king in Naples to grant a constitution (Jan. 27).

March 18. Milanese republicans called a massive demonstration. The Austrian government and the liberals opposed the uprising, but Radetzky, whose troops controlled Milan, was advised to keep the troops out of the demonstration. When people attacked the government palace and forced the government to agree to their demands, **Radetzky was sent in with his troops.** The barricades in Milan proved much stronger than elsewhere in Europe, and Radetzky feared intervention by Piedmont. Students led the revolutionary attacks and drove Radetzky's forces back through the city until he withdrew on March 23.

March 18. A liberal-radical government was established in Milan with Carlo Cattaneo at its head. The government abandoned the more radical and popular causes and also refused to allow dissidents from the countryside to join the urban demonstrations. These peasants and rural dissidents harassed Radetzky's forces outside the walls, but the liberal government of Milan refused to let them into the city. The liberalism of the government helped convince the Piedmontese to intervene on behalf of the Milanese.

March 22. Proclamation of Venetian Republic under **Daniele Manin** as president, after news of the rising in Vienna.

March–April. Italian military intervention. Driven by nationalism, both Charles Albert and Ferdinand of Naples, the latter under pressure from the radicals, supported the Milanese revolution by sending troops after Radetzky's retreat. (**March 22, Piedmont declares war on Austria.**) The pope faced greater difficulty because he could not justify attacking a Catholic nation; he refused to release his troops and published a somewhat ambiguous statement supporting all Catholic peoples.

May 15. Troops put down a new rising in Naples. The rising stemmed from Ferdinand's efforts to resist radical attempts to revise the constitution. Ferdinand, supported by liberals and landowners in southern Italy, drove the radical elements of the revolution out of Naples and dissolved the National Guard.

May 29. Charles Albert intervened because he envisioned a **unified state of Piedmont and Lombardy.** He was opposed by Cattaneo and Mazzini, who feared his recent conservatism and hoped for a more liberal-democratic unity of all Italy. However, a plebiscite carried the attempt at unifying the two states practically unanimously. This action was followed by similar decisions in Parma, Modena, and Venice (the latter was blockaded by the Austrian fleet and needed Piedmont's assistance).

Spring. Radetzky received reinforcements from Austria and began to make considerable progress. Lamartine urged Piedmont to accept French assistance but, backed by Britain, Piedmont declined.

July 24. Radetzky, greatly reinforced by fresh troops, attacked and defeated the Italian troops at the **Battle of Custozza.** He returned to Milan where he promised leniency and signed the **Armistice of Salasco** (Aug. 9) with Piedmont, which gave up Lombardy.

Aug. Popular uprisings in both Tuscany and Bologna were put down by liberal governments, but growing unrest surrounding Pius IX's conservatism proved a larger threat. On Nov. 15, the pope's leading liberal minister was assassinated.

Nov. 16. Demonstrations in the streets of Rome protested the assassination. Crowds were supported by the armed forces, National Guard, and volunteers returning from Lombardy. The pope agreed to support a radical government that called for the election of a constituent assembly. The government abolished the tax on flour and began to create public works to ease the economic hardship.

Nov. 24. The pope fled to Neapolitan protection.

1849, Jan. The constituent assembly was popularly elected in **Rome,** and **new elections in Piedmont** returned a democratic majority. Charles Albert had appointed a democratic cabinet in Dec., which had dissolved the Parliament. In **March,** the Piedmontese government renounced the armistice with Austria and moved into Lombardy.

Feb. 9. The assembly in Rome overthrew papal authority, proclaimed the **Republic** and ended Catholic control of the universities. The pope officially appealed to Catholic powers for assistance (Feb. 18).

March 23. The Austrians defeated Piedmont at Novara, and the Piedmontese had to sue for peace within a week. Charles Albert abdicated in favor of **Victor Emmanuel,** who appointed Massimo d'Azeglio, a liberal, as prime minister. This move, combined with d'Azeglio's willingness to dissolve Parliament until he had a stable majority, established liberalism in Piedmont.

April 24. Gen. Nicolas Oudinot, with a French force of 10,000 men, landed on the Italian coast and marched for Rome. He met no resistance until he reached the gates of the city.

May 4. Austrians began bombarding Venice's garrisons, and food riots broke out in the city in June.

May 15. Neapolitan troops reconquered Sicily.

June 2. Oudinot laid siege to Rome while Roman soldiers were urged on by Mazzini and Garibaldi until, on June 30, the Roman Parliament voted against Mazzini, who left the city with troops loyal to him. These troops were decimated.

July 1. France occupied Rome and reestablished the pope, dissolving the Parliament. The pope, against French wishes, created a conservative government.

July. Austrians began bombarding Venice proper. Cholera and typhus epidemics broke out in the city as famine increased.

July 28. The grand duke of Tuscany was restored.

Aug. 6. The assembly gave Manin leave to negotiate with the Austrians.

Aug. 28. Venice surrendered, and Austria resumed control. The Italian revolutions came to an end.   *(To p. 496)*

e. SWITZERLAND

(From p. 460)

RADICALISM had spread in Switzerland on the heels of the conservative limitations of the press. Radical exiles who fled their own countries often set up print shops in Switzerland and even imported radical literature. The Swiss cantons were divided by the Sonderbund (p. 460), which reinforced the religious distinctions between the Catholics and the Protestants and proved to be the catalyst for the revolution.

1846, Oct. 7. Revolutionaries in Geneva installed a new government. They had gained control following a bloody revolution within the city under the leadership of **James Fazy.** The revolutionaries established barricades and, with the assistance of Catholics from the countryside, overthrew the government. The revolutionary government gave the canton a **new constitution (1847),** which included liberal demands such as freedom of education and election of members to the State Council.

1847, Jan. Diplomats from the conservative powers of Austria, Russia, and Prussia left Berne.

July 20. The Federal Diet **dissolved the Sonderbund** after a radical victory in St. Gall gave the Diet the necessary majority. This move resulted in a protracted struggle between Catholic and radical cantons.

Nov. 4. The Diet declared war on the Sonderbund, with Gen. Dufour in command of the army. In less than a month, the Catholic forces had been defeated, and the Swiss Diet could establish a government on the basis of liberal and radical ideas.

1848, Sept. 12. The **New Constitution** replaced the **Pact of 1815.** It organized Switzerland as a federal union closely modeled on that of the United States. While preserving the historical local government of the cantons, it established a strong central government. Legislative authority resided in two chambers: the **Council of State** *(Ständerat),* consisting of two members from each canton, and the **National Council** *(Nationalrat),* members of which were elected by universal male suffrage in numbers proportional to the population of each canton. The executive was a **Federal Council** *(Bundesrat)* of seven members, elected by the two chambers. Its annual chairman was given the title "president of the Confederation," but he enjoyed no wider powers than his colleagues.

International response to the Swiss revolutions has often been underestimated because of the much longer and well-discussed French revolution of 1848. European newspapers carried news of the Swiss revolution throughout 1847. The Swiss situation received praise from Marx and Engels. Crowds in France and Italy cheered at the Swiss success, and Metternich feared that the radical Swiss victory would spread liberalism and radicalism throughout Europe.   *(To p. 499)*

f. GERMANY

(From p. 462)

Germany faced many of the same problems that Austria and France did. Economic hardship and rising prices had hurt the urban poor and working classes while manorial dues continued to hamper economic growth in the east. Political disunity came under repeated attack with the growing wave of German nationalism, which focused on the German-speaking peoples and sought to unify them in a single country.

Industrial and agrarian unrest. In March and April 1848, artisans and workers employed on the railroads and waterways began to resort to violence in an effort to gain their demands. Workers and crowds in cities broke machines, refused to allow steamships to take on cargo once carried by local boatmen, and attacked and destroyed the Taunus Railroad (April 5). Artisans such as printers organized strikes and demanded higher pay. Especially in the south, the peasantry rose against

manorial dues by looting and burning, which especially targeted ownership records.

Southern Germany. Spurred by the rising in Paris, demonstrations and assemblies in Baden, from late February onward, drew up liberal demands, to which the duke conceded. In Bavaria, the liberals forced the king to abdicate in favor of **Maximilian II.** Baden, Württemberg, and Saxony all included liberal ministers in their governments in an effort to appease the rising tide of revolution. The southern constitutional governments met in Heidelberg and decided to call a national meeting of liberal notables. This decision laid the groundwork for the Frankfurt Parliament.

1848, March 6. In an effort to avoid revolution, Frederick William IV promised to call the Prussian Landtag at intervals and revised the press law (March 8).

March 10. Street demonstrations began in Berlin, which led to a skirmish between the demonstrators and the army in an effort to drive the crowd from the palace square. The artisans and students who made up the crowd erected barricades. Following the street fighting, the king decided to grant concessions.

March 17–21. Frederick William declared in favor of a federal *Reich*. The army, patrolling the palace gardens in anticipation of the announcement, fired on the crowd, which forced Frederick William to withdraw the troops. On **March 19,** the Civic Guard, instead of the army, began policing Berlin, and the government made an effort to restore order in Prussia. Prussian municipalities were authorized to substitute direct taxation, from which the workers were exempt, for duties on cereals, and the city governments established work projects. Censorship was abolished and a **United Landtag** called (**Vorparlament**).

March 31. A **preliminary parliament** opened at Frankfurt-on-the-Main. This parliament, faced with the difficulty of deciding between the radical and liberal programs, chose the latter by refusing to place the radical program on the agenda. The parliament then laid the groundwork for the election of a national assembly. Although the preliminary parliament claimed to support universal male suffrage, the final resolution gave the vote to every "independent" male over age 30. The inclusion of the criterion of independence gave the states a means of excluding the working class.

April 7. The Diet of the Confederation sanctioned the resolutions of the preliminary parliament.

April 15. Prussia, in an effort to encourage economic recovery, passed a **bank law,** which created issuing banks backed by the public treasury.

May 18. Frankfurt Parliament convened. Its delegates, selected under limited suffrage, largely represented the German middle classes.

May 22. Prussian National Assembly convened. The assembly was supposed to cooperate with the government in creating a constitution, but the majority of the delegates took their task to be that of a constituent assembly. The Prussian National Assembly had a stronger left than did the Frankfurt Parliament. The government under Rudolf Camphausen fashioned its own draft of the constitution along the Belgian model. The assembly countered with its own draft, with democratic leanings.

June 2–4. The Assembly of Delegates of the North German Handicraft and Industrial Class meeting in Hamburg called for an artisans' conference to meet in Frankfurt. A committee met to prepare the address that declared the workers' disagreement with industrial freedom and their ability to attempt to solve the social problems.

June 11–14. Printers convened in Mainz and drafted a petition for presentation to the Frankfurt Parliament. The petition demanded regulations of economic concerns such as wages, use of machinery, and employment.

June 28. Archduke John of Austria was appointed provisional executive head, but no real government was set up. Long debates ensued over a rising against Denmark in Schleswig (March 24).

June–July. Prussia sent troops to Schleswig at request of the Frankfurt Parliament. **Armistice of Malmö** (Aug. 28) evacuated Schleswig, but Danish and German nationalists renewed the war on March 31, 1849, until new negotiations (July 1849) led to peace (July 2, 1850), with both sides reserving their rights.

July 15–Aug. 18. The Artisans' Conference met in Frankfurt at the Römer (the coronation hall for the Holy Roman Empire). It included delegates from most of Germany. However, journeymen were excluded from the negotiations at the conference.

July 20–Sept. 20. General German Labor Congress represented the journeymen; they created a program of their own for presentation at the Frankfurt Parliament. Both the conference and the congress agreed with the **Industrial Code** composed by the former. The Industrial Code demanded the end of economic freedom and a return to a corporatist state and traditional guild systems.

July 21. The Frankfurt Parliament assigned a **committee to prepare an industrial code.** The task was not completed until Feb. and never considered by the Parliament. The Parliament remained committed to laissez-faire economics.

Aug. 16–18. Junker Parliament. Alarmed by the Prussian Assembly's debates over the abolition of manorial rights, the Junkers held a conference to protect the rights of property. They managed to obtain widespread support from the countryside.

Nov. 10. The **troops returned to Berlin** under Gen. von Wrangel, and a state of siege was declared all over Prussia. The action met with little popular resistance. It had been sparked by Frederick William's appointment of **Count Frederick William Brandenburg** as prime minister and the latter's subsequent proclamation of the **removal of the Prussian Assembly to Brandenburg.**

Dec. 5. The Prussian Assembly was dissolved, and the Prussian government imposed a constitution. The constitution granted civil rights but highlighted the divine right of the monarchy. It provided for a bicameral legislature with an upper house elected by males over age 30 who could meet a high property qualification and a lower house elected directly by universal male suffrage. The latter would be undermined by a new election law (May 30, 1849), which established a **three-class voting system.** This system divided Prussian voters into three uneven classes based on wealth. These classes each chose an equal number of electors who chose the deputies to the lower house.

1849, Jan. The Frankfurt Parliament completed the first reading of the **new constitution.** One of the major stumbling blocks would prove to be the *großdeutsch* versus *kleindeutsch* (greater Germany versus smaller Germany) issue. Delegates from the Habsburg states wanted provisions to include Austria (großdeutsch) in plans for a unified German state. This problem was resolved after the Austrian government established its own constitution, but the question remained an issue in German politics. The **Frankfurt constitution** (March 27) established a federal system with state governments represented in a parliamentary upper house. The constitution also recognized universal male suffrage and the secret ballot as a concession to the democrats, whose votes were necessary to ensure a liberal majority. Though never in effect, the constitution influenced later German statutes.

March 28. The Frankfurt Parliament elected Frederick William IV as emperor. Frederick William was offered the crown on April 3, but he declined it without refusing to head a German state. Frederick William feared acceptance would tie him to the principles and government of 1848. His move was reinforced when the Prussian government rejected the Frankfurt constitution on April 21. This marked the end of the Frankfurt Parliament. A rump parliament remained in Frankfurt until it was forced to **Stuttgart** and then dispersed (June 18). Radicals continued to stage risings, but the revolutions were over. *(To p. 500)*

6. EUROPEAN DIPLOMACY, 1848–1914

(From p. 446)

The period was marked by the unification of Italy and Germany, constant friction over the Balkans, and a policy of alliances that ultimately involved most of the European powers in one group or another. The effect of technical and industrial advance on warfare resulted in growing anxiety for security on all sides, and consequently to alignments for the event of war, which, in fact, tended to make war more likely. At the same time the expansion of European powers in Africa and Asia greatly extended the field of possible friction.

1849, June 17. Russian troops entered Hungary and ended revolutionary action by Aug. 13. Minor conflict resulted from Constantinople's refusal to extradite the leader, Lajos Kossuth.

1850. The Don Pacifico affair. Don Pacifico was a Moorish Jew, but a British subject. He held large claims against the Greek government, which he pressed with vigor until an anti-Semitic mob burned his house in Athens (Dec. 1849). The British responded with an **embargo on all Greek vessels** in the Piraeus and finally seized them (Jan. 1850). After abortive mediation by the French, the Greeks were eventually forced to comply (April 26).

April 19. Britain and the United States signed the Clayton-Bulwer Treaty regulating their relations with regard to Central America.

1853–56. CRIMEAN WAR (p. 510). The war went very badly for Russia, but all sides saw massive casualties. On March 30, 1856, the **Treaty of Paris** forced Russia to accept the demilitarization and neutralization of the Black Sea, ensuring British dominance in the eastern Mediterranean. The Russians also renounced claims to a protectorate of all Balkan Christians. In the Balkans, Moldavia acquired southern Bessarabia, cutting Russia's access to the Danube (where an international commission was established to ensure safe navigation), and a collective great powers guarantee of Serbia and the Danubian Principalities replaced a Russian protectorate. Britain thwarted French desires to revise the situation of Italy and Poland. The Ottoman Empire was also admitted to the European concert, while Britain, France, and Austria agreed by formal treaty (April 15) to protect Ottoman independence. Finally, the participants adopted **four rules of international law:** (1) privateering remained abolished; (2) the neutral flag covered enemy goods, except contraband; (3) neutral goods, except contraband, were not liable to capture under an enemy flag; (4) blockade, to be binding, had to be effective. More generally, the **impact of the Crimean War** increased British and Russian hesitation to commit further to European affairs. This left France the dominant power, as Austria strove to retain its Italian possessions and Prussia sought to resolve internal problems on the route to German unification.

1858–70. WARS OF ITALIAN UNIFICATION (p. 498).

1860–63. Britain, France and Belgium signed a series of commercial treaties ushering in a period of free trade (p. 492).

1861, Oct. 13. Britain, France, and Spain signed the **Convention of London** to force the new revolutionary government in **Mexico** to fulfill the previous regime's obligations. All three landed troops in December, but Spain and Britain withdrew as Napoleon III's more grandiose schemes to establish a Catholic Latin empire became clear (April 1862). The French attempt to install Archduke Maximilian as emperor failed by 1867 (p. 638).

1863. Representatives from 26 nations signed the **Geneva conventions,** pledging to obey humanitarian rules in time of war and recognizing the neutrality of the Red Cross.

Napoleon III's efforts to intervene against Russia in the **Second Polish Revolution** (p. 513) broke down due to the lukewarm attitudes of the British and the Austrians, and Prussia's support of Russia. Prussia sent four corps (half the army) to the Polish frontier. This resulted in the tsar's support of Prussia during the three wars necessary to German unification.

1863–70. WARS OF GERMAN UNIFICATION.

1863, Aug. A **congress of princes,** summoned by Emperor Francis Joseph to reform the Germanic Confederation (p. 500), but really meant as a bait to German liberalism, miscarried when Bismarck induced King William to refuse to attend. Bismarck's next opportunity to attain German unification under Prussia came in connection with the highly complicated **Schleswig-Holstein question.** A royal proclamation of King Frederick VII of Denmark (March 30, 1863) (p. 507) in substance announced the annexation to Denmark of the duchy of Schleswig. This act was a breach of the **London Protocol** (1852) by which the powers had guaranteed at once the inseparability of the duchies and their personal union with Denmark under the king, and also of the engagement given by Denmark to Austria and Prussia (Dec. 1851) not to incorporate Schleswig or treat it separately. Frederick's act also thrust a new charter on the duchy of Holstein (which retained its autonomy) without consulting its representatives. This flew in the face of the Germanic Confederation, of which Holstein was a member. Expectation of British and Swedish support was an important factor in shaping Danish policy during 1863 and early 1864.

1864, Jan. 16. Austria joined Prussia in an alliance, and the two powers agreed to send an ultimatum to Denmark demanding repeal of the constitution (otherwise they would invade), to settle the future course of the duchies only "by mutual agreement."

Feb. 1. Austrian and Prussian troops invaded Schleswig, resulting in **war with Denmark** (pp. 501, 507).

April 25–June. The **London Conference**, engineered by the British to save the Danes, failed.

June 26. The war was renewed, resulted in a crushing defeat for the Danes and the **surrender of the duchies of Schleswig, Holstein, and Lauenburg** to Austria and Prussia (definitive **Peace of Vienna**, Oct. 30).

Aug. 14. In the **convention of Gastein**, Austria and Prussia agreed to joint sovereignty for the duchies, but Austria was to administer Holstein, Prussia to administer Schleswig (Lauenburg went to Prussia in return for a money payment to Austria). An impossible situation was created: Austrian Holstein became a virtual enclave in unfriendly Prussia. Under the skillful hand of Bismarck, Austro-Prussian relations rapidly deteriorated.

Oct. At Biarritz **Bismarck met Napoleon III** and appears to have dropped vague hints of compensation for France in the Rhineland, in return for which he won a promise of French neutrality from the emperor, convinced that Austria would be victor in the coming war.

1866, April 8. Bismarck, aided by Napoleon III, concluded an offensive and defensive **alliance with Italy:** Italy was to join Prussia if war broke out between Austria and Prussia within three months, with Venetia as a reward.

June 12. Austria, realizing that conflict was inevitable, signed a **secret treaty with Napoleon III.** In return for French neutrality, Austria promised to cede Venetia to Napoleon (who was to retrocede it to Italy), whether Austria won or lost the war. In the event of Austrian victory, Austria was to be free to make what changes it wished in Germany, but if these changes disturbed the European balance of power (as they were bound to do), Austria was to consult with Napoleon before making them. Verbally the Austrians agreed in this case not to oppose the erection of a **neutral buffer state** (client of France) **along the Rhine.**

June 14. On Austria's motion, the Frankfurt Diet voted **federal execution against Prussia** for violating federal (Holstein) territory. Most of the German states, including the larger ones like Bavaria, Saxony, and Hanover, sided with Austria against Prussia. The Prussian government declared the federal constitution violated and the **confederation at an end.**

June–Aug. The **SEVEN WEEKS' WAR.** The war was fought in three theaters. **Italy:** The Italians were defeated on both land and sea (p. 498). **Germany:** On June 27–29 **Gen. Vogel von Falkenstein**, with an army of some 50,000 men, defeated the Hanoverians at **Langensalza** and forced them to capitulate. He turned to the South German allies of Austria, but before he could reach them the die had been cast in **Bohemia.** Using lessons learned from the American Civil War, Moltke concentrated his forces near Gitschin, where he formed three armies and advanced them separately in order to make greatest use of the existing railways. He coordinated their movements from his headquarters in Berlin by telegraph.

July 3. Battle of Königgrätz (Sadowa). The sudden and complete victory of the Prussians was a stunning defeat for the policy of Napoleon III, who had expected a long war that would exhaust both belligerents.

July 26. Napoleon's mediation resulted in the **preliminary peace at Nicolsburg.** Hanover, Electoral Hesse, Nassau, and Frankfurt were to be incorporated into Prussia; Austria was to be excluded from Germany (the Germanic Confederation came to an end); German states north of the Main River were to form a North German Confederation under Prussian leadership, the South German states were to remain independent and to be permitted to form a separate confederation.

Aug. 5. Napoleon advanced his **claims for compensation,** which included the frontiers of 1814 (Saarbrücken, Landau) and possibly the Bavarian Palatinate or Rhenish Hesse (with Mainz) or Luxembourg.

Bismarck brusquely rejected these claims as an offense to German national feeling.

Aug. 9–22. Bismarck took advantage of the French demands to push his peace negotiations with the **South German states** (Baden, Württemberg, Bavaria). They were given very generous terms, but were induced, in return, to conclude with Prussia **military alliances** in the event of French attack.

Aug. 16. Napoleon instructed his ambassador, Count Vincent Benedetti, to ask for Luxembourg and for Prussian support for the **acquisition of Belgium** by France. Benedetti was induced by Bismarck to put these demands in writing, along with the French offer to sanction the union of North Germany and South Germany in return (the **Benedetti Treaty**). Bismarck then took advantage of illness (Sept.–Dec.) to evade a definite reply. The draft treaty was communicated to the British in 1870 and influenced British opinion in favor of Prussia during the war with France.

Aug. 23. The **definitive Treaty of Prague** brought the war to a close.

1867, April. The Luxembourg crisis. This grew out of Napoleon's efforts (winter 1866–67) to acquire the duchy of Luxembourg from the king of the Netherlands, who was suzerain. Bismarck had promised not to oppose the deal, provided it was so engineered that German national feeling would not be aroused. The French mismanaged the affair, the news leaked out, Bismarck was interpellated by the new North German Reichstag, and the king of the Netherlands drew back from the arrangements he had made. There followed a period of acute crisis, which was closed by a compromise.

May 7–11. An **international conference at London,** which finally signed the **Treaty of London** (Sept. 9): Prussia abandoned her previous right to garrison the fortress of the town of Luxembourg. The duchy ceased to be a member of the Germanic Confederation. Its neutrality and independence were guaranteed by the powers. This settlement was a profound humiliation for Napoleon, who henceforth looked upon a final reckoning with Prussia as inevitable, reorganized his army, and initiated negotiations for an alliance with Austria and Italy.

1870–71. FRANCO-PRUSSIAN WAR (pp. 492, 502). The power of Germany, and subsequent French weakness as revealed during the war, drastically altered European relations. Germany became the center of diplomacy as Britain remained aloof.

1872, Sept. 6–12. Meeting of the three emperors in Berlin—William, Francis Joseph, Alexander II of Russia, who invited himself, lest Austria and Germany become too intimate. No political agreements were made at the meeting, but Andrássy, the Austrian foreign minister, and Gorchakov, the Russian chancellor, discussed the Ottoman/Balkan situation and agreed to work to maintain the status quo.

1873, May 6. Military convention between Germany and Russia, concluded during the visit of Emperor William, Bismarck, and Moltke to St. Petersburg. If either party was attacked by another European power, the other was to come to its assistance with 200,000 men.

June 6. Agreement between Russia and Austria (Schönbrunn convention) providing for consultation and eventual cooperation in case of attack on either. These agreements were loose in nature. Together they formed the **Three Emperors' League,** the main aim of which was to emphasize monarchical solidarity against subversive movements and to secure for Germany support in the event of trouble with France (May 1873, overthrow of Thiers by the French monarchists).

Sept. Visit of King Victor Emmanuel II to Vienna and Berlin. Italy loosely associated with the Three Emperors' League, in order to obtain assurance against action by France on behalf of the pope.

Sept. Completion of the evacuation of French territory by German troops. Efforts at alliance with Russia. Friction with Italy and Germany over the question of the papacy and the *Kulturkampf* (p. 502).

1875, April 8. The article **"Is War in Sight?"** published in the Berlin *Post.* This referred to the new French army law and concluded that war was in sight. Panic occurred in France, where the article was regarded as an inspired one. The **Duc Decazes,** French foreign minister, appealed to Britain and Russia for support, with the aim of discrediting Bismarck.

May 10. Visit of Tsar Alexander and Gorchakov to Berlin was marked by warnings of Gorchakov, supported by similar action by the British ambassador, Lord Odo Russell. Acrimonious discussions were held between Bismarck and Gorchakov. The latter's telegram stated,

"Peace is now assured." Results: Bismarck realized the weakness of the Three Emperors' League and the suspicious jealousy of the other powers. France was strengthened by the "moral coalition" that had been formed against Germany and by the knowledge that neither Britain nor Russia would stand idly by if France was attacked by Germany in a preventive war.

July. Outbreak of the **insurrection against Ottoman rule** in Herzegovina and then Bosnia (p. 530). This initiated three years of acute Balkan tension, which profoundly modified the relations of the powers to each other. The **Serbs** at once supported the insurgents, in the hope of acquiring the two provinces for themselves. **Russia** was extremely sympathetic (religious affinity, racial relationship to the South Slavs, Pan-Slav movement and ambitions, secular aims for the destruction of the Ottoman Empire, opening of the Straits to Russian warships, etc.).

Nov. 25. Purchase of the khedive of Egypt's shares in the Suez Canal, a masterstroke of British policy (**Benjamin Disraeli**), which indicated Britain's growing interest in the Middle East.

Dec. 30. The **Andrássy note** was communicated to all powers that were signatories of the Treaty of Paris of 1856. It called for complete religious freedom in Bosnia and Herzegovina, abolition of tax-farming, use of local revenue for local needs, and establishment of a mixed Christian-Muslim commission to supervise these reforms. This program was adopted by the powers and by the sultan (Jan. 31, 1876), but failed in its purpose because it was rejected by the insurgents.

1876, May 13. The **Berlin memorandum,** drawn up by Andrássy, Gorchakov, and Bismarck after a conference at Berlin. It reflected Andrássy's aversion to any policy of annexations (suggested by Bismarck and Gorchakov) and was an expansion of the Andrássy note. It called for a two months' armistice, resettlement of the insurgents, concentration of the Ottoman troops in a few localities, retention of arms by the insurgents, and supervision of reforms by the consuls of the powers. The memorandum was accepted by France and Italy, but was rejected by Britain, partly for technical reasons, but chiefly because of Disraeli's resentment of the failure to consult Britain in the drafting of the program.

May–Sept. Insurrection in Bulgaria (p. 521), suppressed with great severity by Ottoman irregular troops (**Bulgarian horrors**); thousands slaughtered.

June 30. Serbia declared war on the Ottoman Empire, trusting in Russia for support and hoping for the eventual acquisition of the insurgent provinces.

July 2. Montenegro joined Serbia in the war.

July–Aug. The **Serbs,** commanded by the Russian general Chernaiev, were defeated in a series of engagements. Serbia invaded.

July 8. Meeting at Reichstadt of Andrássy and Gorchakov. **Reichstadt Agreement:** the two powers insisted on the status quo ante bellum in the event of the defeat of Serbia and Montenegro, and on the reforms for Bosnia and Herzegovina laid down in the Berlin memorandum. In the event of Serbian-Montenegrin victory, these two powers were to be given parts of Bosnia and Herzegovina, but the larger part of these provinces to be awarded to Austria. Russia was to obtain Bessarabia (lost in 1856). In the event of Ottoman collapse, Bulgaria and Rumelia were to be autonomous states or independent principalities; Greece was to acquire some territory; Constantinople was to be a free city.

Sept. 1. Complete defeat of the Serbs at Alexinatz. They appealed to the powers for mediation. The Ottomans rejected proposals for an armistice, except on very hard terms. Great excitement in Russia and demand for war. Efforts were made by the Russians to secure assurance of German support in the event of war developing between Russia and Austria. Bismarck's reply: Germany would intervene only to prevent either Russia or Austria being mortally wounded or seriously weakened by the other.

Sept. 6. Gladstone's pamphlet: *The Bulgarian Horrors and the Question of the East.* Tremendous agitation in Britain against Ottoman misrule. This greatly hampered the government in a policy of supporting the Ottomans against Russia.

Oct. 31. The Ottomans agreed to a six-week armistice, as a result of a **Russian ultimatum** to check the continued successes of the Ottomans.

Nov. Russian preparations for war against the Ottoman Empire. Bellicose attitude of Disraeli, determined to frustrate the Russian designs.

Dec. 12. First meeting of the **Constantinople conference** (p. 531), convoked at the instance of Britain. Negotiations took place between **Lord Salisbury,** the British plenipotentiary, and **Count Nicholas Ignatiev,** the Russian ambassador. Agreement: Serbia was to lose no territory; Montenegro was to secure parts of Herzegovina and Albania conquered from the Ottomans; Bulgaria (i.e., the regions under the Bulgarian exarchate, extending over most of Macedonia) was to be divided into eastern and western provinces; Bosnia and Herzegovina were to be united as a province, and this, as well as the two Bulgarias, was to have a governor-general appointed by the powers with approval of the Ottoman government, and a provincial assembly; reforms were to be supervised by the powers.

1877, Jan. 18. An **assembly of notables** in Constantinople rejected all demands of the powers, leading to the failure of the Constantinople conference, which closed on Jan. 20.

Jan 15. January convention (Budapest convention) between Russia and Austria, was held to settle disputes as to the terms of the Reichstadt convention: Austria was to remain neutral in an eventual Russian-Ottoman war; Austria was to occupy Bosnia and Herzegovina when it saw fit; Serbia, Montenegro, and Herzegovina were to form a neutral zone. An **additional convention,** signed on March 18 but antedated to Jan. 15, reaffirmed the terms of the Reichstadt convention with regard to the disposition of Ottoman territory; no large state, Slavic or otherwise, was to be erected in the Balkans.

April 24. RUSSIA DECLARED WAR ON THE OTTOMAN EMPIRE, the government yielding to the pressure of the Pan-Slav circles (p. 510).

July 26, Aug. 14. Loose and negative **agreements were made between Britain and Austria,** listing seven points to which they would not agree in the event of a Russian victory. The British cabinet had decided (July 21) to declare war on Russia if the latter occupied Constantinople and did not make arrangements for immediate retirement. The reverses of the Russians at Plevna (July 20 ff.) eased the situation.

Dec. 10. Fall of Plevna, resumption of the Russian advance.

Dec. 12. The Ottomans appealed to the powers for mediation. This was rejected by Bismarck. Disraeli was anxious to act, but his schemes were frustrated by members of his own cabinet (especially Derby). Andrássy contented himself with warning the Russians that Austria and the powers would demand a voice in the peace settlement.

1878, Jan. 9. The Ottomans appealed to the Russians for an armistice.

Jan 31. Armistice concluded; the Russians were to occupy the lines just outside Constantinople. War fever surged in Britain ("We don't want to fight but by jingo, if we do, we've got the men, we've got the ships, we've got the money too").

March 3. The **TREATY OF SAN STEFANO** between Russia and the Ottoman Empire (ratified on March 23): **Montenegro** was to be enlarged and given the port of Antivari; both **Montenegro and Serbia were to be independent,** the latter also receiving some territory; **Romania was to be independent,** Russia reserving the right to give Romania the Dobrudja in return for Bessarabia; **Bosnia and Herzegovina** were to be granted reforms; **Bulgaria** was to be an autonomous state under an elected prince and to be occupied for two years by Russian troops, and it was to include most of Macedonia and to have a seaboard on the Aegean; **Russia** was to receive **Ardahan, Kars, Batum,** and **Bayazid** on the Asiatic front; the **Ottomans** had to pay a huge indemnity.

March 6. Andrássy issued invitations to a congress of the powers to meet at Berlin. Britain and Russia disputed what subjects might be discussed at the congress.

May 8. Mission of Count Peter Shuvalov, Russian ambassador to London, to St. Petersburg. He there imposed a policy of agreement with Britain. He returned on May 23 with the offer to push Bulgaria back from the Aegean, pare it down in the west, and divide it into north and south parts.

May 30. Secret Anglo-Russian agreement, as arranged by Shuvalov.

June 4. Secret Anglo-Ottoman agreement, reluctantly accepted by the sultan. To meet the Russian advance in Asia Minor, the British promised to defend the Ottomans against any further attack on the sultan's Asiatic possessions. In return they were to be allowed to occupy **Cyprus.** The sultan promised to introduce reforms in his Asiatic territories.

June 6. Anglo-Austrian Agreement. The agreement dealt with the future organization of Bulgaria and the length of Russian occupation.

June 13–July 13. The **BERLIN CONGRESS (p. 531): Bismarck,** the "honest broker"; **Gorchakov** and **Shuvalov** for Russia; **Andrássy** for Austria; **Disraeli** and **Salisbury** for Britain; **Waddington** for France; **Count Corti** for Italy; **Caratheodory** (a Greek) for the Ottomans. The main decisions had been made in the preceding secret agreements, but there was much trouble and friction about details, especially after the Anglo-Russian agreement leaked out. **Bulgaria was divided** into three parts: (1) Bulgaria proper, north of the Balkan Mountains, was to be tributary and autonomous; (2) Eastern Rumelia, south of the mountains, was to have a special organization under the Ottoman government; (3) Macedonia, which was to have certain reforms. **Austria** was given a mandate (June 28) to occupy Bosnia and Herzegovina and to garrison the Sanjak of Novi Bazar, a strip lying between Serbia and Montenegro. The territory given to Serbia and Montenegro was reduced. The **Greeks** were put off with promises for the future (p. 516). **Romania** was given the Dobrudja, but had to hand over southern Bessarabia to Russia. **Serbia, Romania,** and **Montenegro** became independent states. **Russia** received Batum, Kars, and Ardahan. Reforms were promised for the sultan's Asiatic provinces. The British occupied Cyprus under the **Cyprus convention.** Objections of the **French** were met by promising them permission to occupy **Tunis.** The **Italians** were put off with suggestions of expansion in Albania. The upshot of the treaty was that it left Russian nationalists and Pan-Slavs profoundly dissatisfied and left the aspirations of Serbia, Bulgaria, and Greece unfulfilled. The Ottoman Empire, wholly at the mercy of the powers, was left with a few fragments of territory in Europe, which were a constant bait for covetous neighbors. The promise of reforms in Macedonia and Asia Minor led to far-reaching agitation and trouble on the part of the Macedonians and Armenians.

Nov. 20. Outbreak of **war between Britain and Afghanistan,** the result of the Russian advance in central Asia and the determination of the British to secure their frontier in India. The British drove out the emir, **Sher Ali,** and put **Yakub Khan** on the throne. In Sept. 1879, the British agent, **Maj. Sir Pierre Cavagnari,** was murdered, and the war flared up anew. **Abd ar-Rahman** entered Afghanistan with Russian support, but made an agreement with the British (July 20, 1880): the British recognized him and gave him a pension.

1879, Sept. 4. Establishment of the **Dual Control** (Britain and France) **in Egypt** (p. 544). This grew out of the heavy investments of Europeans in Egypt and the financial difficulties resulting from the construction of the Suez Canal and many other public works by the **khedive Isma'il.** The dual control was first established in Nov. 1876, but had been suspended in Dec. 1878 when the khedive initiated ministerial government and gave the British and French controllers of finance seats in the cabinet. This plan had not worked, because of the policy of the khedive of retaining power. Britain and France thereupon forced the **abdication of Isma'il** (June 26, 1879) and the succession of **Tewfik,** who restored the dual control.

Oct. 7. ALLIANCE TREATY BETWEEN GERMANY AND AUSTRIA, concluded for five years, but regularly renewed. It remained in force until 1918 and was the foundation stone of Bismarck's alliance system. Provisions: If either party was attacked by Russia, the other should come to its assistance with all forces; if either should be attacked by some other power, its partner should preserve at least neutrality; if some other power should be supported by Russia, then each ally was obliged to aid the other. The alliance was the result of a period of tension between Germany and Russia following the Berlin Congress; the Russian nationalists blamed Bismarck for Russia's diplomatic defeat. There was some thought of bringing **Britain** into the combination; Disraeli was friendly, but the German ambassador, Count Münster, misrepresented the projected alliance as one directed chiefly against France, and Bismarck allowed the matter to drop. The immediate result of the negotiation was the **mission of Count Pierre Saburov** to Berlin, in the effort to effect a Russian-German alliance or the revival of the Three Emperors' League (Sept.–Oct. 1879). For the moment Bismarck evaded these advances.

1880, June–Nov. Montenegrin troubles. The Albanian League, a union of tribes supported by the sultan, vigorously and successfully resisted the efforts of the Montenegrins to take over the Albanian territory assigned them by the treaty of Berlin. A conference of the powers at Berlin (June) decided that Montenegro should receive Dulcigno in lieu

of some of the disputed territory. A naval demonstration of the powers at **Dulcigno** (Sept. 28) had no effect. The British government (under Gladstone since April) took a strong line and threatened to occupy the customs house at Smyrna. The Ottomans finally yielded (Nov. 25).

1881, May 12. Treaty of Bardo, establishing a **French protectorate over Tunis.** This went back to the assurances of Salisbury and Bismarck during the Congress of Berlin, but the French government had not acted because of the indifference of French public opinion in matters of colonial expansion and because of distrust of Bismarck's motives. The question was precipitated by the activity of the Italians, determined to make good their failure to secure gains at the Berlin Congress at Austria's expense. The affair initiated a long period of **Franco-Italian tension** and modified the Mediterranean situation to Britain's disadvantage. Gladstone protested, but the British government was committed by Salisbury's assurances.

May 24. The **Ottomans were obliged to cede to Greece** a considerable part of **Thessaly** and part of **Epirus.** These territories had been promised to Greece at the Berlin Congress, but the Ottomans had temporized. In the autumn of 1880 there was acute danger of war. In the end the Greeks had to content themselves with much less than had originally been envisaged.

June 18. The **ALLIANCE OF THE THREE EMPERORS:** term three years, renewed in 1884 for three more years. Provisions: If one of the contracting powers found itself at war with a fourth power (except the Ottomans), the other two were to maintain friendly neutrality. Modifications of the territorial status quo in the Ottoman Empire should take place only after agreement among the three powers; if any one of them should feel compelled to go to war with the Ottomans, it should consult its allies in advance as to the eventual results; Austria reserved the right to annex Bosnia and Herzegovina when it saw fit; the three powers agreed not to oppose the eventual union of Bulgaria and Eastern Rumelia. This treaty, kept rigorously secret, was the outcome of long negotiations between Bismarck and Saburov, the Russians being anxious for an alliance with Germany as protection against Austrian policy in the Balkans, and equally anxious for recognition of the closure of the Straits against possible British action. Bismarck refused an agreement that would not include Austria, and the Austrians were hostile to the idea until after the advent of the Gladstone government in Britain, which was unfriendly to Austria. The final conclusion of the agreement was delayed by the assassination of the tsar (March 13, 1881).

June 28. Secret treaty between Austria and Serbia, the result of Prince Milan's resentment at being deserted by Russia in 1878 and of his chronic need for Austrian financial support (p. 520). Term ten years. Serbia promised not to tolerate intrigues against Austria. Austria promised to recognize Milan as king.

1882, May 20. TRIPLE ALLIANCE, among Germany, Austria, and Italy, concluded for five years and renewed at intervals until 1915. Terms: If Italy was attacked by France without provocation, Germany and Austria would come to Italy's aid; Italy was to come to Germany's aid if the latter was attacked by France; if one or two of the contracting parties were attacked or involved in war with two or more great powers, the nonattacked member or members of the alliance should come to the aid of the other or others; if one of the allies should be forced to make war on some other great power, the others were to preserve benevolent neutrality. The treaty was the result of Italy's isolation after the French occupation of Tunis and also a reflection of popular demand for security against radicalism and the prospect of intervention by other powers in behalf of the pope. The Italians wanted above all a treaty of guaranty, assuring them of the possession of Rome. Austria was anxious for an agreement that would put an end to **irredentist agitation** (very active since 1876), and Germany was uneasy about the renewed Pan-Slav agitation (speech of Gen. **Skobelev** in Paris, Feb. 1882) and the possibility of a Franco-Russian alliance. The Italians received assurances against attack by France.

1883, Feb.–April. Establishment of the Germans, under Lüderitz, at Angra Pequeña (Southwest Africa), marking the **beginning of German colonialism** (growing agitation from 1875 onward—*German Colonial Society,* 1882) and Bismarck's conversion to imperialism. There followed two years of growing **tension between Britain and Germany,** the dispute extending to East African territory, the Cameroons, and so on.

Bismarck managed to establish a loose **entente with the French** especially in the question of Egypt (financial conference at London, June–Aug. 1884), and thereby to oblige the British to accept Germany as a colonial power.

Oct. 30. Alliance of Romania and Austria, to which Germany adhered. Terms: Austria was to come to the assistance of Romania in case the latter was attacked without provocation; Romania was to come to Austria's aid if the latter was attacked in a portion of its states bordering on Romania (that is, by Russia). The treaty was concluded for five years, but was periodically renewed and remained in force until 1916.

1884, Feb. 26. British agreement with Portugal, recognizing the latter's rights to territory at the mouth of the Congo. France and Germany together protested so vigorously that the British abandoned the treaty (June 26).

1884, Nov. 15–1885, Feb. 26. The **Berlin conference on African affairs** (p. 591), arranged by Bismarck and Ferry. Fourteen nations, including the United States, agreed to work for the suppression of slavery and the slave trade and declared complete liberty of commerce in the basin of the Congo and its affluents and on the adjacent coasts. Freedom of navigation on the Congo and Niger and their affluents was also declared. The Congo basin was declared neutral. The principle of effective occupation to establish a claim on the coasts was set up. At the same time the various powers recognized the **Congo Free State** (p. 595), which had developed under Leopold of Belgium from the **International Association for the Exploration and Civilization of Central Africa** (1876), and later the **International Association of the Congo** (1878), financed by Leopold and exploiting the discoveries of **Henry M. Stanley.**

1885, April. Acute **Anglo-Russian crisis,** resulting from an attack by Russian troops on the Afghan forces at **Penjdeh** (March 30). The question was adjusted by compromise (June 18, 1886).

Sept. 18. Revolution in Eastern Rumelia, initiating another period of tension in the Balkans. The movement was directed at union with Bulgaria (p. 521).

Nov. 13. Serbia declared war on Bulgaria, after it had become clear that an ambassadorial conference at Constantinople would not rescind the union of Bulgaria and Eastern Rumelia.

Nov. 17. Complete defeat of the Serbians in the Battle of Slivnitza.

Nov. 27. Serb defeat at Pirot. **Bulgarian invasion.** This was stopped only through Austrian intervention to save Serbia (**Khevenhüller mission**).

1886, Jan. 4. Greek note to the Ottomans demanding the territorial promises of 1878 by way of compensation for Bulgarian claims.

Feb. 1. Agreement between Bulgaria and the Ottomans (p. 521).

March 3. Treaty of Bucharest: "Peace is restored between Bulgaria and Serbia."

May 10–June 7. Pacific blockade of the Greek coast by an international naval force. The Greeks were obliged to disarm.

1886–87. Rapid development of **nationalist and revenge agitation in France,** the reaction to **Jules Ferry's** policy of understanding with Germany regarding colonial expansion.

1887, Feb. 12. FIRST MEDITERRANEAN AGREEMENT, between Britain and Italy, adhered to by Austria (March 24) and Spain (May 4). The agreement took the form of an exchange of notes (Anglo-Italian; Anglo-Austrian; Italian-Spanish, acceded to by Germany and Austria, May 21). Bismarck had encouraged the combination, exploiting the acute Anglo-French tension (over Egypt) and the Italian-French tension (tariff war, etc.). The notes provided for the maintenance of the status quo in the Mediterranean, including the Adriatic, Aegean, and Black Seas. Italy was to support the British policy in Egypt and Britain the Italian policy in North Africa. The Anglo-Austrian note stressed rather the community of interest of the two powers in the Balkans. Spain promised not to make an agreement with France regarding North Africa that would be aimed at Italy, Austria, or Germany. Britain refused to bind itself to any specific action, but the effect of the agreements was to provide a basis for common action in the event of disturbance in the Mediterranean by France or Russia.

Feb. 20. RENEWAL OF THE TRIPLE ALLIANCE for five years. Negotiations had been carried on since Nov. 1886, the Italians demanding more far-reaching support of their interests in North Africa. This Bismarck was willing to concede, in order to be assured of Italy's friendship in case of a clash with France. But Austria objected, her attention being focused on the Balkans. In the end the old alliance was renewed and additional German-Italian and Austro-Italian agreements made. Germany promised that in the event of French efforts to expand in North Africa, if Italy was obliged to take action or even make war on France, Germany would come to the aid of Italy. If France was defeated, Germany would not object to Italy's taking "territorial guaranties for the security of the frontiers and of her maritime position." The Austro-Italian agreement provided for the maintenance of the status quo in the Balkans and the Middle East. If this became impossible, neither party should occupy territory except in agreement with the other on the principle of reciprocal compensation. This was not to apply to the eventual annexation of Bosnia and Herzegovina by Austria.

May 22. The **Drummond-Wolff convention,** by which Britain agreed to evacuate Egypt within three years but reserved the right to reoccupy in case of disorder. This convention was wrecked by the opposition of France and Russia—the first striking case of Franco-Russian collaboration against Great Britain.

June 18. Signature of a secret **RUSSIAN-GERMAN TREATY** (the Reinsurance Treaty) to replace the expiring Alliance of the Three Emperors, which Russia refused to renew. The two powers promised each other neutrality in the event of either one's becoming involved in war with a third power (but this was not to apply in case of aggressive war of Germany against France, or of Russia against Austria). They were to work for the maintenance of the status quo in the Balkans, and Germany was to recognize Russia's preponderant influence in Bulgaria. The principle of the closure of the Straits was once more reaffirmed. An additional and very **secret protocol** promised moral and diplomatic support "to the measures which His Majesty [the tsar] may deem it necessary to take to control the key of his empire" (i.e., the entrance to the Black Sea). This famous treaty represented Bismarck's effort to keep Russia from France and to buy its friendship by signing away things that he knew Russia could never get on account of British and Austrian opposition. On the Russian side the treaty reflected the victory of the foreign minister, Nicholas Giers, over the extreme nationalist groups.

Dec. 12. SECOND MEDITERRANEAN AGREEMENT among Britain, Austria, and Italy (Bismarck having refused to participate—Bismarck-Salisbury correspondence, Nov.). It restated the principle of the status quo in the Balkans and the importance of keeping the Ottoman Empire free of all foreign domination. The empire must not cede its rights in Bulgaria to any other power or allow occupation of Bulgaria by any other power. Neither must it give up any rights in the Straits or in Asia Minor.

1888, Jan 28. Military agreement between Germany and Italy, providing for the use of Italian troops against France in the event of a Franco-German war.

Feb. 3. Publication of the German-Austrian alliance of 1879. This was intended as a warning to Russia, where nationalist agitation against Germany and Austria continued.

May 15. Italy adhered to the alliance of Germany and Austria with Romania.

July. Crisis in the relations of Italy and the papacy. The pope was on the verge of leaving Rome. The Italians again feared an attack by France and induced the Germans and British to issue warnings.

1890, March 18. DISMISSAL OF BISMARCK, resulting at least in part from the dissatisfaction of the young emperor William II with Bismarck's policy toward Russia (p. 502) and his desire for closer relations with Austria and Britain.

March 23. A German ministerial conference decided, on the advice of **Baron Fritz von Holstein** (long a collaborator of Bismarck, who had recently drifted from him), not to renew the Reinsurance Treaty with Russia. It lapsed on June 18, despite numerous Russian attempts to reopen the question of renewal.

July 1. Anglo-German colonial agreement (Heligoland treaty), by which Germany gave up large claims in East Africa and received in return the island of Heligoland, which Britain had obtained from Denmark in 1815. Since the island at that time was regarded as practically useless, the whole treaty was looked upon as a striking demonstration of German readiness to purchase the friendship of Britain.

1891, May 6. Premature renewal of the Triple Alliance, the three documents being merged in one and Germany assuming somewhat larger obligations to support the Italian claims in North Africa. The renewal of the treaty was due to German fears lest France might force Italy into its orbit. The contracting parties were to do their utmost to associate Britain in support of Italian aspirations.

July 24. Visit of a French squadron under **Adm. Alfred Gervais, to Cronstadt,** included frantic demonstrations of Franco-Russian friendship. The tsar listened to the "Marseillaise" played on one of the French warships. The **Franco-Russian agreement,** which had been prepared by French loans, and so on, began to loom on the horizon, the result primarily of German rejection of the Reinsurance Treaty, the hasty renewal of the Triple Alliance, and the demonstrations of Anglo-German solidarity.

Aug. 21, 27. The **AUGUST CONVENTION** between France and Russia, first fruit of the negotiations. The French desired a hard-and-fast agreement, but this was watered down by the Russians until it was hardly more than an agreement to consult as to what measures should be taken by two powers in case the maintenance of peace was threatened or one of the parties menaced by aggression. All efforts of the French to arrange for mobilization (especially during Giers's visit to Paris, November) proved abortive.

1893, July 13. French ultimatum to Siam, resulting in a short but severe crisis in Anglo-French relations. The French took a strong stand and generally won their point, thereby making a good impression on Russia.

July 15. Passage of the **German military bill,** reducing service in the infantry to two years but increasing the forces. This created much uneasiness in both France and Russia and reminded the Russians of the value of the connection with France.

Dec. 27–1894, Jan. 4. Exchange of notes between the **Russian and French governments,** formally accepting the military convention worked out 18 months before. The agreement was really political as much as military, but was classed as a military convention in order to circumvent the French constitution, which required submission of treaties to the Chamber of Deputies. The convention was to remain in force as long as the Triple Alliance. It provided the following: (1) If France was attacked by Germany, or by Italy supported by Germany, Russia would employ all available forces against Germany; if Russia was attacked by Germany, or by Austria supported by Germany, France would employ all available forces against Germany. (2) In case the forces of the Triple Alliance, or of any one member of it, mobilized, France and Russia should mobilize without delay. Other articles provided for the number of troops to be employed, for specific plans of the general staffs, for secrecy, and so on.

1894, March 16. Conclusion of the **Russian-German tariff treaty,** after years of tariff war and negotiations. This agreement demonstrated the Russian desire not to be drawn into hostilities with Germany.

May 12. Treaty between the British government and the Congo Free State (p. 474) by which the British leased a large tract on the left bank of the Upper Nile, in return for a corridor 25 kilometers in width between Lakes Tanganyika and Albert Edward, which was to serve as a connecting link for the **Cape-to-Cairo telegraph and railway system,** under discussion since 1888. Vigorous protests were made by the French and the Germans, on the basis of earlier agreements. From the European angle it demonstrated once more the rift between Britain and Germany and the renewed tendency of Germany and France to collaborate in colonial affairs against Britain.

1895, June 25. Formation of the **Salisbury cabinet** in England, with **Joseph Chamberlain** at the colonial office. Beginning of the most active phase of British imperialism. In view of Britain's isolation and the situation in the Middle East, Africa, and the Far East, Salisbury tried at first to throw off the danger of French and Russian advance by reconstituting close relations with Germany and the Triple Alliance.

Aug. 5. FAMOUS INTERVIEW BETWEEN WILLIAM II AND SALISBURY AT THE COWES YACHT RACES resulted in profound distrust between Salisbury and the emperor (encouraged by Baron von Holstein), which only served to aggravate relations between the two countries.

Oct. 1. First Armenian massacres in Constantinople, following a great Armenian demonstration (p. 532).

Oct. 17. Under pressure from the powers, the sultan finally accepted the **program of reforms for Armenia.** Nevertheless, the massacres continued, taking place in various cities all over Anatolia.

1896, Jan. 3. The **KRUGER TELEGRAM** was sent by Emperor William to **President Paul Kruger** of the South African Republic (**Transvaal**), congratulating him on the defeat of the raiders led by Dr. Jameson (p. 598). German interests in the Transvaal were considerable, but not decisive. The Germans made themselves the advocates of the Transvaal because they hoped (this was Holstein's plan) to demonstrate the value of German friendship to Britain by annoying the British into better relations. When news of the Jameson raid reached Berlin, the emperor, assuming that the British government was privy to the scheme, demanded strong measures and even military intervention on behalf of Kruger. This created a storm of indignation and recrimination in Britain, especially when it became known that the real purpose of the German government was to beat the British into friendship. Loud demands for an agreement with France and Russia were met by the British government by an agreement with France (Jan. 15) in which the British abandoned many of their claims in Siam, and by approaches to Russia, which, however, led to nothing.

Feb. Limited reconciliation between Russia and Bulgaria. The new tsar, Nicholas II, desired to bring the feud to an end, and Prince Ferdinand expressed his readiness to baptize the crown prince Boris in the Orthodox faith. Russia took the initiative in securing the **recognition of Ferdinand by the powers** (p. 521).

Outbreak of the **insurrection in Crete** (p. 516), fomented by Greeks who were intent on the annexation of the island. Under pressure from the powers, the sultan eventually agreed (July 3) to the restoration of the **Pact of Halepa** (1878), which had introduced a large measure of self-government in the island and had been curtailed after the suppression of a rising in 1889. Greek support of the insurgents continued. The sultan accepted a **new reform scheme** (Aug. 25) drawn up by the ambassadors of the powers (Crete was to have a Christian governor, named by the sultan with the approval of the powers; the Cretan Christians were to have two-thirds of all offices, and the Cretan assembly was to have wide powers; a European commission was to reorganize the gendarmerie, courts, and finances). This program was accepted by the insurgents (Sept. 12).

March 1. Battle of Adua. Disastrous defeat of the Italians by the Ethiopians (p. 592).

March 12. British decision to begin the **reconquest of the Sudan** by an advance on Dongola, to protect the Nile. There was a danger of French advance in that region, as well as from the west (second **Monteil mission,** July 1895; **Marchand mission,** Feb. 1896), despite the famous **Grey declaration** (March 28, 1895) stating that Britain would regard such action as "unfriendly," which obliged the government to reestablish control of the Sudan itself.

1897, Feb. 2. Cretan insurrection resumed (p. 516), supported by the Greek **Cretan Committee** and the **Ethniké Hetairia,** an organization designed for the realization of Greek aspirations in Macedonia. The Greek government was forced by public opinion to send ships and troops to Crete (Feb. 10, following the proclamation of union with Greece, Feb. 6). The powers handed in notes to Greece and the Ottoman Empire (March 2) promising **autonomy for Crete** and demanding withdrawal of the troops on pain of "measures of constraint." The Greek government rejected the note, and on March 18 the **blockade of Crete** was proclaimed. The war in Crete went on and led to **WAR BETWEEN GREECE AND THE OTTOMANS** (April 17). Serbia and Bulgaria were eager to join in the assault on the Ottoman Empire but were deterred by strong warnings from Russia.

May 10. The **Greeks appealed to the powers,** after a series of decisive defeats by the Ottomans. They had first been obliged to recall their troops from Crete and to accept in advance the decisions of the powers. An armistice was arranged (May 19) and a peace settlement reached (Sept. 18). The Cretan question remained open until Nov. 1898, when the powers finally agreed to name **Prince George of Greece** as governor of the island.

1898, March 28. Passage of the **first naval law** by the German Reichstag. This was the work of **Adm. Alfred von Tirpitz,** minister of marine, and laid the basis for Germany's naval expansion (p. 504).

Sept. 18. Beginning of the **FASHODA CRISIS,** between Britain and

France (p. 592). Since March 1896 the Egyptian forces, under **Gen. Sir Herbert Kitchener,** had been advancing up the Nile. The dervishes were decisively defeated on the **Atbara River** (April 8, 1898) and at **Omdurman** (Sept. 2). During the same period British expeditions were trying to reach the Nile from Uganda, all with the object of heading off the French, with whom the Congo government cooperated. The **Marchand mission,** sent out in Feb. 1896, succeeded, after countless delays and hardships, in reaching the Nile at Fashoda (now Kodok) on July 10, 1898, and establishing itself there. After the Battle of Omdurman, Kitchener at once proceeded up the Nile, where he found Marchand. The latter refused to evacuate without orders of his government. There ensued the most acute crisis in Anglo-French relations during the whole prewar period. The British refused to discuss the pros and cons of the French claims until Marchand had evacuated territory that the British claimed for Egypt by right of conquest. The French government, harassed by the Dreyfus affair (p. 494), found itself unprepared for war at sea and, securing no support from Russia (visit of Muraviev to Paris, Oct.), it yielded to a poorly veiled threat of war. On Nov. 3 the **evacuation of Fashoda** was ordered. The French claims were not settled until March 21, 1899, when they were obliged to renounce all territory along the Nile, in return for worthless districts in the Sahara. The episode made more difficult the pursuit of a policy of friendship with Britain, as advocated by **Théophile Delcassé,** French foreign minister from June 1898 to June 1905.

Nov. 21. Commercial treaty between France and Italy, bringing to an end a long and disastrous tariff war. The treaty marked the beginning of the reconciliation of France and Italy and the gradual **defection of Italy from the Triple Alliance** (tacitly renewed for six years in 1896). This policy was necessitated by the collapse of the Italian colonial policy and the instability of the domestic situation (p. 499).

1899, May 18–July 29. FIRST HAGUE PEACE CONFERENCE (p. 423).

Aug. 9. Extension of the Franco-Russian Alliance, during Delcassé's visit to St. Petersburg. The alliance was extended to provide for the maintenance of the balance of power as well as the maintenance of peace, and the term of the military convention was made indefinite.

Oct. 9. Outbreak of the Boer War (p. 488).

Oct. 14. The so-called **Windsor treaty** between Britain and Portugal. The secret agreement renewed older treaties of 1642 and 1661, involving a guaranty of Portuguese territory and including a promise by Portugal not to let munitions pass through **Delagoa Bay** to the Transvaal or to declare neutrality. The agreement was a negation of the spirit of the German-British agreement of August 1898.

Nov. 25. Berlin-Baghdad Railway concession (p. 423). Though primarily an economic enterprise, the railway project quickly became a vital factor in the relations of Germany with Russia and Britain.

Nov. 20–28. Visit of William II and Bülow to England (the first since 1895). Discussion of a possible Anglo-German-American agreement failed to bear fruit, marking a cooling in Anglo-German relations.

1900, June 12. Passage of the **second German naval law,** providing for a fleet of 38 battleships, to be built within 20 years.

Dec. 14. Franco-Italian agreement, dealing with Morocco and Tripoli (p. 423). This marked the full development of the Franco-Italian entente.

1901, July–Aug. Beginning of the negotiations for an **Anglo-Japanese alliance.**

1902, Jan. 30. The **ANGLO-JAPANESE ALLIANCE** (p. 423), marking the end of Britain's "splendid isolation."

March 20. Franco-Russian declaration in favor of the principles enunciated in the Anglo-Japanese Alliance and reserving the right to take counsel to safeguard their interests. This was generally taken as a counterblast to the new combination and an extension of the Franco-Russian Alliance to the Far East, but this was probably an exaggeration.

June 28. Renewal of the Triple Alliance for six years. The demands of the Italians for greater concessions were evaded, but they were given assurances with regard to Tripoli.

Nov. 1. Italian note to France, assuring it that in the event of its being attacked, Italy would remain neutral: "the same shall hold good in case France, as the result of a direct provocation, should find herself compelled, in defense of her honor or of her security, to take the initiative of a declaration of war." Italy also gave assurance that it was

not a party and would not be a party to any military agreement in conflict with this declaration. **Completion of the Italian-French entente. Nadir of the Triple Alliance,** the relations between Italy and Austria being badly strained by irredentist agitation.

Nov. 8. Failure of the **French agreement with Spain** on Morocco. The French had offered the Spaniards a substantial part of northern Morocco as a sphere, but the Spanish government drew back for fear of antagonizing Britain.

1903, Feb. Russian-Austrian program of reform for **Macedonia.** The region had for years been the prey of rival Bulgarian, Serbian, and Greek bands and had broken out in insurrection in 1902. Mild reforms introduced by the sultan (Nov. 1902) had failed to pacify the region. The Russian-Austrian program called for a gendarmerie composed of Muslims and Christians according to population, appointment of foreign officers, and reorganization of the financial system. It was accepted by the other powers.

Oct. 2. The **Mürzsteg program** of reform for Macedonia, worked out by Russia and Austria and approved by the powers. This program was to replace the Feb. program, which had proved inadequate. Austrian and Russian inspectors were to be attached to the inspector general, and a foreign general was to command the gendarmerie. Further administrative and judicial reforms were provided for.

Nov. Anglo-Russian conversations looking toward an understanding. These broke down because of Russia's unwillingness to agree to a partition of Persia into spheres of influence.

1904, April 8. The **ANGLO-FRENCH ENTENTE** concluded. This had been under negotiation since July and especially since Oct. The outbreak of the Russian-Japanese War undoubtedly served to hasten the conclusion. The agreement represented a complete settlement of colonial differences, particularly with regard to Egypt and Morocco: France recognized the British **occupation of Egypt,** but was given guaranties regarding the Egyptian debt; Britain was to make effective the treaty of 1888 providing for the free navigation of the **Suez Canal;** Britain recognized French interests in **Morocco** and promised diplomatic support in realizing them; secret articles envisaged the eventual breakdown of Moroccan independence and the partition of the country between France and Spain; France surrendered ancient rights on the shores of **Newfoundland,** but retained the right to fish; in return, France was given territory near **French Gambia** and east of the **Niger;** British and French spheres of influence were delimited on the frontiers of **Siam,** and disputes regarding **Madagascar** and the **New Hebrides** were adjusted.

Oct. 21. The **Dogger Bank episode.** The Russian fleet, under Adm. Zinovy Rodjestvensky, passing through the North Sea on its way to the Far East, fired upon British trawlers, which they had supposed to be Japanese destroyers. The situation was finally saved through the efforts of Delcassé, and the matter was adjusted by an international commission (Feb. 25, 1905).

Oct. 27–Nov. 23. German-Russian negotiations for an alliance. These arose from the tension between Russia and Britain and from British protests against the coaling of the Russian fleet by German companies. The tsar accepted a German draft treaty (Oct. 30) providing for mutual aid in case of attack by another European power. The plan broke down because of Russia's unwillingness to sign before consulting France, which was expected to be drawn in. Ultimately the two powers agreed (Dec. 12) merely to aid each other in the event of complications arising from the coaling of the fleet.

1905, March 31. VISIT OF THE GERMAN EMPEROR TO TANGIER, initiating the **first Moroccan crisis.** Delcassé had wantonly excluded the Germans from the Moroccan negotiations and had not officially communicated the agreement with Britain. The Germans were uncertain about the Anglo-French entente, but had declared their disinterestedness in Morocco except for the Open Door, regarding which Delcassé had given assurances. The French had thereupon proceeded to capitalize on the free hand secured in the agreements with Italy, Britain, and Spain. After the failure of the German-Russian negotiations, Bülow and Holstein decided to make the Moroccan affair a test of the strength of the Anglo-French entente and carried the unwilling emperor along on this course. At Tangier he proclaimed Germany's adherence to the principles of independence and integrity and declared in favor of the policy of equal opportunity for all. His visit at once created a panic in Paris and led to a loud outcry against Delcassé's policy. Delcassé at once offered to make good his mistake and to buy off the German opposition, but the Germans turned a deaf ear.

May 17, 25. British correspondence with France. The British, apprehensive about German designs on the Moroccan coast, proposed "full and confidential discussion . . . in anticipation of any complications." Delcassé took this as the first step toward an alliance and tried to develop the British advance, but Rouvier objected.

June 6. FALL OF DELCASSÉ, who urged the French cabinet to accept the British offers. He argued that the Germans were only bluffing and that a Franco-British front would be invincible. The cabinet voted unanimously against him, fearing that France was poorly prepared for war, that an agreement with Britain would precipitate war at a time when Russia was rendered helpless by her defeat in the Far East, and that France would bear the burden of German hostility. Rouvier took over the foreign office and renewed his efforts to strike a bargain. The Germans stood by their previous attitude.

July 8. The **French government,** assured of American support against unreasonable demands (the U.S. had agreed to help mediate), accepted the idea of a conference.

July 24. BJÖRKÖ TREATY, signed by Emperor William and the tsar during a visit to each other's yachts. The treaty was essentially a return to the draft of Oct. 1904, excepting that it was to be confined to Europe and was to take effect only after the conclusion of peace between Russia and Japan. Bülow objected to its restriction to Europe and threatened to resign, but was persuaded to remain after an appeal from the emperor. The treaty was vigorously opposed by the Russian foreign office and was ultimately wrecked by the refusal of the French government, estranged by the Moroccan crisis, even to consider joining in such a pact (Oct.).

Aug. 12. Renewal of the Anglo-Japanese alliance for ten years. The treaty was modified to provide for mutual support in the event of attack by *one* other power, and was extended to include India.

Sept. 28. France and Germany finally reached an agreement on the agenda for the **Moroccan conference,** which was to meet in Jan. 1906. Most of the French demands were met, in the hope that France would be disposed to accede to the Björkö treaty.

1906, Jan. 10. Beginning of **Anglo-French military and naval conversations,** which had been unofficially initiated in Dec. The new Liberal government (**Sir Edward Grey, foreign secretary** since Dec. 1905) refused to promise support to France in the event of German attack, but agreed to nonbinding discussions of the modalities of cooperation in case such cooperation should be decided on. Creation of the "moral obligation" of Britain to France. The cabinet as a whole was not informed of these conversations until 1911.

Jan. 16–April 7. Algeciras conference (p. 546) on Morocco. France was supported throughout by all the powers except Austria, which sided with Germany. The **Act of Algeciras** reaffirmed the independence and integrity of Morocco but entrusted the French with the police on the border with Algeria (p. 424).

Feb. 10. Launching of the *Dreadnought* by the British navy, the first all-big-gun battleship (ten 12-inch guns), which revolutionized the world naval situation.

May. The German government decided to increase the tonnage of battleships in the naval program, to add six cruisers to the program, and to widen the Kiel Canal to allow the passage of projected ships of the dreadnought type.

1907, May 16. Pact of Cartagena among Britain, France, and Spain. It provided for the maintenance of the status quo in the Mediterranean and the part of the Atlantic that washes the shores of Europe and Africa. The agreement was directed chiefly at supposed German designs on the **Balearic Islands** and the **Canary Islands.**

June 15–Oct. 18. SECOND HAGUE PEACE CONFERENCE failed to reduce armaments, mainly because of British-German rivalry (p. 424 ff.).

July 30. Russian-Japanese agreement, similar to the Franco-Japanese agreement.

July. Renewal of the Triple Alliance for six years, despite the complete lack of faith on the part of Germany and Austria in Italy's loyalty.

Aug. 31. THE ANGLO-RUSSIAN ENTENTE. This had been discussed at various times since the conclusion of the Russian-Japanese War and was encouraged by the French. Negotiations had lagged because of opposition in Russian court circles, because of the confusion created by the Russian revolutionary movement (p. 511), and because of the fears of **Alexander Izvolski** (Russian foreign minister since May 1906) lest Germany take offense. The agreement was much less extensive than that between France and Britain: **Persia,** the root of the Russian-British antagonism, was divided into three spheres of influence—a large Russian sphere in the north, covering the most valuable part of the country, a neutral sphere in the center, and a smaller British sphere in the southeast. Russia agreed that **Afghanistan** should be outside its sphere of influence and that it would deal with the emir only through Britain; Britain promised not to change the status of the country or to interfere with its domestic affairs. Both governments recognized the suzerainty of China over **Tibet** and promised to respect its territorial integrity. In a separate note (April 1907) the British government had expressed itself as well disposed toward a change in the **Straits agreements** favorable to Russia. In another separate note (Aug. 29) the Russian government recognized Britain's preponderant position in the **Persian Gulf.**

1908, Jan. 27. Count Alois Aehrenthal (Austrian foreign minister since Oct. 1906) announced the intention of the Austrian government to build a **railway through the Sanjak of Novi Bazar** toward Saloniki. The purpose of this was to drive a wedge between Serbia and Montenegro, where anti-Austrian agitation had grown rapidly since the advent of the Karageorgevich dynasty (1903; **Serbian-Austrian tariff war,** 1906–11). The Austrian move was much resented by Izvolski, who claimed it was a violation of the spirit of the Austro-Russian entente of 1897. He brought forward a rival scheme for a railroad from the Danube to the Adriatic. The British were also much concerned about the Austrian step, which they regarded as a bribe by the Ottoman Empire to Austria to induce the latter to oppose further reforms in Macedonia.

March. Grey put forward a scheme of **reform for Macedonia,** which would have given the three provinces virtual autonomy.

April 23. The **Baltic and North Sea conventions,** the first involving Germany, Sweden, Denmark, and Russia, the second involving Great Britain, Germany, Denmark, France, the Netherlands, and Sweden. They provided for the maintenance of the status quo on the shores of the two seas and for consultation among the signatories in case the status quo was threatened.

Sept. 16. BUCHLAU CONFERENCE between Aehrenthal and Izvolski. After long discussion an informal agreement was reached: Russia was not to oppose the annexation of Bosnia and Herzegovina by Austria, and Austria was not to oppose the opening of the Straits to Russian warships, under certain conditions. An international conference was to put the stamp upon these arrangements and other minor modifications of the Berlin treaty.

Sept. 25. Casablanca affair. Three German deserters from the French foreign legion were taken by force from a German consular official. Acute tension in Franco-German relations.

Oct. 6. PROCLAMATION OF THE ANNEXATION OF BOSNIA AND HERZEGOVINA BY AUSTRIA, which gave up the right to occupy the Sanjak militarily. Rage in **Serbia** (p. 520) and **Montenegro,** where the two annexed provinces had long since been looked upon as a future legacy. Military preparations were at once begun, and negotiations were initiated looking toward an Ottoman-Serbian-Montenegrin-Greek alliance against Austria. In **Russia** the event caused hardly less consternation in nationalist circles, where nothing was known of Izvolski's bargain with Aehrenthal. The prime minister, Count Peter Stolypin, at once wrote to Izvolski, instructing him to oppose the Austrian action, and it was this primarily that obliged Izvolski to repudiate his agreement, declare that he had been duped, and take the lead in championing the Serbian claims. The **Germans** supported Austria loyally in order to uphold the alliance. The **French and British,** though they resented Izvolski's underhanded negotiation with Austria, supported Russia and demanded the convocation of an **international conference** to consider the Austrian action.

Oct. 7. Crete proclaimed union with Greece, thereby adding to the crisis.

Oct. 28. The *Daily Telegraph* affair. The publication of the indiscreet utterances of Emperor William to a British nobleman served to create a crisis in Germany and at the same time to accentuate the Anglo-German antagonism.

Nov. 10. Germany and France agreed to submit the **Casablanca affair** to an arbitral board, which rendered a report on May 22, 1909.

Dec. 4. LONDON NAVAL CONFERENCE (p. 424).

1909, Jan. 12. Austro-Ottoman agreement (final form on Feb. 26), by which the Ottomans recognized the annexation and were paid compensation.

March 2. The powers intervened to prevent a war between Serbia and Austria. The powers advised the Serbs to yield, but the Serbian note to Vienna (March 10) avoided any recognition of the annexation and was generally regarded as unsatisfactory.

March 21. German note to Russia, calling upon her to abandon support of the Serbs and to recognize the annexation. Russia complied.

March 31. Serbian note to Austria, recognizing the annexation, declaring that it did not infringe on Serbian interests, and promising to check anti-Austrian propaganda and maintain good neighborly relations in the future.

April 9. The Ottomans recognized the independence of Bulgaria.

Oct. 24. Racconigi agreement between Russia and Italy. Both powers promised to work for the status quo in the Balkans. Italy agreed to support Russian aspirations in the Straits, while Russia agreed not to oppose the Italian designs in **Tripoli.**

Nov.–Dec. Anglo-German negotiations (Gwinner and Cassel) looking toward a general settlement, but dealing chiefly with the **Baghdad Railway.** The Germans were prepared to give up all claims to control the railway from Baghdad to the Persian Gulf, but the British demanded full control (not international) of that section, and were unwilling to act without Russia and France.

1910, Feb. Official **Russian-Austrian reconciliation** based on agreement to maintain the status quo in the Balkans, the Russians being in constant dread of a further move by the Austrians.

Nov. 4–5. Visit of Tsar Nicholas and the new foreign minister, **Sergei Sazonov,** to Emperor William at **Potsdam.** Tentative agreement on the Middle East. The Germans gave the Russians a free hand in **northern Persia,** while the Russians promised no longer to oppose the **Baghdad Railway** and to arrange for the connection of this line with the Persian railways. The British, who had always refused to negotiate without Russia and who were now deprived of their chief support in the Baghdad Railway matter, were disappointed.

1911, April–May. French advance in Morocco, following antiforeign disturbances. The French entered Fez on May 21, despite warnings from the Germans that they were violating the Algeciras Act.

June–Nov. SECOND MOROCCAN CRISIS, resulting from the forward movement of the French and the general dissatisfaction of the Germans with the working of the 1909 agreement. The French government was not unwilling to make compensation to the Germans, and **Jules Cambon,** the ambassador at Berlin, engaged in conversations with the German foreign secretary, **Alfred von Kiderlen-Wächter,** at Kissingen (June 20–21). But the Germans refused to advance demands and took the stand that the French should make an offer. Kiderlen was genuinely anxious to liquidate the Moroccan affair and pave the way to better relations with France and Britain. Negotiations on the French side were hampered by a cabinet change, the result of which was the formation of a **ministry under Joseph Caillaux** (June 28).

July 1. The **German gunboat *Panther* arrived at Agadir** on the Atlantic coast of Morocco, ostensibly to protect German interests, but in reality to frighten the French into action. The French foreign minister, **Justin de Selves,** appealed to Britain to join in sending ships. This action was disavowed by Caillaux and rejected by the British (July 4).

July 15. After much fencing, the Germans admitted to the French that they would require the whole of the **French Congo** as compensation for the abandonment of their rights and interests in Morocco. This was regarded by the French as out of the question, but discussions continued, carried on to a large extent irregularly by Caillaux. Settlement of the French-German issue on Nov. 4 (p. 547).

July 21. Mansion House speech of Lloyd George, in which he declaimed against Britain's being ignored in the Moroccan matter and used threatening language. Nevertheless, negotiations continued between the Germans and French, and by Oct. substantial agreement was reached. By the **convention of Nov. 4,** Germany agreed to leave

France a free hand in Morocco and not to object even to the erection of a protectorate; in return France ceded part of the French Congo, with two strips of territory connecting the German Cameroons with the Congo and Ubangi Rivers.

Sept. 28. OUTBREAK OF THE TRIPOLITAN WAR between Italy and the Ottoman Empire (pp. 499, 551). This was due in large measure to the desire of the Italians to realize the agreements with France and to counterbalance the French gains in Morocco. In one way or another all the great powers were bound not to oppose the Italian action, though they all disapproved of it. The Austrians, however, objected from the outset to all operations that would disturb the status quo in the Balkans and thereby prevented attacks upon the Adriatic or Aegean coasts. Numerous attempts at mediation by the powers broke down through the hasty **annexation of Tripoli** by the Italians, which the Ottomans refused to recognize.

1912, Feb. 8. Haldane mission to Berlin. Haldane suggested that Britain would be willing to support German colonial aspirations in Africa in return for abstention from increase of the fleet. The Germans were unwilling to make naval concessions without a political agreement. German chancellor Theobald von Bethmann-Hollweg demanded a promise of neutrality under certain conditions, whereas Grey refused more than an assurance not to attack or take part in a hostile combination against Germany.

March 8. Publication of the **new German naval bill,** providing for an increase in the number of ships, an increase in personnel, and the establishment of a third squadron in commission. With this the Anglo-German discussions came to an end, though conversations regarding the Baghdad Railway and colonial affairs continued, and an effort was made on both sides to put relations on a better footing.

March 13. Treaty of alliance between Bulgaria and Serbia. This had been under discussion since 1908 and had been warmly supported by the Russians (especially Nicholas Hartwig, the minister at Belgrade). Serious negotiations were initiated in Oct. 1911, in view of the Tripolitan War, but were delayed by the insistence of the Bulgarians that the alliance be directed against the Ottoman Empire rather than Austria and that Macedonia should receive autonomy. The secret *annexe* of the treaty provided for a possible war against the Ottoman Empire. The treaty was supplemented by a **military convention** (May 12). Its general tenor became known to most of the powers at an early date, but it was not taken very seriously. The Russians, who had sponsored it, regarded it chiefly as a defensive bulwark against Austria and relied on their ability to hold back the Balkan states from aggression against the Ottomans.

April 18. The **Italians bombarded the Dardanelles,** which were thereupon closed by the Ottomans. After vigorous protests from Russia and other powers, they were reopened on May 4.

May 4–16. The **Italians conquered Rhodes** and other islands of the Dodecanese, thereby establishing a footing in the eastern Mediterranean and causing much uneasiness in Britain and France.

May 29. Treaty of alliance between Bulgaria and Greece. This had been proposed by Venizelos a year before but had been evaded by the Bulgarians for fear of becoming involved in a war concerning Crete. Such a war was not provided for in the treaty, and the definition of claims in Macedonia was postponed. A **military convention** was concluded on Oct. 5.

July 16. Naval convention between France and Russia, to supplement the military convention of 1893. This was part of Raymond Poincaré's (French premier since Jan. 14, 1912) policy of strengthening the alliance with Russia.

Sept. 18. Bulgaria and Serbia decided for war against the Ottoman Empire, using the demand for reform merely as a blind. The two powers were anxious to take advantage of the Tripolitan War, which was coming to a close.

Sept. 30. Mobilization of the Balkan states. Russia announced a trial mobilization in Poland.

Oct. 8. Austro-Russian note to the Balkan states, demanding respect for the status quo and promising reforms for Macedonia.

Oct. 8. Montenegro declared war on the Ottoman Empire.

Oct. 18. OUTBREAK OF THE FIRST BALKAN WAR, between Bulgaria, Serbia, and Greece on the one hand, and the Ottomans on the other.

Oct. 18. Treaty of Lausanne, between the Ottoman Empire and Italy. This had been under discussion since July and had been forced by an Italian ultimatum (Oct. 12): the Ottomans promised to withdraw their forces from Tripoli, and the Italians promised to withdraw from the Aegean Islands; the Ottomans were allowed to keep in Tripoli a representative of the sultan as caliph.

Oct. 22. Bulgarian victory at Kirk Kilissé, in Thrace, where the Ottomans had rashly taken the offensive.

Oct. 24–26. Serbian victory at Kumanovo.

Oct. 28–Nov. 3. Great Bulgarian victory at Lulé Burgas. Advance of the Bulgarians to the Chatalja lines, last line of defense before Constantinople.

Nov. 3–5. Russian warnings to the Bulgarians against the occupation of Constantinople, which the Russians would resist by the use of their fleet.

Nov. 10. The **Serbs reached the Adriatic** after overrunning northern Albania.

Nov. 15–18. Serb victory at Monastir.

Nov. 17–18. Bulgarian attack on the Chatalja lines, which failed.

Nov. 24. The Austrians announced their unalterable opposition to territorial access to the Adriatic for Serbia and came out for an independent Albania. Acute international crisis. The Serbs remained steadfast and were at first supported by Russia, which was given assurances by France of support in the event of war with Germany. Austria was supported by Italy, which also opposed the appearance of the Serbs on the Adriatic. The Germans, after some hesitation, promised Austria support if it was attacked while defending its interests. Britain was sympathetic to the Austrian position and tried to work with Germany for an adjustment without jeopardizing relations to France and Russia. The crisis was most acute in late Nov. and early Dec., when both Austria and Russia began to mobilize. It was overcome when the Russians, unprepared for war, abandoned the Serb territorial claims.

Dec. 3. Armistice among the Ottoman Empire, Bulgaria, and Serbia. Greece did not join in it. Operations were to continue around **Scutari** (besieged by the Montenegrins), **Janina** (invested by the Greeks), and **Adrianople.**

Dec. 5. Last renewal of the Triple Alliance, for six years from July 1914. This reflected the closer relations between Italy and Austria and the friction between Italy and Britain and France, growing out of the occupation of the Dodecanese.

Dec. 17. Opening of the **London peace conference.** At the same time an ambassadorial conference at London discussed the status and boundaries of Albania, the fate of the Aegean Islands, and so on.

1913, Jan. 6. Breakdown of the London conference, because of the refusal of the Ottomans to give up Adrianople, the Aegean Islands, and Crete.

Feb. 3. Resumption of the war.

March 5. The Greeks took Janina.

March 26. The Bulgarians took Adrianople.

April 16. The Bulgarians and Ottomans concluded an armistice, which was accepted by other belligerents.

April 22. The **Montenegrins took Scutari** (p. 521), despite protests of the powers, who had assigned it to Albania.

May 3. Under threat of war from Austria, the **Montenegrins gave up Scutari,** and the **Serbs evacuated Durazzo** (May 5).

May 7. An ambassadorial conference at St. Petersburg awarded to **Romania the town of Silistria,** without the fortifications, as compensation for the gains of Bulgaria.

May 20. Reopening of the London peace conference. The victorious allies were obliged by an ultimatum from Grey to accept the settlement agreed to by the great powers.

May 30. TREATY OF LONDON, ending the First Balkan War. The Ottomans ceded all territory west of a line between Enos and Midia and abandoned all claim to **Crete;** the status of **Albania** and of the **Aegean Islands** was left to the decision of the powers.

June 1. Treaty of alliance between Serbia and Greece against Bulgaria. This was the result of Serbia's failure to make good its claims on the Adriatic and the unwillingness of Bulgaria to grant Serbia more of Macedonia than had been envisaged in the treaty of March 13, 1912. The Bulgarians were willing to leave the matter to the arbitration of the tsar, which the Serbs tried to evade.

June 29–July 30. SECOND BALKAN WAR. The Bulgarian commander, Gen. Michael Savov, ordered an attack on the Serbian-Greek positions without informing the prime minister, Stojan Danev, who was just leaving for St. Petersburg. The government disavowed the action, but the Serbs and Greeks took advantage of the situation to carry out the attack they had long planned. Romania and the Ottomans entered the war against Bulgaria, which was rapidly defeated.

Aug. 10. TREATY OF BUCHAREST. The Romanians were given the northern **Dobrudja,** from Turtukaia on the Danube to Ekrene on the Black Sea; the Serbs and Greeks retained those parts of **Macedonia** they had occupied (p. 522). Bulgaria retained only a small part of Macedonia, having lost **Monastir** and **Ochrid** to Serbia and **Saloniki** and **Kavalla** to Greece. On the Aegean seaboard the Bulgarians kept only the stretch between the Mesta and Maritza Rivers, with the second-rate port of **Dedeagatch.**

Sept. 23. Invasion of Albania by the Serbs, following Albanian raids into areas assigned to Serbia by the treaty of London.

Sept. 29. TREATY OF CONSTANTINOPLE between Bulgaria and the Ottomans; the Ottomans recovered **Adrianople** and the line of the **Maritza River.**

Oct. 18. Austria demanded **Serbia** evacuate Albania within eight days. Serbia yielded.

Oct. 30. Austro-Italian note to Greece, demanding the evacuation of southern Albania by Dec. 31.

1914, June 15. An **Anglo-German agreement** was initialed. This settled the **Baghdad Railway** problem, the Germans promising not to construct the line south of Baghdad and recognizing Britain's preponderant interests in the shipping on the Euphrates. The agreement reflected a real desire on both sides to remove many outstanding colonial difficulties.

June 28. ASSASSINATION OF THE ARCHDUKE FRANCIS FERDINAND at Sarajevo. The assassin was **Gavrilo Princip.** He and other young Bosnian revolutionaries acted as agents of the Serbian society **Union or Death** (The Black Hand), a terrorist organization founded in 1911 for agitation against Austria on behalf of Serbian aspirations. The Serbian government was cognizant of the plot, but did little to prevent its consummation or to warn the Austrian government. The Vienna government, though convinced of the complicity of Serbia, was intent on making a tight case and sent a legal expert to Sarajevo to collect evidence.

July 5. Mission of Count Alexander Hoyos to Berlin. He took the memorandum of June 24 on the Balkan situation, to which had been added some remarks on the need for settling, once and for all, the intolerable activity of the Serbs. Both the emperor and Bethmann recognized the justice of the Austrian stand, promised support (the Blank Check) and urged that steps be taken while world opinion was favorable. The Germans evidently regarded a localized settlement as possible, and believed the Russians too unprepared to take an extreme stand.

July 7. Austrian crown council. Most of the members favored war against Serbia, but this course was opposed by the Hungarian premier, **Count Stefan Tisza,** who insisted on diplomatic action to avoid larger European complications.

July 13. Baron Friedrich von Wiesner, sent to collect evidence, reported that he had been unable to find conclusive evidence of Serbian complicity, though the part played by members of the Black Hand was clear.

July 14. Austrian crown council. Tisza was won over to a policy of warlike action, on condition that no Serbian territory should be annexed by Austria.

July 20–23. Visit of President Poincaré and Premier René Viviani of France to St. Petersburg. Agreement to invite Britain to join with France and Russia in pressure on Vienna, though the Austrian demands on Serbia were not yet known, except in a vague way. The French apparently disregarded the merits of the case and took the whole matter as a test of the solidarity of the entente in face of action by the Triple Alliance.

July 23. Austrian ultimatum to Belgrade (48 hours). This had been ready on July 20, but had been held back until Poincaré should have left St. Petersburg. It demanded suppression of publications hostile to Austria; dissolution of patriotic organizations engaged in anti-Austrian propaganda; cessation of propaganda in the schools; dismissal of officials accused by Austria of propaganda; collaboration of Austrian with Serbian officials in the inquiry regarding responsibility for the assassination; judicial proceedings against those accessory to the plot; arrest of two Serbian officials known to be involved; explanations and apologies.

July 24. First formulation of **Russian policy:** Serbia must not be attacked and devoured by Austria.

July 25. Austrian assurances to Russia that no Serbian territory would be annexed. A Russian crown council decided on first military measures against Austria, to be followed by war if Serbia was attacked. **French assurances of support** were given to Russia.

The **Serbian reply** to the Austrian ultimatum, generally favorable at first sight, was actually evasive. The crucial point VI was rejected. The Serbian reply may have been due to reports from St. Petersburg of Russia's decision to support Serbia. On reception of the Serb reply, the Austrian minister at once left Belgrade. Serbia had ordered mobilization against Austria even before making the reply. Austria at once mobilized against Serbia.

July 26. Grey proposed a conference to deal with the Austro-Serb issue. France accepted; Austria refused to submit a question of national honor to the decision of others; Germany also refused an international discussion of the Austrian claims, though ready for a conference to deal with the Austro-Russian tension; Russia accepted the Grey proposal in principle, though preferring direct conversations with Vienna, which had been initiated.

July 27. First French preparatory measures. The **British fleet was ordered not to disband** after maneuvers. Grey promised Russia diplomatic support and did nothing to hold Russia back from further steps.

July 28. AUSTRIA DECLARED WAR ON SERBIA. Belgrade was bombarded the next day, though Austria was not ready for real operations until about Aug. 12. The declaration of war was meant to create a fait accompli. Rupture of the Austro-Russian pourparlers. Germany urged the **occupation of Belgrade** as a pawn, to be followed by negotiations with Russia regarding the Serbian reply. This course was also favored by Grey, but was ignored by Berchtold. France renewed assurances of support to Russia.

July 29. Bethmann, resisting pressure from Gen. Helmuth von Moltke, chief of staff, urged the resumption of Austro-Russian negotiations and began to bring **pressure on Vienna.** At the same time he made a bid for **British neutrality:** Germany was ready to promise not to take French territory in Europe, or Belgian territory, if Britain promised neutrality. This was rejected.

The **Russian tsar** yielded to pressure from Sazonov and the military men and agreed to **general mobilization.** The order was recalled, and mobilization against Austria alone decided on when the tsar received a telegram from Berlin telling of Emperor William's efforts to bring the Austrians into line.

July 30. Austro-Russian conversations resumed. Due to technical difficulties the Russian government reversed its action of July 29 and decided for **general mobilization,** despite numerous German warnings.

July 31. Germany proclaimed "**state of threatening danger of war**" and sent a **12-hour ultimatum to Russia,** demanding cessation of preparations on the German frontier.

German inquiry in Paris as to what attitude France would take in a Russian-German conflict.

Germany refused a British request that the neutrality of Belgium be respected.

5:00 P.M. Austria decreed general mobilization.

Aug. 1. French reply to Germany: France would be guided by her own interests.

3:55 P.M. French mobilization.

4:00 P.M. German mobilization. Germany offered Britain a promise not to attack France if Britain would guarantee French neutrality.

7:00 P.M. GERMAN DECLARATION OF WAR ON RUSSIA, no reply having been received to the German ultimatum.

Aug. 2. The **British cabinet,** after many meetings and much disagreement regarding support of France, **voted to give France assurances** to protect the coast against German attack (the "moral obligation" arising from previous naval arrangements).

The **Germans began the invasion of Luxembourg** and submitted to Belgium a demand for permission to cross Belgian territory, in return for a promise to uphold Belgian integrity. This was rejected.

Aug. 3. GERMANY DECLARED WAR ON FRANCE, on the flimsy pretext of frontier violations. In reality the German action was due to military considerations and to the conviction that France would come to Russia's support in any case.

Beginning of the invasion of Belgium.

Aug. 4. BRITAIN DECLARED WAR ON GERMANY, the invasion of Belgium giving Grey a welcome argument in the cabinet and in Parliament.

Aug. 6. AUSTRIA DECLARED WAR ON RUSSIA. WORLD WAR I.

(To p. 650)

7. WESTERN AND CENTRAL EUROPE, 1848–1914

a. SOCIAL, CULTURAL, AND ECONOMIC TRENDS

1. ECONOMIC AND SOCIAL CHANGES
(From p. 441)

THE CONTINUED IMPACT OF INDUSTRIALIZATION. As the problems of industrialization grew, Europe witnessed a concerted effort at **state building.** In nations like Germany, state building meant actual unification and the attempt at centralization in order to enhance economic productivity. In Britain, however, state building was geared more toward solving the social problems resulting from industrialization and urbanization. In all cases, governments became more involved in the daily lives of their citizens through obligatory primary education, military conscription, broad taxation, and social legislation. The result was an increase in state power (despite varying forms of government) and the further erosion of traditional ties to locality and region.

The mid-19th century also witnessed the **rise of consumerism.** Besides being emotional centers, families became centers of consumption. Furthermore, as industry began to look for wider markets, advertising developed. Industry no longer simply catered to a demand, it helped create that demand. This was most visible in the development of **department stores** designed to promote consumption. From the 1870s onward the rise of **kleptomania** reflected the growing psycho-

logical importance of consumerism. Society became more involved in the purchasing of goods than in the actual manufacturing of them.

With the increase in state administrations and the development of a service sector, the European social structure grew to include new **white collar workers.** These workers held an ambiguous position in society; they balked at inclusion with the working classes and had educations that made them similar to the middle classes, yet they could not easily afford the lifestyle of the middle classes. In politics, as part of the **lower middle class,** they frequently played the role of wild card, opting for socialism in some instances, liberalism in others, and nationalism in still other cases. As such, they increased the ambiguities of class conflict.

The latter half of the 19th century also witnessed slower population increases than those of the beginning of the century. In France, where birthrates had begun to fall in the 18th century, depopulation was a major concern, especially after France's defeat in the Franco-Prussian War. By 1870, partly due to the increased availability of **birth control devices** (condoms, diaphragms), birthrates began to drop more widely in Europe among the working classes, as they had earlier among the middle classes. This, along with fewer restrictions on marriage, also contributed to a drop in the rate of illegitimacy, which had exploded between 1750 and 1850.

Emigration continued to reflect population growth, but now it issued more from southern and eastern Europe than from western Europe. The slowing of population growth and the radical decline in

Population of Europe, in Thousands, 1850–1910

	1850	1865	1880	1910
United Kingdom	27,201	29,925	34,623	44,915
France	35,630	38,020	37,450	39,528
Spain	—	15,920	16,859	19,540
Portugal	—	—	4,551	5,958
Italy	—	24,950	28,211	34,377
Belgium	4,426	4,984	5,520	7,422
Netherlands	3,001	3,510	4,049	5,904
Norway	1,392	1,690	1,909	2,353
Sweden	3,462	4,092	4,572	5,499
Denmark	1,422	1,694	1,969	2,702
Germany (boundaries of 1871)	35,310	39,545	45,093	64,568
Austria	17,629	19,650	22,075	28,427
Hungary	—	—	15,697	20,793
Switzerland	—	2,630	2,839	3,735
Russia in Europe (without Finland)	60,000	74,800	85,200	142,500
Finland	1,629	1,835	2,047	3,093
Bulgaria	—	—	2,008	4,317
Romania	—	4,133	4,546	6,966
Serbia	—	1,186	1,724	2,916
Greece	—	1,395	1,702	2,600

birthrates was matched, from 1880 onward, with a **rapid decline of infant mortality.** This **DEMOGRAPHIC TRANSITION** produced the modern demographic regime, with **low birth and child death rates, larger families among the poor than among the middle classes, and a pronounced growth of the percentage of the elderly in the population as a whole.**

Victorian attitudes toward sexuality loosened gradually from the 1870s onward. Sexual respectability was still vitally important for middle-class women, but some men became more open in their **use of prostitutes** and **indulgence of the sexual double standard.** Quietly, many middle-class married couples increased their **use of artificial birth control devices and accepted sexuality as pleasure,** not merely the basis for procreation. At the same time **definitions of homosexuality** became more rigorous from the 1870s onward. Medical and legal writings called new attention to homosexuality as a problem, prompting an unusual belief that people were either homosexual or "normal," with no intermediate behavior; many homosexuals came to share this belief, which heightened their group identity. Famous trials and imprisonments, like those of the Irish writer Oscar Wilde between 1895 and 1898, reflected and furthered anxieties, particularly about male homosexuality.

Finally, by the end of the century, western Europe had become firmly industrial. Only southern and parts of eastern Europe lagged behind. **Urbanization** proceeded at an amazing pace; Paris's population increased from 2 million to 3 million between 1850 and 1914. For Berlin, the increase was from half a million to 2 million in a similar time period. Also, conditions began slowly to improve in the cities. Various reforms reduced the unsanitary conditions.

THE SECOND INDUSTRIAL REVOLUTION. More than the first, this new spurt of industrialization, falling roughly into two periods (1850–70 and 1890–1914), centered on new technology. No longer content to rely on the tinkerings of inventors, industry began hiring engineers and chemists. Scientific research was applied to production, transportation, and communication. Technological advances (p. 443) included **new forms of energy (the internal combustion engine, the development of the electrical industry)** and the creation of the chemical and petrochemical industries (the invention of synthetic dyes and chemical fertilizers).

One of the results of the second industrial revolution was the accelerated decline of artisans and the increase in the number of semi-skilled factory workers. The latter became the majority of the working classes. Additionally, as machines made even more inroads into production, **women and children lost their places in the factories.** This, more than middle-class reforms, explains the increasing disappearance of women and children in industry.

With the **depressions of 1873 and the 1890s,** European industry also sought new ways to survive economic cycles of boom and bust. The depressions differed from previous cycles: they resulted from **speculative investment** and **overproduction** rather than harvest failures. The second industrial revolution thus saw the creation of **big business** (like the Krupps works in Germany). Using the techniques of vertical organization and horizontal integration, European industrialists formed **cartels** designed to control pricing and production. Industrialists also attempted new methods of **scientific management,** designed to streamline the production process and maximize profits. Boards of directors and professional managers and financiers replaced factory owners. In many nations this contributed to the development of a **new upper class,** consisting of industrialists, financiers, and aristocrats.

Besides cartels, industrialists tried to protect themselves by turning away from laissez-faire economics. They supported **government regulation** as a means of protecting industry. Thus, they sought government aid in the forms of tariffs, labor controls, and imperialism (which secured raw materials and new markets).

Government regulation did not always work in their favor, however. As suffrage was extended to include workers, governments became more responsive to their concerns. This was especially true with the advent of large **industrial unions** and the rise of **socialist parties.** Whereas early unions were organized around crafts and controlled by artisans, the persistent decline of artisans and the rise of big industrial complexes convinced working-class activists that only unions organized to include all the workers in one industry could counter the power of the industrialists. Such unions gradually acquired official recognition and had won important victories by the 1890s.

Feeling endangered by working-class radicalism, the middle classes, which had slowly acquired more power as the century wore on, began to address what they labeled **the social question** in earnest after 1870. Some of this concern was also generated by real fears of national degeneration; many English men and boys were rejected for service in the Boer War, for example, because **malnutrition** had caused them to be physically unfit for military service. The result was a series of **social insurance laws,** although not all of Europe embraced this solution.

By 1914, then, Europe was an industrial society wherein big businessmen shared power with the aristocracy in a **new upper class,** while the working classes, having become more militant, were still viewed as a very real threat to the existing social order. The question remained of how to integrate workers in a manner that did not significantly alter middle-class comforts.

(To p. 672)

2. INTELLECTUAL AND RELIGIOUS TRENDS
(From p. 443)

Europe in the late 19th century remained firmly devoted to science; the economy came to rely on the alliance of science and business, and many believed that life would continue to improve thanks to the marvels of modern science. Such views may not have been ill founded. Building on the work of scientists such as **Louis Pasteur** (1822–95), researchers had made great strides by the end of the century against deadly diseases such as typhoid, tuberculosis, cholera, tetanus, and diphtheria.

Yet it was also a time when social, political, and religious thought faced difficult challenges from new theories and discoveries. The most important challenge to preexisting belief came in the form of **Charles Darwin's** (1809–82) **theory of evolution** (based on his book *Origin of Species,* 1859). Darwin argued that the species of the world, including human beings, have evolved over millennia. This represented a strong challenge to religious views of God's creation of the world, contributing to the **secularization** of life in western Europe. Gaining wide acceptance, Darwin's theories were incorporated in other, less scientific, arenas. Many used the concept of **social Darwinism** to justify nationalist animosities and Western imperialism.

Whereas Darwinism contributed to a middle-class view of the 19th century as one of progress amid struggle, **Karl Marx's** (1818–83) and **Friedrich Engels's** (1820–95) use of the scientific method represented a threat to all that the middle class valued. With the publication of the *Communist Manifesto* (1848) and *Capital* (three volumes: 1867, 1885,

1895), Marx established a brand of socialism based on an understanding of history and **class struggle.** He envisioned a world after the social revolution wherein both the state and the social classes would disappear, a view that became central to the socialist parties developing all across Europe. Many experienced battles between "orthodox" Marxists, who wanted only to work toward revolution, and "revisionists," who argued that parties and unions should also work for concrete reforms.

Like Marxism, **anarchism** attacked capitalism and the society it fostered. Anarchists disagreed, however, on the means of attaining a stateless society. Many anarchists were also wary of what Marxists would do after the revolution. Anarchists like **Mikhail Bakunin** (1814–76) favored violent revolt, whereas others like **Georges Sorel** (1847–1922) supported the refusal to cooperate with the state (**general strike**) as a means of causing its downfall. At the end of the century, anarchists were responsible for a number of assassinations and bombings from Paris to Moscow, which caused great concern among European leaders, but overall they were too disorganized to launch a comprehensive revolution.

To meet new challenges, late-19th-century liberals moved to embrace more and more people, gradually extending suffrage to all men. Yet governments faced a new challenge with the rise of **feminism.** Using their accepted positions as moral guardians, women began to move more freely in the public world. It was not long before they called for the right to vote as a means of furthering that role. Only a few women linked their demand for the right to vote to their position as men's equals. Feminists met with little success before World War I, however. Although they were successful in acquiring more rights (English women won the right to own property in 1882, for example), only certain Scandinavian women voted before 1914.

The end of the 19th century (1880–1914) witnessed more profound challenges to accepted notions of progress and science. Philosophers and authors like **Friedrich Nietzsche** (1844–1900), **Fyodor Dostoyevski** (1821–81), and **Henri Bergson** (1859–1941) all questioned the rationality of humankind. Instead of reason, these authors stressed animal instincts as the primary fact of human existence. They were joined by the father of psychology, **Sigmund Freud** (1856–1939). Meanwhile, sociologists **Émile Durkheim** (1858–1917) and **Max Weber** (1864–1920) questioned the benefits of modern society, arguing that the destruction of traditional, agrarian life left society groundless; individuals lost a purpose for living.

Europe on the verge of war in 1914 was thus divided between large segments of the middle class that viewed the development of 19th-century Europe with a sense of smug contentment, the product of evolution, and a growing number of intellectuals who sensed that Europe was about to embark upon a time of turmoil, where many cherished beliefs would provide little comfort.

Some of the important publications and movements that marked the development of philosophical, religious, and social thought from 1848 to 1914 included:

1848. John Stuart Mill's (1806–73) *Principles of Political Economy* was the most logical and persuasive exposition of classical economics, with some concessions to state intervention where private initiative could not work.

1848. Karl Marx (1818–83) and **Friedrich Engels** (1820–95) issued the *Communist Manifesto,* a fiery appeal to the workers of all countries to unite in the struggle against capitalist exploitation; it was a succinct presentation of "scientific" as contrasted with "utopian" socialism.

1851. Herbert Spencer's (1820–1903) *Social Statics,* the first work of the author of *Synthetic Philosophy* (*First Principles,* 1862), was an attempt to organize the corpus of human knowledge and to establish the laws of social evolution.

1851. The *Ensayo sobre el Catolicismo, el Liberalismo y el Socialismo* was published by **Juan Donoso Cortés** (1809–53), the Spanish statesman who clearly reflected the fears inspired by the revolutions of 1848 and the ensuing disillusionment with liberalism and radicalism.

1853–55. Count Joseph de Gobineau's (1816–82) *Essai sur l'inégalité des races humaines* formed the basis for much later writing on racial superiority.

1855. *Kraft und Stoff* by **Ludwig Büchner** (1824–99) was a classic of modern materialism.

1857. Publication of the first volume of **Henry T. Buckle's** (1821–62) *History of Civilisation in England,* a valiant attempt to approach history scientifically.

1860. *Die Kultur der Renaissance in Italien,* by the Swiss historian **Jakob Burckhardt** (1818–97), was a masterpiece of cultural history and a brilliant essay in interpretation. Likewise Burckhardt's posthumous *Weltgeschichtliche Betrachtungen* (1898) was a highly provocative critique of the materialistic, democratic culture in which he lived.

1861. Johann J. Bachofen's (1815–87) study *Das Mutterrecht* explored the matriarchal institutions of primitive man and greatly stimulated anthropological investigations.

1863. Ernest Renan's (1823–92) *Vie de Jésus* was the first of a series of studies of the origins of Christianity. Translated into all European languages, it was a classic of urbane skepticism and rationalism. In his *Réforme intellectuelle et morale* (1871) he questioned the democratic system and envisaged government by an intellectual elite.

1864. The foundation of the **First International Workingmen's Association** by Karl Marx, with headquarters first in London, then in New York. Designed to unite the workers of all countries in support of Marxist socialism, it was eventually wrecked (1876) by the conflict between Marx and Bakunin, who advocated "direct action" to hasten the advent of anarchy. After Bakunin's death, anarchist doctrine was further elaborated by **Prince Peter Kropotkin** (1842–1921) and in the later 19th century gained many adherents, especially in the Latin countries, where a series of assassinations and other attacks were committed in the 1880s and 1890s.

1867, 1885, 1895. *Das Kapital* (three volumes) by Karl Marx, was an elaborate analysis of economic and social history and at the same time the basic exposition of "scientific" socialism.

1879. Wilhelm Wundt (1832–1920) established the first psychological laboratory. **Ivan Petrovich Pavlov** (1849–1936) discovered the "conditioned reflex" and induced "experimental neurosis" in dogs.

1883–88. Provocative and highly original works of cultural criticism were written by **Friedrich von Nietzsche** (1844–1900): *Also sprach Zarathustra* (1883); *Jenseits von Gut und Böse* (1886); *Zur Genealogie der Moral* (1887); *Der Wille zur Macht* (1888). Nietzsche denounced the morality of slaves and called for the utmost development of the individual, even at the cost of much suffering and sacrifice. His doctrine of the "superman" exerted tremendous influence in the early 20th century.

1886–90. The *Lehrbuch der Dogmengeschichte* of **Adolf von Harnack** (1851–1930) was the most outstanding of that scholar's many studies of Christian dogma and of the influence of Greek thought and religion on the development of Christianity.

1889–1914. The **Second International Workingmen's Association** held periodic meetings of representatives of the various national social democratic parties. It never had any central authority and at all times suffered from divergence of interest among its constituents. It was finally discredited by the patriotic participation of the socialist parties in World War I.

1890. Gabriel Tarde (1843–1904) published his *Les lois de l'imitation,* a pioneer work in the field of social psychology. At the same time **Pierre Janet** (1859–1949) carried on studies of hypnosis and hysteria. In 1895 **Gustave Le Bon** (1841–1931) published his *Psychologie des foules.*

1890. William James (1842–1910), the American psychologist, published his *Principles of Psychology,* to be followed by *The Will to Believe* (1897), *The Varieties of Religious Experience* (1902), and *Pragmatism* (1907). James's "pragmatism" viewed thinking and knowledge as aspects of the struggle to live. This school of thought went back to the American logician **Charles Sanders Peirce** (1839–1914) and was espoused also by **John Dewey** (1859–1952) in *How We Think* (1909) and *Democracy and Education* (1916). In Europe the related "logical empiricists" included **Pierre Duhem** (1861–1916), **Ernst Mach** (1838–1916), and **Henri Poincaré** (1854–1912).

1897–1922. The philosophical writings of **Henri Bergson** (1859–1941) stressed intuition and irrational forces: *Matière et mémoire* (1897); *Évolution créatrice* (1906); *Durée et simultanéité* (1922).

1899. The revisionist or reformist current in social democracy was established by **Eduard Bernstein** (1850–1932) in his *Die Voraussetzungen des Sozialismus und die Aufgaben der Sozialdemokratie,* in which he queried Marx's predictions and advocated evolutionary, as distinguished from revolutionary, socialism.

1900. *Traumdeutung*, by **Sigmund Freud** (1856–1939), marked the beginning of the theory of **psychoanalysis.** His other important works include *Über Psychoanalyse* (1910), *Vorlesungen zur Einführung in die Psychoanalyse* (1917), *Das Ich und das Es* (1923), *Die Zukunft einer Illusion* (1927), *Das Unbehagen in der Kultur* (1930), *Neue Folge der Vorlesungen* (1932). Among Freud's early adherents were **Alfred Adler** (1870–1937) and **Carl G. Jung** (1875–1964), both of whom broke away and established schools of their own.

1902. John A. Hobson (1858–1940) published *Imperialism: A Study*, undoubtedly the most comprehensive critique of economic imperialism. Through the German theorists **Rosa Luxemburg** and **Rudolf Hilferding** his arguments found their way into Lenin's famous pamphlet: *Imperialism, the Highest Stage of Capitalism* (1916), which constitutes the official communist view.

1904–5. Max Weber (1864–1920), the eminent German economist-sociologist, published *Die protestantische Ethik und der Geist des Kapitalismus*, in which he concluded that the teachings of Luther and Calvin were among the mainsprings of the capitalist spirit. This thesis was further developed by **Richard H. Tawney** (1880–1962) in *Religion and the Rise of Capitalism* (1926).

1908. Georges Sorel's (1847–1922) *Réflexions sur la violence* supplied a theoretical background for the syndicalist movement, an outgrowth of anarchism that aimed at destruction of the state through a general strike engineered by trade unions.

1912. Gestalt psychology was expounded by **Max Wertheimer** (1880–1943) and developed further by **Kurt Koffka** (1886–1941) and **Wolfgang Köhler** (1887–1967).   *(To p. 673)*

3. CULTURE AND POPULAR CULTURE
(From p. 443)

Corresponding to the increasing value placed on science, art, and literature after 1848, metaphysics was rejected as a means for the detailed examination of everyday life. Romanticism declined as a formal movement. **Realists** like **Charles Dickens** (1812–70), **Gustave Flaubert** (1821–80), and **Gustave Courbet** (1819–77) sought to depict the actual world. **Émile Zola** (1840–1902), **Henrik Ibsen** (1828–1906), and other **naturalists** went a step further, hoping to demonstrate a causal relationship between human character and social environment.

Whereas realism and naturalism reflected the attention placed on the external world by most observers during the middle of the 19th century, the development of **modernism** in the late 19th century reflected an intense introspection. Writers like **Thomas Mann** (1875–1955), **Marcel Proust** (1871–1922), and **Franz Kafka** (1883–1924) probed beneath the surface to uncover a profound reality in the human psyche. In music, modernism was reflected in the dissonance of **Igor Stravinsky** (1882–1971) and **Arnold Schoenberg** (1885–1935).

Modern art also revealed a challenge to existing cultural styles and a search for new forms of expression. The first challenge came in the 1860s and 1870s with the growth of **impressionism.** The followers of **Edouard Manet** (1832–83), **Claude Monet** (1840–1926), and **Pierre-Auguste Renoir** (1841–1919) took the observation of nature a step further by attempting to capture a single moment as the eye perceived it. **Post-impressionists** like **Paul Cézanne** (1839–1906), **Paul Gauguin** (1848–1903), and **Vincent van Gogh** (1853–90); **expressionists** like **Ernst Ludwig Kirchner** (1880–1938) and **Edvard Munch** (1863–1944); and French **fauvists** like **Henri Matisse** (1869–1954) moved farther away from convention by experimenting with space and color to produce an emotional experience dependent on personal impression, not photographic replication. Finally, **Pablo Picasso** (1881–1973) and **Georges Braque** (1882–1963) contributed to a new school, known as **cubism,** between 1909 and 1914. Cubists sought a deeper reality than what the eye first sees by using perspective to capture the experience of seeing in a space of time. By moving away from empiricism, all of these artists represented the growing power and appeal of the nonrational in European thought.

Architecture differed somewhat. Imitations of Gothic, classical, and Byzantine styles continued as European cities expanded. New materials (steel beams, concrete) permitted functional innovations, though

none went as far as the **skyscraper,** developed in the United States. **Antonio Gaudí** (1856–1926) in Barcelona launched the imaginative **modernista** movement with his first building (1886), which linked more directly with other aspects of modern art.

Artistic pessimism departed from the dominant trends in popular culture, where the benefits of industrial life were just starting to be experienced. The belief that this was an age of **progress** was prevalent; people began to view change as a positive, normal occurrence. This belief derived from a faith in science, and, when combined with the popularization of Darwinism, contributed to the growing **secularization** of life in the latter half of the 19th century.

Religious practice declined in western and central Europe, though unevenly. While missionary activity abroad increased, religious leaders retreated still further from mainstream intellectual life. Conflicts with Darwinism, particularly in some Protestant sects, and with socialism weakened organized religion in some quarters.

Consumerism affected not only the middle classes but also the working classes. This was reflected in the growth of new forms of leisure, especially **sports and music halls;** by 1900 there were 50 music halls in London alone. As literacy increased because of public schools, readership also expanded. This resulted in the growth of cheap **newspapers** like London's *Daily Mail*, which, aimed especially for the newly educated masses, sold for only half a penny when it began distribution in 1896. Western Europe after 1870 saw the **birth of modern leisure,** with **commercialized mass outlets, professional athletes and performers,** and **widespread spectatorship.**

Despite such developments, including some improvements in living conditions, life for the working classes remained difficult. Even in industries regulated by the state, the workweek could be as long as 55 hours. States attempted to curb discontent not only through reform, but also through **nationalism and imperialism.** They hoped to attract workers away from unions and socialists by instilling in them an excitement at being part of a growing nation.   *(To p. 674)*

4. SCIENCE AND LEARNING
(From p. 445)

Scientific inquiry underwent great changes by the end of the 19th century. With the discoveries of **Max Planck** (1858–1947) and **Albert Einstein** (1879–1955), the older Newtonian view of the knowable universe was shaken by the new concept of randomness. Physicists demonstrated that in the small-scale world of the electron, scientists can only theorize about probabilities, not facts. Like modern art and Freud's theories of human nature, modern physics introduced feelings of uncertainty, probability, and mystery into a world early-19th-century Europeans felt confident they could conquer.

The major benchmarks in scientific inquiry included:

a. Mathematics, Physics, and Astronomy

1848. William Thomson (Lord Kelvin) (1824–1907) established the absolute thermodynamic scale of temperature, which is named after him.

1849. Armand Fizeau (1819–96) for the first time successfully measured the **speed of light** by observations that did not involve astronomical constants.

1849. Jean Bernard Foucault (1819–68) measured the speed of light accurately in media other than air, and thereby determined that the speed in air is greater than in water. Later, in a famous pendulum experiment, he demonstrated that the earth rotates (1851).

1850. William Cranch Bond (1789–1859), using the Harvard College Observatory's 15-inch refractor, took the first photograph of a star.

1850. Rudolph Clausius (1822–88) announced the **second law of thermodynamics:** heat cannot of itself pass from a colder to a warmer body. In *Über die bewegende Kraft der Wärme* (1865) he introduced the term *entropy*, stating that the entropy of the universe tends to increase.

1851. Bernhard Riemann (1826–66) introduced topological considerations into analysis.

1853. The first **International Statistical Congress** was held at Brussels, organized and inspired by **Adolphe Quetelet.**

1854. Riemann established the mathematical importance of non-Euclidean geometrics, discussing them in his general theory of manifolds. In the same year he gave the most comprehensive and general definition of the classical definite integral, since called the *Riemann integral.*

1854. George Boole (1815–64) published *The Laws of Thought,* an expansion of his 1847 work, *The Mathematical Analysis of Logic,* which marked the beginning of **symbolic logic,** that is, the attempt to express the laws of thought in algebraic symbols.

1856. Karl Weierstrass (1815–97) began to lecture at the University of Berlin. In these lectures, which spanned over 30 years, he gave the modern (delta-epsilon) definition of a limit, eliminated the remaining vagueness in the concepts of the calculus, introduced the notion of uniform convergence, and founded the theory of functions of a complex variable on power series.

1860–77. James Clerk Maxwell (1831–79) and **Ludwig Boltzmann** (1844–1906) developed statistical mechanics, a theory of the behavior of a gas considered as a collection of large numbers of molecules obeying the laws of classical mechanics.

1868. William Huggins (1824–1910), noting a slight shift toward the red in the spectrum of Sirius, calculated the radial velocity of a star for the first time.

1870–83. Georg Cantor (1845–1918) published his major works, founding the **theory of sets** (1870) and the **theory of transfinite numbers** (1883).

1872–82. Richard Dedekind (1831–1916) gave arithmetic definitions of irrational numbers (the *Dedekind cut*), constituting the first rigorous theory of irrationals.

1873. Johannes van der Waals (1837–1923) found an equation of state for imperfect gases.

1873. Maxwell published his *Treatise on Electricity and Magnetism,* in which he described the properties of the electromagnetic field in a series of equations *(Maxwell equations)* that entailed the electromagnetic theory of light.

1877. Giovanni Schiaparelli (1835–1910) observed long, straight, narrow, intersecting, dark lines on Mars, which he called *canali.*

1877–93. Francis Galton (1822–1911) and **Karl Pearson** (1857–1936) developed the major statistical tools of present-day social science, for example, regression (Galton, 1877), correlation coefficients (Galton, 1888), and moments and standard deviation (Pearson, 1893).

1878. William Crookes (1832–1919) showed that cathode rays proceed in straight lines, are capable of turning a small wheel, can be deflected by a magnet, can excite fluorescence in certain substances, and can heat and sometimes even melt some metals.

1884. Gottlob Frege (1848–1925) published *Grundlagen der Arithmetik,* in which arithmetical concepts were defined in logical terms.

1887. Heinrich Hertz (1857–94) demonstrated the existence of electromagnetic waves in the space about a discharging Leyden jar, and found that electromagnetic waves were propagated with the velocity of light as Maxwell had predicted (1873). Hertz's work led to modern radio communications.

1887. Albert Michelson (1852–1931) and **Edward Morley** (1838–1923) announced that they were unable to detect any effect of the earth's motion through the ether in experiments with an extremely sensitive interferometer.

1895. Wilhelm K. Röntgen (1845–1923) announced the discovery of x-rays in *Eine neue Art von Strahlen.*

1895. John W. Strutt (Lord Rayleigh) (1842–1919) and **William Ramsay** (1852–1916) discovered the "inert" or "noble" gas **argon.** Ramsay later discovered the other noble gases: helium, krypton, neon, xenon, and radon.

1895. Henri Poincaré (1854–1912) founded **algebraic topology.** He first applied topology to celestial mechanics (1892–99).

1896. Alfred B. Nobel (1833–96) endowed prizes for outstanding achievements in physics, chemistry, medicine, and physiology. The first prizes were awarded in 1901, to **Wilhelm K. Röntgen** in physics, **Jacobus H. van't Hoff** (1852–1911) in chemistry, and **Emil A. von Behring** (1854–1917) in medicine and physiology.

1896. Antoine H. Becquerel (1852–1908) discovered radioactivity in uranium compounds.

1897. Joseph John Thomson (1856–1940) announced the discovery of the **electron,** the first subatomic particle, and determined experimentally the ratio of its mass to its charge.

1900. Max Planck (1858–1947) stated that energy is not emitted continuously from radiating bodies, but in discrete parcels, or **quanta.**

1902–4. Henri Lebesgue (1875–1941) gave a theory of measure and the Lebesgue integral, extending the notions of integration and area to more general sets.

1904. Marie Sklodowska Curie (1867–1934) showed that pitchblende (uranium ore) contained two new radioactive elements: **radium** and **polonium.**

1904. Ernst Zermelo (1871–1953) published a proof that every set can be well ordered, which made possible the use of transfinite methods in mathematics.

1905. Albert Einstein (1879–1955) announced his **special theory of relativity,** which required a fundamental revision in the traditionally held Newtonian views of space and time, and introduced the celebrated equation $E = mc^2$.

1905. Einstein attributed to radiation itself a particle structure, and by supposing each particle of light **(photon)** to carry a quantum of energy, explained the photoelectric effect.

1910–13. Bertrand Russell (1872–1970) and **Alfred North Whitehead** (1861–1947) published *Principia Mathematica,* carrying out the reduction of arithmetic to symbolic logic. This work is the foundation of the calculus of propositions and modern symbolic logic.

1911. Robert A. Millikan (1868–1953) established that electric charge always consists of an integral multiple of a unit charge, which he determined with great accuracy in his oil-drop experiment.

1911. Ernest Rutherford (1871–1937) introduced the nuclear **model of the atom,** that is, a small positively charged nucleus containing most of the mass of the atom and surrounded by electrons.

1911–13. Ejnar Hertzsprung (1873–1967) studied double stars and their colors, especially in the Pleiades, and with **Henry Norris Russell** (1877–1957) devised the Hertzsprung-Russell Diagram, a graphic way of grouping stars by the relation between their absolute magnitudes and spectral types.

1912. Max von Laue (1879–1960) discovered **x-ray diffraction,** a powerful technique for directly observing the atomic structure of crystals.

1913. Niels Bohr (1885–1962) devised a new model of the atom by applying quantum theory to Rutherford's nuclear atom. Although this model violated classical electromagnetic theory, it successfully accounted for the spectrum of hydrogen.

b. Chemistry, Biology, and Geology

1848. Louis Pasteur (1822–95), in a series of brilliantly conceived and executed experiments, demonstrated the connection between the optical activity of organic molecules and crystalline structure, thus founding **stereochemistry.**

1848. Claude Bernard (1813–78) demonstrated the ability of the liver to store sugar in the form of glycogen. His widely read *Introduction à l'étude de la médecine expérimentale* (1865) influenced the literary world as well as scientists.

1852. Edward Frankland (1825–99) announced his **theory of valency,** that is, each atom has a certain "valency," or capacity for combining with a definite number of other atoms.

1856–64. Bernard evolved the concept of the *milieu intérieur,* envisioning that cells were autonomous physiological units, yet were dependent upon and protected by the internal environment of the whole organism.

1856–66. Hermann Helmholtz (1821–94) extended the doctrine of specific nerve energies developed by **Johannes Müller** to vision and hearing, indicating the penetration of physics and physiology into psychology.

1857–60. Louis Pasteur demonstrated that fermentation was a product of yeast cell activity. This challenged the view of Liebig that the ferment was merely an unstable chemical substance.

1858. Rudolph Virchow (1821–1902) in *Die Cellularpathologie* declared that disease reflects an impairment of cellular organization. Here, too, he stated his famous generalization *"omnis cellula e cellula"* (all cells arise from cells) and described the cell as the basic element of the life process.

1858. Friedrich A. Kekulé (1829–96) published *Über die Konstitution und die Metamorphosen der chemischen Verbindungen und über die chemische Natur des Kohlenstoffs,* in which he recognized that carbon is quadrivalent, and that carbon atoms link together to form long chains that serve as skeletons for organic molecules.

1858. Stanislao Cannizzaro (1826–1910) showed that one could unambiguously determine atomic weights. He was thus able to provide a table giving the correct molecular formulas of many compounds.

1859. Gustav R. Kirchhoff (1824–87) and **Robert W. Bunsen** (1811–99) began researches that made **spectrum analysis** a powerful method for the investigation of matter. They showed that a chemical element was clearly characterized by its spectrum, and by spectrum analysis they were able to discover previously unknown elements.

1859. Darwin amassed 25 years of careful research in *Origin of Species.* Inspired by the evidence in geology, paleontology, zoogeography, and domestic animal breeding, he declared that species evolved through variation and the natural selection of those individuals best suited to survive in given environmental conditions. A similar theory was developed independently by **Alfred R. Wallace** (1823–1913).

1860. Marcelin Berthelot (1827–1907) published *Chimie organique fondée sur la synthèse,* which showed that total synthesis of all classes of organic compounds from the elements carbon, hydrogen, oxygen, and nitrogen was possible.

1861. Alexander M. Butlerov (1828–86) introduced the term "chemical structure" at a chemical meeting in Germany. Butlerov shares credit with **Kekulé** for the development of the theory of the structure of organic compounds.

1861. Pasteur, in a classic paper "Mémoire sur les corpuscles organisés qui existent dans l'atmosphère," described a series of experiments that confuted the doctrine of the spontaneous generation of microorganisms.

1862–77. Pasteur investigated several types of microorganisms to advance the **germ theory of disease.** His evidence encouraged **Joseph Lister** (1827–1912) to initiate the practice of **antiseptic surgery** (1865).

1863. Ivan M. Sechenov (1829–1905) published *Reflexes of the Brain,* one of the earliest attempts to establish the physiological basis of psychic processes. His teaching and research were a decisive influence on the development of physiology in Russia.

1865. Gregor Mendel (1822–84), an Augustinian monk, described crossbreeding experiments with peas, which demonstrated the particulate nature of inheritance. He concluded that many traits were segregated into dominant and recessive alternatives and that combined traits assorted independently. Little attention was paid to his results until 1900, when cytological work suggested such unit characters existed.

1869. Dmitri I. Mendeleev (1834–1907), in *Principles of Chemistry,* devised his periodic table of the chemical elements, which arranged the elements in the order of increasing atomic weight, noted the periodic recurrence of similar properties in groups of elements, and successfully predicted the properties of elements yet to be discovered.

1872–76. HMS *Challenger* made an extended voyage of scientific investigation, led by **Wyville Thomson** (1830–82). The information gathered and reported largely by **John Murray** (1841–1914) gave much impetus to the science of **oceanography.**

1874. Jacobus van't Hoff (1852–1911) and **Achille LeBel** (1847–1930) independently interpreted the 1848 results of **Pasteur** and developed the stereochemistry of carbon.

1878. Josiah W. Gibbs (1839–1903), in his rigorously mathematical thermodynamic study, *Equilibrium of Heterogeneous Substances,* used the concept of chemical potential and introduced the phase rule.

1879. Ivan P. Pavlov (1849–1936) showed the production of gastric juices could be achieved without the introduction of food into the stomach. His work in the physiology of digestion led him to develop the concept of the acquired reflex, or *conditioned reflex.*

1880. John Milne (1850–1913) developed the first accurate **seismograph,** permitting the careful study of earthquakes and opening the way to new knowledge of the earth's interior.

1882. Robert Koch (1843–1910) described the etiology of the **tubercle bacillus.** This discovery led him (1884) to state *Koch's postulates,* a method of isolating microorganisms and proving that they are specific causes, not merely concomitants, of disease.

1883. Ilia I. Mechnikov (1845–1916) described the action of phagocytic cells in transparent starfish larvae. His discovery led to a general explanation of local inflammation.

1883. Edouard van Beneden (1845–1901) described how the chromosomes are derived in equal numbers from the conjugating germ cells. This led to the discovery of reduction division in the formation of the gametes.

1887. Svante A. Arrhenius (1859–1927) announced his theory of electrolytic dissociation, according to which most of the molecules of an electrolyte are immediately dissociated into two ions when dissolved.

1888–91. Wilhelm Roux (1850–1924) destroyed half of the two-cell stage of a frog's embryo (1888). The remaining cell developed into half an embryo. In 1891 **Hans Driesch** (1867–1941), working with sea urchin embryos, got results contradictory to Roux's. This drew attention to the relative roles of the internal and external environments on the development of cells.

1890. Emil von Behring (1854–1917) and **Shíbasaburo Kitasato** (1856–1931) demonstrated that the serum of immunized rabbits neutralized the toxin of tetanus. This discovery opened the possibility that disease could be prevented through the stimulation of specific antibody production.

1892. August Weismann (1834–1914) described in *Das Keimplasma* his theory of the continuity of the germ plasm and a scheme for the unfolding of a particulate hereditary pattern in embryogenesis.

1893. Theobald Smith (1859–1934), in "Investigations into the Nature, Causation and Prevention of Southern Cattle Fever," demonstrated that parasites could act as vectors of disease.

1895. Wilhelm K. Röntgen (1845–1923) discovered x-rays and immediately realized that his discovery had a practical application in medicine.

1897. Eduard Buchner (1860–1917) discovered that *zymase,* a cell-free yeast extract, caused fermentation, thus resolving a long-standing controversy over "vital" and "inorganic" ferments.

1900. Hugo de Vries (1848–1935), **Carl Correns** (1864–1933), and **Erich Tschermak** (1871–1962) independently rediscovered the 1865 work of **Gregor Mendel** while searching the literature to confirm their own experimental results.

1903. Walter S. Sutton (1876–1916) pointed out that the Mendelian ratios could be explained by the cytological behavior of the chromosomes.

1906. Charles Sherrington (1861–1952) described in *The Integrative Action of the Nervous System* the properties of the synapse and the complex integration of reflexes in behavior.

1907. Ross G. Harrison (1870–1959) announced a technique for culturing tissue cells outside of the body.

1909. Paul Ehrlich (1854–1915) showed that the synthetic compound *Salvarsan* was an effective treatment for syphilis. This discovery was a tremendous stimulus to the field of chemotherapy. In 1935 **Gerhard Domagk** (1895–1964) made the fundamental discovery that led to the introduction and widespread use of **sulfa drugs.**

1911. Thomas H. Morgan (1866–1945) claimed that certain traits were genetically linked on the chromosome, thus visualizing a linear arrangement of genes and stimulating the construction of genetic maps.

(To p. 648)

b. BRITAIN

Monarchs: Queen Victoria (r. 1837–1901), Edward VII (r. 1901–10), and George V (r. 1910–36).

Prime ministers: Lord John Russell (1846–52, Whig), Lord Derby (1852, Conservative-Peelite), Aberdeen coalition government (1852–55), Palmerston (1855–58), Derby-Disraeli coalition (1858–59), Palmerston until his death (1859–65), Lord Russell (1865–66), Derby (1866–68), Disraeli (1868), Gladstone (1868–74), Disraeli (1874–80), Gladstone (1880–85), Salisbury (1885–86), Gladstone (1886), Salisbury (1886–92), Gladstone (1892–94), Lord Rosebery (1894–95), and Conservatives, Lord Salisbury (1895–1902), Arthur J. Balfour (1902–5), Henry Campbell-Bannerman (1905–8, Liberal), and Herbert H. Asquith (1908–16, Liberal).

1. ENGLAND, SCOTLAND, AND WALES

Economics. British textile, coal, and iron industries continued to grow but not as rapidly as those of Germany and the U.S. Britain's role as the **leading industrial nation** became superseded by its role as **shipper and financier** in the latter part of the 19th century. Britain also allowed agriculture to decline rapidly, especially after the **Great Depression between 1873 and 1879,** in which agricultural prices plummeted under increasing competition from abroad and good harvests.

1848. The Public Health Act stipulated an annual death rate of 23 per

DESCENDANTS OF QUEEN VICTORIA

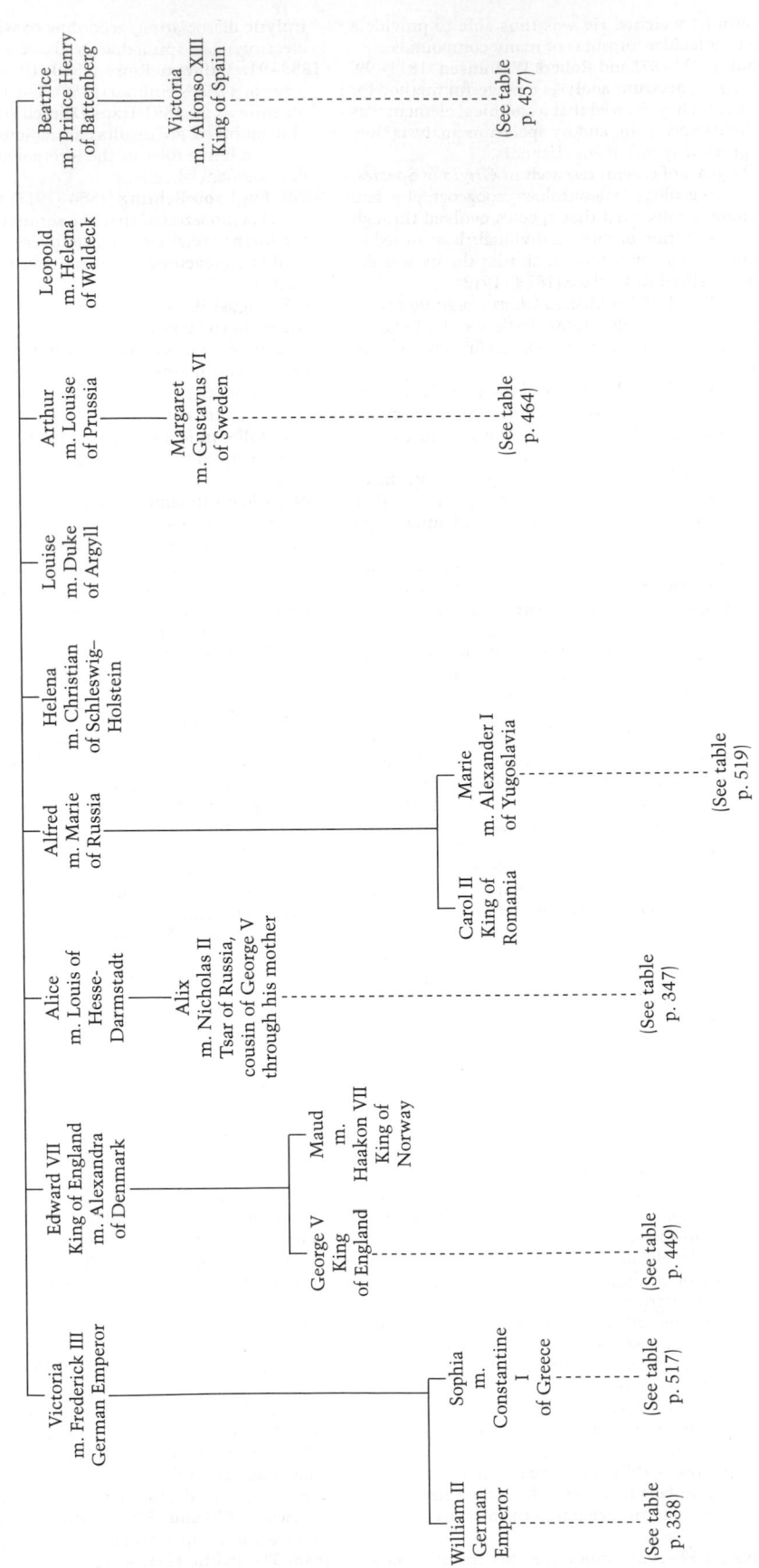

1,000 was unacceptable, but, despite improvements, Britain's death rate remained close to that figure in many cities.

1850. The Factory Act, along with another act in 1853, established a 64-hour workweek for all steam-powered factories and mandated that these factories close at 2:00 P.M. on Saturdays.

1850s. Henry Mayhew (1812–87), a journalist for *The Morning Chronicle,* wrote a series of articles entitled "Labour and the Poor" (1849–50), which appeared in the *Chronicle* and later under the title *London Labour and the London Poor.*

1851. The Great Exhibition in London. The exhibition displayed the most modern machinery and inventions in the glass and iron **Crystal Palace.** Conceived of by **Prince Albert and Henry Cole** (a civil servant), the exhibition spotlighted British superiority and ingenuity. The instigation of **shilling days** helped to calm middle-class fears about the participation of the working class, who, much to the former's surprise, behaved in an orderly fashion.

Formation of the Amalgamated Society of Engineers (ASE). The ASE is perhaps the earliest example of the **new model unionism** of the 1850s and 1860s. The new unions of skilled workers, including organizations for typographers, compositors, boilermakers, spinners, and weavers, were **well organized, national or amalgamated, and funded by dues collected and managed locally.** The unions practiced a policy of cautious bargaining and struck only as a last resort. Many workers began to accept **labor as a commodity,** exchanging less control over their skills in return for shorter hours and higher pay **(instrumentalism).**

1852. The ASE strike was followed by a **three-month lockout.** The engineers returned to work on the employers' terms but demonstrated both strength and persistence.

1853–54. Cholera epidemic in Britain. John Snow, a British doctor, demonstrated that the outbreak could be linked to the water supply.

1853. Vaccination of infants made compulsory. The law bolstered the 1840 Vaccination Act, and further acts in 1858, 1867, and 1871 stipulated various fines and terms of imprisonment for parents who failed to immunize their children.

1854–61. The temperance movement. An act of 1854 forbade the opening of public houses between 2:00 P.M. and 6:00 P.M. on Sundays except to travelers. An **act in 1864** closed the London public houses between 1:00 P.M. and 4:00 P.M. These acts indicated the growing strength of temperance organizations. In 1861, the **Temperance Lifeboat movement,** dedicated to saving people from the ruin of drunkenness, began in Staffordshire.

1855. The Nuisances Removal and Disease Prevention Act allowed local authorities to obtain court orders for the removal of public health dangers at the expense of the property owners involved, if those owners refused to cooperate.

1854–55. THE CRIMEAN WAR (p. 470) caused great hardship for British troops because of inadequate hospital care and lack of supplies due to poor preparation. **Florence Nightingale** and a group of other women became nurses at the front but were unable to make up for the poor planning on the part of the military. As a result, more men died of illness than died in battle.

1855. Civil service reform. The Civil Service Commission was established. In 1859, under the **Superannuation Act,** a certificate from the commission was required to receive a civil service pension.

1856. A banking crisis, caused by fraudulent practices and irresponsibility, led to two acts, in 1856 and 1862, which provided limited liability to banks that followed certain guidelines.

March. The Foreign Service Act forbade new enlistment in the military unless the soldier was willing to serve overseas.

1857. Divorce became possible for both men and women, and a divorce court was established. Adultery by the wife was sufficient grounds for divorce for men, but women could obtain a divorce only for adultery aggravated by cruelty or desertion on the part of their husbands.

1858. Police legislation extended police forces throughout England and Wales and into Scotland in 1869. The new borough and county police forces were continually improved although instances of inappropriate conduct and inadequacy received great attention from the press.

A medical act established guidelines for licensing of physicians and surgeons. It marked not only growing concern about the professionalization of medicine but also the development of numerous organizations to further professional standards.

Jews were given equal legal and political rights.

1858, Feb. 9. Palmerston introduced the Conspiracy to Murder Bill in response to Orsini's attempt to assassinate Louis-Napolean. The bill led to Palmerston's downfall. The short-lived **Derby government** that followed passed bills allowing the **admission of Jews to Parliament and abolishing the property qualifications for M.P.'s.** It also introduced the **Conservative Reform Bill (Feb. 28, 1859).** Despite this, the Derby government fell as the result of the May elections and was replaced by a **coalition of Liberals (Peelites, Irish nationalists, and Whigs) under Palmerston.**

Aug. 2. The India Act, enacted as a result of the Sepoy Mutiny, placed control of India in the hands of a minister directly responsible to Parliament rather than the East India Company (p. 555).

1859. Publication of Darwin's *Origin of Species.*

1860, Jan 23. The Cobden Treaty with France opened up the British market to free trade.

Feb. 10. Gladstone's financial proposals led to a struggle between the Commons and the Lords because they included a **decrease in indirect taxes** and especially because **they abolished the duties on paper**—a long-time demand of the radicals. Gladstone obtained their passage by combining them with the **Budget Bill (1861),** so that the Lords would have to reject the entire budget.

1865, June. The Union Chargeability Act capped Poor Law reforms that attempted to charge uniform rates and establish a consistent system of assessment. The law required that rates be assessed in the same manner throughout the Union and thus forced wealthier parishes to assist the poorer. The Poor Law Board also required all unions to provide adequate medical facilities in workhouses and added a doctor to the inspectorate (1866).

1866. Outbreaks of **bubonic plague** and **cholera** in Bristol, London, and Liverpool.

1867, July 17. THE SECOND REFORM BILL. The Russell cabinet had advanced a reform bill in 1866 that had been defeated by a coalition of Liberals and Conservatives. The Russell government resigned and was replaced by Derby in association with Disraeli. Derby depended on the divisions within the Liberal camp to ensure a Conservative-Liberal majority, and his conservative stance also enabled passage of a bill in both Commons and the Lords.

Provisions: The bill provided a third seat for Manchester, Liverpool, Leeds, and Birmingham but also allowed the electors in those districts to vote for only two M.P.'s, thus providing for a minority seat in each district. Scotland received seven additional seats, but the number allotted to Wales and Ireland remained unchanged. The act also created 11 new boroughs and gave a seat to the University of London. **The bill extended the franchise** to male, adult householders who paid the poor rates in the boroughs. In the counties, the annual value of property required for the vote was decreased from £10 to £5. In doing so it virtually doubled the number of eligible voters, but it did not provide the secret ballot.

Hornby v. Close undermined the legal protection of the trade unions. A boilermakers' union had filed a claim against a dishonest treasurer, but the court ruled that the claim could not be honored because of the union's doubtful legal status as a suitor.

1868. Trades Union Congress (TUC) was formed.

1870. Army reforms under Secretary of War Edward Cardwell reduced the size of the standing army, created a system of reserves, and abolished the system of purchasing army commissions (1871).

June 4. Civil service reforms encouraged competitive examinations.

The First Married Women's Property Act began to extend some rights of property to wives. It was followed by **two more such acts (1882 and 1893),** which, in 1893, provided married women with the same property rights as single women.

Aug. 9. The Education Act enabled local governments, who considered it necessary, to permit elected school boards to **establish public schools** maintained by taxes and fees, which could be remitted for the poor. State aid was also increased for voluntary schools, and **religious instruction in public schools became noncompulsory and nonsectarian.** In 1880, attendance at elementary school was made compulsory, and in 1891, all fees were abolished.

1870 ff. Pronounced decline of birthrate and population growth rate.

1871, June 29. The Trade Union Act provided trade unions with legal status before the law, and the **Criminal Law Amendment Act** attempted to establish clear rules for strikes but disappointed unions with its stringency. In *Regina* v. *Druitt*, the court utilized the inherently uneven **Master and Servant Act** to define intimidation during a strike. This law gave employers a privileged position within the work "contract." The government eliminated these advantages in the Employers and Workmen Act (1875).

1872. Protection of children. The Infant Life Protection Act provided protection to children in foster care by requiring women who fostered more than one child to register with the local authority. Parliament also introduced stricter requirements for the **registration of infant deaths** and legislation making it easier for women to **collect support from the fathers of their illegitimate children.** Poor Law authorities could even start proceedings against the father. Parliament passed the **Agricultural Children's Act (1873),** which forbade the employment of children under age 8 in agriculture.

June 18. The Ballot Act established the secret ballot in British elections.

1873. Judicial reforms. The law consolidated piecemeal reforms throughout the 19th century, combined the common law and equity courts, and rationalized the High Court of Justice and the Court of Appeal. The law also eliminated the House of Lords' judicial role, but an amending act (1876) reversed this provision.

1875. The Public Health Act gave the Local Government Board the right to obtain court orders forcing local authorities to fulfill sanitary obligations. It also enabled local authorities to build **isolation hospitals** if they deemed it necessary.

Aug. 3. The Employers and Workmen Act facilitated trade union bargaining and the use of strikes. **Trade unions** helped secure these acts through a **combination of national associations,** bids for **reformism and respectability,** and the utilization of the TUC. Although trade unions still organized only one-tenth of the workforce and largely ignored the unskilled and women, their importance increased steadily.

Wages continued to improve, albeit unevenly. Wages in England remained higher than those on the Continent. Improved wages did not eliminate poverty or unilaterally improve the standard of living. **Around one-seventh of the population received an inadequate wage. The Great Depression (1873–79)** also struck rural workers because the declining agricultural prices meant a decline in wages in agriculture, while prices for other merchandise did not decline.

White collar unionism did make some progress in the late 19th century. The National Union of Elementary Teachers (1870), the Postmen's Federation (1891), and the Tax Clerks' Association (1892) were products of such efforts, but their unions remained distinct from the working-class unions.

1876, May 1. Queen Victoria was proclaimed empress of India. This move demonstrated the strength of the new imperialism, which had been heralded by Disraeli in his Crystal Palace Speech (1871).

New imperialism. A growing interest in gaining and holding imperial territories in the late 19th century was championed by nationalists like Joseph Chamberlain. English interests abroad grew out of a combination of nationalism, security, and the desire to control trading routes and resources. All of these issues came to a head in the **scramble for Africa,** which Britain became involved in because of economic interests in Egyptian solvency, concerns over access to the Suez Canal, anti-British sentiments in both Alexandria and South Africa, and the adventures of English explorers.

Party reorganization. After the reforms of 1867, both Liberals and Conservatives reorganized their parties and tightened the party control. Disraeli established the **National Union of Conservatives (1867)** and a **Conservative Central Office (1870).** Chamberlain had established a strong municipal party machine in Birmingham. Its success prompted the Liberals to establish a **National Liberal Federation (1877).**

Women began to gain a significant political role. In 1869, female rate payers could vote in borough elections, and from 1870 they could sit on school boards. In 1875, they were allowed to become Poor Law Guardians. The **National Society for Women's Suffrage (1869)** and the **National Union of Women's Suffrage Societies (1897)** preceded the well-known **Women's Social and Political Union** (1903) founded by Emmeline Pankhurst. In general, women's political activities stemmed from the middle class. The Liberals and the Conservatives

also saw the benefit of female organizations and thus organized the Women's Liberal Foundation and its Conservative counterpart, the Primrose League.

1880–81. First Boer War. The Boers in the Transvaal rebelled against British control and waged a guerrilla war (p. 597). In 1881, they attacked **Majuba Hill** and defeated British troops. Gladstone concluded peace negotiations, which guaranteed independence to the Transvaal, subject to British suzerainty. The latter clause was removed at the **Convention of London (1884).**

1880. The Liberal majority in the general election was later undermined by **dissension. Charles Bradlaugh,** a radical M.P. from Northampton, opposed the Church of England, claimed to be an atheist, and advocated birth control. The Liberal majority attempted to stop him from taking his seat by arguing that he could not be bound by the oath that M.P.'s took because of its religious terms. Gladstone allowed Bradlaugh to affirm his loyalty without taking the oath, but Liberals continued to try to keep him from occupying his seat. The creation of a **"Fourth Party"** of opposition Conservatives, including **Lord Randolph Churchill, A. J. Balfour, Sir Henry Drummond Wolf, and Sir John Gorst,** worked in the same manner as the Irish under Parnell to paralyze the Liberal government.

1884, Feb. 28. THE THIRD REFORM ACT extended the vote to adult male householders in the counties and thus increased the franchise to include approximately four-fifths of the entire adult male population. However, it did not assert the franchise on the basis of natural rights or establish the principle of universal male suffrage. The accompanying **Redistribution Bill** proved more sweeping because it created the principle of equal electoral districts and established a Commons of 670 members. **Neither act stopped the practice of plural voting** in which individuals might register as 40-shilling freeholders in several counties.

1885. A political crisis developed after **Parnell,** the leading Irish M.P., grew disenchanted with the Liberals and led a cohort of Irish nationalist M.P.'s into the opposition lobby, defeating Gladstone. Lord Salisbury formed a minority government until the **election of 1885.**

1886. The Irish Home Rule crisis. Parnell gained support from Gladstone while Churchill sided with Conservative Irish M.P.'s who argued that the adoption of Home Rule would leave the Protestant Irish to the whims of the Catholic majority. Gladstone advanced two Home Rule bills, but both were defeated, and his second attempt in 1892 met with a similar fate. Gladstone retired as a result (p. 490).

The creation of a special electoral committee of the Trades Union Congress. The committee, in conjunction with the Liberals, obtained seats for 11 working-class members and established a **"Lib-Lab" alliance,** which continued until 1900. Labor also received an independent voice in 1892 when **Kier Hardie,** influenced by the socialist doctrines of the intellectual **Fabian Society** (1884), broke with the Liberals and sat as a Labour M.P.—even wearing a cloth cap rather than the traditional hat of the middle and upper classes. He founded the **Independent Labour Party (1893),** endorsed by the Trades Union Congress.

1887. The Coal Mines Regulation Act required the presence of men with at least ten years' experience in all mining operations. This requirement strengthened the Miners' Unions against strikebreakers. Unions also obtained the inclusion of a clause in the **Technical Instruction Act (1889)** forbidding the teaching of a particular trade in technical schools.

1889. Dockers' strike (London), following a matchgirls' strike, showed growing organizational power among unskilled workers.

1899, May 31. Naval Defense Act. Against growing naval rivalry, the British planned for their fleet to be as strong as the next two powers' fleets combined.

1899–1902. South African War (Boer War). More soldiers died of illness than of war injuries despite the efforts of female nurses. These nurses were allowed to go to South Africa on the understanding that they would work behind the lines, but, as guerrilla warfare developed, women in nursing capacities found themselves unable to remain "behind the lines." Their service under fire enabled the directors of the **Royal Nursing Corps** to demand recognition and admission as a military unit.

1900. The Labour Representation Committee, established by a group of cooperative societies, socialists, and trade unions that met in London, worked to create a distinct **Labour Party. J. Ramsay McDonald** was elected secretary of the committee, which returned 2 seats in 1900 and 53 in 1906.

1901. The Taff-Vale decision, upheld by the Lords after being overturned by the Court of Appeal, hampered strike activity. The Taff-Vale Railway Company sued the trade union for damages resulting from the strike, which it had encouraged. The decision made strikes virtually impossible by holding the trade union financially liable for any worker's activity. The decision also encouraged union activity in the Labour Representation Committee.

The rise of consumerism demonstrated the growing prosperity of Britain as well as the increasing availability of products. Increased consumption of cigarettes and soap helped encourage advertising. Consumers also had access to a large number of illustrated papers and magazines including those with features meant to appeal to women or children, such as the *Illustrated London News* and the *Boy's Own Paper.*

1902. The Education Act placed full responsibility for education in the hands of the state, replaced local school boards by the authority of local government, and systematized standards and secondary schools. It did maintain voluntary religious education.

1903. The Women's Social and Political Union was organized by **Emmeline Pankhurst,** to launch attention-grabbing tactics to win the vote.

1904. The Licensing Act, recommended by Balfour in the interest of the temperance vote, was passed but also lost him much support. The act closed some of the public houses but compensated their owners out of the licensing fees paid by the remainder of the houses. Temperance crusaders saw this provision as the government's condoning of evil activity.

1906. The Plural Voting Bill eliminated the right to vote more than once even if the voter had more than one landholding.

The Trades Disputes Act reversed the Taff-Vale decision by removing the unions' liability for acts of its agents or members.

1909. The People's Budget, presented by Lloyd George, became the vehicle for **major parliamentary reform.** It proposed to pay for the new social programs with a surtax on incomes over £5,000, a small duty on undeveloped land, and a tax of 20 percent on capital gains in land value. The Lords refused to pass this budget initially. After two elections, and a threat from the new king, George V, to pack the Lords with new peers, the Lords approved a bill that allowed money bills to be passed without the Lords' consent. This law also commuted the Lords' veto on other bills into the right only to delay a bill.

Social legislation. Free school meals (1906) and **medical services (1907)** were made available to poor children, and **secondary schools** were required to keep a quarter of their places available for state elementary school students. In 1908, the Children's Act sought to alleviate cruelty and neglect as well as revising reformatories.

Insurance. The Old Age Pension Act (1909) and the **National Insurance Act (1911)** that followed provided for unemployment and health insurance and for retirement benefits. The National Insurance Act was modeled after the German law of 1889 and was a contributory scheme.

1910–12. Great national strikes by miners, railway workers, transport workers (the **"Triple Alliance,"** 1913), and others attacked various grievances, and along with growing **feminist agitation** for the vote, frightened many politicians. **Suffragist** demonstrations became increasingly militant, with **arson** first used in 1910. *(To p. 679)*

2. IRELAND
(From p. 450)

Economics and society after the famine. The Irish potato famine (1845–47) **decreased the population of Ireland** substantially through death and emigration (the 1841 census listed a population of 8,175,124, but in 1851 the total was 6,552,385). Increases in evictions immediately following the famine furthered land consolidation but also met with increasing agitation by tenant farmers. The results of land consolidation reduced extreme poverty in Ireland but also made land, rents, and tithes a major issue in the years immediately following the famine.

1848, Jan. 3. The pope urged Irish bishops to forbid political activity by clergy.

1849, July 28. The Second Encumbered Estates Act, combined with the First Encumbered Estates Act (1848), accelerated the process of sale of mortgaged land.

Oct. 14. The first tenant protection society was set up in Ireland at Callan, county Kilkenny by two Catholic curates, Thomas O'Shea and Matthew O'Keefe. These societies provided the basis for the **Irish Tenant League,** founded on **Aug. 9, 1850.** They expressed the growing concern among tenants regarding increased evictions following the famine. They received support from the **Irish Presbyterian Church,** which adopted a statute recognizing tenant rights (July 3, 1850).

1850, Sept. 29. Pope Pius IX issued a brief that reestablished Catholic hierarchy in England and Wales. This move prompted a cry of "papal aggression" from Parliament and led to the Ecclesiastical Titles Act.

1851, Aug. 1. Ecclesiastical Titles Act. The act forbade Catholic clergy to take territorial titles. Parliamentary action also sparked Catholic reaction in Ireland.

Aug. 19. Catholic Defense Association of Great Britain and Ireland was founded at a meeting in Dublin. The association expressed Catholic opposition to the Ecclesiastical Titles Act. This association gained parliamentary support from the so-called Irish Brigade—a group of Irish M.P.'s who also opposed the act.

1852, June 30. The act provided for Griffith's valuation of landholdings throughout Ireland, which helped to rationalize the tenant and landholder problems.

Sept. 8–9. Tenant League conference in Dublin. The M.P.'s present adopted a policy of independent opposition to any government that failed to support the Tenant League.

Dec. 13. Independent Irish Party formed at a meeting of Liberal Irish M.P.'s; it agreed to combine the concerns of the Tenant League and the Catholic Defense Association and refuse to support any government that did not commit itself to such a program. During the party's short-lived success, it was able to control the balance within Parliament. However, it failed as a result of attrition of leadership, lack of clarity about how its policy should be translated into action, and gradual economic improvement in Irish agriculture.

1854, May 18. National synod of the Catholic Church approved efforts to regulate the political conduct of clergy. The **bishop of Ossory** subsequently forbade O'Keefe and O'Shea to continue political activity.

Nov. 3. A Catholic university opened in Dublin. The creation of a Catholic university reflected growing concern over the quality of Catholic priests and education in Ireland raised by John Henry Newman, who became the first rector of the university.

1857, Sept. Irish Temperance League founded in Belfast. Organized by Presbyterian clergy, the Temperance League marked the growing concern of the Protestants over the use of drink. The Irish Catholics also included a strong temperance movement, which focused on Father Matthew, who toured Ireland, England, and the United States, asking Catholics to take the pledge.

1858, March 17. The formation of a secret organization that would be called the **Irish Republican Brotherhood (IRB)** in Dublin. The American Irishmen created a counterpart to the IRB in the **Fenian Brotherhood (April 1859)** and the **Clan na Gael (1877),** which followed it.

Fenianism represented the revolutionary and international aspects of Irish nationalism in that it organized radical Irishmen in Ireland and abroad. It focused on physical force as a means of demonstrating its power. The changes it demanded included Irish independence from British rule and the three F's of the land problem—free sale, fixed tenure, and fair rent. Fenianism was **condemned by Archbishop Cullen** because it required a secret oath. Fenians were officially to be denied access to the sacraments until they confessed of their wrongdoing and left the movement.

Agricultural depression, beginning in the 1860s, started to put serious strain on the land system in Ireland. Demands for land reform had declined in the 1850s as agricultural production meant improved earnings. These earnings were curtailed by a series of cold, wet growing seasons followed by a series of droughts in the early 1860s.

1864. Irish National Association was founded. It called for action on disestablishment of the Church of Ireland, the land reform, and Catholic education. Cullen supported this association and called upon his clergy to cooperate with it.

Fenian activity increased. In 1864, James Stephens declared 1865 the **year of Fenian insurrection.**

1866, Feb. 17. Parliament suspended habeas corpus in Ireland. A Fenian council of war decided against an immediate rising, but Fenians continued to be arrested and deported or imprisoned.

1869, July 26. The Irish Church Act disestablished the Protestant Church of Ireland and partially removed its endowment. It also provided funding for both the Presbyterian and Catholic churches.

1870. Isaac Butt launched the Home Rule movement. This movement demanded that Ireland be given the right to govern its own affairs through an Irish Parliament, while remaining part of the British Empire.

Aug. 1. The Landlord and Tenant Act, introduced by Gladstone, extended the **Ulster Custom** throughout Ireland. This custom gave the tenant the right to claim compensation at the end of his tenancy for any improvements he made on property. (**The 1881 Land Act** set up a court to mediate between landlords and tenants.) Agrarian riots increased.

1873–77. The **HOME RULE MOVEMENT** gathered momentum in Ireland despite the failure to win support in Parliament. Butt addressed a meeting in Manchester, which led to the foundation of a **Home Rule Confederation in Great Britain.** Home Rule M.P.'s then decided to form a separate party (1874). Butt initiated debates over Home Rule in the Commons (June 30–July 1, 1876) but failed to obtain his objective. Meanwhile, the IRB adopted a resolution to stop providing support to the Home Rule movement (Aug. 20). **Charles Parnell** replaced Butt as president of the Home Rule Confederation of Great Britain (1877).

1879, April 20. A mass meeting held at Irishtown, county Mayo. Local leaders organized to protest rising rents and thus sparked the **LAND WAR.** It combined refusals to pay unfair rents, intimidation, breaking down fences, and boycotts in an effort to force unfair landholders to lower rents. Tenants renewed demands for fair rents because crop failures and agricultural depressions had decreased their incomes while their rents remained unchanged.

Oct. 21. The Irish National Land League was founded in Dublin. Parnell served as president and Davitt as one of several secretaries. The Land League combined the resources of the IRB with the Home Rulers. Fanny Parnell founded the **Ladies' Land League,** organized in New York (1880) and in the following year in Dublin. The Ladies' Land League violated the long tradition that kept Irish women outside politics.

1884, Oct. 22. The first women ever to receive degrees in Ireland graduated from the Royal University of Ireland.

The growth of Irish nationalism can be seen in the rise in interest in the Gaelic language and Gaelic sports. **The Gaelic Union for the Preservation and Cultivation of the Irish Language** was established in 1880; the **Gaelic Athletic Association, in 1884.** Irish poetry and literature also flourished with Irish writers such as William Butler Yeats (1865–1939).

1885, Oct. 30. The battle over Irish independence intensified as Katherine O'Shea sent Gladstone a draft of Parnell's **Home Rule** constitution (Oct. 30). Gladstone refused to take a stand. The first **Home Rule Bill (1886)** for a separate Irish legislature failed under Conservative attack, joined by former Liberals like Joseph Chamberlain.

1886, Oct. 23. "Plan of Campaign" published in the Republican *United Ireland.* It included withholding rents on some estates, which was declared illegal.

1890–91. Parnell continued to have the support of the Irish Parliamentary Party despite growing rumors about his use of party funds and his being named in divorce proceedings between the O'Sheas. However, in the fall of 1890, the party split, with the majority opposing Parnell. Efforts at reconciliation failed in Feb. 1891. Parnell married Katherine O'Shea (June 1891) after the divorce but died in Oct. 1891.

1893, Sept. 9. The **Second Home Rule Bill was defeated** in the House of Lords after passing in Commons.

1894, April 27–28. The formation of the Irish Trades Union Congress marked the development of trade unionism within Ireland in the late 19th century. Trade unions became particularly effective in the transport industry under the leadership of **James Larkin.** Larkin organized

a dock strike in Belfast in 1907. In 1908, the Irish Transport Worker's Union was founded.

Parliamentary reforms also attempted to address some of the problems in Ireland without dissolving the Union. The Irish Local Government Act (1898) created some elective county and district councils. **The "Wyndham" Land Act (1903) and Birrell's Land Act (1909)** provided the means for tenants to buy out landlords. **The Evicted Tenants Act** allowed estates commissioners to compel landowners to sell land to them for the resettlement of the evicted tenants. Tenants also received grants to repair buildings (1907).

1900, Jan. 30. The reunion of the Irish Parliamentary Party and the foundation of Cumann na Gaedheal by Andrew Griffith marked the continued demands for Irish independence. The latter joined the Dungannon Club (formed in Belfast, 1905) in the Sinn Féin League.

1904, Dec. 2. The Ulster Unionist M.P.'s, meeting at a conference in Belfast, formed the Ulster Unionist Council. Unionism and independence were becoming clearly delineated geographically and confessionally. By the time the Third Home Rule Bill was introduced in 1912, the Unionists had enough support for the debate to include a discussion of possibly excluding Ulster.

1911, Aug. 21. Formation of the Irish Women's Suffrage Federation, reflecting growing demands for voting rights. Women in Ireland had already received the right to sit as Poor Law Guardians.

1914. Home Rule bill passed Commons with an amending bill, which temporarily excluded portions of Ulster. The Lords changed the amending bill to exclude Ulster permanently. After a failed attempt to negotiate the impasse, Parliament turned its interests to the escalating warfare in Europe. It gained a promise of the Irish leader Redmond to support the British war effort, and the Home Rule Bill was suspended for the duration. *(To p. 682)*

c. THE LOW COUNTRIES

1. BELGIUM
(From p. 451)

Monarchs: Leopold I (r. 1831–65), Leopold II (r. 1865–1909), and Albert I (r. 1909–34).

1850 ff. Doctrinaire liberalism gained control in the government under **Charles Rogier. François Laurent** became the major theorist and argued that progress toward individualism was directed by God. *L'Économiste belge* served as the major periodical for the movement.

1850. An education bill increased the number of state grammar and secondary schools, but allowed priests to offer religious instruction in these schools. Nonetheless, the bill met increasing opposition from the Catholics, and priests generally refused to offer such instruction.

National Bank founded.

1852. Walther Frère-Orban adopted a strategy of free trade implemented through a series of bilateral trade treaties and by reducing duties on a number of items.

The Rogier cabinet resigned as a result of domestic crisis and the growing hostility of Napoleon III. Leopold I proved unable to establish a stable conservative government. The doctrinaire Liberals returned in 1857.

1854. L'Affranchissement established. Along with **Les Solidaires (1857),** it combined atheism with socialist ideas. Atheist organizations provided groundwork for socialism in Belgium throughout the 19th century.

1860, July 21. Frère-Orban abolished cities' rights to impose duties on wares brought into towns and established the **Crédit communal,** which provided state loans to municipalities on favorable terms.

1870, Aug. 9, 11. Treaties concluded among Britain, Prussia, and France guaranteed Belgian neutrality during the Franco-Prussian War.

1879, July 1. An education act secularized primary education. No public support was to be given to "free" or Catholic schools. The measure passed with Liberal support but estranged the Clericals.

1880, June. Clericals won a majority in the elections and replaced the Liberals in power until World War I.

1884, Sept. 10. A new education law gave public support for church schools in Catholic districts.

1885. The Workers' Party founded. It soon replaced the Liberals as the primary opposition to the Clericals.

1886. The Depression caused increasing unrest and gains in working-class movements and socialism. A meeting of **anarchists** in Liège (March 18) resulted in demonstrations in the street, and the miners of Charleroi went on strike and forced other workers in the city to join them (March 26). The government sent in troops and restored order. **Alfred Defuisseaux** published *Le Catéchisme du peuple,* which established the principle of universal male suffrage to right social wrongs. The government began an inquiry into the conditions of the workers.

1893, April. Leaders of the Workers' Party called a **general strike** and demanded **universal male suffrage.** The assembly had rejected a bill providing such suffrage but the government introduced a **pluralistic system of universal male suffrage (April 27).** All men over age 24 had one vote, but those men over age 34 with a family and a ratable home received two votes or, if they also had property or professional qualifications, three votes.

1895, Aug. 30. Instruction in Catholic religion was made compulsory in all public schools.

1898. The Belgian socialist party set up a federation to coordinate and organize **trade unions.** This was followed by another period of strike activity (1901–5).

1899, Dec. 24. Adoption of proportional representation for the protection of political minorities.

1902. A **general strike,** in an effort to eliminate pluralistic voting, failed.

1903–4. The Congo scandal over labor conditions under Leopold's rule resulted in a commission of inquiry (1905). The Congo was ceded by the king to the Belgian nation (1908) (p. 595).

1913, April 14–24. A **political general strike** ended on the assurance of the government that the electoral system would be revised, but the revisions occurred after the war.

    Aug. 30. The Army Law was enacted. It established universal military service in place of an earlier system of drafting one son from each family.

1914. Compulsory education was established after rigorous resistance from the Catholics.

    Aug. A German ultimatum to Belgium demanded free passage for German armies. *(To p. 684)*

2. THE NETHERLANDS
(From p. 451)

Monarchs: William III (r. 1849–90) and Wilhelmina (r. 1890–1948).

1848, Nov. 3. A new constitution was proclaimed: William II called upon **Johan Thorbecke** to revise the constitution. The new constitution established two chambers (the upper elected by provincial states and the lower by direct suffrage), asserted ministerial responsibility, and committed education to the government's care.

1850. An election law carried by Thorbecke actually restricted suffrage further, reduced from approximately 90,000 to 75,000 men.

1857. The Primary Education Law retained the religiously mixed school system with state subsidies, but also made it easier to establish "free" schools. The law raised teaching standards and provided for improvement of school buildings.

1863. Slavery was abolished in the Dutch West Indies.

1867, March. The king and France made a treaty for the **sale of Luxembourg,** which resulted in an international crisis, and the sale was not completed.

1878. An education law raised teachers' salaries and required more training. It forced local municipalities to seek financial assistance from the government, helping lead to centralization of the schools.

1881. The various socialist associations were combined into the **Sociaal-Democratische Bond (SDB),** which adopted a program similar to the **Gotha Program** (p. 501) but added a clause regarding women's emancipation. In 1884, the SDB took over the socialist newspaper *Recht voor Allen,* established in 1879.

1886, July. The Eel Revolt, in which Amsterdam police were called upon to stop a popular game involving pulling apart eels, sparked demonstrations and underscored popular hatred of the police. The eventual government inquiry led to the enactment of the first **Child Labor Legislation (1889).**

1887, June 17. Introduction of **suffrage reform,** which approximately doubled the electorate.

1889, Dec. 6. A Calvinist-Catholic coalition passed a law providing financial assistance for all private denominational schools and continued support of nonsectarian public schools.

1890–1948. WILHELMINA (b. 1880). Until 1898, the queen mother, Emma, acted as regent.

1894. Revolt in the Dutch East Indies. Another rising in 1896 was put down only with considerable difficulty.

    Aug. Sociaal-Democratische Arbeiders Partij was founded as alternative to the SDB. The new party grew slowly but would become a major contender in the 20th century.

1896, June 29. A new electoral law again doubled the electorate but still fell short of universal male suffrage and received intense criticism from the working classes.

1897–1901. The Borgesius ministry passed social legislation such as accident insurance, housing improvements, and compulsory education of children.

1901, Feb. 7. The queen married Duke Henry of Mecklenburg-Schwerin.

1903, April. Great railway and dock strikes were broken up by the military.

1907, Aug. 14–21. A **Zionist conference** at The Hague rejected the possibility of establishing an African colony in Uganda, first proposed in 1903, and established **synthetic Zionism**—arguing that a Jewish state could be established only in Israel.

1913, Aug. 25. An extraparliamentary cabinet formed by Cort van der Linden set out to settle the **suffrage and education questions,** but World War I intervened. (**Universal suffrage** and proportional representation were installed in 1917.) *(To p. 685)*

d. FRANCE

1. THE SECOND EMPIRE
(From p. 467)

1852, Jan 1. Louis-Napoleon (Napoleon III) became emperor by decree of the Senate and by plebiscite.

    Jan. 14–15. The constitution of 1852 was signed. It concentrated power in Louis-Napoleon's hands. Louis-Napoleon steered France through moderate economic reforms. He sought mass support by providing for universal male suffrage and confiscating Orléanist estates. He utilized some of the money from these estates for charitable causes. However, his reign was plagued by rumors of assassination plans and attempts on his life.

1850s. Labor reforms. Napoleon III had courted the support of the working classes initially and even won the temporary support of socialist theorist **Pierre-Joseph Proudhon.** However, in 1852, unions and strikes continued to be illegal.

    Social assistance. Napoleon III favored private charity. As such, **his family engaged in philanthropic activities** including the provision of aid to expectant mothers. Empress Eugénie directed maternal charities. An unemployment bureau and rest homes for the elderly and infirm were established. However, **Napoleon III concentrated his efforts on economic expansion,** which he believed would improve the conditions of working classes.

1852. Railroads were organized and consolidated. The government granted railroad concessions between major cities including routes **from Paris to Lyons, Dijon to Besançon, and Sète to Bordeaux.** The state also provided funding for the railroads and guaranteed at least a 4 percent return on capital investment (1856–57). Railroad development boomed in 1853–56 and 1860–64.

    Feb. 17. Government control of the media was decreed. The press was required to register with the government and purchase stamps as well as pay a monthly deposit. The government could refuse to allow even the legal press to be sold on the public way and could suspend newspapers that offended it.

    Nov. 20. The Crédit Mobilier was founded under the direction of **Émile and Isaac Pereire.** The Crédit Mobilier avoided the problems of financing large projects characteristic of small family firms by combining money from numerous small investors. The bank also concentrated on investment banking rather than deposit accounts.

1853. Hardship hit much of France. A **silkworm disease** reduced the value of the silk crop substantially. Poor harvests led to severe food shortages. A **cholera epidemic** hit Paris (Nov. 1853–Dec. 1854). The Parisian authorities established home health care for the poor, but Paris remained plagued by population growth and inadequate water supplies and sanitary services. The problems helped encourage a concerted effort at urban renewal, land reclamation, and economic modernization.

Jan. 30. Louis-Napoleon married Eugénie de Montijo, countess of Téba, daughter of a Spanish grandee. Her rigorous religious training made her an enemy of liberalism and a leader of the Clerical Party in the palace. Napoleon continued a policy favoring the church, begun with the Falloux Law. **Government grants helped fund churches and religious bodies.**

1854. Haussman, prefect of Paris, began plans to rebuild Paris. He was charged with preparing plans for the Paris sewage system, and Belgrand was to begin plans for a Parisian water supply. The two reported to the Paris council (April). **Numerous boulevards, roads, and buildings were completed or renovated.** Rebuilding Paris destroyed traditional meeting places and communities for the working classes and the poor within the city.

June 22. A law required that **workers retain their *livrets*** (worker's passbooks) rather than surrender them to their employers. Other legislation attempted to eliminate some of the worst abuses of the system of *livrets*. Employers were also prohibited from making any notation in the *livrets* and had to register arrivals and departures of their workers. **The law expanded *livret* obligations to include women as well as men,** to aid policing of workers.

1854–56. CRIMEAN WAR. Napoleon III sought a diplomatic solution to the situation in the Crimea because, unlike Britain, France had little interest in the region. **Sixty-three thousand Frenchmen died, out of the 400,000 sent**—the majority from disease, exposure, and improper treatment.

1855, May 15–Nov. 15. The Paris International Exposition marked French economic advances and prosperity.

1856, March 16. The imperial prince was born.

1857, June 23. The right of trademark in France for 15 years was established. This law marked the growing effort to provide protection for French enterprise within the international trade community. Two decrees in 1852 had regulated the rights to artistic and literary property, and the law regarding patents had been codified in 1844. **Diplomats sought reciprocal agreements on copyrights** throughout Europe in the 1850s.

1858, Jan. 14. Felice Orsini launched bombs, which he had obtained in England, at Louis-Napoleon's coach. His attempt on Napoleon's life precipitated the establishment of the Conseil privé.

Feb. 1. The Conseil privé was established to advise the emperor on great occasions and could act in the event of Napoleon III's absence or incapacitation.

Feb. 27. A law permitted the deportation, imprisonment, or exile without trial for anyone who had been found guilty of conspiracy during 1848, 1849, or 1851. Others found guilty of conspiracy could be fined or imprisoned. Newspapers were also repressed.

1859, May 12–July 12. The war of France and Piedmont against Austria (p. 498) resulted in the annexation of Savoy and Nice (March 24). Napoleon sought glory for France by diplomatic and military adventures.

1860–70. "Liberal" Empire.

1860, Nov. 24. A **reform decree** began the extension of powers and more liberal reforms. Napoleon **reinstated the imperial address to the Corps législatif** and authorized the Corps to respond with their own address. Parliamentary debates were to be fully reported.

1861. The government debt, incurred as a result of public works and foreign policy, spurred **heated debate on the 1862 budget.** The budget was finally passed after Napoleon agreed to further reforms and the right to vote the budget by chapters. The session also abolished the sliding scale of tariffs on grain and established free trade. Despite Napoleon's seeming success over the budget, **an opposition coalition rapidly grew up in the country, composed of Catholics, Legitimists, Orléanists, Protectionists, and even Republicans.**

Jan. The **Cobden-Chevalier Treaty** established virtual free trade between France and Britain by lowering or eliminating duties between the countries. The treaty also eliminated French prohibitions on British imports.

1861–67. THE MEXICAN EXPEDITION (p. 638) began as a debt-collecting mission by France, Britain, and Spain, but Napoleon seized the opportunity to establish a permanent French-supported government in Mexico. **France took Mexico City (June 1863)** and declared **Archduke Maximilian** (brother of Francis Joseph I of Austria) as emperor. Under pressure from the United States and in need of troops for his European policies, **Napoleon was forced to withdraw his support.** Maximilian refused to abdicate and was executed by the Mexicans (June 19, 1867).

1864, May 25. The Corps législatif passed the **Coalitions Law,** which legalized strikes in specific cases by revising the Penal Code of 1810. The act of coalition among workers was no longer punishable unless it met certain qualifications. The law effectively eliminated the prosecution of trade unions. The law represented a more lenient government attitude toward strikes during the 1860s.

Sept. 15. The September Convention. Napoleon III promised to remove his troops from the French garrison in Rome, established in 1859, in two years, and the Italians agreed not to invade Rome.

1865, Jan. The Paris branch of the socialist First International was established, to be followed by branches throughout France. The French branch of the International emphasized cooperatives and initially proved hesitant to support striking workers. However, in 1866, it became more radical and allied itself with strikers. The **French government dissolved the International three times** (March 1868, June 1868, and June–July 1870), but it never successfully eliminated the organization.

1866. Members of the government majority **established the Third Party,** demanding that the emperor "further the natural development of the great Act of 1860."

1867, April 1–Nov. 3. The exposition at Paris featured labor history, cheap goods, and displays of workers' houses in the government's growing effort to maintain support from the working classes.

1868, May 11. A **new press law** reduced the stamp tax and eliminated the need for new papers to be authorized.

Labor reforms of 1868 extended a degree of tolerance to trade unions *(chambres syndicales),* and workers' and employers' testimonies received equal weight before the law.

June 11. Limited right of public meeting was granted, provided the meeting was held in a closed building subject to the supervision of a police officer who could dissolve the meeting.

1869, May 23, 24. Parliamentary elections gave the government 4,438,000 votes to the opposition's 3,355,000. The Third Party, in cooperation with 40 deputies of the Left, demanded the creation of a responsible ministry and secured a majority of 116.

July 12. Napoleon III adopted the program of the 116. The Senate (Sept. 6) decreed a new regime and the **Corps législatif could now propose laws,** criticize and vote the budget, and choose its own officers; the Senate became a deliberative body with public sessions. **Ministers were declared responsible** but were to "depend on the emperor alone."

Léon Gambetta's Belleville program, articulated during his bid for election in the Parisian working-class district of Belleville, demanded freedom of the press, right of meeting, right of combination, trial by jury for all political offenses, separation of church and state, and suppression of the standing army. This statement became central in defining republicanism.

1870, Jan. 10. Victor Noir, a Republican journalist, was shot by Prince Pierre Bonaparte, Napoleon III's cousin. Noir's funeral caused a demonstration against the empire and the liberal minister **Émile Ollivier** now faced the problem of saving the empire by concessions. Sweeping constitutional reforms followed.

April 20. The *senatus consultum* created the basis for a new constitution. The Senate became an upper house, sharing legislative power with the Assembly; no constitutional change was to be made without a plebiscite. A plebiscite of May 8 ratified the changes by a vote of 7,358,786 to 1,571,939.

July 19–1871, May 10. The Franco-Prussian War. France declared war on Prussia (pp. 471, 502). The war was sparked by Bismarck's efforts to unify the South German states. Napoleon III assumed the command of the eight French corps at Metz on July 30. The Prussian armies advanced and defeated the French at **Wissembourg (Aug. 4), Spichern**

(Aug. 5), and **Wörth (Aug. 6)**, separating the northern and southern flanks of the French army. The French army, under the command of Bazaine, who replaced the ailing Napoleon III, was defeated at **Colombey-Borny (Aug. 14)** and driven into the forts at Metz. A **council of war met on Aug. 17** and decided that the remnants of the army would fall back to Paris and be reinforced by the National Guard. However, the army was then ordered to advance toward Metz in an effort to relieve the troops there.

Sept. 1. Napoleon III surrendered at Sedan and sought an armistice. He was captured and taken to Wilhelmshöhe. The empire was overthrown (Sept. 4), and Prussia laid siege to Paris (Sept. 19). The army at Metz surrendered (Oct. 27).

1871. Paris fell (Jan. 28), which forced the government to agree to the **Treaty of Frankfurt (May 10).**

2. THE THIRD REPUBLIC

Presidents: Adolphe Thiers (Feb. 1871–May 1873), Maurice De MacMahon (May 1873–Jan. 1879), Jules Grévy (Jan. 1879–Dec. 1887), Sadi Carnot (Dec. 1887–June 1894), Jean Casimire-Périer (June 1894–Jan. 1895), Félix Faure (Jan. 1895–Feb. 1899), Émile Loubet (Feb. 1899–Feb. 1906), Armand Fallières (Feb. 1906–Feb. 1913), and Raymond Poincaré (Feb. 1913–Feb. 1920).

1870, Sept. 4. The empire was overthrown. Crowds entered the Palais-Bourbon and demanded that the Corps législatif establish a republic. The **crowds accompanied the dissenting deputies to the Hôtel de Ville.** Fearful of a radical revolution, the deputies created a **government of national defense,** which included Gambetta, and Gen. Louis Trochu as president. Then, the **republic was declared at the hôtel** in keeping with tradition.

Sept. 19. Paris was besieged while the government tried desperately to muster troops. **Socialists and radicals staged a putsch (Oct. 31)** in an effort to establish a commune, but the movement collapsed. By Jan., the new **German Empire** (p. 502) **had substantially crushed the resistance in the provinces** organized by **Gambetta,** who had escaped from Paris in a hot air balloon, and a young mining engineer, **Charles de Freycinet.**

1871, Jan. 28. Paris capitulated. The Parisian population had only eight days of food left. The armistice yielded the forts to the Germans and disarmed the troops within the city. Bismarck also agreed to permit election of a representative assembly to determine whether the war should be continued or peace made.

Feb. 13. The National Assembly, elected on Feb. 8, met in Bordeaux. The assembly consisted of a majority of monarchists and conservatives who wanted peace (as opposed to the continued support for the war of the Radical Republicans and Socialists). They **elected Adolphe Thiers (Feb. 16)** as chief of executive power.

Feb. 28. Thiers introduced the terms of a **peace treaty negotiated with Bismarck,** providing for the cession of Alsace and part of Lorraine and 5 billion francs' indemnity with an army of occupation to remain until the indemnity was paid, and conceded to the **German march into Paris (March 1–3)** in victory. These negotiations were ratified in the **Treaty of Frankfurt (May 10, 1871).**

March–May. THE PARIS COMMUNE. Causes: The Paris Commune represented Parisians' horror at the conservative government under Thiers and the German march into Paris. However, they also reacted to the lifting of the moratoriums on rents and mortgages that had existed in Paris during the war, the arrest of leaders such as Auguste Blanqui, and press censorship. The precipitating incident was the government's attempt to seize the cannon that the Parisians had made during the war.

March 18. After troops refused to fire on the crowd defending the cannon, the crowd executed Gen. Lecomte and Gen. Thomas. The troops retired, and Paris came under the control of the **Central Committee of the National Guard.**

March 26. The Communal Assembly was elected and took control of the Commune. The Commune sought to decentralize the French state by enlarging the powers of municipalities, to separate church and state, and to substitute the National Guard for a standing army. Under the assembly, the **Commission on Industry and Trade** began plans for workers' cooperatives, and **Édouard Vaillant,** delegate for public in-

struction, began to lay the framework for a more egalitarian educational system.

March–April. Provincial communes. The Paris Commune sparked a series of short-lived efforts at establishing communes in other cities, especially in the south of France. These communes dissolved in the face of the army, but they included risings in **Marseilles (March 23–April 4)** and **Lyons (April 30).**

April 5. Law of hostages. The Commune imprisoned a substantial number of possible political dissidents who were later executed, and created the Committee of Public Safety in April to coordinate the efforts in the civil war.

May 21–28. Bloody Week began when the armies of Versailles attacked Paris. Female Communards aided the militiamen of the Commune in these battles. During the last days, about 100 hostages were killed by Communards; the armies of Versailles executed approximately 25,000 Parisians and held another 36,000 prisoners for trial and deportation.

1871–73. The **monarchist majority** in the National Assembly was determined to settle the question of a new regime for France but were divided among Legitimists supporting the Bourbon line and the count of Chambord; Orléanists supporting the count of Paris, grandson of Louis-Philippe (approximately 200); and a small number of Bonapartists.

1871, July 5. The count of Chambord alienated the Orléanists and the country by declaring that he must rule under the white flag of the Bourbons.

Aug. 31. Law Rivet-Vitet made Thiers president of the republic but declared that the assembly possessed constituent powers. Thiers argued that the conservative republic was **"the government that divides us least"** but met growing opposition from the monarchists.

1872, July 15. The second of two government loans enabled Thiers to pay the German indemnity. **German troops evacuated French territory** (completed on Sept. 16, 1873).

1873, May 24. Thiers resigned, and **Marshal Marie Edmé MacMahon** was elected president. MacMahon was to prepare the way for the restoration. However, an attempted reconciliation between the count of Chambord and the count of Paris (Aug. 5) failed when the count of Chambord again insisted on the white flag (Oct. 27).

Nov. 19. Law of the Septennate. MacMahon was given powers of president for seven years.

1874, Dec. 23. The Roussel Law regulated the wet-nursing industry. **Child labor legislation** limited work for children over age 12 to 12 hours per day and allowed children only between ages 10 and 12 inclusive to work 6-hour days in specific circumstances.

1875. THE "CONSTITUTION OF 1875." The constitution consisted of the **Wallon amendment** accepted on Jan. 30, the **Law on the Organization of Public Powers** (Feb. 25), the **Law on the Organization of the Senate** (Feb. 24), and the **Law on the Relation of the Public Powers** (July 16).

The **Wallon amendment** established the principle of a republic. The president would be elected by an absolute majority of the combined Senate and Chamber of Deputies for seven years. **The president** possessed the usual executive powers but each of his acts required the signature of the relevant minister. Ministers were declared responsible. The **Senate** was to have 300 members, 225 chosen for nine years through indirect election and 75 named by the National Assembly (later by the Senate). The Senate shared the right to initiate legislation (except finance laws) with the **Chamber of Deputies,** elected by universal male suffrage.

1877, May 16. SEIZE MAI CRISIS. The new Chamber of Deputies elected under the constitution consisted of a Republican majority, whereas the Senate remained conservative. MacMahon sought to obtain Republican support by appointing Republican prime ministers, Jules Dufaure (Feb. 1876) and **Jules Simon** (Dec. 1876). Simon proved unwilling to block Republican legislation on issues such as press laws, and MacMahon forced Simon to resign and then called on the Orléanist duke of Broglie to form a government. The duke received a vote of no confidence from the chamber, and MacMahon dissolved the chamber and called for new elections. The elections again returned a Republican majority, and, after the failure of both the Broglie and Rochebouët ministries, MacMahon was forced to retreat and name the Republican Jules Dufaure to the position (Dec. 13).

1879. Parti ouvrier français was established at the third congress of French workers (Marseilles). The congress adopted the **minimalist program** drawn up by Jules Guesde and opposed by the **possibilists**, led by Paul Brousse and Jean Allemane. The minimalist program called for radical reforms but only as agitation for a workers' revolution, whereas the possibilists wished to seek whatever legislation possible to improve the workers' situation and thus adopted a reformist position. The possibilists split with the Parti ouvrier at the **St.-Étienne Congress (1882)** and formed the **Fédération des travailleurs socialistes français** (1883).

Jan 30. MacMahon resigned and was succeeded by Conservative Republican **Jules Grévy.**

1880, March 29, 30. All nonauthorized religious associations were ordered to regularize their positions within three months. This decree also ordered dissolution and dispersion of the Jesuits within three months and dissolution of all religious teaching associations within six months.

July 11. The Communards were granted amnesty. The Communards included numerous radicals who had spearheaded the growing working-class movements before 1870, and their amnesty was thus closely tied to the growth of working-class organizations and socialism.

1880s. Opportunist Republicans increasingly dominated, lacking major issues of principle.

1880–82. Educational reform. Camille Sée established the government's secondary education program for girls, which emphasized women's roles as wives and mothers and sought to strengthen those roles by providing appropriate education (Dec. 21, 1880).

The **Ferry Laws** (June 16, 1881 and March 28, 1882) provided **free, compulsory, public elementary education** without religious content under the aegis of municipal commissions.

1881, March–May. French occupation of Tunis (Treaty of Bardo, May 12) (p. 550).

1882. Brousse's *Le Commune et le Parti ouvrier* was published. It articulated Brousse's anarchism and especially his belief that local activities by workers could allow them to gain substantial control without necessarily overthrowing the state.

1884, March 21. Trade unions were legalized.

July 27. Divorce was legalized. However, it remained expensive, and the law still excluded divorce on the grounds of incompatibility or by mutual consent.

1884–85. The French advance in Tonkin resulted in war with China and the downfall of the second Ferry ministry.

1886. Edouard Drumont's book *Jewish France* signaled the rise of modern anti-Semitism, attacking Jews for capitalism, radicalism, and other "modern problems."

1886–89. THE BOULANGER CRISIS. Gen. Georges Boulanger, protégé of Georges Clemenceau, became minister of war in the Freycinet cabinet (Jan. 4, 1886), where he won popularity in the army through various reforms (improvement of soldiers' food and living conditions, and so on). Boulanger began to receive unsolicited electoral support in special elections for the Chamber of Deputies (1887). The government feared this support and assigned him to an obscure military outpost (Clermont-Ferrand). He resigned to continue his campaigns. Meanwhile, Daniel Wilson, the son-in-law of President Grévy, was discovered to have trafficked in medals of the Legion of Honor, and the so-called **Wilson scandal** forced Grévy from office (Dec. 2, 1887).

1888. Boulanger was elected to the chamber (April 15), where he initiated a campaign for constitutional revision, demanding dissolution of the chamber. He resigned and was returned in three constituencies simultaneously (Aug. 19).

1889, Jan. 27. Boulanger won in Paris, and the government feared he might march on the Elysée Palace and make himself dictator. The **government prepared to try him for treason,** but he fled into exile (April 8) and committed suicide (Sept. 30, 1891).

June 24. A law protected abused and neglected children by removing them from their homes in cases of immorality. An 1898 law gave the judge the right to transfer guardianship to state institutions and punish the parents in cases of abuse.

July 17. A law forbade multiple candidacies; the Republicans triumphed over the Boulangists in the 1889 elections.

1890. Allemanists were expelled from the socialist Fédération as a result of a dispute over control of its elected members. They formed the **Parti ouvrier socialiste révolutionnaire (1891).**

1890–98. The Ralliement. The **Algiers Toast** (Nov. 12, 1890), made by **Charles Cardinal Lavigerie,** primate of Africa, to a banquet of French naval officers, called all citizens to "rally" to support the existing (Republican) government without reservation. The pope issued two encyclicals, *Rerum novarum* (May 15, 1891) on the condition of the workers, and *Inter innumeras* (Feb. 16, 1892), which declared that a government, once accepted, was legitimate. The Ralliement foundered over the struggle over Dreyfus.

1892. Cholera spread from Russia across the Mediterranean to southern France.

Labor legislation set the minimum working age at 13 unless the child had completed schooling by age 12. Children under age 16 were limited to 10 hours of work per day and children between ages 16 and 18 inclusive to 11 hours per day. Women's work was limited in hours and to certain occupations.

Méline tariff made France one of the most protectionist nations.

1892–93. THE PANAMA SCANDAL. French investments had reached approximately 1.5 billion francs in the Panama Company (Compagnie du canal interocéanique) when the company collapsed (Feb. 1889) because of mismanagement and corruption. In the course of government investigation, it was discovered that the company had bribed politicians and journalists to get a lottery loan in 1888. As a result of the investigation, **Ferdinand de Lesseps** (Suez Canal builder) and his associates were condemned (Feb. 9, 1893), but the decree of the court was set aside by the *cour de cassation* because the statute of limitations had expired.

1894, June 24. President Carnot was stabbed at Lyons by an Italian anarchist, **Santo Caserio.**

1894–1906. DREYFUS AFFAIR. When a list of military documents (the *bordereau*) was intercepted by a secret agent on its way to the German military attaché, the handwriting was determined to be that of **Capt. Alfred Dreyfus,** probationer *(stagiaire)* of the General Staff of the army. Dreyfus was arrested (Oct. 15, 1894), charged with treason, tried by court-martial in camera, condemned (Dec. 22), degraded, and deported to Devil's Island in French Guiana. As a Jew, Dreyfus had little support among a military rife with anti-Semitism. **Georges Picquar** demonstrated that the handwriting on the documents matched **Commandant Ferdinand Esterhazy's,** but Esterhazy was acquitted (Jan. 11, 1898). **Novelist Émile Zola** published "J'accuse" in Clemenceau's *L'Aurore* (Jan. 13), which sparked a wave of anti-Semitic riots. Zola was sentenced to one year in prison. Meanwhile, **Col. Hubert Henry** was arrested for forging documents in the case and committed suicide in his cell. Dreyfus returned, was retried and found guilty, but was pardoned by the government (1899). However, he continued to try to clear his name until 1906, when the government overturned the verdict.

1895. Confédération générale du travail (CGT) was founded at the Trade Union Congress at Limoges; it was dedicated to a *syndicalist* program of direct action and the general strike. The program would be given classic formulation by **Georges Sorel's** *Reflections on Violence* (1908).

1896, May 30. Alexandre Millerand called for social unity on the basis of universal suffrage, socialization of production, and support for the international workers' movement without a loss of patriotism. This call failed when Millerand accepted a position (1899) in the Waldeck-Rousseau government, the first socialist in a major government post.

1897–1900. Women's legal position changed. Single women were allowed to witness acts of *état civil* (1897), and businesswomen gained the right to vote for judges of the *tribunaux de commerce* (1898). Women were admitted to the legal profession (1900).

1898–1906. Labor legislation. Laws required employers to provide workers' compensation to employees (1898), established a ten-hour day (1899), and a six-day workweek (1906).

1899. Charles Maurras and Léon Daudet founded *Action française*, a newspaper that sought the restoration of the monarchy and promoted national unity. With **Maurice Barrès's** *Le Roman de l'énergie nationale* (1897–1902), it helped fuel growing nationalism.

1901–5. ANTICLERICALISM AND REPUBLICANISM. The Dreyfus affair resulted in a victory for the more radical Republicans and, with it, increased restrictions on religious associations.

1901, July 1. An associations law stipulated that no congregation could be formed without a law defining its scope and activity, and all congregations lacking authorization were to be dissolved. When Waldeck-Rousseau resigned in the wake of such measures, his successor, **Émile Combes,** proceeded to close some 3,000 unauthorized schools pending their receiving authorization. He prepared 54 bills refusing authorization to as many male congregations (passed, March 1903). All teaching by congregations was forbidden, and such congregations were to be suppressed within ten years (July 7, 1904).

April 8. Conclusion of the **Entente Cordiale** with Great Britain (p. 476). Later (1905), **crisis in Franco-German** relations (p. 476) as a result of the first Moroccan crisis.

1905, March 23–April 6. Unity of the socialists was achieved through the **Parti socialiste section française de l'Internationale ouvrière (SFIO).**

Dec. 9. **Law of separation of church and state,** proposed by **Aristide Briand,** was promulgated. It guaranteed complete liberty of conscience, suppressed all connections between church and state, and allocated all church property to private corporations established for this purpose. This law ended the relationship between the state and the Catholic Church, as well as the state and Protestant and Jewish faiths, that had been established during the 19th century.

1906–11. **Strikes and labor troubles. Vineyard workers** organized in the Confédération générale des vignerons (CGT) (1907). **Postal workers** in Paris struck and demanded the right to unionize and affiliate with the CGT (April–May 1909). The government met the strike with massive firings and denied the right of civil servants to strike. **Railway workers** struck in northern France, and Briand called out the troops (Oct. 18, 1909). The National Union of Railway Workers and Employees then called a general strike but recanted in the wake of a collapse of support.

1906. **Charter of Amiens** established the central tenets of revolutionary syndicalism, including the necessity of the general strike. It became the official doctrine of the CGT.

1907. **Reforms gave women more rights within the family.** Mothers gained the same authority as fathers over their children, and unmarried mothers were allowed to exercise paternal power over their children. Married women also gained control over the monies they had earned.

1909. **Union française pour le suffrage des femmes** was organized by Jeanne-E. Schmahl, Cécile Brunschwicg, and Marguerite de Witt-Schlumberger. Parlement established a committee that drew up a bill to extend the municipal franchise to all women, but women's suffrage would not become a reality until 1944.

1911. **Second Moroccan crisis** (p. 478) and other international problems dominated the ministries of **Joseph Caillaux** (July 27, 1911–Jan. 10, 1912), and **Raymond Poincaré** (Jan. 14, 1912–Jan. 18, 1913).

1913, Aug. **A law increasing military service** from two to three years carried, with vigorous opposition from Radical Socialists and Socialists. Debate over its revocation continued until World War I.

(To p. 686)

e. THE IBERIAN PENINSULA

1. SPAIN
(From p. 456)

1851, March 16. **A concordat** with the papacy recognized the Catholic religion as the sole authorized faith and gave the church sweeping control of education and censorship. The papacy recognized the abolition of ecclesiastical jurisdictions and the sale of confiscated church lands.

1852. A constitutional reform virtually eliminated the powers of the Cortes, established the dictatorship in law, and gave a camarilla financial oligarchy, or complete power.

1854. **Revolution** began in the wake of the introduction of the self-acting mule (spinning machine) and of widespread unrest because of economic hardship culminating in a general strike (1854) among textile workers. Hostility toward workers' organizations increased, and they were suppressed after the revolution. Wheat prices rose due to the loss of supplies from Russia during the Crimean War and a famine in Galicia. **Gen. Leopoldo O'Donnell** overthrew the government, and the Cortes adopted a number of liberal reforms including a law confiscating church lands. Isabella threatened to abdicate, and **Gen. Baldomero**

Espartero resigned (July 15, 1856) in favor of O'Donnell, who reestablished the constitution of 1845. **O'Donnell was dismissed,** and two years of reaction followed. The revolution failed in some respects but did lay the groundwork for economic reforms such as railway expansion.

1856–63. **O'Donnell returned to power** and governed with the support of the Liberal Union, a party organized by him during the revolution.

1856. *The Economist,* a liberal periodical stressing laissez-faire economics, began publication.

1857. **Father Claret** came to Madrid to serve as the queen's confessor. He became the center of the political Catholic movement, seeking to counter rising anticlericalism.

1859. **A budget** created a base for financing public works by extending the disentailing laws.

1859–66. **Foreign policy** concentrated on maintaining and extending the empire. Spanish troops captured Tetuán in their successful **campaign against the Moors in Morocco (1860). Santo Domingo** was annexed but was relinquished after an insurrection on the island (1865). Spain joined France and Britain in **intervention in Mexico (1861)** and engaged in a dispute over the **Chincha Islands with Peru (1864–65). War with Chile (1865–66)** (p. 629).

1863, Sept. 8. **Progressives boycotted politics** (the *retraimiento*) as the government failed to incorporate them.

1868, June 22. In the **mutiny of San Gil,** artillery sergeants shot their officers in protest against exclusiveness of the officer corps and in response to democratic propaganda. O'Donnell ordered the death of 60 sergeants in the aftermath. The mutiny marked the disintegration of the government, which, after the death of O'Donnell, collapsed in revolution.

Sept. 18. **Revolution** was declared by Adm. Juan Topete, followed by a manifesto by the liberal generals.

Sept. 28. **Royal forces were defeated at Alcholea** by Marshal Francisco Serrano. The queen fled to France (Sept. 30) and was declared deposed.

Oct. 5. **The provisional government** established under Serrano accepted the democratic program, including universal male suffrage and freedom of religion and association (Oct. 8).

1869, June 6. **A new constitution,** drawn up by a constituent Cortes (Feb.), was promulgated. It created a constitutional monarchy.

June 15. **Marshal Serrano** was made regent, and the new regime sought a monarch. Prince Leopold of Hohenzollern-Sigmaringen accepted but then withdrew—his candidacy contributed to the war between France and Germany.

1870, June. **The Spanish International** held its first congress at Barcelona and refused to support the Republican program, thus establishing anarchistic opposition to the government.

1870, Dec. 30. The duke of Aosta, son of Victor Emmanuel II of Piedmont, accepted the throne and became Amadeo I.

1871–73. **AMADEO I.**

1871. **Anarchist Congress of Valencia** established the anarchists' position on women, which argued that women should not be required to work, and instigated periodic anarchist risings in Andalusia in the following years.

1872. **The Hidalgo affair** resulting in Amadeo's abdication. Gen. J. Hidalgo was made captain general of the Basque Provinces, despite allegations that he had ordered the sergeants to fire on the officers at San Gil. The artillery officers all protested by declaring they were sick and refusing to take command. The king was forced to sign decrees firing those officers and promoting sergeants to take their places. Following the decrees, **the king abdicated (Feb. 12, 1873).**

July. **Cantonalist risings,** driven by anarchist propaganda, sought to establish independent republics in the south. The cantonal republics were put down forcibly, and the cantonalists were declared criminals.

1873–74. **The FIRST SPANISH REPUBLIC** was proclaimed (Feb. 12) by the radical majority in the Cortes. An elected constituent Cortes was established (May 10). **The Carlists** (p. 456) rose. Don Carlos attempted an invasion that failed but encouraged the government to seek to restore order.

1874, Jan. 2. **Emilio Castelar** was made head of the government in the midst of the Carlist War, but he retired; a military coup established Marshal Serrano as head of a provisional government.

Nov. 24. Alfonso, son of Isabella, came of age and declared for a constitutional monarchy, supported by Liberal Unionists and Moderates.

Dec. 29–31. A group of generals rallied to Alfonso.

1875–85. ALFONSO XII. Continuation of the Carlist War until Don Carlos fled (Feb. 1876). The pope, who had recognized Carlos as king of Spain, supported Alfonso as a result of a governmental increase of the ecclesiastical budget, closing of Protestant schools and churches, and the abolition of civil marriages.

1876, June 30. A new constitution provided a bicameral legislature, a responsible ministry, but limited suffrage. The Cortes was obedient to the ministry, and the ministry was selected by the king. Constitutional forms were observed, and the ministerial power alternated between the Conservatives (led by Canovas del Castillo) and the Liberals (under Práxedes Sagasta). The king's foreign policy followed that of the major powers. Spain associated with Britain, Italy, and Austria in the **Mediterranean Agreements (1887–95)** (p. 474).

Labor organizations developed in the latter quarter of the century. The **Union General de Trabajadores (1882)** was founded as a branch of the Socialist Party (founded, 1879) but soon was rivaled by the anarchist-syndicalist **Confederación Nacional del Trabajo (1911)** and the creation of a **National Federation of Catholic Workers' Syndicates** between 1912 and 1919.

1881. V. Almirall established the **Catalonian national movement** aimed at the creation of a separate Catalonian state. He organized **Catalan congresses** and, in 1882, a political party, the Catalan Center, separated from all parties based in Madrid. The Catalonian movement resulted in a memorial to the king (1885).

1883. Moret established a commission that would become the basis of the **Institute of Social Reform.** The institute advised the government on labor issues and comprised 12 elected members, including 6 workers.

1890, April 30. Universal male suffrage was introduced.

1892. Liberated Women, an anarchist women's organization, was founded. It was followed by the **Feminine Society of Cádiz (1902).**

1898. THE SPANISH-AMERICAN WAR discredited Spain and resulted in further disintegration of the parliamentary regime. Parties now included the Conservatives, Liberal Conservatives, Liberals, Carlists, Republicans, Socialists, and the United Catalans. Naval disasters also resulted in the loss of most remaining Spanish colonies.

1900. Workers' Compensation Act.

1902–31. ALFONSO XIII. He married Princess Eugenia of Battenberg (May 31, 1906).

1908. A law established the basis for arbitration and allowed the Institute of Social Reform to begin to mediate some strikes.

1909. Troops embarked for Morocco, causing protest against inequalities of military service. A general strike was proclaimed at Barcelona and other Catalonian cities under direction of the revolutionary committee.

1910, Dec. 23. The Padlock Law was passed by Liberal premier **José Canalejas** (assassinated, Nov. 12, 1912). It forbade the establishment of more religious houses without the consent of the government. The industrial enterprises of the religious orders were taxed, and public worship of non-Catholic bodies was expressly permitted.

1912. A decree required employers to provide chairs for women who stood at work, one of the earliest pieces of **social legislation dealing with women.**

Nov. 27. Spain's treaty with France defined their respective spheres in Morocco.

1913, Oct. 27. Conservatives returned to power.

1914, Aug. 7. Spain declared neutrality in World War I.   *(To p. 689)*

2. PORTUGAL
(From p. 458)

1851. Fontes Pereira de Melo became secretary of finance. He initiated a series of reforms known as **Fontism,** designed to create a modern economy in Portugal. He encouraged road and railway building and the introduction of the telegraph (1857), and he lowered tariffs.

1852. Direct election of the Chamber of Deputies was reintroduced, with limited suffrage.

1853–61. PEDRO V. Under him and Luis I, the Portuguese government gained some stability. It was ruled alternately by two opposing groups of politicians: the Regenerators (conservatives) and the Progressives (liberals).

1853. Centro Promotor do Melhoramento da Classe Laboriosa became first labor organization concentrating on class struggle.

1861–89. LUIS I.

1867. A civil code was enacted, which included lay marriage for non-Catholics.

1870s–1900s. Labor movements developed in Portugal, including the increase in syndicates, the appearance of a socialist party, and the development of mutual aid societies. In the early 20th century, numerous strikes accompanied growing development of labor organizations.

1878. The first Republicans were elected to the Cortes.

The hereditary peers in the upper house of parliament were abolished. Appointments now were for life. This was reversed in 1896, but hereditary peers were never fully reestablished.

1889–1908. Carlos I.

1901. A law opened Portugal to any religious group coming in the name of education and charity.

1906, May 19. The king appointed João Franco as prime minister. Parliamentary government was suspended (1907).

1908, Feb. 1. Assassination of King Carlos and the crown prince in Lisbon.

1908–10. MANUEL II restored parliamentary government but was forced to flee to England following insurrection in Lisbon (Oct. 5).

1910, Oct. 5. PROCLAMATION OF THE PORTUGUESE REPUBLIC with a provisional government organized under **Dr. Theophilo Braga.** It expelled religious orders, closed their establishments, and confiscated their property. It forbade religious teaching in primary school.

1911, April 20. Separation of church and state.

Aug. 20. A constituent assembly adopted a very liberal constitution.

Aug. 24. Dr. Manuel de Arriaga was elected as first president.

1912, Jan. A serious general strike in Lisbon resulted in the arrest of syndicalists. Workers were discontented with the republic because it failed to give them relief from the hardships of Portugal's slow industrialization.   *(To p. 693)*

f. ITALY AND THE PAPACY

1. THE UNIFICATION OF ITALY
(From p. 469)

1848, March 4. King Victor Emmanuel published the new **Piedmontese constitution,** which provided for a Senate of life members appointed by the king, a Chamber of Deputies elected by limited, direct male suffrage (leaving power in the hands of the nobility and middle class), and a responsible ministry.

1850, March. On the advice of Count Camillo Benso di Cavour, a leading liberal and founder with Cesare Balbo of the periodical *Il Risorgimento,* Piedmontese premier Massimo d'Azeglio appointed Giuseppe Siccardi as keeper of the seals. Under Siccardi, laws abolished ecclesiastical courts, eliminated the right of asylum, limited the number of holidays, and restricted religious bodies' right to acquire real property.

April 12. Pope Pius IX returned to Rome after his exile during the revolutions of 1848. Pius chose to strengthen both the Catholic Church and papal control of it rather than accept opportunities for nationalist leadership.

1852, Oct. Massimo d'Azeglio was forced to resign the premiership over a civil marriage bill his ministry had introduced that roused Catholic opposition. After a brief period of crisis, Cavour became premier (Nov. 4) in exchange for his assurance that he would not turn the civil marriage bill into a vote of confidence. Cavour governed with the aid of a coalition of Liberals of the Right and Left Center. Cavour's government reorganized finances, negotiated commercial treaties and revised tariffs, planned and implemented public works, and helped develop Piedmont's railway system.

1854, Dec. 8. The dogma of the Immaculate Conception became an article of faith. The pope established this dogma unaided by an ecumenical council.

FRANCE

SWITZERLAND

TRENTINO

AUSTRIA – HUNGARY

SAVOY
(to France,
1860)

LOMBARDY
• Milan

VENETIA

Trieste

CROATIA

ISTRIA

Turin •

PIEDMONT

Venice

Po R.

BOSNIA

NICE
(to France,
1860)

PARMA

MODENA

ROMAGNA

DALMATIA

KINGDOM OF
SARDINIA

MASSA
LUCCA

Arno R.

Florence •

TUSCANY

MARCHES

Adriatic Sea

UMBRIA

CORSICA
(France)

PAPAL STATES

Tiber R.

Rome •

SARDINIA

Naples •

Tyrrhenian

Sea

KINGDOM OF
THE TWO
SICILIES

Mediterranean   Sea

Palermo •

SICILY

THE
UNIFICATION
OF ITALY
1860 – 1870

Kingdom of Sardinia

Area added 1860

Area added 1866

Area added 1870

0   20   40   60   80   100
MILES

1855, Jan. 26. Cavour joined France and Britain during the **Crimean War** (p. 470). The Piedmontese regained morale and prestige as well as improving Piedmont's relations with France and Britain.

1856. Foundation of the National Society by Giuseppe Farina, Daniele Manin, and Giorgio Pallavicino. The organization sought the unification of Italy and received the support of Garibaldi and, secretly, Cavour.

1858, July 20. Secret Meeting of Napoleon III and Cavour at Plombières. Spurred by Orsini's assassination attempt (p. 492), Napoleon III agreed to join Piedmont in a war on Austria if it could be provoked in a manner that would justify it in French and European opinion (formalized by treaty, Dec. 10). After the defeat of Austria, Italy would be organized as a federation of four states with the pope as president—(1) an **upper Italian kingdom** of Piedmont, Lombardy, Venetia, Parma, Modena, and the Papal Legations; (2) a **central kingdom** of Tuscany with Umbria and the Marches; (3) Rome; (4) the **kingdom of Naples.** France would receive Savoy and Nice, and Princess Clotilde, Victor Emmanuel's daughter, would marry Napoleon III's cousin, Prince Joseph Charles Bonaparte.

1859, March 8. Piedmontese reserves were called up, including volunteers.

April 19. Austrian ultimatum to Piedmont demanded that the latter demobilize in three days, which supplied Cavour with the provocation he needed.

April 29. The Austrians invaded Sardinia under Gen. Franz Gyulai, but the French had already arrived by this time.

May. Peaceful revolutions in Tuscany, Modena, and Parma.

May 30. Piedmontese victory at Palestro. Allies advanced into Lombardy and engaged the Austrians at the **Battle of Magenta (June 4).** After the indecisive **Battle of Solferino (June 24),** the Austrians withdrew to the Quadrilateral fortresses.

July 11. Meeting of Napoleon III and Emperor Francis Joseph at Villafranca resulted in peace terms, which Victor Emmanuel later agreed to as well. Lombardy (except Mantua and Peschiera) would be ceded to France who could then cede it to Piedmont. Venetia would remain Austrian. Cavour resigned. The agreement was finalized in the **Treaty of Zürich (Nov. 10).**

1860, Jan. 20. Cavour returned to power as premier and negotiated the annexations with Napoleon in return for the cession of Nice and Savoy to France (**Treaty of Turin, March 24**).

March 13–15. Plebiscites in Parma, Modena, Romagna, and Tuscany favored annexation to Piedmont.

May–July. Garibaldi and his Thousand Redshirts sailed from Genoa to Sicily (May 5) after being diverted by Cavour from their intention to go to Nice. Landing at Marsala (May 11), Garibaldi defeated the Neapolitans at Calatafimi (May 15) and took Palermo (May 27), where he set up a provisional government. He defeated the Neapolitans at Milazzo (July 20).

Sept. 7. Garibaldi took Naples after a triumphal march and planned on defeating the remains of the Neapolitan army (Francis II, who succeeded Ferdinand II in May 1859, fled to Gaeta).

Sept. 8. An uprising in the Papal States gave Cavour, who opposed Garibaldi's plans to march on Rome, an opportunity to intervene. Cavour called upon Cardinal Antonelli, papal secretary of state, to disband his "adventurers," and, when the latter refused, the Piedmontese crossed the papal frontier (Sept. 11) where they virtually annihilated the papal forces at Castelfidaro and advanced into Neopolitan territory, joining forces with Garibaldi.

Oct. 21. Naples and Sicily voted by plebiscite for union with north.

Oct. 26. Garibaldi defeated the Neapolitans on the Volturno.

Nov. 3–1861, Feb. 13. Siege of Gaeta.

Nov. 4–5. The Marches and Umbria voted by plebiscite for union with the north.

1861, March 17. The KINGDOM OF ITALY was proclaimed. Victor Emmanuel was its first king, with the government based on the Piedmontese constitution of 1848.

June 6. Cavour died.

1861–62. Ministry of Baron Bettino Ricasoli. He embarked upon a national agitation for the annexation of Rome.

1862, March 9. Society for the Emancipation of Italy was organized by Garibaldi. Garibaldi and his volunteers crossed to the mainland from Sicily and advanced to the north (Aug. 24).

Aug. 29. Battle of Aspromonte. Government troops defeated Garibaldi. Garibaldi was wounded and captured, but his men were amnestied (Oct. 5).

1864, Sept. 15. The September Convention. Napoleon agreed to evacuate Rome within two years (beginning on Feb. 5, 1865), and the Italians promised to move their capital from Turin to Florence.

Dec. 8. Pope Pius promulgated the encyclical **Quanta cura** and the appended **Syllabus errorum.** These documents censured pantheism, naturalism, nationalism, socialism, communism, freemasonry, and so on, and claimed the church's full control of education, culture, and science. Pius denounced freedom of conscience and worship, and claimed church independence from state control and the necessity of the continuance of the temporal power of the Roman See.

1866, May 12. Alliance of Italy and Prussia.

June–July. Italy declared war on Austria (June 18) but Archduke Albert defeated Italy at the second battle of Custozza (June 24). France ceded Venetia, which it had gained from Austria, to Italy (July 3). The Italian fleet was defeated by the Austrians (July 20).

Oct. 12. The Treaty of Vienna ended the war.

Dec. The last French troops were withdrawn from Rome. Garibaldi again led his volunteers and began the invasion of papal territories. He was captured twice but escaped (Sept. 1867).

1867, Oct. 28. A French force landed at Civita and marched to Rome.

Nov. 3. BATTLE OF MENTANA. Garibaldi was defeated by papal troops supported by the French. Garibaldi was captured and sent to the isle of Caprera.

1869, Dec. 8–1870, Oct. 20. THE VATICAN COUNCIL proclaimed the doctrine of papal infallibility. The doctrine marked the final triumph of the papacy over the episcopal and conciliar tendencies of the church and attempted to exalt the papacy above all secular states.

1870. The Jews were emancipated and the Jewish ghetto in Rome abolished.

Aug. 8. Final withdrawal of French troops from Rome.

Sept. 20. Italians entered Rome after a short bombardment.

Oct. 2. After a plebiscite, Rome was annexed to Italy and became the capital.

2. THE KINGDOM OF ITALY

1871, May 13. The LAW OF GUARANTIES defined relations between the Italian government and the papacy. It granted the pope royal honors and prerogatives and full liberty in the exercise of his religious functions; representatives of foreign powers at the Vatican received diplomatic rights and immunities; the pope received an annual income of 3.25 million lire from the Italian treasury and full enjoyment of the Vatican and other palaces with rights of extraterritoriality. Pius IX did not accept this law and posed as the prisoner of the Vatican.

1873–76. Ministry of Marco Minghetti, in which **Quintino Sella,** minister of finance, exercised "economy to the bone" in an effort to balance the budget. The government reorganized the army and recreated the navy.

1876, March 28. First ministry of the Left under Agostino Depretis. He reduced Parliament by corruption and political alliances (transformismo) and defeated the Right in elections through government pressure. Depretis followed the policy of agitation against Austria (**irrendentism**) aimed at acquiring the Trentino and Trieste—Italian-speaking regions still under Austrian rule.

1877. An act made elementary education compulsory for children from 6 to 9 years of age, but it was poorly enforced.

1878–1903. POPE LEO XIII, more liberal than Pius IX, encouraged the renewed study of St. Thomas Aquinas in all Catholic seminaries, which spread the doctrine that no conflict existed between true science and true religion. Leo also fostered the study of church history to increase the prestige of the church by demonstrating its contributions to the progress of Western civilization. He supported experimental science among eminent Catholics. Leo sought collaboration between church and state.

1878, Jan 9. Death of King Victor Emmanuel.

1878–1900. UMBERTO I.

1881. Extension of the franchise (for males only). The age limit was lowered from 25 to 21 and the tax-paying requirement from 40 to 19 lire.

1885. The management of state railways was delegated to three private companies for 60 years, with possible termination at the end of 20 or 40 years. **Employers' liability for accidents** also was introduced but was poorly administered.

Italian occupation of Assab and Massowa on the Red Sea.

1887, July 29. Death of Depretis.

1887–91. First ministry of Francesco Crispi, who adopted an anticlerical policy after abortive negotiations with the papacy. He abolished ecclesiastical tithes and compulsory religious instruction in elementary schools. Crispi also suppressed radical and irredentist organizations.

1887–89. The Ethiopian venture. Crispi attempted to expand Italian influence on the Red Sea and thus engaged in a war with Ethiopia (p. 592). The Italians, despite a setback at **Dogali (Jan. 25, 1887)** backed Menelik, king of Shoa, against the Ethiopian king of kings, Johannes. In the Italian version of the **Treaty of Uccialli (May 2, 1889),** Menelik accepted an Italian protectorate over Ethiopia.

1891–92. Ministry of Marquis Antonio di Rudini, after fall of Crispi (Jan. 31, 1891). Rudini reduced expenditures for the army and the navy in an attempt to balance the budget.

1891. The labor movement celebrated May Day for the first time, and the *Marxist Critica Sociale* was established with Filippo Turati as editor (1891).

May 15. The papal encyclical on the labor question, *Rerum novarum,* though opposed to socialism, applied Christian principles to labor and capital and established that employers had important moral duties to fulfill and that one of the first duties of society was to improve the condition of the workers.

1892, Aug. The Congress of Italian Working Men met in Genoa. Anarchists and Socialists divided at the congress, and the Socialists founded the **Socialist Workingmen's Party (1893).**

1892–93. Giovanni Giolitti's first ministry. Giolitti fell as a result of a banking crisis. He made the managing director of the Banca Romana, Signor Tanlongo, a senator. A parliamentary investigation revealed Tanlongo had issued large sums of duplicate bank notes, and that the two preceding cabinets were aware of these irregularities.

1893, Aug. 10. Bank of Italy established to replace the insolvent Banca Romana. The law forbade state banks to make loans in real estate and limited their powers of discount.

Dec.–1896, March. The second Crispi ministry addressed the banking crisis and growing unrest among the peasants of Sicily and anarchists.

1894. Laws of July 11 and Oct. 22 **suppressed anarchist and socialist organizations.**

1895–96. THE ETHIOPIAN WAR. Menelik had rejected the Treaty of Uccialli and prepared to take on the Italians.

1895, Dec. 7. The Italians were defeated at Amba Alagi. The fortress of Makallé fell on Jan. 20, 1896. Crispi insisted that Gen. Oreste Baratieri secure a victory to save Italian honor.

1896, March 1. Battle of Adua (Adowa). The Italians were completely defeated by the Ethiopians. The Italians sued for peace and signed the Treaty of Addis Ababa (Oct. 26) recognizing Ethiopian independence.

1898. A commercial treaty between France and Italy ended the tariff war between the countries to the detriment of Italy.

May 3–8. THE "FATTI DI MAGGIO." Serious bread riots throughout Italy culminated in Milan where the government declared a state of siege and suppressed the press and political organizations. Heavy sentences by court-martial, especially against socialists, ensued. Rudini resigned.

June 28–1900, June 18. Ministry of Gen. Luigi Pelloux. He presented to Parliament the **Public Safety Law,** which restricted the right of assembly and association, and freedom of the press. The Radicals opposed the law. Pelloux tried to enact it by decree and then to appeal to the country. The vote, however, returned more Radicals, and Pelloux resigned.

1900, July 29. King Umberto was assassinated by an anarchist at Monza.

1900–46. VICTOR EMMANUEL III. He adopted more liberal policies than those of his father.

1900–2. Workers staged a large number of strikes to protest poor working and living conditions. Parliament recognized workers' right to organize and act within the law.

1902, Jan.–Feb. Strike of the employees of the Mediterranean Railway, demanding, among other things, recognition of their union. Gas employees followed with their own strike, and a general strike seemed

imminent. The government called up all railway workers who were reservists but reached a settlement in June.

1903–14. POPE PIUS X carried out an extensive reorganization of the Curia in order to modernize its machinery (1908) and began the codification of canon law (1904–June 28, 1917, under Benedict XV). He vehemently opposed the **Modernists** (including Father George Tyrrell in England, Abbé Loisy in France, and Antonio Fogazzaro in Italy) who sought to bring church doctrine into line with scientific scholarship.

1904, Sept. General strike proclaimed, but it had little lasting consequence. Reformism began to take hold of the Italian working-class movement.

1906. The Confederation of Labor, a reformist socialist organization was established.

May 30–1909, Dec. 2. Ministry of Giolitti.

1907, Sept. 8. The papal encyclical *Pascendi gregis* condemned and censured the Modernist system.

1908. Giolitti sponsored a measure to facilitate religious education by making it available upon demand but optional.

Revived nationalism under **Gabriel d'Annunzio** and others influenced government foreign policy.

Dec. 28. An earthquake struck Calabria and eastern Sicily and destroyed Reggio and Messina. A tidal wave also struck the latter. Loss of life was estimated at 150,000.

1909, Dec. 2. Giolitti's government overturned. Sonnino (Dec. 1909–March 1910) and Luzzatti (March 1910–March 1911) followed.

1911, March 29–1914, March 10. Giolitti became prime minister again.

1911, Sept. 29–1912, Oct. 15. The TRIPOLITAN WAR (pp. 478, 534). Concerned with growing instability in the region as evidenced by the Moroccan crises, the Italians issued an ultimatum to the Ottomans, demanding the right to take Tripoli. The Italians landed at Tripoli (Oct. 5, 1911) and occupied the town. The Italians then proceeded with naval operations in the Red Sea and along the Syrian coast, but Austria's refusal to permit war on the Balkan or Aegean coasts hampered them. The Ottomans closed the Straits after an Italian naval demonstration at the Dardanelles (April 16–19, 1912). The Italians occupied Rhodes and the other Dodecanese Islands (May 4–16, 1912). Peace negotiations opened in July without much success. The Ottomans capitulated under the threat of the Balkan Wars. The **Treaty of Ouchy** (definitive Treaty of Lausanne, Oct. 18) ended the war. The Ottomans gave up Tripoli, but the Italians recognized a representative of the sultan as caliph and restored the Dodecanese Islands to the Ottomans.

1912, June 29. Extension of the franchise increased the number of voters from about 3 million to about 8.5 million. This nearly amounted to universal male suffrage. The bill also provided members of Parliament with salaries.

1913, Oct. The general election gave the Liberals a majority but increased the number of seats occupied by Socialists (78 instead of 41) and Catholics (35 instead of 14).

1914, March 9. A general strike was proclaimed at Rome, which demonstrated popular resistance to tax increases necessitated by the Tripolitan War.

March 10. Cabinet of Antonio Salandra. The revolutionary railway union demanded an increase in wages, but the government and workers compromised.

June 7. Riots broke out in Ancona, and a general strike followed. Enrico Malatesta led the uprising, and **Benito Mussolini,** then editor of the socialist newspaper, took a prominent part.

Aug. 3. Italy proclaimed neutrality in World War I. *(To p. 693)*

g. SWITZERLAND

(From p. 469)

Economic development. The Swiss federal government sought to standardize currencies and weights and measures, expand and regulate postal and telegraph systems, and encourage technological development. While attempting to assure greater federal control, the government continued to face difficulties because the federal system in Switzerland allowed each canton significant independence, including the creation of its own constitution.

1848. The canton of Glarus restricted men to a 13-hour workday, or 10-

hour night shifts, and tried but failed to establish an intercantonal regulatory agreement.

1849. The role of the Swiss as mercenary soldiers in Europe ended as the **Federal Assembly forbade recruiting** in Switzerland on behalf of foreign powers and military capitulations in accordance with the new constitution.

1852. Following a review by English engineers, the Bund lost most of its authority over railway building. The railways became privately owned, and the miles of track grew substantially.

May. The state took control of secondary education in the canton of Ticino. The state abolished several religious institutions responsible for teaching and expelled the monks.

1855. First academic year began for the **federal school of technology,** which provided essential training for the advancement of Swiss industry. The government guaranteed the teachers freedom in their teaching and made certain that all three languages spoken in Switzerland would be represented. It marked a departure from the many problems encountered in efforts to establish a federal university in the midst of differences of religion.

1856–57. The Neuchâtel problem. The royalists seized control of the castle and other territory in the canton of Neuchâtel, seeking to declare a monarchy. The canton had become a republic in 1848, but it was also subject to the sovereignty of the king of Prussia, who threatened to intervene when the canton's militia retook the castle. Napoleon III managed to avert a war between Switzerland and Prussia. In May 1857, the king relinquished his rights in return for a money payment, which he later renounced.

1865, Oct. Revision of the constitution was begun, but burgesses rejected most of the provisions in 1866.

1866. Jews gained equal rights in regard to movement and settlement for both religious and commercial purposes.

July. The Federal Council outlawed export of weapons and war materials.

1870. The Swiss Socialist Party was founded in Zürich as a result of the collapse of the Second International. The socialist platform demanded increased government centralization and a sliding scale of taxation as well as more legislation to be carried out by the people. The Socialist Party was reorganized in 1907, but it never adopted revolutionary programs and remained concerned with Swiss rather than international working-class problems.

1873. Efforts to proclaim **papal infallibility** (p. 498) in Switzerland met with government resistance. In **Berne,** the state called on the clergy to break off relations with the Catholic bishop, and, when they refused, the state fined and imprisoned them—demanding the right to examine and appoint all Catholic clergy. In **Geneva,** a law eliminated religious associational activities within the schools and established the popular election of the clergy. However, these policies led only to growing popular support for the priests.

1874, April 19. A new constitution strengthened the federal government by providing for a better-organized federal militia and introduced a system of **referendum and initiative,** which gave the Swiss people the right to vote on legislation. It also established **civil marriage,** provided compulsory free **education** for both girls and boys with freedom of religion, and allowed individuals to stipulate whether they supported the Catholic or Protestant church or chose to support neither.

Oct. International Postal Congress met at Berne; Switzerland became headquarters for many international conferences and organizations.

1882, May 20. Opening of the **St. Gothard Railway,** first of the great railroad tunnels through the Alps.

1887. A factory law enforced the **11-hour day** and Sundays off, forbade children under age 14 from working in factories, and regulated women's work and the construction and operation of factory buildings.

1889, June. As a result of their position of neutrality, the **Swiss arrested and expelled a Prussian policeman** attempting to capture a spy on Swiss territory. Bismarck immediately demanded an apology and withdrawal of the expulsion from the Federal Council. He threatened to invade Swiss territory and establish his own police force there. The Swiss Federal Council refused, and Bismarck finally dropped the issue.

1890, Sept. 12–14. Radicals rose in Ticino as a result of an election in which, despite a draw, the Conservatives obtained the majority of seats

in the Ticinese Great Council. The Radicals revolted, establishing a provisional government after imprisoning municipal councils in Bellinzona and Lugano. The federal government intervened, sent troops to quell the insurrection, and helped provide proportional representation in the Great Council. The Radicals came to power in Ticino after a **new constitution** was established in 1892, which extended civil rights.

1890–98. Federal powers increased as the federal government received the right to enact social insurance (1890), purchase privately owned railways (1898), and unify and enforce civil and penal codes (1898).

1897, Aug. 21–31. First Zionist conference. Theodor Herzl, author of *The Jewish State,* presided. The conference began the Zionist efforts to establish a Jewish state in Israel.

1907, April 12. A new army bill established an army of 281,000 men with a reserve of 200,000, strengthening the Swiss defensive capabilities. However, the Swiss maintained their neutrality, and, in 1911, the army commanders issued a proclamation indicating their support of this policy.

1911. Federal law provided **mandatory accident insurance** and **subsidized health insurance.**

1914, Aug. 1–4. Parliament granted the executive unlimited powers in the wake of massive mobilization. Neutrality was proclaimed, and Germany was notified that attempts to violate it would be repelled with armed force. *(To p. 696)*

h. CENTRAL EUROPE

(From p. 470)

1. GERMANY

1849–50. After the failed 1848 revolution, **Frederick William of Prussia** and adviser **Radowitz** pushed for more German unity with loose ties to the Habsburg monarchy. A **Prussian Union** scheme (May 26, 1849) won agreement from several North German states, and a **National Assembly at Erfurt** (Oct. 19) was confirmed. Austrian opposition grew, however, and war threatened.

1850, Nov. 29. Olmütz Proclamation. The Prussian president, Manteuffel, and the Austrian prime minister, Schwarzenberg, agreed to joint action in Hesse and Schleswig (dispute between Elector and Parliament) and called for a conference to determine future action among German states. Liberals considered the proclamation a humiliating surrender of Prussian power, but most conservatives, including **Otto von Bismarck,** accepted it. It set the stage for the growing animosity between Austrians and Prussians over the *großdeutsch* and *kleindeutsch* question. The Prussian Union was abandoned and the old Germanic Confederation restored at a conference in Dresden.

Dec.–1851, March. A Dresden conference on German affairs. Revival of conservatism around the newspaper **Kreuzzeitung** (founded in 1848).

1854. The press was stifled; political arrests rose; political clubs were dissolved.

Economy. The German economy experienced rapid growth spurred by heavy industry and chemicals. Germany gained on Britain as a leader in the world economy. Germany also suffered from the short worldwide depression of 1857–59, when agricultural overproduction combined with a wave of financial panic. With the exception of banks in Hamburg that were closely tied to British banking, German banks remained solvent. Agricultural developments included more modern farming techniques, growing use of chemical fertilizers, and an increase in the use of wage labor.

Elite society. The mid-19th century is often considered the age of the **Bürgertum**—the urban economic elites. These elites increasingly **defined culture** during this period by establishing proper values, styles, and educational goals. However, they continued to be overshadowed politically in Prussia by the **Junkers;** a three-class voting system established in 1848 and confirmed in 1866 and 1871 (p. 470) gave the Junkers access to a third of the seats in the Landtag. Bismarck, himself from a Junker family, relied on Junker support after his break with the liberals and created a marriage of "iron and rye." This phrase represented the two major elites in Germany—the industrial and financial capitalists and the large agricultural landowners.

The working classes. The German working class shifted from the craftworkers who had participated in the revolutions of 1848 to the growing number of industrial workers who gradually organized through the efforts of the trade organizations of the socialists, Catholics, and even the industrialists themselves.

Women. German values continued to stress the **importance of the family** and the superiority of men within that family. The family was considered the basis of the state, and therefore **German laws reinforced male legal superiority** through divorce laws, legal control of property, and education. Women continued to balance wage work in and outside the home with the chores of maintaining the household. **Women workers** suffered because they seldom gained seniority at a workplace—changing jobs frequently as a result of pregnancies and the demands of families. Furthermore, the **socialist trade unions** adopted a stance against women in the workplace, which meant that women workers remained unorganized. The **Catholic trade unions** did create women's auxiliaries, but they met with little response and, because of the strong family values of Catholicism, struggled to provide both economic and religious guidance.

1854. The Darmstädter Bank für Handel und Industrie was founded. It was modeled after the Crédit mobilier of Paris. It not only made short term loans, but also assisted in the organization of business and industry. This bank marked the beginning of a German tradition of active participation of banks in industry.

April. Prussia and Austria established a defensive alliance, although Prussian policy still remained unclear with regard to Austria.

1857, Oct. Prince William temporarily took over the government from his ailing brother. He then became the **prince regent (Oct. 1858).** William's regency marked the end of the reactionary conservatism of the 1850s. William supported civil rights as stipulated in the Prussian constitution, and his more liberal stance resulted in increased participation in the elections of 1858.

Liberalization began in much of Germany near the end of the 1850s. In **Bavaria,** King Maximilian established a cautious alliance with the progressives after the conservatives fell in the election of 1858. **Grand Duke Frederick of Baden** cooperated with a liberal majority in the Landtag to create a series of reforms.

1859–62. Bismarck became the Prussian ambassador to Russia and then to France, despite his inexperience. Bismarck also began to place himself on the side of a *kleindeutsch* solution to the unification of Germany. He sent an extended memorandum known as the **Booklet** to the prince. The Booklet argued for a strong Germany led by an independent Prussia.

1859, Sept. Prussian liberals gained support as they formed the Nationalverein (National Union) committed to the *kleindeutsch* option and liberalism. Their support remained much stronger than the Reformverein (Reform Union) organized in Oct. 1862, which supported the *großdeutsch* option.

1860–62. Liberal crisis. Prince William became **King William I** upon the death of his brother (Jan. 1861), and he broke with the Liberals over the military. The Prussian army had remained unchanged since the end of the Napoleonic Wars, and, in 1860, Prince William called upon **Gen. Albrecht von Roon,** minister of war, to reorganize the army. His **Army Bill of 1860** increased the size of the infantry, required expenditures to be raised by one-quarter, and made each draftee serve three years in the army or four in the cavalry and remain in the reserves for another four to five years. The Liberals had no intention of supporting such a bill but passed a **provisional money bill** instead. The latter effectively gave William the means to proceed with the reorganization without the passage of any specific plan.

1861. Formation of the Fortschrittspartei (Progressive Party). King William faced the problem of rising costs for the military in 1861 and managed to receive a 7.3-million-taler grant from the Landtag to defray those costs. The unwillingness of the Liberals to oppose such a grant helped lead to the establishment of the minority Progressive Party, which called for the complete realization of the constitution, continuation of the national guard, two-year military service, and an active policy on unification.

1862, March. The failure of money bills. The Landtag refused to pass another money bill for the military. This action was the result of the electoral success of the Fortschrittspartei in the Dec. elections. The king dissolved the government and formed another cabinet, but the money bill failed again in Sept. He now considered resignation, but his son refused to take the throne.

Sept. 30. Otto von Bismarck was named prime minister and foreign minister. Bismarck relied on **article 99** of the Prussian constitution, which gave the king power to fund government on the basis of existing tax systems if an agreement in the Landtag could not be reached. In doing so, Bismarck made it clear that he intended to govern without the Landtag's approval, if necessary.

1863, May 23. The General German Workers' Association (ADAV) was established under Lasalle. This association was torn between socialism and democracy as its driving forces, and Lasalle soon came into conflict with two other leading socialists, Bebel and Liebknecht. The latter became the leaders in the formation of the Marxist Social Democratic Party.

1864, Jan. 16. Austria and Prussia presented Copenhagen with an ultimatum after agreeing to assist each other in the **war with Denmark** (p. 507) over Schleswig-Holstein. (Denmark had announced virtual annexation of the provinces.) The ultimatum demanded the cancellation of the newly enacted Danish constitution because it included control of Schleswig-Holstein (p. 470). The quickly successful war with Denmark, which followed, resulted in Schleswig-Holstein being ceded to Austria and Prussia.

1865, Aug. 4. The convention of Gastein gave administration of Holstein to Austria, a maneuver by Bismarck to raise new issues with Austria (p. 471).

1866. Austro-Prussian (Seven Weeks') War (p. 471). Prussian troops moved from Schleswig into Holstein (June 9). (On **April 8,** Prussia allied itself with Italy to join in the anticipated war.) The move was calculated to force hostilities to begin between Austria and Prussia, but the occupying Austrian forces managed to withdraw from Holstein without a battle. **Austria made a motion at the Diet** of Frankfurt for the mobilization of all non-Prussian armed forces, which was modified to read all non-Prussian and non-Austrian forces by the Bavarian minister. **The Bavarian motion passed (June 14, 1866).** The Prussian minister declared the Federal Act broken, and war between the South German states and Prussia began; Prussia was victorious. Prussia turned its forces, under the direction of **Helmuth von Moltke,** to Austria. Moltke won the decisive Battle at **Sadowa (July 3).** Successful tactics of the new Prussian army included use of railroads for rapid troop deployment and breech-loading guns.

July 26. The Peace of Nicolsburg established the **North German Confederation** and secured for the south the right to form a southern federation. It also united Prussia by annexing the states formed between the east and the west at the Congress of Vienna (p. 440).

1867, April 16. The North German Confederation accepted a constitution that gave the confederation control over foreign policy and economic policies at home and abroad. It provided for a Parliament elected by universal male suffrage and required that all federal laws be published and discussed within the Parliament. The king of Prussia would serve as **military commander in chief;** the democratically elected **lower house** (Reichstag) would be balanced by the federal council (Prussian-dominated) of state representatives. Most Prussian liberals accepted this incomplete parliamentary monarchy on grounds of nationalism.

1868, July 8. Bismarck decreed industrial freedom, which meant the end of any possibility of guild protection.

1869. The Social Democratic Workers' Party (later to be called the Social Democratic Party, or SPD) was formed at a workers' conference in Eisenach by combining **Bebel's Federation of Workers** and dissenting Lasalleans. This party adopted a Marxist doctrine. Continued mergers among socialist groups led to the adoption of the **Gotha Program (1875),** stating that the SPD would work within any legal means to create a free state and socialist society. It called for the introduction of universal male suffrage, civil liberties and the right of association, and the improvement of working conditions and hours.

1870, July 13. The Ems Telegram was sent to Bismarck. Bismarck had pursued a policy designed to encourage hostilities between Prussia and France in an effort to gain the support of southern Germany. Toward this end, Bismarck encouraged **Leopold of Hohenzollern to take the Spanish throne (March 9, 1869).** William I discouraged such activity, and Leopold declined the throne; William I then decided not to see the

French diplomat, Benedetti, again. Bismarck received the telegram to this effect but stated the terms of the telegram to the press in such a way that it suggested that French and Prussian foreign relations were at a rupture. **As a result, the French government declared war on Prussia.**

1870–71. The Franco-Prussian War (pp. 471, 492) established Prussian military superiority as Prussia advanced on France and laid siege to Paris. The Prussians humiliated the French, and Bismarck secured the support of the southern German states in his efforts at unification. The new Germany gained Alsace and much of Lorraine from France.

1871. German unification. The southern provinces agreed to a stronger federalist system in the **November Treaties (Nov. 15, 1870),** which were followed by the introduction of the constitution of 1871. This constitution established a **federal council** in which Prussia maintained the chair and had an absolute veto. It did give the kingdoms of Bavaria, Württemberg, and Saxony an absolute veto if they voted in unison. The democratically elected (by male suffrage) **Reichstag** was balanced by the council; ministerial responsibility was held by the emperor, not Parliament. The Prussian military organization was extended as the means of maintaining armed forces for the empire. It also established the **Reservatrechte** (maintenance of certain rights such as levying of beer and liquor taxes). This concession had only slight consequences for the stronger federalist state that Bismarck was forging.

1871. Having been given equality (1848). German Jews were guaranteed their rights.

Jan. 18. William I was proclaimed German emperor at Versailles. William I was surrounded by a Prussian show of military force as he ushered in the **Second Reich.**

1870–80. Economic unification began almost immediately with the introduction of the *mark* as the **German unit of currency** (Dec. 1871), the gradual abolition of trade treaties (1873–77) within Germany, and the creation of a **new commercial code** and **imperial bank (1875).**

1872, Dec. 12. Kreisordnung provided for the reorganization of local and county governments within Prussia. The brainchild of minister of interior **Count Friedrich Eulenburg,** the new law took the police out of the hands of local manor lords and placed them in the hands of the provincial high president. It also removed the hereditary right of noble families to representation on the county diet. Nonetheless, the Junkers continued to maintain a majority on those diets and often continued to control the police.

1873–78. The Kulturkampf can be dated from the May Laws of 1873.

1873, May 11–14. The May Laws were introduced by Adalbert Falk, Prussian minister of ecclesiastical affairs. The May Laws allowed only priests who attended German high schools and universities to be appointed to German parishes and eliminated papal jurisdiction over the Catholic Church in Prussia. **The purpose** of such actions was to eliminate the threat to the government posed by the **Catholic Center Party,** which had been formed in 1870.

1875. Civil marriage became obligatory; most Catholic religious orders were dissolved. Bismarck's efforts failed because they turned into a battle against the church rather than the Catholic Center Party. The Catholic Church and its lay associations continued to support the church. The Kulturkampf had only limited impact outside of Prussia and led to deep resentment among Catholics within Prussia. It never weakened the Catholic Center, which remained a force to be reckoned with whenever the government tried to obtain a majority in the Prussian Reichstag. **It came to an end when Pope Leo XIII negotiated the problem in 1878–79;** by 1883, some May Laws had been rescinded and the others were ignored.

1878, May 11. An attempt on William I's life gave Bismarck the opportunity to push for **antisocialist legislation** (Oct. 18, 1878) in an effort to neutralize another threat to his government. The perpetrator, **Max Hödel,** had no clear link with the SPD, but Bismarck succeeded in identifying that party as the origin of the threat. He forced the liberals to support an antisocialist law that outlawed meetings, organizations, and publications of socialists, communists, and democrats. It did not, however, demand the removal from office of the socialists within the government, and it had to be renewed every two and a half years. **Results:** The overt socialist organizations and newspapers were destroyed in Germany, but the SPD maintained a clandestine presence in numerous cultural organizations. Socialist journalists printed newspa-

pers in Switzerland and had them smuggled into Germany, using a network of socialist workers that included a large number of railroad workers. As a result, when **the Reichstag refused to renew the law in 1890,** the SPD emerged stronger than it had been in 1878.

Growth of anti-Semitism. Discrimination and prejudice against the Jews has been a persistent theme in Christian Europe, but a modern, racist attack on Jews developed in the 1870s and 1880s. While anti-Semitic writings spread in several countries, including France (p. 494), a number of organizations targeting the Jews developed in Germany during the last quarter of the 19th century. **William Marr's The Victory of Judaism over Teutonism** (1873) introduced the term "anti-Semitism" into the German language and identified the "Jewish problem" with race rather than religious differences. **Otto Glagau's The Stock Exchange and Founding Swindle in Berlin** claimed links among Manchester liberalism, capitalism, and Jewish efforts at taking over Germany. In 1878, **Adolf Stöcker** organized the **Christian-Social Party,** which combined anti-Semitism with Christian doctrine; the anti-Semitic League of German Students was founded in 1881.

German intellectual life involved growing nationalism. **Heinrich von Treitschke** provided Germany with a strong image of its own history infused with the notion of destiny and the triumph of the German spirit. **Friedrich Nietzsche** indicted the Judeo-Christian tradition for creating weak-willed individuals who refused to take charge of their own destinies. He introduced the concept of the **Übermensch** (superman) whose will triumphs over all emotion and obstacles. The imagery of this "triumph of the will" later became central in the philosophy of Nazism, but it did not represent mere anti-Semitism but a repudiation by Nietzsche of all religious "weakness." **Richard Wagner's** anti-Semitism is well documented, but his music reflected less his personal convictions than the inner torment and struggle within everyone.

Social legislation. In 1883, Bismarck introduced a **health insurance bill,** which provided health care for a large number of wage workers. An **accident insurance bill** followed in 1884, which provided medical coverage and a pension of two-thirds the worker's earnings in the event of full disability. In 1889, the government completed this legislation with **old-age and disability insurance,** which provided modest benefits to workers in most sectors. **The purpose** of such legislation was to alleviate the suffering of many workers while undermining support for socialism. However, it proved unable to stop the increase in such support.

Foreign policy proved to be Bismarck's genius. Bismarck initially established himself as an "honest broker" by convening the **Congress of Berlin (1878)** (p. 472) to settle the disputes surrounding the conflict in the Balkans. Aiming at isolating France and preventing attacks on the 1871 settlement, Bismarck restored the **Alliance of the Three Emperors** (p. 473) among Germany, Austria-Hungary, and Russia (Jan. 18, 1881). **The Triple Alliance (May 20, 1882)** established a defensive treaty among Germany, Austria-Hungary, and Italy. He organized the **Congo Conference of Berlin (1884–85)** to establish some limitations on British imperial power but also to reach an equitable means of partitioning Africa. Bismarck also negotiated the Reinsurance Treaty.

1887, June 18. The Reinsurance Treaty guaranteed friendly neutrality between Russia and Germany in the event that either country went to war with any country other than France or Austria-Hungary.

1888. William II succeeded to the throne. Unlike his father, William II entertained the notion of being his own first minister and so clashed with Bismarck.

1889, May. A miners' strike in the Ruhr was ended through the mediation of William II.

1890, Jan. 25. The Anti-Socialist Law was eliminated. Bismarck had attempted to make this law permanent, but he faced opposition from the Liberals as well as from William II. He also lost support in the election of 1890 as the National Liberals lost seats to the Progressives, and the Social Democratic Party gained more of the popular vote than the resultant 35 seats indicated.

March 18. Bismarck accepted his dismissal and left the government. He was replaced by **Gen. Leo von Caprivi,** whom William hoped would follow the emperor's lead.

1891. Formation of the Pan-German League. This league supported German colonization and the development of German ideals by offering support to Germans who lived abroad. It drew its support from

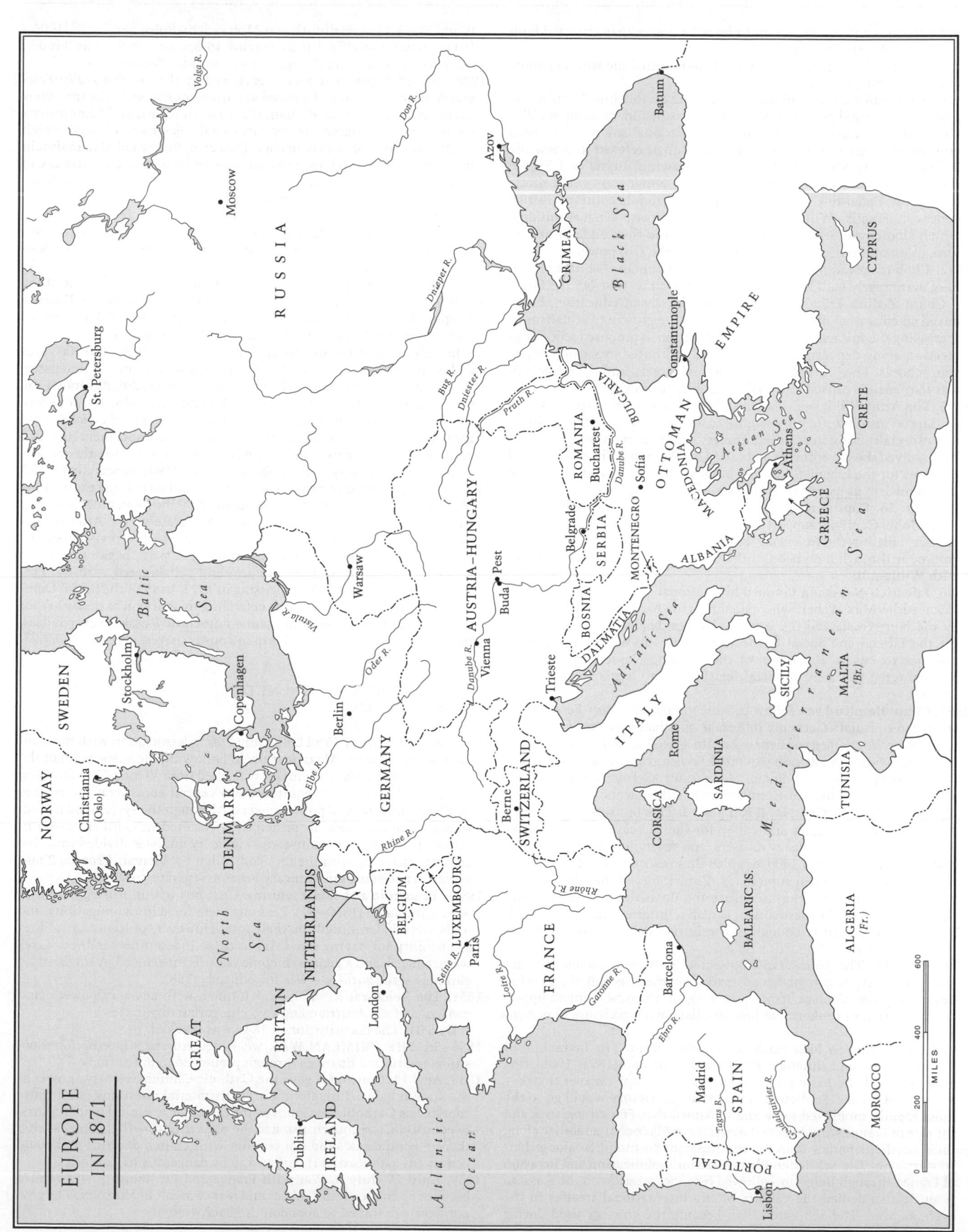

EUROPE
IN 1871

industrialists and academics and adopted a policy that attracted both National Liberals and anti-Semites.

June 1. Laws abolished Sunday work and limited the working hours of women and children.

Foreign policy under William II focused on establishing Germany as a world power and providing for colonial expansion. In doing so, William rode the wave of imperialism and nationalism that had been growing throughout Germany. The government **refused to renew the Reinsurance Treaty with Russia,** thus drawing Russia and France toward an alliance (p. 474). Meanwhile, the Germans supported efforts to **stop the Canal-to-Cape Railroad in Africa** from becoming a British endeavor. Finally, William II engaged in a **massive naval buildup,** which challenged British supremacy at sea and thus undermined efforts to maintain friendly relations between the two powers.

1892. Cholera spread north from France into Germany—hitting Hamburg particularly hard because of poorly treated water from the Elbe.

Count Zedlitz-Trützschler, Prussian minister of education, introduced an education bill that sought to stop the growth of socialism by increasing the influence of Christian education. It proposed school segregation along denominational lines and unlimited expansion of private schools. The bill was opposed by the Liberals, and the bitter contest that ensued caused Zedlitz-Trützschler to resign.

1893. The Army Bill failed (May 6) and then passed after elections (July 8). Caprivi introduced a bill designed to increase the size of the military and especially to increase the numbers of the draft. After its failure, he dissolved the government and called for elections. The elections led to losses for the Liberals, partially because the Conservatives adopted anti-Semitism as part of their platform for the first time.

1894, Oct. 26. Caprivi resigned and was replaced by **Prince Chlodwig Hohenlohe.** Caprivi's support for a subversion bill, which targeted socialists, failed in the Reichstag, and Caprivi considered attempting to enforce it through a revision of the constitution. This led to a break with William II.

1896. Friedrich Naumann founded his National Social Association. Influenced by Max Weber, who called for true participation in politics by the bourgeoisie and the working classes, Naumann attempted to get the Liberal and Social Democratic Parties to work more closely together to ensure the rights of the working classes. In doing so, he countered the lack of social legislation in Germany during the 1890s.

1897. Count Bernhard von Bülow became foreign secretary. **Foreign policy began to isolate Germany in Europe.** German support of the Boers in the Boer War helped to alienate Britain as well as fuel naval buildups in Germany (p. 476). Britain exploited French fears of Germany to establish stronger ties with France. As a result, Germans began to talk about the **encirclement of Germany** by hostile powers.

1898, March 28. The First Naval Bill passed. This bill was drawn up by **Adm. Alfred von Tirpitz** and called for the increase of the navy by seven battleships, two heavy cruisers, and seven light cruisers. A **second naval bill,** passed in 1900, doubled these estimates and thus began to threaten British naval supremacy. Tirpitz argued that the German navy must be in a position to engage the British in a decisive battle that would allow the Germans to continue international trade. Such a battle would destroy enough of the British fleet to eliminate that fleet's supremacy.

1902, Dec. 14. The Bülow tariff protected both grain production and heavy industry, despite higher costs to consumers, as part of a **growing European protectionism.** It was also a sign of the new German **upper-class coalition of Junkers and industrialists,** who made use of nationalist rhetoric.

1905. The Schlieffen Plan reached its classic form. The brainchild of **Count Alfred von Schlieffen,** Prussian chief of staff (1891–1906), this plan provided the basic strategy for fighting a war on two fronts—Russia and France. Schlieffen argued that the **victory would go to the most rapidly mobilized force** and reckoned that French logistics and the size of France would make it easier for the French to mobilize along their northern border than for the Russians to mobilize along their western one. **The Schlieffen Plan called for mobilization and invasion of France through Belgium,** followed by concentration on the Russian front. It also **denied the validity of any international treaties** in the event of war. The Schlieffen Plan became the strategy used during

World War I. Gen. Helmuth von Moltke (chief of general staff [1906–1914]), merely modified it by leaving troops on the Russian border, rather than mobilizing the entire force through Belgium.

1908, Oct. 28. William II was interviewed by the *London Daily Telegraph.* In the interview, he posed as a friend of England. The interview led to severe attacks on William II's personal regime and admonitions for William to observe his constitutional roles more closely, which marked support for the chancellor. However, Bülow **failed to maintain the support of the Reichstag by passing an income and capital tax** to help fund growing expenditures, including those caused by military buildup. **Bülow resigned his position.**

1909, July 14. Bethmann-Hollweg became chancellor. He appointed **Alfred von Kiderlen-Wächter** as foreign secretary. Bethmann-Hollweg tried to appease the British but failed given German refusal to offer concessions on the navy.

1912. The Army Bill allowed for a substantial increase in the size of the army. Spurred by pressure from organizations such as the **Defense League,** the Reichstag expanded the army further in 1913 and passed a special capital bill designed to finance these increases.

Jan. Elections to the Reichstag. The Socialists polled 4,250,000 votes and, with 110 deputies, became the strongest party in the Reichstag. By this time the movement had become much modified through the "**revisionist**" tendency introduced by **Eduard Bernstein.** The revisionists sought to divert interest from the "ultimate goal" of socialism and to fasten attention on the importance of gradual advancement, through parliamentary reforms, toward a new social world. This theory was denounced as a heresy at the **Lübeck congress** (1901, especially by **Karl Kautsky** and **Rosa Luxemburg**), but it nevertheless colored the outlook of the party, which was further influenced by the rapid progress of the trade union movement, dominated by moderate views. After the serious setback of the Socialists in the election of 1907, revisionism became more and more generally accepted. The party began to take an active part in work for social reform and collaborated with the Progressives in organizing the Reichstag in 1912. In 1914 the Social Democrats voted for the war credits, defending their action as necessary for the defense of the fatherland against autocratic Russia. Nevertheless, the socialist rise frightened German conservatives. *(To pp. 650, 697)*

2. THE AUSTRIAN EMPIRE
(From pp. 467, 468)

1849–60. THE BACH SYSTEM, named for its association with the minister of the interior, **Alexander Bach.** Following the suspension of the constitution of 1849, the empire was ruled from Vienna. The abolition of manorialism (p. 467) required a new central bureaucracy to replace landlords' judicial and police powers. Although the system did not advocate **Germanization** in principle, it resulted in Germanization in action. Hungary lost its historical identity and was divided into five administrative "governments" controlled by Vienna. **Croatia, Transylvania, and southern Hungary** became separate provinces.

1850s. Economic and social reforms. Customs within Austria-Hungary were eliminated (1850–51). Peasants were freed from obligations, and lords were indemnified for their loss. However, peasants carried responsibility for paying one-third of these indemnities. Indirect taxes were reduced, and a general income tax was introduced. A single silver currency—the *guilder*—was introduced (1858).

1851. The Reichsrat (council) was formed, with advisory powers, and consisted of six Austrian and two Hungarian dignitaries.

Dec. 31. The constitution of 1849 was revoked.

1854–56. THE CRIMEAN WAR weakened Austria's international position and ruined finances through prolonged mobilization.

1855, Aug. 18. Concordat gave the Catholic Church extensive power as the state religion. Jurisdiction on **matrimonial questions** of all those baptized as Catholics was moved from secular to ecclesiastical courts. In **education,** the church also had the right to ensure that courses other than religion classes did not conflict with church doctrine and could censor any publication it believed to be dangerous to Catholics.

1859, April 29–July 6. War with France and Piedmont (p. 498) ended because of financial difficulties and fear of revolt in Hungary. The government was forced to abandon the Bach system.

1860, Jan. 6–10, Feb. 18. Austrian Jews were allowed to own real estate; oppressive laws were annulled.

1860–61. Constitutional reforms. The emperor enlarged the Reichsrat (March 5, 1860), appointing some Magyars, Croats, and Serbs. The **October Diploma (Oct. 20, 1860)** extended limited legislative powers to this Reichsrat and decreed that its members would be selected by the diets in each land. The **February Patent (Feb. 26, 1861)** established a bicameral legislature with an upper house of aristocrats with hereditary seats and members appointed by the king for life. The lower house consisted of members elected by state diets, but the reforms favored the German bourgeoisie.

1861, April 8. Civil and political rights were granted to Protestants.

April 29. The Reichsrat met, but Magyars, Croatians, and Italians boycotted it. The Hungarian Parliament called for recognition of the Hungarian constitution of 1848. The government continued to try to rule with this rump Reichsrat until the **government suspended the constitution (Sept. 21, 1865).**

1867. Austro-Hungarian Jews were granted legal equality.

AUSTRO-HUNGARIAN COMPROMISE (Ausgleich) of 1867 was developed by **Francis Déak** and recognized two independent states united by common interests and the person of the monarch, thus establishing a **dual monarchy.** The compromise stipulated that if Austria violated the political independence of Hungary by trying to govern both states as a federation, Hungary had the right to declare its own independence from Austrian rule. But the problem of Slavs and other minorities remained unresolved.

Dec. 21. Constitutional laws established a new Austrian constitution, which provided a bicameral legislature; extended basic rights, but also allowed civil rights to be suspended in case of emergency; and guaranteed ethnic equality before the law and in language, including each ethnic group's right to education and church services in its own language. They did not, however, extend political rights or autonomy to each nationality. They extended ministerial responsibility but did not secure the right of approval of the cabinet for the Reichsrat.

3. AUSTRIA-HUNGARY

The dualistic system strengthened Emperor Francis Joseph's position in foreign policy but caused intense problems in domestic policies. It also left unresolved issues of national differences that undermined efforts at solidarity among parties and within social movements.

a. Austria

Ministers: Count Adolf Auersperg (Dec. 1867–Jan. 1870) represented German liberals and stressed anticlericalism. Count Karl Hohenwart (Feb.–Oct. 25, 1871) represented federalist groups and tried to achieve greater autonomy for the various nationalities. Count Hohenwart returned (Nov. 1871–78) and maintained power until the Liberals fell. Count Eduard Taaffe (Aug. 1879–Oct. 29, 1893) ruled with a coalition of Czechs, Poles, German Conservatives, and Clericals (Iron Ring). Count Casimir Badeni (Sept. 1895–97), a Polish landlord, followed. Ernst von Körber (Jan. 1900–Dec. 1904) governed by decree with a ministry of officials and was followed by numerous other ministries without parliamentary majorities.

1868, May 25. The May Laws established secular jurisdiction in marriage issues and the principle of secular control in education.

1869–70. Workers gained a limited right to strike and to organize in unions.

1870, July 30. The 1855 Concordat with the papacy was suspended in reply to the proclamation of the dogma of papal infallibility.

1871. Effort to establish a **Bohemian and Austrian** agreement similar to the Austro-Hungarian Compromise was rejected by the emperor. Hohenwart was forced to resign.

1873, March 10. Electoral reforms introduced direct election to the Parliament.

March. Stock market crash, caused by overconfidence and speculation, exposed corruption within the government.

1874. Legislation provided some **government control of the church** as well as limited supervision of church funds but fell short of achieving equality among religions.

1878, June–July. The Austrian government was given the right to occupy Bosnia and Herzegovina, which were under the administration of the Ministry of Common Finance.

1879–88. Foreign policy. Austria allied itself with **Germany (Oct. 7, 1879)** and joined the **Three Emperors' Alliance** (June 18, 1881) and the **Triple Alliance (May 20, 1882).** The Three Emperors' Alliance not renewed (1887) because of tension with Russia over the Bulgarian problem. Mediterranean agreements with **Britain and Italy** were concluded (1887).

1882, Sept. The Linz Program, drawn up by left-wing Liberals, sought to unify all German-speaking Austrian lands and helped foster the Pan-German movement in Austria. Although the Linz Program did not include anti-Semitic sentiments, the Pan-German movement soon became identified with anti-Semitism.

1883–89. Social reforms shortened the workday and provided accident and other types of insurance, but socialism was repressed vehemently.

1888–89. Hainfield Congress established the platform of the **Socialist Party,** demanding syndicalism, trade unionism, and cooperative movements.

The **Young Czechs,** in existence since the mid-1860s, were also gaining ground. They represented middle-class interests and opposed the partition of Bohemia.

1889, Jan. 30. Suicide of the emperor's son Archduke Rudolf put Archduke Francis Ferdinand in line for the throne.

1896, May 28. Electoral reform extended the franchise on the basis of tax status but also created a pluralistic system. A graduated **income tax system** was also introduced.

1897, April 5. The Badeni Language Ordinances established parity between German and the local language in a district.

April. The Austro-Russian Agreement maintained the status quo in the Balkans.

1898, March. New laws divided **Bohemia into a Czech, German, and mixed linguistic district,** but the compromise failed and the original agreement was restored (Oct. 14, 1899).

1907, Jan. 21. A law introduced **universal, male, equal, and direct suffrage** for parliamentary elections. The law resulted in a return of increasing numbers of Socialists.

1908, Oct. 6. The annexation of Bosnia and Herzegovina by decree ushered in the acute Bosnian annexation crisis. The land of the Bosnian peasants was to be converted to free property through government loans to the peasants.

1912–13. The Balkan Wars (pp. 478, 479). The victories of Serbia and Austrian efforts to block Serbian expansion led to a marked growth of Yugoslav agitation and to a revival of Slavic activity within the monarchy.

1914, June 28. Assassination of Archduke Francis Ferdinand at Sarajevo. He was known to favor a reorganization of the monarchy along "trialistic" lines, that is, giving the Slavic elements a position on a par with that of Germans and Magyars.

b. Hungary

1867, Feb. 17. The **constitution of 1848** was restored in Hungary. **FRANCIS JOSEPH** was crowned king of Hungary at Budapest (June 8).

1868. The Nationality Law recognized the rights of individuals to use their own language in church services and in elementary and intermediate schools.

May 27. Hungarian-Croatian Compromise established the union of Hungary and Croatia as two states but gave precedence to Hungary on issues of joint interest, such as representation. Croatia gained the right to govern itself independently on domestic issues.

Sept. The king permitted the abolition of the military frontier province adjacent to the southern boundary of Hungary, which had served as a safety zone against the Ottomans. The frontier was incorporated into Croatia.

1875, Feb. Formation of the Liberal Party by Kálmán Tisza, which was composed of the larger part of the Independence Party. Elections (Aug.) gave the Liberals a majority.

1894, March 20. Death of Louis Kossuth.

1903. Growing discontent over the unified Austro-Hungarian army. The Independence Party opposed the increase in the number of recruits. The party insisted on the use of the Magyar insignia in the Hungarian regiments and the substitution of Magyar for German as the language of command. Francis Joseph declared he would maintain the army, common and unified, at all costs.

1903–14. Rise of tensions with **Croat, Serb,** and **Romanian** minorities.

1905. The Independents, with 163 seats to the Liberals' 152, renewed demands for the use of Magyar language and refused to recognize the nonparliamentary government established under Baron Géza Fejerváry.

1906, July. A bill stipulating **universal male suffrage** was brought before the Hungarian Parliament but was rejected. The suffrage bill would have broken the strong Magyar and aristocratic influence in the Parliament.

1907. An education bill required extension of the use of Magyar in schools of other nationalities in order for those schools to continue to receive government subsidies.

1912. Labor strife developed, including attempts at a general strike in order to gain universal male suffrage.

1913. New defense law passed.   *(To pp. 702, 704, 706)*

i. SCANDINAVIA

(From p. 463)

Relations among Scandinavian countries played a major role in this period. A **declaration of neutrality** by Denmark, Sweden, and Norway (1853) opened all but seven ports to the warships of any belligerent. This act helped to secure the countries' positions within Europe by gaining French and British support against German claims on territories.

Economics. Sweden was perhaps the most advanced of the countries; its enclosure movement had created a large number of medium-size farms and encouraged more modern agricultural techniques. In **Denmark,** land reclamation in Jutland boosted the agricultural economy. Danish industry also was encouraged by such reclamation as well as trade outside Europe through organizations such as the East Asiatic Company. **Norway** also adopted modern agriculture as more and more land was turned into pasture for dairy cattle. The milk industry was supported not only by the increase in pasturage but also by the development of railways, which made transport of such products much easier. Norway also increased its exports of fish, wood, and metals as well as introducing some processing for these products prior to shipping. **Iceland** was constrained by Danish control, which Icelanders felt drained them of their profits. However, they increased exports of fish and other products from the sea, which in turn helped to boost their economy. **Finland** suffered the greatest hardships during this period as it continued to depend primarily on grain production and timber. Free trade with Russia between 1859 and 1885 did help to stimulate iron and cotton industries, but the reintroduction of tariffs made sustained growth in this area difficult.

Society. With the exception of Finland, all these countries suffered from a labor shortage due to emigration. (Between 1870 and 1914, 1.5 million Swedes emigrated.) This emigration helped to remove excess labor, which in turn meant that wages were high and rising. The scarcity of labor also helped Scandinavia to avoid the problems of urban centers such as London and Paris because the demand for housing did not increase dramatically and the agricultural nature of the countries meant that urban growth was not as rapid. Finland, although it remained primarily agricultural, suffered from rural overpopulation, which depressed wages and led to hardship.   *(To p. 708)*

1. SWEDEN AND NORWAY
(From p. 463)

Revolutions of 1848 elsewhere resulted in King Oscar refusing to continue his support of liberal causes. Franchise reform was delayed until the 1860s.

1848. Norwegian road building, under the direction of Christian Vilhelm Bergh, began. Bergh managed to create roads in the mountainous terrain that maintained a constant grade.

1848–50. THRANE MOVEMENT. Joseph Thrane edited *Drammens Ad-*

resse, a newspaper in which he demanded universal male suffrage and social reforms.

1849, May 5. *Arbeiderforeningens Blad* was founded by Thrane. This newspaper helped establish numerous labor associations, which gathered 30,000 signatures on a petition to the king. The government imprisoned Thrane until 1858.

1850. Johan Sverdrup was returned to the Storting by the Thrane movement. Sverdrup became a leading reformer in his "battle of the fifties." He backed an amendment that helped **eliminate class favoritism** in the army draft system and stopped plans to **combine the Norwegian and Swedish regiments** in a union army. He supported an **amendment that increased the ratio of rural to urban representatives** from three out of four to four out of five. Sverdrup failed to pass legislation for a jury system because he lost the support of Søren Jaabaek, who was leading the farmer group in the Storting.

Women's emancipation. In 1854, a law gave women equal rights to inheritance. It was followed by an 1863 law that eliminated all vestiges of unmarried women's status as minors. The new realist school in the novel, committed to depicting life devoid of any embellishment, was anticipated by the Norwegian Camilla Collett's *The County Governor's Daughters.* This novel depicted the problems that middle-class women faced because of the pressure placed on them to make good marriages.

1859. Karl XV ascended to the throne. Complete religious freedom established.

1860. *Stadholder* controversy. Karl XV had promised to abolish the position of stadholder in Norway. However, the Swedes denied this demand and argued that the Norwegians were bound to the Swedes under the Act of Union (p. 463). As a result, the Swedes claimed the right to amend the Norwegian constitution and act in Norway's best interest. Karl XV supported the Committee on Revision for the Norwegian constitution. **Norwegian nationalism** grew in this period; musical and historical collections were gathered, the **Young Norway Party** was formed by **Henrik Wergeland.**

1865–66. Riksdag reform. Engineered by **Louis De Geer,** prime minister, the reforms replaced the Four Estates with an annual two-chamber legislature elected by a common vote. The **Second Chamber** represented the common people, and thus suffrage was extended to all males at least 25 years of age who owned at least 1,000 riksdalers in real estate, rented farmland valued at 6,000 riksdalers, or had taxable income of at least 800 riksdalers per year. Each eligible voter could serve in the chamber, if elected, and had only one vote. The **First Chamber** had a more elaborate voting structure, which included all men who could vote for town and provincial councils but also had a system of plural voting for numerous enterprises. Women involved in those enterprises could vote. **Karl XV supported these reforms** because he recognized the great impetus for change within Sweden and because De Geer threatened to resign otherwise.

1870s. Wave of strikes. Trade unions had continued to organize in Sweden after the abolition of guilds in 1846. These organizations engaged in a number of strikes during the 1870s but to little avail. The paternalism of the employers resulted in scant progress for workers.

1872. Oscar II ascended to the throne.

1879. The problems of trade unions were emphasized by the **strike at Sundsvall.** Employers in Sundsvall planned to reduce wages in the sawmills. The workers demanded a restoration of their wages, and, when employers refused, they gathered in a nearby field to protest. The governor ordered them to return to work, but they refused. At this point, Oscar II deployed cannon and the military and telegrammed the governor. The workers returned without bloodshed, but their leaders were imprisoned as a result of the strike.

Taxation and tariff reform. Under Oscar II, Sweden reorganized its tax system. Taxes on land became less onerous under a compromise between conservatives and large landowners (1873), and numerous obsolete or cumbersome duties were removed between 1878 and 1911. Sweden enjoyed most-favored-nation status with France (1865), but it began to favor protectionism during the late 19th century. The Farmer's Party split, with the new party demanding protection and the old party continuing to support free trade. After a protracted struggle in the Riksdag, the government provided protection for grain and manufacturing interests in the last decade of the 19th century.

1882. Workers drew up a trial program under the direction of Nyström that urged the establishment of trade unions within each trade, including provisions for pensions, sickness, and unemployment aid, organized on modern principles. The program was made more elaborate in the following years to include liberal demands such as wage and hour legislation.

1884. Norwegian Society for Women's Rights was founded by the journalist Hagbard Berner. Gina Krog succeeded him as president, and under her, the society gained new respect. Its purpose was primarily educational, but it remained committed to attaining for women their full role in society.

1886. A Scandinavian trade union congress in Gothenburg declared a socialist program that would supersede the liberal trade unions in Sweden. After this congress, the social democrats continued to receive support from the trades in the form of the **Landsorganization (LO)**. The Norwegian Labor Party was formed (1887) with support from the trades in Norway.

Suffrage movement. The Riksdag reform had resulted in a broader electorate, but it continued to favor the farmers. As a result, **social democrats, students, and women** all began to demand electoral concessions. Students organized in the liberal-radical society Verdandi, which advocated suffrage and social reforms (1882). Suffrage petitions were drawn up and included the signatures of numerous women (1898).

1889. First Factory Laws (extended in 1900).

1892. Passage of a defense measure presented by prime minister Erik Gustaf Boström. The measure increased training time for recruits, funded by income taxes. The measure marked the beginning of growing concern over military preparedness in Sweden. The movement led to the **adoption of universal military service in 1901**.

1895. Swedish protectionism led to the removal of the free trade agreements between Sweden and Norway.

June 7. The Storting adopted a resolution declaring the willingness of **Norway to negotiate with Sweden on the state of the union.** A committee began work on this union, but the negotiations made no progress. Norway, in the meantime, began to reorganize its military in preparation for independence.

1898. Universal male suffrage passed by Storting.

1899. Passage of the Åkarp law, which provided protection to strikebreakers, angered trade unions. In 1902, a three-day strike for suffrage resulted in the formation of an employers' association, the **Swedish Employers Federation (SAF)**.

General Swedish Cooperative Congress was called, and the Cooperative Union was organized. The congress sought to improve the organization of cooperatives and, after a slow start, began to show substantial growth in 1909. It was endorsed by the Social Democrats in 1901.

1905. Act of Union between Norway and Sweden was dissolved. This dissolution was the result of protracted difficulties in creating any negotiated settlement between the two countries, growing military independence, and the apparent removal of the Russian threat as a result of the Russo-Japanese War.

Nov. 18. The Storting unanimously elected Prince Carl of Denmark as Haakon VII, king of Norway.

1907. Women's suffrage was introduced in Norway. **Parliamentary government** and almost **universal male suffrage** were established in Sweden, with **Gustavus V** as king.

1908. A national retailers' association was formed. Retailers put pressure on wholesalers and bankers to stop the growth of cooperatives by pressuring manufacturers and bankers to refuse services to the cooperatives. The well-published maneuvering of the association backfired, and members clung to their cooperatives because they were being threatened by retailers.

1909, Aug. 4. The Great Strike. This strike was the result of efforts by employers to stabilize or cut wages and the growing animosity between the SAF and workers. The SAF had issued an ultimatum to striking workers and then **engaged in a lockout on Aug. 2.** The LO responded with a **general strike from which only public health and safety workers** were exempted. The strike **ended in failure.** The LO, however, had shown that it could muster a sizable number of workers behind it, and its membership and strength continued to grow after 1909. *(To pp. 708, 709)*

2. DENMARK AND ICELAND
(From p. 465)

Kings of Denmark: Frederick VII (r. 1848–63), Christian IX (r. 1863–1906), Frederick VIII (r. 1906–12), and Christian X (r. 1912–47).

Danish history in the last half of the 19th century focused on struggles for independence by both Iceland and Schleswig-Holstein. **The National Liberals** opposed such independence and, in the **Ejder program of 1846,** argued for a constitution that would extend to Schleswig-Holstein.

1849. The June Constitution, drawn up by a new government, provided for a bicameral legislature, the **Folketing,** divided into the **Herredsting and Landsting**—elected by all men over age 30 who did not receive poor relief. The Folketing was selected by direct vote, but the Landsting would be selected by an electoral college.

1853. Anders Ørsted, chief minister in the Danish government, **carried out a constitution for Schleswig-Holstein by royal decree.** The constitution established a **National Council (Riksdag),** half of which would be appointed by the Riksdag and half of which would be appointed by the provincial assemblies. The Riksdag would make national decisions on foreign policy and defense. These provisions did not assuage concerns in Schleswig-Holstein over restrictions on freedom of speech and use of the German language. As a result of such disputes, the **constitution was suspended in 1858.**

Reforms of the 1850s included **extension of the franchise** in local elections, the **elimination of labor services** on land, and the end of the distinction between privileged and unprivileged land. A **law of 1854 allowed tenants to establish credit associations** so that they could purchase their lands, and in 1861, landlords were allowed to take one holding into their demesne for every ten sold to tenants. Most important, **guild and trade monopolies were ended.**

1863. The March Patent provided Holstein and Lauenburg with separate constitutions. The government also created a **new constitution for Schleswig and Denmark.** The constitutions seemed to promise an end to the territorial problems, except that **King Frederick VII died and was replaced by Christian IX.** Christian IX finally signed the March Patent despite increasing pressure from Prussia and Russia. As a result, Denmark engaged in a war against German troops that had moved into Holstein (pp. 470, 501). The German troops overpowered the Danish, and Denmark lost both Schleswig and Holstein to the German victors.

1866. Enrico Dalgas founded the Heath Society, which was responsible for land reclamation and colonization in western Jutland.

July. I. A. Hansen took advantage of the failure of the Liberals to direct the government to **reform the constitution.** Under the new constitution, the Landsting was reorganized so that it included 12 members appointed by the government, 1 from the Faeroes, and the election of the remainder controlled by electoral colleges split between members popularly elected and members elected by the wealthier taxpayers.

The agricultural crisis of the 1870s hit Denmark particularly hard because of its heavy concentration upon grain production. The Danish responded by **diversifying agricultural development,** particularly by introducing dairy farming. The latter was encouraged by the invention of the **centrifugal cream separator** by the Swede de Laval (1878) and the introduction of **cooperative dairies in the 1880s. Land reclamation** helped to alleviate land pressure, but migration also played a significant role.

1871. Louis Pio founded the Danish branch of the International and began publication of the *Socialisten*. Pio called for a mass demonstration in support of striking building workers (1872), and his violent and revolutionary rhetoric eventually led to his arrest. The International was outlawed as well. **In 1876, the Social Democratic Party was founded.**

Jan. 2. Iceland was given a large measure of home rule.

Realism in literature and art. The works of **Jens Jacobsen** and **Holger Drachmann** contributed to literature, while the "**Skagen School**" of Danish painters, so called because they gathered on the Skaw in the 1870s, followed the style of realism in art.

1874, Aug. 1. A new constitution gave **Iceland independence** in domestic affairs on its 1,000-year anniversary of colonization.

1884. Famine struck Iceland. England sent aid.

1898. Danish Trades Union Congress (Det Samvirkende Fagforbund) was founded. The employers countered with their own organization and staged a lockout (1899). The unions managed to hold on for four months before the employers and workers reached an agreement in the **September Treaty.** The treaty recognized the workers' right to organize but provided for arbitration and defined the conditions for calling strikes.

1899. The government enabled anyone who had saved 10 percent of the value of a piece of land to **borrow from the state annually to help make mortgage repayments.**

1901. The First Reformers' Government was established after a protracted struggle among Moderates, the Left, and the Right in the Folketing. The government **established middle schools,** which would help students in state elementary schools enter the "Latin schools," or gymnasiums. It also **abolished church tithes** and provided for popularly **elected church councils.**

1907. The state granted subsidies to trade unions' unemployment funds and to the poor relief funds of local authorities.

1908. The vote in local elections was extended to all taxpayers, including women.

Defense became a major issue during the years preceding World War I. The government, under J. C. Christensen, sought to reduce defenses to those necessary for security only and defended a neutral status. This goal demanded assessment of the strength of potential invaders while maintaining a position of neutrality in the European theater.

1910. A political scandal and problems over defense necessitated another election. The election brought the Left to power, and, despite their divisions, they sought to establish a new constitution. The constitution was drawn up, but before it could be passed, war broke out in Europe.

1911. University of Iceland was founded.

1914–15. Constitutional amendments regularized parliamentary government, broke the dominance of the upper house, lowered the voting age from 30 to 25, and extended suffrage to all men and most women.

(To p. 708)

3. FINLAND
(From p. 465)

Finland remained under the control of the Russians, but nationalism continued to be strong. The Finnish struggled over the allegiance of the intellectual and professional elites to Swedish and the popular interest in Finnish. The **Censorship Act of 1850** favored the Swedish language for bureaucratic purposes because of the fear of insurrection and confusion as the Finnish language was encouraged.

1855. Alexander II became tsar of Russia (p. 510). Alexander appointed Count F. W. Berg as governor-general, and Berg became sympathetic to those who advocated the use of the Finnish language.

1858. Finnish was decreed the language of local self-government in communes where it was spoken by a majority of the inhabitants.

1860s. A. O. Freudenthal helped create a Swedish language movement among Finnish intellectuals.

1861. The April Manifesto seemed to counter the tsar's friendly posture toward Finland. It postponed calling the Finnish Diet indefinitely and called for the formation of a 48-man committee that would enact laws to be ratified by the tsar. The manifesto **sparked demonstrations in Helsinki,** which led to the statement that the committee could not make laws but merely provide reports for the future Diet.

1863. Alexander II called the Finnish Diet. The Diet established limits to the power of the sovereign by forcing him to call the Diet every five years (**Diet Act of 1869**).

1865. The silver mark was designated as the monetary unit of Finland. This began the process of separating the Russian and the Finnish currencies, which was completed in 1878.

1869. The Church Act, drafted by Bishop Schauman, allowed the laity to participate in ecclesiastical affairs and established the principle of freedom of worship. The latter was not implemented for some time, and only in 1899 did it become legal for a congregation to leave the state church.

1878. The Conscription Act was signed by the tsar. This act established an independent Finnish army.

1880. Liberal Party organized under Leo Mechelin. Prior to that, the Liberals had vied for control in the government with those who supported the use of Swedish, the **Svecomen,** and those who supported the use of Finnish, the **Fennomen.** The Liberals attempted to support the rights of both but spoke Swedish. Language conflict permeated politics, and, in 1884, the administration of justice in anything other than Swedish was challenged by the attorney general.

1898. Nicholas Bobrikov was appointed governor-general. He pursued a policy of Russification of Finland.

1899. Dr. N. R. af Ursin founded an independent Finnish labor party, which helped to provide the working classes with a voice in government. Ursin was a socialist, but the party did not adopt socialism immediately.

Feb. 15. The tsar issued a manifesto that placed the Finnish military under the control of the Russian military. In doing so, he called for a reconsideration of Finnish autonomy. The manifesto was published, but the Finnish estates declared it invalid. Students skied all across Finland, collecting signatures as a protest, and Ursin demanded active defense. The tsar refused to accept the delegation that delivered the petition.

1901, July. The Finnish army was dissolved, and the Finnish conscripts placed in largely Finnish units in the Russian army. Mechelin called for resistance, and people were urged to refuse support for the new law. Those who advocated compliance were to be isolated in society. Continued refusal to accept the new means of conscription resulted in the Russians' eventual abandonment of efforts to impose the law.

1904, June. Bobrikov was assassinated. He had spearheaded the banishment and prosecution of many of the leaders of the resistance to Russification. Bobrikov was shot by a young official, Eugen Schauman.

1905. The strike in Russia spread to Finland (p. 512) but was targeted at the Russian government. The employers did nothing to discourage workers. The **tsar issued a proclamation rescinding the February Manifesto.** The strike also forced the resignation of the Senate, which was replaced by Constitutionalists.

1906. Universal suffrage was established. This reform extended the vote to all women. It also resulted in the failure of the Constitutionalists, who lost seats in the election the following year.

1910, June 30. Finnish autonomy was eliminated by an act of the Russian assembly. In introducing this bill, the tsar had reestablished the principles of the February Manifesto without the problems of illegality. The post of governor-general was filled by F. A. Seyn, a man who had served as chief of Bobrikov's bureau staff. Finland remained under the direct control of the Russian state at the outbreak of war.

(To p. 709)

8. EASTERN EUROPE AND THE BALKANS, 1762–1914

a. RUSSIA

(From p. 349)

Population. With a population of 36 million in 1796, Russia experienced enormous growth during the 19th century, reaching 125 million by 1897. The vast majority of these people were peasants, but urban areas also grew, especially with industrialization.

Society and economics. As Russia's market economy grew in the first half of the century, with rapid expansion of **grain exports** to western Europe, the gentry found its indebtedness increasing. This fact made many hostile to economic and social reforms, creating a situation in which reforms were often limited or highly qualified. Industrialization did nothing to ease these tensions.

Culture. The period 1820–80 is considered the golden age of Russian literature, producing artists such as Dostoyevsky, Chekhov, and Pushkin. As in politics, however, Russian culture retained a tension between Western art forms and ideas and a desire to establish distinctive Russian themes. For many this debate meant little—approximately 45 percent of Russians were illiterate in 1917, despite big literacy gains.

Tsars: Alexander I (r. 1801–25), Nicholas I (r. 1825–55), Alexander II (r. 1855–81), Alexander III (r. 1881–94), and Nicholas II (r. 1894–1917).

1801. Alexander I began his reign by granting an amnesty to political prisoners and exiles, abolishing torture, repealing the prohibition of foreign books, and so on. With a group of intimate friends (the *Informal Committee:* **Czartoryski, Kochubei, Novosiltsov, Stroganov**), Alexander discussed various reforms and the project of a constitution for Russia. Though the constitution was not introduced, the central government was reorganized, and **modern ministries** replaced the old "colleges."

The right to own estates was extended from the gentry to all free Russians.

1803. A law was passed regulating the **liberation of the peasant serfs** of owners who desired to make the change. This was the first move of the government toward the abolition of serfdom. Further reforms were postponed because of the many wars in which Alexander became involved.

1804. Kharkov and Kazan Universities were founded.

1804–13. War with Persia (p. 534) resulted from Russian annexation of the **kingdom of Georgia.** The Russians were victorious, and Persia recognized the annexation, besides ceding to Russia **Deghastan** and **Shemakha.**

1805–12. Russian expansion in North America. Forts were built in Alaska (occupied by Russian pioneers in the late 18th century) and even in northern California.

1805–7. WAR OF THE THIRD COALITION (p. 437) against France. This ended in Russia's defeat and the conclusion of the **Treaty of Tilsit,** by which Alexander and Napoleon became allies.

1806–12. War with the Ottoman Empire (p. 359). This was hurriedly concluded in 1812 by the **Treaty of Bucharest,** which gave Russia not only **Bessarabia,** but rather extensive rights in the Danubian Principalities.

1808–9. War with Sweden, through which Russia acquired **Finland.** Finland was organized as an autonomous grand duchy, with the Russian tsar as grand duke. Constitutional government was guaranteed to the Finns by a special act.

After these wars, Alexander resumed his reform schemes, with **Michael Speransky** as his chief counselor.

1809. An attempt to introduce civil service examinations failed.

1810. A **council of state** was established to draft new laws and watch over the legality of administration. The ministries were also reorganized, and a regular system of state budgets was introduced. Speransky presented a **plan for a constitution,** but it too remained unrealized. Opposition of the conservatives and personal disagreement with the tsar led to Speransky's downfall and temporary exile (1812).

1811. Ministry of the Police was created; it was abolished in 1819.

1812. INVASION OF RUSSIA by Napoleon (p. 438). The formation of the **Grand Alliance** and the campaigns in Germany and France led Alexander to devote himself almost entirely to foreign affairs. He participated in the **Congress of Vienna** (p. 440) and the formation of the **Holy Alliance** (p. 440).

In **domestic affairs,** Alexander continued to discuss constitutional projects, but in practice he became more and more reactionary, demonstrated by his selection of **Gen. Alexis Arakcheiev** as chief adviser and **Prince Alexander Golitsyn,** who, as minister of education, oversaw the purges of several universities. This new departure led to the **growth of opposition,** particularly among the younger army officers who had imbibed liberalism in the West. Before becoming disillusioned, liberal Russians had hoped to work with Alexander by founding various philanthropic and educational societies, but such associations became more political and secret as time passed. They finally took the shape of the **Northern Society** at St. Petersburg (favoring constitutional monarchy and abolition of serfdom) and a **Southern Society** at Kiev (republican and advocating division of land among the peasants) under the leadership of **Paul Pestel.**

1820. Alexander Pushkin (1799–1837) became the first poet to criticize the social order with the publication of *Ruslin i Lyudmila.* His other works included *Boris Godunov* (1825), *Kapitanskaya Dochka* (1832), and *Yevgeni Onegin* (1832).

1825. Alexander Griboyedov (1795–1829) published the most noted play of the time, *Gare ot uma* (*Woe from Wit*), a comedy.

Dec. 26. The **DECEMBRIST RISING,** a military revolt, was started by the Northern Society. This arose out of the confusion following Alexander's death (Dec. 13) and the question of succession. The whole affair was ill planned and halfhearted. Nicholas, Alexander's successor, suppressed it on the same day—his first day as tsar. Several of the leaders were executed, and the rest were sent into exile. An attempted uprising in the south was also frustrated.

1826. In keeping with Nicholas's intolerance of opposition, a political police force (Third Section of Imperial Chancery) was organized. The first comprehensive censorship laws were also drawn up.

1826–28. War with Persia (p. 534) resulted from a Persian attack on Russian possessions in Transcaucasia. The war ended in a Russian victory and in the **Treaty of Turkmanchai:** Russia secured part of **Armenia** with Erivan; Persia recognized Russia's exclusive right to have a navy on the Caspian Sea and granted Russia important commercial concessions.

1828–29. War against the Ottoman Empire (p. 526) grew out of the Greek revolution and conflict between Russia and the Ottomans, over the terms of the Treaty of Bucharest. With the **Treaty of Adrianople** (1829) (p. 526) Russia secured the mouth of the Danube and the eastern coast of the Black Sea.

1832. The government published a **new code of law,** edited by Speransky. This, with some modification, remained in force until the Revolution of 1917. Nicholas, while recognizing the need for reform, sternly opposed all independent public activity. Along with partial measures to alleviate the condition of the serfs and to limit the power of the landlords, this period witnessed the **growth of bureaucracy** and the tsar's personal government. **All manifestations of liberalism** were repressed through the secret police; strict **censorship,** control of the universities, and official championship of **orthodoxy, autocracy, and nationalism** were promulgated. Despite all the repressive measures, strong public opinion nevertheless developed. Two important schools of thought developed: the **Westerners,** who held that Russia must follow the lead of Western countries in political and social development, and the **Slavophiles,** who insisted on the peculiarities of Russian culture and historical evolution and on the need for independent development. But both groups opposed bureaucratic rule and demanded freedom of thought and abolition of serfdom. A third force for change arose in the beginnings of **Russian socialism** (under the influence of the utopian socialists in France) under the leadership of **Alexander Herzen** and **Mikhail Bakunin.** The revolutions of 1848–49 simply resulted in more thoroughgoing repression in Russia, but opposition broke through as soon as Russia began to meet with defeats in the Crimean War.

1833. The **Near Eastern crisis** resulted from Muhammad Ali's victory over the sultan. Russia interfered, and the Treaty of Hunkiar Iskelesi was signed (p. 526).

1835. University statutes were reformed.

1836. After the publication of his *First Philosophical Letter,* Paul A. Chaadayev was declared insane by Nicholas for his critique of Russian backwardness.

First performances of **Nikolai Gogol's** (1809–52) *Government Inspector* and **Mikhail Glinka's** (1803–57) *A Life for the Tsar.*

1837. The first public railroad linked St. Petersburg to Tsarskoe Selo.

1839. Russia possessed the largest telescope in the world and became an important training center for astronomers throughout the world after the construction of the **Pulkovo Observatory** near St. Petersburg.

1839–40. Second Muhammad Ali crisis. Russia cooperated with Britain.

1847. Ivan Turgenev (1818–83) became a leading writer of the realistic novel in Russia with the publication of *A Sportsman's Sketches. Fathers and Sons* followed in 1862. Other Russian proponents of the realistic novel included **Ivan Goncharov** (1812–91); **Fyodor Dostoyevsky** (1821–81) who wrote *Crime and Punishment* (1866) and *The Brothers Karamazov* (1879–80); **Leo Tolstoy** (1828–1910) who wrote *War and Peace* (1869), *Anna Karenina* (1875–77), and *Resurrection* (1899–1900); **Dmitri Merezhkovsky** (1865–1941); **Maxim Gorki** (1868–1936) who also wrote plays and short stories; and **Fyodor Sologub** (1863–1927) who wrote *The Little Demon.*

1848–49. Russia intervened in Hungary to suppress the Hungarian revolutionary movement (p. 470).

Advance in Asia. The Russians were pressing on steadily. During the reign of Nicholas they conquered the Khirghiz Steppe and prepared for the **advance into Turkestan.** In the Far East, **Nicholas Muraviev** (1809–81) became governor-general of Siberia in 1847.

1850. The Russians established a settlement at the mouth of the Amur River.

1851. Opening of **St. Petersburg–Moscow Railway,** the first major rail link in Russia.

1853–56. The **CRIMEAN WAR** was the outcome of the dispute between Russia and France over the holy places in Palestine and of Russian claims to a protectorate over the Christians in the Ottoman Empire. By the **Treaty of Paris** (1856) Russia lost control of the Danube mouth and ceded to the Ottomans the southern part of **Bessarabia** (p. 470). Russia was obliged to accept **neutralization of the Black Sea** and to agree to build no fortifications and to keep no navy in that sea.

1858–60. Advance of Russia in the Far East. By the **Treaty of Aigun** (1858) China ceded to Russia the left bank of the Amur River, and by the **Treaty of Peking,** the Ussuri region (p. 419). **Foundation of Vladivostok** (1860).

1860. Alexander II began his efforts at reform by introducing **rural courts.** Other reforms included the creation of a single state treasury, the publication of the annual budget, and the creation of a state bank to centralize credit and finance.

1861, March 3. The **EMANCIPATION EDICT** liberated the serfs. The subject had been discussed for years by a special committee, which collected huge masses of material from provincial bodies. Temporary freedom of discussion in the press had also produced much information and different viewpoints. The landowners were, on the whole, ready to give the serfs freedom, but not ready to give up much of their land. At the other extreme were the radicals and socialists, who insisted that the land belonged to those who worked it. The final solution was a compromise imposed by the tsar.

Terms: All serfs were given **personal freedom,** together with **allotments of land** for which the owners were paid by the state in treasury bonds. The peasants in turn were to refund the treasury by installments **(redemption payments)** spread over a period of 49 years. The land was not given to individuals, but to the **village communes** (*mir*), which distributed it among the village members according to the size of each peasant family. To ensure equality of treatment, the land was to be redistributed in many communes every 10 or 12 years. The members of the commune were held jointly responsible for the redemption payments. In addition to receiving redemption payments, aristocratic landlords retained some of the best land.

1861–62. Peasant uprisings, student disturbances, and an unexplained rash of fires in St. Petersburg indicated that discontent remained.

1862. The provincial assembly of the Tver gentry, led by Alexis Unkovsky, renounced its gentry privileges and demanded the convocation of a constituent assembly representing the entire people, to establish a new order in Russia.

1864. The **ZEMSTVO LAW** was one of the most important features of the great reforms. The law established a system of local self-government: the nobility, the townspeople, and the peasants were represented (no one class to have a majority of seats) on local boards (*zemstvos*) and were empowered to levy taxes for local economic and cultural requirements (roads, bridges, schools, hospitals, and so on).

Reforms of the judiciary. The old system of class courts was abolished, and a new hierarchy of courts, on the French model, was set up, with thoroughly modernized procedure and jury trial for criminal offenses. **Justices of the peace** were provided to deal with minor civil suits, and the old **peasant courts** were retained for those who wished to use them.

1866. A first attempt on Alexander's life was made.

The Moscow Conservatory was founded.

The appointment of Count Dmitri Tolstoy as minister of education began a gradual process of stricter control.

1867. Sale of Alaska to the United States, more than 20 years after Russian settlements in California were abandoned (1844).

1865–81. Russia advanced in central Asia (p. 419). The conquests of the khanates of **Kokand, Bokhara, and Khiva** were followed by the annexation of the entire Transcaspian region in 1881. This aggressive policy created much friction between Russia and Britain, which was fearful for India.

1869. Peter Ilyich Tchaikovsky's (1840–93) first opera, *The Voyevodye,* was performed. **Dmitri Mendeleev** formulated the periodic table of elements, and the Pan-Slavist **Nicholas Danilevsky** published *Russia and Europe.*

1870. Reform of municipal government, the last of the great reform measures. The old patrician system was abolished, and the towns were given self-government under councils elected by the propertied classes.

1871, March 13. Abrogation of the Black Sea clauses of the Treaty of Paris. The Russian government had taken advantage of the Franco-Prussian War (p. 492) to denounce its obligations. British protests led to the convocation of a **conference at London,** which accepted the fact, but reaffirmed the principle that international obligations could not be abrogated without consent of all signatory powers.

1873. The government ordered Russian students in Switzerland to abandon studies and return to Russia. The anger this generated among many intellectuals (the *intelligentsia*) convinced them to turn to the people as teachers, doctors, and so on, spawning the **"Going to the People" movement.**

1874. Army reform introduced the principle of **universal military liability** in place of the former system of taking recruits only from among the lower classes. The army began to play a growing role in educating recruits.

1875. Cession of the Kurile Islands to Japan, in exchange for the southern part of the island of **Sakhalin.**

1875–78. The **NEAR EASTERN CRISIS,** the Russian-Ottoman War, and the **Treaties of San Stefano** and **Berlin** (p. 531). As a result of the war, the Russians received **Bessarabia** (which had been lost in 1856), **Kars,** and **Batum.**

Growth of opposition to the tsarist regime was due to the incompleteness of the government reforms. The liberal elements demanded a constitution, whereas the radicals and socialists aimed at the complete overturn of the social order and a resettlement of the land question. The radicals soon became avowedly revolutionary. Some, like Bakunin, helped define the doctrines of **anarchism.** Under the leadership of **Herzen, Bakunin, Peter Lavrov,** and **Nicholas Chernyshevsky** they organized a **secret society** (1876) formed under the name **Land and Liberty.** This became the spearhead of the so-called **populist movement** ("Going to the People"). The movement met with a qualified reception from the suspicious peasants and was soon persecuted by the police.

Meanwhile, the unsatisfactory outcome of the war with the Ottoman Empire broadened the base of popular discontent. The liberals were further estranged by the granting of a constitution to the Bulgarians, while the adherents of the new **Pan-Slav movement** (which developed from the foundation of the Slavonic Welfare Society at Moscow in 1857 and the Pan-Slav congress at Moscow in 1867) became extremely critical of the government for its failure to complete the work of liberating the Balkan Slavs. After 1878, therefore, the revolutionary movement secured more popular support.

1877–78. Overt displays of discontent, such as the shooting of St. Petersburg's police chief, resulted in a secret circular published in Sept. that authorized arrest and exile of persons suspected of seditious intent, and mass trials of radicals and revolutionaries.

1878–79. Russia witnessed its first significant **industrial strikes,** in St. Petersburg.

1879. Organization of the society Will of the People, composed of the most radical wing of the older populist group. The new society was overtly terrorist and made carefully planned attempts on the lives of prominent officials, finally of the tsar himself.

1880. Terrorists succeeded in planting a bomb in the Winter Palace. A new department of state police was created.

Appointment of Gen. Mikhail Loris-Melikov as minister of interior. After two abortive assassination attempts, Tsar Alexander decided on a policy of concessions, accompanied, however, with ever more stringent police measures against the terrorists.

1881. Loris-Melikov propounded a scheme for summoning representatives of the *zemstvos* to cooperate with the council of state in the discussion of new laws. This compromise plan was approved by Alexander on **March 13,** but on the very same day he fell victim to the bombs of the terrorists.

ALEXANDER III began his reign determined to suppress the revolutionary movement, and throughout his reign he followed the advice of his former teacher and close friend, **Constantine Pobiedonostsev,** who was made procurator of the Holy Synod. After some debate, Loris-Melikov's plan was dropped and the **autocratic system was reaffirmed**

with the following measures: "temporary laws" gave officials in designated areas broad authority, the reforms of the preceding reign were curtailed, the preeminence of the nobility was restored, all liberal opposition and revolutionary activity were attacked, the **persecution of religious dissenters**—Roman Catholics, Protestants, and especially Jews (beginning with the **pogroms in the Ukraine**)—was established, and **discrimination against national minorities** and attempts at Russification in the border provinces were heightened.

1881–87. **Nicholas Bunge's** tenure at the Ministry of Finance began the **economic changes necessary for industrialization.** These included the creation of the Peasant Land Bank, the abolition of the head tax, and the introduction of an inheritance tax. He also spearheaded the first labor legislation in Russia (1882–86).

1883. The government required peasants to buy out their land allotments.

1884. New university statutes abolished autonomy. A statute on church-parish schools sought to entrust elementary education as much as possible to the church.

1884–87. Continued advance in central Asia (conquest of Merv, 1884) brought the Russians to the frontier of Afghanistan, where a clash of Russian and Afghan troops in 1885 brought Russia to the verge of war with Great Britain. The matter was finally disposed of by agreement on a Russian-Afghan frontier.

1885. The government created the **State Gentry Land Bank** to aid the gentry who had suffered from the growth of a market economy in the first half of the century. This began a series of Alexander's **counterreforms** designed to shore up the position of the gentry. These counterreforms included the establishment of land captains, gentry named by the minister of the interior to provide direct supervision of peasants (1889), and the creation of a distinct group for the gentry in the *zemstvo* system with increased representation (1890).

1887. The government established a limit for the number of Jewish students in institutions of higher education.

1890s. Emergence of a **popular reading public,** which consumed distinctive Russian adventure stories and other materials. Growing urban contacts also began to change **peasant sexuality,** reducing parental controls.

1890. Growing alliance with France (p. 475).

1891. Construction began on the **Trans-Siberian Railway.**

1891–92. Rural discontent, sparked by a **great famine,** obliged the government to abolish the poll tax and reduce redemption payments.

1892. The property requirements for voting in town government were increased.

1892–1903. RUSSIAN INDUSTRIALIZATION was guided by Sergei Witte, minister of finance. The government inaugurated a high protective tariff and began to give extensive support to native industry, while the rapid expansion of railroads and the opening of the coal and iron fields of southern Russia served as an important stimulus. From 1881 to 1894, the state increased the railroad network in length by 40 percent and then doubled it between 1895 and 1905. Witte also established a policy of heavy borrowing abroad, especially in France, in the hope that the increased productive power of Russia would make repayment easy. Many foreign companies established operations in Russia. Estimates place economic growth in this period at an annual average of 8 percent.

But the growth of industry involved also the emergence of an **industrial proletariat,** living in misery and inadequately protected by the first factory laws.

1893. The government abrogated clauses in the Emancipation Edict permitting peasants to leave communes.

1894. Nicholas II, tsar.

1895. Alexander Popov invented the radio (shortly before Marconi).

1897. A law limited the workday in factories with more than 20 employees.

1898. The **Social Democratic Party** was formed among the industrial workers. Marxism had been introduced into Russia by **Georgy Plekhanov,** whose fairly moderate program was, however, soon to be challenged by the more radical wing under the leadership of **Lenin** (Vladimir I. Ulianov). Lenin was the son of a school inspector and the brother of a prominent terrorist who was executed in 1887 for plotting

against the life of the tsar. Lenin himself spent several years in exile in Siberia, but after his escape he became one of the most energetic and uncompromising champions of the workers. The socialists were obliged to operate from abroad (especially from Switzerland).

Appearance of **The World of Art,** a seminal periodical considered to be a cause of the cultural explosion called the "silver age."

1901. Organization of the **Social Revolutionary Party,** which took its inspiration from the earlier populist movement. This party, to which many students adhered, was concerned chiefly with the peasant problem and advocated the nationalization of the land. Its methods were those of **terrorism,** and the years following its birth were marked by an increasing number of assassinations.

1901–3. Sergei Vasilyevich Zubatov, chief of Moscow's public security, founded, with others, the **Society of Mutual Help** for workers in mechanical production. Under police protection, this society flourished, and similar legal trade unions were established in Minsk, Odessa, and St. Petersburg. Zubatov was able to maintain control of the movement in Moscow, but elsewhere the unions got out of control and were used for revolutionary purposes. In 1903 the government withdrew its protection, and Zubatov was dismissed.

1902. A metallurgical syndicate was formed, demonstrating the development of a small capitalist class as industrialization progressed. This was followed in 1904 by a coal syndicate.

1903. Law on labor insurance, holding employers responsible for work-related accidents.

The **Social Democratic Party split** during a party congress in London. The result was two groups: the Mensheviks (moderates) and the Bolsheviks (extremists).

The formation of the **Union of Liberation** created a third opposition party, at the time the most important one. This group consisted largely of intellectuals, members of the liberal professions, and *zemstvo* workers. Its program called for a liberal constitution.

1904–5. RUSSIAN-JAPANESE WAR (p. 568). This was the direct result of the aggressive Russian policy in the Far East: construction of the **Trans-Siberian Railway** (1891–1903), intervention after the **Sino-Japanese War** (1895), **treaty with China** (1896) and penetration of northern **Manchuria,** interference in **Korea,** lease of **Port Arthur** (1898), occupation of **Manchuria** after the Boxer Insurrection (1900–3), and activity of Russian interests in **northern Korea.** Repeated efforts of the Japanese to reach an agreement were treated with disdain by the Russians, so that the lengthy negotiations ended in the outbreak of hostilities (Feb. 8, 1904). The Russians were consistently defeated (**Battle of Liaoyand,** Aug. 1904; **Battle of Sha-ho,** Oct. 1904; **fall of Port Arthur,** Jan. 1905; **Battle of Mukden,** Feb. 23–March 10, 1905; **naval disaster at Tsushima,** May 27, 1905). The government was wholly discredited, and popular protest became ever greater.

1904, July 28. Assassination of Viacheslav Plehve, the ruthless but able minister of the interior. This event induced the government to attempt a policy of conciliation, represented by **Prince Sviatopolk-Mirsky,** but it proved to be too late for halfway measures, and the relaxation of repression gave the opposition better opportunities for organization and expression.

Nov. A great *zemstvo* congress met at St. Petersburg and demanded the convocation of a representative assembly and the granting of civil liberties. Similar demands were advanced by numerous other groups and by the professional classes.

1905, Jan 22. Bloody Sunday was marked by bloodshed and by the emergence of the workers as a factor in the movement. Workers led by **Father Gapon** proceeded to the palace in St. Petersburg to lay their demands before the tsar; they were fired on by troops—70 were killed and 240 wounded. The result was growing indignation, unrest, and an epidemic of strikes.

March 3. The tsar announced his intention to convoke a **"consultative" assembly.** Further concessions included an edict of religious toleration, permission to use the Polish language in Polish schools, relief for the Jews, and the cancellation of part of the redemption payments.

May 8. The organization of the **Union of Unions,** under the chairmanship of **Prof. Paul Miliukov,** brought together all the liberal groups in a renewed demand for parliamentary government and the institution of universal suffrage.

June–Aug. Increasing unrest and disorder continued throughout the country: strikes, agrarian outbreaks, national movements in the border provinces, and mutinies in the army and navy (*Potemkin* episode).

Aug. 19. The tsar yielded to popular pressure and published a **manifesto creating the imperial Duma** (assembly), to be elected by a limited franchise and with deliberative powers only. This concession was far too modest to meet the popular demand, and the revolutionary movement became more widespread until it culminated in a general strike.

Oct. 20–30. The **GENERAL STRIKE** was a spontaneous movement in which elements throughout the country joined.

Oct. 26. The St. Petersburg workers formed the **first** *soviet* (council) to direct the strike. This was essentially a moderate socialist organization and had relatively little influence on the course of events. The strike soon paralyzed the government and forced the tsar to yield further. Pobiedonostsev and other reactionary ministers were obliged to resign, and Nicholas, advised by Witte (who had been disgraced in 1903, but had been restored to favor after the conclusion of the **Treaty of Portsmouth** (p. 573) with Japan), issued the October Manifesto.

Oct. 30. THE OCTOBER MANIFESTO granted Russia a constitution: the projected Duma was to have real legislative power, the franchise was to be greatly extended, and civil liberties were guaranteed. **Witte was appointed the prime minister.**

The manifesto satisfied all the more moderate liberal groups, but appeared inadequate to those who had called for a constituent assembly. The immediate effect of the government's capitulation was, therefore, to split the liberal group; the moderates became known as the **Octoberist Party**, while the progressives took the name **Constitutional Democratic Party** (abbreviated to K.D., *Cadet*). The Social Democrats rejected the whole program of the government, and the St. Petersburg *soviet* (with branches opened in many cities) attempted several times to organize another strike. The sole effect of this policy was to drive more of the liberals into the government ranks. At the same time Witte made every effort to bring back the troops from the Far East.

Dec. 16. When Witte felt sufficiently strong, he had the members of the St. Petersburg *soviet* (about 190) arrested, which led to insurrection.

Dec. 22–1906, Jan. 1. INSURRECTION OF THE WORKERS IN MOSCOW. Severe street fighting and much bloodshed resulted. But the troops remained loyal to the government, and the uprising was finally suppressed. The army undertook vigorous action during the winter to restore order in the provinces (the **Black Hundreds**—punitive raids). Meanwhile, Witte arranged to float a huge loan ($400 million) in France and Britain, so that, when the Duma met, the government would not be dependent on representatives of the people for funds.

1906, May 2. Nicholas **dismissed Witte,** of whom he had never approved and who, he felt, was no longer needed. In his place the tsar appointed **Ivan Goremykin,** a conservative bureaucrat of the old school.

May 6. Nicholas promulgated the **Fundamental Laws,** issued on the very eve of the Duma's first meeting. These extensive regulations decided in advance many of the questions left open by the October Manifesto. The tsar was proclaimed autocrat and retained complete control over the executive office, the armed forces, and foreign policy. Changes in the Fundamental Laws could be made only with his consent. The legislative power was to be divided between the Duma and an upper chamber, the Imperial Council, half of whose members were to be appointed by the tsar, the other half to be elected by various privileged bodies throughout the country. The government reserved the right to legislate by decree when the Duma was not in session. The budgetary powers of the Duma were closely restricted.

May 10. The **FIRST DUMA,** elected by what amounted to universal suffrage, convened. But the radical parties had, for the most part, boycotted the elections, and the Cadets formed the largest party. Profoundly disappointed by the Fundamental Laws, the Cadets criticized the government violently, and this first representative assembly ended in deadlock.

July 21. Nicholas **dissolved the first Duma.** The Cadet leaders adjourned to Viborg and issued the **Viborg Manifesto,** calling upon the country to refuse taxes. The manifesto found but little response in the country, where the revolution was already a thing of the past.

Nov. Agrarian reform act of Peter Stolypin, who had become prime minister in June. Though a conservative, Stolypin was far from being a reactionary. He was eager to maintain the constitutional system and hoped gradually to wean the country from revolutionary sentiment by well-planned reforms. The Agrarian Law put an end to the communal (*mir*) system of landholding and enabled each peasant to withdraw from the commune at will, receiving his own share of the land in private ownership. Any commune was able to end the old system by majority vote. This law was later approved by the third Duma. Under the Stolypin reforms, a group of business-minded peasants emerged, fostering commercial agriculture but disturbing traditional village relations.

In a similar effort at conciliation, unions were allowed, but exclusively on the local, not national, level.

1907, March 5–June 16. The **SECOND DUMA** convened. It was more radical than the first because of the active part taken in the elections by the revolutionary parties. The Cadets were now anxious to cooperate with the government to save the constitutional system (though some of the leaders refused Stolypin's invitation to join the ministry). But these efforts were frustrated by the radicals. The reactionary groups at court, constantly pressing for a return to the simple autocratic system, finally forced the dissolution of the Duma.

June 16. A **new electoral law** was promulgated. It greatly increased the representation of the propertied classes to the detriment of peasants and workers. At the same time it reduced the representation of the national minorities.

1907–12. The **THIRD DUMA,** elected on the new basis, returned a conservative majority. It fostered stern suppression of all revolutionary outbreaks and disorders, formed conservative groups like the Union of True Russian Men and the League of the Russian Nobility, and sponsored drumhead courts-martial. At the same time Stolypin, with cooperation of the Duma, continued his **reform activities:** social insurance, *zemstvo* reform, education, police reorganization, land banks, encouragement of emigration to Siberia. With the restoration of order came the resumption of economic expansion and industrialization.

1907, Aug. 31. The **conclusion of the Anglo-Russian Entente** (p. 477), an important milestone in Russian foreign policy, definitely aligned Russia with Britain and France against the Central Powers.

1908–9. Tensions between Russia and Austria over the annexation of Bosnia and Herzegovina marked the **revival of Pan-Slav, or Neo-Slav, agitation.**

1911, Sept. 14. Stolypin was assassinated by a revolutionary, at Kiev. He was succeeded by **Vladimir Kokovtsev,** an able financier and a moderate statesman, lacking, however, the prestige and willpower of his predecessor.

1912–16. The **FOURTH DUMA** was similar to the third in character and purpose. This period was taken up largely with major questions of foreign policy, notably by the crisis of the Balkan Wars.

1912–13. The Balkan Wars, in which Russia played a very prominent role (pp. 478–79).

Meanwhile, the reforms inaugurated by the government proved insufficient to quiet the political and social unrest. The massacre in the Lena goldfields in April sparked a wave of strikes. The national minorities, too, were antagonized by the policy of the government (especially in Poland and Finland). On the eve of World War I, there was growing dissatisfaction, which spread even to moderate circles. The latter were irritated particularly by the state of affairs at court, where the tsarina, a deeply religious person, had become the center of a group of mystics and magic healers, originally called in to cure the only son of the imperial couple of an incurable disease. Of this group, **Grigory Rasputin** was the most remarkable and powerful, and he was to play a most important role in the history of Russia during the war.

1914, Aug. 1. GERMANY DECLARED WAR ON RUSSIA.

(To pp. 650, 710)

b. POLAND

(From p. 346)

Poland in the 19th century is difficult to characterize, since it was split among three countries that developed differently. For the most important general social and economic trends, refer to the sections on

Austria, Prussia, and Russia. Culturally, the overriding theme during this century remained, however, the reestablishment of an independent Poland and the best means of attaining that end.

1800. Foundation of the Warsaw Society of the Friends of Science, which mixed national preservation with Enlightenment thought. Its most important work was the *Dictionary of the Polish Language*, published in 1806.

1807. Napoleon and Alexander I of Russia created the **DUCHY OF WARSAW,** a constitutional state based on the French model, including the introduction of the Napoleonic Code. The Saxon prince, Frederick Augustus, became the duke.

1809. Polish-Austrian War. The duchy of Warsaw gained new territory in the **Treaty of Schönbrunn.**

1815. The Congress of Vienna (p. 440) accepted limited Polish autonomy through the creation of the **grand duchy of Posen (Poznan),** under Prussian leadership; the **Congress Kingdom of Poland,** in permanent union with the Russian Empire; and the **Free State of Cracow.** Nationalist hopes remained pinned on the kingdom of Poland, where a **constitution** provided for a Sejm (parliament), a separate administration and army, and official use of the Polish language. Gen. Josef Zaionczek (Zajaczek) was made viceroy, and Grand Duke Constantine became commander of the Polish army.

1816. University of Warsaw established.

1817. The first secret society, **Panta Kojna** (Everything in Common), was founded at the University of Warsaw. It was followed in 1820 by the more active Union of Free Poles. Students also founded secret societies at Wilno University, but, as in Warsaw, they did not last long.

Independent of student activity, military officers also formed secret patriotic societies such as the National Freemasonry Society in 1819, and the Patriotic Society in 1821.

1819. Russian tsar Alexander introduced censorship into the Congress Kingdom as his rule became more autocratic in Poland. He refused to call the Sejm between 1820 and 1825.

1822. The publication of **Adam Mickiewicz's** (1798–1855) first volume of poems marked the dawn of Polish romanticism. Mickiewicz's epics *Konrad Wallenrod* (1828) and *Pan Tadeusz* (1834) made him the movement's leader. Other romantic poets and dramatists included **Count Alexander Fredro** (1793–1876, comedies), **Juljusz Slowacki** (1809–49), and **Zygmunt Krasinski** (1812–59). After the November Insurrection, many of the brightest stars of Polish romanticism acquired fame in France, especially the musician **Frédéric Chopin.**

1823. The **Prussian Settlement Decree,** abolishing serfdom (p. 460), was extended to Poles in the grand duchy of Posen. In 1836, however, a royal decree restricted the earlier terms of the settlement to favor the landlords of Posen, retaining a system of large estates as elsewhere in Prussia.

1824. Polish and Russian revolutionaries reached a general agreement, but the Decembrist Revolt (p. 508) of the following year was conducted without Polish support. Nevertheless, the Russian investigation unearthed this connection. The Polish government insisted that the suspects be tried by the Sejm, according to Polish law. In a mark of independence, all conspirators were acquitted of conspiracy and given short prison terms for membership in secret societies in 1828.

1828. Ksawery Lubecki, minister of finance, established the **Bank of Poland,** part of a state effort to increase industrial development (textiles, mining, ironworks).

1830–31. The **NOVEMBER INSURRECTION** in the Congress Kingdom, long prepared by the Polish nationalists, was provoked by the Paris revolution (p. 454) and the tsar's proposal to use the Polish army to suppress new governments in Belgium and France. A Russian garrison was expelled from Poland, a revolutionary government was proclaimed, the Romanov dynasty was declared deposed, and the union with Lithuania was celebrated. Division among moderates and radicals weakened the Poles, however, and the Russians defeated them at **Ostrolenka** (May 26, 1831) and finally took Warsaw (Sept. 8). The revolution collapsed, and most of the Polish leaders escaped to the West, where they formed a powerful revolutionary faction, especially in Paris.

1832. Nicholas I **abrogated the Polish constitution** and replaced it with an **organic statute:** Poland lost its political rights and retained only a small measure of administrative autonomy, beginning the policy of

Russification in Poland. Prussia also took the opportunity to implement Germanification.

Under new conditions of foreign domination and economic development, Polish liberals sought to channel social activity into the concept of **Organic Work,** an attempt through various associations to raise the social, economic, and cultural level of the country without fomenting revolution. It was strongest in the grand duchy of Posen, but spread throughout Poland.

1846, Feb. An uprising in Cracow had been prepared for years among internal and foreign-based patriotic societies. It quickly disintegrated, in part because of the failure to coordinate activity with a **peasant uprising in Galicia.** Austria formally incorporated the Free State of Cracow.

1848. Nationalists in **Posen** took advantage of the revolution in Berlin (p. 469) to establish home rule. As in the rest of Europe, the revolution was quelled as the revolutionaries became divided. Austria suppressed similar events in **Galicia,** but Polish peasants did benefit from the reforms that swept over the entire empire.

1851. The **kingdom of Poland** joined the Russian customs union, fueling expansion in the textile industry near Lódz and in metallurgy near Warsaw.

1861. Austria granted **Galicia** its own **provincial sejm.** Despite the revolution, Galician Poles acquired more autonomy as the Austrian Empire struggled with its ethnic minorities: the school system was infused with the Polish language and culture as were the civil service and law courts.

1863–64. THE SECOND POLISH REVOLUTION. Alexander II attempted to win the support of the Poles with a mild and liberal policy: the arrangements of 1815–30 were substantially restored in 1862. This policy met with support from the Polish moderates (**Marquis Alexander Weilopolski**) but was not enough to satisfy the extreme nationalists (**Reds**), who aimed at complete independence. After considerable disorder the government decided to draft the malcontents (especially students) into the army. This provoked the insurrection of Jan. 1863, which spread rapidly to Lithuania and White Russia. The Poles had no army; most of the fighting was done by guerrilla bands. **Diplomatic intervention by Great Britain, France, and Austria** (in the similar but not identical protests of April, June, and Aug.) produced a strong **nationalist reaction in Russia.** The Russian government was able to ignore the protests of the Western powers because of the support and cooperation of the Prussian government (**Alvensleben Convention,** Feb. 8, 1863). But the insurrection was not finally suppressed until May 1864, and then with great severity. Polish autonomy was again abolished and Russian administration reestablished; the Russian language was gradually made obligatory in Polish schools; the government took steps against the Roman Catholic clergy; relations with the Vatican were ruptured.

The Russians did recognize the need for **agrarian reform,** however, and reaffirmed the results of the revolt by granting Polish peasants the land they cultivated and granting the proprietors compensation from state funds (1864).

1865–80. Industrialization. This was more dynamic in the kingdom, where the railway network was increased from 635 kilometers in 1862 to 2,084 kilometers in 1887. Yet Poland remained far behind western European standards.

1867. Russia eliminated the administrative distinction between the kingdom and the empire. But the Napoleonic Code remained operative in the kingdom, and the *zemstvo* reforms in Russia were not instituted in the kingdom for fear that they would be used for nationalist purposes.

1872. Bismarck instituted the Kulturkampf, with a special anti-Polish emphasis as Germanification intensified.

1873. The Cracow Learned Society became the **Academy of Science and Letters,** one of the few scholarly institutions embracing all of Poland.

1878. The first socialist organizations were formed in Poland, resulting in the first **Polish socialist program** (published in Geneva).

1885, March. Prussia expelled from its eastern provinces **all foreign nationals of Polish descent.** The Colonization Commission was founded in 1886 to enable Germans to buy land from the Poles in an attempt to push Poles out. It was met with the creation of the Polish League, an expatriate organization with strong links to a growing number of secret societies in Poland, especially among the young. This new political awakening was expressed primarily in an illegal campaign of popular education throughout the kingdom, including a course of higher education for women.

1892, May. Troops were called out to suppress a **strike** in Lódz.

In Prussia, Archbishop Florian Stablewski, under the impetus of the *Rerum novarum* (p. 499), began to organize the Societies of Polish Workers, opposed to class agitation.

1893. The **Polish Socialist Party** was founded in the kingdom, led principally by **Józef Pilsudski.** This party was rivaled by the creation of the internationalist **Social Democracy of the Kingdom of Poland,** founded by **Rosa Luxemburg** and **Julian Marchlewski.** They differed substantially over the question of Polish independence, the latter claiming to work solely for social revolution.

1895. The **Peasant Party** was founded in **Galicia.**

1897. The **National Democratic Party** was founded in the kingdom of Poland.

1905, Jan.–Feb. The **October Revolution** in Russia sparked a **general strike** in the kingdom. This was accompanied by a **school boycott,** ending only in Oct., when the government acquiesced to demands for Polish language schools. The movement then developed into a boycott of Russian schools, lasting until 1914.

June. A stike in Lódz led to violence and the first erection of barricades in the Russian Empire.

Dec. A workers' uprising in the kingdom ended in failure, just as it did in Moscow.

1906. The school boycott spread to Posen.

1908. The Prussian Landtag enforced a new **expropriation act,** allowing the government to compulsorily purchase Polish estates in Posen.

1914. On the eve of World War I, Polish nationalists were divided into three groups. One group, led notably by Pilsudski, eagerly sought the war as an insurrectionary measure against the tsar. A second group did not favor the war, but felt that a Russian victory would be more beneficial—allowing for more Polish autonomy. The socialists did not favor war but were prepared to use it to foster social revolution in the event of hostilities.   *(To p. 719)*

c. THE BALKANS

1. THE BALKAN STATES

The 19th century saw the **creation of most Balkan states.** The first national revolutions were not the product of European ideology, the revival of national consciousness among intellectuals, or the rise of an Orthodox merchant class, however, these all played an important role. The immediate cause was the breakdown of Ottoman central authority. In the face of increased brigandage, local governments organized and armed themselves, shifting loyalties and military balances. Moreover, despite general warfare in Europe, Balkan leaders always believed in the possibility of foreign intervention. After independence or autonomy was achieved, these states had to establish the trappings of the modern state. In most cases, divisions arose between advocates of Western-style parliament and partisans of autocratic rule.

The Balkans remained overwhelmingly rural; **industrial development was slow.** Faced with the cost of administration, many Balkan states ran high foreign debts. They were not alone, for as capitalism grew, so did peasant indebtedness. This contributed to a growing chasm between town and country, which would color future developments.

Each of the Balkan nations experienced **cultural revival;** nationalist goals were often tied to linguistic and cultural development. Governments fostered this through the creation of educational systems, yet the bulk of the Balkan population remained illiterate throughout the 19th century.

By the end of the century, the map of the Balkan Peninsula showed a number of new nations. The result was not simply national development, however. The creation of national identities directly countered the Ottoman millet system, which had allowed various ethnic communities to rely on their own local leaders. The creation of new nations alongside areas of mixed ethnicity like Macedonia resulted in increased antagonisms and instability.

2. GREECE

The Peloponnesus offered favorable conditions for a revolution by 1821: the Greeks lived under considerable autonomy under their own church primates, the control of the countryside was more Greek than Ottoman, there was a large concentration of the military in the area, and it was possible to maintain close contact with the islands. Growing trade gave Greek merchants, particularly on the islands, contact with French revolutionary ideas, including nationalism. The time was right in 1821 as the Ottomans concentrated their activities on reining in the disobedient Muhammad Ali Pasha (p. 541). The independence of numerous local governments caused problems for the revolution, however, making unified action difficult.

1821–31. Greek War of Independence. This war resulted directly from growing prosperity of the Greeks in the later 18th century (Black Sea grain trade), the cultural renaissance (Korais, Rhigas), the encouragement of Russia (Catherine's *Greek Scheme*), revolt of 1769–76, and the influence of the French Revolution and the intrigues of Napoleon. A secret revolutionary society, the *Philiké Hetairia*, was founded at Odessa in 1814 and was in close touch with the Russian government (**Count Giovanni Capo d'Istria,** close friend of Tsar Alexander I). At the head of the movement was **Alexander Ypsilanti,** member of a powerful Greek phanariot family from Moldavia and an officer in the Russian army.

The new Greek state included none of the large Greek commercial centers, all of which remained in the Ottoman Empire, and embraced only three-quarters of the empire's 2 million Greeks. The existence of such a large diaspora outside its borders dictated Greece's foreign policy throughout the century, as its leaders strove constantly to expand. **Economically,** Greece suffered chronically from foreign debt. The need for external credit frequently outweighed the need for economic and political reform. The result was a lack of industrialization and high rates of emigration (one-sixth of the population left between 1890 and 1914).

1821, Feb. Outbreak of an **insurrection in Wallachia** against Ottoman-Greek rule. This precipitated action by the Greeks.

March 6. Ypsilanti proclaimed the **revolt in Moldavia** and appealed to the tsar for aid. Tsar Alexander, under Metternich's influence, disavowed him and refused to countenance a revolutionary movement. Ypsilanti lost courage and was defeated by an Ottoman force at **Dragashan** (June 26). He fled but was captured and imprisoned by the Austrians.

At the same time a more imposing insurrection took place in the **Morea,** which was joined by some of the more prosperous islands. The Ottomans, a small minority, were ruthlessly slaughtered, and the movement spread rapidly to the rest of Greece. The Ottomans retaliated by hanging the Greek patriarch and massacring Greeks in Constantinople.

July 27. Russian ultimatum to the Ottomans, demanding restoration of Christian churches, protection of the Christian religion, and so on. The Ottomans rejected this, and relations were severed. War was prevented only through the efforts of Metternich and Castlereagh, who reminded the tsar of the dangers of supporting revolution.

Oct. 5. The **Greeks took Tripolitsa,** the main Ottoman fortress in the Morea. Massacre of 10,000 Ottomans.

1822, Jan. 13. A Greek assembly at Epidauros declared **Greek independence** and drew up an organic statute (constitution) providing for a liberal parliamentary system and an executive directory of five.

Feb. 5. An Ottoman army finally took Janina and brought to an end the career of **Ali of Janina,** one of the most powerful of the pashas. The Ottomans were now free to press the campaign against the Greeks.

April. An Ottoman fleet, under Kara Ali, **took the island of Chios** and either massacred or sold into slavery most of the population.

June 19. The Ottoman fleet was destroyed by the Greeks under Adm. Constantine Kanaris.

July. Invasion of Greece by an army of 30,000, which overran the whole peninsula north of the Gulf of Corinth. The Greek government fled to the islands.

1823, Jan. The **Ottomans were obliged to fall back,** having been unable to take the key fortress of **Missolonghi,** at the entrance to the Gulf of Corinth. The Greeks failed to take advantage of this respite, but de-

Area of Turkey in Europe before Treaty of Berlin, 1878
Area of Turkey in Europe before the Balkan Wars, 1912–1913
Area ceded by Bulgaria to Romania, 1913
Boundaries before the Balkan Wars
Boundaries after the Balkan Wars

Drava R.

BANAT

Sava R.

BESSARABIA

Dniester R.

MOLDAVIA

BOSNIA
*Occupied by
Austria, 1878;
annexed, 1908*

Belgrade •

SERBIA

ROMANIA

Pruth R.

Sarajevo •

HERZEGOVINA

Bucharest •

DALMATIA
(Austria)

MONTENEGRO

Danube R.

BULGARIA

Black Sea

Scutari •

Vardar R.

M A C E D O N I A

Sofia •

Adrianople •

Bosphorus

*Albania
created
from former
Turkish
territory
1913*

ALBANIA

THRACE

TURKEY

Constantinople •

ITALY

Salonika •

*Sea of
Marmora*

Dardanelles

THESSALY

*Aegean
Sea*

TURKEY

*Ionian
Sea*

to GREECE 1881

G R E E C E

Smyrna •

IONIAN
ISLANDS

Athens •

Mediterranean Sea

MOREA

DODECANESE
to Italy, 1912

RHODES

THE BALKANS
1878–1914

to Greece, 1913

CRETE

0   50   100
MILES

voted themselves to personal rivalries (**Theodoros Kolokotronis** against **Lazaros Kondouriottis;** conflict between the executive power and the legislature).

1824. First civil war. Kolokotronis was defeated. The government was established at Nauplia. Meanwhile the sultan had appealed for help to his powerful vassal, **Muhammad Ali,** of Egypt, who possessed a strong army and navy. The Egyptians had already conquered **Crete** (1822–24).

1825, Feb. Ibrahim, the son of Muhammad, effected a landing in the Morea and quickly subdued the whole peninsula. At the same time the Ottomans, under Reshid Pasha, invaded from the north and renewed the **siege of Missolonghi** (finally taken on April 23, 1826).

The Ottoman-Egyptian successes aroused sentiment in Europe, where the Greeks were regarded as descendants of the heroes of old, renewing the struggle against the barbarians. Rapid spread of **Philhellenism** in Germany, Switzerland, France, and England. The governments were obliged to do something, and an ambassadorial **conference at St. Petersburg** (1824–25) discussed projects for establishing Greece as a group of three self-governing but tributary states, but Austria and Britain were unwilling to follow Russia in action against the Ottomans.

July 26. The Greeks put themselves under **British protection** and after the fall of Missolonghi appealed for British mediation.

1826, April 4. St. Petersburg Protocol, signed by Britain (**Wellington mission** to St. Petersburg) and Russia. The two powers agreed to mediate on the basis of complete autonomy for Greece under Ottoman suzerainty. Canning, who was chiefly concerned with preventing separate action by Russia, tried hard to associate other powers.

1827, April 11. The Greek factions, whose rivalries paralyzed all plans of action, united to elect **Capo d'Istria** president for seven years.

May 17. Constitution of Trözene, which practically deprived the executive of all power and vested it in a single chamber, the Senate. Despite the efforts of Englishmen **Lord Thomas Cochrane** and **Sir Richard Church,** united action proved illusory.

June 5. The **Acropolis capitulated** to the Ottomans.

July 6. TREATY OF LONDON. France joined Russia and Britain, and it was provided that if the Ottomans refused an armistice, the three powers would threaten to support the Greeks and use their naval forces.

Aug. 16. Note of the three powers to the Porte, demanding an armistice. The Ottomans refused, whereupon the admirals were instructed to stop all reinforcements and supplies from reaching the forces in Greece.

Oct. 20. BATTLE OF NAVARINO. The British, French, and Russian squadrons entered the harbor, where the large Egyptian fleet was crowded together. The battle was an artillery fight at short range and resulted in the sinking or blowing up of most of the Egyptian fleet. Wild enthusiasm flared in Europe; the indignant Ottomans demanded reparation.

Dec. 28. The allied ambassadors left Constantinople.

1828, April 26. Russia declared war on the Ottoman Empire. The British disapproved (Wellington ministry, Jan. 1828), but the French were friendly to Russia, and Austria did not dare raise too many objections.

Aug. 9. Anglo-French convention with Muhammad Ali provided for the evacuation of the Egyptian forces from Greece. This was carried out by a **French expeditionary force** under Gen. Maison (winter, 1828–29).

1829, March 22. THE LONDON PROTOCOL was drawn up by an ambassadorial conference: Greece, south of a line from the Gulf of Volo to the Gulf of Arta, with Negroponte (Euboea) and the Cyclades (but without Crete) was to be an autonomous, tributary state, under a prince (*not* to be chosen from the ruling families of Britain, France, or Russia).

Nov. 30. The **London conference** decided that Greece should be given complete independence, but the frontier was moved back to the line Aspropotamos–Gulf of Lamia, that is, almost to the Gulf of Corinth. This decision was embodied in a **new London protocol** (Feb. 3, 1830), which the Greeks rejected as inadequate. The powers chose **Leopold of Saxe-Coburg** as prince, but he declined the offer on the grounds that the frontiers of the new state were too restricted. Capo d'Istria ruled the state in dictatorial fashion until his **assassination in 1831.**

1832–62. OTTO I. Otto was a 17-year-old Bavarian prince. A regency of three Bavarian advisers governed during the first three years of his reign, attempting to establish a centralized, bureaucratic system, wholly unsuited to the traditions of local government. Unpopularity, internal dissension, continued brigandage, and economic want marked the entire reign.

1833, July. Otto became head of the Greek Church in a settlement angering many conservative Greeks, followers of the patriarch. The Crown closed over half of the existing monasteries and confiscated their property, contributing to the Catholic king's unpopularity.

1843, Sept. 14. Popular rising in favor of a constitution. Otto yielded and agreed to a fundamental law establishing a bicameral parliamentary regime.

1850, Jan.–March. British blockade arising out of the **Don Pacifico affair.**

Reconciliation between the patriarch in Constantinople and the Greek government.

1854, Jan.–Feb. Greek bands invaded Thessaly and **Epirus,** taking advantage of the war of Russia against the Ottomans. Relations between Greece and the Ottoman Empire were severed (March 28), but the Greeks were prevented from making war by the British and French **occupation of the Piraeus** (this lasted until Feb. 1857).

1862, Feb. Otto suppressed a **military revolt** only to be **deposed** in Oct. after another popular and military revolt; he left the country (Oct. 27).

1863, Feb. 3. The **Greek assembly proclaimed Prince Alfred** of Great Britain as king, after a plebiscite. The election was rejected by the British government.

1863–1913. GEORGE I, a Danish prince (17 years old), was finally chosen with the consent of the powers.

1864, June 5. Britain ceded to Greece the **Ionian Islands** (under British protectorate since 1815).

Nov. 28. A new **democratic constitution** was introduced, providing for male suffrage and a single-chamber parliament (*Boulé*).

1866–68. Cretan revolt; rupture of relations with the Ottoman Empire (Dec. 1868; relations resumed, Feb. 1869) (p. 530).

1878, Jan. 28. Rising in Thessaly, part of the general upheaval in the Balkans resulting from the war of Russia against the Ottoman Empire (p. 510). The Greek government declared war on the Ottomans (Feb. 2), but was constrained by the powers from larger hostilities.

1881, July 2. By convention with the Ottoman Empire, the Greeks acquired **Thessaly** and part of **Epirus,** promised them at the Congress of Berlin.

1886, April 26. Ultimatum of the powers to Greece, to prevent Greek action in harmony with the revolution in Eastern Rumelia. The Greeks refused to disarm, whereupon **the powers blockaded Greece** (May 10–June 7), forcing compliance.

1893. Despite general economic development in the 1880s and 1890s, reflected in the growth of a transportation network (railways increased from 7 miles in 1882 to 568 miles by 1893), the Greek economy remained dependent on a limited number of agricultural exports. The fall in world prices in its leading export, currants, combined with the need to reserve an increasing amount of the national budget for debt service, highlighted the weakness of the Greek economy and forced the government to **declare bankruptcy.**

1896, April. Revival of the **Olympic Games.**

1896–97. Cretan insurrection. Intervention of Greece (Feb. 1896) (p. 532) and resultant **war with the Ottoman Empire** (April 17, 1897). The Greeks were defeated but were treated leniently in the following peace, thanks to pressure from the powers (p. 475).

1898, Feb. An **international commission** was set up to control Greek finances, after the Greek government had defaulted on its obligations.

Nov. Ottoman troops were **forced to evacuate Crete** after attacking the British forces. Contingents from Britain, France, Russia, and Italy remained in occupation of the island.

1905, March 30. Insurrection in Crete, after the powers had repeatedly rejected Crete's appeals for union with Greece. The assembly (leadership of **Eleutherios Venizelos**) decreed union, but the powers, despite attacks upon their troops, remained adamant.

1908, Oct. 7. The **Cretans proclaimed union with Greece,** following the annexation of Bosnia and Herzegovina and the declaration of Bulgarian independence.

1909, July. Britain, France, Russia, and Italy withdrew their forces from Crete.

1910, Jan. The **Military League,** an association of officers, forced the

KINGS OF GREECE: DANISH LINE (1863–)

Christian IX of Denmark

George I King of Greece 1863–1913 ═ Olga of Russia

- George m. Marie Bonaparte
- **Constantine I** 1913–17 1920–22 ═ Sophia of Prussia
- Nicholas m. Helena of Russia
- Marie m. George of Russia
- Andrew m. Alice of Battenberg
- Christopher

Children of Constantine I and Sophia:

- **George II** 1922–23 1935–47 ═ Elizabeth of Romania
- **Alexander I** 1917–20
- Helen m. Carol II of Romania
- **Paul I** 1947–64 ═ Frederika Louise of Brunswick
- Irene m. Duke of Aosta
- Catherine

Children of Paul I and Frederika Louise:

- Sophia b. 1938 m. Juan Carlos of Spain
- **Constantine II** 1964– ═ Anne Marie of Denmark
- Irene b. 1942

Children of Constantine II and Anne Marie:

- Alexia b. 1965
- Paul b. 1967 m. Anne-Marie of Denmark
- Nicolaos b. 1969
- Theodora b. 1983
- Philippe b. 1986

- Maria b. 1996

Greek assembly to agree to revision of the constitution. Thereupon the league voluntarily dissolved itself (March).

Oct. 18. Venizelos became prime minister. He at once undertook the work of military and financial reform. Other reforms reorganized local government and instituted a system of public examinations for civil service. The government also officially recognized trade unions, created free and compulsory primary education, and instituted a progressive income tax. Such reforms met with widespread approval and blunted the development of socialist and agrarian movements more characteristic of other Balkan states.

1912, May 29. Treaty of alliance with Bulgaria.

Oct. 17. THE FIRST BALKAN WAR (pp. 478–79).

1913, March 18. Assassination of King George.

June. SECOND BALKAN WAR.

Dec. 10. Crete officially taken over by Greece.

1913–17. CONSTANTINE I.

1914. A crisis arose from Greek claims in **southern Albania** and from the question of the **Aegean Islands.**

July–Aug. Outbreak of World War I. Constantine rejected appeals from Germany to join in the conflict.

Sept. 7. Resignation of Venizelos, marking the beginning of the crisis of Greek neutrality in the war. (To p. 723)

3. SERBIA

Like most Balkan nations, Serbia in the 19th century expended most of its energies on establishing itself as a European nation, complete with a modern state apparatus; by 1866 Serbia had the largest army in the Balkans. With a population that grew from 368,000 to 2.9 million by 1910, Serbia remained rural; only 10 percent of the population was urban by 1874. The result was land hunger and little industrialization. By 1911, 80 percent of the population was still employed in agriculture. Although Serbian nationalism was built on a cultural revival, at the turn of the century 55 percent of Serbs were still illiterate.

1804–13. First Serbian Revolution, under the local notable **Karageorge Petrovic** (p. 525). The Serbian Revolution grew out of general conditions in the Balkans, especially the breakdown of law and order and the organization of local governments. At the outbreak of the revolution, most Serb leaders wanted only the restoration of peace and security with the recognition of some autonomy. After initial difficulties, the Porte exploited European wars to suppress the Serbs.

1813. The first Serbian **newspaper,** *Srpske Novine,* published in Vienna. It moved to Belgrade in 1834.

1815–17. Second Serbian Revolution, under **Milosh Obrenovich.** The Porte was more willing to find a peaceful solution, fearing European interference.

1817. Milosh was recognized by the sultan as **prince of Serbia** (the pashalik of Belgrade), which was given a measure of self-government. A National Chancery of twelve Serbian notables was to be set up in Belgrade as the highest court. Serbian officials were to collect taxes and to administer local affairs. Milosh followed a cautious policy of bribery, gradually securing larger powers from the Porte. During the Greek War (p. 514), he managed to play a canny game between Russia and the Ottoman Empire.

1829. The Treaty of Adrianople guaranteed the **autonomy of Serbia** and religious liberty.

Vuk Karadzic and **Leopold Ranke** published a history of the Serbian Revolution.

1830. The sultan recognized **Milosh as hereditary prince,** added some territory to his jurisdiction, obliged the Ottoman landlords to sell their holdings, and confined Ottoman troops to a few garrison towns.

1832. A convention signed with Phanar authorities gave Serbia **the right to choose a metropolitan and the bishops.** The bishop of Belgrade became the metropolitan of Serbia.

The first minister of education was installed in office. By 1839 he oversaw 72 primary schools and 5 *lycées.*

1833. Pavle Javanovic became **Petar,** the first metropolitan.

1834. A new **civil code** was promulgated.

The first theater in Serbia was organized in Kragujevac, but the true centers of Serbian culture remained Vienna and Pest.

1835. Opposition of the notables to Milosh's autocratic and oppressive rule (use of bastinado on his opponents, appropriation of forests, con-

trol of the pork business) forced Milosh to grant a **constitution** providing for a Senate of elders with legislative, executive, and judicial powers, and a popular assembly (Skupshtina) with control of the budget.

1835–36. Agricultural laws confirmed village community ownership of forests and pastures. Milosh granted these in an attempt to gain the loyalty of the peasantry, which represented 95 percent of the population. These laws stabilized the conditions of peasant life, making the peasants a community of smallholders.

1838. The sultan, supported by Russia, forced the **abrogation of the constitution** and the appointment of a Senate of Notables with almost complete power.

1839, June 13. Milosh abdicated, in protest against the oligarchic system.

Milan, son of Milosh, came to power. He died after a rule of only a few weeks.

1839–42. MICHAEL, the 17-year-old son of Milosh, became prince. His short rule was marked by constant intrigue on the part of the Karageorgevich faction *(Defenders of the Constitution)* who demanded the convocation of the Skupshtina. Michael was forced to flee.

1842–58. ALEXANDER KARAGEORGEVICH was elected by the Skupshtina. The strong protests of Russia forced the banishment of the popular leaders. Alexander's reign was the quietest in Serbian history, marked by a cautious foreign policy, the spread of Western influence, the growth of trade (especially with Austria), and the development of education (**University of Belgrade,** 1844; Academy of Sciences). Politically it was a period of factional trouble and corruption, the Senate being in complete control.

1843. The public postal system was established as the government concentrated on creating a state bureaucracy similar to Austria's.

1844. Iliya Garasanin, head of Prince Alexander's government, established the Yugoslav idea as Serbian foreign policy, stressing Slav unity. Russia forced his resignation in 1853.

1845. A **regular army was created** for internal security alone.

1847. The **National Museum** and the **National Library** were created.

1856. By the **Treaty of Paris,** Serbia was placed under the **collective guaranty of the powers.**

1858. The criminal justice system was reorganized.

Dec. 23. Alexander was forced to abdicate by an opposition faction, supported by the Obrenovichs and by the Ottoman Empire and Russia.

1858–60. Restoration of Milosh Obrenovich, now 79 years old. He died after wreaking vengeance on his enemies.

1860–68. MICHAEL, son of Milosh, reascended the throne. He was a well-educated and intelligent prince whose great aim was to unite the Balkans in the crusade against the Ottomans. He introduced compulsory service in the army and the gradual development of an efficient administration. But he did so as part of a personal rule, **relegating the Senate to an advisory role in 1861.**

1862, June 15. Bombardment of Belgrade by Ottoman troops, after clashes between the garrison and the populace. Michael appealed to the powers, and the sultan was induced to concentrate his force in three or four places.

1866. Michael appealed again for the **withdrawal of Ottoman troops.** The powers induced the sultan to yield, and the last troops left Serbian territory in April 1867.

Sept. 23. A secret offensive and defensive **alliance was created between Serbia and Montenegro.**

1867, May 26. Secret Serbian-Romanian treaty, with the object of securing independence.

Aug. 26. Serbia and Greece signed a secret treaty (Treaty of Voeslau) by which Serbia was to get Bosnia and Herzegovina; Greece would get Thessaly and Epirus. Action was to be taken against the Ottomans in 1868. A **Balkan confederation** was envisaged as the ultimate goal. Michael organized a far-reaching propaganda campaign in Bosnia and Macedonia, and established close contact with the Bulgarian revolutionary leaders. Widespread nationalist agitation occurred (**United Serbian Youth,** or Omladina, was founded in 1867; it was feared to be too liberal and was suppressed).

1868, June 10. Michael was assassinated by conspirators aiming to restore Alexander Karageorgevich. But Michael's chief adviser, **Iliya Garasanin,** anticipated them, roused the garrison, and had the assassins arrested.

Serbia first minted its own currency.

RULERS OF SERBIA (YUGOSLAVIA, 1804–1945)

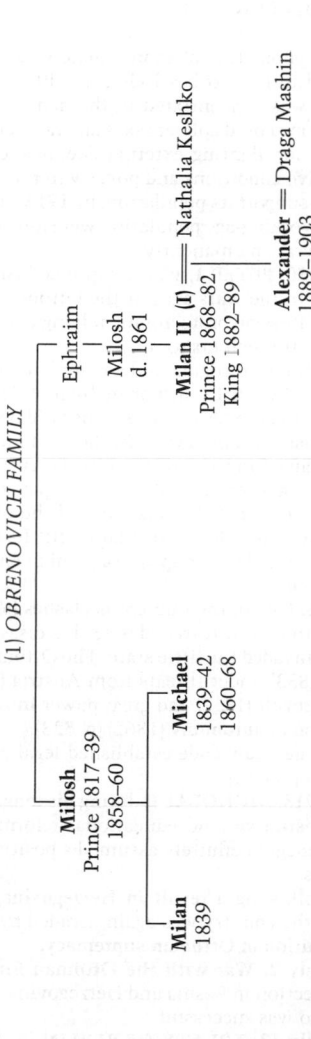

(1) OBRENOVICH FAMILY

Milosh
Prince 1817–39
1858–60

Ephraim

Michael
1839–42
1860–68

Milan
1839

Milosh
d. 1861

Milan II (I)
Prince 1868–82
King 1882–89

Nathalia Keshko

Alexander = Draga Mashin
1889–1903

(2) KARAGEORGEVICH FAMILY

George Petrovich (Kara George)
Hospodar, 1804–13

Persida = **Alexander**
Nenadovich   Prince 1842–58

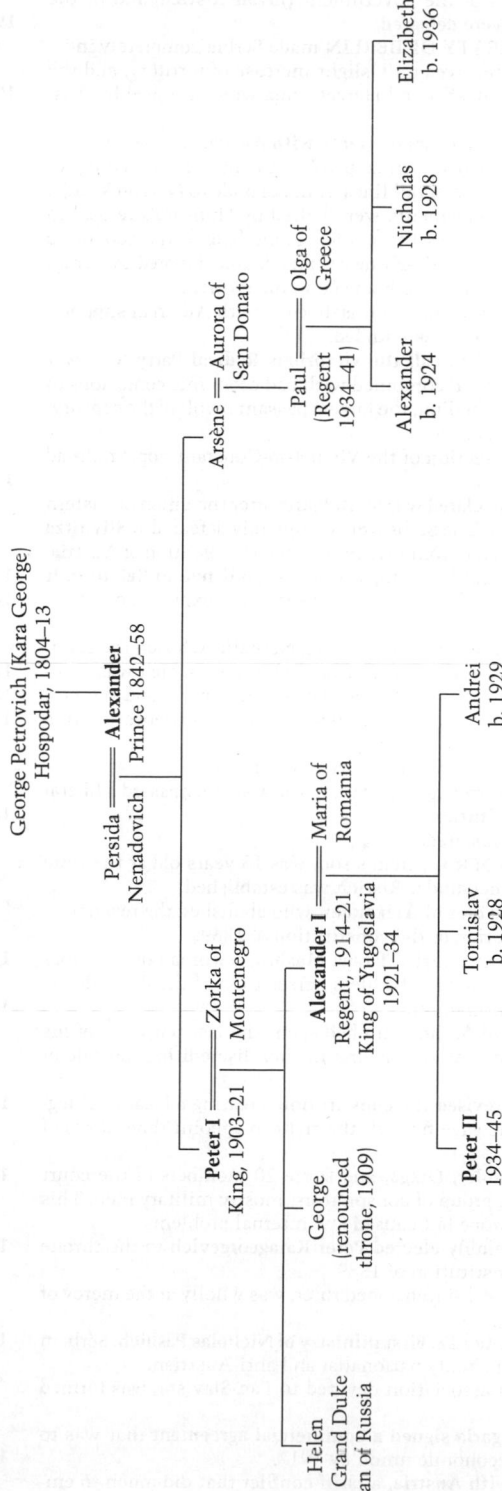

Arsène = Aurora of
San Donato

Paul
(Regent
1934–41)
= Olga of
Greece

Alexander
b. 1924

Nicholas
b. 1928

Elizabeth
b. 1936

Peter I = Zorka of
King, 1903–21   Montenegro

Alexander I = Maria of
Regent, 1914–21   Romania
King of Yugoslavia
1921–34

George
(renounced
throne, 1909)

Helen
m. Grand Duke
Ivan of Russia

Peter II
1934–45

Tomislav
b. 1928

Andrei
b. 1929

1868–89. MILAN, cousin of Michael, was appointed prince with a regency that undertook the **revision of the constitution** (1869) in a liberal sense, to meet the growing demands of nationalist organizations.

1876, July. Serbia declared **war on the Ottoman Empire** (p. 531), following the insurrection in Bosnia and Herzegovina. This unleashed the rampant nationalism of the government (**Jovan Ristich**) and of the country. **The Serbs were defeated.**

1878, July 13. The **TREATY OF BERLIN** made Serbia completely independent, but Serbia received only slight increase of territory, and the coveted provinces of Bosnia and Herzegovina were occupied by Austria.

1881, June 28. Serbia signed a secret treaty with Austria, giving the latter virtually a protectorate over Serbia (p. 473). A commercial accord provided for the construction of rail lines from Belgrade to Nis and Vranje. Further commercial agreements were halted by Hungary's refusal to allow Serbian wheat across the border. Nonetheless, the economic agreements between Austria-Hungary and Serbia favored Austrian manufacturing and retarded Serbian economic growth.

1882, March 6. Milan proclaimed himself king, with Austrian support.

1883, Jan. A national bank was founded.

Nov. Milan's refusal to call the victorious Radical Party to power (**Nicholas Pashich,** leader) combined with bad economic conditions to produce the **Timok Rebellion,** the largest peasant revolt of the century. It was crushed by the army.

1884–85. The Serbian section of the Vienna-to-Constantinople railroad was completed.

1885, Nov. 13. Serbia declared war on Bulgaria after the union of Eastern Rumelia and Bulgaria. The Serbs were completely defeated at **Slivnitza** (Nov. 17) but were saved from invasion by the intervention of Austria.

1887. The **Serbian Industrial Company was established in Belgium.** It represented the power of foreign enterprises in the exploitation of the Timok coal basin.

1888, Aug. Milan divorced his Russian wife, **Nathalia,** who left the country. Milan's increasing unpopularity caused unrest, which was compounded by a growing split between the Austrian party and the pro-Russian nationalist factions, which resulted in the convocation of a constituent assembly.

Dec. 16. The Radicals won a victory in elections.

1889, Jan 3. Despite warnings from Milan, the assembly passed a **liberal revision of the constitution.**

March 6. Milan abdicated.

1889–1903. ALEXANDER I, Milan's son, was 13 years old at the time of accession. A regency under Ristich was established.

1893, April 14. Coup d'état of Alexander, who abolished the regency.

1894, May 21. Restoration of the constitution of 1869.

1899, Aug. 5. Alexander married Draga Mashin, a woman of questionable reputation. This and his ruthless persecution of the Radicals led to increased opposition to him.

1901, Feb. 11. Death of Milan, who had spent the last ten years of his life intriguing behind the throne and further discrediting the rule of his house.

April. Alexander revised the constitution, creating a bicameral legislature, of which he gave himself the right to appoint three-fifths of the upper house.

1903, June 10. Alexander, Draga, and some 20 members of the court were **murdered** by a group of conspirators, mostly military men. This shocked most of Europe but caused few internal problems.

June 15. The **assembly elected Peter Karageorgevich** to the throne and restored the constitution of 1889.

1903–21. PETER I, a well-intentioned ruler, was wholly at the mercy of the conspirators.

1904, Dec. 10–1905, May 22. First ministry of Nicholas Pashich. Serbian policy became outspokenly nationalist and anti-Austrian.

Slovenski Jug, an association devoted to Pan-Slavism, was formed in Belgrade.

1905. Serbia and Bulgaria signed a **commercial agreement** that was to establish a virtual economic union by 1917.

1905–7. "Pig War" with Austria, a tariff conflict that did much to embitter relations. In the end Austria lost by driving Serbia to rely even more on France and Russia.

1908–9. The Bosnian annexation crisis (p. 477) caused an acute danger of war between Serbia and Austria. Serbia was obliged to back down,

but the crisis left a legacy of hate. This spurred the foundation of propagandist societies (Narodna Odbrana, 1908; Union or Death [Black Hand], 1911).

1912, March 13. Treaty of alliance with Bulgaria.

Sept. 12. Pashich was again elected premier.

Oct. 18. Outbreak of the **First Balkan War** (pp. 478, 479).

1913, June 1. Offensive and defensive **treaty of alliance with Greece,** concluded for ten years.

June 29. Outbreak of the **Second Balkan War.**

1914, June 24. Prince Alexander, heir to the throne, was proclaimed regent for the deranged king.

June 28. Assassination of Archduke Francis Ferdinand at Sarajevo.

July 28. Austria-Hungary declared war on Serbia. (To p. 721)

4. MONTENEGRO

With a population of approximately 120,000 people, Montenegro was divided into 36 tribes living in 240 villages. The real power in the nation was concentrated in the hands of the leaders of these tribes, who alone could collect taxes and raise armies. United action, possible only when fighting external enemies, contributed to the continued primitive conditions and poverty in the country. Montenegro was unable to support its population; by 1912 a third or more of Montenegro's male, working-age population were forced to seek foreign seasonal jobs or emigrate permanently.

1782–1830. PETER I, *vladika* (prince-bishop). He was a regular ally of Russia in the wars against the Ottomans. Indeed, Montenegro was a virtual Russian protectorate, relying upon Russian subsidies to replace income through taxation.

1799. Selim III recognized the complete **independence of Montenegro.**

1830–51. PETER II, author in 1845 of *The Garland of the Mountains* and national poet of the southern Slavs. The last years of his reign were disrupted by revolts in the Brda region and by food riots.

1831. In an effort to increase unity, Peter created a senate of 12 members.

1833. The first primary school was opened.

1851–60. DANILO I. He abolished the office of prince-bishop and established himself as a secular ruler. His efforts to reform and modernize the state led to opposition, which ended in **Danilo's murder** (Aug. 12, 1860).

1852–53. One of the numerous clashes between the Montenegrins and the Ottomans threatened to lead to disaster for the former when **Omar Pasha** invaded the little state. The Ottomans were obliged to withdraw (Feb. 1853) under threats from Austria (**Leiningen mission**). A subsequent revolt (1857) and great power intervention produced a new recognition of **autonomy** (1862) (p. 528).

1855. A new law code established legal equality and the protection of private property.

1860–1918. NICHOLAS I, during his long reign, effected many military, administrative, and educational reforms and modernized the state. Montenegro definitely assumed a position among the lesser European powers.

1861. Following a **revolt in Herzegovina,** supported by the Montenegrins, the country was again invaded by Omar Pasha, who forced the **recognition of Ottoman supremacy.**

1876, July 2. War with the Ottoman Empire resulted from the great insurrection in Bosnia and Herzegovina. Despite bad conditions, Montenegro was successful.

1878, July 13. TREATY OF BERLIN (p. 473) recognized the **complete independence of Montenegro,** which doubled in size. Fearing Russian use of the new Montenegrin coast, however, Austria-Hungary was given a type of naval protectorate in the region.

1879. Nicholas reorganized his state. He created a state council that acted as a legislative body, although it was appointed, and he established a council of ministers and a high court. He also divided the country into 12 provinces, further divided into districts headed by captains with administrative and judicial power.

1888. A new law code was introduced, and the army was reorganized along the Russian model.

1905, Dec. 19. Nicholas finally granted a **constitution** with an assembly elected by universal suffrage. He did this mainly to give his nation a modern air and thereby more easily acquire foreign loans.

After the advent of the Karageorgevich dynasty in Serbia (1903), there was growing rivalry for leadership of the southern Slavs, resulting in conspiracy against the life of Nicholas.

1909. An Italian company built **the only rail line in the country,** from Bar to Virpazar.

1910, Aug. 28. NICHOLAS proclaimed himself king.

1912, Oct. 18. First Balkan War (pp. 478–479). Montenegro, though not bound to the other states by formal alliance, was the first power to declare war.

1913, April 10. The European great powers **blockaded the Montenegrin coast** to raise the **siege of Scutari.** Nicholas took Scutari (April 22), but was forced by Austrian threats to evacuate it (May 5).

1914, Aug. 5. Montenegro declared war on Austria.   *(To p. 721)*

5. BULGARIA

By the end of the 19th century, Bulgaria's population had reached **4.3 million,** which served to increase rural discontent. In 1911, 80 percent of Bulgarians were still employed in agriculture, where increasing problems with debt created a growing split between town and country. As a nation, Bulgaria also suffered from debt as it sought to create the trappings of a stable state. Foreign loans curtailed Bulgaria's power as France and other nations forced Bulgaria to assign important sections of its economy, like the growing tobacco industry, to debt service.

1762. The monk **Paiisi Hilendarski** wrote his *History of the Bulgarian People*, marking the beginning of the Bulgarian national renaissance.

1835. Vasil Aprilov founded a Bell-Lancaster school in Gabrovo, the first school to teach in Bulgarian, launching an educational movement that included the foundation of the **first school for girls** in 1840.

May. Velchova rising in Turnovo.

1840. Translation of the Bible into Bulgarian by the monk **Neophytos,** aided by the American missionary **Elias Riggs.**

1841. Risings against the Ottomans in Nish.

1850–51. Risings against the Ottomans in the Vidin area.

1858. Opening of the first **American mission** (Samokov Seminary founded by **James F. Clarke,** 1861).

The Bulgarian national movement grew rapidly, with revolutionary committees at Bucharest and Odessa. The revolutionaries (**George Rakovski** and **Christo Botev**) were connected with Prince Michael of Serbia.

1866. The Bulgarian Secret Central Committee was formed in Bucharest, led by **Liuben Karavelov** and **Vasil Levski.** Levski crossed into Bulgaria in 1868–69 to establish revolutionary committees, but the Ottomans arrested him in 1872 and hanged him in 1873, creating a national hero.

1869. The **Bulgarian Literary Society** was founded in Braila, Romania. It moved to Sofia after liberation and became the Bulgarian Academy of Sciences in 1911.

1870. The Porte established the **Bulgarian exarchate,** a national branch of the Orthodox Church. The exarch was given jurisdiction over large parts of Macedonia and Thrace, as well as Bulgaria. The patriarch of Constantinople refused to recognize the Bulgarian Church, however, and excommunicated it in 1872.

1875, Sept. Abortive rising of the Bulgarians against Ottoman rule.

1876, April–Aug. A great **insurrection in Bulgaria** was planned by the Bulgarian Revolutionary Central Committee and put down by Ottoman irregulars *(Bulgarian Horrors).*

1878, March 3. THE TREATY OF SAN STEFANO (p. 472) provided provision for a large Bulgarian state to include most of Macedonia.

July 13. THE TREATY OF BERLIN (p. 472) established a small Bulgarian principality north of the Balkan Mountains, and an Eastern Rumelia south of the mountains. Both remained under Ottoman suzerainty. Macedonia was left under Ottoman rule, with promises (article XXIII) of reform.

One result of the Treaty of Berlin was Ottoman emigration from Bulgaria, freeing large areas of land. As much as a quarter of the arable land in Bulgaria and Rumelia went to peasant proprietors. Despite population pressures, land availability kept pace with demand throughout this period.

1879, Feb. 22. The Bulgarian constituent assembly adopted a liberal **constitution** providing universal male suffrage and a council of ministers responsible to Parliament. This constitution also called for universal primary education and conscription, and established Orthodoxy as the state religion.

1879–86. ALEXANDER I.

April 29. Alexander of Battenberg was elected prince. He was a favorite nephew of the tsar and was intended to serve as a satrap. He soon became involved in conflict with the national assembly *(Sobranye)*; its liberal members opposed Russian control.

The **National Library** was founded in Sofia.

1881, July 13. Upon Alexander's initiative and with Russian consent, a new constituent assembly, dominated by conservatives after coercive elections, **amended the constitution** and introduced indirect suffrage and restrictions of civil liberties, providing the prince with greater power.

1882. Faced with continued political instability, Alexander appointed a ministry headed by Russian officers.

1883, Sept. 30. Alexander, hounded by Russian concession hunters (demands for a Rustchuk-Küstendil railway) and confronted with the hostility of the liberal, nationalist elements, **restored the constitution of 1879,** thereby winning the enmity of the Russians.

1884, Dec. The Democratic government of **Petko Karavelov** nationalized all rail lines and the Bulgarian bank.

1885, Sept. 18. Bulgarian nationalists staged a coup against the government of Eastern Rumelia in Plovdiv, seeking union with Bulgaria. Alexander, under nationalist pressure, was obliged to assume leadership of the movement, despite violent protests from Russia (p. 532).

Nov. 13. SERBIA DECLARED WAR, demanding compensation (p. 474). A loose force of Bulgarians defeated the Serbs at **Slivnitza** (Nov. 17) and then invaded Serbia and took **Pirot** (Nov. 27), but Austrian diplomatic intervention forced them to withdraw. Peace was made on March 3, 1886. The powers rejected complete union, opting instead for a settlement naming the Bulgarian prince as governor of Eastern Rumelia (Feb. 1, 1886).

1886, Aug. 21. The kidnapping of Alexander by a band of officers was inspired by the Russians. A provisional government was established by **Stephen Stambolov,** an energetic nationalist leader, who arrested the conspirators and recalled Alexander.

Aug. 29. Alexander returned, but left permanently on Sept. 7 after the Russians refused to support his continued reign. He appointed a three-man regency consisting of **Stambolov, Sava Mutkurov, and Karavelov.**

Sept. 25. The Russian general **Nicholas Kaulbars** tried to win over the country to the Russian side, but failed. Acute danger of Russian military intervention ensued, frustrated by opposition from the powers (especially Austria and Britain).

Nov. 10. Prince Waldemar of Denmark was elected prince, but refused the offer.

1887, March. Stambolov suppressed **revolts** in the Silistria, Russe, and Varna garrisons.

July 4. The Bulgarian assembly elected **Prince Ferdinand** of Saxe-Coburg, who accepted and arrived on Aug. 14. Russia protested.

1887–1918. FERDINAND I. Ferdinand was not recognized by any of the powers, but, with the aid of Stambolov and the nationalists, managed to maintain himself, though the first ten years of his reign were punctuated by plots against him and assassinations of his ministers.

1888. Bulgaria completed construction of its section of the Vienna-to-Constantinople railway line.

1890, July. In concessions designed to firm up Bulgarian politics and thereby avoid regional instability, the Ottoman government appointed three Bulgarian bishops to Macedonian dioceses. This bolstered Stambolov's government and the monarchy.

1891. The **Bulgarian Revolutionary Social Democratic Party** was founded with goals similar to the German party's Erfurt program. The party fared poorly, however, due to numerous splits and weak unionization among workers.

1892, Aug. Visit of Stambolov to Constantinople. His policy throughout was one of friendship with the Ottomans and the extraction of concessions in regard to Macedonia. Suggestions by **Charilaos Tricoupis,** the Greek statesman, for formation of a **Balkan league,** were rejected (1891).

Krustiu Krustev became editor of *Misul (Thought)*, the leading literary journal in Bulgaria. This represented the cultural shift since liberation. No longer emphasizing Bulgarian uniqueness, authors such as **Stoyan Mihailovski, Petko Todorov,** and **Petko Slaveikov** sought to link Bulgarian literature to general European trends, highlighting the individual over the national collective.

The Sulzi i Smyah (Tears and Laughter) theater company, the cornerstone of the state-financed National Theater Company to be formed in the 1900s, was founded.

1894, June 12. Dismissal of Stambolov, due in part to peasant dissatisfaction and to Prince Ferdinand's desire to pave the way for reconciliation with Russia, partly to pressure of Macedonian elements dissatisfied with Stambolov's cautious policy.

In reaction to falling world grain prices, the government replaced the tithe with a **land tax. Constantine Stoilov's** government also sought to increase revenues through the first **encouragement of industry bill,** designed to assist Bulgarian manufacturers. The scope of the bill was widened later in 1905 and 1909. Construction also began on modern port facilities in Burgas and Varna (completed in 1903 and 1906 respectively). Finally, this effort was rounded out by commercial reforms built on the 1893 relaxation of banking regulations, such as the creation in 1894 of chambers of commerce, the codification of commercial law in 1897, and the creation of a grain bourse in 1907.

1895, July 15. Stambolov was murdered by Macedonian revolutionaries.

1896, Feb. Reconciliation of Russia and Bulgaria, on the occasion of the conversion of the crown prince, **Boris,** to the Orthodox faith.

Feb. 19. The sultan recognized Ferdinand as prince of Bulgaria and governor-general of Eastern Rumelia, followed shortly by recognition by the great powers.

1899. Forced by the costs of independent administration (state expenditure rose from 20 million leva in 1880 to 181 million leva in 1911), the government secured a loan from France, the first of many foreign loans that plagued Bulgaria's development.

Also, as grain prices began to rise, the government announced plans to return to a tithe in kind for the years 1900 to 1904, replacing the land tax. This gave rise to the **agrarian movement.**

Dec. The Bulgarian Agrarian Union was created in Pleven.

1900. Government troops clashed with **agrarian protesters** in Trustenik and in Daran Kulak. Protests continued, however, and forced the government to resign in Dec. The new government abolished the tithes.

The first opera by a local composer, **Emmanuil Manolov,** was performed.

1901. The Agrarian Union formally entered the political arena as the **Bulgarian Agrarian National Union,** but fared poorly in elections as harvests improved. It became more important under the leadership of **Alexander Stamboliski,** but never acquired more than 15 percent of the vote before World War I.

1902. The government's relaxation of liability laws, coupled the following year with mortgage loan reforms, spurred the growth of the **cooperative movement,** which had begun in 1890. From 1904 to 1911 the number of cooperatives grew from 68 to 1,400. The majority of these cooperatives were credit cooperatives, culminating in the formation of the **Central Cooperative Bank** in 1911.

1905–7. Hellenist activities in Macedonia, sympathy with the Russian Revolution, and poor conditions for urban workers gave rise to growing unrest. The university was closed to prevent student participation in political activity. The unrest culminated in a strike among railway workers at the end of 1906. In Feb. 1907 the government reached a compromise with the railway workers, and the strike ended.

1907, March 11. Prime minister **Petkov** was assassinated in an act of personal vengeance.

The **Bulgarian Operatic Association** was formed. It later became the Bulgarian National Opera.

1908, Jan. Ferdinand appointed **Alexander Malinov,** who reduced tensions by relaxing the earlier government responses to unrest. He spent his main efforts on securing independence, however.

Oct. 5. DECLARATION OF INDEPENDENCE by Ferdinand, who assumed the title of tsar. Beginning of the Bosnian annexation crisis, which overshadowed this action of Bulgaria.

1909, Feb. 21. Visit of Ferdinand to St. Petersburg, where he was received with royal honors.

April 19. Convention with the Ottoman Empire, which recognized

Bulgarian independence. The Ottomans made an agreement with Russia, which assumed responsibility for the financial settlement.

Nov. Draft treaty of alliance between Russia and Bulgaria. Ferdinand avoided committing himself, preferring to balance between Russia and Austria. Efforts of the Serbs to effect an alliance were evaded because of Ferdinand's unwillingness to abandon claim to all of Macedonia.

1911, March 22. Ivan Gueshov's cabinet was formed. Bulgaria began negotiations with Serbia (Oct.) as a result of the Tripolitan War.

1912. Pencho Slaveikov, poet author of *Kurvava Pesen (Song of Blood),* became the only Bulgarian ever to have been recommended for a Nobel Prize in literature.

March 13. CONCLUSION OF THE ALLIANCE WITH SERBIA.

May 29. TREATY OF ALLIANCE WITH GREECE.

Oct. 18. OUTBREAK OF THE FIRST BALKAN WAR (p. 478). Bulgarian victories.

1913, May 30. Bulgaria agreed to cede Silistria to Romania, in compensation for Bulgarian gains elsewhere.

June 14. Formation of the Stojan Danev cabinet. An effort was made to arbitrate the conflict with Serbia regarding division of the spoils.

June 29. OUTBREAK OF THE SECOND BALKAN WAR, following the attack of Gen. Michael Savov and the Bulgarians on the Serbian and Greek positions.

July 15. Formation of the Vasil Radoslavov cabinet.

Aug. 10. Treaty of Bucharest, following Bulgaria's defeat (p. 479).

Oct. 13. Treaty of Constantinople concluded peace between the Ottoman Empire and Bulgaria. The results of the Second Balkan War were disastrous for Bulgaria, which relinquished its most modernized rural areas and acquired areas that were backward and underdeveloped.

1914, July 29. Bulgaria declared **neutrality in World War I.**

1915, Oct. 14. BULGARIA ENTERED WORLD WAR I. *(To p. 724)*

6. ROMANIA

Romania, where the population reached 7 million by 1910, was a nation of large landholders; in 1895, 6,500 Romanians owned half of the agricultural land while landless peasants represented 20 percent of the population. Romania did differ economically from its neighbors in one significant way; its oil reserves had generated much foreign investment by 1900; foreign interests owned 82 percent of Romanian enterprises in 1911. Yet it remained primarily an agricultural state, with 75 percent of Romanians employed in agriculture in 1911. Its large, poor peasant population contributed to an illiteracy rate of 40 percent at the turn of the century.

1774. By the **Treaty of Kuchuk Kainarji, Russia** was given certain rights of intervention in behalf of the Danubian Principalities (**Moldavia and Wallachia**), which were still ruled by *hospodars* (usually phanariot Greeks) appointed by the sultan.

1780. Samuel Micu and George Sincai published *Elementa linguæ daco-romanae sive valachicae.*

1802. Russia forced the sultan to promise to appoint the *hospodars* **for seven years** and not to remove them without Russian consent.

1812. By the **Treaty of Bucharest, Bessarabia** was detached from Moldavia and ceded to Russia.

1821–22. Revolts in Wallachia, led by **Tudor Vladimirescu, and Moldavia,** led by **Alexander Ypsilanti.** Conflicting goals and the lack of Russian support led to an easy victory for the Ottomans, but the boyars (landed gentry) achieved much of what they wanted later, as the Porte accepted the replacement of Greek phanariots with native leaders. The episode continued to poison Russo-Ottoman relations, however, as the Russians felt that native rulers weakened their power in the Principalities.

1829, Sept. By the **Treaty of Adrianople** (p. 526) Russia strengthened her protectorate and secured for the Principalities **complete autonomy.**

1829–34. Russian occupation continued under the enlightened rule of the Russian governor, **Count Paul Kisselev,** who took precautions against the plague, organized a militia, reformed finances, and abolished trade restrictions.

1832. The **ORGANIC STATUTE** was worked out by a group of boyars under Russian auspices: an **assembly of boyars** was to elect the prince from among their own numbers. He was to be elected for life and irremovable without Russian consent. The result was an **oligarchic system,** which continued until 1856.

1832–56. This was a period of great **economic expansion** (demands of western Europe for Romanian grain; development of steamboat traffic on the Danube) and the rapid spread of **French influence** (many Romanian students in France; influence of the Polish emigration). Progressive rule was established under **Prince Michael Sturdza** in Moldavia, but both Principalities continued under strong Russian influence.

1848, June. REVOLUTION IN WALLACHIA demanded a liberal regime (leaders **Constantine Rosseti, Ion and Dmitri Bratianu**). The *hospodars* accepted a liberal constitution and then fled.

    Sept. By agreement with the Ottomans, **Russia invaded the Principalities** and put down the revolution.

1849, May 1. Russia and the Ottoman Empire signed the **Convention of Balta Liman:** the *hospodars* were to be appointed for only seven years; assemblies of boyars were abolished and replaced by *divans,* appointed by the *hospodars.* Russia and the Ottomans were to occupy the country jointly. The Russians stayed until 1851.

1853, July 2. Russia occupied the Principalities following the dispute with the Ottomans, which led to the Crimean War.

1854, Aug. 8. The Russians evacuated and were replaced **by the Austrians** (until March 1857) in agreement with the Ottoman Empire.

1856, Feb.–March. CONGRESS OF PARIS (p. 470). **Napoleon III** favored the union of the Principalities (influence of **Mme. Cornu** and of **Ion Bratianu**). This was opposed by the Ottomans and Austria, but gradually supported by Britain. Russia sided with France. It was finally decided that the sultan should summon popularly elected *divans* to ascertain the wishes of the population. At the same time an **international commission** was to investigate and suggest an organization.

1857, March. Austria evacuated the Principalities. In the election every kind of pressure and corruption was employed to debar the unionists, who were consequently defeated. France at once demanded annulment, which the sultan refused.

    Aug. France, Russia, Prussia, and Sardinia broke off relations with the Ottomans. An acute danger of war arose between France and Britain, the latter supporting the Ottoman Empire.

    Aug. 9. The visit of Napoleon III to Osborne resulted in the **Osborne Pact** between France and Britain: Britain agreed to the annulment of the elections and approved of a system of common institutions under separate princes (broad administrative union).

    Sept. New elections resulted in a great **victory for the unionists.**

Oil production began. By 1913 Romania ranked fourth in the world.

1858, Aug. 19. A conference of the powers at Paris decided to establish the **United Principalities of Moldavia and Wallachia,** with separate but identical administrations; delegates from each of the two assemblies were to form a central commission for legislation.

1859, Jan. 17. Col. Alexander Cuza, a relatively unknown officer, was elected prince in Moldavia.

    Feb. 5. The Wallachians also elected Cuza. Napoleon recognized him at once, and the other powers followed more or less grudgingly, but they recognized the union only for Cuza's lifetime.

1862, Feb. 5. The sultan allowed the **fusion of the two legislatures** (1861) (p. 529) and the union of the Principalities was recognized, with the new name of Romania.

    June 20. Barbu Catargiu, Conservative journalist and politician, was assassinated. Thereafter Cuza, whose sympathy was with the peasant class, appointed a Liberal ministry under **Mikhail Kogalniceanu** and proceeded to a policy of Liberal reform: new civil and criminal codes were based on the Napoleonic Code; a compulsory and free education system was established; two universities were founded in Jassy and Bucharest; and the Romanian Church was declared independent, which the patriarch of Constantinople recognized only in 1885.

1863, Dec. Kogalniceanu nationalized church lands, which represented up to a quarter of the total territory.

1864, March 28. Coup d'état of Cuza, designed to break the Conservative opposition. A plebiscite approved his proposal to strengthen the prince's power by establishing an appointed senate, and so on.

    Aug. Cuza introduced a great **land reform** by decree: manorial dues were abolished with compensation to the landlords, and the peasants were given a small share of the land. Despite its intention, this reform

aided the boyars. The peasantry's position continued to decline throughout the latter half of the century, especially as the population increased.

1866, Feb. 23. Cuza was kidnapped and forced to abdicate by a conspiracy of Conservatives and Liberals who desired a foreign prince. The assembly at once offered the position to the **count of Flanders,** son of Leopold II of Belgium, who declined.

    April 14. The provisional government (with the secret approval of Napoleon III and Bismarck) proclaimed **Prince Charles of Hohenzollern-Sigmaringen.** A plebiscite approved of the action.

    May 22. Charles arrived in Bucharest, having crossed Austria in disguise.

    July. Charles introduced **a new constitution,** based upon the Belgian charter of 1831 (liberal, but not democratic).

    Oct. 24. The **sultan recognized Charles** and the powers followed suit.

1866–1914. CHARLES I (Carol). His reign was characterized by rapid economic development (especially in petroleum). Romanian rail lines were joined to the Austrian and Russian networks, and Romania signed trade agreements with a number of European states.

1868. Romania granted two companies, one Anglo-Hungarian the other Prussian, the exclusive rights to build the first four rail lines from Bucharest to Jassy.

1871. Charles's support of Prussia in the Franco-Prussian War clashed with more popular pro-French sentiments. After demonstrations on the evening of March 22–23, Charles prepared to abdicate, but the formation of a Conservative government under **Lascar Catargiu** convinced Charles to stay.

1877, April 17. Romania and Russia signed a convention allowing Russia to pass over Romanian territory during the war with the Ottoman Empire.

    May 21. Romania entered the war on Russia's side and **proclaimed independence.** The Russians rejected active help until they were hard-pressed at the **siege of Plevna.**

1878, July 13. The **TREATY OF BERLIN** (p. 472) recognized the **full independence of Romania,** but the Romanians were obliged to cede **Bessarabia** to Russia in return for the much less desirable **Dobrudja.** By article XLIV of the Berlin Treaty, the Romanian government was obliged to promise **protection to the Jews,** of whom there were many in Moldavia. With British and French pressure, Romania amended its constitution to allow non-Christians to become Romanian citizens under strict conditions, but, since only Romanians could own land, little changed. The European great powers accepted this, however, and recognized Romanian independence in February 1880. Anti-Semitism became a mainstay of Romanian politics.

1881, May 23. PRINCE CHARLES was proclaimed king.

1883, Oct. 30. ALLIANCE BETWEEN ROMANIA AND AUSTRIA, acceded to by Germany and Italy. This continued in effect until 1914, but was kept a strict secret by the king, so that only a few chosen ministers were ever told of it. The alliance was the result of Romanian fear of Russia, but it failed to overcome the basic antagonism between Romania and Hungary over Transylvania.

1885. In an effort to build trade and industry, the government established protectionist measures and encouraged foreign investment, especially in the Cimpina-Ploiesti oil fields. But industrialization remained limited; in 1901 Romania counted only 37,000 workers in 600 enterprises of more than 25 employees.

1888, April. A serious **agrarian insurrection occurred** over the government's failure to face the vital land question.

1893, Jan. 10. Prince Ferdinand married **Princess Marie of Edinburgh.** Built on the growth of workers' circles since the 1880s, the **Romanian Social-Democratic Party** was founded.

1900–1. Tension in relations with Bulgaria arose from conflicting aspirations in Macedonia and the murder of several Romanians by Macedonian revolutionaries.

1905–11. A rupture of relations with Greece resulted from the friction over the treatment of Kutzo-Vlachs in Macedonia by Greek villagers. Large numbers of Greeks were expelled from Romania.

1907, March–April. A great **insurrection of peasants** in Moldavia had to be put down by military forces. Martial law was proclaimed throughout the country.

1913, May 7. Agreement was reached with Bulgaria by which the latter was to cede **Silistria** as compensation for gains made in the Balkan Wars. The Romanian government demanded more.

July 10. ROMANIA DECLARED WAR ON BULGARIA, joining Serbia and Greece in the **Second Balkan War** (p. 479).

1914, June 14. The visit of Tsar Nicholas of Russia and Sazonov to **Constantza** was taken as evidence of Romania's veering to the side of the Entente powers.

Aug. 4. Romania proclaimed its neutrality in World War I.

Oct. 10. King Charles died.

1914–27. FERDINAND I, nephew of Charles, ascended the throne.

1916, Aug. 27. ROMANIA DECLARED WAR ON AUSTRIA.

(To p. 725)

7. REGIONAL MOVEMENTS

a. Macedonia

As the Ottoman Empire weakened in the 19th century, regions like Macedonia became the scene of nationalist movements based in Bulgaria, Serbia, and Greece. Each saw Macedonia within their natural frontiers. Many of these efforts focused on building national consciousness among the Macedonians through schools and the church. Tensions heightened in the 1890s, however, to include open revolt.

1893. The **Internal Macedonian Revolutionary Organization (IMRO)** was formed to work for an autonomous Macedonia. Unlike the Supreme Macedonian Committee, which favored outright union with Bulgaria, IMRO, as the first indigenous movement in Macedonia, sought autonomy and eventual membership in a Bulgarian federation. IMRO also opposed outside efforts at insurrection in Macedonia, favoring only revolt from the Macedonians themselves.

1894. Formation of the Supreme Macedonian Committee, following a period of repression in Bulgaria. By 1900, IMRO had gained control of this organization.

1895. Formation of the **External Macedonian Revolutionary Organization,** with headquarters in Sofia.

June. Beginning of **raids into Macedonia,** from Bulgaria (**Boris Sarafov,** leader).

1897. Following Greece's defeat at the hands of the Ottomans, the Porte began to favor the Hellenist cause in Macedonia, seeing a weaker threat from Greece than from Bulgarian and Serbian sympathizers.

1901. Arrest of Macedonian leaders, after the assassination of certain Romanians and acute tension between Bulgaria and Romania. They were tried, but acquitted.

1902. In return for a Russian loan, Bulgaria curtailed its support of Macedonian revolutionaries and accepted a Serbian priest as administrator of the Skopje diocese, a blow to the power of the exarch.

Oct. 8. Despite such hindrances, the Supreme Macedonian Committee launched a raid in **Gorna Djumaya** with little result in Macedonia itself. Russia, however, forced both Serbia and Bulgaria to disavow the rebels.

1903, Feb. Bulgaria dissolved all Macedonian organizations in its territory and arrested the leaders.

Aug. 15. Fearing a missed opportunity if they waited, IMRO sponsored the **Ilinden-Preobrazhensko rising.** Like the Supreme Committee's efforts, it ended in Oct. with little result in Macedonia itself.

The heightened tensions, including the possibility of war between the Ottoman Empire and Bulgaria, spurred the European great powers to introduce reform through the **Mürzsteg reform program.** The empire was forced to redraw internal boundaries in an effort to provide more cultural homogeneity within administrative units.

1904. The first Greek bands appeared in central Macedonia, aided by a society in Athens and, secretly, by the Greek government. These bands added to continued skirmishes between pro-Serb and pro-Bulgarian rebels to hinder efforts at a customs union between Bulgaria and Serbia.

1912–13. As a result of the **Balkan Wars** (pp. 478–479), Macedonia was split mainly between Serbia and Greece, but rightful boundaries remained a contentious issue.

b. Albania

The rise of Albanian nationalism began with the **Rilindja,** or Renaissance, in the mid-19th century. Before this, Albania was a region split by religion, with important Catholic, Muslim, and Orthodox populations. Even as a national identity emerged, the nation remained divided, economically backward, and vulnerable to its stronger neighbors.

1850. Naum Vegilharxhi formed the **Albanian Cultural Association** while attempting to establish a national culture by publishing in Albanian.

1864. Demetrio Camarda published an essay on the Albanian language, tracing it back to ancient history.

1871. Zef Jubani attempted to preserve Albanian folk culture in his *Collection of Popular Songs and Albanian Rhapsodies.* **Thimi Mitko** did much the same in his *The Albanian Bee,* published in 1878.

1878. The League of Prizren was formed to promote Albanian nationalism to the European great powers at the Conference of Berlin. The league also established organizations in other sections of the country in an effort to create a de facto government. Their main goal became the prevention of implementation of treaties they felt were harmful to Albania.

April. The failure of the European great powers to recognize Albanian concerns by granting Albanian-inhabited territory to Serbia, Montenegro, and Bulgaria through the Treaty of San Stefano spurred on the political movement. An assembly led by **Abdul Frashëri** convened to petition the Porte for Albanian autonomy. It met with no response.

1881. The League of Prizren, under the continued leadership of Abdul Frashëri, declared a **provisional Albanian government,** which ended in Ottoman suppression. Despite this failure, the league had succeeded in changing the original plans of the European great powers and prevented some lands from falling into the hands of Greece and Montenegro.

1889. With the publication of the epic poem *The History Skanderbeg,* **Naim Frashëri** won his reputation as Albanian national poet.

1897, Nov. Fearing the encroachment of border nations, Albanian leaders met at Pejë to organize in the face of repeated rejections from the Porte of Albanian unity and autonomy.

1905. The **Committee for the Liberation of Albania** was formed and began an active guerrilla campaign in the south against the Ottomans and Greeks.

1908. Albanian leaders met in Bitola and formally adopted the Latin alphabet. They looked to the Young Turks for solutions to their grievances with the Porte, sending the foremost Albanian leader, **Ismail Kemal Vlora,** to the assembly summoned in Constantinople, but they were disappointed with the results.

1910, March. The Kosovo region rose up in rebellion, followed shortly by the population of the northern mountains, led by **Ded Gjo Luli.** The Ottomans suppressed the Kosovo revolt and closed all national organizations after three months of fighting, but faced with internal problems, they could not effectively meet such opposition with force alone. The people in the mountains remained in rebellion.

1912. Following the call for elections, the Ottoman deputies **H. Prishtina** and **Ismail Kemal Vlora** urged a national revolt. Albanian patriots of all three religions met to **declare their independence** and to create the **Vlora government.** In Aug., the rebels took Skopje, but the Ottomans could not respond before the outbreak of the First Balkan War.

1913, July 29. The European great powers meeting in London recognized an independent Albania, but refused to recognize the Vlora government. They chose, instead, to establish a committee with only one Albanian delegate to create a new government. The committee chose **Prince Wilhelm von Wied** to be Albania's first king. His reign lasted only six months. Stability proved elusive as Europe entered World War I.

(To p. 722)

C. THE MIDDLE EAST AND NORTH AFRICA, 1792–1914

(From p. 349)

1. OVERVIEW

The start of the 19th century marks the conventional beginning of modern Middle Eastern and North African history. The region entered a **new course of development** under the **overpowering shadow of Europe,** which increasingly shaped its domestic and international affairs.

By 1914 large parts of the region, including Egypt, Cyprus, Aden, and all of North Africa, had been **occupied by European imperial powers,** primarily Britain and France; the states of the Persian Gulf had accepted one form or another of **British protection;** and Iran and Afghanistan were subject to extensive Russian and British **interference in their internal affairs.** European powers had also helped the Balkan lands shake off Ottoman rule, which was virtually terminated in Europe after a presence of some 500 years.

The looming European threat spurred a dramatic **process of modernization** initiated by regional rulers (primarily in Istanbul and Cairo) in the beginning of the 19th century. Modeling their efforts on Western methods and institutions, they proceeded to **reorganize their armies and centralize their administrations,** and then expanded into new spheres of **social and economic reform** that created European-inspired legal codes, land tenure systems, municipal institutions, secular schools, and public health measures. With the aid of European capital they also promoted **improvements in infrastructure** (irrigation works, roads, railways, telegraph lines, and steam navigation). Governments grew bigger and assumed new social functions, although the ambitious rush to develop led, by the mid-1870s, to the **bankruptcy** of the treasuries of the Ottoman Empire, Egypt, and Tunisia, all of which had defaulted on large loans taken from European bankers. **European financial and political controls** established in the aftermath restricted both the expenditures and sovereignty of regional governments.

Government efforts to modernize were part of a broader **opening up of the region to Western influences.** Newspapers, modern schools (most of them private and communal), translated works, and direct contact with Europeans introduced segments of the public to **new modes of thought.** European dress and architecture spread, especially in the cities. Slavery was abolished, a feminist movement began to emerge, ideas of nationalism and constitutional government took root, and Islamic religious institutions came under attack.

By 1914 the encounter with Western civilization had provoked **serious soul-searching** and questions about the future direction of society. Thinkers tried to explain why a once-flourishing Islamic civilization had become inferior to Europe and how the region could rejuvenate itself. Between those who advocated opposition to Western ways and supporters of wholesale imitation of them, a group of thinkers emerged who sought ways for the region to modernize without being untrue to its own traditions. Many of them were associated with the **movement of Islamic reform,** which supported modernization in the framework of a reformed Islam more suited to the needs of society.

Dramatic transformations occurred also in the demographic and economic spheres. The region's **population increased** during the period between two and three times, from roughly 28 million to about 66 million (in the Middle East from 21 to 54 million, in North Africa from 7 to 12 million). **Improvements in public health and the disappearance of the plague** brought the beginnings of sustained population growth in both city and countryside (the rural population remained at 75–80 percent).

This demographic revolution was accompanied by **economic expansion.** The region's **foreign trade** grew several times as Europeans purchased larger quantities of its agricultural products and found in it ready markets for their mass-produced finished goods. The Middle East and North Africa became **incorporated into the European-dominated world economy,** with a number of mixed results: the colonial pattern of exchange undermined the region's self-sufficiency; there was a large-scale **shift to cash crops** in some areas (such as cotton in Egypt and silk in Lebanon); many local textile workers unable to compete with **cheap European imports** were thrown out of business; **coastal cities** like Beirut and Alexandria, the new contact points with Europe, grew rapidly while the interior cities declined in economic importance; and local **non-Muslim merchants** backed by European favors benefited from the new opportunities at the expense of Muslim traders.

Agriculture, which remained the main sector of the economy, also experienced marked growth. Improved security and irrigation, investments by landowners, and increased demand all helped to expand the cultivated area and agricultural output. Through new laws, large tracts of state land were converted into freehold and came mostly into the possession of **a class of wealthy urban landowners.** Much capital went into land but not into **modern industry,** which was still barely existent in 1914. Manufacturing remained organized around artisanal workshops even as the traditional **guild system was disappearing,** its functions taken over by government and the market. Overall, income and wealth increased, but **the benefits were very unevenly distributed.**

(To p. 751)

2. THE MIDDLE EAST AND EGYPT, 1796–1914

a. THE OTTOMAN EMPIRE

(From p. 359)

1. BEGINNINGS OF MODERNIZING REFORM

1808–39. SULTAN MAHMUD II. In Nov. 1808, just months after his accession, Mahmud faced a **revolt by the Janissaries,** who forced him to abandon plans to create a new army, and in addition killed his reform-minded grand vezir, Mustafa Bayrakdar Pasha. This experience, and the unhappy fate of his predecessor Selim III, prompted the sultan to prepare cautiously for the eventual **destruction of the Janissaries.** A set of decisive actions he took marked the **true beginnings of modernization in the empire.** In addition to creating a **new army** and **restoring central control** in many provinces, he began the **reorganization of the state based on European ideas** of the rule of law, conciliar bureaucracy, and equality of the subjects.

1812–20. Reassertion of Istanbul's control in the Balkans and Anatolia.

Mahmud used political pressures and military expeditions to remove rebellious governors and local notables from their hold over large parts of Anatolia and the Balkans, which were brought under his direct rule. In western Anatolia the central government **eliminated several of the rural notables known as valley lords** (*derebeys*) who ruled over autonomous hereditary principalities, including the Janikli family in the area of Trabzon (1812–13), the Chapanoğlu family around Ankara and Amasya (1814), and the Karaosmanoğlu family in the area of Aydin (1816). The last of the valley lords was subjugated in 1866 when a military expedition removed the Kuchuk Alioğlu chiefs in the area of Adana.

1813. Reassertion of Istanbul's control over the province of Aleppo, after a crackdown on the local Janissary corps and the execution of many of its leaders.

1815–17. The Serbian revolt. In April 1815, two years after the Ottomans suppressed the uprising of Karageorge, a second revolt broke out under the leadership of Milosh Obrenovich. In 1817, Sultan Mahmud conceded a **degree of autonomy to the Serbs** (p. 518), recognizing Milosh as the prince of Serbia and allowing the Serbs to have their own national assembly and army. The Ottomans continued to maintain their governor in Belgrade as well as their garrisons.

1821. First appearance of cholera in the empire. Numerous subsequent epidemics hit the region well into the 20th century (7 between 1821 and 1850). The **estimated mortality** in various cities was 1–4 percent, with higher rates of 6–10 percent among the poor segments of the population. Mecca suffered the highest recorded mortality rates, with cholera epidemics wiping out as many as 10–15 percent of the Muslim pilgrims (the city had 23 epidemics between 1831 and 1912). The **bubonic plague disappeared** in most parts of the region by the 1840s, and cholera took its place as the leading scourge.

1821–23. War with Iran, provoked by border incidents. The Iranians pushed successfully into Anatolia, but agreed to peace after an epidemic ravaged their troops. The **Treaty of Erzurum** (July 28, 1823) reaffirmed the Treaty of 1746 with minor boundary changes in favor of Iran. Provisions were made for the release of the confiscated property of Iranian merchants in Istanbul and for the entry of Iranian traders and pilgrims into Ottoman lands.

1821–30. THE GREEK WAR OF INDEPENDENCE (p. 514). A **revolt against Ottoman rule** in the Morea in March 1821 spread quickly to the Greek mainland and islands, and a Greek assembly declared independence. The Ottomans solicited the **assistance of Muhammad Ali of Egypt,** whose disciplined troops subdued Crete before moving into the Morea in 1825 and defeating the rebels there. When the Ottomans resisted European demands for an armistice, a combined British and French squadron **destroyed the Ottoman and Egyptian fleets at Navarino** (Oct. 20, 1827) in a naval battle that turned the tide in favor of the Greek rebels. The Ottomans refused to settle on European terms, and **war ensued with Russia** (April 1828) in which the Ottomans were soundly defeated. They agreed to a European scheme to establish Greece as an autonomous tributary state ruled by a hereditary prince invested by the sultan (1829), but in 1830 they were forced to accept **full Greek independence.**

1822, Jan. 24. Death of Ali Pasha of Janina, the powerful ruler of Albania and parts of Greece for over three decades, after Ottoman forces occupied his lands and put him to death.

Aug. 13. A major **earthquake** in northern Syria caused extensive damage and loss of life, especially in Aleppo. In 1872 another severe earthquake in that region devastated Antioch (Antakya).

1825, June 10. Abolition of the English Levant Company, by act of Parliament. The final removal of this commercial monopoly **opened up the trade of the eastern Mediterranean** to a wider circle of merchants and transferred responsibility for the appointment and payment of British consular representatives from the company to the government.

1826, June 15. DESTRUCTION OF THE JANISSARIES. Troops loyal to the sultan bombarded the Janissary barracks in Istanbul, killing several thousand soldiers inside. **The corps was abolished,** its garrisons in the provinces were disbanded, and the way was opened to establish new military units and institutions. The episode represented a watershed in the state's struggle to break the obstacles to modernization and became celebrated in Ottoman history as the Auspicious Event (*vakayi hayriye).*

1828. The fez (a rimless cap of North African origin) was officially adopted as the modern headgear of the army. A year later **modern clothing** and the fez were made compulsory also for government servants, with turbans and robes allowed only for the clergy.

1828–1914. The development of steam navigation. A British steamer reached Izmir and Istanbul in 1828, inaugurating the expansion of steam navigation into the region. By 1837 the British, French, and Austrians had **regular services in the eastern Mediterranean,** supplemented in subsequent years by Ottoman, Italian, and Russian lines. **The Suez Canal,** opened in 1869, gave a great stimulus to steam navigation by cutting dramatically the distances from European ports to India and the Far East. Steamers rapidly took over the region's commerce, and by 1914 had almost completely **displaced the sailing ships,** which became confined to coastal trade and a few bulk goods like coal. This technological improvement in sea transport **reduced the traveling time** between the Middle East and Europe by one-half to two-thirds, **promoting the region's foreign trade** and increasing greatly the flow of people and ideas.

1829, Sept. 14. The Treaty of Adrianople, concluding the Russian-Ottoman war of 1828–29. **Russia,** whose forces had advanced as far as Adrianople, abandoned most of its conquests in Europe. It made some gains at the mouth of the Danube, and **acquired substantial territories** in the Caucasus, Georgia, and eastern Anatolia. The Ottomans recognized the **autonomy of Serbia** and agreed to the removal of their troops except for the frontier garrisons and the ending of Ottoman collection of taxes in return for Serbian payment of a fixed annual tribute to the sultan. They also accepted the **autonomy of the Principalities** under Russian protection and the autonomy of Greece (which achieved full independence in 1830). Russia was granted the same **capitulatory rights** enjoyed by the subjects of other European states.

1830, July 5. Surrender of Algiers to the French marked the beginning of the French occupation of Algeria. Although formally part of the Ottoman domains, the province was at the time autonomous. Istanbul protested the occupation but did not break its ties with France.

Aug. The sultan recognized the **hereditary rule of Milosh Obrenovich in Serbia** and agreed to give him six additional districts from the provinces of Vidin and Bosnia. The Serbs occupied these areas in 1833, increasing the size of their country by one-third.

1831. The first modern population census in the empire. It was completed in 1838, and counted the adult male population in most parts of the empire (total 3.6 million).

July. Law establishing an **Ottoman reserve army** *(redif).* Units composed of men between 23 and 32 years of age were set up in the provinces, providing the empire for the first time with a reserve force of at least partly trained men.

Nov. 1. Beginning of the **first Ottoman-language newspaper,** the *Takvim-i Vekayi,* issued by the government on a weekly basis to provide copies of laws as well as news of events. It continued until 1923, with a total of 4,891 issues printed.

1831–38. Reassertion of direct Ottoman rule in Iraq and Kurdistan. In Sept. 1831 an Ottoman expeditionary force entered **Baghdad** after a 90-day siege and took over direct control of the province, which had been under Mamluk rule since 1747. In 1834 the Ottomans restored direct control over **Mosul,** ending the rule of the Jalili family. An Ottoman force then marched through **Kurdistan** and by 1838 broke the authority of the Kurdish chieftains in the areas of Bitlis, the Jazira, and Amadiyya. The Babans of Sulaymaniyya held out until 1850, when they finally submitted.

1831–40. THE EGYPTIAN OCCUPATION OF SYRIA. The army of Muhammad Ali of Egypt occupied Palestine, Lebanon, and Syria (Nov. 1831–July 1832) and then advanced into Anatolia, defeating an Ottoman army near Konya (Dec. 21, 1832) and pushing as far as Kutahya (Feb. 1833). The sultan accepted **Russian military aid,** for which he paid with a defensive alliance in the **Treaty of Hunkiar Iskelesi** (July 8, 1833) (p. 509). The treaty included a secret clause that opened the Dardanelles to the Russians in times of war and closed them to everyone else. Under pressure from France and Britain, the Ottomans and Egyptians reached a **peace at Kutahya** (May 1833) by which Syria, the district of Adana, and Crete were granted to Muhammad Ali's son Ibrahim in return for a yearly tribute.

Egyptian rule in the region became unpopular due to heavy taxation, forced labor, disarmament of the population, and military conscription, which **provoked uprisings** from 1834 onward. In 1839 Sultan Mahmud tried to recapture Syria, but his army was defeated at Nezib (June 24) while his navy defected to Alexandria. With the Ottoman Empire at the mercy of Muhammad Ali, a coalition of European powers led by Britain intervened to impose a settlement (the **convention of London,** July 15, 1840) by which Muhammad Ali was to withdraw from Syria in return for recognition of his hereditary rule in Egypt. When Muhammad Ali refused to comply, **European forces,** combined with a popular uprising, **drove his forces from Syria** in 1840.

For Syria's population, Egyptian rule represented a rude **introduction to features of a modernizing regime** that were to become increasingly common after the return of Ottoman government in 1840 and the gradual application of reforms in the region.

1835, May. Restoration of **Ottoman direct control over Libya,** which lasted until the Italian occupation in 1911.

1835–39. Reorganization of the central government. Mahmud began the process by which the central administration was divided by function into **ministries and departments.** He established, among others, the Ministry of Foreign Affairs (1836), the Ministry of the Interior (1836), and the Ministry of Finance (1838). The ministers (*vekils*) were appointed by the sultan and were responsible to him rather than the **grand vezir, whose powers were reduced.** Several advisory councils were created (1838) to review and initiate legislative proposals. Mahmud also reorganized the bureaucracy, eliminating the traditional practice by which officials had to be reappointed annually and introducing a regular salary system to replace the dependence on fees as the main source of income. This was part of the **development of "big government"** in the empire over the 19th century; the number of scribes in the civil service increased from about 2,000 in 1790 to some 35,000 in 1900.

1835. Creation of the office of **chief rabbi** *(hahambashi)* of the Ottoman Jews. Its holder, based in Istanbul, was responsible for mediating between the authorities and the community and administering the financial and welfare needs of the community, in addition to being its religious head. Similar offices were subsequently created in the provincial towns (the first chief rabbi of Jerusalem was appointed in 1841, and of Baghdad, in 1849).

1836. The introduction of steamboats on the Euphrates River. An expedition under Francis Chesney carried two steamers across the Syrian desert and sailed them down the Euphrates. In 1839–42 four steamboats belonging to the East India Company sailed on the Tigris and Euphrates, surveying the rivers and carrying mail and passengers. **Captain B. Lynch** took over the boats in 1841 and established a **successful transport service** that continued in operation until 1949. An Ottoman government line began operating in 1859. The steamers reduced the journey from Baghdad to Basra to 2–3 days, compared with 5–8 days by sailing boat.

1837. A major **earthquake** in Palestine and southern Lebanon. Its epicenter was near Safed, which was largely destroyed.

1838, Aug. 16. The Anglo-Ottoman Commercial Convention (Balta Liman) prohibited the use of monopolies throughout the empire and severely lowered the level of internal duties. The agreement, to which other European powers soon acceded, was intended to **break the Ottoman and particularly the Egyptian system of monopoly** of the purchase, sale, and export of various agricultural products, and to allow direct business with the peasants. It secured for European merchants uninterrupted access to Middle Eastern agricultural products on favorable terms. In subsequent years most Ottoman internal duties were abolished, **making the empire an open market for European manufactures** while providing little protection for its domestic products.

1839–61. SULTAN ABDULMEJID I. The death of Mahmud (June 30, 1839) and the accession of his son Abdulmejid ushered in the second stage of the **Ottoman reform movement,** a stage commonly known as the **TANZIMAT** (literally, orders or regulations). The Tanzimat program of reforms, which reached its climax in the constitution of 1876, drew its **inspiration from European models** and aimed at rejuvenating the empire through administrative centralization, modernization of the machinery of state, westernization of society, and limited secularization of law and education. The driving spirit behind the reforms was the statesman **Mustafa Reshid Pasha** (1800–58), who served as grand vezir and foreign minister. Two of his protégés, **Ali Pasha** (1815–71) and **Fu'ad Pasha** (1815–69), rose to the same high positions in the government and continued the movement of reform with vigor.

1839. The Imperial School of Medicine was established in Istanbul.

Nov. 3. THE IMPERIAL RESCRIPT (HATT-I SHERIF) OF GULHANE. The proclamation, timed to win British diplomatic support in the crisis with Egypt, spelled out **a set of projected reforms** in the judicial, administrative, and military institutions of the empire. It promised to guarantee **security of life, honor, and property** for all subjects; to establish an orderly system of **fixed taxes** to replace tax farming; and to develop a **regular system of conscription,** with the term of service reduced from lifetime to four or five years. It also adopted for the first time the principle of **equality of all subjects,** regardless of religion.

1840. The Damascus affair. The episode—the most notorious case of **blood libel against Jews** in the empire—began when an Italian Capuchin friar and his native servant disappeared in Damascus (Feb. 5). The local Christians, backed by the French consul, accused the Jews of having the two men murdered in order to use their blood for the rituals of the approaching Passover. Seven leading members of the Jewish

community were arrested, and under torture two died, one saved himself by embracing Islam, and the others were induced to confess. The governor also took 63 Jewish children hostage in order to force their parents to reveal the whereabouts of the two men's blood. The Jewish community became the target of **mob violence,** and it took **international pressure** to rescue it from official harassment and popular attacks. The Austrian consul in Alexandria persuaded Muhammad Ali of Egypt, then still in occupation of Syria, to order his governor in Damascus to protect the Jewish community (May), and a deputation of British and French Jews obtained from him the release of the prisoners (Aug.). The same delegation then interceded with the Ottoman sultan, who issued a **decree denouncing the blood libel** (Nov. 6).

Similar **accusations of ritual murder** recurred many times in the 19th century, coming almost invariably from the Christian population. Such incidents, often accompanied by **outbreaks of violence,** occurred in Damascus (1848, 1890), Aleppo (1810, 1850, 1875), Antioch (1826), Beirut (1862, 1874), Tripoli (1834), Jerusalem (1847, 1870, 1895), Jaffa (1876), Dayr al-Qamar (1847), Istanbul (1870, 1874), Izmir (1872, 1874), Edirne (1872), and more frequently in the Greek and Balkan provinces of the empire.

1840. Restoration of Ottoman authority in the Hijaz, following the withdrawal of the Egyptians. Istanbul pursued a new policy of establishing direct control over the Hijaz through its own governors while curtailing the previously autonomous power of the sharifs of Mecca.

The **first private Turkish newspaper,** the *Jeride-i Havadis*, was founded in Istanbul by the English journalist William Churchill.

May. Adoption of a **modern penal code,** which marked the first attempt at systematizing the criminal laws in the empire. A second revised penal code was published in Feb. 1851, followed in Aug. 1858 by a third code based on French law.

1840–45. Political crisis in Lebanon. The defeat of the Egyptian forces in Lebanon in Oct. 1840 brought the downfall of their local ally, the emir Bashir II. Under his incompetent successor, Bashir III, **fighting broke out between the Christians and the Druze,** driven largely by Druze resentments for their loss of feudal holdings and political influence during the period of Egyptian rule. **The Ottomans intervened** to depose Bashir III and assert their political supremacy (Jan. 1842), and under pressure from the European powers accepted a **plan for communal autonomy** by which Mt. Lebanon would be divided into a northern district administered by a Maronite governor *(kaymakam)* and a southern district administered by a Druze (Dec. 7, 1842).

Continued tensions between the communities erupted in **fresh fighting** in the spring and summer of 1845, leading the Ottomans to impose a general disarmament of the population and an **organic law for the administration of the area** (known as the *Règlement* of Shekib Efendi). The new arrangement, which held until the violent disturbances of 1858–60, provided for representative councils to assist the Druze and the Christian governors, with powers to collect taxes and administer justice. It dealt a **blow to the feudal chiefs** who had traditionally exercised these powers, and marked a first step toward **modernizing Lebanon's administration.**

1841, July 13. Convention of London regarding the Straits, signed by the Ottoman Empire and the five great European powers. The Straits were to be **closed to all foreign war vessels in time of peace,** a regime that survived without major change until World War I.

1843. Reorganization of the army into regional commands for the first time. **Five armies,** charged respectively with the defense of the capital, eastern Thrace, the Balkans, Anatolia, and the Arab provinces, were created. **A sixth army,** charged with the defense of Iraq and the Hijaz, was added in 1848.

1846. Death of **Hammamizade Ismail Dede** Efendi, among the most creative Ottoman musicians of the 19th century. A member of the Mevlevi order, he rose under the patronage of Sultan Selim III and distinguished himself as a singer, flute player, and composer.

1847, May 31. The Treaty of Erzurum with Iran. The agreement **defined the frontier** between the two countries, which had been the source of recurrent disputes. It took many more years of negotiations and adjustments to establish a precise demarcation, which was formally accepted by both sides in Oct. 1914.

1847–90. SUPPRESSION OF THE SLAVE TRADE. Until the 1840s, slave markets existed in all major cities in the empire, and domestic **slavery was common.** Over 10,000 slaves were being imported every year, legally and openly. By the 1890s, the slave trade had been effectively suppressed, the result of a series of **restrictive government measures** taken largely in response to **British pressure.** An Ottoman decree of Jan. 20, 1847, prohibiting the **trade in African** slaves at Basra, was followed in the next decade by the prohibition of the **Circassian and Georgian slave trade** (1854–55) and a general prohibition of the African slave trade throughout the empire, except the Hijaz (decree of Jan. 27, 1857). An **Anglo-Ottoman convention** for the suppression of the slave trade was concluded on Jan. 25, 1880, and in 1890 the Ottomans joined other countries in **signing the Brussels Act** against the African slave trade.

1848. Uprisings in Moldavia and Wallachia (p. 523), which proclaimed their unity and independence as Romania, and the abolition of feudal privileges (June 21). **Ottoman and Russian troops intervened** jointly and suppressed the revolt.

1850. Promulgation of the **Ottoman Commercial Code,** which drew on French law to create rules compatible with international practices. The code was administered by **mixed tribunals** of Ottoman and European judges. It was revised in 1861.

Oct. 17–18. Anti-Christian rioting in Aleppo. Christian neighborhoods were pillaged and several of their residents killed and injured by Muslim mobs resentful of Christian prosperity.

1853. The first **Judeo-Spanish paper** in the empire, *La Luz de Israel,* began publication in Istanbul.

1853–56. The Crimean War (p. 470). The Ottoman involvement in this bloody conflict, which was essentially a European affair, had its roots in a dispute between France and Russia over their respective patronage of Catholics and Orthodox in the **holy places in Palestine,** and the attempts of Russia to extract from the Ottomans further concessions on **Russian claims to protect the Orthodox Christian subjects** of the sultan. Backed by Britain and France, the Ottomans resisted the Russian demands (May–June 1853). Russia responded by occupying **Moldavia and Wallachia** (July 1853), and the war began. The Ottomans engaged the Russians in the Principalities and Caucasus, and suffered some setbacks, including the destruction of a naval squadron anchored at **Sinop** (Nov. 1853). When Russia refused a British ultimatum to withdraw from the Principalities, **Britain and France** signed a treaty with the Ottomans pledging military aid to maintain the integrity of the empire (March 12, 1854) and declared war on Russia (March 28, 1854). The main scene of battle moved to **the Crimea,** where French and British forces along with some Ottoman troops fought bloody battles with the Russians (Sept. 1854–Sept. 1855). Diplomatic negotiations finally led to Russian acceptance of allied demands (Feb. 1856) and the subsequent meeting of a peace conference in Paris.

THE TREATY OF PARIS (March 30, 1856) (p. 470) included a number of important provisions regarding the status and possessions of the Ottoman Empire. All sides agreed to evacuate territory taken during the war. The European powers **guaranteed the independence and integrity of the empire,** and in return the sultan promised reforms and better treatment for his Christian subjects (as proclaimed in his decree of Feb. 18, 1856). **The Straits** were to remain closed to the warships of foreign powers, and the Black Sea was neutralized, open only to merchant ships. **The Principalities and Serbia** were left under Ottoman suzerainty, with their autonomy to be guaranteed by the powers.

For the Ottomans the terms of the treaty meant a welcome **containment of Russia,** but at the cost of substituting the involvement of the powers in concert in the empire's affairs. Inasmuch as the victorious coalition failed to hold together for long or to prevent the Russians from repudiating the Black Sea clauses, what was hailed as a permanent overall solution to the Eastern Question proved **temporary and precarious.**

1854. A municipality was established in Istanbul, with a mayor *(shehir emini)* and a council composed of 12 members. It was the **first major step** toward the introduction of modern municipal government in the capital and later in the provincial towns.

1855–56. Anti-Ottoman revolt in the Hijaz. The sharif of Mecca, Abd al-Muttalib, used an Ottoman order prohibiting the slave trade in the Hijaz to stir up a rebellion against Ottoman rule and to declare his independence. Hostilities broke out, and **the Ottomans suppressed the insurrection** by June 1856 and tightened their hold on the province.

1855. Introduction of the telegraph. The network spread rapidly throughout the empire; by 1914 about 5.5 million telegrams were being sent annually. The new mode of communication expedited the **diffusion of news** and helped the Ottoman **government centralize its control.**

1856, Feb. 18. THE IMPERIAL RESCRIPT (HATT-I HUMAYUN). Worked out by the ambassadors of England, France, and Austria, the sultan's allies against Russia in the Crimean War, the proclamation reiterated and expanded the promised reforms of the 1839 imperial rescript. It stressed in particular the **principle of equality of Muslims and non-Muslims**—in military service, the administration of justice, taxation, admission to state schools, public employment, and social respect. The traditional poll tax *(jizya),* which had symbolized the inferior status of non-Muslims since the early days of Islam, was rescinded. The confessional autonomy of the Jews and Christians was maintained and codified by the recognition of the millets (religious communities) as fundamental corporate entities in society. The decree called for the **constitutional reorganization of the millets,** with greater representation for the lay leaders in the management of their temporal affairs.

1856. Introduction of gas lighting in selected streets of Istanbul. The use of gas lamps spread subsequently in the capital and other cities in the region.

Completion of the **Dolmabahche Palace,** to which the imperial residence was transferred from the Topkapi Palace. The new palace along the Bosphorus was built and furnished extravagantly in a **European style.**

1857. The Refugee Law provided poor immigrant families with plots of state land along with exemptions from taxes and military service for a period of 6 to 12 years, depending on their area of settlement. The law, and the Refugee Commission established in 1860, were intended to deal with the **influx of refugees,** especially from Russian territories after the Crimean War. Between 1854 and 1876 some 300,000 **Tatars from the Crimea** moved into the empire, along with several hundred thousand **Tatars from the Nogay and Kuban,** and about 500,000 **refugees from the Caucasus.**

1857–62. Revolts in Montenegro (p. 520). Prince-Bishop Danilo, the ruler of the predominantly Christian principality, revolted in 1857 and declared his independence from the Ottomans. The Ottomans moved to suppress the revolt, and with the mediation of the European powers a **deal establishing Montenegran autonomy** was made (Nov. 8, 1858). In 1860 Montenegro resumed its agitation and supported a Slav uprising in Herzegovina. The Ottomans again acted to suppress the rebels, but the powers intervened to force a settlement restoring Montenegro's previous boundaries and autonomy (Aug. 31, 1862).

1858, April 21. THE OTTOMAN LAND LAW. The code, and its amendment in 1867, had the dual intention of **reasserting the state's legal right of ownership** in the face of widespread usurpation of its lands and **providing each cultivator with secure title** that would encourage investment. It made provisions for cultivators and others with limited rights over state *(miri)* land to acquire full private ownership confirmed by official titles. Much state land was subsequently converted into private property *(mulk)* by legal and illegal means. But because of the increasing value of agricultural land, the power relations in the countryside, and peasant suspicion of the authorities, the bulk of the land ended up in the hands of wealthy notable families that by the 20th century had accumulated large landed estates and a new source of power.

June. A massacre of Christians in Jidda, in which the British and French consuls were killed along with many others. The Ottomans used the incident to curb further the **power of the sharifs** and to strengthen their control in the Hijaz, which remained paramount until the reassertion of power by the sharifs beginning in the 1890s.

1858–61. CIVIL WAR IN LEBANON. A revolt of Maronite peasants against their Maronite feudal lords in northern Lebanon soon spread into Druze areas where it assumed a communal character, with Maronite peasants, supported by their priests, rising against Druze landlords. **The Druze retaliated violently,** and the Christians were defeated (June–July 1860). Thousands of Christians were killed or died of starvation, and up to 100,000 became refugees. The disturbances **spilled into Damascus,** where about **6,000 Christians were massacred** (July 1860). **France,** which rallied behind the Christians, **landed troops in Lebanon** (Aug. 1860).

Under pressure from the European powers, the Ottomans issued a

new administrative regulation for Lebanon (introduced on June 9, 1861, and modified on Sept. 6, 1864). Mt. Lebanon (not including Beirut, the Biqa', Tripoli, or Sidon) was to be an **autonomous province** *(mutasarrifiyya)* under international guarantee **with a Christian governor,** assisted by an elected council on which all communities were represented. This new regime, which lasted until the reestablishment of direct Ottoman rule in 1914, **brought relative peace** and prosperity to Lebanon. It began the process by which Lebanon evolved into an independent state, and foreshadowed the confessional basis of its modern politics.

1860–70. Ottoman reforms in Bosnia and Herzegovina. Muslim notables in these provinces, who controlled large landed estates and appropriated much of the taxation from the peasantry, resisted vehemently the introduction of the Tanzimat reforms. Following the suppression of a **revolt in Herzegovina** in 1860, the Ottoman authorities began to break up the political and economic power of the landed families and to introduce reforms. They **moved the capital** from Travnik, the center of the landlords' power, **to Sarajevo,** and formed a provincial advisory council composed of representatives of the various social groups. **Secular schools** were opened, **health facilities** were improved, **roads** were built, and the cities were modernized. But Christian peasant discontent in the area continued, exploding in major uprisings in 1875.

1860–62. Constitutional reorganization of the Greek Orthodox community (millet) was stipulated in a series of regulations pressed on the Greek patriarch by the Ottoman authorities. The intent was to increase lay participation in the running of the community's affairs at the expense of the powerful clergy, but in the absence of substantial internal pressure for reform, **communal bodies with only limited lay input** were created, and the patriarch and religious hierarchy in Istanbul succeeded in maintaining their control of the finances and decisions.

1860–1914. Syrian-Lebanese emigration to the Americas. Some 300,000 to 350,000 people, the majority of them **Lebanese Christians,** left Syria by 1914, two-thirds traveling **to the United States** and most of the rest to Brazil and other parts of **Latin America.** Their emigration came in response to population pressure in the mountain areas, social and religious unrest, fear of military service, and a new attraction to the West fostered by the foreign schools. The **remittances** they sent home, and the **skills and capital** brought back by those who returned, contributed significantly to the **economic development of Lebanon.**

Development of the Arab press. Printing in Arabic, which had scarcely existed before the 19th century, spread steadily as presses were established in the major cities, with **Cairo and Beirut** serving as the principal centers of publishing. They issued hundreds of original and translated works directed at a public made more accustomed to reading and more curious about a variety of topics by exposure to **modern schools. Newspapers and periodicals** came into being for the first time, and were more important still in spreading knowledge, discussing current affairs, and opening windows to Western culture. Between 1870 and 1900 some 40 periodical publications and 15 newspapers were founded in Beirut alone. There emerged **a new class of writers and thinkers** such as **Butrus al-Bustani** (1819–83), who produced the first modern encyclopedia in Arabic, and **Jurji Zaydan** (1861–1914), the prolific novelist and journalist. This literary activity created an Arabic vocabulary capable of expressing new concepts and fostered a **pride in the Arab heritage,** which carried over into nationalist ideas.

1861–76. SULTAN ABDULAZIZ. Like his brother Abdulmejid, Abdulaziz was committed to the vigorous pursuit of westernizing reforms in the empire.

1861, Dec. 2. Ottoman official recognition of the **union of Moldavia and Wallachia** (p. 523) developed steadily between 1857 and 1859 with the support of the European powers.

1863. Opening of **the Beirut-Damascus road,** the first major road in the Middle East fit for wheeled traffic. The carriage service reduced the 112-kilometer journey from three days to 13 hours. The road had a considerable effect on the economy of the Syrian interior as well as on the **establishment of Beirut as the main harbor** on the eastern seaboard of the Mediterranean. A similar road between Jerusalem and Jaffa was opened in 1869, but **wheeled traffic** in the region as a whole **remained limited before 1914.**

Robert College was founded by American Protestants in Bebek, Istanbul. The school (which became Boğaziçi University in 1971) has ranked among the leading foreign educational institutions in the region.

Adoption of the **Ottoman Maritime Commerce Code,** which modernized the rules of international trade in conformity with Western practices.

Establishment of the **Ottoman Imperial Bank,** a Franco-British institution that served as the Ottoman state bank.

March 29. Constitution of the Armenian community (millet) was issued. It provided for an assembly of 140 members, most of them laymen, and the election by the assembly of two councils, a religious one to handle spiritual matters and a civil one to deal with taxes, education, and welfare. Alongside these central bodies based in Istanbul were corresponding councils in the provinces. The constitution **strengthened lay participation,** which promoted **communal modernization** and later the pursuit of nationalist goals.

1864. The Provincial Reform Law restructured the system of provincial government. A total of 27 provinces *(vilayets)* were created by the **remodeling of the older provincial units.** They were subdivided hierarchically into districts *(sanjaks* or *livas), kazas,* and *nahiyes,* with the village and urban quarter forming the basic administrative units. The governor and other senior officials were appointed from Istanbul and were to be advised by **councils composed of elected and appointed members** who represented local interest groups. The law, which remained the basis of provincial administration until the end of the empire, **increased the powers of the governors,** provided for central control exercised from Istanbul, and **incorporated local opinion.**

The Alliance Israélite Universelle (founded in Paris in 1860) opened in Damascus and Baghdad its **first schools** in the Ottoman Empire. They were designed to provide Jewish children with a **modern curriculum** of religious and secular studies. Similar schools continued to appear in North Africa and the Middle East, reaching 100 institutions with about 26,000 students by 1900. This Alliance educational network **created cadres of Western-educated Jews** in the region.

The first Hebrew-language newspaper in the empire, *Ha-Lebanon,* began publication in Jerusalem. It was joined by several Hebrew newspapers and periodicals in the following decades.

1865. Constitutional reorganization of the Jewish community (millet). The Organic Statute, drawn up by a committee of reform-minded Jews in Istanbul and approved by the sultan, provided for **limits on rabbinical power,** giving lay leaders, usually more receptive to new ideas, a greater role in running the civil affairs of the community. The **chief rabbi** *(hahambashi)* in Istanbul remained the official head of the empire's Jews, but he was now to accept the advice of **lay and religious councils** selected by an assembly of 80 members, 60 of whom were laymen. Similar arrangements were applied in the provincial towns. **Members of the wealthy lay elite** came to dominate the communal committees and to use their influence to **promote modern education and cultural contacts with the West.**

FORMATION OF THE YOUNG OTTOMANS, a society of liberal intellectuals and activists **opposed to the direction of the Tanzimat reforms.** The approaches of the members to the empire's problems varied widely, but they **agreed on three basic needs: a constitution** that would limit the powers of government and protect the citizens; a representative, **popularly elected parliament;** and the cultivation of **a single Ottoman nationality** with all the subjects having the same rights and obligations regardless of differences of religion or ethnic background. The leading figures of the Young Ottomans included **Namik Kemal** (1840–88), **Ibrahim Shinasi** (1826–71), **Ziya Pasha** (1825–80), and **Ali Suavi** (1838–78). Suppressed by the Ottoman authorities, some members of the group spent several years in exile in Europe, returning home to agitate for the 1876 constitution.

Foundation of the **Palestine Exploration Fund,** which carried out important archaeological surveys, including the investigation of the walls of Jerusalem. It sponsored the first stratified excavation of a *tall* (mound) at Tall al-Hesy (1890).

Sept. 18. A great fire in Istanbul, the most destructive of the century, burned vast areas to the ground. Between 1853 and 1906 the city suffered 229 fires, which resulted in the application of European concepts of urban design to the rebuilt neighborhoods.

1866. The Syrian Protestant College (later to become the American University of Beirut) was established by American missionaries.

1866–1914. The development of railways. The opening in 1866 of two railway lines in Anatolia (Izmir-Aydin and Izmir-Kasaba) introduced the first railways to the region (excluding Egypt, where a railway was started in 1851). By 1914 **over 5,000 kilometers** of railways had been built in Anatolia, Syria, Palestine, and Iraq, **funded largely by European capital** (two-thirds of foreign capital investments in the empire actually went into railway projects). The **Hijaz Railway,** promoted by Sultan Abdulhamid to carry pilgrims to the holy cities and facilitate his control over Arabia, was financed partly by contributions from Muslims. It was started in 1901 in Damascus, and reached Medina (1,320 kilometers away) in 1908.

The overall Middle Eastern network had grave flaws, including a **multiplicity of gauges and wasteful duplication,** but it reduced the costs of transport, cut traveling times sharply, and increased comfort and safety. In 1914, as much as 50 percent of the internal goods traffic of Syria and Anatolia was carried by rail rather than by animals and carriages.

1866–69. The revolt in Crete and its settlement. Some four decades of agitation by the Christian population in Crete against Muslim rule and in favor of union with Greece culminated in a great revolt beginning in May 1866. **Greece,** which sought persistently to annex the island, **coordinated the uprising** and supplied the rebels. Ottoman troops backed by reinforcements from Egypt **suppressed the revolt.** In consultation with Muslim and Christian leaders on the island, the Ottomans drew up **a new organic regulation** (Jan. 10, 1868), which established elected councils at various levels with **equal representation for Muslims and Christians** and reduced taxes; it exempted the Christians from military service as well as the conscription tax. Greece was pressured by the European powers to accept the settlement.

1867. Foundation of the Ottoman Theater, the **first Turkish-language theater,** by an Armenian repertory company directed by Agop Vartovyan, known as Gullu Agop (1840–1902). It performed European as well as new Turkish plays.

April. Consolidation of Serbian autonomy. The Ottomans agreed to withdraw their remaining troops and residents from Serbia, and their authority was confined to the annual tribute and an Ottoman flag flown jointly with that of Serbia over the Belgrade citadel. For all practical purposes Serbia was independent, a status formally recognized in 1878.

June–July. Abdulaziz attended the World Exhibition in Paris and then visited the British royal family in London. He was the **first sultan to travel to the West.**

1868. The **Imperial Museum** was established in Istanbul. It assembled a large collection of artifacts and led the **development of archaeological studies** in the empire.

Sept. Opening of the **Ottoman Imperial Lycée of Galatasaray** in Istanbul, the most famous of the state secondary schools established to provide a modern education. French was the main language of instruction, most of the teachers were foreign, and the student body included members of all religious communities. **Graduates** of the school **played a prominent role in the government** of the empire and, after it, of the Turkish Republic.

1869. Military reorganization was designed to apply the Prussian model of a small peacetime and large wartime force. It systematized three categories of military service: **active service** *(nizamiye)* of four years, **reserve duty** *(redif)* of six years, and service in the **local defense forces** *(mustahfiz)* of eight years. **Financial problems** stood in the way of achieving the target of a wartime army of 700,000, while domestic security tasks continued to require a relatively large standing army.

The **Regulation for Public Education** created the framework for a **modern system of state education** in the empire. It systematized the hierarchy of elementary and secondary schools developed in the previous three decades, laying out their terms of study, curricula, graduating examinations, and modes of funding. The law called for **free compulsory education** for all children until the age of 12. In the succeeding years the number of public schools and students **expanded at a limited pace,** due in part to lack of budgetary resources. **Numerous private schools** established by the religious minorities and foreign missionaries thrived in many parts of the empire.

1870–76. PROMULGATION OF THE OTTOMAN CIVIL CODE (MEJELLE). This was the chief legal achievement of the Tanzimat period, creating a code that endured until the end of the empire and carried over into many of the successor states. Formulated under the direction of the able official Jevdet Pasha, its 1,851 articles were **anchored in the provisions of Islamic law** instead of replacing them with a completely secular code, as some reformers wanted. The Mejelle was to be applied by the new, secular *nizamiye* courts, whereas family law, which it did not cover, continued to be applied by the traditional *shari'a* courts.

1870–1914. Development of **American and French missionary schools.** American Protestant missions set up schools in the empire beginning around 1830, but most actively after 1870. By 1914 there were 23,500 students enrolled in 430 American schools. The French established a considerably larger network of schools, attended by close to 90,000 students in 1914. The foreign schools **catered largely to local Christians.**

1870, March 13. Treaty of London, in which the European powers and the Ottoman Empire essentially accepted the Russian unilateral repudiation (on Oct. 31, 1870) of the neutralization of the Black Sea, established in the Treaty of Paris of 1856. **Russia was allowed to build a fleet on the Black Sea** once again, and in return the Ottomans were permitted to open the Straits in peacetime to warships sent by their friends, if needed to ensure enforcement of the 1856 treaty. With this strategic victory Russia was soon able to pose a **formidable threat to Ottoman interests.**

Sept. 13. Death of **Ibrahim Shinasi** (b. 1826), one of the leading journalists and intellectuals of the Tanzimat period. He was among the pioneers of modern Ottoman literature, and as a member of the Young Ottomans, he served as a prominent voice against the authoritarian direction of government reforms.

1875. The **Université St. Joseph** was founded in Beirut by French Jesuits. A French faculty of medicine was attached to it in 1883.

Completion of the **modern port of Izmir,** built with British and French capital.

July–1876, May. Uprisings in the Balkans. In July 1876 Christian peasants in Herzegovina and then in Bosnia began a **revolt against tax demands,** and more broadly **against their Muslim landlords and Ottoman rule.** The massacres of Muslims, the Muslim retaliations in kind, the influx of arms and volunteers to the rebels from Serbia, Montenegro, and Hungary, and the intervention of the European powers **initiated a complicated international crisis** that lasted for three years and profoundly altered the fortunes of the Ottoman Empire. **Russia and Austria** demanded that the Ottomans abolish tax farming in Bosnia and Herzegovina, reduce the tax burden, provide religious freedom, help peasants purchase land, and establish Muslim-Christian councils to supervise the execution of the reforms, with oversight by the European powers (Dec. 30, 1875). The sultan and other European powers accepted the program, but the rebels did not. **The Ottomans proceeded to suppress the revolt,** setting in motion the flight of thousands of Christian refugees. The European powers renewed their **demands for reforms,** threatening the use of force and occupation of Ottoman territory (May 13, 1876). An **anti-Ottoman revolt in Bulgaria** (April–May 1876), suppressed by the sultan using irregular forces that committed **massacres of Christians,** intensified the crisis (p. 521).

1875–1914. THE OTTOMAN BANKRUPTCY AND PUBLIC DEBT. In 1854 the Ottoman government signed its first foreign loan agreement. It was followed over the next two decades by a succession of **loans taken at increasingly adverse terms from European banks** (primarily French). In Oct. 1875, when the total external debt amassed had reached some 242 million Turkish pounds, with over half the budgetary expenditures going toward its service, the Ottoman government declared its inability to meet its financial obligations. The fall in tax revenues due to **bad harvests and increased expenditure** made worse by the costs of suppressing the uprisings in the Balkans hastened the slide into bankruptcy.

After prolonged negotiations with the European powers, an agreement was reached (published in the Decree of Muharrem in Nov. 1881). It set up the **Public Debt Administration,** consisting of Ottoman and European representatives, to which certain revenues were assigned. This arrangement subjected the Ottomans to **foreign financial control** from which they failed to free themselves, in part because of **continued borrowing.** In 1914 the Ottoman debt in circulation stood at 139.1 million Turkish pounds, and the government was as dependent as ever on the services of European financiers.

1876, May 30. Deposition of Abdulaziz, who was replaced by his nephew Murad. The action, engineered by the war minister Huseyin Avni Pasha, came in the wake of **public protests** against government inaction in the face of the massacres of Muslim peasants in Bosnia and Bulgaria, as well as foreign pressures.

May 30–Aug. 31. SULTAN MURAD V. Although intelligent and open to liberal ideas, the new sultan suffered from a debilitating nervousness that rendered him unequal to the task of leading an empire faced with serious external threats and domestic hardships. The war that broke out during his reign, the **mobilization of the army,** and the **flood of Muslim refugees** from the Balkans put additional strains on the bankrupt treasury. The cabinet arranged **Murad's deposition** on the grounds of mental incapacity and placed his brother Abdulhamid on the throne.

June–1877, March. War with Serbia (p. 520). Serbia declared war on the Ottomans (June 30, 1876), followed by Montenegro (July 2). The two hoped for Russian support and the eventual acquisition of Bosnia and Herzegovina. The Ottomans **inflicted a severe defeat on the Serbs,** but were forced to halt their successful invasion of Serbia by a Russian threat of intervention (Oct. 31, 1876). **Serbia agreed to peace** with the Ottomans, providing for a return to its prewar status (signed on March 1, 1877).

2. AUTOCRACY, REVOLUTION, AND DISMEMBERMENT

1876–1909. SULTAN ABDULHAMID II. Although the new sultan came to the throne promising to support constitutional government, the external and domestic crises early in his reign convinced him that only strong, centralized government could rescue the empire from collapse. In the space of a few years he put in place a **system of autocratic rule** with an almost unprecedented concentration of powers in his own hands. The grand vezirs, whose executive power had grown considerably in the previous half-century, were now reduced to instruments of the sultan's will. State policies were made in the Yildiz Palace by the sultan and a coterie of close associates, and carried out by an **ever-growing bureaucracy** backed by an **elaborate system of internal security,** surveillance, and censorship.

Another feature that distinguished the Hamidian regime from its 19th-century predecessors was its **strong emphasis on Islam. PAN-ISLAMISM,** as this policy is often called, served to rally citizens behind the sultan by presenting him as the chief protector of Muslims against threats by the infidels. **The sultan assumed the title of caliph** (spiritual leader of Muslims everywhere), using this new conception of the caliphate as a powerful diplomatic weapon against European powers that ruled over large Muslim populations, in particular, Russia, France, and Britain. The sultan himself led a life of religious observance and sober frugality, made money available for mosques and religious education, and patronized a circle of religious dignitaries in the court.

Abdulhamid left a **highly unfavorable reputation,** one of a brutal, paranoid despot who violated individual liberties and perpetrated massacres against the Armenians. More recent historical opinion has pointed to other sides of his legacy, including his **accomplishment of many reforms** and improvements during a difficult period when the empire was being rapidly dismembered by separatist movements from within and imperialist powers from without.

1876, Dec. 23. PROCLAMATION OF THE OTTOMAN CONSTITUTION. This document was drafted by a commission appointed by the sultan and chaired by the constitutionalist statesman **Midhat Pasha** (Oct. 7, 1876). In the course of its preparation Midhat was obliged to accept amendments by Abdulhamid that strengthened the sultan's powers, including the removal of clauses regarding ministerial responsibility. But despite considerable bargaining, all parties were eager for an agreement so that the constitution would be ready when the international conference on the Balkans met in Istanbul. The constitution **provided for a bicameral Parliament and protections of various individual rights.** The Parliament voted on laws and on the budget, but the sultan preserved most of his traditional powers: he was responsible to no one for his actions, and it was he who appointed and dismissed ministers, convoked and dismissed Parliament, commanded the army, and signed treaties.

The constitution **functioned for a short period only.** Abdulhamid

soon dismissed its chief architect, Midhat Pasha (Feb. 5, 1877) and **dissolved the Parliament** (Feb. 14, 1878). He ruled with the constitution suspended until forced to restore it by the Young Turk Revolution (July 1908).

Dec. 23–1877, Jan. 20. The Istanbul international conference on the Balkan crisis (p. 472). The European powers came up with proposals involving loss of territories by the Ottomans, reforms in the sultan's administration of his Balkan provinces, and international supervision of Ottoman performance. The Ottomans rejected the various demands, arguing repeatedly that their new constitution (whose declaration was timed to coincide with the opening of the conference) made talk of reforms unnecessary and the acceptance of restrictions on Ottoman sovereignty and territorial integrity unconstitutional.

1877, March 19. Opening of the Ottoman Parliament in Istanbul. It met until June 19, reconvened on Dec. 13, and was dissolved by the sultan on Feb. 14, 1878. During its brief existence the assembly handled some legislation and budgetary matters, but the deputies were **preoccupied mostly with the disastrous war with Russia** and used the new forum for attacking the government's handling of the war.

April–1878, March. War with Russia. Failing to win support for a concerted European action following the unsuccessful conference in Istanbul, Russia declared war on the Ottomans (April 24, 1877) (p. 510). The Russians quickly overran some of the Ottoman defenses in Europe and eastern Anatolia (May–June 1877), but their hopes for a speedy advance on Istanbul and the Straits were frustrated by Ottoman resistance in Anatolia and Bulgaria. In the fall the **Ottoman defenses finally collapsed,** the Russians taking Sofia, Adrianople, and Kars. With Russian troops pressing ahead toward Istanbul, **the sultan asked for an armistice** (concluded, Jan. 31, 1878).

The **Treaty of San Stefano** (March 3, 1878) (p. 472) imposed harsh terms on the Ottomans. **Serbia, Montenegro, and Romania** were to become fully independent, with some additions of territory; a large autonomous **Bulgaria** stretching from the Black Sea to the Aegean was to be created; the government of **Bosnia and Herzegovina** was to be reformed; **Russia** was to gain substantial territories, including Kars, Ardahan, Bayezid, and Batum in eastern Anatolia and Bessarabia in Europe; **reforms** would be introduced in the areas of Anatolia inhabited by the Armenians; and the Ottomans were to pay **a huge indemnity. European pressure forced a revision of these terms** in the Treaty of Berlin (p. 472).

1878, June 4. Transfer of Cyprus to Britain. The Ottomans allowed the British to occupy and administer the island in the name of the sultan in return for a pledge to defend the Ottomans against Russia, and specifically to help revise the Treaty of San Stefano. Formally, the island **remained under Ottoman suzerainty** until Nov. 5, 1914, when it was unilaterally **annexed by Britain.**

July 13. THE TREATY OF BERLIN (p. 472). The European powers, particularly Britain and Austria, opposed certain terms of the Treaty of San Stefano (most notably the creation of a large Bulgaria) and forced Russia to have the entire settlement reexamined in an international congress held in Berlin. In the new treaty, the **independence of Serbia, Montenegro, and Romania** was reaffirmed, but **Bulgaria was carved up** into three parts: an autonomous principality of Bulgaria under Ottoman suzerainty north of the Balkan mountains, a semi-autonomous province of Eastern Rumelia south of the mountains, and Macedonia in the south under direct Ottoman rule. **Bosnia and Herzegovina,** though nominally under Ottoman rule, were placed **under Austrian occupation.** Russia retained Kars, Ardahan, and Batum, but returned Bayezid to the Ottomans. The Ottomans promised to introduce **reforms in areas settled by the Armenians.** The war indemnity to Russia was reduced.

The Ottoman Empire emerged from this settlement, and from the protracted crisis of 1875–78 in general, a much weakened and diminished state. Its **territorial losses** in the Balkans, Anatolia, and Cyprus amounted to some 210,000 square kilometers inhabited by about 5.5 million people (around one-fifth of the empire's population). Its **revenue base shrank** accordingly, compounding the financial hardships caused by the bankruptcy, the costs of the wars, and the influx of Muslim refugees from the lost territories. **The structure of its dominion in Europe was shattered** irreversibly as the old system of autonomous provinces and tributary states gave way to wholly independent countries and a number of autonomous regions now bent on total separation from the empire. The **foreign intervention in the empire's affairs** in the name of protecting minorities and monitoring reforms **reduced Ottoman stature.**

1878. The Commission for Refugees was established to deal with the **influx of Muslim immigrants.** An estimated 1.5 million **Muslims from the Balkans** settled in Anatolia after 1876. Some 500,000 **Circassians from the Caucasus** also entered the empire between 1881 and 1914, and the crisis in **Crete** in 1897 sent thousands of Muslims fleeing to western Anatolia. The various immigrant groups contributed to the economic development of Anatolia while adding ethnic and linguistic diversity that slowed down their assimilation.

1880. Organization of the **Ottoman Ministry of Police,** a central part of Abdulhamid's apparatus of control. The ministry, which was headed by trusted confidants of the sultan, handled not only crime but also the **supervision of society** (including the monitoring of the press, theater, and travel). A separate **secret police organization** operated from the palace under the direct control of Abdulhamid. Its army of spies and informants reported on the activities of officials and citizens, many of whom suffered punishment. A **system of censorship** sought to control information and news. Criticism of the sultan was forbidden as well as the use of suggestive words, such as *liberty, constitution,* and *assassination.* The enforcement of the censorship was often more heavy-handed than efficient.

1881–93. The first comprehensive Ottoman population census included a **count of women.** It arrived at a total of 17.4 million inhabitants (allowing for gaps, the actual figure was probably about 20 million).

1881, April–May. The **French occupation of Tunisia.** The Ottoman government issued protests to the European powers over the violation of Ottoman integrity.

July. Thessaly and parts of Epirus were ceded by the Ottoman Empire to Greece.

1882, Sept. The British occupation of Egypt. Until Dec. 18, 1914, when Britain declared Egypt a protectorate, the legal fiction of **Ottoman suzerainty over Egypt** was maintained. Britain accepted the established practice of the Ottoman investiture of a new khedive, which included the formal issuance at the time of succession of an Ottoman decree that described his autonomous powers and his obligations to the sultan.

1882–1914. JEWISH IMMIGRATION TO PALESTINE. Jewish immigrants from eastern Europe, many of them fleeing persecution in Russia, began to arrive in Palestine in 1882. The **first wave of immigration** (known as the **First Aliyah, 1882–1904**) saw the arrival of some 30,000 settlers and the establishment of 23 new Jewish agricultural settlements. The **Second Aliyah (1904–14)** brought in about 33,000 settlers imbued with Theodor Herzl's political vision of Jewish statehood. It included **David Ben Gurion** and other leaders who became the **founding fathers of Israel.**

With this Zionist effort to encourage immigration, the **Yishuv** (the Hebrew term for the Jewish community of Palestine) **rose dramatically** from 24,000 in 1882 to about 75,000 in 1914, increasing its share of the total from 5 to 10 percent. Starting in 1882 the Ottoman government issued **orders prohibiting Jewish settlement** in Palestine, and after 1892 added restrictions on their purchase of landed property there, but in practice local officials did little to enforce them.

The Jewish settlers directed much of their early colonizing effort toward agriculture, where their socialist ideology **gave birth to the kibbutz,** an innovative communal settlement in which members pooled their energies in the service of the group. In 1909 the settlers **founded the city of Tel Aviv,** the first all-Jewish town in the world. Perhaps their most profound achievement was the **revival of Hebrew as a spoken language,** largely through the untiring efforts of **Eliezer Ben Yehuda** (1858–1922), who campaigned for its exclusive use as the language of Jewish national rebirth. He compiled a comprehensive historical Hebrew dictionary and coined many new words to bring the language up to date. The **schools of the early colonies used spoken Hebrew,** helping its rapid development as the common tongue of the diverse Jewish population of Palestine.

1885, Sept. Bulgarian annexation of Eastern Rumelia (p. 521), following a pro-union revolt by Rumelian leaders. The sultan acquiesced in this overthrow of a central provision of the 1878 Berlin settlement.

1888. Completion of the **Vienna-Istanbul railway line,** which served the Orient Express. The concession for the line was awarded in 1868.

1889. **Insurrection in Crete** led the Ottomans to strengthen their direct rule and suspend previous arrangements for representative institutions (including the **Halepa Pact** of Oct. 1878, which provided for an assembly with a Christian majority).

1889–1907. DEVELOPMENT OF THE YOUNG TURK MOVEMENT. The movement was composed of Ottoman officers, bureaucrats, and intellectuals who **opposed the regime of Sultan Abdulhamid** and were guided by two main aims: the preservation of the empire and the restoration of the 1876 constitution. In July 1908 they succeeded in overthrowing the regime and ruled the empire until the end of World War I. The birth of the opposition movement is dated back to 1889, when students of the military medical school in Istanbul **formed a secret society** to fight the government. Similar secret societies sprang up in other colleges and among junior officers in the army, despite crackdowns by the authorities. At the same time, **opponents of the regime in exile** in European capitals and in Cairo published their ideas and smuggled their works into the empire. In 1899 they were joined by a relative of the sultan, **Prince Sabaheddin,** who from his headquarters in Paris **advocated decentralization** as the key to the empire's salvation. His approach was opposed by another strand in the movement, represented by **Ahmed Riza,** which favored a policy of **centralization** as the only way to prevent the dismembering of the empire.

Much remains obscure about the various groups, their activities, and their links with one another. The best-known group of conspirators within the empire was the **Ottoman Freedom Society** founded in Salonica in the summer of 1906 by army officers and civilian officials. Branches of it spread rapidly in Macedonia, and in Sept. 1907 the group united with Ahmed Riza's group in Europe under the name of **Committee of Union and Progress.** The committee was the leading faction in the Young Turk Revolution.

1890–95. Construction of the **modern port of Beirut** by a French concessionary company.

1894–96. OTTOMAN-ARMENIAN TROUBLES. The empire's Armenian population (concentrated most heavily in eastern Anatolia) experienced a cultural revival and a **growth of Armenian political consciousness** during the 19th century. Along with the development of modern schools and contacts with Europe, there was an emergence of revolutionary groups seeking to stir Armenian agitation against Ottoman rule. From around 1890 **disturbances and acts of terror increased** in eastern Anatolia, and the government employed the **Hamidiye irregular troops** of Kurdish tribesmen stationed in the area to maintain the peace. In the summer of 1894 things reached a head with an **Armenian uprising** in the **area of Sasun.** It was put down brutally by the Hamidiye troops, and the **massacres** led to a great outcry in Europe. On Sept. 30, 1895, a **demonstration of Armenians in Istanbul** provoked attacks by Muslims, and a **massacre** of Armenians in the capital and other towns ensued. Agitation by Armenian revolutionaries continued, especially in the region of Zeytun, culminating in the **seizure of the Ottoman Bank in Istanbul** by armed Armenians of the Dashnak Party (Aug. 26, 1896). This set in motion **large-scale massacres** of Armenians in Istanbul.

The failure of the Armenian activists to bring the European powers to intervene on their behalf, and the high costs of the disturbances, led them to reconsider their strategy. Although some years of relative calm followed, the events of 1894–96 left a **legacy of hostility between Armenians and Muslims** (especially Kurds) in Anatolia and **encouraged close to 100,000 Armenians to emigrate** to the Caucasus and America.

1895, May 25. Death of **Ahmed Jevdet** (b. 1822), one of the leading reforming officials in the Ottoman central government. He served in many ministerial posts, directed the drafting of the Ottoman Civil Code (the Mejelle), and wrote a multivolume Ottoman history.

1896–97. Revolt in Crete and war with Greece (pp. 475, 516). An insurrection in Crete led to large-scale **violence between Muslims and Christians,** a proclamation by the rebels of union with Greece, and the invasion of the island by a Greek force (Feb. 1897). **Greece went to war** against the Ottomans (April 1897) but was **soundly defeated** and had to ask for European intervention to rescue it from Ottoman advances into its territory. The final settlement established **autonomy for Crete under European control,** with only symbolic Ottoman presence. The crisis set in motion the flight of **thousands of Muslim refugees** from Crete and Greece to western Anatolia. **Greece finally annexed Crete** during the First Balkan War in 1912–13.

1897. Death in Istanbul of **JAMAL AL-DIN AL-AFGHANI** (b. 1839), the most famous **Pan-Islamic activist** of the 19th century. Afghani was an **Iranian Shi'ite** who passed himself off as an Afghan to ensure favorable reception among Sunni Muslims. In a turbulent career that took him to Egypt, India, Afghanistan, Iran, and finally to Istanbul, he worked to **awaken Muslims to the threat of European domination,** preaching the importance of Muslim solidarity, opposition to Muslim rulers who abetted European penetration, and the **need to restore the glory of Islam** by reforming it. His inspiring lectures and political agitation stirred people throughout the region and had a profound influence on the **development of modern Islamic thought.**

1898, Oct. Visit of Kaiser William II to Istanbul and Palestine. The trip strengthened the fast-developing ties between the Ottoman Empire and Germany. The Germans became the **chief providers of weapons and training** to the Ottoman army, and by 1914 accounted for 23.2 percent of **foreign capital investments** in the empire, including a major stake in the ambitious Baghdad Railway project.

1899–1914. The Baghdad Railway. As part of a policy of developing railway communications within the empire for military and economic reasons, the Ottoman government promoted the construction of a **railroad connecting Istanbul to Baghdad** and the Persian Gulf. In Nov. 1899 the sultan granted the Deutsche Bank and the German-Anatolian Railway Company a preliminary concession for the extension of the Anatolian railway to Baghdad. A definitive concession was granted on March 5, 1903. The project became the object of **rivalry among German, French, and British companies,** and met with the hostility of Britain, France, and Russia, which feared for their own interests in the region. The diplomatic hurdles as well as technical and financial **difficulties hampered the construction** of the line itself. By 1914 it still had large gaps, which were finished only in 1940.

1900, Aug. 12. The Ottoman Imperial University, the first state university in the empire, was reopened in Istanbul (having been open previously in 1870–71 and 1874–81). It was reorganized as the **University of Istanbul** in 1933.

1901, May 17. Theodor Herzl, leader of the Zionist movement, met with the sultan in Istanbul and presented a proposal for the establishment of a Jewish autonomous region in Palestine (p. 491). Abdulhamid opposed the idea.

1902–3. Insurrection in Macedonia, accompanied by much violence and terrorism by groups representing Macedonian as well as Greek, Serbian, and Bulgarian nationalists. After abortive attempts to find a settlement, Russia and Austria issued a program of reform (Oct. 1903) approved by all the Berlin Treaty signatories. It provided for **Russian and Austrian inspectors** in addition to the Ottoman inspector general, and the introduction of various **reforms** to be supervised by foreign consuls. Political violence in Macedonia continued despite the reforms.

1903. Death of **Abd al-Rahman al-Kawakibi** (b. 1849), a member of a notable family of Aleppo who fell out with Abdulhamid's regime and from exile in Cairo (where he died) wrote two books that **called on the Arabs to take over the caliphate** from the corrupted Turks. His writings were a milestone in the emergence of a distinctly **Arab nationalist ideology.**

1905–6. The second general **Ottoman population census** (a total of 20.8 million inhabitants counted).

1906, Oct. 1. Agreement over the **Ottoman-Egyptian border in Sinai.** The Ottomans made a unilateral attempt to redraw Egypt's eastern boundary by reassigning most of the Sinai to their direct rule. They and the British sent forces to occupy Taba and other points on the Gulf of Aqaba in a struggle to assert their territorial claims (known as the **Taba incident**). The agreement fixed the boundary on an almost straight line from al-Rafah on the Mediterranean to Taba at the head of the Gulf of Aqaba. This line later became the boundary between Egypt and the Palestine Mandate.

1908, July. THE YOUNG TURK REVOLUTION. On July 3 an army officer in the Third Army in Macedonia, **Ahmed Niyazi Bey,** took to the hills with a group of supporters, issuing a **call to rebellion** and the restoration of the 1876 constitution. Acts of insubordination soon

spread throughout Macedonia, and the **Committee of Union and Progress skillfully assumed the leadership role** in this uncoordinated movement of resistance. Agents of the sultan sent to investigate the unrest were assassinated, and troops dispatched from Anatolia to suppress the rebels joined them instead. On July 23 Abdulhamid gave way and proclaimed the **restoration of the constitution.**

This initial success of the Young Turks, which excited celebrations in many parts of the empire, opened the way for a series of profound changes. **The sultan lost much of his power,** the secret police and censorship were dismantled, **parliamentary elections** were set in motion, and the Young Turks, in particular the Committee of Union and Progress, took hold of the reins of power.

Oct. 5. Bulgaria proclaimed its independence (p. 522), renouncing the sultan's suzerainty and stopping the payment of tribute. On the following day, **Austria annexed Bosnia and Herzegovina,** which it had occupied since 1878. After their calls to have the terms of the Treaty of Berlin enforced met with no response from the signatories, the Ottomans reached agreements with Austria (Feb. 26, 1909) and Bulgaria (April 19, 1909), recognizing the **end of Ottoman suzerainty** while providing for the **protection of the Muslim communities** and their religious life.

Dec. 17. Opening of the Ottoman Parliament, after elections in which candidates of the Committee of Union and Progress won a large majority of the seats. Their chief opponents were the **Liberal Party of Prince Sabaheddin,** which promoted decentralization of the empire.

1908–14. Promotion of women's rights. The Young Turk Revolution gave a boost to the movement to improve the status of women. Some Young Turks advocated the emancipation of women as a key to progress in the empire. Various **women's groups** emerged, among them the Association for the Advancement of Women founded in 1908 by **Halide Edip Adivar,** who sought improved education for women. A more radical group, the Society for the Defense of Women's Rights (founded 1912), demanded the economic emancipation of women and their access to employment in the public sector. There were also several **journals devoted to feminist concerns.**

The movement and its **achievements remained modest,** limited largely to the elite. Conservative religious authorities upheld the **prohibitions against the mixing of the sexes** in public, and during the Balkan Wars (1912–13) some even argued that the emancipation of women had contributed to Ottoman defeats.

Development of Turkish nationalism. From the late 19th century, a Turkish cultural consciousness began to take shape as writers promoted an interest in the **history** of the Turkish peoples, in the cultivation of **Turkish literature,** and in the reform of the **Turkish language.** These pursuits and the promotion of the idea of a Turkish nation became more pronounced after the 1908 revolution. Literary clubs such as the **Turkish Homeland Society** and the **Turkish Hearth** emerged, and the most prominent ideologue of Turkish nationalism, **Ziya Gökalp** (1876–1924), celebrated the folk culture of the Turkish people and the notion of **pan-Turkism.** However, the political ideas of Turkish nationalism had **little popular appeal** until the dissolution of the empire, when a predominantly Turkish population was all that was left of what had been a multiethnic mix of peoples.

1908, April. Uprising and political crisis in Istanbul. Soldiers in the capital mutinied on April 13, and with the support of religious students and sympathizers of the **Society of Muhammadan Union** (a conservative Muslim group that condemned the secularist policies of the new leaders) **took control of the city,** attacked known supporters of the Committee of Union and Progress, called for strict observance of Islamic law, and forced the resignation of the grand vezir. Alongside some acts of violence in the capital, the insurrection **provoked the massacre of thousands of Armenians in Adana** (in several days of attacks by Muslims, beginning on April 14). A large army from Macedonia established control of Istanbul (April 24), and the **rebels were put on trial.** On April 27 the Parliament proclaimed the **deposition of Sultan Abdulhamid** on the grounds of his complicity in the insurrection and installed his brother Mehmed on the throne.

1909–18. SULTAN MEHMED V RESIIAD. Unlike his forceful predecessor, Mehmed was essentially a figurehead who posed no threat to the rule of the Young Turks.

1910–12. Albanian revolt and independence (p. 524). A revolt broke out in Kosovo in 1910 in protest against Young Turk plans to impose new taxes, population censuses, Turkish schools, and the Turkish language on the Albanian population. **Harsh repression** measures by the authorities only inflamed nationalist sentiments among both Muslims and Christians and reinforced the drive for Albanian autonomy. The Ottoman government finally conceded to the demands of the Albanian nationalists, granting them **broad autonomy** (Sept. 4, 1912). The Albanian National Assembly proclaimed **Albania's complete independence** on Nov. 28, 1912, at a time when the Balkan War threatened to carve up Albania among the Balkan states.

1911–12. War with Italy (pp. 478–79). Seeking to fulfill three decades of designs on Libya, **Italy declared war** on the Ottomans on Sept. 29, 1911. Its forces **occupied Tripoli** and other port towns, and also **captured the Dodecanese Islands.** The Ottomans were obliged to cede their rights in Tripoli and Cyrenaica to Italy by the **Treaty of Ouchy** (Oct. 15, 1912). Italy recognized Ottoman sovereignty over the Dodecanese Islands, but continued to occupy and administer them.

1912–13. THE BALKAN WARS (pp. 478–79). In Oct. 1912 a coalition of Bulgaria, Serbia, Greece, and Montenegro launched a war against the Ottoman Empire, aimed at partitioning its European territories. The **Ottomans suffered disastrous defeats,** and in the **Treaty of London** (May 30, 1913) had to **give up all of their European lands** with the exception of a narrow strip around Istanbul. Disputes among the Balkan allies over the spoils soon led to the **Second Balkan War** (June–July 1913), and the Ottomans took advantage of Bulgaria's defeat to recover from it Adrianople and most of eastern Thrace.

The Ottoman holdings in Europe were reduced to 27,500 square kilometers and 2 million people (from 162,500 square kilometers and 6 million people before the Balkan Wars). Without its European lands **the empire became a more homogeneous state** in which Muslims, mostly Turks and Arabs, made up the vast majority of the population.

1913, June. At the Arab Congress in Paris, Arab nationalists, mostly from Syria, publicized their political aims: the autonomy of the Arab provinces, Arab participation in the Ottoman central government, and the recognition of Arabic, along with Turkish, as the official languages of the empire. Although some writers and groups began expressing **Arab or Syrian nationalist ideas and demands for political rights** in the late 19th century, in 1914 Arab nationalist sentiments still had **little mass appeal,** and the demands of Arab nationalist societies (such as *al-Fatat* and *Hizb al-Lamarkaziyya*) focused on **greater Arab autonomy** within the Ottoman Empire, **not full independence.** Even in Syria, considered the hub of Arabist aspirations, there was **no extensive Arab nationalist movement,** and most members of the elite remained loyal to the Ottomans until the collapse of the empire.

1913–14. ASCENDANCY OF THE COMMITTEE OF UNION AND PROGRESS. In 1908, when it was widely credited with masterminding the revolution, the committee was little more than a label covering a variety of factions. In the following years it steadily **improved its central organization,** hammered out policies at party congresses, **built up popular support,** won parliamentary elections, and placed its members in prominent government positions. In July 1912 opposition groups forced the replacement of the committee-dominated government, but on Jan. 23, 1913, the committee seized power again in a **coup led by Enver Pasha.** Following this takeover, the committee **suppressed all opposition parties** and by 1914 controlled practically all the seats in the Parliament as well as all government ministries, establishing an **authoritarian regime** that ruled until the end of World War I.

(To p. 752)

b. IRAN

(From p. 363)

1796–97. AGHA MUHAMMAD SHAH, FOUNDER OF THE QAJAR DYNASTY. The Qajars, originally **Turkish tribal chiefs** in Safavid service, consolidated their rule in Iran in the last two decades of the 18th century. The able and brutal Qajar leader Agha Muhammad took advantage of the political chaos to expand his control of the country. In 1796, after crushing the Zand dynasty and taking Khurasan from its Afshar ruler, he was crowned shah in his **capital of Tehran.**

The Qajars, who ruled Iran until 1924, headed a **weakly centralized** regime in which strong provincial tribes and an increasingly independent religious establishment set limits on the power of the state. Growing **European intrusion** also debilitated the government. In the 19th century Iran did not experience the level of modernizing reform of the Ottoman Empire or Egypt. The **population grew** from about 6 million in 1800 to around 12 million in 1920, but close to 90 percent of it remained rural, with a strong nomadic and tribal element (estimated at over a quarter of the population).

1797–1834. FATH ALI SHAH. The shah **deferred to the Shi'ite clergy** in order to enlist their support for the Qajar regime. He contributed state money to them and established many mosques and *madrasas.* At the beginning of Fath Ali's reign, the Qajar bureaucracy was only rudimentary. He created many **additional administrative positions,** such as controller general. Fath Ali Shah had five prime ministers during his reign. Their duties varied according to their abilities and the trust they elicited from the ruler. Always threatened by court intrigue and potentially fatal royal disfavor, no high-level governmental appointee ever felt safe. Fath Ali's many **sons were appointed as governors** of major provinces. Abbas Mirza (d. 1833), the heir apparent, maintained his own provincial army as the governor of Azerbaijan and later Khurasan.

Fath Ali Shah organized the army into two sections, one of which was **based on a European military model** and was directed by French, British, and Russian officers. By 1813 the *nizam-i jadid* **(new army)** included 12,000 regular cavalry and 12,000 regular infantry. Despite this addition, the Qajar army remained dependent on **tribal levies** and the *ghulam*s (military slaves), usually of Christian origin, who formed the shah's personal guard.

1799. Mirza Baba, *naqqash-bashi* (head painter) at the Qajar court, painted one of many life-size portraits of Fath Ali Shah. Mirza Baba mastered oils, miniature illumination, and lacquer, and many of his paintings were designed as presents for European rulers.

1804–13. War with Russia (p. 508). Following its annexation of Georgia in 1801, Russia pushed outward to extend its control in the Caucasus to the Aras River. After nine years of hostilities the **Treaty of Gulistan** (Oct. 12, 1813) confirmed Iran's **loss of Georgia** and districts of **Azerbaijan,** including Baku and Qarabagh. Russia remained dissatisfied, and war resumed in 1826.

1809–11. Appointment of Hajji Mirza Abu al-Hasan Khan as the first Qajar ambassador to Great Britain. He became the object of the satirical work *Adventures of Hajji Baba in England* by James Morier.

1812. Opening of a **printing press.** The press in Iran remained much less developed than that of the Ottoman Empire or Egypt.

c. 1813. Completion of the **Masjid-i Shah** in Tehran. Situated in the heart of the city, the royal mosque is a notable example of the Qajar royal building program, in which members of guilds *(asnaf)* provided the skilled labor for the construction of major architectural projects. In the building trade, as in other crafts, a **system of guilds** with their inner hierarchy of apprentices and masters was in place.

1826. Death of **Sheik Ahmad ibn Zayn al-Din al-Ahsa'i,** founder of the **Shaykhi School of Shi'ism.** The doctrines of the Shaykhi school were regarded as heterodox by the majority of the Shi'ite religious learned. They attempted to **reconcile reason and religion** in order to explain difficult aspects of Shi'ite beliefs. They posited that the hidden twelfth imam, whose return is awaited by all Shi'ite Muslims, was not literally hidden on earth, but existed in an intermediary world of archetypes called Hurqalya. Later members of the Shaykhi School argued that one perfect Shi'ite Muslim might act as an intercessor between this world and the hidden twelfth imam. The Shaykhis retained a **minority following** in Iran and Iraq, but influenced the later Babi movement.

1826–28. Second war with Russia (p. 508). The Russians succeeded in gaining the coveted frontier along the Aras River. Under the **Treaty of Turkmanchay** (Feb. 22, 1828) Iran lost the areas of **Erivan** and **Nakhchevan,** and provided for a Russian diplomatic and commercial presence in Iran.

1829. Death of **Mirza Abd al-Vahhab Isfahani.** A bureaucrat with a flair for poetry and calligraphy, Mirza rose through the administrative ranks. In 1809 he was appointed *munshi al-mamalik* (head of the royal chancery). By 1821, he had control of Iran's foreign affairs. Although never named prime minister, in practice he had a similar influence over Fath Ali Shah in Qajar state affairs until his death.

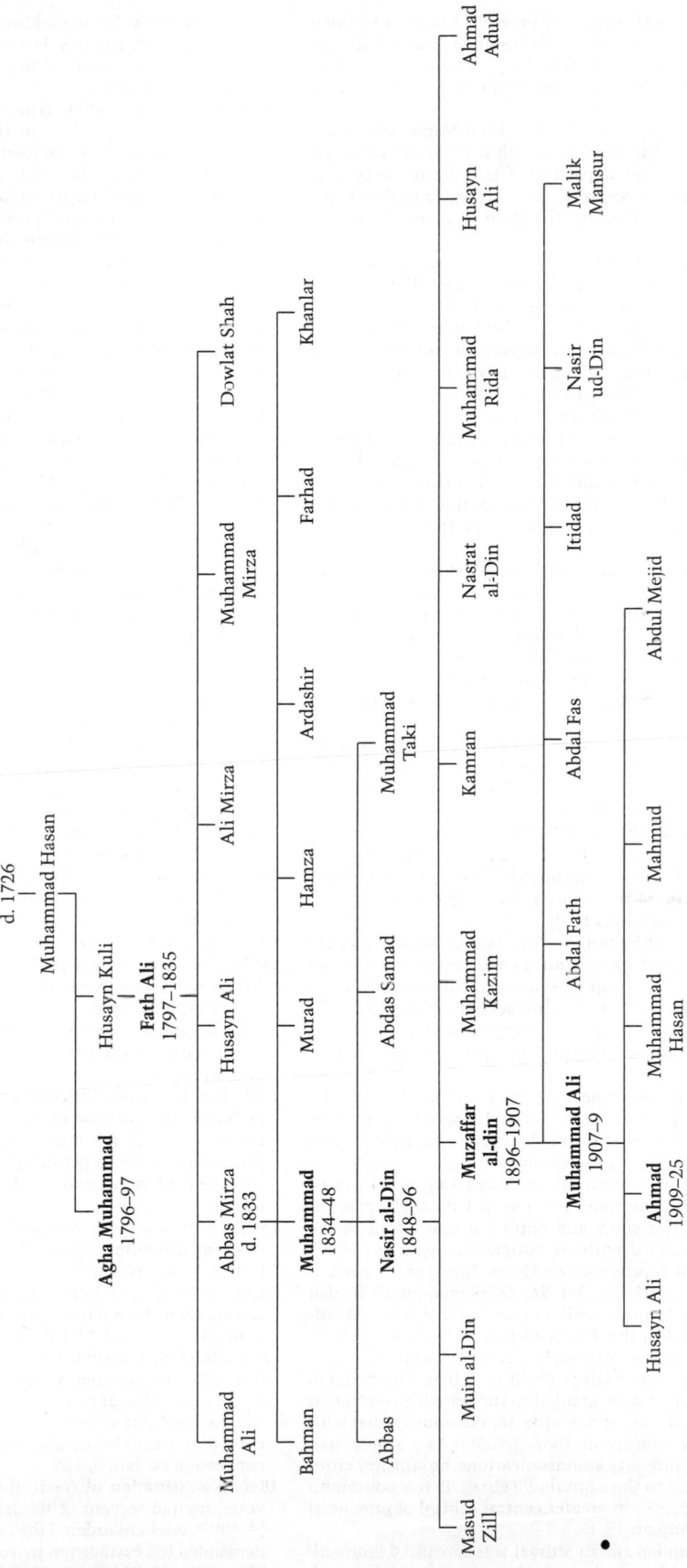

THE QAJAR DYNASTY IN IRAN (1796–1925)

1834–48. MUHAMMAD SHAH. After two previous humiliating Qajar losses to the Russian army, Muhammad Shah sought to **modernize his military forces.** To this end, he utilized European officers as commanders of special brigades, set up a foundry for casting brass cannon, and produced gunpowder.

Under the influence of his prime minister, Hajji Mirza Aghasi, the shah displayed **Sufi mystical tendencies** and thus jeopardized the traditional role of the Qajar rulers as patrons of the Shi'ite clergy. The situation strained relations between the government and the clergy, some of whom articulated the idea that the Qajars were not legitimate political authorities.

1837. First Iranian newspaper was published by Mirza Salih Shirazi, who acquired knowledge of printing and a press in England. With government sanction, the paper continued for a year or two.

1848–96. NASIR AL-DIN SHAH. This son of Muhammad Shah ruled during an eventful period of **reforms,** growing **foreign intervention,** and mounting agitation by constitutionalists and opponents of the regime. The shah attempted to formalize government administration along Russian lines, reducing the dependence on local governors and tribal chiefs. He also sought to strengthen the state by limiting the jurisdiction of the religious establishment and creating new courts. This increased the **tensions between the state and the *ulama*** (members of the religious establishment), which came to a head in the participation of the *ulama* in the great antigovernment protests of 1890–92 over the tobacco concession.

A **new class of westernized intellectuals** emerged during this period. They included people educated in Europe and government officials who shared a belief in the need to **modernize** the country, introduce **constitutional government,** and **limit European interference.** Although their impact on society as a whole was limited, in the 1890s they, along with many *ulama*, became **increasingly opposed to government policies.** Their struggle culminated in the constitutional revolution of 1905–11.

1850. Defeat of the Babi movement, with the execution of **Sayyid Ali Muhammad,** known as the Bab (the Gateway). In 1844, the thousandth anniversary of the disappearance of the twelfth Shi'ite imam, when **messianic expectations** of his return ran high, Sayyid Ali Muhammad had claimed to be the gateway between the imam and the Shi'ite community. In 1848 he even presented himself as the imam. **He denounced the *ulama*** and proclaimed a **new scripture,** the Bayan. The **rebellions** he inspired in various parts of the country were **suppressed.** Some of his followers later joined the Baha'i faith.

1851. Founding of the Dar al-Funun, a state school with a modern **French-style organization and curriculum** as well as some European teachers. It taught engineering, military science, medicine, and foreign languages and served essentially as an **elite school** for training high-level bureaucrats and officers. A **state printing press** was established at the school, where more than 100 titles in history, poetry, and biography were published.

Founding of the official newspaper, *Tarbiyat (Edification),* by the prime minister Mirza Taqi Khan Amir-i Kabir. It was designed to explain government policy and events outside of Iran primarily to state officials, and it featured illustrations beginning in 1860.

1852. Death of the reformist prime minister **Mirza Taqi Khan Amir-i Kabir,** the architect of the state-sponsored Dar al-Funun. His plans to end corruption at the Qajar court and curtail stipends paid to the Shi'ite religious learned ended without noticeable effect, as did his attempts to free Iran from dependence on Great Britain and Russia.

1856–57. Iran's occupation of Herat (Oct. 26, 1856) prompted a **British invasion** of southern Iran from the gulf and several months of hostilities. Peace was concluded in the Treaty of Paris (March 4, 1857), in which Iran gave up all claims to Afghan territory, including Herat.

1858–59. Construction of the **first telegraph lines** in Iran. The rights to this communications project were granted to the British government, whose primary intent in the venture was faster communication with India in the wake of the mutiny in 1857 (p. 555). As a result, Iran received a new system of **intercity communications,** linking key cities such as Isfahan and Shiraz to the capital of Tehran. Better communication with outlying areas meant **greater central control** of provincial authorities by the government.

1864. Mirza Sayyid Muhammad Hasan Shirazi was appointed *marja al-taqlid* (the reference point for emulation). Not only did all other *muj-*

*tahid*s (those skilled in making original, legal opinions) accept his rulings in theology and law, but all Shi'ite Muslims, including the Qajar ruling elite, were required to follow him as the representative of the hidden twelfth imam.

1866. Mirza Husayn Ali Nuri (d. 1892) proclaimed publicly while in exile in the Ottoman city of Edirne that he was Baha Allah (the Splendor of God), the messianic figure foretold by the Bab.

Most of followers of the Bab (Babis) became the followers of this new prophet. The **Baha'i faith** that he founded asserted that Baha Allah, not Muhammad, was the final prophet sent to Muslims as well as to Jews, Christians, and Zoroastrians. It preached **pacifism, equality** between the sexes, and **tolerance** for all religions. The Baha'is made converts in Iran, but were **regarded as heretics and persecuted periodically.** The majority of Baha'is have resided outside Iran.

1868. First Iranian **postage stamps** circulated.

1870. Shah's trip to the Shi'ite holy cities in Ottoman Iraq.

1871–73. A far-reaching **program of reform** was launched by the chief minister, Mirza Husayn. Modeled after the Ottoman Tanzimat, it was intended to reorganize the military, centralize the administration, and reform the law and system of taxation. **Opposition** from vested interests within the government sabotaged the program and procured the **minister's dismissal** in 1873.

1872. The **Reuter Concession** granted the right to build future **railroads** from the Caspian to the south as well as **irrigation projects** to Baron Julius de Reuter, a German-born British subject. The agreement also gave Reuter the right to exploit all Iran's **mineral wealth** and the option to open a **bank.** The British government did not endorse the concession, which was **canceled** by the shah in Nov. 1873.

1876–80. I'timad al-Saltana published a four-volume work, *Mir'at al-buldan,* which is partly a geographical dictionary of Iranian towns and partly a chronicle of Nasir al-Din Shah's reign.

1879. First modern police force established in Tehran under the direction of an Austrian officer.

THE PERSIAN COSSACK BRIGADE was formed at the request of Nasir al-Din Shah, who had been impressed with the Russian Cossack forces on his trip to Russia the previous year. Russian officers organized and commanded the unit, which **promoted Russian influence in Iran.** The brigade, designed to protect the shah and the government, became the **best-trained division** in the Qajar army.

1884. Abolition of the *jizya* (poll tax) on the Zoroastrian minority in Iran. The tax, paid only by non-Muslims in Islamic lands, was removed by pressure on the Qajar government asserted by the Persian Zoroastrian Amelioration Fund founded in Bombay in 1854.

1887. The Qajar bureaucrat **Mirza Muhammad Husayn Farahani** (d. 1912) presented to Nasir al-Din Shah his *Safarnameh (Book of Travels)* describing his pilgrimage to Mecca in 1885–86. One of the few Muslim accounts of the pilgrimage in the 19th century, the work depicted the social and political attitudes of an educated member of the Qajar administration.

1889, Jan. 30. Reuter concession for the formation of the **Imperial Bank of Persia.** The collapse of the comprehensive concession of 1872 still left Reuter with the option to open a bank in Iran, which the shah granted for a 60-year period. The imperial bank had the exclusive right to issue bank notes and was hated by Iranian merchants and moneylenders.

1890–98. Mirza Malkum Khan (1833–1908), a leading proponent of **constitutional reform,** published in London his newspaper *Qanun (Law),* in which he advocated reform and criticized the tyranny and corruption of the Qajar regime. He was one of several advocates of reform, among them **Fath Ali Akhundzadeh** (1812–78), **Mirza Aqa Khan Kirmani** (d. 1896), and **Abd al-Rahim Talibov** (1834–1911).

1890, March 8. The **tobacco concession,** granting a British subject, Maj. G. F. Talbot, a **monopoly** on the production, domestic sale, and export of tobacco. The agreement angered local growers, merchants, and shopkeepers, and aroused a series of **protests,** demonstrations, and boycotts of tobacco, led by major religious figures. The shah **annulled** the concession on Jan. 5, 1892.

1896. Assassination of Nasir al-Din Shah by Mirza Riza Kirmani, devoted Iranian servant of the Islamic activist Jamal al-Din al-Afghani (d. 1897). Afghani ordered the assassination, and the Qajar government demanded his extradition by the Ottoman sultan.

1896–1907. MUZAFFAR AL-DIN SHAH was a weak ruler who attempted moderate reforms in the central treasury, but was undermined by the debt the Qajar court owed to Britain and Russia. He paid for several **lavish trips to Europe** by taking out new loans, which only worsened the fiscal condition of Iran. During his reign small printing presses disseminated more information about Iran and the world outside to more people.

1900-1. Agitation against the government was expressed in the form of *shab-nameh*s (night letters). These **protest leaflets** were distributed at night and urged governmental reform and resistance to imperialist powers.

1901, May 29. D'Arcy Oil Concession. The mineral rights granted to Reuter were withdrawn in 1899, thus opening the way for the new grant to **William Knox D'Arcy,** a British citizen with experience in the Australian gold mines. D'Arcy was granted the right to drill in all of Iran, except the five northern provinces, for 60 years. The **Anglo-Persian Oil Company** was formed in London in 1909 to exploit the concession, a year after the digging of the first commercial well in Iran.

1903. Anti-Baha'i riots in Isfahan and Yazd expressed Muslim anger at foreigners.

1905. Abd al-Husayn Mirza translated into Persian Montesquieu's *On the Spirit of the Law* and Adam Smith's *The Wealth of Nations*.

1905-11. THE CONSTITUTIONAL REVOLUTION. Mounting opposition to the shah erupted in a **wave of protest** and six years of struggle to impose constitutional restraints on the ruler and his ministers. A **coalition of merchants, artisans, and ulama** led the agitation, prompted by increased taxes proposed by the shah's Belgian adviser, Joseph Naus, and a general hostility to the growing foreign intrusion in Iran. **Ideas of constitutional reform,** advocated by westernized intellectuals like Malkum Khan, circulated among the discontented and colored their demands.

The revolution was sparked by the physical punishment of merchants in Tehran for price violations (Dec. 12, 1905). This provoked **protest gatherings** supported by ulama, among them the prominent **Sayyid Muhammad Tabataba'i.** Initially the protesters made amorphous demands for just rule, but a second antigovernment demonstration in July 1906 articulated a clear **call for a constituent assembly (Majlis).** Although the constitutional movement was strikingly small and nonviolent, the government's weakness forced the shah to accept its demands (Aug. 5, 1906).

The **assembly,** which convened in Oct. 1906, consisted of artisans, merchants, *ulama,* and bureaucrats. It drew up a **constitution** (based on the Belgian constitution of 1831), which remained officially in force until 1979. The document subordinated the shah to parliamentary government while maintaining Islam as Iran's official religion. The shah endorsed it, but plotted to overturn it.

1907-9. MUHAMMAD ALI SHAH. A **Russian puppet,** he was kept on the throne by the royal guard of the Persian Cossack Brigade. He **opposed the Majlis** and was supported by conservative Shi'ite members of the *ulama.* His coup against the Majlis ultimately led to further civil unrest and, finally, his deposition.

1907, Aug. 31. Anglo-Russian Convention. It divided Iran, without its consent, into spheres of influence, the north for Russia and a stretch in the southeast for Britain, with the intervening area constituting a neutral zone.

1908, June. The shah closed the Majlis and suspended the constitution, with the aid of the Persian Cossack Brigade. Leaders of the movement for reform were arrested and executed. But the shah **failed to regain control** in the provinces, especially in Tabriz, where the constitutionalists took hold of the government.

1909, April. The Russian army occupied Tabriz, saving it from surrender to the shah's forces.

July. Victory for the constitutionalists, achieved after a force of Bakhtiyari tribesmen from Isfahan and peasants from Gilan occupied Tehran, **deposed Muhammad Ali,** and replaced him with his 9-year-old son, Ahmad, and a regency.

1909-25. AHMAD SHAH. The last Qajar shah was crowned just days before the beginning of World War I. His reign was characterized by an increased **lack of central government** authority and the rise of a plethora of **rebellious groups** from tribes to reformists. **Foreign intervention** in Iran continued, heightened by the world war.

1909-11. THE SECOND CONSTITUTIONAL PERIOD. A new Majlis, dominated by wealthy landowners, convened in Oct. 1909. The **ulama were now less prominent,** and many of them were disillusioned with the demands of the liberal reformers to disestablish Islam and introduce a new system of secular education. **Factional strife** in Tehran and **Russian pressure** undermined the Majlis, which the government **suppressed** in Dec. 1911 under threat of Russian occupation (now extended to much of northern Iran). The constitutional revolution was thus halted, although the restored government of the shah remained weak.

1911. Death of Abd al-Rahman Najjar Zada Tabrizi, author of many popular works on geography, physics, and biology as well as accounts of European social and political institutions. His books emphasized Iran's technological backwardness.

1914, May 20. The British government bought a majority interest in the **Anglo-Persian Oil Company** in order to ensure the purchase of enough petroleum for its naval fleet. *(To p. 754)*

c. AFGHANISTAN

(From p. 364)

1800-3. MAHMUD SHAH (FIRST REIGN). He assumed power during a **period of instability,** when the Afghan territories were fragmented among various family members supported by tribal factions. Affairs of state were directed by the powerful prime minister **Fath Khan** of the Afghan Barakzay clan.

1803-9. SHOJA SHAH (FIRST REIGN). He came to power after he ousted his brother Mahmud.

1809, June 17. A treaty of friendship between the Afghans and the British was signed. Shoja Shah met at Peshawar with the British representative, Mountstuart Elphinstone, to negotiate a joint defense against the **threat of a combined invasion** of India by Napoleon and Alexander I of Russia.

1809-18. MAHMUD SHAH (SECOND REIGN). He was returned to power with the help of Fath Khan, who became immensely powerful. Their efforts to consolidate the state collapsed in 1818 with the **assassination of Fath Khan** by the ruler's jealous son Kamran. This precipitated a *badal* (vendetta) between Afghan clan factions in which the brother of the murdered prime minister, Dost Muhammad, drove Mahmud Shah out of Kabul. Mahmud withdrew to Herat, which he ruled until his death in 1829. His son Kamran continued to rule there until 1842, when the area fell to Iran.

1819. The Sikhs captured Kashmir.

1826-39. DOST MUHAMMAD, FOUNDER OF THE BARAKZAY (OR MUHAMMADZAY) DYNASTY. The collapse of the ruling Sadozay family brought to power the Barakzay clan of the Durranis, whose power had increased since the late 18th century and was to remain dominant into the 20th century.

The chief aim of Dost Muhammad was the **reunification of the country,** a task for which he needed both a stronger Afghan economy and an army reformed according to European example. He turned formerly tax-exempt land grants held by local Durrani clans into prime sources of state revenue through **violent confiscation** and the appointment of special tax agents. Tax collection in the provinces was overseen by his sons. Dost Muhammad was determined to increase the size of his **standing army** to lessen his dependence on unruly clan support.

1834. Capture of Peshawar by the Sikh ruler Ranjit Singh. The **loss of Peshawar** and the fertile land near the Indus River weakened the economy of Afghanistan by severing a lucrative source of revenue. With the loss of its Indian territories, the Afghan kingdom became a **more compact territory** whose difficult mountainous terrain and plateaus made it **easier to defend** against military threats from Iran, Russia, and Britain.

1836. Dost Muhammad took the title *emir al-mu'minin* (commander of the faithful) in preparation for his holy war against the Sikhs. His attempt to recapture Peshawar failed.

1837. Official mission of the Russian diplomat Ivan Vitkevich to Kabul, part of the Russian competition with Britain over influence in Afghanistan.

1839-42. FIRST BRITISH-AFGHAN WAR (p. 553). With the aim of overthrowing Dost Muhammad and reinstalling the Sadozay ruler

THE BARAKZAY DYNASTY IN AFGHANISTAN (1747–1929)

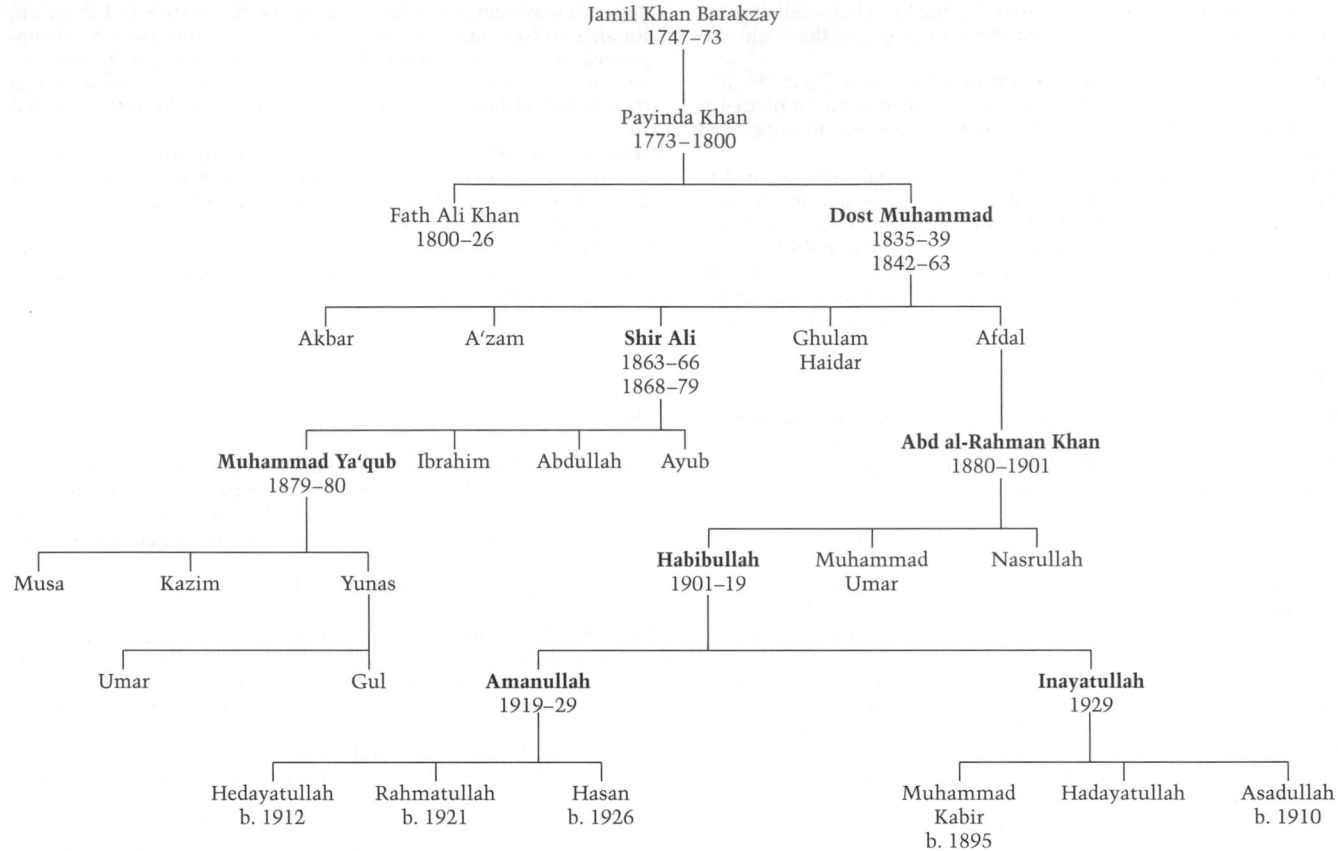

Shah Shoja, the British launched an **ill-fated invasion** of Afghanistan. A British-Indian army took Qandahar and Kabul, **installed Shah Shoja** as a British puppet (Aug. 1839), and deported Dost Muhammad (1840). But Afghan resistance culminated in an uprising in Kabul in Jan. 1842 and a **retreat of the British troops** that ended in their virtual destruction. Shah Shoja was assassinated, and **Dost Muhammad returned to power** in Kabul.

1843–63. DOST MUHAMMAD (SECOND REIGN). The restored Barakzay ruler **reconsolidated the Afghan state** by recapturing Qandahar and then taking Herat from Iran (1863).

1849, Feb. 21. Defeat of Afghan forces and their Sikh allies by the British in the **Battle of Gujrat.** The Afghans had hoped to gain the district of Peshawar in the event of victory. British India proceeded to annex the Punjab and Peshawar, establishing a de facto boundary with Afghanistan that was not formalized for more than 40 years.

1855, March 30. Treaty of friendship with British India, which confirmed the British annexation of Peshawar and the Punjab. Dost Muhammad renounced expansion into British India.

1863–64. The first newspaper was published in Afghanistan.

1863–66. SHIR ALI (FIRST REIGN). The accession of Dost Muhammad's son, Shir Ali, who had been governor of Herat, was opposed by various half-brothers. In 1866, two of them, Muhammad A'zam and Muhammad Afdal, drove him out of Kabul. He retreated to Herat.

1866–68. Rule of Muhammad A'zam (1866–67) and Muhammad Afdal (1867–68). Shir Ali, with the help of his son, Muhammad Ya'qub, recovered Kabul and Qandahar in 1868.

1868–79. SHIR ALI (SECOND REIGN). He instituted the office of *sadr-i a'zam* (prime minister) and established a 13-member **advisory council.** Instead of allowing his sons to oversee provincial taxation, he appointed bureaucrats responsible directly to him. He founded a regular **postal service** between Kabul and the outside world and opened the **first public school** in the capital.

1878–79. SECOND BRITISH-AFGHAN WAR. The acceptance by the Afghans of a Russian diplomatic mission led by Maj. Gen. Stoletov prompted a **British ultimatum** to the Afghan ruler, demanding his agreement to a permanent British diplomatic agency in Kabul (Nov. 2, 1878). The ultimatum was ignored, a British-Indian force entered Afghanistan, and Shir Ali fled to Russian territory after naming his son Muhammad Ya'qub as regent. In the **Treaty of Gandamak** (May 26, 1879) Muhammad Ya'qub agreed to accredit a **permanent British mission** at Kabul, to cede the **Khyber Pass** to British India, and to **surrender to Britain Afghanistan's external sovereignty.** An Afghan uprising led to the renewal of the war a few months later. The British retook Kabul, deposed Muhammad Ya'qub (Oct. 1879), and placed on the throne Abd al-Rahman Khan, a nephew of Shir Ali.

1880–1901. ABD AL-RAHMAN KHAN. His reign tightened Kabul's central control through **4 civil wars** and 100 major and minor rebellions. These military campaigns depended upon a **larger standing army.** To this end, Abd al-Rahman Khan recruited about 79,000 men out of a total population of 6 million. The state budget reflected this priority, with more than half of its revenue being used to pay military salaries. The British government exported guns and gunpowder to the government of Afghanistan during this period.

Abd al-Rahman Khan also **reshaped Afghanistan's state bureaucracy,** detailing specific duties for each section of the government and its appointees. The country was divided into six large provinces and subdivided into districts. A series of internal **highways and bridges** was constructed to further his policy of unification. Most of his efforts to modernize transportation routes were, however, confined to areas close to Kabul.

1884. Conquest of the khanate of Maymana.

1885. At the request of Abd al-Rahman Khan, Mawlawi Ahmadjan Khan, a court official, compiled two handbooks detailing the responsibilities of judges and provincial governors. The chief judge became an employee of the state whose behavior could be closely regulated. In urban areas **Islamic legal courts** were administered by local judges, many of whom were state appointees, but in rural areas **customary tribal codes** continued to prevail.

1893–95. Demarcation of Afghanistan's boundaries. The **Durand Agreement** (Nov. 12, 1893) defined the southern borders, while the northern borders were established by an agreement signed by Britain and Russia (March 11, 1895), describing their respective spheres of influence.

1895. Abolition of slavery in Afghanistan.

1896. Kafiristan, a territory of polytheistic peoples, was conquered. Its inhabitants were forced to convert to Sunni Islam. The province was integrated into Afghanistan and renamed Nurestan (Land of Light).

1901–19. HABIBULLAH KHAN. He renewed ties with the British and opened a wool-weaving center in Kabul. During his reign political exiles were granted amnesty, which allowed the return of Afghan intellectuals from the Middle East and India. The foundation of a group of constitutionalists called the **Young Afghans,** who were anti-British and pro-Turk, formed the basis of **a modern Islamic movement.** They established public education for boys and imported Ottoman doctors and military advisers. **Opposition to their ideas** was promoted by other Afghans who had been exiled in India and were pro-British promoters of secular, technological modernization.

1907. Two schools were founded in Kabul, one civilian and one military.

Habibullah Khan visited British India as a guest of Viceroy Gilbert Elliot.

Aug. 31. British-Russian convention on Afghanistan, in which Russia acknowledged that the country fell within the **British sphere of influence.**

1911. Publication of the Kabul-based Persian language semimonthly *Seraj al-akhbar (Torch of the News)*, which was read widely outside of Afghanistan. The editor, **Mahmud Tarzi** (d. 1933), made popular writing in Afghanistan conform to Middle Eastern rather than Indian journalistic precedent. Raised in Damascus, Tarzi was a nationalist who **supported modernist and Pan-Islamist causes** and helped organize the Young Afghan movement. *(To p. 757)*

d. ARABIA

(From p. 364)

1801. The Wahhabis sacked the Shi'ite holy city of **Karbala** in Iraq, burial place of Imam Husayn, the Prophet's grandson. Their plunder of the shrine and massacre of the population created **outrage among Muslims** everywhere.

1803. The WAHHABIS CAPTURED MECCA, challenging directly the Ottoman sultan's claim to the guardianship of the holy cities. The emir of Mecca fled.

1803–14. Sa'ud ibn Abd al-Aziz ruled as Saudi emir after the assassination of his father (Oct. 1803). He continued his father's militant policies of expansion.

1804. The Wahhabis captured Medina. They destroyed the mausolea and monumental tombs in the cemeteries, which they considered to be polytheistic, and desecrated the Prophet's tomb.

1806–56. Sa'id ibn Sultan ruled Oman and Muscat.

1809–16. Ahmad al-Mutawakkil ruled as imam of Yemen after seizing power from his father, Ali al-Mansur.

1810. The Wahhabis established control over Qatar and Bahrain.

1812–59. Jabir ibn Abdallah ruled as sheik of Kuwait.

1816–35. Abdallah al-Mahdi ruled as imam of Yemen.

1818. END OF THE FIRST WAHHABI STATE. An **Egyptian expedition** ordered by the Ottoman sultan recaptured Medina (1812) and Mecca (1813), reinstated the annual pilgrimage halted by the Wahhabis, returned Hashimite control to the Hijaz, and **destroyed the Saudi capital** of Dar'iyya (1818). The Saudi emir Abdallah was beheaded. Egypt continued to hold the Hijaz and the coastlands of Yemen until 1840.

1820. Treaty between Britain and the Arab tribal peoples of the Persian Gulf, in which the latter **pledged to cease all piracy and slave traffic.**

The agreement marked the formal beginning of British-Indian responsibility for policing the Persian Gulf.

1824. BEGINNING OF THE SECOND SAUDI STATE, with its capital in Riyadh, under the emir **Turki ibn Abdallah** (r. 1824–34). It was destroyed in 1891.

1830. The Saudis recaptured Hasa.

1833, Sept. 21. Treaty of amity and commerce between **Muscat and the United States,** granting extraterritorial privileges to American nationals. This was the sheikdom's first capitulatory treaty with a Western power.

1834–38. Faysal ibn Turki ruled as Saudi emir (first reign), after the assassination of his father (May 1834).

1834, Oct. Death of **Muhammad al-Shawkani** (b. 1760), a leading Yemeni religious scholar, judge, and teacher.

1835. Abdallah Ibn Rashid occupied Hail, the capital of the Jabal Shammar region, **founding the Rashidi dynasty** there (which lasted until 1921).

1835–36. Ali al-Mansur ruled as imam of Yemen (second reign).

1836–40. Abdallah al-Nasir ruled as imam of Yemen, after deposing Ali al-Mansur.

1838. An Egyptian expeditionary force defeated the Saudis, removed the emir Faysal, and installed in his place Khalid ibn Sa'ud (r. 1838–42).

1839, Jan. The British occupied Aden, after fruitless attempts to purchase the port from Sultan Muhsin of Lahij. The sultan acknowledged British possession of Aden in return for an annual subsidy.

1840–43. Muhammad al-Hadi ruled as imam of Yemen.

1842–43. Abdallah ibn Thunayn ruled as Saudi emir.

1843, Feb. 11. Treaty of friendship between the sultan of Lahij and Britain, in which the sultan finally acquiesced to British control of Aden.

1843–65. Faysal ruled as Saudi emir (second reign). He escaped from captivity in Egypt and recaptured the Saudi throne, resuming his **expansionist policies.** He sought to impose his authority on Bahrain, Qatar, the Trucial Coast, and northern Oman, but was **frustrated by the British.**

1844, Nov. 17. Treaty of commerce between Muscat and France, granting France extraterritorial rights and most-favored-nation treatment.

1853, May 4. In the conclusion of a perpetual **maritime truce** among tribal sheiks of the **Persian Gulf,** they prolonged in perpetuity previous agreements to cease all maritime warfare and piracy.

1854, July 14. The ruler of Muscat ceded the **Kuria Muria Islands** to the British Crown.

1856. Thuwayni ibn Sa'id succeeded his father as ruler of Oman and Muscat.

Nov. 17. Muscat leased from Iran the port of Bandar Abbas and the islands of Qishm and Hormuz for an annual payment of 14,000 tomans.

1865–70. Abdallah ibn Faysal ruled as Saudi emir (first reign).

1868–71. Azzan ibn Qays ruled Oman and Muscat.

1870–75. Sa'ud ibn Faysal ruled as Saudi emir, after deposing his brother Abdallah.

1871. Ottoman forces occupied Hasa from the Saudis, as part of a **new policy of Ottoman expansion in Arabia.**

Sheik Abdallah al-Sabah of **Kuwait accepted Ottoman authority** over his country.

1871–83. Turki ibn Sa'id ruled Oman and Muscat.

1872. Ottoman forces occupied Asir and most of Yemen, and set up an Ottoman administration for the area, backed by a large military presence.

1875–89. Abdallah ibn Faysal ruled as Saudi emir (second reign).

1877. Treaty of commerce between Muscat and the Netherlands, granting Dutch nationals extraterritorial rights.

1880, Dec. 22. An agreement between the sheik of Bahrain and Britain, in which the sheik surrendered his external sovereignty to Britain. This was the first in a series of such agreements that over the next 26 years brought the sheikdoms along the Arabian coast of the Persian Gulf into a **British quasi-protectorate system.**

1882, May. The ruler of Hadramawt signed a treaty surrendering his external sovereignty to Britain.

1883–1913. Faysal ibn Turki ruled Oman and Muscat.

1888. A British protectorate established in Hadramawt.

1889–91. Abd al-Rahman ibn Faysal ruled as Saudi emir.

SAUDI ARABIA: THE WAHHABI DYNASTY (1735–   )

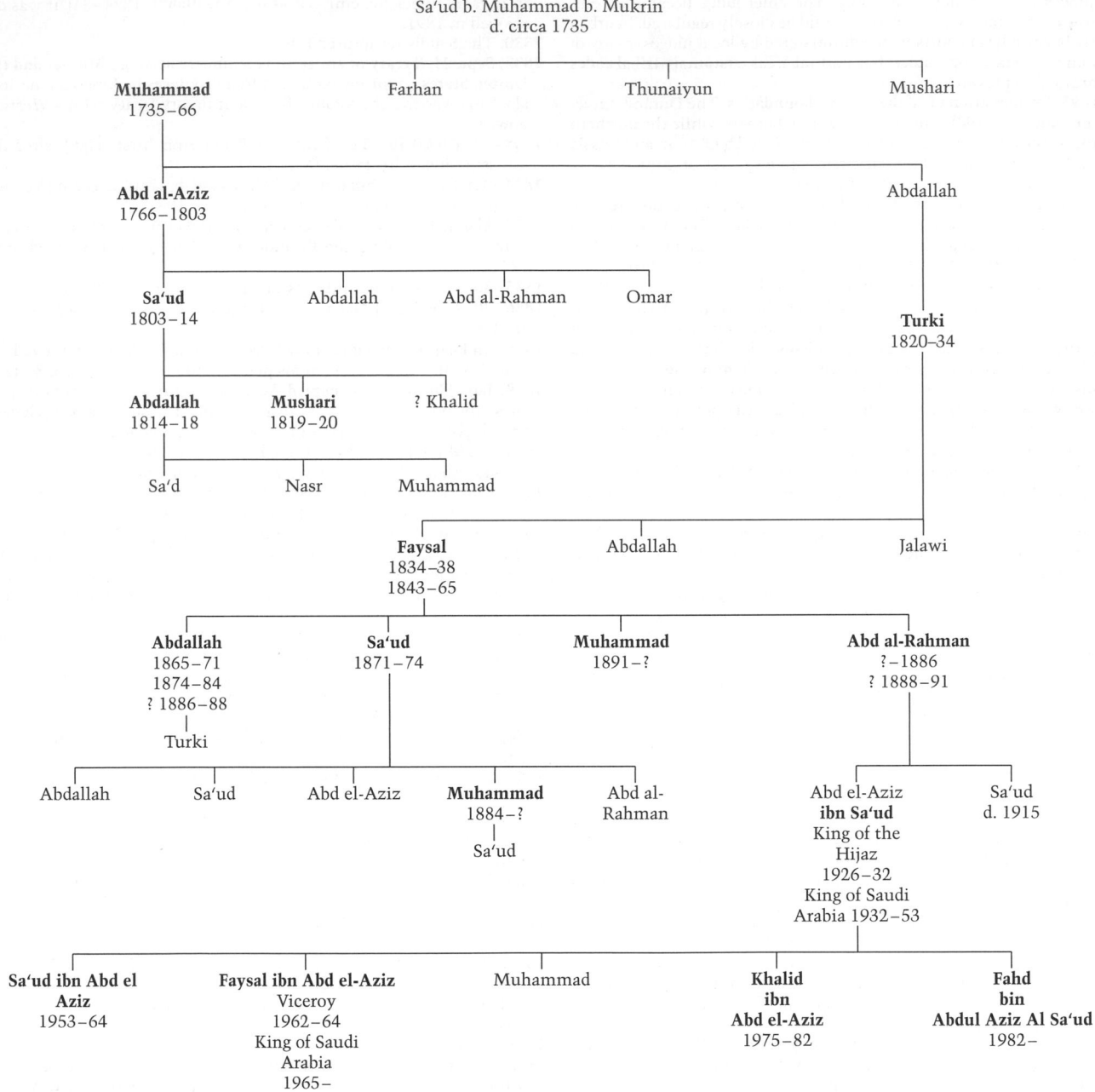

1890–1904. Muhammad ibn Yahya Hamid al-Din ruled as imam of Yemen.

1891, March 19. A commercial treaty between Muscat and Britain replaced the earlier agreement of 1839 and amplified the extraterritorial privileges of British and Indian nationals. Accompanying the agreement was a secret nonalienation bond that **curtailed Muscat's external sovereignty.**

   END OF THE SECOND SAUDI STATE, after its forces were defeated by Muhammad Ibn Rashid of Jabal Shammar. The Saudi family fled to the coast.

1891–92. A large-scale **uprising against the Ottomans in Yemen** was suppressed with difficulty.

1892, March 13. Exclusive **agreement between the sheik of Bahrain and Britain,** in which the sheik reaffirmed in more explicit terms his original **surrender of external sovereignty** in 1880. The sheikdoms of the **Trucial Coast** entered into similar agreements with Britain.

1892–96. Muhammad ibn Abdallah ruled as emir of Kuwait.

1896–1915. Mubarak ibn Abdallah ruled as emir of Kuwait, after assassinating the emir, his half-brother Muhammad. He worked to **regain Kuwaiti independence from the Ottomans.**

1899, Jan. 23. The **Kuwaiti emir** obtained a secret commitment from Britain to protect his dynasty's rule in return for a **surrender of his external sovereignty to Britain.** With British backing he resisted subsequent Ottoman attempts to reassert authority over Kuwait.

1902. BEGINNING OF THE THIRD SAUDI STATE. Abd al-Aziz ibn Sa'ud returned from exile in Kuwait, captured Riyadh from the Rashidis, and acknowledged his loyalty to the Ottomans. He ruled until 1953 and **laid the foundations of the modern kingdom of Saudi Arabia.**

1902–4. Ibn Sa'ud captured more territories from the Rashidis, regaining the whole of southern and central Najd, and assuming the title of **emir of Najd.**

1904. The Saudis defeated an Ottoman force sent against them.

1904–48. Yahya ruled as imam of Yemen. He regained **Yemeni independence** and maintained an authoritarian and conservative regime that shunned foreign influences and restricted modernization.

1905, Feb. The emerging Saudi state became a district *(qada')* of the Ottoman province of Basra, in response to Ottoman pressure.

April. Ottoman-British agreement on the demarcation of the boundary between the British sphere of control around Aden and Ottoman Yemen. The agreement was not ratified by the sultan but helped to reduce tensions between the parties.

1910–12. An anti-Ottoman revolt in Asir in Arabia was led by Muhammad al-Idrisi. The Ottomans failed to remove the rebels from their hold over the lowland areas.

1911. Imam Yahya of **Yemen concluded an agreement with the Ottomans (at Du'an),** restoring to the interior autonomy under nominal Ottoman sovereignty. The Ottomans thereby gave up on their attempts to subjugate the area. Yahya remained loyal to the Ottomans during World War I, and gained **complete independence for Yemen** without a struggle in 1918.

1912. The Saudis established the first of the **IKHWAN SETTLEMENTS,** colonies of nomads who adopted the Wahhabi code, took up agriculture, and served on Saudi military campaigns. Their excessive zeal and militancy led to their suppression in 1929–30.

1913, May. Saudi forces captured Hasa and expelled the Ottoman garrisons.

Oct. Taymur ibn Faysal succeeded his father as ruler of Oman and Muscat.

Oct. 27. A pledge by the sheik of Kuwait to grant Britain exclusive **rights of oil exploration.**

1914, May. In the Ottoman-Saudi Treaty, Ibn Sa'ud **recognized Ottoman sovereignty over Najd** in return for his appointment as governor of a newly constituted province *(vilayet)* of Najd and **hereditary rule** for his family. *(To p. 766)*

e. EGYPT

Egypt remained nominally a province of the Ottoman Empire until Britain declared it a protectorate in 1914, but from 1805 it followed an **increasingly independent** course of development as a separate country. Muhammad Ali and the succeeding rulers detached themselves steadily from Ottoman control, which was reduced to a mere formality after the British occupation in 1882. During the period Egypt underwent **profound changes,** the result of local initiatives and European penetration. Its **population** remained predominantly rural, but **expanded** from about 3.5 million to 12 million.

1805–48. MUHAMMAD ALI PASHA. An officer of Albanian origin from the Macedonian port of Kavalla (b. c. 1770), Muhammad Ali (Mehmet Ali) arrived in Egypt in March 1801 as the second in command of a regiment of Albanian troops sent by the Ottoman government to fight the French. In 1803 he became commander of the unit, which he then employed to undermine the governors sent from Istanbul and the Mamluks who sought to regain their control. He won this **contest for power** and in July 1805 the Ottoman government recognized his authority by granting him a one-year **appointment as governor,** although its hope of replacing him after that with its own appointees was frustrated by the **autonomous power base** he built for himself and his family. He **established a dynasty** that lasted until 1953. Driven primarily by a ruthless desire to consolidate his hold on his adopted country, Muhammad Ali introduced many innovative reforms that **laid the foundation for the modern Egyptian state.**

1807, March–Sept. The British occupation of Alexandria was an abortive effort to restore Mamluk rule and thus forestall a second French invasion. Muhammad Ali made a provisional truce with the Mamluks,

resuming his expeditions against them once the external danger was over.

1811, March 1. MASSACRE OF MAMLUK LEADERS in the Cairo citadel. Invited to an official ceremony by Muhammad Ali, 24 beys and 40 of their subordinates were treacherously killed. This act, and the destruction of the last body of Mamluks in Upper Egypt in the following months, put a **final end to Mamluk power** and established Muhammad Ali as the undisputed ruler of Egypt.

1811–18. The Arabian campaigns. At the request of the Ottoman sultan, Muhammad Ali sent a large expedition **against the Saudi-Wahhabi state,** which was in control of the Hijaz as well as much of central and eastern Arabia. The Egyptian force captured Medina (1812) and Mecca (1813), restored the rule of the Hashimite family in the Hijaz, and after a truce advanced into central Arabia and destroyed the Saudi state (1818). **The campaign was very costly** in treasure and human life, but gave Muhammad Ali a hold on the Hijaz until 1840, along with control over the Red Sea and Arabian trade.

1811–16. Establishment of state agricultural monopolies over grain, rice, sugar, and cash crops. The government purchased the products at a fixed price well below free market level and sold them at its own price while prohibiting private transactions. The system allowed Muhammad Ali to appropriate a larger share of the rural surplus.

1812–14. CONFISCATION OF THE TAX FARMS *(iltizams)* by the state, which thereby reasserted its control over a great part of the cultivated land and the tax income from it at the expense of the powerful tax farmers. Muhammad Ali followed a similar policy with **endowed *(waqf)* agricultural land,** much of which he **confiscated.**

1813. The first student mission was sent to Europe, as part of a government program for the training of Egyptians in technical and professional skills. The **European-trained Egyptians** (a total of some 900 by 1919) provided a cadre of teachers and administrators who **promoted the development of modern institutions** in the country.

1816. The first textile factory was established in Cairo, with machines and skilled workers imported from Europe. It was part of Muhammad Ali's **ambitious policy of import substitution** and was followed by a string of plants for the manufacture of textiles and military equipment as well as the processing of agricultural produce. The factories employed some 30,000 workers. From the late 1830s **many factories were abandoned** because of the financial burdens of reequipping them, and Egypt actually grew more dependent than ever on foreign imports.

1818–73. Improvement of the port of Alexandria. The construction of the **Mahmudiyya Canal** linking Alexandria with the Nile (beginning in 1818) greatly facilitated communications between the port and the interior. The port itself, which was in a bad state of neglect, was deepened and provided with facilities that made it by far **the best port in the eastern Mediterranean.** Alexandria grew from a small fishing town of about 15,000 people to the second largest city in Egypt (over 200,000).

1820. DISCOVERY OF LONG-STAPLE COTTON in a Cairo garden. The new type of cotton (known as Jumel or Mako) was soon introduced by the authorities on an extensive scale, primarily in Lower Egypt, becoming a **major cash crop** that found ready markets in European industrial centers. By 1914 cotton occupied some 23 percent of the cropped area and accounted for about **half of agricultural production** and 90 percent of Egypt's exports. Its cultivation, however, required considerably more labor than did cereal crops and initially involved large-scale coercion of the Egyptian peasantry.

1820–22. Conquests in the Sudan (p. 592). Egyptian military expeditions captured most of northern and central Sudan (the Sennar and Kordofan regions), with the aim of using them as sources of gold as well as slaves for a new army. The thousands of **slaves brought to Egypt** for military training could not adjust and died, and the gold deposits proved a disappointment. However, Egypt gained **control of the trade** with the Sudan. The capital of the Egyptian administration was **Khartum,** founded in 1823.

1822. INTRODUCTION OF MILITARY CONSCRIPTION. On the advice of Frenchmen in his service, Muhammad Ali began the drafting of Egyptian peasants into his newly formed **modern regiments** *(al-nizam al-jadid),* creating the core of an indigenous army that gradually **displaced the traditional mercenary and Mamluk troops.** This innovation provoked **resistance by the peasants,** many of whom fled,

RULERS OF EGYPT (1811–1953)

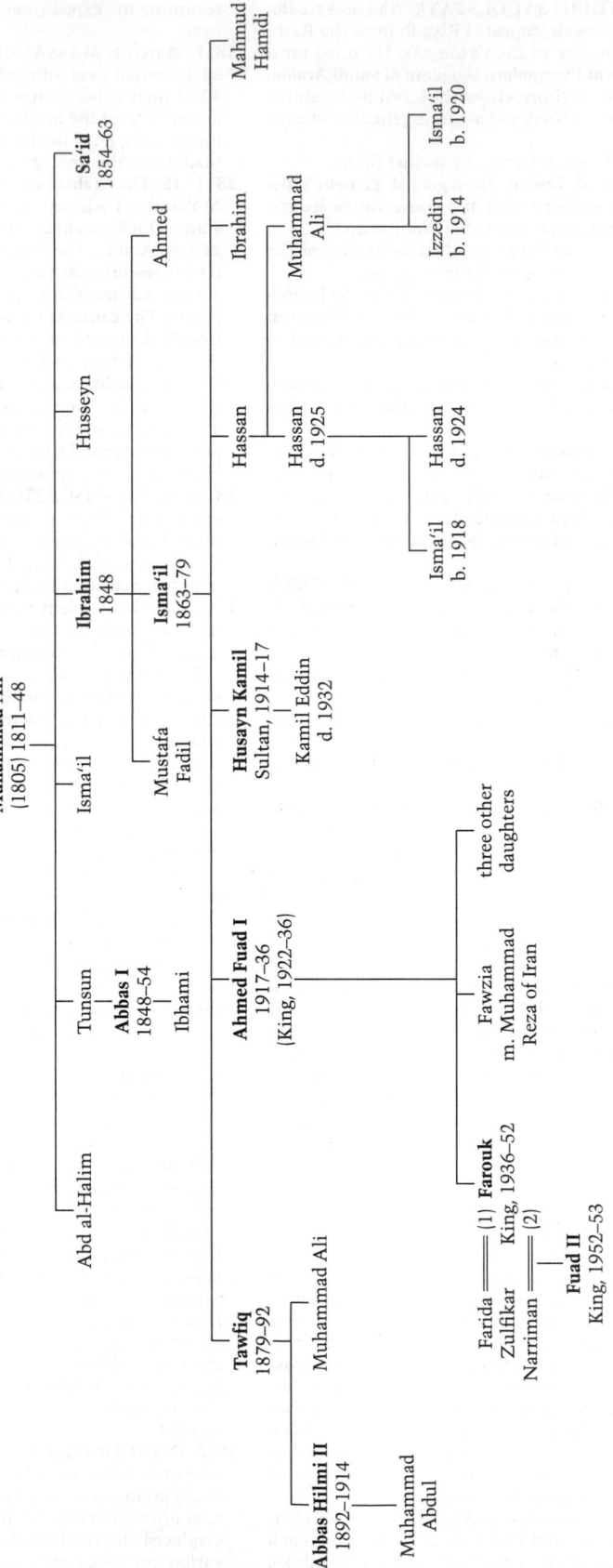

Muhammad Ali
(1805) 1811–48

Tunsun

Abbas I
1848–54

Ibhami

Ismaʻil

Ibrahim
1848

Mustafa
Fadil

Husayn Kamil
Sultan, 1914–17

Kamil Eddin
d. 1932

Husseyn

Ahmed

Ismaʻil
1863–79

Saʻid
1854–63

Mahmud
Hamdi

Ibrahim

Hassan

**Muhammad
Ali**

Hassan
d. 1925

Hassan
d. 1924

Ismaʻil
b. 1918

Izzedin
b. 1914

Ismaʻil
b. 1920

Abd al-Halim

Ahmed Fuad I
1917–36
(King, 1922–36)

Fawzia
m. Muhammad
Reza of Iran

three other
daughters

Tawfiq
1879–92

Muhammad Ali

Abbas Hilmi II
1892–1914

Muhammad
Abdul

Farida ══ (1) **Farouk**
Zulfikar   King, 1936–52
Narriman ══ (2)

Fuad II
King, 1952–53

maimed themselves, or joined antigovernment revolts. Through harsh methods of conscription and rigorous training Muhammad Ali built an army of over 100,000 men that ranked as **the most effective military force in the region.**

Opening of the **government printing press in Bulaq,** the first Arabic press in Egypt. It published numerous Arabic and Turkish works.

1823–28. Campaigns in Greece and the Aegean. At the request of the Ottoman sultan, Muhammad Ali sent his army to assist in suppressing the Greek revolt. The Egyptians **subdued Crete and then the Morea,** both of which were granted as governorships to Muhammad Ali's son Ibrahim. But an allied European fleet dealt a severe blow to the Egyptians by destroying their fleet near **Navarino** (Oct. 20, 1827). The **Egyptian forces withdrew** from the Morea in 1828, but remained in control of Crete until 1840. **Muhammad Ali gained little** from his involvement: he failed in his plans to keep the Morea as a base from which to control the trade of the eastern Mediterranean and in his efforts to persuade the sultan to grant him the promised Province of Damascus.

1825. Death of **Abd al-Rahman al-Jabarti** (b. 1753), one of the last great chroniclers. His *'Aja' ib al-athar* is a major source for the political and social history of Egypt from the 17th century to the early 19th century.

1827. The **Medical School** was founded in Cairo, the first institution for training in modern medicine in Egypt.

1828. The **first Arabic newspaper,** the official *al-Waga'i'al-Misriyya,* began publication. It was a report on government decrees and decisions. The press remained an exclusively state venture until the emergence of independent newspapers in the 1870s.

1831–41. THE OCCUPATION OF SYRIA AND OTTOMAN-EGYPTIAN CONFLICTS. Muhammad Ali coveted Syria from the early years of his rule. During Nov. 1831–July 1832 his son Ibrahim Pasha **occupied Palestine, Lebanon,** and **Syria.** An Ottoman-Egyptian settlement (May 1833) granted Syria, the district of Adana, and Crete to Ibrahim in return for a yearly tribute.

Muhammad Ali now controlled **an empire extending from the Sudan and the Hijaz to Anatolia,** and he was planning to transform the yearly tenure into complete independence. But local opposition, Ottoman refusal to yield, and European intervention combined to undo his empire building. A **coalition of European powers** led by Britain, combined with a popular uprising, **drove the Egyptians from Syria in 1840,** and the sultan reluctantly granted Muhammad Ali **the hereditary viceroyalty of Egypt** (in a decree issued on June 1, 1841). Muhammad Ali was stripped of all his conquests except the Sudan, and his **army was to be reduced** to 18,000 men.

1834. The introduction of steamboats. The East India Company began to use steamships between Bombay and Suez. In the late 1830s steam tugs were employed for towing barges on **the Nile and the Mahmudiyya Canal** linking Alexandria with the Nile. The use of steamboats **spread rapidly** throughout Egypt.

Prostitution was banned by the government but continued to attract poor women. By the 1860s prostitutes were again being taxed and required to undergo regular medical checkups. Many of them were virtual prisoners of their pimps.

1835. The School of Languages was founded by Muhammad Ali, as part of a **state program of translation.** Numerous European works were translated into Arabic by professionals trained in the school. They had a significant impact on the spread of knowledge, the development of education, and the process of westernization.

1848. IBRAHIM PASHA. In 1847 he took over the administration from his senile father, was formally invested by the sultan in July 1848, but died shortly afterward (Nov. 10, 1848). His real legacy was the four decades of energetic service as **military commander and adviser for Muhammad Ali.**

1848–54. ABBAS HILMI I. This grandson of Muhammad Ali **sought to check the rapid pace of reform** and the growing European influence in the country. This orientation won him **many powerful enemies** in the elite and among the Europeans, who worked successfully to demonize him. **Unsympathetic views of him** as a cruel and perverse reactionary have been perpetuated in historical works, often without adequate grounds. Abbas was **murdered** in July 1854.

1849, Aug. 2. Death of Muhammad Ali.

1850–1914. THE INFLUX OF FOREIGNERS. As a result of business opportunities connected with the cotton boom and state projects, the number of **foreigners, primarily Europeans,** in Egypt increased dramatically from about 3,000 in 1850 to about 90,000 in 1882. By the early 20th century the number had reached about 200,000. Although less than 2 percent of the total population, these foreigners **enjoyed extraterritorial privileges** under the Capitulations (commercial treaties with European powers) and held **disproportionate economic power** in the country, controlling the main financial, commercial, and industrial enterprises. Their influence began to decline rapidly after 1915.

1851–1914. Development of railways. A line connecting Alexandria to Suez, built in 1851–58 with government funding, inaugurated the rapid expansion of railways in Egypt. By 1914 the country had a **railway network of about 4,300 kilometers,** which was carrying the bulk of the internal goods traffic.

1854–63. SA'ID PASHA. This son of Muhammad Ali had a **European education,** wore European dress, and was committed to the rapid modernization of Egypt. His lasting contribution was the construction of the Suez Canal, which was to alter profoundly Egypt's political fortunes.

1855, Jan. Abolition of the poll tax *(jizya)* on non-Muslims.

Promulgation of the **Penal Code,** which was based partly on the Ottoman Penal Code of 1851 and partly on various Egyptian codes adopted between 1830 and 1844. In 1875 Egypt adopted a new criminal code, based on the Ottoman Penal Code of 1858, but it was superseded in 1883 by a new code based on the French penal code.

1858. Arabic began to replace Turkish as the main language of administration.

Aug. 5. PROMULGATION OF THE LAND LAW. The measure gave users of state land *(kharajiyya)* the right to own, sell, and mortgage it. It was a major landmark in the development of property rights, resulting in **the conversion of much of Egypt's land to freehold** by the end of the century. But the **distribution of agricultural land grew increasingly unequal:** in 1913, 12,558 large estates constituted 44 percent of the land, while 1,411,000 small owners held 27 percent of the land. Many peasants owned no land and worked as wage laborers or sharecroppers.

1859. Port Said was founded. By 1914 it had grown into a city of about 50,000.

1862–66. Construction of the modern **port of Suez.**

1863–79. KHEDIVE ISMA'IL. This son of Muhammad Ali's son Ibrahim Pasha has figured among the most **controversial** personalities in modern Egyptian history. His **pursuit of rapid development** has ranked him among the leading modernizers of the period, but his excesses, which **drove Egypt into bankruptcy** and then occupation, have occasioned his condemnation as irresponsible and incompetent. He was the first ruler of the dynasty to use the Persian title of khedive, which he acquired from the Ottoman sultan in June 1867 as a way of elevating his status above that of other Ottoman governors.

1863. Founding of the **Egyptian Museum,** which indicated the advancement of the study of ancient Egypt.

1865. The Red Sea ports of Suakin and Massawa were ceded to Egypt by the Ottomans.

1866, May. Change of the **principle of succession** from seniority to primogeniture. Isma'il obtained this privilege from the Ottoman sultan in return for a substantial increase in the annual tribute. Whereas succession had until then passed to the eldest male in accordance with the Ottoman decree of 1841, **all subsequent rulers were descended from Isma'il.**

Nov. Isma'il established the **Assembly of Delegates** *(Majlis shura al-nuwwab),* a parliamentary body of 75 members that began as a rubber stamp for the khedive but gradually developed a degree of independence.

1869, Nov. 17. OFFICIAL OPENING OF THE SUEZ CANAL. Construction of the waterway began in 1859, following **concessions** granted by the Egyptian government in Nov. 1854 and Jan. 1856 to the **Suez Canal Company** established by the Frenchman **Ferdinand de Lesseps.** Egypt supplied the labor for the project and also bought shares in the company (which it sold to the British government in 1875). The canal soon handled a substantial portion of world shipping and proved **a successful private venture:** by 1920 its profits had paid eight times the original investment. **Britain became its main user** and was prompted to occupy

Egypt in 1882 partly by perceived threats to free passage in the water-way.

1869–79. Expansion in Africa. The Egyptians occupied the **Red Sea coast and Harar,** fought a war with Abyssinia, and penetrated **the Upper Nile region,** bringing the regions of Bahr al-Ghazal and Darfur under tenuous Egyptian control.

1870. The **Khedivial Library** (now the Egyptian National Library, or Dar al-Kutub) was founded in Cairo by Khedive Isma'il.

1872. Opening of the **Dar al-Ulum** teacher's college to train Arabic teachers for the state primary and secondary schools. It played a leading role in the development of Arabic studies in Egypt.

1873. Death of **RIFA'A RAFI' AL-TAHTAWI** (b. 1801), one of the leading writers and educators during the first phase of Egyptian modernization. His writings, translations of European works, and teaching activities introduced generations of Egyptians to **Western ideas** and the notion of **Egyptian patriotism.**

Opening of the **first girls' school** by the khedive's third wife.

June 8. An Ottoman decree consolidated various previous grants of privileges to Isma'il, among them almost unrestricted legislative autonomy, full control over nonpolitical external affairs, and the right to enlarge the Egyptian army. The decree affirmed Ottoman suzerainty over Egypt.

1874. The **Coptic Communal Council** was established by Coptic lay leaders. It took over control of the community's endowed property from the clergy, which steadily lost power to secular communal institutions.

1875. The newspaper *al-Ahram* was founded by Salim Taqla, a Greek Catholic immigrant from Lebanon. It marked the beginning of Egypt's modern independent press and has since become Egypt's **most important daily** by far (with present-day circulation of about 1 million copies).

The **Khedivial Geographical Society** (now the Egyptian Geographical Society) was founded by Khedive Isma'il to conduct and sponsor geographical research. It published important findings in areas such as cartography, irrigation, cotton cultivation, and desert studies.

June 28. Establishment of the **Mixed Courts,** a new judicial system for the adjudication of all legal **cases involving foreign nationals.** Based on agreement between Egypt and the great powers, the courts were staffed by both **Egyptian and foreign judges** and applied new codes taken largely from French law. The Mixed Courts were **abolished** on Oct. 15, 1949.

Nov. The khedive, in financial straits, sold his 176,602 **shares in the Suez Canal Company** to the British government for £4 million.

1876, April. EGYPT'S BANKRUPTCY. Faced with an overwhelming **foreign debt** of £68.5 million (incurred mostly under Isma'il), in addition to a **floating debt** of £23 million, the Egyptian government suspended interest payments. The **Caisse de la Dette,** an international body consisting of representatives of the European powers, was put in charge of the country's finances. The **Law of Liquidation** of 1880 fixed the consolidated debt at £98.4 million, of which about 40 percent was owed to French creditors and about 25 percent to British financiers.

1877. Egypt's **first satirical newspaper,** *Abu Naddara,* was founded in Cairo by **James (Ya'qub) Sanua,** an Alexandrian Jew. Its criticism of Khedive Isma'il led to Sanua's exile to Paris, where he died in 1912. Sanua also organized the **first local popular theater** in Egypt (1869–71).

1879, June 26. Deposition of **Isma'il** by the sultan, under pressure from the European powers. For the first time the dynasty's autonomous rule was severely curtailed.

1879–92. KHEDIVE TAWFIQ. Isma'il's son came to power at a time of **great crisis.** The financial stringency due to the bankruptcy, along with the growing European control of Egyptian affairs, caused **widespread discontent.** The influential Pan-Islamic activist **Jamal al-Din al-Afghani,** who lived in Egypt in 1871–79, found many receptive to his agitated calls for Islamic solidarity and action to defeat corrupt regimes and foreign intrusion. Among liberals there was **criticism of the khedive's autocracy** and calls for constitutional limits on it.

Grievances extended also to **the army,** in which the Egyptian officers resented not only their exclusion from ranks higher than colonel (the preserve of the Turkish and Circassian officers), but also their **loss of jobs** due to budget cuts. It was these officers who in 1881–82 took the lead in a popular movement of protest, known as the **Urabi Revolution,**

that challenged both the khedive and the European powers. **Tawfiq lost control** of the situation and chose to **collaborate with the foreign powers** in the hope of restoring order and maintaining his position. During the British occupation of the country he was returned to the throne, although with very limited powers.

1881–82. THE URABI REVOLUTION. In Jan. 1881 Egyptian officers led by **Col. Ahmad Urabi** (1841–1911) presented demands for improvements in their treatment, and following a **mutiny,** secured concessions from the khedive, including the appointment of Mahmud Sami al-Barudi, an officer sympathetic to their demands, as war minister. When Barudi was dismissed, Urabi organized a huge demonstration outside the khedive's palace (Sept. 9), making **broader political demands:** restoring Barudi, enlarging the army, dismissing the prime minister, and reconvening the Assembly of Delegates. Tawfiq again capitulated, and **Urabi emerged as a national hero** with growing control over the government. On Jan. 8, 1882, Britain and France issued a joint note threatening to intervene on behalf of the khedive, but it only emboldened the Urabists. **Urabi became war minister** in a new cabinet headed by Barudi (Feb. 1882), and the two vowed to resist the Europeans. The **popular fervor** they stirred for the defense of Egypt and Islam led to violent **anti-European riots in Alexandria** on June 11 and to a summer of mounting tensions ending in British intervention and the collapse of Urabi's movement.

Urabi's movement is regarded as the **first Egyptian nationalist movement,** although its membership was too diffuse and limited to make it a truly mass phenomenon. It was largely a **movement of social protest** in which **religious sentiments** concerned with defending Islam against injustice and the infidel played a large role alongside genuinely nationalist ideas. Urabi and his associates made remarkable gains at the expense of the khedive, but they **misjudged the determination of the Europeans,** especially the British, to safeguard their interests: the security of the Suez Canal, the repayment of the Egyptian debts, and the safety of the European residents. A more coherent nationalist movement emerged during the occupation and found expression in the 1919 Revolution.

1882, Sept. THE BRITISH OCCUPATION. British troops landed in Egypt in Aug., and on Sept. 13 they **routed Urabi's army** at Tel-el-Kebir and proceeded to occupy Cairo. Urabi surrendered and was exiled to Ceylon, while Khedive Tawfiq, who had put himself under the protection of British troops in July, was restored.

Although intended initially to be short-lived, the British **occupation lasted 72 years.** Until 1914 British control over the country was exercised through **command of the army** and the appointment of **British advisers** in Egyptian ministries. The British consul general exercised a dominant position as de facto governor of the country.

1882–1914. Development of agriculture. The **cultivatable area grew** from 4.8 million to 5.7 million feddans (1 feddan is equal to 1.038 acres). Investment in new dams and barrages, the development of roads and light railways, and the general security **increased agricultural production,** although the doubling of the population during the period (from 6 million to 12 million) made Egypt a net importer of food after 1900. There was little development of modern industry, and agriculture remained the mainstay of the economy.

Limited public investment in education. In 1914 Egypt had 739 private schools, 328 private foreign schools, but only 68 government-supported primary and secondary schools. Government expenditure on education amounted to **only 1 percent of the budget,** leading Egyptians to charge the British with the willful **neglect of Egyptian education.**

Decline of the guild system. The trade and craft guilds into which most of the urban workforce was traditionally organized slipped steadily. By **a series of decrees** beginning in 1881, the government took over their administrative and fiscal functions and abolished their economic monopolies. This, together with the **massive influx of European imports and businessmen,** destroyed most of the guilds by 1914.

1883–1907. Sir Evelyn Baring (later Lord Cromer) served as consul general. An able administrator, he guided the **reform** of Egypt's finances and the development of public works and agriculture. But his **autocratic ways** alienated the khedives and the spokesmen of Egyptian opinion.

1885. Overthrow of Egyptian rule in the Sudan. The forces of the Sudanese Mahdi Muhammad Ahmad, who began his revolt in 1881, defeated an Egyptian expeditionary force under William Hicks in Nov. 1883, and in Jan. 1885 took Khartum after killing the governor-general Charles Gordon and his garrison.

1885–89. FINAL ABOLITION OF FORCED LABOR (the *corvée*). The long-standing official practice of recruiting thousands of peasants annually to work (with pay) on government projects, often far from their homes, had been a source of dislocation for families and much social unrest.

1888, Oct. 29. The **convention on the Suez Canal** was signed by the Ottoman Empire, Britain, and several other European countries. It declared that the **canal should be free and open** to the merchant and war vessels of all powers in time of war as in time of peace. Because of **British reservations** the provision did not become operative until after the British-French entente of 1904. It continued in force until 1956.

1890, Jan. 5. Establishment of the municipality of **Alexandria, the first municipal government in Egypt.** Municipal councils were created subsequently in many towns, but most of their members were government appointees or officials, and their powers remained limited.

1892–1914. ABBAS HILMI II. Tawfiq's son resented **British control,** but his early attempts to resist Cromer and assert himself were so sternly rebuffed that he made no further open attack on Cromer. He turned instead to seeking the support of Istanbul, Europe, and Egyptian nationalists in his persistent opposition to British rule.

1893. Death of **Ali Pasha Mubarak** (b. 1824), a reform-minded administrator who worked to modernize Egypt's educational system as well as its public works. His monumental topographical encyclopedia of Egypt, *al-Khitat al-tawfiqiyya al-jadida,* is a treasury of information.

1895, Nov. 21. The Anglo-Egyptian **Convention for the Suppression of Slavery and the Slave Trade** was signed in Cairo. This measure, along with the growth in the Egyptian free labor force and increasing opposition to slavery among the educated elite, brought an **end to slavery by 1914.**

1896–98. Reconquest of the Sudan was undertaken on **British initiative** primarily to forestall French designs. The mahdist state was destroyed and a **new administration** set up, controlled and staffed at the higher levels by British officials. Although the **Anglo-Egyptian condominium agreement** (Jan. 19, 1899) provided for a joint government, Egypt actually had no real voice in the affairs of the Sudan.

1899. Qasim Amin (1865–1908), considered the **father of feminism** in Egypt, published his book *The Liberation of the Woman,* which called for women's education and their right to work. The work aroused **sharp criticism** from conservatives, leading Amin to challenge traditional views more forcefully in a second book, *The New Woman* (1900).

1902. Opening of the **Aswan Dam** in Upper Egypt, which made it possible to hold up a substantial portion of the Nile's autumn flood and convert much land from basin to perennial irrigation. The dam and a **barrage at Asyut,** also completed in 1902, permitted the **extension of cotton cultivation** to Middle and Upper Egypt.

1903. A **stock exchange** was established in Cairo, following a decade of unprecedented upsurge in investment, primarily in companies involved in business connected with agricultural land and urban real estate.

1904. Beginning of **commercial recording.** The industry, which was dominated initially by foreign companies, soon produced hundreds of recordings by local musicians that sold in Egypt and the surrounding regions.

April 8. Anglo-French entente cordiale. After years of opposition France recognized the special position of Britain in Egypt.

1905. Death of **MUHAMMAD ABDUH** (b. 1849), the leading figure in the modern **Islamic reform movement.** He rose to become the Grand Mufti of Egypt, and in his legal rulings as well as his books, he advocated the reform of Islam to adapt it to modern requirements. His ideas have had an **immense influence** on Islamic thought in the 20th century.

1906, June 13. The **Dinshaway Incident.** A British officer died following a scuffle with Egyptian villagers in a trivial dispute over pigeon shooting. The British imposed heavy punitive sentences on the villagers, including public executions, which stirred widespread indignation and **nationalist feelings** in the country.

1907–11. Sir Eldon Gorst served as British consul general, replacing Cromer. He followed a **more conciliatory policy** of cultivating good relations with the khedive, increasing the Egyptian share in the administration, and putting life into the Egyptian consultative bodies set up shortly after the occupation. He was partially successful, although nationalist opposition to the British was not checked.

1907. Formation of political parties. Mustafa Kamil (1874–1908), a French-educated lawyer, charismatic speaker, and editor of the newspaper *al-Liwa'* (founded 1900), established the **Nationalist Party** (*al-Hizb al-Watani*), which represented uncompromising hostility to British rule. The party declined after his premature death. **A more moderate group** of nationalists founded the newspaper *al-Jarida* and a rival party, *Hizb al-Umma,* which was oriented toward cooperation with Britain to develop constitutional government and Egyptian self-rule. **Sheik Ali Yusuf,** who in 1889 founded the popular journal *al-Mu'ayyad,* established the **Constitutional Reform Party,** which supported the interests of the khedive. The party did not survive his death in 1913.

1908. Establishment of the **first Egyptian university,** financed by voluntary contributions. It was taken over by the state and became King Fu'ad University in 1925.

1910, Feb. 20. Assassination of the Coptic prime minister **Butrus Ghali** by a young Muslim nationalist. One of its repercussions was a new **Coptic mistrust** of the Muslim Egyptian nationalists. A **Coptic Congress** met in Asyut in 1911 to voice specifically Coptic political demands, which were rejected by a rival **Muslim Congress** convened in Heliopolis that year.

1911–14. Lord Kitchener served as consul general, following Gorst's death. He abandoned the policy of conciliation with the khedive and restored strong **autocratic** methods of rule.

1913. Creation of the **new Legislative Assembly,** with wider powers than previous parliamentary bodies. It was dominated by large landowners, but from its members emerged the leaders of the 1919 Revolution, including **Sa'd Zaghlul.**

1914. Death of **Jurji Zaydan** (b. 1861), a Lebanese Christian emigrant who wrote historical novels and biographies and became a **pioneering figure in Egyptian journalism.** His periodical *al-Hilal,* founded in 1892, introduced the popular presentation of topics in different fields of knowledge and gained wide appeal.

Dec. 19. Deposition of Khedive Abbas II (while on a visit to Istanbul) by the British, a day after their declaration of a **protectorate over Egypt.** Abbas was succeeded by his uncle, **Husayn Kamil** (d. 1917), who took the **title of sultan** to signal the end of Ottoman suzerainty over Egypt.
(To p. 757)

3. NORTH AFRICA, 1792–1914

a. MOROCCO

(From p. 366)

1792–1822. MAWLAY SULAYMAN. The Moroccan ruler inherited a decentralized state with a population of 3 million to 4 million inhabitants. Four years of **civil war** with his brothers and a number of **local rebellions** weakened his control, as did the shortage of government funds. During the last decade of his rule he became openly hostile to maraboutism, or **Muslim saint worship,** arguing that the practice deviated from the true faith. By his attack on popular religious practices he sought to curb the growing power of Sufi orders in the country.

1801, June 14. Treaty of peace and commerce with Britain. It built on the progressive development of relations between the two countries during the 18th century, when Britain came to rely on Morocco for food supplies for its troops in Gibraltar in exchange for British arms. The British obtained capitulatory rights, immunity from all taxes, and full jurisdiction for their consuls in legal cases involving their nationals.

1802–4. Berber revolts in various regions. The government launched campaigns to assert its authority over the largely **autonomous tribal territories.** A major revolt of Berber tribes broke out in the Middle Atlas in 1811, continuing until 1820.

1815. Death of **Ahmad al-Tijani,** founder of the **Tijaniyya** Sufi order. He arrived from Algeria in 1789 and was welcomed by Mawlay Sulayman. He lived in luxury and promised his followers both wealth in this world and salvation in the next. His order won many adherents and spread throughout North Africa.

1818. European pressure contributed to the definite **ending of Moroccan piracy.**

1820–22. REBELLION IN FEZ. Various groups, including the ulama, called for an end to Mawlay Sulayman's rule and were joined by the Wazzani Berbers. Sulayman died before completely crushing the uprising.

1822–59. MAWLAY ABD AL-RAHMAN. At the time of his accession the state was an unstable, fragmented collection of cities and tribes. The **army,** badly provisioned and organized, consisted of a few slave contingents and tribal troops who were paid only when they fought. The **administrative machinery** was minimal, and the ruler's income was limited to what he could collect in the lands subject to government authority. The Middle and High Atlas, the Rif, and the southern oases remained largely under **local tribal control.**

1823. Death of **al-Arabi al-Darqawi** (b. 1760), founder of the **Darqawiyya** Sufi order. The movement, which became one of the leading orders in Morocco, exalted poverty and stressed asceticism. It **won widespread support** among the rural inhabitants and the urban lower classes; its popularity was increased by its use of musical instruments in its rituals. In both Algeria and Morocco the Darqawiyya became **involved in political activities** and protest movements.

c. 1830. Beginning of **penetration of European goods** into the Moroccan market. Cheaper European cloth as well as leather products, pottery, candles, tea, and sugar were imported in growing amounts during the 19th century. Some local craftsmen were put out of business, and the country became increasingly dependent on foreign goods.

1830–32. Moroccan troops entered western **Algeria** in the wake of the French invasion (p. 547), looting Tlemcen before returning in 1832 under French military threat. Morocco also gave aid to the Algerian rebel leader Abd al-Qadir, a policy that strained French-Moroccan relations.

1833. Death of **Ahmad al-Zayyani,** Berber statesman and historian. He undertook diplomatic missions to the Ottoman court and engineered government attempts to bring tribes under central authority. His writings include several historical accounts of the Ottoman and Alawi dynasties.

1844. Establishment of the **Pariente Bank** in Tangier, Morocco's **first private business bank.** Various foreign banks opened branches in Morocco in subsequent years, although much of the country's international banking activity was carried out through Gibraltar.

1844. Brief war with France. In an attempt to bring an end to Moroccan support for the Algerian rebel leader Abd al-Qadir, who found asylum in Morocco in 1843, a French squadron bombarded Tangier (Aug. 6) and Mogador (Aug. 15) while French ground troops defeated the Moroccan army at Isly (Aug. 14). In the **convention of Tangier** (Sept. 14) the sultan pledged to outlaw Abd al-Qadir.

1845, March 18. Treaty with France delimiting the **Moroccan-Algerian boundary.** The frontier remained ill-defined, serving later French policies of expansion into Morocco.

1856, Dec. 9. Treaty and commercial convention with Britain. The agreement, which took four years to negotiate, removed **Moroccan trade monopolies** and restrictions opposed by British merchants, and regulated various aspects of British-Moroccan relations.

1859–73. MAWLAY MUHAMMAD IV. Under his rule central authority remained weak despite limited attempts to modernize the army, administration, and economy. **Tribal defiance** continued to pose a challenge to the state, and **European economic penetration** increased.

1859–60. WAR WITH SPAIN. As part of its policy of expansion in Morocco, Spain sent a large force to its outpost in Ceuta, from which it advanced all the way to **Tetuán.** The town fell on Feb. 5, 1860, and remained in Spanish hands for two years. Mawlay Muhammad agreed to pay a **large indemnity** and signed a peace treaty that allowed Spain to expand around Melilla and thus add to its territories at Ceuta and Peñon de Velez.

1862. Foundation of a **school for Jewish boys in Tetuán** by the Alliance Israélite Universelle (founded in Paris in 1860). This Alliance school, the first in North Africa and the Middle East, became the model for similar schools in Tangier (1864), Mogador (1863 and 1868), and Safi (1867). The schools' curriculum combined **religious and modern instruction** in French and Hebrew as well as Arabic, helping the Jewish population (about 100,000) to develop cadres of **westernized leaders.**

1863, Aug. 19. Agreement with France regarding the status of **Moroccan subjects under French protection.** These protégés, who worked in the employ of French diplomats and merchants, escaped taxation, military service, and the local justice system. The agreement, to which other powers later adhered, **formalized the protégé system** for the first time and ended up stimulating rather than checking the growth of foreign protection in the country. An **international convention drawn in Madrid** (July 3, 1880) dealt with the system of native protection and gave a host of European states a voice in the issue. The internationalizing of the problem later complicated the expansionist efforts of France and Spain in Morocco.

1865, June 16. Publication of the **first book printed in Morocco,** under the auspices of the royal press. The **press,** as well as skilled technicians, were imported from the Ottoman Empire. The press became part of the Qarawiyyin religious college and issued mostly religious texts for use in the school.

1873–94. MAWLAY AL-HASAN I. An able ruler, al-Hasan attempted to reform the army. He imposed a fixed levy of recruits on major cities and formed new regiments trained by European instructors.

1881. Currency reform. Mawlay al-Hasan struck **new silver coins** in an attempt to standardize the currency in circulation and halt the continuous depreciation of the coinage. European merchants smuggled the new coins out, draining the country of silver and destabilizing its monetary system. By 1900, Moroccan currency had **depreciated** on the international market by some 140 percent.

1892–93. Second war with Spain. The Moroccan army was defeated at Melilla, and the ruler was forced to pay an indemnity.

1894–1908. MAWLAY ABD AL-AZIZ. He took the throne at the age of 14, and until 1898 the country was effectively ruled by the **chief minister Ahmad ibn Musa.** The ruler relied heavily on **European banks and advisers.** His attempt to institute a single tax (the *tartib*) upon all his subjects, including previously exempt groups, provoked massive opposition and was abandoned.

1897. Death of **Ahmad al-Nasiri** (b. 1835), a prominent scholar and member of the family that founded the Nasiriyya Sufi order in the 17th century. He wrote an important multivolume history of Morocco.

1900–1. French occupation of **Salah and Touat,** two oases that were incorporated into Algeria.

1903–8. Revolt of Abu Himara (Jilali al-Zarhumi), who falsely claimed to be the ruler's missing elder brother Muhammad. He defeated the ruler's troops several times and controlled eastern Morocco until 1908, when he was captured.

1904, April 8. A **French-British agreement,** partly secret, provided the French with a free hand in **Morocco** in exchange for French recognition of British colonial primacy in **Egypt.**

    Oct. 3. Secret convention on Morocco between France and Spain. It divided Morocco into **two spheres of influence** and prepared the ground for their future protectorates. The two powers signed another **secret agreement** on Sept. 1, 1905, setting out joint plans for their management of Moroccan affairs.

1906, April 7. General act issued by the **international conference of Algeciras** (Spain) (p. 477). Thirteen powers participated in the deliberations on the Moroccan question, and despite strong German objections, agreed to entrust to France and Spain the **management of the Moroccan police.** The powers also made arrangements regarding Morocco's state bank, system of taxation, customs administration, and public works.

1907. French occupation of **Casablanca and Oujda,** which was followed by a creeping penetration into the hinterland of both.

1907–8. Rebellion against Mawlay Abd al-Aziz, provoked by his acquiescence in French encroachment on Morocco. The rebels, based mostly in Marrakesh, proclaimed **Abd al-Hafiz,** an older half-brother of the reigning monarch, as the new ruler. Abd al-Aziz failed to rally popular support and **abdicated** in the summer of 1908.

1908–12. MAWLAY ABD AL-HAFIZ. The last ruler of an independent

Morocco, Abd al-Hafiz attempted to repeal the **privileges of foreigners** and ordered the expulsion of French forces. His efforts to bring the Berber tribes under his control resulted in **revolts** throughout the country and increased **violence against Europeans,** providing the French with the pretext for their final occupation of Morocco.

1908, Sept. Battle of Bou Denib, in which French forces defeated Moroccan tribes and occupied the region along the frontier with Algeria.

1909. Muhammad al-Kattani, a member of the ulama of Fez and a Sufi leader, was put to death by order of the ruler for leading a campaign against French encroachment and local passivity.

1911. Completion of a **railway** link between Casablanca and Rabat. During the protectorate the French added about 1,600 kilometers of railway track.

May. French troops entered Fez to provide support for Abd al-Hafiz against a tribal revolt.

Nov. 4. French-German convention on Morocco (p. 478). It settled the crisis provoked by the dispatch of a German warship to the Moroccan port of **Agadir** in July to force the withdrawal of the French military expedition to Fez. Germany finally recognized **French primacy in Morocco** in return for territory in the Congo.

1912, March 30. ESTABLISHMENT OF THE FRENCH PROTECTORATE. A special convention signed by Abd al-Hafiz placed the southern two-thirds of Morocco under **French protection.** A separate Franco-Spanish agreement (Nov. 27) formalized the **Spanish protectorate** over the northern part of the country. The Moroccan ruler retained the appearances of power, but the country's dealings with other countries were transacted through the French government, with the **French resident general** exercising local authority.

The protectorate met with **vigorous resistance** encouraged by Mawlay Abd al-Hafiz. The French resident general, Gen. Lyautey, deposed the ruler and replaced him with his more amenable brother **Mawlay Yusuf** (1912–27). But it was not until 1934 that the last pockets of resistance in the High Atlas were finally suppressed.

Sept. The French defeated the forces of the Mauritanian leader **Ahmad al-Hiba,** who launched a holy war against the French occupation of Morocco.

1914, Sept. 11. A decree *(dahir)* recognized the village councils *(jama'as)* in **Berber areas** as governing councils and Berber customary practices as a system of law. The act was part of a French policy of **cultivating Berber support** by leaving the Berber chiefs and tribes with considerable autonomy. *(To p. 767)*

b. ALGERIA

(From p. 367)

1803–8. Rebellion against the Ottomans in Oran and Kabylia was led by Abd al-Qadir ibn al-Sharif, head *(muqaddam)* of the **Darqawiyya Sufi order.** The founder of the order, al-Arabi al-Darqawi (d. 1823), condemned the uprising. He had stressed asceticism, but the Darqawiyya continued to be linked with religious political movements and became one of the most important Sufi groups in Algeria. The revolt was crushed by the Ottomans, and its leader fled to Morocco.

1807–12. Conflict between Algeria and Tunisia. The Tunisian ruler Hamuda Bey (1782–1814) besieged the Algerian city of **Constantine,** but was unsuccessful. Tunisia ceased to pay tribute to Algeria, and peace was finally agreed upon, with Ottoman mediation, in 1821.

1810–15. Kabyle Berber tribal uprising in Oran was prompted by the taxation demanded by the Turks. The revolt was renewed for similar reasons in 1824.

1811. Decline of privateering. No slaves, potential sources of ransom and labor, were captured in 1811. Only four European ships had been captured in 1801 and one in 1803. After the 1818 Aix-la-Chapelle Congress on the suppression of piracy, the pressure on Algiers had its effects, bringing an end to corsair threats. The loss of revenue meant **increased taxes** for the local population and resulted in a series of uprisings throughout the country, many of which were organized by Sufi brotherhoods.

1812–15. Conflict with the United States. Dey Hajji Ali Pasha (r. 1809–15) declared war on the United States when, in July 1812, the country could not pay its annual tribute. On March 3, 1815, the United States

authorized naval operations against Algiers and captured two of its ships at sea. The Americans dictated the terms of the treaty when they arrived at Algiers and found the city without its fleet (June 30, 1815). On Dec. 22, 1816, the United States signed **a treaty of peace** that confirmed that of the previous year, but added two additional provisions for the immediate release of American prisoners and the end of all tribute previously paid to Algiers. The agreement put an **end to the Barbary Wars,** the assault on U.S. shipping in the Mediterranean that had begun in 1801.

1816, Aug. 27. The British and Dutch naval **bombardment of Algiers** destroyed 33 ships in the harbor and resulted in negotiations for a treaty, signed on Sept. 24, 1816, which released all Christian prisoners and temporarily abolished the slavery of pirate captives.

1818–30. Husayn Dey. The last ruler of Algiers managed to maintain calm in his capital but ruled during a time of relentless rural unrest. He had a series of catastrophic **conflicts with European representatives,** and his expulsion of the British consul led to the **bombardment of Algiers** in 1824.

1820. Tijaniyya Sufi uprising in Oran against the Turkish bey. Opposition, prompted by increased taxation and government encroachment on local autonomy, continued sporadically until 1828. The order had been founded in Algeria in 1782 by Ahmad al-Tijani (d. 1815).

1827, April 29. The fly-whisk incident. Negotiations dragged on over the French grain debt to Algeria incurred by Napoleon (1793–8). In heated discussion, the French consul was struck by Husayn Dey with a fly swatter. The French began a **naval blockade** in June and utilized the incident as provocation for the eventual occupation of Algiers.

1830, July 5. FRENCH OCCUPATION OF ALGIERS. Algiers was captured by a French force of 37,000 troops, and the last dey capitulated. The invasion put an **end to the rule of the deys** of Algeria who had reigned as virtually autonomous representatives of the Ottoman Empire since 1711. The French established a **governor-general** as head of their administration in July 1834. Subjugation of the interior continued until 1890. The French occupation lasted until 1962.

c. 1830. Three *madrasa*s (Islamic religious colleges) existed at the time of the French invasion. They were located in the cities of Algiers, Constantine, and Tlemcen. Under colonial rule they continued to train students but were carefully controlled by French authorities.

1831–47. Revolt of Abd al-Qadir (d. 1883), the son of a Sufi leader, whose uprising was the most sustained and threatening to the French occupation. Abd al-Qadir tapped religious and tribal sentiments to enlist a **highly mobile army** of 10,000. He also benefited from a decade of **support from the sultan of Morocco** (1833–44). In 1833 he captured Tlemcen and the next year signed the **Desmichels Treaty** with France (Feb. 26, 1834), which gave him control over most of the Province of Oran. Armed conflict began again in 1835, when he defeated the French at the Battle of the Macta River (June 28, 1835). The resulting **Treaty of Tafna** (May 30, 1837) ceded Abd al-Qadir control of almost two-thirds of Algeria, but the treaty was broken in 1839. With the loss of Moroccan support (1844) due to French pressure, **the rebellion crumbled,** and Abd al-Qadir surrendered in 1847. He was imprisoned for five years and finally settled in Damascus.

1833. Death of Ibn Mustafa Muhyi al-Din, the father of Abd al-Qadir. He had initiated the holy war against the French by leading attacks on Oran. Ibn Mustafa was an influential *marabout* (holy man), who was head of the Qadiriyya Sufi order in Algeria. He had developed good contacts with the Moroccans, and his influence was critical in the election of his son as a leader of the resistance to the French.

1837, Oct. 13. Ahmad Bey, the last Turkish provincial governor of Constantine, surrendered to the French after an unsuccessful appeal for help to the Ottoman sultan.

1838. The **Tijaniyya Sufi** order resisted Abd al-Qadir's siege of Ayn Madi, the center of their order. They refused to recognize him and by 1839 had made an **alliance with the French.** The Tijaniyya worked actively with the French to recruit other Muslims to acquiesce to their rule.

1841. Reinstitution of the French *bureau arabe,* first organized in 1839 to deal with Muslim affairs in Algeria. French officials who specialized in Algerian issues and culture attempted to govern and to instruct the French government. Members of the bureau initially saw their mission as one of **civilizing the Muslim population.**

1844, Oct. 1. *Habus* land, land left in trust for Islamic charitable or inheritance purposes, was **confiscated** and placed under the control of the French land department. These Muslim trusts were then **made available to French settlers.**

1845–46. The **Tayyibiyya Sufi** order, established at Oran at the beginning of the 18th century, incited the **rebellion** of mountain tribes of Titteri and Hodna by announcing the return of the *mahdi*, the "savior or redeemer" believed by Muslims to usher in the reign of peace and justice.

1846, July 21. Fertile **tribal collective lands,** defined by the French as vacant, were **confiscated** and made available to colonists as part of their *cantonnement* program, which was designed to confine indigenous peoples to specified areas.

1848. Algeria was annexed to France and colonization increased. French colonization introduced new **cash crops** including cotton, roses, tobacco, and grapes for wine production (1878–1903). The most reliable of all colonial agricultural products remained grain.

1848–49. Tax revolt led by the notable Abu Ziyan in the oasis of Za'atsha in the region of Ziban. The siege by the French lasted 52 days and ended in the **massacre** of all the inhabitants. It sparked further uprisings (1851–55) in other oases.

1851, Aug. The **Bank of Algeria** was founded by the French. In April 1852 a **commodities exchange** was also established.

1857. The **first railway system** was constructed.

1857–67. The first **Franco-Arab colleges,** secondary schools for Muslim students of the urban upper classes, were founded in Algiers, Constantine, and Oran. A **teacher training college** opened in 1865, with ten Muslim student teachers in attendance, and a **school of arts** and crafts was opened in Kabylia in 1867. These French innovations did not undo the damage caused by the closure of 2,000 **Islamic primary schools** during the uprisings.

1857–71. The French pacified the Province of Kabylia, home to the Berber Kabyle tribe.

1864–83. The **revolt of the Awlad Sidi Shaykh** of the Oran Province engulfed much of southwestern and south central Algeria. A confederation of tribes organized around *marabouts* rebelled, helped by spies attached to local tribes, who kept track of French officials and supplies and indicated the right times for revolts.

1865, July 14. The **French Sénatus Consulte** allowed Algerians to obtain **citizenship** if they agreed to accept French civil law. Muslims would no longer be governed by Islamic law in matters of marriage, divorce, and inheritance. The latter was particularly important to the French, who hoped to attain legal rights over the lands of new Muslim citizens. The stratagem **failed,** and by 1906 only 1,362 Muslims had received French citizenship.

1866. Death of **Mustafa ibn Azuz,** rebel and leader of the Rahmaniyya Sufi order, who directed **insurrections** in eastern Algeria from his base in Tunisia. His center at the Nafta oasis became a center for Algerian refugees, illegal arms, and propaganda. Due in part to the example of Ibn Azuz, who was known as the Saint of Nafta, the Rahmaniyya order, founded at the end of the 18th century by a Kabyle Berber, attained the largest membership in eastern Algeria.

1867–68. Famine resulted after locusts and animal epidemics hit the interior of the country. With the French export of grain, Algeria no longer had its customary reserves, and at least 300,000 died of hunger and the attendant **epidemics of typhus and cholera.**

1870, Oct. 24. The **Crémieux Decree** granted **Algerian Jews,** who numbered about 40,000, French citizenship. This privilege separated them from the Muslims, who began to associate the Jews with colonists. The Europeans refused to accept the decree in practice, and much of the Jewish population left for France.

1871, March 14. A **Kabyle rebellion** was launched by **Muhammad al-Muqrani** in response to French imposition of rule over previously autonomous tribal areas. Al-Muqrani found 25,000 troops and 100,000 followers. On April 8 the leader of the Rahmaniyya Sufi order, **Sheik al-Haddad,** joined the Kabyle rebellion as a holy war against the French. He mustered 120,000 troops and spread the revolt to the eastern Sahara. Al-Haddad and his Sufi followers were forced to surrender in June 1871. Al-Muqrani was killed and his **uprising suppressed** in Jan. 1872. Eleven million acres of land were seized by the French in retribution to provide additional land for colonists.

1873. The **Warnier Law** promulgated by the French government provided a means for the **dispossession of privately owned Muslim land**

(mulk). Arabs lost their most fertile coastal lands to colonists in a process that continued until 1890.

1881. The native code *(code de l'indigénat)* was promulgated. It imposed a series of **discriminatory laws** upon Algerians, who could be held, charged, and imprisoned without a trial. Algerians could be placed under surveillance and were not allowed to travel in the country without a permit. These laws were enforced until 1927.

1886, Sept. 10. A decree by the French government attempted to obliterate the authority of the **Islamic legal system** by decreeing that in matters of property or criminal proceedings, Algerians were subject to the French legal system.

1896, Dec. 31. The governor-general of Algeria was ceded control of ministries previously located in Paris, and French colonial control was localized in North Africa.

1898, Jan. Anti-Jewish riots by colonists resentful of Jewish commercial success resulted in destruction and looting in urban centers. A number of European anti-Jewish organizations had been established by 1895.

c. 1903. Foundation of the Young Algerians, a group of Muslims exposed to French culture *(evolués)* who promoted a program of assimilation.

1905. French education law introduced. It allowed for minimal religious instruction in either local Qur'anic primary schools or at Sufi lodges. The number of Islamic instructors fell at all levels, and knowledge of classical Arabic declined.

1907. Death of **Si Muhand,** a poet of the Berber tribe of Kabyle. Most of his works were oral, but were later collected and published in French translation.

1912. The reform platform of the **Young Algerians** called for the abolition of the native code, equity in matters of taxation, and automatic French citizenship for conscripts with honorable discharges. The Young Algerians believed that if Muslims were forced to serve in the French army, they would gain increased political rights. Their strategy proved flawed.

1913. Publication of *al-Faruq,* the first weekly Arabic-language journal in Algiers. It advocated Islamic reform in matters of education and economy.

The French Parliament ended restrictions imposed on **Islamic religious celebration,** pilgrimage, and education. Students continued to pursue traditional **Islamic studies** at the advanced level at colleges in Fez, Tunis, and Cairo.

1914. The **European population** in Algeria reached 700,000, with much of the growth occurring from the 1880s, when land became increasingly available to settlers. More than half of these Europeans were **born in Algeria** and formed a group (calling itself the *pieds noirs*) with a conservative and racist outlook. The **Muslim population** numbered about 4.7 million, of whom only 8 percent lived in urban centers. The Muslim and settler communities were **highly polarized,** with great differences in opportunities and circumstances making a meaningful fusion of the two impossible. *(To p. 767)*

c. TUNISIA

(From p. 367)

1800. At the turn of the century Tunisia was ruled by the **Husaynid dynasty,** supported by a Turkish military caste. The estimated population of the country was no more than 1 million, two-thirds of whom were sedentary and the rest tribal nomads. The economy, although largely agrarian, still derived two-fifths of its **income from corsair raiding** activity.

1807–12. War with Algeria. In an effort to end his country's payment of tribute to Algeria, the Tunisian ruler Hamuda Bey (r.1782–1814) besieged Constantine in 1807, but was driven out. After several unsuccessful Algerian counterattacks (1807–12) a peace treaty brokered by the Ottomans was signed in 1821.

1811, Sept. Revolt of the Turkish army contingent (jund). Hamuda Bey used this opportunity to lessen his military dependence on Anatolian recruits and began to draw on members of the Zwawa Berber tribe. The Turkish troops revolted again in 1816 and 1829, forcing rulers to continue attempts to reorganize the composition of the military.

1814–24. MAHMUD BEY. He came to power after assassinating his cousin Uthman Bey and ending his short and ineffective rule (Sept.–Nov. 1814). Together with the chief minister Muhammad ibn Zarruq (d. 1822), Mahmud Bey launched a policy of **increased taxation** that had a negative effect on agricultural production.

1818–20. Bubonic plague, which reduced the population by an estimated one-quarter. Short outbreaks of the disease were almost yearly occurrences throughout North Africa before 1818, but the 1818–20 epidemic was especially severe. There were no further serious instances of the plague after 1822.

1819. Mahmud Bey designated **olive oil a taxable state monopoly.** It was sold to the government at fixed prices and then resold for profit to European exporters.

Sept. 21. Anglo-French naval demonstration. A squadron was sent to notify Mahmud Bey of the European protocol adopted at Aix-la-Chapelle in 1818 demanding the **end of piracy.** Mahmud Bey was forced to agree in writing that he would cease to support corsair activity.

1824–35. HUSAYN BEY II. Economic policy during his reign placed Tunisia in debt to European countries. He maintained neutrality during France's invasion of Algeria (July 1830).

1830, Aug. 17. Commercial treaty with France. The agreement granted France most-favored-nation status and ended the state monopoly on agricultural exports. **Tunisian trade was reoriented toward Europe** and away from Islamic lands, a shift that resulted in a marked decline in the local economy.

1831. Reorganization of the military. Husayn Bey created a small standing army based on the Ottoman precedent of the *Nizam-i Jedid* (New Order), in the first attempt to create a modern army with European technical assistance. Army leadership remained in the hands of Turkish officers.

Jan. A military expedition to Oran to install Husaynid control over the Province of Constantine failed.

1835–37. MUSTAFA BEY. He attempted to maintain ties to Istanbul. While refusing to pay tribute to the Ottomans, he sent troops during their reoccupation of Libya (May 1835) and was ready to recognize Ottoman sovereignty before being dissuaded by his son and heir, Ahmad.

1837. A government **attempt to impose military conscription** in Tunis was abandoned following civil unrest.

1837–55. AHMAD I (AHMAD BEY). The most active and innovative ruler of the 19th century, Ahmad Bey attempted to strengthen Tunisian society against European encroachment through **a series of reforms** often modeled on French precedent. His programs relied on good relations with the ulama and tribal chiefs, who were offered various appointments and gifts. He increased Tunisian participation in high government office, but his military reforms necessitated a new tax on agriculture and state monopolies on tobacco, salt, and leather.

1837–47. Beginning of the modernization of the army. Ahmad Bey's ambitious plans involved the creation of *nizami* (modern) cavalry and artillery regiments garbed in European-style uniforms. He hired French army officers to oversee the training of the troops.

By 1847, 16,000 men were in uniform. The expense of this undertaking forced Ahmad Bey to radically reduce troop strength in 1853 to avoid bankruptcy.

1838. Textile mill founded at Tebourba, as part of Ahmad Bey's attempt to start a series of industries to supply his new army. The water-powered mill opened in 1844, with Tunisian workers instructed by French foremen, but **ultimately it failed.**

1840, March. Establishment of the Bardo Military School. Designed to prepare graduates for employment in the army and administration, the school provided six to nine years of modern training directed by European officers. The school was closed during the reign of Muhammad al-Sadiq (1859–82) for lack of funding.

1841–46. Abolition of slavery. Under pressure from Europe, Ahmad Bey closed the slave market in Tunis (1841), declared all the children of slaves to be free (1842), and finally announced the liberation of all slaves (1846).

1843–44. War scare with Sardinia, caused by a dispute about the delivery of Tunisian grain exports halted during the failed harvest of 1843. The bey was forced to come to terms with Sardinia rather than risk war and an international incident involving Britain, France, and the Ottoman Empire.

1846, Nov.–Dec. State visit of Ahmad Bey to France. Ahmad Bey hoped the trip might gain French support for him at a time when the Ottomans threatened to reincorporate Tunisia into their empire. French civilization deeply impressed him and **spurred his attempts at modernization.**

1847, July. Creation of a state bank in an effort to establish control over money and foreign trade. The bey granted his prominent but corrupt adviser **Mahmud ibn Ayad** the right to issue paper money and the concession to mint silver coins. Ibn Ayad used the opportunity for self-aggrandizement and in 1852 fled to France after driving the state to near bankruptcy. **The bank defaulted** in May 1853.

1849. Death of **Ibrahim al-Riyahi,** a member of the ulama and a poet. He served as head of the Zaytuna mosque and chief jurisconsult *(mufti),* and undertook diplomatic missions to Morocco (1803) and the Ottoman sultan (1838) for the beys. He was pivotal in popularizing the new **Tijaniyya Sufi order** in Tunis. The order, founded by Ahmad al-Tijani (d. 1815) in Fez, gained many followers among government officials and became known for its support of the ruling establishment, even during the French occupation.

c. 1850. The guild that produced the *shashiyya* (fez) was ruined when cheaper copies made in Marseilles undercut markets in the Ottoman Empire. The demise of the prestigious guild reflected the hazards of Tunisia's integration into the European commercial sphere.

1855–59. MUHAMMAD BEY. He sought to assert autocratic control and eschewed the help of local Tunisian authorities at a time when the powers of his office were compromised by foreign interference and the decline of the local economy. The expenses incurred by the military modernization programs of his predecessors forced him to disband most of the modernized army units.

1857. Tax reform. In place of numerous taxes, Muhammad Bey instituted the collection of a single subsidy called the *majba,* a poll tax that accounted for almost half of the government's revenue by the end of the decade.

Sept. 10. Ahd al-aman (Security Covenant). The decree, issued by Muhammad Bey to meet European demands, granted foreigners equality with Muslims before the law and the right to own property, and also abolished government monopolies.

1859. Construction of a **telegraph system** begun by a French company.

1859–82. MUHAMMAD AL-SADIQ BEY. The last truly independent ruler of Tunisia was confronted by two major problems: European encroachment and state debt. **Corruption** in the bureaucracy and his own **extravagance** further weakened the state's finances. His **capitulations** to foreign interests and his repression of civil unrest made him hated by many of his subjects.

1860–83. The **government printing press** published 99 books, including texts on Western subjects as well as Islamic treatises.

1860, March. Publication of the **first Arabic-language newspaper,** the government weekly *al-Ra'id al-Tunisi.*

1861. PROMULGATION OF THE CONSTITUTION, the first in the Islamic world. Issued in response to European demands, it promised a **limited monarchy** with an assembly *(Majlis)* composed of 60 members appointed from among the country's elite families. The Majlis was designed as a check on the bey's administration and had the power to make laws, set taxes, and direct the budget and military.

The constitution appealed to reform-minded government officials, but the ulama viewed it as a European-inspired infringement on their traditional role as advisers to the bey and authorities on Islamic law. It was **abrogated** in 1864 as a result of civil unrest and French pressure.

1863. The government contracted its **first international loan** from the French banking house of Erlanger at an interest rate of nearly 100 percent. Additional loans taken on onerous terms drove the treasury to bankruptcy by the end of the decade.

Dec. 18. Anglo-Tunisian Convention. The agreement allowed British subjects resident in Tunisia, most of whom were Maltese, to own real property.

1864. Tribal rebellion and suspension of the constitution. In 1864 the poll tax *(majba)* was doubled to meet the government's increasing foreign debt, triggering a **rural uprising** led by Ali ibn Ghadhahim (d. 1867), a tribal chieftain. Many tax collectors were killed as the **unrest spread** from farmers and tribesmen to the urban centers of Tunis, Susa, Sfax, and Qayrawan. The ulama and the military, previously tax exempt, also joined the revolt. The uprising was quelled when the bey promised to reduce taxes, retain local authorities as tax collectors, and rescind the constitution.

1866. Death of **Mustafa ibn Azuz,** a prominent member of the Rahmaniyya Sufi order, which he helped promote in Tunisia. At the government's request, he helped mediate an end to the revolt of 1864.

1869, July 5. TUNISIA'S BANKRUPTCY. Tunisia's major creditors—France, Great Britain, and Italy—formed the **International Finance Commission** to ensure Tunisia's repayment of its foreign debt, on which it had defaulted. The French gained a dominant role in the commission, which set up a repayment schedule and pressed for the bey to reduce government spending. The commission signaled Tunisia's loss of economic independence.

c. 1872. Railway service between Tunis and La Goulette was established by a British firm.

1873–77. Reform ministry of Khayr al-Din al-Tunisi, the most prominent statesman of the century. He worked to reform government, education, and the economy, but he was forced out of office and moved to Istanbul in 1877. In 1867, he had published a manifesto called *The Surest Path,* which addressed the issues of European superiority and the importance of applying Western innovations that did not compromise Islamic precedent to strengthen the state.

1874. Death of the historian **Ahmad ibn Abi Diyaf,** known as Bin Diyaf. He had served as a secretary *(katib)* for the beys for more than 30 years. His history illuminates the late 18th and 19th centuries and provides extensive biographical details of noteworthy personages. It is considered a major reference work.

Decree on the rights of sharecroppers *(khammas).* Sharecroppers traditionally received one-fifth of the harvest they worked on as pay, often given as a partial advance. The decree established a **minimum wage,** but bound the sharecropper to the farmer *(fellah)* by ensuring his perpetual indebtedness to his employer. The number of **landless agricultural workers increased.**

1875. Prime minister Khayr al-Din established **Sadiqi College,** the first educational facility not controlled by religious scholars. Instruction focused on European languages, sciences, and mathematics. Graduates assumed government positions previously taken by students of the Zaytuna Mosque college. The nationalist **Young Tunisian movement** was founded by graduates of the school.

1878. Death of **Mustafa Khaznadar,** prime minister under Ahmad Bey, Muhammad Bey, and Muhammad al-Sadiq Bey. A powerful but corrupt minister, he allowed European merchants access to Tunisian resources in return for shares and payments, a policy that earned him great wealth but increased his country's international debt and precipitated its economic decline.

1881, April 24. FRENCH INVASION. Troops advanced in a three-pronged attack on the pretext of a border dispute with Algeria. Muhammad al-Sadiq Bey signed the **Treaty of Bardo** (May 12), by which he retained the title of bey, but with severely curtailed authority. The French were given the right to secure the country's borders with their military forces. French control of the country was completed by 1882 and lasted until 1956.

1882–1902. ALI III (ALI BEY). The first bey to rule under the French protectorate retained only nominal authority.

1883, June 8. The Al-Marsa Convention officially established a French protectorate. Ali Bey renounced his authority and remained solely as a figurehead. The **Husaynid dynasty** continued in name only until the abolition of the monarchy in 1957, whereas real authority was vested in the hands of a **French resident general,** first installed in 1882. By 1884, the French supervised all government business. They left provincial governors in place and worked with cooperative members of the ulama.

1888. Foundation of *al-Hadira,* the weekly newspaper of the reformist followers of Khayr al-Din. This **first private Arabic-language paper** published by Tunisians promoted an **agenda for social change** that included both Western and Islamic components. It continued until 1910.

1889. Death of **Muhammad Bayram al-Khamis** (b. 1840), advocate of Islamic reform. A descendant of one of Tunisia's most prominent ulama families, he studied and taught at the Zaytuna Mosque. He also served as the editor of the official government newspaper and supervisor of the government printing press. His own writings focused on **Islamic reform** as well as the history of 19th-century Tunisia.

Founding of *La Dépêche Tunisienne,* the daily newspaper of French

protectorate policies. It continued until 1961. The views of French colonists were expressed in another paper, *La Tunisie Française* (1892).

1896. Khalduniyya School founded by graduates of Sadiqi College in order to offer those trained at the Zaytuna Mosque education in European subjects necessary for bureaucratic careers.

Beginning of the annual transfer of thousands of acres of *habus* land (property set aside as a trust for the support of a charitable institution or for the maintenance of a family's heirs) to the French Directorate of Agriculture. The **confiscated land** was then **made available to French settlers.** The practice continued until 1956.

1898. Government attempts to **reform the Zaytuna Mosque curriculum** were successfully resisted by the ulama. Traditional Islamic subjects, including Arabic grammar, Qur'anic commentary, and Islamic law, continued to be taught.

c. 1907. FOUNDATION OF THE YOUNG TUNISIAN MOVEMENT. The first nationalist organization originated among a small, **elite group of Sadiqi College graduates** who in the 1880s had begun to discuss the future direction of their country. Their **aims included economic and political modernization,** goals that they argued could be achieved even under the French. They combined support for Western technological development with an insistence on the value of Islamic culture. By 1907, the group established its own newspaper in French, called *Le Tunisien,* which was published until 1911.

c. 1911. The **popularity of tea,** an uncommon beverage in the 19th century, began to increase with the influx of Libyan refugees from the Italian invasion (1911). Tunisians adopted their custom of drinking green tea, which became the **national drink** in the 20th century.

1911. Imposition of martial law by the French. Riots provoked by French encroachment on a Muslim cemetery in Tunis prompted the declaration.

1912. A boycott of the Tunis tram system was organized by the Young Tunisians, who demanded that all non-Tunisians be dismissed and that indigenous employees receive equal pay. **Riots** broke out during the protest, leaders of the Young Tunisian movement were exiled, and the **group was disbanded.** (To p. 768)

d. LIBYA

(From p. 367)

1795–1832. YUSUF PASHA QARAMANLI. Coming to power in the wake of a disruptive civil war, Yusuf Pasha restored order and **revived the economy** of his country, whose population was estimated at about half a million people. For the first 20 years or so of his reign he drew **large revenues from piracy,** a state monopoly on the exportation of agricultural produce and livestock, and the **trans-Saharan trade,** especially in slaves. He reorganized and **expanded the army,** and built an impressive fleet. But the sharp **decline of piracy** by the 1820s caused severe financial hardships that led to an erosion of his authority and a rebellion that forced his downfall.

1795–1805. Expansion of Tripoli's naval power. Yusuf Pasha built a fleet that by 1805 included 24 warships in addition to other vessels. Most of the ships were European and American merchant vessels captured by the pirates and converted to military uses. With this maritime power the pasha's **piratical activities** drew in large revenues in the form of captured property, protection money, and ransom payments for captives.

1801–5. War with the United States (p. 602). The conflict began in May 1801 when Yusuf Pasha Qaramanli, in an attempt to extort more tribute, permitted his corsairs to **attack American merchant vessels.** In 1803 the American frigate *Philadelphia* was captured and its crew imprisoned. President Jefferson permitted the organization of a naval expedition that, together with mercenary troops, captured the city of Darna in April 1805. The **peace treaty** signed on June 10, 1805, allowed the United States to ransom 200 prisoners, but avoided the payment of increased tribute.

1806–11. Yusuf Pasha mounted **expeditions against tribes in Cyrenaica and the Fezzan,** bringing the two areas under his direct control.

1825. Yusuf Pasha began **borrowing** large sums from European merchants to help cover his deficits due to the decline of piracy. The mounting **financial crisis** in the following years led him also to debase the currency several times, to confiscate property, and to impose new taxes. **European pressures** on him to repay his debts combined with a **rebellion** by discontented groups at home led to his **abdication** in 1832 in favor of his son Ali.

1832–35. ALI PASHA QARAMANLI. The last ruler of the dynasty faced a continuing **civil war** at home, with the British and French supporting the two rival parties and the Tunisian government scheming to annex Tripoli. The Ottoman government, which wanted to maintain Qaramanli rule, decided finally to forestall possible outside intervention by taking control of the country.

1835, May 28. RESTORATION OF DIRECT OTTOMAN CONTROL OVER LIBYA. An Ottoman force landed in Tripoli and put an end to the long rule (since 1711) of the Qaramanli family. The move was designed to contain the French penetration of North Africa as well as Tunisian designs on Libya. **Tripolitania** was organized into a province *(vilayet)* under a governor appointed by the Ottomans, while **Cyrenaica** formed a separate subprovince responsible directly to Istanbul. Ottoman sovereignty over Libya lasted until the Italian occupation, but effective Ottoman control was strongest in the coastal areas and major towns, with the **Fezzan** and the **interior of Cyrenaica** enjoying a great measure of autonomy under **tribal and Sanusi authorities.** The Ottomans introduced their program of **Tanzimat reforms** into Libya, setting the foundations for the modernization of the country.

1837. CREATION OF THE SANUSIYYA SUFI ORDER, by **Muhammad ibn Ali al-Sanusi** (1787–1859), an Algerian educated in North Africa and Mecca. He advocated a return to the lifestyle of the Prophet Muhammad and emphasized asceticism and austerity in worship. His movement had the most **appeal for the bedouin in Cyrenaica** where the main lodge was established in 1843. Under al-Sanusi and his son **Muhammad al-Mahdi** (1845–1902) the order established **a network of over 140 lodges** scattered throughout the Libyan desert oases and beyond. These became centers of religious missionary activity and teaching as well as of agricultural settlement and trade. The order acquired **political authority** among the tribesmen by providing services and mediating disputes. The Ottoman government cultivated the support of the order, granting it in 1856 exemption from taxes on its property and recognizing the right of its leaders to tax members.

1842–47. Implementation of the **Ottoman urbanization policy.** Forts were constructed at al-Marj (1842), Bu Nujaym (1844–46), and Gharyan and Murzuq (1847). Each outpost fostered **settlement** and the growth of village populations, particularly in the northern provinces. **Trade** was encouraged by the foundation of numerous trading posts and by the establishment of a route for commerce between the Jabal al-Gharb and Tripoli.

1857. Abolition of slavery. The slave trade had traditionally formed the most lucrative part of Libya's export economy. Slaves were brought to Tripoli from sub-Saharan Africa by caravan routes. The **trade increased** with the abolition of slavery in Algeria and Tunisia a decade earlier. Despite the official ban, **slaves continued to be covertly sold** to markets in Istanbul and Egypt until the 1890s, when the slave trade in the Middle East was finally suppressed.

1857–1900. Ottoman educational reform. In Tripoli a **modern secondary school** was established, and by 1868 Turkish and French were the languages of instruction. Six of these modern secondary schools *(rushdiyya)* were eventually established. A separate **secondary school for girls** was founded in Tripoli by 1900, along with a training school for village primary-level schoolteachers. A **military academy** in Tripoli was established during the governorship of Ahmed Resim Pasha (1881–96); it prepared students in history, engineering, mathematics, and French for further study at the Military College in Istanbul.

1858. Application of the Ottoman land law. It supplanted collective tribal landholding and allowed individuals to register small parcels for a fee in return for a certificate of ownership. Unlike its reception in other parts of the Ottoman Empire, the reform apparently did not create a new class of large landholders or absentee landlords, possibly because agriculture was considered unprofitable because of heavy tax-

ation and high risk. Most wealth remained concentrated in commercial ventures until late in the 19th century. Since 1855 the Ottomans had encouraged the **sedentarization of the bedouin.** The Sanusi leadership supported this objective and was anxious for tribal people to adopt an agricultural lifestyle. In 1914 about half of Libya's population was still pastoral.

1861. A **telegraph line** between Malta and Tripoli was established.

1865. The first Libyan newspaper, *Tarablus al-gharb (Tripoli of the West),* was published. It was a short, government-supported chronicle printed in Turkish and Arabic.

1867–70. Governorship of **Ali Rida Pasha,** an active Ottoman bureaucrat who, with French technical assistance, attempted to improve the **water supply** by digging artesian wells in the capital. He also directed the dredging of the **port of Benghazi** and attempted to make **Tobruk** a more significant site for coastal commerce.

1871. Revised Ottoman law of provincial administration. It established that each city would have its own administrative unit headed by a mayor *(ra'is)* aided by an advisory council responsible for public works. By 1872, Tripoli, Benghazi, Khums, and Darna each had such a program in place for local governance.

1876. Libya became the province of exile for Ottoman political reformers. The policy continued until 1908.

1897. The local newspaper *Taraqqi (Progress)* was started but was suspended after only a few issues because of its reformist views.

1900. A modern police force was established in Tripoli.

1902. Italy obtained from **France** permission to exercise a free hand in Libya, in return for accepting French freedom of action in Morocco.

A branch of the **Banco di Roma** opened in Tripoli as part of the Italian attempt at a peaceful **economic invasion of Libya** through increased trade. Branches were opened after 1907 in Benghazi, Khums, and other cities. The Italians attempted to provide a variety of goods and services ill suited to the local population, including locally available sponges and an ice factory for a population that did not desire it. Local notables were given lavish gifts, but these attempts to buy influence did not succeed. Despite **attempted Italian penetration,** Libya's two greatest trading partners remained England and the Ottoman Empire. The Ottomans, eager to maintain a competitive stance against Italian economic encroachment, opened a branch of the Ottoman Imperial Bank in Tripoli.

1908–10. The Young Turk Revolution of 1908 **lifted press censorship** and resulted in the publication of more than seven **newspapers and journals** during this period. Most, including *al-Asr al-jadid (The New Age)* and *al-Mirsad (The Lookout),* advocated the expansion of industry, compulsory education, and a defense against European encroachment.

1911–12. THE ITALIAN OCCUPATION OF LIBYA. Under the pretext of protecting its citizens in Libya, **Italy declared war on the Ottomans** on Sept. 29, 1911. Its forces invaded Libya and occupied Tripoli (p. 478) and other port towns with 35,000 troops. There were only 7,000 Ottoman soldiers in the province. The local population, with the help of Ottoman officers, offered **considerable resistance,** but the Ottomans were eventually obliged to cede their rights in Tripoli and Cyrenaica to Italy by the **Treaty of Ouchy** (Oct. 15, 1912). Some Libyans, such as the mayor of Tripoli, a member of the Qaramanli family, did not resist the invasion, but instead collaborated with the Italians. By 1914 the Italians had consolidated their control of the coastal areas, but much of the interior, especially the Fezzan, was yet to be conquered. The occupation, which lasted until 1943, fulfilled 30 years of **Italian imperial aspiration** for the last surviving Ottoman province in North Africa.

1912–14. Sayyid Ahmad al-Sharif (d. 1933), head of the Sanusi movement, led the **resistance to the Italian occupation,** claiming to be the heir to the Ottoman authority in Libya. The struggle of the Sanusis to hold on to Cyrenaica continued until 1931, when they were finally defeated by the Italians. *(To p. 768)*

D. SOUTH AND SOUTHEAST ASIA, 1753–1914

1. INDIA, 1800–1914

(From p. 371)

In this period of high empire, Indians and British alike participated in shaping a new understanding of Indian society. As amateur ethnographers, British administrators collected and catalogued data about their colony that, taken together and utilized to support imperial rule, constituted a new sociology of knowledge. In the late 19th century, shaped by the pseudoscience of social Darwinism, the cataloguing of the peoples of India became a way to explain existing social hierarchies (sometimes by measuring the width of noses!) and to place the British at the top of such pyramids. For their part, Indian informants to the British Raj fulfilled their own needs as they described and explained local society and classical texts (as these began to be translated by Orientalist scholars). Many Indians profited by these early interactions with the British. Indirectly, they shaped British understanding of Indian society to fit their own perspectives and situated their caste groups in high-status positions; more directly, they gained control of land, forged lucrative trading relationships, or secured roles for themselves in government advisory groups and, later, representative councils.

Profound changes in local society underlay these interactions. Some were introduced by the British as they imposed their own notions of proper governance, founded on a land revenue–based state, sedentary society, guarantees of property rights, and the "rule of law." But many more changes emerged from processes that had been set in motion as the Mughal Empire declined and aspects of rule passed into the hands of regional rulers and local elites (especially the benefits accruing to those who collected and forwarded the land revenue, and to those who undertook responsibility for cultural patronage). Mechanisms of local self-rule—an important locus of power in a society in which constituent communities held much responsibility for self-regulation—enabled local power holders to advance visions of what Indian society should be that were very different from those held by British administrators.

These conflicting visions were fitted together by the British understanding that local communities (whether defined as caste groups, local villages, or urban neighborhoods) would work through "natural leaders," maintaining order within their boundaries and representing their interests to colonial rulers. In this setup, local religious activity, domestic relationships, and cultural practices could generally be left alone; **only when local practices egregiously offended the colonial state's definitions of morality did the British intervene** (for instance, regarding *satī*, the immolation of a Hindu widow on her husband's funeral pyre). This understanding was a peculiar reformulation of a process under way in western Europe at much the same time, in which "public" life—composed of interactions between an emerging civil society and the state's institutions—was becoming increasingly distinguished from "private" life—in which bourgeois households conducted their domestic affairs as they saw fit. In British India, the state simultaneously created legal structures to deal with individuals *and* with groups, and a unique form of "civil society" grew up in which "representatives" interacted with the state—but no one was considered a citizen.

In British India, the first **nationalist movement** under imperialism emerged between the 1880s and the achievement of independence in 1947. At first a matter of elite petitions for increased employment and political participation, the movement quickened into a **popular campaign** with the partition of Bengal in 1905 and a series of experiments with political festivals in western India, beginning at the turn of the century. From this point on, the nationalist movement reflected an uneasy amalgam of indigenous reformulations of imagined communities and Western-influenced political campaigns targeted at imperial institutions.

At the turn of the century, British **censuses** counted about **238 million people**; these numbers remained stagnant, because of famine and disease, for three decades. From 1921 to 1941, however, the growth rate increased from 1.1 to 1.4 percent annually, setting a trajectory that made **dramatic population increase** one of the greatest problems to be faced by the postcolonial states of the subcontinent when they achieved independence.

1800s. Local communities in India took over more and more self-regulation and **cultural patronage** as an expression of localized political ideologies. Changing relationships between communities and the colonial state (or still independent successor states) led to heightened competition among contenders for local control.

1798–1805. LORD MORNINGTON (later **marquis of Wellesley**) served as governor-general. He developed the system of **subsidiary alliances** by which Britain supplied troops and protection in exchange for territory or monetary grants and was allowed control of the state's foreign affairs but pledged nonintervention in internal government and secured exclusion of every other foreign power from the state's service. The fourth **Anglo-Mysore War** (Tipu d. 1799) led to a protectorate over Mysore: various annexations extended British control over nearly all southern India. The **Maratha leaders,** angered by the **Treaty of Bassein** (1802), which made the Peshwa a subsidiary ally, opened hostilities. Costly but successful warfare (defeat of Sindhia and Bhonsle at **Assaye,** Sept. 23, 1803) led to alarm at home, Wellesley's recall, and temporary abandonment of his policy.

1805. Lord Cornwallis again became governor-general (d. Oct.), succeeded by **Sir George Barlow** (1805–7) and **Lord Minto** (1807–13).

1809. Treaty of Amritsar fixed the river Sutlej as northwestern boundary of the company's territories, checking the advance of a Sikh confederacy under **Ranjit Singh** (d. 1839).

1808–10. Unrest in Banaras To curb French expansion in Asia, Minto made **treaties with Sind, Persia, and Afghanistan,** and captured the French islands in the Indian Ocean and Java, which was under French control (Bourbon was later restored to France and Java to the Dutch).

1810–13. Unrest in Banaras typified the character of change and channels of contention that developed under colonial rule. In 1810 residents of Banaras led a successful protest against the imposition of a house tax which spread to other north Indian cities. In the two years following, conflict among various Hindu communities contending for dominance under the British led to an expansion of the conflict into a Hindu-Muslim riot over processions and sacred space. Those jailed as leaders of the riot (Muslims, Brahmans, and other high-caste Hindus) paradoxically then united in the following year in a jail protest against treatment of prisoners that would force them to lose caste.

1813–23. LORD MOIRA (later marquis of Hastings) served as governor-general, followed by John Adam (acting) and Lord Amherst (1823–28).

1813. Parliament **renewed the company's charter** for another 20 years, but under pressure of free trade interests, **abolished its monopoly of trade with India** and extended the sovereignty of the British Crown over the East India Company's possessions. Missionaries were for the first time allowed to evangelize in the company's territories.

1814–16. Border dispute with Nepal provoked a hard-fought war. The British acquired the Kumaun Division and made permanent peace with Nepal, which retained its complete independence.

1816–18. The marauding **Pindari tribes,** after raiding British territory, were suppressed and broken up by Hastings; hostile Maratha leaders were also defeated, leaving only Nepal, the Sikh state, and Afghanistan independent of direct or indirect British control. (However, **indirect control**—under which Indian princes retained internal control while ceding external control to the EIC—accounted for more than one-third of the land mass.) Pacification of the Pindaris followed a pattern also used to domesticate the **Thags** and large landlords: all three were deprived of their military roles, but in return were rewarded with landholdings as they became sedentarized.

In Bengal, the introduction by the British of **printing** (Wilkins, 1778) stimulated a growing volume of publishing in English, Bengali, Persian, Sanskrit, and Hindustani, and made possible the establishment of schools imparting both modern English-language and vernacular learning. In the field of **higher education,** the combined efforts of British officials and private British and Indian philanthropists led to the founding of the Hindu College (Calcutta, 1816), the Elphinstone Institution (Bombay, origins 1827), the Delhi College (1827), and the Madras University High School (1841), the nuclei of the later universities. **Newspapers** made their appearance in the 1780s in Calcutta, Madras, and Bombay (government controls imposed sporadically, and licensing required, 1823–35).

These developments, and the discoveries by British **Orientalists** active in the Asiatic Society (founded in 1784 by **William Jones**), the **College of Fort William** (founded in 1800 by Wellesley), and the **Serampore Baptist Mission** (founded in 1800 by **William Carey**) stimulated an intellectual renaissance among Bengali Hindu scholars. **Rammohun Roy** published Vedic texts in five languages, condemned idolatry and *satī* as corrupt practices, espoused Christian ethics but ridiculed Christian theology, and established the **Brahmo Samaj** (1828–30), open to all monotheists. An opposing movement, led by **Radhakanta Deb,** organized the **Dharma Sabha** (1830), sponsoring educational change but defending social and religious customary practices. Bengali prose developed rapidly as a literary medium beginning at this time.

1820–31. Various efforts to resist British political and cultural intrusion began to emerge. Mindful of their efforts to supplant the Mughals, the British paid closest attention to movements that attracted Indian Muslims. For instance, some Muslims of northern India, resentful of the new order and hostile to secular education in English as subversive to their faith, responded to the appeal of **Sayyid Ahmad Shahid** of Rae Bareilly (influenced by the reformism of Shah Wali-Ullah and the puritan ideas of Ibn 'Abd-ul-Wahhab of Arabia) for a return to the ways prescribed in the Qur'an and a restoration of Muslim government in India. Mindful of the strength of the British, Sayyid Ahmad preached and organized a jihad (holy war) against the Sikh rulers of the Punjab (1826–31) and was killed in battle against them (1831). His followers, although dispersed, developed a well-knit organization and continued his movement until the 1870s, when by assassinations of British officials they provoked suppression by the government.

In Bengal, **Titu Mir** led a Muslim uprising against oppressive Hindu *zamindars* and was killed by government troops (Nov. 19, 1831). The *Fara'izi* (obligationist) reform movement launched early in the century by **Haji Shari' at-Ullah** became a radical sect under his son **Dudhu Miyan.** The moderate reforms of **Karamat 'Ali,** a disciple of Sayyid Ahmad Shahid, meanwhile attracted widespread support among Bengali Muslims.

1820s–50s. First India-wide police campaign was organized against the Thags (robbers known for ritually strangling their victims). New policing strategies, administrative arrangements, and legal procedures were introduced to suppress what was seen as a direct threat to the British ability to maintain order in their territories. Sir William Sleeman led the new department created for this purpose, the **Thagi and Dacoity Department.** Two legal innovations to control the Thags later paved the way for control of entire caste groups labeled "criminal" and, by the 1920s, of political protesters: the courts agreed to convict those who Sleeman could show had been members of a gang, even if he couldn't demonstrate that they had committed a particular crime; and the role of "approver" was created, in which someone (proved to be involved in a crime) could then give testimony to implicate others as fellow perpetrators.

1824–26. Following Burmese aggression the **first Anglo-Burmese War** led to British acquisition of Assam, Arakan, and Tenasserim.

1827. Pretense of subordination to the Delhi emperor was abandoned, his name was removed from the coinage (1835).

1828–35. LORD WILLIAM BENTINCK served as governor-general. Relative peace favored reform measures: *satī* was made a criminal offense (1829), inland transit duties were abolished (1835), tea and coffee production were added to that of indigo, roads and canals were planned

(Grand Turk Road begun, 1839), and river and ocean steamship lines were encouraged. Administrative costs were cut; revenue settlement was inaugurated in the northwest provinces; more responsibility was given to Indian subordinate officials; and law revision and codification were undertaken by **Thomas B. Macaulay** (law member, 1834–38), whose **Minute on Education** (1835), along with the pressure of Hindu demands and administrative convenience, prompted the momentous decision to subsidize education primarily along Western lines through the medium of English.

1831–81. Mysore state was taken under direct British control, owing to misgovernment.

1833. Parliament renewed the company's charter for 20 years, **abolishing its trade** in India and China and restricting its functions to the administration of its Indian territories. European settlements in India were allowed, and funds for education (first provided, 1813) were substantially increased.

1830s–50s. Export trade relied particularly (in related fluctuations) on opium, raw cotton, indigo dye, and cotton textiles. Around 1850 the fluctuations smoothed out, with cotton textile exports rising dramatically, cotton and opium declining, and raw cotton maintaining a steady rate. Altogether, these exports (and precious metals) yielded some 455 million rupees of surplus available for remittances home to Britain. But the crisis brought about in the 1850s had a long-term impact on the South Asian economy: the risks induced many Indian entrepreneurs to invest in land instead of business, and it ushered in a period of rising food prices that benefited cultivators but created shortages in some places.

1835–36. Sir Charles Metcalfe, governor-general, was followed by **Lord Auckland** (1836–42), **Lord Ellenborough** (1842–44), and **Sir Henry Hardinge** (1844–48).

1837. Persian was abandoned as the language of record and the courts, replaced by English and regional languages, a decision welcomed by the Anglicized Bengali Hindus but deplored by the Muslims, whose numbers in the administration steadily declined.

British officials, now trained initially in England (Haileybury College established, 1805) and increasingly accompanied by their wives, gradually became socially and intellectually more aloof from their Indian subjects.

1839–42. The **FIRST ANGLO-AFGHAN WAR** was a fiasco precipitated by Auckland's exaggerated fear of Russian influence in Afghanistan. Although 16,000 British and sepoy troops succeeded in occupying Kabul (1839–41), popular revolt brought on their evacuation (Jan. 6, 1842) and massacre (121 survivors).

1843. Annexation of Sind, following provocation of hostilities by **Sir Charles Napier.**

1845–48. FIRST AND SECOND ANGLO-SIKH WARS, arising from disorders after Ranjit Singh's death (1839), led to **annexation of the Punjab,** modernization of its government, and permanent loyalty of the Sikhs. **Kashmir** was sold (1846) to a Hindu chieftain who accepted British paramountcy.

1848–56. LORD DALHOUSIE, the governor-general, accelerated public works, developing roads, irrigation canals, and **railways** (first line opened, 1853), introducing telegraph service (Calcutta-Agra line opened, 1854), and fixing uniform postal rates.

Dalhousie adhered consistently to the **doctrine of lapse** (disavowed, 1859), whereby dependent states with no heirs in the ruling line fell to the paramount power; seven principalities were annexed in this manner.

1851. British Indian Association was founded in Calcutta to press for administrative and political reforms in the forthcoming renewal of the company's charter. It had branches in Madras and Avadh (Oudh) and **Debendranath Tagore,** the Brahmo Samaj leader, as secretary. The **Bombay Association** (1852), under Parsi leadership, had similar aims but was short-lived.

1853. Company's charter renewed.

1854. Education dispatch of Sir Charles Wood, president of the Board of Control, laid down the pattern for future government-aided expansion of elementary and secondary schools, and affiliating universities (founded in 1857 at Calcutta, Madras, and Bombay).

1855. The first Indian cotton textile mill was established in Bombay, marking the beginning of a strategy of substituting Indian goods for industrial imports.

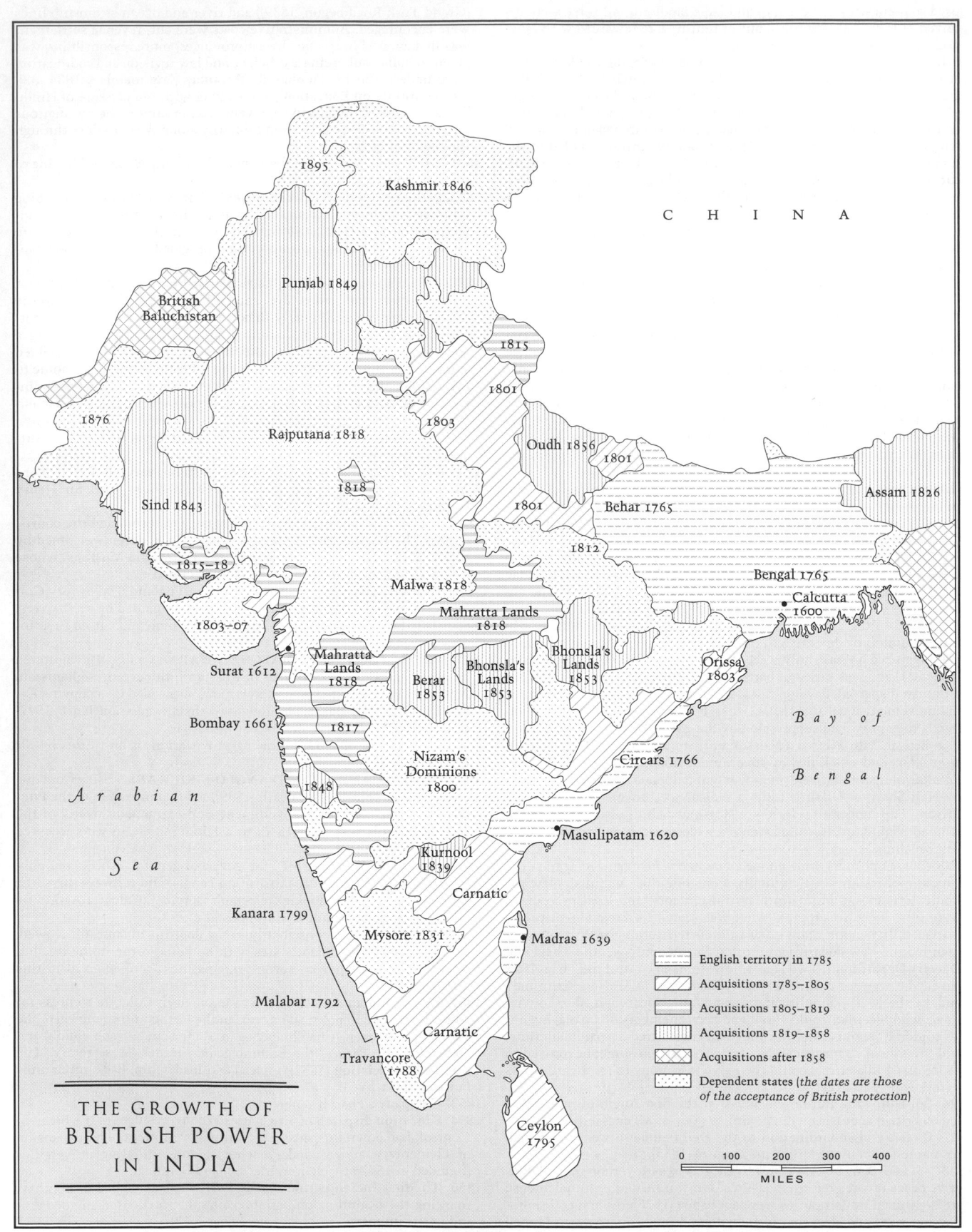

C H I N A

1895

Kashmir 1846

British
Baluchistan

Punjab 1849

1876

1815

1801

1803

Rajputana 1818

Oudh 1856

1801

Assam 1826

Sind 1843

1818

1801

Behar 1765

1815–18

1812

Bengal 1765

Malwa 1818

Calcutta
1600

Mahratta Lands
1818

1803–07

Surat 1612

Mahratta
Lands
1818

Berar
1853

Bhonsla's
Lands
1853

Bhonsla's
Lands
1853

Orissa
1803

Bombay 1661

1817

Bay of

Nizam's
Dominions
1800

Bengal

Arabian

1848

Circars 1766

Sea

Kurnool
1839

Masulipatam 1620

Carnatic

Kanara 1799

Mysore 1831

Madras 1639

Malabar 1792

Carnatic

Travancore
1788

Ceylon
1795

	English territory in 1785
	Acquisitions 1785–1805
	Acquisitions 1805–1819
	Acquisitions 1819–1858
	Acquisitions after 1858
	Dependent states (*the dates are those of the acceptance of British protection*)

THE GROWTH OF
BRITISH POWER
IN INDIA

0   100   200   300   400
MILES

1856. Annexation of Avadh (Oudh), on grounds of misgovernment, aroused deep resentment, especially among the 40,000 Avadhi sepoys in the Bengal army.

1856–62. EARL CANNING, governor-general and (from 1858) first viceroy, was confronted by a short war with Persia (1856–57).

1857–58. REBELLION occurred in northern India, comprising mutinies (beginning at Meerut, May 10) by sepoy troops, popular **uprisings,** and scattered **revolts** by Hindu and Muslim chiefs seeking restoration of canceled privileges. The recapture of Delhi by loyal forces from the Punjab (Sept. 20) marked the turning of the tide, but three expeditions were required to retake Lucknow (March 5, 1858), and guerrilla warfare continued for some months. Although British losses were small, the memory of atrocities committed by both sides (notably the massacre of 211 British women and children at Cawnpore, July 15, 1857) embittered social relations between Indians and Europeans for the next 90 years. The last of the Mughal rulers, **Bahadur Shah II,** having been declared emperor of India by the Delhi rebels, was deposed, tried, and exiled. He died in Rangoon (1862).

1858, Aug. 2. By the **GOVERNMENT OF INDIA ACT,** Parliament transferred the government of India from the East India Company (dissolved, 1874) to the Crown. The governor-general received the additional title of viceroy and was made directly responsible to the secretary of state for India in the British cabinet.

Nov. 1. Proclamation by the queen renounced the policy of annexation of princely states, promised noninterference in religious belief or worship, and opened higher administrative offices to qualified Indians.

1859–62. Paper currency, license fees, income taxes, and a 10 percent tariff were introduced to meet the **heavy debt** left after suppression of the rebellion.

Administrative reforms were undertaken to strengthen the government: cabinet system was introduced; civil service appointments were regulated (competitive since 1853); the army was reorganized, recruited increasingly from the Punjab and Nepal; code of civil procedure (1859), penal code (1860), code of criminal procedure (1861), and high courts (1862) regularized administration of justice; **legislative councils** were appointed (governor-general's, 1853; reorganized and enlarged, 1861; provincial, 1862), containing a small proportion of Indian members.

Public works were pressed energetically: the railway network embraced all major cities by 1875: telegraph service to Europe was opened (1865). Archaeological surveys (1861), famine relief (1861), forestry (1861), and agriculture and sanitation (1864) began to be fostered by official measures.

1862–63. Lord Elgin, viceroy, was succeeded by **Lord Lawrence** (1864–69); **Lord Mayo** (1869–72); **Lord Northbrook** (1872–76); and **Lord Lytton** (1876–80).

1866. Collapse of the cotton boom, which had arisen from increased production during the American Civil War, led to severe economic dislocation, especially in western India where production for external workers had expanded most dramatically.

1868. Security of land tenure granted to peasants by Oudh and Punjab Tenancy Acts, following precedent of Bengal Rent Act (1859), which applied also to Agra and Central Provinces.

Hindu reform movements broadened their influence among the English-speaking middle class: **Keshab Chunder Sen** formed the **Brahmo Samaj of India** (1865), stimulating the establishment of the **Prarthana Samaj** in Bombay (1867); annual meetings of the **Hindu Mela** at Calcutta (1867–80) propagated neo-Hindu and protonationalist ideas; **Arya Samaj** was founded by **Swami Dayananda** (Bombay, 1875), and its headquarters fixed at Lahore (1877).

Muslim reform built momentum in north India through the educational and journalistic work of **Sayyid Ahmad Khan,** who founded the **Muslim Anglo-Oriental College** at Aligarh (1877); in Bombay through the **Aga Khan;** in Calcutta through 'Abdul Latif (**Muslim Literary Society,** 1863) and **Sayyid Amir Ali** (**National Muslim Association,** 1877).

1869. Opening of the Suez Canal eliminated the overland Suez link (regular service opened, 1843), greatly cheapening freight shipments. Both India's overseas trade and the percentage of manufactured goods in its total exports nearly tripled in the following four decades.

1870s. First **railroad systems** opened across India. This new linkage had important implications for economic development, communications, and pilgrimage patterns. The fact that the internal lines were built to a different gauge than those leading to the ports shows that the railroads' first purpose was extractive (that is, the system made it simple to convey goods for export, but almost impossible to recirculate them internally to meet famine needs).

At the same time, **print media** expanded dramatically. Newspaper, journal, book, and pamphlet publication increased significantly; more important, the circulation of these printed materials—including oral transmission through being read aloud in villages and small towns as well as urban neighborhoods—brought ever larger numbers into a world of public information. The movement of people as well as information on the railroads reinforced this expansion of public intelligence and thus the formation of a public opinion that could be brought to bear on the British imperial regime.

1872. Assassination of Lord Mayo by a Muslim.

1875. Peasant uprising in Maharashtra (Deccan) was in part occasioned by the dislocation of cotton growers.

1876. Occupation of Quetta as a safeguard against the Russian southward advance toward Afghanistan.

1876–78. Great famine in the Deccan and adjacent areas took over 5 million lives.

1870–90s. Industrialization was limited under colonial rule for several reasons. The British Indian government refused, for instance, to introduce protective tariffs to protect infant industries. Even the advantage of cheap labor was offset when the Indian government was forced by British industrialists at home to pass a Factory Act in 1882 that restricted the uses of labor in ways similar to restrictions imposed in Britain. Even when entrepreneurs did manage to carve niches for themselves (e.g., cotton textiles), they could not effect linkages with other industries. Textile machinery, for instance, continued to be produced only outside India. But perhaps the greatest disincentive flowed from the enormous appreciation in land values, luring Indian capital out of industry and into nonproductive but more secure investment in the countryside. Some sector industrialization did, however, occur, such as the expansion of the **Tata Iron and Steel Company** (West Bengal), which began during World War I.

1877. On Disraeli's initiative, the **queen was proclaimed empress of India** at a Delhi ceremony *(durbar)* at which the Indian princes were assembled to offer their homage.

Formation of huge **Empress Mill** (for cotton) by **Jamsetji Tata** (1839–1904).

1878–81. The **SECOND ANGLO-AFGHAN WAR,** provoked by Lytton, led to his recall, increased the public debt, but established British control over Afghanistan's foreign relations.

1880–84. LORD RIPON, viceroy, a Gladstonian liberal, introduced local self-government, but fierce opposition by British residents in India defeated the **Ilbert Bill** (1883) by which Indian judges in outlying areas could try Europeans. These developments spurred the growth of nationalist sentiment. Concurrently the spread of higher education, the rise of the daily press, and the ease of travel created by the railway network facilitated the establishment of regional and all-India associations by the English-speaking middle class: **Indian Association** (1876), **Poona Sarvajanik Sabha** (1876), **National Conference** (1883), **Madras Mahajana Sabha** (1884), and **Bombay Presidency Association** (1885), many of whose leaders joined in founding the Indian National Congress.

1885, Dec. 27. The **INDIAN NATIONAL CONGRESS** met for the first time, led by **A. O. Hume.** At successive annual meetings (held at different cities in the last week of each year), the congress demanded expansion and reform of the legislative councils and more rapid Indianization of the civil service. Sayyid Ahmad Khan, fearing Hindu domination of representative institutions, led conservative Muslim opposition to the congress, organizing the Muslim Education Conference (meeting annually from 1887), the Indian Patriotic Association (1888), and the Upper India Muslim Defence Association (1893). The viceroy, **Lord Dufferin** (1884–88), originally encouraging, grew cooler to the congress as its agitation assumed a more aggressive character.

1885–86. Third Anglo-Burmese War ended in annexation of Upper Burma.

1888–94. Lord Lansdowne, viceroy, was followed by **Lord Elgin** (1894–98).

1891. Riot in Banaras typified both resistance to new technology and the "traditionalistic" idiom in which this resistance came to be expressed. Ostensibly provoked by the local administration's decision to let a temple collapse as a new waterworks plant was constructed, the rioting crowd attacked not only the waterworks station (emblematic of the health and public works ethos versus traditionalistic understandings of the purity of water in the sacred pilgrimage site of Banaras), but also the railway station, the telegraph lines, and other forms of new technology.

1892. Dadabhai Naoroji, Parsi business and political leader resident in England, was elected to Parliament on the Liberal ticket. His example of selfless service to India inspired many younger compatriots (notably **Mohandas K. Gandhi** and **Mohammad A. Jinnah**) during their visits to London.

Legislative councils were enlarged and their powers increased. The provision that the nonofficial (European and Indian) members were to be nominated by local bodies gave tacit recognition to the principle of election.

1893. The **Durand Line** demarcated by mutual agreement the border between India and Afghanistan, but bisected the area inhabited by the Pathan tribes.

In this same year the Bengali **Swami Vivekananda,** a disciple of the mystic **Sri Ramakrishna,** became a hero in India by his well-received speeches at the World Parliament of Religions in Chicago; **Mrs. Annie Besant** arrived at Madras to take charge of the growing Theosophist movement; and in the Punjab **Mirza Ghulam Ahmad** was attracting a growing following (later known as the **Ahmadiyas**) by his claims to prophethood. Anti-Christian sentiment and its corollaries, Hindu and Muslim revivalism, grew more pronounced from this time onward, all contributing to the increasingly popular character of the nationalist movement.

Cow Protection Movement represented the first successful political effort to link north Indian city and countryside in the same ideological movement. Focused on protection of the cow (symbol of sacred rites common among many kinds and classes of Hindus, but often used by

Muslims as a sacrificial animal), this movement rested on itinerant preachers and money-collecting networks that knit together villages and cities throughout the Ganges plain. The movement was suppressed only when British administrators, alarmed by the massing of 5,000–6,000 people in various locales in the countryside, put extraordinary pressure on "natural leaders" to keep order.

April. British administrators became alarmed at representations of political figures carried in processions connected to religious and civic ceremonials, including those of Tilak, Gokhale, Lala Lajput Rai—but also the Rani of Jhansi (a heroine in the mutiny and uprising of 1857) and "Bande Mataram" (Mother India).

1896. July. The first **film** shown in India was presented by the Lumiere brothers in Bombay; in the next year it was shown in South India. By 1900 films were presented regularly. The first Indian feature film was made in 1912; Bombay (Urdu films) and Madras (Tamil regional films) became the two largest centers of production. Film conventions rested in large part on public enactments, both popular and classical. (Contemporary India is home to the largest film industry in the world.)

Dec. 12. Coronation *durbar* at Delhi. King-Emperor George V announced **transfer of the capital from Calcutta to Delhi** and **reversal of the partition of Bengal.**

1912, Dec. 23. Lord Hardinge (viceroy, 1910–16) was wounded by a terrorist bomb in Delhi.

1913, Nov. 13. The Bengal poet **Rabindranath Tagore** (1861–1941) was awarded the Nobel Prize for literature.

Dec. At the annual meeting of the Muslim League, Muslim leaders, alienated by the reversal of the Bengal partition and suspicious of British policy toward the Ottoman Empire, carried a resolution calling for the eventual "attainment of self-government for India."

1914, May 21. *Komagatu Maru* incident: 300 Indians arrived at Vancouver to test Canadian immigration laws, but were not admitted; resentment in India and some rioting in Calcutta occurred on return of the vessel (Oct. 2); 16 were killed.   *(To p. 769)*

2. SOUTHEAST ASIA, 1753–1914

(From p. 372)

The conquest and subsequent political domination of Southeast Asia by Western colonial powers were the most outstanding features of this era. In the first half of the period, political entities continued to evolve according to indigenous understandings of power relationships and political centers. Between 1870 and 1910, however, the European colonial powers redrew the map of Southeast Asia, establishing boundaries that would ultimately result in the nation-states that constitute modern Southeast Asia. Even Siam, the only remaining independent Southeast Asian kingdom, was strongly influenced in its actions by the presence of British and French colonial powers in its adjoining territories.

As they redrew the map of the area, the colonial powers profoundly altered local underpinnings of political centers. Rather than being built on relationships among power holders in the area, the new boundaries connected particular power centers with particular European colonial states. Europeans thus created new political frameworks on which they imposed modern bureaucratic systems. Over the decades of their colonial rule they introduced, enlarged, and perfected the apparatus necessary for such systems: transportation systems, including railroads; government departments of all sorts; and modern fiscal and tax systems (including the standardization of currency systems, banking systems, insurance firms, and all-purpose service institutions, i.e., agency houses). In addition, the European colonial powers introduced changes in the education systems that were to have long-range and significant implications for future social and political developments.

The expansion of European political power conjoined imperial economic exploitation of the region; significant economic changes resulted from the new political economy wherein colonial powers ruled directly. After 1870, export industries increased rapidly until they came to dominate the economies of Southeast Asia. **Population steadily and rapidly increased** and was accompanied by significant migrations into and within the area. Statistics show spectacular growth:

Burma's population more than doubled, Java's increased at a rate of almost 1.9 percent per annum, and Siam and parts of French Indochina grew at around 2 percent per annum. A considerable proportion of the growth came from immigration, especially by Chinese and Indian trading groups. The economic changes were based on capitalist, world-market-driven forces. Creation of "national" economic structures served to forge three types of economic linkages: to the world economy in general, to the economies of the various metropolitan powers, and also among the different parts of the new colonies themselves.

Within this context, a number of indigenous reformulations sought to provide ideological and cultural stability. In Thailand, Cambodia, and Laos, Buddhist reform and non-Buddhist solutions were formulated in response to the cultural crisis posed by intrusion of the West. In Indonesia, debate between those espousing revivalist versus modernist reconstructions of Islam prompted social and intellectual changes as well as resistance movements and new political parties. Much of this ferment focused on a new emphasis regarding ethnic identity, in which definitions of community reflected the complex interaction of religious movements, immigration patterns, and the attempt to impose Western sociological assumptions.   *(To p. 772)*

a. MAINLAND SOUTHEAST ASIA

1. BURMA
(From p. 375)

The modern Burmese state was built upon the conquests of **Alaungpaya** (1752–60), who founded Burma's last dynasty, the Konbaung (1752–1885). His successors managed to repulse **invasions by the Chinese** (1766–69) but were unable to maintain themselves in Siam (1771).

1782–1819. Bodawpaya, king. Conquest of Arakan (1784) and further encroachments on Indian territory. **Peace with Siam** (1793).

1819–37. Bagyidaw, king. He continued the advance toward India, seizing Manipur and Assam (1822) and invading Kachar (1824). This policy of expansion soon brought him into conflict with the British East India Company because interests and perceptions were in conflict as to the standards of interstate relations.

1824–26. FIRST BURMESE WAR. Despite vigorous resistance the Burmese were unable to withstand the force of a modern army. The British, under **Sir Archibald Campbell,** took Rangoon, and then Syriam, Tavoy, Mergui, Martaban, and Pegu. An attempt by the Burmese to recapture Rangoon failed (1825). The British advanced up the Irrawaddy and at the same time overran Arakan. On Feb. 24, 1826, by the **Treaty of Yandabu** (near Ava) the British secured Assam, Arakan, and the Tenasserim coast, as well as an indemnity, the conclusion of a commercial treaty, and the right to send a resident to Ava (discontinued, 1837). Humiliation of defeat and terms of peace led to palace revolution and Bagyidaw's loss of throne to his brother, **Tharawaddi Min,** king (1837–46).

1846–52. Pagan Min. Under his reign the friction with the British continued. The Burmese rulers continued to treat the British with contempt and to hamper the development of British trade. Lapse of Anglo-Burmese diplomatic contacts.

1852–53. SECOND BURMESE WAR. Rangoon was again taken by the British. Pegu was also occupied and annexed (Jan. 20, 1853). A revolution in the capital led to the deposition of the king and the elevation of Mindon Min.

1853–78. Mindon Min, attempted to introduce administrative reforms, but the pressure of the looming power of British India made it difficult to introduce a program to revitalize and strengthen the state. He accepted the British gains without concluding a formal treaty and attempted, throughout his reign, to maintain friendly relations with his neighbor, British-controlled "Lower Burma," a designation the British created after announcing this territorial annexation. They were unable to gain official Burmese recognition of this status. British Burma consisted of Arakan, Pegu, and Tenasserim.

1857. Mandalay, built by the king, **became the capital** of the country.

1862. Conclusion of a **commercial treaty with Great Britain.** The customs duty was fixed at 5 percent, and the British were given the right to trade throughout the country.

1878–85. THIBAW became king, following a bloody succession conflict. Unsuccessfully, he attempted to open diplomatic relations with the British on terms of equality as a ruler of a sovereign nation. At the same time he established contact with French interests and negotiated with them for the organization of a royal bank and for the construction of a railroad from Mandalay to the Indian frontier. The British felt threatened by the Burmese king's approaches to its European rivals. This resulted in the Third Burmese War.

1885. THE THIRD BURMESE WAR. The British (Oct. 22) sent an ultimatum demanding that Thibaw receive a British envoy and that his interference with trade be stopped; furthermore, it stated that in the future the foreign relations of Burma would be conducted in accordance with the advice of the Indian government. On the rejection of this ultimatum, a British steamer expedition occupied Mandalay (Nov. 28). Thibaw surrendered and was sent to India. This brought to an end the Konbaung dynasty and Burma's independence.

1886, Jan. 1. UPPER BURMA WAS ANNEXED.

July 24. An **Anglo-Chinese convention** recognized the British position in Burma. Chinese prestige was saved by a continuation of Burmese decennial tribute missions.

1886–90. Monks, among those who served as leaders under the old regime, took more aggressive political roles in their communities. Desultory guerrilla warfare, far bloodier than any palace coup, continued for years. Resistance arose among minority groups who emphasized their ethnolinguistic identities—the Shans, Kachins, Chins, Wa, and other groups who had been rendered increasingly marginal by British and Burmese administrations. The Shan states were not reduced until 1887 and the Chin Hills not until 1891; more remote areas continued through 1895.

1893. Siamese boundary set by convention.

1895. Agreement with France on the boundary with Cochin China.

1900. Agreement with China finally fixed the Burmese frontier on that side.

1906. Founding of **Young Men's Buddhist Association** (YMBA) represented the first efforts by the English-trained new elite seeking to bridge old and new social tenets. The modernist elite used the YMBA to reform and modernize Buddhist beliefs and practices under leadership of laymen rather than monks. For example, the **Footwear Controversy** arose (1916), in which all 50 town branches of the YMBA protested the fact that Europeans and non-Buddhists wore shoes when visiting monasteries and pagodas, seeing this as emblematic of the unequal power relationships embedded in colonialism.   *(To p. 772)*

2. THAILAND (SIAM)
(From p. 376)

1782–1809. RAMA I (Phra Buddha Yod Fa Chulalok), first of the new line. He finally brought to an end the long conflict with Burma (1793), reestablished control over the local potentates throughout the country, and secured part of Cambodia through division of that state with Annam.

1809–24. RAMA II (Phra Buddha Loes Fa Nobhalai).

1824–51. RAMA III (Phra Nang Klao), whose reign was distinguished by the reopening of **contact with the Western nations.**

1826, June 20. Conclusion of a **treaty of commerce** with Great Britain. This was followed (March 20, 1833) by a similar treaty with the United States. Although the Western powers felt the treaties did not satisfactorily meet their needs (the treaties did not even provide for the establishment of consular positions), the Siamese felt they had been forced into granting more concessions than they had wanted to make.

1844. Cambodia passed under the protection of Siam.

1851–68. RAMA IV (Phra Chom Klao Mongkut). As a monk he had made a study of Western governments, and he began the work of modernizing Siam.

1855, April 18. A NEW TREATY WITH GREAT BRITAIN was modeled on the Anglo-Chinese treaty. Consuls were to be established; extraterritorial system was introduced; right to trade throughout the kingdom was established. Similar treaties were concluded with the United States (May 29, 1856) and with France (Aug. 15, 1856), and thereafter with many other powers.

1863. The French established a protectorate over Cambodia. After long negotiations, the Siamese gave up their claims (1867).

1868–1910. RAMA V (Phra Maha Chulalongkorn) was the real founder of modern Siam. After attaining his majority (1873) he devoted himself almost entirely to the reform of his government and the improvement of his country. The feudal system was abolished; slavery was reduced and then stamped out; administrative (central bureaucracy), taxation, and finance reform was effected; postal service was introduced; the army was modernized; the telegraph was introduced (1883); the first railway began service (1893).

1880s ff. Dhammayut, a brotherhood of monks initially established in the 1830s, gained formal status as a separate sect under Chulalongkorn. The movement, which preceded stimulus from the West, had long been interested in a Buddhist modernism, expounding modern religious and social ideas based on a Buddhist rationalism, universalism, and textual study of Buddhist scriptures. This provided a framework for incorporating Western science and the broader world with which Siam began to interact.

1885. Failure of a French **proposal to neutralize Siam** resulted in ever-increasing friction and continuous border disputes.

1893, May–Aug. THE ANGLO-FRENCH CRISIS. The French had been trying for years to extend their dominions westward to the Mekong River, a policy that met with opposition not only from Siam but from Britain, which desired to preserve Siam as buffer between Burma and the French possessions. Border clashes in May 1893 led to the mission of two gunboats to Bangkok in July. The Siamese fired upon them, whereupon the French submitted a stiff ultimatum (July 13). This was rejected, and the French then instituted a blockade (July 31), which led to a short but acute **Anglo-French crisis.** The Siamese were obliged to yield.

Oct. 3. According to the **Franco-Siamese Treaty,** the Siamese abandoned all claim to territory east of the Mekong and paid an indemnity

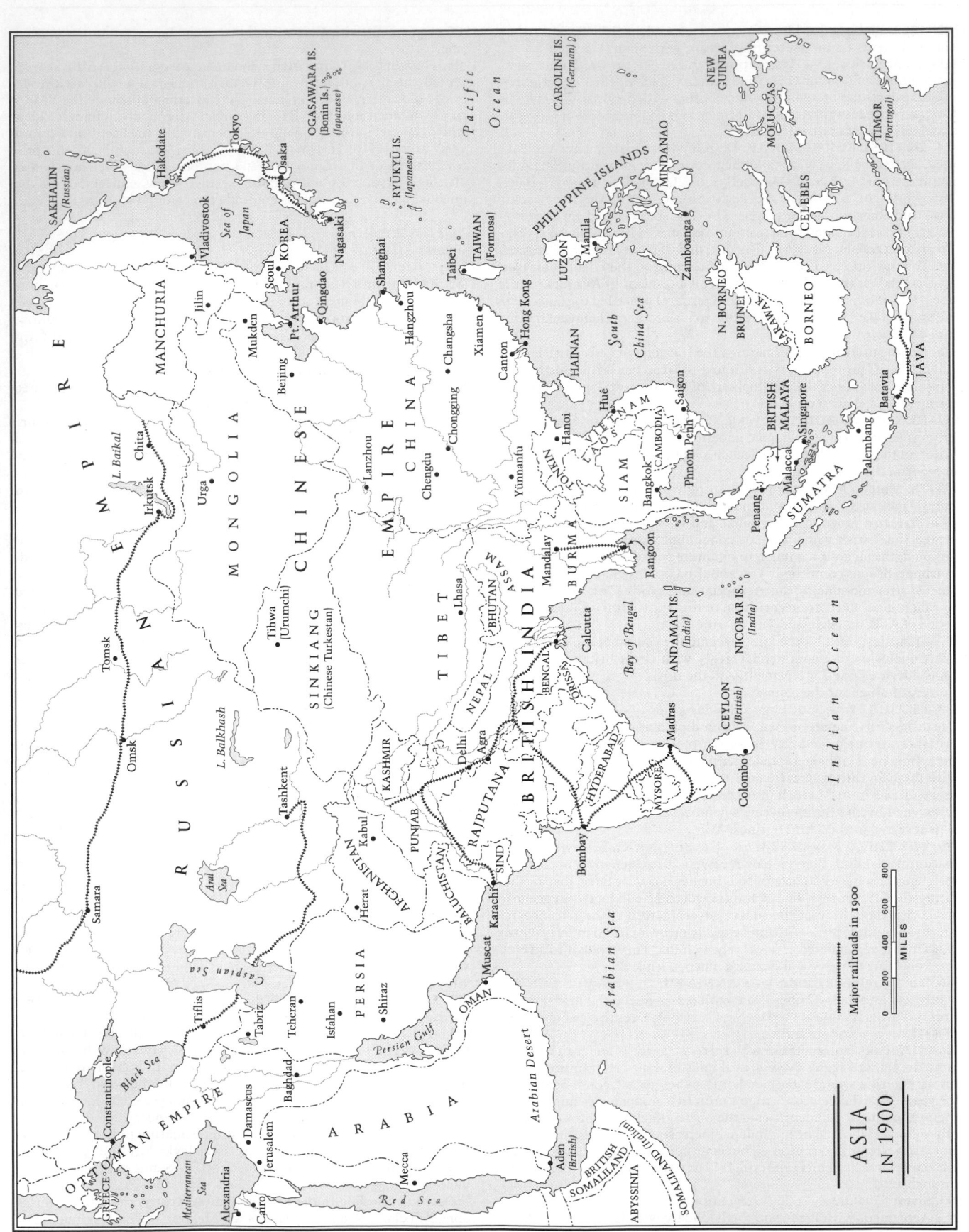

SAKHALIN
(Russian)

Hakodate

Tokyo
Osaka

OGASAWARA IS.
(Bonin Is.)
(Japanese)

Pacific
Ocean

CAROLINE IS.
(German)

NEW
GUINEA

MOLUCCAS

TIMOR
(Portugal)

RUSSIAN EMPIRE

MANCHURIA

Vladivostok

Sea of
Japan

KOREA

Seoul
Pt. Arthur
Nagasaki

Qingdao

Shanghai

RYUKYU IS.
(Japanese)

Taibei

TAIWAN
(Formosal)

PHILIPPINE ISLANDS

MINDANAO

LUZON
Manila

Zamboanga

CELEBES

N. BORNEO
BRUNEI

SARAWAK

BORNEO

JAVA

L. Baikal
Chita
Irkutsk

Jilin
Mukden
Beijing

Urga

MONGOLIA

CHINESE EMPIRE

Hangzhou

Changsha
Xiamen
Canton

Hong Kong

HAINAN

South
China Sea

SUMATRA
Palembang
Batavia

Tomsk

SINKIANG
(Chinese Turkestan)

Tihwa
(Urumchi)

Lanzhou

Chongqing
Chengdu

Yünnanfu

Hué

Hanoi

TONKIN

VIETNAM

LAOS

SIAM

Bangkok

CAMBODIA

Saigon

Phnom Penh

BRITISH
MALAYA

Malacca
Singapore

Penang

Omsk

L. Balkhash

TIBET

Lhasa

NEPAL

BHUTAN

ASSAM

BURMA

Mandalay

Rangoon

Bay of Bengal

ANDAMAN IS.
(India)

NICOBAR IS.
(India)

Indian Ocean

Aral Sea

Tashkent

AFGHANISTAN

Kabul

Herat

KASHMIR

PUNJAB

Delhi
Agra

RAIPUTANA

BRITISH INDIA

Calcutta

BENGAL

ORISSA

CEYLON
(British)

Colombo

Samara

BALUCHISTAN

SIND

Karachi

Bombay

HYDERABAD

MYSORE

Madras

Arabian Sea

Major railroads in 1900

Tiflis

PERSIA

Tabriz
Teheran
Isfahan
Shiraz

Muscat
OMAN

MILES
0 200 400 600 800

Constantinople

Black Sea

OTTOMAN EMPIRE

Baghdad
Damascus

Persian Gulf

ARABIA

Arabian Desert

Aden
(British)

Mediterranean Sea

GREECE
Alexandria
Cairo

Jerusalem

Mecca

Red Sea

BRITISH
SOMALILAND

SOMALI
LAND
(Italian)

ABYSSINIA

Caspian Sea

ASIA
IN 1900

of 3 million francs. The French remained in occupation of Chantabun until 1905.

1896, Jan. 15. An **Anglo-French agreement** ended the long friction between the two countries on the Siamese question. The British recognized the gains made by France in 1893 and abandoned the demand for a buffer between Burma and the French colonies. Both sides guaranteed the independence of Siam.

1897. The king of Siam paid an extended visit to the European capitals.

1904, Feb. 13. A further treaty with France replaced the agreement of 1893. France returned Chantabun, while Siam ceded Bassac, Melupré, that part of Luang Prabang that lay on the right (west) bank of the Mekong, and Krat on the coast.

1907, March 23. By agreement **France retroceded to Siam Battambong, Siemrap, and Sisophon** on the Cambodian frontier, and received in return the region of **Krat and Dansai.** France agreed to **modification of the extraterritorial system,** giving Siam jurisdiction over French Asians.

    April 8. An **Anglo-French convention** confirmed the independence of Siam but established **spheres of influence:** territory west of the Menam River was to be the British sphere, that to the east the French sphere.

1909, March 10. Great Britain gave up the system of extraterritoriality, in return for the cession of Kedah, Kelantan, Trengganu, and Perlis to the Malay States.

1910–25. RAMA VI (Vajiravudh). Educated in England, he continued the policy of modernization and westernization: irrigation projects, education, calendar reform, reduction of compulsory labor, etc. Vajiravudh was a writer, actor, and playwright, and he promulgated his nationalist ideas in public places and through the emerging public press.

1912. An early reaction to Vajiravudh's poor political judgment, however, came when a group of young military officers planned a coup. They claimed that reform was incomplete, and, influenced by developments in Russia (in 1905) and the Chinese revolution of 1911, they planned a revolution for April. Discovered in Feb., however, they were imprisoned.

(To p. 773)

3. LAOS AND CAMBODIA
(From p. 376)

1826–27. The **Anu Rebellion** was suppressed by the Bangkok government, which then forced massive population resettlement. The kingdom of Luang Prabang and its few minor tributary principalities to the east and north were the only remaining independent Lao powers.

1863, Aug. 11. King Norodom of Cambodia, a Hindu state dependent on both Annam and Siam and constantly threatened by these neighbors, accepted a French protectorate.

    From 1872 onward, bands of Chinese (called **Ho**) from Yunnan raided the whole northern region, even reaching Vientiane. The king of Luang Praban was forced to call upon Bangkok, acknowledging Thai suzerainty, for assistance. In the 1870s and 1880s the Siamese government repeatedly sent military expeditions, but these proved ineffectual.

1884, June 17. A new **treaty with Cambodia** gave the protecting power much more extensive control.

1887. Ho sacked Luang Prabang. The king, aided by the French, escaped. Siam lost prestige while the French gained ascendancy in the role of protector.

    Cochin China, Cambodia, Annam, and Tonkin were administratively united as the *Union Indo-Chinoise* (p. 575).

1893. FRANCO-SIAMESE TREATY gave France control of Laos, the interior region along the Mekong that had long been in dispute between Annam and Siam. The French ruled three of the four Lao principalities without Lao princes. Until the end of World War I Laos was governed under a casual ad hoc arrangement: a French regional head *(residente)* in Vientiane exercised indirect French rule in the protected principality of Luang Prabang, ruled by Sisavanvon (r. 1909–59); the *residente* also directly administered the three other Lao principalities of Xieng Khouang, Vientiane, and Champassak. French rule depended on the cooperation of traditional Lao leaders, minimal French economic involvement, the country's isolation, and the compliance of the Lao population. The French administration operated at a deficit in Laos, but this was offset by the French operations in Cambodia and Vietnam.

In the pre–World War II period, the French concentrated resources on public works, primarily the extension of all-weather roads and cultural projects. The French worked through princely families and bureaucratic elites, who went unchallenged because the French-controlled educational system did not produce qualified rivals and also because of the absence of a vernacular press, elected assemblies, and voluntary associations.

(To p. 773)

b. PENINSULAR AND ISLAND SOUTHEAST ASIA

1. BRITISH MALAYA

1795. The **British took Malacca** to hold for the Dutch, who were under French domination at the time.

1800. The **British secured Province Wellesley** from the sultan of Kedah.

1802. Malacca was restored to the Dutch under terms of the **Treaty of Amiens.**

1811. The **British retook Malacca,** which was used as a base for the expedition against Java.

1818. The **Dutch recovered Malacca,** under terms of the **Treaty of Vienna.**

1819. FOUNDING OF SINGAPORE by Sir Stamford Raffles. Practically abandoned for centuries, the city was soon to become the strategic and commercial center of the region, completely overshadowing Malacca. The founding of the city of Singapore signaled a larger development: the new towns created throughout island Southeast Asia focused on export, not local consumption. In addition to trade, these new urban centers served as important communications and administrative centers for the surrounding countryside (from which they extracted goods for export). To facilitate this type of extractive trade, port cities emerged to funnel tin, rubber, rice, and other primary products into world markets. At the close of the 19th century, Singapore may have been the most polyglot city in Asia: residing there were more than 164,000 Chinese, 23,000 Malays from the peninsular states, more than 12,000 Javanese and Sumatrans, as well as at least 1,000 Arabs.

1824, March 17. The **Dutch ceded Malacca** to Britain, in return for Bengkulen in Sumatra.

1826. British treaty with Siam. Under terms of this agreement the sultanates of Perak and Selangor were recognized as independent, while Siamese control of Kedah was acknowledged. At the same time Perak ceded to Britain **Pangkor Island** and the **Sembilan Islands** for use as bases in the fight against piracy.

1850 ff. Steady influx of Chinese laborers into the peninsula. These were employed chiefly in the tin mines, though many also turned to piracy on the coast. Their presence created disturbance in many states and ultimately provoked British interference.

1867, April 1. End of the rule of the British East India Company. The Straits Settlements thenceforth had the status of a Crown colony.

1873, June 20. TREATY OF PANGKOR. After serious Chinese disorders in Perak and a prolonged dynastic conflict, the British obliged the Perak chiefs to accept a British resident and to take his advice on all matters except for religion and custom. The introduction of this system soon outraged the native chiefs.

1875. Revolt of native chiefs resulted in the murder of the British resident, **J. W. W. Birch.** The insurrection was suppressed by a British force, and in the ensuing years further treaties were concluded with the other Malay states.

1885, Dec. 11. British treaty with Johore, regulating relations.

1889. Nine of the smaller states were federated and became **Negri Sembilan.**

1890s. In west coast **FMS (Federated Malay States),** the first census counted 218,000 people, of whom the Malays numbered only 53 percent—reflecting the increased immigration of Chinese and Indian merchants and others. Even in the Unfederated Malay States (UMS), Johore and Kedah both had similar population patterns.

    Traditional rulers (sultans) and the British strove to isolate Malays in villages that continued to operate according to traditional agrarian values. Although this artificial structure in fact deprived the sultans of their autonomy and decision-making control, the fiction of their independence—coupled with the centralized apparatus of government introduced by the British—actually strengthened certain parts of Malay life. In particular, matters relating to Malay religion and custom became protected and reified, so that the ceremonial trappings of Malay life and new administrative establishments for religious practices *(Councils of Muslim Religion and Malay Custom)* became elaborated.

1896, July 1. TREATY OF FEDERATION of Perak, Selangor, Negri Sembilan, and Pahang. Together they were to have one British resident general (the governor of the Straits Settlements), while retaining their separate residents.

1909, March 10. By **treaty with Siam,** Britain secured suzerainty and protection over **Kelantan, Trengganu, Kedah,** and **Perlis.** Protection was proclaimed on July 14, 1909, and treaties were concluded with these states in 1910. Together with Johore they comprised the Unfederated Malay States.

1914, May 12. The **sultan of Johore** accepted a general adviser and a further measure of British supervision and control.

British Malaya was entirely under British rule or control. The different states were organized as follows:

Straits Settlements (Crown colony) comprised Singapore, Penang, Province Wellesley, the Dindings, Malacca.

The Federated Malay States comprised Perak, Selangor, Negri Sembilan, Pahang.

Unfederated Malay States comprised Johore, Kedah, Perlis, Kelantan, Trengganu.   *(To p. 774)*

2. THE MALAYAN ARCHIPELAGO, 1798–1908
(From p. 374)

1798. End of the Dutch East India Company.

1808. The **Dutch subdued Bantam** in western Java. Mission of **Marshal Herman Daendels,** who reorganized the Dutch possessions and began the systematic curtailment of the powers of the princes and feudal lords.

1811. A **British expedition captured Batavia** and took over **Java.** Under the administration of **Stamford Raffles** (1811–16) much of the old system was swept away in an extension of European control that retained native administration. Land leases were given to native peoples.

1814, 1816. Sumatra and then Java were restored to the Dutch, in accordance with the peace treaties.

1824, March 17. The **British ceded Bengkulen** (Sumatra) to the Dutch in return for Malacca: end of British hold in the island.

1825–30. REVOLT OF THE JAVANESE against the Dutch, led by **Dipo Negora.** The rising was suppressed only with great difficulty. The ultimate effect was to oblige the Dutch to conquer the interior and to extend their control. Later revolts (1849, 1888) had the same effect.

1830. Introduction of the forced culture system by the Dutch. This involved government contracts with the native people, crop control, and fixed prices—a system very lucrative to the Dutch.

1839. Native chiefs of Bali acknowledged **Dutch control,** but disorders continued until 1849.

1841. The **sultan of Brunei,** in northern Borneo, **ceded to Sir James Brooke** the region of **Sarawak,** in return for aid against enemies. Brooke became rajah of the region and ruled until 1868, when he was succeeded by his nephew Charles (1868–1917) and the latter's son, Vyner (1917–46). He induced the British government to take an active part in the work of suppressing piracy in the China Sea.

1847. The British secured from the sultan of Brunei the island of **Labuan,** off the northwest coast of Borneo, which, it was expected, would become an important naval base.

1859, April 20. The **Dutch and Portuguese** by agreement **divided Timor** and the neighboring islands between them.

1865. The American government concluded a treaty with the sultan of Brunei, and the **American Trading Company of Borneo** acquired title to lands, but the effort to exploit the region failed.

1870. The Dutch introduced a **new sugar law and a new agrarian law in Java,** which involved a relaxation of the culture system and the gradual extension of private agriculture.

1881. The British government issued **a charter to the North Borneo Company.** This company took over the assets of the American company and secured new concessions from the sultans of Brunei and Sulu. Protests of the Dutch and Spaniards were to no avail (Spanish claims were renounced in 1885).

1888, March 17. Great Britain established a protectorate over Sarawak.

May 12. The British protectorate over North Borneo continued to be held and administered by the North Borneo Company.

1890. Beginning of **resistance movement** in Blora District of Central Java, led by a villager named **Surontiko Samin.** Saminists especially resisted intrusive modern government through reorganizing their villages socially and politically and altering taxation structures. After 1905, Saminists withdrew from the existing social order, refusing to contribute to village rice banks and other communal institutions. They also rejected Islamic marriage forms and insisted that tax payments were "donations" to the Dutch government. Despite the banishment of Samin in 1907, his movement continued sporadically through the 1920s and beyond.

1891, June 20. The British and Dutch by treaty defined their respective **domains in Borneo,** the Dutch retaining by far the larger part.

1900s. Islamic reformism, especially through education and self-reform, came to Indonesia via reformist movements in the Middle East. For example, a reform movement emerged in this decade in Sumatra in Minangkabau, focused on reforming matrilineal custom and traditional Islamic practices. The movement produced important cultural leaders such as the novelist **Hamka** and the political leader **Haji Agus Salim.**

In Java, a conflict arose between those who practiced "Javanese religion" (an amalgam of Islam, Hinduism, Buddhism, and animism) and the *santri,* who distinguished themselves from the others by a more exacting observance of the five daily prayers and fasting during Ramadan.

1907, Dec. The **Dutch,** after many years of warfare, finally **subdued the Achinese** in northern Sumatra (Atjeh), thus completing the pacification of Sumatra.

1908. Direct Dutch rule was established in **Bali,** after a series of native insurrections.

1907–14. Dutch-language **Native System** of education emerged, especially through the establishment of Dutch Native Schools (DNS). In 1915 some 20,000 students were enrolled, making this form of education (conducted entirely in Dutch) the most important early-20th-century educational institution in Southeast Asia and establishing the basis for Indonesian communication with the rest of the world, as well as the stimulus to a nationalist movement. These primary-level institutions were followed by advanced education, such as the Doktor Djawa School that trained medical practitioners.

1908. Within the Doktor Djawa School was founded the first organization to explore redefined ethnic identity, the Budi Utomo. This organization used Javanese culture to create a modern foundation for their own self-respect and to support their claims to participate in civil society. Its moderate stance was typical of organizations founded at this time, and it was peopled by those with traditional elite backgrounds.

More radical organizations, especially those founded by students, emerged in the next decade. A generational split with the older, more moderate party was revealed by these newer groups, all named using the word *jong* (Dutch for "young") in their names—Jong Java, and so on.

1912. Sarekat Islam (Islamic Union) was founded to loosely unite many different kinds of Indonesian Muslims in one mass movement. Initially formed by those with economic interests influenced by changes in China, the group soon included disaffected intelligentsia, Dutch-educated reformist Muslims, and socialists. Relying on a symbolic appeal to a mass audience, these disparate groups all tried to work within Sarekat Islam's format; by 1919 more than 2 million people held formal membership, and the group influenced a great many more.

(To p. 774)

E. EAST ASIA, 1793–1914

1. CHINA, 1796–1914

(From p. 380)

This period embraces China's last imperial dynasty from its initial decline to its end, when it was overthrown by a revolution made in the name of republicanism, though it never took form as such. In addition to the systemic problems of the dynastic form of government, China was subject to natural and secular changes—principally, the disastrous changing course of the Yellow River and the debilitating impact of mass opium addiction—that enervated the Qing dynasty. China's population continued to grow in these years, topping 400 million by the middle of the 19th century. The presence of the Western powers, and later of Japan, and pressing demands on the court exacerbated the Qing's problems. Traditionally, Marxist and many non-Marxist historians dated the beginning of "modern Chinese history" to the Opium War of 1839–42, because the British defeat of the Chinese and the subsequent demands on the Qing government effectively transformed the nature of the Chinese economy. That view has not been seriously defended outside of the People's Republic of China for some time. A more important event signaling the decline of the Qing, and hence of the dynastic system, would be the White Lotus Rebellion, which begins this section.

1796–1820. The **JIAQING REIGN** of Emperor Renzong marked the turning point from the high Qing period into decline. Jiaqing did not actually begin to run the government until the death of the retired Qianlong emperor in 1799. China was faced with threats to the social order from within and without. Little in the way of open pressure was brought to bear on the court.

1796–1804. The **WHITE LOTUS REBELLION,** led by a millenarian Buddhist sect that believed in the return of the Buddha, erupted out of social and economic discontent in the north. It spread across the impoverished three provinces of Hubei, Shaanxi, and Sichuan, before being suppressed by Manchu forces. The fact that it took the armies of the empire eight years to put it down proved to be a harbinger of the declining effectiveness of the State's standing armies; the Qing was saved only by the use of Chinese recruits, the "green standards."

c. 1800–1830s. The **Western powers** had been coming to China for some time; they were allowed to trade only through the strictly limited Canton system. Whereas customers in the West wanted ever greater quantities of tea, silk, and Chinese porcelains, the Chinese wanted nothing the West had to offer, except silver. From about 1800, though, Indian-grown opium found a hungry market in China, despite the fact that it was illegal, and it reversed the silver flow until Chinese coffers were drained. Eventually, this problem would come to a head.

1805. Christian literature was proscribed, and a Catholic priest was strangled for being in China without permission (1815).

1807. Robert Morrison (1782–1834), the first Protestant missionary to China, translator of the Bible into Chinese, and author of the first Chinese-English dictionary, arrived in Guangzhou. He lived there under the aegis of the British East India Company.

1813. A millenarian religious group, the Tianli Sect, rose in rebellion and invaded the imperial palaces in Beijing, before being suppressed.

1816. British ambassador Lord Amherst (1773–1857) was sent away from Beijing without being received, just as British forces were fighting against Nepal, a Chinese tributary.

1820. Li Ruzhen's (c. 1763–c. 1830) satirical novel *Flowers in the Mirror* was completed (first printed in 1828). In it gender roles were reversed, with men binding their feet, applying makeup, and serving women. The novel was in part intended as a critique of the great difficulty many well-educated men were having in finding employment as officials.

1821–50. The **DAOGUANG REIGN** of Emperor Xuanzong marked a tumultuous time in Chinese history, which included a disastrous war and the early beginnings of the greatest rebellion in China's entire history.

1821. The illicit trade in opium, 5,000 chests annually (despite imperial prohibitions of 1800 and 1813), was transferred to Lintin Island near Guangzhou.

1825–28. The kingdom of **Kashgaria** was with great difficulty defended against **Jehangir** (1790–1828) of the Hodja family, which had formerly ruled in Turkestan.

1827. The *Huangchao jingshi wenbian (Essays on Statecraft from the Qing Dynasty)*, compiled by He Changling (1785–1848), appeared. It was a huge compendium of documents dealing with a variety of practical matters and was closely read by many scholar-officials at the time.

1829. The magnum opus of the textual critical movement of the Qing dynasty, the 366-volume *Huangchao jingjie (Qing Exegeses of the Classics)*, was finished under the sponsorship of **Ruan Yuan** (1764–1849). He was also responsible for a definitive edition of the *Shisan jing zhushu (Commentaries and Annotations to the Thirteen Classics)*, reprinted by the Xuehaitang, a private academy, from a Song period original. He had earlier founded the Xuehaitang in Guangzhou, while serving as governor-general of the region (1817–26). Other great critical editors of this era included Sun Xingyan (1753–1818) and Yan Kejun (1762–1843).

1834. The **end of the East India Company's monopoly of British trade** with China removed an important element in the Canton system of commercial regulation. Henceforth, all foreigners could come to China, surely increasing the opium traffic. The assertion of diplomatic equality by the first superintendent of British trade in China, Lord Napier (1786–1834), was followed by the temporary stoppage of trade. Napier died on Oct. 11, and his successors adopted a "quiescent policy."

1836. The Daoguang emperor requested input on how to address the opium issue. Proposals to legalize the importation of opium and concern over the silver drain to pay for it led to heated debates in Beijing with those who wished to crush the traffic and users of the drug. Daoguang decided (1838) to end, once and for all, the opium trade.

1839. Imperial Commissioner **Lin Zexu** (1785–1850) arrived in Guangzhou (March 10), forced the surrender of opium (annual import was 30,000 chests for 1835, 40,000 for 1838), and destroyed it—some 3 million pounds of raw opium. Hostilities soon followed (Nov.).

1840. The British fleet under Adm. George Elliot reached Guangzhou (June), leaving several vessels to block the harbor. Zhoushan Island was occupied (July). An agreement was reached (Jan. 1841) after talks between Capt. Charles Elliot (1801–75), Lord Napier's successor, and **Qishan** (d. 1854), the local governor-general, and both governments repudiated the agreement.

1841–42. The **OPIUM WAR** erupted. British plenipotentiary **Henry Pottinger** (1789–1856) led the British navy along the Chinese coast, capturing several cities. Shanghai was taken (June 1842) and then Zhenjiang (July). The Grand Canal was blocked. The Qing sought peace (Aug.), having received their greatest military defeat to date.

1842, Aug. 29. The **TREATY OF NANJING** was ratified by both parties aboard the British vessel *Cornwallis*. It ended the monopolistic Canton system of trade; **Hong Kong** was ceded to Britain, having already been occupied by British forces (Jan. 1841); five ports were opened to trade: **Guangzhou, Xiamen (Amoy), Fuzhou, Ningbo, and Shanghai;** consulates were to be established there to oversee trade; **indemnities** were to be paid by the Qing to the British; and the treaty established a **uniform import tariff** of about 5 percent ad valorem. Of the four newly opened ports, only Shanghai really grew as a result of the new trading opportunities.

1843, Oct. 8. A **supplementary treaty** was negotiated, also by Pottinger and Imperial Commissioner **Qiying** (d. 1858), conceding most-favored-nation status (later extended to other powers) and amplifying the de-

THE MANCHU (QING) DYNASTY (1796–1912)

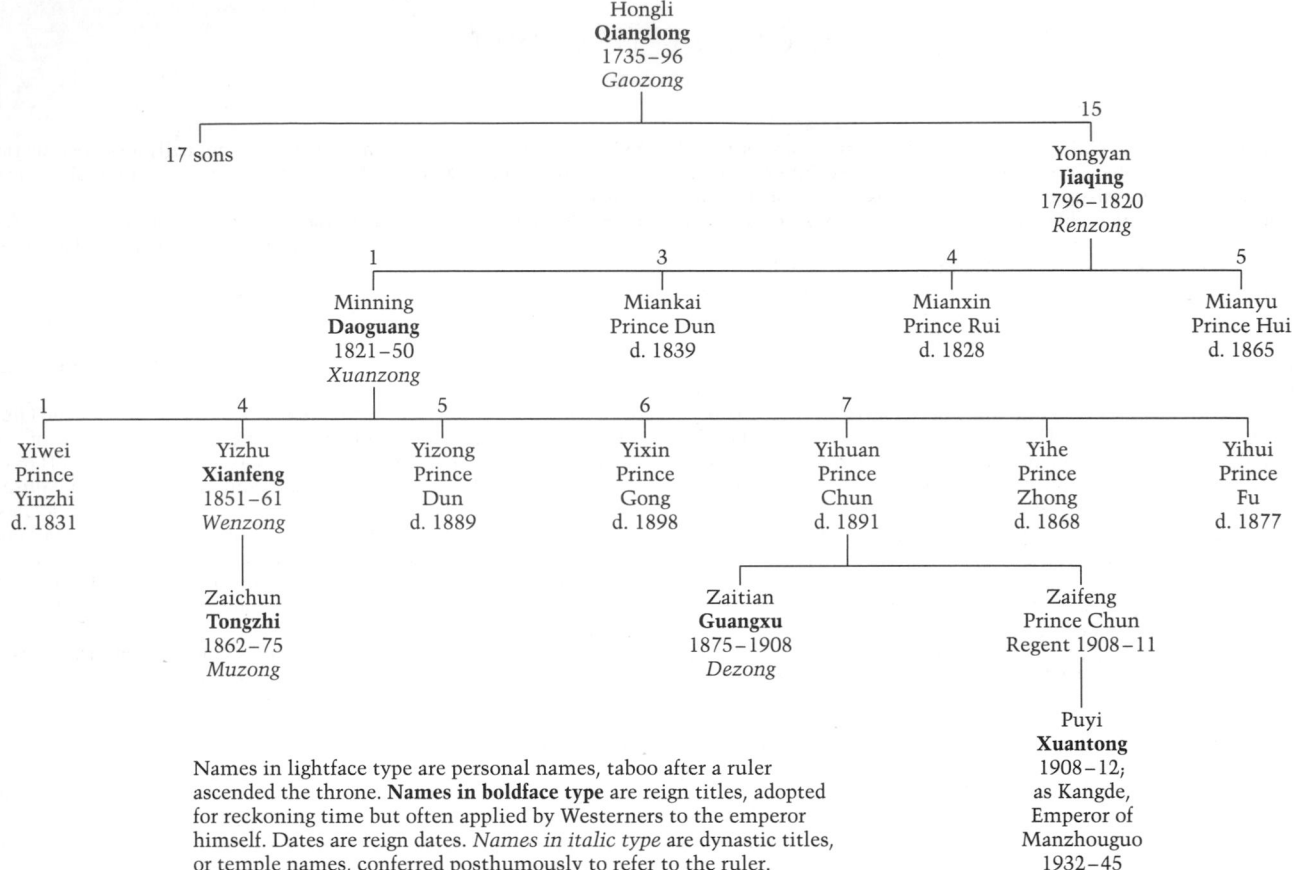

Names in lightface type are personal names, taboo after a ruler ascended the throne. **Names in boldface type** are reign titles, adopted for reckoning time but often applied by Westerners to the emperor himself. Dates are reign dates. *Names in italic type* are dynastic titles, or temple names, conferred posthumously to refer to the ruler.

tails of the new commercial system. Opium traffic, despite remaining illegal, continued.

1844, July 3. The **Treaty of Wangxia,** signed by Qiying and Caleb Cushing (1800–75) for the United States, gave to the U.S. many of the privileges already accorded to Great Britain. In addition, Protestant missionaries gained new advantages, and extraterritoriality was given to U.S. citizens in civil and criminal cases. The study of Chinese also became legal for foreigners. The French **Treaty of Huangpu** (Oct. 24) secured toleration of Catholicism, which was extended (1845) to Protestantism.

1846–48. Popular opposition to foreign entrance into the city of Guangzhou increased friction between China and foreign powers.

1851–61. The **XIANFENG REIGN** of Emperor Wenzong revealed the rapid disintegration of the dynasty. Agrarian unrest due primarily to official exactions, natural calamities, and absentee landlordism fed the movement into antiestablishment causes.

1850–64. REBELLION OF THE TAIPING TIANGUO (Heavenly Kingdom of Great Peace). The Taipings were a Christian-inspired movement founded in Guangxi by **Hong Xiuquan** (1813–64) and **Feng Yunshan** (1832–62). Its core was made up of the Hakka minority. After several failed attempts to pass the civil service examinations, Hong had a fever-induced vision, which he later interpreted as Jehovah calling him to heaven for an audience and to meet his (Hong's) "elder brother," Jesus Christ. In 1847 he joined a Chinese Christian group founded earlier by Feng, the Society of God Worshipers. Two years later their numbers reached 10,000, and twice that number in 1850. Hong soon began to understand his calling from God to be the destruction of the Qing dynasty and all the "demons," as he termed them, who supported it. His followers lived a communal life, sharing every-

thing, strictly segregating the sexes, praying as a group, and forbidding opium and all corruption on pain of death.

Hong was aided by a brilliant strategist, **Yang Xiuqing** (d. 1856), who effectively took over the day-to-day operations of the rebel movement, as Hong became largely a spiritual leader. The government forces attacked them (Dec. 1850) and were badly defeated. The next month Hong announced that he was the "Heavenly King," and the rebellion was launched. Their well-disciplined military fought through Guangxi and Hunan to the Wuhan tri-cities (1852–53) and down the Yangzi River past Nanjing, his capital (1853–64), to the Grand Canal. An expeditionary force sent toward Beijing was deflected through Shanxi by floods of the Yellow River, which shifted its bed north of Shandong (1853), and this force was repelled (1855). The Taipings' failure to provide conquered territory with either protection or constructive administration proved disastrous to their cause. They also failed to work with other contemporaneous rebel bands because of their extremist religious lifestyle. Hong's particular brand of Christianity ultimately alienated the Westerners as well: Hong preached an ascetic Christianity, while he and his fellow Taiping leaders all lived lives of extravagance and debauchery.

Persuaded to come out of ritual mourning, **Zeng Guofan** (1811–72), together with his younger brother Zeng Guoquan (1824–90), Li Hongzhang (1823–1901), Zuo Zongtang (1812–85), and other prominent Han Chinese officials came to the aid of the faltering Manchu dynasty. They were helped by the "Ever-Victorious Army," a group of mercenaries led by Frederick Townsend Ward (1831–62) and, later, Charles George Gordon (1833–85). They retrieved Anqing (1861) from the Taipings, Suzhou (1863), and finally Nanjing (1864). All told, over 20 million perished in this conflict.

1851–68. The **NIAN** were an organized group of rebels from Anhui, northern Jiangsu, Shandong, and later Shanxi, led by Zhang Luoxing (d. 1863), many of whom had joined after losing everything when the Yellow River shifted directions. They took advantage of the Qing troops' preoccupation with the Taipings and the foreigners to rise in **rebellion.** Qing general Senggelinqin (d. 1865) won victories against them and killed Zhang, but he was later killed by them. They were suppressed (1865–68) by the same men who put down the Taipings: Zeng Guofan and later Li Hongzhang were sent to quell the uprising; both had great difficulty. The Nian were finally defeated (Aug. 1868).

1855–73. **Muslims** (Panthays) in **Yunnan revolted,** after years of friction with the local Han Chinese and excessive taxation by the central government, and set up an independent state, "Kingdom of the Pacified South," at Dali, the ancient capital of Nanzhao. There was also a Muslim revolt in the northwest (Shaanxi and Gansu, 1862–73), eventually put down by Zuo Zongtang.

1855–81. Hmong tribesmen in Guizhou seized the opportunity to revolt.

1856, Oct. 8. After several years of efforts by Britain, France, and the United States to secure new rights and privileges through treaty revisions, the **Arrow Incident** in Guangzhou provided the British with an opportunity to force the Chinese militarily. Claiming that the vessel *Arrow* was registered in Hong Kong and had been illegally searched by Qing officials, the British moved and seized Guangzhou in Dec. 1857. British vessels then began to move north to force the central government's hand.

1858, June 26–29. The **TREATY OF TIANJIN** was concluded between China, Great Britain (negotiated by Lord Elgin [1811–63]), France, the United States, and Russia. China opened 11 more ports and permitted legations in Beijing, and trade and Christian missions in the interior; subsequent tariff and rules of trade (Nov.) established a maritime customs service with a foreign inspector general (Horatio N. Lay) and staff, and legalized the importation of opium. The **Treaty of Aigun,** signed by Yishan (d. 1878) and Nicholas Muraviev (c. 1809–81), ceded the north bank of the Amur River to Russia.

1859. The Qing refused British demands for the admission of foreign diplomats into Beijing. The British attacked the Dagu forts (June 25) but were repulsed.

1860, Oct. 12. The result was the **occupation of Beijing** by 17,000 British and French troops. The **Summer Palace (Yuanming yuan) was burned to the ground** (Oct. 18) to punish the court for seizing British envoys under a flag of truce. The emperor had fled the city to the north, and his younger brother "negotiated" the **Beijing Convention** (Oct. 24 with Britain, Oct. 25 with France), which increased indemnities, and the French secured the right of Catholic missions to hold land. Russian envoy Muraviev secured the cession (Nov. 14) of the **Maritime Province.** Now the British became the Qing's strongest ally against domestic rebellion.

1861, Nov. 11. The **Zongli Yamen was created** to handle foreign affairs, under the effective leadership of **Prince Gong** (1833–98). Wheaton's *Elements of International Law,* translated into Chinese by missionary W. A. P. Martin (1827–1916), was accepted by Prince Gong as the foundation for international interaction (1863). A school for interpreters was opened in the capital, with other foreign language schools opening later elsewhere.

1862–75. The **TONGZHI REIGN** of Emperor Muzong witnessed a restoration of Qing control over the empire with the quelling of all the midcentury rebellions. His mother, the Empress Dowager **Cixi** (1835–1908), ruled in conjunction with a prince and several high officials until 1873. Under the leadership of **Zeng Guofan, Zuo Zongtang, Li Hongzhang,** and numerous others responsible for returning the country to Manchu hands, a solid foundation for reform in many areas was put in place. The "Self-Strengthening Movement" (or early Westernization movement) began; by studying Western subjects and skills, it was argued, China would become stronger. Arsenals and shipyards were built and outfitted with machinery from the United States; schools teaching how to use the machines and sail the vessels were attached to the arsenals. When Tongzhi died at the age of 18, Cixi controlled the succession and played a major role in all affairs of state until her death, the most powerful woman in the entire Qing period. Though far from the evil creature that subsequent Chinese and foreign

critics have portrayed her to be, she was conservative and wasted money.

1863–1908. Sir Robert Hart (1835–1911) built up the Imperial Maritime Customs Service as a mainstay of government revenue and credit, with collateral services to train men, light the coast, improve rivers and harbors, and organize a postal service (1896; independent, 1911).

1864–89. Protestant missionaries in China increased from under 200 to nearly 1,300. By the mid-1860s, over 30 different Protestant sects were represented in China.

1868–70. Anson Burlingame (1820–70), former U.S. minister to China, was sent on a goodwill mission with two Chinese associates to Western nations.

1870, June 21. The **"Tianjin massacre"** took place—13 Frenchmen and 3 Russians were killed by an angry mob in response to the shooting of a Chinese by the French consul. Reparations were paid, 16 Chinese were executed, and a mission of apology sailed for France (1871–72).

1871. Cables were laid from Vladivostok via Nagasaki to Shanghai, Hong Kong, and Singapore. A land line was built, Shanghai to Tianjin, in 1881.

The first Sino-Japanese commercial treaty was signed on the basis of equality between the two countries in line with standards of international law.

1872. **Yung Wing** (Rong Hong, 1828–1912), a missionary-trained, English-speaking Yale graduate (class of 1854), led a group of 120 Chinese students, ages 12 to 14, to the United States. Thirty others were sent for technical training to France and Great Britain.

1874. A **Japanese expedition to occupy Taiwan** to punish the murder by locals of Liuqiu (Japanese, Ryūkyū) islanders (1871) was withdrawn in return for an indemnity. The Japanese had claimed control over the Ryūkyūs in 1872; they were annexed several years later.

1875–1908. The **GUANGXU REIGN** of Emperor Dezong. Tongzhi died without an heir, and an infant cousin (b. 1871), a nephew of Empress Dowager Cixi, was adopted as the second son of Xianfeng to carry on dynastic sacrifices, and his prospective offspring was destined to be an adopted son of the late emperor. Prince Gong, his uncle, was named regent under supervision of the empress dowager. He began ruling in person only in 1889.

1875–78. Zuo Zongtang suppressed (1875–76) the Tungans of the northern Tianshan region, who had been in revolt since 1862, and reconquered Kashgaria (1877–78), which had become independent under **Yakub Beg** (c. 1820–77). Both areas were then organized as one territory, **Xinjiang** (literally, "new territory"), with its capital at Urumchi; it became a province in 1884.

1876, Sept. 13. The **Chefoo** (Zhifu) **Convention** was concluded between Li Hongzhang and the British. It was the result of the murder by local tribesmen of interpreter Augustus Margary (1846–75), who had been serving with a British railway survey team in Yunnan near the Burmese border. A large indemnity was to be paid, and ten new ports were to be opened to trade. It was ratified by Great Britain in 1885 with an additional article relating to the importation of opium—its annual average for 1875–85 had reached 82,000 chests, an amount greatly exceeded by production in China.

1877–80. Diplomatic missions, determined in 1875, established legations in London and Berlin (1877), Paris, Washington, and Tokyo (1878), Madrid and St. Petersburg (1879), and Lima (1880).

1881, Feb. 24. The **Treaty of St. Petersburg** was negotiated by **Zeng Jize** (1839–90), Zeng Guofan's son; it returned to China most of the Ili Valley and the passes.

1883, Aug. 25. The **Treaty of Huê** was concluded: Annam became a French protectorate, with the administration of Tonkin handled by French residents in disregard of Chinese suzerainty and protests (1881–82).

1884. Prince Gong and the Grand Council were dismissed by Cixi for failure to repel the French. A preliminary convention signed (May 11) by Li Hongzhang with Capt. François-Ernest Fournier (b. 1842) resulted in misunderstandings, and a French defeat at Baclé (June 23) led to an **undeclared war.** French naval destruction of the new Fuzhou arsenal (Aug. 22) and attacks on Taiwan were balanced by reverses on the Tonkin border (at Lang-son, March 28, 1885). French control over Vietnam was now a fait accompli.

1885, April 18. The **Li-Itō Convention** was agreed upon between Li

Hongzhang (China) and Itō Hirobumi (1841–1909, Japan) for withdrawal of troops by both countries from Korea.

June 9. The **Treaty of Tianjin,** facilitated by Robert Hart, recognized the French protectorate of Tonkin in return for a reciprocal promise to respect China's southern border. On his deathbed, Zuo Zongtang penned a memorial urging modernization and foreign study.

In **Korea,** a tributary of the Qing since 1637 when Manchu armies overran the peninsula, China had evaded responsibility for the persecution of Christianity and for the French punitive expedition that was repulsed from Seoul (1866). China did not protest the **Treaty of Kanghwa,** an unequal treaty imposed by Japan that recognized Korean independence, nor a Korean embassy to Japan. However, Li Hongzhang sent (1882) as "resident" to Seoul **Yuan Shikai** (1859–1916), who was thereafter active in intrigue against Japan.

1886, July 24. A British protectorate in Burma was recognized in return for continuance of decennial tribute.

1887, Dec. 1. The Portuguese secured the cession of Macao on the promise that they would not alienate it.

1888. The **first imperial railway** (Tangshan-Tianjin, 80 miles) was opened and extended to Shanhaiguan (1894) and to Fengtai outside Beijing (1896). **Zhang Zhidong** (1837–1909), governor-general of Hubei and Hunan, opened **coal mines,** the great Daye **iron mines,** and the Hanyang **steel works,** as necessary preliminaries to interior railway construction. Formerly a ferocious conservative, Zhang is credited with formulating a compromise reformist concept of using Chinese learning for the "essence" of reform together with Western learning for "practical utility."

1890. The Board of Admiralty was abolished, and the new and promising Chinese navy fell subsequently into neglect, as a result of the resignation of Capt. William Lang (British) and the death of Prince Chun (1891) and Zeng Jize (1890).

1894. SUN ZHONGSHAN (SUN YAT-SEN, 1866–1925) organized in Guangzhou the first of several **secret revolutionary societies,** with which he tried many times before late 1911 to overthrow the Qing dynasty. After his first failure (1895), he scarcely set foot in China until after the success of the 1911 revolution. During those years, he organized the Chinese in Honolulu and the United States, and was kidnapped and held for ten days by the Chinese legation in London (1896), narrowly escaping execution.

July 23–1895, April 17. The **SINO-JAPANESE WAR** erupted after ten years of rivalry and intrigue concerning Korea. A **revolt of the Tonghak Society** (Eastern Learning Society) in southern Korea afforded the Japanese an opportunity to seize the Korean queen and appoint a "regent" loyal to Japan (July 21). The British vessel *Kowshing,* carrying Chinese troops to Korea, was sunk (July 25) by the Japanese; the Korean regent declared war on China (July 27); China and Japan declared war on each other (Aug. 1). The European powers and the United States attempted in vain to mediate. The Japanese won a string of victories on land and sea: at Bingyang (Sept. 16), off the Yalu River at Lüshun (Port Arthur, Nov. 21), and at Weihaiwei (Feb. 21, 1895). Again, the court turned to Li Hongzhang to negotiate a peace.

1895, April 17. The Chinese were compelled to accept the terms of the **TREATY OF SHIMONOSEKI:** China perforce recognized the independence of Korea and ceded to Japan the island of Taiwan, the Pescadores, and the Liaodong peninsula in southern Manchuria; China was to pay an indemnity of 200 million taels and to open four more ports to foreign commerce. It was a great humiliation for the Chinese.

China's helplessness before a well-armed, small neighbor, upon which it had formerly looked condescendingly, was revealed for all to see. It served as a clarion call to the majority of educated Chinese. Further Chinese demands for reforms were stimulated by the accelerating onrush of the European powers for political and economic concessions and by their efforts to establish exclusive spheres of influence. The Qing government confronted another serious dilemma: native capital for military, railway, and industrial development was not available, and foreign capital could be secured only at the expense of the further extension of foreign control within the empire.

April 23. The **Tripartite Intervention** by Russia, Germany, and France obliged Japan to return the Liaodong peninsula to China in consideration of a further 30-million-tael indemnity. All three intervening powers expected to be well repaid by the Chinese.

June 20. France secured extensive territorial and commercial concessions in the southern provinces.

July 6. A Franco-Russian loan was extended to China (400 million francs at 4 percent interest, to run for 36 years, with the Chinese customs as security).

1896, May 23. An Anglo-German loan (16 million pounds for 36 years at 5 percent interest, secured by the customs revenues) was extended to China.

June 3. A Russo-Chinese treaty was secretly concluded at the coronation of Tsar Nicholas II (1868–1918) at Moscow by Li Hongzhang. In return for a defensive alliance for 15 years, China granted Russia the right to build and operate the **Chinese Eastern Railway** across northern Manchuria, as a link in the Russian Trans-Siberian Railway to Vladivostok.

July 21. A **commercial treaty with Japan,** imposed as part of the peace settlement, gave Japan most-favored-nation status and granted all the treaty powers the right to operate industrial enterprises in the treaty ports.

1897, Nov. 14. The **Germans occupied Jiaozhou Bay** (p. 423) with Qingdao, following the murder of two missionaries in Shandong. The move had been long under consideration and was looked upon by the Germans as the logical consequence of the Tripartite Intervention (1895). Instead, it precipitated the **"scramble for concessions"** the following year, in which most of the European powers participated.

1898, Feb. Britain secured agreements to open inland waters to foreign steamers, to not sell off any part of the Yangzi River valley to any other power, and to employ a British inspector general of customs as long as British trade remained preponderant.

March 6. Germany extracted a convention giving it a 99-year lease on Jiaozhou Bay, with exclusive rights to build railways and develop mines in Shandong (the Qingdao-Jinan Railway opened in 1904). A second Anglo-German loan of 16 million pounds for 45 years at 4.5 percent interest was extended to China.

March 27, May 7. Russia extorted from China a 25-year lease of the southern part of the Liaodong peninsula, including Dalian (Japanese, Dairen; Russian, Dalny) and Lüshun, with the right to construct a railroad from Harbin in the north to the newly leased ports.

April 10. France received a 99-year lease of Guangzhouwan and the vicinity, with the rights to extend a railroad to Yunnan (completed, 1910) and a promise not to sell to any other power any part of the provinces bordering Tonkin.

April 26. Japan secured a promise from China not to sell any part of Fujian.

June 9. Britain secured a 99-year lease for Kowloon opposite Hong Kong, and (July 1) a lease of Weihaiwei to run as long as the Russian occupation of Lüshun.

June 11–Sept. 16. During the **HUNDRED DAYS' REFORM** movement, the Guangxu emperor asserted himself with the issuance of a series of strikingly radical edicts; many of the ideas had been put forth earlier by Zhang Zhidong in his "Exhortation to Study" (1898), by **Kang Youwei** (1858–1927) in many pamphlets and essays, and by others. The edicts called for reforming educational institutions along Western lines and launching vocational schools, reforms in the economy and agriculture, military reforms, and the like. Although they met with general approval, the imperial decrees struck at the vital interests of the civil and military bureaucrats by abolishing sinecures.

Sept. 22. For reasons still not completely understood, the empress dowager, supported by the high-level Manchu military official Ronglu (1836–1903), placed Guangxu under house arrest, ordered the arrest of six of his alleged advisers, and had the latter executed with alacrity. Reforms that were deemed contrary to the best interests of the Manchu and high officials were revoked. Government control reverted to the hands of extreme conservatives. Kang Youwei and his brilliant disciple **Liang Qichao** (1873–1929) escaped by different routes to Japan. Another of his disciples, **Tan Sitong** (1865–98), died a martyr's death as one of the six executed.

1899, Feb. Italy demanded a port and concession in Zhejiang, which China rejected with a show of force and vigorous efforts to strengthen imperial defenses.

In response to notes of Sept. and Nov., **John Hay** (1838–1905), U.S. secretary of state, secured assurances from the great powers that the

Open Door to equal commercial opportunity would be maintained in spheres of special interest in China.

The **BOXERS** (a short form of "Boxers United in Righteousness," the name by which they called themselves), coming together as a military force in 1898 in northwestern Shandong, began in early 1899 to attack Chinese converts to Christianity and their property. They culled from a wide range of religious belief and practiced martial arts, from whence came their name. They were supported in their xenophobia by the Manchu governor of Shandong, Yuxian (d. 1901), who was replaced (Dec. 6) by Yuan Shikai, who then proceeded to suppress the movement.

1900. As the Boxers increased their numbers, the **Boxer Uprising** became more daring. They acquired the support of the empress dowager and a number of high Manchu officials who hoped to use the Boxers as auxiliaries to expel the foreigners from China. The foreign diplomats in Beijing all demanded (Jan.–May) the suppression of the Boxers, which only fanned the flames of resentment. A Boxer **attack on the Fengtai railway station** (May 28) was followed by the admission into Beijing of some 458 legation guards, but a joint naval column of 2,066 men from Tianjin to Beijing was repulsed (June 10–26) by the Boxers. The Westerners' **seizure of the Dagu forts** (June 17) was cited in an imperial declaration of war (June 21), which was disregarded both by the foreign powers and by Chinese officials outside Zhili and Shanxi. The murder (June 20) of the German minister, **Baron Klemens von Ketteler** (1853–1900), opened a **siege of the legations,** which would have succeeded but for Ronglu's protection. An **international expeditionary force** of some 20,000 men (principally from Russia, Great Britain, the United States, Japan, and France) took Tianjin (July 14) and relieved the legations in Beijing (Aug. 14). Elsewhere, especially in Shanxi where Yuxian was now governor, at least 231 foreign civilians (chiefly missionaries) were killed (June 24–July 24). The **court fled** (Aug. 15) to Xi'an, when a rescript (Dec. 26) promptly accepted a joint note embodying the allied demands. Russians at Blagoveshchensk, in retaliation for Chinese bombardments along the Amur (July 14–15) and in fear of attack by the local Chinese, drove several thousand Chinese civilians to their deaths in the river. Russia then quickly seized possession of southern Manchuria (Sept. 4–Oct. 10), without being able to secure ratification of a secret convention extorted at Lüshun (Nov. 11). German troops, arriving late in Beijing, alone carried out 35 of 46 punitive missions (Dec. 12–April 30, 1901).

1901, Sept. 7. After eight months of tough negotiating with the powers, the **Boxer Protocol** was signed by 12 powers. It provided for expressions of regret, punishment of 96 officials, payment over a period of 40 years of 450 million taels, revision of the tariff to an effective 5 percent, fortification of an enlarged legation quarter, the razing of all defensive forts, and the establishment of foreign garrisons along the railway to Shanhaiguan. The immense indemnity was to be met from maritime customs surplus, native customs, and the salt monopoly; the maritime customs under Hart were given charge of the native customs within 50 *li* (c. 17 miles) of all treaty ports.

1902, Jan. The empress dowager and the emperor returned to Beijing by train. Educational, economic, and military reforms were soon undertaken. The **deaths of Li Hongzhang, Liu Kunyi** (1830–1902), and **Ronglu** (1903) left Zhang Zhidong and Yuan Shikai as her ablest advisers. Intermarriage between Han and Manchu was for the first time sanctioned. The earlier trickle of students going to study in Japan became a flood, peaking in 1903–5. The legal code was ordered revised and was eventually promulgated (1910). Military reforms, actually begun the previous year, aimed at building "new armies"; provincial war offices were set up throughout the land (1904); by 1910–11 the reformed Qing army posted impressive victories in Tibet and elsewhere.

1903. Zou Rong (1885–1905), a Chinese nationalist who had studied in Japan, published a fiery tract, *The Revolutionary Army*, which ferociously attacked the Manchus. Arrested in 1904, he went to prison and died of illness there.

The Ministry of Commercial Affairs was created in the central government. The Shanghai Chamber of Commerce was founded. The Guangzhou Chamber of Commerce emerged as a force by 1905.

1904–5. The **defeat of Russia by Japan** (p. 574) again revealed to the Chinese some of the advantages to be gained by learning the lessons of the West. The Treaty of Portsmouth returned Manchuria from Rus-

sian to Chinese control (1907). Japan retained only the leasehold in Liaodong, which had already been definitively conceded to Russia, together with the South Manchurian Railway. Hitherto a Manchu preserve under military government, the "three eastern provinces" (Manchuria) were reorganized (1907) on a civilian basis and thrown open to Chinese settlement.

1905. As a protest against the further exclusion of Chinese immigrants from the United States, a **boycott of goods from the United States** reflected a growing national consciousness.

On Zhang Zhidong's recommendation, a **ministry of education** was founded, and Chinese students continued flocking to Japan. The civil service examination was disbanded as part of a complete overhaul of the educational system.

Sun Zhongshan and associates in Japan organized the Tongmenghui (usually translated as "Revolutionary Alliance"), an amalgam of anti-Manchu groups dedicated to overthrowing the Qing dynasty. They were inspired both by Japan's victory over Russia and the Russian revolution, both of 1905.

1906. Preparation for constitutional government was proclaimed, following the report of a mission sent in 1905 by the empress dowager to study foreign states; the model of the Japanese was especially approved. The reorganization of the state ministries (Nov. 6), together with plans for the eventual convening of a national assembly and provincial assemblies and other political reforms, were ordered.

Provision for a progressive ten-year **suppression of opium cultivation and consumption** was supplemented by an agreement with Britain, which cut imports from 48,530 chests (1907) to 4,236 chests in 1915. At the suggestion of the United States (1909), a series of conferences began in Shanghai and later at The Hague (1912) to establish international control over the world's drug traffic.

A summary of Marx and Engels's *Communist Manifesto* appeared in Chinese for the first time. There was increasing interest among Chinese intellectuals, especially those who had studied in Japan, in socialism.

1908, Jan. 13. Foreign loans for a railway from Tianjin to Pukou (opposite Nanjing) were contracted on the basis of construction, control, and operation exclusively by the Chinese government. The line was completed and opened in Jan. 1912. Foreign involvement in railway construction began a major cause célèbre among nationalist groups throughout the country.

May 13. Remission by the United States of half its share in the Boxer indemnity made possible the establishment of Qinghua (Tsing Hua) University (1911) and the sending of about 1,100 graduates to the United States for advanced study (1911–27).

Nov. 14–15. The deaths of the emperor and empress dowager occurred on successive days. Power passed to the ultraconservative Prince Chun (Zaifeng, 1883–1951) who ruled as regent for the boy emperor, **Puyi,** until the end of the dynasty (1912).

Dec. 3. A **draft constitution** was published, providing for the election of a parliament after nine years. The provincial assemblies were first to meet in Oct. 1909; by early the following year, they pressured the court into convening the cabinet in Oct. 1910.

1908–12. The **XUANTONG REIGN** of Puyi, China's last emperor.

1909, Jan. 2. The **dismissal of Yuan Shikai** and the **death of Zhang Zhidong** (Oct. 4) placed the entire Qing administration in Manchu hands. The provincial assemblies met, and they insisted on the earlier convocation of a national assembly, which was finally promised for 1913.

Scholarship of an extraordinary order continued uninterrupted throughout the last years of the Qing dynasty. Even the memorials of **Zeng Guofan** and **Zhang Zhidong** are considered models of classical Chinese prose. **Wang Xianqian** (1842–1918) compiled a supplement in 320 volumes (1886–88) to the *Huangchao jingjie,* the finest critical edition of the two Han histories (*Han shu* and *Hou-Han shu*) with collected modern commentaries, and the *Donghua lu* (*Records from within the Eastern Flowery Gate,* a selection from the dynasty's historical archives through 1874 in 284 volumes, 1879–87).

Baron Iwasaki Yanosuke (1851–1908) purchased and took to Tokyo (1907) the library of **Lu Xinyuan** (1834–94), a famous critic, archaeologist, bibliophile extraordinaire, and historical scholar; this collection became the basis for the outstanding Seikadō Bunko near Tokyo. **Miao**

Quansun (1844–1919), bibliographer and archaeologist, thereupon persuaded Governor-General **Duanfang** (1861–1911) to buy the extensive library of the Ding family for Nanjing as the **first public library in China** (1909).

Ke Shaomin (1850–1933) authored the *New History of the Yuan Dynasty.* **Yan Fu** (1853–1921) translated into Chinese important Western works such as John Stuart Mill's (1806–73) **On Liberty,** Charles de Secondat Montesquieu's (1689–1755) *L'Esprit des lois,* Adam Smith's (1723–90) *Wealth of Nations,* and Thomas Huxley's (1825–95) *Evolution and Ethics.*

Kang Youwei's *Xinxue weijing kao* (*Study of the Forged Classics of the Xin Era,* 1891) and *Kongzi gaizhi kao* (*Study of Confucius as an Institutional Reformer,* 1897) served to focus on early texts the sort of historical criticism that had not been popular for some time. Kang's foremost intellectual and political opponent in the world of letters was the violently anti-Manchu **Zhang Binglin** (1869–1936) of the old text school; Zhang had gone to prison with Zou Rong (1904) for *lèse majesté.*

Chinese envoys to Japan **Yang Shoujing** (1839–1915) and **Li Shuchang** (1837–97) found there many rare editions of Chinese works, which they reproduced in *Guyi congshu* (*Collection of Old Books Lost,* 1882–84). A profusion of other early documents, both Chinese and central Asian, was recovered in 1907–8 by **Aurel Stein** (1862–1943) and **Paul Pelliot** (1878–1945) from a temple library that had been sealed off (c. 1000) at Dunhuang, the point of bifurcation of medieval caravan routes north and south of the Tianshan mountain range. In 1899 a deposit of oracular inscriptions on bones and tortoise shells was discovered; they dated from the Shang dynasty, and upon decipherment by paleographers already trained in the ancient script from bronze vessel inscriptions, turned out to be the earliest form of Chinese writing.

1911, Oct. 10. The **OUTBREAK OF THE CHINESE REVOLUTION** was precipitated by the discovery of the headquarters of the revolutionary organization in Wuchang. The movement, fueled by provincial distrust of the central railway administration of **Sheng Xuanhuai** (1849–1916), spread rapidly through the west and south, without much shedding of blood.

Nov. 8. Yuan Shikai, who had been recalled to military command by the court (Oct. 14), was elected premier of the provisional National Assembly.

Dec. 4. Yuan signed a truce with the rebel general Li Yuanhong (1864–1928), and he sent Tang Shaoyi (1860–1938) to represent him in negotiations in Shanghai.

Dec. 30. Sun Zhongshan, recently returned from the United States and Europe, was **elected provisional president of the Chinese republic** by delegates from 16 provinces meeting in Nanjing.

The provinces rapidly seceded from the Qing and joined the revolutionary cause after Oct. 10: Jiangsu (Nov. 3), Sichuan (Nov. 22), Shandong (Dec. 12), and so on.

1912, Feb. 12. The **boy emperor, Puyi, abdicated.**

Feb. 15. Yuan Shikai was elected provisional president of the Chinese republic by the National Assembly, just two days after Sun Zhongshan relinquished the position in order to unify the country.

March 10. The **Nanjing provisional constitution,** which aimed at making the bicameral assembly supreme, was completed. Yuan soon came into conflict with the assembly through his own efforts to strengthen his personal power. Several **opposition parties** were soon formed, among them the Jinbudang (Progressive Party of Liang Qichao), advocating a strong executive, and Sun Zhongshan's Guomindang (Nationalist Party, descendant of the Revolutionary Alliance), championing the system of parliamentary government.

Dec. National elections were held for the first time in Chinese history; the results were announced in Jan. 1913.

1913, March 20. Song Jiaoren (1882–1913), a Guomindang stalwart, **was gunned down** on a railway station platform in Shanghai.

April 8. The elected Parliament convened.

April 21. Yuan obtained from Great Britain, France, Russia, and Japan a **"reorganization loan" for 25 million pounds,** secured by the salt tax. It was feared by many former revolutionaries that this measure would strengthen Yuan even more.

July 10. The result was a **"second revolution"** in the southern provinces. The movement was soon put down by Yuan's forces, and Nanjing was taken (Sept. 1).

Oct. 6. Yuan was elected president and Li Yuanhong vice president of the republic. Yuan moved to prevent adoption of the constitution.

Oct. 7. Yuan recognized Tibet's independence, and Britain immediately recognized the Republic of China diplomatically.

Nov. 4. Yuan purged the Parliament of Guomindang members, and soon thereafter **dissolved it.** By the end of the month Sun Zhongshan fled to Japan.

Nov. 5. The Chinese government recognized the **autonomy of Outer Mongolia,** which had been secured by treaty between Outer Mongolia and Russia a year before (Nov. 7, 1912).

1914, May 1. A **"constitutional compact"** promulgated by Yuan Shikai gave him a ten-year term of office with considerable powers.

(To p. 775)

2. KOREA, 1800–1910

(From p. 381)

The long Yi dynasty came to a spiraling end, as Korea in the 19th century fell victim to foreign pressure, domestic rebellion, and Japanese colonial aspirations. The Manchus in China were in no position themselves to assist their vassal Korean state. With the decline and fall of the Chosŏn state, *yangban* society, too, came to a crushing demise.

1800. King Chŏngjo died and was succeeded by **Sunjo** (b. 1790, r. 1800–34), a lad of but ten years.

1812. The **Hong Kyŏng-nae Rebellion** broke out, led by a disaffected "fallen" *yangban.* This was one indication of the trouble brewing in the Chosŏn social order, with the increase of popular uprisings, and local rebellions becoming major affairs.

1834–49. The **reign of King Hŏnjong.**

1849–63. The **reign of King Ch'ŏlchong.**

1857. Ch'oe Han-gi (1803–75), a *sirhak* scholar, completed his *Chigu chŏnyo* (*Descriptions of the Nations of the World*), based on Chinese works of the time. It introduced the countries of the West to Koreans and suggested Korea might want to open its doors to interchange with them. Other *sirhak* scholars—such as Pak Kyu-su (1807–76) and O Kyŏng-sŏk (1831–79)—proposed similar ideas.

1860. The **Tonghak** (Eastern Learning) movement began to attract followers under the leadership of **Ch'oe Che-u** (1824–64). It was a syncretic religion, combining elements from Confucianism, Buddhism, Daoism, and, inadvertently, Catholicism to oppose all Western creeds. Its social thrust was against *yangban* decadence and in favor of improving conditions for the poor masses of Korean farmers; it was also decidedly antiforeign and primarily rural. As the government continued to be unable to prevent foreign humiliation at Korea's expense, it exacerbated antipathy for the government and increased the Tonghak's popularity. Ch'oe was arrested (1863) and executed (1864).

1860. Ch'oe Han-gi finished writing his *Injŏng* (*Personnel Administration*), in which he claimed that the path back to good government was through the appointment of talented men regardless of class background, and that Korea had to abandon its seclusion policy and open up to the outside world.

1862. The **Chinju Uprising** erupted, led by a "fallen" *yangban,* and killed a number of particularly rapacious local officials.

These reigns marked the beginning of "in-law" government, a period in which control over the throne passed between certain in-law factions. It marked a low point in official venality and corruption, which spread to local government as well. In the end, the peasantry suffered most harshly, and the fiscal security of the state was undermined.

Yangban-dominated society was beginning to come apart at the seams. Many *yangban* lineages had become "fallen," meaning they could no longer sustain their families' prerogatives. Members of the **chungin** class, a hereditary rank below *yangban* who had formerly held various technical positions, were on the rise. The number of **slaves** markedly declined, many having been freed in exchange for military service; the government freed its slaves in 1801; slavery was abolished in 1894.

Despite persecutions (in 1801, 1839, and at other times), **Catholicism** continued to attract followers. Its belief that all men and women were equal in the eyes of a supreme deity was an implicit critique of the rigid *yangban*-dominated social order. Executions accompanied the repressions; for example, the first Korean priest, **Kim Tae-gŏn** (1822–46), who had trained in a seminary in Macao, was caught and executed. Under Ch'ŏlchong, the repressions were eased.

Like other religious and intellectual movements, the **sirhak** movement of the 19th century continued its social thrust from the 17th and 18th centuries (p. 381), using practical scholarship as a means of trying to improve the political, economic, and social problems of the day. **Chŏng Yag-yong** (1762–1836) synthesized earlier *sirhak* scholarship. In the Sunjo reign, major compilations of encyclopedic proportions were published on agriculture and other economic and political institutions. Others maintained the strict evidential principles of scholarly methodology characteristic of the contemporaneous *kaozheng* movement in Qing China.

1864–1907. During his **reign, King Kojong** (1852–1919), who ascended the throne at age 12, scarcely ruled outright. His father, Hŭngsŏn Taewŏn'gun, or the **TAEWŎN'GUN (1820–98)**, became regent, ruled directly until 1873, and remained a dominant figure in the political world until his death. He was hostile to foreign influence in Korea, particularly toward Christianity.

While in power, the Taewŏn'gun instituted a series of reforms aimed at reviving the Yi state. Corrupt officials were ousted, and others were appointed solely on the basis of merit; he eased the fiscal burdens on the peasantry, and he closed most of the private academies that owned tax-free agricultural estates.

Although it originated in the early 18th century, the **p'ansori**, literary "one-man operas," came into their own in this period. The librettos came from vernacular Korean novels. The most important figure in this movement was Sin Chae-hyo (1812–84). In addition to novels written in the vernacular, there was an increasing quantity of **literature** written in Chinese, by *yangban* and commoner alike. **Painting** witnessed a new development in expressionism, edging out an earlier move toward naturalism; the most famous painter of the late 19th century was Chang Sŭng-ŏp.

1865. A group of scholars updated the Chosŏn state's code of administrative law with the *Taejŏn t'ongp'yŏn (Comprehensive National Code).*

1866. Responding to revived anti-Catholic activities, a **French expedition** under Adm. Pierre Roze occupied and sacked Kanghwa at the mouth of the Han River but was ultimately unable to continue to the capital, Seoul. After some reverses at the hands of Korean forces, it was obliged to withdraw. It became known as the "French Disturbance of 1866."

1868. An expedition was led by the German **Ernst Oppert** to rifle the royal tombs (supposedly full of gold). The landing force reached the tombs but was unable to open them, and under attack by Korean forces, was compelled to withdraw.

1871, May 16. After the United States vessel, *General Sherman,* had sailed up the Taedong River toward P'yŏngyang and was attacked and destroyed by local Koreans, killing all 24 crewmen on board in 1866, a **U.S. naval force,** under Capt. Robert Shufeldt (1822–95), and the minister to Beijing, Frederic Ferdinand Low, tried to open Korea by force, as Commodore Matthew Perry (1794–1858) had done in Japan (1854) (p. 570). Marines landed at the mouth of the Han River, but hostilities ensued, and the project had to be abandoned. This subsequently became known as the "American Disturbance of 1871."

The Taewŏn'gun held to a strict antiforeign posture in diplomacy, in spite of both China's and Japan's having been opened by force in the preceding three decades.

1873. The **Taewŏn'gun** was forced to give up his authority, his fierce seclusionary policy having been deemed a failure.

1876, Feb. 26. Following a deliberately provocative act (the Unyŏ incident, 1875) in which Japanese vessels had sailed into Korean waters and were fired upon, Japanese ships under the command of **Kuroda Kiyotaka** (1840–1900) moved rapidly to land at Kanghwa Island. He compelled the court to enter into treaty negotiations. The result was Korea's first modern treaty, the **Treaty of Kanghwa,** and the **opening of Korea.** It recognized Korean "independence," implying separation from the Chinese sphere, though there was no protest voiced by Beijing. Pusan and two other ports were to be open to Japanese trade over the following 20 months. Typical of unequal treaties, Japan also acquired extraterritoriality. Japanese-Korean negotiations in the Korean capital led to the opening of a Japanese legation there (1880). From 1879, China's Li Hongzhang (1823–1901) became involved in advising the Korean reformers on self-strengthening measures.

1876. King Kojong sent a high-level official to Japan to observe and report on the impact of the Meiji reform programs on Japanese society. In 1881, several groups of students and observers went to study in Japan.

1880, May 22. The **Korean-American Treaty of Amity and Commerce,** negotiated by Li Hongzhang and Shufeldt, was concluded. This followed a Korean decision to open relations with the U.S. in Oct. 1880 (in response to U.S. pressures to do so) and the creation of a Korean foreign office in the following year. There was no mention of Korean "independence," but the United States secured extraterritoriality and permission to trade. Similar treaties were concluded with Great Britain (Nov. 26, 1883), Germany (1883), Russia (July 7, 1884), Italy (1884), France (1886), and Austria-Hungary (1889).

Meanwhile, those opposed to Kojong and his associates' openings to the outside world and to the king's reform policies generally grew stronger. They began to see the Taewŏn'gun as their only hope, and he was prepared by 1881 to use them to stage a comeback.

July 23. An **attack by this group of Koreans on the Japanese legation** in Seoul led to **intervention by the Chinese.** The following day they found and murdered the head of the Tribute Bureau, Min Kyŏm-ho, whose elder brother was the adopted brother of **Queen Min** (1851–95). On Aug. 26, the Taewŏn'gun was abducted by the Chinese to Tianjin, and the regent was returned to power; there soon developed between him and Queen Min a struggle for control of the government. According to the resultant Treaty of Chemulp'o, the Japanese were compensated and given the right to keep a legation guard. **Yuan Shikai** (1859–1916) was appointed Chinese resident at Seoul and during the ensuing decade devoted himself to strengthening Chinese influence and lessening Japan's.

1884, Dec. 4–6. In the **coup d'état of 1884,** the **Reform Party,** supported by the Japanese, hatched a conspiracy to oust Chinese influence from the peninsula while China was distracted by a war with France during that year. A number of ministers were killed, and the king was seized. The Chinese thereupon dispatched troops to Seoul, recaptured the king and the palace, but provoked further intervention by the Japanese. The reformers also wanted the Taewŏn'gun returned home, all *yangban* privilege abrogated, and power recentralized. The reformist clique of **Kim Ok-kyun** (1851–94) and others escaped with the fleeing Japanese. China and Japan stood on the edge of warfare, which was averted for the time being.

1885, April 18. The Sino-Japanese confrontation was eased by the **Convention of Tianjin** between **Li Hongzhang** and Itō Hirobumi (1841–1909). Both agreed to withdraw their troops and to notify each other if it became necessary to intervene in the future.

April 26. The **British occupied Port Hamilton** (Kŏmun Island) in the course of the Anglo-Russian crisis, for fear that Russia might seize a port on the Korean coast. In spite of Chinese protests, the British remained until Feb. 27, 1887.

Oct. Yuan Shikai was named Director–General Resident in Korea for Diplomatic and Commercial Relations, and he worked to enhance Chinese influence in Korea.

Gradually, Queen Min's clique was growing stronger, and corruption and abuse of privilege was expanding rapidly. As the state needed more money to meet the demands of reform, many of its sources were disappearing through embezzlement. Ultimately, the taxation burden fell on the already suffering peasantry. Japanese economic inroads into Korean commerce were growing by leaps and bounds.

1892. A revival of interest in the Tonghak (p. 566) emerged in the cause to clear the name of its leader, Ch'oe Che-u, executed on trumped-up charges. There was a mass movement in Samnye, and a larger demonstration (April 1893) in Ch'ungch'ŏng.

1894, spring. The Tonghak was now a nationwide movement, and it erupted in armed insurrection in southern Korea.

April 26. Chŏn Pong-jun (1853–95), a local Confucian teacher, took control of the larger Tonghak movement. It prevailed in its initial encounters with government forces.

June 10. The king, flustered by the military successes of the Tonghak, called upon the Chinese for help. Three thousand men were dispatched, and the Japanese were notified (in accordance with the Convention of Tianjin). Chŏn agreed the next day to withdraw his forces, in exchange for assurances that the government would institute reforms.

June 25. The Japanese sent 8,000 men and occupied Seoul. On the suggestion of the Chinese that both forces be withdrawn, the Japanese insisted first on the introduction of extensive reforms. Confrontation was delayed but a week.

July 23–1895, April 17. Hostilities in the **SINO-JAPANESE WAR** broke out when Japan seized the Kyŏngbok Palace (p. 564). Korea was obliged to conclude an alliance with Japan (Aug. 26), and the Japanese soon took control over the government, ousting the pro-Min faction with alacrity and forcing reforms on the Korean government. Japan defeated China quickly and soundly. With the tide flowing in Japan's favor, the Tonghak again rose in rebellion, forming a "righteous army" *(ŭibyŏng)* patterned after the forces formed to fight against Hideyoshi's invasion in the 1590s. Although this rising was the largest peasant uprising in all Korean history, it was quashed by the Korean government's forces and the Japanese, and its leaders were executed. The **Treaty of Shimonoseki** ended the war, leaving Japan in a much stronger position on the mainland.

July–1896, Feb. The **Kabo reforms**, similar to the Meiji reforms, were thrust upon the Korean government by the Japanese. Korea became irrevocably "independent," abrogating all unequal treaties with China; the Korean king was to be elevated to emperor status; efforts were under way to build Korean nationalist pride through the greater use of *han'gŭl*; the government was reorganized into the Japanese cabinet style (Dec. 1894) with a constitutional monarchy; a healthier financial base for the country, with firmer fiscal management, was sought; a modern police force and army were created; the traditional civil service examinations were abolished, and plans were drawn up for a new three-level educational system; a modern independent judiciary was created; and *yangban* class privilege was abolished, enabling commoners access to service based solely on ability or merit. The Taewŏn'gun and his followers were fiercely opposed to these reforms.

1895, Oct. 8. Queen Min was murdered in a plot planned in conjunction with the Japanese legation minister, Miura Gorō (1846–1926). Japan's commanding position was immediately challenged by popular risings. Generally, the country became divided into a conservative, anti-Japanese force and a reformist, pro-Japanese force. The latter was, at first, represented by the **Independence Club.**

1896, Feb. 11. The **king fled to the Russian legation** in the course of another insurrection. Remaining under Russian protection for a year, he was used by the Russians as they supplanted the Japanese as the dominant influence on the peninsula. A mission of Russian advisers and teachers was formed, a Russian-Korean bank was founded, and timber and mining concessions were granted to the Russians. The Japanese felt compelled to conclude with Russia (June 9) the **Lobanov-Yamagata Agreement,** which established a type of condominium: Russia and Japan would cooperate in the reform of the Korean army and finances. In practice the agreement proved virtually worthless, and Russian penetration continued unabated.

July 2. Sŏ Chae-p'il (1864–1951), recently returned from the United States, founded the **Independence Club.** The members were frequently critical of government officials. Among the early members was **Yi Sŭng-man** (Syngman Rhee, 1875–1965). The club became a citizens' forum and popular educational outlet. They issued a newspaper, *Tongnip Sinmun (The Independent),* bilingually in *han'gŭl* and English, edited by Sŏ Chae-p'il. The goals of the club included protection of Korea's independence from foreign imperialism, self-strengthening

reforms to complete the earlier Kabo reforms, and a popular rights movement for eventual popular sovereignty. The club was dissolved in early Nov. 1898; popular action forced the king to allow it to be revived. On Dec. 26, King Kojong, prompted by the club's growing appeal and fears of its intentions, **dissolved the Independence Club** once and for all. Many leaders were arrested, resulting in widespread riots and disorder. The more conservative (pro-Russian) and the more reformist (pro-Japanese) cliques were on the verge of open warfare.

1897, Feb. 20. The king left the Russian legation and moved into the new palace.

Oct. 17. The king took the title of emperor, and Korea became an "empire."

1898, April 25. The **Rosen-Nishi Agreement** was concluded between Russia and Japan. Involved in the international crisis following the occupation of Jiaozhou and Lüshun, Russia was eager to avoid friction with Japan and withdrew many of its advisers and officers. By the new convention, both sides agreed not to intervene in the internal affairs of Korea, but Japan was given a free hand in economic matters.

1900. With the outbreak of the Boxer Uprising in China, both Russia and Japan sent forces in to participate in its quelling. Russia stationed a large force in Manchuria.

March 18. The Russians attempted to secure a **concession** at Masan for a naval station but were foiled by Japan's stiff opposition. Despite all previous agreements, the two powers were gradually moving toward a crisis.

1902, Jan. 30. Determined to exclude Russia from Korea, Japan concluded with Great Britain the **Anglo-Japanese Alliance** (p. 476). Japan recognized Britain's rights in China, and Britain acknowledged Japan's "special interests" on the Korean peninsula. Korean "independence" was again affirmed. Japan now pushed harder for Russian withdrawal of forces from Manchuria. Japan then entered upon negotiations with Russia, which was trying to exploit a great timber concession on the Yalu River in northern Korea (first secured in 1896). The negotiations proved fruitless.

1903, July. A Russian military force crossed the Yalu and occupied a Korean town. Japan then proceeded to military resolution of its differences with Russia.

1904, Feb. 8. A Japanese **surprise attack on the Russian installations at Lüshun** launched the **RUSSO-JAPANESE WAR** (p. 511). Japanese forces immediately occupied Seoul, and Korea was obliged to annul all concessions made to Russia. Korea fell entirely under Japanese control and was forced (Aug. 1904) to accept Japanese diplomatic and financial advisers. Pro-Japanese ministers were placed in important ministerial posts. Japan won a startling and rapid series of victories over the Russians, the first time since the Mongols that an Asian military force had defeated a European power.

1905, Sept. 5. The **Treaty of Portsmouth,** ending the war, was overseen by U.S. president Theodore Roosevelt (1858–1919). Feeling it necessary for Japan to accept U.S. control over the Philippines (as agreed upon in the Taft-Katsura Agreement of July 1905), Roosevelt pushed for Russia's recognition of Japan's preponderant interest—political, military, and economic—in Korea. Russia was further obliged to accept whatever measures Japan deemed necessary for the protection and control of Korea. Britain, too, renegotiated the Anglo-Japanese Alliance (Aug. 1905), recognizing Japan's special place in Korea.

Through an organization established by Japan to push its interests in Korea, the **Ilchinhoe** (Advancement Society), Japan pushed for the establishment of a protectorate over Korea. The treaty was forced by **Itō Hirobumi** on Korean prime minister **Han Kyu-sŏl** (Nov. 17). Through the Protectorate Treaty, Japan acquired complete control over Korea's foreign affairs, presided over by a resident general from Japan. Itō held this position (1906–8).

1906, Feb. 1. Kojong published his opposition to the Protectorate Treaty in an article published in the *Korea Daily News.* This newspaper had been founded by Yang Ki-t'ak (1871–1938) and the British journalist Ernest Bethell (1872–1909) in 1905, and since it was run by an Englishman, Japanese censors could not control it as they did the Korean press. They and others lambasted the Ilchinhoe. After he sent a secret delegation to the Second Hague Peace Conference (1907), **Kojong was forced to abdicate** by Japan (July 19) in favor of his son, Sunjong (1874–1926, r. 1907–10), last king-emperor of the Yi dynasty and a mere figurehead. The administration was placed almost entirely under **Japanese control.**

1907, Aug. The Korean army was disbanded, and many of its soldiers joined *ŭibyŏng* (righteous brigades), which enhanced their fighting organization. This immediately led to widespread uprisings and a war of independence, which was suppressed with great difficulty.

Between 1907 and 1910, nearly 3,000 battles were fought between Japanese forces and Korean guerrilla units. By 1910, nearly 20,000 Koreans had died in the anti-Japanese cause.

1909, Oct. 26. An Chung-gŭn (1879–1910), a Korean patriot involved in *ŭibyŏng* and other anti-Japanese activities, **assassinated Itō Hirobumi** at the train station in Harbin. An was tried and executed in March 1910.

1910, May. Gen. Terauchi Masatake (1852–1919) was appointed resident general and set in motion plans for the annexation of Korea.

Aug. 22. KOREA WAS FORMALLY ANNEXED BY JAPAN.

In the last years of the Yi dynasty, numerous private schools were founded to supply modern Western-style education, and many of these were the work of Protestant missionaries and Korean converts. In the few years prior to annexation, 2,250 such private schools came into existence. Korea's first school for young women, Ehwa Girls School, was founded earlier (1886) through the work of U.S. missionaries; later, many other girls' schools were created by Koreans, and these schools were important agencies for liberating young women from the strictures of *yangban* society. The great attraction of Protestantism from the 1880s forward seems to have been centered in the non-*yangban* sectors.

As use of the **Korean language** became an act on behalf of independence and one of anti-Japanese defiance, new work on Korean grammar appeared. Yu Kil-chun's (1856–1914) *Chosŏn munjŏn (Grammar of Korean)* was the first such work. It was later followed by the work of the great scholar **Chu Si-gyŏng** (1876–1914): *Kugŏ munpŏp (A Korean Grammar)* and *Mal ŭi sori (A Phonology of Korean).* Similar patriotic work of a historical bent was that of Ch'oe Nam-sŏn (1890–1957), founder of the Society for Refurbishing Korea's Literary Legacy, which hunted down and published series of old Korean texts.

In **literature,** the "new novel," written completely in *han'gŭl* and largely in the vernacular, emerged and became a vehicle for the new intellectual trends and especially for independence. They also addressed other social issues, such as women's equality. *(To p. 782)*

3. JAPAN, 1793–1914

(From p. 385)

1793. Lt. Adam Laxman (b. 1776), envoy of Catherine the Great of Russia, arrived at Hakodate but failed to establish friendly relations.

1793–1837. The **personal rule of IENARI** as shogun was characterized by increasing extravagance, inefficiency, and signs of the breakdown of seclusion and the collapse of military rule. During this period lived **Ninomiya Sontoku** (1787–1856), a famous peasant philosopher and agrarian reformer; **Kaiho Seiryō** (1755–1817), a political economist, reformer, and itinerant teacher; **Takizawa Bakin** (1767–1848), an extremely popular author of fiction with a moral bent; **Katsushika Hokusai** (1760–1849), **Andō Hiroshige** (1797–1858), and **Kitagawa Utamaro** (1754–1806), three of the finest *ukiyo-e* woodblock artists.

1795. Capt. William Broughton (1762–1821), a British explorer, visited Hokkaidō, charting parts of the Japanese coast.

1797–1809. U.S. ships traded with Japan nearly every year, on behalf of the Dutch.

1798. The *Kojiki den,* a commentary on the *Kojiki (Record of Ancient Things,* 712), was completed after 35 years of work by **Motoori Norinaga** (1730–1801), one of the finest scholars of the National Learning, or Nativist, school. This achievement marked a significant event in the revival of Shinto and the imperial cause. An earlier figure of considerable importance in this movement was **Kamo Mabuchi** (1679–1769), who worked principally on the *Man'yōshū (Collection of 10,000 Leaves,* 759); a later figure of less intellectual depth but greater popular appeal was **Hirata Atsutane** (1776–1843). All relentlessly attacked Confucianism as alien to things Japanese.

1804, Oct.–1805, April. A Russian ambassador, Capt. Nikolai Rezanov (1764–1807), representing the Russian-American Company, reached Nagasaki but after six months failed to obtain a treaty. In 1806–7, his subordinates raided Sakhalin.

1814. Kurozumi Munetada (1780–1850) founded the **Kurozumi sect,** the first of the modern popular Shinto sects that stressed patriotism and occasionally faith healing. This and 12 similar sects founded over the course of the next century counted in excess of 17 million adherents.

1817–37. A sign of economic problems to come, the *bakufu* (shogunal government) devalued the currency on 19 separate occasions, but did not adequately contain the growing state deficit. Problems were exacerbated by a string of crop failures in the 1820s.

1825. Aizawa Seishisai (Yasushi, 1781–1863) of Mito domain completed his *Shinron (New Proposals,* not published until 1857). He suggested that greater defensive measures be adopted by the feudal domains in preparation for the coming aggressive forces from the West; he felt that even more pernicious than Western force of arms were its Christian religion, its corruptive culture, and its economic incursions. British whaling vessels had landed in Mito the previous year.

1830–44. Although the **Tenpō reign period** witnessed great reform efforts, it also saw severe famines in the mid-1830s and massive social disorders as countless peasants fled rural poverty for the cities. It was an extremely rich era culturally. Planner of the reforms (effected, 1841–43) was **Mizuno Tadakuni** (1794–1851). He abolished the guild system, domainal monopolies, and other institutions, moving toward centralizing Edo power with respect to the domains. The reforms ultimately failed.

1837. Following several years of local famine, inadequate state response, and small-scale risings, Ōsaka witnessed a mass rebellion led by **Ōshio Heihachirō** (1793–1837), a former policeman. He and his followers were angry at the corrupt officialdom and the venal merchants whom they saw as responsible for poverty. The uprising was quelled.

The U.S. vessel *Morrison,* with merchants and missionaries from Macao, visited Naha in the Ryūkyū (Chinese, Liuqiu) Islands, was bombarded at Edo and Kagoshima, and failed to open relations. This was but one of numerous efforts by Westerners to establish more extensive contact with Japan before 1854. One reason for these efforts was that since about 1820 the northern Pacific whaling industry had greatly developed, and more humane treatment of crews of whalers wrecked in Japanese waters was sought, particularly by the United States.

1837–53. IEYOSHI as shogun. The question of opening the country to foreign trade in compliance with the demands of the Western nations became pressing. Sentiment in favor of an imperial restoration was slowly growing, and economic ills were impoverishing many warriors who became *rōnin* (masterless samurai).

1838. Nakayama Miki (1798–1887), a woman, founded the faith-healing **Tenri sect,** the most popular of the modern religious sects.

1839–40. Conservative scholars, in an effort to check the rapid growth of Western learning, had restrictive measures instituted and imprisoned two leading scholars of Western learning (*Rangaku,* "Dutch Learning") who favored the opening of Japan (p. 384), **Watanabe Kazan** (1793–1841) and **Takano Chōei** (1804–50). Another scholar of Western learning, **Sakuma Shōzan** (1811–64), engaged in a wide variety of scientific experimentation and was a student of Chinese philosophy as well; he coined the compromise phrase "Eastern morality and Western technology."

1840. The *bakufu* ordered the Dutch to prepare a full report on the **Opium War** in China.

1844. King William II of Holland warned the shogun by letter of the futility of the seclusion policy.

1846, July. U.S. commodore **James Biddle** visited Edo Bay, but trade was refused him.

1849. Commodore **James Glynn** succeeded in liberating U.S. castaways held at Nagasaki.

1851, June. U.S. commodore **John H. Aulick** was commissioned to open relations with Japan but was removed from his command (Nov.); **Commodore Matthew C. Perry** (1794–1858) was appointed as his successor (March 1852). The Perry expedition was sent on a generally peaceful mission to improve treatment in Japan of U.S. castaways and to open one or two ports for trade and supplies, especially coal for the California-Shanghai steamship service.

1853, July 8. PERRY, with four ships, anchored off Uraga in Edo Bay and remained for ten days, delivering a letter from the U.S. president, which was referred to the emperor and the feudal lords. This unprecedented course of action aroused the nation and elicited, for the most part, an antiforeign response.

1853–58. IESADA as shogun. During these years, the feudal domains increasingly criticized the actions of the shogunate in Edo, and the public became effectively divided into two camps: those in favor of the expulsion of the foreigners *(jōi)*, led by **Tokugawa Nariaki** (1800–60), ex-lord of Mito domain and a devotee of the imperial institution; and those who saw that concessions to the foreigners were necessary to avoid destructive war, led by **Ii Naosuke** (1815–60), a high *bakufu* official. The two groups also diverged over proposed heirs to the childless Iesada. Naosuke favored **Tokugawa Iemochi** (1858–66), lord of Kii; Nariaki favored his own son, **Hitotsubashi Keiki** (Yoshinobu, r. 1866–67), and resorted to the unprecedented stratagem of seeking imperial backing for his candidate.

1854, Feb. 13. Perry returned as promised to Edo Bay with more ships, hastened by fear of Russian and French efforts to acquire treaties, and secured the **Treaty of Kanagawa** (March 31), which opened two ports, permitted trade under regulations, provided better treatment of U.S. castaways, and included a most-favored-nation clause but omitted extraterritoriality. This was followed by treaties with Great Britain (Oct. 1854), Russia (Feb. 1855), and Holland (Nov. 1855, Jan. 1856), which gave further privileges. Japan was not yet, though, really open to trade. These treaties were all signed by the shogun (often called by foreigners *tycoon [taikun]*, based on one of his titles, and incorrectly regarded by them as the "secular emperor").

1854–55. The Dutch aided the Japanese in laying the foundations for a future navy.

1856, Aug. U.S. consul general **Townsend Harris** (1804–78) arrived at Shimoda with instructions to procure a commercial treaty.

1858, March–May. Growing imperial prestige was seen in an extraordinary Edo appeal to the emperor for approval of further interaction, which was refused. The strong antiforeign spirit in the imperial capital of Kyoto became linked with the pro-emperor movement *(sonnō)*.

June. Ii Naosuke was appointed *tairō* (great counselor) and soon became all-powerful in Edo. He secured the appointment of Iemochi as the shogun's heir and the signature (July 29) without imperial approval of the important commercial treaties previously arranged with Harris. This treaty, which went well beyond what Perry had called for, provided for unsupervised trade and permanent residence at five ports, residence at Edo and Ōsaka, an envoy at Edo, extraterritoriality, a conventional tariff, and a prohibition on the import of opium, to be revised in 1872 or later. Treaties followed with Holland (Aug. 18), Russia (Aug. 19), Great Britain (Aug. 26), and France (Oct. 7), all on the model of the Harris treaty. Naosuke commenced a roundup of all those suspected of opposing his moves in the **Ansei Purge** (1858–60).

1858–66. IEMOCHI as shogun. Antiforeign sentiment continued unabated, and the desire for the restoration of the emperor's direct rule increased rapidly.

1859. Despite the fact that Kyoto informed Edo in February that foreigners were to be expelled as soon as possible, **foreign merchants settled in Yokohama.** Yokohama, Hakodate, and Nagasaki were opened as treaty ports. The Dutch abandoned Deshima and established a consulate in Edo. A series of attacks upon foreigners followed and resulted in foreign pressure upon Edo for redress. A silver-gold exchange rate of 5 to 1 led to an outflow of gold.

Nov. Yoshida Shōin (b. 1830), a leading voice on behalf of the imperial institution from the domain of Chōshū (western Honshū), was executed for anti-*bakufu* activities, claiming that the *bakufu's* inability to control the foreigners showed a lack of respect for the imperial institution. His teachings continued to influence the samurai of his native domain. He had earlier studied with Sakuma Shōzan and was strongly influenced by the ethic of the Japanese warrior spirit. He had

unsuccessfully tried to stow away with Perry's ships to the United States.

1860, Mar 24. Ii Naosuke was assassinated by former Mito samurai.

May 17. The **first Japanese embassy** to the United States exchanged commercial treaty ratifications in Washington.

Sept. 17. Nariaki died, and leadership of the antiforeign, proimperial movement passed to the fiefs of **Satsuma** (on Kyūshū), **Chōshū**, and **Tosa** (on Shikoku).

1861, March–Sept. Russia occupied the island of Tsushima.

In the escalating antiforeign violence, Townsend Harris's Dutch interpreter was assassinated.

1862, Jan. A mission to European governments resulted in the signing of an agreement in London (June) that postponed until 1868 the opening of Niigata and Hyōgo and residence in Edo and Ōsaka.

June. The **Senzaimaru** arrived in Shanghai to investigate commercial conditions. This was the first Japanese voyage to China in over two centuries and the first official voyage in over three centuries. Among those on board were several who played important roles in subsequent domestic politics, including **Takasugi Shinsaku** (1839–67) of Chōshū and **Godai Tomoatsu** (1835–85) of Satsuma.

Sept. 14. An Englishman, C. L. Richardson, was murdered by Satsuma men in the village of Namamugi near Yokohama. An indemnity was demanded (Dec.), but Satsuma refused to listen and to turn over the guilty parties. The result was a British squadron attack on Kagoshima (Aug. 15–16, 1863), an event that effectively convinced Satsuma of the impracticality of expelling the foreigners. An agreement was ultimately signed (Dec. 11, 1863). This was one of many similar attacks on Westerners or their employees by antiforeign samurai.

Oct. The system of "alternate attendance," by which all daimyos were compelled to reside half of each year in Edo, was greatly curtailed, and the western lords began to congregate around the court in Kyoto.

Also in 1862, the Institute for the Investigation of Barbarian Books (founded, 1857) was renamed the Institute of Western Books (renamed the Development Office later). A group of 15 Japanese students, including **Inoue Kaoru** (1835–1915) and **Itō Hirobumi** (1840–1901), set sail for Britain.

1863, April. Iemochi went to Kyoto in response to a summons from the emperor. This unprecedented step signified that the political center of the empire was already shifting back toward Kyoto. On June 5, a date (June 25) was chosen for the expulsion of foreigners.

June 24. The *bakufu* paid an indemnity to the British for Richardson and others and announced that negotiations would begin for the closing of ports.

June 25. The Chōshū forts at Shimonoseki fired on a U.S. vessel and later on French and Dutch vessels, resulting in direct reprisals by U.S. and Dutch warships. Chōshū radicals in Kyoto gained supremacy at court and compelled the shogun to evict all foreigners by this date.

Sept. A coup d'état was attempted in Kyoto, and extremist Chōshū forces were expelled.

1864. Internecine strife in Mito eventually robbed it of all its leadership in national affairs.

Aug. Chōshū men who attempted to capture the imperial palace in Kyoto were defeated in pitched battles. The *bakufu* demanded that 35 of the feudal domains join in a punitive expedition against Chōshū.

Sept. An allied expedition of British, Dutch, French, and U.S. ships silenced Chōshū forts at Shimonoseki, thereby breaking the back of the antiforeign movement. Edo agreed to pay an indemnity for Chōshū (Oct.).

1865. The *bakufu* called for a second punitive expedition against Chōshū.

Nov. An allied naval demonstration at Ōsaka secured the imperial ratification of treaties.

1866, June 25. A tariff convention was signed by the United States, Great Britain, France, and Holland. It amounted to 5 percent duty on almost all imports and exports (in force until 1899). This meant that more cheaply manufactured goods from the West could easily undercut the price of items produced in Japan.

July–Aug. The *bakufu* engaged in the second Chōshū expedition to punish it for extremist activities. Satsuma and Chōshū became aligned in their opposition to Edo. Chōshū ultimately defeated the *bakufu's* forces singlehandedly.

In 1866, *Seiyō jijō (Conditions in the West)* by **Fukuzawa Yukichi**

(1835–1901), one of most important figures in the subsequent Meiji era, was published and immediately became extremely popular, selling over 250,000 copies.

Both Shogun Iemochi and Emperor Kōmei died in 1866. They were succeeded, respectively, by Hitotsubashi **Keiki** (Yoshinobu) as shogun and **Meiji** as emperor.

1867. Young leaders, such as **Saigō Takamori** (1827–77) and **Ōkubo Toshimichi** (1830–78) of Satsuma, plotted to undermine the shogunal authorities. A vigorous young ruler, **Mutsuhito (Emperor Meiji,** b. 1852) came to the throne (Feb.). Keiki, who was a Mito scion predisposed to surrender to Kyoto, resigned (Nov.), bringing almost 700 years of feudal military government to an end.

1868, Jan. 1. Hyōgo (Kōbe) and Ōsaka were opened to foreign trade.

Jan. 3. THE MEIJI RESTORATION. The emperor assumed direct control over the nation. Certain of the western clans seized power in Kyoto, and the remaining Tokugawa forces and those domainal forces loyal to the *bakufu* were defeated in a civil war (July 4, **Battle of Ueno** in Edo).

March. The emperor received French, Dutch, and British representatives.

April 6. The **Charter Oath** delivered by the emperor promised a deliberative assembly, the decision of public affairs by public opinion, the dissolution of the feudal system, and the plan to utilize knowledge and information from around the globe, regardless of its origins, to fortify the imperial state.

Nov. The national capital was moved to Edo, renamed **Tokyo** (eastern capital). The next year, the emperor relocated to the shogun's former castle there. Meanwhile, the era name was changed to **Meiji** (enlightened rule), and henceforth there would be only one era name for each emperor, as had been the case in China since the founding of the Ming exactly 500 years earlier.

1868–1912. THE MEIJI PERIOD. The policy of antiforeignism of the Loyalist Party was dropped as soon as it came to power, as Japan entered a reform period that involved great borrowing from the West, comparable only to the much earlier period of borrowing from China. The remnants of military rule and feudalism were systematically dismantled, a strong centralized bureaucratic government fashioned along Western lines was created under the leadership of the Meiji em-

peror, and Japan became a modern world power. **Rapid industrialization** on Western models took place, and, as a consequence, the wealth and population of the land multiplied. In the fields of science, education, philosophy, and even art and literature, great transformations were wrought by the impact of Western civilization, and for a few decades many Japanese traits and institutions were somewhat discredited, if not completely superseded. Shinto was at first declared the state religion; Buddhist elements were to be purged from it, and a Department of Shinto was created, but the department was abolished (1872) in the face of widespread opposition.

1869, March. Kido Kōin (1833–77) and Ōkubo Toshimichi convinced the daimyos of Satsuma, Chōshū, Tosa, and Hizen to offer their lands to the emperor as a step toward the public abolition of feudalism. Others followed this example.

May. The *bakufu*'s navy surrendered to the new government, ending all resistance.

July. Daimyos were appointed as governors of their former estates with one-tenth their former revenue. Representatives of the 276 fiefs, appointed by their lords, met in an assembly *(Kōgisho)*; this body lacked legislative power, was suspended in 1870, and abolished in 1873.

The Yasukuni Shrine was established in 1869 as a memorial to those who had died fighting for the Restoration.

1870. For the first time, commoners were allowed to adopt family names; they were also released from the rigid social and occupational constraints of earlier times.

The first mechanical silk-reeling factory was founded, and others followed through the 1870s. By 1880, roughly 30 percent of Japanese silk exports were machine made. Silk quickly assumed a large percentage of all Japanese exports. Most workers in silk-reeling factories were women, many of them forcibly recruited from the countryside, and they were paid less than men.

1871, Aug. 29. By imperial decree, the fiefs were abolished, and prefectures (*ken,* at first numbering 71, later 44, with three prefectural cities, or *fu*) assumed their place. The first regular governmental postal service was established (Tokyo to Ōsaka). The Ministry of Education was founded to promote universal education. The first daily newspaper commenced publication.

JAPANESE EMPERORS (1867–   )

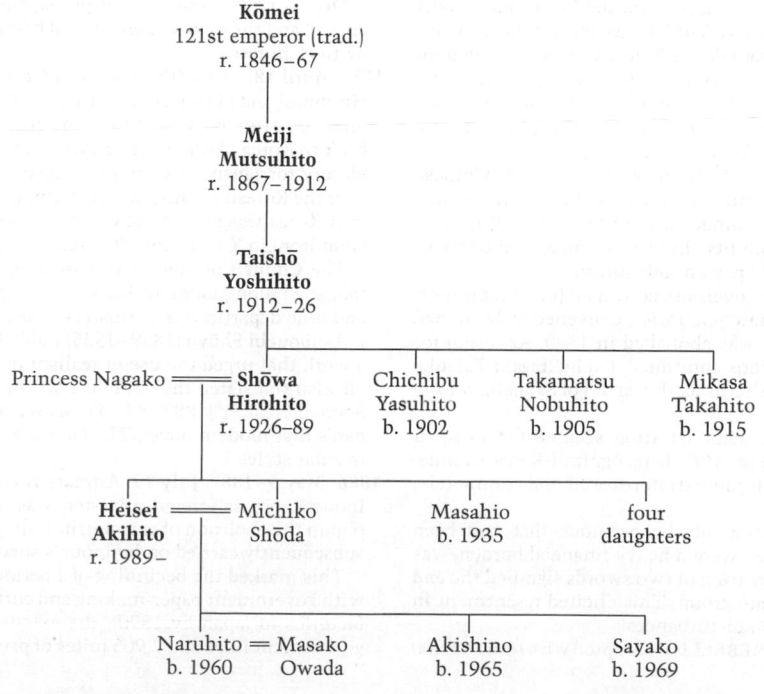

Kōmei
121st emperor (trad.)
r. 1846–67

Meiji
Mutsuhito
r. 1867–1912

Taishō
Yoshihito
r. 1912–26

Princess Nagako ══ **Shōwa Hirohito** r. 1926–89   Chichibu Yasuhito b. 1902   Takamatsu Nobuhito b. 1905   Mikasa Takahito b. 1915

Heisei Akihito r. 1989– ══ Michiko Shōda   Masahio b. 1935   four daughters

Naruhito b. 1960 ══ Masako Owada   Akishino b. 1965   Sayako b. 1969

Sept. 3. The **Treaty of Tianjin was signed with China** as between two equal parties. Japan, thus, did not gain extraterritorial and commercial rights equal to those of the West, nor a most-favored-nation clause.

Oct. The **Iwakura Mission**—including Ōkubo Toshimichi, Itō Hirobumi, and Kido Kōin—led by nobleman **Iwakura Tomomi** (1825–83), departed to seek treaty revisions from the West and to study Western institutions in preparation for reforms necessary to that end. It failed to gain those treaty revisions and returned to Japan in Sept. 1873.

1872. **Universal military service,** primarily the project of **Yamagata Aritomo** (1838–1922), was introduced (adopted as policy in Jan. 1873). The new army was modeled on the French army, and later on that of the Germans. The first railway was opened (Tokyo to Yokohama, 18 miles) at state initiative. National bank regulations were promulgated on the U.S. model. The government issued an ordinance for the establishment of a single, public, nationwide educational system for the entire country to replace the many and varied systems in operation. Four years were initially mandatory, but soon rescinded as unrealistic; the four-year compulsory plan was reinstituted in 1900 and extended to six years in 1902.

1873, Jan. 1. The solar Gregorian calendar was adopted in place of the lunar one. British officers were employed to help reorganize the Japanese navy. A policy of **religious tolerance** called for the removal of signs forbidding Christianity and for the propagation of that religion once again.

Itagaki Taisuke (1837–1919) from Tosa, Soejima Taneomi (1828–1905) from Hizen, Etō Shinpei (1834–74) from Hizen, and Saigō Takamori from Satsuma all left the government and issued an appeal for the promulgation of a constitution.

Oct. After considerable debate, a peaceful policy toward Korea was adopted rather than a bellicose one. Itagaki Taisuke and Saigō Takamori supported war both for nationalist ends and as a means of employment for many samurai who no longer had a hereditary position in society. Opposition to war came from Ōkubo Toshimichi, Kido Kōin, and Iwakura Tomomi. Itagaki and Saigō resigned their posts in the government.

Monetary, banking, and taxation systems were established by 1873, primarily the work of **Ōkuma Shigenobu** (1838–1922) and **Itō Hirobumi.** Although agriculture continued to be the basis of the national economy, taxes were now to be collected in money.

The **Meirokusha** (The Meiji 6 Society) was founded by **Mori Arinori** (1847–89); it was dedicated to the study of Western knowledge. It played an important role in the **"Civilization and Enlightenment"** *(bunmei kaika)* movement, as Japan now took the West as its model for knowledge and reform. Fukuzawa Yukichi, as one prominent voice in this movement and later as founder of Keiō University, argued for basic social reformation; for greater gender equality, including giving women both education and the right to hold property; and for the inadequacy of filial piety in the modern age. Basic to this position were beliefs in natural law and, later, Social Darwinism.

1874, April. An expedition was sent via Xiamen (Amoy) on the Chinese coast to Taiwan to redress the murder by locals there of Ryūkyūan sailors in Dec. 1871; Japan had claimed suzerainty over the Ryūkyūs, and China had avoided responsibility. In Oct., Japan agreed to recall the expedition, and China would pay an indemnity.

1875. An **assembly of prefectural governors** convened (not a representative or legislative body). A senate *(Genrōin),* convened in 1876, had similar advisory duties only; it was abolished in 1890. Agitation for genuine representative institutions continued, led by Itagaki Taisuke and others. Japan exchanged with Russia the island of Sakhalin for the Kurils.

1876, Feb. 26. A Japanese naval demonstration secured the **unequal Treaty of Kanghwa with Korea** (p. 567). It recognized Korea as independent of China and granted Japan extraterritorial and commercial privileges.

Aug. Compulsory commutation of the pensions that had been granted the samurai class, which were a heavy financial burden, was enacted. A prohibition on the wearing of two swords signified the **end of the samurai class** as a separate group. This elicited resentment in many quarters and led to several disturbances.

1877, Jan.–Sept. The **SATSUMA REBELLION** erupted with some 42,000 supporters, partially in anger at the treatment of the former samurai class by the new government. It was led by **Saigō Takamori,** a leader in the Restoration movement, but was quickly crushed by the modern, trained army of commoner conscripts. Saigō committed suicide. A large issue of inconvertible paper currency was used to defray government expenses in quelling the rebels.

Tokyo University was founded, Japan's first national university, then known as the Imperial University.

1878, May. **Ōkubo was assassinated** by followers of Saigō.

Laws for local government under the centralized Meiji state were enacted. Yamagata Aritomo led a major reorganization of the army; it was henceforth to report directly, via a general staff on the German model, to the emperor; a reserve system was established, modern armament purchased, a staff college created, and training methods improved. Similar naval modernization efforts were later adopted.

1879. **Prefectural assemblies,** elected by males over age 20 who paid a land tax of 5 yen or more, were convened with powers to determine local budgets. The Ryūkyū Islands were further incorporated into Japan as a prefecture.

1880, July. A **revised penal code** and a **code of criminal procedure,** based largely on French models, were promulgated.

1881. An imperial decree promised a constitution by 1889 and the convening of a **national assembly** in 1890. The organization of political parties was supported in opposition to the bureaucracy controlled by Satsuma and Chōshū: the *Jiyūtō* (Liberal Party) of Itagaki Taisuke and the *Kaishintō* (Progressive Party) of Ōkuma Shigenobu.

The **Ministry of Agriculture and Industry** was founded. In 1925, the agriculture section split off, and it merged with the forestry ministry; industry remained in its own ministry.

1882, Jan.–July. In a conference on treaty revisions in Tokyo, Foreign Minister Inoue Kaoru failed to secure revisions.

March. Itō Hirobumi was appointed to draft a constitution and traveled to the West. He was particularly impressed by the German political system; he returned in Sept. 1883.

Oct. The **Bank of Japan** was established as the central bank in the European manner.

1883, April 16. The press law was revised, and severe libel regulations were added to it.

1884. A **newly organized peerage** was created with 500 members to provide a basis for an upper house of the Diet; it was made up of former feudal lords and court nobility. The Chichibu rebellion erupted when poor farmers demanding debt relief attacked local moneylenders and bureaucratic offices. The Liberal Party was dissolved.

Dec. A coup d'état by the pro-Japanese liberal party in Korea occurred, and the Japanese envoy and his troops were forced out of Korea by the Chinese.

1885, April 18. The **CONVENTION OF TIANJIN was negotiated** by Itō Hirobumi and Li Hongzhang (1823–1901). Both powers agreed to withdraw their troops and to inform the other of any intention to send them back to Korea. Although negotiated on equal terms, this was clearly a victory for Japan, as China was losing its claim to suzerain control over the Korean peninsula. An attempt by Russia to gain a protectorate over Korea was prevented. Great Britain occupied Kōmun Island (Port Hamilton) in Korea (April 26), but withdrew (Feb. 27, 1887).

The **Council of State** was dissolved, and a **cabinet system** was established along German lines, with a premier (Count Itō Hirobumi) and nine departmental ministers responsible to him.

Tsubouchi Shōyō (1859–1935) published *The Essence of the Novel,* a work that urged the use of realism in writing Western-style fiction. He also translated the complete works of Shakespeare into Japanese. Soon thereafter (1887–89), **Futabatei Shimei** (1864–1909) wrote Japan's first modern novel, *The Floating Cloud,* in a mixed literary-vernacular style.

1886, May 1–1887, July 29. A treaty revision conference, conducted by Inoue Kaoru as foreign minister, was held in Tokyo, but it failed to obtain the abolition of extraterritoriality. Individual negotiations were subsequently carried on by Inoue's successor, Ōkuma Shigenobu.

This marked the beginning of a period of **rapid economic expansion** with government paper-making and cotton-spinning plants (200 steam factories in Japan by 1890), the extension of railroads (959 miles of government lines and 2,905 miles of private lines by 1901), an increase in steamship tonnage (15,000 by 1893 and 1,522,000 by 1905), and the unification of telegraph and postal systems (1886). In addition, a network of police stations was devised for all of Japan.

1887. As work on the constitution neared completion, the government, using the newly enacted Peace Preservation Law, outlawed 570 opposition party leaders from living within three miles of the imperial palace in Tokyo. This restrictive measure was the culmination of over a decade of similar efforts by the government to control the press and the assembly of oppositional elements.

1888, April. The **Privy Council was created** under Premier Itō Hirobumi as an advisory body to the emperor to rule on the constitution and related laws; later, it became the highest organ of state in matters concerning constitutional law. **Kuroda Kiyotaka** (1840–1900) succeeded Itō as premier. The general staffs of the army and navy were detached.

1889, Feb. 11. The **NEW CONSTITUTION WAS PROMULGATED** as an imperial gift to the emperor's people. The emperor's powers were carefully guarded, including the right to declare war and make peace, and the power to issue ordinances having the force of law. There was to be a **bicameral Diet** with an upper house of peers and representatives of merit and wealth (363 members) and a lower house elected through limited suffrage (463 members). The imperial institution was placed at an inviolable level above the Diet. The Diet had a restricted control over state finances.

Dec. Count Yamagata Aritomo became premier and hence leader of the first cabinet under the new constitution.

1890. The emperor formally approved the new civil, commercial, and criminal **codes of law** based on Western models (considered too Western in some circles), in order to eliminate the necessity for extraterritoriality. Mexico had already (1888) granted Japan judicial autonomy over Mexicans in Japan. The civil code was put in force in 1892 and 1898, and the criminal code in 1899.

The **Rescript on Education** was promulgated, revealing a sharply conservative turn in the state's aims for education. Neo-Confucianism was married to loyalty to the throne and state.

July. The **first general elections,** by males age 25 or older who paid direct national taxes of 15 yen or more (460,000 qualified voters out of a population of some 42 million), were held. The Imperial Diet subsequently convened for the first time. The opposition parties won an overwhelming percentage of seats in the lower house; Yamagata Aritomo dissolved it.

1891, May. Premier Yamagata Aritomo resigned and was succeeded by Count **Matsukata Masayoshi** (1835–1924).

1892, June. The cabinet resigned following defeats in the Diet, and Itō became premier. The government had tried to foil opposition parties by using the police, but failed.

1893. An imperial edict was issued to the effect that the Diet would assume the cost of financing the navy.

1894, March. The antiforeign **Tonghak Rebellion** erupted in southern Korea, leading China and then Japan to dispatch troops to Korea.

July 16. The **Aoki-Kimberley Treaty** was signed in London. It revised the treaty with Britain of 1858, abolished extraterritoriality by 1899, and prepared the way for similar treaties with the other powers. By Aug. 4, 1899, all Westerners in Japan were subject to Japanese courts, a new international status for Japan.

In the preceding decade and a half, Japanese agricultural produce had soared by 30 percent because of the introduction of new seeds, new fertilizers, and new farming techniques. Farmland was opened by the state in Hokkaidō. International markets for Japanese goods further aided economic growth. Whereas landlords profited by these and other developments, peasant farmers continued to live in difficult circumstances.

July 23–1895, April 17. The **SINO-JAPANESE WAR** (p. 568) exploded, primarily a struggle for control over Korea. Japan was a rapid and impressive victor.

1895, April 17. The **TREATY OF SHIMONOSEKI** was signed by Itō Hirobumi, Minister of Foreign Affairs Mutsu Munemitsu (1844–97), and Li Hongzhang, the Chinese ambassador extraordinary. China recognized the full "independence" of Korea; ceded to Japan the Pescadores, Taiwan, and the Liaodong peninsula; paid an indemnity of 200 million taels; opened four more treaty ports; negotiated a new commercial treaty (1896); and gained extraterritoriality within China. Japanese ex-

ports to China soared over the next decade or more, as did commercial investment in China, the bulk of the latter in Manchuria. The war with Russia (1904–5) similarly stimulated the domestic economy.

Nov. Japan had no choice but to yield to the **Tripartite Intervention** of France, Germany, and Russia, and relinquish the Liaodong peninsula, receiving instead from China 30 million additional taels of indemnity.

1896. Because of the most-favored-nation clause, a new commercial treaty with China meant additional concessions were granted to the powers. Japan gained domination over the Korean government, which was reorganized following the murder of Queen Min (Oct. 8, 1895).

June 9. The **Lobanov-Yamagata Agreement,** signed in St. Petersburg, recognized Russia's position in Korea.

Sept. Matsukata Masayoshi again became premier.

1897, March 29. Japan adopted the gold standard, ratio of 32.3 to 1.

1898, Jan. Itō Hirobumi again became premier.

April 25. The **Rosen-Nishi Agreement** was signed, by which Russia agreed to Japanese economic penetration of Korea. Both powers were to refrain from interference in internal affairs.

April 26. Japan was assured by the Zongli Yamen, China's foreign office in Beijing, respecting the **nonalienation of Fujian Province** to any other power.

June. Ōkuma Shigenobu and Itagaki Taisuke, now both of the Kenseitō political party, formed a cabinet.

Nov. Yamagata Aritomo formed a cabinet once again.

1899, July 17. The **revised treaties** with foreign nations began to take effect. France and Austria retained consular jurisdiction until Aug. 4.

1900. An electoral tax qualification for voting for the lower house was lowered from 15 yen to 10 yen, resulting in a near doubling of the eligible voting populace.

June 6. The **Boxer Uprising** in China erupted (p. 565), and Japanese joined the international expeditionary force.

Sept. Itō Hirobumi announced the formation of a new political party, the **Rikken seiyūkai,** later known as the Seiyūkai.

Oct. Itō formed a cabinet with his new party, which dominated Japanese politics for many years.

1901, June 2. Viscount **Katsura Tarō** (1847–1913) formed a cabinet.

Aug. Plans for the reorganization of the army and navy were adopted. Civilians became eligible to hold the position of cabinet minister for these departments, but direct responsibility to the emperor was retained.

1902, Jan. 30. The **ANGLO-JAPANESE ALLIANCE** was signed following negotiations in London.

1904. Continued Russian penetration of northern Korea and failure to withdraw from Manchuria, together with the breakdown of Russo-Japanese negotiations, led to the Japanese severance of diplomatic relations (Feb. 6).

1904–5. THE RUSSO-JAPANESE WAR BEGAN (p. 568).

Feb. 8. In a surprise attack, **Japan attacked Lüshun (Ryojun in Japanese, known as Port Arthur in the West),** bottling up the Russian fleet.

Feb. 10. War was declared.

Feb. 23. A treaty was forcibly signed between Japan and Korea, by which Korea became a virtual protectorate of Japan in return for guarantees of integrity.

May 1. Russian forces were defeated at the Yalu River by Japan.

May 30. Japanese forces **occupied Dalian** (Dairen in Japanese, Dalny in Russian). Gen. Nogi Maresuke (1849–1912) began the **siege of Lüshun,** while other Japanese forces moved northward.

Aug. 25–Sept. 4. Japanese troops defeated Russian forces at **Liaoyang.** The latter withdrew to Mukden (Fengtian in Chinese).

1905, Jan. 2. Lüshun surrendered to the Japanese.

Feb. 20–March 9. The Russians were defeated at **Mukden** by five combined Japanese armies.

May 27–29. In the **naval Battle of the Tsushima Straits,** the Russian fleet of 32 vessels, arriving from European waters, was annihilated by the Japanese under Adm. Tōgō.

Aug. 12. The Anglo-Japanese Alliance was renewed for ten years, with *casus belli* defined as an attack by a single power on either party.

Sept. 5. A **peace treaty** was signed at Portsmouth (p. 568), after a conference that began on Aug. 5, through Pres. Theodore Roosevelt's (1858–1919) mediation. Russia acknowledged Japan's paramount interest in Korea, transferred to Japan its leasehold on the Liaodong peninsula and the railroad to Changchun, and ceded the southern half of Sakhalin. Manchuria was to be evacuated by both powers and restored to China, although Japan received control over the South Manchurian Railway and adjacent terrain. Because of failure to obtain an indemnity, the treaty was unpopular in Japan, leading to riots in Tokyo.

Nov. 17. Japan secured by treaty control over the foreign relations of the Korean government.

1906, Jan. Premier Katsura Tarō resigned because of popular dissatisfaction with the Portsmouth treaty. The Kenseitō cabinet was formed by Marquis **Saionji Kinmochi** (1849–1940).

March. A bill passed the lower house for the nationalization of the railways at an estimated cost of $25 million. By 1921 there were 6,481 miles of state-owned railways and 1,993 miles of private lines.

The South Manchurian Railway Company was founded as a semi-private, semipublic company. The first president, **Gotō Shinpei** (1857–1929), former civil governor of the Japanese colony of Taiwan, immediately established a research department, based in Dalian.

1907, June 10. The Franco-Japanese Entente was signed, guaranteeing the "open door" to and the integrity of China, the status quo in East Asia, and a most-favored-nation agreement. There was as well a mutual promise regarding the security of Chinese territory in which each had special interests—for Japan, Fujian, and parts of Mongolia and Manchuria.

July 25. Japan obtained a protectorate over Korea by treaty, with complete control by the Japanese resident-general.

July 30. A Russo-Japanese treaty, similar to the Franco-Japanese Entente (1907), was concluded with an agreement about the Chinese Eastern and South Manchurian Railways and spheres of influence in Manchuria.

1908, Feb. 18. The U.S. minister in Tokyo received the plans for the restriction on emigration of Japanese laborers to the U.S. (Gentlemen's Agreement) to settle existing difficulties between the two countries.

July. Katsura succeeded Saionji as premier.

Nov. 30. An exchange of notes transpired with the United States (Root-Takahira Agreement) on the common policy of the status quo in the Pacific and the "open door" and integrity of China.

1909, June. Itō Hirobumi resigned after confessing his failure to reform the administration of the Korean government.

Oct. 26. Itō was assassinated in Harbin by a Korean patriot angered over Itō's role in the Japanese seizure of his native land and the impending Japanese annexation of Korea.

1910, July 4. A Russo-Japanese agreement demarcated spheres in Manchuria; this was in joint opposition to U.S. proposals (namely, P. C. Knox's scheme of Nov. 1909) for common action in defense of Russian and Japanese interests.

Aug. 22. KOREA WAS ANNEXED by a treaty forced on its government by the Japanese (p. 569). A program of development and attempted assimilation commenced.

1911, Feb. 24. A new treaty with the United States was concluded. It continued the restrictions on emigration of Japanese laborers.

July 13. The Anglo-Japanese Alliance was renewed for ten years without reference to Korea. Neither party was to be drawn into war with a nation with which it had a general arbitration treaty.

Aug. Saionji succeeded Katsura as premier.

The famed social leader Kōtoku Shūsui (b. 1871) and 11 others were hanged for allegedly plotting to assassinate the Meiji emperor, following the Great Conspiracy Trial. The execution sent a chill through those involved in any antigovernment activity.

1912, Feb. 3. An extensive naval program was submitted to the Diet, involving construction of eight dreadnoughts and eight armored cruisers, to begin in 1913.

July 8. A secret Russo-Japanese treaty further delimited spheres in northeast Asia.

July 30. The **Meiji emperor died** and was succeeded by **Yoshihito** (r. 1912–26). The era name was changed to **Taishō.**

1912, Dec. 20. Prince Katsura became premier without a majority when Saionji resigned because of opposition to his retrenchment policy in Korea.

The overwhelming impact of the West influenced Japanese **culture** in the Meiji period as well. **Kobayashi Kiyochika** (1847–1915) continued to work in the *ukiyo-e* woodblock medium, but he used Western painting themes in it. **Okakura Tenshin** (1862–1913) retained an abiding interest in traditional East Asian artistic forms. Others reacted to the predominance of the West in Japan with a return to or search for the Japanese cultural "essence." In **literature,** two especially famous writers were **Mori Ōgai** (1862–1922) and **Natsume Sōseki** (1867–1916). Ōgai studied medicine in Germany; Sōseki studied literature in England. Both wrote powerful novels of life in the changing times of the Meiji era.

1912–26. THE TAISHŌ PERIOD. The movements begun in the Meiji period continued. The personal weakness of the Taishō emperor effectively eliminated the direct control of the imperial institution over practical politics. World War I and economic advance made Japan one of the world's great powers.

1913, Feb. 12. Adm. Yamamoto Gonbee (1852–1933) succeeded Katsura as premier.

May 9. A formal protest was sent to the United States against proposed anti-alien land registration in California. The bill nevertheless was signed into law (May 19), and Japan was assured that treaty rights were not infringed upon.

1914, April. Ōkuma Shigenobu formed a cabinet after Yamamoto resigned because of the defeat of the naval budget.

Aug. Japan issued an ultimatum to Germany, demanding the withdrawal of the German fleet from East Asia and the surrender of Jiaozhou within a week. No reply was received.

Aug. 23. JAPAN DECLARED WAR ON GERMANY and joined the Allies in World War I. *(To p. 784)*

4. VIETNAM, 1802–1902

(From p. 386)

During the early 19th century, the Vietnamese ruler built a Chinese-style court; internally he was called emperor, though in tributary relations with China he was called king. Before long, though, as elsewhere in East Asia, the Western powers exerted increasing pressure to secure rights to trade and proselytize on Vietnamese soil. Vietnam was the only country in East Asia to become a colony of a Western power—France—by century's end, leading to a partition of the country.

1802–20. The reign of **Emperor GIA-LONG** (born **Nguyên Anh** in 1762) began after his rebellious forces took Saigon with French help, won a number of victories, and finally captured Huê (1801). He established the **Nguyên dynasty**—with its capital at Huê—which would last, in name, until 1945. He had been supported in his struggles by the French missionary **Pierre Pigneau de Béhaine** (1741–99), bishop of Adran. He moved to build a centralized monarchy on the Chinese model, with a Confucian bureaucracy, and he instituted sanctions against Buddhist

and Daoist religious practices. Two regional rulers, one in Hanoi and the mighty Lê Van Duyêt (1763–1832) in Saigon, exercised considerable local authority, but their power was withdrawn under Gia-long's successor. The population of the country was roughly 8 million. Administrative sites, aside from those that were major cities or ports, did not become centers for trade; commerce was conducted, as before, at river confluences. The all-important commerce with China tended to be dominated by Chinese émigré merchants, numbering some 40,000 at this time. Land registers were updated annually beginning in 1807 as a part of Gia-long's reforms, but there were still many poor peasants and many with no land to till. Corvée requirements also fell with a heavy burden on the peasantry. Gia-long also enacted a law code (1812) patterned closely after that of Qing China.

Both Gia-long and his successor sought Western technology to build their military capacity as well as to modernize other sectors of the economy. Yet, for all his efforts, the Gia-long reign witnessed roughly 100 uprisings—caused by the devastations of natural disasters and the government's inability to respond.

Catholic missions had been active in the country since the early 17th century (p. 385) and with considerable success. The French, excluded from India by the British, focused their attention ever more on Vietnam. Gia-long, while interested in Western technology, was not open to giving either the French or the British free rein in his country.

1820–41. The **reign of Emperor MING-MANH** (b. 1791) witnessed a continuation of many of the trends set in motion by his father, Gia-long. The power of the government was further centralized, and, as if by exchange, local administrative autonomy grew stronger, especially with the emergence of the **van than** class, a middle-level local stratum of intellectuals who were charged with local administration. Unlike the seemingly similar locally resident *yangban* of Yi dynasty Korea, the *van than* never became wealthy landlords. The state's inability to address problems of the poor masses also continued to plague it. There were over 200 uprisings during Ming-manh's reign. Despite these problems, he furthered use of Chinese-style civil service examinations as the means of bureaucratic recruitment. He fashioned his court in the Confucian Chinese model, and he took measures against Christianity, proscribing it as heterodox, for he suspected that Christians supported rebellious provincial lords. There were some 300,000 Vietnamese converts to Catholicism. Following an uprising in 1833 in which Christians had been involved, he began serious repression, including the execution of missionaries and converts. He was openly derisive of Buddhism as well, and Buddhist-oriented popular religions were frequently responsible for local insurrections. He refused so much as to meet with a British envoy (1822). With the dissolution of the British East India Company's monopoly of trade with China (1834) and the Opium War (1839–1842) (p. 561), commercial relations of the Western powers within East Asia changed.

1840. Ming-manh sent missions to London and Paris to try to reach some measure of compromise with the powers supporting Christianity, but missionary animus crushed these efforts.

1841–47. During the short **reign of Emperor THIÊU-TRI,** the sanctions against Christians continued, as did the will of the ruler not to meet with foreign missions. The party of former missionary Karl Gutzlaff (1803–51) in 1847 was a complete failure. On several occasions during these years, U.S. and particularly French naval commanders intervened militarily on behalf of Catholic missionaries. In 1847 the French bombarded Danang (Tourane).

1848–83. The **reign of Emperor TU-DUC** (b. 1830) witnessed the exacerbation of problems with the Western powers and domestic troubles as well. Despite all of these problems, the deeply Confucian Tu-duc encouraged cultural development to an unprecedented extent, making his reign a high point of literary culture in Vietnamese history. He also relentlessly suppressed Christianity, sanctioning thousands of executions primarily of Vietnamese converts and of 25 Western priests.

1858, Aug. A joint French-Spanish expedition under Adm. Rigault de Genouilly, attempting to end the Nguyên court's intransigence, bombarded Danang on the coast. Unable to proceed by land to the capital at Huê, the expedition turned south and occupied Saigon in early 1859. Britain registered no objections.

1862, June 5. The **Treaty of Saigon** was signed, following French fighting and pressure along the Vietnamese coast. It stipulated that Vietnam would relinquish to the French control over the three southern provinces of "Cochin China," as the French and other Westerners came to call the southern part of Vietnam, and pay an indemnity of 20 million francs over ten years. Long associated by Westerners with the whole of Vietnam, the name Annam became associated henceforth with central Vietnam; and Tonkin (or Tongking) became associated with the north (taken over by the French, 1884). Free exercise of the Catholic religion was to be allowed, and three ports in the central and northern parts of the country were to be opened to French trade. Tu-duc had little choice but to go along with the French; he was fighting to suppress rebellion in the north. There was much popular resistance to the French incursions, such as the "righteous army" of peasants organized by Truong Dinh (1820–64) in the Mekong delta area. Although they and similar forces raided and irritated the French, their efforts failed to sustain an effective movement.

1863–68. Adm. Pierre de la Grandière served as governor of Cochin China. He organized a governmental system through "admirals," but most of the actual governing was done through Vietnamese officials.

1863, Aug. 11. King Norodom (b. 1836, r. 1836–1904) of Cambodia accepted a French protectorate.

1867. The French occupied the three western provinces of Cochin China, after an insurrection.

1868. French explorations were carried out along the Mekong River as far as the Chinese province of Yunnan. It was hoped that this would prove a useful route into southwestern China, but the river was shown to be unnavigable along its upper reaches, and the French therefore began to turn their attention to the Red River of Tonkin. The Mekong delta was to become the site of massive public works projects under the French, with irrigation canals dug and large tracts of land reclaimed for rice agriculture; immense rice plantations emerged, and rice exports grew tenfold between 1860 and 1900.

1872–73. A French merchant active in China, **Jean Dupuis** (1829–1912) explored the Red River region. The residents of Annam objected to French activities in Tonkin.

1873, Nov. Soldier and adventurer **Marie Joseph François Garnier** (Francis Garnier, 1839–73) was ordered by the governor-general of Cochin China to attack Hanoi. Garnier's forces occupied it and other strategic sites of the Red River delta. After his death on the field (Dec.), the French began to press for a second treaty of Saigon the next year.

1874, March 15. The **Second Treaty of Saigon** compelled the Vietnamese emperor to conform his foreign policy to that of France and to recognize the French possession of Cochinchina. Freedom for the Christian religion was again promised. In return France promised protection and offered to supply gunboats and officers to help suppress piracy. France returned Hanoi, but the emperor sought to evade the stipulations of the treaty and now looked to China for possible aid against the French. Both France and China now claimed "sovereignty" over Vietnam. Franco-Vietnamese conflicts continued virtually unabated.

1878. A millenarian rebellion led by one claiming the impending return of the Maitreya (Buddha of the future) was launched by peasants against the French.

1882. After continuous trouble with Chinese troops from the north, who were urged by Tu-duc against the French, the latter seized Hanoi and established a protectorate over Annam.

On Tu-duc's order (1865), the **Dai Nam Nhât Thông Chi,** in 17 volumes, was completed. It was a comprehensive geographical gazetteer of the country. Part of the original was lost (1885) in a battle lost to the French, but it was later (1909) discovered.

1883, Aug. 25. Following the death of Henri Rivière and a small force at the hands of the anti-French Triad guerrilla forces, known as the **Black Flags,** Tu-duc was compelled, under the **TREATY OF HUÊ,** once again to recognize the French protectorate, which now extended to Tonkin and Annam itself. The French, though, still had to deal with pirates and Black Flags in Tonkin who were supported by the Chinese. The result was the Sino-French War (1884), in the course of which the French suffered a setback at Lang-son (March 28, 1885), which in turn led to the overthrow of Jules Ferry, the prime mover for expansion in France.

The year 1883 was marked by severe **domestic strife,** following the death of Emperor Tu-duc. The regents elevated and deposed three emperors in succession, and the fourth, **Ham-nghi** (1872–1947, r. 1884–85, July 5), though just a teenager, joined a guerrilla force and attacked the French. After French control was established, the native ruler became subject to French orders.

1884, June 6. The second **Treaty of Huê** divided Vietnam into thirds and gave France the right to occupy militarily any place in Annam. **Thereby, effective French control was firmly established.**

June 17. A new treaty with Cambodia gave the protecting power much more control than before.

1885–95. The French carried out a program to **pacify Tonkin and Indochina generally.** There were countless revolts in the interior; those in Tonkin were led by the formidable guerrilla insurgent **De Tham** (Hoang Hoa Tham, d. 1913).

1887, Oct. Cochin China, Cambodia, Annam, and Tonkin were administratively united as the **Union de l'Indochine française,** or the Indochina Union, which continued in place until 1945.

1893. France acquired a protectorate over Laos, the interior region along the Mekong River that had long been in dispute between Annam and Siam, after a British armada confronted the Siamese king. In lands under their control, the French colonial administrators pursued a policy of "assimilation," whereby French-speaking Vietnamese would enter the French cultural sphere, ruling at the lower levels of their own society.

1897–1902. Paul Doumer (1857–1932) served as governor-general of French Indochina. He inaugurated the first far-reaching reforms and administrative and fiscal arrangements for the modernization of the region. He resided in Hanoi, ruling Cochin China through its governor and the four protectorates (Cambodia, Annam, Tonkin, and Laos) through French *résidents supérieurs.* The government held monopolies on salt, opium, alcohol, and all public facilities. Coal mines and rice plantations were opened with French funding. The École Française d'Extrême-Orient was established (1898 in Saigon; moved to Hanoi in 1900) as an elite institution for the study of all East Asian cultures and civilizations.   *(To p. 787)*

F. THE PACIFIC REGION, c. 800–1914

1. THE PACIFIC ISLANDS, 1794–1914

(From p. 387)

By the end of the 18th century, the era of European discovery was effectively over, though some significant expeditions, such as the one led by American Charles Wilkes (1838–41), made some further contributions. The 19th century saw the beginning of trade and large trading companies in the islands, the advent of Christian missions, and, most important, the annexation of the islands by European powers. By 1900, all the Pacific islands had come under some form of European control, the sole exception being Tonga, which managed to retain its sovereignty under British supervision. New tools and ideas introduced by European traders brought about profound social and economic change in the island communities and helped destabilize traditional political structures. Large-scale indentured labor migration in the islands was an important legacy of colonial rule. Among the more tragic consequences of increasing contact with the outside world were the introduction of new diseases, depopulation, and large-scale land alienation. As the 19th century ended, the islands had become deeply enmeshed in European political and economic concerns.

1794, Feb. 25. Kamehameha and other chiefs place island of Hawaii under protection of British Crown.

1797, March 6. The **London Missionary Society,** a nondenominational body comprising Congregationalists, Calvinistic Methodists, Anglicans, and Presbyterians, reached Tahiti on the ship *Duff.* It established a major station there and subsequently sent missionaries to Tonga and the Marquesas Islands. **Rev. John Williams,** who arrived in Tahiti in 1817, spearheaded the society's drive in the Pacific.

1801. Pork trade began between Tahiti and the British convict colony of New South Wales, with the active backing of the latter's Governor King. It encouraged colonial entrepreneurs to pursue commercial opportunities in the South Seas and enabled the Pomares of Tahiti to use their new connection to enhance their power.

1804. The discovery of **sandalwood** in Fiji precipitated a rush in 1807 that was over by 1810. A similar short-lived rush in Hawaii began in 1811. A longer-lasting and more significant trade began in Melanesia after the discovery of sandalwood at Eromanga (New Hebrides) in 1829. The trade introduced new tools, which altered the fabric of island society and economy.

1810. Kamehameha I (the Great) achieved the unification of the Hawaiian Islands. Similar efforts on the part of the Pomares of Tahiti and Cakobau of Fiji met with less success.

1814. The **Church Missionary Society** established a station in New Zealand and subsequently in the Pacific islands.

1820. The **American Board of Commissioners for Foreign Missions** sent its first missionaries abroad, to Hawaii. Also, the **Wesleyan Missionary Society** sent its representatives to New Zealand and Tonga.

1828. The Dutch annexed western New Guinea.

1840. The British claimed sovereignty over New Zealand with the Treaty of Waitangi.

1842. The French, led by Dupetit-Thouars, annexed the Marquesas and declared Tahiti and the Society Islands a French protectorate. In 1844, they took Gambier Islands in the Tuamotus, claiming a protectorate over the entire group, which was formally annexed in 1881.

1850. The Hamburg firm of **Godeffroy and Sohn** established a copra trading depot in **Tuamotus** and another more important one in **Samoa in 1857.** From there, they expanded their trading interests to Tonga, Niue, Futuna, the Tokelaus, the Gilbert and Ellice islands, the Marshall Islands, and the Carolines. The company spearheaded German commercial and political influence in the Pacific.

1853. The **French annexed New Caledonia,** with the active support of French Catholic missionaries who had been there since 1843. From 1864 to 1897, the French transported over 30,000 convicts to the island.

1863. The first systematic recruiting of **Pacific islands labor** for Queensland and Fiji. Subsequently, most of the major Pacific islands were involved, with wide social and political ramifications for imperial and local politics. By 1918, some 280,000 Pacific islanders and another 186,000 Asians had been pressed into some form of indentured labor.

1872, April 9. A number of Samoan chiefs petitioned for **annexation by the United States.**

1874, Oct. 10. Ratu Seru Cakobau and other leading chiefs ceded Fiji to Great Britain under the terms of a **deed of cession** that promised to protect Fijian interests while promoting commerce and Christianity in the islands.

1875. King George Tupou I of Tonga promulgated a constitution guaranteeing the civil liberties of all Tongans.

1877. The **Western Pacific Order-in-Council** came into effect, creating the Fiji-based **Western Pacific High Commission,** which administered affairs in those parts of the Pacific under British influence but not under formal colonial rule.

1878, Jan. 16. Leading **Samoan chiefs signed the treaty of friendship and commerce with the United States,** which secured the harbor of Pago Pago as a coaling and naval station.

1879, May 14. The first group of **60,000 Indian indentured laborers** arrived in Fiji on five-year contracts. After the indenture system was abolished on Jan. 1, 1920, most laborers and their descendants decided to stay in Fiji.

1880, March 24. The United States, Britain, and Germany recognized **Malietoa Talavou** as king with an executive council representing the three powers.

1884. Germany annexed the northeast mainland of New Guinea and the Bismarck Archipelago, including the islands of New Britain, New Ireland, New Hanover, and Manus (though not Bougainville) and atolls in the Solomons. The territory was officially known as the Protectorate of the New Guinea Company; the company was a private Berlin-based business firm authorized to administer the territory on behalf of the government. It became a full-fledged colony in 1899.

Britain declared a protectorate over Papua "British New Guinea." Special commissioner general Sir Peter Scratchley arrived in Port Moresby in 1885. It was a British colony from 1888 to 1906.

1885. Germany annexed the Marshall Islands and began to lay the foundations of a German colonial empire in Micronesia.

1887. Unwilling to concede ground to each other, Britain and France asked their Pacific naval commanders to cooperate to maintain order in **New Hebrides** and oversee the affairs of their respective nationals. In 1906, this arrangement was institutionalized in the **Anglo-French Condominium of the New Hebrides,** whereby the two governments agreed to set up a joint administration.

1888. The British established **a protectorate over the Cook Islands.**

1889. Britain, Germany, and the United States arranged for **a joint supervision of the affairs of Samoa.** Britain declared a **protectorate over Tokelau.**

1892. Britain proclaimed a **protectorate over the Gilbert and Ellice Islands,** annexed in 1915. The islands were introduced to the West through the writings of **Sir Arthur Grimble,** a long-time administrator.

After several years of procrastination, Britain declared the **Solomon Islands a protectorate,** to keep other powers out and to secure the islands' labor supply for Queensland and elsewhere. A firmer administrative structure was created in 1896.

1893, Jan. A coup d'état overthrew the monarchy in Hawaii and set up a provisional government under **Sanford B. Dole.** The Republic of Hawaii was proclaimed on July 4, 1894. A reluctant and indignant **Queen Liliuokalani** abdicated her throne.

1898, Aug. 12. Formal **transfer of the Hawaiian Islands to the United States took place.** By the war with Spain, the United States secured the **Philippines** and Guam.

1899. By purchase, the Germans secured from Spain the **Marianas** (Ladrone) and the **Palau Islands.** Through the abolition of the monarchy **and the partition of Samoa,** the United States retained **Tutuila.** With the Anglo-German Treaty, Britain relinquished rights to Savaii and Upolu in favor of Germany. As compensation, Britain secured parts of the Solomons and concessions in Tonga.

1900. Tonga was declared a British protectorate. **Niue** became a British possession.

April 30. Hawaii was organized as a territory of the United States. Unlike Puerto Rico, Hawaii paid its tariff duties, internal revenue collections, and income tax to the federal government. **Large-scale immigration of Asian, particularly Japanese, labor into Hawaii began.** In 1910, its total population was 192,000, of whom only 26,000 were Hawaiians and 12,500 part-Hawaiians; on the other hand, there were 80,000 Japanese and 21,500 Chinese.

1901. The **Cook Islands** were turned over to New Zealand for administration. **Ocean Island** was added to the Gilbert and Ellice Islands Protectorate.

1906. British New Guinea (Papua) was turned over to Australia. Australia's paternalistic colonial policy in Papua was shaped by one man, **Sir Hubert Murray,** who governed the territory from 1906 to 1940.

(To p. 788)

2. THE PHILIPPINES, 1800–1913

(From p. 388)

In the course of the 19th century, corruption in the church and bureaucracy and ethnic discrimination increased social and political discontent in the Spanish colony. A fledgling export economy developed, most notably in sugar, which strengthened ties to the outside world and weakened links with Spain. The number of Chinese in the country grew, and their economic role increased. Most significant, an elite of "Filipinos" emerged, a mixed group of mestizos, indios, and Spaniards born in the archipelago who saw themselves as representatives of a distinct Philippine nation. They spearheaded the movement for overthrow of the Spanish government. Muslim power in the south was still considerable in the first half of the 19th century. Sulu in particular enjoyed the fruits of a large regional market for slaves, which led to conflict with the Spanish and British who sought to halt the slave trade. However, by the 1880s the power of Sulu and the Muslim states of Mindanao had weakened. Partly out of fear of the encroachments of other imperial powers, Spain mounted a push into the Muslim areas and was able to establish its suzerainty over the region, even though it could not exercise real administrative control. With the Philippine revolution and the American takeover, Mindanao and Sulu were effectively incorporated into the Philippine state.

1820. Mexican independence led to a decline in trade, and the Royal Philippine Company became bankrupt. Large numbers of Spaniards and mestizos moved to the Philippines after the independence wars in Latin America. The Spaniards took privileged positions in the bureaucracy, which grew rapidly. Ethnic inequalities intensified.

1823. The Mexican mestizo **Andres Novales** led a revolt in the King's Own Regiment. The uprising, which resulted from tensions between mestizos and Spaniards in the bureaucracy and the military, deepened ethnic divisions and contributed to the development of Philippine nationalism.

1826. A royal decree stated that friars should control most Philippine parishes. Indio and mestizo priests were demoted to curate rank.

1834. Manila was opened to international commerce.

1839. Removal of residence and work restrictions on the Chinese led to an increase in the Chinese population.

1841. Apolinario de la Cruz led a major popular uprising against the Spanish after they refused to acknowledge a religious order he had founded.

1844. The Spanish government outlawed private trading by provincial governors. This gave the Chinese new commercial opportunities, and they became an important economic presence in the colony.

1847. The mercenary **Oyanguren** annexed Davao Gulf on Mindanao for Spain.

1851. Spain attacked Sulu, destroyed the capital at Jolo, and forced the sultan to make concessions, which the Spanish interpreted as an acceptance of Spain's control over Sulu.

1859. Establishment of **Ateneo de Manila,** a school open to all ethnic groups. Such schools contributed to the emergence of an indigenous intellectual elite known as the *ilustrados,* who were instrumental in the formation of Philippine national consciousness.

1861. The government decreed that all parishes in the archdiocese of Manila be given to friars, displacing Filipino clerics. The struggle over religious appointments intensified, adding to Filipino resentment of the friars, who occupied 817 out of 967 parishes by 1898.

Rivalry between Buayan and Magindanao allowed the Spanish to acquire more territory in Mindanao, including Cotabato.

1863. The Spanish Overseas Ministry took over rule of the Philippines from the Council of the Indies.

1864. Mestizo cleric **José Burgos** released a manifesto calling for ethnic equality in the priesthood.

1872. Mutiny amongst the garrison at Cavite Arsenal. The execution of religious nationalists including José Burgos had great influence on the Philippine national movement. A substantial number of *ilustrados* left the country. Filipino intellectuals in Spain later established the **Propaganda Movement,** which sought political representation in the Spanish Cortes and attempted to promote awareness of Tagalog culture and precolonial history. Masonic lodges also played an important part in the nationalist movement.

1876–78. The Spanish attacked Sulu to assert their sovereignty over the sultanate. In 1878 **Sulu's possessions in North Borneo were leased to Britain.** In July 1878 Sulu signed a treaty promising to obey the Spanish ruler. Germany and Britain later acknowledged Spain's rights over Sulu.

1881. Abolition of the tobacco monopoly. Followed by general reform of the tax structure in 1884, this was part of an attempt to transform the archaic fiscal system in the colony.

1886–87. Spanish forces conquered parts of Mindanao, although much of the island retained its independence until the revolution.

1887. The nationalist intellectual **José Rizal** produced the influential novel *Noli Me Tangere* while in exile in Spain. The novel's satire of corruption and injustice in the Philippines aroused government hostility.

1889. *La Solidaridad,* a Filipino nationalist newspaper, began publication in Spain, circulating the views of intellectuals like Rizal.

The Becerra Law set up town councils as part of an attempt to modernize regional organization. In similar fashion, the Maura Law of 1893 reformed urban administration.

1892. Rizal returned to the Philippines and founded the liberal **La Liga Filipina,** which proposed a nonradical program of economic and educational advancement. The government regarded the group as seditious and banished Rizal to Mindanao. The working-class activist **Andres Bonifacio** organized the revolutionary secret society **Katipunan.** Bonifacio attempted to recruit *ilustrados* into Katipunan, but they were generally unwilling to join because of the movement's revolutionary aims.

1896, Aug. 24. Rebellion of Katipunan marked the start of the Philippine Revolution. Economic problems fueled discontent. Inability to gain support from the *ilustrados,* who were the only truly national group in the Philippines, contributed to early failures, as did Bonifacio's military inexperience. The **execution of Rizal** on Dec. 30 intensified popular resentment of the government and widened the scope of the rebellion. The revolt of **Emilio Aguinaldo** in Cavite was the first defeat of the Spanish.

1897. Bonifacio was executed after a power struggle in the revolutionary movement, after which Aguinaldo became leader. The movement suffered military setbacks, and the Spanish began to prevail in the field.

Dec. 15. Biyak-na-bato pact between the revolutionaries and the Spanish, who were anxious to end the war because of the revolution in Cuba. Aguinaldo agreed to stop fighting in return for passage to exile and a money payment.

1898. The United States intervened in the Philippines because of the Spanish-American War (p. 614), destroying the Spanish navy in Manila Bay on May 1. With American backing, Aguinaldo returned to the Philippines and established a government, in cooperation with the *ilustrado* **Apolinario Mabini.** A nationalist platform that guaranteed the property rights of the *ilustrados* was advanced. Aguinaldo's position in the revolutionary movement was weakened by acquiescing to the interests of the *ilustrados.*

June 12. Declaration of independence by Aguinaldo.

Aug. 13. Fall of Manila to American forces.

Dec. 10. Treaty of Paris between Spain and the United States **ceded the Philippines to the U.S.** in exchange for $20 million.

1899, Jan. 21. Proclamation of the **Malolos Constitution** drawn up by *ilustrados* who were concerned about the protection of their own political rights and limiting the powers of Aguinaldo. Similar to the American model, it proposed the separation among the powers of government and separation of church and state.

Feb. 4. Outbreak of fighting between Americans and Filipinos. There was fierce debate in the U.S. government between those in favor of annexation of the Philippines and those opposing it. The former won with a narrow margin. In the ensuing war between the Americans and the Filipino revolutionaries, both sides committed atrocities. **The First Philippine Commission** sent by the U.S. in March promised **self-government under U.S. authority.**

Aug. 20. Agreement between Sulu and the United States granted stipends and religious liberty to Sulu in return for an end to the slave trade and loyalty to the United States. This was the basis for the incorporation of the Muslim south into the modern Philippines. These areas have remained uncertain members of the Philippine state.

1900. The Second Philippine Commission under **William Howard Taft** began to establish American administration. Officially committed to a policy of tutelary colonialism, which envisaged the ultimate independence of the Philippines, the Americans promoted government by conservative, oligarchic Filipino interests. The Partido Federal (Federal Party) was formed, an *ilustrado* party with U.S. backing.

Filipino resistance was outmatched by American military strength, and Filipino leaders favoring a compromise with the United States, such as those in the Federal Party, gained the upper hand. American pressure helped to divide the wealthier and more educated *ilustrados* from the plebeian Aguinaldo.

1901, March 23. Aguinaldo captured by Americans. He later declared support for the U.S.

July 4. Formal **establishment of U.S. civil government** in the Philippines under William Howard Taft. Guerrilla resistance continued until 1902.

1902. Formation of the **Iglesia Filipina Independiente,** an independent national church, under **Gregorio Aglipay,** a priest who had earlier been excommunicated by the Spanish hierarchy for his involvement with the revolutionaries. The Aglipayan church enjoyed considerable support among Filipino Christians. The Catholic Church carried out a number of reforms as a result.

July 1. Philippine Bill passed in the U.S. Senate, providing for a bicameral legislature consisting of an appointed upper house (made up of the Philippine commission) and an elected assembly. The U.S. government retained veto powers. Taft negotiated the purchase of about 410,000 acres of church-owned **Friar Land,** although the distribution of this land to its tenants was never fully carried out.

1906. Formation of the proindependence Partido Union Nacionalista. The Supreme Court ruled that Catholic Church property taken by the Aglipayan church had to be returned. This brought many people into the Catholic Church when it regained control of the places of worship.

1907, July 30. First elections were held for the assembly. Franchise was limited to owners of substantial amounts of property who were literate in English or Spanish (only 2 percent of the population). The proindependence **Union Nacionalista** won 59 of the 80 seats. Rise of **Manuel Quezon** and **Sergio Osmena** as political leaders.

1909, Oct. 6. Payne-Aldrich Act gave the U.S. unrestricted access to the Philippine market and allowed some Philippine exports to enter the U.S. without tariffs, although under quota.

1913, Aug. 21. Francis Harrison was appointed governor. Harrison advocated independence for the Philippines and increased the number of Filipinos in the government and bureaucracy. **Underwood-Simmons Act** (Oct. 3) removed restrictions on importation of Philippine goods into the United States. *(To p. 789)*

3. AUSTRALIA, 1788–1914

(From p. 387)

The 19th century in Australia was characterized by European settlement and political and economic development in European terms. British settlement saw the steady dispossession of some 200 Aboriginal groups: by 1914 only a few desert people remained in control of their country. Between 1788 and 1836, the British government or government-assisted expeditions settled all the sites to become state capitals at federation in 1901, in the east with convicts, in Western and South Australia with free settlers. Despite severe depressions in the 1840s and 1890s, white expansion was confident and prosperous. Stimulated by exports, chiefly gold and wool, by 1901 white Australians enjoyed the world's highest wage levels and living standards and were proclaiming an egalitarian society and an outpost of white civilization in the Pacific.

The later 19th century saw many patterns emerge in Australia similar to those in western Europe and the United States, such as the development of a strong working-class movement. Gender distinctions, including insistence on the domestic responsibilities of respectable women and condemnation of those who seemed to deviate from the respectability model, also followed trends similar to those in Europe. The Australian economy developed industrial centers for the national market along with the potent commercial export economy in agriculture and mining.

The **Dutch,** who discovered and explored the western and parts of the northern and southern coasts of Australia (1613–42), called the land **New Holland. Capt. James Cook,** who discovered and explored the east coast during his first voyage (1768–71), called that part **New**

South Wales. In 1786 the British government decided to use a site Cook had named in New South Wales, Botany Bay, to transport convicts who crowded the British prisons after it became impossible to send them to America. The plan was to set up a **convict colony** that would support itself, although probably strategic considerations also influenced the choice of site.

1788, Jan. 26. Capt. Arthur Philip arrived at Port Jackson (Sydney), with the FIRST CONVICT TRANSPORTS and convoy, 11 ships with 717 convicts, of whom about 520 were men. In the following month 15 convicts and escorts were sent to organize another settlement on **Norfolk Island** (till 1814). Philip remained governor until 1792, during the most critical period of the colony and under difficult conditions: scarcity of food; uncertainty of supplies; laziness, incompetence, and quarrelsomeness of many convicts; prevalence of vice of every kind. The colony was protected by the **New South Wales Corps,** raised in England and itself an unimpressive and insubordinate body. The governor enjoyed absolute power and alone formulated policy. The convicts were supplied from government stores, but on expiration of their terms the more deserving were given 30 to 50 acres of land. Time-expired soldiers were given grants of 80 to 100 acres. The officers were more richly endowed, and some of them, like **John Macarthur,** soon became wealthy and influential.

1792–95. Francis Grose and then **William Paterson** acted as vice governors. As members of the New South Wales Corps, they provided richly for their comrades. The officers were given the service of convicts and were allowed to establish a monopoly of cargoes brought to the settlement. **Importation of rum** was permitted, and rum soon became currency, much to the detriment of the settlement.

1793, Jan. 16. Arrival of the first free settlers (11 in all), who received free passage, tools, convict service, and land grants.

1795–1800. John Hunter, governor. A mild, well intentioned administrator, he was soon at loggerheads with the officers of the corps, through whose influence at home he was ultimately recalled.

1797, May 16. The first merino sheep were imported, leading eventually to the creation of the Australian wool industry.

1800–6. Philip King, governor. His main ambition was to break the power of the officers, wherefore he forbade their trading and prohibited the importation of spirits. Neither policy proved much of a success, and so King, like his predecessor, was in constant conflict with the officers, of whom Macarthur was the leader.

1803–4. Settlement of Tasmania, carried through by the governor for fear that the French might seize it. Settlements were established near present-day **Hobart** and near **Launceston.** In 1810–14 the convicts on Norfolk Island were transferred to Tasmania. From the outset the settlers had much trouble with Aborigines and bushrangers (escaped convicts turned bandits and freebooters).

1804. Insurrection of the Irish convicts, who had been sent in large numbers after the suppression of the revolution in Ireland in 1798. The rising was put down with ruthless vigor.

1806–9. William Bligh, governor. He was appointed in the hope that, as a well-known disciplinarian, he would be able to end the domination of the officer clique and stop the disastrous liquor traffic. But his drastic methods and fiery temperament resulted merely in rebellion.

1808, Jan. 26. Rum Rebellion. The officers, outraged by the arrest of Macarthur, induced the commander, **Maj. George Johnston,** to arrest Bligh as unfit for office and to hold him captive until the arrival of a new governor (1809). Though the home government condemned this action, it removed Bligh.

1821. COL. LACHLAN MACQUARIE, governor. His appointment marked the **end of rule by the naval commanders.** Macquarie took his Highland regiment to Australia and obliged the members of the New South Wales Corps to enlist in the regular force or return home, which about one-half of them did. The new governor devoted himself to the systematic buildup of Sydney, road construction, establishment of orphanages, and unrelenting war on the vice prevalent throughout the colony. **Civil courts** were established (1814) and a bank opened (1817). In 1816 the home government removed all restrictions on free emigration to Australia, thus preparing the way for a change in the character of the colony. But by 1810 there were already 3,000 free settlers, endowed with large blocks of land. These freemen objected violently to **Macquarie's efforts to secure social equality for the emancipists**

(pardoned convicts or those who had served their time) and to discourage free immigration. As a result, Macquarie, like earlier governors, was engaged in constant struggle, though on a different basis.

1813. Gregory Blaxland with two companions (William Lawson and William C. Wentworth) first succeeded in penetrating the mass of mountains along the coast, thus paving the way for the advance to the plateau of the interior.

1815. Bathurst, the first town in the interior, was founded and a road built to it from Sydney.

1817–18. John Oxley began the exploration of the interior, following the Lachlan and Macquarie Rivers. He found the country more or less flooded, but the discovery of great grassy regions stimulated settlement. The government granted land freely to immigrants and to emancipists, in addition to whom large numbers of squatters began to occupy grazing lands. Brutal and rapid **extermination of the native** people, who had become aggressive after many outrages by the whites (kidnapping of women and children, etc.). Rapid **development of bushranging** (lawlessness of escaped convicts and other bandits, who terrorized the more remote areas).

1819–21. Inquiry of John T. Bigge, a London barrister sent out to investigate the government and the general condition of the colony. Bigge, having collected much material, recommended liberal land grants to settlers and extensive use of convict labor to open up the country.

1821–25. SIR THOMAS BRISBANE, the eminent astronomer, served as governor after the recall of Macquarie. The period of his rule was marked by an acceleration of development. Land was granted generously on condition that the grantee take over one convict for every 100 acres. **Sale of Crown lands** ensued, but not more than 4,000 acres to any one person. Systematic clearing of lands was performed by convict gangs, at fixed prices. Organization of large syndicates took place: the Australian Agricultural Company received a grant of 1 million acres and a monopoly of the coal mining near Newcastle. The Van Diemen's Land Company was given a grant of 400,000 acres in Tasmania.

1823. Brisbane's administration was distinguished also by the **establishment of a legislative council,** the first step in the development of representative government. The council consisted of five to seven nominated members, who could act on measures submitted by the governor. In 1828 the council was enlarged by the addition of seven nonofficial members. Beginning of the **agitation for representative government,** inspired by **William C. Wentworth,** editor of *The Australian* (1824).

1824. New convict settlements were opened, to take care of the most dangerous elements. One was established at Moreton Bay, and the town of Brisbane was founded. In 1842 free settlers were allowed into this district. In 1825 (June) **Norfolk Island** was reoccupied and the worst felons were transported there. Brutal treatment led to several serious uprisings, and in 1853 the penal colony on Norfolk was given up.

1824–25. Explorations of Hamilton Hume and William Hovel beyond the mountains west of Sydney. They crossed the upper Murray River and ultimately reached the south coast near Geelong. The rich country discovered by them was soon penetrated by settlers.

1825. Tasmania (Van Diemen's Land) **was separated from New South Wales** and was thenceforth administered by a lieutenant governor and a legislative council. Horrible conditions prevailed in the island, with its large convict population. The bushrangers, under leaders like **Matthew Brady,** were well organized in bands and attacked settlers and native people. In 1828 martial law was declared against Aborigines in the settled districts, leading to the **Black War,** which cost many lives. The lieutenant governor, **Col. George Arthur,** finally managed to track down the bushrangers, many of whom were hanged, but his efforts to corral the native people (the Black Line, 1830) failed. **George Robinson,** a Methodist settler, offered to serve as conciliator. He succeeded in getting the remnants of the native tribes to submit and in 1832–34, the 123 who remained were established on Flinders Island, where efforts were made to "civilize" them. The experiment failed. By 1847 only 47 Aborigines remained, and these were moved back to Tasmania. The last man of full blood in Tasmania died in 1869 and the last woman in 1876.

1825–31. RALPH DARLING, governor of New South Wales. He was

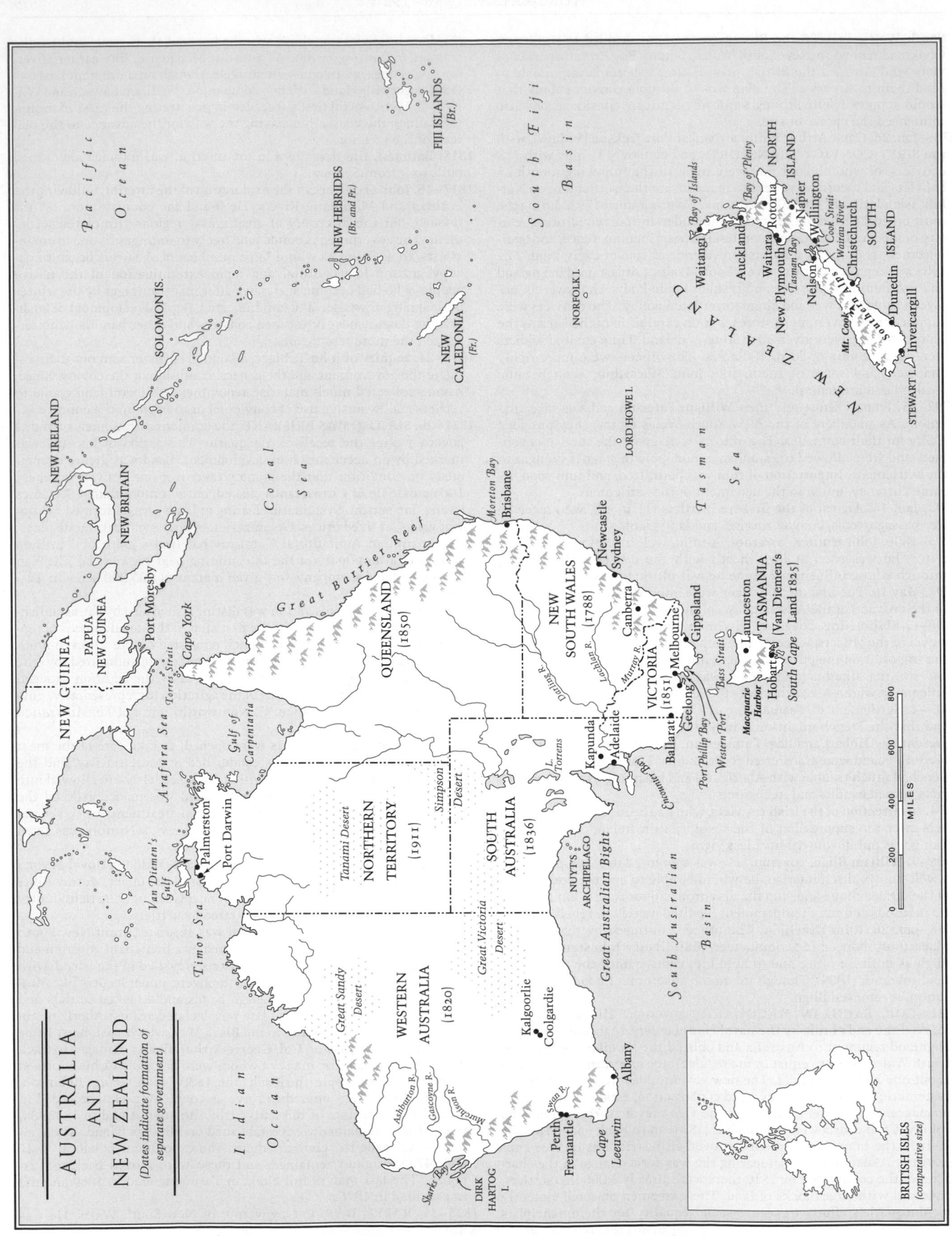

AUSTRALIA AND NEW ZEALAND

(Dates indicate formation of separate government)

Pacific Ocean

FIJI ISLANDS (Br.)

South Fiji Basin

NEW HEBRIDES (Br. and Fr.)

SOLOMON IS.

NEW IRELAND

NEW BRITAIN

NEW CALEDONIA (Fr.)

NORFOLK I.

LORD HOWE I.

Tasman Sea

NEW ZEALAND

Waitangi
Bay of Islands
Bay of Plenty
Auckland
Waitara · Rotorua
New Plymouth · Napier
Tasman Bay · Wellington
Nelson
Cook Strait
Waitau River
Christchurch
Mt. Cook △
Dunedin
Invercargill
Stewart I. △

NORTH ISLAND

SOUTH ISLAND

Southern Alps

NEW GUINEA

PAPUA NEW GUINEA

Port Moresby

Cape York

Arafura Sea

Torres Strait

Coral Sea

Gulf of Carpentaria

Great Barrier Reef

Morrton Bay
Brisbane

QUEENSLAND (1850)

Newcastle
Sydney

NEW SOUTH WALES (1788)

Canberra

Lachlan R.

Murray R.

Darling R.

VICTORIA (1851)

Melbourne
Gippsland
Geelong
Ballarat
Port Phillip Bay
Western Port

Bass Strait

Launceston

TASMANIA
(Van Diemen's Land 1825)

Macquarie Harbor
Hobart

South Cape

Van Diemen's Gulf

Palmerston
Port Darwin

Timor Sea

Tanami Desert

NORTHERN TERRITORY (1911)

Simpson Desert

L. Torrens

Kapunda
Adelaide

SOUTH AUSTRALIA (1836)

Encounter Bay

NUYT'S ARCHIPELAGO

Great Australian Bight

South Australian Basin

Great Sandy Desert

Great Victoria Desert

WESTERN AUSTRALIA (1820)

Kalgoorlie
Coolgardie

Ashburton R.
Gascoyne R.
Murchison R.
Swan R.

Perth
Fremantle
Albany

Cape Leeuwin

Sharks Bay

DIRK HARTOG I.

Indian Ocean

0   200   400   600   800
MILES

BRITISH ISLES
(comparative size)

much more vigorous and autocratic than his predecessor and much less favorable to the emancipists. Conflict with Wentworth occurred over freedom of the press, drastic suppression of disorder, and the **Bushranging Act** (1830)—suspects were to be arrested without warrant and held until proved innocent. On the other hand, Darling's rule was distinguished by the extension of the council and by the introduction of **trial by jury** for criminal cases. Emancipists were permitted to serve on juries, except in special cases. Darling continued the policy of **generous land grants,** and by the end of his period some 4 million acres had been granted in New South Wales, much of it in large blocks.

1825-27. The government, alarmed by the explorations of the Frenchman Dumont d'Urville along the coasts, established **posts at Westernport, at Albany** on the southwest coast, **and at Melville Island** on the north coast, but none of these thrived. In 1829 the British government, however, laid claim to the whole of the continent.

1827-30. Progress of exploration. Allan Cunningham in 1827 discovered the rich Darling Downs, in the hinterland of Brisbane. In 1829 (Feb. 2) **Charles Sturt,** seeking for the great inland sea, which he was convinced existed, discovered the Darling River. On a second journey (1829-30) he descended the Murrumbidgee and Murray Rivers to the sea, returning via the same route to Sydney.

1829. FOUNDATION OF PERTH, in Western Australia. This was the work of **Thomas Peel, James Stirling,** and their associates. A huge tract of land was granted by the government and was divided among the settlers, but dispersal of the population, lack of sufficient labor, etc., led to the collapse of the founders' hopes and investments. Western Australia led a most precarious existence for many years.

1831-38. Sir Richard Bourke, governor. The British government fixed the minimum price of land at five shillings per acre, thus bringing to an end the unrestricted granting of land. Half of the proceeds from land sales was to be devoted to financing of immigration, the other half to public works. In 1832 the New South Wales government began the encouragement and financing of free immigration.

1831, May 15. Arrival of first overseas steamship, *Sophia Jane,* in Sydney. A smaller steamship, *Surprise,* had been built in Sydney in March.

1834-36. FOUNDING OF SOUTH AUSTRALIA. Whalers and sealers from Tasmania and America had for some time maintained stations on the coast, but the establishment of the colony was due to the efforts of **Edward Gibbon Wakefield,** the famous colonial theorist. Wakefield argued that land must be sold at a "sufficient price," which meant a price sufficient to oblige the laborer to work for several years before being able to acquire land for himself. In the interval the proceeds from land sales could be devoted to the importation of further labor, and thus a perpetual turnover of capital, land, and labor could be effected. On Aug. 2, 1834, Wakefield's followers, supported by the duke of Wellington, George Grote, and others, secured for their South Australia Association a charter to found a colony. The first settlers were landed at Kangaroo Island in 1836, but were soon moved to the mainland, where **Adelaide was founded.** Wakefield's theory was not closely adhered to, but the land sales resulted in widespread speculation, which ruined the beginnings of the enterprise. **Sir George Grey** (lieutenant governor, 1841-45) finally succeeded in clearing up the financial muddle and reestablished the colony on the basis of cultivation and grazing.

1834-37. SETTLEMENT OF VICTORIA. This was begun by colonists from other parts of Australia and Tasmania. In 1834 **Edward Henty** from Tasmania began sheep and cattle grazing at Portland Bay, and in the following year **John Batman** and his associates from Tasmania (the Port Phillip Association) concluded a treaty with the native people at Port Phillip and began to open the country. A rival group from Tasmania, led by **John Fawkner,** established itself close by. Batman and his friends were the **founders of Melbourne.**

1834, Oct. 28. The "battle" of Pinjarra, Western Australia. Soldiers led by Gov. Stirling ambushed local Aborigines, killing many.

1837. A British parliamentary committee investigated the whole question of **transportation of convicts** and reached conclusions unfavorable to the system. Beginning of the movement to abolish it.

1838. The **minimum price of land** was raised to 12 shillings per acre (in 1840 to £1 per acre). The government, however, issued **grazing licenses** for a small fee, thereby facilitating the occupation of large tracts in the interior. Between 1840 and 1850 the Darling Downs were opened up and, after a severe depression in the early 1840s, New South Wales began developing its wool industry.

1840, Nov. 18. The **LAST CONVICTS** were landed in New South Wales. Since 1788 about 79,000 had been brought in. In 1840, about 38,400, and in 1850 about 2,360, convicts remained. The free population already greatly outnumbered the convicts and emancipists.

1840-41. Edward J. Eyre explored the barren region north of Spencer Bay as far as Lake Torrens. Thence he and an Aboriginal companion, Wylie, crossed the desert of the Nullabor Plain to Albany (Western Australia).

1842. Reconstruction of the legislative council, which henceforth was to consist of 36 members, of whom 24 were to be elected by the propertied classes. Emancipists were given the vote provided they could meet the property qualifications.

1844-46. Charles Sturt, starting from Adelaide, pushed his way north into the great **Stony Desert** as far as the Diamantina. At the same time the German scientist **Ludwig Leichhardt** explored the region from Darling Downs to the Gulf of Carpentaria and as far as Port Essington (post open, 1838-49).

1847. By order in council the great pastoralists who had occupied land on grazing licenses were transformed into **leaseholders,** thus securing fixity of tenure. The measure acted favorably on the sheep industry, but accentuated the conflict between pastoralists and small farmers.

1848. The **British government resumed transportation of convicts** on the new Pentonville (conditional pardon) system. Convicts who had proved their good behavior for a couple of years in England were transported to Australia and set free on condition that they should not return to England until their sentence was completed. This caused a storm of protest in New South Wales, but 3,340 convicts were transported there before the system was terminated in 1850.

1850-55. Construction of the first railway (Sydney to Goulburn). Railways were built and run by the state.

1850. Convicts were for the first time sent to **Western Australia,** in response to a request from the settlers, who were desperately in need of laborers.

1850, Aug. The **AUSTRALIAN COLONIES GOVERNMENT ACT** was passed by the British Parliament. The colonies were given the right to constitute their own legislatures, fix the franchise, alter their constitutions, determine their own tariffs, all subject to royal confirmation. Thus the Australian states, in conformity with the new colonial policy of the British government after 1837, were given self-government. A committee headed by **William Wentworth** worked out a **constitution of New South Wales,** which received royal assent in July 1855. It provided for a legislative council appointed for life and a legislative assembly elected on a restricted franchise, together with cabinet government on the British model. At the same time the other states (excepting Western Australia) adopted similar constitutions, though for the most part they provided for an elective upper house.

1850, Jan. 1. New South Wales issued Australia's first adhesive postage stamps (Victoria, Jan. 3).

1851, Feb. 12. DISCOVERY OF GOLD in Lewis Ponds Creek, New South Wales. Gold rush began in April, with notable finds at Ballarat (Aug.) and Bendigo (Dec.), in Victoria. Isolated finds had been made ever since 1839, but the government had discouraged the search for fear of the diversion of labor from grazing. From the Victorian fields about £80 million worth of gold was officially taken in the first decade: they were the richest alluvial fields ever found. Tremendous **influx of workers and adventurers** poured in from all over the world. The population of Victoria rose from 77,000 in 1851 to 333,000 in 1855. Recrudescence of bushranging occurred. The government made efforts to secure some part of the new wealth in the form of mining licenses. Growing discontent on the goldfields culminated in Nov.–Dec. 1854 in **open rebellion,** led by German and Irish revolutionaries, who proclaimed the **Republic of Victoria.** The insurrection was put down by government troops without much trouble when they stormed the Eureka Stockade at Ballarat (Dec. 3).

July 1. Port Phillip was separated from New South Wales and became the colony of Victoria.

1852. Foundation of the University of Sydney, followed in 1855 by that of Melbourne and later other state capitals.

1853, May 26. Last convict ship arrived in Tasmania (Hobart). Since 1803 about 68,500 convicts had been landed in the island (about 4,000 a year after 1841). The name *Tasmania* now definitively replaced that of *Van Diemen's Land,* and a constitution not unlike that of New South Wales was adopted.

Nov. The **convict colony on Norfolk Island was abandoned,** after several serious and bloody insurrections.

1855, June. The Victoria government passed an **act to restrict Chinese immigration** (33,000 had come to the goldfields since 1851). The new law provided for a poll tax of £10 on every Chinese immigrant. In 1859 a residence tax of £4 per annum was added. Similar measures were adopted by South Australia (1857) and New South Wales (1861) despite pressure from the British government. The effect was to check Chinese immigration almost completely.

New South Wales, having first adopted a railway gauge of 5 ft. 3 in., changed to the 4 ft. 8½ in. gauge, leaving Victoria with the broader gauge. South Australia, Western Australia, and Queensland, for reasons of economy, adopted the 3 ft. 6 in. gauge, thus producing complete **confusion in the continental railway systems.**

1856. Peninsula and Oriental Steamship Company opened regular service, facilitating travel from England.

March 19. Victoria introduced the **secret ballot,** which later spread to the other Australian colonies and the world.

1859, Dec. 10. QUEENSLAND was established as a separate colony, following agitation against government from Sydney. **Brisbane** became the capital.

1860–1. Robert O. Burke and **William J. Wills** headed a lavishly financed and well-equipped expedition across the desert from Melbourne, using camels for the first time in Australia. The expedition first **succeeded in crossing Australia** from south to north (Gregory River on the Gulf of Carpentaria), but the leaders lost their lives on the return journey.

1861, July. Anti-Chinese riots on the Lambing Flat goldfields, New South Wales.

Oct. 18. In New South Wales the **land selection acts** limited the tenure of leases and permitted **selection of small holdings** for purchase. The measures were intended to help the small farmer (selector), but gave rise to much abuse (selecting of the best part of a large sheep run and "dummying"—purchase by selectors who were mere agents of the large holders). Greater efforts were made in most colonies to restrict and break up the large holdings (resumption of Crown lands on expiration of leases, compulsory resale) culminating (1910) in a heavy tax on unimproved estates of over £5,000 in value. These measures were only partly successful.

Nov. 7. The Melbourne Cup, Australia's premier horse race, was first run.

1861–62. John McDouall Stuart, on his third attempt to cross the continent from Adelaide to Port Darwin, succeeded.

1862, June 15. Bushrangers under Frank Gardiner conducted the most valuable stagecoach robbery in history, at Eugowra Rocks, New South Wales.

1863, July 6. Administration of the Northern Territory (central as well as northern Australia), which, since the separation of Queensland, was no longer contiguous to New South Wales, was **assigned to South Australia,** where there was high hope of fertile territory.

1864. Beginning of the **importation of native (Kanaka) laborers** into Queensland from the Solomons and other islands. The system was intended to meet the labor shortage on the sugar plantations. Though officially a system of contract labor, it soon degenerated into something closely akin to slave raiding, until regulated, to some extent, by the government.

1866. The Victoria Parliament, influenced by the writing of **David Syme,** an influential Melbourne editor, gave up free trade and **introduced protection.** The measure led to a great constitutional conflict between the assembly and the council, which was dominated by the squatter oligarchy. Similar struggles continued until finally the farmer and industrial labor groups secured control of the political situation. The other colonies followed the example of Victoria in adopting protection, with the sole exception of New South Wales, which contented itself with a tariff for revenue only.

1867. The **Public Schools Act** in New South Wales laid the basis for the modern system of compulsory education for the young.

1868, Jan. 10. The **last convicts were landed in Western Australia,** which, since 1850, had received about 9,500. Thus ended the transportation system to any part of the continent.

1870, Sept. 6. The **British government withdrew imperial forces** from Australia, after which the different colonies established militia systems of their own.

1872, Aug. 2. Opening of the telegraph line across the continent from Adelaide to Port Darwin, which in Oct. was reconnected with Java and so with the lines to India and Europe.

1873. Introduction of compulsory, secular schooling in Victoria. At the same time the Victoria government passed the **first factory act,** aimed at protection of children and women and at the maintenance of sanitary and safe working conditions. This pioneer move was improved upon in 1884 and was imitated by the other colonies.

The New Guinea problem. Already in 1867 the New South Wales government had appealed to London for action in the non-Dutch part of New Guinea, but the government had turned a deaf ear. In 1873 **Capt. John Moresby** raised the British flag on the south coast, but the home government repudiated the territorial claim implied.

1874. Crossing of the western half of the continent by **John Forrest,** who made his way from the Murchison River across the desert to the newly constructed south-north telegraph line and thence to Adelaide.

1878. The Queensland government annexed the islands in Torres Strait.

1879. Organization of the **first trade union congress.** Unions had existed for some years previously and had embarked upon a widespread **agitation for the eight-hour day** (one of many points borrowed from the Chartists who had come to Australia after 1848). The unions became powerful factors in New South Wales, Victoria, and South Australia.

1880, June 26–28. Siege of Glenrowan, ending in the deaths of three of the Kelly gang of bushrangers. The leader, Ned Kelly, was hanged in Melbourne on Nov. 11.

1883–84. THE NEW GUINEA CRISIS. The Queensland government, uneasy about German designs, offered to assume the administration of the island if the home government would annex it. On April 3, 1883, the Queensland government, exasperated by delay in London, proclaimed possession, but was disavowed by London. Other colonies joined in the agitation for action. Ultimately, when the home government decided to act, the Germans had already laid claim to the northeastern part, leaving to the British (annexation, Nov. 6, 1884) only the southeastern part. This danger at the door appears to have had much to do with furthering the sentiment for federation in Australia.

1883, Aug. 21. Opening of the Sydney-Melbourne railway line.

1883, Dec. An intercolonial conference in Sydney considered the possibility of federation of the colonies. The idea had been put forward long before by William C. Wentworth and was ardently championed by **Sir Henry Parkes,** the eminent statesman of New South Wales. Homogeneity of race, common tradition, and the needs of defense favored some sort of union, but the colonies were jealous of their independence and in many respects downright hostile to each other.

1885. Victoria established wages boards, empowered to fix wages in sweated industries. These boards, composed of employers and employees, with a neutral chairman, were given extensive powers to regulate entire industries. A daring experiment in labor relations, the system was gradually adopted by other colonies (beginning in 1908) under pressure of the labor parties.

March 3. New South Wales sent 700 troops to the Sudan. This was Australia's first entry into foreign war.

1888. The British privy council upheld the **exclusion of the Chinese** as practiced in Victoria. Thereafter the policy was enforced by all the colonies, and the idea of a "White Australia" met with general acceptance. As a matter of fact, there was growing hostility to any immigration, especially on the part of labor, and the influx of new settlers rapidly declined to a mere trickle.

1890. The Australian colonies and New Zealand agreed to support financially a British naval squadron, to be maintained in Australasian waters.

Aug. 15. Responsible government was established **in Western Australia.**

1891, March–April. The **FIRST AUSTRALASIAN FEDERAL CONVENTION** met at Sydney, under the presidency of **Sir Henry Parkes.** The members were chosen from the colonial parliaments and included most of the outstanding political figures of Australia and New Zealand. The convention worked out a draft constitution, which later served as a basis for the federal system, but the scheme had to be dropped because of the **opposition of New South Wales.** The result was renewed agitation for federation, especially by popular societies and leagues (beginning in 1893). The great **financial crisis of 1893,** the growth of the White Australia sentiment, and the emergence of Australian nationalism contributed further to the desire for union.

1892–94. Great shipping, mining, and shearing strikes resulted in failure, but thereby came to mark an important turning point in the **development of the labor movement.** In several colonies the trade unions embarked upon political activity and soon became crucial factors in the political situation.

1894, Dec. 21. South Australia introduced women's suffrage, which was later adopted by the other states (Western Australia, 1899; New South Wales, 1902; Tasmania, 1903; Queensland, 1905; Victoria, 1909). At the same time South Australia established **compulsory arbitration of industrial disputes,** another experiment in the settlement of labor problems.

1897–1900. THE ACHIEVEMENT OF UNION. A federal convention met at Hobart in Jan. 1897 (ten members from each colony except Queensland). This assembly reconsidered the draft constitution of 1891 and finally evolved the arrangement that was later accepted. The federation drew on the British and U.S. systems of government, although residual powers were kept by the states. The federated states were to be called the Commonwealth of Australia, and the new federal government was to be established in a new capital city to be determined later. The federal government was to have control of foreign affairs, defense, trade, tariffs, posts and telegraphs, currency, naturalization, marriage and divorce, pensions, etc. At the head was to be a **governor-general,** appointed by the Crown. Parliament was to be bicameral: the upper house **(Senate)** was to consist of six members from each state, elected directly for a six-year term, one-half renewable every three years; the **House of Representatives** was to be directly elected on the basis of populational districts. A **high court** was provided for as guardian of the constitution.

On June 3–4, 1898, the draft constitution was submitted to four colonies for popular vote. Victoria, South Australia, and Tasmania were overwhelmingly in favor. New South Wales was opposed, and Queensland and Western Australia did not hold a referendum. In Jan. 1899, **a conference of premiers** agreed on amendments to the proposed constitution, which was then (May–Sept. 1899) passed by referendum in all colonies except Western Australia. After amending the bill so as to allow appeals to the British privy council, the British Parliament passed the Constitution Act, which was given royal assent on July 9, 1900. Western Australia then decided to join the federation (July 31).

1901, Jan. 1. The COMMONWEALTH OF AUSTRALIA came into being. The first cabinet was led by **Edmund Barton,** ardent federationist and protectionist. The opposition, led by **George H. Reid,** favored a tariff for revenue only. The **Labour Party** formed the third group. Led by **John C. Watson** and better disciplined than the other parties, it was able, from the outset, to control the balance, and thus to carry out in the commonwealth the program of state socialism already introduced in the states. In 1901 New South Wales introduced conciliation and arbitration courts and adopted a scheme for old-age pensions. The Labour Party was particularly determined in the matter of immigration restriction, to which all parties, indeed, were committed.

1899–1902. Each colony, and in 1902 the commonwealth, sent troops to the South African War. About 1,400 Australians died.

1901, Dec. 23. The Immigration Restriction Act (federal) provided that an immigrant, on demand, must demonstrate ability to pass a test in a European language (changed in 1905 to "a prescribed language" to spare Japanese susceptibilities). In this way Asians and, if desired, Europeans could be excluded at will. The federal government at the same time put a stop to the importation of Kanakas into Queensland (they were to be repatriated by Dec. 1906). A high tariff on sugar protected the sugar growers from competition from outside.

1902. The **federal tariff** placed the whole continent on the protectionist system.

Women's suffrage was established for all federal elections.

1902–4. Alfred Deakin, Barton's deputy, became prime minister, dependent on support of the Labour Party. When the latter abandoned him, **Watson formed the first Labour cabinet** (1904), which, however, was able to maintain itself for only a few months. Watson was succeeded by Reid.

1904–5. Reid governed with support of the non-Labour representatives. The combination did not work very smoothly and the Reid cabinet was followed by a Deakin ministry.

1905–8. The **Deakin ministry** enjoyed the support of the Labour Party, now led by **Andrew Fisher.**

1906, Sept. 1. British New Guinea became an Australian federal possession and was renamed Papua (the Portuguese name). The territory had been but little developed (white population about 600), but was regarded as vital for defense, especially in view of the rise of Japan and its victory over Russia.

1907, Nov. 8. The "Harvester Judgement" (commonwealth) established the **basic wage,** the basis of Australian wage-fixing systems for the next 60 years.

1908–9. Second Labour cabinet (Fisher). The government was much preoccupied by foreign affairs and defense. The new tariff (1908) gave British goods a 5 percent preference, and other efforts were made to draw closer the bonds to Great Britain, chiefly in view of the rising naval power of Germany and the gradual withdrawal of British naval forces from the Pacific. The Australian colonies had all taken part with the mother country in the South African War, and contributions had been made since 1890 to the maintenance of a naval squadron in the South Pacific. In 1908 the Australian government decided on the **construction of a naval force** of its own and began work on a 22-year program.

1908, Oct.–Nov. The **commonwealth capital** was finally fixed at Canberra (New South Wales), the state government ceding the necessary territory, with a separate strip of coast.

1909–10. Another Deakin government, based on fusion with the following of Reid and his successor, **Joseph Cook.**

1909. Federal old-age pensions were established for those over 65 years of age and resident in Australia at least 25 (later 20) years.

1909–10. Defense Acts. After a visit and recommendations by Lord Kitchener, in 1911 the Australian government introduced a system of **compulsory military training** and began to organize a regular military force.

1910. Australia's first coinage was introduced (first postage stamps, 1913).

1911, Jan. 1. The Northern Territory, administered by South Australia, **became a federal possession.**

April. In the general election the **Labour Party** for the first time **won a clear majority** of seats in the House of Representatives, thus ending the system of three minority parties working in combination. Fisher formed his second government, which lasted until 1913. **Continuation of the social program** (heavy tax on large and absentee properties, etc.). In order to make "White Australia" more secure, the government resumed the **system of assistance to desirable white immigrants,** especially with the view of settling the Northern Territory.

1913, May 31. In the general election the **Liberal Party** (Joseph Cook) **secured a majority** of one. Cook formed a ministry, but legislation was effectively blocked by the Labour Party, which still had a majority in the upper house. To break the deadlock, the governor-general dissolved both houses.

1914, Sept. 5. In the general election the **Labour Party recovered its majority.** Fisher formed his third government, which in 1915 was taken over by his successor, **William M. Hughes.** *(To p. 791)*

4. NEW ZEALAND, c. 800–1913

Archaeological evidence dates the earliest human occupation of New Zealand to around the 9th century C.E. (p. 386). According to Maori tradition, the ancestors of the **Maori people migrated by sea to Aotearoa (New Zealand) from Hawaiki,** thought to be in the eastern Pacific.

Maori artifacts and language show affinities with those of Eastern Polynesia. Many Maori genealogies trace tribal descent from **ancestral canoes,** each of which is associated with a particular area of the country. The Maori had a sophisticated Neolithic culture based on agriculture, fishing, and the hunting of birds. Maori society adapted successfully to New Zealand where the climate was much colder and vegetable food less abundant than in their area of origin. Maori people lived throughout the country but were concentrated in the North Island. Demographers estimate the Maori population was around 100,000 in 1769.

Concepts of prestige *(mana)* and the rules of sacred propriety *(tapu)* have always been fundamental to Maori religious and political life, reflected in sophisticated **carving and oral literature. Land** and **ancestors** were and still remain vital elements in Maori culture. Intertribal relations were intensely competitive and, in response to warfare, **defensive engineering** was highly developed.

1642. The first contact between Maoris and Europeans occurred when the Dutch explorer **Abel Tasman** (p. 387) landed briefly in the South Island and gave the country the name Nieuw Zeeland. Tasman's stay was extremely short and had little impact beyond making the existence of the country known to Europeans.

1769, 1773, and 1777. CAPT. JAMES COOK led expeditions to New Zealand (p. 387). These expeditions transmitted information about the country's geography, flora, fauna, and culture back to Europe. Starting with Cook's expeditions, **European diseases, plants, and animals** entered New Zealand, bringing about important changes in the Maori population and the landscape.

In the 1790s Euro-American **whalers** and **sealers** began to establish permanent stations in New Zealand. Trade in products such as timber and flax, particularly with Australia, brought the Maori into increasing contact with the world economy.

1814–1913. In the first half of the 19th century the Maori remained the dominant culture in New Zealand. Quickly adapting imported technology to their own ends, the Maori exploited the new opportunities brought by contact with foreigners. At the same time, disease, the capitalist economy, and new ideologies transformed Maori society and politics. Relations with Europeans varied from place to place, largely in accordance with tribal political needs. A treaty between Maori leaders and Britain in 1840 established British authority over the country, initiating a rapid growth in immigration from Britain. Despite active political and military resistance by the Maori, Europeans had taken control of most of the country by 1870. Maori population and landholdings both declined, although charismatic leaders helped to maintain communal cohesion. After 1852 New Zealand became a self-governing British colony, and in the late 19th century its politics came to be characterized by a populist form of social democracy. Economic expansion, based on gold and agriculture, was stimulated by ambitious programs of government borrowing and public works in the last quarter of the 19th century. In the 1890s, New Zealand carried out a series of social reforms, including women's suffrage, social welfare measures, and government-controlled industrial arbitration.

1814. Beginning with **Samuel Marsden,** English missionaries attempted to convert the Maori population to Christianity. Marsden established the first Church of England mission in the Bay of Islands. The missionaries also gave the Maori language a written form. In 1815 the **first Maori-English dictionary** was compiled, and more standardized and accurate orthography was developed in 1820. Literacy spread quickly among the Maori.

1820s. Western technology, such as clothing, guns, and metal implements, and food plants like the potato became pervasive among the Maori. Disease and intertribal wars prosecuted by chiefs such as **Hongi** and **Te Rauparaha** disrupted Maori society.

1830s. Maori people were significant participants in the growing commerce with the outside world, marketing flax to Australia in the period prior to 1831 and exporting large quantities of grain and legumes to New South Wales in the 1830s. Another transformation occurring at this time was the growing number of European residents, many of whom purchased land from the Maori. However, the Maori remained the key political force in New Zealand until the middle of the 19th century.

1833. First record of the **Papahurihia millennial movement,** a Maori response to the influx of Christian ideas resulting from increased missionary activity, including the translation of Christian writings. It was the first of many prophetic movements fusing Maori belief and Christianity in the postcontact period.

James Busby became British resident, the first official representative of the British government in New Zealand.

1835. A group of Northern Maori chiefs asserted their political sovereignty by drawing up a **declaration of independence,** later recognized by the British government.

1837. Busby reported to the British Crown that New Zealand was in a state of anarchy. Although a distorted picture of the situation, this prompted the British government to intervene more deeply in the country. Opinion differed among the British in New Zealand; some wanted to safeguard Maori rights, whereas others wished to open the country for settlement. Both groups, however, called for intervention by Britain.

1838. Founding of the **New Zealand Company** in Britain, which proposed sending immigrants to set up a colonial society founded on a strong middle class.

1839. William Hobson was sent by the British government to negotiate with the Maori, paving the way for annexation of New Zealand.

1840. New Zealand Company colonists arrived in Port Nicholson in Jan. The town of Wellington was founded.

Feb. 6. THE TREATY OF WAITANGI was signed between certain Maori chiefs and representatives of the British Crown headed by Hobson. In the English version of the treaty, the Maori ceded sovereignty to the British Crown and gave the British government right of **preemption** to any land the Maori wished to sell. The British promised to **guarantee Maori ownership of lands, fishing grounds, and other items of value. The Maori and English versions** of the treaty **differed in some significant areas,** particularly about **whether or not the Maori had intended to cede sovereignty** to Britain, contributing to subsequent controversy over the treaty. After copies of the treaty had been sent throughout the country (a number of tribes did not sign), Hobson proclaimed British sovereignty and established the capital at Auckland, becoming the first governor of New Zealand (1840–42).

1843. A confrontation between New Zealand Company settlers and Maori over land took place at Wairau, and 20 settlers were killed in the fighting. An inquiry in 1844 blamed the incident on the settlers.

1843–44. The sheep farming industry was established in the South Island, operating on grazing licenses issued by the government.

1844. Hone Heke, the first Maori signatory to the Treaty of Waitangi, cut down the flagpole at Kororareka to protest violations of the treaty and sacked Kororareka settlement. Heke's action was a symbolic attack on British sovereignty over New Zealand.

1845. War broke out between the British and the Maori in the north (the **FIRST NEW ZEALAND WAR**). Initially, the British were severely defeated because of the Maori superiority in defensive engineering. Later minor successes allowed the British to claim victory, although in military terms the outcome of the war was equivocal. There was also fighting in the south of the North Island. The war was over by 1847.

George Grey became governor (his first term lasted until **1854**). Grey was a forceful and talented person and dominated Pakeha (European) politics in New Zealand for much of the 19th century. He was also noted for his scholarship on Maori culture.

1848–50. Establishment of settlements at Otago and Canterbury in the South Island.

1852. THE CONSTITUTION ACT established New Zealand as a self-governing colony of Britain. In addition to the House of Representatives elected by land-owning males, there was an appointed Legislative Council. The act divided the country into six provinces, each with its own council. Power lay more with the provincial councils than with the central government, and New Zealand was essentially disunited until 1875. The relationship between the elected government and the governor appointed by Britain was unclear. The Constitution Act also added to ambiguities about the question of Maori sovereignty.

1854. Meeting of tribes in Taranaki was directed at halting further sales of land to Europeans. This was the first of a series of intertribal political actions in response to growing European dominance.

1858. The European population surpassed that of the Maori.

Through the action of the brilliant Maori leader **Wiremu Tamihana,** the elderly Waikato chief **Te Wherowhero** was elected **Maori king.** The king's election was the culmination of a movement for tribal cooperation to maintain sovereignty, although not all tribes accepted his authority. The alliance over which the king presided was uncertain, but the movement was united in its opposition to land sales. In the same year the government introduced legislation to increase legal control over Maori areas and to change tribal landholdings to individual title.

1859. The government attempted to force a land sale in the **Waitara area** of Taranaki that was opposed by the majority of the local tribe under the chief **Wiremu Kingi.** This substantially increased tensions between the Maori and the government.

1860. War broke out over the Waitara dispute (the beginning of the **SECOND NEW ZEALAND WAR**).

1861. Gold was discovered in Otago, resulting in a great influx of miners; the population of the South Island more than doubled, and it became the most prosperous part of the country. Gold and wool exports formed the basis of the economy over the next decade. George Grey was appointed governor for a second term (until 1867). A temporary peace in the Taranaki area was negotiated by Wiremu Tamihana.

1862. Te Ua Haumene founded the **Pai Marire** millennial movement, which was dedicated to the preservation of Maori identity and sovereignty.

1863. Opening of first railroad (Christchurch to Fernymead).

Government forces invaded the Waikato territory of the Maori king. Despite a series of battles that were either victories for the Maori or ambiguous in their outcome, the Waikato was annexed. The Maori king movement retreated to the central North Island, where it passively resisted government domination until the 1890s.

The government instituted punitive legislation to **CONFISCATE LARGE AREAS OF MAORI LAND.** Land was taken from Maori who had been on the side of the Europeans as well as from the "rebels," adding to the sense of injustice. Confiscation of land has remained a major source of political discontent into the 1990s.

1864. The war extended to the eastern part of the North Island. The British were heavily **defeated at Gate Pa.** Pai Marire became involved in the war, which shifted into a guerrilla phase.

1865. The Native Land Court was established, accelerating the alienation of Maori land in the second half of the 19th century. By 1892 most of the good land was in European hands. The **Native Rights Act** affirmed that the Maori were British subjects, thus denying their sovereignty, and allowing those involved in the war to be treated as rebels rather than as an enemy foreign power. The act also laid the foundations for **Maori male franchise** and the establishment of **four Maori parliamentary seats.** A second **gold rush** occurred, this time on the west coast of the South Island. **The capital was transferred from Auckland to Wellington.**

1867. The first members of Parliament elected to the four Maori seats. These seats have remained into the 1990s. Separate Maori schools were established to facilitate the assimilation of Maori into Pakeha (European) society. The use of Maori language in schools was prohibited in 1871.

1868. Titokowaru and **Te Kooti** waged guerrilla campaigns in different parts of the central North Island.

1870. The last British troops were withdrawn from New Zealand, after which the war was prosecuted by the colonial government. **Hostilities ceased in 1872.**

1871. The first of a series of large **government loans** was initiated by **Julius Vogel,** the colonial treasurer. Money continued to be borrowed through the 1870s for the development of roads, railways, and other public works. European settlement increased steadily through this period. In the 1870s Maori leaders like **Paora Tuhaere** and **Henare Matua** sought redress for unjust land deals and called for greater Maori political participation. Maori led unsuccessful deputations to Queen Victoria to protest violations of the Treaty of Waitangi.

1876. Abolition of provincial governments, putting New Zealand under one government.

1877. Primary schooling made compulsory.

1879. Residence replaced property ownership as the criterion for male suffrage.

1881. Government troops destroyed the passive land protest movement of Maori leaders Te Whiti and Tohu based in the village of **Parihaka. Chinese Immigrant Act** restricted access.

1882. The first shipment of frozen meat to Britain heralded a new age of export. Factory-based production of dairy produce also strengthened the agricultural economy.

1885. The Women's Christian Temperance Union began to campaign for women's suffrage.

1889. Full male suffrage.

1890. New Zealand's first major industrial dispute, a **maritime strike,** took place, involving 8,000 unionists. The strike was defeated, but unions grew rapidly thereafter. Radical political parties began to appear, as party politics replaced the old dominance of local interests.

1891. A **Liberal-Labour Party** government was elected with **John Ballance** as premier. (The Liberals remained in power until 1912.) Taxation on absentee landlords and on the owners of large estates was increased, with the intention of reducing large landholdings.

1892. Kotahitanga Maori parliament was established from an alliance of tribes aiming at autonomy. Meetings of the Kotahitanga continued until 1902, but its authority was never accepted by the Pakeha government.

1893–96. The aggressive populist politician **Richard John Seddon** (King Dick) **became premier.** His administration was associated with a series of social and economic reforms, in particular those sponsored by Minister of Labour **William Pember Reeves.** New Zealand acquired an international reputation for state socialist experimentation. The size of the civil service and state involvement in the economy also increased.

1893. New Zealand granted **women's suffrage,** the first country in the world to do so. Women also gained rights to join the medical and legal professions in the 1890s.

1894. The **Industrial Conciliation and Arbitration Act** established compulsory mediation of industrial disputes and the setting of national wage awards to apply in all parts of a single industry. State arbitration became the basis of the New Zealand industrial relations system, along with rapid trade union growth.

1895. The government secured cheap loans to fund a program of **agricultural expansion.** Small dairy farms expanded in the North Island, forming the mainstay of the agricultural economy there.

1897. The eight-hour working day was established by law. The Te Aute College Students' Association was established, forming the basis for the **Young Maori Party,** a group of leaders including **Maui Pomare, Apirana Ngata,** and **Te Rangi Hiroa (Peter Buck),** who sought to improve Maori conditions by entering mainstream Pakeha institutions, including Parliament. Both Ngata and Pomare became cabinet ministers.

1898. Old age pensions were introduced.

1899. The **New Zealand Farmers' Union** was formed to address the concerns of farmers; it soon came to have political importance and was a rival to radical trade unions.

1899–1900. New Zealand troops were sent to the war in South Africa.

1901. New Zealand **imperialism** in the Pacific began with the **annexation of the Cook Islands** (p. 577).

New Zealand rejected the proposal of **federation with Australia.**

1905. The rugby team **the Invincibles** won all but one of their games in a tour of Britain, becoming a focus for nascent national sentiment.

1907. Foundation of the Royal New Zealand Society for the Health of Women and Children (the Plunket Society) by Dr. Truby King and his wife, an attempt to improve the nation's health by training mothers in "scientific" baby care and child-rearing methods. **By 1947,** 85 percent of all non-Maori children were cared for by Plunket.

New Zealand became a dominion. The **Chinese Immigrant Bill** imposed reading tests on prospective Chinese immigrants, reflecting notions of racial purity and fear of job competition on the part of both trade unions and government.

1909. Formation of the **Federation of Labour,** an alliance of radical trade unions.

1912. The conservative government of the **Reform Party** under **William F. Massey came to power** as a result of disenchantment with the Liberal Party and fear of socialist radicals. Its key support came from urban and rural property owners.

1913. A maritime strike, like the **miners' strike** in the previous year, led to civil disturbances and government action to curb union power. The desire of radical unions to escape the system of compulsory arbitration was a major factor in the dispute. *(To p. 792)*

G. AFRICA, 1795-1917

1. OVERVIEW

(From p. 390)

Given the importance of the transatlantic slave trade for African history during the period 1500–1800, it would seem logical that the abolition of the slave trade, first declared by the Danes in 1792, but enacted by Britain in 1807, would be a major watershed. Indeed it was, but such was the resiliency of African historical process that it took many decades before the abolition of the European slave trade was felt in Africa.

The **abolition of the European slave trade** did not mean the end of slave exports. Britain embarked on aggressive diplomacy to bring the other European nations into the accord. However, as long as there was demand for slaves in the Americas and in the emerging French Indian Ocean plantation islands, African suppliers and European and American carriers would bring slaves to the buyers. Thus, the end of the transatlantic slave trade occurred when Cuba and Brazil began to enforce the prohibition on slave imports in the 1860s. Disguised slave exports persisted well into the 20th century.

However, Britain's prohibition of the slave trade to its nationals in 1807 did signal an important change in the organization and nature of the international economy. Increasingly throughout the 19th century, **industrial capitalism shaped the demand and supply of goods and service on a world scale.** European industries and the mass markets they fed required massive inputs of **tropical raw materials**, including vegetable oils and cotton. Europeans now wanted Africans to remain in Africa, cultivate the tropical commodities they needed, and consume the products of their industries.

European prohibition on the slave trade confronted African political economies in which warfare and enslavement had become deeply embedded. It was not easy to retool the engines of state enterprise. The crisis African states faced was, however, eased by the gradual decline in demand for African slaves in the Americas and by the coincident **expansion of demand for slave labor in Africa** itself. Slavery was a very old institution in Africa, and it had always been a means of increasing the size of domestic groups. In the face of demand for African agricultural commodities, Africans increasingly turned to slave labor to augment the scale of production. By reducing the price of African slaves, the abolition of the transatlantic slave trade paradoxically encouraged the expansion of slavery in Africa.

The **African slave market** had traditionally **favored females.** Female slaves added significantly to the reproductive potential of African households, and most African farming systems relied heavily on female labor. It is not at all clear whether this gender division of labor shaped African preferences for female slaves or whether the presence of female slaves encouraged female farming. Politically ambitious men in matrilineal societies, such as the Yao of East Africa, used female slaves as a means of attracting male followers and as a means of developing junior patrilineages in order to gain control over their own offspring. **Female slaves further encouraged the development of patriarchy and polygyny.** Since most Africans at this time lived in rural settings, additional agricultural labor was always desirable.

Between 1800 and 1914, Africans were drawn into a rapidly changing international economy. The new international economy intersected with ongoing processes of change in Africa. The result was a **speeding up of conflict and change in Africa,** leading increasingly to conflicts between African groups and between Africans and Europeans as Europeans scrambled to claim African territories as colonies. These processes occurred unevenly throughout the continent. By 1914 most of Africa was under **European colonial control.**

In southern Africa, the 19th century opened as Africans pursued their own state-building activities. This was most pronounced among the Nguni-speaking Bantu of southeastern Africa. Increased international commercial activity at Delagoa Bay intersected with human and livestock population growth and led to **ecological crisis.** In the foothills

of the Draksenburg Mountains, Dingiswayo of the Mthwethwa introduced significant organizational innovations that yielded a powerful military machine. Under his successor, Shaka, the Zulu kingdom became a major polity in the region. Its military campaigns unleashed **reverberating cycles of warfare, political consolidation, and political dissolution** (known as the Mfecane), which reached as far north as Tanzania. White Afrikaner pioneers, called the **Trekboers,** entered this area in the 1830s after fleeing from British-controlled areas of South Africa. The better armed Afrikaners became only one more state-building group in this region, whose history over the course of the 19th century was characterized by conflicting but fluid frontiers.

The **discovery of diamonds in 1867 and gold in 1887** profoundly changed both white and black southern African societies and drew them all into an economy dominated by mining enterprises and the need to secure cheap labor. Providing labor for the mines or food for miners initially offered Africans new economic opportunities and introduced a brief period of prosperity. Africans, however, increasingly sought the independence of agriculture in preference to the discipline of the mines. White South Africans and their governments sought to limit Africans' choices and to force them to provide cheap agricultural or mining labor. The South African War (1899–1902) eventually yielded a unified South Africa firmly dedicated to white political and economic superiority.

East Africa was drawn increasingly into a world in which the European economic system was becoming dominant. Deeper patterns of Indian Ocean commerce persisted, but demand expanded for **slaves and ivory,** both essentially predatory activities. Slaves were being drawn to supply demand in the Americas, in the Indian Ocean plantations, the trans-Saharan and Red Sea trade, and in the Swahili slave economies of the coast. Africans and Arab plantation owners began to acquire slaves as agricultural labor in order to service international demand for cloves as well as regional demand for food for the slave and ivory caravans. Long-distance caravans organized by African merchants from the interior and by Swahili merchants from the coast crisscrossed East Africa, pushing ever deeper the **frontiers of international commerce.** These trends coincided with the waves of warfare and state building flowing from the South African Mfecane, yielding increasing cycles of predation and enslavement. In the waning days of the century, rinderpest, jiggers, smallpox, and other epidemics profoundly destabilized African societies. Human and animal populations declined. Rinderpest alone contributed to the loss of up to 90 percent of all large livestock. For cattle-keeping societies, this loss was catastrophic.

In the interlacustrine region, the 19th century witnessed the **consolidation of larger state systems** at the expense of the smaller polities. Buganda emerged preeminent in the region of Lake Victoria, developed a centralized bureaucracy, and began a process of colonization of the outlying regions. The cattle-keeping Tutsi warrior aristocracies emerged successfully in Burundi and Rwanda, structuring the region's economies through their loans of cattle and dependents. In the Sudan, Egyptian forces were trying to impose their authority over the fluid slave-catching frontier, which funneled large numbers of slaves down the river and into the agricultural regions of Egypt. From 1881 to 1885, the Egyptian forces confronted the state-building endeavors of the Mahdi. Intra-European competition for control over the region led to a serious diplomatic crisis in Europe.

In West Africa the century opened as the **militant Muslim forces** were about to embark on the jihad that led to the founding of the Sokoto Caliphate. The waves of Islamic expectancy and militancy reached outward and led to the founding of the Hamdullahi Caliphate in Masina and the Umarian state farther west. Under several of these religious polities, Islamic education and piety made significant advances. The Sokoto Caliphate emerged as one of the strongest states in West Africa.

State building and consolidation were not limited to the interior. In the 19th century, the Asante strengthened a powerful empire in the forest region of what is now Ghana and centralized state power through elaborate **bureaucracies** of state officials. As in the theocratic states of the interior, the forest states were also based upon warfare, conquest, tribute, and the resettlement of captured population.

Perhaps the most striking change to occur in West Africa was the rapid expansion of international commerce in bulk vegetable commodities, especially palm oil and peanuts. For example, the peanut exports from the Gambia rose from a mere 47 tons in 1835 to over 11,000 tons in 1851. Similar patterns of expansion occurred throughout the coastal zones of West Africa and demonstrated how rapidly Africans responded to economic incentives. This has been called the **West African peasant revolution,** and it introduced significant changes in the region's political economy. European merchants established mutually beneficial commercial relations with African middlemen and African producers. Until midcentury, the **barter terms of trade favored African commodity producers,** who benefited both from rising commodity prices and falling prices for manufactured goods. By midcentury, commodity prices began to fall, and by the onset of the European depression of 1867, the international commerce of West Africa was in turmoil. European and African merchants competed for diminishing shares of the market, which led to bankruptcies, fraud, and commercial conflicts. European merchants petitioned home governments for protection. The pace of European colonialism increased, and by the 1870s, the scramble was on.

Until the 1870s, Europeans had neither wanted nor were able to impose themselves on Africans. However, **medical and technological innovations**—including the discovery that quinine provided prophylaxis against malaria, and the invention of the repeating rifle—provided the means for Europeans to defeat Africans in battle and to survive afterward. This window of military superiority closed rather quickly. In 1896, the African army of Menelik II was armed with modern repeating rifles and resoundingly defeated the invading Italian army at the **Battle of Adua** (Adowa). The Battle of Adua marked the end of the "scramble phase" of European colonialism.

By then, however, Europeans had laid claim to all of Africa except for Liberia, which since 1847 had been an internationally recognized republic under the rule of returned African-American freed slaves, and Ethiopia. Europeans' actual control over the land and peoples of Africa was much more doubtful. Indeed, Europeans and their African allies fought widespread resistance movements in the decades immediately following conquest. Some of these **primary resistance movements** drew on well-established forms of organization, such as polities. Others, including the Chimurenga in Southern Rhodesia and Maji Maji in Tanganyika, forged new organizations and networks. Resistance organized by polities was more easily suppressed, since Europeans usually maintained decisive military superiority, and there was usually someone who could surrender. Resistance by acephalous societies proved remarkably difficult to suppress, since each community had to be defeated in turn.

Other forms of resistance, including migration, tax evasion, disobedience, and disrespect, were much less obvious and much more difficult to control. Such forms of resistance continued throughout the colonial period. Even more difficult for colonial officials to understand and to control were the ways in which Africans turned to Christianity and to Western education as means of resisting the power of colonial rule.

The missionary enterprise was an intimate part of European cultural imperialism. Christianity provided Africans with a means of creating a new sense of community. Since the BaKongo prophetess Beatrice Kimpa Vita of the late 17th century, Africans had sought to Africanize European cultural institutions such as the church. Church practices could be shaped to address African concerns more directly. **Breakaway African churches,** which predated colonialism but proliferated under European colonial rule, demonstrated how Africans used Western cultural institutions to resist European domination. Africans also turned to Islam in increasing numbers during the colonial period. African Muslims joined **Sufi brotherhoods** as a means of simultaneously creating new communities and maintaining cultural and political distance from European institutions.

Even European-dominated mission enterprises provided Africans with new opportunities. Particularly in central, eastern, and southern Africa, mission stations formally linked to European churches became sanctuaries to which runaway slaves and oppressed women could flee. Equally important, missions became the primary medium for the **expansion of Western literacy** and thus provided the training for a generation of African nationalists. *(To p. 793)*

2. EUROPEAN EXPLORATION, 1795-1895

(From p. 390)

1795-97, 1805-6. MUNGO PARK explored the **Gambia** and reached the **Niger** at Segu, finally establishing the fact that the great river flowed east. During his second voyage, Park drowned in the Niger near the Hausa state of Yauri.

1798-99. The Portuguese **Francisco de Lacerda** traveled from Tete on the Zambezi northward to **Lake Mweru.**

1802. Pieter Jan Truter and **William Somerville** explored **Bechuanaland** and penetrated the interior almost as far as **Lake Ngami.**

1802-11. The Angolan of color **Pedro Baptista** and **A. José crossed the continent** from Angola to Tete on the Zambezi.

1815. France abolished the slave trade. Other countries (notably Spain and Portugal) followed suit.

1818. Gaspard Mollien discovered the **sources of the Gambia** and the **Senegal rivers.**

1821-25. Walter Oudney, Dixon Denham, and **Hugh Clapperton** journeyed from Tripoli across the desert to **Lake Chad** and thence westward to the **Niger,** proving that the river had no connection with the lake.

1825-26. Alexander G. Laing crossed the desert from Tripoli to **Tuat** and thence to **Timbuktu,** the first 19th-century European to visit that city. Laing was killed on his return across the desert.

1825-27. Clapperton led another Niger expedition from the coast to the interior. All members of the party become ill with malaria and dysentery. Richard Lander accompanied the expedition. Clapperton died in Sokoto in 1827.

1827-28. René Caillié reached **Timbuktu** from Guinea and proceeded thence to Fez.

1830-34. Richard and John Lander explored the lower **Niger** from Bussa to the sea. Richard Lander died along the Niger River.

1837-48. Extensive researches of **Antoine T. d'Abbadie in Ethiopia.**

1840-43. Charles T. Beke mapped much of **Ethiopia.**

1848. Ladislus Magyan explored the Congo River.

1849. DAVID LIVINGSTONE crossed the Kalahari Desert and advanced to **Lake Ngami,** returning (1850) to the upper Zambezi.

1849-55. Heinrich Barth and **Adolf Overweg** crossed from Tripoli to the Niger and Lake Chad, thoroughly studying the country for the first time. Barth made extensive observations of the Central Sudan.

1853-56. Livingstone crossed the continent from the Zambezi to Loanda and returned, discovering the **Victoria Falls.**

1850-65. Paul du Chaillu explored Gabon.

1857-58. Richard Burton and **John Speke** discovered **Lake Tanganyika** and **Victoria Nyanza,** Speke concluding that Victoria Nyanza was the source of the White Nile.

1858-61. Third Expedition of Livingstone, from the Zambezi to the interior. He discovered **Lake Nyasa** (1859).

1861-63. Speke and James Grant passed through Uganda, **reached the Nile,** and descended it to **Gondokoro,** where they met **Sir Samuel Baker** (1863), who had ascended the river to that point.

1864. Baker, continuing up the Nile, **discovered Albert Nyanza** and visited the kingdom of Bunyoro, whence he returned to Gondokoro.

THE PARTITION OF AFRICA–1914

E U R O P E

MADEIRA ISLANDS *(Portuguese)*

CANARY ISLANDS *(Spanish)*

TANGIER

Algiers

Casablanca

ALGERIA

MOROCCO

RIO DE ORO

TUNISIA

Tripoli

LIBYA

Sahara

FRENCH WEST AFRICA

Suez Canal

Cairo

EGYPT *(British Protectorate)*

Red Sea

A R A B I A

ANGLO–EGYPTIAN SUDAN

Khartoum

White Nile *Blue Nile*

Massawa ERITREA

Adua FRENCH SOMALILAND

BRITISH SOMALILAND

ITALIAN SOMALILAND

GAMBIA

Senegal R.

Niger R.

PORTUGUESE GUINEA

SIERRA LEONE

LIBERIA *(Independent)*

IVORY COAST

GOLD COAST

TOGOLAND

RIO MUNI

Lake Chad

NIGERIA

CAMEROUN

FRENCH EQUATORIAL AFRICA

Congo R.

BELGIAN CONGO

ETHIOPIA *(Independent)*

UGANDA

Lake Victoria

BRITISH EAST AFRICA

KENYA

Mombasa

GERMAN EAST AFRICA

ZANZIBAR *(British)*

Lake Tanganyika

NYASALAND

Lake Malawi

E Q U A T O R

ANGOLA

RHODESIA

GERMAN SOUTHWEST AFRICA

BECHUANALAND

PORTUGUESE EAST AFRICA

UNION OF SOUTH AFRICA

TRANSVAAL

ORANGE FREE STATE

NATAL

CAPE COLONY

Capetown

MADAGASCAR

0 200 400 600 800 1000
MILES

EUROPEAN COLONIES IN AFRICA – 1878

Algeria

Senegal

Gambia

Angola

Mozambique

Cape Colony

French	British	German	Italian	Belgian	Spanish	Portuguese

1865–67. Extensive exploration of the **Benuë-Niger region** by **Gustav Rohlfs.**

1866–71. Livingstone traveled from the mouth of the Rovuma inland to Lake Nyasa and thence to Lake Tanganyika and Bangweolu, whence he returned to Tanganyika.

1868–71. Georg Schweinfurth explored the Red Sea coast, and went from Khartum to the interior, where he discovered the Welle River.

1870. Gustav Nachtigal explored the **Chad region** and crossed from there to Egypt.

1871. Henry M. Stanley, searching for Livingstone, found him on Lake Tanganyika. Death of Livingstone (April 27, 1873).

1874–77. Stanley circumnavigated Victoria Nyanza, proceeded thence to Lake Tanganyika, and crossed to the **Lualaba River,** which he **descended to the Congo,** ultimately reaching the Atlantic coast.

1876–78. Pierre Savorgnan de Brazza explored the region of the **Ogowe** and **lower Congo.**

1876. Foundation of the International Association for the Exploration and Civilization of Africa, under the auspices of **Leopold II** of Belgium.

1879–86. Wilhelm Junker demonstrated that the Welle River was part of the Congo system and carried on extensive researches about **Lake Albert.**

1879–84. Stanley, in the service of Leopold, ascended the Congo and established posts in the basin.

1880. De Brazza returned to the Congo River and secured French protectorates from the chief to the north of the river.

1880–83. Hermann von Wissmann explored the **Congo basin** and twice crossed the continent.

1887–89. STANLEY'S EXPEDITION TO RELIEVE EMIN PASHA (Eduard Schnitzer, Egyptian governor of Equatoria, 1877–88). Stanley ascended the Congo and crossed to the great lakes. He found Emin on the upper Nile and induced him to leave for the east coast.

3. REGIONS

a. SUDANIC WEST AND CENTRAL AFRICA

(From p. 391)

1804. The career of **Usuman dan Fodio** (b. 1754) began in the late 18th century, when he traveled throughout the **Hausa kingdom of Gobir** as an itinerant Muslim teacher. He attracted many followers, among whom were newly won converts as well as Hausa farmers and Fulani pastoralists who nursed **grievances against the entrenched Hausa leadership.** In 1804, dan Fodio withdrew his allegiance to the Hausa ruler and launched a major **jihad. Following the model of the Prophet,** Usuman dan Fodio led his followers on a **hijra,** a flight from unbelief, to a rural outpost on the border of Gobir. At first the jihad was designed merely to protect the Islamic community that had grown up around dan Fodio, and was restricted to Gobir, Kebbi, and Zamfara. Later it developed into a **war of conquest,** spilling over into Kano, Zaria, Nupe, and Borno. Dan Fodio's success in spreading Islam constituted one of the most important **Muslim revival movements** of the 19th century.

1808. Sheik Muhammad b. Amin b. Muhammad al-Kanami came to power by leading a resistance movement against Usuman dan Fodio's forces in Borno. In a series of important letters, al-Kanami **challenged the legality of the jihad against Borno,** since Borno was also a Muslim polity. Although Borno lost some of its western provinces to the Sokoto Caliphate, Sheik Muhammad al-Kanami's efforts eventually led to a rejuvenation of Borno's political institutions and a revival of Islam. After having turned back the jihad, al-Kanami gained an enormous following and ousted the ruling Borno dynasty in favor of his own.

1812. Following the success of his jihad, Usuman dan Fodio established the **Sokoto Caliphate,** a powerful Muslim empire.

1810 or 1818. Seku Ahmadu, also known as Ahmadu Lobbo, a former student of Usuman dan Fodio, opposed the mixture of traditional beliefs and Islam so commonly tolerated among West African leaders. In either 1810 or 1818 (the exact date is uncertain), he led a jihad against the Muslim chiefs in Masina; later the jihad expanded to include the Bambara. Seku Ahmadu established an austere Muslim empire ruled from the newly built city of **Hamdallahi.**

1817. Following dan Fodio's death, his son, Muhammad Bello, succeeded. Bello ruled from 1817 to 1837, during which time the caliphate's power was consolidated. Fulani loyalists under nominal allegiance to dan Fodio and Bello then launched successive military campaigns to expand the state's borders. The **walled city of Sokoto** became the capital of the eastern half of dan Fodio's empire. **Ribats,** fortified posts, were erected in newly conquered territory. The Sokoto Caliphate became one of the most dynamic political, religious, and economic regions in Africa. Part of its prosperity came from the **relocation of captured slaves to the core areas of Hausaland,** where they contributed to agricultural, craft, trading, and herding activities. **Indigo-dyed Hausa cloth** fed demand as far west as Senegal and deep into the Saharan desert. Under the Sokoto Caliphate, Arabic became the language of diplomacy, and the aristocracy developed distinctive vernacular poetry. Each year, the Sokoto Caliphate launched new military campaigns to expand the empire or to reclaim territory lost to rebellion.

1848. Having returned from the pilgrimage, where he was introduced into the **Tijanyyia brotherhood** and became the Tijanyyia leader of West Africa, **al-hajj Umar Tal** (b. 1794) launched a jihad. In 1848, Umar Tal, originally from Futa Toro, established an Islamic state in Duinguiray. In 1852–53, he launched a jihad against the Bambara of Kaarta; by 1854, he had established control over the Bambara and Malinke societies of the upper Niger and Senegal basins. Facing increasing pressure from French colonial expansion along the Senegal River Valley, in 1860 he launched a jihad against the Segu Bambara. By 1862, Umar Tal had conquered Masina and established a large empire. At its peak, the Umarian Empire stretched from the lower Senegal in the west to Timbuktu in the east, and from Guemou in the north to Duinguiray in the south. Unlike earlier jihads, that of Umar Tal occurred during the French conquest of West Africa. The Umarian Empire was not stable and suffered from **endemic resistance** and **civil wars.**

1855. The **French** built a fort at Medine to fight against al-hajj Umar.

1856–58. N'Diambour, Sinn, and Salum submitted to the French.

1859. French control over Senegal was expanded.

1862. Al-hajj Umar conquered Masina and occupied Hamdallahi in 1862. During the conquest of Masina, the empire was under the leadership of the original Seku Ahmadu's grandson, who shared his grandfather's name. Umar was killed shortly thereafter during **widespread revolts against the Umarian conquest.**

1864. Umar Tal was killed while trying to quell a revolt in Hamdallahi. Following Umar Tal's death, his son **Sheku Ahamdu,** also known as Ahmad b. Umar, took power. Umar's death led to a series of internecine revolts and a weakening of the political cohesion of the empire.

1854–61, 1863–65. The French appointed **Col. Louis Faidherbe** as governor of Senegal in 1854. Faidherbe was instrumental in reviving French colonialism in Senegal. Based in St.-Louis, Faidherbe built a series of **institutions designed to encourage African loyalty to French colonial ambitions,** including special privileges for African Muslims and schools for chiefs' sons. Under Faidherbe, the French also launched aggressive territorial expansion, using African troops. Gov. Faidherbe laid the foundations for the eventual French conquest of the western Sudan. He left Senegal in 1865. With his departure, the aggressive advance of the colonial frontier was arrested.

1879–93. French conquest of the interior was revived with the appointment of Col. Borgnis-Desbordes (1879–83) to a newly established military command. Under **Col. Louis Archinard,** the French conquered the Umarian capitals at Segu in 1890 and at Nioro in 1893.

1881. The French army's march into the Sahara, as part of the bold vision of **trans-Saharan conquest,** was abruptly halted in 1881 when the **Tuareg** confederation crushed the mission of **Col. Flatters.** As a result of the Tuareg attack, the French abandoned their plans to construct a railway line from Algiers to Timbuktu. Plans for a punitive counter-raid against the Tuareg were never realized.

1883. The French arrived in **Bamako** after several years of gradual European military conquest in West Africa. Sheku Ahmadu, the Umarian ruler, proved unable to stem the erosion of his hegemony at the hands of brothers, who sought power for themselves and the better-armed European adversaries. The French occupation of Bamako signaled their determination to control the upper Niger valley. French conquest was conducted by a small group of French officers and soldiers and a large army of African recruits.

Late 19th century. State-building activities occurred in the upper Niger region under **Almamy Samori.** Born in upper Guinea (c. 1830), the Muslim Almamy Samori began to build up a private army in the late 1860s and early 1870s. Fueled by various grievances against local rulers, his army embarked on wars of conquest and consolidated a power base on the upper Niger. By the 1880s, Samori's empire among the Malinke occupied a vast region, and his soldiers were using modern firearms. The Samorian Empire first clashed with the French in the 1880s, and the conflict continued for over a decade. In 1892, Samori initiated a scorched earth policy as he moved his state eastward, away from his French pursuers. He was captured by the French on Sept. 29, 1898, and was deported to Gabon, where he died in 1900. **Samori's state was one of a handful of MILITARY CONQUEST STATES WHOSE ACTIVITIES YIELDED LARGE NUMBERS OF SLAVES.** Most of these slaves fed demand within Africa.

1875–90s. An **offshoot of the Kong kingdom,** the **kingdom of Kenedugu** consolidated its position of power under the leadership of Tieba Traore (r., c. 1878–93). Tieba was initially an ally of the French and built a strong fortress at Sikasso in present-day Mali. Tieba was succeeded by **Babemba,** who fought against both Samori's forces and the French until he too was captured in 1898.

1893. Umar Tal's forces had begun to clash with the French as early as the 1850s. French conquest of the interior began in 1879, and followed the southern limits of the **Umarian Empire.** The French reached **Bamako** in 1883, gaining ground in their quest to conquer the empire. Umar Tal's son Sheku Ahmadu was defeated by the French in 1893. He fled eastward toward Hausaland, where he died in 1902.

1898. France's eastward advance throughout West Africa gained momentum in the 1890s. In May 1898, the French military occupied the fortress of Sikasso and captured Samori as part of their effort to secure access to Lake Chad.

1890s. Rise of **Mouridiyya under Ahmad Bamba** in Senegal, in the immediate aftermath of French conquest of the interior of Senegal. Ahmad Bamba's Mouridiyya brotherhood brought together peasants, former slaves, and defeated warriors who sought to create a new Muslim community in a period of expanding French colonial rule. As Ahmad Bamba began to be persecuted by the French authorities, his following increased. His group represented a cultural rather than military response to French colonialism and became instrumental in the **expansion of peanut production,** the main export from Senegal.

1895, June 15. In order to impose administrative authority and regularity on vast areas recently conquered, the French minister of colonies established the office of **governor-general of French West Africa,** based in Senegal. His task was to jointly administer the diverse and often competing set of French colonies in West Africa. The governor-general was also charged with facilitating economic cooperation among the territories. In 1895, these territories included Senegal, French Soudan, Guinea, the Ivory Coast, and numerous military districts, which were still not pacified.

1903. Armed with rifles, artillery, and Maxim guns, Britain's Royal Niger Company launched military expeditions in northern Nigeria in the early 1900s to secure territory. In 1903, a small but well-armed force conquered Kano, Sokoto, and Burwuri. Instead of dismantling the Sokoto Caliphate, the British established **a protectorate retaining Muslim Hausa administrative, legal, and fiscal policies.** Northern Nigeria became the premier example of British **INDIRECT RULE POLICY** associated with **Frederick Lugard.**

1915. In response to French efforts to recruit Africans for service in World War I, **recruitment revolts** occurred in Bélédugu and spread throughout French West Africa. *(To p. 794)*

b. FOREST WEST AFRICA

(From p. 392)

1792. Although only a marginal carrier, **Denmark prohibited the slave trade to its nationals, the first European nation to do so.**

1806. The **Asante** defeated the Fante at Abora, near Cape Coast.

1807. By passing the Act for the Abolition of the Slave Trade in 1807,

Britain became the first major slave-trading nation to prohibit the trade. The British government authorized its navy to begin suppressing the human trade and to pursue a diplomatic offense to force other European carriers to abolish the trade. Although the slave trade **continued into the 1880s,** the volume of slaves exported overseas declined. In its place, the **industrializing countries of Europe sought tropical commodities, such as vegetable oils and cotton, to feed their mills.** Shifting European demand from slaves to agricultural produce induced a **peasant revolution** in West Africa, as Africans increased agricultural production.

1808–15. Six thousand slaves were captured at sea by the British Anti-Slavery Squadron and released in Sierra Leone.

c. 1810. The **Yoruba kingdom** was subject to civil wars. Oyo was sacked. Illorin became an independent kingdom.

1811. An **Asante** campaign against the Fante failed.

1814. In 1814 the **Church Missionary Society (CMS)** established a school at Freetown in order to train freed slaves as teachers and missionaries. In 1827 the school was moved to Fourah Bay, east of Freetown. It eventually broadened its focus beyond missionary training and offered a general curriculum in higher education.

1815 ff. The British used the court of admiralty in Freetown to **"liberate"** slaves captured on the high seas. Shortly after the passage of the anti-slave trade act, the **British Anti-Slavery Squadron** began patrolling the West African coast to intercept ships illegally carrying slaves. Intercepted ships were brought to Freetown in Sierra Leone. There a court of vice-admiralty prosecuted crews and freed slaves. Despite the British patrols, the slave trade was not eradicated.

1816. Building of **Bathurst,** Gambia, began.

1817. A jihad was launched in Ilorin, and a Fulani emirate linked to the Sokoto Caliphate was established. The jihad in Ilorin, formerly a dependency of the Oyo Empire, also coincided with **expansion of civil wars in Yorubaland, which led to the destruction of Oyo.** Decades of turmoil and fighting fed the slave trade.

1821. British possessions in Sierra Leone, the Gold Coast, and the Gambia were joined as the **British West Africa Settlements.**

1822. The first settlement for **freed American slaves** was founded in **Liberia** under the auspices of the American Colonization Society (ACS). The ACS was established in Washington, D.C., in 1816 in order to promote the repatriation of freed American slaves to Africa. The first group of freed slaves returning to Africa under ACS sponsorship initially stopped at Freetown, Sierra Leone. From there they proceeded to the new colony of Liberia in Jan. 1822. Liberia (the "land of the free") was a private colony rather than an official territory of the United States. Its capital, Monrovia, was named after U.S. president James Monroe.

1823–31. First war between the British and the Asante.

1824, Jan. 21. Sir Charles Macarthy, British governor, committed suicide to avoid capture by Asante forces.

Osei Bonsu, Asantehene, died.

1827. The **Basel Mission** began work in the Gold Coast.

1831. The Asante made a treaty with the British and the Fante.

1833. Quaker missionaries began work in Gambia.

Methodists began missionary work in the Gold Coast. **American Episcopal Methodists, American Presbyterians, and the American Board of Comissioners for Foreign Missions** began work in Liberia.

1836. The Bible was translated into Mandingo.

1837. First peanuts were exported from Sierra Leone.

1839. Liberian settlers united to form the largely **self-governing Commonwealth of Liberia** in 1839.

1839 ff. Gradual drift of **Saros** (freed slaves from Sierra Leone) back to Yorubaland. "Recaptured" slaves living in Sierra Leone, who were originally enslaved in Yorubaland, began returning to their homeland in 1839. Many Saros brought with them a **taste for international commerce in tropical commodities and a commitment to Christianity.** African Christians established active mission stations in Yorubaland.

c. 1840. The work of **CMS and the Wesleyans** spread rapidly among the freed slaves of Sierra Leone.

1841 ff. In 1841, **Samuel Ajayi Crowther,** a Saro, began the Niger Mission. In 1857, he left Yorubaland to begin missionary work among the societies of the lower Niger and the Niger delta. He led the Church Missionary Society mission among the Niger peoples. Crowther and his followers built a wholly **African-run mission church.** In 1864, Crowther was made the Anglican bishop of West Africa. He was the first African bishop of the Church of England.

1841. Failure of the Thomas Fowell Buston's Niger Missions. Designed for philanthropic and exploratory purposes, the mission was a failure because a large majority of its members died of **malaria.** Only in the 1870s did widespread use of quinine assist in suppressing malaria and permitting Europeans to live longer in the African tropics.

Palm oil exports began from Dahomey.

1842. Saros arrived in Abeokuta.

1845. CMS grammar school was opened in Freetown. By 1849, CMS had opened a girls' secondary school in Freetown.

1846. The British Presbyterian Mission began its work in Calabar along the Nigeria coast.

1847, July 26. The commonwealth became the independent Republic of Liberia. The founders of the republic drafted a declaration of independence and garnered international recognition for their newly established nation. Great Britain was the first to recognize the new nation.

1848. First deputy from Senegal sent to the French National Assembly.

Mid-19th century. Following the abolition of the slave trade, the states of the Niger delta were forced to look elsewhere for commercial opportunities. The development of trade in commodities, known as **legitimate trade, replaced the slave trade** as the economic mainstay of the region. The main trade goods of legitimate commerce included palm oil, ivory, shea butter, indigo, and gum. Demand for these tropical commodities and the decline of the transatlantic slave trade **LED TO THE WIDESPREAD EXPANSION OF SLAVERY IN AFRICA.** Increased use of slaves in Africa augmented production of goods for regional and international trade and contributed to patriarchy because slave wives had fewer rights than freeborn wives. Old elites continued to thrive in the era of legitimate commerce, but new ones were created as a result of the missionary presence and the spread of **Western literacy.** Coastal societies witnessed the rise of a Western-educated African elite in this era. Lagos became a major Christian center in West Africa. Although local African rulers continued to exert political power in the Niger delta in the mid-19th century, their authority was eroded when Europeans established the first **courts of equity** to adjudicate commercial disputes between African and European merchants.

1851. Edward Blyden migrated to Liberia.

Nov.–Dec. The British bombarded Lagos.

1852, Jan. 1. Akitoye, king of Lagos, signed a treaty with the British for the abolition of the slave trade.

1861, Aug. 6. After several decades of resisting new territorial acquisitions in West Africa, **Britain proclaimed Lagos a Crown colony** in order to control the key terminus of Yoruba trade routes. But despite the British move, French and German merchants continued to compete for economic advantage in the region.

1864. By the mid-1860s, the British suspended their antislave trade patrols. The slave trade was not over, but it had declined because of the rise in industrial capitalism and free labor ideologies and the decline of the slave plantation system in the Americas.

1872, April 6. The British gained control over Dutch forts in the Gold Coast.

1873–74. Second Asante War against the British.

1873, Feb 9. Asante forces defeated British troops at Assin Nyankumasi.

1874, Jan. 31. The British defeated the Asante at Amoafo. **Sir Garnet Wolsely** entered the Asante capital of Kumasi on Feb. 4. By the end of that year, the Asante confederation had been severely weakened by British military advances.

Consequent decline of the Asante. Asantehene Kofi Karikari was destooled and replaced by Mansa Bonsu. British incursions **destabilized the Asante,** encouraging palace intrigues and weakening of state power.

1876. Originally a missionary school, **Fourah Bay College,** the first Western institution of higher education in Africa, was established in Sierra Leone and affiliated with the University of Durham. Its students received the equivalent of British degrees.

1878. Under **Cardinal Lavigérie, the White Fathers Mission** was charged with Catholic missionary work in Africa.

1879. Cocoa was introduced into the Gold Coast from Fernando Po and San Tomé.

Sir George Goldie founded the **United Africa Company (UAC).** Under the UAC, Goldie brought together a number of smaller British firms. In 1886, the UAC became the **Royal Niger Company** and was given a charter to rule the region of Nigeria.

1883, Feb. Asantehene **Mansa Bonsu** was deposed by Asante chiefs. Anarchy ensued in the kingdom.

1884, April. Germany occupied Togo.

1884–85. The Berlin West African Conference (p. 474) was held against the backdrop of European territorial advances in Africa, which began to pick up momentum from 1875 onward. The conference established **rules for the "scramble for Africa" in order to prevent armed conflict among Europeans.** Africans were not invited to attend. Both the Belgians and the French moved into the lower Congo basin in this era; the French also expanded their presence along the upper Niger. At the conference, Britain, France, Germany, and Portugal negotiated colonial frontiers in Africa. In doing so, they both regulated and accelerated the scramble.

1888. Prempeh was elected Asantehene. He led the Asante into negotiations with Britain and the establishment of a protectorate, thus maintaining a nominal integrity of the state.

Pope Leo XIII ordered Cardinal Lavigérie to undertake a **crusade against slavery.**

1889, Jan. 10. France established a formal protectorate over the **Ivory Coast.**

1890. France made war with the **king of Dahomey,** who was defeated and forced to recognize a French protectorate.

1890 ff. Expansion of the colonial frontier in West Africa. The Europeans bolstered their presence in West Africa and expanded into new territory by turning increasingly to armed force. The French attacked **Segu** in 1890 and launched military expeditions in the West African interior throughout the decade, occupying African states such as **Mossi and Sikasso.** The British launched an expedition against the **Ijebu** in 1892; in 1897 they conquered Benin. The Germans launched expeditions in **Cameroon and Togo** in the 1890s.

1892. Second French-Dahomey war. King **Béhanzin** was captured, but the French faced continuing resistance.

1893–94. War between the Asante and the British.

1895, Jan. 1. The **Royal Niger Company** proclaimed a protectorate over **Busa and Nikki,** effectively blocking a French advance eastward from Dahomey.

1895–96. Fourth war between the Asante and Britain. A British expeditionary force was sent to Asante.

1896, Jan 20. Asantehene was deposed and imprisoned with other notables. A British protectorate was proclaimed on Aug. 16.

1897, Feb. 18. A British expeditionary force took Benin and plundered its royal art. Most of the art was sent to England, where it formed the core of private and museum collections of Benin art.

1898. Lagos was lit by electricity.

Jan. 1. Hut taxes were imposed in Sierra Leone.

April 27. General uprising against British rule and taxes broke out in Sierra Leone.

1898–1907. Consolidation of Northern Nigeria under Gov. Frederick Lugard. Lugard was appointed the first British high commissioner for Northern Nigeria in 1898. His mission: to establish British authority over the Fulani empires of Sokoto and Gwandu, and to conquer the other independent societies of the region. Lugard led the British military occupation of Kano (Feb. 3, 1903). By March 15, conquest of Northern Nigeria was completed. Serious **famine** broke out following the conquest. Lugard based British colonial administration upon the authority of Islamic rulers in the area, thus instituting **indirect rule.**

1899, Aug 9. The British government revoked the charter of the **Royal Niger Company** and took over possession of Nigerian protectorates and colonies.

1900, Jan 1. A British protectorate was declared over Nigeria, and **Sir Frederick Lugard** was appointed as high commissioner.

Nov. General **uprising of the Asante.**

1901, Sept. 26. The kingdom of Asante was annexed and formally incorporated into the Gold Coast.

1904. Uprising among the **Ekumeku** of southern Nigeria.

1906. Rebellion broke out in Satiru, Sokoto. A British punitive expedition arrived on March 10.

May 1. British colony of **Lagos** was incorporated into Southern Nigeria.

1907–14. Lagos Harbor was improved for ocean-going vessels.

1908–11. Railway linking Kano to Lagos was built.

1909. Teachers Training College opened in Accra.

1912. Uprising in Abeokuta.

1914, Jan. 1. Northern and Southern Nigeria were joined under one administration. **Sir Frederick Lugard** acted as governor-general of Nigeria, 1914–19.   *(To p. 795)*

c. NORTHEAST AFRICA (HORN)

(From p. 393)

1. ETHIOPIA

1800–55. Ethiopian **"Zamana Mesafent" ("era of the princes")** was marked by a breakdown of central power and the **emergence of regionally based feudalism.** During this period the imperial monarchy survived in form but was without substantial authority. There was rivalry among regional feudal lords to become the most powerful in order to dominate the emperor. The Ethiopian Church was also riven by factions. The feudal lords were supported by in-kind payments and corvée labor of the peasantry, who were further undermined by the constant state of war among the regional princes.

c. 1800–20. Galla kingdom of Enarea was founded.

1838. Protestant missionaries were expelled from Tigre.

c. 1842. Lazarist missionaries arrived in Tigre and Eritrea.

c. 1847. Theodore, the future emperor, organized rebels and overran Gondar.

1855–68. The **modern period in Ethiopia** began with the reign of **Tewodros II,** who consolidated and recreated the Ethiopian Empire. Tewodros established a **national army and appointed salaried governors and judges** after defeating feudal lords. Initially he was allied with the church, but he attempted to reform it. Excess church land (beyond that needed to support essential clergy) was redistributed, and Tewodros permitted the introduction of an **Amharic Bible by Protestant missionaries.**

1866. The Gondar region rebelled against **Tewodros,** who imprisoned several British officers.

1867. A **British punitive expedition,** involving 68,000 men under Sir Robert Napier, was sent to release British prisoners held by **Tewodros.**

1868. British forces freed British prisoners, and Tewodros committed suicide. The British expedition demonstrated the power of **modern weaponry.**

1872, Jan. Yohannes IV achieved the Ethiopian throne. He was more successful than Tewodros in bringing about **unification** by following a conciliatory policy toward both the nobility and the clergy. He supported **modernization of the military with imported firearms and a British adviser.**

1876, Feb. Ethiopian army under Yohannes defeated an Egyptian force and captured a huge supply of arms.

c. 1880. The Ethiopian Church forced 50,000 Muslims, 20,000 pagans, and 500,000 Galla to be baptized.

1885, Feb. 3. Italy seized Massawa on the Red Sea coast of Eritrea.

1889, March 10. Death of **Yohannes IV** of Ethiopia in a battle on the Sudanese frontier led to the accession of **Menelik II** as king of kings, shifting the political focus of Ethiopia to the southern region, with the **new capital, Addis Ababa, at its center.**

Italians took advantage of the succession, cattle plague, and epidemics to occupy Eritrea. European powers recognized that Italian claim over Ethiopia was based on a **fraudulent translation of the Uchale Treaty** between Ethiopia and Italy.

1889–1913. Menelik II doubled the size of the Ethiopian Empire. Menelik pursued a **program of modernization,** including the establishment of Addis Ababa as his capital and the starting of a postal service, banking, and a government cabinet.

1890–94. Menelik expanded Ethiopian territory and acquired modern arms.

1891. Menelik denounced Italian claims of a protectorate.

1896, March 1. Menelik and the Ethiopian army of 100,000 men, using modern arms, **inflicted a crushing defeat on Italian invaders at Adua** (Adowa) (p. 475). Italy renounced its claims and recognized the independence of Ethiopia.

1910–14. The Young Ethiopians, led by **Gebre Heywet,** emerged to argue for a program of reform and modernization, and for communications to stimulate the internal economy, not just foreign trade.

1906–13. During Menelik's incapacity, succession struggles were inflamed by European attempts to divide Ethiopia into spheres of influence. **Menelik suffered a series of strokes and died in 1913.**

2. SUDAN REGION

1821. An **Egyptian governor-general** (p. 541) was installed at newly founded **Khartum** to oversee tax collection and slave raiding by the Egyptian army in Sudan, marking the **beginning of Turco-Egyptian domination** there.

1840–54. European, Egyptian, and Sudanese ivory traders on the upper White Nile established *zaribas* (fortified trading posts).

1854. Private armies were established at the *zaribas*. Wars among them led to the capture of slaves and cattle and to a **sizable slave trade.** A ban on slave trading in the Turkish Sudan led to a slave boom in Karka and Shillukland.

1881–85. Mahdist revolution against Turco-Egyptian domination. The revolution was led by the **Mahdi (meaning "restorer of justice sent by Allah"), Muhammad Ahmad ibn Abdallah,** in the form of a **jihad** against the colonial oppressors and "impure" Muslims. The revolt was sparked by a **variety of grievances,** including the appointment of non-Muslim Europeans to administrative posts, among them Englishman **Charles Gordon** as governor-general; the welcoming of **Christian missionaries;** the conquest of **Darfur** in 1874 and the imposition of tax collection there; and the attempt to **suppress the slave trade** in the south.

1883, Nov. The turning point of the Mahdist revolution against Turco-Egyptian rule of the Sudan was marked by the **defeat of the Egyptian force under British officer William Hicks at Shaykan.**

1885, June. The **Mahdi died.** Soon thereafter the Mahdists consolidated their control of the Sudan as the British-Egyptian forces withdrew. **Khalifa Abdallahi,** successor to the Mahdi, created a **centralized bureaucracy** and ended the revolutionary period.

1885–1910. A series of **EPIDEMICS** affecting cattle and people plagued the region, beginning with **rinderpest,** which killed up to **90 percent of the cattle and spread to the Cape of Good Hope by 1897 and west to the Atlantic by 1892.**

1896, March. An **Anglo-Egyptian force under Gen. Kitchener invaded the Mahdist state.** The army had another objective: to keep the Sudan from falling into France's hands.

June. The **Marchand expedition** left France with instructions to advance to **Fashoda** and claim the territory for France.

1897, Feb. A Belgian force under Chaltin reached the Nile at Rejaf, fought battles with Mahdist forces, and occupied Loda and Wadelai.

Aug. Marchand reached the Bahr el-Ghazal region but could not advance because of low water.

1898, July 10. Marchand reached Fashoda and established a post there.

Sept. 2. The **Mahdist army was crushed by Kitchener's** superior weaponry at **Omdurman.**

Sept. 19. Kitchener arrived at Fashoda, raising a serious diplomatic crisis between France and Britain (p. 475).

Dec. 11. France ordered Marchand to evacuate Fashoda, thus defusing the diplomatic crisis.

1899, Nov. 24. Khalifa died at the Battle of **Umm Diwaykrat,** and the Mahdist state collapsed. The British completed their **victory in the Sudan,** marking the beginning of the Anglo-Egyptian Sudan.

1900, Sept. 5. France claimed Chad as a military protectorate.

1904–5. Smallpox epidemic hit the Somali coast and spread to the White Nile. This and succeeding epidemics in humans and animals resulted in **period of declining population** in the region.

1906. Cholera epidemic in Horn.

1900–14. Despite suffering defeat at the hands of the British, **Mahdism persisted, and a number of revolts** occurred in the Sudan. *(To p. 797)*

d. EAST AFRICA

(From p. 393)

1. SWAHILI COAST AND HINTERLAND

1800. Nyamwezi people from the Tanganyikan interior established a **long-distance caravan trade to the Swahili coast,** trading ivory for beads and cloth. Omani authority on the Swahili coast was significant only in Mombassa, Zanzibar, and Kilwa; other towns were dominated by local rulers.

1800–45. Increased long-distance trade initiated change in interior societies, with rise of wealthy traders known as **"BIG MEN"** who used their wealth to attract followers. Regional cultural practices developed, and there was intermarriage among groups. Coastal towns became bigger and more ethnically mixed. **Plantation and domestic slavery** grew at the coast. **Slave concubinage** led to a cultural mix of African and Arab. Trade led to the **spread of Islam and the Kiswahili language** in the interior.

1806–56. Sayyid Sa'id bin Sultan ascended to the Omani throne.

1814. Adballah ben Ahmad al-Mazrui, governor of Mombassa, declared Mombassa independent.

1814–40. Sayyid Sa'id moved to reestablish Omani dominance of Swahili towns, displacing the Mazruis (1822–37) in Lamu, Pemba, and Mombassa.

c. 1818. Cloves were introduced into Zanzibar.

1822. Hamid ben Ahmad al-Busaidi, sent by Sayyid Sa'id, compelled Barawam Lamu, Pate, and Pemba to acknowledge Omani suzerainty.

1827. Sayyid Sa'id visited his domains in East Africa.

1830–80. EXPANSION OF IVORY AND SLAVE TRADE drew East Africa into the capitalist world economic system before the dawn of colonial rule. By the 1870s, most of the East African interior was integrated into the international trade network through Zanzibar. **Swahili-Arab traders** began to trade in the interior for ivory and slaves. Slaves were sought for foreign trade and for clove and other plantations on islands and the coast, while cloth, copper, beads, and guns were traded in the interior. Ivory trade thrived with the Nyamwezi in the central region, while wars encouraged slave trade in the southern region. Interior peoples, especially the Nyamwezi, Kamba, and Shambaa, took an active role in long-distance trade as porters to the coast. **Ivory and slave trades also stimulated interregional trade** in the interior, especially of iron and salt. **The slave trade caused great disruption** among interior peoples but brought wealth to groups acting as raiders and traders. Villages became more compact for defense purposes. Swahili-Arab traders influenced styles of dress and introduced imported goods. **Guns were common by 1860.** Rectangular building styles spread inward from the coast. Trade led to a mixing of ethnic groups at the coast and at interior trading centers. Involvement in trade also led to the emergence of "big men" who amassed followers on the basis of new wealth, unconnected to traditional sources of authority such as religion. Coastal trade also influenced a shift in the interior to **societies based more on military power than on religious authority.**

1840. Sayyid Sa'id moved the Omani capital to Zanzibar and began to reorient the Swahili trading economy toward exports.

1840–45. Ngoni invaders, rippling northward from wars in South Africa, reached southeastern Tanganyika in two main groups. The death of Ngoni leader **Zwagendaba** in 1848 led to a split; offshoots of these groups established **new states,** incorporating local populations, including Mshope and Njelu kingdoms. **Ngoni immigration set off a chain reaction of war and conquest and raiding for cattle and slaves.** Ngoni weapons and tactics were adopted by pastoralist Hehe, Sangu, and Bena peoples in the highlands northeast of Lake Malawi. These disturbances **increased the slave trade** and discouraged ivory traders from infiltrating this region.

1840–70. Sa'id encouraged the establishment of **clove plantations in Zanzibar and Pemba,** which by the 1860s had become the **world's top producers of cloves.** Cloves displaced other crops and gave rise to **plantation slavery** in the islands. By the 1860s, plantations of Zanzibar and Pemba were absorbing 10,000 slaves per year, while the Zanzibar slave market was handling 70,000 slaves per year for export. Sa'id also encouraged the settlement of **Indians, who financed the new interior trade.** About 5,000 Indians were settled in Zanzibar by 1860. European involvement in trade was also encouraged, but Europeans were prohibited from the slave trade from 1822. Trade extended the political influence of the Zanzibari regime through diplomacy and colonies of traders in the interior.

c. 1844. Arabs established a permanent trading post at **Umyanyembe.** By 1851, Arabs had pushed the trading frontier west of the Great Lakes.

1850. Kilwa Kivinje became the most important town on the southern Swahili coast for the export of ivory and slaves, traded by Yao and Bisa from the interior and shipped to Zanzibar.

1854, April 16. Sayyid Sa'id left Zanzibar for Oman.

1860. The minaret of the Malindi mosque was built. **A Catholic mission** was established on Zanzibar.

1862. A United Methodist Free Church mission was established near Mombassa.

1863. A Holy Ghost Fathers mission was established on Zanzibar.

1868. Sir John Kirk began his long-term role as British representative at Zanzibar. Under his influence, the sultan was induced to take measures **against the slave trade.** Kirk was officially consul general from 1873 to 1886.

1870–88. Bargash Sayyid, sultan of Zanzibar. In 1873, he **prohibited the export of slaves by sea.** In 1876, **he prohibited the movement of slaves overland** and closed the Zanzibar slave market.

1875–93. CMS (Church Missionary Society) **missions** were established on Lake Tanganyika.

1878. German African Society established a number of posts in the region between Bagamoyo and Lake Tanganyika.

1884, Nov. Karl Peters signed a number of treaties with native chiefs in the hinterland of Bagamoyo.

1885, Feb. The **German East Africa Company** was chartered to take over the claims established by Peters. The German government established a protectorate over East Africa from the Umba River in the south to the Rovuma River in the north.

Benedictine nuns started work in Dar es Salaam.

Aug. Germans forced the sultan of Zanzibar to recognize a German protectorate over Witu.

1887. The **British East Africa Company** secured from the sultan of Zanzibar a 50-year lease along the coast between the Umba and Tana Rivers. By 1888, the **British East Africa Company** was granted a charter to develop the territory in the British sphere.

1888–90. An insurrection of Arabs in the German territories was organized by **Abu Shihiri.**

c. 1890. An outbreak of **rinderpest epidemic** was followed by pneumonia and smallpox epidemics.

1890, Aug. 1. The sultan of Zanzibar **signed an antislavery decree.**

Nov. 4. A British protectorate over Zanzibar was proclaimed.

1891. Sisal was introduced into German East Africa.

1895, June 18. Following the dissolution of the British East Africa Company, the **British** proclaimed the territory the **East Africa Protectorate.**

1897. Native Courts Regulations in Kenya empowered certain chiefs and headmen.

April 5. Slavery was abolished in Zanzibar by a decree signed by the sultan.

1898–1900. Civil war among the Masai.

1899–1902. General unrest in German East Africa.

1902. East Africa Syndicate received a grant of 500 square miles in British East Africa in order to **promote white settlement in the Highlands.** The grant was further regulated by the First Crown Lands Ordinance (Sept. 2).

Jan. White settlers in Kenya formed the Colonists Association.

1903, June. Lord Delamere settled in Kenya and founded the Kenya Settlers and Farmers Association.

1905–7. The **Maji-Maji rebellion broke out in German East Africa.** Rebellion was sparked by **forced production of cotton in the Rufiji valley,** as well as by issues of taxation and forced labor, but it was carried forward through the spread of the millennial message of the prophet **Kinjikitili** and spurred by drought. Rebellion, though brutally suppressed, forced the Germans to reappraise their white settler policy.

1907–8. Roman script was officially used for Swahili, in place of Arabic.

1914. The **railroad** from Dar es Salaam reached the shores of Lake Tanganyika.

2. UGANDA AND THE INTERLACUSTRINE REGION

1854–84. Rule of **Kabaka Mutesa of Buganda.** Under him, Buganda became an effective **centralized and expansionist state.**

1865–95. Rwanda, like Buganda, engaged in expansionist wars under population pressure. Buganda and Bunyoro participated in ivory and slave trades.

1870–76. Kabaka Mutesa of Buganda moved toward adoption of **Islam,** then purged Muslims in 1875 in the face of an Egyptian threat to his kingdom and began to court **Christian missionaries.** To this date, Islam had made little progress in other parts of the interior. After successful resistance to the Egyptian incursion under Charles Gordon, Mutesa issued a call for **Westerners to come and live at his capital.**

1876–77. First **CMS missionaries** arrived at Uganda, following an invitation by Kabaka Mutesa.

1879. Catholic White Fathers arrived at Mutesa's court.

1884. Death of Kabaka Mutesa. He was succeeded by his son, **Mwanga,** who soon became involved in struggles between various religious factions.

1885–86. Purge of Christian young men of the Buganda court.

1885, Jan. 5. Five **CMS converts were martyred** in Buganda. Religious and political struggles in Buganda were deeply intertwined.

Oct. Murder of **Bishop James Hannington** at the command of Mwanga.

1886, June 3. Catholic and Anglican converts were martyred in Buganda.

1880–1900. Christian missionaries began to penetrate the East African interior, conflicting with the trade-sparked spread of Islam. **Christians attempted to alter African social structure by encouraging monogamy.** Mission stations established communities of liberated slaves and war refugees.

1888–89. Mwanga attempted to decapitate both Muslim and Christian factions at the Bugandan court. His efforts failed and led instead to his defeat and exile, and a series of **religious civil wars.**

1889. Kiwewa succeeded Mwanga as kabaka. By Oct. 18, the Muslim faction was ascendant in Buganda. All Christian missionaries were expelled, and Kiwewa was deposed. Muslim kabaka **Kalema** succeeded him.

1890, Dec. Sir Frederick Lugard, with an armed force, arrived in Buganda. He induced the kabaka to sign a new treaty and attempted to restore peace among the religious factions.

1892, Jan. Outbreak of another round of fighting among religious parties in Buganda. **Lugard** intervened energetically in favor of the **Protestant** faction.

1893, March. Arrival of **Sir Gerald Portal** in Buganda. Despite its reluctance to get involved in Buganda, the **British East Africa Company** was induced to remain because of the intervention and financial support of missionary interests.

1894. Lugard partitioned Buganda among Protestant, Catholic, and Muslim groups. Protestants received the best areas and most important political offices.

1895. CMS started the first schools in Uganda.

1896. Kingdom of Nyoro was added to the Uganda Protectorate.

1897, July–Aug. Rebellion in Uganda was provoked by Kabaka Mwanga. The British defeated Mwanga in Dec.

Sept. Outbreak of the **mutiny of the Sudanese troops in Uganda.** It was finally suppressed by Indian troops in Aug. 1898. Scattered fighting continued until 1901.

1900, March 10. A definitive **treaty between Uganda and Great Britain** regulated the form of government and the **model of indirect rule.** The country was to be ruled by the kabaka, with the advice and consent of the British commissioner.

1901. The **Uganda Railroad** opened, extending from Mombassa to Lake Victoria.

1902–3. Revolt, resistance, and anarchy spread in Burundi.

1909, Jan. A native court system was introduced in Buganda.

(To p. 798)

e. WEST CENTRAL AFRICA

(From p. 394)

1800. Around this time, **Swahili-Arab** traders in **slaves and ivory** established trading posts in northeastern present-day Zambia and southeastern present-day Zaire. These posts came to take on a **military character and supplanted local chiefs in the eastern Lunda Empire.**

1800–73. Consolidation and expansion of the **Lunda Empire** under a succession of rulers: **Yavo ya Mbanyi** in the early part of the century, **Naweji ya Ditende** (c. 1821–c. 1853), and **Muteba ya Chikombe** (c. 1857–73). The empire was ruled through a combination of traditional leaders and an appointed bureaucracy. It was knitted together by an ideology of unity and a balanced administrative structure. The empire was also strengthened by a location suited to agriculture and by the copper and salt trade. Wealth was also based on the **slave trade for export and for domestic slave labor.**

1819–21. Cotton cultivation was introduced into Angola.

1822. Popular **uprising and mutiny** in Luanda.

1834. Angola ignored **antislavery** prohibitions.

1838. The governor of Angola **was removed for trafficking in slaves.**

1839. King Denis, chief of the left bank of the Gabon River, accepted the French treaty.

1840. As part of the **new Portuguese expansion into Angola,** merchants founded the port of **Mocamedes** to tap into the ivory trade of the southern highlands.

1842. King Louis, chief of the right bank of the Gabon River, accepted the French treaty.

1844. Holy Ghost Fathers started missionary work in Gabon. **Protestants** opened a mission station at Bimbia.

1845. Baptist missions opened at Douala.

1848. Baptists were established at Victoria, Cameroon.

1849. The French founded Libreville, using **freed slaves as settlers.**
Portuguese refugees from Brazil introduced sugar and cotton to the Mocamedes area.

1864. King Bell of Douala sought protection from Queen Victoria.

1850–60. Ivory trade led to rapid increase in the supply of guns in southern Central Africa. **Nyamwezi** traders from Tanganyika operated caravans from the coast to the eastern part of the Lunda Empire, trading for copper and ivory. By 1852, **Swahili traders** pushed the East African trading frontier to **Benguela.**

1852–61. Friedrich Welwitsch conducted a botanical survey of Angola.

1856–57. Swahili traders reached Katanga.

1856–65. Tippu Tip established a trading state.

1856–85. The Nyamwezi trader Msiri arrived at Kazembe and used firearms to gain political power among the Lamba and the Sanga. By 1869, Msiri had established the kingdom of **Garenganze** in Katanga, undermining the authority of the Lunda ruler **Kazembe.** By the 1880s he had established authority over much of the former Lunda Empire. Msiri's conquest state revenues were based on an ivory monopoly, the copper trade, and slavery. By 1880, Msiri's kingdom had reached its greatest extent.

1860–70. Portuguese fishermen and market gardeners began to service **whaling fleets at Mocamedes.** The town had by this time become a colony of white settlement, marking a new phase of Portuguese intrusion into Angola, though expansion into the southern highlands continued to be heavily resisted.

1860–90. Expansion of the **slave trade** northward and eastward from the Congo basin.

1875. Slavery and forced labor were abolished in Angola. The new labor regime, however, obligated Africans to provide "free" labor, resulting in a labor-abusive system.

1876, Sept. 12. King Leopold of Belgium, an ardent philanthropist, antislavery advocate, and imperialist, summoned to Brussels an international congress of geographers, explorers, and scientists. The congress led to the founding of the **International Association for the Exploration and Civilization of Central Africa.**

1878, Nov. 25. The Belgian committee of the International Association became the Comité d'Études du Haut-Congo. **Henry Stanley** was engaged to establish stations in the Congo area (1879–84).

1880. The French, alarmed by Stanley's activities, sent **Savargnan de Brazza,** who made treaties with chiefs on the north side of the Congo River. He founded **Brazzaville** and organized a protectorate.

1881–85. Belgian Comité d'Études du Haut-Congo became the **International Association of the Congo,** with the object of establishing claims on territory and expanding trade.

1884, April 22. United States recognized the International Association of the Congo as a **territorial power.**

1884–87. Tippu Tip, acting under the loose authority of the sultan of Zanzibar, claimed the Eastern Congo. In 1887, Tippu Tip was named governor of Stanley Falls District in the Congo Free State.

1885, April. King Leopold of Belgium established the Congo Independent State, operating it as a personal fief and private enterprise. Calling himself "proprietor" of the Congo, he willed it to the Belgian people (Aug. 9, 1890). It remained Leopold's personal fief until 1908.

Dec. 16. Britain recognized the International Association of the Congo. Recognition by Russia and France followed.

1886. A *force publique* was established in the Congo for police and military duties.

Plymouth Brethren mission was established in Katanga.

1888–89. Rescue of **Emin Pasha,** the governor of Equatoria Province, by Henry Stanley. The relief expedition was financed by King Leopold and by William MacKinnon, chairman of the Imperial British East Africa Company. Emin Pasha refused to leave and was murdered in the Congo in Oct. 1892.

1889, Dec. 22. Leopold declared all **"vacant" land to be state land.**

1890, July 2. The **Brussels Act** committed European powers to **prohibit the slave trade and to end the arms trade** in their colonies.

1890–1902. Portugal conquered Ovimbundu kingdoms.

1891, April 15. The **Katanga Company** was formed to exploit the rich copper deposits in Katanga.

Dec. 20. Following the killing of **Msiri,** the Granaganza kingdom collapsed.

1892. Rising of **Arab and Swahili slave traders** in the upper Congo and Tanganyika region. Arabs in the Kasai region were defeated in 1894.

May 8. The *régime domanial* effectively made ivory and rubber products the exclusive property of the state in Congo.

Dec. 5. Introduction of **forced labor** as part of the taxation system in the Congo.

1893. Jesuits started their work in the Congo.

1895–1905. Massive flight away from the Congo to **resist intense labor exploitation** under Leopold's rule. The exploitation involved brutal physical punishments to coerce workers into copper mines and agricultural enterprises.

1895. Slave trade was prohibited in the Cameroon.

1895–97. Revolts and mutinies by members of the *force publique.*

1896. Trappists began their work in the Congo.

1899. Portuguese labor law subjected Africans to "moral obligation to work," including both corvée labor for the government and wage labor. Only chiefs and producers of export crops were exempt.

1902. The Bailundo revolt was spurred by a precipitous decline in the price of rubber, leading to conflict between Portuguese and Ovimbundu traders in Angola. Slave raiding between various Ovimbundu states, however, prevented the formation of a united front. The Portuguese, suppressing revolt, were able to gain control of the central highlands.

June 18–21. Protestant missions in the Congo met to discuss problems and coordinate activities.

1903. Beginning of agitation in Britain, then in the United States and Germany, **against inhumane conditions in the Congo Free State.** Edward D. Morel and Sir Roger Casement were active proponents of this popular movement.

1903–10. A **railway system** was built in the Congo Free State.

1905. Insurrection broke out in the Welle District of the Congo Free State and spread into the French Congo.

1906–8. Congo Reform Association exposed gross and rampant abuses of labor in Congo, leading to the annexation of Congo by Belgium in 1908.

1907. Large-scale **insurrection** in Angola.

1908, Oct. 18. Belgium formally **annexed the Congo Free State.** It became the Belgian Congo.

1910, Jan. 15. The French Congo was renamed French Equatorial Africa and was divided into three colonies (Gabon, Middle Congo, and Ubangui-Shari) under loose confederation similar to that of French West Africa.

May 2. Labor tax was abolished in the Belgian Congo as part of an extensive reform program.

1912. The African Inland Mission began its work in the Belgian Congo.

1913. A BaKongo **uprising** against the Portuguese.

Albert Schweitzer founded a hospital at Lambaréne.

1914. Methodist mission to Central Congo began. (To p. 798)

f. SOUTHERN AFRICA

(From p. 395)

1. NORTH OF THE LIMPOPO

c. 1800–50. Exports of slaves from Mozambique to South America rose to over 15,000 per year. In some years, 25,000 slaves were exported.

1800–40. Lozi state, composed of pastoralist people on the Zambezi floodplain, emerged. The Lozi king acted as the owner of cattle, which he redistributed in return for other goods, generating a kind of internal trade.

1827–29. A **Portuguese garrison** was established in Lundazi District, Zambia.

1840–64. The **Lozi** of the Zambezi floodplain (Zambia) were conquered and ruled by **Kololo** cattle-raiding migrants from Botswana, displaced by the social disruption known as **Mfecane,** who successfully adopted the Lozi canoe-based tributary system. The Kololo also entered the Angolan slave trade with captives generated by cattle raids, beginning in 1850. Soon thereafter they also entered the ivory trade, which brought about tensions leading to the **kingdom's disintegration** in the 1860s.

c. 1840. Ndebele trekked to Matabeleland and defeated the Kalanga and the Rozwi. Kololo migrated across the Zambezi to the Tonga Plateau. **The Ngoni incursions began,** destabilizing wide swaths of the Central and East African interior.

1850–65. Export of slaves from Mozambique declined and then ended.

1859. London Missionary Society mission founded in Inyati, Southern Rhodesia.

1861–64. Failure of the **UMCA** (University Mission to Central Africa) mission to Shire Highlands, Nyasaland.

1862. J. S. Moffat joined the mission at Inyati.

c. 1873. Four hundred white and black pupils attended **schools** in Mozambique.

1875. United Free Church of Scotland mission was established at Blantyre and Livingstonia.

1876. Town of **Blantyre** was founded.

1878. Coffee was introduced into Blantyre.

1879. A **Jesuit mission** was established at Bulawayo.

c. 1881. Regular **caravans** of up to 500 slaves passed through Mwembe to Kilwa.

1881. UMCA resumed its missionary work in Nyasaland.

1882. Trappists founded Marianhill Abbey.

1884. Rebellion against Lewanika, king of the Barotse.

1885. Bechuana territory was organized as Bechuanaland Protectorate.

1888. John Moffat, missionary and agent for Rhodes, concluded a treaty with **Lobengula,** king of the Ndebele, which offered the Ndebele British protection. In a further amendment to this treaty, the **Rudd Concession,** Lobengula ceded exclusive mining rights to Rhodes.

1889. British proclaimed a **protectorate** over the Shire River region. In 1891, **Harry Johnston** was appointed first commissioner of the new British Central Africa Protectorate.

Oct. 29. The British government granted the **British South Africa Company** (BSAC), headed by **Cecil Rhodes,** a charter to develop the territories north of the Zambezi and west of Mozambique. **Leander Starr Jameson** made treaties on behalf of the BSAC.

1890, June 27. The BSAC signed a treaty of protection with **Barotseland.**

The BSAC **Pioneer Column** established posts at Fort Tuli, Fort Victoria, Fort Charles, and Fort Salisbury. On Sept. 12, the British flag was raised.

1891. First **hospital** was opened in Salisbury by the Dominicans.

First **Anglican bishop of Mashonaland** was named.

John Booth started the Baptist Zambezi Mission.

The **Portuguese** government chartered the **Mozambique Company,** financed largely by British capital, to develop the hinterland of Beira.

1892–98. **Pacification** of Ngoni and Arab risings in the British Central Africa protectorate.

1892–93. Ndebele rebellion against British South Africa Company. In Nov. 1893, the BSAC invaded and conquered Ndebele kingdom, forcing King Lobengula to flee.

1894. Rapid development of **Bulawayo.**

1895–99. Risings in Mozambique weakened Portuguese authority. King Gungunhana, chief of the Gaza, was deported to Lisbon.

1897. A Ndebele uprising in Rhodesia was followed by a rebellion by the Shona, who proved much more difficult to pacify. The Shona called their resistance the **Chimurenga.**

1898, Jan. Anglo-Portuguese military operations against Yao chief Mataka.

1901. Portuguese East African administration granted a labor-recruiting monopoly to the **Witwatersrand Native Labour Association** in return for a capitation fee. As a result, the state established authority over the hinterland and was able to profit from a labor migration that it could not prevent.

c. 1906. Beginning of the **Watchtower (Kitawala) movement** in Nyasaland.

1907, May. The government of **Mozambique was reorganized.**

1908. Railway to Blantyre in the Shire Highlands opened the region to British colonization.

First **tobacco** factory was established in Nyasaland.

2. SOUTH OF THE LIMPOPO

c. 1795. Slaves outnumbered Europeans at the Cape.

1799. London Missionary Society began work along the Zak River.

1800–67. This period was characterized by **CONCOMITANT AND CONTRADICTORY STATE FORMATION ENTERPRISES of the Nguni Bantu of the southeastern coast, the expansion of British colonial hegemony, and the creation of Boer Republics.**

1800. The **ivory trade at Delagoa Bay,** from the late 18th century, contributed to political centralization in southeastern South Africa. By this time there were several **large federations of chiefdoms** under paramount chiefs in Phogola-Thukela region—**Zwide's Ndwandwe, Sobhuza's Ngwane** (later the Swazi), and **Dingiswayo's Mthwethwa.** These chiefdoms, in an atmosphere of competition for the ivory trade and grazing, converted male initiation schools into military and state-labor **age regiments** that formed standing armies under royal princes at various capitals.

1803–6. The British left the Cape in the hands of the Dutch **Batavian Republic** by the **Treaty of Amiens.** Batavians continued the British policy on the frontier.

1806. Roman Catholic priests were expelled from the Cape.

Oct. 10. British returned to the Cape with the capitulation of **Papendorp.**

1807. The **abolition of the slave trade** throughout the British Empire caused a serious labor shortage in the Cape.

1809. The Khoikhoi were placed under colonial law.

1811–12. The **British drove 20,000 Xhosa out of Zuurveld** to a line east of the Fish River on the Eastern Cape frontier, opening the area for white settlement.

1814, May 13. By the **Treaty of Paris,** the British secured definitive possession of the Cape.

1815. Slachter's Nek Rebellion against British rule in the Eastern Cape frontier was sparked by a black circuit court that heard complaints of black servants against white farmers.

1816. Protestant missionaries dramatically increased their efforts in the eastern Cape with the intention of converting the Africans. **Wesleyans** arrived.

1817. Dingiswayo was killed by Zwide's Ndwandwe. His protégé, **Shaka,** was quickly installed as chief of the small Zulu chiefdom and took over Dingiswayo's Mthwethwa confederacy under new Zulu paramountcy.

1817–28. Shaka became king of the newly emerged Zulu kingdom. Shaka **militarized and centralized** the state. Men under age 40 remained in active service, serving periodically in central military barracks. They were forbidden to marry and thus establish new homesteads until given permission by the king. The trade and competition that led to state formation in the region, as well as the need to support and employ the army, fueled constant cattle raiding and warfare to exact tribute and incorporate new chiefdoms. **The wars and migrations of this period through the 1840s were known as MFECANE.**

1818–19. The Xhosa war of resistance failed, leading to cession of the area between the Fish and Keiskamma Rivers.

1819–51. Dr. John Philip, the LMS superintendent missionary, proposed protection for Africans. In particular, Philip sought to segregate Africans on land dedicated to them. His proposals met with fierce opposition from the European farmers.

1819–20. Zulus defeated Zwide's Ndwandwe. Remnants scattered northward and established new states from Mozambique to Tanganyika.

1820. Arrival of 10,000 sponsored **British settlers** on small farms in Zuurveld on the Eastern Cape Frontier. They were intended to Anglicize the area and make it defensible, as well as to offset the Dutch population politically. Most of these settlers soon migrated instead to the towns.

1820–30. Basotho kingdom arose under the leadership of Moshoeshoe in a defensive reaction to raiding by the Hlubi and Ngwane offshoots of Mfecane.

1822. A proclamation provided for the **gradual establishment of English** in place of Dutch as the official language.

Mzilikazi, chief of the Khumalo and one of Shaka's generals, defied Shaka by refusing to turn over captured cattle and fled with 200 followers into high veld, leading to the formation of **Ndebele state.**

1824. British traders established a post at **Port Natal** (present-day Durban) under Shaka's goodwill. The Zulu kingdom traded there and through the Portuguese at Delagoa Bay.

Moshoeshoe established a mountain fortress at Thaba Bosiu, which was virtually impregnable, allowing consolidation of a kingdom from various Sotho-Tswana groups straddling the Caledon River.

1825. Ndebele established themselves through raiding and conquest as the dominant kingdom on the high veld.

1828. Shaka was assassinated in a conspiracy by his brothers, including **Dingane,** who became king.

Following the efforts of John Philip, the Cape passed the **Fiftieth Ordinance,** permitting Khoikhoi to hold and to purchase land. The legal system was overhauled, and the court system was replaced by a British judiciary.

1834. Abolition of slavery was gradually introduced and led to the freedom of 35,000 slaves. Dutch slaveholders in particular complained bitterly about the lack of adequate compensation.

Twelve thousand Xhosa attacked Cape Colony outposts.

1836–38. Antislavery legislation and labor regulation under the color-blind British legal system, as well as shortage of land in the Cape for the Boer system of extensive pastoralism, sparked **migration of Dutch-speaking pastoralists** into the South African interior beginning in 1836. This movement was later designated the **Great Trek,** and its participants, the **Voortrekkers.** About 10,000 moved northward. Under **Andries H. Potgeiter,** a group passed beyond the Vaal River and settled in what became known as the Transvaal. Another group under **Piet Retief** crossed the Drakensberg and began to occupy parts of Zululand and Natal in regions depopulated by the **Mfecane.**

1837, Dec. Contingent of **Boer Voortrekkers** under Retief sought **concession of land from Dingane, king of the Zulu.** At a meeting with Dingane, **Retief and 60 followers were murdered.** Zulu forces also attacked trekker encampments. Other Boer Voortrekkers, allied with Tswana and Griqua armies, **defeated Ndebele,** who relocated at Bulawayo in southwestern Zimbabwe.

1838, Dec. 16. Boers under Andreas Pretorius defeated the Zulu army at the **Battle of Blood River** at the Ncome River. The Boers thereupon

settled in Natal, calling it the Republic of Natal, and founded Piet-maritzburg (1839).

1839. Dingane's half-brother **Mpande allied himself with the Boers and defeated Dingane,** becoming king. As a result, Mpande became a vassal of the Boer republic of Natalia.

1842–43. War between the British and the Boers in Natal. Pretorius defeated a British column under Capt. T. Smith in June 1842. By July, the Republic began to collapse, and by May 1843, the British had annexed Natal.

1843, Dec. A treaty with **Moshoeshoe,** powerful leader of the Basuto, led to the recognition of Basutoland under British protection. A similar treaty was made with **Adam Kok,** a leader of the **Griqua.**

1845. British annexation of Natal led to **renewed emigration** of most of the Voortrekkers.

1846–47. Theophilus Shepstone, diplomatic agent to the native tribes (later secretary for native affairs), established **native reserves** in Natal and a system of rule by chiefs under colonial supervision. The "Shepstone system" foreshadowed the British colonial policy of indirect rule.

1848. Sir Harry Smith, British high commissioner, annexed the area between the Fish and Kei Rivers as British Kaffraria; he also annexed the Orange River Sovereignty—the area between the Orange and Vaal Rivers, populated by Sotho and Boer groups. Boers **resisted Smith's annexations,** but they were defeated at the Battle of **Boomplaats.**

1849–52. Sponsored immigration brought British settlers to Natal.

1851–76. Pedi migrants worked in the Cape on farms and, from 1867, diamond fields in order to purchase firearms, under the encouragement of Paramount **Chief Sekukhune.**

1852. The British renounced claims north of the Vaal River in the **Sand River Convention** with Transvaal Boers.

1853, July. A **new constitution** was introduced in the Cape Colony. It provided for an elected Legislative Council and an elected House of Assembly.

1854, Feb. Britain paved the way for formation of the **Orange Free State** by abandoning sovereignty in the **Bloemfontein Convention.** Boer settlers organized a republic with a president and a *volksraad.*

1854–60. Missionary **Robert Moffat** visited Bulawayo, opening a path for Europeans in Zimbabwe, but made no converts.

1856, July 12. Natal was established as a British colony, separate from the Cape, with a legislative council for the settlers. **Civil war in Zulu kingdom** established the supremacy of the Usuthu faction and the right to succession of Cetshwayo, while Mpande remained king.

1857. In a self-defeating effort to resist European incursions, **the Xhosa killed cattle in response to a millennial prophecy.** Perhaps as many as two-thirds of the population died as a result of the killing of cattle and the livelihood they represented.

1859. The first indentured Indian servant arrived in Natal to work especially on **sugar plantations, because of shortages of willing African labor.** By the end of the 19th century, numbers of indentured and voluntary Indian immigrants equaled the white population in the colony.

1860. Republic of Lydenburg joined the South African Republic.

1865–66. War between the Orange Free State and Moshoeshoe's Sotho resulted in cession of most of Sotho state's arable land.

Severe economic depression in South Africa.

1866. The Indian government stopped supply of indentured Indian labor to Natal.

1867, April. DISCOVERY OF DIAMONDS near Hopetown on the Orange River. By 1870 a considerable mining industry had emerged. The discovery of diamonds led to a **profound restructuring** of the relationships among the various communities in South Africa and ushered in an era of **INDUSTRIAL CAPITALISM.**

1868, March 12. Britain annexed Basotholand as a protectorate, following a request by Moshoeshoe, and began the process of establishing white governance over African areas without a substantial white presence.

1868–71. Lobengula became Ndebele king after a civil war over succession to Mzilikazi.

1870. Digger's Republic was proclaimed at Klipdrift.

Diamonds were discovered in the Orange Free State.

1870–80. "Dry diggings" took place in diamond fields of what became **Kimberley** in the northern Cape. By 1875, this region became the larg-est diamond-producing area. **THE MINING ECONOMY TRANSFORMED THE POLITICAL ECONOMY OF ALL PEOPLES IN THE REGION, commercializing agriculture and leading to migrant labor systems, increase in Christian missionary activity, and conquest of independent kingdoms.** Productive mines were increasingly concentrated into a few big conglomerates.

1870–90. Ndebele kingdom maintained dominance in Zimbabwe and exacted tribute from Shona and Rozwi chiefdoms; missionary activities were allowed in the core area of the kingdom, but conversion was discouraged.

1870–1904. Mineral revolution led to white immigration, increasing the white population in South Africa from 225,000 to 1 million.

1871. Kimberley soon became the center of the diamond industry. **Cecil Rhodes** moved from Natal to Kimberley.

April. The **British government annexed** the diamond region (Griqualand West).

Carl Mauch reached Zimbabwe.

1876. Pedi kingdom defeated the Boer South African Republic (Transvaal) army.

1877, March 18. The **British annexed Walvis Bay** on the coast of Southwest Africa.

April 12. Britain annexed the South African Republic under the authority of Theophilus Shepstone. The British intended this annexation to be part of a larger federation of South Africa, but the Afrikaners considered it to be a violation of the Sand River Convention.

1877–78. The last Cape-Xhosa war resulted in famine and defeat for the Xhosa.

1879, Jan. 12–Sept. 1. The British invaded and defeated the Zulu kingdom, after suffering a major defeat in the first battle at Isandlwana. The British rushed in reinforcements and won a decisive victory at Ulundi. Military defeat led to series of civil wars in the former kingdom and finally to annexation by Britain in 1887.

The **Afrikaner Bond** was founded by **Jan Hofmeyer** to promote the Dutch language. It soon rallied most of the Dutch elements in South Africa. The Bond soon developed a political position favoring the elimination of all interference from the British government.

1880–81. Boers in the Transvaal revolted against the British. In Dec. 1881 Boer leaders, including Kruger, Joubert, and Pretorius, declared the **South African Republic.** Boers defeated British forces at Laing's Nek in Jan. and at Majuba Hill in Feb. The British recognized the republic on April 5 in the Treaty of Pretoria.

1880. The **Barnato Diamond Mining Company** was founded by Barney Barnato, and the **De Beers Mining Corporation** was founded by Cecil Rhodes and Alfred Beit.

1883. Britain crushed **Pedi kingdom** and reduced it to a reserve within its former territory.

Germans established settlements in Southwest Africa and at Angora Reqana, between Cape Colony and Angola.

April 16. Kruger became president of the South African Republic.

1883–84. Civil war in Zululand. In May 1884, **Dinizulu,** son of Cetewayo, was made king.

1884. *Imo Zabi Ntgundo,* the first Xhosa newspaper, was published.

Tembu National Church was founded in Transkei.

1886. THE GOLD DISCOVERED on Witwatersrand accelerated the mining revolution; by the end of the century, South Africa was the world's largest producer of gold. Gold increasingly was found only in deep reefs, which required **substantial capital and cheap labor.**

Johannesburg was laid out in Sept. 1886 and before long had a population of over 100,000. **Cecil Rhodes's Consolidated Gold Mines** soon controlled a large share of the business.

1887, June 21. Britain annexed Zululand, and Dinizulu was banished to St. Helena.

1888. De Beers and Barnato amalgamated, which gave **Rhodes a virtual monopoly of the industry.**

1889. Witwatersrand Chamber of Mines was formed.

1889–1918. Seventy-five **Ethiopian** (independent) churches were founded in South Africa.

1890. Cecil Rhodes's British South African Company sent a "pioneer column" of settlers and "police" into **Rhodesia** (Zimbabwe) between Ndebele and Shona areas.

Cecil Rhodes became prime minister of the Cape Colony.

1890–1906. Series of **ecological crises,** including drought, locusts, and cattle disease (rinderpest) undermined the independence of African peasant production, which had been stimulated by the mining revolution.

1892. The first **train** line to link Capetown and Johannesburg was established.

1893. Natal colonists were granted responsible government.

1894. The British annexed Pondoland, thus connecting Cape Colony with **Natal.**

Aug. Glen Grey Act provided for African self-government along the model of indirect rule. It also raised property qualifications and introduced an educational test for black voters of the Cape.

1895, Dec. 29–1896, Jan. 2. Leander Starr Jameson led an unsuccessful raid on Johannesburg, intended to spark an uprising of Uitlander miners as a pretext for British intervention in South African Republic.

1896, Jan. 6. Cecil Rhodes, implicated in the Jameson Raid, was forced to resign as prime minister.

1897. Zululand was incorporated into Natal Colony.

In Natal, it became a **criminal offense for a white man to marry an Indian.**

Aug. Sir Alfred Milner became high commissioner in South Africa.

Nov. Railway from the Cape reached Bulawayo.

1898. Kruger was reelected president of the South African Republic and brought a hardening of Afrikaner attitudes toward immigrants. **Uit-lander** agitation against the Kruger regime increased. Milner was favorably disposed toward Uitlander grievances. In 1899, 20,000 Uitlanders sent a petition to Queen Victoria, recounting their grievances.

1899–1902. South African War (also known as Anglo-Boer War). At the outset, Boers had the military advantage of numbers and knowledge of terrain. Britain had only 25,000 men available. By Feb. 1900, the tide of battle favored British forces. By November, the Boers turned to **guerrilla tactics,** frustrating British army strategy. In Jan. 1901, Gen. Herbert Kitchener used a **scorched earth policy** to counter Boer guerrillas. Some 120,000 **women and children were confined in concentration camps,** where poor sanitation and malnutrition contributed to high mortality (around 20,000 died). British journalist **J. A. Hobson,** covering the war, developed a new **theory of imperialism.** At the end of the war, the British had 300,000 troops in South Africa against 60,000–70,000 Boers. By the **Treaty of Vereeniging** (May 31, 1901) the Boers accepted British sovereignty but were promised representative government. The British promised £3 million to enable the Boers to rebuild their farms.

1900. Willie Mokalapa founded the Basutoland Ethiopian Church.

1902–10. Lord Milner, as high commissioner, **consolidated South Africa** and brought about accommodation among Afrikaner (Boer) leaders and mining and imperial interests.

1903–5. South African Native Affairs Commission endorsed principles of territorial and political segregation for the prospective unified South African state.

1903–7. Sixty thousand Chinese laborers were imported to counter the labor shortage on the Rand mines, undermining the bargaining power of African workers. The Chinese resisted labor conditions and discipline of mine work.

1904–8. The Herero revolt in Southwest Africa required four years and 20,000 German soldiers to suppress.

1905, Jan. Gen. Louis Botha formed the Het Volk organization to agitate for representative government for Afrikaners in the Transvaal. In 1906, the Transvaal was granted responsible government.

1906, Feb. The Bambatha rebellion in Natal and Zululand was sparked by the imposition of a poll tax designed to force men out to work. The rebellion was put down, its leader **Chief Bambatha was killed, and Dinuzulu kaCethshwayo,** heir to the Zulu throne, was convicted and exiled.

1907. The Transvaal government passed the **Asiatic Registration Bill** and provided for restrictions on Asian immigration. **Mohandas Gandhi** began his long campaign of **passive resistance.**

1908, Oct.–1909, Feb. The Constitutional Convention was held first in Durban and then at Capetown. The convention agreed on a scheme for a union of South Africa. There was to be a two-chamber Parliament: in the Senate, composed of eight members from each state, some would be elected proportionally and some appointed; in the House of Assembly, most were to be elected proportionally.

1910. Incident of police violence against **Israelite Church at Bulhoek.**

May 13. The Union of South Africa came into being with white male franchise and property-qualified nonracial franchise in Cape Province. The general election brought **Gen. Botha to power as head of a coalition of Afrikaner parties,** but English speakers were included in the cabinet. Botha's and **Gen. Jan Smuts's** parties merged to form the South African National Party. The opposition was divided among the Unionists, representing business interests, and the small Labour Party.

Native Labour Regulation Act unified laws making breach of contract a criminal offense and outlawed African strikes; it also regulated conditions of employment but had the effect of **depressing wages for Africans.**

1912. The South African Native National Congress (later the African National Congress [ANC]) was founded, composed of educated elites and chiefs but drawn from all ethnic groups and regions. **Rev. John Langalibalele Dube** of Natal was its first president.

The Native Recruiting Corporation was given a monopoly on recruiting for mine labor within South Africa.

1913, June. THE NATIVE LAND ACT ENTRENCHED THE PRINCIPLE OF TERRITORIAL SEGREGATION, restricting African land tenure to 7.3 percent of South Africa (with a promise of more to be added later), mostly in communal tenure reserves and scattered freehold areas. In the long term, this act **crippled the already declining African peasantry;** its antisharecropping and antirenting provisions took effect slowly (except in Orange Free State) but increased the bargaining power of white farmers seeking African labor.

The **Immigration Act** restricted the entry and free movement of Asians. Extensive rioting by Indians followed, during which **Gandhi** was arrested.

July. Troops **fired on striking miners** at Kleinfontein.

1914. Hertzog founded the Nationalist Party in opposition to Botha's South African Party. The Nationalist Party drew its support largely from rural Afrikaners and became an organ for Afrikaner separatism.

(To p. 798)

g. MADAGASCAR

(From p. 395)

1800–10. Andrianampoinimerina (Nampoina), having come to power in 1783, conquered neighboring kingdoms and **reunified Imerina** through strength of imported arms by 1806. Nampoina consolidated power and the authority of the king as owner of land. He inaugurated a system of corvée labor for public works. Wars generated slaves for export and internal use.

1803. A French force established itself at Tamatave.

1810–28. Rule of **Radama I,** son of Nampoina, in Imerina.

1811. The British occupied Seychelles, Madagascar, and Île de France.

1817. Radama I began campaigns of conquest and **reforms to modernize the army with European advisers.** The army reached a strength of 15,000 with modern arms, enabling the conquest of much of Madagascar. This conquest ended the country's isolation, leading to importation of more European goods and ideologies. Under British pressure, **Radama agreed to a treaty to prohibit the slave trade.**

1820. The London Missionary Society (LMS) established a mission station at **Tamatave.**

1822, Feb. 22. Radama I declared sovereignty over all Madagascar.

1826. LMS opened 30 **schools** throughout Madagascar.

1827. Having adopted phonetic Roman orthography for Malagasy, there was a **rapid spread of literacy.** Radama also encouraged the spread of **European building and crafts** in the capital.

1828, July 27. Radama I died, succeeded by his wife, **Ranavalona,** with support of a consortium of chiefs and the Europeanized ruling class. Britain terminated the treaty of protection. Unsuccessful **uprising of Sakalava** against Mcrina.

1830–40. Reaction against Western involvement in Madagascar led to **persecution of Christians** in Imerina.

1831. Jean Laborde established the first **ironworks** in Madagascar.

1845. Ranavalona declared all foreigners subject to local laws. **Christians**

were massacred by Hovas. Merina defeated the Anglo-French force at Tamatave, leading to renewed isolation.

1848. Vicariate apostolic of Madagascar was established.

1861, Aug. 18. Queen Ranavalona died, succeeded by King Radama II.

1883–85. First Franco-Merina war. The treaty ending the war was interpreted by the French (but not the Malagasy) as a declaration of a French protectorate.

1894–95. France occupied Tamatave in 1884. By 1895, France had conquered Madagascar.

1896. Rainilaiarivny, prime minister of Madagascar, was deported to Algeria. Rebellion throughout the island erupted shortly afterward and lasted until 1900.

1897, Aug. France annexed Madagascar. Gen. Gallieni was named resident general. On Sept. 27, slavery was abolished.

1905. The French conquest and economic opportunities for mining, timber extraction, and other exports led to rapid European immigration. By this date, 16,500 immigrants had arrived, half of whom were French. *(To p. 800)*

H. NORTH AMERICA, 1789–1914

1. THE UNITED STATES, 1789–1877

a. OVERVIEW

The period between the new Constitution and Reconstruction is perhaps the most significant phase of American history. This period not only witnessed the gradual growth of respect for American sovereignty abroad, but also entailed dramatic economic, population, and territorial growth at home, including **early industrialization, immigration,** and **urbanization.** Even in rural areas, growing **commercialization** entailed new motivations and anxieties as well as increased production for the market. Commercialization even affected family roles and values, with growing emphasis in the rising middle class on the home as moral haven. In some sectors the **per family birthrate** began to drop.

Closely intertwined with these demographic, economic, and territorial changes were far-reaching cultural and political transformations: the rise of political parties, universal suffrage for white men, and a plethora of new religious and social movements. Although the nation deepened its economic, social, and political independence during the period, it moved only slowly toward cultural independence from the elite traditions of Europe. At the same time, the **removal of Native Americans** from western lands to make way for white settlers and the rapid **spread of slavery** into the Deep South signaled increasing fragmentation along regional, class, and racial lines. These growing socioeconomic, political, and cultural conflicts would culminate in the eruption of the brutal Civil War, followed by the equally painful period of Reconstruction.

Following the establishment of the new constitutional order, the U.S. population increased from **3.9 million in 1790** to **9.6 million in 1820.** The Louisiana Purchase in 1803 added the nearly 2 million people who occupied the nine new states and three territories west of the Appalachian Mountains. The nation's **urban population** increased from less than 550,000 in 1820 to 1.8 million in 1840. By 1870, when the U.S. population reached nearly 40 million, about 25 percent of the total lived in cities, as the urban population grew more rapidly than the population as a whole.

The U.S. population had not only expanded. It had become more ethnically diverse. The Mexican-American War (1846–48) resulted in the acquisition of California and New Mexico, including present-day Utah, Nevada, and Arizona. The Mexican-American population would grow over time. Nearly 2 million Irish immigrants entered the U.S. during the two decades before the Civil War. German immigrants added another million, supplemented by 750,000 immigrants from Canada and Great Britain. Understandably, immigration played a major role in the nation's population growth. It was during the early 19th century that the U.S. became one of the first countries to undergo the **demographic transition**—a sharp decline in the number of births in both urban and rural areas. Among the many factors accounting for the falling birthrate were various methods of birth control.

The War of 1812 strengthened the nation's claim to sovereignty and expanded its role in the market economy. The financing of banks, transportation, and especially manufacturing enterprises escalated. Although the earlier outwork system (which employed manufacturing workers in their homes) persisted in some industries, American manufacturers turned increasingly toward the **factory system** as the primary mode of organizing production. By using new technology and reducing the labor requirements of production, early industrialists undermined the independence of craftworkers and opened the way for the widespread use of common waged labor. Although some master craftworkers benefited from such changes by becoming employers, by 1840 an estimated 50 percent of the nation's free workers labored for wages and found it difficult to acquire property, maintain skills, and move up in the socioeconomic system.

These demographic and economic changes effected a series of political and cultural transformations. As early as the presidential election of 1796, Federalists and Democratic-Republicans (known as Republicans) had adopted party labels in their quest for public office. The rise of Republicans in the election of 1800 signaled the development of a more democratic polity, which culminated in the establishment of **universal white male suffrage** during the 1820s and the triumph of the Democratic Party with the election of Andrew Jackson in 1828. New cultural and social movements both reflected and reinforced these changes. The advent of the **Second Great Awakening,** for example, transformed much of the country into fervent defenders of evangelical Protestantism. Emphasizing piety over theology and education, evangelical Baptist, Methodist, and Presbyterian denominations rapidly expanded. On the one hand, by promoting the virtues of hard work, thrift, discipline, and temperance, the Second Great Awakening reinforced the beliefs and practices of the expanding middle class. On the other hand, its stress on human will and the capacity of people to change their lives helped to stimulate a plethora of reform movements designed to alleviate inequality and democratize American society. The rise of utopian communities like Brook Farm, the Shakers, and the Oneidas; the women's suffrage movement; workingmen's parties; and the abolitionist movement all aimed to reverse diverse forms of inequality and suffering that had increased under the impact of early industrialization.

As the U.S. deepened its socioeconomic and political independence, it also experienced a **cultural renaissance** during the 1840s and 1850s. With the exceptions of Washington Irving (1783–1859) and James Fenimore Cooper (1789–1851), few American artists were known outside the United States before the 1830s; thereafter, however, writers increasingly responded to Ralph Waldo Emerson's (1803–82) call for a declaration of cultural independence from what he called the "courtly muse" of the old western European world. Henry David Thoreau (1817–62), Walt Whitman (1819–92), Nathaniel Hawthorne (1804–64), Herman Melville (1819–91), and others reflected the slow growth of independence in American letters. In short, the impact of republican institutions, the expansion of evangelical Protestantism, the gradual emergence of cultural independence, and rising participation in the market economy all helped to define American nationhood during the period from the establishment of the Constitution through the mid-19th century.

As in earlier periods, however, America remained divided along regional, cultural, and class lines. The westward movement of white settlers continued to remove Native Americans from the land; southerners expanded their dependence on slave labor with the rise of cotton culture in the Deep South; women remained disfranchised and subordinate to white men; growing numbers of Americans found themselves in the ranks of landless wage laborers; and, as Irish and German immigrants entered the country in growing numbers, significant ethnic and religious differences divided white Americans. Although the nation repeatedly worked out compromises (1820, 1850) and saved the nation, the increasing politicization of slavery, sectionalism, and class interests fractured the nation by the 1860s. The U.S. entered nearly five years of brutal military conflict. The Civil War and the era of Reconstruction that followed would liberate some 4 million slaves and define African Americans as part of the body politic, but it was only a partial victory. Region, class, and race would continue to undermine the democratic promise of America. Even as the North and South reunited through the medium of urban industrialization, the fall of Republican governments in the South, the rise of the coercive sharecropping system, and the emergence of white supremacist groups like the Ku Klux Klan reinforced earlier forms of inequality and opened new challenges to America's democratic institutions.

b. THE EARLY NATIONAL PERIOD

1789, March 4. First Congress met at New York.

April 30. WASHINGTON INAUGURATED AS PRESIDENT. Creation by Congress of three executive departments: state, war, and treasury. The **Judiciary Act** of 1789 provided for a system of federal district and circuit courts. The first ten amendments to the Constitution, the so-called **Bill of Rights,** were adopted by the Congress and sent to the states.

1789–90. The **Roman Catholic Church** was established in the new U.S. with the creation of the Diocese of Baltimore and the founding of **Georgetown College** (now Georgetown University) in 1789 and **St. Mary's Seminary** in 1791.

1790, Jan.–1791, Dec. Formulation of **Alexander Hamilton's** fiscal policies. These included the **Funding Bill,** authorizing the treasury to accept old securities at par in payment for new bonds, bearing interest; the **Assumption Bill,** providing for federal assumption of the debts of the states; the **Bank of the United States;** and an excise tax. In his *Report on Manufactures,* Hamilton argued cogently for tariff protection, but the tariff, first imposed in 1789, remained primarily a revenue measure.

1791–1814. Economic developments. In 1791 **Samuel Slater** and **Moses Brown** successfully applied power-driven machinery to the spinning of cotton yarn at **Pawtucket, R.I.** This is commonly considered the introduction of the factory system and the beginning of the Industrial Revolution in the United States. In **1793 Eli Whitney** introduced the **cotton gin,** which, by rendering profitable the cultivation of short-staple cotton in the uplands of the South, had a revolutionizing influence on the South and on the slavery problem.

1792. Political parties made their appearance, largely because of differences of opinion with respect to Hamilton's policies. **Thomas Jefferson,** who became the leader of the **Republican** (later the Democratic) **Party,** felt that Hamilton's policies were designed in the interest of financial and commercial groups and were inimical to the agrarian elements. **Hamilton** and **John Adams** became the leaders of the **Federalist Party.**

Washington and Adams were reelected. With the outbreak of war in Europe between Britain and France, the latter sent **Edmond Genet** as minister to the United States. His efforts to commit the United States to the support of France, even to the point of appealing from the president to the people, forced Washington to ask for his recall. Determined to maintain neutrality in spite of the efforts of Hamilton and Jefferson to influence him in favor of Britain and France respectively, Washington issued his proclamation of neutrality (April 22). The following year (1794) the **Neutrality Act** was passed.

Following defeats at the hands of Indians in the Northwest Territory, **Washington articulated a policy of "civilizing" the Indians,** urging them to adopt white notions of private property, education, and religion.

1794. Whiskey insurrection in western Pennsylvania resulted from opposition to the excise tax on domestic spirits; Washington used some 13,000 men to put down the rebellion of farmers, who had burned the home of the tax collector. The **Eleventh Amendment** closed the federal courts to suits instituted against a state by citizens of another state or citizens or subjects of a foreign state.

Nov. 19. Jay's Treaty was concluded. It provided for the evacuation of the border posts in 1796, permitted trade with the British East Indies, placed trade between the United States and Britain on a basis of "reciprocal and perfect liberty," and admitted American boats of not more than 70 tons' burden to the West Indies. Joint commissions were provided for settling the questions of debt and the northeast boundary. Claims on behalf of loyalists were dropped, balanced by claims for slaves carried away by the British armies. Claims arising from alleged illegal seizures of ships were referred to commissions. The Senate grudgingly ratified it, after striking out the clause with respect to West Indies.

1795, Oct. 27. Treaty of San Lorenzo, or **Pinckney's treaty.** Thomas Pinckney succeeded in negotiating a treaty establishing the southern boundary at the 31st parallel, giving to Americans the right to navigate the Mississippi to its mouth and granting them the *right of deposit* at New Orleans for three years.

1796, Sept. 18. Washington's farewell address.

1797, March 4. JOHN ADAMS became president, with Jefferson as vice president.

The conclusion of Jay's treaty with Britain involved the United States in **difficulties with France,** which regarded the treaty as evidence of a pro-British policy by the United States. The difficulties culminated in the attempt of the French Directory to extort money from the three American commissioners, Pinckney, Marshall, and Gerry, in the so-called **XYZ affair.** Fighting on the sea occurred, a navy department was created, Washington was named commander of the army, and until Sept. 30, 1800, a naval war was carried on. By the **Treaty of 1800,** the treaty of alliance of 1778 with France was abrogated.

1797–1801. Second Great Awakening. Beginning at about the same time in New England and Kentucky, a **new wave of revivals, emphasizing an intensely personal relationship to God,** disrupted established religious practices and helped to break down barriers along sex and color lines. **Baptists and Methodists** were especially receptive to the new wave of religious enthusiasm.

1798. Stung by the criticisms of its opponents (many of them French citizens), the Adams administration enacted a series of repressive measures against them: the **Naturalization Act,** extending the required time of the residence to fourteen years; the **Alien Act; the Alien Enemies Act; and the Sedition Act.** The last act especially represented an attempt to make a crime of political opposition. These acts led to the Kentucky and Virginia Resolutions.

1798–99. The Kentucky and **Virginia Resolutions,** penned by Jefferson and Madison respectively, in effect asserted that a state might nullify the force of an act of Congress within its confines, if it regarded such act as contrary to the Constitution. **These resolutions established grounds for states' rights advocates in subsequent Union crises.**

1798–1801. The first American novelist, Charles Brockden Brown (1771–1810) of Philadelphia, published six novels, but the best-known American writers of this period included **Washington Irving and James Fenimore Cooper.** The literature of the early national era showed many of the characteristics of the **romantic movement** in European literature. Independence from European cultural forms came only slowly.

1799. The Russian-American Fur Company was organized by the Russian government and given a trade monopoly for 20 years (later renewed). A most active period of Russian enterprise ensued under the governorship of **Alexander Baranov** (1790–1819).

1800. In the election, commonly referred to as the **revolution of 1800,** Adams was defeated, but, because Jefferson and Burr had the same number of votes, the election was decided by the House of Representatives, which decided in favor of Jefferson. The tie led to the movement culminating in the **Twelfth Amendment** (1804), which altered the method of electing the president and vice president by requiring that separate ballots be cast for each.

Gabriel Prosser's slave conspiracy. Nearly 1,000 slaves met outside

Lake
of the Woods

*Boundary
undetermined*

CANADA

St. Lawrence R.

L. Superior

Quebec

*In dispute
with
Great Britain*

Montreal

Mississippi R.

L. Michigan

L. Huron

*Claimed
by N.Y.
to
1790*

N.H.

MASSACHUSETTS

Boston

NORTH   WEST

L. Ontario

NEW
YORK

*Mass./N.Y.
claims
adjusted 1786*

CONN.

*Claimed by Virginia to 1784
and by Massachusetts to 1785*

Detroit

L. Erie

R.I.

*Claimed by Virginia to 1784
and by Connecticut to 1786*

WESTERN
RESERVE

*Claimed by
Connecticut to 1782*

N.J.

New York

TERRITORY
Organized 1787

Ohio R.

*Claimed
by
New York
to 1781*

PENNSYLVANIA

Philadelphia

L
O
U
I
S
I
A
N
A

Missouri R.

Claimed by Virginia to 1784

MARYLAND

Baltimore

DELAWARE

St. Louis

Washington

VIRGINIA

DISTRICT OF
KENTUCKY

Richmond

Norfolk

*Claimed by Virginia until
admitted as a state (1792)*

Arkansas R.

TERRITORY SOUTH
OF THE OHIO

NORTH CAROLINA

N. Carolina claims ceded (1790)

Red R.

S. Carolina claims ceded (1787)

*Claimed by Georgia until 1802
Added to MISSISSIPPI
TERRITORY (1804)*

SOUTH
CAROLINA

Wilmington

A t l a n t i c

Savannah R.

Charleston

O c e a n

*Claimed by Spain until 1795
Organized as MISSISSIPPI
TERRITORY (1798)*

Chattahoochee R.

GEORGIA

Savannah

WEST FLORIDA

New Orleans

EAST FLORIDA

St. Augustine

G u l f   o f   M e x i c o

BAHAMA ISLANDS

THE UNITED STATES
DURING THE
CONFEDERATION
PERIOD

CUBA

HISPANIOLA

(France)   (Spain)

0   100   200   300   400

MILES

JAMAICA

Richmond and planned to march on the city in an attempt to secure their freedom. The governor activated some 6,000 troops and put down the rebellion.

1801. John Marshall became chief justice of the Supreme Court.

March 4. **THOMAS JEFFERSON** was the first president to be inaugurated in Washington, D.C., the new capital.

1801–2. Repeal of the internal revenue taxes and of the Judiciary Act of the Adams administration.

1803. Ohio admitted as the 17th state, and the first state to be carved out of the Old Northwest. **It had been preceded into the Union by Vermont (1791), Kentucky (1792), and Tennessee (1796).** The planting of these settlements aroused the Indians to opposition. By the **Treaty of Greenville** (1795), the Indians ceded all but the northwest corner of Ohio, thereby paving the way for the increased settlement leading to the admission to statehood.

Marbury v. Madison became the case in which John Marshall established the principle of judicial review of acts of Congress by declaring a section of the Judiciary Act of 1789 unconstitutional.

April 30. **THE LOUISIANA PURCHASE.** In 1800 Spain had retroceded Louisiana to France. **The failure of Napoleon's army to reconquer Santo Domingo (Haiti), combined with the ominous turn of events in Europe, caused Napoleon to lose interest in a colonial empire in North America.** He therefore sold Louisiana to the United States for 80 million francs, thereby doubling the size of the country. **Louisiana included the area between the Mississippi and the Rocky Mountains, plus the island on which New Orleans stands.** The southern boundary of Louisiana was not finally settled until the Treaty of 1819.

1803–4. New England Federalists, believing the accession of Louisiana would so strengthen the agrarian states as to lead to a decline in New England influence, planned the formation of a **northeastern confederacy,** composed of New England and New York. To carry New York with them, they approached **Aaron Burr,** vice president, who was disgruntled with Jefferson, and proposed that he run for the governorship, with Federalist support. The opposition of Hamilton to this plan was followed by the **duel between Burr and Hamilton (July 11, 1804), in which Hamilton was killed.**

1804–6. Lewis and Clark expedition. Meriwether Lewis (1774–1809) **and William Clark** (1770–1838) were selected by Jefferson to explore the trans-Mississippi country. Leaving St. Louis, they ascended the Missouri to its source, crossed the headwaters of the Snake River, and proceeded down the Columbia River to the Pacific. **Capt. Robert Gray of Boston had earlier entered the mouth of the Columbia in 1792.** Explorations of Lewis and Clark gave the United States another claim to the "Oregon country."

1805. The Tripolitan War (p. 550), which had begun in 1801, brought to close by a treaty.

March 4. **Thomas Jefferson began his second term** as president, with George Clinton as vice president.

On Nov. 11, 1807, **a British order in council blockaded the coast from Copenhagen to Trieste** against neutrals unless they had first entered or cleared from a British port and paid duties there. In December Napoleon replied with his **Milan decree,** which declared that ships lost their neutral character if they obeyed the British order in council of Nov. 11, or if they submitted to search on the high seas by British officers.

1806. Noah Webster (1758–1843) **compiled the first American dictionary.**

1807. Robert Fulton (1765–1815) demonstrated the practicality of **steam-powered boats** and ushered in a new era of water transportation, particularly on western rivers.

June. The *Chesapeake-Leopard* affair. The American ship *Chesapeake* was fired on by the British ship *Leopard,* and four deserters were taken from her. Although Federalists and Republicans put aside their differences in the face of this national insult, Jefferson, opposed to war, merely ordered British ships of war to leave American waters and demanded reparation and the abandonment of impressment.

Dec. 22. **The Embargo Act.** Jefferson, still averse to war, resolved on commercial coercion as a means of forcing France and Britain to withdraw their restrictions on American trade. **The act forbade the departure of ships for foreign ports,** except foreign vessels in port at the time the act was passed. Coasting vessels were required to give bond to land

their cargoes at American ports. **Aaron Burr was tried for treason** and acquitted.

1808. African slave trade was prohibited after Jan. 1.

El Misisipi, **the nation's first Spanish-English newspaper,** was founded in New Orleans during the Napoleonic Wars.

1809, March 4–1817, March 4. JAMES MADISON (1751–1836), the fourth president.

1809, March 15. The **repeal of the Embargo Act** became effective. It had not brought Britain and France to terms, but had fallen with great weight upon American shipping. New England opposition to the policy was reflected in Federalist gains in the election of 1808.

May 20. The **Non-Intercourse Law** permitted commerce with all countries except France and Britain.

1810, May 1. Macon's Bill No. 2 repealed all restrictions on trade with the warring powers and provided that if either should remove its restrictions on American trade, the president should renew nonintercourse with the other. **Napoleon announced revocation of the Berlin and Milan decrees, effective on Nov. 1, whereupon Madison, on Nov. 2, proclaimed the renewal of nonintercourse with Britain within 90 days. Still, Napoleon continued to seize American ships.**

1810–11. Rise of the war party. The election of 1810 brought to power younger men, especially from the West, commonly known as the *War Hawks,* who were especially aroused by the opposition of the Indians, led by **Tecumseh,** to the advance of white settlement in the Northwest. In Nov. 1811 occurred the **Battle of Tippecanoe,** which made **William Henry Harrison** (1773–1841) a hero in the eyes of the frontiersmen. **More and more, the West became convinced that British aid and encouragement from Canada stiffened the Indian opposition.** The result was a growing demand for war with Britain and the conquest of Canada. Reading the lesson of the election of 1810, Madison adopted a firmer tone toward Britain.

1812, April. Ninety-day embargo to ensure that American ships would be safely in port when war with Britain began.

June 18. **War was declared on Britain,** on the grounds of impressment, violation of the three-mile limit, paper blockade, and orders in council.

1812–14. WAR OF 1812. In the naval warfare of the war's first year, the Americans were surprisingly successful—**the *Essex* captured the *Alert;* the *Constitution* captured the *Guerrière* and the *Java;* the *Wasp* captured the *Frolic;* and the *United States* took the *Macedonian.*** Later in the war, however, the American ships were captured one by one or bottled up. Except for the effect on the morale of the people, the victories on the high seas were without influence on the course of the war. For the operations in Canada, see p. 617. In 1814, the British captured and **burned Washington, D.C.,** but were repulsed at Baltimore (Sept. 13), whereupon they launched attacks on the Maine coast and on New Orleans. In the southwest, **Andrew Jackson** broke the military power of the Creek Indians and dismembered their territory (Aug. 9, 1814), whereupon he proceeded to New Orleans to defend it against the British attack. On Jan. 8, 1815, he won the **Battle of New Orleans.**

1814, Dec. 24. The **Treaty of Ghent** brought the war to a close. The treaty was silent on the questions that had been the chief cause of controversy before the war. It restored the status quo ante and provided for joint commissions to determine disputed boundary questions between the two countries.

Dec. **The Hartford Convention.** The New England states, disgruntled since the time of the embargo, formed a convention at Hartford to draw up proposed amendments to the Constitution, designed to safeguard more adequately New England interests.

Francis Cabot Lowell (1775–1817) **established the first major integrated textile mill,** at Waltham, Mass. Lowell and his associates later moved the mill to a site on the Merrimac River and built dormitories to house the workforce, primarily young women from rural New England.

1815. The emergence of "King Cotton" accelerated the westward movement of slaveholders and their human property. The movement west started around 1815 and culminated with the acquisition of Texas in 1845. In two generations more than 835,000 slaves had been moved from the southeast to the new southwest.

1816. The Second **Bank of the United States** was chartered. The **tariff of 1816** provided increased protection.

THE EXPANSION
OF THE
UNITED STATES

Present state
boundaries

MILES
0   100   200   300   400

CANADA

Limit of
British
claim

St. Lawrence R.

L. Ontario
L. Erie
L. Huron
L. Michigan
L. Superior

THE UNITED STATES
1783

ORIGINAL THIRTEEN STATES

Atlantic
Ocean

BAHAMA
ISLANDS
[British]

CUBA

St. Marys R.

FLORIDA
Purchased from Spain, 1819

Perdido R.

Claimed by Spain
to 1795

1810 1813

Ohio R.
Tennessee R.
Mississippi R.

Gulf of Mexico

Mississippi R.

Missouri R.

LOUISIANA PURCHASE
Purchased from France, 1803

Platte R.

N. Platte R.

S. Platte R.

Arkansas R.

Red R.

Sabine R.

REPUBLIC
OF
TEXAS
Annexed, 1845

Missouri R.

ROCKY MOUNTAINS

Area
claimed
by Texas
and ceded
by Mexico,
1848

Rio Grande

MEXICO

OREGON
COUNTRY
U.S. claim recognized
by Great Britain by
Treaty of 1846

Columbia R.
Snake R.

Colorado R.

CEDED BY MEXICO, 1848

Gila R.

Gadsen
Purchase,
1853

Pacific
Ocean

The **American Colonization Society** was organized for the purpose of colonizing free blacks in **Liberia**.

1817, March 4–1825, March 4. JAMES MONROE (1758–1831), the fifth president. An era of good feeling, in which party strife seemed about to disappear, was indicated by the reelection of Monroe in 1820 with but one dissenting electoral vote.

April 28. The **Rush-Bagot Agreement** between Great Britain and the United States limited naval forces on the Great Lakes.

1818, Oct. 20. A **convention between Great Britain and the United States** established the 49th parallel as the boundary between the Lake of the Woods and the Rocky Mountains. Unable to agree on a division of the Oregon country, north of the 42d parallel and west of the mountains, the convention provided for joint occupation for a period of ten years. This was renewed in 1827.

Fugitive slaves escaped to Florida, and raids against settlements in Georgia and Alabama led to trouble. In 1817–18, in the so-called **Seminole War,** Jackson invaded Florida and executed two British subjects. **John Quincy Adams** (1767–1848), secretary of state, demanded that Spain maintain order in Florida or cede it to the United States. Spain chose the latter because of inability to comply with the former demand. The United States agreed to pay an indemnity of $5 million to its citizens for their claims against Spain. The treaty also delimited the western boundary of the Louisiana Purchase and provided for Spain's relinquishment of all claims to territory on the Pacific north of the 42d parallel.

1819. Panic of 1819. The bottom fell out of the market for agricultural products, land, and slaves. Because many new planters and farmers had purchased land and slaves on credit, the West was especially hard hit.

1819–24. The nationalism of the postwar period was emphasized by a series of notable Supreme Court decisions by **Chief Justice John Marshall.** In *McCulloch* v. *Maryland* (1819), *Cohens* v. *Virginia* (1821), and *Gibbons* v. *Ogden* (1824), he gave judicial sanction to the doctrine of centralization of power at the expense of the states. In *Dartmouth College* v. *Woodward* (1819), as in the earlier case of *Fletcher* v. *Peck* (1810), the Court provided judicial barriers against democratic attacks upon property rights.

1820, March 3. The Missouri Compromise. Increasing feeling in the North against the spread of slavery resulted in strong opposition to the **admission of Missouri as a slave state.** The attempt to balance Missouri's admission as a slave state by admitting **Maine** as a free state having failed, a compromise was arranged whereby Missouri was to be admitted without restriction as to slavery; in all the remaining portions of the Louisiana Purchase north of 36° 30′, slavery was to be forever prohibited. **Maine** was admitted (1820) and **Missouri**, after careful scrutiny of its constitution by Congress, was finally admitted as a slave state (Aug. 10, 1821).

The **public land act of 1820** established the minimum price of public lands at $1.25 per acre.

1822. Denmark Vesey's slave insurrection in Charleston, S.C., was uncovered by authorities and defeated. Several thousand blacks were believed to be involved.

1823, Dec. 2. The **MONROE DOCTRINE** was enunciated by the president in his annual message to Congress. The message stated that "the American continents, by the free and independent condition which they have assumed and maintained, are henceforth not to be considered as subjects for future colonization by any European powers," and that European intervention in this hemisphere could not be viewed "in any other light than as the manifestation of an unfriendly disposition toward the United States." It also disclaimed any intention of the United States to take any part "in the wars of the European powers or in matters relating to themselves." By this time America's merchant fleet was the second largest in the world.

1824. Presidential election, in which none of the four candidates, J. Q. Adams, Jackson, Clay, and W. H. Crawford, obtained an electoral majority, although Jackson received a plurality. In the House of Representatives, Adams was elected president.

1825, March 4–1829, March 4. JOHN QUINCY ADAMS, sixth president.

1825. COMPLETION OF THE ERIE CANAL, begun in 1817. The canal made possible the opening of the West and ensured New York's primacy as a port.

1827. Begun in New York, *Freedom's Journal* became the nation's first African-American newspaper.

1828, May 19. The "**tariff of abominations**" (an excessively high tariff) was framed by Jackson men to discredit J. Q. Adams and bring about the election of Jackson. To their surprise it passed Congress, was signed by Adams, and promptly aroused strong opposition, especially in South Carolina, where **John C. Calhoun** (1782–1850) penned his *South Carolina Exposition* (1828), which gave the classic statement of the nullification doctrine.

The **American Peace Society** was founded in New York by **William Ladd. Elihu Burritt** (1810–79) became the chief leader of the American peace movement.

July 4. The **Baltimore and Ohio Railroad was begun,** the first public railroad in the United States.

Cherokee Phoenix, **the nation's first Native-American newspaper,** was established by the **Cherokee Nation** near Calhoun, Ga.

1829, March 4–1837, March 4. ANDREW JACKSON (1767–1845), who defeated Adams in the election of 1828, became the seventh president. The election of Jackson was a triumph of the frontier democracy of the West.

The **spoils system,** the practice of basing appointments on party service, was nationalized by Jackson. The system was already well established in certain states of the North and the West.

1829–50. Rise of the common man and era of reform. By 1829 the principle of **white male suffrage** was established in most states. Opposition to reform was strongest in Rhode Island.

1829. The Workingmen's Party was organized in New York, following the example set in Philadelphia the preceding year. The movement spread to other seaboard states in the North. The program of the movement included social reform, free public schools, banking legislation, and abolition of imprisonment for debt.

The self-educated New York City machinist **Thomas Skidmore** published his *The Right of Man to Property*, which urged workers to gain control over the government and redistribute the wealth on an equal basis.

The free black **David Walker** (1785–1830) of Boston issued his *Appeal to the Colored Citizens of the World*, which exhorted blacks to rise up against slavery at home and abroad.

1830s. Anthracite coal fields were opened in eastern Pennsylvania and stimulated the iron and railroad industries as well as a variety of machine tool industries. By 1860, over 30,600 miles of railroad track traversed the country, nearly equally divided among the Northeast, the South, and the Midwest.

Growing importance of **women writers,** producing realistic fiction, advice manuals, and reform literature.

1830. Organization of the **Mormon Church** at Fayette, N.Y., by **Joseph Smith.** *The Book of Mormon* was first printed.

Revivalists like **Charles Grandison Finney** continued activities known as the **Second Great Awakening.**

Great debate between **Daniel Webster and Robert Hayne** on the nature of the Union. The debate was really begun by Thomas Benton, who protested against New England's attempts to limit the sale of western lands.

Jackson's veto of the **Maysville Road Bill.**

Congress passed the Indian Removal Act, designed to move Native Americans farther west across the Mississippi to make room for migrating white settlers.

1830–34. Controversy arose between Georgia and the Cherokee Indians and led to development of Jackson's **Indian policy.** An act of March 10, 1830, authorized the president to locate on lands west of the Mississippi all Indians who surrendered their holdings east of the river. **The act led to the creation of an area west of Arkansas as the final home for the southern Indians. A commission of Indian affairs was created.**

1831–33. William Lloyd Garrison (1805–79) established the *Liberator* (1831) at Boston to advocate unconditional emancipation of the slaves, marking the beginning of the abolitionist movement. The **New England Anti-Slavery Society** (1832) and the **American Anti-Slavery Society** (1833) were founded. **Oberlin College** opened its doors to Negroes as well as to women (1833).

1831. Nat Turner's Rebellion. Under the leadership of **Nat Turner,** slaves of Southampton, Va., rebelled, killing 60 whites before the militia put the revolt down.

1832. The Sauk and Fox Indians were massacred, when under the leadership of Black Hawk they tried to return to their homes in northwestern Illinois.

July. The Tariff Act of 1832, an improvement over the "tariff of abominations," retained the protective principle that was unsatisfactory to South Carolina and led to the nullification episode.

1832–33. In the **nullification episode,** a South Carolina state convention declared the tariff laws of 1828 and 1832 unconstitutional and void within the state. Jackson repudiated the nullifiers and on Jan. 16, 1833, he asked Congress for additional power to enforce the tariff law. On March 1, 1833, Congress enacted the **Force Bill.** Meanwhile **Henry Clay** had brought forward (Feb. 12, 1833) his compromise tariff, providing for gradual reduction of the tariff until July 1, 1842, when it would reach the 20 percent level.

The bank controversy. Jackson construed his election over Clay as popular approval of his veto of the Bank Bill, and he resolved to crush the institution. In 1833 the **removal of the deposits** began, which entailed the transfer of government funds to certain state banks known as the pet banks.

1833. The **General Trades' Union** linked all the trade societies of New York in one organization. Trade unionism began to supersede the workingmen's parties as the characteristic form of labor activity, until the collapse of the movement in the panic of 1837.

Invented by **Cyrus McCormick** (1809–84) **and Obed Hussey** (1792–1860), **wheat reapers** allowed farmers to harvest 10 to 12 acres per day. At the same time, McCormick's farm implements factories would change the lives of numerous urban workers in cities like Chicago.

1833–37. The **Whig Party** attracted southern particularists who were angered by Jackson's handling of the nullification episode, those who feared the leveling tendencies of Jacksonian democracy, the supporters of the bank, and the industrial and financial groups. It was largely held together by a common hatred for and distrust of Jackson.

1836. Texan independence. The American colonization of Texas had begun in 1821 when **Stephen Austin** (1793–1836) obtained a grant of land on condition that he settle a certain number of families thereon. This was followed by similar grants to other *empresarios* who introduced a substantial number of American settlers. This movement, largely of southerners, was part of the westward movement of the American people. Beginning in about 1830 difficulties developed. In 1836 the **Republic of Texas** was established. The decisive battle was that of **San Jacinto** (April 21, 1836).

1837, March 4–1841, March 4. MARTIN VAN BUREN (1782–1862), eighth president.

1837. Panic of 1837. Fundamentally, this crash was due to the wave of speculation and reckless expansion that swept the country in the years 1833–37. The situation was complicated by the failure of certain great business houses in Britain that had invested heavily in American securities, by poor crops in the West in 1835 and 1837, and by Jackson's **Special Circular** (July 11, 1836), which required that public lands be paid for in "hard" money.

In the face of **declining employment and rising wheat prices,** hungry workers broke into warehouses in New York City and Philadelphia.

John Deere (1804–86) invented the **steel plow,** which would help transform farming in the West by facilitating the breaking of prairie sod.

Mount Holyoke Seminary, first women's institution of college rank, was opened by **Mary Lyon** (1797–1849).

1837–40. Struggle between Van Buren and the Whigs over the **independent treasury** proposed by Van Buren for the deposit of government funds. The Whig leaders favored the establishment of a third United States Bank. Independent treasury plan adopted (1840).

1837–42. Difficulties between the United States and Canada. Alexander McLeod, a Canadian, boasting that he had killed an American, was arrested and tried in New York courts. His acquittal averted the possibility of serious difficulties between the United States and Great Britain.

Difficulty over the northeastern boundary was finally adjusted in the **Webster-Ashburton Treaty** (Aug. 9, 1842).

1838. The **Underground Railroad** was organized. The fugitive slave **Harriet Tubman** (c. 1820–1913) became the most outstanding black conductor on the Underground Railroad. **She returned to the South 19 times and liberated more than 300 slaves.**

One quarter of the **Cherokee Nation** died when the U.S. Army marched them to Indian Territory in what is now the state of Oklahoma.

1838–39. Congress adopted gag resolutions against antislavery petitions.

1840. Samuel F. B. Morse (1791–1872) invented the electric telegraph. By 1860, some 50,000 miles of telegraph wire linked various parts of the country.

1841, March 4–1845, March 4. WILLIAM HENRY HARRISON and **JOHN TYLER** (1790–1862), the ninth and tenth presidents. Harrison died on April 4, 1841.

The Pre-emption–Distribution Act struck a compromise between the **preemption** of public lands and the **distribution of proceeds** from the sale of public lands among the various states.

1842. The **Dorr rebellion** in Rhode Island was occasioned by refusal of conservatives to liberalize the suffrage and to reform representation. It swept away the Charter of 1663, which had served as the constitution of the state of Rhode Island from 1776 to 1842.

1844, April 12. Calhoun's treaty for the annexation of Texas was signed but was defeated in the Senate on June 8.

Presidential campaign. The Democrats nominated **James K. Polk** (1795–1849) on the platform declaring for reannexation of Texas and the reoccupation of Oregon. The Whigs nominated **Henry Clay** (1777–1852). The Liberty Party nominated **James G. Birney** (1792–1857) and took enough popular votes from Clay to enable Polk to carry New York and win the election.

1845, March 1. Tyler brought about the **annexation of Texas** by joint resolution of Congress (p. 637). **John O'Sullivan,** editor of the ***Democratic Review*** and the *New York Morning News,* helped to popularize the term "manifest destiny" to capture the vision of an American empire stretching from the Atlantic to the Pacific. Landscape artists like **Thomas Cole (1801–48)** and Asher B. Durand (1796–1886) inspired the so-called **Hudson River School and Rocky Mountain Painters,** who soon reflected this expansive vision.

March 4–1849, March 4. JAMES K. POLK, 11th president.

The black abolitionist **Frederick Douglass** (1817–95) published his autobiography, ***The Narrative of the Life of Frederick Douglass.*** Two years later he launched the ***North Star*** and broke with the white abolitionist **William Lloyd Garrison.**

1846–48. WAR WITH MEXICO (p. 637). By sending American troops into the disputed area between the Rio Nueces and the Rio Grande, **President Polk** instigated a skirmish that enabled him to say that Mexico had "**shed American blood on American soil.**" An army under Gen. Zachary Taylor (1784–1850) invaded Mexico and won the **Battles of Palo Alto** and **Resaca de la Palma** (May 8 and 9), took **Monterey** (May 24), and won a victory at **Buena Vista** (Feb. 22 and 23, 1847). Col. S. W. Kearny occupied **Santa Fe** (Aug. 18, 1846). Marching inland from Veracruz, **Winfield Scott** (1786–1866) fought the Battles of **Cerro Gordo** (April 17 and 18, 1847), **Churubusco** (Aug. 20), and **Chapultepec** (Sept. 12 and 13), and captured **Mexico City** (Sept. 14). On the Pacific an American squadron seized the California ports.

1846, June 15. Oregon Treaty with Great Britain. By the early 1840s a substantial migration of American farmers to the Willamette Valley was under way, so the Anglo-American rivalry became one of fur trader versus settler. The treaty established the 49th parallel as the boundary on the mainland, and then extending from the middle of the channel to the ocean.

Aug. 8. The **Wilmot Proviso** provided that in any territory acquired from Mexico, slavery should be excluded. Although it never passed in the Senate, it raised the slavery issue and aroused the fears of the South.

Invention of the sewing machine reduced the labor requirements for garment making, but also led to lower wages for the labor force, mostly women who worked at home as "outworkers." When outworkers are included in the number of workers in manufacturing, women made up about 50 percent of the labor force.

1848, Jan. 24. Discovery of gold at Coloma, 60 miles east of Sutter's Fort,

Calif., began the great gold rush. California's population increased from 6,000 to over 85,000 during the next two years.

Feb. 2. The **Treaty of Guadalupe Hidalgo** closed the war with Mexico. Mexico gave up claims to Texas, recognized the Rio Grande as the boundary, and ceded New Mexico and California to the United States in return for $15 million and the assumption of American claims against Mexico.

July 19. The **first women's rights convention** in world history was held at Seneca Falls, N.Y. The women issued a "Declaration of Sentiments," declaring that "all men and women were created equal." They also listed grievances against a male-dominated social order. The movement had started with the visit of Scottish activist **Frances Wright** to America in 1827. Her example moved to action **Sarah** (1792–1873) and **Angelina** (1805–79) **Grimké, Lucretia Mott** (1793–1880), and **Elizabeth Cady Stanton** (1815–1902).

Presidential campaign. The Whig candidate was **Zachary Taylor,** hero of the recent war. The Democrats nominated **Lewis Cass,** who had recently proposed squatter sovereignty as a solution of the problem of slavery in the territories, raised by the Wilmot Proviso. **The Free Soil Party,** favoring homesteading and the exclusion of slavery from the territories, nominated **Van Buren,** who, by splitting the Democratic vote in New York, enabled Taylor to carry the state and win the election.

1849, March 4–1853, March 4. ZACHARY TAYLOR and **MILLARD FILLMORE** (1800–74), 12th and 13th presidents. Taylor died on July 9, 1850.

1850. THE COMPROMISE OF 1850. On Jan. 29, 1850, Clay introduced his compromise resolutions providing that California should be admitted as a free state; that territorial governments should be established in the remainder of the Mexican cession without any action by Congress with respect to slavery; that Texas should yield its claims in the boundary dispute with New Mexico, in return for which the United States would assume the Texan debt; that the slave trade should be abolished in the District of Columbia; and that Congress should enact a more drastic fugitive slave law. **Great debate** in which Calhoun spoke (March 4) against the compromise; Webster (March 7) for the compromise; Douglas for, and Jefferson Davis, Seward, and Chase against. On April 18, the resolutions were referred to a Senate committee of 13, with Clay as chairman. Between Sept. 9 and 20, the separate measures, known collectively as the **Compromise of 1850,** were passed: California was to be admitted as a free state; the remainder of the Mexican cession was to be divided at the 37th parallel into the territories of New Mexico and Utah, to be admitted to the Union ultimately as states, with or without slavery as their constitutions might provide at the time of admission; the claims of Texas to a portion of New Mexico were to be satisfied by payment of $10 million; the slave trade in the District of Columbia was to be abolished; and a more effective fugitive slave law was to be enacted.

Land grants to railways were permitted by Congress. A grant was made to the state of Illinois to help the **Illinois Central Railroad** and another to Mississippi and Alabama in support of the **Mobile and Ohio** line.

1851. The Maine prohibition law was sponsored by Neal Dow. It became the model for all similar legislation of the period restricting the sale of alcoholic liquors.

June 2. The **Erie Railroad** reached Dunkirk on Lake Erie, being the first railway to make connection with the Lakes.

The ex-slave **Sojourner Truth** (c. 1797–1883) delivered her famous **"And Ar'n't I a Woman"** speech at a women's rights convention in Akron, Ohio.

The *Golden Hill's News,* believed to be the first **Asian-American newspaper,** was first published.

1852. The Democratic Party, committed to the **Compromise of 1850** as a solution of the problem of slavery in the territories, fielded Franklin Pierce as presidential candidate.

1853, March 4–1857, March 4. FRANKLIN PIERCE (1804–69), 14th president.

1853. Rail connection established between New York City and Chicago. By 1860 the region north of the Ohio River and east of the Mississippi had been firmly attached commercially to the North Atlantic seaboard. The movement of internal trade, originally north and south

along the Mississippi, now became predominantly a west-east movement, the shift proving of great economic and political significance.

Dec. 30. The **Gadsden purchase** rounded out U.S. possessions in the Far West.

1854–55. The so-called **Know-Nothing Party** emerged. It protested the Kansas-Nebraska Act and appealed to growing anti-Catholic, anti-Irish, and antiimmigrant sentiment in the wake of the massive Irish immigration into the country. Nearly 1.5 million Irish had entered the U.S. by 1860. The **Republican Party** also appeared at this time.

1854. Henry David Thoreau published *Walden, or Life in the Woods,* which followed the lead of the transcendentalist Ralph Waldo Emerson's call for a literary declaration of independence from European cultural forms. The poet **Walt Whitman** and the novelists **Nathaniel Hawthorne and Herman Melville** also responded to Emerson's call. However, the best-known novel of the era was **Harriet Beecher Stowe's** (1811–96) *Uncle Tom's Cabin* (1852), a forceful piece of abolitionist literature. Other women writers of the period included **Sara Parton, Augusta Evans Wilson, and Susan Warner.** In music, songs by **Stephen Foster (1826–64)** were among the first truly American compositions.

March 31. Commodore Matthew Perry (1794–1858) negotiated a **treaty with Japan,** opening the country to commercial interaction with the United States.

May 30. The **KANSAS-NEBRASKA ACT,** which repealed the Missouri Compromise of 1820, opened the Nebraska country to settlement on the basis of **popular sovereignty,** and provided for the organization of two territories, Kansas and Nebraska. The act undid the sectional truce of 1850 and proved to be the deathblow to the Whig Party.

Oct. 18. The **Ostend Manifesto.** The American ministers to Britain, France, and Spain, instructed to confer on the best means of acquiring **Cuba,** met at Ostend and drew up the manifesto saying that if Spain refused to sell Cuba, the United States would be justified in taking it by force. This caused great excitement in the free states.

1854–58. War for "Bleeding Kansas." The opening of Kansas to settlement under the Douglas doctrine of popular sovereignty precipitated a mad scramble for control between proslavery and free-soil elements. In April 1854 the **New England Emigrant Aid Society** was formed to colonize free-soilers in Kansas. This aroused the proslavery people. **Border ruffians** from Missouri interfered in elections in Kansas. A proslavery element attacked the town of Lawrence, and in return **John Brown** (1800–59) staged the massacre at Pottawatomie Creek (May 24, 1856). The **Lecompton constitution** was formed by proslavery forces, but was denounced by Douglas as a fraud upon the people of Kansas and a violation of the popular sovereignty doctrine. This led to a break between Douglas and James Buchanan. The Senate accepted the Lecompton constitution, but the House rejected it. The deadlock was broken by the **English Bill,** enacted on May 4, 1858, providing for resubmission of the constitution to popular vote in Kansas. If accepted, the state would receive a grant of land; if rejected, statehood must await further growth of population. It was rejected, and Kansas did not become a state until Jan. 1861.

1855. Opening of **Soo Canal** between Lakes **Superior** and **Huron** provided cheap transportation of iron ore and laid the basis for rapid development of the steel industry.

1857, March 4–1861, March 4. JAMES BUCHANAN (1791–1868), 15th president.

1857, March 7. The *Dred Scott* decision declared that the Missouri Compromise was unconstitutional because Congress had no right to enact a law that deprived persons of their property in the territories of the United States. Dred Scott, therefore, had not acquired his freedom by being taken into a territory where slavery had been prohibited by the compromise. The decision caused bitter criticism of the court in the North.

Panic of 1857 followed a period of overexpansion and speculation. The economic downturn was especially hard on poor and working-class families. By 1860, 5 percent of all families owned 50 percent of the nation's wealth.

Aug. Lincoln-Douglas debates, seven in number, were part of the campaign for election to the Senate. Stephen Douglas (1813–61) was elected, but Abraham Lincoln (1809–65), by asking Douglas to reconcile his doctrine of popular sovereignty with the *Dred Scott* decision, forced him to enunciate his **Freeport heresy,** which was deeply distasteful to the southern wing of the party.

1859, Oct. 19. **John Brown's raid on Harper's Ferry** further aroused sectional passions.

1860. The **Davis resolutions,** introduced by Jefferson Davis (1808–89) demanded a federal slave code for the protection of property in slaves in the territories.

Presidential campaign. The Republicans nominated **Abraham Lincoln** on a platform opposing further extension of slavery in the territories and supporting homestead and tariff. The Democrats split at Charleston on the question of slavery in the territories. Two platforms were drawn up, one demanding a federal slave code, the other endorsing the Freeport doctrine of Douglas. Subsequently the northern Democrats nominated **Douglas,** while the sourthern Democrats named **John C. Breckinridge.** The Union Party nominated **John Bell.** Lincoln was elected, in a purely sectional contest. He received no electoral support in the slave states.

Dec. 20. South Carolina adopted the **ordinance of secession,** as a protest against the election of Lincoln.

Dec.–1861, Feb. 4. **Futile efforts were made to save the Union:** the **Crittenden compromise resolutions,** proposing the extension of the Missouri Compromise line to the Pacific; conference of governors of northern states; the **peace convention** at Washington, Feb. 4, 1861.

1861, Jan.–May. Mississippi, Florida, Alabama, Georgia, Louisiana, Texas, Virginia, Arkansas, Tennessee, and North Carolina seceded from the Union.

Jan. 9. The ship *Star of the West* was fired upon by a battery at Charleston.

Feb. 4. Delegates of the seven seceding states met at Montgomery, Ala., and formed a provisional government, taking the name **Confederate States of America.**

Feb. 8. Jefferson Davis was elected president and **Alexander H. Stephens** vice president of the Confederacy.

March 4–1865, April 15. ABRAHAM LINCOLN, 16th president.

c. THE CIVIL WAR

1861, March. The **Morrill tariff** marked the beginning of successive tariff increases, which by 1864 reached duties of 47 percent.

MILITARY EVENTS. The Confederates, having seized Federal funds and property in the South, bombarded **Fort Sumter** on April 12–13, just as a relief expedition of the Federalists approached.

March 13. Great Britain recognized the Confederate states as belligerents.

April 15. Lincoln called for 75,000 volunteers to serve for three months and summoned Congress to meet on July 4. On May 3 he appealed for 42,000 men to serve for three years or for the duration of the war. General expectancy of a short conflict. **The North had immense advantages:** 23 states with a population of almost 23 million against 11 states with a white population of 5 million; the North possessed financial strength, manufacturing facilities, and extensive railway communications. The South was largely dependent on cotton growing and badly hampered by the blockade of the Confederate ports (proclaimed on April 19); from the beginning the South was on the defensive. **However, the South was not without some advantages:** Confederate soldiers were fighting on home terrain, slave labor freed a larger proportion of men to fight, and the martial tradition of the slaveholding class gave the South a military edge.

Within the first two weeks of war, women spearheaded the establishment of nearly 20,000 organizations to help supply troops with clothing, food, medicine, and spiritual support. Northern women eventually coordinated their efforts through a central body, the **Sanitary Commission.** Superintendent of nurses for the Union army, **Dorothea Dix** (1802–87) assured officials that she would recruit only women over age 30 and "plain in appearance."

May 23. Gen. Benjamin Butler declared as contraband three slaves who escaped to his lines in Virginia and refused to return them to their master. By Aug., 1,000 contrabands had joined Butler's camp.

July 21. FIRST BATTLE OF BULL RUN. By July there were some 30,000 troops in and around Washington, under command of Gen.

Winfield Scott. At Bull Run the federal army was routed. The effect of the battle was to open the eyes of the federalists and to introduce a period of more extensive and systematic preparation.

Aug. Lincoln signed the **First Confiscation Act,** authorizing the seizure of all property, including slaves, used to support the Confederacy. Also in August, an income tax of 3 percent was levied on all income in excess of $800.

Nov. 1. Gen. **George B. McClellan** (1826–85) was appointed to succeed Scott in command of the federal forces. McClellan's policy was one of cautious, careful preparation and reliance on numbers. He spent the winter training some 200,000 men (the Army of the Potomac) for a march on the Confederate capital, Richmond.

1861–62. NAVAL OPERATIONS. To make the blockade of the southern coasts effective and to prevent privateering, a joint naval and military expedition was sent out in Aug. 1861 to take key positions on the coast.

1862, March 8. The Confederate frigate *Merrimac,* made over as an ironclad, appeared in Hampton Roads and sank the *Cumberland.*

March 9. The federal ironclad *Monitor* (with revolving gun turret) engaged the *Merrimac* and finally forced it to withdraw. Epoch-making development in naval warfare.

March 14. The **capture of New Bern, N.C.,** gave the federal forces a base from which to threaten Richmond, and obliged the Confederates to keep an army near the capital.

April 24–25. A federal force (27 ships and 15,000 troops), under command of Flag Officer (later Adm.) **David G. Farragut** and Gen. **Benjamin F. Butler,** ran the forts below New Orleans and bombarded the city. After the landing of troops, the city was taken (May 1).

April. Congress abolished slavery in the District of Columbia.

The **Homestead Act (1862)** played a prominent part in the settlement of the West and the removal of Native Americans from land east and west of the Mississippi River. It gave to heads of families or individuals age 21 or older title to 160 acres of public land contingent upon 5 years of residence and improvement.

July. The first comprehensive internal revenue act was born of the war. Congress passed the **Second Confiscation Act,** which declared "forever free" all captured and fugitive slaves of the rebels. This bill also authorized the president to use African Americans in the military.

The **Union and Central Pacific Railways** were chartered by Congress and given a large grant of land. They formed the **first transcontinental railway (completed on May 10, 1869).** One result of the new system of transportation was the often violent clashes between Native Americans and white settlers.

The **Morrill Act (1862),** providing for grants of land to states in order to aid the **establishment of agricultural colleges,** opened up more Native American areas for white settlement. In the same year, **Sioux Indians of Minnesota** were defeated by Gen. Henry Sibley at Wood Lake.

THE PENINSULA CAMPAIGN. After long delay, McClellan decided to advance on Richmond, not overland through territory cut by many rivers, but by water to the mouth of the James River. The advance began in April. The Confederates, under Johnston and **Robert E. Lee** (1807–70; Confederate commander in chief after June 1, 1862) were greatly outnumbered and fell back. They were saved in part by McClellan's vacillation and by the operations of **Col. T. J. ("Stonewall") Jackson** (1824–63), who managed to draw a considerable federal force into the Shenandoah Valley and ultimately succeeded in joining Lee with substantial reinforcements. Heavy fighting around Richmond resulted in the withdrawal of the federal forces from the peninsula.

Campaign in Maryland. In the autumn of 1862 Lee began to push on toward Washington. **Federal forces were defeated** in the Second Battle of Bull Run (Aug. 30) and invaded Maryland. The Confederates crossed the Potomac (Sept. 4) and invaded Maryland.

Sept. 17. THE BATTLE OF ANTIETAM was indecisive, but Lee began to fall back into Virginia. **McClellan, as usual, did not take advantage of his opportunities,** did little to pursue him, and did not cross the Potomac until Oct. 26. **Sept. 17 proved to be the single most bloody day in American military history. Total deaths, either during the battle or as a result of it, reached 7,800, with another 15,500 wounded.**

Sept. 22. The president issued a **preliminary emancipation proclamation,** declaring that all slaves in states or parts of states still in rebellion on **Jan. 1, 1863,** should be free, starting on that date. Though

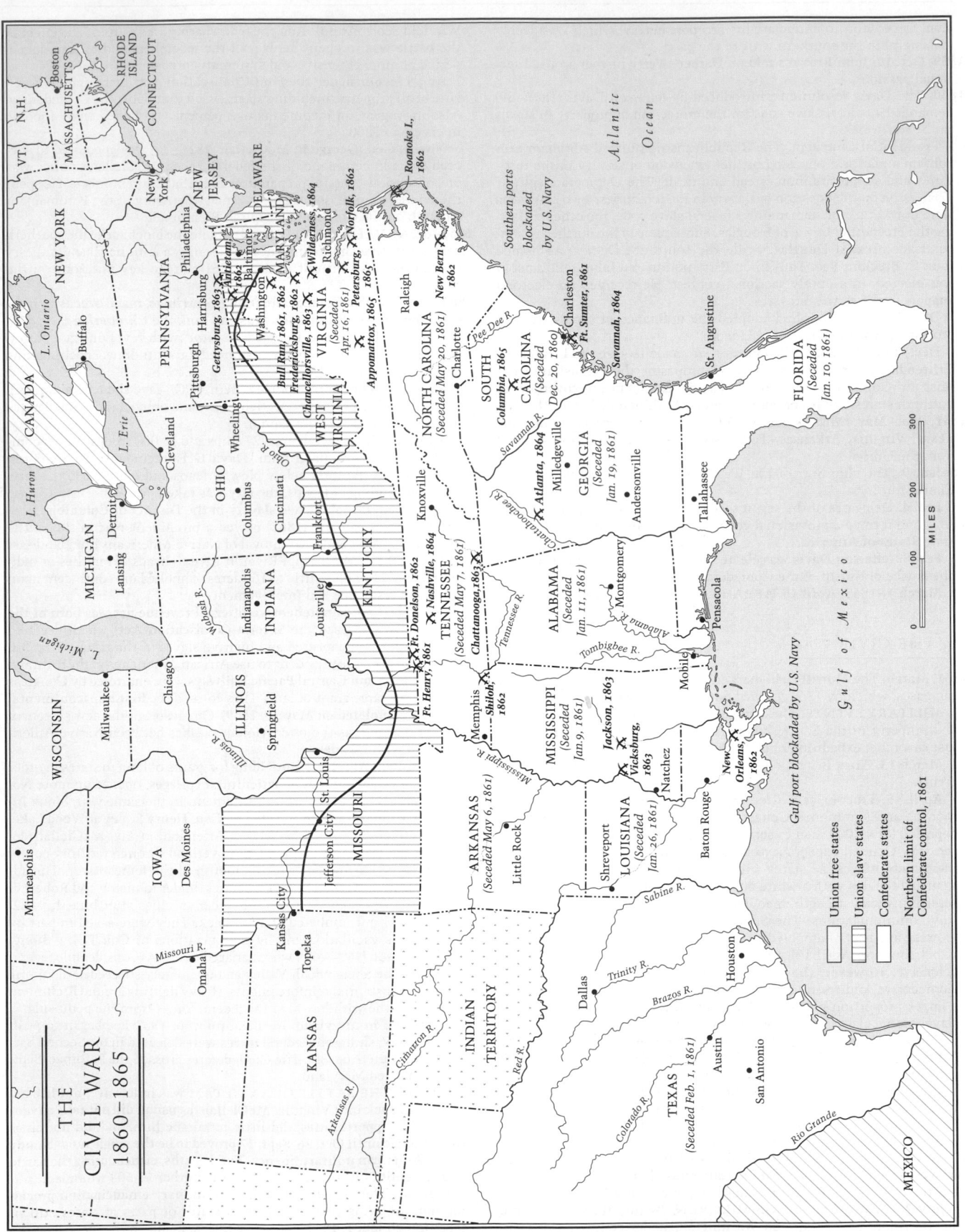

Lincoln decided to free the slaves that summer, he waited for a Union victory before announcing the decision so that the new policy would be taken as a sign of strength rather than one of weakness. **The formal Emancipation Proclamation was issued on Jan. 1, 1863.**

Nov. 7. Gen. **Ambrose E. Burnside** (1824–81) was appointed to succeed McClellan. He pushed the advance in Virginia, but was badly defeated by Lee in the **Battle of Fredericksburg** (Dec. 13). On Jan. 25, 1863, he was succeeded by Gen. **Joseph Hooker** (1814–79).

CAMPAIGNS IN THE WEST. In western Kentucky and Tennessee there was active campaigning throughout the year 1862. Brig. Gen. **Ulysses S. Grant** (1822–85), serving under Gen. **Henry W. Halleck** in command of the federal troops, on Feb. 6 forced the **surrender of Fort Henry** on the Tennessee River, and on Feb. 16 he secured the **surrender of Fort Donelson** on the Cumberland.

April 6–7. Battle of Shiloh. The Confederates, under Gen. **Albert S. Johnston,** attacked Grant's lines at **Pittsburg Landing.** After an initial success the Confederates were driven back. The federal forces commanded the Mississippi as far south as Vicksburg. More than 20,000 soldiers were killed or wounded, making this the bloodiest battle thus far in the war. Also in April the **Confederate Congress introduced the draft.** Some Southerners felt the measure was contrary to the South's notion of state's rights. **The law allowed men to hire a substitute to fight for them, and it exempted from service men who had 20 or more slaves.** Widespread opposition to the draft grew. At the same time many planters volunteered their slaves for service without wages, whereas others hired them out to military officials.

1863. Congress approved creation of the **National Academy of Sciences** to advise the government on science and to promote research.

Feb. 25. National Banking Act was passed to create a market for U.S. bonds, to drive out of circulation the notes of banks chartered by the states, to create a powerful financial support for the government, and to provide for the country a uniform circulating medium. State bank notes were driven out of existence by a tax of 10 percent (1865).

The March Conscription Act created an impartial draft lottery for the North, but also allowed individuals to pay $300 in place of serving. The bill caused enormous anger among the poor, who rioted in cities across the country. **In New York City, implementation of the draft sparked a three-day riot** in which poor whites and immigrant workers attacked the black community and lynched at least a dozen African Americans. In the South, discontent with the government also became apparent in 1863, when the Confederate Congress introduced impressment, allowing the Confederate army to take supplies and animals from farmers while paying a fixed price that was far below market value.

EASTERN CAMPAIGNS.

May 1–4. BATTLE OF CHANCELLORSVILLE. The federal forces were defeated by the Confederates (death of Stonewall Jackson). Gen. **George G. Meade** (1815–72) relieved Hooker as commander of the Army of the Potomac (June 28). Meanwhile Lee had begun the invasion of the North by way of the Shenandoah Valley, establishing himself in southern Pennsylvania. Meade took up his position at Gettysburg.

June 20. West Virginia (the loyal part of Virginia) was admitted to the Union as the 35th state.

July 1–3. BATTLE OF GETTYSBURG. In three days of heavy fighting, Lee was unable to dislodge the federal forces and was obliged to fall back to the Potomac in the decisive battle of the war. Henceforth the Confederates were obliged to remain on the defensive, and the war became a test of endurance. **More soldiers died in this Civil War battle than in any other. More than 50,000 men were killed or wounded.**

WESTERN CAMPAIGNS. The operations in the west centered first on the taking of **Vicksburg,** key to the control of the Mississippi.

July 4. VICKSBURG SURRENDERED, starved out after a short siege. On July 8, **Port Hudson,** farther down the river, surrendered, giving the federal troops command of the entire river and cutting off Texas, Arkansas, and Louisiana from the rest of the Confederacy.

Nov. 23–25. BATTLE OF CHATTANOOGA (Lookout Mountain, Nov. 24; **Missionary Ridge,** Nov. 25). Reinforced by troops from Vicksburg under Gen. **William T. Sherman** (1820–91) and from the Potomac under Hooker, Grant, in command of the armies of the West, fought and drove the Confederates out of Tennessee, opening the road into Georgia.

1863. **Women garment workers** filed hundreds of petitions urging the president and Congress to end the system of subcontracting, which allowed firms with government contracts to hire women in their homes at exceedingly low pay.

In the South women participated in bread riots to protest food shortages that emerged during the war. **Northern women not only participated in bread riots but in antidraft riots as well.** By 1865, Northern women had also formed the **Women's Loyal League** and petitioned Congress to enact a Thirteenth Amendment abolishing slavery.

1864, March 9. **Grant** was made lieutenant general and commander in chief of all the armies; **Sherman** was given command in the West. Grant's plan was to defeat Lee's army. He crossed the Rapidan (May 3) and began the advance from near Chancellorsville through the Wilderness.

May 5–6. BATTLE OF THE WILDERNESS. After a series of reverses, Union forces drove the Confederates from the Shenandoah Valley (**Battle of Cedar Creek,** Oct. 19). Sheridan laid the whole region waste and then rejoined Grant at Petersburg.

The **Cheyennes** resisted the increasing encroachment of white settlers on their land with the aid of the **Arapahoe, Apache, Comanche, and Kiowa.** Troops under **Col. John Chivington** staged a massacre of Indians at Sand Creek, Colo. (Nov. 1864). A commission authorized by Congress persuaded the Apache, Comanche, and Kiowa to relocate in Indian Territory and secured the removal of other groups from the Great Plains to more remote regions.

SHERMAN'S CAMPAIGN. Sherman started from Chattanooga (May 5) with about 100,000 men to march through Georgia to Atlanta. He was opposed by one of the ablest Confederate commanders, Gen. **Joseph E. Johnston,** with 65,000 men. Johnston did what he could to impede Sherman's advance, but wisely refused a general battle. Sherman, however, crossed the Chattahoochee River (July 17), as a result of which Johnston was removed from his command. His successor, Gen. **John B. Hood,** offered battle, but was defeated (**Battle of Atlanta,** July 22).

Sept. 2. Evacuation of Atlanta by the Confederates. Sherman destroyed the factories and stores and urged upon Grant his plan of a march to the sea. Part of the army, under Thomas, was sent north to watch Hood, who was defeated before **Nashville** (Dec. 15–16). Sherman himself, with 60,000 men, started for the southeast (Nov. 16), ravaging the country as he proceeded. He reached the sea (Dec. 12), and the Confederates abandoned **Savannah** (Dec. 20). Sherman then turned north into South Carolina. **Columbia** was taken (Feb. 17, 1865), and the advance continued into North Carolina.

Confederate **general Nathan Bedford Forrest** led his men in a **massacre of black soldiers, at Fort Pillow, Tenn.** The men had surrendered the fort before they were slaughtered.

On the home front, Northern society gradually underwent changes that would greatly transform social life in the postwar years. The **Great American Tea Company** was organized in New York; its name was changed to the **Great Atlantic and Pacific Tea Company** (A & P) in 1869; later it became America's first chain store, with over 500 stores by 1912.

At about the same time, **Marshall Field's of Chicago** pioneered the development of the specialty department store, which utilized fixed price systems.

Nov. 8. Reelection of Abraham Lincoln. The Republican Party had changed its name to the **Union Party** and selected for vice president the loyal Tennessee Democrat **Andrew Johnson** (1808–75).

1865, Feb. 1. Resolution in Congress to submit to the states the **Thirteenth Amendment** to the Constitution, prohibiting slavery within the United States. The amendment was ratified by two-thirds of the states by Dec. 18.

LAST CAMPAIGNS. The Confederate armies, caught between Grant in the north and Sherman in the south and deprived of food supply, were no longer able to withstand the pressure. Sheridan won the **Battle of Five Forks** (April 1) and thus forced the **evacuation of Petersburg** (April 2) and the **surrender of Richmond** (April 3). Grant with all his forces then pursued and surrounded Lee.

March. The Confederacy, experiencing a critical manpower shortage, moved to arm slaves and allow them to serve in the Confederate army. In an executive order, Davis granted freedom to all blacks who served. The move came too late for African Americans to actually enlist in the service.

By war's end, more than 186,000 blacks had enlisted in the Union army. At the same time, as black men enlarged the Union army and others labored behind Confederate lines, **black women and their children had swelled the ranks of contraband camps or took on double duty on southern plantations.**

April 9. LEE'S CAPITULATION AT APPOMATTOX COURT HOUSE. Johnston, with the Southern army, surrendered to Sherman (April 26), and the last Confederate army, under Gen. Kirby Smith, surrendered at Shreveport, La., **on May 26. Jefferson Davis, president of the Confederacy, fled to Georgia, but was captured (May 10) and imprisoned.**

April 14. Lincoln was mortally shot by John Wilkes Booth and died the next day. Andrew Johnson, vice president, succeeded to the office of president.

Cost of the war. National debt in 1860 was $64,842,287; in 1866, $2,773,236,173. This great increase was in addition to the debts incurred by the states and municipalities.

Freedom. Thousands of newly freed people exercised their new status by moving around the country, formalizing long-standing relationships with marriage, searching for loved ones in an effort to recombine families sundered by slavery, seeking education, and establishing churches free of white control. **The freed people also held conventions in a variety of cities, calling for access to full citizenship rights, fair wages, and immediate relief of widespread suffering.**

d. RECONSTRUCTION

1865, March. Congress created the **Bureau of Refugees, Freedmen, and Abandoned Lands.** Known as the **Freedmen's Bureau,** the agency assisted the former slaves and helped them adjust to freedom. Although helpful, the bureau often placed planters' interests above those of the freed people, such as when they coerced blacks to accept unfair labor contracts.

May 29. Pres. Johnson issued a proclamation of amnesty, granting pardon to all ordinary persons who had participated in the rebellion who would take an oath of allegiance.

Dec. Joint Committee of Fifteen on Reconstruction was appointed by Congress.

Dec. 18. Ratification of the Thirteenth Amendment, abolishing slavery.

1865–66. New labor relations. Freedmen refused to work under a gang labor system and forced a compromise, **sharecropping,** between their desire to work for themselves and the planters' desire to control the newly freed people.

1865–67. Black Codes. This series of rigid labor laws, passed throughout the South, were designed to keep freed people immobile, dependent, and lacking labor alternatives.

Former slave owners founded the **Ku Klux Klan** in Tennessee as a means of fighting Reconstruction. By 1870, the group served the Democratic Party as a military force. The Klan murdered and terrorized African Americans and Republican politicians.

1866. The first women's rights convention in the post–Civil War era. Women formed the **American Equal Rights Association** and launched a campaign to gain universal suffrage on the state level, following defeat of such suffrage proposals on the federal level.

Feb. Johnson vetoed a measure extending the life of the **Freedmen's Bureau,** thereby increasing tension between himself and Congress.

April. Congress passed, over Johnson's veto, the **Civil Rights Bill,** declaring all persons born in the United States to be U.S. citizens and entitled to equality of treatment before the law. This was designed to guarantee equal treatment to **African Americans** in southern states.

June 13. FOURTEENTH AMENDMENT was sent to states for ratification. It was declared ratified on July 28, 1868. It incorporated in the Constitution the principle of the Civil Rights Act; gave the southern states the choice of **African-American** enfranchisement or reduced representation in the lower house of Congress; barred from political office those ex-Confederates who had been federal or state officials before the war, until they should be pardoned by a two-thirds vote of Congress; provided that the war debt of the South should never be paid

or that of the Union repudiated; and that former masters should never be compensated for their slaves. It was generally assumed at the time that this amendment was designed solely to safeguard the civil rights of the freedmen, and it was so interpreted by the Supreme Court in the **Slaughterhouse Cases** (1873). In 1886, however, in the case of *Santa Clara County* v. *Southern Pacific Railroad,* the Supreme Court declared that a corporation was a "person" within the meaning of the amendment and thus entitled to its protection. From this time the courts began to apply the **due process clause** of the amendment more and more to shield business and corporations against hostile legislative action by the states. The amendment also disheartened many in the suffrage movement because **for the first time in the Constitution the word** *male* **was used, effectively sanctioning the denial of female suffrage.**

Efforts of federal troops to build an emigrant road from Fort Laramie along the Powder River to the mines of Montana and Idaho led to **war with the Plains Sioux.**

The Civil War years had witnessed the formation of a number of national trade unions, which **William H. Sylvis** (1828–69) attempted to federate into a single nationwide association known as the **National Labor Union.**

1867, March 2. THE BASIC RECONSTRUCTION ACT. This act, as supplemented by regulations of March 23 and July 19, 1867, and March 11, 1868, **divided the southern states into five military districts.** To be restored to the Union, the states had to hold state conventions, whose delegates were elected with the aid of **African-American** suffrage; these conventions had to frame constitutions approved by Congress and ratified by the people of the states; and the legislatures elected under each constitution had to ratify the Fourteenth Amendment. **The act undercut the power of the planter elite and instigated political activity among the freedmen. During the period of Reconstruction politics that followed, numerous African Americans served in state and national offices. State governments modernized state constitutions, increased male suffrage, extended public education, and established hospitals, penitentiaries, and asylums.**

March 2. Tenure-of-Office Act. On March 4, this act was passed over Johnson's veto. **The act aimed to prevent the president from dismissing members of his cabinet without Senate approval.**

March 30. Purchase of Alaska for $7,200,000.

The United States declared a new policy through which it established two great reservations (one in present-day South Dakota and the other in Oklahoma) on which Native Americans were to live until they "learned to walk on the white man's road." Many Native American groups of the West were cajoled, tricked, and coerced into accepting reservation policy. Meanwhile, nontreaty Indians carried out a guerrilla war against white settlers and U.S. troops.

1867–83. The federal government began a concerted policy to destroy the buffalo, the main means of food and shelter for Native Americans on the Great Plains.

1868, Feb. 24–May 26. Impeachment and trial of Andrew Johnson. Johnson and the Congress had disagreed over Reconstruction policy. The immediate occasion for the impeachment proceedings was Johnson's alleged violation of the Tenure-of-Office Act. He was acquitted by a vote of 35 to 19; 36 votes (two-thirds of the senate) were required for conviction.

1861–68. New territories. In the years just before the war, the discovery of precious metals in the Pike's Peak country and in the Washoe Mountains led to mining rushes to those regions, with the result that the territories of Colorado and Nevada were organized in 1861. Mining rushes elsewhere in the years of the war resulted in the organization of the territories of Arizona (1863), Idaho (1863), and Montana (1864). Wyoming was made a territory in 1868.

1869, Feb. 26. The Fifteenth Amendment was adopted by Congress. The radicals, fearing that southern whites might obtain power in their states and repeal the provisions of their state constitutions granting suffrage to **African Americans,** sponsored this amendment, providing that the right to vote shall not be abridged because of "race, color, or previous condition of servitude." It was declared ratified on March 30, 1870. Virginia, Texas, Mississippi, and Georgia were forced to ratify this amendment as a condition of restoration to the Union. **Because the amendment allowed states to continue to deny women the vote,**

its passage split the suffrage movement into two camps. One camp, including **Lucy Stone and Frederick Douglass** and later led by **Rev. Henry Ward Beecher,** supported the Republican Party as the best means of gaining female suffrage. The second camp, led by **Susan B. Anthony** (1820–1906) and **Elizabeth Cady Stanton,** developed a program independent of any political party.

Congress created the **Board of Indian Commissioners** to supervise all government expenditures for the Indians.

African Americans formed the **National (Negro) Labor Union** and sought affiliation with organized white labor without much success.

Uriah Stephens (1821–82) formed the **Knights of Labor,** which attempted to combine all labor, skilled and unskilled, organized and unorganized, into one union.

Serious and recurring epidemics of smallpox, typhus, typhoid, cholera, scarlet fever, and yellow fever in Philadelphia, New York City, Boston, Baltimore, Washington, D. C., Memphis, and New Orleans led to the realization of the need for improved sanitation. **In 1866 a municipal board of health was created in New York City, and in 1869 a state board of health was established in Massachusetts.**

March 4–1877, March 4. ULYSSES S. GRANT, 18th president.

1872. Nov. Reelection of Grant, the Republican candidate, over **Horace Greeley** (1811–72), the Liberal Republican candidate, who was endorsed by the Democratic Party, which had abstained from placing a candidate in the field. Grant received 286 electoral votes to 62 for Greeley.

1873. Crédit Mobilier scandal, resulting from the revelation by congressional investigating committees that **Schuyler Colfax,** the outgoing vice president, and a number of members of Congress, including James A. Garfield (1831–81), held stock, for which they had not paid, in the Crédit Mobilier, the construction company that built the Union Pacific Railway. This was merely one of the numerous instances of corruption in the Grant administration. In 1874 **William A. Richardson,** secretary of the treasury, hastily resigned to escape a vote of censure by Congress. Grant's private secretary, **Orville E. Babcock,** was implicated in the **Whiskey Ring,** while **William W. Belknap,** secretary of war, resigned in 1876 to escape impeachment for bribe taking. **James G. Blaine,** speaker of the house, was compromised through the **Mulligan letters.**

Depression. The depression of 1873 resulted in about 15 percent unemployment among workers; and thousands of farmers were forced to foreclose when the Northern Pacific Railroad financier **Jay Cooke** filed bankruptcy. This economic downturn would persist through the next four years.

The Great Bonanza. Important discovery of silver in Nevada.

1874. Foundation of Women's Christian Temperance Union, a major reform organization that often dealt with labor, health, and international peace as well as temperance issues.

1875. The Civil Rights Act of 1875 prohibited racial discrimination in a wide range of public facilities, including theaters, hotels, restaurants, and barber shops.

Jan. 14. The **Resumption Act** was passed by Congress, providing for the resumption of specie payment (suspended in 1861) on Jan. 1, 1879. The measure made greenbacks redeemable in gold. At the same time, as the price of silver dropped with the expanding output of the **Comstock Lode in Nevada,** western mine owners urged the federal government to adopt a policy of free and unlimited coinage of silver.

1876. National League of Professional Baseball Clubs was formed and ushered in an era of managerial and business practices in the sport.

Johns Hopkins University opened in Baltimore as the nation's first real graduate school. Other universities began to move toward more research training in ensuing years.

Feb. 15. Patent for manufacture of **barbed wire.** This was of the utmost significance in the conquest of the Great Plains.

Nov. The disputed election of Democrat Samuel J. Tilden and Republican Rutherford B. Hayes (1822–93). Republicans required all of the 20 disputed electoral votes in order to win the presidency. Since Congress had to approve the decision, the crisis continued until an informal agreement permitted the election of Hayes in exchange for removal of federal troops from southern soil, greater local control over federal patronage, and federal funds for southern internal improvement projects. The arrangement helped to avert a continuing conflict between the North and South, but at the expense of African-American rights. **Within 20 years, Democrats in the region would control elections, and African Americans would be effectively disfranchised.**

The Granger decisions. These decisions of the Supreme Court came as a climax to the first important farmers' movement in American history. In 1867 the **Patrons of Husbandry, commonly** called the **Grange,** had been formed as a nonpolitical organization of farmers. At this time the farmers in the Middle Western states were incensed because of the unfair practices of railways and grain elevators. Organizing farmers' parties, they proceeded (1870–75) to enact legislation in Illinois, Iowa, Wisconsin, Minnesota, and other states, bringing railways and grain elevators under state control. The Granger decisions established the following principles: (1) a state under its police power has authority to regulate a business that is clothed with a public interest; (2) until Congress acts in the premises, the states may establish rates for interstate shipments; (3) the determination of the reasonableness of rates is a legislative rather than a judicial function. The second of these principles was set aside in 1886 in the case of the **Wabash, St. Louis and Pacific Railroad** v. **Illinois,** whereas the third was undermined and set aside by a series of decisions between 1889 and 1898, the last being the case of *Smyth* v. *Ames.*

1877. Aaron Montgomery opened his mail order business in Chicago with a capital of less than $2,500. By 1883 the company's stock rose in value to over $500,000.

March 3. The Desert Land Act was designed to encourage development of irrigation in arid areas by private effort. The advance of white settlers, slaughter of the buffalo, and the gold rush to the Black Hills caused an uprising of the **Plains Sioux (1876)** under Sitting Bull, which resulted in the crushing defeat of Gen. George A. Custer (1839–76) and his troops by **Chiefs Sitting Bull** (c. 1831–90) **and Crazy Horse** (c. 1842–77) **at the Little Big Horn River.**

March 4–1881, March 4. RUTHERFORD B. HAYES, 19th president.

July. The Great Uprising. In reaction to a depression and numerous wage reductions, railroad workmen instituted a major railroad strike that spread to 14 states in two weeks. The strike left in its wake over 100 deaths and millions of dollars worth of property damage. The work stoppage was the first national strike and the first time the government put the full force of the U.S. Army on the side of business.

Nez Perce Indians under **Chief Joseph** were defeated (Oct. 1877) and removed to Indian Territory.

2. THE UNITED STATES, 1878–1914

a. OVERVIEW

Between the end of Reconstruction and the advent of World War I, America nearly completed its transition from a predominantly agrarian society to a predominantly urban industrial nation. Immigration, urban growth, and the expansion of industrial capitalism proceeded apace. The number of Americans living in cities reached nearly 50 percent, fueled by the arrival of nearly 17 million immigrants, mostly from southern, central, and eastern Europe. The Asian and Hispanic populations also increased. The **birthrate continued to drop,** falling from 39.9 live births per 1,000 people in 1880 to 32.3 by 1900. The nation witnessed the increasing decline of the agricultural sector, the emergence of a progressive movement to reform the worst abuses of industrialism, and the intensification of racism at home and abroad (as the nation expanded beyond its continental boundaries and became an imperial nation with significant overseas possessions). Despite the heightening of nationalistic fervor as the U.S. became a major world power, class, race, and regional differences continued to define the American experience.

The unequal impact of industrialism underlay the emergence of a variety of new social movements. In rapid succession, white workers embarked upon a series of organizing drives: the Knights of Labor in the late 1870s and 1880s, the American Federation of Labor during the 1890s, the Socialist Party of America in the early 1900s, and the Industrial Workers of the World after 1905. Native Americans continued to resist the encroachment of white settlers upon their land, as reflected in the persistence of Indian wars through the 1890s. African Americans, European immigrants, Hispanic Americans, and Asian Americans all intensified their separate institutional and community-building activities, designed to fight the impact of racial, class, and ethnic discrimination on their lives. Likewise, in an effort to arrest the deterioration of their livelihood, farmers launched an aggressive campaign to gain control over state and national economic policy. Their movement gained its greatest expression in the formation of the Populist Party in 1892. For a brief moment, it appeared that farmers would succeed in bridging not only regional differences between the South and the West, but racial and ethnic ones as well. The movement produced some of the most dramatic examples of black-white cooperation in American history.

Under the impact of these diverse social movements, the political system itself underwent significant change. Whereas the period from the fall of Reconstruction through the 1890s represented what some analysts call the "politics of equilibrium," characterized by little disagreement on major issues, the 1890s ushered in a new era of political conflict. Following the decline of the Populist revolt and the triumph of the Republican Party in the election of 1896, the nation experienced a resurgence of reform. Between 1900 and World War I, the Progressive movement sought to control the most exploitative features of industrial capitalism—especially its abuse of men, women, and children. Despite heroic efforts to right outstanding wrongs of the industrial system, failure to address the issue of racial injustice was undoubtedly the movement's greatest shortcoming.

During the late 19th and early 20th century, the system of Jim Crow was consolidated in the South, and its de facto counterpart proceeded apace in the North and the West. Although some whites joined blacks in the formation of the NAACP (1909) and the National Urban League (1910), racial justice represented a low priority for most white Americans. Perhaps it was inevitable that America would stop short of developing a more equitable multiracial society. It was during this period that America completed its continental expansion from the Atlantic to the Pacific. Following the Spanish-American War, the United States also took its place as a new empire with its own colonial claims over peoples of color in Hawaii, Puerto Rico, and Guam.

b. NEW POLITICAL, SOCIAL, AND DIPLOMATIC ISSUES

1878, Feb. The Bland-Allison Act. In 1873 Congress had omitted the standard silver dollar from the list of authorized domestic coins to be minted in the future, commonly referred to as the **Crime of 1873.** The silver producers were supported by the farmers, who believed the free coinage of silver would bring an upturn in the price of farm products. In 1877, the Bland-Allison Act was passed over the veto of Hayes and authorized the secretary of the treasury to purchase from 2 million to 4 million dollars' worth of silver bullion monthly for coinage.

1879. The **U.S. Geological Survey** was founded, consolidating under one office the several surveys that had been gathering valuable information on western North America for over a decade. Under the directorship of **John W. Powell** (1834–1902) after 1881, the survey grew into a powerful agency for the progress of science in the United States.

Frank W. Woolworth established his **five-and-ten-cent store** at Lancaster, Pa. By 1900, the company's volume of business reached over $5 million and continued to rise, reaching $15 million in 1910.

Jan. 1. Resumption of specie payment. The success of the policy was greatly aided by the unusual demand abroad for American agricultural products, which brought gold into the country in large quantity.

1880s. A similar process of invasion separated **Mexican Americans** from their titles to land in the Southwest. At the same time, as irrigation projects transformed the west into fertile lands, Mexican Americans and their immigrant counterparts provided the essential labor supply.

1881, March 4. JAMES A. GARFIELD, 20th president, was **shot by a disappointed office seeker** on July 2 and died on Sept. 19, 1881. He was succeeded by **Chester A. Arthur** (1829–86), his vice president.

May 21. The **American Red Cross Society** was organized, with **Clara Barton** (1821–1912) as president.

William Dean Howells (1837–1920) resigned from his job as editor of the *Atlantic Monthly* and became editor of *Harper's Monthly.* Howells protested against what came to be called the **"genteel tradition"** in American literary and cultural life. He soon published a series of novels that helped to set the tone for a new **realism** in American literature. At the same time, other novelists and writers of short stories had turned to a strong emphasis on local color: **Francis Bret Harte** (1836–1902), **Joel Chandler Harris** (1848–1908), and **Samuel Langhorne Clemens (Mark Twain)** (1835–1910). In music, **John Knowles Paine** (1839–1906) emerged as one of the first American symphonic composers.

1882, May 6. The Chinese Exclusion Act. The increasing immigration of Chinese, especially in California, **caused white workers to riot against the Chinese** as early as 1871. The formation of a workingmen's party in that state in 1877 brought the **anti-Chinese issue** into prominence and to the attention of Congress. The **act of 1882** barred Chinese laborers from entrance into the United States for a period of ten years. In 1902 the exclusion was made permanent, and the same act prohibited the immigration of Chinese to the United States from Hawaii and the Philippines. In 1885 an act of Congress prohibited the entrance of all laborers under contract.

1883, Jan. 16. The Pendleton Act. After more or less continual discussion since 1865, Congress provided in this act for a bipartisan commission to set up and administer a system of **competitive examinations** as a test of fitness for appointment to federal office. It also prohibited the levying of **campaign contributions** upon federal officeholders.

Tariff Act. The protective principle, so securely established by the Civil War tariffs, remained intact.

Sept. 8. The **Northern Pacific Railroad** was completed (it had been chartered and endowed with an enormous grant of land in 1864). This was the second transcontinental line. The **Southern Pacific** was the third, and by 1893 no less than five were completed. Other lines threaded their way across the prairies and plains to the mountains, letting in the tide of population that brought the frontier to an end **and pushed Native Americans increasingly onto reservations.**

U.S. Supreme Court struck down the **Civil Rights Act of 1875,** which had prohibited racially segregated hotels, barber shops, restaurants, theaters, and other public facilities.

1883–90. The problem of the **treasury surplus.** Grover Cleveland (1837–1908) would deal with the surplus by reducing the tariff duties, which he urged in his message to Congress in 1887 and which he made the leading issue in the campaign of 1888. Republicans attempted to remove the surplus by retirement of Civil War bonds, the building of a new navy, and reckless pension legislation.

1884. Presidential race between **James G. Blaine** (Republican) and **Grover Cleveland** (Democrat). The Mugwumps, the reforming wing of the party, deserted Blaine in favor of Cleveland. Cleveland was elected, 219 electoral votes to 182.

1885, March 4–1889, March 4. GROVER CLEVELAND, 22d president.

1886. The **Presidential Succession Law,** providing that in the event of the death of both president and vice president, members of the cabinet should succeed to the presidency in a predetermined order.

The Knights of Labor organized workers across racial, ethnic, and sexual lines. By 1887, the organization claimed nearly 60,000 black members. About the same number of women entered the "ladies' locals" or mixed locals of men and women. After several unsuccessful strikes, the organization began to lose membership and soon gave way to the **American Federation of Labor (formed in Dec.)** as the first permanent national labor movement in American history. The germ of the AFL dated from 1881, when disgruntled members of the Knights of Labor, led by **Samuel Gompers** (1850–1924), formed the **Federation of Organized Trades and Labor Unions.**

The **Haymarket Square Riot** in Chicago. Trade unions announced **May 1, 1886,** as the date for obtaining the eight-hour day in industry. As the deadline approached, a strike wave developed. **Anarchists staged a protest meeting at Haymarket Square on May 4.** When police sought to break up the meeting, someone threw a bomb, which killed seven persons and wounded several others. Eight anarchists were arrested and tried for conspiracy. Four were convicted and hanged.

1886–87. Apache resistance in Arizona and New Mexico dissipated following the capture of **Geronimo** (1829–1909).

1887. The railroad agent **Richard Warner Sears** joined the Chicago watchmaker **Alvah Curtis Roebuck** in a general merchandising business that by 1893, under the name **Sears, Roebuck, and Company,** sold a broad range of goods from a **196-page catalogue.** The mail-order houses helped to nationalize the customs, styles, and manners of the expanding city.

Anti-immigrant sentiment gained sharp expression with the formation of the **American Protective Association (1887),** designed to combat what members perceived as the threat of Catholicism.

Feb. 4. INTERSTATE COMMERCE ACT. The growing realization of the **unscrupulous** practices of the railways led to the appointment by the Senate in 1885 of the **Cullom committee,** which conducted hearings in the principal cities of the country. This was followed by the passage of the **Act of 1887.** It declared that charges of the railways must be reasonable and just, made pooling illegal, contained a long-and-short-haul clause, declared rebates illegal, and created an **Interstate Commerce Commission** with power to inquire into the management of the carriers, summon witnesses, compel the production of papers, and invoke the aid of the federal courts. Up to 1903 the commission was largely frustrated by the courts. In 1897, in the *Maximum Freight Rate* **case,** the Supreme Court denied the commission's authority to prescribe a maximum rate. The long-and-short-haul clause was rendered ineffective, and the commission was left with the duty of collecting railway statistics and requiring the publication of rates by the companies.

Feb. 8. The Dawes Act authorized the president to terminate tribal government and communal ownership of land among the Indians and to divide the land at the rate of a quarter section for each head of a family, full ownership to be withheld for 25 years. Supporters of the act hoped that Native Americans would be transformed into hardworking members of white society. In 1906 the **Burke Act** authorized the secretary of the interior to bestow full property title whenever convinced of the Indians' fitness.

1888. Presidential campaign. Cleveland (Democrat) against Benjamin Harrison (1833–1901) (Republican). The tariff was the dominant issue. Although Cleveland had a popular plurality, he lost the election, receiving 168 electoral votes to 233 for Harrison.

1889, March 4–1893, March 4. BENJAMIN HARRISON, 23d president.

1889. Jane Addams (1860–1935) founded **Hull House in Chicago.** Thereafter, the settlement house movement flourished, particularly after **Lillian D. Wald** (1867–1940) founded the **Henry Street Settlement in New York City in 1895.** Middle-class women hoped to mitigate the difficulties of the working class, particularly immigrants, by acting as amateur social workers.

April 22. Oklahoma was opened to settlement. The territory of Oklahoma was organized in 1890. The movement into the trans-Mississippi country led to the admission of some of the last states to the Union: **Nevada** (1864); **Nebraska** (1867); **Colorado** (1876); **North Dakota, South Dakota, Washington,** and **Montana** (1889); **Wyoming and Idaho** (1890); **Utah** (1896); **Oklahoma** (1907); **New Mexico** and **Arizona** (1912).

Oct. 2. FIRST PAN-AMERICAN CONFERENCE convened at Washington, D.C. The idea of closer relations among the nations of the Western Hemisphere, with the United States playing the role of an elder sister, had long been in the mind of James G. Blaine (1830–93). The conference rejected Blaine's plan of reciprocity and refused to adopt a convention calling for the promotion of peace by arbitration, but established the **Pan-American Union,** a bureau of information.

1890. The **National Woman Suffrage Association** was reorganized as the **National American Woman Suffrage Association (NAWSA),** and continued the campaign for suffrage; by 1900, four states had enfranchised women. By the outbreak of World War I, women exercised the suffrage in 11 states.

The Mississippi Plan. A state constitutional convention met for the primary purpose of disfranchising the black voter. The state imposed a **poll tax, a literacy requirement, and an "understanding" clause,** which virtually removed blacks from the electoral process, while also undermining the political participation of poor whites. Other states soon followed suit.

June 19. The **Force Bill,** providing for federal control of federal elections, was reported in the House of Representatives. It aimed to protect **African-American** voters in southern states against attempts to disfranchise them. It passed the House, but was not adopted by the Senate.

June 27. Disability Pension Act. In reality this was a service pension act since it provided pensions for all veterans of 90 days' service who could claim physical or mental disability, regardless of origin, that precluded the gaining of a livelihood by manual labor. Pensions were to be granted to widows of soldiers without regard to the cause of the husband's death if the marriage had occurred prior to 1890.

July 2. The **SHERMAN ANTI-TRUST LAW** was enacted. After the formation of the Standard Oil Trust in 1879 (revised in 1882), numerous large business combinations made their appearance, thereby raising the specter of monopoly, which led to the demand for legislation by Congress. The **Sherman Act** declared illegal "every contract, combination in the form of trust or otherwise, or conspiracy in restraint of trade or commerce among the several states or with foreign nations."

July 14. The **Sherman Silver Purchase Act.** The act authorized the treasury to purchase 4,500,000 ounces of silver monthly for coinage into dollars and to issue treasury certificates, to be redeemed in either gold or silver at the discretion of the treasury.

Dec. Wounded Knee. Religious adherents of **Wovoka's** (c. 1858–1932) **teachings and the Ghost Dance became increasingly threatening toward white settlers,** who called for army assistance. When Indian police and federal troops attempted to arrest Sitting Bull (Dec. 14), a battle broke out, and 13 people, including the chief, were killed. Two weeks later, more followers of the Ghost Dance surrendered to the military; and they were at the encampment at Wounded Knee when a gun battle occurred between the soldiers and the Sioux, which resulted in the death of 25 U.S. troops and 153 Indian men, women, and children.

1892–95. Labor troubles. A strike of workers in the **Homestead Plant of the Carnegie Steel Company was called by the Amalgamated Association of Iron and Steel Workers (June 30, 1892)** as a result of disagreement over a wage scale. **The entire community—town leaders and women as well as men—rallied to the defense of the union.** The use of Pinkerton detectives by the **Carnegie Company** led to violence, which was followed by the use of state troops to arrest workers and town leaders on charges of riot, murder, and treason. The plant was soon reopened with non-union workers, some of whom were southern blacks. Thereafter, the Amalgamated Association declined as a force in the lives of workers in the steel industry.

On May 11, 1894, a strike occurred in the plant of the Pullman Company, in which the **American Railway Union,** formed the previous year by **Eugene V. Debs** (1855–1926), participated. **Because the strikers refused to handle Pullman cars, the company attached mail cars to the Pullmans. When the strikers refused to handle the trains, the company appealed to the government to protect the U.S. mail.** The government in turn charged the strikers with interfering with the mail, got an injunction against the boycott, and called in federal troops and state militias. Upon disregarding the injunction, Debs was arrested for contempt of court and sent to jail. **The U.S. Circuit Court approved the use of the injunction, sentenced Debs to prison for six months, and approved the use of the Sherman Anti-Trust Act against labor unions.** The next year the Supreme Court sustained the judgment of the lower court. **The use of the injunction gave capital a formidable weapon against labor.**

1892. The **AFL** appointed a woman, **Mary E. Kennedy** of Chicago, to spearhead the organization of women, but denied her full status on the executive board.

Feb. 22. The **People's Party** was organized at St. Louis. For a decade there had been a gathering discontent of the farmers, resulting from the depressed condition of agriculture. Organizations of farmers, known as the **Southern Alliance (including the Colored Farmers National Alliance and Cooperative Union)** and the **Northwestern Alliance,** had appeared and held meetings at St. Louis (Dec. 1889), Ocala, Fla. (Dec. 1890), and Cincinnati (May 1891). They now formed the **People's Party,** or **Populist Party.** In July 1892, at their Omaha convention, they nominated **James B. Weaver** (1833–1912), a veteran inflationist, as their candidate for the presidency and drew up a platform declaring for a national currency without the use of banking corporations, free and unlimited coinage of silver, a graduated income tax, postal savings banks, and government ownership of railways and telephone and telegraph lines. **Populism brought women into the political process to an unprecedented degree.** A woman, **Mary Elizabeth Lease of Kansas,** gave the Populist movement some of its most memorable rhetoric when she exclaimed, **"What you farmers need to do is to raise less corn and more hell."** **Populists also showed a willingness to work across racial lines, and this willingness was partly their undoing.** Democrats were able to put down the Populist movement by charging them with courting "Negro domination." Poor whites, embittered because of their own economic and political plight, turned their anger on African Americans. Southern legislatures soon passed laws requiring rigid segregation in most public facilities. Called **Jim Crow laws,** the new legislation turned the South, for the first time, into a legally segregated society. **The annual number of recorded lynchings of African Americans peaked at about 161 in 1892.** Thereafter lynchings declined but apparently became more sadistic.

Harrison was defeated for reelection by **Cleveland,** who received 277 electoral votes; Harrison received 145, and Weaver, the Populist candidate, 22.

1893–98. On July 7, 1898, **Hawaii** was annexed by joint resolution of the two houses of Congress. U.S. activities in Hawaii during this period symbolized the growing emergence of the nation as a colonial power.

1893, March 4–1897, March 4. GROVER CLEVELAND, president for the second time.

1893. Depression. Nearly 16,000 businesses failed, farm prices plunged downward, and unemployment rose to nearly 3 million workers over the next two years. **Cleveland believed there was just one cause of the depression:** the worldwide fear of American inability to maintain a gold standard was draining off the supply of gold. For this fear he blamed the **Sherman Silver Purchase Act.** He therefore asked the special session of Congress to repeal the act.

Oct. 30. The **Sherman Silver Purchase Act was repealed,** after bitter debate.

The **Anti-Saloon League** founded, a milestone in the development of the prohibition movement. It inaugurated a nationwide campaign in 1895.

1894–96. Government bonds were sold in an effort to maintain the gold reserve. Finding that repeal of the Silver Purchase Act did not stop the outflow of gold, the treasury, to obtain gold, arranged for sale of bonds by banks in Jan. and Nov. 1894.

1894. The opening of **B. F. Keith's New Boston Theater symbolized the arrival of the vaudeville era** in American mass entertainment.

Aug. 18. The **Carey Act** granted 1 million acres of land each to Colorado, Idaho, Montana, Nevada, Oregon, Utah, Washington, and Wyoming to encourage irrigation by state action. In 1908 they each received another million acres.

Aug. 27. The **Wilson-Gorman Tariff Act** retained the protective principle, although duties were lowered to about 40 percent. It contained a provision for a 2 percent tax on incomes above $4,000.

1895. Booker T. Washington (1856–1915) gave his **Atlanta Compromise speech,** which emphasized the virtues of racial solidarity and self-help, and signaled his rise to power.

Frederick Winslow Taylor (1856–1915), a pioneer in the field of scientific management, **published his landmark essay "A Piece Rate System,"** designed to undercut the skills and authority of the workers. This set forth the basic tenets of **scientific management,** reducing workers' decision making on the shop floor in an aggressive drive to increase production and cut labor costs. Skilled workers vigorously resisted such efforts. In 1911, iron molders at the federal arsenal at Watertown, Mass., struck against use of the stopwatch and bonus system.

Increasing popular and medical interest in slenderness and dieting; growing hostility to body fat.

May 20. The income tax was declared unconstitutional in the case of *Pollock* v. *Farmers Loan and Trust Co.,* causing much criticism. An income tax was declared a direct tax, which, in accordance with the Constitution, must be apportioned among the states in proportion to population.

1896. Election of William McKinley (1843–1901), running on a single gold standard platform, over **William Jennings Bryan** (1860–1925), Democratic candidate, supporting free silver. Because of the Democratic espousal of free silver, the Populists supported Bryan. Silver Republicans supported Bryan. McKinley was elected, with 271 electoral votes to 176 for Bryan. **The election of 1896** represented a transformation in American politics—it signaled the demise of populism, the decline of the Democratic Party as a national entity, and the emergence of urban workers and immigrants as pivotal factors in national elections. This election also suggested that Republicans were beginning to lessen their appeals to evangelical Protestants in an effort to attract votes from the multiethnic cities.

Plessy v. *Ferguson.* The Supreme Court upheld the constitutionality of the doctrine of **"separate but equal"** public accommodations for blacks and whites. The law would stand until 1954.

Thomas Edison (1847–1931) invented the **motion picture camera.** The first motion picture was shown in a Pittsburgh auditorium. Movies spread rapidly across the country, helping to transform patterns of leisure and popular culture.

1897, March 4–1901, Sept. 14. WILLIAM McKINLEY, 25th president.

National Federation of Afro-American Women and the Colored Women's League merged to form the National Association of Colored Women. Through the activities of these women, the national settlement house movement entered the black community.

1897–1901. Return of prosperity, to which the increased gold production of the world and the unusual demand abroad for American agricultural products were important contributing factors. This period brought great increases in the gold reserve and great activity in the formation of large combinations in the field of business, despite the Sherman Anti-Trust Act. This movement culminated in the organization of the **United States Steel Corporation** (1901), the first billion-dollar corporation. Great concentration of control by banking interests in the business world.

1898–1900. The National Civic Federation was formed by industrialists and labor leaders to find peaceful solutions to labor management conflicts.

1898. THE SPANISH-AMERICAN WAR (p. 638). The insurrection in Cuba, which broke out in 1895, was increasingly attended by inhuman treatment of the rebels. It aroused the sympathy of various elements in the United States and afforded an opportunity for the new "yellow press" of the United States to influence American sentiment against Spain. On Feb. 15, 1898, the **U.S.S.** *Maine* was mysteriously blown up in Havana Harbor, producing strong feeling against Spain in the United States. In the face of the belligerent attitude of the press and various groups in the country, McKinley finally yielded to the war clamor, despite the fact that Spain had agreed to every condition laid down by his ultimatum with respect to Cuba.

April 11. McKinley sent his war message to Congress, asking for authority to intervene forcibly.

April 20. Congress adopted a resolution authorizing intervention, but disclaiming any intention of annexing Cuba.

April 24–25. War formally declared. The war consisted of five operations: (1) defeat of the Spanish fleet at Manila by Commodore **George Dewey** (May 1); (2) the blockade of Cuba; (3) the search for the main Spanish fleet; (4) the land and sea battles (**Battles of El Caney** and **San Juan Hill** in July, and the **naval Battle of Santiago,** July 3); and (5) the invasion of Puerto Rico (July 25). On Aug. 12 the **peace protocol** was signed, and on Aug. 13 Manila was captured.

Dec. 10. TREATY OF PEACE SIGNED AT PARIS (p. 638). Spain withdrew from **Cuba** and ceded to the United States **Puerto Rico, Guam,** and the **Philippines** (for the loss of the latter, Spain was paid $20 million). The larger effect of the war was to establish the United States as a world power and to extend the sphere of its political interests and contacts.

1899–1902. Philippine insurrection. Although the Filipinos under **Emilio Aguinaldo** (p. 578) had aided the Americans against the Spaniards and had conquered the island of Luzon, they were deeply disappointed when **the Philippines was not given its independence as a part of the peace treaty between the United States and Spain.** Hostilities broke out in Feb. 1899. For the next three years an American army of 60,000 was engaged in the islands. Guerrilla warfare, with all its attendant horrors, developed. Although Aguinaldo was captured (March 1901), it was not until April 1902 that the insurrection was finally brought to an end.

1899, Sept. 6. John Hay (1838–1905), secretary of state, sent his **Open Door** note to London, Paris, Berlin, and St. Petersburg (p. 423), which urged foreign governments to permit free trade in Chinese ports under their influence.

1900–14. **Immigrants** from southern and eastern Europe began arriving in increasing numbers. During the 1890s less than half a million arrived each year. However, more than a million immigrants arrived in six of the years between 1906 and 1914. **Mexican immigration** increased, tripling the country's Mexican population. By 1900, the number of **foreign language papers** increased to over 1,000 before declining in proportion to the English language organs.

1900, March 14. **The Currency Act** declared other forms of money redeemable in gold on demand and provided for a gold reserve of $150 million.

Boxer uprising in China (p. 565). In June the United States participated in the relief expedition against Beijing. Hay made this the occasion for reaffirming the Open Door policy.

Nov. 6. **Bryan,** running on a platform of free silver and anti-imperialism, was defeated by **McKinley,** who received 292 electoral votes to 155 for Bryan.

The **American League of Baseball Clubs** was formed in order to break the monopoly of the **National League** over the game. Baseball now initiated the two-league championship and soon added the World Series.

1901–7. Streetcar segregation. **Only Georgia had a segregated streetcar ordinance before 1901.** Then in rapid succession, such ordinances spread throughout the upper and lower South.

1901. Formation of the **Socialist Party of America** under the leadership of **Morris Hillquit** of New York City, **Victor Berger** of Milwaukee, and **Eugene V. Debs** of the American Railroad Union.

March 2. The **Platt amendment** respecting Cuba was added to the Army Appropriation Bill for 1901–2. The Cuban constitutional convention incorporated the amendment in the Cuban constitution (June 12) as a condition of American withdrawal from the island. Cuba agreed not to impair its independence by treaty with foreign powers, not to assume public debt beyond the ability of its ordinary revenues to liquidate, to permit American intervention for the protection of Cuban independence, and to sell or lease to the United States land necessary for naval or coaling stations.

The Insular Cases decided. The Supreme Court held that territory might be subject to the jurisdiction of the United States without being incorporated into the country. The Constitution was not applicable, in every particular, to all lands over which the country exercised sovereignty. This enabled the United States to develop a distinctive colonial policy and to enact legislation for the government of **colonized peoples.**

Sept. 14. President McKinley died from an assassin's bullet.

Sept. 14–1909, March 4. THEODORE ROOSEVELT (1887–1944), 26th president.

1901–3. Isthmian Canal diplomacy (p. 635).

1902, May 12–Oct. 13. **Strike of anthracite coal miners,** demanding union recognition, a nine-hour day, and wage increase. In the face of a threatened coal shortage, **Roosevelt intervened and threatened to work the mines with federal troops,** whereupon the owners accepted his suggestion of a commission to investigate. The miners returned to work, but when the commission made its award, union recognition was withheld. Not until 1916 did the miners receive union recognition, with an eight-hour day. **Still, for the first time the federal government had intervened in a labor-management dispute without automatically opposing the claims of organized labor.**

June 17. The **Newlands Act** provided for the irrigation of the arid lands of the West.

Maryland enacted the first **state workmen's compensation law.** By 1920 all but five states had enacted such laws.

Oregon adopted the thoroughgoing use of the **initiative and referendum.**

1903. Under the leadership of wealthy women like **Mary Dreier and Mary McDowell,** the **National Women's Trade Union League** was formed. The league played an important role in stimulating the development of working-class leaders like **Rose Schneiderman and Agnes Nestor,** both garment workers.

Jan. 24. **The Alaskan boundary question** was referred to a commission of three Americans, two Canadians, and one Briton. When Lord Alverstone, the British member, voted against the Canadians, the dispute was decided in favor of the United States.

Beginning of effective **state legislation limiting hours of child labor** and establishing state departments of labor or industrial boards. By 1930, 37 states had established the 48-hour week for children in factories.

Wisconsin enacted the first **direct primary** law.

1903–13. **Railroad legislation.** In 1903 the **Elkins Act** was passed to strengthen the Interstate Commerce Act of 1887, which had proved ineffective. The Elkins Act forbade railroads to deviate from published schedules of rates and made railway officers as well as the companies liable in cases of rebating. The **Hepburn Act** of 1906 extended the control of the commission to express companies, sleeping-car companies, and pipeline, ferry, and terminal facilities. The commission was given power to reduce a rate found to be unreasonable. Passes were abolished and a commodity clause included. The **Mann-Elkins Act** (1910) extended the commission's jurisdiction to telephone and telegraph lines, and cable and wireless companies. The long-and-short-haul clause was made effective.

1904, March 14. The **Northern Securities Case** was decided. The efforts of **Edward H. Harriman** to gain control, first of the Burlington system and then of the Northern Pacific, had led to the struggle between Harriman and **James J. Hill,** in which Northern Pacific stock was bid up to fabulous prices, producing the so-called **Northern Pacific Panic (1901).** This was followed by an agreement between the rival groups for the merging of the Northern Pacific, Great Northern, and Burlington systems through the Northern Securities Company. **The Supreme Court declared the merger to be a violation of the Anti-Trust Act and ordered its dissolution.**

Nov. 8. **Roosevelt** was elected president over **Alton B. Parker,** the Democratic candidate, 335 electoral votes to 133.

Dec. 2. Roosevelt enunciated the **Roosevelt corollary of the Monroe Doctrine.** This was occasioned by the debt situation of the Dominican Republic and the pressure of European countries to compel payment. He said that chronic wrongdoing by powers in the Western Hemisphere might compel the United States under the Monroe Doctrine to exercise an international police power as the only means of forestalling European intervention. Under this doctrine the **United States intervened in Santo Domingo** and unofficially collected the customs. On July 31, 1907, the American administration left Santo Domingo.

1905. Roosevelt offered his services as **mediator between Russia and Japan,** and on Aug. 9 the peace conference at **Portsmouth, N.H.,** opened (p. 573). **Roosevelt received the Nobel Peace Prize for his role in ending the Russo-Japanese War.**

The **Industrial Workers of the World** was formed under the leadership of socialists like **Eugene V. Debs** and radical industrial unionists like **William D. ("Big Bill") Haywood** (1869–1928), head of the Western Federation of Miners. The organization's membership never exceeded 100,000, but its influence increased following successful strikes in the textile mills of Lawrence, Mass., and Paterson, N.J.

U.S. Steel Corp. built Gary, Ind., the largest planned community ever constructed by an American manufacturer. Rather than follow the Pullman pattern of company-owned houses, U.S. Steel had private contractors build the houses and then sold them to workers on long-term contracts.

1906, Jan. 16. In Europe, Roosevelt was instrumental in bringing about the **Algeciras conference** (p. 477).

June 30. The **Pure Food and Drug Act** prohibited the mislabeling and adulteration of foods.

Oct. The **segregation of Japanese schoolchildren** in San Francisco schools led to strained relations with Japan; **Roosevelt persuaded the school board to revoke its segregation order. In return,** Japan declared it was not its practice to issue passports to laborers to come to the United States, though passports were issued for Hawaii, Canada, and Mexico, the holders of which in most cases came to the United States. Japan expressed its intention of continuing this policy, and, relying on this **gentlemen's agreement,** Congress inserted in the Immigration Act of 1907 a clause authorizing the president to exclude from the continental territory of the United States holders of passports issued by any foreign government to its citizens to go to any country other than the United States. By the **Root-Takahira Agreement** of Nov. 1908, Japan confirmed *"the principle of equal opportunity for commerce and industry in China"* and agreed to support the *"independence and integrity"* of that empire.

1907. Congress set up the **Dillingham Commission** to study the immigration question. Published in 1911, its report reinforced prejudices against the new wave of immigrants from south, central, and eastern Europe.

1907–10. African Americans and their white supporters launched the **Niagara Movement** in 1907, following the **outbreak of racial violence** in the urban North. The movement resulted in the formation of the **National Association for the Advancement of Colored People (NAACP)** in 1910. The organization pledged itself to fight for full citizenship rights for African Americans.

1908. Oregon adopted the principle of the **recall** of all elective officials. The Supreme Court, in the case of *Muller* v. *Oregon,* upheld the Oregon ten-hour law for women in industry. By 1930 all but five states had laws limiting hours of work for women.

Nov. 3. William H. Taft (1857–1930) **(Republican)** was elected president over **William Jennings Bryan,** by 321 electoral votes to 162.

1909, March 4–1913, March 4. WILLIAM HOWARD TAFT, 27th president.

1909–12. Foreign relations of the United States. In 1909 Taft and **Philander C. Knox,** his secretary of state, interceded with China to secure the participation of New York bankers with British, French, and German capitalists in the loan for the construction of the Hukuang Railways in China. This gave rise to the charge of **dollar diplomacy.**

1909, Aug. 5. The **Payne-Aldrich tariff** disregarded party pledges and maintained protection.

1910. Urbanization. The urban percentage of the U.S. population increased from 19.8 in 1860 to 45.7 in 1910. The number of cities with over 100,000 people increased from 9 to 50, whereas cities of 10,000 to 20,000 rose from 58 to 369. **Special U.S. census data** revealed that of 11.8 million new city dwellers counted between 1900 and 1910, **immigrants** accounted for 41 percent, **American-born** rural-to-urban migrants accounted for 29.8 percent, **natural increase** accounted for 21.6 percent, and incorporation of new territory accounted for the remainder. **Black migration** to cities within and outside the South also gradually increased.

W. C. Handy (1873–1958) wrote **"Memphis Blues"** (1909) and **"St. Louis Blues"** (1914), signaling the movement of African-American music into the mainstream.

Henry Ford's (1863–1947) **Model T** inaugurated a new mode of mass production and the automobile as a new form of mass transportation by bringing it within the financial reach of the average consumer.

Jan. Taft removed **Gifford Pinchot** from the forestry service as a result of the **Ballinger-Pinchot controversy.**

March 19. Insurgent Republicans in the House moved to strip the Speaker of the House of his power by supporting a resolution providing for the election of the Rules Committee and the exclusion of the Speaker from its membership. In 1911 the Speaker was deprived of the right of appointing other standing committees of the house.

Aug. 31. In his speech at Ossawatomie, Kans., Theodore Roosevelt enunciated his doctrine of the New Nationalism. This augured ill for Taft.

c. 1910 ff. Increasing concern about *homosexuality* and new beliefs about homosexual behavior (p. 922).

1911. The Triangle Shirtwaist fire. A tragic fire erupted at the **Triangle Shirtwaist Company** in downtown **New York City.** Forty-seven young women, mostly immigrants, leaped to their deaths, while another 99 died in the flames. This tragedy caused a public outcry that resulted in the creation of the **New York State Factory Commission,** designed to facilitate the spread of safety and health measures.

Labor radicals were charged with killing 20 persons in the dynamiting of the anti-union *Los Angeles Times.*

Jan. 21. The National Progressive Republican League was organized, another step in the split of the Republican Party. Robert La Follette became the leader of the league.

May 1. The Supreme Court, under the Sherman Anti-Trust Act, ordered the **dissolution of the Standard Oil Company** and the **American Tobacco Company.** In the Standard Oil case, the Court enunciated the **rule-of-reason doctrine,** indicating its belief that the government should not attempt to outlaw "every" combination in restraint of trade, but should confine action to those contracts that resulted in an "unreasonable" restraint of trade. The enunciation of this doctrine marked a turning point in the Court's attitude toward the so-called trusts.

Illinois adopted the first statewide law for **assistance to mothers with dependent children.** In 1912 Colorado took similar action; in 1913, 18 other states enacted similar laws.

Several New York City social service organizations joined forces and launched the **National Urban League (1911),** an organization designed to improve the social and economic conditions of blacks as they moved into cities in increasing numbers.

1912. Massachusetts set up a commission to establish **minimum wage schedules** for women and children. By 1923, 14 other states and the District of Columbia had taken similar action, setting up either a statutory minimum or giving commissions mandatory powers. **Such laws were not uniformly favored by working women,** some of whom perceived their own opportunities for work shrinking as a result. In any case, all such laws were dealt a severe blow in the conservative environment of the 1920s.

Socialist candidates captured mayoral offices in major cities, including Milwaukee, Wis.; Schenectady, N.Y.; and Berkeley, Calif. The party's presidential candidate won nearly a million votes.

Feb. 24. Theodore Roosevelt announced he would accept the Republican nomination for president. He carried the preferential primaries over Taft in six states and was successful in four state conventions. In spite of this, the Republican machine managed to renominate Taft.

June 22. Taft's renomination. Roosevelt delegates withdrew and on Aug. 7 nominated **Roosevelt as the candidate of the Progressive Party.**

July 2. Woodrow Wilson (1856–1924) was nominated by the Democratic convention on the 46th ballot.

Aug. American marines landed in **Nicaragua** (p. 636), its fiscal affairs were turned over to an American collector, control of the Nicaraguan Bank was given to New York bankers, and the Nicaraguan government was placed on a monthly allowance.

During 1912 troops were concentrated on the Mexican border, and the revolutionary Madero government of Mexico was warned that it would be held accountable for loss of life and property.

Nov. 5. Wilson was elected with 435 electoral votes; Roosevelt received 88, and Taft, 8.

1913. Over 10,000 employees of **John D. Rockefeller's Colorado Fuel and Iron Company** struck for better working and living conditions. Women as well as men articulated their grievances and joined the strike, which culminated in the **Ludlow Massacre,** in which state militia fired machine guns into a striker's tent, killing 14 adults (2 women) and 11 children. The strikers were finally disarmed by federal troops.

Feb. 25. Sixteenth Amendment to the Constitution, empowering Congress to levy income taxes without apportionment among the states and without regard to any census or enumeration, was declared in effect.

March 4. The Department of Labor was created, with a seat in the cabinet. This was part of a growing set of laws—including the **Federal Mediation and Conciliation Service** and the **Seaman's Act of 1915**—designed to reduce industrial strife and recognize the rights of workers.

March 4–1921, March 4. WOODROW WILSON, 28th president.

May 31. The Seventeenth Amendment to the Constitution, providing for direct election of senators by the people, was declared in effect.

Oct. 3. The Underwood Tariff Act reduced the average rate of duty to 26.67 percent. A graduated surtax on incomes above $20,000 was imposed.

Dec. 23. THE FEDERAL RESERVE BANK ACT. The panic of 1907 had emphasized the weakness of the national banking system. The **Aldrich-Vreeland Act** was passed in 1908 as an emergency measure and **provided for the appointment of a national monetary commission to study the problem.** The report of the commission was submitted (1912), and Wilson asked for legislation that would provide an elastic currency (based on commercial assets rather than bonded indebtedness), mobilization of bank reserves, public control of the banking system, and decentralization. These features were embodied in the **Act**

of 1913. The country was divided into 12 districts, each with a **federal reserve bank.**

1914, April 21–1921. Relations with Mexico (p. 747). Wilson's refusal to recognize the Huerta regime in Mexico led to the seizure of the port of **Veracruz** by American marines (April 21, 1914). In Oct. 1915 an inter-American conference decided to recognize **Carranza,** which prompted Pancho Villa to raid Columbus, N.M. (March 1916). **U.S. expedition against Villa** was commanded by Gen. **John J. Pershing** (1916).

Article 27 of the **Mexican constitution of 1917** led to American businesses' demand for intervention, which Wilson successfully resisted.

1914, Aug. 15. Panama Canal formally opened (p. 635).

Sept. 26. Federal Trade Commission Act abolished the Bureau of Corporations (1903) and established a five-member bipartisan commission, with investigative and regulatory powers in regard to business and corporate practices.

Oct. 15. Clayton Anti-Trust Act, an amendment of the Sherman Act (1890), prohibited price discrimination, exclusive selling or leasing contracts, intercorporate stockholdings, and interlocking directorates in large corporations. It sought to restrict the use of the injunction in labor difficulties and exempted labor, agricultural, and horticultural organizations from the operation of the antitrust laws.

Arizona adopted an **old-age pension system,** which the state supreme court declared unconstitutional. In the 1920s, however, many states would enact such laws.

Dissatisfied with the slow pace of change in the political status of women, **Alice Paul** (1885–1977), a young Quaker woman, spearheaded the formation of the **Congressional Union (later the National Woman's Party)** and escalated the struggle for equal rights for women. At a mass meeting in New York City, women called themselves **feminists** and proclaimed their determination to break from the "separate sphere" into the "human race." *(To p. 726)*

3. BRITISH NORTH AMERICA, 1789–1914

(From pp. 413, 417)

a. OVERVIEW

The period between the American Revolution and the 1880s witnessed major transformations in Canadian society. The country made the transition from a political economy shaped by British mercantilism to a new system of free trade, industrialization, and urbanization. During this period, the nation also attracted large numbers of new immigrants, moved into the western territories, and gradually brought disparate provinces into a larger national union. Significant class, regional, and racial factors nonetheless shaped the nation's history, but they did not erupt into a bloody civil war (between Europeans, as in the United States) partly because they were legally defined and institutionalized from the outset.

Canada's European population increased from an estimated 250,000 in 1791 to over 1.6 million in 1845. By the 1870s, the nation's population had increased to nearly 4 million. Although French-speaking Canadians outnumbered other nationality groups during the early years, by the 1840s English-speaking Canadians surpassed their French-speaking counterparts in numbers. With the repeal of the British Corn Laws (p. 448) during the 1840s and the rise of free trade policies thereafter, the Canadian economy experienced the beginnings of a fundamental reorientation toward industrialism. New manufacturing establishments slowly emerged, cities expanded, and improvements in transportation and communication proceeded apace. By the 1860s and 1870s, new urban industrial elites increasingly displaced an earlier commercial elite with close ties to agricultural production. Nonetheless, for most of this period the old commercial elite dominated the economy, society, and politics of the nation. They controlled the provincial governments and made policies that reinforced their control of the nation's resources. White workers, women, African Canadians, and Native Americans found it difficult to reverse patterns of inequality that subordinated them within the Canadian political economy. Moreover, the cleavage between French- and English-speaking Canadians persisted.

Despite social fragmentation, Canada experienced significant strides toward independence and sovereignty. Although it was divided between Upper Canada and Lower Canada and remained closely anchored to the British Empire following the American Revolution, it gained an expanding measure of autonomy during the 19th century. In 1840, the Union Act brought the two Canadas together in one legislature, and, following the American Civil War, the British North American Act created the Dominion of Canada. Consisting of four provinces—Ontario, Quebec, Nova Scotia, and New Brunswick—the nation moved toward even greater control over its domestic and foreign affairs.

b. THE DOMINION OF CANADA, 1789–1877

1791, June 10. PASSAGE OF THE CANADA ACT through the British Parliament. It went into effect on Dec. 26. Canada was divided at the Ottawa River into **Upper Canada (chiefly English) and Lower Canada (predominantly French).** Each part had a governor, a Legislative Council appointed by him, and an elected Assembly. Colonial laws could be disallowed by the home government within two years of passage. One-seventh of all land granted was to be reserved for the maintenance of the Protestant clergy. All rights of the Catholic Church were reaffirmed.

EXPLORATION OF THE WEST. In 1789 a Spanish expedition from Mexico took possession of the northwest coast, but in 1790 Spain abandoned claims to the region **(treaty of Oct. 28).** In 1792 **Capt. George Vancouver** explored the Pacific coast and circumnavigated Vancouver Island. In 1793 **Alexander Mackenzie** reached the coast after the first overland journey from the east. Meanwhile (1785–95) **David Thompson** had traversed much of the territory along the coast of Hudson Bay north to Fort Churchill, as well as the regions about Lake Winnipeg and along the Saskatchewan and Athabasca Rivers. **Jay's Treaty** between the United States and Great Britain (Nov. 19, 1794) provided for a boundary commission to determine the frontier west of the Lake of the Woods.

By 1810 much of the southern half of present-day Canada had been trekked by various explorers and traders. In 1811 **Lord Selkirk** bought from the **Hudson's Bay Company** 116,000 square miles for settlement in Manitoba, Minnesota, and North Dakota. Scottish settlers arrived there on the **Red River** in 1812. In 1815 an attack was launched on the colony by agents of the rival Northwest Company; colonists were driven out in 1815 and 1816. An investigation in 1817 upheld the claims of Lord Selkirk, and the colony was reestablished.

1791. Estimated population of Canada: French descent, 140,000; British, 110,000; 50,000 Indians in the settled sections of British North America; and a small number of African Canadians. Nearly 50 percent of the 3,000 **black loyalists in Nova Scotia** responded to their lowly position by emigrating to the **African colony of Sierra Leone.**

Despite the support of Indians like Joseph Brant during the American Revolution, Britain offended them by ceding large tracts of Indian land to the U.S.

1796. The arrival of **Jamaican maroons augmented** Nova Scotia's small black population.

1804. The Alien Act was passed, permitting banishment of anyone found guilty of disturbing the peace in Upper Canada.

1807. Napoleon closed off Baltic Sea sources of timber supplies and helped to stimulate the growth of the Canadian timber industry.

1809. An opposition political group called the **Society of Loyal Electors** was formed on **Prince Edward Island.** A similar group known as the **Parti Canadien (later Parti Patriot)** formed in **Lower Canada** at about the same time. They were considered the earliest manifestations of political parties in Canada.

Painter **William Berczy (1744–1813)** produced his masterpiece of early Canadian painting, *The Woolsey Family.*

1812, June 18. UNITED STATES DECLARED WAR ON GREAT BRITAIN. Among the causes of conflict were the continued trouble with the Indians, supposedly instigated and equipped by the British in Canada, and the American desire to conquer Canada. A triple attack was planned: on Montreal; on the region opposite Niagara; and on the region opposite Detroit. On the Montreal front at Niagara, the offensive failed to materialize. At Detroit a short advance was made, followed by retreat. The British, under Gen. Isaac Brock, secured the **surrender of Detroit** (Aug. 16, 1812). Brock then turned to Niagara and fought the successful engagement of **Queenston Heights** (Oct. 13), in which he was killed.

Canada's small **black population** was reinforced by the **arrival of 2,000 ex-slaves from the United States.** By 1860, an estimated 30,000 additional slaves entered Canada via **the Underground Railroad.**

1813. The Americans captured **York** (Toronto) on April 27, but abandoned it soon afterward (May 2). In Ohio the Americans were vigorously attacked by the British, supported by the Indians **(Tecumseh).** On Sept. 10 **Lt. Oliver Hazard Perry,** with an improvised fleet, won the naval **Battle of Lake Erie** and forced the British to abandon Detroit. The Americans, under **Gen. William Henry Harrison,** crossed into Ontario and fought the successful engagement on the **Thames River** (Oct. 5), but were unable to follow up the advantage. The campaign against Montreal was begun on Oct. 17, but the Americans were defeated in the **Battle of Crysler's Farm** on Nov. 11, and the advance was abandoned. On Dec. 10 an American force burned **Newark;** in retaliation, the British and Canadians, after taking **Fort Niagara** (Dec. 18), burned **Buffalo** (Dec. 29–31).

1814, July 5. The Americans, advancing from Niagara, took **Fort Erie** and won the engagement at **Chippewa Plains.** They advanced to Queenston, but then fell back again.

July 25. Sixteen thousand British troops had been sent to Canada, and an invasion was begun by way of Lake Champlain.

Sept. 11. An American naval force under **Lt.** (later Captain) **Thomas Macdonough** won the **Battle of Plattsburg** and forced the retirement of the British.

Sept. 21. The British, having invaded Maine, declared all territory east of the Penobscot annexed to New Brunswick.

Dec. 24. The **Treaty of Ghent** brought the war to a close. All captured territory was returned, and a commission to delimit the northeastern frontier was provided for.

1817, April 28. In an exchange of notes, the United States and Great Britain agreed to **restrict naval forces on the Great Lakes** to one each on Lake Champlain and Lake Ontario and two on the upper lakes.

Bank of Montreal was founded. By 1840, Montreal was the country's largest city, with 40,000 people. Toronto had less than 10,000 as late as 1834.

1818, Oct. 20. Treaty between the United States and Great Britain gave Americans the right to fish on the coasts of Newfoundland and Labrador and to dry fish in unsettled bays. The boundary between the United States and Canada west of the Lake of the Woods was fixed on the 49th parallel to the Rocky Mountains. Territory west of the Rockies was to be jointly occupied for ten years.

John MacLean (Iain MacGhilleathain, 1787–1848) published his famous **collection of poems,** including the works of others as well as his own.

1820–32. Samuel Cunard of Halifax and the Buchanan brothers (Isaac and Peter) symbolized the merchant's role in Canada's changing commercial economy.

The **Lachine Canal** was completed (1821–25), enabling vessels to partially bypass rapids of the St. Lawrence River above Montreal. The **Welland Canal** connected Lake Erie and Lake Ontario (1829), and the **Rideau Canal** linked the Ottawa River at Ottawa with Lake Ontario at Kingston (1826–32). **Masons working on the Lachine Canal struck for shorter hours in 1823.**

1821, March 26. The Northwest Company merged with the Hudson's Bay Company under the latter's name. Rights of exclusive trade to the company in the territory allotted to it was renewed for 21 years.

Bank of Upper Canada was chartered at York.

McGill College was founded on the basis of a gift from Montreal merchant James McGill. **University of King's College** had been founded in 1789 in **Nova Scotia. Dalhousie College** was founded in Halifax by Lord Dalhousie in 1818.

1824. Election of 1824 resulted in an Assembly in **Upper Canada** that for the first time opposed established policies and pushed for significant reforms.

Julia Catherine Hart (1796–1867) published St. Ursula's Convent; or, The Nun of Canada, the first novel by an American-born Canadian of British descent.

1826. Naturalization (or Alien) Bill was passed in **Upper Canada;** the law denied British citizenship to Americans who had lived in the province for less than seven years and who had not declared allegiance to the king and renounced allegiance to the United States.

Disguised as Indians, a group of young Tories destroyed the printing press of the radical **William Lyon Mackenzie.**

1828–32. First **Mechanics Institutes** were formed in British North America. The **York Typographical Society** was formed in 1832.

1834. The Scottish-born radical **William Lyon Mackenzie (1795–1861)** of Upper Canada became the first mayor of **Toronto. Mackenzie** opposed prevailing oligarchies and soon became part of a body of Canadian reformers that included **Louis Joseph Papineau (1786–1871) of Lower Canada; Joseph Howe (1804–73) of Nova Scotia; and William Cooper (1786–1867) of Prince Edward Island.**

1836, July 21. First **Canadian railroad** opened, from Laprairie on the St. Lawrence to St. Johns on the Richelieu.

1837. REBELLION IN UPPER AND LOWER CANADA. Armed rebellion of radicals, supported by discontented farmers, emerged in **Upper and Lower Canada.** Many rebels perished in skirmishes with the government forces, which soon put down the rebellions. Authorities eventually captured 753 men, tried 168, and sentenced 99 to death (12 were actually executed and 58 banished to Australia). This struggle had been brewing ever since 1815 and was also the result of constitutional conflict between the governors and the appointed Legislative Councils; they represented bureaucratic and vested interests (*family compact* in Upper Canada, *château clique* in Lower Canada) on the one hand, and the popularly elected Assemblies on the other. Popular leaders in Upper Canada included **Robert Gourlay** (expelled, 1818), **William Lyon Mackenzie,** and **Egerton Ryerson;** in Lower Canada, **Louis Joseph Papineau.** Grievances included control of judiciary, control of revenue, supply bills, clergy reserves, established churches, executive council.

The situation was worst in Lower Canada, where the British minority, represented by the governor and the Legislative Council, was opposed by the French majority in the Assembly. In 1822 it had been proposed to reunite Upper and Lower Canada, which roused a storm of protest in Lower Canada. A British parliamentary investigation was made in 1828 and led to various administrative reform proposals, but nothing came of them. In 1834 the Assembly of Lower Canada adopted the "92 resolutions," a declaration of rights. By 1837 affairs had reached a deadlock, and the popular leaders decided to resort to force.

In Lower Canada the rebellion was confined to an area around Montreal. There were a number of riots and some fighting at **St. Denis** and **St. Charles.** The rebels were easily defeated, and the leaders fled to the United States. In Upper Canada the rebels, under Mackenzie, attacked **Toronto** (Dec. 5), but were driven off. Mackenzie fled across the border and on Dec. 13 seized **Navy Island** in the Niagara River, where he proclaimed a provisional government.

Dec. 29. A Canadian government force crossed the river and burned the American steamer *Caroline*, which had been supplying the rebels; the incident triggered a famous case in international law.

1838, Jan. 13. Mackenzie abandoned Navy Island and was arrested in the United States.

During the year 1838 the rebels, supported by American sympathizers (Hunters' Lodges), staged several invasions from the United States, but none of these assumed large proportions.

May 29. Lord Durham arrived at Quebec as governor in chief of all the British North American provinces. His lenient treatment of the rebels led to disavowal by the home government. On Oct. 9 he resigned.

The **Cree and Assiniboine Indians** suffered much loss of life from a **smallpox epidemic.**

1839, Jan. Durham's famous *Report on the Affairs of British North America* was published. He proposed the union of Upper and Lower Canada and the grant of responsible government. The imperial government was to retain control only of foreign relations, regulation of trade, disposal of public lands, and determination of the colonial constitution.

June 20. Lord John Russell introduced in the British Parliament a resolution based on the *Durham Report.*

Oct. 19. Poulett Thomson (Lord Sydenham) arrived at Quebec as governor in chief, to prepare the provinces for union.

1840, July 23. THE BRITISH PARLIAMENT PASSED THE UNION ACT. This united Upper and Lower Canada into one government, with one governor, one appointed Legislative Council, and one popularly elected Assembly, in which the former two provinces had equal representation. Various administrative reforms were carried through. The issue of responsible government was evaded, and the principle was not firmly established in practice until the time of **Lord Elgin's governorship** (1847–54), in the course of the crisis arising from the **Rebellion Losses Bill** (1849).

St. John, New Brunswick, emerged as a major shipbuilding center, with the largest merchant fleet of any port in British North America.

1842, Aug. 9. Ashburton Treaty between the United States and Great Britain. Great Britain abandoned more than half of the territory claimed on the northeast frontier.

1845. Estimated population of Canada: British descent, 1 million; French, 600,000; Indian 150,000; and small number of African Canadians.

1846, June 15. Oregon boundary treaty was established between the United States and Great Britain, following a period of acute tension.

Aug. 28. British Possessions Act gave Canada the right to fix tariffs.

Repeal of British **Corn Laws and timber duties** led to a collapse of prices for these commodities and the fall of exports.

1849, June 26. Abolition of the **British Navigation Acts,** removing restrictions on foreign shipping. Following the abolition of the Corn Laws in 1846, this action led to an acute economic depression in Canada and to a short-lived agitation for annexation to the United States (**Annexation Manifesto,** Oct. 10, 1849). Beginning in the 1830s, nearly 40,000 French Canadians left the seigneurial districts for the U.S. The numbers escalated over the next two decades.

Four leading **English newspapers in Montreal pushed for annexation to the U.S.** in the wake of the impact of British free trade legislation on the Canadian economy. The journalists also advocated annexation as a protest against the **Rebellion Losses Bill of 1849,** which compensated **Lower Canadians** for losses in the **rebellion of 1837.**

1854, Jan. The **Great Western Railway** opened, linking Niagara Falls, Hamilton, London, and Windsor.

June 5. The Elgin Treaty established reciprocity between Canada and the United States. This was abrogated by the United States in 1866.

Sept.–Dec. A law converted **clergy reserves** into a special fund to be distributed to counties and cities for secular purposes. Another law abolished **seigneurial tenure;** feudal dues were converted into cash rents.

The **Grand Trunk Railway** was incorporated to build a railroad from Toronto to Montreal.

1856, June 24. The Legislative Council, hitherto appointed, was made elective.

1857. Discovery of gold in Vancouver attracted a variety of new ethnic groups to the area, including Mexicans and Chinese as well as Europeans.

The Canadian legislature passed the **Act for the Gradual Civilization of the Indian Tribes in the Canadas,** which included forced removal of Indians from the path of European settlement.

1858, Aug. 2. British Columbia, having been withdrawn from the jurisdiction of the Hudson's Bay Company, was given separate administration.

1850–60. Hugh Allan (1810–82), president of the **Montreal Board of Trade** (1851–54), was considered the leading financier and industrialist of the period. He formed the **Montreal Ocean Steamship Company** in 1854 and held investments in the Cornwall Woolen Manufacturing Company, the Montreal Rolling Mills, and the Canada Paper Company.

Women and girls soon made up over a third of Montreal's industrial labor force. They made up a majority of workers in the garment and tobacco industries.

1861. The **final Nova Scotia** peace treaty with the **Micmacs** failed to deal with the **land rights of Indians.**

1866. Beginning of the **Fenian** (Irish-American) **raids,** designed to bring pressure on the British government in favor of Ireland. Fenians from Buffalo seized **Fort Erie** (June 1), but were driven out. Other raids took place from Vermont, and Fenian troubles continued to some extent until 1871.

1867, March 29. BRITISH NORTH AMERICA ACT united Ontario, Quebec, New Brunswick, and Nova Scotia in the **Dominion of Canada** (effective on July 1). The movement for confederation was the result of growing difficulty in the government of United Canada (religious and racial differences, problems of representation), as well as of economic (especially railway) considerations and military (defense) problems in the American Civil War period. The movement began in the Maritime Provinces (**Charlottetown conference,** Sept. 1864), but expanded almost at once (**Quebec convention,** Oct. 10–28, 1864, in which all provinces were represented). The 72 **Quebec resolutions** became the basis for the act of confederation. They provided for a federal government and provincial governments, a federal Parliament of two houses (the Senate consisting of 24 members each from Ontario, Quebec, and a third division comprising Nova Scotia and New Brunswick; and an elected lower house). Representatives of the provinces conferred with imperial authorities in London (Dec. 1866) and drew up the **London resolutions,** which were transformed into the final act.

1867–68. Lord Monck, first governor-general. (Sir) **John A. Macdonald** was first premier of the Dominion.

1868, Dec. 29. Sir John Young (Lord Lisgar) was appointed governor-general (1868–72).

"Canada First" movement was initiated with a small group of intellectuals in memory of the parliamentarian **D'Arcy McGee.** The movement emphasized the **"Aryan origins"** of Canada and attacked the Indians and Métis as inferior elements in Canadian culture and history.

1869, Nov. 19. THE DOMINION PURCHASED THE NORTHWEST TERRITORIES from the Hudson's Bay Company for $1,500,000. The company retained one-twentieth of the land. The territories were taken over in 1870.

1869–70. RED RIVER REBELLION. The multiracial Métis, led by **Louis Riel** (1844–85) near Fort Garry (Winnipeg), were irritated chiefly by the belief that surveys being made were to rob them of their land. They set up a provisional government (Nov. 1869) with Riel as president; in their expedition from Portage Laprairie, they were defeated and captured (Feb. 1870). **Thomas Scott** (Orangeman) was executed (March), and great indignation was aroused in Ontario. The rebels were dispersed without a blow before the advance of an expedition under **Col. Garnet** (later Lord) **Wolseley.** Their actions nonetheless led to the **Manitoba Act** (1870), which extended provincial status to the region.

1871, July 1. British Columbia joined the Dominion.

1872, May 22. Marquess of Dufferin was appointed governor-general (1872–78).

July 1. Prince Edward Island joined the Dominion; the Dominion assumed its railway debt.

Nov. 7. Resignation of Macdonald, owing to pressure of public opinion following **transcontinental railway scandal** and charges of corruption in past elections. Alexander Mackenzie formed a Liberal cabinet and won overwhelming victory at general elections.

Toronto Society of Artists was formed to promote research and learning in the arts and sciences.

1869–72. Formation of early Canadian **department stores—T. Eaton Company** (1869) and **Simpson's Ltd.** (1872).

1873. The **North-West Mounted Police** was formed.

1874. Introduction of **ballot voting;** elections were held on a single day.

First Canadian branch of the **Women Christian Temperance Union** was formed at Picton, Ontario, by a public schoolteacher, **Letitia Youmans** (1827–96).

1875. The British Crown disfranchised the Chinese.

1876. Opening of the **Intercolonial Railway,** connecting Ontario with the Maritime Provinces; it was owned and operated by the government.

Toronto Women's Literary Club formed the **first women's suffrage organization** in Canada. *(To p. 621)*

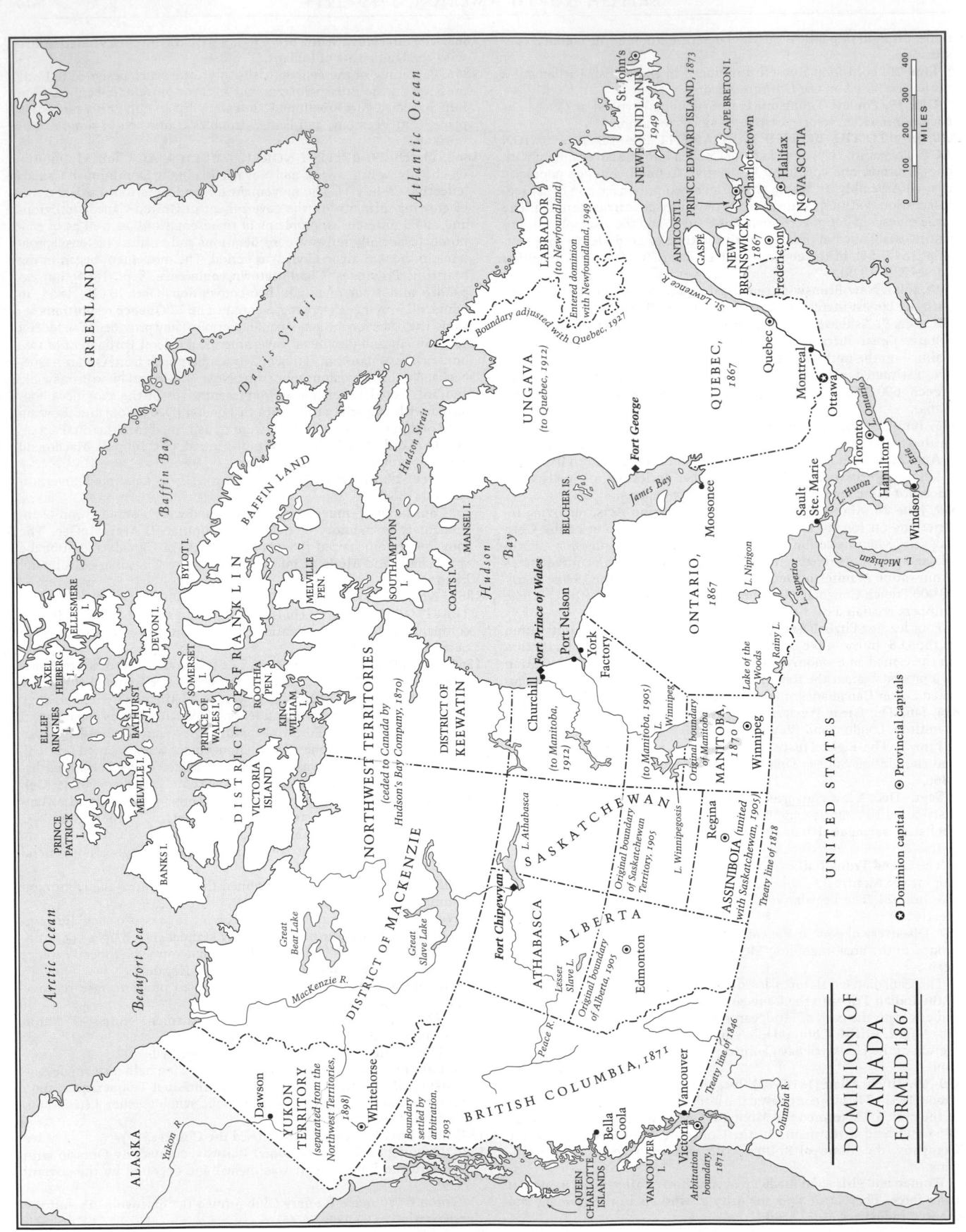

GREENLAND

Atlantic Ocean

St. John's

NEWFOUNDLAND, *1949*

Baffin Bay

LABRADOR
(to Newfoundland)

Entered dominion
with Newfoundland, 1949

CAPE BRETON I.

PRINCE EDWARD ISLAND, *1873*

Davis Strait

ANTICOSTI I.

GASPÉ

Charlottetown

Halifax

NOVA SCOTIA

NEW
BRUNSWICK,
1867

Fredericton

Boundary adjusted with Quebec, 1927

UNGAVA
(to Quebec, 1912)

St. Lawrence R.

QUEBEC,
1867

Quebec

Montreal

Ottawa

DISTRICT OF FRANKLIN

BAFFIN LAND

Hudson Strait

Fort George

James Bay

L. Ontario

Toronto

Hamilton

L. Erie

Windsor

BYLOT I.

ELLESMERE I.

AXEL
HEIBERG
I.

DEVON I.

SOUTHAMPTON
I.

COATS I.

MANSEL I.

BELCHER IS.

Hudson

Bay

Moosonee

Sault
Ste. Marie

L. Nipigon

ONTARIO,
1867

L. Superior

L. Huron

L. Michigan

ELLEF
RINGNES
I.

PRINCE
PATRICK
I.

MELVILLE I.

BATHURST
I.

PRINCE OF
WALES I.

SOMERSET
I.

BOOTHIA
PEN.

KING
WILLIAM
I.

MELVILLE
PEN.

Fort Prince of Wales

Port Nelson

York
Factory

Churchill
(to Manitoba,
1912)

DISTRICT OF
KEEWATIN

Lake of the
Woods

Rainy L.

L.
Winnipeg

(to Manitoba, 1905)

Original boundary
of Manitoba

MANITOBA,
1870

Winnipeg

Arctic Ocean

Beaufort Sea

BANKS I.

VICTORIA
ISLAND

NORTHWEST TERRITORIES
(ceded to Canada by
Hudson's Bay Company, 1870)

DISTRICT OF MACKENZIE

*Great
Bear Lake*

*Great
Slave Lake*

MacKenzie R.

L. Athabasca

Fort Chipewyan

ATHABASCA

*Lesser
Slave L.*

Peace R.

ALBERTA

Original boundary
of Alberta, 1905

Edmonton

SASKATCHEWAN

Original boundary
of Saskatchewan
Territory, 1905

L. Winnipegosis

Regina

ASSINIBOIA
(united
with Saskatchewan, 1905)

Treaty line of 1818

UNITED STATES

● Dominion capital

⊙ Provincial capitals

ALASKA

Yukon R.

Dawson

YUKON
TERRITORY
(separated from the
Northwest Territories,
1898)

Whitehorse

*Boundary
settled by
arbitration,
1903*

BRITISH COLUMBIA, *1871*

Treaty line of 1846

Columbia R.

QUEEN
CHARLOTTE
ISLANDS

Bella
Coola

VANCOUVER
I.

Victoria

Vancouver

*Arbitration
boundary,
1871*

DOMINION OF
CANADA
FORMED 1867

400

300

200

100

0

MILES

c. NEWFOUNDLAND, 1855-1878

1855. Responsible government was granted. The bicameral legislature comprised the Legislative Council (15 members), which was appointed by the governor-in-council, and the House of Assembly (36 members), which was elective. A responsible cabinet was instituted.

1864. Copper was discovered in the north, and mining operations were begun.

1873. Direct steam communication with England and America was established.

d. CANADA, 1878-1914

As in the United States, this period represented the triumph of industrialism in Canadian society. The nation had taken significant steps toward national unification in 1867, but 1885 is considered the crucial watershed in Canadian history during this period. The year 1885 marked the completion of the Canadian Pacific Railway, the nation's first transcontinental transportation network. Like the United States, Canada was now linked by a single rail system from the Atlantic to the Pacific. Moreover, in 1885, Canadian forces defeated the Métis (a multiracial ethnic group) and its Indian allies and opened the way for the unrestricted European occupation of the Canadian west. In the wake of the Métis war, Canada also embarked upon a public debate about its national identity, which revealed deep cleavages between English-speaking (mainly Ontario) and French-speaking (mainly Quebec) Canada. At the same time, this period witnessed the growth of the labor movement, rising demands for women's suffrage, and growing animosities and restrictions against the small Chinese population. Thus, by the eve of World War I, Canada continued to wrestle with significant class, cultural, and regional divisions.

1878, Oct. 5. Marquess of Lorne, governor-general (1878-83).

Oct. General elections were held on the **tariff issue.** Conservatives were victorious in support of protection; Macdonald became premier (Oct. 17), and the protective tariff was instituted.

1880. Queen's Medical School in Kingston opened its doors to women. **Kingston's Women's Medical College** opened three years later.

1881. A charter was given to the newly formed **CANADIAN PACIFIC RAILWAY COMPANY** for construction of a transcontinental railroad, following financial difficulties of older companies. The government granted $25 million, 25,000,000 acres of land, and 670 miles of track already laid; a loan of $20 million was made in 1884 (repaid, 1887). The last spike was driven on Nov. 7, 1885, and the railway formally opened in May 1887; its 2,905 miles of rail joined coast to coast, catalyzing Canadian development. Steamship lines were established, and the flow of immigrants to the west accelerated.

1883, Aug. 18. Marquess of Lansdowne, governor-general (1883-88).

The **Canadian Labor Congress** was formed (name changed to **Trades and Labor Congress in 1892**).

1885, March 26. Outbreak of the **Northwest Rebellion.** It was quickly suppressed by the Dominion government; troops from all the provinces were transported over the new Canadian Pacific Railway. **Riel** surrendered (May 15) and was executed (Nov. 16).

1886. Canadian and Bering Sea fisheries dispute with the United States.

Quebec Board of Health was created by the **Public Health Act** of the province.

1887. Honoré Mercier (1840-91) of Quebec invited the provinces to an **Interprovincial Conference** to reexamine the nature of the federal compact between them and the Dominion.

1888, May 1. Lord Stanley (Earl of Derby), governor-general (1888-93).

1890. Liberals urged policy of "unrestricted reciprocity" to remedy the depression following the U.S. McKinley tariff. **Continental Union Association** was formed. The **Imperial Federation League** (1885) urged preferential trade with the mother country.

Professional hockey was initiated with the formation of the **Ontario Hockey Association.**

1891, June 6. Death of **Sir John A. Macdonald;** he was succeeded by **Sir John J. C. Abbott** (June 16).

1892, Nov. Resignation of Abbott; he was succeeded by **Sir John S. D. Thompson** (Dec. 5).

1892-93. Bering Sea arbitration.

1893, May 22. Earl of Aberdeen appointed governor-general (1893-98).

National Council of Women of Canada advocated broad social reforms, but attracted little attention from working-class women.

1894, June 23-July 10. Second colonial conference was held at Ottawa.

Dec. 12. Death of **Thompson. Mr.** (later Sir) **Mackenzie Bowell** succeeded him (Dec. 21).

1895. Sir Charles Tupper, premier (1895-96).

1896. The offer of Newfoundland to enter the Dominion was refused because of financial disagreement.

April 27. Resignation of **Bowell.**

July 11. Mr. (later Sir) **Wilfrid Laurier** became premier (1896-1911) as a result of a Liberal victory in the general elections (June).

1897. British preferential tariff was instituted. In 1898 the preference was increased to 25 percent and in 1900 to 33.3 percent. Germany retaliated (July 7, 1899) by depriving Canada of most-favored-nation status.

Hubert Brown Ames (1863-1954) published his pioneering sociological study of Montreal, *The City Below the Hill,* modeled on progressive urban reform movements in England and the United States.

1898. Canadian Northern Railway was chartered.

July 30. Lord Minto was appointed governor-general (1898-1904).

1899, Oct. 29. South African (Boer) War (p. 598). The first Canadian contingent was sent to South Africa; a second was sent in 1900. The official contingents were withdrawn before the end of the war, owing to dissatisfaction in Quebec.

Nova Scotia Steel and Coal Corporation (Scotia) and **Dominion Iron and Steel Corporation (Disco)** emerged as major corporations.

1902, Oct. 31. Cable from Vancouver to Brisbane was completed.

The **Trades and Labor Congress** expelled a union connected to the **Knights of Labor** and the **American Federation of Labor.** Expelled unions formed the **National Trades and Labour Congress of Canada.** An estimated 155,000 Canadians belonged to labor unions by World War I.

1903. Alaskan boundary arbitration with the United States (p. 615). High dissatisfaction with the award.

1904, Sept. 26. Earl Grey appointed governor-general (1904-11).

Socialist Party of Canada organized.

1905, Sept. 1. Formation of the provinces of **Alberta and Saskatchewan.**

1905-6. Niagara Falls was developed for hydroelectric purposes for the first time. **Ontario Hydroelectric Commission** was formed.

1908. Civil Service Commission was appointed for the selection of civil officials.

1910. Formation of a small Canadian navy.

1911, Jan. 26. Publication of a **reciprocity agreement** with the United States; ratified by the U.S. Senate (July 22). But in the general elections (Sept. 21), the Liberals were defeated on the issue, and reciprocity was dropped. **Mr.** (later Sir) **Robert L. Borden** formed a Conservative ministry (Oct. 10).

March 21. Duke of Connaught was appointed governor-general (1911-16).

1912. The **social gospel movement** gained expression in the formation of the **Social Service Council of Canada.**

1913, May 30. Defeat in the Senate of a navy bill providing for the contribution of three dreadnoughts to the imperial navy.

1914, April 7. Completion of the **Grand Trunk Pacific Railway.**

May 21. SS *Komagatu Maru* arrived in Vancouver Harbor; 300 Hindus were refused entrance to British Columbia and sent back to India.

May 29. SS *Empress of Ireland* was sunk in a collision in the Gulf of St. Lawrence; 1,023 lives were lost.

Aug. 4. Entrance of Great Britain into **World War I.**   *(To p. 733)*

e. NEWFOUNDLAND, 1878-1914

1880. The government loaned $1 million to create a **railway from St. John's to Hall's Bay**; it was completed to Harbour Grace (1884); after financial difficulties, construction was taken over by Mr. R. G. Reid (1893) and built to Port-aux-Basques.

1888. The Bait Act took effect, after considerable controversy and the protests of the French government. It prohibited capture in Newfoundland waters of bait fish for exportation or sale, except under special license. French retaliations followed until a modus vivendi was enacted (1890). The issue was finally settled in the Anglo-French convention of 1904.

1894-96. Bank failures, insolvency, and severe financial depression. Canadian banks replaced former government institutions. A delegation was sent to Ottawa to discuss union with Canada. Canada objected to assuming all of Newfoundland's $16 million in debt, and negotiations were broken off.

1900. Resignation of **Sir James Winter;** succeeded by **Mr.** (later Sir) **Robert Bond.**

1906, Oct. Modus vivendi with the United States followed difficulties with fishing rights under the Treaty of 1818. The dispute was referred to the Hague tribunal, and an award (Sept. 1910) allowed Great Britain (Newfoundland) the right to make regulations subject to the Treaty of 1818 and defined the "three-mile limit" in bays to be from a line across the bay at a point where a distance of ten miles was not exceeded.

1909. Resignation of premier **Sir Robert Bond;** succeeded by **Sir Edward P. Morris.**

1914, Aug. 4. Declaration of war by Great Britain. Newfoundland, like the other members of the empire, supported the mother country and sent troops. *(To p. 735)*

I. LATIN AMERICA, 1806-1914

(From pp. 405, 407)

1. PERIODIZATION

Latin American history in the 19th century can be divided into several general periods, despite the great diversity of the major regions and nations. **Wars of independence** dominated the decades between 1806 and 1825. The following quarter-century saw the **insecurities of new nations** and the **rise of political forms like** *caudillismo* (strongman rule) in response; manufacturing imports from British industry and political turmoil weakened local economies. Midcentury decades saw some political and economic stabilization and signs of greater cultural vitality as Latin American novelists and other intellectuals began to emerge. **The rise of the export economy and some new foreign interference,** particularly from the United States, marked the decades around 1900.

2. THE WARS OF INDEPENDENCE, 1806-1872

a. CAUSES

(From p. 405)

Political, economic, and social factors inherent in the Spanish colonial system were the fundamental causes that led to the separation of the American colonies from the mother country. The Bourbon reforms prompted widespread discontent in Spanish America. Though export-oriented areas thrived with free trade policies, Spanish American entrepreneurs were excluded from transatlantic trade and shipping, which the Spaniards controlled. The opening of colonial markets to European manufactures affected local industries in certain areas. Popular sectors throughout Spanish America viewed new fiscal exactions as endangering their living standards. Sales taxes and the enforcement of state monopolies affected many ordinary traders and consumers. Tribute and forced sales of goods angered Indian and mestizo peasants.

The Bourbon reforms (p. 402) curtailed the ecclesiastical *fuero,* an institution that placed the clergy outside the control of civil authorities. In areas where the church had grown influential, this measure caused resentment, especially in the lower clergy. In contrast to the weakening of the church, the Bourbon reforms reinforced the military *fuero,* which placed Spaniards and creoles, and even people of color who served in the army, outside civilian jurisdiction. The army created an avenue of social recognition for creoles and nonwhite people, and allowed them to develop military skills that later proved useful in the struggle for independence. The creole aristocracy, however, felt threatened by policies that allowed nonwhites to achieve privileges previously reserved for the elite. The participation of popular sectors, most of them of nonwhite background, in the independence conflicts provoked "caste war" fears, since the elites, considering themselves white, framed any assault on their privileges as a racial attack.

The French Revolution of 1789 influenced the **creole elite intellectuals** of the Spanish colonies, but the slaves in the French colony of St. Domingue (Haiti) made a deeper impact on the creole elite when they destroyed the slave system and achieved independence (1804) through a violent social revolution. Slaveholders of the Americas learned from this defeat of French colonialism that they should avoid those conditions that might aid slaves in their struggle for freedom. **To preserve slavery, creole aristocracies of Cuba and Puerto Rico** remained loyal to the colonial state. The American Revolution was also a source of ideas for creole thinkers favoring independence. Many saw **federalism** as the most appropriate system for the new American republics, where unequal regional resources and political power became an immediate source of civil strife. The United States also provided an example of the coexistence of slavery with a republican state, an attractive model, given the economic benefits that sectors of the Spanish American elites derived from slavery.

Crucial for the growth and timing of the independence movements were the political developments in the metropolis. Napoleon invaded Spain and established his brother Joseph on the throne (p. 438). The American colonies refused to recognize him and proclaimed allegiance to the deposed **Ferdinand VII.** The **Constitution of Cádiz** (1812), issued by Spanish Liberals opposing absolutism, provided for a constitutional monarchy and the election of deputies throughout the Spanish domains. Such measures encouraged the formation of **juntas** in the American cities, which tried to govern in the name of the deposed king. The restoration of Ferdinand VII and his determination to restore the old system propelled the creole movement toward separatism.

The **Wars of Independence** passed through two phases; between 1809 and 1816, movements for separation failed everywhere except in the area of the Río de la Plata; between 1816 and 1825, independence was achieved.

b. THE RÍO DE LA PLATA

The period of independence in the region of Río de la Plata opened with a British attempt to gain possession of a portion of the area.

1806. A British fleet occupied Buenos Aires. The viceroy fled, and **Santiago Liniers,** at the head of the colonial militia, organized the unified war effort of Spaniards and creoles, who defeated the British. Upon his return, a *cabildo abierto* deposed the viceroy and elected Liniers, an act that the Crown approved.

1806-7. The British government dispatched an expedition to conquer Buenos Aires. After taking Montevideo, they advanced on Buenos Aires, where the militia organized by local merchants defeated them. The British agreed to retreat from the Río de la Plata and Montevideo. Urban militia allowed the creole elite to control plebeian mobilization through military organization. Military chiefs gained wider influence in the political arena.

1809-10. In view of the apparent success of Napoleon, a provisional junta of the provinces of the Río de la Plata was established in the name of Ferdinand VII (May 25, 1810). Direct Spanish authority was never restored. The junta included **Mariano Moreno** (1778–1811), a creole lawyer, and **Cornelio Saavedra**, a merchant from Upper Peru.

1810–11. The provisional junta rejected royal authority, suppressed Indian tribute, and sought to extend control over the **Banda Oriental** and **Paraguay.** An expedition sent to liberate Upper Peru was defeated, and Paraguay refused to adhere to the provinces of the Río de la Plata. Moreno and his followers opposed the predominance of militia chiefs. The junta forced Moreno from office, and a triumvirate was installed, with **Bernardino Rivadavia** (1780–1845), an extreme liberal, as secretary. The triumvirate dissolved the junta and reorganized the urban militia.

1812. The triumvirate prohibited slave trade and dissolved the provincial juntas, weakening its popularity in the interior and littoral provinces. Army officers formed the **Logia Lautaro,** a Masonic lodge, which removed the triumvirate and Rivadavia from power. The conflict between centralists *(unitarios)* and federalists *(federales)* intensified. José Gervasio Artigas, leader of the Banda Oriental, pressed for the prompt establishment of a federal system.

1812–13. An expedition to invade Upper Peru failed. An assembly abolished Indian forced labor and gave freedom to all children of slave mothers. It suppressed titles of nobility and disentailed properties, excepting those belonging to the Church.

1814. Royalist military buildup in Montevideo and new defeats in Upper Peru induced pessimism about independence among the leaders of Buenos Aires, who started to consider a reconciliation with Spain. The king, however, refused to accept any compromise with the new leaders.

Buenos Aires forbade foreign merchants to trade freely with the other riverine provinces, creating further enmity toward the main port. Liberal policies hurt Buenos Aires merchants unable to restrain the growing role of the British in provincial trade. Support for federalism also grew within Buenos Aires, since it would allow the province to keep the revenues from foreign trade for itself.

1815. Gen. Alvear (1789–1852) became dictator, while Artigas ruled in the Banda Oriental, and the provinces of Santa Fe and Córdoba announced their own independence. **GEN. JOSÉ DE SAN MARTÍN** (1778–1850) departed for Mendoza to organize an army to liberate Chile and later move by sea to attack royalists in Peru. He became one of the greatest military figures of the independence wars.

1816, July 9. Congress of Tucumán declared the **independence of the United Provinces** and elected **Juan Martín Pueyrredón**, a member of the Logia Lautaro, as supreme chief. In his eagerness to destroy federalism, he allowed the Portuguese invasion of the Banda Oriental (p. 623). Federalists, however, prevailed in the littoral provinces.

c. PARAGUAY

1811. A *cabildo abierto* summoned in Asunción by the intendant swore allegiance to Ferdinand VII. Paraguayans defeated Buenos Aires forces, which attempted to incorporate Paraguay into the United Provinces. **Fulgencio Yegros,** a military chief, led proindependence creoles to depose Spanish authorities. A congress of delegates created a governing junta, which included Yegros, as chief, and **Dr. José Gaspar Rodríguez de Francia** (1766–1840), a creole lawyer of the *cabildo*.

Aug. 14. PARAGUAY PROCLAIMED INDEPENDENCE FROM SPAIN. Dr. Francia withdrew from the junta, condemning the excessive influence of the military in government, but the junta and the *cabildo* called him back. Francia signed a treaty with Buenos Aires, which agreed to the principles of federation and free trade. Thus, Francia obtained a tacit recognition of Paraguay's independence and lower taxes for Paraguayan trade. Again, he retreated from the government to create a following for himself among small landowners, ranchers, and farmers, and a network of informers.

1812. Relations with Buenos Aires declined because of the junta's support for Banda Oriental federalist leader José Artigas. Littoral provinces overtaxed Paraguayan commerce. The Portuguese military attempted to invade Paraguayan territory. The junta urged Francia to return and agreed to create a regiment under his exclusive command. Francia removed civilians accused of being Porteñistas (pro-union with Buenos

Aires) from power. He wanted a Paraguay independent from Buenos Aires, which he saw as incapable of suppressing endemic political disorder.

1814. Francia emerged as the most powerful figure in government. He promoted his followers in the army and removed Spaniards from government positions. Francia's supporters summoned an assembly to change the system of government to one-man rule and voted to make Francia *supremo dictador de la República.*

d. THE BANDA ORIENTAL (URUGUAY)

1811. Montevideo creoles, eager to avoid subordination to Buenos Aires, refused to support the May revolution in that city. In the countryside, however, masses of small landowners, dissatisfied with the expansion of the great estates, rose against Spain. **José Gervasio Artigas** (1764–1850), a man from the *estanciero* (rancher) class, emerged as leader and proclaimed allegiance to the junta of Buenos Aires. He formed a coalition of ranchers and gauchos, and attracted to his army Guaraní Indians led by Andrés Guacarí (**Andresito**). Royalists encouraged the Portuguese military, which invaded the Banda Oriental to incorporate it into the Portuguese Empire. Artigas withdrew his troops. Spontaneously, civilians, fleeing from royalist reprisals and Portuguese brutality, joined him en masse and marched into exile. This **exodus of the "Orientales"** (later Uruguayans) left the Banda Oriental virtually depopulated. When Portugal was forced to withdraw from the Banda Oriental, these exiles returned and, allied with Buenos Aires forces, expelled royalists from Montevideo. Buenos Aires leaders, unable to impose centralism upon the Banda Oriental, withdrew.

1815. Artigas ruled the Banda Oriental. Across the Río de la Plata, the provinces of Santa Fe, Entre Ríos, Corrientes, and Córdoba recognized him as the **Protector de los Pueblos Libres** in their struggle against Buenos Aires centralism. Through the **Reglamento Provisorio,** Artigas promoted free trade and distribution of confiscated properties to poor nonwhite and white people. This measure alarmed the landlords.

1816. The Portuguese invaded the Banda Oriental, with the approval of Pueyrredón, Buenos Aires's centralist leader, who sought to destroy federalism.

1817–20. Montevideo surrendered to the Portuguese army, while Artigas organized guerrilla resistance in the countryside. The Portuguese tried to ally the Banda Oriental elite with the Portuguese Empire, but limited compensation for war damages and the granting of lands to Portuguese created hostility.

1820. The defeat of Artigas and his troops at **Tacuarembó** ended the period known as the **Patria Vieja.** Artigas marched into exile in Paraguay. In later years Artigas acquired greater stature as the founding father of Uruguay and as a man of advanced political vision.

1821. A pro-Portuguese congress voted the incorporation of the Banda Oriental into the Portuguese Empire as the **Estado Cisplatino.** In 1824, the *cabildo* of Montevideo swore the allegiance of the Estado Cisplatino to the constitution of the newly proclaimed empire of Brazil.

1825. Fructuoso Rivera (c. 1788–1854), a *caudillo* who briefly supported Brazilian rule, recruited an army of anti-Brazilian patriots. Revolution against Brazil began in April with the landing of the expedition of **33 Orientales** headed by **Antonio Lavalleja,** a *caudillo* and Artigas's follower. Lavalleja and Rivera became allies, attracting the allegiance of hundreds of cowboys and ranchers. Lavalleja sought the support of the Buenos Aires government, proclaiming the incorporation of the Banda Oriental into the **United Provinces of the Río de la Plata.** War between Argentina and Brazil ensued.

1827. A liberation army composed of Argentine and Banda Oriental soldiers defeated the Brazilian army at **Ituzaingó.** Rivera occupied Brazilian territory in Rio Grande do Sul, forcing Brazilian forces to withdraw from the Banda Oriental in exchange for the land he had occupied.

1828. Lavalleja governed independently while negotiations with British mediation led Buenos Aires and the empire to recognize the independence of the Banda Oriental.

e. CHILE

1810. Upon the apparent triumph of Napoleon in Spain, a junta assumed authority in the name of Ferdinand VII and deposed the captain general. The junta was led by **Juan Martínez de Rozas,** a creole official, who promoted liberal reforms. A **general congress** convened at Santiago.

1811–12. Measures to open commerce provoked opposition from creole merchants and most of the landed elite. **José Miguel Carrera** (1785–1821), a member of a landed military family allied to the antiroyalist deputies, led troops and urban crowds to expel conservatives from the congress. He formed an executive junta that abolished the slave trade and freed all children born from slave mothers subsequent to the decree. The creole ruling class divided into factions organized around powerful landed aristocratic families. Gen. **Bernardo O'Higgins** (1778–1842), although not pro-aristocratic, objected to Carrera's bid for popular support.

1812. The junta promulgated the **Reglamento Constitucional,** which recognized Ferdinand VII while asserting that no orders or laws issued outside Chile should be enforced there. It proclaimed civil rights for all Chileans, freedom of the press, and the subordination of the executive to the congress. These measures caused deep discontent in the aristocracy. Royalist Chileans joined the army sent by the viceroy of Peru to subdue Carrera.

1814. The royal government was established in Santiago. O'Higgins agreed on an armistice with Spanish chiefs, but Viceroy Abascal repudiated the treaty and sent a new expedition, which defeated the proindependence army at **Rancagua,** sealing the end of the period known as the **Patria Vieja.**

1814–17. The retaliatory policy followed by the royalist government alienated creoles. O'Higgins moved to Mendoza to collaborate with Gen. San Martín (p. 623) in preparing the liberation of Chile and Peru. **Manuel Rodríguez,** who had served Carrera, organized guerrillas in the countryside.

1817. San Martín, at the head of the patriot army, crossed the Andes and defeated a Spanish army at **Chacabuco** (Feb. 12). O'Higgins was made supreme director.

1818, Feb. 12. THE INDEPENDENCE OF CHILE WAS PROCLAIMED. San Martín's troops defeated a royalist army from Peru at **Maipú,** thus securing the independence of Chile. San Martín started to organize an army to liberate Peru.

f. PERU AND UPPER PERU (PERU AND BOLIVIA)

1809. The inhabitants of **Chuquisaca** and **La Paz,** declaring loyalty to Ferdinand VII, established juntas in their cities and deposed Spanish authorities. Royal troops soon crushed the movements. Viceroy **José de Abascal y Sousa** (1809–16), with the support of the Limeño aristocracy, made the Viceroyalty of Peru the stronghold of royalism in South America.

1810. Buenos Aires's declaration of independence gained widespread support in Upper Peru, whose population initially welcomed a Buenos Aires military expedition, led by Gen. **Juan José Castelli.** His attempts to suppress Indian tribute, however, antagonized the upper classes. His troops sacked Indian towns and behaved as an occupying force. Royalists defeated Castelli's army and retook control of Upper Peru (1811). They sought Indian support, giving weapons to the *kurakas* to distribute among Indian peasants.

1813. In Cuzco, *kuraka* **Mateo Pumacahua** mobilized a large Indian army on behalf of creole patriots imprisoned in Cuzco. The royalist army defeated and executed him (1815).

1813–15. Two Buenos Aires expeditions invaded Upper Peru but disintegrated as soldiers plundered the countryside and royalists defeated them. Disenchanted with the Buenos Aires–led independence movement, Upper Peru patriots sought to develop their own independence forces, while Buenos Aires military leaders altered their strategy for liberating Peru.

1816–24. Royalists eradicated guerrillas from the countryside, and reestablished their dominance in Upper Peru.

1820. After completing preparations in Chile, **San Martín** transported his forces to Peru by sea. Marquis de **Torre Tagle,** who approved of San Martín's conservatism, promoted aristocratic support for him and proclaimed independence in Trujillo. The viceroy abandoned Lima, and San Martín entered the capital.

1821, July 28. San Martín proclaimed the **INDEPENDENCE OF PERU** and assumed the title of protector of Peru. Peruvian Liberals opposed San Martín's monarchical plans.

1822. After meeting Simón Bolívar (1783–1830) in Guayaquil, San Martín resigned and withdrew his troops.

1823. After struggles among the proponents of independence in Lima, a new government was established and invited **Simón Bolívar** to Peru. **Antonio José de Sucre** (1795–1830), his closest lieutenant, moved to Lima with Colombian troops, and Bolívar followed, being proclaimed dictator.

1824. Bolívar and Sucre led their troops into the highlands, where they defeated the royalist army at **Junín** (Aug. 24) and at **Ayacucho** (Dec. 9), which secured the independence of the new republics of South America. The Spanish leaders agreed to withdraw their armies from Peru. Sucre led his troops to liberate Upper Peru and convened a **congress at Chuquisaca.**

1825, Aug. 6. Anxious to preserve their autonomy from the hegemonic pretensions of Buenos Aires, Upper Peru patriots resorted to Sucre's protection to proclaim the **INDEPENDENCE of the new republic of Bolívar (BOLIVIA).**

g. VENEZUELA, NUEVA GRANADA, AND QUITO (GRAN COLOMBIA)

1808. In Bogotá, a junta convened to govern in the name of Ferdinand VII. Cartagena and other cities of Nueva Granada also formed juntas (1810). The captain general of Caracas blocked attempts by the *cabildo* to establish a junta.

1809. In Quito, a revolt installed a junta in the name of Ferdinand VII, with the support of the Quiteño elite. An army, sent by the viceroy of Peru, suppressed the movement.

1810. In Caracas, an extraordinary *cabildo* created a junta to govern in the name of Ferdinand VII and deposed the captain general. Conservatives in the junta forbade the entry of **Francisco de Miranda** (1750–1816), veteran proindependence conspirator, but the revolutionaries imposed him. The junta decreed free trade and abolition of the slave trade.

1811, July 5. A national congress with representatives from the landed class proclaimed **VENEZUELAN INDEPENDENCE.** It promulgated a constitution restricting the franchise to landowners and included federalist measures to attract provincial support. *Pardos* revolted for full citizenship rights. Violence from the lower classes alarmed the creole landowners, many of whom withdrew from the independence movement. Miranda was given command of the revolutionary forces, and Bolívar became one of his lieutenants. **SIMÓN BOLÍVAR,** born in Caracas of a creole cacao planter family, was a resolute republican. He was the greatest figure of the independence movement.

In Bogotá, the **republic of Cundinamarca** was inaugurated. The other provinces, refusing to join it, formed the **Federation of the United Provinces of Nueva Granada.** Popayán, Pasto, Santa Marta, and Panama remained loyal to Spain. Proindependence provinces favoring federalism waged war against proindependence provinces endorsing centralism.

1812. A royalist army invaded patriot territory. Miranda capitulated. Royalists sent him as a prisoner to Spain, where he died in 1816. Spaniards seized Bolívar's properties but permitted him to go to Nueva Granada.

1813. Bolívar launched the **Campaña Admirable** (Admirable Campaign). He entered Caracas in Aug. to inaugurate the **second Venezuelan republic** and assumed dictatorial powers. He proclaimed war to the death against Spaniards who did not support independence and promised amnesty to royalist creoles. Poorer Venezuelans remained aloof since they distrusted the creole landed elite and slaveholders. **José Tomás Boves,** a peninsular merchant and smuggler, organized a guerrilla war on behalf of the Crown, promising confiscated properties to the men who enlisted in his army. *Llaneros* enthusiastically followed Boves, angered by a law approved by the antiroyalist government of Caracas, which prevented *llaneros* from freely hunting on the plains. The war between patriots and royalists was waged with great violence; the killing of prisoners and the massacre of civilians became common practices on both sides.

1814. Boves's royalist army defeated the revolutionary forces at **La Puerta**, where Boves died but destroyed Bolívar's control of Venezuela. Bolívar escaped to Nueva Granada.

1815. Royalists took Cartagena. Bolívar abandoned Nueva Granada and went to Jamaica where he issued his **"Letter from Jamaica."** In Haiti, he gained support from Pres. **Alexandre Pétion,** to whom he promised to abolish slavery in the future republic.

1816. Royalists took Bogotá, and executed many patriot leaders. Peasants were subjected to forced labor, and Nueva Granada became a supply center for royalist reconquest.

In Venezuela, *llaneros* remained restless under royalist control, since their major demands had not been met. **José Antonio Páez,** a *llanero* chief based in the region of Apure, started to operate against the royalists.

1817. Bolívar returned to the Orinoco region and sought popular support for the creole independence movement promoting *pardo* soldiers and promising freedom to slaves in the patriot army. He issued a decree ordering the distribution of confiscated properties among the patriot troops as payment for their services.

1819. Once **Francisco de Paula Santander** (1792–1840) had organized patriot military support in Nueva Granada, Bolívar led a patriot army across the Andes and defeated the royalist forces at **Boyacá River** (Aug. 9). Patriots occupied Bogotá (Aug. 10). In this campaign, Bolívar definitively liberated Nueva Granada.

Dec. 17. The **congress of Angostura** approved the fundamental law creating **Gran Colombia,** a republic based on the union of Venezuela and Nueva Granada. Bolívar was made president and military dictator.

1820. The **Spanish liberal revolution** caused Ferdinand VII to adopt a more conciliatory policy. A truce ended the war to the death, but the war resumed, since the Crown refused to recognize the independence of Colombia.

1821. Bolívar sent his lieutenant, **Antonio José de Sucre,** to liberate Quito. In Venezuela, Bolívar allied with Páez to defeat the royalist army at **Carabobo** (June 24). This victory assured Venezuelan independence. A proindependence movement in Panama Province promoted union with Gran Colombia.

Aug. 30. A **congress at Cucutá** produced a republican constitution and named Bolívar president. He placed Páez in command of the army in Venezuela. Santander was made vice president.

1822. Moving by sea to Guayaquil, Sucre achieved the liberation of Quito at the **Battle of Pichincha** (May 24). Bolívar moved to Quito and persuaded the provinces of Quito to unite with the Gran Colombia.

July 26–27. San Martín and Bolívar met at Guayaquil to discuss the politics of liberation. Bolívar's republicanism clashed with San Martín's monarchism and impeded cooperation. San Martín chose to withdraw (p. 624).

h. NEW SPAIN (MEXICO)

1808. Following the intervention of Napoleon in Spain, creole elements sought a greater role in the government. With support of the viceroy, a general junta was convened. The *audiencia,* controlled by Spaniards, dismissed the pro-creole viceroy. Four viceroys governed between 1808 and 1813.

1810. **Miguel Hidalgo y Costilla** (1753–1811), a creole priest, initiated a separatist revolt in the town of Dolores, in the Province of Guanajuato. He had limited creole support, but his call galvanized hundreds of peasants and mineworkers who had suffered oppressive conditions in the Bajío region. Although Hidalgo tried to restrict attacks to Spaniards and Spanish properties, his followers destroyed estates indiscriminately, unleashing general rural violence. Massacres committed against wealthy Spaniards and creoles in Guanajuato deeply unsettled the upper class. The rebels threatened Mexico City, but peasants of the region refused to join them. A Spanish army defeated Hidalgo's troops.

1811. A new defeat of revolutionary forces at the **bridge of Calderón,** near Guadalajara (Jan. 17), allowed Spanish authorities to capture Hidalgo. The Inquisition tried him and delivered him to the secular courts for execution (July 31).

1812. **José María Morelos** (1765–1815), a mestizo priest, continued the revolt.

1813. A congress convened at **Chilpancingo** (Sept. 14) made Morelos executive chief and **declared independence** (Nov. 6).

1814, Oct. 22. The **constitution of Apatzingan** was promulgated, establishing male suffrage and abolishing the caste system and slavery, but preserving the prerogatives of the Church. **Agustín de Iturbide** (1783–1824), a creole in Spanish service, forced Morelos to retreat. Morelos was captured and executed (Dec. 22, 1815), and the revolutionary congress was dissolved.

1816–21. Viceroy **Juan Ruiz de Apodaca** instituted a conciliatory policy and secured the surrender of most of the revolutionary leaders. Only a few guerrilla leaders, among them **Vicente Guerrero** (1783–1831), continued resistance.

1820. The **liberal revolution in Spain** (p. 456) threatened the position of the clergy and the upper classes. Conservative creoles and Spaniards decided to secede from Spain to avert reforms. **Agustín de Iturbide** became their leader and with Guerrero formulated the **Plan de Iguala.**

Feb. 24. This proclaimed the **INDEPENDENCE OF MEXICO.** According to the plan, Mexico would be a constitutional monarchy under Ferdinand VII or other European prince, creoles and Peninsulars were declared equal, and the Catholic religion and church properties were to be maintained. Viceroy Apodaca was dismissed. Iturbide assumed authority and created an army.

Aug. 24. A newly arrived viceroy accepted the plan of Iguala by the **Convention of Córdoba.** A regency under Iturbide was formed, pending choice of a sovereign. A constituent congress was convened. The Spanish government refused to accept the Convention of Córdoba.

1822. Iturbide induced his troops to pressure the congress to name him **emperor.** He was crowned **Agustín I** (July 25).

i. GUATEMALA AND CENTRAL AMERICA

1811–18. In the **captaincy general of Guatemala** (Guatemala, San Salvador, Honduras, Nicaragua, Costa Rica, and Chiapas), liberals campaigned for free trade, a more representative government, and the dissolution of *fueros* and monopolies. The captain general repressed them and subdued other rebellions in the provinces of San Salvador, Honduras, and Nicaragua (1811–12). Central American liberals were mainly creole professionals allied to the leading creole families.

1821, Sept. 15. Influenced by the launching of the Plan de Iguala in Mexico, a junta of liberals and moderates convened in Guatemala City to declare independence, with the captain general as leader.

1822. Union with Mexico under Iturbide was discussed in every province. Guatemala and Chiapas decided to join independent Mexico. El Salvador rejected union either with Mexico or Guatemala. Some cities in Honduras and Nicaragua accepted union with Guatemala, but refused to submit to Mexico. Others claimed total autonomy. Costa Rica agreed to separation from Spain and sought union with Colombia. Conservatives were prone to annexation to Mexico, whereas liberals rejected it and favored an independent republican federation.

Iturbide, as emperor of Mexico, sent a Mexican army to advance the annexationist cause.

1823. After military invasion, El Salvador and Costa Rica republicans capitulated.

June 24. Upon learning of the abdication of Agustín I, a Central American congress decided to form the **United Provinces of Central America,** independent from Mexico and integrated by Guatemala, El Salvador, Honduras, Costa Rica, and Nicaragua.

August 20. Mexico recognized the new political entity.

j. BRAZIL

(From p. 407)

1808. As a result of the war in Europe, the king of Portugal, John VI, transferred his court to Brazil, leaving Portugal to be governed by a British-dominated regency. He established his capital in **Rio de Janeiro** and decreed free trade for Brazilian ports. This caused discontent among Portuguese merchants, who were unable to compete with the British.

1817. In **Pernambuco,** a military revolt supported by some planters, merchants, and bureaucrats proclaimed a republic. An army was sent from Bahia, and the rebels surrendered.

1820. The **Portuguese overthrew the regency** in Lisbon and provisionally adopted the Spanish constitution of 1812. The Cortes summoned the king to return and invited Brazil to send representatives to a constituent assembly.

1821. Several military conspiracies in Brazil favored liberal measures and constitutional monarchy. A dispute erupted over the demand for the immediate return of the king to Portugal. A Portuguese faction formed by merchants with Portugal-based interests favored the return as a means to revive monopolies, whereas the "Brazilian" faction, which included Brazilian planters and bureaucrats as well as Brazil-based Portuguese merchants, opposed the departure of John VI. Brazilian deputies in Lisbon rejected attempts by the Cortes to reduce Brazil to colonial status. The king decided to return and leave his son, Pedro, in Brazil as prince regent. **José Bonifácio de Andrada e Silva** (1763–1838) was elected president of the São Paulo provisional junta and was named chief of the first "Brazilian" cabinet.

1822. Brazilian radicals and liberals gave their allegiance to Prince Pedro (1798–1834), who declared (Jan. 9) his determination to remain in Brazil (**"Fico"**—I will stay). He soon convoked a Brazilian constituent assembly. José Bonifácio drew support from large landholders, slaveholders, and merchants in Rio to oppose the principle of popular representation for the assembly, a condition radicals tried to reverse, proposing direct popular elections.

Sept. 7. The **Grito de Ypiranga** (Cry of Ypiranga). While in São Paolo Dom Pedro received dispatches from Portugal, which, although offering concessions, returned Brazil to dependent status. He therefore **proclaimed Brazilian independence.**

Oct. 12. The Senate proclaimed Dom Pedro **constitutional emperor of Brazil.** He pledged acceptance of the constitution to be formulated by the assembly and was crowned **Pedro I** (Dec. 1). Portuguese garrisons and some Brazilians in the northern provinces opposed separation, but the Brazilian navy subdued them. (To p. 634)

3. LATIN AMERICA, 1820–1914

a. OVERVIEW

Spanish colonies emerged from the independence wars divided into republics that briefly cooperated to form broader political units. In Brazil the monarchy held the country together despite strong autonomist and prorepublican movements. By 1850, the countries of Spanish-speaking America had 22.5 million inhabitants, and Brazil had 7.2 million. Most of the population lived in the countryside. As a result of immigration and economic expansion, population grew rapidly in the final decades of the century. In 1900, 44 million people lived in Spanish America, and 18 million in Brazil. This period also witnessed a gradual increase in the size of urban centers, but most of the population still lived in the countryside.

Great Britain asserted dominance over the new nations through its commercial agents and a powerful navy, which proved useful in obtaining better trade conditions for British merchants. **Export economies** developed in the new countries in response to the international market. The resultant expansion of the commercial economy was particularly intense after 1870. The export sector contributed to labor exploitation by encouraging regulations binding laborers to their masters, the expansion of debt peonage, and the use of Chinese indentured servants. **Slavery was in decay** in most countries by the mid-19th century, but it remained the bedrock of a vigorous export economy in Brazil and Cuba until the 1880s. **In the last decades of the 19th century, commercial growth and the first phase of industrialization** led to the expansion of cities and the formation of a working class, in some cases from immigrant backgrounds. An incipient labor movement soon confronted repressive measures against its attempts to improve the lot of workers.

Following independence, elites split into liberal and conservative factions, which clashed over issues such as federalism, free trade, and the status of the church. Liberal measures expropriating church and communal Indian lands encouraged land concentration and, hence, the consolidation of a large landholding class. Territories seized from nomadic Indian tribes also favored latifundia. In some Spanish-American countries, the *caudillos* (civil or military leaders) emerged as the main power brokers. Popular sectors, systematically excluded from political participation, found in the *caudillos* a channel to pressure the elites. In other countries, less disruptive forms of political bossism developed to keep the masses under control. With the consolidation of national states and the emergence of the cities and urban classes, the *caudillos'* role diminished somewhat, giving way to the formation of political parties.

Literature in the 19th century, especially novels and essays, frequently served as a **vehicle to promote cohesive national identities.** Leading writers such as **Domingo F. Sarmiento** (Argentina), **Andrés Bello** (Chile), and **José de Alencar** (Brazil) were prominent political figures who self-consciously used their writings to outline a particular vision of the national "destiny." Novels such as Alencar's *Iracema*

(1865) and *Amalia* (1851) by Argentine writer José Mármol used the romantic genre to allow their characters to form amorous alliances across class, ethnic, and regional lines. Influenced by the romantic canon, intellectuals in the postindependence decades sometimes idealized the indigenous population as the repository of the national essence.

Social Darwinism, however, soon emerged as a major intellectual trend. Cultural elites began to portray Indians and other nonwhite groups as unfit for citizenship in civilized political entities, thus "justifying" the ongoing exclusion of the majority from the formal political system. **Among elites the dominant tendency was to imitate European styles,** including urban architecture, and to foster exclusive institutions that mimicked European high culture. Artists and intellectuals began to seek an alternative to Europeanization in rural popular culture, which some considered a more authentic source of national identity. Meanwhile, waves of immigration from Spain, Italy, and Portugal expanded the ranks of urban popular movements. New forms of association (unions, leagues, mutual-aid societies) and open cultural institutions offered alternatives to political exclusion. Labor activism introduced new ideologies such as anarchism and socialism.

(To p. 736)

b. SOUTH AMERICA

1. ARGENTINA

After independence, the city of Buenos Aires was dominant because of its commercial role, but its place in the broader political system was disputed. Urban elites wanted to make it the national capital and form a central government with control over the provinces. Powerful rural landowners of Buenos Aires Province, in contrast, sought to subject the city to their interests and a federalist framework.

1819. The fragmentation of the territory controlled by Buenos Aires created a general crisis in the region. Gen. **Martín Rodríguez** installed a governing junta.

1821–23. Gen. Rodríguez became governor of Buenos Aires and named an extreme liberal, **Bernardino Rivadavia,** as minister. Liberal policies helped British merchants gain preeminence in the Río de la Plata trade. Native merchants shifted investments and formed a new class of big ranchers *(estancieros).*

Liberals enforced antivagrancy laws to compel peasants and gauchos (free horsemen) to seek fixed employment. Gen. Martínez undertook a campaign against Indians to open new lands for ranching.

1825. Treaty with Great Britain to suppress slave trade. Buenos Aires organized a war against Brazil for the liberation of the Banda Oriental.

1826. Rivadavia was elected president of the **United Provinces of the Río de la Plata.** He made the city of Buenos Aires the national capital, separating it from its province. Ranchers opposed this and united under the **federalist** banner against Rivadavia's **unitarian** policies.

1827. Forces from Buenos Aires and the Banda Oriental defeated Brazil at **Ituzaingó** (Feb. 20), but negotiations with Brazil ended in failure. Rivadavia was forced to resign and was exiled. The congress returned the city of Buenos to its province. **Manuel Dorrego,** federalist leader in Buenos Aires, became its governor. **JUAN MANUEL DE ROSAS** (1793–1877), a wealthy rancher, was named chief of the Buenos Aires militias. **Facundo Quiroga,** *caudillo* of La Rioja, mobilized militias from the interior provinces against the congress. The congress dissolved itself, and the **Confederación del Río de la Plata** (Argentine Confederation) was established.

1828. Brazil and Buenos Aires accepted the independence of the Banda Oriental. Unitarians led by Gen. **Juan Lavalle** protested the accord by occupying Buenos Aires and executing Dorrego, provoking antagonism toward the unitarians.

1829. Rosas, with peasant support, vanquished Lavalle at **Puente de Márquez.** Federalists seized the city of Buenos Aires; Rosas was elected governor of Buenos Aires Province.

1831. Federalists strengthened Buenos Aires's influence in the provinces. Rosas courted support from the urban black population, but he reopened the slave trade.

1833. Rosas led the "Expedition of the Desert" against various Indian cultures of the Pampas. The elite supported this campaign because big ranchers expected to grab Indian lands.

In the city of Buenos Aires, **Encarnación Ezcurra,** Rosas's wife, mobilized plebeian support against Rosas's opponents, patronizing a paramilitary band popularly known as the *Mazorca.*

An English army occupied the Falkland (Malvinas) Islands.

1835–36. The legislature of Buenos Aires, with the assent of the provinces, made Rosas dictator. The ultraconservative Rosas, despite his populist veneer, supported the big ranchers who massively increased their landholdings and secured tight control over the gauchos. The ranching economy offered women few opportunities and led to their migration to the cities to work as domestic servants.

1837. Brief hostilities with Peru-Bolivian Confederation.

1838. The French blockaded Buenos Aires port. Members of the **Generation of 1837,** a group of young intellectuals, conspired against Rosas, established an alliance with Uruguayan *caudillo* **Fructuoso Rivera,** and obtained French support. Rosas signed a treaty with Britain to abolish the slave trade, ensuring his government British support.

1839–40. Rosas suppressed a rebellion in the littoral region and rising dissent in Buenos Aires.

1841. Peace with France. Rosas attempted to negotiate the Falklands (Malvinas) question, offering them as payment for the foreign debt.

1844. The introduction of barbed wire fencing consolidated private claims to land in the countryside. Development of wool exports created a more diversified economy.

1845–50. The British navy blockaded Buenos Aires to pressure Rosas to open rivers to foreign navigation. The blockade ended with a negotiated settlement.

1851. **Justo José Urquiza (1801–70),** *caudillo* of Entre Ríos, withdrew his support from Rosas. The littoral provinces declared war against Rosas.

1852, Feb. 2. The allied army defeated Rosas at **Monte Caseros.** Pact of **San Nicolás** made Urquiza provisional director of the Argentine Confederation. Liberals in the city of Buenos Aires, led by **Bartolomé Mitre** (1821–1906), rejected the pact and seceded. National capital was moved to Paraná for eight years.

1853. Urquiza became chief executive, and a **federal constitution,** to which Buenos Aires refused to adhere, was promulgated (May 1). It extended male suffrage and **emancipated slaves.** The writings of **Juan Bautista Alberdi,** member of the liberal Generation of 1837, were a major inspiration for the constitution.

1859. War between the provinces and Buenos Aires, which was defeated (Oct. 22) and agreed to union with the federation.

1860–61. Mitre promoted riots against Urquiza in the interior. Urquiza retired after the indecisive Battle at **Pavón** (Sept. 17, 1861). Mitre assumed the presidency. Constitution of 1853 was amended to allow the government to intervene in the provinces.

1862. Mitre became head of the national government (Aug. 27); he established a national judiciary, treasury, and customs. The British began financing railroads.

1863. *Caudillo* **Vicente Peñaloza, "El Chacho,"** of La Rioja, rejected unification, but centralist forces defeated him.

1865. Mitre, elected president, adopted a liberal economic policy. **Felipe Varela** rebelled in La Rioja, claiming the provincial right to tax imports to protect local manufactures (1866).

Mitre agreed with Brazil to make war on Paraguay, joining the **Triple Alliance** (Argentina, Uruguay, and Brazil) (p. 630). Named commander in chief of the allied armies, Mitre promised a short war, but it lasted for five years (1865–70) and cost 18,000 Argentine soldiers their lives.

1868. **Domingo F. Sarmiento** (1811–85), Mitre's rival, was elected president. Sarmiento promoted education and European immigration.

1869. First census registered 1,800,000 inhabitants, with 178,000 in the city of Buenos Aires. The growing immigrant population was predominantly composed of male workers from Italy and Spain. Between 1871 and 1914, almost 6 million immigrants came, and half of this figure stayed permanently.

1874. **Nicolás Avellaneda** was elected president (1874–80).

1879–80. Gen. **Julio A. Roca** (1843–1914) directed the **"Conquest of the Desert"** campaign against the Ranquel and Araucanian Indians. Captured Indians were killed or placed in reservations. Land was transferred to local *caudillos.*

1880. Gen. Roca, allied with governors of all provinces—except Buenos Aires—formed the **Liga de Córdoba,** which defeated Buenos Aires's forces. Avellaneda's government collapsed. Roca's triumph marked the beginning of the oligarchy's dominance. This social class controlled the export-oriented sector and the politico-military apparatus. The growing middle class struggled for political reforms.

1881. The victors made Buenos Aires the national capital. The church lost control of civil marriages and education.

1886. Roca imposed his brother-in-law, **Miguel Juárez Celman,** as president (1886–91). Lack of control over monetary emissions depreciated salaries. Labor strikes disrupted Buenos Aires (1888–90). Students opposed Juárez Celman and formed the **Unión Cívica de la Juventud.**

1890–92. To avert financial crisis, Juárez Celman sold public lands and railroads to foreign firms. The **Unión Cívica** organized a massive revolt against Juárez Celman; congress forced him to resign and named vice president **Carlos Pellegrini** president (1890–92). He implemented fiscal austerity. **Leandro N. Alem** and his followers founded the **UNIÓN CÍVICA RADICAL** to struggle for democratic reform.

1892–96. Most of the Misiones territories were given to Brazil as a result of arbitration by the U.S.

Roca and his **Partido Autonomista Nacional (PAN)** backed the election of **Luis Sáenz Peña** (1823–1907), who was soon succeeded by his vice president, Gen. **José E. Uriburu** (1831–1914). Sáenz Peña resigned because of general rebellion in the provinces (1893). General strikes agitated Buenos Aires (1895–96). After the suicide of Leandro N. Alem (July 1, 1896), his nephew **HIPÓLITO YRIGOYEN** (1852–1933) became leader of the Unión Cívica Radical.

1898–1904. During Roca's second term, monetary reform worsened living conditions of workers. The urban working class, almost half of whom were foreigners, concentrated in the new meat-packing plants *(frigoríficos)* and artisanal trades. Workers, often led by anarchists, fought for better living conditions and union rights. The government response was repression.

1904–10. Roca imposed **Manuel Quintana** as president (1904–6). He died in 1906, and vice president **Vicente Figueroa Alcorta** assumed the presidency (1906–10). Anarchism grew more powerful with the foundation of the **Federación Obrera Regional Argentina (FORA).**

1910–14. Administration of **Roque Sáenz Peña.** Congress approved the Law of Social Defense, aimed at dismantling the labor movement. Paramilitary groups attacked working-class neighborhoods. The **Sáenz Peña Law** (1912) established universal suffrage and secret ballot for men over age 18.

1914. A census gave a total population of 7.8 million, 1.5 million in the city of Buenos Aires. Eighty percent of the population were immigrants or children of immigrants. Income per capita was higher than in several European countries, but living conditions in the interior were much poorer. Women in urban and rural areas found few job opportunities; some were coerced into prostitution.

Death of Sáenz Peña; vice president **Victorino de la Plaza** assumed the presidency.

San Francisco

Atlantic

Ocean

M E X I C O

Rio Grande

Mississippi R.

*Gulf of
Mexico*

Mexico

CUBA

HAITI

PUERTO
RICO

BELIZE

CENTRAL
AMERICA

*Caribbean
Sea*

Caracas

PANAMA

NUEVA
GRANADA

VENEZUELA

GUIANA

C O L O M B I A

Bogotá

Amazon R.

Quito

QUITO

Pacific

Ocean

P E R U

B R A Z I L

Lima

BOLIVIA

Sucre

PARAGUAY

Asunción

Rio de Janeiro

UNITED

PROVINCES

OF THE

RÍO

C H I L E

Paraná R.

ESTADO CISPLATINO

Santiago

DE LA

PLATA

Buenos
Aires

Montevideo

Atlantic

Ocean

0   250   500   750   1000

MILES

LATIN AMERICAN
STATES
AFTER THE
REVOLUTIONS

World War I broke out. Argentina remained neutral.   *(To p. 737)*

2. CHILE

The independence wars left Chile's agrarian social structure unaltered. With merchant interests, the Chilean aristocracy preserved the colonial hierarchy and excluded other sectors from power. Control over the land allowed them to compel rural workers, called *inquilinos*, to work hacienda lands and to offer domestic service in exchange for small plots. A centralist state triumphed over federalist proposals.

1818–23. Bernardo O'Higgins was named supreme director by a *cabildo abierto*. He abolished titles of nobility and supported religious tolerance. Such measures and the imposition of new taxes met with widespread resistance. Protectionist measures angered merchants. In 1822, the Chilean elite rejected a constitution sponsored by O'Higgins and forced him into exile.

1823–28. A national junta named Gen. **Ramón Freire** (1787–1851) chief executive. Freire expelled the last Spanish troops from Chilean territory (1826). **Manuel Blanco Encalada** became the first president of the republic. In Sept. he was succeeded by **Augustín Eyzaguirre.**

Conservative classes disliked federalism and liberalism, which they saw as threatening to the social hierarchy. **Diego Portales** (1793–1837) organized the conservative opposition in support of a centralized government and a strong executive.

1828–33. Gen. **Francisco Antonio Pinto** was elected president. Gen. **Joaquín Prieto** (1786–1854) organized a campaign against the government with the support of conservatives. In 1830, Prieto defeated the army led by Gen. Freire at **Lircay** (April 17). In 1831, a congress confirmed Gen. Prieto as president and made Portales vice president.

1830–32. Creation of itinerant commissions of justice to prosecute rural banditry.

1833. A new constitution created a powerful Senate drawn from landed aristocracy. It gave the executive the right to impose states of siege, which it declared in 1840, 1846, and 1858. The franchise was restricted to the propertied and the literate.

Recovery of agrarian economy allowed renewal of trade with Peru, Chile's main market in colonial times.

1835–39. Freire launched a failed invasion into Chile with Peruvian support. The Chilean government declared war on the Peru-Bolivian Confederation. Prieto established a state of siege, giving Portales wide powers to control liberals within the military. Col. **José Antonio Vidaurre** led a movement that ended with the **assassination of Portales at Quillota** (1837). **Chilean forces, commanded by Gen. Manuel Bulnes** (1799–1866), **defeated Confederation armies at Yungay in 1839.**

1841–46. Triumph against the Confederation secured the presidency for Gen. Bulnes.

New mining discoveries were made in the 1840s; exploitation of coal, copper, and silver occurred mainly in the northern regions. A new class of entrepreneurs emerged, and merchants benefited greatly from the mining boom. Symptoms of labor conflict appeared in cities. Tailors organized a strike against employers who hired women at lower salaries. The California gold rush attracted thousands of Chilean workers.

The elite's new prosperity fostered liberal and radical propensities expressed by the **Generation of 1842.** In 1844, **Francisco Bilbao** published his critical essay **"Sociabilidad Chilena."** Bilbao was brought to trial, but a crowd of artisans and students liberated him.

1846–50. Reelection of Gen. Bulnes. The Conservative Party was divided between conciliatory and hard-line factions, the latter led by ultraconservative **Manuel Montt** (1809–80). In 1850, liberal reformers united in the **Sociedad de la Igualdad.** The government declared a state of siege in Santiago (Nov. 5, 1850) and banned the Sociedad.

1851. A civil war erupted in the northern mining districts to protest government fiscal policies and preference for British investors. **Pedro Félix Vicuña Aguirre,** a mine owner and liberal, led the revolt.

1851–61. Administration of Manuel Montt for two five-year terms. A treaty promising revolutionaries amnesty was nullified (1852).

1858. Conservatives and most liberals united against Montt's attempt to make minister **Antonio Varas** his successor. The government imprisoned opposition leaders.

1859. Civil war. Despite popular support for anti-Montt forces, the government defeated rebels. Varas, however, withdrew his candidacy. Montt nominated the more moderate **José Joaquín Pérez** (1800–89).

1861–71. Administration of J. J. Pérez for two five-year terms.

1861. Mapuche Indians rebelled against encroachment by settlers. Regulations to prevent indiscriminate transfer of Indian lands to Chilean and foreign settlers were not enforced.

1866. A brief war with Spain resulted from hostilities between Spain and Peru.

1869. Founding of **Sociedad Nacional de Agricultura (SNA),** which pushed for measures to protect big cattle interests from effects of free trade. Col. **José Manuel Pinto** led the Chilean army in a war of extermination against Mapuche Indians.

1871–75. Federico Errázuriz Zañartu was elected president. He consolidated liberal influence.

1876–81. Aníbal Pinto, president. The depression of 1873 worsened, causing widespread poverty and unemployment.

1879–83. The **WAR OF THE PACIFIC** began when Bolivia unilaterally revoked a treaty exempting Chilean nitrate companies operating in Antofagasta from taxation. The Chilean army took Antofagasta; Bolivia, allied with Peru, declared war on Chile. Chile declared war on Bolivia and Peru (April 1879). The Chilean army was small and poor, but Peruvian and Bolivian armies were even less prepared for war. The Chilean navy controlled the sea. In 1880, after battles in which 5,000 soldiers died, Chilean forces occupied Arica and Tacna. Lima was occupied in 1882, after much bloodshed. To support their army, Chileans confiscated Peruvian properties and levied taxes. They imposed Gen. **Miguel Iglesias** (1830–1909) as president of Peru. Iglesias signed the **Treaty of Ancón,** by which Chile gained Tarapacá from Peru, and Tacna and Arica for ten years. A plebiscite to decide the destiny of these territories was never held. Chile also gained Antofagasta, and Bolivia signed a truce in 1884. Chile acquired nitrate fields and increased its territory by more than a third.

Nitrate regions became a market for foodstuffs as their population grew. Labor conditions were poor and hazardous. Workers founded mutual-aid societies, cultural clubs, and a working-class press.

1881–86. Administration of Pres. **Domingo Santa Maria** (1825–89). Suffrage was extended to all males over 25 years of age (1884).

1883. Army campaign against the Mapuches reduced them to reservations.

1886–91. JOSÉ MANUEL BALMACEDA (1841–91) was elected president. He had sharp conflicts with the congress, which opposed his attempts to strengthen presidential powers. Balmaceda invested in public works and education. British entrepreneurs, meanwhile, sought to consolidate their control over the nitrate industry, provoking Chilean nationalism. In 1889, Balmaceda moved against J. T. North's railway; this British firm monopolized nitrate hauling in Tarapacá. J. T. North, backed by the British Foreign Office, sought support among Balmaceda's opponents.

1891. Civil war. Congress called upon Capt. **Jorge Montt** (1846–1922) to take up arms against Pres. Balmaceda. Montt's forces occupied the north, thus securing nitrate revenues for the congress, and recruiting nitrate workers. Government troops were defeated at **Concón** and **Placilla.** Balmaceda fled to the Argentine embassy and took his own life (Sept. 19).

1891–96. Jorge Montt became president. Balmaceda's partisans were expelled from the army and public service.

Distrust of the political system encouraged many workers to join the anarchist movement. They formed unions and led protests against unemployment and high food prices.

1891–1901. Federico Errázuriz Echaurren was elected president.

1901–6. Germán Riesco Errázuriz assumed the presidency. Bolivia signed peace treaty confirming Chilean possession of Antofagasta. Diplomatic relations reestablished with Peru. U.S. companies started to invest in copper production.

Unionization progressed rapidly under the influence of anarchosyndicalism. Protectionist taxes favoring landowners pushed up prices beyond workers' reach. In 1905, week-long urban riots shook Santiago. In retaliation, elite youths armed by the government massacred hundreds in the capital.

1906–10. Pedro Montt y Montt (1849–1910) from the National Party was elected president. Another wave of strikes shook the nation in

1907. At **Santa María de Iquique,** the army violently repressed striking nitrate workers, killing several thousand people. In 1909, railroad workers founded the **Gran Federación de Obreros de Chile.**
1910–15. Administration of **Ramón Barros Luco.**
1912. **Luis Emilio Recabarren** founded the **Partido Obrero Socialista** at Iquique.
1915–20. Presidency of **Juan Luis Sanfuentes Andonaegui.** He made elementary education compulsory.
1916. Growing labor militancy led to changes in the Gran Federación de Obreros de Chile, which became the **Federación Obrera Chilena (FOCh),** open to all workers. *(To p. 737)*

3. PARAGUAY

At the time of independence, Paraguay was a country of small farmers and ranchers. These settlers had developed military skills because of frequent regional conflicts. International transport was possible only through riverine navigation. Following independence, Paraguay had some 120,000 people, of whom only a tiny minority were whites. Guaraní was the predominant language.
1815–40. The dictatorship of Dr. JOSÉ GASPAR RODRÍGUEZ DE FRANCIA, "El Supremo." Attacks by federalist troops from the Banda Oriental allowed Dr. Francia to claim greater powers. He had a following among the military, and his program for domestic peace gained rural support. Congress made Dr. Francia perpetual dictator (May 31, 1816) and dissolved itself.

Domestic opposition to Dr. Francia was concentrated in the city of Asunción. Abroad the United Provinces of the Río de la Plata sought to annex Paraguay. In 1820, upon learning of an assassination plot, Dr. Francia initiated a campaign of terror against elite families, practically destroying Paraguay's creole elite. Dr. Francia closed the Seminary, the country's only institution of higher education.

Dr. Francia regarded Brazil and the constant strife in the Río de la Plata provinces as threats to Paraguayan sovereignty. He closed Paraguay to foreigners, allowing only authorized merchants to trade in designated ports. Paraguayans exchanged tobacco, yerba mate, and hides for arms and textiles. Buenos Aires's refusal to recognize Paraguay further isolated the country.

Combining repression and isolation, Dr. Francia's dictatorship succeeded in preventing civil conflicts. The financial resources of the Paraguayan state came from its ranches and textile workshops, and from tithes on livestock. The labor force employed on these ranches consisted of peons and slaves. Peasants and militiamen were forcibly drafted to toil on state lands and public works or to serve in the military; many peasant women became independent heads of household.
Dr. Francia died on Sept. 20, 1840.
1841–60. The dictatorship of Carlos Antonio López (1790–1862). A two-man consulate was named (1842), led by **CARLOS ANTONIO LÓPEZ,** who was from a surviving elite family. Successive congresses (1844, 1858) granted López extensions of his presidential term.

López relaxed Dr. Francia's isolationism, hiring foreign technicians, engineers, and artisans to build up his military. But the neighboring countries still refused to recognize Paraguay's independence. Rosas, the Argentine dictator, closed the Paraná River to vessels bound to Asunción. In 1849, tensions intensified, and López prepared for war. Brazil and Uruguay, both in conflict with Rosas, recognized Paraguay. After Rosas's fall, the Argentine Confederation recognized Paraguay's independence and its right to free navigation (1852).

According to the 1846 census, Paraguay had a sedentary population of 238,862, as well as 20,000 nomadic Indians. Twenty percent of all households were headed by women. A law (1852) freed children of slaves and curbed the slave trade. In 1848, a decree divested Indians of their special status and transformed all community lands into state property.

López distributed vast tracts of land to relatives and clients. In 1843, he undertook a bloody campaign against Guaraní Indians who inhabited yerba mate fields. López made yerba mate and exportable lumber property of the state (1846).

Foreign trade tripled between 1850 and 1860. López encouraged textile manufactures and opened new schools but did not allow institutions of higher education.

1862–69. The dictatorship of FRANCISCO SOLANO LÓPEZ (1827–70). Carlos Antonio López died in 1862. His son and vice president, **Francisco Solano López,** assumed the presidency. He continued enriching his relatives and strengthening Paraguay's armed forces, but moved away from the policy of neutrality.
1863. *Blanco* government of Uruguay allied with Paraguay to fight against Colorado Party (p. 631). Argentina and Brazil agreed to invade Uruguay and install *colorados.*
1864. Brazilian troops invaded Uruguay. López protested and then declared war on Brazil.
1865. Paraguayan armies, against Argentina's wishes, invaded Corrientes to attack Brazilian bases. Argentina, Brazil, and *colorado* leaders from Uruguay signed the **PACT OF THE TRIPLE ALLIANCE** to wage war against Paraguay. They expected the war to be short. British foreign ministers favored the pact, and the British helped finance the allied war effort. By the end of 1865, the allies had destroyed the Paraguayan navy and isolated the country, but a war of resistance dragged on for four more years. The resulting carnage produced a demographic catastrophe. The allies plundered Asunción (1869) and abused surviving women and children. The besieged government mobilized women and even male children. López's retaliatory measures against alleged pro-ally conspiracies added to the savagery. During his retreat from the allied armies, he massacred communities suspected of surrendering. In 1871, a census conducted by the victors revealed a population of 221,079, of which barely 13 percent were adult males. Paraguay lost 55,000 square miles of its territory.
1869. Occupation of Asuncíon by allied forces. Brazilian troops remained until 1876. Paraguayan elites split into the **legionaires,** who had come with the ally contingents, and the **lopiztas,** partisans of López. The former were widely resented because of their association with the occupying forces, who did little to reduce rampant starvation.
1870. At **Cerro Corá,** Brazilian troops killed Francisco Solano López in a skirmish. A constitutional convention met; **Cirilo Antonio Rivarola,** with Brazilian backing, was named provisional president. Measures were taken to attract immigrants and to force rural population into full-time labor on large estates.
1872. Presidency of **Salvador Jovellanos.** Demands for withdrawal of Brazilian forces.
1873. Treaty of peace with Uruguay. **Juan Bautista Gill** assumed presidency.
1874. Gen. **Bernardino Caballero,** a hero of the war, founded conservative **Republican** or **Colorado Party,** which was to control Paraguayan politics for 30 years.
1875–76. Withdrawal of Brazilian troops. Negotiations with Argentina resulted in the **Machaín-Yrigoyen Treaty,** which ceded part of the Chaco and submitted Villa Occidental to arbitration. Land sales benefited Uruguayan and Argentine capitalists.
1877. Assassination of ex-president Gill. **Higinio Uriarte** assumed the presidency.
1878–80. Cándido Bareiro was elected president but died in 1880. The U.S. supported Paraguay's claim to the Chaco.
1880–86. Gen. Caballero assumed the presidency after forcing the vice president to resign. Under Caballero, land sales allowed the creation of huge latifundia.
1886–90. Gen. **Patricio Escobar** assumed the presidency. Liberal and Colorado Parties were institutionalized, but *colorados* continued to control elections and repress Liberals.
In 1889, the national university was founded. Railway workers went on strike for higher wages (1889).
1890–94. Repression against Liberals secured the election of *colorado* leader **Juan Gualberto González.**
1894–98. Gen. **Juan Bautista Egúzquiza** assumed the presidency through a coup d'état. He was a moderate *colorado.*
1898–1902. Presidency of civilian **Emilio Aceval** was designated by Egúzquiza.
In 1900, a census demonstrated that demographic balance between the sexes had been reestablished. The total population amounted to 635,571.
1904–8. Liberal revolt unseated *colorados.* Liberals reorganized the army. *Colorados* and Liberals agreed to free elections. **Juan Bautista Gaona** was elected president, but the Liberal *cívico* faction deposed

him and imposed **Cecilio Báez** in 1905. In 1906, **Benigno Ferreira** assumed the presidency as a result of a Liberal coalition. Bolivia occupied Chaco territory. In 1907, Paraguay and Bolivia agreed to arbitration by Argentina. Founding of anarchist **Federación Obrera Regional Paraguaya** (Paraguayan Regional Labor Federation).

1908–12. A series of conflicts between *cívicos*, led by Maj. **Albino Jara,** and radicals of the Liberal Party, caused several regime changes. In 1912, a *cívico* rebellion was defeated at **Paraguarí,** and Jara was killed. **Alberto Schaerer,** a civilian leader of radicals, became president.

(To p. 738)

4. URUGUAY

Uruguay gained independence under the 1828 peace treaty between Brazil and Argentina (p. 634). The city of Montevideo became an important commercial entrepot; a pastoral economy evolved in the countryside, dominated by big ranchers.

1830, July 18. A liberal centralist constitution was adopted by the **República Oriental of Uruguay.** It denied the vote to laborers and illiterates. **Fructuoso Rivera** seized power and led a campaign of extermination against **Charrúa** Indians. From 1835 to 1868, public debt was repaid with land, which encouraged formation of latifundia.

1836–43. Ranchers sought absolute control over the countryside, whereas Montevideo merchants wanted a centralized state. Dispute led to the formation of the **Blanco Party,** connected to rural landlords, and the **Colorado Party,** based mainly on urban groups who favored liberalism and immigration. Rivera was the leader of the *colorados,* and **Manuel Oribe** (1792–1857) the *caudillo* of the *blancos.* In 1842, slavery was abolished, but ex-slaves were compelled to enroll in the partisan armies.

1843–51. With the support of Rosas, the Argentine dictator, Oribe began an eight-year **siege of Montevideo.** The city's foreign population played an important role in its defense. **Giuseppe Garibaldi,** leader of the Italian reunification, organized Basque and Italian defense contingents.

1851–60. Pact of Union (1855) between *colorado* leader **Venancio Flores** and Oribe. A period of economic recovery followed under the administration of **Gabriel A. Pereira** (1856–60). Montevideo merchants prospered as trade intermediaries for the Argentine littoral, Paraguay, and Southern Brazil. Urban population increased because of policies that favored immigration. Foreigners made up 35 percent of a total population of 221,000. Livestock herds, meat salting, and sheep breeding expanded.

1860–68. Administration of Gen. **Bernardo P. Berro,** a *blanco,* ended illegal slavery on Uruguayan estates owned by Brazilians. A *colorado* revolution led by Venancio Flores broke out in 1863. Brazilian forces invaded Uruguay in support of Flores, who became chief executive. The *blancos* sought support from Paraguay's dictator, **Francisco Solano López.** Flores joined with Brazil and Argentina in the **Triple Alliance,** thus entering the war against Paraguay (1865–70) (p. 630).

1868–76. Under the administrations of **Lorenzo Batlle** (1868–71), **Tomás Gomensoro** (1872), and **José E. Ellauri** (1873–75), the Colorado Party stayed in power, despite *blanco* revolts. A military uprising deposed Ellauri in 1875.

1876–86. Merchants and landowners seeking stability gave support to the military regimes of Gen. **Lorenzo Latorre** (1876–80), Gen. **Francisco A. Vidal** (1880–82), and Gen. **Máximo Santos** (1882–86). Fencing of ranches expanded. In 1876, enforcement of the **Rural Code** and the organization of rural police gave ranchers more power over rural workers. Exports of hides and wool increased. In 1877, compulsory primary education was established.

1886–94. Presidents **Máximo Tajes** (1886–90) and **Julio Herrera y Obes** (1890–94) governed during an economic crisis caused by price decline. Montevideo merchants lost their position as commercial intermediaries. Rural workers migrated to neighboring countries or to the city.

1894–1903. An economic recovery was due to the rise in wool sales. *Blanco* leader **Aparicio Saravia** led a revolution in 1896 to secure governorships of the departments. **Juan Idiarte Borda** was elected president in 1894 and assassinated in 1897. **Juan Lindolfo Cuestas** assumed the presidency in 1899 after reaching bi-party accord on elections.

1903–7. JOSÉ BATLLE Y ORDÓÑEZ (1856–1929), a civilian leader of the Colorado Party, assumed the presidency. Labor organization and strike activity increased with anarchist influence. Batlle introduced government mediation in labor conflicts. He challenged the absolute control of *blancos* over some departments, which led to civil war in 1904. The war caused heavy loss of human life. The government defeated the *blanco* army led by Saravia and imposed a centralist program.

Batlle sponsored a divorce law, but massive protest by women and the church stopped its passage for several years. Increasing urbanization and state centralization allowed Batlle to dominate rural elites. **Claudio Williman** succeeded Batlle (1907–11). Under his government, labor protest was repressed.

(To p. 738)

5. BOLIVIA

Bolivia became an independent nation with the support of Bolívar's armies. Disputes among military leaders resulted in pronounced political instability. The majority of the population was made up of Indian peasants organized in hierarchical communities, which controlled land resources and maintained the native languages, Quechua and Aymara.

1825–28. Bolívar decreed the distribution of communal lands to individual Indians and the suppression of Indian tribute, but these measures were not enforced. Peru recognized Bolivian independence (1826). **Antonio José de Sucre,** president after the departure of Bolívar, resigned because of a rebellion of Colombian troops and an invasion by the Peruvian army. An 1828 constitution enfranchised the propertied and literate.

1829–39. Andrés Santa Cruz (1792–1865) became president and, with the collaboration of Orbegoso of Peru, formed the **Peru-Bolivia Confederation** (1835–39), which Argentina and Chile opposed. Chilean troops defeated Confederation forces at **Yungay** (Jan. 20) and brought the union to an end.

1841–47. Pres. Gamarra of Peru attempted to annex Bolivia to Peru; Pres. **José Ballivián** defeated the invaders at **Ingavi** (Nov. 20, 1841). Ballivián applied free trade policy.

1848–55. Manuel Belzú (1808–1865) led a rebellion against the government. He granted artisans protectionist measures. **The 1851 constitution abolished slavery and presidential reelection.** Belzú attracted support from rural and urban masses, who resisted efforts by liberals to depose him. **Jorge Córdova** assumed the presidency in 1855.

1857. José María Linares, with the backing of upper classes, deposed Córdova. Linares attempted an unpopular monetary reform. In 1861, **José María de Achá** deposed Linares. Achá decreed the privatization of communal lands, causing resistance. Massacre of imprisoned Belzú partisans unleashed a popular rebellion in La Paz, which Gen. **Mariano Melgarejo** (1864–70) used to assume the presidency. Melgarejo launched a campaign to expropriate Indian community lands, but an Indian uprising threw him out of power.

1870–74. Agustín Morales became president. He nullified land sales under Melgarejo. Morales was assassinated. **Adolfo Ballivián** took office (1873–74) and formed an alliance with Peru (Feb. 6, 1873).

1874–76. During the administration of **Tomás Frías,** Bolivia allowed Chileans to exploit Bolivian nitrates for 25 years without further taxation. A law dividing Indian communal lands into individual holdings led to their massive transference to mestizo and white landlords.

1876–80. Hilarión Daza became president after a coup d'état. He placed another tax on nitrates (1878), causing British and Chilean protests.

1879, Feb. 14. Chilean troops occupied Bolivian territory (Antofagasta), an act that initiated the **WAR OF THE PACIFIC** (1879–84) (p. 629). Peru allied itself with Bolivia. Chile declared war on the allies (April 5) and occupied all of Bolivia's coastline (1879). Daza was overthrown, and **Narciso Campero** took office (1880).

1884. By the **Treaty of Valparaíso** (April 4), Bolivia and Chile agreed to an indefinite truce. Bolivia lost its nitrate territories and access to the sea.

1888–92. During the administration of **Aniceto Arce,** a railway was opened, affording Bolivia access to the coast. Mining production grew with foreign and native investment. Many landless workers and peasants migrated to the mining zones.

1892–96. Mariano Baptista succeeded Arce.

1896–99. Administration of **Severo Fernández Alonso.** Conservatives sought to make **Sucre** the capital. **José Manuel Pando** led a liberal revolution with support of La Paz. He allied himself with **Pablo Zárate Willca,** an Aymara leader, but soon Indians shifted to rebellion against all white landowners. Liberals and conservatives agreed to unite against the Indians.

1899. Brazilians in the rubber-producing **Acre District** proclaimed an independent state. Under threat of Brazilian military intervention, Bolivia signed the **Treaty of Petrópolis,** ceding the territory of Acre (1903). In return, Brazil built a railroad to transport Bolivian rubber.

In 1900, the Bolivian population reached 1.7 million.

1904-9. Presidency of **Ismael Montes,** who promoted railroad construction.

1904, Oct. 20. A **treaty between Bolivia and Chile** formally terminated the War of the Pacific and recognized Chilean possession of the coast.

1909-17. During the administration of **Eleodoro Villazón** (1909-13) and **Ismael Montes's** second term (1913-17), tin exports increased dramatically. In 1913, the **boundary between Bolivia and Argentina** was adjusted, and efforts were made to determine limits with Paraguay.

(To p. 739)

6. PERU

Peru after independence was riven by conflict between rival military *caudillos.* Exploitation of export commodities stiffened competition among military strongmen. On the coast, mestizo peasants and wage laborers participated in the market economy; in the highlands, Indian communities and mestizo peasants, many speaking Quechua and Aymara, were often subject to coercion by large landowners and state authorities.

1825-29. Bolívar ruled with the apparent support of Peruvian Congress. He abolished Indian communal properties, facilitating their despoilment by landlords. Indian tribute continued to be collected. Liberals resisted Bolívar's plans for confederation with Gran Colombia and forced him to withdraw. They backed Gen. **José de la Mar.**

Marshal **Andrés Santa Cruz** and Gen. **Agustín Gamarra** (1785-1841) sought to unify Peru and Bolivia, but Santa Cruz wanted a federation, whereas Gamarra supported a centralized state. In 1828, Gamarra invaded Bolivia and defeated Bolívar's troops.

In the 1830s, silver mining began to recover. In the Andean south, Arequipa merchants encouraged wool production.

1831-35. Liberals sought to overthrow Gamarra, backing Gen. **Luis José de Orbegoso.** The 1834 constitution favored centralism, subjected the military to civilian control, and enfranchised the propertied.

1835-39. Santa Cruz allied with Orbegoso to establish a confederation. Peruvian exiles allied themselves with Chile against the Confederation, which was defeated by Chilean troops at **Yungay.**

1839-41. During Gamarra's second term, the strongly centralist **Constitution of Huancayo** was approved (1839). Gen. **Ramón Castilla** (1797-1867), acting as minister of the treasury, arranged the first contract (1841) with British capitalists to exploit guano, a fertilizer made from bird dung that accumulated on islands near the coast. Gamarra tried to invade Bolivia but was defeated and killed at **Ingavi.**

1845-79. The **age of guano exports.** Guano became the main source of state revenue. The government leased exploitation rights to a merchant house, receiving in exchange a fixed share of the total sales. Guano revenues served to pay the foreign debt and military and bureaucratic expenses. **Ramón Castilla** emerged as the leading *caudillo* and assumed power (1846-51 and 1854-62). He abolished Indian tribute and African slavery, with compensation for the owners (1854). Castilla inaugurated the repayment of the internal debt. Under his successor, Gen. **José Rufino Echenique** (1851-54), the huge amount of fraudulent claims unleashed protests that led to Echenique's fall.

Firms used conscripts to work in the unhealthy guano islands. Castilla authorized importation of Chinese coolies, who labored virtually as slaves.

Guano benefits concentrated on the coast, while the highlands remained impoverished. Urban artisans protested against free trade policies. Indian peasants suffered from seizure of their lands by hacendados. In 1864, Spain seized the guano island of Chincha, and war between Spain and Peru ensued (1866). Under the administration of **José Balta** (1868-72), peace with Spain was celebrated in 1869, and Peru obtained diplomatic recognition. **Nicolás de Piérola** (1839-1913),

Balta's treasury minister, signed the controversial Dreyfus contract, by which this French capitalist obtained exclusive rights to exploitation of guano islands in exchange for servicing the foreign debt.

Opposition to the military and to Piérola's policies coalesced in the **Civilista Party,** whose leader, **Manuel Pardo,** was elected in 1872. To increase state funds, Pardo nationalized the nitrate industry (1875). The census of 1876 registered a population of 2,651,840, of which 57 percent were Indians.

1879-83. THE WAR OF THE PACIFIC. Due to its treaty of mutual defense with Bolivia (1873), Peru refused to stay neutral in the war between Chile and Bolivia, moving Chile to declare war on Peru (p. 629). Piérola deposed the president, Gen. **Mariano I. Prado** (1872-76). In 1881, Chileans plundered Lima, where they remained until 1882. As the occupying forces advanced along the coast, Chinese workers rose in revolt. In the highlands a united front of Indian peasants and landowners, enraged at Chilean abuses, organized guerrilla resistance.

1883, Oct. 20. The government of **Miguel Iglesias** signed the **Treaty of Ancón,** ceding the nitrate territories to Chile. It also specified that **Tacna** and **Arica** were to be under Chilean control for ten years, after which a plebiscite was to be held.

1884-95. Rebirth of military *caudillismo.* Partisans of **Andrés Avelino Cáceres** (1823-1923), who led highland resistance against Chileans, deposed Iglesias and elected Cáceres president (1885-90). They formed the **Constitutionalist Party,** while Piérola's followers founded the **Democratic Party.** The government ceded all railroads and guano exports to the foreign-controlled **Peruvian Corporation.** Renewal of Indian tribute, along with a salt tax, caused widespread upheaval in the highlands. **Pedro Pablo Atusparia** led an uprising in Huaráz (1885). Cáceres's successor, Col. **Remigio Morales Bermúdez,** continued military rule. Piérola and the *civilistas* unleashed a civil war.

1895-99. Piérola defeated the regular army with his guerrillas and assumed the presidency. He modernized administration and suppressed the Indian tribute. Mining properties were bought up by foreign firms. Workers in Lima agitated for the eight-hour day.

1899-1904. Piérola sought an agreement with the Civilista Party and designated as his successor *civilista* **Eduardo López de la Romaña.**

1904-12. Rule of Civilista Party. José Pardo (1904-8) expanded educational facilities and railroads. North American capitalists started to invest in Cerro de Pasco to extract copper. In the Amazon area, capitalists exploited wild rubber by virtually enslaving the native population; inhuman conditions in the Putumayo provoked international scandal (1912). In 1904, workers in Lima launched a general strike, which the government repressed. **Augusto B. Leguía** (1863-1932) became president (1908-12). Relations with Chile were severed due to disagreements over Tacna and Arica. *(To p. 739)*

7. ECUADOR

Following the disintegration of Gran Colombia, the old presidency of Quito became independent. Persistent regional conflicts were caused by the sharp contrast between the coast, with its cacao export economy, and the highlands, where a traditional aristocracy sought to preserve its political dominance and to maintain Indian peasants' servile status.

1830, May 13. The **Republic of Ecuador** was created with **Juan Flores** (1801-1864), a Venezuelan officer, as president (1830-35). **Guayaquil's** opposition to separation from Colombia was overcome. Flores became the leader of the conservative element: the military, large landholders, and the clergy. Following a civil war between liberals and conservatives, a compromise was reached in 1834, allowing the two groups to alternate in power.

1835-39. Liberal leader **Vicente Rocafuerte** became president. The new constitution separated civil and military authority.

1839-43. Flores succeeded Rocafuerte. A congress convened in 1843 made Flores perpetual president. A poll tax led to riots in urban centers with liberal support. Whites were exempted from the poll tax.

1845, March 6. The liberals forced Flores to resign. A new constitution granted suffrage to all adult males.

1846-60. Liberal **Vicente Roca** became president (1846-50). **Diego Noboa y Astete** assumed the presidency (1851), but was forced out and replaced by Gen. **José María Urbina** (1851-56). A national assembly promulgated a new constitution abolishing slavery, with compensation for owners. Freedom to pursue education and to organize Masonic lodges was proclaimed, offending the church and the conservatives. **Francisco Robles** (1856–59) was elected president through popular suffrage. **GABRIEL GARCÍA MORENO** (1821–75) emerged as the leader of the conservatives, who opposed abolition of Indian tribute. The Congress voted to move the capital from Quito to Riobamba, causing a regional split. A triumvirate headed by García Moreno took control of part of the country. Peru blockaded Guayaquil to protest cession of disputed lands to a British company. Robles conceded territories to Peru in exchange for Peru's support, a measure so unpopular that it precipitated his demise.

In 1850, Ecuador had 1 million people; 80 percent lived in the highlands.

1861–75. The dictatorship of Gabriel García Moreno. García Moreno was formally elected president by a national convention. He allied himself with the church to organize society on a hierarchical and authoritarian structure. He signed a **Concordat** with the papacy, giving wide powers to the church (Sept. 26, 1862). **The constitution of 1869** made Catholicism a condition of citizenship. Indians paid a school tax and were drafted for military service and public works, but repeatedly rebelled against these exactions. In 1871, **Fernando Daquilema** led a great Indian uprising in Chimborazo against forced labor for road work. García Moreno ordered harsh repression. His liberal opponents suffered exile and executions. The leading liberal conspirator was **ELOY ALFARO**, a coastal landlord. In 1875, a young military man assassinated García Moreno.

1875–95. A period of confrontation between liberals and conservatives. The constitution of 1861 was restored, while women of Quito demonstrated on behalf of the church. Gen. **Ignacio Veintimilla** took power (1878–82). His attempt to establish himself as dictator unleashed a civil war in 1882. **José María Caamaño**, a Catholic liberal, became president (1883–88). He supported the church and repressed more radical liberals. **Antonio Flores Jijón** was his successor (1888–92). In 1892, **Luis Cordero** became president, but was forced to resign by liberals who carried out a revolution led by Eloy Alfaro.

1895–1912. Era of liberal predominance. Administrations of Eloy Alfaro (1895–1901; 1907–11) and **Leonidas Plaza Gutiérrez** (1901–5). Church influence was curtailed; church lands were nationalized. Civil registry and marriage, religious freedom, and lay education were established. Construction of the Quito-Guayaquil railway (1900–8). Rivalry between Alfaro and Plaza developed. Alfaro rebelled in 1911 and was imprisoned in Quito, where a mob led by churchmen assassinated him and burned his body.

1912–16. Plaza's second term (1912–16) consolidated oligarchical dominance. Migration by highland peasants to the coastal plantations and cities intensified. In 1900, Ecuador had 1,400,000 inhabitants, with a majority on the coast. Labor movement became more active in Guayaquil.   *(To p. 741)*

8. COLOMBIA (NUEVA GRANADA)

Gran Colombia comprised the viceroyalty of Nueva Granada, the captaincy general of Venezuela, and the presidency of Quito. Despite Bolívar's efforts, separatist movements in Venezuela (1829–30) and Quito (1830) destroyed the confederation.

1831, Nov. 17. Nueva Granada was declared independent. The wars left its social structure intact. The church maintained its power, and regional elites were strong enough to resist attempts to install a centralized state based in Bogotá.

1832–37. Francisco de Paula Santander, a conservative, assumed the presidency. He reduced military influence. Santander gave some protectionist measures to local manufactures and expanded education.

1837–42. Dr. **José Ignacio de Márquez** assumed the presidency with support of the ex-Bolivarian military and defeated a liberal federalist uprising (1839–42). Coffee became the most important export commodity in Santander and Cundinarca, where large landowners engaged rural workers in a debt peonage system.

1841–45. Conservative and centralist administration of **Pedro Alcántara Herrán.**

1845–49. Tomás Cipriano de Mosquera (1798–1878) became president. Liberal measures reduced tariffs and ended state tobacco monopoly.

1849–53. Gen. **José Hilario López,** liberal leader, assumed the presi-

dency. **Slavery was abolished,** with compensation for the owners (1851–52). Artisans in Bogotá formed political clubs, allied to a liberal faction that opposed free trade.

1853–54. During **José Maria Obando's** administration, the constitution of 1853 provided universal male suffrage. In Vélez, liberals enacted female suffrage, which the national supreme court vetoed. Laws separating church and state were approved. Most Indian community lands changed to individual private property.

1854. Provinces demanded greater autonomy. The national army virtually disappeared.

April. Gen. **José María Melo** staged a coup d'état with artisan support. The movement was suppressed, and hundreds of artisans were sent to penal colonies in Panama.

1857–61. Mariano Ospina Rodríguez was elected president. New constitution (1858) designated the republic as the **Granadan Confederation.**

1860–61. Mosquera, now liberal governor of Cauca, declared that state independent. Other states took similar action. A civil war ensued, and Mosquera assumed the presidency (July 18).

1863. The **Constitution of Río Negro** proclaimed the union of nine sovereign states as the **United States of Colombia.** States were permitted to keep their own armed forces. Export economies developed under regional elites. In Antioquia, peasants opened new lands to cultivate coffee on small holdings. In 1871, Colombia had 2,951,111 inhabitants.

Radical liberals and conservatives clashed over the church's role in education, culminating in a civil war (1876–77). Fearing further destruction and misery, the two parties resorted to conciliation.

1878, May 18. A concession for 92 years was granted to a French company to construct a **canal across Panama.**

1880–98. Rafael Núñez (1825–94) became president, with liberal support. The presidency of Núñez, known as the "Regenerator," initiated a half century of conservative rule. During his second term (1884–86), a **civil war** broke out (1885). Núñez, with conservative help, defeated radical liberals. A new constitution (1886) established a centralized government and restored privileges to the church. A cycle of coffee expansion began (1886–96). Núñez was succeeded by **Carlos Holguín** (1888–92) and **Miguel Antonio Caro** (1892–98).

1898–1900. During the presidency of **Miguel Sanclemente,** liberals revolted (1899–1900). Vice president **José Marroquín,** an extreme conservative, deposed Sanclemente and assumed authority (1900–4).

1899–1902. War of the Thousand Days, a prolonged civil war, ended with the victory of conservatives at the cost of massive material destruction and at least 100,000 lives. The country moved to the verge of disintegration. Extremists in both parties were completely discredited.

1902–3. French canal company went bankrupt. **Hay-Herrán Treaty** gave U.S. canal rights and lease of territory (1902). Congress of Colombia refused to ratify the treaty.

Nov. 3. Panamanian elements were supported by the U.S., which proclaimed Panama an **independent state;** Colombia refused to recognize it (p. 635).

1904–9. Gen. **Rafael Reyes** succeeded Marroquín and gave positions to liberals. Protectionist measures allowed a textile industry to develop in Antioquia, which attracted female workers. Labor unions and mutual aid societies formed in Bogotá. Reyes was forced to resign when he recognized Panama's independence.

1910–14. Carlos Restrepo sought to establish a bipartisan government. Gen. **Rafael Uribe y Uribe** reorganized the Liberal Party.

1914–18. José Vicente Concha succeeded Restrepo. An Indian rebellion broke out in Cauca to recover community lands (1914–16). A census of 1912 registered a population of 5,072,604.

1914. With the **Thomson-Urrutia Treaty,** the U.S. agreed to pay Colombia $25 million, and Colombia recognized Panama's independence.

1918. General strike of workers on the Atlantic coast and labor riots in the ports led to a state of siege.   *(To p. 742)*

9. VENEZUELA

The wars of independence shattered the Venezuelan aristocracy. Many great estates passed into the hands of successful *caudillos*, who, allied with merchants, became a new oligarchy based on coffee and cacao production. Popular groups, despite extensive participation in the independence struggle, were excluded from the new political system.

1830, Jan. 13. Gen. **José Páez** (1790–1873) proclaimed Venezuela's separation from Gran Colombia. A constitution (Sept. 24) granted the franchise to propertied residents. Bolívar died in Santa Marta (Dec. 17, 1830).

1831–45. The Conservative Republic. Páez was proclaimed constitutional president (March 31, 1831) and governed as such until 1835. Dr. **José María Vargas** (1835–36), Dr. **Andrés Narvarte** (1836–37), and Gen. **Carlos Soublette** (1837–39 and 1843–47) ruled with his support. Páez controlled a network of *caudillos* who, in turn, controlled the rural population. A labor shortage affected planters expanding coffee production for foreign markets. The government passed antivagrancy laws and laws against rustling, causing deep resentment among *llaneros* (free horsemen). Landlords reenslaved black and *pardo* soldiers who had fought for independence. Under **Gen. Páez's second administration** (1839–43), an opposition led by **Antonio Leocadio Guzmán** coalesced in the Liberal Party (1840).

1846–58. The era of the Liberal Oligarchy was inaugurated by the election of Gen. **José Tadeo Monagas** (1784–1868), an eastern caudillo with liberal sympathies. Monagas's brother **José Gregorio Monagas** succeeded him as president (1851–55), and José Tadeo governed for a second term (1855–58). **In March 1854, Monagas abolished slavery.** The constitution of 1857 centralized power, which unleashed a general civil war.

1859–63. The Federal Wars. Aside from the conflict between conservatives and liberals, popular groups fought against rural repression and confiscations of their properties. Government troops defeated federalist forces at Coplé (Feb. 17, 1860), which led to the **Páez dictatorship** (1861–63). Conservatives lost the war and signed the Treaty of **Coche** (April 24, 1863); Páez went into exile. Liberal leader **Antonio Guzmán Blanco** (1829–99) was recognized as national *caudillo.*

1863–68. Liberal general **Juan C. Falcón** became president. The constitution of 1864 gave states substantial autonomy and granted suffrage to literate males.

1868–90. Era of Gen. Antonio Guzmán Blanco. Backed by a liberal alliance, he was able to control Venezuelan politics for 20 years as provisional and constitutional president (1870–77, 1879–84, and 1886–88), and through his allies Gen. **Francisco Linares Alcántara** (1877–79) and Gen. **Joaquín Crespo** (1884–86). Guzmán Blanco was committed to modernization of the military and communications. Venezuelan foreign debt increased tremendously. In 1870, he decreed free and compulsory primary education and reduced the influence of the Catholic Church. His dictatorial government and personality cult prompted resistance, which Guzmán Blanco suppressed. The first official census of Venezuela registered 1,784,194 inhabitants.

In 1879, Guzmán Blanco was proclaimed **supreme director of the Republic** and governed for a second term. During his third administration, resistance to his rule escalated. In 1888 he fled Venezuela.

1888–90. Administration of Dr. **Juan Pablo Rojas Paúl,** only the second civilian president in a 50-year period.

1890–92. Administration of Dr. **Raimundo Andueza Palacios,** who tried to reform the constitution to expand his presidential term. Legalist revolution forced Andueza to abandon power.

Landless workers migrated to the mountains in search of plots to cultivate, and the Andean region became Venezuela's leading coffee zone. Relations with Britain became strained because of its occupation of Guyana by force.

1892–97. Second administration of Gen. Joaquín Crespo. In 1895, economic crisis paralyzed the economy; workers and artisans protested unemployment. Due to U.S. opposition to British expansionism, Venezuela retained control of the Orinoco region in a boundary dispute (1896).

1898–99. Administration of Gen. **Ignacio Andrade.** Gen. **Cipriano Castro** (1858–1924) forced Andrade to relinquish the presidency.

1899–1908. Dictatorship of Gen. Cipriano Castro.

1902–3. The blockade and bombardment of Venezuelan ports by British, German, and Italian warships was due to Castro's refusal to allow European governments to decide the validity of claims against Venezuela. A Washington protocol forced Castro to allocate 30 percent of customs revenues to repayment of European claims.

1905–8. Gen. Castro was named president, and Gen. **Juan Vicente Gómez** (1864–1935) was named vice president.

1908. Gen. Gómez deposed Gen. Castro. Gómez was to govern Venezuela for the next 27 years.   (To p. 742)

10. BRAZIL

Brazil initiated its independence under a monarchical system, which was instrumental in maintaining unity and preserving a social structure based on slavery. Brazil's population was sharply divided into a minority of wealthy slaveholders and a vast majority of slaves and poor people of color. Rural areas were predominant, and the central government coordinated entrenched regional elites.

1822–31. THE REIGN OF PEDRO I. Brazilian liberals sought to limit the emperor's power. Dom Pedro I dissolved the constituent assembly and proclaimed a strongly centralist constitution with greater powers for the monarch.

1824. In northern provinces, the republican **Confederation of the Equator** was violently suppressed.

1825–28. War between Brazil and Argentina resulted in the independence of the **Cisplatine Province** (Banda Oriental), which eventually became Uruguay (p. 631). The war caused financial havoc in Brazil, and mercenary troops mutinied in Rio (1828).

1826. Britain pressured Brazil into a treaty ending the slave trade by 1830 and granting the British advantageous commercial terms from Brazil. The emperor's close association with Portuguese residents caused deep disaffection among Brazilian elites. Plebeians, including slaves, staged anti-Portuguese riots in cities. Opponents of Pedro I denounced the emperor's involvement in Portugal's dynastic struggles. In 1831, he abdicated in favor of his 5-year-old son, who would become **Pedro II** (1825–1891).

1831–40. The regency. During this period an "Additional Act" gave wider powers to the provinces (1834), and separatist tendencies emerged. The **War of the Farrapos** (1835–45), in Rio Grande do Sul, was inspired by federalist ideas. Revolts also erupted in the Amazon (**Cabanagem**), Maranhão (**Balaiada**), and Pernambuco (**War of the Cabanos**). These usually began as elite disputes but grew into social rebellions as slaves, smallholders, and urban poor joined the uprisings.

1840–89. THE REIGN OF PEDRO II. Frightened by the prospect of prolonged social conflict, liberals and conservatives called for the early coronation of Pedro II to promote stability. **Coffee boom** enriched conservatives in Rio de Janeiro Province. The central government regained full control of the imperial administrative structure. Eager to expand coffee exports, planters purchased African slaves in record numbers from the illegal slave trade. British threats of military action forced Brazil to definitively prohibit the slave trade (1850). In 1872, Brazil had 10,112,000 inhabitants.

In 1864, Brazil invaded Uruguay to support its allies, the *colorados.* López, the Paraguayan dictator, rushed to help his own allies, which created conditions for the **WAR OF THE TRIPLE ALLIANCE** (1865–70) (p. 630). Brazil gained substantial territory as a result of the war, but the conflict proved much longer and costlier in lives and money than originally expected. The war with Paraguay also gave military officers a more prominent role in public life.

Antislavery agitation and debate resumed with the end of the war, resulting in the **Rio Branco Law** (1871), which freed all children of slaves born after that date. Abolitionists like **Joaquim Nabuco** organized a national campaign to emancipate slaves in the 1880s. Free black Brazilians participated prominently in the campaign. Slaves increasingly rebelled against their masters and fled with the help of antislavery activists. In 1885 the **Saraiva Cotegipe Law** gave freedom to slaves over age 65, with no compensation for owners, but specified harsh penalties for those who helped runaways. The imperial government ordered the military to hunt fugitive slaves, but this outraged the military, which in 1887 formally refused to comply. On **May 15, 1888, the GOLDEN LAW, abolishing slavery without compensation to owners, was passed.**

Meanwhile, the **Republican Party** gained strength. Founded by dissident liberals in 1870, with support in São Paulo, Rio Grande do Sul, and the city of Rio de Janeiro, it gained sympathy from military men disillusioned with imperial politics and from federalists who wanted provincial autonomy. Marshal **Deodoro da Fonseca** (1827–1892) led a military coup d'état, forcing the emperor into exile. The republic was proclaimed on **Nov. 16, 1889.**

1889–1930. THE FIRST REPUBLIC. A constituent assembly promulgated a constitution in 1891, according to which the **United States of Brazil** became a federal republic. It enfranchised only literate male Brazilians. Deodoro da Fonseca was named president, but a naval revolt and his own autocratic policies led to his resignation (Nov. 23). Vice president Marshal **Floriano Peixoto** (1839–95) became president (1891–94). Local oligarchies struggled for greater power. The "colonels," rural bosses who manipulated elections at the local level, sought state and national funds for patronage in their areas of influence. State governors became the main power brokers at the national level to decide on the presidency. States of São Paulo and Minas Gerais attained dominance over the federal government. São Paulo developed a strong export-oriented economy, based on coffee and immigrant labor, bought with states subsidies. In the northeast, traditional sugar elites went into decline. Impoverished northeasterners migrated to the Amazon, where the boom in rubber production (1890–1910) created a constant demand for new workers. Brazil had a population of 14,334,000 in 1890.

The new political system fostered frequent conflicts between the federal government and local potentates. Civil war broke out in Rio Grande do Sul (1893–95). In the drought-stricken northeastern backlands, a messianic peasant movement, led by **Antonio Conselheiro**, founded a communal settlement at **Canudos** (1893). Seen as a threat by republican officials, Canudos was assaulted by three unsuccessful military expeditions before being wiped out (with massacres of the surviving residents) by a fourth military campaign. In the south, the messianic **Contestado** movement (1912–15) gathered displaced landowners, squatters, and peasants opposed to colonization projects promoted by a railroad company. The central government violently suppressed it as well. Members of the educated elite justified military violence, describing these religious movements as fanatical and barbaric.

1894–1910. Administrations of **Prudente de Morais Barros** (1894–98), **Manoel de Campos Salles** (1898–1902), **Francisco de Paula Rodrigues Alves** (1902–6), **Affonso Penna** (1906–9), and **Nilo Peçanha** (1909–10). State and federal government revenues, mainly from coffee and wild rubber exports, rose. The valorization agreement of 1906 provided government price supports for coffee. The city of São Paulo emerged as an industrial center. Workers there started to organize and develop a labor press under the influence of immigrant anarchists from Italy and Spain. In Rio, then Brazil's largest city, the working class was predominantly of Brazilian origin. An incipient middle class began to develop in the cities.

Boundary controversies with Argentina (1895), France (1900), Bolivia (1903), Britain (1904), and Holland (1906) were adjusted by arbitration or direct negotiation, resulting generally in the expansion of Brazilian territory.

1911–14. Hermes da Fonseca (1855–1923) assumed the presidency. Factional struggles led to armed federal interventions and imposition of pro-Hermes governors. Cities of Salvador and Manaus were bombarded by federal armies. A financial crisis resulted from the drop in rubber and coffee prices. Brazil proclaimed neutrality at the outbreak of World War I. *(To p. 742)*

11. PANAMA AND THE PANAMA CANAL ZONE

Prior to the revolution of 1903, Panama was a province of Colombia, but geographic isolation allowed Panama to develop autonomously. A small elite of landowners and merchants hoped to exploit the strategic location of their province, envisioning it as a major trade emporium. Foreign entrepreneurs shared this vision, and the area became entangled in a complex international situation that led to its secession from Colombia.

The Panama Isthmus became important at midcentury with the discovery of gold mines in California. A transisthmian railroad was constructed by an American company. Huge numbers of workers died, victims of tropical diseases.

1878, May 18. Colombia granted a French firm, headed by **Ferdinand de Lesseps** (1805–94), builder of the Suez Canal, exclusive rights to construct a canal. The French **Panama Canal Company** began work on a sea-level canal in 1880. Labor was recruited in France and the Caribbean. Malaria and yellow fever took a heavy toll; an estimated 21,000 French, 16,000 Jamaicans, and 8,000 Haitians died. The company reorganized in 1894, and work continued until 1899, when the company declared bankruptcy. **Philippe Bunau Varilla** (1859–1940), the French chief engineer, began to promote Panamanian independence to clear the way for a U.S. purchase of the French concession. U.S. president Theodore Roosevelt approved Bunau Varilla's plans and sent a warship to guarantee the success of the insurrection. Engaged in civil war (1899–1903), Colombia was unable to control events in Panama.

1903, Jan. 22. THE HAY-HERRÁN TREATY between the U.S. and Colombia provided for U.S. acquisition of a canal zone. It was rejected by the Colombian Senate.

Nov. 3. A revolution proclaimed the **INDEPENDENCE OF PANAMA** from Colombia. The U.S. sent troops and recognized the newly independent state.

Nov. 18. Bunau Varilla signed a treaty granting the U.S. control of the canal zone in perpetuity with full jurisdiction. A submissive Panamanian congress promptly approved the **HAY–BUNAU VARILLA TREATY**, though no Panamanians were involved in its formulation.

1904, Feb. 13. Adoption of a Panamanian constitution. The U.S. was given the right to intervene in Panama on behalf of U.S. interests.

1904–8. Manuel Amador Guerrero, first president of the republic. Panama had a sparse population of 50,000 inhabitants.

The U.S. acquired the properties of the French canal company. Construction started in 1903 and ended in 1914. Some 45,000 men and 15,000 women came to work on the canal, mostly from the Caribbean. The labor force was sharply divided by ethnic origin and technical skills; the company favored Europeans and North Americans with higher wages. This became a source of conflict among workers and with management.

Outside the canal zone, Panama developed banana plantations, owned by a landed oligarchy.

1914, Aug. 15. THE PANAMA CANAL WAS OPENED. Its use during the early years was limited due to landslides. Its official opening was postponed until July 12, 1920.

Sept. 2. The **boundaries of the canal zone** were defined, and the U.S. obtained further rights over the zone. *(To p. 744)*

c. CENTRAL AMERICA

1. OVERVIEW

The **United Provinces of Central America** (1823–38) consisted of five autonomous states with their own state assemblies and executives. Guatemala City was the seat of the central government. The constitution outlawed slavery but denied full political rights to Indians and *ladinos* (mestizos). Principal exports were cochineal (a dye stuff), logwood, and indigo.

1825–26. National elections held. The Conservative Party supported the church and the preeminence of the Guatemalan elite. The Liberal Party, seeking to end church influence and merchants' monopolies, imposed its candidate, **Manuel José Arce**, on the central government. Arce deposed the Liberals and named Conservative **Mariano Aycinena** as the new governor of Guatemala, winning Conservative support.

1826–29. In El Salvador, Liberals revolted against the pro-Arce Conservative government, and a three-year civil war ensued, involving Honduras, Guatemala, and El Salvador. **Francisco Morazán** (1792–1842) from Honduras emerged as the victorious Liberal leader.

1830. Morazán became confederation president. He decreed confiscation of church lands and abolition of *fueros*. The federal capital was moved to El Salvador. The British consul wielded great influence.

1831–37. Poll tax for *ladino* and Indian peasants caused such opposition that it was temporarily suspended (1833). Cochineal production increased demand for land and labor in Guatemala. Colonization projects, the new judicial system, and anticlerical measures outraged rural masses.

1837–38. A peasant revolt, supported by rural priests, challenged Liberals. **Rafael Carrera** (1814–1865), a mestizo officer, led the revolt that defeated Morazán. Congress dissolved the Central American Confederation.

1842–52. Morazán tried to reconstitute the confederation but was defeated and executed. Attempts at cooperation among the Central American states failed.

1850. Clayton-Bulwer Treaty. U.S. fear of a British-controlled canal across the isthmus led to an accord by which both nations pledged not to occupy any part of Central America. Belize and the Bay Islands were excluded.

1862–72. Central American states formed the United Army of Central America to expel William Walker's forces from Nicaragua.

1906. After the war of Nicaragua against El Salvador and Honduras, a Central American court of justice was established to resolve regional conflicts. *(To p. 744)*

2. GUATEMALA

1840–65. Rafael Carrera (1814–65) ruled Guatemala. He reinstated ecclesiastical privileges, traditional judicial procedures, and merchant guilds, and abolished the head tax. Carrera's mestizo supporters dominated politics. Indians maintained their communal holdings. In 1848, liberal opponents drove Carrera to resign, but as chief of the army, he was powerful enough to drive liberals into exile. Carrera became president in 1854, backed by the church and the aristocracy.

1865–71. Vicente Cerna continued the conservative rule after Carrera's death. A liberal revolution, led by **Justino Rufino Barrios** (1835–85), deposed Cerna.

1871–85. Dictatorship of Justino Rufino Barrios. His regime promoted economic liberalism, abolishing the merchants' guild and disentailing church properties. Coffee exports tripled in these years. Not only big planters, but also *ladino* and white middling landowners, supported Barrios. The antivagrancy law of 1877 forced Indians to work on local coffee plantations when required. Many Indian communities lost their lands. In 1880, the population was 1,225,000.

1885. Barrios went to war to recreate the Central American Confederation. He was killed in battle.

1885–92. Manuel Lisandro Barillas, a civilian, assumed power at a time of economic crisis. Conservatives gained positions in the government.

1892–98. José María Reina Barrios was named president. He implemented further compulsory measures against rural workers. Large landowners increased their holdings. He was assassinated in 1898.

1898–1920. Manuel Estrada Cabrera (1857–1923) assumed dictatorial powers. He obtained support from German financiers and from U.S. interests linked to the United Fruit Company. A system of police surveillance bolstered Estrada's control of politics. Opposition to Cabrera coalesced around the church hierarchy. The earthquake of 1917, which destroyed Guatemala City, unleashed widespread resistance to his regime. *(To p. 744)*

3. EL SALVADOR

El Salvador was the most densely populated area of the Central American Confederation. Indigo and cochineal were the main exports but were in decline by the mid-19th century. In 1845, laws to promote coffee growing by Indian communities sought to strengthen international trade.

1851–65. During this period El Salvador was under the influence of Guatemala's conservative dictator, Carrera. Liberal **Trinidad Cabañas** (1851–55) was defeated by **Santos Guardiola** (1855–62). In 1863, Carrera imposed conservative **Francisco Dueñas** (1863–65).

1871–1914. LIBERAL ERA. Liberals revolted against Dueñas. Successive liberal *caudillos* ruled as presidents: **Santiago González** (1871–76), **Rafael Zaldívar** (1876–85), **Francisco Menéndez** (1885–90), **Carlos Ezeta** (1890–94), **Rafael Gutiérrez** (1894–98), **Tomás Regalado** (1898–1903), **Pedro José Escalón** (1903–7), **Fernando Figueroa** (1907–11), **Manuel Enrique Araújo** (1911–13), and **Alfonso Quiñonez Molina** (1913–14).

In 1878, the population was 554,000 inhabitants. Liberals decreed the expropriation of Indian communal landholdings (1880). Coffee became the leading export in the hands of large landowners. Peasants revolted against expropriations (in 1872, 1875, 1880, 1885, and 1898).

In 1912 a national guard was created. An urban middle class connected to a modernized army emerged. *(To p. 745)*

4. NICARAGUA

1845–46. Conservatives allied themselves with Salvadoran-Honduran troops and ended liberal control, making conservative **José León Sandoval** president. State monopoly on alcohol led to rebellions against cane planters and the government (1849), and Indians rebelled against land seizures by mestizos and whites. Conservatives defeated liberals in 1849. Coffee cultivation was introduced.

1848. British and Miskito Indian allies occupied San Juan del Norte (Greytown) and proclaimed the kingdom of Mosquitia. The U.S. backed Nicaraguan claims.

1849. Cornelius Vanderbilt obtained a concession from the liberal government to construct an interoceanic canal.

1851–52. Conservative **José Laureano Pineda** was named supreme director.

1853. Conservative leader **Fruto Chamorro** assumed power and supported British interests.

1854. Nicaragua was proclaimed a republic.

1855. Liberals, seeking to overthrow conservatives, obtained aid from a group of U.S. financiers hostile to Vanderbilt. Liberals hired **William Walker** who, with a small army, invaded Nicaragua, quickly defeating his opponents.

1856. Walker discarded his liberal allies, legalized slavery, and sent inquiries to Washington about Nicaragua's joining the Union as a slave state. U.S. legation recognized Walker as president of Nicaragua. An opposition coalition included the British, Nicaraguan conservatives, Vanderbilt, and conservative regimes of the other four Central American nations.

1857. The **Allied Army of Central America,** led by Costa Rica's president **Juan Rafael Mora,** defeated Walker and his allies.

1857–93. CONSERVATIVE ERA. Liberals, discredited by their early association with Walker, remained out of power. Conservatives monopolized the presidency: **Tomás Martínez** (1858–67), **Fernando Guzmán** (1867–71), **Vicente Cuadra** (1871–75), **Pedro Joaquín Chamorro** (1875–79), **Joaquín Zavala** (1879–83), **Adán Cárdenas** (1883–87), **Evaristo Carazo** (1887–89) and **Roberto Sacasa** (1889–93). Coffee growers became the most influential social sector. A law called for the alienation of communal lands (1859). Indians unleashed the **war of the *comuneros*** against encroachment by coffee planters (1881).

1860. Walker attempted reconquest and was executed in Honduras. In 1875, the population comprised 373,000 inhabitants.

1889. A U.S. company began to build a canal through Nicaragua.

1893–1909. José Santos Zelaya (1853–1919), a liberal allied with dissatisfied conservatives, initiated reforms. In 1894, supported by the U.S., he sent troops to occupy Miskito territory and terminated British control of the area. In 1909, however, he refused to grant the U.S. canal rights that included control over Nicaraguan territory. The U.S. sought conservative allies to overthrow Zelaya.

1910–12. Adolfo Díaz led a conservative puppet regime with U.S. backing. The fiscal situation deteriorated. The U.S. intervened in Nicaraguan financial affairs, provoking divisions among conservatives.

1912. Dissident conservatives rebelled against Díaz's rule. A young liberal, **Benjamín Zeledón,** formed an army to fight U.S. intervention. The U.S. government sent a contingent of marines alleging the defense of U.S. properties and lives. Zeledón was defeated and killed. **Twenty-year U.S. occupation of Nicaragua began.** *(To p. 745)*

5. COSTA RICA

1830. Costa Rica became the first Central American country to export coffee. An oligarchy dominated the commercial and financial aspects of the coffee economy, and through them they controlled smaller coffee growers. No forced labor system arose in the coffee areas, so peons and wage laborers enjoyed relatively decent living standards.

Braulio Carrillo Colina (1835, 1838–42) led Costa Rica's secession from the Central American Confederation in 1838 and proclaimed himself dictator in 1841. His enemies allied with Morazán, who deposed him and attempted to return Costa Rica to the confederation.

1847–49. José María Castro Madriz promoted public education and proclaimed Costa Rica a republic.

1849–59. Juan Rafael Mora (1814–60), conservative president, defeated Walker. Coffee merchants benefited from the construction of the Panama railroad (1855).

1870–82. Gen. Tomás Guardia (1831–82) established a liberal dictatorship, drawing support from small landowners. Coffee subsidies were distributed on a more equitable basis. In 1873, confiscation of church land and privatization of communal lands allowed expansion of coffee cultivation.

1885–89. Under presidents **Próspero Fernández Oreamuno** (1882–85), **Bernardo Soto** (1885–89), **Carlos Durán** (1889–90), **José Joaquín Rodríguez Zeledón** (1890–94), **Rafael Iglesias** (1894–98, 1898–1902), **Ascensión Esquivel Ibarra** (1902–6), and **Cleto González Viquez** (1906–10) liberal reforms expanded.

In 1892, the country had 243,000 inhabitants. U.S. entrepreneur Minor Keith obtained land concessions to build a railroad. He displaced local banana growers and secured a monopoly on production. A merger with the United Fruit Company in 1899 led to further land concentration. Workers on banana plantations, many of them immigrants from the Caribbean, were subjected to restrictive systems such as payment in scrip. *(To p. 746)*

6. HONDURAS

1841–47. Conservative hegemony. After Morazán's defeat, Gen. **Francisco Ferrera** assumed the presidency and kept close contacts with conservatives of Guatemala and El Salvador. Allied with the clergy, he reinstated the tithes and colonial legislation. In 1845, he defeated liberal invaders.

1847–51. Juan Lindo attempted to reconstruct Central American unity, going to war with Guatemala (1851). Founding of National University.

1852–56. José Trinidad Cabañas assumed the presidency.

1856–62. Salvadorean **José Santos Guardiola**, with Guatemalan support, invaded Honduras and took power. William Walker attempted to invade Honduras in 1860. British returned the Bay Islands and part of Mosquitia to Honduras. Inhabitants of these areas obtained religious freedom, which led to a proclerical uprising (1861). Guardiola was assassinated in 1862.

1862–72. After a year-long civil war, conservative general **José María Medina,** backed by Carrera, assumed power. A new constitution founded the **Republic of Honduras** (1865).

1872–76. Civil war between conservatives and liberals.

1876–83. Liberal era. Marco Aurelio Soto (1846–1908) initiated liberal predominance by making a pact with conservatives. Foreign investment expanded. The army was reorganized, and mining was developed. **Luis Bográn** succeeded Soto (1883–87 and 1887–91). His reelection provoked divisions among liberal *caudillos.* The Progressive Party, led by Bográn, supported **Ponciano Leiva,** who assumed the presidency (1891–93). His election marked the beginning of constant liberal uprisings. **Domingo Vázquez** (1893–94), **Policarpo Bonilla** (1894–99), **Terencio Sierra** (1899–1903), **Manuel Bonilla** (1903–7), and **Manuel R. Dávila** (1907–11) occupied the presidency. Land concessions to foreign banana firms began, though local growers managed to control production until 1913. Foreign companies controlled shipping and distribution, and interfered in Honduran politics. An agrarian proletariat emerged on banana plantations. Population was 381,938 inhabitants. *(To p. 746)*

d. MEXICO

The wars of independence left the Mexican economy in ruins. Elites were deeply divided between conservatives aiming to preserve the colonial order and liberals trying to reduce the power of the church. *Caudillos* emerged to claim power for themselves, creating further disturbances in the countryside, where many peasants joined irregular armies.

1822. Gen. **ANTONIO LÓPEZ DE SANTA ANNA** (1794–1876) rebelled against the emperor **Agustín I** (Agustín Iturbide) and declared himself in favor of the republic.

1823. Iturbide was forced into exile. A junta of three generals, including liberal **Guadalupe Victoria,** was formed. Conservative **Lucas Alamán** (1792–1853) was named foreign minister.

1824. A constitution maintained military and ecclesiastical *fueros,* and Catholicism remained the official religion. Guadalupe Victoria won the presidency.

1828. Santa Anna imposed **Vicente Guerrero** as president.

1829, Sept. A law abolished slavery, provoking protests from Texas colonizers.

1830. Vice president Gen. **Anastasio Bustamante** (1780–1853) seized power and named conservative Alamán as chief minister. He raised tariffs to protect the textile industry. Guerrero rebelled but was defeated.

1832. Santa Anna rose up against the government. Alamán and Bustamante were exiled.

1833, April 1. Santa Anna was named president. His government was dominated by the liberal federalist minister of education, **José María Luis Mora** (1794–1850). Legislation disentailed some church property; the military lost the *fuero.*

1834. Conservatives called upon Santa Anna to restore "religion and *fueros."* Liberals were expelled from Congress.

1835. Federalist constitution was suspended, moving Yucatán to secede and Texans to revolt against the central government. Santa Anna led his troops against rebels.

1836, April 21. Texans defeated Santa Anna at **San Jacinto** (p. 605), forcing him to accept Texas's independence. Centralists staged a comeback with Bustamante as president.

1840–41. Santa Anna deposed Bustamante.

1843–44. A new constitution assigned unlimited power to the president. Moderates expelled Santa Anna and elected Gen. **Joaquín Herrera.**

1845, March 1. U.S. Congress voted to annex Texas (p. 605). Pres. James K. Polk unilaterally defined the borders of Texas. U.S. troops were deployed.

1846, Jan. Herrera was deposed by Gen. **Manuel Paredes.**

April. MEXICAN-AMERICAN WAR (p. 605). The war began east of the Rio Grande. U.S. troops seized California and Monterrey.

July. A popular liberal uprising led by **Valentín Gómez Farías** deposed Paredes. The constitution of 1824 was restored. Santa Anna deposed Gómez Farías.

1847, March. The U.S. Navy bombarded Veracruz.

Sept. 14. U.S. troops occupied Mexico City.

CASTE WAR IN YUCATÁN. Mayan Indians, rejecting semislave labor on sisal plantations and encroachment on their lands, took control of the countryside.

1848, Feb. 2. Treaty of Guadalupe Hidalgo. Mexico recognized Texas as U.S. territory; Mexico also ceded California and New Mexico. The U.S. was obliged to pay $15 million and assume payment of claims.

July. U.S. troops withdrew from Mexico. Mexican troops defeated Mayan rebels in western Yucatán.

1849. Massive peasant revolt in Querétaro for distribution of land.

1850–54. Gen. **Mariano Arista** was named president but was overthrown in 1853. Santa Anna became dictator with conservative backing. Liberals revolted and put an end to Santa Anna's influence (1854).

1855–61. La Reforma. With the support of liberal *caudillo* **Juan Álvarez,** liberals used state power to abolish corporatist privileges and concessions.

1855, Nov. Minister **BENITO JUÁREZ** (1806–72) issued a law rescinding *fueros.* The clergy protested, and a revolt broke out in Puebla. Álvarez resigned. **Ignacio Comonfort** assumed the presidency.

1856. The Lerdo Law was authored by **Miguel Lerdo de Tejada.** It prohibited corporate ownership of land, but Indian villages could keep some communal holdings *(ejidos).* The law prompted peasant unrest and church opposition.

1857. New constitution granted universal male suffrage, but kept elections to federal offices indirect. The Mexican Church excommunicated anyone who swore allegiance to the new constitution. A coup d'état closed the federal congress.

1858. Benito Juárez was proclaimed president according to the new constitution. Conservatives held Mexico City and proclaimed Miguel Miramón as president.

1858–61. WAR OF THE REFORM. The church, the military, and village Indians supported the conservatives. Liberals had a following among federalist hacendados, unincorporated Indians, and mestizos of the peripheral states.

1859. A law nationalized church property without payment. Separation of church and state was enforced.

1861. Juárez was proclaimed president. A two-year moratorium on all debt payments prompted threats of invasion from Britain, Spain, and France.

1863. French troops entered Mexico (June 7) with conservative support.

1864, April 10. The **Archduke Maximilian of Austria** was crowned emperor of Mexico (p. 492). Foreign capital revitalized the textile industry and railroad building. Conservatives were disillusioned by Maximilian's liberal tendencies. Juárez organized liberals on the border with U.S. support. After Napoleon III withdrew his support from Maximilian, liberals defeated the imperial army and executed Maximilian.

1867, Dec. Juárez returned to power. Disentailment of some communal property was suspended.

1871. Gen. **PORFIRIO DÍAZ** (1830–1915), a liberal officer, revolted unsuccessfully.

1872. Juárez died; vice president **Sebastián Lerdo de Tejada** assumed the presidency.

1876–80. Gen. Díaz rebelled against Lerdo's reelection. Díaz was elected president and signed a constitutional amendment forbidding immediate reelection.

1880–84. Peaceful transfer of power to pro-Díaz Gen. **Manuel Gonzáles.**

1884–1910. THE DICTATORSHIP OF PORFIRIO DÍAZ (The "Porfiriato"). Díaz returned to power. He amended the constitution in order to be reelected, expanded rural police, and adopted a conciliatory attitude toward the church. He allowed expropriation of Indian communal lands, which facilitated encroachment by big landowners. Peasants rebelled against loss of their lands (1878–84), and *agrarismo* emerged as an ideology to redress peasants' grievances. Yaqui Indians in the north suffered extermination campaigns (1880, 1890). Díaz's government encouraged foreign investors, with concessions for railroad construction and mining. Díaz promoted centralization of power. By the turn of the century, the Mexican peasantry was impoverished, and the middle class's opportunities were very limited. Debt peonage was extensive in certain rural areas. Sexual exploitation of women created further outrage against Porfirian authorities. Opponents to Díaz, led by **Ricardo Flores Magón**, an anarchist, organized the **Mexican Liberal Party** in 1905. Mexican workers at the Cananea Copper Company and Río Blanco textile plant protested against labor conditions (1906). **Francisco I. Madero** (1873–1913), a wealthy hacendado, challenged Díaz in the presidential elections of 1910. Díaz claimed victory after imprisoning Madero, who launched the **Plan of San Luis de Potosí,** unleashing a general armed insurrection against Díaz. The census of 1910 indicated a population of 15,150,000.   *(To p. 746)*

e. THE CARIBBEAN

1. CUBA

During the wars of independence, **Cuba** and **Puerto Rico** remained loyal to Spain. Slave labor and fertile soil allowed the sugar economy to flourish, especially after the destruction of slavery in Haiti. In 1827, Cuba had 707,400 inhabitants. The slave population in Cuba increased dramatically between 1790 and 1860. After 1860, slave trade declined, and colonial authorities actively promoted white immigration. Sugar planters, monopolizing land in western Cuba, and tobacco manufacturers formed a powerful elite. In the east, hacendados and free farmers of color predominated.

1868–78. The **TEN YEARS' WAR.** Following the liberal revolution in Spain (1868), eastern small slave owners and farmers unleashed a war for independence with the **Grito de Yara.** Sugar planters of the west supported Spain. Massive participation of slaves in rebel ranks prompted Spain to pass the **Moret Law** of 1870 that freed children of slave mothers and slaves over age 60. The war ended with the **convention of El Zanjón** (Feb. 10, 1878), by which Spain promised amnesty and freedom to slaves and Asian indentured workers who had fought the war on both sides.

1879–86. In the east, **Antonio Maceo** (1845–96) led slaves in a guerrilla war **(Guerra Chiquita).** Slaves resorted to legal and illegal measures to gain freedom. Spanish authorities tried to ensure a gradual process of emancipation. The **Patronato Law** of 1880 regulated emancipation by creating a transitional status for slaves. **Spanish authorities abolished slavery in 1886.**

1895–98. WAR OF INDEPENDENCE. JOSÉ MARTÍ (1853–95) united Cubans to fight for independence. A war without quarter devastated the island. About 10 percent of the population died. The U.S. entered the conflict, alleging Spain's destruction of the *Maine,* a warship stationed in Havana Harbor, thus initiating the **Spanish-American War** (p. 614). Spain was quickly defeated, and by the **Treaty of Paris** (Dec. 10) withdrew from Cuba and ceded Puerto Rico and the Philippines to the U.S. Many Cubans viewed U.S. intervention with distrust.

1899–1902. U.S. occupation of Cuba. U.S. entrepreneurs secured most of the repair and renovation projects in the aftermath of the war. Despite peace and economic recovery, there was extensive discontent with U.S. control of Cuba. The U.S. introduced the **Platt Amendment** (Feb. 12, 1901) by which the U.S. had the right to dictate all of Cuba's international agreements, to intervene in domestic political affairs, and to establish a military base at Guantánamo Bay. Cuba had 1,573,000 inhabitants in 1900.

1903–6. Tomás Estrada Palma, a pro-U.S. candidate, was elected president. U.S. forces withdrew. U.S. investors greatly augmented their ownership of land, industries, and services in Cuba. Popular unrest continued, fueled by electoral fraud. Liberals deposed Estrada Palma.

1906–8. Second U.S. military intervention. Charles Magoon became provisional governor of Cuba. He broadened the franchise and held elections.

1908–13. José Miguel Gómez, a liberal, assumed the presidency. U.S. forces withdrew. Power of foreign investors and local bourgeoisie increased. The **Morúa Law** prohibited political associations based on color or race. Black Cubans tried to resist, but their movement met harsh repression in the eastern provinces (1912). U.S. racism reinforced local prejudices.

1913–17. Conservative **Mario García Menocal** became president. Liberals revolted against his reelection in 1917. The U.S. intervened on behalf of García Menocal.   *(To p. 749)*

2. PUERTO RICO

Columbus claimed **Puerto Rico** for Spain in 1493, and the Spaniards began its colonization in 1506. Spain kept control of Puerto Rico while other American colonies gained their independence. Sugar cane cultivation declined in importance in the mid-19th century, as coffee production rose. Slave labor on the sugar plantations coexisted with wage labor and peasant production. Immigrant workers from Spain gradually replaced slaves in the sugar sector. Population grew from 357,086 in 1834 to 953,000 in 1900.

1868, Sept. 23. The Grito de Lares. A failed uprising against Spanish rule was led by **Ramón Emeterio Betances.** Spanish authorities quickly suppressed the revolt.

1873, March 22. Spain decreed the abolition of slavery. A faction of the elite formed the **Unconditional Spanish Party** to struggle for economic reforms and tax reduction. Another faction, the **Liberal Reform Party,** promoted the extension of the Spanish constitution to Puerto Rico.

1897. Spain granted Puerto Rico autonomy, including the franchise for all literate males. Puerto Rico could establish its own import duties and foreign trade relations.

1898. The U.S. Navy bombarded San Juan de Puerto Rico and invaded the island, canceling the newly acquired autonomy.

1900. Imposition of unpopular **Foraker Act.** It gave the U.S. president the right to appoint the governor, the cabinet, and all judges. Puerto Ricans were allowed to elect only a lower house of 30 delegates and were regarded by the U.S. as unfit for full political participation. Free trade was established between Puerto Rico and the U.S. mainland. An influx of U.S. investment concentrated wealth in fewer hands. The peasant economy was overwhelmed by expanding sugar plantations controlled by U.S. companies.

1901, May 27, Dec. 2. The U.S. Supreme Court decided that Puerto Ricans were not U.S. citizens. **Luis Muñoz Rivera** agitated for definition of Puerto Rico's status and citizenship rights.   *(To p. 749)*

3. DOMINICAN REPUBLIC

1808–21. A revolt in Santo Domingo, aided by British naval forces, established freedom from Haiti and France (1808–9). The **Treaty of Paris** reassigned Santo Domingo to Spain (1814).

1821, Dec. 1. SANTO DOMINGO PROCLAIMED INDEPENDENCE.

1822–44. Haitian president Jean Boyer occupied Santo Domingo (p. 639).

1844, Feb. 27. Haiti's domination ended. **Pedro Santana** established Santo Domingo as an independent republic. His rival, **Buenaventura Báez,** promoted unrest. Tobacco and lumber were the main export products. In 1850 the population was 200,000.

1861, March 18. Santana, fearing another Haitian invasion and seeking to exclude liberals from government, declared Santo Domingo a province of Spain.

1863–65. Dominican liberals waged an independence war against Spain.

1865–82. Spain, confronting internal problems, withdrew from Santo Domingo. Báez took power and unsuccessfully sought annexation by the U.S. (1870–72). Continuous warfare occurred among local *caudillos.* In the mid-1870s commercial agriculture expanded. A process of land concentration occurred in sugar, coffee, and banana production. Wage labor and sharecropping predominated.

1882–99. Ulises Hereaux (1845–99) became dictator. He reformed the army and the bureaucracy, and encouraged export agriculture. U.S. investors formed the **Improvement Company** to refinance Dominican debts upon the guarantee of custom revenues. New loans overwhelmed the nation's financial resources. Population was 700,000 (1900).

1899–1916. Hereaux was assassinated, and a provisional government was installed. European bondholders pressed for the repayment of their loans. In 1907, by an agreement with the government, the U.S. took charge of customs houses to prevent European intervention. In 1916 the U.S. began an eight-year occupation. U.S. military rule encouraged the dislodging of small landowners and favored the interests of large corporations.   *(To p. 750)*

4. HAITI

1697. In the 17th century the French gained control of the western side of **Española,** called St. Domingue, or Haiti. **St. Domingue** became a prosperous plantation colony based on sugar and slave labor.

1789. With the outbreak of the French Revolution (p. 431), free people of color sought greater rights. Wealthy white planters fought smaller planters to represent the colony before the French state. In their struggles, they armed their slaves, who soon started to fight for their own freedom. **TOUSSAINT L'OUVERTURE** (c. 1743–1803) emerged as leader of the slave rising, along with **Jean-Jacques Dessalines** (c. 1758–1806) and **Henri Christophe** (1767–1820).

1794, Feb. 5. The National Convention in France decreed **freedom for all slaves** (p. 433).

1797. Toussaint made himself dictator and established a temporary peace.

1802. Napoleon sent an army to recover Haiti. Toussaint died in exile in France. Haitians waged a general war of resistance against the French army.

1804, Jan. 1. Haitians defeated the French army. **Jean-Jacques Dessalines proclaimed the independence of Haiti.** Revolutionaries either killed white planters or forced them to flee, destroying the plantation economy. Ex-slaves developed peasant production.

Dessalines proclaimed himself Emperor Jacques I (Dec. 8, 1804). After his assassination, Christophe made himself king of Haiti (1811), but **Alexandre Pétion** (1770–1818) kept control of the southern region. Civil war ended with death of Pétion.

1818, March 20. Jean Pierre Boyer (1776–1850) succeeded Pétion, and on the suicide of Christophe (1820), secured control of all Haiti.

1822. Boyer conquered **Santo Domingo,** which had again come under control of Spain (1814), uniting the island as the **Republic of Haiti,** to which France accorded recognition (Feb. 12, 1838).

1843, March 13. Boyer was forced from office.

1844, Feb. 27. Santo Domingo reestablished its independence through a revolution.

1847. Faustin Soulouque became president and proclaimed himself **Faustin I** (1849). He was overthrown after a ten-year rule (Jan. 15, 1859).

1859–67. Fabre Geffrard governed for eight years.

1867–1914. Mulatto and black population was divided into the National Party (blacks) and the Liberal Party (mulattoes). Haiti's population grew from 960,000 in 1888 to 1,270,000 in 1900. U.S. and European firms increased their operations in Haiti. Haitian finances became disorganized, and obligations were contracted abroad.

1914, June 14. The U.S., France, and Germany demanded control of Haitian customs to secure payment.

1915, July 3. The U.S. landed forces. **Philippe Dartiguenave** assumed the presidency under U.S. supervision (Aug. 12). A new constitution allowed foreigners to own land. Peasants rebelled against forced roadwork, and U.S. Marines intervened to repress them. The U.S. established a ten-year protectorate, prolonged until 1936. Under U.S. rule, the Haitian population found itself subjected to harsh racism.   *(To p. 750)*

VI. THE WORLD WARS AND THE INTERWAR PERIOD, 1914-1945

A. GLOBAL AND COMPARATIVE DIMENSIONS

(From p. 424)

Two world wars and a worldwide economic depression of great magnitude provide the global background and foundation for developments in the first half of the 20th century. The globalization of political, economic, and cultural life intensified in a context of the continuing relative domination by the West. However, the core of the West itself spread beyond Western Europe and increasingly, Western Europe became a less central part of the modern industrialized world. By mid-century, world affairs came to be dominated by the two great superpowers of the United States and the Soviet Union. The changing dynamics of world relationships can be seen in two different areas: (1) the emergence of significant patterns of global connections in political, ideological, economic, and sociocultural structures; and (2) the further intensification of international and interstate relationships on a global scale.

1. EMERGING GLOBAL RELATIONSHIPS

Important changing patterns of global connections developed in three areas in the first half of the 20th century: (1) the development of global structures of interstate, economic, and sociocultural relationships; (2) the emergence of globally competing sociopolitical ideologies for shaping the nature of societies in the modern era; and (3) significant experiences with global dimensions in economic life, social transformation, and culture.

a. DEVELOPING GLOBAL INSTITUTIONS AND STRUCTURES

From the beginning of World War I to the end of World War II, many different types of global relationships developed. Three important types of structures emerged: (1) political organizations and relationships among states; (2) multinational economic and business structures; and (3) nongovernmental organizations for cultural, religious, and humanitarian purposes. In all of these areas, foundations had been laid before 1914, but during the era of the two world wars and the "interwar period" there was a significant development of global institutions and relationships in many different areas.

1. 1914-1946. INTERSTATE INSTITUTIONS

At the beginning of the 20th century, relations among the major states primarily represented alliances based on treaties and agreements reflecting relatively temporary arrangements among blocks of powers rather than continuing international institutional structures. Few permanent interstate organizations existed. However, the destructiveness of World War I led to major efforts to create permanent international organizations for the regulation of interstate relations or conflict resolution, as well as for the coordination of international services.

World War I negotiations. In 1914, there was no permanent organization for assembling the prospective antagonists. The existing **International Court of Justice** in The Hague had neither jurisdiction nor power. During the war, occasional efforts at mediation were made, but the war came to an end with a series of armistice agreements that were negotiated often on a bilateral and temporary basis. The major agreements were the armistices between the **Allies** and the Ottoman Empire (at **Mudros,** Oct. 1918), Austria-Hungary (Nov. 3, 1918), and Germany (Nov. 11, 1918). The **PEACE CONFERENCE AT VERSAILLES** (p. 671) began in January 1919 and defined the main lines of international relations for the world war settlement. The **Treaty of Versailles** (signed June 1918) defined the conditions of the peace settlement.

The **LEAGUE OF NATIONS** (p. 671) was created by the Treaty of Versailles to deter war and provide an administrative structure for managing international relations and conflict resolution. The League came into being with a permanent secretariat in **Geneva** in 1920 (**Sir Eric Drummond,** first secretary-general). In the context of the operation of the League, a number of interstate organizations for coordinating important services were created, including the **International Labor Organization (ILO),** created in 1919 as a part of the League of Nations to improve global labor conditions, and the **International Commission for Air Navigation,** created in 1919 to assist in international civil aviation.

The **Permanent Court of International Justice** was created in 1921 in accord with the League's Covenant and established in The Hague as a continuation of the Permanent Court of Arbitration.

Existing international institutions like the **Universal Postal Union,** the **International Institute of Agriculture,** and the **International Meteorological Organization** worked in collaboration with the League of Nations in the continuing process of coordinating important international services.

MULTINATIONAL CONFERENCES continued to be an important instrument for international relations. These enabled major powers to act without the constraints imposed by League of Nations procedures. One major theme for such conferences was arms control and the possible renunciation of war. Some of the most important of these were:

Washington Conference (1921–22), which defined Great Power relations in the Pacific basin and in China, as well as set limits on naval armaments.

Locarno Conference and Treaties (1925) provided for border guarantees in Europe (p. 676).

KELLOGG-BRIAND PACT, signed in Paris in 1928, involved renunciation of war but made no provision for sanctions.

London Naval Conference (1930) (p. 646) dealt with submarine warfare and other naval armament agreements signed by Great Britain, the U.S., Japan, France, and Italy.

Disarmament Conference in Geneva (1932) was attended by 60 states and produced no effective agreements. By the mid-1930s, such major conferences were effectively replaced by the Great Power negotiations that were part of the buildup to World War II.

Other major conferences were held on a variety of subjects. Many were held in the context of European powers' working out the economic implications of the Versailles Treaty and **German war reparations.** Others defined international cooperation in many nonpolitical areas. Important examples of these are the Madrid Conference (1932) of the **International Telecommunication Union,** which merged the

Telegraph Convention (1865) and the Radiotelegraph Convention (1906), and the Havana Conference (1928), creating the **Pan American Convention on Air Navigation.**

2. REGIONAL INTERSTATE INSTITUTIONS

During the interwar period, some groups of states developed important permanent interstate structures. The British Empire made significant steps in the direction of the **BRITISH COMMONWEALTH OF NATIONS.** The earlier extension of dominion status to Canada (1867), Australia (1901), New Zealand (1907), and the Union of South Africa (1910) laid the foundation for the establishment by the **Imperial Conference** in 1926 of the association of equal states united by "common allegiance to the crown." In the Western Hemisphere, conferences had been held by the independent republics throughout the 19th century. **PAN-AMERICANISM** was institutionalized with the creation of the **International Union of American Republics** in 1890. Four International Conferences of American States were held before World War I, and the Fifth International Conference of American States, held at Santiago, Chile, in 1923, reorganized the structures, establishing the **Pan-American Union** as the permanent organization for the association of American republics. The Eighth International Conference (Peru, 1938) issued the Declaration of Lima affirming solidarity in defense of the hemisphere against foreign intervention. At the Ninth International Conference (Colombia, 1948), the organization was restructured as the **ORGANIZATION OF AMERICAN STATES** as a regional grouping under the United Nations.

World War II negotiations. The structures for the peaceful resolution of international conflicts did not prevent significant fighting in the 1930s leading up to World War II. The Japanese occupation of **Manchuria** (1931–32) and invasion of China (1937), the Italian invasion of **Ethiopia** in 1935, and the German reoccupation of the **Rhineland** (1936) and steady expansion through negotiation and attack were signs of the failure of institutions of international political cooperation. Following the declarations of war by the world's major powers in 1939–41, structures of international political coordination were organized for the efforts of a world war. Two major groupings of powers emerged: the **AXIS POWERS,** led by Germany, Japan, and Italy; and the **ALLIED POWERS,** led by Great Britain, France, the U.S., and China.

Axis international cooperation was defined by the German-Italian-Japanese Treaty of 1940. However, Germany and Japan did not coordinate efforts significantly, and Japan never attacked the Soviet Union.

Allied international coordination was more intensive, and a series of conferences during the war defined the foundations for the postwar international system. Among the most important of these were: **Atlantic Conference** of Franklin Roosevelt and Winston Churchill (Aug. 1941), which issued the **ATLANTIC CHARTER** (p. 732) as a declaration of British and American peace aims. **1943 SUMMIT CONFERENCES** (p. 810) of heads of major Allied states to define war aims and goals: **Casablanca** (January; Britain, the U.S., and France); **Quebec** (August; Churchill and Roosevelt); **Cairo** (November; Britain, the U.S., and China); **Tehran** (November–December; Churchill, Roosevelt, and Stalin). **1945 CONFERENCES** coordinated the final **Allied war** efforts and established a new international organization to succeed the League of Nations. Summit conferences of heads of the governments of Great Britain, the U.S., and the Soviet Union took place at **Yalta** (February) and **Potsdam** (July–August). The **San Francisco Conference** (April–June) completed the charter of the **UNITED NATIONS ORGANIZATION,** which succeeded the League of Nations, and the first session of the U.N. General Assembly took place in January 1946. A **peace conference** in Paris in 1946 drafted treaties of peace between the Allies and Italy, Romania, Hungary, Bulgaria, and Finland, but the Allies could not agree on the major treaties with Germany and Japan. The creation of the **United Nations** represented the beginning of a new era of global interstate institutions.

3. MULTINATIONAL ECONOMIC INSTITUTIONS

The worldwide experiences of the two world wars and the Great Depression provided the framework for the development of interstate and private economic institutions whose operations were increasingly global in nature.

International financial institutions became increasingly important for economic life. In the 19th century, a truly global market had developed for goods and services and was based on an increasingly integrated financial and monetary system. The common acceptance of the **gold standard** meant that the major currencies were convertible. By 1914, Europeans had substantial investments throughout the world. **World War I** forced major changes in economic organization. Governments became increasingly involved in the operation of economies through control of production, trade, and labor. Following the war, international economic issues like **German reparations payments** and repayment by European powers of **war loans** made by the U.S. had important effects on world economic activities. In this context, financial operations became more globally integrated. Major **stock markets** became more closely interconnected, with the result that the **crash on the New York Stock Exchange** in October 1929 had an impact throughout the world. Similarly, in banking, the failure of the **Austrian Credit-Anstalt** in 1931 began a series of major bank failures throughout the world.

The Great Depression of the 1930s caused many governments to institute policies of economic nationalism and protectionism. The impacts of these policies moved in waves across the globe, emphasizing the integrated nature of the global economy even in contexts of conflict. Great Britain went off the **gold standard** in 1931 and was followed by more than 20 other countries. The United States did so in 1933, and by 1937, no country in the world was on the full gold standard. Economic nationalism resulted in the imposition of high **tariffs** on internationally traded goods. The U.S. enacted the very high **Hawley-Smoot tariff** in 1930, and rapidly countries throughout the world, even traditionally free-trade-oriented Great Britain, enacted similar protective tariffs. The **London International Economic Conference of 1933** attempted to develop arrangements for stabilization of currencies and regulation of international debts but failed.

World War II arrangements. The outbreak of World War II brought an end to the conditions of the 1930s, and during the war, Allied negotiators worked on establishing less anarchic international economic conditions as a part of the postwar reorganization. Major international economic institutions were established in the chief problem areas of international finance, monetary issues, and trade. At the **BRETTON WOODS CONFERENCE** in 1944, representatives from 44 Allied states met to establish rules for trade and international economic relations in the postwar period. As a result of conference recommendations, the **International Monetary Fund** was created in 1945 and the **International Bank for Reconstruction and Development** (the "World Bank") began operations in 1946 as institutions to stabilize currency and international financial relations.

Nongovernmental economic associations. Private international associations and organizations developed in the 19th century as an important part of global economic activities. However, it was in the first half of the 20th century that such structures grew rapidly in number and became more institutionalized. In 1907, the first comprehensive listing by the **Union of International Associations** named 185, and by the middle of the 20th century, more than a thousand international organizations were in operation. Their activities were especially important in the economic and scientific areas. The **International Chamber of Commerce** had roots in 19th-century structures but was created as a permanent organization in 1920 as a confederation of national commercial associations and other business groups. It played an important consultative role in economic conferences in the interwar period and, after World War II, received consultative status with the UN. **INTERNATIONAL EXPOSITIONS,** or World's Fairs, were important events in the 19th century, beginning with the **Crystal Palace Exhibition** of 1851 in London. They provided major international opportunities to exhibit new trade goods and the most advanced technologies of the time. Throughout the 19th century, they were organized by individual countries. In 1928, a convention signed by 35 countries created the **Bureau of International Expositions** to regulate the holding of world's fairs. The New York World's Fair (1939–40) was the last major fair before World War II, and the next did not take place until the Brussels Exposition of 1958. Individual industries coordinated standards and activities through organizations like the International Hotel Alliance (1921), the International Wool Textile Organization (1929), the International Broadcasting Union (1925), and the International Shipping Conference (1921). A large number of other associations reflected the increasing globalization of all significant areas of human activity.

Multinational corporations. The interwar period was an important time in the development of global business structures. International companies have existed since ancient times, but truly multinational corporations are recent creations. In the 19th century the major international companies were generally involved in import-export trade or exploitation of raw materials. Possibly the first truly multinational corporation was **Singer,** an American company that manufactured and mass-marketed a product (sewing machines) internationally. By 1914, the idea of a multinational corporation was established through the development of a number of major companies, but their share in the economic activity of industrialized societies was still limited. In the first half of the 20th century, this situation was transformed. In those industries involving production of mass consumer goods or new advanced technologies, there was a significant internationalization of enterprise. **Ford** and **General Motors** led in internationalizing the automobile industry, and other important examples of emerging multinational corporations were **Philips Electrical** (originally Dutch), **Courtaulds** in synthetic fibers, and the German **I. G. Farben** chemical trust. In some major industries, **CARTELS,** groups of large companies that coordinated their efforts, emerged as an important form of multinational economic enterprise. Major cartels emerged in the chemical, steel, and synthetic fibers industries. The most successful was the **oil cartel,** in which the seven largest oil companies in the world, led by **Standard Oil (New Jersey), Royal Dutch–Shell,** and **Anglo-Persian** (now British Petroleum), set conditions of pricing and production for most of the world's oil industry. Cartels flourished in the first half of the 20th century but became less important as a result of the transformations of the global economic context created by World War II and postwar developments. However, by mid-century, the large multinational corporation had emerged as a very important part of the global economy.

4. MULTINATIONAL CULTURAL INSTITUTIONS

Nongovernmental organizations for cultural, religious, and humanitarian purposes have long been internationally active. Religious communities like the **Roman Catholic Church** have been significantly transnational institutions since the classical period of world history. However, in the 19th century, modern associations began to emerge as important international agents. During the first half of the 20th century, these organizations joined the more traditional structures in becoming a major element in the globalization of modern societies.

Religious organizations. During the 19th century, the intensification of global relationships also involved religious groups. In the era of Western domination, this frequently involved **Christian missionary** activities in non-European areas. In the first half of the 20th century, the interactions became more cosmopolitan. In the **Roman Catholic Church,** especially under **Pope Pius XI** (1922–39) and **Pope Pius XII** (1939–58), there was a significant effort to create local clergies and indigenous hierarchies in the mission lands. The **ECUMENICAL MOVEMENT** was especially strong among Protestant Christians. Competition among Christian missionary bodies led to a world conference of missionary societies in Edinburgh in 1910 which laid foundations for the modern ecumenical movement. In 1921 the **International Missionary Council** was created for global coordination of missions, and it held five major international conferences that redefined the ecumenical Protestant understanding of mission in multinational terms. The **Commission on Life and Work** and the **Faith and Order Commission** were established in the 1920s. In a conference at Utrecht in 1938 they voted to merge in order to create a **World Council of Churches,** a process that was completed following World War II at a meeting at Amsterdam in 1948. Individual church organizations also became more explicitly global in the first half of the 20th century with the creation of organizations like the **Lutheran World Federation** in 1947.

HINDU organizations of a modern multinational style also emerged. During the late 19th century, the **Ramakrishna Mission** gained international prominence through the travels and lectures in the West of **Vivekananda** (1863–1902) and the establishment of Vedanta Societies. The teachings of **Aurobindo Ghose** (1872–1950), presented as Integral Yoga, gained followers throughout the world organized in special meditative communities or *ashrams.* **BUDDHISM** was also a source of new movements in many different areas. A number of Buddhist missionary organizations were active in the West, and Buddhism became a fully global religion during the first half of the 20th century.

ZIONISM emerged in Judaism during the late 19th century in a distinctively modern organizational format. The first Zionist Congress was held in 1897, and it created the **World Zionist Movement,** whose goal was to create an independent Jewish state. During World War I, the Zionist movement secured international recognition. The interwar period saw the development of a formal Jewish community in British-controlled **Palestine** and the development of Zionism as a significant global movement. Following World War II, Zionism achieved its goal with the creation of the **State of Israel** in 1948.

Humanitarian organizations. Nongovernmental organizations were established to deal with humanitarian issues in many different fields. The more prominent of these associations often worked closely with interstate and national governments. During the first half of the 20th century, the **Red Cross** continued to grow as an international force. In 1919 the various national societies joined together in what came to be called the **International Federation of Red Cross and Red Crescent Societies,** which provided relief in disaster situations. **The Society of Friends** (Quakers) also formed a number of humanitarian agencies in the first half of the 20th century. Although they were nationally organized, like the **American Friends Service Committee,** established in 1917, they worked internationally. The American committee and the Service Council of the British Society of Friends shared the Nobel Peace Prize in 1947 in recognition of this worldwide activity.

Women's associations grew in international importance during the first half of the 20th century. Ten of the first 32 organizations admitted to "category B" consultative status at the UN in 1946–47 were explicitly international women's organizations, including the International Federation of Business and Professional Women.

b. GLOBALLY COMPETING IDEOLOGIES

The first half of the 20th century was a time when major modern comprehensive ideologies were developed as the basis for sociopolitical identities and political systems. In the social, economic, and political transformations framed by the two world wars and the Great Depression, world visions and broad programmatic perspectives were an important part of the global scene. The most comprehensive statements of the emerging ideologies were made by movements and thinkers in more industrialized societies. These helped to shape the options defining transformations taking place outside of Europe and North America. Two important lines of experience shaped the developing global competition of ideologies in the first half of the 20th century: (1) the definition and conflict of explicitly modern ideologies in the Western world, and (2) the evolution of options for guiding transformations in the emerging nationalist context of societies dominated by the major powers.

1. WESTERN IDEOLOGICAL COMPETITIONS

At the beginning of the 20th century in Europe, comprehensive ideological positions defining the basic nature of society tended to be politically marginal. The nationalist unifications of Italy and Germany had avoided becoming ideologically liberal, and Great Britain and France maintained a practical adherence to parliamentary liberalism. Democratic liberalism, in an explicitly capitalist format, as it was emerging in the U.S., was also pragmatic in orientation. World War I destroyed the stability of the politically evolutionary acceptance of change, and following the war, the alternatives were more sharply defined in ideologically programmatic terms.

a. Democratic Liberalism

The victorious powers in World War I were committed to differing forms of democratic liberalism. The **World War I settlement** reflected this ideological position. The global terms were set by the U.S. president **WOODROW WILSON**, in an ideological liberal internationalism committed to the **self-determination** of peoples, **democratic** political systems, relatively **capitalist** market economies, and peaceful resolution of international conflicts by public negotiation. The **League of Nations** was the manifestation of this ideology. Although Great Britain and France were less committed to the international aspects, they maintained their own democratic parliamentary systems and supported efforts to create and maintain them elsewhere in Europe. Germany was reconstituted in the **Weimar Republic,** and in the other new states established in Central and Eastern Europe, parliamentary systems were established. Significant economic difficulties in all of the democracies and growing political divisions among the parties led to increasing pressures for more authoritarian leaders, and in a number of countries dictators came to power. In the continuing democracies, the Depression forced major changes involving significant government intervention in the economy. **Democratic socialism** became a major force in Britain and France, and the **New Deal** of President Franklin Roosevelt, beginning in 1933 in the U.S., was a major transformation of the economy of the U.S. The economies of the liberal democracies were increasingly **mixed economies**, combining aspects of capitalism and socialism in an emerging **democratic welfare state** system. During World War II, the **Axis powers** represented the authoritarian alternative to liberal democracy. When they were defeated, the **Allied powers** established constitutional democratic systems in **Italy, Japan,** and the parts of Germany under occupation by American, British, and French forces. In the Western world, after major setbacks during the interwar period, liberal democracy, in modified capitalist and socialist economic systems, emerged after World War II as the dominant sociopolitical ideology.

b. Communism

The philosophy and sociopolitical ideology of **Karl Marx** (1818–83) provided the basis for the major ideological alternative to liberal democracy in the 20th century. Building on a materialist interpretation of history, Marxists developed a vision of a society in which production and distribution were controlled by the community in a collectivized economy. The working class was to be the major vehicle for achieving this goal, and class interests rather than national identities were seen as primary. When the member parties of the **Second International** supported their national governments in World War I, the International was dissolved. An explicitly **communist alternative** was defined by **LENIN** (Vladimir I. Ulianov), who led a radical faction of the **Social Democratic Party** that had been formed in Russia in 1898. In the **Russian Revolution of 1917,** Lenin's faction, the **Bolsheviks,** came to power and was reorganized as the **Communist Party** in 1918, which was the sole party in the emerging Soviet Union. Lenin created the **THIRD INTERNATIONAL** (Comintern) in 1919 as the structure for organizing global revolution and coordinating efforts of Communist parties around the world. Parties of the extreme left from 37 countries attended the second congress of the Comintern in 1920. During the 1920s, formal Communist parties were founded in many countries of Asia, including Turkey, Iran, India, China, and Japan, in Latin America, in the Middle East, and in most European countries. Although no other countries became Communist systems in the interwar era, the Soviet Union emerged as a major world power. **Leninist communism** became a major alternative to and competitor with **Wilsonian liberal democracy.**

Communist-democratic conflicts quickly developed. Great Britain, France, and the U.S. intervened militarily in the Russian civil war in 1918–19 to prevent the consolidation of Bolshevik rule of Russia but failed. In the efforts to establish new states and create a new international system at the end of World War I, there were important but unsuccessful Communist efforts to gain control in many places. In **Germany,** the **Spartacist group,** which advocated a Communist state, led a series of uprisings in 1919–20 against the emerging Weimar Republic and was defeated. Communist attempts to gain power in the

new republic of **Austria** (1919) and **Bulgaria** (1923–25) were unsuccessful. The Communist dictatorship of **Béla Kun** in Hungary lasted only a few months in 1919. In **Iran (Persia)**, Persian nationalists and social democrats received support from the Bolshevik regime in establishing a short-lived **Soviet Republic of Gilan** in 1920. The new Communist Party in **China** cooperated with the Kuomintang regime until a major split in 1927, and the Communists went into revolutionary opposition.

Communist "threat." Although Communist parties did not succeed in winning control of any countries in the interwar era, they represented the most visible global opposition to **democratic liberal** regimes. This led at times to periodic waves of fear of Communist revolutions in democratic countries. In the U.S. during the **Red scare of 1919–20,** thousands of people were arrested as suspected Communist revolutionaries. In Great Britain, the publication of the so-called **Zinoviev letter** in 1924, exposing an alleged Communist conspiracy, contributed to the overwhelming electoral victory of the Conservatives over the more socialist Labour Party. Fear of communism was an important reason why many people supported the emergence of the authoritarian regimes of **Mussolini** in Italy and **Hitler** in Germany. In 1933, Hitler charged the Communists with setting the **Reichstag fire** (p. 699), which partly destroyed the German parliament building. The alleged danger of a Communist revolution was the rationale for the suspension of constitutional liberties and the granting of special powers to Hitler. The most effective response to Communist threats, real and imagined, was thought by many, even in the liberal democracies, to be more authoritarian policies. By the 1930s, the real ideological competition was frequently seen as being between communism and various forms of fascism, with liberal democracies believed to be in decline. This situation was strengthened by the economic conditions of the Great Depression.

c. Fascism

Fascism developed as the third major competing ideology of the first half of the 20th century. It was not simply an assertion of dictatorial or military rule, nor was it a socially conservative perspective, although many conservatives preferred it to either communism or democratic liberalism. **Fascist movements** that emerged after World War I took a number of different forms, but they shared an ideological perspective that **subordinated the individual** to the state, opposed class struggle, and affirmed **nationalist identities** and a **corporate state.** Structures were **elitist** rather than egalitarian, and there was an emphasis on the role of the **great leader.** The first major Fascist leader to come to power was **MUSSOLINI** in Italy, who became prime minister in 1922 and seized full power by 1926. Other states came under the control of dictators in the interwar period, including Poland (1926), Lithuania (1926), Portugal (1932), and Estonia (1934). The most important Fascist-style regime was established in Germany during the 1930s by the **NAZI MOVEMENT** led by **HITLER.** Fascist-style governments also came to power in **Greece** in 1936 under General **Johannes Metaxas,** and in **Spain** with the victory in 1939 of the Falange led by **Francisco Franco** in the **Spanish Civil War.** In **Argentina,** a group of military officers impressed by Nazi achievements seized power in 1943, and their dominant leader, **Juan Perón,** established a Fascist-style dictatorship in 1945. In **JAPAN** a distinctive statist authoritarian regime developed in the interwar era, and it established ties with the major European Fascist states in the late 1930s. Fascist-style movements also developed in a number of countries: the **Iron Guard,** founded in Romania in 1927; the "Black Shirts" of **Oswald Moseley** in Great Britain (formed in 1932); **Young Egypt** (the "Green Shirts"), formed in Egypt in 1933. Elsewhere, including in the U.S., many people became convinced that some form of authoritarian fascism was necessary in the face of the Communist challenge and the difficulties of the Depression.

d. Victory of Democratic Liberalism

The defeat of the **Axis powers** in World War II brought an end to the appeal of Fascism, as the major examples of Fascist-style regimes were defeated and were forced to experience the establishment of **liberal democracies.** While authoritarian dictatorships continued in many parts of the world, only **Franco** in Spain and **Perón** in Argentina advocated Fascist-style ideologies on which to base their legitimacy. Most dictators after World War II appealed to popular sovereignty and the concepts of democracy. This created the conditions for the main ideological conflict of the second half of the 20th century, the competition between **democratic liberalism** and **communism,** which took the concrete form of the **COLD WAR** between the emerging superpowers of the **U.S.** and **the Soviet Union.**

2. NATIONALIST OPTIONS

In the areas dominated by the major powers and empires, the first half of the 20th century was a time when nationalist movements began to be important throughout the world. In the 19th century, nationalist movements had been most effective and active in Europe. The advocacy of the right of **self-determination** which was part of the World War I settlement created a number of new nationally identified states in Europe but maintained imperial control in much of the rest of the world.

MIDDLE EAST. Movements for assertion of national identities had developed in the late 19th century in **Egypt** and **Persia** (Iran), and among **Turks** in the Ottoman Empire. In the **Arab lands** of southwest Asia and French North Africa, there was little Arab nationalism until World War I. Following World War I, major nationalist movements developed in Turkey under **Mustafa Kemal Atatürk** (p. 752), in Persia under **Reza Shah Pahlevi,** and in Egypt under the **Wafd Party** of Sa'd Zaghloul. In French North Africa, the **Destour Party** and then the **Neo-Destour Party** in Tunisia and less well structured efforts elsewhere presented nationalist programs, as did intellectuals in the states that had been created as League of Nations **mandates** in the Middle East—Syria, Lebanon, Iraq, Jordan, and Palestine. All of these nationalist movements tended to express their goals in terms of **Wilsonian liberal democracy.** They sought self-determination, recognized popular sovereignty, and tried to create independent parliamentary political systems. All also advocated programs of rapid modernization following explicitly Western European models. Fascism and communism had limited appeal or support. The real conflict was between nationalist aspirations and imperialist power. Only in the new Turkish republic under **Atatürk,** and, to a lesser extent, in Persia (Iran), were nationalists able to achieve effective political independence and implement modernization programs of their own rather than an imposed definition.

AFRICA. The interwar period was from some perspectives the heyday of European imperialism in Africa. Major concepts of imperial governance like **Indirect Rule** were developed by the British, and there was little expectation that imperial rule would end before a long period of time had elapsed. The units of imperial control had been created by the processes of European imperial expansion and had little relationship to the ethnic and cultural identities of the subject peoples. In the interwar period there were, however, small groups of educated Africans who began to call for independence and did so in nationalist terms, calling for the independence of the existing imperialist-created state. In the **Anglo-Egyptian Sudan** a Graduates Congress was formed in 1938 and advocated nationalist aims, presenting a list of demands to the British in 1942. In **Kenya** during the 1920s there was the Kikuyu Central Association, which sought the return of land taken by British settlers, but its leaders, like the later nationalist **Jomo Kenyatta,** were not actively nationalist in the interwar era. In general terms, educated Africans in all colonies expressed desires for self-determination and effective political participation, but effective nationalist movements did not emerge until after World War II.

PAN-AFRICAN movements did not have much support in Africa itself, but in the U.S., African-American organizations supported various types of Pan-Africanism and possible return to Africa. The most important advocates of these ideas were **W. E. B. Du Bois** early in the century, and **Marcus Garvey** in the Universal Negro Improvement Association in the 1920s. A religious form of American black nationalism was formulated by **Elijah Muhammad** in the organization of the **Nation of Islam** in the 1930s.

SOUTH ASIA. In **India,** there was a well-established nationalist movement by the beginning of the 20th century. The **Indian National Congress** had been founded in 1885 with the goal of securing for Indians a greater role in their government. In the interwar period, especially under the dramatic nonviolent leadership of **Mahatma Gandhi,** the nationalist movement gained great strength. The **Muslim League,** founded in 1906, originally worked closely with Congress to secure Indian self-government. During the interwar period, Indian Muslim feelings of identity and fear of Hindu domination in an independent India led the Muslim League to advocate establishing an independent Muslim state in South Asia to be called **Pakistan.** Following World War II in 1947, when British India became independent it was partitioned into Pakistan and the Republic of India.

EAST ASIA. In the colonial areas of East Asia there were some beginnings of modern nationalism. In the **Philippines,** the period of rule by the U.S. began with a bloody war of Philippine resistance (1898–1901) and ended with the establishment of commonwealth status in the late 1930s and the Japanese conquest during World War II. Nationalist resistance to French rule in **Indochina,** Dutch rule in **Indonesia,** and British control in various southeast Asia lands began to be expressed in the interwar era but with only limited success until World War II, when the defeat of the imperial powers by **Japan** inspired local nationalists.

Japan's role. Japan had an important international role in the development of nationalist movements during the first half of the 20th century. The success of the program of rapid modernization set in motion by the **Meiji Revolution** in the 19th century inspired reformist nationalists like Atatürk in Turkey. Japan's victory in the **Russo-Japanese War of 1905** had a major impact in showing that European imperial powers could be defeated. In **World War II,** the Japanese conquest of the French, British, Dutch, and American possessions in East and Southeast Asia opened the way for wartime puppet states to set precedents for later demands for independence. In addition, the expansion of Japan's own imperial strength aroused the fears of Japan's historic rivals, China and Korea, and provided a negative impulse for the development of nationalism in China under the **Kuomintang** led by **Jiang Jieshi.** In **Korea,** following its annexation by Japan in 1910, nationalist resistance took a number of forms, including the establishment of a Korean provisional government in exile whose president in 1919 was **Syngman Rhee,** who became the first president of South Korea in the republic created by the U.S. following World War II.

Nationalist ideologies in the first half of the 20th century tended to be based on the **Wilsonian liberal democratic** vision of the world. It was not until the time of the Cold War following World War II that more Communist-style perspectives became important in developing nationalist movements and visions.

a. GLOBALIZATION OF CULTURE

The period between the two world wars was a time when many aspects of human life and experience became more global in style or mode of operation. The Great Depression showed the global nature of important economic aspects of life, but this was also part of many aspects of social and cultural life. These tendencies could be seen in sports, entertainment, and literature.

1. SPORTS

The organizational and social context of sports became significantly globalized in the first half of the 20th century. The sports involved the establishment of significant international organizations both of athletes and of competitions. The **International Amateur Athletic Federation (IAAF)** (founded 1913) became a major global institution by mid-20th century. **THE MODERN OLYMPIC GAMES** became major global events in the interwar era. The **Berlin Olympics of 1936** were an attempt by **Hitler** to glorify the new racist Nazi state but this failed when an African-American athlete, **Jesse Owens,** won four gold medals. The Olympics were extended to include winter games in 1924. The **London Olympics of 1948** were a celebration of the Allied victory in World War II as well as an athletic event.

Major individual sports also became globalized, with the world's most widely viewed sport of **SOCCER**, or Association Football, reflecting the broader history. Following World War I, association football became a major feature of social recreational life, especially in Europe and Latin America. The first **World Cup** competition was held in 1930 and was won by Uruguay. International competitions were interrupted by World War II but quickly resumed following the war.

2. CINEMA

The development of the technology of motion pictures and the large movie industry is an important global phenomenon of the first half of the 20th century. The ability to present "moving pictures" was the result of work by people in a number of different countries in the 1890s. Louis and Auguste **Lumière** in France developed equipment using machines made by **Thomas Edison,** and the Lumières first presented motion pictures to a paying audience in a Paris café in 1895. The **film industry** developed rapidly in the U.S., with **D. W. Griffith** making more than 400 films between 1908 and 1913, transforming the art and the business. World War I inhibited the development of the film industry in Europe, but in the interwar period cinema spread rapidly throughout the world, both in terms of audience and film production. In the 1920s, large film companies grew in the U.S., especially in **Hollywood, California,** and major film industries developed in Ger-

many, France, and Sweden. In the new Soviet Union, major directors like **Sergei Eisenstein** created films like *Potemkin* (1925), which had an international impact. Cinema sometimes became an important medium for political propaganda, as in the films of **Leni Riefenstahl** in Nazi Germany in the 1930s. Outside of Europe and the U.S., important film industries also developed, showing the global impact of the new medium. In **Egypt,** film shows for Allied troops during World War I created great local interest, and local production efforts began after the war. The first full-length Egyptian film was produced in 1927, and in 1934 the large Studio Misr was founded. World War II stimulated further interest and opportunity, so that the Egyptian film industry emerged as an important part of the postwar Arab world. Other major film industries producing large numbers of films began in the interwar era in **JAPAN** and **INDIA,** and after World War II movies like **Akira Kurosawa's** *Rashomon* (1950) and **Satyajit Ray's** *Pather Panchali* (1955) gained major international recognition. The expansion of the movie industry was a part of the Westernization and industrialization of the modern world. It also provided modern means for the expression of distinctive cultural identities in the context of increasingly global means of presentation and communication.

The **globalization of human experience** in the first half of the 20th century is seen in the development of political institutions, economic structures, ideological competitions, and cultural areas. This shows the continuing influence of Western forms and structures but also the expansion beyond the traditional West of modern forms and ideas. In the process, the **modern world** emerged from the **Western-dominated world.**

3. INTERNATIONAL RELATIONS

The era between the two world wars was a period of complex interrelations among states and involved a variety of other institutions. The major dividing point in the two decades is the beginning of the Great Depression, which can be dated from the collapse of the New York stock market in 1929. The interwar period may be divided chronologically into two phases: (1) the postwar period of adjustment and building, and (2) the era of the Great Depression.

a. THE POST–WORLD WAR I ERA

The main lines of development of international relations during the 1920s were to implement the Versailles Treaty, to organize international relations among the major powers in the changing global context, and to adjust to the globalization of many different types of activities.

1919. Creation of the **International Labor Organization** and the **International Commission for Air Navigation** as a part of the development of the League of Nations organizational structures. Creation of the **International Federation of Red Cross Societies,** joining the various national societies into a single world federation. The formation of the **Third International (Comintern)** by Lenin.

1919, Nov. 19. U.S. Senate refused to ratify the **Versailles Treaty** (p. 728) and the defensive treaties among the U.S., Great Britain, and France. This significantly weakened the whole structure of the international peace structure established at Paris.

1919–24. Conflicts over borders of peace settlement (p. 674). Numerous disputes in **Eastern Europe** took place, contesting control of Vilna (between Poland, Lithuania, and Russia), Teschen (Poland and Czechoslovakia), Bergenland (between Austria and Hungary), Fiume (between Italy and Yugoslavia), and Upper Silesia (between Germany and Poland). In the **Middle East,** there was a **Turco-Greek War** (1919–22) for the control of Western Anatolia, which the new Turkish nationalist movement won, driving Greek forces completely out of Anatolia.

1920. Creation of the **International Chamber of Commerce.**

Olympic Games resumed, after eight-year break, in Antwerp. Finnish distance runner Paavo Nurmi was major star.

1920, Jan. 10. Official **birth of the League of Nations.** The assembly met for the first time Nov. 15.

April 19–26. The **San Remo Conference** of the Allied powers to discuss territorial arrangements and to assign League of Nations Class A Mandates.

June 19–22. Conference of Hythe and Boulogne to discuss the Middle Eastern situation and reparations issues.

1921. Establishment of the **International Hotel Alliance** and the **International Shipping Conference.** Christian church organizations established the **International Missionary Conference.**

1921, Aug. 24, 25. U.S. peace treaties with Austria and Germany made separately.

Oct. 20. The Aaland Islands convention signed in Geneva providing for the neutralization and nonfortification of the islands.

1921, Nov. 12–1922, Feb. 6. The **WASHINGTON CONFERENCE,** which met at the invitation of the U.S. government to consider naval armaments and East Asian questions. Great Britain, France, Italy, Belgium, the Netherlands, China, Japan, and Portugal were represented. Soviet Russia, not yet recognized by the U.S., was not invited, despite its major interests in East Asia. The conference resulted in (1) the **four-power Pacific Treaty,** Dec. 13 (the U.S., Great Britain, France, and Japan), by which the signatories guaranteed each other's rights in insular possessions in the Pacific and promised to consult if their rights were threatened. The Anglo-Japanese alliance came to an end; (2) **the Shantung Treaty** (Feb. 4), by which Japan returned Kiaochow to China; (3) two **nine-power treaties** (Feb. 6), guaranteeing the territorial integrity and administrative independence of China and reiterating the principle of the "Open Door"; (4) the **naval armaments treaty** (Feb. 6), providing for a ten-year naval holiday during which no new capital ships (defined as ships over 10,000 tons with guns larger than eight-inch) were to be built, and establishing a ratio for capital ships of 5–5–3–1.67–1.67. This meant that Great Britain and the U.S. were each allowed 525,000 tons, Japan 315,000, and France and Italy each 175,000. Total tonnage of aircraft carriers was restricted and a maximum size fixed for capital ships, aircraft carriers, and cruisers.

1922, Feb. 15. The **Permanent Court of International Justice** was opened at The Hague.

April 10–May 19. Genoa Conference, including Germany and Russia, called to consider the Russian problem and the general economic questions of the world. The conference broke down on the insistence of France that Russia recognize its prewar debt.

April 16. Rapallo Treaty of alliance between Germany and Soviet Russia in which both renounced reparations (p. 675).

June 30. The new **Danube statute** went into effect.

Aug. 1. Lord Balfour, the British foreign secretary, sent a note to the Allied powers indebted to Great Britain offering to abandon all further claims to payment and all claims to reparations, provided a general settlement could be made that would end the "economic injury inflicted on the world by the present state of things." If the U.S., which had not demanded a share of reparations payments, should refuse to cancel the debts owed by European governments, then Great Britain would have to insist on receiving enough from its debtors to pay its own obligations to the U.S. The American attitude was that reparations and interallied debts were not connected problems, so that German default on reparations would not excuse default on Allied payments to the U.S.

Aug. 7–14. London Conference. Poincaré demanded, as conditions for a moratorium, a series of "productive guarantees," among them appropriation of 60 percent of the capital of the German dyestuff factories on the left bank of the Rhine, and exploitation and contingent expropriation of the state mines in the Ruhr. The British rejected Poincaré's scheme, and Poincaré refused to grant a moratorium.

1922, Nov. 20–1923, Feb. 4. First Lausanne Conference, to conclude peace between Turkey and Greece (p. 753).

Dec. 9–11. Second London Conference. The British offered to cancel Allied debts to Great Britain even if Britain had to continue to pay the U.S. Poincaré refused, since the reparations expected from Germany were theoretically greater than the French debt to Great Britain.

1923, Jan. 9. Germany declared in default on coal deliveries.

April 23–July 24. Second Lausanne Conference. The **TREATY OF LAUSANNE** (p. 753) replaced the harsh Treaty of Sèvres (1920), which had been imposed on the defeated Ottoman Empire, while the Lausanne negotiations were with the new **Turkish Republic.** The treaty brought an end to Allied (including Greek) occupation of Turkish republican territories and abolished the old Capitulations privileges of Europeans in Turkey.

1924, March 3. The office and title of **CALIPH,** which had been assumed by the Ottoman sultans, were abolished by the new **Turkish Republic.**

April 9. THE DAWES PLAN. The committee chaired by the American **Charles G. Dawes** presented its report. The plan provided for a reorganization of the German Reichsbank under Allied supervision. Reparation payments of 1 billion gold marks were to be made annually, increasing by the end of five years to 2 billion 500 thousand. Germany was to receive a foreign loan of 800 million gold marks.

April 16. The Germans accepted the Dawes Plan.

July 16–Aug. 16. A **conference in London** adopted the Dawes Plan, and the Reichstag passed the necessary legislation. The U.S. took up $110 million of the loan.

Oct. 2. The **Geneva Protocol** for pacific settlement of international disputes was an attempt to strengthen international institutions and overcome the problems caused by the absence of the U.S., Germany, and the Soviet Union in the League of Nations. The **British dominions** opposed the compulsory arbitration aspects, and the British ultimately rejected the protocol.

1924. Britain, France, and Spain signed the **Tangier convention,** providing for permanent neutralization of the Tangier zone and government by international commission.

1925, Feb. 9. The German government proposed a Rhineland Mutual Security Pact. The British supported the idea as a replacement for the failed Geneva Protocol, and **Aristide Briand,** who became the French foreign minister in April 1925, accepted the suggestion on the condition that Germany join the League.

Feb. 11, 19. International opium convention provided more effective control of production and trade in opium.

June 17. Arms traffic convention dealing with international trade in arms and munitions. A protocol was signed that prohibited the use of poison gas.

1926, May 16–18. First meeting of the **Preparatory Commission for a Disarmament Conference.** The U.S. was represented. The commission held many meetings in the next few years.

Sept. 8. Germany admitted to the League and given a permanent seat on the Council.

1927, May 4–23. Geneva economic conference attended by representatives of 50 countries.

June 20–Aug. 4. Three-power naval conference in Geneva attended by Great Britain, Japan, and the U.S. The conference failed to reach an agreement.

Nov. 30–Dec. 3. Russian proposal to the preparatory committee on disarmament by **Maxim Litvinov** for complete and immediate disarmament was rejected as a Communist ploy.

1928, April 13. Frank B. Kellogg, U.S. secretary of state, submitted a plan for the **renunciation of war** to the Locarno powers.

April 21. Aristide Briand, for France, presented a draft of a treaty for outlawing war.

June 23. An explanatory note on the proposed **Kellogg-Briand Pact** was circulated among major powers, and all supported the concept.

July. RED LINE AGREEMENT among the major oil companies participating in the **Iraq Petroleum Company,** a consortium established as the boundaries of the British mandate of Iraq were determined. The companies agreed to coordinate all oil exploration in the former Ottoman lands.

Aug. 27. The **KELLOGG-BRIAND PACT** was signed in Paris. It involved renunciation of aggressive war but had no provisions for sanctions. The League of Nations passed resolutions implementing the pact, with an optional clause for compulsory arbitration.

Dec. 6. Beginning of conflict between Bolivia and Paraguay over the **Chaco region** (p. 738)). Mediation efforts by the League of Nations and the Pan-American Union were not successful in resolving the dispute, although open hostilities were avoided until 1932.

1929, Jan. 5. General act of **Inter-American arbitration** similar to the optional clause for compulsory arbitration in the **Kellogg-Briand Pact** signed at the Pan-American conference in Washington.

June 7. The Young Plan. The Young Committee (appointed Jan. 1929) revised arrangements for German reparations. Germany was to assume responsibility for transferring payments from marks into foreign currency, to be done under a new institution, the **Bank for International Settlements** in Basel. All principal central banks were represented in the new bank's directorate. The total proposed annuities to be paid by Germany were less than what Germany had been paying under the **Dawes Plan,** so diplomats thought that the Young Plan represented a permanent settlement.

June 3. The dispute between Chile and Peru over the districts of **Tacna and Arica,** which had lasted for more than two decades, was settled. The U.S. had aided negotiations.

Aug. 6–31. Hague Conference on the Young Plan. The Germans accepted the plan, and it was agreed that the **Rhineland** would be evacuated by June 1930.

Oct. STOCK MARKET CRASH in New York began a series of economic difficulties, creating the worldwide **Great Depression.**

b. THE ERA OF THE GREAT DEPRESSION

During the 1930s, the major themes of global history were the continuing efforts to resolve the problem of war, first in terms of continuing the effort to find ways of eliminating war, and then in terms of limiting actual prospects of the major war that was clearly looming; and the efforts to cope with the economic conditions of the global depression.

1930, Jan. 21–April 22. LONDON NAVAL CONFERENCE. It led to a treaty signed by Great Britain, the U.S., France, Italy, and Japan, regulating submarine warfare and limiting the tonnage and gun caliber of submarines. The limitation of aircraft carriers, provided for by the Washington Treaty, was extended. Great Britain, the U.S., and Japan agreed to scrap certain warships by 1933 and allocated tonnage in other categories. Increased tonnage was allowable under specified conditions. The agreements were to operate until 1936.

Nov. 6–Dec. 9. Final meeting of the **Preparatory Commission on Disarmament.** It adopted by a majority vote a draft convention to be discussed at a disarmament conference called by the League Council for February 1932. German and Russian representatives did not approve, and Swedish and American delegates had strong reservations. The major problems involved clauses preserving obligations from previous treaties, especially those barring German equality in armament.

1931, June 20. President Hoover proposed a **one-year moratorium** on all intergovernmental debts as a way of easing the crisis. This followed the failure of the Austrian Credit-Austalt (p. 676) and worldwide fears of government and corporate bankruptcies. French opposition caused a significant delay.

July 6. Acceptance of the moratorium by all major creditor governments was announced by President Hoover. European leaders saw the moratorium as an American acknowledgment that inter-Allied debts and reparations were closely connected.

Aug. 19. The **Layton-Wiggin report** by an international committee of bankers meeting in Basel called for a six-month extension of all foreign credits to Germany. After this, Germany did not become fully solvent in international transactions.

Sept. 21. The **Bank of England** went off the **GOLD STANDARD** despite credits from the Federal Reserve Bank of New York and the Bank of France and the formation of a national coalition government to balance the budget. Great Britain experimented with a managed paper currency, and all of this created significant instability among those currencies that had been tied to the pound sterling. Eventually almost all countries were forced into currency devaluation. International trade greatly contracted in the absence of a major fixed medium of exchange.

Sept. 18. Japanese occupation of the Manchurian towns of Mukden, Changchun, and Jilin (p. 778) took place in the context of the world economic disorder and Chinese internal instability. This was the informal beginning of a long war between Japan and China.

1932–35. The **Chaco war** between Bolivia and Paraguay broke out despite efforts by the League of Nations and the Pan-American Union to resolve the conflict. Paraguay announced its withdrawal from the League of Nations in 1935, and a truce was finally arranged in 1935 by the U.S. and five South American governments.

1932, Jan 4. Occupation of Shanhaikwan by Japanese troops completed Japanese military control of southern Manchuria.

Feb. 2–July. Meeting of the **Disarmament Conference** at Geneva, with 60 states represented, including the U.S. and the Soviet Union. France proposed a system of international police and insisted that security must precede disarmament. Germany demanded equality. Various other plans were proposed but none accepted.

June 16–July 9. Lausanne Conference on German reparations. Representatives of Germany, France, Belgium, Great Britain, Italy, and Japan reached an agreement that set aside the German reparation debt and substituted for it 5 percent bonds for Rm. 3 billion to be deposited with the Bank for International Settlements and issued when and if it became possible to market them at an appropriate price. Ratification was contingent upon acceptance by the U.S., the major creditor of the associated powers. The U.S. refused to accept the new plan, which technically meant a return to the Young Plan. In practice, Germany made no payments, and the Nazi government repudiated what it termed "interest slavery." Britain and France made small token payments to the U.S. until the U.S. Congress ruled against such payments. Only **Finland** paid the full installments.

Oct. 4. The **Lytton Commission of Inquiry** of the League of Nations determined that the Japanese occupation of **Manchuria** was not an act of self-defense and that the creation of an independent **Manchukuo** under Japanese domination was not a case of genuine self-determination. The report recommended nonrecognition by the League and urged Japanese withdrawal.

1933, Feb. 25. The **Lytton Report** was adopted by the League of Nations despite Japanese protests. Japan gave notice of **withdrawal from the League** (May 27), and the effect was to weaken the prestige of the League as a peacekeeping force.

Feb. 2–Oct. 14. Meeting of the **Disarmament Conference** following the **No Force Declaration** (Dec. 11, 1932), in which Germany, France, Great Britain, and Italy promised not to attempt to resolve any future disagreements among them by resort to force. The coming to power of **Hitler** in Germany (Jan. 20) changed the framework of disarmament discussions. The issue of German armaments was central to discussions, with Britain, France, Italy, and the U.S. insisting on postponing German equality in arms and the Germans insisting on having at least defensive weapons at once.

June 12–July 27. International Economic Conference at London. Discussions disregarded war debts and reparations and tried to secure agreement on currency stabilization. This was blocked by President Roosevelt's repudiation of it in his message to the conference (July 3). The conference failed.

Oct. 14. Germany announced its withdrawal from the **disarmament conference** and the **League of Nations** (Oct. 23).

1934, Feb. 9. The **Balkan Pact** among Turkey, Greece, Romania, and Yugoslavia (p. 677) concluded.

May 29–June 11. The **disarmament conference** had a brief and fruitless session.

Sept. 18. The **Soviet Union** joined the **League of Nations,** reflecting growing fear of the new Germany.

Dec. 19. Japan renounced the **naval agreements** of 1922 and 1930.

1935, Jan. 7. Franco-Italian agreement granted concessions to Italy in Africa, opening the way for the invasion of **Ethiopia,** in return for possible Franco-Italian cooperation against Germany.

March 16. GERMANY FORMALLY DENOUNCED THE CLAUSES OF THE TREATY OF VERSAILLES CONCERNING GERMAN DISARMAMENT (p. 677).

April 17. The **League** formally condemned Germany's unilateral repudiation of the Versailles Treaty.

October–1936, May. THE ETHIOPIAN CRISIS (p. 797). The Italian invasion of Ethiopia began on Oct. 3 and was condemned by the League of Nations. The League voted to impose **sanctions on Italy** (Oct. 11). The sanctions had little impact, especially since the states could not agree to apply the **oil sanction** (February 1936). Italian forces occupied **Addis Ababa** (May), and Ethiopian resistance collapsed.

1936, March 7–12. DENUNCIATION OF THE LOCARNO PACTS. Germany denounced the Locarno Pacts and reoccupied the **Rhineland area.** Great Britain, France, Belgium, and Italy denounced the German action, but Britain was unwilling to invoke sanctions, so the League of Nations' response was limited. The reaction was also influenced by developments in the Ethiopian crisis.

March 25. London naval agreement among Britain, France, and the U.S.

July 18. BEGINNING OF THE CIVIL WAR IN SPAIN (pp. 691–92). Foreign powers intervened, with Italian and German support for the "Insurgents" and Liberals and Communists supporting the "Republicans" in **a battleground of the major international ideological forces.**

July 20. The **Montreux Conference** approved the Turkish request for permission to fortify the Straits.

Oct. 25. The **BERLIN-ROME AXIS** established by a German-Italian pact.

Nov. 25. A **German-Japanese agreement** followed by an **Italian-Japanese agreement** (Nov. 6, 1937) completed the alliance structure of the **Axis powers** of World War II.

1937, July. Undeclared war between Japan and China began with a major Japanese military campaign in northern China.

Sept. 10–14. The **Nyon Conference** and agreement to deal with piracy in the Mediterranean in connection with the Spanish civil war. Nine powers adopted a system of patrol zones, with Britain and France assuming major responsibilities.

Nov. 3–15. Conference of the powers in Brussels failed to find a way to settle the war in China.

1938, Dec. 24. The **Declaration of Lima** was adopted by 21 American republics. It reaffirmed their solidarity and opposition to any foreign intervention or activity that might threaten their sovereignty.

April 7. Italian invasion of Albania.

1939, June 23. Treaty between France and Turkey allowed Turkey to take control of the Alexandretta district of northern Syria (**Hatay**) in return for a pledge of mutual aid in case of aggression.

Aug. 23. Russo-German pact (p. 679).

Sept. 1. GERMANY INVADED POLAND (p. 800).

Sept. 3. BRITAIN AND FRANCE DECLARED WAR ON GERMANY, and the European phase of World War II began. *(To p. 800)*

4. SCIENCE

(From p. 485)

Science and technology became increasingly international but major developments were concentrated in Europe and the U.S. Throughout the interwar years, physics remained the center of most scientific activity, illuminating a universe that lacked any absolute reality. In 1919 **Ernest Rutherford** (1871–1937) showed that the atom could be split. By 1944 seven subatomic particles had been identified. Although few nonscientists understood the revolution in physics, the implications of the new theories and discoveries, as presented by newspapers and popular writers, were disturbing to millions of men and women in the 1920s and 1930s.

The major benchmarks in scientific inquiry follow.

a. MATHEMATICS, PHYSICS, ASTRONOMY

1915. Einstein announced his **general theory of relativity,** which explained the advance of Mercury's perihelion and predicted the subsequently observed bending of light rays near the sun.

1918. Harlow Shapley (1885–1972), from an extensive study of the distribution of globular clusters and cepheid variable stars, increased the estimated size of our galaxy about ten times. He envisioned the galaxy as a flattened lens-shaped system of stars in which the solar system occupied a position far from the center.

1919. Rutherford found that the collision of alpha particles with nitrogen atoms resulted in the disintegration of the nitrogen and the production of hydrogen nuclei (protons) and an isotope of oxygen. He was the first person to achieve artificial transmutation of an element.

1919. Arthur S. Eddington (1882–1944) and others, by studying data obtained during a total solar eclipse, verified Einstein's prediction of the bending of light rays by the gravitational field of large masses.

1919–29. Edwin P. Hubble (1889–1953) detected cepheid variable stars in the Andromeda Nebula, a discovery that allowed him to determine the distances between galaxies.

1924. Louis-Victor de Broglie (1892–1987) determined from theoretical considerations that the electron, which had been considered a particle, should behave as a wave under certain circumstances. Experimental confirmation was obtained in 1927 by **Clinton Davisson** (1881–1958) and **Lester H. Germer** (1896–1971).

1925. Wolfgang Pauli (1900–1958) announced the **exclusion principle** (in any atom no two electrons have identical sets of quantum numbers). This principle was an important aid in determining the electron structure of the heavier elements.

1925–26. Werner Karl Heisenberg (1901–76) and **Erwin Schrödinger** (1887–1961) independently, and in different ways, laid the theoretical foundations of the new **quantum mechanics,** which, though violating classical notions of causality, successfully predicts the behavior of atomic particles.

1927. George Lemaître (1894–1966), in order to explain the red shift in the spectra from distant galaxies, introduced the concept of the **expanding universe. Eddington** pursued research in this subject from 1930.

1928. Paul A. Dirac (1902–84), by combining quantum mechanics and relativity theory, devised a relativistic **theory of the electron.**

1930. Vannevar Bush (1890–1974) and his associates placed into operation a "differential analyzer," the first modern analog computer.

1931. Ernest O. Lawrence (1901–58) invented the **cyclotron,** a device for accelerating atomic particles, which has become the fundamental research tool in high-energy physics and has made possible the creation of transuranium elements.

1931. Kurt Gödel (1906–78) published *Uber formal unentscheidbare Sätze der Principia Mathematica und verwandter Systeme,* showing that in any formal mathematical system in which elementary arithmetic can be done, there are theorems whose truth or falsity cannot be proved.

1932. Karl Jansky reported the reception of radio waves from cosmic sources, making **radio astronomy** possible.

1938–39. Otto Hahn (1879–1968) and **Otto Strassmann** bombarded uranium with neutrons and found an isotope of barium in the product (1938). **Lise Meitner** (1878–1968) and **Otto Frisch** (1904–79) explained this result by assuming the fission of the uranium nucleus (**nuclear fission**).

1939. Nicolas Bourbaki (pseudonym assumed by a group of mathematicians) published the first of a long series of expository works on modern mathematics.

1939. Hans A. Bethe (b. 1906) and **Carl von Weizsäcker** (b. 1912) independently proposed two sets of nuclear reactions to account for stellar energies: the carbon-nitrogen cycle and the proton-proton chain.

1939–45. World War II research needs stimulated the formation of large groups or teams of research workers to concentrate effort on single problems, such as radar and the atomic bomb. Such group research has become a common feature of postwar science.

1940. Gödel, in *The Consistency of the Axiom of Choice and of the Generalized Continuum Hypothesis with the Axioms of Set Theory,* proved that transfinite methods could not introduce inconsistencies into mathematics.

1942. Enrico Fermi (1901–54) and associates built the first controlled self-sustaining **nuclear reactor.** Fermi was one of the chief architects of the theory of the atomic nucleus.

1944. Mark I, the Harvard-IBM Automatic Sequence Controlled Calculator, was put into operation at Harvard University. This was the first large-scale digital calculating machine.

1945. Vannevar Bush issued the report *Science: The Endless Frontier,* recommending the creation of a U.S. foundation for the support and encouragement of basic research and education in science. In 1950 the U.S. Congress established the **National Science Foundation** to implement this recommendation.

b. CHEMISTRY, BIOLOGY, GEOLOGY

1915. Alfred Wegener (1880–1930) gave the classic expression of the controversial theory of continental drift in *Die Entstehung der Kontinente und Ozeane.*

1921. Hans Spemann (1869–1941) postulated an organizer principle that was responsible for the formative interaction between neighboring embryonic regions. He stimulated contemporary embryologists to search for the inductive chemical molecule.

1927. Hermann J. Muller (1890–1967) announced that he had successfully induced mutations in fruit flies with x-rays. This provided a useful experimental tool, yet in retrospect gave warning to generations of the 1940s and 1950s of a danger in the release of atomic energy.

1929. Alexander Fleming (1881–1955) announced that the common mold *Penicillium* had an inhibitory effect on certain pathogenic bacteria. It was not until 1943 under the pressures of World War II, however, that the first antibiotic, penicillin, was successfully developed.

1930. Ronald A. Fisher (1890–1962) established in *The Genetical Theory of Natural Selection* that superior genes have a significant selective advantage, thus testifying that Darwinian evolution was compatible with genetics.

1941. George W. Beadle (1903–89) and **Edward L. Tatum** (1909–75) described an experimental assay that evaluated the exact relationships between specific mutant genes in mold and particular stages in the metabolic process.

1944. Ostwald T. Avery (1877–1955) and collaborators announced they had transmuted one type of pneumococcus bacteria into a second type by the transfer of DNA molecules.   *(To p. 818)*

5. TECHNOLOGICAL DEVELOPMENTS

(From p. 428)

The major achievements in technology follow.

a. ENERGY AND MATERIALS

1921. Tetraethyl lead, gasoline antiknock additive, produced by **Thomas Midgley** (1889–1994).

1930–35. Development of first commercially practicable **catalytic cracking system** for petroleum by **Eugene J. Houdry** (1892–1962).

1930–37. Development of gas turbine unit for jet propulsion in aircraft by **Frank Whittle.**

1942. DAWN OF THE NUCLEAR AGE. The first self-sustaining **nuclear chain reaction** achieved at Stagg Field, Chicago, by **Enrico Fermi** (1901–54). The first full-scale use of nuclear fuel to produce electricity occurred at Calder Hall (England) in 1956.

b. MATERIALS AND CONSTRUCTION

1928. The first steel-frame, glass-curtain-wall building completed. By 1960 this technique was practically universal for high buildings; developed particularly by **L. Mies van der Rohe** (1886–1969).

1941. Shell molding, a revolutionary process producing more accurate castings cheaply, invented by **Johannes Croning.** Powder metallurgy, although known since Wollaston's work at the beginning of the 19th century, achieved extensive application in mid-20th century.

1945. Industrial development of silicones proceeded apace for a wide variety of applications, including lubricants for exceedingly high and low temperatures; binding of fiberglass; water-repellent agents; etc.

c. MACHINES AND INDUSTRIAL TECHNIQUES

1914. Conveyer-belt mass production employed in the U.S. most dramatically in Henry Ford's assembly line for Model T Ford automobile, which became the symbol for American industrial technique.

1915. Development of **tank in warfare** by British (Sir Ernest Swinton).

1920. J. C. Shaw developed **a sensing device,** controlled by a servomechanism, for a milling machine. Hydraulic trace of J. W. Anderson (1927) allowed the reproduction of complex shapes. Machine tools further supplemented by electrolytic and ultrasonic machines, and cutting machines guided by an electron beam. **Development of laser** (light amplification by simulated emission of radiation) by Theodore N. Maiman (1960); laser also used for precision cutting.

1920 ff. Managerial techniques improved through development of "scientific management," whose principles were first enunciated by **Frederick W. Taylor** (1856–1915) in the first decade of the century. Taylor concentrated on time-motion studies. Other proponents of "rationalized" production were Frank Gilbreth and Charles Bedaux. Quality control developed 1926 ff.

1923. First mill for hot continuous wide strip rolling of steel, based on work of John B. Tytus.

1938. Ladislao J. and George Biro patented the **ballpoint pen.**

1941–45. Development of **rockets and missiles** during World War II.

1944. Harvard IBM Automatic Sequence Controlled Calculator, the first automatic general-purpose **digital computer,** completed, ENIAC (electronic numerical integrator and calculator), the first electronic digital computer, built in 1946. Development of special-purpose computers and data processors (1950 ff.), including programmed **teaching machines.**

d. AGRICULTURAL PRODUCTION AND FOOD TECHNOLOGY

1917. Clarence Birdseye (1886–1956) began development of method for quick **freezing of foods** in small containers; placed on market in 1929.

1939. Paul Muller synthesized DDT for use as an insecticide. Othmar Zeidler had prepared DDT in 1874, but its insecticidal qualities had not been suspected.

1940 ff. Development of **artificial insemination** to improve livestock breeding.

1945 ff. Unit **packaging of foodstuffs** improved by development of plastic packaging films. Trend toward prepared "convenience" foods for household use.

e. TRANSPORTATION AND COMMUNICATION

1920. Frank Conrad (1874–1941) of the Westinghouse Co. began broadcasting radio programs in Pittsburgh, marking the **beginning of radio** as a mass communication medium.

1922. Herbert T. Kalmus developed **Technicolor,** the first commercially successful color process for motion pictures.

1926. Sound Motion Pictures. Although Edison had attempted to put together his phonograph and motion picture inventions for sound movies as early as 1904, it was 1923 before de Forest successfully demonstrated his phonofilm system for recording sound on the motion picture film. The first motion picture with sound accompaniment was publicly shown in 1926, the first talking picture in 1927.

1926 ff. John L. Baird (1888–1946) successfully demonstrated **television** in England. His mechanical system of television, similar to that of C. F. Jenkins in the U.S., was based on Paul von Nipkov's rotating disk (1886) but had technical limitations; modern electronic television developed from the cathode-ray tube (1897) of Ferdinand Braun and A. A. Campbell-Swinton's proposals (1911) for use of a cathode ray to scan an image. The crucial invention was the Iconoscope of the Russian American **Vladimir Zworykin** (1889–1982), the device that transmits television images quickly and effectively. Philo Farnsworth of the U.S. contributed the image dissector tube (1927). General broadcasting of television began in England in 1936, in the U.S. in 1941, but languished until after World War II. Peter C. Goldmark of Columbia Broadcasting System (CBS) demonstrated (1940) a sequential method of color television, which gave way to a compatible electronic system developed by RCA in the 1950s.

1932. Edwin H. Land (1909–91) invented the first practical synthetic light-polarizing material (**polaroid glass**), found useful in sunglasses, cameras, and scientific optical instruments. In 1947 he invented the **Polaroid Land camera,** which developed the film inside the camera and produced a photograph print within one minute; in 1962 he introduced color film for his camera.

1933. Fluorescent lamps introduced for floodlighting and advertising. Developments leading up to this included experiments by George Stokes (1852) and Alexandre Becquerel (1859) to excite fluorescent materials by ultraviolet rays or in a discharge tube; Peter Cooper-Hewitt's invention of the mercury vapor lamp (1901); the introduction of the **Neon lamp** by Georges Claude and the work on cathodes by D. M. Moore and Wehnelt in the 1900s; and J. Risler's application of powder to the outside of tubular discharge lamps (1923). Subsequent developments have included increased cathode life and improved fluorescent powders.

1933. Edwin H. Armstrong (1890–1954), pioneer radio inventor (regenerative, that is, feedback, circuit, 1912, and superheterodyne circuit, 1918), perfected **frequency modulation (FM),** providing static-free radio reception.

1937. Chester Carlson patented a new dry photographic process (Xerography) based upon principles of photoconductivity and electrostatics.

1939. Igor Sikorsky (1889–1972) flew the first **helicopter** of his design. The first helicopter capable of flight was the work of Ellehammer of Denmark (1912), based on C. Renard's articulated rotor blade (1904) and G. A. Crocco's cyclic pitch control (1906). Juan de la Cierva invented the autogiro (1922), differing from the helicopter in that its rotor autorotated and the engine drove a normal propeller. Further development work was done (1934–36) by Louis Breguet and Heinrich Focke.

1939. First test flight of a **turbo-jet airplane** (Heinkel) with an engine designed by Hans von Ohain. Simultaneous and parallel work on jet airplanes in Britain, based on turbo-jet engine designed by Frank Whittle (1930). In 1958 **jet-powered transatlantic airline** service was inaugurated by BOAC and Pan-American Airways. In 1962 the British and French governments announced plans to cooperate on the production of a jet-propelled supersonic transport plane (the Concorde), and the U.S. government proposed American production of a supersonic commercial plane the following year. The first plane to exceed the speed of sound in level flight was the American rocket-propelled Bell X-1, which reached Mach 1.06 (approximately 750 m.p.h.) on October 14, 1947.

1940–45. Development of radar ("radio-detection-and-ranging") stimulated by World War II, for detection of aircraft, blind-bombing techniques, and naval search equipment. Based on Heinrich Hertz's demonstration (1887) that radio waves are reflected similarly to light rays, the technique was first applied by Edward Appleton in Britain (1924)

and G. Breit and M. A. Tuve in the U.S. (1925) for investigating ionization in the upper atmosphere. Robert A. Watson-Watt showed the possibilities of employing radio waves to detect aircraft (1935); J. T. Randall and H. A. H. Boot developed the cavity magnetron for high-power microwave transmission. Simultaneously, radar development had been going on in Germany and the U.S., including the development of equipment by Robert H. Page of the Naval Laboratory. After 1940 Britain and the U.S. cooperated in radar development, much of the work being done at the Radiation Laboratory in Cambridge, Mass.

1941–45. Construction of 2,500 miles of large-diameter (20-inch–24-inch) **pipelines** to deliver petroleum from oil-producing regions in southwest U.S. to East Coast depots. Development of welding of steel-pipe sections (1913–14) cut leakage and made possible large-scale pipeline construction. *(To pp. 818, 836)*

B. WORLD WAR I, 1914–1918

Declarations of War

1914
July 28	Austria on Serbia
Aug. 1	Germany on Russia
Aug. 3	Germany on France
Aug. 4	Germany on Belgium
	Great Britain on Germany
Aug. 5	Montenegro on Austria
Aug. 6	Austria on Russia
	Serbia on Germany
Aug. 8	Montenegro on Germany
Aug. 12	France on Austria
	Great Britain on Austria
Aug. 23	Japan on Germany
Aug. 25	Japan on Austria
Aug. 28	Austria on Belgium
Nov. 4	Russia on Turkey
	Serbia on Turkey
Nov. 5	Great Britain on Turkey
	France on Turkey

1915
May 23	Italy on Austria
June 3	San Marino on Austria
Aug. 21	Italy on Turkey
Oct. 14	Bulgaria on Serbia
Oct. 15	Great Britain on Bulgaria
	Montenegro on Bulgaria
Oct. 16	France on Bulgaria
Oct. 19	Russia on Bulgaria
	Italy on Bulgaria

1916
March 9	Germany on Portugal
March 15	Austria on Portugal
Aug. 27	Romania on Austria
Aug. 28	Italy on Germany
	Germany on Romania
Aug. 30	Turkey on Romania
Sept. 1	Bulgaria on Romania

1917
April 6	U.S. on Germany
April 7	Panama on Germany
	Cuba on Germany
April 13	Bolivia severs relations with Germany
April 23	Turkey severs relations with U.S.
June 27	Greece on Austria, Bulgaria, Germany, and Turkey
July 22	Siam on Germany and Austria
Aug. 4	Liberia on Germany
Aug. 14	China on Germany and Austria
Oct. 6	Peru severs relations with Germany
Oct. 7	Uruguay severs relations with Germany
Oct. 26	Brazil on Germany
Dec. 7	U.S. on Austria
Dec. 8	Ecuador severs relations with Germany
Dec. 10	Panama on Austria
Dec. 16	Cuba on Austria

1918
April 23	Guatemala on Germany
May 8	Nicaragua on Germany and Austria
May 23	Costa Rica on Germany
July 12	Haiti on Germany
July 19	Honduras on Germany

1. THE WESTERN FRONT, 1914–1915

(From p. 480)

GERMAN STRATEGY was based on the **Schlieffen Plan,** which provided for the concentration of the main German forces on the French front, the passage through Belgium, and a huge wheeling movement to encircle Paris. This plan required a massing of forces on the German right flank, but even before the outbreak of war the German chief of the general staff, **Gen. Helmuth von Moltke** (1906–Sept. 14, 1914), had transferred some divisions from the right to the left (Lorraine) wing in order to block an invasion of south Germany. The Germans concentrated about 1.5 million men organized in seven armies. On the eastern (Russian) frontier, German forces were relatively few in number and were intended merely to delay the invaders until a decisive victory could be won in the west.

The **French plan of campaign** (Plan 17) had been drawn up in 1913

by **Gen. Joseph Joffre** (chief of general staff, July 28, 1911–Dec. 12, 1916) under the influence and teaching of **Gen. Ferdinand Foch.** The plan ignored the danger of a great German advance through Belgium and depended entirely on a vigorous French offensive on the right wing and center. The French reckoned on a Russian advance in the east with about 800,000 men on the 18th day of mobilization. **Britain** was expected to contribute about 150,000 men.

1914, Aug. 4. In the night the **Germans crossed the frontier** of Belgium, forcing Belgian troops back to Brussels and Antwerp.

The **French offensive** (five armies) developed in the region between Mézières and Belfort, Joffre hoping for a breakthrough on either side of Metz.

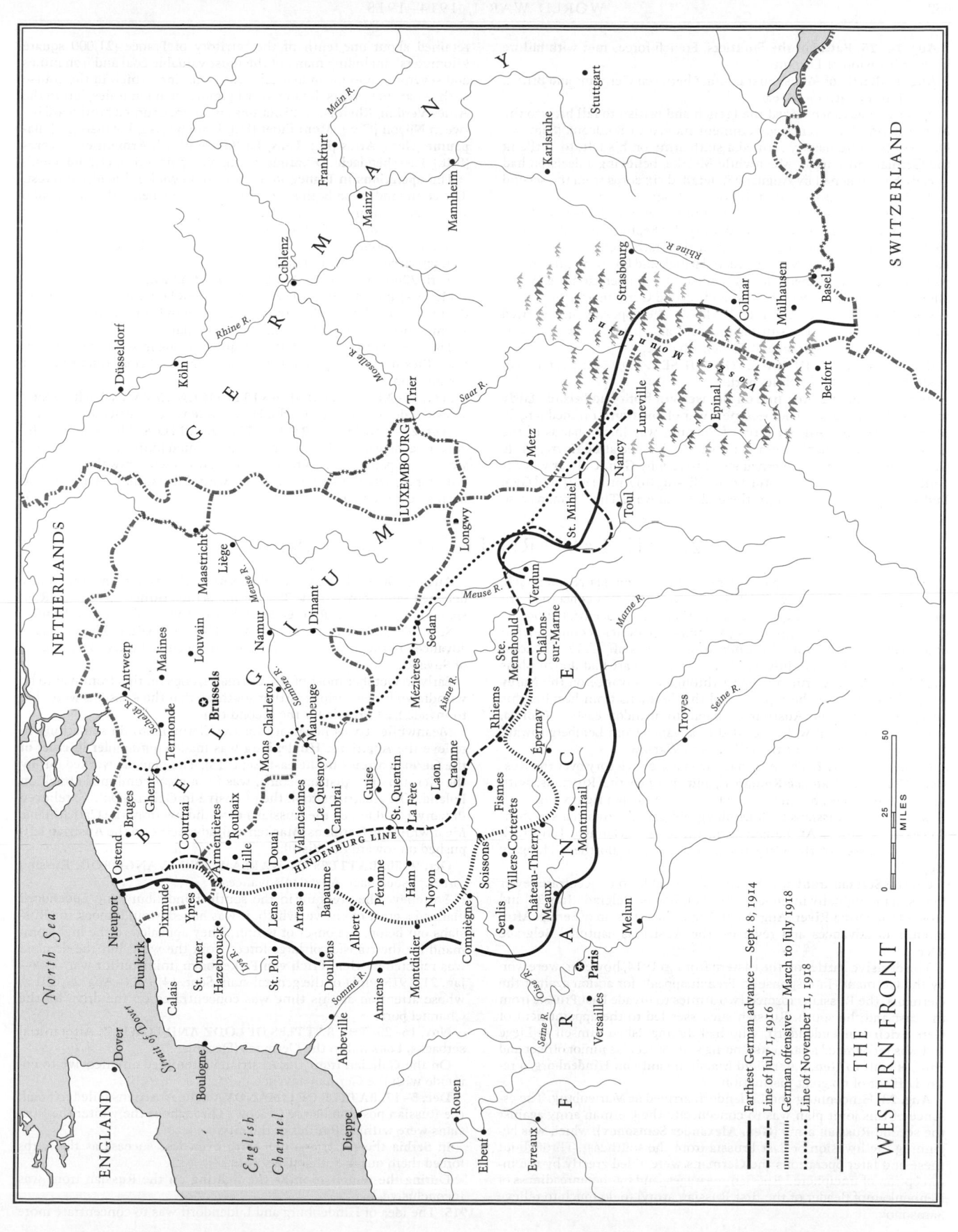

THE
WESTERN FRONT

North Sea

English Channel

ENGLAND

Dover
Boulogne
Dieppe
Elbeuf
Evreaux
Rouen

NETHERLANDS

Düsseldorf
Köln
Coblenz
Frankfurt
Mainz
Mannheim

G E R M A N Y

Stuttgart
Karlsruhe

Rhine R.
Main R.
Moselle R.
Saar R.

Trier

LUXEMBOURG

Düsseldorf

Maastricht
Liège
Namur
Dinant
Sedan
Mézières
Longwy

BELGIUM

Antwerp
Malines
Louvain
Brussels
Ghent
Bruges
Ostend
Termonde
Charleroi
Mons
Maubeuge

Scheldt R.
Sambre R.
Meuse R.
Aisne R.

Strasbourg
Colmar
Mülhausen
Basel

SWITZERLAND

Belfort
Epinal

Vosges Mountains

Luneville
Nancy
Toul
St. Mihiel
Metz
Verdun

Meuse R.

Ste. Menehould
Châlons-sur-Marne
Epernay
Rhiems
Craonne
Laon
La Fère
Guise
St. Quentin

Marne R.

Troyes

Seine R.

F R A N C E

Montmirail
Meaux
Château-Thierry
Villers-Cotterêts
Soissons
Fismes
Senlis
Compiègne
Noyon
Ham
Péronne
Bapaume
Albert
Cambrai
Le Quesnoy
Valenciennes
Douai
Lille
Roubaix
Armentières
Courtrai
Ypres
Dixmude
Nieuport

HINDENBURG LINE

Lens
Arras
Doullens
Montdidier
Amiens
Abbeville
St. Pol
Hazebrouck
St. Omer
Calais
Dunkirk

Lys R.
Somme R.
Oise R.
Seine R.

Melun
Versailles
Paris

Strait of Dover

————— Farthest German advance — Sept. 8, 1914
– – – – Line of July 1, 1916
·············· German offensive — March to July 1918
············· Line of November 11, 1918

MILES
0   25   50

Aug. 14–25. Battle of the Frontiers. French forces met with failure in their invasion of Lorraine.

Aug. 23. Battle of Mons. First contact between Germans and British resulted in the latter's retreat.

A German advance forced the French and British to fall back to the **Marne River.** The French government moved to Bordeaux (Sept. 3–Dec. 1914). Joffre hastily formed a sixth army on his left, to outflank the German fifth army. Meanwhile Moltke, believing a decision had already been reached by August 25, detailed six corps from the second and third armies to serve on the Russian front.

Aug. 30. Kluck gave up his advance to the west of Paris in order to keep contact with Bülow's second army. By September 4 Kluck realized the danger threatening him from the sixth French army before Paris. On the same day Moltke ordered Kluck and Bülow to turn southwest to meet this danger. In the course of the operation a gap was allowed to open between the first and second German armies.

Sept. 5–12. BATTLE OF THE MARNE. The opposing armies tried to outflank each other, resulting in a German withdrawal west of Verdun and a cautious British and French advance.

Oct. 10–Nov. 10. THE RACE FOR THE SEA. The Germans failed to push through to the **Channel ports.**

By the end of 1914 the line on the western front had become fairly **well fixed** and the war had become a **war of position,** confined largely to **trench warfare.** All but a tip of Belgium was in the hands of the Germans. The Belgian government was established at **Le Havre,** while the occupied area was governed successively by **Gen. Colmar von der Goltz** (to Nov. 1914), **Gen. Moritz von Bissing** (to April 1917), and **Gen. Ludwig von Falkenhausen** (to the end of the war). The Germans also retained about one-tenth of the territory of France (21,000 square kilometers), including many of the most valuable coal and iron mines and several important industrial areas. The line, which in the course of the next three years did not vary by more than ten miles, left to the Allies **Verdun, Rheims,** and **Soissons** and thence turned northward between **Noyon** (Ger.), **Montdidier** (Fr.), **Peronne** (Ger.), **Albert** (Fr.), **Bapaume** (Ger.), **Arras** (Fr.), **Lens, La Bassée** (Ger.), **Armentières, Ypres** (Brit.), **Passchendaele, Dixmude** (Ger.), **Nieuport** (Brit.), **Ostend** (Ger.).

The operations in France in 1915 were devoid of broader interest. The commanders on both sides persisted in the belief that a decision was to be won in this area, and consequently devoted as many men and guns as possible to renewed efforts to break through the opponents' line. None of these "offensives" had a notable effect. All were characterized by appalling loss of life.

April 22–May 25. SECOND BATTLE OF YPRES.

May 9–June 18. SECOND BATTLE OF ARTOIS. After an unprecedented bombardment, the French succeeded in breaking through on a six-mile front north of Arras and facing Douai.

The western front was unusually quiet during most of the summer, the Allies using this period for preparation of a "great offensive" for the autumn.

Sept. 22–Nov. 6. SECOND BATTLE OF CHAMPAGNE. After many weeks of desperate fighting the French offensive revealed little gain.

Sept. 25–Oct. 15. THIRD BATTLE OF ARTOIS. The failure of the great offensive of the French and British, which Joffre had hoped would work like a pair of pincers to force the German withdrawal from northern France, left the situation in the west substantially where it had been a year previously. *(To p. 659)*

2. THE EASTERN FRONT, 1914–1915

The Russian plan of campaign (**Grand Duke Nicholas Nicolaievich,** commander in chief, Aug. 3, 1914–Sept. 5, 1915) was concerned primarily with Austria; large forces were therefore concentrated on the Galician frontier. The Austrians (**Archduke Frederick,** commander in chief, **Gen. Conrad von Hötzendorff,** chief of staff, 1912–17, commander in chief, 1917–July 16, 1918) on their part had drawn plans that depended on German support through an advance on the **Narev River.** Pressure elsewhere prevented the Germans from keeping this engagement, but the Austrians, unable to abandon eastern **Galicia,** with its valuable oil wells, decided to advance from **Lemberg** toward **Lublin** and **Cholm** to cut the railways to Warsaw.

1914, Aug. 26–Sept. 2. The Austrians won a great victory over the Russians (**Battle of Zamosc-Komarov**), but at once the Russians, with much larger forces, began to drive back the Austrian right wing.

Sept. 13. The Russians took Lemberg, obliging the Austrians to abandon eastern Galicia. At the same time the Russians launched an attack upon the passes of the Carpathians leading into northern Hungary (Sept. 24).

On the **Serbian front** the Austrians were able to concentrate fewer forces than originally intended. They bombarded **Belgrade** (July 29) and crossed the **Drina River** (Aug. 13) to begin the invasion of Serbia. After months of advances and reverses, the Austrians captured **Belgrade** (Dec. 2).

The decisive battles on the eastern front in 1914, however, were won by the Germans. In response to French appeals for action against the Germans, the Russians formed two armies to invade **East Prussia** from the east and the south. Russian successes led to the appointment of **Gen. Erich von Ludendorff,** who had distinguished himself at Liège and was recognized as an outstanding staff officer, as junior officer and chief of staff to **Gen.** (later Field Marshal) **Paul von Hindenburg,** a retired officer of no great distinction.

Aug. 23. Hindenburg and Ludendorff arrived at Marienburg. The essence of this joint plan was to concentrate the German army against the second Russian army (**Gen. Alexander Samsonov**), which was beginning the invasion of East Prussia from the southeast. Throughout these and later operations the Germans were aided greatly by the interception of unciphered Russian messages, and by the unreadiness of Rennenkampf (leader of the first Russian army) to do much to relieve Samsonov.

Aug. 26–30. BATTLE OF TANNENBERG. The Germans completely defeated Samsonov's army. The Germans then turned on the first Russian army (**Gen. Paul Rennenkampf**), which was obliged to fall back.

Sept. 6–15. BATTLE OF THE MASURIAN LAKES. The Germans advanced to the lower Niemen River and occupied the *gouvernement* of Suvalki.

Early in October most of the German troops on this front had to be withdrawn for operations farther south, so that the Russians were able to invade **East Prussia** for the second time.

Meanwhile it was necessary for the Germans to do something to relieve the Austrians. **Hindenburg** was made **commander in chief of the German armies in the east** (Sept. 18). The plan, as worked out by the German and Austrian staffs, was for a great combined attack on Poland. The Austrians took the offensive in Galicia (Oct. 4), relieved **Przemysl,** and forced the Russians to withdraw from the Carpathians. Meanwhile the Germans (**Mackensen**), advancing on the Austrian left, pushed on toward the Vistula.

Oct. 9–20. BATTLES OF WARSAW AND IVANGOROD. Russian forces pushed back Austrian advances.

To relieve the pressure in the south, Hindenburg and Ludendorff planned a great offensive, which, it was hoped, would knock the Russians out before the onset of winter. They appealed to the high command for the transfer of large forces from the west, but the demand was rejected by **Gen. Erich von Falkenhayn** (minister for war, 1906–Jan. 21, 1915; chief of the general staff, Sept. 14, 1914–Aug. 29, 1916), whose attention at this time was concentrated on the drive for the Channel ports.

Nov. 16–25. THE BATTLES OF LODZ AND LOWICZ. After initial setbacks, **Lodz** fell to the Germans (Dec. 6).

On the **Galician front** the Austrians attempted an offensive to coincide with the German advance.

Dec. 5–17. BATTLE OF LIMANOVA. The Austrians failed to break the Russian position before Cracow. Throughout the winter the Russians were within 30 miles of the city.

In **Serbia** the Austrians met with even less success as the Serbs forced them out of Serbia (Dec. 3–6).

During the winter months the fighting on the Russian front was inconclusive.

1915. The idea of Hindenburg and Ludendorff was to concentrate more

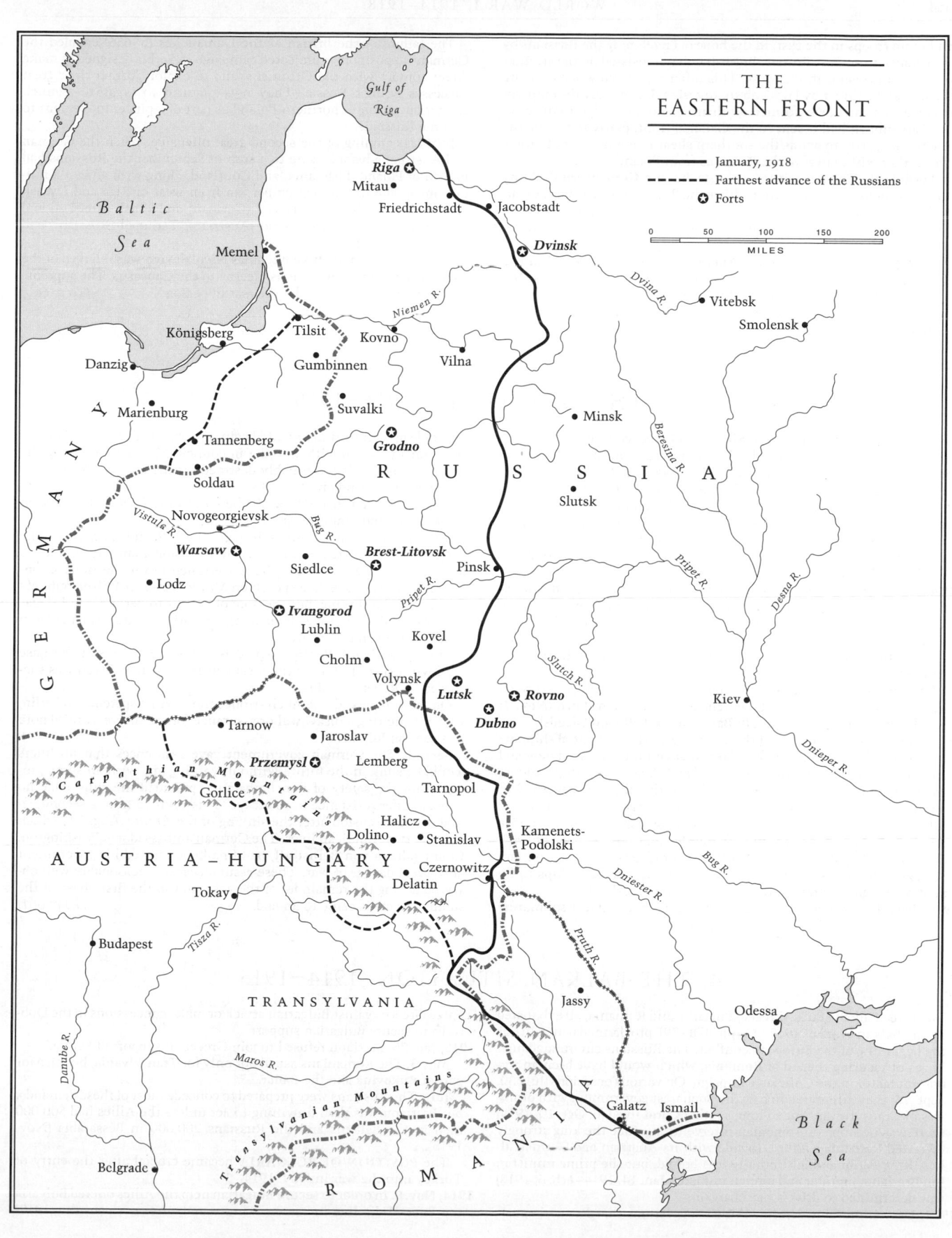

THE EASTERN FRONT

——— January, 1918
– – – Farthest advance of the Russians
✪ Forts

0   50   100   150   200
MILES

Baltic
Sea

Gulf of Riga

Riga ✪
Mitau •
Friedrichstadt • Jacobstadt •

Dvinsk ✪

Dvina R.

Vitebsk •
Smolensk •

Memel •

Niemen R.

Königsberg •
Tilsit •
Kovno •

Vilna •

Danzig •

Gumbinnen •

Minsk •

Beresina R.

Marienburg •

Suvalki •

Grodno ✪

R   U   S   S   I   A

Tannenberg •

Soldau •

Slutsk •

Vistula R.

Novogeorgievsk •

Bug R.

Warsaw ✪

Siedlce •

Brest-Litovsk ✪

Pinsk •

Pripet R.

Pripet R.

Desna R.

Lodz •

Ivangorod ✪
Lublin •

Kovel •

Slutch R.

Cholm •

Volynsk •

Lutsk ✪

Rovno ✪

Kiev •

Tarnow •

Jaroslav •

Dubno ✪

Dnieper R.

Carpathian Mountains

Przemysl ✪

Lemberg •

Gorlice •

Tarnopol •

A U S T R I A – H U N G A R Y

Halicz •
Dolino •
Stanislav •

Kamenets-
Podolski •

Bug R.

Czernowitz •

Tokay •

Delatin •

Dniester R.

Budapest •

Tisza R.

Jassy •

Odessa •

Pruth R.

T R A N S Y L V A N I A

Maros R.

Danube R.

Transylvanian Mountains

R   O   M   A   N   I   A

Galatz •
Ismail •

*Black
Sea*

Belgrade •

and more troops in the east, in the hope of enveloping the Russians by an advance from East Prussia. But Falkenhayn insisted on the attempt to reach a decision in the west. This difference of view led to acute tension and a threat by Hindenburg to resign. Ultimately the emperor decided that the newly formed tenth army should be sent to the east, but Falkenhayn had it sent to the Galician front, partly to relieve the Austrians, partly to act as the southern shear in a movement to force the further withdrawal of the Russians from Poland.

April 2–25. The **Austrians,** with the aid of a **German South Army** (Gen. Alexander von Linsingen), drove the Russians back from the Carpathians. An 11th army, under Mackensen, was then formed to cooperate with the Austrian forces from the region southeast of Cracow, in the direction of Przemysl.

May 2. Beginning of the great **Austro-German offensive in Galicia.** By the end of June the Austro-German forces had advanced almost 100 miles, had liberated **Galicia** and **Bukovina,** and had taken huge numbers of prisoners. The Russian armies on this front were completely demoralized.

The failure of the British at the Dardanelles (p. 656) enabled the Germans to postpone a projected campaign in Serbia designed to make direct contact with the Ottomans, and to exploit further their great successes against Russia. They now planned to organize a much greater operation in northern Poland as part of a pincer movement to trap the Russians.

July 1. Beginning of the **second great offensive.** When the German and Austrian advance came to a stop in September the Russians had lost all of Poland, Lithuania, and Courland, along with almost a million men. The line in September ran from west of Riga and Dvinsk almost due south to Baranovici (German) and Pinsk (Russian) and thence farther south to Dubno (Austrian), Tarnopol (Russian), and Czernowitz (Austrian).

Sept. 5. The **Grand Duke Nicholas Nicolaievich** was relieved of the supreme command and sent as viceroy to the Caucasus. The supreme command was taken over by the tsar in person. *(To p. 660)*

3. THE WAR AT SEA, 1914–1915

The **British Grand Fleet (Adm. Sir John Jellicoe,** commander, Aug. 4, 1914–Nov. 29, 1916) consisted of 20 dreadnoughts and a corresponding number of battle cruisers, cruisers, destroyers, and other craft. The fleet was based on **Scapa Flow, Cromarty,** and **Rosyth,** with Harwich as base for destroyers and submarines. A second fleet, consisting largely of pre-dreadnought types, guarded the Channel. The **Germans** had a **High Seas Fleet** of 13 dreadnoughts, based in the North Sea ports. The Germans remained in port, despite the efforts of **Adm. Alfred von Tirpitz** to bring about a more active policy.

1914. The Germans devoted their attention to mine-laying and **submarine work.** After an attempted German submarine raid on **Scapa Flow** (Oct. 18), the Grand Fleet was withdrawn from that base and concentrated, for a time, on the west coast of Scotland.

Apart from occasional sinkings, the war in the North Sea was restricted to raids.

The largest naval battles occurred between German ships in foreign stations and the Allied fleets assigned to hunt them down **(Nov. 1: naval action off Coronel; Dec. 8: Battle of the Falkland Islands).**

From the very beginning of the war the question of **neutral shipping** had arisen. Both the British and French governments issued new and more rigorous **interpretations of contraband** (Aug. 20, 25, 1914), adding greatly to the list of contraband goods. To this the U.S. government replied (Oct. 22) that it would insist on the observance of the existing rules of international law. Nevertheless the British continued to revise the list of contraband and to modify the Declaration of London of 1909. On Nov. 2 they declared the North Sea a military zone, and on Jan. 30, 1915, the British admiralty ordered British merchant ships to fly neutral ensigns or none in the vicinity of the British Isles.

1915, Feb. 4. The German government announced that a submarine

blockade of Great Britain would begin on Feb. 18. To this the London government replied with an order in council (March 11) ordering the seizure of all goods presumably destined for the enemy. Cotton was declared contraband on March 18.

May 7. *LUSITANIA* SUNK off the coast of Ireland, with a loss of 1,198 lives, including 139 Americans.

The sinking of the *Lusitania* brought the U.S. and Germany to the verge of war and created much greater tension than had developed between the Americans and Allied governments over questions of contraband and blockade. In a speech on May 9 **President Wilson** publicly denounced the sinking, but the note of protest to Berlin (May 13) was somewhat milder in tone, demanding reparations and abstinence from such practices in the future.

June 8. William J. Bryan resigned as U.S. secretary of state because of unwillingness to follow the president in his policy. Bryan was succeeded by **Robert Lansing.**

On the very next day a much stronger note was dispatched to Berlin, without eliciting a disavowal or assurance for the future. A third note was sent on July 21.

Sept. 1. The German government gave assurances that no liners would be sunk in the future without warning and without some provision for the safety of noncombatants, provided the ship made no effort to offer resistance or to escape. This resulted from a second period of acute tension after the sinking of the *Arabic* (Aug. 19), which claimed two American lives. The German ambassador at Washington, **Count Johann von Bernstorff,** had finally convinced his government of the real danger of war. These assurances were reasonably well observed during the remainder of the year, and so the first phase of the submarine crisis came to an end. *(To p. 661)*

4. THE BALKAN SITUATION, 1914–1915

The three Balkan states, Greece, Bulgaria, and Romania, all exhausted by the Balkan Wars of 1912–13 (pp. 478–79), proclaimed neutrality at the beginning of the European conflict. The Russians entertained high hopes of securing the aid of **Romania,** which would have been an important factor in the Galician campaign. On various occasions (July 30, Sept. 16) they attempted to bait the Bucharest government with promises of Transylvania, but so long as **King Carol** lived (d. Oct. 10, 1914) there was no hope of Romanian intervention, since the king strongly regretted Romania's failure to side with its Austrian and German allies. **King Ferdinand** felt morally less bound, but the prime minister, **Ion Bratianu** (premier and foreign minister, Jan. 14, 1914–Feb. 6, 1918) was determined to drive a hard bargain.

1914, Dec. 6. Bratianu rejected Allied suggestions that Romania guarantee Greece against Bulgarian attack or make concessions in the Dobrudja to secure Bulgarian support.

1915, Jan. 25. Bratianu refused to join Greece in support of Serbia.

May 3. The Romanians asked not only for **Transylvania,** but also for part of **Bukovina** and the **Banat.**

July. The Russians were prepared to concede most of these demands, but Bratianu was then unwilling to act unless the Allies had 500,000 men in the Balkans and the Russians 200,000 in Bessarabia (Nov. 1915).

The **POSITION OF BULGARIA** became crucial after the entry of Turkey into the war in Nov. 1914.

1914, Nov. 9. In order to secure Bulgarian help the Allies offered Bulgaria the **Enos-Midia line** in eastern Thrace and, after the war, the (1912)

uncontested zone of Macedonia, this territory being in the possession of Serbia.

It was clear almost from the outset, however, that such an offer would not prove attractive, since the Bulgarians aspired not only to part of **Thrace,** but also to most of **Macedonia,** the **Kavalla-Drama-Seres** region of western Thrace, and that part of **Dobrudja** lost to Romania in 1913.

1915, Jan. As the Dardanelles campaign was being decided on, the Allies offered to **Greece** the Turkish city of **Smyrna** and its hinterland, on condition that the Greeks cede the **Kavalla** region to Bulgaria and join a Balkan bloc in support of Serbia. **Venizelos** favored this policy strongly, but **King Constantine** preferred the sparrow in the hand to the pigeon on the roof (Jan. 24, 29).

March 6. Venizelos fell from power when the king refused to adopt his policy of aiding the Allies at the Dardanelles (p. 656). His successor, **Demetrios Gounaris** March 9–Aug. 22), was less favorable toward the Entente.

April 12. Gounaris rejected a second offer of the Smyrna region, on the plea that the Allies would not guarantee Greek territory (i.e., against Bulgaria).

May 7. The **Allies,** more eager than ever to secure the aid of Bulgaria in view of their failure at the Dardanelles, gave **Serbia** a conditional guarantee of the eventual acquisition of Bosnia and Herzegovina and "a wide access to the Adriatic," as compensation for the part of Macedonia required to bring in Bulgaria.

May 29. A definite offer along these lines was made to **Bulgaria.** The Sofia government treated these advances dilatorily, and was already leaning to the Central Powers, which were prepared to promise whatever Bulgaria wanted, in view of the fact that Bulgarian aspirations were directed chiefly to Serbian and Greek territory.

July 22. The **Germans** persuaded the **Turks** to cede to Bulgaria a strip of territory along the **Maritza River** (definitive agreement Sept. 22). On Aug. 8 the Bulgarian government secured from Germany and Austria a loan of 400 million francs.

Sept. 6. Bulgaria concluded an alliance and military convention with Germany and Austria, providing for mutual aid against attack by a neighboring state, for a German-Austrian campaign against Serbia within 30 days, and for Bulgarian participation five days later. Bulgaria was to receive **Macedonia,** and, if Romania joined in the war, **Dobrudja** also; if Greece proved hostile, Bulgaria was to receive the **Kavalla** region as well.

Sept. 21. The **Bulgarians began to mobilize.** The Serbs, being directly threatened, appealed to Greece for aid under the terms of the treaty of

May 1913. **Venizelos,** who had returned to power on Aug. 22, was as eager as ever to intervene, but made it a condition that the Allies furnish the 150,000 troops that Serbia was required to supply under the treaty terms.

Sept. 24. The British and French governments gave a promise to this effect. Venizelos then secured the secret consent of the king to the landing of the Allied forces at **Saloniki,** but publicly the request of the Allies to land was rejected (Sept. 28).

Oct. 3–5. One **British** and one **French** division were **landed at Saloniki,** followed by two more French divisions at the end of the month. King Constantine now refused to support Venizelos to the extent of joining in the war; the prime minister resigned (Oct. 5, 1915) and was succeeded by **Alexander Zaimis** (Oct. 6–Nov. 5, 1915).

Oct. 6. Beginning of the **great Austro-German campaign in Serbia (Gen. von Mackensen).** Belgrade fell (Oct. 9), and then **Semendria** (Oct. 11).

Oct. 14. Bulgaria and Serbia declared war on each other. Britain and France declared war on Bulgaria (Oct. 15, 16), and so did Russia and Italy (Oct. 19). The Allies made great efforts to induce Greece to join, the British offering them the island of **Cyprus** (Oct. 16), but this offer too was rejected (Oct. 20).

Oct. 22. The Bulgarians began a string of victories, forcing the British and French to remain on Greek territory. The British were, by December, prepared to give up the whole Saloniki adventure, but the French, under **Gen. Maurice Sarrail,** insisted on staying. The result was that ever greater forces were tied up at Saloniki.

Nov. 5. Zaimis resigned and was succeeded by **Stephanos Skouloudis** (Nov. 6, 1915–June 21, 1916). The Greek government then declared its benevolent neutrality (Nov. 8) and agreed not to interfere with the Allied forces at Saloniki, in return for the guarantee of the eventual restoration of Greek territory (Nov. 24).

Dec. 2. The **Austrians** took **Plevlje** and the **Ipek** (Dec. 6). **Mt. Lovchen,** guarding Montenegro, was stormed (Jan. 10, 1916) and **Cettinje** taken (Jan. 13). **King Nicholas** laid down his arms and retired to Italy.

1916, Jan. 11. The **French occupied Corfu** as a refuge for the Serbian troops. The Greek government refused its consent, but the Serbs were landed nevertheless (Jan. 15).

Feb. 24. The **Albanian provisional government,** under Italian protection at Durazzo, left for Naples. Mountain warfare between the Austrians and the Italians in Albania continued until the end of the war.

(To p. 660)

5. THE INTERVENTION OF ITALY, 1915

On the plea that the Austrian action against Serbia was an offensive action and therefore incompatible with the terms of the **Triple Alliance,** the Italian government in July 1914 refused to join the Central powers and declared neutrality (Aug. 3). But almost from the outset the Italian government maintained that under Art. VII of the Triple Alliance, Italy was entitled to some compensation to counterbalance the Austrian gains in the Balkans. These claims were advanced the more persistently when the foreign ministry was given to **Baron Sidney Sonnino** (Nov. 3), following the sudden demise of **Marquis Antonio di San Giuliano** (Oct. 16).

The necessity of making some concession to Italy in order to keep it neutral was fully recognized in Berlin, but the Austrian foreign minister **(Baron Leopold von Berchtold)** refused to entertain suggestions of territorial cessions.

1914, Dec. 20. Prince Bernhard von Bülow, former German chancellor, arrived in Rome on a special mission. He admitted the Italian claim to the Trentino, and the German government made every effort to persuade the Austrians to give in (mission of Count Betho von Wedel to Vienna, Jan. 16, 1915).

1915, Jan. 13. Count Stephen Burian appointed Austro-Hungarian foreign minister to replace Berchtold. Burian finally agreed to the cession of territory (March 9) but was willing to cede the **Trentino** only after the conclusion of peace. This was not enough to satisfy the Italians, who were already negotiating with the Entente powers. Sonnino de-

manded of Austria the immediate cession of the **South Tyrol,** the district of **Gorizia** and **Gradisca,** the establishment of **Trieste** and its neighborhood as a free state, the cession to Italy of the **Curzolari Islands** off the Dalmatian coast, and full sovereignty over the island of **Saseno** and over **Valona** on the Albanian coast (Italian occupation of Saseno, Oct. 30, 1914; "provisional" occupation of Valona, Dec. 26, 1914). These demands were exorbitant, from the Austrian point of view, but the Germans finally (May 10) induced their allies to agree to substantially all the Italians were holding out for. As it turned out, the Austrians yielded too late.

April 26. Britain, France, Russia, and Italy concluded the **secret Treaty of London. Antonio Salandra,** the Italian prime minister, had envisaged Italian intervention on the Entente side almost since the beginning of war, but the noninterventionists, led by **Giovanni Giolitti,** were too strong to make that at first a practicable policy. During the winter, however, the interventionist movement gathered strength (**Mussolini** broke with the Socialist Party and became an active proponent of intervention). The western powers, meeting with failure on the western front, were ready to offer much. Negotiations were embarked upon in Feb. 1915 but were delayed by the opposition of the Russian foreign minister, Sazonov, to the assignment of the Dalmatian coast to Italy, in view of Serbian aspirations in that region. Under the terms of the treaty as finally concluded, a military convention was to be drawn up to protect Italy against the full force of Austrian attack.

The political clauses promised Italy the **South Tyrol** and **Trentino, Gorizia, Gradisca, Trieste, Istria,** the most important **Dalmatian Islands** and the southern part of the province of **Dalmatia, Saseno** and **Valona,** and full sovereignty over the **Dodecanese Islands** (occupied since 1912). Moreover, in the event of the partition of Turkey, Italy was to have the province of **Adalia;** and in the event of Britain and France enlarging their empires by the addition of German colonies, Italy was to receive extensions of its territory in **Libya, Eritrea,** and **Somaliland.** Italy was further to receive a loan, and ultimately part of the war indemnity. The Entente powers were to support Italy in preventing the Holy See from taking diplomatic steps for the conclusion of peace. Italy was to commence hostilities within a month of the signature of the treaty.

May 3. The Italian government denounced the Triple Alliance.

May 10. Conclusion of a **naval convention** among Britain, France, and Italy.

May 23. Italy mobilized and declared war on Austro-Hungary. Germany at once severed diplomatic relations (May 24), but for various financial reasons Italy did not declare war on Germany until Aug. 28, 1916.

1915. FIRST FOUR BATTLES OF THE ISONZO. The first two years of Italy's participation in the war were taken up with the fighting of 11 successive battles on the Isonzo, along a front of only about 60 miles. The Italians never advanced more than 10 or 12 miles.

(To p. 660)

6. THE MIDDLE EAST, 1914–1918

1914, Aug. 2. Conclusion of a **secret Ottoman-German alliance** by top-ranking officials, including prime minister **Said Halim** and minister of war **Enver Pasha.** A majority within the Ottoman cabinet, however, favored neutrality and delayed the empire's entry into the war.

Aug. 10–11. Arrival of the **German warships** *Goeben* and *Breslau* at the Dardanelles after a long chase through the Mediterranean by the British navy. The Ottoman government allowed the ships into Istanbul and later purchased them.

Oct. 29–30. BOMBARDMENT OF RUSSIAN PORTS in the Black Sea by **Ottoman warships.** The **OTTOMANS** thereby **ENTERED THE WAR** on the side of the **Central powers.**

Nov. 1. Declaration of neutrality by the Iranian government.

Nov. 2. RUSSIA DECLARED WAR ON THE OTTOMAN EMPIRE. Great Britain and France followed on Nov. 5. The **British immediately annexed Cyprus.**

Nov. 7. Proclamation of a jihad (holy war) against the Entente by the Ottoman sultan in his capacity as caliph. The announcement had no material effect on the course of the war.

Nov. 22. British **occupation of Basra** in Iraq.

Dec. 17. Beginning of the **Ottoman offensive in the Caucasus** against the Russians.

Dec. 18. Imposition of a British protectorate over Egypt, which was officially detached from the Ottoman Empire. The British also **deposed the khedive, Abbas Hilmi II,** and replaced him with his uncle, **Husayn Kamil,** who assumed the title of sultan.

1915, Jan. Defeat of the Ottomans in the Caucasus at the **Battle of Sarikamish.** The victorious Russian forces advanced and took the fortress of Erzurum on Feb. 15.

Feb. 3–4. Failed Ottoman attack on the Suez Canal.

March 4–April 10. The Constantinople Agreement. Britain and France formally promised that in the event of a complete Entente victory, Russia would receive Istanbul and the Straits.

April. Armenian revolt in Van. Russian forces reached the city in May.

April 25. Opening of the **BATTLE OF GALLIPOLI,** which the Entente eventually lost. The **British and French landed troops in the Straits** with the goal of capturing Istanbul. After suffering heavy losses from fierce Ottoman resistance, they were **forced to withdraw** (Dec. 1915–Jan. 1916).

April 26. The Treaty of London. The British recognized Italian claims to the Dodecanese Islands and the province of Adalya in Anatolia.

July–March 1916. THE HUSAYN-McMAHON CORRESPONDENCE. Husayn, sharif of Mecca, offered to **revolt against the Ottomans** if, after the war, the British would recognize him as the ruler of all Arab lands in the Fertile Crescent and Arabia. **Sir Henry McMahon, British high commissioner in Egypt,** welcomed Husayn's overtures, but with several reservations. Within the future Arab state, **he demanded "special administrative arrangements" for the regions of Baghdad and Basra** to protect British interests in the Persian Gulf. McMahon further **excluded Alexandretta and Mersin and the lands west of the "districts of Damascus, Hama, Homs, and Aleppo"** from the proposed state. Within Arabia, all existing political arrangements would be preserved. Finally, McMahon warned Husayn that Britain would not commit itself to any actions that compromised French interests. The British treated all their promises as mere declarations of intent, but Husayn—and later many Arab nationalists—viewed them as binding agreements.

July. Russian occupation of Erzinjan, which marked the farthest penetration of Russian arms into Ottoman territory.

Aug. Ottoman recapture of Van.

Aug. 21. Italy declared war on the Ottoman Empire.

Sept. 22. Ottoman territorial concession to Bulgaria. Under pressure from Germany, the Ottomans ceded all claims to Thrace west of the Maritsa River so that the Bulgarians could have a direct outlet to the Aegean Sea. This concession was Bulgaria's price for entering the war (Oct. 1915) on the side of the Central powers.

Nov. Movement of Russian forces toward Tehran in response to German-Iranian talks.

Nov. Raids from Libya into Egypt by Sanusiyya tribes, penetrating as far as Marsa Matruh. The tribes were receiving advice and supplies from the Ottoman military. British counterattacks drove them back to Libyan territory by March 1916.

Nov. 22–24. Defeat of the British army in Iraq at the **Battle of Ctesiphon.** British forces **retreated to Kut** and eventually **surrendered to the Ottomans** on Apr. 29, 1916. The Ottomans then sent troops into Iran during the summer of 1916.

1916. Organization of the **South Persia Rifles** by Sir Percy Sykes. The unit operated under British command and purely in the service of British interests.

Jan. 7. Creation of the **Arab Bureau** in Cairo. Originally conceived as a center for the development of war policy, the agency quickly became the heart of the British intelligence network in the Middle East.

April 26–Oct. 23. THE SYKES-PICOT AGREEMENT. Secret negotiations between Britain and France prepared for the partition of the postwar Middle East. **France received Cilicia, Lebanon, coastal Syria, and a sphere of influence** stretching from the east of these territories to Mosul. **Britain secured the areas around Baghdad and Basra, the ports of Haifa and Acre,** and a **sphere of influence** between Palestine and Iraq. **Palestine** itself, however, was to be placed under an **international administration.** The agreement assigned the **remaining lands,** as well as the territory within the European spheres of influence, **to one or several Arab states.** Arab nationalists later charged that, after the promises of an independent state contained within the Husayn-McMahon correspondence, the British betrayed them in these negotiations. The Arabs were particularly sensitive over the **question of Palestine.** Since Palestine did not lie to the west of the "districts of Damascus, Hama, Homs, and Aleppo," they believed that it ought to have been included in an Arab state as the Husayn-McMahon correspondence provided.

May 22. Departure of the **Niedermeyer mission** from Kabul. Niedermeyer, a German agent, sought Afghan support for the Central powers in World War I. Despite German overtures, Amir Habibullah maintained **Afghanistan's neutrality** for the duration of the war.

June 5. THE ARAB REVOLT. The sharif of Mecca, **Husayn, proclaimed independence and attacked Ottoman garrisons in the Hijaz.** Jedda surrendered on June 16, and Mecca on July 4. Medina, however, held out for the duration of the war.

Aug. Failure of the second Ottoman attack on the Suez Canal.

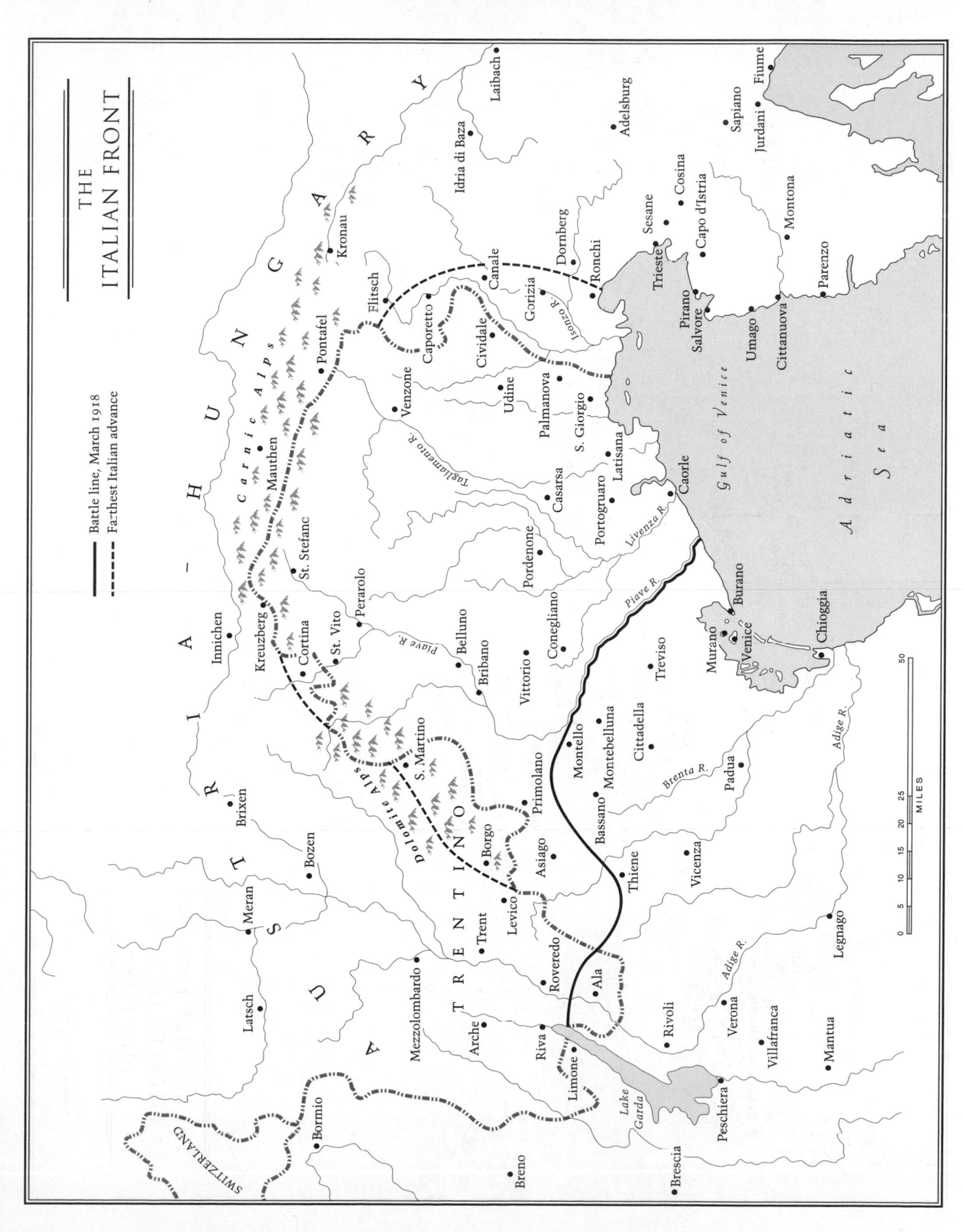

THE
ITALIAN FRONT

Battle line, March 1918
Farthest Italian advance

MILES
0   5   10 15 20 25   50

A U S T R I A — H U N G A R Y

SWITZERLAND

Carnic Alps

Dolomite Alps

TRENTINO

ISTRIA

Tagliamento R.

Piave R.

Isonzo R.

Livenza R.

Brenta R.

Adige R.

Lake Garda

Gulf of Venice

Adriatic Sea

Laibach
Adelsburg
Sapiano
Fiume
Jurdani
Idria di Baza
Cosina
Montona
Sesane
Capo d'Istria
Parenzo
Dornberg
Trieste
Ronchi
Kronau
Flitsch
Canale
Gorizia
Pirano
Salvore
Umago
Cittanuova
Pontafel
Caporetto
Cividale
Venzone
Udine
Palmanova
S. Giorgio
Latisana
Caorle
St. Stefanc
Casarsa
Portogruaro
Innichen
Kreuzberg
Cortina
St. Vito
Perarolo
Belluno
Bribano
Vittorio
Conegliano
Pordenone
Burano
Chioggia
Murano
Venice
Treviso
Brixen
S. Martino
Montello
Montebelluna
Cittadella
Bozen
Primolano
Bassano
Padua
Borgo
Asiago
Thiene
Vicenza
Latsch
Levico
Meran
Trent
Roveredo
Ala
Rivoli
Verona
Villafranca
Legnago
Mantua
Mezzolombardo
Arche
Riva
Limone
Peschiera
Bormio
Breno
Brescia
Mauthen

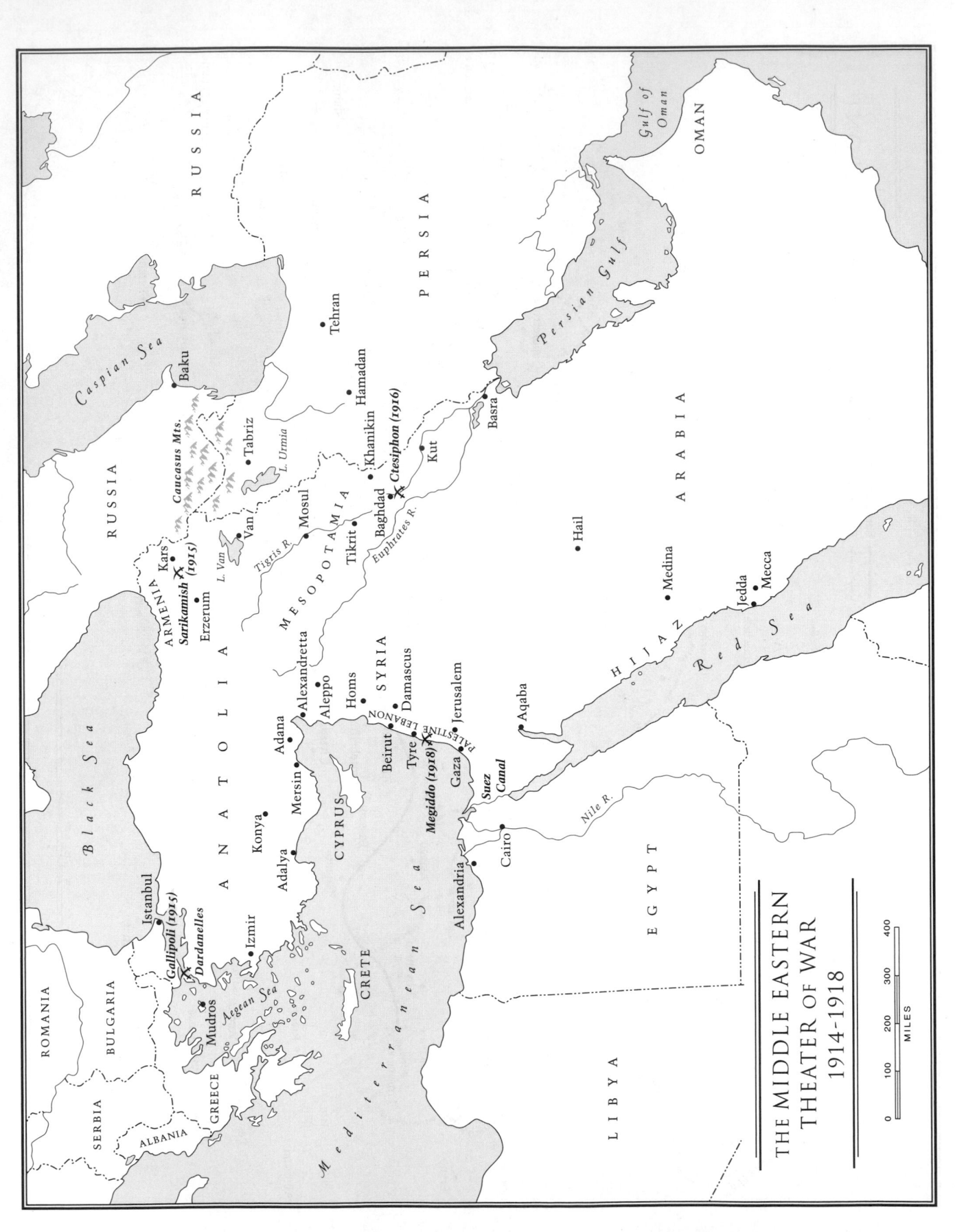

RUSSIA

Gulf of Oman

OMAN

Caspian Sea

PERSIA

Baku

Tehran

RUSSIA

Caucasus Mts.

Tabriz

Hamadan

Khanikin

Persian Gulf

L. Urmia

Basra

ARABIA

Kars

Sarikamish (1915)

Erzerum

Van

L. Van

Mosul

Tigris R.

Tikrit

Baghdad

Ctesiphon (1916)

Euphrates R.

Kut

Hail

ARMENIA

MESOPOTAMIA

Medina

Jedda

Mecca

ANATOLIA

Alexandretta

Aleppo

Homs

SYRIA

Damascus

HIJAZ

Red Sea

Black Sea

Adana

Mersin

CYPRUS

Beirut

Tyre

LEBANON

PALESTINE

Jerusalem

Gaza

Megiddo (1918)

Suez Canal

Aqaba

Konya

Adalya

Cairo

Alexandria

EGYPT

Nile R.

Istanbul

Gallipoli (1915)

Dardanelles

Izmir

CRETE

Mediterranean Sea

Aegean Sea

Mudros

ROMANIA

BULGARIA

SERBIA

GREECE

ALBANIA

LIBYA

THE MIDDLE EASTERN
THEATER OF WAR
1914–1918

0   100   200   300   400

MILES

Dec. Advance of the British army into the **Sinai Peninsula** to establish a forward defensive position. By early January, it had reached Rafah.

Dec. Formal British recognition of Husayn as king of the Hijaz.

1917, March 11. The British capture of Baghdad. British forces would move another 80 miles north to Samarra by late April. Meanwhile, the Ottoman army in Iran had to fall back.

April. The British capture of **Gaza.**

April 19–Sept. 26. St. Jean de Maurienne Agreement. In return for recognizing the Sykes-Picot Agreement, **Italy was to receive** the Anatolian territories of **Izmir, Adalya, and Konya** in the postwar settlement.

April 20. The Ottoman Empire severed diplomatic relations with the U.S.

June 16. British Declaration to the Seven, issued to a delegation of seven Syrians resident in Cairo on the future of the Arab Near East. The British promised to uphold the principle of self-determination in all Arab lands located within the Ottoman Empire which British troops were occupying.

June 29. Sir Edmund Allenby replaced Sir Archibald Murray as **commander of British forces** in the Middle East.

July 6. Capture of Aqaba by an Arab force, assisted by **Col. Thomas E. Lawrence (Lawrence of Arabia).** Operations began against the now vulnerable Hijaz railway. The Ottomans withdrew all forces from Arabia except their garrison at Medina.

Nov. Russian withdrawal from Iran after the Bolshevik seizure of power. In December, the **Russians renounced all claims to Ottoman** territory. Through the **Treaty of Brest-Litovsk** (March 3, 1918), the **Ottomans regained** the districts of **Kars and Ardahan** (which Russia had annexed in 1878), and Russia renounced its capitulatory privileges.

Dec. 9. British occupation of Jerusalem.

1918, April. Creation of the **Federated Transcaucasus Republic** (including Georgia, Armenia, and Azerbaijan) for joint defense against the Ottomans. The **federation collapsed** in May as a result of internal differences and an **Ottoman offensive** in the Caucasus. Throughout the summer of 1918, the Ottoman army made extensive gains in Azerbaijan.

Sept. The **Battle of Megiddo,** which opened Britain's great offensive in Palestine. The Ottoman lines broke, and the British advance into Syria, supported on its right flank by the **Arab army,** quickly gained pace.

Sept. 14. Ottoman occupation of **Baku.**

Oct. 1. Occupation of Damascus by Arab troops under the leadership of Husayn's son, Faysal (the British arrived two days later). **Homs** fell on Oct. 15 and **Aleppo** on Oct. 26.

Oct. 30. THE ARMISTICE OF MUDROS. By the terms of this ceasefire, the **Ottomans demobilized their armies, severed relations with the Central powers, and opened their territory, especially the Straits,** to the Entente powers for military operations.

Nov. Deployment of British troops in northeastern Iran to block possible Russian encroachment. Meanwhile, a British flotilla drove the Ottomans out of Baku.

Nov. 7. British occupation of Mosul.

Nov. 13. Arrival of the British fleet at Istanbul. (To p. 752)

7. THE WESTERN FRONT, 1916–1917

(From p. 652)

Both **Joffre** and **Falkenhayn** were still convinced, at the end of 1915, that a military decision could be reached only on the French front. Joffre planned for a great Anglo-French offensive to begin in the summer, to be supported by simultaneous Russian and Italian offensives. **Sir Douglas Haig** (who succeeded Sir John French as commander in chief of the British forces, Dec. 19, 1915) would have preferred to arrange for an offensive in Flanders, but Joffre insisted on operations in the Somme area, where the British and French could collaborate more easily.

Meanwhile Falkenhayn, having disposed of the threat from the east, was able to bring almost half a million men to the western front. The plan was not so much for a breakthrough as for mere attrition. The French were to be bled white at Verdun, a salient with poor communications and hard to hold and yet a place that, for sentimental reasons if for no other, would have to be fought for to the end. The French, having lost faith in forts, had taken away most of the guns about Verdun, and Joffre, intent on preparations for the Somme offensive, ignored the warnings of danger in that area.

1916, Feb. 21. THE BATTLE OF VERDUN. The immediate effect of the assault on Verdun was felt in the preparation for the Somme offensive. The French were obliged to reduce their contribution from 40 divisions to 16 and their front attack from 25 miles to 10, so that the operation was in the main a British one.

July 1–Nov. 18. THE BATTLE OF THE SOMME. The Allies conquered about 125 square miles of territory but nothing of prime strategic importance. The maximum advance was about seven miles. British losses were over 400,000, and French almost 200,000. The German losses were between 400,000 and 500,000.

The British first used **tanks** (Sept. 15). These had been suggested long before, but the military authorities had been hostile to the idea, and even when they were finally used there were far too few (only 18 on the field) to gain the fullest advantage.

Oct. 24–Dec. 18. The **French counterattacked at Verdun,** making a total advance of about two miles.

The operations of 1917 were prefaced by important changes in the German and French high commands. On Aug. 29, 1916, **Hindenburg succeeded Falkenhayn** as chief of staff of the German field armies, with **Ludendorff** as quartermaster-general. Despite their constant advocacy of a concentration of forces on the eastern front, both Hindenburg and Ludendorff now came to share the opinion of Falkenhayn that a decision could be reached only on the French front.

On Dec. 12 **Nivelle succeeded Joffre** as commander in chief of the French armies. Nivelle had distinguished himself in the fighting at Verdun. His energy and dash made a profound impression, and it was hoped that his appointment would lead to a more fruitful campaign.

Nivelle, like his predecessor, hoped to effect a breakthrough and planned a great French offensive in the direction of Laon, to be introduced by a preliminary Franco-British advance on both sides of the Somme. The execution of this plan was delayed by **disagreement between Nivelle and Haig,** who himself would have preferred an offensive in Flanders and resented being put more or less under Nivelle.

In the interval **Ludendorff** had decided that the western front could be made stronger and more defensible if some of the bulges were eliminated. A strong new position was therefore constructed, which became known as the **Hindenburg Line.** After completely destroying the area between, and after mining the roads, the Germans withdrew.

1917, Feb. 23–April 5. The Germans abandoned **Bapaume, Péronne, Roye, Noyon,** and **Chauny.**

Though this move on the part of the Germans dislocated the French plans, Nivelle was still optimistic. The new **cabinet of Alexandre Ribot** (succeeded Briand, March 20) and Paul Painlevé (minister of war) brought pressure upon him to give up the plan but yielded when Nivelle threatened to resign.

April 9–May 4. BATTLE OF ARRAS. Despite some advances, a breakthrough eluded Allied forces.

April 16–20. SECOND BATTLE OF THE AISNE and THIRD BATTLE OF CHAMPAGNE. Heavy losses for the French with only minor territorial gain spread discontent. Mutiny became widespread, affecting 16 corps (May–June).

May 16. Nivelle was dismissed and replaced by **Pétain,** who did what he could to redress the grievances of the troops and wisely decided to stand on the defensive until American reinforcements could make themselves felt. At the same time the government proceeded with the greatest rigor against socialist and pacifist agitators. Twenty-three leaders were executed.

The collapse of the Nivelle offensive gave **Haig** greater freedom to act. In view of the great destructiveness of the submarines, based on the Belgian coast, Haig was more determined than ever to start an **offensive in Flanders** and to roll up the German right flank. The French command was not enthusiastic about the plan, and pointed out that it could cooperate only to the extent of launching lesser attacks on the Verdun and Champagne fronts.

July 31–Nov. 10. THIRD BATTLE OF YPRES (Passchendaele). Despite the opposition of Lloyd George and the skepticism of some of his subordinates, Haig proceeded hopefully to the main offensive. No breakthrough was effected, costing the British about 400,000 men. The British forces were almost as demoralized by this operation as the French were by the Nivelle offensive.   *(To p. 664)*

8. THE EASTERN FRONT, 1916–1917

(From p. 654)

1916, June 4. The great **BRUSILOV OFFENSIVE,** initiated somewhat prematurely in order to meet the Italian appeals to distract the Austrians in the Trentino. Brusilov (appointed to the command of the Russian southern front, April 4) had planned the offensive for June 15, to coincide with Joffre's great offensive on the Somme. But the Brusilov offensive was meant to be followed by an even larger operation farther north. After heavy fighting and initial gains, the Russians failed to reach either Kovel or Lemberg. Their losses were about a million men, and the whole operation left the army demoralized and discontented.

The situation in the east was dominated, in 1917, by the developments of the **Russian Revolution** (p. 711). The provisional government (**Paul Miliukov,** foreign minister, March 15–May 16, 1917) was strongly in favor of prosecution of the war in the hope of realizing the national aspirations. The same was true of **Alexander Kerensky** (minister of war, May 16, prime minister, July 20), who hoped to combat disruptive tendencies and galvanize the country by a new military effort.

1917, July 1. Brusilov began a **great offensive on the Galician front.**

Aug. 1. Brusilov was succeeded by Gen. Lavr Kornilov.

Sept. 8–14. Kornilov marched on Petrograd as leader of a counter-revolutionary movement, which failed.

Nov. 7 (Oct. 25 Old Style). BOLSHEVIK COUP D'ÉTAT IN RUSSIA.

Nov. 28. The new Bolshevik regime offered the Germans an armistice and peace.

Dec. 15. ARMISTICE CONCLUDED ON THE EASTERN FRONT.

(To p. 663)

9. THE ITALIAN FRONT, 1916

(From p. 656)

The Austrian chief of staff, **Conrad von Hötzendorff,** had for some time been urging upon the German high command the desirability of massing troops in the Trentino for an attack upon the Italian rear and flank, but **Falkenhayn** had flatly refused to contribute forces that he needed for the operations at Verdun. The Austrians decided to make the try alone. As many troops as possible were withdrawn from the Russian front and prepared for an advance on the Asiago plateau.

1916, May 15–June 3. The Austrian offensive in the Trentino. After initial setbacks, the Italians recovered lost territory, but at a cost of 150,000 men.

During the first part of 1917 the Italian effort continued to center on the Isonzo (tenth battle [May 12–June 8] and eleventh, and last, battle [Aug. 17–Sept. 12]). As result of two years of operations the Italians had advanced only about ten miles, or halfway to Trieste.

In part the Italian failure was due to inadequate artillery and ammunition. **Gen. Luigi Cadorna** had urged Britain and France to send supplies and men in large numbers, so that a knockout blow might be delivered against war-weary Austria. Foch and Lloyd George favored this plan, but Haig had his way and proceeded to the offensive in Flanders.

Meanwhile **Ludendorff** decided to follow the annihilation of Serbia and Romania with a similar assault on Italy. Six divisions of German troops were sent to reinforce the nine Austrian divisions on the Isonzo front. It was decided to attack on the Upper Isonzo, near Caporetto, in the hope of breaking through and advancing as far as the Tagliamento River.

Oct. 24–Dec. 26. THE CAPORETTO CAMPAIGN. After a complete rout of the Italians on the first day, Italian forces, bolstered by British and French troops, held firm at the Piave River. The Italians had lost almost 300,000 men taken prisoner and even more than that in deserters.

Nov. 7. Cadorna was replaced by Gen. Armando Diaz, who devoted himself to establishing a defensive position and above all to restoring the morale of the troops.

10. THE BALKAN FRONT, 1916–1917

(From p. 655)

a. GREECE

Throughout the summer and autumn of 1916 the **Greek situation** continued to be most unsatisfactory from the Entente viewpoint.

1916, May 26. A **Bulgarian-German** force occupied **Fort Rupel** in Greek Macedonia, this action enhancing the suspicion that King Constantine was secretly bound to the Central powers.

June 6–22. The **"pacific blockade" of Greece** by the Entente powers. France and Britain sent Greece an ultimatum (June 21) demanding demobilization of the Greek army and the institution of responsible government. The Greek government yielded. The **Skouloudis ministry resigned** and a Zaimis cabinet was organized. The army was put on a peace footing (June 27) and new elections were arranged for.

July 25. The reconstituted Serbian army, which had been shipped from Corfu to Saloniki, came into action on that front. Russian troops from France and an Italian contingent also arrived (July 30, Aug. 11).

Aug. 30. A Venizelist, pro-Ally movement, fostered by Gen. Sarrail, took place at Saloniki.

Sept. 29. Venizelos and Adm. Paul Condouriotis **established a provisional government** in Crete. Venizelos then (Oct. 9) went to Saloniki, where the **provisional government declared war on Germany and Bulgaria** (Nov. 23).

Oct. 10. The **Entente powers,** incensed by the surrender of the Greek forces at Kavalla, **submitted an ultimatum** to Athens demanding the surrender of the Greek fleet. The Athens government (**Lambros ministry,** Oct. 10–May 3, 1917) yielded (Oct. 11), whereupon the Entente powers demanded (Nov. 19) the dismissal of the representatives of the Central powers at Athens and the surrender of war materiel. These demands were rejected (Nov. 30), and in consequence **French and British** landing parties **debarked at Piraeus.** They withdrew again on Dec. 1 after conflicts with the Greeks.

Dec. 8. Blockade of Greece. The Allies demanded (Dec. 14) the complete withdrawal of Greek forces from Thessaly. The Athens government once more gave in (Dec. 15), but on Dec. 19 the British government decided to recognize the provisional government of Venizelos.

The Macedonian front was quiet during the winter of 1916–17.

1917, May 5–19. Battle of the Vardar (or **Doiran**). These engagements were inconclusive but served to convince the Allied powers that success on this front hinged on the Athens government.

June 11–12. The newly arrived French envoy **(Charles Jonnart)** presented an Allied ultimatum, demanding the abdication of King Constantine and the renunciation of the claims of the Greek crown prince. At the same time Allied troops invaded Thessaly and a French force occupied the Isthmus of Corinth.

June 12. Constantine abdicated in favor of his second son, Alexander.

June 26. Venizelos became premier, replacing Zaimis.

June 27. The **Greek government** severed relations with the Central powers and **entered the war on the Allied side.**

b. ROMANIA

Since the spring of 1916 the Russian government had been redoubling its efforts to bring Romania into the war. The success of the Brusilov offensive and the readiness of the Russian government and its allies to recognize the Romanian claims to the Bukovina and Banat as well as to Transylvania resulted in the conclusion of a political and military agreement (Aug. 18).

1916, Aug. 27. ROMANIA DECLARED WAR ON AUSTRIA-HUNGARY. Germany declared war on Romania, and Italy finally declared war on Germany (Aug. 28). Turkey and Bulgaria declared war on Romania a few days later (Aug. 30, Sept. 1, respectively).

Dec. 1–5. The Romanian government was hastily moved to Jassy, and the capital, **Bucharest, fell into the hands of the enemy** (Dec. 6).

1917, Jan. By the middle of the month the Romanians had reached the Sereth River, where the campaign came to a stop. Most of Romania, with important wheat- and oil-producing areas, was in the hands of the Central powers. *(To p. 663)*

11. THE WAR AT SEA, 1916–1917

(From p. 654)

The second half of 1915 and the first half of 1916 were not marked by any striking events of naval warfare. The Germans continued their efforts to reduce British preponderance by submarine and mine destruction, and at the same time extended their operations against merchant shipping.

1916, Feb. 21. The German government notified the U.S. government that thenceforth armed merchantmen would be treated as cruisers. **The "extended" submarine campaign** began March 1.

March 24. The *Sussex* sunk by torpedo in the English Channel with the loss of American lives. Acrimonious debate between Washington and Berlin, culminating in an American ultimatum. The Germans agreed to give up unrestricted submarine warfare for the time being (May 10).

Meanwhile (Jan. 1916) **Adm. Reinhardt Scheer** had succeeded Adm. Hugo von Pohl in the command of the German High Seas Fleet. The famous minister of the navy, **Adm. von Tirpitz, resigned** (March 14) in protest against the emperor's unwillingness to make full use of German sea power. He was succeeded by **Adm. Eduard von Capelle.**

May 31–June 1. BATTLE OF JUTLAND (SKAGERRAK).

The German high command reckoned confidently on winning the war through the destruction of the British food supply. The prospects were indeed excellent. Already in the last months of 1916 German submarines had destroyed 300,000 tons of shipping a month. By the beginning of 1917 the Germans had about 120 submarines, the number being increased to 134 by Oct. 1917.

1917, April. Submarine warfare reached the high point. In this month alone 875,000 tons of shipping were destroyed, more than half of it British. This figure exceeded the German estimates (600,000) and brought the British admiralty to the point of despair. Finally, owing largely to the insistence of Lloyd George, the admiralty agreed to try **convoying** merchant ships (first convoy, May 10). The system proved to be an unqualified success. At the same time the British increased the numbers of their destroyers and submarine chasers, and developed the depth bomb and the system of scouting with hydroplanes. Shipbuilding was pushed to the very limit.

By Oct. 1917 the Germans had destroyed about 8 million tons of shipping, but they had lost 50 submarines and their campaign was becoming less and less effective. By the beginning of 1918 the Allies were building more new tonnage than was being destroyed. The German gamble on the submarine had failed.

Naval operations during the years 1917–18 were confined largely to submarine and destroyer activities.

12. THE WAR IN THE AIR, 1914–1918

Although only France had done much before the war to develop the military use of the airplane, throughout the war the British and the Germans were the main antagonists.

1914, Aug. 30. The First German airplane raid on Paris.

Sept. 22, Oct. 8, Nov. 21. British airplanes raided the German flying-fields at **Düsseldorf, Köln,** and **Friedrichshafen.**

Dec. 21. The first German air raid on England (Dover).

On the western front, and on other fronts to a lesser extent, the airplane was used for reconnaissance, but almost immediately (Sept. 1914) experiments were made by the British in wireless communication between airplanes and artillery, in aerial photography, and in bomb-dropping. There was not much aerial combat until the middle of 1915.

1915, Jan. 19. First German airship raid on England.

Oct. The Germans began the use of the **Fokker** plane, equipped with a device allowing the pilot to shoot through the propeller. This gave the Germans **mastery of the air,** though the British, with a greater number of planes, kept carrying the fight over the German lines. Renowned German fighters of this period were **Oswald Boelcke** (d. Oct. 28, 1916) and **Max Immelmann** (d. June 1916).

Oct. 13. The worst of the **Zeppelin raids** on eastern England and London. There were 19 such raids in 1915 and 41 in 1916. But by the end of 1916 the British had elaborated a fairly good defense against airships (fighting planes, antiaircraft guns, searchlights, sirens, etc.).

1916, April. Battle of Verdun, including heavy air fighting between Germans and French. The French, with the **Nieuport 3** and the **Spad 3,** succeeded in securing mastery of the air. Great French fighters were **René Fonck** and **George Guynemer** (d. Sept. 1917).

July. Battle of the Somme. The British, with the new **De Havilland** and **Farman Experimental** planes, definitely put an **end to German Fokker supremacy.** Great British fighters: **Albert Ball** (d. May 7, 1917), **J. T. B. McCudden** (d. July 1918), **W. A. Bishop,** and **Edward Mannock** (d. July 1918).

Sept. The Germans introduced the **Albatross** and **Halberstadt planes** and developed formation flying. This reestablished something like a balance on the British front, though the British had a distinct superiority in numbers and continued to take the offensive.

Nov. 28. First German airplane raid on London. There were a great many of these in the course of 1917–18, first by daylight, then by night. There was a considerable loss of life and property, but the raids do not appear to have achieved any marked strategic results.

1917. The British began to use the **Scouting Experimental** and **Bristol**

Fighter. This period was marked by the spectacular achievements of **Manfred von Richthofen** (d. April 21, 1918) and by the development of ever larger formations and more intricate tactics.

1918. The Allied superiority became more marked, and American air squadrons began to take part (April). The British did much in the development of large-scale bombardment, especially of munitions cen-

ters. At sea much use was made of the airplane for scouting and submarine-chasing.

During these years the Germans continued their raids on England, first with **Zeppelins,** then with airplanes, with the object of drawing back British air forces from France, of interrupting industry, and of demoralizing the civil population.

13. THE WAR IN THE COLONIES, 1914–1918

Most of the German colonies were seized by the British and French during the first months of the war (p. 793).

1914, Aug. 8. The British opened hostilities in German East Africa by bombarding the coast towns of **Bagamoyo** and **Dar-es-Salaam.** Indian forces were then brought to East Africa for the campaign. But the German commander (**Gen. Paul von Lettow-Vorbeck**) defeated a greatly superior landing force in the **Battle of Tanga** (Nov. 2–5, 1914). The campaign remained desultory until in Nov. 1915 the British secured naval control of **Lake Tanganyika,** and landing forces took **Tanga** (July 7, 1916) and **Bagamoyo** (Aug. 15, 1916). **Gen. Jan Smuts,** with a force of Afrikaners and Portuguese, now began to push the operations. **Dar-es-Salaam** fell (Sept. 4), then **Lindi** (Sept. 16) and **Tabora** (Sept. 19). Lettow-Vorbeck and his troops were obliged to fall back to the southeast corner of the colony. The campaign was resumed in 1917, when the Germans defeated their enemies at **Mahiwa** Oct. 15–18, 1917) and began the invasion of Portuguese East Africa. Lettow-Vorbeck advanced almost to the mouth of the Zambezi but then fell back to **Lake Nyasa.** On Nov. 2, 1918, he began the invasion of **Rhodesia.** The armistice went into effect on Nov. 14, 1918, at which time the Germans were still in the field.

Aug. 23. **Japan** declared war on Germany and began to land forces in Shantung for an attack on the German position at **Tsingtao.** The

Japanese were joined by a British detachment. The bombardment of **Tsingtao** was begun in October, and was accompanied by an attack from the land side. On Nov. 7 the fortress was obliged to capitulate. During this same period the Japanese naval forces occupied a number of the German islands (**Marshall Islands, Marianas, Palau, Carolines**).

Aug. 26. **Togoland** defense force capitulated to an Anglo-French force. The colony was divided between the British and the French in agreements of Aug. 26, 1914, and Dec. 27, 1916.

Aug. 30. A New Zealand expeditionary force occupied **Samoa.**

Sept. 11. An Australian force landed on the **Bismarck Archipelago.** German forces in **New Guinea** surrendered to Australians (Sept. 21).

Sept. 7. A British force from Nigeria invaded the **Cameroons** and took **Duala** (Sept. 27). The French invaded the colony from the south and east. The Germans were obliged to fall back and ultimately crossed into Spanish territory (Feb. 9, 1916).

Sept. 19. A British force landed at **Lüderitz Bay,** German Southwest Africa. The Union of South Africa decided to prosecute the war in the German colony, and **Gen. Louis Botha** crossed the Orange River, taking **Swakopmund** (Jan. 14, 1915). He defeated the German forces at **Riet** and **Treckkopje** (April 26, 1915), took **Windhoek** (May 12, 1915), and finally forced the 3,500 German and colonial troops to capitulate at **Otawi** (July 9, 1915).

14. PEACE NEGOTIATIONS, 1916–1917, AND THE INTERVENTION OF THE UNITED STATES, 1917

From the very outbreak of the war, **President Wilson** appears to have believed that ultimately the opportunity would present itself for the U.S. government to step in as mediator.

1916, Jan.–Feb. The president's close friend and intimate adviser **Col. Edward M. House** visited Europe and consulted with leading statesmen. His conferences with Sir Edward Grey resulted in the so-called **House memorandum** of Feb. 22, which stated that the president was ready, whenever Britain and France thought the time opportune, to propose a peace conference. If the proposal were accepted by the Allies but rejected by Germany, the U.S. would *probably* enter the war on the Allied side. The terms on which the U.S. would mediate would include the restoration of Belgium and Serbia, the retrocession of Alsace-Lorraine to France, the acquisition of Constantinople by Russia, and the transfer of the Italian-speaking parts of Austria to Italy. Poland was to be independent. Germany would retain some colonies and perhaps be given more.

Public opinion in the U.S. was still distinctly divided, but sentiment for peace was prevalent except in the eastern states, where there was some feeling for intervention on the Allied side (influence of British propaganda, etc.). The president was re-elected (Nov. 7, 1916) very largely on a platform of peace, but he applied himself almost at once to the resumption of his mediatory efforts.

Dec. 12. The **German government** appealed to the U.S. to inform the Entente governments that the Central powers were **prepared to negotiate peace.** Failure of the Germans to mention any specific terms, and the fact that all the advantages were on their side, made it relatively easy for the Allied governments to reject the German advances (Dec. 30).

Dec. 18. President Wilson transmitted his own proposals to the warring powers. He suggested that the belligerents state their terms for peace and for arrangements to guarantee the world against renewal of conflict. The German, Austrian, and Turkish governments replied (Dec. 26) in an appreciative way, but reiterated their opinion that the

best method would be to call a meeting for exchange of views. No definite terms were mentioned. The Allied powers in their reply (Jan. 10, 1917) named specific terms. These included the restoration of Belgium, Serbia, and Montenegro; the evacuation of French, Russian, and Romanian territory, with just reparation; the reorganization of Europe on the basis of nationalities; the restoration of territory previously taken from the Allies; the liberation of Italians, Slavs, Romanians, and Czechoslovaks from foreign rule; the freeing of subject nationalities under Turkish rule; and the expulsion of the Turks from Europe.

The far-reaching nature of the Allied terms, at a moment when the military situation was by no means in their favor, estranged even Wilson, who still stuck by the idea of **"peace without victory"** (speech to the Senate, Jan. 22). The first step, however, was to elicit from the Germans a concrete statement of aims. These were confidentially communicated to the president on Jan. 29: restitution of the part of Alsace occupied by the German forces; acquisition of a strategic and economic zone between Germany and Poland on the one hand and Russia on the other; return of colonies and the granting to Germany of colonial territory in accord with its population and economic needs; restoration of occupied France; renunciation of economic obstacles to normal commerce; compensation for German enterprises and civilians damaged by the war; freedom of the seas, and so on.

Though this program was anything but hopeful, the president and the German ambassador, **Count Johann von Bernstorff,** continued to negotiate. But these discussions were cut short by the decision of the Germans to begin unrestricted submarine warfare.

1917, Jan. 8. A **meeting** of the highest military and civil officials of Germany, **at Pless,** finally concluded that the unrestricted use of the submarine was the only method by which Britain could be brought to its knees. It was understood that the decision would probably mean war with the U.S., but it was felt that the conflict would be over before the full weight of America could be thrown in. The chancellor, Bethmann-Hollweg, and men like Helfferich were not convinced of the soundness of the policy but offered no other solution. To counterbalance the hostility of the U.S., the foreign minister, Arthur von Zimmermann, sent instructions to the German minister in Mexico to work for an **alliance with Mexico and Japan** directed against the U.S. (Jan. 19).

Jan. 31. The U.S. was notified that **unrestricted submarine war** would begin on Feb. 1 (p. 697).

Feb. 3. The **U.S. government severed relations** with the German government. In response to an appeal from Wilson, Brazil, Bolivia, Peru, and other Latin American states followed suit. So did China (March 14).

The president had decided not to declare war until the Germans had committed an overt act. Several American ships were in fact sunk during February and March. At the same time the British secret service intercepted and deciphered the **Zimmermann note,** revealing German plans against the U.S.

April 6. The **U.S. DECLARED WAR ON GERMANY,** following the president's war message to the Senate (April 2). War was not declared on Austria-Hungary until Dec. 7, 1917.

1917, Feb.–June. Secret negotiations between **Emperor Charles** of Austria and his foreign minister, Count Ottokar Czernin, **and the French and British governments.** The emperor seems to have been determined, from the time of his accession (Nov. 1916), to make peace, even without Germany. The negotiations were carried on through his brother-in-law, **Prince Sixtus of Bourbon,** who was serving in the Belgian army. After several secret meetings in Switzerland, Prince Sixtus went to Vienna, with the full knowledge and approval of the French foreign office, and had a conference with the emperor and Czernin. He returned to Paris with a letter from Charles (dated March 24) in which the writer promised to use his influence with his allies to support "the just French claims relative to **Alsace-Lorraine.**" Belgium was to be restored, with compensation for its losses; so also Serbia, which was to have access to the Adriatic. The emperor was also not opposed to Russia's acquisition of Constantinople.

This offer was well received by **Poincaré** and **Briand** and also by **Lloyd George.** The one flaw was the failure to offer adequate gains to Italy. In the ensuing negotiations, which continued until June (second visit of Prince Sixtus to Vienna, May 6–8), it became clear that the Austrians were willing to turn over the **Trentino** to Italy but not **Trieste,** and that the Italians (statement of Sonnino at the **St. Jean de Maurienne conference,** April 19–21) were unwilling to accept anything short of the full terms of the Treaty of London (p. 656). Efforts continued to be made by Poincaré and Lloyd George, but the French prime minister, **Alexandre Ribot** (succeeded Briand, March 20), took a hopeless attitude, and indeed the Italians made no move in the direction of concessions.

Aug. 1. Outline **proposals for peace** submitted to the warring parties by the pope. These included disarmament, arbitration, freedom of the seas, renunciation of indemnities, evacuation and restoration of occupied territories, and examination of conflicting territorial gains. Prolonged negotiations proved futile.   *(To pp. 664, 671)*

15. THE SETTLEMENTS IN EASTERN EUROPE, 1917–1918

(From pp. 660, 661)

While discussion of peace among the western powers led to an impasse, the winter of 1917–18 produced a settlement in the east.

1916, Nov. 5. The **Germans,** in occupation of Poland, announced the formation of an **independent Polish state.** The object of this move, inspired by the military men, was to win over the Poles and induce them to enlist on the German side. This hope was sadly disappointed.

1917, March 30. The Russian provisional government recognized the independence of Poland.

April 5. The British government adhered to the principle of an independent and united Poland.

Sept. 12. The Central powers granted a constitution to what was formerly Russian Poland and appointed a regency council (Oct. 15).

Nov. 7. The **Bolshevik Revolution in Russia** (p. 711). **Lenin** and his followers, who regarded the war as a capitalist and imperialist venture, were in favor of a peace without annexations or indemnities, and were determined to make peace, which the Russian people yearned for. The old Russian Empire, indeed, was already dissolving.

Nov. 20. The Ukrainians proclaimed the **Ukrainian People's Republic.**

Nov. 21. The Bolshevik government, having invited all belligerents (Nov. 8) to make peace on the basis of no annexations and no indemnities, and having elicited no reply, opened separate discussions with the Central powers.

Nov. 28. The local Diet proclaimed the **independence of Estonia.**

Dec. 3. Opening of peace conference at Brest-Litovsk. Germany (Kühlmann), Austria (Czernin), and their allies negotiated an armistice with Russia (represented by **Leon Trotsky**).

Dec. 6. Finland proclaimed its independence.

Dec. 23. Proclamation of the **Moldavian** (Bessarabian) **Republic.**

Dec. 25. The Central powers accepted the principle of no annexations and no indemnities on condition that the Allied powers accept it within ten days. Trotsky's appeals brought no response, and there was nothing to moderate the German demands (these were laid down by the German general staff and were regarded as too extreme by Kühlmann).

1918, Jan. 4. Beginning of the peace discussions at Brest, after a suspension of ten days. Trotsky refused to recognize the new Baltic states without a plebiscite, and much acrimonious discussion ensued.

Jan. 12. Latvia declared its independence.

Feb. 1. The Central powers recognized the independence of the Ukraine.

Feb. 9. TREATY OF PEACE between the **Central powers** and the **Ukraine** signed at **Brest-Litovsk.**

Feb. 10. Trotsky declared the war ended, without peace having been made.

Feb. 18. The Germans at once resumed hostilities. They took **Dvinsk** (Feb. 18), **Dorpat** (Feb. 24), **Reval** (Feb. 25), **Pskov** (Feb. 25), and **Narva** (March 4), advancing to within 100 miles of Petrograd.

Feb. 28. The Russians, at the insistence of Lenin, renewed negotiations at Brest.

March 2. At the request of the Finnish government the **Germans occupied the Aaland Islands.**

March 3. The **Russians signed the TREATY OF BREST-LITOVSK,** abandoning Poland, Lithuania, the Ukraine, the Baltic provinces, Finland, and Transcaucasia.

March 3. In order to clear the Bolsheviks out of the Ukraine, the Germans and Austrians sent an expeditionary force. They occupied **Kiev** (March 3), **Odessa** (March 13), **Nicolaiev** (March 17), and **Kharkov** (April 8), and then invaded the Crimea, taking **Sevastopol** (May 1). The Ukraine henceforth became an important granary for the Central powers, though the returns were never as great as anticipated. Under German direction **Gen. Paul Skoropadski was proclaimed hetman of the Ukraine** (April 29).

April 3. German forces landed in Finland itself. They took **Helsingfors** (April 13) and **Viborg** (April 30). After a five-day battle the **Whites,** supported by the Germans, **defeated the Reds** and the Finnish civil war came to an end (May 7).

June 4. The Lithuanian assembly elected Duke William of Württemberg king.

Oct. 8. The Finnish assembly proclaimed Prince Frederick Charles of Hesse king. German troops remained in Finland until Dec. 16, 1918.

ROMANIA was likewise obliged to make peace in the winter of 1918.

1917, Aug. 6–Sept. 3. Battle of Putna. After the failure of the Brusilov offensive (p. 660) the Germans and Austrians began the invasion of northern Moldavia. Though it had been reorganized by the French general **Henri Berthelot,** the Romanian army was forced to fall back.

Dec. 6. Truce of Focsani. Hostilities between the Central powers and Romania ceased.

1918, Feb. 6. A German ultimatum demanded the opening of peace negotiations at once. **Bratianu resigned** and was succeeded by **Alexander Averescu** as premier and foreign minister.

April 9. The **Moldavian Republic** (Bessarabia) proclaimed its union with Romania. The Russian government protested against this (April 23), but the union was recognized by the Central powers in the treaty of Bucharest.

May 7. TREATY OF BUCHAREST. Romania was obliged to cede **Dobrudja** to Bulgaria and to turn over the Carpathian passes to Austria-Hungary. The Germans took a 90-year lease on the Romanian oil wells.   *(To p. 672)*

16. THE END OF THE HABSBURG MONARCHY

By the summer of 1918 the **Habsburg Monarchy** was already in full process of dissolution. Disorders were common in the larger centers, parliamentary government had had to be given up, and desertions from the army had reached a large scale. In Russia, in France, and in Italy there had been formed Czech, Polish, and Yugoslav legions that were fighting for the Allies, while national councils of these subject nationalities were springing up not only in the provincial capitals but also in Paris and London.

1918, April 10. Meeting of the **Congress of Oppressed Austrian Nationalities** in Rome. Here the Czech, southern Slav (Yugoslav), Polish, and Romanian representatives proclaimed the right of self-determination, denounced the Habsburg government as an obstacle to free development of the nations, and recognized the need for fighting against it.

April 21. The Italian government recognized the Czechoslovak National Council as a de facto government.

May 29. Secretary **Lansing** declared the sympathy of the U.S. for the Czechoslovaks and Yugoslavs.

June 3. Allied declarations were made supporting the national aspirations of Poles, Czechoslovaks, and Yugoslavs.

June 15–24. Battle of the Piave. The Austrians crossed the river but were unable to maintain their position. They withdrew again after losing some 100,000 men. From this time on there was steady demoralization of the army.

June 30. Italy and France officially recognized the **independence of Czechoslovakia.** Britain followed suit on Aug. 13, and the U.S. on Sept. 3.

In view of the rapid disintegration of the monarchy, the Austrians made a last bid for military victory.

Sept. 15. The Austrian government appealed to President Wilson to call an informal conference to discuss peace. This plea was rejected by Wilson.

Oct. 4. The Austrians joined the Germans in appealing for an armistice (p. 666).

Oct. 16. Emperor Charles proclaimed the reorganization of the non-Hungarian part of **the monarchy as a federal state,** with complete self-government for the subject nationalities. This move was patently belated.

Oct. 24–Nov. 4. BATTLE OF VITTORIO VENETO. Diaz attacked the Austrian front all the way from the Trentino to the Adriatic. The Austrians held out for a week on the Monte Grappa, but on the lower Piave they collapsed completely. The Italians advanced to **Vittorio Ve-**

neto (Oct. 30), by which time the Austrian armies were in a state of dissolution, several hundred thousand men being captured and the remainder streaming back toward home. The **Italians took Trieste** (Nov. 3) and **Fiume** (Nov. 5).

Oct. 27. Count Julius Andrássy (succeeded Burian as Austrian foreign minister, Oct. 25) notified Wilson that Austria was willing to recognize the rights of the subject nationalities and to make a separate peace.

Oct. 28. THE CZECHOSLOVAKS DECLARED THEIR INDEPENDENCE.

Oct. 29. The **YUGOSLAV NATIONAL COUNCIL** at Agram (Zagreb) **proclaimed the independence of the Yugoslavs.**

Oct. 29. The Austrians offered to surrender unconditionally to the Italians.

Meanwhile disorders in both Vienna and Budapest had resulted in revolutionary changes.

Oct. 30. Formation of a **German National Council in Vienna,** for the German provinces.

Nov. 1. Establishment of an independent Hungarian government, under **Count Michael Károlyi.**

Nov. 3. CONCLUSION OF AN ARMISTICE between the Allied powers and Austria-Hungary: complete demobilization of the armies and withdrawal of troops fighting with the Germans; surrender of half the equipment; evacuation of territories still occupied and of territory in dispute among Austrians, Italians, and Slavs; Allied occupation of strategic points; surrender of the fleet; and so on.

Nov. 7. A Yugoslav conference at Geneva decided for the **union of Croatia and Slovenia with Serbia and Montenegro.**

Nov. 11. Emperor Charles stepped down but never formally abdicated.

Nov. 12. PROCLAMATION OF THE AUSTRIAN REPUBLIC.

Nov. 16. PROCLAMATION OF THE HUNGARIAN REPUBLIC.

Nov. 24. PROCLAMATION OF THE UNITED KINGDOM OF THE SERBS, CROATS, AND SLOVENES at Zagreb. King Peter of Serbia became king, with Prince Alexander as regent.

Dec. 1. King Nicholas of Montenegro, having opposed union, was declared deposed by the parliament, which then voted for union with the new kingdom.

A national assembly of the Romanians of **Transylvania** and the Banat at Alba Julia **voted for union** of these regions with **Romania.**
                                                                 (To p. 672)

17. OPERATIONS IN THE WEST, 1918

(From pp. 660, 663)

The tremendous gains made by the Germans in the east did not serve to improve the situation with respect to the Western powers. On the contrary, it was generally felt that the terms imposed on Russia and Romania were irrefutable proof of Germany's expansionist aims. In the West the demands for peace died away and the allied governments were able to take a stronger line than ever.

1917, Nov. 27. The **Supreme War Council** had been established, consisting of the leading statesmen, with their military advisers (first Sir Henry Wilson, Foch, Cadorna, and Bliss). Even this new board was unable to establish harmony.

The **Germans,** now disillusioned about the submarine campaign, fully cognizant of the war-weariness of their allies, and feeling acutely the pinch of the blockade, decided to stake everything on a decision

in the west, which it was hoped could be reached before the Americans arrived in great force. **Ludendorff** planned a series of crushing blows to be delivered against the British on a 60-mile front south of Arras, by which he hoped to break through, roll up the opposing forces, and drive them westward to the sea.

The British expected an attack but not along the southern part of their front, so that the fifth army (Gen. Sir Hubert Gough) was left holding an extensive front with relatively few forces.

1918, Jan. 5. Lloyd George, in an address to the Trades Unions Congress, **formulated the British war aims.** These included the restoration of Belgium, Serbia, Montenegro, and the occupied parts of France, Italy, and Romania. In addition, a "reconsideration" of the great wrong done to France in 1871; the establishment of an independent Poland "com-

TERRITORIAL
CHANGES
FOLLOWING
WORLD WAR I

NORWAY

SWEDEN

FINLAND

*North
Sea*

*Baltic
Sea*

ESTONIA

DENMARK

LATVIA

NORTH
SCHLESWIG

MEMEL

DANZIG

LITHUANIA

SOVIET
UNION

EAST
PRUSSIA

MEMEL

GREAT
BRITAIN

POLISH
CORRIDOR

POLAND

NETHERLANDS

GERMANY

UPPER
SILESIA

BELGIUM

GALICIA

EUPEN-
MALMÉDY

CZECHOSLOVAKIA

BESSARABIA

LUXEMBOURG

SAAR

ALSACE-
LORRAINE

AUSTRIA

HUNGARY

TRANSYLVANIA

ROMANIA

SWITZERLAND

FRANCE

ISTRIA

SOUTH
TYROL

YUGOSLAVIA

BULGARIA

*Black
Sea*

SPAIN

ITALY

ALBANIA

TURKEY

*Mediterranean
Sea*

GREECE

AFRICA

	Territory lost by Germany
	Territory lost by Russia
	Territory lost by Bulgaria
	Territory lost by Austria-Hungary

0   200   400
MILES

prising all those genuinely Polish elements who desire to form part of it"; genuine self-government of the nationalities in the Austro-Hungarian monarchy; satisfaction of the Italian national claims, and of Romanian aspirations; and "recognition of the separate national conditions" of Arabia, Armenia, Mesopotamia, Syria, and Palestine. Lloyd George envisaged further some future organization to limit armaments and prevent war.

Jan. 8. In an address to Congress **President Wilson outlined** a peace program consisting of **Fourteen Points,** as follows: (1) Open covenants openly arrived at. (2) Absolute freedom of navigation alike in peace and war, except as the seas might be closed by international action to enforce international covenants. (3) The removal, so far as possible, of all economic barriers. (4) Adequate guaranties that armaments would be reduced to the lowest point consistent with domestic safety. (5) An impartial adjustment of all colonial claims on the principle that the interests of the population must have equal weight with the claims of the government. (6) The evacuation of Russian territory and the free determination of its own political and national policy. (7) Evacuation and restoration of Belgium. (8) Evacuation and restoration of French territory and righting of the wrong done to France in the matter of Alsace-Lorraine. (9) Readjustment of the frontiers of Italy along clearly recognizable lines of nationality. (10) Opportunity for autonomous development for the peoples of Austria-Hungary. (11) Evacuation and restoration of Romanian, Serbian, and Montenegrin territory, together with access to the sea for Serbia. (12) The Turkish parts of the Ottoman Empire to be given a secure sovereignty, but the other nationalities to be given an opportunity for autonomous development, and the Dardanelles to be permanently opened to the ships of all nations under international guaranties. (13) An independent Poland, to include territories indisputably Polish, with free and secure access to the sea. (14) A general association of nations to be formed to afford mutual guaranties of political independence and territorial integrity to great and small states alike.

The Allied war aims could be realized only through military victory, and prospects for this were not very good at a time when the Germans were able to transfer troops from the east to the west and when the American forces were not yet numerous enough to make much difference. Some efforts had been made, however, to establish greater coordination of effort among the Allies.

1918, March 21–April 5. THE GREAT MARCH OFFENSIVE. In a few days the Germans drove the British line to a depth of 40 miles. The hasty and generous supply of reserves by the French helped to check the advance.

March 26. In the midst of the crisis a **conference at Doullens** named **Gen. Ferdinand Foch** to coordinate operations on the western front.

April 14. Foch named **commander in chief of the Allied armies in France.** In practice the national commanders (Haig, King Albert, Pershing) retained extensive control.

April 9–29. Battle of the Lys.

May 27–June 6. (THIRD) BATTLE OF THE AISNE. Taking the French by surprise, the Germans reached the Marne River, only 37 miles from Paris.

June 9–14. Battle of the Matz. Ludendorff, astounded at his own success, gave up the idea of an offensive in Flanders and undertook to join up the Soissons and Noyon salients by an attack toward Compiègne.

June 4. The **American forces at Château-Thierry,** collaborating with the French, managed to break the German advance. In this engagement the Americans first played a substantial role.

July 15–Aug. 7. (SECOND) BATTLE OF THE MARNE. The Allied counteroffensive was of importance because it frustrated Ludendorff's plan for a great attack in Flanders, and because it enabled Foch to take the initiative in the months to come.

After the **second battle of the Marne** the Allied forces, together with the Americans, gradually went over to a sustained offensive, consisting at first of a series of local attacks but later merging into a general movement.

The resulting blows, together with the news of the surrender of Bulgaria, shook the nerve of Gen. Ludendorff, who, in something of a panic, demanded (Sept. 29) that the government initiate armistice and peace negotiations while the army could still hold out.

Sept. 30. Hertling and his fellow ministers resigned.

Oct. 4. Prince Max of Baden, a Liberal, named chancellor and foreign minister, with support of the Center, Progressive, and Socialist Parties. On the same day the **German and Austrian governments appealed to President Wilson for an armistice,** accepting the **Fourteen Points** as a basis for peace. There followed an exchange of notes between Berlin and Washington extending over several weeks, Wilson demanding evacuation of occupied territories, insisting that the Allies could negotiate only with a democratic government, and so on. In the interval Ludendorff regained some of his composure and began to talk of resistance, renewal of the war in the spring, and so forth. The home situation, however, was bad and the democratic tide strong. The government (Oct. 27) accepted **Ludendorff's resignation.** He was succeeded as quartermaster-general by **Gen. Wilhelm von Gröner.**

During October the British continued to advance in the north. By that time the American troops also resumed the advance. The Germans began to withdraw rapidly, and by Nov. 10 the Americans were at **Sedan.** Foch was then planning still another thrust east of Metz and arranging for the mission of a force through Austria to attack Bavaria.

Oct. 28. Mutiny broke out in the **German fleet** at Kiel, the crews refusing to put to sea on a series of cruiser raids planned by Adm. Scheer. The mutiny spread rapidly to Hamburg, Bremen, and Lübeck and thence to the whole of northwestern Germany.

Nov. 7–8. Revolution broke out in Munich. The king abdicated. In Berlin the ministry convinced itself that the abdication of William II was imperative if the monarchy was to be preserved. The emperor, who was at Spa, resisted the suggestion, but Prince Max, feeling unable to wait, made the announcement.

Nov. 9. THE ABDICATION OF WILLIAM II ANNOUNCED IN BERLIN BY PRINCE MAX. Philipp Scheidemann, the Socialist leader, then **proclaimed the German Republic.**

Nov. 10. William II, having been told by Hindenburg and Gröner that they were unable to guarantee the loyalty of the army, took their advice and **fled to Holland.**

Nov. 8. The **German armistice commission,** headed by **Matthias Erzberger,** the leader of the Center Party, was received by Foch in his railway coach near Compiègne. The terms submitted by the Allies were designed to make Germany helpless and to ensure the acceptance of the peace terms. The armistice provided for immediate evacuation of occupied territory on the western front and of all territory west of the Rhine, which was to be occupied by Allied forces. The **treaties of Brest-Litovsk** and **Bucharest** were to be renounced and German troops were to be withdrawn from Romania, Austria-Hungary, Turkey, and eventually Russia. Germany was to surrender 5,000 locomotives, 5,000 trucks, and 150,000 freight cars. It was to turn over 160 submarines and a large number of other warships. The armistice, harsh though the terms were, had to be accepted. It was concluded for a period of 30 days, but was periodically renewed until peace was signed.

Nov. 11. AT 11:00 A.M. HOSTILITIES CEASED ON THE WESTERN FRONT. The Allies at once began to take over the occupied and western German territories. French troops occupied Strassburg on Nov. 25, while British and American troops began the occupation of Germany on Dec. 1.

World War I Losses

The number of known dead has been placed at about 10 million men, the wounded at about 20 million, distributed among the chief combatants as follows (round numbers):

	Dead	Wounded	Prisoner
Great Britain	947,000	2,122,000	192,000
France	1,385,000	3,044,000	446,000
Russia	1,700,000	4,950,000	2,500,000
Italy	460,000	947,000	530,000
United States	115,000	206,000	4,500
Germany	1,808,000	4,247,000	618,000
Austria-Hungary	1,200,000	3,620,000	2,200,000
Turkey	325,000	400,000	

The total direct cost of the war has been figured at $180.5 billion, and the indirect cost at more than $151.6 billion.

MILITARY SUMMARY

The Western Front

1914

Aug. 4   The Germans crossed into Belgium. Armies one and two were obliged to pass through a narrow strip between the Netherlands and the Ardennes, heavily guarded by the fortifications of Liège. The Germans got past the forts in a night attack (Aug. 5–6), which were then reduced by heavy artillery (Aug. 6–17). The Belgians fell back on Brussels and then Antwerp, destroying the bridges on the Meuse.

Aug. 20   Gen. Kluck entered Brussels after the battle of Tirlement (Aug. 18–19).

Aug. 14–15   **Battle of the Frontiers** (Lorraine). The French invasion was checked almost at once and the French armies driven out of Lorraine with heavy losses. The third and fourth armies were also driven back from Luxembourg. Germans captured Namur (Aug. 25), Longwy (Aug. 27), Malmédy (Aug. 30), Soissons (Sept. 1), Laon (Sept. 2), Rheims (Sept. 3), and Maubeuge (Sept. 7).

Aug. 23   **Battle of Mons.** First contact between Germans and British. The latter were obliged to fall back with the French fifth army. Further delaying action fought by the British (Gen. Horace Smith-Dorrien) at Le Cateau (Aug. 26).

Sept. 5–12   **Battle of the Marne.** The opposing armies tried to outflank each other (**battle of the Ourcq**). Strongly urged by **Gen. Joseph Gallieni** (military governor of Paris), Joffre (commander in chief of the French armies) decided to order a general counteroffensive (Sept. 5) in the hope of breaking in on the right and rear of Bülow's second army. Sept. 6–9, no decision. Kluck's efforts to outflank the French increased the gap between the German first and second armies, but the British and French failed to take full advantage of this. On Sept. 9, Kluck and Bülow began to fall back (oral instruction of **Col. Hentsch**, from German headquarters). The whole German line began to withdraw west of Verdun. The British and French advanced cautiously.

Sept. 15–Oct. 10   All efforts to dislodge the Germans from north of the Aisne River ended in failure: battle of the Aisne (Sept. 15–18), battle of Picardy (Sept. 22–26), battle of Artois (Sept. 27–Oct. 10).

Sept. 22–25   Repeated German assaults at Verdun. Germans captured St. Mihiel.

Oct. 1–9   Germans forced the Belgian army and a small British force to evacuate Antwerp.

Oct. 10–Nov. 10   **The Race for the Sea.** The Germans captured Ghent (Oct. 11), Bruges (Oct. 14), and Ostend (Oct. 15), but failed to reach the Channel ports as the Belgians flooded the district of the Yser (battle of the Yser, Oct. 18–Nov. 30). The Germans also captured Lille (Oct. 12), but failed to take Ypres (first battle of Ypres, Oct. 30–Nov. 24).

Dec. 14–24   The Allies launched a major offensive along the whole front from Nieuport to Verdun, but no substantial gains.

1915

Feb. 16–March 30   After bombarding the German positions in Champagne, the French attacked but made no significant advances.

March 10–13   British attacks near Neuve Chapelle succeeded in breaking through the German line for a short distance.

April 22–May 25   **Second Battle of Ypres.** The original Allied plans for a major offensive were more or less frustrated by the **use of gas** (chlorine) by the Germans (April 22). Though the French had advance information of what was coming, they had made no preparation for it. The troops fled, leaving Ypres exposed. The Germans gained some ground at first, but were apparently themselves skeptical of the effect of the new weapon and were unprepared to take full advantage of the situation.

May 9–June 18   **Second Battle of Artois.** After an unprecedented bombardment, the French (**Gen. Henri-Philippe Pétain**) succeeded in breaking through on a six-mile front north of Arras and facing Douai.

Sept. 22–Nov. 6   **Second Battle of Champagne.** This was the key operation in Joffre's great offensive. The French attacked on a front between Rheims and the Argonne. The Germans, however, held their own on the heights between Rheims and St. Menehould, so that after many weeks of desperate fighting Joffre had little to show.

Sept. 25–Oct. 15   **Third Battle of Artois.** This was the British contribution to the great offensive in Champagne. The British here first used gas. Greatly outnumbering the Germans, they succeeded in driving the enemy back toward Lens and Loos, but then failed to capitalize on this advantage.

The Eastern Front

1914

Aug. 17–21   **Battle of the Tser and the Jadar.** Serbian forces repulsed an Austrian invasion.

Aug. 19–20   **Battle of Gumbinnen.** The first Russian army defeated **Gen. Friedrich von Prittwitz's** eighth German army, resulting in a German retreat to the Vistula. On learning of this, the German high command dismissed Prittwitz.

Aug. 26–30   **Battle of Tannenberg.** German forces led by **Gen. Hermann von François** surrounded Gen. Samsonov's Russian forces from the west and defeated them. The Germans took over 100,000 prisoners. Samsonov, in desperation, shot himself.

Aug. 26–Sept. 2   Battle of Zamosc-Komarov. Under **Gen. Moritz von Auffenberg-Komarow**, the Austrians won a great victory over the Russians (**Gen. Alexei Brusilov**).

Sept. 6–15   **Battle of the Masurian Lakes.** The Germans (**Gen.**, later Field Marshal, **August von Mackensen**) drove the enemy into the difficult lake country and succeeded in capturing 125,000 men. Completely demoralized, the Russians fell back, while the Germans advanced to the lower Niemen River and occupied the *gouvernement* of Suvalki.

Sept. 8–17   **Battle of the Drina.** Austrian forces again crossed the **Drina** into Serbia as the Serbs invaded Syrmia. The Serbs captured Zemlin (Zemun) on Sept. 10, but were unable to continue the advance into Austrian territory. The two opponents fought a long series of desultory engagements on the heights along the river. The Serbs were ultimately forced to retreat and surrender Belgrade (Dec. 2).

Sept. 8–12   **Battle of Lemberg.** Austria abandoned eastern Galicia. The Russians also captured **Czernowitz** in the Bukovina (Sept. 15) and **Jaroslav** (Sept. 21). At the same time the Russians invested the key fortress of **Przemysl** (Sept. 16) and launched an attack upon the passes of the Carpathians leading into northern Hungary (Sept. 24).

Oct. 9–20   **Battles of Warsaw and Ivangorod.** Mackensen advanced as far as Warsaw (Oct. 12), but was obliged to fall back when the Russians counterattacked farther east. The Austrians retreated to Cracow, while the Russians commenced the second investment of Przemysl (Nov. 10) and renewed the invasion of northern Hungary (Nov. 15). Heavy fighting also continued around Cracow (Nov. 16–Dec. 2).

Nov. 16–25   **Battles of Lodz and Lowicz.** For a time the Russians, having brought up reinforcements, threatened to surround the Germans, but in early December the Germans were themselves strengthened by the arrival of new divisions from the western front. Lodz fell to the Germans on Dec. 6.

Dec. 3–6   **Battle of Kolubara.** The Austrians were forced to recross the Serbian frontier as Serbs recaptured Belgrade (Dec. 15), ending the second invasion of Serbia.

Dec. 5–17   **Battle of Limanova.** The Austrians failed to break the Russian position before Cracow.

1915

Feb. 4–22   **Winter battle in Masuria.** The Germans advanced and took Memel (Feb. 17), but a further German offensive in East Prussia (battle of Augustovo Forest, March 9–10) met with strong Russian resistance.

March 22   The Russians captured Przemysl and were in a position to break through the Carpathian passes into northern Hungary, but Austrian forces drove them back (April 2–25).

May 2   Beginning of the great **Austro-German offensive in Galicia.** The Russians, already suffering severely from lack of rifles, artillery, ammunition, and clothing, gave way at once **(battle of Gorlice-Tarnow).** The Austro-German armies crossed the Dunajec (May 3–5) and took **Jaroslav** (May 14). By May 15 they had reached the San and forced a crossing **(battle of the San,** May 15–23). **Przemysl** was retaken (June 3), and gradually the whole Russian south front collapsed. **Lemberg** fell (June 22), and farther east **Zuravno** (June 5) and **Stanislav** (June 8). The Dniester River was crossed on June 23–27. By the end of June the Austro-German forces had advanced almost 100 miles, had liberated **Galicia** and **Bukovina,** and had taken huge numbers of prisoners.

July 1   Beginning of the **second great offensive.** The **Austrians** (Archduke Joseph Ferdinand) took **Lublin** and **Cholm** (July 31) and stormed **Ivangorod** (Aug. 4). In Courland the **Germans** took **Windau** (July 18) and **Mitau** (Aug. 1), while in northern Poland they (Gen. Max von Gallwitz with the 12th army) advanced to the Narev and took **Warsaw** (Aug. 4–7). The Germans took **Kovno** (Aug. 18) and stormed the key fortress of **Novo-Georgievsk** (Aug. 20). **Brest-Litovsk** fell into their hands (Aug. 25) and **Grodno** (Sept. 2). In the south the Austrians took **Lutsk** (Aug. 31) and **Dubno** (Sept. 8). The capture of **Vilna** (Sept. 19) marked the end of the great offensive.

The War at Sea

1914

Aug. 28   British cruisers, supported by battle cruisers **(Adm. Sir David Beatty),** raided **Heligoland Bight.** The German cruisers came out and drove the British fleet off, but Beatty was able to sink three enemy ships.

Aug.   When the war broke out, there were eight German cruisers on foreign stations, mostly on the China station. When **Japan** declared war (p. 574), the German commander, **Adm. Maximilian von Spee,** left for the South American coast with the cruisers *Scharnhorst, Gneisenau,* and *Nürnberg.* He bombarded **Papeete** (Sept. 22) and destroyed the British cable station at **Fanning Island.** At **Easter Island** (Oct. 12–18) Spee was joined by the cruisers *Dresden* (from the West Indies) and *Leipzig* (from the California coast). Together they proceeded to the Chilean coast. Meanwhile **Adm. Sir Christopher Cradock,** with three old ships, had been ordered to hunt down Spee.

Sept. 10–Nov. 9   The *Emden* **(Capt. Karl von Müller)** left the China station for the Indian Ocean, bombarding **Madras** (Sept. 22) and capturing several ships before being sunk at Cocos Island.

Sept. 22   The *U.9* sank three old cruisers, *Hogue, Cressy,* and *Aboukir.*

Oct. 18   After an attempted German submarine raid on **Scapa Flow,** the Grand Fleet was withdrawn from that base and concentrated, for a time, on the west coast of Scotland. **Naval action off Coronel.** Spee destroyed two of Cradock's ships (the *Monmouth* and the *Good Hope;* the *Glasgow* escaped). To meet the danger from the German squadron, all available Allied warships were assembled off the southeast coast of South America. Three battle cruisers were hastily dispatched from the Grand Fleet to the South Atlantic.

Nov. 3   **Adm. Franz von Hipper** raided Yarmouth.

Dec. 8   **Battle of the Falkland Islands. Spee** made the fatal decision to attack the **Falklands** on his way homeward. The British squadron **(Adm. Sir Frederick Sturdee)** came upon the Germans unexpectedly and sank four of their five ships *(Scharnhorst, Gneisenau, Leipzig,* and *Nürnberg).* A total of 1,800 men died, including Spee and his two sons. The *Dresden,* having escaped from the Falklands, engaged in commerce-destroying until cornered at Juan Fernandez, where the ship was blown up by its own crew (March 14, 1915).

Dec. 16   German forces bombarded Scarborough and Hartlepool.

1915

Jan. 24   Naval action occurred off the **Dogger Bank** between the British and German battle-cruiser squadrons. Hipper, though outnumbered, did much damage to the British flagship and ultimately got away, losing only his poorest ship, the *Blücher.*

March 28   A German submarine sank the first passenger ship.

May 1   The first American ship *(Gulflight)* was sunk without warning.

May 7   *LUSITANIA* SUNK off the coast of Ireland. Before the ship left New York, a warning against sailing on it had been inserted in the newspapers by the German embassy, but it is not true that a submarine was sent out specially to sink it. The captain failed to observe instructions to zigzag his course, and so came within range of the submarine. The *Lusitania* carried a part-cargo of small arms and munitions.

Aug. 19   German submarine sank the *Arabic.*

The Balkans

1915

Oct. 6   Beginning of the **great Austro-German campaign in Serbia. Belgrade** fell (Oct. 9) and **Semendria** (Oct. 11).

Oct. 22   The **Bulgarians** (Gen. Jekov) took **Üsküb** (Skoplje), and then (Oct. 28) **Pirot. Nish** fell (Nov. 5). A British and French attempt from Saloniki to block the Bulgar advance on the Strumitsa (Nov. 3–5) and on the Cerna (Nov. 12) was brushed aside. The Allies were again repulsed on the lower Vardar (Dec. 4–10) and forced to retreat to Greek territory.

Nov. 16   The Bulgarians took **Prilep,** then **Pristina** (Nov. 23), **Prizrend** (Nov. 29), and **Monastir** (i.e., Bitolje, Dec. 2). The Serbs were now in full flight into Albania, the Bulgars pursuing them and taking **Dibra** and **Okhrid** (Dec. 8), and ultimately **Elbasan** (Feb. 2, 1916).

1916

Jan. 23   The Austrians took **Scutari,** then **San Giovanni di Medua** (Jan. 25) and **Berat** (Feb. 17). Durazzo was also taken by the Austrians from the Italians (Feb. 27).

The Italian Front

1914–1915

Dec. 20   **Durazzo** occupied by the **Italians.**

1915, June 29–Dec. 10   **The first four battles of the Isonzo.** The Austrians (commander **Archduke Eugene**) held the two important bridgeheads at **Gorizia** and **Tolmino.** The Italians **(Gen. Luigi Cadorna,** commander in chief, May 23, 1915–Nov. 7, 1917) tried to force the passage, but their total advance never exceeded 10 or 12 miles. The Isonzo battles were the first (June 29–July 7); second (July 18–Aug. 10); third (Oct. 18–Nov. 3); and fourth (Nov. 10–Dec. 10).

The Western Front

1916

Feb. 21 **Battle of Verdun.** The Germans concentrated 1,400 guns on a short front of eight miles on the right bank of the Meuse. After a devastating bombardment they took Fort Douaumont (Feb. 25). French reinforcements were rushed to this sector, but the defense was hampered by the bottlemouth of the salient.

March 6–April 10 Renewal of the attack, this time on both sides of the salient. Gen. Robert Nivelle replaced Gen. Pétain, and the French began a series of vigorous counterattacks (May).

June 2 The Germans finally took Fort Vaux, and before the end of the month the works of Thiaumont (June 23). Heavy attacks continued until July 11, when the Germans went over to the defensive. The French losses have been estimated at about 350,000, the German at somewhat less.

July 1–Nov. 18 **Battle of the Somme.** After a long and intensive bombardment the British advanced on a front of 15 miles toward Bapaume, while the French objective was Péronne. Though the Germans were outnumbered at least six to one at first, the British had but little success. The heavily laden infantry was unable to move fast enough to keep up with an extraordinarily rigid time schedule. British losses on one day were 60,000, heavier than in this or any other war.

Oct. 24–Dec. 18. The French (Gen. Charles Mangin) counterattacked at Verdun and recaptured Forts Douaumont and Vaux (Nov. 2).

1917

April 9–May 4 **Battle of Arras.** The British third army **(Gen. Edmund Allenby)** began the advance after a heavy gas attack (use of the gas projector). **Canadian troops took Vimy Ridge,** and the British made a total advance of about four miles, without, however, effecting a breakthrough. On the Somme they advanced to near St. Quentin.

April 16–20 **Second Battle of the Aisne** and **Third Battle of Champagne.** Nivelle's plans had been so well advertised that the Germans were able to concentrate large forces in the area of attack. The French took only the **Chemin des Dames,** and this with very heavy losses.

June 7–14 **Battle of Messines.** The British second army **(Gen. Herbert Plumer)** launched a surprise attack on **Messines Ridge,** and was entirely successful in straightening the Ypres salient.

July 31–Nov. 10 **Third Battle of Ypres (Passchendaele).** This was a series of eight heavy attacks, carried through in driving rain and fought over ground waterlogged and muddy. The total gain was about five miles of territory, which made the Ypres salient more inconvenient than ever.

Aug. 20–Dec. 15 **Second Battle of Verdun.** Intended to serve as relief for the British in Flanders. The French gained several key positions, even on the east bank of the Meuse.

Oct. 23–Nov. 1 **Battle of Malmaison.** The French, attacking along the Chemin des Dames, cut off a German salient northeast of **Soissons.** The Germans fell back to the Oise-Aisne Canal.

Nov. 20–Dec. 3 **Battle of Cambrai,** the first great tank raid. Without preliminary bombardment the British launched a surprise attack with 380 tanks. They penetrated the three German lines and were on the point of breaking through into open country, but the exhausted troops were unable to take advantage of the situation. The British advanced five miles in the direction toward **Cambrai** on a six-mile front, but on Nov. 30 the Germans suddenly counterattacked on both flanks of the salient and forced the British to give up much of the ground they had conquered.

The Eastern Front

1916

March 19–April 30 The Russians fought the inconclusive **Battle of Lake Naroch,** intended only to relieve pressure at Verdun.

June 4 The great **Brusilov offensive.** The objective in the south was **Kovel,** an important railway center, but the advance extended over a front of 300 miles. The Austrians, taken by surprise, fell back, leaving many prisoners in Russian hands. The **Russians took Lutsk** (June 8) and **Czernowitz** (June 18). Heavy fighting continued about Kovel, Tarnopol, and Baranovici (**battles of the Strypa,** June 11–30; **Baranovici,** July 2–9; **Kovel,** July 28–Aug. 17) until September. The Russians advanced from 25 to 125 kilometers in the region from Pinsk south to Czernowitz and took half a million prisoners, but the offensive was stopped by the arrival of 15 divisions of Germans from the western front. The Russians had failed to take either Kovel or Lemberg.

1917

July 1 A Russian offensive on the Galician front began.

July 18–28 **Battle of East Galicia.** The Germans and the Austrians drove the Russians back and retook **Halicz, Tarnopol, Stanislav** (July 24–26), and **Czernowitz** (Aug. 3).

Sept. 3–5 The Germans captured **Riga.**

Oct. 11–20 The Germans, having overrun much of Latvia, **conquered the Baltic Islands.**

The Italian Front

1916

Feb. 15–March 17 The **fifth battle of the Isonzo,** which, like the previous engagements, led to no substantial change.

May 15–June 3 **The Austrian offensive in the Trentino.** The Italians were taken by surprise and yielded **Asiago** and **Arsiero** (May 31). But the Austrians lacked sufficient forces to break through, the more so as the Italians hastily brought up reserves from the Isonzo front. The Italian lines held, and by June 17 a counteroffensive was launched. When this came to a close (July 7), most of the territory had been recovered.

Aug. 6–17 **Sixth battle of the Isonzo.** The Italians finally took **Gorizia** (Aug. 9).

Sept. 14–18 **Seventh battle of the Isonzo.**

Oct. 9–12 **Eighth battle of the Isonzo.**

Oct. 31–Nov. 4 **Ninth battle of the Isonzo.**

1917

May 12–June 8 **Tenth battle of the Isonzo.**

Aug. 17–Sept. 12 **Eleventh and last battle of the Isonzo.**

Oct. 24–Dec. 6 The **Caporetto Campaign** (sometimes called the **12th battle of the Isonzo**). The German-Austrian forces attacked after a short bombardment, but in a heavy fog. The Italian forces, worn down by long and inconclusive fighting, broke at once. The Austro-German advance on the first day was fully ten miles. In three days they were through the hills and almost prevented the completely demoralized enemy from crossing the Tagliamento. **The Italians fell back to the Piave.** French and British troops were rushed to Italy to help hold the front (Nov. 3, 4). The Austro-German forces, outrunning their supply system, were obliged to slow down. The line became fixed on the Piave River.

The Balkan Front

1916

Aug. 2–21 **Battle of Doiran.** The Allies began to advance against the Bulgarians on the Saloniki front.

Aug. 17–19 **Battle of Florina.** The Bulgars and Germans counterattacked and pushed back the Saloniki forces. They took **Seres** (Aug. 19), **Drama,** and **Kavalla** (Sept. 18), where the fourth Greek army corps voluntarily surrendered.

Aug. 28   The Romanians began the **invasion of Transylvania** and took **Kronstadt** (Brasov) and **Hermannstadt** (Sibiu).

Sept. 27–29 **Austro-German forces,** hastily assembled in Transylvania and commanded by Falkenhayn, counterattacked and surrounded the Romanians at Hermannstadt (**battle of Sibiu**).

Sept. 26–Nov. 23 A Bulgarian-German force under Gen. August von Mackensen began operations in **Dobrudja.** Silistria was taken (Sept. 10), then **Constantza** (Oct. 22) and **Cernavoda** (Oct. 25).

Oct. 5–Dec. 11 The Allied forces under Sarrail began a great offensive in Macedonia (**first battle of Monastir**). Monastir (Bitolje) was taken (Nov. 19), and the Allies pushed forward as far as Lake Okhrid.

Oct. 7–9   **Battle of Kronstadt** (Brasov). The Austro-German forces retook the city and advanced to the Carpathian passes.

Nov. 10–14 **Falkenhayn forced the Vulcan Pass** into Romania and began the invasion of Wallachia.

Nov. 23   Mackensen's troops crossed the Danube at Sistova and advanced toward Bucharest, as did Falkenhayn coming from Craiova.

Dec. 1–5   A Romanian counterattack on the Arges River failed (**battle of Argesul**).

Dec. 6   **Bucharest fell to the Central powers.**

1917

Jan. 5   **Braila** fell to Austro-German forces, as did **Focsani** (Jan. 8).

March 11–19 **Second battle of Monastir** and **battle of Lake Presba.**

May 5–19   **Battle of the Vardar** (or **Doiran**).

The War at Sea

1916

April 24–25 A **German squadron** raided and bombarded **Yarmouth** and **Lowestoft.** Submarines also appeared off the Scottish naval bases.

May 31–June 1 **Battle of Jutland.** On May 30, **Adm. Franz von Hipper** with the German battle cruiser squadron had been sent to show himself off the Norwegian coast. On May 31, he came into contact with **Adm. Sir David Beatty** and the British battle cruisers, running southeast before the Grand Fleet. Though decidedly outnumbered, Hipper and the Germans, through superior marksmanship, sank two of Beatty's ships. Beatty, sighting the German High Seas Fleet (Scheer) in battle order, turned north to join Jellicoe and the Grand Fleet. The German Fleet, having been drawn in, met the Grand Fleet just before 6:00 P.M. Jellicoe tried to deploy across Scheer's line of retreat, but **Scheer** turned about suddenly and made away to the south and then to the east, coming up on the flank of the British, in pursuit. Scheer turned right, launching a torpedo attack, which obliged Jellicoe to fall back. Scheer then sent Hipper and the battle cruisers to attack while the High Seas Fleet effected its escape. Night fell, leaving the two fleets steaming southwest about six miles apart. But at 9:00 P.M. Scheer turned east and made for Horns Reef, forcing his way through the tail end of Jellicoe's forces, still steaming south. The German fleet reached Horns Reef in safety at 3:30 in the morning. Each fleet lost six ships in the Jutland engagement, but the British ships lost totaled twice the tonnage of the Germans. Scheer had to yield to the superiority of the British in capital ships, but in battle cruiser warfare the Germans were completely victorious.

Aug. 19, Oct. 26–27 **German raids** on the English coast. At the same time German light cruisers slipped through the blockade and ravaged commerce in the Atlantic. The German submarine *Deutschland* made a trip to the U.S. and back (July 10, 1916, at Norfolk, Va.).

1917

April 20, 26 The **Germans raided** the English coast.

Oct. 17, Dec. 12 The **Germans attacked British convoys** in the North Sea.

Nov. 17   A **British light cruiser attack off Heligoland** was beaten back.

1918

Jan. 14, Feb. 15 The **Germans raided** the English coast.

April 23   The **British attacked the mole at Zeebrugge** while three old cruisers were run in and sunk in the canal entrance. A similar operation at Ostend was unsuccessful, and even at Zeebrugge the blocking was not complete.

The Western Front

1918

March 21–April 5 **The great March offensive.** After cleverly concealed preparations, the Germans began with a bombardment of 6,000 guns and a heavy gas attack. They advanced from **St. Quentin** in a thick fog, which recurred for several days. The Germans captured **Péronne, Ham, Bapaume, Chauny, Noyon,** and even **Montdidier,** before being checked.

April 9–29 **Battles of the Lys.** The second great German blow, delivered south of Ypres on a short front. The Germans opened up a wide breach in the British front, but a lack of reserves made it impossible for them to take full advantage of the situation. The Germans stormed **Messines Ridge** and took **Armentières.**

May 27–June 6 **(Third) Battle of the Aisne.** Ludendorff, in order to draw the French reserves from Flanders preparatory to the main offensive there, arranged an attack upon the French between Soissons and Rheims, along the strong and therefore weakly held **Chemin des Dames.** The French were taken by surprise and driven back 13 miles on the first day. The Germans took **Soissons** (May 29) and on May 30 reached the Marne River, only 37 miles from Paris. The new salient was 40 miles deep.

June 4   **American forces at Château-Thierry** (second division), collaborating with the French, managed to break the German advance.

June 9–14 **Battle of the Matz.** The Germans advanced about six miles, but the move had been hastily prepared and the French were able to contain it.

July 15–Aug. 7 **(Second) Battle of the Marne.** Ludendorff threw his weary troops into yet another attack. East of Rheims no progress was made, and west of the city, though the **Germans crossed the Marne,** they made little progress against strong French and American forces. **On July 18, Foch ordered a counterattack,** in which nine American divisions took part. The Germans were forced back over the Marne to the Vesle River, while the French retook **Soissons** (Aug. 2).

Aug. 8–11 **Battle of Amiens.** The British attacked with 450 tanks. They advanced about eight miles the first day, after which the German lines tightened.

Aug. 21–Sept. 3 **Second battles of the Somme and of Arras.** The British and French gradually extended their attacks. They took **Roye** (Aug. 27), **Bapaume** (Aug. 28), **Noyon** (Aug. 28), and **Péronne** (Aug. 31), and obliged the Germans to fall back to the Hindenburg Line.

Sept. 12–13 American forces, attacking on both sides of the **St. Mihiel** salient, pinched out that area, capturing some 15,000 of the enemy.

Sept. 26–Oct. 15 **Battles of the Argonne and of Ypres** (Sept. 28–Oct. 2). Foch's plan was to execute a pincer movement with an American thrust north through the Argonne and a British thrust eastward toward Cambrai and farther north toward Lille. If successful, this would have cut the main lateral German railway and forced a general withdrawal. But at both ends the advance was much slower than expected. By mid-October. the Americans had gotten through part of the Argonne, while the British had taken **St. Quentin, Lens,** and **Armentières** (Oct. 1–2).

Oct. 18   British troops took **Ostend, Zeebrugge, Roubaix, Lille,** and **Douai.** They also captured **Bruges** (Oct. 19) and **Valenciennes** (Nov. 1).

18. THE PEACE SETTLEMENTS

(from p. 663)

a. THE TREATY OF VERSAILLES

1919, Jan. 18. The peace conference was formally opened at Paris, with 70 delegates representing 27 of the victorious powers. The Germans were excluded until the terms were ready for submission. The German request for a peace on the basis of Wilson's **Fourteen Points** (p. 666) had been granted by the Allied note of Nov. 5, 1918, with two reservations, but the Fourteen Points receded into the background as the conflict of views and interests developed at the conference. **President Wilson,** received with the wildest enthusiasm when he arrived in Europe in mid-December, represented the new idealism in international relations and was intent primarily on securing the adoption of a plan for a **League of Nations,** to be included in the peace treaty. **Lloyd George,** the chief representative of Great Britain and the empire, was disposed to make a moderate peace, but was deeply committed by promises made in the general election recently held, to the effect that the war criminals would be brought to justice and that Germany would be made to pay for the war. **Clemenceau,** in turn, was frankly the exponent of the old diplomacy, being intent on the interests of France, and on provisions for the security of France. Both Britain and France were bound further by their agreements with Italy, by commitments in the Near East, and so on. The Italian prime minister, **Vittorio Orlando,** played a secondary role, but the foreign minister, **Sidney Sonnino,** stood forth as an unbending champion of Italian claims against Austria and against the new Yugoslav state.

The plenary sessions of the conference were of little significance, for the decisions rested from the start with the **Supreme Council,** the **Big Ten,** composed of President Wilson and the prime ministers and foreign ministers of the five chief powers (Wilson, Lansing, Lloyd George, Balfour, Clemenceau, Pichon, Orlando, Sonnino, Saionji, Makino). Russia was not represented, though the Russian situation was of vital import. The wars of the counterrevolution were in full swing and the fate of the new states on Russia's western frontiers depended on the outcome. Clemenceau having refused to invite delegates of the warring parties to Paris, a conference was arranged for at the Prinkipo Islands. The Bolshevik government was apparently anxious for some kind of adjustment, but **Kolchak** and **Denikin,** the two leading generals of the counterrevolution, refused to enter into discussion, and the whole project fell flat. Public opinion in both France and Britain was violently anti-Bolshevik, and it seems hardly likely that an agreement could have been reached.

Jan. 25. The conference unanimously adopted a resolution for the **creation of a League of Nations.** A committee was appointed to draft a constitution, and other committees were organized to deal with reparations and various territorial questions.

Feb. In the middle of the month **President Wilson returned** for a time to the U.S. and **Lloyd George** to London.

March 25. After the return of Wilson and Lloyd George to Paris, the statesmen devoted themselves to the working out of the German treaty. The Council of Ten was replaced by the **Council of Four,** for the expedition of business.

April 28. The **Covenant of the League of Nations** (p. 640) (worked out by a committee consisting of Wilson, House, Cecil, Smuts, Bourgeois, and Venizelos) was presented in final form. The League was to consist of the signatory states and others admitted by two-thirds vote. The members were to afford each other mutual protection against aggression, to submit disputes to arbitration or inquiry, and to abstain from war until three months after a ruling. All treaties between members which were incompatible with these obligations were declared abrogated; all subsequent treaties were to be registered with the League. The League was to devote itself to problems of disarmament, labor legislation, health, international administration, and so on.

The drafting of the peace terms was marked by violent conflict among the members of the Council of Four. Clemenceau insisted on the separation of the **left bank of the Rhine** from Germany, and desired also the annexation of the **Saar Basin** to France. These demands were opposed by Wilson and Lloyd George, and French security was finally

arranged for otherwise, Wilson having ordered preparations for his return home (April 7). Other disputes arose from the demands of Britain and France that Germany be required to meet the **costs of the war,** a proposition to which Wilson objected. The **Polish claims,** supported by France, also caused friction, as did the **Japanese pretensions** in Shantung and the **Italian claims** in Dalmatia, neither of which Wilson was prepared to recognize. All these questions were finally settled by compromise in order to keep the conference together (the Italian delegates left the conference on April 23 and did not return until May 6).

May 7. The **treaty was submitted to the German delegation,** which had arrived on April 29. The Germans (**Count Ulrich von Brockdorff-Rantzau,** chief of the delegation) protested vigorously that the terms were not in keeping with the conditions on which Germany had laid down its arms and that many of the clauses were impossible to fulfill. Nevertheless the victorious powers made only slight modifications in the draft, and the Germans, after an acute domestic crisis, decided that they were unable to resist and that their only possible course was to sign.

June 21. The **German fleet** (ten battleships, nine armored cruisers, eight smaller cruisers, 50 torpedo boats, 102 submarines, totaling about 500,000 tons) **was scuttled** by the crews under the command of Adm. Ludwig von Reuter, **at Scapa Flow,** where the fleet had been interned. This act of defiance made the victors more determined to enforce the terms of the treaty draft.

June 28. SIGNATURE OF THE TREATY OF VERSAILLES at Versailles. The treaty provided for the **League of Nations** and for the following territorial cessions by Germany (see map on p. 665): **Alsace-Lorraine** to France; **Moresnet, Eupen,** and **Malmédy** to Belgium, with a plebiscite in Malmédy after cession; **the Saar** area to be under international administration for 15 years, after which a plebiscite was to be held, France exploiting the coal mines in the meanwhile; northern and central **Schleswig** to decide their allegiance by plebiscite; in the east, Germany to cede the larger part of **Posen** and **West Prussia** to Poland; a plebiscite to be held in **Upper Silesia; Danzig** to be a free city within the Polish customs union; plebiscites to be held in parts of **East Prussia** to decide whether they should go to Poland or remain with Germany; **Memel** ceded to the Allies; and the **German colonies** to be ceded to the Allies, to be organized as mandates under supervision of the League. Germany, in **Article 231,** accepted sole responsibility for causing the war. It was henceforth to keep an **army of not more than 100,000 men,** was to have no large guns and only a limited number of smaller ones. The **navy** was limited to six warships and a corresponding number of other craft; Germany was to have **no submarines or military aircraft**; the fortifications of **Heligoland** were to be dismantled; the Allies were to occupy the **Rhineland** for 15 years, and longer if necessary, and a belt 30 miles wide on the **right bank of the Rhine** was to be **demilitarized.** The **Kiel Canal** was opened to the warships and merchant shipping of all nations, and the **German rivers** were internationalized. The former **emperor** and other offenders were to be tried. The Germans were required to pay for all **civilian damage** caused during the war, the final bill to be presented by May 1, 1921; in the interval Germany was to pay $5 billion, the rest to be paid in 30 years. Germany was to hand over all **merchant ships** of more than 1,600 tons, half of those between 800 and 1,600 tons, and a quarter of its **fishing fleet.** It was to build 200,000 tons of shipping for the victors annually for five years. Large quantities of **coal** were to be delivered to France, Belgium, and Italy for ten years. Germany was to bear the **cost of the armies of occupation.** It bound itself further to agree to the sale of German property in Allied countries.

July 7. The **German government ratified the treaty,** as did France (Oct. 13), Great Britain (Oct. 15), Italy (Oct. 15), and Japan (Oct. 30). The U.S. government never ratified it, the Senate having first proposed amendments, which failed of the necessary votes. The U.S. government also refused to ratify the **treaty of alliance signed with Great Britain and France** (June 28) (p. 728) providing for assistance in case of attack by Germany. This treaty thus also failed of effect.

(To p. 674)

b. THE TREATY OF SAINT-GERMAIN

1919, Sept. 10. Austria signed the treaty that had been submitted on July 20. This merely registered the breakup of the Habsburg monarchy, at the same time penalizing the new Austrian Republic as the representative of the old regime. Austria recognized **the independence of Czechoslovakia, Yugoslavia, Poland, and Hungary,** these states being obliged to give guaranties of protection of minorities. **Eastern Galicia,** the **Trentino, South Tyrol, Trieste,** and **Istria** were ceded by Austria. The **army** was limited to 30,000 men, and Austria, like Germany, was to pay **reparations** for 30 years. The **union of Austria with Germany** was forbidden, except with consent of the Council of the League.

(To p. 702)

c. THE TREATY OF NEUILLY

1919, Nov. 27. The Bulgarians signed the treaty of peace, which deprived them of a seaboard on the Aegean and gave them only an economic outlet. Bulgaria recognized the **independence of Yugoslavia.** It agreed to pay **reparations** of $445 million. Its **army** was reduced to 20,000 men, and it was obliged to surrender most of its war materiel.

(To p. 724)

d. THE TREATY OF TRIANON

1919, March 21. The Hungarian government headed by **Count Károlyi** was overthrown by a **Bolshevik coup,** headed by **Alexander Garbai** and **Béla Kun.** This government became involved in war with most of Hungary's neighbors when it became known that territory was to be assigned to them. Ultimately the **Romanians invaded and took Budapest** (Aug. 4) just after the Bolsheviks had been overthrown (Aug. 1). The monarchists then regained control and appointed **Adm. Miklos Horthy as regent** (March 1, 1920). The Romanians were finally induced to withdraw (Nov. 14, 1919), under pressure from the Allies, but only after they had carried away most of what was movable.

1920, June 4. The **Hungarians signed the treaty of Trianon,** by which the old Hungary was shorn of almost three-quarters of its territory and two-thirds of its inhabitants. Czechoslovakia was given **Slovakia,** Austria received **western Hungary,** Yugoslavia took **Croatia-Slavonia** and part of the **Banat of Temesvar,** and Romania received the rest of the **Banat, Transylvania,** and part of the **Hungarian plain.** Hungary agreed to pay **reparations,** to keep an **army** of only 35,000 men, to assume part of the old Austro-Hungarian debt, to hand over war criminals, and so on.

(To p. 706)

e. THE TREATY OF SÈVRES

In the settlement of the Turkish question the Allies were much hampered by the downfall of the tsarist regime in Russia, the withdrawal of Russian claims to Constantinople, and the publication by the Bolsheviks of the **secret treaties** revealing the Allied plan of partition. President Wilson in particular opposed the former program, while American opinion showed little interest in assuming responsibility for either the Straits area or Armenia. The question dragged on through 1919, while in Turkey a nationalist movement under **Mustafa Kemal** (p. 752) was building up a strong opposition to the Allied plans.

1919, May 15. The Greeks, with the support of the Allies, **landed troops at Smyrna,** acting as agents for Allied interests. The Italians also landed troops in southwestern Anatolia.

1920, April 18. At a **conference** of the Allied prime ministers at **San Remo** the main lines of the Turkish treaty were agreed upon.

Aug. 10. The feeble and helpless government of the sultan, protected by an international force of occupation at Constantinople, signed the **Treaty of Sèvres.** By this treaty the sultan's government renounced all claims to non-Turkish territory. **The kingdom of the Hijaz was recognized as independent. Syria** became a mandate of France, and **Mesopotamia** (with Mosul), as well as **Palestine,** became British mandates. **Smyrna** and its hinterland were to be administered by Greece for five years, after which a plebiscite was to be held. The **Dodecanese** and **Rhodes** went to Italy, while **Thrace** and the remainder of the **Turkish islands** in the Aegean were assigned to Greece. **Armenia** was recognized as independent. The **Straits** were to be internationalized and the adjoining territory demilitarized. **Istanbul** and the strip of territory to the Chatalja lines remained Turkish, as did the remainder of **Anatolia.** This treaty was not recognized by the Turkish nationalists, who, under Mustafa Kemal's leadership, continued to build up a military force in Anatolia and to organize a government in defiance of the sultan and the victorious Allied powers. As a result of nationalist successes the Treaty of Sèvres was ultimately replaced by the **Treaty of Lausanne.**

(To p. 752)

C. EUROPE, 1919–1945

1. ECONOMIC AND SOCIAL CHANGES
(From p. 481)

Three events define this period in European history: World War I, the Depression, and World War II. **The impact of the First World War** was truly revolutionary. The total number of casualties, including killed, wounded, and missing, is figured at 37.5 million. The greatest burden of war dead and wounded, about 6 million, was suffered by Germany. France's losses were 5.5 million, but with a population less than two-thirds that of Germany, France suffered proportionally more. An outbreak of **influenza** in the autumn of 1918 compounded the death toll as it swept through populations already weakened by the nutritional privations of total war.

Economically, Europe was in ruins. Governments had borrowed heavily to fund the war, and had responded to this debt after the war by printing more money. The result was **inflation,** felt most disastrously in Germany. Yet the victors, especially France, depended upon German reparations to revive their economies. Germany's inability to pay led first to confrontation, as in the **French and Belgian occupation of the Ruhr,** and later to peaceful settlements, like the **Dawes and Young plans.** Wartime disruption helped cause a sharp **recession** in 1920–21, and some longer-term trends toward agricultural overproduction. For most nations, prosperity returned only in the mid-1920s. Ongoing economic uncertainty prompted many families to continue trends toward **lower birth rates.**

The catastrophic toll of the war also resulted in **a new, looser code of morality,** especially in a growing urban environment. A new generation, decimated by war, felt betrayed by their elders and rejected the more austere standards of conduct they had been taught as children. In the age of jazz and the flapper this was most notable in **changing attitudes toward sexuality.** While in France contraception became illegal because of population concerns, women like **Marie Stopes** in England actively supported contraception and a more open attitude toward sex. In Berlin, **Mangus Hirshfeld** opened the Institute for Sexual Science in 1919, an institution designed to further the study of sexuality and promote understanding, including gay rights. Sexuality became the subject of great popular interest, reflected in prescriptive literature, but this also fueled the impression among conservatives and rural populations that this was a degenerate age.

The devastation of the war also produced a strong **pacifist movement,** questioning duty to the state. Many argued that there was no suitable reason ever to reproduce the amount of bloodletting witnessed during World War I, "the war to end all wars." Though the League of Nations was unable to develop this into a concrete system to avoid war, this sentiment helps explain the policy of appeasement Western Europe followed in the face of Nazi aggression.

On the political stage, the revolutionary dream of national unity first introduced by the French Revolution became reality in Eastern Europe. The creation of **new nation states** heralded the end of multinational empires, though one was to reemerge in the Soviet Union. Throughout the 1920s **democracy** also triumphed. Not only did working-class men gain suffrage, but in most nations women too acquired the vote. France and Italy were notable exceptions.

Government also became **"big government"** during the war and afterward. The demands of total war necessitated government involvement in all walks of life. Governments established minimum and maximum wages and prices, curtailed production in industries not deemed necessary to the war effort, and introduced rationing when necessary. Administrations grew as liberal notions of free trade gave way to **planned economies.** Since morale on the home front was as important as in the trenches, governments also attempted to influence behavior through **extensive propaganda campaigns.** With the problems of demobilization and continued economic hardships, governments did not readily decrease their activities with the war's end. Indeed, administrations continued to grow as various states instituted the early trappings of the **welfare state,** such as unemployment insurance, housing allotments, and accident insurance for workers.

The success of the **Communist Revolution** in Russia also entered a new element into European politics. For many in Eastern Europe it justified early shifts to right-wing governments and the end of democracy. In Western Europe the impact of the Russian Revolution was a split in the Socialist parties, as Communists formed their own parties, allied closely to the Third International, and revisionists gained control of the Socialist parties. Throughout Europe the "specter of world Communism" was also the force behind domestic policies, such as social and land reforms, designed to integrate workers and peasants into noncommunist political and economic systems.

The next defining event in interwar Europe was the **world depression** that followed the U.S. stock market crash of 1929. Europe did not feel the full brunt until the early thirties, but when it did, whole economies were devastated. Peasants were unable to acquire credit or obtain loans as world market prices plummeted. Unemployment reached disastrous proportions throughout Europe, making insecurity a reality for millions. While factory workers suffered most, the growing **white-collar and professional** sectors also experienced massive loss of jobs. Many were now willing to support radical attempts to deal with the crisis by both democratic leaders and dictators.

The responses to the Depression differed significantly. In Britain, for example, the government followed orthodox economic theory by balancing its budget, but unemployed workers did receive enough welfare simply to survive. **In Scandinavia, however, a cooperative tradition and strong Socialist influence in government** since the end of the war generated a reformist socialism that responded to economic crisis with deficit spending and vast public works programs. In nations with weak democratic traditions, however, the response to economic crisis was dictatorship. This was a result not so much of the economic solutions proffered by various totalitarian leaders, but of the general fear that economic insecurity generated, a fear of disorder and revolution that only force could prevent. Millions surrendered civil liberties for such security.

The rise of **fascism** (p. 643), which depended on an aggressive foreign policy and the glory of conquest, led to expansionist policies that resulted first in the disappearance of countries like Albania, Austria, and Czechoslovakia, and eventually in the outbreak of **World War II** in 1939. As in World War I, the demands of modern warfare dictated total war. As men were conscripted into the armed services, **women were conscripted into the workforce.** In England, the Women's Power Committee was able to win equal insurance and benefits for women workers in 1943, but the government consistently fought demands for equal pay. Rationing once again became a fact of life as governments planned every aspect of the economy. Civil liberties were curtailed in the name of security, and governments launched more extensive propaganda campaigns to retain popular support.

Occupied nations responded differently to the Nazis. In the western portions of the Soviet Union, for example, the invading Germans were first greeted as liberators. In Western Europe, **resistance** developed quickly to Nazi occupation, growing in intensity with the influx of Communists after the Nazi invasion of the Soviet Union. The combination of various political beliefs among resistance fighters sometimes led to violence within resistance movements and set the tone for postwar political battles. In all occupied nations, industry was retooled for the German war effort, while forced labor led many into slave conditions in German factories. The Nazis also transported their racist policies into occupied areas, forcing Jews, Gypsies, and others into ghettos and later into concentration camps. *(To p. 834)*

2. INTELLECTUAL AND RELIGIOUS TRENDS

(From p. 483)

The most important development in thought after World War I was the rejection of the rational. While a few philosophers had moved in this direction in the last years of the 19th century, the barbarism of world war convinced many that the previous century's faith in reason and progress was misplaced. This revolt went in two directions. On the Continent, **existentialism** rose to prominence. Although it truly came into its own after World War II, the interwar years witnessed its birth in the works of **Martin Heidegger** (1889–1976), **Karl Jaspers** (1883–1969), and the early works of **Jean-Paul Sartre** (1905–80). Existentialists held that human beings simply existed in an absurd world without a supreme being, left to define themselves only through their actions. Any sense of hope could come only by "engaging" in life and thereby finding meaning in it.

Logical empiricism found more supporters in England, though its main proponent was the Austrian philosopher **Ludwig Wittgenstein** (1889–1951). Wittgenstein argued in 1922 that philosophy is only the logical clarification of thoughts, and therefore its study is the study of language, which expresses thoughts. Gone were the days when primary philosophical topics were God, freedom, and morality; the new scope of philosophy was greatly reduced to only those things that could be proved. To talk of anything else was a waste of time.

Still others turned to **religion.** But unlike the theologians of the late 19th century, who attempted to merge religion with science by portraying Christ primarily as the greatest moral teacher, theologians of interwar Europe stressed the frailty of humankind and the "supernatural" aspects of God. Building on the works of Søren Kierkegaard

(1813–55), leading scholars like **Karl Barth** (1886–1968), **Gabriel Marcel** (1887–1973), **Jacques Maritain** (1882–1973), **C. S. Lewis** (1898–1963), and **W. H. Auden** (1907–73) saw in religion and God's grace the answers to a world of terror and anxiety.

Others seeking security in an insecure world turned to political philosophies. The two most important in interwar Europe were **communism** and **fascism.** While communism was not new to the 20th century, the existence of a Communist society did propose changes in the philosophy as well as an example for other nations. **Joseph Stalin** (1879–1953) produced the most important change with his concept of **socialism in one country.** Despite the argument that socialism was a stage of development that must occur in all of the industrial world and that Soviet Russia must await the revolution while promoting it through such organizations as Comintern, Stalin argued that socialism could be developed in a single nation, a belief built on a strong base of Russian nationalism. That philosophy was a prime component in the great pace of Russian industrialization in the thirties.

Fascism can be difficult to define because its proponents often tried to make it everything to everybody. As presented by **Adolf Hitler** (1889–1945), **Benito Mussolini** (1883–1945), and **Italo Balbo** (1896–1940), it embodied a rejection of socialism and class warfare, presenting the nation as the most important unifying element that transcended all differences. At the same time, it promoted **a corporatist notion of capitalism and a planned economy.** It drew on the threat of world communism, on the economic problems recurring throughout the period, and on the war experiences of its adherents, expounding a brotherhood akin to that found in the trenches. It fed on fear and resentment to promote a picture of social order and national grandeur.

In the realm of economics, **John Maynard Keynes** (1883–1946) published his *General Theory of Employment, Interest, and Money* in 1936. This work explained how and why an economy might fail to maintain a level activity required for full employment. Though dealing primarily with short-run phenomena, "Keynesian economics" became crucial in the development of theories of economic growth.

Other important events in the development of interwar thought included:

1916. Vilfredo Pareto (1848–1923), in his *Trattato di Soziologia Generale*, provided a comprehensive mathematical analysis of economic and sociological problems, based on the distinction between the fundamental motivations of human natures *(residues)* and their outward appearance or rationalization *(derivations)*.

1918–22. Oswald Spengler (1880–1936), in *Der Untergang des Abendlandes*, produced a cyclical interpretation of history and forecast the eclipse of Western civilization as inevitable.

1929. Marc Bloch (1886–1944) and **Lucien Febvre** (1878–1956) founded the journal *Annales d'histoire économique et sociale*, which became an influential international forum for the new social history, a new form of history turning away from political narrative to focus upon economic structures, social institutions, and mentalities in a historical context.

1934–54. *A Study of History* (ten volumes), by **Arnold J. Toynbee** (1889–1975), constituted an exhaustive reexamination of human development in the light of an idealist philosophy of history.

(To p. 835)

3. CULTURE AND POPULAR CULTURE

(From p. 483)

Literature articulated **the general intellectual climate of pessimism, relativism, and alienation.** While 19th-century novelists had adopted the more general stance in their novels of all-knowing narrators, 20th-century authors tended to take on the narrower viewpoint of a single individual. This was notable in the works of **Marcel Proust** (1871–1922), **George Orwell** (1903–50), **Franz Kafka** (1883–1924), **James Joyce** (1882–1941), and **Virginia Woolf** (1882–1941). The two latter authors also became famous for a style of writing known as **stream of consciousness,** a technique that demonstrated the impact of psychology on the arts.

As with the postwar generation in general, interwar artists rejected the rules and forms handed down from their elders. In architecture, **Walter Gropius** (1883–1969), founder of **Bauhaus,** broke with the past in his designs of clean and light buildings of glass and iron. **Le Corbusier** (1887–1965) epitomized the new turn to functionalism in his designs. In art, modern painters rejected French impressionism, becoming more abstract and nonrepresentational. Like the early 19th-century romantics, they wanted to portray unseen, inner worlds of emotion and imagination. This can be seen in the art of **Henri Matisse** (1869–1945), **Pablo Picasso** (1881–1973), and **Wassily Kandinsky** (1866–1944).

As abstract painters arranged lines and color but did not draw identifiable objects, so modern composers arranged sounds without creating recognizable harmonies. Such composers were led by the Viennese composer **Arnold Schönberg** (1874–1951).

In popular culture, the long-declining traditional arts and amusements of people in villages and small towns almost vanished, replaced by standardized, commercial entertainment. In the cities, the prosperity of the late 1920s and the growth of leisure among the working class, resulting from the legalization of the eight-hour day, brought a growth in the leisure industry. **Cabarets and music halls** did a brisk business, centers of society's loosening sense of morality. Playing to crowded rooms, the American **Josephine Baker** (1906–75) brought an exotic African eroticism to Parisian music halls in 1925.

For many, leisure also found outlets in the development of **radio** and **cinema. Charlie Chaplin** (1889–1978) became a world icon, the king of the "silver screen." The great appeal of cinema was its ability to offer people a temporary escape from the hard realities of everyday life. While the U.S. dominated the industry during the First World War, destroying young German studios in the early 1920s, the advent of "talkies" resuscitated national film industries in the 1930s, particularly in France.

Radio became possible with the transatlantic "wireless" communication of **Guglielmo Marconi** (1874–1937) in 1901 and the development of the vacuum tube in 1904, which permitted the transmission of speech and music. But only in 1920 were the first major public broadcasts of special events made in Great Britain and the U.S. On June 16, 1920, Lord Northcliffe, the Briton who had pioneered in journalism with the inexpensive, mass-circulation *Daily Mail*, sponsored a broadcast of the soprano Nellie Melba, which was heard simultaneously all over Europe. Every major country quickly established national broadcasting networks. The typical pattern was direct control of the medium by the government. By the late 1930s, more than three out of every four households in both democratic Great Britain and dictatorial Germany had at least one cheap, mass-produced radio, a powerful tool for political propaganda. *(To p. 836)*

4. EUROPEAN DIPLOMACY AND THE DEPRESSION, 1919–1939

(From p. 671)

European diplomacy between the two world wars involved the following **major problems:** (1) the attempt to establish collective security by means of new international bodies, the League of Nations, and the World Court, without creating any form of superstate; (2) the unwillingness of the non-European powers, the U.S., Japan, and the British Dominions in particular, to assume responsibility for anything outside their respective spheres of interests; (3) the competition between French efforts to maintain the position of leadership on the continent of Europe established by the peace settlements, and German endeavors to evade or revise the terms imposed in 1919; (4) the attempts to attain security and prosperity by neomercantilist ideas imposed as emergency measures.

The era between the wars can be divided chronologically into three phases: (1) the period of settlement (from the peace treaties to the Dawes Plan, 1924); (2) the period of fulfillment (1924 to the evacuation of the Rhineland, 1930); (3) the period of repudiation and revision (1930–39).

1919, June 28. Conclusion of **defensive treaties among France, Britain, and the U.S.** Britain and the U.S. were to come to France's assistance in case of aggression by Germany. The U.S. Senate refused to ratify this agreement and also rejected the Versailles treaty (Nov. 19), thus knocking out one of the keystones in the international peace structure established at Paris.

1919–22. The **Vilna dispute,** between Poland and Lithuania. Polish forces took the town from the Bolsheviks (April 4, 1919). The **Curzon line** (Dec. 8) established a boundary depriving Poland of the city, which was retaken by the Bolsheviks (June 15, 1920). The Lithuanians took it when the Russians evacuated (Aug. 24), but were driven out by Polish freebooters under **Gen. Lucien Zeligowski** (Oct. 9). By decision of the League a plebiscite was to be held to decide the fate of the city, but this was later abandoned (March 3, 1921). A **plebiscite** (Jan. 8, 1922) held by Zeligowski decided for Poland, and the Vilna Diet voted for union. On April 18 it was incorporated with Poland, though Lithuania refused to recognize this disposition of the question.

1919–20. The **Teschen conflict** between Poland and Czechoslovakia. The Czechs had occupied the disputed area (Jan. 1919) and serious clashes took place (May). The supreme council decided for a plebiscite

(Sept. 27), but disorders continued (March, May 1920) until the conference of ambassadors divided the territory (July 28). (In these and other Eastern European disputes, France, eager for stable powers on Germany's eastern borders, took the lead in organizing ambassadorial negotiations.)

1919–20. The **Polish-Russian War,** resulting from the effort made by the Poles to push their frontier east to the frontier of 1772. The Poles, in agreement with the Ukrainian leader **Gen. Simon Petliura,** attempted to wrest Ukraine from the Bolsheviks. They quickly overran the country, taking Kiev (May 7), but the Bolsheviks launched an energetic counterattack and drove the Poles out of Kiev (June 11) and Vilna (July 15). By Aug. 14 the Russians were on the outskirts of Warsaw. But the Poles, vigorously aided by the French **(Gen. Maxime Weygand)** made a stand and were soon able to turn the tables. The Bolsheviks were forced to fall back and abandon their Polish conquests. The preliminary treaty of Riga (Oct. 12) was followed by the definitive **Treaty of Riga** (March 18, 1921), which defined the frontier between the two countries.

1919–21. The **Burgenland dispute** between Austria and Hungary. The strip of territory had been assigned to Austria by the peace treaties, it being only 15 miles from Vienna. The population, too, was predominantly German. But Hungarian irregulars were in occupation and refused to evacuate (Aug. 1921). Through Italian mediation a plebiscite was arranged for. This was held (Dec. 1921) and gave Austria most of the area, though Ödenburg went to Hungary.

1919–22. The **Greek invasion of Anatolia** (p. 752).

1919–24. The **Fiume question.** President Wilson had rejected the Italian claim to the town and the coast south of it (April 14, 1919), whereupon the Italians had withdrawn from the peace conference. A compromise, suggested by **André Tardieu,** which would have created a buffer state of Fiume (May 30), was rejected by Yugoslavia. **Gabriele d'Annunzio** led a filibustering expedition that occupied the town and set up a visionary government (Sept. 12). The matter was finally left to Italy and Yugoslavia to settle (March 6, 1920). The **Treaty of Rapallo** (Nov. 12) made Fiume an independent city and gave Italy Zara and a number of Dalmatian islands. But a Fascist coup (March 3, 1922) overthrew the local government, and government troops took control (March 17). By a treaty of Jan. 27, 1924, Yugoslavia abandoned claims to Fiume but received **Porto Barros** in return.

1919–22. The **Upper Silesian question.** The peace treaties had provided for a plebiscite in this valuable area. It was held on March 20, 1921 (p. 719), and returned 717,122 votes for Germany, as against 483,154 for Poland. But an armed rising under the Polish commissioner **Adalbert Korfanty** (May 4, 1922) was acquiesced in by the French commander acting for the League. In Aug. 1922, the council of ambassadors referred the matter to the League, and the League council accepted **a scheme of partition** by which a majority of the population and more than half of the territory were awarded to Germany, while Poland was given the principal mining and industrial districts.

1919, July 29. Italy signed a treaty with Greece supporting Greek claims in Thrace and Eprius, Greece to support an Italian protectorate over Albania and Italian claims in Anatolia. Italy was to keep Rhodes for 15 years, and the **Dodecanese Islands** were to be ceded to Greece. Italy denounced these treaties on Oct. 8, 1922.

1920, Jan. 23. The Dutch government refused to surrender the **former emperor William,** though it later agreed to intern him.

Feb.–March. The **plebiscites in North Schleswig** gave the northernmost zone to **Denmark** and the remainder to Germany.

April 19–26. The **San Remo conference** of the Allied powers, to discuss various territorial problems and to assign the Class A mandates.

June 19–22. Conferences of Hythe and Boulogne, to discuss the Near Eastern situation and the reparations problem.

July 5–16. The **Spa conference,** where the Germans submitted a scheme of reparations payments and signed a disarmament engagement. The Allies decided to apportion reparations money as follows: France, 52 percent; British Empire, 22 percent; Italy, 10 percent; Belgium, 8 percent; the smaller powers to receive the rest.

Aug. 14. Treaty between Czechoslovakia and Yugoslavia, which became the foundation of the **Little Entente.** Its purpose was to enforce observance of the peace treaty by Hungary and to forestall a possible restoration of the Habsburgs.

Nov. 12. Treaty of Rapallo between Italy and Yugoslavia, regarding Fiume and other Adriatic issues.

1921, Jan. 24–30. Paris conference, to discuss reparations.

Feb. 19. Treaty between Poland and France, providing for mutual assistance in case of attack.

Feb. 21–March 14. London conference, dealing with reparations. Schedules of payment were worked out for the Germans, who made counterproposals.

March 3. Offensive and defensive **treaty between Poland and Romania.**

March 8. The **French occupied Düsseldorf, Duisburg,** and **Ruhrort,** after an ultimatum to Germany had been evaded.

March 24. The reparation commission declared **Germany in default,** though the Germans, reaching other figures on payments already made, denied the default.

April 23. Romania joined Czechoslovakia in the Little Entente.

April 27. The reparations commission announced that Germany should pay a **total of 132 billion gold marks.**

April 29–May 5. London conference on reparations. It sent an ultimatum to Germany demanding 1 billion gold marks by the end of the month on penalty of occupation of the Ruhr. The Germans raised the money by borrowing in London, and accepted the payment schedules.

June 7. Treaty between Yugoslavia and Romania, completing the Little Entente.

Aug. 24, 25. By separate treaties the **U.S. made peace with Austria and Germany.**

Oct. 6. The **Loucheur-Rathenau agreement,** arranging for payments in kind.

Oct. 20. The Aaland Islands convention signed at Geneva. It provided for the neutralization and nonfortification of the group.

Oct. 20. The former **king Charles arrived in the Burgenland** by airplane and began a march on Budapest (p. 706). Czechoslovakia and Yugoslavia mobilized, and the Hungarians, unable to face another war, did not dare restore the Habsburg king.

1922, March 13–17. Conference at Warsaw of the Baltic states and Poland; provided for arbitration and a defensive league in the event of attack by another power.

March 17. Poland concluded treaties with Latvia, Estonia, and Finland which provided for maintenance of the treaty settlements and neutrality in case one of these powers should be attacked.

April 16. The **TREATY OF RAPALLO** between Germany and Soviet Russia. The agreement provided for economic cooperation and established close political connections. Despite the indignation of the other powers, Russia and Germany, as outcast powers, held steadfastly to the pact, which was supplemented by a commercial treaty (Oct. 12, 1925) and a treaty of friendship and neutrality (Treaty of Berlin) of April 24, 1926, which remained technically in effect until Hitler's attack in 1941. During the 1920s the German high command made secret agreements with its Russian counterpart that enabled Germany to manufacture munitions and carry out training in violation of the Treaty of Versailles.

May 31. The reparations commission, despite protests from France, granted Germany a moratorium for the remainder of the year, it having become clear that payments were resulting in the collapse of the mark and creating an impossible transfer problem.

Oct. 23. Italy and Yugoslavia signed the **Treaty of Santa Margherita,** reaffirming the 1920 Treaty of Rapallo. This was followed on Jan. 27, 1924, with a treaty of friendship, following the settlement of the Fiume problem. This was not renewed in 1929.

Dec. 26. After several conferences failed to resolve reparations and war debts issues (p. 646) the reparations commission again declared **Germany in default** on the motion of Louis Barthou, the French representative. The point at issue was a minor delay in deliveries of timber.

1923, Jan. 2–4. Paris conference. British and Italian schemes for bond issues, and so on, were rejected by the French.

Jan. 9. Germany declared in default on coal deliveries.

Jan. 11. French and Belgian troops began the **OCCUPATION OF THE RUHR DISTRICT.** The British government refused to take part in it and in a note of Aug. 11 declared that the "Franco-Belgian action . . . was not a sanction authorized by the treaty." The Italian government, though technically associated, took no active part. The activities of the M.I.C.U.M. (mission interalliée de contrôle des usines et des mines), sent into the heart of Germany to supervise business enterprises under military protection, were not, according to the Franco-Belgian note (Jan. 10), to disturb the normal life of the civilian population. But the German government urged **passive resistance** on the people of the Ruhr and recklessly inflated the currency to defray the expense of supporting idle workers and compensating their employers. The French fomented a **separatist movement** in the Rhineland, which failed, after some bloodshed, to establish an independent buffer state.

Aug.–Sept. THE CORFU INCIDENT. Gen. Enrico Tellini and four members of his staff were assassinated (Aug. 27) while engaged in delimiting the Greek-Albanian frontier. The Italian government sent a stiff ultimatum to Greece (Aug. 29) and on Aug. 31 bombarded and occupied Corfu. Greece appealed to the League of Nations and agreed to accept the decision of the council of ambassadors. The latter sent a note to Greece embodying most of the Italian demands. Under considerable pressure from Britain and other powers, the Italians evacuated Corfu (Sept. 27).

Sept. 26. End of passive resistance in the Ruhr. German paper marks had sunk to the point of being worth less than the paper they were printed on. The effect of the financial collapse could not be confined to Germany. The French franc fell about 25 percent, and by November the French were willing to make an agreement directly with the Ruhr mine operators to secure deliveries. **Stanley Baldwin,** British prime minister, secured a promise of American cooperation to avert a more global economic and financial collapse.

Nov. 1, 2. Latvia, Lithuania, and Estonia concluded defensive treaties, which paved the way for close relations and the ultimate construction of a Baltic bloc (1934) (p. 715).

Nov. 30. Two committees were organized to investigate the German economic problem as it touched reparations.

1924, Jan. 25. France signed a treaty of mutual aid, in the event of unprovoked attack, with Czechoslovakia.

Jan. 27. Treaty with Yugoslavia, Fiume ceded to Italy.

April. A conference between Romania and Russia on Bessarabia broke down when Romania refused to hold a plebiscite.

April 9. THE DAWES PLAN. The committee under the chairmanship of the American **Charles G. Dawes** presented its report. Based on the slogan "Business, not politics," this Dawes Plan provided for a reorganization of the German Reichsbank under Allied supervision (p. 646).

1925, Feb. 9. The German government proposed **a Rhineland mutual guaranty pact.** The idea was taken up by the British, who were seeking some European arrangement to replace the Geneva protocol. **Aristide Briand,** who became French foreign minister in April 1925, accepted the suggestion on condition that Germany join the League.

July 26. France and Spain reached an agreement for common action in Morocco.

Aug. 25. The French **evacuated Düsseldorf, Duisburg,** and **Ruhrort.**

Oct. 5–16. LOCARNO CONFERENCE AND TREATIES (signed Dec. 1). The treaties included (1) **a treaty of mutual guaranty** of the Franco-German and Belgo-German frontiers (signed by Germany, France, Belgium, and by Great Britain and Italy as guarantors); (2) **arbitration treaties** between Germany and Poland, and Germany and Czechoslovakia; (3) **arbitration treaties** between Germany and Belgium, and Germany and France; (4) a **Franco-Polish** and a **Franco-Czechoslovakian treaty for mutual assistance** in case of attack by Germany. The effect of the treaties was far-reaching. For some years the "spirit of Locarno" gave the European powers a sense of security, though Britain had guaranteed only the western frontiers of Germany and Germany had not specifically bound itself to refrain from aggression to the east and south. Realizing this, France secured itself by alliances with Poland and the states of the Little Entente, and proceeded with a program of fortifying the German frontier (Maginot line) and reorganizing the army.

1926, March 17. The **admission of Germany to the League** was postponed because of complications raised by Spain and Brazil regarding seats on the council.

March 26. Romania and Poland concluded a treaty of alliance.

June 10. Spain announced withdrawal from the League but later rescinded this decision.

Aug. 7. Italy concluded a treaty of friendship with Spain. This was followed by similar treaties with Ethiopia (Aug. 2, 1928) and with Greece (Sept. 23, 1928).

Aug. 17. Yugoslavia concluded a treaty with Greece, settling the question of the Yugoslav **free zone at Saloniki.** Yugoslavia gained more extensive privileges at Saloniki in a later treaty (March 17, 1929). This was followed by a treaty of friendship between the two nations on March 27, 1929.

Sept. 8. Germany was admitted to the League and given a permanent seat on the council.

Sept. 18. Yugoslavia and Poland concluded a treaty of friendship.

1927, Jan. 31. End of the **Inter-Allied commission of military control** in Germany. Problems of German armament were henceforth put under jurisdiction of the League.

April 5. Italy and Hungary concluded a treaty of friendship, beginning the Fascist policy of rallying the "revisionist" states against the Little Entente and its supporter, France. With a similar treaty signed with Austria (Feb. 6, 1930), Mussolini began to assert himself more openly as the champion of revision of the peace treaties.

Nov. 11. Yugoslavia concluded a treaty of friendship with France, intended as a reply to the Italian advance in the Balkans.

1928, Jan. 29. Germany and Lithuania signed treaties regarding the frontiers and the status of Memel, and providing for arbitration.

Sept. 23. Greece signed a pact of friendship with Italy, a first step in restoring Greece's international position.

1929, Jan. 19. Appointment of the Young committee to reexamine the reparations problem and make final disposition of it.

Feb. 9. Litvinov protocol, an eastern pact for renunciation of war, signed at Moscow by the Soviet Union, Poland, Romania, Estonia, and Latvia.

April 12. Report of the Young committee, to which the Germans made some counterproposals.

June 7. THE YOUNG PLAN (p. 646).

Sept. 5–9. Briand proposed a European federal union. The plan was discussed by the League, but nothing came of it.

1930, Oct. 5–12. First Balkan conference at Athens. These conferences met annually for several years and were the basis for the **Balkan Entente.**

The years following 1930 were dominated by the great international **economic depression,** which almost ruined world trade and brought many nations to the verge of bankruptcy. The tension in domestic affairs led to a marked turn toward dictatorial forms of government and to widespread repudiation of financial and moral obligations in the effort to solve domestic problems. A number of less favored nations embarked frankly upon a policy of territorial expansion.

1931, March 21. Publication of a **project for a German-Austrian customs union.** This met at once with vigorous protest from the French government and its satellites, the protest resting on the claim that a customs union involved infringement of Austrian sovereignty and was therefore contrary to earlier obligations assumed by the Austrian government. Under pressure, Germany and Austria voluntarily renounced the project (Sept. 3) on the eve of an adverse decision by the World Court (Sept. 5).

May 11. The **failure of the Austrian Credit-Anstalt,** caused largely by the artificial and impracticable restrictions on commerce and finance imposed by the succession states of the old monarchy, precipitated an alarming financial and diplomatic crisis in Central Europe which threatened to involve the whole continent. A guaranty of the Credit-Anstalt's foreign debts by the Austrian government, backed by a foreign exchange credit from ten of the largest central banks (arranged through the Bank for International Settlements), failed to check the panic. Foreign funds were rapidly withdrawn from Germany. The Bank of France, actuated by the purely political motive of forcing the abandonment of the proposed customs union between Austria and Germany, refused financial support for the Austrian bank.

June 16. The Bank of England, despite difficulties at home, advanced 150 million schillings to the Austrian National Bank. Everywhere, from Austria to Australia, governments, banks, and corporations were exposed to immediate bankruptcy and were in terror of Fascist or Communist uprisings.

July 6. "Hoover moratorium" on intergovernmental debts (p. 646).

1932, June 16–July 9. LAUSANNE CONFERENCE (p. 647).

1933, Feb. In view of the danger from the new nationalist Germany and increased Hungarian irredentism, the **Little Entente was reorganized** and given a permanent council.

March 17. Conclusion of the Rome protocols among Italy, Austria, and Hungary. They provided for closer trade relations, consultation, and common policy, and in general represented the organization, under Fascist auspices, of a Danubian bloc to counterbalance the Little Entente and the French influence.

July. Romania and Russia concluded a nonaggression pact, involving tacit recognition of Romania's possession of Bessarabia. It was the direct result of Hitler's victory in Germany and Russia's preoccupation with the Far Eastern situation.

July 15. Conclusion of the four-power pact among Britain, France, Germany, and Italy; backed by Mussolini as an alternative to the League, but of no significance.

Sept. 15. Greece and Turkey signed a ten-year nonaggression pact. The two countries agreed to close cooperation in foreign policy.

Oct. 14. German withdrawal from the disarmament conference and from the League of Nations (Oct. 23).

1934, Jan. 26. Conclusion of the **German-Polish nonaggression pact,** the first break in the French alliance system.

Feb. 9. Conclusion of the Balkan pact among Turkey, Greece, Romania, and Yugoslavia. It was the counterpart of the Little Entente and was designed to protect the Balkans from encroachment by other powers. The great weakness of the pact was the absence of Bulgaria.

May 5. The Soviet Union's nonaggression pacts with Poland and the Baltic states were extended into ten-year agreements.

Sept. 18. The Soviet Union joined the League of Nations, another reflection of fear of the new Germany.

Dec. 19. Japan denounced the naval agreements of 1922 and 1930.

1935, Jan. 7. Franco-Italian agreement, dealing with conflicting interests in Africa, but meant to pave the way to Franco-Italian cooperation in the event of action by Germany. Italy was given more or less a free hand in Ethiopia, which it soon used by sending a large force to Eritrea (Feb. 23) (p. 797).

Jan. 13. Plebiscite in the Saar Basin, resulting in an overwhelming vote for union with Germany. Ninety percent of the electors voted for reunion with Germany, as against union with France or continuation of League administration.

March 16. GERMANY FORMALLY DENOUNCED THE CLAUSES OF THE TREATY OF VERSAILLES CONCERNING ITS DISARMAMENT, reintroduced conscription, and announced that its army would be increased to 36 divisions. This step was based on the failure of the other powers to disarm as provided in the peace treaties and on the steady growth of French and Soviet military establishments.

April 11. Stresa conference among Britain, France, and Italy, establishing a common front in view of the German action.

May 2. Franco-Russian Alliance concluded for five years. For some time the French government had labored not only to resuscitate its alliances with the Little Entente powers and Poland, but also to bring Germany, Poland, and Russia into an eastern pact guaranteeing the status quo. Both Germany and Poland evaded this suggestion, and after the announcement of German rearmament, the French government hurried into the alliance with Russia. Each promised the other aid in case of unprovoked aggression.

May 16. Conclusion of a **pact of mutual assistance between Russia and Czechoslovakia,** together with an air convention. By the terms Russia was obliged to come to the aid of Czechoslovakia in case of attack, provided that France did likewise. The agreement followed the breakdown of French efforts to engineer an eastern pact, and the conclusion of the Franco-Russian Alliance.

June 18. Anglo-German naval agreement by which Germany promised not to expand its navy beyond 35 percent of that of Britain. By this pact Hitler did much to reassure the British and drive a wedge into the Anglo-French entente.

Sept. THE ETHIOPIAN CRISIS. By this time Italian preparations for invasion were complete, and Mussolini no longer concealed the fact that only the annexation of Ethiopia would satisfy him. League action against Italy ended in failure (p. 797).

1936, March 7. DENUNCIATION OF THE LOCARNO PACTS AND GERMAN REOCCUPATION OF THE RHINELAND. The Germans took advantage of the Ethiopian crisis and pleaded the danger from the Franco-Russian combination. Acute international crisis, influenced by the British attitude not to resort to military action in defense of the treaties.

March 12. Great Britain, France, Belgium, and Italy denounced the German violation of the Locarno treaties, but no concrete action resulted (p. 647). Hitler's vague proposals for a new agreement came to naught, through his refusal to consider the extension of the agreement to Eastern Europe.

March 25. London **naval agreement** between Britain, France, and the U.S.

May 5. The **Italian army occupied Addis Ababa,** bringing to an end the Ethiopian war. **Complete collapse of the League as a political instrument.** Ethiopia, though a member of the League, was abandoned to its fate, and Italian aggression, like that of the Japanese in Manchuria, proved successful in the face of world opinion and even the application (though incomplete) of sanctions.

July 18. BEGINNING OF THE CIVIL WAR IN SPAIN (p. 691). The Spanish war divided Europe into Fascist and non-Fascist groups, with the intervention of Germany, Italy, and Russia.

Oct. 25. A GERMAN-ITALIAN PACT established the Berlin-Rome Axis, marking the division of Europe into contending groups, with the Axis powers pressing for changes in the status quo.

Nov. 9–12. Vienna conference of representatives of the Rome protocol states, marking the gradual consolidation of the Italian position in the Danube Basin.

Nov. 14. Germany denounced international control of its waterways. Only France, Czechoslovakia, and Yugoslavia protested.

Nov. 25. A **German-Japanese agreement,** followed by an Italian-Japanese agreement (Nov. 6, 1937), directed against communism and the Third International (the anti-Comintern pact).

1937, Jan. 2. An **agreement between Great Britain and Italy** for mutual respect of interests and rights in the Mediterranean and the maintenance of the independence and integrity of Spain. This failed to affect the situation materially.

Jan. 24. Signature of the **Bulgarian-Yugoslav treaty of friendship and perpetual peace,** bringing to an end the long antagonism between the two states.

March 25. Conclusion of a **nonaggression and neutrality pact** for five years **between Italy and Yugoslavia.** The latter agreed to recognize Italian possession of Ethiopia, while Italy made extensive trade concessions. The agreement brought to an end the long-standing feud between the two powers and reflected Premier Stoyadinovich's anxiety to establish a middle position between the French and the Italians.

Nov. 17. Visit of Lord Halifax, member of the British cabinet, **to Hitler,** with the aim of discovering the German objectives and, if possible, striking some peaceful settlement. Halifax returned deeply impressed with the magnitude of the German program, especially in Central and Eastern Europe.

1938, March. The **AUSTRO-GERMAN CRISIS** and the annexation of Austria by Germany (p. 704) created remarkably little tension in international relations. Italy, which might have been expected to offer stiff opposition, was so bound up with Spanish and Mediterranean affairs that Mussolini had to accept the inevitable as graciously as possible. France, at the moment, was in the midst of a cabinet crisis. The British appear to have been reconciled to the German move from the outset. Beyond a few half-hearted attempts to revive the Stresa front of 1935, the powers acquiesced and accepted the fait accompli.

March 16–19. The Polish-Lithuanian crisis (p. 720).

April 16. Conclusion of the **Anglo-Italian pact,** which had been under negotiation for some time. The British being eager to free themselves of Italian hostility in the Mediterranean and Middle East and Mussolini apparently desiring some counterweight to the oppressive friendship of Hitler, the two parties succeeded in liquidating their differences. Great Britain was to recognize Italian sovereignty over Ethiopia and use its influence to induce other states to do likewise. Italy was to respect Spanish territory and withdraw its "volunteers" at the end of the war (at that time regarded as very near). Italy was to desist from hostile propaganda in the Middle East, and both powers were to collaborate in maintaining the status quo in the Red Sea. The provisions of the agreement were to come into force as soon as the Spanish affair had been settled.

May 19–20. First Czech crisis (p. 705).

July 19–21. State visit of King George VI and Queen Elizabeth to Paris, clearly meant as a counterdemonstration of Anglo-French solidarity.

Aug. 21–23. Meeting of the Little Entente statesmen at Bled (Yugoslavia). The three powers **recognized Hungary's right to rearm** and arranged for the conclusion of nonaggression pacts.

Relations between Germany and Czechoslovakia grew seriously strained again in August and produced a **second crisis in September.** that brought the powers to the verge of war.

Sept. 7–29. Height of the **GERMAN-CZECH CRISIS** (p. 705). The Sudeten leaders broke off negotiations with the government (Sept. 7) after an affray at Moravska Ostrava. Discussions were resumed (Sept. 10), but disorders, provoked by extremists, became more and more frequent. On Sept. 12 Hitler, in a speech at Nürnberg, first demanded in no uncertain terms that the Sudeten Germans be given the **right of self-determination.** This address was the signal for widespread disorders and the proclamation of martial law by the government (Sept. 13). Henlein and other leaders fled across the frontier (Sept. 15). To meet this dangerous situation, Prime Minister Chamberlain, in agreement with the French government, proposed a personal conference to Hitler.

Sept. 15. CHAMBERLAIN-HITLER CONFERENCE AT BERCHTESGADEN. The German chancellor baldly stated his demand for annexation of the German areas of Czechoslovakia on the basis of self-determination, and did not conceal his readiness to risk a war to attain his end. Chamberlain returned to London, as did Runciman from Prague. On Sept. 18 Premier Édouard Daladier and Georges Bonnet (French foreign minister) arrived in London. Decision reached to advise and urge the Czech government to accept Hitler's terms, promising an international guaranty of the rump state. After long deliberations, the **Czech government** (Sept. 20) suggested arbitration on the basis of the German-Czech Locarno treaty of 1925. This proposal was at once rejected by Britain and France as inadequate. After further pressure and threats of desertion by France and Britain, the **Prague government finally yielded** (Sept. 21), despite the fact that Poland and Hungary had both put in additional claims for territory. The **Hodza cabinet resigned** (Sept. 22), and a new government was formed by **Gen. Jan Sirovy,** a popular military leader.

Sept. 22–23. CHAMBERLAIN'S SECOND VISIT TO HITLER AT GODESBERG. Further demands of the German chancellor: surrender of the predominantly German territories at once, without removal or destruction of military or economic establishments; plebiscites to be held in areas with large German minority by Nov. 25, under German-Czech or international supervision. These terms were regarded by Chamberlain as quite unacceptable, and as an unwarranted extension of the original German demands.

Sept. 24–29. ACUTE INTERNATIONAL CRISIS, the most serious since 1918. The Czech government ordered full mobilization, and the Great Powers took precautions of every kind. Italy, however, came out more and more definitely on the German side. Daladier and Bonnet again came to London (Sept. 26), and the decision was evidently reached to support Czechoslovakia in resisting the extended German demands. Chamberlain appealed to Hitler for a conference so that the cession of Sudeten territory, already agreed on by all, might be effected by discussion, not by force. **President Roosevelt** also appealed to Hitler and urged a conference (Sept. 27). Finally (Sept. 28) Hitler, apparently persuaded by Mussolini (to whom both Chamberlain and Roosevelt had appealed), agreed to a conference.

Sept. 29. THE MUNICH CONFERENCE AND AGREEMENT. Hitler, Ribbentrop, Mussolini, Ciano, Chamberlain, and Daladier conferred during the afternoon and evening, Czechoslovakia being unrepresented. The agreement (dated Sept. 29) was actually signed just after midnight. Hitler secured about all that he had demanded: evacuation to take place between Oct. 1 and Oct. 10, under conditions arranged by an international commission, which should also determine the plebiscite areas. Britain and France undertook to guarantee the new frontiers of Czechoslovakia against unprovoked aggression. When the

Polish and Hungarian minorities questions were solved, Germany and Italy would give a like guaranty. The Czech government felt impelled to acquiesce in this settlement on Sept. 30.

The statesmen, returning from Munich, received warm ovations from their peoples, and there could be no doubt that the will to peace was strong, not only in Britain and France, but also in Italy and Germany. The crisis, however, soon led to much dispute. Many felt that the democratic powers had not only deserted the one democratic outpost in Central Europe, but that they had suffered a tremendous defeat, which might have been avoided if the strong stand taken just before the Munich conference had been maintained. Others believed that the German case in Czechoslovakia was too strong to justify war against Germany, and that Hitler, far from bluffing, was determined to march. In any event, the final outcome established **German hegemony in Central Europe** and opened the way to domination of the entire Danubian area.

THE SETTLEMENTS:

(1) *GERMAN.* The occupation was carried through as scheduled at Munich, taking over all the vital Czech frontier fortresses. The predominantly German regions were determined by the Austrian census of 1910. The international commission caused Germany no trouble, and in the end there were no plebiscites. Germany acquired about 10,000 square miles of Czech territory, with about 3.5 million inhabitants, of whom about 700,000 were Czechs. By agreement with the Czechoslovak government (Nov. 20, 1938), Germany was given **rights to a highway across Moravia to Vienna, and to a canal connecting the Oder and the Danube Rivers.** The truncated Czechoslovak state, without defensible frontiers, became of necessity a satellite of the Reich.

(2) *POLISH.* During the crisis the Polish government had renewed its long-standing **claims to the Teschen region.** On Sept. 29 a virtual ultimatum was submitted to Prague, to which the Czech government yielded. On Oct. 2 Polish forces occupied the Teschen area, and Czechoslovakia lost about 400 square miles of territory with some 240,000 inhabitants (less than 100,000 Poles).

(3) *HUNGARIAN.* The Hungarian **claims to Slovakia** were to be settled by negotiation, and delegates of the two countries met on Oct. 9. Agreement proved impossible, and serious clashes took place on the frontier. Ultimately the matter was adjusted by joint decision of Germany and Italy. Hungary received a broad strip of southern Slovakia and Ruthenia, almost 5,000 square miles, with a population of 1 million. The Hungarian claim, supported by Poland, for a common frontier with Poland was denied.

As a result of Hitler's immense victory, the **Little Entente disappeared as an important factor** in international relations. What remained of Czechoslovakia fell entirely under German influence. Much the same was true of Hungary and the other Danubian countries. The Czech alliances with Russia and France became all but valueless, and the Franco-Russian alliance of 1935 lost most of its significance. Germany now emerged as the strongest power on the Continent.

Nov. 16. The **Anglo-Italian agreement of April 16 was put into force,** despite the fact that the conditions of enforcement had been only very imperfectly fulfilled.

Nov. 26. Poland and Russia suddenly renewed their nonaggression pact. Poland, directly exposed to the German advance eastward, now required closer relations with Russia and, indeed, made efforts to build up a barrier of Baltic and Balkan states to join with Poland in the interest of the status quo.

Nov. 30. Anti-French demonstrations in the Italian chamber of deputies (demands for Corsica and Tunisia, which were then taken up by the government-controlled press) ushered in a period of acute **tension between France and Italy,** which became even more accentuated with the Fascist victories in Spain.

Dec. 6. France and Germany concluded a pact by which they guaranteed the inviolability of the existing frontier and provided for consultation with the aim of settling any disputes pacifically.

Dec. 17. An Italian note to France declared the agreement of 1935 invalid because ratifications had not been exchanged. France rejected this argument.

1939, March. The **SLOVAK CRISIS** and the **ANNIHILATION OF THE CZECHOSLOVAK STATE** (p. 705). None of the great powers made a move to check the German annexation of the rump Czech state or the Hungarian conquest of Ruthenia (Carpatho-Ukraine). Yet Hitler's action served to disillusion those who held that his aims were restricted to German territories.

March 21. German annexation of Memel (p. 701).

April 7. Italian invasion and conquest of Albania (p. 722).

April 15. Letter of President Roosevelt to Hitler and Mussolini asking assurances against aggression on 31 named nations and suggesting discussions on reduction of armaments.

May 12. Announcement of an **Anglo-Turkish mutual assistance pact.**

May 22. Conclusion of a political and **military alliance between Germany and Italy** marking the full development of the Rome-Berlin Axis.

June 17. Sweden, Norway, and Finland rejected a German offer of a bilateral nonaggression pact, preferring to maintain a rigid neutrality. Denmark, Estonia, and Latvia, however, accepted the German proposal.

June–Aug. Triangular negotiations among Britain, France, and the Soviet Union for a "peace front" to block further Nazi expansion. The Soviets insisted on a complete alliance and military convention, in addition to clear guarantees for the Baltic states. Negotiations dragged on through the summer and were marked by growing Soviet distrust. Eventually the Soviets insisted on the right to send troops through Poland in the event of German aggression. Since the Poles themselves objected violently to such an arrangement, a deadlock ensued.

Aug. 20–Sept. 1. THE DANZIG-POLISH CRISIS. After months of agitation and recrimination, punctuated by incidents on the Danzig-Polish frontier, the long-anticipated crisis broke when Albert Forster, Nazi leader in Danzig, announced publicly that the hour of deliverance was near. At the same time the world was startled by the conclusion of a trade treaty between Germany and Soviet Russia.

Aug. 21. The trade treaty was followed by the announcement that Germany and Russia were about to conclude a nonaggression pact. Coming after months of negotiation, this move was regarded in the West as a demonstration of Soviet perfidy. Discussion of Russia's inclusion in a peace front was at once dropped. In Britain and France as well as in Germany military preparations were initiated, the Germans concentrating forces in Slovakia as well as along the Corridor.

Aug. 22. The British government reiterated its pledges to Poland, but at the same time appealed to Germany for a truce in Eastern Europe and negotiation of German claims.

Aug. 23. The **German-Russian pact** was signed at Moscow by the German foreign minister, Ribbentrop, artisan of the anti-Comintern pact of 1936. It provided not only for abstention by either party from attack on the other, but for neutrality by either party if the other were attacked by a third power. A secret protocol attached to the pact provided for the partition of Poland, while Finland, Estonia, and Latvia were assigned to the Soviet sphere of influence.

Aug. 24. President Roosevelt appealed to King Victor Emmanuel, to Hitler, and to President Moscicki of Poland, suggesting direct negotiations between Germany and Poland, arbitration, or conciliation. Poland agreed to conciliation by a third party.

The British parliament met in special session and voted the government practically dictatorial powers; at the same time **Britain and Poland signed a pact of mutual assistance.** Poland began to call up reserves.

Aug. 25. In discussion with the British ambassador, Hitler renewed his demand for a free hand against Poland. Roosevelt again appealed to Hitler to seek a peaceful solution.

Aug. 26. Premier Daladier of France appealed to Hitler, receiving in reply (Aug. 27) a plea for German-French peace but also a reiteration of the German demands on Poland.

Aug. 28. The British government replied to Hitler, again urging a truce and repeating former warnings of British action in case of German aggression. British shipping was recalled from the Baltic and Mediterranean. In Germany emergency rationing was introduced. On all sides military preparations were accelerated.

Aug. 29. Hitler reiterated to Britain his extreme demands on Poland and refused to negotiate until these demands were met. He called for arrival of a Polish plenipotentiary in Berlin within 24 hours.

Aug. 30. The **Poles decreed partial mobilization**, while in Germany a six-man "cabinet council for defense of the Reich" was set up under the presidency of Hermann Goering.

Aug. 31. The German government published a **16-point proposal to Poland.** This was of rather moderate tenor, but before it could be transmitted to Warsaw, communications were cut off. On this same day the Russian Supreme Soviet ratified the pact with Germany, and Hitler, claiming his proposals to Poland had been rejected, gave the order to march.

Sept. 1. GERMAN ATTACK ON POLAND on land and in the air. Forster proclaimed the **reunion of Danzig and Germany.** Britain and France mobilized but expressed readiness to negotiate if German forces were withdrawn from Poland. Italy declared its intention of remaining neutral.

Sept. 2. Italy proposed a five-power conference to discuss the situation, but Britain refused negotiation so long as the Germans remained on Polish soil. Hitler having failed to reply to the Anglo-French notes, these two powers sent an ultimatum, to which Hitler replied by a note blaming Britain for encouraging the Poles in a policy of persecution and provocation. The German government rejected the Anglo-French demands for withdrawal from Poland.

Sept. 3. BRITAIN AND FRANCE DECLARED WAR ON GERMANY, thus signaling the second great war of the 20th century.

(To p. 800)

5. THE BRITISH ISLES

a. GREAT BRITAIN

(From p. 489)

Monarchs: George V (r. 1910–36); Edward VIII (r. 1936); George VI (r. 1936–52).

Prime Ministers: Herbert H. Asquith (1908–15, Liberal); Herbert H. Asquith (1915–16, coalition); David Lloyd George (1916–19, coalition); David Lloyd George (1919–22, coalition); Andrew Bonar Law (1922–23, Conservative); Stanley Baldwin (1923–24, Conservative); J. Ramsay MacDonald (1924, Labour); Stanley Baldwin (1924–29, Conservative); J. Ramsay MacDonald (1929–31, Labour); J. Ramsay MacDonald (1931–35, National); Stanley Baldwin (1935–37, National); Neville Chamberlain (1937–40, National); Winston Churchill (1940–45, coalition).

Impact of World War I. The most significant results of Britain's wartime experience were the **expansion of state planning** and **disillusionment.** Beginning with the **Defense of the Realm Act** (1914) and continued through the creation of the **War Committee** (1915), British leaders recognized that only central control could lead to victory. This was especially true of the economic sector, where the creation of the ministries of munitions (July 2, 1915) and blockade (Feb. 23, 1916)

aided government management of shipbuilding, food production and distribution, and the supply of wool and cotton. **War socialism** placed munitions, coal, iron, steel, and railroads under state control. This also brought trade unions into government planning activities. Such control was also extended over manpower through the **compulsory military service bill** (Jan. 6, 1916) and the creation of a ministry of labour (1916). Finally, the government became increasingly involved in influencing public opinion, including the distribution of newsreels and **propaganda films** that contributed to the later popularity of commercial cinema. Gradually, the nation became accustomed to such extensive state planning, shaping the course of interwar Britain.

Disillusionment was evident primarily in cultural life, as in the plays of **Noel Coward** (1899–1973), the novels of **Aldous Huxley** (1894–1963), and the poetry of **T. S. Eliot** (1888–1965). Disillusionment bred a search for new styles, witnessed in the stream-of-consciousness works of **Virginia Woolf** (1882–1941) and **James Joyce** (1882–1941). Another impact of the war was a loosening of moral standards, personified by the flapper, and seen in the spread of jazz, the popularity of commercialized sports and movies, and an increase in sexual freedom. **Increased wages and shorter work hours** after the war allowed a greater number of Britons to spend more time in leisure activities, in which cinemas, pubs, and dance halls came to share top billing. In the 1930s intellectual attention turned more to social concerns, as the condition of England became a theme to such authors as J. B. Priestley (1894–1984) and George Orwell (1903–50).

Popular authors throughout the interwar years included Thomas Hardy (1840–1928), Joseph Conrad (1857–1924), Arthur Conan Doyle (1859–1930), James M. Barrie (1860–1937), Rudyard Kipling (1865–1936), H. G. Wells (1866–1946), Hugh Walpole (1884–1941), D. H. Lawrence (1885–1930), and Katherine Mansfield (1888–1923). The greatest popular success was reserved for the authors of thrillers, especially John Buchan (1875–1940), and detective stories, like Agatha Christie (1890–1975).

Great Britain's losses in the First World War were almost 1 million killed and over 2 million wounded. The total expense exceeded £8 billion, and the burden of domestic and foreign debt was ten times what it had been in 1914. Britain was faced with the problem of returning soldiers to industry and introducing social reforms loudly demanded by the laboring classes, and confronted at the same time by increased competition in foreign trade. In Ireland, India, Egypt, and Palestine it faced almost insoluble problems. Even the self-governing dominions demonstrated enhanced national feeling and reluctance to be committed to any share in future European wars.

Economics. As women were forced out of wartime employment to make way for demobilized soldiers (rapid demobilization between 1919 and 1920), immediate economic disaster was averted by the economic boom of 1919–20. The government responded by returning to prewar laissez-faire policies, resulting in inflation, strikes, and wage increases. But Britain had lost its position in the world economy and could not maintain this boom, which failed in late 1921. The recession was triggered by a decrease in government expenditures, increased taxes, and the overproduction of primary products. The old specter of class war loomed on the horizon as trade unions threatened a general strike. The government responded with the Emergency Powers Act (1920), restoring its wartime emergency authority. In addition, the government subsidized the building of more than 200,000 houses, making housing another social service of the government. Such assistance was continued by subsequent governments, and by 1928 houses built with public funding made up 40 percent of the total housing construction.

Aside from the economy, Britain's other pressing problem in the immediate postwar years was a solution to the Irish question (p. 682). The result in domestic politics was a Unionist defection from Lloyd George's government, causing its collapse (Oct. 19, 1922), and a weak Conservative government (general election, Nov. 15, 1922), bolstered by a split between the Liberal followers of Asquith and Lloyd George. **The Labour Party became for the first time His Majesty's Opposition.** The interwar years were dominated by the insecurity of three-party contests.

1918. Reforms of 1918. The **Representation of Peoples Act** widened suffrage by abolishing practically all property qualifications for men and **by enfranchising women over 30 who met minimum property qualifications.** The enfranchisement of this latter group was accepted as recognition of the contribution made by women defense workers.

An **Education Act** made elementary education compulsory between the ages of 5 and 14. Children who left school at 14 were supposed to attend continuation schools for 320 hours a year until they were 18. Those who continued their regular schooling until they were 16 were under no further obligation. Furthermore, child labor was sharply limited, halting a large number of children from leaving school at age 12 and becoming unemployed because of lack of skills.

The **Labour Party adopted a new constitution** designed to recruit more members, admitting local Labour parties (constituency parties), which individuals could join without first becoming affiliated with a trade union or a socialist group.

Dec. 14. The Khaki election. The coalition government won a huge majority on a platform promising punishment of the German "war criminals," full payment by the defeated powers of the costs of war, and the prevention of dumping of foreign goods in Great Britain. These promises greatly hampered Lloyd George's freedom of action at the Paris peace conference (p. 671).

1919. Parliament passed the **Arbitration Act,** calling for unions and employers to submit to court decisions. The only important application of this act occurred a year later when the Transport and General Workers Union (dockers), led by Ernest Bevin, won a favorable court settlement.

Nov. 28. Lady Astor became the first woman elected to the House of Commons.

1920. The **British Board of Film Censors** was established.

Oxford University allowed women to take degrees.

Feb. The first **public broadcasting station** was opened by G. Marconi at Writtle.

March 31. Parliament decreed the official **disestablishment of the Anglican Church in Wales.** This was previously legislated in 1911 but postponed due to the war; the Welsh Anglican Church was now organized under its own archbishop.

Aug. 8. British Labour organizations appointed a Council of Action to arrange a general strike if Britain declared war on the USSR.

1921, March 3. The **Emergency Unemployment Act** increased unemployment payments to 20 shillings a week for men and 18 shillings for women. There were at this time almost 1 million unemployed. Lloyd George's reforms in unemployment insurance compromised the insurance principle itself by advancing payments against future contributions—the precursor to welfare.

March 28. The Labour Party refused to affiliate with the Communists.

March 31. Great coal strike began as government control of the mines ended and proposals for nationalization had been rejected. The Triple Alliance of miners, railway, and transport workers all went on strike, but railway and transport workers returned to work on April 15, known in labor history as "Black Friday." The strike ended July 1 when the miners accepted a government offer of subsidy and increased wages.

1922. The **British Broadcasting Company** was licensed as a monopoly, and nationalized in 1926 as the British Broadcasting Corporation (BBC).

Lady Rhondda was permitted to take a seat in the House of Lords by the Committee of Privileges, but this judgment was later reversed. During the same year, Marie Stopes held a series of meeting in Queens' Hall, London, advocating **birth control.** Discussion of women's sexuality increased.

Oct. 17. Unemployed workers in Glasgow began a **hunger march** on London.

1923, Oct. 1–Nov. 8. Imperial Conference. This recognized the right of the dominions to make treaties with foreign powers.

July 18. The **Matrimonial Causes Act** gave women equality in divorce suits.

Dec. 6. A **general election** to pass upon Baldwin's scheme for a protective tariff to relieve unemployment resulted in a heavy loss for the Conservatives and a decided gain for Labour.

1924, Jan. 22. With Asquith's refusal to form a coalition government with the Conservatives, **J. Ramsay MacDonald** formed Britain's **first Labour government.** His largely inexperienced cabinet was unable to deal effectively with unemployment and other domestic issues. Their one success was the **Housing Act,** which followed the pattern of the Conservative housing program.

Feb. 1. De jure recognition of Soviet Russia.

Oct. 29. The **general election** turned out a great victory for the Conservatives, owing largely to the so-called **Zinoviev letter** (Oct. 25), by which the Third International allegedly instructed British subjects to provoke revolution.

Nov. 21. The new government **denounced earlier commercial treaties with Russia** (Aug. 8).

1925, May 1. Cyprus (annexed in 1914) **made a crown colony.**

May 5. Britain returned to the **gold standard,** overvaluing the pound and making it more difficult to sell British-made goods abroad.

July 31. The **Unemployment Insurance Act.**

1926. In a move to expedite the creation of a "national grid" for the efficient transfer of electric power from one area of the country to another, the government, under the auspices of the **Central Electricity Board,** took over the wholesale distribution of electric power, but not its generation or retail distribution.

Adoption was legalized.

May 1. Strike of coal miners, a reaction to a commission report adverse to the continuation of government subsidy and mineowners' plans to slash wages.

May 3–13. GENERAL STRIKE, in sympathy with coal miners. It involved about 2.5 million of the 6 million trade union members in Great Britain. Volunteers, largely from the upper classes, maintained essential transport and other services. The Trade-Union Council called off the strike on May 13 with an understanding that negotiations on wages and hours would be resumed. But the miners' union continued to strike until Nov. 19, when it surrendered unconditionally. Baldwin's government responded with the **Trade Unions Act of 1927.** The act declared all general strikes illegal and prohibited the use of trade union dues for political purposes unless so requested in writing by a member. As a result, union membership dropped almost 50 percent.

Oct. 19–Nov. 18. Imperial Conference. Its report declared that Great Britain and the dominions "are autonomous communities within the British Empire, equal in status, in no way subordinate one to another in any aspect of their domestic or external affairs, though united by a common allegiance to the crown and freely associated as members of the British Commonwealth of Nations."

1928. Sir Alexander Fleming discovered penicillin.

The **Revised Prayer Book of the Church of England** was rejected by Parliament, sparking controversy over Parliament's power to dictate rules to the Anglican Church.

July 2. An act of parliament extended the **franchise to women** on the same terms as men.

1929. Presbyterian Churches in Scotland united, creating the **Church of Scotland.**

The **Local Government Act** reorganized county councils, giving them wider powers, and reformed the ancient Poor Law structure by transferring the care of the poor to local government bodies. Relief was given directly through public assistance committees of the local councils. Local taxes on much agricultural land and industry were wholly or partially lifted to encourage greater stability, with the loss of revenue made up by central government grants out of general taxation.

May 30. In the **general election** the Labour Party was victorious, securing 288 seats, against 260 for the Conservatives.

Oct. The **Depression** hurt Britain less severely than other countries, but the collapse of raw-material prices quickly closed down many of Britain's export markets (by 1931 exports stood at a little more than half what they were in 1929); the loss of confidence shut off new investment; and unemployment, persistently high, rose from over a million to 2.5 million by the end of 1930.

The Labour government responded with a coal mines act in 1930 that shortened the work day and reorganized the industry, the Greenwood Housing Act (1930), and the creation of agricultural marketing boards. A bill to nationalize London transport failed, however, as did Labour attempts to repeal the Trade Union Act of 1927.

The National government responded principally with the **Protective Tariff Acts.** Aside from a few large subsidies to the shipbuilding industry, for example, the government preferred a policy of benevolent support of industry's own recovery scheme. Parliament did pass the **Special Areas Act (1934),** however, which provided grants and public works projects to economically distressed areas.

After 1933 Britain witnessed a **gradual recovery,** which contributed in the middle of the decade to a **rise in living standards** for those with work and a **drop in the unemployment rate.** The index of industrial production stood 75 percent higher in 1935–38 than in 1910–13.

1931, Feb. Oswald Mosley broke from the Labour Party to form the New Party but failed in the general elections. In 1932 he founded the **British Union of Fascists.**

July. Report of the **May Committee** of financial experts. They claimed the deficit for the fiscal year would be over £100,000 sterling and suggested drastic economies, including a cut in the dole to the unemployed. This report caused **a split in the cabinet,** the majority rejecting the proposals as too burdensome to the workers. There were, at this time, over 2 million unemployed.

Aug. 24. Resignation of the MacDonald cabinet, the result of the financial crisis and disagreement as to remedies.

Aug. 25–Oct. 27. A NATIONAL COALITION GOVERNMENT formed to include Conservatives, Liberals, and Labour members, with MacDonald as prime minister. The Labour Party opposed this coalition and expelled those of its leaders who favored it. MacDonald,

Snowden, Thomas, and others formed a new **National Labour group.** Henderson became leader of the old Labour Party.

Sept. 10. The government's measures in the face of worldwide depression (cuts in unemployment pay and government salaries, a rise in taxes, and a balanced budget) sparked **riots in London and Glasgow.** Sailors in Invergordon also mutinied over pay cuts (Sept. 15).

Sept. 21. England forced to abandon the gold standard. The pound sterling fell from par (\$4.86) to \$3.49.

Oct. 27. A **general election** gave the coalition government a majority of almost 500 seats over the combined opposition.

Dec. The **STATUTE OF WESTMINSTER** passed by Parliament, giving force of law to the changes in empire relations worked out by the Imperial Conference in 1926 (p. 734).

1932. Sir Thomas Beecham founded the **London Philharmonic Orchestra.**

Feb. 29. Protective Tariff Acts, including a new "corn law," which guaranteed British farmers about \$1 a bushel for a specified quantity of homegrown wheat. Abandonment of free trade.

July 21–Aug. 20. Ottawa Imperial Economic Conference. A series of agreements for a carefully limited measure of imperial preference led to the resignation (Sept. 28) of the free-trade Liberal members of the cabinet, who went into opposition under the lead of **Sir Herbert Samuel.** The Liberals who remained in the government were led by **Sir John Simon.**

1933, June 12–July 27. World Economic Conference at London. The failure of this conference led the British government to extend its neomercantilist policy of economic nationalism. Campaign to "buy British." Managed paper currency; control of foreign exchanges through an exchange equalization fund. Gradual but slow recovery took place.

1934. A highly publicized **Peace Ballot** demonstrated overwhelming support in Britain for disarmament and the League of Nations.

1935, June 7. Reconstruction of the cabinet, following a general election that continued the majority of the coalition government. **Stanley Baldwin succeeded MacDonald as prime minister,** and Sir Samuel Hoare became foreign secretary.

Nov. In a **general election** the Labour Party gained 95 seats, but the Unionists retained a majority of 385.

1936. John Maynard Keynes published *General Theory of Employment, Interest and Money,* advocating government interference in the economy to moderate the business cycle. His theories were not incorporated into government policy in Great Britain, however.

Allen Lane founded **Penguin Books,** starting the **paperback revolution.**

As a result of the collaboration of Guglielmo Marconi with the Russian-born researcher **Isaac Schoenberg,** the world's first **regular television service** was opened by the BBC at Alexandra Palace.

April 30. The government announced plans for the construction of 38 warships, the largest building program since 1921.

Dec. 10. Abdication of Edward VIII, the first voluntary abdication in British history. The Baldwin ministry and the dominion governments had refused to consent to a morganatic marriage between the king and **Mrs. Wallis Warfield Simpson,** an American-born woman whose second divorce had not yet become final. Edward, apparently at odds with his ministers on other matters also (social policy, etc.), insisted on his right to shape his own life and abdicated rather than abandon his plan. He became **Duke of Windsor** and in June 1937 married Mrs. Simpson in France.

1937. Billy Butlin set up the **first commercial holiday camp** at Skegness, as traveling during annual holidays and regular bank holidays became more popular.

Lewis Ltd. signed the first **comprehensive wages agreement** in Britain.

May 28. Neville Chamberlain became prime minister on the retirement of Stanley Baldwin. Chamberlain had been chancellor of the exchequer. He was confronted at the outset with a most difficult and dangerous European situation, which overshadowed all issues of purely domestic character. Abandoning the rather aimless, opportunist policy of Baldwin, Chamberlain held that peace, in order to be secured, would have to be definitely worked for. He therefore sought to reach agreements with Germany and Italy, even at the expense of considerable concessions. This became known as the **policy of appeasement.**

July 8. Publication of the Peel Report recommending the ending of the **Palestine mandate** and the division of the country into Arab and Jewish states, Britain to retain a mandate only over Jerusalem, Bethlehem, and a corridor to the sea. Parliament refused to commit itself to this scheme, and the opposition to it on the part of both Jews and Arabs resulted in its reconsideration (p. 763).

July 23. The **Matrimonial Causes Act** facilitated divorce proceedings in England and Wales.

Nov. 17. Visit of Lord Halifax to Chancellor Hitler at Berchtesgaden. This was the first concrete step in the policy of appeasement.

1938. The British Ministry of Labour Committee recommended **a week's holiday with pay as a national standard.**

Feb. 20. Resignation of Anthony Eden, British foreign secretary and outstanding champion of the system of collective security and action. He resigned in protest against the prime minister's determination to seek an agreement with Italy without waiting for a settlement of the Spanish problem. Lord Halifax became foreign secretary in his place.

April 25. Conclusion of a three-year **agreement with Ireland,** bringing to an end a feud that had continued for years (p. 684).

Dec. 1. Opening of a **"national register"** for war service. This was entirely voluntary but was looked upon as an important item of preparedness. After the crisis of 1938 the British government pushed its preparations to the utmost, going so far as to buy large numbers of planes in the U.S.

1939, March 31. British-French pledge to Poland (p. 720), marking the end of the policy of appeasement. After the Italian conquest of Albania, guarantees were given to Greece and Romania, a mutual assistance pact was concluded with Turkey, and the British government finally embarked on the arduous task of bringing Russia into the "peace front."

April 27. The **British government introduced conscription** for men 20–21 years old, in order to increase the forces by 300,000 men.

May 17. The British published a **new plan for Palestine** (p. 763), after abortive negotiations with both Arabs and Jews.

King George and Queen Elizabeth **arrived in Canada** for an extended visit, followed (June 8–11) by a **visit to the U.S.** obviously intended to strengthen Anglo-Saxon ties in the face of threatening war in Europe.

Aug. 20–Sept. 1. The Danzig-Polish crisis.

Aug. 24. Parliament approved the **Emergency Powers Bill.**

Sept. 3. OUTBREAK OF WAR BETWEEN GREAT BRITAIN AND GERMANY.

Nov. 17. Britain and France agreed to coordinate their economic efforts.

1940, Jan. Food rationing began.

Feb. 21. Women were granted old-age pensions at 60 years of age.

May 13. Churchill's "blood and toil" speech rallied the British war effort and won confidence in his government.

May 22. Parliament granted the government wide emergency powers.

Aug. 23. The first all-night raid on London began the "blitz." By Sept. 7 **intensified bombing of London** raised the casualties to 300–600 a day killed and 1,000–3,000 injured.

1941. Great Britain became increasingly dependent for arms, food, and raw materials upon the U.S. as the German sea and air blockade was extended. President Roosevelt had proposed (Nov. 1940) an equal division of the American arms output between the U.S. and Britain. British credit in dollar exchange, which had amounted to $6.5 billion, was exhausted by Jan. 1941, however, and British purchases had to be curtailed. This situation was eased by the signing (March 11, 1941) of the **LEND-LEASE ACT** (p. 804). The first shipments of food for Britain (April 16) came just in time to avert a critical shortage there. Between April and Dec. 1941, 1 million tons of foodstuffs reached Britain from the U.S.

March. Pacifists, including leading Communists, organized a People's Convention to end the war.

Dec. 9. The **National Service Bill** lowered the age of call-up to 18.5 and rendered single women aged 20–30 liable to military service.

1942. Beveridge Report. This report, authored by Sir William Beveridge, called for an **extension of social services** from "cradle to grave" and for the systematic maintenance of full employment as a postwar government policy.

1943, March. Growing support in by-elections for candidates of the **Commonwealth Party,** founded by Richard Acland, indicated dissatisfaction with the government's social policy. Churchill's broadcast of March 22 advocating a four-year plan for postwar reconstruction revived the government's popularity.

Nov. 11. Lord Woolton was appointed the first **minister of reconstruction.**

1944, April 11. As social conditions created growing discontent, Aneurin Bevan began a fight for the annulment of powers conferred on the minister of labour for dealing with strikes. *(To p. 845)*

b. IRELAND

(From p. 490)

1914, Aug. 8. Press censorship decreed, remaining in effect until 1922.

1916, April 21. Sir Roger Casement landed on the Irish coast from a German submarine to start a rebellion.

April 24–29. The **EASTER REBELLION,** led by Patrick H. Pearse and the Irish Republican Brotherhood, despite the failure of German aid. After a week of fighting the British suppressed the insurrection (May 1). Several of the leaders were tried and executed (May 3). Casement was hanged on Aug. 3.

1917, April. The **Ford Motor Co.** began construction at Cork of a factory for the production of Fordson tractors.

June 15. Amnesty granted the rebels of 1916.

Oct. 25–27. A Sinn Fein convention at Dublin adopted a constitution for the Irish Republic and elected **Eamon De Valera president.**

1918, March 6. Death of John Redmond, leader of the Irish Nationalist group in the British Parliament.

April 18. Adoption of **conscription for Ireland.** The Irish Nationalists thereupon deserted the British Parliament and organized opposition to the measure (one-day general strike, except Ulster, April 23), forcing its abandonment (June 25).

May 18. De Valera and other Sinn Fein leaders again arrested.

Dec. 14. Great victory of the **Sinn Fein** candidates in the elections for the British parliament.

1919, Jan. 21. The **Sinn Fein members** of Parliament, having decided not to attend, **organized a parliament** of their own for Ireland (the dáil Éireann) and declared Irish independence.

Jan. 25–Feb. 20. Workers of the Federation of Engineering and Shipbuilding Trades in Belfast went on strike for a 44-hour work week. Shipyards, gas works, electricity stations, tramways, and the like, all closed. The strike ended when workers won a 47-hour work week.

April 14–25. General strike in Limerick resulted in the creation of the Limerick soviet.

July 4. Sinn Fein and other organizations **suppressed** in Tipperary and later in other troubled areas. Thus began a war between the Sinn Fein and British forces: attacks on the constabulary, arson, and so on.

Sept. 12. The **dáil was suppressed** and the headquarters of the Sinn Fein party raided.

1920, May 15. Arrival of British reinforcements (Black and Tans) and initiation of **a policy of reprisal.** There followed several months of ferocious conflict.

May 23. Railway workers in Dublin launched a **munitions strike,** which spread soon to most of the country. It was extended to the transportation of armed troops as well. Workers resumed normal handling of government traffic as an alternative to government closure of the railways on Dec. 21.

Dec. 23. PASSAGE OF THE GOVERNMENT OF IRELAND ACT by the British Parliament: **Northern Ireland** and **Southern Ireland** each to have its own parliament, and each to retain representatives in the British Parliament. A **Council for Ireland,** representing the two parts, was to attempt to effect common action in common affairs.

1921, May 13. Elections: In the north the Government of Ireland Act was generally accepted and the new system went into effect. In Southern Ireland the **Sinn Fein won 124 out of 128 seats.**

June 28. The parliament for Southern Ireland was opened, but only the four delegates not members of the Sinn Fein attended. The Sinn Feiners declared themselves the dáil Eireann and rejected the settlement proposed.

July 11. Britain established a truce with Sinn Fein that was rejected by the dáil (Aug. 23).

July 14–21. Conferences of De Valera and **Sir James Craig** (representing Northern Ireland) with Lloyd George and other British representatives. De Valera rejected offers of dominion status for Ireland.

Oct. 11–Dec. 6. Second conference with the British leaders; De Valera did not attend, and the negotiations for the Sinn Fein were conducted by **Arthur Griffith** and **Michael Collins.**

Dec. 6. The IRISH REPRESENTATIVES SIGNED A TREATY with the British government which granted Ireland **dominion status** as the **Irish Free State** (Northern Ireland retained the right of keeping the existing arrangement).

Dec. 8. De Valera denounced **the settlement** made by Griffith.

1922, Jan. 7. The **dáil Eireann accepted the settlement,** 64–57.

Jan. 9. Resignation of De Valera. Griffith became president of the executive council and Collins prime minister. The dáil ratified the treaty (Jan. 14).

March 15. De Valera organized a new Republican Society and began an **insurrection** against his former colleagues; irregular forces resumed the methods of assassination and arson formerly used against the British.

March 30. Collins and Craig signed a peace pact at the Irish conference in London. This was followed the next day with the passage of the Irish Free State (Agreement) Act, giving force of law to treaty articles and providing for the transfer of powers to the provisional government within four months.

April 7. The **Civil Authorities (Special Powers) Act** for Northern Ireland went into effect for one year. It was renewed annually until May 9, 1933, when it became permanent.

April 14. Rebels seized the Four Courts, Dublin, from the Free State government.

May 31. The **Royal Ulster Constabulary** created.

June 16. Government forces won a great victory in general elections.

June 28. Government troops laid siege on rebel forces at Four Courts, beginning a civil war. The rebels surrendered two days later, but heavy fighting continued in Dublin (June 30–July 5). Limerick and Waterford were captured by government troops on July 20, Cork on Aug. 11.

Aug. 12. Death of Arthur Griffith.

Aug. 22. Assassination of Michael Collins by the Republicans.

Sept. 9. WILLIAM T. COSGRAVE BECAME PRESIDENT of the executive council and, aided by **Kevin O'Higgins,** began a policy of rigorous repression of the Republicans.

Oct. 25. The DÁIL ADOPTED A CONSTITUTION, providing for a two-chamber parliament (a senate, with a 12-year term, one-fourth renewable annually, with suspensive veto; a chamber of deputies, popularly elected and with exclusive power in financial affairs; the lower chamber to elect the president).

Dec. 6. The constitution went into effect, and the **Irish Free State was officially proclaimed.**

Dec. 7. Northern Ireland's parliament voted for noninclusion in the Irish Free State (IFS).

1923, April 27. Irish rebels suspended offensive operations against the Free State.

June 22. The **Northern Ireland Education Act** established nondenominational schools, which were opposed by Presbyterians and boycotted by Catholics.

Aug. 15. De Valera was arrested by government forces and imprisoned without trial; he was interned until July 16, 1924.

Sept. 10. Ireland was admitted to the League of Nations.

Nov. 14. W. B. Yeats (1865–1939) was awarded the Nobel Prize for Literature.

1924, March 6–19. An **army mutiny** resulted from the proposed reorganization (Feb. 18).

June 5. The **Old Age Pensions Act** reduced pensions from 10 shillings to 9 shillings a week.

Aug. 5. The **Military Pensions Act** provided pensions for those who served in government forces in 1922–23 and in the Irish Volunteers and in their successor, the Irish Republican Army (IRA) in 1916–21.

1925. The **Peacock Theatre** founded for experimental productions and performances by the Abbey School of Acting.

Feb. 11. The Irish Free State effectively **prohibited divorce.**

Dec. 3. Boundary between the Irish Free State and Northern Ireland fixed after long negotiations.

1926, March 11. De Valera resigned as head of Sinn Fein and subsequently founded **Fianna Fáil.**

Nov. 11. George Bernard Shaw (1856–1950) was awarded the Nobel Prize for Literature.

Nov. 19. Public Safety Act in the **Irish Free State** empowered the government to proclaim a state of national emergency with consequent powers of arrest and detention on suspicion.

1927, July 10. Assassination of Kevin O'Higgins, dominant figure of the government. Popular condemnation of the tactics of the Republicans. A drastic **public safety law** enacted (Aug. 11) and repealed (Dec. 28, 1928).

Aug. 11. De Valera and other Republican leaders **agreed to take the oath** and assume their seats in the dáil.

Sept. 15. Elections. The government party had 61 seats, against 57 for the Republicans, but failed to secure a clear majority and had to rely on the support of the Independents.

1929, July 16. The **Censorship of Publications Act** provided for the censorship in the Free State of any publication for obscenity or other reasons.

Dec. 20. The **Housing Act** authorized grants and loans for housing in Irish-speaking areas.

1930, March 27. Resignation of Cosgrave, who was soon reelected (April 2: 80 votes against 65 for De Valera).

1931, Oct. 17. Passage of a **new public safety law** to meet the revival of Republican agitation and activity, stimulated by economic stress. The Republican army was declared illegal, and military tribunals were set up to deal with sedition, illegal drilling, and so on.

1932, Feb. 9. The **Army Comrades Association** (Blue Shirts) was founded, organizing ex-members of the IFS army. Renamed the **National Guard** (July 20, 1933), under the leadership of **Gen. Eoin O'Duffy,** and proclaimed an unlawful association by the government on Aug. 22, 1933.

Feb. 16. Elections. The **Republicans won** 72 seats against 65 for the government. The Labour deputies supported the Republicans, thus giving them a majority.

March 9. DE VALERA ELECTED PRESIDENT, with a program of abolishing the oath to the king.

July. Outbreak of tariff war with Great Britain, following long abortive negotiations.

1933, Jan. 2. De Valera dissolved the dáil and in the ensuing elections (Jan. 24) secured for his party a clear majority of one.

Jan. 30–April 10. Railway workers in Northern Ireland went on strike.

May 3. The dáil abolished the oath of loyalty and soon afterward voted that the approval of the governor-general should no longer be necessary to put legislation into effect; appeals to the British privy council were made illegal.

June 11. The **Communist Party of Ireland** was founded.

Sept. 2. The **Center Party** (Cumman na nGaedheal) fused with the **National Guard** to form the **United Ireland Party** (later known as Fine Gael). After some initial infighting under the leadership of O'Duffy, Cosgrave became leader of the party.

Nov. 16. The Irish Free State enacted the **Unemployment Assistance Act** of 1933.

1934–35. Continuation of the tariff war with Great Britain. Ireland suffered tremendously from the loss of its export markets, and much discontent developed.

1934, Jan. 17. The "loop line" at Greenisland, Co. Antrim, was opened. It had been built as part of a government scheme of public works to relieve unemployment.

Dec. 21. The IFS and Great Britain concluded a **coal and cattle agreement** that enabled the Irish to sell at least some of their meat.

1935, Feb. 28. Under the Criminal Law Amendment Act the IFS forbade **the sale or importation of contraceptives.** The age of consent was also raised from 16 to 17.

1936, April 26. The IFS census noted a population of 2,968,420. In Feb. 1937 a census of Northern Ireland noted a population of 1,279,745.

This was a net decrease of 3 percent for the island, which had a total population of 4,381,951 in 1911. Taken separately, the IFS faced a declining population while Northern Ireland saw a population increase.

June 18. The IRA declared illegal in the IFS.

1937, June 14. The dáil approved a constitution bill and dissolved.

July 16. The **elections resulted in a stalemate,** the De Valera party winning exactly one-half of the seats.

Dec. 29. The IFS became **Eire** by terms of the **new Irish constitution.**

1938, Feb. 9. The **elections in Northern Ireland** resulted in an overwhelming victory for the Unionists, thus blasting any hope of merger of the Free State and Northern Ireland.

April 25. CONCLUSION OF AN AGREEMENT WITH GREAT BRITAIN for three years. The Ulster (Northern Ireland) problem had to be shelved, but other outstanding questions were adjusted. All recent tariff barriers were thrown down. Great Britain turned over to the Free State (Eire or Ireland in the new constitution) the coast defenses of Cobh, Bere Haven, and Lough Swilly. This agreement, restoring close, friendly relations between Ireland and Britain, was approved by the Irish opposition.

June 17. The elections resulted in a great **victory for De Valera,** who became prime minister under the new system.

June 25. DOUGLAS HYDE INAUGURATED THE FIRST PRESIDENT OF IRELAND. Hyde was one of the leaders of the Gaelic cultural revival and a Protestant. His election was taken as a persuasive gesture toward Northern Ireland.

1939, Jan 16. After issuing an ultimatum on the removal of all British troops from Irish soil, the **IRA began its first series of bomb attacks in England** (ended May 1940).

July 4. The **Matrimonial Causes Act** in Northern Ireland gave the supreme court the power to grant divorce for adultery, desertion, cruelty, or incurable unsoundness of mind.

Sept. 2. De Valera announced Ireland's intention of remaining neutral.

1940, Jan. 3. The government introduced emergency legislation to combat the IRA.

Nov. 25. J. M. Andrews became **prime minister of Northern Ireland** upon the **death of Sir James Craig.**

1941, Sept. 23. The **Trade Union Act** set up a tribunal with the power to license unions with the greatest number of members in a given industry as the sole negotiators for workers.

1943, April 28. Upon the resignation of J. M. Andrews, **Sir Basil Brook** became **prime minister of Northern Ireland.**

1944, Jan. 14. The **Labour Party split** as the **Irish Transport and General Workers' Union** seceded to form the **National Labour Party.**

Feb. 23. The **Children's Allowances Act** provided for grants of 2 shillings 6 pence per week for third and further children under 16.

1945, May 2. De Valera expressed formal condolences to German embassy on death of Hitler.

June 16. SEAN T. O'KELLY was elected president of Ireland.

Dec. 13. The **Family Allowances Act** of Northern Ireland provided grants of 5 shillings per week for second and further children.

(To p. 851)

6. THE LOW COUNTRIES

a. BELGIUM

(From p. 491)

Monarchs: Albert I (r. 1909–34), Leopold III (r. 1934–44).

1914. The government fled the German invasion and went into exile in Le Havre (Oct. 14). Faced with the prospect of starvation, since the Germans refused to supply civilians in occupied areas, Belgians established the **Comité national de secours et d'alimentation,** which, although neutral, became a center for patriotism.

Hoping to win support, Germany courted the Flemings by establishing a **Flemish university at Ghent** (1916) and promising **administrative separation** of the Flemish and Walloon provinces (creation of the **Council of Flanders** in 1917). The German policy of systematic massive deportation (120,000 men and boys) roused much resistance, however, sparking riots in Antwerp that killed 200 on Nov. 30, 1916. The deportations ceased in 1917.

While German efforts were largely unsuccessful, Flemish separatism caused greater concerns in the Belgian army. Unrest among Flemish soldiers aroused fear of mutiny in 1917 and 1918 (formation of Flemish study circles and their abolition, an open letter to King Albert listing grievances and cautiously defending Flemish activists in the occupied territories, and a demand by some Flemish leaders for self-government after the war). But such fears proved unfounded.

Of all the countries involved in the First World War, **Belgium** suffered most. The total damage was estimated at over $7 billion, but the country showed extraordinary recuperative power and soon returned to a peace basis. Politically the country was ruled by the Catholic and Socialist Parties. One of the major questions at issue was the demand of the Flemish for recognition of their language.

1918, Nov. 21. Roman Catholics, liberals, and Socialists formed a new government of national solidarity after the German evacuation. This was followed the next day by King Albert's promise of radical reforms: universal male suffrage, equal rights for language groups, the foundation of a Flemish university at Ghent, and the repeal of Belgium's obligatory neutrality.

1919. The first commissions paritaires were established by the government to quell a wave of strikes. These commissions were consultative bodies representing employers and workers on the national level. By 1923 there were 23 of them. They helped in negotiations and advised the government, but acquired legislative authority only in 1945.

April 7. A total of 160,000 women signed a petition demanding suffrage.

May 9. A **new electoral law** introduced **universal manhood suffrage** and gave the franchise to certain classes of women.

May 30. By agreement with Great Britain, later confirmed by the League of Nations, Belgium was given the **mandate over part of German East Africa** (Ruanda and Urundi).

June 28. By the Treaty of Versailles, Belgium acquired the German districts of **Eupen, Malmédy,** and **Moresnet.**

Nov. 17. Belgian claims to Limburg and part of the Scheldt river were thwarted as **Belgium and the Netherlands reached agreement on the River Scheldt.**

1920, Aug. 14. The VII Summer Olympic Games opened in Antwerp.

Sept. 7. Military convention with France. In the following years Belgium acted closely with France in most questions of international import.

1921. The constitution was revised to legalize new electoral regulations and to alter the composition of the Senate.

The eight-hour workday was made obligatory.

July 25. Belgium and Luxembourg signed a 50-year economic pact.

1922, Jan. 1. A law went into effect putting **Flemish on a par with French** as an official language.

1923, Jan. 11. Invasion of the Ruhr by French and Belgian troops.

May 23. Sabena, the national airline of Belgium, was founded.

1924. Under Flemish pressure, the Chamber rejected a commercial treaty with France.

Old age pensions became obligatory. Other forms of social legislation remained voluntary, but as government subsidies increased, the number of insured persons rose.

1925, April 3. A treaty with the Netherlands settled a long-standing dispute regarding the **navigation of the Scheldt.**

1926, May 22. A treaty with Britain and France formally abrogated the treaty of 1839.

July. Financial crisis. The king was given dictatorial powers for six months to solve the problem. Devaluation and stabilization of the Belgian franc through the creation of a new unit of currency, the belga.

1932, July 18. Enactment of **new language regulations.** Henceforth French was to be the administrative language only of the Walloon provinces, while in Flanders the Flemish language was to be official.

July 19. Conclusion of the **Ouchy convention** between Belgium,

Luxembourg, and Holland. The three parties agreed to gradual reduction of economic barriers between them.

Sept. 14. The **government was granted extraordinary power** to deal with the alarming budget deficits. The worldwide depression struck Belgium very hard in view of the cessation of German reparations payments. In response to a series of strikes, the government pressured employers to stabilize falling wages.

1933, March 16. The victory of the National Socialists in Germany obliged the government to take precautionary measures. One hundred fifty million francs were devoted to **fortifications along the Meuse** and Belgium thenceforth constantly increased appropriations for defense. In Dec. 1936 the term of service for the infantry was extended from seven to eighteen months.

1934, July 12. The government prohibited the formation of military units and the wearing of uniforms by political organizations. This law was directed at the **growing fascist movement** and also at the **Labor Defense Militia.** Both organizations were dissolved.

1935. Belgium abandoned the gold standard.

March 25. Paul Van Zeeland, eminent financier, formed a **Government of National Unity,** which was given decree powers for a year to cope with the desperate financial situation.

The **Office de redressement économique** was established to stimulate economic growth through government subventions. This office became permanent in 1937 but was abolished in 1939.

1936. The 40-hour work week and paid holidays were made obligatory.

May 24. Parliamentary elections. The Fascists, led by **Léon Degrelle,** and generally called Rexists, won 21 seats.

June 24. Social improvement program, roughly the equivalent of the Popular Front program in France.

Oct. 14. BELGIUM DENOUNCED THE MILITARY ALLIANCE WITH FRANCE AND RESUMED LIBERTY OF ACTION. This step resulted from the German reoccupation of the Rhineland and was generally taken as a reflection of Belgium's determination not to become embroiled with Germany through connection with the Franco-Russian alliance.

1937, Oct. 13. GERMANY, in a note to Brussels, **guaranteed the inviolability and integrity of Belgium** so long as the latter abstained from military action against Germany.

Oct. 24. Resignation of Van Zeeland, following charges of corruption in connection with the National Bank. After a prolonged cabinet crisis, **Paul Janson** (Liberal) formed a new coalition government.

1938, May 13. This government gave way to a coalition headed by **Paul Spaak** (Moderate Socialist).

1939, Feb.–March. A prolonged **cabinet crisis** resulted from the failure to construct a parliamentary majority.

April 2. The **elections** brought no great change, though the Rexist deputies dropped from 21 to only 4.

April 18. Hubert Pierlot formed a **Catholic Liberal government.**

Aug. 23. King Leopold issued an **appeal for peace** on behalf of Belgium, the Netherlands, and the Scandinavian states. This proved of no avail. Belgium mobilized but proclaimed neutrality in the European war that broke out on Sept. 3.

1940, May 10. GERMAN ARMED FORCES INVADED BELGIUM (p. 800).

May 28. Leopold III ordered the Belgian forces to **cease fighting.** Leaders of the Belgian government on French territory declared **Leopold deposed.**

Oct. 31. A Belgian government in exile was formed in London.

1942, March 7. The Nazis decreed the deportation of Belgians to alleviate worker shortages.

1944, Sept. 2. Brussels was liberated.

Sept. 5. The Belgian, Dutch, and Luxembourgeois governments in exile agreed upon the formation of **Benelux** after liberation.

(To p. 853)

b. THE NETHERLANDS

(From p. 491)

Monarchs: Wilhelmina (1890–1948).

Though the Netherlands took no part in the First World War, the nation suffered considerably through interference with trade. Toward the end of the war the government was obliged to submit to stringent regulations by the Allies and to permit the requisitioning of Dutch shipping. The Dutch merchant fleet was seized by the Allies on March 20, 1918.

1917, Dec. The revised constitution granting universal manhood suffrage and proportional representation was promulgated. Financial equality between state and private schools was also established.

1918, Sept. The **Ministry of Labor** was created.

Oct.–Nov. A wave of strikes led many to **fear a social revolution,** a fear the Socialists fostered. This generated massive support for the monarchy and the government, and a great loss in prestige for the Social Democratic Workers' Party (SDAP).

1919. The government responded to worker discontent by focusing on social insurance: the Disability Insurance Act of 1913 was finally implemented and a voluntary old age pension scheme was established with substantial government financing.

The **Supreme Labor Council** was established as a consultative body comprising workers and employers.

The **Labor Act of 1919** shortened the workday to eight hours.

1920. All initiatives in social legislation were halted as the Netherlands entered a **depression.** The government responded by reducing expenditures, including civil servants' salaries. Rapid recovery began in 1925.

Women's suffrage was instituted.

Jan. 23. The Dutch government refused the Allied demand for the surrender of the **former German emperor, William.** He lived in retirement first at Amerongen, then at Doorn.

1925, April 28. The Netherlands returned to the gold standard.

1926, Nov.–1927, July. A **Communist revolt** in the East Indies was suppressed only with difficulty (p. 774).

1928, April 4. Palmas Island, near the Philippines, in dispute between the Netherlands and the U.S., assigned to the Netherlands by arbitration.

1930, Dec. 22. Conclusion of the **Oslo agreements** between the three Scandinavian countries, the Netherlands, Belgium, and Luxembourg. The contracting parties promised not to raise tariffs without notification and consultation. On July 19, 1932, the Netherlands, Belgium, and Luxembourg concluded the **Ouchy convention** arranging for more specific reduction of tariffs. The Oslo agreements were renewed in 1937, but on July 1, 1938, the trade agreement had to be dropped.

1931, Dec. 22. The **Dutch government began to increase the tariff** and to set up import quotas, in order to help the agricultural and dairying interests, hard hit by the world depression.

Throughout the depression the parliament voted the government piecemeal powers to handle the crisis, such as the Agricultural Crisis Act of 1933, which empowered the government to regulate agriculture.

1933, April 26. Following the elections, **Hendryk Colijn constructed a crisis cabinet** that attempted to deal with the serious financial situation and to check the growth of extremist movements on both Right and Left.

1934, May. The government was granted **emergency powers** to regulate trade and industry. **Drastic measures against extremists:** National Socialists, Revolutionary Socialists, and Socialists barred from holding office. Despite these measures, the National Socialists continued to increase their numbers and influence throughout 1935.

1935. *In the Shadow of Tomorrow,* **Johan Huizinga's** (1872–1945) condemnation of contemporary European civilization, was published.

1936. In view of developments in Germany, the government felt obliged to strengthen its defenses.

Sept. 26. The Netherlands abandoned the gold standard.

1937, Jan. 7. Marriage of Princess Juliana (heiress to the throne) to **Prince Bernhard of Lippe-Biesterfeld.**

May 26. The elections proved to be a **setback for the National Socialist movement.** The Liberal Democratic Party showed a marked gain.

1939, June 30. Resignation of the Colijn government, which was reformed amid much party dissension.

1940, May 10. GERMAN ARMED FORCES INVADED THE NETHERLANDS (p. 800).

May 14. The Dutch army surrendered as the government and Queen Wilhelmina escaped to London (May 13).

Aug. 18. The **German commission** in the Netherlands **suppressed all representative bodies** in the country. Instead of being under direct military control, the Netherlands became a protectorate (Schutzstaat).

Nov. Resistance was first organized nationwide by the Order Service (Orde Dienst), which concerned itself mainly with maintaining calm until the peace. The National Organization for Assistance to Divers (those who went underground), founded in 1942, and the National Action Groups, founded in 1943, focused upon the protection of those who went into hiding. The **Council of Resistance in the Kingdom of the Netherlands,** founded in 1943, concerned itself primarily with armed resistance. The government in exile attempted to organize these groups and others in 1944 under the Netherlands Forces of the Interior.

1941, Feb. The Dutch responded to raids on Jewish neighborhoods with a strike organized by the Communist party. The Nazis responded with a declaration of martial law on March 8.

1942. The **deportation of Jews** began in the Netherlands first with foreign Jews and then Dutch Jews. In the summer the Catholic and Prot-

estant Dutch Reformed churches organized a joint public denunciation, sparking Nazi threats of reprisals. When the Catholics proceeded alone with denunciations, the Nazis began to deport Jews who had converted to Catholicism too.

June 17. A consultative board for the affairs of the **Netherlands East Indies** was set up in London to assist the minister for the colonies of the Netherlands government in exile.

1943, April–May. Another wave of strikes swept the Netherlands in protest of the occupation.

1944, Sept. 5. In hopes of setting the stage for liberation, railway workers went on strike.

The Belgian, Dutch, and Luxembourgeois governments in exile agreed upon the formation of **Benelux** after liberation.

Nov. 3. Though Antwerp (Belgium) was reopened to shipping, the Allies were unable to liberate the heart of the Netherlands until the spring of 1945, leaving many Dutch to suffer starvation over the winter.

(To p. 854)

7. FRANCE

(From p. 495)

The Third Republic: Presidents: Raymond Poincaré (1913–20), Paul Deschanel (1920), Alexandre Millerand (1920–24), Gaston Doumergue (1924–31), Paul Doumer (1931–32), Albert Lebrun (1932–40).

Leading Premiers: Georges Clemenceau (1917–20), Raymond Poincaré (1922–24), Aristide Briand (1925–26), Raymond Poincaré (1926–29), Léon Blum (1936–37), Edouard Daladier (1938–40).

The French State (Vichy): Head of State: Marshal Philippe Pétain (1940–44).

Leading Premiers: François Darlan (1941–42), Pierre Laval (1942–44).

1914, Sept. 3. Fearing that Paris might fall to the advancing German armies, the **French government moved to Bordeaux.** This temporary withdrawal made it more difficult for the civilian ministers to control the army commanders, and the French general staff displayed a spirit of independence that sometimes verged on insubordination.

Although French political parties relaxed their feuds in a *union sacrée,* discontent and division brought down successive cabinets.

In the spring of 1917 the inability of both sides to win a decision on the battlefield and the victory of the revolution in Russia led to widespread defeatism and pacifism. These sentiments became more widespread after the disastrous Nivelle offensive.

1917, Nov. 16. Formation of the great **ministry of Georges Clemenceau,** in which the prime minister was also minister of war, while **Stephen Pichon** was given the foreign office. Clemenceau's policy was one of victory *sans phrase.* He set out at once to hunt down the preachers of disaffection (**Malvy, Humbert, Bolo Pasha, Caillaux**) and to organize the country for victory.

Under the leadership of Clemenceau (second ministry, Nov. 1917–Jan. 1920), France survived the final year of the war. Clemenceau took a leading part in shaping the peace that followed.

WAR LOSSES. The acquisition of Alsace-Lorraine and of mandates in Africa and Syria did not compensate victorious France for its losses in the war, which had been fought largely on French soil. The 1,385,000 French soldiers known to be dead; 700,000 seriously wounded; 2,344,000 other wounded; and 446,000 prisoners or missing meant a loss of manpower proportionately greater than that suffered by any other belligerent. Of Frenchmen who in 1914 were aged 20–32, more than half were killed. This heightened French concerns over **depopulation.** In 1920 a statute strictly **prohibited artificial contraception and abortion** and even punished advocacy of these practices. A growing number of **pronatalist advocates** also opposed the employment of married women. Even as the percentage of French women employed fell slowly from 1921 to 1936, however, the proportion of women in the French labor force remained among the highest in the Western world. Meanwhile, in the 1920s large firms began active campaigns to recruit **foreign labor** as France replaced the United States as a leading recipient of immigration.

Property damage in the war zone in the north and east of France included 300,000 houses destroyed, and as many more damaged; 6,000 public buildings and 20,000 workshops and factories destroyed or badly damaged; 1,360,000 head of livestock killed or confiscated; thousands of acres of farm land and forest ravaged by shell fire. These figures explain the intensity of the postwar demand for security and reparation.

Public finance became another problem in postwar France. The wartime governments had preferred to borrow to finance the war. While an **income tax** had been instituted in 1916, revenue remained low. When peace returned, financial crisis followed: the depreciation of the franc reached 50 percent one year after the victory. The crisis in public finance thus gave the postwar era the appearance of financial crisis, despite the general health of the overall economy.

On the whole, as one historian notes, "the war's effect on France's social and economic structure was to shake it up without producing really revolutionary or fundamental changes. . . . on the one hand, an increased stability approaching stagnation; on the other hand, a growth in stresses and tensions within this rigidified social and economic structure."

1919. The end of the war brought various social concerns to the fore as railway and other transport workers went on strike (Jan.) and the acquittal of Raoul Villain, the man who assassinated Jean Jaurès (Aug. 1914), sparked massive demonstrations (March). The government responded with the long-awaited law making the **eight-hour workday obligatory** (April 23), but worker dissatisfaction continued to manifest itself in strikes through May and June.

Feb.–April. The Chamber and Senate passed two remunerative bills, one on the damages caused by the war and the other on veterans' pensions, thinking that German reparations would cover the costs.

July 4. The government announced its intention to complete demobilization by Oct. 30. Over 3 million men were returned to their homes.

July 12. A **new electoral law** introduced the *scrutin de liste* and a measure of proportional representation. The effect of this was to make it more difficult than ever for any one party to secure a majority.

Nov. 16. Elections. The coalition that had governed under Clemenceau split into a Right Bloc National (Clemenceau, Millerand, Poincaré, Briand) and a Cartel des Gauches, led by Herriot. The Royalists, Socialists, and Communists were not included in either group. The elections gave a majority to the Bloc National, which was also victorious in the senatorial elections of Jan. 1920.

These elections registered a great victory of the Right (loosely composed of royalist reactionaries, more compromising conservatives, and radical nationalists), but on the whole they remained unable to work efficiently in the realm of mass politics. Their electoral resurgences were due often to continued splits on the Left, those times when the

Radicals chose to work with conservatives rather than accept Socialist economic and social programs.

1920, Jan. 17. Presidential election. Clemenceau was defeated by Paul Deschanel, a reflection of public opinion that held the Treaty of Versailles too lenient.

April 23. Joseph Caillaux, former prime minister, sentenced to three years' imprisonment and other penalties after conviction of dealings with the enemy. He was amnestied in Nov. 1924.

Sept. 15. Resignation of President Deschanel on account of ill health.

Dec. Having already voted to leave the Second International (Feb.), **the Socialist Party at its party convention in Tours split over joining the Third International.** Over three-fourths voted for adhesion, leaving a minority led by Léon Blum to secede. The majority renamed themselves the **French Communist Party.**

1921. Jean Cocteau (1889–1963) staged his play *Les Mariés de la Tour Eiffel,* a farce that mirrored the prevailing surrealist sentiment of the times. Music for the play was composed by Les Six, a group of composers who introduced modern music to France in the 1920s. Les Six included **Georges Auric** (1899–1983), **Louis Durey** (1888–1979), **Arthur Honegger** (1892–1955), **Darius Milhaud** (1892–1974), **Francis Poulenc** (1899–1963), and **Germaine Tailleferre** (1892–1983).

Other popular playwrights included **Jean Anouilh** (1910–87), **Eugène Bireux** (1858–1932), **Henri Bernstein** (1876–1953), **Paul Claudel** (1868–1955), **Sacha Guitry** (1885–1957), and **Jean Giraudoux** (1882–1944).

Jan. 13. The **General Confederation of Labor was dissolved** by court order after having attempted a failed general strike in May 1920. It survived the court order but lost many adherents. Its position was further eroded by **schism** and the creation of two new organizations, the Catholic CFTC and the Communist CGTU. Throughout this period 90 percent of French workers remained unorganized, however.

Nov. 10. Anatole France (1844–1924) received the Nobel Prize in literature. Novelists of the time included **Marcel Proust** (1871–1922), **André Gide** (1869–1951), **Romain Rolland** (1866–1944), **André Malraux** (1901–76), **Jules Romain** (1885–1972), **Colette** (1873–1954), and **François Mauriac** (1885–1970).

1922, Jan. 15–1924, June 1. Cabinet of Raymond Poincaré, with a program of forcing reparations payments from Germany, chiefly to meet the expense of restoration of the devastated regions, on which 20 billion francs had already been spent.

1923, Jan. Invasion of the Ruhr (p. 675).

April 1. Compulsory military service reduced to one and a half years.

1924. André Breton (1896–1966) gave definition to the new artistic movement **surrealism** in his *First Surrealist Manifesto.* Other surrealists included **Louis Aragon** (1897–1982) and **Paul Eluard** (1895–1952).

Jan. A flight in capital caused the franc to fall drastically in the world market, creating an **economic crisis.** This was caused mainly by the government's refusal to raise taxes enough to cover the continued rise in expenditures. Instead, France handled its debt by securing ever larger loans from the Bank of France. Poincaré was given extraordinary powers to handle the crisis on Feb. 8. The franc regained stability on March 10, but an atmosphere of crisis remained until 1926.

Jan. 6. The **Catholic Church** was given the right to reoccupy its former property under a system of *diocesan associations.*

April 12. The National Assembly voted to revise the laws on civil and military pensions, widening the number of pensioners.

May 11. The **elections** gave the Cartel des Gauches a majority in the chamber, as a result of the failure of Poincaré's policy of coercing Germany. Poincaré resigned.

The rise of the Left spurred movement on the Right, including the formation of a new conservative paramilitary group, the **Jeunesses patriotes,** and the first openly Fascist party, the **Faisceau.** These entered into competition with existing Rightist groups like the Action française, which were more royalist in conviction. Membership declined in such groups after economic recovery began in 1926.

June 11. Resignation of President Millerand. This was forced by Édouard Herriot, leader of the Radical Socialist Party, the strongest group in the chamber, who refused to form a government while Millerand was president, charging that the president had abandoned the traditional neutrality and had openly sided with the Right.

Nov. 23. Jean Jaurès' remains were transferred to the Panthéon.

1925. Catholics united to form a **Fédération nationale catholique** in hopes of later creating a larger Catholic party. By July the federation counted 1.8 million members.

Jan. 17. The Herriot government created the **Conseil national économique consultatif** in order to stimulate cooperation between the government and unions. Herriot also attempted to sponsor closer contacts with employers through the **Comité consultatif supérieur du Commerce et de l'Industrie.**

1926, April–May. The franc began another rapid fall, declining to the value of 2 cents. The budget could not be balanced despite the imposition of new taxes and increases of income and other taxes. War debts, postwar extravagance, and the failure of reparations made a partial repudiation of the debt inevitable.

1926, July 28–1929, July 26. National Union ministries of Poincaré. The new government voted new taxes and drastic economies that balanced the budget.

Aug. 10. The two chambers, sitting as a national assembly, incorporated **a sinking-fund measure** in the constitution. Income from the tobacco monopoly and from inheritance taxes was to be used to redeem part of the national debt.

1927, July 13. The system of *scrutin d'arrondissement* restored for the elections.

1928, April 5. After years of discussion, the National Assembly adopted a system of **social insurance.** Recognizing some problems in the law, however, the government announced plans for two follow-up laws, the final law of which established France's system of welfare (April 30, 1930). The final **National Workmen's Insurance Law** insured 9 million workers against sickness, old age, and death. Workers contributed 3 percent of wages, employers an equal amount. The state contributed in some cases.

June 24. The **franc was devalued** from 19.3¢ to 3.92¢, this being a disguised repudiation of about four-fifths of the national debt. The measure hit the *rentier* class hardest and explains later opposition to further devaluation.

1929, July 27. Resignation of Poincaré, on account of ill health. There followed a series of short-lived cabinets, based on shifting parliamentary blocs rather than on genuine party groupings.

1930, June 30. End of the evacuation of the Rhineland.

1931, June–1932, May. PRESIDENCY OF PAUL DOUMER. Briand was passed over, since his efforts at international conciliation had estranged the Right. Death of Briand (March 7, 1932).

1931. The French economy, having experienced a boom between 1926 and 1931, went into a downswing as the effects of the **depression** were finally felt. While France weathered the depression better than many other nations because of its continued reliance on small farms, a traditionally conservative business approach, and the government's policy of sending home foreign workers, **the downswing lasted until 1935 and the recovery was slower than in almost any other country.**

The government's response to economic crisis was the isolation of France behind **high tariffs and quotas.** At the same time, the government let industry take care of itself through **domestic cartel arrangements,** in which industry agreed to cut production, share the home market, and keep prices at predepression levels. The government also reduced the number of people liable to income taxes. This combination favored weaker companies and traditional farmers, however. The most notable economic failures were often those industrialists, like André Citroën, who had been more dynamic before the depression.

1932. The Chamber established a system of **family allowances** to aid poor families and fight the low birth rate *(dénatalité).*

May 6. President Doumer assassinated by a Russian émigré.

May. The **elections** gave the Left parties a majority.

June–Dec. Second **ministry of Édouard Herriot.** He resigned because the government proposal to pay the scheduled debt installment to the U.S. was voted down by the Chamber. There followed five short-lived ministries in the next 13 months. All were concerned with keeping France on the gold standard and with balancing the budget without resorting to inflation.

1933, Dec. The Stavisky case. Alexandre Stavisky, a Russian promoter involved in the floating of a fraudulent bond issue by the municipal pawnshop of Bayonne, fled to escape arrest and when cornered was alleged to have committed suicide. Royalists and Fascists stirred up an agitation against the republic which recalled the Dreyfus case. It was believed that important officials and politicians were involved and that their guilt was being concealed. The full facts were never made known.

1934, Feb. 6–7. SERIOUS RIOTS IN PARIS and other cities, resulting from the Stavisky case.

Feb. 8. A **coalition cabinet** under ex-president **Doumergue,** including leaders of all parties except Royalists, Socialists, and Communists, formed to avert civil war. The Chamber voted the government the right to rule by decree on economic matters (Feb. 28).

Feb. 12. The General Confederation of Labor (CGT) organized a **general strike** in a call for unity on the Left.

July 27. The **Socialists and Communists signed an agreement** to end mutual attacks and form a united front. The prominent Communist Maurice Thorez first called for a Popular Front against fascism, uniting Socialists, Communists, and Radicals, in October.

Nov. Fall of the Doumergue ministry, Doumergue having proposed a constitutional reform by which a change of ministry should, as in Britain, necessitate a new election. The coalition was reorganized under **Pierre Flandin.**

1935, May 31. The **Flandin cabinet was overthrown** when it demanded quasi-dictatorial powers to save the franc. A **Laval ministry** followed. Like the Doumergue government, Laval too acquired the right to rule by decree until Oct. 31 (June 7). Laval's program called for severe deflation to get the French price level down to the world level. He also used his special powers to cut state expenditures drastically.

July 14. The **Popular Front** (Rassemblement populaire) was formally initiated. The official adhesion of the Radical Socialists came at the end of the year. The Popular Front produced its electoral program in January.

1936, Jan. 22. Downfall of the Pierre Laval government, which was thoroughly discredited by its half-and-half attitude toward Italy during the Ethiopian crisis and further suspected of supporting the reactionary currents. There followed a **cabinet under Albert Sarraut** which was nothing more than a stopgap.

March. The **CGT and CFTU merged,** with leadership remaining mainly in the hands of the CGT.

May 3. The **parliamentary elections gave the Popular Front a majority** in the Chamber of Deputies.

June 5. FIRST POPULAR FRONT MINISTRY, under **Léon Blum,** leader of the Socialist Party. The cabinet was composed of Radical Socialists and Socialists, and enjoyed the support of the Communists. A great **wave of sit-down strikes** (300,000 workers out) accompanied this important change (resolved by the **Matignon Agreements** on June 7–8) and led at once to the introduction of a far-reaching **program of social reform:** establishment of the 40-hour week (June 12); reorganization and ultimately nationalization of the Bank of France; nationalization of the munitions industry (July 17); compulsory arbitration of labor disputes, vacations with pay, and so forth. These measures, hailed by the workers as marking the dawn of a new era, at once aroused the hostility of the employing classes. Rapidly rising costs of production brought with them rising prices. The franc began to sink steadily, and capital started to flee the country in large amounts. To the increasing financial difficulties was added the **enhanced tension in international affairs** following the German reoccupation of the Rhineland, the Italian victory in Ethiopia, the collapse of the League system (on which France had depended so much), and the outbreak of civil war in Spain. The government was obliged to expend huge sums on further rearmament and, after Belgium's resumption of neutrality, to undertake the **fortification of the Belgian frontier.** In the Spanish affair Blum felt impelled to follow the British lead and adopt a policy of nonintervention. **Anglo-French relations** had grown so cool as a result of Laval's Italian policy that Blum looked upon revival of close relations as worth any cost.

June 30. The government suppressed Fascist groups. Most of these groups responded by re-forming as political parties. The Croix de feu, for example, became the **Parti social français** (PSF). Jacques Doriot also founded the **Parti populaire français.** An attempt was made later in 1937 to create an electoral front called the **Front de la liberté,** but the PSF refused to join.

Oct. 2. A **bill devaluing the franc,** but not definitely fixing its gold content, was finally passed. Cooperation of Great Britain and the United States averted violent fluctuations in the foreign exchanges.

1937. Roger Martin du Gard received the Nobel Prize for literature. He was most famous for his multivolume novel *Les Thibaults* (1922–40).

Feb. 7. A new French defense plan created a ministry of defense, extended the **Maginot Line,** which had been constructed in the late 1920s, and nationalized the Schneider-Creusot arms factory.

Feb. 13. Blum was obliged to announce a "breathing spell" in the work of social reform, in order to reassure capitalist groups and make possible the flotation of huge defense loans.

This pause divided the extreme Left from the rest of the coalition and sparked worker unrest (the Clichy massacre, March 16, 1937). In September and December 1937 and June 1938 strikes erupted that tested the glue of the Popular Front, which finally dissolved in October 1938.

June 19. The Senate refused Blum's demands for emergency fiscal powers, whereupon **the cabinet resigned.** The government was reformed with **Camille Chautemps** (Radical Socialist) as premier and Blum as vice-premier. The new government secured the necessary powers and devoted itself to the Herculean task of financial reconstruction. At the same time the foreign minister, Yvon Delbos, embarked upon an extended visit to France's eastern allies (Dec.), without finding much prospect of active collaboration against Germany.

Nov. 18. Discovery of a **royalist plot** against the republic. The Cagoulards (Hooded Ones) appear to have been a terrorist group within a larger revolutionary (Fascist) movement. Secret plans, fortified dugouts, and caches of weapons and munitions were discovered.

1938. Frenchwomen who had married under the separate property or dowry regimes gained their legal majority as a result of pressure from women's rights activists such as Maria Véronne, Suzanne Grinberg, and Yvonne Netter.

Jan. 14. The **Socialists deserted the cabinet,** which was reorganized by Chautemps as a Radical Socialist ministry. This the Socialists at first tolerated.

March 10. Chautemps's government fell, however, when the Socialists rejected a demand for full powers.

March 13–April 10. Léon Blum, after trying in vain to organize a national coalition cabinet to face the acute international situation, formed a **new Popular Front government.** Like its predecessor it was frustrated by the Senate, which refused Blum all confidence. Forced out of office, Blum made way for Daladier.

April 10. The **cabinet of Édouard Daladier** (Radical Socialist) was formed, who stood further to the Right. Daladier was given decree powers until July 31, and proceeded to devalue the franc and end a new strike movement. Blum and the Socialists supported him.

Sept. THE GERMAN-CZECHOSLOVAK CRISIS (p. 705).

Oct. 4. The **Daladier government broke definitely with the Socialists and Communists** when the former abstained from the vote of confidence on the Munich agreements and the Communists voted in opposition. **End of the Popular Front.**

Oct. 28. Senatorial elections confirmed the solid shift to the Right evident in the policies of the Daladier government.

Nov. 12. The government promulgated a large number of decrees aimed at improvement of the desperate financial situation. Among other things the 40-hour week, retained in principle, was to be much modified in practice. This departure created much ill-feeling, especially in the ranks of the CGT (Confederation of Labor) with its 5 million members. A new strike epidemic was launched by the workers.

Nov. 30. A **general strike of protest,** called for 24 hours, was the culmination of this epidemic. The government had prepared to meet the threat, had put railway workers under military orders, and had otherwise requisitioned services. Under threats of punishment the whole movement collapsed, with relatively few workers going on strike.

1939, March. The continued expansion of Germany to the east produced ever greater tension. Daladier asked for and received from Parliament power to govern by decree without express limitations, a situation unprecedented under the Third Republic. The premier used his power to speed up rearmament and to effect partial mobilization. France assumed an attitude of quiet determination, but at the same time joined with Britain in guarantees to Poland and Greece, and used all its influence to draw Russia into the nonaggression system (p. 678).

Aug. 20–Sept. 1. The Danzig-Polish crisis. The French government throughout stood shoulder to shoulder with Britain.

Sept. 3. France declared **WAR ON GERMANY.**

Nov. 17. Britain and France agreed to coordinate their economic efforts.

1940, May 12. GERMAN ARMED FORCES INVADED FRANCE.

June 16. Marshal Pétain replaced Paul Reynaud as premier and sued for peace (June 17).

June 22. FRANCE CONCLUDED AN ARMISTICE WITH GERMANY.

July 2. French government seat established at Vichy (p. 801).

July 9. The **National Assembly** voted to establish an **authoritarian government,** granting Pétain almost dictatorial powers.

Aug. 7. Britain signed an agreement for cooperation with the Free French leader Charles de Gaulle. His government was established later on Oct. 27.

Dec. 14. Pétain excluded Pierre Laval from the council of ministers. Laval favored a closer working arrangement between Vichy and Berlin.

1941, Oct. 21. The assassination of a German officer in Nantes was punished by the execution of **50 French hostages.**

1942, April 14. Pétain reinstated Laval under German pressure.

July 16. The Vichy government ordered a massive raid on the Jewish population of Paris. More than 13,000 Jews were arrested and then gathered at the **Vélodrome d'Hiver** to await transfer to Auschwitz.

Sept. 14. The Vichy government decreed **compulsory labor** for men between 18 and 65 and for unmarried women between 20 and 35. This move was regarded in France as an enforcement of German demands for labor collaboration.

Nov. 11. In retaliation for the Anglo-American invasion of French North Africa, **German forces moved into the hitherto unoccupied portions of France.** At Toulon, where most of the surviving ships of the French navy were stationed, the **ships were sunk by their crews** (Nov. 27) to frustrate German efforts to seize them.

Nov. 17. Pétain appointed Laval his successor and assigned him the power to make laws and issue decrees. This step reflected the increased German control over the Vichy regime.

Dec. 1. Adm. Jean-François Darlan assumed authority as **chief of state in French North Africa,** with the approval of the British and U.S. governments. He was assassinated three weeks later (Dec. 24).

1943, March 15. Gen. Henri Giraud, successor to Darlan as head of the French government in North Africa, declared that legislation passed since 1940 was without effect, restored representative government, and promised that France itself would regain the right of self-determination after victory.

May. Various groups in the French resistance, including the principal political parties and trade unions, agreed to the creation of a **National Resistance Council,** under the leadership of **Jean Moulin.** The underground paramilitary forces were also united under a single command and were given the label **French Forces of the Interior.** These guerrilla units were already beginning to play an effective role, especially in railroad sabotage.

June 4. A **Committee of National Liberation** was formed, including both **Gen. de Gaulle** and **Gen. Giraud.** It was recognized by the Allies on Aug. 24.

1944, June 6. The liberation of France began with the invasion of Normandy.

Aug. 25. De Gaulle entered liberated Paris. On Aug. 30 the seat of the French provisional government was relocated to Paris from Algiers.

Oct. 23. The Allies recognized de Gaulle's administration as the provisional French government. *(To p. 855)*

8. THE IBERIAN PENINSULA

a. SPAIN

(From p. 496)

Though Spain was spared the horrors of the First World War, the effects of the conflict made themselves felt. The demands of the combatants for iron, munitions, and other goods led to a striking **development of Spanish industry,** centering in Catalonia. The growth of industry in turn resulted in increased tension between the semifeudal upper classes, supported by the Church and the army, and the new forces of **socialism** and **anarchism.** The volatility of this mixture was exacerbated by the uneven economic and social development of Spain and subsequent strong regionalist sentiment. The movement for **autonomy for Catalonia,** which had survived the centralizing policies of the 19th century, flared up anew, and the government was throughout confronted with the additional **problem of Morocco,** where constant native risings required a great military effort and the expenditure of much money. Politically the prewar system extended through the First World War and immediate postwar periods, with repeated changes of ministry and the rotation of Liberals and Conservatives in power.

1917. The **crisis of 1917** resulted from the waning economic benefits of the war and a rise in the cost of living. It began in May with military unrest that became more general social unrest by the end of July with strikes in Valencia, Bilbao, and Santiago. The result was a period of insecurity between 1917 and 1923.

June. The **Junta of Defense of the Infantry** forced the government to **suspend constitutional guarantees.**

July 5. The **Catalan deputies and senators** in the cortes **demanded the convocation of a constituent assembly** to consider home rule for Catalonia.

Aug. 13. A **general strike** was called to protest economic, social, and political conditions.

1919, Jan. 24. A **Catalonian Union** met at Barcelona and drafted a program for home rule. The government appointed a commission to consider the question, but its carefully circumscribed report was rejected by the Catalonians as inadequate.

1921, July 21. DISASTER AT ANUAL, Morocco, culmination of the troubles there. **Gen. Fernandez Silvestre** and 20,000 Spaniards were defeated by the Riffians under **Abd-el-Krim** and 12,000 were killed. Silvestre committed suicide. The disaster precipitated a political crisis and a widespread demand for an investigation of responsibility. A parliamentary commission was established, but its report, when submitted to the cabinet in 1922, was at once suppressed.

1922. The dramatist **Jacinto Benavente y Martinéz** (1866–1954) won the Nobel Prize. Other literary figures of interwar Spain included the poet **Juan Ramon Jiménez** (1881–1958), the novelist **Vicente Blasco Ibáñez** (1867–1928), and the essayists **Miguel de Unamuno y Jugo** (1864–1936) and **Ortega y Gasset** (1873–1955). In the world of music **Manuel de Falla** (1876–1946) gained recognition for his orchestral works, especially ballet music.

1923, Sept. 12. Mutiny of the garrison at Barcelona and outbreak of a separatist movement.

Sept. 13. MILITARY COUP OF GEN. MIGUEL PRIMO DE RIVERA, who acted with the approval of the king. He took Barcelona, formed a military directorate, proclaimed martial law throughout the country, dissolved the cortes, suspended jury trial, and instituted a rigid press censorship. Liberal opponents were imprisoned or harried out of the land (**Miguel de Unamuno, Blasco Ibáñez**). The military government tried to bolster the economy through public works programs like the **Confederaciones Sindicales Hidrográficas,** running up a budget deficit of a billion pesetas by 1928. These were largely ineffectual, however, as industrialists remained cautious and farmers had little capital. The government was equally ineffective in its social policies, such as the creation of **compulsory arbitration boards.**

1924, Nov. 19–28. Visit of Alfonso XIII and Primo de Rivera to Rome, in return for a visit of the king and queen of Italy (June). This exchange of visits marked the dictator's efforts to establish a close understanding with Fascist Italy, culminating in the **treaty of friendship** of Aug. 7, 1926.

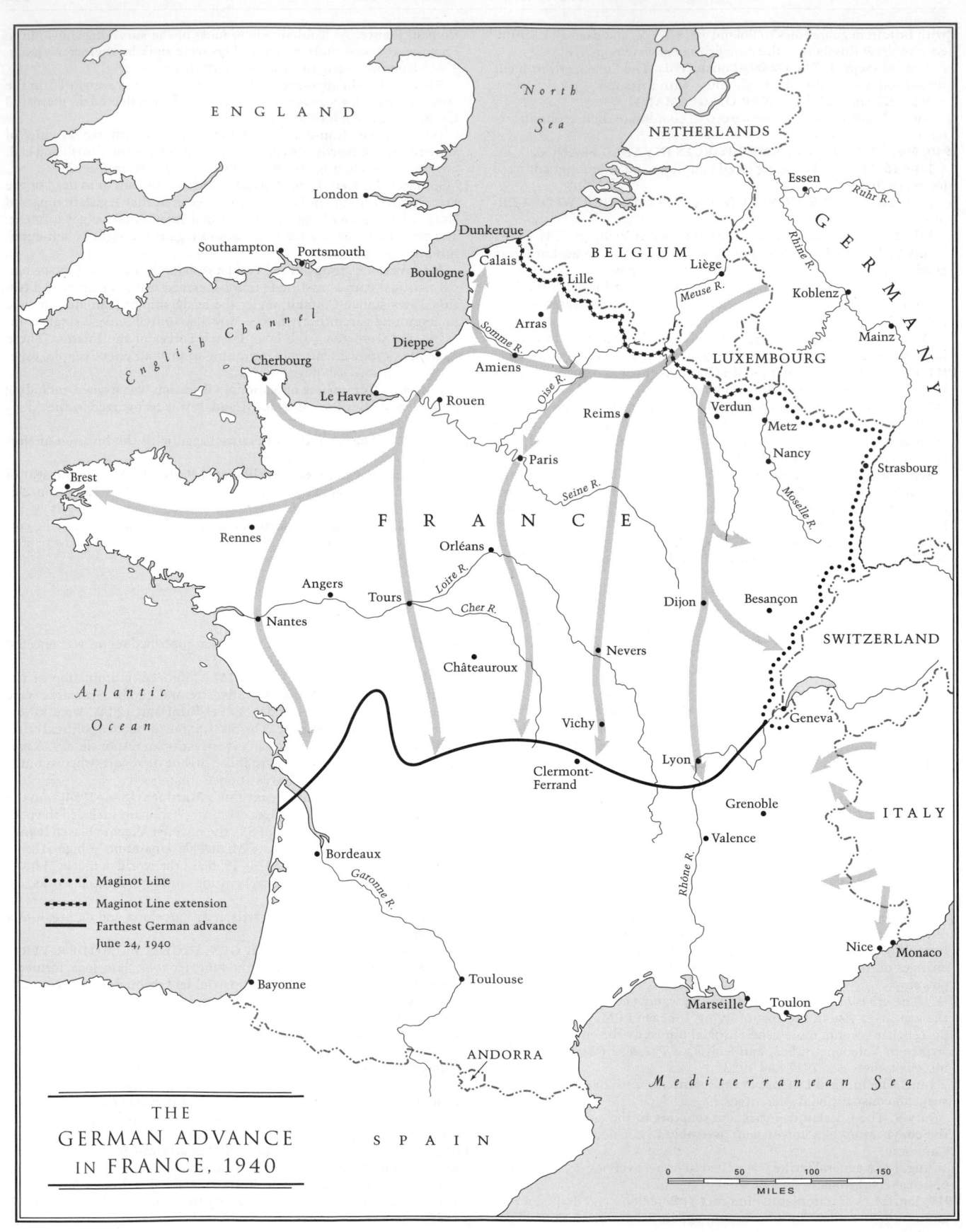

ENGLAND

North Sea

NETHERLANDS

Essen

Ruhr R.

GERMANY

London

Dunkerque

Southampton Portsmouth

Calais

BELGIUM

Liège

Rhine R.

Boulogne

Lille

Koblenz

English Channel

Dieppe

Arras

Somme R.

Amiens

Meuse R.

LUXEMBOURG

Mainz

Cherbourg

Le Havre

Rouen

Oise R.

Reims

Verdun

Metz

Nancy

Strasbourg

Paris

Brest

Seine R.

F R A N C E

Moselle R.

Rennes

Orléans

Loire R.

Dijon

Besançon

Angers

Tours

Cher R.

SWITZERLAND

Nantes

Châteauroux

Nevers

Atlantic Ocean

Vichy

Geneva

Lyon

Clermont-Ferrand

Grenoble

I T A L Y

Valence

Bordeaux

Garonne R.

Rhône R.

Nice

Monaco

Bayonne

Toulouse

Marseille

Toulon

ANDORRA

Mediterranean Sea

SPAIN

••••• Maginot Line

••••• Maginot Line extension

—— Farthest German advance
June 24, 1940

THE
GERMAN ADVANCE
IN FRANCE, 1940

0   50   100   150
MILES

1925, Dec. 3. End of the dictatorship, because of widespread and increasing popular discontent. But Primo de Rivera was at once named prime minister, with a predominantly military cabinet.

1926, June 10. Spain resigned from the League of Nations, but the resignation was later withdrawn (March 22, 1928).

Nov. 2. Attempted **coup in Catalonia** by conspirators operating from France.

1927. Discontent continued to grow as the Federation of University Scholars and then the students became more active. The creation of a **petroleum monopoly** also fed popular protest.

1929, Jan. 29. Military revolt at Ciudad Real, indicating the spread of dissatisfaction to military groups.

March 17. The University of Madrid and other universities were closed in order to put an end to the agitation of the students and intellectuals.

1930, Jan. 28. RESIGNATION OF PRIMO DE RIVERA, discouraged and in ill health (died March 16).

Jan. 30. Government of Gen. Damaso Berenguer, who attempted a policy of conciliation. An amnesty was granted, Primo de Rivera's assembly was dissolved, local government organs restored, juridical rights recognized. The government promised early elections for a national parliament. But the students continued their agitation, and **Republican leaders openly denounced the monarchy** as responsible for national disasters and dictatorship. After the removal of censorship (Sept.), criticism and demonstrations became the order of the day.

Aug. Antimonarchist groups signed the **Pact of San Sebastian** declaring their unity in the fight for a republic.

Dec. 12–13. Mutiny of the garrison at Jaca, demanding a republic. This was suppressed only with difficulty.

1931, Feb. 8. The king announced the **restoration of the constitution** and fixed parliamentary elections for March. Popular demand for a constituent assembly. **Berenguer resigned.**

March. The government called for municipal and provincial elections and promised a constituent assembly.

April 12. The **municipal elections** resulted in an overwhelming victory for the Republicans. Niceto Alcalá Zamora, the Republican leader, called for the king's abdication.

April 14. KING ALFONSO LEFT SPAIN without abdicating, stating that he would await the expression of popular sentiment. In Eibar, Barcelona, and San Sebastian the Republic was proclaimed. Alcalá Zamora at once set up a provisional government, with himself as president.

June 28. Elections for the constituent assembly gave the Republican-Socialist coalition a huge majority.

Nov. 12. A committee of the assembly declared **Alfonso XIII guilty of high treason** and forbade his return to Spain. The royal property was confiscated.

Dec. 9. The **new constitution** was adopted. It provided for universal suffrage and a single-chamber parliament (cortes), to be elected for four years. The president of the republic was to be chosen by an electoral college consisting of parliament plus an equal number of electors chosen by popular vote. His term was to be six years. No army officer or member of the clergy was to be eligible. The ministry was to be responsible to parliament. The constitution proclaimed complete religious freedom and separated Church and State; education secularized; church property nationalized; the Jesuit order dissolved (Jan. 1932) and its property taken over. Catalonia was given a measure of local autonomy. The government was granted power to expropriate private property, to socialize large estates, and to nationalize public utilities.

Dec. 10. Alcalá Zamora elected first president. He had resigned in October in protest against extremist anticlerical legislation, and was succeeded by **Manuel Azaña,** who became first prime minister under the constitution. The national assembly continued to function as the first regular parliament.

The government began a policy of high wages, ignoring the problems this posed during a world depression. Spending became difficult to control, and the government stopped publishing a budget in 1932. The result by 1936 was deflation and economic decline, which, ironically, helped the Left come back to power after its 1934 election losses.

1932, Aug. 10. Revolt of Gen. José Sanjurjo, who seized Seville. The movement was quickly suppressed by loyal troops, but was indicative of conservative opposition to the radical legislation of the new regime.

Sept. 25. CATALAN CHARTER OF AUTONOMY. The home rule leaders had drawn up the charter soon after the revolution and had secured Catalan approval by a plebiscite (Aug. 1931). After much agitation and disorder in the province, the Republican government was obliged to accept it. Catalonia was given its own president, parliament, and government, with extensive taxing and other powers. The Catalans were to have their own flag, and Catalan was made the official language. The Catalan parliament met for the first time in December. Success of the movement led to similar demands by the Basques and other regionalists.

1933, Jan. 8. Great radical rising (anarchists and syndicalists) in Barcelona, which spread to many other large cities. It was successfully suppressed by government troops, but indicated the impatience of the lower classes with the social reform movement.

Jan. 12. Government forces suppressed a revolt in the village of **Casas Viejas.** It severely tarnished the prestige of the government and indicated that the peasantry too was unhappy with the pace of agricultural reform.

April 23. Municipal elections reflected a distinct veering of opinion to the Right.

May 17. An **Associations Law** required that heads of all religious orders be Spaniards; members of religious orders were forbidden to engage in industry or trade; church schools were abolished and all secular education by religious orders prohibited; church property was nationalized, though left in the custody of the clergy. Vigorous protests of the pope (encyclical *Delectissimi nobis*).

Sept. 8. Elections for the Tribunal of Constitutional Guaranties (a body to test the constitutionality of legislation and protect civil liberties) showed a further trend toward the Right.

Oct. 29. José Antonio Primo de Rivera launched the program of his Fascist organization, the **Falange.**

Nov. 19. The **first regular elections** for the cortes gave the Right parties 44 percent of the seats, the Left parties only 21 percent. There followed a series of coalition ministries, all of them more or less helpless and unpopular.

Dec. 9. Syndicalist-anarchist rising in Barcelona, put down only after ten days of fighting.

1934, Jan. 14. Catalan elections, resulting in a victory for the moderate Left groups; a protest against the swing to conservatism in Spain generally. **Luis Companys president** of Catalonia.

April. A **great strike in Barcelona,** led by Socialists, created further tension with Madrid and was suppressed only with difficulty.

Oct. 4. Cabinet of Alejandro Lerroux, in which the Catholic Popular Action Party of **Gil Robles** was represented. This party, allied with the monarchists, was outspokenly clerical.

Oct. 5. The Left parties called a **general strike** in protest against the rising opposition to the democratic, social republic.

Oct. 6. President Luis Companys of Catalonia proclaimed the **independence of Catalonia.** This separatist uprising was suppressed by government troops, as was also an **insurrection of the miners in the Asturias,** where a Communist regime had been proclaimed. As a result of the rising in Catalonia, the Catalan statute was suspended preparatory to revision (Dec. 15).

1935, Sept. The **Lerroux cabinet fell,** and was succeeded by several ephemeral ministries, all more or less at the mercy of the Right.

1936, Jan. 6. The cortes was dissolved.

Feb. 16. Elections. The Left parties (Republicans, Socialists, Syndicalists, Communists) combined in a Popular Front and won a decisive victory over Conservative Republicans, Clericals, and Monarchists. **Manuel Azaña** formed a new cabinet (Feb. 19), which at once proclaimed an amnesty and undertook the **restoration of Catalan autonomy.** The social reform program (distribution of land, development of schools, etc.) was resumed, as was the anticlerical policy.

April 10. The **cortes voted to remove President Alcalá Zamora** for exceeding his powers.

May 10. Manuel Azaña was regularly **elected president.**

July 18. THE SPANISH CIVIL WAR. The conflict began with a revolt of the army chiefs at Melilla in Spanish Morocco. It spread rapidly to the garrison towns of Spain (Cadiz, Seville, Saragossa, Burgos, and others). In Madrid and Barcelona the government held its own, thus making early success of the Insurgents impossible. All the parties of the Left united in resistance, and the government declared the **confiscation of all religious property** (July 28). The Insurgent leaders, **Gen. Francisco Franco** and **Gen. Emilio Mola** (**Gen. Sanjurjo** was killed at the very outset in an airplane accident), were supported by the bulk of the army and air force, and had at their disposal large Moorish contingents. On July 30 they set up a **Junta of National Defense** at Burgos. At an early stage in the war **foreign powers began to intervene, and Spain became the battleground of rival ideologies.** Italian and German "volunteers" joined the Insurgents, while Russia supplied the government with equipment and advisers.

Aug. 15. The **rebels captured Badajoz** and began a great advance eastward up the Tagus Valley through Talavera and **Toledo** (relieved Sept. 28 after a ten-week siege of the famous Alcazar fortress by the Loyalists).

Sept. 4. The **rebels captured Irun** in the north. On the same day a Popular Front government was formed in Madrid under **Largo Caballero,** with Catalan and Basque Nationalists represented. In November anarchist-syndicalists were included. On Sept. 12 the Insurgents took San Sebastian.

Oct. 1. GEN. FRANCISCO FRANCO was appointed by the Insurgents as Chief of the Spanish State.

Oct. 8. The government adopted **home rule for the Basque provinces,** which established the first autonomous Basque government under President José Aguirre.

Nov. 6. Beginning of the siege of Madrid by the Insurgents. The government moved to Valencia. Despite heavy fighting in the suburbs of the city and appalling air bombardments, the Loyalist troops held the capital, and the Insurgent assault ended in deadlock.

Nov. 18. Germany and Italy recognized the government of Gen. Franco. Great Britain and France continued their ban on supplies to the republican government and attempted to unite the powers on a **policy of nonintervention,** for fear that the war might expand into a general conflict. Twenty-seven nations, including Germany and Italy, agreed to participate in a **nonintervention committee,** sitting in London. A scheme for supervision was introduced, but this, like other methods adopted, failed to prevent participation by those powers that cared to intervene. The Italian government came out more and more openly in support of Franco, and ultimately had from 50,000 to 75,000 troops in Spain.

1937, Feb. 8. The **rebels captured Malaga** with Italian aid but failed to cut the road from Madrid to Valencia.

March 18. Loyalist forces defeated Italian troops at Brihuega, capturing large stores. The Insurgents, frustrated in the effort to cut off Madrid, turned to the north and concentrated on Bilbao.

April 26. The Basque village of **Guernica** was bombed, a battle made internationally famous by the most celebrated Spanish artist of the century, **Pablo Picasso** (1881–1973).

May 17. A new government, under Juan Negrin, replaced that of Largo Caballero. Negrin represented the Socialists but took in members of other Left parties (except the Anarcho-Syndicalists). The new cabinet took the view that the war must be won before the social revolution could be carried further. All defense ministries were unified under **Indalecio Prieto.**

June 18. Bilbao fell to the Insurgents after weeks of heavy fighting and countless air bombardments. Basque resistance soon collapsed, and the rebels pushed on to Santander.

June 23. Germany and Italy quit the neutrality patrol off the Spanish coast in protest against the unwillingness of the other powers to secure satisfaction for the attack on the *Deutschland.* At the same time they refused to accept patrol by Britain and France. Acute international tension, the French being held back from opening the frontier to supplies for the Loyalists only by pressure from Britain. Meanwhile "piracy" became rife in the western Mediterranean, with mysterious submarines attacking British ships and even warships. Thereupon the British government convoked the **Nyon conference,** and, with French support, organized a new and drastic antipiracy patrol.

Oct. 21. Franco's troops finally captured Gijon, breaking the resistance in the Asturias and **completing the conquest of the northwest.**

Oct. 28. The **Spanish government moved from Valencia to Barcelona,** having taken over control of the Catalan government (Aug. 12).

Nov. 28. Franco announced a **naval blockade** of the entire Spanish coast, using the island of Majorca as a base.

Dec. 5. Beginning of a great **Loyalist counteroffensive around Teruel,** which was taken on Dec. 19. This move served to divert the Insurgents from operations to the northeastward. But the government forces, much less adequately supplied and equipped than their opponents, were unable to sustain the offensive.

1938, Feb. 15. Franco's forces recaptured Teruel and made a spectacular drive toward the sea.

April 15. The **Insurgents took Vinaroz,** on the seacoast, thus severing Loyalist territory in Castile from Barcelona and Catalonia. A tremendous battle developed along the Ebro River, where the contestants were deadlocked during most of the summer. In accordance with the **Anglo-Italian agreement,** Mussolini withdrew some troops from Spain, but there still remained a substantial force estimated at 40,000.

Dec. 23. Beginning of the great **Insurgent drive in Catalonia.** Despite valiant resistance, the Loyalist forces were gradually driven back toward Barcelona.

1939, Jan. 26. BARCELONA WAS TAKEN BY FRANCO'S TROOPS, with Italian aid. The Loyalist resistance now collapsed, and within a couple of weeks the Insurgents had overrun all of Catalonia, with some 200,000 Loyalist troops crossing the French frontier, where they were disarmed.

Feb. 27. Britain and France finally recognized the government of Gen. Franco, without conditions.

Feb. 28. President Azaña, who had taken refuge in Paris, thereupon **resigned** his position. Efforts of Britain and France to bring the civil war to an end met with the opposition of Premier Negrin, who enjoyed the support of the more radical elements in Republican Spain.

March 6. A military coup in Madrid, led by **Gen. Segismundo Casado,** resulted in the removal of Negrin and his colleagues. They fled to France by air, while at Madrid a new National Defense Council was organized, with **Gen. José Miaja** (defender of Madrid in 1936–37) at the head. The Republican fleet escaped from Cartagena and took refuge in the Tunisian port of Bizerte, where it was interned by the French authorities. The new Madrid regime was committed to a policy of "peace with honor," but this policy at once led to **conflict with the Communists** in the capital, producing a civil war within the larger civil war. The Communists were finally defeated, and Miaja then devoted himself to the task of reaching a compromise with Franco. Failing to secure assurances of leniency, the National Defense Council was finally obliged to accept unconditional surrender.

March 28. END OF THE CIVIL WAR came with the **SURRENDER OF MADRID** and Valencia. Members of the defense council fled. The war had cost about 700,000 lives in battle, 30,000 executed or assassinated, 15,000 killed in air raids. Franco and his government at once set up special tribunals that convicted hundreds of Loyalist leaders, despite the efforts of Britain and France to ensure moderation. The United States recognized the new regime (April 1).

April 7. Spain announced **adhesion to the German-Italian-Japanese anti-Communist pact** (p. 677).

May 20–June. Withdrawal of Italian and German forces from Spain after an imposing victory parade in battered Madrid. As it turned out, the Germans had some 10,000 men in Spain, mostly in the aviation and tank services. Together with the Italian "volunteers" they had aided Franco greatly in transporting troops from Morocco in the early days of the war, and had played a major role in many later engagements.

Sept. 3. Spain indicated its intention of remaining neutral in the great European conflict over Danzig and Poland. Spain remained neutral throughout the war.

1942, July. The **cortes** was reestablished by **Gen. Franco,** but on Fascist lines. It was to form the supreme organ of the state and to be composed of 438 members, almost all selected by virtue of the fact that they had qualified for administrative or juristic posts.

1944, May 3. Under Allied (especially U.S.) economic pressure, the Spanish government agreed to restrict the **shipment of minerals to Germany** and to limit the **activities of Axis agents** in Spain. *(To p. 860)*

b. PORTUGAL

(From p. 496)

1914, Nov. 23. The **Portuguese national assembly voted to join Great Britain** and France in the war against Germany, but action in accord with this vote was delayed by a coup.

1915, Jan. 28–May 14. The insurrection and **dictatorship of Gen. Pimenta de Castro,** representing a pro-German faction in the army. This coup had the support of President Arriaga. He in turn was overthrown by a democratic revolt on May 14.

1915–17. Bernardino Machado became president on the resignation of President Arriaga.

1916, March 9. GERMANY DECLARED WAR ON PORTUGAL after the seizure of German ships in the harbor of Lisbon. The Portuguese organized an expeditionary force, which arrived in France on Feb. 3, 1917, and took over a small sector of the front.

1917, Dec. 5. Gen. Sidonio Pães led another pro-German uprising, arrested and deported the president, and **made himself president-dictator.**

1918, Dec. 14. Pães was assassinated by a radical, whereupon the democratic regime was reestablished. The situation in the country continued to be utterly confused. In a land that was still 65 percent illiterate the democratic system did not function well. One cabinet relieved another, the average duration of governments being about four months. Insurrections and coups were hardly less numerous. The financial condition of the country, long parlous, went from bad to worse. Multiplication of offices, widespread political corruption, and appalling inefficiency characterized the decade from 1918 to 1928.

1919, Jan. 19–Feb. 14. A **royalist uprising** in the north assumed substantial proportions but was ultimately suppressed.

May 6. The Allied supreme council assigned to Portugal the **mandate for part of German East Africa,** known as the Kionga Triangle.

Aug. 5. Antonio José de Almeida became president.

1920, April 8. Portugal joined the League of Nations.

1923, Aug. 6. Teixeira Gomes succeeded as **president.**

1925, April 18–19. An **attempted military coup** directed against the democratic regime led to some shooting and bloodshed in Lisbon but then collapsed from want of leadership.

Dec. 16. Bernardino Machado was again elected **president.** The general situation was improving: the budget tended to be balanced, the currency became stable again, public works were on the rise, and agrarian reforms and social welfare were being actively discussed in government circles. But it was too late; Republicans were tending toward radicalism, but their traditional supporters, the middle- and lower-class people of Lisbon, were tired of the constant instability.

1926, May 28. OVERTHROW OF THE EXISTING REGIME by an army movement inspired by **Mendes Cabeçadas** and led by **Gen. Gomes da Costa.** The revolt broke out in the north and was supported by most of the army. Gomes da Costa, an audacious, vain, and politically innocent leader, became a national hero. Machado and the cabinet of Antonio Mara da Silva were overthrown, parliament was dissolved, and parties were broken up.

July 9. Gen. Antonio de Fragoso Carmona deposed the utterly incompetent Gomes da Costa, who was honorably exiled to the Azores.

1927, Feb. 3–13. Insurrection against the military dictatorship broke out at Oporto and then (Feb. 7) at Lisbon. This was described as "Communist," but was really inspired by a group of intellectual reformers around the journal (*Seara Nova*). After some severe fighting the movement was defeated.

1928, March 25. Gen. Carmona was elected president. The new regime, which had no very specific program, proved itself not much different from its predecessors, excepting that the spoils were in the hands of the military clique rather than in those of the parliament.

April 27. ANTONIO DE OLIVEIRA SALAZAR became minister of finance, with extraordinary powers. Born in 1889, he had been educated for the priesthood, had then turned to law, and had finally become a professor of economics. In a remarkably short time he solved the long-standing financial muddle (using old-fashioned methods of economy and strict accountancy). Before long he became the dominant figure in Portugal, a retiring, studious statesman, proponent of a national renaissance.

1930, July 30. Foundation of the National Union, a political-social party of a Fascist type. This was the only party permitted by the government and was designed to prepare the way for the Estado Novo. By 1936 the National Union had all of the trappings of a Fascist party, including the Portuguese Legion, a body of volunteers for the defense of the regime, and the Portuguese Youth, a compulsory paramilitary framework for the young.

1932, July 5. OLIVEIRA SALAZAR BECAME PREMIER and to all intents and purposes dictator. He ruled with a strong hand, but opposition to Fascism and dictatorship continued to smolder, as shown by occasional uprisings and attempts on the life of the dictator.

1933, Feb. 22. The government promulgated a **NEW CONSTITUTION,** which was approved by plebiscite on March 19. Provisions: a **president** elected for seven years; a **cabinet** appointed by the president and responsible to him alone; a **national assembly** elected by heads of families possessing a certain degree of education; a **corporative chamber** representing occupations (on the Italian model), but with only advisory power.

1934, Jan. 18. A **revolutionary movement** led by the General Confederation of Labor and by the Communists was suppressed and the leaders imprisoned.

Dec. 16. In the **elections** the voters were allowed to choose among candidates put forward by the National Union; no others were permitted. The first national assembly of the new regime met on Jan. 10, 1935.

1935, Feb. 17. President Carmona was elected for another term.

1936, July–1939. With the **outbreak of the civil war in Spain** (p. 691) the Portuguese dictatorship at once sided with the Insurgents against the Republican government. Portugal became one of the main routes by which supplies reached Franco from Germany and elsewhere. This continued until in April 1937 the British government persuaded the Portuguese to permit a British border control. By that time Franco was able to get his supplies through the northern Spanish coast towns. The British were obliged to strain themselves to the utmost to uphold the traditional alliance with Portugal, the latter country having become of immense strategic importance because of its location athwart the routes from Africa to Britain and France.

1939, March 18. Portugal concluded a nonaggression pact with Fascist Spain.

May 22, 26. Portugal and Britain reaffirmed their traditional alliance, Portugal thereby demonstrating the desire to stand well with both Fascist and democratic powers.

1940. Salazar's regime reached its apogee with the ceremonies surrounding the tricentennial of independence, fêted with typical Fascist displays.

1943, Oct. 13. Portugal allowed the Allies to establish military bases in the Azores with little or no compensation. *(To p. 863)*

9. ITALY AND THE PAPACY

(From p. 499)

When World War I commenced in Aug. 1914, the Italian cabinet, headed by **Antonio Salandra,** chose neutrality despite Italy's membership in the Triple Alliance. After weighing offers from both camps, the Italian government turned against the **Central Powers** and joined the **Allies** on May 23, 1915 (p. 656).

1914, Sept. 3. BENEDICT XV (Giacomo della Chiesa) was elected pope on the death of Pius X (Aug. 20). During the war he appealed to the belligerents for peace, submitting outline proposals on Aug. 1, 1917.

1916, Dec. 12. The **Salandra cabinet** resigned and was succeeded by a new ministry led by **Paolo Boselli.**

1917, Oct. 29. The **Boselli cabinet** fell as a result of the **Caporetto disaster** (p. 660). A new cabinet under **Vittorio Orlando** took office and remained in power until June 1919.

Italy had entered the war primarily to gain territory and wrest control of the Adriatic from Austria-Hungary. Its military achievement proved far below Allied expectations and as a result Italy was given but little say at the peace conference. President Wilson took a hostile stand toward the provisions of the **Treaty of London** (p. 655), and Italy, in return for 600,000 lives lost, received only 9,000 square miles of territory with a population of 1.6 million. None of the former German colonies was assigned to Italy as a mandate. The war, then, left Italy loaded with debt, suffering from high costs of living, and generally restless and discontented. The governments enjoyed no prestige. The political situation was complicated by a rapid spread of Communism and by the emergence of an organized clerical party. Efforts of the government to meet the situation by social legislation had little success.

By the end of the war **Italian economic bifurcation** was becoming more evident as modern industry grew in the north. Industrial wealth centered in the triangle between Turin, Genoa, and Milan, where union activity was especially strong. Workers were split among a socialist union, a Catholic union (which appealed to the peasantry as well), and an anarcho-syndicalist union. As for the peasantry, still the majority of the Italian population, they were disappointed after vague promises of land redistribution during the war were ignored by the government.

1919, Jan. 19. Formation of the Partito Popolare, a Catholic party.

March 23. Formation of the first Fascio di Combattimento by **Benito Mussolini** (b. 1883), former socialist and editor of *Avanti*, who had turned violently interventionist and nationalist.

April 24. The Italian delegation left the Paris peace conference after the public appeal of President Wilson against the Italian territorial claims on the Adriatic. The Italian delegation returned on May 5.

June 19. The Orlando cabinet resigned. A new ministry was formed by **Francesco Nitti**, with **Tommaso Tittoni** at the foreign office.

Sept. 2. A **new electoral law** introduced universal suffrage and the French system of *scrutin de liste* (election by departmental lists) and proportional representation.

Sept. 12. Gabriele d'Annunzio, eminent writer, ardent nationalist, and world war hero, **seized Fiume** with a band of volunteers (p. 675).

Oct. 5–8. The Socialist Congress at Bologna voted for adherence to the Third International.

Nov. 11. The pope definitely lifted the prohibition against participation by Catholics in Italian political life.

Nov. 16. Elections for Parliament. The Socialists secured 160 seats; Catholics 103; Liberals 93; Radicals 58.

1920, April 26. The **San Remo conference** decided to leave the Fiume question to settlement by Italy and Yugoslavia.

June 9. Fall of the Nitti cabinet, after it had been twice reconstructed. A new government was formed by the veteran **Giovanni Giolitti**, with **Count Carlo Sforza** at the foreign office.

Aug. 2. Agreement with Albania to evacuate the country, with the exception of the island of Saseno. The Albanians had attacked the Italian forces and made their position untenable.

Aug. 31. A general lockout in the metallurgical factories led to the **occupation of the factories** by the workers, the beginning of a far-reaching movement. By September **factories all over Italy were occupied by workers.** Despite popular support, a Socialist revolution did not occur; the workers never attempted the seizure of government buildings. The government therefore refused to use force against them and eventually the factories returned to former management.

Nov. 12. Treaty of Rapallo with Yugoslavia (p. 675).

Dec. 1. D'Annunzio declared war on the Italian government.

Dec. 27. Italian troops bombarded Fiume and forced D'Annunzio to evacuate. Disorders continued in the city between the autonomists and the nationalists.

1921, Jan. 13–22. Congress of the Socialist Party at Livorno. The party split into a moderate and a radical wing, the latter frankly Communist. Their main theoretician was **Antonio Gramsci** (1891–1937), the publisher of *Ordine Nuovo* in Turin.

Feb. 27. Communist and Fascist riots at Florence, inaugurating a period of repeated clashes that ultimately approximated civil war between the two factions. Central in this disorder were the Fascist **Arditi**, gangs of strike-breaking thugs.

May 15. Elections, the first held under a system of universal suffrage. The Liberals and Democrats won a resounding victory and secured 275 seats, as against 122 for the Socialists and 107 for the Popular (Catholic) Party. The Communists had only 16, the Fascists 22.

June 26. Fall of the Giolitti cabinet, the result of dissatisfaction with its foreign policy. A new ministry was organized (July 5) by **Ivanhoe Bonomi.**

1922, Feb. 6. PIUS XI (Achille Ratti) was elected pope on the demise of Benedict XV (Jan. 22). His reign proved to be one of the most critical in the modern history of the papacy. Although the long-standing quarrel with the French republic was gradually adjusted by compromise (May 12, 1923; Jan. 18, 1924), the pope took a strong **stand against communism,** which he condemned publicly on many occasions (as in the encyclical of March 19, 1937). The anticlerical policies of the Mexican government drew similar condemnations in 1926, as did those of the Spanish republic in 1931.

Feb. 9. The Bonomi cabinet resigned. The new government (Feb. 25) was led by **Luigi Facta,** supported by Liberals and Democrats.

March 3. A Fascist coup overthrew the Fiume government. The town was then occupied by Italian troops (March 17).

May. Fascists drove out the Communist city government of Bologna. The conflict between the factions extended to all the larger cities.

Aug. 3–4. Fascists seized control of the Milan city government. The government seemed quite unable to cope with the aggressive action of the bands.

Oct. 16. Formation of a quadrumvirate under Mussolini (Michele Bianchi, Italo Balbo, Gen. Emilio De Bono, Dino Grandi).

Oct. 24. Fascist congress at Naples. Mussolini, having refused a seat in the cabinet, demanded the resignation of Facta and formation of a Fascist cabinet. Facta refused, apparently underestimating the power of the Fascist movement, which was, to be sure, a minority movement but one led aggressively and supported by nationalist elements and by business interests that feared communism.

Oct. 28. The MARCH ON ROME by the Fascists. The king refused Facta's demand for the proclamation of martial law, whereupon Facta resigned. The Fascists occupied Rome.

Oct. 31. Mussolini, summoned by the king from Milan, **formed a cabinet** of Fascists and Nationalists.

Nov. 25. Mussolini was granted by the king and the Parliament **dictatorial powers** until Dec. 31, 1923, to restore order and introduce reforms. He then appointed prefects and subprefects of Fascist sympathies and, with the support of the army, gradually established control of the government machinery. He still professed the intention of governing constitutionally, and the constitution remained technically in force.

1923, Jan. 14. A voluntary **Fascist militia** authorized by the king.

March 24. Reform of the judicial system.

May. After having supported Mussolini in 1922, those members of the Popular (Catholic) Party who had taken office with him were forced out. **Don Luigi Sturzo,** leader of the party's left wing, resisted the Fascists, but Pius XI helped Mussolini by denouncing Sturzo and his followers.

July. Initiation of a rigid policy of **Italianization in South Tyrol** (Upper Adige).

Aug.–Sept. THE CORFU INCIDENT (p. 675).

Nov. 14. A new electoral law. Before the expiration of his dictatorial powers, Mussolini forced through parliament a law providing that any party securing the largest number of votes in an election (provided it had at least one-fourth of the total) should receive two-thirds of the seats. The remaining seats were to be divided according to proportional representation. This arrangement would avoid the difficulty of coalitions and blocs in a parliament where no party had a majority.

1924, April 6. In the **elections** the Fascists, through government control of the machinery and through liberal use of "squad" methods, polled 65 percent of the votes and were given 375 seats in the chamber (as against the 35 they had previously had).

June 10. MURDER OF THE SOCIALIST DEPUTY GIACOMO MATTEOTTI, who had written a book, *The Fascisti Exposed*, containing detailed case histories of hundreds of acts of violence illegally carried out by Fascists. The murderers were Fascists, some of them prominent in the party. When tried in 1926 they were either acquitted or given light sentences.

June 15. Most of the non-Fascist third of the new chamber seceded (Aventine Secession) and vowed not to return until the Matteotti affair had been cleared up and the complicity of the government disproved. The opposition demanded the disbanding of the Fascist militia and the cessation of violence. Mussolini, faced by a major crisis (the most serious during his rule), disavowed all connection with the affair and dismissed all those implicated. A rigid **press censorship** was introduced (July 1) and meetings of the opposition group were forbidden (Aug. 3). The support of part of the Liberal group, under Salandra, helped to break the force of the opposition, which never returned to parliament.

1925. Continuation of the crisis, marked by revival of Liberal and Communist demonstrations in various parts of the country. Mussolini twice reorganized the cabinet (Jan. 5, Aug. 30) and extended the work of repression through the Legge Fascistissime, which tightened control of the press, forbade **Freemasonry** and similar secret organizations (May 19), and established government control of local government through the appointed podestàs. Many political opponents of the regime were arrested and transported to the Lipari Islands.

1926, April 3. Recognition of a number of **labor syndicates** and establishment of compulsory arbitration in industrial disputes. Lockouts and strikes made illegal.

April 3. Organization of the Ballilla, a Fascist youth association to train the rising generation.

April 7. Mussolini wounded in the nose by Violet Gibson, a deranged Irish noblewoman. Two other attempts were made to assassinate the Duce (Sept. 11, Oct. 31).

Sept. 25. Beginning of the **campaign against the** Mafia, a loose criminal organization that had dominated Sicilian politics and life for 50 years.

Nov. 27. Treaty with Albania, establishing what amounted to an Italian protectorate.

1928, May 12. A new electoral law. Universal suffrage abolished and franchise restricted to men of 21 and over who paid syndicate rates or taxes of 100 lire. Electorate reduced from almost 10 million to about 3 million. Four hundred candidates for election to be submitted to voters by the Fascist grand council, to be voted for or rejected in toto by the electorate.

Nov. 15. The **Fascist grand council** made an official organ of the state and charged with the duty of naming candidates for the chamber and/ or coordinating all government activities.

1929, Feb. 11. The **LATERAN TREATIES** with the papacy (ratified June 7).

Of these agreements the **Lateran Treaty** proper restored the temporal power of the pope, who was to rule over **Vatican City,** a small section of Rome (108.7 acres) around St. Peter's and the Vatican, in full sovereignty. **A concordat with the Italian government** defined the position of the Church in the Fascist state, while a **financial agreement** involved the payment by the Italian government of an indemnity of 750 million lire in cash and 1 billion lire in government bonds. Under the new conditions, the pope gave up his status of voluntary prisoner and on July 25 for the first time left the Vatican. The agreements by no means ended friction between the Church and the government. Much dispute arose regarding the activities of the Catholic youth organization, the Azione Cattolica.

March 24. Elections. The 400 official candidates received almost 100 percent of the votes.

April 21. National Council of Corporations established to adjust disputes between various groups in the interest of national production. The council was composed of representatives from the syndicates and from the government. Despite much official oratory about the Corporate State it does not appear that much actual power was entrusted to the syndicates or corporations.

1930, April 30. Great naval program, the result of failure to secure recognition of Italian parity from France.

Oct. 25. Marriage of Princess Giovanna to King Boris of Bulgaria. Bulgaria was brought more and more within the orbit of Italian influence.

1930–35. The **economic depression,** aggravated for Italy by lack of basic raw materials and constant adverse trade balance. Great efforts were made to increase the production of food and to reclaim swamp areas for agricultural exploitation (Pontine marshes, for example), as well as to develop hydroelectric power. Industrial production was increased and cost of production reduced by cuts in wages and other devices. Italy, like many other countries, tried to stave off the worst effects of the depression by the conclusion of **trade pacts,** rigid control of foreign exchange, conversion of the public debt, and so on. The result was almost complete government control of finance and industry.

1931, May 15. The pope issued the **encyclical** *Quadragesimo anno,* to supplement the famous encyclical *Rerum novarum* of Leo XIII (1891). The pope called for social and economic reform, condemned the maldistribution of wealth, and strongly urged fundamental changes to give the workers a fairer share in the product of their labor. At the same time he once more condemned communism and socialism.

1933, Jan. The advent of the National Socialist government in Germany at once raised the **prospect of Italo-German cooperation,** which would have involved an immeasurable strengthening of Italy's position with respect to Great Britain and France.

1934. Luigi Pirandello (1867–1936), novelist and dramatist, was awarded the Nobel Prize for literature.

Nov. 10. Establishment of the **Central Corporative Committee,** a type of economic parliament intended to complete the structure of the corporative state.

Dec. 5. CLASH OF ITALIAN AND ETHIOPIAN TROOPS AT UAL-UAL, on the disputed Ethiopian-Somaliland frontier. This was seized upon by the Italian government as the point of departure for the conquest of Ethiopia (p. 797).

1935, Oct. 3. THE ITALIAN FORCES BEGAN THE INVASION OF ETHIOPIA. They took **Adua** on Oct. 6.

Oct. 7. The **LEAGUE COUNCIL DECLARED ITALY THE AGGRESSOR** in the Ethiopian affair and began to arrange for sanctions.

Nov. 18. The League of Nations voted the **application of sanctions** against Italy (prohibition of import of Italian goods, arms embargo, financial embargo, etc.). Italy thereupon ended all economic relations with the sanctionist powers and adopted a system of rigid control of food and raw materials to meet the emergency.

Italy weathered the sanctionist storm, the more so as the nations could not agree to apply the **oil sanction** (Feb. 1936), which might have proved decisive, but which might also have involved armed conflict. The reoccupation of the Rhineland by Germany (March 1936) diverted the attention of Britain and France and made all prospects of further action against Italy illusory.

1936, May 5. The Italian forces finally occupied **Addis Ababa,** and the resistance of the Ethiopians collapsed (p. 797).

May 9. The **ITALIAN GOVERNMENT FORMALLY PROCLAIMED THE ANNEXATION OF ALL ETHIOPIA,** the king of Italy assuming the title emperor of Ethiopia. Gradual pacification of the country (p. 797).

July 4. The League council voted to discontinue sanctions.

July. OUTBREAK OF THE CIVIL WAR IN SPAIN (p. 691). From the very outset Mussolini took an active part in supporting the Insurgents with men and equipment, on the theory that Italy could not permit the establishment of a "Communist" government in the Mediterranean. The expense of sending 50,000–75,000 "volunteers" to Spain, added to the cost of the Ethiopian campaigns and the demands for ever greater armaments, necessitated the **devaluation of the lire** (Oct. 5) and the introduction of various forms of levy on capital. At the same time the Italian action in Spain aroused the apprehensions of Great Britain and France and served to increase the tension in the Mediterranean. Mussolini, under these circumstances, was obliged to draw closer to Germany.

Oct. 25. The **Italian-German agreement regarding Austria was concluded** (p. 677). It served as a foundation for Italo-German cooperation and may be taken as the beginning of the **Rome-Berlin Axis.**

1937, Aug. 27. The papacy recognized the Insurgent regime in the Spanish civil war.

Dec. 11. The withdrawal of Italy from the League of Nations.

1938, Jan. 7. The Italian government announced a huge **naval construction program,** to supplement the great rearmament plan introduced a year earlier.

March. The German annexation of Austria (p. 703). The world was astounded at Mussolini's calm acceptance of a situation that involved the breakdown of the Rome protocol system and brought the powerful German Nazi state to the Brenner Pass.

Aug. 3. The Italian government, despite past policy and assurances, introduced a **"racial" program** directed against the Jews, who were few in Italy. Various regulations barred foreign Jews from Italian schools, ordered all Jews who had taken up residence in Italy since 1919 to leave within six months, discharged Jewish teachers and students from schools and universities, and prohibited marriage between Italians and non-Aryans. Despite such official policies, Italy earned the anger of its Nazi allies for the lax enforcement of anti-Semitic laws throughout the war. Pius XI also criticized German and Italian racial policies.

Sept. In the **Czechoslovak crisis** (p. 705) Mussolini remained in the background until the tension reached the breaking point. He delivered a series of threatening speeches, but in the last resort did his utmost to bring about the Munich meeting.

Oct. 8. The Fascist grand council abolished the chamber of deputies, last vestige of the old constitution, and replaced it with a **chamber of fascist unions and corporations.**

Nov. 30. A great **demonstration in the Italian chamber,** with loud demands for the cession of Corsica and Tunisia by France.

1939, Feb. 10. Pope Pius XI died with the reputation for firmness against any regime threatening religion. His successor, **PIUS XII** (Eugenio Pacelli), was elected pope on March 2. He had served for years as papal secretary of state and chief adviser to Pius XI and was generally recognized as a man of strong will, great astuteness, and diplomatic skill. He devoted himself at once to efforts for the pacification of Europe but introduced no basic change of policy.

April 7. Italian invasion and **conquest of Albania,** which voted personal union with Italy (p. 722).

May 22. Conclusion of a political and **military alliance with Germany.** The closest cooperation was now established, with much coming and going of military men and technical experts.

Aug. Conferences of Count Galeazzo Ciano with the German leaders were kept extremely secret, but were taken to presage the international crisis that broke on Aug. 20 (p 679). Throughout Germany's dispute with Poland the Italian press strongly supported the German position, though Mussolini used his influence to effect a pacific solution. When the storm broke on Sept. 1–3, Italy surprised the world by maintaining **neutrality.**

1940, June 7. Italy ordered its ships to neutral ports.

June 10. ITALY DECLARED WAR ON FRANCE AND BRITAIN.

June 12. The British government announced a complete **blockade of Italy.**

1941, June 22. ITALY DECLARED WAR ON THE SOVIET UNION.

Dec. 11. ITALY DECLARED WAR ON THE UNITED STATES.

1943, July 10. Allied invasion of Sicily (p. 806).

July 25. Mussolini resigned and was placed under arrest. **Marshal Pietro Badoglio replaced him and declared the Fascist Party dissolved** (July 28).

Sept. 3. The **Badoglio cabinet accepted terms of surrender for Italy.** Upon the announcement of surrender (Sept. 8), German forces seized control of the leading cities, including Rome, Milan, Trieste, Genoa, Bologna, Verona, and Cremona.

Sept. 15. Mussolini, rescued from captivity by German troops, **proclaimed a Republican Fascist Party** and achieved some authority in the areas of Italy still under German control.

Oct. 13. The Badoglio government of Italy declared war on Germany.

1944, Feb. 11. Parts of **southern Italy, with Sicily and Sardinia, were returned to the jurisdiction of the Italian government.** After occupation these areas had been administered with the aid of an **Allied Control Commission,** an **Allied Military Government** (AMG), and an **Advisory Council** for Italy composed of representatives of the United States, Great Britain, the Soviet Union, and the French Committee of National Liberation.

June 4. The **U.S. Fifth Army entered Rome.** Marshal Badoglio resigned as Italian premier and was succeeded by **Ivanoe Bonomi.**

1945, April 28. MUSSOLINI WAS CAPTURED AND EXECUTED by Italian anti-Fascist forces. *(To p. 864)*

10. SWITZERLAND

(From p. 499)

1914, Aug. 1. The **Swiss Confederation mobilized** its forces in view of the international crisis and remained on a war footing throughout the conflict. On Aug. 4 the government announced its **neutrality,** and its readiness to defend it no doubt had something to do with respect for Swiss territory on both sides. The war resulted in ever-increasing authority of the federal as against the cantonal governments (the federal council was given exceptional powers on Aug. 3, 1914). Switzerland suffered much from food shortages and was obliged to establish highly **centralized control of economic activity.** The demands of the combatants and the need for food resulted in a striking **development of Swiss industry,** with a corresponding growth of industrial labor and a spread of socialist and radical thought.

1915. The all-Swiss **Metalworkers' Association merged with the Watchmakers' Association.** By 1919 membership in the Swiss Metalworkers' and Watchmakers' Association (SMUV) was over 84,000.

1918, Nov. 11. A **general strike** began in Zurich. The causes resembled those in most of Europe at this time: demobilized workers faced unemployment, food prices and rents had doubled during the war, and workers' wages had only slightly increased. The strikers capitulated after three days of demonstrations. Of the nine demands put forth by the strikers, one became law by 1919: proportional voting was introduced in the election of the Nationalrat.

Dec. 8. Switzerland broke off relations with Soviet Russia, which was suspected of subversive propaganda.

1919, April 11. Geneva was chosen as the seat of the League of Nations. The Swiss, though long interested in international collaboration, were nevertheless primarily concerned with maintenance of their neutrality, and were anxious to avoid dangerous commitments.

April 11. The people of **Vorarlberg voted** by a large majority **for union with Switzerland,** but the federal government ignored the opportunity to extend the confederation.

June 28. In the Treaty of Versailles the powers recognized the **perpetual neutrality of Switzerland,** while the Swiss gave up their treaty right to occupy northern Savoy in the event of war (this right or obligation had not been exercised). The intricate **problem of the free zones** of Upper Savoy and Gex, so important for the defense of Geneva, was left to direct Franco-Swiss negotiations.

Nov. 19. The Swiss parliament voted to join the League of Nations, but the federal government first secured from the League council the declaration of London.

1920, Feb. 13. The **declaration of London,** by which the League council agreed that Switzerland should not be obliged to take part in military sanctions under the terms of the covenant.

March 8. Switzerland formally joined the League.

May 16. Nevertheless, a plebiscite arranged to decide the issue showed a vote of only 416,000 in favor as against 323,000 opposed to joining the League.

1921, Aug. 7. Agreement with France with respect to the free zones. Switzerland gave up former treaty rights, but this arrangement was repudiated by a Swiss plebiscite (Feb. 18, 1923). Thereupon the French government took unilateral action, moving its customs stations forward to the political frontier (Nov. 10, 1923). The Swiss government protested, and it was finally decided to investigate the legal aspects of the problem and to arbitrate the dispute (Oct. 30, 1924, March 18, 1925).

1923, March 29. Conclusion of a **customs union between Switzerland** and the little principality of **Liechtenstein,** which before the war had been closely associated with Austria-Hungary.

May 10. Vaslav Vorovsky, Russian delegate to the Lausanne conference, **was assassinated by Maurice Conradi,** a Swiss who had suffered under the Soviet regime in Russia. Conradi was acquitted by the courts (Nov. 16), and the incident brought Switzerland and Russia to a state of extreme tension.

1927. A federal law prohibited government officials from striking.

1930, April 13. The Swiss and French governments having failed to reach agreement on the **free zones,** the Permanent Court of International Justice was appealed to.
1932, June 7. The court decided the question in favor of Switzerland. The French government was directed to withdraw its customs stations by Jan. 1, 1934.

 Nov. 9. Serious labor disturbances at Geneva resulted from the growing pressure of the world crisis. The government proceeded with vigor against all extremists.
1933, May 12. The wearing of party uniforms was forbidden.
1934. The **Swiss government bitterly opposed the admission of Russia to the League of Nations** and voted against it in the League council.

 A planned reduction in wages threatened to cause a major dispute between workers and employers but was averted when the Federal Ministry of Economics created an arbitration commission. This led to a 1936 federal decree giving the ministry the right to resolve as final arbiter all collective wages disputes that could not be solved between the parties. Neither employers nor employees responded favorably.
1935, Feb. 24. By plebiscite the people voted to extend the period of military training. The Swiss embarked upon an **extensive armament program** (June 5, 1936), which involved thorough modernization of frontier defenses, mechanization of army units, development of air defense, and other measures.
1936, Feb. 4. Assassination of the National Socialist leader **Wilhelm Gustloff** by a Jew at Davos. The government at once forbade continuation of a national organization of National Socialists.

 Sept. 26. The **government decided to devalue the Swiss franc,** in keeping with the policy of France.

1937. A peace agreement was signed between the Employers Association and the unions in the Swiss engineering and metalworking industries. This agreement long served as the basis for employer-employee relations and contributed to the relatively small number of strikes that occurred after 1937.

 Dec. 7. Romansch was recognized as a fourth national (though not official) **language.** This was a step designed to win renewed support from the cantons most directly exposed to Italian designs.
1938, April 30. The **government appealed to the council of the League of Nations to recognize Switzerland's unconditional neutrality,** pointing out the great change that had come over Europe since 1919 and stressing the particularly exposed position of Switzerland between the League powers and those of the Rome-Berlin Axis. The **League council accepted the Swiss view** (May 14), thus freeing Switzerland from all obligation to take part even in economic sanctions against a future aggressor.
1939, Sept. 1. Switzerland proclaimed its neutrality and successfully preserved it throughout the Second World War. But, as a protective measure, the parliament granted special wartime authority to the Federal Council for the duration of the war. Under this authority the Federal Council introduced an **insurance plan** to give financial relief to persons liable for military service. This served later as an operating model for postwar old-age and survivors' insurance (AHV), disability or invalidity insurance (IV), and the family allowance plan for agricultural employees and small farmers.
1940, Nov. 19. The **government dissolved the Swiss Nazi Party** on the ground that the activities of the party were "of a nature to endanger public order and create conflict." *(To p. 868)*

11. GERMANY
(From pp. 504, 666)

Theobald von Bethmann-Hollweg, chancellor since 1909, remained in office until July 1917, but German policies were increasingly influenced by the military leaders.
1917, Jan. 8. The German government decided to resume **unrestricted submarine warfare.** Bethmann-Hollweg opposed but was unable to prevent this decision (p. 662).

 By 1917 growing unrest led to certain important promises by the government.

 April 7. Emperor William II, as king of Prussia, announced in an **Easter message** the end of the famous three-class system of voting in Prussia. The introduction of a system of equal, direct, and secret suffrage was announced somewhat later (July 11).

 July 14. Bethmann-Hollweg, having lost the support of the Conservatives, National Liberals, and Center, and having long since become objectionable to the military, **was allowed to retire.**

 July 14–Oct. 30. Chancellorship of George Michaelis, an almost unknown official, who was the appointee of the high command and served chiefly as a cloak for the **power of Ludendorff.**

 July 19. Under the leadership of **Matthias Erzberger** and his Catholic Center Party, the **Reichstag passed a resolution in favor of a peace of understanding,** without annexations (212 Centrists, Majority Socialists, and National Liberals against 126 Conservatives, National Liberals, and Independent Socialists). The new chancellor declared that his aims were attainable within the limits of the resolution as "he understood it."

 Oct. 28. Mutiny of sailors at Kiel, caused by orders from the admiralty to go to sea and fight the British. "Further than Heligoland we will not go."

 Oct. 29. Emperor William II, alarmed at demands in the **Reichstag** for his abdication, left Berlin for army headquarters at Spa.

 Nov. 4, 5. The revolt at Kiel spread to other seaports. **Councils of workers and soldiers formed.**

 Nov. 7. Revolt at Munich, led by **Kurt Eisner,** an Independent Socialist, led to the proclamation of a republic in Bavaria (Nov. 8).

 Nov. 9. ABDICATION OF THE EMPEROR announced in Berlin by Prince Max (the chancellor since Oct. 4). **REPUBLIC PROCLAIMED.** Government turned over to Majority Socialists, led by **Friedrich Ebert**

and **Philipp Scheidemann.** The emperor fled to Holland in his special train. His abdication was not signed until Nov. 28, by which time all other German rulers had abdicated.

 Nov. 10. A joint **ministry of Independent and Majority Socialists** took control in Berlin. Struggle between the extreme Left, or **Spartacist,** group, led by **Karl Liebknecht** and **Rosa Luxemburg,** who favored a Communist regime, and the Social Democrats (Majority Socialists), who wanted a gradual and not a violent abandonment of capitalism.

 Nov. 25. A conference of representatives of the new state governments met at Berlin and agreed that a **national constituent assembly** should be elected. The Spartacists opposed the plan for a national assembly.
1919, Jan. 5–15. Spartacist revolt in Berlin, crushed by the provisional government with the aid of the regular army. The Independent Socialists sided with the Spartacists, now avowed Communists. Rosa Luxemburg and Karl Liebknecht were killed while under arrest (Jan. 15).

 Jan. 19. Election of a national assembly to draw up a constitution. The Communists refused to take part, but all other groups both Right and Left were represented. Majority Socialists won 163 seats, Center 88, Democrats 75, Nationalists 42, Independent Socialists 22, others 31.

 Feb. 6. National assembly met at Weimar.

 Feb. 11. Friedrich Ebert chosen as first president of the German Republic, by the national assembly.

 Feb.–March. Further **Communist uprisings** in Berlin, Munich, and elsewhere, suppressed by **Gustav Noske,** acting for the government.

 Feb. 21. Assassination of Kurt Eisner by a conspiracy to reestablish the monarchy.

 April 4–May 1. Soviet Republic established in Bavaria. This was overthrown by armed forces of the federal government.

 June 1. Proclamation of a Rhineland Republic, instigated and supported by France. After some months the movement collapsed because of the hostility of the inhabitants.

 June 20. The **Scheidemann ministry resigned** rather than sign the peace treaty dictated by the Allies.

June 21. The **German fleet was scuttled at Scapa Flow** by its crews.

June 23. The new cabinet, under **Gustav Bauer** (**Matthias Erzberger,** vice chancellor; **Count Ulrich von Brockdorff-Rantzau,** foreign minister), **accepted the peace treaty unconditionally** after the Weimar assembly had voted 237 to 138 for conditional acceptance in order to avoid invasion of the country.

July 12. The **Allied blockade** was finally lifted after a large part of the population had been brought to the verge of starvation.

July 31. ADOPTION OF THE WEIMAR CONSTITUTION. The president, elected for a seven-year term, was to appoint a chancellor who in turn chose a cabinet that could command a majority in the Reichstag. By Articles 25 and 48 the president was empowered to suspend constitutional guaranties and dissolve the Reichstag in periods of national emergency. The Reichsrat, composed of delegates from 18 states (no one of which was to have more than two-fifths of the seats), could delay but not prevent legislation. The members of the Reichstag were elected not as individuals or as representatives of districts but by party lists for all Germany. A system of proportional representation ensured the representation of minority parties but also necessitated coalition governments.

The new republic faced many problems. Germany was in financial ruins, the dead and wounded from the war numbered about 6 million, and returning soldiers found no jobs. Facing a crisis in confidence, the government turned to Paul von Hindenburg and the military. The latter, seeing in the republic the lost hope of maintaining German unity, lent its support by putting down rebellions and giving the new regime legitimacy. This alliance won over the majority of civil servants, many of whom remained loyal to the monarchy, who eased the transition to peace. The alliance also prevented significant social change, however. Landlords and industrialists retained their traditional power. Discontent and instability resulted; those on the Left sought the social changes promised by a republic and those on the Right sought a return to the prestige of the past. **The result was a republic with over 11 governments in 13 years,** as governments vacillated in their search for partners on the Left and on the Right.

There was change, however, in the cultural life of Germany. Socialists who controlled the city governments of many large cities eagerly sought to demonstrate Germany's new beginning through architecture. Schools, hospitals, public offices, and low-cost housing for workers reflected the rise of **Walter Gropius** (1883–1969) and his **Bauhaus** school of design, which emphasized functionalism. In other arts the absence of social stability fostered social criticism, as in the works of dramatist **Bertolt Brecht** (1898–1956) and novelist **Thomas Mann** (1875–1955). Finally, the amusement industry flourished for those who had profited from speculation during the inflationary crisis of 1923. The **cabaret** became the center of new freedoms, seen especially in new expressions of sexuality. This remained an urban phenomenon, however, leaving rural Germans to reflect upon the "moral decay" of their nation.

Territorial changes. Aside from the union of eight central German states to form the new state of **Thuringia** (April 30, 1920), many areas around Germany held plebiscites to determine union or were reallocated by the Allies. These included plebiscites in **Allenstein** and **Marienwerder** (July 11, 1920), **Upper Silesia** (March 20, 1921), and the southern zone of **Schleswig** (March 14, 1920), all of which voted for union with Germany.

Sept. 22. The government was obliged by the Allies to strike out provision for the **representation of Austria** and to promise to respect Austrian independence.

1920, March 13–17. The **KAPP PUTSCH,** a monarchical coup, led to seizure of government buildings in Berlin. The government fled to Stuttgart, but the movement collapsed as result of a general strike of the trade unions.

March 19. A great **Spartacist rising** took place in the Ruhr mining districts.

April 3. Government troops, having entered the Ruhr, put down the revolt with great severity.

April 6–May 17. **French troops occupied Frankfurt** and some of the Ruhr towns as a reply to invasion of the Ruhr by German government troops.

June 6. **General elections,** to replace the national assembly by a reg-

ular Reichstag. The Weimar coalition lost its majority, and a new coalition was formed of the People's Party (Liberal), Center, and Democrats. The Müller cabinet resigned (June 8), and a new government was formed by **Konstantin Fehrenbach,** leader of the Center Party (June 25). The Socialists were excluded.

July 5–16. Spa conference (p. 675). The Germans signed a protocol of disarmament and arranged for reparations payments.

1921, March 8. Allied occupation of Düsseldorf, Duisburg, and **Ruhrort,** because of alleged German default in reparations payments.

May 11. Germany accepted the Allied **reparations terms** (p. 675).

July 16. Trial of war criminals at Leipzig.

Aug. 29. Assassination of Matthias Erzberger by reactionary conspirators, who escaped.

1922, June 24. Assassination of Walther Rathenau, Jewish industrialist and cabinet minister, by reactionary nationalists. The assassins committed suicide and their accomplices were mildly dealt with by the government.

June 30. Membership in monarchist organizations made a criminal offense.

Aug. Beginning of the **collapse of the mark,** due to heavy reparations payments.

1923, Jan. 11. OCCUPATION OF THE RUHR by French and Belgian forces, after Germany had been declared in default (p. 675). The government suspended all deliveries to the Allies, but the Franco-Belgian commission arrested the recalcitrant mine owners and took over mines and railroads. The government supported the population in a policy of **passive resistance** by printing currency to aid striking miners and railroad workers. This resulted in **massive inflation** and fueled the collapse of the mark. The workers were hard hit because their wages, although steadily increased, did not keep up with rising prices. The middle classes, especially those relying on pensions, rents, or investment in government loans, were hardest hit. Their faith in the republic was severely undermined.

Aug. 12. Gustav Stresemann, leader of the People's Party, formed a new government with the support of the Socialist, Center, and Democratic Parties. His goal was to **end passive resistance,** which he did on Sept. 16, and restore the economy.

Oct. 21. A **Rhineland Republic** was proclaimed at Aachen, with Belgian and French support. The government was faced also with Communist troubles in Saxony and with monarchist plots in Bavaria.

Nov. 8–11. "BEER HALL PUTSCH" in Munich, occasioned by the general crisis resulting from the Ruhr occupation and the financial collapse. **General Erich Ludendorff** and **Adolf Hitler,** leader of a growing National Socialist Party, attempted to overthrow the Bavarian government. The rising was poorly organized and was easily put down. Hitler was arrested and sentenced to five years in prison. While serving his term he wrote *Mein Kampf,* a book outlining his career, his theories, and his program. He was released after serving less than a year, and at once resumed his propaganda and organizing activity.

Nov. 15. Opening of the Rentenbank. Hjalmar Schacht, appointed special currency commissioner, undertook the difficult task of substituting a new monetary unit for the worthless paper currency. The new *Rentenmark,* theoretically secured by a blanket mortgage on all land and industry to the amount of 3.2 billion gold marks, was exchangeable for 1 trillion of the old marks. **Hans Luther,** as minister of finance, tried by drastic economies, including the dismissal of more than 700,000 government employees, to balance the budget. But the Dawes Plan (p. 676) and the foreign loan that went with it were what really made it possible for Germany to emerge from bankruptcy. In the process most of the internal debt, public and private, was wiped out. The businessmen, who tended to dominate the various coalition governments, were, however, convinced that Germany, in need of raw materials, markets, and new capital, must remain on good terms with Britain, the United States, and possibly France. Hence the **policy of fulfillment** represented by **Gustav Stresemann,** who remained in every cabinet until his death in 1929. The policy made possible the flotation of large bond issues, largely in the United States, which helped pay reparations and brought on a fictitious prosperity.

1924, Jan. 31. Collapse of the separatist movement in the Rhineland, after the assassination (Jan. 9) of **Heinz,** the president of the autonomous Palatinate government.

May 4. Reichstag elections. Gain of Nationalists and Communists at the expense of the moderate parties.

Dec. 7. Reichstag elections, in which the Socialists regained some of their losses.

1925, Feb. 28. Death of President Ebert.

March 29. Presidential election. None of the seven candidates received the needed majority, but the Nationalist candidate, **Karl Jarrès,** was in the lead, with 10,416,655 votes against 7,802,496 for **Otto Braun** (Socialist). The constitution provided for a second election, in which the candidate receiving the largest number of votes should be elected. The Socialists and Democrats supported **Wilhelm Marx,** leader of the Center, while the Right parties abandoned Jarrès in favor of Field Marshal **Paul von Hindenburg,** in retirement since 1919. The Communists put forward **Ernst Thälmann.**

April 26. HINDENBURG ELECTED PRESIDENT, with 14,655,766 votes against Marx's 13,751,615. Thälmann polled almost 2,000,000 votes.

Nov. 29. The Prussian government settled the **Hohenzollern claims,** leaving the former emperor large tracts of land and many estates.

Dec. 5. Resignation of the Luther cabinet. This caused a deadlock that was broken only by Hindenburg's threat to invoke Article 48. Luther ultimately reformed his cabinet.

1926, Feb. 10. Germany applied for admission to the League, in accord with the Locarno treaties. Its admission was postponed because of a dispute regarding seats on the council. Germany was admitted to the League with a permanent seat on the council on Sept. 8.

May 12. Resignation of the Luther cabinet, following its instructions that the old imperial colors should be used in the diplomatic service.

1927, Sept. 18. President von Hindenburg, in a memorial speech dedicating the Tannenberg monument, **repudiated German responsibility for the war** (Article 231 of the Versailles treaty).

1928, May 20. Reichstag elections. The Socialists so strengthened their number that they had to be included in the government. The Nationalists lost heavily.

1929, Sept.–1930, June. Evacuation of the Rhineland.

Dec. 22. A referendum upheld the decision to adopt the **Young Plan.** This marked a defeat for the Nationalists, led by **Alfred Hugenberg.**

1930, July 16. The Reichstag having rejected a **budget bill,** President Hindenburg authorized it by decree. This act was condemned by the Reichstag, which was thereupon dissolved, the budget being put into effect by decree.

Sept. 14. Reichstag elections. Emergence of Hitler's National Socialists as a major party (107 seats as against their previous 12). The Communists returned 77 candidates. The Socialists retained 143 seats, but all the moderate parties lost heavily. This was probably a reflection of the world economic situation and the cessation of loans by the United States. The election ushered in a period of disorder, with numerous **clashes between National Socialist (Nazi) and Communist bands.**

Dec. 12. Completion of the evacuation of the Saar by Allied troops.

1931, May 11. The failure of the Austrian Credit-Anstalt marked the beginning of the financial collapse of Central Europe, including Germany. With the financial collapse came a great economic crisis and depression. By the beginning of 1932 the number of unemployed was already more than 6 million. Economic hardship brought greater social tension: rapid growth of communism and of its opponent, national socialism.

1932, March 13. Presidential election. Hindenburg secured 18,651,497 votes as against 11,300,000 for Hitler and 4,983,341 for Thälmann (Communist). Hindenburg fell just short of the required majority. In the second election (April 10) he secured a plurality of only 6 million out of a total vote of 36 million.

May 30. Brüning, who had been obliged to govern largely by emergency decrees issued by the president, **resigned** when the president refused to sanction a decree that would have divided bankrupt East Prussian estates into allotments for small farmers. Hindenburg, himself of the Junker class, seems to have felt that the Brüning regime was no longer popular with the public or with the army.

May 31. Franz von Papen was asked by the president to form a ministry responsible to the executive alone. This **ministry of barons** in-

cluded **Constantin von Neurath** (foreign minister) and **Gen. Kurt von Schleicher** (minister of defense). National Socialists were excluded.

June 16. The government lifted a ban on Nazi storm troops, which had been imposed by Brüning (April 13). The National Socialist movement now gained great momentum. Disorders and clashes of rival groups became the order of the day.

July 20. Coup d'état in Prussia. Papen removed the Socialist prime minister and other officials. Berlin and Brandenburg were put under martial law, because the activities of Nazi storm troops had made it difficult for civil authorities to maintain order.

July 31. Reichstag elections, following a dissolution (June 4). The National Socialists returned 230 candidates, Socialists 133, Center 97, Communists 89. Since neither the Nazis nor the Communists would enter a coalition, no majority was possible.

Aug. 13. Hitler refused Hindenburg's request that he serve as a vice chancellor under Papen. He demanded all or nothing.

Sept. 12. The Reichstag dissolved. After a presidential decree had been read, a vote was taken, contrary to rules, on a Communist motion of "no confidence." This was passed by 512 votes to 42, indicating the impossibility of securing popular support for the Papen ministry.

Nov. 6. An election failed to break the Reichstag deadlock. The National Socialists lost some seats, while the Communists gained.

Nov. 17. Resignation of Papen.

Nov. 24. Hitler rejected the offer of the chancellorship on certain conditions. His demand for full powers was refused by Hindenburg.

Dec. 2. Gen. Kurt von Schleicher formed a new presidential cabinet.

1933, Jan. 28. Schleicher forced to resign after his efforts to conciliate the Center and Left had failed and Hindenburg had rejected a demand for another dissolution.

Jan. 30. ADOLF HITLER, CHANCELLOR. Papen, vice chancellor; **Hermann Goering** (Nazi), without portfolio; **Wilhelm Frick** (Nazi), interior; **Gen. Werner von Blomberg,** defense; **Constantin von Neurath,** foreign affairs. **Hugenberg** and **Franz Seldte,** Nationalists, were included. The ministry, regarded as a coalition of National Socialists and Nationalists, with important posts assigned to nonparty men of the old governing class, lacked a majority so long as the Center stood aloof. But Hitler refused to compromise with **Mgr. Ludwig Kaas,** the Centrist leader, and the Reichstag was dissolved. The new elections were set for March 5.

The **National Socialist German Workers' Party** appealed to prejudices widely held in Germany against Jews, intellectuals, pacifists, Communists, Socialists, and liberals. Hitler exacted unquestioning obedience from his followers but promised in return to make Germany strong, self-sufficient, respected. His denunciations of the Versailles treaty had brought him much support. The middle classes, ruined by inflation and economic depression, were offered the elimination of Jewish competition in business and the professions. Thousands of unemployed and hopeless young men were put into uniform as storm troopers, with the support of which the lieutenants of Hitler, such as Goebbels, were able to organize an unusually effective propaganda and imposing demonstrations. The movement was financed by many in the well-to-do classes and big business interests against communism. Hitler's fanatical patriotism and extreme nationalism, combined with asceticism, his vague denunciations of capitalism, and his extraordinary powers as a popular orator secured him the backing of many in various classes deeply discontented with things as they were.

Feb. 27. A violent **election campaign** culminated in **a fire that partly destroyed the Reichstag building.** Hitler denounced this as a Communist plot, and President von Hindenburg issued emergency decrees suspending the constitutional guaranties of free speech and free press, as well as other liberties. The Nazi storm troopers were able to intimidate and bully their opponents with impunity.

March 5. The **Reichstag elections** gave the Nazis only 44 percent of the votes and their Nationalist allies (party of big business and of the old aristocracy) only 8 percent. The Center Party elected 74, the Socialists 120, the Communists 81, and other non-Nazi parties 23 members. There were 288 Nazis and 52 Nationalists. The vote cast exceeded all preceding ones.

March 23. Passage of the Enabling Act by the Reichstag and Reichsrat. The National Socialists and the Nationalists found support among deputies of the Catholic Center. The Communist Party had already been outlawed after the Reichstag fire. Only 94 votes (all Social Democratic) were cast against the crucial **Enabling Bill,** which gave the government dictatorial powers until April 1, 1937. Thereby the **Nazi dictatorship** was firmly established.

The **Nazi revolution** proved to be one of the greatest overturns in German and European history. It affected almost every phase of life. The policies of the first years may be briefly summarized as follows:

(1) *CONSTITUTIONAL CHANGES.* The German states were allowed to continue, but the state governments were gradually shorn of effective power. Statthalter were appointed for all the states (April 7, 1933), and the Reichsrat, representing the states, was abolished (Jan. 30, 1934). Thereby the sovereignty of the states came to an end, and **Germany became a national rather than a federal state.** Relations between the state governments and the local party organizations (Gaue) were not clearly defined, but the tendency was to identify them more and more.

(2) *ADMINISTRATIVE.* By the **Civil Service Law** of April 7, 1933, all non-Aryan (Jewish) officials of national, state, and municipal governments could be retired, as could notaries, teachers, and other semipublic servants. Thenceforth no opponents of the Nazi regime could hope to retain their positions.

(3) *JUDICIAL.* The entire legal system was overhauled, all traditional concepts of law being discarded and the welfare of the state and the Nazi regime becoming the sole deciding considerations. The **People's Court** (May 3, 1934) was set up to try cases of treason (which was given an extremely wide definition); the proceedings were made secret and there was no appeal except to the Führer. A secret state police, the **Gestapo,** also gained prominence as the ruthless protectors of Nazism. Summary execution of sentences became the usual thing. **CONCENTRATION CAMPS,** in which thousands of opponents were detained without trial, became standing institutions.

(4) *POLITICAL.* All opposing parties were liquidated under government pressure. Socialist parties were prohibited on May 10, 1933; the Nationalist Party dissolved itself (June 27, 1933); the Catholic parties were obliged to dissolve (July 5, 1933); all monarchist organizations were forbidden (Feb. 2, 1934). In the same way such nonpolitical organizations as the *Stahlhelm* were incorporated with the Nazi party (June 21, 1933) and ultimately disbanded (Nov. 11, 1935). The **National Socialist Party was declared the only political party** on July 14, 1933.

(5) *RACIAL.* From the very outset the new regime aroused indignation throughout the world for its ruthless **persecution of the Jews.** A national boycott of all Jewish businesses and professions (April 1, 1933) introduced a long series of outrages. As quickly as possible Jewish businesses were liquidated and lawyers and doctors barred from practice. By the famous **Nürnberg Laws** (Sept. 15, 1935) Jews (including all those of one-quarter Jewish extraction) were deprived of rights of citizenship and all intermarriage with Jews was strictly forbidden. Many Jews left the country, though they were required to sacrifice almost all of their property in so doing. After the annexation of Austria the same measures were extended to the new state and, on June 16, 1938, Jews were required to register all their property, at home and abroad, within a couple of weeks. Early in Nov. 1938 the persecution came to a head when, following the assassination of a German diplomat by a Jew in Paris, well-organized attacks upon synagogues and Jewish property took place throughout the Reich (**Kristallnacht,** Nov. 9, 1938). The government levied a fine of 1 billion marks upon the Jewish community, which amounted to a capital levy of 20 percent on property above 5,000 marks. No secret was made of the determination of the government to drive all Jews out of the country. In view of this desperate situation an **international refugee committee** was organized to arrange ways and means of effecting the emigration of so large a number as soon as possible. One great obstacle to a satisfactory arrangement was the unwillingness of the German government to allow the emigrants to take money or property with them.

(6) *RELIGIOUS.* Though both Catholics and Protestants gave the Nazis considerable support at the outset, it soon became evident that the new regime was bent on coordinating all religious organizations with the state machinery. **Neopagan movements,** which were many, were countenanced and even encouraged by the government, while the Christian churches were exposed to great pressure. The Protestant state churches amalgamated to form a new **Evangelical Church** (July 11, 1933), but when the government appointed as national bishop **Lud-**

wig Müller, many pastors who objected to him broke away and formed the **German Confessional Church,** which soon found itself in conflict with the authorities. On Sept. 28, 1935, the Protestant Church was placed under state control, and **Hans Kerrl** was made minister of Church affairs with decree powers. The opposition was led by Pastor **Martin Niemoeller,** who was finally arrested (July 1, 1937). Though acquitted after trial (March 1938), he was at once rearrested by the secret police and returned to a concentration camp. How many other recalcitrant pastors suffered the same fate can only be guessed at. The **Catholic Church** had an equally hard time. On July 20, 1933, the government signed a new **concordat** with the Vatican, replacing the older agreements with separate German states. The Catholic clergy was forbidden to take part in politics, and future diocesan appointments were to be made by the Holy See only after consultation with the German government. On the other hand Catholic schools and societies were to be permitted so long as they did not meddle in public affairs. Despite this agreement the government brought pressure to bear to prevent parents from sending children to confessional schools (Catholic or Protestant), and furthermore brought children into the **Youth Movement,** where doctrines wholly objectionable to many Christian parents were freely taught. The policy of the government led to many protests by Catholic leaders (notably **Card. Faulhaber** of Munich). But these proved futile. On the contrary, the government took the offensive (1937), brought many monks to trial on charges of immorality and the like, and in general did its utmost to discredit and break the influence of the Catholic Church.

(7) *ECONOMIC.* The workers' parties, after dissolution, were replaced by the **Nazi Labor Front,** which was given a new constitution (Oct. 24, 1934). Strikes and lockouts had already been forbidden (May 17, 1933), and under the new constitution the employers (as leaders in their respective factories and industries) were given extensive control; wages remained low. On the other hand the new regime succeeded, within a remarkably short time, in **eliminating all unemployment** (chiefly through opening of labor camps for young men and even women, by public works and rearmament, etc.). Many of the workers were won over to the Nazi Party by the establishment of the organization Kraft durch Freude (**Strength through Joy),** which provided for cheap entertainment, vacations, and so on. In the larger sphere the government brought to an end the reparations problem and embarked upon a **policy of self-sufficiency** (autarchy) which would make the country independent (especially in raw materials) in the event of war. This underlay the famous **Four-Year Plan** of Oct. 19, 1936. Germany suffered greatly from the parlous condition of world trade, and considerably also from the boycott of German goods resulting from the anti-Jewish policies. The great costs of government and rearmament were met by internal loans, more forced than voluntary. Industry was brought under considerable government control, just as the peasants were more and more attached to their land.

(8) *MILITARY.* The government restored **universal compulsory military service** on March 16, 1935, and from that time on made rapid progress in rearmament. By 1938 Germany had not only an impressive land army, equipped with the latest weapons, but an air fleet superior to that of any other country. In the course of 1938 the western frontier was heavily fortified, giving the country further assurance against attack from France.

(9) *SOCIAL.* The Nazi regime believed firmly in the "traditional" family. By the Law to Reduce Unemployment (June 1, 1933) newlywed husbands became eligible for **marriage loans,** provided that the wife had been a worker and had given up her job. Moreover, parts of the loan were forgiven upon the births of a first and second child. The cult of motherhood received official sanction through women's and girls' organizations. Those who could not contribute Aryan families to the development of the Reich, such as non-Aryans and homosexuals, were ruthlessly persecuted. The desire to push women out of the workplace was reversed at the beginning of the war, but by then many middle-class women had accepted Nazi propaganda that established the home as their true place and refused employment. Working-class women were forced to accept much lower pay as gender became the sole factor in determining wages. In all, sexual divisions of labor, eugenics, better conditions for mothers, and sterilization and birth control for "inferior" groups made up the Nazi position on sexuality and reproduction.

1933, Oct. 14. WITHDRAWAL OF GERMANY FROM THE DISARM-

AMENT CONFERENCE AND FROM THE LEAGUE OF NATIONS. This marked the beginning of an independent policy in foreign affairs.

Nov. 12. Election of a new Reichstag. Ninety-three percent of the voters approved the government's action in withdrawing from the League; 92 percent voted for the Nazi list of candidates. There were no opposition candidates, but opponents of the regime, despite intimidation, cast about 3 million invalid ballots, the only way of registering disapproval. The Reichstag itself, under the new system, lost all importance and became little more than an assembly of Nazi leaders occasionally convoked to hear addresses by the Führer.

1934, June 30. The GREAT BLOOD PURGE, in which, according to Hitler's own admission in the Reichstag (July 13), 77 persons, many of them leaders high in the party, were summarily executed because of an alleged plot against Hitler and the regime. In reality this dramatic move was directed against representatives of the more radical, social revolutionary wing of the party, which aimed at incorporation of the storm troopers (i.e., party forces) in the army, and at far-reaching property changes. Outstanding among the victims were **Gen. von Schleicher** and his wife (later said to have been shot by mistake); **Ernst Roehm,** one of the ablest organizers in the movement; **Gregor Strasser,** one of the earliest and most energetic but also one of the most radical of the Nazis; and **Erich Klausener,** prominent Catholic leader.

Aug. 1. Law concerning the head of the state, combining the presidency and chancellorship.

Aug. 2. Death of President von Hindenburg (age 87).

Aug. 19. A plebiscite approved **Hitler's assumption of the presidency** and of sole executive power (88 percent of the votes affirmative). Hitler, however, preferred to retain the title Der Führer.

1935, Jan. 13. PLEBISCITE IN THE SAAR BASIN (p. 677). The return of the Saar to the Reich (March 1) marked the beginning of German expansion under the Hitler regime.

March 16. Hitler startled the world by denouncing the clauses of the Versailles treaty providing for German disarmament. Under French lead, Great Britain and Italy joined in a strong protest against the German action (p. 677).

1936, March 7. The GERMAN GOVERNMENT DENOUNCED THE LOCARNO PACTS of 1925 **and reoccupied the Rhineland** (p. 677).

Nov. 14. Hitler denounced the clauses of the Versailles treaty providing for international control of German rivers.

Nov. 18. The German government recognized the Insurgent government of Gen. Franco in Spain. From the beginning of the civil war in Spain, the Germans had openly sided with the rebels, supplying Franco with armaments and technical experts, as well as with some troops (p. 692).

1937, Nov. 24. Walther Funk replaced Schacht as minister of economics, Schacht remaining president of the Reichsbank. Schacht had done much to develop German trade through **bartering agreements** with the Balkan and Near Eastern countries. But his methods, however clever, were not in accord with the more extreme theories of Nazi circles. In Oct. 1936 the **Four-Year Plan** had been introduced and Goering had been made economic dictator. Funk's advent marked a further advance of the more extreme Nazi elements.

1938, Feb. 4. Reorganization of the military and diplomatic command. Hitler assumed the ministry of war, while Gen. Wilhelm Keitel became his representative at the supreme command and Gen. Heinrich von Brauchitsch became commander in chief of the army. In the foreign office the place of **Constantin von Neurath** was taken by **Joachim von Ribbentrop.** Definitive subordination of both the army and the foreign service to the Nazi Party. The new men were known to be exponents of a bolder, forward policy.

March 12–13. GERMAN INVASION AND ANNEXATION OF AUSTRIA. Thereby over 6 million people were added to the Reich and the way paved for future expansion in the Danube Valley.

May 19–20. The first Czech crisis arose after a Hitler speech promising protection to German minorities in Czechoslovakia.

Sept. 12–29. The GREAT CZECHOSLOVAK CRISIS (p. 705), as a result of which Hitler annexed to Germany over 3 million people of the Sudeten region.

1939, Jan. 20. Dismissal of Schacht, whose place as president of the Reichsbank was taken by Walther Funk. Schacht had supposedly warned that the huge armament program would have to be curtailed if catastrophic inflation were to be averted. Germany's adverse trade balance in 1938 was 432 million marks, and by standards of bourgeois capitalism the country had been bankrupt since 1931.

March 15. German occupation of rump Bohemia and Moravia, and extinction of the Czechoslovak state (p. 705). Bohemia-Moravia became a German protectorate; Slovakia remained nominally independent.

March 21. German annexation of Memel. At the same time extensive demands were made on Poland with regard to Danzig and Pomorze. The firmness of the Poles and the alarm of Britain and France, which guaranteed Poland against attack (p. 720), induced the German government to hold back.

April 28. Hitler's Reichstag speech in reply to President Roosevelt's appeal (p. 679). He denounced the Anglo-German naval convention of 1935 and the German-Polish agreement of 1934 because of the new policy of "encirclement" supposedly followed by Britain and Poland. At the same time he renewed his demands on Poland and offered any state assurance against aggression. Specific offers of **bilateral nonaggression pacts** were made to the Scandinavian and Baltic states, but only Denmark, Latvia, and Estonia accepted.

During the summer the **dispute with Poland** over Danzig and Pomorze rapidly came to a head. Despite repeated warnings from Britain and France, the Germans reiterated their demands and their determination to secure satisfaction at any cost. At the end of June German "volunteers" began to arrive in Danzig and a "free corps" was organized. Border incidents became frequent.

Aug. 20, 21. The crisis finally broke when the German government succeeded in arranging a **pact with Russia** that marked a complete reversal of the anti-Communist policy that had underlain National Socialist theory. Throughout two weeks of tension (p. 679) the Berlin government refused to negotiate directly with Poland.

Sept. 1. German forces invaded Poland, without formal declaration.

Sept. 3. DECLARATION OF WAR BY GREAT BRITAIN AND FRANCE quickly followed.

1941. By the fall 70,000 people suffering from incurable illnesses had been killed through a policy of **euthanasia** instituted in Oct. 1939. When word of this became public, Bishop Wurm of Württemberg and Bishop Count Galen of Münster condemned the policy publicly. It is the only major case in which public indignation stopped Nazi practices.

1942, Jan. The WANNSEE CONFERENCE. Reinhard Heydrich, commissioned in July 1941 to develop a plan for the **"final solution"** of the Jewish question, convened a group of high-ranking Nazis. Agreement was reached on the collection of all the Jews of Europe into ghettos and then into extermination camps in Poland. From this point to the war's end, more than 6 million Jews were killed **(the HOLOCAUST).**

1943, Jan. 27. As the war began to go badly for Germany, the government ordered the civil conscription of women to fill labor demands.

Feb. 3. A broadcast from Hitler's headquarters conceded that the **Battle of Stalingrad** had ended in a German defeat.

May. The air offensive on Germany became more destructive. Berlin and other cities began to experience heavy damage. The saturation bombing of German cities disrupted communications and thereby strengthened Nazi control. The government maintained control of roads, railroads, telegraph and telephone lines. While the population suffered great hardships, it is believed that the Nazi apparatus alone maintained awareness of the situation as a whole.

1944, Jan. 20. The British Royal Air Force dropped 2,300 tons of bombs on Berlin.

March. American bombers began daylight attacks on Berlin.

July 20. A group of liberals, Socialists, high civil servants, and generals all conspired to **assassinate Hitler,** hoping to clear the way for peace negotiations with the Allies. Their failure met with strong retribution.

1945, April 30. ADOLF HITLER COMMITTED SUICIDE. *(To p. 869)*

12. AUSTRIA
(From pp. 506, 672)

The strain of war intensified the divisions and weaknesses of the Habsburg Empire and prepared the way for its dissolution.

1916, Oct. 21. The Austrian prime minister, **Count Karl Stürgkh,** was assassinated. His place was taken (Oct. 28) by **Ernst von Körber.**

Nov. 21. The old emperor, **Francis Joseph, died,** and was succeeded by his grandnephew, **Charles, emperor** to Nov. 11, 1918.

1918, Jan. 14. A reduction in the flour ration sparked a series of strikes throughout Austria. The workers were joined by the Fifth Fleet, which mutinied on Feb. 1. Both movements were suppressed.

Oct. 21. The delegates of the German parties who had been elected to the 1911 Reichsrat convened as the provisional **National Assembly of the "independent state of German-Austria."**

Oct. 30. A provisional government was formed under **Karl Renner.** This government coexisted with the imperial government until November.

Nov. 11. Emperor Charles stepped down but never formally abdicated.

Nov. 12. The provisional government declared AUSTRIA A REPUBLIC AND A CONSTITUENT PART OF THE GERMAN REPUBLIC.

1919. The larger part of the year was one of confusion, marked particularly by **Communist disorders, the difficult process of negotiating peace, and the shattered economy.**

Feb. 16. Election of a constituent assembly. The Socialists secured 72 seats, the Christian Socialists (agrarian, clerical) 69, the German Nationalists 26.

April 17. A Communist-led demonstration resulted in street fighting and the burning of the parliament. Order was restored when units of the newly created Volkswehr and Social Democratic leaders took control. The incident demonstrated that the army would stand by the legal government against revolutionary action.

The government, under pressure from the Socialists, also attempted to secure working-class loyalty between 1918 and 1921 by introducing much **social welfare legislation.** The eight-hour day was made standard, and regulations were issued concerning vacations, social insurance, and the employment of women and children.

Sept. 10. Austria signed the **Treaty of Saint-Germain** (p. 672), in which union with Germany was expressly forbidden. The name of the state had to be changed from German-Austria to Republic of Austria.

The republic, with a population almost entirely German, was the most unfortunate creation of the peace conference. Of less than 8 million population, 2 million lived in Vienna, a great industrial center, which was cut off from the former territories of the monarchy and shut in by the high tariff walls of the new neighbors. The economic viability of the country was in question from the outset. Despite the principle of self-determination, Austria was forbidden to unite with Germany for political reasons. The history of the country after the peace treaty centered on the conflict between the countryside (conservative and clerical) and the metropolis, controlled by the Socialists; on the question of union with Germany (Anschluss); and on the question of subsistence.

1920, June 11. The **Renner cabinet resigned** and was followed by a ministry of all parties under **Michael Mayr.**

Oct. 5. A new constitution created a federal state on the Swiss model with eight provinces (Vienna a separate province) and a two-chamber legislature.

Oct. 10. A dispute with Yugoslavia over the **Klagenfurt** area was decided by plebiscite in favor of Austria.

Oct. 17. The first regular elections resulted in a victory for the Christian Socialists (84 seats). The Socialists gained 69 seats, and the newly created Grossdeutsche Volkspartei (Greater German People's Party) won 20 seats. Michael Mayr retained the post of chancellor, and **Michael Hainisch** became the first president of the republic.

1921. Acute food shortage, leading to much suffering and unrest. This was aggravated by inflation and high unemployment. These troubles forced many to question the viability of this new state.

April 24. Plebiscite in the Tyrol, which voted for union with Germany.

May 29. Salzburg voted for union with Germany. The movement of separation was stopped by Allied threats.

June 21. New cabinet of **Johann Schober,** supported by Christian Socialists and German Nationalists.

1922, May 31. CABINET OF IGNAZ SEIPEL (Christian Socialist).

Oct. 4. The **League of Nations** took over the problem of Austrian reconstruction, following the earnest appeal of the chancellor. An international loan, under guaranty of the League, was accorded and a League commissioner appointed to supervise Austrian finance. Outside pressure forced the government to cut expenditures: about 85,000 civil servants were fired or pensioned, taxes were raised, and social service benefits were curtailed.

1923, Oct. 20. In the elections the **Christian Socialists won a victory** over the Socialists.

1924, Nov. 17. Resignation of Seipel because of ill health. His place was taken by his follower **Rudolf Ramek.**

Dec. The government introduced a new unit of currency, the schilling. This helped halt inflation, but the general economic condition of the country remained poor. By 1926 unemployment was over 240,000.

1925, Sept. 10. The League voted to discontinue control of Austrian finance in July 1926, the reconstruction scheme having put Austria on its feet.

1926, Oct. 15. The Ramek cabinet gave way to a new **Seipel ministry.** During this period there was a marked recrudescence of agitation in favor of union with Germany, and a growing antagonism between the Christian Socialist government and the Socialist government of Vienna, which established costly programs, including the construction of hospitals and large apartment complexes to provide low-cost housing. By providing resources for education and cultural activities, the Socialists created an environment in Vienna wherein a worker could live in a world organized by his party from housing to recreation to newspapers.

1927, July 15. The acquittal of three Nationalists of the murder of two Socialists led to riots and a **general strike in Vienna.** The mob burned the Palace of Justice, destroying many valuable records. The disorders were put down with some bloodshed. In the succeeding years clashes between the factions became more and more frequent in various parts of the country, each organizing private armies (the Christian Socialists the Heimwehr, the Socialists the Schutzbund).

1928, Dec. 5. Wilhelm Miklas elected second president.

1929, Sept. 26. Second Schober cabinet, supported by Christian Socialists and Nationalists, with a program of restoring order.

Dec. Growing internal instability fostered support for a constitutional change strengthening the position of the president, who was now given the power to dissolve parliament and to issue emergency proclamations. The presidency also became a directly elected office.

Aside from political instability, the government also had to contend with growing economic crisis due to the world depression. By June 1931 there were over 350,000 unemployed, a figure that rose to 480,000 by 1938, undermining the democratic basis of the First Republic.

1930, May. With the declaration of the **Korneuburg Oath** the Heimwehr moved further right by accepting a political program similar to that of the Italian Fascists, denouncing parliamentary democracy and capitalism.

Sept. 30. Cabinet of Karl Vaugoin.

Nov. 9. The elections gave the Socialists 72 seats as against 66 for the Christian Socialists.

Dec. 3. Cabinet of Otto Ender (Christian Socialist), including Schober and Vaugoin.

1931, March 20. The Anschluss problem culminated in a projected **customs union with Germany.**

May 11. Collapse of the Austrian Credit-Anstalt, due in part to the withdrawal of short credits by France to force the abandonment of the customs union with Germany. The Austrian government attempted to save the bank but was ultimately obliged to appeal for aid abroad. France refused support except on the most burdensome terms, but at the last moment (June 16) the British government offered a necessary loan. On the same day the **Ender cabinet resigned.**

June 21. Karl Buresch (Christian Socialist) **formed a new government,** concerned primarily with saving the desperate financial situation.

Sept. 13. The Fascist Heimwehr attempted **a coup in Styria** and proclaimed **Walter Pfrimer** "dictator." This was suppressed by the army.

Oct. 9. President Miklas was reelected.

1932, April. The National Socialists made impressive gains in local elections in Vienna, Lower Austria, Salzburg, Styria, and Carinthia.

May 20. A CABINET UNDER ENGELBERT DOLLFUSS (Christian Socialist) replaced that of Buresch. Like its predecessor, the new government represented a coalition of Christian Socialists and Agrarians.

July 15. The **League of Nations finally agreed to a loan** of 300 million schillings, Austria agreed not to enter into political or economic union with Germany before 1952.

1933, March. Growing antigovernmental agitation in Austria, following the victory of the National Socialists in Germany. To meet the situation, **Dollfuss suspended parliamentary government** (March 7) and prohibited parades and assemblies; freedom of the press was also curtailed (March 8). Nevertheless the Austrian Nazis staged a great demonstration and riot in Vienna on March 29, and the Styrian branch of the Heimwehr became frankly Nazi. The government (May 4) forbade the wearing of uniforms by all political parties. Nazi agitators were harried from the land, and relations with Germany became tense. On June 1, Hitler imposed a charge of 1,000 marks on Germans desiring to visit Austria, thereby completely ruining the Austrian tourist business.

June 14. The **Austrian government expelled Theodor Habicht,** Hitler's "inspector for Austria." The Germans retaliated with a series of **terrorist outrages.**

June 19. The **Nazi Party** in Austria **was dissolved.** Agitation and terrorism continued, encouraged by a virulent Nazi radio campaign. On Oct. 3 an attempt was made to assassinate Dollfuss.

1934, Feb. 11–15. DESTRUCTION OF THE AUSTRIAN SOCIALISTS. This followed a decree dissolving all political parties except Dollfuss's Fatherland Front. Raids by government forces and the Heimwehr on Socialist headquarters led to an uprising and the bombardment of the Karl Marx Hof, the Socialist housing unit, where the leaders had concentrated. These leaders were either captured or forced to flee. By this drastic action Dollfuss and the Christian Socialists permanently antagonized the working classes of Vienna and deprived themselves of what might have been the most effective support against the Nazi threat.

March 17. Signature of the Rome protocols, effecting close relations among Austria, Hungary, and Italy. Dollfuss was obliged to rely more and more upon Italian support against a hostile Germany.

April 1. Promulgation of a **new constitution for Vienna,** which deprived the capital of most of its powers of self-government.

April 30. A complicated **constitution for Austria** was accepted by the national assembly. Parliamentary democracy was replaced by a corporative system. Dollfuss assigned influential government posts to the pro-Fascist Heimwehr.

May 1. A concordat with the Vatican gave the Church in Austria wide control of education.

July 25. NAZI COUP. A band of Nazis seized the radio station in Vienna and forced the staff to broadcast Dollfuss's resignation. They then entered the chancellery and (probably unintentionally) **shot and killed Dollfuss.** The whole affair was badly mismanaged, and the conspirators were routed by Heimwehr troops. Action by Germany on behalf of the Nazis was made impossible by the strong stand of Italy and Yugoslavia, which concentrated large forces on the frontier. Thereupon the German government disavowed all connection with the affair and recalled its ambassador to Vienna.

July 30. Kurt Schuschnigg, close collaborator of Dollfuss, **formed a new cabinet** committed to the same policies. Twice in the course of the autumn he visited Mussolini. Economic agreements with Italy and Hungary led to some improvement in the situation, and political agitation died down somewhat.

1935, July 4. Repeal of the anti-Habsburg laws and restoration of part of the imperial property. This move was symptomatic of increased sen-

timent for return of the Habsburgs, advocated by Prince Rüdiger von Stahremberg and supposedly encouraged by Mussolini. The opposition of the Little Entente and of France served, however, as an effective damper.

1936, April 1. Reintroduction of conscription, in violation of the provisions of the Treaty of Saint-Germain. The Austrian step followed similar action by Germany (p. 700) and was intended to give the Austrian dictatorship an armed force more reliable than the Heimwehr. On May 14 Schuschnigg forced **Prince Stahremberg,** commander of the Heimwehr, out of the offices of vice chancellor and leader of the Fatherland Front, thus removing his only serious rival.

July 11. German-Austrian agreement, ending the feud between the two countries at least temporarily. Germany engaged to respect the independence of Austria, and Schuschnigg promised to pursue a policy befitting a German state. The agreement was evidently inspired by Mussolini during a visit by Schuschnigg to Rome (June 1), Mussolini being anxious, on the eve of the Ethiopian campaign, to secure the goodwill of Germany.

Oct. 10. Schuschnigg disbanded the Heimwehr and had the members absorbed into the Fatherland Front militia. He dropped the remaining Heimwehr members from his cabinet, and on Oct. 18 had himself proclaimed Front Führer.

1937, Feb. 14. Schuschnigg publicly claimed the right to decide the **question of Habsburg restoration.** All indications were that he was veering more and more in that direction. This was highly objectionable to Hitler and to the entire Nazi party, and probably accounts for the **recrudescence of Nazi demonstrations** and mutual recrimination (Feb.). Schuschnigg's position was further weakened by the conclusion of the Rome-Berlin Axis (p. 677) and by Mussolini's preoccupation with the Spanish civil war.

April 22. Schuschnigg visited Mussolini at Venice, where he was warned that Italy could not be counted on to give armed support against Germany. Mussolini seems further to have opposed the projected restoration of the Habsburgs and to have objected to a suggested alliance between Austria and Czechoslovakia for common defense. His advice was that Schuschnigg make his peace with Hitler and admit Nazis to the government. Schuschnigg rejected this advice but continued throughout the year to further **negotiations with Czechoslovakia** and the Little Entente. Indications were that, deserted by Italy, he was seeking and finding a measure of support from France and its allies. This policy, on the other hand, led to much dissatisfaction in Germany and to ever more outspoken demands on the part of the Austrian Nazis and Pan-Germans.

1938, Feb. 12. Schuschnigg paid a visit to Hitler at Berchtesgaden, and under pressure was obliged to promise an amnesty to Austrian Nazis who had been imprisoned, and furthermore to agree to take certain Nazis into the cabinet. On Feb. 16 **Arthur Seyss-Inquart** (Nazi) became minister of the interior. **Full amnesty** was granted, and (Feb. 19) the Fatherland Front was opened to Nazis.

Feb. 24. Schuschnigg, replying to a speech of Hitler (Feb. 20) promising protection to 10 million Germans outside the Reich, **reaffirmed the independence of Austria** and appealed for support against further demands. This speech called forth a good deal of enthusiasm in Austria, but the Nazis, confident of success, assumed the offensive. On March 1 serious **disorders broke out at Graz,** and soon all Styria, as well as other places, was in a state of revolution. The government was unable to cope with the situation without offending Nazi Germany. Last-minute efforts of Schuschnigg to arrange a reconciliation with the Socialist working classes came to nothing. As a last resort, Schuschnigg suddenly announced (March 9) that a plebiscite would be held on the following Sunday on the question of Austrian independence; only Yes ballots were to be distributed (those who desired to vote No would have to supply their own ballots, of specified form). This announcement drove the Nazis to extremes and plunged the country into chaos. Hitler seized the opportunity.

March 11. Germany submitted an ultimatum demanding postponement of the plebiscite and the resignation of Schuschnigg. German troops began to concentrate on the frontier. Unable to resist, **Schuschnigg resigned and Seyss-Inquart became chancellor.**

March 12. The German army began the **invasion of Austria.** No resistance was offered. **President Miklas resigned.**

March 13. SEYSS-INQUART PROCLAIMED THE UNION (ANSCHLUSS) WITH GERMANY. Hitler arrived in Vienna on March 14 and took formal possession. He had already decreed a plebiscite to be held on April 10. Meanwhile the most ruthless revenge was taken on all opponents of the Nazis, many of whom committed suicide and most of whom, unable to get away, were thrown into concentration camps. Schuschnigg allowed himself to be arrested and was kept in confinement without trial. The Jews suffered assault and humiliation of all kinds.

April 10. The **plebiscite in Austria** revealed a vote of 99.75 percent in favor of the union with Germany. Austria was incorporated with the Reich not as a new state but as seven separate districts (Gaue). The union was carried through with such speed and energy on the part of the Germans that no international complications ensued. Britain and France protested, but these powers were too deeply involved in Mediterranean and Far Eastern problems to be able to take further action, the more so as Italy refused to join in protest. Mussolini, though his ally's success brought a powerful state to the Brenner Pass, could only acquiesce as gracefully as possible.

From 1938 to 1945 Austria formed a part of the German Reich. There was relatively little resistance to the Nazi regime in Austria, most potential advocates of resistance having been destroyed earlier under the Dollfuss regime. Discontent began to rise only in 1943 when Austria became the target of large-scale air raids. No government in exile had been formed, however.

Oct. Members of the Hitler Youth and Sturm Abteilung (SA, Stormtroopers) stormed the residence of the archbishop in Vienna. Despite original assurances that the Church would retain prominence in education and family issues, the Nazis soon challenged the Church's authority in Austria.

1939, June. By an agreement signed by Hitler and Mussolini, German inhabitants of the Tyrol were forced to decide whether to stay in the province and accept full Italian citizenship, or migrate to German territory.

1943, Nov. At a meeting of foreign ministers in Moscow the Allies agreed on the restoration of an independent Austria after the war.

1944, April. Vienna experienced the first significant raid of the war. In subsequent attacks more than 9,000 Viennese were killed. Industrial centers were also severely damaged.

1945, April 13. Vienna fell to the Red Army.

At the end of the war Austrians faced a ruined country. The loss of human life was devastating: 247,000 members of the armed forces were killed or missing or had died in captivity; 29,000 civilians also died. Of the 220,000 Jews in Austria in 1938 only about 5,000 remained in 1946. Finally, the essentials of life, such as food and fuel, were exhausted, and transportation had broken down everywhere. *(To p. 876)*

13. CZECHOSLOVAKIA

(From pp. 506, 672)

The new state, with a population of about 15 million, inherited the most valuable part of the old Austro-Hungarian monarchy, with most of the industrial areas. Levels of urbanization and the social structure, particularly in the Czech lands, were more similar to those of the industrialized Western European countries than to those of most other countries in the region. The literacy rate was also very high. Again, this tended to be particularly true of the Czech lands, causing some friction among regions of the country. Its political life after the war was dominated by the ethnic problem and the resulting multiplication of political parties.

However, Czechoslovakia earned a reputation as the most democratic nation in the region. Because of the strength of Czechoslovak democracy, for example, the Czechoslovak Communist Party, which was founded in 1921, was allowed to develop fully as a mass-based party, differing significantly from those parties based on the Soviet model.

The state of the economy also promoted stability. Since Czechoslovakia had coal and iron mines and modern brewing and textile industries, its economy was better balanced between industry and agriculture than that of any other country in this area. This too, however, varied regionally. Attempts to industrialize Slovakia failed, partly as a result of the world depression. Even with recovery in the mid-1930s, Slovakia's level of development remained far below that of Bohemia and Moravia.

1918, Oct. 14. The Czechoslovak national council in Paris organized a **provisional government,** with **Thomas Garrigue Masaryk** as president and **Eduard Beneš** as foreign minister.

Oct. 28. DECLARATION OF INDEPENDENCE, by the national council.

Oct. 30. The Slovak national council voted for union with the Czechs.

1919, April 16. The Land Reform Bill. This involved the confiscation, with compensation, of the large estates and their partition among the peasants in lots of about 25 acres, with state aid, ensuring peasant support for the new republic.

The new government also solidified working-class support with laws establishing an eight-hour workday, special insurance schemes, and unemployment benefits.

1920, Feb. 29. Adoption of the constitution, closely modeled on that of France.

April 18. The first regular elections. There were numerous parties, representing ethnic groups and social strata. The country had to be ruled by various coalitions, representing chiefly the bourgeois, democratic elements. The first government, headed by the Social Democrats, faced crisis soon after these elections, however. As the Social Democrats split between Communists and reformists (the latter, while representing the minority of the party, controlled the government), the Communists attempted to take over the party. The more conservative elements beat off the challenge, but the Communists responded by turning against the system and calling for a general strike. President Masaryk then stepped in, instituting repressive measures to prevent the strike and replacing the Social Democratic head of the government. After the crisis passed in 1921, Czechoslovakia returned to parliamentary government and the Czechoslovak Communist Party accepted its place in the electoral system.

1927, May 27. President Masaryk reelected. Eduard Beneš remained foreign minister in all cabinets and took an active part in the work of the League of Nations.

July 1. An **administrative reform** gave a greater measure of self-government to the provinces. This was designed to meet the constant complaints of the Slovaks and Ruthenians that their districts were ruled from Prague by Czechs. In both areas there was an active movement demanding autonomy.

1928, Dec. The arrest and **conviction of Voitech Tuka,** a Slovak deputy accused of irredentist agitation in favor of Hungary, caused much ill feeling in Slovakia.

1929. Klement Gottwald became head of the Czechoslovak Communist Party and began to Bolshevize the party.

1933, Feb. 14–16. The powers of the **Little Entente,** meeting at Geneva, **concluded a pact of organization,** providing for a standing council and a permanent secretariat, as well as for coordination of policies and for economic collaboration. This step toward greater solidarity was provoked partly by revival of irredentist agitation in Hungary, in part by the advent of Hitler's National Socialist government in Germany. In the course of the year **Nazi agitation** spread rapidly among the more than 3 million Germans living along the frontiers of the republic. These areas, largely industrial, were particularly hard hit by the depression, so that economic grievances were added to the earlier cultural and political ones.

Oct. 4. The **Sudeten National Socialist Party dissolved itself,** on the eve of a government order prohibiting it. Led by **Konrad Henlein,** the party soon emerged again as the Sudetendeutsche Partei, Nazi in its program but officially not directed at the disruption of the state.

1934, May 24. President Masaryk was once again reelected.

1935, May 19. In the **general elections** the government coalition secured 149 out of 300 seats in the chamber. The Sudeten Party won a sweeping victory in the German areas and, with 44 seats, became the strongest single party, with the exception of the Czech Agrarians.

Nov. 5. Milan Hodža, a Slovak and the leader of the Agrarian Party, **formed a new cabinet.**

Dec. 13. Resignation of President Masaryk, who had reached the age of 85. He was succeeded by his close friend, the foreign minister, Beneš.

1935–38. EDUARD BENEŠ, president. He continued to guide the republic's foreign policy, though on Feb. 29, 1936, **Kamil Krofta,** well-known Czech historian, became foreign minister.

1936, March 9–10. Premier Hodža visited Vienna. On April 2 a trade treaty was concluded between Czechoslovakia and Austria. This rapprochement reflected the Austrian desire for support in the face of German hostility and Italian uncertainty, as well as the hope of the Czechs, backed by France, to bring Austria, and perhaps Hungary, into association with the Little Entente. The Czech government had already embarked upon an extensive **program of armament** and had undertaken the construction of a strong line of fortifications along the German frontier.

Sept. 10. Joseph Goebbels, the German minister of propaganda, publicly **accused Czechoslovakia of harboring Soviet army planes** and permitting Soviet aerodromes on Czech soil. Despite Czech protests, these accusations were repeated, and there developed a Nazi campaign of denunciation and recrimination reminiscent of the Nazi campaign against Austria.

1937, Sept. 14. Death of President Masaryk.

Oct. 16. The Czech police suppressed a meeting of the Sudeten German Party at Teplitz. Some violence having occurred, **Henlein** protested against the government's methods and **demanded complete autonomy** for the Germans in the republic. In view of the general excitement and tension, the government postponed the elections scheduled for Nov. 14. All political meetings were forbidden.

Nov. 29. The **Sudeten German deputies left Parliament,** declaring that they had been beaten by the police.

1938, March–May. The first German-Czech crisis. Hitler's speech of Feb. 20 promising protection to German minorities outside the Reich was answered by Premier Hodža (March 4) by a firm declaration that Czechoslovakia would defend itself against outside interference. But the **German annexation of Austria** (March 13) completely changed the position of the Czechoslovak Republic, now surrounded on three sides by the new German Empire. The German government gave Prague assurances of its desire to improve German-Czech relations (March 14), and both the French and Russian governments categorically declared their intention to honor their treaty obligations. Nevertheless the situation rapidly grew worse. The **German Activists** (i.e., German parties that had joined the cabinet) **all withdrew** (March 22–25) and Hodža's announcement of a forthcoming **Nationality Statute** made but little impression on the German elements. On April 24 the Sudeten leader, Henlein, put forward his demands (the **Carlsbad program:** full equality of status for Germans and Czechs; delimitation of the German areas; full autonomy; removal of all injustices and reparation for damages suffered by the Germans since 1918; full liberty for the Germans to proclaim their Germanism and their adhesion to "the ideology of Germans"; furthermore, Henlein demanded complete revision of Czech foreign policy). These demands were rejected by the Prague government, despite strong urging by France and Britain that the utmost concessions be made. Henlein then paid visits to London and Berlin, where he posed as the soul of moderation. On his return disorders began to break out in the German districts. This situation and rumors of German troop concentration on the frontier led the Czech government to mobilize 400,000 men. France and Britain took a strong stand, and the crisis blew over. Shortly afterward Henlein began negotiations with the Czech government with regard to the Nationality Statute, but Hitler, with feverish haste, began the fortification of the German-French frontier and ordered a huge increase in the German air forces.

July–Aug. The summer was filled with **negotiations between the government and the Sudeten leaders,** but little progress was made. On July 26 the government finally published a draft Nationality Statute, based on the principle of proportionality but falling short of Henlein's Carlsbad program. At the same time it was announced that a British mediator, **Lord Walter Runciman,** would come to Prague. He arrived on Aug. 3 and held many conferences with Sudeten leaders. By the beginning of September the situation was clearly critical; various Czech proposals for cantonal organizations were flatly rejected by Henlein after visits to Hitler. The Carlsbad program was insisted on as a minimum.

Hitler's demands on Czechoslovakia (Nürnberg speech, Sept. 12) produced an international crisis in **Sept. 1938,** which eased only after Britain and France yielded to the German chancellor's belligerence in a final gesture of appeasement. For the Munich conference and the subsequent dismemberment of Czechoslovakia, see p. 678.

CZECH LOSSES THROUGH THE DISMEMBERMENT: In all the republic lost 5 million inhabitants (retaining 10 million), distributed as follows: Germans, 2,850,000; Hungarians, 591,000; Poles, 77,000; Jews, 60,000; Ruthenians, 37,000; Czechs and Slovaks, 1,161,000. In territory Czechoslovakia lost 16,000 square miles (retaining 38,500).

Oct. 5. Resignation of President Beneš, who had been the target of German attack throughout the crisis. He left the country almost at once, going eventually to the U.S. His departure was the signal for a violent campaign directed against him and Masaryk and the policies that had led to Munich.

Oct. 6. Slovakia was given the full autonomy that Slovak leaders had demanded for a long time. **Mgr. Joseph Tiso** became premier of Slovakia.

Oct. 8. Ruthenia was given full autonomy and was renamed Carpatho-Ukraine. This remote region of Europe at once assumed crucial importance as the base for Ukrainian agitation, supposedly inspired from Berlin. The Polish government made every effort to arrange for its partition among Poland, Hungary, and Romania, but all such plans were frustrated by German opposition.

Oct. 20. The **Communist Party was outlawed** in Czecho-Slovakia (so spelled after the federal reorganization). This was merely one move in the direction of the new policy planned in conformity with Germany. **Persecution of Jews** and others soon followed.

Nov. 30. EMIL HACHA, judge of the high court, **was elected president. Rudolf Beran** (Agrarian), an opponent of Beneš, became prime minister.

1939, March 10–16. THE ANNIHILATION OF THE CZECHOSLOVAK STATE. The crisis began when the Prague government deposed Mgr. Tiso, premier of Slovakia, for allegedly working for separation, with support of the Fascist Hlinka Guards. Tiso appealed to Hitler and during a visit to Berlin was given assurances of support. Hitler summoned President Hacha and foreign minister František Chvalkovsky to Berlin and induced them to "place the fate of the Czech people . . . trustingly in the hands of the Führer." **Slovakia and Carpatho-Ukraine declared independence.** On March 15 Bohemia and Moravia became a German protectorate, which was promptly occupied by German forces, the Czechs offering no resistance. On March 16 Tiso put Slovakia also under German protection. **Constantin von Neurath,** former German foreign minister, became **protector of Bohemia and Moravia,** Hacha continuing as "head of the state." The disappearance of Czechoslovakia was momentous, inasmuch as it demonstrated Hitler's readiness to extend his claims beyond German ethnic areas and base them on German needs for "living area" (Lebensraum). The small states were thrown into a panic, and Britain and France promptly adopted a policy of guarantees to prevent further German expansion.

1940, July 21. Britain recognized the **Czechoslovak National Committee** in London as the provisional government.

Resistance was difficult in the Czech lands, where German occupation was directed at extinguishing all vestiges of Czech culture. Although human losses among the population as a whole were not on the order of those in countries like Poland, the Jewish community was virtually destroyed. As occupied regions whose task was to produce industrial products for Germany and the war effort, Bohemia and Moravia also suffered heavy economic losses.

In Slovakia the new state set up in 1939 emulated Nazi Germany in its policies and organizations. Extreme nationalism and anti-Semitism led to the persecution of Czechs and the deportation of Slovak Jews to concentration camps. More dramatic resistance occurred in Slovakia, however. Democratic and Communist forces cooperated in an armed uprising in Aug. 1944. The Germans eventually reasserted their control, but it took them four months to do so.

1942, June 10. In retaliation for the assassination of Gestapo leader **Reinhard Heydrich** by Czech resistance fighters parachuted in from London, the Nazis destroyed the Bohemian village of **Lidice,** killing the male inhabitants and deporting the women and children.

1945, May 9. The Red Army entered Prague, followed the next day by Eduard Beneš's government. The American army had had an opportunity to enter the city three weeks earlier but was ordered to halt.

(To p. 886)

14. HUNGARY

(From pp. 506, 672)

Hungary, left a country of some 8 million population by the peace settlements, was predominantly agricultural, socially still organized on a semifeudal basis. Much of the political history after 1918 had to do with the successful efforts of the landholding classes to secure and retain control, and with the agitation for revision of the peace treaties and the restoration of the monarchy. Conservatives effectively cast the blame for postwar misery on Communists and Jews. The bulk of the middle class and the peasantry was favorably inclined toward conservative-nationalist rule, and there was a growing mass of disillusioned working people who isolated themselves from public life and wanted order and consolidation. Furthermore, antiquated political arrangements effectively kept the lower classes from exerting much influence.

Hungary was economically devastated by the war. Agricultural production dropped by two-thirds, and industrial output was down to one-fifth of its prewar level. The crown was also one-third its prewar value. Of the 3.8 million men mobilized for the war, 660,000 were killed and 745,000 were wounded seriously. Like the other successor states, Hungary compounded these economic problems by following a postwar policy of economic isolation rather than attempting to rebuild the more profitable economic union that existed under the Habsburg Empire. By the 1930s Hungary was hard-hit by permanent unemployment and a marketing crisis that made fascism appealing.

1918, Oct. 17. The **Hungarian Parliament,** in reply to Emperor Charles's declaration of reorganization of the monarchy, declared **complete independence from Austria,** except for the personal union.

Oct. 31. REVOLUTION IN HUNGARY. Count Mihaly Károlyi, grand seigneur of liberal, republican, and pacifist views, made prime minister in the hope of securing satisfactory peace terms and maintaining the unity of the monarchy.

Nov. 16. The national council proclaimed **Hungary a republic.**

1919, Jan. 11. Károlyi appointed president of the republic. The government at once proceeded to the work of dividing the large estates among the peasants.

March 21. Károlyi resigned in protest of the Allied decision to assign Transylvania to Romania.

March 21. Formation of a **Socialist-Communist government** under **Alexander Garbai** (president) and **Béla Kun** (foreign affairs). The Socialists were soon crowded out and a Communist dictatorship established under Béla Kun.

March 28. Hungary declared war on Czechoslovakia and proceeded to the reconquest of Slovakia.

April 10. Romanian troops began to invade Hungary to forestall reconquest of Transylvania. A provisional government was set up by **Count Julius Károlyi** (brother of Mihaly), **Count István Bethlen, Adm. Miklós Horthy,** and **Archduke Joseph** at Szeged (under French occupation). **Beginning of the counterrevolution.**

June 24. Communist constitution.

Aug. 1. Béla Kun fled to Vienna in the face of the Romanian advance. The Revolutionary Governing Council resigned.

Aug. 4. The **Romanians occupied Budapest** (until Nov. 14).

Aug. 6. Archduke Joseph took control as state governor but was forced by Allied protests to resign. A new government was formed under the industrialist István Friedrich. But chaos reigned. This was a period of "white terror" in which roving gangs of counterrevolutionary officers targeted socialists, radical democrats, and Jews.

1920, Jan. Elections to the national assembly resulted in a victory for the conservative National Smallholder's Party and the Christian National Union.

Feb. 25. Final evacuation of the country by the Romanians, who took with them all that was movable.

March 1. Adm. Miklós Horthy, commander in chief of the forces, appointed **regent and head of state.**

March 23. He proclaimed **Hungary a monarchy,** with the throne vacant.

June 4. SIGNATURE OF THE TREATY OF TRIANON. The treaty was followed by **Count Pál Teleki's** new government's attempts to restore order. He **suppressed roving officer-gangs** by "reconciling" anti-Semitism with order. The government limited the number of Jewish students allowed in university, for example. But the most important step in stability was **land reform.** Four hundred thousand landless peasant families received small plots of land. The poor were also allotted 250,000 building lots. This eased some of the tensions over land possession, but because it forced many to undertake labor tenancy, it was an insufficient response to the problem of rural poverty.

1921, March 27. King Charles returned to Hungary and called on Horthy to give up his powers. Owing to the threatening attitude of the neighboring states, the national assembly voted against restoration, and Charles was obliged to return to Switzerland.

April 14. CABINET OF COUNT ISTVÁN BETHLEN, who remained in power until 1931.

Oct. 21. Second arrival of King Charles, at Ödenburg. With an improvised force he marched on Budapest. Czechoslovakia and Yugoslavia began to mobilize, and a government force was obliged to turn back and capture the king, who was exiled to Madeira (d. April 1, 1922).

Nov. 4. A **Dethronement Act** abrogated the rights of Charles.

1922, June 2. Elections, held under a system of carefully restricted suffrage and open voting, gave the government a strong majority. Bethlen proceeded on a conservative policy designed to maintain the status quo. He did, however, soften the government's anti-Semitism by allowing open entry to universities and encouraging the Jewish middle class to participate in public life. Efforts of the extreme royalists and Fascists (Awakening Magyars, for example) to overthrow the government were summarily dealt with.

Sept. 18. Hungary was admitted to the League of Nations.

1923, Dec. 20. The League of Nations adopted a **plan for economic reconstruction** of Hungary, not unlike the one successfully applied in Austria. This continued until June 1926.

As the economy improved in the late 1920s, the government implemented new social policies. While broadening the areas of compulsory accident and health insurance, and raising the duration and amount of sickness benefits, the Bethlen government also introduced old-age, disability, and widows' pensions. Over a million workers were included in insurance programs. Under Minister of Culture Kunó Klébelsberg, education also improved. With increased numbers of students and teachers, literacy increased to 90 percent.

Moderate reforms were also introduced in the election process of municipal governments. And, while the restoration of the upper house of the national assembly gave more power to the landed aristocracy (Nov. 11, 1926), the majority of this house was now elected, not appointed. This political, economic, and social consolidation of limited parliamentarianism was halted, however, when the depression hit Hungary.

1927, April 5. Treaty of friendship with Italy, initiating a period of close relations. This was reflected in the growing **agitation for treaty revision,** which was ardently supported in Britain by the Rothermere press. It also signified an end to Hungarian isolation.

1930, Sept. 1. Social conflicts resulting from the depression culminated in a **mass demonstration** in Budapest. With the economic collapse of Eastern Europe, agricultural workers saw their salaries drop over 50 percent, the debts of small landholders tripled, and over one-third of industrial workers were unemployed. Those who could find work received salaries 25–30 percent below 1929 averages. In this atmosphere opposition to the government resurfaced on the Left and Right.

1931, Aug. 15. France granted a loan to Hungary, evidently on condition that revisionist agitation should cease.

Aug. 19. Resignation of Count Bethlen, officially because of ill health, actually because of inability to cope with the financial situation. His friend, **Count Julius Károlyi,** took his place.

1932, Oct. 4. Gyula Gömbös, former reactionary and anti-Semite, took Károlyi's place. Gömbös was not averse to a measure of agrarian and electoral reform, but was above all an ardent nationalist and revisionist. He opposed the restoration of the Habsburgs but sought further realization of Hungary's territorial claims by **close cooperation with Fascist Italy.**

1933. The advent of Hitler and the National Socialists in Germany led to the **rapid spread of Nazi agitation** to Hungary, where there were large-scale demonstrations already in April.

1934, March 17. SIGNATURE OF THE ROME PROTOCOLS.

Oct. 9. Assassination of King Alexander of Yugoslavia (p. 722). The assassins had operated from Hungary. Acute danger of conflict developed, but the matter was finally adjusted by the League of Nations, which, in a masterpiece of diplomatic circumlocution, mildly rebuked the Hungarian government (Dec. 10).

1935, April 11. In the **parliamentary elections** the opposition groups polled 1,041,000 votes as against 908,000 for the government, but the intricate electoral system enabled the government to retain 166 seats in the chamber as against 25 for the Agrarians, 14 for the Christian Socialists, and 12 for the Social Democrats.

Electoral "success" encouraged Gömbös to launch a comprehensive social and cultural movement. Following his desire for a corporatist state, he envisioned national youth, social, and athletic associations, paramilitary organizations, and a cultural movement. A few writers obliged by creating the **New Intellectual Front,** hoping to enlist the aid of a new "populist" *(népiek)* group of intellectuals **(Zoltán Szabó, Géza Féja, Ferenc Erdei, Gyula Illyés, László Németh, Imre Kovács, József Darvas).** This attempt failed, however.

June 1. Count Bethlen and his followers joined the most important opposition group, the **Agrarian Party** of **Tibor Eckardt.** This party resented the dictatorial methods of Gömbös and suspected him of designs against the constitution. At the same time it advocated land reform on behalf of the 3 million landless peasants, and electoral reform as a stage on the road toward real democracy.

Oct. 6. Death of Premier Gömbös, who was succeeded by **Kálmán Darányi.** Darányi tried to follow a somewhat more conciliatory course. Hungary's position became steadily worse through international developments. Under the circumstances, Darányi, during 1937, drew closer to Austria, and both Austria and Hungary began to seek contact with the nations of the Little Entente. This policy of necessity estranged Germany (Hungary's most important customer) and was vigorously opposed by the Hungarian Nazis.

1937, March 5. The existence of a widespread **Nazi plot** was revealed. The Nazi leader, **Ferenc Szálasi,** and other conspirators were arrested but treated rather mildly. The Nazi elements had a most effective weapon against the government, namely, the promise of land reform and relief for the agrarian proletariat. The government resorted to strenuous methods to repress agitation, but without avail.

Oct. 11. Eckardt and his Agrarian Party **joined the Legitimists.** Even the Social Democrats became friendly to the idea of Habsburg restoration as the most effective way to block the Fascist elements.

Oct. 16. Various Fascist groups united to form the **Hungarian National Socialist Party** (the Arrow Cross), under the leadership of Szálasi. Efforts were made to glorify the regent, Adm. Horthy, and to further his candidacy for the throne. Horthy himself discountenanced these efforts.

1938, Feb. Szálasi was again arrested, with 72 associates. He was sentenced to prison, and drastic steps were taken to stamp out the Fascist-Nazi movement. But with the **annexation of Austria** by Germany (March 13), the large German element in Hungary (c. 500,000) became more and more restless.

May 13. A new cabinet was formed by Béla Imredy, eminent financier, who was regarded by the ruling classes as the strong man needed to manage the situation. Imredy did, indeed, rule with a strong hand. At the same time, however, he initiated certain **political and economic reforms** (a part of all large estates to be distributed to the peasantry, etc.) and undertook the **limitation of Jewish activity** in business and the professions. In this way he hoped to steal the thunder of the Nazi agitators. For the rest he tried to maintain good relations with Germany.

Nov. 2. ACQUISITION OF SOUTHERN SLOVAKIA, as a result of the dismemberment of Czechoslovakia. Hungary was given 5,000 square miles of territory, with 1 million inhabitants.

1939, Jan. Imredy's government announced the creation of the Hungarian Life Movement in the hope of imitating the success of Fascists in other countries.

Feb. 15. Resignation of Premier Imredy. The Nazis, whom he had tried to outdo in his anti-Semitic policy, had taunted him with his own Jewish ancestry.

Feb. 24. The **new government of Count Pál Teleki** suddenly suppressed the leading Fascist organization, yet at the same time, to placate Germany, **joined the Anti-Comintern Pact** of Germany, Japan, and Italy.

March 15. HUNGARY OCCUPIED CARPATHO-UKRAINE and annexed it after heavy fighting with the inhabitants, who had driven out the Czechs and, under Augustin Volosin, had enjoyed independence for one day.

April 11. Hungary withdrew from the League of Nations, revealing further influence of German pressure.

May 3. Introduction of drastic **anti-Jewish laws** providing for rigorous limitation of Jews in professions and business, expulsion from government service, and eventual emigration within five years.

May 28. In the **elections** the government secured 180 seats out of 260, but the Nazis increased their representation from 6 to 53, while the Agrarians had 14 seats as against a previous 23.

1940, Sept. Hungary refused permission for the German army to pass through its territory but permitted the movement of 130,000 Polish soldiers into Hungary as refugees. Hitler reacted by canceling war contracts with Hungary.

Nov. 20. The Hungarian government endorsed the Rome-Berlin-Tokyo Axis and joined it against the Allies.

1941, April 3. Teleki committed suicide. He had realized that he could not prevent Horthy's decision to side with Germany in war with Yugoslavia. **László Bárdossy** formed the next government. On June 26 Hungary also joined the Nazi invasion of the Soviet Union.

Aug. New anti-Semitic laws prohibited intermarriage and punished extramarital sexual relations between Jews and gentiles.

1943, May 5. The Hungarian Parliament was adjourned indefinitely.

1944, March 19. The German army occupied Hungary and began the systematic extermination of its last Jewish enclave. Approximately 75 percent of Hungary's Jewish population was killed during the war.

Oct. 15. Horthy proclaimed an armistice with the Soviet Union and withdrew from the war. The Nazis responded by occupying the royal castle and installing the leaders of the Arrow Cross. The Hungarian army did not respond to this aggression and accepted new leadership.

Dec. 21. A provisional assembly and government were established in Debrecen.

Dec. 24. The Red Army encircled Budapest, but the Germans and Arrow Cross offered strong resistance. The fighting did not end in Hungary until April 1945. *(To p. 889)*

15. THE SCANDINAVIAN STATES

(From p. 506)

a. OVERVIEW

The Scandinavian states were all able to preserve neutrality during World War I, though they were obliged to accept various Allied regulations and restrictions made necessary by the Allied blockade of Germany. After 1918 they all took an active part in the development of collective security, in which obviously they had a great interest. For the rest they all became thoroughly democratic states and leaders in social reform. In politics the situation in most cases was rather unstable, due to the relative strength of conservative, liberal, agrarian, and social democratic parties and the difficulty of establishing majority government. In foreign policy efforts were made consistently to develop a program of close cooperation and solidarity, which became all the more necessary after the resurgence of Germany as a powerful military state.

1914, Dec. 18–19. Meeting of the kings of the three Scandinavian states at Malmö was the first such effort at collaboration. They discussed various problems of the war, neutrality, and so on.

1926, Jan. 14, 15, 30. Agreements were made among Denmark, Sweden, Norway, and Finland providing **for the pacific settlement of all disputes.** These countries began to suffer severely from the world economic crisis in 1931.

1931, Sept. 6. Prime ministers of the Scandinavian states met for discussion of economic problems.

1932, Feb. 7. As a result, the **Oslo convention** came into force, by which the Scandinavian states joined with the Netherlands and Belgium in a scheme of economic cooperation, albeit on a modest scale.

1938, April 5–6. The four Scandinavian foreign ministers met for a discussion of the **defense problem.** In view of the unwillingness of Denmark to challenge Germany, the specific question of armament and defense had to be left to the individual governments.

July 1. The Oslo mutual trade agreements came to an end. Nevertheless, relations among the so-called Oslo powers continued to be cordial and even close.

1939, June 17. Sweden, Norway, and Finland declined the **German offer of a mutual nonaggression pact,** an offer provoked by President Roosevelt's suggestion, in his letter to Hitler, that Germany's neighbors felt threatened by aggression.   *(To p. 878)*

b. DENMARK

(From p. 508)

1912–47. CHRISTIAN X, king.

1915, June. A **new constitution** was adopted, instituting universal suffrage and more popular representation in the Landsting. The new electoral laws made it difficult to form governments, however, and a rapid succession of ministries followed.

1916, Aug. 4. Sale of the Danish West Indies to the United States. The transaction was approved by a Danish plebiscite on Dec. 14.

1918, Feb. Protesting the rising cost of living, the unemployed, led by the syndicalist trade unions, staged an attack on the stock exchange in Copenhagen.

April 22. Elections. Under the new system the Conservatives secured 23 seats, the Left (Liberals) 45, the Radicals 33, and the Socialists 39. The government was formed by a coalition of Radicals and Socialists.

1920, Feb. 10, March 14. By the plebiscites provided for in the Treaty of Versailles, **a northern zone of Schleswig** went to Denmark by popular vote. It was officially incorporated on July 9.

March. The Easter Crisis. When the government refused the king's call for new elections, on the grounds that no election should occur before electoral reform, it was dismissed, causing popular demonstrations. The Social Democrats and the unions called for a general strike. The king was forced to yield and appoint a caretaker ministry acceptable to all parties. This ministry would propose electoral reforms that would take effect before the new elections.

March 8. Denmark joined the League of Nations.

1924, April 11. In the elections the Socialists increased their representation from 39 to 55. Thereupon **Thorvald Stauning** (Socialist) formed a government.

1926, March 12. The Danish parliament voted for almost complete **disarmament,** which was subsequently carried through.

Dec. 2. A Liberal government was formed by **Thomas Madsen-Mygdal** after a severe setback to the Socialists in the elections.

1929, April 24. Stauning organized another government after Socialist successes at the polls. His party acted in coalition with the Radical Left.

1931, July. A serious **dispute with Norway** developed over the problem of sovereignty over East Greenland.

1932–33. Unemployment reached 42.8 percent. Farmers were also increasingly unable to make loan payments. Economic problems led to an agreement between the Socialists and the leaders of the Vestre Party (Agrarian) that promised a 10 percent devaluation, the government purchase of surplus cattle, lower taxes on farm property, a one-year ban on strikes and lockouts, a large program of public works, and various social reforms.

1933. Agitation of the Germans in North Schleswig followed on the victory of the National Socialists in Germany. National socialism itself made but little progress in Denmark, although Denmark, practically disarmed, remained more or less at the mercy of its powerful neighbor.

1939. Denmark signed a nonaggression pact with Germany.

1940, April 9. GERMAN FORCES OCCUPIED DENMARK (p. 800). Stauning remained head of the government and Christian X remained in Copenhagen.

1941, April 9. The people of **Greenland,** while affirming their loyalty to Christian X of Denmark, **accepted the protection offered by the United States.**

1943, Aug. 29. After increasing acts of sabotage, **Denmark was placed under a state of emergency.** The Danish army was disarmed, and the government was replaced by an administration of civil servants who exercised legislative powers when necessary to avoid direct German rule.

Sept. Resistance was coordinated by the Freedom Council, which aided in the smuggling of almost all of Denmark's 7,000 Jews to Sweden.

1945, May 4. Denmark was liberated.   *(To p. 878)*

c. NORWAY

(From p. 507)

1905–57. HAAKON VII, king. Norway, much more dependent on trade and fishing than either Denmark or Sweden, alone among the Scandinavian powers revealed a tendency toward expansion overseas.

1919. The government established the **8-hour workday** and the **48-hour week.**

Sept. 25. The Allied supreme council awarded Norway sovereignty over **Spitsbergen,** which was thereupon annexed (Feb. 9, 1920).

1920, March 5. Norway joined the League of Nations.

1921. The Storthing established **prohibition** after a plebiscite in 1919 showed great popular support. A second popular vote in 1926 swung the opposite direction, and prohibition was repealed in 1927.

1924, Oct. 20. In the **elections** the Conservatives emerged victorious, with 54 seats as against 34 for the Radicals, 22 for the Agrarians, 24 for the Labor Party, and 8 for the Socialists.

1927, Oct. 17. In the next **elections,** however, the Labor Party for the first time became the strongest group (59 seats as against 31 for the Conservatives and 31 for the Liberals). The **first Labor government** was organized by **Christopher Hornsrud** but was soon forced out by its opponents (Feb. 10, 1928). Thereupon **Johan Mowinckel** (Liberal) formed a cabinet.

1928. Novelist **Sigrid Undset** (1882–1949) won the Nobel Prize for literature.

The government instituted a state-controlled grain monopoly, which meant both price regulation and subsidies to farmers. Throughout the 1920s the Norwegian economy struggled. During the last half of the decade bankruptcies ran into the thousands. Unemployment rose to 25 percent in 1927 and, when Norway went back on the gold standard in 1928, causing deflation, attempts to reduce wages in proportion to falling prices caused serious labor disturbances.

Jan. 18. Annexation of Bouvet Island.

1929, Feb. 2. Annexation of Peter Island. Both Bouvet and Peter islands, in the South Atlantic, were important as whaling stations.

May 8. Annexation of Jan Mayen Island in the Arctic.

1929–30. Explorations of Capt. Hjalmar Riiser-Larsen in the Antarctic continent.

1931, May 8. Peter Kolstad (Farmers' Party) formed a government.

July 10. Annexation of the East Greenland coast between 71° 30′ and 75° 40′ north latitude. The Permanent Court of International Justice ruled against this, however, and Norway complied.

1932, March 5. On the death of Premier Kolstad, his place was taken by **Jen Hundseid.**

1933, Jan. 25. Mowinckel organized another Liberal cabinet, which continued in power even after the elections of Oct. 16 gave the Labor Party 69 seats (Right 30; Left 24; Farmers 23).

1935, March 20. A second Labor government was formed by **Johan Nygaardsvold,** with **Halvdan Koht,** an eminent historian, at the foreign office. This government was successful in overcoming the economic crisis, and became noteworthy for its extension of social security legislation (1937, Jan.: **Workers' Security Law** and **Seamen's Security Law**).

1939, Jan. 14. Norway laid claim to 1 million square miles of **Antarctic territory** extending from 20° west longitude to 45° east longitude (Coats Land to Enderby Land, about one-fifth of the entire Antarctic coast).

1940, April 9. GERMAN FORCES INVADED NORWAY (p. 800). The government fled to England on June 7.

1942, Feb. 1. The German commissioner for Norway, **Joseph Terboven,** appointed **Vidkun Quisling "minister-president"** of a puppet regime. Quisling abolished the Norwegian constitution (Feb. 7) and made himself **virtual dictator.** His plan to create a chamber of corporations on the Italian model was thwarted by mass resignations from the trade unions.

1945, May 6. With the comprehensive surrender to Eisenhower, **Norway was liberated.** (To p. 879)

d. SWEDEN

(From p. 507)

1907–50. GUSTAVUS V, king.

1917, Dec. 29. The **Aaland Islands,** following the Bolshevik Revolution in Russia, **voted to join Sweden,** but later (June 24, 1921) the League of Nations council assigned them to Finland, with the proviso that they should be demilitarized.

1918, Nov. 13. Worker demonstrations in Stockholm demanded a general strike, establishment of a socialist republic, and organization of workers' and soldiers' councils. The government moved quickly to introduce sweeping suffrage reform. By 1919 tax restrictions, property restrictions, and gender restrictions were all abandoned, except for people on poor relief, and the voting age was set at 23.

1920, March 4. Sweden joined the League of Nations.

March 10. Hjalmar Branting formed the first purely Socialist cabinet. From 1920 to 1926 the Socialists formed three governments that ruled for all but approximately two and a half years. These Socialist cabinets enacted a large body of **social reform legislation** for both workers and peasants, and greatly reduced the military establishment. After the downfall of the Socialist government in June 1926, there followed a number of Liberal and Conservative governments.

1923. The Tenants' Savings and Building Society (HSB) was founded in Stockholm. In its first decade it built 8,000 dwelling units, demonstrating the strength of the **cooperative movement** in Sweden (as in the rest of Scandinavia).

1924. Sweden became the first country in Europe to return to the gold standard after economic recovery had begun rapidly in 1922.

1931. The depression caused worker discontent, culminating in a rare episode of violence during a labor dispute in Adalen, where soldiers killed five workers.

1932, May 12. Economic conditions worsened with the news of **Ivar Kreuger's** suicide and the subsequent financial collapse of his vast financial empire. Thousands of investors were wiped out, and the political scandal that followed forced Prime Minister Carl Ekman's resignation in August.

Sept. 24. Per A. Hansson became premier of a Socialist government. This government did much to combat the depression by introducing large-scale public works, drastically economizing in administration, and passing a long-term **unemployment insurance act** (May 1934). The government also undertook a **program of rearming,** which appeared essential after the rise of Hitler and the rapid deterioration of German-Russian relations.

1936, June 13. Axel Pehrsson (Agrarian) formed a cabinet.

Sept. 28. Hansson again became premier, after the elections of Sept. 20 (Socialists 112 seats; Conservatives 44; Agrarians 36; Liberals 27), his government representing a coalition of Socialists and Agrarians.

1939, Sept. 3. Sweden preserved its neutrality throughout World War II, and suffered fewer privations than during World War I. Greater self-sufficiency and careful planning avoided desperate food shortages, though the lack of fuel did create hardships. Sweden became a haven for war refugees, accepting Norwegians, Finns, and Balts.

1941, June 25. In response to a demand from Germany and Finland the Swedish government allowed the **passage of one division of German troops** from Norway to Finland.

1942, Nov. 7. The Swedish foreign minister announced that **Sweden was determined to maintain neutrality** but regarded a free Finland and a free Norway as essential for the survival of a free Sweden.

1943, Aug. Sweden placed new restrictions on freight traffic via Sweden between Germany and Norway, and from Sept. 1944 only hospital cars could pass from Finland through Sweden to Germany. Trade was increasingly curtailed. (To p. 880)

e. FINLAND

(From p. 508)

1917, March 21. The Russian provisional government recognized Finland as an **independent state** within the proposed Russian federation.

Dec. 6. FINNS PROCLAIMED THEIR COMPLETE INDEPENDENCE of Russia, and this was recognized by the Soviet government (Jan. 2, 1918) as well as by Sweden (Jan. 4), France, and Germany (Jan. 6).

1918, Jan. 28. CIVIL WAR ensued in Finland. Finnish Communists (Reds), supported by the Russian Bolsheviks, seized Helsingfors (Helsinki) and overran much of southern Finland.

April. The Whites (opponents of Bolshevism), led by **Baron Karl Gustav Mannerheim** and supported by a German force under **Gen. Rüdiger von der Goltz,** retook the capital (April 13) and drove the Reds out of the country (**Battle of Viborg,** April 30).

Oct. 8. The Finnish Diet elected Prince Frederick Charles of Hesse as king. After the defeat of the Central powers, Frederick Charles renounced the crown (Dec. 31).

Oct. The first **agrarian reform law** was enacted, enabling tenants on land owned by private persons to purchase that land at prices fixed by public authorities. Parish and state landholders were added to this scheme in 1921 and 1922, respectively. About 117,000 new independent holdings were thereby created. With the 1922 Law Providing Land for Settlement (Lex Kallio), the state provided funds for those to whom the 1918 law did not apply but who wanted to purchase a farm. In 1918 the farming population was approximately 66 percent; it was still over 50 percent by 1938.

Dec. 11. Baron Mannerheim had become **head of the state** in the interval, and the last German forces had departed (Dec. 17).

1919, June 6. War with Russia broke out again, over conflicting claims to Karelia. Hostilities were concluded by the **Treaty of Dorpat** (Tartu) of Oct. 14, 1920, by the terms of which the independence of Finland was reaffirmed and Finland was given a narrow strip of territory between Murmansk and the eastern frontier of Norway, with the ice-free port of **Pechenga.**

June. Prohibition became law in Finland.

July 17. A **democratic constitution** was adopted. Finland had a unicameral parliament elected by universal suffrage.

July 25. KAARLO J. STAHLBERG was elected president for six years.

1920, Dec. 16. Finland joined the League of Nations.

1921, June 24. The League council assigned to Finland **sovereignty over the Aaland Islands,** on condition that the islands be given an autonomous regime.

1923. The **University of Helsinki** became a bilingual institution in an attempt to ease tension between the Swedish and Finnish linguistic communities.

1925. Jean Sibelius (1865–1957), composer, wrote his last major work, *Tapiola.* Sibelius was hailed as a national treasure in Finland, where his birthdays were national celebrations.

Feb. 16. LAURI RELANDER succeeded Stahlberg as president.

1928. The secretary of the Federation of Labor Unions was convicted of treason and jailed for five years. The labor movement was split between Social Democrats and Communists throughout the 1920s. The federation collapsed in 1929 when the Communists called for a general strike that failed without Social Democrat support. Communism was later outlawed in 1930, and a new non-Communist Confederation of Finnish Trade Unions (SAK) was founded.

1930, Oct. 14. **Attempted coup of Gen. Kurt Wallenius** and his Fascist Lapua organization.

1931, Feb. 16. PEHR SVINHUFVUD became president. During his term of office he threw his influence in the direction of conservatism, encouraging the Fascist elements.

1932, Feb. 27–March 7. Another Lapua uprising. Once again the movement failed. Wallenius was arrested, and on Nov. 21 more than 50 leaders were convicted. The organization was disbanded, but in 1933 there emerged the Patriotic National Movement, similar to the Lapua.

1933, May 4. The government forbade the military organization of political parties and groups.

1934, April. The wearing of uniforms and political emblems was prohibited.

1935, Aug. 28. The Finnish foreign minister for the first time joined in the meeting of ministers of the other Scandinavian states. Thereafter Finland regularly participated in these meetings. In view of the changed conditions in the Baltic after Hitler's rise to power, Finland attempted to form a **bloc of Scandinavian and Baltic states** to hold a balance between Germany and Russia. In close collaboration with these states Finland proceeded to **refortification of the Aaland Islands,** despite the opposition of the inhabitants.

1937, Feb. 15. KYOSTI KALLIO, premier and leader of the Agrarian Party, **was elected president,** with support of the Social Democrats.

1938, Nov. 22. The **government dissolved the Patriotic National Movement,** which was the spearhead of fascism.

1939. Novelist **Frans Eemil Sillanpää** (1888–1964) won the Nobel Prize.

Jan. The interwar development of social legislation culminated in the implementation of **old-age and invalidity insurance,** covering all persons 18 years and over.

Sept. 1. Finland announced its neutrality.

Oct. 5. The Soviet Union invited Finland to enter political discussions. The Finns mobilized (Oct. 9) and replied to Soviet proposals to garrison certain positions in Finland by offering counterproposals (Oct. 23). The talks were broken off (Nov. 13), and the Soviet Union **denounced the Soviet-Finnish nonaggression treaty,** which had been renewed on April 7, 1934.

Nov. 30. SOVIET FORCES INVADED FINLAND (p. 800), **and Finland appealed to the League of Nations** (Dec. 3), which responded (Dec. 14) by **expelling the Soviet Union from the League.** The **SOVIET-FINNISH WAR** lasted from Nov. 30, 1939, to March 12, 1940, when **Finland yielded territory and concessions to the Soviet Union.**

1941, June 22. Finland attacked the Soviet Union in collaboration with the surprise attack launched by the Germans.

Sept. 22. Requests from Great Britain and subsequently (Oct. 3) from the **United States that Finland cease its war with the Soviet Union were rejected by the Finns.**

1944, Aug. 1. Risto Ryti, president of Finland, **resigned** his office, and the Finnish parliament voted **Marshal Karl Gustav Mannerheim** to succeed him.

Nov. 10. Juho Paasikivi formed a new cabinet. The Finnish **Communist Party,** having secured recognition, prepared to contest the elections.

1945, March 3. FINLAND DECLARED WAR ON GERMANY.

(To p. 881)

f. ICELAND

1918, Nov. 30. By the Act of Union, **Iceland was recognized as a sovereign state,** united with Denmark only in the person of the ruler. But until 1944 certain affairs were to be handled jointly.

1920. A **Supreme Court** was established. By World War II Iceland controlled most of its own affairs: a postal system, a banking and money system, tariff laws, and a penal system. Denmark retained control over foreign relations and protected fishing rights in Icelandic waters.

1923. The Althing passed the **Cultivation of Soil Act,** granting subsidies for agricultural improvements. With the aid of modern equipment, this revitalized Icelandic agriculture.

1937. The Althing proclaimed that it would not seek a renewal of the treaty binding Iceland with Denmark.

1940, May 10. A British garrison was accepted under protest to prevent a German invasion.

1941, May 17. The **Althing announced that Iceland would separate from Denmark.**

July. After an agreement, American forces replaced British forces in Iceland.

1944, June 17. After a plebiscite (May 20–23), **Iceland declared itself a republic,** with Sveinn Björnson as its first president. *(To p. 882)*

16. RUSSIA (UNION OF SOVIET SOCIALIST REPUBLICS)

(From p. 512)

On Germany's declaration of war (Aug. 1, 1914), the opposition parties in Russia declared their readiness to put aside domestic quarrels and support the government. Since the government failed to respond, political discontent developed rapidly.

1915, May. The **Russian defeat in Galicia** deeply stirred public opinion (p. 654), and the government was openly accused of inefficiency in failing to supply the armies.

June 25. The tsar was obliged to dismiss Gen. **Vladimir Sukhomlinov,** the minister of war (tried and convicted by the provisional government in 1917), and to admit representatives of the duma and other public bodies (the Union of Zemstvos and Municipalities, the War Industry Committee, and others) to direct participation in the work of army supply and the mobilization of industry. Tsar **Nicholas** refused, however, to comply with the demand of the progressive bloc in the duma for an entirely new ministry that would enjoy the confidence of the country and be committed to a more liberal policy.

Sept. 5. The situation was aggravated when the tsar dismissed the popular commander-in-chief Grand Duke Nicholas and assumed the command himself. The tsar's absence from the capital opened the way for **domination by Empress Alexandra,** known to be bitterly hostile to the duma and under the influence of **Gregory Rasputin.**

1916, Feb. 3. Boris Stürmer, arch-conservative and allegedly pro-German, replaced Ivan Goremykin as **chief of the cabinet,** which led to the government's being completely discredited in the eyes of the public. On July 23 Stürmer took charge of the foreign office. Rumors of treason in high places undermined the morale of the army and the population generally. To all this was added a **grave economic problem**: shortage of labor, due to repeated mobilizations; disorganization of railroad transport; and failure of food and fuel supplies in the cities.

Nov. 18. Meeting of the duma. In a turbulent session the leaders denounced the "dark forces" in the government and warned the country of impending disaster unless there was an immediate change of policy.

Nov. 24. Alexander Trepov replaced Stürmer as president of the council of ministers, and the government embarked upon a policy of repression of dissatisfaction. But opposition continued.

Dec. 30. Rasputin was assassinated by Prince Felix Yusupov and other aristocrats. Even these drastic measures were barren of results, and in some political and military circles there was discussion of a palace revolution.

1917, March 8. Strikes and riots broke out in St. Petersburg (named Petrograd at the beginning of the war).

March 10. A **general mutiny of the troops** in the capital, which sealed the fate of the old regime.

March 11. The duma refused to obey an imperial decree ordering its dissolution.

March 12. A **PROVISIONAL GOVERNMENT,** headed by **Prince George Lvov** (chairman of the Union of Zemstvos and Municipalities), was established by the duma. The new government included **Paul Miliukov,** leader of the Constitutional Democrats (as minister for foreign affairs); **Alexander Guchkov,** leader of the Octobrists (minister of war); and **Alexander Kerensky,** the only Socialist (minister of justice).

March 15. Nicholas II abdicated for himself and his son in favor of his brother Michael, who in turn (March 16) abdicated in favor of the provisional government pending election by a constituent assembly.

March–Nov. THE RULE OF THE PROVISIONAL GOVERNMENT. At the outset the new regime proclaimed **civic liberties** and recognized equality of all citizens without social, religious, or racial discrimination. **Finland** was recognized as independent within a Russian federation (March 21); **Poland's** complete independence accepted (March 30); **Estonia** granted autonomy (April 12). At the same time the government announced a program of far-reaching **social reforms,** including distribution of land among the peasants (confiscation of imperial and monastery lands, March 30). But the decision on these and other matters was reserved for the **constituent assembly.** From the outset the provisional government, essentially liberal and bourgeois, found itself in **conflict with the Petrograd Soviet** (Council of Workers' and Soldiers' Deputies), which had been organized by the Socialists (March 12). The government pledged itself (March 18, May 1) to continuation of the war against the Central powers, in common with the Allies, until the attainment of a "victorious end." It attempted to maintain the efficiency of the army and proceeded, but cautiously, toward its democratization. The Soviet leaders, on the other hand, insisted on a radical revision of war aims, renunciation of secret diplomatic agreements concluded by the tsarist government (and promising Russia Istanbul), and the speedy conclusion of a "general democratic peace," without annexations or indemnities. Suspecting the generals of counterrevolutionary tendencies, the Soviet issued (March 14) **Order No. 1,** which deprived the officers of all authority except for strategic operations, and entrusted the administration of the army to committees elected by both officers and men. The counterorder of the provisional government was virtually ignored, and the committee system was subsequently introduced in all army detachments. The antagonism of the Soviet to the government soon became more outspoken.

April 16. Lenin, Gregory Zinoviev, Karl Radek, Anatoli Lunacharski, and other **Bolshevik leaders arrived in Petrograd** from Switzerland, having been transported through Germany in a sealed carriage, the German high command having calculated that these extremists would soon undermine the pro-Allied provisional government. **Lenin's program** was (1) transfer of power from the "bourgeois" provisional government to the Soviets; (2) immediate cessation of the war, if necessary by the acceptance of a separate peace with the Central powers; (3) immediate seizure of land by the peasants, without awaiting the decision of the constituent assembly; (4) control of industry by committees of workers. Lenin was ably supported by Leon Bronstein, who adopted the name **Trotsky.** Trotsky returned from the United States and England early in May, but Lenin's program was not accepted by

the more moderate (Menshevik) wing of the Social Democratic Party or by the Social Revolutionaries.

May 14, 16. Guchkov and Miliukov were obliged to resign from the provisional government as a result of agitation over war aims and army organization. The government was remade and now accepted a policy of no annexations and no indemnities, though still declaring against a separate peace. Several Socialists were included in the cabinet, and **Kerensky became minister of war.** He undertook to revive the war spirit and the fighting power of the army on the basis of the new "revolutionary discipline."

June 29–July 7. A **Russian offensive** against the Austro-German forces was ordered by Kerensky after a spectacular visit to the front and a stirring appeal to the soldiers. After a brief initial success the offensive collapsed, and the disorganized Russian troops were completely defeated (p. 672). The radicals now took the initiative.

July 16–18. The **Bolsheviks attempted to seize power** in Petrograd, but the effort proved premature. The movement was suppressed by the government, and many of the leaders (including Trotsky) were arrested. Lenin went into hiding in Finland.

July 20. The **resignation of Prince Lvov,** whose place was taken by Kerensky, was caused by this coup and by disagreement between ministers regarding the burning question of land reform and the status of national minorities (assumption of power in Ukraine by the local rada, June 26; establishment of Gen. Alexis Kaledin as hetman of the Don Cossacks, June 30; Finnish declaration of complete independence, July 20). The position of the government, however, remained precarious in view of the growing restlessness of the masses, who suffered from war-weariness and material privations, and were all too ready to listen to Bolshevik propaganda. On the other hand, the conservative elements opposed the government because of its alleged weakness in dealing with the Bolsheviks. The advocates of a strong line found a champion in **Gen. Lavr Kornilov,** recently appointed commander in chief.

Sept. 9–14. The **Kornilov attack** upon the government was brought about by a rift between Kerensky and Kornilov. Kerensky had dismissed Kornilov, who refused to obey and ordered his troops to advance on Petrograd, his avowed aim being to destroy the Soviet and liberate the provisional government from Socialist domination. The movement broke down because of defection on the part of many soldiers and because of mobilization of the radical elements in the capital, to whom Kerensky appealed for support against the "counterrevolution" (Trotsky and some other Bolshevik leaders were released from prison).

Kornilov was defeated, but Kerensky now found himself under the domination of his Bolshevik allies. The masses had come to suspect not only the army command but the provisional government also of counterrevolutionary designs. Bolshevik influence made rapid progress among the factory workers and soldiers of the Petrograd garrison. In October the Bolsheviks secured a majority in the Soviet, Trotsky becoming its chairman. Thereupon Lenin decided to attempt a coup.

Nov. 6. (O.S. Oct. 24.) **THE BOLSHEVIK REVOLUTION.** The Bolsheviks, led by the military revolutionary committee, the soldiers of the Petrograd garrison, the sailors from Kronstadt, and the workers' Red Guards, captured most of the government offices, took the Winter Palace by storm, and arrested the members of the provisional government. **Kerensky managed to escape,** and, after a futile attempt to organize resistance, went into hiding and subsequently into exile abroad.

Nov. 7. The **Second All-Russian Congress of Soviets,** from which the moderate Socialists bolted, approved the coup and handed over power to the Bolsheviks.

The history of Russia (Union of Soviet Socialist Republics) from 1917 to 1941 may be conveniently divided into **three periods**: (1) the **Period of Militant Communism** (1917–21); (2) the **Period of the New Economic Policy** (1921–27); and (3) the **Period of the New Socialist Offensive** (1928–41).

The new government (organized Nov. 9) assumed the name Council of People's Commissars. It was headed by **Lenin** and included **Trotsky** (commissar for foreign affairs) and **Joseph Stalin** (commissar for national minorities). To protect itself and to crush opposition, the council organized (Dec. 20) the Extraordinary Commission to Combat Counter-Revolution (the Cheka, later known as the GPU).

Nov. 25. The **elections to the constituent assembly** returned 420

Social Revolutionaries as against only 225 Bolsheviks. When the assembly met in Petrograd (Jan. 18, 1918) it was dispersed at once by the Red troops. Therewith one of the most influential elements of the opposition was disposed of. Some of the Social Revolutionaries joined in the anti-Bolshevik movements that soon began to form.

1917–21. SOCIAL AND ECONOMIC POLICY. The victorious Bolsheviks at once undertook the reorganization of society along collectivist lines. A **Land Decree** (Nov. 7) ordered immediate partition of the large estates and distribution of the land among the peasants. But on Feb. 19, 1918, the **nationalization of the land** was proclaimed (all land to be the property of the state, and only those willing to cultivate it themselves to be permitted to use it). No further efforts were made in the direction of collectivization, but when the civil war brought the cities and the armies into danger of starvation, the peasants were ordered (Dec. 14, 1920) to turn over to the government their entire surplus (the **food levy**). As they were reluctant to do so, and saw no prospect of any return in consumer goods, the government was driven to adopt **forcible requisitioning,** which created widespread discontent.

On their advent to power the Bolsheviks at once declared all **banks nationalized,** confiscating private accounts. The **national debt was repudiated** (Jan. 28, 1918). The workmen were given **control over the factories** (Nov. 28, 1917), and by the summer of 1918 all the larger plants (and subsequently the smaller ones) were nationalized (law of June 28, 1918). The workers were instructed to join **government-controlled trade unions** and were denied the right to strike. In emergencies the government resorted to a system of **compulsory labor.** Private trade was gradually suppressed, and the government undertook the distribution of food and other commodities among the urban populations, introducing **a rationing system** and making use also of the cooperatives. All **church property was confiscated** (Dec. 17, 1917), and all religious instruction in the schools was abolished. Only civil marriages were thenceforth to be recognized. The **Gregorian calendar** was introduced on Jan. 31, 1918.

1917–18. CONCLUSION OF PEACE WITH THE CENTRAL POWERS (p. 663).

March 9. The government moved the capital from Petrograd (renamed Leningrad, Jan. 26, 1924) **to Moscow.** This was partly because of the exposed position of Petrograd with relation to the Germans and their satellites, and partly because of the threat of counterrevolution emanating from the borderlands. Monarchists and members of the propertied classes, who favored political and economic restoration, as well as Liberals and Moderate Socialists who were opposed to the Communist dictatorship, were all more or less united in their refusal to accept the disastrous Brest-Litovsk treaty. The British and French, who regarded the Bolsheviks as tools of the German general staff and were eager to keep supplies and munitions from falling into the hands of the Germans, encouraged and supported movements among the opponents of the Bolsheviks. **Independent governments** were established all along the Russian frontiers (**Lithuania,** Dec. 11, 1917; **Moldova,** Dec. 15; **Republic of the Don,** Jan. 10, 1918; **Ukraine,** Jan. 28; **Transcaucasia,** April 22; etc.). The revolt of the Don Cossacks, led by Gens. **Kornilov** and **Kaledin,** Dec. 9, 1917, may be said to mark the beginning of the civil war.

1918–20. GREAT CIVIL WAR. The Bolshevik government was at first faced with the prospect of war without anything like an adequate, trained force. During the first period of the war it suffered one reverse after another, but gradually a new **Red Army** of volunteers was organized. Under the leadership of Trotsky (who had become commissar for war) it developed into a regular army based on conscription and subject to strict discipline. The Bolsheviks had the advantage of fighting on the inside lines and derived a certain measure of support from the fact that they were defending Russian territory. At the same time the lack of cohesion among the counterrevolutionary movements and the fitful attitude of the Allied powers constantly hampered the operations of the Whites.

(1) **The war with the Cossacks.** Operations began with the new year. **Kaledin** committed suicide after a defeat (Feb. 13), and **Kornilov** was killed in battle (April 13). The command in the south was taken over by **Gen. Anton Denikin,** supported by **Gen. Peter Krasnov** (hetman of the Don Cossacks, May 11).

(2) **The struggle for Ukraine.** Ukraine had declared its independence

of Russia (Jan. 28, 1918), and the Moderate Socialist government at Kiev had concluded a separate peace with the Germans and Austrians (Feb. 9). Thereupon the Bolsheviks attacked and took **Kiev** (Feb. 18), but they were soon ejected by the Germans (March 2), who then also took Odessa (March 13) and overran the whole of Ukraine, from which they tried, rather unsuccessfully, to secure much-needed food supplies. With German aid, a more conservative government, under **Gen. Paul Skoropadsky,** was set up, but after the end of the world war, Skoropadsky was overthrown (Nov. 15) by the Ukrainian Socialists, under **Gen. Simon Petliura.** The French occupied **Odessa** (Dec. 18), but the Bolsheviks, having assumed the offensive, took Kiev (Feb. 3, 1919) and expelled the Allied forces from Odessa (April 8). **Ukraine became a Soviet Republic,** which was conquered by the White armies of Gen. Denikin (Aug.–Dec. 1919) only to be retaken by the Bolsheviks (Dec. 17) and then invaded by the Poles (May 7, 1920). The Bolsheviks managed to drive the Poles back and on Dec. 28 concluded a treaty with the Ukrainian Soviet government, recognizing the latter's independence. On Dec. 30 Ukraine joined with the other Soviet Republics to form the Union of Soviet Socialist Republics.

(3) **The war in Belarus (White Russia) and the Baltic region.** Most of this area continued to be occupied or dominated by the Germans down to and beyond the conclusion of the world war armistice. In the autumn of 1919 a White army under **Gen. Nicholas Yudenitch** advanced on Petrograd (Oct. 19) but was forced back by the Bolsheviks. The Soviet government recognized the **independence of Estonia** (Feb. 2, 1920), **of Lithuania** (July 12), **of Latvia** (Aug. 11), **and of Finland** (Oct. 14). Belarus continued to be a Soviet Republic until its union with the other Soviet Republics in 1922.

(4) **Allied intervention in northern Russia.** The British landed a force at Murmansk on June 23, 1918, primarily with the object of holding German forces in the east and protecting Allied stores from falling into hostile hands. On Aug. 2 the **British and French took Arkhangelsk** and began to support a puppet **government of northern Russia.** The Americans also sent a force, and during the spring of 1919 there was considerable fighting between the Allies and the Bolsheviks. The French were the most ardent advocates of more extensive intervention against the Bolsheviks, but neither the British nor the Americans were willing, after the armistice, to go beyond financial and other support for the anti-Bolshevik movements. On Sept. 30, 1919, the Allies abandoned Arkhangelsk and then (Oct. 12) Murmansk. These territories were quickly taken over by the Bolsheviks.

(5) **Campaigns of Denikin and Wrangel in the Caucasus and southern Russia.** The Caucasian states (**Georgia, Armenia, and Azerbaijan**) declared their independence on April 22 and May 26, 1918. After the withdrawal of the Germans and Austrians from southern Russia, the Bolsheviks made an effort to reconquer this territory, so valuable for its oil, but **Denikin** defeated them (Jan. 1919). After a rather spectacular advance northward, Denikin was himself driven back to the Black Sea coast (April), where he maintained himself until the autumn. In another swift offensive he then captured Odessa (Aug. 18) and took Kiev (Sept. 2), only to be forced to retreat again (Dec.). By March 27, 1920, his last base fell to the Bolsheviks, and he turned over the command to **Gen. Peter Wrangel.** The Bolsheviks meanwhile advanced into the Caucasus and took Baku (April 28), but Wrangel, starting from the region north of the Sea of Azov, began to overrun much of southern Russia (June–Nov.). Finally, however, the Bolshevik forces, freed by the conclusion of the war with Poland, were able to concentrate against Wrangel, who was forced back to the Crimea (Nov. 1) and then obliged to evacuate his army to Constantinople (Nov. 14). Early in 1921 **Soviet governments were set up in Georgia** (Feb. 25) **and in Armenia** (April 2). By the treaty with Turkey (Oct. 13) **Batum was restored to Russia.** On March 12, 1922, the Soviet governments of Georgia, Armenia, and Azerbaijan were combined to form the **Transcaucasian Soviet Socialist Republic,** which on Dec. 30 became part of the larger Union of Soviet Socialist Republics.

(6) **The war in Siberia and eastern Russia. Japanese forces** were landed at **Vladivostok** on Dec. 30, 1917, at a time when the **Czech legions** (organized before the revolution out of large numbers of Austrian war prisoners) had already started their march toward Vladivostok with the purpose of ultimately joining the Allied forces in Europe. Disagreement between them and the Soviet government led to armed

conflict (June 1918), in the course of which the **Czechs seized control of the Trans-Siberian Railway** and formed an alliance with local anti-Bolshevik forces. An **autonomous Siberian government** had already been formed at Omsk. This government later merged with the directory organized in Ufa by former members of the constituent assembly (mostly Moderate Socialists). Meanwhile the Czechs extended their operations to the Volga region, taking Ekaterinburg (July 26) and other places. At Omsk the military and conservative elements executed a coup (Nov. 18) by which the Socialists were forced out of the government, and **Adm. Alexander Kolchak was proclaimed Supreme Ruler of Russia.** His Siberian White army then staged an **advance into eastern Russia,** capturing Perm (Dec. 24) and Ufa. But the Bolsheviks initiated a vigorous counteroffensive, taking Orenburg and Ekaterinburg (Jan. 25, 27, 1919) and gradually forcing Kolchak back into Siberia. They recaptured Omsk (Nov. 14) and drove the White army back on Irkutsk. Kolchak gave way to **Gen. Nicholas Semenov** (Dec. 17) and was subsequently captured and executed by the Bolsheviks (Feb. 7). The Bolsheviks attempted to take Vladivostok by a coup (Jan. 30) but were obliged to yield to the greater power of the Japanese. In order to avoid conflict, the Soviet government of Russia set up a buffer state in eastern Siberia (April 6). This was known as the **Far Eastern Republic,** with its capital at Chita. When the Japanese finally evacuated Vladivostok (Oct. 25, 1922), the city was occupied by troops of the Far Eastern Republic, which was itself annexed to Soviet Russia on Nov. 19, 1922.

Other important developments of this confused and crucial period were as follows.

1918, July 10. PROMULGATION OF THE SOVIET CONSTITUTION, which was adopted by the Fifth All-Russian Congress of Soviets. The main lines of the soviet system were these: (1) **local soviets** elected representatives to the **provincial congresses of soviets,** which in turn sent delegates to the **All-Russian** (subsequently **All-Union**) **Congress of Soviets;** (2) the latter elected the **Executive Committee,** a permanent body that acted in the intervals between sessions of the congress; the congress also elected the **Council of People's Commissars;** (3) elections were held on an occupational and not on a territorial basis: the factory workers were more generously represented than the peasants, while the "nontoiling" bourgeois classes (including the clergy) were disfranchised; (4) all elections were open, with no provision for secret ballot. In practice this system of "soviet democracy" was dominated by a **dictatorship of** (or for) **the proletariat,** and this in turn was exercised by the Bolshevik Party (renamed the **Communist Party** in March 1918). No other parties were permitted, and the press and other channels of expression were put under sweeping government control. The Communist Party was governed by the **Central Committee,** within which there was a smaller group called the **Political Bureau** (Polithuro). This latter was the real governing body of the country. Lenin's authority remained supreme in both party and government until his death.

July 16. Murder of Nicholas II, Tsarina Alexandra, and their children in a cellar at Ekaterinburg, where they had been kept in captivity. On the outbreak of the revolution the imperial family had been confined first in the palace of Tsarskoe Selo. Thence it had been moved to Tobolsk and finally (April 1918) to Ekaterinburg. The murder was ordered by Bolsheviks who feared the imminent capture of the city by the advancing Czechs and Whites.

Aug. 30. An attempt was made by a Social Revolutionary to assassinate Lenin. Coming at the time of severe crisis, this move inaugurated a systematic **reign of terror** by the Bolsheviks, in the course of which huge numbers of intellectuals and bourgeois of all types were wiped out.

1919, March 2. Foundation of the Third International (Comintern), an organization for the propagation of Communist doctrine abroad with the purpose of bringing about the world revolution, on which Lenin and his associates reckoned with confidence in the stormy period following the end of the war.

1920, April 25–Oct. 12. WAR WITH POLAND.

The effects of the Allied blockade (p. 712) and of the devastating civil war, together with the revolutionary economic policy of the government, led to an almost complete **collapse of the Russian economy** by 1921. There was a sharp decline in production in both industry and agriculture, widespread disorganization of transport, and acute shortages of food and fuel, especially in the cities. Popular discontent found expression in numerous **peasant uprisings** during 1920 and in rioting of the factory workers in Petrograd.

1921, Feb. 23–March 17. The **mutiny and uprising of the sailors at Kronstadt,** which was put down only with difficulty and after much bloodshed. This situation finally forced the Communist Party to adopt a new economic policy.

March 17 et seq. The **NEW ECONOMIC POLICY** (often spoken of as the NEP), sponsored by Lenin himself. To placate the peasants, the **food levy was abolished,** and in its place there was introduced a limited **grain tax,** thus leaving the peasants at least part of the surplus. To enable them to dispose of this surplus, **freedom of trade** within the country was partially restored. Subsequently (1922) **a new land statute** was passed which made possible reconstruction of small individual farms and even permitted, under certain conditions, limited use of hired labor and lease of land. In industry some of the small plants were returned to former owners and licenses were given to private persons to start new enterprises.

Private commercial establishments were also permitted in the cities. In course of time the **financial system** was recast on a semicapitalistic basis: the state bank was given the right to issue bills backed either by goods or by foreign bonds; attempts were made to stabilize the currency (the devaluated paper money was replaced by the new *chervonets* bills). Large industry and transport, however, remained nationalized, and foreign trade continued to be a government monopoly.

The NEP was declared to be a "temporary retreat" from Communism, necessary for purposes of economic reconstruction. After the **great famine** of 1921–22 (caused by drought but aggravated by the economic collapse that preceded it), the national economy recovered at a rapid pace. Production in industry and agriculture reached the prewar level, and there was marked improvement in living standards both in the cities and in the countryside. Along with this recovery went an **abatement of the Red terror** and a slight relaxation of governmental censorship and repression. With the end of the civil war, more attention could be given to cultural work, and the government introduced an ambitious **educational program** aiming at a speedy elimination of illiteracy.

Throughout the interwar period the **party continued to grow,** reaching the million-member mark by the late 1920s and continuing despite the purges. In addition to the party proper, there existed huge youth organizations. The party also worked with and directed many other institutions and groups: professional, social, cultural, athletic. In the 1920s, however, many sectors of society, including women's groups, advocated various reform programs. During this decade the Bolshevik regime **experimented with innovation in the family.** Divorce could be obtained simply. **Abortions were legal** and extremely common. Officially, women were emancipated by the revolution and enjoyed complete equality. **Education became more available;** by 1939 81.1 percent of the population was literate. The arts also prospered under a great deal of freedom in the early years of the Soviet Union. Experimental approaches flourished under such artists as **Wassily Kandinsky** (1866–1944) and the poet **Boris Pasternak** (1890–1960).

Much of this changed, however, as Stalin solidified his power in the 1930s. Communist efforts to reshape Russian society and culture became more monolithic. In keeping with Stalin's belief in **"socialism in one country,"** Russian nationalism dictated a new relevance for the Soviet family, which was the subject of much propaganda. Women thus took on the task of running a household as model Soviet mothers while working full-time outside the home in order to further Soviet industrialization. Non-Russian national movements were suppressed, as were all cultural endeavors that did not reflect the official style of **socialist realism** (adopted at the first all-union congress of Soviet writers in 1934). Art was to be the truthful, historically concrete presentation of reality in its revolutionary development. Many artists responded by emigrating, like **Igor Stravinsky** (1882–1971), or by ceasing to create, like Pasternak. Others may have tried to prove their loyalty to the state through their works, like the composer **Sergei Prokofiev** (1891–1953) and the filmmaker **Sergei Eisenstein** (1898–1948) in their collaboration on *Alexander Nevsky* (1938). The result was also a great wave of proletarian novels, propaganda designed to build support for such government endeavors as collectivization. In the sciences, Soviet progress was hindered by the official acceptance of **Trofim Lysenko's**

(1898–1976) incorrect theories on heredity and by official condemnation of Einstein's "petty bourgeois" theories.

1922, April 10–May 19. Russia took part in the **economic conference at Genoa,** thus for the first time indicating a readiness to collaborate with non-Bolshevik countries for common ends.

    April 16. THE TREATY OF RAPALLO.

    Dec. 30. The **Union of Soviet Socialist Republics** was organized, bringing together Russia, Ukraine, Belarus, and Transcaucasia in one federation. The member states retained a large measure of cultural autonomy, but political control was exercised from Moscow through the All-Union Communist Party organization.

1924, Jan. 21. THE DEATH OF LENIN. This important event marked the beginning of a **struggle for power** within the inner councils of the party and the government. The chief contestants were **Trotsky** and **Stalin.** The latter at first allied himself with **Leo Kamenev** (whose given name was Rosenfeld) and **Gregory Zinoviev,** but these two soon quarreled with Stalin and adhered to the opposition bloc of Trotsky. Open conflict of the factions broke out in 1926.

    Feb. 1. Great Britain recognized the Bolshevik regime, and was soon followed by most of the other European and some extra-European powers (Italy, Feb. 7; France, Oct. 28).

1925, Jan. 21. Japan recognized the Soviet government and agreed to withdraw from northern Sakhalin (evacuation April 4).

    May 12. Revision of the federal constitution. A number of new republics were added to the federation (**Uzbekistan, Turkmenistan, Kazakhstan,** and others).

1926, July–Oct. Victory of Stalin over the Leftist opposition bloc led by Trotsky. This bloc insisted on discontinuation of the NEP policy, the speeding up of "socialist construction," and the active resumption of work for the world revolution. Trotsky held that a Communist regime in one country was an anomaly and that the proletarian revolution could be safe only when the whole world had been directed into the same channel. Trotsky, Zinoviev, Radek, and other leaders were now expelled from the political bureau of the party.

1927, Dec. 27. Definitive victory of the Stalin faction over the Trotsky group, when the fifteenth All-Union Congress of the Communist Party condemned all "deviation from the general party line" as interpreted by Stalin. Trotsky and his followers were banished to the provinces after expulsion from the party. In Jan. 1929 **Trotsky was expelled from the Union** and was obliged to take refuge in Constantinople. Later he moved to Norway and ultimately to Mexico. The same party congress made several decisions that signified the end of the NEP.

1928. NEW SOCIALIST OFFENSIVE INAUGURATED. A program of speedy industrialization was introduced in the form of several successive **five-year plans** (beginning Oct. 1, 1928). Considerable success was achieved in the **development of heavy industries** (primarily for purposes of national defense). The manufacturing labor force swelled with new workers from the countryside; huge new industrial cities grew up (Magnitogors in the Urals; Kuznetsk in Siberia. **Over 1,500 new factories** were built in the 1930s, as **industrial output expanded 12–14 percent annually.** But production of manufactured products still lagged behind the needs of the population, and the government was constantly faced with inefficiency, to say nothing of ill-will (in 1930 a series of **trials of technicians** began for mismanagement and sabotage). In the field of agriculture the government now returned to a policy of socialization by pooling individual peasant farms in large concerns, such as the **collective farms** *(kolkhoz)* and the **state farms** *(sovkhoz).* The collectivization campaign in the villages was carried out by means of both propaganda and coercion (drastic measures against the recalcitrant peasants and especially against the well-to-do farmers, or *kulaks,* who were completely wiped out). The objectives of the government were substantially achieved, and within a few years the great majority of the peasants were collectivized, the government controlling the output of the new farms.

1929, Nov. 17. Expulsion of Nicolai Bukharin and other members of the Rightist opposition. This group had advocated further concession to the peasants along the lines of the NEP. Stalin was now undisputed master of the situation and dictator of Russia.

    Dec. 22. An **agreement with China** brought to an end a prolonged dispute over the conflicting claims to the **Chinese Eastern Railway.**

1932–33. Collectivization was completed amid deliberate starvation (especially in Ukraine and the northern Caucasus). Villages and entire regions were surrounded by elite state security troops and deprived of all food reserves, which resulted in the death of more than 10 million people. The government did its utmost to conceal the famine from the world. Eventually, the amount of foodstuffs taken by the state was reduced, and collective farms were permitted to sell at least part of their surplus produce.

1932, July 25. Conclusion of **nonaggression pacts with Poland, Estonia, Latvia, and Finland,** followed by a similar **agreement with France** (Nov. 29).

1933. Purge of the Communist Party. About one-third of the members (1 million) were expelled for one reason or another. In April a number of British engineers were put on trial for sabotage. The British government protested and put an embargo on Soviet goods. Though convicted, the engineers were permitted to leave the country, but Anglo-Soviet relations continued to be distant.

    Nov. 17. Recognition of the Soviet government by the United States brought to an end a long period of estrangement. Trade relations were opened, and the Soviet government promised to abstain from propagandizing in the United States.

1934. The opening of *Lady Macbeth of Mtsenk,* an opera by **Dmitry Shostakovich** (1906–75), led to an accusation of formalism, yet the composer remained one of the great stars of Soviet music.

1934. In view of the National Socialist victory in Germany and the openly expressed hostility of the new German regime to communism, the Soviet Union felt more than ever endangered. Trade relations with Germany continued and even expanded for a few years, but the Moscow government at once embarked upon an extensive **program of armament** on land, sea, and air. Within a few years the Soviets had a formidable air fleet and had made considerable progress toward the construction of a powerful navy (especially submarines).

    Sept. 18. The **SOVIET UNION JOINED THE LEAGUE OF NATIONS,** which earlier it had roundly denounced. Russia's far-reaching goal was to make the League of Nations an anti-German and anti-Japanese alliance. France was supported in the plan for an eastern pact to cover an anti-German alliance by a regional system of collective security.

    Dec. 1. The **assassination** of Stalin's close collaborator **Sergey Kirov,** who had begun to be regarded by a significant number of Communists as a possible alternative to Stalin's leadership. The assassination was probably inspired by Stalin himself and marked the beginning of the **"great purges."** In a series of spectacular trials many of the most prominent of the older Communist leaders were convicted.

1935. Alexei Stakhanov, a Donets miner, developed a new extraction method. **Stakhanovite** program set up to reward and motivate productive workers with bonuses and hero-of-labor pins.

    Jan. 15–17. Zinoviev, Kamenev, and several other leaders were **tried for treason** and conspiracy. They were convicted and imprisoned for terms of five to ten years.

    May 2. CONCLUSION OF THE FRANCO-RUSSIAN ALLIANCE (p. 677).

    July 25–Aug. 20. The **Seventh Congress of the Third International** ordered Communists all over the world to form Popular Fronts with other "anti-Fascists." However, the ultimate goals remained unchanged; the "historical mission" of the "working class at the head of all working people" was to unite "in a million-strong revolutionary army, led by the Communist International."

1936, Aug. 19–23. Zinoviev, Kamenev, and a group of their followers were put on trial again, this time as Trotskyists, accused of plotting with enemy powers against the existing regime. They openly confessed to most of the charges brought against them, much to the astonishment of the world. On conviction, 16 of them were at once executed.

    July. On the outbreak of the **civil war in Spain** (p. 691), the Russian government at once took the side of the Madrid government and sent airplanes and other supplies to the Loyalists.

    Dec. 5. ADOPTION OF A NEW "DEMOCRATIC" CONSTITUTION. The Soviet Federation was recast and the Union thenceforth was composed as follows: (1) **Russia;** (2) **Ukraine;** (3) **Belarus;** (4) **Azerbaijan;** (5) **Georgia;** (6) **Armenia;** (7) **Turkmenistan;** (8) **Uzbekistan;** (9) **Tajikistan;** (10) **Kazakhstan;** (11) **Kirghizstan.** Russia and subsequently all other states of the Union adopted an **electoral system** from which no elements in the country were any longer debarred: all votes were to be equal; elections to the higher assemblies were made direct; votes were to be cast on a territorial, not on an occupational, basis; the secret ballot was introduced. The place of the congresses of soviets was taken by a two-chamber parliament (the **Supreme Soviet**), consisting of a **Council of Nationalities** (i.e., a federal chamber) and **a Union Council.** This parliament was to appoint **a Presidium** to act while the council itself was not in session. All civic rights were guaranteed, but the Communist Party continued to be the only political group permitted in the country.

1937, Jan. 23–30. George Piatakov, Karl Radek, and other leaders were put on trial and convicted, 13 of them suffering the death penalty. The various "purges" continued throughout the year and extended through the entire administration, ultimately reaching also the army and the diplomatic service. Political commissioners were appointed to watch over the army commands. On May 31 **Marshal Ian Gamarnik** was reported to have committed suicide.

June 12. Marshal Michael Tukhachevski and seven other generals of the highest rank were executed after a secret court-martial. They were accused of conspiracy with the Germans and the Japanese. There followed further purging, in the course of which all "Trotskyists" and others objectionable to Stalin were "liquidated." These trials and executions did much to discredit Russia as a reliable factor in international relations.

Dec. 12. The **first elections** under the new constitution were held. Most of the candidates elected were those of the Communist slate, so that no significant change resulted from the new system. The Supreme Soviet met for the first time on Jan. 12, 1938, and appointed to the key positions those who were already dominant in the government.

1938, March 2–15. Nicolai Bukharin, Alexei Rykov, Genrikh Yagoda, and other prominent Bolsheviks were put on trial, accused of wanting to restore bourgeois capitalism and of joining with Trotsky in treasonable conspiracy. They were **convicted and executed.** More and more, Stalin trusted to the younger generation, which had never known anything but the Bolshevik regime and which was therefore less apt to criticize.

July 11–Aug. 10. Open warfare broke out between the Russians and the Japanese on the frontier of eastern Siberia and Manchukuo (p. 780).

Sept. The great Czech crisis (p. 705). The Russian government publicly announced its readiness to come to the assistance of the Czechs if France did so.

1939, May 3. Maxim Litvinov was suddenly dismissed from the post of commissar for foreign affairs, after 18 years of service. Premier Vyacheslav Molotov took his place.

Aug. 20, 21. A trade pact was concluded with Germany, and an announcement was made of a forthcoming **nonaggression pact** (concluded on Aug. 23) (p. 679). When Germany made war on Poland (p. 800), Bolshevik Russia stood by as a benevolent neutral.

Sept. 17. Soviet troops moved into Poland (p. 800).

Sept. 29. By agreement, the **Soviet Union and Germany divided Poland** between them.

Nov. 26. The government of **Finland rejected Soviet demands,** leading to the **RUSSO-FINNISH WAR** (Nov. 30, 1939–March 12, 1940).

1940, July 21. Incorporation of **Estonia, Latvia,** and **Lithuania** into the Soviet Union after Moscow, with German aid, had secured military bases in those countries (ultimatums of June 15, 16, charging hostile activities), had occupied them militarily, and had arranged for pro-Soviet administrations to request admittance to the Soviet Union.

1941, April 13. THE SOVIET UNION AND JAPAN CONCLUDED A NEUTRALITY PACT.

June 22. GERMAN ARMIES INVADED THE SOVIET UNION WITHOUT WARNING (p. 802).

Some of the most bloody battles occurred in the Soviet Union. Leningrad underwent a two-and-a-half-year siege, virtually cut off from the rest of the country; its population was decreased from 4 million to 2.5 million by starvation, disease, and war. In some areas like the Baltics, Belarus, and Ukraine the Nazi invaders had been greeted as liberators, but their treatment of the inhabitants soon destroyed that support. Throughout the war, however, government control remained effective, and morale did not break on the home front. With the war against the Nazis hailed later as the **Great Patriotic War,** Soviet victory came at a tremendous price: the estimated loss of population was 20 million, of which 7 million were military fatalities.

Sept. Russian agricultural supplies were seriously reduced by the loss of Ukraine and the North Caucasus region, for these areas had produced half the Soviet wheat and pork output. The grave deficiency was met in part after Sept. 1942 by increasing the shipments of canned meats, butter, fats, oils, dehydrated fruits, and vegetables from the U.S. By July 1943 the Soviet Union had received 15 million tons of foodstuffs under this arrangement.

1943. In an attempt to bolster patriotism, the Russian Orthodox Church was allowed to elect a patriarch, Sergius. The last patriarch, Tikhon, had died in 1925, and the Church had been forbidden to elect anyone in his place.

May 23. The Third International was dissolved. Moscow announced that **Communist parties** in other countries would be **autonomous** henceforth.

1944, Feb. 1. An amendment to the constitution granted separate commissariats for defense and for foreign affairs to each of the constituent republics. Each could thus maintain its own army (which would form, however, a component element in the army of the USSR) and could conduct its own negotiations with foreign countries and conclude treaties with them.

July 24. Soviet forces drove the Germans from the last large Russian city by **liberating Pskov.** This opened the war for a Soviet drive against the German divisions holding Estonia.

1945, April 5. The Soviet Union denounced its five-year nonaggression pact with Japan.

June 29. The **Soviet Union acquired Ruthenia** from Czechoslovakia.

Aug. 8. THE SOVIET UNION DECLARED WAR ON JAPAN.

(To p. 902)

17. THE BALTIC STATES

a. OVERVIEW

The development of the three Baltic states after World War I was more or less along a common line. All were previously part of Russia; they were, during the war, occupied by the Germans, who ruled them through puppet regimes; after Germany's collapse, efforts were made by the Bolsheviks to recover these territories, which gave access to the Baltic. Through German and Allied aid, and by their own efforts, the Baltic forces drove out the Bolsheviks and established independent governments. In all three states there was a German minority of landed wealth and influence, against which **agrarian legislation,** involving the breakup of large estates, was directed. The democratic systems set up after the war gave rise to considerable confusion, with much party wrangling among Social Democrats, Agrarians, and others. **Communism** was an ever-present force, against which all the governments took vigorous measures. But after the victory of National Socialism in Germany, the Baltic states hastened to improve their relations with Soviet Russia in order to forestall German intervention on behalf of the German minorities. To present a common defense the Baltic states also signed the **TREATIES OF THE BALTIC ENTENTE** (Sept. 12, 1934).

By 1939 all three of the Baltic states had gone over to some form of **dictatorship,** not from deference to the German system, but rather to forge a stronger regime for ultimate resistance to Germany.

1940, July 21. Incorporation of Estonia, Latvia, and Lithuania into the Soviet Union after Moscow, with German aid, had in 1939 secured military bases in those countries (treaties of Sept. 29, Estonia; Oct. 4, Latvia; Oct. 10, Lithuania). Ultimatums of June 15, 16, 1940, charged hostile activities; Russia had occupied the Baltics militarily and had arranged for pro-Soviet administrations to request admittance to the Soviet Union.

Most political and military leaders were deported soon after annexation. The discovery of the bodies of some of those arrested and executed was well publicized by the Germans and contributed to the level of mass support for them during the first months of their occupation, and to atrocities against the Jews, accused of backing Soviet rule.

THE GERMAN ATTACK
ON THE SOVIET UNION
1941–1943

Axis-occupied areas and Finland,
June 22, 1941

Areas retaken by Soviet Union after
November 19, 1942

Area retaken by Axis,
March 15, 1943

Soviet areas held by Axis,
April 15, 1943

Battle line as of April 15, 1943

Battle line as of November 19, 1942

NORWAY

SWEDEN

FINLAND

Barents Sea

Murmansk

White Sea

Archangel

L. Onega

Vyborg

Leningrad

L. Ladoga

ESTONIA

Novgorod

L. Ilmen

Vologda

Sverdlovsk

Riga

LATVIA

Kalinin

Gorki

Kazan

Ufa

Velikiye Luki

LITHUANIA

Mozhaisk

Dmitrov

Vilna

Vitebsk

Vyazma

⊛ Moscow

Ryazan

Minsk

Smolensk

Tula

Kuibyshev

Bialystok

Michurinsk

Volga R.

POLAND

Brest-Litovsk

Orel

Kursk

Voronezh

Saratov

Kiev

Don R.

Zhitomir

Kharkov

Tarnopol

Stalingrad

Dnieper R.

HUNGARY

Dniester R.

Dniepropetrovsk

Stalino

Rostov

Prath R.

Odessa

Tanganrog

Astrakhan

ROMANIA

CRIMEA

Kerch

Danube R.

Sevastopol

Novorossiisk

Maikop

Makhachkala

BULGARIA

Tuapse

Grozny

Black Sea

Caspian Sea

Istanbul

Batum

Tiflis

Baku

TURKEY

IRAN

Baltic Sea

0   100   200   300

MILES

In all three republics, **German invasion** (June 1941) was accompanied by Baltic revolt. Provisional governments were set up in all three states but were soon closed by the Germans. Thousands in each state were recruited into police battalions, while the Germans formed SS legions in Latvia and Estonia. The Germans fostered cooperation with vague promises about the future of the Baltics. The Jewish population was herded into ghettoes and massacred. In July 1944 **Jewish resistance** in the remnant of the Vilna ghetto launched a revolt, but the ghetto was destroyed. The Balts who resisted the Germans did so as Baltic nationalists, not Soviet resisters; partisans were sometimes responsible for atrocities against Communists. In the summer of 1944 the Balts attempted to restore their national governments. By then the Red Army was pouring into the Baltic states, and these provisional governments lasted for only a few days. Hundreds of thousands of Balts fled with the Germans or across the Baltic to Sweden. Their places were taken by Russian-speaking immigrants and demobilized military personnel, securing the place of the Baltic states in the postwar Soviet Union.

b. LITHUANIA

1917, Sept. 18–22. A Lithuanian conference at Vilna led to the **establishment of a national council** and a demand for independence from Russia (Dec. 11). The movement was encouraged by the Germans.

1918, Feb. 16. A FORMAL DECLARATION OF INDEPENDENCE resulted. The new state was at once invaded by the Bolsheviks.

March 3. The treaty of Brest-Litovsk (p. 663), however, obliged Russia to recognize Lithuanian independence. The Germans also recognized the new state (March 23) and drew it into alliance with Germany (May 14).

June 4. Duke William of Urach as king was elected by the Lithuanian government. But when German power collapsed in November, this election was rescinded.

Nov. 11. Augustinas Voldemaras formed a national government, the first of many short-lived cabinets. The Germans were obliged to withdraw, whereupon the Bolsheviks again invaded the country.

1919, Jan. 5. The Bolsheviks took Vilna, which they lost soon afterward to the Poles (April 4).

April 6. Antanas Smetona was elected president of Lithuania in Kaunas.

Dec. 8. The Allied powers defined the Polish-Lithuanian boundary by the Curzon Line, which left **Vilna to Lithuania.**

1920, July 12. The **Treaty of Moscow** brought to an end Russian-Lithuanian hostilities. The Bolsheviks, at war with Poland, hastened to recognize Lithuania and its possession of Vilna, which was taken over by the Lithuanians on the evacuation by the Bolsheviks (Aug. 24).

Oct. 9. Gen. Lucien Zeligowski and his Polish freebooters seized Vilna by surprise. The Lithuanians refused to give up their claims, and the League of Nations arranged for a plebiscite. Meanwhile the Lithuanian capital was fixed at **Kaunas** (Kovno).

1921, Sept. 22. Lithuania joined the League of Nations.

1922, Jan. 8. The **Vilna plebiscite,** supervised by Zeligowski and his Poles, resulted in a majority vote for union with Poland. The Lithuanians refused to accept this as a valid vote and all intercourse between Lithuania and Poland was cut off.

Feb. 15. The constituent assembly passed the **land reform** law. Less far-reaching than similar laws in Estonia and Latvia, it was directed against Polish landowners.

Aug. 1. Adoption of the constitution that had been worked out by a constituent assembly convoked in May 1920. Lithuania became a democratic republic, recognized by the United States on July 27 and by Britain, France, and Italy on Dec. 20.

Dec. 21. Antanas Stulgenskis became president of the republic.

1923, Jan. 11. INSURRECTION IN MEMEL, engineered by Lithuanians. The city, which was predominantly German, had been under inter-Allied control since 1918. Lithuanian troops now occupied it, obliging a French garrison to withdraw. An inter-Allied commission was sent out to investigate.

Feb. 16. The council of ambassadors decided to grant Lithuania sovereignty but to constitute **Memel an autonomous region** in the Lith-

uanian state. Lithuania accepted (March 16), and the Memel Statute was signed by Britain, France, Italy, and Japan on May 8, 1924.

May 12–13. Elections for a second Seimas (parliament) took place after dissolution of the first Seimas when no party was able to form a government. These elections led to a coalition government of Christian Democrats and Peasant Populists. The new government passed a number of important pieces of legislation: the tax system was normalized, health protection was improved, central banks were established, and work and industrial laws were introduced, including a workmen's compensation law. The government also established the land bank in 1924, to extend credit to farmers, and a social insurance administration in 1926.

1926, Dec. 17. COUP D'ÉTAT OF ANTANAS SMETONA, who arrested the president and cabinet and had himself made president, with Augustinas Voldemaras as premier. The constitution was suspended and the Seimas dissolved, Smetona becoming virtual dictator (new constitution, May 25, 1928) with the support of the **Nationalist Union.**

1929, Sept. 19. Voldemaras forced to resign. He was later (May 1930) tried for high treason, exiled to a village, and ultimately convicted and imprisoned for a term of 12 years (June 1934).

1931, May 6. A treaty of friendship with Russia (first concluded in 1926) was renewed for another five-year term.

Dec. 11. Smetona was reelected for another seven-year term.

1932, Feb. 6. The **arrest of Herbert Boettcher,** head of the Memel directorate, for alleged treasonable correspondence with Germany, ushered in a period of continued German protests and recrimination. Britain, France, and Italy periodically made efforts to hold Lithuania to respect the spirit as well as the letter of the Memel Statute, but with little success.

Dec. 16. The **Nationalist Union,** supporting Smetona, frankly adopted a Fascist (of course not German Fascist) program.

1934, Sept. 12. CONCLUSION OF THE BALTIC PACT.

1935, March 25. Conviction of almost a hundred Memallanders on a charge of plotting the return of Memel to Germany.

1935–36. The depression led the government to institute a price control law in 1935. With the fall in prices the farmers were unable to pay loans. Discontent was fanned into strikes and disorders. The strikes were at first of an economic nature, but later they assumed a political hue when opposition parties became involved.

1936, Feb. 6. The government suppressed all political parties except the Nationalist Union.

June 9–10. Elections were held for a new Parliament along Fascist lines. Only Nationalist candidates were presented, and these were elected by local authorities. The parliament met on Sept. 1.

1938, Feb. 11. The Seimas adopted a **new constitution** that legitimized the status quo.

March 16. The **Polish government sent a stiff ultimatum to Lithuania** demanding reopening of the frontier and regularization of relations. After a short crisis the Lithuanian government yielded (March 17).

Dec. 11. The **elections in Memel** brought a vote of more than 90 percent for the National Socialists. In view of the resurgent power of Germany, the Lithuanian government was obliged to leave the Nazis practically a free hand in Memel.

1939, March 23. The **Germans took Memel** after extorting an agreement from Lithuania. In return they guaranteed Lithuanian independence and integrity and concluded a commercial treaty.

March 28. Gen. Jonas Cernius, the chief of the general staff, formed a new **National Coalition cabinet** in which the outlawed opposition parties were represented. On April 8 Cernius resigned so that the government might not have a military character.

Sept. 1. Lithuania declared its neutrality.

1940, June 15. Soviet troops began the occupation of Lithuania.

c. LATVIA

1917, Oct. 29. Formation of the **Latvian national council,** following the Soviet seizure of power in Russia. Since German forces remained in the country, the national council was unable to assert its authority or build up an effective national army. For more than a year German efforts to organize a **Baltic duchy** continued.

1918, March 3. According to the **Treaty of Brest-Litovsk** (p. 663) the Bolsheviks were obliged to accept loss of the Baltic states.

Nov. 17. A people's council was set up by the Latvians after the defeat of Germany, with **Karlis Ulmanis** as prime minister.

Nov. 18. The council proclaimed the independence of the **Republic of Latvia.**

1919, Jan. 3. Almost immediately, however, a Bolshevik army invaded the country and took **Riga** (Jan. 4). A Soviet government was set up, but German-Latvian forces, with the approval of the Allies, drove the Soviet troops back (March).

June 28. The **Treaty of Versailles** (p. 671) required the Germans to withdraw from the Baltic states. Gen. von der Goltz was recalled (Aug. 16) at Allied insistence, but fighting between Germans and Latvians continued (German attack on Riga, Oct. 8) until about Nov. 20, when the country was finally cleared of German forces.

1920, Jan. The last of the Bolshevik troops were also expelled.

Feb. 1. An **armistice** was concluded between the Latvian and Soviet governments.

May 1. The Latvian **constituent assembly** met and drafted a constitution.

Aug. 11. By the **Treaty of Riga** the Soviet government recognized Latvian sovereignty and renounced all rights to the territory.

Sept. 16. The constituent assembly passed the **Agrarian Reform Bill,** creating a state land fund of almost 3.5 million hectares from governmental, municipal, and church property and private estates exceeding 110 hectares. The German land barons were most hurt by this. In further moves to aid farmers in this primarily agricultural nation, the assembly established a state monopoly on flax. In general, the state also attempted to increase economic activity by taking over the railways and undertaking the repair of destroyed ports and harbor installations. Finally, on Aug. 3, the assembly passed a financial bill creating the lat as the Latvian unit of currency, thereby curtailing inflation.

1921, Jan. 26. The Allied powers recognized the new state, and on **Sept. 22** Latvia joined the **League of Nations.**

1922, May 1. The new constitution went into effect. It provided for a single-chamber parliament (**Saiema**) and ministerial responsibility.

Oct. 8. The elections resulted in a victory for the **Social Democrats.**

Nov. 14. Jānis Chakste became president.

1927, April 8. Gustav Zemgalis, president.

1928, Jan. 14. The conservative parties for the first time formed a government.

1930, April 9. Albert Kviesis, president.

1931. The credit crisis in Germany led to a sudden withdrawal of gold and credit reserves from Latvian banks. On July 22, the government imposed a banking moratorium to prevent Latvia's financial collapse and continued with more emergency legislation.

1932, July 25. Conclusion of a **nonaggression pact with Soviet Russia.**

1934, May 15. COUP D'ÉTAT OF KARLIS ULMANIS, the prime minister, assisted by **Gen. Jānis Balodis.**

The new Government of National Unity dissolved the Saiema and all political parties. The government fostered **corporatism** with the formation, in Jan. 1936, of a national economic council, made up of the elected boards of the newly created chambers of commerce, industry, agriculture, artisans, and labor. A state cultural council was also created, consisting of the boards of the Chamber of Professions and the Chamber of Literature and Art. The president also convoked a joint state council, which acted much like a consultative legislature. Finally, municipal and rural self-government switched over to a system of elections along guild, rather than political, lines. Martial law, however, continued until Feb. 1938, when the government replaced it with a new law for the defense of the state. Civil liberties remained curtailed.

Sept. 12. Latvia joined the Baltic pact with Lithuania and Estonia (p. 715).

1936, April 11. Ulmanis succeeded Kviesis as **president.**

1939, May. Latvia, directly exposed to the German advance to the east, became an object of great concern to Russia. In the negotiations for an Anglo-Russian pact, the Moscow government insisted on a guaranty of the independence of all the Baltic states, but the Latvian government, ever suspicious of the Soviets, accepted the German offer of a mutual nonaggression pact (June 7) (p. 679).

1940, June 15. In response to an ultimatum, Red Army troops occupied Latvia.

d. ESTONIA

1917, Nov. 28. The **Estonians,** taking advantage of the Bolshevik revolution in Russia, **proclaimed their independence,** but the Soviet government at once undertook the reconquest of this strategically important area. To block the Russian advance, the Germans occupied the country (Dec.).

1918, Feb. 24. The independence of Estonia was again proclaimed, under German protection. A provisional government was formed by **Konstantin Päts,** who was to play a prominent role throughout the entire postwar period.

March 3. By the **Treaty of Brest-Litovsk** (p. 663), Russia was obliged to recognize Estonian independence.

Nov. 11. The Germans began the withdrawal from the country, following the end of World War I. They ceded complete power to Päts.

Nov. 22. The **Russians began a second invasion** of the country. The Estonians put up a valiant resistance and were supported by a British fleet.

1919, Jan. The **Bolsheviks were finally driven out,** and the Estonian government was able to establish its control throughout most of the land.

Oct. 10. A constituent assembly passed a sweeping **agrarian law** that inaugurated the breakup of the large estates of the (German) Baltic barons and the distribution of the land among the peasants.

1920, Feb. 2. The **Treaty of Tartu** (Dorpat) with Russia brought Estonia definitive recognition as an independent state.

June 15. Adoption of a constitution. Estonia became a democratic republic with Tallinn as the capital. The constitution established parliamentary superiority with a unicameral state assembly that selected a state elder who served as prime minister.

Despite gaining the **right to vote** and taking an active role in political life, women remained subordinate in the family, especially in terms of property rights and decision-making.

1921, Sept. 22. Estonia joined the League of Nations.

1924, Nov. 27. Trial of 150 Communists, most of whom were convicted and imprisoned. Estonia continued to be particularly exposed to Communist agitation.

Dec. 1. A Communist uprising was the culmination; however, it was suppressed.

1933, Oct. 14–16. A **plebiscite in favor of constitutional revision,** providing for the election of a president (thus far the premier had acted as head of state), to whom wide powers were to be assigned.

The popularity of reform was the result of worsening economic conditions (the depression hit its low point in Estonia in 1932–33) and parliamentarianism's seeming inability to solve the nation's economic problems.

1934, Jan. 24. The **new constitution** went into effect. The **League of Veterans,** which had sponsored the constitutional revision, attempted a badly organized coup, but this was suppressed.

March 12. KONSTANTIN PÄTS, aided by **Gen. John Laidoner,** set up a virtual dictatorship. Martial law and restrictions on civil and political rights were continued throughout 1934–38.

Sept. 12. Estonia joined in the Baltic pact (p. 715).

1935. Labor unrest grew significantly, but in the last half of the decade the state increasingly intervened in labor matters and placed legal limits on the right to strike.

1936, Feb. 23–25. In a plebiscite, the nation voted 3 to 1 in favor of abolishing the **constitution of 1934** and returning to the democratic system. In December a national assembly was convoked to work out a new constitution.

May 6. About 150 leaders of the League of Veterans were put on trial for attempting another coup in Dec. 1935. Only seven of them were acquitted. Päts continued to be irreconcilably opposed to fascism and national socialism, as he was to communism.

1937, July 29. The **new constitution,** providing for a president and a two-chamber parliament, was adopted. Restoration of civil liberties was provided for, as were democratic elections. But under the new system the president (to be elected for six years) was to enjoy great authority, with power to appoint and dismiss the cabinet, dissolve both houses of Parliament, and rule by decree in national emergencies.

1938, Feb. 24. The **election** resulted in a chamber containing 63 deputies of Päts's National Front and 17 of opposition groups.

April 24. Päts was elected president. Although Päts returned to constitutionalism in 1938, there proved to be little change from the authoritarianism of the post–March 1934 period. Political parties re-

mained proscribed, the government continued to issue legislation by decree, and the new parliament played a minor role in public life.

1939, May. Estonia concluded a mutual **nonaggression pact with Germany,** acting together with Latvia (see above).

1940, June 17. Gen. Laidoner, commander in chief, signed the order permitting the passage of Soviet troops into Estonia.

18. POLAND

(From p. 514)

During World War I Poland was a pawn in the conflict between Russia and the Central powers. The Russian government made appealing promises in order to hold the loyalty of the Poles.

1914, Aug. 14. Russia promised that Poland should be **restored as an autonomous kingdom.** This policy secured the support of an important faction of Polish nationalists, led by **Roman Dmowski,** who, on Nov. 25, formed the Polish National Committee at Warsaw.

Aug. 16. On the other hand, **Gen. Joseph Pilsudski** (a Russian Pole by birth and several times convicted and imprisoned in Russia for radical, revolutionary activity) founded the **Supreme National Committee** at Kraków, under Austrian protection. The Austrian government permitted the formation of Polish legions to fight against Russia. In the course of 1915 most of Poland was conquered by the Germans and Austrians, who for a time divided the administration of the territory between them. Ultimately, however, the German high command took almost complete control of the country.

1916, July 25. Pilsudski resigned from his command in protest against the failure of the Central powers to establish a Polish kingdom. The Polish legions were incorporated with the Austro-Hungarian army.

Nov. 5. The German and Austrian governments joined in the proclamation of an **"independent" Polish kingdom** and set up a council of state, which adopted a constitution (Jan. 30, 1917). Pilsudski accepted a seat on this council.

1917, March 30. The **Russian provisional government declared in favor of an independent Poland,** to include all lands in which the Poles composed a majority of the population.

July 2. Pilsudski resigned from the council of state in protest against continued German control. He was thereupon arrested and imprisoned at Magdeburg (until Nov. 2, 1918).

Aug. 15. Dmowski **established the Polish national committee at Paris,** the French government having given permission (June 4) for the formation of a Polish army in France.

Oct. 15. The Germans set up a regency council in Poland that exercised effective control under German supervision.

1918, Oct. 12. The **regency council took charge** of affairs on the collapse of the Central powers. But the Ukrainians had already begun the invasion of Galicia.

Nov. 1. Poland soon made war on Ukraine, reconquering Galicia for the new Polish state.

Nov. 3. The **POLISH REPUBLIC WAS PROCLAIMED** at Warsaw. This soon fell under the control of Pilsudski, who returned from his German captivity on Nov. 10 and was granted full military power by the regency council, which thereupon resigned (Nov. 14). Under Pilsudski's direction the Poles continued their advance in Galicia, taking Lemberg (Nov. 23). At the same time they attempted to realize their aspirations in the west.

Dec. 27–28. Polish forces **occupied Posen** (Poznan) with their troops. Pilsudski succeeded in reaching agreements with other provisional governments (that of **Ignace Daszynski** at Kraków and that of **Dmowski** and **Ignace Jan Paderewski** at Paris).

1919, Jan. 17. Paderewski formed a coalition cabinet, Pilsudski acting as provisional president. A constituent assembly was elected (Jan. 26) and worked out a temporary constitutional system. Meanwhile the entire effort of the government was devoted to the conquest of the territories belonging to Poland at the time of the first partition of 1772. This brought the Poles into conflict with the Bolsheviks in Belarus and with Lithuania (p. 712).

June 28. The **TREATY OF VERSAILLES** established the Polish fron-

tier in the west, Poland receiving **a corridor along the Vistula** to the sea (the **city of Danzig** to be a free city under supervision of the League of Nations but economically connected with Poland) and large parts of **West Prussia** and **Posen.** A plebiscite was to determine the frontier in Upper Silesia. Poland was obliged to accept a **minority treaty** guaranteeing full rights and numerous religious, educational, linguistic, and other privileges to the minority peoples.

July. Conditions at the end of the war bred discontent, making **social reform** a great concern to the constituent assembly. In the summer of 1919, the most important issue under discussion was land reform. On July 22 a central land office was created to oversee the division of large estates. Shortly afterward the Sejm passed a number of laws affecting the workers, introducing an eight-hour workday, compulsory insurance, and rights of persons renting houses. In an attempt to build support in the war against Russia in 1920, the Sejm passed a more radical land reform law, but this was never fully implemented.

Dec. 7. Paderewski resigned as premier. Pilsudski, now marshal of Poland, remained as chief of the state.

Dec. 8. The supreme council laid down the so-called **Curzon Line** for Poland's eastern frontier. This line deprived Poland of Vilna.

1920, March 27. The Poles demanded of the Russians the **boundaries of 1772** with a plebiscite in the region west of that boundary. This the Bolsheviks would not accept, though they made many efforts to effect a compromise. Breakdown of negotiations led to war.

April 25–Oct. 12. THE RUSSIAN-POLISH WAR (p. 674).

1921, Feb. 19. Conclusion of the **Polish alliance with France,** followed shortly by a similar alliance with Romania and less extensive pacts with Czechoslovakia, Yugoslavia, Estonia, and Latvia. Poland had a hostile Germany and a hostile Russia on its frontiers and for that reason was bound to France and the French system. The French supplied large sums of money for armaments and for reconstruction of the country.

March 17. ADOPTION OF THE CONSTITUTION, which provided for a president, elected for seven years by a two-chamber parliament (**Senate** and **Sejm**) chosen by popular vote. The whole system was modeled closely on that of France.

March 20. The **plebiscite in Upper Silesia** resulted in a victory for the Germans.

May 4. The Poles under **Adalbert Korfanty,** however, occupied some of the disputed areas. The matter was referred to the League of Nations, which finally decided, on the plea of economic necessity, to partition the region (Oct. 12).

1922, Jan. 8. The **Vilna plebiscite** showed a majority in favor of Poland, and the city and district were incorporated on April 18. The result was a bitter **feud with Lithuania.**

Nov. 5. The elections resulted in a victory of the Rightist parties. Pilsudski resigned as chief of state and became chief of the army staff.

Dec. 9. Gabriel Narutowicz was elected president by the Parliament, but he was assassinated on Dec. 18.

Dec. 20. STANISLAS WOJCIECHOWSKI became president.
The next few years were devoted to the work of reconstruction. The nation's finances were in bad condition; the parliamentary system was characterized by bitter strife between the more conservative and nationalist parties and the Socialists and peasants. At the same time there was much friction with the minorities (especially the Ukrainans and the Germans). Cabinets changed with great suddenness.

1923. Inflation resulted in the fall of real wages and a bitter strike movement began as a result of the rise of prices. In October a strike of railway workers occurred to which the government replied by the conscription of the workers. In November the Socialist Party declared a general strike. The government replied by introducing a state of siege. Bloody disturbances took place on Nov. 6 in Kraków. While these events undermined the government's authority, it was the question of land reform that caused its downfall on Dec. 15.

Dec. 19. Ladislav Grabski formed a nonparliamentary ministry of experts, which managed to stabilize the currency by creating the Bank of Poland and establishing a new unit of currency, the zloty. He also attempted to revive the Polish economy by launching the construction of a port at Gdynia. The government made some concessions to the demands of the minorities (including Jews) and regulated Polish relations with some of the neighboring states. On Grabski's downfall (Nov. 13, 1925) there followed another period of political confusion.

1924. The novelist **Wladyslaw S. Reymont** (1868–1925), best known for *Chlopi* (*The Peasants*, 1904–6), won the Nobel Prize for literature. Poland's prominent literary figures also included the lyric poet **Jan Kasprowicz** (1860–1929).

1925, Dec. 28. An important **land law** was passed, providing for the distribution of about 500,000 acres of land to the peasants annually for ten years.

1926, May 10. Vincent Witos, the leader of the Peasant Party, formed a government.

May 12–14. PILSUDSKI LED A MILITARY REVOLT against the government. After two days of fighting Pilsudski took the capital, forcing Witos to resign. President Wojciechowski also resigned (May 15), whereupon Pilsudski was elected to take his place. Pilsudski declined.

June 1. IGNACE MOSCICKI, friend of Pilsudski, **became president.** Pilsudski was the real ruler of the country, though he acted through the president.

Aug. 5. A revision of the constitution gave the president much greater power.

Oct. 2. Pilsudski assumed the premiership, which he retained until June 27, 1928. His coup and practical dictatorship had aroused great resentment and opposition among the parties of the Left. Under Pilsudski the government resorted to the most **drastic methods of repression.** The Sejm was dissolved and 54 opposition deputies arrested (Nov. 28, 1927), but new elections indicated the continuance of strong opposition to the rule of the military **(rule of the "colonels").**

1930, Aug. 25. Pilsudski again took over the premiership (until Nov. 28) in order to break the Leftist opposition. Many of the radical leaders were tried and imprisoned (including Witos).

Nov. 16. Finally, the elections returned a majority of deputies supporting the government bloc. Pilsudski's control was complete, but the country began to suffer severely from the world depression, and the unrest attending general want produced an ever greater tendency on the part of the ruling group to turn to more conservative policies.

1932, March. Parliament granted the president **decree powers** for a period of three years, and these were later extended.

1933, May 8. Moscicki was reelected for a second term of seven years.

Aug. 5. An **agreement with the city government of Danzig** (which had recently fallen under National Socialist control) assured the Poles in Danzig fair treatment while guaranteeing to Danzig a certain percentage of Poland's seaborne trade. By this time the new Polish **port of Gdynia** (constructed after 1920 because of the constant friction between Poland and Danzig) had already outstripped its older German neighbor as a trade center.

1935, April 23. A NEW CONSTITUTION was adopted after years of planning and discussion. The new regime, railroaded through the Sejm while the opposition stayed away, brought to an end the democratic, parliamentary system.

May 12. Death of Marshal Pilsudski. He was succeeded as head of the army by **Gen.** (later Marshal) **Edward Rydz-Smigly,** the new power behind the presidential system.

Sept. 8. The elections, in which only 45 percent of the electorate took part, produced a Sejm dominated by the deputies of the government bloc. The Socialists and Peasant Party persisted in demanding a return to genuine democracy. The Ukrainians became bolder and bolder in their claims for autonomy or independence.

1937, March 1. Col. Adam Koc organized the Camp of National Unity, intended to be an all-inclusive union of those supporting the govern-

ment. Its program called for maintenance of the constitution of 1935, popular support for the army as the shield of national existence, anti-Communism, distribution of land to the peasants, Polonization of minorities, and so on. In reply to this move the workers and peasants in the same month joined in a Workers', Peasants', and Intellectuals' Group, opposed to Koc and his camp. Peasant strikes became widespread and led to some bloodshed.

1938, Jan. 11. Col. Koc resigned leadership of the camp to **Gen. Stanislas Skwarczynski,** who represented a somewhat more conciliatory wing of the government group. On April 21 the camp broke definitely with the Union of Young Poland, an out-and-out Fascist and violently anti-Semitic organization founded by Koc.

March 16–19. The Polish government, taking advantage of the international situation created by the German annexation of Austria, sent an **ultimatum to Lithuania** demanding an end to hostility and an early regulation of relations between the two countries.

Sept. 29. A POLISH NOTE was sent **to Czechoslovakia** demanding the cession of the Teschen area (seized by the Czechs during the Polish-Russian War of 1920). The Czechs, face to face with the threat of German invasion and deserted by their friends, were obliged to yield. On Oct. 2 **Polish forces occupied Teschen.**

1939, March–April. A **Polish-German crisis** ensued after the German action in Czechoslovakia and the annexation of Memel (p. 717). At the end of March the German government submitted extensive demands to Warsaw, including the cession of Danzig to Germany and the right to construct an extraterritorial railway and automobile highway across Pomorze (the "corridor"), in return for a guarantee of Polish frontiers and a nonaggression pact. The demands were rejected but resulted directly in the guarantee from Britain and France.

March 31. Anglo-French guarantee of aid to Poland in the event of aggression (expanded April 6 into a mutual pact of assistance "in the event of any threat, direct or indirect, to the independence of either").

April 28. In reply **Hitler denounced the agreement of 1934** with Poland. Relations continued to be tense, with much friction in Danzig. In view of this situation the Poles gave up opposition to a proposed guarantee by Russia and approved the British efforts to bring the Soviet government into the new "peace front."

The Danzig problem developed rapidly during the summer, and frontier incidents became frequent. The Germans began to send troops into Danzig, and the Poles began to take countermeasures while reiterating their determination to oppose any effort to change the status quo by force. Finally the crisis broke on Aug. 20 (p. 679). The British and French stood by Poland while the Germans refused to engage in direct negotiations. Two weeks of tension ended with the German invasion.

Sept. 1. GERMAN FORCES INVADED POLAND, and 17 days later **Soviet troops marched in** from the east.

Sept. 28. GERMANY AND THE SOVIET UNION agreed to divide Poland between them.

The Nazis lost no time in putting their **racist doctrines** into effect. Many thousands of Polish officers, professionals, and intellectuals were rounded up and executed out of hand, and many more were sent off to Germany to work in factories or to perform menial tasks. Large numbers of Poles, as an "inferior race," were moved from their homelands into less desirable areas to make room for German settlers, who were to occupy the new territory for the Reich.

The large Jewish population of Poland was herded into cities and concentrated in **ghettoes,** where many, deprived of means of livelihood, perished of hunger or disease. With the implementation of the "final solution" (p. 701), these Jews were later moved to concentration camps established all over Poland, where most of them were destroyed by the Nazis..

Sept. 30. Polish exiles formed a provisional **government in exile** in Paris.

1940, June 19. The government in exile transferred from Paris to London.

1941, Dec. 11. The government in exile **declared war on Japan.**

1943, April 16. The government in exile asked the International Red Cross to investigate a German report that **10,000 Polish officers,** allegedly slain by the Soviets, had been **found near Smolensk.**

April 18. Soviet radio declared that the slaughter and burial of **Polish officers** near Smolensk could be traced to the **German Gestapo,** and (April 27) suspended relations with the Polish government in London.

April 19–May 16. **WARSAW GHETTO UPRISING.** The ghetto, originally containing 400,000 Jews, was populated by only 60,000 survivors when the Nazis decided to destroy it. A force of 2,000 German soldiers aided by Lithuanian militia members and Polish police and firefighters met heroic resistance by Jews armed with only a few pistols, rifles, machine guns, and homemade weapons. The Nazis countered by setting the ghetto on fire block by block and then flooding and smoke-bombing the sewers when the Jews attempted to use them as escape routes. Similar uprisings occurred in the ghettoes of Kraków, Vilna, Kaunus, Minsk, and Slutsk.

1944, Aug. 1. Polish underground forces in Warsaw under Gen. Tadeo Bor attacked the German forces of occupation. Soviet troops, although they had almost reached Warsaw, failed to support the uprising, which was suppressed by Oct. 2.

1945, Jan. 17. The Red Army liberated **Warsaw** and swept into **Tarnow, Kraków,** and **Lodz** two days later (Jan. 19). *(To p. 882)*

19. THE BALKAN STATES

a. YUGOSLAVIA

(From pp. 520, 521)

The history of the new state, composed of Serbia, Montenegro, Croatia, Slovenia, and Dalmatia, was marked chiefly by the efforts of the Serbs to establish a centralized Serb state and by the vigorous resistance of the Croats and Slovenes (Roman Catholic and much more Westernized than the Serbs) to secure some type of autonomy.

1917, July 20. The **PACT OF CORFU,** signed by Serbian, Croatian, Slovenian, and Montenegrin representatives, declared that the Serbs, Croats, and Slovenes formed a **single nation,** to be organized under the Serbian dynasty.

1918, Oct. 29. The Croatian diet announced secession of Croatia and Dalmatia from the Austro-Hungarian Empire and handed over supreme authority in the new state to the **national council.** The council then proclaimed the desire for union with Serbia and Montenegro without specifying further conditions.

Nov. 26. A **national assembly in Montenegro proclaimed union** with Serbia and declared **King Nicholas,** who had resisted previous efforts at union, **deposed** (d. March 1, 1921, in exile).

Dec. 1. Prince Alexander of Serbia accepted the **regency** of the new state and **THE KINGDOM OF THE SERBS, CROATS, AND SLOVENES FORMALLY PROCLAIMED.**

The new state had numerous economic and social problems resulting mainly from the union of different systems. The old manorial system was abolished and one in four peasant families obtained land, but the holdings remained small. The Serbs represented 39 percent of the population, the Croats 24 percent, the Slovenes 8.5 percent, and the rest was an amalgam of Germans, Magyars, Albanians, Macedonians, and Bosnian Muslims. Finally, Yugoslavia had to contend with border disputes with six neighboring states, including Italy (p. 675).

1919, June 13. The peace conference decided that the **Banat of Temesvar,** in dispute between Yugoslavia and Romania, should be divided between them.

1921, Jan. 1. The **new constitution** provided for a centralized form of government. Nicolas Pashich became premier of a coalition of Serbian Radicals and Democrats. The Croats continued in opposition, boycotting the Skupština.

July–Aug. The Skupština (Parliament) reacted to the minister of the interior's assassination by a Bosnian Communist by passing decrees for the defense of the state which authorized drastic measures against terrorists. The government took this opportunity to remove the 58 members of the Communist Party from the Skupština, and the party was forced to go underground. The government continued to define treason very loosely, making open opposition difficult.

Aug. 16. Death of King Peter.

1921–34. ALEXANDER I. He was a hard-working, intelligent ruler whose aim was to consolidate the kingdom despite opposition from Croats and other groups.

1922. The government quickly dealt with a financial crisis and inflation by stabilizing the dinar. Despite political instability, Yugoslavia experienced economic progress in the 1920s: in 1924 exports exceeded imports for the first time, and by 1926 Yugoslavia had paid all of its war debt.

April. Centralization was strengthened by a law detailing the administration of the new nation along French lines. Historic provinces were eliminated, as the nation was broken into districts administered by crown-appointed prefects.

1924, Dec. The government outlawed the most important Croat party, the Peasant Party, and imprisoned its leader, **Stephen Radich.** In March, after the government failed to win a majority in elections (Feb.), Radich, realizing he could garner Serbian support, accepted the constitution and agreed to work within the political system he had earlier fought to overthrow. He was released from prison and, making a deal with Pashich, joined a coalition government with long-time foes, the Radicals.

1927, June. Rupture of relations with Albania, following repeated frontier incidents (p. 722).

1928, June 20. Stephen Radich, leader of the Croatian Peasant Party, and his associates were **fired upon** in Parliament by a Radical deputy. **Radich died** on Aug. 8. The Croat deputies withdrew from Parliament.

Aug. 1. The **Croats** once more demanded the institution of a federal regime as the price of their cooperation. They then set up a separatist "parliament" at Zagreb and refused to have anything more to do with the Belgrade government (Oct.). All efforts of the king to effect a compromise ended in failure.

1929, Jan. 6. After a series of 23 governments between 1918 and 1928, **KING ALEXANDER PROCLAIMED A DICTATORSHIP.**

Jan. 21. The Croat and all other parties were dissolved.

Feb. 17. A **legislative council,** with only advisory powers, was set up to replace Parliament.

Aug. Amid the flood of legislation dealing with religious, legal, and administrative affairs, the crown established the **Privileged Agrarian Bank,** chartered to issue loans to farmers at 10 percent or less, with easy terms of repayment and with a dividend of 6 percent guaranteed by the state to the shareholders.

Oct. 3. The **name of the kingdom** was officially changed to Yugoslavia, another indication of the king's effort to wipe out the old historic divisions. The traditional provinces were divided into nine new *banats,* with purely geographical names.

Dec. 4. In an effort to build unity, the king promulgated the Sokol Law, dissolving Croatian, Slovene, Catholic, and Serbian *sokols,* or physical training societies. They were replaced with a single Yugoslav *sokol* under government control. At the same time, the government continued to imprison all who opposed the regime by accusing them of terrorism.

1931, Sept. 3. The king announced the **end of the dictatorship** and introduced a **new constitution** (two-chamber parliament). The **electoral law** left no place for purely local parties; two-thirds of the seats were to go to the party receiving the largest number of votes; voting to be open. While the constitution also promised extensive civil liberties, they were all circumscribed by the draconian laws established under the dictatorship.

Adding to the political discontent aroused by the new constitution, **Yugoslavia's economy began to deteriorate** in 1931. After a run on the banks in September, the government gained control of the banks. An attempt to create a government grain monopoly ended in disaster for taxpayers.

Nov. 9. Farcical **elections.** The government named most of the candidates and therefore won a great victory; most of the opposition groups boycotted.

1932, March. In an attempt to ease economic conditions for the peasantry, the government declared a six-month moratorium on peasant debt. This increased misery, however, as creditors began to refuse loans at a time when most peasants normally expected them. Nevertheless, the government extended the moratorium until Nov. 1933.

The government also responded to a drop in export trade by making it illegal for money to leave the country. Foreign trade was paralyzed as a result.

Nov. 14. The Croat Peasant Party denounced the regime and again demanded autonomy, following the imprisonment of the Croat leader, Vladko Machek (Oct. 17).

1934, Oct. 9. ASSASSINATION OF KING ALEXANDER and **Louis Barthou** at Marseilles. The assassin was a Macedonian revolutionary, working with Croat revolutionists having headquarters in Hungary. The assassination led to **danger of war between Yugoslavia and Hungary** (deportations on both sides), which was finally avoided (Dec. 10) through the good offices of the League of Nations.

1934-45. KING PETER II (b. 1923). **Prince Paul** (cousin of Alexander) chief regent.

1935, May 5. Despite police interference and widespread fraud, the opposition won 37.4 percent of the votes. The opposition boycotted the Skupština. The regents reacted on June 23 by inviting **Dr. Milan Stojadinovic,** a member of the Radical Party, to form a cabinet. The new government was composed of Slovenes, Croats, and Muslims. Stojadinovic created a new government party, the **Yugoslav Radical Union,** and proceeded cautiously to relax censorship. On Dec. 1 the government issued a general amnesty for political offenses, affecting some 10,000 people. Attempts at agreement with the Croats were fruitless, however.

1936, May. Conclusion of **a barter agreement with Germany.** This was made necessary by the falling-off of trade with Italy subsequent to Yugoslavia's imposition of sanctions during the Ethiopian crisis. Ever closer trade relations with Germany brought in their train a political rapprochement.

1939, Aug. 26. DEMOCRATIC GOVERNMENT WAS REESTABLISHED in Yugoslavia and new elections by secret ballot arranged for. The state was to be reorganized on a federal basis, the Croats receiving complete autonomy in all cultural and economic matters. Machek became vice premier, and five other Croats joined the cabinet.

1941, March 25. The Yugoslav government, under the regent Prince Paul, announced the **adherence of Yugoslavia to the Axis pact.**

March 27. The **government was overthrown** by a military coup and the young king, Peter II, was installed. This defiant move led to an **invasion of Yugoslavia** (April 6) **by German forces.** Belgrade was occupied by the Germans on April 20.

1943, Oct. 9. Yugoslav guerrilla forces commanded by **Marshal Tito** (Josip Broz) **opened an offensive** against Axis troops in the region of Trieste.

1944, Oct. 20. Belgrade was occupied by Soviet and Yugoslav forces.

As the war ended, Yugoslavia was still theoretically a monarchy. The actual power, however, was wielded by Marshal Tito and his **National Liberation Movement.** *(To p. 891)*

b. ALBANIA

(From p. 524)

The major concern of Albanian patriots during World War I was to retain independence and the borders agreed upon before the war (1912 proclamation of independence and provisional government, recognized by Treaty of London, May 30, 1913). In this effort they were aided by Albanian Americans, who underwrote lobbyists in the major capitals of Europe. The newly independent Albania was invaded and overrun by most of its neighbors during the war.

1918, Dec. 25. A national assembly elected **Turkhan Pasha president.** The government had to deal with the incursions of the Yugoslavs in the north and the Italians on the coast.

1920, Aug. 2. Italy agreed to evacuate Valona while retaining the island of **Saseno.** The Italians left on Sept. 2. But Greece and Yugoslavia maintained troops in Albania until 1922.

Dec. 17. Albania was admitted to the League of Nations.

1921, Nov. A conference of ambassadors reaffirmed the 1913 boundaries of Albania.

1921-24. As its international position solidified, Albania experienced a period of political instability revolving mainly around the necessity of social and economic reform before modernization.

1924, June. Fan Noli seized control of the government following a short-lived uprising and announced a comprehensive reform plan, including land distribution and the establishment of national legal and educational systems. His government lasted only six months, however, falling to a new government under **Ahmet Zogu.**

1925, Jan. 21. The NATIONAL ASSEMBLY PROCLAIMED ALBANIA A REPUBLIC. Ahmet Zogu became its first president. Opposition to Zogu was manifested in a series of narrowly based antigovernment uprisings in 1925, 1926, 1935, 1936, and 1937. Zogu managed to put these down without difficulty. Outside opposition centered on Noli's National Liberation Committee, which was financed by Comintern. Noli's opposition ended by the mid-1930s, however, and Zogu faced few external antiregime groups after that.

March 2. A **constitution was promulgated,** providing for parliamentary government but granting the president almost dictatorial powers. Zogu's priority was establishing order by creating a national bureaucracy and police force, by disarming the northern tribesmen (except his own), and by eliminating to a large extent the practice of the blood feud. Between 1928 and 1931 he also promulgated civil, commercial, and criminal law codes based on Western European models.

1926, July 30. A **final act fixing the frontiers** was signed by Great Britain, France, Italy, Greece, and Yugoslavia.

Nov. 27. TREATY OF TIRANA, between Italy and Albania. The two powers promised each other support in maintaining the territorial status quo, and Italy promised not to interfere in Albania except by request.

1927, May-July. A **rupture of Albanian-Yugoslav relations** was finally patched up by the powers.

Nov. 22. SECOND TREATY OF TIRANA, establishing a defensive alliance for 20 years and providing for military cooperation. It marked the beginning of what became practically an Italian protectorate. The Italians granted Albania substantial loans and in return secured valuable concessions (notably oil), supervision of military affairs, construction of roads, educational privileges, and so on.

1928, Sept. 1. Ahmet Bey Zogu was proclaimed king.

1928-39. Zogu ruled as **ZOG I.** Throughout he acted as the champion of the modernization of the country (building of Tirana as a modern capital, language reform, educational development, religious independence, and so forth).

Nov. 22. The assembly adopted **a new monarchical constitution.** The constitution discouraged political activity. By 1938 there were still no organized political parties in Albania, and manipulation of elections by the king and his associates fostered political apathy.

1931, June. An **Italian loan,** spread over ten years and subject to Italian supervision, established Italian economic control of the country. This was essential to the Albanian economy, the least developed in Europe. Industrial production in 1938 was only 4.4 percent of total output, and agricultural production continually failed to meet domestic requirements, generating chronic budget and trade deficits.

1932. King Zog rejected a proposal for a customs union with Italy; beginning of Albanian opposition to too great extension of Italian influence.

1934, June 23. After further disputes an **Italian fleet** suddenly appeared at **Durazzo** and frightened the government into submission. The Italian control of the army was strengthened, Italians were given the right to colonize certain areas, and so on.

1936, March 19. Further agreements between Italy and Albania provided for even closer financial and trade relations.

1937, April. Over the opposition of the Greek government, the patriarch of Istanbul (formerly Constantinople) decreed the autocephalous status of the Albanian Orthodox Church.

May 15-19. Insurrection of the Muslims in the southern sections. The immediate cause was the government's decree forbidding the veiling of women, but in the larger sense it was another expression of discontent with King Zog's dictatorial rule.

1939, April 7. END OF ALBANIAN INDEPENDENCE. The Italians, long irritated by Albanian resistance to their direction (prohibition of a Fascist Party, etc.), took advantage of the confusion produced by the German absorption of Czechoslovakia. They bombarded the coast towns and landed an army, which, after some resistance by the natives, overran the whole country. **King Zog and his queen fled to Greece** and then Turkey. On April 12 an Albanian constituent assembly voted personal union with Italy, and King Victor Emmanuel graciously accepted the crown. On June 3 Albania was given a constitution providing for a superior Fascist corporative council over which the king, however, retained extensive control. **From April 1939 to Sept. 1943, Albania remained under Italian control.**

1941, Aug. In order to win over the Albanians, Germany and Italy agreed to the incorporation of the Kosovo region of Yugoslavia into Albania.

Nov. 8. The **Albanian Communist Party** was formed clandestinely in Tirana under the leadership of **Enver Hoxha.**

1942, Sept. At the Peza Conference of anti-Fascist forces, the National Liberation Movement was formed. It was dominated by the Communists. Its only rivals were the republican Balli Kombetar, formed in November, and the pro-Zog Legality Organization.

1943, Sept. With the Italian surrender, German forces occupied Albania.

1944, May. With southern Albania liberated, the National Liberation Movement convened a congress in Permet, where the movement was renamed the National Liberation Front and Hoxha became the supreme commander of the Albanian National Liberation Army. King Zog was formally deposed, and all treaties concluded by the Albanian government since 1939 were nullified.

Oct. When the National Liberation Front had consolidated its power over most of Albania (German troops withdrew completely by late November), it convoked a congress at Berat. Hoxha was named the head of a new **provisional government** dominated by Communists.

(To p. 896)

c. GREECE

(From p. 518)

Greece entered the war only in June 1917 after a virtual civil war between the prime minister, **Eleftherios Venizelos,** and **King Constantine I.** The latter went into exile without formally abdicating and was replaced by his son, **ALEXANDER I.** The subsequent purge of the Greek military, administration, and judiciary of Constantine's supporters set the stage for the instability of interwar Greece.

1920, June 22. Beginning of the **Greek offensive in Anatolia** (p. 752).

Aug. 10. The **TREATY OF SÈVRES:** Greece obtained Smyrna, the Dodecanese (except Rhodes), eastern Thrace, Imbros, and Tenedos.

Oct. 25. Death of King Alexander. Regency of Queen Olga.

Nov. 14. Defeat of the Venizelists in the election, due to dissatisfaction with the Anatolian adventure. **Venizelos resigned.**

Dec. 5. A **plebiscite,** held despite Allied warnings, showed an almost unanimous vote for King Constantine. The Allies thereupon withdrew all support from Greece.

1920–22. CONSTANTINE I, restored. He announced continuation of the war with Turkey.

1921, Aug. Battle of the Sakarya. The Greeks failed to reach Ankara (p. 752).

1922, Aug. 18. Turkish counteroffensive. Taking of **Smyrna,** Sept. 9.

Sept. 26. A revolutionary committee formed from the defeated army, led by colonels **Nikolas Plastiras** and **Stylianos Gonatas,** assumed power. It set up a token civilian government, which was replaced by a military government in November, and demanded Constantine's abdication. Venizelos declined to participate in the revolution.

Sept. 27. Abdication of Constantine (d. Jan. 11, 1923).

1922–23. GEORGE II, a mere puppet in the hands of the military men.

Nov. 13. Trial for treason of the ministers and commanders of Constantine. **Demetrios Gounaris and five others convicted and shot** (Nov. 28).

1923, July 24. TREATY OF LAUSANNE (p. 753). Exchange of populations: in the period until 1930 some 1,250,000 Greeks repatriated, with the help of the League of Nations and of the Near East Relief Commission; great financial and other problems were connected with this huge transfer, but Greece was enriched by the influx of artisans and farmers.

The Greek population rose from 2.6 million in 1907 to 6.2 million by 1928. Moreover, the population exchange eased tensions between Turkey and Greece and made Greece a more homogeneous nation, as refugees resettled in territories with previously few ethnic Greeks. In rural areas, the influx of settlers hastened the pace of land reform be-

gun in 1917; large landed estates like those owned by the monasteries of Mount Athos were expropriated and broken up.

Dec. 16. Great victory of the Venizelists in the elections.

Dec. 18. George II left Greece, under pressure from the military junta.

1924, Jan. 11. Venizelos premier. He opposed the deposition of the king, but, failing to convince the military men, resigned (Feb. 3) and retired from Greece.

April 13. A plebiscite resulted in an overwhelming **vote for a republic.**

May 1. GREECE PROCLAIMED A REPUBLIC. Adm. Paul Kondouriottis made provisional president. Instability remained, however. From Jan. 1924 to June 1925 six governments were formed.

1925, June 25. Coup d'état of Gen. Theodore Pangalos.

Oct. 22–23. Clash of Greek and Bulgarian forces on the frontier, followed by the invasion of Bulgaria. The matter was settled by the League of Nations (Dec. 14), which fined Greece.

1926, Jan. 3. Pangalos made himself dictator.

Aug. 22. Pangalos overthrown by Gen. George Kondylis, who recalled Kondouriottis.

Nov. 7. The Republicans won a bare majority in the elections. A **coalition government** formed by **Alexander Zaimis.**

1927. As some measure of stability returned, a **new constitution was promulgated.** It established a republic with two houses (a *gerousia* and a *vouli*), with the government dependent on the majority of the lower house. But the president, with a five-year term, was given about the same powers as were previously allotted to the king.

1928, May 31. Return of Venizelos, who formed a cabinet (July 4).

1929. The world depression hit Greece severely. The total value of Greek exports fell from a yearly average of $125 million between 1922 and 1930 to only $49 million in 1933. By 1934 the value of Greek exports amounted to only half the value of imports. Moreover, emigrant remittances and revenue from shipping, the principal means by which Greece had traditionally overcome its chronic balance of payments deficits, decreased. By 1933 virtually two-thirds of state expenditures were devoted to servicing Greece's foreign debts. Ultimately, Greece was forced to default on interest payments. The severe strains this placed on Greek society were met with limited reform and government repression. The government introduced a program of public works, established an agricultural bank to help peasants gain credit, and increased the number of primary schools. But the government also passed the 1929 "idionym" law making attempts to undermine the existing social order illegal.

Dec. 10. Retirement of President Kondouriottis. Zaimis provisional **president.**

1932, Sept. 25. The Venizelists failed to secure a majority in the election. **Growing power of the Royalists,** strengthened by general economic stringency.

Oct. 31. Venizelos resigned and was followed (Nov. 4) by a moderate Royalist cabinet under **Panyotis Tsaldaris,** who declared his loyalty to the republic and was therefore tolerated by the Venizelists.

1933, Jan. 13. Fall of the Tsaldaris cabinet, defeated on its financial policy.

Jan. 16. Venizelos became premier again.

March 5. After dissolving Parliament, he suffered defeat in the elections. **Nicolas Plastiras,** an ardent Republican general, attempted a coup d'état, which failed.

March 10. Tsaldaris premier again, despite Venizelist opposition.

1934, Oct. 19. Zaimis elected president for five years.

1935, March 1. Rising of the Venizelists in Athens, Macedonia, and Crete as a protest against royalism. The movement was put down, after some fighting, by **Gen. George Kondylis.** Venizelos fled to France, during a purge of his supporters.

June 9. In the elections the followers of Tsaldaris and Kondylis secured most of the seats, the Republicans having abstained from voting.

Oct. 10. By a coup, **Kondylis ousted Tsaldaris** and induced Parliament to vote for the **recall of the king.**

Nov. 3. A farcical plebiscite resulted in an almost unanimous call for restoration of the monarchy.

Nov. 24. Return of George II, from exile in England. The king was supported by Britain (Ethiopian crisis) but was at the mercy of Kondylis.

1935–47. GEORGE II, RESTORED. He insisted on a general amnesty (Dec. 1).

1936, Jan. 26. The elections were **a victory for the Venizelists,** who, however, failed to secure a majority.

April 13. Gen. John Metaxas, premier. Paralyzed over its inability to establish a coalition government and divided over the reinstatement of Republican officers purged after the 1935 coup, parliament accepted Metaxas's proposal that it disband for five months. Legislative functions were transferred to a commission of 40 proportionately representing each party in Parliament.

May 9. Demonstrations by tobacco workers in Salonica resulted in the deaths of 12 strikers. The Communists called for a 24-hour general strike on Aug. 5 to protest against proposed legislation to impose compulsory arbitration in labor disputes. Social unrest and political stalemate bolstered cries for strong government.

Aug. 4. COUP D'ÉTAT OF METAXAS, who made himself dictator, proclaimed martial law, and dissolved the Parliament. Institution of a regime of rigid repression (parties abolished; censorship; persecution of opponents). The Metaxas regime rested squarely on the army, but real efforts were made to conciliate the population by wage increases, social security legislation, artificially low bread prices, and other measures, as well as by cancellation of agricultural debts. A huge **public works program** (especially rearmament) necessitated a substantial increase of taxation and domination of business by government. In **foreign affairs** Metaxas drew closer to Germany (barter agreements) but at the same time attempted to retain the goodwill of Britain and France. **Relations with Turkey** continued to be close.

1938, July 29. A revolt in Crete was quickly suppressed. Despite widespread dissatisfaction with the dictatorship, the regime became more and more firmly entrenched.

July 30. Metaxas became premier for life.

1939, April 13. Britain and France guaranteed Greek independence and integrity following the Italian conquest of Albania (p. 722).

1939, Sept. 3. Greece **remained neutral on the outbreak of World War II.**

1940, July 1. The **Italian government** threatened to take **action against Greece** on the ground that British warships were using Greek territorial waters in their attacks on Italian ships.

Oct. 28. Italian forces attacked Greece, creating a state of war. The Greeks offered a stout defense.

1941, April 6. Germany attacked Greece.

April 23. The **Greek army surrendered unconditionally** to the Germans and Italians. A government in exile was formed and fled to London with King George. The **British forces** that had been landed in Greece to aid in its defense were withdrawn on May 1.

Resistance to the Germans was strong but hindered by ideological disputes between groups. Despite a National Bands agreement negotiated in 1943 attempting to set up a common front, relations among the resistance groups remained hostile throughout the war, setting the stage for the Greek civil war.

1943. A series of strikes in February and March effectively put an end to German plans to draft Greek workers for compulsory labor service.

1944, Oct. 13. Athens was occupied by Allied forces.   *(To p. 897)*

d. BULGARIA

(From pp. 522, 672)

Defeated in World War I, Bulgaria not only failed to recover any of the territory lost in the Second Balkan War, but was also deprived of some further areas on the Serbian frontier and of all access to the Aegean. The country was flooded with **thousands of refugees** from Thrace and Macedonia, whom the government, loaded with debt and heavy reparations payments, was unable to settle. They formed a huge mobile element, easy converts to the revolutionary program of the **Macedonian committees** or to **Bolshevik agitators.** The drastic policy of nationalization pursued by the Yugoslav and Greek governments in Macedonia stimulated the unrest in Bulgaria, which the government was

unable to control. **Raids of revolutionary bands** across the frontiers became the order of the day, creating a state of chronic tension between Bulgaria and its neighbors.

1918, Oct. 4. Abdication of **Tsar Ferdinand.**

1918–43. BORIS III, son of Ferdinand, tsar.

1919, Aug. 17. The **Peasant Party won a great victory** in the elections.

Oct. 6. Alexander Stamboliski, leader of the Peasant Party, became premier.

The Communist Party, formed in 1919, not only did not join the government (despite winning 18 percent of the vote) but soon clashed with the Agrarians. Communist leaders were very active in labor agitation and in the organization of strikes, the most important of which was the **general strike** of Dec. 1919. Stamboliski opposed these actions by forming the Orange Guard, composed mainly of peasants armed with clubs, which was used to break up demonstrations. After the arrest of the leaders, the strikes collapsed.

Nov. 27. Bulgaria signed the Treaty of Neuilly (p. 672).

1920, March. Hoping for a clear majority, Stamboliski held new elections, which, after invalidating a number of mandates, gave him a majority of four. With a completely Agrarian cabinet, Stamboliski began his reforms aimed at making Bulgaria a "model agricultural state." These included restricting bureaucracy, reducing government pensions, and altering the tax system to aid peasants. Most of these reforms were aborted when he fell from power. He was, however, able to pass important measures covering land reform, the introduction of labor service, and the improvement of education on the village level.

Dec. 16. Bulgaria became a member of the League of Nations.

1921, Oct. Operatives of the Macedonian terrorist organization IMRO assassinated Stamboliski's close adviser Alexander Dimitrov.

1923, April. Through repressive measures the Agrarians won a great electoral victory. It was rumored that Stamboliski planned to use this opportunity for more reforms, including the abolition of the monarchy.

June 9. STAMBOLISKI WAS OVERTHROWN by a conspiracy of officers with the support of a number of political parties, affected by his attempt to deprive them forever of a say in government. A new cabinet was formed by **Alexander Tsankov.**

June 14. Stamboliski was shot and killed, allegedly in an effort to escape. Tsankov and the new government proceeded with great vigor in a policy of revenge.

Sept. On instruction from Moscow, the Bulgarian Communist Party staged a badly organized revolt, which was easily suppressed.

1924, April. The **Communist Party was outlawed** for terrorist activity. Communist activity continued through front organizations.

Aug. 31. Assassination of Todor Alexandrov, the result of infighting among Macedonian nationalists. The conflict was between federalists, who wanted an autonomous Macedonia in Balkan federation, and centralists, who wanted annexation with Bulgaria. Their continuing internecine warfare contributed to the instability in Bulgaria.

1925, April 16. A bomb exploded in the Sofia cathedral. The Communists were held responsible, and mass arrests followed as the government made an effort to destroy the movement.

Oct. 22. Greek invasion of Bulgaria, following serious frontier incidents. The matter was settled by the League.

1926, Jan. 4. A cabinet of Andrey Liapchev followed that of Tsankov and initiated a policy of reconciliation.

1927, Feb. The Communists were allowed to reenter political life under the guise of the **Bulgarian Workers' Party.**

1930, Jan. 20. The **Hague agreement** greatly reduced the Bulgarian **reparations payments.** Like the other Balkan nations, Bulgaria began to feel the impact of the depression. Unemployment rose in urban centers as farmers' earnings fell. Economic distress convinced many to accept the radical solutions offered by the extreme Left and Right.

Oct. 25. Marriage of Tsar Boris and Princess Giovanna, daughter of Victor Emmanuel III of Italy. Gradual **rapprochement between Italy and Bulgaria.**

1931, June 21. In the elections a coalition including the **Peasant Party** and the **Democratic Party** won a victory over the Democratic Entente, which had supported Tsankov and Liapchev. A new cabinet was formed (June 29) by **Alexander Malinov,** who was soon replaced by another Democrat, **Nikola Mushanov.**

1932, Feb. 8. Bulgaria denounced further reparations payments.

Sept. 25. Striking success of the Communists in the Sofia municipal elections. But in the communal elections (Nov.) the Democrats and Agrarians won an overwhelming victory.

1933, June 24. The government arrested over a thousand Communists and Macedonians.

1934, May 19. Coup d'état of army officers under **Kimon Georgiev,** who put an end to 55 years of parliamentary rule. The coup, staged by an organization called the **Military League,** had the support of a civilian association called Zveno (Link). The new government proclaimed a program of social renewal through force of law. It abolished the 1879 constitution, dissolved the national assembly, banned all political parties and activities, and disarmed IMRO.

1935, Jan. 22. In a bloodless coup, Boris III established a more personal government; Georgiev was forced out and his place was taken by Gen. Petko Zlatev.

April 18. A purely **civilian cabinet** was formed by **Andrey Toshev,** the officers' group having been weakened by factional dissension.

Nov. 23. A **new cabinet** was formed by **George Kiosseivanov.**

1936, Feb. Trial and conviction of a number of military men, including **Damyan Veltchev,** supposed to be the leader of the military party.

March. The **Military League was dissolved.** For all intents and purposes Tsar Boris was master of the situation.

1937, Jan. 24. CONCLUSION OF THE PACT OF FRIENDSHIP WITH YUGOSLAVIA, bringing to an end the long period of hostility and opening the way for closer relations between Bulgaria and the other Balkan powers.

Oct. 13. More than 40 political leaders petitioned the tsar for free elections and a return to constitutionalism. Thereupon the tsar promulgated a **new electoral law** providing for free voting by men and married women but forbidding candidates to run as representatives of the old parties.

1938, March. The **elections** resulted in victory for a number of opponents of the government.

May 22. Parliament met for the first time since the military coup of 1935. Its powers were considerably reduced.

July 31. AGREEMENT WITH GREECE (acting for the Balkan Entente) **recognized Bulgaria's right to rearm.** By this time Bulgarian rearmament (in contravention of the treaties) had already made considerable headway, Germany supplying much of the material. This did not, however, imply acceptance of National Socialism by the Bulgarian government. On the contrary, the pro-Nazi and pro-Fascist organizations were outlawed in the same way as the other political parties. Moreover, the government readily accepted an **Anglo-French loan** of $10 million to support the rearmament program (Aug.). In the growing international tension of 1938–39 Bulgaria, like most of the lesser states, was pulled this way and that. Great efforts were made to bring it into the Balkan Entente, but this courting merely enabled the government to demand more insistently a revision of the treaties. Claims to the Dobrudja created rather tense relations between Romania and Bulgaria in the spring of 1939.

1939, Sept. 3. Bulgaria remained neutral on the outbreak of World War II.

1940, Feb. 15. A new cabinet was organized under **Bogdan Filov.**

June 18. Bulgaria demanded Dobrudja and an outlet to the Aegean Sea. A Bulgarian-Romanian agreement whereby Romania ceded this territory was concluded on Sept. 8.

1941, March 1. Bulgaria joined the Rome-Berlin Axis (p. 802), and German troops occupied Sofia.

April 6. Bulgaria joined Germany and Italy in attacking Yugoslavia. It annexed parts of Yugoslavia (July 31).

Sept. 12. Bulgaria received a **warning from the Soviet government** that its activities did not reflect a friendly attitude.

Nov. 25. Bulgaria joined the Rome-Berlin-Tokyo alliance.

Dec. 13. Bulgaria declared war on the United States.

1943, Aug. 29. King Boris III died suddenly and was succeeded by his six-year-old son, **Simeon II.** A **council of regency,** including **Prince Cyril, Bogdan Filov, and Gen. Nichola Michov,** was established and approved by the Bulgarian Parliament (Sept. 9).

1944, Sept. 8. Bulgaria accepted armistice conditions laid down by the Soviet government in accord with other Allied nations.   *(To p. 899)*

e. ROMANIA

(From p. 524)

1914–27. FERDINAND I.

1916, Aug. 27. Romania declared war on Austria-Hungary, but the Romanian armies were decisively defeated before the end of the year.

1918, May 7. Treaty of Bucharest (p. 664).

Nov. 10. Romania reentered the war, and Romanian forces occupied **Transylvania.**

Dec. 2. A government, headed by **Julius Maniu,** Transylvanian peasant leader, was soon (Dec. 14) obliged to give way to a cabinet under **Ion Bratianu,** leader of the Liberal Party, representing the industrial, commercial, and professional classes of the old kingdom.

Romania's main problems after the war were economic recovery and internal consolidation of the state, primarily by the unification of legislation throughout the country. To alleviate economic problems **land reform** was partially introduced in Dec. 1918, when a decree was issued expropriating a considerable part of the great landed estates. Reform became more definite in 1921; almost 7 million acres were divided among nearly 1.5 million families, and the remainder of over 4 million acres of grassland and forest became village property to be used by the peasants on payment of a tax. As in the rest of the Balkans, reform was not enough to end rural poverty, and peasants actually cut back commercial production in favor of local subsistence. Urban conditions were also difficult, sparking frequent strikes culminating in a countrywide **general strike** in 1920.

1919, April. Beginning of the **Romanian advance into Hungary.** The Romanians ultimately occupied Budapest (Aug. 4) and did not evacuate until Nov. 14 (p. 672).

May 18. Russia declared a state of war.

May 28. The **Jews were emancipated** and given full citizen rights, but **anti-Semitism** continued to be rampant, especially in the universities, which had to be closed repeatedly because of anti-Semitic riots.

1920, March 2. Armistice with Russia.

Sept. 5. The Trancu-Iasi Law banned the organization of workers in trade unions overtly directed by a political party.

Sept. 14. Romania joined the League of Nations.

Oct. 28. Britain, France, Italy, and Japan recognized the Romanian possession of Bessarabia. This treaty was not ratified by Britain and France until 1924, and not by Italy until 1927.

1923. After 1922 industry and the economy as a whole developed more rapidly, and there was comparative political stability. By 1928 industrial output had gone up 56 percent as against 1919; consumer and extractive industries still predominated. Romania remained primarily agricultural, however. Moreover, despite economic growth, conditions for both workers and peasants remained difficult.

March. The **new constitution** abolished the three-class system of voting and introduced the direct, secret ballot. Substantial civil liberties were also instituted such as freedom of the press and equality of all ethnic groups.

1924, July 27. The fledgling Romanian Communist Party and its affiliated groups (founded in May 1921) were dissolved by the government.

1925, Dec. 28. Prince Charles (Carol) renounced his right of succession to the throne and preferred to live in exile with his mistress, **Magda Lupescu.** Bratianu and the Liberals were actively hostile to the prince.

1926, March 25. A **new electoral law** provided that the party polling 40 percent of the votes should have one-half of the seats in Parliament.

Sept. 16. Treaty of friendship with Italy, which made a large loan in return for oil and other concessions.

Oct. Fusion of the peasant parties to form the new **National Peasants' Party,** under Maniu's leadership.

1927, July 20. Death of King Ferdinand.

1927–30. MICHAEL (b. 1921). Principal regent **Prince Nicholas,** brother of Prince Charles, the father of Michael.

1928, May 6. Congress of the National Peasants' Party at Alba Julia, demanding representative government, decentralization, and reform.

Nov. 9. JULIUS MANIU became premier. He set out to purge the administration, make easier the influx of foreign capital, improve the lot of the peasants, and so on.

1930, June 6. Prince Charles arrived by airplane and was accepted by Maniu. The parliament (June 8) revoked the law excluding him from the throne. Michael was put aside in favor of his father.

1930–40. CAROL (CHARLES) II. He soon fell out with Maniu, brought back Mme. Lupescu, and attempted to establish his personal rule.

1931, April 18. The king appointed a coalition **(National Union)** cabinet under Nicholas Iorga, his former tutor. This was regarded as a prelude to a royal dictatorship.

1932, Jan.–May. Negotiations with Russia, held under Polish auspices at Warsaw, failed to effect a settlement of the Bessarabian question.

May 31. Iorga resigned after failure to secure a loan from France.

June 6. A **new cabinet** was formed by **Alexander Vaida-Voevod,** Peasant leader.

July 17. The **Peasants won** a great victory in the elections. But their position was weakened by the inability of Maniu to get along with the king and by rivalry between Maniu and Vaida-Voevod. On Oct. 20 Maniu took over the premiership (until Jan. 5, 1933).

1933, Jan. A system of **League of Nations supervision of Romanian finances** was introduced for four years.

Jan.–Feb. Strikes by the oil and railway workers were ended in bloodshed, but the government was forced to give up a planned third wage cut. The government had dealt with the depression by promoting foreign investment, decreasing wages, and increasing taxation.

1934, April. Parliament passed a law on "the defense of order within the state" which enabled the government to dissolve any political group that jeopardized the political and social order.

1936, Feb. The anti-Semitic **Christian League,** headed by A. C. Cuza, and the **National Christian Party,** led by the poet Octavian Goga, united with one wing of the National Peasants' Party, under Vaida-Voevod, to form a reactionary bloc not much different from the Fascist Iron Guard.

The liberal government under **Tatarescu** proved to be helpless in the face of a series of terrorist acts, committed by the fanatically anti-Semitic **Iron Guard** under **Corneliu Z. Codreanu.**

1937, Dec. 21. Thanks to surprising preelectoral pacts of the National Peasants' Party with the Iron Guard and the Communists, the elections resulted in a **defeat for the government.** Thereupon the government resigned (Dec. 26) and King Carol, once more astounding the world, appointed Goga his prime minister.

Dec. 28. OCTAVIAN GOGA made prime minister, despite the fact that his National Christian Party had gained only 10 percent of the vote in the election. Goga at once embarked upon an orgy of **anti-Semitic legislation,** forbidding Jews to own land, depriving those naturalized after 1920 of their citizenship, barring Jews from the professions, and so on. At the same time Goga aimed at the establishment of a dictatorship by sending his party troops into all localities.

1938, Jan. 18. King Carol dissolved the parliament, which had not yet met. For contradictory reasons, this unconstitutional procedure led to protests from all the other parties, while the anti-Semitic policy quickly brought the country to the verge of business collapse.

Feb. 10. The **king dismissed Goga,** using as a pretext the fact that the courts had invalidated several of the anti-Semitic laws. Goga and his followers had thoroughly discredited themselves and had really strengthened the position of the king, who now assumed complete control of the situation. A new "concentration" cabinet, containing seven former premiers, was established under the leadership of the patriarch, **Miron Cristea. The constitution was suspended and all political parties were suppressed.** Rigid censorship was instituted. These moves were violently opposed by both the Iron Guard and the National Peasants' Party of Maniu.

Feb. 24. A **plebiscite,** however, properly managed by the government, **approved Carol's action** by an overwhelming vote (only 5,300 opposed).

April 19. The leader of the Iron Guard, **Corneliu Codreanu, was condemned** to six months' imprisonment for libel, and then (May 27) to ten years at hard labor for treason. The government's **attack upon the Iron Guardists** now assumed major proportions. Many of Codreanu's followers were arrested and imprisoned after discovery of an alleged plot against the king.

Oct. Trade unions were dissolved by decree and replaced with guilds, which were considered as vocational bodies subordinate to the aims of the royal dictatorship.

Nov. 30. DEATH OF CODREANU. He and 13 other Iron Guardists were reported shot by their guards while being moved from one prison to another.

1939, March 6. Armand Calinescu became premier on the death of Patriarch Cristea.

April 13. Great Britain and France guaranteed Romanian independence and integrity following the German annihilation of Czechoslovakia and rumors of a German ultimatum to Romania. But the Bucharest government nevertheless concluded a **commercial agreement with Germany** giving the latter broad scope for expansion of Romanian industry. In short, the government attempted to straddle the two groups of powers in Europe.

Sept. 21. Premier Calinescu was assassinated by members of the **Iron Guard. Gen. George Argeseanu,** who succeeded him, was replaced (Sept. 28) by **Constantine Argetoianu,** and he was followed in turn by **Jorge Tatarescu** (Nov. 24).

1940, June 26. The **Soviet Union** demanded the return of **Bessarabia** and the cession of northern **Bukovina.** The disputed territory, 19,300 square miles with a population of 3.5 million, was occupied by Soviet troops on June 28.

July 1. Romania renounced the Anglo-French guarantee of its integrity.

Aug. 30. Under pressure from Berlin and Rome, the government agreed to yield an area of 16,642 square miles with a population of almost 2.4 million to Hungary (**Vienna conference**).

Sept. 6. Under pressure from the Iron Guard, **King Carol fled** and was replaced by his son, **Michael.**

Sept. 8. A further territorial cession of some 3,000 square miles (**southern Dobrudja**) was demanded by, and yielded to, Bulgaria (**Treaty of Craiova**).

Oct. 8. German troops entered Romania to "protect" the oil fields.

Nov. 23. Romania joined the Rome-Berlin-Tokyo tripartite pact.

Nov. 27. The **Iron Guard executed 64 former officials** of King Carol's government while rioting spread throughout Romania.

1941, Dec. 12. Romania declared war on the United States.

1944, Aug. 23–24. King Michael dismissed the cabinet of **Gen. Ion Antonescu** and **accepted armistice terms** from the United Nations. The **Russians occupied Bucharest** (Aug. 31) (p. 803). (To p. 900)

D. NORTH AMERICA, 1915–1945

1. THE UNITED STATES

(From p. 617)

The two world wars and the Great Depression completed the urban industrial transformation of America. The changes of this era accelerated the rise of the United States as a world power; heightened the process of democratization; and increased the role of the state in shaping the economy, culture, and society. After World War I **isolationism** defined most American foreign policy, but the nation's international economic role continued to expand; periodic intervention in Central America and the Caribbean also continued (pp. 745, 750). During this period the rise of new forms of **mass culture**—e.g., movies, radios, and automobiles—would also help to transform American attitudes and values. **New sexual attitudes,** including growing belief in the centrality of sex for marriage, accompanied rising consumerism. This development joined growing acceptance of **artificial birth control** devices for married couples (particularly middle class) and also new sexual suggestiveness in advertisements and movies. With radio and movies, more standardized cultural fare became available. Following the introduction of sound to feature-length films in 1927, for example, movie attendance increased by nearly 30 million people over the next three years. The cultural differences among Americans would appear less apparent than in previous years.

Still, by the end of World War II, the dynamics of class, race, and region continued to shape definitions of American nationality. Participation in two world wars expanded the federal bureaucracy, which gained expression in a number of wartime agencies: the National War Labor Board (World Wars I and II), the Selective Service system (World Wars I and II), and the War Industries Board (World War I), to name only a few. Under the leadership of Democratic president Franklin D. Roosevelt, a variety of New Deal social welfare programs reinforced the growing role of the state in the political economy. The Social Security Act, the National Labor Relations Act, and the Works Progress Administration were among the many measures that signaled the changing role of the state in American society. Supporting these developments was the rise of a new political coalition of urban workers, ethnic groups, blacks, and women. These constituents of the so-called **New Deal Coalition** demanded relief and security from the vagaries of industrial capitalism. Significantly, FDR appointed the first woman to hold a cabinet-level position, Francis Perkins, secretary of labor.

The rise of the welfare state was by no means unproblematic. Corporate elites dominated the development of American society during this period. Following a brief recession during the early 1920s, the industrial sector (except for coal, textiles, and a few other so-called sick industries) soon recovered and prospered. Corporate mergers accelerated, and by the stock market crash of 1929 the number of such combinations had exceeded the record set during the late 19th century. As industry recovered during the mid-1920s, however, agriculture continued to face the destructive impact of competition with European products. New Deal programs had limited impact on the fortunes of American farmers. The Agricultural Adjustment Act, for example, encouraged the concentration of agricultural production in the hands of large landowners, hastened the demise of the small farmer, and reinforced the movement of African Americans from the Jim Crow South to the urban North and West.

Despite the passage of New Deal labor legislation, industrial workers faced stiff resistance to their quest for equal rights. In 1936, it took a 44-day sit-down strike to produce victory for the CIO's United Automobile Workers. While large companies like General Motors and U.S. Steel negotiated contracts with their workers, others like the so-called Little Steel companies held out and refused to recognize the union until 1941. Women and ethnic and racial minorities also faced persistent patterns of inequality. Even during the acute labor shortages of World War II, for example, employers were reluctant to train women for available skilled jobs. Only when African Americans launched the March on Washington movement (1941) did they gain access to heretofore racially restricted defense industry jobs. Indeed, Native, Hispanic, African, and Asian Americans faced special problems, which culminated in the internment of Japanese Americans during World War II. Racism not only challenged America's domestic tranquility, but questioned its growing claims as leader of the free world. Along with new forms of repression unleashed by the cold war, fear of Communism, and the threat of nuclear annihilation, racism and questions of social justice would emerge as key issues of the post–World War II years.

1915. *The Birth of a Nation* heralded as a modern cinematic triumph, although it inflamed racial hatreds by portraying African Americans as inferior and black men as threats to white womanhood. The **Ku Klux Klan was revived in Georgia during the same year** and flourished as a national movement during the early postwar years, as membership rose to over 2 million and covered urban as well as rural America.

1915–17. The Woman's Peace Party formed following the international women's congress at The Hague. **At the same time women escalated their demands for suffrage,** which they received in 1920 with passage of the **Nineteenth Amendment.**

1916. Alice Paul spearheaded the formation of the militant **National Woman's Party** and advocated a constitutional amendment to enfranchise women in one stroke.

Under the leadership of the Jamaican **Marcus M. Garvey,** the **Universal Negro Improvement Association** established a Harlem chapter and spread rapidly among the African-American population. Emphasizing race pride and "Africa for Africans," the organization struck a responsive chord among black Americans in the racial environment of wartime and especially postwar America.

1916–18. With the assistance of **Harriet Stanton Blatch,** the **Food Administration** launched an extensive consumer education program and became one of the most successful wartime regulatory agencies.

1917. The AFL argued for a no-strike rule for the duration of the war. In exchange for its loyalty, it received federal support for its collective bargaining efforts.

Thirty-nine black men, women, and children lost their lives in an outbreak of racial violence in East St. Louis, Illinois.

April 6. WAR DECLARED ON GERMANY (p. 663). Diplomatic relations with Austria-Hungary were terminated on April 8, but war was declared on Dec. 7. Diplomatic relations with Turkey were severed on April 20, but war was never formally declared on either Turkey or Bulgaria.

May 18. Selective Service Act passed providing for the registration of those between 21 and 31 years of age, inclusive. On June 5 local draft boards registered 9,586,508 men. **The U.S. ended its traditional dependence on volunteer units for defense and used conscripts almost exclusively.** Seventy-two percent of the nation's armed forces were draftees: 13 percent black, 18 percent immigrant, and the remainder American-born. **Nearly 400,000 African Americans served in the war.**

1917–18. When some Americans resisted the draft, officials broke up antidraft meetings, arrested several individuals, and imprisoned such activists as **Emma Goldman, Eugene V. Debs, A. Philip Randolph, and Chandler Owens.** The U.S. Supreme Court upheld such limitations on free speech in the case of *Schenck* v. *United States.*

Great Migration. Nearly a million **African Americans** moved into American cities of the north, south, and west. At the same time, many **Hispanic Americans** moved not only into cities of the South and West, but into the urban Midwest as well, particularly the steel cities of Indiana and Ohio, as well the meatpacking centers of Illinois.

1917, June 15–1918, May 6. The Espionage Act, the Trading-with-the-Enemy Act (Oct. 6, 1917), **and the Sedition Act** (May 6, 1918). Radical groups like the **Industrial Workers of the World** became special targets of this legislation. In Bisbee, Arizona, local officials rounded up over 1,000 striking miners, one-third of them Mexican Americans, and about 50 recent members of the Industrial Workers of the World, and shipped them into the desert of New Mexico without food or water.

July. War Industries Board created and placed in complete charge of all war purchases.

Aug. 10. The Lever Act, establishing control over food and fuel. **Herbert Hoover,** food administrator.

Sept. 1. Grain Corporation inaugurated, which fixed price of grain and financed the 1917, 1918, and 1919 crops.

Oct. 3. War Revenue Act, greatly increasing income tax and imposing an excess profit tax on business earnings of corporations and individuals.

Nov. 2. Lansing-Ishii agreement, reaffirming the assurances of the Root-Takahira agreement (1908), with the admission by the U.S. that "territorial propinquity" gave Japan special interests in China.

Dec. William G. McAdoo, secretary of the treasury, made director-general of the railroad administration.

Dec. 18. Under stress of war conditions and the need for food conservation, Congress had in Aug. 1917 prohibited the use of food products in the making of distilled beverages. Ownership of large numbers of breweries and distilleries by persons of German origin accentuated popular resentment against liquor traffic. As a result Congress adopted the **Eighteenth Amendment,** prohibiting the manufacture, sale, and transportation of alcoholic liquors, and sent it to the states for ratification. It became part of the Constitution on Jan. 29, 1919.

1918. Average real wages for manual labor rose by about 20 percent in industries like steel, textiles, shipbuilding, and munitions between 1914 and 1918.

National War Labor Board created to mediate labor-management disputes. AFL membership rose from 2.7 million to 4 million between 1916 and 1919.

Jan. 8. Fourteen Points set forth by President Wilson in an address to Congress defining war aims of the U.S. (p. 666).

April. When **an anti-German mob wrapped a German American in an American flag and lynched him** near St. Louis, Missouri, a local judge called the lynching a "patriotic murder." The phrase "100 percent American" became a watchword for squashing dissent.

April 5. War Finance Commission created with fund of $500 million for financing essential industries.

April 10. Webb-Pomerene Act exempting export associations from the restraints of the antitrust laws, with a view to encouraging export trade.

June 13. First division embarked for France.

July 18–Nov. 11. American troops participated in six prolonged assaults upon German positions. Two of these were conducted wholly by American forces: the **Battle of St. Mihiel** (Sept. 12–16) and that of the Meuse-Argonne (Sept. 26–Nov. 11), in which 1.2 million men were engaged (p. 672).

Nov. 11. Armistice signed (p. 666).

Dec. 13. Arrival of President Wilson in France for the peace conference.

1919. The wartime suppression of civil rights underlay the founding of the **American Civil Liberties Union.**

Racial violence erupted in dozens of cities. The worst confrontation flared in **Chicago,** where nearly 500 persons were injured and more than 38 died during the so-called **Red Summer of 1919.**

The **Communist Labor Party and the Communist Party of the United States** formed. Although the two groups could claim little more than 70,000 members, they became the target of a vigorous **anti-Red campaign.**

When 450,000 coal miners went on strike, the **Wilson administration used the wartime Lever Act to break the strike.**

March 2. Senate round-robin, declaring the opinion of 39 senators that only after the establishment of peace should the League of Nations concern the negotiators.

July 10–1920, March 19. Treaty of Versailles (p. 671) before the Senate. Strong objections developed to the treaty. Wilson refused to accept amendments or reservations. On Nov. 19 the Senate defeated the treaty with and without reservations. Finally on March 19 (1920) the treaty with reservations was rejected by a vote of 49 to 35. Wilson then vetoed a joint resolution of Congress declaring war with Germany at an end. A similar resolution was passed in July 1921 and signed by Harding.

Sept. 22–1920, Jan. 8. Steel strike. Although the public sympathized with the steel workers, the strikers were defeated.

Oct. 28. The **National Prohibition Act,** commonly known as the **Volstead Act,** passed, over President Wilson's veto. It was strengthened by amendments of 1921 and 1929.

Dec. As part of a federal campaign to rid the country of radicals, 300 persons were deported to the Soviet Union, including the activist **Emma Goldman.**

1919–20. Cost of living increased to 77 percent of prewar level in 1919 and to 105 percent a year later.

Numerous **strikes** erupted involving 4 million workers. **The largest strike involved 350,000 steelworkers who walked out in September.** The union demanded a reduction in the number of hours and workdays; the U.S. Steel Corp. responded by hiring Hispanic- and African-American workers as strikebreakers, who for their part resented the discriminatory practices of steel unions.

Growing corporate and service sector employment in the 1920s created new pressures for **emotional restraint** in the work place. Various kinds of employees were told to manipulate emotions to please customers, bosses, or subordinates.

The combination of machine-produced interchangeable parts and the moving assembly line helped to stimulate the **emergence of a consumer-oriented society.** Automobile sales, mainly of **Ford's famous Model T,** soared to 5 million by 1929, rising from about 1.5 million in 1921. The rapid expansion of electric power and equipment companies also spurred the development of electric home appliances. From the launch of **KDKA in Pittsburgh** in 1920 to the onset of the Great Depression, radio stations rose in number to about 800 in 1929, with

nearly 40 percent of all families owning receiving sets. At the same time, the **movie industry** introduced the **"star system"** and pushed weekly movie attendance from about 40 million in 1922 to over 100 million less than a decade later. Other forms of leisure, education, social services, health care, and media also witnessed rapid growth.

1920s. The Lost Generation. The mass destruction of human life during World War I embittered large segments of postwar American artists and intellectuals. They linked the war to what they saw as the debilitating impact of materialism and the onslaught of consumer culture. Some of these writers, like **T. S. Eliot,** left the U.S. and settled permanently overseas. Others, like **Ernest Hemingway** and **F. Scott Fitzgerald,** frequently traveled to Europe, particularly Paris, and even lived there for long periods of time. In Paris these artists came under the influence of the "modernist movement" in cultural expression and took a highly critical posture toward the recent impact of science, technology, and urbanization on American life. Writers like **Sherwood Anderson, Sinclair Lewis, and Theodore Dreiser** wrote scathing indictments of American culture. The 1920s were an unusually rich era of artistic creation. **Edith Wharton** won a Pulitzer Prize for her novel *The Age of Innocence* (1920); African Americans launched the **Harlem Renaissance,** which the critic **Alain Locke** promoted in an anthology, *The New Negro* (1926); **William Faulkner** explored Southern life in his novel *The Sound and the Fury* (1929); and Sinclair Lewis received the **Nobel Prize** for literature (1930). Major composers included **Aaron Copland, Howard Hanson, and George Gershwin.** Both Copland and Gershwin appreciated the growing popularity of African-American jazz and sought to adapt it to symphonic forms. One of the leading big band composers was **Edward Kennedy "Duke" Ellington** (1899–1974).

1920, Feb. 28. Transportation Act signed by President Wilson, giving the Interstate Commerce Commission power to establish and maintain rates that would yield a "fair return upon the aggregate value of the railway property of the country," and power to prescribe minimum rates. Prosperous roads were to share profits with the less prosperous. The commission was empowered to draw up a plan for the consolidation of the railway lines into a limited number of systems, such combinations to be exempt from operation of the antitrust laws.

March 1. The railroads were returned to their owners.

June 5–1928. Merchant Marine Acts. Under the act of 1920 the Shipping Board was to dispose of the wartime merchant fleet to private parties, and to operate those ships that it could not sell; to establish new shipping routes; and to keep ships in these services until private capital could be attracted to them. In effect the act of 1928 provided for subsidies to the merchant marine.

June 20. Water-Power Act passed, creating a federal power commission composed of the secretaries of war, interior, and agriculture and subordinate appointive officers. Its authority extended to all waterways on public lands and to all navigable streams, including falls and rapids. It could license power companies to use appropriate dam sites for periods not exceeding 50 years.

Aug. 28. Nineteenth Amendment, providing for women's suffrage.

Sept. 8–11. Transcontinental air mail service established between New York and San Francisco.

Nov. 2. The Westinghouse Electrical Company arranged the **first general radio broadcast** for the national election. On Nov. 30 the same company broadcast the first regular evening program.

Warren G. Harding (Republican) elected president over **James M. Cox** (Democrat), 404 electoral votes to 137.

1921, March 4–1923, Aug. 2. WARREN G. HARDING, 29th president.

April 20. Colombian Treaty (p. 742) ratified by the Senate; the U.S. was to pay Colombia $25 million for the loss of Panama and to grant free access to the Panama Canal.

May 19. Immigration Act signed, limiting the immigrants from a given country to 3 percent of the number of foreign-born persons of such nationality resident in the U.S. according to the U.S. Census of 1910.

May 27. Emergency Tariff Act, raising duties on agricultural products, wool, and sugar. It placed an embargo on German dyestuffs; those products that could not be made in the U.S. were put on a licensing basis.

Aug. 24. Treaty of peace signed with Austria.

Nov. 12–1922, Feb. 6. WASHINGTON CONFERENCE. On Aug. 11 President Harding issued a call to Great Britain, France, Italy, and Japan to meet for discussion of naval limitation, and to the same powers, plus Belgium, Netherlands, Portugal, and China, for discussion of questions affecting the Pacific and the Far East.

1922–28. The real earnings of American workers continued to increase, rising by an estimated 22 percent between 1922 and 1928. The work week also declined by nearly 4 percent.

1922, Feb. 11., April 1–Sept. 4. Strike of coal miners in protest against wage reductions and in support of the check-off system by which the unions required employers to deduct union fees from wages. **Herrin riots** in Illinois.

July 1–Sept. 13. Railway shopmen's strike in protest against wage reductions set by Railway Labor Board.

Aug. 2. CALVIN COOLIDGE became 30th president upon death of Warren G. Harding.

Sept. 19. Fordney-McCumber Tariff Act passed. Contained highest rates in American tariff history.

Nov. 20. An American observer sent to the Lausanne conference. This break with the administration's policy of noninterference in European affairs was largely caused by the concern of American oil interests over the oil situation in the Near Eastern fields, where a British monopoly was feared.

1923–30. Refunding of debts owed the U.S. by Allied powers. During and immediately following the war the U.S. lent to foreign powers a total of $10.35 billion. The first refunding agreement was with Great Britain, which was to pay over a period of 62 years, with interest at 3.3 percent. By May 1930 17 nations had come to terms with the United States.

1924, Feb.–March. Teapot Dome oil scandal. On April 7, 1922, **Albert Fall,** secretary of the interior, leased the Teapot Dome oil reserve to Harry F. Sinclair, and by agreements of April 25 and Dec. 11, 1922, he leased the Elk Hills reserve to Edward L. Doheny. Secrecy attending the leases, combined with the sudden opulence of Fall, led to Senate investigation under the direction of Senator Thomas J. Walsh. It was shown that Sinclair had personally befriended Fall, while Doheny had "loaned" $100,000 to Fall without security or interest. As a result, Edwin Denby, secretary of the navy, resigned (Fall had previously resigned), and in 1927 the Supreme Court ordered the reserves returned to the government.

May 19. Soldiers' Bonus Bill for veterans of the First World War passed, over the president's veto.

May 26. Immigration Bill signed, limiting annual immigration from a given country to 2 percent of the nationals of the country in the U.S. in 1890. A further provision of the law stipulated that from July 1, 1927 (later deferred to 1929), the annual immigration should be limited to 150,000, to be apportioned among the different countries in proportion to the relative strength of the various foreign elements represented in the American population in 1920. The bill provided for the total exclusion of the Japanese, thereby abrogating the gentlemen's agreement. Protest from Japan and resulting ill feeling.

Nov. 4. Calvin Coolidge elected president over John W. Davis (Democrat) and Robert M. La Follette (Progressive) by 382 electoral votes to 136 for Davis and 13 for La Follette.

1925, March 4–1929, March 4. CALVIN COOLIDGE president.

1925–29. Agricultural legislation. In Feb. 1922 the **Capper-Volstead Act** granted to agricultural associations and cooperatives the right to process, prepare, handle, and market their goods in interstate commerce. In March 1923 the **Federal Intermediate Credit Act** provided for the creation of a system of federal intermediate credit banks for the purpose of handling agricultural paper exclusively. The **McNary-Haugen Bill,** a measure designed to make the tariff on agricultural products effective, was vetoed by Coolidge when it passed both houses of Congress in 1927 and again in 1928. This measure, as well as the export debenture plan, was opposed largely because of price-fixing and subsidy features. In June 1929 the **Agricultural Marketing Act** of the Hoover administration was enacted with its plan for the redemption of agriculture through voluntary cooperation and self-discipline under governmental auspices. A **Federal Farm Board** was created with a revolving fund of $500 million for loans to cooperatives and with power to create stabilization corporations. Grain and cotton stabilization corporations bought extensively with a view to sustaining prices of farm products, but to little avail.

1925, May 20–21. Charles A. Lindbergh made the **first nonstop New York to Paris flight** alone in the monoplane *Spirit of St. Louis.* His time was 33 hours, 39 minutes.

June. Secretary of State Frank B. Kellogg charged the Calles government in Mexico with failure to protect American lives and property rights, creating tension between the two countries that was increased by the enactment of the Mexican Petroleum Law and the Alien Land Law in Dec. 1925 (p. 748).

1925. Scopes trial. The civil liberties lawyer **Clarence Darrow** defended **John T. Scopes,** a young high school teacher who faced charges of violating Tennessee's law that banned the teaching of evolutionary theories in public schools. **William Jennings Bryan,** the recurring presidential candidate for the Populist Party before its demise, served as counsel for the prosecution and won the case; nonetheless, antievolutionist forces compiled few additional gains, including their efforts to gain more state legislation barring evolutionary doctrines in the schools.

1927, Oct. Dwight W. Morrow appointed ambassador to Mexico.

Dec. By his tact and understanding Morrow secured the amendment of the **Mexican Petroleum Law,** improving markedly relations between the U.S. and Mexico.

1927. Nicola Sacco and Bartolomeo Vanzetti executed for allegedly killing a factory paymaster during a robbery in Braintree, Massachusetts. The trial lasted seven years and represented the culmination of widespread attacks on persons of foreign birth.

1928, Aug. 27. The Pact of Paris (Kellogg Pact) signed.

Nov. Herbert Hoover (Republican) elected president over **Alfred E. Smith** (Democrat) by 444 electoral votes to 87.

1929, Jan. 15. Pact of Paris ratified by the Senate, with the declaration that it did not curtail the country's right of self-defense; that the treaty was not inconsistent with the Monroe Doctrine; and that it did not commit the U.S. to engage in punitive expeditions against aggressor states.

March 4–1933, March 4. HERBERT HOOVER, 31st president.

Oct. STOCK MARKET CRASH, the culmination of the boom market and unrestrained speculation of the Coolidge era. It ushered in a prolonged depression that gradually settled upon the country with increasing unemployment, bank failures, and business disasters.

1930, Jan. 21–April 22. London naval conference, resulting in a three-power treaty signed by the United States, Great Britain, and Japan (p. 646).

March. CLARK MEMORANDUM ON THE MONROE DOCTRINE made public by the State Department. Written by J. Reuben Clark, undersecretary of state two years before, the memorandum declared: 1. The Monroe Doctrine is unilateral. 2. "The Doctrine does not concern itself with purely inter-American relations." 3. "The Doctrine states a case of the United States versus Europe, not of the United States versus Latin America." 4. The United States has always used the doctrine to protect Latin American nations from the aggression of European powers. 5. The Roosevelt corollary is not properly a part of the doctrine itself, nor does it grow out of the doctrine.

June 17. Smoot-Hawley Tariff Act signed by Hoover in spite of protests of more than 1,000 trained economists. Duties higher than ever. This led to widespread reprisals and retaliation by other countries. By the end of 1931 some 25 countries had taken steps to retaliate.

1930. Under the leadership of **Hallie Q. Flannigan,** the **Federal Theater project** staged plays throughout the nation.

1930–32. Federal authorities deported thousands of Mexicans as illegal aliens. At the same time, Puerto Ricans gradually moved to the U.S., particularly New York, adding greater complexity to the Hispanic-American population.

1930–39. Blacks and their white allies campaigned for an **antilynching bill,** which failed passage during the entire period.

1931. Scottsboro case. When nine young blacks faced a summary trial and were sentenced to hang for allegedly raping two white women near **Scottsboro, Alabama,** the **Communist Party** launched an international campaign that blocked the execution of the young men.

June. Debt and reparations moratorium (p. 646).

Wiley Post and Harold Gatty circumnavigated the globe by air in eight days, 15 hours, 51 minutes.

1932, Jan. 7. Stimson Doctrine enunciated by the secretary of state. Stimson, in notes to Japan and China, stated that the U.S. would not "recognize any situation, treaty or agreement which may be brought about by means contrary to the covenants and obligations of the pact of Paris." This was in protest against Japanese occupation of Manchuria.

Feb. Norris Anti-Injunction Act, declaring "yellow-dog" contracts unenforceable before the federal courts, and providing that certain types of activity in labor conflicts should be immune from injunctions. It provided that "no person participating in, or affected by, such disputes shall be enjoined from striking, or from striking for the success of the strike by customary labor-union effort, short of fraud or violence." The immunity extended to all persons "in the same industry, trade, or occupation" rather than merely to employers and their own employees.

Feb. 2. Reconstruction Finance Corporation created with a fund of $500 million and the right to borrow more money, for the purpose of making available government credits to release the frozen assets of financial institutions and to provide aid for the railways.

Nov. Franklin D. Roosevelt (Democrat) elected president over Herbert Hoover (Republican) by 472 electoral votes to 59.

Dec. 15. Default of various European governments in payment of war debts owed to the U.S.

1932. The Communist Party's presidential candidate proposed a Marxist program for transforming American society in the book *Toward Soviet America.*

1933–45. Under **Commissioner John S. Collies,** executive secretary of the **American Indian Defense Association,** the **Bureau of Indian Affairs** emphasized **"autonomy and self-determination"** over the earlier policy of forced assimilation.

1933. Following the suggestions of **Charles S. Johnson** of Fisk University, FDR organized a cluster of black advisers called the **"black cabinet."**

Feb. 6. Twentieth Amendment to the Constitution proclaimed. It provided that after Oct. 15, 1933, senators and representatives should take office on Jan. 3 following the election and that Congress should convene annually on that date. The president and vice president were to take office on Jan. 20, after election.

Feb. 14. Closing of all banks in the state of Michigan gave warning of an impending **banking crisis.** Bank holidays spread from state to state until the climax was reached on the night of March 3.

March 4. FRANKLIN D. ROOSEVELT, 32d president. Banks closed and business virtually at a standstill.

March 6. Banks closed for four days by proclamation of the president, and an embargo was placed on the export of gold in order to protect the gold reserve.

March 9. Congress convened in special session. It legalized the president's action with respect to banks and authorized the comptroller of the currency to take charge of insolvent banks. Within a week after the president's proclamation the sound banks began to reopen.

May 18. The **Tennessee Valley Authority Act** created the Tennessee Valley Authority to maintain and operate Muscle Shoals and to develop the water-power resources of the Tennessee Valley. Also to improve the economic and social status of the valley population.

June 16. The **Emergency Railroad Transportation Act** created a federal coordinator of transportation.

The **National Industrial Recovery Act** created a national recovery administration to supervise the preparation of codes of fair competition and to guarantee to labor the right to organize and bargain collectively; it also made provision for a program of public works. The act was declared unconstitutional by the Supreme Court on May 27, 1935.

Dec. 5. Ratification of the Twenty-first Amendment, repealing the Eighteenth, or Prohibition, Amendment.

1933–36. NEW DEAL AGRICULTURAL LEGISLATION. On May 12, 1933, the **Agricultural Adjustment Act** became law. Its aim was the establishment of the parity for farm products that had existed in the period 1909–14. This was to be achieved through removal of the agricultural surplus by means of compensated crop curtailment, financed through the licensing and taxing of the processors of farm products. Provision was also made for the refinancing of farm mortgages.

The **Farm Credit Act** (approved June 16, 1933). **The Farm Mortgage Refinancing Act** (approved Jan. 31, 1934). **The Farm Mortgage Foreclosure Act** (approved June 12, 1934). **Frazier-Lemke Farm Bankruptcy Act** (approved June 28, 1934). The **Crop Loan Act** (approved Feb. 23, 1934) permitted the Farm Credit Administration to make loans to farmers in 1934 for crop production and harvesting.

The **Cotton Control Act** (approved April 21, 1934) placed the production of cotton on a compulsory rather than a voluntary basis.

The **Jones-Costigan Sugar Act** (approved May 9, 1934) included among the basic crops of the original Agricultural Adjustment Act sugar beets and sugar cane.

Tobacco Control Act (approved June 28, 1934) placed the production of tobacco on a compulsory basis.

The **Frazier-Lemke Farm Bankruptcy Act** was subsequently declared unconstitutional, while on Jan. 6, 1936, the **Agricultural Adjustment Act** met a similar fate. The objective of the latter act was then achieved by the **Soil Conservation Act,** by which farmers were paid for planting soil-conserving crops in lieu of the ordinary staples.

1933–34. NEW DEAL BANKING LEGISLATION. The **Emergency Banking Relief Act** (approved March 9, 1933) gave the president power to regulate transactions in credit, currency, gold and silver, and foreign exchange. It also authorized the secretary of the treasury to require the delivery of all gold and gold certificates, and provided for the appointment of conservators of national banks in difficulties.

The **Banking Act of 1933** (approved June 16, 1933) extended federal reserve open market activities; created the **Federal Bank Deposit Insurance Corporation** to insure deposits; and regulated further the operations of member banks and separated security affiliates.

The **Bank Deposit Insurance Act** (approved June 19, 1934) amended deposit features of the Banking Act and raised the amount eligible for insurance of each depositor to $5,000.

NEW DEAL HOME FINANCING. The **Home Owners' Refinancing Act** (approved June 13, 1933) created the **Home Owners' Loan Corporation** to refinance home mortgages.

The **Home Owners' Loan Act** (approved April 27, 1934) guaranteed the principal of the HOLC's bond issues and permitted loans for repair of dwellings.

NEW DEAL MONETARY LEGISLATION.. The **Gold Repeal Joint Resolution** (approved June 5, 1933) canceled the gold clause in all federal and private obligations and made them payable in legal tender.

The **Gold Reserve Act** (approved Jan. 30, 1934) authorized the president to revalue the dollar at 50–60 cents in terms of its gold content; set up a $2 billion stabilization fund.

The **Silver Purchase Act** (approved June 19, 1934) authorized the president to nationalize silver.

NEW DEAL SECURITIES LEGISLATION.. The **Securities Act of 1933** (approved May 27, 1933) provided for filing with the Federal Trade Commission and for transmission to prospective investors of the fullest possible information, accompanied by sworn statements, about new security issues sold in interstate commerce or through the mails.

The **Securities Exchange Act** (approved June 6, 1934) provided for the regulation of securities exchanges and established the Securities and Exchange Commission.

1933–35. NEW DEAL RELIEF LEGISLATION. The **Federal Emergency Relief Act** (approved May 12, 1933) authorized the RFC to make $500 million available for emergency relief to be expended by the **Federal Emergency Relief Administration** created by the act.

The **Civil-Works Emergency Relief Act** (approved Feb. 15, 1934) appropriated an additional $950 million, available until June 30, 1935, for continuation of the civil-works program and for direct relief purposes under the FERA.

The **Emergency Relief Appropriation Act** of April 8, 1935, was designed to provide relief and work relief and to increase employment by providing for useful projects; it appropriated $4 billion to be used nominally at the president's discretion. It further appropriated unexpended balances of several earlier appropriations aggregating about $880 million.

1933–35. NEW DEAL LABOR LEGISLATION. The **Labor Disputes Joint Resolution** (approved June 19, 1934) abolished the National Labor Board and created a federal agency for the investigation and mediation of labor disputes growing out of the **National Industrial Recovery Act** (NIRA).

The **Railway Pension Act** (approved June 27, 1934) provided a comprehensive retirement system for railway employees based on employer and employee contributions. This act was subsequently declared unconstitutional.

The **Crosser-Dill Railway Labor Act** (approved June 27, 1934) provided for the settlement of labor disputes on the railroads and outlawed company unions.

The **Wagner-Connery Labor Relations Act** of July 5, 1935, was designed to satisfy the complaints of labor organizations against provisions of the Recovery Act of 1933 as it affected them, and also to remedy their disappointment at losing the advantage of these provisions by the invalidation of that act. The act declared it the policy of the U.S. to encourage collective bargaining and to protect employees' freedom of self-organization and their negotiating as to their employment through representatives of their own choosing. New **National Labor Relations Board** created.

OTHER NEW DEAL LEGISLATION. The **Beer-Wine Revenue Act** (approved March 22, 1933) levied a tax of $5 on every barrel of beer and wine manufactured; reenacted portions of the Webb-Kenyon Act as a protection to states whose laws prohibited liquors with alcoholic content in excess of 3.2 percent. The states were left in control of the sale and distribution of liquor.

1933–36. FOREIGN POLICIES of the New Deal. On Nov. 17, 1933, diplomatic **relations with Russia** were resumed, ending the policy of nonrecognition which had prevailed since the overthrow of the Kerensky government in 1917.

The **Johnson Debt Default Act** (approved April 13, 1934) prohibited financial transactions with foreign governments in default in payment of obligations to the U.S.

The **Cuban Treaty** (ratified May 31, 1934) abrogated the Platt Amendment.

Pan-American conference, convened at Buenos Aires on Dec. 1, 1936, was addressed by President Roosevelt in person, who outlined his American peace program. Secretary Hull presented the plan for a neutrality pact for American nations.

1934. Dennis Chavez of New Mexico, the only Hispanic in the U.S. Senate, served as an adviser to FDR on Hispanic affairs.

June 12. Reciprocal Tariff Act, authorizing the president, for a period of three years, to negotiate trade agreements with foreign countries without the advice and consent of the Senate; gave the president the power to raise and lower tariff rates by not more than 50 percent.

June 19. The **Communications Act** created the Federal Communications Commission to regulate interstate and foreign communications by telegraph, telephone, cable, and radio. It abolished the Federal Radio Commission and transferred its functions, and those of the Interstate Commerce Commission, with respect to telephone and telegraph, to the new commission.

1935. Eleanor Roosevelt championed minority and women's rights in the White House and lobbied extensively on their behalf. Partly under her influence, FDR appointed **Francis Perkins secretary of labor,** the first woman to hold a cabinet-level post.

Aug. 9. The **Motor Carrier Act** placed interstate bus and truck lines under control of the Interstate Commerce Commission.

Aug. 14. Social Security Act. Its primary objects were: (1) to provide, in cooperation with each of the states, systems in the states for the payment of support to the needy aged; (2) to pay sums to persons during limited periods after their loss of employment. Provision was also made for federal aid toward states' aid for needy, dependent children, for crippled children, for neglected children, for the vocational rehabilitation of the disabled, for health-service agencies, and for the blind. The purpose of the old-age pensions was to be effected in the first instance by the government's matching states' allowance to needy persons over the age of 65 years, up to $15 a month for each case. A tax on employees and a tax at an equal rate on the payrolls of employers was to be levied starting in 1937 at 1 percent, and rising by steps to 3 percent in 1949, to provide a fund out of which, not before Jan. 1, 1942, qualified employees retiring at 65 would receive to the end of their lives payments of from $10 to $15 per month.

To help states pay allowances to persons losing employment the act created a separate tax of 1 percent the first year, 2 percent the second, and 3 percent the third and thereafter, on employers' payrolls, starting with the payrolls of 1936.

Aug. 26. Public Utility Holding Company Act. Purpose: (1) doing away with holding companies among the public-utility enterprises serving communities with electricity except where such companies might be needful; (2) regulating the relations of remaining holding companies and their relations with the subsidiary companies that they controlled. The **Federal Power Commission** was made the administrative agency for these purposes. It was charged to proceed after Jan. 1, 1938, to limit each holding company system to a single integrated public-utility system, save for minor and appropriate transgressions of the exact limit.

Aug. 30. Guffey-Snyder Bituminous Coal Stabilization Act. Provisions of the act followed in great measure those of the bituminous coal code under the NRA. A national Bituminous Coal Commission was created to administer the act, particularly to establish a code for the industry, embodying mandatory features detailed in the law obliging employers to accept labor organizations and negotiate with representatives of the employees' own choosing. Declared unconstitutional in May 1936.

Wealth-Tax Act. Use of federal power of taxation as a weapon against "unjust concentration of wealth and economic power." Increased surtaxes on individual yearly incomes of $50,000 and over.

1936, Nov. 3. Franklin D. Roosevelt reelected president over **Alfred M. Landon** (Republican) by 524 electoral votes to 7. He carried every state except Maine and Vermont.

1937, Jan. 20. FRANKLIN D. ROOSEVELT inaugurated for second term.

Jan.–June. Widespread labor troubles resulting from efforts of the CIO to organize the workers in the automobile and steel industries on the basis of industrial unionism. The **sit-down strike** made its appearance in the General Motors strike as a weapon of labor. The strike spread to Chrysler Corp. employees and to those of the Republic Steel Corp., the Youngstown Sheet Steel and Tube Co., the Inland Steel Co., and the Bethlehem Steel Corp. A strike among workers of the U.S. Steel Corp. was avoided when the company signed a contract with the CIO on March 2. The strike of the employees of the Republic Steel Corp. resulted in bloodshed. Although the sit-down strikes and the aggressiveness of the CIO in this period seriously divided public opinion, labor, through the application of the collective-bargaining provisions of the Wagner Labor Relations Act by the National Labor Relations Board, made substantial progress in the unionization of the mass-production industries, where the principle of collective bargaining had never before been admitted by employers.

Feb. 5. President Roosevelt in a special message to Congress recommended the enactment of legislation empowering him to appoint **"additional judges in all federal courts without exception, where there are incumbent judges of retirement age who do not choose to resign."** This proposal aroused widespread opposition in and out of Congress as an attempt on the part of the president to "pack" the **U.S. Supreme Court,** whose adverse decisions on various items of New Deal legislation had greatly displeased Roosevelt. After months of debate and controversy the bill failed of enactment, due largely to opposition by members of the president's own party in the Senate.

April 26. The president signed the **Guffey-Vinson Act,** successor to the Bituminous Coal Stabilization Act of 1935, largely invalidated by the Supreme Court. The act created a **Bituminous Coal Commission,** to administer a code covering "unfair" practices, fixing minimum and, in some cases, maximum prices for coal, and dealing with arrangements for marketing.

May. Neutrality Act, reaffirming and somewhat enlarging statutes of Aug. 1935 and Feb. 1936. Whenever the president proclaimed a state of war outside of the Americas, the export of arms and munitions to the belligerents was to be prohibited. Certain materials designated by the president would have to be paid for before leaving the U.S., and would have to be carried in foreign ships. All other trade with the combatants was subject to the cash, but not to the carry, restriction. In addition the act prohibited American citizens from traveling on belligerents' ships and barred loans to warring powers.

Sept. 2. President Roosevelt signed the **Wagner-Steagall Act,** declaring a federal policy of employing government funds and credit to help states and their subdivisions to remedy the housing shortage.

Oct. A **business recession,** the gradual onset of which had been evident for several months, brought sharp declines in the stock market.

By November the recession had become general throughout the country.

1938, Oct. 24. Wages and Hours Law became operative. It provided for minimum wages and maximum weekly hours in industries affecting interstate commerce; it also prohibited child labor.

Nov. 8. State and congressional elections, showing substantial Republican gains for first time since 1928.

1939. John Steinbeck published his renowned novel *The Grapes of Wrath.*

Jan. 12. President Roosevelt asked Congress for $552 million for defense. Preparations were made for extensive fortifications in the Pacific and in the Caribbean (Puerto Rico and Virgin Islands). More and more openly the president expressed the sympathies of the U.S. for the European democracies. France was permitted to buy large numbers of military planes, and the U.S. government itself embarked upon construction of 600 additional airplanes. After German annexation of Czechoslovakia the United States refused to recognize the change and imposed countervailing duties on imports from Germany.

April 15. The danger of a German-Polish conflict led to **Roosevelt's letter to Mussolini and Hitler** asking for assurances that they would refrain from aggression against 31 named nations (p. 679).

June. King George VI and Queen Elizabeth paid a four-day visit to the U.S., the first reigning European sovereigns to set foot on American soil.

Despite all efforts of the administration, Congress refused to modify the **Neutrality Act,** which provided for an embargo on arms to belligerents. The president publicly stated that, indirectly at least, the Neutrality Act constituted an encouragement to a would-be aggressor. Then, in August, the German-Polish conflict came to a head (p. 679). Roosevelt appealed to Victor Emmanuel, Hitler, and Moscicki, but without avail. The American government secured from the belligerents a promise not to bombard open cities.

Sept. 5. Upon the outbreak of the Second World War the U.S. announced its neutrality.

Nov. 4. The Neutrality Act (p. 731) was amended, repealing the embargo on arms and placing exports to belligerents on a cash and carry basis.

1940s. Nearly 300,000 women served in the armed forces. They took advantage of the new policies that accepted female volunteers as enlisted personnel and officers.

1940, June 22. The Congress passed a **National Defense Tax Bill** to produce $994,300,000 a year, and raised the national debt limit from $45 billion to $49 billion.

June 28. The Republican National Convention at Philadelphia nominated **Wendell L. Willkie** and **Charles L. McNary** as candidates for the presidency and vice presidency.

July 18. The Democratic National Convention at Chicago nominated **Franklin D. Roosevelt** as presidential candidate for a third term, and **Henry A. Wallace** as candidate for vice president.

July 20. President Roosevelt signed a bill providing for a **"two-ocean"** navy as part of a vast defense plan.

Sept. 16. The **Selective Training and Service Act** was adopted. The act provided for the **registration of all men between the ages of 21 and 36 years** of age, and for the training, for one year, of 1.2 million troops and 800,000 reserves. On Oct. 16, 16.4 million men were registered, and the draft lottery commenced on Oct. 29.

Sept. 26. President Roosevelt placed an **embargo on the export of scrap iron and steel.**

Nov. 5. FRANKLIN D. ROOSEVELT WAS REELECTED PRESIDENT for a third term.

1941–42. U.S. secretary of war removed about 120,000 Japanese citizens as well as noncitizens from the West Coast to detention camps in seven states of the Rocky Mountains region. Evacuees were forced to leave behind valuable property and endured the deprivation of their civil and human rights. The U.S. Supreme Court sanctioned the use of racial criteria and the removal process in *Hirabayashi* v. *U.S.* (1943) and *Korematsu* v. *U.S.* (1943), but modified its decision in ex parte *Endo* in Dec. 1944. Still, Japanese Americans remained interned until Jan. 1945.

1941. African Americans formed a March on Washington movement and demanded an end to racial discrimination in defense industries. Fear-

ing an interruption of the war effort, FDR issued **Executive Order 8802,** establishing the **Fair Employment Practices Committee.** Nearly a million blacks served in the armed forces during World War II. They made up about 10 percent of all service men and women.

Native Americans supported the war effort by contributing to Red Cross campaigns, and in the case of the six nations of the Iroquois Confederacy, in New York, declaring war on the Axis powers. Moreover, nearly 30,000 Native Americans joined the armed forces. A special unit of Navajos gained widespread recognition when they used their language to develop secret communications that confused the Japanese.

Mexican Americans gained defense jobs in growing numbers and also joined the armed forces in disproportionately large numbers. As recognition of the increasing importance of Hispanic Americans, FDR appointed **Carlos Castaneda** of the University of Texas to serve as special assistant on Latin American affairs and as assistant to the chairman of the Fair Employment Practices Committee. The **Spanish-speaking people's division of the Office of Inter-American Affairs** also worked to ease discrimination against Hispanic Americans.

Jan. 8. President Roosevelt appointed a four-person **Office of Production Management** to coordinate defense activities.

March 11. The Congress passed the **Lend-Lease Act,** empowering the president to provide goods and services to those nations whose defense he deemed vital to the defense of the U.S.

May 27. President Roosevelt proclaimed an unlimited state of national emergency.

June 16. The government ordered German consulates throughout the country closed. Three days later the German and Italian governments asked that U.S. consulates in Axis-controlled areas of Europe be closed.

Aug. 14. THE ATLANTIC CHARTER. President Roosevelt and Prime Minister Churchill, representing the United States and Great Britain, issued a joint declaration of peace aims. They announced that their countries sought no aggrandizement, desired no territorial changes contrary to the wishes of the people concerned, respected the right of nations to choose their form of government, and wished to see sovereign rights and self-government restored to peoples who had been forcibly deprived of them. They likewise favored equality of economic opportunity with access to essential raw materials for all nations; they sought to promote friendly collaboration among the peoples of the world, fair labor standards, social security, freedom from fear and want, free traverse on the high seas, the abandonment of force, and the disarmament of aggressor nations.

Aug. 18. President Roosevelt signed a bill permitting the army to keep men in service 18 months longer.

Sept. 20. A revenue measure designed to provide for **defense expenditures** of $3,553,400,000 became law.

Sept. 24. Fifteen governments (nine in exile) **endorsed the Atlantic Charter.**

Nov. 6. The U.S. extended a $1 billion lend-lease credit to the Soviet Union.

Nov. 10. The National Defense Mediation Board ruled against John L. Lewis and the United Mine Workers of America in the captive coal-mine dispute, but the UMW soon won a closed-shop agreement (Dec. 7).

Dec. 2. President Roosevelt asked the government of Japan for a definition of its aims in Indochina and appealed (Dec. 6) to Emperor Hirohito to help in preserving peace.

Dec. 7. THE JAPANESE OPENED HOSTILITIES with a surprise attack on Hawaii, the Philippines, Guam, Midway Island, Hong Kong, and Malaya.

Dec. 8. THE U.S. CONGRESS DECLARED A STATE OF WAR WITH JAPAN.

Dec. 11. GERMANY AND ITALY DECLARED WAR ON THE UNITED STATES.

Dec. 15. Congress voted an appropriation of $10,077,077,005 for the defense of the U.S. and for lend-lease aid. Four days later it **extended the draft** for military service to men from 20 to 44 years of age.

1942. Although **defense industries and training programs initially barred women,** by mid-1942 most companies reversed their policies and accepted women workers in growing numbers. **By war's end more than**

2 million women worked in heavy industries. At the same time, as the number of men enrolled in colleges dropped, the number of women gaining access to higher education also increased.

Jan. 13. Donald M. Nelson became chief of the War Production Board, created to speed the armament program.

Jan. 30. President Roosevelt signed the **Price Control Act,** which was intended to limit inflation.

Feb. 10. President Roosevelt established as a wartime measure a **minimum 48-hour work week** for areas where there was a labor shortage.

April 4. The **War Production Board** halted all nonessential building in order to conserve materials.

April 27. President Roosevelt proposed that the American people **combat inflation** by a seven-point program: (1) heavier taxes, (2) a ceiling on prices, (3) wage stabilization, (4) price control on agricultural products, (5) increased purchase of war bonds, (6) the rationing of essential commodities if scarce, and (7) reduction of installment buying.

May 29. The **Office of War Mobilization,** directed by James F. Byrnes, became the supreme federal agency for the prosecution of the war effort on the home front.

June 26. The **Smith-Connally Anti-Strike Bill** made anyone who instigated or aided in promoting strikes in government-operated plants or mines subject to criminal penalties.

June 30. The Congress voted a **record appropriation of $42 billion** for the defense of the U.S.

July 16. The **War Labor Board** decreed that in the interest of **wage stabilization,** wage increases would be granted equivalent to the rise in living costs between Jan. 1, 1941, and May 1942. This was known as the **Little Steel Award.**

Oct. 3. James F. Byrnes was appointed Director of the **Office of Economic Stabilization.**

Oct. 12. Attorney General **Francis Biddle** announced that 600,000 **unnaturalized Italians** in the U.S. would no longer be classed as enemy aliens.

Nov. 8. U.S. **FORCES LANDED IN FRENCH NORTH AFRICA** (p. 806).

1943. Beginning of **baby boom.** Birth rates began to rise in middle-class families, to over three children per family. Concomitant **reduction in average marriage age.**

June. The "zoot suit" riots. A group of sailors from the Chavez Ravene Naval Base attacked **Hispanic and black youths.** The violence involved over 1,000 youths and lasted two days before it subsided; similar attacks on the so-called zoot-suiters occurred in San Diego, Long Beach, Chicago, Detroit, and Philadelphia.

June 23. Detroit race riot. Twenty-five blacks and whites died in the riot. The conflict required nearly 6,000 National Guardsmen before order was restored. **Two months later race riots erupted in New York City,** which resulted in the deaths of six blacks and more than 300 injuries.

July 16. The **Office of Economic Warfare** superseded the Board of Economic Warfare and assumed some functions of the Reconstruction Finance Corporation. Later (Sept. 25) the new organ was named the **Foreign Economic Administration.**

Aug. 11–24. Quebec Conference of Prime Minister Churchill and President Roosevelt (p. 805).

Nov. 28–Dec. 1. TEHRAN CONFERENCE (p. 810).

1944, June 6. INVASION OF NORMANDY (p. 807).

July 21. Franklin D. Roosevelt was nominated for a **fourth term** as president of the United States by the Democratic National Convention at Chicago. **Harry S. Truman** was named candidate for vice president. They won the subsequent election of Nov. 7.

Nov. 27. Cordell Hull resigned as secretary of state and was succeeded by Edward R. Stettinius.

1945, Feb. 7–12. YALTA CONFERENCE (p. 807).

April 12. PRESIDENT ROOSEVELT DIED SUDDENLY at Warm Springs. Vice President Truman became president.

May 18. President Truman informed the French ambassador that the U.S. **would relinquish part of the American zone of occupation in Germany to the French.**

Aug. 6. The U.S. military dropped an atomic bomb on Hiroshima, Japan, on orders of President Truman. On Aug. 9, a second bomb dropped, on Nagasaki, Japan (p. 809). **The Japanese accepted terms on Aug. 14.**

Nov.–1946, March. Large-scale strikes in several leading industries, after seriously curtailing production, led to a first round of wage increases.

Dec. 4. The Senate approved U.S. **participation in the United Nations.** *(To p. 916)*

2. THE DOMINION OF CANADA

(From p. 621)

As in the U.S., the interwar years accelerated the urban industrial transformation of Canadian society. Mobilization of resources to address the demands of World War I, the Great Depression, and World War II all increased the role of the government in Canadian life. In 1931 Canada broke its ties to imperial Great Britain and gained an independent place in the new commonwealth. The emergence of Canada as a significant world power during these years, however, was fraught with difficulties. Before the nation could consolidate its position as an independent actor in world affairs, it came increasingly under the influence of the U.S. As early as the 1920s, American companies like Ford, Chrysler, and General Motors dominated the Canadian automobile industry, which produced the second largest number of cars during the period and became a major exporter. The depression and two world wars also revealed the persistence of deep regional, class, and cultural divisions within the nation. During both world wars, Anglo-Canadians imposed conscription policies, which French Canadians fiercely resisted. Despite the enfranchisement of women and the increasing democratization of the Canadian polity during the period, women remained subordinated to men in the political economy; workers faced hostile opposition to their efforts to organize until government recognition of their right to collective bargaining occurred in 1944; and ethnic and racial groups faced stiff patterns of antagonism, including the rise of Canadian chapters of the American-based Ku Klux Klan during the 1920s and the removal of Japanese Canadians from the west coast to designated inland areas during World War II.

1914. Nationalization of the Canadian Northern Railway forced by fear of imminent failure and a collapse of national credit. The **Grand Trunk Railway** was nationalized in 1920. The government operated about 23,000 miles of railway representing a capital investment of $1,652,000,000, known as **Canadian National Railways.** Gradual coordination of lines occurred. Sir Henry Thornton appointed in 1922 as the nonpolitical head of the system.

Aug. 4. Entrance of Great Britain into the First World War. Message of Canada to the mother country: **"If unhappily war should ensue, the Canadian people will be united . . . to maintain the honor of the empire"** (Aug. 2). Special session of Parliament called (Aug. 18) and a war budget voted. Thirty thousand volunteers embarked for England by the end of September.

1915, Dec. 3. Internal war loan of $50 million subscribed twice over; others for $100 million (1916) and $150 million (1917) were also oversubscribed.

The **Imperial Munitions Board** set up under the direction of businessman **Joseph Flavelle** (1858–1939).

1916, Feb. 3–4. The Parliament buildings in Ottawa destroyed by fire.

Nov. 11. The DUKE OF DEVONSHIRE, governor-general.

1917, Sept. 26. Compulsory Military Service Act became law, conscripting men between ages of 20 and 45.

Oct. 6. Parliament dissolved and a **coalition cabinet** formed. The Liberal Party was split, with **Sir Wilfrid Laurier** opposing conscription. **French Canadians** were dissatisfied with conscription and with English-language requirements in the schools and failed to enlist. The elections (Dec. 17) resulted in a sweeping victory for the coalition; Quebec was unrepresented in the cabinet.

Dec. 6. Explosion in Halifax harbor, with heavy loss of life and destruction of property.

Wartime Elections Act. The new **Union government** ensured support of the war by Anglo-Canadians without French Canadian participation.

National Hockey League created from the **National Hockey Association.**

1918, March. Woman Franchise Bill passed, extending the federal vote to all women over 21 years of age.

April. Riots in Quebec due to enforcement of conscription; several civilians killed.

Nov. 11. Armistice declared (see World War I). Canada had supplied 640,886 men for the war; cost to Canada, over $1.5 billion.

1919, Feb. 17. Death of Sir Wilfrid Laurier.

May 15. The Winnipeg General Strike. Strikers closed down city services. Violence erupted when Mounties on horseback met the strikers, leaving two dead and injuring many others.

1920, May 10. Official announcement that Canada would be represented in Washington by a Canadian resident minister; **new international status;** no appointment made until 1926, but treaties with the U.S. on North Pacific halibut fisheries (March 1923), and for mutual assistance to prevent smuggling (June 6, 1924), both signed by a Canadian official (Ernest La Pointe).

July 10. Resignation of Sir Robert Borden. **Arthur Meighen** prime minister.

Urbanization. Over 50 percent of Canadians now lived in urban centers.

1921, Aug. 11. Arrival of **Lord Byng of Vimy** as governor-general (1921–26).

Dec. 6. General elections resulting in Liberal (opposition) victory. **W. L. Mackenzie King** prime minister.

1923. Redistribution Bill increasing seats in House of Commons from 235 to 245, with the loss of two seats by the eastern provinces and the gain of 12 by the western.

1924, March 21. A liquor treaty between Great Britain and the United States was ratified by the Dominion House of Commons, and on April 4 by the Senate.

Communist Party legalized.

1925, Oct. 29. National elections. Liberal platform called for an adequate but moderate tariff, the reform of the Senate, a strong immigration policy, government steps to develop the foreign trade of the Dominion, completion of the Hudson's Bay Railway, and the reduction of grain rates. Conservatives advocated higher tariff. Liberals had 101 seats in the House of Commons, Conservatives 118, Progressives 23, Labor 2, Independent 1. The Progressives held the balance of power.

1926. King maintained a precarious hold on the government until June 28, when he resigned because of customs scandal. **Arthur Meighen** then organized a cabinet that was defeated on the first government measure placed before Parliament.

Sept. 14. National elections. Liberals had 119 seats, but not a majority.

Sept. 25. Liberal cabinet, with King as prime minister.

Oct. 2. Lord Willingdon, new governor-general, came into office.

Nov. 10. Vincent Massey appointed **first Canadian minister to Washington.**

1927, Feb. William Phillips appointed **American minister to Ottawa.**

Nov. 15. Election of Canada to a seat on the **council of the League of Nations.**

1928. Appointment of **Canadian diplomatic representatives to Japan** and **France,** further evidence of Canadian nationhood. Proposal made that a British diplomatic representative to Ottawa be appointed since the governor-general was merely the personal representative of the king.

1929, April 9. Canadian minister in Washington protested the sinking of the Canadian ship *I'm Alone* in the Gulf of Mexico by a U.S. Coast Guard Prohibition patrol boat. On April 25 it was announced the case would be settled by arbitration.

Growing irritation in Canada at the threat of hostile American tariff legislation against Canadian agricultural products.

Dec. 15. Agreement between Dominion government and the governments of **Alberta** and **Manitoba,** subject to ratification by Dominion Parliament and provincial legislatures, providing for return of natural resources to the two provinces and for continuation of the annual subsidies previously received by the provinces.

The U.S.-based **Ku Klux Klan** had spread to Canada, with over 125 local chapters in Saskatchawan.

1930, May 2. Dunning tariff became effective; most drastic tariff revision since 1907. Gave expression to uneasiness and resentment aroused in Canada by the high duties on Canadian articles in the Smoot-Hawley tariff of the U.S. Imports from Great Britain given preferential treatment.

July 28. National election. Basic issue the economic depression and the failure of the Liberal government to provide a policy for relief of unemployment. Conservatives had 139 seats, a clear majority. **Richard B. Bennett** and the Conservative cabinet took office on Aug. 7.

Sept. 8–22. Special session of Parliament to enact emergency unemployment and tariff legislation. Public works appropriation of $20 million voted as an unemployment relief measure, supplemented by a similar amount from the provinces, substantial contributions by the municipalities, and $521 million by the railways, making a total of between $80 million and $90 million available for expenditure within the next 12–18 months. Tariff duties increased on about 125 classes of goods, including textiles, shoes, paper, agricultural implements, cast-iron pipe, fertilizers, electrical apparatus, jewelry, and meats.

Oct. 1. Transfer of natural resources to Alberta and Manitoba.

1931. In accordance with the decision of the federal-provincial conference held in Ottawa, on April 7 and 8, the **statute of Westminster** (p. 681) stipulated that the British North America Act should remain unchanged. The statute of Westminster, providing that laws of the United Kingdom do not apply to any dominion unless that dominion so requests, was adopted by Parliament without a division.

June 18. Tariff of 1930 revised upward. It was estimated that the new duties would cut off two-thirds of the goods previously imported from the U.S.

1932, July 21–Aug. 21. IMPERIAL ECONOMIC CONFERENCE IN OTTAWA. Seven bilateral treaties signed by Great Britain, one of them being with Canada, gave raw material of the Dominion a preference of about 10 percent in the British market. The U.K. imposed new duties on wheat and other imports in order to give dominions this preference. British preferential tariffs also imposed on foreign meat, butter, cheese, fruit, and eggs. For Canada's benefit, Great Britain removed the restriction on Canadian live cattle, placed a tariff of four cents on copper, and promised that the 10 percent ad valorem tariff on foreign timber, fish, asbestos, zinc, and lead would not be reduced unless Canada agreed. In return, Great Britain received concessions on manufactured goods entering Canada. Canada also signed new treaties with South Africa, Rhodesia, and the Irish Free State, and began the revision of existing treaties with Australia and New Zealand.

Formation of the **Canadian Radio Broadcasting Commission** (name changed to **Canadian Broadcasting Corporation** in 1936).

1933. Railway legislation embodying the recommendations of the royal commission in the report of Sept. 1932. Three trustees for CNR and cooperation between it and the Canadian Pacific.

May 12. Trade agreement with France signed, going into effect on June 10. It provided for reciprocal tariff preferences on 1,148 items.

Aug. 25. Canada joined in **wheat agreement** with the U.S., Argentina, Australia, and the Soviet Union. The countries agreed to export a maximum of 560 million bushels for 1933–34, and, except for the Soviet Union and Danubian states, promised to reduce either acreage or exports by 15 percent.

1934, July 3. The **Natural Products Marketing Act** assented to. It provided for the creation of a Dominion marketing board with powers to form local boards and to cooperate with marketing boards created by the provinces; and it authorized the regulated marketing of any natural products, control by license of the export of any regulated products, and control of interprovincial marketing.

Aug. 4. Henry H. Stevens, minister of trade and commerce, in a privately printed pamphlet, made revelations that transformed widespread popular demands for governmental action to alleviate the depression into a demand for regulation of big business in Canada. Stevens resigned his cabinet position on Oct. 27.

Oct. 1. The **Dominion Companies Act** went into force. It repealed the Companies Act of 1927 and established stringent regulations safeguarding the security of investors, shareholders, and creditors.

1935, Jan. Prime Minister R. B. Bennett announced his Canadian version of the U.S. **New Deal.**

March 11. The **Bank of Canada** opened its doors, making effective the **Bank of Canada Act of 1934.** This privately owned but government-supervised institution served as a central bank.

Prime Minister Bennett early in the year proposed a **platform of social legislation** as the only means of escaping defeat in the face of growing popular dissatisfaction. Before adjourning on July 5, Parliament enacted a comprehensive series of laws designed to cope with the economic situation. Among them were: the **Wheat Board Act,** establishing a board to buy wheat at a fixed minimum price, the government to absorb the loss if the board failed to sell the wheat at a profit over the fixed minimum; an act providing for a **Dominion trade and industry commission** to administer the **Combines Investigation Act,** prohibiting monopolies operating to the detriment of the public; the **Fair Wages and Hours of Labor Act,** guaranteeing fair wages on public works and a 44-hour week; the **Employment and Social Insurance Act,** providing for contributory unemployment insurance for workers receiving less than $2,000 per year, with certain industries excepted, equal premiums to be paid by employers, employees, and the federal government; the **Minimum Wage Act,** authorizing the establishment of a federal agency to fix minimum wages in manufacturing and commerce; the **Limitation of Hours of Work Act** providing for an eighthour day and a 48-hour week for industrial workers.

Aug. 14. **Dissolution of Parliament** and call for general election.

Aug. 22. Victory of the Social Credit Party in Alberta, under the leadership of **William Aberhart,** promising to every adult citizen of the province a regular income of $25 per month, funds for which were to be provided by a turnover tax of about 10 percent on domestic products. Death blow to Alberta's credit.

Oct. 14. General election. A **Liberal landslide** gave Liberals 171 seats, with eight seats held by independent Liberals who would ordinarily support the party.

Oct. 23. King prime minister for third time.

Nov. 15. Prime Minister King signed in Washington the **reciprocal trade agreement with the U.S.** The treaty granted Canada lower rates or other concessions on two-thirds of its exports by volume to the U.S. The U.S., in turn, received concessions on three-fourths of its dutiable exports to Canada.

Dec. 9–13. Conference of federal and provincial governments agreed unanimously that it was "imperative" to amend the Constitution, and that Canada should have the power to amend its own Constitution.

1936, June 17. Supreme Court of Canada invalidated most of "New Deal" legislation enacted by the Bennett government in 1935.

Canada only country in the Commonwealth to give Hitler a Nazi salute at the **Berlin Olympic games.**

1937, Jan. 28. The Judicial Committee of the Privy Council in London, England, declared unconstitutional the bulk of the "New Deal" legislation of the Bennett government, sustaining the decision of the Supreme Court of Canada.

April. The **demand of the CIO for recognition of the local branch** of the National Automobile Workers Association (an affiliate of the CIO) in the Oshawa, Ontario, plant of the General Motors Corp. led to a **sitdown strike.** More than 4,000 workers struck for an 8-hour day, higher wages, and better working conditions. Premier Hepburn of Ontario intervened, denounced the CIO, and brought about an agreement (April 23) granting concessions to workers on wages and working conditions but withholding recognition of the NAWA.

The Dominion minister of justice announced (March 24) that the sit-down strike was wholly illegal in Canada and that all the powers of the government would be used to prevent its use in the Dominion.

Aug. 15. Prime Minister Mackenzie King appointed a royal commission (Rowell Commission) to study **amendment of the British North America Act,** which now seemed imperative in view of the court decisions on social and economic legislation. The commission was charged specifically to consider the economic and financial relations between the federal and provincial governments, but was given wide powers to investigate all phases of the confederation.

1939, May. Visit of King George VI and Queen Elizabeth to Canada. They were the first reigning sovereigns to visit the Dominion and were given an enthusiastic reception.

Sept. 3. Britain's declaration of war on Germany (p. 679) brought forth expressions of solidarity in Canada, and the government at once took steps to aid the mother country in the great conflict.

Sept. 10. Canada followed the British action of Sept. 3 and DECLARED WAR ON GERMANY.

1940, March 26. The **Liberal Party** won a decided victory in the Canadian elections.

1941, Dec. 8. CANADA DECLARED WAR ON JAPAN. The government soon relocated Japanese Canadians to the interior of British Columbia.

1942, Nov. 8. Canada severed relations with the French Vichy regime on the grounds that there no longer existed in France any government with effective independent existence.

1945, June 11. National elections held a **majority for Prime Minister Mackenzie King's Liberal Party,** thus endorsing the government's conduct of the war. The Progressive Conservatives came out second, and the Co-operative Commonwealth Federation (Socialist) third.

(To p. 928)

3. NEWFOUNDLAND

(From p. 622)

1917. Resignation of Premier Sir Edward Morris, who was succeeded by **Sir William F. Lloyd.**

1919, May 23. Michael P. Cashin, premier. Elections (Nov. 1) resulted in the overthrow of the Cashin ministry, and **Sir Richard A. Squires** became premier.

1923. William R. Warren, premier.

Dec. 26. Grave **charges of misappropriation of funds** brought against Sir Richard Squires and others (later acquitted) by Premier Warren. Warren was defeated in the assembly following the arrest of Squires (April 22, 1924), and he resigned. He was succeeded by **Walter Munroe.**

1933. NEWFOUNDLAND LOST ITS STATUS AS A DOMINION, reverting to that of a crown colony because of debt resulting from incompetence and corruption. A **royal commission** (appointed in March) reported (Nov.) the following **recommendations:** (1) Replacement of the existing form of government by a special commission consisting of three British representatives and three Newfoundlanders, with the

governor as president. This commission was to have legal and executive authority subject to the supervisory control of the British government. (2) Readjustment and lowering of tariffs. (3) Assumption by the United Kingdom of responsibility for Newfoundland finances until the island should become self-supporting. These recommendations were approved by the Newfoundland Parliament on Nov. 29 and received the royal assent on Dec. 21.

1934. Substantial progress toward economic and financial recovery.

Oct. 1. The commission announced that on Jan. 1, 1935, import duties would be revised, generally downward.

1936–37. The commission continued to devote itself to the problem of **economic rehabilitation,** giving particular attention to the development of alternative sources of employment, to the encouragement of subsistence farming, to the relief of poverty, and to the improvement of medical and educational facilities.

E. LATIN AMERICA AND THE CARIBBEAN, 1914–1945

1. OVERVIEW

Though most Latin American nations, at the suggestion of the U.S. government, either declared war on Germany or broke off diplomatic relations, they played no part militarily in World War I. Nevertheless, the war period was important for the entire region because the demand for raw materials made a **phenomenal expansion of trade** possible. Except for the slump of 1920–21, this expansion continued from 1916 to 1929. It was accompanied by **large capital investments**, especially by the U.S. after the war, and by the emergence of local industries in the more developed countries. In spite of this growth, Latin America's **dependence on exports came increasingly under attack** during these years. The liberal export model of development had already led to major crises in Mexico, and by the 1920s **growing numbers of nationalists** throughout the region were questioning the social and economic costs of the export boom. Nationalists believed that too many of the benefits of economic progress had gone into foreign hands, and that it was time to reassert national control over the wealth and resources of the region.

The population of Latin America more than doubled from the turn of the century to 1940, reaching a total of 126 million. The influx of European immigrants and, after 1930, the growing wave of internal migrants expanded the political and economic weight of the cities. **Emerging urban middle classes** struggled against the great landholders and oligarchic elites for control of national governments. At the same time, the efforts of the rural workers, or campesinos (on coffee, sugar, and other plantations), were reinforced by those of workers from the oil fields, mines, and factories. These groups demanded **social legislation** to protect their interests, and sought to organize the lower classes (in many instances in alliance with the middle classes, at least for a time). **Left-wing political parties,** drawing their support from these dissatisfied groups, became an important political force in the region. These parties were often very nationalistic, and in some cases began to support the cause of **women's suffrage.** Between 1914 and 1945 women gained the vote in eight Latin American countries. These basic social issues fermented throughout the continent, the world depression after 1929 further stimulating unrest.

Among the Latin American states and between Latin America and the U.S. cooperation along various lines increased, interrupted by moments of profound distrust between Latin America and its neighbor to the north. Despite Nazi propaganda campaigns prior to and during World War II, most Latin American nations severed diplomatic relations with the Axis powers. With the exception of Argentina, Latin American nations contributed to the Allied war effort.

(To p. 931)

a. REGIONAL DIPLOMACY

1915, May 24. The first **Pan-American financial conference** met in Washington.

   May 25. Conclusion of an **arbitration treaty among Argentina, Brazil, and Chile** (the ABC powers).

1916, April 3. A **Pan-American high commission,** meeting in Buenos Aires, worked out a scheme for improvement of telegraph and railway communication. A permanent high commission was created to elaborate uniform commercial laws.

1923, March–May. The **fourth Pan-American conference** at Santiago resulted in accords providing for fact-finding commissions in cases of disputes, in addition to many resolutions touching health, education, etc.

   May 3. Signature of the Pan-American Treaty for the pacific settlement of disputes.

1928, Jan.–Feb. The **sixth Pan-American conference** met at Havana. The Pan-American Union was placed on a treaty basis, and various conferences arranged for matters of common interest. The U.S., however, opposed a resolution directed against intervention in the internal affairs of other states.

1928, Dec.–1929, Jan. The **Pan-American conference on conciliation** and arbitration met in Washington, revised the treaty of May 3, 1924, declared for conciliation and arbitration of all disputes, and set up commissions to deal with cases as they should arise.

1930, Sept. Meeting of the **first Pan-American conference on agriculture** in Washington.

1933. Seventh Pan-American conference, in Montevideo. Secretary of State Hull did his utmost to remove distrust of the U.S. and impress upon the American states the need for confidence and collaboration.

1936, Dec. 1–23. Pan-American conference (p. 731) for the maintenance of peace, in session at Buenos Aires. This conference marked the end of unilateral intervention by the U.S. in Latin America (Good Neighbor Policy). The American governments for the first time accepted the principle of consultation in case the peace of the continent should be threatened. A convention was drawn up to provide for a common policy of neutrality in the event of conflict between American states.

1938, Dec. 24. The Pan-American conference, meeting in Lima (21 states represented), adopted the Declaration of Lima, which reaffirmed the absolute sovereignty of the various American states, but also expressed their determination to defend themselves against "all foreign intervention or activities that may threaten them." It provided further for consultation in case the "peace, security, or territorial integrity" of any state should be menaced. The declaration was a reflection of growing uneasiness, especially in the U.S., over possible designs of the European Fascist powers upon Latin American territory.

1939, Oct. 2. The Pan-American conference proclaimed a **safety zone** around the Western Hemisphere (p. 803).

1942, Jan. 15. In Rio, the Pan-American conference discussed possible joint action against aggression.

1945, Feb. 21. The Inter-American conference, at a meeting in Mexico City (p. 804), agreed to work out a general hemispheric defense treaty.

b. CULTURAL DEVELOPMENTS

(From p. 626)

Latin American society and culture flourished in the early 20th century. Writers, poets, artists, architects, and other intellectuals regularly used their modes of expression as vehicles for critically examining their societies. Mexican poets **Enrique González Rubio** (1871–1952) and **Ramón López Velarde** are early examples of this. Peruvian essayist **Francisco García Calderón** argued that Latin American art was a key arena in which the region might find its ancient heritage and express its independence from the colonial powers. Latin American novels as well, such as **Mariano Azuela's** (1873–1952) *The Underdogs* (1916), were harshly critical of the social problems and inequities that pervaded the region. These critiques also reflected a new **"cultural" nationalism** that was growing in the region, as evidenced by the novels of Venezuelan **Rómulo Gallegos** (1884–1969). The quality of the literature and poetry from the region was shown when Chilean poet **Gabriela Mistral** (1889–1957) won the 1945 Nobel Prize in literature.

Latin American art took on a distinctive flavor in the early 20th century. Mexican visual artists such as **José Clemente Orozco** (1883–1949), **Diego Rivera** (1886–1957), and **Frida Kahlo** (1907–54), along with Brazilian **Cándido Portinari,** received worldwide acclaim for their distinctive syntheses of European and indigenous techniques. In Brazil, novelist **Oswald de Andrade** and painter **Tarsila do Amaral** led a modernist movement beginning in the early 1920s which rejected 19th-century European doctrines and sought inspiration in Brazil's "primitive" Indian past. Along with their contemporaries in other arts, they produced work that was very critical of their societies. Composers like Mexican **Carlos Chávez** (1899–1978), Brazilian **Heitor Villa-Lobos** (1887–1959), and the Argentine-born **Alberto Williams** (1862–1952) and **Alberto Ginastera** (1916–83) likewise integrated a variety of artistic traditions to produce world-renowned music.

This period also saw the rise, for the first time, of **urban working-**

class culture in Latin America. As an emerging group, urban workers sought new forms of entertainment and expression in Latin American cities. Dances such as the **tango** and **samba**, along with the increasingly important role that **Carnaval** played in many Latin American nations, became forums for these groups to express their views and opposition to entrenched elites in a relatively nonconfrontational way. **Soccer** as well became an important arena for the working classes to express their loyalties and antagonisms. *(To p. 931)*

2. SOUTH AMERICA

a. ARGENTINA

(From p. 629)

1916–22. HIPÓLITO YRIGOYEN, leader of the Argentine Radicals, was **elected president** after an electoral reform (1912) granted the secret ballot and suffrage to all males over 18 years of age. Yrigoyen introduced **modest social reforms** (factory acts, regulation of hours, pensions, etc.), but eventually gave up efforts to win over the labor movement and turned to repression to control workers. Large landowners retained their dominance, and the patronage and corruption of earlier regimes persisted. Yrigoyen refused to give up neutrality during the First World War, although diplomatic relations with Germany were strained after the sinking of Argentine ships by German submarines (1917). Argentine supplied huge quantities of wheat and meat to the Allies.

1918. Entrance of middle-class immigrants' children into universities fueled **La Reforma,** a movement for student participation in university governance and curricular reform. It began with student strikes in Córdoba and soon spread to campuses in Buenos Aires and La Plata. Yrigoyen supported the movement, which also inspired student political activity elsewhere in Latin America.

1919, Jan. SEMANA TRÁGICA (the Tragic Week). **Police and the army opened fire first on striking workers** and then on the funeral for those killed in the massacre. Perhaps **thousands were killed** in the worker riots that followed. In the aftermath, the "Patriotic League," an anti-Communist, anti-Semitic nativist organization, aided in the identification and persecution of surviving strikers and supporters.

1920. Argentina became an original **member of the League of Nations,** but withdrew from the assembly in 1921 on rejection of an Argentine resolution that all sovereign states be admitted to the League.

1922–28. MARCELO ALVEAR, Radical candidate, **elected president.** His attempts at fiscal austerity caused a split in the Radical Party (1924). His presidency also witnessed a growing wave of conflicts between the federal government in Buenos Aires and anti-Radical governments in the provinces.

1928. Yrigoyen was again elected to the presidency.

1930, Sept. 6. General José Uriburu forced Yrigoyen from office. Yrigoyen's assumption of wide personal powers had aroused much criticism, while the distress created by the world depression had provoked a demand for further relief measures. With Uriburu the landowning and big business and other conservative groups returned to power. This began the period (1930–43) known alternatively as either the "**Conservative Restoration**" or the "**Infamous Decade.**" Modeling themselves on the fascistic style of Mussolini's Italy, Uriburu and his followers used fraud and severe repression to decimate the radical Left. Although the Radical Party initially boycotted elections during the Infamous Decade, in 1936 they struck a deal with the conservatives (the **Concordancia**) for some power sharing.

1932–37. Agustín Justo was elected president. The regime maintained a system of fraud and intimidation to ensure conservative victories in the elections. Political and social unrest continued and culminated in an unsuccessful **radical revolt** in the northeastern provinces (1933–34).

1932, Nov. 17. Carlos Saavedra Lamas, the foreign minister, published a proposed **South American antiwar pact,** which had already been accepted by several states. Argentina also resumed full membership in the League of Nations (1933).

1933. The government launched a program of national economic recovery, which achieved some success. Part of this was the **Roca-Runciman treaty with Great Britain,** which was designed to safeguard Argentina's export markets by guaranteeing the purchase of British goods and ensuring the profitability of British firms in Argentina.

1935. Conflict between the Conservative government of Justo and the opposition Radical and Socialist parties, which represented the majority of voters. **Fascist organizations** also opposed the government and formed a common front of the extreme Right (Oct.).

1936, March. In congressional elections, the Radical Party, under the leadership of former president Alvear, triumphed. A **Leftist Popular Front** was organized (May 1), but Fascist groups continued to gain ground. The rightist elements supporting the government formed a **National Front,** favoring a conservative dictatorship (May 31). The **Communist Party was declared illegal** (Nov. 10).

1937, Sept. 5. Presidential elections, bitterly contested. **Roberto M. Ortiz, candidate of the government, was elected** over the nominee of the Radical Party, Alvear. Efforts of the leftist parties to prevent a quorum in a joint session of congress to confirm the election failed, and Ortiz was proclaimed elected.

1938–40. Roberto M. Ortiz, president.

1939, Sept. 4. Argentina proclaimed neutrality in the Second World War.

1942, July 6. President Ramón S. Castillo announced that the republic would maintain its **policy of neutrality.**

1943, June 5. The isolationist regime of **President Castillo** was **overthrown by a military junta.** The congress was dissolved and a new government formed by **Gen. Pedro P. Ramírez** (June 8).

Oct. COL. JUAN DOMINGO PERÓN (1895–1974) **took over the Department of Labor** and elevated it to the Ministry of Labor and Welfare. From this position he orchestrated a meteoric rise in popularity, especially among the workers. Using strongly nationalist sentiment and granting concessions to the labor movement, he forged an alliance with the unions, while trying to avoid alienating big business.

1944, Jan 27. The discovery of an **espionage plot** involving agents of the Axis powers led the Argentine government to sever **relations with Germany and Japan.** *(To p. 933)*

b. CHILE

(From p. 630)

Chile remained neutral in the First World War despite violation of its neutrality by both German and British warships. The war **demand for Chilean nitrate in large quantities generated a brief boom,** but the discovery of the **Haber process** for fixing nitrogen from the air in 1914 spelled the end for this industry. In the meantime, however, Chilean **copper was emerging** as an immensely important industry. U.S. firms dominated this extremely profitable enterprise. From an investment of merely $15 million in 1912, American investments in Chilean copper totaled almost $500 million by the late 1920s.

1919, Aug. Increasingly militant organized labor staged **a demonstration of 100,000 people** in Santiago, protesting inflation, declining wages, and government repression.

1920, Jan. 10. Chile became a member of the League of Nations.

1920–21. Chile suffered severely from the general world slump and the cessation of the demand for nitrate. The lower classes demanded a more democratic regime and extensive social legislation.

1920–24. ARTURO ALESSANDRI (1869–1950) **elected president** after a disputed election. Candidate of the **Liberal Alliance Party,** he advocated wide political and social reforms. His election represented a **victory for the middle classes, supported by labor elements.** But during his term, Alessandri, impeded by the elite-dominated parliamentary system, was unable to make much progress. At the same time many military officers, seeing the ineffectiveness of repression, began to pressure the government for social reforms. They did gain child labor laws, recognition for unions, and increases in army salaries. When in 1924 the government began to return to more traditional ways, the military forced Alessandri from office.

1925, Jan. 23. After control by a military junta under **Gen. Luis Altamirano,** in a climate of increasing labor militancy and widespread strikes, a **coup d'état** engineered by pro-reform officers and **led by Maj. Carlos Ibáñez** (1877–1960) resulted in the **recall of Alessandri.** At this point military leaders believed they needed to co-opt labor movements to maintain order.

June. In a reversal of his earlier stances, **Alessandri cracked down on striking nitrate workers.** This initiated a period of severe government repression of labor movements.

Sept. 18. New constitution, providing a stronger executive, broader suffrage, separation of Church and State, provincial autonomy, etc.

Oct. 1. Alessandri resigned, in view of the continued disorder and uncertainty.

1925–27. He was succeeded by **Emiliano Figueroa Larrain.**

1927–31. Larrain was in turn forced out by Gen. Carlos Ibáñez, who made himself **dictator-president,** and then promoted many of the social reforms and public works that Alessandri had advocated.

1929, June 3. Settlement of the Tacna-Arica question, which had embittered the relations of Chile and Peru for many years (diplomatic relations severed 1910). Efforts of the U.S. (1922–26) to mediate a settlement through a plebiscite led to no result, but served to bring about direct negotiations and the final agreement, by which **Chile received Arica and Peru was awarded Tacna,** Chile agreeing to accede Peru port and transportation facilities at Arica. Chile retained all territory taken from Bolivia, but granted Bolivia a railway outlet to the Pacific. Thenceforth Chile and Bolivia drew closer.

1931. Ibáñez resigned because of high unemployment, riots, challenges from the extreme Left and Right, and finally a general strike. In many ways a victim of the Great Depression, he fled to Argentina.

Juan Montero, representative of the conservative elements, was elected in opposition to Alessandri. Political and social unrest continued.

1932, June 4. Montero was overthrown. Numerous coups followed, including one, led by **Air Force Comdr. Marmaduke Grove,** which declared Chile a socialist republic during its 12-day tenure. Eventually a junta headed by **Carlos Dávila** assumed power and proclaimed Chile a socialist republic, which survived only ten days.

Sept. 13. Dávila was overthrown by a military coup and Alessandri became president once more, after an election (Dec. 24).

1932–38. The Alessandri government, supported by a coalition of Conservative and Liberal parties, assumed greater control of economic activity, enacting far-reaching social reforms. Marked improvement of economic conditions after 1933 did not, however, relieve the political tension. Alessandri faced severe **challenges from Chilean Nazis as well as from a growing Left-Center movement.** In both instances he used repression to reduce the opposition. After 1936 a growing number of Left and centrist parties coalesced into the Chilean Popular Front.

1938, Sept. 5. A Fascist (Nacista) **uprising** proved abortive.

1938–41. In the ensuing elections the parties of the Left elected **Pedro Aguirre Cerda, Radical, president.** The **POPULAR FRONT** ticket consolidated movements from the Left and center (the Radicals, Communists, and Socialists), and was supported by small shopkeepers, professionals, public employees, traditional liberals, feminist organizations, and the working classes. Generally backing Radical candidates in public office, it also led the call for state-subsidized industrialization in Chile. The new regime embarked on a policy of helping the worker (low bread prices, housing, education), despite strong protests from large landholders, who retained control of politics in rural areas.

1943, Jan. 20. Chile severed diplomatic relations with Germany, Italy, and Japan. *(To p. 936)*

c. PARAGUAY

(From p. 631)

1912–16. The **presidency of Edward Schaerer** saw economic development and relative political stability. Industry, ranching, and agriculture expanded, transportation and communications were improved, and foreign capital was invested. **Paraguay remained neutral during the First World War,** and in 1920 it became an **original member of the League of Nations.**

1916–19. Manuel Franco, president.

1919–20. On Franco's death, **José Montero,** the vice president, succeeded.

1920–21. Manuel Gondra, president. He was forced to resign by a revolutionary group.

1924–28. After the short presidencies of **Eusebio Ayala** (1921–23), **Eligio Ayala** (1923–24), and **Luis Riart** (1924), **Eligio Ayala was elected president.** Representing the Liberal groups, he inaugurated a policy of social legislation.

1928–31. José Gugiari, president.

1928–30. During Gugiari's administration, the **dispute with Bolivia over the Chaco territory came to a head.** Despite earlier agreements (1913, 1915), claims on the potentially oil-rich territory were still unsettled. In Dec. 1928, the forces of the two states clashed and war seemed inevitable. Diplomatic relations were severed and Paraguay appealed to the League of Nations, but the Pan-American conference at once offered to mediate. Direct negotiations were agreed to, but skirmishes in the contested area continued until a **temporary arrangement** (return to status quo ante) was arrived at (April 2, 1930).

1932–35. THE CHACO WAR. The League of Nations and the Pan-American Union both called upon the two parties to desist from hostilities and accept neutral arbitration, but to no avail. **Standard Oil of New Jersey** and **Royal Dutch Shell,** supporting Bolivia and Paraguay respectively, fueled the conflict because of a belief in rich oil deposits in the region. The Paraguayans, after a series of major campaigns, occupied the larger part of the Chaco but failed in their attempts to invade Bolivian territory. During the war the **relations between Paraguay and Chile became badly strained** because of the service of Chilean officers with the Bolivian army and employment of Chilean workmen by Bolivia.

1935. At the suggestion of the League of Nations, some 20 nations lifted the embargo on arms in favor of Bolivia, while retaining it against Paraguay. Thereupon **Paraguay announced withdrawal from the League.**

June 14. Paraguay and Bolivia concluded a truce, at the instigation of the U.S. and five South American governments. A peace conference at Buenos Aires met in July. A **definitive peace treaty** was not signed until July 21, 1938 (approved by plebiscite on Aug. 10). The treaty provided for arbitration of boundaries between American states. The territorial award assigned the **greater part of the Chaco to Paraguay,** but provided Bolivia with an outlet to the sea by way of the Paraguay River.

1936, Feb. 17. A **military revolt,** provoked by the army's criticism of the supposed weakness of the government in the peace negotiations, led to the **overthrow of President Ayala. Rafael Franco became provisional president.** Supported by a junta of officers, and by radical and nationalist elements, he made himself a military dictator.

March 11. Franco proclaimed a totalitarian state, and introduced economic, social, and financial reforms. These policies antagonized Paraguayan and foreign interests, which resented the heavy taxation.

1937, Aug. 15. Franco was forced to resign as a result of a bloodless coup d'état. **Felix Pavia,** of the Liberal Party, became provisional president and suppressed a number of counterrevolutionary movements.

Oct. 11. Pavia was elected constitutional president.

1939, April 30–1940. General José Félix Estigarribia was elected president.

1940, Feb. 14–18. The cabinet and Parliament resigned, and President Estigarribia took over the functions of government.   *(To p. 938)*

d. URUGUAY

(From p. 631)

In the first decades of the 20th century, Uruguay enjoyed comparative stability and affluence. Massive waves of immigration in the late 19th century and increased trade with Britain brought a great deal of prosperity. After 1910 **JOSÉ BATLLE Y ORDÓÑEZ** (1856–1929) created a two-party system to prevent factionalism. The majority party, the **Colorados** (representing the middle and working classes), fought the **Blancos** (a mainly rural party) in subsequent elections.

1907–11. Claudio Williams administration.

1911–15. José Batlle y Ordóñez administration.

1915–19. Feliciano Viera administration.

1919–23. During the administration of **Baltasar Brum,** as in those of his three predecessors and his successors, many **social and administrative**

reforms were initiated and the internal development of the country was rapid. Immigration and urbanization continued throughout the period.

1917. On the entry of the U.S. into the First World War, Uruguay expressed solidarity and later **severed relations with Germany.**

1919, March 1. A new constitution curtailed the powers of the president, created the **National Council of Administration** (nine members elected by popular vote and endowed with important functions), and **disestablished the Roman Catholic Church.** The council was designed to assuage Blanco opposition to continued Colorado rule and prevent them from seeking nonelectoral means of gaining power.

1920. Uruguay joined the League of Nations.

1923–27. José Serrato, president.

1927–31. Juan Compisteguy, like Serrato before him, continued and accelerated the policy of social reform until Uruguay began to feel the pinch of the Great Depression.

1931–38. GABRIEL TERRA (1873–1942), president. He represented the more advanced wing of the Liberal Party, and soon found himself in conflict with the National Council of Administration concerning the division of executive authority. This period began Uruguay's experiment with state-subsidized import substitution industrialization, funded mainly with revenues from livestock exports.

1932. National women's suffrage recognized.

1933. In view of the political and social unrest and the consequent threat of civil war, **Terra established a temporary dictatorship.**

1934, April 19. A new constitution provided for a strong executive, restricted the powers of Parliament, and established compulsory voting. Terra was reelected president.

1935. A revolt against Terra was crushed.

1935–38. The **Terra government** continued the work of social and economic reform, and Uruguay gradually experienced economic recovery.

1938–43. Alfredo Baldomir elected president to succeed Terra.

1942, Feb. 23. President **General Alfredo Baldomir** dissolved both chambers of the legislature and created a state council with members drawn from all parties, except Communists and Herreristas. In the aftermath, outlawed factions of the dominant two parties were reincorporated into the political process, strengthening the two-party system.

(To p. 938)

e. BOLIVIA

(From p. 632)

1913–17. Ismael Montes president, for his second term in office. Increasingly, tin was outstripping silver and other products as Bolivia's main export.

1917, April 13. Bolivia severed relations with Germany but did not declare war.

1917–20. José Gutiérrez Guerra, president.

1920, Jan. 10. Bolivia became an original member of the League of Nations.

March 16. In the **Tacna-Arica dispute,** Bolivia took the stand that neither Chile nor Peru was entitled to the provinces. The Bolivian government appealed to the League of Nations (Nov. 1) for access to the Pacific, but the effort failed.

July 11. A coup d'état led to the overthrow of Gutiérrez Guerra.

1921–25. Juan Bautista Saavedra became president. By this time Bolivia was producing one quarter of the world's tin supply. The largest tin mining concerns were owned by three Bolivian families: the Hochschilds, Patiños, and Aramayos, known collectively as **La Rosca.** This period was marked by massive development of the tin industry, some public improvements, and flotation of large loans in the U.S. By the mid-1920s, Bolivia (having had no foreign debt in 1908) owed $40 million to foreign creditors. Americans controlled Bolivia's mining and customs bureaus and had claims on more than half of the government's revenue. Civil unrest grew as miners created a large anarchosyndicalist union movement, which was only fueled by army massacres of striking workers in 1918, 1919, and 1923.

1925, May 2. José Cabino Villanueva, president. His election was annulled (Sept. 1) by congress because of fraud. Villanueva fled the country.

1926–30. Hernando Siles became president.

1927. Women's Labor Federation founded.

1928–29. Dispute between Bolivia and Paraguay over the Chaco region.

1929. Settlement of the Tacna-Arica question. Bolivia definitively lost Atacama but obtained the right to use the Chilean-built railway between La Paz and Arica.

1930, May 28. Overthrow of President Siles, whose regime had become unpopular through economic depression, a fall in the price of tin, closing of the mines, and resulting labor unrest. A brief military rule, led by Gen. Carlos Blanco Galinda, followed.

1931. Daniel Salamanca was elected president. Salamanca outlawed unions.

1932–35. The **CHACO WAR,** between Bolivia and Paraguay. The war was fought over the eastern lowlands of Bolivia, known as the Chaco Boreal. Thousands of workers and peasants from both countries died in the bloody conflict, which was fueled by a belief in rich oil deposits in the region. Bolivia lost 20,000 square miles of territory in the conflict but retained some of the land richest in oil.

1934, Dec. President Salamanca was overthrown by a military coup, following serious defeats of the Bolivian forces. The vice president, **Luis Tejada Sorzano,** assumed the presidency.

1936, May 17. Urban trade unionists and miners, in cooperation with returned veterans of the Chaco War, led a broad-based general strike that toppled the government. The **"Veterans of the Chaco"** would become an important voice for social change in Bolivia in subsequent years. Tejada Sorzano was replaced by a joint civil-military junta under **David Toro,** who then established a dictatorship. Measures to promote economic revival were adopted (virtual state monopoly over the petroleum industry; **confiscation of Standard Oil properties, March 1937;** efforts to control mining and banking). Toro's policies aroused much opposition.

1937, July 14. Toro was driven from office by fellow army officers.

1938–39. German Busch succeeded as president. He endorsed attempts to promote **"military socialism"** but was unable to co-opt or control emergent labor, veteran, and peasant movements. These groups supported change, but would not accede to simple "top-down" reform.

1939, April 24. Busch assumed dictatorial powers, dissolving Congress and suspending the constitution. All connection with European totalitarianism was, however, denied.

Aug. 22. Death of President Busch. **Gen. Carlos Quintamilla** assumed power.

1940. Enrique Peñaranda became president.

1941. A group of middle-class intellectuals and lawyers founded the populist **NATIONALIST REVOLUTIONARY MOVEMENT** (MNR).

1942, June. Founding of the **National Agrarian Party** (PAN). An offshoot of the MNR, PAN called for valorization of Bolivia's Indian heritage along with major agrarian reform.

1943, Dec. 21. President Enrique Peñaranda was unseated by an MNR-army alliance headed by **Maj. Gualberto Villarroel.** The new regime was not recognized diplomatically except by Argentina. The U.S. refused recognition because of the ruling faction's Fascist sympathies.

1945, May 10. Opening of the **National Indigenous Congress** in La Paz. Reflecting a growing politicization among Bolivian peasants (highlighted by increased confrontations with landlords since the 1930s), delegates to the congress called for more education, agrarian reform, and an expansion of peasant rights.

(To p. 939)

f. PERU

(From p. 632)

1914, Feb. 4. A military revolt led to the **overthrow of President Guillermo Billinghurst.**

1914–15. Col. Oscar Benavides served as provisional president.

1915–19. José Pardo, president.

1917, Oct. 5. Peru severed relations with Germany, after attacks on Peruvian ships.

1919, Jan. Workers led a three-day **general strike,** winning an eight-hour-day law for Peru's urban workers.

July 4. A coup d'état led to the **resignation and imprisonment of President Pardo.**

1919–30. He was succeeded (Aug. 24) by **AUGUSTO LEGUÍA** (1863–1932), **president.** Leguía's administration, known as the **Oncenio,** was

Caribbean Sea

Panama

PANAMA

Caracas

Orinoco R.

VENEZUELA

Georgetown

Paramaribo

Cayenne

DUTCH
GUIANA

BRITISH
GUIANA

FRENCH
GUIANA

Bogotá

COLOMBIA

Negro R.

Amazon R.

Quito

ECUADOR

Belém

Madeira R.

B R A Z I L

PERU

Araguaya R.

São Francisco R.

Lima

*Lake
Titicaca*

Salvador

BOLIVIA

Sucre

Paraguay R.

Paraná R.

TACNA

ARICA

CHACO

Pilcomayo R.

São Paulo

PARAGUAY

Rio de Janeiro

Asunción

Pacific

Ocean

Paraná R.

Uruguay R.

CHILE

URUGUAY

Santiago

ARGENTINA

Buenos
Aires

Montevideo

Atlantic

Ocean

▨ Territories in dispute

SOUTH AMERICA
IN 1930

0   250   500   750   1000

MILES

Atlantic

Ocean

noteworthy for great material changes and widespread corruption. American companies, which had been investing in northern agriculture and mining since the early 1900s, moved extensively into Peruvian agriculture at this time. Firms such as **Cerro de Pasco combined mining interests with large landholdings** to take over some of the country's best land. By the late 1920s, most of the principal sources of Peruvian wealth were in foreign hands. During this time, the Peruvian government secured large loans in the U.S. (1924, 1927, 1928) to develop the economy, build public works, and expand education. Leguía also revised Church-State relations. He initially courted the support of labor and leftist groups, designing his 1919 constitution on the nationalist-socialist model in Mexico. Once in power, however, he repressed worker, student, and peasant movements.

1919, Dec. 27. A new constitution (went into effect Jan. 18, 1920) introduced compulsory primary education, compulsory labor arbitration, income tax, etc.

1920, Jan. 10. Peru joined the League of Nations at the very outset.

1921–29. The long, drawn-out **dispute with Chile over Tacna and Arica,** when finally settled, assigned Tacna to Peru.

1924, May. Peruvian **VICTOR RAÚL HAYA DE LA TORRE** (1895–1979) founded the **American Popular Revolutionary Alliance** (APRA) in Mexico City, where he was living in exile. Inspired by the socialist, anti-imperialist ideas of the Mexican Revolution, Haya de la Torre sought to unite all the proletarian elements of "Indo-America" in a mass revolutionary movement. A follower of Mexican education minister **José Vasconcelos** and **Manuel González Prada** (an anarchist teacher at the University of San Marcos in Lima), he believed that the only source of regeneration for Latin America would be its indigenous peoples. In practice his party called for selective nationalization, protection of human rights, state control of the economy, and protection of the middle and lower classes.

June 21. Signing of a protocol with Ecuador, envisaging negotiations concerning the old boundary dispute, and providing for arbitration in the event of failure of direct discussion.

1927. Publication of *Tempest in the Andes,* by **Luis E. Valcárcel.** Along with *Seven Interpretive Essays on Peruvian Reality* (1928), by **José Carlos Mariátegui** (1894–1930), this text was representative of a growing body of literature published by members of the *indigenista* **movement.** The movement, represented politically by APRA, looked to Peru's Inca (supposedly socialist) past for solutions to the current social problems, promoting an Indian-led socialism as the answer to crisis. Following from the tradition of González Prada, these writers called for rebellion by the Indian proletariat or peasantry.

1928. José Carlos Mariátegui, known as the father of Latin American Marxism, founded the **Peruvian Socialist Party.** A writer and journalist, as well as a supporter of *indigenismo,* Mariátegui proposed a revolutionary path to social change predicated on an alliance between Peruvian workers and peasants in order to overthrow the imperialist order.

1929. Mariátegui founded the **General Confederation of Peruvian Workers** (CGTP).

1929–32. The Great Depression caused Peruvian exports to fall by more than two-thirds. Massive numbers of workers were laid off in the mines and on the sugar and cotton plantations. APRA, growing in popularity both within and outside of Peru, decided it would run candidates in Peruvian elections.

1930, Aug. 25. Resignation and flight of Leguía, following a revolt led by **Col. Luis Sánchez Cerro.** Leguía was captured and tried for corruption, but was acquitted. Sánchez Cerro became provisional president.

1931, Feb.–March. A series of revolts obliged Sánchez Cerro to give way to **David Samanez Ocampo.**

Oct. 11. Sánchez Cerro was elected president. Haya de la Torre ran as the APRA candidate, but lost under suspicious circumstances.

1932, July. Pro-APRA peasants took control of the northern city of Trujillo for four days, killing a number of captured military personnel. After their defeat by the military, **thousands were taken prisoner and massacred** in the military retaliation. This incident created long-standing enmity between APRA and the armed forces.

1932–33. Threat of war with Colombia over the disputed territory of **Leticia.** Peru took a strong line and prepared for war, though accepting proffered mediation of the League. The question was finally settled by agreement on Nov. 2, 1934.

1933, April 9. A new constitution was introduced.

April 30. Assassination of Sánchez Cerro.

1933–39. OSCAR BENAVIDES (1876–1945) **succeeded at once as president.** Social and political unrest continued, despite the gradual recovery of the country from the depression. Strikes, including several clashes between miners and management at the **Cerro de Pasco** complex, were common. Benavides, supported by conservative and clerical elements, was opposed by the radical APRA, which had strong student support. The Aprista opposition was held down with an iron hand.

1936, Oct. 11. The elections resulted in the **defeat of Benavides's candidate** by the leftist groups, and in a Socialist's being chosen president. Benavides had the **elections declared null** and had his own term prolonged for three years.

Dec. 8. The constituent assembly was dissolved and Benavides became virtual dictator. The radical opposition was suppressed (**Public Security Law** of Feb. 21, 1937), and efforts were made to counteract radicalism by the extension of social reforms.

1938, June. The **boundary dispute with Ecuador** threatened to end in war when the troops of the two states clashed on the frontier. On Oct. 12, Ecuador appealed to several American presidents to mediate, but Peru took an uncompromising attitude toward Ecuadorian demands for cession of territory.

1939–45. Manuel Prado Ugarteche, president.

1942, Jan. 24. Peru severed diplomatic relations with Germany, Italy, and Japan.

1945, June 10. José Luis Bustamante was elected president, supported by Liberal and Aprista forces. *(To p. 941)*

g. ECUADOR

(From p. 633)

1916–20. Alfredo Baquerizo Moreno, president.

1917, Dec. 7. Ecuador severed relations with Germany because of the submarine campaign, but did not follow most other Latin American states in joining the League of Nations at the conclusion of the war. During the war and the immediate postwar period much progress was made in education, social legislation, and above all sanitation (work of the American **Col. William Gorgas** at Guayaquil, long a center of bubonic plague).

1920–24. José Luis Tamayo, president.

1924–25. Gonzalo Córdova succeeded Tamayo. He was driven from office by a military revolt led by **Gen. Francisco Gómez de la Torre** (July 9, 1925).

1926–31. ISIDRO AYORA, president.

1929, March 28. A new constitution ended the military regime set up in 1925, but paved the way for endless disputes between the executive and the legislature. Ayora had elaborate social and labor laws enacted, including **female suffrage,** and adopted many financial reforms.

1931, Aug. 25. Ayora resigned. Col. Luis Alba became provisional president but was forced to flee after a coup d'état (October). There followed a period of utter confusion, marked by conflict between the executive and legislature and between the conservative and liberal groups. After the suppression of a revolt (Aug. 1932), **Martínez Mera** became president, only to be replaced in Dec. 1933 by **José M. Velasco Ibarra.**

1932–34. The **Leticia dispute** between Peru and Colombia (p. 742) gave Ecuador an opportunity to assert claims to portions of the Amazon Basin.

1934, Sept. 28. Partly motivated by these aspirations, **Ecuador entered the League of Nations.**

1935, Aug. 20. President Ibarra was overthrown by a military junta after he attempted to assume dictatorial powers. He was replaced by **Antonio Pons,** who, in turn, was forced to resign.

Sept. 26. A military dictatorship under Federico Páez was set up, to prevent the election of a Conservative (the dominant Liberal Party was split by dissensions).

1935–37. DICTATORSHIP OF PÁEZ. He suppressed a number of movements directed against his regime.

1937, Oct. 22. After a conflict with a constituent assembly, convened to promulgate a new constitution, **Páez was forced to resign.**

1937–38. Gen. G. Alberto Enríquez became provisional president. With the support of the army he adopted strong measures to maintain his authority. At the same time he liberated many political prisoners, abrogated objectionable repressive legislation, and embarked upon the work of financial and legal reform.

1938, June–Oct. Growing tension in relations with Peru (p. 741), due to the long-standing dispute about the boundary.

Dec. 2. The congress elected **Aurelio Mosquera Narváez president.**

1942, Jan. 29. Ecuador severed diplomatic relations with Germany, Italy, and Japan. On the same date an agreement was signed to settle boundary disputes between Ecuador and Peru.   *(To p. 942)*

h. COLOMBIA

(From p. 633)

1914–18. José V. Concha, president. He represented the conservative groups (whose rule became known as the **Regeneración**) that had been in power since 1884 and continued to rule the country until 1930. Even the conservative administrations of Colombia were obliged to initiate a measure of social legislation to meet growing pressure from the lower classes. **Colombia remained neutral during the First World War,** but joined the League of Nations (Feb. 16, 1920).

1918–21. Marco Fidel Suárez, president.

1919, Aug. 15. Signature of a **contract with the Tropical Oil Company** for exploitation of the Colombian oil fields, one of the most important sources of national wealth.

1921, April 20. The U.S. Senate finally ratified the **Thomson-Urrutia Treaty** (concluded 1914) (p. 728) with certain modifications, thus ending the long dispute with regard to Panama. The Colombian Congress ratified it on Dec. 22.

1922–26. Pedro Nel Ospina, president.

1922, March 24. An award by the Swiss federal council ended a long-standing **boundary dispute with Venezuela** in favor of Colombia. A boundary treaty with Peru settled the frontier on that side.

1924. Banana workers struck against the United Fruit Company (UFCO) in the Santa Marta region on the Caribbean coast. UFCO, which had set up plantations in Colombia beginning in 1901, employed over 30,000 Colombian workers (most under miserable conditions) at this time. Poorly organized, the workers were ignored by the company, which claimed that they were not really employees of UFCO but contracted labor.

1926–30. Miguel Abadia Méndez, president. During his administration the growing social tension found an outlet in a number of **major strikes,** in the course of which many were killed by the police and government forces.

1927. Colombian elites, centralizing their power around coffee, founded the **National Federation of Coffee Producers** (FNC). This association combined the power of small producers into one group that could prioritize spending, control prices, and support certain projects.

1928, Dec. UFCO banana workers, better organized after their 1924 failure, struck again. On Dec. 6, the military, in cooperation with UFCO, **opened fire on workers and villagers gathered in the town square at Ciénaga.** Perhaps thousands were slaughtered in the attack. After the massacre the government arrested numerous left-wing leaders and suppressed the unions. This incident would become an important symbol in the 1930s as the depression generated more and more support for labor militancy.

1930–34. The election of ENRIQUE OLAYA HERRERA (1881–1937), a moderate liberal, brought to an end the long domination of the conservative groups. **The world depression brought with it a rapid decline in coffee prices,** and necessitated heavy borrowing.

1932–34. The Leticia dispute with Peru. Occupation of Leticia by armed Peruvians brought the two countries to the verge of war. Under pressure from the Latin American powers and the U.S., the disputants finally permitted supervision of the area by a League of Nations commission. In the final settlement (1934) Peru and Colombia proclaimed peace and amity and renounced armed action.

1934–38. ALFONSO LÓPEZ PUMAREJO (1886–1959) became president, continuing the rule of the Liberal Party. He attempted a Colombian version of Roosevelt's American "New Deal." With the support of labor and the Left, the government embarked upon far-reaching **social reforms,** aiming at government control of subsoil riches, agrarian reforms, etc. **Primary education** was made free and compulsory, and the Catholic Church was disestablished. All these policies called forth the opposition of the conservatives and clericals, who were further aided by the **split in the Liberal ranks** into moderate and progressive or even radical wings.

1938. Nevertheless, in the election the Liberals were able to maintain a majority.

1938–42. Eduardo Santos, a moderate Liberal, **became president.** The Liberals won in the congressional elections of March 19, 1939.

1941, Dec. 8. Colombia broke diplomatic relations with Japan, citing the Havana Resolution.

1942. Liberal Alfonso López was reelected president.

Nov. 26. Colombia severed diplomatic relations with (Vichy) France.   *(To p. 943)*

i. VENEZUELA

(From p. 634)

1909–35. Dictatorship of JUAN VICENTE GÓMEZ (1857–1935), who served during this period as either president or chief of the army. Gómez pursued a policy of nepotism and took care to have a congress entirely subservient to him. The period was marked by striking **material progress:** administrative reforms were adopted, finances stabilized (national debt liquidated, 1930), schools built, and commerce and industry encouraged. At the center of this development was the opening of the **Venezuelan oil fields** in 1918, which soon made the country a leading oil producer. Oil quickly supplanted coffee and other agricultural products as the main source of Venezuelan wealth. It also allowed new oil-based elites to challenge the old agricultural oligarchy for political power. At the same time, the oil and industrial development led to the creation of new working and middle classes. Oil workers organized the **Syndicalist Labor Federation of Venezuela** in 1928, which found support among many student groups. The latter became active opponents of the dictatorship.

1920, March 3. Venezuela maintained neutrality during the First World War, but **joined the League of Nations.**

1928. The government arrested a group of **radical students,** leading to numerous worker and student demonstrations and to an abortive general strike. The incident became an important symbol for future radicals and moderates.

1929, 1931. Revolts led by Gen. **Arévalo Cedeño** were put down, as were other opposition movements directed against the Gómez regime.

1935, Dec. 18. Death of President Gómez ended the dictatorship. **Gen. Eleazar López Contreras** became provisional president and succeeded in suppressing the strikes and movements that broke out after the death of the strongman.

1936, April 25–1941. Gen. Eleazar López Contreras was elected president.

1936, July 16. A **new constitution** provided that the president's term should be limited to five years, with no eligibility for reelection.

1937, Jan. Elections were held for about one-third of the seats in Congress. These turned out to be a decisive victory for the Left parties, whereupon (Feb. 4) the government arrested many of the leaders of the Left (including newly elected congressmen) on the charge of Communism. Most of these leaders were exiled, and most of the leftist organizations (including the **Federation of Students**) were dissolved. The president then undertook to suppress the Left, but at the same time embarked on a far-reaching program of social reform designed to meet the needs and demands of the lower classes and to check the spread of support for leftist movements.

1940–45. The Second World War greatly increased demand for Venezuelan petroleum, causing a boom in oil-industry profits and revenues.   *(To p. 944)*

j. BRAZIL

(From p. 635)

1914–18. Wenceslau Braz Pereira Gomes, president. The temporary unavailability of manufactured imports during World War I expanded the demand for domestic industrial goods, mainly produced in São Paulo and Rio de Janeiro. Large textile factories, mainly employing women and children, opened in both cities, coexisting alongside smaller plants and workshops. The war also spurred a shift from Britain to the U.S. as the major source of Brazilian imports and financing.

1915, May 25. Agreement with Argentina and Chile (ABC treaty) providing for arbitration of disputes.

1917, 1919. Faced with rising prices for basic goods, **Brazilian workers, including women textile operatives, declared general strikes** in the major industrial centers. The agro-export oligarchies, which also had interests in Brazil's burgeoning manufacturing industries, generally refused to recognize the unions and called upon the military to crush the strikes. **Socialist and anarchist leaders were exiled as result of the strikes,** and the oligarchic power holders refused to give in to demands for greater representation.

1917, Oct. 26. BRAZIL DECLARED WAR ON GERMANY. Relations had been severed on April 11 after the sinking of Brazilian ships. During the war Brazilian warships cooperated with the Allies, and Brazil furnished large stocks of food and raw materials.

1918. Rodrigues Alves, president. He died (1919) before assuming office.

1919–22. Epitácio Pessôa succeeded Alves as president. He was the only civilian from Brazil's declining northeast to serve as president during the First Republic.

1920, Jan. 10. Brazil joined the League of Nations as an original member.

1922. The Brazilian Communist Party (PCB) was founded.

1922–26. Artur da Silva Bernardes, president. During this time **political and economic power was beginning to shift to the new industrialists of São Paulo and their allies.** These emerging leaders began to form economic associations to promote their interests.

1922–24. Young nationalist military officers, known as *tenentes* since many held the rank of lieutenant, revolted on several occasions against the government, calling for social reform and a stronger central state. These movements were all defeated, but left an important legacy for reformist movements in the 1930s.

1924, July. Formidable *tenente* revolt in São Paulo and Rio Grande do Sul, led by Gen. Isidoro Lopes. After suppression of the insurrection, which involved aerial bombing of neighborhoods in São Paulo, the government undertook certain economic reforms.

1924–26. Luis Carlos Prestes (1898–1990) led a column **(Prestes Column)** of former *tenentes* across the length of the Brazilian interior and then over the mountains and through the jungles to Bolivia. Soldiers in the column called for universal suffrage, freedom for unions, nationalism, and socialism.

1926, June 14. Brazil announced withdrawal from the League of Nations after failure to secure a permanent seat on the council.

1926–30. WASHINGTON LUÍS PEREIRA DE SOUZA (1869–1957), **president.** He maintained order and tried, without much success, to improve the nation's finances. Washington Luís undermined the traditional alliance between the coffee elites in Minas Gerais and São Paulo by favoring Paulistas, generating deep divisions in the ruling classes. Social unrest developed rapidly during this period and resulted in **drastic measures against strikes and Communism** (strikes illegal, Aug. 13, 1927).

1930, March. After Washington Luís broke with tradition by choosing another Paulista as his successor, urban groups, landowners from Rio Grande do Sul, and disaffected politicians from Minas Gerais formed the **Liberal Alliance** under **GETÚLIO VARGAS** (1883–1954) to contest the elections. In the election **the official candidate Júlio Prestes was named president.**

May. Opposition candidates from Minas Gerais and Paraíba were refused permission to take their seats in the congress.

July. Vargas's running mate, **João Pessôa,** was assassinated.

Oct. REVOLUTION OF 1930. A great revolt erupted in the southern provinces, led by **Getúlio Vargas,** governor of Rio Grande do Sul. With the coffee market devastated by the depression and widespread discontent over the presidential elections, Vargas was able to build support based on the social groups that supported the Liberal Alliance. Military leaders, sensing collapse, deposed Washington Luís on Oct. 24, and turned the presidency over to Vargas a week later. Seeking to centralize power, Vargas moved quickly against regional politicians. He replaced all the governors but one with personally chosen **"interventors."** He also set out to promote state-directed industrialization

in Brazil, passing labor laws, exchange controls, tax incentives for industry, and lowering duties on imported machinery.

1931. Establishment of the National Coffee Department, which year after year supervised the destruction of large quantities of coffee, in the hope of maintaining a good price in the world market. As coffee was Brazil's chief export, the collapse of coffee prices during the depression created much financial difficulty.

1932, Feb. Vargas announced a new **electoral code,** introducing the secret ballot, lowering the voting age to 21, and giving the **vote to women.**

July–Oct. A revolt broke out in São Paulo, led by agrarian and industrial elites who demanded that Vargas fulfill his promise to call a constitutional assembly. Vargas, who sought either to co-opt social and political movements or to crush them, quickly suppressed the revolt but also sought a rapid conciliation. In the end, this regionalist revolt served to strengthen the cause of centralism in Rio.

1933. The government introduced a program of economic rehabilitation, with numerous social and political reforms.

1934, July 16. One such reform was a **new constitution,** which, although similar to the Constitution of 1891, decreased the autonomy of the states vis à vis the federal government. The president and bicameral legislature were to be directly elected, and some modest restrictions were put on foreign ownership of land and participation in the economy. The constitution also legally recognized unions and the right to strike, allowed the government to fix minimum wages, and established a labor tribunal system. Later decrees introduced social security, an eight-hour workday, educational innovations, and civil service reforms.

1934–37. Vargas elected president by the constitutional assembly. Economic conditions gradually improved, but social and political unrest reached a fevered pitch. Among the industrial and plantation workers radical and Communist propaganda made marked progress, while among the middle classes a Fascist **(Intergralista) green shirt movement** gained many adherents. The **Communist Party** had ties to Moscow and the Comintern, while the new Nazi government in Germany promoted Fascism and pro-Nazi sentiment. Agents of the Third Reich actively spread propaganda among the many German immigrants in the southern provinces. Barter arrangements with Germany yielded greatly expanded trade between the two nations.

1935, Nov. A revolt of Communists and some military radicals, led by **Luis Carlos Prestes,** broke out in Pernambuco and then in Rio de Janeiro. This uprising by the "National Liberation Alliance" (ANL), though suppressed within a week, gave the government an excuse to introduce martial law. The president was granted almost dictatorial powers, strict censorship was inaugurated, and special tribunals were set up to try Communist leaders. Vargas used this process to suppress Brazil's independent labor unions as well.

1937, Nov. 10. Vargas canceled upcoming presidential elections and declared himself dictator of an *ESTADO NÔVO*. A new constitution gave the president full dictatorial powers, dismantled the local political machines, and established a corporative state structure (including a national economic council). The president announced that the new regime was not Fascist, but in both its name and its constitution it appeared strongly influenced by the Fascist regimes of Portugal and Italy. Vargas did outlaw the Intergralista movement, along with all other political parties.

1938, May 11. An Intergralista rising was put down by the government without much difficulty.

1939, March 9. Brazil concluded a series of agreements with the U.S., thereby obtaining financial aid and support in the work of **general economic development,** including expansion of the modern steel industry.

1942, Jan. 28. Brazil broke off diplomatic and trade relations with the Axis nations.

Aug. 11. The U.S. and Brazil agreed to set up a **joint defense board,** similar to those established with Canada and Mexico.

1943. After **declaring war on the Axis in Aug. 1942** (p. 804), Brazil agreed to send troops to fight alongside U.S. soldiers in Italy. Citing the country's state of war, the Vargas regime suspended or ignored much of the labor legislation it had recently issued in the "Consolidation of Labor Laws" (CLT).

Feb. 6. Brazil announced its formal **acceptance of the declaration of the United Nations.**

(To p. 946)

3. CENTRAL AMERICA

a. OVERVIEW

(From p. 636)

After the declaration of war on Germany by the U.S., the states of Central America severed relations with Germany and ultimately declared war, mostly in 1918 (**Panama,** April 7, 1917; **Costa Rica,** March 23, 1918; **Nicaragua,** May 8, 1918; **Honduras,** July 19, 1918; **Guatemala,** April 23, 1918). After the war almost all of them became **members of the League of Nations** (**El Salvador** joined in 1924, the others in 1920).

In the political sphere most of these states continued in unstable conditions, with numerous insurrections and regime changes. Common to all of them was the growing class consciousness of the laborers on banana, coffee, and sugar plantations which came to constitute an ever more formidable challenge to the ruling groups. Despite representative machinery, the governments in many states were essentially dictatorships. During the 1920s the **U.S. government intervened frequently** (including several **prolonged occupations of Nicaragua, Cuba, and Haiti**) to protect American interests and property. This policy, among other things, aroused much hostility toward the United States throughout Latin America, and was later replaced by the **Good Neighbor Policy** (1930s), which eschewed intervention.

1918, March 10. The **Central American Court was dissolved** after denunciation by Nicaragua and failure of the members to renew arrangements.

1921–22. The **PACT OF UNION** among **Costa Rica, Guatemala, Honduras, and El Salvador,** signed at San José (Jan. 19, 1921). The agreement set up an indissoluble and perpetual union, to be called the **Federation of Central America.** A provisional federal council was organized (June 17), and **Vicente Martínez** of Guatemala became president. On Oct. 10 the federal constitution was completed, but once again the project of union was to be frustrated. On Dec. 8 a revolution broke out in Guatemala, directed against the government's policy of federation. With the success of this uprising the whole scheme fell through and the **federation was dissolved** (Jan. 29, 1922). In the ensuing years there was chronic trouble over borders between the different states, with occasional danger of war.

1922, Dec. 4–1923, Feb. 7. A **Central American conference** met in Washington at the insistence of the U.S. government, which hoped to terminate the dangerous friction between Nicaragua and Honduras. A general **treaty of neutrality** was drawn up, provision was made for the creation of a Central American Court of Justice, and measures to limit armaments and to further economic development were envisaged. The majority of the states ratified the treaties by 1926, but little was done to put them into effect.   *(To p. 803)*

b. PANAMA

(From p. 635)

1914. After more than ten years, and the deaths of over 5,000 workers, the **Panama Canal was opened.** Construction of the canal radically altered both the ethnic makeup of Panama (introducing thousands of Caribbean immigrants into the population) and the economy of the country. Panamanian elites, backed by the presence of thousands of U.S. troops in the Canal Zone, based their newfound prosperity on the international commerce associated with the canal. On numerous occasions they invited U.S. troops into the country to put down popular protests that called for improved social and economic conditions.

1921. A **boundary dispute with Costa Rica,** inherited from the period of Colombian sovereignty, threatened to provoke war when Panamanian troops occupied disputed territory and armed clashes ensued (Feb.–March). The U.S. government induced Panama to evacuate the area involved, which was then occupied by Costa Rica (Aug.)

   April 20. By the **THOMSON-URRUTIA TREATY** (p. 742), Colombia recognized the independence of Panama. The boundaries, hitherto disputed, were adjusted, diplomatic relations established, and various accords signed (1924–25).

1925. **U.S. troops entered Panama City** to put down striking workers who were calling for lower rents. Numerous workers were killed in the incident.

1926, July 28. Treaty with the United States, designed to protect the canal in time of war. It required that Panama consider itself at war when the U.S. was belligerent, and that Panama permit peacetime maneuvers by U.S. forces on Panamanian territory. Opposition by the Panamanian assembly because of infringement of sovereignty prevented ratification (Jan. 26, 1927). The question of sovereignty over the Canal Zone then arose, Panama denying that the U.S. possessed such sovereignty. Panama appealed to the League of Nations to determine the question, but the League took no action and the president of Panama disavowed the appeal.

1931. President Florencio Harmodio Arosemena was forced to resign as a result of revolution (Jan. 2). A military government was set up.

1932–36. HARMODIO ARIAS (1886–1962) then became president.

1933, Oct. 17. President Arias conferred with President Roosevelt in Washington regarding the treaty relations between the two countries. The result was a declaration that Panama should be permitted all the commercial rights of a sovereign nation in the Canal Zone, and that there should be no U.S. economic enterprise detrimental to Panama in the Canal Zone, concessions to rising nationalist sentiment among Panamanians.

1934–35. Panama opened negotiations with the United States to secure modification of the treaty of 1903, so as to eliminate the U.S. guarantee of Panama's independence, which gave the U.S. the right to intervene.

1936–39. JUAN AROSEMENA, president. The negotiations with the U.S. continued.

   March 2. A new treaty was reached with the U.S. which met many of the objections raised by Panama to the earlier treaty.

1939–40. Augusto S. Boyd, president.

1940–41. Right-wing nationalist **Arnulfo Arias** (1901–1988) **became president.**

1941, Oct. 9. President Arias overthrown by U.S.-supported Panamanian police and national guard forces, which installed **Ricardo Adolfo de la Guardia as president.**   *(To p. 949)*

c. GUATEMALA

(From p. 636)

1920, April 8. MANUEL ESTRADA CABRERA, president since 1898, was deposed by the assembly because of his opposition to the scheme of Central American federation.

1920–21. Carlos Herrera, president. He was overthrown by a revolution (Dec. 5, 1921) led by **Gen. José Orellana,** who rejected the Central American federation scheme.

1922–26. Orellana, president.

1926–30. Lázaro Chacón, president.

1930. Bautillo Palma, president. He was overthrown (Dec. 16) by **Gen. Manuel Orellana,** who was not recognized by the U.S. and who soon resigned.

1930–31. José M. Andrade, president.

1931–44. GEN. JORGE UBICO (1878–1946) made himself president-dictator. He established close contact with the dictators of Honduras and El Salvador for the suppression of all opposition. Posing as a friend of the Indians, Ubico also oversaw the end of state-imposed forms of debt peonage in the country. In actual fact, however, the government then used vagrancy laws as a means of recruiting laborers for the coffee economy. This period also saw major railroad, land, and port concessions granted to a small number of foreign interests, with the United Fruit Company in the lead.

1935, June. By "plebiscite" **Ubico's term was extended** until 1943, and subsequently (1941) a constitutional convention extended it to 1949, but he was expelled in 1944.

1941, Dec. 8. Guatemala declared war on Japan, "thus expressing the solidarity of the Guatemalan government and people with the United States." On Dec. 11 Guatemala also declared war on Germany and Italy.

1944, June. **Ubico was forced to resign** after a student and then general strike elicited strong support for the opposition from progressive military officers and urban middle-class groups. He was followed by a brief right-wing regime, however, pushing dissident groups to arm in preparation for revolutionary struggle.

Oct. A coalition of urban middle-class groups, junior army officers, and working-class activists united to launch the **DEMOCRATIC REVOLUTION OF 1944**. **JACOBO ARBENZ GUZMAN (1913–71), Francisco Arana, and Jorge Toriello** established a military-civilian junta, which called for free elections in December.

Dec. 17–19. In Guatemala's first free elections, **JUAN JOSÉ ARÉVALO** (1904–90), a university professor, was **chosen president** to succeed dictator Jorge Ubico, who had been expelled. The new president followed a program of economic and labor reform, which met with growing opposition from large landowners, foreign investors (particularly the United Fruit Company), and the military. Arévalo was an anti-Communist, but he did promote social, educational, and health care reform, and introduced a **1947 Labor Code** that provided workers with social security and the right to unionize, bargain collectively, and strike. The latter greatly angered UFCO executives, who fought against the code. *(To p. 950)*

d. EL SALVADOR

(From p. 636)

1914. **Alfonso Quiñones Molina became president.** He represented the **Meléndez-Quiñones family**, which would control the presidency through several members until 1927, ruling under a state of siege after 1917.

1922. Several thousand **women marching in San Salvador** on behalf of opposition politicians were attacked and **many killed by soldiers.**

1923. Signing of a **loan agreement between U.S. banks and El Salvador.** The agreement, which gave the U.S. control of customs in the event of default on loans, accelerated the emergence of the U.S. as the dominant investor in El Salvador.

1927. Pío Romero Bosque, president.

1929. Founding of the **Communist Party of El Salvador** (PCES).

1931. Amid high rural unemployment and a growing rural protest movement led by the founder of El Salvador's Communist Party, **Agustín Farabundo Martí,** the populist engineer **Arturo Araujo was elected president.**

Dec. 2. A coup d'état enabled Maximiliano Hernández Martínez (1883–1966) to make himself president.

1932, Jan. 22. **Simultaneous uprisings,** organized by Farabundo Martí and his followers, were set to begin throughout the countryside. Martínez, however, was informed of the plan, and suppressed the rebellion easily. In the aftermath, in a series of actions known as **LA MATANZA** (The Massacre), perhaps as many as 30,000 people were hunted down and killed by government forces on the pretext of their Communist or otherwise subversive tendencies. These actions set the tone for the **Martínez dictatorship.**

1937, Aug. 10. El Salvador withdrew from the League of Nations.

1939. Salvadoran women were granted the vote.

Jan. 20. A constitutional congress **abrogated the constitution of 1886** and adopted a new regime, headed by **Gen. Andrés I. Menéndez.**

1944, April 19. In a highly charged climate, labor leaders called a **general strike, which paralyzed the national economy.** The crisis emerged from long-standing conflicts created by the increasing concentration of land in the hands of a small number of coffee magnates, and the military government's practice of catering exclusively to elites. The strike forced Gen. Menéndez to flee the nation, and opened the way for discussions of democratic and social reform. Fearing social unrest, hard-line military officers moved quickly to install **Gen. Salvador Castañeda** as president. After his ascension, Castañeda dissolved political parties, labor unions, and student groups, and meted out harsh treatment to their leaders. *(To p. 952)*

e. NICARAGUA

(From p. 636)

1912. Liberal revolts against the conservative regime of **Adolfo Díaz** were on the point of victory when U.S. troops were sent to Nicaragua to help put them down. After the entry of **American Marines,** the U.S. would essentially rule the country until 1925 through a series of puppet dictators.

1914, Aug. 5. Conclusion of the Bryan-Chamorro treaty with the United States by U.S. puppet Adolfo Díaz, giving the U.S. the right to construct a canal across Nicaragua and lease sites for naval bases. The treaty signified a concession for continued U.S. support of the Conservative regime. Costa Rica and El Salvador at once protested against what they claimed was an infringement of their sovereignty.

1916, April 13. The treaty was ratified by the U.S., with the inclusion of a declaration that its provisions were not intended to affect the rights of other states.

1916–21. EMILIANO CHAMORRO (1871–1966), president.

1917, March 2. El Salvador submitted the question of the Bryan-Chamorro treaty to the Central American Court of Justice, which declared the treaty to be a violation of the treaties of 1907. Nicaragua and the U.S. refused to abide by the ruling, and in the process helped to undermine the authority of the court.

1917–24. An American financial commission, in collaboration with the collector-general of customs, stabilized Nicaraguan finances, increasing U.S. control of the economy.

1921–23. Diego Chamorro, president.

1923–25. Martínez Bartolo, president.

1925, Aug. 3. Carlos Solórzano elected president. Like his predecessors he was a Conservative, but the new vice president, **Juan Sacasa (1874–1946),** was a Liberal. After the U.S.-supervised elections, the **Marines were withdrawn for a brief time.**

Oct. 25. A revolt, led by **Emiliano Chamorro,** forced Sacasa and other Liberals out of the government.

1926, Jan. 14. Solórzano resigned and **Chamorro became president.** The U.S. refused him recognition.

May 2. When a **Liberal insurrection** was started by **GEN. AUGUSTO CÉSAR SANDINO (1895–1934),** the U.S. government hastily landed forces. Dedicated to freeing the country of foreign domination and improving the lot of Nicaraguan peasants, **Sandino would fight a war against U.S. Marines and the National Guard for the next eight years.** A brief armistice was effected by the U.S. (Sept. 23); Chamorro then resigned.

Nov. 11. The Nicaraguan Congress elected Conservative **Adolfo Díaz** president.

Dec. 2. But **Sacasa returned** from exile in Mexico and set up a rival Liberal government recognized by Mexico. During the civil war that ensued, the U.S. government supported Díaz.

1927, May 4. Henry L. Stimson, representing the United States, succeeded in bringing the two factions together. President Díaz was to complete his term of office, the opposition was to disarm, and the U.S. was to supervise the forthcoming elections.

1928, Nov. 4. José Moncada (Liberal) was elected, with the U.S. government supervising the polling. Sandino, who had continued the fighting on his own account and who had gone so far as to attack American troops, withdrew to Mexico, but in 1931 he resumed the struggle.

1933, Jan. 1. With the Sandino forces numbering over 3,000, the U.S. Marines gave up the fight in Nicaragua. In keeping with the turn toward a less interventionist policy, initiated by Herbert Hoover and made official by Franklin Roosevelt, the U.S. created a **National Guard,** staffed and directed by Nicaraguans. U.S.-educated **GEN. ANASTASIO SOMOZA GARCÍA (1896–1956)** was appointed head of the guard, which was conceived as a peacekeeping force that would remain politically neutral.

1933–36. JUAN SACASA, president.

1934, Feb 21. During a U.S.-mediated negotiation between the government and Sandino, **Somoza ordered Sandino's execution.** In the following weeks scores of Sandino's followers were rounded up and executed, crushing the movement.

1936, June 2. Sacasa was deposed by the National Guard, led by Gen. Anastasio Somoza.

1937–47. ANASTASIO SOMOZA, president. Somoza undermined U.S. intentions in creating the National Guard by assuming the presidency, but the U.S. recognized his government nonetheless. He made himself virtual dictator and proceeded with the utmost vigor against sources of dissent. The introduction of rigid exchange controls was designed to help the country economically, but it met with indifferent success.

1939, Mar. 23. A constituent assembly approved a **new constitution** and reelected Somoza.

1941, Dec. 11. Nicaragua declared war on Japan, Germany, and Italy. Somoza was a strong supporter of the U.S. throughout the war.

1944. Somoza declared a new labor code because of severe unrest, briefly winning the support of the Nicaraguan Socialist Party (PSN).

(To p. 953)

f. COSTA RICA

(From p. 637)

1917, Jan. 27. President Alfredo González Flores was overthrown by a military coup led by **Federico Tinoco.** The U.S. refused recognition to the new regime.

1919, May 6. Tinoco was deposed by the Flores party. **U.S. Marines were landed** (June 4) to protect American interests.

Dec. 9. Election of Julio Acosta as president; the U.S. government granted recognition (1920).

1921. Conflict with Panama over the boundary.

1924–28. Ricardo Jiménez (1859–1945), president.

1924, Dec. 24. Costa Rica withdrew from the League of Nations.

1928–32. Cleto González Víquez, president.

1932–36. Ricardo Jiménez again president. During this time the country went through a series of crises due to falling coffee prices and the decline in the Caribbean banana industry (which had peaked in the 1910s). The economy was dominated by two groups: the white or mestizo medium-size coffee growers of the uplands, and owners of the large banana plantations of the coasts. Both of these industries employed mainly black Caribbean immigrants, who organized into leftist labor movements in the late 1920s. With the onset of the crisis of the 1930s, major confrontations between these workers and the landowners were forestalled by a series of laws that allowed unemployed or underemployed workers to occupy public lands and colonize them.

1936–40. Léon Cortés Castro, president.

1941, Dec. 8. Costa Rica declared war on Japan as a consequence of the Japanese attack on the U.S. *(To p. 954)*

g. HONDURAS

(From p. 637)

1916, March. Francisco Bertrand became president following a successful revolution.

1919, Aug. Insurrection of Rafael López Gutiérrez, a Liberal. President Bertrand was obliged to flee, and U.S. Marines were landed (Sept 11). Through American mediation a civil war was avoided.

1920–23. Gutiérrez became president. The elections of 1923 proved to be indecisive, however.

1924, Feb. 1. Gutiérrez then established a dictatorship. The Conservatives, under **TIBURCIO CARÍAS ANDINO (1876–1960),** rose in revolt and marched on the capital. The U.S. severed relations with Gutiérrez and landed more troops. Gutiérrez was killed (March 10).

March 31. The insurgents occupied the capital. Through U.S. mediation **(mission of Sumner Welles)** agreement was reached between Honduras and its neighbors, depriving insurgent bands of their bases **(pact of Amapala,** May 3). **Vicente Tosta** became provisional president, and he suppressed an attempt at further revolution by **Gregorio Ferrara** (Aug.–Oct.). A new constitution was then framed.

1925. MIGUEL PAZ BARAHONA became president, U.S forces having prevented revolutionary leaders from becoming candidates. The United States supported Barahona against further attempts at revolt by Ferrara.

1928. Vicente Mejía Colindres, president.

1933. Gen. Tiburcio Carías, president. He assumed practically dictatorial powers.

1936, Apr. 15. The constitution was amended to enable the president to retain power until 1943. The growing unrest in the country led to numerous outbreaks and revolts.

1937, Jan.–Feb. A serious uprising, led by **Gen. Justo Umana,** was crushed. The government drove all opponents of the regime into flight or else imprisoned them.

1939, Dec. 23. Parliament extended Carías's term to 1949.

1941, Dec. 8. Honduras declared war on Japan and four days later (Dec. 12) on **Germany and Italy.** *(To p. 955)*

4. MEXICO

(From p. 638)

The **REVOLUTION** that convulsed Mexico, beginning with the **insurrection against Díaz in 1910,** brought the country to total civil war by 1914. During the 34-year rule of **Porfirio Díaz** the country had gone through enormous economic changes, benefiting members of the elites and a small emergent middle class, but at the same time creating massive unrest in the countryside. The development of the railways, mines, commercial agriculture, and small-scale manufacturing transformed Mexico into a modern economy, but large numbers of subsistence peasant villages and other peripheral cultures lost their autonomy to centralized powers as well as access to their lands. During the late **Porfiriato,** unrest mounted and rural rebellions increased in frequency. By 1910 a number of factors—the depression that had begun in 1907, explosive misery and instability in the countryside, the decay and corruption of the regime, a weakened military, and discontent among affluent but disenfranchised middle-class and elite groups—came together to produce a massive social revolution.

In regions such as **Morelos,** where plantation agriculture had made great advances during the Porfiriato, campesinos under **EMILIANO ZAPATA** (1879–1919) remained rebellious for more than a decade, demanding a return of usurped land. In **Chihuahua,** where Porfirian progress had turned the frontier into a commercialized region, cross-class coalitions under leaders such as **FRANCISCO (PANCHO) VILLA** (1877–1923) also struggled for almost a decade against Porfirian and

other centralizing forces. These groups represented the most radical elements of the revolution. They sought to recreate Mexican society in a way that empowered the lowest classes. By Dec. 1914, with Villa and Zapata in control of Mexico City, their victory seemed possible.

At the same time, members of the middle classes, foreigners, and the elites that had grown rich during the Porfiriato reacted decisively against the radical revolution. In 1914, more moderate leaders, such as **VENUSTIANO CARRANZA** (1859–1920) and **ALVARO OBREGÓN** (1880–1928), organized coalitions of old Porfirian interests and middle-class and urban working-class groups to stem the tide of the revolution. With the help of an infusion of American arms, these groups took control of the revolution by 1916, and proceeded to place all reforms within a very restrictive context.

1910–11. Liberal **FRANCISCO I. MADERO** (1873–1913), after being defrauded of the presidency in the 1910 election, led a broad insurrectionary movement that **overthrew Porfirio Díaz** (May 25, 1911) and installed Madero as provisional president.

1911, Nov. 6. Madero elected president. Scion of a wealthy landed family, Madero soon alienated his more radical supporters with his indifference to demands for land reform. At the same time, Madero's political reforms antagonized Porfirian military officers and the U.S. ambassador, **Henry Lane Wilson.**

Nov. 28. Emiliano Zapata issued the PLAN DE AYALA, which proclaimed that all lands, waters, and woods seized by *hacendados*, political bosses, and others during the Porfiriato due to **"tyranny and venal justice"** would be returned by his revolutionary government; he then proceeded to implement that plan in the areas under his control.

1913, Feb. 9. The **military garrison at Tacubaya rebelled against the Madero presidency,** attacking the National Palace. The first counterrevolutionary attack failed, but the rebels retreated to the Citadel, and began a ten-day artillery battle—the *Decena Trágica*—in Mexico City, during which most of the victims were civilians.

Feb. 18. With the support of U.S. ambassador H. L. Wilson, **VICTORIANO HUERTA** (1854–1916), Madero's military commander, **ARRESTED AND MURDERED THE PRESIDENT AND VICE PRESIDENT.** Huerta then assumed leadership of the government.

1913–14. Outraged by the murder of Madero and regarding Huerta's regime as a restoration of the old order, **revolutionary forces led by Villa, Carranza, Obregón, and Zapata rose in revolt against Huerta.**

1914, April 9. A group of U.S. Marines was arrested by Huerta's forces at Tampico. The U.S. demanded satisfaction (especially a salute). On the refusal of Huerta to meet American demands, **U.S. troops occupied Veracruz** (April 21). Huerta broke off relations with the U.S. South American states attempted to mediate, and on Nov. 23 U.S. forces evacuated Veracruz.

July 5. Victoriano Huerta was elected president. He resigned almost at once (July 15), largely because of the refusal of the U.S. government to recognize him, which made his position untenable.

Aug. 15. Alvaro Obregón and a Constitutionalist army took Mexico City, and **Venustiano Carranza became president.** The Constitutionalists, at this point, held only part of the country. In the north **Pancho Villa** was virtual dictator. He at once declared war on the Carranza regime, installing **Eulalio Gutiérrez** as president (deposed Jan. 17, 1915).

Dec. After Carranza failed to resign by a Nov. 10 deadline, the armies of **Villa and Zapata fell on Mexico City,** occupying it.

Dec. 4. Villa and Zapata held their first meeting in Mexico City, agreeing on a radical course for the future revolution under the provisional leadership of Gutiérrez. Villa and Zapata, however, proved unskilled at politics and foreign relations, and these weaknesses soon proved their downfall. At the same time that they were occupying the capital, **Carranza** was planning his comeback, **reformulating the Constitutionalist movement** in order to broaden its appeal to workers and peasants.

1915, Jan. 27. Obregón recaptured Mexico City for the Constitutionalists.

March 29. Carrancista forces under **Gen. Salvador Alvarado** entered Mérida, Yucatán, deposing **Abel Ortíz Argumedo.** The region had been quiet up to that point, largely because the rural peasantry had been devastated by the **Caste War** of the 1840s and was living in such restrictive, slavelike conditions that organization was nearly impossible. Initiating reform from the top down, Alvarado freed labor by ending debt peonage and engaged in limited mobilization of the workers, encouraging urban unions and peasant leagues.

April. Pancho Villa's 25,000-strong army was defeated at the **Battle of Celaya** by forces under the command of Alvaro Obregón. Using techniques gleaned from the battlefields of Europe, and arms supplied by the U.S., Obregón devastated Villa's forces, killing 5,000 and wounding 6,000 more, while losing only a few hundred men. The battle marked the beginning of the end for Villa and the emergence of Carranza as the ultimate victor in the war.

Oct. 19. The **U.S. government and a number of Latin American states recognized Carranza** as de facto president. Great Britain followed suit (Nov. 16).

1916, March 9. Villa's forces raided across the border into **Columbus, New Mexico.** A U.S. punitive expedition pursued him into Mexico (March 15). Carranza protested the violation of Mexican territory and authorized resistance. Clash of Americans and Mexicans at **Carrizal** (June 21). Ultimately conferences were arranged to arrive at some settlement. American troops departed on Feb. 5, 1917.

1917, Jan. 31. The **NEW CONSTITUTION** was adopted by the Mexican congress (promulgated Feb. 5). This instrument had been worked out by a constitutional convention, in session since Nov. 21. Representing **advanced nationalist and radical social views,** the Constitution of 1917

at once became the charter of the new Mexico. It provided for universal male suffrage (delegates to the constitutional convention at Querétaro were hostile to female political participation). The most significant sections included **Article 3,** which (reflecting strong anticlerical sentiment) restricted the power and property of the Church and monastic orders and called for **free, secular, and obligatory primary education for all Mexican children. Article 27** called for the **return of peasant lands** seized illegally during the Porfiriato (providing the complainant possessed written title), made private ownership of land a privilege and not a right, and curbed foreign ownership of land and subsoil rights. **Article 123,** the **labor code,** called for an eight-hour day, a minimum wage, labor arbitration, and the **right to strike.** Though radical for the time, the articles calling for redistribution of land and labor reform were not initially implemented because of conservative opposition.

Under the new constitution Obregón also created a government **Office of Anthropology,** under **Manuel Gamio.** As part of a new effort to assert the valuable contributions of Indian culture to Mexico, the office promoted cultural and social studies of indigenous Mexico.

March 11. Carranza was elected president for a four-year term, being barred from running for reelection. During the next three years he consolidated Constitutionalist rule and swung the **revolution far to the right.** While he remained strongly nationalist regarding foreign interests, he redistributed very little land, suppressed workers' movements, and ignored calls for free education. During this period his armies also continued to **repress any remaining resistance in the countryside.**

1918. Formation of the **Regional Confederation of Mexican Labor** (Confederación Regional Obrera Méxicana, popularly called the CROM) by **Luis N. Morones.** The confederation was the counterpart of the American Federation of Labor and was an important factor in the constitutional and social reform movement. Morones, as CROM leader, eschewed confrontation for a conciliatory attitude toward the government, and accepted generous government donations. Notorious for enriching himself at the expense of the union, he would later accept the position of **secretary of labor** under **Plutarco Elías Calles.**

Jan. Textile workers in Veracruz won 80–100 percent pay raises in the wake of a series of strikes. Strike actions on the part of Veracruz and Puebla textile workers over wage issues multiplied between 1917 and 1925, peaking at over 300 in the early 1920s.

Feb. 19. Oil was declared an inalienable national resource, a tax was levied on oil lands and contracts, and titles to oil lands were to be transformed into concessions. American and British companies, supported by their governments, protested. The matter was settled by compromise, but the episode was only the first move in a long campaign to break the power and wealth of foreign companies.

1919, April 10. After struggling to defeat Zapatista forces for years, Carranza approved a plan to lure Zapata into a phony meeting with a "defecting" officer. Upon arrival **Zapata was executed by federal soldiers.**

1920–26. Initial enthusiasm over the radical articles in the Constitution of 1917 waned. Conservative governments refused to implement land and labor codes, eschewing reform in favor of proforeign and procapitalist economic and social policies to jumpstart a devastated economy. With the original revolutionaries largely destroyed, new regional leaders emerged who continued the battle for social revolution. **Primo Tapia,** a Tarascan peasant, led a series of agrarian revolts for land in **Michoacán.** The sentiment in these revolts, which were echoed by leaders such as **Adalberto Tejada in Veracruz,** represented **continuing discontent** with the slow and uneven pace of land and political reform in rural Mexico. In some cases these movements also promoted a strong sense of **Indian ethnic identity,** aligning with Mexico's growing **Indigenista movement.**

1920, April 9. Three of the leading generals (Adolfo de la Huerta, Alvaro Obregón, and Plutarco Elías Calles) joined forces against Carranza, who was accused of attempting to dictate the presidential succession. The opposition, an alliance of Sonoran generals from the north, proclaimed **the Plan de Agua Prieta** and took to the field.

May 8. Obregón took Mexico City and thereafter many of the cities on the east coast. **Carranza was killed** (May 21), **and Villa surrendered** to the victorious insurgents (July 27); he was endowed with a handsome estate, which he enjoyed until his assassination in 1923.

Sept. 5. OBREGÓN elected president. He was recognized by the U.S.

(Aug. 31, 1923) upon agreement to respect titles to land acquired before 1917 and to accept an adjustment of American claims.

1922, Jan.–1924, Jan. The Marxist **Felipe Carrillo Puerto** was **governor of Yucatán.** Diverging from the conservatism of his predecessors, he initiated widespread agrarian reform, extensively redistributing land. Turning the revolution into a distinct regional movement, he mobilized campesinos around his **Southeast Socialist Party** (PSS). His regional radicalism aroused opposition from Obregón, and Carrillo was deposed and killed during the de la Huerta revolt.

1923, Dec. 6. Adolfo de la Huerta led a revolt against the government of Obregón and the latter's candidate for the presidency, Calles. The U.S. government supported Obregón, who was able to crush the insurrection (1924).

1924–28. PLUTARCO ELÍAS CALLES (1877–1945), president. The authoritarian Calles ruled Mexico directly or indirectly for a decade, a period known as the **MAXIMATO.** After a long and serious controversy with the U.S. regarding the application of the constitution to foreign properties, Calles agreed that American oil companies would not need to apply for new concessions (1927, **Calles-Morrow agreement**).

Because of the prosperity of the mid-1920s Calles was able to continue some agrarian and educational reform, but soon came into **conflict with the Roman Catholic Church** over the application of constitutional provisions.

1926, July 31. The **archbishop** of Mexico declared a **strike** against the state, leading to a **GREAT INSURRECTION,** known as the **"CRISTERO REVOLT,"** which soon affected a dozen provinces. The Cristeros called for an end to the oppressive measures the government had implemented against the Catholic Church, and a return to the religious and ethnic autonomy of earlier years. In the struggle **Calles proved himself the strongman** of Mexico by proceeding with great vigor against the rebels. Most of the **leaders were defeated, captured, and executed** by late 1927, but several areas remained in revolt beyond the end of Calles's term in 1928.

1927, Feb. The Church publicly repudiated the Constitution of 1917, but the government (Feb. 11) ordered **nationalization of Church property** and began to close Church schools. Foreign priests, monks, and nuns were deported.

1928, July 1. Obregón was reelected president, but was **assassinated** a few weeks later (July 17) by a devout Catholic. He was the fourth key revolutionary leader (besides Zapata, Carranza, and Villa) to be assassinated.

1928–30. Emilio Portes Gil served as provisional president. Calles, however, remained the real power in the regime.

1929, March–April. Calles put down another **insurrection, provoked by political and religious discontent** and led by **Gens. Jesús María Aguirre** and **Gonzalo Escobar.**

June 21. A compromise agreement was reached **with the Church.**

Aug. 11. Promulgation of an **extensive labor code,** in accordance with the 1917 constitution: eight-hour day, six-day week, right to strike, minimum wage, compulsory insurance, etc.

1930–32. Pascual Ortiz Rubio, president. Calles remained the dominant figure, and the new administration continued the policy of its predecessors.

1931, Sept. 9. Mexico joined the League of Nations.

1932, Sept. 3. President Ortiz Rubio resigned after a difference with Calles, who had (1931) assumed the ministry of war.

1932–34. Gen. Abelardo Rodríguez served as provisional president.

1933. Adoption of a **six-year plan** of social legislation and economic development, which really signified a move to the right on the part of Calles and the National Revolutionary Party, insofar as it deferred some of the more radical measures earlier envisaged.

1934, July 2. GENERAL LÁZARO CÁRDENAS (1895–1970), the choice of Calles, was **elected president** for a six-year term (recently extended by constitutional amendment). Cárdenas was a former revolutionary general who had had some success with land reform as governor of Michoacán between 1928 and 1932. Conflict soon developed between Calles and the new president, who represented the advanced wing of the party and regarded Calles as too conservative. In 1935 he **forced Calles into exile.** Thereafter Cárdenas, undisputed master of the country, embarked upon an **accelerated program of reform,** in which he was supported by the new Confederation of Mexican Workers (Feb. 1936), led by **Vicente Lombardo Toledano.**

Within a few years twice as much **land was expropriated** as in the years 1917–34. This was **distributed to the peasants on the communal (ejido) basis.** Cárdenas gave out over **49 million acres** of land to these communities, and established a bank to provide them credit. Cárdenas used the *ejido* as the symbol of Mexico's indigenous heritage, focusing his vision on a reconciliation between the noble Indian past and the need for modernization. With regard to the Church, Cárdenas adopted a more conciliatory attitude, though he insisted on the **elimination of the Church from politics** and upheld the nationalization of its property.

1936. Mexican workers engaged in a **series of strikes against foreign-owned oil companies,** demanding better wages and working conditions. Although relatively well paid, the workers were angry about the excessive oil profits that left the country and the refusal of the companies to engage in serious labor negotiations.

Feb. 26–29. At a **National Unification Congress** called by various unions, participants agreed to create the **Confederation of Mexican Workers (CTM)** under the leadership of **Lombardo Toledano.** Reflecting the reemergence of a powerful labor movement, the CTM was a **Communist**-backed alternative to the corrupt CROM, and totaled over 1 million members by 1938.

Nov. 23. A new **expropriation law empowered the government to seize private property** when necessary for the "public or social welfare."

1937, June 23. Thereupon the **National Railways of Mexico were taken over by the workers.**

Nov. 1. As the conflict between the foreign oil companies and Mexican workers began to endanger the economy, the **government nationalized the subsoil rights of Standard Oil and several other companies.** Cárdenas also submitted the dispute to the Industrial Arbitration Board, which ruled in favor of better wages and benefits for the workers. U.S. and British oil interests refused to abide by the decision. The government, representing labor, appealed to the Mexican Supreme Court, which decided for the government in the wage dispute (March 1). Oil companies again rejected the judgment.

March 18. The **Mexican government took over the properties of the U.S. and British oil companies,** which the companies valued at $450 million. The measure was extremely popular in Mexico, leading to massive public demonstrations, but the foreign governments strenuously protested. The U.S. government (which under Franklin Roosevelt had had very friendly relations with Mexico) discontinued silver purchases from Mexico as a retaliatory measure. The British government suspended diplomatic relations.

May–June. Cárdenas proceeded against Gen. Saturnino Cedillo, "boss" of the province of San Luis Potosí, who was reported on the verge of revolt in the interest of conservative groups. The movement was easily broken.

July 21. The **U.S. government proposed arbitration of claims against Mexico** for oil expropriations. Although the Americans insisted that their properties were worth over $200 million, the Mexican government argued that the companies had recovered their investment in Mexico many times over, and offered only $10 million. Eventually a compromise figure of $24 million was agreed upon.

Sept. 5. Mexico concluded oil barter agreements with Germany, Italy, and other nations, by which the oil would be exchanged for manufactured goods (previously imported chiefly from the U.S. and Britain). The U.S. strongly opposed these agreements.

Nov. 12. Finally the **U.S. and Mexico reached an accord on the land question.** Commissioners were to appraise the value of the properties and the Mexican government was to pay compensation at the rate of $1 million per annum until claims were liquidated. Efforts to reach an agreement on the oil issue failed to produce results.

1939. Cárdenas oversaw the **creation of the Party of the Mexican Revolution (PRM),** which had representation from the military, agrarian groups, labor, and popular movements. This reflected Cárdenas's move away from more radical politics, and toward creating a broad-based political process in Mexico. With this in mind, Cárdenas then threw his support behind **Manuel Avila Camacho,** a Conservative Catholic, for the 1940 election.

1940, July 7. Avila Camacho was elected president of Mexico. His ascension in December marked a move by the revolutionary party to the right.

1942, May 22. Mexico declared war on Germany, Italy, and Japan.

Nov. 19. Mexico reestablished diplomatic relations with the Soviet Union. *(To p. 956)*

5. THE WEST INDIES

a. CUBA

(From p. 638)

1917, April 7. Cuba declared war on Germany. The war period was one of great prosperity for the sugar industry, large quantities being shipped to the U.S. But after the war the market collapsed, with serious results for Cuba.

1920, March 8. Cuba joined the League of Nations.

Nov. 1. Dr. Alfredo Zayas, candidate of the coalition National League, elected, but his opponent, José Gómez (Liberal), launched accusations of fraud. To prevent conflict the U.S. government sent **Gen. Enoch Crowder,** who arranged for new elections (March 15, 1921), which resulted in another victory for Zayas.

1921–25. Alfredo Zayas, president. Crowder was recalled (1923). Crowder's meddling in Cuban politics, however, combined with rampant government corruption and a collapse in Cuba's monocultural sugar economy, helped to revive Cuban nationalism. Under Zayas the Cuban government gradually adopted a policy of opposition to U.S. interference.

1925–33. Liberal **GERARDO MACHADO** (1871–1939), **president.** He attempted to solve the problems of the sugar industry by restricting production; also stimulated industrial development with higher tariffs, and promoted public works and sanitation. This period saw a marked increase in political violence and unrest. Machado used assassinations and strong-arm tactics to silence opposition leaders and striking workers on several occasions. In 1928 he extended his political control by outlawing the opposition party of **Carlos Mendieta** and having himself reelected. This move aroused much opposition, which was enhanced by economic difficulties arising from the world depression. Workers' movements, based in urban factories and on the rural sugar plantations, grew in both size and militancy in response to this situation.

1930, May. A **general strike** led by radical workers and student groups failed to topple the Machado government. In the aftermath political assassinations and repression increased.

Sept. After the killing of a student leader, students at the University of Havana organized a demonstration, which led to the closing of the university and firing of hundreds of teachers.

1930–31. A **revolt led by Mario Menocal** was suppressed and various restrictive measures were introduced, but unrest and disorders continued (1931–33). During this time student groups, labor unions, and Communist organizations grew more popular as bases of opposition to Machado. The U.S. had, at the outset, declared its intention not to intervene except in case of extreme anarchy, but it did attempt to mediate.

1933, Aug 12. After a **bus drivers' strike in Havana expanded into a general strike** that led to numerous major demonstrations and police massacres, an **army revolt** forced Machado out of office. **Carlos Manuel de Céspedes became president,** but disorder continued and the U.S. sent warships to Cuba.

Sept. 5. Céspedes was driven from office by another army coup, known as the **"sergeants' revolt,"** led by FULGENCIO BATISTA (1901–73), a sergeant himself, who became virtual dictator, though he eschewed political office.

Sept. 10. Ramón Grau San Martín (1887–1969) became president and established a reformist government, which was not recognized by the U.S. since he was regarded as too nationalist. Grau San Martín had only a tenuous hold on power, however, and quickly faced the ire of leftist groups, which were unhappy with the pace of his reforms, as well as right-wing groups, which opposed all reform.

1934. Cuban women granted the vote.

Jan. 20. Overthrow of Grau San Martín. Carlos Mendieta became president.

May 29. An AGREEMENT TO RESCIND THE PLATT AMEND-MENT and thus all formal limitations on Cuban sovereignty was concluded with the U.S. by Mendieta. Somewhat later (Aug. 24) the U.S. and Cuba signed a reciprocal trade agreement favorable to the latter.

1935, Dec. 10. Mendieta resigned.

1936, Jan. 10. Miguel Mariano Gómez was elected president.

Dec. 23. Gómez was forced from office by Batista.

Dec. 24–1940. Federico Laredo Bru became president. Batista remained the real dictator, and his regime, after 1933, embarked on a policy that apparently aimed at a corporatist state along Fascist lines. All political and social opposition was dealt with in drastic fashion. At the same time the government threw itself into radical social legislation and adopted (July 25, 1937) a **three-year plan** that involved state control of the sugar and mining industries, the reorganization of agricultural schools, the distribution of land, etc.

1939. Batista legalized the **Popular Socialist Party** (PSP), the Cuban Communist party.

1940, Feb. A convention assembled to draft a new constitution, which came into force on Oct. 10, with Fulgencio Batista as head of the government (July 14).

July 14. Fulgencio Batista was elected president of Cuba. He invited two Communists into his cabinet in order to garner the support of left-wing movements and labor groups.

1941, Dec. 9. Cuba declared war on Japan and also (Dec. 11) on Germany and Italy.

1942, Oct. 16. Cuba established diplomatic relations with the USSR.

1944, May 31. Ramón Grau San Martín was elected president for a four-year term. His new regime was notorious for its corruption. Some reform occurred, and labor and women's movements were very active, but the regime responded to activism with repression. *(To p. 958)*

b. PUERTO RICO

(From p. 638)

1915. Santiago Iglesias founded the **Puerto Rican Socialist Party (PS).** As part of a growing militant labor movement, based in both the urban and the rural sectors, Iglesias led strikes, helped found labor unions, and struggled against the invasion of U.S. goods and capital.

1917, March 2. The JONES ACT, making Puerto Rico a territory and granting U.S. citizenship to its inhabitants. Voting was made compulsory. Proportional representation was established by means of a "limited vote" for certain senators and representatives. It was further provided that U.S. internal revenue collections on the island should be paid into the Puerto Rican treasury. (Subsequently permission was accorded the island to collect U.S. income tax for the benefit of the local treasury.) With such assistance, the budget of the insular government increased from about $2 million in 1901 to $11 million in 1924. More than half of these funds were derived from what would normally be federal taxation. At the same time, however, the island continued to be run by appointed governors from the mainland United States with little experience or knowledge of Puerto Rico.

May. The U.S. having declared war on Germany, the **selective draft was extended to Puerto Rico** by request of the insular government. Some 18,000 men were inducted into service.

1918, June 2. The war, thus far rather distant, was suddenly brought home to the Puerto Ricans when a German submarine sank the *Carolina* on its voyage from San Juan to New York.

1924, March. A delegation, including Gov. Horace Towner, came to the U.S. with the request that Puerto Rico be granted the **rights of statehood** without representation in Congress.

1928. The **Puerto Rican legislature petitioned President Coolidge for the grant of autonomy** without statehood. Autonomy was desired to provide homesteads for the peasantry, to free the island from U.S. tariff restrictions, and to deal with the problem of absentee landlordism.

During the same year **Dr. Pedro Albizu Campos** founded the Nationalist Party, a small but militant proindependence organization.

1930. Gov. Theodore Roosevelt, Jr., was forced to appeal to Congress and to private philanthropy to aid the depressed population, of whom 60 percent were without employment. By this point the Puerto Rican economy had been radically transformed by the arrival of the Americans. Coffee, once the island's predominant crop, was supplanted by sugar, which was grown on nearly 50 percent of the island's cultivable land by 1930. American industrialists as well were increasingly exploiting the labor of the island in harsh, low-paying sweatshops.

1933. The Democratic administration in the United States took a greater interest in the Puerto Rican situation. Unemployment on the island was massive, and conditions in general were much worse than on the mainland. The government used measures resembling those employed in the U.S. to deal with the crisis, but relief measures in Puerto Rico were very limited and ineffective. Meanwhile, ever stronger demands for redefinition of status developed in the island. Apart from widespread prostatehood sentiment, a growing and militant nationalist movement aimed at independence.

1936. After the **assassination of American police captain Francis Riggs** (who a year earlier had been involved in the deaths of the Nationalist Party's labor secretary and several students), Dr. **Albizu Campos** (who was a great supporter of Franco's Spain and was accused of being a Fascist sympathizer) and the rest of the Nationalist Party leadership were **arrested** and charged with attempting to overthrow the government. During the ensuing trials and protests that accompanied it, sympathy for the nationalist cause continued to grow.

1937, March 21. During a rally protesting the imprisonment of Dr. Albizu Campos and his leadership, **U.S. troops opened fire, killing 20 and wounding many more.** In the aftermath, over 2,000 supporters of the Nationalist Party were jailed.

1939. LUIS MUÑOZ MARÍN founded the **Popular Democratic Party (PPD)**, a populist reform party more moderate than the Nationalist Party. The PPD, led by U.S.-educated professionals and intellectuals, and supported by elements of the labor movement, moved away from direct demands for independence and focused its energies on economic and social reform.

June 4. A committee of the legislature brought forth a demand for statehood and in the interval **"demanded" an elective governor with power to appoint officials.**

1941–46. Rexford G. Tugwell, governor. An economist and supporter of the New Deal, Tugwell promoted a **"peaceful revolution"** on the island in which the profits from the wartime boom in rum were reinvested into public corporations and industry. Unlike his predecessors, Tugwell worked closely with Muñoz Marín in achieving his goals, and strongly advocated free elections for governor. *(To p. 960)*

c. THE VIRGIN ISLANDS

1916, Aug. 4. AMERICAN-DANISH TREATY, by which Denmark agreed to cede the Danish West Indies (about 100 islands with a total area of 132 square miles) to the United States for $25 million. The treaty was ratified on Jan. 17, 1917, and formal possession was taken on March 31 of the same year. Danish laws were allowed to remain in effect.

The population (c. 26,000 in 1917) suffered much from economic distress. The **sugar industry** of St. Croix had been in a process of concentration and many small sugar mills had been abandoned. Ultimately all grinding was done in three large "centrals." Many laborers were thereby thrown out of employment. The loss of free port status, which had existed under Danish rule, reduced the trade of the islands, especially of St. Thomas. The American Prohibition law (1919) further destroyed the market for sugar products, though bay rum continued to be manufactured. The main achievement of the U.S. administration was the **development of education.**

1931, Feb. After a succession of governors from the U.S. Navy, the U.S. established a **civil government** for the islands, making St. Thomas the capital. **Paul M. Pearson** became the first civil governor.

March. The **depression** became so pronounced in the islands that President Hoover referred to them as "an effective poorhouse," with 90 percent of the population dependent upon the bounty of the U.S.

1933. The **Roosevelt administration** began **relief measures** in the islands. Development of the tourist trade, expansion of the **rum industry,** etc., did much to ameliorate economic conditions.

1936, June 22. The **Organic Act** revised the political arrangements of government. The governor was to be assisted by a territorial legislative assembly, composed of the elected municipal councils of St. Thomas and St. Croix.

1938, Jan. 1. Universal suffrage went into effect under the new arrangements.

d. THE DOMINICAN REPUBLIC

(From p. 639)

1914, June 26. Fearing for the safety of U.S.-owned sugar estates, **the U.S. government intervened in Dominican struggles** to restore order.

1916, May. Further outbreaks resulted in further intervention.

Nov. 29. U.S. MARINES INVADED AND OCCUPIED THE COUNTRY. Immediately the American occupying force took over banks and customs houses and broke up small-scale peasant holdings to protect and expand U.S.-owned enterprises. U.S. administrators devastated traditional landholders by imposing modern landownership regulations in the country. This generated opposition in the republic as well as in the U.S., and made the Americans anxious for an early withdrawal of the occupying force.

1922, June 30. Agreement between the Dominican government and the United States. Because of mounting opposition in the U.S. and an aggressive guerrilla campaign against American forces, the withdrawal of American troops was set for an early date. American rule ended on Oct. 21, and the last marines were withdrawn on Sept. 18, 1924. A provisional government was set up.

1924–30. Horacio Vásquez became president.

1924, Sept. 29. The Dominican Republic joined the League of Nations as soon as the last American forces had left.

1929, April. A **U.S. commission,** headed by Charles G. Dawes, at the request of the Dominican government investigated its finances and made recommendations.

1930, Feb. 23. An **uprising** led by National Guard commander **Rafael Trujillo** toppled President Vásquez.

1930–38. RAFAEL LEONIDAS TRUJILLO (1871–1961), president. An avowed advocate of U.S. interests and commander of the U.S.-sponsored Dominican National Guard, Trujillo would rule the Dominican Republic as a ruthless dictator for 31 years. Over the period of his dictatorship increased sugar and mineral exports allowed Trujillo to pay for expanded public works and other construction projects. Political control, however, was maintained through extensive intelligence networks and brutal suppression of any perceived opposition.

1936. Trujillo had the name of the capital changed to **Ciudad Trujillo.** Always one for self-aggrandizement, Trujillo constructed countless monuments to himself.

1937, Oct. The Dominican government **drove a large number of immigrant Haitians back over the border, killing as many as 20,000 people** in the process. This led to protests and demands for reparation from the Haitian government, which invoked American conciliation treaties for settlement of the dispute. By this method an agreement was arrived at (Jan. 31, 1938).

1938, May 17. Jacinto B. Peynardo was elected president after Trujillo announced his forthcoming retirement.

1941, Dec. 8. The Dominican Republic declared war on Japan, and shortly after (Dec. 11) on Germany and Italy.

1942. Dominican women received the vote. *(To p. 961)*

e. HAITI

(From p. 639)

1914, Dec. 17. Fearing German designs on Haiti, and wanting to protect American commercial interests there, U.S. Marines landed at Port-au-Prince and seized $500,000 in gold coin from the National Bank. These actions marked the beginning of a 20-year period during which American troops would occupy Haiti (permanent occupation began in July

1915). The country had been in a state of constant unrest for several years, following upon a century of economic and environmental decline due in part to the inefficiency of Haiti's peasant-based agriculture. Unrest was intensified by the tensions between Haiti's small (10 percent) mulatto population, which held most of the power and wealth, and the large black population, which lived in extreme poverty. During the occupation the U.S. controlled Haitian customs and the police.

1915–22. Philippe Dartiguenave, president.

1915, Sept. 16. Due to a fear that Haitian instability would make the nation an easy target for outside powers, the **U.S. Marines occupied Haiti** (to stay there until 1934). The U.S. also **took over the financial administration** of the country and the customs houses in order to ensure timely payment of the Haitian foreign debt. Over the next three decades the U.S. would come to control most aspects of Haitian political life, from the organization of the military to the choice of political leaders.

1918, June 19. A **new constitution** was introduced.

July 12. Haiti declared war on Germany.

1918–19. A **revolt against the U.S. occupation** led by **Charlemagne Perlate** caused much trouble but was eventually suppressed.

1920, June 30. Haiti joined the League of Nations.

1922–30. Luis Borno, president.

1929, Dec. Opposition to his rule led to **serious disorders.** Larger U.S. forces were sent to the island, where they were attacked by mobs. One of the root causes of the anti-U.S. sentiment was the American practice of giving preference to Haitian mulattos (because of their light skin) over blacks in government and other arenas of power.

1930, Feb.–March. In view of the widespread anti-American feeling, **a commission of investigation,** headed by **W. Cameron Forbes,** was sent out by the Washington government. This commission recommended administrative reforms, the replacement of the military high commissioner by a civilian, and the continuation of the treaty relationship until 1936. It also persuaded Borno to relinquish office.

1930–41. Stenio Vincent (1874–1959) became president. With American aid, order was restored, finances and administration were reformed, public improvements introduced, and education developed. At the same time a series of agreements was made providing for eventual termination of U.S. control. These were blocked by the Haitian assembly, which insisted on immediate withdrawal. After the advent of the Roosevelt administration, arrangements were quickly made for complete termination of U.S. control and liquidation of the Haitian foreign debt.

1934, Aug. 6. The American forces were withdrawn. After a plebiscite and under executive pressure, the Haitian assembly approved the agreements with the U.S.

1935, June 17. The Haitian assembly adopted a **new constitution,** which endowed the president with broad executive powers. Vincent's term was extended to 1941.

1937, Oct. An acute crisis developed in **relations between Haiti and the Dominican Republic,** because of the massacre of Haitians who had migrated there to work. The Vincent government sought a peaceful solution and requested the good offices of the U.S., Mexico, and Cuba. An agreement was finally reached on Jan. 31, 1938.

1941, Dec. 8. Haiti declared war on Japan and later (Dec. 12) on Germany and Italy.

(To p. 962)

F. THE MIDDLE EAST AND NORTH AFRICA, 1914–1945

1. OVERVIEW

(From p. 525)

Between the two world wars, several forces—both internal and external—combined to produce **unprecedented change** in the societies, cultures, economies, and political systems of the Middle East and North Africa. The most disruptive of these forces was **European imperialism,** which reached its zenith during these decades. **Britain and France** (together with Italy in Libya and Spain in part of Morocco) possessed extensive **colonial dominions** and wielded considerable **influence** even in countries that they did not rule directly. Only **central Arabia** escaped formal **European administration and/or occupation** for the entire length of the interwar period. But European domination did not go entirely unchallenged. In several countries, **nationalist movements** emerged for the first time and forced the Europeans to **cede a degree of power** to native elites or even to grant **nominal independence.**

The most far-reaching consequence of European intervention was the **destruction of the Ottoman Empire** after World War I. In lands that had formerly been unified, the Europeans laid the foundation for an entirely **novel system of states** that, in spite of its artificiality, persisted into the late 20th century with few modifications. The **ruling elites** of these states were generally drawn from **great landowning families.** They modeled their regimes on the Western democracies and created **Western political institutions** such as **constitutions, parliaments,** and **political parties.** In reality, power was concentrated in the hands of the elites. Democratic institutions were subject to constant **manipulation,** whether from the **elites** or from the **European powers.** The abuses of the political system bred **disillusionment,** which expressed itself in the rise of **Fascist organizations, Muslim political movements,** and **pan-Arab ideologies** during the 1930s. At the same time, a **new generation** composed of young professionals, bureaucrats, and junior army officers began to appear on the political scene. These men grew increasingly disenchanted with the political establishment but were not yet prepared to challenge the ruling elites.

In economic affairs, the interwar period was marked by **economic stagnation.** The **Great Depression** was a devastating blow to the region, but many areas partly recovered during the boom generated by World War II. Within the world economy, the Middle East and North Africa essentially maintained their roles as suppliers of raw materials to and importers of finished goods from industrialized countries. As in the 19th century, Europeans occupied **critical positions in the economy** through their **banks, commercial houses, and insurance firms.** Overall, the region's economy continued to be dominated by **agriculture.** Though several countries founded modern **industries,** development in this sector proceeded slowly (except in Turkey). Outside Turkey and Iran, no regimes engaged in economic planning. The **oil industry,** operated by foreign firms, was still moving through the developmental phase. The few oil fields in production supplied a negligible proportion of total world output.

The modes of **transportation and communication** underwent a revolution during the interwar period. **Automobiles** made their first appearance but remained the exclusive possession of the well-to-do. More important was the spread of trucking, which gradually replaced camels for the hauling of goods. **Rail networks** were still growing and received heavy investment, but generally remained inadequate except in Turkey and Egypt. **Air service,** provided mostly by foreign firms, became available for the first time for both passenger and commercial traffic. In communications, **radio and film** quickly established themselves as popular sources of news and entertainment.

The **population** of the region was **expanding** rapidly, over 1.5 percent per year. The increases resulted from a high fertility rate coupled with improvements in hygiene, diet, and medical care. In 1914 the total number of inhabitants stood at about 66 million (54 million for the Middle East and 12 million for North Africa). These figures reached approximately 101 million by the end of World War II (81 and 20 million, respectively). Most of the population still lived in the **countryside** (over three-quarters in most places), but the proportion of urban dwellers was rising fast. **Pastoralists** were rapidly disappearing, usually settling down as farmers.

The **educational system** steadily expanded under government supervision. Yet **illiteracy** remained rampant, for education was largely restricted to a privileged minority. Through the educational system, as well as the various media, the elites gained exposure to **Western ideas, attitudes, and tastes,** which they eagerly adopted. They actively sought (most radically in Turkey) to **secularize** their societies, particularly in law and education. Another sign of Western influence was the emergence of a fledgling **feminist movement,** which demanded modest reforms in the legal and educational systems.

All the new ideas and social reforms were bitterly opposed by **members of the religious establishment.** In this respect, the men of religion expressed the views of the great majority, who professed an unshakable **devotion to religion and custom.** Traditional attitudes held out even as the forces of modernity inexorably reshaped the societies of the region. *(To p. 965)*

2. THE MIDDLE EAST

a. THE OTTOMAN EMPIRE AND TURKEY

(From pp. 534, 659, 672)

1914. Production of the **first Turkish film,** a documentary entitled *The Demise of the Russian Monument in Ayestefanis.*

Sept. 9. Abolition of the Capitulations by the Ottoman government.

Oct. 29. OTTOMAN ENTRY INTO THE FIRST WORLD WAR as one of the Central powers. The huge military effort placed a **great strain on Ottoman society and the economy.** Large-scale **conscription** affected some 3 million men (more than half of whom may have deserted). The general population had to contend with rampant **inflation** and the shock of a 2500 percent increase in the **cost of living** between 1914 and 1918. **Trade and communications** were disrupted, and consumers faced **widespread shortages** of basic goods. Some areas of the empire experienced **disastrous famines,** such as the one that struck Syria and Lebanon in 1915–16 and claimed an estimated 100,000 victims.

1915, March. The first **deportations of Armenians** from eastern Anatolia. The Ottoman government organized these relocations to reduce the likelihood of Armenian insurrections behind the eastern front. Many of the deportations turned into **death marches and massacres.** It is estimated that **between one and one and a half million Armenians perished** in 1915–16. A substantial number of **refugees** fled east into the **Caucasus** and south into **Syria and Lebanon,** where many settled permanently. Armenians have accused the Ottoman central government of directing the attacks, a claim denied by successive Turkish governments.

March 25. Administrative reform of religious institutions. All Islamic courts were placed under the jurisdiction of the ministry of justice. *Vakif* (endowed) property was put in the hands of the finance ministry, and supervision of religious schools was transferred to the ministry of education.

1916. Death of **Najib Azoury,** a prominent Christian writer who articulated the **idea of an Arab nation** in which both Muslims and Christians stood on an equal footing. In the decade prior to the First World War, he was among a handful of activists who demanded independence for the Arabs from the Ottoman Empire.

Reform of marriage laws. Women were permitted to seek divorce if their husbands committed adultery, violated the terms of the marriage contract, or took an additional wife without the first wife's consent.

1918, Dec. 8. Allied military administration established in Istanbul.

1918–22. SULTAN MEHMED VI. He succeeded **MEHMED V** (who died July 3, 1918) and served as the last Ottoman sultan. During his brief reign he repeatedly tried to reassert the authority of his office. His government ultimately came into **conflict with the rival Kemalist regime** in central Anatolia, which led directly to his downfall.

1918–23. TRANSFER OF POPULATION BETWEEN GREECE AND TURKEY. Approximately 1.2 million "Greeks" (actually Turkish-speaking Christians) were forced to leave Turkey while, in an identical process, the Greek government expelled about 600,000 "Turks" (actually Greek-speaking Muslims).

1919, March 7. Formation of a new Ottoman cabinet under Damad Ferid Pasha, who agreed to cooperate with the Allies.

April 29. Landing of Italian troops at Antalya. Ever since the conclusion of the secret wartime agreements among the Allies, the Italians had intended to occupy this region. The troops eventually **withdrew in July 1921.**

1919–22. THE GREEK-TURKISH WAR. Greek forces landed at Izmir on May 15, 1919. Like the Italians, the **Greeks had colonial ambitions** in Anatolia and wished to incorporate most of western Asia Minor into the Greek state. The Greek army soon became the tool of the British cabinet under Lloyd George, who wanted to force the Turks into accepting the Treaty of Sèvres.

The **first Greek offensive** began in June 1920. The Greeks defeated Turkish forces at Alashehir (June 24) and took Bursa (July 9) and Edirne (July 25). A **second offensive** was launched in March 1921 but was brought to a halt by the **Turkish victory at Inönü. The Greeks attacked again** in July 1921 and captured Eskishehir (July 17), but their drive into the interior **stalled at the Sakarya River** (Aug. 24). Attempts to mediate a Greek-Turkish settlement broke down in March 1922.

The decisive **Turkish counteroffensive** commenced on Aug. 18. Turkish forces liberated Afyun (Aug. 30) and Bursa (Sept. 5). Greek resistance rapidly disintegrated into a disorderly retreat to the coast. On Sept. 9, **Turkish troops occupied Izmir and completed the reconquest of Anatolia.** The Greek-Turkish armistice concluding the war was signed on Oct. 14, 1922.

1919, May 19. Arrival of **MUSTAFA KEMAL** (who later took the name **ATATÜRK**) at the port of Samsun on the Black Sea. The sultan had appointed him inspector of the Ottoman Third Army in Anatolia for the purpose of eventually disbanding it. Instead, Kemal quietly **defied his superiors** and set about reorganizing his troops **to resist the Western forces** occupying parts of Turkey. The sultan officially dismissed him on July 8, and three days later he was declared an outlaw.

July 23–Aug. 17. In Erzurum, a congress of delegates organized by the **Association for the Defense of Rights of Eastern Anatolia,** under nationalist leadership, proclaimed an original version of what later became the **National Pact.** The nationalists vowed to **resist the partition and foreign occupation** of Anatolia. The nationalist resolve was reiterated at the **Congress of Sivas,** convened on Sept. 4.

Oct. Nationalist victory in elections for the **Ottoman Parliament.** The sultan's new cabinet (formed Oct. 5), under Ali Riza, adopted a policy of reconciliation with the nationalists.

1920, Jan. 28. Proclamation by the Ottoman parliament of the Turkish **National Pact,** which set out the goals of the Turkish nationalist resistance. The nationalists, who had won a strong majority in the Dec. 1919 elections, vowed **never to submit to the partition and foreign occupation** of Turkey (which they took to mean as Anatolia and eastern Thrace). Among the **main demands of the National Pact** were Turkish self-determination, the security of Istanbul, the opening of the Bosphorus and Dardanelles straits, and the abolition of the Capitulations.

March 16. Allied occupation of Istanbul in response to a perceived threat from the nationalists, many of whom were arrested and deported. The Allies offered reassurances that they had no intention of keeping Istanbul for themselves, but were merely acting for the safety of the minorities and the security of the straits. A new Ottoman cabinet under Damad Pasha was formed and the **Parliament was dissolved** (April 11).

April 23. First meeting of the **National Assembly.** The organization had been formed in March, when elections were staged in response to the dissolution of the Ottoman Parliament, which was never to meet again. By this act, the **nationalists created,** in effect, **a parallel government** in relation to the regime in Istanbul under the sultan. The latter actively tried to topple the nationalist government by organizing irregular military forces in central Anatolia.

Aug. 10. Signing of the **Treaty of Sèvres** (p. 672), which **divided western Anatolia** among Greece, France, and Italy. The sultan at first had protested the harsh terms but eventually signed the pact anyway. **The nationalists** in Ankara unconditionally **rejected all terms.**

Oct. 21. Turkish capture of Kars from forces of the Armenian Republic. **A peace treaty with the Armenians** concluded on Dec. 3 gave the Turks Kars and Ardahan. Armenia, which was later to become a Soviet republic, was reduced to the province of Erivan.

1920–50. Growth of the educational system. The number of students alone rose from some 400,000 to 1.8 million by the end of this period. Yet, overall, these gains represented small strides. The general **literacy rate** hovered around 35 percent as late as 1950 (though it had improved from 11 percent in 1927).

1921, Jan. 20. Passage of the **Fundamental Law** by the National Assembly in Ankara. Among its guarantees were an **elected parliament** equipped with a responsible ministry and a **presidency** invested with broad powers.

March 16. Conclusion of a **treaty with the Soviet Union by the Kemalist government.** The pact acknowledged the Kemalist regime as the official government of Turkey and settled the international borders between the two countries. The Soviets also began to provide material aid to the Kemalist resistance.

Oct. 20. The Ankara Agreement between Turkey and France. The **French permanently withdrew** their forces from Anatolia and renounced all their territorial claims north of Syria.

1922, Oct. 11. Armistice between British forces and the Kemalist government. French and Italian troops had already withdrawn from the Straits, and the British agreed to do the same. The treaty also guaranteed eastern Thrace for the Turkish state.

Nov. 1. ABOLITION OF THE SULTANATE by the National Assembly. **The sultan was left only with the title of caliph,** supreme spiritual leader of the Muslim world. Sultan **MEHMED VI was deposed** (Nov. 13), and his cousin **ABDULMEJID** was appointed the new caliph. The **OFFICE OF CALIPH WAS ABOLISHED** in 1924.

1923, July 24. THE TREATY OF LAUSANNE. Turkey formally won recognition for its independence within almost all its current borders. Other terms of the treaty included the **abolition of the Capitulations, guarantees for the security of the minorities, and the demilitarization of the straits** (except if Turkey were at war). Though Turkey was not required to pay reparations, the country was saddled with two-thirds of the old **Ottoman debt,** the remainder being divided among the states that had been provinces of the empire in 1914. The Turkish portion of the debt was finally liquidated in 1948.

Aug. Formation of the **People's Party** under **Mustafa Kemal.** It later changed its name in Nov. 1924 to the **Republican People's Party.** The party immediately established itself as the center of political power in Turkey and **ruled single-handedly until 1950.**

Oct. 2. Departure of the last Allied troops from Istanbul.

Oct. 13. Transfer of the Turkish capital from Istanbul to Ankara. The move was an open symbol of the government's desire to break with, and if possible to bury, the Ottoman past.

Oct. 29. DECLARATION OF THE TURKISH REPUBLIC. This act put an **official end to the Ottoman Empire. MUSTAFA KEMAL** (1881–1938), who later took the name **ATATÜRK,** became the **first president** of the Republic.

Atatürk's decisive leadership in Turkey's war of independence and his **program of modernizing reforms established him as the most important figure in 20th-century Turkish history.** His policies were largely responsible for defining the shape of the future Turkish state. Instead of diverting resources toward campaigns to reclaim former Ottoman lands, he contained Turkish ambitions within Anatolia and eastern Thrace and **concentrated on building a distinctly Turkish state** within these borders. He left his imprint not only on politics but also on the direction and spirit of society and culture. He dreamed of creating a fully modernized and secular society, and in pursuing this goal he **ruthlessly imposed social reforms** whose main objective was to sweep away the Ottoman past.

1924–28. SECULARIZATION CAMPAIGN. The abolition (Mar. 3, 1924) **of the caliphate,** the office of the supreme spiritual leader for Sunni Muslims worldwide, represented the first move in the **government's campaign to secularize Turkish society.** At the same time, the **position of Sheik ul-Islam** (the highest ranking religious official in the Ottoman Empire) **was dissolved, religious schools were closed,** and the **administration of all** *vakifs* (religious and charitable endowments) was placed **in the hands of the prime minister.** In addition, the **Islamic law courts were dismantled** by a decree of April 8, 1924. Other secularizing measures followed: **all Sufi orders and lodges were shut down** (1925); a **civil code of law,** based on Swiss civil law, superseded Islamic law in personal matters (1926); and a **constitutional amendment dropped Islam** as the state religion (1928).

The policy of secularization was **most successful in the cities,** particularly among the well-educated elites. The people of the countryside remained rooted in older attitudes that favored a wide and public role for religion in society.

1924. Founding of the **Iş Bank,** funded by private investors and operated by the state, to promote industry. The following year, the government created the **State Bank for Industry and Mining.**

April. Electoral reform. All male Turkish citizens over 21 became eligible to vote. Property qualifications were permanently abolished.

April 20. Proclamation of the **Republican Constitution.** One of the most notable features of the new constitution was its **commitment to separating religion from political life.**

Oct. 25. Death of **Ziya Gökalp** (b. 1875), author famed for his work as a sociologist, philosopher, and folklorist. The guiding principle of his thought was **nationalism:** Ottomanism in his early writings and Turkish nationalism in his later years. He advocated **selective modernization** on the Western model, but wished to **preserve the Turkish cultural heritage.**

1925–27. The **Independence Tribunals** in operation. These courts were established ostensibly to crush enemies of the state. In practice, they became the instrument by which the government terrorized and eliminated many of its political opponents.

1925. Opening of the **University of Ankara.**

Founding of the **Turkish Historical Society.** One of its chief responsibilities was the preparation of **new history textbooks** for the national school system. From the beginning, the organization was an important ideological weapon for the state, which was determined to inculcate nationalist beliefs in students.

Feb. The **Revolt of Sheik Sa'id,** named for the Kurdish tribal leader who instigated it. The uprising involved Kurdish tribes throughout a large area west of Lake Van. Sheik Sa'id himself was quickly captured in April and executed with other leading rebels on June 30. By November the revolt had been completely put down.

March 5. In the wake of the Revolt of Sheik Mustafa Sa'id, **Kemal assumed sweeping emergency powers.** Civilian rule was not restored until March 1929.

June 3. Proscription of the opposition **Progressive Republican Party,** organized the previous year. The measure removed any semblance of a multiparty system from Turkish political life.

Aug. Abolition of polygamy.

Nov. 25. Reforms in dress. The fez (a brimless hat widespread in the Middle East) was banned, and Turks were required to wear Western-style hats. Another law prohibited religious dress outside mosques.

Dec. 17. Soviet-Turkish treaty of friendship. The agreement was not, however, a result of pro-Communist leanings in the government. The Turkish Communist Party was banned the same year.

Dec. 26. Adoption of the Christian Gregorian calendar.

1926, March. The **first civil service reforms.** Government bureaucrats were to receive regular salaries based on a fixed scale. The act also established official regulations for functionaries and raised the number of posts filled by competitive recruitment.

June 5. Anglo-Turkish Treaty on the status of Mosul. In 1924 the Turks had submitted a claim to the region before the League of Nations. The League's ruling awarded most of the territory to Iraq, including the big oil fields. By this treaty, the Turks officially accepted the League's decision.

Sept. 1. A new law made **civil marriage compulsory.**

1927. The **first Turkish census.** The population had fallen by about 30 percent, to around 13.6 million, a drop that resulted primarily from the wars in which Turkey was embroiled between 1912 and 1923. Muslims accounted for 98 percent of the total population, about 85 percent of whom spoke Turkish as their first language. About three-quarters of the inhabitants lived in the countryside. Despite losing about a third of its 1914 population, Istanbul remained by far the largest city at about 700,000 residents.

May 28. Law for the Encouragement of Industry. Determined to promote native industry, the government set aside free land for privately owned factories and mines and exempted them from land, property, and profit taxes. The Turkish government was required to make purchases from these firms regardless of their products' quality or cost.

1928, Nov. 10. ADOPTION OF THE LATIN ALPHABET for Turkish. Writing had previously been done in Arabic script. In 1932 the process of reform was extended even further. An official committee called the **Turkish Linguistic Society,** which was set up specially for the project, began to purge non-Turkish grammatical structures and—far more radical—Arabic and Persian vocabulary from the existing language at a rapid rate. Since approximately 80 percent of Ottoman Turkish consisted of words drawn from Arabic and Persian, this reform represented a **radical linguistic transformation.** The process has continued unabated throughout the 20th century.

1929. Removal of Arabic and Persian as subjects taught in Turkish elementary schools. The measure simultaneously struck at the religious establishment and reoriented the curriculum further in the direction of secular studies.

1930–50. The ERA OF ÉTATISM in economic planning. The state assumed the leading role in developing Turkish industry, but without large-scale nationalization of existing firms. The state economic programs **allowed private enterprise in industry and commerce** and proposed no radical agrarian reforms such as collectivization schemes. Nor did the economic planners in the government favor the establishment of any state monopolies. The function of the state was to provide leadership, capital, and management where the Turkish private sector, due to its internal weaknesses, was unable to do so.

As part of its long-term vision, the state implemented a **Five-Year Plan,** modeled on Soviet lines, in Jan. 1934. It was the **first state-directed economic program** of its kind in the Middle East. The main goals of the project were to develop consumer industries, particularly textiles, and to provide the foundations for heavy industry (for example, iron and steel plants).

1930. Suspension of payments on the Ottoman debt in the wake of the world financial crisis. Negotiations led to a reduction of the debt in 1933.

March 28. Only **Turkish names** were henceforth to be used for Turkish cities (for example, Istanbul for Constantinople, Edirne for Adrianople, etc.).

April 3. Women won the right to vote in municipal elections. In Dec. 1934 they were permitted to vote in national elections and to sit in parliament.

April 3. Law of municipalities, which incorporated all of Turkey's cities and provided them with an official municipal structure. (Turkey's villages had already received a similar status and administrative apparatus in 1864.)

July. First labor law, which provided for mandatory labor inspections, arbitration committees for labor disputes, and the establishment of minimum working conditions.

Aug. 12–Nov. 17. Life span of the **Free Republican Party,** which existed briefly as a closely supervised opposition party. The government soon grew uneasy with the new party and suppressed it.

Dec. 30. Turkish-Greek treaty of friendship. The two countries formally settled their border disputes and agreed to naval equality in the eastern Mediterranean.

1931. The **state** took over responsibility for **paying the salaries of all religious functionaries.** The decision made all religious positions in effect government jobs subject to government supervision. The change further **reduced the independence of the religious establishment.**

1932, Jan. 22. First public recitation of the Qur'an in Turkish despite the opposition of conservative Muslims. The following year, a government decree required the Muslim call to prayer to be chanted in Turkish instead of Arabic.

Jan. 23. Official demarcation of the Turkish-Iranian frontier.

July 18. Admission of Turkey to the **League of Nations.**

1933. The formation, under state supervision and control, of the **Sumer Bank** to promote and manage industry. In 1935 the state organized the **Eti Bank** for mining projects.

Reorganization of the Ottoman University as the **University of Istanbul.**

1934, Feb. 9. Conclusion of the **Balkan Pact** by Turkey, Yugoslavia, Greece, and Romania. The signatories promised to respect one another's independence and territorial integrity.

June 28. Legal requirement of **Turks to use surnames,** like Westerners. Prior to this law, Turks had mainly used patronymic names, like most other Middle Easterners.

1935. Sunday replaced Friday as the weekly day of rest.

1936, July 20. Signing of the **Montreux Convention,** which permitted the Turkish government to move troops back onto the straits of the Bosphorus and Dardanelles. In the event of war, the straits were left entirely to the disposal of Turkey.

1937, July 8. Signing of the **Sa'dabad Pact,** a nonaggression treaty, by Turkey, Iran, Iraq, and Afghanistan.

1938, Nov. 10. Death of Atatürk, who was succeeded as president by **Ismet Inönü.**

1939, June. ANNEXATION OF THE HATAY, the area surrounding the cities of **Iskenderun** (Alexandretta) and **Antakya** (Antioch). It had formerly been a semiautonomous part (1920–38) of the **French mandate for Syria.** After hostilities between the Arabs and Turks inside the Hatay, French and Turkish negotiators set up elections, which resulted in the establishment of the autonomous **Republic of Hatay.** Because the Hatay was politically dominated by ethnic Turks (even if they constituted only some 40 percent of the population), it was soon absorbed into Turkey. Another factor leading to annexation was the overriding desire of France to secure a military alliance with Turkey even at the price of sacrificing the Hatay.

1942, Nov. 11. Passage of the **Varlik Vergisi Tax,** a large-scale capital levy. The **burden fell disproportionately on the Greek, Armenian, and Jewish minorities.** Many businessmen were assessed at rates far exceeding the worth of their firms. Those who could not pay lost their fortunes and were sent to forced labor camps. The program lasted until the end of July 1943, when all prisoners were finally released. Perhaps the greatest long-term result of this campaign was the **destruction of a large number of minority businesses.**

1944. Death of **Mehmet Emin Yurdakul** (b. 1869), one of the most important poets in modern Turkish literature. He was noted for incorporating folk meters and Turkish themes into his work. *(To p. 970)*

b. IRAN (PERSIA)

(From p. 537)

1919. Arrival of the **Iranian delegation** at the **Paris peace conference.** The Iranian representatives sought the termination of the Capitulations, war reparations, and the cancellation of the 1907 Agreement. In addition, they demanded that the western border of Iran be fixed at the Euphrates River in the west and that it extend to the Oxus River in the northeast. At British insistence, **the delegation was not officially recognized** in Paris.

Aug. 9. Anglo-Iranian agreement, amounting in reality to the establishment of a British protectorate. The British promised to guarantee Iran's independence and territorial integrity, and offered material and technical aid to the government.

Within Iran, **opposition to the treaty quickly mounted.** The national assembly (Majlis) never approved it, and in 1921 the government officially repudiated it.

1920–22. Suppression of rebellions in Gilan, Khurasan, Azerbaijan, and Kurdistan.

1920. The population of Iran reached **12 million.** Muslims (about 80 percent of whom were Twelver Shi'ites) made up 95 percent of the total. Approximately 80 percent of the inhabitants lived in the countryside.

RIZA KHAN assumed command of the **Cossack Brigade,** the main military organization of the Iranian government.

Jan. 10. Iran became one of the charter members of the **League of Nations.**

May 18. Bolshevik occupation of most of Gilan, where the Soviet Republic of Gilan operated until Oct. 1921.

1921, Jan. 18. Beginning of **British evacuation** from northern Iran. Later

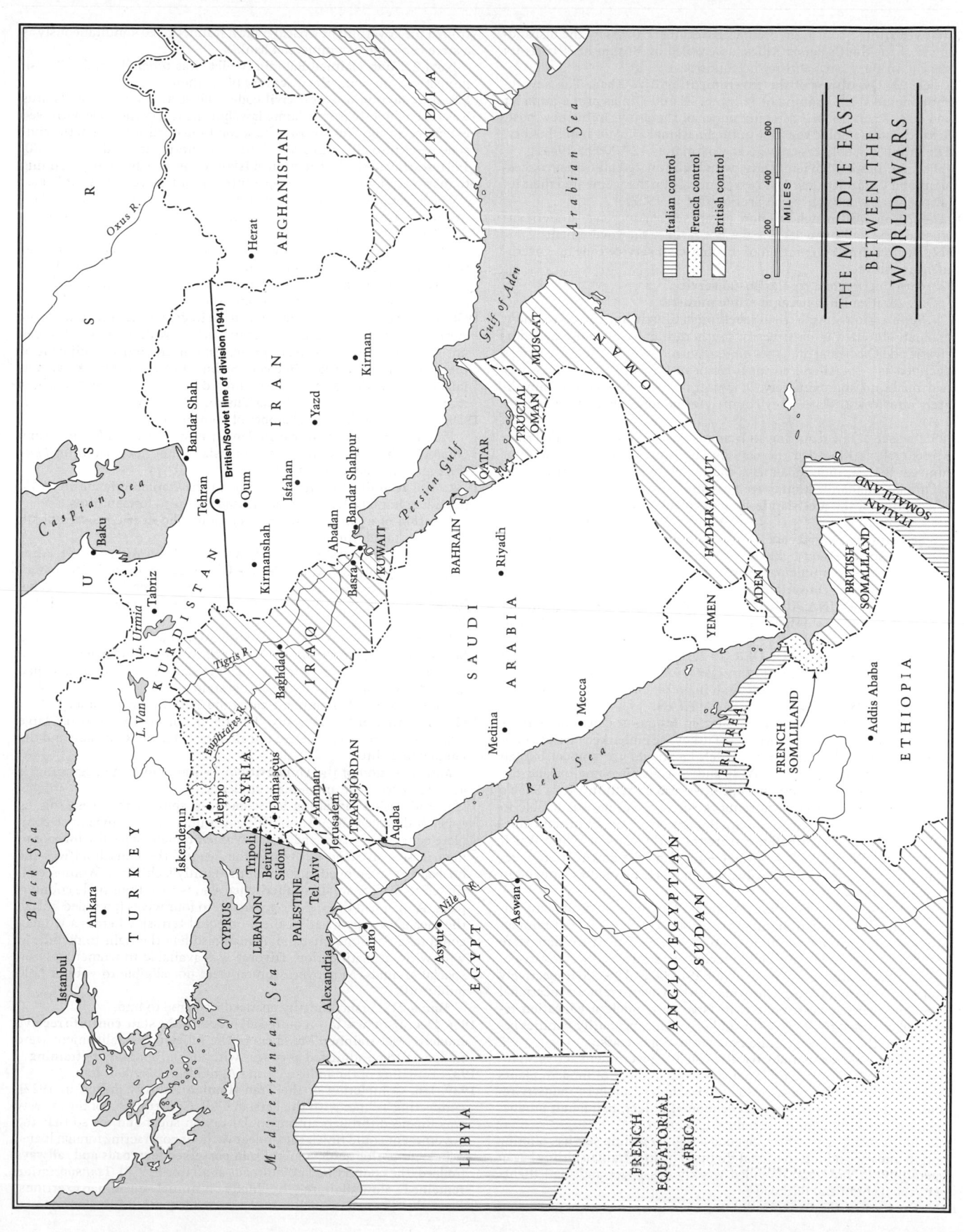

THE MIDDLE EAST
BETWEEN THE
WORLD WARS

Italian control

French control

British control

MILES

0   200   400   600

Black Sea

Istanbul

Ankara

TURKEY

Iskenderun

CYPRUS

Mediterranean Sea

Aleppo

Tripoli

Beirut

LEBANON

Sidon

Tel Aviv

PALESTINE

Jerusalem

Alexandria

Cairo

EGYPT

Asyut

Nile R.

Aswan

LIBYA

FRENCH
EQUATORIAL
AFRICA

ANGLO-EGYPTIAN
SUDAN

Red Sea

Aqaba

Amman

TRANS-JORDAN

Damascus

SYRIA

Euphrates R.

Baghdad

Tigris R.

IRAQ

KURDISTAN

L. Van

L. Urmia

Tabriz

Baku

Caspian Sea

U S S R

Oxus R.

Herat

AFGHANISTAN

Bandar Shah

Tehran

Qum

Isfahan

I R A N

Kirman

Yazd

British/Soviet line of division (1941)

Kirmanshah

Abadan

Bandar Shahpur

Basra

KUWAIT

Persian Gulf

BAHRAIN

QATAR

SAUDI
ARABIA

Riyadh

Mecca

Medina

MUSCAT

TRUCIAL
OMAN

O M A N

HADHRAMAUT

ADEN

YEMEN

Gulf of Aden

Arabian Sea

I N D I A

ERITREA

FRENCH
SOMALILAND

BRITISH
SOMALILAND

ITALIAN
SOMALILAND

Addis Ababa

ETHIOPIA

that year in the south, the Iranian government oversaw the disbandment of the **South Persia Rifles,** assembled by Britain in 1916 as its special military force within the country.

Feb. 21. Overthrow of the government by Riza Khan. The new regime included the prominent reformer Zia ud-Din as prime minister and Riza Khan himself as commander of the army. In his new post, Riza Khan assembled the first unified national army in Iran's history. The number of soldiers grew to approximately 127,000 by 1941.

Feb. 26. Iranian-Soviet Treaty, which eliminated all tsarist concessions and Capitulations. The two countries further cemented their relations with a nonaggression pact on Oct. 1, 1927.

1922–27. The **Millspaugh mission,** composed of American advisers, entrusted by Riza Khan with the fiscal reform of the government.

1922, Dec. 12. Implementation of the **first civil service code** for government employees.

1923. Introduction of a **regular postal service.**

Oct. 28. Riza Khan became prime minister.

1924. Suppression of Arab tribal rebellion in Khuzistan. The government gradually brought other tribes in southern Iran (principally the Bakhtiyaris and Qashqais) under its direct control by 1930. Hereafter **tribes declined** as a social and political factor in Iranian life. Whereas they had made up approximately 20 percent of the population immediately after World War I, they counted for no more than 10 percent by 1941.

1925. Passage of law requiring all **Iranians to adopt family names.** Prime Minister Riza Khan led the way by choosing the name *Pahlavi* for himself. By law, individuals also had to obtain birth certificates.

Official standardization of weights and measures.

Adoption of the pre-Islamic Iranian calendar to replace the Islamic system of dating.

The **first commercial code.** A revised version appeared in 1932.

Installation of street lights in Tehran. By 1929, homeowners in the city had access to municipal electricity.

June 6. Military conscription for males at age 21.

Oct. 31. TERMINATION OF THE QAJAR DYNASTY. At the behest of Riza Khan the Majlis (parliament) **deposed Ahmad Shah,** who was away in Europe.

1925–41. RIZA SHAH, FOUNDER OF THE PAHLAVI DYNASTY. The Majlis revised the constitution in Dec. 1925 to make Riza Khan the new shah. He crowned himself shah in an official ceremony on April 25, 1926, and became known as **RIZA SHAH.**

Riza Shah was the dominant figure in Iranian society and politics until World War II. Like Atatürk in Turkey, he embarked on a **program of sweeping modernization** by which he sought to remodel Iranian society in the image of the West and to centralize and expand the power of the Iranian state. But unlike Atatürk's reforms, Riza Shah's **policies failed to strike deep roots** in society, and he was unable to broaden his base of support among the Iranian elites. In the end, **miscalculations in foreign policy** during the early years of World War II brought an Allied invasion of the country and the downfall of his regime. Following his **forced abdication in 1941,** he died as an exile in South Africa (1943).

Expansion of the educational system. The number of modern primary schools jumped from more than 600 to over 2,300. The number of secondary schools rose from 74 to nearly 350. In 1925 there were about 55,000 primary and 14,500 secondary students; by comparison, the number of students grew to about 287,000 and 28,000 respectively in 1941. Yet the accomplishments of the government's educational programs were at best modest. In large part, **modern education remained confined** to the wealthy and privileged, primarily families belonging to the landowning and new professional classes.

Expansion of Iranian industry. Riza Shah's government actively promoted the modernization of industry. The number of modern plants rose from about 20 to nearly 350. Nevertheless, **modern industry remained a small part of the total economy.** In fact, handicraft production still accounted for most industrial output.

1926. Junkers, a German firm, opened a **regular airline service,** offering both domestic and international flights. The **first Iranian airline** began operations in 1937 and provided weekly passenger and mail flights between Tehran and Baghdad.

1927. Creation of the **Bank Melli Iran,** which issued currency and controlled the government's fiscal policy. It functioned simultaneously as a state bank and a commercial bank.

Nov. 22. Iran claimed Bahrain, which was officially under British protection, following the discovery of oil there.

1928. Introduction of a new civil code. The section on personal status was taken directly from Islamic law, but the rest of the code **borrowed extensively from French law.** The second and third volumes of the civil code went into effect in 1935. A further reform, enacted on Nov. 30, 1931, **restricted the jurisdiction of Islamic courts** to matters pertaining to marriage, divorce, and the appointment of trustees and guardians.

The government took over the function of certifying *ulama* and religious students with its own system of examinations. In 1931 it imposed a standard syllabus on all religious schools *(madrasas).*

Clothing reform. A new law required all Iranians, except *ulama,* to wear Western clothes. Western hats were made mandatory in 1935.

May 10. Abolition of the Capitulations, the special legal and economic privileges that Westerners enjoyed.

1930–60. Experimentation and innovation in Persian fiction. A new generation of writers emerged who began working with themes and genres not found in classical Persian prose. Among the most significant of these authors were **Sadiq Hedayat, Sadiq Chubak, Buzurg Alavi, and Jalal al-e Ahmad.** A similar spirit entered Persian poetry and was best exemplified in the work of **Nima Yushij.**

1930. Founding of the first chamber of commerce.

Production of the **first feature-length film,** *Avi va Rabi,* by Avans Ohanian. The first movie to have a Persian soundtrack, *Dukhtar-i Lur (The Lur Girl),* appeared in 1932.

1932. The **technique of dubbing** entered the Iranian cinema in 1946, providing Iranians with unprecedented access to foreign films.

Creation of a navy in the Persian Gulf. The fleet consisted of six ships purchased from Italy.

Unilateral **cancellation of the D'Arcy Oil Concession** of 1901. After negotiations with the **Anglo-Persian Oil Company** in 1933, the Iranian government accepted a compromise through which it was to receive higher royalties. In return, the company's concession was extended to 1993.

March 17. A new law required **all legal and property documents to be registered in state courts.** The reform came **at the expense of the ulama,** who lost the substantial income that these transactions had generated within the Islamic court system.

June–July. Kurdish uprising along the Turko-Iranian border.

1934. Abolition of the land tax. The reform primarily benefited large landholders and strengthened the alliance between Riza Shah and the landowning elite.

May. Creation of the **University of Tehran.** From the beginning, it accepted both male and female students.

1935. Prohibition of veiling for women. In spite of the Westernizing spirit of this measure, Riza Shah's government never envisioned complete equality between the sexes. **Women remained legally inferior** to men in several respects. By law the head of the household was the husband, who enjoyed custody of the family's children. Women continued to receive smaller **inheritance** shares than their male counterparts. A man had the right to marry up to four wives (provided he had the means to support all of them on equal terms), whereas a woman could take only one husband. A man also had the right to divorce at will, without justification. **Divorce** was available to women only on special grounds. Moreover, women were not eligible to vote or hold public office.

March 21. Persia officially changed its name to Iran.

1936, Dec. 27. A new law required **all judges in the state courts to receive modern legal training.** Members of the religious establishment were no longer to be admitted as judges without the appropriate training.

1937. Founding of the Industrial and Agricultural Bank of Iran.

1939, Jan. Completion of the **Trans-Iranian Railway** (begun in 1927), connecting Tehran with the Persian Gulf. Construction of the railway was financed through an unpopular tax on sugar and tea so that the government could finish the project without contracting foreign loans.

In spite of this achievement, **Iran possessed few roads and railways** (indeed, the country had no railroads at all until 1928). **Transportation remained a slow affair,** relying chiefly on animal and human exertions. Even the Trans-Iranian Railway was inadequate. Most commercial traffic in Iran flowed east-west, whereas the rail line ran north-south. By 1941 the government had built about 14,000 miles of highway, but these roads primarily served military purposes and did little to improve the overall speed of transportation within the country.

1940. The first Iranian radio station, **Tehran Radio,** began broadcasting.

1941, Aug. 25. INVASION OF IRAN by Soviet and British forces (p. 806). The Allies occupied Tehran on Sept. 16. **Riza Shah abdicated and was succeeded by his son, MUHAMMAD RIZA SHAH.** The presence of Soviet and British troops, and after 1942 of American advisers, sharply reduced the power of the shah and the government for the duration of **the Allied occupation (1941–46).**

Sept. Founding of the **TUDEH PARTY,** which became a left-wing organization espousing Marxist ideology. In 1944 it helped to organize the **Council of Federated Trade Unions (CFTU),** which planned and executed labor strikes throughout Iran. Membership in the Tudeh peaked at around 50,000 in 1946; it could also claim another 350,000 adherents through the CFTU at around the same time.

1942, Jan 29. Signing of the **Tripartite Treaty of Alliance** by Iran, Great Britain, and the Soviet Union. The treaty provided a legal front for the Anglo-Soviet occupation of Iran during the war. *(To p. 973)*

c. AFGHANISTAN

(From p. 539)

1919, Feb. 20. Murder of AMIR HABIBULLAH, which touched off a **struggle for the succession.** His brother, Nasrullah, was proclaimed emir by conservative factions that had opposed Habibullah's modernization program and his acquiescence to British foreign policy in the region. But the emir's third son, **AMANULLAH,** won the backing of the army and soon **emerged as the new ruler.**

1919–29. EMIR (KING) AMANULLAH. The emir, who assumed the title of king in June 1926, **embarked on a modernization program** that became the central theme of his reign. He **introduced a series of reforms** that tried, often with little effect, to reshape the government, the national infrastructure, and the legal system. The reckless pace of these reforms led ultimately to his undoing.

1919, May–Aug. The Third Afghan War. Afghan troops invaded the Indian frontier but were soon driven back. An armistice was signed at the end of May. In the **Treaty of Rawalpindi** (Aug. 8), the British formally recognized the sovereignty of the Afghan state, but also terminated their annual subsidies to the Afghan treasury.

1921. Enactment of **a new family code,** which banned child marriage and marriages between close relatives (on the grounds that they were contrary to the teachings of Islam). The new law also put a cap on wedding expenses, including the value of the dowry.

Feb. 28. Soviet-Afghan Treaty of mutual recognition. The two countries signed a nonaggression pact on Aug. 31, 1926. To the Afghan government, the Soviets represented a counterweight to the pressure from British India.

March 1. Signing of a Turkish-Afghan treaty of friendship, as Amanullah tried to cast himself as a pan-Islamic leader. A similar treaty with Iran followed on June 22.

Nov. 22. Anglo-Afghan Treaty, by which Afghanistan secured full and formal independence.

1922. Institution of the first national budget.

1923, April 9. Promulgation of **a constitution.** The emir retained all executive powers. A legislature (half of which was appointed by the emir) was established, but its functions were mainly consultative.

1924–25. Promulgation of **a new penal code,** which was a **combination of secular law, aspects of tribal law, and a systematized version of Islamic law.** The new code **antagonized leaders of the religious establishment,** who perceived it as an attempt by the emir to undercut their authority and prestige.

1924, April. The **Khost Rebellion,** led by the Mangal tribe in response to the government's modernizing reforms. The revolt was put down by Jan. 1925.

1925. Appearance of the first Afghan radio station.

1927. Founding of the first regular daily newspaper, *Aman-i Afghan.*

1928, July. Inauguration of a **second wave of reforms,** inspired by Turkish and Iranian precedents, which ultimately **caused the downfall of Amanullah.** Among the projects the king put forward were the expansion of the army and the introduction of military conscription, the modernization of the country's communications, and the promotion of secular education. To finance these measures, the king declared a new tax on all mature males. But by far his **most controversial proposals involved social policy.** The king publicly came out in opposition to **polygamy and women's veiling,** and imposed Western dress on all Afghans visiting or residing in Kabul. His reforms particularly incensed the religious establishment, the bastion of conservatism in the country.

Nov. Outbreak of an extensive **antigovernment revolt** brought on by the king's latest round of reforms. By Jan. 1929 fighting had reached the outskirts of Kabul.

1929, Jan. 14. ABDICATION OF AMANULLAH. His older brother, Inayatullah, became the new king, but he too abdicated three days later under mounting rebel attacks inside Kabul.

Jan. 17. Assumption of power by **BACHA-I SAQAO,** a bandit chieftain of Tajik descent, who declared himself emir and took the name **HABIBULLAH GHAZI.** He immediately denounced Amanullah's reforms and sided with the conservatives. Nevertheless, his rule was short-lived. Forces led by Gen. **MUHAMMAD NADIR KHAN,** former commander in chief of the Afghan army, **occupied Kabul** in Oct. 1929 and **brought down Bacha's regime.**

Oct. 16. MUHAMMAD NADIR SHAH became ruler of Afghanistan. He immediately established a **policy of reconciliation** with tribal chieftains and conservative religious leaders. Although he committed himself to a modernization program, he promised, unlike Amanullah, to move slowly and to avoid social legislation.

1931. Establishment of **Afghanistan's first bank,** which, after being reorganized the following year, was named the **Afghan National Bank.**

Oct. 31. Promulgation of **a new constitution. A bicameral legislature** was established, consisting of an elected lower house and royally appointed upper house. All executive powers were vested in the king, who also had the right to veto all legislation. Several clauses guaranteed the social and legal **position of Islam** and the religious establishment.

1933, Nov. 8. Assassination of **NADIR SHAH,** to avenge the execution of a political notable the previous year. **Nadir** was succeeded by his son, **MUHAMMAD ZAHIR SHAH,** but real political power lay in the hands of Zahir's uncle, **Hashim Khan,** who carried on with Nadir Shah's policies.

1934. Admission of Afghanistan to the League of Nations. *(To p. 976)*

d. EGYPT

(From p. 545)

1917–36. SULTAN (KING) AHMAD FU'AD. He succeeded his father, **HUSAYN KAMIL,** who died on Oct. 9, 1917. In March 1922, Fu'ad assumed the title of king. His reign was marked by the unceasing **ambition to acquire** real as well as nominal **power.** He used his constitutional authority to manipulate the political system and undermine popularly elected governments. Nor was he averse to cooperating with the British in order to further his own political aims. His boldest move was the dismissal of the Sidqi government (1933), after which he attempted for over a year (until Nov. 1934) to rule through palace officials and cronies.

1917. Death of **Shibli Shumayyil** (b. 1860), an author of Syrian Christian background. He became a vocal champion within the Arab world for **science and the scientific outlook,** and believed that societies organized on scientific principles would eventually supersede those based on religion.

1918, Oct. 17. Death of **Malak Hifni Nasif** (b. 1886), the **first outspoken female writer on women's issues.** Her ideas resembled the reforms first proposed by Qasim Amin, but her thought was generally more conservative. Among her chief demands were compulsory primary education for women, the opening of higher education to women who wished to pursue their studies, the retention of the veil, and a ban on marriages in which members of the prospective couple had not met each other beforehand.

Nov. 13. A **delegation (wafd)** led by **SA'D ZAGHLUL** requested permission to leave for London to begin negotiations on the postwar status of Egypt.

1919, March 8. THE EGYPTIAN REVOLUTION OF 1919. Strikes and demonstrations broke out throughout the country **following the deportation of Sa'd Zaghlul** and other Wafdist leaders. This represented the **first genuine mass movement of national self-assertion** in modern Egypt. The British were compelled (April 7) to release Zaghlul and his colleagues, who promptly made their way to the peace conference in Paris.

Oct. 17. Appointment of Gen. **Edmund Allenby** as British high commissioner in Egypt to replace Sir Reginald Wingate.

Dec. 7. The arrival of **Lord Milner** at the head of a **commission to investigate the uprisings of 1919.** The Egyptians staged a **unanimous boycott** of the proceedings, and as a result Milner was unable to talk to any Egyptian representatives. Having made little headway, the commission departed for Britain in March 1920. Its report (published Dec. 9, 1920) **recommended independence for Egypt** contingent upon guarantees for the protection of British interests.

1920–22. Abortive negotiations with Britain. In intermittent talks the Wafd failed to win British agreement to full Egyptian independence. The Wafd proclaimed a policy of passive resistance to British rule on Jan. 23, 1922.

1920. The **population** stood at about 13 million, over 90 percent of whom were Sunni Muslims. About one-quarter of the inhabitants resided in cities and large towns. The biggest cities were Cairo (900,000) and Alexandria (500,000).

Founding of **BANK MISR** under the guidance of **Tal'at Harb,** one of the country's most prominent businessmen. The purpose of the project was **to promote economic development,** particularly in industry, and to encourage investment in Egyptian-owned businesses.

Harb was one of the few visionaries among the Egyptian leadership who recognized the **need to diversify and expand the country's economy,** which was largely reliant throughout the interwar period on the export of cotton. Egypt's first burst of industrial growth occurred during the 1930s, mainly in light industries such as textiles and food processing. Overall, though, **industry remained a small sector of the economy,** which continued to be dominated by agriculture.

Jan. 12. Creation of the **Wafdist Women's Central Committee** at a nationalist convention in St. Mark's Cathedral which drew over 1,000 upper-class women. It was the first women's political organization in Egyptian history.

1921. Establishment of the **Egyptian General Agricultural Syndicate,** whose main purpose was to improve the bargaining position of the great Egyptian landholders in the international cotton market. Throughout the interwar period, **cotton remained Egypt's biggest and most lucrative export,** accounting for around 70 percent of total exports into the 1930s. Figures would reach about 80 percent for the 1950s, but never approached the peak of 90 percent for the earlier period of 1910–14.

1922–52. Ministerial instability and party politics. During this period, 32 different governments ruled Egypt. Nevertheless, the pool of cabinet members remained fairly stable throughout the reshuffling. Political life was dominated by a class of large landholders who formed most of the political leadership.

The **Wafd** was the **most important party** and enjoyed the greatest popularity as well as the only true grassroots organization in the country. Because of the widespread support for the party, the Wafdist leadership claimed not only a popular mandate to govern, but the exclusive right to speak for the Egyptian nation. As a result, the Wafd showed little inclination to compromise or join political alliances. The party had two leaders prior to 1952, **Sa'd Zaghlul** (until his death in 1927) and **Mustafa al-Nahhas.** Other leading personalities who later broke away from the party were **Isma'il Sidqi** (founded the **People's Party** in 1930), **Ahmad Maher** and **Mahmud Fahmi al-Nuqrashi** (the **Sa'dist Party** in 1937), and **Makram Ubayd** (a Copt who formed the **Independent Wafd** in 1942).

The **first major opposition party** to the Wafd was the **Liberal Constitutional Party** (1922), led by **Adli Yegen** and drawing its intellectual inspiration from the thought of **Ahmad Lutfi al-Sayyid** and **Muhammad Husayn Haykal.** The **Union Party,** directed by **Hasan Nashat** and mainly representing wealthy landowners, soon followed (1925) and proved eager to cooperate with the palace. None of the Wafd's main-

stream rivals ever attracted a large following. On the other hand, less conventional opposition, namely the **Young Egypt Party** (1936) and, above all, the **Muslim Brotherhood** (1928), successfully appealed to much larger and more enthusiastic constituencies.

1922. Creation of the Egyptian **Communist Party.** The Communists never acquired a significant following, even at the height of their activities in the late 1940s.

An archaeological team under **Howard Carter** discovered the **tomb of King Tutankhamen** near Luxor.

Feb. 28. EGYPTIAN INDEPENDENCE unilaterally granted by **Great Britain,** which nevertheless **retained control over Egyptian foreign affairs and defense, the Suez Canal, and the Sudan** (which Egypt had ruled until the British occupation). The **British also insisted on the maintenance of the Capitulations,** the system of special laws and courts that applied to foreigners. Into the late 1930s, **these four reservations proved a constant source of irritation to Anglo-Egyptian relations.** Because the declaration was a unilateral act and because it did not really provide Egypt with full independence, the Egyptian leadership never really accepted it. Up to the revolution of 1952, **Anglo-Egyptian relations became the dominant issue in Egyptian politics** to the near exclusion of all the other problems facing the country.

1923, March 16. Establishment of the **Egyptian Women's Union** by several leading upper-class women, the most prominent among them **Huda Sha'rawi.** The organization and its affiliates carried out most of their work in **promoting health and education.** The Union's leadership called for the reform of marriage and divorce laws, including a ban on polygamy and the abolition of a man's right to a summary divorce. It also demanded that women receive full legal and political equality.

Huda Sha'rawi drew further attention to herself by **publicly unveiling** at a Cairo railway station upon her return from a women's conference in Italy. Her act scandalized public opinion. It should be noted, however, that veiling was generally an upper-class practice. For most Egyptian women, her gesture was entirely symbolic.

April 21. Proclamation of the **Egyptian constitution.** Egypt became a monarchy equipped with a bicameral legislature. **Power was officially shared between the king and the cabinet, but British influence remained substantial.** Although the form of government was parliamentary, the king appointed the cabinets and scheduled the elections. In the coming years, the king often abused this power by dismissing popularly elected governments and installing minority cabinets to rule until new elections were unavoidable. Behind the scenes, the British usually encouraged the king in these intrigues, especially in thwarting the designs of the Wafd.

Sept. 15. Death of **Sayyid Darwish** (b. 1892), one of the leading Egyptian musical figures in modern times. In his short career he composed dozens of songs that portrayed the experiences of ordinary people and have remained part of the musical lore of the region.

Sept. 27. In the **first elections** held under the new constitution, the Wafd Party scored an overwhelming victory. Sa'd Zaghlul became the **first prime minister** in Jan. 1924.

1924, Nov. 20. Murder of Sir Lee Stack, *sirdar* (commander in chief) of the Egyptian army. In the ensuing crisis, which the British exploited to demand indemnities and the withdrawal of Egyptian troops from the Sudan, the first **Wafdist government fell from power.** Sa'd Zaghlul would never serve as prime minister again.

1925. Law making elementary education free and compulsory. The program largely failed through a lack of resources. As late as 1950, only 30 percent of Egyptian children attended elementary school despite a 500 percent increase in government expenditures on education over the previous 25 years. **Illiteracy remained widespread** among both sexes.

Within a larger framework, the period 1920–50 did show some **modest successes in the field of education.** The number of students rose from about 600,000 to 1.6 million, and the number of primary and elementary schools from some 600 to over 4,500. But this expansion was counterbalanced by a general inability to open enough schools, to support an adequate number of trained teachers, and to keep students in school beyond the elementary levels.

Official opening of **Fu'ad I University,** the first state university, which later became **Cairo University.** It incorporated many previously existing schools, such as **Dar al-'Ulum,** into one large institution.

Publication of *Islam and the Principles of Political Authority,* by

Sheik Ali Abd al-Raziq, who contended that Islam was merely a religion and did not require a particular system of government. His ideas **outraged conservative opinion,** which considered his book an attack on the very basis of Islam. His membership in the religious establishment was later revoked.

First issue of the **political weekly** *Rose al-Yusuf* under the auspices of Fatma al-Yusuf.

Feb. 26. Appointment of **Lord Lloyd** as the new high commissioner.

1926. Publication of *Pre-Islamic Poetry,* by TAHA HUSAYN. The book, which applied modern literary criticism to the study of pre-Islamic poetry, cast doubt on the standard Muslim dating for many of these works. Conservative readers viewed the book as an indirect and highly subversive attack on the traditional interpretation of the Qur'an. **The book had to be withdrawn shortly after publication.** In large part due to this controversy, Husayn lost his teaching position at Cairo University five years later.

Writers like Taha Husayn belonged to an **intellectual movement that looked to Europe** for its guiding ideas and cultural models. Among their chief concerns was **the attempt to construct a unique Egyptian identity,** extending back to pharaonic times, in politics, language, religion, and culture. The intellectuals who were most active in formulating these ideas were (apart from Taha Husayn) **Ahmad Lutfi al-Sayyid** (1872–1963), **Muhammad Husayn Haykal** (1888–1956), **Salama Musa** (1887–1958), **Muhammad al-Aqqad** (1889–1964), and **Isma'il Mazhar** (1891–1962). The movement reached its peak during the 1920s before losing ground to Islamic and pan-Arab ideologies in the following decade.

Jan. 21. Opening of the **Makwar (Senaar) Dam** in the Sudan, which roused fears among Egyptian landowners over the potential diversion of water from the Nile.

May 13–19. The **Cairo Caliphate Congress,** an international conference (though attended mostly by Egyptian and Palestinian delegates) to discuss the possibility of reviving the caliphate, which the Turkish government had abolished in 1924. Poorly organized, the congress quickly became bogged down in procedural issues. In the end, nothing came of it and **the movement to reestablish the caliphate faltered completely.**

1927. Founding of the **Young Men's Muslim Association** by **Abd al-Hamid Sa'id.** The organization, modeled on the YMCA, was formed in part to counter Christian missionary activity.

Production of *Layla,* the **first full-length film** in the Arab world. The first talking movie appeared in 1932. The **first Arab movie studio,** Studio Misr, was founded in 1934, and Egypt immediately assumed **cinematic leadership** of the Arab world.

April 18. Appointment of Tharwat Pasha as the new prime minister.

Aug. 27. Death of **SA'D ZAGHLUL,** the leader of the delegation *(wafd)* that first tried to make Egypt's case for independence at Versailles and then undertook negotiations with the British government. Upon independence, Zaghlul emerged as **undisputed leader of the Wafd Party** and, following elections, became **Egypt's first prime minister.** By the end of his career, he had become the **living symbol of the Egyptian independence movement** and its aspirations. His death left a political vacuum that no succeeding politician was able to fill and further weakened an already divided national leadership.

1928. Establishment of the **Egyptian Radio and Television Corporation.**

Formation of the **MUSLIM BROTHERHOOD** in Ismailiyya by **HASAN AL-BANNA.** The organization began as a **religious and educational society** that sponsored public meetings and lectures on Islam. In general, its program stressed the need to defend Islam from corrupting forces and outside threats (e.g., missionary activity), and to reform Egyptian society and politics according to Islamic principles.

In 1932, the headquarters of the Muslim Brotherhood moved to Cairo. By the late 1930s, it had become **increasingly involved in Egyptian and Arab politics.** Openly proclaiming an anti-Zionist and anti-British platform, the Brotherhood sent aid (and, in 1948, fighters) to Palestine and plotted during World War II with anti-British politicians (and in 1951–52 staged a guerrilla campaign against the British in the Canal Zone). By the late 1940s, the Brotherhood had become **one of the most powerful political organizations in the country.** At this stage, the leadership **adopted violent methods,** a decision that had profound consequences for the regime and for the Brotherhood itself.

March 16. Appointment of **Mustafa al-Nahhas,** the new leader of the Wafd, as prime minister.

June 25. Appointment of **Muhammad Mahmud** (from the Liberal Constitutional Party) as premier.

July 19. Suspension of Parliament. The government also did away with freedom of the press and the right of public assembly. Constitutional government was restored on Oct. 31, 1929.

1929. Admission of the first female students to **Cairo University.** The first female graduates (there were four) received their diplomas in 1933.

May 7. The **Nile Waters Agreement** with the Sudan. The treaty allocated all White Nile water to Egypt and Blue Nile water to the Sudan, allaying the anxieties of Egyptian landowners.

Aug. 8. Arrival of **Sir Percy Loraine** as the new British high commissioner.

Dec. 21. A resounding **Wafdist victory** in national elections. **Mustafa al-Nahhas** took office as prime minister on Jan. 1, 1930.

1930, Feb. National tariff autonomy. The government immediately set high duties on a large number of imports to encourage indigenous industry.

June 21. Appointment of **Isma'il Sidqi** as prime minister. The move was an attempt by the king to circumvent parliamentary authority and rule through his followers. The Wafd announced its opposition to the new government and organized protests around the country.

Oct. 22. Imposition of a **new constitution** by the Sidqi government in collusion with the palace. The system of parliamentary elections, already indirect, was made even more so, to the disadvantage of the popular Wafd. The announcement of the constitution was followed by popular protests throughout Egypt.

1931. Founding of **Misr Air,** the national airline of Egypt.

May. Rigged parliamentary elections resulted in a victory for Sidqi's newly formed **People's Party.**

1932. Deaths of **Ahmad Shawqi** (b. 1869) and **Hafiz Ibrahim** (b. 1871), the two leading practitioners of the **neoclassical style** in **poetry.** Poets of this school combined classical forms (e.g., in meter, rhyme, and language) and contemporary subjects.

Founding of the **Arab Language Academy.**

March 14–April 3. Meeting of the **Congress of Arab Music in Cairo,** attended by leading musicians and musicologists from the Arab world as well as Turkey and Europe. The congress marked the first organized effort in the region **to promote the traditional musical heritage** by codifying the theory, establishing a standard notation system, and encouraging musical research and education.

1933. Ahmad Husayn created the **Young Egypt Party** (Misr al-Fatat), which became a full-fledged political organization in 1936. It favored aggressive state activity in economic development and rapid expansion of the armed forces. The party's ideology originally emphasized Egyptian nationalism, but switched to more Islamic themes after it was renamed the Nationalist Islamic Party (1940). The party exercised its strongest appeal in Cairo and the surrounding suburbs, where more than half its members lived.

The **party organized** many of its young members into **paramilitary squads,** known as the **Green Shirts,** who became notorious for their hooliganism. On the political scene, such behavior was hardly isolated. The rival **Wafd Party assembled** its own bands of thugs, the **Blue Shirts,** who engaged in many of the same violent and lawless practices.

The **first labor laws,** which prohibited factories from working adolescents (ages 12–16) and women more than nine hours a day.

June 21. Resignation of the Sidqi government. In the aftermath, the **king tried to rule without Parliament** through a palace council of ministers, but gave up the attempt in Nov. 1934 and appointed Tawfiq Nessim as prime minister.

1934, Nov. 30. The government of Tawfiq Nessim **revoked the constitution of 1930,** but under pressure from the British did not reinstate the original constitution of 1923.

1935. Founding of the **National Theatre,** under the direction of prominent authors including **Taha Husayn** and **Khalil Mutran.** By this time, **Egypt had assumed leadership of Arabic drama.**

Death of **RASHID RIDA** (b. 1865), probably the most renowned disciple of the great Muslim thinker **Muhammad Abduh.** Like Abduh, Rida believed in the **compatibility of Islam and modern civilization.** He is best known as the leading proponent of the **Salafiyya,** a movement to purify Islam. He advocated a **pan-Islamic political ideology** to help unify Muslims around the world and fend off European domination. Rida's **later thought** became more stringent as he drifted toward a **strict orthodoxy** that criticized such practices as Sufi ritual.

Dec. 12. Restoration of the constitution of 1923.

1936–52. KING FARUQ. Upon the death of King Fu'ad (April 28, 1936), his young son, Faruq, ascended the throne, but he was not invested with full royal powers until the end of the regency period in July 1937. **Early in his reign,** Faruq was an extremely **popular figure** among the Egyptian public. **One of his biggest supporters was the religious establishment,** which received generous patronage from the palace and looked to Faruq as its champion against the secularist politicians. Like his father, Faruq was **constantly at odds with the politicians** and tirelessly schemed to undermine the constitutional system of government in order to acquire supreme power. His authority and prestige were briefly eclipsed after a humiliating confrontation with the British ambassador (Feb. 1942), but by the end of World War II he had returned to the political scene with the same ambitions and penchant for intrigue.

1936, May 2. A **great victory for the Wafd** in national elections. **Mustafa al-Nahhas** again became prime minister.

Aug. 26. Signing of the **ANGLO-EGYPTIAN TREATY,** which arranged for the **abolition of the Capitulations** and **removed direct British interference in foreign affairs and defense.** The British garrison of 10,000 men in the Canal Zone was allowed to stay another 20 years, and the British kept the right to use Egyptian facilities in the event of war. **No agreement was reached on the status of the Sudan,** but Egyptian troops were allowed to return there. Egypt was furthermore to be **admitted to the League of Nations.**

Among the Egyptian public, the treaty **failed to generate enthusiasm.** Essentially a compromise, it was a disappointment even for moderate members of the Wafd and seemed like a betrayal for hard-liners. The government had hoped that by finally signing an independence treaty with Britain it could move on to more pressing domestic issues. Instead, the **new treaty merely inflamed the politicians' preoccupation with Anglo-Egyptian relations.**

1936–37. Expansion of the Egyptian army. A further measure established **a new recruitment policy,** which admitted candidates from the middle and lower classes to the officers' training school for the first time. Within the army, the new policy soon created **divisions between junior officers,** who came from modest circumstances, **and their superiors,** who had been born into elite families. The reform was to have important consequences for Egyptian politics in the early 1950s.

1937. Public rift within the Wafd Party over the terms of the treaty of 1936. Prominent politicians **Ahmad Maher** and **Mahmud Fahmi al-Nuqrashi,** unhappy with the settlement, broke away and formed the hard-line **Sa'dist Party** in 1938.

New system of taxation. Concessions within the treaty of 1936 allowed the government unrestricted freedom in levying taxes. For the first time, **members of minority communities and foreigners** resident in Egypt **assumed a full tax burden.** These groups had formerly received fiscal protection from the Capitulations, which had denied the Egyptian government the additional revenues.

May 8. Conclusion of the **Montreux Conference,** which formally phased out the Capitulations over the next 10 years and the Mixed Tribunals over a period of 12 years.

Dec. 30. Dismissal of Nahhas's Wafdist government. The king replaced it with a minority government under Muhammad Mahmud.

1938, Feb. 2. The king dissolved Parliament. Elections ending on April 2 led to a **disastrous defeat for the Wafd.**

1942. Foundation of the **University of Alexandria.**

Trade Union Act. The government (under the Wafd) recognized the right of workers to organize trade unions (except in agriculture).

Feb. 4. British ultimatum to the king to appoint a Wafdist government. Driven by anxieties over the presence of Axis sympathizers in the palace and government, **the British turned to the Wafd** as the only party they could trust to govern wartime Egypt. When the king, who disliked the Wafd, tried to defy the ultimatum, the British ambassador, **Sir Miles Lampson, sent tanks to surround Abdin Palace,** the royal residence. Faced with abdication or submission, **the king capitulated and appointed a Wafdist government.** Though officially neutral for most of the war, the government cooperated with the British.

1943. Final repayment of the **foreign debt,** which had burdened the economy since the mid-19th century. Egypt's creditors were now (at least until the late 1950s) entirely Egyptian.

Publication of the **Black Book,** by former Wafdist **Makram Ubayd,** detailing **corruption** within the party. The book further eroded the credibility of the Wafd among nationalists.

1944, Oct. 7. Signing of the **Alexandria Protocol,** by which Egypt committed itself to **joining the ARAB LEAGUE** as a charter member. The decision was the culmination of a slow **drift in Egyptian foreign policy toward pan-Arabism.** Henceforth Egypt acted as the leading state in the Arab world.

1945, Feb. 24. Assassination of prime minister Ahmad Maher at the Parliament building on the same day Parliament approved a **declaration of war against Germany.** *(To p. 987)*

e. SYRIA

(From p. 545)

1919, July 2. The **General Syrian Congress** in Damascus passed a resolution affirming its **opposition to a French mandate in Syria.**

Oct. 9. Appointment of **Gen. Henri Gouraud,** an official in the French administration of Morocco, as **French high commissioner for Syria.** The ideas for early French policy in Syria were drawn largely from French experience in Morocco, where conditions were quite different. This led to misunderstandings.

1920. Death of **Tahir al-Jaza'iri** (b. 1851), one of the leading scholars on Arabic language and literature. He was responsible for saving many of Aleppo's Islamic manuscripts and storing them in the Zahiriyya Mosque.

March 8. The second General Syrian Congress in Damascus declared **Syrian independence** and chose **FAYSAL,** son of Sharif Husayn of Mecca, as the king of Syria.

April. France was awarded the mandate over Syria.

July 22. Military defeat of the Arab government in Syria at the Maysalun Pass. The French army ousted the Arab regime of Faysal from Damascus, paving the way for French rule under the League of Nations mandate. Aleppo was occupied the same month. Armed resistance continued in the Alawi region around Latakia and in the western portion of Aleppo's hinterland, but by the end of 1921 these movements had been quelled. **Faysal left Syria** in Aug. 1920, and a year later **became king of Iraq.**

Sept. 1. Establishment of **the Syrian administrative territories** under the mandate. The area of Lebanon was originally part of Syria, but in 1922 **Lebanon was split off to form a separate country** under French mandatory control (p. 761). **The population** of the newly created country of Syria numbered about 2.2 million, 85 percent of whom were Muslim (about four-fifths of them Sunni). One-quarter of the inhabitants lived in urban centers, of which Aleppo and Damascus were the largest.

1920–50. Growth of the educational system. Figures for students attending schools increased from 50,000 to about 300,000. But as elsewhere in the Middle East, educational opportunities for the overwhelming majority of people remained scarce.

1921, Oct. 20. The Ankara Agreement between France and the Kemalist government in Turkey, in which France gave up all territorial claims north of Syria.

1922. Approval of the French mandate for Syria by the **League of Nations.**

1923. Abolition of the Capitulations.

April. Arrival of the new French high commissioner, **Gen. Maxime Weygand,** who served until Jan. 1925.

1925, Jan.–Nov. Gen. Maurice Sarrail served as French high commissioner. He was popular with leftist politicians in France, but his anticlerical attitudes **antagonized the Christian population throughout Syria.**

June. Organization of the **People's Party.** The leadership was composed mainly of **nationalists** who had been **active in Faysal's Arab government** before the arrival of the French. Taking advantage of a laxer political climate under Sarrail, the party openly **demanded the unification of Greater Syria and its ultimate independence.** It was also outspoken in denouncing Zionist settlement in Palestine.

1925–27. THE GREAT REVOLT. An **uprising** broke out in July 1925 **among Druze tribes in Jabal Druze,** a mountainous area southeast of Damascus. The main aims of the revolt were the appointment of a Druze governor for the region, the evacuation of the French garrison, and permission for the Druze to remain armed. The revolt quickly **gained the support of nationalist politicians** and spread to other parts of southern Syria, including the cities of Damascus and Hama. Although the insurrection was put down by early 1927, it had a **lasting effect on French policy,** which became less high-handed and more conciliatory. The **French administration henceforth sought the cooperation of Syrian notables** and rewarded them with a share of the colonial government.

Oct. 14. **Uprising in Damascus,** which forced the French military to withdraw from the city. The French returned on Oct. 18 and staged a two-day attack on the city using artillery and aircraft. The disturbances in Damascus were the first signs of **links between the Druze rebels and urban politicians.**

Nov. 6. **Henri de Jouvenel** became the new high commissioner. He immediately **abandoned the unpopular policies** of his predecessor, who was blamed for inciting the Great Revolt.

1926. Enactment of **compulsory land registration.** The measure, the centerpiece of a French program for **land reform,** aimed at **encouraging and protecting small landholders** while undermining the power of the great landlords. Implementation of the policy was slow and inefficient, and the wealthy landowners, by lending money to peasants at usurious rates, soon reclaimed much of the land that had been redistributed. Indeed, the **long-term effect** of the reform was actually **to increase the amount of land held by the wealthiest families** and to lower the percentage of small landowners.

Organization of the **first trade union** under the leadership of **Subhi Khatib.** Under French rule, **Syrian industry was severely neglected,** and the country was turned into a cheap market for French products. The standard of living among Syrian workers fell sharply and by the 1930s had dipped below late Ottoman levels.

In 1935 the government passed a **law authorizing trade unions,** but only as joint employer-employee associations. Labor officials organized the **Federation of Trade Unions of Syria** (March 1938) to agitate for workers' rights. Labor did not officially win the right to establish independent organizations (that is, without employer participation) until 1939.

May 7. Druze attack on Damascus. French forces bombarded the city for the second time (May 8–19).

Oct. 12. Appointment of **Henri Ponsot** as the new French high commissioner.

1927. Formation of the **NATIONAL BLOC,** a **large group of Syrian notables** who represented most of the country's political leadership. After witnessing the defeat of the Great Revolt, they decided that it was necessary to **cooperate with the French authorities** in order to win greater autonomy. The **membership** of the front was drawn mostly from the **commercial and absentee landowning classes.** The leaders of the National Bloc held sway in Syrian politics until new groups began to challenge their authority and legitimacy in the 1940s. Among the most prominent politicians during the mandate were **Abd al-Rahman Shahbandar, Shukri al-Quwwatli,** and **Jamil Mardam.**

1928, June. Elections for a national assembly. Most of the delegates turned out to be ardent nationalists who promptly drafted a constitution that rejected the mandate and called for the unity of Greater Syria. The **high commissioner** refused to accept the constitution and **suspended the assembly** indefinitely (Feb. 5, 1929).

1929. Excavation of **ancient Ugarit** (modern Ras Shamra) near Latakia. A team led by **Claude Schaeffer** found tablets in an alphabetic script and a hitherto unknown language which threw new light on Canaanite mythology and ritual.

1930, May 22. A **new constitution,** imposed by the French high commissioner. It remained in effect until 1950. Syria received a **unicameral parliament** and a **president** who, though chosen by the parliament, was not responsible to it.

1933, July. Arrival of **Damien de Martel,** the new high commissioner.

1936, Jan. Outlawing of the **Nationalist Party,** which had been organized by nationalist politicians in 1935. The measure was followed by violent protests in the major cities. French authorities imposed martial law.

Feb. A **nationwide general strike** in protest of French policy. The French relented and allowed the formation of a Nationalist cabinet (Feb. 23).

Sept. 9. **Franco-Syrian Treaty.** All Syrian **administrative units,** with the exception of Alexandretta, were consolidated and made **into a single Syrian state.** France was given supervision of Syrian foreign affairs and defense and received the right to use Syrian bases upon the outbreak of war. Syria was also promised admission to the League of Nations within three years.

Because of divisions among the Syrian leadership and opposition to the treaty within France, **the pact remained unratified.**

Nov. Under French auspices, a **Syrian government assumed partial power.** During its short tenure in office, the government was hampered by a combination of political feuding inside Syria, an ailing economy, the Palestinian crisis, and growing French uneasiness with the new political arrangements. The **French suspended the Syrian regime** in 1939 after the French Parliament rejected the treaty of 1936 and French diplomats ceded Alexandretta to Turkey.

1937, July. Outbreak of a **two-month revolt among the Kurds** in northeastern Syria. The leaders of the movement were Kurdish separatists who demanded special legal status and political autonomy for Syrian Kurds.

1939, June. FRANCE CEDED THE HATAY (the region surrounding Alexandretta and Antioch) to Turkey, **outraging Syrian opinion. Syrians viewed the Hatay** and its Arab majority **as an integral part of Syria.** The Syrian territorial claim has remained a constant source of friction in relations with Turkey.

1940, June. Installation of a Vichy administration.

1941, June. INVASION OF FREE FRENCH AND BRITISH FORCES, which overthrew the Vichy administration. The French commander, **Gen. Catroux,** promised a grant of independence.

1943, July. Prodded by the British, the Free French regime reluctantly **restored the constitution of 1930** and authorized elections.

1944. Founding of the **Syrian Muslim Brotherhood,** a branch of the religious organization that originated in Egypt. Most of the leadership was well educated, coming from the professional and religious ranks. The rank and file was centered mostly in the bazaars and among new immigrants to the cities. In its early years, the organization did not become actively involved in politics, preferring to focus on social issues.

1945, Feb. Syrian **declaration of war** against Germany.

March. **Syrian membership** in the newly created **Arab League.**

(To p. 977)

f. LEBANON

(From p. 534)

1918, Oct. 7. French landing in Beirut following the Ottoman evacuation of Lebanon. **British forces** entered the city the next day and formally imposed a military administration under French supervision.

1919, Nov. 10. The French government under Clemenceau announced its **support for a separate Lebanese state.**

Nov. 21. Arrival in Beirut of **Gen. Henri Gouraud,** the high commissioner for the French mandate.

1920, Sept. 1. CREATION OF GREATER LEBANON, an administrative district within the French mandate for Syria. The new territory included the **former autonomous district of Mt. Lebanon along with the Biqa and the environs of Tripoli, Sidon, and Tyre.**

With the exception of the **Christians** living around Mt. Lebanon and in Beirut, **the inhabitants of the new district did not wish to be included in it.** Throughout the mandate, Muslims called for **reintegration into Syria.**

1922. Approval of the **French mandate** by the **League of Nations.** Greater Lebanon thereby became a separate administrative territory from French Syria.

Death of **Farah Antun** (b. 1874), a Christian journalist who spent much of his career in Cairo and New York. He was most noted for publishing *al-Jami'a,* a widely read political journal. The central idea in his political writings was the demand for **separation of religion and** state so that all citizens, regardless of their religious affiliations, could participate equally in political life.

1923. Abolition of the Capitulations.

1926, May 23. Promulgation of the **Lebanese constitution,** which formally established the Lebanese Republic. The centerpiece of the constitution was the creation of a **confessional system** by which **power and representation in the political system were apportioned to various religious groups according to their share of the total population.** Among Christians, the major groups were the **Maronites,** who formed the biggest constituency in Lebanon (29 percent in 1932), and the **Greek Orthodox** (10 percent) and the **Greek Catholics** (6 percent). **Muslims** were divided primarily among **Sunnis** (23 percent), **Shi'ites** (20 percent), and **Druze** (7 percent). The remainder of the population consisted of miscellaneous Christian factions like the **Armenians.**

The constitution provided for a **bicameral legislature** in which the lower house was popularly elected and the upper house (permanently dissolved the following year) was appointed by the French high commissioner. It also established a **presidency and a cabinet.** On May 26, the legislature elected **Charles Dabbas,** a Greek Orthodox, the first president of Lebanon.

According to the constitution, the Lebanese government exercised **control only over domestic affairs.** Foreign relations were left to the French authorities. In practice, the French high commissioner also enjoyed extensive power through his right to appoint advisers to the various Lebanese ministries.

1926–33. Henri Ponsot served as French high commissioner.

1932. Founding of the **Parti Populaire Syrien** by **Antun Sa'ada.** In organization and discipline, the party resembled the many Fascist groups that were surfacing throughout Europe. The party's central demand was the **reunification of Lebanon with Syria** and ultimately, the creation of a state embracing all of Greater Syria.

Last official census. The survey determined that **51 percent of the population was Christian** and the remainder Muslim. The data further showed that **the Muslim population was growing at a higher rate** than the Christian. To protect the dominant position of Christians in Lebanese society, the authorities decided to forgo future censuses. The independent government of Lebanon later adopted the same policy of intentional oversight.

May 9. Fearing the possible election of a Sunni Muslim, **Muhammad al-Jisr,** as president, the **French high commissioner dissolved the legislature and suspended the constitution of 1926.** Upon the request of the French, **Charles Dabbas** remained as acting president.

1933, Jan. 31. Appointment of **Habib al-Sa'd** as the new president.

1934, Feb. 1. Introduction of a **code of civil procedure,** which largely **replaced Ottoman law.**

1936, March 10. The **Conference of the Coast,** at which several leading Muslim politicians denounced the partition of Lebanon from Syria. The meeting reflected the lingering resentment within much of the Muslim community over Lebanon's separate status.

Nov. Formation under **Pierre Jumayyil** of the **Phalanges Libanaises,** a Christian youth society that in practice functioned as a **paramilitary group.** The organization fervently **supported the detachment of Lebanon from Syria.** In 1937 **Muslims responded** by creating their own paramilitary organization, the **Najjada (Muslim Scouts).**

Nov. 13. Franco-Lebanese Treaty, in which the French recognized Lebanese independence, but retained ultimate control over foreign affairs and defense. **Most Muslims adamantly opposed the treaty, and the French National Assembly never ratified it.**

1937, Jan. 4. The restoration by French authorities of the constitution and the domestic political system.

1939, Jan. Arrival of **Gabriel Puaux** as the new French high commissioner.

Sept. 21. Suspension of the constitution and the dismissal of Parliament due to the outbreak of World War II. **Emile Eddé** remained as official president, but he wielded very little power.

1940, Dec. Gen. **Henri Dentz,** the new Vichy high commissioner, assumed office.

1941, April. Resignation of **Emile Eddé** as president. French authorities appointed **Alfred Naccache (Naqqash),** a Maronite, to replace him.

June 8. Free French and British forces invaded Lebanon and toppled the Vichy administration. **Gen. Georges Catroux** afterward took office as the Free French high commissioner.

Nov. 26. The Free French administration formally proclaimed Lebanese independence. The French nonetheless kept working to hold on to the reality, if not the legality, of their supremacy within the country.

1943, March 25. Restoration of the constitution by French authorities, under pressure from the British.

July. Formulation of the **NATIONAL PACT,** the **informal understanding** reached by Christians and Muslims on **the internal division of power.** According to this agreement, **the president was to be a Maronite, the prime minister a Sunni, and the speaker of the lower house a Shi'ite. The proportion of seats in the lower house would be distributed according to a ratio of six Christians to five Muslims.** The cabinet was to be divided along similar lines: two (or three) Maronites, two (or three) Sunnis, and one each for the Shi'ites, Greek Orthodox, Druze, and Greek Catholics. On the whole, **the arrangement overrepresented the Christian communities** and heavily contributed to later political instability.

Sept. 21. Election of **Bishara al-Khuri** as the new president. The government immediately undertook negotiations to end the French Mandate.

Nov. 11. Arrest of leading Lebanese officials (including President Bishara al-Khuri and Prime Minister Riyad al-Sulh) after they tried to amend the constitution without consulting French authorities. Great Britain forced the colonial administration to release them (Nov. 22), and thereafter **French rule began to wind down.**

1945, May 17. The arrival of Senegalese troops in Beirut to reinforce the French. **The deployment** of these reinforcements **roused fears among Lebanese** that France was bent on **re-establishing the mandate.** Violence ensued between French troops and Lebanese protesters. The staunch Lebanese resistance soon persuaded the French government to evacuate its forces.

Aug. 1. The *troupes speciales,* Lebanese troops who had formerly served under French command, were **transferred to Lebanese control.**

(To p. 978)

g. PALESTINE

(From p. 534)

1917, Nov. 2. Publication of the **BALFOUR DECLARATION by Britain.** The document later became the **foundation of British policy in Palestine** and the **basis of Zionist claims for settling in the territory.** The text stated that the British government would support "the establishment in Palestine of a national home for the Jewish people, and will use their best endeavours to facilitate the achievement of that object, it being clearly understood that nothing shall be done which may prejudice the civil and religious rights of existing non-Jewish communities in Palestine."

Dec. 9. Entry of British troops into Jerusalem. Palestine was immediately placed under a British military administration.

1919, June 19. Arrival of the **King-Crane Commission** (composed of two Americans) under the auspices of the **League of Nations.** The commission conducted extensive interviews throughout Syria and Palestine. With respect to Palestine, it concluded that the **overwhelming majority** of Muslim and Christian inhabitants **were opposed to the Zionist program** of establishing a Jewish national home. The commission's report also revealed **strong sentiment against the British proposal to separate Palestine from the rest of Syria.** The British ignored the report's findings.

1920–48. Extensive Jewish immigration, far surpassing the total since 1882. The number of new arrivals reached 452,000 (four-fifths from Europe) by the time of Israeli independence. In 1947 the Jewish population in Palestine amounted to about 610,000, representing 32 percent of the total population. The numbers contrasted sharply with the composition of the Palestinian population around 1920. The total had stood at about 700,000, approximately 80 percent of whom were Muslim; the remaining 20 percent was divided fairly evenly between Christians and Jews.

1920. Founding of the **Histadrut,** the Jewish Federation of Labor. The organization **promoted a Jewish labor agenda** and demanded that Jewish businesses hire only Jewish workers. It remains an important economic and political force in the state of Israel.

Formation of the **HAGANA,** the Jewish militia, which became the

military backbone of the Zionist movement in Palestine and later, of the Israeli Defense Forces.

April. Nomination of Britain for the mandate of Palestine at the **San Remo Conference.**

April 4–10. Anti-Zionist rioting in Jerusalem.

July 1. Assumption of power by a **British civil administration,** which relieved the army of political duties. **Herbert Samuel,** a Jewish and pro-Zionist politician, became the **first British high commissioner** and served until 1925.

Oct. Creation of an **advisory council** consisting of 21 members appointed by the high commissioner. Among these, four members were Muslim, three were Christian, and three were Jewish. The council possessed no real power.

1921. Al-Hajj Muhammad Amin al-Husayni became **mufti** (chief religious official) **of Jerusalem.** He played a leading role in the politics of Palestinian Arabs, but encountered increasing difficulty in unifying the resistance movement under his direction. Throughout the mandate, relations within the Palestinian leadership remained fractious and turbulent. **Husayni tended to represent the policies of more extreme groups, whereas his chief rivals, the Nashashibi family, adopted a more accommodating position toward the Jews and the British.**

May 1–6. Anti-Zionist riots in the region of Jaffa. Government troops were called in and forcibly restored order.

1922, July 1. Issuing of the **Churchill White Paper,** an attempt by the Colonial Office **to clarify British policy in Palestine.** It promised support for the Zionist cause as outlined in the Balfour Declaration, but **favored restrictions on immigration,** contingent upon "the economic capacity of the country at the time to absorb new arrivals." The statement further promised that the **rights of the Arabs would be upheld** and that the inhabitants of **Palestine would eventually receive self-government.**

July 24. The **League of Nations** officially entrusted the **Palestine mandate** to Great Britain.

Aug. Promulgation of a **constitution** for the mandate. The **Arabs organized a boycott** of elections, and the British abandoned the plan.

1923. Arab rejection of the proposed **Arab Agency,** a formal advisory council that would have represented Arab interests to the high commissioner. It was designed to function as a parallel institution to the **Jewish Agency,** which served the interests of Jewish settlers.

Abolition of the Capitulations.

1925–28. Lord Plumer served as British high commissioner.

1925, April 1. Official opening of the **Hebrew University** in Jerusalem, with **Lord Balfour** in attendance. The **Institute of Technology (Technion)** was opened the same year in Haifa.

1927. Introduction of the Palestinian pound (in Transjordan as well) to replace the Ottoman and Egyptian currencies that were still in use.

1928, July 6. Sir John Chancellor became British high commissioner.

1929, Aug. Western (Wailing) Wall riots. Disputes over Jewish access to the Western Wall of the second Jewish Temple complex escalated into Arab-Jewish rioting, which claimed the lives of approximately 250 Arabs and Jews. The fighting ended only after the intervention of British troops. In the aftermath of the clashes, **Arab-British relations sharply deteriorated** because of the excessive violence (including the bombing of villages) the British used in quelling the disturbances and the harsh collective punishments they imposed on parts of the countryside. As a result of British severity, Palestinian notables, many of whom had tried to cooperate with the British during the conflict, lost much of their credibility and influence within the Arab community.

1930, March 31. Report of the **Shaw Commission,** formed **to investigate the causes of the Wailing Wall riots.** The committee concluded that the hostility of Arabs to the British mandate grew out of fears that the Zionist program would deprive them of their lands, throw them out of work to open jobs for Jews, and ultimately reduce them to a subordinate class within their own country.

Oct. Publication by the British government of the **Passfield White Paper,** which called for the creation of a legislative council (first intimated in the 1922 White Paper) and restrictions on Jewish immigration and land purchases. The White Paper **generated heated debate within Britain, Palestine, and the world Jewish community,** leading to the suspension of the immigration restrictions (Feb. 1931) by the British Parliament. The long-promised legislative council never materialized.

1931, July 14. Appointment of **Sir Arthur Wauchope** as high commissioner.

1932. The first **Maccabiah Games** (often described as the Jewish Olympics), which have since become the most important events in the Israeli sports calendar.

1933–36. Peak of Jewish immigration to Palestine. In these three years, 166,000 Jews entered Palestine. By 1936, the total Jewish population was approximately 400,000, 30 percent of the general population.

1933. Production of *Oded the Wanderer,* the **first Hebrew feature film shot in Palestine.**

The construction of modern harbor facilities at Haifa was completed.

Oct. Anti-British rioting by Arabs in Jaffa spread to other towns. British troops quickly put down the protests and occupied several towns.

Dec. Jewish protests against restrictions on immigration, following the rise of anti-Semitism in Germany and the flight of thousands of Jews.

1934. Death of **Haim Nahman Bialik,** one of the greatest Hebrew poets. His rich and extensive work, grounded in Jewish experiences and aspirations, has exerted a lasting influence on Hebrew poetry.

Opening of the **Weizmann Institute of Science** in Rehovot.

1936, April. The **Palestine Broadcasting Service** began operating from Jerusalem.

Beginning of a **national strike by Arab workers.** The protest was marked by widespread demonstrations, which often turned violent, and guerrilla warfare in the countryside. Palestinian leaders organized the **Arab High Committee,** which announced the strike and assumed responsibility for sustaining it. The **strike finally ended on Oct. 10,** due in part to the appeals of Arab states. In an attempt to mollify the Arab leadership, the British announced the formation of the **Peel Commission,** which proceeded to Palestine in October **to investigate social and political conditions.** The commission was boycotted by Arab politicians.

1937, July 7. The **Peel Commission declared the Palestine mandate to be unfeasible.** It recommended the **partition of the territory into three sections: a Jewish state** (about one-third of the territory), extending from the Syrian borders down along the coast to Jaffa; a **British section,** containing a few specified territories (such as the cities of Jaffa and Jerusalem) deemed essential to British interests; and **all other lands,** which were to be Arab and united with Transjordan.

The **World Zionist Congress** (Aug. 2) accepted the plan in principle, but demanded modifications in favor of the Jewish settlers. The **Arabs rejected** outright the idea of **partition.** At the Bludan Pan-Arab Congress in Syria (Sept. 8) delegates called for the abrogation of the Balfour Declaration, suspension of Jewish immigration, and British recognition of Palestinian independence.

Sept. 26. Assassination of Yelland Andrews, British district commissioner for Galilee. The British responded by **outlawing the Arab High Committee** and arresting many of its members. The chairman of the committee, **Hajj Amin al-Husayni,** eluded capture and eventually made his way to Syria, which became the committee's new base of operations. In the absence of the established leadership, more radical politicians assumed control of the resistance movement within Palestine itself. Anti-Zionist and anti-British attacks rapidly increased.

Oct. Beginning of the **GREAT ARAB REVOLT,** which in most areas was merely a resumption of fighting that had broken out the previous year. **Mostly a rural phenomenon,** the revolt was **centered primarily in three areas:** the settlements south and west of Jerusalem, the Galilee, and the area surrounding Jenin, Nablus, and Ramallah. Many Arab notables whom the British had not already detained fled the country. As a result, the guerrillas had to fight without the benefit of a coordinated leadership inside the country. **The main target of the attacks was the British administration,** which responded with mounting military force until it finally subdued the resistance in late 1939.

1938. Appearance of the Irgun, a militant Zionist organization that began a terrorist campaign in response to anti-Jewish attacks.

March 3. Arrival of **Sir Harold MacMichael,** the new high commissioner.

Nov. 9. The **Woodhead Commission,** established to **determine the feasibility of partition schemes,** published its report, which **declared**

them all to be impractical. The British government then announced it would convene an international conference on the Palestine question.

1939, Feb.–March. The Palestine Conference in London. Jewish and Palestinian Arab representatives refused to compromise. Delegates from outside Arab states were more flexible, but were unable to sway the Palestinians. The conference ended inconclusively.

May. Publication of the **WHITE PAPER**, which effectively **repudiated the Balfour Declaration.** It promised independence for Palestine after ten years. The British **envisioned the creation of a binational state** in which power would be shared between Arabs and Jews. In the meantime, **Jewish immigration was to be restricted** to 15,000 per year over the next five years and subject to Arab control thereafter. The administration was also charged with maintaining close supervision over all sales of land. Due mainly to the outbreak of war in 1939, the British **never fully implemented this program.**

The **Zionists rejected the White Paper** and ultimately came to the realization that they could no longer depend upon the British to uphold their aims for a Jewish homeland. They turned increasingly to the U.S. for protection and patronage. On the other side, **the Palestinians— with few exceptions—greeted the new British policy with similar hostility and apprehension.** Most guerrilla bands vowed to fight on.

1940, Nov. 25. Sinking of the *Patria*, a ship carrying Jewish immigrants, in the harbor of Haifa. Jewish agents secretly carried out the operation to publicize the Zionist cause around the world.

1942, May. The Biltmore Declaration. American Jewish organizations threw their weight behind the establishment of a Jewish state in Palestine. By the end of World War II, the horrors of the Nazi Holocaust (p. 701) had persuaded most American Jews to back the Zionist program.

1944, Nov. 6. Assassination of Lord Moyne, Britain's minister resident in the Middle East, by Zionist terrorists.   *(To p. 979)*

h. TRANSJORDAN

(From p. 534)

1920. The best available estimates have put the **population** at around a quarter of a million inhabitants, 90 percent of whom were Muslim. Nearly half the people were nomads, and there were no large towns.

Nov. 11. Arrival of the Hashemite emir ABDALLAH at the city of Ma'an. **ABDALLAH** had previously been promised the throne of Iraq, but it went to his brother Faysal after the latter was driven from Syria by the French. The territories that would later compose Transjordan were remnants of Faysal's Syrian kingdom which lay outside the French mandate for Syria and the British mandate for Palestine.

1921, March 27. The British recognized ABDALLAH as provisional ruler of Transjordan, which at that time was still included within the Palestine mandate (though not subject to the Balfour Declaration). Abdallah chose Amman, previously little more than a large village, to be his capital.

April. Appointment of **Albert Abramson** as British adviser to Abdallah. He was soon replaced by **H. St. John Philby** (Nov. 21).

1922, Oct. Abdallah requested independence for his territory. The British responded by offering him autonomy within the Palestine mandate.

1923. British advisers began **reforming the administration of Transjordan,** most notably in the fields of taxation and land registration. At roughly the same time, the government began converting many prominent tribal sheiks into large landholders, who became allies of the regime. To help prop up Abdallah's government, the British offered annual subsidies and agreed to provide military aid.

Creation of the **ARAB LEGION,** built up from the earlier unit known as the **Reserve Force.** The legion acted as Transjordan's **army and main police force,** and trained and operated under the direction of a British officer (the first British commander was **Frederick Peake**).

May 25. Anglo-Jordanian Treaty. The British transformed the provisional government in Transjordan into a permanent one and separated Transjordan from the Palestine mandate. In return for administrative recognition, **the British demanded that Transjordan adopt a constitution, maintain an efficient administration, and leave its foreign policy in British hands.** Although the Transjordanian administra-

tion was set up immediately, the new arrangements were not officially ratified until Feb. 20, 1928.

The British were soon disappointed with Abdallah's regime. In Aug. 1924, they issued an **ultimatum,** accepted by Abdallah, **that imposed greater British control over his administration,** which was henceforth supervised by **Henry Cox,** who served as British representative in Amman (1924–39).

1924. Tribal sheiks received official legal powers through the **Tribal Courts Law.**

1925, Nov. 2. Treaty of Hadda, which defined the border between Transjordan and Saudi territory. Beduin raids from Saudi territory had been a constant irritation to Abdallah's government.

1928, April 16. Promulgation of a constitution, which created a **Legislative Council** (two-thirds of its members elected) and a cabinet to be appointed and dismissed by Abdallah himself. The first elections were held in Feb. 1929.

1930. Organization of the **Desert Mobile** Force under the command of British officer **John Glubb.** The new unit, operating as part of the **Arab Legion,** relied primarily on Beduin recruits. During World War II, it became a mechanized force of some 3,000 soldiers.

Not only did the **Desert Mobile Force** strengthen the army, it also helped to create lasting links between the state and the desert tribes. Henceforth tribesmen formed one of the main bulwarks of Abdallah's regime.

1931–32. Demarcation of Transjordan's borders with Syria and Iraq.

1939, March. Appointment of **Alec Kirkbride** as British resident in Amman.   *(To p. 982)*

i. IRAQ

(From p. 534)

1920, May 5. The League of Nations mandate for Iraq was formally accepted by Britain. The newly created country, made up of the former Ottoman provinces of Baghdad, Mosul, and Basra, had a **population of around 3 million,** about 80 percent of whom spoke Arabic as their first language (some 15 percent were primarily Kurdish speakers). About 90 percent of Iraqis were Muslims, the majority of them (60 percent) Shi'ites. Four-fifths of the population was rural, and Baghdad ranked as the largest urban center, with some 200,000 residents.

June. Anti-British revolt in northern and central Iraq, which lasted most of the summer.

Oct. 1. Arrival of Sir Percy Cox as **British high commissioner** in Iraq.

1920–47. Growth of the state bureaucracy from some 3,000 positions to about 18,000. Despite this unprecedented expansion, the government remained weak and ineffectual.

1920–50. Expansion of the educational system. Whereas in 1920 Iraq had only about 10,000 students, by 1950 the total had climbed to 240,000. Against these figures, the general state of education was much bleaker. The great majority of Iraqis had no access to good schools even if they managed to attend school at all.

Through its educational system, **Iraq emerged at the forefront of Arab nationalist ideology** in the 1920s and 1930s. Textbooks and curriculum were designed to emphasize notions of Arab identity. The most influential figure in disseminating these ideas was **SATI' AL-HUSRI,** the chief official in the educational system during the mandate and one of the most vocal spokesmen for the cause of Arab nationalism.

1921–58. Ministerial instability. For this period there were no fewer than 59 separate governments in power. **Yet the political elite remained fairly constant,** drawn largely from urban notables of Arab and Sunni Muslim background and former Ottoman army officers and bureaucrats. Among the most influential notables were **Nuri al-Sa'id, Ali Mumtaz al-Daftari, Yasin al-Hashimi, Tawfiq al-Suwaydi, Umar Nadhari,** and **Abd al-Muhsin al-Sa'dun.**

1921–33. KING FAYSAL I. The son of **Sharif Husayn of Mecca,** he was installed as king of Iraq after the French expelled him from Syria. Throughout his reign, **he tried to strike a delicate balance** among the constraints imposed by the British presence in Iraq, his own ambitions as king, and Iraqi aspirations for independence. He was acutely aware that the Iraqi monarchy attracted little support within Iraq, and he worked to bind Iraqi society more closely to his **Hashemite dynasty.**

1922. Abolition of the Capitulations.

June. Kurdish tribal revolt in northern Iraq led by **Sheik Mahmud al-Barzinji,** who declared himself **king of Kurdistan.** The uprising had a predominantly tribal character, but its leadership aimed at the creation of an **independent Kurdish state,** or at the very least an autonomous zone for Kurds. The revolt was not suppressed until July 1924.

Oct. 10. Anglo-Iraqi Treaty, by which Great Britain managed Iraq's foreign affairs and defense, placed advisers in other departments inside the Iraqi government, and gave the country a constitution. The effect of the treaty was to **secure indirect British rule of Iraq** without the expenses of a direct administration.

1924. The **Tribal Disputes Regulation,** which **bolstered the power of the tribal sheiks** by upholding their tribal laws, expanding their legal jurisdiction, and funneling money to them through government projects and land grants. Throughout the period of the monarchy, they operated as an important buttress to the political establishment.

July 10. Adoption of a **constitution** that provided for a **parliamentary government** under a **monarchy.** The political system was to prove more democratic in theory than in practice. Parliament consisted of two chambers, the lower one elected by restricted male suffrage and the upper house filled by royal appointment. The king was also responsible for appointing the cabinet, but did not have the power to dismiss it. The chief result of this constitutional constraint was **political intrigue between the palace and the government** as the king secretly tried to subvert governments that displeased him. The other crucial power in Iraqi politics, not named in the constitution, was of course the **British administration,** which usually sought to bolster the position of the king against the politicians.

1925, March. Conclusion of an oil concession with the **Iraq Petroleum Company,** a British firm that was to develop the **oil fields around Mosul.** The company received the concession on favorable terms extending over 75 years. Production began in 1927, but royalties to the government did not become significant until the 1950s.

1926, June 5. Anglo-Turkish Treaty, which **awarded** most of the region surrounding **Mosul** to Iraq. Included in the Iraqi territory was the biggest prize, the northern oil fields near Kirkuk.

1927. First development of the **Kirkuk oil field.**

1929, Oct. 3. Appointment of **Sir Francis Humphreys** as British high commissioner.

Nov. 13. Suicide of prime minister Abd al-Muhsin al-Sa'dun, a pro-British politician, because of his government's frustrating inability to negotiate a new treaty with the British. In the transformed political atmosphere afterward, **Nuri al-Sa'id** came to power as prime minister for the first time. In what became a trademark of his political style, he immediately imposed restrictions on the political opposition and press. His government then undertook a **new round of negotiations with the British** which eventually bore fruit.

1930, June 30. ANGLO-IRAQI TREATY, which provided for **full Iraqi independence.** The British were to receive two air bases and the right to use Iraqi facilities in time of war. **The mandate officially ended on Oct. 3, 1932.** Iraq was then admitted to the **League of Nations.**

Sept. 11. Kurdish tribal revolt, which was suppressed by April 1931.

1932. Land settlement law, which created a new category *(lazma)* of land ownership in addition to the old Ottoman *(tapu)* holdings. The law allowed all settled tribesmen who had been cultivating, without title, the same piece of land for over 15 years to claim the rights to it. The only restriction was that the peasants not alienate the land from their tribe. **The intent of the law was to prevent tribesmen from losing their land and to confirm their position on it.** But urban notables and tribal sheiks—the latter of whom had already become large landlords—scrambled to snap up the available land by securing deeds from the government committees in charge of the reform. **A large number of the tribesmen became** little more than **sharecroppers,** and some were completely dispossessed. Tensions rose in the countryside, and were violently released shortly thereafter.

April–June. Third Kurdish tribal uprising. The Iraqi army crushed the revolt with help from British air units. The surviving rebels retreated into Turkey.

Nov. Establishment of a fixed border with Syria through the mediation of the League of Nations.

1933, Aug. 4. Outbreak of the Assyrian Rebellion. The Assyrians (Nestorian Christians) wanted to establish an **autonomous zone in northern Iraq** and had even presented their case to the League of Nations. A large number of them had fled to Syria, where French authorities refused to let them settle. While they were recrossing the border, **fighting broke out** between the refugees and a unit of the Iraqi army. Violence spread to other districts, and **hundreds of Assyrians lost their lives.** Public sentiment strongly backed the army.

1933–39. KING GHAZI. He succeeded his father on Sept. 7, 1933, and became popular for his Arab nationalism and reputed hatred of the British. Nevertheless, he carried little political weight.

1934, July 14. Opening of the **oil pipeline** from Mosul to Tripoli in Lebanon. A second line to Haifa was put into operation on Jan. 14, 1935. From this time forward, **pipelines were crucial to the Iraqi oil industry** as its chief outlet to the world market.

1935–36. Tribal revolts in southern Iraq, which the army successfully suppressed. For the first time, the government had effective control over the tribes in the region.

One of the repercussions of the revolts was **widespread discontent among the military leadership** with civilian rule. According to rumor, prominent opposition politicians had encouraged the tribes to revolt. At the same time, the army feared that it was becoming a tool of the government for stamping out political opposition. Some officers began to think that, in view of civilian incompetence and treachery, direct military rule would be better for both the army and the country.

1936. Creation of the Industrial and Agricultural Bank of Iraq. **Most of the economic projects** undertaken by the Iraqi government in the 1920s and 1930s **benefited agriculture.** This bias toward agrarian development was no accident in a regime that relied heavily on the support of rural notables and tribal sheiks, especially in southern Iraq.

Oct. 29. An **army coup,** the first of many in Iraqi history, **overthrew the civilian government** of Yasin al-Hashimi. The chief plotters were the disgruntled politician **Hikmat Sulayman** and the army chief of staff, **Bakr Sidqi.**

1937, Aug. 11. Assassination of army chief of staff Bakr Sidqi. Six days later Hikmat Sulayman, lacking the army's support, resigned as prime minister. All the social reforms proposed by his government were shelved and ignored until after the revolution of 1958.

1939–58. KING FAYSAL II. He was not yet four years old when he succeeded his father, Ghazi, who died in an automobile accident (April 4). **Abd al-Ilah,** the young king's uncle, served as regent until 1953 and remained active in Iraqi politics up to the revolution of 1958.

1940, Feb. Another **coup d'état under the leadership of the Golden Square,** four young **Arab nationalist colonels (Salah al-Din al-Sabbagh, Muhammad Fahmi Sa'id, Mahmud Salman, and Kamil Shabib).** With the backing of the palace, they kept **Nuri al-Sa'id** in power as prime minister just as his government was on the verge of splitting up. Over the next two years, the **Golden Square** became the **dominant force in Iraqi politics.** This group increasingly tilted the government toward a **strident pro-Arab, anti-British policy** that had disastrous consequences for Iraq during World War II.

1940 March. Formation of a new government under **RASHID ALI AL-GAYLANI.** The **Golden Square** stood in the background as the real power brokers, directing an anti-British policy that led to a **British ultimatum** (Nov. 1940) and the subsequent **resignation of** Rashid Ali as premier (Jan. 31, 1941).

1941, April 10. THE RASHID ALI COUP. An army coup, organized by the **Golden Square,** brought Rashid Ali back to power as prime minister. His government immediately opened contact with the Axis powers. In response to the government's anti-British activities, **the British intervened militarily,** forcing the coup leaders to flee the country (May 29). A **pro-British government was established,** and prominent supporters of the coup were executed, jailed, or deported.

June 1–2. Anti-Jewish pogrom *(Farhud)* in Baghdad. Soldiers, paramilitary youth gangs, and crowds of citizens went rampaging through Jewish neighborhoods and business districts. The toll was high: 179 Jews killed, 586 businesses looted, and 911 buildings housing more than 12,000 people pillaged. The episode profoundly undermined the confidence of Iraq's Jews.

1945. Death of **Ma'ruf al-Rusafi** (b. 1875), a leading poet in the neoclassical style.   *(To p. 983)*

j. STATES OF THE ARABIAN PENINSULA

(From p. 541)

1914. Nov. 3. Kuwaiti independence under British protection.

1915, Dec. 26. Treaty between IBN SA'UD and the colonial government of India. The Indian government recognized Najd and several territories along the Persian Gulf as the independent possessions of Ibn Sa'ud.

1916, Nov. 3. British treaty with **Qatar**, making it a **veiled protectorate.**

1918, Dec. Surrender of the Ottoman garrison in Yemen, which had successfully repelled all British attacks and reached within 20 miles of Aden. Several members of the former Ottoman bureaucracy agreed to stay in Yemen and work for **IMAM YAHYA**, who was maneuvering to become ruler of the northern half of Yemen.

1919. After being rebuffed in negotiations by Imam Yahya, the British awarded the region of Tihama, including the city of al-Hudayda, to the tribal ruler of Asir.

1920. Treaty of Sib, mediated by Great Britain. The sultan of Oman relinquished the right to intervene in tribal affairs in the Omani interior.

Aug. Saudi conquest of Asir.

1921. Sheik Ahmad became ruler of Kuwait and reigned until 1950.

Creation of the **Muscat Levy Force**, a small military unit that served as the police force for the Sultanate of Oman.

Nov. Saudi conquest of Hail.

1922, May 5. The **Treaty of Muhammara**, a diplomatic agreement brokered by the British, which fixed the boundaries between Kuwait, Iraq, and Ibn Sa'ud's domains.

1923. British removal of **Sheik Isa** as ruler of Bahrain. The new regime admitted a British adviser and set about reforming the administration, primarily in law, finance, and the collection of customs, to suit British wishes.

1924. Appearance in Mecca of the **first official Saudi newspaper**, the weekly *Umm al-Qura*. Additional publications joined it after 1932.

March 5. Proclamation of KING HUSAYN of the Hijaz as Muslim caliph. The decree was announced two days after the Turkish parliament abolished the Ottoman Caliphate. **Husayn's pretensions were greeted with a mixture of skepticism and hostility** around the Muslim world.

March 31. Ending of British subsidies to the Hijazi and Saudi governments.

Oct. 3. Abdication of HUSAYN following military defeats at the hands of Saudi forces. **His son, ALI, was declared the new king.** Saudi units occupied Mecca on Oct. 12.

1925, March. Yemeni forces loyal to **IMAM YAHYA reoccupied** the port of **al-Hudayda.** The following year, the imam seized the territory of Tihama. By the end of the decade, he had secured control over the whole of northern Yemen and subdued the region's tribes.

Dec. The Saudis completed the **conquest of the Hijaz.** This event marked the **fall of the Hashemite dynasty in Arabia.**

1926, Oct. 21. Agreement on a **Saudi protectorate for the territory of Asir.** The ruler of Asir, Sayyid Muhammad ibn Ali, formally handed over control of foreign affairs to the Saudis to protect himself from the incursions of Yemeni forces. On Nov. 20, 1930, the **Asir was absorbed** into the larger Saudi kingdom. By this point, the borders of Saudi Arabia had assumed their present shape.

1927, Feb. IBN SA'UD assumed the title of **king of the Hijaz and Najd.**

May 20. Saudi-British Treaty, which formally established the **independence of Ibn Sa'ud's domains.**

1928–30. Removal of the British garrison from Aden. The move was made possible by the success of the RAF in policing the tribes of the interior.

1928. Expulsion of Yemeni troops from the protectorate of Aden.

Founding of the **first periodical in Kuwait,** the monthly magazine *al-Kuwait.*

1929. Collapse of the pearling industry in the Persian Gulf. The competition of Japanese cultured pearls and the onset of the Great Depression together spelled the end for pearl diving in the region, which had been the chief support of the economy. **Only Bahrain,** which began to exploit its oil reserves, **was saved** from complete economic devastation during the Great Depression.

1929–30. Suppression of the Ikhwan. Ibn Sa'ud organized a campaign to defeat rebellious tribesmen who, originally with his encouragement, had settled on cultivable land and organized themselves into **religious communities** based on a strict Wahhabi interpretation of Islam. Their frequent **raids into neighboring states**—to fight "infidels"—had become a **serious diplomatic problem** for the Saudi dynasty. Ibn Sa'ud was able to rally broad support and mount an offensive against them only after they had begun to attack towns and tribes within Arabia itself. The Ikhwan communities were not entirely disbanded, but they never again presented a threat to the Saudi state.

1930, Feb. 24. Treaty of friendship between the Iraqi and Saudi governments.

1931. Beginning of **oil exploration** in Arabia.

1932. OFFICIAL ESTABLISHMENT OF THE KINGDOM OF SAUDI ARABIA. Ibn Sa'ud's oldest son, Sa'ud, was selected to be crown prince and heir to the throne.

Discovery of oil in Bahrain. Export began in 1934. The country opened its own oil refinery in 1937.

Death of Omani sultan **Taymur ibn Faysal** (r. 1913–32). His son, **Sultan Sa'id** (r. 1932–70), succeeded him on the throne.

May 23–24. Anti-Jewish riots in Aden, resulting in numerous injuries and extensive property damage.

1933. Standard Oil of California was awarded an oil concession by the Saudi government. Ibn Sa'ud made the grant despite opposition from conservative religious quarters. His **primary concern** at this time and over the next 20 years was **internal security.** Yet he had **difficulty raising sufficient funds** to police his kingdom, a predicament that led him to seek commercial and diplomatic subsidies.

July 27. Treaty of friendship between Transjordan and Saudi Arabia. The agreement ended years of hostility and tension between the two states.

1934. Feb. 11. Treaty of San'a between Yemen and Britain. The British recognized **IMAM YAHYA** as **king of Yemen,** and the imam accepted the Anglo-Ottoman line of 1905 as the border separating Yemen from the Aden protectorate.

April. WAR BETWEEN SAUDI ARABIA AND NORTH YEMEN. The Saudis launched an invasion of Yemen and nearly conquered it, but were forced by the British and the Italians to give up their gains. The **Yemeni state was fully restored,** but in the Treaty of Ta'if accepted Saudi control of three provinces formerly claimed by Yemen: Asir, Najran, and Jizan.

1938. Start of oil production in Arabia.

1938–39. Abortive move toward political reform in Dubai. The ruling dynasty set up a council of finance, composed mainly of local notables whom it wished to exclude from power. The existence of the council proved intolerable to the regime, which abolished it a year later.

1943. Development of irrigation projects in southern Yemen, particularly for the cultivation of cotton.

1944. Organization of **ARAMCO**, an American oil company that was established to operate a huge oil concession in Saudi Arabia.

Creation of the **Free Yemen Party** in Cairo. The membership of this opposition group consisted mainly of Yemeni intellectuals from prestigious families who had been exposed to the writings of Islamic modernists and the message of the Muslim Brotherhood. The appearance of the party was one of the first signs of growing fissures within Yemen's ruling elites.   *(To pp. 984, 985, 986)*

3. NORTH AFRICA

a. MOROCCO

(From p. 547)

1914. Publication of **decree that divided all lands into alienable and inalienable property.** The first category comprised private holdings and all public lands. The second consisted chiefly of collectively owned tribal lands.

In 1919 a related decree was issued by which the French sought **to reclassify a large part of the collective tribal lands.** An office was created to determine what portion of these lands was needed by the tribes. The remainder was turned over to the state, which in practice sold large plots to European settlers. By these methods and others, the **amount of land held by the French rose** to 675,000 hectares by 1932, most of it lying in fertile plains.

Sept. 11. Decree by Resident-General **Lyautey** empowering **local Berber village councils to function as courts and to use their customary law as the official legal code.** The French tried to present this policy as a defense of local traditions, but both measures were in fact innovations. In the short term, **the French sought to avert possible Berber insurrections** as French troops were being moved to fight the Germans. Looking further ahead, the French authorities hoped to foster a separate Berber identity within Morocco and thus create divisions within the local population.

1915. The Spanish recognized **Raisuli,** the powerful Berber tribal leader, as governor of the Jabala district.

1919, July 11. First **attacks by Raisuli's tribesmen** on Spanish possessions in Morocco. The Spanish immediately began military operations against him. By the following year, they had sharply reduced his power.

1921–26. THE RIF WAR, a rebellion against French and Spanish rule in Morocco which at one point tied down some 700,000 French and Spanish troops. The war opened with the **Battle of Anwal** in Spanish Morocco (July 21, 1921). Berber forces under **MUHAMMAD ABD AL-KARIM AL-KHATTABI** annihilated a large contingent of Spanish troops and declared a rebellion within the Spanish sector of Morocco. The **Rif Republic** was established in 1922, and **Abd al-Karim** assumed the title of **president.**

1922, Sept. 22. Final **submission of Raisuli** to the Spanish authorities, thereby bringing hostilities in the western part of Spanish Morocco to an end.

1923, Dec. 18. Treaty to establish an **international administration,** under the supervision of the British, French, and Spanish, **for the city of Tangier.** Negotiations on details continued until Jan. 1929.

1924, Dec. Spanish withdrawal from the interior of Morocco in order to concentrate their forces on the coast. The retreat followed a series of military setbacks against the Rif army under Abd al-Karim.

1925, Feb. 7. Abd al-Karim captured Raisuli, who had been fighting alongside the Spanish. Raisuli died soon afterward in captivity.

Feb. A *fatwa* (legal opinion) from the **Qarawiyin Council of Learning** condemned the Sufi author **Muhammad al-Nazafi** for a book in which he contended that a prayer in the order's ritual was part of God's eternal speech. **The ruling served both religious and political motives.** The members of the council were predominantly modernist scholars who wished to purify Islam of doctrines and practices (such as those found in Sufism) that they viewed as corruptions. On the other hand, the Sufi orders had thrown in their lot with the French regime and urged Muslims to obedience. Since many members of the council were part of the growing Moroccan opposition to the existing French administration, they wanted to discredit the Sufi leadership.

April 13. Abd al-Karim opened an offensive against French forces operating along the frontier of the Rif Republic.

July 26. Franco-Spanish military alliance against **Abd al-Karim.** The colonial offensive, commanded by Marshal **Henri Pétain,** got under way on Sept. 9, and the Rif army began to fall back.

Sept. 24. Resignation of Louis Lyautey, the French resident in Morocco.

1926, May 26. Final defeat and surrender of Abd al-Karim, putting an end to the Rif Rebellion. He was later exiled to the island of Reunion.

1927, Nov. 17. Death of **MOULAY YUSUF,** sultan of Morocco. He was succeeded by his son, **SIDI MUHAMMAD III.**

1930. Establishment of a **Federal Bank** whose primary task was to provide settlers with reasonable loans. In comparison, native farmers had great difficulty in securing credit.

Formation of the **Zawiya,** a small group of leaders within the National Group (al-Jama'a al-wataniyya) who, by 1932, had broken away and formed the **National Action Bloc.** The group's chief objective was to win the sultan over to the nationalist cause. In 1934 it issued a **"Plan of Reform"** that criticized administrative abuses and economic and educational failures, and called for legal reforms. The authors of the proposal, published in France, were careful to express their admiration for French culture and the French political system. **Their plan did not denounce the protectorate itself,** but demanded a more faithful application of its principles. The nationalists had not yet reached the point of insisting on complete independence.

May 16. Intensification of French assimilationist policy. The French authorities transferred the tribal courts created in 1914 to newly formed "customary tribunals," which operated under French supervision. **The law was highly unpopular, and the French finally rescinded the order** in April 1934—but they did not renounce the policy of assimilation itself.

1931. Death of **Abdallah ibn Idris al-Sanusi,** a religious leader of modernist *(salafi)* intellectual leanings. He had studied in Egypt during the 1870s and come under the **influence of Muhammad Abduh's thought.** One of his most significant contributions was his lifelong campaign against *ta'wil,* the allegorical interpretation of the sacred texts by Sufis. He held these ideas responsible for what he considered to be the degeneration of Islam in Morocco.

Dec. 29. Administrative reorganization of Spanish Morocco, which was put under the civil and military authority of a high commissioner.

1932–34. French suppression of **tribal unrest in the interior.** This campaign marked the **final stage of the French conquest of Morocco** and gave the colonial authorities complete control over the interior.

1933, Nov. 28. Opening of the **Moroccan-Tunisian Railway,** which connected all of French North Africa. The French administration valued the railway for its efficiency in transporting troops from one end of the Maghrib to the other.

1936, July 18. Spanish troops under Gen. **Francisco Franco** revolted and seized the city of Melilla, opening the **Spanish civil war.**

1937, March 18. Outlawing of the National Action Bloc, which had begun recruitment among Muslim workers.

Nov. A wave of popular demonstrations led to the **arrest of leaders within the National Party** (the National Action Bloc under its new name).

1940, Nov. 9. Incorporation of Tangier into Spanish Morocco.

1943, Dec. Founding of the **ISTIQLAL PARTY,** which officially demanded independence for Morocco. *(To p. 990)*

b. ALGERIA

(From p. 548)

1919, Feb. 4. Extension of **French citizenship to all Muslim veterans** of World War I in Algeria. Under the previous law, French citizenship was unobtainable without conversion to Christianity. Yet this proposal affected few Algerians directly and became moot anyway when the **French government,** under heavy pressure from the colonists, **later withdrew the offer.**

1926. Founding in France of the **Étoile Nord-Africaine** by **Messali al-Hajj.** The purpose of this organization was to coordinate the political activities of Algerian workers residing in France. It quickly assumed a nationalist character and **opposed all forms of union with France.**

1931. Creation of the **Association of Ulama** under the guidance of **Abd al-Hamid ibn Badis,** a modernist *(salafi)* religious leader whose ideas owed much to the thought of Muhammad Abduh. The program of the organization had **two main goals: the reform of Islam,** namely the purging of Sufi doctrines, which were held to be superstitious corruptions of the pure faith; and **the cultivation of the Arabic language in schools and the general promotion of Arabic culture** throughout the country.

1934, Aug. 3-5. Violent Muslim attacks on Jews in Constantine caused widespread damage to Jewish property and the loss of 23 Jewish lives.

1936, June. An **Islamic congress** in Algiers. Following the electoral victory of Leon Blum's Popular Front in France, Algerian activists believed they could wrest key concessions from the new government. Among their demands were universal male suffrage irrespective of religion, the complete administrative absorption of Algeria into France, permission for Muslims in matters concerning personal status to live by Muslim law, and the abolition of all legal restrictions on Muslims. On the whole, the program of the congress represented **the last attempt by Muslim leaders to take seriously French promises of full assimilation and equality.**

Dec. Defeat of the Blum-Viollette Bill in the French Chamber of Deputies. The bill would have conferred full French citizenship on a minority of Muslim Algerians, namely former officers in the French army and university graduates. **Conservative and colonial opposition** to the legislation kept the matter from ever being debated by French deputies.

1937. Founding of the **Parti du Peuple Algérien (PPI)** by **Messali al-Hajj.** The party immediately adopted an antiassimilationist platform.

1944, March 7. A Free French decree granted **full French citizenship to a small minority of Algerians** (about 20,000 men), mainly those who had received an advanced education in France or had served under French arms.

March 17. Creation of the **Amis du Manifeste de la Liberté (AML)** by **Farhat Abbas.** The organization demanded an **Algerian republic federated with France.**

1945, May 8. Riots in Sitif involving Muslim demonstrators and colonial police. Disturbances soon spread to the entire region surrounding Constantine. Afterward the colonial authorities banned the AML in retaliation. *(To p. 991)*

c. TUNISIA

(From p. 550)

1919, Sept. 12. A Franco-Italian agreement ceded several oases in southeastern Tunisia to Libya. In addition, all Italians residing in Tunisia received the same legal status as Frenchmen.

1920, June 4. Creation of the **DESTOUR PARTY** (Tunisian Liberal Constitutional Party), which was dominated by the landed and religious elites. The party called not for independence but for **a reform of the colonial government** to permit greater Tunisian participation. The bey, **MUHAMMAD AL-NASIR,** threw his support behind the party's program in April 1922.

1921, Nov. 8. Grant of **French citizenship to all French residents of Tunisia** who had at least one parent who had been born in the country. The government simultaneously bestowed citizenship on all children of Tunisian-born Europeans. French authorities considered this ruling necessary because of the legal fiction by which the Tunisian government formally—if not actually—exercised internal sovereignty. Under the previous arrangement, Tunisian-born Europeans had been viewed only as Tunisian citizens. Following British protests, the **law was modified** (May 24, 1923) to allow the children in question to choose the European nationality they preferred.

1922, July 13. Administrative reforms in response to the demands of Tunisian nationalists for greater participation in the government. The French created a **network of councils** composed of both Frenchmen and Tunisians, but the jurisdiction of these bodies extended only to economic matters.

1924, Oct. 12. Organization of the **Confédération Générale des Travailleurs Tunisiens** by political activist **Muhammad Ali,** who was arrested soon afterward.

1926, Jan. Restrictions on political activity and the press.

1932, Dec. Controversy over the burial of Muslim apostates. The mufti of Bizerte declared that Tunisians who had obtained French citizenship—and by doing so had necessarily renounced Islam—were not allowed to be buried in Muslim cemeteries. Most prominent religious officials concurred with this ruling. As a result of the widespread furor,

the colonial government had to set aside special cemeteries for the Christian converts.

1934. Death of **Abu al-Qasim al-Shabbi** (b. 1909), one of the most notable Romantic poets in the Arab world. Poetry in this style was characterized by a desire to innovate and break with classical and neoclassical expression. The Romantic poets often looked to the cultural scene in Europe for inspiration and guidance. Other leading poets of this school outside Tunisia were, to name only a few, **Ahmad Zaki Abu Shadi** (1892-1955), **Khalil Mutran** (1872-1949), **Abd al-Rahman Shukri** (1886-1958), and **Abbas Mahmud al-Aqqad** (1889-1964). Romanticism flourished in Arabic poetry throughout the interwar period.

March 2. Establishment of the **NEO-DESTOUR PARTY,** of which **HABIB BOURGUIBA** became the leader. Membership in the party appealed to those who had grown up in Tunisia but received an advanced education in France, giving them an appreciation of and ambivalence toward both cultures.

The party was outlawed only six months after its appearance. The colonial regime jailed Bourguiba and did not release him until 1936.

1938, April 9-10. Riots in Tunis following the arrest of neo-Destour activist Ali al-Balhawan. A decision by police to fire on demonstrators left 112 dead.

Dec. Rising calls within Italy for the annexation of Tunisia. The French premier, Édouard Daladier, visited Tunis (Jan. 1939) and refused to consider any possibility of withdrawing from Tunisia.

1942. MUNSIF became the new bey of Tunisia.

1943, May 14. Deposal of Munsif by the new Free French administration. The bey was accused of collaborating with the Axis, but the French more likely viewed him as a threat to colonial rule. *(To p. 992)*

d. LIBYA

(From p. 551)

1918, Nov. 18. Proclamation of the **Tripolitanian Republic** by an alliance of tribal leaders and *ulama.* The new government had a highly provisional character, which became evident in negotiations with the Italians. The Tripolitanian delegation expressed its willingness to drop the demand for independence in exchange for internal autonomy and full legal equality for its people with Italians.

1919, June 1. Fundamental Law of Tripolitania. The Italians promised to grant Italian nationality and full civil and political equality to Libyans.

Aug. Dissolution of the Tripolitanian Republic.

Sept. 12. A Franco-Italian agreement transferred several oases in southeastern Tunisia to Libya.

1920, Oct. 25-Dec. 21. The **al-Rajma Agreement** between the **Sanusiyya** and the **Italians.** It created an **autonomous zone for the Sanusiyya confederation** around several oases in Cyrenaica and recognized **AL-SAYYID IDRIS,** the Sanusi leader, as emir of this region.

1922. July 18. By decree **all uncultivated lands became state property.** A further decree (Feb. 10, 1923) set the terms by which Italian settlers could lease or purchase these lands.

After the war with the Sanusiyya, colonial authorities seized all Sanusi estates. In a later decree, **the government appropriated additional lands** belonging to the tribes. If the tribes did not officially object to government seizure of their lands, it was assumed that they had renounced them. Many tribesmen lost their land before they had even heard of these proclamations.

Dec. Secret departure of Al-Sayyid Idris to Egypt. He did not return permanently to Libya until 1947.

1923, May 1. Start of the **war between the Italians and the Sanusiyya.** The Italian governor of Cyrenaica declared all agreements with the Sanusiyya to be void.

1927, March 9. Termination of the local administrations in Cyrenaica and Tripolitania. The Italians permanently abandoned the principle of self-government for the Libyans.

1928, June. A decree made **all public lands suitable for agriculture available only to Italian settlers.**

1929, Jan. 24. Union of Tripolitania and Cyrenaica under one colonial administration.

1931, Sept. 11. Capture and execution (Sept. 16) by Italian authorities of **al-Sayyid Umar al-Mukhtar,** local leader of the Sanusiyya resistance. This event marked **the end of the eight-year Sanusiyya insurrection** in the Libyan interior.

1940, June. **Al-Sayyid Idris** agreed to organize a Sanusi force to fight with the British in Cyrenaica.

1942, Jan 8. The British promised that Libya would not be returned to Italian rule after the war.

1943, Feb. Completion of the **British occupation of Cyrenaica and Tripolitania,** where separate administrations were set up. The French had already established themselves in Fezzan. *(To p. 993)*

G. SOUTH AND SOUTHEAST ASIA, 1914–1945

1. INDIA

(From p. 556)

The period encompassing the two world wars marked more than the worldwide conflict between Fascism and democracy or socialism/Communism. This was also the period in which imperial powers were profoundly challenged by colonized areas demanding to become nation-states in their own right. British India, as the **first locus of a full-blown nationalist movement,** created a model—the **Indian National Congress**—soon to be followed across the colonized world, from Southeast Asia to Africa.

Nationalist ideology arose from a complex set of interactions in British India, producing a number of side effects that still loom large in postcolonial South Asia. The general process involved the identification of "imagined communities" and mobilization of public support around these ideological constructions. The dominant pattern involved an all-India, nationalistic definition of community—in which M. K. Gandhi played a key role—which, because of the symbolic vocabulary used, was evocatively Hindu and north Indian in nature. The Indian National Congress, while not the only actor on this nationalist stage, managed to remain the key organization in directing resistance to the British through nationalism.

In part prompted by these same processes, and in part as a reaction to the vocabulary invoked by congress, other definitions of community also emerged. Many Indian Muslims, for instance, regardless of the stark differences among them, were led by these developments to define a separate but overlapping identification for themselves. Similarly, in south India, a regional movement grew up around the Tamil language which collapsed into one community identity a range of cultural, religious, and linguistic markers. In most of these movements, proto-class distinctions were deliberately downplayed in favor of other shared characteristics; in the west and the south, however, the domination of the nationalist movement by Brahmans led to "non-Brahman" movements essentially focused on lower-class or caste interests.

It is possible to argue that these "imagined communities" emerged especially in response to government institutional changes, in which the identification and, especially, the counting of people as part of one community or another became increasingly important as constitutional changes allowed for more democratic participation in governance. But equally important were movements aimed at religious reform which, for the first time, emphasized individual action as the basis for identity; the passionate activism attached to devotionalism was extended to various movements in defense of other forms of community as well.

Events in the larger world helped to shape both the demands by Indians for greater autonomy and British reactions to these demands. Indeed, the interests of the British Indian government were often at odds with those of the British government at home. Moreover, the question of Indian support for British war efforts was much more straightforward during World War I than it was by the time of World War II, when little progress seemed to have been made toward self-rule, and the impact of the world depression had underscored the disadvantages of India's links to the larger world. Rapid population growth from 1921 (1.1–1.4 percent annually) exacerbated social and economic tensions.

1914, Aug. 4. Britain at war with Germany, making India automatically a combatant. Indian leaders responded loyally, and during the first two years of the war the political situation in India was comparatively quiet. The imperial legislative council voted a gift of £100 million toward Britain's war effort. British India and the Indian states provided about 1.2 million troops (combatants and laborers), who took part in the campaigns in Europe, Mesopotamia, Palestine, Egypt, and East Africa. During the second half of the war unrest became more and more prevalent, with rising prices and heavy taxation adding to popular discontent.

1915. **Madan Malaviya, Sir Sundar Lal, and Annie Besant,** the Theosophist leader, founded the Benares Hindu University. Besant organized the Home Rule League outside the Indian National Congress. The return from imprisonment (since 1908) of **Tilak,** and the deaths of **Gokhale** and **Pherozeshah Mehta** opened the way for a reunion of the moderate and extremist groups in congress. Meanwhile the Muslim leaders **Abul Kalam Azad** and **Mohammed Ali** were interned for opposing Muslim participation in the war against the Ottoman Empire.

1916–21. **Baron Chelmsford,** viceroy. He was met at once with a demand for increased self-government made by 19 Indian elected members of the imperial legislative council. This was elaborated in the scheme, approved in December by the Indian National Congress and the All-India Muslim League meeting simultaneously at Lucknow, calling for dominion status, extension of the franchise, 80 percent of legislative councilors to be elected rather than government-appointed, and half the members of executive councils to be responsible to the legislatures. The efforts of Tilak and **M. A. Jinnah** produced the **Lucknow Pact** between the congress and the league, recognizing separate electorates for the Muslim minority, giving them more seats in the legislatures than their numbers required ("weightage"), and allowing three-fourths of the Hindu or Muslim legislators to veto any measure affecting their communal interests.

1917. Tilak and Besant carried on a vigorous agitation for home rule. To forestall serious trouble, and embarrassed by the revelation of maladministration of the Indian forces in Mesopotamia, the British government, through the new secretary of state for India, **Edwin Montagu,** made an important policy change in August.

Aug. 20. The British government announced a policy of developing **self-governing institutions** in India, with a view to introducing responsible government. Montagu visited India in 1918 and together with Lord Chelmsford worked out a report (April 22, 1918) for limited self-government, presented to Parliament in July, which was denounced by the congress as "disappointing and unsatisfactory" and similarly condemned by the Muslim League. The moderate members of the congress seceded and formed the **National Liberal Federation** (Nov. 1918), pledged to cooperate with reforms.

1918–19. Influenza epidemic caused 5 million deaths.

1919, March 18. The **ROWLATT ACTS,** two antisedition measures that enabled the government to intern agitators without trial and entitled judges to try cases without juries, became law despite the united dissent of the Indian members of the imperial legislative council. Angered at this, **Mohandas K. Gandhi** (1869–1948), saintly leader of the Indians in South Africa (1893–1913), having loyally supported the war effort, now proclaimed a day of fasting and work stoppage *(hartal)* throughout India, but ignorance of his pacifist program led to rioting. At Amritsar in the Punjab, five Englishmen were killed and an Englishwoman beaten (April 10).

April 13. THE AMRITSAR MASSACRE. Gen. Reginald Dyer, aiming to terrorize the populace, ordered his Gurkha troops to fire on an unarmed assembly caught inside a walled garden until their ammunition was exhausted; 379 persons were killed and 1,200 left wounded. Gandhi (April 18) suspended his civil disobedience *(satvagraha)* campaign, calling it a "Himalayan miscalculation." Mounting agitation throughout India followed, aggravated by belated and mild official censure of Dyer's action.

May 3–Aug. 8. The **third Anglo-Afghan War** (p. 757), begun by the new emir **Amanullah,** who appealed to India's Muslims to rise against the British.

Dec. 23. The **GOVERNMENT OF INDIA ACT** introduced the **Montagu-Chelmsford reforms.** The Indian Parliament (opened at Delhi in Feb. 1921) was to consist of the viceroy, **council of state** (60 members, of whom 26 were to be officials), and **legislative assembly** (140 members, of whom 100 were to be elected). The **provincial governments** were to have Indian as well as British ministers. Under the "dyarchy" principle, important matters were "reserved" for the governor and the appointed British members of his executive council; the less important (sanitation, education, agriculture, etc.) were to be "transferred" to the Indian members. **Provincial legislative councils** were to be 70 percent elective, with an extended franchise limited by property qualifications. The Indian National Congress rejected the new system but members of the National Liberal Federation cooperated with the government and in many places worked the new system with considerable success.

1920. Seeking to unite Hindus and Muslims, Gandhi joined the **Ali brothers** and **Azad** in organizing the **KHILAFAT MOVEMENT** to protest the treatment of the Turks by the victorious Allies.

Aug. 1. Death of Tilak, who had been pressing for further constitutional advances. On the same day, Gandhi, accompanied by the Ali brothers, began a nationwide speaking tour to enlist support for a great **noncooperation movement,** involving a boycott of foreign goods, schools, law courts, official functions, legislatures, and overseas military service. A special session of the congress at Calcutta (Sept. 4–9) approved Gandhi's program, and the regular session at Nagpur (Dec.) reaffirmed it, converted the congress into a mass organization under a hierarchy of full-time leaders, and defined its aim as "the attainment of *swaraj* [self-rule] by peaceful and legitimate means."

1920s. Definite **change in foreign trade** for India. A negative balance of trade with Britain characterized the period leading up to the Great Depression, prompting the metropole to look for other outlets, and for India to increase its trade with Germany, Japan, and the U.S. Britain survived the depression in India by using a high exchange rate, a deflationary monetary policy, and discriminating protection. These policies, while ensuring that India was part of the world market, did not allow India to participate in it. Seriously damaging the Indian economy and prolonging the impact of the depression, such policies transmitted external disturbances but gave no benefits. Indian peasants suffered most severely.

1921–26. LORD READING, viceroy.

1921. Height of the noncooperation movement. Despite Gandhi's insistence on nonviolent action, terrorist outbreaks were frequent, and in some parts of the country serious peasant risings against landlords and moneylenders took place: **peasant movement** in Gangetic plain (**Kisan movement**) linked claims to higher status with resistance to landlords and government; **rising of the Akalis** (Sikh peasant puritans) in the Punjab, March 1921; **rising of the Moplahs** (Muslim peasants of Malabar) in Aug. 1921, with forced conversions and slayings of Hindu landlords. The last episode set off a decade of chronic clashes between Hindus and Muslims, with much bloodshed. Other kinds of conflict—especially class conflict as exemplified by landlord-peasant tensions in areas where they shared religious identity—were denied outlet by Gandhi. He and Jawaharlal Nehru disagreed on the relationship between class protest and the nationalist struggle; Nehru eventually acceded to Gandhi's strategy of postponing such struggle in the interest of winning national independence.

Nov. 2. The Ali brothers were convicted and sentenced to two years in prison for calling on Muslim troops to desert. As more and more first-line (male) leaders were imprisoned, women took on additional responsibilities in running the nationalist struggle. In the Khilafat movement, for instance, the mother and wife of an Ali brother became the main spokespersons. Large sums were raised from women, who contributed their jewelry (often their main dowry goods); economic boycotts, because they focused on domestic goods, succeeded essentially because women decided to support them. Although Gandhi tried to distinguish between male and female roles in support of nationalism, many strong women leaders acted outside that dichotomy.

Dec. 24. The Indian National Congress gave Gandhi sole executive authority. Gandhi denounced all violence and introduced a **campaign of civil disobedience** toward the law. Despite his great authority, violence continued to spread.

1922, Feb. 4. The Chauri Chaura affair. Insurgent peasants, led by Indian nationalists, attacked the police station at Chauri Chaura (United Provinces) and killed 22 policemen. Gandhi at once ordered suspension of noncooperation and civil disobedience, but the government took drastic measures.

March 10. Gandhi was arrested and sentenced to six years' imprisonment. The leaders in Chauri Chaura were presented in courts not as political protesters but as ordinary criminals.

1923, Sept. 25. Victory of the moderate element in the Indian National Congress. This group (the **Swaraj Party**), led by **Chitta R. Das** (prominent Bengali leader), favored participation in the elections with the aim of using its representatives in the legislature to obstruct government and so force the granting of home rule. In the elections the nationalists did, in fact, win an impressive victory, but many of the elected deputies soon forgot about obstruction and began cooperating with the government (tariff autonomy bill passed, 1923). The leaders, Das and **Motilal Nehru** (father of Jawaharlal), began to advocate the granting of **dominion status** to India.

1924, Feb. 4. Gandhi was released from prison because of his precarious health. A **united conference at Delhi** (Sept. 26) brought together representatives of the Hindus, Muslims, Parsis, Sikhs, and Christians, who agreed to set up local committees to prevent religious clashes. The militant activities of the Hindu Mahasabha (founded 1915) and the Arya Samaj (Swami Shraddhanand murdered by a Muslim, Dec. 23, 1926) nevertheless continued to aggravate Hindu-Muslim relations.

1925, Sept. 7. The nationalists in the Indian Legislative Assembly called for the establishment of round-table conferences to frame a scheme for responsible government.

1926–31. LORD IRWIN, viceroy.

1926, Nov. 8. The British parliament appointed the **Statutory** (Simon) **Commission,** with members from all British parties, to study the situation in India and the working of the Montagu-Chelmsford system. Most Indian parties voted to boycott the commission because no Indians were included. The total effect of the move was to revive agitation and call forth further disorder during the commission's tour of India (1927–28).

1928. India was swept by a **great series of strikes** among the Bombay textile workers, railway employees, etc., marking the emergence of the industrial proletariat as an important factor (All-India Trade Union Congress founded 1920), and the growing influence of the Communist Party of India (origins 1923).

Aug. 28. All-parties conference at Lucknow adopted the **Nehru report,** a proposed constitution that would give India dominion status under a representative government. Muslim leaders, although divided, disliked the omission of the safeguards for minorities agreed on 12 years earlier in Lucknow. Extremists, led by **Jawaharlal Nehru** (chairman of the constitutional committee), **Subhas Chandra Bose** of Bengal, and **Srinivasa Iyengar** of Madras, rejected the dominion status provision.

Aug. 30. These leaders then organized the **Independence of India League,** calling for complete independence. Their demand clouded the central issue of Hindu-Muslim cooperation.

Dec. 22–1929, Jan. 1. That cooperation broke down at the **all-parties national convention** at Calcutta and the concurrent **Calcutta session of the congress** (Dec. 29–1929, Jan. 1), at which Gandhi emerged from virtual retirement to heal the extremist-moderate rift with a compromise resolution calling on the government to grant dominion status within one year, failing which the congress goal would become complete independence and another noncooperation campaign would be inaugurated.

1929–31. Religious reform movements linked personal behavior to public statements of community. The **Tanzim** movement urged Muslims to become good, practicing Muslims through marches, prayer, and charitable activities. The **Tabligh** movement linked training in physical fitness for community defense with being a good Muslim. The Arya Samaj fostered equivalent movements for many Hindus: the **Shuddhi** movement provided new rituals for lapsed Hindus (especially Untouchables or Muslims) to reenter the Hindu fold (and hence to be counted as "Hindus" for political purposes); the **Sangathan** movement trained Hindus for militant community defense.

1929, March 15. Thirty-one Communist leaders arrested for sedition: their trial, the **Meerut conspiracy case,** lasted four years and aroused widespread public sympathy.

Oct. 31. The viceroy announced that a **round-table conference** would be opened with the objective of dominion status, but Conservative opposition in Britain prevented his making a firm pledge.

1930, Jan. 1. Accordingly, **the congress declared the Nehru report to have lapsed and empowered Gandhi to begin civil disobedience.**

March 12–April 6. The **salt march** inaugurated the campaign. Gandhi marched to the Gujarat seacoast to make salt illegally as a symbol of defiance. The government remained inactive until violence broke out.

April 18. Chittagong armory raid, eight guards killed.

April 23–May 4. Peshawar in revolt after government troops fired on an unarmed crowd, killing at least 30.

May 5. Gandhi arrested and imprisoned without trial, but his followers continued the movement: altogether 60,000 were jailed in this year, 103 killed and 420 injured by police firings. Again, women took increasingly prominent roles in the nationalist movement.

Nov. 12–1931, Jan. 19. The **first round-table conference** held in London, attended by representatives of the Indian princes, the Liberals, and the Muslim League.

Dec. 29. Muhammad Iqbal, president of the Muslim League, proposed the formation of a separate state for the Muslims of northwestern India.

1931, Jan. 26. Gandhi was released from prison, and, at Lord Irwin's request, entered upon discussions with the government.

March 4. The Delhi pact resulted. Gandhi agreed to discontinue civil disobedience and promised that the congress would recognize the round-table conferences; in return Lord Irwin agreed to release political prisoners who had not been guilty of violence.

March 24. A civil **strike** called by the congress to protest the execution of bomb-throwing Bhagat Singh turned into a Hindu-Muslim riot of unprecedented scale in Kanpur, United Provinces.

Sept. 7–Dec. 1. Second round-table conference. Gandhi went to London as sole representative of the congress, but the conference broke up without reaching agreement on the representation of religious and other minorities.

1931–36. Earl of Willingdon, viceroy, whose unwillingness to negotiate led Gandhi to resume civil disobedience soon after his return to India (Dec. 28).

1932, Jan. 4. Gandhi was again arrested, the congress was declared illegal, and repressive measures were instituted to crush the nonviolent demonstrations that followed.

Aug. 16. The round-table conference having failed to settle the question of minority representation under a new constitution, Prime Minister MacDonald announced the **communal award,** retaining the principle of separate communal electorates and extending it to embrace the depressed classes (Untouchables). Gandhi, in prison, condemned the latter provision and embarked on a "fast unto death" (Sept. 20–26), ended when he and the Untouchable leader **B. R. Ambedkar** agreed on the **Poona Pact,** giving the depressed classes a larger number of representatives, chosen by themselves in a primary election but elected by the general Hindu electorate. Gandhi's fast, and a second one (May 8–29, 1933), did much to arouse public sentiment against caste restrictions.

Nov. 15–Dec. 24. Third round-table conference confined to minor matters.

1933, April–1934, Nov. 22. A **parliamentary joint committee,** reviewing the material of the Simon Commission and of the round-table conferences, worked out a draft constitution.

1933, May–1934, May. Gradual suspension of the civil disobedience movement. Gandhi now devoted all his efforts to raising the status of the depressed classes, whose members he renamed Harijans ("children of God").

1934, Oct. 21. All-India Congress Socialist Party founded.

Oct. 24. To free the hands of its younger leaders, **Gandhi resigned from the congress,** but remained the supreme arbiter of its policies.

1935, Aug. 2. The **GOVERNMENT OF INDIA ACT** passed by the British parliament. **Burma and Aden were separated from India.** British India was divided into 11 provinces, each under an appointed governor and an appointed executive council. Each province was to have an elected legislature (bicameral in six provinces and unicameral in five), with a ministry responsible to it. Representation was to be based on the communal award. The **provincial governments** were to enjoy wide autonomy, though the governors retained certain emergency powers. The ultimate objective was the establishment of an **All-India Federation,** to include the Indian states as well as the provinces of British India, but this arrangement was doomed by the fierce opposition of the congress and the states' refusal to join. A **central legislature** at Delhi consisted of an upper house (council of state) composed of 34 elected members and 26 appointed members, and a lower house (legislative assembly) of 105 members elected by the provincial assemblies and 40 appointed members. The governor-general retained control of defense, foreign affairs, etc.

1930s. Talkies, and the **technology of sound** added to cinema, changed the nature of the Indian film industry dramatically. It also reinforced the movement, under way in other forms of cultural and political production, toward more regionally focused activities. Before sound, any movie could be shown with title cards in different regional languages. After sound, all cinema production became tied in to indigenous language centers (making the Tamil production companies among the most secure). Sound also enabled the continuities with folk and other drama traditions to be felt more directly; song and dance became a central part of all films.

1936–43. MARQUESS OF LINLITHGOW, viceroy and governor-general.

1937, Jan.–Feb. Elections for the provincial assemblies. The **All-India Congress** (chiefly Hindu and demanding complete independence) was the only well-organized party and so won absolute majorities in six provinces and pluralities in three others. The objective of the party having been to force the abrogation of the new constitution and secure the convocation of an Indian constituent assembly, the leaders were now confronted with the problem of whether to make use of such power as had been gained in the elections.

July. After prolonged negotiations, the congress agreed to form ministries in six provinces (and in two more by 1938).

1937–39. Deepening conflict between the Muslim League and the congress, touched off by a congress ultimatum to the United Provinces League to disband, which was rejected.

Once in power, the congress ministries liberated many political prisoners and restored civil liberties. Attention began to turn more and more toward extensive social and agrarian reform. However, policies by provincial congress governments permitted only congress members to participate in governing (effectively shutting out most Muslims). Particular policies also alarmed many people—e.g., the introduction of cow protection measures, and the adoption of Hindi as a major language to be taught in the schools. The war in China and the revelation of Japanese imperial designs contributed to the greater cordiality and collaboration between the nationalists and the British authorities.

1938, Feb. 19–21. At the congress session in Haripura the radical leader **Subhas Chandra Bose** was elected president.

April 28. After a lengthy correspondence, Gandhi met Jinnah in Bombay to discuss the Muslim League's demand that it alone represent India's Muslims. Gandhi and the congress executive rejected this demand, and further attempts to reach an understanding were finally abandoned by both parties (Oct. 1938).

1939, Jan. 29. Bose was reelected congress president, defeating Gandhi's candidate. The delegates to the ensuing congress session (Tripuri, March 10–12) rejected Bose's proposal to send the British government an ultimatum demanding independence within six months, and reiterated their faith in Gandhi's nonviolent policy and program. Unable because of Gandhi's opposition to form a working committee (the congress executive), Bose resigned (April 29) and formed his own party, the **Forward Bloc** (May 3), outside the congress.

During the Great Depression the peasantry was adversely affected by the fall of prices on the world market, but business interests were able to expand in areas left vacant by the shortage of investment capital from abroad. The standard of living remained pitifully low for the vast mass of the people, 85 percent of whom lived in rural areas, and 90 percent of whom were illiterate. By 1940 the total population had grown to about 385 million from an estimated 160 million in 1800.

Sept. 3. India declared war on Germany.

1940, Aug. 8. Great Britain offered India partnership and a new constitution after the war.

1942, April 11. The Indian Nationalist leaders rejected a **British offer of autonomy** for India after the war, with the right to secede, conveyed to them by **Sir Stafford Cripps** as emissary of the British government.

Instead, they demanded **immediate independence.** Disturbances developed in India, and **Mohandas K. Gandhi, Jawaharlal Nehru,** and **Abdul Kalam Azad,** leaders of the independence movement, were arrested, but were released later in the year.

July 3. The British government announced a **reorganization of the government,** giving the Indians a large majority on the viceroy's council.

1943–47. FIELD MARSHAL VISCOUNT WAVELL, viceroy.

1945, June 29. The **All-India Congress** failed to agree on a common list of ministers for the new government, and the **deadlock between the Muslim leaders and the Hindu leaders** continued.

Sept. 19. The new British Labour government proposed to discuss with Indian representatives the offer for Indian autonomy made in 1942.

Sept. 20–23. The **All-India Congress,** meeting in Bombay, declared this plan to be unsatisfactory, and called on Great Britain to "quit India."

Dec. 27. Elections to the **central legislative assembly** gave the largest number of seats to the **Congress Party** and the **Muslim League.**

(To p. 994)

2. SOUTHEAST ASIA

(From p. 556)

The period between the two world wars saw significant social change, including the emergence of nationalism throughout the region. The course of events during World War II significantly heightened these changes because they strengthened the demands for independence.

Peasant rebellions punctuated the period. Seldom if ever "nationalist" in their ideology, they nevertheless responded to the increasing interference of Western colonial rule in peasant welfare and social values via administrative, economic, and social changes. Such peasant uprisings continued a historical pattern that had preceded the colonial era. **Common characteristics** among peasant revolts included a rural and agrarian setting; highly localized frames of reference; a leadership characterized by emphasis on return to "traditional" values; and, often, strong religious overtones. Representing resistance to changing times and seldom espousing far-reaching aims, these movements therefore differed in character and intent from urban-based nationalism, which they often paralleled. Eventually, however, they were absorbed into the urban-based nationalist movements.

The emergence of nationalism during this period owed much to the hastened process of urbanization. Part of this process related to the establishment of new urban centers: these developed primarily in response to demands of alien trade and commerce but also as important communication and administrative centers for the surrounding countryside. Part of the process also related to the emergence of new elites: as traditional elites were displaced by colonial changes, new urban elites grew up to serve the administrative and commercial needs of the colonial powers. Because of their exposure to Western education, members of this elite had aims and ideas that owed a great deal to Western ideas and organizational forms. Social change thus resulted, as well, in new social security networks and new interest groups: the formation of "voluntary associations" proved especially significant in influencing the patterns of nationalist activities. Beginning with recreational gatherings, especially football clubs, these voluntary associations soon expanded to include cultural and intellectual societies focused on self-improvement and ranged from debating clubs to literary circles, study groups, religious reform societies, and language improvement associations.

This period witnessed an increase in the importance of what had been a persistent feature of Southeast Asian society because of the needs of the colonial powers: since many of the commercial and trading functions were in the hands of foreigners, the diaspora of Chinese and Indians into Southeast Asia grew rapidly. This pattern became more pronounced because the indigenous "middle class" (the new bourgeoisie in most of Southeast Asia) concentrated on roles as bureaucrats and government servants, while commercial and trading ac-

tivities remained the exclusive domain of nonindigenous immigrants. Since most Chinese lived in towns, they represented a majority of the population in most of the urban centers of Southeast Asia.

In the early decades of the 20th century the Chinese were politicized by events in mainland China which strengthened a sense of internal Chinese cohesion and distinctiveness and prevented further assimilation into the indigenous Southeast Asian cultures. This in turn prompted suspicion and hostility on the part of the indigenous Southeast Asian populations, with long-term ramifications for developments in the region in the face of nationalist demands for independence.

(To p. 1008)

a. MAINLAND SOUTHEAST ASIA

1. BURMA
(From p. 557)

1918. Tentative scheme of reform by the British in the process of separating Burma from India. Local self-government was to be strengthened.

1920. The **Young Men's Buddhist Association split** reflected the generational divide between conservatism and activism. Younger members renamed the organization the **General Council of Burmese Associations,** making explicit their nationalist and political purposes. First activities focused on student strikes regarding the proposed rulers of the University of Rangoon; soon the GCBA began encouraging the organization of village-level nationalist organizations (*wunthanu athin,* "own race societies") to boycott government officials and refuse to pay taxes and rent.

1923. Dyarchy (British system created in India to divide governance responsibilities between colonial administration and indigenous representatives) introduced. **Legislative Council** with 80 elected members (of 103 total) was created, with communal constituencies that reinforced Burma's awareness of ethnic identities (categories included Indians, Karens, Anglo-Indians, British). Working the institutions introduced under dyarchy underscored the very different interests of urban and rural participants.

1928–34. The **impact of world depression** led to a fall in rice prices by one-half, while peasants' costs (land rents, payments on indebtedness, taxes, and prices of imported necessities) remained steady or declined only slightly. Almost 20 percent of the mortgages on agricultural land were foreclosed between 1928 and 1934.

1930, May. Anti-Indian riots began in Rangoon as a response to world economic pressures; these spread to the countryside in the year following. General anticolonial disorder followed.

Dec. Peasant revolt, led by Hsaya San in Tharrawaddy District. Hsaya San was a former monk practitioner of indigenous medicine and a GCBA organizer. His arguments gave voice to peasant grievances (which he had surveyed in the countryside in the late 1920s), as he asserted that colonial rule had destroyed rural life through taxation, increased crime, and led to rising rice prices, land alienation, Indian immigration, unemployment, and the denigration of Buddhism. Although this kind of insurgency had no hope of ultimate success, it provided martyrs and an example of anticolonial activism much romanticized by later resisters.

1942, March 8. The **Japanese occupied Rangoon.** For the campaigns in Burma during World War II, see p. 808.

1945, May 17. A British White Paper promised Burma dominion status after the war. (To p. 1008)

2. THAILAND (SIAM)
(From p. 559)

1917, July 22. Siam declared war on Germany and Austria-Hungary, and in the summer of 1918 sent a small expeditionary force to Europe. The war enabled the government to inaugurate the work of freeing the country of extraterritoriality and tariff restriction. By the peace treaties Germany, Austria, and Hungary were obliged to abandon their claims in these matters.

1920, Jan. 10. Siam became an original member of the League of Nations.

Sept. 1. A TREATY WITH THE UNITED STATES did away with American extraterritorial rights and granted Siam tariff autonomy.

1924, March 10. By **treaty with Japan** the latter power also gave up extraterritorial and tariff rights.

1925, Feb. 14. TREATY WITH FRANCE. France followed the example of the U.S. and Japan, gave up all special rights, arranged for arbitration of disputes, and finally agreed (Aug. 25, 1926) to the establishment of a demilitarized zone along the Indochinese frontier. Britain concluded a similar treaty on July 14, and the other European powers followed suit, so that by 1926 Siam had secured full jurisdiction and tariff autonomy.

1925–35. RAMA VII (Prajadhipok), king, succeeding his brother. He appointed a council of state, composed of five royal princes, to aid him in government, and at once initiated a policy of economy.

1927, March 25. With the ratification of the last treaties with the powers, the **consular courts came to an end** and the Siamese government established a new tariff.

1932, June 24. A coup d'etat put an **END TO ABSOLUTE GOVERNMENT** in Siam. The movement was organized by a group of young radicals, educated in Europe or imbued with European democratic theory, who formed a **People's Party.** The king, held captive for a short time, at once agreed to a constitution and the organization of a senate. The definitive **constitution** was adopted on Dec. 10: provision for popular sovereignty; the council of state, though appointed by the king, to be responsible to a national assembly, half the members of which were to be appointed while the other half were to be elected by universal (male and female) suffrage. This kept the pressure on the government to fulfill democratic ideals. Indirect elections were held in 1933 and 1937.

1933, April 3. Nevertheless, the king, convinced that the country would support him against the radicals, **suspended the new constitution** and set up a new council of state.

June 20. This led to a new coup d'etat, led by **Col. Phya Bahol Sena** and other army officers. While affirming their loyalty to the king, they forced the resignation of his council of state and recalled the national assembly. Phya Bahol Sena became prime minister.

Oct. 11. Attempted counterrevolution by a number of princes and nobles, **led by Prince Bovaradet,** failed; several of the leaders were captured and the others fled the country.

1934, Jan. 12. The king left for a prolonged visit to Europe, from which he did not return.

1935, March 2. Abdication of King Prajadhipok, who was dissatisfied with the new regime and disagreed with the government over the execution of the counterrevolutionary leaders.

1935–46. ANANDA MAHIDOL, the ten-year-old nephew of Prajadhipok, became king, and a council of regency, headed by **Prince Aditya Dibabha,** was set up on his behalf. The young ruler was being educated in Europe and did not even visit his kingdom until Nov. 1938. Meanwhile the country was governed by a **triumvirate** consisting of the prime minister (Phya Bahol Sena), the minister of defense (**Col. Luang Phibun Songgram),** and the foreign minister **(Luang Pradit).**

1938–44. First government under popular Col. Phibun, who strongly espoused Thai (not just Siamese) nationalism. In a world context in which the ultranationalist and militarized state of Japan was seen as very attractive (alliance, 1941—see p. 809), Siamese politics turned to the right, glorifying the army and national values while attacking Western culture and imperialism. The name of the kingdom was changed to Thailand to reflect territorial claims and nationalist identity (reverted briefly to Siam, 1945–47).

1941, Dec. 21. Thailand concluded a ten-year treaty of alliance with Japan.

1942, Jan. 25. Thailand declared war on Great Britain and the U.S.

(To p. 1010)

3. LAOS AND CAMBODIA
(From p. 559)

The situation after the First World War in Indochina and Malaysia was comparatively quiet, marked by rapid expansion of administrative control, development of sanitation and education, and above all by increase of population and productivity. The extension of rubber plantations in particular had a profound effect on the economic setup in many of the states. Some progress was made toward the introduction of a popular element in government, and in all parts of the region (least in the Malay states) there was a growing demand for national recognition. The Great Depression after 1930 struck all states equally hard, led to the adoption of economic control measures by the governments, and called forth a considerable amount of labor agitation, with some communistic tinges. The great Asian crisis after 1931 revealed the exposed position of the whole area, and in all states measures were taken to strengthen defenses. The completion of the harbor works, dry dock, airfield, and fortifications of Singapore (June 1937) made that crucial port what was considered to be one of the strongest places in the world.

1922. Elected members added to **colonial council** that assisted the governor-general. The council was reorganized along functional lines in a system similar to British dyarchy. Three high positions were awarded to Lao elite, who had charge of the interior; justice, education, and religion; and finance, public works, commerce, and agriculture. The elite, including **King Sisavangvong** (r. 1904–54), had been trained in the French educational system as engineers and lawyers; such persons could serve as technical staff for the French colony.

1930. Buddhist Institute founded in Phnom Penh (Laos established its own institute in 1937) to counter the influence of Thai newspapers, books, radio, and Buddhist education of monks in Siam. Founded under the joint patronage of the Cambodian monarch, the king at Luang Prabang in Laos, and the French to encourage Buddhist studies in Cambodia and Laos, the institute in fact led to an intensification of the relationship between the Cambodian monarch and his people. As the institute began printing Buddhist texts in Pali and Cambodian, and organizing conferences, it became the center of intellectual life in the region.

1936. Founding of **Cambodian-language newspaper,** *Nagarasvata (Angkor Wat).*

1940–41. INDOCHINA WAR resulted in the French losing sizable portions of territory to Thailand (p. 808). As a result the French had to renegotiate with the king of Laos at Luang Prabang to strengthen and expand his powers. This state of affairs initiated an awareness on the part of the Laotian elite of the possibility of freedom from French control. At the same time, since France had to cede to Thailand the Lao provinces on the west bank of the Mekong, reaction against Thai culture followed as well.

1941. The French started weekly newspaper and radio broadcasts in Lao; the Laotian elite attempted to break with Thai culture by introducing romanized script for Lao language, to replace the Thai script previously used.

Oct. The Cambodian monarch, **Sisowath Monivong** (r. 1927–41) died; to strengthen their hand against the Thai, the French passed over the heir apparent in favor of **Prince Norodom Sihanouk,** then 18 years old and in a French school in Saigon, to succeed.

1941–45. Under Vichy government direction, the French maintained day-to-day control.

1942. Demonstration led by monks in Cambodia. Under the vigorous young resident who took up the post in 1943, the influence of the Buddhist sangha was reduced, and Prince Sihanouk was made more visible (through sponsorship of paramilitary youth organizations encouraged by the Vichy government).

1945, March 9. The **Japanese** imprisoned all French military and civilian personnel, turning day-to-day administration over to unprepared Cambodians, Lao, and Vietnamese.

March 10. The Japanese told King Sihanouk that Cambodia was independent, inaugurating a new era in Cambodian nationalism.

(To pp. 1012, 1014)

b. PENINSULAR AND ISLAND SOUTHEAST ASIA

1. THE MALAYAN ARCHIPELAGO
(From p. 560)

1915. Peasant rebellion in Pasir Puteh district of Kelantan, although localized, panicked the British into thinking that the revolt was potentially widespread. The protest targeted the substitution by the British of a fixed land rent for an earlier tax on crop production. The uprising was led by To' Janggut (or Haji Mat Hassan), an elderly landowner and peddler who had the support of the territorial chief.

1920s and 1930s. Despite attempts by the British to isolate Malays in a stable village society, a nascent Malay nationalism began to appear, appealing first to religious, racial, and linguistic loyalties.

Three new elite groups fostered this nationalism. Those active in the Islamic-educated religious reform movement brought anticolonial ideas back from Egypt. They joined a Malay-educated intelligentsia (made up primarily of peasants who had been educated to become teachers, journalists, engineers, and the like) who espoused radical, secular ideals. In using a town-based vernacular press to put forward a **Greater Indonesia ideology** around **Malay language** and identity, these two elements of the new elite joined with a third group: those drawn from the traditional elite who had become English-educated in order to serve in the bureaucracy. This third group reacted especially to the local-born activists among the Chinese and Indian communities who were agitating for a greater share in governance and public life.

1927. Periodic gatherings of (traditional Malay) rulers, begun as a token of the devolution of authority from the British to the states, became by the late 1930s occasions on which local rulers would take nationalistic positions—e.g., to encourage Javanese immigration and limit Chinese influx; to strengthen Malay landowning rights, etc.

1930. Malayan Communist Party founded, almost wholly Chinese in composition (but with links to Indonesia and Vietnam).

1930s. Impact of economic **depression** began to undermine the concept of a plural society in Malaya, pitting economic and political interests of one group against another. (For example, Chinese and Indian workers, thrown out of mine and estate employment, sought to become agriculturalists, previously a niche occupied solely by Malays.)

1938. Kesatuan Melayu Muda (Young Malay Union) formed by radicals as a new political organization with pan-Indonesian aims. **Malay Associations** were also organized within each state as organizations loyal to local rulers, conservative in outlook, and even supportive of British colonial rule; these served as a bulwark against more outspoken resistance to Western imperialism, and were the only organizations that had any mass support. The growth of a genuine Malay nationalism after the war drew on the ideology, structure, and leadership of the Malay Associations movement.

1941, Dec. 7. The Japanese attacked Malaya (p. 808).

1942, Feb. Singapore fell to the Japanese. As the tide of war turned against them, the Japanese tried to enlist local leadership in support of their activities. They released persons like the Malay radical **Ibrahim Yacob** who had been imprisoned under the European colonial regimes.

1943, July. Four northern Malay states (Perlis, Kedah, Kelantan, and Terengganu) were handed over to Thailand as a reward for its support of the Japanese.

1945, Sept. The British resumed control.   *(To p. 1016)*

2. INDONESIA (NETHERLANDS EAST INDIES)
(From p. 560)

1910s and 1920s. A battle raged over religious reformism. Traditionalists *(santri)* founded modern Islamic schools and modern organizations, especially the Nahdatul Ulama (founded 1926), to be used against the modernists. Modernists pulled back from more extreme secularist and Islamic reformist positions.

1916–18. A **legislative council** (Volksraad) was created and met, finally, in 1918. Composed of 24 nominated and 24 elected members, the latter were chosen by local councils. Ethnically there were 30 Dutchmen, 25 "East Indians," and five members of other groups (Chinese, et al.). This body was given advisory powers in budgetary, military, and other matters.

1921. Two movements created that were internationalist in orientation: the **PKI,** or **Indies Communist Party** (Perserikatan Komunis di India), joined the Comintern. At much the same time, Muslim socialists gained control of the **Sarekat Islam Party (SI),** forcing the PKI out, and, as a counterweight to the Communist movement, they supported the pan-Islamic movement of the time, focusing on restoration of the Ottoman caliph as leader of all Islam. (This movement was thus connected to the Khilafat movement under way in India.)

1922. The **Volksraad** became a genuinely legislative body when its assent was made obligatory for all government ordinances.

1925. The entire **administrative system was overhauled,** and in 1929 it was decreed that in the future the Volksraad should have 30 "East Indians" (out of the total 60).

1926. A **revolt** emerged in scattered areas, led generally by local PKI members. The government repression that followed broke the PKI for the next generation, and left the SI with only the lost cause of the caliphate.

1927–28. A **new idea of Indonesia** emerged out of this wreckage. Small groups led by **Achmed Sukarno** founded the **PNI, the Indonesian National Party** (Partai Nasional Indonesia). In Oct. 1928, the congress of youth organizations created an ideological slogan that showed the tenor of this great leap of the imagination: "One nation—Indonesia, one people—Indonesian, one language—Indonesian."

Connected to these developments was the emergence of a national language and its own literature. "Revolutionary Malay" was the home language of only a few scattered peoples, thus giving it the political advantage of belonging to no one. Since this language had served as the argot of both commerce and Islam for centuries across the entire archipelago, it also belonged to everyone. It possessed flexibility, a "democratic" character (because it lacked elaborate status distinctions), and a simplicity that made it possible to introduce modern terms and concepts. This language was renamed "Indonesian," and literary works in the language began to appear in the 1920s. Writers, especially those connected to the government-run publishing house Balai Pustaka and to the literary journal *Pudjang Baru,* actively developed literary Indonesian. Most of these writers, however, were Sumatran; Javanese and others found it more difficult to write creatively in the national language.

1930s. The **National Indonesian Party** emerged in this period; in 1937 the Volksraad unanimously petitioned the Dutch government to grant dominion status within ten years.

1940, April 15. Japan announced that should hostilities in Europe be extended to the Netherlands, Japan wished to see the **status quo in the Netherlands East Indies** preserved.

1941, June 18. Japan broke off negotiations with the Netherlands East Indies for an **economic accord.**

Dec. 8. The Netherlands government in exile and the Netherlands East Indies declared war on Japan.

1942, Jan. 11. Japanese forces invaded the Netherlands Celebes, and presently occupied the entire Indies (p. 809).

1945, Aug. 17. Two days after the Japanese surrender, the Indonesian leaders **Achmed Sukarno** and **Mohammed Hatta** proclaimed the **IN-DEPENDENCE OF THE REPUBLIC OF INDONESIA.** The Dutch refused to recognize the new government.

Sept. 29–Oct. 3. British and Dutch troops arrived in Batavia to disarm and repatriate the Japanese. Before long, fighting was under way between these troops and the **"Indonesian People's Army."**

Oct. 12. The Dutch government offered to negotiate with those Indonesians who were ready to agree to a self-governing Indonesia within the Netherlands kingdom.

Nov. 13. Soetan Sjahrir, a young Socialist, became premier of the new republic while **Sukarno** became president.

1945. Although the idea of "Indonesia" as an imagined community had captured the enthusiasm of the educated elite, and a number of movements and cultural developments explored the implications of this idea, the vast majority of peasants were still living in the fragmented rural worlds characteristic of the area for centuries.   *(To p. 1018)*

H. EAST ASIA, 1902–1945

1. OVERVIEW

During the interwar years, the population of the nations in the region continued to rise. Always the most populous, China topped 400 million, while Japan (the second most populous) exceeded 55 million by the early 1920s. An industrial economy was emerging in China's cities, especially Shanghai with its many foreign concerns, as well as in Japan under the influence of World War I. Japan continued to penetrate the entire East Asian region, with the exception of Vietnam, prior to the 1940s. By the end of the interwar period, Japan would be at war with China and Vietnam, while continuing to maintain an increasingly brutal colonial policy over Korea.

2. CHINA, 1914–1945
(From p. 566)

1914, May 1. Having convened a session of 66 men drawn from his cabinet and other provincial posts, **Yuan Shikai** (1859–1916) had the provisional constitution replaced with a "constitutional compact," which afforded Yuan nearly complete powers.

July. Sun Zhongshan (Sun Yat-sen, 1866–1925) changed the name of his party, the Guomindang (Nationalist Party), to Gemingdang (Revolutionary Party) in Tokyo; its first manifesto came out in September. In 1919 it reverted to its original name.

Aug. 23. The Japanese declaration of war against Germany was followed by **violation of China's neutrality** (Sept. 2) and the capture of the German concession area of Qingdao in Shandong province (Nov. 7).

By 1914, under the government of Yuan Shikai, the total investment of the foreign powers in China soared to U.S.$1.61 billion. Yuan encouraged the development of a strong judiciary, as China's best hope against the continuation of extraterritoriality, pushed for agricultural development, and tried to crush the opium trade.

1915, Jan. 18. JAPAN SECRETLY PRESENTED THE TWENTY-ONE DEMANDS to China. An ultimatum extracted from the Yuan government (May 8) modified acceptance of the first **four groups:** (1) Japanese succession to German rights in Shandong; (2) extension to 99 years of the leases in southern Manchuria, with commercial freedom for Japanese there; (3) a half interest in the Hanyeping Co., which operated iron and steel mills at Hanyang, iron mines at Daye, and a colliery at Pingshan; and (4) a declaration that no part of China's coast be leased or ceded to any power. The **fifth group,** calling notably for Japanese police and advisers in the political, financial, and military affairs of China, and railway concessions in the Yangzi River valley (Great Britain's sphere of interest), was set aside. When news of these demands leaked out, widespread anti-Japanese boycotts and rallies erupted.

Dec. 9. Yuan Shikai, following a well-orchestrated monarchist campaign by the **Chouan hui** (Plan for Peace Association, Aug. 14), and election by a hand-picked "representative assembly," **accepted the imperial institution** (Dec. 12) for the following Jan. 1, and adopted the reign title of **Hongxian.** He was immediately faced by a **rebellion in Yunnan** (Dec. 25) led by **Cai E** (1883–1916), declaring Yunnan's secession, followed by Guizhou (Jan. 1916) and Guangxi (March 1916).

1916, March 22. In response to the unpopularity of his plan to revive the monarchy, **Yuan canceled his imperial plans** and organized a republican cabinet under **Duan Qirui** (1865–1936), senior general in the Bei-

yang militarist clique. Yuan died on June 6 and was succeeded as president by **Li Yuanhong** (1864–1928), who promptly restored the constitution of 1912 and convoked the original parliament of 1913.

1917, Jan. 23. Japan exacted special rights in Manchuria and Inner Mongolia and sought China's declaration of war against Germany (so as to shore up its hold on the former German leasehold in Qingdao) in exchange for a "loan" of 5 million yen.

March. China broke diplomatic relations with Germany.

May 23. The **dismissal of Duan** led to an uprising of northern military governors. **Zhang Xun** (1854–1923) was called to intervene.

July 1. In Beijing, Zhang Xun declared, with the help of Kang Youwei (1858–1927), the **restoration of the Manchu dynasty.** It was quickly overthrown again (July 12) by Duan Qirui who thereupon resumed the premiership. Twice-deposed former emperor Puyi returned to the Forbidden City, where he lived until 1924. Li Yuanhong resigned, leaving the presidency to Vice President **Feng Guozhang** (1857–1919, elected Oct. 1916). **Sun Zhongshan** headed a secessionist government in Guangzhou (Sept.), from which he was expelled by militarists in 1918.

Aug. 14. CHINA DECLARED WAR AGAINST GERMANY AND AUSTRIA-HUNGARY. Labor battalions were sent to France, Mesopotamia, and Africa (mostly to northern France)—54,000 Chinese in late 1917, 96,000 by late 1918. China secured the termination of German and Austrian extraterritoriality and Boxer indemnity payments, and the return of their concessions in Tianjin and Hankou. The Allies postponed Boxer payments for five years. Japan lent the Duan regime 140 million yen.

1918, Jan. Following the Russian Revolution of Nov. 1917, a Guomindang newspaper congratulated the Bolsheviks, and Sun Zhongshan cabled his compliments to Vladimir Lenin (1870–1924) personally.

May 16. A Japanese defensive alliance against any Soviet threat provided for action by Japanese-trained Chinese troops in Siberia under Japanese direction (notes March 25, treaty May 16, clarified Sept. 6). **Loans** of perhaps 250 million yen for Manchurian projects were contracted, about half through Premier Terauchi Masatake's (1852–1919) agent, **Nishihara Kamezō** (1872–1954), with Premier Duan and his clique, now called the **Anfu** (Anhui-Fujian) **Club.**

June. Li Dazhao (1889–1927), appointed librarian of Beijing University in February, wrote his first essay in support of the Russian Revolution. Later in the year, Li organized a Marxist Research Society, among whose members were **Mao Zedong** (1893–1976), **Zhang Guotao** (b. 1897), and **Qu Qiubai** (1889–1935).

Aug. 12. A newly elected parliament convened and elected **Xu Shichang** (1858–1939) **president** (Sept. 4–June 1922). Chinese political affairs continued, however, to be dominated by personal ambitions and the schism between the governments of Beijing and Guangzhou.

Oct. Duan resigned, stronger than ever with Japanese support. Japan let it be known that in the previous month Duan had promised in secret to allow Japan to set up police and military garrisons in Jinan and Qingdao (both in Shandong), as well as deals in Shandong for railroads that Japan planned to construct. The armistice ending World War I was concluded (Nov. 11).

The Wuhan-Changsha section of the main rail line to Guangzhou was finished in 1918. The population of the country was roughly 450 million, the overwhelming majority being farmers; the small urban working class was notoriously underpaid and worked under harsh conditions, although in both respects they were better off than their fellows in the countryside. Women worked especially in textile factories, outnumbering men there two to one and earning even lower pay.

1919, March. The Communist International **(Comintern)** held its first congress, charged with the task of coordinating the world revolution. At its second congress (July 1920), it was argued that nonindustrialized, agrarian countries might skip the capitalist stage of social development by forging ties with "bourgeois democratic" parties and if supported by the Soviet Union.

April 30. Despite anticipation in China to the contrary, U.S. president Woodrow Wilson (1856–1924) came to agreement with his counterparts in Great Britain and France to allow the transfer of former German holdings in Shandong to Japan. When news that the delegates to the **Versailles Peace Conference** would act accordingly reached China (May 1), a sense of betrayal spread among the urban classes.

May 1. In a special issue on Marxism in the journal *New Youth*, Li Dazhao published his essay "My Marxist Views," thus becoming the first Chinese to declare for Marxism.

May 4. Demonstrations exploded in Beijing; some 3,000 students gathered at Tiananmen Square and marched toward the foreign legation quarter. Like demonstrations occurred elsewhere as well. The homes of officials involved in negotiations with the Japanese or regarded as pro-Japanese were attacked, and several men were beaten unconscious. The Chinese delegates refused to sign the peace accords (June 28). Boycotts of Japanese goods ensued.

June. Students from other cities met in Beijing to form a student union of the Republic of China.

July. The Soviet Union, through Lev M. Karakhan (1889–1937), renounced all special rights in Manchuria and all secret treaties negotiated during the tsarist era, including all indemnities.

The **New Culture movement,** which began in the mid-1910s and is often considered coterminous with the **May Fourth movement,** surged ahead in the months following the incidents of May 4, 1919. Its proponents were younger professors, many at Beijing University and most of whom had studied overseas: **Chen Duxiu** (1879–1942), a dean at Beijing University; **Li Dazhao,** the librarian; **Cai Yuanpei** (1868–1948), the chancellor; **Hu Shi** (1891–1962), professor of philosophy; and **Lu Xun** (pseud., Zhou Shuren, 1881–1936), the finest short story writer of the era; and many others. They published numerous journals and magazines, although *Xin Qingnian (New Youth)* was considered the core publication of the movement. Lu Xun published his two most famous pieces—"Diary of a Madman" (1919) and "The True Story of Ah Q" (1921)—in it. Proponents of this movement called for an end to the social and customary restrictions placed on people's lives by Confucianism, patriarchy, and other Chinese practices out of touch with the modern world. **They were especially outspoken on the issue of gender equality,** in favor of coeducation, and opposed to arranged marriages; **women entered Beijing University for the first time in 1920.** These thinkers wrote in, and vigorously argued that all publications should be written in, the vernacular language, not the extremely complex literary language. Already by 1919, though, divisions were becoming apparent within the movement. Li and Chen became Communists, Lu Xun a nonparty leftist, and Hu a Deweyan liberal. In the summer of 1919 Hu assailed Chen and other radicals in an article entitled "Study More Problems, Talk Less of 'Isms.'" Between 1919 and 1923

such eminent figures as John Dewey (1859–1952), Bertrand Russell (1872–1970), Albert Einstein (1879–1955), Margaret Sanger (1876–1966), and Rabindranath Tagore (1861–1941) all visited China.

1919–20. A work-study program for Chinese students in France commenced, with over 1,000 Chinese taking part. Among the participants were **Zhou Enlai** (1899–1976) and **Deng Xiaoping** (1904–97), the youngest member of the group. Both became Communist activists in France. In 1920 Comintern agent Grigorii Voitinsky (1893–1956, or before) traveled to China and met with Li Dazhao in Beijing, and later with Chen Duxiu in Shanghai (May).

1920–26. The **WARLORD PERIOD** (so named because groups of militarists were in constant contests for power and warfare was nonstop) left no real power in the hands of the national government, which struggled to maintain its envoys abroad. Revenues from customs and salt were already pledged and administered for service of foreign loans. Those from the railways and land taxes were absorbed by local armies for which the civilian population felt no concern because no local interests were served by them. After the death of Yuan Shikai, there was no charismatic personality, no concrete cause strong enough to direct or to claim the loyalty of the majority of Chinese.

1920–21. The northern Chinese provinces of Hebei, Shandong, Henan, Shanxi, and Shaanxi farther to the west experienced a severe famine. Half a million people died; nearly 20 million were living in dire poverty.

1921, July. The **CHINESE COMMUNIST PARTY was founded** in a school in the French Concession in Shanghai. Neither Chen Duxiu nor Li Dazhao was there, but Mao Zedong, as representative of his native Hunan province, and 11 others were in attendance. Chen was elected secretary-general. The Comintern was represented by the Dutch agent Maring (pseud. Hendricus Sneevliet, 1883–1942).

1922, Jan. Some 40 delegates from China were invited by the Soviet Union to a session of the "Toiler of the Far East" in Moscow. Qu Qiubai, who had gone to Moscow in 1920, served as one of the interpreters at the meeting.

Some 30,000 Chinese sailors and dock workers in Hong Kong and Guangzhou went on strike. Local sympathy strikes raised their numbers to 120,000 (March). The owners gave in and awarded them significant pay raises.

Feb. 4. The **Washington Conference** resulted in a nine-power treaty to respect China's sovereignty, independence, and territorial and administrative integrity; to maintain the "open door"; and to afford China the opportunity to develop a stable government. There was also a nine-power treaty (Feb. 6) to grant an immediate customs revenue increase to an effective 5 percent, and to call a conference to prepare for Chinese tariff autonomy; and a **Sino-Japanese Treaty** (Feb. 4) to evacuate Japanese troops from Shandong, and restore to China all former German interests in Qingdao and the railway to Jinan, in return for their assessed value plus Japanese improvements. The mines were to be operated by a joint company. Britain announced (Feb. 1) the **return of Weihaiwei** (actually effected Oct. 1, 1930). A joint resolution by eight powers (Dec. 10, 1921) called for reexamination of Chinese law and its administration in relation to extraterritoriality. Sun Zhongshan disavowed all agreements made at the Washington Conference, because the regime in Beijing, and not his in Guangzhou, had been party to them.

May. Li Lisan (1900–67) and **Liu Shaoqi** (1898–1969) began organizing "workers' clubs," fronts for union organization among workers in the Anyuan coal mines and the Daye steel foundry.

Aug. The Chinese Communist Party (CCP) held its second congress in Hangzhou. Following Comintern policy, Maring strongly encouraged aligning with the Guomindang (GMD), designated a "bourgeois democratic party," for the tasks of ridding China of the divisive militarists.

Aug. Sun Zhongshan was forced out of his base in Guangzhou by "reformist" militarist Chen Jiongming (1878–1933), who from the previous year had given Sun his protection. There Sun had created a Chinese People's Government and become its president. He thereupon revived the Guomindang (GMD) and entrusted two close supporters, **Hu Hanmin** (1886–1936) and **Wang Jingwei** (1883–1947), with the task of composing plans for the reform of the GMD. Sun had been assisted in his getaway from Guangzhou by a young military man in the GMD,

JIANG JIESHI (Chiang Kai-shek, 1887–1975). Sun had met with Maring in 1921 about an alliance with the CCP, and he met with Soviet diplomat Adolf Joffe in Jan. 1923. By Feb. 1923, Chen Jiongming had been forced out of Guangzhou, and Sun was back, appealing to the Soviets for financial help.

The CCP, with only about 300 members, was ordered by the Comintern to join with the GMD, though not relinquishing CCP membership, to complete the national revolution. Both GMD and CCP leaders were being supported by the Soviet Union. Li Dazhao was much more sanguine about the partnership than Chen Duxiu. When Comintern agent **Borodin** (pseud. Mikhail Gruzenberg, 1884–1953, or before), arrived in China (Oct. 6, 1923), he worked with Sun Zhongshan to seal the CCP-GMD bond.

1923, Feb. 4. The newly founded (Feb. 2) general union of railway workers along the Wuhan-Beijing line called a general strike. Militarist **Wu Peifu** (1874–1939) sent his troops in to break it up; 35 workers were killed (Feb. 7), and the strike ended (Feb. 9).

1924, Jan. 21. The **first Guomindang national congress** convened in Guangzhou, with Sun as president, admitted Communists into the party, and accepted Soviet advisers, notably Borodin, who proceeded to reorganize the GMD along Soviet lines of democratic centralism, which tended to strengthen the leader and party discipline. Lenin's death that month was announced, and Sun hailed him. **Jiang Jieshi,** himself trained in Japan, was named to head German and Soviet instructors in the new **Huangpu** (Whampoa) **Military Academy** (June) near Guangzhou; **Zhou Enlai** was named head of the political department of that institution. Sun presented his platform in a series of lectures entitled **"Three Principles of the People"** (*"San min zhuyi"*), namely, nationalism, democracy, and people's livelihood, which he had initially laid out in 1907 and which now became the GMD's official line.

May 31. The **Soviet Union,** in fulfillment of its repudiation (July 1919 and Sept. 27, 1920) of the tsar's ill-gotten gains at China's expense, **gave up extraterritoriality, concessions** at Tianjin and Hankou, and the rest of the **Boxer indemnity,** to be used for education under Russian veto. The Chinese Eastern Railway was placed under joint management.

Despite Japanese objections to competition with the South Manchurian Railway, the Chinese built two lines, Dahushan to Dongliao, and Jilin to Hailong.

Sept. 17. The China Foundation for the Promotion of Education and Culture was created with the U.S.$6 million remitted by the United States (May 21) from the Boxer indemnity balance. The foundation made annual grants for scientific education, and housed and built up the national library extensively.

1925, March 12. Having learned in January of his incurable liver cancer, **Sun Zhongshan died.** Already the new alliance and Soviet expert help were showing signs of success in battles against the militarists.

May 30. Following a lockout and demonstration of laborers at a Japanese textile mill in Shanghai, a worker was killed, leading to massive demonstrations of Chinese workers at the International Settlement. The British police fired on the demonstrators, killing 11 and wounding 20. Widespread demonstrations erupted throughout China in the **May Thirtieth Movement.**

Sentiment against the unequal treaties and against the British, for their deadly actions in Shanghai in May and against laborers in Guangzhou (June 23), found effective expression in a strike and boycott of British goods and ships which lasted 16 months in Guangzhou (until Oct. 1926).

Aug. 20. Liao Zhongkai (1878–1925), GMD leader, **was murdered.** Antileftists within the GMD, upset at the pro-Soviet direction of the party, were suspected. Later, the right wing within the GMD formed a "Western Hills" faction aimed at ridding the party of Borodin and the Communists.

1926, March 20. The gunboat *Zhongshan,* commanded by a Communist, was seen near Jiang Jieshi's headquarters. On the pretext that he was to be kidnapped, Jiang arrested the crew and 30 Soviet advisers in the city of Guangzhou. He and Borodin later (April) worked out an arrangement.

July–Aug. The **northern expedition of Jiang Jieshi's National Revolutionary Army,** with the aid of Soviet general **Vasili Blyukher** (1889–

1938, then using the name Galen), followed the old Taiping route from Guangdong through Changsha in Hunan (July 11) to Hankou (Sept. 6) and Wuchang (Oct. 10, captured on the 15th anniversary of the Republican Revolution).

Nov. Having taken Nanchang, Jiang set up his base, while the Communists and leftist members of the GMD established a base in Wuhan.

1927, Jan. 11. As the Wuhan-Nanchang standoff grew ever more troubled, Jiang went to Wuhan to try to resolve the differences, but he was snubbed and sent packing.

Feb. 19–20. From the British, who were tired of the Chinese boycott and hopeful of wooing the Chinese away from the Soviets, the GMD extracted the **rendition of the concessions at Hankou and Jiujiang.**

Feb. The Shanghai General Labor Union and labor leaders called for a general strike to support the surging National Revolutionary Army, which had just taken Hangzhou. Militarist armies broke up the strike, executing 20 and arresting many more.

Having observed on several trips to his native Hunan province the rising tide of peasant unrest, Mao Zedong published in a Communist journal his essay **"Report on an Investigation of the Peasant Movement in Hunan"** (Feb.). He lauded the radical actions of the peasants, seizing landlords' lands and property, and forming "poor peasants associations." He allotted 70 percent of the leftist movement's success up to that point to the peasantry, not the urban proletariat, and he praised the especially difficult predicament of women peasants, who strove against all the same things the men did, as well as against male oppression. Most of these associations were later destroyed by militarist or GMD forces.

March 21. The CCP and the Shanghai General Labor Union called a general strike. Some 600,000 workers participated. On March 22, troops of the National Revolutionary Army began to enter Shanghai. The General Labor Union held a meeting of delegates (March 27). The workers were effectively in control of the city at the end of the month. Jiang Jieshi entered the city at the end of the month.

April 12. Members of the underworld Green Gang attacked the offices of all the major unions in the city, often with the help of Jiang's military forces. Numerous workers were murdered. Protests the next day led to more killings.

April 18. Jiang and the rightist members of the GMD split with the leftists, based in Wuhan, and set up a new government in Nanjing. The CCP was commanded by the Comintern now to try to continue working with the **"left" GMD,** under the leadership of **Wang Jingwei,** who felt he (not Jiang) was heir to Sun Zhongshan's mantle and who publicly asserted the CCP-GMD alliance. Surface harmony was restored by a purge of Soviets and Communists from the Wuhan regime in return for the (temporary) retirement of Jiang from public life (Aug. 8). Chen Duxiu was blamed for the year's catastrophes and dropped from his leadership position in the CCP; he was later expelled from the CCP altogether. Qu Qiubai was named to replace him.

April. Zhang Zuolin (1875–1928), the right-wing militarist in control of southern Manchuria (since 1911 and later with Japanese assistance) who had his headquarters in Beijing, sent his troops to attack the Russian embassy and arrest all the Chinese holed up there. **Li Dazhao and 19 others were taken and hanged.**

Sept. Mao, with a force of some 2,000 men, attacked villages around Changsha in the **"Autumn Harvest Uprisings."** They were quickly put down. Mao took the remnants (about 1,000 men) into the secluded Jinggang Mountains at the Hunan-Jiangxi border (Oct.). He was joined there by a larger force under the command of Zhu De (1886–1976). Mao was dropped from the CCP's Central Committee (Nov.).

Dec. 11. Under orders from the Comintern (Stalin needed a victory in China to bolster his attacks against Trotsky), the CCP attempted to capture the city of Guangzhou. The so-called **Guangzhou Commune** (Canton Commune) was decimated within two days, and countless lives were lost in the wholesale executions following it.

Dec. Jiang Jieshi married Song (Soong) Meiling (b. c. 1897; Wellesley College class of 1917) in Shanghai.

1928, Jan. After several months of "retirement," Jiang resumed his position as military and civil head of the GMD. His new wife's brother, Song Zewen (T. V. Soong, 1894–1971), became the GMD government's head financier.

April 7. Jiang commenced a fresh northern expedition, this time in conjunction with **Yan Xishan** (1883–1960), militarist ruler of Shanxi province since 1912; **Feng Yuxiang** (1882–1948), a magnetic but erratic northern militarist since 1920 who had thrown in his lot with the GMD after a visit to Moscow in 1927; and two militarists from Guangxi, **Li Zongren** (1891–1969) and **Bai Chongxi** (1893–1966).

April 30. The farther advance of the National Revolutionary Army to Beijing was blocked as it entered Jinan, Shandong, by 5,000 Japanese troops, sent to protect residents there. After conflict (May 3–11) with the Japanese forces in Jinan, Jiang's army withdrew and moved directly on Beijing. The Japanese troops withdrew from Jinan in May 1929, as a vigorous Chinese boycott (1928–29) protested Japanese intrusions.

June 2. Zhang Zuolin, seeing his hold on Beijing slip through his fingers, left the capital by rail heading north; the train was bombed and Zhang **assassinated by Japanese officers** opposed to the less radical policies of their own government and angry at Zhang's growing sense of independence.

June 8. Beijing captured by the National Revolutionary Army. It was renamed Beiping ("northern peace"; *Beijing* means "northern capital"), for the capital remained in Nanjing ("southern capital"). **Zhang Xueliang** (b. 1898) inherited the command of his father, Zhang Zuolin, and joined forces with the GMD (Nov.).

Oct. 10. The Central Executive Committee of the GMD promulgated a **temporary organic** law that provided for a state council headed by the president (also the highest military authority), heading **five administrative divisions** *(yuan):* executive, legislative, judicial, civil service, and censorial. All appointments to these offices were to emanate from the Central Executive Committee and the Party Congress.

Toward the end of the year, Mao's forces, constantly under attack, were compelled to give up their base in the Jinggang Mountains, moving westward toward Fujian province. In the Jiangxi town of **Ruijin** at the Fujian-Jiangxi border, he established his new base, which would subsequently become the center of the **Jiangxi Soviet** government (until 1934). Among the many more radical policies adopted by the Jiangxi Soviet was a new marriage law that prohibited arranged marriages and made divorce contingent merely on the will of either partner. **Li Lisan** replaced Qu Qiubai as head of the CCP, but was himself ousted in 1930. Mao and Li never got along.

A series of **treaties with 12 countries** (July 25–Dec. 22) **recognized the Nanjing government** and its right to **complete tariff autonomy,** provided it did not discriminate against foreign nationals. The Chinese in turn did away with domestic transit duties and other taxes imposed by Sun Zhongshan's Guangzhou regime. Customs revenues soon skyrocketed.

The extremely harsh realities of rural life continued unabated, probably worsening with the worldwide Great Depression; many thousands starved to death when international markets in the crops or goods they produced dried up.

1929–30. The Japanese were concerned over the certainty of rapidly losing a large market for its cotton goods if the Chinese textile industry received protection; this dragged out treaty negotiations until May 6, 1930. Tariff autonomy, a substantial revenue source, was regained on May 16. By 1930 nine nationalities had lost extraterritorial privilege in China, and several more had by treaty agreed to its end when it should be universally abolished, but the privilege was still retained (1939) by France, Great Britain, Japan, and the U.S.

1930, March. Mao's premature obituary appeared in the principal Comintern serial. In addition to the Jiangxi Soviet, there were many other smaller base areas under CCP control throughout China.

Oct. 1. Weihaiwei was restored to China by Great Britain.

Late in the year, forces under the command of **Deng Xiaoping** joined those of Mao and Zhu De in the Jiangxi Soviet.

1931, Feb. 7. The GMD executed 23 leading Chinese Communists, who were probably betrayed by fellow Communists of a different clique. Among the dead was writer and poet Hu Yepin (b. 1907).

May 5. A National People's Convention of the GMD in Nanjing adopted a **provisional constitution** that confirmed the separation of the five branches within the government, transferred the power of executive appointment to the chairman of the State Council, established the autonomy of the county *(xian)* under provincial authority, and guaranteed personal freedom. The government pledged itself to free education and social insurance. A national congress to inaugurate full

constitutional government was to be called when autonomous county organization was completed in a majority of the provinces.

July 1. Serious anti-Chinese riots in Korea, stimulated by a false report of a minor affair at Wanbaoshan in Manchuria, resulted in the renewal of the boycott against Japanese goods. A report of a murder (Aug. 17) by Chinese troops of a Japanese officer in western Manchuria (June) inflamed Japanese opinion.

1931–32. THE JAPANESE OCCUPATION OF MANCHURIA (p. 647). Japan's Guandong Army, engaged in night maneuvers at Mukden (Sept. 18), set off an explosion on a nearby rail line and alleged it to be the work of Chinese forces—the **Manchurian Incident.** With this excuse, they commenced a preconcerted seizure before morning of the arsenal as well as of Andong, Yingkou, and Changchun; Jiang Jieshi ordered his troops to withdraw, as he could not sustain a major battle with the Japanese. Amid foreign office statements of intention to localize the incident, **Jilin was captured** (Sept. 21) and the whole of the **three eastern provinces** (Manchuria) soon occupied (Feb. 5, 1932). The League of Nations sent (Nov. 1931) the **Earl of Lytton** (1876–1947) on a **commission of inquiry** into Japanese actions in Manchuria. Floods in the Yangzi River Valley and Communist pressures prevented any Chinese military efforts to save Manchuria, but an immediate and more intensive boycott cut Japanese exports to one-sixth of their usual figure.

1932, Jan. 7. U.S. Secretary of State Henry Stimson (1867–1950) notified all signatories to the nine-power treaty of Feb. 4, 1922, that the U.S. would recognize no gains achieved through armed force contrary to the Pact of Paris of Aug. 27, 1928.

Jan. 28–March 4. To compel the Chinese to abandon their economic war against Japan, **70,000 Japanese troops landed at Shanghai** and drove the Chinese 19th Route Army from the vicinity of the International Settlement, destroying Zhabei through bombardments (Jan. 29), costing many lives. The Chinese fought back well. An agreement (May 5) was reached establishing a demilitarized zone about the settlement and the termination of the boycott.

Feb. 18. INDEPENDENCE FOR MANZHOUGUO (Manchukuo, the "Manchu state," Manchuria) was proclaimed; it consisted of the former three eastern provinces and Rehe (Jehol), with a capital at Xinjing ("new capital"), formerly Changchun. **Henry Puyi** (1906–67), the deposed (1912) last emperor of the Qing, was installed as "chief executive" (March 9) and advanced (March 1, 1934), as he had initially insisted in negotiations going back several years, to **emperor with the Kangde reign title.** Japanese advisers and military men ran all important matters from the start.

Sept. 15. A protocol established a close protectorate of Japan over Manzhouguo.

Oct. 2. The **report of the Lytton Commission** found that Japanese actions on Sept. 18–19, 1931, were not self-defensive as claimed, and that the creation of Manzhouguo did not flow from a "genuine and spontaneous independence movement." It recommended establishment in Manchuria of an autonomous administration under Chinese sovereignty with international advisers and police, and recognition of Japanese economic interests.

1933, Feb. 24. Approving the Lytton Commission report, the **League of Nations assembly adopted the Stimson formula on nonrecognition,** and indicated that Japanese military pressure should cease. The League debated the issue and ultimately accepted the Lytton report, condemning Japan's claims that the establishment of Manzhouguo was a grassroots independence movement. **Japan announced its withdrawal from the League** (May 27).

Jan.–Feb. Japanese forces fought into Rehe, occupying the region and controlling access south of the Great Wall at the Shanhaiguan pass (April).

May 31. This necessitated the **Tanggu Truce,** forced upon the Chinese, by which Chinese troops were to be evacuated from the Tianjin area of Hebei province.

After two unsuccessful GMD campaigns (1931, 1932) at "bandit suppression," that is, to dislodge and destroy the Communists in the Jiangxi Soviet, a third campaign (July–Oct. 1932) proved moderately more successful. New roads, airfields, and blockhouses were constructed for the fourth (1933) and fifth (1934) campaigns, the last of these in an effort additionally to strangle the Jiangxi Soviet economically. Jiang Jieshi was assisted by Reichswehr Gen. Han von Seeckt (1866–1936), who arrived in China in May 1933 on leave from Nazi Germany.

1934. Early in the year, Jiang Jieshi launched the GMD's New Life movement, an effort to forge "a new national consciousness and mass psychology." He sought to militarize the entire Chinese populace so as to be prepared for dangers and adversity. He was inspired by many creeds, from Confucianism to Fascism. Another movement of GMD party stalwarts, supported by Jiang, from the early 1930s was the arch-reactionary Blue Shirts; ferociously devoted to their "leader," Jiang Jieshi, they formed a special corps for military and secret police actions.

Oct. 16. Faced with an onslaught from air and land of GMD troops far in excess of their own numbers, the Communist leaders of the Jiangxi Soviet decided (Aug.) to leave their base, prepared to break through the GMD encirclement to the southwest (Sept.), and finally **commenced the Long March,** one of the longest retreats in military history, subsequently treated as a heroic event. The two advance armies, the First Army Corps and the Third Army Corps, were under the commands, respectively, of **Lin Biao** (1908–71) and **Peng Dehuai** (1898–1974). The total number of "marchers" was 80,000. Their decimated numbers, perhaps no more than 10 percent of the original "marchers," reached Shaanxi province just over one year later (Oct. 20, 1935), after a march of nearly 6,000 miles over rugged and perilous terrain.

1935, Jan. 15–18. At a **conference** held in the town of **Zunyi** (Guizhou province), blame for the defeats leading to the Long March was laid upon the shoulders of Mao's opponents in the CCP leadership, and Mao's position was subsequently strengthened.

March 23. The Soviet Union sold to Manzhouguo its interest in the Chinese Eastern Railway after negotiations begun in May 1933.

April. The government decreed one year of military training for all male high school and college students in order to provide 100,000 reservists each year.

June 9. The Japanese army extracted the **He-Umezu Accord** for withdrawal from Hebei of troops objectionable to the Japanese.

The continuing excessive cost of the occupation of Manzhouguo, in which bandits and irregular guerrillas prevented any durable pacification, led the Japanese army to attempt to force, without actual invasion, the formation of a local puppet Chinese government willing to afford Japan opportunities for the exploitation of resources and markets in north China. Efforts to secure the secession of five provinces (Shandong, Hebei, Shanxi, Chahar, and Suiyuan) had failed.

In the middle of the year, the Long March troops with Mao Zedong linked up with those of **Zhang Guotao** in northern Sichuan. Although they had been acquaintances for many years, Mao and Zhang never got along well.

Nov. 24. An **East Hebei Autonomous Council** was established between Tongzhou (outside Beijing) and the sea. Japanese goods were smuggled wholesale into China through this area, and narcotics were poured from it upon the world market.

Dec. 9. Thousands of student demonstrators in Beijing protested Japan's growing authority in China and the GMD's inaction. When they were suppressed by the GMD police, over 30,000 marched in a sympathetic demonstration the next week.

Dec. 18. A **Hebei-Chahar Political Council** was established at Beijing (Beiping) under **Gen. Song Zheyuan** (1885–1940), who rendered lip service to the Japanese but made no vital concessions.

1936, July 19. Jiang succeeded in gaining control over Guangdong, in spite of Japanese aid to his adversaries, and of Guangxi (Sept. 6), where the local leaders were loudly demanding war against Japan, for which he was still unprepared so long as the Communist menace remained. The same demand for a united front was constantly voiced by the Chinese Communists, who had now set up an orderly government in the town of Yan'an in northern Shaanxi province.

Sept. Japan presented seven secret demands (known Oct. 1) under threat of immediate invasion of both north and central China. The most serious were: brigading of Japanese with Chinese troops against Communists everywhere, employment of Japanese advisers in all branches of government, autonomy for five northern provinces, and reduction of tariffs to the level of 1928. Although Japan dispatched troops to Shanghai, Nanjing steadfastly refused.

Dec. 12–25. JIANG JIESHI WAS KIDNAPPED and held in Xi'an by **Zhang Xueliang** until he agreed to stop the civil war and join forces with the CCP to fight Japan. Zhang Xueliang had returned to China from abroad in early 1934 and was assigned by Jiang to carry out anti-Communist actions in the Hubei-Henan-Anhui border area. Later he was sent to Xi'an, capital of Shaanxi province, to join in the assaults on the Yan'an Soviet, and the CCP was active from Jan. 1936 working on the anti-Japan line among his troops, many of whom had come with Zhang from Manchuria, now firmly in Japanese control. Zhang held several secret meetings with Communist leaders. After the Anti-Comintern Pact was signed by Japan and Nazi Germany (Nov. 25), many suspected that Jiang would become even more pro-Japanese. Zhang resolved to act. Zhou Enlai arrived in Xi'an (Dec. 16) and argued the Communists' position in favor of a united front against Japan under Jiang's leadership, the latter point coming at Stalin's insistence. Jiang left on Dec. 25, and arrived back in Nanjing (Dec. 26) before an immense audience of supporters.

1937, Jan. 28. Negotiations terminated the long anti-Communist campaign and brought the Yan'an government into surface harmony with Nanjing.

The Hankou-Guangzhou Railway was completed with help from British Boxer indemnity funds, and a new Hangzhou-Nanchang Railway was opened.

June 1. Sichuan was brought into the new national union, made effective by telegraph, long-distance telephone, and radio communication.

The achievement of political unity and a measure of stability (1927–37, the "Nanjing decade") supplemented and accelerated fundamental changes that had been in progress since 1912 in many areas of life, often led by students who had returned from study abroad. Vital to China's clearly approaching struggle with Japan was the introduction of **modern finance and banking.** Finance Minister Song Zewen in 1932 announced a balanced budget and abolition of the *lijin* transit dues which had been a vexation since the Taiping Rebellion. Substitution (Nov. 1934) of paper silver certificates for the new standard silver dollars (minted March 1, 1933) served to concentrate in the treasury large deposits of silver bullion. The U.S. treasury under the Putman Act agreed (July 9, 1937) to exchange these for gold, thus affording a large volume of credits abroad just when they were urgently required for the purchase of arms.

Scholarship was profoundly stimulated by contact with Western thought and literature. An official commission (1914–28) wrote up from the state archives the *Qing shi gao (Draft History of the Qing Dynasty)* to complete the standard series. **Wang Guowei** (1877–1927) was a traditional scholar brilliant in deciphering and elucidating Shang oracle bone inscriptions, as well as in textual and historical scholarship. His older friend **Luo Zhenyu** (1866–1940) was as well known for his work on the oracle bones as he was for his loyalty to the Qing dynasty. Younger scholars brought Western methodologies into every domain of the humanities and social sciences. **Hu Shi,** professor at Beijing University, played a major role in developing a **written style in the vernacular,** which would be easier to learn and would enable larger numbers of people to become literate. It won general acceptance, though not without difficulties, for scholarly, literary, and practical purposes. The introduction of Western-style punctuation facilitated understanding of both ancient and modern texts, and the preparation of indexes made their content accessible to a greater degree than ever before. Hu Shi's disciple **Gu Jiegang** (1893–1980) did important work opening up China's high antiquity to modern scholarly criticism. A flood of periodicals of all sorts afforded a medium for scholarly publication and interchange of current views scarcely present in 1912.

Education was altered as much in content and method as in diffusion. Elementary school pupils increased (1912–35) from 2,793,633 to 11,667,888, and high school students from 52,100 to roughly 500,000. In place of four colleges in 1912, there were (in 1933) 40 universities, 40 colleges, and 29 technical schools, with 43,000 students, libraries totaling 4.5 million volumes, and a budget of over U.S.$20 million silver.

Literature flourished and became highly politicized under the harsh realities of these years, as well as under the stimulus of realism, especially among Chinese novelists and short story writers. **Ding Ling**

(1904–86) launched her literary career with "The Diary of Miss So-phie" (Dec. 1927) and stressed themes in defense of feminism and free-dom. **Lao She** (1899–1966) was a master of both symbolic satire (*Cat Country,* 1932) and realistic tales of great sadness and tragedy (*Rick-shaw,* 1937). **Lu Xun** (p. 776) ceased writing short stories and concen-trated instead on piercingly critical essays of a topical nature. **Mao Dun** (1896–1982) wrote realistic novels about life in Shanghai (*Midnight,* 1932) and elsewhere.

1937–45. JAPANESE ATTACKS ON CHINA PROPER BEGAN WORLD WAR II IN EAST ASIA. There was no Japanese declaration of war until 1941. The conflict had long been in the offing, at least since the Manchurian Incident of 1931. Most Japanese historians date the beginning of the war to 1931, and certainly no later than July 7, 1937.

1937, July 7. The Marco Polo Bridge Incident (near Beijing) erupted. Japanese troops on night maneuvers clashed with Chinese. The fight-ing spread rapidly and led to the **seizure of Beijing** (July 28) and **Tianjin** (July 29) by the Japanese. A large-scale campaign was begun in north China. Without meeting much resistance, the **Japanese took Zhang-jiakou** (Kalgan, Sept. 3), **Baoding** (Sept. 24), **Shijiazhuang** (Oct. 10), **Gui-sui** (Oct. 14), and **Taiyuan** (Nov. 9). By this time the Chinese had be-come better organized and managed to slow down the advance, though inferior equipment told heavily against the Chinese throughout.

Aug. 8–Nov. 8. The **Shanghai campaign,** in which a Japanese naval force landed (Aug. 11) in Shanghai, resulted from the killing of two Japanese marines at a Chinese military airdrome; the Japanese force soon found itself endangered by vastly superior Chinese forces. The Japanese were obliged to send an army, which, after ferocious resis-tance by the Chinese and severe fighting, ultimately forced the Chi-nese back from the city (Nov. 8). The **fall of Shanghai** was followed immediately by the **taking of Suzhou** (Nov. 20) and by an energetic drive up the Yangzi River. Merciless **bombing of Chinese cities** by the Japanese outraged world opinion. Jiang's forces sustained 250,000 dead or wounded; the Japanese suffered some 40,000 casualties.

Aug. 25. The **Japanese naval blockade** of south China was extended (Sept. 5) to the entire coast, but Qingdao, Hong Kong, Macao, and Guangzhouwan were excepted, out of consideration for foreign pow-ers.

Aug. 29. A **nonaggression treaty between China and the Soviet Un-ion** was concluded.

Oct. 5–6. This treaty led to the sale of military aircraft to China and to the shipment of large quantities of munitions, especially after the **League of Nations and the U.S. condemned Japanese actions in China.** A conference of powers at Brussels (Nov. 15) failed to effect mediation.

Nov. 20. The **GMD capital was moved inland from Nanjing to Chongqing** (Chungking), though the executive power was, for the time being, established in Hankou. Jiang arrived on Dec. 8.

Dec. 12. The *Panay* **Incident** occurred, in which Japanese bombers attacked U.S. and British ships near Nanjing, producing heightened tension between the powers. The U.S. government ultimately ac-cepted Japanese explanations, but the Japanese government continued a high-handed policy toward foreign property and rights in China and evaded all protests from the United States, Great Britain, and France. The tense situation in Europe enabled Japan to pursue its aims without running the serious risk of intervention.

Dec. 13. The **fall of Nanjing** followed heavy Japanese bombing. Great atrocities were committed by the Japanese troops in the **Rape of Nan-jing** over the following seven weeks: thousands, perhaps more, were raped, and tens of thousands were murdered. The Chinese fell back, denying the Japanese a decisive victory. The first six months of the war demonstrated to the world the unity of the Chinese against the external aggressor. All factions, Communists and GMD alike, acted on the orders of the central government of the united front under Jiang Jieshi.

Dec. 24. The Japanese took Hangzhou and, advancing from the north, occupied Jinan (Dec. 27).

There were disastrous droughts and famines throughout China (1936–37), adding starvation to the causes of death among ordinary Chinese people. Food riots, brigandry, and mass migrations took place in certain locales.

1938, Jan. 10. The Japanese captured Qingdao, after the Chinese had destroyed the Japanese mills in that area. The Japanese then began their advance south along the Hankou Railway and through Shanxi. They reached the Yellow River (March 6), but mobile Chinese forces restricted the Japanese to the railway zone. It was becoming ever more evident that the Japanese could capture the large cities and important communications, but that the countryside would remain in the hands of Chinese guerrillas. During the spring of 1938, the Japanese forces suffered serious reverses at the hands of the Chinese.

March 28. The **Japanese installed a puppet government of the Re-public of China** at Nanjing under Liang Hongzhi (1882–1946). Earlier (1937), a puppet regime had been established in Inner Mongolia, and another was established in Beijing under Wang Kemin (1873–1945) in late 1937.

In Yan'an **Mao Zedong** announced his theory on "protracted war"—that is, that victory was certain to be China's, but it would take a long time and would require sacrifices.

April. Li Zongren defeated the Japanese in the ferocious **Battle of Taierzhuang,** in which 30,000 Japanese were killed, considered a turn-ing point in the war.

May. The Japanese military resumed its advance, taking Xiamen (May 10), Xuzhou (May 20), Kaifeng (June 6), and Anqing (June 12). As the Japanese marched toward Kaifeng, Jiang Jieshi ordered the dikes of the nearby Yellow River blown up to try to halt Japanese advances. Over 4,000 Chinese villages were destroyed and countless farmers killed in the flooding.

July 11–Aug. 10. Japanese and Soviet forces clashed at Zhanggufeng Hill, on the borders of Siberia, Manzhouguo, and Korea. After severe fighting a truce was finally arranged, with the Soviets retaining their position.

Sept. 22. The Japanese managed the creation of a United Council for China. The Japanese made even less a secret of their intention to over-throw Jiang and his GMD regime and transform China into a Japanese protectorate, as part of the projected "new order" in East Asia.

Oct. 12. The Japanese landed forces at Bias Bay, near Hong Kong, evidently intending to capitalize on the acute crisis in Europe arising from the Czechoslovak affair.

Oct. 21. Advancing inland, **Japanese troops took Guangzhou,** almost without a struggle. The city had been mercilessly bombed for months, and a large part of the population had already fled. Capture of the city enabled the Japanese to cut the Guangzhou-Hankou Railway, the most important line for transporting supplies from abroad to the Chinese forces in the interior.

Oct. 25. Hankou fell to the Japanese after extensive fighting and casualties. The Chinese government and army withdrew up the Yangzi to Chongqing. Japanese control over the Yangzi below Hankou became ever more rigid, leading to repeated and insistent protests by the West-ern powers. U.S. secretary of state Cordell Hull (1871–1955) reasserted the validity of the nine-power treaty (Nov. 4) and was supported in his attitude by the British government. These protests, however, made little impression in Tokyo.

Dec. 2. The Burma Road was opened, enabling supplies to reach Kun-ming in Yunnan from the south.

1939. The fighting continued in an inconclusive way over a large area. There was no indication of any slackening of Chinese determination, and Jiang's government continued to receive supplies from the Soviet Union and other powers, often by the most devious routes. Both the United States and Great Britain made substantial loans to the GMD government. The Japanese, unable to force a decision, developed an indirect attack on the position of the foreign powers in China, de-manding a larger share in the Shanghai International Concession and challenging foreign rights everywhere.

June 14. The Japanese established a blockade of the British conces-sion at Tianjin (and, incidentally, also of the French), following a re-fusal by the British authorities to surrender four Chinese accused of "terrorism." Japanese spokesmen publicly announced that Britain had to give up support of the Chinese Nationalist regime and cooperate with Japan in establishing the "new order" in East Asia.

In accordance with the united front policy (1937–39), the Commu-nist forces had been integrated into the overall GMD military struc-ture, though as independent units. The Red Army in Yan'an became the Eighth Route Army, and Communist forces in central China became the New Fourth Army. In addition, they set up the Shaan-Gan-Ning border government (at the borders of Shaanxi, Gansu, and Ningxia provinces) and the Jin-Cha-Ji border regime (at the borders of Shanxi, Chahar, and Hebei). CCP membership rose greatly during the war years, from some 40,000 in 1937 to 20 times that number only three years later. Radical CCP policies toward landlords and land reform were tempered to accommodate the GMD and the discredited policies of the Jiangxi Soviet. Mao's power in Yan'an was threatened within the party by Zhang Guotao, his earlier rival, and Wang Ming (pseud. Chen Shaoyu, b. 1907), the leader of a group of Russian-trained, Stalinist ideologues who were never overly pleased by Mao's independent course. But Mao overcame them both.

Sept. 3. The outbreak of World War II in Europe gave the Japanese a chance to press their undeclared war in China. War was not formally declared by China against Japan until Dec. 9, 1941, after the attack on Pearl Harbor.

By this time, **Jiang Jieshi** and the **Nationalists (Guomindang, GMD)** were firmly ensconced in their wartime base in **Chongqing** (Chungking, Sichuan province); **Mao Zedong** and the followers of the **Chinese Communist Party** were in their base in **Yan'an** (Shaanxi province). Although accommodation had been made between the two sides and a united front to end their civil war and jointly fight the Japanese invaders was in place, the relationship was tense from the very start. Following their escape from Jiangxi and the Long March to Yan'an, the Communists had grown considerably in strength: membership was roughly 800,000 in 1940. The CCP became more popular because they tempered their earlier harsh land policies, as agreed in their united front pact, they demonstrated a greater intent to focus on the external enemy, and they did not allow their troops to abuse the local populace, something the GMD troops were notorious for doing. An anti-Japanese university was established in Yan'an as an institute to instill Party values.

1940. The Communists embarked on a series of assaults on strategic Japanese points in north China; these were known as the **Hundred Regiments Offensive**, led by **Gen. Peng Dehuai** (1898–1974). The Japanese took heavy casualties but beat back the Communists, often committing acts of immense destructiveness against the local communities.

March 30. A puppet Chinese government headed by **Wang Jingwei** (1885–1944) was established at Nanjing with Japanese support.

Dec. Jiang Jieshi demanded that all Eighth Route Army forces (CCP) be north of the Yangzi River by the end of the year; and all New Fourth Army forces (CCP) retreat north of the Yangzi River by the end of Jan. 1941. The latter opposed Jiang's ultimatum.

1941, Jan. 7–13. Nationalist troops ambushed the New Fourth Army, killing some 3,000 Communist soldiers; this was later known as the **New Fourth Army Incident.**

The **Japanese forces** committed acts of appalling brutality in China, with a policy of **"three-alls": kill all, burn all, destroy all.** The populations of entire villages, frequently numbering in the thousands, were on many occasions exterminated in mass slaughters, their homes burned to the ground, and often all farm animals put to death. Such a policy was meant to deter people from aiding either the Communists or the GMD.

The Japanese bombing of Pearl Harbor brought the United States into the war against Japan, opening a second front of sorts in the Pacific. The U.S. soon awarded China $630 million in lend-lease, followed by another $500 million loan—all to the Chongqing regime.

1942, March 8. The governments of Great Britain and the United States, to check the serious inflation in China, provided credits of £50 million and U.S.$500 million.

April. After tough fighting with the Japanese in Burma, Chinese and British troops withdrew, and the Burma Road closed.

Oct. 9. Great Britain and the U.S. announced their **relinquishment of extraterritorial rights** and special privileges in China (ratified by treaties, Jan. 11, 1943).

During the fighting, thousands of Chinese flocked to Yan'an and the Communists, and in 1942 the Party tried to weed out less than completely dedicated revolutionaries with a **"Rectification Campaign."** Certain persons were severely criticized and drummed out of the Party, with some committing suicide; Mao's position was thus further secured. The writer **Ding Ling** (1904–86) was one such object of criticism; her stories frequently singled out male Communists for mistreating women, views now deemed bourgeois feminism.

May. Mao called the **Yan'an Forum on Art and Literature** and laid down strict literary guidelines for socialist art and literature.

1943, Sept. 13. Gen. Jiang Jieshi was elected **president** of the Chinese Republic by the Central Executive Committee, which also permitted him to retain his post as commander in chief of the Chinese army. The committee announced that democratic, responsible government would be established in China as soon as the war ended.

Dec. Jiang Jieshi was invited to join Franklin Delano Roosevelt (1882–1945) and Winston Churchill (1874–1965) at the **Cairo Conference** (p. 810), where it was decided that after the war, Taiwan and Manzhouguo would revert to Nationalist control.

1944, June. Chinese pilots bombed Japanese rail yards in Bangkok, flying from airfields constructed with U.S. and British help. They then bombed a Japanese steel plant in Kyūshū, Japan's southernmost island (June 15), as well as sites in Manchuria and Taiwan.

June–July. U.S. missions to "observe" operations in Yan'an by Vice President Henry Wallace (1888–1965) and others came back strongly suggesting closer ties with the CCP, as opposed to the corruption-ridden GMD. Patrick Hurley (1883–1963), a Roosevelt envoy, returned with similar impressions from a trip in November.

April. Japanese forces launched the **Ichigo Campaign** in northern and central China. Changsha was taken; later (Nov.) Guilin and Liuzhou (in Guangxi province) were captured as well.

Oct. Gen. Joseph Stilwell (1883–1946), adviser to the Chinese forces and frequent critic of Jiang Jieshi, **was recalled** to Washington and replaced by Gen. Albert Wedemeyer. Roosevelt wanted Stilwell to take control over all Chinese forces, and Jiang vociferously refused.

Dec. 31. Gen. Jiang promised the Chinese people that a **constitutional government** would be established before the end of the war.

1945, Feb. Roosevelt, Churchill, and Joseph Stalin (1879–1953) met at Yalta (p. 807), excluding Jiang and not even informing him of their decisions, indicating a serious drop in Jiang's international popularity.

April. The **Seventh National Congress of the Chinese Communist Party** met in Yan'an. CCP membership was 1.2 million, and troop strength was 900,000.

Aug. 8. With the war now over in Europe for several months, immense numbers of Soviet troops poured into Manchuria, just two days after the bombing of Hiroshima. Within the week, Japan had accepted unconditional surrender.

Aug. 14. Song Zewen concluded a treaty of friendship and alliance with the Soviet Union for the GMD. In return for Soviet recognition of the Nationalists as the "central government of China," the Nationalists agreed to the independence of Outer Mongolia, gave the USSR joint 30-year ownership of the South Manchurian Railway and the port of Dalian (Japanese, Dairen), and agreed to the conversion of Lüshun (Port Arthur) into an exclusively Chinese and Soviet naval base.

The end of the war found China still divided between the Guomindang forces of Jiang Jieshi and the Communist forces of Mao Zedong.

Aug.–Sept. U.S. forces captured Shanghai, Qingdao, Dagu, Guangzhou, and Pusan (Korea) and sent troops into Beijing and Tianjin. The U.S. then flew GMD forces into these cities to have them accept Japanese surrender. The Japanese were instructed to surrender only to Jiang's, and not CCP, troops. The Communists' military commander, **Zhu De** (1886–1976), demanded that the Japanese surrender wherever his troops found them. Over 2 million Japanese troops were in China and Manchuria, with another 1.75 million Japanese civilians. There was a rush to accept Japanese surrender, both to gain hold over the territory and to seize the weaponry. Frequently, the GMD used former puppet troops to retain control over an area, a highly unpopular move among the populace at large. Fantastic inflation ensued, and food prices soared.   (To p. 1020)

3. MONGOLIAN PEOPLE'S REPUBLIC, 1911-1926

1911. During the Chinese Revolution of 1911, northern Mongol princes, with the support of tsarist Russia, proclaimed an autonomous Outer Mongolia, with Bogdo Gegen, the Living Buddha, as the khan, thus ending the suzerainty of China over Outer Mongolia. But Chinese troops reoccupied Mongolia during 1919–20 after the Russian Revolution.

1921. The First Congress of the Mongolian People's Party (Communist, renamed as the Mongolian People's Revolutionary Party in 1924) was held in Kyakhta on March 1, and the basic task of the Party program was national liberation and the establishment of an independent state. The Mongolian People's Army defeated Chinese occupying forces in March. Mongolian and Soviet troops overcame the Urgen White Guard bands, and a permanent People's Government of Mongolia was formed in July 1921. Serfdom and the institution of hereditary feudal rulers were abolished in 1922.

1924. After the death of the Living Buddha in May, the People's Revolutionary Party and the People's Government adopted a resolution to abolish the monarchy and introduce the republican system in June. The first Grand People's *Hural* legally proclaimed the Mongolian People's Republic and approved its constitution in November.

1925, Oct. The Fourth Party Congress adopted the second Party program, which centered on the social and political consolidation of the revolution as the basic task. Beginning in 1929, large landholdings of feudal lords were confiscated and those of monasteries in 1938.

1926, Sept. Enactment of a law on separation of the Church and the State. *(To p. 1028)*

4. KOREA, 1910-1945

(From p. 569)

1910, Aug. 22. KOREA WAS FORMALLY ANNEXED BY JAPAN, when the Treaty of Annexation was signed by Prime Minister Yi Wan-yong (1858–1926). Emperor Sunjong (1874–1926, r. 1907–10) proclaimed (Aug. 29) the end of the Yi dynasty. For the next 35 years, Koreans lived under often brutal Japanese colonial domination. Ultimately, the independence movement against Japan aroused Korea's national identity but at a heavy price. Over the course of the period 1910–40, Korea's population rose from 15 million to over 24 million.

Oct.–1916. The first governor-general of the Korean colony was Gen. Terauchi Masatake (1852–1919). The colonial regime was known as the Government-General of Chōsen (Korea), which had tight, centralized authority over every aspect of life in Korea. The governor-general effectively had complete power, civil and military. Terauchi's period as governor-general, along with that of his successor, was dubbed "the period of military rule." The bureaucracy in 1910 employed some 10,000 officials; by 1937, it encompassed 87,552 officials (over 60 percent of them Japanese). The number of police in the employ of the governor-general rose from 6,222 in 1910 to 20,771 in 1922, and to over 60,000 by 1941; about half were Koreans. The stated policy of the regime was to assimilate the Koreans into the Japanese empire, eventually; in fact, Koreans fell victim to sharp discrimination.

Under Terauchi, a land survey bureau was set up to rationalize the land distribution and land-tax systems. The state remained the largest landowner in the colony, holding nearly 40 percent of it in 1930. The Oriental Development Company, a semipublic corporation set up by the colonial authorities and much hated by nationalist Koreans, held 269,500 acres of land by itself. The land survey (1910–18) ultimately firmed up the existing state of affairs. Japan also constructed extensively on preexisting Korean telecommunications and rail lines.

Despite great antipathy for their new overlords, Koreans were prevented, by arrests and police intimidation, from voicing opposition. Guerrillas were active in the countryside, although already in the period between 1907 and 1910, 17,600 guerrillas had been killed. The new regime disbanded all Korean publications, political groups, and meetings of any sort.

The government-general sharply reduced the number of private schools and moved to develop a nationwide system of education to accompany assimilation to Japanese ways. In 1910 there were 110,800 Korean students in public schools; by 1941 there were 1,776,078 enrolled. Few Koreans received higher education, although some studied in Japan (3,171 by 1912) or the U.S. Japanese became the national language, and Japanese language acquisition soared, so much so that it virtually became a work of nationalism to try to preserve the Korean language. **Chu Si-gyong** (1876–1914) and his students continued their work standardizing vernacular grammar and spelling; the Korean Language Research Society was founded in 1921. Such writers as Yi In-jik (1862–1916) and Yi Hae-jo (1869–1927) began to write in new literary forms. **Yi Kwang-su's** (b. 1892) novel *Mujŏng* (*The Heartless*, 1917) was extremely popular.

Dec. A conspiracy to assassinate Terauchi, implicating An Myŭng-gŭn (brother of An Chung-gŭn, 1879–1910, who had assassinated Itō Hirobumi, 1841–1909), was uncovered, and 600 people were arrested; 105 of them were indicted the following year, including such vital leaders of the **Sinminhoe** (New People's Association, a moderate group founded in 1907 by An Ch'ang-ho, 1878–1938) as Yun Ch'i-ho (1865–1945), Yang Ki-t'ak (1871–1938), and Yi Sŭng-hun (1864–1930). It was known thereafter as the **"Case of the One Hundred Five."** Despite a show trial, it was clear that the Japanese used the incident to destroy the Sinminhoe.

From 1910, the Japanese Daiichi Bank became the Bank of Korea in the colony, becoming also its central bank. Together with the Japanese Shokusan Bank, it controlled much of Korean finance.

The number of Korean expatriates living in Manchuria rose to 109,000 from some 65,000 in 1894. By 1912 this number reached 169,000. Some among them organized (1911) the Military School of the New Rising to prepare young Koreans to fight against Japan; others later (1914) founded the Government of the Korean Restoration Army. Neither got far. Thousands of Koreans also moved to the Maritime Province in the Russian Far East. Many also lived in the U.S. and Hawaii, where Yi Sŭng-man (Syngman Rhee, 1875–1965) founded the Korean National Association (1909).

The **Company Law** was enacted, by which any corporation, public or private, needed prior approval by the government-general.

1912. Preempting any opposition to its control, the government-general made some 50,000 arrests of a political nature, having already shut down the newspapers and presses. There were 140,000 arrests in 1918.

1916, Oct.–1919. Hasegawa Yoshimichi (1850–1924) replaced Terauchi as **governor-general** of Korea. He resigned in the midst of the March First movement (1919).

1919, March 1. The **MARCH FIRST MOVEMENT** was an explosion of nationalist pride that erupted after nearly a decade of brutal repression. Inspired by Woodrow Wilson's (1856–1924) pronouncement on behalf of self-determination, Koreans (like Chinese and Vietnamese) expected big things from the Versailles Peace Conference. **Syngman Rhee** attended on behalf of the Korean National Association. The Korean Young Independence Corps, founded by students in Japan, had ratified (Feb. 8, 1919) a statement written by **Yi Kwang-su** calling for independence. Christian and Buddhist leaders in Korea were stimulated by these and other actions and planned a movement at home. The date was set for March 3, when the **funeral for King Kojong** (d. Jan. 22) was scheduled, a timely date inasmuch as it was to be a focus of nationalistic feeling. Later it was changed to March 1. A "declaration of independence" (penned by **Ch'oe Nam-sŏn,** 1890–1957) was drawn up, as were various other documents for the international community. That morning, the signers of the "declaration" met at a restaurant in Seoul, delivered a copy of it to the governor-general's office, and announced their plans. Mass demonstrations and marches were held throughout the country: only seven of Korea's 218 counties had no "disturbances" that day; well over 1 million people participated.

May. The Japanese called for military backup and crushed the movement everywhere. Japanese records reported 533 dead, 1,409 wounded, and 12,522 arrested (between March and Dec.). Korean figures were far higher: over 7,500 killed, some 15,000 injured, and 45,000 arrested. The Western powers did nothing and showed no interest. Despite its failure, the March First movement was a great spur to the independence movement and became a legendary event in modern Korean history.

April 9. The **Provisional Government of the Republic of Korea** was founded in Shanghai; it brought together all the expatriate Korean communities. Syngman Rhee became president, and cabinet posts went to An Ch'ang-ho, Yi Tong-hwi (1873–1928 or 1935), Kim Kyusik (1881–1950), Mun Ch'ang-bŏm, and Ch'oe Chae-hyŏng.

Sept. When Hara Takashi (Kei, 1856–1921) became Japan's prime minister, he instituted a less draconian style to the government-general of Korea under the slogan of "harmony between Japan and Korea." Adm. **Saitō Makoto** (1856–1936) was chosen as the new governor-general.

1919–27. Saitō's task was to reform the government-general, and he selected well-trained men to help carry out this job. Some of the anti-Korean discriminatory laws were altered, and Saitō formed an advisory council of Koreans which, although it had no real power, attempted to have some measure of input. Because he eased restrictions in the areas of education, the press, publication, religion, and the like, his reforms were known as the **Cultural Policy.** These included economic plans as well. It was a far more flexible era that the decade preceding it.

1920. The two Korean-language newspapers, **Chosŏn ilbo** (*Korea Daily News*) and **Tong-A ilbo** (*East Asia Daily News*), were allowed to publish in Korean. In addition, the number of vernacular language publications mushroomed, with 409 permits given in 1920, as compared with fewer than 40 for the entire 1910–19 period.

April. The **Company Law was abolished.** Corporations no longer required the government-general's approval; they merely had to register.

June. The **Korean Youth League was founded** when some 600 smaller groups coalesced.

The number of police stations, meanwhile, increased from 151 in 1919 to 251 by late 1920 (substations rose from 686 to 2,495). The institution of a High Police for intelligence and control over the press was also founded.

Among the many thousands of Koreans living in Manchuria, the **Korean Independence Army** under Hong Pŏm-do (1868–1943) linked up with the troops of the **Military Directorate** under the command of Ch'oe Tong-jin and attacked Japanese forces in several border towns; 160 Japanese were killed and 300 were wounded. In another encounter, over 1,000 Japanese troops were killed. Retaliation came swiftly and was harsh.

The first **Korean Communist Party** (Koryŏ Kongsandang) was founded by Yi Tong-hwi in Shanghai. Yi had organized a Korean Socialist Party in Khabarovsk in 1918, which he moved to Shanghai in 1921 when the Communist Party was created; in 1920 (some say 1919) a Korean section of the Bolshevik Party was organized in Irkutsk, which also joined the Korean Communist Party. The Shanghai and Irkutsk groups soon splintered into warring factions.

Numerous magazines, often with mass circulation and frequently dealing with hot social or political themes, began publication.

1922, May. After returning to Korea from China earlier in the year, **Yi Kwang-su** published his essay "A Treatise on National Reconstruction" in the popular magazine *Creation*. It described a cultural nationalist agenda.

Nov. The Society for the Establishment of a National University was founded, and a fund-raising drive was instituted. The Japanese soon proclaimed their intention to build **Keijō Imperial University** by 1926, which sapped the energies behind the Korean movement.

Dec.–1924. The **Korean production movement** was launched as a means of developing a self-sufficient national economy. Among its leaders were Yi Sŭng-hun, Cho Man-sik (b. 1882, Korea's Gandhi, founder of the Society for the Promotion of Korean Production in July 1920), Yi Kwang-su, and Yŏm T'ae-jin. They encouraged all Koreans to buy only domestic products.

Numerous modern novels were published in the 1920s. Among the more famous writers of the day were **Kim Tong-in** (1900–51), Yŏm Sang-sŏp (1897–1963), Han Yong-un (1879–1944), and Yi Pyŏng-gi

(1892–1968). The 1920s are generally considered a period of cultural renaissance, though many leftist publications were censored or closed down by the Japanese police.

1923, Sept. 1. Following the **Great Kantō Earthquake,** which leveled the Tokyo area, several thousand Koreans living in Japan were murdered by xenophobic Japanese.

1925, May. A new **Peace Preservation Law** was enacted, and the police rounded up a group of Korean Communists and other leftists (Nov.).

1926, March. Pak Yŏl (1902–74), an anarchist and radical activist in the Korean community in Japan, was arrested for plotting the assassination of the Japanese emperor. He was condemned to death, but amnestied the next month, spending the next 20 years in prison. Many similar terrorist acts were attempted in Korea and China against Japanese.

April 17. The **Korean Communist Party** (Chosŏn Kongsandang, with a different word for "Korea" in its title) was founded in Seoul and received recognition by the Communist International in Moscow (spring 1927).

June 10. In conjunction with the funeral for King Sunjong, **anti-Japanese riots** erupted throughout the colony.

1927, Jan. The **Sin'ganhoe** (New Korea Society) was founded as an organization representing all the various nationalist and anti-Japanese groups. By 1930 it claimed nearly 77,000 members in numerous branches nationwide. It remained active until May 1931, when its radical wing took control of the leadership and voted to disband. There was as well a parallel women's organization, the Kunuhoe.

1929, Jan.–April. Although defeated, the **Wonsan general strike** and the **Kwangju student movement** (Nov. 1929–spring 1930) were the only major exceptions to a period of quiet in the independence movement.

1931, July. Gen. **Ugaki Kazushige** (1868–1956) took up the post of governor-general of Korea. He had served briefly in this capacity in 1927, with several others following him, serving short terms in the post. He remained there until the summer of 1936. While the economy developed under Ugaki, the nationalist movement was suppressed.

From 1931, as Japanese ambitions on the northeast Asian mainland grew, Korea was drawn further into plans linking its economy with that of Japan and Manchuria. Ninety-five percent of all Korean exports in 1931 went to Japan; 80 percent of all Korean imports came from Japan. **As the Korean economy grew industrially in the 1930s,** many new jobs became available in industrial plants, and peasants most often filled them just as rural misery was growing as well.

1934, May. The **Chindan Study Society** for research into Korean history and literature was founded by Yi Pyŏng-do (b. 1896), Kim T'ae-jun (1904?–49), and Son Chin-t'ae (b. 1900). It worked to preserve scholarship on Korea in the face of the government-general's plans for cultural assimilation. It was eventually suppressed.

1935. Governor-General Ugaki began to require Korean students and government bureaucrats to participate in Shinto rituals. Unrest among Korean Christians exploded, leading to the expulsion of some missionaries and arrests of many Korean Christians (1935–38).

1936, Aug.–1942, May. During the period when **Gen. Minami Jirō** served as the Japanese governor-general of Korea, **forced assimilation** of Koreans and their mobilization for the war effort were local policy. From 1937 all Korean organizations were closed, and in 1938 the government-general set up its own organizations to expedite Japan's war needs. In late 1939, Koreans were required to change their names to Japanese ones, considered a great humiliation. By the early 1940s, the Korean language was all but completely banned, with even banks and other businesses compelled to use Japanese alone. Concomitant with "assimilation" came suffrage, passed in the Japanese Diet in the late 1930s and 1941; the program never saw fruition because of Japan's surrender. As a result of the countless mass organizations in which Koreans were forced to participate and the difficult circumstances of everyday life during the long period of colonial rule, the Japanese produced numerous **Korean "collaborators."**

The number of Koreans mobilized to fight on Japan's behalf or to engage in labor to that end outside the borders of Korea reached 4 million by 1944, or 16 percent of the population. There was a general conscription for Koreans from 1943, and a group of **"comfort women"**—so-called because they were forced into prostitution for the Japanese troops at the front—was dragooned. The number of women so humiliated remains unknown. Some Korean guerrillas allied with the Chinese fighting against Japan.

In exchange for Soviet participation in the Asian war, the Allies (at Yalta and Potsdam) were ready to allow Soviet control over Korea (and Manchuria). The Red Army invaded Manchuria in the final days of the war. The U.S. was able to negotiate a dividing line at the **38th parallel** for the two occupation zones. The U.S. zone in the south contained Seoul; the Soviets' to the north had P'yŏngyang.

1943, Dec. The U.S., China, and Great Britain agreed at the Cairo Conference that Korea should become independent "in due course."

1945, Aug. 15. Japan's unconditional surrender spelled the end of colonial rule in Korea. *(To p. 1028)*

5. JAPAN, 1914-1945

(From p. 574)

1914-18. During the years of **World War I**, the Japanese manufactured and sent to Europe large quantities of munitions (especially to Russia). At the same time, Japanese merchants took advantage of the conflict to supplant German commerce in East Asia. **Heavy industry** in particular grew in the postwar years, with considerable investment from the *zaibatsu* conglomerates, which increasingly dominated the economy. In the 1920s they set the stage through planning with greater efficiency for the rapid expansion of the 1930s, following the government's shift in financial policy.

Domestically, the **Taishō period** (1912-26) is usually considered an era of opening to liberal and Western trends in many areas of society and the arts, the so-called Taishō democracy. This is usually to distinguish it from the political authoritarianism of the preceding Meiji era and from the militarism and the crackdown on domestic liberalism of the subsequent Shōwa era. Western influence was felt in the **visual and literary arts**, both in theme and technique.

1914, Aug. Japan declared war on Germany. Within a three-month period, German possessions in Shandong and the Pacific were in Japanese hands.

Nov. 7. Jiaozhou surrendered to the Japanese after a two-month siege.

1915, Jan. 18. JAPAN SUBMITTED TO CHINA THE TWENTY-ONE DEMANDS, initiating a policy of increasing Japanese dominance in East Asia at China's expense.

Oct. 19. Japan formally joined the pact of London (Sept. 5, 1914), binding itself not to conclude a separate peace.

1916, July 3. A Russo-Japanese convention was concluded by which Russia accepted the extension of Japanese influence in China under agreements of 1915, and Japan recognized the Russian advance into Outer Mongolia.

Sept. 3. Fresh demands made on China, increasing Japanese rights in southern Manchuria and Inner Mongolia, followed a clash between Japanese and Chinese troops at Zhengjiadun (Aug.). China acquiesced (Feb. 1917).

Oct. 9. Terauchi Masatake (1852-1919) succeeded **Ōkuma Shigenobu** (1838-1922) as prime minister, with a slight minority in the lower house of the diet.

1917, April 20. The **general election** proved a victory for the government.

Nov. 2. Notes were exchanged with the U.S. (**Lansing-Ishii Agreement**) by which the latter recognized the special interests of Japan in China, and Japan gave pledges of good faith in the maintenance of China's integrity, independence, and the "open door."

1918, April 5. British and Japan marines landed at Vladivostok.

May, 16. A Sino-Japanese treaty was signed.

July 6. Japanese commanders took control of Vladivostok and the eastern terminus of the Trans-Siberian Railway. An announcement of intervention (Aug. 3) was issued. The **Siberian Expedition was launched** (p. 712) with 75,000 Japanese troops. The other troops sent by France, Great Britain, Canada, and the United States left by early 1919; the Japanese stayed over four years.

Aug. Rice riots erupted in towns and cities throughout Japan, spurred by the rise in the price of foodstuffs (rice principal among them) during the boom of World War I. They were mercilessly crushed.

Sept. 29. The Terauchi cabinet resigned because of its inability to cope with the unrest of the rice riots. **Hara Takashi (Kei,** 1856-1921), the first common prime minister, formed a government. Corruption and refusal to consider universal suffrage caused alienation among the populace toward party politics.

1919, Jan. 18. The **Versailles Peace Conference** began (p. 666). Japan was favorable toward the League of Nations, but its demand for a statement of racial equality was rejected.

Feb. 14. Acrimonious **debate over universal suffrage** took place in the Diet. The franchise was then limited to men over 25, paying a direct tax of 3 yen, thus excluding agricultural and industrial labor, as well as all women. Organized demonstrations in Tokyo led to the dissolution of the Diet (Feb. 26).

March 1. Rioting and **rebellion in Korea** (p. 782), following the March First Movement, was mercilessly suppressed. There followed a reform of the Korean government-general promising larger powers of self-government should Koreans abandon their independence movement.

March 25. A reform act increased the electorate from 1.5 million to 3.0 million.

May 10. A general election, with universal suffrage a dominant issue, resulted in 283 seats for the government party (Seiyūkai), which was opposed to it, 108 for the Kenseikai, and 68 for other parties.

1920, Jan. 10. Peace was formally reached with Germany by the exchange of ratifications. Japan, after initial satisfaction, became chagrined over the failure to secure recognition of its special position in East Asia.

Dec. 17. Japan received as mandates from the League of Nations the former German islands in the Pacific north of the equator (Caroline, Marshall, and Marianas [Ladrone] archipelagoes).

Dec. 31. The first **imperial census** revealed a population of 55,191,140; including Sakhalin, Taiwan, and Korea, the total came to 77,005,112.

1921, March-Aug. The world tour of Crown Prince Hirohito marked the first time a member of the imperial family had been abroad.

Nov. 4. Prime Minister Hara was murdered by a political fanatic.

Nov. 12. Takahashi Korekiyo (1854-1936) became prime minister.

Nov. 12-1922, Feb. 6. The Washington Conference met. Adm. Katō Tomosaburō (1861-1923), Shidehara Kijūrō (1872-1951), and Prince Tokugawa were the delegates from Japan. By these accords, Japan agreed to build no more three vessels for every five constructed by the U.S. and five by Great Britain.

Nov. 25. Crown Prince Hirohito became regent because of the illness of the emperor.

A shipyard strike in Kōbe succeeded in winning an eight-hour workday, which was later extended to laborers in other heavy industries.

1922, Feb. 23. Serious riots erupted over the issue of universal suffrage.

June 2. The Sino-Japanese agreement over Shandong was ratified, resulting in friendlier relations with China and the return of Jiaozhou (Dec. 10).

June 11. Katō Tomosaburō succeeded Takahashi Korekiyo as prime minister.

July 6. Treaties from the Washington Conference (p. 645) were ratified by Japan, and Japan's naval budget was reduced by 117 million yen.

Sept. 6-24. The Changchun Conference with the Soviet Union was a failure, and Japan continued to occupy northern Sakhalin.

Oct. The last of the Japanese troops left Siberia, over four years after the first ones had arrived, having failed to defeat the Bolshevik Revolution.

Frank Lloyd Wright (1869-1959) built Tokyo's Imperial Hotel.

1923, March 2. A universal suffrage bill was defeated.

Aug. 28. Yamamoto Gonbee (1852-1933) succeeded Katō Tomosaburō as prime minister.

Sept. 1. The **GREAT KANTŌ EARTHQUAKE** was followed by fierce fires in Tokyo, Yokohama, and neighboring cities, with tidal waves and repeated aftershocks. Over 100,000 were killed, with U.S.$1 billion worth of damage. Relief was sent from abroad, especially from the U.S. In the immediate aftermath, frenzied mobs killed several thousand Koreans; the police used the occasion to arrest leftists, torturing and killing some.

Dec. 29. The government resigned; this event was followed by an attack on the life of the prince regent. Kiyoura Keigo (1850–1942) became prime minister.

1924, April–June. High feelings were aroused by the United States' abrogation of the gentlemen's agreement and the total exclusion of Japanese. Demonstrations and boycotts of U.S. products resulted.

May 10. General elections were held, and the Kiyoura government fell. **Katō Takaaki** (Kōmei, 1860–1926) became prime minister, and **Shidehara Kijūrō** became foreign minister (June 1924–April 1927), with **conciliatory policies toward China.** Labor unions were legalized, and there were other labor reforms; a peace preservation law was enacted that put a serious damper on freedom of speech.

1925, Jan. 20. A Russo-Japanese convention reestablished diplomatic relations: Russia recognized the Treaty of Portsmouth of 1905; the fisheries convention of 1907 was to be revised; and Japan received oil and coal concessions in northern Sakhalin and agreed to evacuate its troops. This and subsidiary agreements formed a general settlement of issues between the two countries.

March. A bill passed the Diet granting **universal suffrage for men** aged 25 and over; the number of eligible voters increased from 3 million to 14 million. Although this development ought to have strengthened party government, the increased size of the electorate necessitated more expensive campaigns and led to more extensive corruption.

1926, Jan. 28. Prime Minister Katō Takaaki died and was succeeded by the new leader of the Kenseikai, Wakatsuki Reijirō (1866–1949), the second commoner to become prime minister.

Dec. 25. The **Taishō emperor died,** and the prince regent succeeded him to the throne. The reign period was changed to **Shōwa.**

1926–89. The **SHŌWA PERIOD** was the longest reign in Japanese history. After a few more years of the liberalism and internationalism of the Taishō period, a sudden and sharp **militaristic and imperialistic reaction** set in after the Manchurian Incident (Sept. 18, 1931). There was a partial repudiation of popular intellectual and cultural aspects of Western civilization and a revival of older Japanese ideologies. Politicians lost their influence, and the army and, to a lesser extent, the navy became the dominant forces in the government, with the farming populace more often than not supporting the military against the urban bourgeoisie and the large economic combines or *zaibatsu.* Under this leadership, the nation embarked on a daring program of territorial expansion on the continent. Meanwhile, Japanese industry was growing rapidly, and Japanese manufactured goods began to flood the world market.

1927, April 17. The Wakatsuki cabinet fell, and **Tanaka Giichi** (1863–1929), leader of the Seiyūkai, became prime minister, pursuing an "activist" policy toward China.

May–June. Japanese troops intervened in Shandong to block the northern advance of the Chinese National Revolutionary Army upon Beijing in the Northern Expedition.

1928, April. Japan intervened again in Shandong, allegedly to protect Japanese nationals there, leading to the following events in early May.

May 3–11. Sino-Japanese clashes erupted in Jinan: Japan temporarily seized control of the railways in Shandong; a Chinese boycott movement against Japan lasted for over a year; the incident was settled on March 28, 1929; China agreed to pay damages but not an indemnity; and Japanese troops withdrew on May 20, 1929.

June. Zhang Zuolin was assassinated by a clique of officers within the Guandong army, in order to make his forces in Manchuria and north China more cooperative. This policy backfired; Tanaka was compelled to recognize the Nanjing-based regime (Guomindang) of Jiang Jieshi (Chiang Kai-shek); and the Tanaka cabinet ultimately fell (July 2, 1929) when the emperor intervened to note Tanaka's failure to prosecute the murderers of Zhang.

1929. The growth of **labor unions,** begun particularly during 1915–20, reached a total of 600 associations with a third of a million members. There was also an increase in labor disputes (576 in 1929).

July 2. The Tanaka cabinet fell. Hamaguchi Osachi (1870–1931) of the Minseitō formed a cabinet, and Shidehara Kijūrō returned as foreign minister. To redress Japan's balance of payments problem, Hamaguchi tried to reduce government expenditures; he also strengthened the yen by moving Japan again to the gold standard. The coming Great Depression undid much of his success.

The international depression hit Japanese labor, although the government's reflationary policies helped to alleviate some of the pain after 1932, and the speedy recovery of the 1930s together with continued expansion in both heavy and light industries served actually to enlarge the labor pool considerably.

1930. The **population** of Japan, estimated at 26.5 million in 1726 and 34.8 million in 1872, doubled in the following 63 years (69.2 million in 1935), the rate of increase accelerating steadily to a peak of 15.3 per thousand in 1930 before beginning to decline (14.4 in 1935). This rate of increase (roughly 1 million per year by 1930) created a problem because of the already high density of the Japanese population in the Tokugawa period. Public concern over the population question after 1922 and the failure of emigration to provide a lasting solution led to an emphasis on manufacturing and foreign trade as a means of providing employment.

May 6. A Sino-Japanese tariff agreement was signed in Nanjing by which Japan recognized China's tariff autonomy and received certain commercial safeguards and recognition of Japanese loans to former Chinese governments.

Oct. Japanese ratification of the London Naval Treaty (signed April 22) followed acrimonious debate in which the Seiyūkai attacked the policies of Hamaguchi and Shidehara, arousing anger in ultranationalistic quarters.

Nov. 14. Prime Minister Hamaguchi was shot by an assassin in Tokyo.

1931, March. The **Cherry Society,** an ultrarightist group of army officers, planned a coup in Tokyo but failed.

The Japanese military was itself not united. In addition to endemic differences between the army and the navy, there were serious rifts within the army. One antidemocratic clique, the Imperial Way Faction, called for direct rule by the emperor; among its leaders were future war minister **Gen. Araki Sadao** (1877–1966) and **Gen. Mazaki Jinzaburō** (1876–1956). Another group, the Control Faction, called for all-out war and the complete militarization of Japan to that end; its members included **Gen. Nagata Tetsuzan** (1884–1935), **Ishiwara Kanji** (1889–1949), and **Tōjō Hideki** (1884–1948). The factions fought each other, and often with deadly force.

April. Hamaguchi was succeeded as prime minister by Wakatsuki Reijirō, the new leader of the Minseitō.

Sept. 18. The **Manchurian incident in Mukden** (p. 778), masterminded by rogue elements of the Guandong Army, erupted, leading to Japanese occupation of key sites in Manchuria.

Dec. The Wakatsuki government fell, and a new government was formed by Inukai Tsuyoshi (1855–1932), with Gen. Araki Sadao as war minister.

By this year, 80 percent or more of all Japanese foreign investments went to China, amounting to over one-third of all foreign investments there. Most of it went to Manchuria and Shanghai. Japanese textile manufacturing in China was substantial, nearly 40 percent of the Chinese textile industry being owned by Japanese in 1930.

1932, Jan. 28–March 2. Sino-Japanese hostilities erupted in Shanghai (p. 778); local Chinese forces beat back the Japanese.

Feb. 18. The **independence of Manzhouguo** (Manchukuo) was proclaimed by the puppet regime set up there by the Japanese military.

May 15. Inukai Tsuyoshi was assassinated in a military coup that was quickly crushed. A cabinet primarily of nonparty members was formed under Saitō Makoto (1856–1936), with Araki Sadao as war minister and Takahashi Korekiyo as finance minister. This marked the **end of party government** in prewar Japan.

1933, May 27. Following the report to the League of Nations of the Lytton Commission, Japan announced its **withdrawal from the League** (to take effect in two years).

May 31. The Japanese invasion of Rehe (Jehol, Jan.–March) led to a truce signed at Tanggu which created a demilitarized zone in eastern Hebei province under Japanese domination.

1934, April 18. A Japanese foreign office statement asserted a virtual Japanese protectorate over China's relations with the Western powers.

July 7. The Saitō government was succeeded by that of Adm. Okada Keisuke (1868–1952). Hirota Kōki (1878–1948) continued to serve as foreign minister.

1935, June 9. The He-Umezu Accord was concluded.

Oct. 28. Foreign Minister Hirota enunciated his "three points": the establishment of a Japan-China-Manzhouguo bloc, the suppression of anti-Japanese activities in China, and the organization of a joint Sino-Japanese front against Communism.

Nov. Japan's effort to create an autonomous north China collapsed. Instead, the East Hebei Autonomous Council was created (Nov. 24). This led to student demonstrations in Beiping (Beijing, Dec. 9).

1936, Feb. 20. The more liberal Minseitō regained the leading position in the Diet, following elections.

Feb. 26. Prime Minister Saitō, Finance Minister Takahashi, and others were assassinated in an uprising of young army officers of the Imperial Way Faction in Tokyo, aiming at establishing a military dictatorship; this was subsequently known as the **February 26th Incident.** Seventeen of the rebellious officers were sentenced to death (July 7) by a military tribunal.

March 9. Hirota became prime minister, forming a cabinet dominated by the military. The budget was greatly increased, and development of heavy industry was pushed.

Nov. 25. The **Japanese-German anti-Comintern pact** was concluded, Japan having already abandoned the naval limitation agreements.

1937, Jan. 23. The Hirota cabinet fell. Gen. Ugaki Kazushige (1868–1956) was prevented from forming a cabinet by army leaders. A cabinet was formed (Feb. 2) by Hayashi Senjūrō (1876–1943).

April 30. The general election went in opposition to the Hayashi cabinet, which resigned (May 31). **Prince Konoe Fumimaro** (1891–1945) formed a "national union" cabinet with Hirota Kōki as foreign minister (June 3).

July 7. SINO-JAPANESE HOSTILITIES erupted following the Marco Polo Bridge Incident (p. 780).

The establishment of the **cabinet advisory council** (Oct.) and the **imperial headquarters** (Nov.) centralized the conduct of the war in the hands of the military and naval leaders, acting under direct authority of the emperor. Persons suspected of liberal or radical tendencies were arrested (371 on Dec. 14).

Nov. 3. The Brussels Conference opened.

Dec. 13. After Japanese troops took Nanjing in fierce fighting, they began committing acts of mass murder and rape: **the Rape of Nanjing.** Over 50,000 Chinese men and women were murdered, and many thousands more women were raped.

1938, March 26. Passage of the National Mobilization Bill allowed the state to dictate almost all phases of economic life.

May 26. The cabinet was reorganized, giving military and naval officers six portfolios.

Sept. 29. Gen. Ugaki resigned as foreign minister.

Oct. 29. Arita Hachirō (1884–1965) was appointed foreign minister.

1939, Jan. 4. Prince Konoe resigned as prime minister. He was succeeded by Hiranuma Kiichirō (1867–1952), who formed a cabinet that included Konoe.

April 2. A sharp dispute between the Soviet Union and Japan over fishing rights was settled by agreement for one year, Japan to participate on Soviet terms in an auction of the fishing areas.

May. Serious fighting between Soviet forces and the Japanese Guandong Army at Nomonhan broke out on the Manchurian–Outer Mongolian border. Over the course of the summer, Japan lost 18,000 troops. A peace was reached in mid-September.

Aug. 21. The Nazi-Soviet Nonaggression Pact was concluded, proving to be a tremendous shock to Japan, which at once scrapped the anti-Comintern pact and resumed freedom of action.

Aug. 25. The Japanese government protested the Nazi-Soviet pact of August 21.

Aug. 28. The Hiranuma cabinet resigned, and a new government under Gen. Abe Nobuyuki 1875–1953) was formed to put the new policy into effect.

Sept. Japan signed the Tripartite Pact with Nazi Germany and Fascist Italy.

Cultural Trends

The interwar period as a whole witnessed remarkable developments in literature and the arts. In **literature,** modernist themes could be found in the fiction of **Shiga Naoya** (1883–1971), particularly in his autobiographical writings, contrary to the earlier naturalism. **Akutagawa Ryūnosuke** (1892–1927) wrote numerous short stories, often picking up on themes from older times but with new psychological twists; he is most famous for "Rashōmon." Perhaps the most popular Japanese writer of the century was **Tanizaki Junichirō** (1886–1965), whose novels deal with the problems of assimilating "modernity" in Japan; his best-known work remains *The Makioka Sisters.* The writing of **poetry** also went through a period of readjustment in conflict and interaction with new themes and styles from the West.

There was a movement, begun in the early Shōwa years, to invest dignity in Japanese handicraft or folk art, the ***mingei*** movement, advocated by **Yanagi Sōetsu** (1889–1961). In the 1930s, the enthnographer **Yanagida Kunio** (1875–1962) carried out an immense national survey of Japanese folklore.

The individualistic trend that flowed to Japan with Western cultural forms found expression in the **"modern girl"** movement. Young women dressed in fashions from the West, styled their hair like matinee idols, and behaved in decidedly autonomous ways.

In **scholarship,** Western philosophical trends—Hegelianism, Marxism, phenomenalism, and other schools—found interested Japanese. **Yoshino Sakuzō** (1878–1933), who coined the term *Taishō democracy,* was a Christian and a liberal who argued strongly on behalf of democracy. **Nishida Kitarō** (1870–1945) attempted to merge Buddhist ideas with European ones. Socialism, Marxism, anarchism, and Communism all attracted followers in the Taishō and Shōwa years, until the government clamped down on them. A Japan Communist Party was founded in the 1920s, but it never achieved much distinction; many of its members recanted their views to avoid prosecution during the 1930s. **Feminism** flourished briefly in the Taishō era; women sought the franchise, in vain, and greater control over their own lives, but until after World War II they were completely excluded from political life. **Censorship** became ever more serious from the mid-1930s forward; authors of censored books not only had to face the government, but they were frequently threatened by fanatical terrorists on the extreme right as well.

The most famous critic of trends in Japan from the right was **Kita Ikki** (1883–1937); he merged seemingly leftist attacks on the bankrupt party system and the *zaibatsu,* as well as calls for equality and nationalization of industry, with imperialistic adventurism and imperial autocracy. He became a hero for the emerging extreme right, and he was executed in 1936 for his alleged role in the February 26th Incident. There were ultranationalist organizations dedicated to such ventures in these years who concentrated their attentions on China and especially Manchuria.

1940, Jan. 14. Adm. **Yonai Mitsumasa** (1880–1948) formed a new cabinet.

March 30. The Japanese supported the establishment of a **puppet regime at Nanjing under Wang Jingwei** (1885–1944).

July 16. Prince KONOE FUMIMARO (1891–1945) was named **prime minister** of Japan to direct a program of consolidation and defense.

Sept. 23. Japanese forces commenced the **occupation of French Indochina** after the French government yielded consent for the use of three airfields and made other concessions.

Sept. 27. Japan joined Germany and Italy in a tripartite pact whereby all pledged total aid to each other for ten years (p. 808).

Oct. All political parties were consolidated into the **Imperial Rule Assistance Association,** with the aim of building a mass party along Nazi lines. It never achieved that end. Efforts were made to eradicate all Western influences from Japanese life and culture and to indoctrinate the people in traditional, nativistic values.

1941, June 23. The Japanese, who had demanded the concession, obtained the consent of the French government at Vichy for **Japanese military control over French Indochina.** Here, as elsewhere in Southeast Asia, Japan used the anticolonialist slogan "Asia for the Asians" to try to turn the local populace against the West and toward the Japanese. They were in fact exchanging one master for another, Japanese colonialism being often even more brutal than what had preceded it.

Oct. 17. The Konoe cabinet was forced to resign, and **Gen. TŌJŌ HIDEKI (1884–1948),** who was more pro-Axis in his views, became both prime minister and minister of war.

Nov. 29. Prime Minister Tōjō declared that the influence of Great Britain and the U.S. must be eliminated from East Asia.

Dec. 7. JAPAN COMMENCED HOSTILITIES WITH THE UNITED STATES AND GREAT BRITAIN BY SURPRISE ATTACKS ON PEARL HARBOR (HAWAII), THE PHILIPPINES, GUAM, MIDWAY ISLAND, HONG KONG, AND MALAYA (p. 808).

Dec. 8. The U.S. declared war on Japan.

Dec. 11. Germany and Italy, in accord with the pact of Sept. 27, 1940, **supported Japan by declaring war on the United States.**

Dec. 21. Japan concluded a ten-year **treaty of alliance with Thailand. Thailand declared war on the U.S. and Great Britain** a month later (Jan. 25, 1942).

1942, March 8. The **Japanese occupied Rangoon** in Burma.

June. At the **Battle of Midway,** Japan's initial successes in the Pacific theater were thwarted by an important U.S. victory.

1943, July 5. The Japanese government announced that it had approved the **cession of six Malayan states to Thailand.**

1944, July 18. Gen. Tōjō Hideki and his entire cabinet resigned and was replaced by **Gen. Koiso Kuniaki** (1880–1950) as prime minister and **Adm. Yonai Mitsumasa** as deputy prime minister.

1945, March. U.S. planes **firebombed Tokyo,** killing tens of thousands. Similar attacks were carried out in May.

April. Koiso was replaced by **Adm. Suzuki Kantarō** (1867–1948) as prime minister.

July 10–19. The **Japanese home islands were attacked** with mounting intensity. Over 1,000 carrier planes raided Tokyo (July 10); the U.S. fleet moved in to shell Honshū and Hokkaidō (July 14–15); the British fleet joined in carrier raids against Japanese centers (July 17); and U.S. and British fliers sank some of the last remnants of the Japanese navy in Tokyo Bay (July 19). On July 26, the U.S., Great Britain, and China demanded that Japan surrender unconditionally, but the demand was ignored.

Aug. 6–14. The **WAR IN THE PACIFIC ENDED** in a week of disaster for Japan. An **atomic bomb** (p. 809), the formula for which had been secretly perfected by U.S. and British scientists, was dropped on the Japanese city of **Hiroshima** (Aug. 6). It killed or injured some 200,000 people and leveled four square miles of houses and factories, roughly 80 percent of the city. Two days later, the **Soviet Union declared war on Japan,** and Soviet troops swept into Manchuria (Aug. 8). On Aug. 9, a **second atomic bomb** shattered **Nagasaki.** The Japanese government offered to surrender if Emperor Hirohito were permitted to retain his throne (Aug. 10), and on receiving this assurance the **Japanese accepted terms of surrender** (Aug. 14).

Aug. 28–Sept. 2. U.S. forces landed in Japan to occupy strategic centers while the disarmament of Japanese military forces and the surrender of navy ships and aircraft proceeded rapidly. **Formal terms of surrender** were signed by the Japanese envoys on board the USS *Missouri* in Tokyo Bay (Sept. 2). *(To p. 1032)*

6. VIETNAM, 1902–1945

(From p. 576)

This period began with the entirety of Vietnam under French colonial control. Resistance movements led by the *van than* class in the mountains had been mollified by the French colonial administration's willingness to allow *van than* local control and village autonomy, creating a sort of feudal system. Aside from guerrilla leaders like **De Tham** (d. 1913), insurgency in the Red River delta came to an end. In Cochinchina to the south, the rice plantation economy grew rapidly and produced widespread tenancy among the farming populace. Both systems were typical of colonial regimes in the 20th century.

Following World War I, foreign investment in Vietnam mushroomed. As a result, coal mines in the north, rubber plantations in central and south Vietnam, and the rapid increase of production for rice farmers in the south spawned a working class, as well as a landlord class, rice exporters in Saigon, and a modern intelligentsia.

1902. Japan's conclusion of the Anglo-Japanese Alliance, together with its victories over China (1894–95) and Russia (1904–5), was extremely impressive to many Vietnamese in that an East Asian state had successfully modernized, become technologically sophisticated, and forged equal ties with Western states.

1903. A knowledge of French became a necessity for entrance into the traditional civil service in Annam and Tonkin.

1904. Phan Boi Chau (1867–1940), influenced by the reformist movements of late Qing China, especially that of Kang Youwei (1858–1927), founded the Viêt Nam Duy Tan Hoi (Vietnam Restoration Party) with the aim of building a constitutional monarchy in Vietnam. The next year he traveled to Japan, where he met Liang Qichao (1873–1929), and wrote *The History of the Demise of Vietnam.* He began the Eastern Travel movement to get Vietnamese students to come and study in Japan, there to be trained to promote reform back home.

1905. Phan Chu Trinh (1871–1926), having earlier passed the civil service examinations and awaiting bureaucratic appointment, became disaffected by the system and began traveling primarily in southern Vietnam, calling for the revival of the country. The next year (1906), he went to Japan and met Phan Boi Chau, but they differed on many things, tactics among them: Chau was readier to adopt revolutionary means, while Trinh's thinking was more in the enlightenment reformist vein. Also, Chau still wanted to use the monarchy as a symbol of the united anti-French movement, while Trinh was a republican much

taken with aspects of French culture. Trinh then returned to Vietnam and proposed an educational system based on the vernacular, *quôc ngu,* which was effected when the **Tonkin Free School** opened that year. The school was shut down by the colonial authorities the same year. For his participation in an antitax movement of Vietnamese farmers (1908), Trinh was transported to a penal colony on Poulo Condore Island. He was later released (1910).

1909. When Japan signed a treaty with France, **Phan Boi Chau** was expelled from Japan, and he took refuge in Thailand. From that point, he showed sympathy for the populist thought of Sun Zhongshan (Sun Yatsen, 1866–1925).

1912. After the success of the 1911 revolution in China, **Phan Boi Chau** traveled to Guangdong (China), where he met the Chinese revolutionary leader Hu Hanmin (1886–1936) and founded the **Viêt Nam Quang Phuc Hoi** (Vietnam Restoration Society), with the intent of creating a republic in his native land. Japan was rapidly discrediting itself as a model, after seizing Taiwan (1895) and Korea (1910) as colonies. The Chinese revolution seemed the next best hope for Vietnamese radicals. With help from the Chinese Revolutionary Alliance, Chau planned for an armed revolution in Vietnam. He was arrested and imprisoned in 1914 by the governor of Guangdong, and when released in 1917 he worked out of Shanghai and Hong Kong, still planning to rise in revolt.

1914–18. During World War I, some 100,000 Vietnamese troops and workers were sent to France. Through contacts with Europeans and their writings, some acquired a taste for current ideas of national autonomy, revolutionary struggle, and the like.

1915. By this time, all three sectors of Vietnam had daily newspapers written in the romanized *quôc ngu* script.

1918. The University of Hanoi, founded by Vietnamese, was permitted by the French.

1919. The **Confucian examination system,** traditionally used as the means for entrance into the civil service, **was finally abolished** throughout the entire country.

1925, June. The **Vietnamese Revolutionary Youth League** was secretly founded by **HỒ CHI MINH (1890–1969)** in Guangzhou (Canton). Through it, the basis was laid in many areas for the founding of the Indochina Communist Party (1930). The Youth League issued a propaganda organ, *Thanh nien (Youth),* weekly for nearly two years and had a political training institute in Guangzhou. Hô had been in France prior to World War I and had participated in the founding of the French Communist Party (1920); in 1923 he traveled to Moscow and took part in the Fifth Congress of the Communist International (Comintern, 1924) before returning to Guangzhou in 1925.

The young **Bao Dai** (b. 1914) acceded to the Nguyên throne. He "reigned" until 1945.

1926. The **Cai Dai** sect, an amalgam of various East Asian religious traditions, was founded as a new religion by Lê Van Trung. He soon attracted tens of thousands of followers from the urban lower middle classes and the farming populace in the south.

1927. Nguyên Thai Hoc (1902–30) founded the **Viêt Nam Quoc Dan Dang** (Vietnamese Nationalist Party) on the model of the Chinese Guomindang, with the intent of fighting for Vietnamese independence. It grew rapidly in the north among urban, educated classes, small businessmen, lower-level officials, and soldiers. Hoc was executed by guillotine (June 17, 1930) with other party leaders for participating in an armed uprising at Yen Bai (Feb. 9).

1930, Feb. 3. At a meeting in Hong Kong called by **Hô Chi Minh** of all factions of Indochinese Communists, the **Vietnamese Communist Party was founded.** The Comintern insisted (Oct.) that the name be changed to the less nationalistic sounding **Indochina Communist Party.** As the Great Depression hit Vietnam, social and economic problems were exacerbated. Rural uprisings occurred in the middle of the year in Nghe An and Ha Tinh provinces.

Sept.–1931. The Communist Party established the **Nghe-Tinh Soviet** (some argue that it joined the movement later) at this provincial border region in north-central Vietnam. It frequently attacked outposts of the French colonial authorities and was eventually crushed by the French in 1931. However, it represented the first large-scale struggle led by the Communists. It also made it clear that Vietnam's revolutionary potential was in the countryside, not among its tiny urban proletariat. Hô Chi Minh was imprisoned in Hong Kong (1931–33).

1931–35. In the troubled times after the smashing of the Nghe-Tinh Soviet, **Trân Van Giau** (1910–69?) worked as secretary of the Indochina Communist Party. When **Ta Thu Tau** (d. 1945), a Trotskyist active in the south, returned to Vietnam from France in 1933, they formed a united front, running for Saigon city office in 1935. He was forced underground in 1938 during a period of repression by the authorities.

1933. The Self-Reliance Literary Group urged all educated Vietnamese to the cause of a simpler writing style, egalitarianism, nationalism, and individualism, and attacked what it deemed outmoded Confucian notions. Its first journal was banned by the French (1936).

1939, May. The **Hoa Hao** sect, a syncretic religion combining various East Asian strains, was founded by **Huynh Phu So** (b. 1919). Early on, it became especially popular in the Mekong River delta as a prognosticating faith.

Aug. 23. The announcement of the Nazi-Soviet nonagression pact led soon to war in Europe and the fall of France the next year. With the installation of the collaborationist Vichy regime, Indochina fell under its nominal control.

1940, June 19. On the eve of the Franco-German armistice (June 22), Japan announced that it would oppose any change in the status quo of the French (Vichy) possessions in Indochina. Japan would thus rule through the colonial institutions already in place. Although this policy violated the "liberator" image Japan painted for itself in Southeast Asia, allegedly freeing those countries from the colonial rule of European imperialists and returning Asia to the Asians, the policy remained in place until it was clear, early in 1945, that Japan was going to be defeated in the war. Many French puppets under the Japanese then switched sides, effectively destroying the colonial structure of rule.

Sept. 23. Japanese troops invaded Lang Son province in northern Vietnam from southern China. Pressure on Hanoi forced the French troops to flee, and in the anarchy that followed, a **Communist-led, anti-French rebellion** in the mountainous region of **Bac Son in northern Vietnam** broke out on Sept. 27.

1941, Feb. With the anti-Fascist united front policy from the previous year, the Bac Son commando units, as they were renamed, were reorganized into the First Company of the National Salvation Army. They were destroyed in an ambush by French troops that September, but they created a tradition and a powerful legacy in the anticolonial fight.

July 21. Although France was obliged to yield effective military control of Indochina to the Japanese, the French Indochinese government still retained some political, economic, and military sovereignty.

During the war years, **Hô Chi Minh,** like his Chinese allies to the north, formed a united front organization known as the **VIÊT MINH** (the shortened name of the Viêt Nam Doc Lap Dong Minh, or the League for the Independence of Vietnam). During the major famine of 1944–45, exacerbated by Japanese military confiscations of goods and destruction of property, the Viet Minh orchestrated the relief work; some 2 million people, however, starved to death. Guerrilla troops were based in a "liberated area" near the Chinese border and were under the command of **VO NGUYÊN GIAP (b. 1912)**, who had been trained under the Chinese Communists in their main anti-Japanese base in Yan'an. In Vietnam, in contrast to other parts of Southeast Asia, the Viêt Minh's anticolonialism meant that they never allowed themselves to be compromised by the Japanese.

1945, Feb. 9. With the liberation of Paris in 1944 and the consequent rise of the de Gaulle faction within the Indochinese regime, the **Japanese army** began to fear the arrival of Allied forces in Indochina, and thus carried out a **coup d'état** in which they attacked French forces in Saigon, Hanoi, and other cities. Two days later, Emperor Bao Dai declared the independence of the Vietnamese Empire. On April 7, Trân Trong Kim (1883–1953) became prime minister and picked a cabinet (April 17). This thoroughly puppet regime collapsed when Japan did in mid- to late August.

Aug. 2. Following the defeat of the Axis powers in Europe and Asia, **Hô Chi Minh,** Nationalist Communist leader of the native resistance to Japan in Tonkin, and Gen. Giap established a provisional government in Hanoi under Hô. **Bao Dai** abdicated as emperor (Aug. 23).

(To p. 1036)

I. THE PACIFIC REGION, 1914–1945

1. THE PACIFIC ISLANDS

(From p. 577)

Until 1939 this was a fairly quiet period in the islands, though in some of the major islands, there were protests over aspects of colonial rule. In 1914, Apolosi Nawaii formed the Viti Company to circumvent the European intermediaries and trading companies. In the 1920s, the nationalist **Mau movement** in Western Samoa reacted against New Zealand paternalism and advocated independence for the island; in 1929, the murder of **District Officer William Bell** on Malaita in the Solomons led to official campaigns of pacification. In the 1920s and 1930s, a series of laws was passed in Papua designed to **"preserve white standards"**; industrial and political protests by Indo-Fijians were carried out against the European-dominated colonial order in the 1920s.

1914. In the early months of World War I, British ships with Australian and New Zealand forces conquered the **German island colonies** south of the equator, while in Oct. 1914 the Japanese took possession of those north of the equator (Marianas, Carolines, and Marshalls). Australia captured German New Guinea. At the war's end, Japan, Australia, and New Zealand favored outright annexation of these territories, but because of American objections, these were finally classified as class C mandates to be governed as an integral part of the administering power.

1918–19. The influenza epidemic wrought havoc in several islands, killing 21 percent of the Samoan population and 6 percent of the indigenous Fijian population. Discontent at New Zealand's handling of the epidemic in Samoa increased resentment against colonial rule and helped the Mau movement.

1919, May 7. The Supreme Council of the Allied Powers assigned **German New Guinea** and the neighboring German islands (Bismarck Archipelago) to Australia; **German Samoa** (Western Samoa) became a New Zealand possession. The rich phosphate island of **Nauru** was given to the British Empire, and by agreement the administration was divided among Great Britain, Australia, and New Zealand. Japan received the **German islands north of the equator** as a mandate. These arrangements were confirmed by the League of Nations on Dec. 17, 1920.

1922, Feb. 6. The **naval treaty** (p. 645) among the five great powers included an agreement to maintain the status quo with regard to fortifications and naval bases in the Pacific (the American and Alaskan coasts excluded).

April. The Japanese government established **civil administration** in the mandated islands (over 1,400 of them, with a total area of only 836 square miles, scattered over an immense area of water). The capital was set up at **Korror Island** (Palau group) with six branches in the major island groups. Indigenous people were involved in subsidiary government positions. The Japanese approached their task of colonial administration seriously and attempted a large-scale program of social and economic development. Economically, the development of the **sugar industry,** under the leadership of **Matsue Haruji,** in the Marianas was the most important. This development brought a considerable influx of Japanese immigrants. By 1935 there were **50,000 Japanese in Micronesia, 40,000 in the Marianas.**

1933, May 27. Japan announced **withdrawal from the League of Nations** (p. 785), to become effective in two years. At the same time, the Japanese government made it clear that it had no intention of abandoning the mandate.

1936, Jan. 1. With the **expiration of the international naval limitation treaties,** the provisions for maintenance of the status quo of fortifications in the Pacific collapsed. Since 1932 there had been rumors of Japanese fortifications and submarine bases, subsequently found to be exaggerated. Australia and New Zealand were very active in coastal preparations, and the U.S. government projected a great scheme of fortifications extending from the Alaskan coast and Aleutian Islands to Midway Island, Guam, and Samoa.

1937. Samuel King, the Hawaiian delegate in the U.S. Congress, introduced a bill to change the status of Hawaii from that of a territory to that of a state. A congressional committee advised against it.

1939. The **Hawaii Equal Rights Commission** was created by an act of the territorial legislature to further claims for equal treatment and to oppose federal legislation discriminatory toward the territory.

1941, Dec. 7. Japanese attack on Pearl Harbor, Hawaii (p. 808)

1942, Jan. Japanese advance in the Philippines and the Dutch East Indies.

May 7. Battle of the Coral Sea blocks possible Japanese access to Australia.

Aug. 7. U.S. landing on the Solomon Islands.

1943, July. Allied offensive in the South Pacific.

Nov. 22. Allied landing on the Gilbert Islands.

1944, Feb. 2. Allied invasion of the Marshall Islands.

Oct. 21–22. Second Battle of the Philippine Sea. Reconquest of the Philippines. *(To p. 1041)*

2. THE PHILIPPINES

(From p. 578)

In this period profound social and economic changes occurred, against a background of American control and constant agitation for independence. The Philippines became more urbanized, and the educated section of the population grew, following the promotion of English-language education by the administration. A large number of Filipinos joined the bureaucracy. National consciousness spread, crossing regional and class lines.

Free trade with the U.S. produced export-led economic growth, but led to dependence on the American market. At the same time, socioeconomic disparities increased, and the political and economic power of the oligarchic Filipino elite was consolidated.

1916. A **council of state** was created, consisting of the governor-general, the presidents of both houses of the legislature, and the heads of executive departments. The U.S. Senate passed the **Jones Act,** which promised independence to the Philippines once there was a stable government. It replaced the Philippine Commission with a 24-member elected senate.

1919. Quezon and other Filipino notables led an independence mission to Washington.

1921. The **Wood-Forbes mission** sent by the U.S. government opposed immediate independence for the Philippines, and advocated increased powers for the governor. The appointment of the conservative **Francis Wood** as governor-general increased tensions between nationalist Filipinos and the U.S. government.

1922. Manuel Quezon replaced Sergio Osmena as leader after a power struggle within the Nacionalista Party.

1923. Quezon attacked Wood for interference in the elected government. Filipinos on the council of state resigned in protest at Wood's behavior, and the legislature unsuccessfully called for his replacement.

1924. Filipino leaders appealed to the U.S. for independence, but this was rejected by President Coolidge. Further requests for independence were made in 1925 and 1926.

1930. Establishment of the Philippine Communist Party, which was outlawed two years later.

1931. The **Os-Rox mission** to Washington led by Sergio Osmena and **Manuel Roxas** proposed that independence be accompanied by the preservation of free trade with the U.S. for ten years and a restriction on Filipino immigration to the United States. Support for Philippine independence increased in the U.S. during the 1920s because free trade with the Philippines was considered unfavorable to American economic interests.

1933, Jan 13. The U.S. Congress passed the **Hare-Hawes-Cutting Bill,** advocating independence after 12 years of transitional government, retention of U.S. military bases, and restrictions on immigration and on Philippine sugar and coconut exports. The Philippine legislature rejected the bill because of the restrictions on exports and immigration, the ill-defined nature of the powers of the U.S. high commissioner, and the retention of U.S. military bases.

1934, March 24. The U.S. government adopted the **Tydings-McDuffie Act,** which proposed gradual introduction of tariffs on Philippine exports to the U.S. in the period leading up to independence. This was reluctantly accepted by the Philippine legislature.

July 30. A commission of 202 members was elected to draft a constitution. Suffrage was to be given to literates over 21 (which meant that only 14 percent of the population was eligible to vote in 1940). The constitution was approved on May 14, 1935.

1935. Sakdalista revolt of activists who thought the new constitution would favor entrenched interests. A plebiscite that ratified the constitution was held a few days after the revolt's suppression. **Quezon was elected president** in June, with Osmena as vice president.

A **COMMONWEALTH GOVERNMENT** established in November. The U.S. retained control of currency and foreign relations, including defense. The U.S. and the Philippines negotiated the formation of a national army, with the U.S. seeking to preserve its security interests in Asia.

1937. The Communist Party legalized again, merging with the Socialist Party in the following year. **Tagalog made the national language.** Formation of the **Partido Nacionalista,** a fusion of the parties of Osmena and Quezon.

1938, Nov. 8. Quezon reelected despite criticism of his dictatorial practices. Calls for immediate independence declined, partly because of fear of Japanese expansionism.

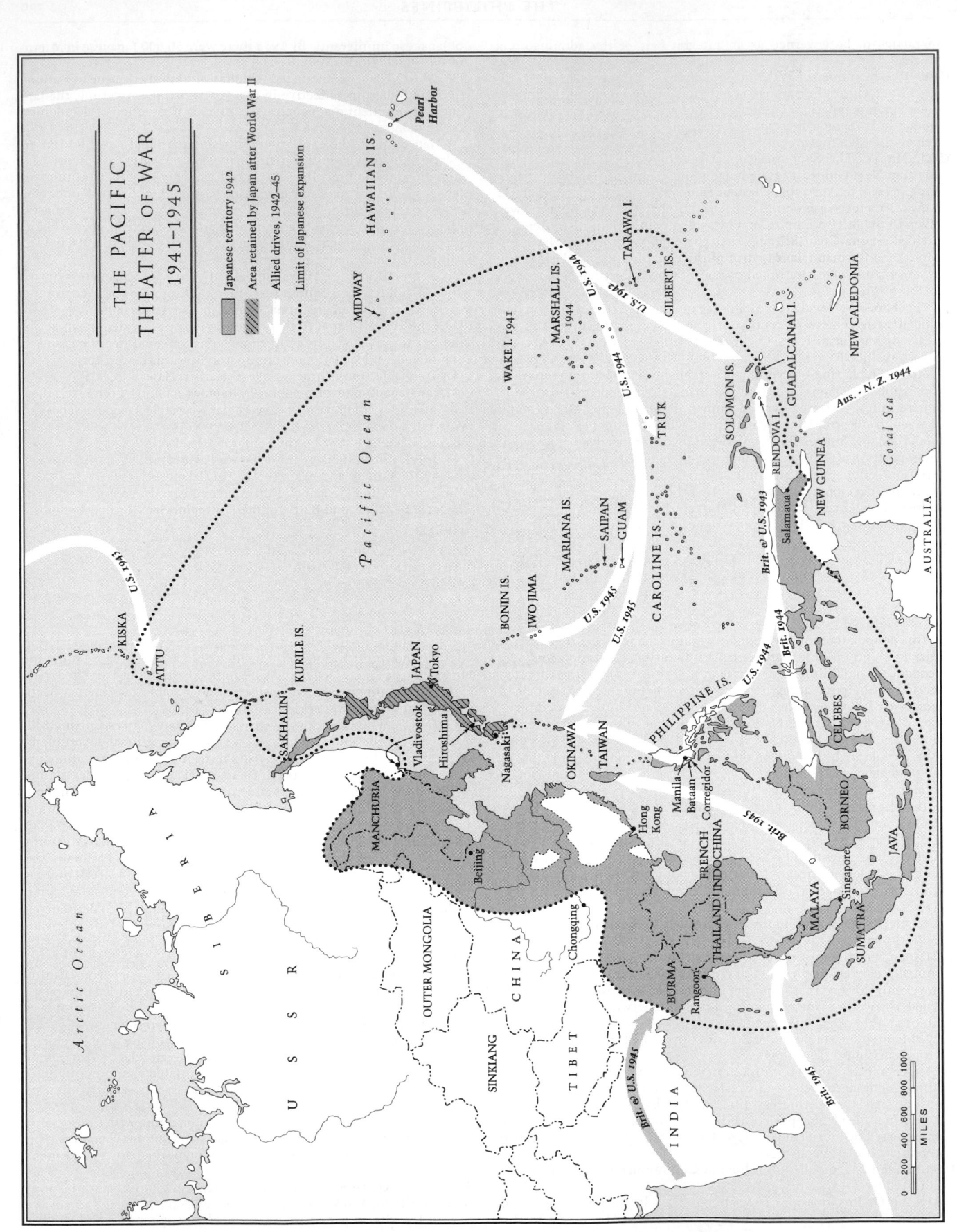

THE PACIFIC
THEATER OF WAR
1941–1945

Japanese territory 1942

Area retained by Japan after World War II

Allied drives, 1942–45

Limit of Japanese expansion

Pearl Harbor

HAWAIIAN IS.

MIDWAY

TARAWA I.

GILBERT IS.

U.S. 1942

MARSHALL IS.
1944

U.S. 1944

WAKE I. 1941

NEW CALEDONIA

GUADALCANAL I.

RENDOVA I.

SOLOMON IS.

Aus. - N. Z. 1944

Coral Sea

TRUK

U.S. 1944

Pacific Ocean

CAROLINE IS.

Brit. & U.S. 1943

Salamaua

NEW GUINEA

AUSTRALIA

MARIANA IS.

SAIPAN

GUAM

U.S. 1945

BONIN IS.

IWO JIMA

U.S. 1943

Brit. 1944

KISKA

U.S. 1943

ATTU

KURILE IS.

SAKHALIN

JAPAN
Tokyo

Vladivostok

Hiroshima

Nagasaki

OKINAWA

TAIWAN

PHILIPPINE IS.

U.S. 1944

CELEBES

BORNEO

JAVA

Manila

Bataan

Corregidor

Hong
Kong

FRENCH
INDOCHINA

Brit. 1945

MALAYA

Singapore

SUMATRA

Arctic Ocean

S I B E R I A

MANCHURIA

Beijing

U S S R

OUTER MONGOLIA

SINKIANG

C H I N A

Chongqing

T I B E T

I N D I A

BURMA

Rangoon

THAILAND

Brit. & U.S. 1945

Brit. 1945

0   200   400   600   800   1000
MILES

1939. Suffrage extended to women.

1941. Constitution amended to establish a bicameral system. The presidential term was extended to permit two terms of four years, allowing Quezon to hold on to power.

Dec. 8. Japan attacked the Philippines.

1942, Jan. 2. The Japanese took Manila.

Quezon and Osmena were evacuated from the Philippines and formed a government in exile. Most of the political elite joined the Japanese-sponsored government, while the majority of the population supported the guerrilla resistance to the Japanese.

1944. Quezon died in the U.S. in August. American troops landed in the Philippines in October. *(To p. 1042)*

3. AUSTRALIA

(From p. 583)

The two world wars were Australia's largest national enterprises, and were fought at great cost in lives and suffering. The interwar period (1918–39) was stagnant economically, troughing in the Great Depression of 1929–32, when perhaps a third of Australian men were out of work. Confidence in Australia's long-term prosperity was not shaken. The economy industrialized further, but depended heavily on agriculture and mining, with 35 percent of the nation's export income up to 1950 generated by sheep grazing.

The outbreak of World War I revealed all Australian parties united in loyalty to the mother country and in readiness to contribute to its defense. During the war Australia sent 331,000 men overseas, who took a prominent part in the Dardanelles campaign, the Palestine campaign, and the fighting in France (after 1916). In May 1918 the five Australian divisions in France were organized as an **Australian army corps,** under the command of **Sir John Monash,** an Australian. The war was financed chiefly by borrowing and was accompanied, in Australia as elsewhere, by a great extension of government control, economic as well as political. Rising prices together with a decline in real wages led to much **labor unrest** and a very extensive strike in Aug.–Sept. 1917. The failure of this strike resulted in stricter organization of the trade unions and greater concentration on economic rather than political aims. In the military field the Australian government took advantage of the opportunity to seize the German island colonies south of the equator.

1915. Construction of **major steel mill** by BHP, Australia's largest company for decades.

April 25. Australian and New Zealand Army Corps (**ANZAC**) landed on Gallipoli Peninsula, Turkey. The place was soon called Anzac Cove, and the day Anzac Day. In the 1920s, April 25 was made a public holiday, and many Australians consider it Australia's most important national day. Anzac Cove was evacuated in Dec. 1915, and the Anzacs transferred to France or Egypt.

Oct. 27. William M. Hughes as prime minister and leader of the Labour Party. Hughes became the embodiment of Australian and British patriotism, and, after a visit to England in the summer of 1916, he began to advocate **conscription** of men for service overseas. The suggestion roused much opposition.

1916, Oct. 28. Conscription was defeated by a narrow margin in a popular referendum. The result was an open **rift in the Labour Party,** which ejected Hughes and several of his colleagues. The cabinet was reconstructed.

1917, Feb. 17. Hughes organized a **national war government,** relying on the new **Nationalist Party,** which was composed of Labour leaders who followed Hughes and by a large section of the Liberal opposition. The new party received a popular mandate in the elections of May 5.

Oct. 17. Completion of the **railway from Port Augusta to Kalgoorlie,** thus first attaching Western Australia by rail to the other states.

In order to meet the steady decline in voluntary enlistment, the prime minister, unable to enforce conscription by parliamentary action, decided to refer the matter once more to popular vote.

Dec. 20. Conscription was again defeated by referendum. Through the exertions of influential leaders voluntary enlistment was increased to some extent, but not enough to satisfy Hughes and his associates. In the summer of 1918 Hughes went to England and in the spring of 1919 took part in the Paris Peace Conference. There, with the support of the other Dominion statesmen, he succeeded in excluding from the covenant of the League of Nations any recognition of the principle of race equality. At the same time he intervened actively in the problem of the German colonies.

1919, May 7. THE SUPREME COUNCIL ASSIGNED TO AUSTRALIA

THE MANDATE FOR THE GERMAN COLONIES SOUTH OF THE EQUATOR, excepting Nauru Island and Samoa (which went to New Zealand). This arrangement was confirmed by the League on Dec. 17, 1920. By agreement with Britain and New Zealand (July 2, 1919), Australia was given the administration of Nauru Island, which the three held together as mandatories.

Dec. 10. Sir Ross Smith arrived at Port Darwin by air, completing the flight from England in 27 days.

Dec. 23. The elections resulted in a victory for the Nationalist Party and the Hughes government continued in power.

1920. In a famous decision (**Engineers' case**) the Australian high court gave the Commonwealth Conciliation and Arbitration Court authority to regulate the conditions of labor of state employees.

Jan. 10. Australia became an original member of the League of Nations with the full status of an independent nation.

1921, Dec. 15. Adoption of a higher tariff, chiefly to protect the industries that had been born of the war. All parties were more or less united on the tariff issue.

1922. By the **Empire Settlement Act,** the British government undertook to assist in the promotion of emigration to Australia and in the settlement of emigrants on the land.

Dec. 10. The elections resulted in 27 seats for the Nationalist Party, 29 for Labour, and 14 for the **Country Party** (founded 1919), led by **Earle Page** and representing farmers. The Country Party held the balance of power and was hostile to Hughes.

1923, Feb. 3. Resignation of the Hughes government forced by the Country Party. The Nationalist Party began to disintegrate.

Feb. 9. Stanley Bruce, together with Page, formed a coalition cabinet composed of Nationalists and Country Party representatives.

1925, Sept. 23. A new immigration restriction act gave the governor-general authority to prohibit the entrance of aliens of any specified nationality, class, race, or occupation, either for economic or racial reasons. This act was never systematically applied, but it made possible restriction of Italian immigration, which had begun to arouse objections, especially among the labor groups.

1926. The **Northern Territory was divided** along 20° S.L. into **Northern Australia** and **Central Australia.** The division was repealed in 1921.

1927, May 9. Parliament House was officially opened at **Canberra.** Thus far Parliament had sat at Melbourne while numerous schemes for the new capital were under debate. In a competition among architects, **Walter B. Griffin** of Chicago received first prize, and his plan became the basis for the new city.

June 8. Financial agreement between the Commonwealth government and the state governments, following years of dispute concerning continued federal support to the states (the federal government having gradually appropriated most of the best springs of revenue).

1928, June 9. Capt. Charles Kingsford-Smith arrived at Brisbane after his trans-Pacific flight from California.

1929, Oct. 12. The Labour Party won in the elections.

Oct. 22. James H. Scullin formed a Labour cabinet. For the most part Labour had remained moderate in its policy, though in 1921 the party had adopted a program of socialization, and in 1927 the Council of Trade Unions had been organized as a left-wing group associated with Moscow.

1930–36. The **Great Depression** made itself acutely felt in Australia, where the government tried to combat it by drastic economy and other obvious devices. The rising price of gold and (after 1933) of wool, however, enabled Australia to recover more readily than many other countries.

1931. Foundation of the **United Australia Party,** composed of a number of dissident Labourites together with remnants of the Nationalist Party. The leader of the group was **Joseph A. Lyons.**

Dec. 19. The Labour Party was badly defeated in the elections, and a new **Lyons cabinet** was formed.

1932. The **Financial Agreement Enforcement Act** further strengthened the power of the federal government as against that of the states.

March 19. The Sydney Harbour Bridge was opened.

May 13. In New South Wales, the governor dismissed the Labour premier, John Thomas Lang.

July 1. The Commonwealth government established the Australian Broadcasting Commission (ABC).

Nov. 18. The notorious "bodyline" cricket tests between Australia and England began in Melbourne. "Bodyline" was an English tactic of bowling fast at the batsman's body, designed to curb the brilliant batting of Australia's Don Bradman.

1933, April 8. Western Australia voted 2–1 to secede from the commonwealth. Together with South Australia and Tasmania, the other agricultural states, Western Australia had long protested against the "incidence of federation" and had demanded abatement of taxes or some form of federal relief. The government thereupon appointed a **grants commission** to investigate the claims of aggrieved states and to decide on compensation. Meanwhile (1934, March) Western Australia sent a petition to the king asking for legislation to effect secession. The British Parliament, however, refused to accept the petition without the previous approval of the Australian people as a whole.

May 26. The Australian government assumed authority over about one-third of the Antarctic continent (an area roughly the size of Australia itself).

1934, Nov. 9. The Lyons cabinet was replaced by a **Lyons-Page combination,** representing a coalition between the United Australia Party and the Country Party.

Dec. 8. Inauguration of **weekly airmail service** between England and Australia.

1936–45. Baron Gowrie, governor-general.

1936, May 23. A new and **higher tariff** was introduced, to replace the more modest tariff of 1932. The new schedule led to considerable **friction with Japan,** whose textiles were hard hit, but by an agreement of Dec. 27 the Australian government agreed to take as many Japanese textile products as in 1934, in return for Japanese purchase of a specified amount of Australian wool.

1937, Oct. 23. The **Lyons-Page government** won a sound victory in the elections (United Australia Party 28 seats; Country Party 17; Labour 29). The outstanding issue of the elections was the **defense problem,** the government advancing a program of naval construction, Labour calling for emphasis on air armaments and less dependence on Great Britain. Establishment of the first airplane factory. Appointment of an Australian counselor at the British embassy in Washington.

1939, April 7. Death of Lyons, who was succeeded by Sir Earle Page.

April 24. Robert G. Menzies formed a new government.

Sept. 3. When **Britain declared war on Germany,** Australia unhesitatingly joined the mother country and arranged for assistance of all kinds.

1940–45. Australian troops fought in the Middle East, Greece, and North Africa, notably at Tobruk and El Alamein, and from 1942 in Malaya and New Guinea, notably on the Kokoda Track and along the New Guinea north coast. Australian aircrews served in the Pacific and in Europe, especially in Bomber Command, in which over 5,000 Australians died. Australia's war dead totaled 19,000 (World War I, 63,000).

(To p. 1044)

4. NEW ZEALAND

(From p. 585)

In the aftermath of World War I, government investment and tariff protection strengthened agriculture, which came to dominate the economy. An economic regime founded on the export of wool, meat, and dairy produce to Britain emerged. Partly as a result of this dependency, the global economic crisis in the 1930s affected New Zealand severely. In response to the depression, the Labour government of 1935 established one of the most comprehensive welfare programs in the non-Communist world.

Despite continuing alienation of land, the Maori population began to increase, and there were modest improvements in Maori health and socioeconomic position. A number of Maori leaders joined the government or were active in other areas of national politics. New Zealand's political ties to Britain remained strong, reflected in the large numbers of New Zealand troops participating in World War I. New Zealand continued to practice petty imperialism in the South Pacific through the period, violently suppressing the independence movement in Samoa in the 1920s. New Zealand sent 117,000 men overseas in World War I, most of whom were volunteers. New Zealand troops fought in Turkey, Palestine, and France, often in company with Australians. Casualties were very high. Participation in World War II was also extensive.

1914. New Zealand annexed Samoa from Germany (p. 788).

1915. New Zealand and Australian troops **(ANZACs)** participated in the ill-fated **Gallipoli campaign.** This became a symbol of **emergent nationalism.**

1916. The Maori prophet **Rua Kenana** was arrested for sedition. **Formation of New Zealand Labour Party by socialists and trade unionists.** Heated political debate took place over the issue of conscription, which was opposed by the Waikato tribes and by the Labour Party.

1918. Foundation of **Ratana** church by the Maori prophet **Tahupotiki Wiremu Ratana.** This fusion of Maori and Christian beliefs appealed to many Maori in the lower socioeconomic stratum. **Samoa was given to New Zealand as a trust territory of the League of Nations.**

1919. The conservative **Reform** government won a resounding victory

in the general election. The subsequent elections in the 1920s were all characterized by competition among the three parties of Reform, Liberal (later United), and Labour. Women gained the right to stand for Parliament.

Throughout the 1920s the government provided assistance to farmers through credit and price controls. The establishment of a dairy board (1923) helped in the marketing of dairy products.

1925. Election of a Reform Party government under **Gordon Coates.** The government engaged in a program of public works construction, and borrowed heavily overseas.

1928. The United Party, formed out of the remains of the Liberals, won the election. Its leader, **Joseph Ward,** promised extensive borrowing for public works.

1929. New Zealand troops attempted to suppress the nationalistic **Mau** movement in Samoa, killing a number of its leaders.

New Zealand suffered severely from **the depression,** being essentially a producer of primary materials. The unemployed were compelled to do laboring work in return for government compensation.

1931. A **coalition government** was formed from the Reform and United Parties. Prime Minister Coates reduced civil service salaries and introduced legislation to allow the arbitration court to cut wages.

1932. Riots involving unemployed people occurred in each of the four main cities.

The first Ratana member of Parliament was elected, beginning the Ratana dominance over the Maori seats. Ratana established a political alliance with the Labour Party. The government made arbitration in industrial negotiations voluntary, but kept conciliation compulsory, so that unions could be forced to accept employers' terms. This weakened union power. Tariffs on New Zealand exports to Britain worsened the economic situation.

1935, Nov. 27. ELECTION OF THE FIRST LABOUR GOVERNMENT under Michael Joseph Savage. Savage became one of the best-loved prime ministers in New Zealand history.

Expansion of social welfare provisions and state support for savings and loans, including mortgages for home purchases. Government controls in banking and internal transportation increased.

1936. Wage rates cut during the depression **were restored,** working hours limited, and **minimum pay set.** Union membership became compulsory. The **Reserve Bank** was **nationalized,** ensuring low-interest loans for national development schemes. The government undertook to buy farm produce at a guaranteed price, with deficits being made up from Reserve Bank credits. The government undertook an extensive program of **public housing construction.**

1937, May 12. Foundation of the National Party, a merger of the old Reform and United Parties. It opposed the government's socialistic program, favoring private enterprise.

1938. Universal free health care established. National superannuation scheme was introduced.

Oct. 15. Labour won with a convincing majority in elections. Foreign exchange and import controls were introduced which remained in place until the 1980s.

1939, Sept. 3. New Zealand supported Britain's declaration of war. In 1940 Savage died and was replaced by **Peter Fraser.** The war enabled the Labour government to negotiate favorable export arrangements for New Zealand's agricultural products. New Zealand troops, including a **Maori battalion** that became a focus for Maori pride, fought mainly in Europe and the Middle East. A war cabinet containing ministers from both parties administered the country. *(To p. 1045)*

J. AFRICA, 1914–1945

1. OVERVIEW

(From p. 587)

The 30 years between World War I and the end of World War II represented simultaneously **the high-water mark of colonialism in Africa and its dissolution.** Even though formal decolonization did not begin until 1956, the **roots of African independence** were planted during this period.

Looking back at the period from military conquest to 1914, European colonial officials could point to significant but limited accomplishments. Colonial regimes had defeated their African political opponents, suppressed the armed resistance movements, installed rudimentary administrations, and constructed railways and harbors. Despite the promises of tropical bounty awaiting colonial entrepreneurs, metropolitan countries could point to few clear economic advantages their colonies provided. Nor did Africans unequivocally embrace European cultural institutions, including missionary Christianity. Islam seemed to be making more progress in northeastern and West Africa than Christianity. The outbreak of World War I arrested the development of colonial administrations even as African manpower, mineral, and agricultural resources became crucial to metropolitan war economies. The war made clear just how important colonies actually were.

Military campaigns took place where Germany had colonies (p. 662): in Togo, Cameroon, Southwest Africa, and East Africa. The Germans in Togo and Cameroon were quickly defeated. The Germans in Southwest Africa surrendered to a British imperial army commanded by the South African general Smuts. Fighting in East Africa was longer and bloodier, although relatively few European troops were killed in the fighting. Many more were incapacitated and slain by disease.

Few Africans actually fought. Most Africans in East Africa were recruited into the carrier corps. Without adequate roads, it fell upon Africans to carry the vast military and logistical arsenal for the troops. Officially, the British reported that 44,991 recruits in the carrier corps died, compared with 3,500 imperial troops who died from battlefield wounds and 6,500 from disease. The mortality rate for Africans in the carrier corps was roughly 2 percent per month; an additional 15 percent were incapacitated by disease and poor nutrition each month. At least one historian of East Africa estimated that **between 200,000 and 300,000 Africans died** directly or indirectly because of the military campaigns in East Africa as their crops and herds were requisitioned and as their male kinsmen were forcibly recruited. Knowing what was in store for them, it is not surprising that as European military recruiters approached their villages, Africans raced off to the bush to hide.

Fighting was limited in West Africa, but recruitment was widespread, especially by the French. All able-bodied men were liable for recruitment into the French military service. In 1915 and 1916, **recruitment revolts** broke out in many French West African colonies. The black Senegalese representative to the French National Assembly, Blaise Diagne, helped recruit Africans for the war effort, but only in exchange for symbolic gains (he rode in the same railway car as the governor-general) and legal ones (specific voting and religious rights were clarified). Although the Germans were defeated and the recruitment revolts suppressed, the experience unleashed significant social, political, and cultural changes.

For those who survived, the **experience of World War I was important and lasting.** Africans saw that Europeans were not invincible. Recruitment brought Africans from a great number of different ethnic groups and backgrounds together; they turned to English, French, Portuguese, Lingala, and Swahili as **common languages.** Africans participated in **new organizations,** which provided models for future nationalist mobilization. Moreover, the defeat of Germany and the subsequent mandating of German colonies to European victors provided **opportunities for Africans with Western literacy** to fill administrative positions left vacant. And finally, the politics surrounding the Treaty of Versailles introduced two important ideas into the language of emergent African nationalism. The first was derived from President Woodrow Wilson's Fourteen Points and spoke of **"self-determination."** Although the idea was not intended for colonized Africans, Africans and Pan-Africanists would use it as a lever against colonial rule. The second came from the League of Nations mandate terms, which provided for **"trusteeship,"** not colonial dominion. Africans would see this term as providing them with important political and economic rights, as well as underscoring the temporary nature of the colonial rule.

The role of African manpower and natural resources during the war demonstrated the importance of African colonies. During the interwar years, most European colonies embarked on **ambitious economic development programs,** which were fueled by rapidly rising commodity prices. During this period, the de facto division of African colonies into **four main economic clusters** became clear: colonies where African peasants were predominant (mostly West Africa), colonies where agricultural concession companies predominated (mostly Central Africa), colonies where mining capital dominated (mostly southern Africa), and colonies of white settlement (mostly East, Central, and southern Africa). Several colonies shared two or more of these economic orientations, but the impact of colonialism on African societies was shaped more by these broad economic orientations than by differences in colonial administrative policy.

The practical differences between **direct rule,** where European colonial officials ruled over administrative districts, and **indirect rule,** where "indigenous authorities" were empowered to rule with European officials gently modernizing "traditions," have been exaggerated. Direct rule has been associated with the French and indirect rule with the British, although all colonial powers employed both methods and **all relied on African collaboration in order to administer as cheaply as possible.**

There were, nonetheless, important outcomes to these different styles of colonial rule. Elevated to the level of formal colonial policy by Frederick Lugard and applied vigorously to Nigeria, indirect rule **heightened ethnic differences**, since indigenous authorities were to emerge from identifiable communities. If, as in the case of the Igbo, there were no identifiable indigenous rulers, the British simply appointed willing collaborators and gave them a "warrant" to rule. Customs were invented to demonstrate the age-old practices of these indigenous authorities. Empowering indigenous authorities led to significant abuses of power, as chiefs used their positions to accumulate wealth and power. Because even those practicing direct administration needed African collaborators, the French, Belgians, and Portuguese appointed provincial chiefs to assist them. Provincial chiefs also used their positions to enhance their power to accumulate wealth. The **invention of tradition** in colonial Africa helped undergird the power of African chiefs to determine access to agricultural resources and to increase the power of older men over both women and younger men.

Younger men and women often resisted the power of chiefs and elderly men. Young men migrated to cities, to the mines, and to other agricultural regions. Many went in search of an independent income in order to establish their own households. If women could not escape their "arranged" first marriages, divorce and subsequent marriages, especially among Muslims, often provided women with more choice regarding their spouses. Some women also fled to the emerging urban centers and became prostitutes. Others fled to the mission communities, where marriage among Christian converts occasionally provided greater choice.

Some women responded collectively to what they considered the erosion of their customary rights. In 1929, Igbo women in southeastern Nigeria rose up against the appointed warrant chiefs and against British colonial officials in **protest against the erosion of women's secret societies** (the British banned all secret societies, although many were indeed the "indigenous authorities") and the proposed tax on women's property. The women of Aba (p. 797) used well-established techniques to express their anger, including bawdy songs and dances. When they sang and danced before the British headquarters, officials panicked, troops were brought in, and many African women were martyred. In response to these events, the British held an inquiry and appointed anthropologists to study Nigerian societies more thoroughly.

Among the most significant social and cultural changes to occur during this period were the **development of African nationalism and Pan-Africanism, the expansion of Western education, and the growth of cities.** Pan-Africanism was a movement born in the African diaspora of the New World. As a political movement, it was a coalition of a wide variety of African-American and later African nationalist groups. They shared a vision of a great African homeland, but little else. Nonetheless, Pan-Africanist political agitation influenced a variety of nationalist groups in colonial Africa, ranging from youth associations, protonationalist associations (such as the South African Native Peoples Congress), labor unions, and literary self-help societies, which drew from Pan-Africanist rhetorical models for the empowerment of colonized African peoples. These groups sought gradual, political reforms within the context of colonialism. Others, such as the influen-

tial **Négritude** movement formed in Paris by French-speaking African and Afro-Caribbean intellectuals, sought cultural recognition and presented only vague political goals.

Collective action by railway workers and dock workers, who engaged in a series of strikes in the 1920s and 1930s, had an important impact in the continent. Influenced by the Comintern (p. 713) and by metropolitan socialist parties, African workers began to understand and exercise their power. Strikes along the major rail arteries and at the harbors had the potential to strangle colonial economies. So too did the **African cocoa planters** of Ghana, whose supply holdups in 1937 caused a crisis in the Gold Coast economy and led to colonial reassessment of commodity markets. In response, the British colonies established commodity marketing boards, which acted as sole buyers of commodities, in an effort to even out the wide fluctuations in commodity prices. Although intended to serve the interests of producers, these commodity boards evolved into powerful bureaucracies controlling vast sums of money. Other Africans turned to African independent churches as a means of expressing their religious and nationalist sentiments. Cities expanded dramatically during this period; the **urban areas provided fertile ground for the establishment of new forms of community.**

The expansion of African nationalism coincided with the **consolidation of white settler domination** in South Africa, Southern Rhodesia, Kenya, Angola, and Mozambique. In the 1920s and 1930s white settlers exerted increasing control over the affairs of their colonies through the grant of "responsible government" to British settlers. British settlers used their power to impose harsh economic and political restrictions on Africans, which in turn only fueled African nationalist sentiments. In the Portuguese colonies, changes in metropolitan politics were felt as a second colonial occupation under a much more interventionist colonial development policy.

The **Great Depression** profoundly affected world commodity markets and African social life. The continent's role as a producer of primary agricultural and mineral resources made Africans especially vulnerable to economic deceleration. Misery stalked the cities and rural villages alike. In the late 1930s, mobilization for another war stimulated African commodity markets and ushered in a sustained period of economic growth. As before, Africa continued to produce agricultural and mineral resources that were largely processed in Europe. The only exception was in South Africa, where manufacturing and secondary processing helped create a wide industrial base.

In contrast with World War I, when fighting occurred in many parts of sub-Saharan Africa, fighting during World War II was limited to the Horn of Africa. Most Africans participated in the war effort through their agricultural and mining labor. Africans were also recruited for the war overseas. In West Africa, Charles de Gaulle rewarded Africans for their support of the Free French by introducing a series of **political reforms** agreed upon at the 1944 Brazzaville meeting. In British West Africa, efforts were made to introduce constitutional changes permitting greater representation of Africans in the legislative councils. However, colonial governments controlled by white settlers imposed ever harsher laws to prevent the expression of African political grievances and to hinder African economic progress. (To p. 1046)

2. REGIONS

a. SUDANIC WEST AND CENTRAL AFRICA

(From p. 590)

1913–14. The **drought** in the *sahel* devastated local communities. Thousands died in the middle Niger region; those who survived saw their livestock herds largely destroyed. French colonial policies stirred up resentment during the drought, and contributed to armed unrest beginning in 1915.

1914–16. World War I military movements in Togo and Cameroon. In Aug. 1914 the Germans administering Togo retreated northward from the coast in the face of advancing French and British troops. Shortly thereafter the **Germans surrendered,** leaving France and Britain in control of Togo. The military conflict in Cameroon was more prolonged,

lasting from 1914 to 1916. The Germans finally fled Cameroon for Spanish Guinea in Feb. 1916. In March 1916 the French and British agreed to the **partition of Cameroon for administrative purposes.**

1915–17. French efforts to **recruit Africans for service during World War I** led to rebellions in French West Africa. In order to avoid conscription, many Africans fled toward the Gambia, Portuguese Guinea, Sierra Leone, Liberia, and the Gold Coast. Elsewhere, armed rebellions broke out. In 1915 the Bambara staged an anticonscription revolt; another rebellion occurred in the western Volta region. In 1916 Africans staged a popular revolt in northern Dahomey. The French suppressed the revolts by force. However, with the assistance of **Blaise Diagne, the Senegalese African member of the French National Assembly,** larger numbers of Africans joined the French armed forces.

1916–17. The Tuareg living in Air (in present-day Niger) retained their independence up until the First World War. In 1916 the **Tuareg chief Kawsen ag Muhammad** and his followers rebelled against the French presence in their territory, laying siege to the French fort at Agades. Bitter reprisals followed. Although the French captured and executed Kawsen in 1919, instability in the region continued into the early 1930s.

1917. Returning African soldiers formed local sections of the League for the Rights of Man to protest colonialism. The League for the Rights of Man was particularly active in Guinea and Gabon, where French West African ex-soldiers pressed for the establishment of a new dispensation. Demobilized African soldiers would play a leading role in anticolonial movements in the years to come.

1919. The French reorganized the West African colonies, creating the colony of **Upper Volta.**

1920. Lycée Faidherbe, a secondary school, founded in St.-Louis, Senegal.

1921. Katsina Training College founded.

1924. Polo introduced into Katsina, becoming the sport of the Northern elite.

1925. Africans elected members of the *conseils administratives* in the French colonies of Soudan, Guinea, Ivory Coast, and Dahomey.

1928. First **school for girls** in Northern Nigeria opened in Ilorin.

1930. Elementary Training College for Teachers established in Katsina.

1931–34. Numerous small **risings throughout the southern Sahara** against the French.

1934–35. Branches of French **Social and Labor Parties** established in Senegal.

1936. First **airmail** service between London and Kano introduced.

1938. Twenty thousand troops in French West Africa recruited for the war effort. Seven thousand were sent to France to augment the 18,000 regular *tirailleurs* troops stationed in West Africa and the 29,000 already in France.

French West African officials first recognized African trade unions in 1937. The following year, African **railway workers at Thies staged a strike** on the Dakar-Niger line. Authorities reacted by calling in French troops to crush the strike. The violence that followed left six dead and at least 30 wounded.

1940. For military service **130,000** French West Africans were recruited.

German occupation of France and the establishment of the Vichy government fractured colonial political alliances. Dakar originally sided with Vichy.

Anglo–Free French expedition to Dakar failed.

July 8. The **British** attacked battleship *Richelieu* in Dakar Harbor.

Nov. 26. Niger and Chad declared themselves in favor of the Free French.

1941. Second Anglo–Free French expedition to Dakar also failed.

1942. All of **French West Africa broke with Vichy** and sided with the Allies. *(To p. 1049)*

b. FOREST WEST AFRICA

(From p. 592)

1901–14. Development of indirect rule as British colonial policy. **Sir Frederick Lugard** developed indirect rule in Northern Nigeria while serving as British high commissioner there from 1901 to 1906. Lugard believed that the British could best govern Africa through indigenous authorities. Under Lugard's system, British authorities delegated to African chiefs the responsibilities of law enforcement, labor recruitment, and tax collection. In principle, British colonial officials sought to modernize "traditional" African political institutions by gradually modifying their practices. In practice, indirect rule led to conflict over traditions and favored Africans loyal to the colonial rulers. Indirect rule was continued in Northern Nigeria following Lugard's departure, and was eventually adopted in other British colonies in West Africa, such as Southern Nigeria, the Gold Coast, Sierra Leone, and the Gambia. In one form or another, indirect rule was adapted throughout British-controlled Africa. Variations of this policy were applied by all European colonial powers as a way of reducing the costs of administration.

1905–39. EXPORTS FROM AFRICA INCREASED BY APPROXIMATELY FIVE TIMES IN VALUE AND VOLUME. Among the most important export crops in forest West Africa were **coffee, cocoa, and peanuts.** The Ivory Coast successfully produced and exported forest-grown coffee. The Gold Coast became one of the leading suppliers of cocoa, producing almost half the world's supply by 1925. Revenue from cocoa exports made the Gold Coast the wealthiest colony in tropical Africa.

1909. The coal discovered at Udi in eastern Nigeria in 1909 proved to be the only deposit of its kind in West Africa. The British colonial government built a railway to link the coal works to export facilities at Port Harcourt on the coast.

1911–13. In 1911 both colonial officials and the British Cotton Growing Association expected the Nigeria railway to boost dramatically the profitability of **cotton cultivation in central Hausaland. But Hausa farmers found peanut cultivation more attractive.** Their decision to concentrate on peanuts—which were edible and easier to grow than cotton—took the British by surprise and demonstrated how quickly Africans responded to economic opportunities and how little colonial powers actually controlled Africans' economic lives. Nigerian peanut exports rose from under 2,000 tons before 1911 to almost 20,000 tons in 1913.

1914, Jan. Lugard, who was recalled to Nigeria in 1912, managed the amalgamation of the colonies of Northern and Southern Nigeria and the Nigerian Protectorates into one colony, Nigeria. Lugard became governor-general.

1918–21. Massive **outbreak of influenza** with very high mortality.

1919. Following the First World War, Germany's African colonies became mandates of the **League of Nations.** In May 1919 **Togo** was declared a mandate and transferred to the French for administrative purposes. France obtained the portion of **Cameroon** that had been ceded to the Germans in 1911; the rest was transferred to Britain.

1920s–1930s. Expansion of the **African Christian independent churches.** Throughout sub-Saharan Africa, Africans flocked to breakaway, often ecstatic Christian movements. Yoruba Anglicans began to form independent prayer groups as early as 1918. These prayer groups, known as *aladura*, proliferated in the 1920s and 1930s. The *aladura* groups sought to adapt Christianity to African traditional beliefs and practices. They conducted their own healing sessions and baptisms, built their own churches, and developed their own liturgies. They helped spread Christianity into areas untouched by European missionaries, who strongly disapproved of their activities. First **Church of the Lord (Aladura)** founded at Ogere, Western Nigeria, c. 1930.

1920. National Congress of British West Africa founded in Accra.

1921. Gold Coast cocoa holdup. When the price for Gold Coast cocoa dropped sharply in 1920, African farmers suddenly found themselves in debt and unable to obtain credit. They reacted by staging a "holdup" in 1921. Their refusal to deliver their produce to market led to an eventual rise in the cocoa price and an end to the boycott. The holdup strategy thus provided a way for African farmers to defend their interests in a collective manner. In the Gold Coast, withholding cocoa provided a defense against international market forces and the collusion among expatriate cocoa exporters.

Establishment of a **legislative council** in Nigeria with some elected members.

1922. Achimoto College founded near Accra.

1923–25. The onset of Gov. Clifford's administration in Nigeria in 1921 led to the introduction of major **new constitutional reforms.** Clifford established a legislative council in 1923, thus giving Nigerians **electoral representation** for the first time. The establishment of legislative councils followed in Sierra Leone in 1924 and in the Gold Coast in 1925. In each of these colonies, the franchise was limited to wealthy Africans residing in urban centers; the percentage of Africans eligible to vote was very small. Traditional leaders and chiefs, handpicked by the colonial administration, outnumbered elected members of the legislative councils as well. The African elite eventually became disillusioned with the ineffectiveness of the "legco" system.

1925. A new **constitution** for the Gold Coast, implemented along the Clifford model. The Prince of Wales visited Nigeria.

1926. Sierra Leone railway strike. British West Africa was the scene of an increasing number of strikes and protests following World War I. The 1926 strike called by railway workers in Sierra Leone resulted in considerable violence. African workers called the strike to protest

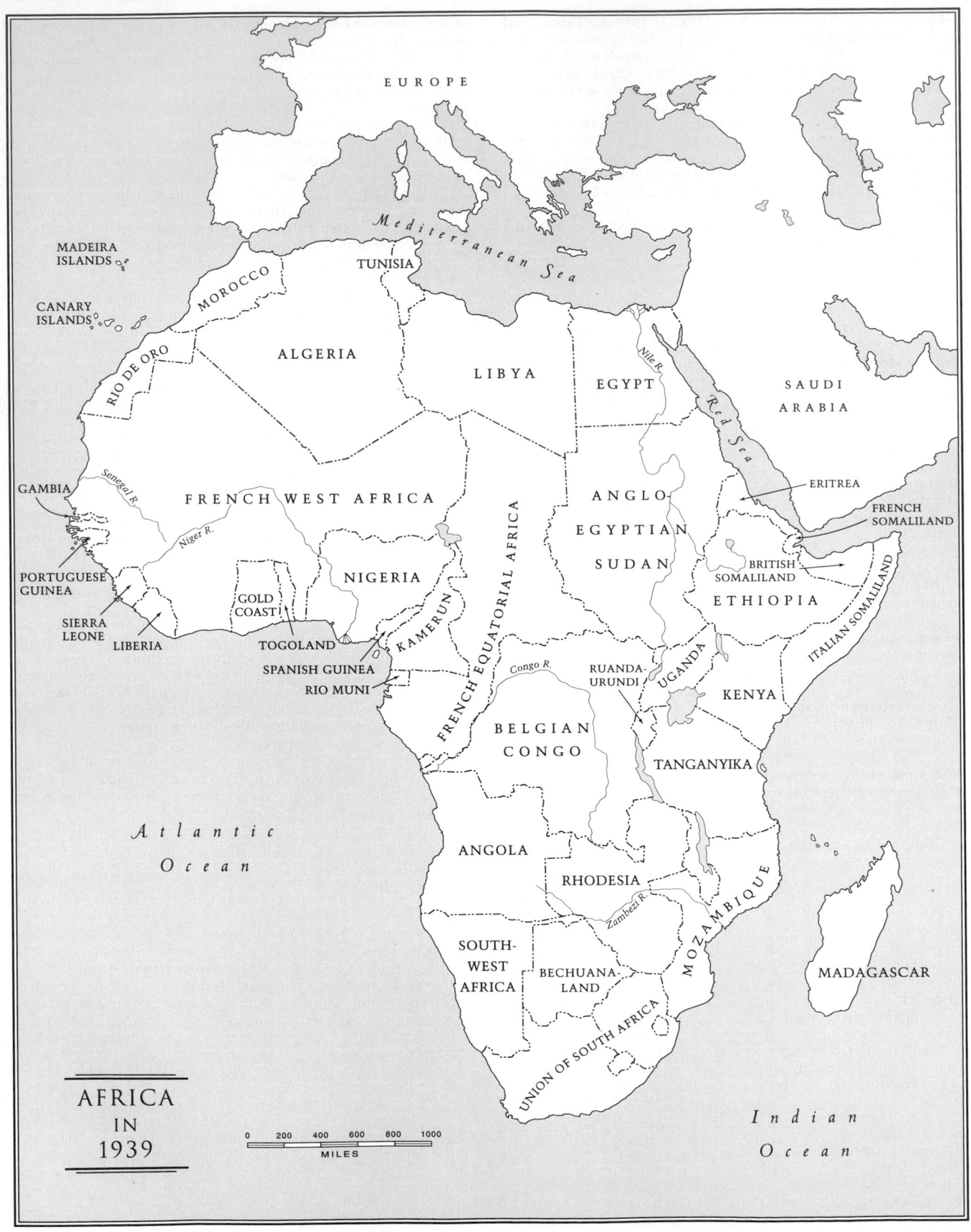

EUROPE

MADEIRA
ISLANDS

Mediterranean Sea

CANARY
ISLANDS

TUNISIA

MOROCCO

RIO DE ORO

ALGERIA

LIBYA

EGYPT

Nile R.

SAUDI
ARABIA

Red Sea

GAMBIA

Senegal R.

FRENCH WEST AFRICA

Niger R.

ERITREA

ANGLO-

FRENCH
SOMALILAND

EGYPTIAN

PORTUGUESE
GUINEA

SUDAN

BRITISH
SOMALILAND

SIERRA
LEONE

NIGERIA

ETHIOPIA

LIBERIA

GOLD
COAST

TOGOLAND

SPANISH GUINEA

RIO MUNI

KAMERUN

FRENCH EQUATORIAL AFRICA

Congo R.

RUANDA-
URUNDI

UGANDA

ITALIAN SOMALILAND

KENYA

BELGIAN
CONGO

TANGANYIKA

*Atlantic
Ocean*

ANGOLA

RHODESIA

SOUTH-
WEST
AFRICA

Zambezi R.

MOZAMBIQUE

MADAGASCAR

BECHUANA-
LAND

UNION OF SOUTH AFRICA

*Indian
Ocean*

AFRICA
IN
1939

0   200   400   600   800   1000
MILES

against a discriminatory salary plan, and received support from Western-educated Africans both at home and as far away as Lagos and Kumasi. Colonial authorities used armed force to crush the strike.

1927. Slavery declared abolished in Sierra Leone.

Firestone Rubber secured a 99-year lease on 1 million acres of Liberian land for its rubber plantation. Liberian leaders initially balked at the Firestone proposal, but finally accepted the agreement under pressure from the U.S. government. Rubber prices fell sharply soon after the plantation was established.

1928. First Roman Catholic priest ordained in Dahomey.

1929–30. The League of Nations launched an inquiry into the **Liberian labor scandal** after it received reports that Liberian laborers were virtually enslaved while working on Spanish plantations on Fernando Po. The League's report incriminated top Liberian officials who had supported involuntary labor recruitment schemes. Following the League's inquiry, Liberian president King and vice president Vancy were forced to resign. The U.S. resisted calls from Firestone that it intervene in Liberia following the scandal.

1929. The **Aba Women's War (Ogu Umunwanyi)** occurred in eastern Nigeria in response to British indirect rule policy. In the course of their administration of Igboland, the British colonial authorities concentrated power among newly created warrant chiefs, breaking with local tradition. New tax policies introduced by the British in 1928 aggravated African resentment in the region. Igbo women were particularly incensed by the chiefs' new authority, the decline of their own political associations, and the imposition of new taxes. In 1929 women in the Owerri province staged a mass protest, leading to the dismissal of the resident warrant chief and a government pledge of no new taxes. But the revolt spread despite official assurances. In southern Nigeria, **women protesters destroyed native courts, burned property, and forced chiefs to flee.** British troops were ordered to quell the protests, leaving 50 African women dead and 50 injured.

1931–35. Introduction of **colonial political reforms in Nigeria** under Gov. Donald Cameron. In response to the Aba Women's War and other protests against indirect rule, Cameron introduced councils of elders and notables in an effort to make African administration more responsive to local conditions and needs. The **Cameron Reforms** nevertheless failed to satisfy the political aspirations of younger Nigerian men and women.

1931–37. Dr. Nnamdi Azikiwe returned from the U.S. and founded the *African Morning Post,* which became a leading nationalist forum. Before returning to West Africa, Azikiwe had studied and taught in the U.S., where he was exposed to radical black journalism. In 1933 he became the editor of the *African Morning Post* in Accra, Gold Coast. He used the paper to **agitate against the colonial system,** and soon became known as a leading African nationalist. Following his stint as editor of the *African Morning Post,* Azikiwe established the *West African Pilot* newspaper in Lagos. By 1937 the paper's nationalist sentiments drew a readership of at least 9,000 people. The 1930s also saw the establishment of several **African-owned newspapers** in French West Africa, especially in Senegal and the Ivory Coast. Many positioned themselves against the colonial order. Youth clubs arose simultaneously with the nationalist press. After his return to Nigeria in 1937, Azikiwe lent support to the Nigeria Youth movement, which soon won control of the Lagos town council. Other **youth movements** in Nigeria, Sierra Leone, and the Gold Coast brought together young, Western-educated Africans impatient for change. They provided a training ground for the nationalist activists of the years to come.

1934–35. A Marxist trade unionist born in Freetown, **I. T. A. Wallace-Johnson** was deported from Lagos in 1933 because of his union activities. He then moved to the Gold Coast, where he attacked the colonial system through his articles in the *Negro Worker.* He established the nationalist **West African Youth League** in the Gold Coast between 1934 and 1935. The colonial administration there charged Wallace-Johnson with sedition in 1936, a charge of which he was eventually acquitted. He was deported to Sierra Leone in 1938.

1940. Enactment of the **Colonial Development and Welfare Act, designed to spur economic development in British colonies.** The passage of the act marked a turning point in the relationship between Britain and its colonies. No longer viewing its colonies purely in terms of economic self-interest, Britain began **efforts to promote African edu-**cation and welfare. This act set aside £5 million per year for economic aid to British colonies. British colonial officials came to believe that improving the educational, social, medical, and economic infrastructure of its colonies would lay the foundation for increased African participation in colonial administration.

1943. First Africans appointed to the executive council of the Gold Coast.

1940s. The Second World War further stimulated **nationalist sentiments** that had already begun to develop by 1939. Wartime inflation and restrictions exacerbated African grievances. Africans largely supported the British war effort, but expected major concessions in return, especially the **application of the Atlantic Charter** to West Africa. The rise of African trade unions during the war considerably increased agitation for change. The **DECOLONIZATION MOVEMENT** began to build up momentum immediately following the end of the war in 1945.

1944, Jan. 30–Feb. 8. Brazzaville Conference called by the Free French to redefine colonial status and introduce administrative reforms following the end of the war. *(To p. 1049)*

c. NORTHEAST AFRICA (HORN)

(From p. 593)

1914. The early 20th century witnessed a **boom in commodity production,** especially **coffee,** in Ethiopia. The boom was spurred in part by the **development of railways,** reaching Addis Ababa in 1916. **Drought** in Sudan, and the failure of the Nile flood, led to famine. The famine was offset by grain imported from India.

1914–22. Partial British authority in southern Sudan led to **ethnic conflict** between those under that authority and those not under it.

1915–18. Good rains brought about high agricultural production for export in Sudan.

1916. Tafari (later Haile Selassie; 1891–1975) joined a conspiracy that put Menelik's daughter **Zawditu** on the throne, with Tafari as regent.

1919–20. Inauguration of **Gezira Scheme** in Sudan for tenant farmer production of cotton under large-scale irrigation. Initially excellent results were followed by a rapid fall in production.

1920–30. Rise in exports, especially coffee, equal to contemporaneous rise in imports.

1921–22. Opposition to British rule became widespread in **southern Sudan** under **Prophet Ariandhit,** leading the British to impose more effective administration there from 1922.

1925. Completion of **Sennar Dam for the Gezira Scheme,** leading to an increase in acreage under cultivation to 700,000 by 1931.

1928–30. Ras Tafari took control following a coup d'état in 1928. He was crowned *negus* by Empress Zawditu and gained land and power. Zawditu and the conservative leaders resented Ras Tafari's prominence. Zawditu's husband, Ras Gugsa, led a rebellion in 1929. Following Zawditu's death, on April 3, 1930, **Haile Selassie** was crowned emperor. Thereafter he led a campaign to defeat rebels using **air power.**

1929–30. Tafari obtained airplanes and training for Ethiopian pilots from France, increasing central authority. A program of road building and the importation of trucks improved communication between the capital and the provinces.

1930–31. Collapse of cotton price and production in Gezira Scheme aggravated the effects of the **Great Depression** in Sudan.

1931. Haile Selassie declared a new constitution, modeled on Japan's, designed to increase imperial authority with the support of rural commoners. He opened a Parliament of members appointed by the emperor and elected by notables.

1934, July. Fascist Italy invaded Ethiopia (p. 677). The League of Nations initially ignored Ethiopian protests.

1935. By this date, production recovered in the Gezira Scheme, which continued to be an important producer of revenue for Sudan.

July. Haile Selassie obtained arms from Germany after being turned down by the U.S.

1936, May 1. Haile Selassie fled to Djibouti, and then to Britain; the **Italians occupied Addis Ababa** four days later.

1936–41. The Italians expanded their control over Ethiopia and the Horn. Italy emphasized the importance of ethnic-linguistic regions to dislodge loyalty to the imperial center. The education of children was redirected from academics to trades and crafts. **Italians** numbering 200,000 immigrated to work mostly in towns and in road construction.

1937–39. Sporadic **resistance** became a general but uncoordinated revolt.

1938, April. Britain recognized the Italian annexation of Ethiopia.

1940. The revolt reached a stalemate, but Britain and France joined the war against Italy, thus becoming allied with the Ethiopian resistance.

1941, Jan. The Allies invaded Ethiopia to dislodge the Italians.

> **May 5.** Haile Selassie returned to Addis Ababa.

> **Nov.** The Allies completed the defeat of the Italians in Ethiopia.

1942, Jan. Anglo-Ethiopian Agreement. Britain recognized the independence of Ethiopia but retained special powers, including the administration of Somali areas of Haud and Ogaden.

1942–43. Rebellion in **Tigre** province of Ethiopia, put down with British military assistance.   *(To p. 1058)*

d. EAST AFRICA

(From p. 594)

1914–18. World War I led to fighting between German and British forces, using African troops and porters, in Tanganyika (German East Africa). War proved **disastrous for East Africans,** who were forced to supply food, soldiers, and porters to the armies. Ten percent of the soldiers and 20 percent of the porters died, mostly from disease and malnutrition, totaling 100,000 deaths. **War resulted in famine and disease** throughout the region; cattle disease depleted the stored wealth of stock.

1917, Oct. The British defeated the German commander Lettow-Vorbeck at Mahiva; the Germans withdrew to Mozambique.

1918. Resident Natives Ordinance in the Kenya colony forced African tenants to work for white landlords at least six months each year.

1918–19. Just as the British occupation of Teso and Lango was completed, **serious famine and rinderpest epidemic** broke out in Uganda.

1920. Native Registration Ordinance enacted to ensure tighter labor and tax controls over Africans, who were now required to carry a pass *(kipande).* Wages declined as the postwar boom ended.

> **Jan. The British mandate over German East Africa** went into effect. The name of the territory was changed to Tanganyika.

> **July.** British East Africa was renamed **Kenya** and made into a crown colony.

1921. A meeting concerning Indian rights was held in Nairobi. A government **trade school** opened in Makerere, Uganda.

> **June.** Harry Thuku, a telephone operator, founded the **Young Kikuyu Association** to oppose *kipande,* tax increases, forced labor, and alienation of land to settlers.

1922, March. Thuku was arrested and exiled to the coast, causing a riot in Nairobi in which 20 Africans died.

1923. Poll tax introduced in Tanganyika.

> **Kavirondo Tax Payers Welfare Association** founded; **Kilimanjaro Native Planters Association** established.

1924. Formation of **Kikuyu Central Association** (KCA), to support education in government, rather than mission, schools, and to support African traditional practices, which were being undermined by missions.

1925. Cotton cultivation expanded in Uganda.

1926. Native Authority Ordinance formalized indirect rule policy in Tanganyika.

1929. The KCA, supported by its secretary, newspaper editor **Jomo Kenyatta,** clashed with missions over the Kikuyu practice of **clitoridectomy.**

1929–32. The depression led to the collapse of international commodity markets, hurting incomes from production of sisal, coffee, maize, and hides from the region.

1933, March. Kenya's **white settlers** sent an anti–income tax petition to London.

1934. The **Kenya Land Commission Report** established **African reserves and exclusive white farming areas.**

1936. Tribute to Ugandan chiefs was outlawed and replaced by salaries.

1940. The first **African doctor** entered government service in Tanganyika.

1941. Kitawala revolt in Uganda.   *(To p. 1061)*

e. WEST CENTRAL AFRICA

(From p. 595)

1912. Discovery of diamonds in Lunda area of Angola. Mining of diamonds in Angola began in 1916, and first exports in 1920.

1914–18. Troops of the Belgian Congo assisted the French and the British in coordinating the **war against Germany.**

1916. Holy Ghost Fathers replaced German Pallottine Fathers in Cameroon. **Seventh Day Adventists** began work in the Belgian Congo.

1917. Female slavery prohibited by the French in Cameroon.

1920. Extensive reorganization of **local government** in the Belgian Congo.

> **Bwiti cult** began in Gabon; **Kiyoka cult** started in Angola.

1921. Simon Kimbangu, a BaKongo peasant and catechist, declared that he was an emissary of God, chosen to lead his people from under the yoke of Belgian colonialism. He was arrested that year, but his movement persisted in rural areas for more than 30 years despite concerted persecution.

1922, July. Two hundred forty-four followers of Simon Kimbangu were deported from the Huri district.

1923. Many **Kimbanguist churches** opened in the Belgian Congo.

> **Slavery abolished in Cameroon.**

1925. Kimbanguists banned in Kasai. Watchtower movement (Kitawala) introduced by Romo Nyirenda Mnyasa into Katanga.

> The University of Louvain established **medical and agricultural** institutes in the Belgian Congo.

1926, May 28. A Military coup in Portugal led to the Estado Novo, and the accession to power of **Antonio Salazar** in 1928. Estado Novo revived colonial development policies, especially with respect to cotton, forcing many peasants in Angola and Mozambique to convert to cotton production instead of food crops, at great cost to their living standards.

1929. Electric lighting introduced into Douala.

1930. The French in the Congo spent 3 million francs to combat **sleeping sickness.**

1930–33. Great suffering in Angola from the depression, aggravated by drought and locusts.

1933. It was estimated that there were more than 1 million **Catholics** in the Belgian Congo.

1935. The Salvation Army began work in the Belgian Congo.

1939. One hundred thousand students were attending school in Cameroon.

1940. Mvungi cult emerged on the River Congo. **Tonsi movement** began in western Angola.

> **Aug. 27. The Free French took control of Cameroon.** Brazzaville was taken the next day.

1940–45. The Belgian Congo remained loyal to the Belgian government in exile and to World War II Allies under the forceful leadership of **Pierre Rykmans.** Demands for increased production for the war effort **increased the corvée labor** requirement from 60 to 120 days and more, in addition to forced rubber tapping. These stresses led to a series of urban and rural disturbances.

1941. Sixty killed in **uprising** in Luluabourg.

> **Dec. Miners' strike** in Elizabethville (Lubumbashi).

1944. Rural **religious-based uprising** in Kivu province, Congo.

1945, Nov. Dockworkers' strike at Congo port of Matadi.   *(To p. 1064)*

f. SOUTHERN AFRICA

(From p. 598)

1. NORTH OF THE LIMPOPO

1915, Jan. John Chilembwe, an American-trained pastor, led a brief **uprising** against colonial rule in Nyasaland (Malawi), sparked by forced conscription into World War I and by complaints of labor tenants.

1917–19. Widespread rebellion in Zambezi region of Mozambique, over wartime labor demands; not finally pacified in **Barwe** area until 1919.

1920–30. Growth of **religious and cultural movements in Southern Rhodesian mining compounds,** including Watchtower movement, called Kitawala, and **Beni dance associations.** Beni dance associations were a syncretic mix of African dance and European marching bands.

1923. White settlers in Southern Rhodesia (Zimbabwe) gained self-governing status.

1925, April. White women in Southern Rhodesia granted suffrage.

1927. African workers called a strike in Southern Rhodesia.

1930. Land Apportionment Act in Southern Rhodesia reserved half of the land, and most of the good farming land, for whites, and confirmed the status of African reserves, while requiring African tenants to work for white landlords.

Makape "cleansing" cult emerged in Nyasaland.

c. 1930. Welfare societies or self-help groups established amongst Africans in Northern Rhodesian mines.

1933. Tshekedi Khama, regent of Bamangwato, deposed by the British for exceeding his powers. Tshekedi subsequently reinstated.

Native authorities in Nyasaland instructed on model of indirect rule.

1935, May. Strike by African mineworkers on Copperbelt of Northern Rhodesia (Zambia), sparked by changes in poll tax administration which worked to the detriment of urban areas.

1936. Native authorities and courts established in Northern Rhodesia.

1940. White miners' strike on Copperbelt, caused by wartime inflation. The white strike led to a **second African mineworkers' strike** for higher wages and against color bar.

2. SOUTH OF THE LIMPOPO

1914, Jan. J. B. Hertzog became the leader of the **Nationalist Party,** composed of "Afrikaners," defined as those who placed South Africa's interests first. Imperial and mining interests were represented by the ruling South African Party under Botha. **Strike by white miners** in Natal and on Rand was put down by the army, drawing Nationalist and (white) Labor parties closer.

Aug.–Dec. South Africa entered World War I as part of the British Empire and invaded German South West Africa (SWA), prompting an Afrikaner rebellion in the Orange Free State, led by Gen. De Wet; the rebellion was put down by December.

1914–18. South African troops, white and "colored" (mixed race), fought in Europe and, under **Gen. Smuts,** in East Africa; Africans served as noncombatants.

1915, July. South Africa defeated German forces in SWA.

Oct. The war gave an electoral boost to the opposition Nationalists, who won 30 percent of the vote in the general election.

1918. Up to **200,000 Africans died in South Africa** from a worldwide influenza epidemic.

1919. South Africa given a League of Nations mandate to rule SWA.

The **African National Union** organized burning of passes as protest.

Aug. South African prime minister Botha died; **Gen. Jan Smuts became prime minister.**

1919–20. Formation of **Industrial and Commercial Union** (ICU) by **Clements Kadalie** among dockworkers in Cape Town. ICU led dockworkers out on strike in December. ICU quickly spread among workers in other urban centers.

1919–21. Severe drought coincided with postwar boom and collapse of agricultural prices in South Africa, driving many **Afrikaners off the land** to become urban workers.

1920. Nationalists won the largest number of seats in the general election, but Smuts stayed in power by an alliance with the Unionists; election showed the growing **appeal of Afrikaner nationalism.** The **Native Affairs Act** provided for local councils in reserve areas and a permanent (white) Native Affairs Commission, furthering the **doctrine of segregation** in the political sphere.

Witwatersrand University chartered. Students at **Fort Hare** burned buildings in protest against school policies.

1921–36. Doubling of the urban black population and a significant increase in the **numbers of black women in towns.**

1921, May. The South African army massacred **Enoch Mgijima's Israelite sect** at Bulhoek in Eastern Cape, killing 163.

1922, Jan. White mineworkers' strike to maintain monopoly of skilled jobs for whites, leading to white workers' insurrection. Communist Council of Action briefly gained control of the Rand.

March 10. Smuts declared martial law and launched a military assault against the strikers, killing up to 220.

May. Bondelswarts Rebellion in SWA, sparked by imposition of a dog tax, was put down, killing more than 100.

1923. Natives (Urban Areas) Act provided for urban segregation and regulation of conditions in black areas.

Africans held conferences at Bloemfontein and Pretoria to protest changes in their rights.

1924, June. General election brought **Hertzog to power in a pact with the Labour Party** under the banner of "civilized labor" to protect white employment.

1925. The Native Tax and Development Act replaced hut taxes with a uniform poll tax of £1 per African adult male, plus 10 shillings per annum for reserve dwellers, earmarked for development projects.

Afrikaans recognized as an official language of South Africa, on a par with English and Dutch. **Areas Reservation Act** segregated Indians.

1925–29. A wave of **rural radicalism** in eastern South Africa was marked by the rise of the ICU and other radical or millenarian movements.

1926. Hertzog's **Native Bills to further establish territorial and political segregation** were introduced, but were not passed until after the fusion of white political parties in 1933 due to the need for a two-thirds majority to interfere with the Cape African franchise.

1926–27. The African National Congress adopted a more radical line under the leadership of **J. T. Gumede,** influenced by the example of the USSR and by the Comintern's call for a black republic in South Africa.

1927. Native Administration Act furthered implementation of administrative and legal segregation and indirect rule.

1928, May. Strike of South African Native Clothing Workers' Union and Witwatersrand Tailors' Association.

1929. The Riotous Assemblies Act gave the government power to deport those promoting "racial hostility"; the act was a tool for clamping down on radical movements.

Word *apartheid* was used.

1929–32. Severe **depression** caused the collapse of agricultural prices, leading to government institution of price supports and other aid to white farmers.

1930. The ANC returned to a moderate stance under the leadership of **Pixley Seme.**

1931. Revision of South Africa's **Urban Areas Act** further restricted Africans' rights to residence in cities and towns.

1932–40. Abandonment of the gold standard led to a steep rise in the price of gold and to a boom in secondary industry, **vastly increasing urbanization and labor migration.**

1933. Fusion of Smuts's SAP and Hertzog's Nationalists gave electoral victory; **D. F. Malan** led Afrikaner republicans into the **Purified Nationalist Party.**

1935. In emulation of Nazi Brown Shirts, **Grey Shirts** emerged in South Africa.

Dec. All-African Convention of black organizations met in Bloemfontein to **oppose Native Bills,** especially the **withdrawal of the Cape franchise.**

1936, April 7. Passage of **Natives Representation Act** removed the Cape African franchise and set up the advisory Natives Representative Council (NRC); simultaneous passage of Natives Trust and Land Act added land to native reserves and required six months' service of African tenants on white-owned land.

1937. Marketing Act extended farm price subsidies, increasing agricultural output and use of African labor, in competition with better-paying industrial jobs.

1938. Electoral gains by the Purified Nationalist Party. **Centennial of the Great Trek** used to galvanize Afrikaner nationalism. **Census of urban areas** used to enforce segregation.

1939, Sept. South Africa joined World War II on the side of Britain, leading to the resignation of Hertzog; Smuts became prime minister; Purified Nationalists emerged as the main Afrikaner party.

1940, Jan. 1. **Price controls** introduced in South Africa.   *(To p. 1067)*

g. MADAGASCAR

(From p. 599)

1914–18. Forty-one thousand Malagasy served in European war; war stimulated the demand for labor and production of rice, other foods, and graphite.

1914–30. The economy depended largely on the export of rice, hides, and meat.

1929–35. The depression led to the collapse of commodity prices and forced government aid to settler agriculture. Weakened settler agriculture was an encouragement of Malagasy production.

1935–39. Successful commodity production in rural areas and **organization of workers** led to beginnings of modern nationalist movement.

(To p. 1072)

K. WORLD WAR II, 1939–1945

(From pp. 647, 679)

1. THE CAMPAIGNS IN POLAND AND FINLAND, 1939–1940

1939, Sept. 1. POLAND WAS INVADED by German forces estimated at 1 million men. Headed by mechanized divisions and supported by overwhelming air power, the German thrusts disorganized and defeated the poorly equipped Polish armies. Though the latter had a numerical strength of 600,000 men, they were unable to mobilize effectively or concert their resistance.

Sept. 17. In accordance with the secret protocol of the Soviet-Nazi nonaggression pact (p. 679), **Russian troops invaded Poland** from the east, meeting the advancing Germans near Brest-Litovsk two days later.

Sept. 27. After heroic resistance and destructive bombing, **Warsaw surrendered** and Polish organized opposition came to an end. The Blitzkrieg had lasted less than four weeks and the outcome had been determined in the first ten days.

Sept. 29. The German and Russian governments divided Poland. Germany annexed outright the Free City of Danzig (population 415,000) and 32,000 square miles between East Prussia and Silesia. In addition an area of 39,000 square miles, known as the Gouvernement Général, remained under German protection. The total German gains were estimated at 72,866 square miles, with a population of 22,140,000. The Russians occupied 77,620 square miles of eastern Poland, with a population of 13,199,000. Lithuania and Slovakia received small cessions of Polish territory.

Nov. 30–1940, March 12. RUSSO-FINNISH WAR. Russian armies attacked on three fronts: below Petsamo on the Arctic Sea, in central Finland, and on the Karelian Isthmus.

Dec. 14. Russia was expelled from the League of Nations (p. 710) for acts of aggression against Finland.

1940, March 12. After three months of varying success but increasing pressure, the Russians breached the Mannerheim Line. **Finland accepted peace,** negotiated at Moscow, ceding to the USSR the Karelian Isthmus, the city of Viipuri (Vyborg), a naval base at Hangö, and territories totaling 16,173 square miles, with a population of 450,000. Most of the Finns in the ceded areas were to be resettled in Finland.

2. THE INVASION OF DENMARK AND NORWAY, 1940

1940, Feb. 16. British naval forces entered Norwegian waters to rescue 299 prisoners of war from the German ship *Altmark.* The Norwegian government protested (p. 804).

April 8. The French and British governments announced that Norwegian waters had been mined to prevent the passage of German ships.

April 9. German sea and airborne forces descended on Norway. Oslo, Bergen, Trondheim, Stavanger, and Narvik were rapidly invaded. At the same time German forces entered and occupied Denmark without more than pro forma resistance.

April 9. A German destroyer squadron landed at Narvik and held the town even after destruction of the German ships by the British (April 13). On May 28 a British force recovered the town but was withdrawn on June 10 in view of the German attack in the west.

April 11. Rallying from the surprise attack, Norwegian forces offered growing resistance. Three German cruisers and four troopships were lost in the invasion.

April 16–19. Anglo-French expeditionary forces landed in southern Norway, but were compelled to withdraw after two weeks (May 3).

April 30. The Germans, reinforced steadily, captured Dombas, a key rail center, and **Norwegian resistance was broken,** though military operations were carried on until June 10.

Sept. 25. The German reich-commissar for Norway set aside the legal administration, dissolved all political parties except the Nasjonal-Samling, and entrusted the government to 13 commissars.

3. THE CONQUEST OF THE LOW COUNTRIES AND THE FALL OF FRANCE, 1940

1940, May 10. German armies, without warning, **invaded the Netherlands, Belgium, and Luxembourg.**

The French and British governments dispatched expeditionary forces into Belgium to cooperate with the Belgian army in its resistance. The Germans captured Fort Eben Emael, a key Belgian defense position.

May 12. The **Germans crossed the Meuse** at Sedan.

May 13. Rotterdam surrendered to the Germans after part of the city had been blasted by an exterminating air attack. The **Netherlands army capitulated** on May 14.

May 17–21. German mechanized divisions drove deep into northern France, racing down the Somme Valley to the English Channel at **Abbeville.** The British and Belgian forces in Flanders were thus separated from the main French armies. **Gen. Maxime Weygand** replaced Gen. Gustave Gamelin as French commander in chief, but he was unable to arrest the French collapse. The **fall of Brussels** and Namur forced the British and Belgian armies back upon Ostend and Dunkirk.

May 26. Boulogne fell to the Germans. The Belgian armies, disorganized and short of supplies after 16 days of fighting, could not sustain further attacks, and Leopold III ordered them to capitulate.

May 28. Exposed by the capitulation of the Belgians, the British expeditionary force of some 250,000 had to be withdrawn, chiefly from the beaches of **Dunkirk.**

June 4. By heroic efforts some 200,000 British and 140,000 French troops were rescued, but were forced to abandon almost all equipment. British losses including prisoners totaled 30,000.

June 5. Having secured their right wing, the German invaders launched a wide attack against the French on an arc from Sedan to Abbeville.

June 10. ITALY DECLARED WAR AGAINST FRANCE AND GREAT BRITAIN. Italian forces invaded southern France.

June 13. Paris was evacuated before the continued German advance.

June 15. The French fortress of **Verdun was captured.**

June 17. Marshal Henri-Philippe Pétain asked the Germans for an armistice.

June 22. The **armistice was signed at Compiègne.** It provided that the French forces be disarmed, and that three-fifths of France be surrendered to German control.

June 24. An armistice was concluded between France and Italy.

July 3. Battle of Mers-el-Kebir. The British, to prevent the battle cruisers *Dunkerque* and *Strasbourg* and other naval forces from falling into enemy hands, called upon the French commander to join the British or sail to British or West Indian ports to be disarmed. The French commander, on orders from Vichy, resisted, whereupon the British opened fire and destroyed or damaged three battleships. The *Strasbourg* escaped to Toulon. The *Dunkerque* (26,000 tons), the *Provence* (22,000), the *Bretagne* (22,000), and an aircraft carrier (10,000) were damaged, and French losses in men were 1,300 dead.

July 4. All French ships in ports under British control were seized.

July 5. The **French government** at Vichy **severed relations with the British government.** On Nov. 11, 1942, German forces entered unoccupied France, following the Anglo-American invasion of North Africa. (For the liberation of France, see p. 807.)

4. THE BATTLE OF BRITAIN, 1940

1940, June. The **fall of France** and the loss of war materiel in the evacuation from Dunkirk led the British prime minister, Winston Churchill, to appeal to the U.S. government for military supplies. These were released by the War Department (June 3), and three weeks later a first shipment, including 500,000 rifles, 80,000 machine guns, 900 75-mm field guns, and 130 million rounds of ammunition, reached Britain.

July. On the fall of France the Germans occupied islands in the English Channel and intensified their air attacks on British cities, communications, and shipping.

Aug. 8. German bombers opened an **offensive designed to destroy British air strength** by blasting the airfields and vital industries.

Aug. 15. One thousand German planes ranged as far north as Scotland. Croydon airfield was bombed. The British retaliated with heavy raids on Berlin, Düsseldorf, Essen, and other German cities.

Aug. 17. The German government proclaimed a **total blockade** of the waters around Great Britain.

Sept. 2. An important **defense agreement** was concluded **between Great Britain and the United States.** Fifty American destroyers were transferred to Britain to combat the air and submarine menace. In exchange the U.S. received a 99-year **lease of naval and air bases** in Newfoundland, Bermuda, the Bahamas, Jamaica, Antigua, St. Lucia, Trinidad, and British Guiana.

Sept. 11. The **British bombed Continental ports,** including Antwerp, Ostend, Calais, and Dunkirk, to frustrate German invasion preparations.

Sept. 16. Improved British defense measures inflicted heavy losses on German air raiders, 185 invading planes crashing in one day.

Sept. 27. A **GERMAN-ITALIAN-JAPANESE PACT** was concluded at Berlin providing for a ten-year military and economic alliance. The three contracting powers further promised each other mutual assistance in the event that any one of them became involved in war with a power not then a belligerent.

Oct. 10. Resuming the **air assault** with full intensity, the German Luftwaffe raided London heavily. Some Italian air squadrons joined in

the attack. But shorter days, stormy weather, and improved defenses diminished the effectiveness of the air arm.

Nov. 10. In a supreme effort at crushing British industrial resources and demoralizing the population, the Germans blasted the industrial city of **Coventry** with destructive effect. Thereafter the air attacks became more sporadic. The British had survived the worst of the aerial Blitzkrieg, and after November the winter weather made any attempt at invasion less likely. German losses in aircraft had been heavy: an official estimate placed them at 2,375 German to 800 British planes destroyed in the period Aug. 8–Oct. 31. But many British cities had been severely shattered and burned, and 14,000 civilians had been killed in London alone. British losses at sea had also been heavy. On Nov. 5 Churchill declared that the **submarine boat** had become a greater menace than the bombing plane.

Nov. 20. The **Stimson-Layton agreement,** arranged between Sir Walter Layton, for the British Ministry of Supply, and Henry L. Stimson, U.S. secretary of war, provided for a partial **standardization of military weapons and equipment** and initiated a general policy of pooling British and American technical knowledge, patents, and formulas in armament production.

1941, March 11. The British war effort was aided by the signature of the **LEND-LEASE ACT** (p. 804).

May. Intensified German air attacks, facilitated by longer days and clearer skies, culminated in a shattering assault on London (May 10) that damaged the houses of Parliament and the British Museum. Thereafter, however, secret German preparations for the invasion of Russia (June 22) reduced the number of bombers available for raids on Britain. Enormous damage had been endured by the British with remarkable courage. One home in every five was damaged or destroyed, factories shattered, and transport, gas, and water systems disrupted.

June 22. The **Battle of Britain subsided** with the opening of the Russian front in June 1941. But the German submarine blockade remained a grave menace to British supply services throughout 1941 and 1942. It was gradually curbed by air and sea patrols, improved detection devices such as radar, and the extension of the convoy system.

5. THE BALKAN CAMPAIGNS, 1940–1941

1940, June. The **fall of France** and the desperate position of Great Britain in the summer of 1940 caused a shift in the European balance. In the Balkans Romania, which had won territory from all its neighbors in the 20th century, was particularly menaced. By September the Romanian government had ceded territory to the Soviet Union, Hungary, and Bulgaria, yielding to threats and Axis pressure. In all, Romania lost about 40,000 square miles and a population of 5 million (p. 726).

Oct. 4. Hitler and Mussolini conferred at the Brenner Pass. The failure to break British resistance and increasing activity in the Balkan

and Mediterranean areas forecast a shift in Axis strategy. Hitler also conferred with the French vice premier, **Pierre Laval** (Oct. 22), with **Gen. Francisco Franco** of Spain (Oct. 23), with **Marshal Henri-Philippe Pétain,** head of the Vichy French government (Oct. 24), and again with Mussolini, in Florence (Oct. 28).

Oct. 8. German troops entered Romania to "protect" the oil fields.

Oct. 28. Greece rejected a demand of the Italian government for the use of Greek bases. Thereupon the Italians invaded Greece from Albania.

Oct. 30. British reinforcements were landed on Crete and other Greek islands. The Russian government delivered 134 fighter planes to Greece in accord with existing agreements.

Nov. 12. Vyacheslav Molotov, Soviet commissar for foreign affairs, **conferred with Hitler** in Berlin. Soviet troops were massed on the Romanian border.

Nov. 13. British bombing planes destroyed or damaged half of the Italian fleet anchored in the inner harbor at **Taranto.** At the same time Churchill announced the addition of five 35,000-ton battleships to the British navy.

Nov. 20. Hungary joined the Berlin-Rome-Tokyo pact.

Nov. 23. Romania joined the Berlin-Rome-Tokyo pact.

Dec. 3. The **Greeks broke through the Italian defenses** in Albania, captured Porto Edda, and claimed a total of 28,000 prisoners. Agyrokastron was likewise captured five days later, and the Greeks overran one-fourth of Albania. The Germans dispatched 50,000 troops to reinforce the Italian armies. Combined with temporary successes of the British against the Italians in Africa, the Greek victories marked a blow to Axis prestige.

1941, Jan. 10. German air squadrons, transferred to Italy, attacked British naval forces off Sicily.

Feb. 10. The **British government severed diplomatic relations with Romania.**

March 1. Bulgaria joined the Rome-Berlin Axis, and German troops occupied Sofia. The British delegation had left on Feb. 24, and the Soviet government warned the Bulgarians not to expect Soviet aid.

March 25. Yugoslav envoys signed the Rome-Berlin-Tokyo pact at Vienna, but a Yugoslav coup reversed this, declaring Yugoslav neutrality (p. 722).

April 6. German troops, who had been massing on the Hungarian, Romanian, and Bulgarian borders, **poured into Yugoslavia and Greece.** In Moscow official journals laid the responsibility for the spread of war upon the Germans.

April 13. RUSSIAN AND JAPANESE DIPLOMATS SIGNED A MUTUAL NONAGGRESSION PACT AT MOSCOW.

April 17. The **Yugoslav government capitulated** after a campaign of 12 days. Resistance against the Germans and Italians was maintained by guerrilla forces.

April 23. Greek resistance was broken and an **armistice signed.** King George II fled to Crete.

April 27. The Germans entered Athens. Of the British expeditionary force in Greece 48,000 of the 60,000 men were evacuated, but much valuable equipment was abandoned.

May 2. In **Iraq** a pro-Axis regime under **Premier Rashid Ali** invited German aid, whereupon British forces entered the country.

May 20. German parachute troops invaded Crete and superior German air power inflicted serious losses and damage on the British cruisers and destroyers in Cretan waters.

May 31. Surviving **British forces in Crete were evacuated** to Cyprus and Egypt. The Axis position in the eastern Mediterranean was greatly strengthened by the possession of Greece and Crete, which made the Aegean Sea unsafe for British ships. **Rebellion in Iraq** ended when British troops entered Baghdad after Iraqi airfields had been bombed. Mosul was occupied June 4. An armistice was concluded and a government friendly to Great Britain installed. Iraq later declared war on Germany, Italy, and Japan (Jan. 16, 1943).

July 12. Confused **fighting in Syria** ended with an armistice after British and Free French forces moved on Beirut and Damascus. British naval units landed troops on the Lebanon coast. This occupation terminated the authority of the French Vichy government over Syria and Lebanon and defeated the attempts of the Germans to obtain control of these territories. Possession of Syria and Iraq enabled the British to exert increased **pressure upon Iran,** the government of which was persuaded to cooperate (Aug. 28) after British and Soviet forces entered the country. The danger that the German successes in the Balkans would bring Istanbul and the Straits under Axis control was fully realized in Moscow and the possibility that a Soviet offensive might threaten the German flank explains in part why Hitler attacked Russia on June 22.

6. THE CAMPAIGNS IN THE SOVIET UNION, 1941–1944

1941, June 22. GERMAN ARMIES INVADED THE SOVIET UNION, opening hostilities on a front of 2,000 miles, from the White to the Black Sea. The German invaders, with their allies, the Italians, Romanians, Hungarians, and Finns, were estimated at over 3 million men. The Russians were credited with 2 million men under arms, and an indefinite reserve. Churchill promised that Great Britain would extend all possible aid to the Russians. The German invasion of the Soviet Union, combined with conquests in Poland, Hungary, Czechoslovakia, and the Balkans, brought millions more Jews under Germany's influence. The Nazis already practiced extermination against "Bolsheviks," and special "intervention squads" *(Einsatzgruppen)* accompanied German attack forces with orders to liquidate Communist Party officials and Jews.

June 29. The Germans reached Grodno, Brest-Litovsk, and Vilna.

July 1–2. Riga, capital of Latvia, **was occupied by German troops,** and the Russian retreat continued with heavy losses, especially around Bialystok.

July 13. A pact promising mutual aid was concluded between Great Britain and Russia.

July 16. The Germans captured Smolensk.

Aug. 1. Britain severed relations with Finland, which the Germans were using as a base for their invasion of Russia.

Aug. 19. The **Germans claimed all Ukrainian territory** west of the Dnieper except Odessa.

Aug. 25–29. British and Soviet forces invaded Iran (p. 757).

Sept. 4. The Germans commenced the **investment of Leningrad,** a state of partial siege that was not ended until Jan. 1943.

Sept. 19. Kiev and Poltava were stormed by the Axis forces, which continued their victorious advance to Orel (Oct. 8), Bryansk (Oct. 12), Viazma (Oct. 13), Odessa (Oct. 16), Tanganrog (Oct. 19), and Kharkov (Oct. 24). By the end of October the Germans had **entered the Crimea** on the southern end of the vast front and had commenced the **siege of Moscow** in the north. The Soviet government transferred its headquarters to Kuibyshev.

Oct. 1. The **FIRST SOVIET PROTOCOL,** signed at Moscow, provided that Great Britain and the U.S. would supply materials essential to the Russian war effort for nine months. Purchase of American supplies was speeded by extending the Soviet government a credit of $1 billion (Oct. 30). This was supplemented (June 11, 1942) by a **master lend-lease agreement** whereby the U.S. promised to supply the Soviet Union with such materials and services as the president might authorize. In return the Soviet government pledged that such articles or information would not be transferred to a third party without the consent of the president. The arrangement was to continue until a date agreed upon by the two governments and materials unconsumed were to be returned to the U.S. at the end of the emergency.

Nov. 15. The **siege of Sevastopol,** a heroic epic of the war on the eastern front, commenced.

Nov. 16. The **Germans captured Kerch.** Rostov, entered by the invaders (Nov. 22), was retaken by the Russians a week later (Dec. 1). A counterthrust temporarily relieved the pressure on Moscow (Dec. 6), and the Russians were also able to retake Kalinin (Dec. 16).

1942, Jan. 20. Continuing their **winter offensive,** the Russians recaptured Mozhaisk. Dorogobuzh also fell to them (Feb. 23) and Rzhev (March 20). In addition they scored advances toward Kursk (April 29) and Kharkov (May 12).

May 26. The **mutual aid pact** between Great Britain and Russia was extended to a **20-year treaty.**

July 2. The Germans, who had opened a new **summer offensive** in southern Russia, captured Sevastopol, which had sustained a siege of eight months. Driving powerfully toward the Caucasus, the Germans claimed Voronezh (July 7), Millerovo (July 15), and Rostov (July 24).

Aug. 9. Maikop fell to the invaders, who crossed the Don River (Aug. 20) and opened a vital **offensive against Stalingrad** (Aug. 22). This city was important as a communications center through which Volga River traffic, especially oil from the Caspian region, reached Russian distribution points. The Germans hoped not only to obtain needed supplies of petroleum for themselves, but to cripple the Soviet war effort by cutting a major line of supply.

Sept. 1. The **Germans crossed the Kerch Straits** and captured Novorossiisk (Sept. 6). Farther north, a week later, they penetrated the city of Stalingrad (Sept. 14). Their summer offensive appeared on the point of succeeding, but they had overstretched their lines. **Soviet forces counterattacked** northeast of Stalingrad (Sept. 21) and ten days later (Oct 1) opened a second thrust from southeast of the city.

Nov. 19. Without permitting the Germans time to entrench or to withdraw, the Russians intensified their pincer attack on the **Stalingrad front** while opening new drives toward Rzhev (Nov. 25) and Kharkov (Dec. 16).

1943, Jan. 1–18. The list of **German defeats** mounted to a **debacle.** Soviet forces recaptured Velikiye Luki (Jan. 1), entered Mozdok (Jan. 3), and relieved **Leningrad** from a 17-month siege. Twenty-two German divisions, cut off at Stalingrad, and reduced to 80,000 men, were forced to capitulate by Feb. 2. This second Soviet winter offensive then rolled on, with the capture of Kursk (Feb. 8), Belgorod (Feb. 9), Rostov (Feb. 14), Kharkov (Feb. 16), Rzhev (March 3), and Viazma (March 12). The losses of the Germans and their allies, in killed and captured, exceeded 500,000 for three months of winter fighting.

March 15. Despite these casualties the Germans were able to open a **spring drive,** wresting Kharkov from the Russians once more (March 15), and retaking Belgorod (March 21). This checked the Russians temporarily, and the lines were more or less stabilized. The Axis armies had been driven back halfway from the Don to the Dnieper. When they attempted to open a summer offensive in July, they found that the Russians had also been gathering men and materiel for a renewal of the struggle.

July. Military supplies from Great Britain and the United States helped materially to arm the Soviet forces for the campaigns of 1943. The U.S. shipped 4,100 planes, 138,000 motor vehicles, shiploads of steel, and industrial machinery for Soviet arms factories. Part of the equipment went by northern **convoy routes** to Arkhangelsk, part in Russian ships to Vladivostok, part via the Persian Gulf. Shipments through Iran increased to 100,000 tons a month by July 1943.

The Soviet summer campaign of 1943. The Germans and their allies had 240–60 divisions, the Soviet armies had grown to 250–75, and the advantage in materiel had passed to the Russians. Anglo-American bombing was crippling German industry, greatly reducing the output of German planes, and this unhinged the plane-tank combination of mechanized warfare which had won earlier successes for the Wehrmacht. The output of Russian factories had increased greatly, and the

U.S. shipments of planes to Russia, mounting to a total of 6,500 by the autumn of 1943, deprived the Germans of their superiority in the air.

July 5. The **Germans opened an offensive** in the Orel-Belgorod sector but were checked after a week's fighting.

Aug. 23. Broadening and gathering momentum, the Soviet drive swept on to **Kharkov.** In the south, Tanganrog fell (Aug. 30); in the center, Bryansk was recaptured (Sept. 17), as was Smolensk (Sept. 25). By October the **Russians had reached the Dnieper** at several points, capturing Kiev (Nov. 6). The year closed with the reconquest of Zhitomir (Dec. 31).

1944. In January Novgorod in the north fell to the Russians (Jan. 20), and by February they had penetrated Estonia and were on the borders of prewar Poland.

Feb. 17. Ten German divisions, trapped in a pocket near Cherkassy, were largely destroyed, and the survivors made prisoner.

March 26. The **Ukrainian drives** carried the Russians to the Romanian border. Odessa fell to them on April 10 and Tarnopol on April 15. By May 9 they had taken Sevastopol, and the Crimea, like Ukraine, was cleared of invading forces.

June 20. An **offensive against the Finns** delivered Vyborg into Soviet hands. Farther south Vitebsk fell to them (June 26) and Minsk (July 3). The opening of an Allied front in the west, following the **invasion of Normandy** (June 6), prevented the Germans from strengthening the eastern front, and July and August brought an almost unbroken series of Soviet triumphs. By the end of August they had reached the borders of East Prussia and were invading Poland and Romania.

Aug. 24. The **ROMANIAN GOVERNMENT SURRENDERED** when Soviet troops reached the mouth of the Danube and captured Jassy and Kishinev. The capitulation of Romania trapped major units of the German Black Sea naval forces, although some of the smaller craft escaped up the Danube before the Russian advance closed that route. Soviet domination of the Black Sea opened a new and important supply route whereby cargoes could reach the Soviet Union.

Sept. 5. The Soviet Union declared war on Bulgaria. Three days later the Bulgarian government asked for an armistice (Sept. 8), and Soviet columns moved into Sofia (Sept. 16).

Oct. 20. German forces of occupation in Yugoslavia were harassed increasingly by the partisans and failed to halt the advance of the Russians, who entered Belgrade (Oct. 20). Two weeks later they were at the gates of Budapest, but the Hungarian capital resisted savagely for over two months and was not conquered until Feb. 18, 1945.

Victorious in the Balkans, with their central armies pressing into Poland, and their northern (right) end of the line anchored on the Baltic after the **capture of Tallinn** (Sept. 22) **and Riga** (Oct. 13), the Russians opened their final drives into Germany (Jan. 1945). These maneuvers, synchronized with the Allied drives across the Rhine, merged into the **Battle of Germany** (p. 807).

7. DEFENSE OF THE WESTERN HEMISPHERE, 1939–1945

1939, Oct. 2. A **Pan-American conference at Panama** declared that the waters surrounding the Western Hemisphere for a distance of 300 miles from shore and as far north as Canada constituted "sea safety zones" and must be kept free from hostile acts by non-American belligerent nations. The conference also issued a **general declaration of neutrality** of the American republics.

Nov. 4. President Roosevelt signed an **amendment to the Neutrality Act** which repealed the embargo on the sale of arms and placed exports to belligerent nations on a **cash-and-carry** basis.

Dec. 13. Three British cruisers attacked the German battleship *Graf Spee* and drove it into the harbor of Montevideo. When forced to leave harbor, it was scuttled by the German crew (Dec. 17). In the name of the American republics the president of Panama protested to Great Britain, France, and Germany at this and other belligerent acts committed in American waters.

1940, May 16. President Roosevelt asked the Congress to appropriate $2.5 billion for **expansion of the army and navy** and proposed a production goal of 50,000 airplanes a year. This program of expansion was to be supervised by a **defense advisory commission.**

June 16. Congress authorized the sale of munitions to the government of any American republic. This measure, known as the **Pittman Act,** was extended by provisions authorizing the Export-Import Bank to lend the American republics up to $500 million (Sept. 26) and permitting them to procure munitions of a total value of $400 million for their defense. These programs were taken over by the **Lend-Lease Administration** after its creation in March 1941.

June 17. The **U.S. Department of State notified European governments that it would not recognize the transfer of any geographic region of the Western Hemisphere from one non-American power to another non-American power.**

July 20. President Roosevelt signed a bill providing for a **two-ocean navy** as part of a vast defense plan for the U.S. in particular and the Western Hemisphere in general.

July 30. The republics of the Pan-American Union approved a convention setting up an **Inter-American commission on territorial administration** to guard the sovereignty of the states of the Western Hemisphere. At this meeting at Havana, the delegates also approved the **Act of Havana** providing that the American republics, jointly or individually, should act as their own defense and that of the continent required.

Aug. 18. President Roosevelt and Prime Minister Mackenzie King of Canada agreed to set up a **joint board of defense.**

Sept. 2. The **U.S. obtained naval and air bases** in Newfoundland, Bermuda, the Bahamas, Jamaica, St. Lucia, Trinidad, Antigua, and British Guiana on 99-year leases from Great Britain. In exchange Britain acquired 50 overage destroyers from the U.S. The facilities at these bases were extended to the Latin American governments in conformity with understandings reached at the conferences of Lima, Panama, and Havana.

Sept. 16. The U.S. Congress passed the **Selective Service Act** providing for the registration of all men between 21 and 36 years of age, and for the training, for one year, of 1.2 million troops and 800,000 reserves.

Dec. 20. The president named a defense board headed by **William A. Knudsen** to prepare defense measures and speed armament production.

1941, Feb. 1. The **U.S. patrol force** in the Caribbean area was raised to fleet status. Naval bases at Guantanamo Bay, Cuba; San Juan, Puerto Rico; and St. Thomas, Virgin Islands, were developed rapidly. A third set of locks was designed for the Panama Canal.

March 11. The **LEND-LEASE ACT** was signed by President Roosevelt. It had passed the Senate by a vote of 60 to 31 and the House of Representatives by 317 to 71. Under this enactment "any country whose defense the president deems vital to the defense of the United States" became eligible to receive any defense article by sale, transfer, exchange, or lease.

March. The **Republic of Panama** granted the U.S. the right to extend its air defenses outside the limits of the Canal Zone. A **Pan-American highway,** to extend ultimately from Mexico City through Central America to Santiago, Chile, and thence across the Andes to Buenos Aires, and up the Atlantic coast to Rio de Janeiro, was two-thirds completed by Dec. 1941. A highway from the state of Washington to Alaska was also undertaken.

Nov. 24. The U.S. sent forces to occupy **Dutch Guiana,** to protect the resources and prevent possible activities by agents of the Axis powers.

Dec. 7. THE JAPANESE ATTACKED HAWAII AND THE PHILIPPINES.

Dec. 8. THE CONGRESS OF THE UNITED STATES DECLARED WAR ON JAPAN.

1942, Jan. 15. Representatives of the American republics met for an **Inter-American conference at Rio de Janeiro.** It was convoked to concert measures for defending the Western Hemisphere against aggression.

Jan. 21. The representatives of 21 American republics, assembled at Rio de Janeiro, adopted unanimously a resolution calling for severance of relations with the Axis powers.

March. An inter-American defense board was established to promote working cooperation among the American states in defense of the Western Hemisphere.

June 28. Eight German agents who had landed from a submarine on the shore of Long Island were captured by agents of the Federal Bureau of Investigation.

Sept. Ecuador granted the U.S. naval bases in the Galapagos Islands and the Santa Elena Peninsula.

1943, Jan. 29. President Roosevelt visited President Getúlio Vargas of Brazil. They announced the joint determination of the governments of the U.S. and Brazil to safeguard the sea lanes of the Atlantic Ocean (p. 743).

March 11. The **Lend-Lease Act was extended** for one year by a vote of 82 to 0 in the Senate and 407 to 6 in the House of Representatives.

April 21. President Roosevelt visited President Avila Camacho of Mexico. They emphasized the good relations existing between the U.S. and Mexico as an example of the Good Neighbor policy.

1944, Sept. 29. President Roosevelt called attention to the "growth of Nazi-Fascist influence" in **Argentina** and the failure of the Argentine government to fulfill its inter-American obligations. U.S. ships were forbidden to call at Argentine ports.

The **Mexican government** agreed to pay $24 million with interest at 3 percent for the property of U.S. oil companies expropriated in 1938.

1945, Feb. 21–March 8. Inter-American conference on problems of war and peace met in Mexico City. The United States offered an "economic charter for the Americas," to promote orderly reconversion and raise the standard of living. In addition, the U.S. government guaranteed for the duration of the war to aid any American state if its political independence or territorial integrity were attacked by a neighbor.

March 3. The **Act of Chapultepec** was approved by the delegates of 19 American republics, providing for joint action to guarantee each American state against aggression. The states of the Western Hemisphere were to act collectively in their own defense unless and until the World Security Council should take effective measures to deal with an attack.

March 27. The **Argentine republic declared war on Germany and Japan.** One week later (April 4) the governing board of the Pan-American Union admitted Argentina to membership and the Argentine regime was recognized (April 9) by the United States, Great Britain, and France.

8. NAVAL WARFARE AND BLOCKADE, 1939–1944

The gross tonnage of the merchant fleets of the leading nations in 1939 reflected the overwhelming advantage that Great Britain and its subsequent allies enjoyed on the sea. The ships of Norway, the Netherlands, and Belgium, most of which escaped when these countries were overrun by the Germans in 1940, took service with the British and helped to build up the pool of **United Nations** shipping.

Merchant tonnage, 1939

Great Britain	21,001,925	Japan	5,629,845
United States	11,470,177	Germany	4,482,662
Norway	4,833,813	Italy	3,424,804
Netherlands	2,969,578		
France	2,933,933		
Belgium	408,418		
Total	43,617,844		13,537,311

In 1939 the **world tonnage** for merchant ships of 100 tons or over was 68,509,432. More than half of this was destroyed, largely by submarine or air attack, in the course of the next five years. Yet, so energetic was the shipbuilding program, carried out largely in American yards immune to air attack, that by May 1945, Britain and the U.S., through the **war shipping administration,** disposed of over 4,000 ships with a

deadweight tonnage of 43 million. The Germans, Italians, and Japanese, on the other hand, found it increasingly difficult to make good their losses, and by 1945 their fleets, merchant and naval, had been almost completely eliminated.

1939, Sept. 3. The British government proclaimed a **naval blockade of Germany.**

Nov. 21. The British tightened the blockade on German imports and announced that German exports likewise would be halted.

Dec. 1. From this date neutral shippers were advised to obtain a "navicert" or certificate from British consular officials. These navicerts enabled a cargo to be passed through the patrols established by the British government in concert with its allies. Italy, the Netherlands, Belgium, and Japan protested against the British blockade measures.

Dec. 8. The U.S. Department of State questioned the British practice of seizing German goods on neutral vessels, and challenged (Dec. 14) the diversion of U.S. ships to British and French control bases. The State Department also protested (Dec. 27) against the British **examination of neutral mail** in the search for contraband.

Dec. 17. The German battleship *Graf Spee* was blown up by order of the commander.

1940, Feb. 16. A **British destroyer invaded Norwegian coastal waters** to attack the German ship *Altmark*, which was attempting to reach Germany with British prisoners of war aboard. The Norwegian government protested to London.

April 8. The British and French governments announced that Norwegian waters had been mined to prevent the transit of German ships.

July 3. BATTLE OF MERS-EL-KEBIR. British naval forces destroyed part of the French fleet stationed at Oran to make certain the ships would not be available for the Germans. The French crews had refused to surrender.

Sept. 2. Britain received 50 overage destroyers from the U.S.

Sept. 6. The U.S. Congress passed a **defense measure** appropriating $5,246,000,000 and providing for 201 ships of war, seven to be battleships of 55,000 tons each.

1941, March 30. Battle of Cape Matapan. Three Italian cruisers and two destroyers were sunk by British naval forces in the waters between Crete and Greece.

April 10. The U.S. declared **Greenland** under its protection and established naval and air bases there.

May 24. The giant battleship *Bismarck* escaped into the Atlantic, where it sank the British dreadnought *Hood,* but was itself destroyed by combined British air and naval attack (May 27).

July 7. U.S. troops landed in Iceland to relieve British occupying forces, provide for the defense of the island, and develop air and naval bases.

Sept. 16. The U.S. Navy assumed protection of all shipments as far as Iceland.

Oct. 17. The U.S. destroyer *Kearny* was torpedoed off Iceland but reached port. The destroyer *Reuben James,* likewise torpedoed in the Atlantic, was lost (Oct. 31).

Dec. 7. THE JAPANESE OPENED A SURPRISE ATTACK ON HAWAII, THE PHILIPPINES, MALAYA, AND HONG KONG. (For developments in the Pacific area, see p. 809).

1942, Nov. 8. American and British expeditionary forces landed in French North Africa in the greatest amphibious invasion hitherto attempted (p. 806).

Nov. 27. The greater part of the **French navy,** which had been rated the fourth largest in the world in 1939, was scuttled by the crews in **Toulon** harbor to prevent the Germans from obtaining the ships.

1943, March 17. The U.S., Britain, and Canada issued official assurances that their governments agreed on the most effective methods for combating the **U-boat menace.**

July 10. American, British, and Canadian forces invaded Sicily in the second mass amphibious invasion of the war. Over 2,500 vessels were involved.

July 16. President Roosevelt created the new **Board of Economic Warfare.**

Aug. 24. At the **Quebec Conference,** which ended on this date, Prime Minister Churchill and President Roosevelt announced important progress in curbing German submarine activity. "In the first six months of 1943 the number of ships sunk by U-boats was only half that of the last six months in 1942, and one-quarter that of the first six months of 1942." Figures subsequently released by the **Office of War Information** (Nov. 29, 1944) revealed that the tonnage of Allied and neutral merchant ships lost through enemy action between Sept. 1939 and Jan. 1, 1944, aggregated 22,161,000 gross tons. This was replaced by the output of U.S. shipyards alone, which launched 4,308 ships with a deadweight tonnage of 44,082,000 in the same period.

Aug. 29. When the Germans attempted to seize the Danish naval vessels anchored in the navy yard at Copenhagen, the crews scuttled 29 of the 48 ships. Some of the smaller craft, 13 in all, escaped to Sweden, and six fell into German hands.

Sept. 3. With air and naval support **ALLIED FORCES CROSSED THE STRAITS OF MESSINA AND LANDED IN SOUTHERN ITALY.** This marked the first successful amphibious invasion of continental Europe in the course of the war.

Sept. 12. The major part of the **Italian fleet** escaped to the Allies after the Italian government of Marshal Pietro Badoglio surrendered.

Oct. 13. Portugal granted Great Britain the use of the **Azores Islands** as an Allied naval and air base.

1944. By 1944 the Allied nations had achieved a position of **naval supremacy** that increased monthly and could no longer be seriously challenged. Despite improvements in submarine construction, 500 U-boats had been destroyed and merchant ship losses from this cause sharply reduced. The Germans no longer had any capital ships in fighting condition and had all but ceased to build or repair shipping. What warships survived of the Italian and French navies were wrecked or in Allied control, part of the French fleet having been repaired at a cost of $200 million. The Japanese still possessed a respectable navy, including 17 capital ships, but it was inadequate to protect the long route to the East Indies and Malaya, threatened increasingly by American and British aircraft and submarines. **Japanese air power** in particular was seriously reduced, and fewer than ten **Japanese** carriers survived, a fatal deficiency when the British carrier list had risen to 40 and the U.S. Navy possessed over 100. Inability to maintain air protection for warships even in harbor was to doom the remnants of the Japanese navy in 1945.

1944, Jan. 22. The **Allies landed forces on the Italian coast south of Rome** in a second amphibious invasion of the Italian mainland (p. 806).

June 6. ALLIED FORCES LANDED AT SEVERAL POINTS ON THE COAST OF NORMANDY, with strong naval support, an armada of 4,000 ships, and over 10,000 aircraft (p. 807). (For naval activities in the Pacific areas, see p. 809.)

9. THE CAMPAIGNS IN THE MIDDLE EAST AND AFRICA, 1939–1943

1939, Sept. 3. Egypt severed diplomatic relations with Germany, but remained neutral.

Oct. 19. Turkey signed a **treaty of alliance with Britain and France.** The Turkish government promised to enter the war when Italy did, but **remained neutral** even after the Italian declaration of war. Turkish diplomats spent much of the war struggling to keep Turkey out of the fighting.

1940, June 10. ITALY DECLARED WAR ON FRANCE AND GREAT BRITAIN.

Aug. 6. Italian forces invaded British Somaliland from Italian East Africa, completing their conquest by Aug. 19.

Aug. 27. Free French forces under Leclerc took possession of **Duala** on the Cameroon Coast, West Africa.

Sept. 13–15. An **Italian army invaded Egypt** from Libya.

Sept. 22–25. British naval forces and Free French troops under **de Gaulle** tried unsuccessfully to occupy **Dakar** in French West Africa.

Dec. 1. The British opened a **surprise drive against the Italians** in North Africa. From Mersa Matruh in Egypt, to which they had retreated, imperial troops outflanked the Italians, captured 1,000 prisoners, and advanced so rapidly that they were in **Sidi Barrani** and had begun the invasion of Libya by Dec. 12.

1941, Jan. 5. The **Italian garrison at Bardia surrendered** to the imperial forces, which took 25,000 prisoners and valuable war materiel.

Jan. 15. British forces from the Anglo-Egyptian Sudan and Kenya opened **drives into Italian East Africa** (Ethiopia) and also penetrated **Eritrea** (Jan. 19).

Jan. 22. Tobruk fell to the imperial forces invading Libya. **Darna** surrendered (Jan. 24); **Benghazi,** capital of Cyrenaica, was entered (Feb. 7); and advance units reached **El Argheila** (Feb. 8). In a campaign of two months the imperial divisions, commanded by **Gen. Sir Archibald Wavell,** had captured over 114,000 prisoners at a cost of 3,000 casualties.

Feb. 26. Mogadishu, capital of Italian Somaliland, fell to the imperial forces.

March 22. Neguelli in southern Ethiopia was occupied by the British and Ethiopian forces, and the capital, **Addis Ababa,** capitulated (April 6). Italian resistance in Eritrea collapsed by June, and before the end of 1941 all of Italian East Africa was under British control.

April–May. British invasion of Iraq and subsequent overthrow of pro-Axis government under Rashid Ali al-Gaylani.

April 3. The Italians, reinforced by German divisions trained for desert fighting, and brilliantly commanded by **Gen. Erwin Rommel,**

opened an attack against the imperial outposts in Libya. Weakened by the dispatch of 60,000 troops to Greece, the British were forced to abandon their recent conquests in a costly retreat.

April 14. The Germans reoccupied Sollum and Bardia.

April 20. Tobruk was encircled, but the imperial garrison held out with naval support. The drive of Axis mechanized divisions stopped at the Egyptian frontier (May 29). Through the summer the British prepared for a counteroffensive.

May. Trial of retired chief of staff **Aziz Ali al-Masri** and several other Egyptian officers for attempting to reach Axis lines in western Egypt and defect to the enemy.

Axis forces at Marsa Matruh in western Egypt.

June 8. BRITISH AND FREE FRENCH INVASION OF SYRIA AND LEBANON, which removed the Vichy administration.

June 18. German-Turkish nonaggression pact, signed partly to foil Soviet ambitions on Turkish territory. Another compelling motive was the close proximity of German troops, who had recently occupied Greece. For the Turks, one of the benefits of the treaty was a lucrative wartime trade with the Germans, particularly in the export of chrome.

Aug. 16. Soviet-British ultimatum to the Iranian government, demanding the expulsion of all Germans. **The shah,** whose ties with Germany had been growing closer since the late 1930s, **refused to comply. Iran remained neutral.**

Aug. 25. BRITISH AND SOVIET INVASION OF IRAN. Tehran was occupied on Sept. 16, and the country remained under **Allied occupation until 1946 (p. 757).**

Oct. Anglo-Russian ultimatum to Afghanistan, similar to the one issued earlier to the Iranian government, to expel all Axis nationals. The Afghan government grudgingly complied (Oct. 19), but **insisted on preserving its neutrality** throughout World War II.

Dec. 10. Second British drive into Libya. After relieving Tobruk, Imperial troops reached **Benghazi** for the second time (Dec. 25), but stopped short of **El Argheila** (Jan. 18, 1942). Rommel's reserves in Africa had been depleted because of the opening of the German drive on Russia (p. 802).

1942. Anglo American Middle East Supply Center, coordinated Middle Eastern economies to meet Allied war needs.

April–May. British invasion of Iraq and subsequent overthrow of pro-Axis government under Rashid Ali al-Gaylani.

May 26. Second Axis drive on Egypt. Reinforced, Rommel opened a powerful drive that captured **Tobruk** (June 21) and swept on to **Bardia** and **Bir-el-Gobi.** The victorious advance of the Axis troops was finally checked at **El Alamein,** only 70 miles from Alexandria. A four-month lull followed.

Oct. 23. Third British offensive in North Africa. The British Eighth Army under **Gen. Bernard L. Montgomery** drove from **El Alamein** and expelled Rommel's divisions from Egypt by Nov. 12.

Nov. 8. INVASION OF FRENCH NORTH AFRICA. An Anglo-American invasion force, commanded by **Gen. Dwight D. Eisenhower,** disembarked in French Morocco and Algeria. This amphibious operation, on a scale hitherto unequaled in history, required 850 ships. The French garrisons at Casablanca, Oran, and Algiers were overcome after brief fighting, and an armistice arranged (Nov. 11) by **Adm. Jean-François Darlan,** who was in Algiers. Darlan, whose role as representative of the Vichy government was ambiguous, aided the Anglo-American forces in assuming control of French North Africa and West Africa.

Dec. 1. Darlan retained his post as chief of state in North Africa with Anglo-American approval. On his assassination (Dec. 24), **Gen. Henri Giraud** was designated to succeed him.

1943, Jan. 24. Tripoli was occupied by the British Eighth Army, which pursued the retreating Axis forces into Tunisia.

Jan. 14–23. Conference at Casablanca, Morocco, with President Roosevelt, Prime Minister Churchill, Gen. Giraud, and Gen. de Gaulle attending. The relationship between **Giraud** and the **de Gaulle** "Fighting French" Party remained undefined, and Eisenhower took command of the unified North African operations. Plans for reducing the Axis powers to "unconditional surrender" were discussed at Casablanca but not disclosed.

Feb. 22. The Germans, who had rushed reinforcements to Tunisia, sought to hold this protectorate, and seized **Kasserine Pass.** The Americans reoccupied it four days later.

Feb. 25. Activation of Allied supply route through Iran to Soviet Union; 100,000 tons per month by July.

March 15. Giraud at Algiers restored representative government in French North Africa, declared legislation introduced there since 1940 void, and promised that after victory the French nation should decide its own form of government.

March 18. American forces, striking east from Algeria, captured **El Guettar** in Tunisia.

March 30. The British Eighth Army broke through the **Mareth Line** into southern Tunisia, meeting the advancing American Second Army Corps between Gabès and El Guettar on April 8.

May 8–12. End of Axis resistance in North Africa. British and U.S. forces captured the cities of **Tunis** and **Bizerte.** Possession of the whole North African coast opened the central Mediterranean to Allied shipping and exposed Italy to invasion. The threat to Egypt and the Suez Canal was ended, and the Italian dream of a great African empire had proved a costly failure. Fighting in Africa was estimated to have drained the Axis powers of 950,000 men, killed or captured, 8,000 airplanes, and 2.4 million tons of shipping.

Sept. 9. Iran declared war on Germany.

1945, Jan. 6. Turkey severed diplomatic relations with Japan. The Turkish government declared war on Germany on Feb. 23.

Feb. 24. Egypt declared war on Germany.

10. THE INVASION OF ITALY, 1943–1944

1943, July 10. U.S., British, and Canadian forces invaded Sicily under the command of Gen. Dwight D. Eisenhower. Over 2,000 vessels were employed to convoy 160,000 men, and landings were effected along the southern coast. The Americans seized Gela; the British Eighth Army and Canadian troops, disembarking at Cape Passaro, drove along the east shore.

July 14. Port Augusta was captured.

July 19. Allied **bombing planes wrecked Naples,** and, after repeated warnings, attacked railway terminals and military objectives in Rome (July 20).

July 22. Half of Sicily was occupied, the Allied front stretching from Catania to Mazzara. Palermo fell on July 24.

July 25. BENITO MUSSOLINI WAS FORCED TO RESIGN with his cabinet, and his place was taken by **Marshal Pietro Badoglio,** who opened negotiations for an armistice.

Aug. 18. Resistance in Sicily collapsed with the fall of Messina. The campaign had cost the Allied armies an estimated 22,000 casualties, the Axis forces 167,000. At a loss of 274 planes, the Allied airmen accounted for 1,691 enemy aircraft.

Sept. 3. British and American forces crossed the Straits of Messina and landed in southern Italy.

Sept. 3. An **armistice was signed** at Algiers, ending hostilities between the Anglo-American forces and those of the Badoglio regime. It was announced (Sept. 8) that the Italian surrender was unconditional. The actual terms were not disclosed.

Sept. 15. Ex-premier Mussolini, who had been held prisoner near Rome, was rescued by German troops (Sept. 12), who seized the leading cities, including Rome.

Oct. 1. After **landing near Salerno** (Sept. 9), American troops entered Naples. Thereafter, however, winter weather, the mountainous countryside, and stubborn German resistance stopped the Allied advance on a line south of Cassino.

1944, Jan. 22. Allied forces landed at Anzio in an attempt to outflank the German lines. The beachhead proved costly to hold and changed the situation little.

March 15. The Allied armies launched a heavy **assault against Cassino,** which fell on May 18.

June 4. Anglo-American troops entered Rome.

Aug. 12. Florence was captured after bitter fighting, and the Allies controlled Italy north to a line running from Livorno to Ancona. Thenceforth the Italian front remained a tense but unprogressive field of action until the final collapse of Germany in April and May 1945.

The German divisions in Italy were forced to capitulate (April 29–May 1, 1945). **Mussolini** was seized when he attempted to escape to Switzerland and was shot by his anti-Fascist captors without formal trial (April 28, 1945) (p. 696).

11. THE LIBERATION OF FRANCE AND BELGIUM, 1944

1944, June 6. INVASION OF NORMANDY. For many months careful and elaborate plans had been matured by the Supreme Headquarters of the Allied Expeditionary Force (SHAEF) for invading France. Command of this greatest amphibious operation in history was entrusted to **Gen. Dwight D. Eisenhower.** The British Isles provided the chief base for the concentration of men and war materiel, and the plan of campaign to follow the invasion date (D-Day) was rehearsed in exhaustive detail. **Air control** was to be maintained by the U.S. Eighth and Ninth Air Forces and the British Royal Air Force, with a combined strength of over 10,000 planes. An American naval task force and a British naval task force were assembled to support the assault, and the invasion was planned to proceed under cover of an intense and accurately directed bombardment by 800 guns on 80 warships. To convey the troops and supplies across the channel, 4,000 other ships were used, and the lack of port facilities for disembarkation was overcome by a dramatic improvisation in engineering. **Artificial harbors** were to be constructed on an exposed coast by sinking lines of blockships and concrete caissons to form breakwaters, with floating pierheads and pontoon causeways to serve as wharves and docks.

June 6. U.S. and British forces succeeded in **landing on the Normandy coast** between St. Marcouf and the Orne River. Within a week a strip of beach 60 miles long had been occupied and the artificial harbors constructed.

June 18. An unusually **severe gale** with high waves delayed landing operations for three days and wrecked the major causeways of one artificial harbor. It was abandoned and traffic diverted to a British-built harbor that was less exposed and had suffered less severely.

June 27. The **capture of Cherbourg** placed a major port in Allied control. During the first hundred days following D-Day 2.2 million men, 450,000 vehicles, and 4 million tons of stores were landed. This extraordinary achievement was rendered possible by perfecting the services of supply, on the basis of experience gained in the First World War and in the amphibious landings in Africa and Italy. The enormous output of Allied factories and shipyards, which made it possible to duplicate all wrecked or damaged equipment, was also an important factor.

July 9. British and Canadian troops captured Caen. Allied tanks broke through German defenses near **St. Lô** and fanned out, disorganizing enemy resistance. Persistent bombing of all bridges and railways severely crippled the German attempts to bring up adequate forces to halt Allied drives.

Aug. 15. In another amphibious operation the Allies effected successful **landings on the French Mediterranean coast** between Marseilles and Nice.

Aug. 24. The citizens of **Paris** rioted against German forces of occupation as Allied armed divisions crossed the Seine and approached the capital. **French Forces of the Interior (FFI)**, which had been organized for underground resistance and supplied with arms, rose against the retreating Germans.

Aug. 25. Paris liberated.

Sept. 2. Allied forces, which had penetrated into Belgium, **liberated Brussels.**

Sept. 12. The **American First Army crossed the German frontier** near Eupen, and American armored forces entered Germany north of Trier. The Germans, however, manning their **Westwall** defenses, offered firm resistance, and the Allied advance was halted. An Allied attempt to outflank the Westwall through the flat Dutch territory to the north (Sept. 17–26) failed, and survivors of an Allied airborne division that was dropped at **Arnhem** had to be withdrawn.

Sept. 15. The American Seventh and the French First Armies, sweeping up the Rhone Valley from beachheads won (Aug. 15) on the Riviera, joined the American Third Army at Dijon. The American, British, and French forces were then reorganized in liberated France for a projected assault on Germany.

Dec. 16–25. BATTLE OF THE BULGE. The German supreme commander in the west, **Gen. Karl von Rundstedt,** under orders from Hitler, dislocated Allied preparations by a sudden drive against thinly held American lines in the Belgian and Luxembourg sector. Suffering heavy losses, the Allied forces were driven back to the Meuse, but they rallied to attack strongly on both sides of the "bulge," and the Germans were checked before the close of December.

With the opening of 1945, the American, British, and French drives into Germany from the west, coordinated with the rapid and powerful Russian thrusts from the Danube Valley, Poland, and East Prussia, fused into one vast combined operation.

12. THE BATTLE OF GERMANY, 1945

THE ROLE OF AIR POWER. In 20th-century warfare the assembly line became as important as the battle line and consequently an equally vital target for attack. The strategy of blockade adopted by the Allied governments was designed primarily to starve not the German population but German industrial and military machines, chiefly by cutting off fuel and essential raw materials. This aim could best be achieved by supplementing the naval blockade with a systematic **bombing of German factories, power plants,** and **transportation centers.**

At the commencement of the Second World War, in 1939, the Germans possessed the strongest air force in the world. By the close of 1943, however, their bombing squadrons were depleted, though they still had a peak force of 3,000 first-line fighters. In 1944 the Allied air offensive was sharply intensified and German air strength declined decisively. Over 1,000 Luftwaffe planes were destroyed in January and February, and vital machine plants in **Essen** and **Schweinfurt** were crippled. **Gen. Henry H. Arnold,** commanding general of the U.S. Army air forces, later characterized the week of Feb. 20–26, 1944, as "probably the most decisive of the war" because of the shattering damage inflicted upon German installations in six days of favorable flying weather. By the end of hostilities the Germans had received 315 tons of explosive in retaliation for every ton of aerial bombs they had launched against Britain. Their loss in planes, by Jan. 1, 1945, had passed 50,000, in comparison with a total loss of 17,790 suffered by the U.S. air forces on all fronts. During the last four months of fighting, Allied air squadrons roamed Germany almost at will, destroying communications, obliterating plants and stores, and wrecking many of the remaining German aircraft on the ground, where they lay helpless for lack of fuel and repairs.

1945. The **military collapse of Germany** was consummated in four months by simultaneous drives launched by Soviet armies in the east and south and by American, French, and British imperial forces in the west. Concentration camps were liberated during the Allied invasion.

Jan. 12. Opening a powerful **drive into Poland,** the Russians took **Warsaw** (Jan. 17), swept into **Tarnow, Cracow,** and **Lodz** two days later (Jan. 19), and forced the Germans to abandon the whole **Vistula defense line.** By Feb. 20 Russian mechanized units, spearheads of the encroaching Soviet host that numbered 215 divisions, were within 30 miles of Berlin.

Feb. 4–12. Yalta Conference. While President Roosevelt, Prime Minister Churchill, and Marshal Stalin met at Yalta in the Crimea to plan the final defeat and occupation of Germany, the U.S. Third Army crossed the German frontier at ten points. British and Canadian divisions opened an offensive southeast of **Nijmegen** (Feb. 8).

Feb. 22. The Third Army continued its progress, crossing the **Roer River.** American advance forces drove toward the **Ruhr Valley** (Feb. 23) and entered **Trier** (March 2) and **Köln** (March 5). Supreme Headquarters announced that 954,377 German prisoners had been taken since D-Day (June 6, 1944).

March 7. The U.S. First Army **crossed the Rhine at Remagen,** and the German defense system on the east bank collapsed. By April 11 the U.S. Ninth Army had reached the **Elbe River;** eight days later the Russians fought their way into **Berlin** (April 20); and advance units of the **American and Soviet armies met on the Elbe at Torgau** (April 25).

April 28. German resistance in northern Italy broke as American and British forces swept into the Po Valley (p. 806).

May 1. BATTLE OF BERLIN. Soviet forces continued to shell Berlin and fight their way into the capital. A German radio announcement from Hamburg declared that **Adolf Hitler had died** defending the Reichschancellery, and that **Adm. Karl Doenitz** had succeeded him.

One million German and Italian soldiers in Italy and Austria laid down their arms.

May 4. The **dissolution of the German National Socialist regime** continued, with local military commanders making their own offers of capitulation. German divisions in northwestern Germany, the Netherlands, and Denmark surrendered.

May 7. A group of **German army leaders** sent envoys to Reims, where they **signed terms of surrender.**

May 8. President Truman for the United States and Prime Minister Churchill for Great Britain proclaimed the **end of the war in Europe (V-E Day).**

May 9. Marshal Stalin announced the end of the war to the Russian people. German army chiefs completed the formula of surrender in Berlin.

May 9–23. While German forces were being disarmed, the Allied governments transmitted orders through a **provisional German government** headed by Doenitz. After two weeks this provisional regime was superseded. Doenitz, with several colleagues, and members of the German high command and the general staff, were taken into custody.

June 5. An **Allied Control Committee,** including **Gen. Dwight D. Eisenhower, Field Marshal Sir Bernard L. Montgomery,** and **Marshal Gregory K. Zhukov,** assumed full control throughout Germany. German territory, as of Dec. 31, 1937, was delimited in four **zones of occupation** under American, British, Soviet, and French military administration.

13. THE WAR IN ASIA, 1939–1941

1939. Economic penetration and **military intervention** enabled the Japanese to bring a widening area of China under their control after 1931, and especially after 1937. They forced the Chinese Nationalists to establish a new capital at **Chongqing** (p. 780). At the same time, the outbreak of war in Europe compelled the British, French, and Soviet governments to concentrate their forces in that quarter, and left the United States the only great power in a position to oppose Japanese expansion.

Dec. 31. Russia and Japan reached an accord concerning the renewal of fishing rights and the settlement of debt claims between Russia and Manchukuo.

1940, March 30. The Japanese supported the establishment of **a puppet government under Wang Ching-wei** at Nanking to administer the areas of China under their control.

April 17. Secretary of State **Cordell Hull** warned the Japanese that the U.S. would oppose any attempt to change the status quo of the **Netherlands East Indies** by other than peaceful means.

June 9. Russia and Japan reached an accord regarding the disputed frontier of Manchukuo.

June 25. With the **collapse of France,** the Japanese demanded the right to land forces in **French Indochina.** Japanese warships arrived at several ports there.

July 18. The British government closed the **Burma Road.** This was the main route by which the Chinese Nationalist armies under **Gen. Jiang Jieshi (Chiang Kai-shek)** could obtain foreign war materiel. The Japanese agreed to discuss peace terms with the Chinese Nationalist government.

Aug. 9. British garrisons at Shanghai and in northern China were withdrawn.

Sept. 4. Secretary of State Hull warned the Japanese government that aggressive moves against Indochina would have an unfortunate effect upon public opinion in the U.S.

Sept. 26. After the French government at Vichy had conceded the use of three airfields and several ports in Indochina, Japanese forces began the **occupation of Indochina** and crossed into China 120 miles from Hanoi. The U.S. government placed an embargo on the export of iron and steel scrap after Oct. 15 to countries (except Great Britain) outside the Western Hemisphere. The Japanese ambassador at Washington described this (Oct. 8) as an "unfriendly act."

Sept. 27. JAPAN JOINED ITALY AND GERMANY in a ten-year tripartite pact (p. 801).

Oct. 18. Great Britain reopened the Burma Road.

1941, Jan. 31. Under Japanese auspices an armistice was arranged to end hostilities that had broken out between **Thailand and French Indochina.** The Japanese obtained rice, rubber, coal, and minerals from Indochina and confirmed their military occupation.

March 11. France and Thailand concluded a convention, later signed at Tokyo (May 9) whereby Thailand acquired the section of Laos province west of the Mekong River, three-fourths of the Campong-Thom province, and territory in northern Cambodia.

April 13. JAPAN AND SOVIET RUSSIA CONCLUDED A NEUTRALITY PACT.

July 26. All Japanese credits in the U.S. were "frozen" by a presidential decree. Great Britain took similar action regarding Japanese assets in that country. All armed forces in the Philippine Islands were placed under the control of the U.S. with **Gen. Douglas MacArthur** as commander in chief in East Asia.

Aug. 17. President Roosevelt warned the Japanese ambassador, Adm. Kichisaburo Nomura, that any further policy of military domination in Asia by the Japanese would force the U.S. "to take immediately any and all steps necessary" to safeguard legitimate American rights and interests. **Prime Minister Churchill** declared a week later (Aug. 24) that Great Britain would support the U.S. if negotiations with Japan failed.

Nov. 17. Ambassador **Joseph C. Grew** at Tokyo cabled a warning to the U.S. that the Japanese might make a sudden attack.

Nov. 20. At Washington **Nomura** and a special Japanese envoy, **Saburo Kurusu,** proposed that the U.S. and Japan reopen trade relations and cooperate in securing the commodities of the Netherlands East Indies.

Nov. 26. Secretary Hull proposed as a **basis of agreement** that the Japanese withdraw their forces from China and Indochina, recognize the territorial integrity of these countries, and accept the Chinese Nationalist government. The U.S. and Japan could then negotiate a liberal trade treaty. Kurusu declared such proposals practically "put an end to the negotiations." Three days later (Nov. 29) Hull informed the British ambassador that diplomatic conversations between the U.S. and Japan had virtually broken down.

Dec. 6. President Roosevelt cabled a personal message to the emperor of Japan urging him to use his influence to preserve peace.

Dec. 7. JAPANESE ATTACK ON PEARL HARBOR (below).

After Dec. 7, when Japan was **at war with the United States and Great Britain,** the conflict in China was overshadowed by developments in the Pacific and the East Indies. Japanese **conquest of Burma** (1942) closed the Burma Road, the last practicable route by which military supplies could reach Chongqing, for only a few tons a month could be flown in by air. Chinese armies remained in the field, and the Japanese kept an army of 1 million men as an occupying force to protect towns and railway lines. The ultimate fate of these Japanese armies in Asia, and their communications with the Japanese home islands, depended upon the outcome of the war at sea.

14. THE WAR IN THE PACIFIC, 1941–1945

1941, Dec. 7. The JAPANESE SEA AND AIR FORCES LAUNCHED A SURPRISE ATTACK ON THE UNITED STATES BASE AT PEARL HARBOR, HAWAII, ON THE PHILIPPINES, and against British forces in **Hong Kong** and **Malaya.** The U.S. forces were caught unprepared. At Hawaii five battleships and three cruisers were sunk or seriously damaged, three battleships less severely damaged, many smaller vessels sunk or crippled, and 177 aircraft destroyed. The casualties included 2,343 dead, 876 missing, and 1,272 injured.

Dec. 8. THE UNITED STATES DECLARED WAR ON JAPAN. Japanese air and naval forces attacked **Guam** and **Wake Island.** Resistance on Guam ended on Dec. 13 and on Wake Island on Dec. 20. **Great Britain declared war on Japan.**

Dec. 10. The British battleship *Prince of Wales* and the battle cruiser *Repulse,* which had been dispatched to Singapore, were sunk by Japanese aircraft off the Malay coast.

Dec. 11. GERMANY AND ITALY DECLARED WAR ON THE UNITED STATES.

Dec. 21. A **ten-year treaty of alliance** was signed at Bangkok **between Japan and Thailand.** The Thai government agreed to aid Japan and declared war (Jan. 25, 1942) against Great Britain and the U.S.

Dec. 25. British forces at **Hong Kong surrendered** to the Japanese.

1942, Jan. 2. Manila and Cavite were captured by the Japanese. U.S. and Philippine forces fortified their position on **Bataan Peninsula** and held out until April 9. The island fort of **Corregidor** at the entrance to Manila Bay did not fall until May 6.

Jan. 11. Japanese forces commenced an **occupation of the Netherlands East Indies,** landing on Celebes, at Rabaul (Jan. 23), New Ireland (Jan. 25), the Solomon Islands (Jan. 26), and Amboina (Jan. 31).

Jan. 24–27. Allied forces sank five Japanese transports in a naval engagement in the **Macassar Straits.**

Feb. 15. Japanese forces, which had penetrated Malaya, captured **Singapore** from the north by land, taking 60,000 prisoners.

Feb. 27–March 1. Battle of the Java Sea. Naval units of the Allied powers were largely destroyed, opening the way for the Japanese conquest of the East Indies. Batavia fell on March 6.

March 7. The **British evacuated Rangoon,** and the Japanese rapidly occupied Burma. **Lashio** was taken (April 30), closing the Burma Road at that point, and **Mandalay** fell on May 2.

March 9. The **conquest of Java** was virtually completed by the Japanese, who **had won Timor** (Feb. 20) also. The growing threat to Australia was checked in the jungles of New Guinea, and **Gen. Douglas MacArthur** assumed command of the combined Allied forces in the southwest Pacific (March 17).

April 18. U.S. carrier-based bombers, commanded by **Col. James H. Doolittle,** raided Tokyo and landed on Chinese bases.

May 5. To avert possible Japanese penetration, British forces landed at **Diego Suarez,** the naval base on the north end of Madagascar, and proceeded to occupy this French colony, entering the capital, Tananarive, on Sept. 23.

May 7. BATTLE OF THE CORAL SEA. Allied naval and air power frustrated a possible Japanese invasion of Australia or the New Hebrides by destroying 100,000 tons of Japanese shipping between New Guinea and the Solomon Islands.

June 4–7. A Japanese naval force attacked **Midway Island** and was dispersed with heavy losses by U.S. naval and air units.

June 12. Japanese invaders occupied Attu in the Aleutian Islands and later landed on **Kiska.** The Japanese tide of conquest was at its height, coinciding with the German drive for the Caucasian oil fields.

July 9. The Chinese Nationalist armies won a major success over the Japanese in Kiangsi Province.

Aug. 7. U.S. Marines landed in the Solomon Islands. Tulagi and Japanese airfields on **Guadalcanal** were captured.

Nov. 12. A three-day **naval battle in the Solomon Islands** ended in a victory for U.S. forces. One Japanese battleship and five cruisers were reported sunk, and 12 transports destroyed.

1943, March 4. Allied air squadrons destroyed a Japanese convoy approaching New Guinea.

July 1. Opening a **concerted offensive** in the South Pacific, Allied

forces captured **Rendova Island** (July 2), while Australian troops linked up with American troops at **Salamaua** (July 3). The Japanese base and airfield at **Munda** on New Georgia Island fell on Aug. 7. In September a Japanese force of 20,000 was encircled near **Lae** (Sept. 6–7), the airfield at Salamaua was captured (Sept. 13), and **Finschhafen** occupied (Oct. 3). Allied forces disembarked on **Bougainville Island** (Oct. 31). Landing on the **Gilbert Islands** (Nov. 22), U.S. forces crushed Japanese resistance in three days' fighting, and marines captured the important air base at **Cape Gloucester** on Dec. 31.

1944, Feb. 2. Invasion of the Marshall Islands. Roi (Feb. 3), **Kwajalein** (Feb. 6), and an air base in **Eniwetok** (Feb. 20) were seized by the U.S. troops. On March 1 American troops landed on the **Admiralty Islands,** and new landings were achieved in **New Guinea** (April 24) at **Hollandia** and **Aitape.** The **Schouten** group was invaded (May 28) and the **Marianas** (June 16).

June 16. U.S. superfortress bombing planes raided the Japanese home island of Kyushū, opening a campaign of destructive attacks on Japanese cities which ended only with the Japanese capitulation.

Aug. 11. The **reconquest of Guam** was completed. On the Indian frontier the last Japanese invaders were driven back to Burma.

Sept. 14. American forces disembarked on **Morotai** in the Molucca Islands, and on the **Palau Islands** in the Carolines (Sept. 15).

Oct. 19. U.S. invasion groups, commanded by MacArthur, **landed on the island of Leyte,** opening the campaign for the **reconquest of the Philippines.**

Oct. 21–22. SECOND BATTLE OF THE PHILIPPINE SEA. The Japanese fleet, having failed to halt the invasion, withdrew from Philippine waters (Oct. 25). It had suffered 40 ships sunk, 46 damaged, and 405 planes destroyed. More U.S. forces were promptly landed on the island of **Samos** (Oct. 26).

Nov. 26. A new phase of the Pacific war opened with the initiation of **raids on Japan** by U.S. land-based B-29 bombers operating from **Saipan** in the Marianas.

1945, Feb. 19–March 17. The stubborn and protracted **battle for Iwo Jima** gave the U.S. air forces a base 750 miles from Yokohama, at a cost of 19,938 American casualties.

March 21. U.S. carrier aircraft, penetrating Japanese inland waters, attacked principal units of the Japanese fleet, damaged 15 warships, and destroyed 475 planes. No U.S. ship was lost.

April 1. U.S. Marines and Army troops invaded Okinawa. An attempt by the Japanese fleet to check this amphibious operation resulted in the sinking by American aircraft (April 7) of the Japanese battleship *Yamato,* two cruisers, and three destroyers. The last bitter resistance on Okinawa did not end until June 21, but the island provided an airbase 325 miles from Japanese cities.

April 30. In Southeast Asia the 14th British Imperial Army **(Adm. Lord Louis Mountbatten),** with support from U.S. and Chinese forces, completed the destruction in 15 months of the Japanese 15th, 28th, and 33d Armies. Total Japanese casualties were set (May 5) at 347,000.

May–Aug. In the **greatest air offensive in history** U.S. land-based and carrier-based aircraft destroyed or immobilized the remnants of the Japanese navy, shattered Japanese industry, and curtailed Japanese sea communications by submarine and air attack and extensive minefields. U.S. battleships moved in to shell densely populated cities with impunity and the **20th Air Force** dropped 40,000 tons of bombs on Japanese industrial centers in one month.

After the collapse of Germany in May (p. 807) the Japanese were left without allies, and the British and American resources in men and materiel were redirected toward the Pacific theater of war. Japanese strength was already half broken and Japanese morale was beginning to disintegrate when three terrible strokes within one week hastened the conclusion of the war.

Aug. 6. An **ATOMIC BOMB,** secretly prepared by American and British scientists, was dropped on the Japanese city of **Hiroshima** with obliterating effect. The city was more than half destroyed.

Aug. 8. SOVIET RUSSIA DECLARED WAR ON JAPAN and commenced **invasion of Manchuria.**

Aug. 9. A **second atomic bomb** was dropped by the Americans on Nagasaki.

Aug. 10. The Japanese cabinet decided to make an **offer of surrender.** The Allied terms of capitulation were communicated to Tokyo and accepted four days later (Aug. 14). **U.S. forces of occupation landed in Japan on Aug. 26.**

Sept. 2. The **FORMAL TERMS OF SURRENDER WERE SIGNED** by the Japanese officials and military leaders on board the USS *Missouri* in Tokyo Bay.

15. THE ORGANIZATION OF PEACE

The **League of Nations,** formed at Versailles in 1919, failed to curb powerful aggressors or to protect its weaker members from attack. It was never a well-balanced, truly supranational league, and proved itself unfit to deal with economic problems or to enforce its decisions. When the Second World War opened in 1939, the League of Nations had lost almost all its prestige and influence.

The **international anarchy,** repudiation of treaties, acts of aggression, and final outbreak of a general war that marked the 1930s brought home to peaceful nations the need for an organization better adapted to adjust international tensions and disputes.

Three **projects for international federation** took form in the war years 1939–45. In Europe, Germany, Italy, and their satellite states forged an anti-Comintern, antidemocratic bloc that Adolf Hitler called his **"New Order."** In Asia and the East Indies the Japanese extended their power over a widening area, which they termed a **"Coprosperity Sphere"** and in which they promulgated the doctrine of Asia for the Asians. Both the German and the Japanese hegemony had contracted and finally collapsed in defeat by the summer of 1945.

The third international federation formed in the war years came to be known as the **United Nations Organization.** It was based ideologically upon the foundations of the **Atlantic Charter** (p. 732); structurally upon the wartime solidarity of the "Big Three," Britain, the Soviet Union, and the United States; and financially upon the credits ($43 billion) made available by the lend-lease policy of the U.S. government to nations that opposed the Axis. The victory of the United Nations, achieved in large measure through the effective mobilization of world resources, left their leaders in a position to write the peace treaties.

1942, Jan. 1. Declaration by the United Nations at Washington to cooperate, on the basis of the Atlantic Charter, in employing their full forces against Germany, Italy, and Japan. The declaration was signed by the U.S., Great Britain, Soviet Russia, and 23 other nations at war. Subsequently 19 other nations adhered.

1943, Oct. 19–Nov. 1. Moscow conference of British, U.S., and Soviet foreign ministers, who agreed (China adhering) to establish an international organization for peace and security, to set up a European advisory commission on terms of German surrender, to separate Austria from Germany, and to destroy the Italian Fascist regime.

Nov. 9. The **United Nations Relief and Rehabilitation Administration (UNRRA)** was established at Washington. This international body was to aid countries subjugated by the Axis powers.

Nov. 22–26. Cairo conferences (Roosevelt, Churchill, Jiang Jieshi [Chiang Kai-shek] and **Cairo Declaration** on postwar treatment of Japan (Manchuria to be returned to China; Korea to be independent).

Nov. 28–Dec. 1. Tehran Conference (Roosevelt, Churchill, Stalin): discussion of landing in France and of cooperation in the peace settlements. Agreement to set up a **European Advisory Commission** to study European problems.

Dec. 4–6. Second Cairo Conference: futile efforts of Roosevelt and Churchill to induce Turkey (President Inönü) to enter the war.

1944, April. A **United Nations Organization for Educational and Cultural Reconstruction** was proposed by the ministers of education, meeting in London.

July 1–22. A **United Nations Monetary and Financial Conference** (Bretton Woods Conference) met for three weeks. To improve world economic conditions, the delegates of the UN proposed to create an **International Monetary Fund** and an **International Bank for Reconstruction and Development,** the first with a credit of $8.8 billion, the second with a capital of $10 billion. The major purpose was to avert currency disorders and stabilize exchange rates, and the plans, worked out by the financial experts of 44 nations, were referred to the governments concerned for approval.

Sept. 16–26. The **council of the United Nations Relief and Rehabilitation Administration** held its second session, at Montreal. The allotment of $50 million to Italy, partly for medical supplies, marked the first extension of aid by the UN to a former enemy country. Plans were laid to provide for a budget of $11.5 million for 1945, by assessing member states.

Oct. 9. Dumbarton Oaks Conference. Delegates representing the U.S., the British Commonwealth, and the Soviet Union, after meeting from Aug. 21 to Sept. 27, published proposals for a permanent international organization to be known as the **United Nations.** The aim of the new society of nations was the preservation of world peace and security.

1945, April 25–June 26. SAN FRANCISCO CONFERENCE. Delegates of 50 nations met at San Francisco to complete a **charter for the United Nations Organization.** A preliminary draft was submitted to the conference on June 22 by U.S. secretary of state **Edward R. Stettinius.** It provided for four organs in the new body: (1) **a General Assembly** as the major policy-shaping forum; (2) a **security council** to supervise military and political problems; (3) an **economic and social council** to deal with problems of economic and social conflict; and (4) an **international court of justice** for the adjustment of international disputes. The administrative work of the United Nations Organization was to be handled by a general **secretariat** directed by a secretary-general.

July 17–Aug. 2. POTSDAM CONFERENCE. President Harry S. Truman, Prime Minister Winston Churchill, and Generalissimo Joseph V. Stalin met in Potsdam to confer on plans for reestablishing peace. After July 28, **Clement R. Attlee,** head of the new British Labour cabinet, replaced Churchill at the conference. An agreement was reached to establish a **council of foreign ministers,** representing the U.S., Great Britain, the Soviet Union, France, and China, to continue the drafting of peace settlements. Its first session was held in London (Sept. 11).

For **Germany** the decisions reached at the Potsdam Conference implied: (1) disarmament and demilitarization; (2) dissolution of National Socialist institutions; (3) trial of war criminals; (4) encouragement of democratic ideals; (5) restoration of local self-government and democratic political parties; (6) freedom of speech, press, and religion, subject to the requirements of military security.

Economic restrictions drafted by the conference for Germany included: (1) prohibition of the manufacture of war materiel and implements of war; (2) controlled production of metals, chemicals, and machinery essential to war; (3) decentralization of German cartels, syndicates, and trusts; (4) emphasis upon agriculture and peaceful domestic industries; (5) control of exports, imports, and scientific research. The methods whereby the victors would enforce these conditions were to be worked out in detail later.

The **conference further ordained** "that Germany be compelled to compensate to the greatest possible extent for the loss and suffering that she caused to the United Nations." The members of the conference agreed in principle on the disposal of the German navy and merchant marine, but in this matter likewise the details were not worked out.

Peace treaties with Finland, Bulgaria, Hungary, Romania, and Italy were to be drawn up as promptly as possible.

Sept. 2. FORMAL TERMS OF SURRENDER were signed by the Japanese civil and military envoys aboard the USS *Missouri* in Tokyo Bay. The Japanese home islands were placed under the rule of a U.S. army of occupation, but the emperor remained as the head of the state and the Japanese political and police officials continued to fulfill their functions. The high command and the military organizations were progressively disbanded. American forces also occupied island possessions regained or newly captured in the Pacific Ocean.

Korea was placed under Soviet and U.S. occupation, pending establishment of a Korean democratic government. The **Kurile Islands** and the southern part of **Sakhalin** were ceded to Russia, **Outer Mongolia** was recognized as part of the Soviet sphere of control, and Russia shared with China the facilities and supervision of **Port Arthur** and the Manchurian railroads.

Sept. 9. Capitulation terms for Japanese forces in China (estimated at 1 million men) were signed at Nanking by Japanese commanders and representatives of Jiang Jieshi.

China regained sovereignty over **Inner Mongolia** and **Manchuria**, as well as the islands of **Formosa** and **Hainan**. **Hong Kong** was reoccupied by the British, who likewise accepted the formal surrender at Singapore (Sept. 12) of all Japanese forces (585,000 men) in Southeast Asia and the East Indies.

1946, July 29–Oct. 15. A **PEACE CONFERENCE** of the 21 nations that waged war against the Axis in Europe met at Paris to discuss the draft treaties for peace with **Italy, Romania, Hungary, Bulgaria,** and **Finland.** These treaties had been prepared by the foreign ministers' council of Great Britain, France, the U.S., and the Soviet Union.

1947, Feb. 10. The **peace treaties were signed** in Paris. **Italy** lost four small border regions to France, its Adriatic islands and most of Venezia Giulia to Yugoslavia, and the Dodecanese Islands to Greece. It also renounced sovereignty over its North African colonies and agreed to the creation of the **Free Territory of Trieste.** Its armed forces were reduced to 300,000 men, and it agreed to pay $360 million in reparations. **Romania** lost Bessarabia and northern Bukovina to the Soviet Union, but received back all of Transylvania. **Hungary** was left with its 1938 borders, except for a minor frontier rectification in favor of Czechoslovakia. **Bulgaria** retained the southern Dobrudja. **Finland** ceded the port of Petsamo to the Soviet Union and granted the Russians a 50-year lease of a naval base at Porkkala.   *(To pp. 824, 837)*

VII. THE CONTEMPORARY PERIOD, 1945–2000

A. GENERAL AND COMPARATIVE DIMENSIONS

(From p. 650)

In the second half of the 20th century, the rivalry of two superpowers, the **United States** and the **Soviet Union,** dominated world political affairs. Within this political framework, **the globalization of virtually all aspects of human life continued.** Yet the intensification of global interactions resulted in neither a peaceful "one world" society nor a world filled with identical technological dictatorships. Instead, local anarchies and assertions of special identities coexisted with global

communications and economic networks and new transnational and regional structures. The major global dynamics of the second half of the 20th century can be seen in two broad dimensions: the evolution of global relationships in political, economic, social, and cultural structures, and in scientific and environmental interactions; and the intensification and diversification of concrete international relationships of institutions and movements.

1. CHANGING GLOBAL PATTERNS

Global relationships evolved in a number of important ways in the second half of the 20th century. The developments were reflected in three important areas: the changing nature of global power structures and conflicts; the impact of globalization on economics, science, and technology, and responses to the environment; and the emerging complex relationships among global, regional, and local aspects of culture and society. By the 1990s, there was considerable awareness of many different possibilities for the formation of "new world orders."

a. CHANGING STRUCTURES OF GLOBAL POWER

The basic nature of global power structures, and even the nature of the most important conflicts, changed significantly during the second half of the 20th century. Such changes were clearly visible in 1) the transformation of **imperialisms** and the development of **nationalisms;** 2) the evolution of the **cold war** and the basic framework for world politics; 3) the development of **international institutions** for conflict management and resolution.

1. IMPERIALISMS AND NATIONALISMS

At the end of World War II, a number of major European states still controlled significant overseas empires. In the postwar years, the main transformation was the **decline of the older empires** and the **emergence of two superpowers** that replaced them as the major world powers. During the war, **Allied** promises and **Axis** conquests had raised hopes of national independence in many areas. After the war, growing nationalism and European weakness, sometimes furthered by cold war rivalries for Asian and African allegiances, led to **decolonization.**

1945–54. Reestablished empires and new states. In the immediate postwar era, the major empires attempted to reestablish control in many areas but also granted independence to particular states. The empires faced movements of armed opposition and growing political nationalism.

Armed opposition to empires. In many of the areas that had been conquered by the **Axis powers** during World War II, there was armed nationalist opposition to attempts to reestablish European imperial control. In **INDOCHINA,** the **Viet Minh,** originally a movement of resistance to Japanese control, declared **Vietnamese independence** in 1945 (p. 1036). However, the **French** attempted the reconquest of its Indochinese colonies; in the long **first Indochina war,** the French ultimately lost and withdrew after their defeat at **Dien Bien Phu** in 1954. In **INDONESIA,** the **Dutch** attempted to reestablish control after the Japanese defeat, in opposition to the independence declared in 1945 by nationalists led by **Sukarno** (p. 774). After a costly war, **Indonesian**

independence was recognized in 1949. In **SYRIA** and **LEBANON,** French attempts in 1945 to reverse wartime agreements giving independence to the two countries were met with nationalist opposition. Under pressure from the United States, Great Britain, and the United Nations, French troops were withdrawn in 1946.

Negotiated independence in the immediate postwar era. The imperial powers and local leaders in a number of countries were able to negotiate arrangements for independence. In **SOUTH ASIA** negotiations led to independence for **Ceylon** (now Sri Lanka) from the **British** in 1947, and for **Burma** in 1948. **INDIA** was partitioned and, in 1947, became the independent states of **Pakistan and India.** Britain also withdrew from **PALESTINE,** where a United Nations–defined partition resulted in the establishment of **Israel** in 1948 and in the emergence of a **Palestinian** nationalist movement seeking to create an Arab Palestinian state. Both partitions resulted in bloody conflicts, but Great Britain was not involved directly in either postindependence war. However, **Jewish guerrilla** warfare during and immediately after World War II had put added pressure on the British to withdraw from Palestine. **JORDAN** received formal independence from its mandate status in 1946, although it maintained a special treaty relationship with Britain until the 1950s. **The Philippines** were proclaimed independent in 1946, shortly after their reconquest by the **United States** from Japan. **Former Italian colonies** were special cases. After considerable disagreement among the major powers, the United Nations established the independent Kingdom of **LIBYA** in 1951, and voted in 1950 to affirm the independence of **SOMALIA** under the trusteeship of Great Britain and Italy. **Eritrea** was included in the newly liberated **Ethiopia** with some autonomy, which was later lost in the 1950s.

1954–69. Victory of nationalism. In the 1950s and 1960s, the classic struggles between nationalism and imperialism reached a climax. By the end of the 1960s virtually every major colony in the large European overseas empires had gained its independence, and only smaller dependencies remained. This was achieved both through costly wars of **nationalist revolution** and **continuing negotiations.** The end of the European empires was often overshadowed by the tensions of the cold war, which threatened nuclear global destruction rather than costly local conflicts. Nevertheless, the end of the old empires marked a major transition, and the newly independent states became important members of the emerging **THIRD WORLD,** between the communist world and the West.

Wars of nationalist liberation. In a number of countries, independence came only after a fierce fight. In contrast to the nationalist wars of the late 1940s, these later wars did not build on structures developed as a result of World War II so much as they were the products of distinctive local developments involving imperial policies and nationalism. In **ALGERIA,** there was a large French settler community, and the French claimed that Algeria was part of France, not a colony. The Algerian war for independence (p. 991) began in 1954, under the leadership of the **Front de libération nationale (FLN).** The war involved counterrevolutions by conservative French Algerians and a transformation of the French political system itself. Finally, in 1962, after perhaps more than one million war deaths, Algeria became independent under an FLN government.

The **British** faced three major colonial conflicts in the 1950s. In **CYPRUS,** Greek Cypriot nationalists sought union with **Greece** and engaged in sometimes violent opposition to both the British and Turkish Cypriots. After negotiations that included Greece and Turkey, Cyprus became independent in 1960. In **KENYA,** local Kenyan resistance, especially to British settlers, led to the violent **Mau Mau uprising,** which was suppressed in 1955 (p. 1061). However, the uprising increased pressures for negotiations, and Kenya achieved independence in 1963. In **MALAYA,** the British reestablished control at the end of the war, but a **communist revolt** began in 1948 among some Chinese Malayans. This conflict was costly, but it encouraged the British and the Malayan nationalists to move toward agreement on independence. The suppression of the revolt by 1955 was followed by Malayan independence in 1957 (p. 1016) and the formation in 1963 of the **Federation of Malasia** which included Singapore, Sarawak, and North Borneo, as well as Malaya.

The achievement of independence in the **PORTUGUESE COLONIES** involved wars of national independence following the **revolution of 1974** in Portugal itself. In **ANGOLA,** a number of nationalist groups with essentially regional identities emerged by the 1960s. In 1961 a multisided conflict began in which three major groups fought against the Portuguese and each other. Negotiations after the 1974 revolution resulted in the proclamation of Angolan independence in 1975. Agreement among the liberation movements was brief, and the **Movimento Popular de Liberatação de Angola (MPLA)** formed a regime that received much international recognition. A postindependence civil war followed, which continued into the 1990s. In **MOZAMBIQUE,** the **Frente de Libertação de Mozambique (FRELIMO)** began a revolution in 1964 against the Portuguese that resulted in independence in 1975. In the small Portuguese colony of **Guinea-Bissau,** a remarkable, ideologically radical movement led by **AMALCAR CABRAL,** who was murdered in 1973, began a guerrilla war in 1963. By 1973, the movement controlled much of the territory and declared independence, which was recognized by the Portuguese after the 1974 revolution.

In **SOUTHWEST AFRICA (NAMIBIA)** a long war of national liberation was begun by the **South-West African Peoples' Organization (SWAPO)** in 1966. The **Republic of South Africa** received a League of Nations mandate granting control over the former German colony at the end of World War I, and it continued to control the area in defiance of the United Nations after World War II. **SWAPO** received considerable international support, but **Namibia** became independent only in 1990, after almost 24 years of nationalist guerrilla warfare.

Negotiated independence. During the 1950s and 1960s an extraordinary transformation took place, especially in Africa. In the 1950s, a few countries were the harbingers of a flood of new countries to come. **Sudan** (1956); **Ghana,** the former Gold Coast (1957); and **Malaysia** (1957) received independence from Great Britain. France agreed to the independence of **Morocco** and **Tunisia** in 1956. In 1958, **GUINEA,** under the leadership of **Sékou Touré,** voted to become independent rather than to be a member of the French Community. Then, 1960 was a **year of independence** in Africa. Thirteen former French colonies became independent members of the French Community; **Nigeria, Togo,** and **Somalia** received independence from Great Britain, and the Belgian Congo **(Zaire)** became independent and almost immediately was plunged into civil war. By 1969, another 15 African states had become independent, including **Southern Rhodesia,** whose white regime made a unilateral declaration of independence that received little international recognition. In the **Caribbean region,** four dependencies had become independent by 1969; elsewhere there were also the new island states of **Malta** (1964), the **Maldives** (1965), and **Mauritius** (1968).

Newly independent states became a significant feature in global affairs. In 1945, 51 states had signed the **Charter of the United Nations.** Then, between 1954 and 1969, 53 newly independent states also be-

came members of the United Nations. This reflected the **triumph of nationalism** and the end of the age of the European overseas empires.

1970–90s. Changing nature of new states. In the final decades of the 20th century, the status of the remnants of the European overseas empires was defined, with a number of newly independent **ministates** being established. However, additional new states emerged as nationalist movements developed in response to other types of multinational and multiethnic structures, such as the Soviet Union. By the 1990s, a new process of national state formation had replaced decolonization as the major source of new state structures.

The remnants of overseas empires. In the 1970s and 1980s, most of the last small colonial holdings of European powers gained independence. Island groups in the **PACIFIC BASIN** that had come under imperial control in the 19th century had their political status defined. Some had been colonies; the former German colonies had been League of Nations **mandates** and United Nations **trusteeships** placed under the control of various powers. Among the first to gain permanent status were **Hawaii,** which became the fiftieth state of the United States, and **Western New Guinea,** which became a part of Indonesia in 1963. Independence was gained by **Western Samoa,** a New Zealand trusteeship, in 1962, and by **Nauru,** an Australian trusteeship, in 1968. Between 1970 and 1990, eight additional independent Pacific basin states were established. **East Timor** was annexed by Indonesia in 1976, following the Portuguese withdrawal, but a guerrilla movement fighting for independence emerged. In the 1990s, some island groups remained under the control of the United States, France, Australia, and New Zealand. In the **PERSIAN GULF** region, **Kuwait** had already become independent in 1961, and Britain formally withdrew from **Bahrain, Qatar,** and the small states that joined together in the **United Arab Emirates** in 1971. In the **CARIBBEAN,** nine new independent states emerged from British and Dutch control, though some islands, like the Caymans, opted for continued colonial status qualified by local autonomy. Between 1970 and 1990, 34 more new states joined the United Nations.

Postcolonial new states. In the final decades of the 20th century, **SEPARATIST MOVEMENTS** had little success in many areas, but the establishment of independent **Bangladesh** in the former East Pakistan, as a result of a civil war in 1971, was an important exception. Before the late 1980s, there had been a number of civil wars in newly independent states in which regions attempted to secede. In **AFRICA,** the newly independent nations maintained their imperially defined boundaries, despite their often arbitrary nature. As a result, there were regional factions that wished to break away from countries they did not feel themselves to be a part of. Regions that attempted to secede in unsuccessful wars included **Katanga** in **Congo** (1960–63), **Biafra** in **Nigeria** (1967–70), and southern **Sudan** (1955–72, 1981–90s). The only successful African secessionist movement was in **ERITREA,** where the Eritrean liberation movement fought against a series of different Ethiopian regimes and finally succeeded when a dictatorial Marxist regime collapsed in 1991; a referendum confirmed its independence in 1993. Elsewhere, **KURDS** failed to create an independent state from the Kurdish areas of **Iraq, Turkey,** and **Iran,** although a short-lived Kurdish republic was created by the Soviet Union in northern Iran (1945–46) and an autonomous Kurdish region in northern Iraq received international protection after the Persian Gulf War of 1990–91. **TAMIL** separatists in **Sri Lanka** began a revolt in 1983 that continued into the 1990s, and **Philippine Muslims** fought for autonomy or independence in some southern islands throughout much of the second half of the 20th century.

REDEFINED STATES. In the early 1990s, there was another burst of new states. Most of this activity was the result of a redefining of the political status of ethnic and national groups in the wake of the **collapse of the Soviet Union** and its Eastern European empire, and of the new ways in which existing political identities were recognized. From 1990 to the end of 1993, 28 states were admitted to the United Nations. Eighteen new members were former republics of the **Soviet Union,** four had been part of **Yugoslavia,** and two new states emerged out of the former **Czechoslovakia.** The other new members were two **Pacific island groups, North and South Korea,** and the two African states whose wars of liberation were finally successful, **Namibia** and **Eritrea.** In addition, four old European ministates that had been dependent on larger neighbors for representation (**Andorra, Liechtenstein, Monaco, and San Marino**) became independent members of the United Nations. The new states reflected the **end of centralized, multinational empires** of the old style, even the continental empire of Russia, and the emergence of a new era of **smaller ethnic states** and **larger unions of states** of a Common Market or confederation type. At the same time, larger structures of international coordination were being built. Not only the European Common Market but also the Confederation of Independent States, loosely linking most former states in the Soviet Union, and the North American Free Trade Association (1993), suggested new regional coordination. The domination of global affairs by European empires or by the two great superpowers had come to an end by the 1990s.

2. THE RISE AND END OF THE COLD WAR

The **United States** and the **Soviet Union** had been allies in World War II but by the end of the war, the two strongest powers in the world were already in competition in many different areas. This competition was both a **military-security rivalry** and a continuation of the **ideological competition** between **Leninism** and the **Wilsonian worldview,** or between communism and capitalism, which was first visible after World War I. Because the two superpowers avoided a world war, their competition came to be called the **COLD WAR.** The conflict affected all parts of the world, often in different ways. On a global scale, the conflict can be seen as having three major phases: the initial phase of an actually **bipolar world** (1945–60); a phase of superpower competition in an increasingly **diversified global arena** (1960–75); and a phase of **declining relevance** and importance of the cold war to basic issues of global affairs (1975–90), leading finally to the end of the cold war.

1945–62. Cold war in a bipolar world. In the years immediately following World War II, the **United States** and the **Soviet Union** were the only major powers capable of effective independent action. The old European empires were being dismantled and the Axis powers were destroyed. The global nature of the U.S.-Soviet rivalry was already emerging in 1945. In **EUROPE,** the **Soviet Union** established a position of dominance in the east, taking control of the **Baltic states** and establishing communist regimes, with the aid of the Soviet armies of occupation, from **Poland** to **Bulgaria.** By 1947 the **United States** had instituted the **Marshall Plan** for the reconstruction of noncommunist Europe and helped to reduce the influence of large communist parties in France and Italy. **GERMANY** was divided and occupied by the four Allied powers of the war. The **Berlin blockade** by the Soviets in 1948 increased tensions. In 1949 the zones occupied by U.S., French, and British forces were combined in the new **Federal Republic of Germany,** and the **German Democratic Republic** was established in the Soviet zone, thus splitting postwar Germany into two countries. The United States established the **North Atlantic Treaty Organization (NATO)** in 1949 for the coordination of Western military forces against the Soviet Union. Rapidly, the European continent was divided into two parts by what Winston Churchill, in 1946, had called the **IRON CURTAIN.**

The rivalry between the emerging **communist world**—referred to in cold war terms as **the East**—and **the West** extended far beyond Europe, even at the beginning of the cold war. In the **Middle East,** Soviet forces in northern **IRAN** at the end of World War II established autonomous republics and evacuated the areas only under strong pressure from the United States in the **Azerbaijan crisis** of 1945–46 (p. 973). Soviet pressures on **TURKEY** for new rights in the Straits and the cession of some territory in the Caucasus, as well as Soviet aid for communist guerrillas in **GREECE,** were important factors leading to the articulation of the **Truman Doctrine** (p. 917) of 1947 and the U.S. policy on the containment of communism. The Soviet Union was seen as providing support for the communist insurgency in **Malaya.** In **CHINA,** the long conflict between the **nationalists,** supported by the United States, and the communists led by **MAO ZEDONG** came to an end with the communist victory in 1949, and the establishment of the **People's Republic of China.** In **KOREA,** the United States and the Soviet Union agreed in 1945 to a temporary Soviet occupation of the north and a U.S. occupation of the south. It was expected that a unified Korea would soon be established, but Soviet-American disagreements led to the creation of the **Republic of Korea** in the south and the **People's Democratic Republic** in the north. North Korean armed forces attacked the south

in 1950, initiating the **KOREAN WAR** (p. 1029), in which the United States, through the United Nations, and the People's Republic of China intervened.

The bipolar division of the world became relatively fixed by the middle of the 1950s. The Soviet Union was able, without significant Western response, to crush major **anti-Soviet demonstrations** in East Berlin in 1953 and the **HUNGARIAN REVOLUTION OF 1956.** At the same time, the United States established a series of **regional military pact organizations,** including the **Central Treaty Organization** in the Middle East (p. 967) and the **Southeast Asia Treaty Organization** (p. 1037) as a part of its broad policy of containment. The Soviet Union became a nuclear power in 1949 and developed a hydrogen bomb by 1953, so the **balance of terror** of a global nuclear war helped to enforce the stability of the bipolar world. The **FOUR-POWER SUMMIT CONFERENCE** in Geneva in 1955 showed that some efforts at tension management were possible. Occasionally, as in the **Suez Crisis** of 1956, when both the Soviet Union and the United States opposed the Anglo-French-Israeli invasion of Egypt, the interests of the superpowers would coincide, but this was rare. Soviet advances in missiles and space technology were shown in the launching of ***Sputnik I*** (1957), the first satellite to orbit the earth. By the early 1960s, cold war tensions reached a climax. In central Europe, the communists built the **BERLIN WALL** in 1961, emphasizing the East-West conflict. Soviet support for the revolutionary regime of **Fidel Castro,** who came to power in **CUBA** in 1960, brought the cold war openly to the **Western Hemisphere.** The placing of Soviet missiles in Cuba in 1962 brought the two superpowers to the brink of war in the **CUBAN MISSILE CRISIS** (p. 959). However, the general framework of the cold war changed significantly soon after the resolution of the Cuban crisis.

1962–75. Cold war in a diversified global arena. By the early 1960s, many changes had taken place in the broader global context of the cold war. In both the West and the East, new centers of power emerged, altering the bipolar structure of the cold war. The **communist world** had appeared to be united under Soviet leadership, but it became clear that regimes could be communist in ideology and reject Soviet domination. **Yugoslavia** had broken with the Soviet Union as early as 1948, for example. But the major break in communist unity came with the **SINO-SOVIET SPLIT,** which became visible through mutual public condemnations and the abrupt withdrawal of Soviet economic and military advisers from China in 1960. In 1961, **Albania** followed China in its opposition to the Soviets. In the nationalist and radical movements and the new states of Asia, Africa, and Latin America, a major competition for followers developed between **MAOISTS** and more Soviet-oriented leftists. **This undermined Soviet influence in many areas.**

Decentralization of power was also visible in **the West** by the early 1960s. **France** withdrew its troops from NATO's combined forces in 1966, although it did not withdraw from NATO itself. The beginnings of the **European Common Market** (1957) provided a rival for U.S. economic domination, and by the 1970s, **West Germany** and **Japan** emerged as major economic powers.

In broad global terms, the newly independent states and powers that were not directly allied with either the United States or the Soviet Union began the **NONALIGNED MOVEMENT.** This group represented a **Third World,** which had limited military or economic power but, in the context of the cold war, represented a major arena for competition between the Soviet Union and the United States. The precursor of the more formal nonaligned movement was the **Bandung Conference** in 1955, which was attended by representatives of 29 states. The next major conference was hosted by **Marshal TITO** in **Yugoslavia** in 1961, and major conferences of the nonaligned movement were held occasionally in the following years. Major figures in the movement included prominent leaders in Africa and Asia, such as **Nehru** of India, **Sukarno** of Indonesia, and **Nasser** of Egypt. **Chinese** communist leaders also played an important role in the early years of the movement. During the 1960s the nonaligned forces were important on the global political scene, because they emphasized the **diversification of power.** The Soviet Union and the United States engaged in a major competition to win the support of the nonaligned nations, using **military and economic aid** to do it. During the 1960s **Egypt,** for example, was closely tied in military and economic terms to the Soviet Union, but Soviet advisers were expelled in 1972, and the United States emerged as

Egypt's primary patron. In **Ethiopia,** the United States gave strong support to the conservative emperor, **Haile Salessie,** until he was overthrown in 1974. His radical successor, **Mengistu Haile Miriam,** received aid from the Soviet Union. In many areas, the superpower rivalry provided a way for smaller countries to obtain arms and economic aid, and this competition set the tone for the second era of the cold war.

Superpower negotiations between the Soviet Union and the United States were also an important part of the global politics of the 1960s and 1970s. Soon after the **Cuban missile crisis,** the two powers negotiated and ratified the **Nuclear Test Ban Treaty** of 1963. Despite regional wars of competition between the United States and communist powers, such as the **Vietnam War,** negotiations continued in the era of **DÉTENTE,** leading to the **Strategic Arms Limitation Talks (SALT)** and the arms reduction agreements of 1972 and 1974. In this same time, U.S. president **Richard Nixon** extended formal diplomatic recognition to the **People's Republic of China** and, in 1972, made a highly publicized trip to China, emphasizing the mood of the new era. While their major conflicts had not been resolved, **normalization of relations** between Western and communist states was still possible. A culmination of these developments was the **Conference on Security and Co-operation in Europe** held in Helsinki (1973–75). The **HELSINKI AC-CORDS,** signed by the Soviet Union, the United States, Canada, and 32 European states, recognized the validity of the **existing borders** in Eastern Europe, especially the post–World War II borders of Germany and Poland. The signatories also pledged to respect **human rights,** giving human rights organizations and Helsinki Watch Committees a legal basis for protesting violations of human rights in all of the countries involved. By the late 1970s, relations between the superpowers became strained again, but the old cold war concerns were increasingly irrelevant to the major global issues.

1975–90. Declining relevance of cold war concerns. In the final decades of the 20th century, the old power conflicts between the Soviet Union and the United States and the ideological competition between the ideologies of Lenin and Wilson no longer dominated global affairs. The rise of **economic superpowers** like **Japan** and **Germany,** the resurgence of **ethnic nationalism** and **religious revivalism** in many areas, the global pressures for **democratization,** and other developments transformed the global scene from the early days of the cold war. The United States and the Soviet Union were still powerful rivals. The Soviet invasion of **Afghanistan** in 1979 aroused old fears of Soviet expansionism, but the successful response of the **Mujahidin,** the Afghan religionational resistance fighters, and the eventual Soviet military withdrawal in 1989 showed the weakness of the Soviet military force. In the 1980s, there were **Strategic Arms Reduction Talks** (1982) but the U.S. movement toward a major arms buildup through the **Strategic Defense Initiative** and Soviet support for groups like the **Sandinistas** in Nicaragua revealed a continuing high level of mistrust and tension. The situation changed significantly with the coming to power in the Soviet Union of **MIKHAIL GORBACHEV** in 1985. His vigorous efforts for internal reform in the Soviet Union and openness in foreign relations helped to set in motion the transformation of the communist world of Eastern Europe and the end of the Soviet Union. In these efforts, the United States became the ally rather than the enemy of the leadership of the Soviet Union.

Between 1989 and 1992, the communist world was transformed. The **Berlin Wall** was destroyed (1989) and **Germany was unified** (1990). In every communist state in **Eastern Europe,** the regime was overthrown and the Communist Party formally disbanded. In the **Soviet Union** itself, 15 independent states emerged from the structures of the old communist state. In the new state of **Russia,** elections were held, and the United States made significant efforts to provide economic support in an era of difficult transition. By 1992, the one remaining major communist state was **CHINA,** where the preservation of administrative stability and economic growth were more important than ideological concerns. Economic liberalization and a greater openness in foreign affairs raised expectations of political liberalization in China. Large student demonstrations in 1986 and 1987 were suppressed, and then a movement for **democratic reform** erupted in the spring of 1989 with huge demonstrations in a number of cities. The largest, which lasted for a number of weeks, was in Beijing in **TIANANMEN SQUARE.** Al-

though the prodemocracy movement received much international visibility and sympathy, the government forcibly crushed the demonstration in June 1989, with many casualties. Despite some international protests, the Chinese government soon resumed normal diplomatic and economic relations with the major world powers. The success of efforts to encourage Western investment in China in the 1990s and China's continued **most-favored-nation status** for trade with the United States, despite U.S. protests about human rights abuses, along with the transformed nature of U.S.-Soviet relations, proved that by the early 1990s the world had witnessed the **end of the cold war.**

The final phase of the cold war also saw the increasing **spread of democracy** beyond its previous centers in Western Europe, North America, India, and Japan. Democratic regimes began to spread in Latin America from the late 1970s onward, becoming the standard political form for the first time. Democratic shifts also affected the Philippines and South Korea, and then the states of Eastern Europe from 1989 onward. An increasing move toward democracy reached sub-Saharan Africa in the early 1990s, though it remained incomplete. The major regions resisting the democratic trend were China, Vietnam, North Korea, and some of the Middle East.

3. INTERNATIONAL CONFLICT RESOLUTION

At the end of World War II, the victorious Allies created a system of international organizations roughly combined under the aegis of a central structure, the **UNITED NATIONS.** Some of the organizations, like the International Labor Organization (ILO) and the International Court, were continuations of earlier bodies that had been part of the **League of Nations.** The United Nations itself was viewed as the successor to the League of Nations, and its primary political bodies were the **General Assembly,** in which all members participated, and the **Security Council,** on which the major powers served as permanent members with veto power along with rotating participation by other member states. The primary organization for crisis resolution was the **Security Council.** Economic, health, social, and cultural matters were handled by separate agencies that had varying degrees of autonomy. In the second half of the twentieth century, the **United Nations** was an active global political force with an important role in a number of areas, including conflict-resolution negotiations, creating multilateral military responses to aggression, and organizing peacekeeping forces to help stabilize conflict situations. In addition, the **International Court of Justice** provided an effective forum for resolving disputes involving international law. In these activities, the United Nations proved to be more effective than the League of Nations had been.

Conflict-resolution mechanisms. The United Nations provided mechanisms for dealing with conflicts and either avoiding war or assisting in bringing it to an end. These mechanisms were less effective, however, with conflicts involving the major powers, which had the **veto** in the Security Council. The United Nations also had only limited jurisdiction to become involved in civil wars and the internal affairs of member states. Nevertheless, within these limits the United Nations performed important services in conflict resolution. At the end of World War II, there were issues that needed resolutions based on international agreement. When the four Allied powers were unable to agree on the disposition of the **former Italian colonies,** the matter was referred to the United Nations and was resolved by the creation of an independent **Libya,** trusteeships for **Somalia,** and the inclusion of **Eritrea** within liberated Ethiopia. When the British were unable to resolve the question of the future of the **PALESTINE MANDATE,** the issue was referred to the United Nations, and the General Assembly, after study and debate, approved a partition plan in 1947. Following the establishment of **Israel** in 1948, there was an Arab-Israeli War. The armistice agreements at the end of the war were negotiated by United Nations officials. The United Nations was not able to resolve the **ARAB-ISRAELI CONFLICT,** but it provided structures for negotiating cease-fires and interim agreements to prevent fighting. The ending of the **Arab-Israeli wars** of 1948, 1956, 1967, and 1973 involved significant United Nations mediation. United Nations agencies also played important roles in many of the conflicts that emerged in the process of decolonization. UN officials worked in the **Congo conflict** (1960–63) and in **Cyprus** (1964), and played an important role in coordinating international responses to white regimes of control in **southern Africa.** When the white government of **Southern Rhodesia** made a unilateral declaration of independence in 1965, the United Nations helped to define sanctions and to bring about the end result of multiracial elections in 1980. When the white regime in **South Africa** maintained its control over **southwest Africa,** the United Nations took the lead in providing the legal basis for an independent **Namibia** in 1968 and in organizing the negotiations that ultimately led to South African withdrawal from the country (1988) and the formal independence of Namibia in 1990.

Although the United Nations was active in helping to resolve many conflicts, critics noted that its effectiveness was limited by the ability of the superpowers to restrict UN actions. As the cold war came to an end, the United Nations emerged as an increasingly effective force, aiding in the end of the **Iran-Iraq War** of the 1980s; mediating conflicts in **Cambodia, Angola,** and the **western Sahara** in 1988; assisting in the Soviet withdrawal from **Afghanistan** in 1989; and monitoring the elections that brought an end to the civil war in **Nicaragua** in 1990. **FORMAL OBSERVER GROUPS** were among the most important mechanisms created by the United Nations to help monitor agreements. **Major United Nations observation missions** played a role in Palestine (1948), India and Pakistan (1949), Lebanon (1958), Yemen (1963), the Dominican Republic (1965), Afghanistan (1988), the Iran-Iraq ceasefire (1988), and Kuwait (1991).

Multinational responses to aggression. The United Nations was the organizational framework for two major military mobilizations in response to aggression. This function was limited by the cold war rivalries, which meant that either the United States or the Soviet Union could prevent UN responses to attacks. However, in 1950, when **North Korea** invaded **South Korea,** the Soviet Union was temporarily boycotting the United Nations. This enabled the Security Council to pass without veto the appropriate resolutions calling on member states to contribute forces for a UN **police action** to stop the aggression, with the United States providing the major source of military power for the action. The second major United Nations military response was in 1990, when **Iraq** invaded **Kuwait.** In the **PERSIAN GULF WAR** of 1990–91, the United States again provided the major source of military power, and the United Nations provided the international authority for the multinational response to Iraqi aggression. Such a multilateral action had become possible by the end of the cold war.

UN peacekeeping and security forces. In a number of conflict situations, the United Nations created multinational military forces to supervise a truce or administer arrangements that had been established as part of the conflict's resolution. Such peacekeeping forces were an important part of many efforts at conflict resolution, and by the 1990s they had become an accepted resource for conflict management in global affairs. **United Nations peacekeeping forces** were sent to the **Sinai** Peninsula following the Suez crisis (1956–67); the **Congo** (1960–64); **West Irian,** New Guinea (1962–63); **Cyprus** (1964–90s); the **Sinai** again (1973–79); the **Golan Heights** in Syria (1974–90s); **southern Lebanon** (1978–90s); territories in the former **Yugoslavia** (beginning in 1992); **Cambodia** (beginning in 1992); **Mozambique** (beginning in 1992); and **Somalia** (beginning in 1993).

International Court. The jurisdiction of the International Court of Justice was limited, but in its rulings and advisory opinions, the court played an important role in resolving some conflicts and further defining the rights and obligations of states under international law. Some of the rulings that reflect the wide variety of issues dealt with by the Court include the **Corfu Channel** case (1949), in which a settlement was reached between Great Britain and Albania concerning damages resulting from mining the Corfu Channel; the case dealing with the **Anglo-Iranian Oil Company nationalization** (1951–52), in which the court declared its jurisdiction was limited and affirmed Iran's right of nationalization under specified conditions; and the case brought by New Zealand and Australia in 1974 to prevent **nuclear testing in the Pacific** by France. The court had difficulty imposing its decisions on major powers, but it provided an important forum for international debate even in issues involving a superpower, as was seen in *Nicaragua v. the United States* (1984), in which it declared that the mining of Nicaraguan harbors by the United States was a violation of Nicaraguan sovereignty. The court played an important role in resolving

border disputes, as in its decisions defining the U.S.-Canadian maritime boundary in the **Gulf of Maine** (1984) and resolving a dispute in 1992 between **Honduras and El Salvador** that dated back to 1839 and had been the cause of considerable conflict.

By the 1990s it was clear that international organizations still could not prevent wars, but that the international conflict resolution mechanisms of the United Nations were more effective than those that had been available to the League of Nations. At the end of the 20th century, such mechanisms were an accepted part of the structure of global political power.

4. TERRORISM

A variety of conditions from the 1950s onward promoted acts of terrorism in various parts of the world. Opponents of colonialism often used terror because they lacked the power to confront established military forces outright; terrorism in some of these cases grew out of guerrilla warfare tactics. Brutal police responses sometimes encouraged further terror. Left-wing movements of various sorts, particularly after the failure of the 1968 uprisings in Europe, sometimes used terror to dramatize their cause. Terrorist acts included bombing buildings and vehicles; hijacking and planting bombs on airplanes; kidnapping and hostage taking. Major terrorist movements included the Irish Republican Army's attacks on Great Britain; Algerian rebels' campaign against France in the 1950s (with bombings both in Algeria and in France); Arab, particularly Palestinian, attacks on Israelis and Americans after the defeat in the 1967 war (murder of Israeli athletes at the 1972 Munich Olympics); larger Muslim attacks on the West during the 1980s, with the involvement of governments such as Libya's (explosion of French passenger plane over Africa, 1989; American jet exploded over Scotland, 1988; frequent hostage taking in Lebanon). Antiterrorist measures had some impact, particularly tighter airport inspections. UN action against terrorism was hampered by the frequent unwillingness of communist countries and former colonies to condemn the movements too vigorously.

b. GLOBALIZATION OF MATERIAL LIFE

During the second half of the century, many important aspects of individual and societal life developed patterns of global interaction. This was visible in a number of important areas: in the evolution of state and private economic structures; in developments in science and technology; and in response to the changing physical environment.

1. EVOLUTION OF INTERNATIONAL ECONOMIC STRUCTURES

Major changes took place in the international structures of economic life. These were visible in the institutions regulating international finance and international trade and in the further development of nongovernmental multinational economic institutions.

International finance: The **Bretton Woods system (1945–71).** A conference of the Allied powers was held near the end of World War II in Bretton Woods, New Hampshire. At that meeting, the major institutions for the management of the international monetary and financial order were agreed on, and the result was the creation of the **International Monetary Fund (IMF)** in 1945 and the **International Bank for Reconstruction and Development** (the World Bank), which began operation in 1946. The Bretton Woods system involved the easy convertibility of the major currencies, with the foundation being the **U.S. DOLLAR** and the guarantee by the U.S. government that dollars could be exchanged for **gold** at a rate of $35 per ounce. The U.S. dollar became the major medium of international financial exchange. A large U.S. **balance-of-payments deficit** resulting from transfers of funds to support reconstruction and development in programs like the **Marshall Plan** (1947) and direct U.S. investment overseas provided the **liquidity** necessary for rapid global economic development and growth. However, by the 1960s this system began to have difficulties: dollar holdings outside of the United States began to exceed the total value of U.S. gold reserves, creating a destabilizing **dollar overhang;** in 1971, for the first time in the century, the value of U.S. imports exceeded that of its nonmonetary exports; while the U.S. economy was still clearly the world's largest, other major economies had developed as powerful rivals or partners. In an effort to supplement the role of the dollar, a new reserve asset called **special drawing rights (SDR)** was developed in 1969, but a major change in the international system was required.

International finance: Post–Bretton Woods. A series of measures significantly changed the international monetary system. The United States ended its commitment to exchange gold for dollars in 1971, and the **Smithsonian Agreement** (1971) began the process of international monetary reform. In 1973, the United States ended fixed exchange rates between the dollar and other major currencies; the most important feature of the post–Bretton Woods system was **flexible exchange rates** among all major currencies. Instability of currency values was lessened by the efforts of major governments to coordinate their economic policies. This was aided by the meetings of financial policy leaders from the **GROUP OF SEVEN (G-7)**, the seven largest Western economies (the United States, Japan, Germany, France, Britain, Italy, and Canada). These meetings began in 1976 and became annual events that ranged over a host of international issues, including currency. In this new system gold had a less important role, and **SDRs**, defined as a weighted mixture of major currency values, became by the 1980s an important unit of accounting; the system as a whole was more volatile and more openly related to politics as well as economics. By the 1990s, JAPAN emerged as a major international financial center, with nine of the world's ten largest banks in terms of assets; in 1987 it had surpassed the United States as the world's major creditor. The post–Bretton Woods system was not as centralized as the earlier system, but global interactions were of increasing importance to all levels of economic life throughout the world.

Both the IMF and the World Bank also played recurrent roles in providing **investment aid** to developing (not yet fully industrial) nations. In return for investment capital, both organizations typically tried to require more stringent national fiscal policies, including less government expenditure, which posed potential political problems for the nations involved—as in parts of Latin America and Africa in the 1980s and 1990s (p. 1050).

International trade regulation, 1945–93. At the end of World War II, the Allied powers were anxious to avoid the trade wars and protectionism that had been an important part of the Great Depression of the 1930s. Following the war, the UN Economic and Social Council convened a committee to draft a charter for a proposed International Trade Organization. That organization was not created, however; instead, the preliminary **GENERAL AGREEMENT ON TARIFFS AND TRADE (GATT)** was adopted by 23 states and became the basic instrument for regulating international trade in the second half of the 20th century. With a secretariat in Geneva, the **GATT** supervised **eight "rounds"** of multilateral trade negotiations to reduce tariffs and encourage international trade. The first were held in Geneva (1947); Annency, France (1949), Torquay, England (1951–52); and Geneva (1955–56). The Dillon Round (1961–62) was named for U.S. secretary of the treasury Douglas Dillon, and the Kennedy Round (1963–67) for President John F. Kennedy. The **Kennedy Round** involved across-the-board industrial tariff reductions, and in 1965 the signatories added a new section to the agreement addressing positive encouragements for the international trade of **less-developed countries.** The **TOKYO ROUND** (1973–79) dealt with a major restructuring of trade in response to the transformation of the international monetary system with the end of the **Bretton Woods arrangements** in 1971, and a comprehensive set of agreements was approved. The eighth round, the **URUGUAY ROUND**, began in 1986 and dealt with many new areas. Negotiations were suspended in 1990 as a result of disagreements relating to agricultural subsidies in the European Community. Discussions were resumed in 1991, and a major new pact was completed in 1993 that was signed by officials from 125 states at a meeting in Morocco in 1994. The agreement represented a significant further liberalization of global trade regulations. It also established the **WORLD TRADE ORGANIZATION** as the successor to GATT, with increased powers to mediate trade disputes and enforce adherence to existing agreements.

GATT began in 1947 with 23 members, and by 1994 its membership had grown to 117. At that time, reflecting the end of the cold war,

Russia was seeking formal membership along with China, whose membership had been suspended in 1950. GATT negotiations had transformed the conditions of international trade. They had succeeded, for example, in reducing average tariffs on industrial goods from about 40 percent in the years following World War II to about 5 percent of their market value in the 1990s. The globalization of trade regulation helped the world economies to avoid a repeat of the economic crises of the era between the two world wars. This was accomplished in the context of a profound expansion of international trade and of its importance in the life of every society.

Multinational corporations. In the second half of the 20th century, private corporations became an increasingly important part of global economic life. Following the lead of older commercial trading companies and the relatively small number of large internationally active companies in the first part of the century, companies of all sizes began to participate in international investments and enterprises after World War II.

1945–71. Era of American predominance. Following the war, multinational corporations based in the United States tended to dominate global international business. This reflected the importance of the U.S. dollar and the strength of the U.S. economy in the era of the **Bretton Woods system** in international finance. American corporations were a major mechanism for the circulation of dollars in the global economy, and they made significant investments in many different countries, especially in Europe. The book value of direct foreign investments by U.S. companies rose from $7.2 billion in 1946 to almost $71 billion in 1969. Much of the U.S. international investment in this period was made by large, already internationally established corporations like **Ford, General Motors,** and **Standard Oil (New Jersey),** and in such industries as the **auto industry, oil,** and **chemicals,** where a few large companies dominated the market. The international nature of much of the corporate activity was in **finance** and **management** rather than in actual production. Multinational corporations would buy or establish **subsidiaries** or establish **production facilities** in other countries, and these organizations would then operate as they might have in the "home country" of the corporation.

By the late 1960s, this situation was changing. Growing numbers of smaller U.S. companies were establishing overseas facilities, and investment by European companies in the United States increased. In 1969, the merger of **British Petroleum (BP)** with **Standard Oil (Ohio)** and the takeover of **Wyandotte Chemicals** by the German chemical giant **BASF** signaled the beginning of an era of major foreign corporate involvement in the U.S. economy. As the Bretton Woods system came to an end in the early 1970s, the world of multinational corporations was also changing significantly, with many new participants becoming involved in the global economy.

Transformation of the petroleum industry. The evolution of the petroleum industry in the second half of the 20th century illustrates the changing nature of the global world of business. In the first half of the century, the industry was dominated by a **cartel** of seven large oil companies that set global prices and production levels while competing actively among themselves. These companies were among the largest multinational corporations, and direct foreign investment in petroleum industries was a major part of global business. Following World War II, this domination continued. When one member of the cartel, the **Anglo-Iranian Oil Company (AIOC),** half owned by the British government, was nationalized by the **Iranian government** in 1951, the cartel was able to respond successfully through sanctions and a boycott. It reestablished control over Iranian oil through a consortium arrangement in 1953, and AIOC was reorganized as **British Petroleum.** The real challenge came with the creation of the **ORGANIZATION OF PETROLEUM EXPORTING COUNTRIES (OPEC)** in 1960, whose initial goal was to limit the ability of the major companies to reduce oil prices. By 1970, OPEC members began to work together to coordinate production and thus control supply and, ultimately, prices. For a short period (1971–73), prices were set by consultation between OPEC and the oil companies. The **Arab-Israeli War of 1973** and changing market conditions were the occasion for an **Arab oil embargo** on sales to allies of Israel and a significant increase in oil prices. By the end of the crisis, basic prices were no longer set by the companies. In terms of investment, in 1960 more than 40 percent of U.S. direct foreign investment was in petroleum industries, but this was reduced to 14 percent by 1990. These changes coincided with a significant restructuring of the international oil industry. In the first half of the century, oil companies had been granted **concessions** by governments to explore for and produce petroleum. Governments were paid **royalties** on a per-barrel basis. After World War II, there was a change to **profit-sharing** arrangements in the 1950s and then to the gradual assumption of ownership of production facilities by the governments of the producing countries. In **SAUDI ARABIA**, the original exploration and production concession was granted to **Standard Oil of California (SOCAL)** in 1933. SOCAL's concession became the basis for Arabian American Oil Company (**ARAMCO**), a consortium of four major American oil companies, which developed the Saudi oil industry. In 1950, ARAMCO agreed to the shift from per-barrel royalties to profit sharing. In the early 1970s, participation was accepted by ARAMCO; the Saudi government acquired 25 percent of ARAMCO in 1973, 60 percent in 1974, and became the full owner in the early 1980s. The major oil companies maintained close relations with the Saudi-owned company and became global distributors for its products. This evolution of control occurred in most other oil-exporting countries as well. It reflected the broader trends of the final decades of the century, with a clear globalization of activity but a decentralization of control. The old cartel of oil companies was replaced by an organization of governments that had less control over the dynamics of the world markets but was operating in a more globalized economic situation.

1971–93. New world of multinational corporations. In the final decades of the century, the nature of multinational business operations changed in significant ways. **INTERNATIONAL INTEGRATION OF PRODUCTION** reflected the globalization of economic enterprise. Increasingly, multinational corporations developed diversified production facilities in which parts were made in many different places and then assembled, rather than setting up comprehensive production facilities in different countries. In the multinational automobile industry, for example, by 1980 cars like General Motors' J-car were built of parts produced in many different countries, and by the 1990s virtually no automobile could be said to have been completely produced within one country. This integration was seen in many different types of multinational operations; as major **fast-food companies** like McDonald's became global in operation by the 1980s, French-fried potatoes were prepared and frozen in one country and shipped to another for consumption. The **GLOBAL SPREAD OF MULTINATIONAL OWNERSHIP** was another important feature of the changing nature of multination business operations. The business world went from being dominated by a few large companies in the United States and Western Europe involved in a small number of industries to a global distribution of companies large and small in virtually every industry. By the 1980s there were more than 10,000 significantly multinational corporations, including important firms from developing countries, such as India, South Korea, Taiwan, Singapore, and Brazil, as well as the older industrial states. This is reflected in the **automobile industry,** where U.S. companies produced more than two-thirds of the world's motor vehicles in 1950 but barely one-fifth in 1980. In the 1950s, Britain was the second largest producer; it was displaced by West Germany in the 1960s; and **Japan** became the second largest producer in the 1970s and passed the United States in production in the 1980s. Other countries—such as South Korea, Brazil, and Mexico—became important producers in the 1980s. By the 1990s, ownership of production was also more diversified, as seen in many different countries. More than 10 percent of the production capacity in North America was owned by non-U.S. corporations, and an important factor in the revitalization of the British auto industry was the establishment of production facilities in Britain by Japanese companies like **Toyota, Nissan,** and **Honda.** In Iran, an auto industry was developing around Iran Khodro, a joint venture with the French company Peugeot, and a second joint venture was established with Daewoo, the third largest automaker in South Korea.

The **NORMALIZATION OF GLOBALIZED ECONOMIC ENTERPRISE** was firmly established by the 1990s. Significant foreign participation in or ownership of local enterprises around the world became an accepted fact. Complex interconnections on both very large and very small scales created global economic networks that became a nor-

mal part of local and multinational business enterprise. In a typical situation, Kirin Brewery, a Japanese corporation, became the parent company of a Coca-Cola Bottling Group in a small northeastern state in the United States. Multinational corporations had a growing impact on daily life, as can be seen in the expansion of consumer food companies. Soft drink firms became highly visible participants in the expansion of multinational business enterprise in the second half of the century. **COCA-COLA** was an early multinational corporation, and its soft drink products could be found in many countries even before World War II. By 1994, with the establishment of a bottling plant in Albania, Coca-Cola was made in 197 countries. By the 1990s, the rivalry between **Pepsi-Cola** and **Coca-Cola** was strong in Russia and Vietnam as well as in most of the rest of the world. **Fast-food chains** had a significant impact on world eating habits by standardizing products and expectations and providing new concepts of service. **McDonald's** became an economic power, encouraging some countries to reorganize agricultural production to provide potatoes and meat for the chain. By 1994, McDonald's had more than 4,700 overseas stores in 71 countries (having doubled its total in about five years). The **Kellogg Company,** a U.S. producer of breakfast cereals, opened a plant in Latvia in 1994 and began an effort to transform the concept of breakfast in the former communist world.

The diversity of multinational economic affairs was reflected in the changing topics of debate in the **GATT rounds.** Important debates in the final Uruguay Round involved not only the usual discussions of tariffs on industrial and agricultural products, but also talks on opening domestic markets to foreign legal services, accounting, and computer **software** concerns. U.S. officials were disappointed that there was no agreement on opening **audiovisual** markets, especially in television programming and videocassettes, since **entertainment** had become the second largest U.S. export industry in terms of dollar value. The world of multinational business was global in nature and had become an important factor in the daily life of every society, reflecting the complex, interconnected nature of human life at the end of the 20th century.

2. SCIENCE AND TECHNOLOGY

Scientific discoveries and the development of technologies emphasized the globalization of material life during the second half of the century. Global communication networks and the exchange of ideas, ranging from espionage to formal associations of scholars and international institutions, played an important role. The worldwide nature of scientific enterprise and technological development was reflected in many fields, including the development and use of nuclear power, the exploration of space, world health and disease control, and in communication and information technologies themselves.

NUCLEAR POWER. The immense amounts of energy created by atomic processes of **nuclear fission** and **nuclear fusion** had long been recognized. During World War II, the major combatants worked to develop **atomic bombs.** The United States succeeded, testing the first successful major nuclear military device in 1945, and then dropping atomic bombs on the Japanese cities of **HIROSHIMA** and **NAGASAKI** in an effort to hasten the end of the war. The U.S. action was subject to much international debate, but the **ATOMIC AGE,** both in military and in civilian terms, had begun. The development of nuclear weapons and efforts to prevent nuclear war were very important aspects of global life in the second half of the 20th century.

Spread of nuclear weapons. For a short period, the United States was the only state with employable nuclear weapons. Efforts to create international structures to control nuclear weaponry interacted with the development of the weaponry itself. In 1946 the **United Nations** worked to establish an Atomic Energy Commission, and the United States, in the **Baruch Plan** (1946), proposed the creation of an international atomic development authority with a virtual monopoly over all forms of nuclear energy production, military or civilian. Developing **cold war** tensions made international control impossible, and other countries gained nuclear weapons capacities: the **Soviet Union** in 1949, **Great Britain** in 1952, **France** in 1960, and the **People's Republic of China** in 1964. By the 1970s, a number of other countries were believed to have fission weapon capacities, including India, Israel, South

Africa, and Brazil. Concern over **nuclear proliferation** resulted in many conferences, negotiations, and some success in global nuclear arms limitation and agreement on broader issues of disarmament. The United Nations established the **International Atomic Energy Agency** in 1957 to promote the peaceful uses of atomic power. In 1963 **a nuclear test ban treaty** was signed by the United States, the Soviet Union, and Great Britain, and more than 100 states subsequently adhered to it, and in 1968, 62 states ratified the **NUCLEAR NON-PROLIFERATION TREATY**, which limited the spread of atomic weapons. Other treaties banned nuclear weapons in space (1967) and on the ocean floor beyond the 12-mile national limit (1971). The major reduction in the threat of nuclear war involved the changing conditions of the **cold war.** The United States and the Soviet Union began serious arms reductions negotiations in the 1970s with the **Strategic Arms Limitations Talks (SALT)** in 1972 and **SALT II** (1972–79), which resulted in an agreement that was largely implemented although never formally ratified. In the 1980s, the **Strategic Arms Reduction Talks (START)** moved beyond limiting the arms race to an actual reduction in the existing weapons arsenals of the superpowers. The resulting treaty was signed in 1991. With the dissolution of the Soviet Union, the major concern regarding nuclear weapons was no longer global nuclear war so much as the possible development and use of nuclear weapons by smaller powers in regional wars. Some of the newly independent states of the former Soviet Union, such as **Ukraine** and **Kazakhstan,** came into possession of substantial nuclear arsenals, and after 1992 engaged in long negotiations, with support from the U.S., for denuclearization and the implementation of their areas of the START treaty. The possible development of nuclear weapons by **India** and **Pakistan** was a long-standing dispute that assumed new importance in the post–cold war world. And one of the major areas of tension in the Middle East following the Persian Gulf War of 1990–91 was monitoring **Iraq** for the production of weapons of mass destruction. By the 1990s, nuclear weapons and their control had, however, lost much of their importance as a source of international concern.

Nuclear power for both military and civilian use became very significant. Energy produced by nuclear facilities came to be used in many different ways, from providing power for running large ships to producing electricity. The United States developed the first nuclear-powered submarine, the *Nautilus,* by 1954. Nuclear submarines, capable of remaining submerged for many months, transformed the nature of underwater warfare. Also nuclear submarines undertook important explorations under the Artic ice cap in 1958, demonstrating their utility. A nuclear-powered merchant cargo ship, the *Savannah,* was launched in 1959, and the nuclear-powered aircraft carrier *Enterprise* was launched in 1960. The most important use, in global terms, of nuclear power was in the production of electricity. Nuclear power plants were built in the **Soviet Union** (1954), **Great Britain** (1956), and **France** (1957), and the first commercial nuclear power plant was opened in the **United States** in 1957. By the early 1990s, almost one-fifth of the world's electricity was produced by nuclear power plants. Although nuclear power had many advantages in terms of cost of fuel, efficiency, and availability, by the end of the century, there was a growing awareness of important risks. Problems of disposing of radioactive waste had not been solved by the early 1990s as some of the early plants were beginning the decommissioning process. Accidents and malfunctioning equipment posed major dangers as well. The first serious accident was at a British weapons production facility in 1957. A more serious accident occurred at the **Three Mile Island** reactor in 1979 in Pennsylvania. The worst known nuclear accident took place at the **CHERNOBYL REACTOR** in the former Soviet Union in 1979. The radioactive pollution from this event illustrated important international dimensions of nuclear power and its management.

SPACE EXPLORATION. The exploration of the earth's upper atmospheric regions and of outer space represented an important part of global affairs in the second half of the century. Many things, like space travel in general and human travel to the moon in particular, which had been the subject of science fiction and were believed even at mid-century to be in the distant future, were accomplished by the 1990s. Initially space exploration was associated with the development of military capacity, especially for building more effective rockets and space station technology. Space programs were national in organiza-

tion but by the 1990s had become significantly multinational and increasingly civilian in nature. Orbiting satellites became essential not just for military surveillance but also in global communication networks. Following World War II, most major powers undertook programs for rocket development and possible space exploration. Important events in the history of human activity in space include the launching of the first successful human-made satellite, the Soviet *Sputnik I,* in 1957, and the first human orbit of the earth, by Soviet astronaut **Yuri Gagarin,** in 1961. By the 1960s, both the Soviet Union and the United States were involved in serious efforts to explore the earth's **moon** and other parts of the solar system. Soviet and U.S. probes of **Mars** and **Venus** were begun in 1960–64, and rockets were sent to other planets as well during the 1960s and 1970s. A climax of these efforts was the **first landing of humans on the moon,** in 1969, as a completion of the priority program set by U.S. president **John Kennedy** in 1961. Other important specific **U.S. SPACE PROGRAMS** were the **Mariner** spacecraft (ten flights between 1962 and 1973 exploring Mercury, Venus, and Mars), the **Pioneer** program (*Pioneer 10,* launched in 1973, was the first human-made object to leave the solar system, which it did in 1986), and the **Voyagers** (launched in 1977 for exploration of the outer planets of the solar system). **SOVIET SPACE PROGRAMS,** in addition to the early Sputniks, included the **Lunas,** which in 1959 sent the first space vehicle to reach the moon; the **VEGAS,** which were deployed on Venus in 1985; and the **SALYUT** program of large space stations (1971–91) for human operation in earth's orbit. Orbiting **space stations** and **satellites** were major parts of the developing programs. In 1958, the first attempt at establishing a communications receiver and transmitter in space was made, and by 1963 the United States established the **Communications Satellite Corporation (COMSAT)** to utilize the new communications technologies. In 1964 the United States provided the initiative for the formation of the **International Telecommunications Satellite Organization (INTELSAT)** as a vehicle for providing access for all countries to space communications satellites. Initially the consortium had 12 members, but by the 1990s there were more than 100 states involved in INTELSAT. The Soviet Union also established a multinational network, utilizing its **MOLNIYA** satellite systems. By the 1980s satellites played an increasingly important role in virtually all aspects of global communications. A U.S. shuttle mission in 1983, for example, deployed or worked with communications satellites from West Germany, Canada, and Indonesia, and in 1985 a consortium of Arab states established a special Arab-world communications satellite system. By the early 1990s more than 200 countries relied in some significant way on satellites to meet their needs for communications services.

HEALTH AND DISEASE CONTROL. The globalization of human life in the 20th century had an important impact on issues of health and disease control. Humans have always been subject to interregional outbreaks of disease that have spread across continents. The **Black Death** plagues seen in postclassical Eastern Hemisphere societies are important examples, as is the spread of **smallpox** into the Western Hemisphere in the early era of European expansion. However, by the second half of the 20th century, conscious human activity on a global scale had transformed the world health situation, as had the involuntary consequences of intensified human interactions.

Conscious disease control made important advances in the 20th century. Expanded research facilities made it possible to lessen and sometimes even eliminate major historical illnesses. Research on the crippling disease **poliomyelitis** resulted in the development of vaccines by **Jonas Salk** in 1953–54 and of an oral vaccine by **Albert Sabine** in 1960, significantly reducing the incidence of this disease. In the case of **SMALLPOX,** a vaccine had already been developed in the 19th century, but the disease was still relatively common in the 20th. In 1967, the **World Health Organization (WHO)** announced the beginning of a program aimed at the total eradication of smallpox, and in 1979 WHO officially declared that the world was **smallpox free.** This represented a notable turning point in the world history of human health, since smallpox had been one of the most deadly diseases in history. Other major historic diseases have also been affected by 20th-century developments. **MALARIA** is an ancient and widespread disease whose causes were discovered in the late 19th century. It is transmitted by mosquitoes, so mosquito control was an important part of combatting the disease. Following World War II, the development of the highly effective insecticide **DDT,** and its extensive use in regions with a high incidence of malaria, lead to a reduction in the number of people infected. On the basis of the growing effectiveness of insecticides, the **World Health Organization** announced in 1955 the initiation of a program for the worldwide eradication of malaria. Throughout Africa, Asia, and Latin America, extensive use of insecticides was part of the eradication program, and there was a reduction in the incidence of malaria. However, migrations of people, especially in Africa, the emergence of DDT-resistant strains of mosquitoes, and the discovery of the disastrous environmental consequences of using DDT were important factors in making the total eradication of malaria impossible. The modern history of other major diseases also involves the development of powerful drugs for effective treatment and the subsequent emergence of drug-resistant variants of the disease. Effective drug treatment of **TUBERCULOSIS (TB)** had been readily available in the industrialized world since the 1950s. However, in the 1980s the number of cases of TB rose significantly. While much of this increase could be attributed to increasing poverty in many areas and to the rise of **AIDS,** which made people more susceptible to TB, the number of drug-resistant strains of TB had doubled within the decade as well. Overuse and misuse of the powerful drugs created by medical research had the potential to create dangerous versions of many ancient diseases.

New diseases also were encouraged by the globalization process. Great continental pandemics are a part of world history, but throughout most of history, the spread of diseases, even in pandemic conditions, was a relatively slow process tied to the speed of the transportation facilities available. In a globalized world of high-speed transport, diseases can spread around the world in remarkably short time periods. **FLU VIRUSES** develop new strains rapidly, and this makes immunization and treatment difficult. The great **influenza pandemic** in 1918–19 began as a result of the coming together of soldiers from North America, Europe, and Africa in northern France at the end of World War I. The disease spread rapidly throughout the world, killing possibly as many as 20 million people. Such great flu pandemics are always possible, because of the constant interaction of global populations, but modern research facilities enable a rapid response in recognition of new virus strains and the creation of appropriate vaccines. In the second half of the century, there have been many instances of the rise and spread of a new flu virus followed by a relatively rapid global response, so the catastrophe of the influenza epidemic of 1918–19 has not been repeated. There have, however, been widespread epidemics, like the epidemics of **Asian flu** in 1957 and the **Hong Kong flu** in 1968. The development and spread of the **HUMAN IMMUNODEFICIENCY VIRUS (HIV),** which causes **ACQUIRED IMMUNODEFICIENCY SYNDROME (AIDS),** was the single most important new disease epidemic in the second half of the 20th century. The disease spread widely in parts of Africa (p. 1049). The first cases were reported and identified in the United States in 1981, and by mid-1993 almost 200,000 deaths from **AIDS** had been reported in the United States alone. World Health Organization estimates in mid-1993 were that more than 25 million cumulative AIDS cases had occurred in the world by that date. More than 80 percent of the estimated cases were in developing countries, but the disease had spread throughout the world. Despite major efforts, vaccines and cures had not been found by the end of the century.

On June 23, 2000, the U.S. announced that its Human Genome Project scientists had completed a draft of the **entire sequence of the human genome.**

AGRICULTURE AND FOOD RELIEF. Agricultural production remained a regional issue for the most part, though food exports continued to increase. **International food aid,** developed in response to famine conditions in Europe after World War I, increased after 1945. The United States provided food relief to postwar Europe. Private organizations and governments organized food relief in a number of subsequent famine situations, such as that in Somalia in 1993. The agricultural arm of the United Nations, the Rome-based Food and Agriculture Organization, sponsored many studies and development projects to promote greater agricultural productivity in many areas. As part of the cold war rivalry, the United States and its allies provided agricultural experts to promote food production in many areas. Agricultural experts from the United States contributed greatly to the

GREEN REVOLUTION that improved food conditions in India and other parts of Asia by the 1960s. High-yield Mexican wheat (Sonora 64) and Taiwanese and Philippine rice (Taichung Native I and Tainan II and IR 8), developed by the United States, greatly increased India's food grain production. Greater food production helped account for a longer life expectancy (to 51 years in India by 1969) in many Third World countries.

INFORMATION TECHNOLOGIES. The development of new means of communication and information management created a revolutionary transformation of virtually every aspect of human life in the second half of the 20th century. The wireless **radio** and the **telephone** were already widely used by the middle of the century, changing the way people around the world gained information and communicated with each other. **Motion pictures** had already begun to transform entertainment. Following World War II, technologies in these media developed significantly. Telephones became increasingly automated and mobile, with the handheld, wireless telephone of the 1990s being representative of the changes. New technologies rapidly became available for mass public use in virtually every part of the world. **TELEVISION** was conceived during the 19th century, and the first public broadcasts in black and white were made in the 1930s. However, it was in the post–World War II period that television rapidly became a major medium for communication. In the United States in 1949, there were approximately 1 million TV sets in use. By 1951 that number was 10 million, and in 1975, the number of TVs in use had risen to more than 100 million. The first television transmissions in Japan were made in 1953, and by 1975 television reached more than 90 percent of all Japanese households. Similar expansions of television took place throughout the world. By the 1990s, a global network of television stations, such as the **Cable News Network (CNN),** could broadcast via satellite to any country in the world. Direct, live broadcasting of events made them known immediately around the world. The beginning of the U.S. bombing of Baghdad in 1991 during the **Persian Gulf War** was viewed by the worldwide CNN television audience as it happened. In 1992 it was estimated that even in relatively isolated countries, like Papua New Guinea, there were ten thousand TVs, or 1 for every 383 persons, while in countries like Panama, there was 1 for 12 and in Poland, 1 for 7. In the United Kingdom, the ratio was 1 television receiver for every 2.9 persons, and in France, 1 per 1.9 persons. The immediacy of the visual images of television was an important force in the increasing sense in the 1990s that the world is a "global village." The technologies for **duplication and transmission of documents** also created important new conditions for communication. A special method of **xerography,** a form of electrostatic printing, made possible the rapid reproduction of exact copies in a convenient dry-printing process. This process was developed by Chester Floyd Carlson in the 1930s and was commercially developed by the **Xerox Corporation** by the late 1950s. The ease of the reproduction process transformed many administrative, business, and scholarly activities. Another important development was in fascimile, or **FAX TRANSMISSION,** of exact copies over telephone lines. Basic transmission methods had been developed early in the 20th century and were used by newspapers and police forces. However, these were slow and inefficient until they were combined with computer technology and digitalization processes. In 1980 common standards for transmission methods and equipment were established, and the **fax machine** rapidly became an important vehicle for international communication. In the rise of revolutionary movements in the late 1980s, fax technology was important in that it provided an uncensorable vehicle for communication. The **ELECTRONIC COMPUTER** is in many ways the symbol of the new technological age of the second half of the 20th century. For centuries, people had developed various calculating machines and other mechanical devices, and in the early 20th century "business machines" performed accounting and calculating functions. However, during World War II the first truly **electronic digital computers** were designed. By the 1950s, the first commercially available computers were the **UNIVAC,** produced by the Sperry Rand Corporation, and the **EDVAC.** Through the 1950s and 1960s, computers were large and expensive, and only highly trained experts could operate them. Even at this stage, the great magnitude of calculations that could be performed meant computers had a major impact on military technology and scientific research. By the 1970s, important changes were taking place. Miniaturization of component parts and greater sophistication of theory and design meant that corporations like **Cray Research** and **Control Data** could produce small **SUPERCOMPUTERS** capable of very large numbers of operations. At the same time, small **PERSONAL COMPUTERS** began to be developed, and companies like **Apple Computer** and **Commodore** led the field in creating computers for home use and computer games. By the 1990s, in most industrialized countries the computer had transformed important aspects of daily life and had become a powerful tool for military defense and scientific research.

New modes of international communication, along with larger international business organizations, produced **more intense global cultural interactions.** Most of these built on previous trends in Western Europe and the United States. Western-based political groups like **Amnesty International** (founded in London, 1961) monitored human rights violations in many countries and tried to mobilize world public opinion. The **"international" architectural style,** implemented by practitioners from many regions, created similar kinds of buildings in various cities. **Western rock music,** disseminated through cable television and world concert tours, had a strong impact in Africa, Latin America, and parts of Asia. Popular culture also changed under the influence of U.S. exports of films, television shows, fashions (such as blue jeans) and fast-food chains. **AMERICANIZATION** affected Western Europe as well as other parts of the world. Called "coca-colonization" by French critics in the 1950s, it brought new-style supermarkets to many areas, reduced the filmmaking industries of many countries, particularly at the popular level, and gave rise to imitations—like the spread of television game shows—even where American products were not directly used. **English increased in importance as the most commonly learned second language. Yet no single world culture formed.** Western influences were variously used—Japanese game shows, for example, involved a distinctive level of shaming—and rejected. The rejection of these influences played a role in **nationalist and religious revivals** by the 1970s.

3. ENVIRONMENTAL ISSUES

During the second half of the century there was an increasing awareness of changes in the physical environment caused by industrialization and other aspects of the modern era. This development tended to transform basic economic life and enterprise from seeking to exploit natural resources to seeking to preserve resources being destroyed by the normal activities of modern life. In the years immediately following World War II, concern for environmental preservation was limited. **International environmental problems increased nevertheless.** Industrial pollution (**acid rain**) from Germany's Ruhr Valley and the United States' industrial Midwest worsened water quality in Scandinavia and Canada, respectively. Shoreline pollution in major oceans spread beyond national boundaries. The twin sources of growing global pollution were **rapid population growth,** with attendant increases in human waste, and **heightened industrialization** (including automobile emissions) both in established industrial nations and in developing newcomers like South Korea, China, Mexico, and Brazil.

A major turning point came in the 1960s when some environmental issues reached crisis levels and events like the publication of **Rachel Carson's** *Silent Spring* increased broader public awareness of problems. By the 1960s, serious problems had become apparent in many areas. The dangers of radioactive atmospheric pollution from the extensive testing of nuclear devices first aroused the concerns of popular organizations and then played a role in providing incentives for intergovernmental actions like the **Nuclear Test Ban Treaty** of 1963. The dangers of extensive use of **DDT,** even when used for benevolent purposes such as malaria prevention, led to the banning of its use in the United States in 1972. In the second half of the century, **voluntary and private organizations** played an important role in environmental action. Some were long-established groups, like the **Sierra Club** in the United States, which had been established in 1892 to encourage wilderness activities and preservation and by the 1960s was a major political activist group. New groups ranged from small, single-issue associations to international activist organizations. **Greenpeace** was

founded in 1969 by a group of Canadians, to take direct nonviolent action against threats to the environment, the hunting of whales and baby seals, and nuclear testing in the Pacific. In 1985 the sinking of *Rainbow Warrior*, a Greenpeace ship, by French agents in New Zealand caused a major international incident. In Europe, the **GREEN MOVEMENT** became a visible political force in a number of countries. In the 1980s there were formal Green parties in at least six European countries, and the Green Alliance was an important force in the European Parliament. **INTERGOVERNMENTAL ACTIONS** also played an increasingly important role. By the 1970s, conferences were held regularly to deal with both specific issues and more general concerns. The **UN CONFERENCE ON THE HUMAN ENVIRONMENT** (1972) in Stockholm was important in this development. Specific conferences and conventions often created administrative structures to implement international agreements, as was the case with the **Convention on International Trade in Endangered Species** (1973). Other organizations, like the **International Whaling Commission,** were involved in environmental affairs but represented particular industrial or economic interests. By the 1990s, regular international conferences dealing with environmental issues and involving high-level officials had become an accepted part of international affairs. Limitations on global environmentalism included national sovereignty, resistance by major private companies, and the concern that established industrial powers were trying to impose expensive environmental measures on poorer, developing nations.

Nevertheless, many groups recognized the international dimensions of pollution problems. Conventions and multinational treaties regulating activities ranging from the use of seabed resources to use of outer space became established parts of international law. The **UN CONFERENCE ON ENVIRONMENT AND DEVELOPMENT** (UNCED), or the **Earth Summit,** held in Rio de Janeiro in 1992, was a symbol of the globalized environmental context. Leaders of 178 countries attended, making it the largest summit meeting ever held. Representatives and observers from more than 2,000 nongovernmental organizations at the meeting revealed the global scope of private activity as well. Major conventions relating to biodiversity, **global warming** (including the much-discussed destruction of tropical rain forests), forestry, and environmental policy principles were adopted, and later the UN General Assembly created the **Sustainable Development Commission** for implementation of the agreements.

4. POPULATION TRENDS AND MIGRATIONS

World population grew at an unprecedented rate after 1945, though regional trends varied:

	Estimated population (in thousands)		
	1900	**1950**	**1991**
North America	106,000	166,000	279,000
Latin America, Caribbean	—	166,000	458,000
Europe	400,000	392,000	502,000
Asia	932,000	1,368,000	3,046,000
Africa	—	180,000	293,000
World	1,600,000	2,564,000	5,423,000

Massive population growth resulted from **improved public health measures** and successful attacks on many traditional diseases. Infant mortality generally declined, which also meant more people reached childbearing age, and life expectancy rose (despite major regional variations). Food supplies largely kept pace. Most regions saw a decline in the rate of population growth by the 1980s, and there were some dramatic **demographic transitions** (Japan in the 1950s, Mexico in the 1960s). Overall however rapid growth is expected to continue into the 21st century. By the 1990s, the annual natural population increase (births over deaths) averaged 2.1 percent in developing countries and .5 %percent in industrial countries.

Concern about world **overpopulation** gained ground. Many Western experts in the 1950s and 1960s argued that population control was essential for industrialization (lest too many resources be expended on sheer survival). Some remnants of racist concern about the growth of nonwhite populations may have entered in to this view. **United**

Nations agencies largely accepted the argument that population control was an essential goal, and worked to distribute birth control information. By the 1980s, concern about the environmental effects of population growth exceeded the older focus on the impact on industrial development. **A concerted international approach to population issues was hampered,** however, by the opposition of the Catholic Church and, under Republican administrations, of the United States; these factors limited United Nations action by the 1980s. Most birth control policies were national; they varied by region and time period (China's policy changed several times) and also varied in effectiveness.

Population issues relating to public health, birth control, and family planning became major subjects of international debate. Early international conferences on population—**World Population Conference in Rome** (1954) and the **Second World Population Conference** in Belgrade (1965)—dealt with scientific and technical issues. The United Nations designated **1974 as WORLD POPULATION YEAR,** and the first major intergovernmental World Population Conference was held in Bucharest. The debates involved in drafting the *World Population Plan for Action* reflected international differences. **China,** the **Soviet Union,** and a number of developing countries, despite their own domestic policies, opposed international commitments to **birth control** as a new form of imperialism. The **Roman Catholic Church** and many predominantly Catholic countries opposed birth control and population planning on ideological grounds. The **UN International Conference on Population** in Mexico City in 1984 reached greater agreement on general issues. The issue of **abortion** was heatedly debated, and funding for population programs that allowed abortion was opposed by the U.S., reflecting the position of the **Reagan administration,** and the **Roman Catholic Church.** The final conference statement involved support for a commitment to global population control. The draft of the action program of the **1994 UN INTERNATIONAL CONFERENCE ON POPULATION** in Cairo reflected the continuing evolution of population concerns. While older ideological reservations about abortion remained in the debate, of greater concern were emerging global issues relating to improving the **role of women,** and the relationship among population, **environmental conditions,** and **development,** in achieving sustainable development that does not do irreparable environmental damage.

Population problems varied in intensity in different regions. **FAMINES** resulting from natural causes and civil wars resulted in major loss of life in the **Sahel region** in Africa in the 1970s, in **Ethiopia** and **Sudan** in the 1980s, and in other parts of the world. **Refugees** from famine, poverty, and wars grew in number by the 1990s. In mid-1993, it was estimated that there were more than 18 million international refugees and an additional 24 million who were displaced within their own country.

World population and economic trends created **new patterns of emigration** (though some of these had begun to take shape between the world wars). After the postwar dislocations (including movement of European Jews to Israel), emigration from Europe became insignificant. Africa (particularly North Africa), Central America and the Caribbean, Pakistan, Turkey, Thailand, China, the Philippines, and the Koreas became the largest sources of international migration, both legal and illegal. Destinations were most often the United States and Canada, Western Europe, Australia, and, to a limited extent, Japan—centers of industrialization. Changes in U.S. law (p. 918) facilitated non-European immigration, which came mainly from Asia and Central America; overall, 6 million Mexican workers, both legal and illegal, entered the country. **By the 1970s the United States was experiencing the highest absolute rate of immigration in its history.** By 1990, immigration had brought more than 12 million non-European people into the European Community. Japan had received about 600,000 foreigners, mainly from the Koreas and Southeast Asia. In all cases, most immigrants were unskilled laborers and were often badly treated, though there was an important if small outpouring of professionals (doctors, engineers) from places like India as well. An important subsidiary pattern of immigration involved oil-rich states in the Middle East such as Saudi Arabia and Kuwait, which received migrants from other parts of the Middle East (Egyptians, Palestinians) and also from Pakistan, India, and parts of Southeast Asia. International migration plus ongoing rural-to-urban migration increased city size. Several predominantly rural areas in 1945 had a majority urban population by the 1990s. **MEGACITIES** with huge populations developed; by the 1990s, 14 metropolitan areas had a population above 10 million, 9 of them in the Third World.

A rough periodization described the new international migration patterns. Rapid industrial growth in Europe and the United States prompted favorable reception, and in some cases active recruitment, of immigrants during the 1950s and 1960s. Slower growth, more frequent recessions, and a tendency toward growing unemployment, particularly among the unskilled, produced **new hostility to immigration** from the 1970s onward. This new environment included legislative limits, attempts to force some migrants to leave, and increased racist incidents.

c. GLOBALIZATION AND SPECIAL IDENTITIES

During the second half of the 20th century, a complex relationship developed between two major historical dynamics. One was the intensification of the globalization of all aspects of human life and the other was the continuing affirmation of special human identities. By the 1990s, globalization had not resulted in the emergence of either a single, global society or a network of fundamentally similar societies. Instead, special identities coexisted with global communications and economic networks and new transnational and regional structures. These developments are clearly visible in two major areas: 1) the development of ethnic and national identities, and 2) the evolution of identities based on particular ideologies and religions.

ETHNIC AND NATIONAL IDENTITIES. The emergence of nationalist opposition to the old empires in the period following World War II was an important factor in the nature of nationalist identities. Old ethnic and special cultural identities were associated with particular languages or historical traditions. However, the state boundaries that had been created by the imperial powers often did not match the regional boundaries of those old identities. When **NATIONALISM** developed, it did so within the framework of the imperially created political units, and it was those states that became nationally independent; **existing state identities** were the basis for the most effective nationalist movements. Movements for broader unity had only limited success. **ARAB NATIONALISM** developed in the first half of the 20th century as a broad regional sentiment, but nationalist movements in the Arab world were identified with the individual imperially created states, such as Algeria, Syria, and Palestine. The formation of the **Arab League** in 1945 was an important manifestation of Arab unity, but it was a coordinating organization of sovereign states. During the 1950s, enthusiasm for substantive Arab unity was encouraged by Egyptian president **Gamal Abdel Nasser** and resulted in the creation of the **United Arab Republic (UAR),** joining Egypt and Syria. However, the UAR only lasted for three years (1958–61), and other projects for Arab political unity remained unimplemented. **PAN-AFRICAN NATIONALISM** had roots in movements in the first half of the 20th century, and as many African states became independent, there was a hope of greater African unity. When the British colony of the Gold Coast became independent as **Ghana,** under the leadership of **KWAME NKRUMAH** in 1957, it assumed a leading role in African unity. Nkrumah was host to two pan-African congresses in 1958, but when the **Organization of African Unity** (OAU) was formally created in 1963, its charter affirmed the independence and territorial integrity of the individual member states. The OAU was effective in mediating disputes between African nations, and it coordinated expression of African views in international bodies, but the **pan-African vision** of a unified Africa was not realized. In the period from 1945 until the early 1970s, **state-based identities** remained the most effective, even when the states had been arbitrarily created by imperial and political settlements. Along with broader unification efforts, separatist movements also generally failed, as was the case in **Congo (Kinshasa)** (1960–64), **Nigeria** (1967–70), and among the **Kurds** in the Middle East. States created by partitions that were assumed to be temporary following World War II were still in existence at the beginning of the 1970s: the **two Germanies,** the **two Koreas,** and the two states in **Vietnam.**

1970–93. Ethnic revival and nationalism. In the early 1970s, increasing attention began to be given to cultural-linguistic sources of identity, and ethnic groups in new forms emerged as important elements in individual societies and on the global scene in general. The development of groups like the **Black Panthers** in the United States during the 1960s was an early signal of the change. Movements affirming black identity in the U.S. were not necessarily separatist or nationalist, but they strongly affirmed a distinctive ethno-cultural identity in the face of pressures for uniformity in modern society. In countries where there was a strongly established "national" identity, there was a rise in the importance of local ethnic traditions. In Great Britain, **Welsh nationalism** succeeded in achieving parity for Welsh with English in governmental matters in Wales in 1967. The **Scottish National Party** had been organized in the interwar period but remained unimportant until the 1960s. By the 1990s, the party had become a small but important part of the British political scene, regularly electing members to Parliament. In Canada, there was a major revival of **French-Canadian separatism** in Quebec. In many countries, activist—and sometimes violent—movements of ethnic identity gained strength after the early 1970s. A number of cultural-linguistic groups began to have more success asserting their identity in political ways. In 1971 the Bengali eastern part of Pakistan seceded and formed the new state of **Bangladesh**, and **Vietnam** was reunited by the communist victory in 1975. In the late 1980s a major political reorganization of countries based on historic cultural identity began as the **Soviet Union** and **Yugoslavia** broke up into their constituent republics, and the **reunification of Germany** also took place. By the 1990s, throughout the world there were active movements affirming their cultural and linguistic identity in many different ways. These included continuing separatist movements among the **Tamils** in Sri Lanka, the **Basques** in Spain, on **Timor** in Indonesia, and among many groups in the former Soviet Union, such as the **Abkhazians** in Georgia. Tensions between Hutu and Tutsi peoples in **Rwanda** resulted in 1994 in one of the bloodiest of these conflicts. Other groups affirmed their special identity in other ways—by reviving older customs or seeking cultural autonomy—as was seen among some **Native Americans** in the Western Hemisphere, the Swedish-speaking minority in **Finland**, and in the continuing definition of the relationship between the **Flanders** and **Wallonia** in Belgium. By the 1990s it was clear that the social and technological globalization of the second half of the 20th century had not dissolved cultural-linguistic boundaries between peoples. Instead, through new media for communication and interaction, the conditions of the new, globalized world societies seemed to encourage affirmations of special identity and made such affirmations more effective.

IDEOLOGICAL AND RELIGIOUS IDENTITIES. Some of the major global conflicts in the 20th century were drawn along lines of ideology and worldview. The competition between the world visions of Wilson and Lenin and the rise of fascism in the interwar era are part of this. In the era of the **cold war,** the conflict had a major ideological dimension as a conflict between communism and democratic capitalism. The main ideologies of the 20th century were global in their scope and vision. As nationalism developed, it reflected the different ideological frameworks; nationalism emerged in democratic, liberal forms or in Marxist, radical forms in the era following World War II.

1945–70s. Global political ideologies. In the era of the active cold war, the framework for ideological competition was the conflict between Marxist radicalism and Western liberalism. Movements asserting distinctive national identities expressed their nationalism in terms of these conflicts. As the **Third World** emerged by the 1960s, the **Nonaligned movement** developed, at the core of which was a group of nationalists strongly influenced by Marxist political radicalism. The new and most visible Third World leaders of the 1960s were **Nasser** in Egypt, **Sekou Touré** of Guinea, **Nkrumah** of Ghana, **Fidel Castro** of Cuba, and **Sukarno** of Indonesia, all of whom developed and advocated an ideologically radical nationalism. Their more conservative rivals, like **Muhammad Reza Pahlavi** in Iran, **Ferdinand Marcos** in the Philippines, and **Houphouët-Boigny** in the Ivory Coast, also expressed their visions in terms of politically ideological nationalisms. Leninism, Wilsonianism, Maoism, radical nationalism, and conservative nationalism all shared the character of being **political ideologies of modernization.** They were not clearly identified with existing religious traditions and accepted many of the modern assumptions about progress, modern science, and rationalism that were the basic character-

istics of Western European thought as it emerged from the 18th century. By the early 1970s, the cold war entered the full **détente stage,** making the Soviet-U.S. rivalry less acute in the Third World, and important new ideological changes took place in many areas. The student demonstrations in **Paris** in 1968 (p. 858), the **antiwar movement** in the U. S., and other demonstrations in the late 1960s reflected the growing disillusionment with all of the major ideologies. The **New Left** rejected much of Soviet-defined Marxism; radical nationalisms in the Third World had created repressive states; modernization and economic "progress" was beginning to be recognized as disastrous for the environment; leaders like the Shah of Iran and Marcos of the Philippines, who received support from democratic liberalism, were creating oppressive dictatorships. There was a gradual shift in worldview to a less ideological pragmatism and also to activist approaches more explicitly tied to the major religious traditions.

1970s–93. Global religious revival. In many areas of the world, changing conditions and attitudes supported a revival of religions. Some of this took the simple form of increased adherence to existing rules and greater sensitivity to the message of religion in the modern context. The **ROMAN CATHOLIC CHURCH** was an early leader in this revival of religious activism. The great Ecumenical Council, **VATICAN II** (1962–65) (p. 867), issued many important documents defining the Roman Catholic Church and its role in the modern world. Vatican II had a worldwide impact and was especially important in the development of political ideology in Latin America. A 1967 papal encyclical, *Populorum progressio,* and a major conference of the Latin American bishops in 1968 in Medellin, Colombia, clearly defined a position of opposition to social injustice and oppression. Building on this foundation, a movement of **LIBERATION THEOLOGY** developed that presented a clearly defined theological position in the writings of people like **Gustavo Gutierrez** and advocated and worked for significant social change. This brought some Catholic leaders into open conflict with social and political conservatives, and in the civil war in El Salvador, **Archbishop Oscar Romero** was murdered in 1980. Priests like **Ernesto Cardenal** in Nicaragua were active in developing new structures, such as "base communities," and participated in the **Sandinista** revolutionary movement.

Movements of religious activism and revival developed in virtually all major religious traditions. Many of these took a form that is frequently referred to as **fundamentalism,** calling for a return to traditional beliefs and moral codes. Fundamentalists were not always literally traditional—for example, many were less tolerant than their religions had previously been—and they often used new methods of propaganda. **Protestant fundamentalism** became more assertive in the United States in the 1980s, and also spread rapidly in Latin America; after 1989 there was also growing missionary activity in Russia. In the **ISLAMIC WORLD,** many revival movements developed. Some, like the **Muslim Brotherhood** (p. 759) in Egypt and the **Jamaat-i Islami** in South Asia, already had a long history. Others emerged as important forces in the 1970s, and by the 1990s, explicitly Islamic organizations were either the largest opposition group or an important part of the government in virtually every country where the majority of the population was Muslim. The **ISLAMIC REVOLUTION IN IRAN** (p. 974) in 1978–79 overthrew the Shah and established a republic that became the most visible Islamic government in the world. An Islamic movement also came to power in **Sudan** through a military coup in 1989. In **Algeria** the Islamic party was about to win the parliamentary elections of 1991–92 when a military coup prevented the completion of the elections. A **HINDU** religious revival became an important part of Indian history by the 1980s. In the early 1990s, the **Bharatiya Janata Party,** which supported an actively Hindu program, emerged as the largest opposition group in the Parliament. In 1992, Hindu extremists destroyed a mosque in **Ayodhya,** and hundreds of people were killed in the subsequent Hindu-Muslim rioting. Also in India, the **SIKHS** experienced a revival. In its militant form, the revival involved the demand for an independent Sikh state in the Punjab. The formation of **Akali dal** in 1980, an organization advocating Sikh independence, began an era of conflict. **BUDDHISM** experienced revivals in a number of areas as well. In the conflicts in Southeast Asia, Buddhist priests were sometimes involved, and with the disintegration of the communist world, some areas, such as **Mongolia** and **Laos,** experienced a revival of interest in Buddhism. In Japan, **Soka Gakkai,** a major Buddhist organization, grew significantly as did Buddhist groups in North America.

At the same time that some aspects of the religious revival emphasized distinctive identities, globalization of religious organizations also occurred. The **Roman Catholic Church** had long been a global organization, but its most rapid expansion has been outside of the West. In 1974, less than 15 percent of the world's Roman Catholics were in Asia and Africa, but by 1994, more than 25 percent of the estimated membership in the Church was on those two continents. Among the other Christian churches, the formation of the **World Council of Churches** in 1948 created a global organization that continued to be a voice throughout the rest of the century. The global nature of religious life, as well as the continuing importance of the distinctive traditions, was emphasized by the convening of the **Parliament of the World's Religions** in Chicago in 1993. This was held on the centennial of a similar parliament convened during the Chicago World's Fair in 1893, emphasizing that the processes of globalization were long-standing in religion. The parliament was basically a gathering of representatives of different traditions rather than a convention of believers sharing a common creed, reflecting the complex interactions between the processes of globalization and maintenance of distinctive identities in the 20th century.

2. INTERNATIONAL RELATIONS

(From p. 811)

International relations in the 50 years following World War II were dominated by the **cold war** between the two superpowers, the **Soviet Union** and the **United States.** The half century was a time of increasing globalization in all areas of life, so international relations also reflected those transformations in social and religious life, changes in the networks of economic relations, the rise of nationalism and decline of the old empires, and many other developments. The period can be **divided into two eras, with the beginning of the 1970s marking a time of transition** in the cold war, a change in the global economic system, and a shift from the old empires to newly transformed nationalisms.

a. RISE OF THE COLD WAR AND END OF EMPIRES

The main lines of development in the period following World War II involved the organization of international institutions to manage global affairs, the U.S.-Soviet rivalry, the rise of nationalism, and the growing globalization of human life.

1945, April 25–June 26. SAN FRANCISCO CONFERENCE. Drafted the Charter for the **United Nations Organization,** an international body that would be the successor to the **League of Nations** as the main organization for international relations on a global scale.

July 17–Aug. 2. POTSDAM CONFERENCE. The leaders of the United States, Great Britain, and the Soviet Union, **Harry S. Truman, Winston Churchill, and Joseph Stalin,** met to discuss postwar arrangements in Europe. These involved the disarmament and occupation of Germany and trials of war criminals.

Sept. 2. FORMAL SURRENDER OF JAPAN with the signing of terms on the U.S.S. *Missouri* in Tokyo Bay. The Japanese home islands were placed under U.S. military occupation, but the emperor remained as the head of state. **Korea** was placed under Soviet and U.S. occupation, pending the establishment of a democratic government. The **Kurile Islands** and the southern part of **Sakhalin Island** were ceded to the Soviet Union.

Oct. 24. United Nations formally came into existence when the twenty-ninth member government ratified the Charter. New York City was chosen as the site for the permanent seat of the organization.

Dec. 27. The **International Monetary Fund** was established (p. 816).

1946. Cold war tensions involved Soviets' continued occupation of northern Iran. Soviet troops withdrew by May.

The **Nuremberg Tribunal** for Nazi war criminals reached its verdicts, sentencing ten Nazis to death.

Feb. 1. Trygve Lie of Norway was elected secretary general of the United Nations for a five-year term.

June. The **International Bank for Reconstruction and Development** began operation.

1947. Cold war developments included the initiation of the **Marshall Plan** and the direct commitment by the United States to oppose Soviet expansion in **Greece** and **Turkey.**

The **Dead Sea Scrolls,** manuscripts dating back two thousand years, were discovered in Khirbat Qumran in Jordan. These proved to be of major importance for the understanding of Jewish and Christian history at that time.

The **Kon-tiki** expedition led by the Norwegian explorer Thor Heyerdahl provided that it had been possible for ancient peoples to travel by raft from South America to the Pacific Islands.

Nov. The UN General Assembly approved a plan for the partition of **Palestine** into a Jewish and an Arab state.

1948. Cold war tensions involved the Soviet restrictions on transport to Berlin and the resulting **Berlin blockade and airlift** (p. 870).

The **World Council of Churches** held its organizational meeting in Amsterdam. Representatives of 147 churches in 44 countries attended.

The **Olympics** in London revived major international athletic competitions after the interruptions caused by World War II.

The publication of **Alan Paton's** novel *Cry, the Beloved Country* brought the problem of relations between blacks and whites in **South Africa** to a worldwide audience.

The murders of **Mahatma Gandhi** (the Hindu nationalist advocate of nonviolence) in January by a Hindu extremist and **Count Folke Bernadotte** (the UN mediator in the Arab-Israeli war) in September by a Zionist extremist emphasized the violence accompanying the partitions of Palestine and British India.

Dec. The UN General Assembly adopted the **Universal Declaration of Human Rights** and the **Convention on the Prevention of Genocide.**

1949. Cold war developments included the victory of communist forces in China and the establishment of the **People's Republic of China** under the leadership of **Mao Zedong.** The Roman Catholic primate in Hungary, **Cardinal Mindszenty,** was sentenced by the communist government there to life imprisonment for treason. The treaty creating the **North Atlantic Treaty Organization (NATO)** was signed in Washington.

The publication of **George Orwell's** novel *Nineteen Eighty-four* articulated the growing fear of bureaucratic totalitarianism aided by modern technology.

The publication of **Simone de Beauvoir's** *Le Deuxième Sexe (The Second Sex)* provided a major statement for women's rights movements and feminism.

April. The **International Court of Justice** issued its first decision as the successor to the Permanent Court of International Justice, ruling against Albania and awarding damages to Great Britain in the **Corfu Channel case.**

1950. Cold war developments included the invasion of South Korea by North Korean forces, initiating the **KOREAN WAR.**

Akira Kurosawa, the noted Japanese film director, received his first major international recognition with the release of *Rashomon.*

July. The UN established a **unified command** of armed forces from 16 member countries to defend **South Korea.**

Nov. 3. UN General Assembly passed "Uniting for Peace" resolution allowing for emergency action if Security Council failed to achieve unanamity.

1951. Cold war developments included the continuation of hostilities in the **Korean War.** In the United States, **Julius and Ethel Rosenberg** were sentenced to death for espionage; executed in 1953.

The **IRANIAN OIL NATIONALIZATION CRISIS** (1951–53). **Mohammed Mossadegh** became premier of Iran in April 1951, and the Iranian government nationalized the **Anglo-Iranian Oil Company.** The

International Court of Justice ruled (1952) that it did not have jurisdiction because this was an internal matter. The matter was not resolved until the shah, **Mohammad Reza,** was restored to full power by a military coup aided by the U.S. Central Intelligence Agency in 1953.

1952. Cold war developments included the announcements that Great Britain had produced an atomic bomb and that the United States had tested **hydrogen bombs.** The Soviet Union vetoed admission of Japan and three Indochinese states to UN. Cold war vetoes, particularly by the Soviets, frequently marked UN debates.

July. EGYPTIAN REVOLUTION brought to power a group of young military officers advocating radical reforms; the most important of such revolutions in the Middle East.

Oct. The **Mau Mau revolt** in Kenya began with attacks on white settlers, and a state of emergency was declared by the British.

1953. Cold war developments included the successful explosion of a **hydrogen bomb** by the Soviet Union, the suppression by Soviet forces of major demonstrations in **East Berlin,** and the end of the Korean War.

April. DAG HAMMARSKJÖLD elected secretary general of the United Nations.

Oct. The **Federation of Rhodesia and Nyasaland** was established to unify the major British territories in central Africa and begin the transition to a multiracial, independent political system.

1954. Cold war developments included the agreement of the Western powers on the rearmament of **West Germany** and its admission to **NATO,** and the establishment by the United States of the **Southeast Asia Treaty Organization (SEATO).**

The second meeting of the assembly of the **World Council of Churches** was held in Evanston, Illinois.

Jonas E. Salk, developer of an antipoliomyelitis serum, begins inoculation program in Pennsylvania.

Nautilus, the first nuclear-powered submarine, was launched by the United States.

May. Defeat of the French at **Dien Bien Phu** in Vietnam brought an end to French rule in Indochina. The **Geneva Agreements** (July) defined the partition of Vietnam.

1955. Cold war developments included the **FOUR-POWER SUMMIT MEETING IN GENEVA** (July) in which U.S. president **Eisenhower** met directly with Soviet premier **Bulganin** for discussions on Germany and other matters.

Feb. The **BAGHDAD PACT,** which created the basis for the **Central Treaty Organization** in the U.S. system of regional alliances, was signed by Turkey and Iraq. Great Britain, Pakistan, and Iran soon joined as well.

April. The **BANDUNG CONFERENCE OF ASIAN-AFRICAN STATES** was attended by leaders from 29 countries, including **Tito** of Yugoslavia, **Nehru** of India, **Zhou Enlai** of the People's Republic of China, and **Nasser** of Egypt. The conference was the effective beginning of the **nonaligned movement** in world affairs.

1956. Cold war developments included the anti-Soviet **HUNGARIAN REVOLUTION** (Oct.) which was crushed by Soviet armed forces (Nov.)

SUEZ CRISIS. The Egyptian government under **Nasser** (p. 966) nationalized the **SUEZ CANAL** following the announcement by the United States and Britain that they would not participate in financing the **Aswan High Dam** (July). Egypt took control of the operation of the canal (Sept.) following the withdrawal of foreign technicians. A series of international conferences failed to resolve the issues. A coordinated **invasion of Egypt** by Israeli, French, and British forces resulted in the occupation of **Sinai** and the canal zone. U.S. and Soviet opposition to the invasion resulted in the creation of a **UN Emergency Force** (Nov.), which supervised the withdrawal of forces (completed by Jan. 1957).

1957. Cold war developments included the promulgation (Jan.) of the **Eisenhower Doctrine** on the use of U.S. armed forces in the event of communist aggression in the Middle East, and the test explosion of a **hydrogen bomb** by Britain. **SPUTNIK,** the first successful artificial satellite, was launched by the Soviet Union. UN **International Atomic Energy Commission** established to encourage the peaceful use of atomic power.

March. The **Treaty of Rome** established the **EUROPEAN ECONOMIC COMMUNITY,** creating a major new economy in the global markets.

June. The **International Geophysical Year** began. Thousands of scientists from more than 60 countries engaged in a massive coordinated research effort coinciding with a period of maximum solar activity. Among the achievements was the discovery of the **Van Allen radiation belts** around the earth.

Dec. The **Afro-Asian People's Solidarity Conference** convened in Cairo and established a permanent secretariat in Egypt. It worked to define the principles of **positive neutralism** in the cold war but was viewed in the West as being procommunist.

1958. Cold war developments included extensive discussions on discontinuance of **nuclear weapons testing,** leading to the opening of a Geneva conference on the issue. Russian author **Boris Pasternak** received the Nobel Prize for Literature. The nuclear-powered submarine *Nautilus* undertook major Arctic explorations and passed under the ice cap at the **North Pole.** The **First UN Conference on the Law of the Sea** produced four major conventions dealing with the use of the seas and their natural resources.

Jan. The **Federation of the West Indies** was established, bringing together ten British territories in the Caribbean. The federation was dissolved in 1962, following the withdrawal of Jamaica and Trinidad-Tobago.

Feb. The **UNITED ARAB REPUBLIC (UAR)** was created, joining Egypt and Syria in a major experiment in **pan-Arab nationalism** under the leadership of **Nasser.** Syria withdrew in 1961.

Oct. Cardinal Roncalli elected as Pope, taking the name of **JOHN XXIII,** beginning an era of major change in the Roman Catholic Church.

1959, Feb. FIDEL CASTRO became **premier of Cuba** following the victory of the revolutionary forces, and Cuba became a radical force in the Western Hemisphere.

Sept. The Soviet rocket *Luna 2* became the first space vehicle to reach the moon.

Dec. The **ANTARCTIC TREATY** reserved the Antarctic for scientific and other peaceful activities in an important action of international cooperation among all interested major powers. The **UN** established a permanent committee for the **peaceful uses of outer space.**

1960. Cold war developments included plans for a summit meeting between Eisenhower and Khrushchev; it was cancelled when a U.S. **high-altitude spy plane,** a U-2, was discovered and shot down by the Soviets.

Independence achieved by 17 countries in **AFRICA** during the year.

UN peacekeeping force deployed in the newly independent **Congo** following the outbreak of severe civil strife. The force was finally withdrawn in 1964.

The **Second UN Conference on the Law of the Sea** added to existing agreements on the use of ocean resources.

1961. Cold war developments included the **VIENNA SUMMIT CONFERENCE** (June) between U.S. president **Kennedy** and Soviet premier **Khrushchev,** at which many issues were discussed; the construction of the **BERLIN WALL** (Aug.) revealed the continuing tension over Germany and Soviet concern about the large numbers of refugees fleeing to the West.

The **World Food Program** for dealing with problems of hunger and famine relief was established.

The Assembly of the **World Council of Churches** met in Delhi, India, and the International Missionary Council was formally integrated into the organization.

April. Yuri Gagarin, Soviet astronaut, became the **FIRST HUMAN TO ORBIT THE EARTH.**

Sept. The **Conference of Non-Aligned Nations** in Belgrade was attended by 25 states and established a continuing organizational structure. UN secretary general **Dag Hammarskjöld** was killed in an airplane crash in the Congo.

Nov. U THANT OF BURMA named acting secretary general of the UN and subsequently elected (1962) to a four-year term.

1962. Cold war developments included the **CUBAN MISSILE CRISIS** (Oct.–Nov.), a major U.S.-Soviet confrontation over the Soviet placement of missiles in Cuba that brought the superpowers close to war.

A 17-nation **Disarmament Conference** opened in Geneva (March) but was finally adjourned (Aug. 1963) without reaching any agreements.

July. The completion of the **DILLON ROUND** of tariff negotiations in Geneva under the **General Agreement on Tariffs and Trade (GATT)** resulted in significant reductions in obstacles to international trade.

Oct. Pope John XXIII opened the **Twenty-first Ecumenical Council (VATICAN II)** of the Roman Catholic Church in Rome. By the time the council finished in 1965, many major decrees had been issued that changed the life of the Church.

1963. Cold war developments included the agreement by the United States, the Soviet Union, and Great Britain on a Limited **NUCLEAR TEST BAN TREATY** (Aug.). A **UN Observation Mission** was sent to **Yemen** when a civil war developed there with possible involvement of foreign forces. The mission was ended in 1964.

June. Valentina Tereshkova, a Soviet astronaut, became the first woman in space as the prime pilot of *Vostok 6*.

1964. UN Peacekeeping force for CYPRUS established as fighting developed between Greek and Turkish Cypriots.

Martin Luther King, Jr., civil rights leader in the United States, received the Nobel Peace Prize.

The **Olympic Games** were held in Tokyo.

Jan. The **Federation of Rhodesia and Nyasaland** was dissolved. Northern Rhodesia became independent **Zambia,** Nyasaland became independent **Malawi,** and Southern Rhodesia came under the control of an all-white government.

March. The **Afro-Asian Solidarity Council** met in Algiers.

March–June. UN CONFERENCE ON TRADE AND DEVELOPMENT (UNCTAD) met in Geneva, attended by 120 states. It established a permanent organization with special concern for the trade needs of developing countries.

Oct. Conference of Non-Aligned Nations met in Cairo with 47 members and 10 observers represented. Declarations affirmed opposition to foreign bases and Western colonialism.

Nov. Special **UN committee report on South Africa** called for total economic sanctions.

1965. RHODESIA became a problem area, with the white government of **Ian Smith** demanding independence and then issuing a **Unilateral Declaration of Independence** (Nov.). The UN Security Council called for nonrecognition, and **international economic sanctions** against the white government were organized.

Feb. Malcolm X, a major American Muslim leader, was murdered in New York.

Aug.–Sept. Second World Population Conference met in Belgrade.

Sept. UN Security Council and U Thant were able to implement a cease-fire in the **India-Pakistan fighting** in the continuing conflict over **Kashmir.**

Nov. The UN General Assembly established the **United Nations Development Program (UNDP)** to merge a variety of activities and organizations.

Dec. The UN General Assembly recommended **mandatory sanctions against South Africa.**

1966. SOUTHERN AFRICA. The UN Security Council authorized the British use of force to maintain an oil embargo on **Rhodesia** (April), and the General Assembly terminated the South African mandate for **Southwest Africa (Namibia).**

Soft landings on the moon were successfully made by the Soviet *Luna 9* and the U.S. *Surveyor 1.*

Jan. The first block from the ancient Egyptian temple of **Abu Simbel** was placed in its new location to avoid flooding by the Aswan Dam. The huge temple-moving project was coordinated by **UNESCO** and was the result of a global effort to preserve **major historic monuments.**

March. The **Archbishop of Canterbury** visited **Pope Paul VI,** initiating efforts to reconcile the Anglican and Roman Catholic Churches.

1967. ARAB-ISRAELI CRISIS. Tensions between Israel and its neighboring Arab states increased significantly in the early months. The **UN Emergency Force** was withdrawn from Sinai. The **SIX-DAY WAR** in June between Israel and the Arabs resulted in a major **victory for Israel** and the Israeli occupation of Sinai, the Golan Heights, the Gaza Strip, and the West Bank territories. United Nations played a major role in organizing international discussions. At the **Khartoum Conference,** Arab heads of state agreed on a position of "no negotiation" with Israel. **UN SECURITY COUNCIL RESOLUTION 242** provided an agreed-upon base, with international support, for a general peace settlement. Little progress was made in actual peace negotiations undertaken by the UN special envoy **Gunnar Jarring** in 1967–69.

EXPO 67, the world exposition in **Montreal,** celebrated the centennial of Canada's dominion status.

The People's Republic of **China** exploded its first **hydrogen bomb.**

Jan. Treaty of Principles Governing the Activities of States in the Exploration and Use of Outer Space was negotiated by the United States and the Soviet Union and signed by 62 states. It prohibited orbiting weapons of mass destruction and forbade separate claims to celestial territories.

May. The completion of the **KENNEDY ROUND** of negotiations under the **GATT** provided for significant tariff reductions and greater awareness of the trade problems of developing countries.

July. French president **Charles de Gaulle** promised French support for the separatist movement in **Quebec** during a state visit to Canada.

Nov. UN General Assembly unanimously adopted a declaration on the elimination of discrimination against women.

Dec. Dr. Christiaan Barnard in South Africa performed the first human heart transplant operation. The patient lived for 18 days. In 1968 another heart transplant patient of Barnard's lived for 19 months.

1968. MAJOR STUDENT AND URBAN UNREST surfaced in many countries. In the **United States,** there were **student demonstrations** in many cities in opposition to U.S. involvement in Vietnam, and in the summer there were **urban riots** in Cleveland (July) and violent street demonstrations during the **Democratic National Convention** in Chicago (July). There were civil riots in **Northern Ireland** (Oct.) and a near revolution in **FRANCE** following violent student outbreaks and strikes by workers in a number of industries (May–June). Similar disturbances took place in **West Germany** (April), **Poland, Mexico** (Sept.), **Brazil** (March–April), **Pakistan** (Oct.), and **Japan.** The **"Prague Spring,"** involving political liberalization in Czechoslovakia, was crushed by a Soviet invasion (Aug.).

Yusanari Kawabata, the Japanese novelist, received the **Nobel Prize for Literature.**

The **Olympic Games** were held in **Mexico City.**

June. The UN General Assembly approved the **NUCLEAR NON-PROLIFERATION TREATY** submitted by the UN Disarmament Committee, and 62 states ratified the agreement.

July. Pope Paul VI issued the encyclical *Humanae vitae,* which upheld the Church's traditional opposition to **artificial methods of birth control,** despite recognition by the papal advisory commission of the problems of global overpopulation.

Dec. The U.S. spacecraft *Apollo 8* was the first manned spacecraft in circumlunar orbit.

1969. July. The U.S. spacecraft *Apollo 11* landed a lunar module on the surface of the **MOON. Neil Armstrong** and **Edwin "Buzz" Aldrin** became the **FIRST HUMANS TO WALK ON THE MOON.** *Apollo 12* completed the second manned lunar landing mission (Nov.).

Nov. United States and Soviet Union ratify the **Nuclear Non-Proliferation Treaty.** The United States also unilaterally pledges not to utilize **germ or chemical weapons,** except in self-defense.

Nov.–Dec. STRATEGIC ARMS LIMITATIONS TALKS (SALT) between the United States and the Soviet Union began.

1970. Jan. The **International Monetary Fund** announced the completed allocation of **special drawing rights (SDR),** as part of a major revision of the Bretton Woods system.

Feb. Surrender of **Biafra** brought an end to the **Nigeria civil war.**

March. EXPO 70, the World Exposition, opened in **Osaka, Japan.** Foreign ministers from 24 Islamic countries held their first conference on cooperation in Jiddah and laid the foundation for the **ISLAMIC CONFERENCE ORGANIZATION.**

May. South Africa was expelled from the **International Olympic Committee.**

July. Pope Paul VI met with three leaders of independence movements in **Portuguese** African territories, and Portugal recalled its ambassador to the Vatican in protest.

Sept. UN Conference of the Committee on Disarmament approved a draft treaty banning nuclear weapons from the ocean floor. **Conference of Non-Aligned Nations** at Lusaka, Zambia, attended by delegates from 54 states. Resolutions were passed supporting **liberation movements** and in opposition to South Africa, Israel, and U.S. policy in Vietnam. Soviet unmanned spacecraft *Luna 16* returned from the moon with rock samples. Death of **Gamal Abdel Nasser** removed a major figure from Arab and Third World international politics.

Oct. The Twenty-fifth session of the United Nations General Assembly reflected the significant changes taking place: a majority (but not the necessary two-thirds) approved the membership of the People's Republic of **China;** resolutions condemning **colonialism** dealt with small remnants of empires and were approved by many newly independent states and postindependence white regimes in **southern Africa.** Economic discussions were focused on the new world of developing countries, and the issues were those of development and **neocolonialism** rather than imperialism.

b. NEW GLOBAL RELATIONSHIPS

By the 1970s, the continuing processes of globalization had taken many complex forms. At the same time that the networks of relationships in all areas of life were increasingly determined by global contexts, several older international structures were breaking down. The clearly structured world of the **Bretton Woods system** was replaced by a more global but anarchic international monetary system (p. 817); the old **bipolar world** of the early **cold war** was rapidly being replaced by a **polycentric world order.** These trends were visible in culture and society as well.

1971. Bangladesh became an independent state in place of East Pakistan after postelection fighting brought the Pakistan army into conflict first with Bengali followers of **Mujibur Rahman** (May) and then with invading Indian armed forces (Dec.).

U.S.-Chinese relations transformed. Informal contacts like the visit of the U.S. table tennis team to China ("Ping-Pong diplomacy") were combined with the U.S. announcement that it was lifting the embargo on trade with China (June). In October, the United States supported the admission of the **People's Republic of China** to the United Nations, and in November it was announced that U.S. president **Richard Nixon** would visit China.

Petroleum industry changes. Representatives of the **Organization of Petroleum Exporting Countries** (OPEC) met with major oil companies to discuss oil prices (Jan.–Feb.). **Algeria** took control of 51 percent of French oil companies' operations in **Algeria.**

West German chancellor **Willy Brandt** received the **Nobel Peace Prize** for his work in lessening East-West tension.

June. International Court of Justice declared that South Africa's administration of **Namibia** was illegal and should be surrendered to the UN.

Oct. The changing context of global politics was revealed in the state visits of the Ethiopian emperor **Haile Selassie** to China, where he was welcomed by **Mao Zedong,** and of Soviet premier **Kosygin** to Morocco, where he was welcomed by King **Hasan II.**

1972. Reduction of East-West tension continued. U.S. president **Nixon** visited the People's Republic of **China** (Feb.). In May **Nixon** made the first official visit of a U.S. president to the **Soviet Union,** giving an unprecedented televised address directly to the Soviet people and negotiating a number of agreements with Soviet leader **Brezhnev.**

Important **international monetary system modifications.** In April the **U.S. dollar** was officially devalued, and discussions continued throughout the year regarding modifications of the international system. The **IMF Committee of Twenty** opened formal negotiations on reforming the monetary system (Nov.).

May. The Third **UN Conference on Trade and Development (UNCTAD)** met in Chile and reached little agreement.

June. The **UN Conference on the Human Environment** in Stockholm adopted a declaration of 26 international environmental guidelines; an important landmark in international environmental policy.

Aug.–Sept. The **Olympic Games** were held in **Munich.** "Black September" Palestinian terrorists seized 11 Israeli athletes as hostages. All were killed, and a West German police attack ended the incident.

1973, Jan. VIETNAM PEACE AGREEMENT was signed in Paris by representatives of North and South Vietnam, the United States, and the Viet Cong. Considerable fighting continued in the broader region, but a second agreement strengthening the cease-fire was signed in June.

International monetary instability continued throughout the year. Japan permitted the **yen** to float (Feb.)

March. Treaty outlawing trade in endangered species is signed by 80 countries in Washington.

Mar.–May. American Indian Movement occupied **Wounded Knee**

in South Dakota, protesting the U.S. government's treatment of Native Americans and demanding rights and recognition.

Sept. Fourth Conference of Non-Aligned Nations, in Algiers, urged the establishment of a new world economic order.

Oct.–Dec. FOURTH ARAB-ISRAELI WAR. Egypt and Syria attacked territories occupied by Israel during the 1967 war in a new war that was costly to both sides and ended in an unstable cease-fire established under pressure from the Soviet Union and the United States. Arab petroleum-exporting countries placed an **EMBARGO ON OIL SHIPMENTS** to the United States, Western Europe, and Japan in retaliation for their support of Israel. The unstable oil situation resulted in shortages and price increases throughout the world. The immediate crisis ended with the convening of a **peace conference** between Israel and Arab states in Geneva (Dec.).

1974. ARAB-ISRAELI CONFLICT continued to be an important international issue. With the aid of the "shuttle diplomacy" of U.S. secretary of state **Henry Kissinger,** Egypt and Israel signed a disengagement agreement for the **Suez Canal zone** (Jan.), and Syria and Israel signed a disengagement agreement for the **Golan Heights** (May). The **Palestine Liberation Organization** was recognized by the UN as the representative of the Palestinian people (Oct.) and granted observer status (Nov.).

WORLDWIDE ENERGY CRISIS began with the Middle East conflict. OPEC did not reduce prices. A **conference of 13 oil-consuming states** in Washington (Feb.) agreed that the countries would cooperate in dealing with the energy crisis. In March, seven major oil-exporting countries agreed to lift the oil embargo on the United States.

International monetary adjustments. International financial instability continued with the devaluation of the **yen** and **franc** (Jan.). The final meeting (June) of the **IMF Committee of Twenty** was able to adopt only interim rules, because of global inflation and balance-of-payments problems.

Feb. Islamic summit conference in Lahore was attended by representatives from 38 Islamic countries.

May. India exploded a **nuclear device,** making it the world's sixth atomic power. **Portuguese Revolution** overthrew the government, opening the way for democratization in Portugal and the independence of its colonies. **Guinea-Bissau** became independent in Sept.

June. THIRD UN LAW OF THE SEA CONFERENCE convened in Caracas, with delegates and observers from 148 countries attending.

Sept. Haile Selassie was overthrown in the **ETHIOPIAN REVOLUTION.** The radical regime that ultimately came to power transformed Ethiopia from an ally of the United States into an ally of the Soviet Union.

1975. Separatist movements. A number of countries saw the rise of important regional and ethnic separatist movements. In **CYPRUS, Turkish Cypriots** declared the northern part of the island to be a separate state (Feb.). Although the new state received no international recognition, it was supported by the Turkish Army, which controlled the area. In **ETHIOPIA,** the movement for the liberation of **Eritrea** continued, despite the change of regimes, and fighting intensified in some areas. In **ANGOLA,** rival liberation movements representing regional-ethnic groups fought each other as **Portugal** sought to grant independence to the country.

ARAB-ISRAELI NEGOTIATIONS. As a result of the first Egyptian-Israeli disengagement agreement, the **Suez Canal** was reopened for shipping (June). A **second disengagement agreement** was signed by Egypt and Israel, expanding the area of Sinai from which Israeli forces withdrew.

End of the Portuguese empire was virtually complete as independence was gained by **Mozambique** (June), **São Tomé and Principe** (July), the **Cape Verde Islands** (July), and **Angola** (Nov.).

Aug. CONFERENCE ON SECURITY AND COOPERATION IN EUROPE adopted a charter that was signed in **Helsinki** by the leaders of 33 European states, the United States, and Canada. It represented formal acceptance of the territorial changes at the end of World War II, and all signatories agreed to support human rights in their countries.

Nov. Meeting of the Assembly of the **World Council of Churches** in Nairobi, Kenya. The Assembly took strong positions on racism and sex discrimination, and elected two women, a Ghanaian jurist and a U.S. psychologist, to the six-member presidium.

1976. Southern Africa. International actions regarding white regimes in **Rhodesia** and **South Africa** continued. U.S. secretary of state Henry

Kissinger attempted to mediate, and a conference of Rhodesian leaders in **Geneva** (Oct.–Dec.) failed to produce agreements. Riots in **Soweto** (June) spread to other black townships in **South Africa,** drawing international attention. **Transkei** became the first independent black homeland in South Africa (Oct.), but it did not receive international recognition.

Jan. International monetary reform. Finance ministers from countries belonging to the IMF met in Jamaica and agreed on an arrangement in which values of currencies would "float" in the world market according to supply and demand.

June. ECONOMIC SUMMIT of the leaders of the seven major industrial countries (United States, Japan, West Germany, Great Britain, France, Italy, and Canada) met in Puerto Rico to coordinate policies. This was the first meeting of what was to become the **GROUP OF SEVEN** (p. 817).

July. Indonesia launched a communications satellite, *Palapa,* into permanent orbit over the country. Indonesia joined the United States, Canada, and the Soviet Union as the only countries with **domestic satellite systems** for coordination of national communications systems. The summer **Olympic Games** were held in **Montreal.** Thirty-one countries did not participate, in protest against **apartheid** in South Africa, and the Canadian government excluded athletes from **Taiwan.**

Aug. Fifth Conference of the Non-Aligned Nations was held in Colombo. The major emphasis was on the **economic world order,** demanding better economic terms for developing countries.

Oct. Arab League summit conference in Cairo approved the establishment of an **Arab peacekeeping force** to assist in implementing a cease-fire in the growing civil war in **Lebanon.**

Dec. OPEC, meeting in Qatar, was divided over the prices to be set for oil for the first half of 1977. The deliberations showed that the producing countries, rather than the major companies, **set global oil prices.**

1977. SOUTHERN AFRICA continued to be a focus of global attention. The **Roman Catholic Church** defied apartheid in South Africa by admitting blacks into previously all-white schools (Jan.), and South African bishops denounced government policies (Feb.). A UN-sponsored conference in Mozambique (May) urged **self-determination for Zimbabwe and Namibia** and an end to regimes of racial separation. The death of **Steven Biko,** a South African black leader, while in police custody (Sept.) led to major demonstrations and international protests, and 13 official representatives of Western states attended his funeral.

ENERGY CRISIS. The global energy crisis was dealt with in many different ways. U.S. president **Jimmy Carter** announced a national energy program that aimed at, among other things, reducing U.S. reliance on **imported oil.** Nuclear power was an important subject discussed at the **Group of Seven** meeting in London.

May. Meeting of the **Group of Seven** in London was attended by the heads of the member governments and confirmed the plan to hold such meetings regularly.

June. The sixth assembly of the **LUTHERAN WORLD FEDERATION** was held in Tanzania. Bishop **Josiah M. Kibira** of Tanzania became the first African elected president of the federation. The **Southeast Asia Treaty Organization (SEATO)** dissolved itself; members agreed that it had outlived its usefulness as a cold war weapon.

Sept. Panama Canal Accords signed by the United States and Panama, arranging for Panama's eventual control of the canal and the Canal Zone.

Nov. The United States formally cancelled its membership in the **International Labor Organization (ILO)** because of the ILO's political positions. (The United States returned to the ILO in 1980.) A major **Arab-Israeli peace initiative** began when Egyptian president **ANWAR SADAT** traveled to Israel and addressed the Knesset. Active Egyptian-Israeli negotiations began following the address. Other Arab states opposed the Sadat initiative.

1978. MIDDLE EAST PEACE NEGOTIATIONS between Egypt and Israel continued throughout the year. When they became deadlocked, U.S. president **Carter** intervened and hosted intensive negotiation sessions at **CAMP DAVID** (Sept.). The accords provided the basis for a later peace treaty.

SPACE MILESTONES included the successful docking of Soviet spacecraft with the *Salyut 6* **manned space laboratory** (Jan.) and a new endurance record of 139 days and 14 hours in space, set by two **Soviet astronuats** (Nov.).

ROMAN CATHOLIC CHURCH experienced changes in leadership. **Pope Paul VI** died (Aug.) and Cardinal Luciani was elected his successor as **Pope John Paul I.** The sudden death of the newly elected Pope in Sept. led to the election of Cardinal Wojtyla as **Pope John Paul II.** Wojtyla, the archbishop of Kraków, was the **first non-Italian** to be elected pope since 1522.

ISLAMIC REVOLUTION IN IRAN began with a series of antigovernment demonstrations throughout the year. By the end of the year, the shah, **Muhammad Reza Pahlavi,** had clearly lost control, and power passed to the revolutionary movement led by **AYATOLLAH KHOMEINI.** This revolution marked the emergence to global prominence of **Islamic revivalist forces** and a major change in Middle Eastern and global power relationships.

May–June. Special session of the UN General Assembly convened to consider **DISARMAMENT.** UN organizations dealing with disarmament were restructured.

July. The first documented birth of a **"test-tube baby,"** a human conceived outside of its mother's body, occurred in England. The **Organization of African Unity (OAU)** met in Khartoum. The presence of foreign troops in African conflicts dominated discussions, with radical states supporting **Cuban** and **Soviet** military involvement in Ethiopia, Angola, and elsewhere.

Nov. A religious commune in **Guyana** led by **Jim Jones** came to an end with the mass suicide of more than 900 followers. The San Francisco–based sect had established the commune, called **Jonestown,** in the mid-1970s.

1979. Middle Eastern peace negotiations continued, and a **PEACE TREATY** between Egypt and Israel was signed in March. Other Arab states continued to oppose the Egyptian action, imposing an economic boycott on Egypt and severing diplomatic relations.

The **ISLAMIC REPUBLIC OF IRAN** was established with the departure of the shah (Jan.) and the return of **Ayatollah Khomeini** from exile (Feb.). The international effect was increased when militants seized the **U.S. embassy** in Tehran and held U.S. diplomats hostage. The **UN Security Council** and then the **International Court of Justice** called for the release of all hostages.

Pope John Paul II made a series of international trips and affirmed a more conservative vision for the Church. He visited **Latin America** (Jan.), **Poland** (June), **Ireland** (Sept.), and the **United States** (Oct.).

March. A major accident occurred at the **Three Mile Island nuclear power plant** in the United States, reflecting the potential dangers of utilizing nuclear energy for electricity production.

April. The **TOKYO ROUND OF NEGOTIATIONS UNDER THE GATT** was completed, with agreement on significant reductions of tariffs. **Rhodesian elections** were held on the basis of universal suffrage, and **Bishop Abel Muzorewa's party** won a majority of seats in the Parliament. The election was repudiated by the UN Security Council (May). International negotiations continued, and a **peace agreement** allowing for political participation by the **Patriotic Front** was signed by all parties in December.

May. A draft treaty resulting from the seven years of **SALT II** negotiations between the United States and the Soviet Union was completed and signed by **Carter** and **Brezhnev** in Vienna (June).

July. The **International Whaling Commission** banned all whale hunting in the Red Sea, the Arabian Sea, and much of the Indian Ocean.

Sept. The Sixth Summit Conference of the Non-Aligned Nations was held in Havana. Vietnamese occupation of Cambodia and foreign troops in Africa were important areas of disagreement.

Dec. The price of **gold bullion** on the London exchange closed the year at $524 per ounce. This reflected the transformation from the Bretton Woods system (which came to an end in 1971), in which gold was fixed at $35 per ounce.

1980. U.S.-Soviet Relations entered a period of increased tension following the Soviet invasion of **Afghanistan** (Dec. 1979). The United States limited **grain sales** to the Soviet Union (Jan.) and led a **boycott of the Olympic Games in Moscow** (July). The Soviet invasion was also condemned by the **UN General Assembly** (Jan.) and the **Islamic Conference Organization** (May).

March. ROBERT MUGABE and the Zimbabwe African National Union (ZANU) won the new national elections in **ZIMBABWE.** Zimbabwe became the one hundred fifty-third member of the UN in August. **Archbishop Oscar Romero,** a major defender of human rights in **El Salvador,** was murdered while saying mass.

May. The **World Health Organization** announced the total eradication of **SMALLPOX.** The **Mediterranean Action Plan** of the UN Environment Program was expanded by a protocol in which all bordering states agreed to limit pollution from land sources.

Aug.–Oct. Labor unrest in **POLAND** led to the creation of independent unions and a national federation called **SOLIDARITY,** which advocated a program of political and economic reforms. The United States, **NATO,** and the European Community warned the **Soviet Union** not to intervene militarily in Poland. The formation and success of Solidarity was a major turning point in the end of communist rule in Eastern Europe.

Sept. Saudi Arabia became full owner of **Aramco,** the largest company producing Saudi oil.

Nov. The U.S. spacecraft *Voyager 1* sent important photographs and data about **Saturn.**

1981. AIDS (acquired immunodeficiency syndrome) first identified and diagnosed as the cause of a deadly illness. Originally it was identified with homosexual males, but it was soon recognized that all elements of the population around the globe were susceptible. **AIDS** resisted all attempts at cures.

Drug Trade. Under the Reagan and then Bush administrations, increasing attempts were made to intercept drug traffic and shut down drug growing and processing centers in Latin America.

Space shuttle. The United States launched the first space shuttle, *Columbia,* in April, and then successfully relaunched it in November.

Jan. U.S. hostages were released by the Iranian government after 444 days in captivity.

May. The World Health Organization voted overwhelmingly to discourage the use of **baby formulas** in Third World countries.

July. The leaders of the **G-7 countries** held a summit in Ottawa to coordinate economic policies.

Sept. After 300 years of British control, **Belize** (former British Honduras) became independent.

Oct. ANWAR SADAT was killed by Muslim terrorists in Cairo because of his peace initiative and his secular policies. His successor, **Hosni Mubarak,** affirmed his dedication to continuing the policies of Sadat.

1982. REGIONAL WARS were an important part of international affairs. The **FALKLAND ISLANDS/MALVINAS WAR** (March–June): **Argentina** invaded the Falkland Islands (March), asserting its claim to the British colony. In response the **British** sent a major military force, which defeated the Argentine forces and recaptured all territories. The **LEBANESE WAR:** In the course of a continuing civil war in Lebanon and continuing Israeli-Palestinian conflict across the southern Lebanese border, **ISRAEL** invaded southern Lebanon (June) and rapidly gained control of the region. The invasion and then bombardment of Beirut aroused large-scale international protest. After many incidents, Israel pulled back from Beirut but maintained an occupation force in much of the south at the end of the year. **IRAN-IRAQ WAR:** the war that had begun with Iraq's invasion of Iran in 1980 entered a new phase in 1982 with a successful Iranian counteroffensive and a shift in the balance of fighting.

International meetings of many different types showed some of the difficulties in developing coordinated policies and actions on a global scale. A conference on **East-West cooperation** in Madrid (March) adjourned when discussions reached an impasse. The **Second General Assembly Special Session on Disarmament** (July) was unable to reach any agreement. Despite a meeting at the ministerial level of **OPEC** regarding prices and production quotas (July), the states remained strongly divided. The regularly scheduled summit conference of the **Organization of African Unity** was canceled because of a dispute over Chad's representation.

May. The completion of the **LAW OF THE SEA TREATY** was a major success for international negotiations. The **Third UN Conference on the Law of the Sea** drafted the treaty, which represented eight years of negotiations (1973–82) and was a comprehensive agreement governing the use of the seas and their resources.

June. The eighth summit of the leaders of the **G-7 countries** dealt with political issues, like the wars in the south Atlantic and in Lebanon, as well as economic issues.

Sept. *Conestoga 1,* the first successful privately developed launch vehicle, completed a suborbital flight.

1983. SEPARATIST MOVEMENTS were important elements in international affairs. In **INDIA,** Sikh militants in Punjab, Muslims in **Kashmir,** and activists in **Assam** all mounted serious opposition to the government. An Armenian militant group, the **Armenian Secret Army for the Liberation of Armenia** was responsible for a series of bombings, including one in a Paris airport that killed five people (July). Violence involving **Tamil separatists** in Sri Lanka resulted in nearly 400 deaths in July and August. The French banned the **Corsican Liberation Front,** a separatist group that had taken credit for many bombings during 1982.

Feb. U.S. and Soviet negotiators resumed **Strategic Arms Reduction Talks (START)** in Geneva.

March. Summit Meeting of the Conference of the Non-Aligned Nations in Delhi reflected the lessening influence of pro-Soviet radicals.

June. The U.S. spacecraft *Pioneer 10* crossed the orbit of Neptune and became the first human-made vehicle to pass out of the solar system.

July–Aug. The Sixth General Assembly of the **World Council of Churches** met in Vancouver. Deliberations gave attention to matters of shared worship and approved a document on war and peace.

Sept. Soviet fighter planes shot down a South Korean commercial airliner, **Korean Air Lines flight 007.** An international diplomatic incident followed.

Oct. Lech Walesa, the leader of Poland's Solidarity movement, received the **Nobel Peace** Prize.

Dec. The **United States** gave formal notice of its intention to terminate its membership in **UNESCO** by the end of 1984.

1984. The U.S. Goddard Spaceflight Center estimated there were 1,462 spacecrafts and satellites in space.

Jan. The summit meeting of the **Islamic Conference Organization** in Morocco voted to invite **Egypt** to return to the organization. Egypt's membership had been suspended when it signed peace accords with Israel.

May. The **International Court of Justice ruled** on a complaint brought by Nicaragua that the United States should cease and refrain from mining Nicaraguan ports.

July. The summer **Olympic Games** were held in **Los Angeles.** Athletes from a record 140 countries participated.

Aug. The **UN International Conference on Population** convened in Mexico City with representatives from 149 countries. The most disputed subject was **abortion.** The **United States** actively opposed proposals including abortion and had announced (June) that it would not provide aid for international population programs that included abortion.

Oct. Soviet cosmonauts set a new record, spending 237 days in space. The **famine in Ethiopia** aroused a global relief effort led by governmental and nongovernmental agencies. **Violent Sikh separatism** continued throughout the year, and in October a **Sikh extremist** murdered INDIRA GANDHI, the prime minister of India.

Nov. Morocco withdrew from the **Organization of African Unity** because of its recognition of the **Western Sahara nationalist group.**

Dec. A toxic gas leak from a **Union Carbide** plant in Bhopal, India, killed 2,500 (or more) people. The catastrophe initiated much debate about the role of **multinational corporations** and their responsibilities in developing countries.

1985, Jan. Pope Shenuda III was allowed to return to Cairo to resume his duties as leader of the **COPTIC CHURCH.** In 1981 he had been ordered by the Egyptian government to go to a desert monastery. The **United States** announced that it would cease to participate in the case brought against it by **Nicaragua** in the **International Court of Justice.**

Feb. New Zealand refused to allow a **U.S. warship** to visit New Zealand unless the United States certified that it did not carry nuclear weapons. This was viewed by the United States as weakening the AN-ZUS ALLIANCE.

April. A special meeting of **nonaligned states** was held in **BAN-DUNG,** Indonesia, to mark the thirtieth anniversary of the original conference of nonaligned states. Representatives from 80 countries attended, in contrast to the 29 at the original conference.

July. LIVE AID CONCERTS in London and Philadelphia were watched on television by more than 1.5 billion people worldwide and raised more than $71 million for the **Band Aid Fund** to combat starvation in Africa. The show was arranged by rock musician **Bob Geldof.** A meeting of **OPEC oil ministers** was unable to agree on prices or production quotas. **OPEC's share** of the world market had gone down in the past decade, from 53 percent to 30 percent, because of increased competition from non-OPEC producers in the **North Sea** and **Mexico.** In a later meeting (Dec.) the oil ministers agreed to abandon quotas and compete directly in the world market. *Rainbow Warrior,* a ship belonging to the activist environmental group **GREENPEACE,** was sunk by French agents in an effort to prevent protests against **French nuclear testing** in the Pacific. The UN Conference to mark the end of the **UN DECADE FOR WOMEN** was held in **Nairobi.** The record of the past decade was assessed, and goals were set for future action.

1986. Wole Soyinka, Nigerian playwright and poet, received the Nobel Prize for literature.

Jan. The U.S. space shuttle *Challenger* exploded shortly after it was launched. All seven persons aboard were killed, including **S. Christa McAuliffe,** a schoolteacher who was the first private citizen to fly on a shuttle.

Feb. The **Dalai Lama,** exiled Tibetan Buddhist leader, met with **Pope John Paul II** in India. The U.S. **Senate** ratified the **UN Convention on the Prevention and Punishment of the Crime of Genocide,** 37 years after it had been submitted by President Truman.

Mar. The *Giotto* spacecraft launched by the European Space Agency sent back data about the nucleus of Halley's Comet.

April. U.S. **warplanes** bombed **Libya** in retaliation for terrorist attacks against U.S. citizens. The **CHERNOBYL NUCLEAR POWER PLANT** in the Soviet Union (Ukraine) experienced a **major accident.** Severely high levels of radioactivity were detected throughout northern and eastern Europe.

May. The annual economic summit of the leaders of the **G-7 countries** was held in Tokyo.

June. The UN General Assembly approved a **Program of Action for African Economic Recovery and Development.** It was the first time that such action had been taken for a specific region.

July. The leader of the Turkish republic in **northern Cyprus** rejected UN efforts to unseal the border that divided the island.

Sept. Summit meeting of the **Conference of Non-Aligned Nations** in Zimbabwe. It issued a call for selective sanctions against **South Africa.**

Sept.–Oct. The **U.S. Congress** overrode a veto by President Reagan, legislating strict U.S. economic sanctions against **South Africa.**

Oct. World Day of Prayer for Peace in Assisi, Italy, was attended by leaders of 12 different religious traditions.

1987. The UN secretary general declared a Yugoslavian boy born in 1987 to be the world's **five billionth inhabitant.**

June. Thirteenth annual summit meeting of the leaders of the **G-7 countries** was held in Venice. There was some discussion of the need to protect oil tankers in the **Persian Gulf,** because of the continuing Iran-Iraq War.

Aug. UN Conference on Trade and Development (UNCTAD) discussed debt problems of developing countries and the need for encouraging trade.

Sept. La Francophonie, a new organization of 41 French-speaking states and territories, met in Quebec. The province of **Quebec** was recognized in a Canadian constitutional revision (May) as a **distinct society** within the confederation.

Oct. The **Commonwealth of Nations,** meeting in Vancouver, remained divided over the issue of sanctions on **South Africa.**

Dec. Summit meeting between U.S. president **Reagan** and Soviet general secretary **Gorbachev** in Washington. They signed the **Intermediate-Range Nuclear Forces (INF) Treaty,** providing for demolition of intermediate-range missiles and continuous mutual verification inspections. The **Association of Southeast Asian Nations (ASEAN)** held

its first summit meeting, in Manila, in more than a decade and only the third in its 20-year history.

1988. Naguib Mahfouz, the Egyptian novelist, received the **Nobel Prize for literature.**

United Nations peacekeeping forces received the **Nobel Peace Prize.** A new novel, *The Satanic Verses,* by **Salman Rushdie** was banned in some Muslim countries because censors thought it dealt blasphemously with the Prophet Muhammad.

May. U.S. president **Reagan** and Soviet leader **Gorbachev** held their fourth summit meeting, during Reagan's visit to Moscow. U.S. and Soviet representatives signed nine different agreements on subjects ranging from student exchanges to fisheries to arms control. The formal documents of ratification of the **INF TREATY** were exchanged.

June. The **G-7 summit** met in Toronto and discussed farm subsidies and the economic needs of developing countries.

July. U.S. missiles mistakenly shot down an **Iranian commercial airliner** in the Persian Gulf during U.S. naval escort operations to protect oil shipping. **Ayatollah Khomeini** accepted the UN Security Council cease-fire resolution relating to the **Iran-Iraq War.** Hostilities came to an end on August 20 in a war in which more than one million people had been killed.

Sept. Growing global interest in environmental affairs was reflected in **Sweden.** In national elections, the **Green Environmental Party** won 20 seats in the 349-seat Swedish Riksdag. It was the first new party to win representation in 70 years.

Oct. The U.S. government formally charged the **Bank of Credit and Commerce International** with conspiracy to launder drug money in a huge global financial network. BCCI operated in more than 70 countries, with assets of more than $20 billion. The charges had an impact on financial institutions around the world.

Dec. Southern African agreement signed by Angola, Cuba, and South Africa. The accord granted independence to **Namibia.** South Africa agreed to withdraw from Namibia in return for Cuba's withdrawal from Angola.

1989. YEAR OF POLITICAL TRANSFORMATION. In a remarkable series of rapid changes, many of the established political systems and seemingly permanent networks of relationships experienced significant alterations. **END OF COMMUNIST SYSTEMS IN EASTERN EUROPE.** In the countries of Eastern Europe, popular demonstrations brought an end to the rule of the **Communist Party.** In East Germany, the old rulers were out of power by October, and by the end of the year the **Berlin wall** was being torn down. **Hungary** had its first free, multiparty elections in 42 years (Nov.). In **Czechoslovakia,** communist leaders stepped down, and in December, the dissident playwright **Vaclav Havel** was elected president. **Solidarity** won a decisive victory in the elections in **Poland** in June. Communist regimes also came to an end in **Bulgaria** (Nov.) and **Romania** (Dec.). In the **SOVIET UNION** itself, the Baltic republics were beginning to assert their independence, and the core political system was being rapidly reformed by **Gorbachev.**

Feb. Ayatollah Khomeini in Iran issued a ruling condemning **Salman Rushdie,** the author of *The Satanic Verses,* to death for blasphemy. Many Muslims around the world opposed the sale or display of the book. Other groups defended Rushdie's freedom of expression.

April–May. Pro-democracy demonstrations in CHINA brought thousands of students and workers to **Tiananmen Square** in Beijing. The demonstrations were suppressed by military force after they had captured the world's attention for a number of weeks.

May. Egypt resumed its membership in the **Arab League;** it had been suspended after the signing of a peace treaty with Israel in 1979.

Sept. Summit meeting of the Conference of Non-Aligned Nations held in Belgrade. Declarations were less radical than in previous years.

1990. Tim Berners-Lee, a British engineer, launched what became the **WORLD WIDE WEB** for information retrieval.

1990 ff. Intensification of economic globalization.

1990. POLITICAL TRANSFORMATIONS CONTINUED. Dramatic political change continued to be a major theme in global affairs during 1990. Significant changes in rulers or in political systems occurred in widely different areas. In **SOUTH AFRICA,** steps were taken to end the **apartheid system. Nelson Mandela,** the leader of the African National Congress, was freed from prison (Feb.) and began significant negotiations with the government. Following the end of communist rule in East Germany, **GERMANY WAS REUNITED** (Oct.). Previously authoritarian regimes agreed to significant **democratization in Nepal** (April), **Chile** (March), **Mongolia** (March), **Zambia** (Oct.), and **Bangladesh** (Dec.). Free elections were also held in **Myanmar** (formerly Burma) and **Haiti** (Dec.), although subsequent events made democracy short-lived in these countries. Throughout the year, the **Soviet Union** and **Yugoslavia** continued to break up into their constituent parts.

March. **Japan** became the third country, after the United States and the Soviet Union, to place a satellite in orbit around the **moon.**

April. **EARTH DAY** celebrated by an estimated 200 million people from 140 countries in a major global expression of concern for the environment.

Aug. **PERSIAN GULF WAR** began when Iraq invaded and occupied Kuwait. An international response led by the **United States** and coordinated through the **United Nations** developed. By the end of the year, a large multinational force was set to enforce UN resolutions calling for **Iraqi withdrawal.**

1991. NEW STATES EMERGING. In the **Soviet Union,** the process of disintegration was relatively orderly. Early in the year, **power-sharing** arrangements were developed and these were quickly passed. By September the **Baltic republics** were already new members of the **United Nations.** The remaining republics signed an agreement of economic cooperation (Oct.), and in December created the **Commonwealth of Independent States.** In **YUGOSLAVIA,** the disintegration involved conflict. **Croatia** and **Slovenia** declared independence by the end of the year, and open civil war among the various ethnic groups began in some areas.

Aung San Suu Kyi, the leader of the democratic opposition in Myanmar, received the **Nobel Peace Prize.**

Nadine Gordimer, South African novelist and opponent of apartheid, received the **Nobel Prize for literature.**

Jan.–Feb. In January the UN forces, led by the United States, attacked Iraqi positions in Kuwait and bombed targets throughout Iraq. The military victory of the UN forces came rapidly, and at the end of February U.S. president **Bush** declared the war to be over.

Feb. The **Warsaw Pact states** voted to dissolve the organization's military structures.

Aug. **Ontario Native Americans** and **Ontario provincial officials** signed an agreement recognizing the right of self-government for the Native Americans in the province.

1992. Divisions of states. The breakup of existing states was an important aspect of world affairs. The **Soviet Union** completed its transformation into a group of independent states that had been republics in the former union. **Yugoslavia** experienced increasingly violent conflict among the constituent parts of the former federation. **Serbian** opposition to the other groups was a main theme, and Serb forces attacked **Bosnia and Herzegovina,** which voted for independence in February. **Czechoslovakia** peacefully moved toward becoming two separate republics, the **Czech Republic** and the **Slovak Republic,** by the beginning of 1993. Throughout the year, **CANADA** debated constitutional changes that included self-government for Native Americans and special status for Quebec, but the issues were not resolved by the end of the year.

Jan. **Boutros Boutros-Ghali,** an Egyptian, became the sixth secretary general of the United Nations. An agreement bringing peace to **El Salvador** after 12 years of civil war was signed in Mexico City. Outgoing UN secretary general **Javier Pérez de Cuéllar** had successfully mediated the resolution to the conflict.

Feb. U.S. **president Bush** and **Russian president Yeltsin** signed a statement of general principles that brought a formal **END TO THE COLD WAR.**

June. **UN Conference on Environment and Development** held in Rio de Janeiro. Leaders from 178 countries attended, signing agreements that emphasized the necessity of global approaches to environmental issues.

July–Aug. Summer **Olympic Games** were held in Barcelona. They were the first summer games since 1972 to be unaffected by a political boycott, and South African athletes competed for the first time in 32 years.

Sept. Meeting of the **Conference of Non-Aligned Nations** was held in Jakarta. Delegates from 108 states discussed the role of the **nonaligned movement** in the post–cold war era. It was concluded that the movement still had an obligation to represent the poorer countries of the world. The **International Court of Justice** resolved a border dispute between **Honduras** and **El Salvador** that had lasted more than a century.

Dec. U.S. troops acting in the name of the United Nations arrived in **Somalia** to assist in the distribution of emergency famine relief. Because of anarchic civil war conditions, there was no functioning government in Somalia.

1993. The **Nobel Peace Prize** was awarded jointly to **NELSON MANDELA** and **F. W. DE KLERK** for their achievement in bringing about a peaceful transition to nonracial democracy in South Africa.

Jan. U.S. president **Bush** and Russian president **Yeltsin** initialed the second **Strategic Arms Reduction Treaty,** which called for significant reductions.

Feb. The **World Trade Center** in New York City was bombed by terrorists. A group of people from a number of Muslim countries were arrested.

April. **Eritreans** by referendum overwhelmingly approved of total independence from Ethiopia.

May. The **International Whaling Commission** rejected Japanese proposals for limited whaling in its coastal waters.

June. A UN-supervised election in **CAMBODIA** brought **Norodom Sihanouk,** the former monarch, to power at the head of a coalition government as a part of the ending of the long-lasting civil war.

July. **Sheik Omar Abdel-Rahman,** an Egyptian Muslim cleric, was detained by the United States for possible involvement in the bombing of the World Trade Center and a major terrorist plot for other attacks.

Sept. **ISRAEL** and the **PALESTINE LIBERATION ORGANIZATION,** with the assistance of the U. S., signed a peace agreement bringing a formal end to decades of conflict and beginning a process of creating structures for peaceful coexistence.

Nov. The **TREATY ON EUROPEAN UNION** (Maastricht Treaty) officially took effect following ratification by each of the twelve members of the European Community, which was transformed into the **EUROPEAN UNION.**

Dec. The **Uruguay round** of negotiations in GATT was concluded with an agreement by 117 states which transformed the structure of GATT into the **WORLD TRADE ORGANIZATION** as well as making major changes in trade regulations.

1994, Jan. 25. International **talks began** in Geneva **on banning the testing of nuclear weapons.** The five nuclear powers of Great Britain, China, France, Russia, and the U.S., as well as 32 other states, participated.

Feb. 1. The UN appointed its first human rights chief, Jose Ayala Lasso of Ecuador. This position is responsible for monitoring human rights violations and discussing them with relevant governments.

April 15. One hundred twenty-five countries of GATT signed a pact to liberalize international trade regulations in hopes of boosting international trade; environmental and labor groups opposed these initiatives.

Aug. 7–11. The tenth International Conference on AIDS was held in Yokohama, Japan. Participants discussed the lack of an imminent cure, the importance of preventive measures, and the increased threat posed by the disease in Asia.

Sept. 5–13. The UN held its third International Conference on Population and Development in Cairo, Egypt, discussing the threat of overpopulation, particularly in developing countries. Major abortion debates occurred. In the majority report emphasis was placed on improving women's access to education.

1995, Jan. 3. The World Health Organization (WHO) announced that there were more than a million AIDS cases worldwide.

Feb. 26. The Bank of England announced the bankruptcy of Barings PLC, Britain's oldest merchant bank, founded in 1762. A force in international banking and, earlier, in imperial finance, the bank failed because of unauthorized speculation by Nicholas Leeson, an employee in Singapore.

March 6–13. The UN held its first World Summit on Social Development in Copenhagen, Denmark. Discussion centered around the eradication of poverty and the hoped-for achievement of full employment. Secretary General Boutros Boutros-Ghali urged patience. An action plan for upholding workers' rights was created.

March 14. Norman Thagard became the **first U.S. astronaut to go into space on a Russian rocket,** showing the commitment of Russia and the United States to a new joint exploration of space.

March 28–April 7. The UN held a **summit on global warming** called the Conference of the Parties to the UN Framework Convention on Climate Change. More than 120 countries attended the conference, which took place in Berlin, agreeing to set specific goals for reducing emissions of carbon dioxide by the year 2000.

Aug. 4. For both environmental and peace reasons, the UN set an international pact to lower fishing rates and decrease conflicts over fishing areas.

Sept. 4–15. The UN held its fourth World Conference on Women in Beijing, China. The delegates endorsed a "Platform for Action" to work on stopping violence against women, giving women economic and political power, and funding programs to support these initiatives.

Oct. 22–24. The largest gathering of world leaders convened at UN headquarters to celebrate the **UN's 50th anniversary.** Crime and conflict were discussed.

1996, March 1–2. The first trade summit of 25 European and Asian nations met in Thailand to discuss strengthening trade ties; they avoided any conversation on human rights.

June 27. United Nations International Criminal Tribunal in The Hague indicted eight Bosnian Serbs on charges of rape. **This was the first time that rape was officially identified as a war crime.**

July 7–11. The 11th International Conference on AIDS was held in Vancouver, Canada. Discussions centered around significant research gains and new drug treatments recently discovered, as well as the growing threat of AIDS in India.

July 30. The G7 countries, the world's seven largest economies, met to discuss increasing measures to prevent terrorism on an international basis and to impose punitive measures on terrorists.

Sept. 24. The U.S., Great Britain, China, France, and Russia signed the **Comprehensive Test Ban Treaty,** forbidding any testing of nuclear weapons.

1997, Jan. 1. Kofi Annan, a native of Ghana, was sworn in as the **UN's new secretary general,** replacing Boutros Boutros-Ghali, who was not reelected due in large part to pressure from the United States.

Feb. 13. Ian Wilmut and colleagues at the Roslin Institute in Scotland announced the **first successful cloning of an adult mammal,** a sheep named Dolly.

Feb. 15. More than 65 countries agreed to a global telecommunications accord that opened their markets to foreign competition.

April 27. The G7 met and expressed concern over the continuing rise of the U.S. dollar, especially in relation to the Japanese yen. The group threatened to intervene in international currency markets to stabilize the dollar.

May 11. Deep Blue, a computer program developed by IBM, defeated world chess champion Garry Kasparov in a highly publicized match by a score of 3½ to 2½ games.

June 23–27. Sixty heads of state and delegates from 180 countries attended a **UN conference on the environment** called **Earth Summit.** Considerable tension between richer and poorer nations heightened divisions, however, and little was actually decided.

July 16. Kofi Annan announced a reform package restructuring the internal organization of the UN.

Sept. 17. Eighty-nine countries met in Oslo and agreed to a treaty banning the use, production, transfer, and stockpiling of landmines.

Dec. 1–11. The UN held a global warming summit in Kyoto, Japan, setting the first global limits on greenhouse gas emissions to standards below then-current levels.

1998. In Angola, war raged between the Popular Movement for the Liberation of Angola (MPLA) and the National Union for the Total Independence of Angola (UNITA). Although the UN had spent some $1.6 billion between 1994 and 1998 in peacekeeping funds, the terrible fighting continued, and the UN withdrew its forces.

Feb. 13. Nigerian troops defeated the Sierra Leonese military government, previously led by rebel militant Lt. Col. Johnny Paul Koromah, and ousted him from power. This Nigerian intervention helped restore Pres. Kabbah to power after ten months of exile. However, Si-

erra Leone remained a problem for the UN and other international organizations, because the two main rebel forces continued fighting government forces in Sierra Leone's civil war.

Feb. 23. Former ANC leaders P. W. Botha and F. W. de Klerk appeared before the South African Truth and Reconciliation Commission, created by Pres. Nelson Mandela, to be questioned concerning their roles in the old apartheid system.

April 19. Leaders of the Western Hemisphere signed a joint declaration regarding the Free Trade Area of the Americas (FTAA), originally brokered in 1994. In addition to trade issues, human rights, education, and drug trafficking, the conference agreed to give greater agency to the Organization of American States (OAS) to monitor the progress of efforts to control the illegal drug trade and passed measures to strengthen Latin America's weak judicial systems.

May 6. A brutal border war broke out between Ethiopia and Eritrea as conflicts over the 150-mile border area known as Badame carried over from struggles surrounding Eritrean independence in 1993.

May 11–13. India caused international controversy by conducting five successful nuclear-weapons tests. Meanwhile, many of the world's other nuclear powers were engaged in negotiations to gradually disarm and to ban the testing of nuclear weapons. India faced reproach and sanctions from the UN and the United States.

May 11 and July 13. The Organization of American States (OAS) was successful in intervening as an outside observer in elections in Paraguay and Ecuador, respectively. Argued as fraudulent by opposition parties within each country, both elections met OAS standards for fairness.

May 28–30. Pakistan conducted atomic-weapons testing (p. 1004).

June 21. A temporary cease-fire was called in Burundi's five-year-old civil war (p. 1062). The death toll by late 2000 rose to over 200,000. On Aug. 28, 2000, a short-lived peace accord was witnessed by former South African president Nelson Mandela and U.S. president Bill Clinton.

Aug. 20. In response to the Aug. 7 bomb attacks on U.S. embassies in Kenya and Tanzania, the U.S. sent cruise missiles and destroyed a pharmaceutical manufacturing facility in Sudan that was allegedly producing chemical weapons. Simultaneously, the U.S. attacked military targets in Afghanistan.

Sept. 4. A UN tribunal sentenced former prime minister of Rwanda Jean Kambanda to a life sentence for his role in the Rwandan genocidal killing of nearly half a million people between 1994 and 1999.

Oct. 23. In a historic peace agreement, Israeli prime minister Netanyahu, Palestinian National Authority (PNA) president Yasir Arafat, King Hussein of Jordan, and U.S. president Bill Clinton convened to sign the Wye River Peace Accords. The agreement established a preliminary plan for the gradual transfer of the West Bank to Palestinian control and the freeing of some 750 Palestinian prisoners in the process.

Oct. 26. A long-standing border dispute between Peru and Ecuador was resolved through the signing of a treaty.

Nov. 2. A two-week-long **environmental conference** opened in Buenos Aires, attended by delegates from over 160 nations, most of them members of the UN. Aimed at implementing the Kyoto Protocol of 1997, the conference ended on Nov. 14 with the "Buenos Aires Action Plan." This was a proposal in which industrialized nations agreed on worldwide strategies for carrying out emissions reductions for vehicles with internal combustion engines.

1999, Jan. 1. Pres. Charles Taylor of Liberia was internationally exposed by the UN as a supporter of rebels in Sierra Leone's civil war through his illegal diamonds-for-arms trading (p. 1055).

Jan. 13. In a huge international human rights advance, Senegal banned female circumcision.

March 11. In a UN summit, U.S. president Clinton announced equalization plans for immigration restrictions on Central Americans wishing to enter the U.S. This plan would allow for about 240,000 additional legal refugees to reside in the U.S.

April 5. The international embargo of Libya was ended as Pres. Qaddafi handed over two men suspected of perpetrating the 1988 bombing of a Pan American World Airways plane during flight 103. The aircraft exploded over Lockerbie, Scotland, leaving at least 270 persons dead.

April 21. The U.S. Congress accused China of stealing nuclear secrets from its classified reports over the past twenty years. Sino-American relations further deteriorated when on May 7 U.S. forces mistakenly bombed the Chinese embassy in Belgrade, killing 3 and wounding 27 more. The U.S. had been engaged in an attack on Yugoslavia.

April 23–25. The North Atlantic Treaty Organization (NATO) celebrated its 50th anniversary.

April 30. The Organization of African Unity (OAU) imposed diplomatic and economic sanctions on Comoros, a nation of small African islands, after a military coup led by Col. Azzaly Assoumani overthrew the government (p. 1063).

May 26–June 10. The India-Pakistan conflict that had prompted recent nuclear displays escalated as international peace talks concerning Jammu-Kashmir stalled. The Indian Air Force launched air strikes, and the army sent in ground troops to Jammu-Kashmir. By July 26 Pakistan was forced to withdraw the troops it had supplied to the Kashmiri rebels. Intermittent fighting between Indian troops and Islamic rebel forces in Jammu-Kashmir continued.

June 2. Nelson R. Mandela retired from the presidency of South Africa, establishing himself as one of the world's most recognized and revered statesmen.

June 29. A two-day international summit was held in Rio de Janeiro, Brazil. Representatives met from Mercosur (South American Common Market) and the European Union to discuss gradual free-trade efforts between the two continents. A tentative objective was to establish some sort of free-trade agreement by the year 2005.

July 9. Japan reached a comprehensive trade agreement with China, lowering duties on various important commodities and securing Japanese backing for China's application to join the World Trade Organization (WTO).

July 10. Pres. Lee Teng-hui of Taiwan announced the island's abandonment of the longstanding "One China" policy in a declaration of Taiwanese autonomy. Lee now held that Taiwan would deal with China on a "state to state basis" (p. 1026).

Aug. 30. In a UN-led referendum, the people of East Timor voted by an overwhelming majority for independence from Indonesia.

Aug. 31. After the signing of a weak peace accord by the six involved nations (Rwanda, Uganda, Democratic Republic of the Congo, Namibia, Angola, and Zimbabwe), the civil war in the Democratic Republic of the Congo intensified when conflict erupted between the previously allied nations of Uganda and Rwanda on Congolese soil. The violence and military occupation did not end until UN peacekeeping intervention was successful on July 19, 2000 (p. 1067).

Sept. Australia was the leading military force when the UN intervened in East Timor to prevent violence by pro-Indonesian forces against the East Timorese in reaction to independence votes.

Sept. 12–16. Zambia hosted the Eleventh International AIDS Conference in the capital city of Lusaka. Southern Africa continued to be the region most devastated by HIV/AIDS in the world, with UN estimates citing Botswana as the world's most afflicted country, 36 percent of the country's population being infected with HIV/AIDS. One-fifth to one-fourth of the populations of Zambia, Mozambique, Malawi, Zimbabwe, Namibia, South Africa, and Swaziland were also infected, according to UN estimates.

Sept. 14. The Pacific island nations of Nauru and Kiribati were admitted to the UN. Tuvalu attained UN membership the following year.

Oct. 12. The UN applied heavy sanctions and showed great disdain as Pakistan's government was taken over in a bloodless military coup. This occurred after Prime Minister Nawaz Sharif attempted to dismiss his army chief of staff, Gen. Pervez Musharraf. In a situation that would soon lead to charges of terrorism and hijacking against Sharif, Musharraf took control through martial law and suspended the powers of the Pakistani constitution. This takeover marked the first time in world history that a military regime had gained control over an affirmed nuclear power.

Nov. 6. In a national referendum, voters in Australia elected to cut the last ties with Britain and become a completely independent republic.

Nov. 14. Refusing to turn over ex-Saudi millionaire and terrorist leader Osama bin Laden to the U.S. for prosecution, Taliban-led Afghanistan faced increased UN and U.S. economic sanctions.

Nov. 30. Riots against World Bank meetings in Seattle, Washington united environmental, labor, and other protesters against globalization. In the following year disruption also occurred in Switzerland, Washington, D.C., and the Czech Republic.

Dec. 20. Macao was returned to Chinese sovereignty after 442 years as a Portuguese colony.

Dec. 31. Panama formally took control over the Panama Canal from the U.S.

2000, Jan. 21. In Ecuador, an Indian-supported army coup overthrew Pres. Jamil Mahuad Witt, who was replaced by V.P. Gustavo Noboa Bejarano the following day. This was the first military coup to overthrow a government in Latin America in almost ten years (p. 933).

Jan. 20. Turkish foreign minister Ismail Cem and Greek foreign minister George Papandreou signed six peace accords, greatly improving foreign relations between Turkey and Greece. This marked the first visit by a Greek foreign minister to Turkey in 38 years.

March 2. After extradition from Britain, former Chilean leader Augusto Pinochet Ugarte, who faced charges of torture, murder, and other serious war crimes, was returned to Chile. Pinochet was stripped of his immunity from prosecution by the Chilean Supreme Court on Aug. 8, and preparations for his internationally awaited trial were made. In addition to facing fourteen charges in Chile alone, Pinochet was sought for prosecution by Argentina, Uruguay, Spain, and Paraguay.

May 7. The RUF rebel forces in Sierra Leone's civil war took 500 UN peacekeeping troops hostage; it was not until July 15 that the last of these hostages were rescued. The UN created an international tribunal to begin trying war criminals in Sierra Leone on Aug. 14.

May 24. Southern Lebanon suddenly came under Hizbollah control when Israeli forces and 3,000 Christian militiamen withdrew from the area after 22 years of occupation.

June 13–15. South Korean president Kim Dae Jung and North Korean president Kim Jung Il met for peace and unification talks in Pyongyang. Greatly calming tensions between the two nations, the summit marked the first meeting of the leaders of those countries.

Aug. 15–18. Peace conferences throughout the summer allowed dozens of families that had been separated since the war to be reunited in Seoul, South Korea. As a result of his efforts to promote peace, Kim Dae Jung was awarded the 2000 Nobel Peace Prize.

July 8–14. The Thirteenth International AIDS conference was held in Durban, South Africa.

Aug. The U.S. government approved aid of $1.3 billion to Colombia in order to fund efforts to constrain drug trafficking in that nation.

Sept. 6–8. More than 150 world leaders met at the Millennium Summit, marking the largest gathering of international heads of state in world history.

Sept. 28. After Palestinian-Israeli talks had failed in late July due to disagreement over problems in East Jerusalem, the worst violence seen in the region since 1996 erupted and continued through the end of the year.

Nov. 20. In Peru, the internationally criticized president Alberto Fujimori finally resigned and was replaced by Valentin Paniagua Corazao (p. 942).

Dec. 10. Pursuing the goals of the 1997 Kyoto Protocol, delegates from 122 nations met in Johannesburg, South Africa to discuss a treaty that would ban 12 highly toxic chemicals that have historically proved detrimental to humans and the environment. Clean-up funds were pledged. The meeting was considered by some to be an unsuccessful reiteration of the Kyoto Protocol, but it was agreed that the resultant proposed treaty would take effect only when 50 or more nations had ratified it.

B. EUROPE, 1945–2000

1. ECONOMIC AND SOCIAL CHANGES

(From p. 673)

As in 1918, Europe after the Second World War was in ruins. **Estimates of the dead range as high as 50 million,** although national tolls varied greatly, from 20 million Russians to 460,000 British and Commonwealth subjects. Overall, the losses in Central and Eastern Europe far outnumbered those in Western Europe. As for the survivors, roads and major cities were clogged with displaced persons, resulting in great migrational flows. Throughout the Continent material costs were also staggering: cities had been reduced to rubble, transportation networks had been destroyed, and farms and coal mines were wastelands. Finally, the war left a divided Europe in its wake. The course of reconstruction and the features of the postwar economy and society thus differed between Western and Eastern Europe.

Despite such destruction, Western Europe experienced virtually unprecedented prosperity within 15 years; by 1963 it was producing more than two and a half times as much as it had before the war. Economic growth rates soared for almost two decades, particularly in Germany, France, and Italy, and standards of living reached unprecedented levels. France, for example, attained an 8 percent annual growth rate by the end of the 1950s, continued at a somewhat slower rate during the 1960s, and rose again, to 7 percent, in the early 1970s. Meanwhile real wages in France experienced a sixfold increase between 1950 and 1980. The base of this growth was consumer goods—cars, radios, televisions, and the like—prompting many to label this period in European history the **consumer society.** Much of this economic growth developed out of the European Recovery Program, or the **Marshall Plan.** The plan, announced by the United States in June 1947, provided billions of dollars to European nations to help them rebuild their economies. By 1959, the United States had spent more than $74 billion in aid. This represented both a desire to avoid the errors of post–World War I Europe and an acceptance of **Keynesian economics** (p. 674). Governments became more active in economic planning, and a number of key industries were **nationalized.** Moreover, as a precondition to receiving U.S. aid, Western European nations began to coordinate their economic activities for maximum effectiveness. This led to the establishment of the **Organization of European Economic Cooperation,** the first step toward European unity.

Not all of Europe benefited from the Marshall Plan, however. The nations of Eastern Europe, those under Soviet domination, followed Stalin's lead and refused U.S. aid. Instead the Soviet Union and its allies founded **COMECON** (Council for Mutual Economic Assistance) in 1949 (p. 838). Designed to align socialist economies, in reality the satellite economies of Eastern Europe were all geared to the reconstruction of the Soviet Union first, and then of their own country. In keeping with socialist thought, Eastern Europe witnessed mass nationalizations of private industry. Agriculture was also collectivized, with the exception of Poland. While a measure of prosperity did rise in Eastern Europe, unlike in Western Europe, it was not built on consumer goods. The economies of the Soviet Union and its allies remained predominantly geared for heavy industry and defense.

The devastation of two world wars within 30 years brought forth new ideas about the state, especially about its relations with other states and with its citizenry. The end of the war ushered in a new **push toward European unity,** especially in Western Europe. The first steps were taken with the OEEC and the **Council of Europe,** but such attempts at attaining European federalism via a direct political approach foundered. The economic approach was more successful. Under the auspices of the French politicians Jean Monnet (1888–1979) and Robert Schuman (1886–1963), six European nations (France, West Germany, Italy, Belgium, the Netherlands, and Luxembourg) began to integrate their economies through the **European Coal and Steel Community,** founded in 1951, and, with the Treaties of Rome signed in 1957, through the **European Economic Community** (p. 840). The

goal of the Common Market, as it became known, was just that, the creation of a single free-trade area, with free movement of goods, capital, and workers. This goal was attained in 1992, after the Common Market had grown to 12 member states.

The rise of European unity brought with it a decline in the power of individual states to control the hearts and minds of their citizens. **Nationalism,** seen as a major cause of destruction in European history, began to wane. Indeed, most Europeans gave up their old dreams of glory and empire as a wave of **decolonization** swept through Asia and Africa. Instead, what bound citizens to their state was the vast array of services the new **welfare states** provided for their citizens in need. These services ranged from old-age pensions and unemployment insurance to free health services and low-income housing. In demanding such services, citizens came to accept not only larger government bureaucracies, which also provided many white-collar jobs, but also the fact that government was a much larger presence in their lives. In a short time, Europeans came to expect the government to provide services deemed necessary to daily living, making it difficult in the 1980s for those governments forced to implement austerity plans and for the citizens of Eastern Europe, who had come to expect a greater range of social services from their now-defunct communist states.

In all of Europe these economic and political changes accompanied social change. In Western Europe the class structure changed significantly as the **importance of the nobility declined** due to high taxes, and the **peasantry virtually disappeared** with further urban migration and new, commercial practices among the remaining farmers. The middle classes grew more diversified, open, and democratic as bureaucracies developed, and education, rather than property, became the basis of social and economic position. Thus, while businesses and governments became more complex, allowing middle-class managers to rise to positions of importance, the middle class lost the ability to pass these positions on to their children like capital. Meanwhile the **traditional manufacturing working classes ceased to expand,** due to technological change. Instead, the number of workers in service and white-collar positions grew rapidly, creating a large segment of the working class that had many similarities to members of the middle classes. Overall, Western European society became more mobile and more democratic as rigid social divisions softened.

There were limits on mobility, however. Education, the key to mobility, fell short of the egalitarian ideal. Although the number of **university students** had risen sharply to 24 percent of the 20 to 24 age group in Western Europe in 1978, up from less than 4 percent in 1950, children from the lower strata continued to be underrepresented in higher education. In France the proportion of university students from working-class families actually fell from 13 percent in 1974 to 9 percent in 1979. A similar division could be found in secondary education. Despite increasing enrollments, in most countries secondary education remained sharply divided into vocational and academic tracks. **Immigrants** were another group for whom mobility was difficult. In the 1950s and 1960s, at the height of economic prosperity, Western European nations welcomed immigrants (from Turkey, North Africa, Pakistan, the West Indies), but this came to an end in the 1970s. The children of these immigrants, not immigrants themselves, often faced the prospect of poverty, underemployment, discrimination, police harassment, and inadequate housing and schooling. They also became the object of a renewed xenophobic, anti-immigrant movement on the far Right.

In Eastern Europe, the social structure was altered by communist policy. The nobility lost its influence and property, as did all property owners, while most peasants became either collectivized agricultural workers or industrial workers. Officially, the middle class ceased to exist. Yet even in the presumably classless society, social distinctions developed. Instead of property, the distinguishing factor became relation to the party. Party members became the new elite, while government bureaucrats became a quasi-middle class.

Europeans also experienced alterations in their family life. From 1945 to the early 1960s Europe experienced a **baby boom,** with populations growing by 1 percent to 1.5 percent per year in many countries. These rates dropped sharply in the 1960s, however, and most countries experienced zero population growth. On the other side of the aging spectrum, Europeans were urged to think of their later years as a "third age," in which they expected to be healthy and to engage in a host of activities they had been too busy to enjoy during their working years. This became possible as life expectancies rose and the old-age pensions provided a measure of security. But rising numbers of elderly citizens burdened the welfare state.

Women became more central to the economy, as both consumers and workers. Whereas it used to be that working-class women left the workforce after childbirth, taking only work they could do at home, women in postwar Europe remained in the workforce. This was due mainly to the fact that women were marrying and having all their children earlier than their mothers and grandmothers had. By the late 1960s the age at marriage for European women had dropped to 23. At the same time, women were having 80 percent of their children before they were 30. This helps to account for growing feminist dissatisfaction by the late 1960s and 1970s; women found that their traditional role as mother no longer absorbed the energy of a lifetime, yet new roles in the male-dominated world outside the family were slow to open. Nevertheless, even for middle-class wives, work outside the home became more common.

These economic and social developments in Western and Eastern Europe brought, for the most part, a period of stability and prosperity that lasted throughout much of the 1950s and 1960s. By the late 1960s new forms of protest began to emerge, however. Older protest movements, such as trade unionism, had periodically mounted large (and usually short) strikes to win concessions from business and government, and left-wing parties led demonstrations, but none of these forms of protest did much to disturb a Western Europe remarkable for its political stability and rapid economic recovery. Class divisions ceased to be a major source of protest. **Disaffection grew, however, in the late 1960s, blossoming into student protests, feminist demonstrations, and, in the 1970s, terrorism.** Student movements called into question the structure of authority and the materialism of advanced industrial societies. **Feminism** rejected conventional assumptions about gender. By the 1970s an **environmentalist movement** had gathered considerable strength in several countries, as had a surprising **new wave of regional and ethnic activism,** which disputed the authority of central governments and in some cases even long-standing assumptions about the immutability of existing nation-states. Racial and ethnic conflict also gave rise to riots, racial attacks, antiracist demonstrations, and divisive debate over citizenship rights and immigration, especially in the 1980s.

While none of these developments led to the kind of general political crisis that toppled regimes in the interwar years, they signaled the end of a period of postwar complacency. This was followed shortly by **economic crises** in 1973 and 1979 caused by European dependence on foreign, especially Arab, oil. Most Western European nations suffered from a combination of economic stagnation and rapid inflation dubbed "stagflation." Unemployment rose while productivity and living standards declined. Governments responded at first by borrowing, to maintain the vast systems of social services implemented after the war, but in the 1980s they turned increasingly to austerity measures. It is important to note, however, that the welfare measures implemented after the war were effective, by and large, in preventing the mass suffering that might have occurred earlier in similar circumstances. After a brief economic upswing in the mid-1980s, Europe continued to deal with sluggish national economies and their social implications.

In Eastern Europe, protest came earlier, and while it had economic and social undercurrents, it remained primarily political in nature. The overriding focus of discontent was Soviet domination. To be sure, not all nations experienced Soviet-brand communism similarly. After its 1956 uprising, Hungary, for example, experimented with an economy based more on consumer goods. Poland, too, took a separate path, with little collectivized agriculture and a strong Roman Catholic presence. Yet discontent emerged regularly. In Poland, the Soviet-supported government faced popular demonstrations in the 1950s and, more seriously, in the 1980s. Troops were called on to quell protests in Hungary in 1956 and in Czechoslovakia in 1968. Despite such protest, real change came only after the rise of **Mikhail Gorbachev** in the Soviet Union in 1985 (p. 905). His policies of glasnost and perestroika led to far-reaching economic, social, and political reforms. By 1989 these policies had given the satellite nations of Eastern Europe enough security to break their bonds with the Soviet Union. One by one, they toppled their communist-led governments and instituted democratic reforms. Most of these revolutionary transformations were peaceful; Romania was the notable exception. This period of "revolution" came to an end in 1992 with the collapse of the Soviet Union.

Europe clearly entered a new and uncertain period in 1989. East and West Germany were unified, but many former East Germans lost their jobs. The other nations of Eastern Europe sought economic aid in building market economies. Meanwhile, old national and ethnic rivalries long suppressed by the communists resurfaced; these caused the most damage in the former Yugoslavia. In Western Europe, economic problems muted the promise of 1992, when the 12 member nations of the Common Market became one free-trade zone and curtailed their ability to help the struggling states in the East. Finally, immigration became a problem as unemployment spurred discontent among European nationals who competed for jobs with the descendents of immigrants who had first arrived in Europe in the 1950s, when governments had eagerly accepted this needed influx of labor.

2. RELIGIOUS AND PHILOSOPHICAL THOUGHT

(From p. 674)

In the realm of religious thought, **secularism** continued to make great strides as divorce and contraception, for example, became more commonplace. But the churches did not stand still in this period. Pope John XXIII (1881–1963) convened **Vatican II** (1962–65), the world Catholic council that updated the Church. Later popes, while remaining traditionalists in matters like priestly celibacy, the ordination of women, and birth control, continued to campaign for social justice. In the Protestant churches, two theological movements emerged. Under the leadership of the Swiss theologian **Karl Barth** (1886–1968), some Protestants dismissed the notion that reason could save the soul, arguing instead for the primacy of revelation and the powerlessness of humans without God's grace. Others, following the British theologian John **Robinson,** built on 19th-century liberalism to argue that the Bible must be interpreted in a modern context. Robinson believed modern Christians had to extract the inner meanings from the old biblical

myths and apply them to each situation of modern life, a stark difference from Barth's fundamentalism.

For many, however, the notion that God was dead was as true after World War II as it had been after World War I. Indeed, philosophical thought in postwar Europe continued along trends established in the interwar period that highlighted the absurdity and meaninglessness of life. The philosophical school that best expressed this view was **existentialism,** led by French philosophers **Jean-Paul Sartre** (1905–80), **Simone de Beauvoir** (1908–86), and **Albert Camus** (1913–60). These theorists argued that there were no absolutes or eternal truths for humankind. In the 1960s a new school of thought, known as **structuralism,** rose to challenge this view (p. 858). Major figures, including anthropologist **Claude Levi-Strauss** (b. 1908) and literary critic **Roland Barthes** (1915–80), grounded their theories on structural linguistics and the science of signs to assert that human consciousness was the helpless victim of objective structures implied in the laws of language syntax. In the late 1960s and early 1970s other intellectuals, such as **Jacques Derrida** (b. 1930) and **Michel Foucault** (1926–84) challenged the linguistic stability and systematic function of structuralism. Their emphasis on textual analysis and relativist positions was instrumental in the formation of **poststructuralism** and **deconstruction** in the post-1968 intellectual community.

3. CULTURE AND POPULAR CULTURE

(From p. 674)

In the fine arts, it was difficult to discern any great changes from trends established in the interwar period. Private expression continued to underpin the work of most artists; artists were freed from learned convention to explore all avenues of self-expression. In painting, as in architecture, the postwar period witnessed the continued development of the main ideas of the interwar period. In the 1960s some artists created **pop art,** using bits of comic strips and commercial art to bridge the gap between commercial mass culture and fine art. In literature, while the traditional novel continued to thrive, the **"new novel"** of French writers like Alain Robbe-Grillet (b. 1922) and Natalie Sarraute challenged this form by concentrating on concrete details without plot or character development. Film also became an important medium as directors like Jean-Luc Godard (b. 1930), François Truffaut (1932–84), Michelangelo Antonioni (b. 1912), and Bernardo Bertolucci (b. 1940) made Paris and Rome centers of experimental filmmaking. The works of Ingmar Bergman (b. 1918) and Rainer Werner Fassbinder (1946–82) also provided dark commentary on modern life. In music, the application of computers and electronic instruments like the Moog synthesizer aided composers in their search for new sounds. And in architecture, major figures like Ludwig Mies van der Rohe (1886–1969), a Bauhaus disciple, carried on functionalism, while Paris and Barcelona remained at the forefront of modern architecture with a variety of new buildings in the "international style," plus a new interest in Barcelona's earlier Modernista movement.

In the realm of popular culture, the most striking feature was the spread of a worldwide culture, influenced heavily by the Americans. This was made possible by the availability of cheap transistor radios, television, films, and recordings, and by inexpensive travel opportunities. Popular culture was thus the product of a society where such technologies were commonplace, a society based on prosperity and consumption. The new culture glorified youth, and film stars like Marilyn Monroe (1926–62) and James Dean (1931–55) became international symbols. Perhaps the most famous purveyor of this culture was the **Beatles,** a popular British rock and roll band. The band members clearly represented the new international, youthful culture of carefree, good-humored hedonism. This youth culture flourished easily in Western Europe, but even Soviet youth clamored for blue jeans and Western music.

Popular culture changed in certain other respects. The new hedonism among young people; greater freedom from adult supervision, including more public opportunities for young women; and the development of the birth control pill in 1960 produced **new sexual behavior and a more open sexual culture.** Representations of sexuality in European films and television, the advent of stores that sold sexual items, and new behaviors, including increased premarital intercourse, signaled this growing change. While rates of illegitimate births increased for a time, public acceptance of birth control for young people stabilized that trend by the 1970s.

Leisure time increased greatly in Europe, with many groups gaining as much as five weeks in annual vacation time. Those in the north made massive annual migrations to Italy, Spain, and southern France. New vacation organizations developed, and many Europeans bought summer homes. Club Med was founded in 1950 by Gerard Blitz, and its resorts ultimately spread around the world, providing a European atmosphere for vacationers. At the same time, **television watching** became the most common leisure pastime. Consumeristic values led to a heightened interest in material possessions, such as household appliances, motor scooters, and automobiles. Shopping patterns changed, away from community-based stores and toward supermarkets and other glossy settings. Most Western European countries permitted **television advertising** by the 1970s, another consumeristic change.

European manners became less stiff. Parent-child relations became less formal. Divorce rates varied, rising in Britain to approximately one in every three marriages and generally increasing. With growing numbers of women working, use of **daycare centers for children,** usually government-sponsored, grew rapidly. While a minority maintained important religious attachments, church attendance overall continued to decline in Europe. Only in Eastern Europe, particularly after the fall of communism, were there signs of new interest in Christianity.

4. SCIENCE AND TECHNOLOGY

(From p. 819)

The most important development in these two arenas was their continuing merger after World War II. During the war, scientific research and technical expertise were both directed at solving practical military problems. After the war, this cooperation between pure science and applied technology continued, giving rise to what many called **"big science."** The war had demonstrated the effectiveness of directed research, a trend continued after the war. This required a great deal of organization, however, and became very expensive. Indeed, scientific research became the province of large, well-defined bureaucratic organizations, and funding could be maintained only by governments and corporations. By 1960, for example, when governments in Western Europe created the European Council for Nuclear Research to build an accelerator outside of Geneva, the cost was $30 million. The cost of research resulted in a "brain drain" in Europe, as many scientists emigrated to the United States, where both the government and large corporations spent vast sums of money. European nations responded to this challenge, however, by pooling their energies, as in the Franco-British collaboration on the Concorde, the supersonic passenger airliner, and Airbus, the airline manufacturing consortium created by Great Britain, France, West Germany, and Spain among others.

Much of what was accomplished in technology built on what had existed before World War II; jets, radar, and electronic computers were all developed before the war and were adapted to more consumer-centered uses afterward. Microwave technology, for example, was perfected for military purposes during the war, but generated endless applications afterward in the telecommunications industry. This continued after the cold war as well, as technology developed for the space race between the United States and the Soviet Union gave rise to the use of French Arianne rockets to launch commercial satellites.

At the same time, the vigorous environmental movement began to question the results of rapid technological change. In 1969, for example, millions of fish died in the Rhine River two years after the disappearance of two 50-pound canisters containing the insecticide Thiodan. Concerns over such environmental tragedies developed into political movements, especially in Germany, where the **Green Party** gained enough power to win a considerable number of votes in elections in the early 1990s. Disasters like the 1986 meltdown at the Chernobyl nuclear power plant in the Ukraine tempered society's belief in the potential benefits of modern technology.

Some of the major scientific and technological developments that have occurred since 1945 follow.

1947. The word *automation* was coined by John Deibold and D. S. Harder, to define "a self-powered, self-guiding and correcting mechanism," and it was later extended to include all elements of production—"automated factory"—and office and clerical procedures.

1950s. The basic-oxygen process for the manufacture of steel was developed in Austria.

1953. Francis H. C. Crick (b. 1916) and **James D. Watson** (b. 1928) offered a model for the structure of DNA that accounted for gene replication and posited a biochemical code that could transmit a great variety of genetic information. **Electronic computers** with feedback mechanisms (servomechanisms) made possible the new field of **cybernetics,** defined by **Norbert Wiener** (1953) as "the study of control and communication in the animal and the machine."

1961. The first manned spaceship circled the earth April 12 in 89.1 minutes, at an altitude of 187.7 miles. Soviet astronaut **Yuri Gagarin** (1934–68), made the orbit in the space vehicle *Vostok I*, and astronaut (cosmonaut) Gherman Titov orbited the earth 17 times less than four months later.

1962. Neil Bartlett (b. 1932) announced that he had combined xenon with platinum and fluorine to form xenon-platinum hexafluoride; other compounds of xenon and radon were found, thus destroying the notion that the noble gases are all nonreacting.

July 10. *Telstar I* was launched. The new satellite was used to transmit the first live transatlantic telecasts between the United States and Great Britain.

1965. *Early Bird* was put into orbit by the three-year-old Communications Satellite Corporation (COMSAT) to relay telephone messages and television programs between Europe and North America. The world's first commercial satellite, it was the first link in a global network of space communications planned by COMSAT.

1967. The electronic quartz wristwatch was announced in December by the Swiss Horological Electronic Center. Thirty-one Swiss firms pooled $7 million in 1962 to develop the watch.

1968, Dec. 31. Aeroflot demonstrated the Tu-144, the first supersonic airliner.

1969, Oct. 1. The Concorde supersonic airplane made its first flight.

1974. The Airbus A300B, assembled in Toulouse, France, began to challenge Boeing for the world jet aircraft market. Airbus Industrie was a consortium of government-owned British and French aircraft makers with some private German companies and 4 percent Spanish participation.

The computerized axial tomography (CAT) scanner, developed in England by EMI, Ltd., with money from sales of Beatles records, gained wide use not only for diagnosing brain damage but also for whole-body scanning.

1977, May 22. The Orient Express, which had begun service in 1883, made its last trip into Istanbul from Paris. Most travelers now preferred to cover the 1,900 miles in 3 hours by air rather than taking 60 hours by rail.

1978, July 25. The world's first "test-tube baby," Louise Brown, was born.

1979. The British Post Office inaugurated a Prestel system that gave subscribers access to 160,000 pages, or television screenfuls, of information. Using telephones, computers, and TV sets, subscribers could obtain information such as rail and air schedules and stock and commodity quotations, buy airline tickets, reserve hotel rooms, and book theater seats by remote control. The government spent $30 million to develop the system. A Prestel set, which could also receive ordinary TV programming, cost at least $2,000, and the subscriber was also billed for the amount of time the set was used.

A similar French system, Minitel, was launched in a two-year development effort in 1980. The sets were free, and a charge was made for use.

1980. The steroid abortifacient drug RU486 was developed by French endocrinologist Etienne-Emile Baulieu.

1981, Sept. 22. France's TGV train began service from Paris to Lyons. Powered by electricity and capable of going 236 mph, it was Europe's first super-high-speed passenger line.

1983. Dr. Luc Montagnier and a team of researchers discovered the putative cause of HIV and AIDS.

1986. Superconductivity made news in January as Swiss physicist K. Alex Müller and German physicist J. Georg Bedornz of IBM's Zurich Research Laboratory discovered zero resistivity in a ceramic material that permits superconductivity at $-397°$ F—a much more extreme temperature than was ever before possible.

1998, Nov. 20. Zarya, the first module of a planned international space station, was launched into orbit by Russia. On Dec. 4 the U.S. sent Unity, the second module, into space to join the Russian module in the first international connection, from which the space station was planned to expand.

2000, June 26. Two separate organizations, the internationally funded Human Genome Project and the U.S.-based Celera Genomics Corp., jointly announced that each had compiled a working map of the human genome. The achievement was hailed as a revolution for science and medicine and the dawn of a new era for human biology.

5. DIPLOMATIC RELATIONS AND EUROPEAN PACTS

(From p. 811)

1946, Sept. 6. U.S. Secretary of State **James F. Byrnes,** in a speech in Stuttgart, announced a more lenient American policy toward Germany and called for a unified German economy.

1947, March 4. An **Anglo-French treaty of alliance** was signed at Dunkirk.

March 10–April 24. The **council of foreign ministers,** meeting in Moscow, failed in its effort to draft peace treaties for Germany and Austria.

July 12–15. The **MARSHALL PLAN** (p. 917), a program for European recovery proposed by U.S. secretary of state George Marshall, was discussed by delegates of 16 European nations meeting in Paris. A committee was set up to draft a **European Recovery Program.** The Soviet Union and its satellites refused to participate in a program of European reconstruction.

Oct. 5. The **COMMUNIST INFORMATION BUREAU (Cominform)** was established by the Communist parties of the Soviet Union, Yugoslavia, Bulgaria, Romania, Hungary, Poland, France, Italy, and Czechoslovakia. With headquarters in Belgrade, the bureau was to coordinate the activities of European Communist parties.

Oct. 29. Ratification of the **customs union among Belgium, the Netherlands, and Luxembourg.**

Nov. 25–Dec. 16. A conference of the Big Four foreign ministers in London again failed to agree on solution of the German problem.

1948, March 17. The **BRUSSELS TREATY,** signed by Great Britain, France, Belgium, the Netherlands, and Luxembourg. It constituted a 50-year alliance against attack in Europe, and provided for economic, social, and military cooperation.

April 16. The subscribers to the European Recovery Program met at Paris and set up the permanent **Organization for European Economic Cooperation (OEEC).**

May 7. The first **Congress of Europe** convened in The Hague under the honorary chairmanship of Sir Winston Churchill, to discuss **plans for European Union.**

June 1. A **six-power agreement** among the Western powers and the Benelux countries was reached, calling for **international control of the Ruhr,** German representation in the **European Recovery Program,** closer integration of the three Western zones, the drafting of a **federal constitution** for Western Germany, and the creation of an **Allied military security board.**

June 28. Yugoslavia was expelled from the Cominform for alleged doctrinal errors and hostility to the Soviet Union.

July 30–Aug. 18. The future **status of the Danube River** was discussed at a ten-nation conference at Belgrade. The Soviet delegate introduced a new statute, to replace that of 1921, restricting membership on the Danubian Commission to the riparian states, thus excluding Great Britain, France, and the United States. Such a commission was set up (Nov. 11, 1949) despite the protest of the three Western powers.

1949, Jan. 25. COUNCIL FOR MUTUAL ECONOMIC ASSISTANCE (COMECON) set up by the Communist governments.

March 13. Belgium, the Netherlands, and Luxembourg agreed to organize full economic union at an early date. France and Italy made a similar agreement (March 26).

April 4. The **NORTH ATLANTIC TREATY ORGANIZATION** (NATO) founded by signature of the **North Atlantic Treaty** in Washington, by the foreign ministers of the United States, Great Britain, France, Belgium, the Netherlands, Luxembourg, Italy, Portugal, Denmark, Iceland, Norway, and Canada. The treaty provided for withdrawal at the end of 20 years, on one-year notification. It provided, further, for mutual assistance against aggression within the North Atlantic area and for cooperation in military training, arms production, and strategic planning. The **North Atlantic Council,** consisting of the foreign ministers of all members, was to meet semi-annually and to serve as the directing body. A **defense committee,** consisting of the ministers of defense, and a **military committee,** consisting of the chiefs of staff, was to deal with military problems. A **standing group** (United States, Britain, and France) was to provide general guidance. This organization was completed in Sept. 1949.

April 23. Thirty-one minor **rectifications of West German borders** were carried out.

May 5. The **Statute of the Council of Europe** was signed in London. It provided for an executive committee of ministers and a consultative assembly. Headquarters were fixed at Strasbourg.

Sept. 21. The **Allied Occupation Statute came into force.** The functions of military government were transferred to the **Allied High Commission.**

Sept. 27. The Soviet Union denounced its treaty of friendship with Yugoslavia, and other communist governments presently did likewise. For some time there seemed to be an acute danger of an attack on Yugoslavia by its former allies, despite the Tito government's firm adherence to communism.

Nov. 24. In the **Petersberg agreement,** the Allied High Commission made further economic concessions, to Western Germany, in return for German membership in the International Ruhr Authority. Despite the fact that industrial production had reached 93 percent of the 1936 level, the influx of more than 8 million Germans from the East had caused widespread unemployment.

1950, Jan. 6. The NATO council approved the **"master defense plan"** prepared by the defense committee.

Jan. 29. In a series of bilateral agreements, the United States contracted to supply arms and other equipment to the members of NATO.

March 3. A **French agreement with the Saar,** confirming the region's autonomy and its economic union with France, created consternation in West Germany and led Chancellor Konrad Adenauer to demand (May 30) that the Saar be allowed freely to choose between France and Germany.

March 30-April 1. The **Council of Europe** decided to invite West Germany and the Saar to be associate members.

May 9. The **SCHUMAN PLAN** for the integration of the Western European coal and steel industries was proposed by French foreign minister **Robert Schuman.**

Sept. 12-19. A three-power conference in New York agreed on a **more liberal policy toward Western Germany.** The **Western powers** announced that they would consider any attack against the Federal Republic or against Berlin as an attack on themselves, and that they would strengthen their military forces in Germany. At the same time, they **agreed to revise the Occupation Statute,** to relax economic controls, lift the limit on steel production, and permit the Bonn government to establish diplomatic relations with foreign countries. A special security police force was authorized to meet the threat of the much larger Soviet-sponsored People's Police of Eastern Germany. The Western Allies also began considering the possibility of **German participation** in a Western army under the **North Atlantic Treaty.** This announcement signaled the start of the rapid process during the 1950s

in which **West Germany's status changed from that of former enemy to future ally,** largely as a result of the Korean War.

Oct. 20-21. The West's new liberal German policy was denounced by a Communist conference at Prague.

Nov. 16-22. The second **World Peace Congress** (Communist-inspired and directed) met in Warsaw, with 60 countries represented.

Dec. 18. General of the Army Dwight D. Eisenhower was named supreme Allied commander, Europe, with headquarters near Paris.

Dec. 20. The Brussels treaty powers decided to merge their military resources with those of NATO.

1951, Jan. 20. In notes to Britain and France, the USSR forcefully reaffirmed its charge that Germany's remilitarization was a prime threat to peace and security in Europe.

Feb. 21. The British government indicated opposition to a U.S. suggestion that **Spain** be associated with NATO. The hostility of labor governments and organizations against Spain continued generally unabated through the years. U.S. bases in Spain drew the nation toward NATO unofficially, but full membership was not granted until 1982 (p. 862).

April 18. France, West Germany, Italy, Belgium, the Netherlands, and Luxembourg signed a treaty embodying the Schuman Plan and set up a **single market for coal and steel.** An important first step toward European economic union.

May 2. West Germany became a full-fledged member of the Council of Europe.

Sept. 6. The **Azores** became integrated with the NATO defense plan, by agreement between the United States and Portugal.

Sept. 10. The foreign ministers of Great Britain, France, and the United States met in Washington, for a two-day conference on measures to contain Soviet aggression. They agreed on plans for a German "peace contract" to replace the Occupation Statute and on the use of West German troops in a European army.

Tito offered to negotiate a general settlement of all outstanding problems with the Italian government.

Sept. 15-20. Meeting in Ottawa, the **NATO council decided to invite Greece and Turkey** to become members of NATO.

Sept. 24. The three Allied high comissioners, meeting with Chancellor Adenauer, informed him that the Occupation Statute would be abrogated and the Allied High Commission abolished only after Germany agreed to contribute to the defense of Europe.

Nov. 14. The Yugoslav government signed an **agreement with the United States,** which undertook to supply military equipment, materials, and services to the armed forces of Yugoslavia.

Dec. 31. The **Marshall Plan** came to an end as the Economic Cooperation Administration was replaced by the **Mutual Security Agency.**

1952, Jan. 18. Prime Minister Churchill and President Truman agreed on the appointment of an **American admiral as supreme commander of NATO naval forces in the Atlantic.**

Jan 25. The French government decided to substitute a diplomatic mission for the **High Commissariat of the Saar.** The action created a furor in West Germany where Chancellor Adenauer demanded that the Western powers consult German wishes on the Saar question (Feb. 4).

Feb. 20-25. Greece and Turkey were formally admitted to NATO at a meeting of the council in Lisbon. The council also voted to provide 50 divisions for the defense of Western Europe by the end of 1952. (This figure was never attained).

April 4. General Lord Hastings Ismay took office as secretary general of NATO.

April 15. The British government aligned Britain with the **European Army project** and accepted the extension of its commitments under the Brussels treaty to cover military assistance to West Germany and Italy.

April 28. General Matthew B. Ridgway succeeded General Eisenhower as supreme allied commander, Europe.

May 27. A **EUROPEAN DEFENSE COMMUNITY** (EDC) was created by a Paris conference to establish a single unified command and bind West Germany to the Atlantic defense plan. The EDC charter was signed by Italy, the Netherlands, Belgium, Luxembourg, France, and West Germany. These six countries signed a treaty with Great Britain by which the latter agreed to aid any EDC member if attacked. A

NATO protocol extended that alliance's guarantees to West Germany. In a declaration signed by Britain and the United States, these powers agreed to regard any threat to the EDC as a threat to their own security.

July 6. Tito declared his government's willingness to cooperate with Greece, Turkey, and Austria, but ruled out pacts and alliances.

Aug. 1. French-German negotiations on the **question of the Saar Valley.** The French desired it to be "Europeanized" and made it the seat of the Schuman Plan.

Aug. 10. The first session of the high authority of the **European Coal and Steel Community** took place at Luxembourg.

Sept. 10. The members of the Coal and Steel Community, meeting in a supranational assembly, voted unanimously to establish a **European federal political community.**

Nov. 14. Control of Tangier. The United States, Britain, and France agreed to set aside the 1945 agreement and restore police powers in the Tangier zone to Spain.

Nov. 18. Objecting to the alleged political domination of the Saar by France, the Bundestag's major parties supported a Bundestag declaration denying the **legality of the Saar election** (Nov. 30) and refusing to recognize any Saar government so elected.

Nov. 26. The French cabinet approved terms for revising the French-Saar conventions to permit the enlargement of the Saar's economic independence. Saar premier **Johannes Hoffman** praised the step as a concession by France of equal rights to the Saar.

Nov. 30. The **Saar election** resulted in a victory for the autonomists and the French, as most voters rejected German appeals to boycott the polls or invalidate the votes.

Dec. 4-7. Prime Minister Churchill, President Eisenhower, and **Premier Joseph Laniel** of France met in Bermuda to discuss the **relations of the Big Three with Soviet Russia,** the problem of Germany and Austria, and the defense of the free world.

Dec. 17. Tito's government broke **diplomatic relations with the Vatican** to protest the latter's refusal to settle the church-state conflict in Yugoslavia.

1953, Feb. 23. Meeting in Rome, the members of the Coal and Steel Community voted unanimously to support ratification of the EDC and gave tentative approval to a Dutch proposal to create a single market through tariff reductions.

March 10. A "constituent assembly" voted 50–0 to approve that draft of a **charter for a European Union.**

April 23–25. The regular ministerial council of NATO agreed that Soviet policy had not changed, despite the launching of a "Peace Offensive." It was therefore decided that six more divisions would be added to the NATO forces by the end of 1953.

May 13. General Alfred M. Gruenther succeeded General Ridgway as supreme allied commander, Europe.

Oct. 8. The **Trieste problem.** The United States and Britain, abandoning their 1945 promise to restore all of Trieste to Italy, announced plans to withdraw their forces from Zone A, which was to be returned to Italy, while leaving Yugoslavia in control of Zone B. Italy favored the plan, but Yugoslavia denounced it. Tito threatened to send his troops into Zone A the minute the Italians attempted to occupy it (Oct. 11).

Oct. 12–15. Tito called for an international conference on Trieste, while the Soviet Union sought action by the UN. On Oct. 18 the foreign ministers of Britain, France, and the U.S. proposed a conference with Italy and Yugoslavia.

Nov. 1. The **Trieste crisis was averted** when Yugoslavia and Italy agreed (Nov. 21) to attend such a conference and (Dec. 5) to withdraw their troops from the disputed area.

Dec. 14. U.S. **secretary of state Dulles,** irked by the failure of some NATO members to meet their military commitments, warned a NATO conference in Paris that unless a European army were established "soon," his government would be forced to undertake **"an agonizing reappraisal"** of its own basic policies.

1954, Jan. 25–Feb. 18. A Big Four foreign ministers conference in Berlin discussed the **German and Austrian problems** and considered a Soviet proposal for a European security organization. The conference ended in deadlock, but decided to hold a further conference in Geneva to discuss East Asian questions, and to invite Communist China to attend.

Jan. 31. The **Yugoslav government** declined the invitation of the Cominform to "restore the ancient bonds" with Soviet Russia, arguing that political and economic decentralization had reached such a point that restoration of centralized communist control would lead to "convulsion."

March 26. West German president Theodor Heuss signed the constitutional amendment permitting the Federal Republic **rearmament as a member of the EDC,** if established.

April 13. Great Britain completed an agreement to associate itself with the **EDC.**

June 3. Yugoslav **president Tito** and Greek **premier Papagos** were reported in "complete agreement" on a **tripartite alliance with Turkey.**

July 30. The U.S. Senate unanimously authorized the president to take direct action for the restoration of German sovereignty if France did not ratify the EDC treaty.

Aug. 30. The **FRENCH NATIONAL ASSEMBLY REJECTED THE EDC** treaty of 1952, thus sounding the death knell for an integrated European army.

Sept. 30. Pierre Mendès-France, speaking before the European assembly at Strasbourg, announced French agreement to link West Germany with West European defense arrangements, provided that Britain joined the alliance.

Oct. 3. Nine powers (Britain, France, Italy, Belgium, the Netherlands, Luxembourg, West Germany, the United States, and Canada) reached agreement on an alternative to the EDC.

Oct. 5. The **Trieste issue was settled** by agreement between Italy and Yugoslavia. Italy was accorded Zone A, including the city of Trieste, and Yugoslavia, Zone B. American and British troops were to be withdrawn shortly.

Oct. 6. Soviet foreign minister V. M. Molotov urged immediate four-power talks regarding German unification, neutralization, and evacuation, but British prime minister Winston Churchill firmly rejected the proposal (Oct. 26).

Oct. 20–23. A **NATO ministerial conference** in Paris voted to terminate the occupation of West Germany but provided for the retention of foreign troops there; to admit West Germany into NATO; and to expand and revise the Brussels treaty so as to create a **Western European Union (WEU)** by adding West Germany and Italy and by controlling armaments of the member states.

Nov. 13. The Soviet Union, Poland, and Czechoslovakia invited the European nations and the United States to a conference on European security in Moscow (Nov. 29). Washington denounced the proposal as an attempt to forestall ratification of the Paris agreements.

Nov. 29. At a conference of Communist nations in Moscow, **Foreign Minister Molotov** declared that the rearmament of West Germany required the Communist governments to take common measures for defense.

Dec. 21. An agreement signed in London defined **Great Britain's relations with the European Coal and Steel Community.**

1955, May 9. At a conference of NATO foreign ministers in Paris, **West Germany was formally admitted to membership in NATO.**

May 14. The **WARSAW PACT,** signed by eight European Communist governments, was the reply to the integration of West Germany with NATO. **Marshal Ivan S. Koniev** became chief of the joint military command. **A political consultative committee** was to serve as the directing organ.

Dec. 14. Bulgaria and Hungary entered the UN in a 16-nation "package deal."

1956, Jan. 27–28. Meeting of the Warsaw Pact consultative committee in Prague. It called for immediate agreement among the great powers to prohibit the placement of nuclear weapons in Germany. A new **East German army** was to be added to Koniev's command.

April 17. The Cominform was officially dissolved.

May 4. "Three Wise Men," a subcommittee of NATO, were appointed to "advise the Council on ways and means to improve and extend NATO co-operation in non-military fields and to develop greater unity within the Atlantic Community." The members were **Lester Pearson,** Canadian secretary of state for external affairs, **Gaetano Martino,** the Italian foreign minister, and **Halvard Lange,** the Norwegian foreign minister.

June 24. In his first official visit to a Soviet satellite since 1948,

President Tito journeyed to Romania for **talks with Romanian leaders,** concluding agreements (June 26) for closer Yugoslav-Romanian ties.

Nov. 20. General Lauris Norstad succeeded General Gruenther as supreme allied commander, Europe.

Dec. 14. Paul-Henri Spaak succeeded Lord Ismay as secretary general of NATO.

1957, Feb. 7. General Hans Speidel of West Germany was appointed **commander of NATO land forces in Central Europe.**

March 20. Representatives of Yugoslavia, Greece, and Turkey met to discuss "activation" of the Balkan alliance.

March 25. The **ROME TREATY** established the **European Economic Community,** often known as the **Common Market.** Its members were France, West Germany, Italy, Belgium, the Netherlands, and Luxembourg. Another treaty set up a **European Atomic Community (Euratom).** Both organizations were to come into effect on Jan. 1, 1958.

July 28. The **Berlin Declaration,** signed by the United States, Britain, France, and West Germany, called for a free and reunited Germany as a requisite to a European settlement.

Sept. 13. The **UN General Assembly** approved a resolution condemning for the second time Soviet intervention in Hungary in 1956. The resolution also included the appointment of Thailand's foreign minister, **Prince Wan,** as the UN's "special representative on the Hungarian problem." Hungary announced its refusal to admit Prince Wan (Sept. 14).

Nov. 14–16. Meeting of delegates from 13 communist countries in Moscow. It called for unity in opposing imperialism and capitalism abroad and for the elimination of deviationism at home. Mao Zedong, for Communist China, recognized Soviet Russia as the head of the "socialist camp."

Dec. 19. Establishment of **missile bases in Europe** was decided on by a top-level meeting of NATO in Paris. The United States was to retain basic control of the weapons, but assured its allies of its readiness to discuss "any reasonable proposal" for "comprehensive and controlled disarmament."

1958, Feb. 3. A 50-year treaty, signed in The Hague, united Belgium, the Netherlands, and Luxembourg in a **Benelux Economic Union.** The union came into force Nov. 1, 1960.

Feb. 8. The Albanian government signed an **agreement with the Greek government** for the joint removal of mines between Corfu and the Albanian mainland. The two governments signed a joint declaration (July 30) that the straits were safe for navigation.

March 19. Opening meeting of the **European Economic Assembly** (the deliberative body of the Coal and Steel Community, the Common Market, and Euratom). **Robert Schuman** was elected president.

May 21–23. The **Communist COMECON,** meeting in Moscow, pledged increased economic cooperation. Four Asian nations (Communist China, North Korea, North Vietnam, Mongolia) agreed to integrate their economies with COMECON.

May 24–27. Meeting of the Warsaw Pact countries in Moscow. They agreed on early **withdrawal of Soviet forces from Romania and of one Soviet division from Hungary.**

Sept. 3. The **European Court of Human Rights** came into existence when Austria and Iceland completed the necessary ratifications.

Dec. 2. The **Benelux** (Belgian, Dutch, Luxembourger) foreign ministers decided that their three countries should become a single economic unit early in 1959.

Dec. 13–16. The NATO council, meeting in Paris, supported the **determination of the United States, Britain, and France not to abandon West Berlin** and to reject the Soviet contention that it could withdraw unilaterally from the international agreements concerning Berlin.

1959, Jan. 27–28. The **Twenty-first Congress of the Soviet Communist Party** ended in agreement for common opposition to the Tito-led "revisionist" movement.

Feb. 19. An agreement signed in London provided for the **independence of Cyprus** (p. 973).

March 14. Beginning of **French defection from NATO** precipitated by President De Gaulle's refusal to put one-third of France's naval forces in the Mediterranean under NATO command. Disagreement between the United States and France on the **stockpiling of nuclear weapons.** The U.S. decided to transfer 200 airplanes from French to British and West German bases.

1960, May 3. The **European Free Trade Association** (EFTA) of Great Britain, Sweden, Norway, Denmark, Switzerland, Austria, and Portugal (the *"Outer Seven"*) was established as a counterpart to the Common Market.

Sept. 23. NATO members agreed to establishment of a unified **West European air defense command** and related measures to strengthen the alliance.

Nov. 19. Twenty nations agreed on a charter for the **Organization for Economic Cooperation and Development** (OECD) to replace the Organization for European Economic Cooperation (OEEC). The United States and Canada joined the older organization to form the new OECD, the objective of which was to expand trade, provide aid to underdeveloped countries, and so on. The convention was signed on Dec. 14.

Dec. 5. A manifesto, signed by leaders of 81 Communist parties meeting in Moscow (since Nov. 7), pledged a world Communist victory by peaceful means and reaffirmed the leadership of the Soviet Communist Party as against Chinese claims.

1961, Jan. 31. Dirk U. Stikker of the Netherlands **succeeded Paul-Henri Spaak** as secretary general of NATO.

April–May. Recall of Soviet technicians from Albania and termination of all aid to that country, in response to Albania's support of the Chinese position.

July 25. U.S. president John F. Kennedy spoke on **U.S. preparedness in the Berlin crisis** (p. 872).

Aug. 10. The British government formally applied for membership in the Common Market after the House of Commons, by a vote of 313–5, approved the move (Aug. 3).

Oct. 27. At the **22nd Congress of the Soviet Communist Party,** Khrushchev abused the Albanians and called for the ouster of Prime Minister Hoxha and Interior Minister Shehu (p. 896).

Nov. 7. Premier Khrushchev declared his willingness to postpone a settlement of the Berlin issue.

Dec. 7. Agreement between the Common Market members to admit 18 African states as "associates."

1962, April 10. Edward Heath, leading Britain's negotiations on the **Common Market,** declared that Britain planned to play its "full part" in the political and economic future of the Common Market.

June 6–7. The **COMECON conference** in Moscow adopted the principle of the "internationalist socialist division of labor."

June 14. Ten Western European governments set up a **European Space Research Organization,** devoted to space experiments.

July 25. General Lyman L. Lemnitzer was appointed to **succeed General Norstad** as supreme allied commander, Europe.

Aug. 5. Negotiations for **British entry into the Common Market** foundered on the relationship of the Commonwealth to the European market, but British prime minister Macmillan and French president De Gaulle agreed (Dec. 15) to continue examination of the problem.

Aug. 8. Foreign Minister Schroeder indicated that Bonn would break diplomatic relations with any country endorsing a peace treaty between East Germany and the USSR.

Aug. 22. The USSR abolished the office of Soviet commandant in East Berlin. The United States declared that the action would not affect the rights of Western commandants in Berlin.

Dec. 12. State visit of Marshal Tito to Moscow, during which Premier Khrushchev, addressing the Supreme Soviet, angrily attacked the Chinese Communists, who in reply began to call on Communists the world over to revolt against Soviet domination.

1963, Jan. 29. FRANCE VETOED BRITAIN'S APPLICATION FOR MEMBERSHIP IN THE COMMON MARKET.

Feb. 5. Walter Hallstein, the executive head of the Common Market, castigated De Gaulle's plan for transforming Europe into a "Third Force" and sharply criticized French obstruction of Britain's entry into the Common Market.

May. The seven members of the European Free Trade Association voted to eliminate all tariffs on nonfarm products by the end of 1966.

June 21. The French government announced its intention to withdraw its Channel and Atlantic naval forces, except for some submarines, from the NATO command.

July 24–26. A **communist interparty conference** in Moscow shelved a Soviet plan for integration of the Communist states and reaffirmed the principles of "equality, strict observance of sovereignty, and mutual comradely assistance."

Oct. 11. Delegates from the United States, Britain, West Germany, Italy, Belgium, Greece, and Turkey began discussions looking toward an **integrated atomic fleet** for the defense of Europe.

Oct. 14–24. The COMECON decided to establish among communist states a **multination payments system** and an **International Bank of Economic Collaboration.**

1964, Feb. 21. Danish Premier Krag, on a **state visit to the Soviet Union,** stated that he hoped to increase trade with the USSR.

March 3–10. A high-level Romanian delegation arrived in Peking (Beijing) in an effort to bridge the Soviet-Chinese rift.

March 31. The U.S. Air Force announced that training flights in a 70-mile zone along the East-West German border would be prohibited in the future. Three U.S. airmen shot down March 10 had been released earlier by the Soviet Union.

April 22. The Romanian Communist Party asserted in the strongest terms its claims to full equality and independence.

May 4. France withdrew its officers from the NATO naval commands.

May 13. Manlio Brosio of Italy was **elected to succeed Dirk Stikker** (Aug. 1) as secretary general of NATO.

June 12. Signing of a 20-year **treaty of friendship and mutual assistance between the Soviet Union and East Germany.** The treaty included a guarantee of the frontiers of the German Democratic Republic.

July 22. Celebration of the **twentieth anniversary of the Polish Republic.** Khrushchev, Walter Ulbricht, and Antonín Novotný joined in casting aspersions on Romanian nationalism.

Sept. Prime Minister Ulbricht, in a parliamentary speech, asked for East German membership in the UN and **proposed a treaty between NATO and the Warsaw Pact** and a general reduction of forces in Germany.

Dec. 15. Members of the **Common Market,** after prolonged debate, agreed on a **common wholesale price for wheat.** German farmers were to be compensated for substantial losses vis-à-vis their French counterparts.

Dec. 16. British prime minister Harold Wilson's counterproposal for a broader **Atlantic nuclear force.** The U.S. proposal for a **NATO multilateral nuclear force** of 25 mix-manned surface ships, equipped with Polaris missiles, had met with a favorable response only from West Germany.

1965, Feb. 21. De Gaulle announced his intention to modify the arrangements between France and its NATO partners.

March 2. Decision of the Common Market countries to merge the Common Market, the Coal and Steel Community, and the Atomic Energy Community, with headquarters in Brussels.

July 27. Reconvening of the UN disarmament committee in Geneva.

1966, March 11. De Gaulle, describing NATO as outmoded, yet desiring to retain membership, stated the **decision of the French government to withdraw all French troops from the integrated NATO command** and requested that all NATO bases and headquarters be removed from French soil by April 1, 1967.

April 21–27. Visit of Soviet foreign minister Andrey Gromyko to Italy and reception by the pope. Beginning of closer economic and cultural relations between the two countries.

June 20–July 1. Visit of President Charles De Gaulle to Russia, following visits of French foreign minister **Couve de Murville** to other Eastern European capitals. The French envisioned a "Europeanized Europe" free from both American and Soviet domination.

July 1. Allied supreme headquarters in Europe moved from Paris to Casteau, Belgium.

July 4–6. Meeting of the Warsaw Pact powers at Bucharest. Romanian **premier Ceauşescu** proposed the dissolution of both the NATO alliance and the Warsaw Pact, as well as the withdrawal of all foreign troops from the territory of other nations.

July 6–8. Conference of British prime minister Wilson and French premier Georges Pompidou: decision to proceed with construction of a Channel tunnel and to collaborate in the design and development of a supersonic airliner, the Concorde.

1967, Jan. 15–March 8. Prime Minister Wilson's tour of Common Market countries and extensive discussions of the conditions of British membership.

Jan. 31. Diplomatic relations established between West Germany and Romania, the initial move in the development of better relations between Central and Eastern Europe.

Feb. 9. Soviet premier Aleksey Kosygin, addressing the House of Commons during a visit to England, called for a treaty of friendship and nonaggression, the dissolution of NATO and the Warsaw Pact, the denial of nuclear weapons to Germany, and a declaration that the European frontiers were to be regarded as unalterable and inviolable.

May 2. Prime Minister Wilson announced the **British government's decision to apply for membership in the Common Market.** The Commons supported him, 487–26 (May 8).

May 11. The **British government formally applied for admission to the Common Market.** Denmark, Ireland, and Norway did likewise.

May 16. De Gaulle once more vetoed the British application on grounds of British insularity, ties to the United States, and so on.

June 18–20. A visit of Prime Minister Wilson to Paris failed to move De Gaulle, who called upon Britain to undergo a **"profound transformation"** before attempting to enter the Common Market. Nevertheless, the council of ministers of the Common Market voted (June 27) five to one (France) in favor of the British application.

July 5. The new **European Community** (EC), consolidating former entities, went into effect. **Jean Rey** (of Belgium) became president.

July 7. Marshal Ivan I. Yakubovsky became supreme commander of the Warsaw Pact forces.

1968, Jan. 19. British-Soviet agreement to cooperate in applied science and technology.

March–June. A new period of **harassment and obstruction of traffic between West Germany and West Berlin by the East German authorities.**

June 15. Extensive **Soviet and Warsaw Pact maneuvers** in Poland, East Germany, and Czechoslovakia.

July 1. The **EC became a single trading area** for all industrial produce, with a common external tariff.

Aug. 20–21. Occupation of Czechoslovakia by Warsaw Pact forces, creating an acute international crisis (p. 887).

Sept. 12. Albania formally withdrew from the Warsaw Pact.

Oct. 16. Soviet agreement with the new Czech government permitting the stationing of troops in Czechoslovakia.

1969, March 17. The Warsaw Pact powers proposed a European security conference, a proposal reiterated by Foreign Minister Gromyko on July 10. The Western powers, shocked by the Czech affair, exhibited little enthusiasm.

May 6. General Andrew J. Goodpaster became supreme allied commander, Europe, **replacing General Lemnitzer.**

May 28. The **NATO defense planning committee** decided to organize an "on call" naval force in the Mediterranean, in response to the constant strengthening of Soviet naval forces in the eastern Mediterranean.

June 3. Conclusion of a **British-Soviet trade treaty.**

Aug. 2–3. Visit of U.S. President Richard Nixon to Romania.

Dec. 4–5. The NATO council endorsed the idea of a security conference, provided it were carefully prepared and that the United States and Canada be included.

1970, Feb. 6. Conclusion of a **trade agreement between the Common Market and Yugoslavia,** the first such agreement with an Eastern European country.

March 26. First meeting of the delegates of the four great powers (U.S., Britain, France, and USSR) to canvas possible improvements in the West Berlin situation.

April 11. Visit of Chancellor Willy Brandt to Washington, where he found approval for his program of *Ostpolitik.*

May 27. The NATO council, meeting in Rome, called for discussions with the Soviet Union and the Warsaw Pact governments, looking to the reduction of forces in Central Europe.

Aug. 12. West German chancellor Brandt in Moscow for the signing of a **TREATY BETWEEN WEST GERMANY AND THE SOVIET UNION** recognizing the **inviolability of all postwar European boundaries,** including specifically the **Oder-Neisse line.** The Soviet Union disclaimed opposition to the reunification of Germany, provided it could be achieved by peaceful means. West Germany reserved all its ties with the West, but agreed to develop economic, scientific, and cultural ties with the Soviet Union. **Ratification of the treaty,** which was seen as a possible milestone in East-West relations, was made conditional on successful conclusion of negotiations regarding the status of West Berlin.

Oct. 19. Romanian president Ceauşescu, in his address to the UN General Assembly, reiterated his demand for the abolition of military blocs, the dismantling of bases on the territory of other nations, and the withdrawal of armed forces from foreign territories.

Nov. 19. Members of the European Community adopted measures aimed at the coordination of their foreign policies. A newly created **political committee** was to hold monthly meetings.

Dec. 1–4. The **NATO council and defense ministers** meeting in Brussels announced plans for the European members to contribute more than $1 billion during the ensuing five years to improve bases, forces, and weapons to counterbalance increases in the strength of the Warsaw Pact forces. The United States disclaimed any intention of reducing its own forces in Europe. In a concluding statement, the conference declared that even the first steps toward a European security conference depended on satisfactory improvements in the **status of West Berlin,** about which talks had been initiated in March.

Dec. 7. Visit of West German chancellor Brandt to Warsaw for signature of a **treaty with Poland** (p. 873). Both sides renounced the use of force for settling disputes, and West Germany conditionally recognized the Oder-Neisse line as the western frontier of Poland. In return Poland was to allow some 90,000 ethnic Germans to leave for Germany. This treaty, too, was to be ratified only after settlement of the problem of West Berlin.

1971, Jan. 1. The International Investment Bank set up by COMECON in 1970 began operations.

April. COMECON countries signed agreements on the establishment of seven new scientific centers.

July 27–29. The twenty-fifth session of COMECON adopted a **"Complex Program,"** which aimed at the attainment of greater economic cooperation and integration among the COMECON members in the next 15 to 20 years.

1972, Jan. 22. The Treaty of Accession to the European Communities was signed by the prime ministers of the United Kingdom, Ireland, Denmark, and Norway. A Norwegian referendum rejected membership in September, while the other three countries ratified the treaty, to go into effect Jan. 1, 1973.

April 19. A convention to establish the European University Institute in Florence was signed, following the agreement reached in Brussels Nov. 16, 1971.

1973, Oct. 30. Warsaw Pact and NATO countries began a conference on mutual and balanced force reduction in Central Europe.

Dec. 11. The Social Action Program 1974–76 of the EC defined three broad objectives: equal pay for men and women, a standard 40-hour work week, and four weeks of annual paid holidays.

1974, March 22. Denmark and Sweden signed an agreement with Finland, East and West Germany, Poland, and the Soviet Union aimed at the reduction of pollution in the Baltic Sea.

Nov. 28. Greece was readmitted to the Council of Europe after its withdrawal in December 1969.

1976, April 7. The council of the European Free Trade Association approved the statutes for a **$100 million Industrial Development Fund to help Portuguese industry** over a five-year period.

Sept. 22. Portugal admitted to the Council of Europe.

Nov. The Warsaw Pact's draft treaty on a pledge against the first use of nuclear weapons and a proposal for "freezing" the membership of the two military alliances were both rejected by NATO.

Nov. 10. A 16-article **Convention on the Suppression of Terrorism** was adopted by the Committee of Foreign Ministers of the Council of Europe and signed by all members except Ireland and Malta. The convention was to facilitate the extradition and persecution of perpetrators of terrorist acts. Ireland and Malta finally signed the convention in 1986 (on Feb. 24 and Nov. 5, respectively).

1977, Feb. Euratom and the International Atomic Energy Agency (IAEA) concluded a Safeguards Agreement to prevent the "diversion of nuclear energy from peaceful uses to nuclear weapons or other explosive devices."

April–Sept. COMECON held its first top-level preliminary talks with the EC for future negotiations on economic cooperation.

July 1. Free trade in industrial products (the European Industrial Market) began between all EC and EFTA members.

Nov. 24. Spain joined the Council of Europe.

1978–79. To alleviate the crisis in energy supplies, COMECON members agreed on plans to diversify the production of nuclear plant equipment, to bring about increased nuclear output.

1978, June 19–20. Yugoslavia and the EFTA established a full joint committee to promote intensified economic cooperation between the two sides.

Nov. 23. Liechtenstein was formally admitted to the Council of Europe.

1979, March 13. Inauguration of the European Monetary System (EMS). All EC members except Britain began implementing the EMS exchange mechanism, a joint floating of eight of the nine EC currencies.

June 7 and 10. Universal suffrage was used for the first time **in European parliamentary elections.** The European Parliament was first directly elected by citizens of the member states (July 17).

June 26. Spain signed a multilateral free trade agreement with the seven members of the EFTA, effective in May 1980.

1980, July 21. The Council of the Western European Union unanimously agreed to **abolish with immediate effect WEU protocol restrictions on the permitted size of West German warships.** The Soviet Union strongly criticized the decision to lift the restrictions.

1981, Jan. 1. Greece became the tenth member of the EC.

Oct. 2. The French government ratified Article 25 of the European Convention for the Protection of Human Rights and Fundamental Freedoms—providing for the right of individual appeal to the European Human Rights Commission—and the **Second Protocol,** empowering the European Court of Human Rights to give advisory opinions on observance of the convention.

1982–83. Disagreement increased between COMECON members over questions of mutual trade, particularly over the prices and quantity of crude oil deliveries from the Soviet Union. The Soviet Union had steadily increased its oil price and decreased oil supplies to its COMECON partners in the wake of the 1979 oil price increase by the Organization of Petroleum Exporting Countries (OPEC).

1983, Jan. 4–5. A Warsaw Pact summit meeting resulted in a proposed nonaggression pact with NATO and arms reduction talks between member states of the two organizations.

April 28. A **protocol on abolition of the death penalty** to be added to the Convention for Human Rights was opened for signature and was signed by 12 of the 21 members that day.

Nov. 24. The Committee of Ministers of the Council of Europe declared illegal the Turkish Republic of Northern Cyprus and called for Turkey's withdrawal.

1984, June–Oct. The defense and foreign ministers of the WEU agreed that the postwar controls on West German conventional rearmament, as monitored by the WEU's Agency for the Control of Armaments, should be entirely lifted by Jan. 1, 1986.

July 16. The abolition of customs formalities for EC citizens at the Franco-German border came into effect for the French and Germans and, later, for other EC citizens (Aug. 1). The ultimate aim was to end all routine formalities at the border by 1986, and to rely thereafter on spot checks only.

1985, June 25–27. The communiqué of the fortieth COMECON session confirmed a **proposal for the establishment of relations between COMECON and the EC.**

Dec. A Comprehensive Program for Scientific and Technological Progress, going up to the year 2000, was approved at COMECON's forty-first session. Portugal ended its membership in the EFTA in expectation of becoming an EC member on Jan. 1, 1986.

1986, Jan. 1. Spain and Portugal became full members of the EC, thus enlarging the community to 12. **Finland became a full member of the EFTA.**

Jan. The Council of Industry Ministers began **dismantling the controls on the system of monitoring and production quotas** for the EC steel industry. (In June 1988 the council announced **the end of steel production quotas system, effective July 1, 1988.**)

June 30. The EC approved the **Eureka high-technology research program,** which included more than 60 projects.

1987, Feb. 17. Sixteen NATO and seven Warsaw Pact nations met in Vienna for the first session of roundtable discussions on European conventional arms talks.

May 14. The Council of Education Ministers approved the **Erasmus program,** designed to provide grants for EC students to study in other member countries and to establish a European university network.

July 1. The Single European Act went into force. The act included measures to provide the EC with its own "adequate, stable and guaranteed" resources by allowing the EC to access a percentage of member countries' gross national product (GNP).

Nov. 26. The Convention for the Prevention of Torture was signed by all members of the Council of Europe except Ireland and Turkey.

1988, Jan. 25. The Convention on Mutual Administrative Assistance in Tax Matters, which sought to exchange information between tax authorities on suspected tax evasion, was opened for signature of the member states of the Council of Europe.

April. A 17-member committee under chairman **Jacques Delors** (president of the EC commission) approved a **three-stage plan leading to the European Economic and Monetary Union (EMU).** According to the plan, policies were to be managed jointly with a view to attaining common macroeconomic objectives. Stage one, which went into force July 1, 1990, involved the strengthening of monetary policies among member states through the existing exchange rate mechanism of the European Monetary System; stage two, which started Jan. 1, 1994, involved the creation of a European Monetary Institute; and stage three, beginning Jan. 1, 1999, involved the introduction of one single currency and the complete liberalization of banking transactions.

May 24. An EC foreign ministers meeting announced that **the EC and COMECON would formally recognize each other in a joint declaration (June 25).**

Nov. 14. Spain and Portugal signed an accession protocol to **join the Western European Union.** Formal accession occurred in April 1989, when the document was ratified by the Parliament.

1989, May 5. Finland became a full member of the Council of Europe.

Oct. 26–27. A communiqué from a **Warsaw Pact** foreign ministers meeting confirmed the effective **renunciation of the Brezhnev Doctrine** and recognized the absolute right of each state to determine its own sociopolitical development.

Dec. 8–9. The European Council meeting in Strasbourg agreed to establish a **European Bank for Reconstruction and Development** to aid Eastern Europe.

1990, March 27. COMECON member countries agreed to **abolish two of the organization's most important functions: multilateral cooperation and the coordination of economic planning.** Trade relations between member countries were to be conducted primarily on a bilateral basis.

June 7. Warsaw Pact meeting in Moscow focused on transforming pact given collapse of European communism. Hungary prepared to leave the Pact.

June 13. Joint declarations of cooperation were signed by the **EFTA and Czechoslovakia, Hungary, and Poland.**

June 19. The Schengen Agreement. Belgium, France, West Germany, the Netherlands, and Luxembourg signed an agreement in Schengen on the abolition of mutual border controls. The agreement to advance the introduction of a single internal market within the EC was joined by Italy in November and by Spain and Portugal in June 1991.

Nov. 6. Hungary became the first Eastern European country to join the **Council of Europe.**

Nov. 8. The **Convention on Money Laundering and Confiscation of the Proceeds of a Crime** was signed by half of the member states of the Council of Europe. The convention aimed at simplifying the exchange of evidence and information, and making the laundering of drug money a crime.

Nov. 19–21. Warsaw Pact member countries and NATO member countries signed an unprecedented treaty on Conventional Armed Forces in Europe and endorsed a joint declaration renouncing the use of force.

Dec. The Rome Summit and European Political Union (EPU). Heads of state of the 12 members of the Council of Europe established a broad framework for negotiations at parallel intergovernmental conferences on political union and on economic and monetary union. On political union, key issues included strengthening the role of the European Parliament and the concept of European citizenship, and possible security and defense policies.

1991, Jan. 5. The executive committee of COMECON agreed to disband the council and replace it with a new body, the **Organization for International Economic Cooperation (OIEC).**

Feb. 21. Czechoslovakia joined the Council of Europe.

March 31. End of military alliance features of the Warsaw Pact.

May 22. Liechtenstein became a full member of the EFTA.

June 27–28. Hungary and the EFTA signed a free trade agreement to be implemented by January 1992.

June 29. COMECON was formally dissolved.

July 1. The Warsaw Pact was formally dissolved by its members.

Oct. 23. The EFTA and the EC reached an agreement on the **creation of a common European Economic Area (EEA).** The agreement was signed on May 2, 1992, but due to rejection in a Swiss referendum, modification had to be made with a target date of mid-1993 for the agreement to go into force.

Nov. 26. Poland joined the Council of Europe.

Dec. 11. The MAASTRICHT TREATY on European Union. Heads of state of the EC concluded their year-long intergovernmental conferences with a treaty framework for the European Union, incorporating the EPU and the EMU agreements. The Treaty on European Union was formally signed on Feb. 7, 1992. The Danish electorate rejected the treaty in a referendum (June) but reached a "national compromise" (Oct. 27) on additions to the treaty. By the end of 1992, the treaty had been ratified by all 12 member countries except Denmark and the United Kingdom.

1992, May 7. Bulgaria joined the Council of Europe.

June 19. Defense and foreign ministers agreed to set up a **joint military force of the WEU** that could be deployed in response to requests from the Conference on Security and Cooperation in Europe or from the UN.

Sept. 17. The **EFTA signed a free trade agreement with Israel,** the first with a non-European nation, to go into effect on Jan. 1, 1993.

Nov. 5. The Convention on Minority and Regional Languages, designed to preserve regional languages and promote their official use, was opened for signature by the member states of the Council of Europe and was signed that day by 11 of the 27 members.

Nov. 20. The **WEU extended full membership to Greece** and observer status to Denmark and Ireland. The WEU extension policy tied in with its growing role as the forum for Western European defense cooperation and its strengthening links with the EC.

Dec. 10. The EFTA concluded free **trade agreements with Poland and Romania,** and signed a **declaration on cooperation with Albania.**

1993, Jan. 1. A **single European Market was established,** instituting the free movement of goods, services, capital, and persons throughout the 12 member states.

Jan. The council and the secretariat of the WEU moved from Paris and London, respectively, to Brussels as the WEU continued to strengthen and develop specific relations with the European Union and NATO.

July 23. The British Parliament voted to ratify the Maastricht Treaty of European Union, making Britain the last EC member to complete the voting process.

Oct. 12. The German Federal Constitutional Court unanimously declared the Maastricht Treaty to be in conformity with the German Basic Law (constitution), whereupon President Richard von Weizsäcker signed it, officially making Germany the last nation to ratify the treaty despite overwhelming parliamentary approval in Dec. 1992.

Nov. 1. The Maastricht Treaty of European Union entered into force.

Nov. 8. The EC's Council of Ministers decided to call itself in future the Council of the European Union. This caused some confusion, since the EU had no "legal personality" and thus treaties with third parties could only be done formally in the name of the EC. Officially the Union embraced the EC (with its enhanced powers under the Maastricht Treaty) and the opportunity for foreign and security policy coordination and cooperation on issues of justice and domestic affairs. The council of 12 ministers conducted both EC and EU business, depending on subject matter.

1994 ff. Unemployment rose in most European countries, reaching figures like 12 percent in France and straining welfare systems **despite continued overall economic growth.**

Jan. 10–11. NATO held a summit in Brussels and offered limited association to former members of the Warsaw Pact, beginning an initiative called **Partnership for Peace.** Hungary, Slovakia, the Czech Republic, and Poland approved the plan, which gave the countries offices at NATO headquarters and also changed the structure of NATO so that it no longer needed U.S. approval to respond to European crises. The summit also agreed to mount air strikes against Bosnian Serbs should it become necessary.

March 29. The EU agreed to admit Austria, Sweden, Norway, and Finland pending referenda in each country.

June 9–12. The 12 nations of the EU held elections; leftist parties kept the largest position in the European Parliament.

July 21. After an earlier deadlock, the EU summit agreed on Jacques Santer, the premier of Luxembourg, for president of the European Commission.

Sept. 29. All 16 countries of NATO agreed to name Willy Claes, the foreign minister of Belgium, as NATO's secretary general. On Dec. 1, however, NATO picked **Javier Solana,** Spain's foreign minister, as its ninth **secretary general,** replacing Willy Claes, who resigned due to charges of corruption.

1995, May 31. The **EU** issued plans to implement an Economic and Monetary Union (EMU), including the **establishment of a single currency for all members by 2003.**

Dec. 15. The EU leaders agreed to call the new currency the *euro* and to put it into use in trade debts as soon as possible after its launch on Jan. 1, 1999. They planned to introduce the currency itself by 2002.

1996. On June 3, NATO agreed on a plan to strengthen European armies.

1997, July 8. NATO formally invited Poland, Hungary, and the Czech Republic to join.

1998, March 30. At a ceremony in Brussels, Belgium, the EU formally began membership talks with Poland, Estonia, Cyprus, Hungary, Slovenia and the Czech Republic. This planned EU expansion effort marked the first time that formal negotiations would include former Soviet-bloc nations.

May 3. After an extended summit, the difficult decision of choosing the future president of the European Central Bank (ECB) was finalized with the selection of Wim Duisenberg, former president of the Dutch Central Bank. Duisenberg was chosen over French nominee Jean-Claude Trichet. With this decision, the EU was free to proceed with plans to launch its Economic and Monetary Union (EMU) by 1999.

May 28. Denmark citizens voted in favor of adopting the EU's Treaty of Amsterdam, a modified version of the Maastricht Treaty that Denmark had rejected in 1992.

June 8. As tensions rose in Yugoslavia, Serb forces were detected as using "excessive force" in the Kosovo region. The EU passed several sanctions on the government of Slobodan Milosevic and gave support for a future NATO force to intervene in the area if peaceful relations were not quickly restored between Serbs and ethnic Albanians.

June 15–16. The EU heads of state met in Cardiff, Wales and agreed that negotiations should begin with a group of six nations applying for membership in the EU. These countries were Poland, Czech Republic, Cyprus, Estonia, Slovenia, and Hungary. The EU heads of state also agreed that Bulgaria, Latvia, Lithuania, Romania, and Slovakia were possible EU members in the future but that each would require more economic and political reforms before the EU would extend formal membership invitations to them. Turkish representatives voiced extreme disgust at the EU's decision to include Cyprus—the Aegean island shared by Turkey and Greece—yet to exclude Turkey in membership negotiations.

July 6. Spain and Britain signed an agreement allowing NATO extensive use of the Mediterranean island nation, Gibraltar (p. 864).

July 13. The EU banned 130 Belarusan officials from traveling to EU countries (p. 910).

Aug. 28. The Russian stock market was in a free fall and the government halted trading of the ruble on international currency markets. The extended economic crisis that ensued led Pres. Yeltsin to replace his government several times before resigning on Dec. 31, 1999, and leaving the presidency to his hand-picked successor, Vladimir Putin.

Nov. 2. An EU summit was held to discuss environmental issues worldwide. A special focus was the question of global warming.

Nov. 23. The EU ban on beef from Britain, barred from European sale for three years because of possible infection with bovine spongiform encephalopathy (BSE), commonly known as mad cow disease, was lifted; sale of young British beef was resumed on the continent.

Dec. 8–23. In multiple referendums, Latvia, Bulgaria, and Lithuania changed national legislation in accordance with EU standards. Latvia voted to ease its difficult language requirements for citizenship that had been mainly directed at the ethnic Russians living there (p. 912). Bulgaria and Lithuania abolished the death penalty.

1999, Jan. 1. In the EU's greatest economic victory in its 40-year history, the euro, a single European currency, was launched. The nations participating in this inauguration of the Economic and Monetary Union (EMU) were France, Finland, Belgium, Austria, Luxembourg, Germany, Ireland, Italy, the Netherlands, Portugal, and Spain.

March 12. Poland, Czech Republic, and Hungary became full members of NATO.

March 24–26. In a summit of the EC, former Italian prime minister Romano Prodi was chosen as the new president of the EU executive body.

March 24–June 10. Realizing that its military powers were insufficient in the face of a crisis, the EU agreed to back NATO in bombing Yugoslavia in order to combat oppression and attempted genocide against ethnic Albanians in its southern province of Kosovo. A pact was signed on June 3, and 50,000 NATO troops entered the region on June 12 to secure peace. The Kosovo Force (KFOR) consisted of soldiers from many EU countries, including Italy, France, Britain, and Germany. Although uncooperative with NATO and EU officials, Russia was also intimately involved in the conflict and peace agreement. Russia insisted on inclusion in the Yugoslav intervention after having shown significant support for the Serb government of Slobodan Milosevic, sending food and other aid during the fighting.

April 23. NATO celebrated its 50th anniversary in member countries all across Europe.

June 3. The EU banned the sale of Belgian poultry and dairy products after an economic and political crisis arose in Belgium because of the accidental poisoning of the nation's chicken supply. It was believed that the cancer-causing chemical, Dioxin, had contaminated Belgian poultry through poisoned animal feed.

June 10–13. Although a larger number of left-wing candidates had dominated in 1998, the 1999 elections for the EC saw a substantial gain for rightists in the EU.

Aug. 7–Dec. 26. Russia initiated a massive military assault on Islamic uprisings in Dagestan and Chechnya, reviving the war of 1996. By Feb. 6, 2000, Russia had taken control of Grozny, the Chechen capital.

Sept. 13. After over a decade of sanctions against Libya, economic penalties against the country were lifted after Pres. Qaddafi handed over two Libyans suspected in the 1988 bombing of a Pan American World Airways 747 airplane over Lockerbie, Scotland (p. 969).

Nov. 4. In environmental talks, the EU progressed toward its goal of getting more countries to sign the Kyoto Protocol, a 1997 pact aimed at reversing the effects of global warming and other worldwide threats to the environment.

Nov. 22–Dec. 8. Although lifted by the EU one year earlier, the ban on British beef, which had been implicated in cases of mad cow disease, continued in France. An economic battle developed between the two countries as the lucrative French market remained closed to the British beef industry (p. 851).

Dec. 10. At an EU summit in Helsinki, Finland, seven nations were formally invited to begin the processes of applying for future EU membership. Along with Bulgaria, Lithuania, Romania, Malta, Latvia, and Slovakia, Turkey was tentatively invited to participate in negotiations. EU officials urged Turkey to improve its human rights record, as well as its economic and political systems, in order to qualify the nation for future inclusion in the European organization (p. 972).

2000, Feb. 7. The EU passed sanctions against a right-wing government after Austrian elections, held Feb. 4, left Nazi sympathizer Joerg Haider's Freedom Party in a prominent position within the coalition government. Haider later resigned his position as party leader and on Sept. 12 the EU sanctions were lifted. The U.S. and Israel had been included in the resistance to bilateral diplomatic relations with Austria (p. 878).

June 14. Georgia became the 137th nation to join the World Trade Organization (WTO).

June 26–27. In Warsaw, Poland, representatives from 108 nations and 12 international organizations attended a two-day conference that was aimed at supporting democracy worldwide.

Aug. 12. Raising serious questions in the EU about Russia's political, military, and economic stability, the Russian nuclear submarine *Kursk* sank in the Barents Sea; all 118 sailors aboard died. Russia was severely criticized by many European diplomats for its handling of the disaster.

Sept. 11. As the Asian economic crisis, along with huge protests against high petroleum prices, threatened to spill over into countries belonging to the EU, the euro hit a record low in exchange value.

Sept. 26. More than 15,000 delegates from 182 countries met in the Czech Republic capital of Prague for the annual conferences of the IMF and World Bank. Violent protests against IMF and World Bank policies in developing countries were staged outside the center where the conference was held (p. 889).

Sept. 27–28. The EU met with OPEC nations to discuss making changes in OPEC policy. EU officials stressed that it was OPEC supply limitations on oil that had contributed to the massive gas crisis plaguing EU countries during Sept. 2000.

Oct. 3. Amid neo-Nazi violence and anti-foreigner demonstrations in the southern part of the nation, Germany celebrated its tenth year of East–West unification.

Oct. 9–14. Directly following the ousting of Yugoslav dictator Slobodan Milosevic, who had lost a Sept. 24 election to Vojislav Kostunica but refused to yield power, the EU lifted sanctions against Yugoslavia and promised economic aid to the new government.

Oct. 24. Although Colombian president Pastrana requested $1 billion, the EU pledged only $321 million in anti-drug aid to Colombia.

Dec. 6–7. Further talks between EU countries broke down when agreement eluded conference members on issues concerning the 1997 Kyoto Protocol.

Dec. 11. In a summit held in Nice, France, the EU government was revamped and a new rights charter approved for EU member nations. In light of EU military inadequacies that had led to NATO-directed forces intervening in the 1999 Kosovo crisis, a greater emphasis was placed on developing substantial military forces that would be part of the EU.

6. WESTERN EUROPE, 1945–2000

a. BRITAIN

(From p. 682)

Monarchs: George VI (r. 1936–52); Elizabeth II (r. 1952–).

Prime ministers: Clement Atlee (1945–51, Labour); Winston Churchill (1951–55, Conservative); Anthony Eden (1955–57, Conservative); Harold Macmillan (1957–63, Conservative); Sir Alec Douglas-Home (1963–64, Conservative); Harold Wilson (1964–70, Labour); Edward Heath (1970–74, Conservative); Harold Wilson (1974–76, Labour); James Callaghan (1976–79, Labour); Margaret Thatcher (1979–90, Conservative); John Major (1990–97, Conservative); Tony Blair (1997– , Labour).

1945, May 7. Germans surrendered unconditionally to representatives of the U.S., USSR, France, and Great Britain in **Reims**, France. Britain lost a total of **398,000 military personnel** over the course of **World War II.**

May 23. Prime Minister Winston Churchill resigned in the face of the collapse of the wartime coalition, established in 1940, of the **Conservative** and **Labour Parties.**

July 5. In an unexpected victory in the first general parliamentary elections in ten years, the **British Labour Party** won 388 seats out of 640.

July 26. A new **Labour cabinet,** with **Clement R. Atlee** as prime minister, was formed. **Atlee replaced Churchill** for the later sessions of the **Potsdam Conference** (p. 810). The new government immediately embarked on an ambitious **program of socialization.** A brief period of postwar optimism was followed by an extended regime of **economic austerity,** due chiefly to the profound disruption of Britain's economy caused by the war. To facilitate the reconversion to peacetime production, demobilization of manpower and industry was carried out only gradually.

Oct. 15. The House of Commons voted to extend the government's **wartime emergency powers** for five years, to make up for the **cessation of lend-lease,** which came as a deep shock to Britain's economy.

Dec. 6. The **United States** granted a **loan** of $3.75 billion to Great Britain. **Canada** subsequently provided a loan of $1.25 billion. However, both these loans were exhausted by the end of 1947 due to high prices on the American market.

1946, Feb. 13. Parliament repealed the **Trades Disputes Act of 1927,** which had made certain strikes illegal and had hampered the political activities of labor unions.

Feb. 14. The **Bank of England** was brought under public ownership.

May–July. In a burst of socialist legislation, Parliament passed a bill providing for the **nationalization of the coal industry,** a **National Insurance Bill** (consolidating existing schemes of social insurance and extending them to a larger section of the population), a **National Health Service Bill** (to make free medical services available to everyone) and a **Cable and Wireless Act,** nationalizing imperial communications.

July 1. British transatlantic passenger flights between London and New York began.

July 21. Britain's export difficulties and a world shortage of wheat combined to necessitate **bread rationing** (a measure never taken during the war). This was followed by restrictions on most other staple foods.

Aug. 15. India gained independence from Great Britain.

1947, Jan. 1. The **nationalization of the coal mines** went into effect.

Jan.–April. The fiercest winter in decades caused severe fuel shortages across the nation. A serious **coal shortage** led to drastic **fuel restrictions** and curtailment of industrial production. At the same time, Parliament continued its socialization programs by adopting the **Transport Act,** which created the British Transport Commission to regulate rail and trucking systems and other modes of transport, as well as to plan for the repair of war damage and the expansion of the nation's transportation infrastructure. Parliament also adopted the **Electricity Act,** nationalizing 550 private electricity companies, and the **Town and Country Planning Act,** which set up a new planning system to regulate the growth of communities.

June 1. Minister of Labour George Issacs urged that more **British women** should take paid employment outside the home.

Aug. 12. Britain accepted 20,000 **refugee women** from the U.S. zone in Germany, to help in filling the **labor shortage.**

Nov. 20. Princess Elizabeth and **Philip Mountbatten,** duke of Edinburgh, were married in Westminister Abbey.

1948. Football (soccer) **betting pools,** launched in the 1930s, began drawing 7 to 8 million participants.

Jan. 1. The British railways passed into public ownership.

Jan. 12. The London Cooperative Society inaugurated the first full-size supermarket in England.

March. Aid from the Marshall Plan (p. 837) began to arrive.

April 1. The **British Electrical Authority** took over the electricity industry.

July 30. The **British Nationality Act** received royal assent. It gave each Dominion the right to determine who its citizens were, while at the same time conferring the status of British subjects on all citizens of the Commonwealth.

August. The first **Olympic Games** since 1936 were held in London. A total of 6,005 contestants from 59 nations participated.

Dec. The **National Service Act** conscripted all men between the ages of 18 and 26.

1949, Feb. 1. Rationing of clothing was discontinued, but meat, dairy products, and sugar continued to be on the list of restricted items.

April. North Atlantic Treaty signed (p. 838).

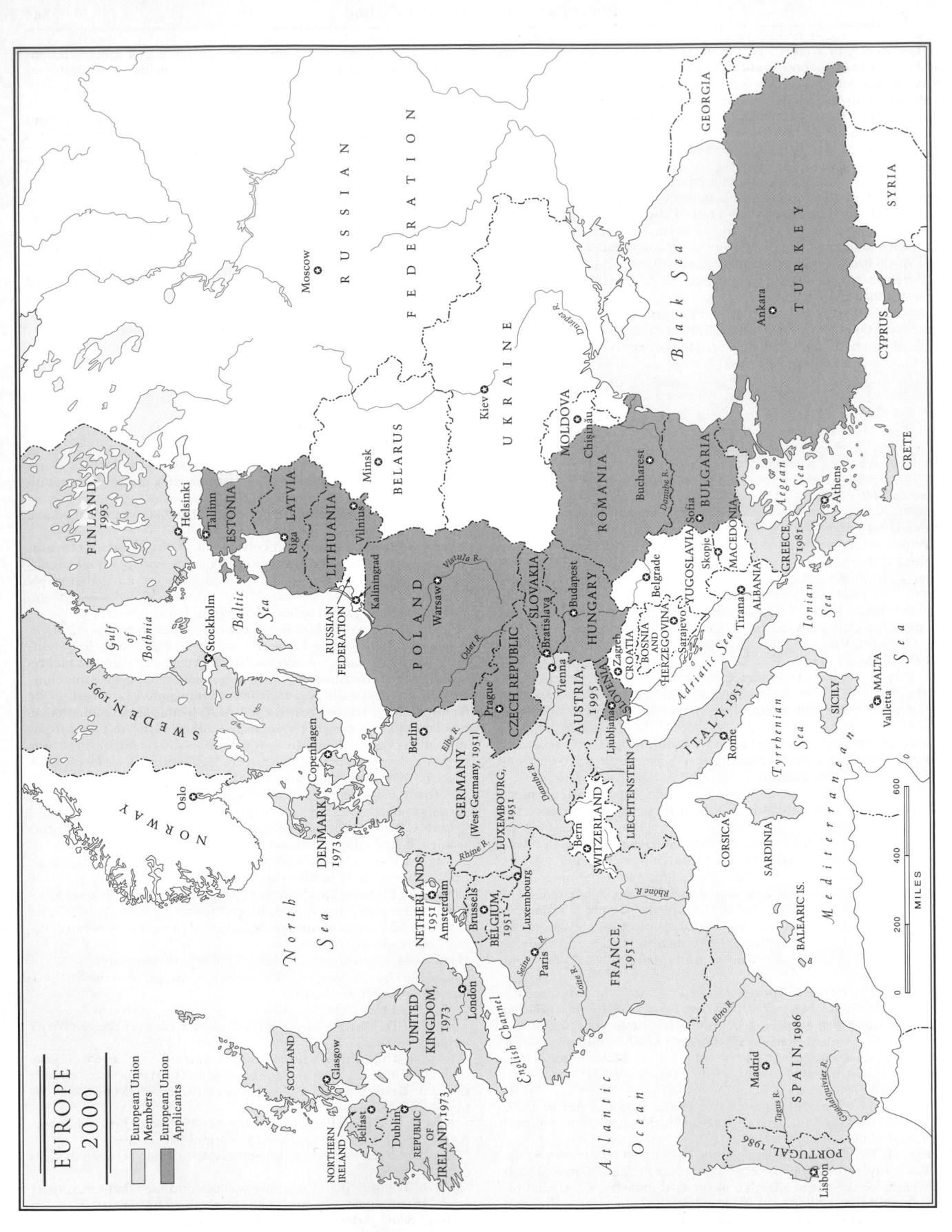

EUROPE
2000

European Union
Members

European Union
Applicants

NORWEGIAN

NORTH SEA

ATLANTIC
OCEAN

SCOTLAND
Glasgow

NORTHERN
IRELAND
Belfast
Dublin
REPUBLIC
OF
IRELAND, 1973

UNITED
KINGDOM,
1973
London

English Channel

FRANCE,
1951
Paris

Seine R.
Loire R.

SPAIN, 1986
Madrid

PORTUGAL, 1986
Lisbon
Tagus R.
Guadalquivir R.
Ebro R.

BALEARIC IS.

CORSICA

SARDINIA

Mediterranean Sea

NETHERLANDS,
1951
Amsterdam
BELGIUM,
1951
Brussels
LUXEMBOURG,
1951
Luxembourg
Rhine R.

GERMANY
(West Germany, 1951)
Berlin
Elbe R.
Rhône R.
Bern
SWITZERLAND
LIECHTENSTEIN

DENMARK,
1973
Copenhagen

Oslo
NORWAY

Stockholm
SWEDEN, 1995
Gulf of Bothnia

FINLAND
1995
Helsinki

Baltic Sea

RUSSIAN
FEDERATION
Kaliningrad

ESTONIA
Tallinn
Riga
LATVIA
LITHUANIA
Vilnius
Minsk

POLAND
Warsaw
Vistula R.
Oder R.
Prague
CZECH REPUBLIC
Danube R.
Vienna
AUSTRIA,
1995
SLOVENIA
Ljubljana
CROATIA
Zagreb
BOSNIA
AND
HERZEGOVINA
Sarajevo
ITALY, 1951
Rome
Tyrrhenian Sea
SICILY
MALTA
Valletta

SLOVAKIA
Bratislava
Budapest
HUNGARY
Belgrade
YUGOSLAVIA
Skopje
MACEDONIA
ALBANIA
Tirana
Adriatic Sea
Ionian Sea

MOSCOW

RUSSIAN
FEDERATION

BELARUS
Kiev
UKRAINE

Dnieper R.

MOLDOVA
Chişinău
ROMANIA
Bucharest
Danube R.
Sofia
BULGARIA

Black Sea

GEORGIA

TURKEY
Ankara

SYRIA

CYPRUS

CRETE
Athens
GREECE, 1981
Aegean Sea

MILES
0   200   400   600

April 2. Advertising lights went on again after a ten-year restriction in the use of electrical energy for such purposes.

June–July. A major **dock strike,** which effectively closed the nation's ports, led to the proclamation of a state of emergency before a settlement was finally reached.

July 27. The de Haviland Comet, world's **first jet airliner,** made its premiere flight from Hatfield, England.

Sept. 18. To meet the rapid decline of British exports and to remedy the growing dollar deficit, the **British government devalued the pound sterling** from $4.03 to $2.80. This set in motion a widespread devaluation of other European currencies.

Nov. 24. The **Iron and Steel Bill,** calling for the nationalization of these key industries, passed both houses of Parliament, after raising considerable opposition. It was not to go into effect until 1951.

Dec. 16. Despite opposition from the House of Lords, the **Parliament Bill,** restricting the powers of the upper house to veto legislation, was enacted into law.

1950, Feb. 13. PARLIAMENTARY ELECTIONS reduced the Labour Party's majority from a high of 148 in 1945 to 7 in 1950. The final count gave Labour 315 seats, the Conservatives and their allies 297, and the Liberals 9. The government of Prime Minister **Clement Atlee** remained in office, although its position was precarious. As a result, few controversial measures were introduced into Parliament.

April 19–May 1. London dock workers went on strike.

June 25. The outbreak of **war in Korea** found Great Britain on the side of the United States and the United Nations against the North Koreans. It subsequently contributed naval and ground forces to the UN cause and embarked on increased defense production and an expansion of the armed services.

Nov. 28. The **Columbo Plan** to aid India, Pakistan, Ceylon, Sarawak, and Borneo was presented at the British Commonwealth meetings; it envisaged an 8-billion-pound economic program over six years, from July 1, 1951.

Dec. 13. It was announced that **Marshall Plan aid to the United Kingdom** would be suspended on Jan. 1, 1951.

1951, Jan. 29. Prime Minister Atlee announced a **three-year armament program,** to cost 4.7 billion pounds.

March 9. Herbert Morrison succeeded **Ernest Bevin** as foreign secretary.

April 22. Aneurin Bevan, labour minister since Jan. 17, resigned in protest against a decision to give defense priority over social service needs.

June 26. Defense ministers of the British Commonwealth discussed the **situation in the Middle East.** The Egyptian foreign minister announced (Aug. 6) that the **Anglo-Egyptian Treaty of 1936 would be abrogated** (Oct. 27).

Sept. 12. After the failure of earlier discussions (Aug. 22), the **Iranian government sent an ultimatum to Great Britain** and subsequently **occupied Abadan** (Sept. 27) (p. 974). The British appealed to the UN Security Council without result and then completed the evacuation of Abadan (Oct. 4).

Oct. 25. After six years in power, the **Labour Party was defeated** in a general election, and the **Conservatives** won a majority of 16 seats in the House of Commons. WINSTON CHURCHILL BECAME PRIME MINISTER and minister of defense (Oct. 27), with **Anthony Eden as foreign secretary** and **Richard Austen Butler** as chancellor of the exchequer. Most of the social programs introduced by the Labour government remained in place.

Dec. 10. The government of **Iran** agreed to submit its oil dispute with Britain to the **International Court of Justice.**

1952. Attendance at football (soccer) games declined in favor of television viewing.

Feb. 6. KING GEORGE VI DIED. His daughter **Elizabeth,** who was on a visit to East Africa, flew back to take the oath as **QUEEN ELIZABETH II** (Feb. 8).

Feb. 26. Churchill announced that the British had produced an **atom bomb.** It was tested successfully in the Monte Belo Islands near Australia (Oct. 2). Britain joined the U.S. and the USSR, becoming the **world's third atomic power.**

1953, Jan. 5–9. On a visit to Washington and New York, **Churchill** conferred with **President Harry Truman** and **President-elect Dwight Ei-** senhower on European defense, the Korean War, and Anglo-American relations. Two months later (Mar. 4–7) **Foreign Secretary Eden** visited Washington to discuss U.S. **air bases** in Britain, British relations with **Iran,** and other problems.

May. Road transport and the steel industry were denationalized.

June 2. Coronation of Elizabeth II.

Dec. 5. The governments of **Great Britain** and **Iran** announced that they would renew diplomatic relations and seek a negotiated settlement of their **dispute over Iranian oil.**

1954, July 28. The British government offered **Cyprus limited self-government** but refused to consider a change in its sovereignty.

Oct. Rationing finally ended.

1955, April 5. CHURCHILL RESIGNED for reasons of age and health; **Sir Anthony Eden,** former secretary for foreign affairs, succeeded him.

May 26. A national election returned a **Conservative government** to power with a **majority of 67** seats in the House of Commons.

June 15. Great Britain and the United States concluded an agreement in Washington to cooperate **in the peaceful use of nuclear power.**

Oct. The **London Clean Air Act** banned the burning of untreated coal. The new law was aimed at preventing a recurrence of the "killer smog" of 1952 and saving the estimated $4.5 million dollars spent annually to repair damage and clean up the effects of soot raining down on the city.

Dec. 7. Hugh Gaitskell replaced **Clement R. Atlee** as leader of the **Labour Party.**

1956, April. First protest march against atomic weapons research, at Aldermaston.

July 26. President Gamal Abdel Nasser of Egypt announced that the **Suez Canal would be "nationalized."** This threat to British communications with the East produced a critical situation in which the cabinet considered **military intervention.**

Aug. 20. The **first turbine using nuclear fuel to produce electricity** went into operation at Calder Hall. In addition to generating some 90,000 kilowatts of power, the facility was also designed to manufacture plutonium for military purposes.

Oct. 30. Following the Israeli attack on Egypt (Oct. 29), **Britain and France invaded the Suez** (p. 966).

Dec. 17. Petrol (gasoline) rationing went into effect as a result of the **Suez crisis.**

1957, Jan. 9. Discredited by the failure of his policy in the Suez Canal crisis, **Eden resigned** and was replaced by **Harold Macmillan** (Jan. 10).

March 21–24. To mend the strain in Anglo-American relations that resulted from the Suez debacle and other disagreements, Prime Minister Macmillan and Foreign Secretary Selwyn Lloyd conferred with U.S. president Eisenhower and Secretary of State John Foster Dulles in Bermuda. The British announced their intention to reduce their armed forces and rely on greater mechanization. The United States promised to supply them with intermediate-range guided missiles.

April 11. An **agreement was made with Singapore,** that it would attain internal self-government on Jan. 1, 1958.

May 15. British scientists exploded a **hydrogen bomb** at Christmas Island in the Pacific Ocean. Further tests were carried out on May 31 and June 19, and in Australia (Sept. 14–Oct. 9).

June 6. The government decontrolled most rents, despite opposition from the Labour Party.

Sept. A report issued by the **Committee on Homosexual Offences and Prostitution** recommended abolishing punitive laws against homosexuality "between consenting adults in private." **The Church of England** supported the recommendations.

Oct. 23–25. Macmillan and Lloyd visited Washington to discuss the new situation created by the Russian success in putting a manned space vehicle, *Sputnik I,* into orbit. The conferees arrived at a Declaration of Common Purpose.

1958, Feb. 22. The United States agreed to supply Britain with 60 Thor missiles carrying atomic weapons.

Feb. The **Campaign for Nuclear Disarmament** was founded by Bertrand Russell and (Anglican) Canon Collins.

Aug. 4. An agreement for Anglo-American **cooperation on nuclear defense** projects went into effect.

1959, May 24. An Anglo-Russian trade agreement, to last five years, was signed in Moscow.

1960, Nov. 1. Macmillan announced that Britain had agreed to allow the United States to use Holy Loch on the Firth of Clyde as a base for **nuclear-powered and nuclear-armed submarines.**

Nov. 4. Hugh Gaitskell retained his leadership of the **Labour Party** over an opposition that favored unilateral nuclear disarmament.

1961, Feb. 2. Forty thousand persons petitioned Parliament, protesting British possession of nuclear weapons.

July 25. Selwyn Lloyd, chancellor of the exchequer, introduced his **austerity program** to combat excess of imports over exports. The plan included a wage freeze and an increase in bank rates from 5 to 7 percent.

Aug. 10. The British government formally **applied for membership in the Common Market** after the House of Commons approved the move by a vote of 313 to 5 (Aug. 3).

1962, Dec. 21. Prime Minister Macmillan and President John F. Kennedy, at the end of a four-day meeting in the Bahamas, announced plans to replace Britain's Skybolt missiles project with U.S. Polaris missiles.

1963. First big hit song for the **Beatles:** "I Want to Hold Your Hand." The musical group from Liverpool went on to become a major influence on the development of popular music and youth culture.

Jan. 29. Britain's entry into the Common Market was vetoed by France at a Brussels meeting (p. 840). The French were suspicious of British good faith, including its "special relationship" with the United States.

Feb. 14. The Labour Party elected Harold Wilson as leader, succeeding Hugh Gaitskell, who had died on Jan. 18.

June 5. John Profumo resigned as secretary for war, after admitting that he had lied (Mar. 22) in his denial of any impropriety with Christine Keeler. One of a recurrent series of sex scandals affecting postwar British politics.

July 31. A bill permitting peers to disclaim their titles and relinquish membership in the House of Lords went into effect.

Aug. 10. Britain again applied for **membership in the Common Market.**

Oct. 19. PRIME MINISTER MACMILLAN RESIGNED because of ill health. **Sir Alec Douglas-Home** (formerly the earl of Home) was named to succeed him.

1964, Feb. 13. The government reported its decision to maintain an independent nuclear deterrent, and announced a record peacetime $5.5 billion defense budget.

April 1. The government created a new ministry of education and science to replace previous separate ministries.

Oct. 15. In general elections the **Labour Party** won a four-seat majority in the House of Commons. Sir Douglas-Home resigned and (James) **Harold Wilson** became prime minister and formed a new cabinet.

Nov. 19. Establishment of a secretary of state for Wales.

1965. The **Rolling Stones** had their first international hit, "(I Can't Get No) Satisfaction." The band reflected and encouraged a growing rebelliousness in international youth culture.

Jan. 24. Death of Sir Winston Churchill after a stroke. Impressive state funeral Jan. 30.

April. Corporation tax introduced.

May 6. Decision of the Labour government to nationalize 85 to 90 percent of the **steel industry.**

July 28. Edward Heath elected leader of the Conservative Party, to succeed Sir Alec Douglas-Home (resigned July 22).

Dec. Mary Quant, owner of a bazaar in Chelsea, won international notoriety for her design of **the miniskirt,** which came to six inches above the knee. Adaptations of Quant's design changed women's fashion profoundly.

1966. First knighthood granted to a professional footballer, a sign of the growing acceptance of popular culture.

Feb. 22. The Labour government's decision to **reduce defense expenditures** resulted in the resignation of the secretary for the navy and the first sea lord in protest against the decision to abandon aircraft carriers as the main strike force and to put future emphasis on short-based F111A planes, to be purchased from the United States.

March 23. Visit of the archbishop of Canterbury, Arthur M. Ramsey, **to Pope Paul VI.** They agreed on efforts to bring the Anglican and Roman Catholic churches together.

March 31. Elections greatly strengthened the position of the Labour Party, which thenceforth had a majority of 97 in the house and was freer to embark on economic planning and the development of social services.

May 16–July 1. Strike of the National Union of Seamen, the most serious labor dispute since 1926. The government declared a state of emergency (May 23), but finally agreed to a compromise settlement.

July 1. Introduction of a **freeze on wages, salaries, and prices** for one year, in an effort to check inflation and improve the balance-of-payments situation.

July 14. A Welsh nationalist for the first time defeated all other candidates in a by-election, reflecting the growing spirit of nationalism in both Wales and Scotland.

July 31. Abolition of the Colonial Office, whose responsibilities for the remaining dependencies were to be taken over by the Commonwealth Office.

Oct. 5. The Gibraltar issue became acute when the Spanish government closed the customs facilities at La Linea and rejected a British offer to submit the question of sovereignty to the International Court of Justice (Dec. 14) (p. 864).

1967. Abortion laws liberalized (among the earliest in Europe). The 1967 Abortion Act authorized abortions up to the twenty-eighth week of pregnancy (in certain special cases) and provided for abortion under the National Health Service.

Feb. 6–13. Soviet Premier Aleksey Kosygin visited Britain. Discussions of a possible British-Soviet treaty of friendship and cooperation were hampered by continued differences over American policy in Vietnam.

April 10–15. The Conservatives won a large majority of the seats on the Great London Council, reflecting rapidly developing dissatisfaction with the Labour Party.

May 11. Formal application of the British government for membership in the **European Common Market** again vetoed by French president Charles de Gaulle (May 16).

Nov. 18. Devaluation of the pound sterling, from $2.80 to $2.40, in the hope of checking the decline in balance of payments.

1968, Jan. 16. Large cuts in public expenditures were announced, including government **plans for accelerated withdrawal of military forces east of Suez.**

March 1. The Commonwealth Immigrants Act drastically restricted the immigration of Asians holding British citizenship—applying chiefly to 200,000 Asians from Kenya being expelled by the Kenyan government.

March 17. A student demonstration held in London against the Vietnam War led to mob violence.

1968. Immigration levels to Great Britain had risen sharply since 1948. Between 1951 and 1961, the enumerated population that was of West Indian, Indian, Pakistani, and Far Eastern origin rose from 63,100 to 297,700. Though immigration laws were tightened in 1962, problems relating to the integration of immigrant populations into British society continued. On April 23, 1968, Parliament passed the **Race Relations Act** prohibiting discrimination in employment, housing, and such on the basis of color, race, or national origin. Still, growing popular resentment at the continued **influx of immigrants to Great Britain** resulted in protests and demonstrations.

April 23. First **decimal coinage** went into circulation as legal tender; full changeover to decimal currency was set to take place on Feb. 15, 1971 (Decimal Day, or "D-Day").

Oct. 5. The growing **crisis in Northern Ireland** was marked by civil rights riots in Londonderry, where the Catholic majority claimed that rank discrimination was practiced by the Protestant-controlled local government in matters of employment, housing, and the like. Tension had been rising since the summer of 1966, when the **Reverend Ian Paisley** and his ultra-Protestant **Free Presbyterian Church** had denounced any concessions to Roman Catholics and staged a riot in Belfast.

Oct. 16. The **Commonwealth Office** was merged with the Foreign Office to form the new **Foreign and Commonwealth Office.**

Oct. 27. A large-scale and mostly peaceful demonstration against the Vietnam War was held in London; it represented one of a series of **student demonstrations** protesting U.S. policy in Southeast Asia as well as problems in the university system.

Nov. 22. The Belfast government's program of moderate reforms again aroused the opposition of Paisley and his extremists.

1969, Jan. 1. In Northern Ireland, Catholic students held a 73-mile civil rights march from Belfast to Londonderry to protest discrimination. They were attacked by Protestant demonstrators.

Jan. 7–15. At a meeting of Commonwealth prime ministers in London, there were sharp discussions of British immigration restrictions, as well as of the Rhodesian and Nigerian situations.

Jan. 17. A new **Trade Union Bill** was passed, designed to check wildcat strikes. The government proposed a Permanent Commission on Industrial Relations but, after long and acrimonious discussions, yielded to the pressure from the trade unions and abandoned the bill (June 18) in return for the Trade Union General Council's promise to set up machinery to forestall and control strikes.

Jan. 27. The Protestant leader **Paisley** was sentenced to three month's imprisonment for actions against Catholics in Northern Ireland.

Feb. 27. Victory of the Unionists in **Northern Ireland** (the ruling party since 1921; advocates of the Union of Ireland and Great Britain), but there was a heavy vote for Paisley and the Protestant extremists.

April. Franchise extended to 18-year-olds.

April 20. Major **religious conflicts in Belfast and Londonderry,** following the election to parliament of **Bernadette Devlin,** a fiery 22-year-old Catholic leader. On the request of the Belfast government, the British government decided to send troops to help guard key utilities.

April 23. The Northern Ireland government accepted the demand for universal adult suffrage in local elections, thus breaking the power of Protestant minorities in some localities.

April 28. Resignation of Prime Minister Terence O'Neill of Northern Ireland, who was succeeded (May 1) by **Major James Chichester-Clark.**

Aug. 2–4. Huge **riots in Belfast,** the worst in 30 years, were followed by similar disturbances in Londonderry and other towns. Rejecting Ireland's peace-force bid, **British troops took control over Ulster security** and urged reforms.

Aug. 18. Conferences held between British prime minister Wilson and Prime Minister Chichester-Clark of Northern Ireland. It was decided that a British commander should assume control of security and that the largely Protestant part-time security force should be phased out. The British government was to have a voice in Northern Ireland's affairs and press for further reforms.

Dec. 18. The British Parliament voted to **abolish the death penalty.**

Dec. 22. Bernadette Devlin was convicted of incitement to riot and sentenced to six months in prison.

1970. The **feminist movement** in Great Britain gained momentum in the 1970s. Serving as impetus for its organization were the anti-Vietnam campaigns, the campaign for nuclear disarmament, and, to some extent, the feminist movement in America. In 1970 the British national women's liberation movement held its **first conference** at Oxford. The participants called on the government to provide 24-hour-a-day child care, equal pay and equal education for women, and free contraception and abortion on demand. Although the women's movement suffered from a conflict between its radical and socialist factions, it succeeded during the decade in exerting pressure for the passage of a series of laws (beginning with the **Equal Pay Act of 1970**) designed to guarantee women's rights and to improve the conditions under which women lived, worked, and bore children.

June. Britain reapplied for membership in the **Common Market.**

June 18. DEFEAT OF THE LABOUR PARTY in general elections. The Conservatives won a majority of 30 in the House of Commons, and **Edward Heath became prime minister,** with Sir Alec Douglas-Home as foreign secretary.

June 26–28. Further violent outbreaks between Protestants and Catholics in **Northern Ireland** resulted in the dispatch of more British forces. These disturbances frequently involved loss of life as well as widespread destruction of property.

1971, Sept. 24. Britain expelled 105 Soviet officials, the single largest strike ever made against Soviet spies.

Oct. 28. The House of Commons ended a 14 year debate and **approved membership in the European Common Market.** Britain formally entered the market on Jan. 1, 1973.

1972, Jan.–March. On **Jan. 30,** 13 unarmed civilians were shot in Belfast as British troops clashed with Catholic demonstrators. Retaliation

against British forces followed. In Dublin, the British embassy was razed with fire bombs. In Parliament, Home Secretary **Reginald Maudlin** was struck by parliament member Devlin of Northern Ireland.

March 30. Britain ended 51 years of semi-autonomous rule by the Ulster government of Northern Ireland and appointed **William Whitelaw** to the new post of **Secretary of State for Northern Ireland.** Catholic moderates welcomed this move and Protestant extremists opposed it.

1973, March 8. A heavy Protestant vote and a Catholic boycott resulted in a "yes" vote in a referendum on whether Ulster should remain part of the UK. On March 20 the British government released a **white paper on constitutional proposals for Northern Ireland,** including a more just representation for Catholics in government and measures for reducing anti-Catholic discrimination. Catholic moderates supported the proposals, and Protestants and extremists in the Irish Republican Army (IRA) opposed them.

Nov. 21. William Whitelaw and Northern Ireland's political leaders reached a **compromise plan for a coalition government** in which Protestants and Catholics would share power. This executive body was to control all affairs of Northern Ireland except security, justice, foreign relations, and some financial matters.

1974, March 4. Prime Minister Heath failed to form a coalition government with the Liberal Party, leaving **Labour Party leader Harold Wilson** to form the nation's **first minority cabinet in 45 years.**

May 29. Following the collapse of the Protestant-Catholic coalition, the British government resumed direct rule in **Northern Ireland.** Violence continued, despite the arrival of more British forces.

Oct. In general parliamentary elections, Labour won 319 seats, Conservatives 277, Liberals 13, and others 26.

Nov. 29. The House of Commons approved emergency legislation to **outlaw the IRA** and to give police absolute powers of arrest and detention as well as stricter control over travel between England and Ireland.

1975, Spring. Formation of the **National Abortion Campaign,** an organization charged with defending the 1967 Abortion Act. Also in 1975, the **women's movement scored a series of victories** with the enactment of important legislation affecting women, including the **Sex Discrimination Act,** which established an **Equal Opportunities Commission** to enforce new laws, and the **Employment Protection Act,** which gave women a statutory right to paid maternity leave, protection from unfair dismissal during pregnancy, and the right to regain their job up to 29 weeks after giving birth. These gains were followed in 1976 by the **Domestic Violence Act,** which strengthened the procedures by which women could obtain an injunction to restrain a violent husband.

July. Unemployment reached 1 million.

1976, March. Faced with severe inflation, which under his administration had reached an unprecedented 17 percent, **Prime Minister Harold Wilson resigned.** He was replaced the following month by his former foreign secretary **James Callaghan.**

1977, March. Liberals entered into a parliamentary coalition with the Labour Party to keep Callaghan's government in power.

May 7–8. Leaders of the world's seven major industrialized nations, the Group of Seven (G-7) (p. 817) held an economic summit conference in London to coordinate policies on global inflation and recession and to create a multibillion-dollar cushion, through the International Monetary Fund, against trade deficits caused by rising oil prices.

1978–79. Winter of discontent: six weeks of widespread labor strikes led to **defeat of Callaghan's Labour government in the May 1979 general elections.**

1979, May 3. Margaret Thatcher, leader of the Conservative Party, became the **first female prime minister** in the history of England and Europe. As prime minister (until 1990), Thatcher initiated radical conservative policies and became one of the most influential political figures of the late twentieth century. **"Thatcherism,"** as her policies were dubbed, represented a sharp move away from Britain's mixed economy of private capitalism and government planning. It was also an effort to curtail the welfare state, and included cuts in government spending, the sale of nationalized industries, a curb on the power of trade unions, and strict monetarist policies. Though Thatcher succeeded in bringing the inflation rate down to 5 percent in her first term, unemployment rose to nearly 14 percent. In foreign policy, Thatcher was both vehemently anticommunist and nationalistic. She was highly critical of the EC but also displayed a streak of pragmatism—evident, for example, in the fact that she was the first Western leader to meet with Soviet president Mikhail Gorbachev.

1980s. Recurrent, sometimes vicious **riots by spectators at professional football matches.**

1980, Oct. The number of unemployed in England rose to more than 2 million.

1981, April. Race riots in South London resulted in 191 arrests.

May 5. In Belfast's Maze Prison, IRA gunman and member of Parliament **Bobby Sands died as a result of a hunger strike;** nine other fasters died later.

Oct. 24. In one of a series of mass demonstrations occurring across Europe, 50,000 marched for nuclear disarmament in London.

1982, Feb. 25. The European Court of Human Rights ruled that British parents might refuse to allow corporal punishment of their children in public schools.

April–June. The Falkland Islands/Malvinas War. Although Britain and Argentina reached agreement on **opening the Falkland Islands to sea and air links** on July 1, 1971, Argentine forces invaded the islands on April 2 (p. 935). Because the British had claimed the Falklands as a colony for 150 years, they responded by sending troops there on May 21, securing a surrender from Argentine forces by June 4.

1983, June. In a **general election,** the Labour Party received only 28 percent of the vote, its worst showing since 1918. The Social Democratic–Liberal Alliance received 26 percent. **Conservatives maintained their majority in the House of Commons, and Margaret Thatcher won re-election as prime minister.**

Nov. First cruise nuclear missiles arrived at Greenham Common air base, Berkshire.

Dec. Thirty thousand women demonstrated against the nuclear presence at Greenham Common.

1984, July 26. Trade Union Bill was enacted to ban union membership at government communications headquarters.

Oct. A miners' strike, begun in February 1981, was spread throughout the entire British coal industry by the National Union of Mineworkers, in opposition to pit closures. Thatcher's hard line against the miners added to bitterness and social, economic, and political polarization in British society.

Oct. 12. In an attempt to assassinate Thatcher and her cabinet members, the **IRA** bombed the Grand Hotel in Brighton.

1985, Nov. 15. Britain and Ireland signed the **Anglo-Irish Agreement (Hillsborough Accord),** a framework for resolving the problem of Northern Ireland. The agreement affirmed that any change in the status of Northern Ireland should have the consent of the majority of the people of Northern Ireland.

1987, June–Sept. The **Social Democratic Party** (founded in 1981 after a Labour Party split) and the **Liberal Party merged** into the **Liberal Democratic Party.**

July 29. Ratification of the **Channel Tunnel Treaty** between the United Kingdom and France.

1990, March–April. The unpopular community charge (poll tax) replaced property taxes ("rates") in England and Wales, beginning April 1, leading to protests and riots. The popular backlash against this new system of taxation represented a major political setback for the Thatcher government.

Oct. 5. Another setback for the Thatcher government occurred when Sir Geoffrey Howe, longtime Thatcher supporter and senior government official, resigned because Thatcher had publicly denounced the plan for monetary integration with Europe, a plan that all other EC nations and many conservatives supported.

Nov. 28. Thatcher resigned over domestic and European monetary issues. Her chancellor of the exchequer and protégé, **John Major, succeeded** her as Conservative Party leader and as prime minister. While Thatcher's policies had brought about a rise in the standard of living for many in Britain, they had also brought higher unemployment, recurring inflation, and social unrest in many inner cities.

1991, April. The **Conservative Party,** led by Prime Minister **Major,** won **a fourth consecutive term of office,** the first such instance since the early 19th century.

1992, April 10. Three people were killed and more than 90 injured in an explosion in London's financial district. The IRA claimed responsibility.

July 18. John Smith was elected **leader of the Labour Party** to replace Neil Kinnock, who had resigned in April.

Nov. 11. The General Synod of the **Church of England** approved a measure to permit the ordination of women priests.

Dec. 21. The High Court ruled that the government's decision of Oct. 13 to close ten pits was illegal and had "unlawfully" ignored the right of mineworkers and trade unions to be consulted.

1993, Feb. 11. Prime Minister Major announced to the House of Commons that the **Queen would be charged personal income taxes and capital gains taxes.**

March 8. Prime Minister Major suffered a political setback when Labour and Liberal Democrat members of Parliament won approval of an amendment to the bill to ratify the Maastricht Treaty on European Union (p. 843). The amendment had the result of slowing down approval of the treaty.

March 29. John Treshman and his Rescue America group, plus its British supporters, organized a **series of anti-abortion protests in London and Birmingham,** resulting in 21 arrests.

May 17. In the most conflictive labor dispute since the 1981–85 miners' strike, 38 demonstrators were arrested outside the U.S.-owned Timex Electronics plant in Dundee. Timex staff had been dismissed after striking on Jan. 29 and had been replaced by nonunion employees. On May 28, the International Labor Organization called for the United Kingdom to extend explicit protection against the blacklisting of any worker.

May 26. The High Court ruled that British Coal could in fact close any of the ten pits it had attempted to shut down in October 1992. British Coal offered 14 other pits for licensing to private individuals.

June. A series of revelations about alleged improprieties in the funding of the ruling Conservative Party caused a scandal in the public media.

July 23. Prime Minister Major won a vote of confidence in the House of Commons (339 to 299) for his handling of the **Maastricht Treaty.** The vote finalized the legislative ratification after a year and a half of debate.

Aug. 8. The Home Office announced that procedures used in deportation cases that required arrests would be reviewed, as a result of the death of a 40-year-old Jamaican woman in a struggle with police officers in her home during a predawn raid.

Nov. The British government revealed that it had been engaged in secret negotiations with the IRA for several months. This was followed (Dec. 15) by a joint British-Irish offer to negotiate openly with the IRA on the status of Northern Ireland, if the IRA would agree to renounce violence.

1994, Jan. The minister for the environment, Tim Yeo, resigned because of scandal; he was replaced by Robert Atkins.

March 9–13. The **IRA launched mortar attacks at a London airport,** disrupting air traffic and constituting the most aggressive IRA action on British land since June 1993, making an imminent peace initiative appear unlikely.

Aug. 11–15. British health services came under fire for their attempted reforms. Hospital services were criticized; in particular, complaints concerned the long waits for treatment.

1995, Feb. 22. Britain and Ireland presented a framework for peace negotiations over Northern Ireland and Ulster.

Feb. 26. Barings PLC, the biggest bank in Britain, declared bankruptcy due to the actions of a trader who had lost a great deal of money making unauthorized transactions in Singapore.

June. John Major resigned as leader of the incumbent Conservative Party and called for elections because of doubts regarding his leadership capabilities by a more right-wing group called the Euroskeptics. On July 4 he won the leadership back.

1996, Feb. 9. An IRA bomb killed 2 and injured 100 in London. John Major broke off contact with Sinn Fein and demanded a cease-fire.

1997, Feb. 23. Researchers in Scotland reported having **cloned an adult sheep,** something that was previously thought impossible. This report sparked an international debate on the possibility and desirability of human cloning.

May 1. After 18 years of conservative rule, the Labour Party won

British elections. Its leader, Tony Blair, became the new prime minister.

May 6. In an unprecedented move, the Labour Party **granted the Bank of England autonomy in establishing interest rates.**

May 16. Tony Blair dropped the ban on British government contact with Sinn Fein.

Sept. 15. Sinn Fein participated in Northern Ireland peace talks for the first time.

Sept. 11. In a referendum, **Scotland voters approved plans to form their own parliament** to control issues of local and regional concern.

1998, Oct. 16–2000, March. In London, **British police arrested Gen. Augusto Pinochet Ugarte,** the former military dictator of Chile, after Spanish officials requested his extradition on charges of human rights abuses such as torture and genocide, allegedly committed when his military regime ruled Chile. In Oct. 1999 a court reversed an earlier ruling, saying that Pinochet could be extradited to Spain and face prosecution. However, British doctors in Jan. 2000 concluded that Pinochet was medically unfit to stand trial. By March 2000 the British authorities decided to extradite Pinochet to his home country of Chile, where he also faced numerous charges for war crimes committed during his reign.

Dec. 19. Along with the United States, Britain launched air strikes against Iraq after Saddam Hussein had permanently expelled UN arms inspectors earlier in the year. Periodic attacks on Iraqi military and arms-producing targets continued for the next two years as Iraq refused compliance with UN calls for the admittance of inspections teams into Iraq to confirm that all chemical, biological, or nuclear weapons production had ceased in the country.

1999, March 24–June 12. British diplomatic and military power played a crucial role in the NATO intervention in Kosovo, Yugoslavia. Negotiated by British forces, a peace agreement was signed on June 3; **NATO peacekeeping troops began entering Kosovo** on June 12.

May 6. After separate parliaments had been formed in Scotland and Wales, mostly due to constitutional reforms by **Prime Minister Tony Blair,** Scotland elected its parliament for the first time since 1707. The **Scottish National Party (SNP) was effectively defeated by the Labour Party** in elections. In its first year, the new legislature experienced mixed results, but many Scottish citizens hoped that giving the Parliament even more autonomy would improve its overall performance. Queen Elizabeth opened the new parliament on July 2.

July 1. Though holding fewer powers than their Scottish counterparts, **delegates in Wales opened its National Assembly,** which was planned to have a limited jurisdiction over local affairs in the Welsh region. A small step toward greater political autonomy, this was the first real self-government enjoyed by Wales in over 600 years.

July 14. The EC ended its three-year ban on British beef, which had been linked to bovine spongiform encephalopathy (BSE), commonly known as mad cow disease. This reinstatement of British beef into European markets was fraught with controversy, and key nations such as France refused to purchase British beef. As a result, economic relations between Britain and France were strained.

Dec. 2. Through hard-fought compromise between Protestant and Catholic leaders, Britain's parliament was able to officially pass political authority over Northern Ireland to the new provincial government, establishing Northern Irish home rule for the first time in several decades.

2000, Feb. 7. Britain suspended the new government in Northern Ireland after the IRA allowed the arms deadline to pass without beginning the process of removing and destroying its weapons supplies. Direct rule over Northern Irish affairs was returned to London.

Sept. World oil prices reached the high level of $35 per barrel, which prompted massive strikes on fuel providers across Europe and throughout Britain. Nearly 3,000 service stations were closed in the chaotic gridlock created by vociferous British protestations. Surprised by the situation, **Prime Minister Blair** significantly damaged his popular support by refusing to lower fuel taxes. However, emergency measures were taken to ensure that those whose lives would be at risk without the fuel, such as elderly homeowners or the hospitalized, would be supplied with sufficient gas.

b. IRELAND (EIRE)

(From p. 684)

1945, June 4. Elections in Northern Ireland favored continued Irish partition.

June 25. President Douglas Hyde retired and **Seán T. O'Kelly became second president of Eire.**

1948, Feb. 4. In a general election, de Valera's Fianna Fáil Party lost its majority.

Feb. 18. James A. Costello of the Fianna Fáil Party was nominated prime minister.

Dec. 21. President O'Kelly signed the Republic of Ireland Bill calling for complete independence of Ireland at an early date.

1949, Feb. 8. The Irish government declared that participation in the North Atlantic Treaty was impossible so long as Ireland remained divided.

Feb. 10. Elections in Northern Ireland showed that at least two-thirds of the population favored continued union with Great Britain.

April 18. The **REPUBLIC OF IRELAND** was officially proclaimed in Dublin on the anniversary of the Easter Rebellion of 1916. King George VI sent his good wishes.

May 17. The British House of Commons adopted the Ireland Bill, recognizing the independence of the republic but affirming the position of Northern Ireland within the United Kingdom. This provision met with protest from the Republic of Ireland.

1950, Jan. 26. Ireland concluded a treaty of friendship, commerce, and navigation with the United States.

1951, May 4. The cabinet headed by Prime Minister Costello resigned. An election (May 30) gave a majority to the Fianna Fáil Party, and a new cabinet with Eamon de Valera as prime minister came to office on June 13.

1954, May 18. After de Valera's defeat in national elections, Costello formed a coalition government.

1955, Dec. 14. Ireland admitted to the United Nations.

1959, June 17. Eamon de Valera was elected president of Ireland, resigning the post of prime minister he had earlier regained.

June 23. Deputy Prime Minister Sean Lemass was elected prime minister by the dáil (Parliament).

1960, Sept. 20. Frederick H. Boland, the representative from Ireland, was elected president of the fifteenth session of the General Assembly of the United Nations.

1961, Oct. 11. The new Parliament (chosen on Oct. 4) reelected Lemass prime minister.

1965, Jan. 14. Meeting of the prime ministers of Northern Ireland and the Irish Republic at Belfast and later (Feb. 9) at Dublin. Efforts of the two governments to improve relations, at least in the economic and cultural spheres.

March 1. State funeral for Sir Roger Casement (executed in 1916 for participation in the Easter Rebellion). His remains were repatriated by the British government.

1967, Dec. 11. Visit of Prime Minister John Lynch to Northern Ireland for further discussions on trade, tourism, and the like. The visit was returned by **Prime Minister Terence O'Neill** of Northern Ireland in Jan. 1968.

1969, Aug.–1970, June. Different views of policy toward Northern Ireland resulted in **resignations from government and expulsions from Fianna Fáil Party.** Moderate nationalist groups formed a **Social Democratic and Labor Party.**

1970, Oct. 23. Charles Haughey, former finance minster of the Irish Republic, was acquitted of secret dealings to supply arms to the Catholics of Northern Ireland. Haughey was an **opponent of Prime Minister Lynch** and of the policy of peaceful rapprochement between the two Irelands.

Dec. 4. The Irish government threatened to invoke the Offenses Against the State Act if necessary to forestall plans of radicals and nationalist extremists to assassinate or kidnap officials to force the reunion of the two Irelands. The activities of the outlawed Irish Republican Army (IRA) in Northern Ireland were virtually an open secret.

1972, Sept. Ireland officially entered the European Community.

Dec. 1. The Irish Parliament voted for a bill to suppress the outlawed IRA.

Dec. 7. Referenda favored changing the voting age from 21 to 18, and removing from the constitution the "special position" of the Roman Catholic Church.

1973, Sept. Ireland established formal diplomatic relations with the Soviet Union.

1976, July 21. The British ambassador to Ireland, Christopher Ewart-Biggs, and his secretary were killed when an IRA land mine exploded beneath their car on the outskirts of Dublin.

1979, Dec. 7 and 11. Charles Haughey was elected **leader of Fianna Fáil Party and prime minister** after **Jack Lynch** announced his resignation from both positions on Dec. 5.

1983, Sept. 7. National referendum approved constitutional amendment on banning abortion in the Republic of Ireland.

1985, Nov. The two largest unionist parties in Northern Ireland, the **Official Unionist Party** and the **Democratic Unionist Party,** strongly **denounced** the **Hillsborough Agreement.** This agreement, signed Nov. 15 between Britain and Ireland, affirmed that no change be made in the status of Northern Ireland without majority consent while setting up an Anglo-Irish Intergovernmental Council to discuss political and security issues and cross-border cooperation. Irish nationalists also denounced the agreement, but the dáil approved it, as a step toward peace, on Nov. 21.

1986, June. With the help of a campaign by the Roman Catholic Church against a government proposal to legalize divorce, a **referendum confirmed a constitutional ban on divorce.**

1987, Nov. 8. IRA terrorism: 11 were killed and more than 60 injured in an IRA bombing in Northern Ireland when hundreds were gathering for ceremonies on Britain's Remembrance Day in Enniskillen.

1988, Dec. The Irish government settled a dispute with the UK over extradition and ratified the European Convention on Terrorism.

1990, April. A government bill proposed a formal abolition of the death penalty and a 40-year mandatory prison term.

May 17. The general synod of the Church of Ireland voted in favor of the ordination of women as priests and bishops.

Nov. President Brian Lenihan was brought down by scandal; **Mary Robinson** was elected the **first female president of Ireland.**

1991, March 14. The Irishmen serving life sentences in prison for the killing of 21 people in bomb attacks in Birmingham, England, in Nov. 1974, were released. It was the latest in a series of convictions in cases arising from the IRA's 1974 public house bombings in England that had been overturned, the Guildford Four having been freed in Oct. 1989, and the Maguire Seven in June 1990.

1992, Jan. 30. Charles Haughey announced his resignation on Feb. 6 as prime minister and leader of Fianna Fáil; former finance minister **Albert Reynolds succeeded** Haughey.

Feb. 17.–Nov. Abortion issues: the High Court in Dublin sparked a huge abortion controversy after it ruled against granting permission for a 14-year-old girl, who had become pregnant after being raped, to travel to the UK for an abortion. In November, referendums approved the right to receive information about abortion services and the right to travel to other EC states for abortions.

Nov. 5. The Fianna Fáil–Progressive Democratic coalition government, led by Prime Minister Albert Reynolds, collapsed following a no-confidence vote in the dáil. In the general elections, the Labor Party made sweeping gains.

1993, Jan. 12. Seven weeks after the general elections, the Fianna Fáil and the Labor Party formed a coalition headed by Albert Reynolds, outgoing prime minister.

March 31. Paul "Dingus" Magee, one of the IRA's best-known gunmen, was sentenced to life in prison for the murder of a special constable and the attempted murders of three other police officers in North Yorkshire, England.

May 26. The European Court of Human Rights ruled that the security situation in Northern Ireland justified UK legislation allowing the detention of terrorist suspects for up to five days without charge.

June 24. The dáil approved the legalization of homosexual acts between consenting adults over age 17.

Dec. 15. The UK and Irish prime ministers, John Major and Albert Reynolds, signed a 12-point "Downing Street Declaration" in London,

outlining general principles for holding peace talks on Northern Ireland. The initiative was described as "the first step on a road which will remove the bullet and the bomb forever from our small island" by Northern Ireland Social Democratic and Labor Party leader John Hume.

1994, Aug. 31. The IRA declared a cease-fire in Northern Ireland in hopes of advancing a more democratic peace process. On Sept. 6 Irish prime minister Albert Reynolds met with IRA leader Gerry Adams regarding the establishment of a permanent truce. On Nov. 17 Reynolds resigned because of a split within his party that posed a threat to the peace process. Conservative John Bruton was elected on Dec. 15. Bruton stated that peace in Northern Ireland was his major priority.

1996, June 10. Peace talks began in Northern Ireland; Sinn Fein, the political wing of the IRA, was excluded. A car bomb exploded on July 14 in Northern Ireland, injuring 17 and destroying a hotel after a week of violence in Ulster.

1997, June 26. Ireland elected right-winger **Bertie Ahern** as the **new prime minister.**

July 19. The IRA declared a cease-fire in Northern Ireland.

1998, Feb. 20. Sinn Fein was briefly suspended from Northern Ireland's peace talks after the British government connected the organization to two murders that had been committed earlier that month. Sinn Fein resumed its participation in the negotiations on March 23.

April 10. After some 20 months of arbitration, negotiators in Northern Ireland approved the historic **Good Friday Accord,** a peace agreement involving eight of the ten political parties in Northern Ireland. The conference was headed by former U.S. senator George Mitchell, and the team of international mediators included British prime minister Tony Blair, Irish prime minister Bertie Ahern, and U.S. president Bill Clinton. The accord established that Protestants would share political power with the minority Catholics, giving the Republic of Ireland a hand in the affairs of Northern Ireland.

May 22. The Good Friday Accord was overwhelmingly approved by referendums in the Irish Republic and in Northern Ireland.

July 12. The slaying of three Catholic boys in the town of Ballymoney during a Protestant march through Catholic neighborhoods dampened the spirit of peace that had followed the April 10th peace agreement.

Aug. 15. In the town of Omagh, 28 people died in a bomb attack that was attributed to a splinter group calling itself the Real IRA.

Sept. 14. The **Northern Ireland Assembly** met at the Stormont building in Belfast for its first working session. Four days later **Northern Ireland freed the first 24 prisoners** who were to benefit from the terms of the recent peace settlement.

Oct. Sinn Fein leader John Hume and Ulster Unionist David Trimble were awarded the 1998 Nobel Peace Prize for their efforts to find a peaceful solution to the conflict in Northern Ireland.

Dec. 18. Protestant and Catholic leaders reached an agreement on the organization and structure of the new coalition government and met to further develop the dual political authority in Northern Ireland.

1999, July 16. While Sinn Fein desired an IRA disarmament after the formation of the new government, Ulster Unionist opposition insisted that weapons removal begin before the new coalition was allowed to take power. The start of Northern Ireland's new government was thus stalled.

Nov. 27. The **Protestant Ulster Unionist Party,** headed by David Trimble, decided to allow Sinn Fein into the coalition cabinet before its IRA had begun disarming.

Dec. 2. Through hard-fought compromise between Protestant and Catholic leaders, Britain's parliament was able to officially pass political authority over Northern Ireland to the new provincial government. This established **home rule in Northern Ireland for the first time in several decades.** Two Sinn Fein leaders, Gerry Adams and Martin McGuinness, took their seats in the 12-member, four-party parliamentary body. A deadline of Jan. 31, 2000 was set for the start of the IRA disarmament.

2000, Feb. 7. Britain suspended the new government in Northern Ireland after the IRA allowed the arms deadline to pass without beginning the process of removing and destroying its weapons supplies. Direct rule over Northern Irish affairs was returned to London.

May 30. Finally able to agree on the disarmament issue, **Britain re-**

turned home rule powers to the Northern Ireland Assembly. Agreeing to "completely and verifiably put IRA arms beyond use," the organization promised to allow periodic inspections of its arms dumps by neutral third parties. Inspections began on July 26.

c. THE LOW COUNTRIES

1. BELGIUM
(From p. 685)

1944, Sept. 2. Brussels was liberated from German occupation by the 2nd British Army.

Belgium, after its liberation, was governed by coalitions of the main political parties, with **Prince Charles** as regent. Its major domestic issue was the return of **King Leopold** (deposed in 1945), which the Catholics favored and the Socialists opposed. On July 17, 1945, parliament passed a bill making Leopold's return dependent on parliamentary approval.

1946, Feb. 17. A general election gave the Catholic **Christian Socialists** the largest number of votes, but continued disagreement over the future of the monarchy prevented the formation of a coalition cabinet.

1947, March 19. Paul-Henri Spaak was able to form a coalition government of Catholics and Socialists, thus assuring greater stability in the handling of pressing economic problems.

Nov. 1. A **customs union** with Holland and Luxembourg (**Benelux**) became effective.

1948. The franchise was extended to women.

1949, June 26. In a **general election,** the Christian Socialists came within two seats of an absolute majority.

Aug. 10. Gaston Eyskens (Christian Socialist) formed a coalition cabinet with Liberal support. The Socialists refused to join.

1950, March 12. A **popular referendum** voted 57.7 percent in favor of King Leopold's return.

June 4. General elections gave the Catholics an absolute majority, thus upholding the verdict of the referendum.

June 8. The first all-Catholic government in 30 years was formed by **Jean Duvieusart.**

July 22. KING LEOPOLD RETURNED after years of exile and was greeted by violent protests from the Left, notably the Socialists. To avoid violence, Leopold decided to abdicate when his son, **Prince Baudouin,** came of age in September 1951.

Aug. 11. Prince Baudouin was invested with the royal powers as prince royal.

Aug. 18. Julien Lahaut, head of the Communist Party, was **assassinated.**

1951, July 16. LEOPOLD III ABDICATED, and his son **Baudouin** became king the following day.

1952, Jan. 9. Premier Joseph Pholien resigned, and a new cabinet, likewise **Christian Socialist** in composition, was formed (Jan. 15) under **Jean van Houtte.**

1954, April 23. After an indecisive election (April 11), a Socialist-Liberal coalition cabinet took office with **Achille van Acker.**

1958, June 1. The Christian Socialist Party won 104 out of 212 seats in the Chamber of Deputies and a Senate majority. **Gaston Eyskens** established a minority government (June 2) and a stronger Social-Liberal government Nov. 6.

1959. After years of national debate over the role of the Church in education, Parliament passed a law giving each school administrating authority (national government, commune, or church) the right to devise its own curriculum, so long as it met the minimal requirements of the ministry of education. Political propaganda and proselytizing were banned.

1960, Sept. 2. Premier Eyskens organized a new coalition cabinet to deal with the **crisis in the Congo** (p. 1066).

Nov. 1. The Benelux Economic Union Treaty, signed Feb. 3, 1958, came into force.

Dec. 20. Socialist-led strikes, centered in Liège, broke out to protest the government's austerity program, which was designed to compensate for the economic loss caused by Congolese independence.

1961, Feb. 17. Liberal members of the coalition government of Premier Eyskens **resigned** in disagreement over the application of a new economic reform measure. King Baudouin, on Feb. 20, refused to accept their resignation, but dissolved Parliament and scheduled new elections, March 26. Premier Eyskens resigned (March 27), and on April 25 **Theo Lefevre,** president of the Christian Social Party, was installed as premier and Paul-Henri Spaak as vice premier and foreign minister.

1962, Oct. 14. Demonstrations by Flemish-speaking Belgians, to protest the denial of their cultural and political equality by the French-speaking (Walloon) community, and to demand that Dutch replace French as the language of business.

1963, July 3. King Baudouin rejected Premier Lefevre's resignation, offered on July 2, following a **renewed outbreak of the Flemish-Walloon** language dispute.

On July 6 Lefevre announced a settlement of the dispute, and on July 12 the lower house of Parliament approved a **new boundary line between the Walloon and Flemish areas,** to take effect Sept. 1.

1964, April 1–18. Physicians went on strike protesting a new national health insurance law, which established a fixed low fee schedule.

Renewed agitation for the reorganization of Belgium as a federal state. Conferences of the government with representatives of both nationalities broke down over the demand of the Walloon minority for a veto over any future legislation in the field of nationality.

1966, July 11. Language riots, focusing on the insistence of the Flemings that the Walloon section of the **University of Louvain** be moved to some location on Wallonia.

1968, Feb. 7. Resignation of the Vanden Boeyants government over continued agitation on the issue of Louvain University.

March 31. In the **national elections,** the traditional parties managed to hold their own against the extremist groups, the Flemish **Volksunie** and the **Rassemblement Walloon.**

June 18. A new coalition of Center-Left parties was formed by **Gaston Eyskens,** who embarked on a program of expanded regional autonomy, especially in cultural matters, between the Flemish and the Walloon areas. The new government was committed also to a gradual division of the University of Louvain between the two nationalist factions. In an effort to diffuse the language dispute, the French-language faculties of the Catholic University of Louvain were moved to nearby French-speaking areas, but a new dispute soon arose over the allocation of university funds.

1969, May 28. A linguistic and cultural compromise reestablished French faculties at Louvain and **provided for a new Flemish Free University of Brussels.**

1970, Dec. Parliament introduced constitutional amendments (implementation of which began in July 1971) to **ease friction between the French-speaking and Flemish communities.** Bills connected with these amendments included laws on setting up and defining the powers of **cultural councils** for the two major language groups.

1973, July. Parliament passed a bill for the establishment of a **cultural council for the German-speaking community.**

1979, July–1980, July. REGIONAL DEVOLUTION AIMED AT CREATING A FEDERAL STATE. The government of Wilfried Martens introduced a three-phase plan for the devolution of extensive central government powers and the establishment of regional parliaments based on linguistic groups. In August 1980 Parliament approved **limited autonomous rule for Flanders and Wallonia.** The devolution plan, which aroused political ire and caused the collapse of Martens's government, began to be carried out in the late 1980s. The first stage of devolution took place in August 1988, when the three regions (French-speaking Wallonia, Flemish-speaking Flanders, and bilingual Brussels) were given control over their own education, economic policy and development, and public works. In January 1989 Parliament approved a second stage of devolution whereby the regions acquired financial resources. The final phase of devolution, specifying the powers of the national government, was completed in 1993.

1981, July. The voting age for parliamentary elections was lowered from 21 to 18.

Aug. 27. The government announced the **abolition of the death penalty.**

1986, July. The government approved **new restrictions on immigration,** making asylum seekers ineligible for social assistance.

1990, April 4. Parliament, during a joint session, signed the **abortion bill** into law. The new law replaced the previous law of 1867, and allowed abortion during the first 12 weeks of pregnancy for women who were deemed to be "in a state of distress."

1991, June 12. Parliament approved a **constitutional amendment allowing female members of the royal family to succeed to the throne.** The monarch would nevertheless continue to be known as the king, regardless of gender.

1993, July 14. A final vote in the Chamber of Deputies completed constitutional reform begun in 1970, as **Belgium officially became a federal state comprising three regions (Wallonia, Flanders, and bilingual Brussels) and three linguistic communities.**

The Senate also gave final approval to an environmental tax imposed from April 1994 on a range of goods, depending on the amount of pollution caused in their production.

Aug. 9. ALBERT II BECAME KING OF THE BELGIANS on the sudden death of his brother King Baudouin (July 31).

1999, Jan. 1. Along with ten other European countries, Belgium participated in the **implementation of the euro.** Joining Belgium in adopting the single European currency were Austria, France, Germany, Finland, Italy, Ireland, Luxembourg, Portugal, Spain, and the Netherlands.

May 28. A Belgian political crisis arose from a disaster within the nation's food supply. Dioxin, a cancer-causing chemical, leaked into batches of chicken feed, effectively contaminating Belgium's poultry, eggs, and dairy products. Government officials later admitted to keeping the public uninformed of the chemical leak for months after they had realized the existence of a possible public health danger. The Democrat-Socialist coalition government toppled as **Prime Minister Jean-Luc Dehaene resigned** on June 14 under the weight of the scandal.

June 13. While the ruling party's image suffered, new **prime minister Guy Verhofstadt** and his free-market Liberal Party won control over the government with a coalition of the Liberal, Socialist, and Green Parties from both the French- and Flemish-speaking regions of the country. The Flemish Christian People's Party and the French Christian Social Party were not included in the Belgian government for the first time in 41 years. This election also marked the Green Party's entry into Belgian government affairs.

2. THE KINGDOM OF THE NETHERLANDS
(From p. 686)

1945, May 3. QUEEN WILHELMINA RETURNED.

June 24. Willem Schermerhorn formed a coalition government.

1946, May 17–30. Parliamentary elections gave first place to the Catholic People's Party, with Socialist Labor running a close second. **Louis J. M. Beel** formed a new coalition cabinet.

1948, July 7–8. General elections lost the government some support, and a new coalition was formed under Labor's leader, **Willem Drees.**

Sept. 4. Queen Wilhelmina abdicated for reasons of health and was succeeded on Sept. 6 by **QUEEN JULIANA.**

1949, Aug. 3. Holland's upper chamber ratified the **North Atlantic Treaty.**

1951, Jan. 24. A proposal offered by Foreign Minister **Dirk Stikker** that the Netherlands share **Western New Guinea** with the republic of Indonesia brought on a prolonged cabinet crisis (Mar. 14).

1952, June 25–26. Elections for Parliament gave the **Labor Party** and the **Catholic Party** equal strength in the second chamber.

Sept. 1. Drees of the Labor Party formed a coalition cabinet.

1954, Aug. 10. THE UNION OF THE NETHERLANDS AND INDONESIA WAS DISSOLVED.

Dec. 15. Surinam and the Netherlands Antilles won autonomy in a statute signed by Queen Juliana.

1956, June 13. The **Labor Party** won a small margin in the second chamber in a general election.

After the longest cabinet crisis in Netherlands history, Willem Drees of the Labor Party formed **a new coalition cabinet.**

1957, Dec. 1. Netherlands citizens in Indonesia, and property owned by Netherlands nationals there, suffered because of **Indonesian indignation** over the status of **Netherlands New Guinea,** which the Dutch refused to surrender.

1958, Dec. 11. The coalition cabinet headed by Drees resigned and was succeeded (Dec. 22) by a coalition cabinet under the leadership of **Louis J. M. Beel** of the People's Party.

1959, May 19. A 68-day government crisis ended with the swearing in

of **Jan Eduard de Quay,** the new premier, and his coalition cabinet. For the first time since World War II, the Labor (Socialist) Party was excluded from the government.

1961, Jan. 2. A 12-day cabinet crisis ended when Premier Jan de Quay withdrew his resignation after Queen Juliana asked him to remain in office.

1962, Nov. 28. Queen Wilhelmina died at the age of 82.

1963, May 15. Premier de Quay's **Catholic People's Party** won the general elections to Parliament with 50 seats in the 150-member lower house. The Labor Party won 43 seats, the Protestants 26, and the Liberals 11.

May 20. Queen Juliana asked Catholic Party member **Carl P. M. Romme** to form a coalition government.

1966, June 13–15. The Netherlands, like many other countries, was confronted with serious **youth demonstrations and riots.**

1967, Feb. 15. General elections.

April 5. Petrus de Jong, of the Catholic Party, formed a new government.

1971, Jan. 19–29. The lower house of the Parliament approved a bill to reduce the voting age from 21 to 18. The age of eligibility for election to public bodies was also reduced, from 25 to 21. These provisions came into force after the 1971 general election.

1974, May. European Airbus, a French, West German, Dutch, and Spanish project, **entered into service.**

1975, Nov. 25. The Netherlands granted **Surinam independence** (p. 948), leaving the Netherlands Antilles as the only remaining possession of the once vast Dutch Empire.

1980, April 30. Beatrix was crowned Queen of the Netherlands, following the abdication of her mother, Queen Juliana.

1983, Feb. 17. Constitutional reform: citizens' basic "social rights" were **extended and redefined,** making it illegal to discriminate on the grounds of political and religious affiliations, sex, and race. Citizens were explicitly entitled to social welfare; foreigners were given voting rights in local elections. **The death penalty was abolished. Succession to the throne was to pass to the monarch's eldest child, whether male or female.**

1986, Oct. 4. The **Öostercheldedam,** the world's most advanced sea storm barrier, **was inaugurated.** In 1990, it held off the highest flood waters since 1953.

1987, April 11. Parliament approved **new restrictions on immigration** to stem a surge in the number of refugees seeking asylum.

1992, May 26. Prostitution was legalized, requiring prostitutes to register and to pay income tax and social security contributions. Prostitutes would also qualify for state benefits such as pensions and sick pay.

1993, April 24. In response to increased concern over the cost of the social security system, the government adopted a program of spending cuts, including reductions in unemployment and other benefits, a public-sector wage freeze, and increases in direct and indirect taxes.

Sept. 7. A parliamentary commission proposed radical reforms of the social security systems, replacing the concept of maximum collectivization of risks with an individual legal guarantee of minimum social protection.

Nov. 30. The upper house of Parliament approved legislation under which **euthanasia remained illegal, but doctors would not be prosecuted for administering it.**

1998, May 6. In parliamentary elections, the **Labor Party** made significant gains and retained power when the ruling coalition returned **Wim Kok** to his position as prime minister.

1999, Jan. 1. The Netherlands participated in the **implementation of the euro,** a single European currency. Ten other nations introduced the euro: Spain, Portugal, Luxembourg, Italy, Ireland, Germany, Austria, Belgium, Finland, and France.

May 19. A proposal to introduce the limited use of popular referenda for policy-making in the Netherlands induced Premier Wim Kok's entire cabinet to resign. This drastic move came after conflict flared along party lines in the government coalition, dividing the cabinet into two parts. This ended Wim Kok's government.

2000, Sept. 12. The Netherlands became the first country to legalize same-sex marriages.

Nov. 28. The lower house in the Netherlands voted in favor of legalizing euthanasia under specified conditions.

Dec. The two Libyans accused in the **1988 bombing of a Pan American aircraft during flight 103** over Lockerbie, Scotland, went on trial in the Netherlands.

3. LUXEMBOURG

1948, Jan. 1. After suffering German occupation in two world wars, the **grand duchy of Luxembourg** abandoned its policy of unarmed neutrality and joined in **a customs union with Belgium and the Netherlands.** Ten years later (Feb. 3, 1958) the accord was expanded into the **Benelux Economic Union.**

1952, July 2. Pierre Dupong organized a new cabinet.

1953, Dec. 22. On Dupong's death, his place was taken by **Joseph Bech** (Christian Social Party).

1954, May 30. The Christian Social Party won 26 seats and the socialist parties 17 seats in the 52-member Chamber of Deputies. **Bech remained in power** as head of a new coalition cabinet that took office on June 29.

1958, March 26. Bech resigned with his cabinet but became foreign minister in a new cabinet headed by **Pierre Frieden,** also of the Christian Social Party. The Frieden government resigned Dec. 10.

Dec. 18. Grand Duchess Charlotte dissolved Parliament and scheduled elections.

1959, Feb. 1. After the elections, **Pierre Werner** became premier.

1964, Nov. 12. ABDICATION OF GRAND DUCHESS CHARLOTTE in favor of her son, who ascended the throne as **Grand Duke Jean.**

1964–68, Oct. Pierre Werner continued as prime minister, supported by a coalition of the Christian and Socialist parties.

1968. A rapid increase in the number of children attending school, known as the **"Explosion Scolaire,"** sparked educational reforms.

1968, Dec. 15. Following the elections, Werner retained the premiership, but with a coalition of Christian and Democratic parties.

1972, Jan. 13. The Chamber of Deputies approved a constitutional amendment to reduce the voting age from 21 to 18 and the qualifying age for election from 25 to 21.

1974, May–June. The Christian Social Party, which had been in government since 1919, **lost power. A Liberal-Socialist coalition government was formed** under Gaston Thorn, chairman of the Democratic Party. Thorn's new government proposed the **liberalization of abortion and divorce law,** increased participation of workers in management, and the indexing of incomes to the cost of living.

1975. A slump in steelmaking led the government to encourage electronics and other industries.

1979, May 17. The Chamber of Deputies approved the **abolition of the death penalty.**

1982–83. The government announced a series of plans for the **modernization and restructuring of the Arbed Steel Concern** (Luxembourg operation). The plans included spending $500 million (U.S.) on redevelopment up to 1987, an increase in the state holding of the concern from 2 percent to 20 percent, and the reduction of the workforce to 10,500 while cutting salaries by 10 percent over a period of two years.

1992, Dec. Luxembourg was admitted as the twenty-second member of the Development Assistance Committee of the Organization for Economic Cooperation and Development.

1999, Jan. 1. Along with ten other European nations, Luxembourg participated in the implementation of the euro. Also involved were Ireland, Austria, Italy, Spain, Belgium, Portugal, Finland, Germany, the Netherlands, and France.

June 15. Grand Duke Jean asked **Premier Jean-Claude Juncker** to create a new government following the poor showing by the Socialist Party in general elections two days earlier. The Democratic Party was expected to join the Social Christians in a new coalition government.

2000, Oct. 7. After serving as head of state for 36 years, **Grand Duke Jean abdicated the throne** and was replaced by his son, **Crown Prince Henri.**

d. FRANCE

(From p. 689)

Postwar provisional government: Gen. C. de Gaulle (1945–46), F. Gouin (1946), G. Bidault (1946–47).

Fourth Republic presidents: V. Auriol (1947–53), R. Coty (1953–58).

Fifth Republic presidents: Gen. C. de Gaulle (1958–69), G. Pompidou (1969–74), A. Poher (1974, April–May, interim), V. Giscard d'Estaing (1974–81), F. Mitterrand (1981–95), J. Chirac (1995–).

1944, Aug. 23–24. German forces in Paris were compelled to capitulate as Allied armies approached and armed citizens liberated the city. The administration was turned over to **Charles de Gaulle** with the approval of the Allied commanders.

Through the 1940s and beyond, the **issue of collaboration** remained a central question in French political life. French society was divided on the degree to which those who had collaborated with the Nazis should be punished. Communists favored harsh sentences; Catholic groups advocated forgiveness in the name of national reconstruction; prominent existentialists and socialists took a more moderate approach.

The *épuration*, or **purge,** of persons known or suspected to have collaborated with the Germans began during the war itself but intensified in the immediate postwar period. Some nine thousand summary executions were carried out by the population, three-quarters of them before the Allied landing or during the fighting, the remainder occurring as a result of popular impatience with the slowness of the court system. An additional 767 executions were carried out in the years following the war by state authorities, after prosecution and conviction of the accused.

Sept. 27. The first phase of **nationalizations** designed to restore prewar levels of production in the transport, fuel, and heavy-machinery sectors of the economy began when de Gaulle's government took over the coal fields of the Nord and Pas-de-Calais departments.

Oct. 4. The French state seized control of Renault automobile factories.

Nov. 7. A **consultative National Assembly,** summoned by de Gaulle, held its first session. Municipal and departmental elections for the 89 *départements* were set for February 1945, and the franchise was extended to all citizens, male or female, older than 21.

Dec. 10. A **Franco-Soviet treaty of alliance and mutual security** was negotiated. It was to run for 20 years.

Dec. 18. Nationalization of the French merchant fleet.

1945–1950. Increasing prominence of **existentialist philosophers** and novelists, headed by Jean-Paul Sartre and Albert Camus.

Jan. 1. France joined the United Nations in full partnership three years after the Free French government in exile had offered adherence.

May 21. The governments of **Syria and Lebanon broke relations** with the French. The French denied (June 2) that they were using lend-lease equipment against the Syrians and Lebanese.

May 29. The government nationalized the Gnome et Rhône aircraft engine works and, on June 26, reorganized air transport into what would become, by 1948, Air France.

June 30. The **French Communist Party** voted for union with the Socialist Party.

Aug. 15. Henri-Phillipe Pétain, head of the **Vichy regime,** was sentenced to death for treason, but his sentence was commuted to life imprisonment. Pétain's political prestige had been on the wane since February 1942, when the Vichy regime's trials of Third Republic leaders at Riom had turned into a condemnation of military rule.

Oct. 4. The French government reorganized the various existing social security schemes into a general system and, in an Oct. 19 ordinance, formulated the principle that social security benefits should be extended to the entire population.

Oct. 9. Pierre Laval was sentenced to death for collaborating with the Germans. He was executed on Oct. 15.

Oct. 21. Elections for the constituent assembly showed a swing to the Left, the Communists receiving 152 seats, the Socialists 151, and **Mouvement Républicain Populaire (MRP),** a new Catholic party, 138.

Nov. 16. Gen. Charles de Gaulle was unanimously elected **president of the provisional government** by the Assembly and on Nov. 21 formed a cabinet of National Union.

During the fall of 1945, the French government created the **Commissariat Général du Plan (CGP)** to coordinate economic recovery and expansion. In the decades that followed, the CGP engaged in extensive central planning of the French economy. The first plan was announced in January 1946 and covered the period from 1947–52, laying emphasis on increasing output in the coal, electricity, steel, cement, tractor, and transport sectors.

The second phase of the French **nationalization** process began in mid-1945 and extended through the first half of 1946, with the aim of forcing industrial output to increase as quickly as possible. On Dec. 2, 1945, the banking and credit industries were nationalized, and the state became the sole shareholder of the Banque de France and of the four principal deposit banks. In April 1946, the state partially nationalized the insurance industry and completely nationalized gas and electric industries.

1946. The population of France in 1946 was 40 million.

Jan. 20. DE GAULLE RESIGNED abruptly because of continued leftist opposition.

Jan. 22. Socialist **Félix Gouin** was elected **president.**

May 5. A **popular referendum rejected the draft constitution** that the Assembly had approved on April 19.

June 2. Elections for a new **Constituent Assembly** resulted in a victory for the MRP, with the Communists in second and the socialists in third place.

June 19. Georges Bidault was elected **president of the provisional government.**

Aug. 22. The Constituent Assembly revised the *code de la famille* of July 29, 1939, and put into effect the present system of **family allowances,** the cornerstone of the French social security system, providing financial aid for families with numerous children.

Oct. 13. The revised **draft constitution** was **adopted** by a vote of 9,120,576 to 7,980,333, with 7,938,884 abstentions. The new constitution closely resembled that of the Third Republic, except that the Senate was replaced by the Council of the Republic (the National Assembly, also called Chamber of Deputies remained the lower house of Parliament), France's relations to her overseas possessions were revised by creating the **French Union,** and **suffrage was extended to women.**

Nov. 10. Elections for the National Assembly gave the Communists 186 seats, the MRP 166, and the Socialists 103. The resulting deadlock between communists and the MRP left a Socialist premier as the only choice.

Dec. 16. After vainly trying to form a coalition, **Léon Blum formed an all-Socialist cabinet and became prime minister.**

1947, Jan. 16. VINCENT AURIOL was elected first PRESIDENT of the FOURTH REPUBLIC. BLUM resigned as prime minister for reasons of health.

Jan. 28. Paul Ramadier became prime minister after forming a **coalition cabinet.**

March 4. An Anglo-French treaty of alliance was signed at Dunkirk.

April 14. Gen. de Gaulle assumed control of the nationwide **Rassemblement du Peuple Français** (Rally of the French People, RPF) to rally noncommunists to the cause of unity and reform.

May 9. The growing split between Communist and other members of the government, increased by economic difficulties and a wave of strikes, led to the exclusion of the **five Communist ministers from the cabinet.** An unbalanced budget, a poor harvest, and the refusal of many peasants to deliver their grain further aggravated the situation in the summer and early fall.

Oct. 19–26. De Gaulle's RPF emerged as the strongest group in the **municipal elections,** followed by the Communists. In the face of this growing extremism, the government and middle parties decided to cooperate and created a new **Third Force.**

Nov. A **series of strikes,** sparked by the postwar economic situation and affecting nearly two million workers, was overcome by firm governmental action and a growing rift among workers over the Communist-dominated leadership of the union **Confédération Générale du Travail (CGT).** The noncommunist members of the executive committee, on Dec. 19, seceded and formed the Force Ouvrière as a socialist union.

Nov. 13. Nobel Prize for literature awarded to André Gide.

Nov. 19. At the height of the crisis resulting from the strike, **Ramadier resigned as prime minister.**

1947, Nov. 23–1948, July 19. The cabinet of Robert Schuman, supported by a Third Force coalition of Socialists, MRP, and Radicals. After a brief period of economic stability, a renewed rise in prices and corresponding demands for higher wages temporarily deprived the government of Socialist support and thus led to its fall. **André Marie and Schuman both tried unsuccessfully to form a lasting cabinet.**

1948, Sept. 10. The Radical Party leader **Henri Queuille** formed a government, with Schuman as foreign minister.

Oct.–Nov. To exploit the country's economic difficulties, the CGT initiated another **wave of strikes.** Its cause was weakened however, as the political, pro-Communist motivation of the strikes became obvious and the government took strong countermeasures.

Nov. 7. Elections to the Council of the Republic continued the swing to the Right, as de Gaulle's RPF gained the largest number of seats.

1949. Publication of **Simone de Beauvoir's** *The Second Sex,* in which women's social subjugation is credited to patriarchal rather than biological or psychological structures. Her book became one of the seminal treatises of the modern feminist movement.

Feb. 22. Communist leader **Maurice Thorez** stated that French Communists would refuse to defend France against a Soviet army.

Oct. 5. Economic difficulties led to the **resignation of Henri Queuille.** Jules Moch and René Mayer tried unsuccessfully to form a cabinet.

Oct. 28. The Assembly approved a coalition under **Georges Bidault.**

Nov. 3. French forces withdrew from the northern border of Indochina (p. 1036).

1950. The French inaugurated Le Mistral, a new luxury electric train line linking Paris and Nice. Le Mistral marked the beginning of French leadership in railway technology and investment in the postwar world.

The **birth rate** increased markedly between 1946 and 1950, to 20.9 per 1,000 from the 14.9 per 1,000 rate of the 1935–1939 period.

March 8. The Chamber of Deputies adopted a strict **antisabotage bill,** primarily directed against Communist-inspired activities.

June 24. The **Bidault government** was **defeated,** and was followed by a short-lived (June 30–July 13) cabinet under Henri Queuille.

July 11. René Pleven succeeded in forming a coalition based on economic compromise with the Socialists.

Aug. 6. The French government announced that it planned to create **15 new and fully equipped army divisions** in the following three years. After conversations in Washington, **Jules Moch,** minister of defense, and **Maurice Petsche,** minister of finance, declared (Oct. 15) that the United States would furnish more than **$2 billion in aid to France,** and that this would include aid for the war in Indochina.

Oct. 26. Premier Pleven recommended the creation of a **European ministry of defense** (known as the Pleven Plan) rather than the rearmament of (West) Germany.

1951. The population of France in 1951 was 42 million.

Feb. 28. The cabinet of **René Pleven** resigned, and **Henri Queuille** formed a coalition cabinet (March 10).

April 18. France signed the **Schuman Plan Treaty providing for the creation of the European Coal and Steel Community.**

May 24. The **French National Assembly was dissolved.** A general election held June 17 gave the **Communist Party** 26.5 percent of the popular vote and the **Rally of the French People** 21.7 percent. In the Chamber of Deputies, however, the RPF won 118 seats to 103 for the Communists.

July 10. The **Queuille cabinet resigned,** and **René Pleven** again constructed a ministry (Aug. 11).

Dec. 13. The **French Assembly** approved the **Schuman Plan Treaty.** Five days later (Dec. 18), Premier Pleven and Prime Minister Winston Churchill announced that France and Britain would support the Schuman Plan, the proposals for a European army, and the ideal of European unity.

1952, Jan. 7. The **Pleven cabinet was overthrown** and supplanted by a new coalition cabinet headed by **Edgar Faure** (Jan. 22). The Faure cabinet lasted only five weeks, and that of **Antoine Piany,** which won approval from the Assembly on March 11, resigned on December 23.

1953, Jan. 7. A two-week cabinet crisis ended with **René Mayer** organizing a new cabinet.

May 20. France and the Saar concluded an accord that gave the Saar autonomy but provided for its economic union with France.

May 21. The **Mayer cabinet resigned,** and **Joseph Laniel** won approval for a new cabinet on June 26.

July 22. Founding of the Union de Défense des Commerçants et Artisans (its members were known as Poujadists) a right-wing, antiparliamentary, nationalist movement that reacted to industrial modernization, the growth of large firms, and decolonization.

Aug. 6–28. Public services were disrupted by a **wave of strikes.**

Dec. 23. RENÉ COTY WAS ELECTED PRESIDENT of the French Republic to succeed **Vincent Auriol,** and assumed office Jan. 17.

The CGP announced its second national economic plan, for the years 1954–1957, which, in addition to focusing on the traditional bases of industry, targeted food production and housing for growth.

1954, June. The disastrous **defeat of French forces at Dien Bien Phu** on May 7 **led to the withdrawal of France from Indochina** (p. 1037).

June 12. The cabinet headed by Joseph Laniel suffered defeat, and **Pierre Mendès-France** formed a new cabinet June 18.

July 22. The Geneva settlement of the Vietnamese-French conflict was ratified by the National Assembly.

Aug. 27. The National Assembly approved a government plan to grant a greater measure of **self-rule to Tunisia and Morocco.**

Aug. 30. The **National Assembly rejected the European Defense Community** Treaty.

Nov. 1. Beginning of the **Algerian insurrection (p. 991).**

Nov. 10. An **antialcoholism campaign** was initiated by Mendès-France.

1955, Feb. 5. Pierre Mendès-France alienated many of his fellow deputies with his attempts to solve the conflict between France and the insurgent forces in **French North Africa.** The National Assembly overthrew the Mendès-France cabinet (Feb. 5) and approved a cabinet led by **Edgar Faure** (Feb. 23). The Faure cabinet lasted until Nov. 29, and when it fell Faure ordered the Assembly dissolved (Nov. 30).

1956, Jan. 2. In the resulting elections, the Left (Communists) and Right (**Poujadists**) gained strength.

Jan. 24. Faure's cabinet resigned, and a Socialist, **Guy Mollet,** organized a new government.

Feb. 29. The government legislated that all French workers would receive three weeks of paid vacation.

March 7–20. The French government granted **independence to Tunisia and Morocco** (pp. 990, 993).

July 26. The Suez Crisis began (p. 966).

1957, May 21. The cabinet of Guy Mollet was succeeded by a coalition government of Socialists and Radicals under **Maurice Bourgès-Maunoury** that carried through a 20 percent **devaluation of the franc** but suffered defeat (Sept. 30) over the Algerian issue. After more than five weeks' delay, **Félix Gaillard** organized (Nov. 6) a combination of the center parties to form the twenty-third cabinet France had seen since the Second World War. The war in North Africa, following the long struggle in Indochina, had placed a heavy strain on the French government's finances. The national economy, however, benefited from the **creation of the Common Market** (p. 840), promoted by the treaties concluded in Rome (Mar. 25).

Oct. 7. Albert Camus received the Nobel Prize for literature.

1958, Jan. 30. France was promised more than $655 million in aid from the United States, the European Payments Union, and the International Monetary Fund.

The **third economic plan of the CGP,** for the years 1958–1961, reflected growing protectionist attitudes at the highest levels of French society. It sought to hold imports to 1956 levels and raise exports by one-third.

Jan. 31. The National Assembly passed an **Algerian Reform Bill** that failed to satisfy the Algerians. (War with Algeria from 1954 to 1962.)

April 16. The cabinet of Félix Gaillard was overthrown (again over the North African deadlock) and **Pierre Pflimlin** of the Mouvement Républicain Populaire **headed a new cabinet** on May 13. Because they believed that Pflimlin would negotiate with the Front de Libération Nationale (FLN), a **committee of public safety,** headed by **Brig. Gen. Jacques Massu** and **Commander-in-Chief Raoul Salan,** seized control in Algeria and threatened France with **civil war.** The Pflimlin cabinet resigned after two weeks in office that had witnessed a virulent pro-Gaulist movement, and President Coty named **GEN. CHARLES DE GAULLE PRIME MINISTER** (May 31).

June 1. De Gaulle headed an emergency regime with the approval of the Assembly (329 to 244), rallied the people of metropolitan France to his support, and prepared to reorganize the French government.

Sept. 28. The **CONSTITUTION FOR A FIFTH FRENCH REPUBLIC** was approved by more than four to one in a popular referendum, and the Fifth Republic was inaugurated Oct. 5. Elections (Nov. 23 and 30) gave the Gaullist Union for the New Republic control of the assembly, and a special college (Dec. 21) named **DE GAULLE AS THE FIRST**

PRESIDENT OF THE FIFTH REPUBLIC, for a seven-year term commencing Jan. 8, 1959. Under the new constitution, the **office of the presidency** was vested with greater powers than those accorded by the constitutions of either the Third or the Fourth Republic. New presidential powers included the right to appoint the prime minister (or premier), to dissolve the National Assembly, to hold popular referendums, and to assume emergency powers. The new constitution also granted French overseas possessions six months to decide whether to remain as they were, to become *départements* closely integrated with France, or to become autonomous member states of a French Community. Government censorship of the press was ammended as a new article in the Fifth Republic's constitution. Newspapers expressing disagreement with the Gaullist government were seized and impounded until March 1965.

Under the Fifth Republic, national health insurance was extended to cover the whole population, regardless of employment status.

1959. By 1959, French steel production was double that of 1929. The nation's consumption of electricity had quadrupled in those 30 years, and automobile and truck manufacturing had nearly quintupled.

Jan. 10. Michel Debré became prime minister.

Feb. 3–4. Premiers of the 12 African autonomous republics of the French Community conferred with President de Gaulle in Paris in the first meeting of the community's Executive Council.

Sept. 16. President de Gaulle made an offer of self-determination to Algeria.

1960, Feb. 13. France exploded its **first atomic bomb** in the Saharan areas of southwestern Algeria and became the fourth nation to develop nuclear capacity (after the United States, the Soviet Union, and Great Britain). France undertook a series of atmospheric nuclear tests over the years that followed, in Africa and the Pacific.

April 25. The Gaullist Union ousted one of its founders, **Jacques Soustelle,** who was a strong believer in Algeria's integration with France.

1961, April 11. President de Gaulle announced his government's unwillingness to take part in any **United Nations activities** and reiterated his refusal to pay the French share of UN costs in the Congo. A year later (March 5, 1962), the French government refused to send a representative to the Geneva disarmament conference, and, as of 1966, it withdrew from its military commitments to NATO.

April 23. French leaders alerted the nation to a possible invasion by rightist military **insurgents from Algeria** (p. 991); President de Gaulle assumed full powers to deal with the crisis.

1962, March 23. After the Evian Agreement providing for peace between France and the Algerian rebels (March 18), de Gaulle instructed the French army to wage all-out war against the Organisation de l'armée secrète (OAS) resistance.

April 8. In a **national referendum on the Algerian settlement** of March 18, 90 percent of the valid ballots approved.

April 14. On the resignation of Michel Debré, de Gaulle named **Georges Pompidou** as the next prime minister.

May 20. French authorities organized an airlift to evacuate Europeans from Algiers.

May 23. As OAS terrorism continued in Algeria, OAS leader **Raoul Salan was sentenced** by a military tribunal in Paris **to life in prison.**

Oct. 5. Parliament censured the proposal, announced on Sept. 20, to elect the president by popular vote, but a national referendum (Oct. 28) approved it. Pompidou's cabinet resigned, but he was reappointed premier (Nov. 25).

1963, Jan. 14. De Gaulle declared his **opposition to Britain's entry into the Common Market,** and rejected proposals for a **multilateral nuclear force** within NATO.

Jan 22. A **Franco-German treaty of reconciliation** was signed in Paris by de Gaulle and West German chancellor Konrad Adenauer.

July 29. De Gaulle declared that France would not sign the Limited Nuclear Test Ban Treaty.

1964, Jan. 27. France agreed to establish **diplomatic relations with the government of Communist China.** The French denied that this step implied a disruption of relations with Taiwan (Jan. 28) or recognition of East Germany (Feb. 4).

Jan. 28. France and the USSR agreed to negotiate a five-year trade agreement to increase French-Soviet trade.

Feb. 10. Nationalist China broke diplomatic relations with France.

March 14. Twenty-one **administrative regions** were established, each headed by a coordinating prefect who presided over a Commission of Regional Economic Development, to stimulate economic growth.

March 15–24. De Gaulle visited Mexico and the French territories in the Western Hemisphere.

April 16. In a radio and television address, de Gaulle declared that France would build its own **nuclear striking force,** and that he favored continued French economic **aid to the poorer nations,** thus providing an alternative to U.S. and Soviet aid.

April 28. The government ordered the **removal of French naval officers from NATO commands** in the Mediterranean and the English Channel.

June 9. The French government, retaliating against Tunisia's nationalization of foreign-owned farmlands, announced that, beginning Oct. 1, Tunisian products would no longer enter France on preferential terms, thus abrogating the 1959 trade agreement.

Sept. 20–Oct. 16. President de Gaulle, during an unprecedentedly long absence from France, **visited ten South American countries** in an effort to strengthen economic and cultural relations.

Oct. 22. Jean-Paul Sartre refused to accept the Nobel Prize for literature, lest extraneous influences unfairly affect the power of a writer's words.

1965. All projections of the **fourth national economic plan,** covering the years 1962–65, were met or exceeded, except those set for productive investment, as economic growth advanced rapidly.

Dec. 19. In a runoff election, **President de Gaulle defeated François Mitterrand** and began his second term as president.

Dec. 23. The law providing all French workers with a **fourth week of paid vacation** went into effect.

1966. The **fifth national economic plan** of the CGP, covering the period 1966–70, placed new emphasis on the future growth of industry and on regional development.

March 10. France announced its **decision to withdraw from NATO.**

June 20–July 1. President de Gaulle visited the Soviet Union. Discussion of a program for cooperation in the exploration of space and in general technological development.

Sept. President de Gaulle toured Asia. In a speech at Phnom Penh, he called on the U.S. to withdraw from Vietnam.

1967. Birth control was legalized in France.

March 5, 12. In **national elections,** the Gaullists lost 25 seats and were left with a majority of 1 in the Assembly. They could usually count on the support of **Valéry Giscard d'Estaing's** Independent Republican Party.

May 16. President de Gaulle for the second time vetoed the admission of Great Britain to the Common Market.

Aug. Social security was extended to cover all non–wage earners in France.

1968. France lagged behind Great Britain in **television set ownership.** While the British owned 19 million sets by 1968, the French owned only 10 million.

Half of the French labor force was now in the **service sector.**

May–June. Violent **student outbreaks** at the University of Nanterre quickly spread to the Sorbonne and other institutions and ultimately involved hundreds of thousands of students. After widespread street fighting and occupation of buildings, the **universities were closed.** The crisis was aggravated by a **series of strikes**—involving millions of workers in various industries—that paralyzed the economy. In this truly revolutionary atmosphere, President de Gaulle appealed to the country for restoration of order in a radio address (May 24). He promised the drafting of reforms that would be submitted to popular referendum. On May 30 **Parliament was dissolved** and new elections were proclaimed.

June 23, 30. The Gaullist Party won an outright majority of seats in the elections, while the Communists and other radicals suffered losses. It was obvious that the country at large was opposed to revolution and desired an end to disorder.

July 11. Couve de Murville succeeded Georges Pompidou as **prime minister.**

1969, April 28. RESIGNATION OF PRESIDENT DE GAULLE after an unexpected defeat in a popular referendum (April 27) on various proposed administrative reforms. **The student movement had hastened de Gaulle's departure from power;** he died the next year, Nov. 9, 1970. **Alain Poher,** president of the Senate, acted as interim president.

June 1, 15. In a runoff election, **Pompidou,** a Gaullist, **defeated Poher** and became president of the republic (June 20). **Jacques Chaban-Delmas** was appointed prime minister.

Aug. 18. The new administration undertook a limited **devaluation of the franc,** long resisted by de Gaulle. In other respects, too, an effort was made to soften previous French positions, notably with regard to NATO and to the problem of Britain's admission to the Common Market.

1970. Beginnings of the French civilian nuclear energy program, which expanded rapidly with surprisingly little opposition.

Implementation of the CGP's **sixth national economic plan,** covering the years 1971–75.

Oct. 13. President Pompidou visited the Soviet Union and concluded an agreement "to extend and deepen political consultations on major international problems of mutual interest," though without prejudice to the commitments of either party to other nations.

Nov. 3. Administrative reform in the direction of further decentralization: local authorities were thenceforth able to decide on local projects without reference to Paris ministries.

Cultural developments: existentialist philosophy, which held that individuals, in the absence of any absolute moral law, create their own moral values and therefore should be held responsible for their actions, dominated the French intellectual community in the first postwar decades. Beginning in the 1960s, **structuralism** emerged as a reaction to existentialism. Major figures in the structuralist movement included anthropologist **Claude Levi-Strauss** and literary critic **Roland Barthes,** who grounded their theory on the structural linguistics of **Ferdinand de Saussure** (1857–1913) and the science of signs. Structuralism drew on linguistic theory for a mathematical rationalism and asserted that human consciousness was dependent on objective structures implied in the laws of language syntax. In the late 1960s and early 1970s, other intellectuals, such as **Jacques Derrida** and **Michel Foucault,** challenged the linguistic stability and systematic functions of **structuralism.** Their emphasis on textual analysis and relativist positions was instrumental in the movement of **poststructuralism** and **deconstruction** in the post-1968 intellectual community.

1971, Jan. 7. Establishment of a new government department, the **Ministry of the Environment.**

May. President **Pompidou** and British Prime Minister **Edward Heath** reached an agreement that allowed **Britain's entry into the European Common Market.**

June. François Mitterrand assumed **leadership of a new Socialist Party** following the Epinay congress.

1972, April 29. In a referendum, the French people approved the **enlargement of the European Economic Community.**

June. The French Socialist Party and Communist Party established a Common Program.

July 5. Pierre Messmer became prime minister.

1973. This year marked the end of the postwar period of rapid economic growth.

April 8. Death of Pablo Picasso, who had long resided in France.

Sept. 13–17. President **Pompidou** made an **official visit to the People's Republic of China.**

1974. The Messmer Plan accelerated the development of the French civilian nuclear industry.

April 2. DEATH OF GEORGES POMPIDOU.

May 5, 19. Finance Minister **VALÉRY GISCARD d'ESTAING narrowly defeated François Mitterrand in presidential elections.** After taking office, Giscard d'Estaing began a series of liberalization measures that included reducing the voting age from 21 to 18, establishing a secretary of state for the condition of women, liberalizing the divorce law, legalizing abortion, decentralizing the broadcasting system, and banning telephone tapping.

May 27. Jacques Chirac became prime minister.

June 27. France and Iran signed a $4 billion ten-year development pact that included France's sale to Iran of five nuclear reactors.

1975, Nov. 15. The French and Italian Communist Parties, the two largest ones in Europe, issued a joint statement asserting that the road to power was through their democratic systems and declaring their opposition to "all foreign interference," specifically by "American imperialism" and by implication by the Soviet Union.

1976. The **seventh national economic plan,** covering the years 1976–80, emphasized the development of new technologies, electronics, information systems, robotics, biomedical products, and energy-saving equipment.

Feb. 4, 8. At its twenty-second congress, the French Communist Party renounced the notion of the "dictatorship of the proletariat."

Aug. 25. Raymond Barre became prime minister, and the following month he announced an extensive plan to fight inflation.

1977, July 31. Antinuclear protesters demonstrate in Isère.

Sept. Differences on revising the Common Program of government led to the **rupture of** the union of the Left among the **Socialists, Communists, and left-wing Radicals.**

Oct. Giscard d'Estaing's administration was rocked by **scandal** when it was discovered that as finance minister in 1973 he received $250,000 in diamonds from **Emperor Bokassa** of the Central African Republic.

Nov. 3. President **Giscard d'Estaing** made Quebec premier René Levesque a grand officer of the Legion of Honor. His support of Quebec's right to self-determination angered the Canadian government.

1978, March 16. The *Amoco Cadiz* **oil spill occurred off of the coast of Brittany.**

1979. Statistics on crime in France indicated that in 1979 there were 1,645 homicides, compared with 21,456 for the same period in the United States.

July 7. The first French nuclear attack submarine was launched.

1980s. By this point, 22 percent of all restaurant dining was occurring in fast-food outlets.

1980, March 6. Marguerite Yourcenar was the first woman elected to the Académie Française.

April 15. Death of Jean-Paul Sartre.

Oct. 3. A bombing outside of a synagogue on rue Copernic in Paris killed four persons and injured ten. The terrorist attack raised fears that nascent anti-Semitism in French society could burgeon. President Giscard d'Estaing responded by launching a campaign against neo-Nazi and other racist organizations.

1981, May 10. Socialist Party leader **François Mitterrand's defeat of President Giscard d'Estaing in national elections** led to turmoil in financial markets: the stock exchange suspended trading for 48 hours, and extra customs officials were posted to prevent the smuggling of money and other valuables out of the country. In the June 14–20 National Assembly elections, the socialists won by a landslide, assuring Mitterrand of full power as **the first Socialist president of the Fifth Republic.** Mitterrand appointed four Communist members to his cabinet and began an **economic austerity program** that included nationalization on a scale unprecedented since the immediate postwar period, devaluation of the franc, and tax hikes for the rich. Mitterrand also proceeded to end nuclear tests and abolish the death penalty.

May 21. Socialist **Pierre Mauroy became prime minister.**

1982. The eighth national economic plan was abandoned, and the interim plan of 1982–83 was implemented instead. These plans, along with the ninth plan, covering the years 1984–88, were followed much less closely by government and industry, because increased ministerial stability had largely replaced the need for a separate administrative planning office.

Feb. 1. France established a **fifth week of paid vacation and a 39-hour work week.**

Feb. 13. The French Parliament passed the **nationalization law** providing for the nationalization of most of the remaining privately owned portions of the banking sector, as well as the largest firms in the chemicals, steel, aviation, electronics, and telecommunications industries that had not been nationalized earlier.

Aug. 8. An anti-Semitic terrorist attack was carried out on the rue de Rosiers in Paris.

1983. The high-velocity rail system known as TGV (Train à grande vitesse) began operating between Paris and Lyons, offering passenger service at speeds up to 168 miles per hour.

March 25. The government announced a **second austerity plan.**

April 5. The French government expelled 47 **Soviets accused of espionage.**

Oct. 15–Dec. 3. A series of **demonstrations against racism** were carried out by the youth of France.

1984, March 28. Mitterrand's government published its plan for the steel industry, which included the loss of 20,000 jobs over three years.

June–July. Called by Catholic action groups, more than one million people demonstrated in Paris on June 24 against the **reform of private schools** *(écoles libres).*

July 12. President Mitterrand announced the **repeal of the Savary law,** which legalized the integration of private schooling into the state system. Mitterrand's action **led to the resignations of Education Minister Alain Savary and Prime Minister Pierre Mauroy.**

July 17. Laurent Fabius became prime minister.

Sept. 23. Former President **Valéry Giscard d'Estaing** was elected to the National Assembly.

1985, July 11. The **Greenpeace ship** *Rainbow Warrior* **was sunk** by French frogmen on orders of the Defense Ministry; the so-called **Greenpeace Affair** led to the resignation of Defense Minister Charles Hernu and the firing of the head of the External Security Agency, Admiral Pierre Lacoste.

1986, Jan. 20. The Franco-British Channel Tunnel Treaty was signed by President Mitterrand and Prime Minister Margaret Thatcher. Also called the "chunnel," work on the Channel tunnel was begun at both ends, and the two halves of the service tunnel met on Dec. 1, 1990. The Chunnel, actually three tunnels, was **completed in 1994.**

March 20. Jacques Chirac, a Gaullist, became prime minister, and **cohabitation between Socialists and Gaullists** began; his government programs, presented in April, included a privatization plan.

April 14. Death of Simone de Beauvoir.

June. A public opinion poll taken after the Chernobyl nuclear reactor accident in the Soviet Union indicated that the French population's approval for the further development of the domestic nuclear power industry was declining. In December 1985, the approval rating for nuclear power was 62 percent; by June 1986 it had dropped to 51 percent.

Sept. A wave of terrorist attacks in Paris was linked to French policy in the Middle East; in November, Renault chief **Georges Besse was assassinated** by the group **Action Directe.**

Sept. 2. In a speech to the United Nations General Assembly, Prime Minister Chirac declared that France would not give up its goal of replacing all oil-fired electricity generating stations with nuclear-powered plants.

Nov. 17–Dec. 10. Student demonstrations against university reforms proposed by education minister Alain Devaquet led to Devaquet's resignation on Dec. 6.

1987, May 11–July 4. Former Nazi SS officer Klaus Barbie was tried in Lyons.

Oct. 19. Stock markets crashed in New York, Paris, and other major financial centers.

1988, Jan. 22. France and West Germany established a Defense and Security Council and an Economic and Finance Council during German prime minister Helmut Kohl's visit to France.

April 24, May 8. François Mitterrand won a **second term** in the presidential elections in a landslide victory.

April–May. Jean-Marie Le Pen, leader of the radical right-wing **National Front,** received a high level of support in presidential elections (more than 14 percent in the first round). Since the advent of Socialist government in 1981, Le Pen had been a leader in the opposition, concentrating on issues of immigration and "insecurity" and thus gaining increasing political influence and media coverage. Though he won substantial percentages of votes in municipal elections in the mid-1980s, his racist remarks about Jews and immigrants caused widespread controversy and protest.

May 9. Michel Rocard became prime minister.

Nov. 25–26. On a visit to the Soviet Union, Mitterrand watched the launching of a French-Soviet space mission.

1989, July 14. The Bastille Day celebration in France attracted the world's attention as the culmination of a year-long celebration of the **bicentennial of the French Revolution.**

Sept. 20. The state-owned TGV Atlantique railway began operating between Paris and Le Mans, offering passenger service at up to 186 miles per hour. TGV lines to Tours and the Loire Valley began the following year.

Dec. 31. Mitterrand called for a European Confederation, reminiscent of de Gaulle's call for a united Europe, from the Atlantic to the Urals.

By the late 1980s, 70 percent of electricity in France was produced by nuclear reactors and France had the second largest nuclear power industry in the world.

1990, April 25–26. A Franco-German summit concentrated on the issue of **German unification.**

May 13–14. In Paris and other cities, thousands demonstrated to protest the desecration of a Jewish cemetery in Carpentras.

1991, Jan. 3–5. With the failure of the French peace initiative to Baghdad, war against Iraq followed (p. 969). France participated in Operation Desert Storm during the **Gulf War.**

May 15. Edith Cresson became **the first woman prime minister of France.**

Nov. 10. With a view to 1993 legislative elections, **Mitterrand** announced **plans to reform the constitution,** including a reduction in the presidential term from seven to five years, the strengthening of parliamentary powers, and the enhancing of judicial authority.

1992, April 2. Pierre Bérégovoy became prime minister.

May 22. France and Germany agreed to form a joint army corps of at least 35,000 soldiers. The force, known as the **European Corps,** was to be operational by October 1995, was intended to operate under the umbrella of the Western European Union (p. 839), and was to be open to other WEU members.

1993, March 21, 28. Legislative elections for the National Assembly, held in two rounds, **cut the ruling Socialist Party's share of the vote by half.** The Socialist Party lost all but 54 of the 252 seats it had held in the National Assembly, while the Gaullist Rassemblement pour la République (Rally for the Republic, RPR) increased its representation from 126 seats to 247. The Center-Right Party, the Union for French Democracy (Union pour la Démocratie Française, UDF), became the second strongest party in the National Assembly by acquiring 213 seats, as compared to the 131 which it had held previous to the election.

March 29. President Mitterrand named **Edouard Balladur** of the RPR as prime minister.

July 22. Entry into effect of a new nationality law directed toward curbing immigration.

Oct. Beginning on Oct. 12 with rail workers, industrial unrest spread through the public sector and brought the operation of the national airline to a virtual standstill. The industrial strikes and protests were in reaction to Balladur's economic policy and plans to reform employment.

Nov. 19. As part of Balladur's conservative immigration policies, the National Assembly and Senate approved an ammendment to the constitution strengthening control over asylum seekers.

1994, Jan. 12. France freed two Iranian murder suspects who had been part of a group in a Geneva suburb; Switzerland was unhappy with this action.

May 6. The **Channel tunnel** connecting Britain and France **was inaugurated.** It opened officially to traffic on Nov. 14.

Sept. 28. The European Court of Justice in France proclaimed that women and men doing equal work must get equal pension benefits.

1995, May 7. The mayor of Paris, **Jacques Chirac,** defeated his Socialist rival for the **presidency of France,** vowing to reduce unemployment.

Sept. 5. Despite international protests, France resumed its nuclear testing, setting off a nuclear device in Tahiti.

Oct. 2. France conducted the second of these tests.

Oct. 17. A bomb exploded on a Paris subway train, injuring 29. The bomb was set by an Algerian terrorist organization called the Armed Islamic Group.

Oct. 27. France exploded a third nuclear device, stating that it would test three more.

Dec. 4–7. France faced **huge union strikes** over government plans to reform welfare, trim social security, and bring the public service sector almost to a standstill.

1996, Jan. 29. Chirac announced the **end to France's nuclear testing.**

1997, April 21. Chirac dissolved the lower chamber of the French Parliament and announced elections. This was seen as a measure to solidify and affirm French support of the upcoming EU currency. On June

3 French leftist parties won the elections. Socialist leader Lionel Jospin took office as premier. The extreme right party National Front also recorded gains.

1998, Feb. 27. France, Finland, Germany, Italy, and the Netherlands reported qualifying economic statistics for the EU's Economic and Monetary Union (EMU). Six other countries had economic reports strong enough to probably be eligible to join in the implementation of the euro in 1999.

July 1–16. France hosted the World Cup soccer tournament; the French team won the world title for the first time in tournament history, with a multiracial team.

1999, Jan. 1. France adopted the euro as its currency. The successful test of the euro also involved the participation of ten other countries: Austria, Belgium, Finland, Germany, Ireland, Italy, Luxembourg, the Netherlands, Portugal, and Spain.

May 25. The Jospin government narrowly survived a censure motion against French governmental policy on separatist violence in Corsica.

June 21. France sent 7,000 troops as part of the NATO effort to contain violence and ethnic cleansing in Kosovo, Yugoslavia. These soldiers served as part of NATO's Kosovo security force (KFOR) to occupy the region over an extended period.

Nov. 22–Dec. 8. An economic dispute arose with Britain when France, leery of contaminated beef that might possibly be infected with bovine spongiform encephalopathy (BSE), commonly known as mad cow disease, refused to import British meat, even though the EU had lifted its three-year ban on British beef in July 1999.

Dec. 13–23. Negotiations began with Corsican representatives concerning the ongoing separatist uprisings in the island territory. Talks ended with an unconditional cease-fire being declared by spokesmen for the militant National Front for the Liberation of Corsica (FLNC).

2000, March 27. Prime Minister **Lionel Jospin** responded to public criticism of his Socialist-led government's inability to implement reforms by replacing four of his cabinet ministers.

Sept. 4. Protests over rising fuel prices began in France; truckers and other motorists blockaded refineries and service stations. The spirit of rebellion spread, and protests broke out across Europe.

Sept. 24. In a national referendum in which only 30 percent of the French electorate participated, voters approved a proposal to reduce the term of the president from seven to five years.

Dec. 20. The French National Assembly voted to reverse the order of spring 2002 elections, placing the presidential vote before the one for Parliament.

e. THE IBERIAN PENINSULA

1. SPAIN
(From p. 692)

Heads of state: Gen. Francisco Franco (1939–75), King Juan Carlos de Borbon (1975–   ).

Prime ministers (post-Franco): Carlos Arias Navarro (1975–76), Adolfo Suarez (1976–81), Leopoldo Calvo Sotelo (1981), Felipe Gonzalez (1981–   ), José Maria Aznar (1996–   ).

After the defeat of the Axis powers in World War II, **Gen. Francisco Franco** began moving away from the fascist ideology that had underpinned his regime during its first years in power. Still, policies of economic autarchy were not abandoned until the later 1950s, the political system remained strictly authoritarian, and civil liberties were not fully restored until after the *caudillo*'s death in 1975. The **transition to democracy** in Spain that took place thereafter was distinct from that of other European nations in that it was a gradual process, with figures from the former regime remaining in positions of military and civilian authority through the 1980s.

1945, March 22. Don Juan, the Bourbon claimant to the Spanish throne, called for the resignation of Gen. Franco and the restoration of the monarchy.

May 8. Spain broke off diplomatic relations with Germany.

May 12. Falangist officials attended a requiem mass for Adolf Hitler. Spain continued to give refuge to large numbers of Germans, despite Allied demands for their repatriation.

June 20. The San Francisco (Calif.) Conference on the United Nations Charter excluded Spain from membership in the UN. A similar exclusion was contained in the report on the Potsdam Conference (Aug. 2).

July 20. Gen. Franco made changes in his cabinet, filling several government posts with reputedly royalist sympathizers, and stated that the **monarchy would be restored at a future date.**

1946, March 4. The United States, Britain, and France appealed to the Spanish people to oust the Franco regime and prepare the way for democratic elections.

Dec. 11. The United Nations General Assembly voted to bar Spain from all UN activities and urged members to break off diplomatic relations with Spain.

1947, March 31. Gen. Franco announced a bill of succession (ratified on July 6 by national referendum), according to which Spain again became a monarchy, the choice of the monarch being left to Franco as head of the state.

April 2. Don Juan condemned the bill of succession and maintained his opposition to Franco.

1948, Sept. 20. The treaty of friendship and nonaggression concluded with Portugal in 1939 was extended for ten years.

1949, Oct. 22–27. Gen. Franco paid a visit to Lisbon, demonstrating the close relations between Spain and Portugal.

1950, Sept. 6. The U.S. Congress recommended, with certain restrictions, a **$62.5 million Marshall Plan loan for Spain.** The loan represented a first step in the normalization of relations between the United States and Spain, and the beginnings of U.S. attempts to draw Spain into its Western anticommunist alliance.

Nov. 4. The UN adopted a resolution, sponsored by several Latin American states and supported by the United States, that rescinded the earlier resolution of Dec. 11, 1946, thus opening the door to Spain's admission to the postwar international community of nations.

1951, April 23. After a decade of economic difficulties, some 250,000 workers went on strike against **rising living costs.**

During the 1950s, Spain experienced some **economic growth:** by mid-decade it finally regained its 1936 levels of industrial and agricultural production.

1953, Sept. 26. In agreements with the United States, Spain gave the U.S. the right to establish naval and air bases on its territory in return for military and economic aid.

1954, Dec. 29. Don Juan of Bourbon and Gen. Franco met and discussed the future regime of Spain.

1956, April. Spain terminated its Moroccan protectorate.

1959, Feb. 1. Liberal and rightist foes of the Franco regime joined to organize the Spanish Union, an illegal action, since all political parties except the Falange Party had been forbidden.

May 14. A liberal Catholic group organized the Christian Democratic Left Party, in opposition to the ban on political parties.

June. Franco's government announced an **Economic Stabilization Plan,** which brought an official end to what remained of the fascist policies of autarchy. The plan liberalized the economy, contributed to a recession, and set the stage for the dramatic economic recovery of the 1960s.

1960–74. The Spanish economy grew at an unprecedented rate, second in the world only to Japan. Employment in the agricultural sector dropped from 42 percent of the labor force in 1969 to 23 percent) in 1975, while employment in the industrial sector rose from 32 percent to 37 percent in the same period. The formal end of Franco's policies of economic autarchy brought massive increases in foreign investment: from $40 million in 1960 to $697 million in 1970. The number of tourists visiting Spain also contributed to economic recovery. In 1960, 6 million tourists visited Spain; in 1982, 42 million did. Spaniards working abroad and sending money back to their families further added to the nation's growing prosperity. Whereas emigrant remittances had been $362 million in 1965, by 1973 they were $1.1 billion. Prosperity, coupled with the expansion of welfare benefits for the nation's working classes, acted to provide a measure of legitimacy to Franco's rule.

1960, June 13. In a letter to their bishops, 342 Basque priests protested police brutality toward political prisoners and violations of civil rights. In the Basque provinces as well as Catalonia, a good portion of the opposition to the regime had its origins in lay organizations and the lower levels of the church hierarchy.

1963, Aug. 10. The government announced plans to grant some autonomy to the provinces of Rio Muni and Fernando Po, comprising Spanish Guinea.

1964, Dec. 14. A new constitution, mildly liberal, was approved by an overwhelming vote in national elections.

1969, July 22. PRINCE JUAN CARLOS DE BORBON, son of Don Juan, was named by Gen. Franco as his eventual successor and heir to the Spanish throne.

Oct. 2. Visit of U.S. President Richard Nixon to Spain, in the course of a Mediterranean tour. Relations between the U.S. and Spain had remained close in view of the use of Spanish bases by American air and naval units, in return for which the United States had provided large sums of money for Spain's economic and military development.

1970, Aug. 6. Renewal of U.S.-Spanish agreements on military bases, for a period of five years.

Dec. THE BASQUE PROBLEM. On Dec. 1 the honorary West German consul at San Sebastian was kidnapped by Euzkadi Ta Askatasuna (ETA), a Basque nationalist group demanding independence for the Basque provinces. The kidnapping was to protest the court-martialing at Burgos of 15 Basque nationalists charged with having assassinated a hated police official in 1968. The incident led to widespread protests on the part of Spanish intellectuals and church authorities and signaled the beginnings of a long terrorist campaign for Basque independence from Spanish rule.

Dec. 4. On opening the court-martial, the government proclaimed a three-month state of emergency in Guipúzcoa province that permitted searches without warrants and the indefinite detention of suspects. Emergency measures were extended to all of Spain on Dec. 14 and represented a move away from the state's limited policies of political liberalization in the 1960s.

Dec. 28. The court-martial's verdict, in which six of the Basque prisoners were sentenced to death and nine others to unusually long prison terms, led to widespread unrest in the country and induced Franco to commute the death sentences and reduce the prison terms.

1972, May–Oct. A revised law of public order restricted freedom of thought and association. University officials and staff members in Madrid, Salamanca, and Valencia quit in protest of the new government rules.

1973. Franco resigned his premiership but remained head of state. **Carlos Arias Navarro** was made prime minister. Although in 1973–74 his government **began reforms** to reduce press censorship, allow some limited political associations, reform the Cortes (parliament), make local government more democratic, and revise labor laws, a new law issued in December 1974 put political association under state control again.

The assassination of Premier Carrero Blanco by ETA contributed to the retrenchment of the Spanish state in its commitment to authoritarianism and provided new momentum for the organization of real and widespread opposition to Franco's rule.

1975, Nov. 20. DEATH OF GEN. FRANCISCO FRANCO. JUAN CARLOS I WAS CROWNED AS KING on Nov. 22.

Nov. 25. King Juan Carlos issued a decree pardoning certain political prisoners, as a gesture of goodwill to mark the beginning of his reign. The pardon fell short of leftist demands for a more sweeping pardon of prisoners of the Franco regime.

Dec. 5. King Juan Carlos requested that the sitting prime minister, Carlos Arias Navarro, form a new government.

1976. In the spring of 1976, a number of well-known **exiled writers, historians, and political figures returned to Spain,** including Salvador de Madariaga and Claudio Sánchez Albornoz. Throughout the year, strikes and demonstrations put pressure on the new post-Franco regime to implement democratic reforms, release all political prisoners, and grant regional autonomy to areas such as Catalonia and the Basque provinces.

July 3. After asking Arias Navarro to step down, King Juan Carlos named **Adolfo Suarez prime minister** and requested that he form a new cabinet. Suarez created the Democratic Center Union and ruled as prime minister until 1981. Somewhat unexpectedly, Suarez moved away from his previous rightist political inclinations and presided over the first phases of Spain's democratic reforms.

1977, Jan. 4. Press **censorship** was **abolished.**

March 12. The poet **Vicent Aleixandre was awarded the Nobel Prize for literature.**

April. The Communist Party was legalized after its leaders promised Premier Suarez that the party's interest was in peaceful changes.

June 15. In the first free national elections since 1936, Suarez's Democratic Center Union won a majority of the seats in the Cortes.

Aug. 4. A sweeping **political amnesty** was granted. Jailed Communist Party members were freed on Aug. 30.

1978, Sept. 28. A **new constitution** was approved by the Cortes. It recognized constitutional monarchy as the basic form of government, provided for regional autonomy, and disestablished the Church. It was approved by 87 percent of the vote in a national referendum in December (though with 32 percent abstention by conservatives).

Oct. 5. Prime Minister Suarez and parties on the Left arrived at the **Moncloa Pact,** which promised to index wage increases to inflation, raise welfare benefits, and introduce the progressive income tax. By February 1978, Suarez said the **pact was "virtually dead"** when the Left challenged his cabinet's weak economic efforts. In 1979 a government wage ceiling provoked new labor unrest, and **national economic difficulties led to an unsuccessful censure motion in the Cortes against Suarez.**

Nov.–Dec. The new monarchy enacted the first constitutional reform, the **Political Reform Law.** The law included the acceptance of popular sovereignty, universal suffrage, and political pluralism. The law created a bicameral Cortes, composed of a Congress of 350 deputies elected by proportional representation and a Senate of 207 elected by a simple majority. The law also stipulated that the king could submit bills, dissolve the Cortes, and call new elections. In a national referendum, the law was affirmed by 90 percent of the vote. In February 1979, the Cortes amended the law by barring the military from politics.

1979, July 18. A **Basque statute of autonomy,** providing for fiscal independence from the central state, the right to form a separate police force, and guarantees for the use of Basque as the official language, was approved by the Cortes.

Aug. 13. A **Catalan statute of autonomy,** providing for the reinstitution of the Generalitat government, regional control over education, and the normalization of the Catalan language, was approved by the Cortes (provisional restoration of the Generalitat and pre-autonomous status had been granted in 1977). The 1979 Catalan statute of autonomy further provided for the establishment of a new regional television channel (TV3), which ultimately had a profound impact on the **renaissance of the Catalan language.**

1980, Oct.–Dec. Prime Minister Suarez faced increasing criticism, both from within his party and by the opposition, for his handling of economic problems, terrorism, and issues of regional autonomy.

1981, Jan. 29. Prime Minister **Suarez resigned unexpectedly,** and before his replacement, Leopoldo Calvo Sotelo, was sworn in, Lt. Col. Antonio Tejero and a group of Civil Guards seized control of the Cortes building on Feb. 23 in an attempt to effect a **MILITARY COUP.** Tejero held the deputies to the Spanish Cortes hostage for 18 hours while Gen. Milans de Bosch declared a state of emergency in Valencia and sent tanks out into the streets. The insurrection was quelled by the firm action of the king in securing pledges of personal loyalty from key military leaders.

Feb. 25. Leopoldo Calvo Sotelo was confirmed as prime minister.

March 27. A demonstration march involving an estimated one million persons was organized in Madrid by the political parties and the trade unions, in support of "liberty, democracy, and the Constitution." Similar demonstrations occurred simultaneously across Spain, with the largest number of participants in Catalonia, Andalusia, and Valencia.

June 22. The Cortes passed the first **divorce bill** since the 1930s. It went into force on July 20.

July 10. Autonomy statutes for Valencia, Murcia, and La Rioja entered into force.

Aug. 16. Autonomy statutes for Aragon, Castile–La Mancha, Canary Islands, and Navarre entered into force. Autonomy statutes for other states were subsequently passed as well, completing the post-Franco redrawing of the Spanish administrative map.

Oct. 25. Unveiling of Picasso's *Guernica* (housed in New York since 1939), at the Prado Museum in Madrid.

1982, May 30. Spain became an official member of NATO.

Oct. 28. Socialists won an overwhelming victory in the elections and **formed a new government headed by Felipe González.** They won 47 percent of the vote, the greatest electoral victory in Cortes history. They also won the three elections in 1986, 1989, and 1993. González served as premier from December 1982 onward.

1983. The Spanish Supreme Court ruled that **regional autonomous governments should control administrative areas such as education, linguistic, and health policy.** Nevertheless the balance of power between the center and the periphery in Spain (most notably between Catalonia and the Basque country and the central government) remained a contentious political, social, economic, and cultural issue well into the 1990s.

Feb. 18. After a poor showing in the 1982 elections, party leaders dissolved the Union of the Democratic Center (UCD) and authorized those 12 deputies that had been elected to the Cortes to join other parties.

Nov. Abortion law: the Cortes passed a bill legalizing abortion under certain circumstances. The bill was strongly opposed by the Church and the rightest Popular Alliance and did not enter into force until August 1985.

Nov. 30. A bill was passed that, while maintaining the king's role as commander of the armed forces, established overall political control of the military under the office of the prime minister.

1985, July 23. A bill was passed in the Spanish Cortes to reduce pension entitlements by 8 percent. It produced an unprecedented rift between the ruling Socialist Party and the General Union of Labor (UGT), the socialist trade union, including a 24-hour national general strike on June 20.

Sept. 11. Spain joined the European Economic Community, though its formal membership did not begin until Jan. 1, 1986.

1986–92. Communist and Socialist labor groups recurrently **protested** the economic policies of **Gonzalez's government** with general strikes as negotiations failed to bring any settlement.

1986, March 12. In a national referendum, preceded by acrimonious debate, Spanish voters chose to continue membership in NATO.

July and Oct. The first two rounds of the negotiations to reduce the U.S. military presence in Spain were held in Madrid.

Nov. 21. A liberalization of the laws on abortion allowed private clinics to perform abortions in the first 12 weeks of pregnancy with the approval of two physicians rather than a five-person commission, as had previously been required.

Dec.–1987, Mar. Students demonstrated for university reform and open admissions. It was the largest protest in recent years. Students and labor groups increased their hostility toward the González government.

Dec. 1. The opening of the third round of negotiations to reduce the U.S. military presence in Spain.

1987. Growing conflict between the ruling Socialist Party and the socialist trade union, UGT, over the government's policies to reduce inflation. The UGT demanded wage increases and policies to reduce the 20 percent inflation rate.

1988, Jan. 15. Agreement in principle to withdraw the U.S. Tactical Air Wing from Spain within three years of the ratification of such an agreement, and to reduce U.S. military and civilian personnel on the Torrejón base to fewer than 300, and on the Zaragosa base to fewer than 200.

Dec. 14. After a one-day general strike, negotiations between the ruling Socialist Party and the UGT broke down.

1989, April 7. A three-month unilateral cease-fire initiated by ETA ended when the government refused to acknowledge that a "political solution" had been under negotiation between the two sides in Algiers.

Oct. 29. In general elections, the United Left (Izquierda Unida, IU), a leftist coalition that included the Communist Party, trebled its representation in the Cortes, and the ruling Socialist Party saw its majority reduced to one seat. Twenty percent fewer voters supported the party than in 1982; 10 percent fewer voted for the party than in 1986.

1990, June 21. After a protracted national debate, the Spanish Constitutional Court ruled that the four Herri Batasuna deputies (the political arm of ETA) elected to the Cortes in 1989 could take their seats by swearing an ammended oath to the constitution.

1991–92. A massive industrial crisis came to a head with widespread unrest in steel, coal, shipbuilding, and other sectors, as a result of government efforts to restructure the economy in preparation for the 1993 EC single market.

1991, Nov. 17. Ten thousand neofascists from Spain and elsewhere assembled in Madrid's Plaza Oriente to commemorate the sixteenth anniversary of Franco's death. Throughout the year, right-wing extremist groups, particularly skinheads in Barcelona and Madrid, became increasingly active and vocal, engaging in numerous acts of violence against foreigners residing in Spain.

Dec. 10. Illegal immigrants numbering 110,000 (half of whom were from Morroco) met a deadline for amnesty by showing that they had arrived in Spain prior to May 15, 1991, had gainful employment, or were able to set up independent business enterprises.

Early 1990s. The ruling Socialist government sustained increasing levels of criticism as several ministers were forced to resign due to their involvement in a series of scandals and corruption cases.

1992, April 20. Opening of the Universal Exposition in Seville to commemorate the five hundredth aniversary of the "discovery" of America.

July 25. Opening ceremonies were held for the Olympic Games in Barcelona. After investing billions in preparation for the event, the city and the country plunged into an economic recession in the aftermath of the games. The draft budget proposed for the following fiscal year, introduced in the Cortes in the fall of 1993, was the most restrictive in two decades.

1994, May. Spanish premier Felipe Gonzalez of the Socialist Workers Party was called to resign because of charges of corruption involving various financial and ethical scandals. He refused.

1996, March 3. In general elections in Spain the Center-Right Popular Party under leader José María Aznar gains the most votes.

May 4. Aznar officially becomes the premier.

1998, May 3. Formal plans were launched for the formation of the EU's Economic and Monetary Union (EMU) that would include the participation of 11 nations, including Spain, in the Jan. 1, 1999, adoption of the euro.

July 29. Although former prime minister Felipe Gonzalez Marquez was not implicated in the probe, 12 officials from his government received jail sentences for crimes in the anti-Basque "dirty war" that went on during the prime minister's term of office.

Sept. 16. The militant Basque separatist group ETA announced a "total and indefinite" cease-fire. The Spanish government remained highly skeptical of the extremist group's unconditional truce.

1999, Jan. 1. Spain participated in the implementation of a single European currency, the euro. The ten other countries initiating the euro were France, Finland, Austria, Belgium, the Netherlands, Portugal, Ireland, Italy, Luxembourg, and Germany.

Nov. 28. Despite the release of several Basque prisoners and progressive talks with the Aznar government, the ETA announced an end to its truce of Sept. 1998, resuming its violence with bombings and assassinations.

2000, March 12. In a general election, Prime Minister José María Aznar and his Center-Right Popular Party easily yet unexpectedly won an absolute majority in the lower house of Parliament, known as the Congreso.

Sept. 4–14. When fuel crises erupted throughout Europe due to extremely high petroleum prices on the world market, Spain also saw widespread protests against taxes on fuel.

2. PORTUGAL
(From p. 693)

1945, Oct. 7. Premier **Antonio de Oliveira Salazar** permitted the formation of opposition parties. Censorship was removed on Oct. 12, and a **political amnesty** was granted. Yet on Oct. 14, because of immediate attacks against his government, Salazar reimposed the censorship of the press.

Nov. 18. The first **general election** in years, because of a boycott by the opposition, brought victory for the **National Union Party** and the paternalist regime of Premier Salazar.

1946, June 2. The United States and Great Britain returned the bases they had held in the Azores during the war.

1949, Feb. 13. **President Antonio Carmona,** 79, was reelected after the single opposition candidate withdrew.

April 4. Portugal signed the North Atlantic Treaty. It still was excluded from the United Nations, however, by Soviet veto.

1950, Sept. 26–27. **Spain's general Franco** and **premier Salazar** discussed questions of peninsular strategy and emphasized the solidarity of their two countries.

1952, April 14–15. Premier Salazar and Gen. Franco agreed on an intensification of their political and military collaboration to defend their countries, "within the general framework of Western defense," against Soviet aggression.

1957, Nov. 15. The 1951 **Azores common defense pact** with the United States was extended to 1962.

1959, June 18. The National Assembly approved government-sponsored legislation to abolish the system of direct presidential elections by universal suffrage.

1962, Jan. 3. Premier Salazar severely condemned Britain and the United States for not strongly supporting Portugal in the UN when **India seized three of its enclaves.**

1964–70. The Portuguese government was exposed to increasing and more threatening protests against **continuance of its colonial rule** in Africa, both by the United Nations and the Organization of African Unity.

1968, Sept. 16. Premier Salazar suffered a brain hemorrhage and sank into a coma.

Sept. 27. Dr. **Marcello Caetano** was named to succeed Salazar in the premiership.

1970, July 27. Death of former Premier Antonio de Oliveira Salazar.

Dec. 2. Caetano announced plans to accord the **African colonies** additional seats in the legislature and extensive autonomy in planning and administration of their local and social affairs, but all within a system of complete racial equality.

Dec. 9–11. The ministerial council of the **Organization of African Unity,** meeting at Lagos, condemned "those states, particularly the NATO powers, who sustain Portugal in her colonial aggression by their continued assistance to her." The council directed its **liberation committee** to afford substantially increased financial and material aid to **Amilcar Cabral** and his **Party for Independence of Guinea and Cape Verde.**

1974–75. After granting **independence to Guinea-Bissau on Aug. 26, 1974,** Portugal recognized in 1975 the independence of **Cape Verde Islands (July 5), Mozambique (June 25), São Tomé and Principe (July 12), and Angola (Nov. 11)** (p. 1065).

1974, April 25. A military coup established a junta under Gen. Antonio de Spinola.

Sept. 30. Gen. Francisco da Costa Gomes replaced **Spinola** as **president,** a position he held until July 1976.

1975, Feb. 15. A **divorce amendment to the 1940 Concordat** was signed to legalize the right of couples married in the Church to obtain a civil divorce.

March. The leftist military **government nationalized banks and insurance companies.**

April 25. In the first free elections in 50 years, voters **elected a constituent assembly to revise the constitution.**

June. Portugal applied for membership in the European Community.

1976, April 2. A **new constitution** was adopted to replace the 1933 constitution. It **envisaged the construction of a "socialist society" for Portugal.**

June 27. A moderate Socialist, Gen. Antonio Ramalho Eanes, was **elected president** in the first free elections in decades, and **a Socialist government was formed.** In the 1979–80 parliamentary elections, however, the **Center-Right Democratic Alliance Coalition** won 45 percent of the vote.

1980, Dec. 8. Gen. **Eanes** was **reelected** and served until March 1986.

1982, Oct. The 1976 **constitution was revised** to abolish the Council of the Revolution, exclude the military from politics, reduce presidential power, and extend the private sector's role in the national economy.

In **1989,** the 1976 constitution was again revised, to remove its Marxist elements.

1984, Jan. 27. The assembly approved an **abortion law** despite strong opposition from the Church and the Democratic Social Center. Although the law did not legalize abortion, it waived persecution for abortion in the first 12 weeks of pregnancy under certain circumstances.

1985, Nov. Anibal Cavaco Silva **formed** a minority **Social Democratic Party (PSD) cabinet** with independent members. In 1987 the PSD won a majority, and Silva's new government started **reform programs** that included increased reliance on free market forces in the economy, the revitalization of agriculture, and a new labor law to reduce protection of employees against dismissal. These free market policies encouraged private-sector growth.

1986, Jan. 1. Portugal formally entered the EC.

March. Mário Soares succeeded Gen. Eanes as president.

1989, Sept. A draft law was introduced to facilitate a **large-scale privatization program** for the following five years. It was also in preparation for the single European market by January 1993. The program gave rise to constant labor unrest, and the government agreed with unions in October 1990 to increase wages no more than 13.4 percent, to reduce the workweek from 48 to 44 hours, and to solve labor disputes through negotiations rather than industrial action.

1992, Feb.–Mar. A series of student strikes and demonstrations demanded reform in the Portuguese education system.

1993, July 7. In response to growing concerns over the economy, the government announced a major regional development plan involving the investment of 6,500 million *escudos* over a six-year period, with part of the funding to be provided by the EC.

1995, Oct. 1. Socialists won the general elections in Portugal, making **Antonio Guterres** the new premier.

1996, Jan. 14. Jorge Sampaio was elected president of Portugal, giving the country its **first Socialist premier and president since democracy was restored in 1974.**

1998, May 3. The admission of Portugal as a founding member of the EU's Economic and Monetary Union (EMU) was a sign of the country's stable and expanding economy.

June 28. In a public referendum, the first of its kind in Portuguese history, voters rejected a proposal to loosen the country's tight restrictions on abortion. However, because voter turnout was less than 50 percent, the referendum was declared null and void.

1999, Sept. 20. Portugal urged the UN to send peacekeeping forces into its former colonial territory of East Timor when Indonesian forces wreaked havoc in the recently independent state.

Dec. 20. Portugal returned rulership of Macao to China after 442 years of colonial dominion over the island nation.

3. GIBRALTAR

1964, Sept. Ongoing **tension over Gibraltar.** Spanish protests against the new constitution promulgated for the base that granted more self-government, followed by restrictions on vehicular traffic and on the free movement of workers to and from the mainland to Gibraltar.

1965, July 8. A new **coalition government** on Gibraltar proclaimed its desire for free association with Great Britain.

1966, May–Oct. Anglo-Spanish discussions of the Gibraltar situation in London. On Oct. 5 the Spanish government ordered the **closing of the customs post** at La Linea.

Dec. 14. Spain rejected the British proposal to submit the question of sovereignty over Gibraltar to the International Court of Justice.

1967, Sept. 10. A **plebiscite on Gibraltar** registered 12,762 votes. Of these, 12,138 favored remaining a British possession, while 44 voted for union with Spain.

1968, May 5. The Spanish government **closed the frontier** to all but residents and daily workers employed on Gibraltar.

1969, May 30. A **new Gibraltar constitution** declared the city "part of Her Majesty's dominions" until Parliament should decide otherwise, but in no case contrary to the wishes of the inhabitants.

June 5. By **further measures of closure,** the Spanish government threw 4,800 Spanish workers on Gibraltar out of employment.

June 27. The **ferry service** from Algeciras to Gibraltar was terminated.

July 30. Gibraltar elections. Formation of a government of the Integration with Britain Party together with the Independents, with **Maj. Robert Peliza** as chief minister (Aug. 6).

Sept. 29. Spanish naval demonstration off Gibraltar.

1977–80s. Talks between Spain and the United Kingdom opened in Madrid in 1977, and restrictions were eased in 1980. Continued talks led to an agreement signed in Brussels in 1984 and the reopening of the border in 1985. In the late 1980s, Gibraltar began to portray itself as a center for offshore investment, in hopes of reviving its economy following a downturn caused by a cut in British troops.

1998, July 6. The governments of Britain and Spain signed an agreement in which it was stated that NATO would be authorized to use the tiny island of Gibraltar, claimed by Britain, as a point of exchange and organization for economic, communications, and military NATO activities.

f. THE ITALIAN REGION

1. ITALY
(From p. 696)

Presidents: Enrico de Nicola (1946–48); Luigi Einaudi (1948–55); Giovanni Gronchi (1955–62); Antonio Segni (1962–64); Guiseppe Saragat (1964–71); Giovanni Leone (1971–78); Alessandro Pertini (1978–85); Francesco Cossiga (1985–92); Oscar Luigi Scalfaro (1992–   ).

1945, Nov. 30. The leader of the Christian Democrats, **Alcide de Gasperi,** formed a new government supported by all major parties.

1946, Jan. 1. With the **transfer of Bolzano** province by the Allies, the whole country, except for Venezia Giulia (claimed by both Italy and Yugoslavia), was under Italian sovereignty.

May 9. KING VICTOR EMMANUEL III ABDICATED. His son proclaimed himself **King Umberto II.**

June 2. Elections to the **Constituent Assembly** gave 207 seats (out of 556) to the Christian Democrats, 115 to the Socialists, and 104 to the Communists. At the same time, a referendum rejected the monarchy, 12,717,923 votes to 10,719,284, thus making **ITALY A REPUBLIC.**

June 11. The prime minister, **Alcide de Gasperi,** was made temporary head of state.

June 13. King Umberto, while refusing to accept the popular verdict against the monarchy, **left the country** to prevent the outbreak of violence.

1947, Feb. 10. The **PEACE TREATY** with Italy was signed in Paris. Greece acquired the **Dodecanese Islands,** France gained the **Briga** and **Tenda** areas of northern Italy, and **Trieste** became a free territory. A final decision on the future of **Italy's colonies** was postponed. Italian **reparation payments,** after the Western Allies had waived their claims, were set at $360 million.

Dec. 22. The Constituent Assembly adopted the **new constitution,** which called for far-reaching decentralization of the government, a Chamber of Deputies, and a popularly elected Senate. Relations between Church and state remained unchanged. While ministerial instability became a fact of Italian political life, the industrialist- and Church-supported Christian Democrats remained strong, supplying the premiers for every government between 1948 and 1981. Meanwhile, the Italian Communist Party (PCI) retained the largest membership of all Italian parties and fostered an important subculture in Italian life.

Dec. 28. Ex-king **Victor Emmanuel died** in exile.

1948, Feb. 2. Italy signed a treaty of friendship, commerce, and navigation with the United States.

April 18. In the crucial first **national elections** under the new constitution, with Communist control as the main issue, the **Christian Democrats won an absolute majority.** The Popular Front of Socialists and Communists received 30.7 percent of the votes cast.

May 23. Prime Minister **de Gasperi** formed a new government that was severely hampered by Communist-inspired unrest, such as the **general strike** proclaimed by the Communist-dominated Federation of Labor (CGIL) in protest against an attempt on the life of Communist leader **Palmiro Togliatti** (July 14), who was shot and seriously wounded by a student.

June 28. Italy was allocated $601 million under the **Marshall Plan** to aid her economic rehabilitation.

Economically, Italy had suffered less damage from the war than other countries; only 15 percent of industrial installations in the north had been destroyed. Despite its ability to restore production quickly, however, the Italian economy suffered from the wide disparity between the industrial north and agricultural south. As a whole, **the postwar Italian economy began to prosper only in 1956,** and the price for prosperity for many was internal migration from the south to the north. The continued economic, political, and social differences between the north and south remain a source of tension in Italian life to this day.

Oct. 18. The noncommunist elements in the CGIL seceded and formed a separate trade union.

1949, April 4. Italy signed the **North Atlantic Treaty** despite strong opposition from the Left.

Nov. 21. The UN General Assembly decided for **eventual independence of Italy's former colonies.** Until such time, they were to remain under UN supervision.

1950, Jan. The government announced a **ten-year economic plan,** designed to wipe out Italy's large-scale unemployment. Some progress was made during 1950 with plans for much-needed agricultural reform, especially in the south, where the Christian Democrats created the Cassa del Mezzogiorno (Bank of the South) to finance development.

April 1. Italy assumed **trusteeship** under the United Nations over **Somaliland,** although it remained barred from UN membership by veto of the Soviet Union.

1951, May 1. A new **Socialist Party** emerged as a result of the union (April 4) of the right-wing Socialists, led by **Giuseppe Saragat,** and the Unitarian Socialists, led by **Giuseppe Romita.**

July 26. Premier Alcide de Gasperi's seventh cabinet was sworn in, following a decision on July 3 that the government needed more liberal members.

1953, Jan. 1. Civil rights were restored to several thousand former fascists, previously barred from voting and holding office.

Aug. 15. Veteran financial expert **Guiseppe Pella became premier** as fears spread that a Yugoslav seizure of Trieste was imminent.

1954. The state broadcasting monopoly RAI began regular television service. It was tightly controlled by the Christian Democrats and became a major factor in creating a more unified, modern Italian culture.

Jan. 5. An extended cabinet crisis began with the resignation of the Pella cabinet.

Feb. 10. Mario Scelba became premier of a government of Christian Democrats, right-wing Socialists, and Liberals.

Aug. 19. Alcide de Gasperi died.

Oct. 5. An **agreement was signed with Yugoslavia** that ended the Trieste dispute.

1956. In a sign of increased secularization, a couple married in only a civil wedding unexpectedly won a slander suit against the bishop of Prato after he had denounced them as "public concubines." The outcome spurred Cardinal Lercaro of Bologna to order his cathedral to be dressed in mourning for a month, and church bells tolled throughout the land.

April 23. A **constitutional high court,** similar to the Supreme Court of the United States, was inaugurated as the nation's supreme judicial body.

1957, Oct. 11. The 12-year rule of **San Marino** by Communists ended with the inauguration of **Federico Bigi** as the head of the government.

Nov. 14. The left-wing Socialists, led by **Pietro Nenni,** approved "unity of action" with the Communists.

1958. Giuseppe Di Lampedusa's novel *The Leopard* became the most popular novel in Italian history.

May 25–26. The center parties, led by the Christian Democrats, were victorious in the national elections.

June 25. Amintore Fanfani, secretary of the Christian Democratic Party, **became premier.**

1960, April 25. After two months of governmental crisis, President Gronchi ordered Ferdinando Tambroni, a Christian Democrat, who had resigned (April 11), to continue as prime minister.

July 27. Amintore Fanfani headed a new Christian Democratic government.

1961, Sept. 12. The government formally protested to Austria over terroristic acts by persons demanding autonomy for the **German-speaking populace of Alto Adige** province (formerly Austrian South Tyrol).

1962, Feb. 2. Premier Fanfani and his cabinet resigned to prepare for a **Center-Left government** with outside support from Pietro Nenni's left-wing Socialists. This ushered in a period in Italian politics known as the *apertura alla sinistra,* or opening to the Left, during which time Christian Democrats turned to the Left in forming their governments.

Feb. 21. Fanfani government was formed, composed of Christian Democrats, Democratic Socialists and Republicans, with left-wing Socialist parliamentary support.

1963, May 16. The Fanfani cabinet resigned following the results of parliamentary elections (April 28) in which the Christian Democrats lost 13 seats and the Communists gained 25.

1964, Jan. 11. The left wing of the Socialist Party, representing about 40 percent of the membership, announced that it would form a new group, the **Italian Socialist Party of Proletarian Unity.**

1964–68. A period of **political instability** and **social unrest.** The Center-Left cabinets, of which **Aldo Moro** headed three in this period, were unable to attack and solve major problems, because of conservative opposition even within Moro's dominant Christian Democratic Party and because of continuing dissension in socialist ranks.

1968, May. Following significant losses in the elections, the Socialists refused to participate further in the Center-Left alliance.

June 5. Resignation of the Moro cabinet following withdrawal of the Socialists.

June–Nov. Giovanni Leone headed an interim minority Christian Democratic cabinet.

Dec. 13. Mariano Rumor (Christian Democrat) managed to reconstruct the Center-Left combination and formed a cabinet with a program of sweeping reforms. It seemed impossible, however, to attain political stability. Despite growing unrest in student and worker circles, the government fell (July 5, 1969) following a split in the Socialist Party and desertion of the cabinet by the Socialist ministers.

1969, Aug. Mariano Rumor tried to carry on with a purely Christian Democratic government.

Oct.–Dec. Influenced by the student movement, **the labor movement** demonstrated the most persistent and violent conflict between workers and employers since 1920. With the government putting pressure on the employers, organized labor gained the highest settlement ever achieved at any one time, including large wage increases (about 25 percent in the early 1970s), the implementation of a 40-hour week, and limits on overtime work. Finally, the passage of a **Labor Relations Act** (1970) protected workers from employer control.

Despite these gains, the moderation of the PCI and the quick demise of the student movement in Italy contributed to the emergence of **terrorist violence** on both the extreme Right and the extreme Left.

Nov. 20. Agreement between Italy and Austria on a system of self-government for **Alto Adige** (South Tyrol).

1970, Feb. 7–March 27. Another prolonged cabinet crisis, following the **resignation of the Rumor government** and various vain attempts to construct a new coalition. Such a government was announced by Rumor on March 27, but lasted only until July 6.

Aug. 6. Emilio Colombo (Christian Democrat) presented a new coalition cabinet, renewing the Center-Left combination. Meanwhile **student riots, strikes, and demonstrations** of all kinds became almost endemic in several of the large cities (Dec.), making early action for reform all but imperative.

Dec. 1. After long and heated debates, the chamber of deputies passed the **first Italian divorce law,** despite vigorous opposition by the Catholic hierarchy and conservative organizations of many kinds. The law was upheld by a divorce referendum in May 1974. Divorce became a mobilizing issue for Italian **feminists,** bolstered by a younger generation of educated women no longer content to stay at home. The movement became a powerful force in Italy and pushed for more legislative changes throughout the 1970s.

1973, Sept. The secretary general of the Italian Communist Party, **Enrico Berlinguer,** proposed the "**historic compromise**" between the PCI and the Christian Democrats, reminiscent of Popular Front governments of the 1930s. After 1975, this policy garnered six regional governments and most big city governments for the Communists, and Parliament could not function without them. Ministerial positions remained elusive, however. The policy of reconciliation cost the party much of its rank and file, and it returned to a more militant stand by 1979.

Oct. The international oil embargo caused petroleum prices to sky-rocket, hitting the auto industry hardest. **Double-digit inflation began** and continued through the mid-1970s. The economic crisis resulted in low investment and high unemployment. At the same time, how-ever, an **unofficial economy** began to develop and thrive. This econ-omy was based on moonlighting on a massive scale. In this rebirth of "cottage industry," industrialists saved costs through decentraliza-tion, lower wages, and lower health and safety costs; workers made less money but did not declare this income on their taxes.

1975–77. The central government revised regional laws first developed in 1968–70. Thenceforth, Italy's 15 regions controlled most of the na-tional or local agencies on which Italian public administration rested. By 1980 the regions were spending 18 percent of the national budget and had become the main bodies responsible for health and social ser-vices. These changes greatly altered Italian politics, allowing new par-ties to build bases in various regions and creating patronage networks and new groups of elites.

1975. The government extended the state insurance fund (Cassa Inte-grazione Guadagni), guaranteeing laid-off workers at least 80 percent of their pay for up to a year. This increase in government spending worsened economic conditions.

The government revised **family legislation** to create equality within families. The new laws abolished dowries, allowed wives to retain their maiden names, and secured for married women the right to live where they chose. The minimum age for marriage was also reduced to 18 for both sexes, and illegitimate children were granted equal status with legitimate children.

1976. The Constitutional Court ended the state's broadcasting monop-oly, causing hundreds of local radio and television stations to spring up immediately. This change in broadcasting reflected the greater cul-tural changes Italy underwent in the 1970s; consensus was now even more difficult to achieve on issues of values and morality.

July. Giulio Andreotti formed a minority Christian Democratic gov-ernment after the Socialists withdrew parliamentary support. During the general elections that followed, the Communists gained several important posts in the Parliament.

1978, March 16. Red Brigade terrorists kidnapped former prime minister **Aldo Moro.** This left-wing terrorist organization had waged violent campaigns against the political and business establishment of Italy since the early 1970s. After the government refused to release a num-ber of prisoners as demanded, Moro's body was found in Rome (May 9). Terrorism began to wane in the late 1970s as the government passed new antiterrorist measures that allowed the police greater powers.

April–May. Parliament passed a liberal **abortion law,** which allowed free termination during the first 90 days of pregnancy for any woman older than 18. A referendum in May 1981 favored the law and rejected broad changes proposed by the Roman Catholic Movement for Life. The **Constitutional Court confirmed** (April 1988) the right of women to undergo abortion without the knowledge of their husbands.

Dec. 12. Italy decided to **join the European Monetary System** from its proposed inauguration in 1979.

1979, Jan. 31. The Communists withdrew from the official five-party parliamentary majority formed in 1978, bringing down the govern-ment of Giulio Andreotti.

1980. The Fiat company angered unions with the announcement of 23,000 layoffs. A protest strike, in which 40,000 Fiat automobile work-ers marched through Turin defying union leaders and demanding a return to work, ended in failure. This signaled a change in the country; for the first time since the demonstrations of 1968, management began to reassert its control.

Aug. After years of inactivity, right-wing terrorists blew up a restau-rant in the Bologna train station, killing 84 people and wounding 200 more.

1981, June 28. The Christian Democrats lost control of the office of prime minister for the first time since 1945, as Giovanni Spadolini, a Republican, formed a new government.

1982, Sept. In a campaign to eradicate the Mafia, Parliament passed an **anti-Mafia law,** specifying for the first time that association with the Mafia was a criminal offense. The campaign, which generated large

popular demonstrations against the Mafia, lasted into 1988, when 342 people were convicted of illegal activities.

1983, Aug. Bettino Craxi, leader of the PSI, became prime minister. He would hold the office longer than anyone since De Gasperi.

1985, Oct. The Italian government reasserted its sovereignty in a dispute with the United States over Italian-held terrorists responsible for the seizure of the ocean liner *Achille Lauro* and the murder of an American citizen.

1990, Feb. Parliament passed **tougher immigration laws,** to encourage illegal immigrants to register with the police and to ensure control of future immigration from outside the EC. The law brought Italy into line with the majority of EC member states.

1991, Oct. The government approved the formation of a new anti-Mafia investigation department that would coordinate the efforts of the po-lice, the military police, and the customs police.

Nov. 21. The Chamber of Deputies approved a **bill on the optional use of minority languages** in primary schools, government offices, and broadcasting.

1992–93. An investigation into corruption in Milan led by Judge Anto-nio di Pietro gained national attention as the web of those under investigation grew to include prominent members of all the major parties, including former prime ministers Bettino Craxi and Giulio An-dreotti. Throughout this period popular discontent grew against the *partitocrazia,* the system of rule under Italy's major parties.

1992, April. In parliamentary elections, both the Socialists and the Christian Democrats suffered setbacks, while a group of conservative regional parties known as the **Northern League** emerged as the fourth-largest party in the nation.

April 25. President Cossiga's resignation caused a government crisis, leaving Italy with neither a president nor a new government for nearly two months.

May 23. Judge Giovanni Falcone, who had been expected to lead a new anti-Mafia drive, was assassinated.

Aug. 7. The Chamber of Deputies approved special powers for the police to search and question Mafia suspects and also introduced better protection for witnesses and new rules for evidence in Mafia trials.

Sept. 17. Following Britain, Italy pulled out of the European Mone-tary System.

1993, April 18–19. Voters approved a new system of elections to the Senate by referendum, and voted to end state funding for political par-ties.

May 27. A bomb explosion attributed to the Mafia damaged the Uffizi Museum in Florence, generating popular anti-Mafia demon-strations throughout Italy.

1994, March 27–28. A conservative coalition party called the Alliance for Freedom won Italian elections. The group, led by Silvio Berlusconi, included a group labeled as neo-Fascist.

July 13–27. A financial scandal involving Berlusconi emerged. On Dec. 22 Berlusconi resigned to avoid a no-confidence vote.

1995, Jan. 13. The Italian president named **Lamberto Dini** the new pre-mier; Dini pledged economic and political reforms including pension cuts.

1996, Jan. 11. Dini resigned to avoid a no-confidence vote.

Feb. 1. The Italian president, **Oscar Luigi Scalfaro,** appointed a new government to be headed by Antonio Maccanico. On Feb. 16 Scalfaro dissolved Parliament because of Maccanico's failure to form a coali-tion government.

April 21. A coalition of Center and leftist parties came to power under the leadership of **Romano Prodi.**

1998, Feb. 3. Italian relations with the United States suffered a blow when a low-flying U.S. military aircraft severed a gondola cable at a ski resort in Northern Italy. Twenty people were killed.

May 3. After substantial economic rearrangement by Prime Minister Prodi in order to qualify, Italy joined the EU's Economic and Monetary Union (EMU).

July 7. Former premier Silvio Berlusconi was convicted of bribing government tax inspectors to protect his business interests. On July 13 Berlusconi was also found guilty on an unrelated charge of appro-priating illegal donations money worth nearly $12 million.

Aug. 19. Italy's largest insurance company, Assicurazioni Generali SpA, tentatively agreed to pay $100 million to the victims and surviving families of the Nazi Holocaust. These claimants had previously been denied access to policies that had been purchased from Generali before and during World War II.

Oct. 16. Prime Minister Romano Prodi's government fell after losing a vote of confidence by one vote in the Chamber of Deputies. Stemming from a dispute with the hard-line Marxist Reconstructed Communist Party, this vote ended the second-longest tenure of any Italian administration since World War II. Prodi was replaced later that month by Massimo D'Alema, head of the Democratic Party of the Left.

1999, Jan. 1. Along with France, Belgium, Germany, Luxembourg, Spain, the Netherlands, Ireland, Finland, Portugal, and Austria, Italy adopted the euro, a single European currency, as its monetary unit.

March 24. Former prime minister Prodi became the new president of the European Commission.

May 18. The popular treasury secretary Carlo Ciampi was elected president, replacing Oscar Luigi Scalfaro.

June 24. Nearly 2,000 Italian troops joined KFOR, a NATO-led security force, and entered Kosovo as a peacekeeping army.

Dec. 18. Prime Minister D'Alema's Center-Left coalition faltered, and the prime minister briefly resigned. Four days later D'Alema formed a new coalition government that was accepted by the Italian Parliament.

2000, April 16. In municipal elections, D'Alema's Democratic Party of the Left lost numerous posts nationwide. As a result, Prime Minister D'Alema resigned on April 19 and was replaced by former Socialist Party member Giuliano Amato and his new Center-Left coalition.

Sept. 26. As internal strife rocked the ruling Center-Left coalition, Premier Giuliano Amato stepped down from his position. He was replaced by the mayor of Rome, Francesco Rutelli, who vowed to run again in the April 2001 elections. This established Italy's 58th government since World War II.

2. THE VATICAN
(From p. 696)

1946, Feb. 18. Pope Pius XII ordained 32 new cardinals.

1949, July 13. A **Vatican** decree **excommunicated all Catholics who followed** and taught the **Communist doctrine** and denied the sacraments to those who "consciously and freely" supported Communist activities.

1950, June 30. A papal decree excommunicated all plotters against legitimate ecclesiastical authorities.

Nov. 1. As climax of the twenty-fifth Holy Year, **Pope Pius XII pronounced the dogma of the corporeal Assumption of the Virgin Mary.**

1954, May 29. Pope Pius XII officiated at a ceremony canonizing **Pope Pius X.**

1958, Oct. 9. Pope Pius XII died at Castel Gandolfo at the age of 82.

Oct. 28. The college of cardinals elected **Angelo Giuseppe Cardinal Roncalli as supreme pontiff.** Taking the name **John XXIII,** he was enthroned Nov. 4.

1961, July 14. Pope John XXIII issued the encyclical *Mater et magistra,* stressing the need to search for social justice and condemning materialism. He appealed for aid to underdeveloped areas and asked that workers be given a greater voice in industry at all levels.

1962, Oct. 11. Pope John XXIII opened the **twenty-first Ecumenical Council** of 2,700 Roman Catholic prelates at Vatican City.

1963, April 10. The pope issued the encyclical *Pacem in terris,* which called for a world community of nations to ensure the peace.

May 11. The **pope called on Italian President Segni,** in the first visit by a pope to a president of the Italian Republic.

June 3. Pope John XXIII died in Vatican City at the age of 81, after one of the most notable pontificates in the history of the papacy.

June 22. The sacred college of cardinals elected **Giovanni Battista Montini** pope (**Paul VI**). He was crowned on June 30 as the 262nd Roman Catholic pope.

Sept. 29. Pope Paul VI reopened the Ecumenical Council with an **appeal for the unity of all Christians.**

Dec. 4. The Vatican Council ended its second session after authorizing the **use of vernacular languages** in the mass and sacraments.

1964, Jan. 4. Pope Paul VI and Ecumenical **Patriarch Athenagoras I** of the Eastern Orthodox Church conferred in Jerusalem, during the pope's **visit to the Holy Land.**

Sept. 14. Opening of the **third session of the Ecumenical Council (Vatican II).** It ended on Nov. 21 with the constitution *(De ecclesia)* providing for the sharing of power in the Catholic Church between pope and bishops. It furthermore pronounced in favor of eventual Christian unity and recognition of autonomy for the Eastern churches.

1965, Sept. 14. Opening of the **fourth** and last **session of Vatican II.** The pope announced that a synod of bishops would collaborate in the governance of the Church.

Oct. 4. Visit of the pope to New York to address the United Nations General Assembly and to throw the weight of his authority behind the struggle for peace.

Oct. 28. The pope declared the decrees of Vatican II to be **Church doctrine.** He **denounced anti-Semitism** and **absolved the Jews of the charge of collective guilt** for the crucifixion of Christ.

1966, March 23. Visit of the archbishop of Canterbury to the pope, the first step in the attempt to reconcile the Anglican and Roman Catholic churches.

1967, Jan. 9–12. Meeting of Roman Catholic and Anglican delegations at Gazzoda, Italy, to explore the possibilities of unity.

July 25–26. Visit of Pope Paul to Istanbul, where he conferred with **Patriarch Athenagoras I** of the Greek Orthodox Church. The pope's efforts in behalf of ecumenism were rewarded by the return visit of the patriarch to the Vatican (Oct. 26).

1968, July 29. The pope, in an encyclical *(Humanae vitae),* condemned all **artificial methods of birth control,** despite the fact that a papal commission, after long deliberations, had recognized the threat of overpopulation to the world and had recommended approval of certain methods of birth control. The papal encyclical came as a great shock to world opinion and caused considerable consternation in Roman Catholic circles.

1970, June 5. Henry Cabot Lodge was named U.S. president Richard Nixon's **personal envoy to the Vatican,** reviving a connection established by President Franklin Roosevelt.

Sept. 12–17. The World Congress on the Future of the Church brought some 700 theologians to Brussels. Demands were advanced for a more democratic organization of the Church and Church procedures, a greater role for women, etc. In general it was felt that the Church needed a fundamental restructuring in the direction of greater decentralization.

Oct. 12. The pope, in a message to a convention of Roman Catholic physicians, declared **legal abortion** the equivalent of infanticide and called for "absolute respect for man, from the first moment of his conception to his last breath of life."

Nov. 23. By a *Motu Proprio,* the pope decreed that officials of the Curia should resign voluntarily on reaching the age of 75, and that cardinals, on passing the age of 80, should no longer have a vote in the papal elections.

Nov. 26–Dec. 6. A lengthy journey by air took Pope Paul on visits to **Southeast Asia, the Philippines, Samoa, and Australia.** In Manila, an attempt to assassinate him was unsuccessful.

1971. With the dissolution of the Vatican gendarmerie and the previous disbanding in 1968 of the Noble Guard and Palatine Guard of Honor, the Swiss Guard became the sole guarantors of internal security and public order in Vatican City, though Italian police continued to patrol St. Peter's Square.

1973, Dec. Pope Paul VI offered to collaborate on a solution to the Middle East problem. Arab and African leaders visited the Holy See to put forward their views on the future of Jerusalem and the holy places.

1978, Aug. 6. Death of Pope Paul VI. His successor, Albino Luciani (**John Paul I**), was elected on Aug. 26 and reigned only briefly, until his unexpected death on Sept. 28.

Oct. 16. Karol Cardinal Wojtyla (Pope John Paul II) of Kraków became the first non-Italian pope in 450 years. During his pontificate, he would travel more extensively than any of his predecessors, preaching to millions of people on six continents and in more than fifty nations.

Pope John Paul II's pontificate was shaped by two goals: a commitment to justice and peace, and a desire to affirm the unambiguous identity of Roman Catholicism since Vatican II. In implementing this second goal, he did not hesitate to use the Church's strong disciplinary rules against those who disagreed with him.

1981, May 13. Pope John Paul II was shot and wounded in an assassination attempt. The Bulgarian assailant, Mehemet Ali Agca, was arrested immediately and was sentenced on July 22 to **life imprisonment,** after a three-day trial.

Sept. The pope published an encyclical on human work *(Laborem Exercens)* that analyzed the place of work in human life and proposed a new economic order (neither capitalist nor Marxist) based on the rights of workers and the dignity of work.

1982, Jan. 16. Full diplomatic relations were established between the Vatican and the United Kingdom, ending the long-standing diplomatic rift.

1984, Jan. 10. The United States and the Vatican reestablished diplomatic relations, which had been broken off in 1867.

1986, April 13. In the first visit by a **pope to a synagogue,** John Paul expressed his abhorrence of the genocide of the Jewish people during World War II at Rome's central synagogue.

1988. The pope excommunicated **Marcel Lefebvre,** head of a Roman Catholic traditionalist movement, for consecrating four bishops against the Vatican's wishes and thereby causing a schism.

Feb. 19. The pope published his seventh encyclical *(Sollicitudo rei socialis)* to address the question of international solidarity and development needs.

1990, Jan. The Vatican banned **Fr. Leonardo Boff,** a renowned Brazilian liberation theologian who advocated the necessity of political action for gaining social justice, from preaching and theological teaching.

June. Nelson Mandela met with the pope during a visit to Europe.

1991. At year's end the pope convened a special synod on the problems in Europe caused by the collapse of communism, such as the rise of nationalism and anti-Semitism. Protestant and Anglican delegates accepted a papal invitation to attend, but the Orthodox Church sent only one emissary, reflecting the growing rift between the two churches over proselytism in Central and Eastern Europe.

Dec. The final report of the Anglican–Roman Catholic International Commission was declared not in accord with the fullness of the Catholic faith by the office of Joseph Cardinal Ratzinger, the doctrinal watchdog. This added considerable strain to attempts at bringing the two churches closer together.

1992. The **Universal Catechism,** after nine drafts, was finally completed. Such new sins as terrorism and offenses against ecology were condemned, but the most significant changes were that the term "grave" sin replaced "mortal" sin and that an attempt was made to understand the psychological factors that could lead to sexual sins.

March. Orthodox Church officials accused the papacy of seeking converts in its territory, worsening the increasing divisions between the Orthodox and the Roman Catholic churches.

May. The Most Rev. George Carey, archbishop of Canterbury, criticized the birth-control policy of the Roman Catholic Church.

1994, April 15. The Vatican began allowing girl altar servers to assist Roman Catholic priests during services.

1995, March 30. The pope made a strong encyclical statement against abortion, birth control, in vitro fertilization, genetic manipulation, and euthanasia.

July 10. The pope issued an informal letter **condemning bias against women and apologizing for the Church's own history of sex discrimination.**

3. MALTA

1947. Malta, a British base since Napoleonic times, was granted self-government. This was revoked in 1959 and restored in 1962.

1964, Sept. 21. The island became a **completely independent monarchical state,** at the request of the local government. According to a ten-year **mutual defense pact,** Britain retained the right to station armed forces there.

1966, March 26–28. In elections the **Nationalist Party** was victorious over the **Malta Labour Party.** The Nationalist leader, **Dr. Borg Olivier,** became prime minister.

1967, Jan.–March. The **Anglo-Maltese crisis** developed, deriving from the decision of the British government to accelerate the withdrawal of

military forces as a matter of economy. Since this was a major threat to the economy of the island, which depended largely on the British defense system, the Maltese government protested. An agreement was eventually reached (March 12) by which the British government slowed down its withdrawals and promised larger grants to cushion the rate of unemployment.

1968. Establishment of **a standing consultative group of NATO** to deal with any eventual threat to Maltese security.

June 13–16. Visit to Malta of the prince and grand master of the Sovereign Military Hospitaler Order of St. John of Jerusalem, Rhodes, and Malta, to renew the ties forcibly severed by Napoleon's conquest of the island in 1798.

1971–87. The Labour Party, under **Dominic Mintoff** and then **Carmelo Mifsud Bonnici,** dominated Maltese politics.

1971. Malta adopted a new comprehensive contributory insurance scheme, integrating a variety of earlier legislation. The new plan included an annual pension amounting to two-thirds of an individual's salary at the time of retirement.

1974, Dec. 13. MALTA BECAME A REPUBLIC within the British Commonwealth. The new constitution provided for a president, a prime minister, and a unicameral legislature.

1979. The British military presence ended in Malta.

1987. **Eddie Fenech Adami** led the Nationalist Party to electoral victory and became prime minister, a post he would retain after the 1992 general elections as well.

1989. A "neutrality and nonalignment" amendment to the constitution forbade any foreign military base or nuclear-weapons-carrying ship in Maltese territory.

April. Vincent Tabone was elected president.

1990. Malta applied for membership in the European Community.

1993, June 30. Malta's membership application was favorably reviewed, with EC concerns centering on the adjustment of the nation's economy and distinctive features of its legal structure.

1998, Sept. 5–6. In parliamentary elections, the Nationalist Party took back power and returned Eddie Fenech Adami to his position as prime minister. After the Labor Party had shunned many international pursuits during its reign from 1996 to 1998, the Nationalists showed renewed interest in EU membership and involvement in the NATO Partnership for Peace program.

g. SWITZERLAND

(From p. 697)

1946, April 2. Switzerland announced its decision to stay outside the **United Nations,** so as not to endanger its traditional neutrality.

1947, Oct. 28. General elections brought no important changes in the lineup of parties. The Progressive Democrats received 51 seats, the Social Democrats 48, the Catholic Conservatives 44, and the Labor Party (Communist) 7 of the total 194 seats in the Parliament (Federal Assembly).

1950s. Spread of **self-service stores,** displacing older shops; growing consumerism.

1950, Feb. Switzerland embarked on a **five-year plan of military preparedness** and announced that it would fight to defend its neutrality.

Sept. The executive **Federal Council (Bundesrat) expelled all Communists from government service.**

1952, Nov. 28. The Federal Council directed the Finance Ministry to draft a **constitutional amendment providing for a direct federal tax.**

1953, Dec. 6. After the Nationalrat (National Council, the popularly elected lower house) (March) and the Council of States (June) had modified a Finance Ministry draft, the voters rejected the constitutional amendment for a federal direct tax.

1956, Dec. 12. Reviewing Swiss foreign policy, **foreign minister Max Petitpierre** told Parliament that the Swiss could best keep the world and themselves secure by maintaining their traditional neutrality and by keeping their armed services strong.

1958, July 11. The federal government decided to equip the Swiss army with **nuclear weapons,** as the most effective way "to maintain our independence and protect our neutrality."

1959, Feb. 1. Male voters defeated a **constitutional amendment to allow women to vote** in national elections and to run for national office.

1960, March 6. Geneva citizens voted to give women the ballot in local elections.

March 23. Parliament ratified **Swiss membership in the European Free Trade Association (EFTA).**

1962, Sept. 24. Switzerland formally applied for **membership in the Common Market,** reserving the right to withdraw if Swiss neutrality were prejudiced.

1965, Feb. 28. A national referendum approved the continuance of the **anti-inflationary regulations** of the government.

Sept. The federal Parliament voted to continue for five years the **ban on the holding of land** and other property **by foreigners.** There was much concern over the fact that there were more than 800,000 foreigners, chiefly Italian workers, in Switzerland, and systematic efforts were made to effect a gradual reduction in their numbers.

1968, June. Agitation of the Catholic, French-speaking **population of the Jura** (part of the canton of Berne) for the establishment of the area as a separate canton. A federal special commission was set up (Aug.) to seek a solution to the problem.

1970. Women's suffrage: During the period from June to September, Parliament approved a **constitutional amendment on female suffrage for federal affairs and the eligibility of women for election to the federal Parliament.** The new constitution was endorsed by a national referendum held on Feb. 7, 1971. At the same time, a number of cantons also held referenda on the extension of the same rights in cantonal matters. Although in certain cantons these rights of women were restricted, progress on giving the franchise to women on cantonal and local levels continued in the following years.

1970-85. Immigration restrictions: Following the introduction of a new permit system in March 1970 to stabilize the number of foreign workers employed in Switzerland, the Bundesrat approved more stringent measures in 1973 through 1975 to limit the size of the foreign workforce, especially Italian workers. In 1983 and 1984, a law was passed on the revised rules of political asylum, under which the refugees had to prove they were not economic migrants.

1977, April 20. The Bundesrat decided to **join the Nuclear Suppliers' Group,** which was made up of states exporting nuclear equipment and materials and thus bearing a particular responsibility for the prevention of proliferation of nuclear weapons.

Sept. 25. Abortion issues: A national referendum narrowly rejected a proposal to allow the termination of pregnancy within the first 12 weeks.

A referendum in the canton of Zurich accepted a proposal to initiate **federal legislation to permit euthanasia** to be carried out by doctors at the request of a terminally ill patient.

1979, Jan. 1. The **Republic and Canton of the Jura was created,** bringing the total number of cantons to 23 (20 full cantons, 6 half cantons). Jura was the first new canton to be formed since the establishment of the Swiss Confederation in 1848.

1981, June 14. A national referendum approved a **constitutional amendment on the guarantee of equality of rights and opportunities for men and women.** On the same day, the Swiss electorate also approved a constitutional article on the protection of consumers.

1984, March-Dec. The Parliament voted in favor of Switzerland's joining the United Nations. But on **March 16, 1986, a national referendum rejected full Swiss membership in the UN,** though it kept its observer status and its membership in various UN organizations.

Oct. 2. For the **first time in Swiss history, a woman, Dr. Elisabeth Kopp, was elected to the Bundesrat,** serving as head of the Federal Department of Justice and Police.

1985, June 9. A national referendum rejected a new constitutional amendment that was intended to ban all abortions except when the mother's life was in danger, and all forms of birth control that destroyed the embryo after conception.

Sept. 22. Marital law: A national referendum approved the **reform of the 1907 marital law,** effective Jan. 1, 1988, which described husband and wife as "equal partners," gave a spouse not in paid employment the right to an income from his or her partner, and, in cases of divorce, established the wife's right to half of the family wealth.

1986, Nov.-Dec. Thirty tons of toxic waste were released into the Rhine in a fire at Sandoz Company's chemical warehouse in Basel; the spill was considered the worst environmental disaster in Europe in decades.

1988, Oct. The government further tightened immigration laws, banning political asylum seekers from working for the first three months.

1991, March 3. A national referendum approved a reduction of the voting age from 20 to 18.

Sept. 16. The government **abolished the death penalty** for wartime offenses, almost 50 years after it was abolished for civilian offenses.

1992, May. The government announced its decision to **apply for EC membership,** but a referendum voted against it.

Dec. 9. The Federal Assembly elected Adolf Ogi and Otto Stich as president and vice president, respectively.

1993, March 10. Ruth Dreifuss was elected to the Bundesrat, in what was described as "a rare triumph over Swiss male chauvinism." She was the second woman elected to the Bundesrat.

Dec. 8. The Federal Assembly carried out the annual presidential elections for 1994, in which vice president Otto Stich became president and Kaspar Villiger became vice president.

1994, March 16. The lower house of Parliament approved legislation, effective July 1, giving police increased powers to arrest foreigners who were unable to identify themselves, the power to imprison them for up to three months, and sweeping powers to search homes.

1998, Aug. 12. The two largest Swiss banks, Credit Suisse Group and UBS AG, reluctantly agreed to pay $1.25 billion in reparations to victims of the Nazi Holocaust and other tragedies wherein stolen or "lost" assets had been unrecoverable since World War II.

Dec. 9. Ruth Dreifuss, leader of the Social Democratic Party, became Switzerland's first female president as well as its first Jewish president. She took office on Jan. 1, 1999, and replaced Pres. Flavio Cotti.

1999, June 13. In a national referendum, Swiss voters supported a proposal to further restrict the influx of foreign refugees seeking asylum in mountain-protected Switzerland.

Oct. 24. In elections for the National Council, the nativist Swiss People's Party had the largest total vote and won the second-largest number of seats, which threatened to destabilize Switzerland's four-party ruling coalition. The party's campaign platform opposed immigration and advocated European isolationism.

2000, Sept. 24. The Swiss electorate rejected a plan to limit the number of foreigners in the country to 18 percent of the population. This was the fourth referendum of its kind since 1970; all of them failed to pass the restrictive plan.

h. GERMANY

(From p. 701)

Chancellors (Federal Republic): Konrad Adenauer (1949–63, Christian Democrat); Ludwig Erhard (1963–66, Christian Democrat); Kurt Kiesinger (1966–69, Christian Democrat–Christian Social Union); Willy Brandt (1969–74, Social Democrat); Helmut Schmidt (1974–82, Social Democrat); Helmut Kohl (1984–98, Christian Democrat); Gerhard Schroeder (1998–, Social Democrat).

The end of World War II brought profound changes to Germany. The fighting itself left the country in ruins, the outbreak of cold war hostilities led to **partitioning** in 1949, and in East and West Germany the dismantling of traditional structures of power by occupation forces produced very different cultural shifts as well as contrasting economic trajectories. After four decades of development along separate paths under divided statehood, Germany unified in 1989. One country again, Germany began to face a series of new challenges that tested not only its economic strength, but also the nation's cultural integrity and social cohesiveness.

1945, April 30. ADOLF HITLER COMMITTED SUICIDE IN BERLIN as Soviet forces captured the city.

May 8. Terms of **unconditional surrender, signed at Reims** on the previous day, became effective and **ended the Second World War in Europe.** Surrender terms were also signed in Berlin between German and Soviet commanders.

With the total defeat of the Hitler regime, no German government remained. Instead, supreme authority was vested in an **Allied Control**

Council of Great Britain, France, the United States, and the Soviet Union. Each of these powers administered its own occupation zone, with the Soviet Union holding the region east of the Elbe. The former capital, Berlin, was likewise divided into four sectors. Future policy toward Germany had been outlined at the Potsdam Conference, though its implementation varied in the different occupation zones. The victors' most immediate measures were concerned with the liquidation of the Nazi system, the transformation of Germany's economy to peacetime production, and the transfer of administrative functions into German hands. On Nov. 20 the trial of major Nazi leaders opened at Nuremberg before an inter-Allied tribunal. In addition, thousands of lesser Nazis were removed from office and held for trial. Also on Nov. 20, the Control Council approved the transfer of 6,500,000 Germans from Austria, Hungary, Czechoslovakia, Poland, and the German region beyond the Oder-Neisse line, which had been handed to Poland at the Potsdam Conference, pending a peace settlement. In the months that followed, Germany's industrial power was drastically reduced by the dismantling of the war plants and the removal of equipment for reparations purposes. At the same time, large stores of food were imported to maintain a minimum ration. In all occupation zones, political parties were authorized by the end of 1945. In the Soviet zone administrative authority was vested in the provincial councils, which immediately initiated far-reaching land reforms. In the three Western zones, German self-government was initiated on local and provincial levels.

1946, Jan. 27. Local elections in the U.S. zone resulted in victory for the Christian Democrats, with the Social Democrats in second place.

March 26. The Allied Control Council limited the future level of German production to half its 1938 volume, with German steel capacity set at 7.5 million tons. These limitations soon proved unworkable, since they seriously hampered German recovery.

April 21. The Social Democrats and Communists in the Soviet zone merged into the Communist-directed Socialist Unity Party (SED), which received majorities in all subsequent elections. The Liberal Democrats and the Christian Democrats continued to exist but had no power.

May. The closing of the American zone to any further Soviet extraction of industrial equipment marked the rapid deterioration of discussions on the issue of reparations.

June 30. Elections for constituent assemblies in the American zone brought victories for the Christian Socialists in Bavaria, the Christian Democrats in Wuerttemberg-Baden, and the Social Democrats in Greater Hesse.

July 2. The first of several political amnesties was declared by the Americans, to help overcome some of the difficulties of large-scale denazification.

Sept. 30. The International Tribunal at Nuremberg announced its decisions. The Nazi Leadership Corps, the Schutzstaffel (SS), the Security Police, and the Gestapo were found to have been criminal organizations, while the SA (Sturm Abteilung), the cabinet, and the general staff were acquitted. Of the 22 defendants, 3 were acquitted and the rest received sentences ranging from ten years' imprisonment to death. Shortly before his scheduled execution, Hermann Göring committed suicide (Oct. 15).

Dec. 2. U.S. secretary of state James F. Byrnes and British secretary of state for foreign affairs Ernest Bevin signed an agreement for the economic fusion of the U.S. and British zones (Bizonia), inviting France and the Soviet Union to join.

1947, March 10–April 24. The Moscow conference of the Big Four foreign ministers revealed considerable disagreement between the Soviet Union and the West on the German question. Notably, the Soviet demand for $10 billion in German reparations, to be paid from current production, ran counter to the U.S.-British policy of making western Germany economically self-supporting. The only agreement reached was on the formal abolition of the state of Prussia.

June 2. A German Economic Council was created to direct bizonal economic reconstruction.

Aug. 29. A revised plan for western German industry set the 1936 production level as the ultimate goal and raised the yearly figure for steel production.

Oct. 5. Elections in the Saar brought victory to the Christian Peo-

ple's Party and the Socialists, and was seen as a popular endorsement of the new Saar constitution adopted previously by these parties.

Nov. 25–Dec. 15. Another unsuccessful meeting of the Council of Foreign Ministers in London ended in open disagreement over German peace terms. Economic issues in general, and reparations in particular, constituted the main stumbling block in formulating a coordinated plan for the administration of the four Allied zones.

1948, Feb. 6. A new bizonal charter made the economic fusion of the British and American zones, Bizonia, a reality.

Feb. 13. As a countermove, Soviet authorities conferred extensive powers on a German Economic Commission in the Soviet zone. Subsequently the British, French, and Americans agreed to proceed with plans to draft a separate constitution to revive German political authority in the West.

March 20. The Soviet delegates walked out of the Allied Control Council, after charging the Western powers with undermining the quadripartite administration of Germany.

April 1. Alarmed by the degree to which the city was becoming a capitalist outpost within eastern Germany, the Soviets began interfering with traffic going between Berlin and western Germany.

June 18. The Western powers announced the introduction of currency reform in western Germany, establishing the stable deutsche mark, and initiating a process of rapid economic recovery.

June 23. Soviet authorities introduced a currency reform for the Soviet zone.

July 24. Disagreement between the Soviet Union and the West over the latter's program of economic and currency reforms brought complete Soviet stoppage of rail and road traffic between Berlin and the West. To circumvent this blockade, the Western powers began a large-scale airlift of vital supplies (BERLIN AIRLIFT).

Nov. 30. After ousting the democratic majority in the Berlin municipal assembly, the Communists set up a new administration, claiming authority over the whole of Berlin.

Dec. 5. In response to the Communists, elections in the western sectors of Berlin gave the Socialists 64.6 percent of the vote, and Socialist Ernst Reuter became lord mayor.

Dec. 28. The United States, Great Britain, France, and the Benelux countries constituted themselves (and eventually Germany) as an International Ruhr authority with far-reaching powers of control.

1949, Jan. 17. The Western Allies established a military security board to supervise German disarmament and demilitarization.

March 19. The Soviet-sponsored People's Council in eastern Germany approved a draft constitution for a Democratic Republic of Germany and called for the election of a People's Congress.

April 8. The three Western powers agreed on an Occupation Statute for western Germany, which assured the Germans considerable self-government while reserving far-reaching powers to the occupation authorities. Simultaneously, dismantling provisions were eased and numerous industrial restrictions were removed, to meet the German demand for greater economic freedom.

1. THE GERMAN FEDERAL REPUBLIC (WEST GERMANY)

1949, May 8. The western parliamentary council adopted the Basic Law (Grundgesetz) for the FEDERAL REPUBLIC OF GERMANY. While following the Weimar Constitution in many respects, the Basic Law tried to avoid the main shortcomings of its predecessor. The new constitution provided for freedom of association, banned forced labor, guaranteed private property, and declared that men and women had equal rights. Representing a political compromise, the Basic Law left the federal legislature with far-reaching powers to define economic structures and specific labor rights. It was subsequently ratified by all states except Bavaria. The Federal Republic, with Bonn as its capital, came into existence on May 23.

The creation of two separate nations in Germany was one of the first tangible political results of the outbreak of the cold war. Because the Allies did not carry their wartime cooperation into the postwar period, no general peace treaty to deal with the defeated German state could be agreed on. Two very different German states emerged. West Germany had more than twice the population of its counterpart in the

East (45 million versus 18 million), and it possessed, without question, the bulk of the nation's industrial capacity. These structural features contributed to the West German "economic miracle," a term used to describe the economic takeoff that Germany experienced after 1951.

May 12. The **Berlin blockade** was officially lifted.

Aug. 14. Elections for the Bundestag (lower house) in **West Germany** gave the Christian Democratic Party a small lead over the Socialist Party, with the Free Democrats holding the balance. The division of Berlin, the traditional base of support for the Social Democrats, contributed to the Christian Democrats' success in 1949, and to the party's ability to function as the ruling political power in West Germany for two decades to come. Also on Aug. 14, a **U.S. court at Nuremberg** concluded the last of its **war crimes trials** with the sentencing of 19 German government officials and diplomats.

Sept. 12–15. THEODOR HEUSS (Free Democrat) was **elected president**, and **KONRAD ADENAUER** (Christian Democrat) was elected **CHANCELLOR** of the **Federal Republic.**

Sept 30. The **Berlin airlift ended** its operation after 277,264 flights.

Nov. Industrial production reached 93 percent of the 1936 level, but the influx of more than 8 million Germans from the East caused widespread unemployment.

Dec. 15. West Germany received the first allotment of funds from the Economic Cooperation Administration, and thus **became a full participant in the Marshall Plan.**

1950s. During the 1950s, West Germany experienced **spectacular economic growth.** Real output climbed by about 8 percent per annum (a rate higher than anywhere else in Europe during the decade), inflation remained low, and by 1960 the unemployment rate had fallen to less than 1 percent.

German writers in the 1950s focused on events in the period between 1933 and 1945. A new generation of more aggressively critical writers experienced increasing popularity. The most noted works in this movement included **Günter Grass's** novel *The Tin Drum* and **Rolf Hochhuth's** play *The Representative.*

1950, Jan. 16. The last rationing restrictions ended in West Germany.

May 9. The **Schuman Plan** was welcomed by the Bonn government (p. 838).

May. The Socialist opposition, under **Kurt Schumacher,** strongly criticized the growing collaboration of the Bonn government with the West on issues of military security. Schumacher's opposition to remilitarization found strong popular support, as was shown in the **Landtag elections** in the American zone (Nov. 19–26) that resulted in noticeable **Socialist gains.**

1951, Jan. 25. Industrialists agreed to trade union demands for a "**codetermination**" law, giving labor a share in the management of the coal and steel industries.

Dec. 6. Both the East and West German governments agreed to send representatives to the United Nations to discuss the holding of free elections in Germany. On Dec. 19 a five-nation commission was approved to inquire into the possibility of such elections. Soviet opposition made the prospect unlikely.

1952, Jan. 11. The West German Bundestag ratified the **Schuman Plan** by a vote of 232 to 143. The Communists and Socialists voted against it.

March 10. The USSR, in notes to the United States, Great Britain, and France, called for a four-power conference to discuss the **unification and rearmament of Germany.** On March 23 the Western powers replied that they would consider the establishment of an all-German government only on the basis of **free elections;** that such a government should not be empowered to rearm but could enter security agreements with other powers; and that the German borders drawn at the 1945 Potsdam Conference were subject to revision.

April 10. The USSR continued the exchange of notes on Germany that had begun on March 10. The new note proposed that all-German elections be held under a four-power commission rather than United Nations supervision. It rejected Western views on the rectification of Germany's 1945 frontiers.

May 26. Nine months of negotiations with Britain, France, and the United States ended in the **signature at Bonn of the contractual agreement giving West Germany internal independence.**

1953, March 4. The combined steel group of the Allied High Commission lifted its controls from the **Krupp industrial empire,** in exchange for Alfred Krupp's pledge to liquidate his iron, steel, and coal holdings, and not to return to those industries.

Aug. 16. The USSR proposed a **Big Four conference** within six months on a German peace treaty. Moscow suggested that East and West Germany meet first to set up a provisional all-German regime.

Sept. 6. In **general elections,** Chancellor Adenauer's coalition won a sweeping victory. The extent of Adenauer's political support was in large part attributable to the success of his regime's **economic policies.** Under the direction of **Ludwig Erhard,** Adenauer's economics minister, the Christian Democrats turned away from demand-stimulus policies and implemented what was to a large extent a **free market policy,** albeit one with a "social conscience." Specifically, the state provided insurance for all paid workers, who accepted lower wages in exchange for a sense of security and the benefits that accrued from the overall growth in the economy.

1954, Oct. 23. After France and Germany reached agreement on the Saar question, French prime minister Pierre Mendès-France joined the other Allies in signing the **protocols to make West Germany a sovereign and equal member of the Western alliance.**

1955, May 3. The Free Democratic Party broke with Chancellor Adenauer over the issue of German unification.

May 5. The **WEST GERMAN FEDERAL REPUBLIC GAINED SOVEREIGN STATUS** as the final instruments of ratification of the Paris treaties were deposited in Bonn; it joined NATO four days later (p. 839).

June 6. Adenauer resigned from his post as foreign minister, and **Heinrich von Brentano** succeeded him.

July 18–23. The **Geneva conference** discussed German unification among European and world problems, and provided for a Big Four Foreign Ministers Conference, which failed to agree on a solution to the German problem (Oct. 27–Nov. 16).

July 22. A **rearmament bill** was enacted that authorized the immediate enlistment of 6,000 officers and men to form the nucleus of a future army of half a million.

Sept. 9–13. During **Chancellor Adenauer's visit to Moscow,** West Germany and the USSR decided to establish diplomatic relations, and the USSR promised to release German war prisoners.

Oct. 23. Saarlanders voted **overwhelmingly to reject Europeanization,** agreed on by France and Germany (Oct. 5), and in a parliamentary election (Dec. 18) gave a majority to pro-German parties.

1956, July 25. Compulsory military service became law.

Oct. 27. A Franco-German agreement was signed for the **transfer of the Saar Basin to West Germany.** Also, France, Germany, and Luxembourg agreed to canalize the Moselle River, connecting the Lorraine steel industry with the Ruhr Valley.

1957, Jan. 1. The **Saar returned to Germany,** becoming the Federal Republic's tenth state.

June 18. A new **law of equal status** expanded on the constitutional dictum that men and women were to have equal rights by regulating matrimonial property laws and shaping the control that husbands and wives had over their children toward more equality.

July 1. The first 3 of 12 West German divisions formally joined the NATO command.

Sept. 15. In parliamentary elections, Chancellor Adenauer's Christian Democratic Union (CDU) obtained an absolute majority in the Bundestag.

1958, March 28. The Bundestag, after a heated debate, approved the government's **atomic armament policy,** and rejected a Soviet offer of a peace treaty and reunification with East Germany.

Nov. 27. Soviet premier Nikita Khrushchev's demand that the **four-power occupation of Berlin be terminated** created tension, which was eased by the visits of Soviet deputy premier A. I. Mikoyan to Washington (Jan. 4–19, 1959) and British prime minister Harold Macmillan to Moscow (Feb. 21–Mar. 3, 1959).

Dec. 14. The foreign ministers of Britain, France, and the United States reasserted their determination to maintain their **rights and duties in West Berlin,** including the "right of free access," and rejected Soviet proposals for the demilitarization of the city. On Dec. 31 they called for talks on Berlin within the context of German unity and European security.

1959, Jan. 10. The Soviet government rejected the Allied proposal of Dec. 31, 1958, and proposed, instead, **a draft peace treaty** providing for a demilitarized Germany and East German control over all access points to a free Berlin. It also recommended that 28 nations meet within two months in Prague or Warsaw, to establish a peace treaty with a neutralized but divided Germany.

March 26. Britain, France, and the United States invited Soviet participation in a Foreign Ministers Conference on the question of a German peace treaty and the ending of Berlin's occupation. The USSR accepted on March 30.

April 30. The United States revealed its decision to halt flights to Berlin above the 10,000-foot ceiling, as the Soviet Union had earlier requested.

May 11–Aug. 5. The **Foreign Ministers Conference in Geneva** on Berlin made no progress toward narrowing the gap between the Soviet demand for a peace treaty with both West and East Germany and the Western insistence on the reunification of Germany based on free elections.

July 1. **Heinrich Luebke,** the CDU candidate and minister of agriculture since 1953, was **elected president,** succeeding Theodor Heuss.

Sept. 28. At the end of Khrushchev's tour of the United States, U.S. president Dwight Eisenhower reported that the Soviet premier had promised not to set a deadline for the solution to the Berlin problem.

1960s. The slower economic growth rates that Germany experienced during the 1960s (compared with the previous decade) were due in part to labor shortages. In an effort to combat this problem, the German government in the 1960s recruited **"guest workers"** (Gastarbeiter) from Italy, Spain, Greece, Yugoslavia, and Turkey. Guest workers from southern and southeastern Europe numbered about 250,000 in 1960; by 1970 their numbers had grown to 1.8 million. While facilitating economic growth, guest workers, especially those from Turkey, faced **problems of social and cultural integration.** Problems relating to the integration of foreign workers in German society persisted in the following decades.

On the cultural front, writers and social commentators in the 1960s continued to explore the peculiarities of German history that could be drawn on to explain the acquiescence of the population in the atrocities of the Hitler regime. Increasingly, German culture aligned itself with wider European trends. One area in which this made itself evident was in **childrearing practices,** which moved away from an earlier emphasis on authoritarianism and obedience toward encouraging the self-expression and individuality of children.

1960, April 25. Khrushchev stated that a **separate peace treaty with East Germany** would terminate Allied entry rights into West Berlin "by air, land or water." He warned that any Allied attempt to maintain its rights in Berlin by force would be matched by Soviet force.

April 27. President Eisenhower reaffirmed that Western troops would not evacuate West Berlin.

1961, June 4. A **Soviet memorandum** called for a peace treaty with East and West Germany and the demilitarization of Berlin as a free city; and Khrushchev declared (June 15) that the USSR would conclude a treaty by the end of the year, and would "rebuff" any Western move to enforce its rights of access to West Berlin.

July 17. Britain, France, and the United States rejected Soviet proposals to hold a peace conference on Germany and make Berlin a free city, and a month later a U.S. force of 1,500 troops entered West Berlin to reinforce the Western garrison.

Sept. 17. In **parliamentary elections,** Adenauer's Christian Democratic Union lost its majority with 241 seats while the Free Democratic Party, with 66 seats, made great gains, and the Social Democrats won 190 seats.

Oct. 26–28. A **crisis arose over the right of U.S. civilians to enter East Berlin** when the East German government demanded that they must submit identity papers to East German border guards.

Nov. 4. After two weeks of negotiations, the CDU and the Free Democratic Party agreed on a **coalition government.** After the Bundestag approved Adenauer as chancellor (Nov. 7), the new government took office (Nov. 14) with **Gerhard Schroeder** as foreign minister in place of Heinrich von Brentano, who had resigned at the insistence of the Free Democrats.

1962, Nov. 2–28. A prolonged government crisis arose over the Free Democratic Party's demands for changes in the cabinet, ending with Adenauer's agreement to drop Defense Minister **Franz Josef Strauss** from a reconstructed government. **Kai-Uwe von Hassel** replaced him on Dec. 14.

1963, June 24. U.S. **president John F. Kennedy,** during a **four-day visit to West Germany,** pledged with Adenauer joint efforts to reunify Germany, achieve European unity, and defend West Berlin from Communist encroachment, and on June 26 electrified West Berlin with his statement in a public address: "I am a Berliner."

Oct. 16. Adenauer stepped down as chancellor and **Ludwig Erhard** succeeded him.

1964, Feb. 16. West Berlin **mayor Willy Brandt** became leader of the Social Democratic Party.

May 26. The **Moselle Canal** was opened by President Charles de Gaulle of France, Grand Duchess Charlotte of Luxembourg, and President Heinrich Luebke of the German Federal Republic.

July. **Agreement with Yugoslavia** on trade and cultural relations, the first step in a policy of improving and developing relations with Eastern European countries.

July 1. **Reelection of Heinrich Luebke as president** of the German Federal Republic.

Sept. Agreement between West Germany and East Germany allowing West Berliners to visit their relatives in East Berlin at four specified times of the year. Before long, these times were restricted to Christmas and New Year's, and presently the agreement became an additional bone of contention between the two Germanies.

Dec. Negotiations held within the Common Market in an effort to establish an acceptable price for grain finally led to an agreement on a low price to meet French requirements; this involved government subsidies for the West German farmers.

1965. The **Statute of Limitations,** which fixed July 1965 as the final date for the trials of Nazi war criminals, was extended to Dec. 31, 1969, in view of the large number of cases still to be tried.

April 7. The West German Bundestag held a one-day session in West Berlin, despite East German and Soviet protests and harassment.

Sept. The national elections once again proved a victory for the Christian Democrats and the Christian Social Union (CSU), despite a substantial gain by the Social Democrats. Ludwig Erhard remained chancellor, and a new coalition of the Christian Democrats and the Free Democrats assumed power.

1966, Oct. Defection of the Free Democrats from the government left Erhard and the Christian Democrats in a minority in Parliament.

Nov. 8. The Christian Democrats and the Christian Social Union chose **Kurt Kiesinger,** prime minister of Baden-Würtemburg, as their leader. **Erhard resigned** (Nov. 30).

Dec. 1. Kiesinger was named chancellor and undertook the formation of a **GRAND COALITION GOVERNMENT,** combining the Christian Democrats, the Christian Social Union, and the Social Democrats. **Franz Josef Strauss** of the Christian Social Union became minister of finance, and **Willy Brandt,** former mayor of West Berlin and the leader of the Social Democrats, became minister for foreign affairs.

Dec. 13. In a programmatic speech, Kiesinger emphasized his intention to revivify the **relationship with France** and to attempt improvement of relations with Eastern European countries—all, however, without prejudice to West Germany's position in NATO.

1967, Jan. 31. Establishment of **diplomatic relations with Romania,** the first achievement of the new **Ostpolitik,** with its emphasis on better relations with eastern Europe.

April 19. Death of former Chancellor Konrad Adenauer, at the age of 91.

June. Serious **student outbreaks** growing out of protests against the visit of the shah of Iran. The **Socialist Students' League** was particularly radical and violent and soon paralyzed work in many of the universities.

Nov. Rise of conservative nationalism in Germany. The **National Democratic Party,** under **Adolf von Thadden,** gained consistently in various state elections and gave rise to fears of a recrudescence of Nazism in Germany.

1968, April 11. An attempt to assassinate **Rudi Dütschke,** the leader of the Socialist Students' League, resulted in widespread violence, with demands for university reforms rapidly growing into demands for abolishing the existing democratic regime, establishing student and worker soviets, and opposing the passage of the emergency laws.

May 30. The Bundestag passed the **Emergency Powers Bill,** which, among other things, allowed the use of armed forces to help police in the event of insurrection.

Sept. Formation of a **new Communist Party.** The old party had been banned in 1956, and the new one was obliged to conform to requirements of the security laws.

1969, March 5. The **Socialist Party replaced the Christian Democratic Party as the dominant party for the first time since World War II. GUSTAV HEINEMANN** (Social Democrat) **was elected president** of the Federal Republic by the Bundestag, which was meeting in West Berlin despite protests and threats and obstructions to travel on the part of East German and Soviet authorities, who steadfastly maintained that West Berlin was not a part of the Federal Republic.

Sept. 28. In the **national elections,** the Social Democrats registered substantial gains (42.7 percent of the total votes cast).

Oct. 21. Foreign Minister **Willy Brandt** (Social Democrat) succeeded in arranging a coalition with the Free Democrats and **became chancellor** in succession to Kurt Kiesinger. The largest party, the Christian Democrats, was out of the office for the first time since the war.

Oct. 24. German mark revalued upward by 8.5 percent, a step that had been resisted by the Kiesinger government.

Oct. 28. The new chancellor outlined an extensive program of **domestic reforms** and spoke at length on the new government's **objectives in foreign policy.** For the first time, a chancellor recognized that **two German states actually existed,** even though West Germany did not and would not officially recognize the East German state. Brandt indicated his readiness to discuss ways to improve relations between East and West Germany, and also indicated his intention to push on with the West German **Ostpolitik,** while safeguarding West Germany's position in NATO.

Nov. In notes to Moscow and Warsaw, the West German government suggested the initiation of discussions looking toward an agreement on major areas of dispute including border questions. The Soviet government responded at once, and a start was made before the end of the year.

Nov. 28. West Germany signed the Nuclear Non-Proliferation Treaty.

Dec. Walter Ulbricht, the East German Communist Party leader, **sent proposals to Bonn** for improving relations. Discussions were to begin soon.

Dec. 16. The United States, Britain, and France, in identical notes to Moscow, proposed talks reviewing the **status of West Berlin,** with the objective of improving and stabilizing the situation in the disputed city.

1970, March 19. First meeting of Chancellor Willy Brandt and the East German prime minister Willi Stoph, at Erfurt. Though inconclusive, the meeting marked an important departure.

May 21–22. Second conference of Brandt and Stoph, at Kassel (p. 875). Discussions still failed to overcome West Germany's refusal to formally recognize East Germany as a state, and East Germany's refusal to accept the status of West Berlin.

Aug. 12. SIGNATURE OF THE WEST GERMAN–SOVIET TREATY of friendship and cooperation, a possible landmark in the development of the European international situation. The negotiations had been long and difficult, but agreement was evidently much desired by both sides. With the treaty, the West German government recognized the **inviolability of all postwar European boundaries,** including specifically the **Oder-Neisse line** as the western boundary of Poland. The Soviet Union undertook not to oppose the **reunification of Germany,** provided it could be achieved by peaceful means. Other provisions touched on cooperation in economic, scientific, and cultural matters, but the West German government made **ratification** of the entire treaty **dependent on the achievement of substantial improvements in the status of West Berlin.** Chancellor Brandt went to Moscow personally for the signing of this epochal document.

Dec. 7. Chancellor Brandt went to Warsaw for the signing of a **SIMILAR PACT BETWEEN WEST GERMANY AND POLAND.** The two parties renounced the use of force, and West Germany conditionally recognized the Oder-Neisse line as Poland's western frontier. They

further pledged to respect each other's territorial integrity and to settle all differences by peaceful means. **Brandt was awarded the Nobel Peace Prize in October 1971.**

1972, June. Leaders of **Baader-Meinhof Gang,** the **terrorist Red Army faction** that had emerged from the radical Left of the 1960s student movements, were **arrested.** But terrorist activities continued and reached their height in 1977 when the Red Army kidnapped and murdered H. M. Schleyeer, and hijacked a Lufthansa 747 jet (the Mogadishu hostage crisis). In February 1978 the Bundestag passed antiterrorist laws. With the suicides of Baader-Meinhof Gang members in a Stuttgart prison, German terrorism abated. Terrorism emerged again in the early 1980s, shifting to NATO and American personnel and installations as the primary targets.

Dec. 11. A **treaty between West Germany and Czechoslovakia** was signed, making the **Munich Agreement** of 1938 **void.**

Dec. 21. The **Basic Treaty** between East and West Germany was signed, with the recognition of each German state as an independent sovereignty. The Bundestag ratified the treaty on May 11, 1973.

1974, May 16. Brandt resigned as a result of an East German spy scandal; **Helmut Schmidt succeeded** him as federal chancellor. Under Schmidt, a series of progressive social policies was implemented, including the passage and ratification of a codetermination law that allowed equal numbers of representatives of owners and employees to form a supervisory body in each company. Simultaneously, the feminist movement contributed to a notable increase in the number of women attending German universities. Schmidt was reelected as chancellor in 1976 and again in 1980.

1975, July 25. The Bundestag approved the accords of the Helsinki Conference, which finalized the borders of European signatory states and guaranteed human rights in Europe.

1977–79. Rise of Green Party (later known as the **Greens**) in *Länder* (state) elections. It gained enough popular support to enter federal elections in 1980. The Greens offered themselves as an alternative to the so-called generation of '45, which had ruled Germany since the end of the war.

A **"second enlightenment"** affected West German theater in the 1970s, which turned the stage into a forum of social and political consciousness-raising by means of "total theater," with extensive audience involvement. **Peter Stein** was a representative director of this decade.

1981, June 11. Richard von Weizsäcker was elected governing mayor of West Berlin after the Christian Democratic Union's victory at the polls. He was elected federal president in 1984.

1982. Collapse of the SPD-FDP coalition in government since 1969. In mid-1982 Schmidt's Social Democrats (SPD) clashed with Genscher's Free Democrats (FDP) over economic strategy. On **Sept. 17,** four FDP ministers left Schmidt's cabinet.

Oct. 1. Helmut Kohl (Christian Democrat) was **elected chancellor** after a successful constructive vote of no confidence in the Bundestag. His CDU-CSU-FDP coalition obtained a clear majority in national elections in March 1983.

1984, spring. Lengthy and **major industrial dispute** over a 35-hour workweek in the printing and metal industries.

Aug. The Ministry of Labor and Social Affairs announced that roughly 300,000 persons had taken advantage of the year-old legislation designed to encourage guest workers to return to their country of origin, in response to growing unemployment.

1986, June. A new Ministry of Environment, Nature Conservation, and Reactor Safety was created. The move was in direct response to the public unease that followed the nuclear reactor accident at Chernobyl in the Soviet Union.

1987, March 11. Helmut Kohl was reelected as chancellor with CDU-CSU-FDP coalition. Kohl was reelected chancellor for the fourth time on Jan. 17, 1991.

1990. Beginning of German reunification. In **March, Chancellor Kohl campaigned for national unity** in East Germany with the promise to exchange East German marks one-for-one for West German marks when the country was reunified. On July 1, German monetary union was established with parity **between East and West German marks.**

June 21. West and East German Parliaments ratified the treaty reunifying the nation. The two German states signed the unification treaty on Aug. 31, with Oct. 3 set as the date for unity. On Sept. 12 the four Allied powers and the two Germanies met in Moscow and verified the Treaty on the Final Settlement with Respect to Germany.

July 16. Chancellor Kohl met Soviet president Mikhail Gorbachev and agreed to pay the costs of withdrawing and rehousing Soviet troops stationed in East Germany by 1994, while Gorbachev accepted a reunified Germany in NATO. In addition, West Germany assumed all of East Germany's commercial obligations to the USSR.

Oct. 3. Germany was reunified, with the former East Germany becoming five separate *Länder* (states) of the Federal Republic of Germany. **Berlin** was restored as the **capital** and the **seat of the united German legislature and government.** Moving the government from Bonn to Berlin was scheduled to take 8 to 12 years. Unification became known as *die Wende,* the turning point.

2. THE GERMAN DEMOCRATIC REPUBLIC (EAST GERMANY)

The outbreak of the cold war left eastern Germany in the Soviet sphere of influence. The new German state that emerged east of the Elbe, constructed in conformity with Soviet social, economic, political, and cultural patterns, became one of the Eastern European bloc of countries known in the Soviet Union as people's democracies, referred to in the West as satellites of the USSR. With a largely agricultural economic base and a peripheral relationship to the Soviet Union, East Germany's economic recovery in the postwar decades was far less meteoric than West Germany's. Still, held up in comparison with Eastern Europe generally, the economy in East Germany during the 40 years after the Second World War was one of the most successful in the region.

1948, May 16. Elections for a People's Congress in eastern Germany, despite official pressure, gave only 66.1 percent backing to the single list of Communist-approved candidates. On May 30 the Congress adopted the draft constitution of the **Democratic Republic.**

1949, Oct. 7. As a countermove to developments in the West, the **GERMAN DEMOCRATIC REPUBLIC** was established in eastern Germany without an election and with **WILHELM PIECK** as **PRESIDENT** and **OTTO GROTEWOHL** as **MINISTER PRESIDENT** (a figurehead role for an aging Social Democrat), and with a predominantly Communist cabinet. The Soviet military government was replaced by a **Soviet Control Commission.**

1950, June 6. An **agreement between East Germany and Poland** recognized the **Oder-Neisse line** as the final German-Polish frontier and evoked protests from West Germany.

Oct. 15. Elections to the East German legislature brought the expected "victory" for the official list of candidates.

1952, May 1. President Pieck announced that **East Germany would be forced to rearm** if West Germany became integrated with Western Europe. On May 7 the government announced plans to form an army to defend the Soviet zone "against aggression."

May 26–June 5. Increased pressure on West Berlin coincided with the signing of the **Bonn agreement,** as the East German government ordered new restrictions on communications between East and West Germany.

1953. The slow pace of economic recovery across Eastern Europe contributed to mounting popular discontent, which, in the absence of any organized opposition to the existing regimes, was expressed as nationalist resentment toward the Soviet presence. The death of Stalin in 1953 was viewed by many Eastern Europeans as an opportunity to reduce levels of Soviet control, thus de-Stalinization was accompanied by a degree of social volatility across the region. The most serious disorders in the wake of Stalin's death occurred in East Berlin, where the government had loosened some restrictions on worker protests.

May 28. The Soviet Union abolished the **Soviet Control Commission** in East Germany and created the post of **high commissioner,** to which **Vladimir Semyenov** was appointed.

June 16. The government's announcement of new norms for construction workers led to a strike by East Berlin workers and then, on the following day, to a full-fledged revolt.

June 17. The Soviet Union sent tanks and troops against the 30,000 East Berlin rioters. Twenty-five persons died in the violence.

June 22. As arrests continued, the Communist government offered a **ten-point reform program,** including provisions for pay increases, reduced work, and improved living conditions. Despite these government concessions to workers, **600 persons were subsequently executed** for their involvement in the uprising.

1954, March 7. Walter Ulbricht emerged as the new strongman, when President Pieck and Premier Grotewohl were relieved of their chairmanship positions on the Communist Party's Central Committee.

March 25. The USSR granted **"full sovereignty"** to East Germany and announced the end of its occupation, although Soviet troops would remain there "temporarily," for security reasons.

1955, Sept. 20. East German–Soviet agreements were signed conferring sovereignty on East Germany as well as control over civilian traffic between Berlin and West Germany.

1956, July 17. Premier Otto Grotewohl and Soviet Premier N. A. Bulganin, meeting in Moscow, declared that **German unification** must proceed via East-West German negotiations.

1957, Nov. 14. East and West Germany reached an **agreement to trade** $260 million in goods in 1958.

1959, Nov. 24. East and West Germany agreed on $548 million in trade for 1960.

1960, Sept. 8. East Germany announced that **travel by West Germans to East Berlin** was under permanent restriction; West Germans would thenceforth have to obtain a Communist police pass before entering East Berlin. The Allied powers declared that this was the most serious infringement to date of the four-power agreement on Berlin.

Sept. 30. The West German cabinet decided to break off trade relations with East Germany after Jan. 1, 1961, if East Germany did not lift its travel restrictions, but later (Nov. 25) announced that it would reopen trade talks despite the restrictions, and finally (Dec. 29) agreed to extend the trade pact.

1961, Aug. 13. The **East German government closed the border between East and West Berlin** and began (Aug. 15) to build a wall between the two zones. These actions followed publication of a communiqué by the Warsaw Pact nations, appealing to the East German Parliament to halt the **mass flight of refugees** to the West. While the **Berlin Wall** represented a crucial cold war symbol in the West, historians have also noted that by halting the flight of refugees to the West, East Germany was able to stabilize its economy and eventually become one of the most prosperous communist countries in the world.

1963, Dec. 19. After being granted permission by the East German government, more than 500,000 West Berliners visited relatives in East Berlin during the holidays, through Jan. 5, 1964.

1964, Sept. 21. Death of Otto Grotewohl, who was succeeded as prime minister by **Willi Stoph.**

1965, April 7. Closure of the autobahn between West Germany and West Berlin in protest against the meeting of the West German Parliament in Berlin. Higher tariffs were also imposed on rail and water traffic from West Germany to Berlin.

1966, Feb. Ulbricht suggested talks between the West German Social Democratic Party and the East German Communist Party. The plan for an exchange of views finally broke down over legal details.

April. Professor Robert Havemann, a critic of the Ulbricht regime, was dismissed from membership in the Academy of Sciences in East Berlin, a clear warning that the East German regime would allow no more free expression than the Soviet Union.

1967. East Germany signed treaties of friendship with Poland, Czechoslovakia, and Hungary, involving promises on the part of these powers not to open diplomatic relations with West Germany unless the latter were prepared to recognize the existence of two German states.

April. Chancellor Kurt Kiesinger of West Germany submitted suggestions for improving relations with East Germany. Ulbricht responded by proposing a meeting between Kiesinger and Stoph and the negotiation of a treaty "between the two German states."

May 10. Stoph formally proposed talks, which the West German government agreed to (June 13), but only on condition that formal recognition of the German Democratic Republic would not be involved.

Sept. 18. Stoph sent the Bonn government a detailed draft treaty that set forth such extreme demands that the draft was ignored by the West German government.

1968, April. A **new constitution** for "the Socialist State of the German

Nation" was approved by referendum. It claimed East Berlin as the state's capital.

Aug.–Sept. Soviet intervention against the Czech regime of Alexander Dubček. The East German attitude was harshly anti-Czech, and East German troops participated in the occupation of Czechoslovakia.

1969, Dec. 18. New **Ulbricht proposals** to Bonn, asking for full diplomatic relations, the recognition of West Berlin as an independent unit (not part of West Germany), and so on.

1970, March–May. The **first meetings** between West German chancellor **Willy Brandt** and the East German chairman of the Council of State (prime minister) **Willi Stoph** (p. 873). Though inconclusive, their meetings marked an important departure from their previous relationship and led to their mutual diplomatic recognition in 1973.

1971, May 3. Walter Ulbricht, first secretary of East Germany, **resigned;** his successor was **Erich Honecker,** who also became the chairman of the Council of State and the general secretary of the East German Communist Party (a change of title from first secretary) in 1976.

1972, Nov. Some **30,000 political prisoners were released in an amnesty.**

1973, Sept. 18. Both East and West Germany became members of the United Nations after they recognized each other's sovereignty.

1981, April 11–16. At the Tenth Congress of the Socialist Unity Party (SED), Honecker expressed a will to maintain and improve relations with West Germany. Prime Minister Willi Stoph stressed the development of heavy industry in a new five-year plan.

1984, Sept. 4. Honecker postponed a visit to West Germany scheduled for October after Soviet attacks on his perceived willingness to improve relations with West Germany.

Mid-1980s. A preoccupation with the German past again emerged as part of what the intellectual community referred to as the **"historians' debate"** *(Historikerstreit).* Extensive discussion centered around the effort to reckon with Germany's National Socialist heritage.

1986, Feb. 19–22. East German Parliament president Horst Sindermann visited Bonn. A cultural agreement was signed between East and West Germany.

1987, July. The Council of State announced the **abolition of the death penalty** and a general amnesty, effective on Oct. 8, for all prisoners except those sentenced for war crimes, espionage, or murder.

Sept. 7–11. Honecker visited West Germany. The visit was the first undertaken by an East German head of state. Several agreements were signed between the two German states.

1988, May. The Communist Party's renunciation of one-party rule in Hungary and the subsequent opening of the Hungarian-Austrian border led thousands of East Germans to pour into Hungary before going on to West Germany.

1989, spring. Throughout the spring, the Honecker regime expressed open hostility toward Soviet president Mikhail Gorbachev's reform movement.

Sept. Despite Gorbachev's requests for political and economic reforms, the Honecker regime resisted, insisting that change was unnecessary. Popular opposition to the Communist government began to mount very quickly. In the five months following September 1989, party membership shrank from 2.3 million to 890,000. Thousands of East Germans either burned or sent back their party booklets.

Oct. 6–7. Soviet president Gorbachev's visit to East Germany for its fortieth anniversary acted as the catalyst for the **resignation on Oct. 18 of Erich Honecker,** who had been in power for 18 years. Egon Krenz was elected to succeed him.

Nov. 5. As popular discontent against Communist rule mounted, so did the exodus to West Germany. On the weekend of Nov. 5, 10,000 East Germans left for the West via Czechoslovakia.

Nov. 9. A revolutionary atmosphere took hold in East Berlin. Acting independently, some Politburo members authorized that a few border crossings to West Berlin be opened for a limited time. Thousands of East Germans streamed to the Wall, and local authorities found it impossible to stem the tide. **The Berlin Wall was broken open, and East Germany opened its borders to West Germany.** The Wall was torn down in the following months.

Nov.–Dec. The Communist government and the Politburo resigned; the Communist Party renounced its leading role.

1990, Jan. The Socialist Unity Party became the Party of Democratic Socialism as the mass exodus to West Germany continued.

March 18. The Alliance for Germany, a three-party coalition backed by West German chancellor Helmut Kohl, **won 48.1 percent of the vote in East Germany's first general election.** The Social Democratic Union won 21.8 percent, the second largest vote.

Aug. 23. After bitter debate, the East German Volkskammer **voted for the reunification with West Germany, set for Oct. 3.**

3. GERMANY, 1990–2000

1990, Dec. 2. The **first all-German elections** in almost 60 years took place. The ruling West German coalition of the Christian Democratic Union, Christian Social Union, and Free Democratic Party won the election. The SED, the former East German Communist Party, also won representation in the Bundestag. The federal government rapidly began to unify and improve schools, roads, and communication systems, while at the same time organizing sales of formerly state-owned industries in the East. Widespread pollution damage added to economic revitalization problems. With government resources strained, unemployment rose in the eastern states and stood near 14 percent in 1992.

1991, March. Former General Secretary of the East German Communist Party **Erich Honecker** fled to the Soviet Union and then, in December, sought refuge in the Chilean embassy in Moscow. He was forced to go back to Germany in July 1992 to face trial for alleged brutalities under his regime. In January 1993, Honecker was released from jail and exempted from prosecution for reasons of ill health. He immediately joined his wife in Chile.

Oct. 3. Racist violence: The first anniversary of unification was marred by about 50 attacks on immigrants throughout the country. In the first eight months of 1991, 4 people were killed and 169 injured in attacks on foreigners by neo-Nazis and other right-wing elements. The first year of unification was accompanied by an increase in membership in neo-Nazi organizations, from 1,200 to 6,000. Right-wing assaults increased from 270 in 1990 to 1,300 in 1991. Opinion polls also indicated a **substantial decline in support for parties of the governing coalition,** especially among eastern Germans, many of whom said they were made to feel like "second-class citizens" in the unified Germany.

1992, April. Major setbacks for Kohl government: Kohl's party lost in two *Länder* elections, there were public-sector strikes, and Foreign Minister Hans-Dietrich Genscher (FDP) resigned after 23 years in the cabinet.

June 26–July 10. Parliament approved **abortion legislation** applicable to the whole country, by which women had the right to an abortion during the first 12 weeks of pregnancy.

Aug. 22–26. Five nights of rioting at a reception center for asylum seekers near Rostock marked a resurgence of antiforeigner violence in eastern Germany. On each of these nights, several hundred neo-Nazis and skinheads attacked the reception center. Antiracism marches followed in Berlin, Frankfurt, Rostock, and other German cities.

Nov. 22–23. A racist arson attack was carried out on two houses occupied by Turkish families. Two young girls and their grandmother were killed as a result of the fire. The violence led to the government's banning (Nov. 27) of the neo-Nazi Nationalist Front. During the course of 1992, 2,285 extremist right-wing attacks were recorded, including 77 on Jewish cemeteries, memorials, and other buildings.

Dec. The German government moved to ban three more extremist right-wing organizations and to impose harsher sentences on those attacking foreigners.

1993, May 28. The Constitutional Court ruled that a woman's right to abortion on demand up to the twelfth week of pregnancy was not constitutionally guaranteed. Ruling that abortion in the first 12 weeks of gestation is not a criminal offense, the court left specific legislation on the issue to be enacted in the federal legislature.

May 29. In the wake of debate in the Bundestag over a constitutional amendment to limit political asylum, arsonists attacked a house in Solingen, killing five female Turks, aged 4 to 27. Three days of demonstrations by Turks and Germans against racist violence followed in Solingen and other German cities.

July. Unemployment figures for Germany indicated a considerable rise over the previous year's rates. In western Germany, unemployment reached 2,300,000, or 7.5 percent of the total workforce; in the former East Germany, 1,170,000, 15.3 percent of the workforce, found themselves unemployed.

July 1. A constitutional amendment to Article 16 of the Basic Law came into force. The new Article 16a imposed greater restrictions on the extension of political asylum to persons arriving from other countries.

Nov. 25. Amid the rising unemployment, Volkswagen and the metal workers' union agreed to introduce a four-day, 28.8-hour workweek beginning Jan. 1, along with 10 percent pay cuts, as an alternative to proposed layoffs of 30,000 of the 100,000 German Volkswagen workers.

Nov. 26. The Bundestag approved a federal budget that included significant cuts in social security payments, child allowances, and unemployment benefits.

1994, May 23. Germany elected Roman Herzog as president, making him the **first federally elected president since German reunification.**

1995, March 30. The Central Bank in Germany increased its cuts in order to help slow the depreciation of the U.S. dollar. On Aug. 24 the Bundesbank cut two of its important interest rates in order to slow the increasing value of the mark in hopes of stimulating the economy.

1998, Jan. 1. Unemployment in Germany, soaring to 12.6 percent, reached its highest level since before World War II.

Sept. 27. The Christian Democrats (CDU) were defeated in parliamentary elections by new chancellor Gerhard Schroeder's SPD. This ended Helmut Kohl's 16-year run as chancellor of Germany, the longest rule by any German chancellor in the 20th century. Kohl's government fell as a result of growing public discontent over Germany's economy. Schroeder had campaigned on a centrist platform, promising to lower taxes, reform the German welfare system, and increase pension and welfare payments, which had been cut under Kohl's government.

Oct. 27. The SPD formed a coalition government with the Green Party. Holding 345 of 669 seats in the Parliament, the new 16-member cabinet was made up of a few centrists and several left-wing reformists. The major objectives of the coalition included reductions in Germany's income tax, creation of 100,000 jobs, and a disputed plan to phase out German reliance on nuclear energy.

1999, Jan. 1. Germany joined ten other European nations in the implementation of the experimental single European currency, the euro.

Jan. 14. A government proposal was announced that would alter German law, allowing for the gradual reduction of nuclear energy sources. However, the plan was postponed indefinitely on Jan. 25.

Feb. 4. Germany's largest bank, Deutsche Bank AG, admitted to having helped finance the World War II Nazi death camp, Auschwitz.

March 11. Left-wing German finance minister and SPD leader Oskar Lafontaine resigned after several months of political struggle against Schroeder and several government-backed German business leaders. Lafontaine was replaced by Hans Eichel.

June 24. Germany contributed 8,500 soldiers to the NATO security force (KFOR) that entered Kosovo to maintain peace in the region. Prior to the 1998 NATO involvement in Yugoslavia, Germany had not participated in an armed conflict since World War II.

Sept. The German Parliament returned to its historic seat in Berlin.

Nov. 30. In a huge political scandal, former chancellor Kohl admitted that during his last five years in office he had accepted more than $1 million in political donations from unidentified sources. Kohl also admitted to violating German campaign finance laws by depositing the illegal contributions into secret bank accounts. Investigations of the scheme subsequently broadened to focus on activities of other prominent members of the CDU from 1982 to 1998.

2000, Jan. 18. Surrounded by charges of illegal fund-raising, Helmut Kohl resigned as honorary chairman of the CDU. Kohl refused to name any of the donors. The once-dominant CDU was almost ruined by the scandal.

April 10. Replacing former chancellor Helmut Kohl, who had led the CDU for eighteen years, Angela Merkel was chosen as the new party head for the Christian Democrats. Merkel was viewed as a very promising new personality who might save the party from its disastrous involvement in recent scandals.

July 14. Chancellor Schroeder by a narrow margin passed tax reform legislation that would cut taxes for the rich and eliminate the capital gains tax on German companies that sold shares in other companies.

The latter reform was expected to spur corporate mergers by German businesses.

Oct. 3. Though concerned about recent uprisings of anti-Semitic violence, Germany celebrated the tenth anniversary of the unification of East and West Germany.

i. AUSTRIA

(From p. 704)

1945, April 25. A **provisional government** was set up with **Karl Renner** of the Socialist Party as **chancellor.**

May 14. THE DEMOCRATIC REPUBLIC OF AUSTRIA was reestablished.

Aug. 8. The division of Austria and Vienna into **four occupation zones** was completed. The **Allied Council for Austria** assumed authority over matters affecting the whole of Austria.

Nov. 25. The first **general election** since 1930 gave the **People's Party** a majority over the Socialists and Communists.

Dec. 18. Leopold Figl (People's Party) formed a coalition cabinet with the Socialists.

Dec. 20. KARL RENNER was unanimously elected **PRESIDENT OF THE REPUBLIC** by the National Assembly.

1946, Jan. 7. The **occupying powers officially recognized the Austrian Republic** within its 1937 frontiers.

June 28. The Austrian government was given a large measure of authority by the Allied Council.

July 6. The **Soviets claimed,** as German assets, important **industrial establishments** in their zone of occupation.

Sept. 6. An **Austro-Italian agreement** gave considerable autonomy to South Tyrol (Alto Adige).

1948–50. Repeated **attempts to reach a peace settlement for Austria failed** because of Soviet and Yugoslav demands against Austria. To facilitate negotiations, the Western Allies renounced their own claims for German assets in Austria and made far-reaching concessions to Soviet claims for such assets, but the **deadlock continued through 1949 and 1950.**

1949, Oct. 9. General elections brought losses to both the **People's Party** and the **Socialists,** as many former Nazis rallied behind the new **Union of Independents.** Communist strength remained negligible. The coalition government of People's Party and Socialists remained substantially unchanged, despite their basic disagreement on economic questions.

1950, Dec. 31. Death of President Karl Renner.

1951, May 27. Theodore Koerner, Socialist mayor of Vienna, was **elected president.**

1952, June 14. After seven years, the Soviet government agreed to **reopen to Austrian shipping** that part of the Danube running through the Soviet zone.

1953, Feb. 6. A **deputy foreign ministers' conference** on an Austrian peace treaty was quickly deadlocked.

Feb. 22. In general elections the extreme Right and Left suffered serious losses, while the militant anti-Communist Socialist Party made substantial gains.

April 2. Julius Raab, formerly president of the chamber of commerce, formed a People's Party–Socialist Party coalition government.

June 8. The Soviet Union lifted its control measures along the border between the Soviet and Western zones.

July 30. The Soviet government announced it would pay its own **costs of occupation** in Austria after Aug. 5, as the United States had been doing since July 1947.

Aug. 17. The three Western powers withdrew their **proposal for a "short" Austrian treaty** and proposed a London meeting, Aug. 31, to prepare a full peace treaty for Austria, but the USSR rejected the invitation (Aug. 29).

1955, April 11. Chancellor Raab arrived in Moscow to discuss Soviet proposals for a treaty, and he agreed on terms (April 15) calling for the withdrawal of all occupation forces from Austria by Dec. 31.

May 15. After a fortnight of negotiations, a **peace treaty** with Austria was agreed on by the four-power Foreign Ministers Conference in Vienna.

July 27. AUSTRIA FORMALLY REGAINED ITS SOVEREIGNTY,

and the Allied Council for Austria held its final meeting in Vienna. Austria pledged **neutrality.** Western and Soviet occupation forces were withdrawn.

1956, May 13. Chancellor Julius Raab's People's Party won in the national elections.

1957, Feb. 8. The government gave Italy assurances of its intention to abide by the 1946 **agreement on South Tyrol.** Italy offered a continuation of talks with Austria on the problem.

May 5. Adolf Schaerf, **leader of the Socialist Party and vice chancellor, was** elected as Austria's third postwar **president.**

1959, July 10. The People's Party and the Socialist Party agreed to form a coalition government, thus ending a nine-week rift over the division of ministries within the cabinet. The coalition government, under Chancellor Julius Raab, was sworn in on July 16.

Sept. 13. Demonstrations in the Austrian Tyrol **protested Italian violation of the rights of Austrian Tyrolese, as guaranteed in the Italian-Austrian Tyrol agreement of 1956.**

1960, Sept 21. Foreign Minister **Bruno Kreisky** asked the UN General Assembly to discuss the status of the German-speaking minority in South Tyrol.

1961, April 11. Alfons Gorbach, head of the People's Party, was sworn in as chancellor, succeeding Julius Raab, who had resigned for reasons of health.

1963, April 28. Adolf Schaerf was reelected president.

Sept. 20. The People's Party elected former finance minister **Josef Klaus** chairman, to succeed Gorbach.

1964, Feb. 26. Chancellor Gorbach resigned, and on April 2 Josef Klaus succeeded him at the head of a People's Party–Socialist Party coalition government.

1965, Feb. 28. Death of President Adolf Schaerf.

March–Dec. Intermittent **negotiations with the Common Market,** with a view to Austria's admittance, were systematically opposed by the Soviet Union and made no progress because of uncertainty on the side of the EC.

May. Franz Jonas, former mayor of Vienna, was **elected president.**

Oct. 23. The government resigned as a result of recurring party wrangles.

1966, March. The **national elections** resulted for the first time in an **absolute majority for the People's Party.**

April 19. End of the coalition government. Josef Klaus became chancellor with a strictly People's Party cabinet. He at once introduced an extensive program of economic, educational, and other reforms.

Aggravation of the **situation in the South Tyrol,** where Austrian terrorists engaged in numerous bombings and other outrages.

1967, March. Visit of Chancellor Klaus to Moscow. The Soviet government refused to abandon its opposition to Austrian membership in the Common Market but signed a cultural agreement with Austria. During the year, the chancellor visited a number of Balkan countries and established better relations, even with Hungary.

1968, Nov. 13. A **constitutional amendment** reduced the voting age from 21 to 19.

1969, Nov. The South Tyrol People's Party accepted the **Italian proposals for autonomy** of the province of Bolzano, from then on to be known as South Tyrol. Official approval was given to this settlement by the Italian government (Dec.) and the Austrian government (Dec. 16).

1970, March 1. Victory of the Socialist Party in the national elections. **Bruno Kreisky** replaced Klaus as chancellor and restored the traditional coalition between the Socialist and People's Parties.

1970–1983. Socialist rule. Bruno Kreisky, chairman of the Socialist Party, was **chancellor.** After winning an overall majority in general elections on Oct. 10, 1971, the Socialist Party became the dominant party after a long rivalry with the conservative People's Party. The Kreisky government adopted pragmatic policies and emphasized the creation of a welfare state and the continuation of neutrality in international affairs. In April 1983 Kreisky announced his resignation from the post of federal chancellor after the Socialist Party lost its absolute majority in general elections.

1970, Nov.–1971, July. The National Assembly (Nationalrat) approved a bill reducing compulsory military service from nine to six months.

1978, Nov. 5. Austrians participating in the first national referendum since 1938 voted against the commissioning of a nuclear reactor at Zwentendorf.

1983–86. Small Coalition: the Socialist Party and the Freedom Party formed a coalition under the chancellorship of Alfred Sinowatz of the Socialist Party after the 1983 elections. In June 1986, Franz Vranitzky was nominated chancellor. On **Jan. 14, 1987, he formed a coalition of the Socialist Party and the People's Party, and thus began the Grand Coalition of 1987–93.** Vranitzky emphasized modernization of the economy, democratization, and improvement of the environment as key issues in government programs. In July 1987, the Parliament adopted a privatization bill as part of a long-term plan to rescue the heavily indebted state sector.

1983, May. Environmental policies and the Greens: the government set up an "environmental management and protection fund"; programs on such issues as purifying the country's rivers, reducing acid rain's effects, and using lead-free petrol were announced thereafter. **The Greens** (the **United Green Party of Austria,** which contested the 1983 general elections, and **Green Alternative) made their way into the Parliament in the 1986 elections,** when they came together under the banner of Green Alternative. Green Alternative became their official party name in February 1987. The alliance broke down on Dec. 1, 1987, and the United Green left.

1986. The Waldheim affair: Kurt Waldheim was elected (July 8) to a six-year term as president despite the controversy over his wartime activities and his alleged involvement in war crimes in and outside of Austria. Western countries and Israel continued condemning him throughout his presidency.

1988–93. Immigration issues: the opening of Eastern European borders led to a massive influx of those seeking work and political asylum. To slow down the flow, the Austrian government imposed visa requirements in March 1990 on Romanians, Bulgarians, and Turks.

1989, July 17. Austria applied for EC membership. (Membership would be approved, after detailed negotiations, in 1994).

1992, May 24. Thomas Klestil (the Austrian People's Party) **was elected president.**

1993, Jan. 23. In the largest rally since 1945, 200,000 people demonstrated against zenophobia and racism in Vienna.

Feb. An initiative against foreigners launched by the right-wing Freedom Party of Austria (FPO) in Nov. 1992 gained 417,000 signatures, well surpassing the 100,000 needed to launch a parliamentary debate.

July 1. A **Residence Act** came into effect, limiting the number of immigrants to a maximum of 30,000 a year, excluding asylum seekers.

Sept. 29. Gottfried Kussel, 35, was sentenced to ten years' imprisonment for organizing a neo-Nazi group, the Volkstreue Ausserparlamentarische Opposition (People's Extraparliamentary Opposition).

1995, Oct. 12. The ruling government coalition in Austria collapsed because of its inability to agree on a budget for 1996. The Parliament dissolved pending general elections.

1997, Jan. 18. Austrian chancellor Franz Vranitzky stepped down, declaring his successor to be finance minister **Viktor Klima** of the Social Democratic Party.

1998, Sept. 29. Austria discussed returning the hundreds of art objects that had been stolen by the Nazi regime from their former, primarily Jewish, owners.

1999, Jan. 1. Austria joined ten other European nations in the implementation of a single European currency, the euro. The other countries launching euro use were Belgium, Finland, France, Luxembourg, Italy, Ireland, the Netherlands, Germany, Portugal, and Spain.

Aug. 25. In Vienna, Austrian police arrested Gen. Momir Talic, a Bosnian Serb military leader wanted by the UN for war crimes.

Oct. 3. In a general election during which the Social Democrats won only one-third of the votes, the right-wing anti-immigration Freedom Party upset traditional Austrian politics by tying for second place with the Center-Right People's Party. Shocking the European political establishment, this election marked the strongest popular support for a Far-Right Western European party since the end of World II. Wolfgang Schuessel of the conservative People's Party became chancellor.

2000, Feb. 4. When the People's Party and the Freedom Party formed a coalition government, massive domestic and international cries of protest erupted, beginning in Vienna and echoing throughout Europe. Some EU members threatened to sever ties with Austria entirely. The bulk of the criticism was focused on Freedom Party leader and alleged Nazi sympathizer Joerg Haider. Resigning his position as party head in late February, Haider retained his post as the governor of Austria's southern province of Carinthia.

Sept. 12. Most member nations of the EU lifted sanctions against Austria. The 14 nations (in addition to the U.S. and Israel) that had cut off bilateral diplomatic relations restored contact with Austria.

j. THE SCANDINAVIAN STATES

(From p. 708)

A chief concern of the Scandinavian countries during the postwar period was with military security. Negotiations among Denmark, Norway, and Sweden in 1948–49 on a joint defense pact broke down when Denmark and Norway (together with Iceland) decided to join the North Atlantic Treaty, while Sweden was determined to do nothing that might impair its traditional neutrality. Finland likewise tried to maintain a middle course, constrained by Soviet overtures for more cordial relations.

In economic and cultural matters, however, the Scandinavian states drew ever closer together. On Feb. 12, 1953, all of them except Finland organized the **Nordic Council,** which Finland joined two years later. The council consisted of members of the various parliaments, meeting annually for discussion of common problems and general consultation; committees were set up to deal with economic, social, financial, and cultural matters. In 1967 the council set up the **Nordic Cultural Foundation,** and in 1969 it endorsed plans for a **Nordic Economic Union.** Various foundations were established for scientific and other purposes.

1. DENMARK
(From p. 708)

1945, May 5. Vilhelm Buhl, a Social Democrat, formed the first postwar cabinet.

Oct. 30. General elections for the first time gave 18 of the 148 seats in the lower house to the Communist Party. The Social Democrats lost an equal number but still emerged as the strongest party. Since no coalition was possible, **Knud Kristensen** formed a Liberal Party minority government.

1947, April 20. Death of King Christian X. He was succeeded by his son, who ruled as **KING FREDERICK IX.**

Oct. 28. General elections brought an increase in Socialist strength and a corresponding decline for the Communists.

Nov. 13. Hans Hedtoft formed a Social Democratic minority cabinet.

1949, April 4. Denmark signed the North Atlantic Treaty.

1950, Sept. 5. In a **general election,** the Socialists showed further gains.

Oct. 28. The leader of the Liberal Agrarian Party, **Erik Eriksen,** formed a coalition cabinet of Liberals and Conservatives.

1951, April 27. A 20-year **agreement with the United States** was signed, providing for the joint **defense of Greenland** against the threat of attack or invasion.

1953, April 21. Following a setback in the April 21 elections, Premier Eriksen's coalition Agrarian-Liberal-Conservative government announced its resignation. King Frederick asked members of the Social Democratic Labor Party to form a new cabinet.

June 5. King Frederick signed a **new constitution** that abolished the upper house of the Parliament and enlarged the lower house (Folketing).

Sept. 30. Hans Hedtoft formed a new Social Democratic minority cabinet.

1955, Jan. 29. Death of Prime Minister Hedtoft, who was succeeded by **Hans Christian Hansen.**

1957, May 15. After losing their parliamentary majority in the May 14 elections, **Prime Minister Hansen** and his Social Democratic government **resigned.**

May 27. Hansen formed a **coalition government** of nine members of the Social Democratic Party, four from the Radical Liberal Party and three from the Single Tax Party.

1960s. In the early 1960s, 50 percent of all married women in Denmark worked outside the home.

1960, Feb. 19. Death of Prime Minister Hansen. Finance Minister **Viggo Kampmann,** also a Social Democrat, succeeded him.

Nov. 19. Premier Kampmann formed a new minority coalition government made up of Social Democrats and Radicals.

1962, Aug. 31. Premier Kampmann resigned for reasons of health. The majority Social Democratic Party named Foreign Minister **Jens Otto Krag** as his successor.

1968, Jan. 23. In national **elections,** Premier Krag and the Social Democrats retained their lead, but more conservative parties made significant gains, and a **new government was formed by Hilmar Baunsgaard** (Radical Liberal Party), supported by a coalition of Conservatives, Agrarian Liberals, and Radical Liberals.

1970. Major reforms of divorce law expanded the grounds for divorce and separation.

1971, Sept. Premier Baunsgaard resigned after his coalition government lost its majority in national elections.

1971–73. Social Democrats in power. A minority government led by **Jens Otto Krag** was sworn in on **Oct. 11, 1971.** A year later, **Anker Jorgensen,** leader of the General Workers Union, **succeeded Krag.** The Social Democrats were badly **defeated in elections in December 1973** because of policies for high taxes, and the **Jorgensen government resigned.**

1972, Jan. 14. Death of King Frederick IX. Princess Margrethe, his eldest daughter, **was proclaimed Queen Margrethe II** on Oct. 5.

Oct. 2. The Danes voted overwhelmingly to join the European Economic Community. Denmark officially became an EC member on Jan. 1, 1973.

1973–75. Moderate Liberals in power. Poul Hartling, leader of the Agrarian Liberal Party, was sworn in **as premier on Dec. 19, heading a minority government.** On Jan. 1, 1974, he announced a temporary **freeze on prices, wages, and profits** to last until Feb. 28. In November, more than 100,000 workers demonstrated in Copenhagen and other cities to protest the government's economic policies and demand the resignation of Hartling and his government.

1973, April 5. The Folketing approved a defense reform program reducing military service from 12 to 9 months.

April 9. Workers and employers accepted a new two-year collective wage agreement, ending a labor crisis that had involved 260,000 workers since March 21. The agreement provided a reduction of the workweek from 41.75 to 40 hours by the end of 1974, a 7.5 percent wage increase, equal pay for male and female industrial workers, and automatic cost-of-living adjustments.

May 24. Abortion Bill: the Folketing approved a bill, effective on Oct. 1, permitting women to obtain an abortion up to the end of the twelfth week of pregnancy.

1975–82. Social Democrats in power. Anker Jorgensen returned to office as **premier** and **formed a coalition government** of Social Democrats and Liberal Democrats in February 1975. His government retained Danish membership in the EC and NATO, and took measures to fight unemployment and inflation. In Sept. **1979,** Jorgensen's coalition government failed, due to disagreements on price and income policies. He set up a **minority Social Democratic government** after his party won limited gains in general elections, and **began the toughest price and wage freeze since the war.** In September **1982** Jorgensen's government resigned after failing to secure parliamentary passage of economic austerity measures.

1978, April 28. The Folketing passed a bill for the **complete abolition of the death penalty,** effective on June 1.

Sept. 19. The voting age was reduced from 20 to 18.

1979. Denmark granted Greenland home rule.

1980, June 1. The Danish government declared a **200-mile economic zone** off the east coast of Greenland.

1982–93. Conservative Party in power. Poul Schlüter took office as premier and **formed a four-party coalition government** on Sept. 10, 1982. He became **Denmark's first Conservative Party prime minister since 1901.** His severe austerity measures in the following years brought about a subsequent economic recovery.

1983. Denmark led the Common Market countries in the number of married women working outside the home; by 1983, 80 percent of married Danish women were employed. The Danes also led EC nations with its number of illegitimate births (40.6 percent of all births in 1983).

1985, March 24–31. A **major private-sector strike** broke out over a collective wage agreement. The Folketing approved a series of emergency measures requiring a return to work and imposing wage increases of 2 percent and 1.5 percent, respectively, in each of the next two years.

1985, Dec.–1986, Oct. The Folketing approved **restrictive immigration legislation limiting the admission of refugees** and **those seeking political asylum.**

1989, May 26. Matrimonial law: marriage laws were revised so that all **civil rights of married couples were extended to both heterosexuals and homosexuals** who had previously lodged an official registration of their relationship.

Oct. 1. Eleven male couples were married in the first wedding ceremonies governed by Denmark's Registered Partnership Law.

1991, Aug. 27. Sweden and Denmark reached an agreement to construct a road bridge between Copenhagen and Malmö.

1992, June 2. In a national referendum, 50.7 percent of voters voiced their opposition to the Maastricht Treaty on European Union (p. 843).

1993, Jan. 14. Prime Minister Poul Schlüter resigned due to a scandal surrounding his statements regarding permission for family members of Tamil refugees to join relatives living in Denmark.

Jan. 25. Social Democrat Poul Nyrup Rasmussen was appointed prime minister and formed a coalition government with the Center Democratic Party, Radical Liberal Party, and Christian People's Party. The main problem faced by Rasmussen's government was growing unemployment.

May 18. In a second national referendum, **56 percent of Danish voters supported the signing of the Maastricht Treaty,** though with numerous so-called opt-outs that acted to exclude Denmark from taking part in the planned monetary union, common defense endeavors, and common citizenship policies. Public contention over issues surrounding the Maastricht Treaty led to the outbreak of numerous riots; it was **the most intense domestic conflict in Denmark since the end of World War II.**

1998, March 11. The ruling Center-Left coalition of Denmark narrowly won a victory in general elections. Following his victorious Social Democratic Party, Premier Poul Nyrup Rasmussen retained his position as head of the Danish government.

May 28. Denmark citizens voted in favor of adopting the EU's Treaty of Amsterdam, a modified version of the Maastricht Treaty, which Denmark had rejected in 1992.

2000, July. The long-awaited ten-mile bridge and tunnel connecting Sweden and Denmark was opened; it linked Copenhagen, Denmark with Malmö, Sweden.

Sept. 28. Danes voted in a national referendum not to join the euro currency zone. Scorned by both right-wing nationalists and liberal Socialists, the single European currency received very limited support from the Danish people. This vote marked the first time that any EU member nation had directly consulted its electorate at large to consider the euro.

2. NORWAY
(From p. 709)

1945, June 26. The leader of the Labor Party, **Einar Gerhardsen,** formed the first postwar coalition government.

Sept. 10. Nazi collaborator **Vidkun Quisling** was sentenced to death and **executed** on Oct. 24.

Oct. 7. The first **general elections** since 1936 gave a majority to the Labor Party, and **Einar Gerhardsen** formed a Labor government.

1947, March 3. Parliament rejected a Soviet request for military bases in **Spitsbergen.**

1949, April 4. Norway signed the North Atlantic Treaty.

Oct. 10. General elections increased the majority of the Labor Party, while the Communist Party lost all of its seats in the lower house.

1950, Jan. 6. A serious imbalance of imports over exports necessitated shelving the **project of a customs union with Sweden and Denmark.**

1951, Nov. 13. Resignation of Prime Minister Gerhardsen.

Nov. 19. Oscar Torp, the Labor Party's leader in Parliament, **formed a new government.**

1955, Jan. 14. Prime Minister Torp resigned, to be succeeded (Jan. 21) by Gerhardsen.

1957, Sept. 21. Crown Prince Olaf succeeded to the throne as **KING OLAF V,** following the death of his father, King Haakon VII.

1960, Sept. 28. An **agreement with Britain** was signed in Oslo allowing British trawlers to fish within 6 miles of the Norwegian coast for ten years; thereafter the limit would be 12 miles offshore.

1962, April 28. Parliament approved the government's decision to apply for full **membership in the EC.**

1963, Aug. 2. For the first time in 28 years, the **Labor Party was ousted** when Parliament voted no confidence in the government of Premier Einar Gerhardsen. King Olaf V asked **John Lyng,** leader of the Conservative Party in Parliament, to form a government. On Aug. 27 a four-party coalition government led by Premier Lyng took office.

1965. The long rule of the **Labor Party was supplanted** by a coalition of four nonsocialist parties under **PER BORTEN.**

1970. Norway's second university was founded at Bergen.

1971, March 17. Labor Party leader Trygve M. Bratteli became premier when scandal forced the **resignation of Per Borten. Bratteli formed a minority government** after he failed to construct a four-party nonsocialist coalition cabinet.

1972, Sept. 24–27. The Norwegians rejected entry into the EC in a national referendum, and **Brattelli's government announced its resignation** in October.

March 2. The Storting (parliament) voted 45 to 2 to reject a constitutional amendment to abolish the monarchy and create a republic.

1972, Oct. 17. Lars Korvald formed a new minority **coalition government,** consisting of the Christian People's, Liberal, and Center Parties, all of which opposed EC membership.

1973, Sept. 9–10. The **Socialist Election Alliance** won a **one-seat majority** in the elections for the Storting.

1973–81. Labor Party in power. Trygve M. Brattelli formed a minority government to replace Lars Korvald's on Oct. 16, 1973. His new government canceled gasoline rationing, restricted the activities of foreign oil companies, set up a national oil company, and imposed price freezes to reduce inflation.

1975. The discoveries of North Sea oil and gas fields began to stimulate the economy.

Feb. 1. The government **banned most categories of foreign immigration** for a year, and then extended the ban without setting a time limit.

Oct. 2. King Olav announced that Norway would extend its fishing limits by creating a **200-mile "economic zone."** In June 1981 the government declared a 200-mile zone around Jan Mayen Island.

1976. Norway introduced an official nutritional policy that included both price subsidies and state educational campaigns designed to promote better eating habits.

Jan. Odvar Nordli (Labor Party) **succeeded Brattelli** as prime minister.

1978, Nov. 28. The Storting adopted a proposal to **reduce the voting age from 20 to 18.** It also passed a liberal **abortion law giving women the right to choose,** though the Christian People's Party insisted on limiting abortion to special circumstances.

1979, May 31. The Storting approved the **complete abolition of the death penalty.**

1981. Gro Harlem Brundtland became the first female prime minister of Norway, heading a minority government.

1981–86. Conservative Party in power. In general elections, parties of the Center-Right obtained an overall majority in the Storting. **Kaare Willoch formed a minority Conservative government and became the first Conservative Party prime minister since 1928.** In June 1983, Willoch was able to form a new three-party, nonsocialist coalition, but his government resigned after he failed to obtain parliamentary approval of his austerity economic measures in April 1986.

1986–93. Labor Party in power. Gro Harlem Brundtland formed a new cabinet in which 8 of the 18 members were women. When Jan P. Syse's Center-Right coalition collapsed over the EC issue after a year in power, Brundtland returned to office, heading a minority government for the third time. The **Norwegians continued to oppose EC membership.**

1991, Jan. 17. Death of King Olav V. His son Harald was sworn in as King Harald V (Jan. 21).

April 20. Kaci Kullmann Five was elected leader of the Conservatives; by then **women held positions as leaders of three out of the four**

major parties, and they represented one-third of the Storting and one-half of the cabinet members.

1992, Nov. 19. The Norwegian Storting approved application for EC membership after a national referendum on the issue showed majority support.

1993, Sept. 12. Effective measures to reduce unemployment contributed to the victory of the Norwegian Labor Party in national elections. Gro Harlem Brudtland was again named prime minister.

1994, Nov. 28–29. Norway voted against joining the EU, saying that they had enough economic strength on their own.

2000, March 9. The coalition government of the Christian Democrats, the Center Party, and the Liberal Party lost a confidence vote that had been called by the Labor Party in response to the government's opposition to the building of gas-powered electrical plants in Norway. Opposition to the power plants originated in environmental concerns.

Sept. 4–14. To protest exorbitant fuel prices, truckers and other Norwegian motorists blockaded oil terminals; the blockades failed to gain gasoline tax cuts from the government. With 70 percent of the price coming from taxes, gas costs more in Norway than in most other countries in the world.

3. SWEDEN
(From p. 709)

1945, July 31. The coalition government of **Per A. Hansson** was replaced by a Social Democratic cabinet under Hansson.

1946, Oct. 5. Death of Premier Hansson, who was succeeded by **Tage Erlander.**

1948, Dec. 19. General elections maintained the Social Democratic Party as the strongest party, while the Communist Party lost 7 of its 15 seats.

1950, Oct. 29. Death of King Gustav V. He was succeeded by his son, **KING GUSTAV VI ADOLF.**

1954, July 1. The inauguration of a **common labor market** with Norway, Denmark, and Finland placed workers on the same footing with respect to employment.

1955. A national health insurance system, financed by the state and employer contributions, was established to provide medical, sickness, and parental benefits to all Swedish citizens and alien residents.

1957, Oct. 26. Premier Tage Erlander's Social Democratic Party and Agrarian Party government resigned, following the withdrawal of the Agrarians on Oct. 24. On Oct. 26, Erlander's **all-socialist minority government** took office.

1961, Aug. 22. Premier Erlander said his government could not join the **Common Market** because the views of that organization could not be reconciled with Sweden's policy of neutrality, but he declared Sweden's willingness to negotiate with Common Market countries (Aug. 28), so long as any compromises did not affect Swedish neutrality.

1968, Sept. 15. The ruling Social Democratic Party gained 12 seats in the election for the lower house of the Riksdag, the **first clear Social Democratic majority in the Riksdag since 1940.**

1969, Jan. Sweden established diplomatic relations with North Vietnam and became an asylum for deserters from the U.S. forces. The Vietnam War contributed to a rise in anti-American sentiment among Swedes.

Feb. 18. Parliamentary system reform: the Riksdag approved legislation to change the existing **bicameral Parliament into a unicameral system.** The single chamber was established on **Jan. 1, 1971,** with 350 members serving three-year terms, and it became constitutional on Jan. 1, 1975.

Sept. 28–Oct. 14. Olaf Palme succeeded Erlander as **chairman of the Social Democratic Party and prime minister.**

Dec. 3. The "Seven Crowns Reform" legislation, making most doctors salaried employees of the state, was introduced in the Riksdag.

1970, Sept. 20. The **elections brought substantial losses to the dominant Social Democratic Party,** while the Communist Party and the Center Party registered gains. Premier Palme, though his party was now in a minority, continued in office, with approval of the Communists. Palme was faced with widespread discontent, despite the prosperity of the country, because of drastic legislation affecting the status and incomes of the educated and upper classes.

1971, Jan. 1. Reform of administrative units: 132 cities and towns, including Stockholm as well as 716 municipalities and rural districts,

were reorganized into 464 *Kommuner,* or local districts. These local districts were later reduced to 272.

Sept. 15. Death of King Gustav VI. His grandson **Carl Gustaf was installed as King Charles XVI** on Sept. 19.

Sept. 16. The **Socialist and non-Socialist groups were tied in the election,** each winning 175 seats in the 350-member unicameral Riksdag.

1973. No-fault divorce was introduced into the Swedish juridical code. Childless couples were given the right to divorce immediately on the request of either partner. Couples with children under the age of 16 were required to wait six months to secure a divorce.

1974, Feb. 27. The Riksdag gave final approval to a **new constitution,** effective on Jan. 1, 1975, **which withdrew most of the monarch's residual powers.** On **April 20, 1978,** the Riksdag approved the **abrogation of Salic Law in Sweden,** which since its introduction in 1810 had limited the succession of the throne to male heirs only. Final endorsement of the abrogation came on Nov. 7, 1979.

1975. Restrictions on abortions up until the twelfth week of pregnancy were abolished. Women seeking to abort pregnancies between the twelfth and eighteenth weeks were required to discuss their decision with a social worker.

1976. The 40-year rule of Social Democrats ended, and a Center-Right coalition assumed power until 1983. The defeat of Social Democrats in general elections led to the resignation of Palme's government on Sept. 20, and **Thorbjorn Fälldin, leader of the Center Party** and endorsed as prime minister by the Riksdag, **formed a three-party coalition** government. Fälldin's government collapsed amid differences over nuclear policy in 1978, but he returned to power in Oct. 1979, heading a new nonsocialist coalition government.

1979. The Swedish antispanking law went into effect. Under this new legislation, parents were forbidden to subject their children to corporal punishment or other injurious or humiliating treatment.

1980, May. The **most serious labor conflict in Sweden's history** occurred when one-fourth of the total labor force went on strike. A compromise made between trade unions and the employers' federation brought an end to the countrywide paralysis that had resulted from the strike.

1983–91. Social Democrats returned to power. The Social Democrats obtained 12 more seats in the 1983 general elections, and **Olaf Palme took office as prime minister on Oct. 8. He was shot dead on Feb. 28, 1986, and was succeeded by Ingvar Carlsson.**

1983. The Health and Medical Services Act mandated that county councils promote the health of residents in their area and provide equal access to good medical care for all. Since the mid-1960s, county councils had taken over the management and planning of all outpatient services and psychiatric care in Sweden.

1984. Social Democrats, with the support of the Center Party, introduced the Dagmar Reform, which sought to control and limit the number of part-time private practitioners of medicine.

1985, March. The Swedish government adopted a wide-ranging program to strengthen the position of women in the labor market.

1986. A Ministry of Environment and Energy was created to tackle energy questions in the aftermath of the Chernobyl nuclear disaster in the Soviet Union.

1987. A new **Marriage Code** went into effect that strengthened the financially weaker spouse's position on divorce or the death of the other partner. The new law also defined the limits of joint property for unmarried cohabitating couples.

1990, March. Ingmar Bergman received the D. W. Griffith Award from the Directors' Guild of America for his contribution to film. Bergman's films include: *Wild Strawberries* (1957), *Through a Glass Darkly* (1961), *Persona* (1966), *The Passion of Anna* (1969), and *Fanny and Alexander* (1983).

1991. Formation of the "bourgeois" coalition government: Carl Bildt, leader of the conservative Moderate Party, formed a four-party coalition under his prime ministership on Oct. 4, after the resignation of Carlsson's Social Democratic government. Bildt declared the end of the age of collectivism, and proposed a "New Start for Sweden" program, which featured significant decreases in government spending.

July. Sweden **applied for EC membership.**

1992, Sept. 20. Prime Minister Carl Bildt and the opposition agreed to measures to cut the budget deficit by increasing taxes and restricting the provision of social benefits.

Nov. 30. Two nationalist marches in Stockholm and Lund, involving several hundred **neo-Nazis,** resulted in conflicts with police and leftist groups.

1993, Feb. 1. Sweden and Finland opened **formal negotiations with the EC** regarding their entry.

July 1. The new proposed budget introduced by the Finance Ministry cut significantly into the areas of unemployment benefits, education, health insurance, and housing subsidies.

1994, Sept. 18. The Social Democratic Labor Party led by **Inguar Carlsson** won the Swedish elections. On Nov. 13 Sweden voted to join the EU.

1998, Sept. 20. The Social Democrats won a slight majority in the Swedish Parliament, known as the Riksdag. The Social Democratic Party continued its control of the government only through a coalition with several smaller left-wing parties. Goran Persson was reinstalled as prime minister.

1999, Dec. 17. After almost 500 years as the established religion of Sweden, the Lutheran Church was stripped of its official connection to the Swedish government.

2000, July. Malmö, Sweden, and Copenhagen, Denmark, were connected by a bridge and tunnel that crossed the ten miles of water separating the two nations. The $2.6 billion bridge was expected to significantly enhance Sweden's economic future.

4. FINLAND
(From p. 710)

1945, March 3. FINLAND DECLARED WAR AGAINST GERMANY.
March 17–18. The **general election** brought a swing to the Left.
April 17. Juho Paasikivi formed a new coalition cabinet.

1946, Feb. 21. A number of wartime leaders, among them ex-president **Risto Ryti,** were sentenced to prison for involving Finland in the war or preventing the conclusion of peace. They were pardoned, over Soviet protests, in 1949.
March 4. President **C. G. E. Mannerheim resigned** for reasons of health.
March 9. JUHO PAASIKIVI was elected president.
March 24. Mauno Pekkala formed a new coalition government.

1947, Feb. 10. The **FINNISH PEACE TREATY** was signed at Paris. The Soviet Union received the **Pestamo** area, a 50-year lease on a naval base at **Porkkala,** and substantial reparations.

1948, April 6. The USSR and Finland concluded a treaty of friendship and **mutual assistance,** directed primarily against Germany.
July 1–2. In the **general election,** the Communists lost one-fourth of their parliamentary seats.
July 29. Karl-August Fagerholm formed a Social Democratic cabinet.

1949, Aug.–Sept. A wave of Communist-instigated strikes was defeated by firm government action and the loyalty of the noncommunist workers.

1950, Jan. 16–17. Parliamentary elections gave a majority to the parties supporting President **Paasikivi,** who was reelected on Feb. 15 for a term of six years.
March. Urho K. Kekkonen became premier and also minister of the interior (until Jan. 1951).

1954, May 5. Ralph Törngren, the leader of the Swedish People's Party, representing an ethnic minority in Finland, **formed a coalition government** with the Social Democratic Party and the Agrarian Party. Kekkonen became foreign minister.
Oct. 14. Törngren resigned in the face of a threatened general strike protesting the high cost of living. On Oct. 20 Kekkonen formed a coalition government of Social Democrats and Agrarians.

1955, Sept. 19. A treaty signed with the Soviet Union provided for the return to Finland of the **Porkkala naval base.** The Soviet government also agreed to permit all Finnish nationals, including war prisoners, to leave Russia if they wished. Porkkala was restored to Finland Jan. 26, 1956.

1956, Feb. Urho Kekkonen became president.

1957, Nov. 29. President Kekkonen ended a 43-day crisis with the appointment of Rainar von Fieandt, chairman of the Bank of Finland, to head a business government.

1958, Aug. 29. A four-week crisis ended with the approval of a new coalition cabinet, led by Social Democrat **Karl-August Fagerholm.**
Dec. 4. The resignation of five Agrarian Party members of the cabinet touched off a crisis, resulting in the collapse of Premier Fagerholm's coalition Socialist government. On Dec. 10 President Kekkonen, in a broadcast to the people, declared that "the overriding question" for Finnish foreign policy was good relations with the Soviet Union.

1961, July 14. Martti J. Miettunen, governor of Lapland, was named premier of a new Agrarian Party minority government. He succeeded **Vieno Sukselainen,** who resigned after being found guilty of administrative irregularities.
Oct. 30. The USSR, in a note to Finland, declared that the threat of aggression by West Germany was grounds for invoking the Soviet-Finnish mutual defense treaty of 1948. Consultations were requested.
Nov. 23–25. A communiqué, issued after a two-day **meeting between Kekkonen and Soviet leader Nikita Khrushchev** in Novosibirsk, Siberia, declared the Soviet Union's willingness to postpone military talks. On Nov. 26 Kekkonen reported to the Finnish people on his talks with Khrushchev, stating that all political opposition leaders who had earned Moscow's enmity should leave politics.

1962, Jan. 15–16. President Kekkonen received an overwhelming majority of the popular vote in the two-day presidential election. His Agrarian Party received 145 seats in the 300-seat electoral college, which was scheduled to meet on Feb. 15 to select the president.
Feb. 4–5. In parliamentary elections, President Kekkonen's Agrarian Party replaced the Communist Party as the largest single parliamentary group.
March 1. President Kekkonen was inaugurated for his second six-year term.
April 13. Ahti K. Karjalainen formed a new coalition government.

1963, Aug. 30. Karjalainen's coalition government resigned following a cabinet disagreement on how to finance increases in farmers' incomes, but President Kekkonen requested the cabinet to remain in office.
Dec. 18. Reino R. Lehto was appointed as caretaker of the government.

1969. The first Finnish automobile factory opened as industry boomed.

1970, July 14. A **new coalition government** of Socialists and nonsocialists was formed by former **Premier Karjalainen.**

1972. Finland concluded **trade agreements with the European Economic Community.**

1973, May 16. In Moscow, **Finland signed** economic, scientific, and technological **cooperation agreements with the Council for Mutual Economic Assistance (COMECON) of the Eastern European communist countries.** The agreement was the first between COMECON and a country with a free-market economy.

1975, Aug. 1. The Helsinki Conference and Accords (p. 815): an attempt by 35 nations to achieve East-West cooperation; the accords set out basic, worldwide human rights standards.

1981, Oct. President Urho Kekkonen **resigned** because of ill health.

1982, Jan. 26–27. Mauno Koivista, a Social Democrat, was **appointed president by the Electoral College.** He failed to win the necessary overall majority for reelection in Finland's first direct election for the presidency in January 1988, but the Electoral College reelected him in February for his second six-year term.

1984, Dec. 5. Reform of the constitution: proposals were presented to the Eduskunta (Finnish Diet) regarding the changes of presidential election procedures, the restriction of the presidency to a maximum of two successive terms in office, the strengthening of the Eduskunta's powers vis-à-vis the president in the formation of government, the exercise of the president's right of veto, and the dissolution of the Eduskunta. The proposals were ratified in mid-1987.

1986, Jan. 1. Finland became a full member of the European Free Trade Association (p. 842).

1987, April 30. Harri Holkeri, of the conservative National Coalition Party, **formed a four-party coalition** and was **the first conservative to become prime minister after World War II.**

1990, Feb. 1–March 4. A strike and lockout closed most of Finland's banks, causing numerous problems for small businesses.
April 29. The splintered Communist and Left-Socialist forces formed **a new party, the Left-Wing Alliance.**

1991, March 17. The Center Party, led by Esko Aho, **won the elections** by focusing on the problem of high unemployment. **Fourteen more women became members of Parliament,** bringing the total number to 77.

Sept. 23. The government announced the decision to **end the 1948 treaty with the Soviet Union** that had prevented Finland from joining any organization that could be construed as harmful to the Soviet Union.

1992, March 18. Finland applied for membership in the EC, despite several domestic protests.

April 22. Two hundred thousand demonstrators protested cuts in pensions, unemployment, and children's benefits.

May 22. Finland and Russia signed a treaty of good neighborliness and mutual cooperation to replace the abrogated treaty of 1948.

Nov. 5. The EC Commission endorsed Finland's application, but discussions over the obstacles to full membership presented by Finland's policy of neutrality continued through 1993. Full agreement would be reached in 1994.

1994, Feb. 6. Martti Ahtisaari became the president of Finland; he favored a Finnish application to the European Union. On Oct. 16 the people voted in a referendum that Finland should join the EU.

1995, March 19. Social Democrats won Finnish elections under the leadership of **Paavo Lipponen,** who said he was dedicated to working on economic troubles such as unemployment.

1999, Jan. 1. Finland, along with ten other European countries, adopted the euro as its official currency. The uniform monetary unit was also implemented in France, Austria, Germany, Luxembourg, Italy, Ireland, Belgium, the Netherlands, Portugal, and Spain.

March 21. The Social Democratic Party won a majority in parliamentary elections but the opposition Center Party, separated by only three seats in the legislature, came extremely close to overtaking the Social Democrats. As negotiations continued on the formation of a new government, Paavo Lipponen retained the position of premier.

2000, Feb. 6. Social Democratic Party leader and foreign minister Tarja Halonen was elected and became Finland's first female president. Publicly admired as a single mother and social activist, Halonen narrowly defeated former premier Esko Aho of the Center Party. Halonen succeeded fellow Social Democrat Martti Ahtisaari.

5. ICELAND
(From p. 710)

1944, July 17. ICELAND WAS ESTABLISHED AS AN INDEPENDENT REPUBLIC.

1950, April. The Danish parliament passed a law annulling the Act of Union between Denmark and Iceland.

1951, April 7. At the government's request, the **United States sent a contingent of its armed forces** to aid in Iceland's defense in the cold war.

May 5. A U.S.-Iceland agreement was signed providing for the use by NATO nations of defense facilities in Iceland.

1952, July 1. Asgeir Asgeirson was elected president.

1956, March 28. Parliament called for the **withdrawal of foreign forces** from the country.

July 21. A new coalition was formed by the Progressive Party, the Social Democrats, and the Communist People's Alliance, with the latter filling two cabinet posts.

Dec. 6. The U.S. government announced that Iceland had **canceled its requests for the withdrawal of U.S. forces.**

1958, Dec. 4. Premier Hermann Jonasson's coalition government of Progressive, Social Democratic, and Labor Alliance Parties collapsed in disagreement over economic policy.

1959, Nov. 19. Premier Emil Jonsson resigned, and Independence Party leader **Olafur Thors** formed a coalition government.

1963, June 11. Returns from the **parliamentary elections** (June 9) revealed that the coalition of Premier Thors's Independence Party and the Social Democratic Party had won 32 seats in the 60-seat Parliament.

1968, June 30. Kristjan Eldjarn was elected president of Iceland. He was reelected in 1972 and 1976.

1970, March 1. Iceland became a full member of the European Free Trade Association (p. 840) and also a party to the Finland-EFTA agreement.

1976, May 30–June 1. The "cod war" between Britain and Iceland (1972–76) over fishing limits ended in compromise.

1980, Aug. 1. Vigdís Finnbogadóttir took office as president of Iceland after she won a closely contested election on June 29. She was **the world's first popularly elected female head of state.** She was reelected in 1984, 1988, and 1992.

1985, May. Iceland declared itself a nuclear-free zone after mounting opposition to the U.S.-NATO base on the island.

1986, June. Iceland became a participating **member of the "Eureka" high-technology cooperation program;** thus all the members of the Organization for Economic Cooperation and Development became participants.

1989, March 1. The sale of beer was legalized in Iceland after a ban that had lasted 74 years.

1991, April 23. The outgoing Progressive Party prime minister Steingrímur Hermannsson resigned after elections held on April 20.

April 30. Davíd Oddsson of the Independence Party formed a coalition government with the Social Democratic Party.

1992, March 30. *Children of Nature* was the first Icelandic foreign language film nominated for an Academy Award.

1993, Dec. 14. The EC created the European Economic Area, which extended the Economic Community's single market legislation to Iceland, Finland, Norway, Sweden, and Austria.

1996. On June 29 **Olafur Ragnar Grimsson** won the presidency of Iceland despite continuing controversy over his leftist tendencies.

1999, May 8. The ruling Independence Party, headed by conservative prime minister David Oddsson, won the most seats in parliamentary elections.

6. GREENLAND

Greenland achieved internal autonomy under Danish sovereignty in May 1979. It withdrew from the European Community in 1985. Greenland followed Denmark's policy of a nuclear weapons–free zone; in the late 1980s there was a dispute over the installation of advanced radar equipment at the U.S. airbase in Thule. Greenland signed a fishing cooperation agreement with Denmark and Russia in March 1992.

7. EASTERN EUROPE, 1945–2000

a. POLAND

(From p. 721)

1945, April 21. The **Soviet government** and a **Polish provisional government** set up in Moscow agreed on a **20-year treaty** of mutual aid.

June 12. The British and French, who favored the Polish government in exile in London, persuaded the USSR to agree to a **tripartite commission** that would aid in the **organization of a Polish government.**

At the Yalta Conference, Poland's eastern territories were reduced approximately to the "Curzon line" of 1919, while its western border, pending a final peace settlement, was extended to the **Oder-Neisse line** in eastern Germany. The leadership of postwar Poland was claimed by two rival groups, the Soviet-sponsored **provisional government at Lublin,** and the Polish **government in exile in London.**

June 28. After lengthy negotiations, a **government of national unity** was formed, under Socialist **premier Eduard Osobka-Morawski** of the Lublin administration. It was recognized by the Western powers, though its leanings turned out to be decidedly pro-Soviet. For this reason, many Polish citizens who, as displaced persons or members of Poland's armed forces, were still in Western Europe refused to be repatriated.

1946, Jan. 6. The government announced the **nationalization of all industries** employing more than 50 workers.

June 30. A **popular referendum** approved the government's program of nationalization and land reform, and the establishment of a one-house parliament, as advocated by the communists.

1947, Jan. 19. The first **general election,** preceded by repressive measures against Deputy Prime Minister **Stanislaw Mikolajczyk's Peasant Party,** gave the government bloc 394 seats and the Peasant Party 28. Both

Great Britain and the United States charged that the Yalta provisions for free and honest elections had been violated.

Feb. 4. Boleslaw Bierut was elected **president of the republic,** and Josef Cyrankiewicz formed a new coalition cabinet.

Feb. 19. The Diet approved an **interim constitution** and proclaimed liberty and equality for all citizens.

Sept. Mikolajczyk was forced to resign.

Sept. 14. Poland **denounced its concordat** and entered on a series of conflicts with the Catholic Church.

Oct. 24. A campaign among progovernment members of the Peasant Party for his dismissal led to **Mikolajczyk's flight to London** and the purge of his followers from the ranks of the Peasant Party.

1948. The **transformation of Poland into a Communist-dominated Soviet satellite** made further headway as the Socialist Party was fused with the Communist Party, and became the **Polish United Workers' Party (PUWP).** The Peasant Party joined the government bloc, a compulsory youth organization was set up, and the judiciary was changed along communist lines.

June 26. A five-year **trade agreement** was signed with the **Soviet Union** to counterbalance the Marshall Plan, in which Poland had refused to participate.

Sept. 5. The secretary general of the PUWP, **Wladyslaw Gomulka,** was forced to resign because of ideological deviation from the Soviet line.

1949, Jan. 25. Poland joined the **Council for Mutual Economic Assistance** (p. 838).

Sept. 30. Poland again showed its adherence to Soviet and Cominform policy when it **renounced its treaty of friendship with Yugoslavia.**

Nov. 7. Marshal Konstantin Rokossovsky of the Soviet Union was appointed **minister of defense and commander-in-chief of the Polish army.** The army was thoroughly reorganized along Soviet lines.

Nov. 11–13. The **Central Committee of the United Workers' Party** expelled a number of prominent members for **Titoist** leanings.

1950. Poland's relations with the Western powers—having deteriorated steadily since the war—**came close to the breaking point** as several Western diplomats and correspondents were accused of hostile acts against the Polish government.

March 20. Hostility between Church and state led to the **confiscation of Church lands** and other restrictions on Catholic activities.

June 6. The **East German Democratic Republic recognized the Oder-Neisse line as the final border.** Most Germans east of this line had been expelled, and the region had been thoroughly polonized.

1951, May 22. The deputy prime minister met with Soviet foreign minister A. Vishinsky and signed an **agreement to cede territory in the Lublin area** to the USSR in return for part of Drohobyca province, which reportedly contained enough oil wells to increase Polish oil production by 20 percent.

1952, Nov. 20. With the abolition of the presidency by the **new constitution,** President Boleslaw Bierut stepped down to become premier. The **Council of State** became the nation's highest political organ.

1953, Sept. 8. Cardinal Jozsef Wyszynski, head of the **Polish Catholic Church,** was arrested for alleged conspiracy against the state; he was held in a monastery for years.

Dec. 18. On the radio in Warsaw it was reported that all **Roman Catholic bishops** in Poland had taken an oath of loyalty to the state.

1954, March 19. Josef Cyrankiewicz succeeded Bierut as prime minister.

1956, April 6. Wladyslaw Gomulka, who had been arrested in 1951, and other Polish Communists were reported to have been **freed and rehabilitated.**

June 28. Rioting, leading to more than one hundred deaths, broke out **in Poznan** after workers demonstrated for better social and economic conditions.

Oct. 10. Signs of an approaching storm occurred when the **trials of Poznan rioters** ended abruptly and (Oct. 16) several Communist leaders urged that Soviet officers be removed from the Polish army.

Oct. 20. Gomulka reentered the Polish Communist Party. While Khrushchev and other Soviet leaders hastened to Poland to plead for the continuation of pro-Soviet policies, Defense Minister and Commander-in-Chief Rokossovsky, a former Soviet officer, ordered troops to take positions near Warsaw. **Polish and Soviet frontier troops exchanged fire.**

Oct. 21. Gomulka became first secretary of the Polish Communist Party. By not electing Marshal Rokossovsky to the new Politburo, the Polish Communist Party gained some **independence from interference by the Soviet Union.**

Oct. 24. Gomulka announced that **Soviet troops** stationed in Poland **would return to their regular bases** "within two days." But the Soviet troop removal, which began on Oct. 25, did not include the three or four Soviet divisions from East Germany that had entered Poland a few days earlier. Polish militia used tear gas to quell **Polish attacks on Soviet army installations** at Legnica (Liegnitz).

Oct. 28. Marshal Rokossovsky returned to the USSR when an investigation unearthed evidence of his plot to stage a military coup against Gomulka.

Oct. 29. Cardinal Wyszynski was released from custody.

Oct. 30. The Gomulka government decided to present the Soviet Union with a bill for Poland's fair share (15 percent) of the **German reparations payments** to the Soviet Union.

Nov. 18. Gomulka and Premier Cyrankiewicz signed an **agreement** in Moscow with Khrushchev and Nikolay Bulganin **for equality in Soviet-Polish relations.**

Dec. 17. A Polish-Soviet agreement limited the **role of Soviet troops** in Poland.

1957, Jan. 20. The **National Front,** led by Gomulka, was victorious in the national elections.

Feb. 27. Parliament approved the new government of Premier Josef Cyrankiewicz.

May 1. Subject to U.S. congressional authorization, the **United States** formally agreed to provide $95 million in aid in the form of commodities and mining machinery, and a month later (June 7) arranged two **loans to Poland** amounting to $48,900,000.

1958, Dec. 6. The government revealed plans for building an **oil pipeline** from Russian fields to Poland and East Germany.

1959, March 31. The **repatriation of Poles from the Soviet Union** to East Poland, under the agreement of November 1956, ended, after some 250,000 Poles had been repatriated.

1960s. While the Polish government remained a reliable partner of the Soviet government, especially in the ideological conflict between Moscow and Beijing, growing unrest among intellectuals and artists obliged the government to relax measures of repression and to accept greater academic and business contacts with the West.

1964, Aug. 12. Edward Ochab, a veteran Polish Communist, was elected president by the Sejur to replace Aleksander Zawardzki, who had died.

1966, May 3. Celebration of 1,000 years of Polish Christianity. The projected attendance of Pope Paul VI was vetoed by the Polish government.

1968. Growing **dissatisfaction with the Gomulka regime.** Student demonstrations and outbreaks were accompanied by much factional struggle in government ranks. This led to a **purge of "Zionist" elements** and the emigration of many Jews. Gomulka, however, retained the support of the Soviet authorities.

Aug. The invasion and occupation of Czechoslovakia. Gomulka fully supported the Soviet position, and Polish troops participated in the military operations.

Nov. 11–16. The **Polish Communist Party Congress** failed to shake Gomulka's position.

1970, Dec. 7. Signature of the **TREATY WITH THE GERMAN FEDERAL REPUBLIC,** by which the latter at least provisionally recognized the **Oder-Neisse line** as Poland's western frontier and the Polish government assented to the repatriation of Germans still living in the area east of that line.

Dec. 14. Outbreak of serious **RIOTS IN GDANSK AND OTHER PORT CITIES,** resulting from food shortages and increased prices on food and other commodities. Police and troops were able to quell the disturbances only with difficulty and with considerable loss of life.

Dec. 20. With their regime badly shaken by the riots, **Gomulka and other members of the Politburo were obliged to resign.** Edward Gierek, chief of the party in Upper Silesia, succeeded to Gomulka's offices.

Dec. 23. President Spychalski and Prime Minister Cyrankiewicz also resigned. Cyrankiewicz then became the **new president and Piotr Jaroszewicz became the new prime minister;** they formed a cabinet that same day. The new government immediately announced a price freeze on food for at least two years, minimum wage increases, family allowance and pension increases, and credit increases for peasants and small businesses.

1971–72. Church-state relations improved. In June 1971, the Roman Catholic Church was granted full ownership of nearly 7,000 church buildings in the territories acquired from Germany after World War II. In February 1972 the government exempted the Church from paying tax on its farms and repealed its 1962 decree that the Church keep inventories of all its property for taxation purposes. In June, four new dioceses were established in western Poland, and the former "apostolic administrators" were appointed as bishops of the new sees.

1971, Sept.–1972, Feb. As a sign of a more liberal policy toward intellectuals under Gierek's regime, **liberal writers were released in 1971 and allowed to publish their works.** Meanwhile, six leaders of an underground political organization known as Ruch (Movement) were tried and sentenced to several years of imprisonment.

1972, Sept. 13–14. Poland established full diplomatic relations with West Germany. In June, the Polish and German parliaments had ratified the Normalization Treaty.

1974, Oct. The PUWP adopted a long-term **program for the modernization of agriculture and the food industry,** with the aim of tripling production by 1990. The program made no proposal for nationalization or collectivization of the currently private-owned land.

1976, June 25. The government canceled its proposed food price increases, due to workers' protests and intellectuals' open criticism of the government.

1977, March 3. The government ratified the UN Covenants on Civil and Political Rights and on Economic, Social, and Cultural Rights.

1978, Oct. 16. Cardinal Karol Wojtyla of Poland was made Pope John Paul II. When Pope John Paul II visited Poland (June 2–10, 1979), it was the first visit by a pope to a communist country. Hundreds of thousands gathered to see him.

1980, July–Sept. Industrial unrest and government crisis. A wave of industrial **strikes and protests in Gdansk and other areas** in northern Poland, over price rises and political dissatisfaction, led to the **resignations of First Secretary Edward Gierek and Prime Minister Edward Babius.** By August more than 120,000 workers were on strike. A major reorganization of the cabinet and the PUWP leadership took place when **Jozef Pinkowski became prime minister on Aug. 24** and **Stanislaw Kania became first secretary of the PUWP on Sept. 6.** Government approval of the right to strike and the right to form unions independent of the Communist Party finally ended the strike.

Sept. 14. The Soviet Union provided a loan of $260 million and consented to the postponement of repayment of a previous $280 million loan. The United States provided a $670 million loan for food.

Sept. 21. Catholic Mass was broadcast on the radio for the first time in 35 years.

Sept. 24. Independent unions formed during the industrial unrest organized themselves into a national confederation of independent trade unions known as **Solidarity** and elected **Lech Walesa as its chairman.**

Oct. 24. The government officially recognized **Solidarity** as an independent trade union.

Nov.–Dec. Warsaw Pact troops maneuvered **on the Polish border** as a reaction to the political situation in Poland. To avert invasion, **Solidarity called off strikes.**

1981, Jan. 31. The **government agreed** to the demands of striking **Solidarity** for a **41.5-hour, five-day workweek** and the publication of a **Solidarity-sponsored daily newspaper** and its nationwide distribution.

Feb. 9. Gen. Wojciech Jaruzelski replaced Pinkowski as prime minister.

Feb. 12. Solidarity expressed a willingness to comply with Jaruzelski's request for "3 months of honest work, 90 days of calm, **to put some order into the economy."**

Feb. 14. Solidarity began negotiations with the government but reached no agreement. In the summer, strikes continued throughout Poland, as did negotiations between the union and the government, and between the Polish government and the Warsaw Pact leadership.

April 17. The government agreed to allow **farmers** to form **independent trade unions.**

April 27. The Polish government narrowly averted bankruptcy when Western nations made new arrangements for its repayment of their loans.

July 23. The government announced **food price hikes** and **cuts in rations.** Protests led to a **general strike** on Aug. 5.

Aug. 30. The price of bread tripled.

Sept. 5–10. Solidarity held its first national meeting in Gdansk. The union had gained more than 9 million members.

Sept. 17. The Soviet Union issued an ultimatum against **Solidarity.**

Oct. 18. Jaruzelski became the leader of Poland's Communist Party, replacing **S. Kania.**

Nov. 10. Poland applied for membership in the International Monetary Fund and the World Bank. Its **acceptance** was delayed until **June 1986** because of the imposition of martial law.

Nov. Relations between Solidarity and the government deteriorated severely when the government used armed police to move protesting occupants away from a Warsaw officers' training academy. **On Dec. 12–13 Gen. Jaruzelski declared a state of martial law and established a Military Council for National Salvation.** Almost the entire leadership of Solidarity was arrested immediately after the declaration of martial law, and **Solidarity went underground.**

1982, Jan. 8. The Military Council issued a decree on the resumption of lectures in universities by Feb. 15, the **suspension of student and faculty organizations,** and a ban on independent student associations.

March 19. The independent **Association of Polish Journalists was dissolved** and replaced by the Association of Journalists of the Polish People's Republic.

May 3–4. The government arrested numerous participants in huge demonstrations in Warsaw.

Oct. 8. Two new laws, though condemned by union members and the Polish Roman Catholic Church, effectively **dissolved all existing unions** and created a framework for new and closely controlled unions to replace them.

Nov. 12. Solidarity leader **Walesa was released from internment** amid a general easing of social tensions.

Dec. 18. Parliament passed laws to close the **internment centers** and to release thousands of internees, although many of them were rearrested for illegal trade union activities.

Dec. 30. Gen. Jaruzelski suspended martial law.

1983, Jan. Officially sponsored trade unions were formed to replace Solidarity.

May–June. Pope John Paul II visited Poland, met with Jaruzelski and Walesa, and **criticized the authorities for imposing martial law.**

July 21. President Henryk Jablonski declared the end of the emergency and introduced an amnesty proposal in Parliament. Solidarity and Social Self-Defense Committee members were not included in the amnesty.

Oct. The Nobel Peace Prize was awarded to Lech Walesa.

1984, July 21. The government announced **broad amnesty** and brought about an important change in the political situation by **releasing all but a handful of political prisoners.**

Oct. 19. A Catholic priest in Warsaw who supported Solidarity, **Jerzy Popieluszko,** was kidnapped and murdered.

Oct. 27. A member of the government confessed to killing Father Popieluszko. In December, four suspects went on trial.

Nov. 24–25. Representatives of **official trade unions voted to establish the National Trade Union Accord (OPZZ)** to make the unions more effective. The government immediately sanctioned OPZZ and turned over to it funds that had been impounded on the suspension of Solidarity in Dec. 1981.

1984, Dec.–1985, Aug. Solidarity and OPZZ protested against price increases by calling for strikes. Activists were arrested and sentenced to prison terms.

1985, Feb. 7. A secret police colonel and captain received jail sentences for the murder of Jerzy Popieluszko.

Nov. 6. The government underwent a reshuffling, with **Gen. Jaruzelski elected president and Zbigniew Messner prime minister.**

April 23. A **bill on joint venture was approved** to allow foreign capital investment in Polish enterprises.

1987, April. Mikhail Gorbachev and Jaruzelski signed an accord on Soviet-Polish cooperation.

June 8–14. Pope John Paul II attracted large crowds during his third visit to Poland and **gave vocal support to the banned Solidarity.**

Oct. 10–24. Prime Minister **Messner presented an economic reform**

proposal involving greater autonomy for state-owned enterprises, expansion of private labor, a reduction in bureaucracy, and increases in salaries and prices.

Nov. 29. A referendum on reforms that called for economic austerity was not endorsed by voters.

1988, Jan. 30. The government announced large **price increases** meant to accelerate a transition to a market economy. Wage increases of nearly 40 percent were intended to partially offset the price increases.

April 25. Local transportation union leaders in Bydgoszcz led a strike and subsequently bargained for a 63 percent wage increase. Labor unrest began to spread throughout Poland.

May–Aug. Workers in Gdansk went on strike in support of steel strikes in May. In August strikes of mine workers in southern Poland spread to shipyards, including Gdansk. This **strike wave prompted talks between Walesa and Interior Minister Kiszczak** and led to the promise of roundtable talks.

Sept. 19. Prime Minister Messner offered his own and his government's resignations after Parliament endorsed a report highly critical of the government's progress in implementing the economic reform program.

Sept. 28. Mieczyslaw Rakowski was elected by the Parliament to be the **new prime minister.**

Oct. The government announced that the Lenin Shipyard in Gdansk was to close on Dec. 1 because it was unprofitable. Solidarity supporters interpreted the government move as politically motivated and designed to wreck the prospects of roundtable discussions between the government and Solidarity.

1989, Feb. 6. Roundtable talks began between the government and Solidarity with the aim of reaching an agreement on a program of economic stabilization and political reform, including Solidarity's reauthorization. By April, Solidarity and the government came to an agreement that some parliamentary seats were to be contested at the polls.

Feb. 15. The journal *Odrodzanie* reprinted a report, originally published in 1943, on the murder of Polish officers by Soviet secret police, called the **Katyn massacre.**

April. Parliament passed laws on constitutional changes to create a bicameral Parliament and a presidency, on new electoral regulations, and on rights of associations. **Solidarity and Rural Solidarity were formally granted legal status.**

May 10. Lech Walesa received the Council of Europe's Human Rights Prize for 1989.

June 4, 18. National elections. Solidarity and independent candidates won all contested seats for a new National Assembly, beating the ruling Communist Party candidates. Solidarity-supported candidates won 92 of 100 seats in the Senate and 160 of 161 seats in the Sejm (the lower house).

July–Aug. Gen. Jaruzelski was elected by the two chambers of the National Assembly to the new post of **executive president of Poland on July 19.** On his recommendation, **M. Rakowski was elected first secretary of the PUWP.** Jaruzelski's strong suggestion that the government form a "grand coalition" of all parties was rejected by Solidarity, which intended to seek a mandate to constitute a government of its own or form an opposition government. On Aug. 24, after Kiszczak failed to form a coalition government, the lower house of the National Assembly elected **Tadeusz Mazowiecki,** a leading member of Solidarity, as **prime minister** and mandated him to **form a Solidarity-led coalition government** embracing all four main parties in the Assembly— the first non-Communist government in 44 years.

1989, Aug. 16. The Senate unanimously adopted a resolution condemning the Warsaw Pact members' invasion of Czechoslovakia in 1968.

Lech Walesa told the Polish press that Solidarity was prepared to form a coalition government without the Communists.

Sept.–Oct. The Mazowiecki government began a plan to progressively replace the command economy with a market economy by removing restrictions on private ownership of land and property and privatizing state enterprises.

Dec. The government presented to the Sejm a budget and economic reform package, effective Jan. 1, 1990, that involved reducing wages by 25 percent, removing price controls, cutting government subsidies, and restricting credit. The package, **aimed at moving toward a market economy,** incorporated the measures necessary to secure International Monetary Fund (IMF) agreement on a $700 million standby credit over 13 months. The **Sejm passed the package on Dec. 29** after prolonged debate.

Dec. 29–30. New constitutional amendments removed the PUWP from its leading role and **changed the country's name** from the Polish People's Republic **to the Polish Republic.**

1990, Jan. Walesa joined Czech and Hungarian leaders in calling for the withdrawal of Soviet troops.

Jan. 29. The Polish Communist Party dissolved and formed again as the Social Democratic Party.

March 1. Inflation dropped from 78 percent in January to 10 percent in February.

April 11. The Sejm abolished censorship.

May 8. Poland sought rescheduling of its foreign debts (which reached $40,000 million at the end of 1989) by cutting 80 percent of its debt-servicing obligations to secure safe transition to a market economy.

May–July. Solidarity divided. A major dispute arose between Walesa and Mazowiecki on the future structure of the union. On July 16, the **Citizens' Movement for Democratic Action Party (ROAD)** was formed as a counter to Walesa's **Center Alliance,** formed in May.

July 19. Gen. Jaruzelski agreed to resign as president to make way for a successor. He officially resigned on Sept. 19.

Sept.–1991, May. The abortion issue. On May 16, 1991, the Sejm voted to halt the passage of the controversial antiabortion bill, passed by the Senate in September 1990. The antiabortion bill, backed by the Roman Catholic Church, was designed to replace the 1956 abortion laws that made abortion free and available on demand.

Dec. Lech Walesa won a landslide victory in the second round of voting in the presidential election held on Dec. 9. He resigned his leadership of Solidarity on Dec. 12 and was sworn in as president of Poland for a five-year term on Dec. 22. He nominated Jan Krzysztof Bielecki, a 39-year-old economist, as the new prime minister.

1991, Jan. 11. The issuing of shares for five showcase state-owned enterprises was finalized. Investment was sluggish, and the government began to rethink its approach to privatization.

Jan. 21. Poland decided to cease all cooperation with the Warsaw Treaty Organization on July 1, 1991.

Feb. 23. Marian Krzaklewski replaced **Lech Walesa** as chairman of the Solidarity trade union.

April 18. The IMF approved additional loans for Poland in support of its economic program.

June. Government-union talks throughout June failed to reach a settlement on union demands for higher wages, outstanding overtime pay, reform of the wage tax, and compensation for the 140 percent and 110 percent increases, respectively, in gas and electricity costs.

June 27. The government announced plans to privatize 400 state-owned companies by the end of the year.

July. Presidential aide Maciej Zalewski secretly visited the United States to win IMF approval for the introduction of a state of emergency so that the economy could be run by decree.

Aug. 5. Finance Minister Leszek Balcerowicz, author of Poland's "shock therapy" introduction to a market economy, announced he would resign in October. Tension between Balcerowicz and Walesa had been building throughout the summer, due to Poland's severe economic difficulties.

Sept. 23. The former president of the National Bank of Poland, Grzegorz Wojtowicz, was arrested and charged with gross mismanagement.

Oct. 4. The Sejm voted to abolish the state farms and allow farmworkers to organize themselves as trading companies and rent the land as individuals.

Oct.–1992, April. Tense relations between the president and the National Assembly. After the elections on Oct. 27, Mazowiecki, who had disagreements with Walesa, was authorized by the winning Democratic Union to start talks on forming a coalition government. On Oct. 29, **President Walesa** (who had the right to nominate the prime minister) **proposed that he be the prime minister for a guaranteed two years, to provide stability in the government.** His government failed to broaden its coalition negotiations in April 1992, and Walesa considered forming a nonparty government with greater presidential powers, along the lines of the French system.

Nov. 26. Poland became a **member of the Council of Europe.**

Dec. The government succeeded in forming a new coalition cabinet under Prime Minister **Jan Olszewski.**

1992, Jan. 13. Solidarity trade union members struck over energy price rises.

Feb. 17. The government unveiled its socioeconomic policy, which called for, in part, an increase in the money supply to curb inflation. Finance Minister **Karol Lutkowski** resigned over the policy, and the Sejm approved **Andrzej Olechowski** to replace him. The Sejm rejected the economic policy on March 5.

May 26. Lech Walesa announced that he was withdrawing his support of the government and proposed the formation of a new cabinet, citing a lack of cooperation between the government and the head of state over defense and national security issues.

June 4–5. The Sejm passed a no-confidence vote against the minority government of Prime Minister Olszewski.

July 11. The Sejm approved a new government, consisting of **Hanna Suchocka** as prime minister with a majority cabinet.

July–Aug. A copper workers' strike, which had started on July 20, was supported by six other unions. The unions called for a national general strike on Aug. 18 against Poland's economic reforms.

Sept. 10. The Senate passed a "small constitution" passed by the Sejm on Aug. 1. The new constitution clarified the powers and relationship between the National Assembly and the president.

Oct. 9. Prime Minister Suchocka announced her government's socioeconomic program, which provided for new taxes to cut the budget deficit, measures to speed up privatization of state-owned enterprises, and measures to sustain the export-led recovery in industrial output. On Oct. 17 the Sejm approved the program.

Dec. A strike by the country's coal miners during the second half of December posed a serious threat to the government's economic and industrial policy.

1993, Jan. 7. Parliament approved an abortion bill that restricted the availability of abortion, but removed the original clause making a woman criminally responsible for her own abortion.

Jan. 21. Lech Walesa presented the Sejm with a Charter of Rights and Freedoms that would forbid censorship, grant the right of privacy, ban forced assimilation of minorities, and give citizens the right to examine their personal files held by the authorities. The **Sejm passed the proposed charter by 251 votes to 72.**

Feb. 28. Janusz Rewinski, chairman of the Polish Beer Lovers' Party, which had won 16 seats in the Sejm in October 1991, was expelled from the party and accused of embezzling party funds.

April 19. Ceremonies were held commemorating the fiftieth anniversary of the Warsaw Ghetto uprising. Among those present were Itzhak Rabin, the Israeli prime minister, and U.S. vice president Al Gore.

May 28. Prime Minister Suchocka was given a no-confidence vote by the Solidarity parliamentary group. She tendered her resignation, but Walesa did not accept it. **Walesa formally dissolved the Sejm on May 31** and on June 2 said elections to both the Sejm and the Senate would be held on Sept. 19.

April 30. The Sejm approved privatization of more than 600 enterprises, to take effect June 14.

May 5. More than 600,000 teachers and health care workers went on strike for higher wages.

June 1. The **Council of Ministers approved a concordat with the Vatican,** under which the state recognized religious marriages and accepted the teaching of religion in schools.

Sept. 17. The last remaining **Russian troops withdrew from Polish soil** on the fifty-fourth anniversary of the Soviet invasion of Poland.

Sept. 19. General elections. The **Democratic Left Alliance (SLD)** and the **Polish Peasant Party (PSL)** won a majority of seats in the Sejm. The SLD took 171 and the PSL took 132 out of a total of 460 seats. Both parties had roots in the former communist regime. The results appeared to be a protest against the social and economic costs of the transition to a market economy.

1994, April 8. Poland applied to the European Union.

1995, Feb. 7. Poland nominated the former Communist Jozef Oleksy as its next premier.

Nov. 9. A presidential runoff was won by former Communist **Aleksander Kwasniewski, defeating Lech Walesa,** who had served as president since 1990.

1996, Jan. 24. Jozef Oleksy resigned because of allegations of espionage, although he denied all of the allegations. On Feb. 7 Poland swore in former Communist **Wlodzimierz Cimoszewicz as its new premier.**

1998, March 30. At a ceremony in Brussels, Belgium, the European Union formally began membership talks with Poland. Also invited to apply for membership were Estonia, Cyprus, Hungary, Slovenia, and the Czech Republic. The ceremony included preliminary discussion about possible future membership processes with Bulgaria, Latvia, Lithuania, Romania, and Slovakia. **This EU expansion effort marked the first time in EU history that formal negotiations would include former Soviet-bloc nations.**

1999, March 12. Poland became a full member of the North Atlantic Treaty Organization (NATO). Also joining were the Czech Republic and Hungary.

June 5–17. Polish-born **Pope John Paul II** visited Poland for what some speculated would be the last time. The Pope stopped in 21 cities in the course of his eighth visit to Poland. This was the longest tour of a country that he had made during his 20-year papacy.

Sept. 2. Deputy Premier and Interior Minister Janusz Tomaszewski resigned following a court investigation of illegal police activities that dated back to the time before the country had been lifted from Communist rule.

2000, June 6. The smaller of two coalition parties, the Freedom Union dropped out of the coalition government, leaving the Solidarity Electoral Action without a majority in Parliament. The coalition split came after internal discord over policy arguments concerning Poland's entry into the EU.

June 26–27. Representatives from 108 nations and 12 international organizations attended a two-day conference on democracy in Warsaw. The two-part conference was meant to encourage the proliferation and protection of democratic ideals such as rule of law, freedom of the press, freedom of religion, and fair elections on a worldwide level.

Oct. 8. Pres. Kwasniewski was elected to a second five-year term; he secured 53.9 percent of the vote and was the only political figure in post-Communist Poland who while in office had experienced a rise in popularity. With the help of progressive policies by Pres. Kwasniewski, Poland was expected to become the next country officially accepted into the EU, although completion of this process was not anticipated until 2005 or 2006.

b. CZECH REPUBLIC AND SLOVAKIA (CZECHOSLOVAKIA)

(From p. 706)

1945, April 5. Klement Gottwald, vice prime minister of Czechoslovakia and a leader of the **Czechoslovak Communist Party,** declared that the new Czechoslovak state would be based on the **equality** of **Czechs and Slovaks.**

May 10. The new **government moved to Prague.** In a sweeping political purge, many collaborators were tried and executed. **Former president Emil Hácha** died in prison; **Konrad Henlein** committed suicide.

June 6. Edvard Beneš, president of Czechoslovakia, declared that the **German and Hungarian minorities had to be expelled** from his country.

June 29. Czechoslovakia ceded Ruthenia to the Soviet Union.

Aug. 3. All **Germans and Hungarians** in Czechoslovakia were **deprived of their citizenship** and subsequently **expelled from the country.**

Oct. 14. A provisional **National Assembly** was elected by indirect suffrage.

Oct. 18. The government embarked on a far-reaching program of **industrial nationalization and agricultural reform.**

1946, Feb. 27. The Czechoslovak and Hungarian governments agreed that **ethnic Slovaks from Hungary** and **ethnic Hungarians from Czechoslovakia** who volunteered to return to their native countries **would be exchanged** in equal numbers.

May 26. Elections to the National Assembly gave the **Communists** 2.7 million of the total 7.1 million votes and 114 out of 300 seats. As a result, Communist leader **Klement Gottwald** formed a new coalition cabinet.

June 19. The Assembly unanimously **reelected President Beneš.**

1947, April 16. Josef Tiso, former president of Slovakia, was condemned to death and **executed.**

July 7. Czechoslovakia first accepted but later, under Soviet pressure, **rejected an invitation** to participate in the **Marshall Plan conference** in Paris.

1948, Feb. 25. COMMUNIST COUP. The **Communists,** having infiltrated most government services and trade unions, and enjoying Soviet support, **threatened a coup d'état** and thus secured President Beneš's signature to a **predominantly Communist government under Gottwald.** In a drastic purge, lasting several months, democratic **Czechoslovakia was transformed into a Communist-run people's democracy and a Soviet satellite.**

March 10. Foreign Minister **Jan Masaryk** was killed in a fall from his office window; reported as suicide.

All industrial firms, banks, and retail trade companies were nationalized. In addition, all estates of more than 50 hectares were confiscated, without compensation to the owners.

May 9. The National Assembly adopted a new constitution.

May 30. National elections resulted in a victory for the single list of candidates from the Communist-dominated **National Front.**

June 7. President Beneš resigned on grounds of ill health. He died on Sept. 3.

June 14. KLEMENT GOTTWALD was elected president.

June 27. The Czechoslovak Social Democratic Party was forced to merge with the Communist Party.

Oct. 25. Forced-labor camps were set up to punish reactionaries and saboteurs.

1949, Jan. 1. A **five-year plan** of industrial development was started, to make Czechoslovakia economically independent of the West.

June. In an **attempt to destroy the influence of the Catholic Church,** the government founded its own **Catholic action committee** to take the direction of Church affairs away from **Archbishop Joseph Beran** and the Catholic hierarchy.

June 20. The **Vatican,** as a countermeasure, **excommunicated all active supporters of communism in Czechoslovakia.**

Oct. 14. The **government assumed full control over Church affairs** and required all clergy to swear an oath of loyalty to the state. Most of the lower clergy complied.

1950. In an uninterrupted **series of political trials,** the government prosecuted not only its foes but also some of its own members, who were accused of anti-Soviet, pro-Western leanings. In addition, several **Western diplomatic representatives were charged with espionage,** and most Western correspondents were barred from Czechoslovakia.

April. The **new minister of defense, Čepička,** after dismissing several leading officers, announced a thoroughgoing **reorganization of the army along Soviet lines.**

1951, March 2. Reports indicated that the Czech Communist Party was undergoing a **purge of "Titoist" elements.**

1952, June 7. Premier Antonin Zapotocky announced a **"desperate coal shortage"** and the complete failure of the state farms.

Nov. 20. A **mass treason trial** opened in Prague, with **Rudolf Slansky,** former secretary general of the Czechoslovak Communist Party, pleading guilty to treason, espionage, and sabotage.

Nov. 27. Slansky and ten other prominent Communists were sentenced to be hanged; their execution took place on Dec. 3.

1953, Jan. 1. President Gottwald announced a lag in industrial production and a scarcity of food.

March 21. Following President Gottwald's death (March 14), Premier **Zapotocky** was unanimously **elected president** by Parliament. He was succeeded as premier by **Viliam Siroky. Antonin Novotny** retained his earlier post as deputy premier and assumed leadership of the Communist Party Secretariat.

June 7–8. Rioting occurred against currency reform designed to stop inflation.

1954, Dec. 13. Viliam Siroky formed a new government.

1957, Nov. 17. Following the **death of President Zapotocky** on Nov. 13, Parliament elected Antonin Novotny to replace him. Novotny retained his post as first secretary of the Communist Party.

1958–68. For a decade, Czechoslovakia to a large extent disappeared from the international scene, being an obedient satellite of the Soviet Union and a key member of the Council for Mutual Economic Assist-

ance (COMECON), whose important industries contributed greatly to the economy of the communist bloc. Czech armaments production was used in many Soviet military-aid arrangements in various parts of the world.

1960, July 11. In a new, thoroughgoing **communist constitution,** Czechoslovakia was designated a "socialist republic," in recognition of the progress it had made in the direction of communism. Nonetheless, **forces of discontent** were rapidly developing, and pressure rose for relaxation of the repressive system imposed by the Soviets.

1968, Jan. 25. The first break in the Soviets' grip came when **President Novotny was replaced as first secretary of the Communist Party by** Alexander Dubček, a young and attractive Slovak leader.

March 22. President Novotny resigned at the behest of the National Assembly, the first important move along the road to democratization.

April 6. General Ludvik Svoboda was elected president, and **Oldrich Černik** was appointed premier. The reorganization of the Communist Party was undertaken and a **new party program** published, pledging freedom of speech, press, assembly, and religion. Slovakia was to be given a greater measure of autonomy. These changes evoked widespread enthusiasm throughout the country but were viewed with much concern and distrust by Moscow and some other communist capitals.

June 27. Czechoslovak intellectuals criticized the Czechoslovak Communist Party's policies in an open letter entitled **"Two Thousand Words."**

July. The **Soviets increased the pressure on Dubček** to check the liberalizing tendencies of his regime. Dubček declined invitations to attend conferences in Warsaw or Moscow (July 15), whereupon the Soviet government announced the **mission of the entire Soviet Politburo** to Prague (July 22). At the same time, Soviet forces were concentrated on the Czech frontiers, ostensibly for maneuvers (July 23–Aug. 10). The Soviet Politburo arrived at the border town of Cierna on July 29.

Aug. 9–11. Visits of President Tito of Yugoslavia and of **President Ceaușescu of Romania** (Aug. 15–17) to Prague, in a demonstration of support for Dubček and his party and if possible to forestall Soviet intervention.

Aug. 20–21. THE INVASION OF CZECHOSLOVAKIA by 200,000 Soviet and satellite troops (Romania abstained) to crush the **"Prague Spring,"** under the pretext of defending socialism. Popular protests and demonstrations threatened to lead to revolution, and the invading forces were soon raised to 650,000. Dubček disappeared for several days, evidently summoned to Soviet headquarters. On Aug. 23 President Svoboda was called to Moscow.

Aug. 27. Dubček and Svoboda returned to Prague and announced the annulment of several important reforms.

Sept. 6. Soviet **deputy foreign minister Kuznetsov** arrived in Prague, whereupon political clubs were banned, a preventive censorship system was introduced (Sept. 13), and Czech foreign minister **Jiri Hajek,** who had presented the Czech case at the UN, was forced to resign (Sept. 19).

Sept. 11. Soviet troops left Prague.

Oct. 3–4. The **Czech leaders were summoned to Moscow** and obliged to promise to abandon reforms as well as to accept Soviet military occupation "temporarily."

Oct. 27. A **new federal constitution** was introduced giving **Slovakia complete autonomy** as an equal partner with Bohemia-Moravia. Each partner was to have its own institutions, and only foreign affairs, defense, and foreign trade were to be dealt with in common. In Bratislava (Pressburg or Pozsony) a **Slovak Socialist Republic** was proclaimed.

1969, April. The **Central Committee** of the Czech Communist Party **removed Dubček, Smrkovsky,** and other liberal leaders from office. **Gustáv Husák** replaced **Dubček** as first secretary of the party.

Sept. 28. Dubček was ousted from the presidium of the Central Committee and forced to resign as chairman of the National Assembly. These were merely discrete steps in the process of eliminating him entirely from Czech public life. On Dec. 15 he was appointed Czech ambassador to Turkey, the remaining steps being his resignation as a member of the Central Committee (Jan. 28, 1970), his expulsion from the Communist Party (June 26, 1970), and, finally, the loss of his seat in the Assembly (July 8, 1970).

1970, Jan. 29. The Central Committee replaced Černik as premier with

Lubomir Strougal. Černik was later (Dec.) expelled from the Communist Party.

The attempt of the Czechoslovak leaders to bring about a relaxation of the communist system was watched with keen anticipation throughout the world, and the Soviet–Warsaw Pact invasion and occupation of the country once again revealed the determination of Moscow to maintain that system. The Soviets charged that the Czech leaders were flirting with the West Germans and their "imperialist" allies and thereby endangering the entire communist bloc.

June. Alexander Dubček was expelled from the Czechoslovak Communist Party.

1973, June 20. Following a protracted series of talks and negotiations, **Czechoslovakia and West Germany initialed a treaty normalizing their relations.** The treaty contained the mutual recognition that the **Munich Agreement of 1938,** by which Czechoslovakia had conceded Sudetenland to Germany, was **"null and void."**

1975, May 29. Gustáv Husák was elected president of Czechoslovakia, a position he held till 1989. He was also the general secretary of the Czechoslovak Communist Party from 1969 to 1987.

1977, Jan. The **"Charter 77" manifesto** appeared in Western newspapers, **exposing the nonobservance of human rights in Czechoslovakia.** Many journalists and writers had lost their positions and some had been imprisoned in the purge of 1968-reform supporters. The manifesto was drawn up by Czechoslovak intellectuals after Czechoslovakia ratified UN Covenants on Civil and Political Rights and Economic, Social, and Cultural Rights. A total of 242 people initially signed the manifesto demanding compliance with human rights provisions of the Helsinki Agreement. In February, 208 more added their signatures to the manifesto. The government declared the document to be against the social and political order. Police interrogated and arrested those who had signed the manifesto. The arrests continued into the 1980s.

1980s. Church-state relations strained. Judicial action increased against clerics and clandestine religious groups, leading to several imprisonments. Worsening relations between the Catholic Church and Czechoslovak authorities were affected by the development of Solidarity in Poland in August and September 1980, as the government was concerned about the possible growth of militant Catholicism in its own country. In December 1987, after a break of four years, Czechoslovak representatives and Roman Catholic officials in the Vatican resumed talks to ease the strained relations and to resolve the dispute over ten vacant bishoprics. Progress, though slight, was made when the government endorsed three new bishops in May 1988.

1986, Sept. 2. The police arrested seven leaders of the **Czechoslovak Musician's Union Jazz Section,** searching and confiscating their papers.

Oct. An abortion law was approved by the Czech and Slovak Councils (Parliaments); it entered into effect on Jan. 1, 1987. The law allowed women to choose abortion, provided they notified a doctor within the first 12 weeks of pregnancy.

1987, Dec. 17. Milos Jakes replaced **Gustáv Husák** as head of the **Czechoslovak Communist Party.**

1988, Oct. 10. Jakes named **Ladislav Adamec** premier after the **resignation of Lubomir Strougal,** who had been premier for 18 years. Adamec wanted change at a slower pace.

1989. THE 1989 REVOLUTION (Velvet Revolution). On **Jan. 15,** 5,000 demonstrators in Prague's Wenceslas Square commemorated Jan Palach, who had burned himself in 1969 in protest against the Soviet invasion. **Václav Havel and other dissidents were arrested;** Havel was sentenced to nine months' imprisonment on Feb. 21.

1989, Feb. 2. More than a thousand artists demanded the release of all political prisoners in the country.

Feb. 9. Milos Jakes declared that the government would not discuss matters with "anti-Socialist" groups.

May 13. Withdrawal of Soviet troops from Czechoslovakia began. It was to be completed by June 1991.

May 17. Václav Havel was released from prison after serving half his sentence.

Aug. 14. Two Slovakian human rights activists were detained by the police after a search of their homes.

Nov. Opposition groups formed Civic Forum, and hundreds of thousands of people demonstrated against the Communist govern-

ment. On **Nov. 24,** the Communist Party **Politburo resigned;** on **Nov. 28** the National Assembly approved and promulgated constitutional changes on the **abolition of the Communist monopoly in power.**

Dec. 17. Opening of border with Austria. The wire fencing between Czechoslovakia and Austria was cut ceremonially by foreign ministers of both countries. This followed the decision of the Czechoslovak government on Nov. 30 to open the border and remove all fortifications. Tens of thousands of Czechoslovakian citizens crossed the border in the next few days.

Dec. 28. Alexander Dubček, the 1968 reformist leader, **was elected chairman of the National Assembly.**

Dec. 29. Václav Havel was elected president, thus becoming the **first noncommunist head of state since 1948.** He was reelected in July 1990.

1990, Jan. 1. President Havel declared amnesty for a large number of common prisoners.

Jan. 30. The **Czechoslovak Communist Party lost** more than 100 seats in the Federal Assembly when a total of 120 new deputies were sworn in, only 9 of them Communists.

Feb. 26. The Red Army began withdrawing its troops.

March. Constitutional and political Reforms: new laws allowed citizens to form associations without approval of the Interior Ministry and to gather or hold demonstrations without approval of the local government. New law regarding the press abolished censorship and allowed individuals to publish newspapers and magazines.

March 29. Czechoslovakia adopted a new name to represent the Czech and Slovak Federative Republic: **Czecho-Slovakia,** written in Slovak.

May. The secret police agency was dismantled, and the death penalty was abolished.

June 8–9. The **Civic Forum** and its Slovak parallel party, **Public Against Violence,** took 46.3 percent of the vote and 170 seats in the 300-member **Federal Assembly.** The Communist Party took 47 seats.

Oct. 25. The **Slovak parliament** approved a law declaring **Slovak the official language** of the state.

Dec. 12. The **Czechoslovak Federal Assembly** approved legislation that would lead to **power sharing between the central government and the Czech and Slovak republics.**

1991. Privatization: a new national economic strategy took shape as the government introduced measures on price deregulation, denationalization, and privatization. The first round of "large" privatization started in May 1992 with the voucher system, in which holders of vouchers were able to apply for shares in the privatizing companies.

Feb. Czechoslovakia was admitted to the Council of Europe.

Sept. Slovak sovereignty and the split of Czechoslovakia: the Slovak National Party put forward a motion for Slovakian sovereignty but failed to gain majority support.

1992, May. The majority (73–59) of the Slovak National Council favored independence.

Aug. The Czech prime minister and the Slovak prime minister agreed to abandon the federation because there was "no chance of maintaining the present state of affairs." The timetable for the formal partition of the country was Jan. 1, 1993.

Sept. 1. The Slovak National Council adopted a draft constitution for a Slovak Republic, and on Dec. 16, 1992, the Czech National Council adopted a constitution for the Czech Republic. As scheduled, Czechoslovakia **peacefully split into two countries on Jan. 1, 1993: Slovakia and the Czech Republic.**

1993, Jan. 26. Václav Havel was elected president of the **Czech Republic;** he was sworn in on Feb. 2.

Jan. 12. The **Slovak cabinet** formally took office.

Feb. 8. Two separate currencies came into force for the Czech Republic and Slovakia.

Feb. 15. Michal Kovac was elected president of **Slovakia.**

March 8. The Czech Republic tightened borders between itself and Slovakia and Germany to prevent illegal immigrants to Germany.

March 17. The International Monetary Fund (IMF) approved **credit for the Czech Republic** based on its 1993 economic program.

March 30–31. Michal Kovac made his first official visit to the Czech capital as president of Slovakia.

April 26. In Bratislava, 4,500 people protested against the Slovak government's economic and social policies.

July 7. The **National Council in Slovakia** approved legislation allowing the use of foreign first names and surnames and allowing women to drop the Slavic suffix "-ova" from their surnames.

July 9. The **Czech Republic's Chamber of Deputies voted the former communist regime illegal,** thus allowing prosecutions for crimes committed for political reasons.

July 27. The IMF approved a loan to assist the transformation of the Slovak economy.

Sept. 20. A readmission treaty was signed between Slovakia and Romania, allowing each country to repatriate illegal aliens.

1994, March 16. The **new Slovakian cabinet, led by Premier Jozef Maravcik,** was sworn in after the government of Vladimir Meciar fell on March 11 due to a no-confidence vote by Parliament.

1998, Jan. 20. Pres. Václav Havel of the Czech Republic was reelected by Parliament.

March 2. Pres. Kovac of Slovakia stepped down after his official term ended, leaving the nation without a president.

June 19–21. In the Czech Republic, the Center-Left **Social Democrats (CSSD)** won a minority of seats in the House of Representatives and with 32.3 percent of the vote remained the most successful party.

July 9. In a surprising development, the new government did not form a coalition in order to secure a legislative majority but instead made a deal with the rival **Civic Democrats (ODS).** Part of the deal was that the ODS promise to refrain from bringing any no-confidence votes on the minority government of the CSSD. In return, the CSSD would allow the ODS to appoint the speakers of both houses, the budget and secret service committee chairs, and the head of the Supreme Audit Office.

Sept. 25–26. Legislative elections in Slovakia saw nationalist prime minister Vladimir Meciar's supporters suffer a substantial defeat when the ruling **Movement for a Democratic Slovakia (HZDS)** was ousted. A four-party coalition formed to secure a majority in Parliament; **Mikulas Dzurinda** was established as the new prime minister, ending Meciar's tenure.

Nov. 13–21. In the Czech Republic Senate elections the ODS gained three more seats than the CSSD. However, both of these two largest parties in the Czech Republic lost seats in the Senate during the election.

1999, Jan. 15. The planned budget anticipated the young government's first deficit, which would be a result of the lingering economic recession. Meanwhile, unemployment rose to nearly 10 percent.

March 12. The Czech Republic became a full member of NATO, along with Poland and Hungary.

May 29. After the constitution of Slovakia had been changed to allow for a direct vote, **Vladimir Meciar was defeated by Rudolf Schuster in a presidential runoff vote.** Schuster became the first president in Slovakian history to be elected by popular rather than parliamentary vote. The election also ended the 15-month period during which the largely ceremonial position of president had remained vacant. Analysts predicted that the pro-West Schuster would speed Slovakia toward greater levels of democracy and entrance into the EU.

Dec. 3. More than 50,000 protestors gathered in Prague to demand the removal of the Czech Republic's premier, Milo Zeman, and Speaker of Parliament Václav Klaus. Similar demonstrations were held in 20 other cities throughout the nation, but the government leaders refused to step aside.

Dec. 10. Slovakia was one of seven nations to receive a first invitation to join the EU in the near future. The other invited countries were Bulgaria, Latvia, Romania, Malta, Turkey, and Lithuania.

2000, April 20. After a three-week standoff at the home of Slovakia's former prime minister Meciar, a commando force finally used dynamite to locate and arrest him on charges of fraud and abuse of power. Meciar was accused of giving illegal bonuses to his cabinet ministers while he was in office.

July 3. Pres. Schuster of Slovakia struggled with an ongoing illness as his cabinet **transferred presidential power to the prime minister, Mikulas Dzurinda,** and the speaker of Parliament, Jozef Migas.

Sept. 23. A meeting was held peacefully between IMF and World Bank officials and representatives from opposition organizations, many of whom criticized IMF and World Bank policies as elitist, racist, and harmful to the environment.

Sept. 26–27. More than 15,000 delegates from 182 countries met in the Czech Republic capital of Prague for the annual conference of the IMF and the World Bank. Conference delegates were trapped in the convention center for several hours by thousands of protestors. The demonstrators, reflecting the rising anti-globalization movement, turned violent on Sept. 26 after having resisted bloodlessly for more than a week.

c. HUNGARY

(From p. 707)

1945, Nov. 3. The first **general election** gave an absolute majority to the anticommunist **Smallholders' Party,** whose leader, **Zoltan Tildy,** formed a coalition cabinet. The Communists gained the Interior and Justice Ministries and thus controlled the secret police.

The economic situation of the country was desperate as a result of the war, with serious food shortages and an unprecedented currency inflation. Large-scale Soviet requisitions further aggravated the situation.

1946. About 150,000 ethnic Germans were expelled; another 100,000 were expelled in 1947.

Feb. 1. A republic was proclaimed with Zoltan Tildy as president. Ferenc Nagy of the Smallholders' Party became **premier** on Feb. 4.

1947, Feb. 10. The **HUNGARIAN PEACE TREATY** was signed in Paris. It called for the **return of Transylvania to Romania,** a small frontier rectification in favor of Czechoslovakia, reparations, and the reduction of armed forces.

Feb. 25. The **arrest of Béla Kovács,** secretary general of the Smallholders' Party, for alleged plotting against the occupation forces, ushered in the gradual purge of the party's anticommunist wing.

May 31. Premier **Imre Nagy,** accused of conspiracy by the Communists, **resigned** and was replaced by **Lajos Dinnyes;** the Communist Party soon won complete control over the country.

Aug. 1. A **three-year plan** went into effect, calling for a planned economy and nationalization of the banks.

Aug. 31. A **general election** gave the **Communists the largest number** of seats. **Premier Dinnyes** continued in office at the head of a coalition cabinet of 15 members, including five Communists.

1948, Feb. 13. A Soviet-Hungarian treaty of cooperation and mutual aid was signed.

June 12. A fusion of Communists and Social Democrats into the **United Workers' Party** was engineered by the Communists.

July 30. President Tildy was forced to resign and was replaced by the chairman of the United Workers' Party, former Socialist **Arpád Szakasits.**

Dec. 9. After completing its purge of anticommunist members, the Smallholders' Party called for **Premier Dinnyes's** resignation and put procommunist **István Dobi** in his place. The real power, however, was in the hands of the Communist deputy premier, **Mátyás Rákosi.**

Dec. 27. The refusal of the Catholic Church to make concessions to the government led to the arrest of **Josef Cardinal Mindszenty** and other dignitaries on charges of conspiracy to overthrow the government. Cardinal Mindszenty was found guilty and sentenced to life imprisonment (Feb. 8, 1949). He sought asylum in the American embassy.

1949, May 15. A **general election** with open voting **gave complete victory** to the Communist-controlled **National Independence Front.**

June 16. The **arrest of Communist foreign minister László Rajk** on charges of conspiracy **set off a wholesale purge of Hungarian Communists** accused of deviating from the pro-Soviet line.

Aug. 7. A **new constitution** was proclaimed that followed **very closely that of the Soviet Union.**

Dec. 28. The government decreed the **nationalization of all major industries** and announced the start of a **five-year plan.**

1950, May–June. The remaining former **Socialists,** among them **Arpád Szakasits,** were **dismissed** from the government. Hungary, in its domestic and foreign affairs, had come completely under Communist and Soviet domination.

1951, June 28. Archbishop Josef Groesz was convicted of conspiring to overturn the government.

July 21. The **Roman Catholic bishops** took an oath of allegiance to the "people's republic," after having refused to do so for two years.

1952, Aug. 14. István Dobi **formally resigned** as premier and was succeeded by **Mátyás Rákosi.**

1953, Feb. 21. A purge, reportedly dictated by a visiting Soviet group, took a toll of 30 Jewish Communist leaders.

July 2. Following a shakeup of the top Communist leadership, the government resigned. The next day, parliament reelected István Dobi to the presidency and Imre Nagy to the vice presidency. On July 4 **Prime Minister Rákosi resigned,** as a concession to the farmers and consumers, to make way for the new premier, **Imre Nagy.**

1955, April 18. Parliament, endorsing Communist Party action, named **Andras Hegedus** to the premiership, replacing Imre Nagy, who had been accused (Apr. 14) of right-wing deviationism.

1956, March 29. László Rajk, who had been executed in 1949 after being prosecuted, along with other leaders, for treason and Titoism, was posthumously cleared, according to an announcement by Mátyás Rákosi.

July 18. Mátyás Rákosi was replaced as first secretary of the Hungarian Workers (Communist) Party by **Erno Gero,** a first deputy premier.

Oct. 21. University students threatened to strike if their demands for freedom were not met, and a revolutionary situation rapidly developed.

Oct. 24. **Imre Nagy,** who had been readmitted to the Communist Party (Oct. 13), **became premier,** as anti-Russian rioting developed in Budapest and Soviet forces sought to quell the uprising.

Oct. 25. **Anti-Russian rioters** won a concession in the replacement of Stalinist Erno Gero with **János Kádár** as head of the Hungarian Communist Party; the rioters pressed for further concessions.

Oct. 27. As the **revolt** began to spread throughout the country, the Central Committee of the Hungarian Communist Party promised to work for the withdrawal of Soviet troops as soon as the rioting ended, and Nagy appointed leaders of the illegal Smallholders' Party to his cabinet.

Oct. 30. **Soviet forces withdrew from Budapest,** and Premier Nagy, in a radio speech, promised Hungarians free elections and a prompt ending of one-party dictatorship.

Nov. 2. **Nagy denounced the Warsaw Pact** and asked the UN to take up the Hungarian situation; it had already voted (Oct. 28) to discuss the Hungarian problem.

Nov. 4. **Soviet forces reversed their withdrawal** and moved in to smash the revolt. Nagy was ousted as premier and replaced by Kádár. The **UN General Assembly adopted a resolution condemning the Soviet assault on Hungary** and calling for an investigation.

Nov. 14. **Soviet forces** crushed the last rebel stronghold on Csepel Island, and later (Nov. 22) **seized Nagy** as he left the Yugoslav embassy in Budapest.

Dec. 12. While a general strike protested the Kádár regime, the UN General Assembly adopted a resolution that condemned Soviet repression in Hungary, called on the USSR to withdraw its forces, and urged that Hungarian independence be reestablished.

1957, Feb. 10. The government initiated measures to restore the status quo ante, making Russian language compulsory in the schools, giving workers piecework payment rather than fixed wages, and repudiating the promised religious education.

March 28. Premier Kádár signed **agreements in Moscow** providing for Soviet economic aid and the continued presence of Soviet troops in Hungary to guard against a repetition of the 1956 uprising.

1958, Jan. 27. János Kádár **resigned** as premier but kept his post as first secretary of the Hungarian Socialist Workers Party. He took a post in the cabinet as minister without portfolio. On Jan. 28, First Deputy **Ferenc Muennich** succeeded Kádár as premier.

June 17. Budapest announced the **executions,** after a secret trial, of **former premier Imre Nagy, General Pal Malater,** and two other leaders of the 1956 revolt. Others received prison terms.

1959, Nov. 30. Kádár, Hungarian Communist Party secretary, said Soviet troops would remain in Hungary as long as the international situation required.

1962, Aug. 19. An official announcement disclosed that 25 "Stalinists," including Erno Gero and Mátyás Rákosi, had been **expelled from the Socialist Workers Party.**

1964, April 1–10. Nikita Khrushchev visited Hungary. In a joint statement, Hungary declared its support of the Soviet Communist Party in its dispute with the Chinese.

1965, June. Kádár resigned as premier (he had begun a second term in 1961) but remained as first secretary of the Socialist Workers' Party. Though **Gyulla Kállai** became premier, Kádár remained the effective ruler of the country, following the Soviet lead in all matters of foreign policy and accepting the presence of Soviet troops on Hungarian territory but trying, in return, to lighten the repression characteristic of Communist rule. Cautious liberalization dominated Kádár's approach in the 1960s.

1966, Oct. A new electoral law gave the voters a somewhat larger measure of choice between candidates on the official list.

Nov. 28–Dec. 3. The Ninth Congress of the Hungarian Socialist Workers Party met and discussed economic reforms.

1967. Jeno Fock succeeded Gyulla Kállai as premier.

1968, Jan. 1. The regime initiated **a series of reforms known as New Economic Mechanism,** decentralizing authority. Liberal economic policies led to increases in agricultural production. **More market mechanisms and small businesses** were allowed in most Communist countries.

Aug. **Hungarian troops participated** with other Warsaw Pact countries **in the invasion of Czechoslovakia.**

1970, Nov. 23–28. The Tenth Congress of the Hungarian Socialist Workers Party reaffirmed the party's policy of full support for the Soviet Union in international affairs combined with cautious liberalization and economic reform at home.

1975, May 15. György Lázár replaced Jeno Fock as **prime minister** and Hungary was reported to be continuing its economic cooperation with the West—especially West Germany—in establishing more joint ventures and increasing trade.

1977, June 7–9. János Kádár, the first secretary of the Hungarian Socialist Workers Party, **met with Pope Paul VI at the Vatican.** The meeting marked a "new progress" in **improvement between state and Roman Catholic Church relations in Hungary.**

1978, Jan. 6–7. The U.S. authorities returned to Hungary St. Stephen's Crown and Regalia, which had been in U.S. custody since the end of World War II.

May 22. The U.S. House of Representatives approved the granting of **most favored nation (MFN) status to Hungary.** Hungary thus was the fourth Eastern European state to have MFN status with the U.S., following Romania, Yugoslavia, and Poland.

July 5. **Hungary and Austria signed an agreement on the mutual abolition of visa requirements,** effective Jan. 1, 1979. This was the first agreement of its kind concluded between a Warsaw Pact country and a noncommunist direct neighbor.

1981, Nov. 4. Hungary applied for membership of the International Monetary Fund (IMF) and of the World Bank. It was **admitted to IMF in May 1982 and to World Bank in July 1982.**

1986, July–1987, Oct. Censorship and dispute within the Writers' Union. The government banned the publication of dissident writer István Csurka and the literary magazine *Tisza Táj.* Dispute arose within the Hungarian Writers' Union, with some claiming it was "anti-Communist" and others, "anti-arts."

Sept. 14. **Imre Pozsgay,** a member of the Political Committee of the Hungarian Socialist Workers Party, published an article in the journal *Magyar Nemzet* declaring that the 1956 events had been a popular uprising against oppression, not a counterrevolution.

1987, June 25. Karoly Grósz succeeded Grörgy Lázár as chairman of the Council of Ministers (prime minister).

July 1. Amendments to laws on **marriage, family, and guardianship were introduced to tackle Hungary's rising divorce rate, the highest in Europe.** The new laws included raising the marriageable age of women from 16 to 18, increasing the compulsory waiting period for couples registered to marry from one to three months, and ensuring the equal rights and responsibilities of divorced parents with respect to alimony and the child's interests in custody.

1988, June 22. Political reform and shift of positions: János Kádár, leader of the ruling Hungarian Socialist Workers' Party since 1956, was **replaced by Karoly Grósz.** Nearly a third of the Politburo members were replaced by advocates of reform. The new members included Imre Pozsgay, leader of the Patriotic People's Front, and Reszö Nyers, a main architect of the 1968 economic liberalization who had been ousted from the Politburo in 1975.

1989, Feb. 11. The government approved the formation of independent parties in a multiparty system.

April 12. János Berecz and three other conservative opponents of reform were expelled from the Central Committee of the Hungarian Socialist Workers Party.

May. Dismantling of the border fences built in the mid-1960s began.

May 5. János Kádár lost his positions as party president of the Hungarian Socialist Workers Party and member of the Central Committee after **Mária Ormos,** a historian, delivered a speech to the Hungarian Academy of Sciences denouncing him as a Soviet puppet.

June 8. Minister of Culture and Education **Ferenc Glatz** announced that, as of September, **Russian language** would no longer be required in Hungarian schools and universities.

1989, June 16. The body of former prime minister Imre Nagy was exhumed and reburied with state honors on the thirty-first anniversary of his execution.

Oct. The **Hungarian Socialist Workers Party** renamed itself the **Hungarian Socialist Party** and renounced Leninism.

Nov. 15. Hungary applied for full membership in the Council of Europe.

1990, Jan. 5. The Parliament adopted a resolution calling for the **withdrawal of Soviet troops** from Hungary by the end of 1991.

Jan. 23. The Hungarian Democratic Forum pushed for an investigation of the secret service.

March 10. The Soviet Union agreed to a complete withdrawal of troops from Hungary and finished the withdrawal by June 19, 1991.

March–April. Formation of a noncommunist government: Hungarian voters favored the Center-Right Hungarian Democratic Forum and its appeal to nationalism over other parties in general elections; it won nearly 60 percent of the seats in Parliament. The **Democratic Forum formed a three-party coalition government with József Antall as prime minister.** In May, Antall presented a government program that emphasized privatization and foreign investment.

June. Parliament voted for Hungary's total withdrawal from the Warsaw Pact by the end of 1991.

July 22. The governing coalition agreed to the reprivatization of farmlands.

Aug. 3. The National Assembly elected **Arpad Göncz,** a member of the Alliance of Free Democrats, as **national president.**

Oct. 14. The opposition was victorious in municipal elections.

Oct. 23. Parliament declared Oct. 23 a national holiday in honor of the revolution of 1956.

Dec. 11. The government signed a trade agreement with the Soviet Union.

1991, May. Former Communists **Imre Pozsgay and Zoltán Biró formed** a new Hungarian party, the **National Democratic Alliance.**

June. The **National Assembly** approved a bill to **recompensate** those whose property had been expropriated under the Communist regime.

Dec. 3. The National Assembly voted to host the 1996 World Exposition.

1992, March 3. The Constitutional Court ruled unconstitutional a bill passed in 1991 that would have allowed prosecutions of political crimes committed under the Communist regime.

March 11. The State Property Agency launched the second phase of its privatization program.

April 7. The National Assembly approved the second compensation law for state-caused damages that occurred between 1939 and 1949.

April 25. Jozsef Torgyan, leader of the rump of the Independent Smallholders' Party, organized between 15,000 and 20,000 people to demonstrate in Budapest, calling for resignation of the government for betraying the anticommunist revolution.

May. Hungary was admitted as a participant in the Eureka initiative on high-technology projects.

May 13. The National Assembly passed the third compensation for expropriations from 1939 to 1989.

June 11. Jozsef Torgyen was suspended as chair of the Independent Smallholders' Party.

June 23. Zoltan Kiraly announced the formation of a new left-wing party, the Social Democratic People's Party.

Aug. 19–21. The World Federation of Hungarians held its third congress in Budapest, after an interval of 54 years. More than 15,000 Hungarians, living in Hungary and abroad, attended.

Sept. 19. Several thousand supporters of right-wing ideologue Isatvan Csurka protested outside the National Assembly to demand the resignation of President Árpád Goncz.

Sept. 24. A major counterdemonstration organized by the Democratic Charter Movement marched against the recent rise of the far right and related racist attacks.

Sept. 29. A bill of rights to protect national and ethnic minorities was introduced in the National Assembly.

Nov. 10–11. Hungary settled several outstanding claims with Russia during a visit by Boris Yeltsin.

Dec. 17. The National Assembly voted in a new abortion law that allowed abortion on demand.

1993, Feb. 3. The government announced the privatization of national utilities.

April 14. Parliament approved legislation banning the wearing or display of either Nazi or Communist symbols.

Sept. 15. The IMF approved a standby credit to support the government's economic program.

1994, Feb. 28. Hungary launched a massive program to privatize all of its industry.

April 1. Hungary applied to the European Union.

June 4. After a Socialist resurgence due largely to the hardships of economic reform, the Hungarian Parliament chose Socialist Gyula Horn as its new premier.

1998, March 30. The EU formally began membership talks with Hungary. Other nations considered in this largest planned expansion of the EU in its 40-year history were Cyprus, Estonia, Poland, the Czech Republic, and Slovenia.

May 24. In Hungarian parliamentary elections, only 134 of 386 available seats went to the Socialist Party. The Fidesz-Hungarian Civic Party, a Center-Right faction that won only 20 seats in 1994, controlled the new government by means of 148 seats in a coalition with other Right parties. The major objective of the new Hungarian government was admission to the EU in the near future. Fidesz leader Viktor Orban was chosen prime minister of the coalition government.

1999, March 12. Along with Poland and the Czech Republic, Hungary became a full member of NATO. Weeks later, on April 11, Hungary was called upon by NATO to block attempts by its former ally Russia to ship fuel and food to Yugoslavian Serbs during the Kosovo crisis.

2000, June 6. In a third round of legislative voting Hungary's Parliament elected **Ferenc Madl** as president.

d. YUGOSLAVIA AND SUCCESSOR STATES

(From p. 722)

1945, May. As the war ended, Yugoslavia was still theoretically a monarchy. The actual power, however, was wielded by **Marshal Tito** and his **National Liberation Movement.**

Nov. 11. Elections for a constituent assembly gave a substantial majority to Tito's Communist-dominated National Front.

Nov. 29. The assembly proclaimed a **FEDERAL PEOPLE'S REPUBLIC OF YUGOSLAVIA.**

1946, Jan. 31. A new constitution was adopted, closely resembling that of the Soviet Union. The new government was recognized by the Western powers, though its leanings, from the start, were decidedly pro-Soviet.

March 10. General Drazha Mihailovich, wartime resistance leader, was captured, tried for collaboration with the enemy, and, despite Western protests, **shot on July 17.**

Sept. 18. Archbishop Aloysiye Stepinac, Catholic leader of Croatia, was arrested on similar charges and **sentenced to 16 years' hard labor.**

1946–47. Yugoslavia concluded a series of **political and economic agreements with Poland, Czechoslovakia, Albania, Bulgaria, and Hungary.** It also became one of the founding members of the **Cominform.**

1947, April 27. Marshal Tito announced a **five-year plan** for industrial development.

Despite Yugoslavia's close outward association with the Soviet Union, Tito repeatedly asserted Yugoslavia's own interests. Differences between the two countries became more frequent.

1948, March 18. The Soviet Union recalled its military and technical advisers from Yugoslavia.

June 28. The **COMINFORM EXPELLED YUGOSLAVIA** from membership for doctrinal errors and hostility to the Soviet Union.

July 21–29. Tito denied the Cominform charges before a congress of the Yugoslav Communist Party and received a vote of confidence. The party was later purged of Cominform supporters.

1949, June–July. The Soviet Union's Eastern satellites broke off all economic relations with Yugoslavia. As a countermove, Tito concluded a series of economic agreements with the West, notably the United States.

1949, Sept. 27. As a final gesture, the **Soviet Union denounced its treaty of friendship with Yugoslavia** (p. 903). Its satellites subsequently followed the Soviet example.

1950, March 25. General elections, in methods and results, differed little from those in other Communist-controlled countries and **brought an overwhelming endorsement** of the single list of **People's Front candidates.** Still, the rapprochement between Yugoslavia and the West spread from the economic to the political sphere, as Yugoslavia opposed Chinese intervention in the Korean War, resumed diplomatic relations with Greece, and improved its relations with Italy, which had been disturbed by conflicting claims over Trieste. In the ideological arena, Marshal Tito continued to adhere to his own brand of anti-Russian communism, known as **Titoism.**

1952, July 13. The United States announced its decision to equip the Yugoslav armed forces with tanks, heavy artillery, and jet aircraft.

1953, Jan. 14. Parliament, in joint session, formally appointed **Marshal Tito as president** of the Federal People's Republic.

Jan. 20. Turkey's foreign minister arrived in Belgrade for talks regarding the formation of a formal **Balkan defense alliance.**

March 31. After a five-day **visit to Britain** (March 16–21), President Tito announced that Prime Minister Winston Churchill had promised to protect Yugoslavia, and that he had pledged resistance to any aggression.

June 14. President Tito disclosed that the **USSR had requested a resumption of normal diplomatic relations,** a "great victory" for Yugoslavia.

Dec. 22. Agreement in principle was reached by Yugoslavia, Greece, and Turkey to arrange a **defense alliance,** providing that an attack by or through Bulgaria on any one of the three would be regarded as an attack on all.

1954, Jan. 17. The Communist Party condemned Vice President **Milovan Djilas** for criticizing party policy and stripped him of his party position. Djilas's widely translated book, *The New Class,* attacked the privileges of Communist Party officials.

April 16. A joint **statement with Turkey** reaffirmed the objectives of a Balkan military alliance and gave Greece assurances that its approval would be sought on "all questions of principle."

Aug. 9. Yugoslavia, Greece, and Turkey signed a **20-year treaty of alliance,** political cooperation, and mutual assistance.

1955, May 26. Nikita Khrushchev arrived in Belgrade with an apology for Soviet treatment of Yugoslavia in 1949 and called for a renewal of close ties. Tito secured recognition of Yugoslavia's independence in domestic and international affairs.

June 2. A joint communiqué, issued at the end of the Khrushchev-Tito meeting in Belgrade, called for a European collective security treaty, the banning of nuclear weapons, and UN membership for communist China.

1956, Jan. 3. An agreement with the Soviet Union provided for Soviet construction of an **experimental reactor** in Yugoslavia.

June 20. President Tito concluded a three-week Moscow visit.

1957, Feb. 19. Khrushchev confirmed the rift that had developed since the previous autumn by stating that Yugoslavia could not expect any more economic favors from the Soviet Union.

July 29. Reconciliation talks in Moscow resulted in an agreement providing for the restoration of $250 million in Soviet aid.

Aug. 3. At a secret meeting in Romania, Yugoslav and Soviet leaders agreed on closer cooperation.

Oct. 7. Tito recognized East Germany.

1958, Dec. 22. An **agreement with the United States** provided for Yugoslavia's purchase of surplus agricultural goods amounting to $95 million.

1959, Dec. 28. The government announced the completion of its first nuclear reactor.

1962, July 23. Speaking at the close of a two-day meeting of the Communist Party's Central Committee, Tito declared that liberalism and deviation from official ideology would no longer be tolerated in politics, economics, or literature.

1963, April 7. The parliament unanimously approved a **new constitution** permitting President Tito to remain in office for life. Future presidents, however, were to be elected by Parliament for a maximum of two consecutive four-year terms. The new constitution, naming the country the **Socialist Federal Republic of Yugoslavia,** provided for a Communist-controlled state and created the post of premier.

Nov. Romanian Communist leader **Gheorghiu-Dej visited Yugoslavia** and signed an agreement with Tito on the construction of an "Iron Gate" hydroelectric navigation system on the Danube.

1965. The government relaxed various controls over the economic life of the country. This tendency to abandon the system of strict regulation and approach the principles and practices of a free economy was later continued, though with some caution. **Workers' councils** were developed to maintain social responsibility and some democracy in key economic units.

1966, July. Ouster of Vice President Aleksander Rankovic, alleged to have opposed the liberalizing tendencies. The office of vice president was abolished and its functions assigned to the president of the Federal Assembly.

1967, April. Constitutional amendments tended to strengthen the parliamentary system and expand the powers of the six local republics that constituted the federal state.

1968, Dec. Further constitutional changes laid greater emphasis on the Chamber of Nationalities and the federal structure of the country.

1969, Jan. A **new electoral law** permitted voters to reject the candidates on the official party list and to propose candidates of their own. This was simply the latest evidence of Yugoslavia's gradual evolution in a somewhat more pronounced liberal, democratic direction. In the world at large, Marshal Tito had over the years made himself a **leader of the nonaligned and anticolonial states** (p. 814). He traveled widely and established close relations with President Gamal Abdel Nasser of the United Arab Republic and with India, and enjoyed much prestige throughout Africa.

1970, Dec. 29. Death, in exile, of former king Peter.

1971, June 30. The Federal Assembly adopted **constitutional amendments that limited the powers of the federal government, increased powers for republics** comprising the federation, and **established a Collective State Presidency** of 22 members, in which all the republics were equally represented.

July 30. Dzemal Bijedich replaced Mitja Ribichich as **premier** of the federal government.

1972, July–Nov. Croatian nationalists were **tried and sentenced** for antistate offenses. Leaders of the League of Communists of Croatia were purged from the Yugoslav party and state posts because of connections with nationalist activities.

1973, Feb. 21. A **new constitution promulgated major changes,** including the replacement of the existing five chambers of Parliament with a Federal Chamber and a Chamber of Republics and Provinces, the introduction of a "delegational system" of representation at all levels, and the expansion of the powers of Yugoslav **workers' councils.** It also recognized the sovereign status of the republics and granted to the republics and provinces the right to veto federal decisions.

1974, May 16. Tito was elected president of the Federal Republic for an unlimited time. After his death, an annual rotating presidency was established to prevent unrest among various ethnic groups.

1980, May 4. Death of Marshal Tito at age 88.

1981–84. Church-state relations: popular interest in religion was renewed and was allegedly **linked with nationalism.** Several Catholic clergymen and a number of Muslim fundamentalists were sentenced to imprisonment for political offenses. After late 1984, religious activities were more tolerated and the first mosque in Zagreb was opened.

1981, March–Sept. A state of emergency in Kosovo was declared in April because **ethnic Albanians rioted for independence.** Albanian secessionists were sentenced to prison terms ranging from 7 to 13.5 years. A political purge was conducted in June through September in connection with the nationalist riots.

July 3. The Federal Assembly approved a series of **constitutional amendments that reaffirmed the system of collective state and party leadership** and the system of one- and two-year terms of office that came into full effect after Tito's death.

1982–84. Industrial output and external trade were improved, but **high inflation and food and fuel shortages remained.** In 1983 the federal government adopted **programs of austerity measures for economic stabilization,** including correlating pay levels to productivity, taxing income earned through "moonlighting," and increasing property taxes. At the same time, the federal government negotiated with Western governments and banks for a "rescue package" to repay foreign debt ($4 billion to $5 billion in 1983) and for further loans.

1985, Aug.–1986, July. The federal court reduced prison sentences for the dissident intellectuals of the so-called Belgrade Six, indicating some government tolerance for criticism.

1988, May 16. The government began wage controls in response to an International Monetary Fund agreement granting Yugoslavia $430 million in credits and rescheduling more than $21 billion in loans.

Nov. 23. In Kosovo province, Serbian authorities banned all public assemblies and demonstrations conducted by ethnic Albanians.

1989, Sept.–1990, Dec. Independence of Slovenia. On Sept. 27, the Slovenian Assembly adopted constitutional amendments declaring Slovenia "an independent, sovereign, and autonomous state" that had the right to veto any federal decision prejudicial to Slovenia's welfare. In July 1990, the Assembly proclaimed the full sovereignty of the Slovenian Republic, despite the opposition of the federal government and other republics. A referendum in Slovenia approved the declaration of independence on Dec. 23, 1990.

1990, Jan. 2. In response to slowed production and increased inflation, the government introduced new economic measures.

Jan. 23. The Yugoslav League of Communists met and voted to relinquish the party's political monopoly. The Slovenian delegation demanded greater autonomy for the republics.

Feb. 4. The Slovenian League of Communists declared itself independent from the Yugoslav Communist Party.

May–Dec. Formation of noncommunist governments: Lojze Peterle, chairman of the Slovene Christian Democratic Party, formed a new Slovenian government on May 16, after his party had won the election. Franjo Tudjman, leader of the Croatian Democratic Union (HDZ), was elected president of Croatia, and the government of Stjepan Mesic of the HDZ was approved on May 31. In December, noncommunist governments were also formed in Bosnia-Herzegovina and Macedonia.

July 2. Rejecting the new constitutional proposals of Serbia, the Kosovo Assembly **declared Kosovo independent** of Serbia and **a full constituent republic within the federation of Yugoslavia.** In retaliation, Serbia permanently dissolved Kosovo's provincial assembly, took over its responsibilities, and terminated the contracts of all Kosovo parliamentary officials.

July 17. The ruling Serbian Communist Party renamed itself the Serbian Socialist Party.

Aug. 18. In Croatia the Serbian minority voted on an unofficial referendum for political autonomy. The government declared the ballot illegal.

Oct. 1. Serbs in Croatia declared those areas where they were the majority **"autonomous regions."** Violence occurred between police and residents. The government of Serbia called on the federal authorities to intervene to defend Serbs from what it called "repression in Croatia."

Oct. 3. The presidents of Slovenia and Croatia met in Zagreb to work together to obtain full autonomy from Yugoslavia.

Oct. 30. Slovenia imposed customs duties on Serbian goods, effectively ending a unified Yugoslav internal market.

Dec. 21. A new Croatian constitution proclaimed Croatia's sovereignty and its right to secede from Yugoslavia, though this was boycotted by ethnic Serbian deputies to the Croatian Assembly.

1991, Feb. 20. Slovenia voted for secession from Yugoslavia.

March 9. Severe political crisis ensued after the suppression in Belgrade of an anticommunist demonstration. **Slobodan Milosevic,** hardline leader of the Socialist Party of Serbia (SPS) and president of Serbia, began to try to undermine the power of the Collective State Presidency by influencing representatives to resign. Presidents from Montenegro and Vojvodina, an autonomous Serbian province, withdrew from the collective because of its problems. Milosevic implied that military intervention was the only thing that could save the Yugoslav federation.

March 28. The presidents of Yugoslavia's six constituent republics (Slovenia, Croatia, Serbia, Macedonia, Bosnia-Herzegovina, Montenegro) began a series of meetings to negotiate Yugoslavia's future.

April 1. The self-proclaimed Serbian Autonomous Region of Krajina, made up of municipalities in Croatia with a majority Serb population, seceded unilaterally from Croatia and decided to become part of Serbia. The Serbian Assembly did not endorse this move.

April 16. Nearly 700,000 textile, leather, and metallurgical workers went on strike in Serbia for guaranteed minimum wages. The government agreed within hours, and the strike was called off after 24 hours.

May. Ethnic Serbs living in Croatia **voted** overwhelmingly **for union with Serbia.**

Civil war and the disintegration of Yugoslavia: the deteriorating federal-republic relations were exacerbated in May 1991 when Serbia and Montenegro failed to endorse Stjepan Mesic, a Croat, as head of the Collective State Presidency. Yugoslavia slid into **civil war** when Croatia and Slovenia declared independence on June 25, 1991, and the federal government refused to recognize them. Fighting began in Croatia and Slovenia between the Serbian-dominated federal army and the republics, and between ethnic groups. Although a cease-fire was declared in Slovenia in July, fighting continued in Croatia, where Serbian soldiers backed by the federal army had taken almost one-third of Croatian territory by Sept. 1991. In the ensuing months and years, several attempts by the European Community to broker a peace failed.

May 9. The Collective State Presidency gave the Yugoslav National Army greater power within Croatia because of the intensified fighting between Serbs and Croats within the Serbian Autonomous Region of Krajina.

Aug. 13. A **Serbian Autonomous Region of Western Slavonia** was established.

Sept. Croatia lost almost one-third of its territory to Serbian nationalist forces as the civil war escalated. The Yugoslav National Army now openly identified itself with the Serbian nationalists, but was growing weaker because non-Serbs refused to join.

Oct. 22. Kosovo, a province of Serbia, passed a referendum for sovereignty with 87 percent voter turnout and 99 percent of voters in favor of the referendum.

Nov. 27. The UN Security Council began preparing to deploy peacekeeping troops as requested by both Serbia and Croatia.

1992, Jan. Bosnia-Herzegovina was embroiled in civil war between ethnic groups. Little progress had been made toward peace, despite the efforts of the international community and the presence of UN peacekeeping forces.

Jan. 15. The Collective State Presidency condemned the EC decision to recognize Croatia and Slovenia as independent states, saying it violated the principles of the UN Charter by changing the borders of Yugoslavia.

Mar. 1. In **Montenegro,** voters overwhelmingly approved a measure keeping the republic part of Yugoslavia.

March 9–12. In **Serbia,** mass protests in Belgrade called for the resignation of Serbian president Milosevic.

March 26. Yugoslav National Army troops withdrew from **Macedonia** as it prepared for independence from Yugoslavia.

April 27. A new **Federal Republic of Yugoslavia was formed,** with only two of the six members of the former socialist Yugoslavia: **Serbia (together with its provinces of Kosovo and Vojvodina) and Montenegro.** This was effectively a recognition of the separate states of Croatia, Slovenia, Bosnia-Herzegovina, and Macedonia.

June. The UN Security Council sent troops to **Bosnia-Herzegovina** in efforts to secure a cease-fire between Bosnian and Serb forces in Sarajevo.

June–July. Dobrica Cosic was elected president of the Federal Republic of Yugoslavia, and U.S.-born **Milan Panic** was elected prime minister on July 14.

June 9. The Serbian Democratic Movement called for the resignation of Serbian president Slobodan Milosevic.

Aug. 13–14. In an extraordinary session of the UN Human Rights Commission, a resolution was passed unanimously condemning the policy of forced expulsions, or "ethnic cleansing," being practiced by the Bosnian Serbs against the Muslims and Bosnian Croats.

Oct. 11. In the Federal Republic of Yugoslavia, the Serbian government staged a referendum to call for early elections. The voter turnout was too low, due to a boycott.

Dec. 20. Elections took place in the Federal Republic of Yugoslavia. Hard-liner **Slobodan Milosevic** was reelected to the Serbian presidency, and his party made gains in the Serbian legislature. In a runoff election on Jan. 10, **Momir Bulativic** was reelected as president of Montenegro.

1993, Feb. 9. Radoje Kontic, a Montenegrin, accepted his nomination as prime minister of Yugoslavia.

Feb. 10. A new Serbian government proposed by Nikola Sainovic, prime minister–designate of Serbia, was approved by the Serbian Assembly.

March 2. Prime Minister Kontic named a new coalition government.

March 26. Serbian trade unions staged a strike in Belgrade over falling living standards, as the authorities began to print ration books and coupons for staple foodstuffs.

June 1. Milosevic agreed to remove Dobrica Cosic, president of the Federal Republic of Yugoslavia, because he had exceeded his constitutional powers. Zoran Lilic was elected president on June 25. The removal of Cosic caused demonstrations in Belgrade.

Aug. 13. A 500-million-dinar banknote, worth $6.00, was introduced as spiraling hyperinflation destroyed the value of the currency. The official monthly inflation rate increased from 430 percent in July to 1,800 percent in August.

Sept. 22. In a move toward centralization, a new law on defense was passed that empowered the Federal Assembly to declare a state of emergency in a republic without the consent of its own assembly.

1997, July 23. Slobodan Milosevic is sworn in as the president of Yugoslavia, the Federation of Serbia and Montenegro.

1998, Feb. The Yugoslav military began battling the Kosovo Liberation Army, a pro-independence rebel faction in Yugoslavia's southern province of Montenegro.

May 31. Montenegro elected reformist Milo Djukanovic as its president. An outspoken opponent of Yugoslav president Slobodan Milosevic, Djukanovic even went so far as to publicly discuss ideas of secession to Albania for Montenegro, 90 percent of whose population is comprised of ethnic Albanians. The Serbs under Milosevic brutally resisted pro-independence forces in Montenegro. As substantial evidence of "racial cleansing" tactics reached NATO, the organization expressed concern that the conflict would lead to human rights violations similar to those that had been committed against Bosnian citizens two years earlier. Agreeing to intervene in Kosovo, NATO involved itself for the first time in the affairs of a sovereign nation and its people.

Oct. 12. A truce mediated by American diplomat **Richard Holbrooke** was signed by Pres. Milosevic, who agreed to withdraw his military forces, faced with the threat of a NATO air strike. Fighting continued, nevertheless, and neither side would agree to the compromises proposed by Washington: Kosovars wanted independence and Serbia wanted strictly limited autonomy for Kosovo.

1999, March 24–June 3. After U.S. and NATO pressure on the Yugoslav government failed to slow Serbian assaults on ethnic Albanians in Kosovo, **NATO launched an air war against Yugoslavia.** In a terrorizing Serb retaliation, hundreds of thousands of Kosovars fled to neighboring Albania and Macedonia. An estimated 850,000 refugees fled from the attacks.

June 9. After 78 days of air attacks by NATO, **Yugoslavia signed an accord;** Milosevic promised to withdraw his troops from Kosovo. Making peacekeeping efforts more difficult to manage, Russia insisted on participating in the peace deal while ignoring NATO jurisdiction over the matter.

June 11. An international force (KFOR) of 50,000 troops entered Kosovo; by Sept. 1 most of the Kosovar refugees had returned to the country. During the conflict, NATO had changed its intervention objective from that of preventing a Balkan war to that of stopping ethnic cleansing in Kosovo. However, throughout the conflict NATO withheld deployment of its ground troops out of concern that such an action early in the conflict might lead to international discord within NATO countries.

2000, Feb. 2–13. Violence broke out between Serbs and ethnic Albanians

in **Mitrovica, Kosovo,** greatly challenging the abilities of NATO peacekeeping forces to maintain order in the region. In a reversal of roles, it was now the minority Serb population of Kosovo that fled Albanian retaliatory attacks.

June 11. Local elections in Montenegro resulted in a slight majority of municipal posts going to pro-independence leaders.

Sept. 24–28. Slobodan Milosevic was defeated in the first round of a presidential election by opposition leader Vojislav Kostunica. Kostunica refused to agree to a second round of voting as national and international observers declared him the rightful winner of the referendum. Milosevic initially refused to yield power to the new government; approximately one million protestors began to bombard the capital of Belgrade in violent opposition to Milosevic.

Oct. 5–6. Under a wave of violent mass demonstrations, **Milosevic resigned his position and Kostunica was sworn in as president.** Throughout the two-day period, various government powers had renounced their loyalty to Milosevic and called for his resignation. The U.S. and EU immediately began lifting economic sanctions from the battered nation of Yugoslavia when Kostunica took power.

Oct. 28. In Kosovo elections that were monitored by the UN, moderates won decisive municipal posts, and the reformist Democratic League of Kosovo (LDK) took 21 of 30 seats.

Nov. 1. The United Nations General Assembly unanimously approved Yugoslavia's application for UN membership. This ended eight years of UN opposition to the Yugoslav government.

1. BOSNIA-HERZEGOVINA

1991, Oct. Bosnia-Herzegovina declared its independence.

1992, March 1. A vote approved the republic's declaration of independence.

April 6. The **EC recognized** the independence of the new state.

May. Sarajevo, in Bosnia-Herzegovina, was under intensive attack from Serbian forces throughout May.

June 6. A new government was formed.

1993, Jan. 2. Peace talks concerning the war in Bosnia-Herzegovina took place in Geneva between the three warring parties: the Bosnian Serb leader, Bosnian president Alija Izetbegovic, and a Bosnian Croat delegation.

Jan. 21. Amnesty International reported that women from all sides in the Bosnian conflict, but mainly Muslims, had suffered horrific sexual violations, including rape. These assaults appeared to be carried out in a systematic way by the military.

Feb. 10. The U.S. agreed to become involved in peace efforts in Bosnia-Herzegovina.

April 25–26. The Bosnian Serb Assembly rejected the Vance-Owen peace plan for Bosnia, after it had been endorsed by Bosnian Croats and Muslims.

June 4. The UN Security Council adopted a resolution that allowed the UN to use force to enforce cease-fires in protected areas.

June 15. A provisional agreement was reached in Geneva on a three-way division of Bosnia-Herzegovina into Muslim, Serb, and Croat areas.

July–Nov. Cease-fires failed to hold as fighting intensified, especially around Sarajevo. Continued peace talks were unsuccessful.

1994, Jan. 4–5. In Vienna, European countries ran informal negotiations over possible partitions of Bosnia-Herzegovina. In February, in order to obviate threatened NATO air strikes, Bosnian Serbs got rid of guns around Sarajevo; Russia sent mediators to assist with the situation.

March 18. Bosnian Muslims signed a charter to create a federation with the Croats; U.S. president Clinton expressed hope that Serbs would join in these efforts.

March 29–April 7. Bosnian Serbs began assaulting a Muslim enclave in and around the town of Gorazde, just southeast of Sarajevo. NATO sent aircraft to bomb Serbian positions in Bosnia so as to interrupt this move. As Serbs continued to advance into Gorazde, Clinton supported the use of greater force by the UN, and NATO air strikes induced Serbs to pull back.

May 13. The U.S. and six European countries, including Russia, announced a plan to partition Bosnia, giving Serbs 49 percent of the land and the Muslim-Croat Federation 51 percent. Factions in Bosnia signed a month-long cease-fire agreement on June 10, but in July and August, Serbs rejected three peace and partition plans.

Aug. 5. NATO launched an air strike against the Serbs in Bosnia. Yugoslavia closed its Bosnian borders. On Sept. 16 Serbia agreed to allow inspections on the Bosnian border.

Oct. 26–Nov. 3. Bosnian Croats and Muslims started to make gains against the Serbs, seizing the previously Serbian town of Kupres.

Dec. 8. Harassment of UN forces by Serbs led the UN to consider withdrawing its troops from Bosnia. On Dec. 9–10 an EU summit decided that UN forces were still needed in Bosnia.

Dec. 20. Former U.S. president Jimmy Carter visited Bosnia and negotiated a cease-fire. The Bosnian government and the Serbs agreed to start a truce to the 33-month war as of New Year's Day.

1995, Jan. 1. The four-month truce went into effect.

Feb. 19. Serbian president Slobodan Milosevic rejected a peace proposal for Bosnia. In the ensuing months, Muslims and Serbs periodically broke the truce, and Bosnian Serbs periodically harassed UN forces.

Aug. 1. NATO threatened another air strike on the Serbs if they would not stop attacking safe zones.

Aug. 4. Croats invaded the Serb republic of Krajina, committing many human rights violations.

Aug. 14. The U.S. proposed a new peace plan for Bosnia, giving more territory to the Serbs than the original plan had allotted.

Aug. 30–31. NATO bombed Serb positions near Sarajevo in the biggest military action by NATO to date.

Sept. 8. Bosnian factions agreed to the U.S. peace plan to partition the country and rid Sarajevo altogether of heavy weaponry. On Sept. 26 Serbs, Croats, and Muslims agreed to establish a collective presidency and parliament in Bosnia. On Oct. 12 the formal cease-fire went into effect in Bosnia. Peace talks began between the various leaders on Nov. 1 in the United States. On Nov. 21 the Balkan presidents finally agreed to a peace accord, with NATO acting as a peacekeeper in the split state. On Nov. 27 Pres. Clinton asked the U.S. public and Congress to allow U.S. forces to assist NATO peacekeepers.

Dec. 14. Leaders of the Bosnian factions signed a peace treaty in Paris.

1996, Feb. 18. At a conference in Rome, the Balkan presidents reaffirmed their commitment to a peace treaty. On March 19, after the final Serbian military withdrawal, Sarajevo was reunited under a Muslim government. The first elections held in Bosnia since the civil war left **Alija Izetbegovic,** a Muslim, as the chairman of a three-man collective presidency (Sept. 14).

Nov. 11–12. Fighting occurred between Serbs and Muslims in the Bosnian town of Gajevi. Clinton announced on Nov. 15 that 8,500 U.S. troops would remain in Bosnia until June of 1998 to keep the peace.

1997, Jan. 3. The Bosnian parliament met for the first time, approving the new cabinet. Many opposition politicians won seats in the Sarajevo city council on Feb. 4. Serbian president Slobodan Milosevic accepted this.

Feb. 10. Croats and Muslim pilgrims battled in the village of Mostar.

1998, Sept. 12–13. Elections to two-year terms were held for the various government institutions, including the Muslim-Croat Federation, the Serb Republic, the three-member presidency, the Chamber of Representatives, and the Chamber of Peoples. The new executive authority was shared by Zivko Radisic, Alija Izetbegovic, and Ante Jelavic. Hardliners won out over more moderate candidates, and Nicola Poplasen became the new president of the Serb Republic. The Coalition for a Unified and Democratic Bosnia-Herzegovina won the most support in the Chamber of Representatives, and Milorad Dodik remained prime minister.

1999, March 5. On the same day that the president of the Serb Republic, Poplasen, was deposed, a Western "arbitrator" passed control of the strategically important town of Bracko to the Muslim-Croat Federation. These circumstances resulted in the effective withdrawal of the Serb Republic from Bosnia-Herzegovina. As tensions heightened in the region, NATO considered postponing its plans to reduce the number of occupying troops in the year 2000.

2000, April. Local elections resulted in victories for many of the national parties that had been in power before NATO intervened in Bosnia-Herzegovina. In view of that development, a reduction from 30,000 to 21,000 troops was considered less likely for NATO forces in the near future.

2. CROATIA

1991, June 25. Croatia **declared its independence,** but the federal government refused to recognize it.

1992, Jan. Croatia gained international recognition of its independence.

Jan. 15. The **European Community recognized Croatia as an independent state.** The Yugoslav Collective State Presidency condemned the EC decision as violating the principles of the UN Charter by changing the borders of Yugoslavia.

Aug. 2. President **Franjo Tudjman** and his ruling Croatian Democratic Community (HDZ) secured an overwhelming victory in Croatia's first presidential and legislative elections since secession from Yugoslavia.

1993, Jan. 22. Croatian forces penetrated UN peacekeeping lines in a resurgence of fighting, attempting to recover Croatian territory from the Serbs.

Feb. 7. The first elections to the Chamber of Districts (upper house) of the Croatian Assembly gave the ruling HDZ 31 seats.

March 12. A warning strike by the three main trade union confederations over low wages and high prices demanded that the government resign.

April 3. A new government was sworn in with Prime Minister Nikica Valentic, who promised to return refugees from the Bosnian war and strengthen the democratic process through freedom of the press and privatization of the media.

1998, Jan. 15. Through UN intervention, **Croatian sovereignty was returned to Eastern Slavonia,** the last traditionally Croatian territory that had been held under militant Serb occupation.

1999, Dec. 10. Pres. Franjo Tudjman died after a long battle with stomach cancer. He had been replaced by Speaker of Parliament Vlatko Pavletic two months earlier in a ruling by the Croatian Supreme Court that Tudjman was incapacitated.

2000, Jan. 3. In parliamentary elections, an alliance of the Social Democrats and the Social Liberal Party won 47 percent of the vote, substantially overpowering the HDZ. When **Social Democrat Ivica Racan was selected to be premier,** the change of power was hailed worldwide as a step toward positive political and economic reform in Croatia.

Feb. 7. Temporary leader Pavletic was succeeded by the moderate Stipe Mesic after Mesic won a runoff presidential election. One of Mesic's first acts as head of state was to invite the 300,000 exiled Serbs to return peacefully to Croatia.

3. SLOVENIA

1991, June 25. Slovenia **declared independence,** but the federal government refused to recognize it.

1992, Jan. Slovenia gained international recognition of its independence.

Jan. 15. The **European Community recognized Slovenia as an independent state.**

April 22. The Slovene Assembly passed a vote of no confidence in the **Slovenian** government.

Aug. 13. The Federal Republic of Yugoslavia recognized the independence of Slovenia.

Dec. 6. Janez Drnovsek of the Liberal Democratic Party was reelected prime minister and confirmed by the National Assembly on Jan. 12.

1993, July 23. A cache of 120 tons of arms, hidden in humanitarian aid containers, was discovered at Slovenia's largest airport, causing a scandal for the president, the prime minister, and the interior and defense ministers, who were accused of engineering the delivery.

1998, March 30. The EU invited Slovenia and five other nations to apply for membership.

1999, Sept. 19. Pope John Paul II visited Slovenia for the second time since the predominantly Roman Catholic nation gained independence from Yugoslavia in 1991.

2000, Nov. Eight-year veteran **prime minister Janez Drnovsek** was voted out of office in favor of the more conservative leader **Andrej Bajuk.**

4. MACEDONIA

1991, Sept. Macedonia **declared its independence.**

1992, Aug. A new government was formed by the Social Democratic Alliance of Macedonia, with **Branko Crvenkovski** as prime minister.

Nov. 6. Three protesters were killed by police during riots in Skopje over police brutality.

1993, Jan. 7. The government formally submitted an application for membership in the UN.

Feb. The Greek government agreed to international arbitration over the issue of Macedonia's name. Greece objected to the use of "Macedonia," because it was historically associated with ancient Greece, it was already the name of a Greek province, and it could encourage Slavic territorial ambitions against northern Greece.

1994, Feb. 9. The **U.S. recognized Macedonia,** which had formerly been a part of Yugoslavia, **as an independent republic. Greece protested,** placing a trade embargo on Macedonia to which the European Union in turn objected.

1998, Nov. 1. The ruling **Social Democrats** were defeated in general elections by the **Internal Macedonian Revolutionary Organization (VMRO)** and its coalition with a new pro-business party, the **Democratic Alternative (DA).** The new coalition won 62 of 120 seats.

1999, March 24–June 3. After heavy NATO air strikes ignited a massive campaign of ethnic cleansing by Serb forces in Kosovo, **over 240,000 Kosovar refugees fled into Macedonia.**

Dec. 5. The ruling Center-Right VMRO candidate, **Boris Trajkovski, won a presidential runoff vote over Tito Petkovski.**

e. ALBANIA

(From p. 723)

1945, Nov. 10. The Communist-dominated government of **Premier Enver Hoxha was recognized** by the Soviet Union and the Western powers. It was upheld in **general elections, which returned the single list of official candidates** (Dec. 2).

1946, Jan. 11. The **constituent assembly** proclaimed the **PEOPLE'S RE-PUBLIC OF ALBANIA.** Its domestic and foreign policy followed closely the communist, pro-Soviet line taken by other Russian satellites. Relations with the West, and notably Great Britain, rapidly deteriorated.

May–Oct. Two naval incidents in the Corfu Channel, caused by Albanian coastal batteries and mines and resulting in the loss of British lives, further **increased British-Albanian tension.**

1948–49. Relations between Albania and Yugoslavia, which had been particularly close, **were broken off as a result of the latter's exclusion from the Cominform.**

1949, June 10. Koci Xoxe, the Communist former vice premier, and a number of other high officials, were convicted of being Yugoslav agents. Xoxe was executed on June 11. As arrests for sabotage and espionage continued, large numbers of Albanians fled the country.

1950, May 28. A general election confirmed the regime of Marshal Enver Hoxha. Albania fell completely under Soviet domination, **joining the Cominform and concluding a treaty of friendship with the USSR.**

1953, July 24. A government shuffle stripped Hoxha of his posts as minister of defense and foreign affairs but let him remain premier. **Lt. Gen. Mehmet Shehu,** Hoxha's rival, remained as interior minister and head of the police, but lost his post as secretary of the Central Committee of the (Communist) Labor Party.

Dec. 22. Diplomatic relations between Albania and Yugoslavia resumed, having been disrupted since 1948.

1954, July. The principle of **collective leadership** was adopted, involving a separation of the premiership (government) from the post of first secretary (party). Gen. Hoxha, the prime minister, resigned to become the first secretary of the Central Committee, and Interior Minister **Shehu formed a new government.**

1956, Jan. 11. The government announced an **amnesty for all Albanian exiles,** to expire Dec. 31, 1957.

1957. Albania's only university, the **State University of Tirana,** was founded.

1961, April–May. The **USSR withdrew all Soviet technicians,** terminated economic aid, and recalled Soviet naval units from Vlore, as a result of Albania's refusal to adopt the Soviet "division of labor" policy, which relegated Albania to supplying raw materials, stifling its industrial growth. **Albania maintained closer relations with China than with the USSR.**

Dec. 10. The USSR recalled its diplomatic mission from Albania and ordered the Albanian embassy in Moscow closed.

1962, Jan. 19. A one-year **trade pact was signed with Poland,** the only European communist state that had not recalled its ambassador from Albania.

July 16. Parliament unanimously reelected Mehmet Shehu as premier.

1964. **Enver Hoxha** implemented Albania's **"ideological and cultural revolution,"** which aimed to eliminate the influences of religion, excessive family loyalty, and bourgeois economic and social outlooks. The **women's emancipation campaign** tried to eliminate socially conservative attitudes, for the betterment of the state.

1964–70. Albania remained a communist dictatorship, ruled by the same politicians who had emerged after 1945. Only in foreign relations did it occupy a notable position, one of uncompromising **opposition to Soviet policies** and complete **devotion to Communist China.** The latter's protection not only inhibited attack by neighboring powers but also provided the economic and technical aid needed for the gradual development of the country.

1967. The government proclaimed Albania an **atheist state.** Full **collectivization of farming** was completed.

1968, Sept. 12. Albania **formally withdrew from the Warsaw Pact,** thus terminating all official identification with the Soviet bloc.

1971–76. Hoxha purged numerous high-level economic and political leaders to **maintain** hard-line **Marxist-Leninist purity.**

1973. Hoxha cracked down on the **League of Albanian Writers and Artists** and the **Union of Albanian Labor Youth,** thus stifling Albania's cultural life for more than a decade.

1976, Dec. 27. The People's Assembly adopted a **new constitution** to replace its 1946 version. The new constitution renamed the country the **Socialist People's Republic of Albania** and **rejected reconciliation with the "revisionist" Soviet Union.** It also set up equal rights for both sexes, eliminated religious activities, and abolished private enterprises, property ownership, and tax payment by citizens.

1978, Sept. China withdrew its military and economic advisers and **terminated economic assistance to Albania** after more than a year of criticism of its post-Maoist policies by the Albanian government.

1982, Jan. 14. **Adil Carcani** succeeded Shehu as **chairman of the Council of Ministers** after **Shehu committed suicide in December 1981** following a dispute with party leader **Hoxha.**

1985, April 11. Enver Hoxha, leader of Albania since 1944, **died** and was **succeeded by Ramiz Alia.** Under Alia's leadership, Albania **relaxed its isolationist policies** and began to establish diplomatic and trade relations with Western and neighboring states.

1986, March 1. **Nexhmije Hoxha,** widow of Enver Hoxha, was elected to **chair the Democratic Front of Albania (DFA),** a political umbrella organization whose functions included organizing election campaigns and nominating candidates. **She remained a strong influence on government policies.**

1987, June. Wage differentials were introduced as a means of providing **incentives** for workers.

1988, June. After Alia's criticism of the inefficiency of cadres, the government introduced a **new system to change cadres' responsibilities every five years,** to ensure high standards of administration and contain bureaucratic excess.

1990, May. The People's Assembly approved a **wide range of judicial reforms,** which included rescinding capital punishment for statements against the government, legalizing religious activities, and giving all Albanians the right to a passport for foreign travel.

June 28–July 6. Thousands of Albanians took refuge in foreign embassies in Tirana, fearing renewed repression. After preventing food deliveries to the embassies, the government bowed to international pressure and ordered them evacuated.

July. The government announced **extensive educational reforms** designed to expand the system and eradicate illiteracy.

July 30. Albania and the Soviet Union agreed to normalize their re-lations and reopen their respective embassies.

Aug. 16. Albania joined the Nuclear Non-Proliferation Treaty.

Nov. Alia called for changes to the 1976 constitution, including a redefinition of the leading role of the Communist Party and freedom of religious beliefs.

Nov. 14. A new electoral law was approved that **promised a secret ballot** and the possibility of **independent candidates along with nom-inees of the Communist Party.**

Dec. Formation of the opposition party: on **Dec. 12, intellectuals and students** in Tirana announced the formation of the **Democratic Party,** the first opposition party in 46 years. A week later, the parliament adopted a decree permitting the establishment of political parties, and the new party was registered.

Dec. 20. Nexhmije Hoxha, who opposed these party changes, was **replaced by Adil Carcani as president of the Democratic Front.**

1991. Freedom of religion replaced official atheism.

March. The first multiparty general elections resulted in a Com-munist victory, though the opposition Democratic Party dominated in the cities.

June 12. Government of national stability: Ylli Bufi of the ruling Communist Party **formed a coalition government,** including, for the first time, opposition parties and independent members.

June 13. The **Albania Party of Labor** (Communist) renamed itself the **Socialist Party of Albania.**

June 19. Albania became a **member of the Conference on Security and Cooperation in Europe (CSCE).**

Aug. Land privatization: following the enactment of a land privati-zation bill at the end of July, the government began to measure out land, to **return holdings to peasants** dispossessed under Hoxha's rule. Killings occurred when disputes arose among peasants over rights to land ownership.

Oct. Albania became a member of the **International Monetary Fund** and the **World Bank.**

Dec. 4. Nexhmije Hoxha was arrested to stand trial for corruption.

1992, March–April. The **Democratic Party won the general elections** and secured an overall majority in the People's Assembly (March 22 and 29). On April 3, **Ramiz Alia resigned** as president and **Sali Berisha,** leader of the Democratic Party, became the **new president.** On April 19, a Democratic Party–dominated government was sworn in under **Prime Minister Alexander Meksi,** definitively ending the communist era.

1993, March 31. The **People's Assembly** approved legislation to protect **human rights and freedoms,** as part of a future new constitution.

July 30. Fatos Nano, leader of the **Socialist Party** and **prime minister in 1991,** was **arrested** in Tirana and charged with mishandling $8 mil-lion.

1994, July 2. Ramiz Alia, the last Communist leader of Albania, **was convicted for human rights violations and abuses of power.** He was sentenced to nine years in prison.

1998, Sept. Domestic struggles erupted into violence between support-ers of the Albanian Democratic Party and the Socialists (formerly the Communist Party of Labor). By Sept. 28 **Prime Minister Fatos Nano had resigned his position.** He was replaced by Pandeli Majko.

1999, March 24–June 3. As many as 465,000 ethnic Albanian refugees from Kosovo flooded into Albania when NATO bombing sparked vi-olence and ethnic cleansing by Serb forces in the region. By the end of the summer, most of the Kosovar refugees had returned to their home-land.

Oct. 25. Premier Pandeli Majko resigned after losing a vote to retain leadership of the ruling Socialist Party. Two days later, **Deputy Pre-mier Ilir Meta succeeded Majko.** The thirty-year-old Meta moved rap-idly forward in his first year in office, reforming the tax and judiciary systems, privatizing business, and modernizing the economy.

f. GREECE

(From p. 724)

1944, Dec. 25. British prime minister **Winston Churchill** and his foreign secretary, **Anthony Eden,** arrived in Athens to arrange a **settlement in**

the civil war that had developed between Greek factions. A **regency government** was proclaimed, and **Archbishop Damaskinos** sworn in as regent after his appointment (Dec. 30) by the Greek king, **George II.**

1945, Jan. 11. The **Greek civil war** ended with a truce between the Brit-ish forces and the leftist factions opposing British intervention.

The war left Greece a legacy of economic ruin, starvation, and do-mestic strife. The end of the **civil war** did not bring political stability. The regent, **Archbishop Damaskinos,** supported by British occupation authorities, appointed six different ministries during 1945, none of which was able to bridge the gap between moderates and left-wing resistance groups.

1946, March 31. The first **general election** won an **overwhelming ma-jority** for the royalist **Popular Party.** The National Liberation Front (Ethniko Apeleftherotiko Metopo, EAM) and other leftist groups re-fused to participate in the voting.

April 18. Populist leader **Panyoti Tsaldaris** formed a cabinet.

May–1949, Oct. Several thousand communists, supported by Greece's communist neighbors, engaged in extensive guerrilla activi-ties that soon developed into a regular **civil war.**

Sept. 1. A **plebiscite decided** 69 percent **in favor of the monarchy,** and **King George II returned to Athens** (Sept. 28).

1947, March 12. U.S. president Harry Truman announced a far-reaching program of economic aid to Greece and Turkey (**TRUMAN DOC-TRINE**) (p. 917).

March 31. The **Dodecanese Islands were returned to Greece.**

April 1. Death of King George II, who was succeeded by his brother, **Prince Paul.**

Sept. 7. Themostokles Sophoulis formed a **coalition government** of Liberals and Populists.

Oct. 21. The **UN General Assembly called on Greece, Yugoslavia, Albania, and Bulgaria** to settle their disputes by peaceful means, and set up a Balkan Committee to observe compliance with the resolutions.

Dec. 24. "**General Markos,**" leader of an estimated 20,000 guerrillas, proclaimed the establishment of the **First Provisional Democratic Government of Free Greece.**

Dec. 27. The Greek government dissolved the **Communist Party and EAM.**

1949, June 30. Death of Prime Minister Sophoulis, who was succeeded by **Alexander Diomedes.**

Aug. The remnants of the defeated Democratic Army fled into Al-bania.

Oct. 16. After three years of fighting, the **civil war ended** with the **defeat of the rebel forces.** This was made possible partly by American aid and partly by the closing of the Yugoslav frontier as a result of Tito's quarrel with the Cominform (p. 892).

1950, Feb. Martial law, in force since 1947, was lifted.

March 5. A **general election** gave the largest number of votes to the Populists, but the majority went to the Center and moderate Left. This distribution of forces, together with the aftermath of the civil war, greatly contributed to the instability of the government, as was shown in the rapid succession of five cabinets during the remainder of 1950.

Nov. 28. Full **diplomatic relations with Yugoslavia** were restored.

1951, Feb. 15. In a speech to the Vouli (parliament), **Premier Veniselos** called on Britain to permit **Cyprus** to unite with "Mother Greece."

Sept. 24. The result of **general elections** held on Sept. 9 gave the conservative **Greek Rally Party** of Field Marshal Alexander Papagos a clear plurality. But a parliamentary deadlock ensued, because no party had an absolute majority.

Sept. 29. King Paul broke the political deadlock by appointing **Gen. Nicholas Plastiras** of the Progressive Union of the Center to head a coalition cabinet with the Liberals.

1952, April. Death sentences left over from the civil war were com-muted, and many political prisoners were freed.

Nov. 16. Papagos's conservative Greek Rally Party won a sweeping victory in **general elections,** accounting for at least two-thirds of the members of the new parliament.

1954, June 3. Premier Papagos and Yugoslav president Tito reportedly agreed on a **tripartite alliance with Turkey.**

Dec. 14. U.S. resistance to Greek efforts in the UN to establish the "principle of self-determination" for Cyprus touched off anti-Ameri-can riots in Athens.

1955, Oct. 4. Death of Premier Alexander Papagos, at age 71.

1956, Feb. 19. The **National Radical Union,** led by **Premier Constantine Karamanlis,** won a narrow victory in parliamentary elections. These were the first national elections in which **women voted.**

1958, March 3. King Paul named former minister of education **Constantine Georgakopoulos** to head a caretaker government, following the resignation of Karamanlis.

> **May 17.** The new government of Constantine Karamanlis was installed following the victory of his National Radical Union in the Chamber of Deputies.

1959, June 4. Greece rejected a Soviet note urging that no missile bases be established on Greek soil.

1961, Oct. George Papandreou launched a bid to overturn Constantine Karamanlis's election victory.

> **Nov. 4.** Karamanlis, whose National Radical Union had been victorious in the Oct. 29 elections, again headed the government.

1962, Nov. 1. Greece became an **associate member of the Common Market.**

1963, June 11. Premier Karamanlis resigned, and King Paul asked **Panayoti Pipinelis,** a member of the National Radical Union, to form a caretaker government (June 17).

1964, Feb. 19. After the Center Union Party won the national elections (Feb. 16), its leader, **George Papandreou,** became premier.

> **March 6. Death of King Paul,** who was succeeded by **Crown Prince Constantine.** During the spring and summer, acute tension developed between Greece and Turkey as a result of the renewed Cyprus question.

1965, July 15. Forced **resignation of Premier Papandreou,** believed by the court to be planning to take over the Ministry of Defense and purge the army of conservative elements. The fall of the Left-Center coalition led to popular riots (July 19–21) and a general strike (July 27).

> **Aug.** Papandreou's **Center Union Party,** still commanding a majority in the parliament, rejected the king's nominations to the premiership.

> **Sept. 25.** Following the defection of a number of Papandreou's followers, Parliament voted approval of a **cabinet headed by Stephanos Stephanopoulos** that was a Center Union government with the support of the conservative National Radical Union.

1967, April 21. COUP BY A GROUP OF RIGHTIST ARMY OFFICERS, led by **Col. George Papadopoulos** and **Brig. Gen. Styliano Pattakos.** The cabinet was overthrown and leftist leaders, such as Papandreou and his son Andreas, were arrested. The constitution was suspended, and strict censorship was enforced. The United States imposed an **embargo on military supplies** to the new regime.

> **Oct. 7. Release of George Papandreou** and several other political leaders, but Andreas Papandreou and hundreds of others remained under arrest.

> **Dec. 13. Failure of King Constantine's appeal** for popular support in restoring democratic institutions. On Dec. 14 **the king fled to Rome,** while the military junta appointed a new cabinet with George Papadopoulos as premier.

> **Dec. 25. Andreas Papandreou was freed** in a Christmas amnesty. He went into exile in Paris, where he denounced the Greek dictatorship and called on democratic countries to aid in its overthrow. The Greek dictatorship was regarded with much aversion throughout most of the Western world.

1968, Sept. 29. A **new constitution,** drafted by the military government, was approved by an overwhelming popular vote. It greatly reduced the royal power, though it still defined Greece as a "crowned democracy." The parliament was to be deprived of most of its authority, which was vested instead in the military. Civil rights and political rights, though recognized, were kept in abeyance.

> **Oct.** The United States partly lifted the embargo on military supplies, chiefly because of Greece's importance in the developing naval tension in the eastern Mediterranean.

> **Nov. 24.** The **right to form trade unions** and the **right to assembly** were restored, to demonstrate the intention of the dictatorship eventually to reestablish representative institutions. Additional rights were restored in April 1969.

1969, Oct. 3. The government announced the **abolition of the Censorship Department and the restoration of freedom of the press.**

1970, April. Constitutional rights against arbitrary arrest and detention were restored when the government relaxed controls imposed in 1967.

> **Sept. 22. Termination of the U.S. embargo** on the shipment of heavy armaments and equipment.

1971, Dec. 18. Martial law was lifted throughout the country (Jan. 1, 1972) except in Athens, the Piraeus, and Salonika.

1973, June 1. Greece abolished the monarchy and proclaimed itself a republic. In a referendum on July 29, voters favored this constitutional change, and **George Papadopoulos was elected the first president of the Greek Republic.**

> **Nov. 25. The Papadopoulos government was overthrown in a bloodless coup d'état. Phaidon Ghizikis became president and Adamantios Androutsopoulos prime minister.**

> **Feb.–Dec.** Students and workers clashed with security forces, resulting in the closure of universities and the proclamation of martial law in November, when students took over Athens Polytechnic. Universities were reopened in December.

1974, July 23. In the wake of Turkey's invasion of Cyprus, the military junta collapsed (p. 972). President **Ghizikis called on prominent civilians to form a new government for national emergency. Konstantinos Karamanlis was reinstated as prime minister,** thus restoring democratic civilian government.

> **Nov. 17. General elections** took place for the first time since 1967. Karamanlis's **New Democracy Party** took 54 percent of the vote, thus a majority in the parliament.

1975. A series of trials of those held responsible for the dictatorship were held. Col. Papadopoulos, Col. Makarezos, and Brig. Gen. Pattakos were sentenced to death, but Karamanlis quickly commuted their sentences to life imprisonment.

> **June 7.** A **new constitution** was adopted, **reinforcing the powers of the president.** On June 19, **K. Tsatsos was elected president** by the parliament.

> **July 29.** The **Greek Orthodox Church broke off relations with the Vatican** after the Vatican violated its agreement not to appoint a new Uniate bishop in Greece.

1979, Feb. 9. Parliament passed a **law to permit divorce on the grounds of six years' separation on the petition of one spouse** only. The Orthodox Church opposed both the law and the proposals for legalizing civil marriages that were under government discussion.

> **May 28.** Greece joined the **European Common Market.**

1980, May 6. Karamanlis resigned his premiership after being **elected president.** A new government was subsequently formed, with **George Rallis as prime minister.**

1981, Jan. 1. Greece entered the European Community. The opposition Pan-Hellenic Socialist Movement (PASOK) won a first direct election to the Parliamentary Assembly of the European Community in October.

> **Oct. 18. PASOK heavily defeated the New Democracy in general elections. Andreas Papandreou formed Greece's first Socialist government** (remaining in office until 1989) and **emphasized decentralization of government roles,** the strengthening of a democratic basis in national life, protection of trade union activities, and even distribution of social income and wealth. In 1985 **Papandreou** was reelected for a second term.

1984, Jan. 10. Parliament approved a law that legalized **equal pay for equal work by women and men.**

1985, March 10. President Karamanlis resigned after the ruling Socialist Party withdrew support for his reelection. **Christo Sartzetakis was elected president** on March 29.

1989, June 18. A general election in which no party won an overall majority led to a **temporary Conservative-Communist coalition, with Tzannis Tzannetakis (New Democracy) as prime minister. PASOK suffered a serious political defeat** because of its involvement in a bank scandal (the Koskotas affair) and other political corruption.

> **Nov. 5.** Another election was called. New Democracy increased its share of the vote, and PASOK increased its share as well, but the left-wing alliance fell. None had a clear majority in the parliament, and an all-party alliance was formed, led by Zenophon Zolotas, a nonpolitical former governor of the Bank of Greece. He would stay in office until the April elections.

1990, April 8. Konstantinos Mitsotakis's New Democracy secured 150 out of 300 seats in the Parliament, and he was able to **form the first single-party government** since 1981. His government began privatizing state-owned industrial companies to stimulate the national economy. This election signaled the end of the rule of PASOK and Papandreou.

May 4. Konstantinos **Karamanlis** of New Democracy **was elected president** again for a five-year term.

1991, Jan. 9. After a teacher's murder by right-wing elements, the teachers' unions ordered an immediate strike in all schools. In Athens, violence erupted and more than one hundred people were hospitalized.

Feb. 27. Aleka **Papariga,** a moderate, was elected general secretary of the Communist Party of Greece, the first woman to hold the post.

March 18. Maria Damanaki, who began her career as a student involved in the 1973 polytechnic uprising, was elected president of the Left Alliance coalition.

March–1992, May. Andreas Papandreou's trial. The televised trial of Papandreou and three other politicians for illegal arms dealings with the Middle East opened on March 11 and dominated the political scene in Greece throughout the year. As the accusations were subsequently discredited, Papandreou was acquitted on Jan. 17, 1992. In May the parliament voted to drop the charges against Papandreou.

Nov. 7. A **24-hour general strike** was called, in reaction to the government's economic policy, by two principal unions and supported by PASOK. Thirty thousand workers marched on the Parliament building calling for action against unemployment and the increasing cost of living.

Nov. 29. The government presented the 1992 budget, which called for an intensification of the austerity program.

1992, Aug. 27. A nationwide **general strike** by all public-sector workers was ordered by the General Confederation of Greek Workers against the privatization of public transport in Athens, which had been approved by the Vouli (parliament) on Aug. 7.

Dec. 2. Prime Minister Constantine Mitsotakis dismissed his entire cabinet after facing dissent over his austerity policies. He appointed a new cabinet on Dec. 3.

1995, March 8. Greece elected conservative **Costis Stefanopoulos** to the presidency.

Sept. 13. Greece ended its 19-month trade embargo on Macedonia, formally recognizing the country.

1996, Jan. 22. The new Greek government under **Premier Costas Simitas** was sworn in. Simitas called for governmental restructuring and the broadening of relations with the U.S.

1998, March 30. Cyprus was named as a nation and formally invited to begin talks with the EU and to apply for membership. This move angered Turkey, the only country actively aspiring to attain EU membership that was not invited to the negotiations (p. 844). Subsequent relations between Turkey and Greece suffered as the two nations continued conflicts over the shared island nation of Cyprus (Turkey controlled northern Cyprus; Greece claimed southern Cyprus).

March 31. Greece's economy failed to fulfill the EU's qualifications for participation in the European Monetary Union. The next opportunity for Greece would be in 2002. However, international estimates were that it might be 15 years or more before Greece's per capita GDP would approach the current EU average.

1999, March 24–June 3. Because of potential economic and political instability that might result from mass migrations of refugee Kosovars and also because of religious ties with the Serbs, Greeks were the most vocal opponents of NATO intervention in Kosovo.

Aug. Following a devastating earthquake in Turkey, Greece greatly improved its relations with that country by devoting substantial financial and humanitarian assistance to the most damaged regions.

2000, Jan. 20. Turkish foreign minister Isma'il Cem and Greek foreign minister George Papandreou met in Ankara, Turkey; talks ended with an accord for economic cooperation and promises of peace in Cyprus. This summit marked the first visit by a Greek foreign minister to Turkey in 38 years.

Feb. 8. Pres. Constantinos "Costis" Stefanopoulos was reelected by the Chamber of Deputies to his second five-year term.

April 9. The PASOK Party became the first Greek party to win a majority in three consecutive legislative elections, taking 158 seats in the Parliament. This was Greece's closest parliamentary election to date, inasmuch as PASOK's main rival, the New Democracy Party,

won 125 seats. PASOK leader **Costas Simitas was reinstalled as prime minister.**

g. BULGARIA

(From p. 725)

1945, Nov. 18. The first **general election gave overwhelming support** to the single list of the **Fatherland Front,** a wartime coalition of major parties, by this time under Communist control.

1946. In a sweeping purge, more than 1,500 high-ranking men and ten times as many minor figures in the old regime were killed.

March 31. Premier Kimon Gueorguiev formed a Communist-dominated government.

Sept. 8. A **referendum decided against the monarchy.**

Sept. 15. Bulgaria was proclaimed a PEOPLE'S REPUBLIC. Young Tsar Simeon II went into exile.

Oct. 27. General elections for a **constituent assembly,** carried on with considerable governmental interference, **resulted in a Communist majority.**

Nov. 21. Veteran Communist **Georgi Dimitrov returned from Moscow to become premier.**

1947, Feb. 10. The BULGARIAN PEACE TREATY was signed in Paris. Bulgaria retained the southern Dobrudja, but had to pay reparations and reduce its armed forces.

April 1. A **two-year plan** was announced, followed by **nationalization of banks and industries** (Dec. 26).

June 6. Nikola Petkov, leader of the Agrarian Party, was arrested, convicted of treason, and executed (Sept. 23).

Aug. 26. An extended campaign against the opposition culminated in the **dissolution of the Agrarian Party.**

Nov. 27. Bulgaria and Yugoslavia signed a treaty of friendship and **mutual aid.**

Dec. 15. Soviet occupation forces left Bulgaria.

Dec. 26. The government **nationalized** all banks, mines, and industry.

1948, Aug. 11. The **Bulgarian Social Democratic Party** and the **Communist Party** declared their merger as the **Bulgarian Communist Party.**

1949, Jan. 1. A **five-year plan** was inaugurated.

June 25. Communist deputy premier **Traicho Kostov was arrested and charged with ideological deviation and treason.** Together with ten associates, he was later found guilty; he was **executed on Dec. 16.**

July 2. Premier Dimitrov, who earlier had gone to Russia for medical treatment, **died in Moscow.** He was succeeded by **Vassil Kolarov.**

Oct. 1. Bulgaria denounced its treaty of friendship with Yugoslavia.

1950, Jan. 23. Death of Premier Kolarov, who was succeeded by **Vulko Chervenkov,** head of the Communist Party. A **large-scale purge of government officials** charged with complicity in the Kostov conspiracy continued throughout the year.

Feb. 21. Similar charges of complicity against U.S. diplomatic representatives in Bulgaria led to a **break in U.S.-Bulgarian diplomatic relations.**

April 1. The Communist Party revealed that **92,500 of its members had been expelled** during the previous 12 months.

1951, April. The government announced a **six-year plan** for the collectivization of the Dobrudja in order to turn the area into a vast collective farm.

1953, Feb. 13. The government decreed that all persons who left the country without permission were subject to the death penalty, and their families, to internment in concentration camps.

1956, April 17. Vulko Chervenkov, a protégé of Stalin, was **succeeded as premier by Anton Yugov.**

1959, Feb. 16. First secretary of the Bulgarian Communist Party, **Todor Zhivkov,** issued new directives calling for a 100 percent increase in industrial production and providing for decentralization of the administration and the economy.

1960, March 7. U.S. diplomat **Edward Page, Jr.,** arrived in Sofia, terminating a nine-year break in U.S.-Bulgarian diplomatic ties.

1964–70. Bulgaria might have been described as **the perfect Soviet satellite.** Its economy was closely integrated with that of the Soviet Union, and the USSR supplied the financial support to implement development plans. Bulgaria worked toward increases in heavy industry, particularly steel. Through electrification, mechanization, and automation of production, the government planned to increase production more than 200 percent, all in line with Soviet needs.

1968, Aug. Bulgarian troops took part with other Warsaw Pact forces **in the invasion and occupation of Czechoslovakia.**

1971, March 30. A **new constitution** emphasizing Bulgaria's socialist political and economic system was issued for nationwide discussion, to replace the 1947 constitution. A national referendum approved the new constitution on May 16.

July 7-8. Todor Zhivkov was elected **chairman of the State Council** (president) and **Stanko Todorov, chairman of the Council of Ministers** (prime minister) by the newly elected National Assembly.

1975, June 27. Todor Zhivkov's talk with **Pope Paul VI** at the Vatican resulted in an agreement that led to the appointment of a Roman Catholic bishop and a vicar-apostolic for the first time in more than 20 years. Eighty percent of Bulgarians were estimated to be followers of the Roman Catholic Church.

1976, Jan. 27-28. The Central Committee of the Communist Party proposed **intensification of political and economic integration with the Soviet Union,** with which Bulgaria had more than 50 percent of its total foreign trade. Russian language began to be taught in the third grade instead of the fifth in all schools.

1980, June. New legislation was passed to permit, for the first time, the **establishment of joint economic ventures** involving Bulgarian and noncommunist foreign enterprises.

1981, June 16. Grisha Filipov replaced Todorov as **chairman of the Council of Ministers.**

1984, Sept. Under Soviet pressure, **Zhivkov canceled a visit to West Germany.**

1984-89. Turkish minority problems: an alleged "Bulgarization" campaign was launched by the government in **1984-85** to force ethnic Turks to change their names to the Bulgarian (Slav) form. Clashes occurred when the campaign met resistance in certain areas.

1986, April. Amnesty International reported that more than a hundred ethnic Turks had been killed. Defections to the West and an exodus to Turkey continued into 1989 (it was estimated that more than 3 percent of the total population fled the country), causing serious disruption to Bulgaria's already shaky economy.

1987, July-Aug. Reform proposals: at a party plenum of the Central Committee, **Zhivkov** presented **proposals for wide-ranging constitutional and economic reforms,** including multicandidate elections, a major reorganization of state and government bodies, and devolution of economic management.

1989, June 7. Thousands of ethnic Turks were expelled from the country.

Nov.-Dec. The fall of Zhivkov. Todor Zhivkov, the longest-serving leader in Eastern Europe, **was forced to resign on Nov. 10.** He was **replaced by** former foreign minister **Petur Mladenov,** who promised reform and began sweeping personnel changes in the government. In December Zhivkov and his close associates were expelled from the party and the National Assembly. In early 1990 **documentary evidence** showed that Zhivkov had secretly agreed in 1972 with Soviet leader Leonid Brezhnev to create conditions for **Bulgaria's annexation by the Soviet Union. Zhivkov** and his second-in-command, **Milko Balev,** were **indicted** on Dec. 7, 1990, on charges of "gross embezzlement" and abuse of power. The trial of Zhivkov was indefinitely adjourned because of his ill health.

Dec. 7. The **Union of Democratic Forces (UDF)** was formed as an umbrella organization to coordinate political activities. It began to dismantle the totalitarian political system.

Dec. Mass demonstrations in Sofia demanded democratic reforms and talks between the authorities and the opposition.

Dec. 13. The **Communist Party renounced its constitutionally guaranteed "leading role"** and called for free elections in June 1990.

1990, Jan. 2. A decree **abolished the secret police** department in the Ministry of Internal Affairs.

Jan. 15. The **National Assembly** voted to **revoke** the **Communist Party's** constitutionally guaranteed **monopoly** on power.

March 5. The National Assembly adopted a bill that **entitled all Bulgarian citizens to choose their own names,** thus allowing ethnic Turks and Pomaks to reassume their original names.

March 6. Strikes were legalized for the first time in Bulgarian history. On the same day, a **new property law** removed limitations on real estate ownership.

April 3. The Bulgarian Communist Party renamed itself the **Bulgarian Socialist Party.**

April-July. Petur Mladenov was **elected president on April 3 by the National Assembly.** But on July 6 he was **forced to resign** when the opposition made public a videotape showing him suggesting the use of tanks to crush antigovernment demonstrations in Dec. 1989.

June 10 and 17. In a general election, the first free multiparty election since 1946, the **Socialists (former Communists) won a prevailing majority in the National Assembly.**

Aug. 1. Opposition leader Zhelyu Zhelev was elected president. He would be reelected in January 1992 for a five-year term.

Sept. 20. After the opposition refused to participate in a grand coalition government, the **Socialists formed a cabinet** with independent members under **Prime Minister Andrei Lukanov.** In October Lukanov announced a plan for the **transition to a market economy.** However, student demonstrations, general strikes, and an opposition boycott of parliament, in protest against the government's economic reform programs and its association with the former Communists forced **Lukanov to resign on Nov. 29.**

Dec. 20. The Grand National Assembly approved a **transitional coalition government led by an independent, Dimitur Popov.** The coalition included the Bulgarian Socialist Party, the Union of Democratic Forces, and the Bulgarian Agrarian People's Union.

Sept. 25. Bulgaria became a member of the International Monetary Fund and the World Bank.

Nov. 15. The Grand National Assembly voted to **change the country's name** from the People's Republic of Bulgaria to the **Republic of Bulgaria.**

1991, Oct. 13. The **Union of Democratic Forces defeated the Bulgarian Socialist Party** by a margin of 1 percent of the vote in the second free election since 1989. Following the party's victory, UDF leader **Filip Dimitrov formed the first noncommunist cabinet** and took office on Nov. 8.

1992, April 9. Despite the opposition of the Socialists, **the government adopted a decree restoring private ownership of land and property that had been nationalized during 1947 to 1962.**

Dec. 30. The formation of a new government of nonparty figures, with the economist **Lyuben Berov as prime minister,** ended a two-month-long governmental crisis following the collapse of the UDF government.

1993, June. The **Union of Democratic Forces** organized a series of **protests** around Sofia and other cities, aimed at President Zhelyn Zhetev.

Aug. 2. The government approved a plan to **privatize more than 500 medium-size to large state enterprises.**

1994, Oct. 17. Bulgarian **president Zhelyu Zhelev dissolved the Parliament** and appointed Reneta Indjova premier of an interim government until elections could be held.

1996, Nov. 3. Presidential runoffs were won by Petar Stoyanov of an opposition party called Union of Democratic Forces.

1998, Aug. 5. Bulgarian Communist dictator **Todor Zhivkov,** who ruled the country for 35 years, the longest of any Soviet-bloc head of state, died at age 86.

1999, Dec. 10. At the European Union's Helsinki Summit in Finland, Bulgaria was invited to apply for future membership, along with Lithuania, Romania, Malta, Latvia, Turkey, and Slovakia.

h. ROMANIA

(From p. 726)

1945, March 2. King Michael asked Petru Groza, leader of the left-wing Plowman's Front, **to form a government.** Based largely on the National Democratic Front, from the start the new government showed its Communist, pro-Russia leanings.

1946, Jan. 7. As a result of British and American pressure, **representatives of the opposition parties were included in the government,** although the important posts continued to be in Communist hands.

May 17. Gen. **Ion Antonescu,** wartime premier, was **condemned to death.**

Nov. 19. The **general election,** preceded by a campaign of violence against the opposition, **resulted in a majority for the Communist government.**

1947, Feb. 10. The **ROMANIAN PEACE TREATY** was signed in Paris. It called for reparations, reduction of armaments, and the **return of Transylvania** to Romania.

July 15. Julius Maniu, leader of the National Peasant Party, was **arrested,** together with some one hundred members of the opposition, on charges of espionage and treason. He was sentenced to solitary confinement for life.

July 28. The National Peasant Party was dissolved.

Nov. 5. Foreign Minister Tatarescu, a noncommunist, resigned and was **succeeded by veteran Communist Anna Pauker.**

Dec. 19. Romania and Yugoslavia signed a treaty of friendship and mutual aid.

Dec. 30. KING MICHAEL ABDICATED under Communist pressure.

1948, March 28. In a **general election,** the official **People's Democratic Front** received 91 percent of the votes. **Petru Groza** continued as premier.

April 13. A **new constitution** was adopted, modeled on that of Soviet Russia.

1949. The **transformation of Romania into a full-fledged Soviet satellite** made further progress. An uninterrupted **series of trials** purged the country of all political opponents and the Communist Party of "deviationists." **All religious organizations were subjected to state control.** Catholic opposition led to the arrest of the remaining bishops and the **dissolution of all Roman Catholic congregations.** There was **collectivization of agriculture and nationalization of industry,** and the death penalty was imposed for even minor offenses against the state. Relations with the Western powers further deteriorated as several Western diplomats were accused of espionage.

Oct. 21. Romania denounced its treaty of friendship with Yugoslavia.

1950, July. The Romanian Communist Party announced the expulsion of 192,000 members in the previous two years.

1952, May 29. Foreign Minister **Anna Pauker was removed** from the Politburo and the secretariat of the Central Committee.

1955, Aug. 12. Premier **Gheorghe Gheorghiu-Dej** announced that Soviet troops would stay in Romania until U.S. forces pulled out of Western Europe and NATO was abolished.

1956, Jan. 3. A **trade agreement** was completed **with Communist China.**

Aug. 25. Diplomatic relations were resumed **with Greece** for the first time since the war.

1958, July 26. The government announced the **withdrawal of Soviet occupation forces.**

1960, Sept. 30. Gheorghiu-Dej, first secretary of the Communist Party in Romania, affirmed the continued possibility for a **neutral buffer zone** in the Balkans, to be composed of Romania, Hungary, Bulgaria, Albania, Yugoslavia, Greece, and Turkey.

1961, March 21. Bucharest radio announced a new government structure under which the presidium would be replaced by a 17-person **State Council.** Gheorghiu-Dej was elected council president.

1964, April 22. The Communist Party issued a declaration bluntly insisting on the full equality and independence of all communist parties and nations, and noninterference in Romania's industrialization program. Subsequently the Romanian government, while halfheartedly supporting the USSR in the ideological dispute with communist China, embarked on economic negotiations with the U.S., France, and other countries.

1965, March. Death of Premier Gheorghiu-Dej, who was succeeded by **Nicolae Ceaușescu** as chief of the party.

Ceaușescu became president of the council and thus head of state. He continued his predecessor's policy of maintaining strict internal controls, but in international affairs insisted on the full sovereignty of all nations, which meant full independence within the Communist bloc.

1966, May 10–13. Visit of the secretary of the Soviet Communist Party, **Leonid Brezhnev,** to Bucharest. Ceaușescu stood firm by Romanian claims and even argued for the withdrawal of Soviet troops from Poland, East Germany, and Hungary. Romania regularly objected to having Warsaw Pact maneuvers taking place on its territory.

1967. Romania established diplomatic relations with West Germany, the first country in the Eastern bloc to do so.

1968, Aug. Romania, alone among the Warsaw Pact countries, **refused to contribute troops to the invasion and occupation of Czechoslovakia.** It firmly rejected the Soviet doctrine of "limited sovereignty" for the communist countries.

1969, June. At the meeting of the Communist Parties in Moscow, the Romanian representative voted against the condemnation of Communist China, stressing again the full sovereignty of all countries.

Aug. 2–3. Visit of U.S. president Richard Nixon to Bucharest, a demonstration of Western interest in Romania. The gesture was later returned when President Ceaușescu visited Washington (Oct. 1970).

1972, May 16. The Iron Gates hydroelectric and navigation project on the Danube, built jointly by Romania and Yugoslavia, was **inaugurated.** It was one of the five largest hydroelectric systems in the world.

Dec. 15. Romania became a member of the International Monetary Fund and the World Bank.

1973, June 26–30. Nicolae **Ceaușescu visited West Germany,** the first such visit by the head of state of an Eastern European country.

Dec. 4–5. Ceaușescu paid a state visit to the United States and signed an agreement on economic, industrial, and technological cooperation. In Aug. 1975, Romania was granted **most-favored-nation status** for trade with the United States.

1974, March 25–26. Ceaușescu was elected to the newly created office of the president.

March 29. A new press law abolished preliminary censorship and made the editor-in-chief solely responsible for the publication.

1976, Nov. 22–24. Brezhnev visited Romania and signed a statement on the further development of cooperation and friendship.

1977, Aug. 1–2. More than 35,000 coal miners went on strike to protest a new pension law, food shortages, and overtime work.

1980s. Foreign debts and economic difficulties: in Sept. 1981 Romania asked Western banks to roll over a large portion of its short-term hard-currency debt. An economic slowdown since the mid-1970s had resulted in price increases and large hard-currency debts (estimated at $10–14 billion at the end of 1982) owed to Western creditors. Serious economic difficulties, including energy and food shortages, continued into the late 1980s.

Ideological controls: Restrictions of cultural and press freedom became increasingly repressive. From the early 1980s, government policies also discouraged religious activities, especially non-Catholic religious groups. Discrimination was alleged against ethnic minorities, such as Germans, Hungarians, and Jews.

1981, Oct. 9. Citizens who were hoarding food were persecuted, and only official stores were designated for groceries.

1984–86. Measures to stimulate the birth rate: in February 1984 the government introduced measures making abortion illegal for women under the age of 42. In early 1986 increased taxation was imposed on childless couples.

1987, Nov. 15. Thousands of workers across the country protested wage cuts and food and energy shortages.

1988, March. Ceaușescu announced a **systematization policy,** under which about eight thousand villages were to be demolished and their inhabitants forcibly resettled in new **"agro-industrial centers."**

1989, Feb. 24. More than 13,000 Romanians emigrated to Hungary.

March 17. An editorial in the daily Communist Party newspaper, *Scinteia,* declared that anyone criticizing the current situation within Romania would be guilty of espionage and treason.

April 13. Ceaușescu declared that Romania had the capability to produce and use nuclear weapons.

Aug. 9. László Tökés, a Calvinist minister from Transylvania, was arrested for criticizing the Ceaușescu government on Canadian television. (He was later released.)

Dec. The fall of Ceaușescu and the formation of a provisional government. The clash of demonstrators and the Ceaușescu government led to violence in Timișoara and Bucharest that turned into a brief but bloody civil war, ending with the **execution of Ceaușescu and his wife on Dec. 25.** In the following days, **the National Salvation Front (NSF)**

formed a provisional government, with its leader, Ion Iliescu, as provisional president. The provisional government abolished the death penalty and promised elections.

1990, Jan. 27. Thousands demonstrated against the National Salvation Front, accusing it of maintaining Ceaușescu's communist policies.

Feb. 11. The U.S. provided food aid, but Secretary of State James Baker, visiting Romania, announced that longer-term aid would depend on free elections.

May. The NSF won the elections, and Iliescu was elected president. He would win another four-year term as president in Sept.–Oct. 1992.

Sept. 27. Romania was denied observer status in the **Council of Europe** because of continued human rights abuses in the country.

Dec. 16. Workers and students began a general strike, demanding the resignation of the president and the government in Timișoara; the strike lasted through January.

1991, Feb. 8–21. A strike was called by 20,000 railway workers around Iași city, and subsequently by those in Timișoara. They demanded improved salaries and stricter employment laws.

March 18. The Romanian Supreme Court convicted **Col.-Gen. Iulian Vlad,** the former head of the secret police under the Ceaușescu regime, on charges of taking dissidents into custody illegally. Four other officers received prison sentences.

April 1. The government introduced the second stage of its price liberalization program, which took away governmental subsidies, and the cost of foodstuffs doubled overnight.

Aug. Severe floods in the Bacău region north of Bucharest caused a dam to burst and swept away 17 villages, killing 70 people and leaving 43 missing.

Aug. 14. President Ion Iliescu signed a law privatizing all state enterprises except utilities.

Sept. 26. Prime Minister **Petre Roman resigned** amid demonstrations and violent riots in Bucharest by thousands of striking miners. Former finance minister **Theodor Stolojan** was asked by the president to **form a new broad-based coalition government.**

Nov. 21. Parliament endorsed **a new constitution,** which **guaranteed pluralism, human rights, and a free market economy.** A national referendum approved the new constitution on Dec. 8.

1992, April 7. The ruling **National Salvation Front** (mostly made up of former Communists) **split** when the **NSF–22 December Group** (supporting President Iliescu) elected a national council and **described itself as a "social-democratic" party.**

Sept. 27. The **second general election** since 1989 took place. The Democratic Convention of Romania (DCR), a Center-Right coalition, did well in urban areas, and the Democratic National Salvation Front (DNSF), the party of incumbent president Iliescu, did well in rural areas.

Oct. 11. Ion Iliescu (of the DNSF) won another four-year term as president in a runoff election, defeating Emil Constantinescu (of the DCR).

Nov. 4. President Iliescu appointed **Nicolae Vacaroiu as prime minister.**

1993, Jan. 17. After electing the writer **Bela Marko** as its leader, **the Hungarian Democratic Union** of Romania called on the government to help the Hungarian minority preserve its identity, culture, language, religion, and education.

Feb. 15. Thousands of Romanian workers demonstrated in Bucharest against rising prices, unemployment, and inflation.

March 19. The government defeated a no-confidence vote brought against it for its economic program.

April 12. Tens of thousands of workers across the country struck for higher wages and price controls. Strikes had been called for by the National Free Trade Union Confederation.

Aug. Striking miners in the Jiu Valley and striking train engineers protested inflation and demanded large salary increases. The miners won their demands, while the engineers were forced back to work by the threat of losing their jobs.

Sept. 28. The **Council of Europe** approved the admission of Romania.

1998, March 30. Prime Minister Ciorbea was forced to resign as a result of public dissatisfaction with his attempts to implement much-needed economic reforms. He was replaced by presidential appointment on April 1 when Radu Vasile took over as prime minister. On the same day, Romania was named as one of five nations to begin talks about future membership in the European Union.

1999, Jan. 5–22. Nationwide, violent protests were staged by mine workers in reaction to a government austerity plan that proposed the closing of many of Romania's mining operations.

Dec. 10. Romania was officially invited to apply for EU membership along with Bulgaria, Slovakia, Latvia, Lithuania, Malta, and Turkey.

2000, Nov. 26. In Romania's parliamentary elections, the moderate Party of Social Democracy won a legislative majority.

Dec. 10. Former president and leader of the Party of Social Democracy **Ion Iliescu won the presidency** by an overwhelming majority in a runoff election against ultranationalist Corneliu Vadim Tudor.

May 7–9. Pope John Paul II visited Romania.

i. RUSSIA (UNION OF SOVIET SOCIALIST REPUBLICS AND SUCCESSOR STATES)

(From p. 715)

1. SOVIET UNION

1944, Feb. 1. An amendment to the constitution of the Union of Soviet Socialist Republics granted **separate commissariats for defense and for foreign affairs** to each of the constituent republics. Each could thus maintain its own army (which would form, however, a component element in the army of the USSR) and conduct its own negotiations with foreign countries, and conclude treaties with them.

1946, Feb. 10. The first **general elections** since 1937 for the **Supreme Soviet** returned the official list of approved candidates.

March 15. The fourth **five-year plan,** designed to increase industrial output by more than 50 percent over prewar levels, was adopted by the Supreme Soviet. Much of the necessary industrial equipment was collected from Soviet-occupied regions in Eastern and Central Europe.

March 19. In a series of governmental changes, **President Michael Kalinin** resigned because of ill health and was **succeeded by** the former trade union leader **Nikolai Shvernik. A Council of Ministers** (with **Joseph Stalin** as chairman and Foreign Minister **V. M. Molotov** as deputy chairman) **replaced** the former **Council of People's Commissars.**

June 28. The **Ministry of State Control** announced widespread dismissals in industry for incompetence and dishonesty. This was followed in August by a similar purge of agricultural offenders.

Nov. 18. Marshal Koniev replaced **Marshal G. K. Zhukov** as **commander-in-chief** of the Soviet armed forces.

1947, March 3. Stalin was succeeded as minister of defense by Gen. N. A. Bulganin.

March 5. The **Soviet Union rejected** the report of the UN Atomic Energy Commission on **atomic control.**

July. The **Soviet Union** and its satellites refused to participate in European economic reconstruction under the **Marshall Plan** (p. 917).

Oct. According to official reports of the Soviet **State Planning Commission** (Gosplan), Russia's industrial output under the **five-year plan** had failed to reach its yearly goal in 1946 but had surpassed it in 1947. A shortage of labor continued to be the main economic drawback. A severe food shortage, resulting from drought and crop failures in 1946, was relieved by an excellent harvest in 1947.

Dec. 15. The government was able to abolish food rationing.

Dec. 16. A drastic **currency devaluation,** at the rate of ten to one, brought renewed hardships to most people, but served to further strengthen the Soviet economy.

1948, Feb.–March. The USSR concluded treaties of friendship and mutual assistance with **Romania, Hungary,** and **Bulgaria.**

Feb. 10. The **Central Committee of the Communist Party of the Soviet Union** (CPSU) accused Soviet composers, including **Dmitri Shostakovich, Sergei Prokofiev,** and **Aram Khachaturian,** of losing touch with the masses by showing bourgeois influences in their works. The accused confessed and repented.

April 6. The USSR concluded a military assistance pact with **Finland.**

Aug. A further ideological shake-up occurred when the biologist **Trofim Lysenko,** backed by the Central Committee, condemned the generally accepted "formal genetics," based on the findings of **Gregor Mendel,** and substituted the outmoded teachings of **Ivan Michurin,** as being in complete accordance with Marxian doctrine.

Aug. 31. Death of Andrei Zhdanov, deputy premier and one of the party's leading ideologists.

1949, March 4. A series of governmental changes was initiated with the replacement of Foreign Minister **Molotov** by A. Vishinsky and of Minister of Defense Marshal **Bulganin** by Marshal **A. M. Vassilievsky.** Both Molotov and Bulganin continued as members of the Politburo.

Sept. 27. The USSR **repudiated** its 1945 treaty of friendship with Yugoslavia (p. 892).

Dec. 31. Stalin's seventieth birthday was the occasion for worldwide Communist celebrations. The announcement of several Stalin peace prizes was seen as a move in the Soviet **"peace offensive,"** which had become the main Communist propaganda weapon in the cold war.

1950, Jan. 12. The **death penalty,** abolished after the war, was **reintroduced** for espionage, treason, and sabotage.

Feb. 14. The USSR and the **People's Republic of China** signed a 30-year **treaty of alliance.**

Oct. 20–21. Molotov and the foreign ministers of East Germany, Poland, Bulgaria, Hungary, and Romania met in Prague, denounced the agreement of the Western Big Three to liberalize their German policy, and called for German unification and a German peace treaty.

1951, Jan. 5. After a two-year stalemate, the USSR agreed to reopen talks with the United States on Jan. 15 for a settlement of its $11 billion **lend-lease aid account** in accord with the 1942 agreement, but negotiations were suspended indefinitely on Jan. 31.

Feb. 22. The Soviet press announced that in recent elections to the Supreme Soviet, the Stalinist bloc had won a popular majority of 99.6 percent.

April 16. Moscow radio announced the **successful completion of the fourth five-year plan;** production had increased by 73 percent over 1940.

Oct. 5–14. The 19th Party Congress gave special attention to outlining the **transition from socialism to communism;** the Presidium replaced the Politburo and assumed wider functions.

1953, Jan. 31. A *Pravda* announcement of the **"doctors' plot"** to kill leading Soviet commanders presaged a purge, especially of Jews, which ended with Stalin's death (March 5) and the release of the doctors arrested (April 4).

March 5. Death of Joseph STALIN. He was interred in Lenin Mausoleum on March 9.

March 6. G. M. Malenkov became head of the Soviet government, with the following first deputy chairmen of the Council of Ministers: **Laurenty Beria, Molotov** (also foreign minister), Marshal **Bulganin, and Lazar Kaganovich.** Vishinsky, formerly foreign minister, became a permanent Soviet representative at the UN.

March 20. Nikita Khrushchev succeeded Malenkov as first secretary of the CPSU Central Committee.

June 22. The government lifted most of its **curbs on travel by foreigners,** including diplomatic personnel.

July 10. Beria's expulsion from the party and dismissal as minister of internal security was announced. His execution, along with six associates (Dec. 23) followed his conviction of treason by the Soviet Supreme Court.

Aug. 8. Premier Malenkov declared that "the United States no longer possesses a monopoly on the hydrogen bomb."

Nov. 16. The **International Labor Office** rejected a Soviet application for membership.

1954, Feb. 26. The government decreed a change in the **status of the Crimea,** making it a part of the Soviet Ukraine.

May 3. The government, with one reservation, ratified the **Genocide Convention** (adopted by the UN General Assembly, Dec. 9, 1948), making illegal the destruction of religious, racial, ethnic, or national groups.

June 27. The world's first **nuclear-generated power plant** opened in Russia.

Nov. 22. Death of Andrei Y. Vishinsky, chief Soviet delegate to the UN.

1955, Jan. 15. The Soviet Union recognized the **sovereignty of West Germany.**

Feb. 8. Malenkov resigned as chairman of the Council of Ministers and was succeeded by **Marshal Bulganin.**

Feb. 9. In his inaugural address, Premier Bulganin emphasized the Sino-Soviet tie. **Marshal Zhukov** was appointed minister of defense.

March 2. The government decreed a **decentralized system of agricultural planning** to provide farmers with greater initiative and independence.

May 7. The Presidium of the Supreme Soviet annulled the **treaties of friendship with Britain and France.**

Aug. 12. During a relaxation of international tension after the Geneva Conference, the government announced it would **reduce its armed forces** by 640,000 men by Dec. 15.

Oct. 10. The government announced a plan to offer industrial and agricultural equipment and technical assistance to any underdeveloped Arab or Asian nation.

Nov. 18. Bulganin and Khrushchev arrived in New Delhi to begin a visit to India, Burma, and Afghanistan.

Dec. 29. In addresses in Moscow, Bulganin and Khrushchev denounced Western **"colonialism,"** and Khrushchev criticized the **aerial inspection plan** proposed by U.S. president Dwight Eisenhower.

1956, Feb. 14. At the opening of the 20th Congress of the Communist Party of the Soviet Union, Khrushchev launched an **ATTACK ON STALIN** and the **"cult of personality."** He also declared that **coexistence** was now the goal of Soviet foreign policy. The Congress, sitting until Feb. 25, adopted the **sixth five-year plan.**

April 17. The government announced the **disbanding of the Cominform.**

April 23. Khrushchev, on a **visit to England** (April 18–27), announced that the USSR would produce a **hydrogen-guided missile.**

May 14. The government announced a **reduction in the armed forces** by 1.2 million men, by May 1, 1957.

June 1. Foreign Minister Molotov resigned his post and was succeeded by **Dmitri T. Shepilov,** editor of *Pravda.*

July 17. Despite its friendship with Arab countries, the Soviet government signed an **agreement to step up its oil deliveries to Israel.**

Oct.–Nov. Soviet forces were involved in the **Hungarian revolt** (p. 890).

Dec. 26. The state of **war with Japan was ended.**

1957, Feb. 11. A Jan. 9 decree provided for the **rehabilitation of five minority groups:** the Balkars, Chechens, Ingush, Kalmyks, and Karachais, who had been accused of disloyalty and exiled to Central Asia and Kazakhstan during World War II.

Feb. 15. Foreign Minister Shepilov was replaced by **Andrei Gromyko.**

May 7. Khrushchev presented a plan to the Supreme Soviet for a sweeping **reorganization of industrial production,** including the establishment of 92 economic regions.

July 3. The Soviet news agency Tass reported the **ouster of Molotov, Malenkov, and Kaganovich** from the Central Committee and from its Presidium because of antiparty activities; **Shepilov** was ousted on July 4.

Sept. The overly optimistic sixth five-year plan was replaced by a **seven-year plan** (1959–65), the goals of which were to be worked out by mid-1958.

Oct. 5. THE SOVIET UNION FIRED AN EARTH SATELLITE, *Sputnik I,* into orbit. It circled the globe at 18,000 mph.

Oct. 26. Marshal Zhukov was dismissed as defense minister and succeeded by **Marshal Rodion Y. Malinovsky.** Later (Nov. 2) Zhukov was ousted from the Presidium and Central Committee for promoting his own "cult of personality" in the army.

Nov. 3. With a live dog aboard, *Sputnik II,* the second earth satellite, was fired into outer space.

1958, March 27. NIKITA KHRUSHCHEV SUCCEEDED MARSHAL BULGANIN AS PREMIER. On March 31 the Supreme Soviet approved all of Khrushchev's political appointments, including those of **Anastas I. Mikoyan** and **Frol R. Kozlov,** who were both given the title of first deputy premier.

March 31. Foreign Minister Gromyko announced the Soviet **suspension of nuclear weapons tests.**

Oct. 29. The writer **Boris Pasternak** informed the Swedish Academy of his "voluntary refusal" to accept the **Nobel Prize** for literature, which was awarded him on Oct. 23.

1959, Jan. 27–Feb. 5. The 21st Party Congress in Moscow adopted a new **seven-year economic plan.**

Feb. 21–March 3. British **Prime Minister Harold Macmillan visited Russia.**

June 6. Khrushchev stated that unless the Western powers agreed to a **nuclear-free zone** in the Balkans, Soviet rocket bases would be set up in Albania, Bulgaria, and Romania.

July 24. United States **vice president Richard Nixon** opened the American national exhibition in Moscow, engaging in an informal debate with Khrushchev.

Sept. 13. Russia launched the first man-made object to land on the moon, *Lunik II.*

Sept. 15–27. Khrushchev visited the United States (p. 919).

1960, Jan. 14. Khrushchev announced that the Soviet Union would **reduce its standing armed forces** by a third in 1960–61.

Jan. 14. Talks reopened with the United States, **on lend-lease debts,** after a lapse of seven years, but again broke off without agreement (Feb. 23).

Feb. 13–March 5. Khrushchev toured Asia.

March 29. A **trade pact with China** provided for an exchange of goods totaling 7.9 billion rubles.

May 1. A high-altitude United States reconnaissance plane, a **U-2, was shot down over Soviet Russia.** Khrushchev used this incident to break up the **Paris summit conference.**

May 7. Leonid Brezhnev replaced Marshal K. Y. Voroshilov as president of the Soviet Union.

May 30. The Soviet defense minister announced that Soviet rockets had been ordered to fire on any foreign base from which an Allied plane took off for a flight over the USSR.

Aug. 17. American U-2 pilot **Francis Gary Powers** pleaded guilty before a high Soviet military tribunal to charges of having flown an intelligence mission over the Soviet Union. On Aug. 19 he was found guilty of espionage for the United States and sentenced to ten years' loss of liberty.

1961, April 12. Maj. Yuri A. Gagarin, in the spaceship *Vostok I*, became the first man successfully to **orbit the earth;** he circled the earth for 108 minutes at a maximum altitude of 203 miles.

July 8. Khrushchev announced the **suspension of planned Soviet reductions in the armed forces** and an increase in defense expenditures as a result of the Berlin crisis (p. 872).

Aug. 31. The **resumption of nuclear testing** was announced.

Oct. 17. Khrushchev, in an address opening the CPSU's 22nd Congress in Moscow, offered to delay the year-end deadline for signing a **German peace treaty,** declared that the USSR would "probably" test a 50-megaton hydrogen bomb, and attacked Albania for pursuing Stalinist policies.

Oct. 30. A **50-plus-megaton bomb** was detonated in the Arctic.

Oct. 31. Stalin's body was removed from Lenin's Tomb in Red Square.

1962, Feb. 10. The Soviet Union released **Francis Gary Powers,** U.S. pilot of the U-2 aircraft that crashed in the USSR in May 1960, in exchange for **Col. Rudolf Abel,** a Soviet spy convicted of espionage by the United States in 1957.

March 21. Khrushchev accepted President John F. Kennedy's proposal for Soviet-American **cooperation in outer space exploration** and research. Discussions regarding the possibility of such cooperation began on March 27.

Aug. 5. The USSR resumed its **nuclear tests** with a high-altitude blast thought to be in the 40-megaton range.

Nov. 21. The government announced the **end of the state of alert** that had been called for Warsaw Pact and Soviet forces because of the Cuban missile crisis.

1963, March 8. Khrushchev declared that de-Stalinization policies did not permit individual **political liberties** or artistic **deviations from socialist realism.**

Aug. 5. A **Limited Nuclear Test Ban Treaty** was signed in Moscow.

Nov. 1. The government announced the launching and successful performance of *Polyot I*, the first **maneuverable unmanned satellite.**

1964, Jan. 1. In a message to the world capitals, the Soviet Union proposed the **renunciation of force in all territorial disputes.**

Feb. 10–15. A meeting of the Communist Party's Central Committee called for the use of more scientific and technological methods to increase **agricultural production.** Problems with agriculture, including the failure of expensive plans to expand cultivation in Siberia, brought growing criticism of Khrushchev.

April 3. *Pravda* confirmed the **expulsion of Malenkov, Molotov, and Kaganovich from the Communist Party** for "antiparty" activity directed against Khrushchev.

April 12. Khrushchev called on all Communist governments to join in a "resolute rebuff" of Chinese claims to a special place in the socialist world. He insisted on the **equality of all Communist countries.**

May 11–25. Khrushchev visited Egypt and inspected work on a projected Aswan Dam. He promised Soviet aid and support of Egypt in times of crisis.

June 16–July 4. Khrushchev visited the Scandinavian countries and suggested that they resign from NATO.

Oct. 12–13. Three men in a Soviet spacecraft completed 16 orbits of the earth.

Oct. 14–15. DEPOSITION OF KHRUSHCHEV, charged by his opponents with hasty decisions, phrase mongering, personality cult, and so on. The new first secretary of the Communist Party was **Leonid I. Brezhnev** and the new premier, **Aleksei N. Kosygin.**

1965. Efforts to revitalize the Soviet economy: in the industrial sphere, more freedom of decision was given to management, and a system of profit sharing was introduced. More emphasis was placed on increased production of consumer goods. In agriculture, the collective farmers were assured of a monthly wage and an old-age pension. Use of fertilizers was expanded and improved varieties of seed were introduced.

Feb. 11–15. Kosygin visited North Vietnam and North Korea: proclaimed Soviet support to strengthen the defenses of North Vietnam.

March 1–15. A meeting of representatives **of Communist Parties** was boycotted not only by the Chinese, but also by the North Vietnamese, the North Koreans, the Indonesians, the Japanese, and the Romanians and Albanians. All efforts to bridge the rift between the USSR and Communist China proved unavailing.

March 18–19. Lt. Col. Aleksei A. Leonov, in the Soviet spacecraft *Voskhod II*, became the **first human being to walk in space.**

1966, Feb. 14. Conviction and imprisonment of Andrei Sinyavsky and Yuli Daniel for arranging the publication of anti-Soviet writings in the West. In literature and art, the Soviet authorities frowned on the extension of freedom of expression. (Neither **Boris Pasternak** nor **Alexsandr Solzhenitsyn** was able to go to Stockholm to accept his Nobel Prize for literature.) At the same time, prominent scientists, such as **Andrei Sakharov** and even **Pyotr Kapitsa,** being essential to the Soviet military effort as well as the space program, went unpunished despite their repeated pleas for greater freedom of thought and expression and improved relations with the West.

March 29–April 8. The 23rd Congress of the CPSU. The Chinese Communists not only rejected an invitation to attend but also seized the occasion for delivering a new blast against Soviet policies.

April 21–27. Foreign Minister Gromyko visited Italy and the Vatican. His visit led to the conclusion of an agreement for the construction of a Fiat automobile factory in Russia.

June 20–July 1. French president **Charles de Gaulle visited Russia.** The visit resulted in an agreement on improved trade and cultural relations.

1967, Jan. 27. Signature of the **Treaty for the Exploration and Uses of Outer Space.**

June. Outbreak of the **Arab-Israeli War** (p. 967). The USSR, which had for years supplied the United Arab Republic with military equipment and training, immediately began replacing materiel (especially planes) that had been wiped out in the Israelis' surprise attack. At the same time, the Soviet government began to strengthen its **naval units in the eastern Mediterranean** and even in the **Indian Ocean,** presaging a fundamental change in the balance of power in the Middle East and Indian Ocean areas.

July 7. Marshal Ivan I. Yakubovsky was named supreme commander of the Warsaw Pact forces.

1968, June 3. Conclusion of a **Soviet-British trade treaty.**

June 4. Signature of the Nuclear Non-Proliferation Treaty, ratified Nov. 24, 1969.

Aug. Invasion and occupation of Czechoslovakia by Soviet and other Warsaw Pact forces (p. 887).

1969, March 2, 5. Serious **border clashes** between Soviet and Communist

Chinese troops on the Ussuri River raised the possibility of a major conflict (p. 1024).

June 15–17. Conference of Communist Parties held in Moscow, with 75 parties represented. The chief subject of debate was the deepening division of the Communist world, but in the end the conference refused to condemn and outlaw Communist China. The conference revealed much criticism of the Soviet action in Czechoslovakia.

Sept. 11. Brief **conference of Premier Kosygin** (returning from North Vietnam) **and Chinese premier Chou En-lai** at the airport in Beijing.

1970, Aug. 12. Signature of the important **SOVIET TREATY WITH THE GERMAN FEDERAL REPUBLIC.** It reflected, among other things, the keen desire of the Soviet government to secure more technical aid from Germany.

Oct. 6–14. President Georges Pompidou of France visited Russia and discussed means to increase trade and collaborate in the exploitation of Soviet mineral resources. An agreement was concluded for closer political and cultural consultation.

Nov. 17. Beginning of **Strategic Arms Limitation Talks** (SALT) between the United States and the Soviet Union, in Helsinki.

Nov. 23. Signature of a new **trade pact with Communist China,** reviving a trade relationship that had become all but nonexistent. There were indications of slight improvement in relations as China emerged from the Cultural Revolution (p. 1024) and began to reestablish its position in the world.

Oct. Dissident writer **Aleksandr Solzhenitsyn was awarded the Nobel Prize** for literature. In Feb. 1974 **he was expelled from the USSR** after publication of *Gulag Archipelago.*

1971, Feb. The **ninth five-year plan called for a greater increase in production of consumer goods** rather than producer goods.

April. The 24th Party Congress emphasized the need for a new European security settlement.

1972, May 22–30. President **Richard Nixon visited Moscow, signing the first SALT anti–ballistic missile treaty,** an interim agreement on offensive missiles, and establishing a U.S.-USSR Commercial Commission.

1973, June 17–25. Brezhnev visited the United States, signing agreements on the prevention of nuclear war and the promotion of trade. He made a televised speech to the American people during his visit.

June 27–July 3. Agreements on nuclear arms control were signed between the U.S. and the USSR during Nixon's second visit to Moscow.

1975, July 17–21. The first joint Soviet-U.S. space flight, involving Soyuz and Apollo spacecraft, was made.

Aug. The Soviet Union agreed to the Helsinki Accord and **allowed the establishment of dissident "Helsinki groups" in the country to monitor human rights.**

Oct. 9. Scientist **Andrei Sakharov was awarded the Nobel Peace Prize.**

1976, May 28. The USSR and the U.S. signed the Treaty on Underground Nuclear Explosions.

1977, June 16. Brezhnev replaced N. Podgorny as chairman of the Presidium of the Supreme Soviet, becoming the first Soviet leader to act as both party leader and head of state.

Oct. 7. A new constitution was adopted to replace the "Stalin" constitution of 1936; the Communist Party was specifically named as ruling party of the Soviet Union.

1979, July 18. SALT II was signed by Brezhnev and U.S. president Jimmy Carter in Vienna.

Dec. Soviet Union invaded Afghanistan (p. 976). Tension between the two superpowers increased and détente deteriorated. **The United States imposed an embargo on grain shipments to the USSR in January 1981.**

Early 1980s. Economic difficulties. The decline of economic growth in the 1970s (after strong growth rates in the 1950s and 1960s) **presented serious problems in agricultural and energy sectors in the 1980s.** A shortage of food supplies and consumer goods became an increasing national problem. To raise farm productivity, the central government expanded the material and technical base of agriculture and related industries, but the problems in the agricultural sector were overcome only very slowly, because of bureaucratic and political corruption. In the early 1980s, the energy sector also suffered a serious decline in the production of oil, gas, and coal. The USSR faced growing problems because of prior **environmental damage,** some deterioration in public health, increasing alcoholism, and difficulties with worker morale and motivation. By the early 1980s, **death rates** were surpassing birth rates as the population declined.

1980, Jan. 22. Andrei Sakharov and his wife, Elena Bonner, were banished to the city of Gorki for his criticism of the Afghan invasion.

July 19–Aug. 3. The **Olympic games** were held in Moscow but 62 countries refused to attend in protest of the Afghan invasion.

Oct. 23. Aleksei Kosygin, the longtime premier of the Soviet Union, **resigned** because of ill health; he **died in December.**

1981, Sept. 4. Russia began massive military exercises.

Nov.–Dec. The **Strategic Arms Reduction Talks (START) began** with the United States.

Nov. 10. Death of Leonid Brezhnev, at age 76. He was replaced by **Yuri Andropov,** former head of the KGB (Committee for State Security), the secret police.

Dec. 9. Andrei Sakharov ended his hunger strike, begun on Nov. 22, when his daughter-in-law was issued an exit visa.

1983, Jan. Andropov, party leader of the Soviet Communist Party, was **elected chairman of the Supreme Soviet Presidium.**

1984, Feb. Death of Yuri Andropov. **Konstantin Chernenko was elected to succeed Andropov as party leader** (Feb. 13).

May 8. The Soviets boycotted the Olympic games in the U.S. in retaliation for the 1980 boycott of the games held in Moscow.

Oct. 1. The section of the Transbaikal-Amur Railway from Lena to the Pacific was opened.

1985, March 10. Death of Konstantin Chernenko. He was **succeeded by Mikhail Gorbachev as party leader in April,** the first Soviet chief born after 1917.

July 2. Andrei Gromyko was elected chairman of the Presidium of the Supreme Soviet. The new foreign minister was **Eduard Shevardnadze,** a friend of Gorbachev.

1986, Feb. 25–March 6. At the 27th Party Congress, **Mikhail Gorbachev stressed the need for radical change.** Complaining that the economy had been stagnating since the 1970s, he called for a restructuring (**perestroika**) of Soviet society. The party adopted his suggestion and called for greater openness (**glasnost**) in public dealings. Perestroika and glasnost thereafter became words frequently used in Soviet reforms.

Boris Yeltsin also caused strong reactions with his speech that decried party privileges and abuses of power.

April 26. The Chernobyl atomic power station exploded. Thirty-two people were killed at once; a fallout cloud drifted westward over Europe; parts of Belorussia and the Ukraine were permanently evacuated. On Oct. 2 the remaining Chernobyl atomic reactor was buried under a security mound of metal and concrete. Four years later, there was still a 30-mile exclusion zone around the site.

June 27. Glavlit, the official censoring agency, was disbanded and its ten thousand workers were reassigned.

1987, June 29–30. The **Supreme Soviet approved the restructuring of the national economy,** with new laws on state enterprises and on procedures for suing officials who infringed on citizens' rights.

Nov. 11. Boris Yeltsin was discharged as head of the Moscow Communist Party for blaming Gorbachev for the slow pace of reforms.

1988, Feb. 23. Unrest was reported in Azerbaijan in a region that was 80 percent Armenian.

April 15. Soviet troops began **withdrawing from Afghanistan.** The withdrawal was completed in February 1989.

May 17. More than 100,000 protesters in Yerevan, the capital of the Armenian Soviet Socialist Republic, were dispersed by Soviet troops.

June 13. Gorbachev opened a dialogue with the Vatican, ending years of hostility.

Dec. 7. In a speech to the United Nations General Assembly, **Gorbachev promised to cut Soviet forces in Europe by 500,000.** Marshal Sergei Akhromeyev, head of the forces, resigned after Gorbachev's speech, though he later publicly supported the military cut. In **January 1989 Gorbachev announced** that the **Soviet military budget was to be cut by 14.2 percent and personnel, by 12 percent.**

Dec. 7. An earthquake destroyed part of northern Armenia, killing 11,000 people in Spitak and leaving half a million homeless.

1989, Jan. Azerbaijan and Armenia remained under martial law in response to intercommunal violence.

Jan. 5. In a continuing process of de-Stalinization, the Communist

Party of the Soviet Union called for the annulment of hundreds of thousands of verdicts handed down during the Stalinist purges from the 1930s to the 1950s.

Jan. 23. An earthquake rocked the republic of **Tajikistan,** causing landslides and killing more than 274 people.

Feb. 3. Twenty more villages were evacuated in Belorussia (Belarus) because of continuing high levels of radiation contamination from Chernobyl.

March. New presidents were appointed in the republics of **Uzbekistan, Kazakhstan,** and **Georgia.**

April 8. The Supreme Soviet amended Article 70 of the criminal code, which had been used to punish dissidents, drastically decreasing the maximum prison term and fine. The move was likely a result of numerous nationalist outbreaks.

April 9. In **Tbilisi, Georgia, Interior Ministry troops and the army** used gas and clubs to **attack a massive protest.** Twenty were killed and more than 4,000 were injured. On April 14, the party leadership of Georgia resigned, accepting blame for the shootings in Tbilisi.

April 25. Gorbachev secured the "retirement" of 74 "old guard" party members, in another step toward his reforms.

May 22. Gorbachev was officially elected to the new post of **chairman of the Supreme Soviet** (state president). He had been de facto Soviet president since October 1988.

May 18. Estonia voted to give itself full control over its economy, introducing its own currency, the koru, to replace the ruble. On the same day, **Lithuania** declared itself "sovereign."

May 31. Boris Yeltsin, the most prominent radical of the Congress of People's Deputies, criticized Gorbachev for the failures of perestroika (restructuring) and put forth an alternative economic program to cut capital spending. He also warned the congress of the increasing threat of Gorbachev's powers and the possibility of a "new dictatorship."

July. Thousands of striking miners demanding better working and living conditions in the Donbass and Kuzbass coalfields and in other areas posed what Gorbachev called the most serious threat yet to perestroika.

July 2. Death of Andrei Gromyko, foreign minister from 1957 to 1985 and then chairman of the Presidium until 1988.

July 30. An **unofficial opposition in the People's Congress,** the "interregional group," **was formed by more than 200 Soviet deputies, with Boris Yeltsin as leader.**

Aug. 16. A draft law was published giving workers the right to strike.

Aug. 23. Two million people formed a chain across Estonia, Latvia, and Lithuania to mark the fiftieth anniversary of the Soviet occupation of the Baltic states.

Sept. 8–10. The People's Movement of the Ukraine, called **Rukh,** held its congress in Kiev, where it called for the restoration of Ukrainian language and cultural traditions.

Sept. 23. The Azerbaijan Supreme Soviet adopted a new law defining the republic's sovereignty.

Oct. 2. The Supreme Soviet imposed a ban on all strikes in key industries.

Oct. 7–8. The second annual congress of the Latvian Popular Front endorsed the goal of Latvia's complete independence from the Soviet Union. It also called for a common market of the three Baltic republics.

Oct. 7. More than 20,000 demonstrators in Moscow supporting an acceleration of the Soviet reform process formed a human chain stretching from Gorky Street to the northwestern suburb of Zelenograd.

Nov. 10. The Presidium of the USSR Supreme Soviet declared that certain recent legislation (nationalist legislation) adopted by Lithuania, Latvia, Estonia, and Azerbaijan was at variance with the USSR constitution and had to be modified.

Nov. 17–19. The Georgian Supreme Soviet amended the Georgian constitution, giving itself ownership of all natural resources and the right to "suspend Soviet laws and regulatory enactments" if they "run contrary to Georgian interests."

Nov. 29. Direct rule in Nagorno-Karabakh, the Armenian enclave, was ended, and the region was returned to Azerbaijani administration.

Dec. 1. Gorbachev met Pope John Paul II in the Vatican, the first encounter between the leader of the world's Catholics and the head of an officially atheist superpower.

Dec. 3. Gorbachev met with U.S. president **George Bush,** and they **declared the end of the cold war.**

Dec. 14. Death of Andrei Sakharov, the Soviet Union's foremost human rights campaigner.

Dec. 19–20. The Lithuanian Communist Party declared itself independent of the CPSU, providing the most serious nationalist challenge to date to President Gorbachev.

1990s. Economic crisis: increasing economic crisis characterized the Soviet Union from the late 1980s until 1993. The decline of the Russian economy intensified in the 1990s with the loss of control over monetary circulation. Cash in circulation in 1991 increased 4.8 times over that in 1990, and sharp price increases reduced the purchasing power of savings by 2.4 times in the same 12-month span. The GNP in 1991 was 83 percent of that of 1990. **Profiteering and crime** increased rapidly.

1990, Feb.–March. Elections for local soviets (councils) and legislatures took place in most of the Soviet Union's 15 republics. In many regions they proved to be the most open elections to take place under Soviet rule. Victories for radical reformers, nationalists, and candidates from the political opposition took place in the Baltic republics, Moscow, Leningrad, and Kiev, demonstrating the waning power of the CPSU.

Feb. 13. The Communist Party **Central Committee issued revised policies,** including guarantees of human rights with a high court to protect them, emphasis on the production of consumer goods, and the development of a market economy. In addition, government was to be based on an electoral system with multiple political parties and a presidential head of state who was responsible to the Congress of People's Deputies but with powers to ensure the functioning of the state. The federation of nations within the Soviet Union was a "unity in diversity," and attempts at secession were opposed.

Feb. 28. The Congress of the People's Deputies passed a **law to redefine rights to own property and land.** Peasants could choose to be in *kolkhozes* (collectives) or to receive their own allotment of land. On **March 6** the Congress passed a further **law on property,** giving Soviet citizens the right to own assets and shares in enterprises and to pass these on to heirs. These changes were intended to provide the ground for a new market economy.

March 11. Lithuania declared its independence and voted to drop the words "Soviet Socialist" from its name. On **March 14** the all-Soviet **congress passed a resolution** by a large majority that the **Lithuanian declaration of independence had no legal force.** On **March 22** Gorbachev, using his new powers as president, **increased pressure on Lithuania by forbidding the ownership of guns** and tightening immigration and customs controls on the republic. There was also a show of strength in the capital, Vilnius, as the **Red Army patrolled the streets in armored cars.** On **April 21** the **Soviet Union imposed an economic blockade on Lithuania,** including the reduction of oil and gas supplies.

March 14. The **Congress of People's Deputies voted to elect Mikhail Gorbachev president of the USSR,** a new post with extensive executive powers. The **Congress** also **voted (March 13) to abolish the Communist Party's guaranteed monopoly** of political powers.

May 1. The traditional May Day parade in Red Square was followed by more than 40,000 people from political opposition groups denouncing both Communist rule and Gorbachev.

May 4, 8. Both **Latvia and Estonia passed independence resolutions.** Gorbachev issued decrees (May 14) outlawing the independence declarations and asserting that they violated the USSR constitution and the laws of April 30, 1990.

May 29. Boris Yeltsin was elected chairman of the Russian Supreme Soviet by the Russian Congress, making him de facto president of the Russian Federation.

June 2. Ethnic unrest broke out in the Kirghiz Republic among the minority Uzbeks, leaving 48 dead and many wounded. A **state of emergency was declared, and the border with Uzbekistan was closed.**

June 8. The **Warsaw Pact** organization declared its intention to become mainly a political body.

June 12. The **USSR Supreme Soviet passed a law on the press and mass media,** featuring detailed guarantees of **press freedom and the abolition of censorship.** The law came into effect on Aug. 1.

June–Aug. 13. Market economy reform plan: the USSR Supreme Soviet ordered major revisions to a program that aimed at accelerating the introduction of a market economy. The price rises the program entailed had aroused fierce opposition among politicians and the public. In August Gorbachev and Yeltsin agreed to sponsor a commission of experts working on the transition to a market economy. On Aug. 9 the USSR Council of Ministers passed a resolution to legalize small businesses and to allow private individuals to establish, buy, or sell a business and to hire labor.

June. Sovereignty Declarations by Russian Federation, Uzbekistan, and Moldova. On June 12 the **Russian Federation,** the largest and most powerful republic of the Soviet Union, **declared itself a sovereign state** with the right to determine its own economic and political future and "the right to freely leave the USSR." On June 20 **the Uzbek Supreme Soviet adopted a declaration of Uzbekistan's sovereignty** within a "renewed Soviet federation" and of the supremacy of Uzbekistan's laws in its territory. On June 23 **Moldavia (Moldova) declared its sovereignty** and asserted the supremacy of the Moldavian constitution and laws throughout the republic now called Moldova.

July 2–13. The 28th Congress of the CPSU. Even in the face of resurgent conservatism, Gorbachev was able to sway some key votes his way. **Gorbachev was reelected general secretary** on July 10.

July 16. The Ukraine declared its sovereignty. Going further than Uzbekistan or Moldova, it declared the right to have its own armed forces, internal security troops, and state security bodies.

July 27. Belorussia (Belarus) declared itself sovereign, giving itself the right to voluntary unions with other states and the freedom to withdraw from such unions.

Aug. Independence and sovereignty declarations: Armenia declared its independence (Aug. 23) and changed its name to the **Republic of Armenia** (a referendum in Sept. 1991 favored independence). **Turkmenistan** (Aug. 22) **and Tajikistan** (Aug. 25) joined the list of republics **declaring their sovereignty** and the precedence of their constitutions and laws over those of the Soviet Union.

Aug. 9. The Council of Ministers passed a resolution allowing private individuals to establish, buy, and sell businesses and to hire labor. This represented the first departure from Marxism's prohibition on private ownership.

Aug. 15. Gorbachev restored Soviet citizenship to many intellectuals who had been exiled, including writers Aleksandr Solzhenitsyn and Vladimir Voinovich, poet Irina Ratushinskaya, historian Lev Kopelev, chess player Viktor Korchnoi, and physicist Yury Orlov.

Sept. 24. The Supreme Soviet granted Gorbachev emergency presidential powers, which gave him the ability to dictate economic reforms, manage the state budget, and supervise law and order.

Oct. 1. The improvement in church-state relations since 1988 culminated in the passage of a **law on freedom of conscience and religious organizations,** marking the end of state persecution of believers.

Oct. 19. The USSR Supreme Soviet approved an outline program to create a market economic system. This momentous decision to abandon the 60-year-old centralized, state-controlled economy was overshadowed by unresolved, bitter arguments over how to proceed. The plan included abandonment of direct state participation in economic activity, price freedom, competition between producers, and full responsibility of organizations, enterprises, and workers for better economic results. The Supreme Soviet also adopted a law that for the first time in Soviet history allowed workers the right to strike.

Oct. 25. Kazakhstan declared its sovereignty.

Oct. 30. Kirghizstan declared itself sovereign.

1991, Jan. Soviet forces intervened in the newly independent Baltic republics by seizing key buildings and installations. The crackdown caused deaths and provoked an international outcry. On Jan. 7, the USSR Defense Ministry ordered paratroopers into Lithuania, Latvia, and Estonia, as well as into Armenia, Georgia, Moldova, and parts of Ukraine under the excuse of enforcing conscription. On Jan. 10, President Gorbachev ordered the restoration of the Soviet constitution in Lithuania. On Jan. 31, Iceland became the first country to recognize Lithuania as an independent state.

Jan. 22. A presidential decree outlawed 50- and 100-ruble banknotes (the highest denominations). The decree was intended to wipe out the illegal cash holding of black marketeers, who supposedly had been draining 20 percent of the money supply. On Feb. 12 Prime Minister Valentin Pavlov announced that the January withdrawal of the notes was the result of a Western plot to flood the Soviet economy and create artificial hyperinflation.

Feb. 19. In a TV broadcast, Russian Federation leader **Boris Yeltsin launched a personal attack on Gorbachev and demanded his immediate resignation.** He accused Gorbachev of bringing the country to dictatorship and "absolute personal power." The Gorbachev-Yeltsin rivalry continued with Yeltsin campaigning for a "no" vote in the all-union referendum and Gorbachev working for a "yes," to "preserve the integrity of the state which is a thousand years old."

March 17. The **all-union referendum on the preservation of the Soviet Union took place, and 76.4 percent of the voters voted "yes"** according to the official report. Six republics (Armenia, Estonia, Georgia, Latvia, Lithuania, and Moldova) refused to participate in the referendum.

March 31. The military alliance of the Warsaw Pact ended.

April 9. The **Georgian Supreme Soviet adopted a formal declaration of the "restoration of state independence"** after a favorable referendum on March 31.

April 23. President Gorbachev signed a pact with 9 of the 15 union republics (the Russian Federation, Azerbaijan, Belorussia, Kazakhstan, Kirghizstan, Tajikistan, Turkmenistan, the Ukraine, and Uzbekistan). The pact gave broad support to the central government's proposed measures to stabilize the economy, including a clampdown on political strikes.

May 20. The Supreme Soviet of the USSR passed a law allowing free travel and emigration from the Soviet Union.

June 12. Boris Yeltsin was elected president of the Russian Federation (RFSFR) **in the first general election in Russian history,** and was sworn in on July 10.

In a poll, the people of Leningrad voted (55 percent to 43 percent) to change the name of the city to St. Petersburg. It had been called St. Petersburg in 1703, after Peter the Great, and in 1924 had been renamed in honor of Lenin.

July 1. The Supreme Soviet passed a **bill on the basic principles of destatization** (transfer of state assets to joint stock companies) and **privatization** (the sale of shares to private individuals) of enterprises. The law envisaged denationalization of 40 to 50 percent of state assets by the end of 1992 and of 60 to 70 percent by 1995.

July 2. The Supreme Soviet passed **legislation allowing republics to draft their own criminal codes** within certain guidelines.

July 23. The Soviet Union decided to apply for full membership in the International Monetary Fund and the World Bank.

July 30–31. In a summit meeting between President Gorbachev and President Bush, **the USSR and the U.S. signed a Strategic Arms Reduction Treaty (START),** which committed each side to reducing its nuclear weapons by 30 percent. Meanwhile, the U.S. granted the USSR most-favored-nation status.

Aug. 19. Conservatives attempted to depose Gorbachev in a three-day coup. The coup was strongly opposed by the prodemocratic forces led by Yeltsin. Opposition of the armed forces was a major reason for the failure of the coup. The Supreme Soviet suspended all activities of the Communist Party (Aug. 29), effectively dissolving it.

Aug.–Sept. Independence declarations: Estonia and Latvia declared their independence on Aug. 20 and 21, respectively. Soviet security forces and troops began to withdraw. The CPSU was banned in Estonia, Latvia, and Lithuania. The RSFSR recognized Estonian and Latvian independence (Aug. 24). **The State Council of the Soviet Union recognized the independence of the three Baltic republics** (Sept. 6), and they were also admitted to the United Nations on Sept. 17. **Moldova declared its independence on Aug. 27,** which Romania recognized; Romania set up formal diplomatic relations with Moldova on Aug. 29. **Azerbaijan declared its independence on Aug. 30. Uzbekistan declared its independence on Aug. 31** and changed its name to the **Republic of Uzbekistan. Ukraine adopted an independence resolution on Aug. 24,** pending a referendum on Dec. 1. The **Belorussian Supreme Soviet voted to declare political and economic independence on Aug. 25** and changed its name to the **Republic of Belarus. Tajikistan became the twelfth Soviet republic to declare its independence (Sept. 9);** only the Russian Federation, Kazakhstan, and Turkmenistan had not done so.

Oct. 11. The State Council decided to **abolish the KGB** (Committee for State Security) and to form instead units concerned with border defense, intelligence, and counterintelligence.

Oct. 21. The first session of the new USSR Supreme Soviet was convened, but with only seven republics—the Russian Federation, Kazakhstan, Belarus, Uzbekistan, Kirghizia, Tajikistan, and Turkmenistan.

Nov. 4. The abolition of union ministries and the agreement to form a union of sovereign states. The State Council, attended by the leaders of all 12 republics except Moldova and Armenia, agreed on the abolition of all union ministries except those for the railway, atomic power, and electricity, as well as the defense and foreign affairs ministries.

Dec. 21. The end of the Soviet Union and the formation of a Commonwealth of Independent States (CIS). Eleven of the former constituent republics of the Soviet Union (Georgia was absent) signed a protocol at Alma Ata on the formation of the CIS. This loose alliance had no central governing bodies, and the Russian Federation took over many of the functions of the former union. **Gorbachev resigned as president of the Soviet Union on Dec. 25.**

1992, March 13. The CIS agreed on repayment of the former Soviet Union's foreign debt.

April 1. Seven CIS states agreed to establish an interparliamentary assembly for further coordination.

2. POST-SOVIET SUCCESSOR REPUBLICS IN EUROPE AND ASIA

a. Armenia

1990, Aug. 23. Armenia declared its independence and changed its name to the **Republic of Armenia.** (A referendum in September 1991 favored independence.)

Oct. 5. Paruir Airikyan, an exiled Armenian nationalist, was restored to citizenship and returned to Armenia in early November.

Nov. 30. Stepan Pogosyan was elected first secretary of the Armenian Communist Party.

1991, Sept. 21. In a referendum on independence, voters—in a 95.5 percent turnout—voted over 94 percent in favor of secession. And on Sept. 23 **the republic was declared an independent state.**

1992, June 11. Parliament adopted a law on privatization and denationalization.

Oct. 16. Foreign Minister Raffi Hovhannesyan resigned at the request of President Levon Ter-Petrosyan over "apparent policy disagreements," and on Nov. 10 Arman Kirakosyan was appointed acting foreign minister.

1993, Jan. 23. The entire republic was without power when, in a territorial dispute with Azerbaijan, Azeris in the Marneulskiy region of Georgia blew up a section of pipeline bringing gas to Armenia. This epitomized the country's worsening energy shortage, which continued through January.

Feb. 2. President Ter-Petrossian dismissed Prime Minister Khosrov Haroutunian for criticizing the government's draft budget and economic plan.

Sept. 17. Prime Minister Hrand Bagratian declared Armenia's food shortage "catastrophic." Armenia's neighbors, Iran and Turkey, had stopped trade in protest of Armenia's role in its dispute with Azerbaijan.

Nov. 1. Government opposition parties, along with some progovernment deputies, attacked the government's proposed privatization plans. In a compromise, the opposition Communists voted in favor of a plan that provided that 20 percent of the state enterprises would be turned over to the workers' collectives before privatization.

1995, July 5. Armenia held its first parliamentary elections. The progovernment Republican party won the most seats.

1997, March 20. Armenia named **Robert Kocharyan,** a former war hero, as its new **premier.**

1998, Feb. 3. As a conflict arose with Premier Robert Kocharyan over the disputed Nagorno-Karabakh region, Pres. Ter-Petrossian resigned from office.

March 30. Runoff elections for the presidency were won by Premier Robert Kocharyan, an Armenian nationalist who was born in the Nagorno-Karabakh enclave.

1999, July–Aug. The presidents of Armenia and Azerbaijan met to discuss peace in the Nagorno-Karabakh territory, an area of conflict between the two nations.

Oct. 27. Prime Minister Vazgen Sarkissian and seven others were murdered when five armed assailants entered the Armenian Parliament building and began firing.

Nov. 3. Pres. Kocharyan named Sarkissian's brother, Aram Sarkissian, as the new prime minister.

b. Azerbaijan

1990, Dec. 1. Ayaz Mutalibov, president of Azerbaijan, announced the adoption of the new name **Republic of Azerbaijan** to replace the Soviet Socialist Republic of Azerbaijan.

1991, Aug. 30. Azerbaijan declared its independence from the Soviet Union.

Oct. 10. The Azerbaijani Supreme Soviet voted to establish a republican defense force.

1992, Feb.–March. Fighting intensified around the regional capital, Stepankert, in **Nagorno-Karabakh,** a disputed area between Armenia and Azerbaijan within the Armenian enclave in Azerbaijan. A cease-fire was reached in September but was frequently violated.

March 6. President Mutalibov resigned after an all-night demonstration outside the Parliament building over his failure to defend Azeri lives in Nagorno-Karabakh.

June 7. Abulfez Elchibey, leader of the Azerbaijani Popular Front, was elected president with more than 59 percent of the vote in an election with 76 percent voter turnout.

1993, June 15. Heydar Aliyev, leader of the Nakhichevan autonomous region, was elected chair of the Azerbaijan Supreme Soviet.

June 18. President Elchibey was forced to flee Baku in the face of a rebellion led by Col. Surat Guseinov. Guseinov claimed for himself "all the powers of a head of state and responsibility for the future of the republic" (June 21).

Oct. 3. Heydar Aliyev secured 98.8 percent of the vote in the presidential election, with 97 percent voter turnout.

1997, Nov. 12. A pipeline running through Azerbaijan was opened to transport oil from the Caspian Sea to the Russian port of Novorossiysk.

1998, Oct. 11. In an election deemed fraudulent by international observers, Pres. Heydar Aliyev was reelected as the Azerbaijan head of state.

1999, April 17. A 515-mile pipeline running through Azerbaijan and Georgia was opened. Pipeline construction over a two-year period cost $1.5 billion. The Azerbaijan government and three major oil corporations signed a deal worth an estimated $10 billion.

2000, Nov. 6. Amid charges by opposition leaders of fraud and vote-rigging, the Central Election Commission gave a victory in parliamentary elections to the ruling New Azerbaijan Party. Though widespread protests followed, **Pres. Heydar Aliyev's son, Ilham, was named prime minister.**

c. Belarus

1990, July 27. Belorussia declared itself sovereign, like the Ukraine, giving itself the right to "voluntary unions with other states, and free withdrawal from such unions."

Dec. The Belorussian Communist Party elected its first secretary, Antoly Malofeyev.

March 1. Miners in the Donbass, Vorkuta, and Karaganda coalfields began a strike, demanding 100- to 150-percent pay increases. The strike extended into April and came to an end May 10 without any settlement.

Aug. 25. Belorussia's president, Nikolai Dementei, resigned, and the Supreme Soviet voted to declare "the political and economic independence of Belorussia."

Sept. 18. The Supreme Soviet of Belorussia announced that the republic would be renamed the **Republic of Belarus,** and Stanislav Shushkevich was elected as the new chair of the Supreme Soviet—the de facto president of the republic.

1992, May 25. The government introduced its own internal currency, the ruble.

1993, Feb. 3. The Supreme Soviet lifted the bans imposed in August 1991 on the Communist Party of the Soviet Union (CPSU) and on the Communist Party of Belarus.

June 5. The Federation of Trade Unions threatened a strike after the government announced a package of price increases for food, electricity, and municipal services.

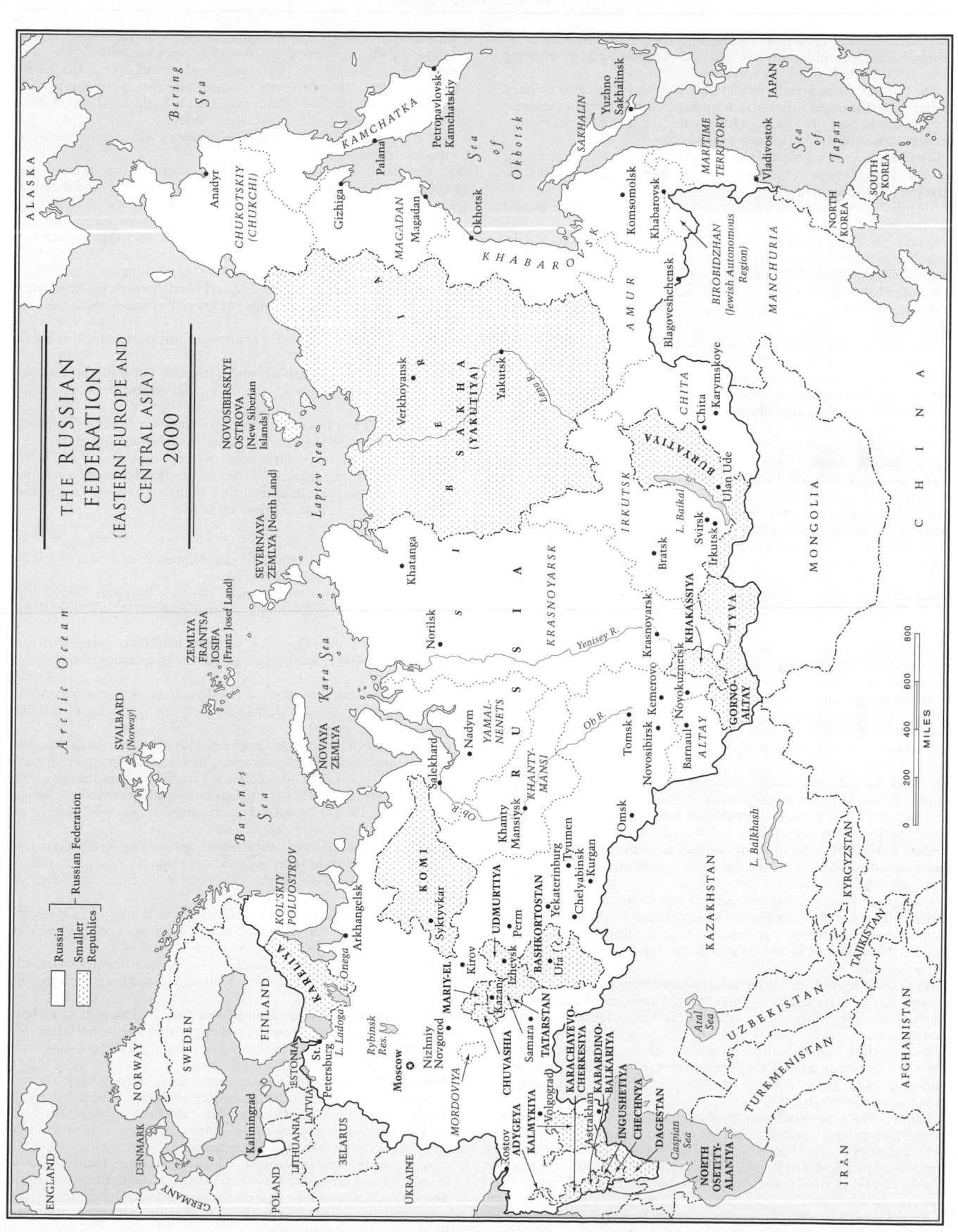

1994, Jan. 5. Belarus set an economic union with Russia, instantly transferring 1.6 trillion rubles into the Belarusan economy and threatening to destabilize the Russian economy.

Jan. 26. The Belarusan head of state, **Stanislav S. Shushkevich,** a liberal, was **dismissed because of his support for free market reforms** and his **opposition to aligning with Russia.** On Jan. 28 former Communist **Mechislav Grib was elected** in his place.

June 23. Alexander Lukashenko, a populist known for speaking out against corruption, won the first round of presidential elections. He **won the presidency** on July 10.

1997, April 2. Belarus signed a treaty **agreeing to become more closely integrated with Russia.**

1998, July 13. The 15 nations of the EU banned 130 high-level Belarusan officials from traveling to EU countries. A response to Belarus's efforts to expel numerous foreign diplomats from its borders, the ban on officials included Belarus president Alexander Lukashenko. Belarus rescinded its diplomatic eviction order on Oct. 28.

Sept.–Dec. Highly dependent on Russia to import its goods—Russia buys nearly 70 percent of Belarus's exports—the economy of Belarus plummeted as a Russian recession set in.

1999, July. Authoritarian president Lukashenko canceled planned elections that would have challenged his regime; he cited a 1996 amendment to the constitution that he claimed extended his term into 2001. Governmental turmoil ensued in Belarus, and Lukashenko soon disbanded the Parliament.

July 20. Semyon Sharetsky was chosen as acting Belarusan president by a group of 35 members of the disbanded Parliament. This secret referendum came in light of Pres. Lukashenko's cancellation of elections earlier in the year. Still claiming his position as head executive, Sharetsky fled for safety.

Oct.–Dec. Demonstrators in Minsk protested the mysterious disappearances of opposition leaders and the proposed reunification with Russia. On Dec. 8 Pres. Lukashenko signed an agreement in Moscow that further connected Belarus with Russia, economically and militarily.

2000, Oct. 15. In parliamentary elections, pro-government candidates were overwhelmingly victorious, although Western governments, opposed to Lukashenko's regime for some time, remained highly skeptical and refused to recognize the election as legitimate.

d. Estonia

1989, Nov. The Estonian Supreme Soviet declared the republic "sovereign."

1990, May. Estonia moved toward independence. On May 8, the **Estonian Supreme Soviet restored** five key articles of its **1938 constitution** and changed its name to **the Republic of Estonia.** It also abolished the state emblem, flag, and anthem of Soviet Estonia. On May 14, **Gorbachev issued decrees outlawing the independence declaration of Estonia,** asserting that it violated the USSR constitution and the laws of April 30, 1990.

1991, March 3. The Estonian government refused to take part in the all-union referendum held by the Soviet Union and held its own, asking if voters were in favor of a restoration of state independence. The official results showed nearly 78 percent in favor with an 83 percent voter turnout.

Aug. 20. Estonia declared its independence from the Soviet Union.

Sept. 6. The State Council of the Soviet Union voted unanimously to recognize the independence of the republics of Lithuania, Latvia, and Estonia.

Nov. 6. The Estonian parliament voted to reinstate the 1938 Law on Citizenship, which gave automatic citizenship to all Estonians, set a two-year waiting period for immigrants, and granted citizenship to those married to Estonians.

Jan. 23. The government resigned after failing to convince the Supreme Council (parliament) to impose a state of emergency because of severe shortages of oil, grain, and raw materials. Food rationing was introduced as a result of Russia's failure to maintain agreed supplies. A new caretaker government was created under Prime Minister Tiit Vahi (Jan. 30).

April 6. Jaan Manitski was endorsed by the Supreme Council as the new foreign minister, replacing Lennart Meri.

June 28. The Constituent Assembly drafted a constitution that provided for a parliamentary system with a strong presidency.

Sept. 20. In Estonia's first postindependence elections, the right-wing nationalist fatherland group (Isamaa) and other right-wing parties won a strong position in the Supreme Council. In the presidential elections, no candidate gained an overall majority.

Oct. 5. Lennart Meri, former foreign minister, was elected president by the Supreme Council.

1993, June 21. The government passed a measure that **defined the 500,000 former Soviet citizens in Estonia as "foreigners"** and required them to apply for a residence permit or face expulsion.

Oct. 26. The Riigikogu (legislature) adopted a law on cultural autonomy for ethnic minorities, which entitled minorities that included at least 3,000 citizens to establish cultural, religious, and educational institutions, for which state funding was made possible.

1994, July 26. Estonian president **Lennart Meri** came to an agreement with Yeltsin mandating the **pullout of Russian troops** from Estonia **by August 31.**

1995, March 5. Estonia ousted its ruling government, replacing them with former Communists.

Oct. 11. The Estonian **cabinet under Premier Tiit Vahi resigned because of a scandal** involving the wire-tapping of official conversations.

1998, March 30. The EU invited Estonia to apply for membership along with Poland, Cyprus, Hungary, Slovenia, and the Czech Republic.

1999, March 7. In Estonia's parliamentary elections, a coalition of three Center-Right parties regained control of the legislature by a narrow margin. For the second time, free-market supporter **Mart Laar of the Fatherland Party was named prime minister.**

e. Georgia

1990, Nov. 11. Elections to the Georgian Supreme Soviet were won by the pro-independence nationalist bloc.

Nov. 14. In a constituent session, the new Supreme Soviet proclaimed the Republic of Georgia, dropping "Soviet" and "Socialist" from its name.

Dec. 8. The Georgian Communist Party ended its congress with the announcement that it was seceding from the Communist Party of the Soviet Union.

1991, Feb. 1. Interethnic unrest in the autonomous oblast (region) of South Ossetia continued with the suspension of supplies of electricity and water to the region.

March 31. The Georgian government refused to take part in the all-union referendum held by the Soviet Union and held its own in conjunction with local council elections, asking if voters thought that state independence should be restored on the basis of the independence act of May 26, 1918. The official results showed nearly 99 percent in favor with a 90.5 percent voter turnout.

April 9. The Georgian Supreme Soviet adopted unanimously a formal declaration of state independence and elected Zviad Gamsakhurdia, a strong nationalist, to the new post of executive president of Georgia.

Sept. 2. The Georgian National Guard opened fire on 2,000 demonstrators in Tbilisi who were demanding the resignations of President Gamsakhurdia and the Georgian Supreme Soviet.

Sept. 6. Akaky Asatiani, chair of the Georgian Supreme Soviet, announced that Georgia had broken off all official relations with the Soviet Union.

1992, Jan. 6. President Gamsakhurdia fled after four months of violent conflict between his government and opposition forces in Tbilisi.

Feb. 10. Prime Minister Tengiz Sigua announced a grave economic situation, including food and fuel shortages.

March 6. Eduard Shevardnadze, former Soviet foreign minister and first secretary of the Central Committee of the Communist Party of Georgia, returned to Georgia for the first time in three years. The Military Council transferred legislative and executive powers to a newly created State Council led by Shevardnadze.

Aug. Tension between Georgia and its autonomous republic of Abkhazia escalated into armed conflict, causing more than 100 deaths.

Oct. 11. In elections for a new parliament, Eduard Shevardnadze was elected parliamentary chair with more than 95 percent of the vote (effectively a presidential role).

1993, Aug. 20. Otar Patsatsia was confirmed as Georgia's new prime minister.

Nov. 2. President Shevardnadze introduced the punishment of summary execution for rebels loyal to the deposed former president, Zviad Gamsakhurdia.

1994, Jan. 13. Georgia signed a peace agreement with its secessionist region of Abkhavia.

Feb. 3. Under **President Eduard A. Shevardnadze,** Georgia signed a military treaty and other cooperation pacts with Russia in hopes of improving their previously strained relations.

1998, Feb. 9. As several gunmen attacked his motorcade, **Pres. Eduard A. Shevardnadze** survived an assassination attempt, the second since 1995.

Oct. 19. A military mutiny of over 200 soldiers in opposition of the Shevardnadze government was put down by the Georgia military forces.

1999, Oct. 31. Pres. Shevardnadze's ruling Citizens Union Party won a majority in parliamentary elections. This victory was a surprise to most observers and analysts, who predicted that the Citizens Union would lose its legislative majority.

2000, April 9. Pres. Shevardnadze was reelected to his third term, winning nearly 80 percent of the vote.

June 14. Georgia became the 137th nation to join the WTO.

f. Kazakhstan

1990, Oct. 25. Kazakhstan declared itself sovereign. It was one of three new republics (with Belarus and Ukraine) with nuclear weapons.

1991, Aug. 28. The Kazakh Communist Party dissolved itself and created an organization uniting progressive forces. Former party officials were banned from holding senior state posts.

Sept. 8. The Kazakh Communist Party voted to withdraw from the Communist Party of the Soviet Union and become the independent Socialist Party of Kazakhstan (SPK).

Dec. 1. Nursultan Nazarbayev, running unopposed, was elected president of Kazakhstan by popular mandate.

Dec. 16. The Supreme Soviet passed a law declaring Kazakhstan's independence, which was recognized by Russia on the following day. On Dec. 10 the Supreme Soviet had changed the republic's name to **Republic of Kazakhstan,** dropping the words "Soviet Socialist."

1992, Feb. 24–25. A riot of more than 17,000 construction workers took place at the Baikonur space center in Leninsk over poor living conditions and maltreatment by officers.

May 8. The president transferred all military property of joint Commonwealth of Independent States (CIS) armed forces on Kazakh territory to the jurisdiction of Kazakhstan.

June 2. A new draft constitution was adopted by the Supreme Soviet.

Oct. 11. Three Kazakh opposition parties, the Azat (Freedom) Party, the National Democratic Party Jeltoksan, and the Republican Party, merged to form the Republican Party, Azat. Kamal Ormantayev, a member of the Kazakh Academy of Sciences, was elected chair.

1993, Jan. 28. The Supreme Kenges (Parliament) voted to adopt a new constitution.

Feb. 6. The People's Unity Union, a progovernment party, assembled in Alma Ata and adopted a program backing radical economic reform and political pluralism.

March 18. The government's new economic program for 1993 through 1995 was announced. A nationwide privatization program was introduced, as well as new rules on hard currency disposal and a state monopoly on alcohol and tobacco.

Nov. 2. The first round of mass privatization began with the free distribution of vouchers in some parts of the country.

1994, Jan. Kazakhstan and Uzbekistan signed an economic agreement at Tashkent, abolishing tariffs and border customs between them.

Feb. The International Monetary Fund lent Kazakhstan $225 million in order to assist and encourage economic and financial reforms.

March 7. Kazakhstan held its **first parliamentary elections.**

1995, Feb. 10. Commonwealth of Independent States leaders met in Kazakhstan and signed an informal pact to work toward encouraging and maintaining peace and stability in their region.

March 11. Nursultan Nazarbayav, the president of Kazakhstan, **dissolved the Parliament** and declared himself ruler until the next elections.

1998, June 9. Formerly known as Akmola, the remote city of Astana was made Kazakhstan's new capital, possibly for reasons of national security.

July. Pres. Nazarbayev signed a pact with Russia, resolving the disputed territorial rights to the oil-rich northern Caspian Sea.

1999, Jan. 10. In a referendum held 18 months ahead of schedule, **Pres. Nazarbayev was elected to his second term as president.** His main opposition, former prime minister Akezhan Kazhegeldin, was barred from the election on a technicality.

Oct. 12. Kasymzhomart Tokayev was sworn in as Kazakhstan's new prime minister following the Oct. 1 resignation of Nurlan Balgimbayev.

Dec. Nine oil companies and the governments of Kazakhstan, Oman, and Russia signed an agreement worth $2 billion to build a 900-mile pipeline from western Kazakhstan to Russia's Black Sea port, Novorossiysk.

g. Kirghizstan

1990, Oct. 28. Aksar Akayev, president of the Academy of Sciences, was selected as the new executive president.

Oct. 30. Kirghizstan declared itself sovereign.

Dec. 13. The Kirghiz Supreme Soviet announced the republic's new name, the **Republic of Kirghizstan.**

1991, Aug. 28. President Akayev left the Communist Party of the Soviet Union, and the Kirghiz Communist Party Politburo and secretariat were retired. Party property was nationalized and funds frozen. Finally, the party's activities were suspended for six months (Aug. 30).

Oct. 12. Askar Akayev, a democrat eager to develop contacts with capitalist countries, was elected president with more than 95 percent of the vote and 90 percent turnout.

1992, June 22. A constituent congress of the Party of Communists of Kirghizstan was attended by about 250 delegates, including many young people.

June 25. An economic reform program developed with International Monetary Fund advice (lower budget expenditures, tighter credit policy, the formation of a banking system, and accelerated privatization) was approved by a joint session of the presidential State Council and the government.

Aug. 20. An earthquake centered in the Susamyr Valley, measuring 7.5 on the Richter scale, killed 50 people and injured more than 200.

1993, April 3. Several centrist parties announced that they had agreed to form a bloc "for the sake of political stability."

May 5. The first postindependence constitution was formally adopted.

May 10. The government adopted a new currency, the som, which replaced the ruble.

Oct. 30. Kirghiz president Askar Akeyev issued a decree reversing the government censorship allegedly introduced in August.

1994, Feb. Kirghizstan, under its leader **Askar Akayev,** joined the **economic union of former Soviet Central Asian Republics,** including Kazakhstan and Uzbekistan, with a view toward **resisting Russian political influence and demands.**

Sept. 5. The **government** under Akayev **resigned** because of political infighting in the Parliament. Akayev called for new elections.

1998, Oct. 17. Through a national referendum, the **Kirghizstan Constitution was amended to allow for private land ownership.** The amendments also sought to further restrict the powers of the Parliament.

2000, Feb. 20. Under close observation by international monitors, parliamentary elections were held in Kirghizstan with the Communist Party taking 28 percent of the vote and the pro-government Union of Democratic Forces securing 17 percent. The Organization for Security and Cooperation in Europe (OSCE) noted several violations that tainted the election. Under diminishing public approval, Pres. Akayev was accused by the opposition of cheating. Most of the prominent opposition parties were kept out of the election through various judiciary rulings.

h. Latvia

1990, May. Latvia moved toward independence. On May 4, **the new Supreme Soviet in Latvia passed an independence resolution** by restoring the pre-1940 constitution of the independent Latvian republic, and changed its name to the **Republic of Latvia.** Its independence move, however, did not reject the validity of the Soviet constitution and laws. On May 14, **Mikhail Gorbachev issued decrees outlawing the independence declaration of Latvia,** asserting that it violated the USSR constitution and the laws of April 30, 1990.

May 3–4. Demonstrators, both pro- and anti-independence, gathered outside the Latvian Supreme Soviet building. On May 14, army cadets protested against independence outside the Supreme Soviet building.

1991, Jan. 2. The OMON or Black Berets, a paramilitary police force formed by the Soviet Interior Ministry in 1987, seized Riga's main press building. This was part of a crackdown by the USSR on the Baltic republics, initiated by President Gorbachev.

March 3. The Latvian government refused to take part in the all-union referendum held by the Soviet Union and held its own, asking if voters were in favor of an independent Latvian republic. The official results showed nearly 74 percent in favor, with 87 percent voter turnout.

Aug. 21. Latvia declared its independence from the Soviet Union.

Sept. 6. The State Council of the Soviet Union voted unanimously to recognize the independence of the republics of Lithuania, Latvia, and Estonia.

1992, May 6. The Latvian Currency Reform Committee introduced a Latvian ruble to circulate in parallel with the former Soviet ruble.

Aug. 9. Latvia joined the World Bank. It was admitted to the **International Monetary Fund in May.**

1993, March 5. The government introduced a new currency called the lat, which replaced the ruble.

Oct. 6. The government banned three procommunist organizations, the Latvian Union of Communists, the Union to Secure Veterans' Rights, and the Latvian Association of Russian Citizens, alleging 22 acts of conspiracy.

1994, Jan. Latvia and Lithuania agreed to build an oil terminal at the Baltic Sea port of Liepaja, Latvia, so that Lithuania's Mazeikiai refinery would not have to depend only on Russian resources.

April 30. Latvia signed a treaty with Russia saying that **Russian troops would completely withdraw from Latvia, leaving Estonia the only remaining Baltic state to be occupied by Russian forces.**

1997, Jan. 20. Latvian premier **Andris Skele resigned** after making a controversial appointment for the position of finance minister and being accused of conflict of interest violations.

1998, Oct. 3. In response to international pressure from the U.S. and the EU, **Latvia voted to ease its citizenship requirements** that had excluded from citizenship over one-half million ethnic Russians who inhabited the country. However, competency in the Latvian language remained a requirement for official naturalization and citizenship.

In another referendum, parliamentary elections saw great division between various parties, and none were even close to gaining a legislative majority. Former premier Andris Skele regained the premiership briefly when his People's Party formed a coalition government. Skele succeeded Guntar Krasts as premier, who had held the position for less than a month. In November, Skele was replaced by Vilis Kristopanis.

1999, June 17. The legislature elected Vaira Vike-Frieberga as Latvia's first woman president, the only female president ever elected in an ex-Soviet republic.

July 16. The Kristopanis government failed when agreement waned within his ruling coalition. The succeeding government, led by Andris Skele, collapsed on April 12, 2000.

Dec. 10. Latvia was one of seven nations to receive an invitation from the EU to apply for membership. The other countries were Slovakia, Bulgaria, Romania, Malta, Turkey, and Lithuania.

2000, April 25. Riga mayor Andris Berzins was nominated to succeed Andris Skele as prime minister.

i. Lithuania

1989, May 18. The Lithuanian Supreme Council passed a declaration of sovereignty.

Dec. 19–20. The Lithuanian Communist Party split from the Soviet Party.

1990, March 11. Lithuania declared its independence after all 124 delegates to its new parliament voted in favor. They also voted to change the republic's name by dropping the words "Soviet Socialist." **Vytautas Landsbergis** was elected chair (head of state).

March 14. The all-Soviet **Congress passed a resolution** by a large majority that the **Lithuanian declaration of independence had no legal force.**

March 17. Kazimiera Prunskiene was elected prime minister.

March 22. Mikhail Gorbachev, using his new powers as Soviet president, **increased pressure on Lithuania by forbidding the ownership of guns** and tightening immigration and customs controls on the republic. There was also a show of strength in the capital, Vilnius, as the **Red Army patrolled the streets in armored cars.** On Apr. 21 the **Soviet Union imposed an economic blockade on Lithuania,** including the reduction of oil and gas supplies.

June 23. The Lithuanian Supreme Council accepted in principle a moratorium on the declaration of independence, and the Soviet economic blockade ended.

Dec. 8–9. The Lithuanian Communist Party reorganized itself as the Lithuanian Democratic Labor Party.

1991, Jan. 6. Prime Minister Prunskiene announced steep price increases. Parliament refused to approve them and forced her resignation.

Jan. 11. Soviet forces seized the headquarters of the Lithuanian Defense Council, the day after President Gorbachev ordered the restoration of the Soviet constitution in Lithuania.

Jan. 13. Soviet troops seized the television center and tower in Vilnius. Fifteen people were killed, shot to death or crushed by tanks.

Feb. 9. A referendum regarding independence produced an overwhelming majority in favor.

June 4. Soviet troops surrounded the Parliament building in Vilnius and set up checkpoints around the city, raising fears of a forced takeover.

Sept. 6. The State Council of the Soviet Union voted unanimously to recognize the independence of the republics of Lithuania, Latvia, and Estonia.

Oct. 10. Lithuania formally established diplomatic relations with the Soviet Union.

Nov. 5. The Lithuanian Parliament adopted a law on issuing currency, the litas.

Nov. 11. Retail prices of consumer goods were liberalized and food prices went up. On Nov. 19 industrial prices were also freed.

1992, July 4. Prime Minister Gediminas Vagnorius was forced to resign by the Lithuanian Supreme Council. He was replaced by Aleksandras Abisala, a right-wing independent.

Oct. 25. Algirdas Brazauskas and the Lithuanian Democratic Labor Party (formerly the Communist Party) won an overwhelming victory in the parliamentary elections. When Parliament met in November, Brazauskas was elected chair, replacing Landsbergis, and Bronislovas Lubys, a Liberal and former deputy premier, was elected prime minister.

1993, Feb. 14. Algirdas Brazauskas was elected president, beating the rightist candidate, Stasys Lozoraitis.

March 10. President Brazauskas appointed **Adolfas Slezevicius** as prime minister. Slezevicius subsequently announced a new government (March 16).

1996, Feb. 8. The Lithuanian Parliament voted to dismiss premier Adolfas Slezevicius because of his involvement in a banking scandal. On Feb. 15 **Mindavgas Stankevicius** was appointed in his place.

1998, Jan. 4. In a runoff election, **Lithuanian-American Valdas Adamkus won the presidency.** Adamkus was strongly backed by the former leader of the Communist Party, Algirdas Brazauskas.

1999, May 18. With pressure from Pres. Adamkus, Premier Vagnorius resigned and was replaced with pro-Adamkus leader Rolandas Paksas.

Oct. 27. After the cabinet agreed to privatize Lithuania's Mazheikiu Nafta oil refinery, Paksas resigned in protest and was replaced by Irena Degutiene.

Dec. 10. Lithuania was one of seven nations to be officially invited to apply to the EU. Also named in the EU announcement were Latvia, Slovakia, Bulgaria, Romania, Malta, and Turkey.

j. Moldova

1990, June 23. Moldavia declared its sovereignty and asserted the supremacy of the Moldavian constitution and laws throughout the republic, now called **Moldova.**

1991, Feb. 21. Moldova's president, Mircea Snegur turned in his resignation, citing increased media attacks on him by the Moldovan Communist Party.

Aug. 27. Moldova declared its independence from the Soviet Union.

Dec. 8. Mircea Snegur was elected president in popular elections. With a turnout of more than 82 percent, 98 percent voted for Snegur.

1992, March 28. President Snegur imposed a state of emergency following a month of skirmishes and fighting in the self-proclaimed Dnestr republic. The mainly Russian and Ukrainian people in the region wanted to separate because they believed the Moldovan government was drawing closer to Romania and imposing Romanian culture and language on the whole republic.

July 21. An agreement was signed between Russian President Boris Yeltsin and Moldova's Snegur in an attempt to halt fighting in the Dnestr republic. The agreement gave special status to the Dnestr region and the right to self-determination in the case of Moldova's unification with Romania.

1993, May 7. The government announced a massive privatization program and introduced a new national currency called the leu—the same name as the Romanian currency.

Sept. 9. The presidium of the Moldovan parliament voted to legalize the Moldovan Communist Party, which had been banned following the August 1991 Soviet coup attempt.

1998, March 22. Although the Communists won the most seats in legislative elections, a coalition of three Center-Right parties joined to garner a majority and form the new government.

Sept.–Dec. The Russian financial crisis spread quickly through the largely agricultural region of Moldova. With a desperately ailing economy and a growing number of impoverished citizens, **some 600,000 Moldovans fled the country.**

1999, Feb. 1. In the face of a stagnating economy, Prime Minister Ion Ciubuc resigned and was replaced by Ion Sturza on March 12.

March 22. Pres. Petru Lucinschi proposed a constitutional amendment, which was to be approved through referendum, that would substantially increase presidential powers.

k. Russian Federation

1990, June 12. The **Russian Federation,** the largest and most powerful republic of the Soviet Union, **declared itself a sovereign state** with the right to determine its own economic and political future and "the right to freely leave the USSR."

1991, June 12. Boris Yeltsin was elected president of the Russian Federation (RFSFR) in the first general election in Russian history; he was sworn in on July 10.

1992, March 31. A Federation Treaty was signed by 18 of the 20 autonomous republics within the Russian Federation, delimiting powers between the center and the regions.

April. Confrontation between the Russian Congress and the Yeltsin government: the 6th Russian Congress of the People's Deputies, led by chairman Ruslan Khasbulatov, criticized the government's economic reforms. The criticism provoked the resignation of the government (made up of young economists), but Yeltsin refused to accept it. Compromise was eventually reached when the Congress declared its support for economic reforms. The conflict between the Congress and Yeltsin continued and reached a critical climax in March 1993, when Yeltsin claimed emergency powers and suspended the Congress. In an April 25 referendum, the majority voted confidence in Yeltsin and thus strengthened his position as president.

May 7. President Yeltsin issued a decree to establish Russian Federation armed forces and made himself commander-in-chief. All former Soviet Union troops on Russian territory and those outside of Russia but under its jurisdiction were included in the armed forces.

June. Progress of economic reform in the Russian Federation: the Congress passed mass privatization legislation on June 11 to enable citizens to purchase shares in state property. A presidential decree on June 14 permitted the sale of land to private owners and allowed state enterprises to declare bankruptcy for liquidation.

Dec. 1–14. The 7th Congress of Russian People's Deputies (Russia's supreme legislature) met, following months of political maneuvering between President Boris Yeltsin and the Civic Union.

1993, Feb. 11. President Yeltsin and Supreme Soviet chair Ruslan Khasbulatov held a round of talks in Moscow but failed to reach any agreement. The two were locked in confrontation during February, essentially over whether supreme political power in post-Communist Russia resided with the presidency or the legislature.

March 20. President Yeltsin addressed the nation on television, saying he had signed a series of decrees introducing a special regime and had scheduled April 25 for a national vote of confidence in the president and a vote on the new constitution. The Congress of People's Deputies would cease to exist under the new constitution. On March 22 the Constitutional Court began examining the legality of Yeltsin's address and decreed that Yeltsin had exceeded his authority. The climax came on March 28 with a motion to dismiss Yeltsin as president, which was voted on by secret ballot. The tally was 617 votes in favor and 268 against, but this fell short of the necessary two-thirds majority of the 1,033 deputies.

April 25. In a **special referendum,** President Yeltsin received an important personal vote of confidence and secured support for his reform programs.

May 1. Up to 600 demonstrators and police were injured in clashes in Moscow, in the worst violence since the failed coup attempt of August 1991, during a protest march organized by pro-Communist and nationalist opponents of President Yeltsin.

May 10. President Yeltsin dismissed **Yury Skokov** from his post as secretary of the Security Council of the Russian Federation. Skokov, one of the most powerful politicians in Russia, had criticized Yeltsin for his introduction of special rule in March.

Sept. 21. President Yeltsin declared the suspension of all "legislative, administrative, and control functions" of the Russian Parliament and called elections to the State Duma (lower house).

Oct. 3–4. Serious armed clashes occurred in Moscow between forces loyal to President Yeltsin and rebels protesting against his suspension of the Parliament.

Nov. 9. Russia's draft constitution was published, to be submitted for approval in a national referendum in December. The constitution included increased presidential powers and decreased parliamentary power.

Dec. 11. In parliamentary elections, Russia's ultranationalist Liberal Democratic Party, described by reform-minded critics, unexpectedly led the popular vote by a wide margin. Party leader Vladimir Volfrovich **Zhirinovsky** commanded 24 percent of those votes cast for parties.

Voters also **approved the new constitution,** with 57 percent in favor.

1994, Jan. The Russian government banned the use of hard currency with the exception of credit cards in an effort to stabilize the ruble; as a result, inflation began to slow. Russia also announced that **15 percent of its territory suffered from serious ecological damage, mostly because of radiation contamination.**

Jan. 11. The **new bicameral Parliament in Russia opened,** and Yeltsin urged them to **establish a legal basis for democracy.**

April 20. The IMF released a loan of $1.5 billion to support economic reform and the building of democracy in Russia. Yeltsin issued a decree on May 23 to increase foreign investments in Russia in the hope of boosting the economy. Russia then announced its desire to participate in the NATO Partnership for Peace initiative, enrolling on June 22. At the EU summit on June 24–25, Russia signed an economic and human rights accord.

July 21. Renowned author **Aleksandr Solzhenitsyn returned to Moscow after living in exile in the United States for 20 years.**

Sept. 5. Forces from the Loyalist government of Chechnya, a secessionist republic in southern Russia, **captured a rebel stronghold,** cutting off links with Russia. Massive violence erupted. On Sept. 15 Chechen **president Dzhokhar Dudayev declared martial law** and imposed a curfew.

Dec. 11. Russian forces invaded Chechnya, launching a full-scale attack on Grozny, the Chechen capital on Dec. 31.

1995, Jan. 3. Russia launched a second full-scale attack. A cease-fire was declared on Jan. 10, to no avail. **The intensity of the attacks increased.** On Jan. 19 Russian troops captured the presidential palace, and in February Pres. Dudayev left Grozny. On March 30–31 the Russians captured the Chechen towns of Gudermes and Shali.

Feb. 23–24. Iran signed an agreement with Russia to have a nuclear reactor for commercial purposes, in spite of objections from the U.S.

June 19. Chechen rebels released Russian hostages they had taken while raiding the Russian town of Budennovsk.

July 11. Yeltsin was hospitalized with serious heart problems. He was hospitalized again on Oct. 26.

July 30. Russia and Chechnya reached an accord to end the war after six weeks of peace talks. Russia agreed to withdraw its troops.

Dec. 17. In elections, **Communists made huge gains in the Russian Parliament,** possibly because of popular protest against Yeltsin's economic reform policies.

1996, Jan. 15. Russian forces assaulted separatist guerrillas in the Chechnya-held village of Pervomayskoye.

March 31. Yeltsin unveiled a peace plan for Chechnya.

April 2. Russia and Belarus signed a treaty joining in an economic and political union called the **Community of Sovereign Republics.**

May 27. Russia and Chechnya signed a peace accord.

July 3. Yeltsin was reelected in a runoff, thwarting the possible resurgence of communism under Gennadi Zyuganov.

Aug. 6. Separatist rebels in Chechnya launched new attacks in Grozny.

Aug. 22. Russia and Chechen rebels signed a cease-fire.

Oct. 17. Yeltsin fired his security chief, Aleksandr Lebed. Earlier Lebed had encouraged NATO to consult with Russia before including more Eastern European nations. He was also actively involved in the conflict with Chechnya. On Oct. 19 Yeltsin named **Ivan Rybkin** as his new Security Council secretary; Rybkin said he would continue the peace negotiations with Chechnya.

1997, Jan. 5. Russia completed its withdrawal from Chechnya.

Jan. 20. Negotiations toward forming a charter between Russia and NATO began.

Jan. 27. Chechnya elected Gen. Aslan Maskhadou president. Russia did not object to these election results.

April 17. Russian finance minister **Anatoly B. Chubais** announced a huge budget crisis, calling for emergency cuts in spending.

May 12. Russia and Chechnya signed a formal peace treaty.

May 14. Russia announced that it would agree to NATO's expansion into former countries of the Soviet bloc.

1998, March 23. Pres. Boris Yeltsin dismissed Prime Minister Viktor Chernomyrdin and replaced him with the little-known **Sergei Kiriyenko.** The Russian government became increasingly unstable throughout 1998, and the economy plummeted into a deep recession.

Aug. 23. Pres. Yeltsin sacked Kiriyenko. The Russian Parliament (the Duma) saw increased friction in the face of economic crisis. The third prime minister in six months, former foreign minister Yevgeny Primakov took office on Sept. 11. Pres. Yeltsin remained in poor health at this time, undergoing a series of treatments and surgeries that took him out of the political sphere for weeks at a time.

Aug. 27–31. The value of the ruble rapidly fell, and Russia defaulted on its debt. Meanwhile, the Russian stock market was in a veritable free fall, and the government halted trading of the ruble on international currency markets. This financial disaster led to an extended economic crisis and its subsequent political upheavals. Economic recession spread throughout the rest of Asia and much of Eastern Europe.

1999, March 24–June 10. NATO conducted a heavy bombing campaign against Pres. Slobodan Milosevic's forces in Yugoslavia (p. 894). As refugees fled into neighboring Macedonia and Albania, Russian relations with NATO and the United States cooled considerably. Because of Russia's support for the Yugoslav government with shipments of food and supplies, NATO tried with little success to keep Russian influence out of the subsequent peace settlement signed on June 3 in Kosovo.

May 13–15. The Duma attempted to impeach Pres. Boris Yeltsin on five charges, but the impeachment was quickly abandoned; consensus held that most of the complaints brought against Yeltsin were not legitimated offenses that could be used for impeachment. The five charges that stood briefly against him were for provoking the 1991 collapse of the Soviet Union, using force to dissolve the Parliament in 1993, initiating the bloody war with Chechnya in 1994, ruining the Russian military, and causing the severe recession through ill-conceived economic policy.

May 19. Prime Minister Primakov was stripped of his position by Pres. Yeltsin and replaced with Sergei Stepashin. The Stepashin government lasted only a few weeks; on Aug. 9 Yeltsin again shuffled legislative leaders by naming former KGB agent Vladimir Putin as the premier. Many saw Putin as Yeltsin's hand-picked successor to power, especially in light of Yeltsin's failing health and the timing involved: an election was scheduled for the spring of 2001.

Aug. 7–Dec. 26. Russia used military force to subdue uprisings of Islamic rebels in Dagestan. As violence spread, neighboring Chechnya experienced serious conflicts, and Russia launched a full-scale assault. Several terrorist bombings in Moscow and other Russian cities provoked the attack. Fighting had resumed three years after the end of the bloody Chechen-Russian War (1994-1996).

Nov. 28. Russian troops surrounded Grozny, Chechnya's capital, pushing some 215,000 Chechen refugees into nearby Ingushetia.

Dec. 6. The Russian government issued an ultimatum that stated that all 40,000 people still inhabiting Grozny must evacuate the city. Because Western nations condemned Russia's harsh tactics in Chechnya, the terms of the ultimatum were eased somewhat.

Dec. 19. The pro-government Unity Party won a strong majority in Russia's parliamentary elections.

Dec. 31. Claiming political but not health considerations, **Pres. Yeltsin unexpectedly announced his resignation** with six months remaining in his term. After having served as Russia's leader since the fall of the Soviet Union in 1991, Yeltsin named Premier Vladimir Putin to be his successor.

2000, Feb. 6. Russian troops took control of Grozny. Although fighting continued in the region, the Grozny takeover was a huge military and political victory for Russia and for Pres. Putin, whose hard-line stance against Chechnya had greatly improved his political popularity.

March 26. Running on persistently vague campaign promises about specific reform policies, **Pres. Vladimir Putin defeated ten opponents and won his first presidential election.** Garnering 53 percent of the vote, Putin moved to centralize power in Moscow by diminishing the influence of local and regional governments and Russian business leaders. Meanwhile, the Center-Right Unity Party most closely associated with Putin allied itself with the Communists in the Russian legislature. Announcement of the multiparty pact prompted nearly one-fourth of the Duma to walk out of the Russian Parliament building in protest.

April 14. The **Duma approved the second Strategic Arms Reduction Talks Treaty (START II).**

April 21. The Russian Parliament ratified the Comprehensive Test Ban Treaty, which renounced the testing of nuclear weapons throughout the world.

May 17. In a surprising decision by the Duma, a set of Putin-supported legislative changes that diluted the authority of Russia's 89 regional governors and local legislative leaders was passed by a cautious parliament. The laws were modified so that, instead of filling the seats themselves, local legislatures would elect senators to represent them in the upper house of Parliament, known as the Federation Council. The new legislation also gave Putin the power to remove governors and dissolve local legislatures if they violated the law.

June. Vladimir Gusinsky, media tycoon and owner of Russia's only independent television network, was arrested for his alleged embezzlement of government property. Gusinsky's station had criticized the Kremlin for its harsh policies in Chechnya. Other millionaires came under investigation in the mining, oil, and auto industries and faced government prosecution for alleged tax violations.

Aug. 12. Off the northern coast of Russia, **the Russian nuclear submarine Kursk sank in the Barents Sea;** all 118 sailors aboard perished. Raising questions about Russia's political and military stability, the international community severely criticized Moscow's handling of the disaster. The accident was the worst Russian peacetime naval catastrophe in history.

l. Tajikistan

1990, Aug. 25. Tajikistan joined the list of republics that **declared sovereignty** and the precedence of its constitution and laws over those of the Soviet Union.

Nov. 30. Kakhar Makhkamov was elected executive president by the Tajik Supreme Soviet.

1991, Aug. 29. The Tajik Communist Party resolved to leave the Communist Party of the Soviet Union, and the republic dropped "Soviet Socialist" from its name, to become the Republic of Tajikistan.

Sept. 1. President Makhkamov resigned after a vote of no confidence.

Sept. 9. Tajikistan became the twelfth Soviet republic to declare its independence.

Nov. 24. Rakhmon Nabiyev was elected president with 58 percent of the vote and a voter turnout of more than 84 percent.

1992, March 6. The Tajik Supreme Soviet approved a land reform law giving all citizens the right to lifetime ownership of land and to lease and inherit land.

May 8. Demonstrations throughout April and the first part of May by activists opposed to President Nabiyev's regime culminated in the formation of a new coalition government. Nabiyev remained president, however.

Sept. 7. President Nabiyev was forced to resign as a result of serious political confrontations reflecting the regional divisions within the republic.

Nov. 10. Acting President Akbarsho Iskandarov and his coalition government resigned and called for a cease-fire as procommunist militias laid siege to Dushanbe and occupied much of Tajikistan.

1993, June 21. The Tajik Supreme Court banned four opposition parties, the Democratic Party, Lale Badakshon, the Nazdate Islamiye Tajikistan (Islamic Renaissance Party of Tajikistan), and the Rastokhez People's Front (Rebirth). The court accused the parties of fomenting civil war, illegally forming militias, and killing or kidnapping legislators.

1994, Jan. 4. Tajikistan announced that it would no longer accept Soviet era rubles but would accept Russian ones, making it the **only former Soviet state to share the Russian ruble.**

Nov. 6. Tajikistan held its first elections, voting in **President Imamali Rakhmonov** and approving a new constitution.

1997, Jan. 8. The government attacked rebel forces, claiming they had stolen important weapons.

1998, May 2. Although a cease-fire had been signed in 1997, three days of fighting left some 45 people dead and 80 wounded in the capital city of Dushanbe. The fighting halted when the Tajikistan army and Islamic opposition forces agreed to withdraw from the city.

1999, Sept. 26. In a national referendum, Tajikistan voters approved constitutional changes that legalized the formation of Islamic political parties. The vote also extended the presidential term from five to seven years.

Nov. 6. In an election that was highly criticized as illegitimate by international human-rights observers, Pres. Imomali Rakhmonov won the presidency with 96 percent of the vote.

m. Turkmenistan

1990, Aug. 22. Turkmenistan declared its sovereignty.

Oct. 27. Saparmurad Niyazov, first secretary of the Turkmen Communist Party, was unopposed in a direct election for the new post of executive president.

1992, May 18. A new constitution that gave more power to the president was adopted unanimously by the Supreme Soviet.

June 21. Saparmurad Niyazov, former Communist and the sole presidential candidate, was voted into the presidency.

1998, April 23. Pres. Saparmurad A. Niyazov visited the United States and met with Pres. Clinton for talks on the global economy. While on his U.S. tour, Niyazov reached agreements with several U.S. energy firms to research the possibility of a gas pipeline that would pass through Turkey and reach markets in the West.

1999, Dec. 28. Pres. Niyazov (also referred to as Turkmenbashy, or Leader of All Turkmens) **was unanimously elected president for life of Turkmenistan.** Niyazov had created what some international analysts noted as a cult of personality, developed through vigorous self-promotion, propaganda, and an iron-fisted authoritarian reign.

n. Ukraine

1990, July 16. Ukraine declared its sovereignty, which went further than that of Uzbekistan and Moldova. It declared the right to have "its own armed forces, internal security troops, and state security bodies."

Nov. 14. The Ukrainian Supreme Soviet voted to confirm Vitold Fokin, a liberal compromise candidate, as prime minister.

1991, Feb. 12. The Ukrainian Supreme Soviet voted to restore the status

of autonomous Soviet socialist republic (ASSR) to the Crimea within the Ukraine.

March 30. Cardinal Miroslav Lubachivsky, 77, the spiritual leader of 5 million Ukrainian Catholics (known as Uniates), returned after 52 years in exile in Rome. His return marked the rejuvenation of the Uniate Church, which had been outlawed by Stalin.

Aug. 24. The Supreme Soviet of the Ukraine adopted a resolution declaring its independence from the Soviet Union, pending a referendum on Dec. 1.

Aug. 31. The chairman of the Ukrainian Supreme Soviet, Leonid Kravchuk, banned the republic's Communist Party because of its support for the abortive coup in Russia.

Sept. 20. The Ukrainian KGB (secret police) was dissolved and replaced by a security service under the control of the republican government.

Oct. 23. The Ukrainian Supreme Soviet created a legal basis for the formation of the country's own army, air force, and navy.

1992, May 5. The Crimean Supreme Soviet declared its independence from Ukraine. The Ukrainian Parliament voted to annul the independence declaration as against the constitution.

Aug. 3. In Yalta, Ukrainian president Leonid Kravchuk and Russian Federation president Boris Yeltsin signed an agreement on the division of the Black Sea fleet. The issue of control of the fleet had been a source of tension between the two states since the collapse of the Soviet Union in December 1991.

Sept. 25. The government announced a new economic reform program that called for mass privatization as well as more central control over wages and prices. Prime Minister Vitold Fokin tendered his resignation on Sept. 30 over economic and political issues.

Oct. 1. The Ukrainian parliament passed a vote of no confidence in the cabinet for its mishandling of the country's economy. Parliament elected Leonid Kuchma, head of the Yuzhmash missile factory in Dnepropetrovsk, as the new prime minister.

Nov. 12. The government replaced the ruble with the karbovanets currency coupon as the republic's economic crisis continued.

1993, June 7. A strike began in the coal mines in the city of Donetsk and spread throughout the Donbass region and across industrialized eastern Ukraine, prompting a political crisis and raising fears of economic collapse and ethnic conflict between western Ukraine and the Russian-speaking eastern half of the republic.

1994, Jan. 14. Ukraine **president Leonid Kravchuk signed a disarmament agreement with Clinton and Yeltsin;** the U.S. and Russia pledged security to Ukraine in the event of an attack.

Feb. The autonomous republic of Crimea elected **Yuri A. Meshkov president.** This move was supported by ethnic Russians but opposed by Ukraine. Tension was alleviated on June 3, when negotiators signed a pact reaffirming that Crimea is part of Ukraine.

July 10. Ukraine elected **Leonid D. Kuchma** as president.

1996, April 23. Forest fires spread atomic ash left over from the Chernobyl disaster.

June 28. Parliament approved a new constitution creating a strong presidency and a unicameral legislature.

1997, July 16. Approval of **Valery Pustovoitenko** as Ukraine's new **premier.**

1998, Aug. The **IMF agreed to grant loans of $2.2 billion** to assist the Ukranian government and its failing economy.

1999, Nov. 14. In a runoff election against Communist candidate Petro Symonenko, **Pres. Leonid Kuchma won reelection** to a second five-year term.

2000, April 17. A proposal initiated by Pres. Kuchma to expand presidential powers was approved through a public referendum by a wide margin. However, the four-part proposal still faced a vote in the Ukrainian Parliament before it could begin to be implemented.

Dec. 15. Pres. Kuchma officially closed the Chernobyl nuclear plant, site of the 1986 occurrence of the worst nuclear power accident in world history. Plans, including construction of a $750 million concrete shell to cover the disaster area, were made to secure the site.

o. Uzbekistan

1990, June 20. The Uzbek Supreme Soviet adopted a declaration of Uzbekistan's sovereignty within a "renewed Soviet federation," and the supremacy of Uzbekistan's laws on its territory.

Nov. 1. The Supreme Soviet abolished the republic's Council of Ministers and replaced it with a cabinet attached to Executive President Islam Karimov.

1991, Aug. 31. The Supreme Soviet declared the independence of Uzbekistan and changed its name to Republic of Uzbekistan.

Dec. 29. In presidential elections, incumbent president Islam Karimov won with 86 percent of the vote. The opposition party was banned from participating.

1992, June 29. Increased harassment of Uzbekistan's opposition parties culminated in an attack on two leaders of the Birlik (Unity) movement.

Aug. 7. The government established a Central Bank of Uzbekistan.

Dec. 8. The Supreme Soviet adopted a new constitution promising freedom of thought, conscience, and religious convictions; a multiparty democracy; and respect for human rights.

1993, Jan. 29. The head of Uzbekistan's Human Rights Association, Abdumannob Pulatov, was released from prison, but moves against the outlawed Birlik (Unity) movement showed that the regime was tightening its grip on political opponents.

1999, Feb. Uzbekistan declined an opportunity to renew its collective security treaty with the CIS. Meanwhile, bombings and other violence killed hundreds as militant Islamic rebels continued fighting to overthrow the secular, Russia-backed government.

C. NORTH AMERICA, 1946–2000

1. THE UNITED STATES, 1946–2000

(From p. 733)

The post–World War II era brought a plethora of changes to American life. The country claimed leadership of the "free world" and entered a sustained period of cold war with the Soviet Union and its allies. In order to combat the spread of communism, the government embarked upon an unprecedented period of peacetime military expansion. Federal support for the development of advanced military technology played a role in research development that undermined the old blue-collar sector of the economy. The increasing application of computer technology helped to transform the nation from a predominantly goods-producing society to a mainly service-producing one. The postwar **baby boom** (p. 733), **increasing suburbanization,** and the continuing spread of American consumer culture all reflected as well as reinforced these trends. Following the end of the Vietnam War, the economy deteriorated, unemployment increased, and Republicans returned to power with a firm determination to end the New Deal social welfare order. By the early 1990s, with the collapse of communism in Eastern Europe, the nation sought to craft new policies for a post–cold war world.

The cold war not only influenced American foreign policy and the economy, but also helped to transform domestic social and political relations as well. The nation's aggressive posture toward communism abroad was accompanied by equally vigorous attacks on suspected Communists at home. Sen. Joseph R. McCarthy's investigations, the Korean and Vietnam Wars, and wiretaps on the phones of civil rights leaders such as Martin Luther King, Jr., all reflected the destructive impact of the cold war at home and abroad.

Beginning with the Montgomery bus boycott in 1955 and culminating in the March on Washington for "freedom and jobs" in 1963, civil rights emerged as the most pressing domestic issue facing the nation. By the late 1960s, the U.S. had moved to dismantle the system of Jim Crow, to enfranchise African Americans, and to address the "unfinished revolution" of full citizenship rights for African Americans. Women, Hispanics, Native Americans, and eventually gay rights and environmental activists accelerated their assault against various forms of injustice and inequality, including racial, ethnic, gender, and sexual-preference barriers. Until the late 1960s, the Democratic Party remained committed to the New Deal welfare state and helped push provisions for social services beyond the limits established during the 1930s. During the 1970s and1980s, however, the U.S. undertook a dramatic reordering of its national priorities.

Following the election of 1968 and the nation's defeat in and retreat from Vietnam, the U.S. entered a prolonged crisis of economic and political restructuring. This period also signaled the end of American dominance in the world economy. The U.S. experienced the painful transition from a creditor to a debtor nation, with the world's largest foreign debt and a rising foreign trade deficit that peaked at $171 billion in 1987. The nation's increasing dependence on Middle Eastern oil played a major role in the eruption of the Persian Gulf War in 1990. Beginning with Republican president Richard M. Nixon in 1968, and accelerating with the election of Ronald Reagan in 1980, the nation turned away from its commitment to social welfare spending and undercut measures for translating civil rights laws into social practice. Dubbed "Reaganomics," this movement caused the federal government to disband the Office of Economic Opportunity (1971), weakened support for affirmative action in *Bakke* v. *University of California–Davis* (1978), and enacted a vigorous policy of tax cuts with the Economic Recovery Tax Act of 1981 and the Tax Reform Act of 1986. Under the Republican administrations, numerous groups—labor unions, women, racial and ethnic minorities, and environmentalists—experienced the impact of increasingly conservative policies.

Despite strong reactions against social programs and grassroots social movements, however, the U.S. continued to witness vigorous forms of activism during the period. The environmental movement and the gay rights movement (with intensified motivation after the outbreak of AIDS) represented important centers of activism. At the same time, African Americans increasingly channeled their efforts into the electoral arena. Civil rights activist Jesse Jackson mounted important challenges to the established Democratic Party with his "Rainbow Coalition" in the elections of 1984 and 1988. With the presidential election of Democrat William "Bill" Clinton in 1992, the nation seemed prepared to reassess the desirability of Reaganomics. Yet Clinton's first year in office revealed the nation's deep resistance to social change, including the lifting of bans on gays in the military. The conservative tide of the Reagan years would turn only slowly.

The postwar economy. Both founded in 1944, two institutions—**the International Bank of Reconstruction and Development, or World Bank, and the International Monetary Fund**—fueled the nation's postwar economic growth. Along with the **General Agreement on Tariffs and Trades (GATT),** a multinational trade agreement, these economic arrangements represented what became known as the **Bretton Woods system** of postwar economic development.

1946–60. The baby boom generation. During these years the nation's **birth rate soared.** The 20 percent population growth rate in the 1950s resulted particularly from an increase in middle-class birth rates. **The boom peaked in 1957.** Because of their numbers, the children, called "baby boomers," greatly influenced U.S. public, private, and cultural behaviors. Dr. Benjamin Spock published his best-selling *Baby and Child Care* (1946) and influenced a generation of baby boom mothers. **Technological changes** continued to transform American life and promote the expansion of consumerism. Consumer credit rose from $8.4 billion in 1946 to $45 billion in 1958. At the same time, the emergence of the first **McDonald's restaurant** in San Bernardino, Calif. (1954) and the **Holiday Inn** motel chain in Memphis, Tenn. (1952), signaled the rise of the fast food, vacation, and recreation industries. Although fewer than 7,000 **television sets** existed in the entire nation in 1947, by 1955, 66 percent of American families owned one.

1946, March. Winston Churchill delivered his "iron curtain" speech in Fulton, Mo., which helped set the tone for the cold war.

April–May. The U.S. labor movement could claim a greater membership than at any other time in its history; **nearly 40 percent of the labor force was unionized. A second wave of strikes** hit the soft-coal mines and the railroads. Before the strikes were settled, the government had taken control of the railroads (May 17) and the coal mines (May 20). **Pres. Harry Truman angered labor leaders by threatening to draft striking workers into the armed forces.** Congress passed the **Employment Act** to initiate federal fiscal planning on a permanent basis, to ensure economic growth as well as to curb inflation.

June 25. The Senate passed a measure extending **Selective Service** until March 31, 1947. Prior to this, public pressure had brought about the **hasty demobilization** of close to 9 million men.

July 1–25. Scientists at Bikini in the Pacific demonstrated the effect of an atomic explosion in experiments detonated on warships and under water.

July 15. Pres. Truman signed a bill extending a **credit of $3.75 billion to Great Britain.**

Sept. 20. Secretary of Commerce **Henry A. Wallace was asked to resign** following his criticism of the government's increasingly firm policy toward the Soviet Union.

Nov. 9. Following a futile battle with Congress to maintain price and wage controls, **Pres. Truman removed virtually all controls** except those on rent and some foods.

1947, Jan. 7. James F. Byrnes resigned as secretary of state and was succeeded by **Gen. George C. Marshall.**

Feb. 2. The U.S. and Canada announced the continuation of their defense cooperation under the **Permanent Joint Defense Board** of 1940.

March 12. Pres. Truman, in a message to Congress, outlined the **TRUMAN DOCTRINE** of economic and military aid to nations threatened by communism. He specifically requested urgently needed **aid for Greece and Turkey.** The Greek-Turkish Aid bill went into effect on May 22.

Federal Employee Loyalty Program. Truman issued an executive order empowering the attorney general and the FBI to investigate and dismiss employees suspected of disloyalty to the U.S. All levels of government, colleges and universities, and private organizations soon followed suit.

The House Un-American Activities Committee escalated its campaign against so-called subversives in government, which led to the conviction and imprisonment of **Alger Hiss** (1950), a former State Department official, on the basis of flimsy evidence.

June 5. Secretary of State George Marshall, in a speech at Harvard University, called for **a European recovery program,** initiated by the European powers and supported by American aid (**the MARSHALL PLAN**).

June 23. Congress, over the president's veto, passed the **Taft-Hartley Act,** which prohibited the use of union funds for political purposes, introduced a 60-day notice before a strike or lockout, outlawed the closed shop, and empowered the government to serve injunctions against strikes likely to cripple the nation's economy. Labor unions were especially troubled by **Section 14b,** which permitted states to pass **"right to work" laws** and to prohibit the union shop.

July 26. Congress approved the **unification of the armed services** under a secretary of defense (James V. Forrestal was the first).

Truman's Civil Rights Commission (formed in 1946) delivered a report entitled *To Secure These Rights.* The report helped to sanction the expanding civil rights movement by advocating the extension of full citizenship rights to all Americans regardless of race, color, creed, or national origin.

Americans for Democratic Action, a right-wing group, was formed; it waged vigorous attacks on Communists.

1948. Invention of the transistor, which would soon revolutionize computers and the entire electronics field. The **U.S. Census Bureau purchased the first commercial computer system** in 1951 (called the Universal Automatic Computer).

March 14–31. Congress passed **the Foreign Assistance Act (Marshall Plan)** and authorized an initial $5.3 billion for European recovery. **Paul G. Hoffman** was appointed chief of **the Economic Cooperation Administration (E.C.A.)** on April 6.

April–July. Strikes in the coal, railway, and steel industries were stopped by government action, and a third round of wage increases was implemented to meet the constantly rising cost of living.

General Motors offered the United Automobile Workers a cost of living adjustment clause to protect workers against inflation.

United Electrical Radio and Machine Workers of America refused to purge Communists from their ranks and broke with the Congress of Industrial Organizations (CIO).

June 19. Congress passed a peacetime **Selective Service Bill** for men between ages 19 and 25.

July 26. The president issued an executive order to desegregate the military.

Aug. 22. Jackie Robinson broke the color line in major league baseball.

Aug. 25. The Soviet Union broke off all consular relations with the U.S. when the latter refused to surrender a Soviet citizen against her will.

Nov. 2. Contrary to most predictions, **HARRY S. TRUMAN WAS REELECTED** president over **Thomas E. Dewey** (Republican) by 303 electoral votes to 189. Truman lost four southern states to **"Dixiecrat" Strom Thurmond of South Carolina,** but the increased number of black voters in the urban North helped to offset the loss.

1948–49. Berlin airlift (p. 870). The Soviet Union imposed a **land and sea blockade** on the city of Berlin. For **321 days** American planes flew food and supplies into the city. **Joseph Stalin lifted the blockade on May 12, 1949.**

1949. Growing fear of communism. The spread of communism in Eastern Europe and the Far East created a growing fear among many Americans of a possible Communist danger at home. The trial and conviction for espionage of **Judith Coplon,** employee of the Justice Department; the revelations made in connection with the trial of **Alger Hiss,** formerly of the State Department; and the trial of the leaders of the American Communist Party were only the more prominent among a large number of investigations and restrictive measures conducted by federal, state, and local authorities to uncover or prevent Communist infiltration, espionage, and sabotage. The best-known proponent of the Red scare tactics, **Republican senator Joseph R. McCarthy, held hearings to investigate Communist infiltration in the government and numerous industries.** Though **McCarthy's charges were often false,** he became one of the most feared politicians of the 1950s.

Jan.–Oct. In one of its longest peacetime sessions, **Congress,** largely because of the opposition of the southern Democrats, **failed to give support to the major points of Pres. Truman's "Fair Deal" program—** the repeal of the Taft-Hartley Act and the enactment of federal civil rights legislation. In the field of foreign affairs, on the other hand, Congress on the whole shared the administration's international orientation.

Jan. 7. Secretary of State Marshall resigned for reasons of health and was succeeded by Dean Acheson.

Jan. 20. HARRY S. TRUMAN was inaugurated for his second term. In his inaugural address, he presented a four-point plan for American foreign policy, **point four** of which called for "a bold new program" of assistance to economically underdeveloped areas.

April 4. THE NORTH ATLANTIC TREATY (p. 838) was ratified by the Senate on July 21 and signed by the president on July 25.

Aug. 10. Pres. Truman signed a bill establishing **the Department of Defense,** including broader and more well-defined powers for the secretary of defense.

Oct. 6. Pres. Truman signed **the Mutual Defense Assistance Act,** appropriating more than 1 billion dollars for military aid primarily to members of the Atlantic pact.

Oct. 14. The leaders of **the American Communist Party** were convicted of conspiracy to advocate the violent overthrow of the U.S. government and sentenced to fines and imprisonment.

1950s. During this decade, **the white population in the nation's largest cities dropped, while the population in the suburbs exploded.** Municipalities launched aggressive **urban renewal programs** that demolished nearly 150,000 structures and displaced nearly a half million people between 1949 and 1961. Although government-sponsored, low-income **public housing units** also helped to transform the face of the inner city, the units proved insufficient to meet the needs of incoming and displaced residents, mainly nonwhite minorities. The decade also saw the beginning of a major **influx of women into the workplace.**

Television entered millions of U.S. homes in the 1950s, dramatically altering American life.

1950, Jan. 25. Alger Hiss was found guilty of perjury for having denied his Communist affiliations and his role in the transfer of State Department secrets to the USSR prior to the war.

Created by the National Security Act of 1947, the Central Intelligence Agency (CIA) moved beyond its original mission as a strictly data-gathering agency to become actively involved in foreign affairs, including the overthrow of foreign governments.

Jan. 31. Pres. Truman instructed the Atomic Energy Commission to proceed with its work on **the hydrogen bomb.**

June 5. Pres. Truman signed **the third foreign aid bill,** appropriating close to $3 billion for the European Recovery Program and the Point Four Program.

June 25. The invasion of South Korea by North Korean forces led to calls for U.S. intervention.

June 27. THE U.S. INTERVENTION IN THE KOREAN WAR, described as "police action," was launched to support the UN (p. 1029).

June–Sept. The administration's Korean War policy found immediate support in Congress. Selective service was extended, the military budget was almost doubled, and far-reaching military aid was appropriated under the Mutual Defense Assistance Program.

July 8. Gen. Douglas MacArthur was appointed commanding general of U.N. forces in Korea.

July 20. The charges made by **Sen. Joseph McCarthy** of large-scale Communist infiltration into the State Department were found to be untrue by a Senate committee. The senator's careless accusations brought great hardship to many people.

Sept. 23. Congress, over the president's veto, adopted **the Internal Security Bill,** which called for the registration of Communists and Communist "front" organizations.

Oct. 15. At a meeting at **Wake Island, Pres. Truman and Gen. MacArthur** tried to clarify differences regarding America's policy in eastern Asia. On several occasions, MacArthur had without authorization openly advocated a pro-Nationalist and anti-Communist policy in China. Although such views were applauded by critics of the government's Far Eastern policy and of Secretary of State Acheson, the general's interference in matters outside his military sphere had caused considerable embarrassment to the administration's conduct of foreign policy.

Dec. 16. Reversals suffered by UN troops in Korea led to **the proclamation of a state of national emergency** by Pres. Truman. **Charles E. Wilson** was made head of the newly created **Office of Defense Mobilization.**

1951, Jan. 4. Pres. Truman stated in his weekly news conference that the U.S. probably would not bomb China without a formal congressional declaration of war.

Jan. 5. The Senate opened the **"great debate" on American foreign policy** with an attack on the administration by **Sen. Robert A. Taft.**

Jan. 6. It was revealed that U.S. **arms and ammunition were being sent to Nationalist China** to strengthen the defenses of Taiwan.

Feb. 26. The 22nd Amendment to the Constitution, limiting the presidency to two terms, came into force.

March 12. The Senate committee to investigate organized crime in interstate commerce **(the Kefauver Committee)** held its first public hearings in New York City. Two weeks of sensational disclosures followed.

April 4. After three months of debate, the Senate approved (69–21) a resolution expressing the "sense" of its members on the issue of **sending troops to Europe.** It affirmed the president's plan to send four divisions to Europe, but served notice that no additional divisions should be sent without further congressional approval.

April 11. Gen. Douglas MacArthur was relieved of all his commands in the Far East, to be **succeeded by Gen. Matthew B. Ridgway** (p. 1029). In an address to a joint session of Congress on April 19, MacArthur presented his arguments against the administration's policies. On

April 24 the Senate voted to conduct an investigation of the U.S. Far Eastern policy and the dismissal of MacArthur. Hearings during May 3–June 25 ended in approval of a limited war in Korea.

April 25. Secretary of State Acheson revealed a U.S. commitment, undertaken ten weeks earlier, to give **military aid to the Chinese Nationalist government** for "the legitimate self-defense of Formosa."

June 4. The Supreme Court upheld (6–2) the Smith Act and the conviction of 11 Communists.

June 19. Pres. Truman signed **a military manpower bill** extending the draft until July 1, 1955; lowering the draft age to 18; and authorizing universal military training to take effect at an unspecified date.

1952, March 20. The Senate ratified the peace treaty with Japan and approved Pacific security agreements contracted with Japan, the Philippines, Australia, and New Zealand.

April 8. The president ordered **government seizure of the nation's steel industry** to avert a strike. On April 29, the district court of Washington, D.C., ruled that the seizure was unconstitutional. On June 2 the Supreme Court upheld the ruling.

May 23. The government returned the railroads to private owners after 21 months of government management.

June 26. The McCarran-Walter Immigration and Nationality Act, passed over the president's veto, permitted **naturalization of Asians** and established a quota for further admission, but also provided for exclusion and deportation of aliens and control of citizens abroad. Increasing numbers of **Mexicans were admitted to the U.S. under the bracero (temporary, or "day worker") program. Puerto Rican immigration also increased** without legal restrictions.

July 24. A White House agreement ended the 54-day **strike of steel workers.**

Nov. 5. Dwight D. Eisenhower (Republican) carried 39 states to defeat **Adlai Stevenson** (Democrat) for the presidency.

1953, Jan. 20. DWIGHT D. EISENHOWER WAS INAUGURATED as the 34th president. **Richard M. Nixon** became vice president.

July 7. J. Robert Oppenheimer, former director of Los Alamos Laboratory, was barred from access to classified material in the continuing McCarthy-led campaign against communism.

1954, Jan. 12. Secretary of State John Foster Dulles declared that the basis of U.S. defense policy was **"a great capacity to retaliate"** against an aggressor "instantly by means and at places of our own choosing."

March 1. A hydrogen bomb was exploded in the Marshall Islands testing grounds.

March 16. Secretary of State Dulles declared that the NATO and Rio treaties empowered the president, without needing to consult Congress, **to order instant retaliation in Europe and the Western Hemisphere** if an ally was attacked.

May 7. Secretary of State Dulles declared that a distinct possibility existed that the U.S. might be forced to intervene militarily in Indochina, in association with other free nations.

May 17. The Supreme Court, in *Brown* v. *Board of Education of Topeka,* unanimously held that **public school segregation was unconstitutional** under the 14th Amendment.

May–June. McCarthy climaxed his campaign against communism with 35 days of televised hearings before his subcommittee on "investigations" of government operations.

June 1. The Atomic Energy Commission's personnel security board unanimously found **Dr. J. Robert Oppenheimer** "loyal" and "discreet" in handling atomic secrets, but recommended, in a 2–1 decision, that he not be reinstated as a government consultant.

June 25–29. Pres. Eisenhower and Secretary of State Dulles conferred with Sir Winston Churchill and Foreign Secretary Anthony Eden on Anglo-American differences, particularly concerning **Communist action in Southeast Asia.** The British agreed not to approve or condone Communist conquests, nor to press at this time for the admission of Communist China to the UN.

Aug. 9. The Senate passed **the Agriculture Act,** which set up a flexible scale of price supports for farm products.

Aug. 24. Pres. Eisenhower reluctantly signed the bill **outlawing the Communist Party.**

Sept. 9. The Agricultural Trade Development and Assistance Act went into effect; it authorized sale or gift of surplus farm products to needy foreign nations and American families.

Dec. 2. The Senate passed a resolution, 67–22, condemning some of Sen. McCarthy's actions. The November elections, by returning a Democratic majority, deprived him of his chairmanship of the Senate Internal Security Committee.

Dec. 20. Defense Secretary Charles E. Wilson announced an **accelerated reduction of military manpower,** cutting the armed forces from 3,218,000 men to 2,815,000 men over a period of 18 months.

Dr. Jonas Salk perfected the polio vaccine and thereby increased the health of children.

1955, Jan. 25. Pres. Eisenhower asked Congress to authorize the **use of armed force to defend Taiwan,** the Pescadores, and certain "closely related localities." Congress granted his request by a large majority.

The U.S. sent advisers and increasing amounts of military aid to Vietnam, replaced France as the dominant foreign power in the area, and **set the stage for the Vietnam War.**

Feb. 9. A joint **AFL-CIO** unit committee announced agreement on unification, which was formally consummated in the following December. The new organization represented over 90 percent of the nation's 17.5 million union members. Contracts shifted toward emphases on workers as consumers rather than producers.

Mechanization of industry continued apace during the 1950s. In 1952, **the Ford Motor Co. introduced drilling machines** in its Cleveland engine facility, which permitted 41 workers to perform a job that previously had required 117 workers.

March 23. Pres. Eisenhower declared that the U.S. would not use nuclear weapons in a "police action."

May 31. The Supreme Court ruled that STATES MUST END RACIAL SEGREGATION IN THE PUBLIC SCHOOLS "with all deliberate speed."

June 15. An accord with Great Britain on **the peaceful use of nuclear power** was concluded.

July 11. The U.S. Air Force Academy near Denver, Colo., was dedicated.

Nov. 25. The Interstate Commerce Commission issued **an order to end,** after Jan. 10, 1956, **racial segregation** on buses and trains that crossed state lines.

Dec.–1957, Jan. African Americans fought the segregated policies of the Montgomery city bus line with a 13-month boycott. Though the bus company nearly went bankrupt, the city did not desegregate the buses until mandated to do so by a **Nov. 1956 Supreme Court ruling. The boycott is credited as the impetus for the modern civil rights movement.**

1956. The percentage of American workers employed in white-collar jobs exceeded those in blue-collar positions for the first time. Service-producing employees began to outnumber goods-producing employees.

Rock 'n' roll icon Elvis Presley burst onto the popular culture scene after appearing on the *Ed Sullivan Show.* Also, since 1954, disc jockey **Alan Freed** of Cleveland, Ohio, had been helping to spread the influence of black music to white America with his prime-time radio show.

Jan. 28. Pres. Eisenhower rejected Soviet premier Nikolay Bulganin's proposal for a friendship pact.

May 4. A new series of atomic tests began in the Pacific. On May 21, **the first airborne H-bomb** was exploded.

May 9. Secretary of State Dulles explained that the U.S. had refused to supply **arms to Israel** in order to avoid a U.S.-USSR war by proxy.

May 28. The president signed **the Agriculture Act,** which embodied the "soil bank" plan in an effort to reduce surpluses.

June 29. The Federal Aid Highway Act authorized a 42,500-mile network linking major urban centers; 90 percent of the cost would be borne by the federal government.

Aug. 14. The government established the **Middle-East Emergency Committee** to assure western Europe of U.S. oil supplies if the Suez crisis interrupted shipments.

Nov. 6. The Eisenhower-Nixon Republican ticket won the presidential elections by a landslide, but the Democrats won a majority in both houses of Congress. Pres. Eisenhower was inaugurated on Jan. 21, 1957.

The Interstate Highway Act provided federal support for expansion of the nation's highway system, which was designed to accommodate the rapidly growing automobile culture, suburbanization, recreation, and defense needs during an era of great fear of nuclear war.

1957. Albert Sabin's oral vaccine against poliomyelitis proved effective in mass tests.

March 9. A joint congressional resolution empowered the president to use up to $200 million for **economic and military assistance to any Middle Eastern nation** desiring it; it asserted vital U.S. interest in the integrity and independence of all Middle Eastern countries (**"Eisenhower Doctrine").**

Sept. 3. At Little Rock, Ark., National Guardsmen blocked African-American students from entering Central High School. A federal court injunction required **Gov. Orval Faubus** to remove the National Guard (Sept. 20), and on Sept. 24, Pres. Eisenhower sent federal troops to prevent "mob rule."

Sept. 9. A **CIVIL RIGHTS ACT** set up the bipartisan **Civil Rights Commission** to investigate infringements of voting and other rights, and strengthened executive and court procedures. The commission was appointed on Nov. 7.

The Southern Christian Leadership Conference was formed to coordinate the expanding civil rights movement.

1958, Jan. 27. The U.S. and the USSR signed an agreement to expand cultural, educational, technical, and sports exchanges.

April 28. Nuclear tests began on Eniwetok, an atoll in the Pacific.

July 15–19. Eight thousand U.S. troops landed in Lebanon (p. 978).

Aug. 3. The USS *Nautilus* completed the first **undersea crossing of the North Pole.**

Sept. 2. The president signed **the National Defense Education Act,** which provided loans to college students, grants to schools for facilities in the sciences and foreign languages, and fellowships for graduate students intending to teach.

1959, Jan. 3. Pres. Eisenhower signed the document **making Alaska the 49th state** in the Union.

Jan. 4. Soviet first deputy premier **Anastas I. Mikoyan arrived in Washington, D.C.,** on a two-week visit to the U.S. On Jan. 19 he suggested a reduction of U.S. barriers to Russian trade, but the State Department rejected the suggestion.

Aug. 21. Pres. Eisenhower proclaimed Hawaii the 50th state.

Sept. 14. The **Labor-Management Reporting and Disclosure Act** (Landrum-Griffith Act), passed to end corruption and place new limitations on labor unions, became law.

Sept. 15–27. Premier Nikita Khrushchev toured the U.S. (p. 904). During the last three days he talked with Pres. Eisenhower at Camp David and agreed to hold further discussions on **the Berlin issue** and to expand the U.S.-USSR exchange program (The Spirit of Camp David).

Nearly 500,000 **Cubans left their country in the wake of Fidel Castro's rise to power.** Miami became a major center for the new Cuban population.

1960. Introduction of **the birth control pill** easily and reliably helped women control their fertility and curtail the baby boom. This helped lead to the so-called **sexual revolution.** Encouraged by a rise in marriage, **sexual activity before marriage increased** (notably among middle-class women), and age of first sexual intercourse decreased. **Illegitimacy rates increased** as well.

Jan. 5. After six months during which Pres. Eisenhower had invoked the Taft-Hartley Act to end the steelworkers' strike, steel companies and unions came to an agreement on wages, benefits, and work rules.

Feb. 1. Four black college students staged a "sit-in" at a segregated lunch counter in Greensboro, N.C. More than 50,000 people, mostly African Americans, participated in sit-ins throughout the country that winter and the following spring.

April 21. Congress passed **the Civil Rights Act** of 1960, which provided voting referees in areas where **African Americans** were barred from the polls by state barriers. Pres. Eisenhower signed it on May 6.

July 20. A Polaris missile was launched from a submerged submarine.

Nov. 8. JOHN F. KENNEDY DEFEATED RICHARD M. NIXON for the presidency. Kennedy was inaugurated on Jan. 20, 1961. Four televised debates between the two presidential candidates had signaled the growing importance of television in American politics.

1961, March 1. Pres. Kennedy issued an executive order creating the

Peace Corps, a coterie of trained American men and women who used their skills to help various developing countries.

April 17. An attempt by CIA-sponsored Cuban nationals to foment an anti-Castro rebellion in Cuba failed. The botched invasion embarrassed the new Kennedy administration and strained U.S.-Soviet relations.

May 4. "Freedom rides" by black and white members of the Congress of Racial Equality (CORE) sought to test recent court rulings that banned segregated coaches and facilities on interstate bus lines. Pushed by news clips showing the brutality to which the riders were subjected, **Atty. Gen. Robert Kennedy** intervened to help the riders. At **Montgomery, Ala.** (May 20), mob action against the riders led to the dispatch of several hundred federal marshals.

June 3–4. Pres. Kennedy conferred with Premier Khrushchev in Vienna.

July 25. Pres. Kennedy, in a national address on **the Berlin crisis** (p. 872), proposed an increase in armed forces by 217,000 men and in defense spending to total $3.4 billion, in order to meet the Soviet "worldwide threat."

Sept. 22. The Interstate Commerce Commission ordered the **desegregation of all interstate bus and railroad terminals,** effective on Nov. 1.

1962, Jan. 11. In his **State of the Union message** to Congress, **Pres. Kennedy** called for a reduction of tariff barriers, expansion of welfare programs, and measures to help the economy.

Publication of Rachel Carson's book *Silent Spring* helped to launch **the environmental movement.**

Feb. 20. Lt. Col. John H. Glenn, Jr., became **the first U.S. astronaut to make an orbital flight,** circling the earth three times.

April 25. The U.S. resumed **nuclear testing** by exploding a nuclear device at the Christmas Island test site in the Pacific Ocean.

July 10. Telstar, a 170-lb. communications rocket, **was put into orbit** in a joint effort by the government and the American Telephone and Telegraph Company.

Atty. Gen. Robert Kennedy authorized wiretaps on the Atlanta home of civil rights leader **Martin Luther King, Jr.;** the government believed King was linked to Communists.

Oct. 15–28. Cuban missile crisis (p. 959). For 13 days, the U.S. and the Soviet Union stood at the brink of nuclear war after aerial photography showed Soviet missile bases, complete with missiles, under construction in Cuba. **The U.S. quarantined Soviet ships from Cuba until the missiles were removed.**

Oct. 23. Pres. Kennedy signed the $3.9 billion **foreign aid bill,** clauses of which forbade aid to 18 Communist nations and to any country shipping arms to Cuba.

1963. Betty Friedan kicked off the modern movement for women's rights with her book *The Feminine Mystique,* which debunked the assumption that homemaking and childbearing were the sole means of fulfillment in a woman's life.

End of the baby boom. Birthrates began to decline rapidly.

Spring. The Birmingham Movement. The battle to desegregate Birmingham, Ala., made headlines around the world. **When civil rights leaders decided to use children in protest marches, the city's police force responded by using high-power fire hoses and police dogs to break up the marchers.**

May 15–16. Astronaut **Maj. L. Gordon Cooper, Jr.,** orbited the earth 22 times in the Mercury capsule *Faith VII.*

June 10. Pres. Kennedy delivered a speech at American University, emphasizing his desire to **"make the world safe for diversity"** and laying the groundwork for **détente.**

June 17. The Supreme Court ruled that **local governments could not require recitation from the Bible or prayers in the public schools.**

June 20. An agreement with the USSR was signed to set up an **emergency communications link** ("hot-line") to reduce the risk of accidental war. The Soviet Union had accepted the proposal on April 5.

Aug. 28. March on Washington for Freedom and Jobs. In the largest protest assembled up until that time, about **250,000 blacks and whites** marched on Washington, D.C., in a peaceful demonstration in support of the civil rights bill requested by Pres. Kennedy (June 19).

The U.S., the USSR, and Great Britain agreed to ban testing of nuclear weapons in air or on sea.

Nov. 22. Upon the **ASSASSINATION OF PRES. KENNEDY** in Dallas, Tex., **V. P. LYNDON BAINES JOHNSON** was sworn in as the 36th president of the U.S.

1964. The Beatles appeared on *The Ed Sullivan Show* and electrified American teenagers.

Jan. 10. Export licenses increased **wheat sales** to the USSR, an initiative first approved by Pres. Kennedy on Oct. 9, 1963.

Feb. 13. At the end of a two-day conference, **Pres. Johnson and British prime minister Alec Douglas-Home** issued a joint communiqué endorsing each other's **policies in Malaysia and South Vietnam.**

Feb. 25. To end a 90-day longshoremen's ban on loading Russian-bound wheat, Pres. Johnson ordered that the government honor its commitment to ship 50 percent of the wheat in U.S. vessels.

April 28. Pres. Johnson asked Congress for $228 million to fund a program, for fiscal year 1965, aimed at wiping out poverty in the ten Appalachian states.

May 28. A consular agreement was completed with the USSR to protect tourists and other travelers.

Freedom Summer. Leaders of **CORE and the Student Non-Violent Coordinating Committee (SNCC)** got hundreds of students from northern states to volunteer to help in a **black voter registration drive in Mississippi.** In mid-June, three of the civil rights workers, **James Chaney, Andrew Goodman, and Michael Schwerner,** were reported missing. After a major search, federal officials found the bodies of the three men, two of whom were white.

June 15. The Supreme Court ruled that both bodies of a bicameral legislature must be apportioned on the basis of population.

June 19. Civil Rights Act. The Senate passed the **Civil Rights Bill** (73–27), which greatly **increased federal powers to combat racial discrimination.** The law guaranteed **equal access to public accommodations and schools, and banned discrimination by both employers and labor unions.** Previously (June 10), the Senate had voted cloture to end the filibuster carried on since March 30.

July 18–21. Racial violence. This marked the first of several **"long hot summers"** during which blacks expressed growing dissatisfaction with life in the urban North. The first major eruption occurred in **Harlem** after police shot a black criminal suspect. In August, violence spread to several cities in **New Jersey** as well as to **Chicago and Philadelphia.**

July 26. James R. Hoffa, president of the International Brotherhood of Teamsters, was convicted of fraudulent use of union funds and efforts to bribe a jury. He was sentenced to 15 years in prison (Aug. 17).

July 28–31. The U.S. spacecraft *Ranger VII* relayed numerous close-up pictures of the moon's surface before plunging into it.

Aug. 7. Gulf of Tonkin Resolution (p. 1038). **Congress passed a resolution authorizing Pres. Johnson to take any measure necessary to repel or prevent aggression against U.S. forces. The resolution prepared the way for escalation of the Vietnam War.**

Autumn. Berkeley student organizations, feeling that their rights to free speech had been abridged, banded together and **held a sit-in at the main administration building.** The action persuaded university officials to drop the ban on political activity, which had ignited the student action. **The Berkeley sit-in started the nation's student protest movement.**

Sept. 3. The Wilderness Preservation Act placed over a million acres of wilderness under federal jurisdiction.

Sept. 27. The voluminous report of the **Warren Commission,** investigating the assassination of Pres. Kennedy, was released. The report held that **Lee Harvey Oswald** was solely responsible for the act. Oswald had been shot and killed (Nov. 24, 1963) by Jack Ruby while being transferred from one jail to another.

Nov. The election gave Pres. Johnson the popular mandate and the congressional majority to push his "Great Society" program. In a rush of liberal legislation, Johnson expanded the social welfare functions of the federal government. **The Office of Economic Opportunity** established by the **Economic Opportunity Act** became the centerpiece of the administration's **"War on Poverty."** Headstart, Neighborhood Youth Corps, and Volunteers in Service to America (VISTA) were only a few of the programs initiated under the Johnson administration.

1965. United Farm Workers (UFW), the first successful union to represent migrant workers, went on strike at the Delano vineyards. The grape pickers, led by **Cesar Chavez,** encouraged a national boycott of table grapes. In 1968, Chavez fasted for 25 days to protest the increasing violence in the fields. **In 1970, the strike ended when the California grape growers recognized the UFW.**

Jan. 18–23. Voter registration drive in Selma, Ala. After a black voting-rights advocate was killed, **Martin Luther King, Jr., and others called for a major march from Selma, Ala., to the state capital.** The march turned violent when mounted state troops attacked the marchers.

Jan. 20. LYNDON B. JOHNSON AND HUBERT H. HUMPHREY INAUGURATED as president and vice president.

Feb. 21. Assassination of Malcolm X, former Black Muslim leader, in New York City. He had justified the use of defensive violence as an alternative to the prevailing nonviolent direct action approach of Martin Luther King, Jr.

March 8. The first **U.S. Marines entered South Vietnam** (p. 1038), signaling the escalation of U.S. involvement in the fight against the Viet Cong. By year's end, nearly 190,000 U.S. soldiers were in Vietnam. The deepening involvement of the U.S. in the Vietnam War led to growing opposition and protest not only at home but abroad.

March 9–25. The second civil rights march from Selma to Montgomery, Ala., was led by **Rev. Martin Luther King, Jr.** The march was temporarily halted by a federal restraining order, but following Gov. George Wallace's statement of inability to protect the marchers, Pres. Johnson federalized the Alabama National Guard and ordered federal troops to the scene. From March 21 to March 25, King, with over 3,000 blacks and numerous white participants from all over the country, completed the march to Montgomery. Gov. Wallace finally agreed (March 30) to meet with a delegation demanding equal civil rights.

March 11–25. The deaths of white civil rights activists **Rev. James J. Reeb and Viola Liuzzo,** at the hands of Ku Klux Klansmen on the road from Selma to Montgomery, helped galvanize white support for the civil rights movement.

March 13. Conference of Pres. Johnson and Gov. Wallace of Alabama. The president insisted on protection of the civil rights of all people. On March 17 the president called on Congress for legislation to end discrimination in registration and voting.

April 14–15. Visit of Prime Minister Harold Wilson to Washington, D.C. He reiterated British support of U.S. policies in Vietnam.

July 30. Passage of **MEDICARE LEGISLATION,** which involved medical care for the aged. The program would be financed with Social Security funds.

The Water Quality Act provided for federal cooperation with the states in the struggle against pollution.

Aug. 6. The Voting Rights Act suspended literacy tests and other examinations designed to exclude people, especially blacks, from voting.

Aug. 11. Racial violence erupted in the Watts section of Los Angeles, where 60 percent of all adults were on relief. Thirty-four people died, and property damage reached $200 million in the worst case of urban racial violence since 1943.

Sept. 29. The National Foundation of the Arts and Humanities was established to encourage and aid the arts and artists.

Oct. 3. New immigration laws fixed the annual quota of immigrants at 120,000 from the Western Hemisphere, without establishing national quotas, and at 170,000 from the rest of the world, not more than 20,000 to come from any one country. This spurred a new wave of largely non-European immigration; by 1985, only 10 percent of immigrants would be of European origin, in contrast to 90 percent in 1965.

Oct. 20. The Higher Education Act for the first time provided federal scholarship aid for undergraduates.

Griswold v. *Connecticut.* The U.S. Supreme Court overturned state laws against the sale of contraceptives to married adults.

1965–66. The drug culture. Drugs became a prominent part of student culture in the late 1960s, and **marijuana** seemed to be the students' drug of choice. Others began experimenting with drugs such as **lysergic acid diethylamide (LSD).**

1966. After 1965, **the antiwar movement and draft protests increased in intensity.** The most explosive expressions of unrest came in 1970 after Pres. Richard Nixon ordered American troops to invade Cambodia.

Betty Friedan and 27 other professional women started **the National Organization for Women (NOW).** Formed by women radicalized by civil rights and student protests, **the women's liberation movement** soon gained momentum.

Black power movement. Stokely Carmichael, head of the Student Non-Violent Coordinating Committee (SNCC), helped to usher in a new African-American movement when he proclaimed the need for "black power." **The Black Panther Party** was only one of the many black power organizations that soon emerged. Building upon the legacy of **Malcolm X,** the Panthers urged African Americans to take pride in their blackness and to take up arms and defend themselves "by any means necessary."

May 5. Sen. J. W. Fulbright, chairman of the Senate Foreign Relations Committee, began to attack the administration's Vietnam policy.

June 5–26. African Americans marched on the capitol at Jackson, Miss., in a drive to induce African Americans to register to vote.

July. Race riots occurred in Chicago, Brooklyn, Cleveland, and in other cities.

July 1–4. At the convention of the **Congress of Racial Equality (CORE)** at Baltimore, the organization endorsed the objective of black power, rejected the doctrine of nonviolence, demanded the withdrawal of U.S. forces from Vietnam, and supported resistance to the draft.

July 4–9. The National Association for the Advancement of Colored People (NAACP) convened in Los Angeles and rejected black power as a separatist movement.

Oct. 15. The Department of Transportation was created to exercise control over air, rail, and highway transportation.

Oct. 19–Nov. 2. Pres. Johnson visited New Zealand, Australia, the Philippines, South Vietnam, Thailand, Malaysia, and South Korea. At a conference in Manila (Oct. 24–25) leaders of the allied nations pledged support for the war in Vietnam.

1967, Feb. 10. The 38th state (Colorado) ratified the 25th Amendment to the U.S. Constitution, which concerned the problem of presidential infirmity and succession.

Feb. 13. Furor erupted in academic circles over the revelation that **the Central Intelligence Agency** had secretly financed **the National Student Association** in certain of its activities.

March 16. A **consular agreement with the Soviet Union** was concluded.

April 15. Huge marches in New York City and San Francisco **protested the war in Vietnam** and demanded peace.

Summer. Hippies, alienated youth, captured the nation's attention and helped to shape contemporary culture by professing to have dropped out of mainstream culture to practice peace and love.

In the worst summer of urban violence to date, African-American discontent with life in the cities reached a boiling point. In July and August, violence broke out in 22 cities.

July 1. The treaty restricting the proliferation of nuclear weapons (p. 819) was concluded.

July 15. Initiation of **direct air service between the U.S. and the Soviet Union.**

Oct. 2. Justice Thurgood Marshall became the first **African American** to serve as an associate justice of the Supreme Court.

Oct. 21–22. A huge **peace march on Washington** drew participants from all over the country and culminated in clashes between demonstrators and army troops protecting the Pentagon.

Nov. 7. Inauguration of **the Corporation for Public Broadcasting,** a nonprofit public corporation that allocated funds to noncommercial radio and television stations to assist them in creating high-quality programs.

Dec. 1–8. Stop the Draft Week was organized by 40 antiwar groups. An enormous demonstration in New York City was followed by mass arrests.

1968. Native Americans from Minnesota formed the American Indian Movement (AIM).

Jan. 30. The Tet Offensive, a surprise attack by the Viet Cong on South Vietnamese installations (p. 1039), was begun. **The Viet Cong's strength belied reports that they were being defeated.** Between 1965 and 1968, the U.S. had dropped a million tons of bombs on North Vietnam. **In May, peace talks opened between the U.S. and North Vietnam in Paris.**

Feb. 29. The voluminous report of the president's **National Advisory Commission on Civil Disorders** held white racism primarily responsible for the riots of the summer of 1967 and made numerous detailed recommendations for dealing with racial antagonisms, warning that American society threatened to divide into separate and unequal white and black sections.

March 31. Pres. Johnson announced that he would neither seek nor accept nomination for a second term.

April 1. The Open Housing Law. This law forbade discrimination in the sale or rental of about 70 percent of all the housing in the country.

April 4. ASSASSINATION OF REV. MARTIN LUTHER KING, JR., the influential leader of the nonviolent civil rights movement, in Memphis. This act led at once to an epidemic of urban violence affecting some 125 cities, including Washington, D.C. In many places the National Guard and even army troops had to be called out.

April 11. A civil rights act banned racial discrimination in housing and made it a federal crime to injure civil rights workers or even to cross state lines with the intention of inciting to riot.

April 23–May 6. A crisis at Columbia University epitomized the political unrest in academic circles. The radical **Students for a Democratic Society** protested the building of a gymnasium in an area needed for low-income housing and also denounced the University's Institute of Defense Analysis as an agency of the military establishment and American imperialism. Protesting students eventually occupied the university library and sacked the president's office. After much hesitation, the administration called on the police to clear the protesters from the buildings (April 30). Hundreds were arrested and allegedly were abused by the police. Similar disturbances took place at many other institutions.

May 3–June 23. Poor People's March on Washington. Thousands of poor people of various races attempted to set up **Resurrection City** on the Potomac. **Rev. Ralph D. Abernathy,** successor to Dr. King, hoped to impress Congress with the needs of millions of Americans for food, clothing, and jobs.

June 5. ASSASSINATION OF SEN. ROBERT F. KENNEDY, presidential candidate and brother of the late president, in Los Angeles. The assassin was a young Arab, **Sirhan Beshara Sirhan,** evidently outraged by the pro-Israeli utterances of the senator.

July 23–24. Riots in Cleveland resulted from sniper attacks on the police. The disorders led to some loss of life and heavy property losses through looting.

Aug. 8. The Republican National Convention at Miami **nominated Richard M. Nixon and Spiro T. Agnew** (the governor of Maryland) for president and vice president.

Aug. 26–29. The Democratic National Convention at Chicago nominated **Hubert H. Humphrey and Sen. Edward S. Muskie** of Maine for president and vice president. The convention, extremely disorderly itself, was accompanied by violent street demonstrations and fighting. Police, in what was later termed a **"police riot,"** dispersed protesters with mace, tear gas, and clubs.

Oct. 4. The nomination of Justice Abe Fortas to be chief justice of the Supreme Court was withdrawn by Pres. Johnson in view of the vigorous and widespread opposition to his confirmation in the Senate.

Nov. 5. THE NATIONAL ELECTIONS resulted in a narrow margin of **victory for Nixon** and the Republicans. Nixon's popular vote was 31,770,237 against Humphrey's 31,270,533. The third-party candidate, **Gov. George C. Wallace** of Alabama, polled 9,906,141 votes.

1969, Jan. Unrest in the universities and other schools continued unabated, centering on violent opposition to the Vietnam War, but including various other demands.

Feb. 23–March 2. Pres. Nixon visited Europe to strengthen and revitalize NATO. His trip included a visit to the Vatican.

March 28. Death of former president Dwight D. Eisenhower.

March. Hispanic activists came together in a Denver conference of **La Raza Unida** (The United Race), a new political party, to reaffirm the heritage of Latin American cultures and the Spanish language.

June. The gay liberation movement was born, following a riot between police and the gay customers at **the Stonewall Inn in New York City.** From about 1900, scientists and the popular media had characterized homosexuality as a deviant and socially threatening lifestyle.

July 20. Neil Armstrong and Edwin Aldrin, Jr., walked on the moon.

Summer. Woodstock. About 400,000 young people gathered at White Lake in **Bethel, N.Y.,** for a rock festival.

Sept. 10. Oil leases on the newly discovered Alaskan North Slope fields netted over $900 million.

Sept. 24. The trial of eight radicals (the "Chicago Eight") began. They were charged with conspiring to incite riots in Chicago during the Democratic National Convention in Aug. 1968. The trial produced so much disorder in the courtroom that ultimately **Bobby Seale,** the Black Panther leader, was ordered bound and gagged. On Nov. 5, Seale was cited for contempt of court and sentenced to four years in prison.

Oct. 2. Thurgood Marshall became the first African American to sit on the U.S. Supreme Court.

Oct. 15. Moratorium Day was observed, expressing nationwide opposition to the Vietnam War and demanding that the troops be brought back immediately. There was, however, no agreement as to the best and quickest means of achieving peace.

Oct. 30. The Supreme Court ordered an immediate end to separate school systems for blacks and whites.

Nov. 13, 20. V.P. Agnew charged television networks and newspapers with presenting biased versions of the news and misrepresenting the government's policies.

Nov. 15. In the second Vietnam Moratorium, 250,000 war protesters marched in Washington, D.C., and about 100,000 in San Francisco.

Nov. 21. The U.S. and Japan agreed on **the return of Okinawa to Japan** in 1972.

Nov. 26. The Selective Service Act of 1967 was amended to provide for selection by lottery.

Dec. 4. Black Panther leader Fred Hampton died in a Chicago police raid.

Following a White House conference on food, nutrition, and health, Pres. Nixon ordered **the extension of the food stamp program** and substantial increases in allowances.

Dec. 9. Secretary of State William Rogers **proposed a settlement of the Arab-Israeli War.**

Dec. 12. The final report of the **National Commission on the Causes and Prevention of Violence** warned that the tide of violence would continue to rise and called for massive expenditures on social reform programs.

Dec. 16. Pres. Nixon endorsed a Senate amendment prohibiting **the use of combat troops in Thailand and Laos,** which had been included in a military appropriations bill.

In 1969, **AIM** (the American Indian Movement) seized control of **the island of Alcatraz,** turning it into an area free of government control. The siege lasted for 18 months.

1970s. Deindustrialization. The nation's industrial base entered a long period of decline. By the end of the 1970s, the nation's capital was being invested in speculative and foreign investments, rather than in the country's basic industries. **Estimates suggest that the U.S. lost between 32 million and 38 million jobs.** By the end of the decade, the 100 largest multinational corporations and banks earned more than one-third of their profits outside the U.S.

1970, Jan. 1. The three-person **Council on Environmental Quality** was established, a crucial step in the fight against pollution.

Jan. 26. Pres. Nixon vetoed a $19 billion appropriation for health, education, and antipoverty measures on grounds that such expenditure would aggravate inflation. The House of Representatives failed to override the veto.

Feb. 20. Five of the **"Chicago Eight"** were convicted of crossing state lines to incite riots and were sentenced to five years in prison.

March 6. The president signed a revised appropriations bill for the Department of Health, Education, and Welfare, and the Department of Labor.

April 22. The first Earth Day. Environmentalism was becoming a mass movement; on this day, 22 million people across the country gathered to show their support for the ecology of the planet.

April 30. The president announced the commitment of U.S. troops in the **war in Cambodia** (p. 1039) against the Vietnamese Communists. This announcement, involving an escalation of a war that Nixon had promised to conclude, caused a storm of indignation in the country and rekindled the peace movement.

May 4. At Kent State University in Ohio, four students were killed when the National Guard opened fire on a demonstration. Added to the outrage felt over Cambodia, the Kent State incident, regarded by most people as indefensible for any reason, produced such disorder that many universities and colleges were temporarily closed.

May 8. Construction workers attacked antiwar demonstrators in New York City.

May 9. Huge antiwar protest demonstration by students in Washington, D.C.

May 11–12. In Augusta, Ga., violence followed the beating death of a black prisoner.

May 12. After failing to confirm two earlier candidates, the Senate finally confirmed a presidential nomination for the Supreme Court, **Justice Harry A. Blackmun.**

May 14. Two black students were killed and nine wounded when police opened fire on a dormitory at **Jackson State College** in Mississippi.

June 10. Creation of the new **Office of Management and Budget** replaced the Bureau of the Budget.

June 13. The Commission on Campus Unrest was appointed, with former governor of Pennsylvania **William W. Scranton** as chairman.

June 15. The Supreme Court ruled that exemption from the draft on grounds of **conscientious objection** need not be based on religious belief but might be granted for moral or ethical reasons.

June 22. The Voting Rights Act was extended to 1975, and the voting age reduced to 18, to begin in 1971.

June 24. The Senate voted overwhelmingly to **repeal the Gulf of Tonkin Resolution** of 1965, on which the government's involvement in the Vietnam War was largely based.

June 30. The evacuation of Cambodia by American troops was completed as promised by the president.

July 9. Creation of the independent Environmental Protection Agency and the National Oceanic and Atmospheric Administration.

July 24. A new law provided for the construction of 1.3 million new housing units.

Aug. 12. The U.S. Postal Service was established as an independent government agency that would take over the U.S. Post Office and operate the postal service as a business enterprise.

Aug. 18. Congress overrode the president's veto of the $4.4 billion appropriation for the Office of Education.

A government ship loaded with nerve gas was scuttled in the Atlantic, 280 miles off the coast of Florida.

Aug. 24. The bombing of the U.S. Army Mathematical Research Center at the University of Wisconsin resulted in the loss of one life. The building was wrecked, and many neighboring buildings were badly damaged. Responsibility was assumed by **the Weathermen,** a radical, violent faction of the Students for a Democratic Society. This incident was followed by many less serious bombings in various parts of the country and led eventually to punitive legislation.

Aug. 26. Thousands of women celebrated **the 50th anniversary of the 19th Amendment** and called attention to persistent gender inequality in the nation's social, economic, and political life.

Sept. 3–7. A congress of African people, mainly African Americans, at Atlanta studied problems of culture and ideology.

Oct. 12. The U.S. Commission on Civil Rights, in a comprehensive report, concluded that because of a lack of interagency coordination and adequate supervision, a major breakdown had occurred in the implementation of the voluminous legislation designed to ensure equal rights for all. Civil rights issues were becoming less of a national priority, as indicated in **Daniel Patrick Moynihan's advice to Pres. Nixon** that "the issue of race could benefit from a period of benign neglect."

Oct. 15. The Organized Crime Control Act established federal jurisdiction over major gambling operations, control over the interstate sale of explosives, and so on. The death penalty was made mandatory for bombings resulting in loss of life.

Oct. 22. The Merchant Marine Act provided for the construction of 300 ships over the next ten years and the extension of operating subsidies in order to restore the U.S. to the position of a first-rate maritime power.

Oct. 24. Pres. Nixon repudiated **the report of the National Commission on Obscenity and Pornography,** declaring its conclusion—that pornography was not a contributing factor to crime and that it ought to be freely available to adults—to be morally bankrupt. Many called Nixon's judgment a biased interpretation of a generally sound report.

1971. Lt. William L. Calley was court-martialed for atrocities committed in the Vietnamese village of My Lai. Retaliating for the casualties of their comrades, soldiers in 1968 **allegedly killed 350 Vietnamese villagers.**

June. Daniel Ellsberg leaked classified documents (the so-called Pentagon Papers) to the *New York Times;* the documents detailed numerous instances of governmental wrongdoing in the prosecution of the Vietnam War. The officials tried unsuccessfully to stop the story from running.

The National Women's Political Caucus was formed to promote the election of women to public office.

The Office of Economic Opportunity was dismantled in the wake of conservative reactions against government spending on social welfare programs.

In *Swann* v. *Charlotte-Mecklenburg Board of Education,* the U.S. Supreme Court supported busing to achieve racial balance in the nation's public schools.

1972, Feb. 21. Pres. Nixon visited the People's Republic of China in what he called "a journey for peace."

June 17. Watergate. A break-in at the Democratic National Headquarters was carried out by Republicans, at least one of whom was on **the Committee to Reelect the President.** Nixon denied knowledge of the burglary. It became clear, however, that **the White House was engaging in a cover-up.** Nixon apparently feared an investigation into Watergate would expose his dubious fundraising methods and the **"dirty tricks"** (political sabotage) used by his reelection campaign. Eventually, several people in the White House, including Nixon and his closest advisers—**John Erlichman,** his chief domestic adviser; **H. R. Haldeman,** the chief of staff; and **John Dean,** White House counsel—resigned or were fired.

Equal Rights Amendment. Congress passed a proposed constitutional amendment stating that **"Equality of rights under the law shall not be denied or abridged by the United States or any state on account of sex."** Thirty-five states quickly ratified the amendment, but it needed 38 states for passage. By 1982, it was clear that the amendment would not be ratified.

Baird v. *Eisenstadt.* The U.S. Supreme Court permitted single persons to purchase contraceptives.

The Occupational Safety and Health Administration (OSHA) and the Consumer Product Safety Commission were established to protect the health of workers and consumers.

1973, Jan. 27. A Vietnam cease-fire agreement was signed in Paris by the U.S., North and South Vietnam, and the Viet Cong (p. 1040). The agreement provided for the return of U.S. prisoners of war in exchange for unilateral withdrawal of American troops from South Vietnam. North Vietnam freed 590 U.S. prisoners of war by April 1, and the last U.S. troops left Vietnam on March 29.

March. AIM activists occupied Wounded Knee, the site of the 1890 Indian massacre, and declared it liberated territory. Despite major gun battles with the government, the activists held out for 71 days before negotiating a truce. **Wounded Knee, along with the takeover of Alcatraz, symbolized growing Native American activism and consciousness.**

Oct. 10. V.P. Spiro T. Agnew was forced to resign after being indicted for allegedly accepting kickbacks on construction contracts while he was governor of Maryland. **Gerald Ford** replaced Agnew and became the first appointed vice president under the 25th Amendment.

The U.S. Supreme Court legalized abortion in the case of *Roe* v. *Wade.* The decision would spark major controversy. The vigorous **"Right to Life Movement"** to overturn the decision soon developed.

1973–74. The Arab oil embargo caused gas shortages throughout the U.S. and **forced Americans to recognize their dependence on foreign oil.**

1974, Aug. 9. Facing sure conviction in a Senate trial, **Nixon became the first U.S. president to resign. Gerald Ford assumed the office and a month later gave Nixon a full pardon.**

1974–75. Busing. In the 1970s, the government began to enforce, more vigorously than before, the school desegregation order. The government pushed first in the South, which eventually complied, and then in the rest of the country. **Desegregation of city school systems, generally achieved by busing students, became a controversial and violent issue.** By the late 1970s, the federal government had backed away from busing as a means to achieve racial balance in schools.

1975. Recession. The economy entered its deepest downturn since the Great Depression. Production declined by more than 10 percent, and nearly 9 percent of the workforce was unemployed.

1976. Jimmy Carter defeated Gerald Ford in the presidential election. Walter Mondale was elected vice president.

1977. Jimmy Carter pardoned Vietnam-era draft evaders.

An estimated 20,000 women gathered in **Houston, Tex.,** as part of the **U.N. International Women's Year.**

Sept. 7. The U.S. agreed to turn over control of **the Panama Canal** to Panama on Dec. 31, 1999.

Introduction of **Apple II personal computer.** The personal computer made computer technology affordable for home use.

Completion of the controversial 800-mile **trans-Alaska oil pipeline** from Prudhoe Bay to the port of Valdez. Environmental groups had waged a long legal fight to stop the pipeline.

1978. Pres. Carter mediated a treaty between Israel and Egypt after persuading Egyptian president **Anwar Sadat and Israeli prime minister Menachem Begin** to agree on a framework for peace.

Bakke v. *University of California.* **Allan Bakke,** a white man, sued the University of California Medical School at Davis, focusing attention on the controversy surrounding affirmative action. He charged that the school rejected him while admitting less-qualified minorities. First implemented in 1968, affirmative action was intended to correct racial and gender imbalances by giving preference to minorities. The Supreme Court accepted Bakke's charge of **"reverse discrimination"** and ordered his admission to the school. At the same time, **the Court also upheld the concept of affirmative action,** though it ruled against the use of strict quotas.

1979. The U.S. established diplomatic relations with **the People's Republic of China** (p. 1025).

In response to the Carter administration's decision to allow the deposed **shah of Iran, Muhammad Reza Pahlevi,** to enter the U.S. for medical treatment (the shah suffered from incurable cancer), **Islamic fundamentalist students seized the U.S. embassy in Tehran, Iran** (p. 975). The students, under the direction of **religious leader Ayatollah Khomeini,** released 19 hostages—primarily women, black marines, and the seriously ill—and kept 52 others. **The students kept the hostages for 14 months.** Six months into the crisis, the White House launched a rescue attempt, which failed when the rescue helicopters broke down in the desert. **The hostages were released on Jan. 20, 1981, at the exact moment Carter turned the presidency over to Ronald Reagan.**

March 30. The Three Mile Island nuclear power plant in Pennsylvania came close to having a major nuclear accident when its central core reactor threatened to melt down. The incident undermined the public's faith in nuclear technology by seeming to confirm long-standing fears about the safety of nuclear power.

1970s–1980s. A profound change in immigration took place as millions of **Hispanics, Asians, and Caribbeans** poured into the U.S. Asians had increased their proportion of the total U.S. population from 1.6 percent in 1980 to 3.0 percent in 1990; the Hispanic population rose from 6.4 percent to 9.8 percent during the same period.

1980, Nov. Ronald Reagan defeated Jimmy Carter in the presidential election. George Bush was elected vice president. Reagan's election ended almost a half century of government activism begun by the New Deal. **Reagan moved to redefine government priorities by instituting tax cuts, reducing the domestic budget, and increasing the military budget by $1.7 trillion over a five-year period.** Soon dubbed "**Reaganomics,**" the new policies resulted in a ballooning national deficit.

1980s. Religious fundamentalism. A large number of people began to identify with a fundamentalist Christian religious movement. Overtly political and right-wing, this religious revival was led by several **television evangelists,** the most powerful of whom was **Jerry Falwell, leader of the Moral Majority.** Falwell's organization was a major factor in Ronald Reagan's candidacy and election. Toward the end of the decade, the fundamentalist influence began to wane, as some of its leaders faced various legal charges, including misuse of funds.

More than 7 million immigrants entered the country. Asians and Hispanics represented the major groups involved in this new immigration movement.

Cable television and satellite dishes changed the face of television by expanding station options.

The environmental movement gained greater momentum when New York State relocated families from the **Love Canal housing development,** which had been built over a chemical waste site.

1981. Sandra Day O'Connor became the first woman to sit on the Supreme Court.

The Professional Air Traffic Controllers Organization union (PATCO) struck to protest a two-tier pay system and overly stressful working conditions. **Pres. Reagan fired the more than 10,000 striking members of PATCO,** about three-quarters of the nation's air traffic controllers. Reagan's get-tough policy began an era of business antiunionism.

The first case of AIDS was reported. Initially, **Acquired Immunodeficiency Syndrome** received little research funding or government attention. Some charged that the inaction was because the disease first surfaced in the gay community. After mid-decade, this fatal, often sexually transmitted disease began appearing more frequently in the heterosexual community, particularly among bisexuals and intravenous drug users and their partners. **During the AIDS crisis, the U.S. began to see a growth of violence against homosexuals.**

1981–82. Recession. Industrial growth dropped, raising the unemployment rate to 10.7 percent, the highest since the Great Depression.

Deindustrialization. In 1982 more than 1.25 million jobs were lost through 2,700 mass layoffs and plant shutdowns.

1982, Jan. 8. A 13-year Justice Department lawsuit against **the American Telephone and Telegraph Company (AT&T)** was settled. **AT&T gave up 22 of its Bell System companies in exchange for approval to expand into new areas,** including data processing, telephone and computer equipment sales, and computer communication systems.

June 30. States failed to ratify **the Equal Rights Amendment** despite the extended deadline of June 30, 1982. **Phyllis Schlafly,** a conservative activist, spearheaded an antifeminist movement to block the measure.

Vincent Chin, a Chinese American, was killed in a Detroit bar. His assailants, unemployed autoworkers, blamed **Japanese competition** for the troubles of the auto industry and generalized their resentment to include all Asians.

1983. American troops invaded the Caribbean island of **Grenada** (p. 964).

Oct. Two hundred and forty-one American soldiers died in **Beirut, Lebanon,** after their barracks were rammed by a car laden with explosives.

1984. Ronald Reagan defeated Democratic candidate **Walter Mondale** and was reelected as president. **George Bush** was reelected as vice president. Democratic candidate Mondale broke precedent when he selected **Geraldine Ferraro** as his vice presidential running mate. Ferraro was the first woman to be nominated to the national ticket of a major party. Civil rights activist **Jesse Jackson** also ran for president. Though Jackson was not the first African American to run for the office, he was the first to make a strong political showing, mobilizing large numbers of neglected constituents.

1985. Congress passed **the Gramm-Rudman Balanced Budget and Emergency Reduction Control Act.** The measure aimed to balance the budget by 1991 through a program of automatic budget cuts.

1986. Iran-Contra Affair. The Reagan administration had secretly sold arms to Iran, which was at war with Iraq, hoping to gain Iran's cooperation in freeing American hostages. The negotiations took place with the same revolutionary government that Reagan had denounced in the early 1980s and resulted in only one hostage release. The arms sales, however, generated large profits, most of which were sent as military aid to **the Contras in Nicaragua** (p. 954). The illegal diversion of funds to the Contras seemed to have been the idea of **Marine Lt. Col. Oliver North,** who had been assigned to the National Security Council. North destroyed numerous incriminating memos to cover up the scandal, but he missed one that linked the White House to the plan.

Congress passed **the Immigration Reform and Control Act,** which permitted some people who had immigrated illegally to the U.S. before 1982 to gain legal status.

1987. Savings and loan crisis. The nation's "thrifts," as the S&Ls were called, were **deregulated in the early 1980s to allow them to invest in commercial real estate and business.** However, the thrifts became unstable because many of their investments reflected the growth in the 1980s of high-risk **"junk bonds,"** which were speculative or fraudulent. In 1987, the instability of these investments became apparent as stock prices plummeted and with them the solvency of the thrifts. **The losses were so great that many of the thrifts lost their depositors' funds, requiring the government to cover the federally insured deposits.** The bill to American taxpayers to bail out the industry was projected at $200 billion.

1988. Republican George Bush defeated Democrat Michael Dukakis in the presidential elections. **Dan Quayle** was elected vice president. **Jesse Jackson** ran for president for a second time and again made a strong showing with his **"Rainbow Coalition."**

1989. Poverty. Close to 12.8 percent of all Americans, about 31.5 million people, were classified as poor by federal standards; that is, they sustained an income of $12,675 or less for a family of four. This group included 10 percent of all whites and over 25 percent of African Americans and Hispanics. **Poverty was most common among families headed by women.** Also, in the 1980s **homelessness** became a problem. By the end of the decade, families with children made up one-third of the urban homeless population. On the other hand, largely because of Social Security and Medicare, **the elderly,** who used to be among the poorest segments of society, **were comparatively well off.**

1990. The U.S. Census Bureau released figures showing a total of **246.9 million Americans.** One in four Americans now claimed non-European ancestry.

1991, Jan. 16. Persian Gulf War. The U.S. led a multinational force to liberate Kuwait from Iraq (p. 969). The war lasted for 42 days and was a success for the U.S.-led coalition forces. Pres. Bush called for a **"new world order"** in which nations recognized and shared responsibility for "peace and justice."

March 3. Black motorist **Rodney King** was arrested and brutally beaten by members of the **Los Angeles Police Department.** A civilian video of the arrest and beating led to criminal charges against the officers. The case gained wide publicity when **news stations throughout the nation picked up the story and repeatedly aired the violent scene.**

Clarence Thomas, a black conservative nominee for the U.S. Supreme Court, received confirmation despite the allegations of former assistant **Anita Hill** that he had sexually harassed her on the job at a federal agency that he had headed.

1992, April. Los Angeles riots. Five days of violence erupted among African Americans after the acquittal (of all but one charge) of four white police officers accused of excessively beating **Rodney King.** Three months after the riots, the officers were charged in **federal court** for violating King's civil rights. **The officers were found guilty of that charge and were sentenced to two and one half years in prison.** The L.A. riots occurred against the backdrop of an increasingly hostile racial environment in American cities. By the 1980s, **unemployment** rates in the inner city rose as high as 60 percent. In 1986, the **life expectancy** of African-American men and women began declining, and by 1989, 66 percent of all **black children** were born out of wedlock.

Nov. Democratic candidate William ("Bill") Clinton was elected president over George Bush. Albert ("Al") Gore, Jr. was elected vice president.

1993. Clinton sparked major controversy when he attempted to lift the ban on **gays in the military.** Eventually, he opted for the compromise of permitting gays to stay in the military if they did not engage in homosexual conduct.

Feb. After being vetoed twice by Pres. Bush, **the Family and Medical Leave Act** was signed into law. The act required major companies to provide up to 12 weeks of annual unpaid leave for medical or family emergencies.

Feb. 26. Six died and more than 1,000 were injured when a car bomb exploded in New York City's World Trade Center; several Muslim fundamentalists were arrested as possible perpetrators.

April 22. The U.S. Holocaust Memorial Museum was dedicated in Washington, D.C.

April 23. A U.S. Department of Defense report revealed that at least 117 naval officers could face disciplinary action growing out of sexual assaults on some 90 people at a 1991 Las Vegas convention of the Tailhook aviators group.

April 25. More than 300,000 people marched on Washington, D.C., to demand equal rights for homosexuals.

Sept. 22. The president revealed his health care plan. He promised that details of the plan were negotiable, but that the goal of health care for all Americans was not.

Oct. 3. American troops who went to Somalia for humanitarian reasons in 1992 (p. 1059) came under fire—twelve were killed, and more than 75 were injured. Pres. Clinton sent in more troops but promised to bring American troops home by March 1994.

Oct. 7. Toni Morrison became the first African American to receive the Nobel Prize for literature.

Nov. 9. The U.S. Supreme Court unanimously decided to expand the definition of **sexual harassment** to enable employees to win **without having to prove psychological damage.**

Nov. 20. The Congress passed **the North American Free Trade Agreement (NAFTA),** which would significantly reduce trade barriers between the U.S., Canada, and Mexico.

Nov. 24. After seven years, Congress passed gun control legislation. **The so-called Brady Bill mandated a waiting period of up to five days for handgun purchases.**

Dec. 8. Pres. Clinton signed NAFTA into law. The agreement would eliminate most tariff and trade barriers between the U.S., Canada, and Mexico over a 15-year period.

The government began to disclose information about **radiation experiments** conducted from the 1940s through the 1970s on people who had no knowledge of the experiments.

1994, Jan. Pres. Clinton was subpoenaed for possible dealings with the Whitewater Development Corp., which was part of the savings and loan scandal of 1989. On June 14 the U.S. Congress approved the beginning of hearings on this issue.

Jan. 7. A well-known polluter barge was responsible for an oil spill 500 yards off of the coast of San Juan, PR.

Jan. 25. The U.S. launched its ambitious Clementine space project. A joint effort between the Strategic Defense Command and NASA, this lunar exploration lasted seven months, costing at least $175 million.

Feb. Clinton arranged for a visa for IRA leader Gerry Adams to visit the U.S. He had previously been denied a visa because of his links to IRA violence. On Oct. 3 the **U.S. lifted the ban on communications** between the U.S. government and Sinn Fein, the political wing of the IRA, **because of Sinn Fein's Aug. 31 cease-fire declaration.**

Feb. 15. The chief of naval operations, Admiral Frank B. Kelso II, announced his plans for early retirement over charges stemming from the Tailhook sexual harassment scandal.

June 10. The **U.S. extended its sanctions on Haiti** in order to emphasize its desire to get rid of the military regime in power there.

June 12–14. The **National African-American Leadership Summit** met in Baltimore. The meeting attracted a broad cross section of black civil rights and political leaders.

Aug. 19. The U.S. announced an end to allowing Cuban refugees to enter the country, though many continued to try. On Sept. 9 the U.S. agreed to accept a limited number of Cuban refugees per year.

Sept. More than 300 Republican candidates for the U.S. House of Representatives met outside the Capitol building in Washington, DC, and signed what they called a **"Contract with America,"** a 10-point **plan of conservative reforms** designed to reverse expenditures for social welfare, "get tough on crime," and add a balanced budget amendment to the constitution, among other objectives. GOP candidates for the U.S. Senate endorsed a similar plan.

Oct. 17. After the buildup of Iraqi troops on Iraq's border with Kuwait, the U.S. announced plans to send its troops there.

Nov. 8. Republicans won control of Congress for the first time in 40 years.

Dec. 15. Dee Dee Myers, the first woman and the youngest person to hold the post of White House press secretary, resigned, citing the difficulties confronting women and particularly young women in top-level government positions.

1995, Jan. 4. The 104th Congress convenes. The new Speaker of the House, Newt Gingrich (R., Ga.), broke precedent, moved beyond the usual ceremonial opening, and held a 14-hour session designed to implement the Republican Party's proposed Contract with America.

Jan. 20. The U.S. said it would ease its 44-year trade embargo on

North Korea to ensure North Korea's cooperation in reducing its nuclear arsenal.

Jan. 31. Clinton authorized an emergency loan of $20 billion to Mexico.

Feb. 4. The U.S. **imposed huge tariffs on imports** from China in an effort to **punish the Chinese government for its continued manufacture of pirated goods.** On Feb. 26 the U.S. and China signed a negotiation pact because China agreed to crack down on piracy. The pact was expected to be a big boost to trade. The U.S. and China signed trade accords on March 12.

Feb. 19. Clinton announced his refusal to participate in a planned May summit in Russia because of the situation in Chechnya.

March 7. The U.S. dollar plunged to a record low since World War II against the Japanese yen and the German mark, due in part to the loan made to help with the Mexican economic crisis.

March 15. Clinton signed a ban on the participation of U.S. companies in petroleum production activities in Iran because of the U.S.'s perception of Iran as a terrorist country.

April 19. A huge car bomb exploded in Oklahoma City, Oklahoma, destroying the Alfred P. Murrah Federal Building and killing more than two hundred people, including approximately 24 children. On April 21 **Timothy McVeigh,** a citizen with strong anti-government views, **was arrested** for planting the bomb.

April 30. Pres. Clinton **put an end to all U.S. trade with Iran,** citing the country's record of terrorism and its acquisition of nuclear power as the reasons.

July 11. Clinton formally **reestablished diplomatic ties with Vietnam.**

July 19. Pres. Clinton defended affirmative action programs at the conclusion of a five-month-long review of federal affirmative action programs designed to prevent or redress discrimination against women and minorities.

Aug. 31. The U.S. Immigration and Naturalization Service (INS) announced "Citizenship USA," a plan to reduce the amount of time between an immigrant's application for citizenship and the swearing-in process.

Oct. 2. The **acquittal** of African-American football star **O.J. Simpson for the murder of his ex-wife** sparked a tremendous race debate in the U.S.

Oct. 3. Clinton signed an order easing restrictions on trade with and travel and humanitarian aid to Cuba.

Oct. 16. An estimated one million black men attended the **Million Man March** in Washington, DC, where the principal organizer, **Louis Farrakhan of the Nation of Islam,** promoted what he called a "holy day of atonement and reconciliation."

Oct. 31. In a suit against Las Vegas Hilton and its parent company, the Hilton Hotels Corp., a federal jury awarded Tailhook victim Paula A. Coughlin, a navy helicopter pilot, $16.7 million in damages.

Nov. 5. An estimated 1,000 members of the United Automobile Workers union (UAW) agreed to end a four-day strike at Chrysler Corporation's McGraw Glass Division in Detroit, Michigan.

1996, Jan. 26. The U.S. Senate voted to ratify **START II, the second Strategic Arms Reduction Talks Treaty,** which would get both the **U.S. and Russia down to one-third of their 1993 nuclear arsenal levels.**

March 27. In *Seminole Tribe of Florida* v. *Florida,* the U.S. Supreme Court voted 5–4 to overturn the 1988 Indian Gambling Regulatory Act, which allowed American Indians to file federal law suits against any state that failed to negotiate "in good faith" the establishment of gambling casinos on Indian land.

April 9. United Airlines flight attendants rejected a four-year contract proposal offered by the union and United. The attendants opposed the creation of foreign crew bases, which they believed would erode U.S. jobs.

July 31. Clinton agreed to sign a sweeping plan **overhauling the American welfare system** and making enormous **cuts in welfare.**

Aug. 6. NASA research on a meteorite from Mars **suggested evidence of life existing or having evolved in a place other than Earth.**

Sept. 3–4. The **U.S. launched missile attacks on Iraqi military sites** to counter Iraq's recent moves against Kurdish enclaves.

Sept. 30. Pres. Clinton signed into law the new **Illegal Immigrant Reform and Immigrant Responsibility Act,** which aimed to reduce the

number of illegal immigrants, partly by limiting immigrant access to welfare services.

Nov. 5. Clinton was reelected as president of the United States. The Republican Party maintained control of Congress.

Nov. 15. Texaco, Inc., a major oil producer, **agreed to a $176.1 million settlement with black employees** who had lodged a federal suit against the company in 1994 for **discrimination in promotions and pay.** The company settled following disclosure (Nov. 4, 1996) of a tape-recorded conversation in which executives made racist remarks and discussed the destruction or alteration of documents pertinent to the lawsuit.

Dec. 5. Clinton chose **Madeline K. Albright** as the **first woman secretary of state for the U.S.** Prior to obtaining this position, she served as the American ambassador to the UN.

Dec. 21. A U.S. House ethics subcommittee found that Speaker **Newt Gingrich violated House ethics rules** by accepting tax-exempt donations and using the funds for political purposes.

1997, Feb. 4. A **civil jury** in Santa Monica, Calif., **ordered** the former football star **O.J. Simpson to pay $8.5 million in compensatory damages for the wrongful death of Ronald L. Goldman,** a friend of Simpson's ex-wife, Nicole, who was also murdered. Simpson had been acquitted of murder charges in a 1995 criminal trial, which had generated a great deal of discussion and conflict over issues of race in American society. A separate trial was set for punitive damages in the death of Nicole Simpson.

June 14. Pres. Clinton announced the formation of a new panel on race, headed by the distinguished historian John Hope Franklin of Duke University. Clinton charged the panel to **launch a "great and unprecedented discussion about race" in U.S. society.**

June 20. The **tobacco industry reached an agreement with dozens of claimants in lawsuits** against the industry. When implemented, the plan would result in the payment of a landmark $368 billion in damages and imposition of stricter rules on the marketing of cigarettes; it would also free the industry from a variety of pending legal claims against it.

June 24. Federal district court judge James Lawrence King of Miami blocked the deportation (from three southern states) of thousands of refugees from Nicaragua and other Central American countries. Critics of Clinton's Citizenship USA policy claimed that thousands of immigrants had been wrongly naturalized under the program.

July 4. The U.S. probe *Pathfinder* landed on Mars to examine the landscape there.

July 27. A **bomb exploded at the Olympic Games in Atlanta, Ga.,** taking the life of one person and injuring 111 others. Pres. Clinton described the bombing as "an evil act of terror."

Oct. 22. Clinton unveiled plans to **fight global warming** by giving industries **financial incentives to decrease their greenhouse gas emissions.**

Oct. 25. An estimated 300,000 to 500,000 black women held a Million Woman March in Philadelphia at the Benjamin Franklin Parkway, where they adopted a 12-point platform for improving life in the black community.

Oct. 27. The U.S. stock market plunged by 554 points, the largest single-day decline in its history; analysts credited a series of internal "corrective" measures in the market's speedy rebound.

Oct. 29. Chinese president Jiang Zemin visited the U.S. and met with Clinton for the first U.S./China summit in eight years.

Nov. 13. The U.S. Senate Judiciary Committee blocked Pres. Clinton's nomination of Bill Lann Lee as assistant attorney general for civil rights. Conservative members of Congress opposed Lee because of his vocal support for affirmative action. Lee's appointment would have made him the highest ranking Asian American in the Clinton administration.

1998, Jan. 28–Nov. 4. The Justice Department indicted 14 fund-raising members of the Democratic Party over the course of the year in its probe of 1996 campaign finance abuses. No independent counsel probes were provided by Attorney General Janet Reno on Pres. Clinton or V.P. Al Gore.

March 27. The U.S. Food and Drug Administration approved Viagra, a prescription pill to counteract impotence. In its first two years, the medicine was prescribed more than any medicine in history, particularly in such a short amount of time.

June 17. A proposed $516 billion nationwide settlement of smoking-related lawsuits against the tobacco industry failed in the Senate. On Nov. 20 the 46 states and tobacco industry involved that had not reached prior settlements agreed to a much smaller deal.

June 25–July 3. Pres. Clinton became the first U.S. president to visit China since the violence at Tiananmen Square erupted in 1989.

July 22. Pres. Clinton signed a bill reforming the Internal Revenue Service (IRS).

Aug. 6. Although bipartisan support passed it in the House, a substantial campaign finance reform bill was blocked by a Republican majority in the Senate.

Aug. 7. Bombs exploded at U.S. embassies in Kenya and Tanzania, killing over 250 people and injuring thousands more. The bombings were thought to be organized by Islamic extremist and terrorist leader Osama bin Laden, who had been hiding in Afghanistan for some time (p. 976). On Aug. 20 in a largely retaliatory attack the U.S. destroyed several weapons-manufacturing facilities in Afghanistan and the Sudan with cruise missile assaults.

Sept. 30. The 1998 fiscal year ended with the U.S. government having its first federal budget surplus in three decades.

Oct. 19. Microsoft Corp., a software company owned by Bill Gates, went on trial for two antitrust lawsuits filed on May 18 by 20 states and the U.S. Justice Department. The lawsuits accused Microsoft of abusing its quasi-monopoly in the market for computer operating systems.

Oct. 23. At a Camp David, Maryland, summit that included Israeli prime minister Benjamin Netanyahu, Palestinian leader Yasir Arafat, and U.S. president Clinton, the Wye Memorandum was signed as a reinforcement of a peace accord created earlier in the year. The pact set a three-stage plan for Israel to withdraw from the West Bank; the plan represented some of the greatest progress made in Middle East peace negotiations in many years.

Oct. 29–Nov. 7. Senator John Glenn, who had in 1962 been the first American to orbit the Earth, returned to space at age 77 on a mission in the shuttle *Discovery*. Two other important space flights were launched on Nov. 20 and on Dec. 4 when the Russians and Americans, respectively, sent their first modules for the planned international space station into orbit.

Nov. 3. The Democratic Party gained five seats in the House of Representatives during midterm elections. Despite impeachment proceedings against party leader president Clinton, the election gains were enough to cause GOP House Speaker Newt Gingrich to resign on Nov. 6.

Nov. 30. Riots and demonstrations took place against the World Bank, which was holding a meeting in Seattle.

Dec. 16–19. United States and British aircraft conducted an extensive bombing attack on Iraq because of Saddam Hussein's refusal to comply with UN inspections teams throughout the previous year. In an effort to deplete a possible Iraqi arms buildup, the U.S. and Britain conducted frequent attacks on military targets in Iraq during 1999 and 2000.

Dec. 19. The Republican-led House of Representatives voted to impeach Pres. Bill Clinton for the Monica Lewinsky sex and perjury scandal. The vote to impeach was made largely along party lines, following an eight-month investigation by independent counsel Kenneth Starr. It was alleged in the impeachment proceedings that in trying to cover up a recent sexual relationship with Lewinsky, Clinton lied under oath and obstructed justice in a court of law. Pres. Clinton became the second president in U.S. history to be impeached.

1999, Feb. 12. The U.S. Senate voted to acquit Pres. Clinton of impeachment charges.

March 24–June 10. United States forces played a key role in NATO bombing missions against the Serb government in Yugoslavia.

March 29. The Dow Jones industrial average closed above 10,000 for the first time in U.S. history. By Dec. 31 the Dow had reached a closing level of 11,497.12.

April 12. Pres. Clinton was held in contempt of court for giving "intentionally false" information about his relationship with Lewinsky during the Paula Jones sexual harassment trial, which had been settled out of court in Nov. 1998.

June 23. In three important cases, the U.S. Supreme Court upheld the notion of states' rights, protecting states from facing lawsuits for failing to comply with federal laws. The three cases involved the Americans with Disabilities Act: the Court ruled that the law did not include individuals whose disabilities had been corrected by mechanical devices.

Aug. 11. The Kansas Board of Education removed Darwin's Theory of Evolution from the state's science curriculum.

Aug. 17–19. The United States and Russia began discussion of a third Strategic Arms Reduction Talks treaty, START III.

Oct. 7. In a defeat for the Republican majority, the House passed a bipartisan bill supporting patients' rights with regard to medical and insurance benefits and laws.

Oct. 13. The U.S. Senate rejected ratification of the Comprehensive Test Ban Treaty, which would bar nuclear weapons testing in any form.

Oct. 18. Investigator Kenneth Starr, whose inquiries since 1994 had largely led to Pres. Clinton's impeachment, stepped down from his duties as independent counsel. Mr. Starr, whose independent counsel statute was set to expire on June 30, 2000, had been accused of overzealousness and blatant partisanship in his legal pursuit of Pres. Clinton.

Nov. 5. In the Microsoft antitrust lawsuit, a judge concluded that Microsoft held a monopoly power that it had used to the detriment of its competitors.

Dec. 20. The Supreme Court in Vermont ordered state legislators to grant to homosexual couples benefits that were held by heterosexual married couples. Many saw this as a first step toward fully recognized same-sex marriages in the U.S.

Dec. 30. Leading Republican presidential candidate and Texas governor George W. Bush announced that his campaign had raised a record $67 million in 1999 that was intended to go toward his presidential campaign expenses.

Dec. 31. The United States passed full control of the Panama Canal over to the Republic of Panama.

2000, Feb. 6. First Lady Hillary Rodham Clinton announced her intention to run for a Senate position for the state of New York in the 2000 elections.

April 13. In an antitrust lawsuit filed by the federal government and 19 states, Microsoft was found to be in violation of antitrust law by having used monopoly power to disable its competition. In a landmark case for the corporate United States, it was ordered on June 7 that the corporation split into two smaller companies in order to dilute its monopoly powers. After an appeal of prior rulings, the U.S. Supreme Court refused on Sept. 26 to take the Microsoft case.

April 26. The state of Vermont passed a bill recognizing same-sex civil unions as legitimate under state law. Vermont was the first state to enact such a bill.

June 26. Two separate organizations, U.S.-based Celera Genomics Corp. and the internationally funded Human Genome Project, jointly announced that each had compiled a working map of the human genome. The remarkable achievement was expected to revolutionize the fields of science and medicine.

June 26. The U.S. Supreme Court surprisingly upheld the 1966 Miranda decision that required a suspect to have been informed of his or her rights before confessions could be admissible in court. In *Dickerson* v. *United States*, the Court judged a 1968 statute that largely negated the Miranda decision as unconstitutional. Other important precedents upheld by the Supreme Court in the year 2000 were state sovereignty in age-discrimination lawsuits, separation of religion and public education, and the unconstitutionality of state laws banning partial birth abortions.

Aug. 23. Attorney General Janet Reno ruled against a fund-raising probe on Democratic presidential candidate and vice president Al Gore.

Sept. 1. Amid some criticism by Republican opponents, Pres. Clinton postponed a 20-year-old proposal to begin construction of a national missile defense system. The planned project was aimed at protecting the U.S. from nuclear attack.

Sept. 20. In the Whitewater probe, Pres. Clinton and First Lady Hillary Rodham Clinton were cleared of any criminal wrongdoing. The independent counsel cited a lack of evidence against the First Lady and Pres. Clinton, who had been plagued by the scandal throughout his presidency.

Sept. 22. As the U.S. faced remarkable worldwide increases in oil prices, Pres. Clinton approved the allotment of surplus oil from the Strategic Petroleum Reserve in order to increase the oil supply and bring U.S. gas prices under control.

Oct. 12. In an attack that was apparently orchestrated by Yemeni Islamic terrorists, the Navy warship *U.S.S. Cole* was bombed while harbored in Aden, Yemen; seventeen sailors were killed and dozens more injured.

Nov. 2. The international space station project that was initiated with its first module launches one year earlier reached another milestone when its first crew members were sent into space to occupy the station.

Nov. 7. The presidential election remained undecided, the narrowness of the vote margin, particularly in the key electoral state of Florida, being still too close to declare either V.P. Al Gore or Texas governor George W. Bush a definite victor. Congressional elections to the 107th Congress resulted in Republicans retaining a slight majority in the Senate as well as in the House of Representatives. In state elections nationwide, the Republican Party made crucial gains in the state legislatures with the tally of state governorships remaining nearly the same, only one state changing hands.

Dec. 13. After several court battles, the Supreme Court halted recounts and Gore conceded to Bush.

2. CANADA, 1946-2000

(From p. 735)

The cold war shaped Canadian history no less than it did U.S. history. Located between two superpowers, both with nuclear capabilities, Canada supported the U.S. and became a major architect of the North Atlantic Treaty Organization. Through its treaty agreements as well as through trade arrangements, the nation became increasingly linked to the political economy of the U.S. Most of its trade went to the U.S., while American businesses expanded their investments in the Canadian economy. Foreign corporations (mostly U.S. companies) owned most of the nation's petroleum and discouraged Canadian-controlled research and development projects; this ensured Canada's exclusion from the microchip computer revolution that transformed American technology and industries during the period. Although some Canadian policy makers soon complained of the growing dependence of the Canadian economy on foreign companies, the pattern persisted and placed Canada in an increasingly precarious position in the world market. When the Middle Eastern oil crisis struck Western countries in the 1970s and 1980s, the Canadian economy was particularly hard hit.

Despite heavy dependence on the U.S. for economic development and defense, Canada experienced unprecedented economic growth and prosperity until the early 1970s. Production and consumption rose, as the nation's population not only increased but continued to urbanize, and then suburbanize, in growing numbers. A variety of forces fueled the development of Canadian cities, suburbs, and consumer culture: the baby boom, relatively low rates of unemployment, and an overall rise in the standard of living. Yet, as in earlier eras, the country's prosperity was unequally distributed. Inequality persisted between the troubled agricultural sector (and the maritime provinces) and the vibrant urban economies of Montreal, Toronto, and Vancouver. French-speaking Quebec only slowly gained parity with English-speaking Canada. And the problems of Native Americans, African Canadians, women, and homosexuals received little attention until these groups organized and exerted increasing pressure on the Canadian government. By the late 1980s and early 1990s, Canada was also attracting increasing numbers of new immigrants from Europe (especially Italy), Africa, Asia, and the Americas. Although French-speaking Quebec voted to remain in the Dominion in 1980, the new wave of immigrants challenged the nation's ability to maintain an increasingly multiracial as well as multicultural nation.

1946, April 12. Field Marshal Sir Harold Alexander succeeded the earl of Athlone as **governor-general.**

July 1. The proclamation of **the Canadian Citizenship Act** clarified the definition of Canadian citizenship but retained the status of British subjects for Canadians. It went into effect on Jan. 1, 1947.

July 15. A royal commission investigating the activities of a **Soviet spy ring** in Canada reported the disclosure of important secret information by Canadian officials and the existence of a Communist fifth column in Canada, directed by Soviet agents. Among the Canadians involved was the one parliamentary delegate of the Labour-Progressive (Communist) Party.

Aug. 3. An Anglo-Canadian wheat agreement provided for British purchases of large amounts of Canadian wheat at prices considerably below the world market.

1947, Feb. 12. Prime Minister William King announced continued **military cooperation between Canada and the U.S.**

1948, July 22. A referendum in **Newfoundland** to decide between future self-government and confederation with Canada voted in favor of confederation by a narrow margin (78,408–71,464). On March 31, 1949, Newfoundland joined Canada as the tenth province.

1949, April 4. Canada signed the North Atlantic Treaty.

June 27. National elections gave the Liberal Party an overwhelming majority of 193 of the 262 seats in the House of Commons.

Nov. 22–Dec. 2. The British Parliament passed **The British North America Bill** granting the Parliament of Canada the right to amend Canada's constitution.

1950, June–Dec. Upon the outbreak of the Korean War (p. 1029), Canada immediately rallied to the support of the UN. The first Canadian troops arrived in Korea on Dec. 19. Earlier in the year, the Canadian government had placed three destroyers at the disposal of the UN for action in Korean waters. Defense appropriations were more than doubled, and a 40 percent increase of Canada's armed forces was authorized by Parliament. The **Essential Materials Act,** adopted in September, gave the government extensive control over defense industries.

1951. Marshall McLuhan (1911–80) published his first book, *The Mechanical Bride: Folklore of Industrial Man.* He soon became the leading international expert on mass media.

1952, Jan. 24. Vincent Massey was **appointed governor-general** of Canada, to succeed Viscount Alexander of Tunis. His was the first appointment of a Canadian to that post.

Aug. 13. The government announced its decision to provide about $150 million in 1952 as a **mutual aid gift to Britain.**

The Canadian Broadcasting Corporation opened the country's **first two television stations,** in Toronto and Montreal.

1953, Aug. 10. In national elections, the Liberal Party, under **Prime Minister Louis S. St. Laurent,** won its fifth consecutive victory.

1955, Oct. 11. An agreement with the USSR, negotiated by **Sec. Lester B. Pearson** in Moscow, granted most-favored-nation trade privileges and **cooperation in Arctic research.**

1956, May 23. Sir Saville Garner was appointed to succeed **Sir Archibald Nye** as British high commissioner.

Dec. 14. The national convention of the Progressive Conservative Party elected **John Diefenbaker** as its new leader, succeeding **George Drew.**

The Trades and Labour Congress of Canada and the Canadian Congress of Labour merged into one body, **the Canadian Labour Congress (CLC).**

1957, June 17. Following the Conservatives' victory in the June 10 parliamentary elections, **John Diefenbaker formed a new cabinet,** the first Conservative government in 22 years.

1958, Jan. 16. Lester B. Pearson succeeded St. Laurent as leader of the opposition Liberal Party.

March 31. Prime Minister Diefenbaker and the Conservative Party won **the greatest election victory in Canada's history,** securing 202 seats of the 265 in the federal House of Commons.

April. The **Gordon Commission report** was released. It expressed concern over the growing level of U.S. investments in the Canadian economy since 1945.

July 10. U.S. president Dwight D. Eisenhower and Prime Minister Diefenbaker agreed in Ottawa to establish **the Canada–United States Committee on Joint Defense.**

1959, June 26. Pres. Eisenhower and Queen Elizabeth II officially opened **the St. Lawrence Seaway,** linking the Great Lakes with the Atlantic Ocean.

1961, Jan. 17. U.S. president Eisenhower and Prime Minister Diefenbaker signed a treaty in Washington, D.C., for the joint **development of the Columbia River Basin.**

May 2. The government announced that Canada and Communist China had negotiated **a grain sale agreement.**

The National Indian Council was formed to promote better Indian–non-Indian relations.

George Woodcock founded *Canadian Literature,* the first review devoted solely to Canadian writers.

Marie-Claire Blais published her novel *La Belle Bête,* which launched her prolific career as a writer.

1962, June 18. The ruling Conservative Party lost its parliamentary majority in national elections

1963, Jan. 31. Prime Minister Diefenbaker reacted to the U.S. State Department's criticism (Jan. 30) of Canada's lack of plans to equip its defense forces with nuclear weapons by denouncing it as an unwarranted intrusion.

Feb. 6. Following a **defeat of the Diefenbaker government on its nuclear weapons policy** (Feb. 5), Parliament was dissolved and elections were scheduled.

April 8. The Liberal Party won the **general elections** by receiving a plurality of 129 seats in the House of Commons. **Lester B. Pearson** took office on April 22 as Liberal **prime minister.**

May 11. U.S. president Kennedy and Prime Minister Pearson agreed to **equip Canadian missiles with U.S.-supplied nuclear warheads.**

Front de libération du Québec (FLQ) was formed. The organization soon protested Quebec's dependent status within the Dominion by placing bombs in mailboxes.

1964, Jan. 22. An agreement signed with the U.S. provided for the multimillion-dollar **power and flood-control development of the Columbia River Basin.**

Sept. 18. The Columbia River treaty was signed by British Columbia, Canada, and the U.S., providing for the development and distribution of hydroelectric power.

Oct. 5–13. Visit of Queen Elizabeth and Prince Philip. They were greeted in Quebec by deserted streets, a form of protest by the advocates of autonomy for French-speaking Quebec.

1965, Aug. 11. Huge sales of **Canadian wheat to the Soviet Union and to Communist China.**

Nov. 8. National elections. The Liberal Party failed to secure a majority of seats in Parliament, and the government of Lester Pearson became dependent on the **New Democrats,** who had polled 18 percent of the vote, for support.

Hubert Aquin published *Prochain Episode,* which received acclaim as the great novel of Quebec's revolutionary period.

1966. In the **Quebec provincial election, Daniel Johnson's Union Nationale defeated Jean Lesage's Liberal Party,** which held power. The Union Nationale favored the concept of two nations within the Canadian confederation.

1967, April. The navy, army, and air force were consolidated to form the **Canadian Armed Services.**

The death penalty was abolished for a five-year trial period, though it could be instated for the murder of a police officer or prison guard.

April–Oct. Celebration of the **centennial of Dominion status.** The great world exposition (Expo 67) brought millions of visitors to Montreal.

July 24–26. State visit of French president Charles de Gaulle. He openly promised French support for Quebec's efforts to become master of its own destiny; in a speech at Montreal, he shouted, "*Vive le Québec libre.*" For this amazing outburst he was rebuked by Premier Pearson and abruptly canceled his projected visit to Ottawa, returning directly home. There seems no doubt that de Gaulle's interference in Canadian affairs encouraged the **growth of a separatist movement** in the Province of Quebec, despite the disapproval of the principal parties. The separatist leader was **René Lévesque.**

Nov. Confederation for Tomorrow. In conferences of federal and provincial officials, Premier Johnson of Quebec opposed separatism but called for greater provincial autonomy and complete equality within the confederation for Quebec.

1968. Parti Québecois was formed in Quebec and called for political independence, while retaining economic ties to Canada.

The National Indian Council was dissolved. **The Canadian Métis Society** (which became the Native Council of Canada in 1970) was formed; it represented Métis and nonstatus Indians. **The National Indian Brotherhood was formed** to represent the Assembly of First Nations, or status Indians.

Feb. The former African French colony of **Gabon invited the Quebec minister of education** to attend a conference and treated him as representative of a sovereign state. The Canadian government broke off relations with Gabon and blamed France for using Gabon as a front.

Further **conferences on constitutional questions** were attended by premiers of all ten provinces. They discussed linguistic rights for French-speaking minorities outside Quebec Province.

April 6. Pierre Elliott Trudeau was elected leader of the Liberal Party, following the resignation of Pearson.

April 20. TRUDEAU BECAME PRIME MINISTER.

June 25. The decisive victory of the Liberal Party in the national elections indicated the tremendous popular appeal of Trudeau.

The Broadcasting Act of 1968 replaced the **Canadian Radio-Television Commission (CRTC);** the new body emphasized the ownership and control of media by Canadians.

July 5. Trudeau organized an all–Liberal Party cabinet.

1969, Feb. 10–12. The federal-provincial conference on constitutional reform grappled with the question of **the allocation of revenues** among the federal and the provincial governments.

Students protested racism by occupying the computer center of **Sir George Williams University in Montreal.** Forty-one blacks were among the 90 students arrested.

April 3. The Canadian government announced its intention of carrying out a phased **reduction of its forces in Europe,** while remaining faithful to its obligations under NATO.

May. The Criminal Code Amendment Act liberalized laws on abortion, homosexuality, lotteries, and so on. **The first gay liberation organizations** soon developed in Vancouver, Montreal, Toronto, and Ottawa.

July 9. The Official Languages Act. The English and French languages were made equally official in federal administration. **Bilingual districts** were to be established anywhere in Canada where the English or French population exceeded 10 percent of the total.

Sept. 19. The government announced that the forthcoming **reduction of forces in Europe** involved a 50 percent decrease and that Canada's nuclear role would be ended by 1972.

Oct. 7. Police officers and firefighters in Montreal went on strike to demand higher pay. The city soon became the prey of criminals and arsonists, and the Canadian armed forces had to be brought in. On Oct. 8, the Quebec provincial parliament ordered the strikers back to work.

1970, Oct. 5. James R. Cross, a British trade official, and (Oct. 10) **Pierre Laporte,** Quebec minister of labour, were abducted by terrorists of **the Front for the Liberation of Quebec.** The men were held hostage to force the liberation of 23 political prisoners and payment of a large ransom. The governments of Quebec and of Canada rejected the demands.

Oct. 13. Establishment of diplomatic relations with Communist China and severance of relations with Nationalist China. Canada recognized the People's Republic of China as "the sole legal government of China" but did not recognize its claim to the possession of Taiwan.

Oct. 16. Prime Minister Trudeau invoked the **War Measures Act** for six months, to meet the threat of insurrection in Quebec. While army units were assigned to preserve order in the Province of Quebec, police forces pressed the search for Cross and Laporte, arresting hundreds of members of the outlawed front and other suspects.

Oct. 18. The murdered **body of Laporte was found** in the trunk of an abandoned automobile.

Oct. 19. The House of Commons approved Trudeau's invocation of emergency legislation, 190–16.

Dec. 1. The House of Commons passed **the Public Order (Temporary Measures) Act** to replace the more stringent War Measures Act. The new law still outlawed the secret Quebec nationalist society and authorized the police to arrest without warrant and hold suspects for as long as a week without bringing charges.

Dec. 3. Cross was rescued after 59 days in captivity, but only after the government had provided three kidnappers and four of their relatives with a Canadian army plane on which to escape to Cuba.

Dec. 28. Arrest of three additional suspects in the Laporte murder.

1972–84. Under the leadership of Trudeau, Liberals held the reins of power in a series of close elections (except in 1979, when a minority Tory regime seized control under Joseph Clark). **Headed by David Lewis, the New Democratic Party** held the balance of power in the liberal minority government.

1973, Oct. 6. Arabs placed an embargo on oil to nations supporting Israel and thus disrupted the Canadian economy, shaping subsequent political events.

1975. Postal Service Workers' strike led to better benefits.

1980, May 20. In a referendum on separation, the Province of Quebec rejected separation by a majority of nearly 60 percent.

1981. Passage of **the Constitution Act** gave Canada full power over its own constitution within the Commonwealth.

1982. The Laboratory Centre for Disease Control in Ottawa began tracking incidence of **AIDS.**

1983, May 10. The Nova Scotia Court of Appeal overturned the 1971 murder conviction of Native American **Donald Marshall.** The court revealed a gross miscarriage of justice in the earlier case and ordered Marshall's release, after he had served 11 years in prison for a crime that he did not commit.

1984–93. John Turner replaced Trudeau as prime minister, dissolved Parliament, and called for new elections, which he lost to the **Progressive Conservative Brian Mulroney,** who served through 1993.

1986. The West Edmonton Mall was completed—the largest in the world—symbolizing the growing triumph of consumer culture in Canadian society.

1987. The Mulroney government negotiated a free trade agreement with the U.S.

1988. Mulroney and the Progressive Conservatives returned to office.

The Supreme Court of Canada declared abortion law to be in conflict with the nation's Charter of Rights. **Dr. Henry Morgentaler** had helped polarize Canadian opinion on the subject when he defied earlier legal constraints and continued to perform abortions.

April 3. The Meech Lake Agreement to protect Quebec's autonomy gave Quebec veto over most amendments to the constitution, but failed passage (June 1990) after **Manitoba's Indian leader Elijah Harper and Newfoundland's Clyde Wells** refused to endorse the measure.

1990. Jean Chrétien replaced John Turner as Liberal leader.

Aubrey McLauglin (b. 1936), a former social worker from the Yukon Territory, became **the first woman party leader in Canada** when she replaced **Ed Broadbent** as leader of **the National Democratic Party.**

June. Failure of the Meech Lake Agreement led to violent confrontation between the Mohawks of Oka and the government of Robert Bourassa of Quebec. The government responded by bringing in federal forces.

1991, Jan. 1. The government instituted **the Goods and Services Tax (GST),** designed to increase federal revenue by imposing a 9 percent across-the-board tax on goods and services. The measure met stiff resistance from citizens, who often crossed the border, shopped in the U.S., and smuggled goods back into Canada.

The Aboriginal Justice Inquiry in Manitoba concluded that the justice system itself had become abusive.

A parliamentary **bill to recriminalize abortion** failed passage after a tie vote.

1992. A survey of cigarette smokers revealed that Canada was the only country in the world with more women than men smokers. Terry Fox had initiated the **Marathon of Hope** (1980) in Canada to demonstrate the need for cancer research and education.

The **Toronto Blue Jays** reached the **World Series** in baseball and won

against the **Atlanta Braves.** The Blue Jays were the **first non-U.S. team to win the series.**

1993, Jan. 7. Unitel Communications Toronto completed a deal that gave the **American Telephone and Telegraph Company** 20 percent of its stock.

March 9. The Canadian Immigration Board adopted new guidelines that broadened the opportunities of women seeking admission to the country.

March 29. Catherine Callbeck of Prince Edward Island became the first woman elected as a Canadian provincial premier. Callbeck had gained leadership of the province's Liberal Party in January.

April 20. Two senior managers were charged with criminal negligence and manslaughter in Nova Scotia's **Westray coal mine disaster, which killed 26 miners.**

May 25. The federal government, the Northwest Territories, and **the Inuit (Eskimos)** of the eastern and central Arctic region signed a new "native land claims agreement."

May 27. The House of Commons approved the proposed **North American Free Trade Agreement (NAFTA).** Canada became the first of the three countries (which included the U.S. and Mexico) to approve the arrangement.

June 25. Kim Campbell became Canada's first woman prime minister, following her election to the head of the ruling Progressive Conservative Party. Campbell resigned after serving for only 134 days (Nov. 4). Her chief rival, Jean Charest, soon replaced her as interim head of the party (Dec. 13).

Nov. 4. Jean Chrétien was sworn in as the nation's 20th prime minister

Nov. 16. Finance Minister Paul Martin reported the nation's 1992–93 **budget deficit** to be at $40.5 billion, the largest in the country's history.

Dec. 20. Fisheries minister Brian Tobin reported plans to close all but one of Canada's **Atlantic cod-fishing grounds.** The closure was expected to result in the loss of some 5,000 jobs.

1994, Jan. 18. In Ottawa, Canada held its first parliamentary session since the Liberal Party of Prime Minister **Jean Chrétien** took power over a year earlier. The government made job creation and economic growth its top priorities.

April 29. Nearly 400 construction workers forced the Nova Scotia legislative assembly to close its session. The workers protested pending legislation that would have allowed the hiring of nonunion workers on construction sites.

1995, May 25. In a vote of 5–4, the Supreme Court of Canada ruled that the country's **Charter of Human Rights and Freedoms also protected homosexuals,** but the court **refused to sanction homosexual marriage** as a basis for allocating state-supported social welfare benefits.

Oct. 30. A referendum in Quebec to make the province its own state, independent of Canada, was rejected by just 1 percent.

1996, Oct. 24–27. The country's ruling Liberal Party held its biennial convention in Ottawa and announced that it had achieved 78 percent of the 197 goals referred to in its 1993 Red Book. Opposition parties soon disputed the claim.

Nov. 13. Canada proposed a UN plan to provide a relief mission to refugees in Zaire; Africans requested a UN presence.

1997, April 27. Prime Minister Jean Chrétien's Liberal Party called for an early parliamentary election, nearly a year and a half before the party's existing mandate expired. The party claimed that it was ahead of schedule and needed a new mandate to forge ahead with reforms, including efforts to balance the budget.

1998, Aug. 20. The Canadian Supreme Court ruled that the province of Quebec could not secede from Canada until it had negotiated the terms of its secession with both the central government and each of Canada's other individual provinces.

Nov. 30. Parti Québecois (PQ) won a reduced plurality in Quebec's parliamentary election. This ruling party of Quebec premier Lucien Bouchard took 76 seats in the 125-seat National Assembly.

1999, Aug. 20. Premier Bouchard publicly stated that his PQ would pursue a third Quebec secession vote before Nov. 2003.

April 1. Canada officially created a new autonomous territory called Nunavut in part of its arctic and subarctic region. The territory was to be governed solely by the Inuit tribe, who comprised more than 85 percent of the 25,000 inhabitants that occupied this sparsely populated 772,000 sq. mi. of land. The creation of Nunavut was the first Canadian territorial change since 1949 and the product of more than 30 years of land-claims negotiations and Inuit activism.

Oct. 20. A Quebec court judge overturned several parts of a law that stated that French must be the predominant language on government and road signs in the region.

2000, March 25. A newly formed political party, the Canadian Reform Conservative Alliance, emerged as a strong opposition force to the ruling government. Alliance leader Stockwell Day and his supporters were expected to challenge the current administration in 2001 elections. The new party replaced the Reform Party as the official opposition to the Liberal Party government of Prime Minister Jean Chrétien.

Sept. 28. Former Canadian prime minister Pierre Elliott Trudeau (Joseph Philippe Pierre Yves Elliott Trudeau) died at age 80. Trudeau had been the leader of Canada from 1968 to 1984.

Nov. 27. After Prime Minister Chrétien called for elections 18 months ahead of schedule, his ruling Liberal Party won a plurality in parliamentary elections for the third straight time, gaining nine seats in the legislature. Nevertheless, this election established the recently organized Alliance Party as the most legitimate conservative opposition to the Liberal Party. The election began Canada's 37th House of Commons.

D. LATIN AMERICA, 1945–2000

1. OVERVIEW

(From p. 736)

In the years since World War II, Latin America has undergone major cultural, economic, and political changes. **Industrialization and urbanization** have transformed the region. Long-standing **conflicts over land use and control** were supplemented by the struggle for industrial development, the desire for **regional self-sufficiency and integration,** and the fight against imperial domination. New political movements, ranging from the extreme Right to the extreme Left, reflected Latin America's changing international and internal situation.

Beginning in the 1950s, **hyperurbanization** produced megalopolises in cities such as São Paulo, Rio de Janeiro, and Mexico City. **Declining economic opportunities** and land scarcity in the countryside have driven ever larger numbers of *campesinos* into urban areas, looking for work. By the 1980s these cities, surrounded by countless **squatter settlements,** were among the largest in the world. Rapid population growth was simultaneously felt in rural areas, where inhabitants continued to struggle against the onslaught of commercial agriculture and **environmental destruction.**

In some regions the urban middle and working classes have also expanded rapidly. **Import substitution industrialization** and public employment supported the expansion of these classes in the years after 1945. As these groups grew, so did demands for social welfare and health programs, expanded educational opportunities, and growth in the role that the state played in regulating the economy and society. Before the crises and privatizations of the late 1980s, the state in nations such as Brazil, Mexico, and Argentina was heavily involved in commerce and society, and often **the state owned important national industries.** In other less-developed countries, where a small number of people were able to maintain control of the political apparatus, **right-wing repressive tactics** were often maintained.

The nationalist and populist politics that dominated the 1940s and 1950s gave way to a more socialist-oriented politics in some areas by the 1960s and 1970s. This trend produced the **socialist revolutions** in Cuba (1959) and Nicaragua (1979), and the election of a socialist president in Chile (1970). However, harsh **authoritarian regimes** and extremely reactionary governments dominated much of the region. Many movements identified with the Left were ruthlessly suppressed. During this time, Latin American **militaries, often with U.S. support, played a growing role in politics,** occasionally as social reformers (as in Peru in 1968), but most often as representatives of the Right.

By the late **1980s** both **military interventions in politics and the power of the Left were in steep decline.** Years of brutal dictatorships and the horrors of Argentina's "dirty war" and Augusto Pinochet's Chile had helped to bring Latin America's militaries into deep disregard, while the obvious failures of Fidel Castro's Cuba and the decline of socialism abroad forced the region's leaders to look elsewhere for solutions to their problems. The new, mostly civilian governments of the region are currently resorting to **neoliberalism** and considering the policies of the newly industrializing nations of the Far East for answers to their problems with staggering debt and economic stagnation.

Larger political movements have also reflected certain profound changes in the internal power relationships in Latin American society. The **role of women** has changed radically in Latin America over the past 50 years. From simply receiving the vote to demanding (and finding) expanded roles in politics, business, and other fields, **feminist movements** have had some startling successes in the region. **Native, mestizo, and black movements** have also made great strides in their **demands for representation and for ethnic and racial equality.** The Catholic Church in the region has recently taken up the cause of the poor and dispossessed, highlighted by conferences in 1968 and 1979 wherein **the church abandoned its traditional noninterventionist stance** and openly advocated action to empower the poor and change the plight of the dispossessed. Religious life, meanwhile, has become more diverse, with evangelical Protestant sects attracting numerous converts from poor urban neighborhoods. African-influenced religions, such as Santería (Cuba), Vodun (Haiti), and Candomblé (Brazil) have also thrived in the rapidly expanding cities.

a. CULTURAL DEVELOPMENTS

In the years since World War II, Latin American art, literature, and film have assumed a prominent international status. Many Latin American **artists of the postwar era have used their work to engage in social and political struggles.** Poets such as Nobel Prize–winner **Pablo Neruda** (1904–73), whose most famous work, *Canto General* (1950), explores the history of Latin America from the point of view of the workers and peasants, examined issues and social groups that had been all but ignored. Cuban poet **Nicolás Guillen,** too, used traditions drawn from **Afro-Cuban folk culture** to attack imperial domination in Latin America.

Over the past 50 years, the novel and short story have emerged as the two dominant art forms of the region. In the 1940s, the Argentine **Jorge Luis Borges** (1899–1986) rose to international prominence with works such as *Ficciones* (1944), which used magic and fantasy as its primary vehicle. The Mexican Nobel laureate (1990) **Octavio Paz** published his major work, *The Labyrinth of Solitude* (1950), in the immediate postwar period. During the same years, writers such as **Miguel A. Asturias,** who wrote *Men of Maize* (1949), were developing the school of magical realism in Latin America. These authors blended myth, fantasy, and native imagery to produce works that might be understood from the perspective of Indian cultures or as rejections of the "logic" of Western literary narratives.

The boom in Latin American fiction began in the 1960s. During this decade, the Mexican **Carlos Fuentes** (*The Death of Artemio Cruz,* *1962*), the Peruvian **Mario Vargas Llosa** (*Conversations in the Cathedral, 1970*), and the Colombian **Gabriel García Márquez** (*One Hundred Years of Solitude, 1967*) gained international prominence. García Márquez (b. 1928), perhaps the most prominent Latin American author, used **magical realism** to retell some of the most tragic events in Colombian history, mixing fantasy with reality, making the two part of everyday life. García Márquez was awarded the Nobel Prize for literature in 1982.

In the postwar period, the Latin American film industry also grew significantly, but it was not until the 1960s that Latin American filmmakers emerged as major artists. **Cinema Nôvo** in Brazil produced a wealth of films exploring poverty in the region, focusing particularly on the *favelas* (urban slums) of Brazil's cities. During the 1960s the Cuban film industry, led by figures such as **Tomás Gutiérrez Alea** (*Memories of Underdevelopment, 1968*) launched a concerted assault against the dominance of Hollywood in the region. Elsewhere in Latin America, efforts at independent filmmaking have been frustrated by the lack of public and private funding.

b. REGIONAL DIPLOMACY

1945, Feb. Latin American and American leaders met in Mexico City for the **Chapultepec Conference** to discuss postwar cooperation. The U.S. indicated that European recovery had top priority and that, although it intended to protect its own producers, it wanted an open door for investment and trade in the region. The Latin Americans opposed the U.S. position.

1947, Sept. 2. The Inter-American Mutual Assistance Treaty was adopted by the Inter-American conference meeting at Rio. It provided for mutual assistance against aggression.

1948, April 30. The Ninth Pan-American Conference, at Bogotá, established the **Organization of American States (OAS)** as a regional grouping under the UN. The Inter-American Conference became the supreme authority of the OAS, and the Pan-American Union its secretariat.

Dec. 13. The OAS charter went into effect upon ratification by Colombia, the 14th state.

1954, March 12. The Inter-American Conference, meeting at Caracas, adopted a U.S. resolution calling for **action to exclude Communism from the Western Hemisphere.** Guatemala dissented.

1958. In a "goodwill" trip to eight Latin American nations, **V.P. Richard Nixon of the U.S. was repeatedly attacked by protesters** unhappy with U.S. policies. The demonstrations, which at times threatened the vice president's life, received worldwide press coverage and were a blow to U.S. prestige in the region. They also prompted Washington to rethink its Latin American policies.

1959, Aug. 12–18. The Declaration of Santiago, signed by the foreign ministers of 21 American states, condemned not only dictatorial regimes, but also efforts by other governments to overthrow them.

Sept. 30. A South American free trade zone was agreed to by Brazil, Argentina, Bolivia, Chile, Paraguay, Peru, and Uruguay.

1960. Creation of the **Central American Common Market.** El Salvador, Guatemala, Honduras, and Nicaragua signed initially, with Costa Rica joining later in 1962. Within the next decade it eliminated interstate tariffs and vastly increased reciprocal trade.

Aug. 28. In the **declaration of San José,** foreign ministers condemned the efforts of the Soviet Union and Communist China to spread Communism in the Western Hemisphere. The Cuban delegation walked out of the meeting.

1961, Jan. 4. The OAS council voted 14–1 (with 6 abstaining) to impose an **economic boycott on the Dominican Republic.**

March 13. The Alliance for Progress to aid Latin American countries was proposed by U.S. president John F. Kennedy.

Aug. 17. THE ALLIANCE FOR PROGRESS CHARTER was signed by the U.S. and all Latin American governments except Cuba, at Punta del Este (Uruguay). A ten-year program involving $20 billion in public and private investment, it was designed to raise the per capita income of Latin American populations by 2.5 percent annually.

1962, Jan. 23–31. A conference of OAS foreign ministers at Punta del Este voted that Cuba had in effect excluded itself from OAS activities, though it retained its membership.

Nov. 15–17. Foreign ministers from El Salvador, Guatemala, Honduras, and Nicaragua met to create the new **Organización de Estados Centro Americanos (ODECA),** with an economic council, a foreign ministers council to maintain collective security, and a court of justice.

1963. At the behest of the U.S. Southern Command, **presidents of Central American countries established the Central American Defense Council (CONDECA),** a joint military council designed to aid in defense against Communist aggression from Cuba.

1964, July 21–26. The OAS conference of foreign ministers voted to invoke **sanctions against Cuba** and called on all members to sever diplomatic and trade relations. Only Mexico and Jamaica refused to do so.

1965, April–1966, Oct. OAS intervention in the Dominican civil war.

1965–70. This period of **increasing crisis** was fueled by a dramatic rate of population increase, widespread unemployment, steadily mounting inflation, and general prevalence of poverty. **Politics became polarized,** and authoritarian regimes became a major feature of the region. Military dictatorships sought to silence opposition and promote capitalist agendas that disregarded the claims of the dispossessed. Many workers, students, and peasants turned to **leftist ideologies** to express their dissent. As tolerance for peaceful activism disappeared, **urban guerrilla groups** emerged, which resorted to the kidnapping of officials and foreign diplomats as a means of struggle.

1966, Jan. A tricontinental conference of Asian, African, and Latin American Communists founded the Organization for Latin American Solidarity, which held its first meeting at Havana in 1967 (July 31– Aug. 10).

1967, Feb. 14. Fourteen nations of Latin America and the Caribbean signed a **treaty prohibiting** the manufacture, use, or possession of **nuclear weapons** on their territory.

April 12–14. A meeting of 19 American chiefs of state **at Punta del Este** (Uruguay) discussed economic problems and laid plans for a Latin American common market.

1968. The General Conference of Latin American Bishops (CELAM) held its second conference at Medellín, Colombia, with Pope Paul VI in attendance. The key issue at the conference was the role the Catholic Church should play in the region's current structural crisis. In the end, the conference blamed neocolonialism and institutional violence for Latin America's problems, and **called for a radical redistribution of wealth** in underdeveloped areas. **Pope Paul VI affirmed the role of the church in liberating the poor** from inequitable social, economic, and political structures.

Oct. 8. Death of Ernesto "Che" Guevara (1928–67), Argentine-born Cuban revolutionary, in a clash with Bolivian troops.

1969, May 26. An agreement for ANDEAN INTEGRATION, creating a common market, was signed in Bogotá by Colombia, Ecuador, Bolivia, Peru, and Chile.

June–July. OAS intervention in the Salvadoran-Honduran War.

1976, June 4–18. The OAS General Assembly in Santiago, Chile, mainly addressed one major issue: the rising tide of **human rights abuses** in Latin America. Delegates to the assembly pressured the Chilean government of Augusto Pinochet to curtail torture and murder of dissidents.

1977, June 14–23. The OAS General Assembly met in Grenada. Human rights violations again dominated the agenda, and the U.S. decision to suspend aid to Uruguay and Argentina because of human rights abuses was much debated. Delegates split over this apparent interference in the internal affairs of Latin America.

1978, Oct. As the insurrection in Nicaragua intensified, the U.S. sought to mediate a compromise in the civil war through a **committee of the Organization of American States.** This effort failed because Anastasio Somoza refused to resign, and the liberal opposition felt the OAS was too sympathetic to entrenched interests.

1979, March. The Third CELAM Conference was held at Puebla, Mexico. Conservatives attacked the liberationist agenda set in Medellín by preparing a paper that called for resignation on the part of the poor and a hope for a better afterlife. Progressive church elements were highly critical of this line of thought and sought the intervention of the new pope, John Paul II, in the dispute. At this point John Paul II sided with more progressive elements, continuing the precedent of Medellín.

Oct. 30. The OAS General Assembly unanimously adopted **the Declaration of La Paz,** which called for democracy, respect for human rights, and disarmament in the region.

1983–84. Colombia, Mexico, Venezuela, and Panama worked out a 21-point peace plan for Central America known as **Contadora.** The plan was supported by most nations of Latin America (including Nicaragua), the European Common Market, and Japan, but it was blocked by the U.S.

1984, June 21–22. At the **Conference of Foreign and Finance Ministers** of Latin America in Cartagena, Colombia, the presidents of Argentina, Brazil, Colombia, and Mexico released a joint statement condemning First World protectionism and rising interest rates. The conference adopted **the Declaration of Quito,** which proclaimed that negotiations over debt payments must consider the social and developmental aims of the debtor nations, and that creditor nations should accept some responsibility for Third World debt.

1986, April 25. Twenty-two nations met in Rio de Janeiro to sign an agreement to create **the Inter-American Drug Control Committee** to set out strategies for controlling drug trafficking.

1987, Aug. In the aftermath of the failure of Contadora, the presidents of Guatemala, El Salvador, Honduras, Nicaragua, and Costa Rica met in Guatemala City to sign a set of peace agreements proposed by Costa Rican president **Oscar Arias. The Arias Peace Plan** called for an end to outside assistance to insurgent forces, democratic reforms, the release of political prisoners, and fair elections. The U.S. initially opposed the treaty but in the end reluctantly endorsed it. Arias won the 1987 Nobel Peace Prize for his efforts.

1991, March 26. Representatives of Brazil, Argentina, Uruguay, and Paraguay met in Asunción to create **the Southern Cone Common Market (Mercosur).** This free trade agreement was due to come into effect by Jan. 1, 1995.

1994, Jan. 1. The **North Atlantic Free Trade Agreement (NAFTA)** went into effect, covering a population of more than 360 million people and making it one of the world's two largest free trade zones.

Dec. 9–11. Thirty-four leaders from North and South America, with only Cuba absent, held a conference and decided to establish a full free trade zone by the year 2005.

Dec. 17. Brazil, Argentina, Paraguay, and Uruguay signed a pact **creating Mercosur.**

1995, Jan. 2. Chile and Bolivia requested membership in Mercosur.

Oct. 16–17. Leaders from Spain, Portugal, and Latin America met for the fifth annual **Ibero-American summit** in Argentina. They **condemned the U.S. embargo on Cuba.**

1998, April 19. Leaders of the Western Hemisphere signed a joint declaration regarding the Free Trade Area of the Americas (FTAA), initiated in 1994. In addition to trade issues, the challenges of human rights, education, and drug trafficking were major concerns of Western Hemisphere nations. The talks led to the creation of a press advocate position in the Organization of American States (OAS), judicial education ideas for undertrained Latin American court systems, anti-drug monitoring powers in the OAS, and international loans to fight poverty.

May 11, July 13. Observers from OAS approved allegedly fraudulent elections in Paraguay and Ecuador, internationally legitimizing these new governments.

Oct. 26. The 50-year-old border dispute between Ecuador and Peru that sent the nations to war in 1995 was resolved. It was the last conflict of its kind in Latin America to date (pp. 942, 943).

Nov. 2. In Buenos Aires, Argentina, 160 nations met at an environmental conference that lasted two weeks and was aimed at implementing the 1997 UN Kyoto Protocol, a program by which industrialized nations hope to reduce fossil fuel emissions and global warming (p. 936).

Dec. 9. Chile, Argentina, Brazil, Paraguay, Uruguay, and Bolivia signed a joint declaration backing Chilean state sovereignty in arresting and prosecuting alleged war criminal and former military leader of Chile, Augusto Pinochet Ugarte. After his extradition from Europe (p. 851), Pinochet's prosecution was one of the most formidable legal movements against human rights violations in recent South American history.

1999, June 29. In a two-day international summit in Rio de Janeiro, Brazil, the European Union and Mercosur joined to discuss trade liberalization efforts between the two continents with an eye to establishing free trade by 2005 (p. 948).

Nov. 15–16. The Ninth Ibero-American Summit was held in Havana, Cuba, yielding lengthy international discussion over the U.S. embargo on Cuba and human rights violations in Cuba and in Central and South America.

Dec. 31. The Panama Canal was formally handed over by the United States to Panama.

2000, Jan. 21. In Ecuador the government lost power to an Indian-supported military coup, the first seizure of power by the armed forces in Latin America in over ten years. Internal and diplomatic pressure led to a quick restoration of civilian rule.

Aug. 31–Sept. 1. The presidents of South America's 12 countries met for an economic summit in Brasilia, Brazil (p. 948). Headed by Pres. Cardoso of Brazil, the conference focused again on the goal of establishing free trade in South America by 2005.

2. SOUTH AMERICA, 1945–2000

a. ARGENTINA

(From p. 737)

1945, Oct. 9. With the country polarized over Juan Perón's labor concessions and advocacy of the poor, the military (supported by big business, the landed elites, as well as Socialists and Radicals) mounted a coup. **Perón was jailed.**

Oct. 17. A rally of more than a quarter of a million workers in Buenos Aires, supported by **the General Confederation of Labor (CGT),** forced the release of Perón. He then formed the **Labor Party** and vowed to run for president. During this time **EVA DUARTE DE PERÓN** (1919–52), Perón's wife, grew to national prominence for her activism and advocacy for the lower classes.

1946, Feb. 24. Against a united opposition, **PERÓN WAS ELECTED PRESIDENT.** His supporters won a majority in both houses. During the campaign, the U.S. accused Argentina and Perón of collaboration with the Axis powers. Yet Perón's popularity was reaching an all-time high among workers. As minister of labor he had raised workers' wages by nearly 20 percent, and his political style was uniquely **suited to a populace disillusioned by decades of corruption and repression. He mixed his populist ethos with a strong nationalist message,** producing a style of politics not easily described as right- or left-wing. Once president, Perón nationalized numerous foreign-owned firms, and he was able to use foreign exchange reserves built up during and after the war to increase workers' wages by an additional 20 percent, while at the same time keeping industry profitable.

1947, Jan. 1. A five-year plan of economic reform and industrialization went into effect.

Sept. 23. Under pressure from Eva Perón and the newly formed **Peronist Women's Party,** women were granted the vote. This created another forum in which to mobilize support for Perón, as well as further legitimating Eva's role in the regime. Popular particularly among the poor, "Evita" was Peronism's most charismatic symbol.

1948, July. Using profits from the war boom, **Perón paid off Argentina's entire foreign debt and issued a "Declaration of National Independence."** During the next two years he would nationalize British-owned railways and assume control of the international marketing of Argentina's beef exports.

Aug. 13–14. The Chamber of Deputies gave **unlimited powers to Perón** in case of a national emergency and voted to reform the constitution. Elections for a constituent assembly (Dec. 5) gave the Peronist Party a large majority.

1949, March 8. The new constitution, approved by the assembly, confirmed Perón's policies of **land reform and nationalization of industries,** and made the president eligible for reelection. Although democratic institutions remained in place, there was a growing tendency toward repression of dissidents.

1951, April 13. In an effort to stamp out public criticism of his regime, Perón suppressed the newspaper *La Prensa.*

Nov. 11. In spite of a deteriorating economy, **Pres. Perón won another six-year term** of office, garnering 67 percent of the vote.

1952, July 26. The president's wife, **Eva Perón, died** of cancer. Her death was nationally mourned and deprived Perón of one of his most important political assets.

1952-55. In a deteriorating economic climate, **Perón was forced to scale back his support for worker demands** and to begin suppressing labor agitation. He increased repression considerably and at the same time sought to increase his appeal by calling for *justicialismo,* social justice for all. Peronist attacks against the Catholic Church further divided the country, offering military rivals a pretext to force him out of office.

1955, May 17. Supporters of Perón introduced a bill in the Senate to deprive the Roman Catholic Church of its tax exemption. On May 13, the House of Deputies had **prohibited religious instruction in the schools.**

May 26. On Independence Day, **demonstrations by Roman Catholics** resulted in a wave of arrests.

June 16. Climaxing several days of clashes between demonstrators and the police, **the pope excommunicated Pres. Perón;** naval officers seized outlying towns, and planes bombed government buildings in the capital.

July. Perón called for a truce (July 5), but the strongest opposition party, the Radicals, rejected his plea. On July 18 Perón promised to give up all dictatorial powers.

Sept. 19. A four-man military junta ousted Perón. Gen. Eduardo Lonardi became provisional president.

Oct. 5. The position of the provisional president was strengthened by **the dismissal of the Supreme Court** and by **an anti-Perón revolt** of a dissident minority within the General Confederation of Labor.

Nov. 13. Following a **bloodless military coup,** which ousted the Lonardi regime, **Gen. Pedro Aramburu was installed as president.** Aramburu decided to purge the nation of Peronism, outlawing the Peronist Party, firing Peronists from their posts, and suppressing all Peronist propaganda. Still, Peronism remained extremely popular among workers.

1956-59. In spite of repression, a Peronist resistance emerged, especially in union organizations such as the CGT, which remained predominantly loyal to the deposed president.

1956, June 10. Government forces smashed a **Peronist revolt.** In the aftermath, **40 of the rebels were executed.**

1957, Sept. 24. The constituent assembly voted to **restore the 1853 constitution.**

1958, Feb. 22. After negotiating with Perón to gain the votes of his 2 million supporters, **ARTURO FRONDIZI** was elected president.

1962, Feb. 8. The government severed diplomatic ties with Cuba.

March 18. Peronist parties polled **35 percent** of the votes and won ten governorships. This brought to a head the growing dissatisfaction with Pres. Frondizi's moderation and his encouragement of foreign investments.

March 28. Military leaders **deposed Pres. Frondizi;** on March 30 president of the Senate **José María Guido** became Argentine president with the endorsement of the armed services.

April 24-25. Under pressure from some extreme anti-Peronist military leaders, **Guido nullified the recent provincial and legislative elections,** and established **rule by decree.**

July 24. The government issued **four decrees banning the Peronist and Communist Parties** and providing controls for the internal affairs of all parties.

Sept. 6. Pres. Guido dissolved the rump congress and signed a decree scheduling presidential and congressional elections for Oct. 27, 1963.

Sept. 18. Dismissal by war secretary of three generals sparked an **army revolt** that led to the seizure of Buenos Aires on Sept. 23.

1962-66. Emergence of Augusto Vandor as leader of the CGT's 62 Peronist unions. **Vandorism** was characterized by a more conciliatory attitude toward government and management; unions were integrated into the system and became more bureaucratic and authoritarian.

1963, May 12. Eleven cabinet members resigned in protest against the interior minister's demand for authority to purge Peronists. The minister resigned on May 13.

May 17. A presidential order forbade the **Unión Popular Party** (Peronist front) to nominate candidates for the presidency or governorships; it could seek only legislative posts.

July 7. Dr. Arturo Illia and his Popular Radical Party won power in presidential elections with a mere 25 percent of the popular vote.

1964, Dec. 2. Perón's attempt to return from his exile in Spain was thwarted when Brazil refused him passage and obliged him to return to Spain.

1965, March. In congressional elections, the recently legalized Peronist Party won 30.3 percent of the vote, whereas Illia's Radical Party won 28.9 percent.

1966, June 28. A MILITARY COUP, backed by the chiefs of the armed services and supported by Augusto Vandor, obliged Pres. Illia to resign and named **Gen. Juan Carlos Onganía as president.** Congress and political parties were disbanded, new governors of the provinces were appointed, and all power was concentrated in the office of the president. Unrest in the universities was ruthlessly suppressed.

July 15. The U.S. government recognized the Onganía regime.

Sept. Creation of state councils, one for economic development and one for national security. The new regime **encouraged foreign investment,** allowing foreign companies to gain an ever-larger foothold in the Argentine economy. Growth rates were high, but domestic bankruptcies doubled, and inflation depleted workers' frozen wages.

1967, March. Devaluation of the peso, from 250 to 350 pesos to the U.S. dollar. Foreign exchange controls were abolished, and more liberal economic policies were adopted.

1968. Stabilization of the economy, control of trade unions and regulation of strikes, and the freezing of wages took place.

1969, May 13. Major student demonstrations were followed by labor protests and strikes lasting for several weeks. A limited state of siege was proclaimed (May 28), and nine out of ten state universities were closed.

June. Under pressure from reformists in the military and growing unrest, Minister of the Economy **Adalbert Krieger Vasena** resigned.

Aug. A general strike in Córdoba followed major **student-worker demonstrations** in Rosario, Corrientes, and Córdoba. Participants in the uprising, known as the **Cordobazo,** briefly managed to take over the city and declare a socialist revolution before it was put down by the military.

1970, May 29. THE KIDNAPPING AND EXECUTION OF FORMER PRESIDENT PEDRO ARAMBURU by the left-wing Peronist **Montoneros,** one of several new guerrilla groups that reflected the growing militancy of labor and the Left. Leftists were increasingly responding to government violence with violence. The country stood on the verge of civil war.

June 8. Pres. Onganía was deposed by military leaders, who appointed **Brig. Gen. Roberto Marcelo Levingston** as president.

Aug. 27. The assassination of José Varela Alonso, a prominent labor leader and Peronist, was apparently perpetrated by rightist terrorists.

1971, March. After renewed rioting in Córdoba and a downturn in the economy, Gen. Levingston was deposed in a coup headed by **Gen. Alejandro Lanusse.** Lanusse continued repression of the growing left wing but sought to liberalize the political climate.

1972, Nov. 17. Fearful of the growing power of the extreme Left, the Lanusse government agreed to allow Perón to return to Argentina to rally support for a rightist Peronist party.

1973, March. Perón's presidential candidate, **Dr. Hector Cámpora, won the presidential elections** with 49 percent of the vote. Cámpora immediately initiated social reforms and sought to build an alliance among the social classes, but he was faced with escalating political violence.

July. Cámpora stepped down. He was replaced by **Raúl Lastiri,** who scheduled presidential elections for September.

Sept. Perón was elected president with 60 percent of the popular vote. He moved to eradicate left-wing elements from the Peronist movement, leading to a rupture in the movement between left- and right-wing organizations.

1974, April 26. Carlos Mugica, priest and leader of Argentina's **Third World Priests movement,** was murdered by a right-wing death squad.

Over the next three years, more than 20 dissident priests, including a bishop, were killed.

July 1. Pres. Perón died at the age of 78. He was succeeded by his vice president and widow, **María Estela (Isabelita) Perón.** Her regime faced **extreme economic problems** and was plagued by corruption and violence. Her chief adviser, the ultrarightist **José Lopez Rega,** was reported to head the AAA (Argentine Anti-Communist Alliance), death squads responsible for killing over 2,000 people during the winter of 1974.

Sept. The Montoneros denounced the government and went underground. Political kidnappings and assassinations increased.

1975, Feb. The government authorized the military to wage full-scale war against leftist guerrillas.

1976, March 23. Facing growing violence, general strikes, and economic chaos, **the military, with substantial civilian support, overthrew Pres. Perón** and installed **Gen. Jorge Rafael Videla** as president of a three-man junta. The junta then began the **PROCESS OF NATIONAL RE-ORGANIZATION (EL PROCESO),** which aimed to stamp out all traces of the Left and recreate economic and political order.

March–1979. ARGENTINA'S "DIRTY WAR." Somewhere between 10,000 and 24,000 Argentines—mainly students, young professionals, and labor activists (including pregnant women and even small children)—were abducted by security forces, **"disappeared,"** tortured, and murdered. Approximately 2 million Argentines were driven into exile. The junta's economic policies, crafted by neoliberal economic minister **José Martínez de Hoz,** aimed at stabilization. Wage cuts and austerity measures pleased foreign financiers, but the slowdowns associated with the program led to considerable deindustrialization and outflow of capital.

1977. In the Plaza de Mayo in Buenos Aires, groups of women began assembling with photographs of missing relatives pinned to their chests. These **"Mothers of the Plaza de Mayo"** began as a small group protesting the human rights abuses, but soon numbered in the thousands. They mobilized international criticism of the regime.

1980, Oct. 13. **Adolfo Pérez Esquivel,** the human rights activist, was awarded the Nobel Peace Prize.

1981, March 29. Retired major general **Roberto Viola** succeeded Videla as president.

Nov. 20. Unable to deal with massive inflation, spiraling debt, and economic chaos, Pres. Viola was forced out of office by a coup that replaced him with army commander in chief **Gen. Leopoldo Galtieri** (Dec. 11).

1982, Feb. A column of trade unionists marched into the Plaza de Mayo to join the mothers and grandmothers in their protest against the regime. Increasingly, **all sectors were turning against the junta.**

April. Argentine troops invaded the British-held Malvinas Islands (also known as the Falklands) to shore up support for the regime in the face of economic crisis. The islands had long been claimed by Argentina. Popular support for the regime briefly revived.

May–June. In response to the invasion, Prime Minister Margaret Thatcher of Britain sent an overwhelming military force to the islands (p. 850) that routed the poorly equipped Argentine military, killing over 1,000 Argentine soldiers. The humiliated Argentine military leadership decided to hand over power to civilians.

June 17. Galtieri was forced out by the junta and replaced by retired general **Reynaldo Benito Antonio Bignone,** who promised elections in 1983.

Dec. Massive rallies in Buenos Aires protested any continued role for the military in politics, demanding unconditional national elections for president.

1983, Oct. 30. After granting itself amnesty for human rights violations, the military allowed presidential elections, won by **RAÚL ALFONSÍN** (b. 1927) of the moderate **Radical Party.**

Dec. 16–1984, Sept. 20. Hearings were held before the **Commission on the Disappearance of Persons (CONADEP).** Nine thousand people testified before the commission, which investigated military and right-wing terrorism during the "dirty war." With the release of the commission report, some 2 million exiles began to return to Argentina.

1985, March. In Buenos Aires, 50,000 people rallied to protest the lack of action against former torturers and murderers. Pres. Alfonsín moved trials of officials from military to civilian courts, resulting in life sentences for **Adm. Emilio Massera** and **Gen. Jorge Rafael Videla.**

June 14. Facing 1,000 percent inflation and a foreign debt near $50 billion, Alfonsín replaced the peso with a new currency unit, **the austral.** The plan froze prices but also cut wages by 30 percent and decreased public spending.

1986. Fearing military reprisals for convictions against torturers, **Pres. Alfonsín decided to end further prosecutions** related to torture.

1987, April. Military officers close to former torturers launched **the Easter coup,** almost managing to overthrow Alfonsín. Nearly 1 million civilians rallied for democracy in the Plaza de Mayo in opposition to the coup. **Pres. Alfonsín agreed to grant amnesty** to all but 50 officers still under charges.

Sept. In elections, Peronists won 41 percent of the vote and took the governorship of Buenos Aires and several other provinces.

1988. Argentina's population reached 31.5 million.

April. Unable to meet interest payments, **Alfonsín stopped payments on a nearly $60 billion debt.**

1989, May 14. After massive monetary devaluations in March and April and amid growing unrest, Peronist **Carlos Saúl Menem** (b. 1935) was elected president.

May 23–June 2. In the wake of major cuts in social spending and a 12,000 percent inflation rate, food riots broke out across the country. **Rioters sacked supermarkets** in major cities but usually took only food and not money.

July 8. Pres. Alfonsín stepped down five months early, handing power over to Menem. Pres. Menem, much to the surprise of his followers, initiated a **"shock treatment"** for the economy, designed to privatize state industries and move the economy toward the free market. He also curbed the right to strike and fired dissident union leaders.

Oct. 7. Calling for **national reconciliation,** Menem pardoned 277 "dirty war" veterans.

1990, March 4. Menem unveiled a **new austerity plan,** calling for more privatizations and curbs on the right to strike. Pleased with these measures, **the International Monetary Fund (IMF) approved new loans** (May 25).

Dec. 30. Pres. Menem pardoned several top military officials and former presidents serving prison terms for atrocities committed during the "dirty war," despite public opposition.

1991. After a brief respite, inflation returned to high levels. One-third of the workforce remained unemployed or underemployed, and Argentina's key industries continued to operate at less than 50 percent capacity.

Jan. 3. New austerity measures were aimed at controlling inflation and cutting 20,000 state sector jobs, including massive sale of state-owned industries.

Oct. 31. Sweeping deregulation measures were introduced in several state-dominated sectors.

1992, Jan. 1. Menem introduced a **new peso,** equalling 10,000 australs. Inflation fell to 84 percent, down from 1,440 percent in 1990.

1994, April 10. The Peronist Party won the assembly vote in Argentina despite disaffection due to ongoing charges of financial corruption within the party. The left-of-Center Broad Front (Frepaso) did surprisingly well in the capital.

July 18. In the **worst terrorist attack in Argentina's history,** a bomb exploded in the Buenos Aires headquarters of several Jewish organizations, killing at least 96 people. Suspicion fell on Islamist groups. A subsequent car bombing at the Israeli embassy (July 26) caused a dozen injuries.

Aug. 2. A one-day general strike was called to protest Pres. Menem's neoliberal policies.

Aug. 22. A new constitution allowed Pres. Menem to seek a second consecutive term as chief executive.

1995, Feb. 27. The government unveiled a new austerity plan to narrow the budget deficit and restore investor confidence.

March 3. A retired naval officer alleged in an interview that between 1,500 and 2,000 disappeared persons had been thrown from airplanes during the military's **dirty war** of the late 1970s. Cmdr. Adolfo Francisco Scilingo claimed that top-ranking officers ordered the killings.

June 23. Riots erupted in Córdoba, Argentina's second largest city, prompted by the provincial government's failure to pay salaries and pensions.

July 8. Pres. Menem was sworn in for a second term in office following his reelection (May 14) by a wide margin.

1996, Sept. 26–27. The **CGT,** Argentina's largest labor federation, **called a 36-hour general strike to protest Menem's austerity measures. Between 80 and 90 percent of the workforce stayed home,** bringing the country to a virtual standstill.

1997, Jan. 25. Police discovered the body of a prominent journalist, **José Luiz Cabezas,** gruesomely murdered. The discovery sparked allegations that Cabezas had been **executed in retaliation for an article on corruption in the Buenos Aires police force.**

May. A series of protests erupted throughout Argentina to express dissatisfaction with government policies widely blamed for the 17 percent unemployment rate.

Oct. 26. In midterm elections the ruling Peronist Party lost its legislative majority to the Alliance, a Center-Left coalition.

1998, July 21. Threats of civil unrest deterred President Menem from changing the Argentine constitution to allow him to run for a third term in 1999. Menem's Peronist Party dramatically lost popularity as unemployment rose to 15 percent and a scandal concerning alleged presidential links with organized crime was uncovered.

Nov. 2. A two-week-long environmental conference opened in Buenos Aires, attended by delegates from over 160 nations. Aimed at implementing the UN-sponsored Kyoto Protocol of 1997, the conference ended on Nov. 14 with the "Buenos Aires Action Plan," an agreement between industrialized nations on strategies for carrying out emissions reductions programs and other measures to slow global warming.

Dec. 21. Peronist candidate José Manuel de la Sota won the governorship of Córdoba, a long-time stronghold of the opposing Radical Civil Union Party.

Dec. 28. Former naval commander and alleged kidnapping ring leader Ruben Franco was arrested in connection with the abduction of infants for political reasons between 1976 and 1983.

1999, March 14. Following a partial repeal of the United Kingdom's arms embargo on Argentina in late 1998, Prince Charles visited the nation and paid tribute to the Argentine soldiers who died in the Falkland (Malvinas) Islands conflict of the early 1980s.

July 14. International leaders signed a pact restoring commercial air connections between Argentina and the Falkland Islands.

Oct. 24. Fernando de la Rua, opposition party leader and mayor of Buenos Aires, won Argentina's presidential election. He took office on Dec. 10.

2000, Aug. 8. Former Chilean president Augusto Pinochet was stripped of immunity and faced charges in Argentina, Chile, and Spain for war crimes committed under the Argentine military junta between 1976 and 1983 (p. 938).

Sept. 8. A political scandal emerged surrounding a labor-reform bill that had passed with an overwhelming majority as part of President Fernando de la Rua's plan to rescue Argentina's ailing economy. Eleven senators were implicated in vote-buying activities.

b. CHILE

(From p. 738)

1946, Sept. 4. Gabriel González Videla was elected president by a leftist bloc to succeed **Don Juan A. Ríos** (1942–46). His cabinet included Socialists and Communists, who later dropped out as the regime moved to the Right.

1947, Oct. Communist-led strikes brought the arrest of 200 Communists and a **break in diplomatic relations with the Soviet Union.**

1948, Sept 2. The Communist Party was outlawed, but strikes and disorders continued.

1949. Women were granted the vote.

March. Parliamentary elections gave the government coalition a majority.

1952, Sept. 4. Voters gave an overwhelming victory to conservative-populist **Gen. Carlos Ibañez** in presidential elections.

1953–58. Period of increased political activity. Left-wing parties united and formed the **Popular Action Front (FRAP),** supported by the newly formed **Unified Workers Central (CUT).** A new **Christian Democratic Party (PDC)** under **EDUARDO FREI MONTALVA** (1911–82) also emerged, appealing to Catholic workers, urban white-collar employees, and the rural poor.

1955, May 21. As inflation mounted, Pres. Ibañez blamed the problem on political opposition.

1957, March 3. General elections revealed discontent with the president's economic program.

1958, Aug. 5. The Communist Party was legalized after a ten-year ban.

Sept. 4. In presidential elections, a former finance minister, conservative senator **Jorge Alessandri,** won a plurality of the vote, beating **SALVADOR ALLENDE GOSSENS** (1908–73) of the FRAP by a mere 33,500 votes. Alessandri vowed to restore free enterprise and seek out foreign capital.

1961, March 5. In the congressional elections, the Communists and Socialists made gains, the centrist Radicals retained their strength, and the rightist Liberals and Conservatives suffered substantial losses.

1964, Sept. 4. In the presidential elections, Eduardo Frei, candidate for the PDC, secured 55.7 percent of the popular vote, whereas **Sen. Allende,** candidate of the FRAP, polled 38.5 percent. Fear of an Allende victory prompted both the Right and Center to support the Frei candidacy, which was heavily financed with $20 million in CIA funds. Frei advocated a policy of gradual economic and social reform.

1966, Jan. Establishment of the **National Copper Corporation.** This independent agency controlled the production and sale of copper, forging partnerships whenever possible with foreign-owned copper-mining corporations **(Chileanization).**

1967, July. Passage of the **Agrarian Reform Act** ensured distribution of land to needy peasants.

1969, March. In the congressional elections, the Christian Democrats lost their majority in both houses, while the National Party on the Right and the FRAP on the Left registered gains. The results reflected dissatisfaction with the gradual reform program of the Frei government and the continuing rise in the cost of living.

June. Large-scale **student and worker protests** led the government to cancel the projected visit of Gov. Nelson A. Rockefeller of New York.

June–July. Chileanization of the holdings of the Anaconda Company and renegotiation of agreements with the Kennecott Corporation.

1970, May 26. Failed military coup against Frei.

Aug. 26. Seizure of land near Santiago by organized Marxist groups **(Revolutionary Junta of the Homeless).** Political tension made the government hesitant to interfere.

Sept. 4. Presidential elections. Sen. Allende of the **Popular Unity (UP)** coalition won 36.3 percent of the popular vote, while Jorge Alessandri Rodríguez of the National Party secured 34 percent. The six-party UP included Communists, Socialists, and radical elements from the PDC and the **United Popular Action Movement (MAPU).** Support for the UP came from urban and rural workers, some middle-class elements, and intellectuals. Since no candidate had a majority, it was left to the Congress to choose. Despite an effort by the U.S. to bribe congressmen to fix the outcome, the PDC supported Allende in return for guaranteed civil liberties. Allende asserted that while he intended to achieve dramatic reforms, he would adhere to constitutional norms.

Oct. 22. Gen. René Schneider Chereau, commander in chief of the army, was attacked and fatally wounded in a CIA-supported coup attempt by right-wing extremists hoping to block the election of Allende.

Oct. 24. ALLENDE WAS ELECTED by a joint session of the Congress, by a vote of 153–35.

Nov. 12. Reestablishment of diplomatic relations with Cuba, the first step in Allende's policy of rapprochement with the Communist countries. **Allende was the first overt Marxist popularly elected in an American state.** His government called for the expropriation of large foreign companies and financial, commercial, and industrial monopolies. He also planned to redistribute all landholdings over 80 hectares.

1971–73. During his 1,000 days in power, Pres. Allende introduced **far-reaching social and economic reforms.** An initial price and wage freeze, along with massive public spending in housing, sanitation, and health, led to a short-run boom in consumer spending and income redistribution. Highly popular through 1971, even among middle-class groups, **Allende nationalized copper, coal, and steel production, and most private banks.** Workers in some cases occupied their firms, refusing to leave until expropriation was announced. Factories, such as the Yarur textile works, were turned into cooperatives with or without government approval. Pressures mounted from the Left in the UP and the rural sector (where peasants took over land on their own) for more rapid reform. By 1972 the latifundia system (large agricultural estates with low productivity) had been dismantled, but under the reform, agricultural production had declined by 29 percent. **By 1973 the government had lost control of the reform** in many areas. At the same time, **opposition on the Right and Center** was growing. Runaway inflation (300 percent by 1973), widespread strikes, disinvestment, sabotage, and protests were destroying the economy. **CIA initiatives also helped cause serious problems for the regime** by 1973. The U.S. stopped the flow of needed spare parts and supplies and cut off aid and loans to the government (**destabilization**), while still funding the military.

1971, July 16. Congress unanimously approved the **expropriation of the foreign-owned copper mines.** Although allowing for compensation, Allende later claimed that excess profits carned by Anaconda and Kennecott denied them the right to recompense. The firms protested the ruling and called for retaliatory measures.

1972, March. Press reports revealed **joint plans on the part of International Telephone and Telegraph and the U.S. government to overthrow the Chilean government.**

Oct. A CIA-subsidized truck drivers' strike developed into a full-scale lockout by capitalists trying to pressure the regime into reversing reforms.

1973, June 29. With the backing of the U.S., dissatisfied elements of the military launched an abortive coup attempt.

July 26. In a renewed right-wing offensive, private truckers launched a strike. In the following weeks business and professional groups formed a "civic front" calling for Allende's overthrow. Meanwhile, factory occupations and mass demonstrations (calling for the arming of workers) continued as the country moved to the brink of civil war.

Sept. 11. PRES. ALLENDE OVERTHROWN in U.S.-backed military coup. Anti-Allende forces claimed he had committed suicide during the siege of the presidential palace. **GEN. AUGUSTO PINOCHET** (b. 1915) emerged as head of a four-man junta. In the next month perhaps as many as 30,000 dissidents were rounded up and tortured, and approximately 2,000 were murdered. Political parties and labor unions were banned, and Pinochet moved quickly to adopt a free market strategy to "regenerate" the Chilean economy and society.

1973–78. Under a declared **state of siege,** Pinochet ruled the country with a mix of terror and radical free market ideology. Pinochet established a secret police, **the National Intelligence Directorate (DINA),** which used national information networks and concentration camps to implement its terror. The economy was put under the control of the **"Chicago boys,"** free market economists trained under Milton Friedman at the University of Chicago. They applied a "shock treatment" to the economy, which, after lowering wages and reducing the GNP, did lead to growth rates of about 8 percent between 1977 and 1980. The recovery was fueled by massive loans from abroad.

1974, Dec. Pinochet assumed the presidency.

1976, Sept. 21. A car bomb exploded in Washington, D.C., killing **Orlando Letelier,** former Allende government official and lobbyist against U.S. aid to Pinochet.

1978, Jan. In a tightly supervised plebiscite, the Pinochet regime gained the endorsement of the electorate.

1980, Sept. Pinochet decreed a **new constitution,** guaranteeing his position until 1989.

1981, Nov. 2. The government stepped in and took over eight of the nation's largest banks, which were facing collapse.

1982–86. With foreign exchange reserves dwindling as copper prices fell, **bankruptcies multiplied, and unemployment grew by 30 percent.** By 1986 the GNP was close to 1970 levels, with consumption actually below that of 1970.

1983, May 12. In the first **National Day of Protest,** the 22,000-member Copper Workers Confederation, led by **Rodolfo Seguel,** launched a strike. In the following months, clashes between police and protesters multiplied, with membership in the newly formed **Democratic Workers Union (UDT)** reaching over one-half million. These protests were supported by a growing Chilean exile community, led by writers such as **Ariel Dorfman** and **Isabel Allende.**

1984, Oct. 30. After the arrests of several **Democratic Alliance (AD)** and **Popular Democratic Movement (MDP)** leaders, a general strike was called in Santiago.

Nov. Pinochet reinstated a state of siege. Abductions and torture intensified to postcoup levels. International condemnation mounted.

1985, March 3. Santiago was hit by a major **earthquake,** seriously damaging the urban slums.

Aug. Eleven political parties, including representatives of the Right, signed an accord calling for Pinochet's removal and a transition to democracy.

1986. Economic recovery, based largely on timber and agricultural exports, resulted in 5.7 percent growth in 1987, but few gains went to workers. Women employed in new agricultural processing plants were paid especially low wages. Stifled by foreign debt, Pinochet agreed to trade ownership of industry for debt remissions.

Sept. After a barely foiled attempt on his life by guerrillas of the **Patriotic Manuel Rodríguez Front,** Pinochet reinstated the state of siege.

1987, Oct. Labor leaders launched a successful one-day general strike opposing repression. A month later **200,000 attended a protest rally.**

1988. Chile's population reached 12.8 million.

Oct. 5. In a plebiscite deciding continuation of one-man rule, PINOCHET WAS REJECTED BY 55 PERCENT OF THE VOTERS (43 percent supported him).

1989, Dec. 14. Presidential and congressional elections. PDC candidate **Patricio Aylwin Azócar** won the presidential bid. His **Democratic Concordance** coalition gained a majority of seats in the Congress.

1990, March 11. Pres. Aylwin assumed power as the first democratically elected president since 1970. He vowed social and economic reforms but had to promise to maintain both a free market economy and amnesty for the military. Pinochet remained in charge of the military and security forces.

March 12. Pres. Aylwin freed all political prisoners.

1991, March 4. Aylwin released the report of the **"Commission of Truth and National Reconciliation,"** charging the previous regime with massive human rights violations and confirming at least 2,279 disappearances.

1992, Nov. 9. In the first human rights prosecution since the return of democracy, **Gen. Manuel Contreras Sepúlveda** and **Col. Pedro Espinoza** were charged with the 1976 murder of Orlando Letelier.

1993, Nov. 12. The Chilean Court sentenced Gen. Contreras Sepúlveda and Col. Espinoza to six and seven years in prison, respectively, for their roles in the Letelier murder.

Dec. 11. Eduardo Frei Ruiz-Tagle, son of the former president, won the **presidential election** by a landslide. He pledged to continue free market economic policies.

1994, March 11. Eduardo Frei Ruiz-Tagle sworn in as **president.** It was Chile's **first normal democratic transfer of office since 1970.**

1995, March 17. Signaling the economic success of Chile's neoliberal policies, the United States declared its support for Chile's inclusion in NAFTA.

1997. Former dictator Gen. Augusto Pinochet, required by the constitution to retire as armed forces head by March 1998, sparked protests by announcing plans to become a senator for life—an honor awarded by the constitution to former presidents.

1998, March 10. Augusto Pinochet retired as army commander-in-chief.

April 18–19. The second Summit of the Americas was hosted in Santiago, Chile. Attended by the leaders of 34 Western Hemisphere nations, the summit began discussions focused on establishing the Free Trade Area of the Americas (FTAA) by the year 2005.

Oct. 16. Pinochet was arrested and detained in England, where he was receiving medical treatment. Facing charges for his leadership role in the ruling military junta of Chile from 1973 to 1990, Pinochet was declared unfit for trial by the U.K. on Jan. 11, 2000.

Dec. 9. Chile signed a joint declaration with Argentina, Brazil, Paraguay, Uruguay, and Bolivia backing Chilean state sovereignty in arresting and prosecuting alleged war criminal and former dictator Augusto Pinochet.

1999, Dec. 12. The first round of elections for the Chilean presidency resulted in plans for a runoff vote on Jan. 16, 2000, between Ricardo Lagos Escobar, a member of the Socialist Party, and Joaquín Lavín, the right-wing candidate.

2000, Jan. 16. Lagos was elected president, becoming the first socialist president to run Chile since the overthrow of Salvador Allende in Sept. 1973. Lagos took office on March 11.

March 2. Augusto Pinochet was returned to Chile, temporarily avoiding prosecution by Spain on charges of torture.

March 15. In a speech just days after his inauguration, Pres. Lagos promised to seek a constitutional amendment to shift more control of the previously independent military into the hands of the civilian government.

Aug. 8. Pinochet was stripped of immunity by the Supreme Court of Chile. With 14 cases pending against him in Chile alone, he faced additional prosecution in Spain and Argentina.

c. PARAGUAY

(From p. 738)

1946, July 26. Gen. Higenio Morinigo formed a two-party cabinet, thus ending a six-year dictatorship.

1947, March–Aug. Civil war between the government and left-wing forces under former president Rafael Franco ended with the latter's defeat.

1948–49. The retirement of Pres. Morinigo ushered in a procession of presidents: **Manuel Frutos** (June 6, 1948), **Natalicio González** (Aug. 5, 1948), **Raimundo Rolón** (Jan. 30, 1949), **Molás López** (Feb. 27, 1949), and **Federico Chávez** (Sept. 12, 1949).

1954, May 4. A revolution led to the installation of a government junta headed by ALFREDO STROESSNER (b. 1912).

1956. Stroessner introduced an **austerity program** in the style of the International Monetary Fund (IMF), driving down wages and provoking unrest. All opposition and the strikes that followed were repressed.

1961. Paraguayan women were granted the vote.

1963, Feb. 10. Gen. Alfredo Stroessner, president since 1955, met only token opposition in his bid for **reelection.** Stroessner, a champion of foreign interests, organized the political life of the nation around his **Colorado Party;** opposition meant possible torture, exile, and murder.

Aug. 15. Stroessner was sworn in for a third term as president.

1965. The U.S. House of Representatives passed the **Selden Resolution,** authorizing U.S. troop movements to Paraguay in the event of a Communist threat. Over the next two decades, more than **1,000 Paraguayan troops were trained at U.S. installations.**

1967, May. Elections for a constituent assembly resulted in a victory for the ruling Colorados.

1968, Feb. Pres. Stroessner was reelected for his fourth term. He developed a system of **"preventive repression,"** by which any opposition, real or imagined, was crushed. Other South American dictators viewed his **"culture of fear"** as a model for their own repressive activities in the 1970s.

1973, April 26. Paraguay and Brazil signed the **Treaty of Itaipu,** providing for construction of a 12,600-megawatt dam in the border region. Construction took place under police guard and dangerous conditions; the region's population was exploding to over a half million, and peasants in the area were forcibly relocated.

1973–82. Led by cotton, soybean, and timber exports, **the economy grew at an annual rate of 6 percent** during the 1970s. Most profits were exported, however, and benefits reached only a few friends of the regime. There was also a **boom in smuggling,** much of it by government officials.

1979. Paraguay hosted the congress of **the World Anti-Communist League,** noted for its ultrarightist stance and Fascist overtones. Stroessner made Paraguay a safe haven for ex-Nazis and other exiled right-wing extremists.

1984, March. Amid rising protests against the regime and a general economic slowdown, Stroessner closed down the country's largest newspaper, *ABC Color,* which had criticized high-level corruption.

1987, June 21. Domingo Laino, leader of the **Authentic Radical Liberal Party (PLRA)** and recently returned from exile, spoke at an opposition rally attended by 30,000 people. In the following months, political activity increased, leading to an even larger **silent march against repression led by Archbishop Ismael Rolón** on Oct. 30.

1988. Paraguay's population reached 4 million.

Feb. 14. Amid growing internal divisions in the Colorado Party concerning Stroessner's continued rule, Stroessner was reelected in a campaign marked by repression.

1989, Feb. 2–3. Stroessner was overthrown in a bloody coup led by Gen. Andrés Rodríguez (who had suspected ties with the drug trade). Rodríguez immediately ended press censorship, legalized political organizations, released many political prisoners, and allowed exiles to return. He also launched **neoliberal reforms.**

May 1. Rodríguez was elected president in a disputed election.

1992, June 20. A new constitution, calling for democracy, was approved.

1993, May 9. Juan Carlos Wasmosy, a wealthy neoliberal and candidate of the Colorado Party, was elected president in the country's first multiparty elections.

1997, Oct. 3. Pres. Juan Carlos Wasmosy ordered the arrest of Lino Cesar Oviedo, a former army chief selected to be the ruling Colorado Party's candidate in the upcoming presidential election, citing "accusations he [Oviedo] has made against the president."

1998, May 10. Raúl Cubas Grau was elected president of Paraguay following a banking scandal that involved former president Wasmosy and his entire staff, including the Central Bank president.

May 11. Observers from OAS approved allegedly fraudulent elections in Paraguay, internationally legitimating the new government.

Aug. 18. Gen. Oviedo, whom Cubas succeeded as head of the corrupt Colorado Party, was freed from jail by the newly inaugurated president Cubas.

1999, March 23. Paraguay vice president **Luis Maria Argana** was assassinated by unidentified gunmen. The vice president had publicly disagreed with Pres. Cubas in his decision to release Oviedo from prison; Argana's murder was largely attributed to Pres. Cubas and his supporters.

March 28. Pres. Cubas was forced out of office because he was allegedly involved in the assassination of his vice president. Cubas had publicly refused to jail Gen. Oviedo, his political mentor, who was convicted of leading a failed coup against Pres. Wasmosy in 1996. Both men fled the country as they lost control of the government. Senate leader **Luis Angel Gonzalez Macchi** was sworn in as president.

2000, May 18. A military coup attempted by Oviedo was subdued by the new government. Three weeks later, Oviedo was arrested in Brazil.

Aug. Julio Cesar Franco was elected vice president, marking the first major victory for the Liberal Party in over 50 years.

d. URUGUAY

(From p. 739)

1946, Nov. 24. Tomás Barreta was elected president. He died on Aug. 2, 1947 and was succeeded by **V.P. Luiz B. Berres,** fellow Liberal Colorado. Pres. Berres promoted import substitution industrialization (with the help of U.S. loans), expanding the industrial workforce from about 50,000 to over 140,000.

1950, Nov. 26. Andres Martínez Trueba was elected president to succeed Berres.

1952, March 1. A nine-man federal council replaced the presidency, from which Trueba had resigned. The new system called for elections every four years. The two-party system, based largely on political clubs and patronage networks, continued to dominate politics.

1955. Beginning of an **economic downturn.** Landowners and business leaders criticized the inflated bureaucracy and economic controls; organized workers increasingly supported the Left.

1959, March 1. The defeated Colorados, after 93 uninterrupted years in office, handed over the executive to the **Nationalist (Blanco) Party.** The Blancos moved to support large landholders and the private sector in an IMF-approved plan.

1963, March 1. Blanco **Daniel Fernández Crespo** became president of the nine-man national council. The economy continued having serious problems, leading to massive capital flight.

1964. Founding of the National Labor Convention (CNT), drawn from various trade union groups.

1966, Nov. 27. The election of **Gen. Oscar Diego Gestido** as president signified the resurgence of the conservative wing of the Colorado Party. Diego Gestido was inaugurated on March 1, 1967, at which time a constitutional amendment marked the abandonment of the council system and the return to the presidency.

1967, Nov. Devaluation of the currency.

Dec. 6. Death of Pres. Gestido, who was succeeded by **V.P. Jorge Pacheco Areco.** The new administration took a hard line in the face of economic crisis.

1968, June. Conflict with trade unions. A state of emergency was proclaimed, and a wage and price freeze was imposed. In response, the unions launched several hundred strikes.

1969, March. Security restrictions were removed. However, the increasing actions of urban guerrillas (the **Tupamaros,** who directed their efforts against authoritarianism and corruption) led to the reimposition of security measures (June 24). Wages fell to World War II levels, press censorship spread, and labor activists and leftists were suppressed.

April 23. Signature of the five-nation treaty for joint development of the Río de la Plata basin.

1970, July 31. Dan Mitrone, a U.S. official who trained police in repressive activities, **was captured and executed by the Tupamaros.** The execution highlighted U.S. complicity in the terrorist methods used by the regime, but also tarnished the Tupamaros' "Robin Hood" image.

The Tupamaros kidnapped one Brazilian and two American officials, whom they held hostage pending release of 150 political prisoners. Pacheco Areco refused to negotiate with them.

1971, Feb. 14. Progressive factions from the two ruling parties formed the **Frente Amplia** (Broad Front) to contest the 1971 elections. Unhappy with the traditional parties' rightward drift, the Frente included Socialists, Communists, and Christian Democrats. The Tupamaros called a cease-fire and declared their support for Frente Amplia presidential candidate **Gen. Líber Seregni Mosquera.**

Nov. 28. In elections widely believed fraudulent, ultraconservative Colorado candidate **Juan María Bordaberry** was elected and declared president (Dec. 2).

1972, April. Responding to widespread strikes, protests, and continued guerrilla activities, the Congress declared a **"state of internal war."** The act gave the military (aided by the U.S.) unlimited powers to stamp out the Tupamaros, who were decimated within a year.

1973, June 27. The military dismissed Congress, formalizing military rule with the consent of Pres. Bordaberry. Left-wing parties were banned, the Colorados and Blancos dismissed, the National University closed, and censorship increased. **The following 12-year dictatorship was the bloodiest in Uruguayan history.**

1976, June 14. After three years as presidential figurehead, Bordaberry was dislodged by the military, and **Aparicio Méndez** was installed (July 14). All political parties were banned and dissidents imprisoned. By this time Uruguay, once known as the Switzerland of Latin America, had more political prisoners per capita than any other Latin American nation. Torture was widespread, arousing international condemnation.

1980. After seven years of dictatorship, one-seventh of the population had left the country because of political repression and declining wages.

Nov. 30. The military held a plebiscite to approve a new constitution that would give legitimate power to the military. The document was rejected by a 57 percent to 43 percent margin.

1983. Political and strike activity increased.

Aug. 25. Hundreds of thousands took to the streets of Montevideo in the first **national day of protest,** supporting the **Interpartidária,** a new alliance calling for the release of political prisoners and a return to democracy.

1984, June 27. A general strike succeeded in shutting down the national economy.

Nov. 25. After negotiations, the military allowed presidential elections and a return to civilian rule. **Julio María Sanguinetti** of the Colorado Party was elected president.

1985, March 1. Pres. Sanguinetti assumed office.

1986. Fearing military intervention in politics, Pres. Sanguinetti granted a **general amnesty for human rights violations** by the military.

1988. Uruguay's population reached 3 million.

1989, Nov. 26. Luis Alberto Lacalle, a moderate conservative of the National Party, was elected president.

1990, March 1. Pres. Lacalle was sworn in. He promised inflation controls, debt reduction, and social welfare improvements.

1995, March 1. Julio María Sanguinetti was sworn in as **president.** He vowed to reform the nation's social security system, which had been consuming 37 percent of the federal budget.

1999, Oct. 31. In a remarkable election for the General Assembly, the Colorado Party was ousted, securing only 32 seats while the Progressive Encounter Party took 40.

Nov. 28. Jorge Batlle won 54.1 percent of the votes in a runoff presidential election in Uruguay, securing the position for the Center-Right Colorado Party.

2000, Aug. An investigative commission began its inquiry into the disappearances of 160 people during the military regime that ruled Uruguay from 1973 to 1984.

e. BOLIVIA

(From p. 739)

1946, July 21. Amid economic crisis caused by falling tin prices, **Pres. Gualberto Villarroel was killed and his regime overthrown** by rebellious workers, soldiers, and students. The provisional government was recognized by Argentina and the U.S.

Nov. Delegates to the fourth annual meeting of the **Union Federation of Mine Workers of Bolivia (FSTMB)** signed a Trotskyist declaration that proclaimed their desire for revolution through an alliance with the National Revolutionary Movement (MNR) and the peasants.

1947, Jan. 5. Enrique Hertzog, leader of the Republican Socialist Union Party, was elected president. Several attempts by the MNR to overthrow the government were unsuccessful.

1949, May 1. A strike in the tin mines in May and a rebellion by the outlawed MNR in September were put down by the army, but they left the country on the verge of bankruptcy.

Oct. 19. Pres. Hertzog resigned because of ill health and was succeeded by **V.P. Mametro Urriolagoita.** Disturbances from the Right and the Left continued.

1950, April 10. The Communist Party was outlawed.

1951, May 16. After **Victor Paz Estenssoro** (b. 1907) of the MNR won presidential elections on a platform calling for agrarian reform and nationalization of the mines, a military junta led by **Gen. Hugo Balliván** seized power.

1952, April 9. A revolt in La Paz led by students, workers, and the national police, and bolstered by tin miners from the countryside, overthrew the junta of Gen. Ballivián after three days of bloody fighting. The revolt, which became known as the **BOLIVIAN REVOLUTION,** was organized by the middle-class-based MNR. Paz Estenssoro, MNR leader, was sworn in as president on April 16 and began a series of major reforms. Universal suffrage (including **women's suffrage**) was introduced. The military was largely dismantled, and weapons were distributed to a **civilian militia** composed mainly of peasants and miners. **Land seizures** initiated autonomously by peasant groups were officially approved and eventually totaled over 10 million hectares. Indian and peasant groups asserted their identity as political actors. **Mines of the tin oligopoly were nationalized** into the state-controlled Mining Corporation of Bolivia (COMIBOL).

Despite strong initial backing from worker, peasant, and middle-class groups, the MNR's base weakened as the leftist workers sought more state reform and as middle-class leaders, under pressure from the U.S., sought to minimize the reforms. Solidarity among mineworkers and peasants evaporated as poor peasants were enlisted to break up labor strikes. Although briefly creating a system of joint labor-state management, Victor Paz Estenssoro soon **ended worker participation in COMIBOL, invited foreign participation in the economy, and sought U.S. aid** (much of it used to rebuild the army).

1956, June 17. The candidate of the ruling MNR, **V.P. Hernán Siles Suazo,** was elected president. Suazo used U.S. aid to form a new conservative army that would offset the power of the revolutionary civilian militias.

1960, June 5. Victor Paz Estenssoro succeeded Siles Suazo as president. During his second term he increasingly used the new army to suppress the Left, students, and workers, fracturing the MNR even further.

1962, April 16. Bolivia canceled diplomatic ties with Chile because of a 23-year fight concerning the use of the waters of the Lauca River.

1963, June 17. Bolivia formally withdrew from the OAS council because of the body's "mishandling" of the border dispute with Chile.

Dec. 12. After several miners were kidnapped by government agents, miners and members of the miners' **Housewives Committee** seized a U.S. labor attaché and several others at a COMIBOL meeting. After long negotiations, the Housewives agreed to release the Americans.

1964, May 31. Victor Paz Estenssoro was reelected to a third term as president.

Nov. 3. Pres. Paz Estenssoro was overthrown by a military faction, which set up a junta headed by **GEN. RENÉ BARRIENTOS ORTUNO.** Popular groups, disillusioned with the MNR's move to the Right and repressive measures, initially supported the junta.

1965, May 17–24. Tin miners struck against the government and occupied the mines. The government sent in troops and began to draft insurgent workers into the army.

1966, July 3. Military-controlled elections gave victory to Pres. Barrientos, whose promilitary **Bolivian Revolutionary Front** controlled Congress.

1967, March–Oct. A formidable **guerrilla movement emerged in southeast Bolivia,** led by the Cuban revolutionary **Che Guevara.** Bolivian forces, with U.S. training, captured Guevara and managed to suppress the movement. **Guevara died** of his wounds (Oct. 8).

Sept. 24. Government troops led a **daybreak massacre** of hundreds of men, women, and children at the Siglo XX mine. The victims were accused of being guerrilla sympathizers.

1968, July. Violent rioting followed the revelation that a former minister of the interior had maintained contacts with Fidel Castro. **The cabinet was obliged to resign, and the government suspended constitutional rights.**

1969, April 27. Death of Pres. Barrientos in a helicopter accident. He was succeeded by **V.P. Adolfo Siles Salinas.**

Sept. 26. Pres. Siles was overthrown by a military coup and was followed by **Pres. Alfredo Ovando Candia,** commander in chief of the armed forces, who introduced a more liberal policy: political prisoners were released, troops were withdrawn from the mines, and restrictions on trade unions were rescinded.

Oct. 17. The government **nationalized the U.S.-owned Bolivian Oil Company.**

1970, Oct. 4. An army coup forced Pres. Ovando to resign (Oct. 6). **Gen. Rogelio Miranda,** army chief of staff, appointed a ruling junta. But air force officers, led by leftist **Gen. Juan José Torres** and supported by students and workers, claimed the presidency and began to attack army posts. The junta capitulated, and **Torres became president** (Oct. 7).

Oct. 14. Workers began to seize the properties of the state mining corporation and to expel the officials and the police guards.

1970–71. Pres. Torres briefly revived the revolutionary movement by nationalizing numerous foreign firms and expanding ties with the Soviet bloc.

1971, Aug. Supported by the extreme rightist **Socialist Falange, Col. HUGO BANZER SUÁREZ** (b. 1926) overthrew Torres. Over the next seven years, Banzer used his U.S.-trained special forces to brutally repress all dissidents and opened the country to massive foreign investment.

1974, Nov. 9. Banzer outlawed all political parties and trade unions. His **Department of Public Order (DOP)** terrorized all dissenters.

1978, July 9. Banzer's handpicked successor was elected in fraudulent elections. In the turmoil that followed, **Gen. Juan Pereda Asbun** seized power and called for a **democratic transition.** Intense mobilization on the Left made Pereda's hold on power tenuous.

Nov. 24. Through a coup, **Gen. David Padilla** seized power, promising elections for 1979.

1979, July 1. Presidential elections did not produce a clear victor. The Congress appointed an interim president and planned new elections.

Nov. 25. The military again seized power, but fell in a few weeks after a general strike and protests destabilized the regime. Congress elected **Lydia Gueiler Tejada** (Bolivia's first woman president) to serve in the interim.

1980, June 29. Hernán Siles Suazo, candidate of the leftist **Popular Democratic Union (UDP),** won presidential elections.

July 17. In what was known as the **"cocaine coup,"** military hard-liners under **Gen. Luis García Meza Tejada** seized power. The new regime escalated corruption and repression to new levels, and **maintained close links with the exploding international cocaine trade. By 1981, cocaine was Bolivia's main export.**

1981, Aug. 4. Under pressure from all sectors, Gen. García Meza passed power to another junta, which convened Congress to certify the election of Siles Suazo.

1982, Oct. 2. Siles Suazo was sworn into office. He faced disastrous economic conditions: 75 percent underemployment and unemployment, extremely low tin prices, and a spiraling foreign debt of nearly $4 billion. The military command was dismissed, measures were taken to control galloping inflation, and Siles Suazo announced plans to increase worker participation.

1984, Nov. With the economy racked by 1,000 percent inflation and facing drug scandals, Siles Suazo acceded to pressures to call an election one year ahead of schedule.

1985, Aug. 5. After presidential elections produced no clear victor between right-wing Gen. Hugo Banzer Suárez and MNR candidate Victor Paz Estenssoro, Congress elected Paz Estenssoro (who polled fewer votes). Banzer threatened a coup, and the International Monetary Fund demanded a severe austerity program, pushing the new regime to the Right.

Sept. Workers launched a general strike. The army crushed the protesters and arrested over 1,000 of them. Paz Estenssoro, working with Banzer, declared a state of siege and continued a neoliberal plan for economic stabilization.

1986, July. Paz Estenssoro announced **Operation Blast Furnace,** a military venture assisted by U.S. forces and designed to eradicate the coca industry. At the time, coca sales generated $600 million annually.

Aug. Attending **the March for Bread and Life,** thousands of workers and peasants, including many women (who had mobilized in **Peasant Leagues and Housewives Committees** of the mining unions during the 1980s), called for the protection of mines, farms, and wages, along with the removal of U.S. troops.

Sept. The Paz Estenssoro government was forced to make concessions to striking mineworkers, who had occupied mineshafts and launched a hunger strike. Mine closures were halted, and workers were released from custody. **Neoliberal policies** continued, however, and by the end of the year 25,000 miners were out of work.

1988. Bolivia's population reached 6.9 million.

1989, Aug. 5. After presidential elections produced no clear victor, Hugo Banzer made a deal to allow **Jaime Paz Zamora of the Movement of the Revolutionary Left (MIR)** to assume the presidency. Paz Zamora maintained neoliberal policies, closing down public enterprises.

1990, Sept. 22. The government reached an agreement with Indian groups to stop deforestation in indigenous areas, following a six-week, 400-mile march by 500 protesters.

1992, June 10. Paz Zamora privatized 66 state-owned companies.

Nov. 13. Bolivia signed a free trade agreement with Peru, eliminating tariffs on 6,000 items.

1993, June 6. Neoliberal **Gonzalo Sánchez de Lozada** defeated Hugo Banzer in presidential elections.

1995, April 18. The Bolivian government declared itself to be in a state of siege because of huge labor strikes and the collapse of government talks with the unions.

1996, April 20. The government signed an agreement ending a month-long general strike by public sector employees.

Dec. 17. Argentina, Brazil, Paraguay, and Uruguay voted to admit Bolivia to Mercosur.

1997, July 12. The Bolivian government confirmed that remains of leftist guerrilla leader Ernesto Che Guevara were discovered in a mass grave near Vallegrande.

Aug. 5. The Bolivian congress confirmed former military ruler and leader of the right-wing Democratic Nationalist Action Party, Hugo Banzer Suárez, as the new president.

1999, Feb. 9. Bolivian and Brazilian leaders inaugurated a natural gas pipeline between Rio Grande, Bolivia and São Paulo, Brazil. The pipeline was 1,830 miles long and was expected to net $1.6 billion for Bolivia over a period of twenty years.

2000, April 26. A strike by the Workers Confederation and a plan for increased water rates incited riots throughout Bolivia. The government of former military dictator and current president Banzer quickly suppressed the insurrections.

f. PERU

(From p. 741)

1945, June 10. José Luis Bustamente was elected president, supported by Liberals and Apristas.

1948, Oct. 29. Pres. Bustamente's government was overthrown and replaced by a military junta under **Gen. Manuel Odría** (1897–1974). The APRA (American Popular Revolutionary Alliance) and the Communist Party were outlawed.

1950, July 2. Using a populist style reminiscent of Juan Perón of Argentina and running unopposed, **Gen. Odría was elected president.**

1951, Aug. 13. Peru asked the U.S., Argentina, Brazil, and Chile to investigate border incidents with Ecuador. Fighting had begun on Aug. 11 over the long-standing issue of access to certain Amazon tributaries.

1955. Peruvian women were granted the vote.

1956, June 17. Manuel Prado Ugarteche was elected president for a second term.

1958–62. As the land problem became more acute, members of Indian sierra communities organized and initiated land invasions on highland haciendas. In the region of **La Convención** valley, the seizures developed into a full-scale insurrection under **Hugo Blanco** before being brutally repressed.

1962, July 18. A military junta overthrew and imprisoned Pres. Prado. It also closed Congress and suspended constitutional guarantees. The U.S. suspended diplomatic relations and on July 19–20 halted all aid.

Aug. 17. The U.S. resumed diplomatic relations with Peru.

1963, July 28. FERNANDO BELAÚNDE TERRY (b. 1912), elected with great promises of agrarian reform and support for *indigenista* causes, was inaugurated as president, ending one year of military rule. Land invasions accelerated, moving to occupation of cultivated lands. In response, Belaúnde called upon the army to suppress the peasant movement, killing over 8,000 people and leaving nearly 20,000 homeless.

1964, May. AGRARIAN REFORM LAW provided for the distribution of virtually all state lands and church-owned agricultural property among Indian communities and landless tenant farmers.

1968, Aug. A compromise was reached with the U.S.-owned International Petroleum Company (IPC). The IPC gave up its claims on the nearly depleted La Brea–Pariñas oil fields in return for new concessions in the Amazon.

Oct. 3. Pres. Belaúnde was overthrown by a military coup, following widespread discontent with his economic policies. Congress was dissolved, and a revolutionary government was formed, with **GEN. JUAN VELASCO ALVARADO** (1910–1977) as president. Schooled in **dependency theory,** the regime's **Plan Inka promised to end the "unjust social and economic order"** that had concentrated the national wealth in a few hands. Velasco favored industrialization and channeled funds into this sector rather than into rural development. Popular mobilization was briefly encouraged, but the regime favored control from the top down, paying lip service to popular demands but rarely considering them seriously. Peasant and worker organizations soon opposed the regime.

1969, Feb. 6–13. Seizure and expropriation of the properties of the IPC, after repudiation of the earlier compromise agreement. The Velasco government claimed that $690 million in oil profits had been exported since 1924. The expropriated properties were turned over to a new agency, **Petroleos Peruanas** (Aug.). In the aftermath, U.S. aid to Peru was briefly frozen.

Feb. Establishment of diplomatic and trade relations with the USSR and other Communist bloc countries.

June 24. Announcement of a far-reaching program of **land distribution.** Seeking to end the semifeudal agrarian system and foreign enclaves, Velasco **expropriated the coastal sugar plantations along with the highland haciendas,** parceling them out into small and medium-size commercial units and peasant cooperatives. During the reform, over **20 million hectares of land were distributed,** ending the power of the *hacendados* and putting 75 percent of Peru's productive land under cooperatives. However, inefficient planning and undercapitalization limited the benefits of the reform. Rural unemployment and landlessness remained endemic.

1970. SENDERO LUMINOSO (the Shining Path), a Maoist movement, was founded by the philosophy lecturer **Abimael Guzmán Reynoso** in Ayacucho.

1971. Velasco created **the National System for the Support of Mobilization (SINAMOS).** Founded in response to the growing problems of squatter communities around Lima, which the regime renamed *"pueblos jovenes,"* SINAMOS gave the new residents title to the land they occupied. Over the next decades, more than 4 million people would migrate to Lima's shantytowns.

1973, Dec. 31. As part of an economic reform process, the regime nationalized the **Cerro de Pasco** mining complex.

1975, Aug. In economic crisis due to the rising price of oil and **a fall in the value of Peruvian exports,** the nationalist wing of the Velasco regime was ousted by conservatives, replacing Velasco with **Francisco Morales Bermúdez.** The new leadership sought to promote private enterprise and support a free market economy. Austerity measures caused widespread rioting.

1976, June. The regime announced an end to the land reform.

1977, July. Morales Bermúdez announced June 1978 elections for a **constituent assembly** to write a **new constitution** in preparation for a return to civilian rule.

1978, May 22–23. A million workers participated in a general strike.

June 18. In constituent elections, APRA won a plurality of seats, followed by the rightist **Popular Christian Party (PPC),** with whom they formed a coalition majority. They produced a constitution that ensured a free market economy with a protected private sector.

Aug. 7. The regime reached agreement with the IMF for **a new austerity program,** including massive cuts in the state sector, further price increases, and wage controls.

1980, May 19. In presidential elections, **Fernando Belaúnde Terry,** of the **Popular Action Party (AP)** was declared the victor.

July 28. Belaúnde was sworn in as Peru's first civilian president in 12 years. He pledged to return agriculture to the free market and reduce government involvement in the economy.

1981, Jan. 15. In the midst of severe and ineffective austerity measures, all of the major labor unions joined in a general strike.

1982–83. Guerrilla attacks by Sendero Luminoso increased precipitously. Pres. Belaúnde dispatched the military to crush the uprising. Although they numbered only about 2,500, Sendero had strong regional peasant support, and over the next ten years this guerrilla organization would come close to overthrowing the government. Strategic acts of terrorism, combined with revenue from the drug trade and the ill effects of government repression, made the movement a critical national force.

1983, Nov. 13. Angry over austerity measures, voters elected leftist **Alfonso Barrantes** as mayor of Lima.

1985, July 28. Alan García Pérez, APRA candidate, assumed the presidency after Alfonso Barrantes dropped out of a runoff election. **García promised to protect the agrarian reform and rejected dealing with the IMF.** He restricted debt payments, made efforts to prevent capital flight, and raised wages.

1986, June 16–20. Pres. García sent the military to end **riots begun by Sendero Luminoso** members in prisons in Lima and Callao. In the operation, 267 prisoners were killed, raising a storm of public protest.

Oct. In retaliation for the prison killings, Sendero soldiers carried out several attacks, including the murder of **Adm. Geronimo Cafferata** and several APRA officials.

1987, Feb. In an effort to stem the growth of Sendero Luminoso, the government raided five university campuses. By this point there were over 2,000 political prisoners in the country.

April 13. The regime passed a law officially recognizing 3,642 peasant communities, which exempted them from taxes and allowed them to enter into business contracts.

Sept. 29. Fearing capital flight due to a collapsing economy, **García enacted plans to nationalize the banking system.** His measures failed to stabilize the economy, and over the next two years the GDP declined by 20 percent.

1988. Peru's population reached 20.7 million.

1988-90. Sendero Luminoso plunged the country into civil war. The only economic sector immune to crisis was the cocaine trade, which amounted to a billion-dollar industry by 1990.

1989, July-Aug. Sendero Luminoso **renewed bombing attacks** of electrical stations and urban areas, and assassinated certain peasant and political leaders, severely damaging the economy. The group controlled the Upper Huallaga Valley (where one-half the cocaine consumed in the U.S. was grown, earning Sendero $500 million annually in drug taxes), as well as parts of the economically vital Huánuco, Pasco, and Junín regions.

1990, April. In the first round of presidential elections, novelist **Mario Vargas Llosa,** pledging economic "shock therapy," won 30 percent of the vote to **Alberto Fujimori's** 29 percent. Fujimori opposed shock therapy, insisting that the people's basic needs must be met.

June 10. FUJIMORI WON RUNOFF ELECTIONS easily. After the election, to the dismay of his followers, he initiated severe austerity measures that came to be known as **"Fujishock."**

1991, Feb.-May. Emergence of cholera epidemic. By May, 1,300 were dead.

Feb. 11. Other Latin American nations banned food imports from Peru.

1992, April 5. Pres. Fujimori seized near dictatorial powers to facilitate the fight against Sendero Luminoso. Congress was dissolved, the constitution suspended, the press censored, and opposition leaders arrested. The move had widespread support.

Sept. 12. SENDERO LUMINOSO LEADER ABIMAEL GUZMÁN WAS CAPTURED. After a trial he was sentenced to life imprisonment. Other arrests followed.

Nov. 13. Failed coup attempt against Fujimori.

Nov. 22. Fujimori supporters won a clear majority in the new Congress, which had been assembled to rewrite the constitution.

1993, Oct. 31. A new constitution approved by voters strengthened the executive and bolstered Fujimori's free market agenda.

1994, Dec. 28. Peruvian Indians filed a class-action lawsuit against Texaco, seeking $1 billion in damages. The suit, filed in New York City, alleged environmental damage due to improper oil disposal in neighboring Ecuador.

1995, Jan. 26. Fighting erupted on the border between Peru and Ecuador over land that Ecuador ceded to Peru in 1941. Though the border issue remained unresolved, Peru and Ecuador signed a truce on Feb. 17.

April 9. Pres. Alberto K. Fujimori was easily reelected to a second five-year term.

Nov. 30-Dec. 1. Peruvian police killed three alleged members of **Tupac Amaru Revolutionary Movement (MRTA)** in a 2-day **siege of a house in a Lima suburb.** Police also arrested Lori Helene Berenson, a U.S. citizen who rented the house occupied by rebels.

1996, Aug. 23. Peru's congress approves an interpretation of the constitution that would allow Pres. Fujimori to run for a third term in the year 2000.

Dec. 17. Marxist guerrillas from the **MRTA stormed the Japanese ambassador's residence in Lima, holding hundreds hostage and demanding help for impoverished Peruvians.**

1997, April 22. Peruvian commandos stormed the Japanese ambassador's residence, freeing 72 hostages and **ending the 126-day-long crisis.** In addition to one hostage and two soldiers, all 14 rebels were killed in the raid. Pres. Fujimori's approval ratings soared to 67 percent as a result of the action.

1998, Aug. 7. Liberal premier **Javier Valle Riestra resigned his position,** remarking on Pres. Fujimori's totalitarian governmental policies.

Aug. 20. In a surprising change of his cabinet, Pres. Fujimori replaced his armed forces chief Nicholas Hermoza Rios, who was widely considered one of Peru's three most powerful people.

Oct. 26. A treaty with Ecuador was signed, ending a 50-year-long border dispute with Peru. The cause of a 1995 war between the two countries, the border dispute was the last unresolved conflict of its kind in Latin America.

1999, July 14. The last of the commanders of the Sendero Luminoso (Shining Path), Oscar Ramirez Durand, was captured. He was later sentenced to life imprisonment without parole. Membership in the Peruvian Maoist guerrilla force reportedly dwindled to under 1,000 by the year 1999.

Dec. 27. Pres. Fujimori announced that he would seek a third presidential term. Because of legislation passed in 1996, Fujimori was able to evade a two-term limit to the presidency that was delineated in Peru's 1993 constitution.

2000, April 9. Congressional elections in Peru yielded a majority for Pres. Fujimori's Peru 2000 Party, but Fujimori failed to get a majority of votes in the presidential election. A runoff was scheduled for May 28.

May 21. Fujimori's only remaining opponent for the presidency, Alejandro Toledo, withdrew, claiming the election was a fraud. International election observation teams, including one from OAS, abandoned the Peruvian elections in protest of voter irregularities and computer imprecision in counting the ballots. Apparently winning the election by only one percentage point, Fujimori's July 28 inauguration saw widespread rioting in Lima, leaving many of the buildings in flames and six people dead.

Sept. 14. A videotape of Fujimori's closest political advisor, Vladimiro Montesinos, was released to the public and indicated that bribery may have played a part in Montesinos's campaign activities. Shortly thereafter, Montesinos went into hiding, and there was widespread fear that he would organize a military coup if Fujimori's government were overthrown.

Sept. 16. Fujimori agreed to cut his presidential term short in light of the scandals but refused to hand power over to a transitional government before new elections, planned for March or July 2001, could take place. Meanwhile, opposition leader and presidential hopeful Alejandro Toledo led the calls for Fujimori to step down.

Nov. 20. With mounting civil unrest over the whereabouts of the fugitive Vladimiro Montesinos, Pres. Fujimori flew to Japan and resigned, along with both of his vice presidents. Two days later, the Peruvian Congress swore in legislative leader **Valentin Paniagua Corazao** as interim president, he being Peru's next-highest remaining elected official.

g. ECUADOR

(From p. 742)

1946, Aug. 11. PRES. JOSÉ VELASCO IBARRA (1893-1979) was reelected by the assembly.

1947, Aug. 23. Col. Mancheno, in a successful revolt, ousted Pres. Velasco Ibarra, only to be overthrown himself on Sept. 3 by a Conservative counterrevolution. **Carlos Arosemena** became acting president.

1948, June 6. In the first popular elections since 1940, **Galo Plaza Lasso was elected president.**

1949, Aug. 5. An earthquake in central Ecuador killed more than 4,000 people.

1952, June 1. Voters gave the Liberal candidate, **Velasco Ibarra,** an upset victory over the Conservative candidate in the presidential vote.

1961, Nov. 6-9. The government resigned as a result of riots and military unrest. **Carlos Arosemena was installed as president.**

1963, July 11-12. A military junta, headed by **Capt. Ramón Castro Jijón,** overthrew the government, outlawed the Communist Party, and promised to wipe out pro-Castro guerrilla bands.

1966, March 29. The military junta was overthrown and a civilian government established under **Clemente Yerovi Indaburu.**

Oct. 16. A constituent assembly named **Otto Arosemena Gómez** as president pro tem.

1968, June 2. In the elections, **Dr. José Velasco Ibarra,** four-time former president, led the field with about one-third of the popular vote. He assumed the presidency (Sept. 1).

1969, March. Establishment of trade relations with the USSR.

1970, Oct. 27. Kidnapping of **Gen. César Rohan Sandoval,** chief of the air force, by guerrillas. Martial law was proclaimed, and Gen. Rohan was released a few days later (Nov. 1).

1972, Feb. 15. Fearing that popular candidate **Assad Bucaram** would be elected president, the military installed **Gen. Guillermo Rodríguez Lara** as president. Rodríguez Lara then expelled the American military mission and initiated a minor agrarian reform.

1974, June 6. Rodríguez Lara **expropriated 4 million hectares of oil holdings** from Texaco and Gulf. Although initially these expropriations and Ecuador's membership in OPEC led to a jump in government revenue, the foreign companies retaliated and forced reductions in the price and taxes on oil.

July 11. All political parties and elections were suspended for a five-year period of **"national development."**

1975. Urban groups, mobilizing to demand social reform amid massive migration from the impoverished countryside to the cities, carried out a successful **general strike.**

1976, Jan. 11. Rightist military leaders led a coup under **V. Adm. Alfredo Poveda Burbano.** The regime moved to the Right, inviting massive foreign investment and initiating an International Monetary Fund (IMF) austerity program.

1979, April. After the military, unable to deal with economic problems, agreed to turn power over to civilians, **Jaime Roldós Aguilera,** candidate of the **Confederation of Popular Forces (CFP),** won presidential elections. He promised social and economic reform but was consistently stifled by the Congress.

1980–90. Growing protest by the **National Federation of Peasant Organizations (FENOC)** and the **Confederation of Indigenous Nationalities of Ecuador (CONAIE)** against government promotion of agribusiness and Amazonian oil development at the expense of rural communities.

1980, May. Roldós's CFP won a majority in Congress, opening the way for a massive program of rural investment and reform.

1981, May. Pres. Roldós was killed in a plane crash and was succeeded by the conservative **Osvaldo Hurtado Larea,** who adopted austerity measures favoring big business. The collapse of the oil economy, the growing debt ($5.5 billion in 1982), and student and labor protests led to several **states of emergency.**

1984, May 6. Ultraconservative **León Febres Cordero** was narrowly elected president. In late 1984, Febres signed an **agreement with the IMF** to defer the $7 billion debt and promote foreign and private investment. He also **removed subsidies** on basic foodstuffs, cut back loans to small farmers, and limited wages.

1987, March 5. The country was hit by a devastating **earthquake,** leaving 2,000 dead and over 50,000 injured. The earthquake also severely disrupted the oil industry.

March 25. For the second year in a row, labor organizations launched a general strike to protest the government's neoliberal policies. Protesters were suppressed by security forces through widespread arrests, beatings, and torture.

1988. Ecuador's population reached 10.2 million.

May 8. Presidential elections were won by **Rodrigo Borja Cervallos of the Democratic Left (ID).** Borja promised to secure greater economic independence and to give social needs priority over debt payments, but he was forced to accept an IMF austerity program. Opposition to the regime mounted quickly.

1990, June. Hundreds of thousands of Indians joined a protest over government policies and the development of the Amazon basin for foreign oil companies. The protesters demanded a constitutional amendment recognizing the multiethnic nature of Ecuador and promulgating major land reform.

1991, Jan. Labor groups called a **general strike** protesting IMF-imposed austerity measures.

1992, May 13. One hundred forty-eight Indian communities were granted title to 1.2 million hectares of land in the Amazon basin. Commercial development was banned in the area, but the regime reserved oil exploration rights.

July 5. Conservative **Sixto Durán Ballén** of the **United Republican Party** won a runoff election for president. He vowed to privatize state sector companies.

1994, June 13–20. Tens of thousands of Indians protested a new land law that they claimed ignored their traditional land and water rights. Indigenous communities barricaded highways, causing severe food shortages in several cities.

1996, July 7. Abdala Bucaram Ortiz of the Center-Left Roldosista Party defeated a rightist Social Christian Party candidate for the presidency.

1997, Feb. 6. In response to several episodes of bizarre public behavior, Congress voted to **oust Pres. Bucaram,** claiming that he was **mentally incapable of handling the presidency.** On Feb. 11 **Fabian Alarcón,** president of Congress, was **named the interim leader.**

1998, July 12. Popular Democracy Party candidate and mayor of Quito **Jamil Mahuad Witt won the presidential election** in a second-round runoff, following the **Feb. 1997 removal of Pres. Abdula Bucaram Ortiz by Congress for bizarre behavior and mental incapacity.** Far closer than analysts expected, the final results of the runoff showed Mahuad with 51 percent of the vote and opponent Alvaro Noboa with 49 percent.

July 13. Observers from OAS approved an allegedly fraudulent election in Ecuador, internationally legitimating the new government.

Oct. 26. Ecuador resolved its border conflict of over 50 years' duration with Peru. The presidents of the two nations signed a treaty to peaceably end conflicts over a portion of the Amazon jungle.

Nov. 9. In tax reforms put forth by the government of Pres. Mahuad a two-year suspension of the income tax was proposed; the economy and citizens of Ecuador struggled to remain afloat.

1999, Feb. 17. As he was exiting the Congressional building in Quito, Jaime Hurtado, a legislator and founding member of the Popular Democratic Party, was assassinated.

March 11. Pres. Mahuad took emergency economic measures to lower inflation and stabilize the economy. His austerity plan was widely protested with massive national strikes by military leaders and Indian groups.

Sept. 26. Ecuador defaulted on part of its international debt by failing to make a $44.5 million payment on its internationally borrowed money in Brady Bonds. Continuing devaluation of the sucre pulled Ecuador into its worst economic crisis since the 1920s.

2000, Jan. 21. An Indian-supported army coup overthrew Pres. Mahuad; through Congressional ratification he was replaced the following day by the vice president, **Gustavo Noboa Bejarano.** This was the first successful military coup in Latin America in over ten years.

March 3. Though it was the cause of Mahuad's overthrow, Pres. Noboa proceeded with a plan to replace the sucre with the American dollar as the official national currency. This action was part of a larger effort to privatize state-owned industries and restructure Ecuador's foreign debt.

h. COLOMBIA

(From p. 742)

1946, May 4. Conservative leader **Mariano Ospina Pérez** became president. He organized the new **political police,** used by the Conservatives to terrorize and murder Liberals.

1948, April 9. The assassination of left-wing Liberal JORGE ELIÉCER GAITÁN (1903–48), who was expected to win the 1950 presidential elections, touched off a **major upheaval (known as the Bogatazo), interrupting the Ninth Pan-American Conference in Bogotá.** Thousands died in the insurrection, which saw widespread rioting in the cities, occupation of foreign-owned oil installations, and hacienda takeovers by peasants in the highlands. Elite Liberals and Conservatives, frightened by the violence, initially decided to join together in a group called the **National Union** to protect their interests. This alliance soon broke down, and in the ensuing months a reign of terror that would last until the 1960s (known as **LA VIOLENCIA**) was instituted against the Liberals and all other opposition groups. As many as 300,000 died in the violence. Terrorist actions by the political police were widespread. Clashes between peasants and landlords increased in frequency, and well-organized guerrilla movements emerged in the countryside in support of oppressed groups. As shown in the writings of **Gabriel García Márquez** (*One Hundred Years of Solitude,* 1967), La Violencia profoundly affected the tenor of Colombian political and social life.

1949, June 5. Congressional elections gave the Liberals a reduced majority.

Nov. 27. Following a violent campaign costing over 1,000 lives, the Conservative **Laureano Gómez** was elected president. The Liberals boycotted the election.

1953, June 14. GEN. GUSTAVO ROJAS PINILLA (1900–75) seized power, ousting Pres. Gómez. He escalated political violence, using conservative vigilante gangs to wreak terror on former and current opponents.

1955, April. The regime declared the **Sumapaz** region a war zone, sending in major military formations to stamp out opposition.

1957. Women were granted the vote.

May 8. Despite a constitutional provision against reelection, **Gen. Rojas Pinilla** was **reelected** by 76 members of the legislative assembly meeting under military control.

May 9. The Roman Catholic Church accused the Rojas regime of murder in its suppression of student riots. On May 10, **Rojas resigned** before the completion of his first term, and a military junta took control.

July 26. Amid popular demonstrations, the ruling **military junta dissolved the constituent assembly** and announced presidential and congressional elections for May 4, 1958.

Dec. 1. Colombians voted to **amend their 1866 constitution** to provide for joint rule by Conservatives and Liberals for 16 years.

1958, May 4. **Alberto Lleras Camargo** was elected president and was inaugurated on Aug. 7.

1959, March 24. Pres. Lleras Camargo announced a cabinet composed of six Liberals, six Conservatives, and one military figure.

1961. Fearing social revolution, the government launched a heavily publicized but insubstantial **land reform.** The reform coincided with new military efforts, with U.S. aid, to eradicate guerrilla movements in the countryside.

1962, May 6. **Guillermo León Valencia,** endorsed by the National Union Coalition, won the presidential election.

1965, May–1969, Dec. A state of siege was instated to control student unrest and disturbances resulting from the economic crisis.

1966. Founding of the **Revolutionary Armed Forces of Colombia (FARC).** This organization, along with others such as the **National Liberation Army (ELN)** and the **April 19 Movement (M-19),** had ties to the peasant mobilizations of the 1950s and continued to grow despite repeated efforts at suppression.

May. In the presidential elections, the candidate of the National Front, **Dr. Carlos Lleras Restrepo,** was successful.

1968, Jan. Resumption of **diplomatic relations with the USSR.**

Dec. Adoption of constitutional reforms that provided for the progressive termination of joint-party rule.

1969, May 26. Signing of the agreements to establish **ANDEAN INTEGRATION** among Colombia, Ecuador, Bolivia, Peru, and Chile.

1970, April 26. **Misael Pastrana Borrero** was declared victor in the presidential election. The result was contested by former president Rojas Pinilla but was confirmed after a recount (July 15). After the elections, supporters of Rojas Pinilla, claiming electoral fraud, launched the April 19 Movement (M-19), which kidnapped several prominent leaders.

1974, April 21. Electoral competition was restored in the presidential election won by **Alfonso López Michelsen of the Liberal Party.**

1975. **Cocaine emerged** as an important Colombian export. Centered around the **Medellín and Cali cartels,** Colombia became a major processing center for cocaine by the mid-1970s. By the 1980s this industry generated $6 billion annually, contributing to massive government and banking corruption and expanding violence, but also providing some relief to an economy beset by the declining coffee industry and massive foreign debt.

1977, Sept. 14. A coalition of urban poor, workers, peasants, and students launched the first nationwide **civic strike,** protesting government policies. In the repression that followed, 50 people were killed and thousands arrested.

1978, Jan. Congress granted the police and the military a **"license to kill"** in dealing with violence and drug traffickers.

June 4. Liberal **Julio César Turbay Ayala** was elected president. He reimposed a state of siege.

1982, May 31. Conservative nationalist **Belisario Betancur** won the presidential election on a platform calling for talks with guerrilla groups and greater independence from U.S. interests.

Nov. The Betancur government negotiated a **cease-fire and amnesty with the FARC and the M-19.** After increases in death squad activities, however, **the accord broke down.** Operating in concert with the drug lords, military leaders sought to undermine the peace process.

1983, Nov. The FARC, the M-19, and the ELN formed a political alliance.

1984, April 30. Justice Minister **Rodrigo Lara Bonilla** was assassinated by drug traffickers. Pres. Betancur then imposed a **state of siege,** declaring war on the drug trade.

May–Aug. New cease-fires were signed with several guerrilla groups. In spite of violations of the agreement by military attacks on the FARC in December, the peace process continued.

1985, May. Amnesty was granted to most guerrillas.

June 20. The **National Civic Movement (MCN)** led a massive general strike, calling for wage hikes, social reform, and a debt moratorium.

Nov. M-19 commandos attacked the Palace of Justice. One hundred people were killed in the ensuing battle, including 11 Supreme Court justices. In the following months, political murders on the Left and the Right escalated.

1986, May 25. Liberal candidate **Virgilio Barco Vargas** was elected president. Barco, under heavy pressure from the U.S., vowed to wage effective war against drug traffickers.

Sept. The labor movement formed the **Single Workers' Central (CUT),** which broke away from traditional politics, forming an association of worker, Indian, peasant, and religious groups.

Dec. Newspaper publisher **Guillermo Cano** was assassinated.

1987, Oct. **Jaime Pardo Leal,** 1986 presidential candidate of the **Popular Union (UP)**—the political arm of the FARC—was **assassinated** by a rightist death squad. During its first two years, over 1,000 Popular Union members were murdered by death squads.

1988. Colombia's population reached 30 million.

1989. Increasingly turning against the political elites whom they had once worked with in repressing peasant and worker groups, the drug cartels assassinated the governor of Antioquia, the attorney general, and the Medellín police chief.

Aug. 18. Sen. **Luis Carlos Galán,** Liberal presidential candidate, was murdered by the drug lords. Thousands attended his funeral, calling for an end to **narco-terrorism.** Within days the Barco government launched a major crackdown on the drug lords.

1990, Feb. 15. U.S. president George Bush and the presidents of Peru, Colombia, and Bolivia signed an agreement in Cartagena pledging **cooperation in the drug war.**

March 19. M-19 signed a **peace accord** with the government, giving its members amnesty and a right to political representation. This left six major rebel groups with 10,000 members.

March 22. **Bernardo Jaramillo,** Popular Union presidential candidate, **was assassinated** in the Bogotá airport. A month later, M-19 candidate **Carlos Pizarro was murdered.**

May. Liberal **César Gaviria** won the presidential elections. He faced the task of dealing with both guerrilla groups and the drug lords.

Dec. 18. After months of negotiations, Medellín drug cartel leader **Fabio Ochoa Vásquez** surrendered to authorities.

1991, Feb.–June. A national **constituent assembly** was convened to write a **new constitution.** Written with the participation of some guerrilla groups, it aimed at creating popular elections at all levels, limiting terms and restricting power to declare a state of siege, and granting special rights to Indian groups and minorities.

March 1. The ELN disarmed, accepting political party status.

June 19. Hours after the new constitution banned extradition of Colombian-born nationals, Medellín drug cartel leader **Pablo Escobar** surrendered to authorities.

1992, July 22. Pablo Escobar escaped from police custody.

Nov. 7. The FARC killed 26 policemen and bombed 30 buildings.

Nov. 8. Due to a wave of escalating drug and insurgent violence, the government declared a 90-day state of emergency.

1993, Dec. 2. Medellín drug cartel boss **Pablo Escobar** was killed by government forces.

1994, Jan. 12. Colombian military officials acknowledged that **250 U.S. troops,** previously said to be on a humanitarian mission, **were helping the Colombian government track guerrillas and drug traffickers.**

Jan. 17. In one of a series of attacks by leftist rebel groups, an assassination attempt was made against the Colombian finance minister in Bogotá.

June 19. **Ernesto Samper Pizano** of the ruling Liberal Party **won the presidency.**

July 2. The soccer world was stunned by the **shooting death** in Medellín **of Andrés Escobar,** the player who had inadvertently scored an "own-goal" for the U.S. in Colombia's World Cup match (June 22).

1995, Aug. 16. Pres. Samper announced a 90-day state of emergency, claiming it would enable the government to more effectively combat guerrilla, paramilitary, and organized crime groups. In justifying the decree, Samper noted that **19,450 people had been killed and more than 700 kidnapped since January.** Critics claimed the decree was intended to divert attention from **mounting evidence that the Cali drug cartel had contributed to Samper's presidential campaign.**

1996, April 15. Leftist rebels ambushed an army convoy near the Ecuadorian border, killing 31 soldiers and injuring 18. The ambush, attributed to the Revolutionary Armed Forces of Colombia (FARC), was the first in a series of major offensives by the rebels, including several attacks (Aug. 30) that left at least 96 soldiers, police, rebels, and civilians dead.

Sept. 10. Vice President Humberto de la Calle Lombana submitted his resignation, claiming that Pres. Samper had lost credibility due to allegations that he accepted a $6 million campaign donation from the Cali drug cartel.

Nov. 25. A report by Human Rights Watch claimed that right-wing paramilitary groups had been incorporated into the Colombian armed forces to conduct a "dirty war" against leftist guerrillas.

1997, March 16. Colombian defense minister Guillermo Alberto Gonzalez resigned due to allegations that he accepted a campaign contribution from a drug trafficker.

July 21. More than 30 people were killed in the remote village of Mapiripan in a massacre allegedly perpetrated **by a right-wing paramilitary group.**

1998, March 2. The FARC attacked and defeated an army battalion in the jungle near Cartagena del Chaira. At least 62 of the 150 soldiers in the battalion were killed in the worst single defeat the army had suffered at the hands of leftist rebels in over 30 years.

March 8–9. The ruling Colombian Liberal Party retained a majority in both congressional houses during the legislative elections.

June 21. Andres Pastrana Arango, son of former president Miguel Pastrana Borrero, **was elected president** in a runoff election and promised to clean up corruption in the government. The second round of voting was the result of an almost perfect tie in the first election, held on May 31.

Aug. 3–7. The FARC and ELN initiated their fiercest killing and kidnapping operation in recent memory just prior to the inauguration of new president Pastrana.

1999, Jan. 15. Pres. Pastrana and Venezuelan president Hugo Chavez Frías visited Cuba to meet with Fidel Castro in an effort to improve relations with the Communist nation.

Oct. 24. Over five million people in 700 towns and cities protested the persistent violence and human rights abuses in Colombia. In Dec. 1999 the Colombian military reported 2,787 people kidnapped for that year, the most of any country in the world. The murder rate was also very high in 1999; right-wing paramilitaries, leftist guerrillas, drug traffickers, and other criminals were blamed for the abductions and violence that claimed some 23,000 lives and created over 100,000 refugees. In two years, approximately two million people had fled the country.

Dec. 20. The FARC announced its first cease-fire since 1984, but the promised stoppage of violence lasted only twenty days, through Jan. 10, 2000.

2000, Jan. 11. In response to intensified fighting among the military, paramilitary, and FARC beginning on this date, Pres. Clinton visited Colombia in August, stressing the need for massive reforms to combat violence, drug trafficking, and human rights abuses. The U.S. government approved $1.3 billion in anti-drug-trafficking aid for Colombia, despite fears in Colombia and the U.S. that these funds might escalate human rights abuses by the Right.

June. Southwest of Bogota, an oil field was discovered containing up to 300 million barrels of oil, a valuable product for quickly increasing the exports and income of Colombia at a time of severe economic recession.

Oct. 10. Colombia was chosen by the UN to be one of five new nonpermanent members of the 15-member UN Security Council. This status was determined in the international governing body's most recent referendum.

Oct. 24. The European Union (EU) offered an anti-drug package worth up to $321 million, far short of the $1 billion requested by the Pastrana government.

i. VENEZUELA

(From p. 742)

1945. Venezuela ranked third among the nations of the world in **petroleum production** when World War II commenced, but wealth remained concentrated in too few hands. A majority of the people remained impoverished, while a high birthrate caused a rapid rise in population.

Oct. 18. Pres. Isaias Medina was overthrown by a revolt of army officers, and **RÓMULO BETANCOURT** was made provisional president on Oct. 22.

1946, Oct. 27. Elections for the constituent assembly gave a majority to the Democratic Action Party (AD).

1947. Venezuelan women were granted the vote.

Dec. 14. Rómulo Gallegos (1884–1969), well-known literary figure, was elected president, and his Democratic Action Party maintained an overwhelming majority.

1948, Nov. 24. The government was overthrown, and a military junta under **Col. Carlos Delgado Chalbaud** took control.

1948–57. This period is known as **Venezuela's oil boom.** Oil production more than doubled, and massive foreign investment rolled in. Urbanization exploded, massively expanding Caracas and making Venezuela among the most urbanized nations in Latin America. Over a million foreigners also immigrated to the country's burgeoning cities.

1950, May 13. The Communist Party was outlawed.

Nov. 13. Pres. Delgado Chalbaud was assassinated, and Germán Suárez Flammerich became president of the junta (Nov. 27).

1951, Oct. 13. The government quelled a **revolt in Caracas** led by members of the outlawed **Communist and Democratic Action Parties.**

1954, Jan. 9. In the wake of charges of fraud concerning the Nov. 30 election results, **Col. Marcos Pérez Jiménez** was named provisional president by the National Assembly to serve "until constitutional government is reestablished."

1957, Nov. 4. Facing a severe recession, capital flight, and widespread political mobilization, Pérez Jiménez canceled the presidential election scheduled for Dec. 15 and announced a **plebiscite** instead. On Nov. 8, the government announced its readiness to initiate its own aid program for Latin America.

Dec. 31. A revolt against Pres. Pérez Jiménez broke out.

1958, Jan. 23. A military junta, led by **Adm. Wolfgang Larrazabal ousted Pres. Pérez Jiménez.** The junta assumed power after army units defeated the secret police in Caracas.

May 13. During U.S. vice president **Richard Nixon's goodwill tour** of South America, mobs in Caracas stoned his car. Pres. Dwight Eisenhower demanded that Nixon's safety be ensured by Venezuela and ordered marines to Caribbean bases as a "precautionary measure."

Dec. 7. Rómulo Betancourt (1908–81) of the Democratic Action Party was elected president. Betancourt promised gradual reform. He raised the tax rate on oil profits to 65 percent and initiated moderate agrarian and social reforms.

1960, April. Leftist AD elements, unhappy with the slow pace of reform, Betancourt's move to the right, and his opposition to Cuba, broke away and formed the Marxist **Movement of the Revolutionary Left (MIR).**

Aug. 15. A five-nation investigative committee reported to the OAS that it had conclusive evidence that the attempted June 24 assassination of Pres. Betancourt was linked to officials of the Dominican Republic.

Nov. Amid renewed recession, protests broke out among the poor and students in Caracas.

1963, Feb. 13. Nine Communists were reported to have hijacked a Venezuelan freighter in the Caribbean as part of a **terrorist campaign** against the Betancourt government.

Dec. 1. Voters elected **Raúl Leoni** of the ruling AD to succeed Betancourt as president.

1964–69. PRESIDENCY OF RAÚL LEONI (1906–72). He used shifting coalitions with the **Republican Democratic Union (URD)** and **National Democratic Front** to maintain a measure of stability. At the same time, industry mushroomed because of investment of oil remittances and foreign capital in manufacturing. Urban and rural unrest also escalated, with expansion of **guerrilla activity and urban terrorism.**

1968, Dec. 1. The presidential elections resulted in a narrow victory for

Dr. Rafael Caldera Rodríguez, the leader of the opposition Social Christian Party (COPEI).

1971, July 3. The Hydrocarbons Reversion Law passed amid protest over the power of foreign oil companies. It called for nationalization of all oil concessions by 1983.

1973, Dec. 9. CARLOS ANDRES PÉREZ (b. 1922) of the AD was elected president. Pérez, a leading architect of OPEC, discarded agrarian reform and promoted large-scale agriculture. Pérez benefited from OPEC, which raised the price of oil from $2 per barrel in 1970 to over $14 per barrel in 1974, expanding state revenue.

1974–78. The government initiated large-scale public works projects paid for with oil revenues and foreign loans. Pérez combined concessions to labor and rural groups and repression of dissident groups to solidify his regime. By the late 1970s, however, growing debt and an ever-increasing dependence on oil was severely hurting the economy.

1975, Aug. 29. Pérez signed a decree nationalizing the oil industry and creating the state-owned PETROVEN, which would accrue approximately $10 billion in annual sales.

1978, Dec. 3. COPEI candidate **Luis Herrera Campins** was elected president. He initiated privatization, cuts in public spending, and an end to many price controls. Rampant inflation followed, and unemployment tripled.

1983, Dec. 4. With the national debt at $27 billion and the economy in ruins, AD candidate **Jaime Lusinchi** was elected president.

1986, Feb. Lusinchi reached an accord with creditors, rescheduling foreign debt payments.

1988. Venezuela's population reached 18.8 million.

Dec. 4. Carlos Andres Pérez, AD candidate, was returned to the presidency. Contrary to his election promises, he quickly moved to implement an IMF austerity program in order to secure a $4.5 billion foreign loan.

1989, Feb. 27–28. Tens of thousands rioted in Caracas after the announcement of a rise in bus fares. Between 200 and 600 people were killed in the riots and repression that followed.

1992, Feb. 4. A coup attempted by military officers opposed to corruption in the regime failed. Martial law was declared.

June 21. For the first time since nationalization of oil production, private foreign firms were invited into the oil industry.

Aug. 23. New austerity measures were introduced, leading to a freeze on public sector hiring and acceleration of privatization.

Nov. 27. Military leaders, concerned with poverty and corruption, launched another **failed coup attempt.** Two hundred thirty people were killed in the violence and the widespread antigovernment rioting.

1993, May 21. The Senate voted unanimously to **suspend Pres. Pérez** on charges of embezzlement and misuse of public funds. **Octavio Lepage** of the AD was sworn in as acting president amid widespread popular celebration.

Dec. 5. Rafael Caldera Rodríguez, age 77, regained the presidency as an independent candidate. The vote was considered a negative reaction to free market policies.

1996, May 30. Former president Carlos Andrés Pérez convicted by the Venezuelan Supreme Court of mismanaging government funds and sentenced to 28 months in prison.

1998, Jan. 3. Pres. Rafael Caldera signed a law reforming the nation's electoral system to make the process less vulnerable to abuses by political parties.

Dec. 6. HUGO CHAVEZ FRÍAS, an unsuccessful coup leader in Feb. 1992, **was elected president** on a populist ticket called the Patriotic Pole Coalition. This election saw the decline of the Social Christian Democrats (COPEI) and Democratic Action parties, which had controlled Venezuelan politics for over 40 years. Chavez called for the privatization of the government oil company, wealth redistribution, and the abolition of Congress. A distant second in the election was Henrique Salas Romer of Project Venezuela, an opposing coalition.

1999, Jan. 15–18. Pres. Chavez and Pres. Pastrana of Colombia visited Cuba on a foreign relations trip and meeting with Fidel Castro that proved very unpopular in international diplomatic circles.

July 25. Chavez supporters elected a constitutional assembly of 131 members, 121 of whom were strong proponents of Chavez's policies. Forming to rewrite the Venezuelan constitution, the members of the assembly had replaced the existing elected Congress with their own

appointees by August, while Chavez retained strong public support. In reaction to Chavez's pledge to dramatically close the gap between rich and poor, critics predicted the establishment of a left-wing dictatorship under his rule.

Aug. 30. With public and Assembly support, Pres. Chavez took the last of the opposition-controlled legislature's powers. On Nov. 11, the Assembly suspended 75 judges and dismissed 5 others, further tightening its grip on national power.

Dec. 15. Venezuela's 26th constitution since 1821 was adopted by the Assembly.

2000, July 30. Chavez won the presidential election amid substantial protests over its validity in numerous cities. Rioting ensued and national troops were called in to quell the uprisings. Many wealthy Venezuelans were uneasy about Chavez's ties to Communist Cuba and his leftist political goals.

Aug. 7–14. In an effort to rally with other OPEC nations, Chavez traveled to Libya, Iran, Iraq, and several other OPEC countries despite strong criticism from the U.S. He was the first foreign head of state to visit Iraq since the Gulf War (1991).

Sept. 27–28. The leaders of many OPEC nations gathered in Caracas, Venezuela's capital. The meeting was the first of its kind since 1975. Although efforts were made to instill unity and uniformity of policy, the goals of those attending the conference—to limit petroleum production and increase oil prices worldwide—were stifled somewhat by external calls from the U.S. and the U.K. for greater production.

j. BRAZIL

(From p. 743)

1945, Oct. 29. The general demand for a more liberal government led to the forced resignation of **Pres. Getúlio Vargas** after almost 15 years of dictatorship. He was succeeded by **Chief Justice José Linhares.** Despite his resignation, Vargas retained a large popular following and easily won election as a senator.

Dec. 2. With the endorsement of ex-president Vargas, conservative **Gen. Eurico Dutra** of the Social Democratic Party (PSD) was elected president. The new government pledged cooperation with the U.S. abroad and the elimination of "extremist ideologies" at home.

1946. Massive strike wave, particularly in São Paulo. **Dutra outlawed most strikes and stepped up government intervention in unions.**

Sept. 17. A new constitution authorized the government to outlaw any antidemocratic party.

1947, May 1. The Communist Party was outlawed.

Oct. 20. Brazil broke off diplomatic relations with the Soviet Union.

1950, Oct. 3. Calling for accelerated industrialization and strengthened social welfare legislation, **GETÚLIO VARGAS WAS REELECTED PRESIDENT.** His nationalist-populist program and rhetoric garnered wide support among discontented industrialists, workers, and urban middle-class groups.

1953. Three hundred thousand **workers struck in São Paulo,** Latin America's leading industrial center, for increased wages and benefits.

June. In the aftermath of the strike, Vargas appointed **JOÃO GOULART** as minister of labor. Sympathetic to labor's demands, **Goulart moved to double the minimum wage.**

Oct. After two years of pressure by Vargas and popular groups, Congress passed a law creating **Petrobrás,** a mixed public-private company giving the state a monopoly over new oil refineries and drilling.

1954, Aug. 24. Tarnished by repeated scandals and ordered to resign by the armed forces, **PRES. VARGAS COMMITTED SUICIDE.** He was succeeded by his vice president, **João Café Filho.**

1955, Oct. 3. In national elections, Social Democrat **Juscelino Kubitschek** (1902–76) and Laborite **João Goulart** (1919–76) won the presidency and vice presidency. Fueled by expansion of heavy industry, during the next five years the **economy grew by nearly 7 percent annually.** State enterprises combined with massive private multinational investment to produce the growth.

1959. Facing debt service payments that took up more than half the value of Brazil's exports, Kubitschek refused IMF demands for stabilization and expanded the money supply. This caused rampant inflation.

1960, April 21. Brasília was inaugurated as the new capital.

Oct. 3. Presidential elections resulted in victory for **Jânio da Silva Quadros,** an independent moderate.

1961, Aug. 25. Pres. Quadros resigned, saying that the forces of reaction blocked his effort to achieve economic and social progress.

Sept. 7. V.P. João Goulart succeeded Quadros, after initial opposition by Brazil's three top military chiefs. Goulart supported agrarian reform, selected nationalizations, and legalization of the Communist Party, but he was circumscribed by a congressional amendment weakening the executive.

Sept. 29. The regime introduced a law requiring the **registration of foreign capital** and banning profit remittances of more than 10 percent. Foreign, particularly American, investors opposed the measure, and during the next year **investment dropped sharply.**

1961–64. A period of **increasing labor militancy** (urban and rural) ensued in the face of declining economy and widespread inflation. Strikes increased, and over 2,000 peasant leagues were organized among the smallholders and the landless of the northeast.

1963, Jan. 1. Goulart won a plebiscite that returned full powers to the executive. His victory sparked **cuts in U.S. aid and capital flight** among Brazilian elites. Annual inflation soon reached 100 percent.

1964, Feb.–March. Pres. Goulart ordered **distribution of federal lands** to peasants, doubled the minimum wage, and expropriated land adjacent to federal highways. His actions aroused conservative opposition.

March 31–April 2. Military leaders and several state governments **revolted against Goulart.** He fled to Uruguay. Repression followed.

April 11. Congress elected army chief of staff **Gen. Humberto Castelo Branco** (1900–67) as president, to serve for the remainder of Goulart's term. The new military dictatorship reversed the Goulart reforms, freezing wages, banning strikes, and facilitating foreign takeovers of the economy.

1965, Oct. 27. PRES. CASTELO BRANCO ASSUMED DICTATORIAL POWERS with Institutional Act No. 1, abolishing political parties, packing the Supreme Court, suspending constitutional rights, and suppressing opposition. Henceforth, popular election of the president was to be replaced by a majority vote in Congress.

1966, Oct. 3. Marshal Arthur da Costa e Silva, former minister of war, was **elected president** by the Congress.

Nov. 15. In general elections, the government-sponsored **Aliança Renovadora Nacional (ARENA)** won a resounding victory and was transformed into a political party. Only one opposition party, the **Movimento Democrático Brasileiro (MDB),** was permitted.

1967, Jan. 22. Congress approved a **new constitution** greatly strengthening presidential powers and federal control over the states.

1968, March–April. Widespread student protests were waged against the repressive policies of the government and firings of dissident professors.

April. Fifteen thousand metalworkers in Minas Gerais struck after taking several factory managers hostage. After this and other wildcat strikes during 1968, the labor movement was brutally crushed and its leaders exiled or imprisoned.

April 4. Police assaulted a crowd of 30,000 attending the funeral of a student slain by security forces.

June 28. The March of the 100,000 took place in Rio de Janeiro, rallying the opposition.

Dec. 13. ESTABLISHMENT OF BLATANT AUTHORITARIAN REGIME. Hard-liners in the military won out as Pres. Costa e Silva suspended Congress indefinitely, assumed power to rule by presidential decree, and instituted drastic censorship. The new **Institutional Act No. 5** gave the president power to proclaim a state of siege and to suspend political rights. The government made mass arrests of dissenters and began using torture systematically.

1969–73. Brazil underwent its **"economic miracle,"** involving denationalization of key sectors. State industries were used to provide cheap steel, power, and raw materials to foreign firms, leading to massive increases in exports (12 percent annually between 1969 and 1972). There was, however, no concomitant jump in domestic consumption. Income remained concentrated in relatively few hands as real wages fell. Imports of oil and other goods also created a trade deficit and increased the debt.

1969, July 13. Destruction of the TV station in São Paulo by leftist bombing. Rapid development and **spread of urban guerrilla movements** were marked by kidnappings and bombings.

Aug. 31. Pres. Costa e Silva was incapacitated by a stroke. A triumvirate of military chiefs assumed control.

Sept. 4. C. Burke Elbrick, the U.S. ambassador, was **kidnapped by guerrillas** and threatened with execution unless the Brazilian government released 15 political prisoners within 48 hours. The ambassador was released when the government complied (Sept. 7). This was followed in 1970 by similar **kidnappings of Japanese, West German, and Swiss diplomats.**

Oct. 7. The military junta named hard-liner **Gen. Emilio Garrastazú Médici as president.**

1970, June 21. Brazil won an unprecedented third **World Cup** in soccer (Brazil had also won in 1958 and 1962), boosting the government's campaign to make Brazil a world power. Soccer star **Pelé** emerged as an informal spokesman for the regime.

1973–74. The jump in oil prices and antidumping laws abroad combined to **devastate the economy. Unemployment soared;** despite gains for some urban groups, malnutrition and disease were widespread. The period also saw **expansion of peasant agriculture and ranching in the Amazon basin,** devastating large portions of the rain forest and threatening remaining indigenous groups.

1974, Jan. 15. Gen. Ernesto Geisel was elected president. He initiated some intermittent relaxation of authoritarian rule. Torture and imprisonment remained tools of the regime.

Oct. 15. The Brazilian Democratic Movement (MDB), the legal opposition, won 62 percent of the popular vote in elections for Congress, giving it a majority in the Senate.

1975, Oct. 25. The death of well-known journalist Vladimir Herzog in police custody galvanized the opposition. At the University of São Paulo 15,000 students went on strike.

1976, Nov. 15. In spite of new laws designed to stifle the opposition, **the MDB made significant gains in municipal elections.** This prompted a temporary closing of Congress to change the constitution. Divorce was legalized when Congress reopened.

1976–79. Continued decline in living standards coincided with a growing **antimilitary movement** with strong participation by the Catholic Church and grassroots Christian communities. Emerging **women's movements** protested specific injustices, and a small feminist movement took shape; also, renewed militancy among the African-Brazilian population challenged Brazil's image as a **"racial democracy."** Most significant in terms of popular protest was labor insurgency. Militant trade unionists appeared in key industries.

1978–80. In a series of massive metallurgical workers' strikes, 500,000 workers struck in 1978 and another 3.2 million in 1979. LUIZ INÁCIO (LULA) DA SILVA emerged as leader and head of the newly formed **Workers' Party.**

1978, Sept. 30. Thirty-three unions issued a joint manifesto demanding the right to strike.

Oct. 15. Military candidate Gen. João Baptista Figueiredo was declared the victor over MDB candidate Gen. Euler Bentes Montero in presidential elections.

1979, Jan. 19. Gen. Figueiredo declared an *"abertura"* (opening) and vowed to oversee a gradual transition to civilian rule. General amnesty was given to most political prisoners and exiles. Censorship was eased.

1982, Nov. 15. In spite of right-wing military violence against the political opening, **direct elections** for governors, municipal officials, and Congress took place. The opposition, led by the PMDB (Party of the Brazilian Democratic Movement), won 62 percent of the vote, ten governorships, and control of the lower house.

Dec. 20. Brazil signed a **rescue loan agreement** with the IMF concerning its $89 billion debt. Relief was predicated on removal of subsidies on gas and basic food items and cuts in government spending.

1984, April. Massive demonstrations in Rio (April 10) and São Paulo (April 15, with 1.5 million marchers) called for immediate direct popular elections for the presidency; nevertheless, the military insisted on indirect election.

1985, Jan. 15. Moderate opposition businessman **Tancredo Neves** (1910–85) of the PMDB was elected president but died of cancer before his inauguration.

April 22. Vice president–elect **José Sarney** (a long-time supporter of the military regime and very recent convert to the PMDB) assumed the presidency. He promised land reform and a voice for the workers in government.

Nov. Congress passed a **land reform bill** providing for distribution of 88 million acres to 1.4 million families by 1989. The move proved ineffective as large landowners stalled the program by hiring armed thugs to intimidate and murder peasants in the affected regions.

1986, Feb. 28. The government introduced the **Plan Cruzado,** aimed at stopping inflation (which stood at 230 percent in 1985) by wage and price freezes. After some initial success, rampant inflation resumed.

Nov. 20. The regime introduced **Plan Cruzado II.** The new austerity program led to devaluation of the currency and price hikes.

Dec. 12. Two major union confederations, the Single Workers' Central (CUT) and the General Workers' Command (CGT), launched a **general strike** opposing the austerity plan.

1987, Feb. Pres. Sarney **suspended payments on the debt** to foreign banks. After much international pressure, payments were resumed one year later.

1988. Brazil's population reached 144.4 million.

Oct. Pres. Sarney announced "**Our Nature,**" a program designed to protect the rain forest while allowing limited development of the Amazon basin.

Oct. 5. Progressive in nature, **the new constitution** solidified democratic institutions, abolished presidential rule by decree, gave the vote to illiterates, protected Indian rights, and created a new labor code.

Dec. 22. Murder of Francisco "Chico" Mendes, renowned leader of the **National Rubber Tappers Council,** by local cattle ranchers in the Amazonian village of Xapuri. Seeking to take over forest and convert it to pasture, ranchers used such extreme measures to silence opposition.

1989, Feb. 20–24. Indians in Altamira led a **protest against a proposed dam on the Xingú River** that would flood 15 million acres.

March–April. Over 300 strikes (including a two-day general strike, March 14–15) were called to protest inflation (which stood at 988 percent in 1988) and wage freezes.

Dec. 17. Francisco Collor de Mello of the conservative **National Reconstruction Party** won presidential elections, narrowly defeating Workers' Party candidate Luiz Inacio (Lula) da Silva. He promised to fight corruption, privatize the $110 billion debt, and fight the 1,300 percent annual inflation rate with a neoliberal program.

1990, Feb. 8. Food riots broke out in Rio in the midst of continued inflation and recession.

Nov. 15. Plans were finalized for a 36,000 sq. mi. reserve for the Yanomami Indian nation in the Amazon basin. The government planned to create 278 reserves by 1994.

Nov. 30. Thirty-five hundred children marched through the streets of Rio to protest the murder of some 5,000 street children by police since 1983.

1992, June 3–14. Brazil hosted **the Earth Summit** (p. 821).

Sept. 29. Impeachment proceedings were initiated against Pres. Collor on charges of corruption. He was indicted on Nov. 12.

Oct. 2. V.P. Itamar Franco was sworn in as acting president.

Dec. 29. On the eve of his conviction in the Senate for corruption, **Pres. Collor resigned.** Itamar Franco was sworn in as president immediately. He promised to pay more attention to social problems but faced continuing economic crisis.

1993, Oct. 20. A congressional inquiry into corruption began after police discovered millions stashed in the home of a former government accounting official. Two cabinet ministers and 19 members of Congress were implicated.

1994, Jan. 21. A special investigative committee of the Brazilian congress recommended the expulsion of 19 fellow lawmakers for involvement in a multi-million-dollar kickback scheme.

Oct. 3. FERNANDO HENRIQUE CARDOSO became president of Brazil and vowed to end high inflation rates. Cardoso's landslide victory over Workers' Party candidate Luis Inácio Lula da Silva (favored in early polls) was attributed to the success of the "Real Plan" (July 1) in ending hyperinflation; the plan was developed while Cardoso was serving as minister of the economy.

1995, Aug. 9. At least 10 killed, 75 missing, and 350 arrested when **police**

violently evicted 1,300 landless farmers who had occupied a 40,000-acre estate in the northern state of Rondônia and ignored a court order to vacate the property. The level of police violence created **public sympathy for the growing Landless Movement.** Later in the year (Dec. 16) **Manoel Ribeiro,** a politician in Rondônia known for his support of the landless, was **shot dead.**

1996, April 17. Police in the Amazonian state of Pará opened fire on a group of protesters belonging to Brazil's **Landless Movement (MST),** killing at least 19 and injuring at least 50 others. Police claimed protesters fired shots first but a video of the attack aired nationwide (April 18) contradicted police accounts.

1997, April 17. Two-month-long march by members of the Landless Movement culminated in Brasília, where marchers were joined by tens of thousands of demonstrators calling for land reform.

May 21. Preliminary congressional approval of an amendment to allow reelection was marred by evidence that two deputies accepted bribes to vote for amendment. Despite scandal, the amendment became law (June 5), opening the way for Pres. Cardoso's reelection.

Nov. 10. Pres. Cardoso announced a stringent austerity program of tax hikes and spending cuts aimed at reducing budget deficit and restoring investor confidence.

1998, Oct. 4. Fernando Henrique Cardoso was reelected president of Brazil for another four-year term.

1999, Jan. The Asian economic crisis began to spread through Brazil. During 1999 Brazil let its currency devaluate by as much as 40 percent. As Cardoso tightened Brazil's economy, the austerity measures greatly damaged his voter popularity; yet Brazil saw a strong economic rebound in 2000.

April 22. After the IMF had released the remaining funds from its 1998 aid package one month earlier, more steps were taken to bolster Brazil's weakening economy. Brazil sold $2 billion in bonds on the world market to try to strengthen international confidence in its currency; former president of the Central Bank Francisco Lopes was arrested and later freed on charges of corruption, alleged to have taken place prior to his January removal from office.

June 29. A two-day international summit between the EU and Mercosur met in Rio de Janeiro, Brazil, to discuss gradual free-trade efforts between Europe and South America. The target date for establishing a Free Trade Area of the Americas (FTAA) was 2005.

Aug. 26. Tens of thousands marched on Brasilia, the nation's capital, protesting Pres. Cardoso's austerity efforts and calling for his resignation. Popular support remained low for Cardoso, even with the relative improvement of the economy during the year 2000.

2000, Aug. 31–Sept. 1. The presidents of South America's 12 countries met for an economic summit in Brasilia. The conference was headed by Brazilian president Fernando Henrique Cardoso; the talks focused both on anti-narcotics initiatives in Colombia and the expansion of free trade throughout the continent.

k. SURINAM

1975, May. Riots by Hindustanis protested the impending independence from the Netherlands. Hindustanis, then the largest ethnic group in a population of 348,000, feared political dominance by proindependence black creoles. After the riots, a majority of the Hindustanis emigrated from Surinam.

Nov. 8. Surinam, under the leadership of Prime Minister Henk Arron, was granted independence. Creole groups achieved a majority in Parliament, but the **constitution** (Nov. 21) guaranteed ethnic representation in the army. The Surinamese economy depended heavily on **bauxite exports,** which accounted for 92 percent of foreign exchange earnings.

1977, Oct. 31. In the country's first national elections, Henk Arron was returned as prime minister. Arron promised economic reform to reduce Surinam's dependence on bauxite exports.

1980, Feb. 25. Surinamese army sergeants deposed Prime Minister Arron and installed the **National Military Council (NMC)** under Lt. Michel van Rey, with **Chin A. Sen** as president.

1982, Feb. 5. Pres. Chin A. Sen was deposed by a leftist military coup led by **Lt. Col. Deysey Bouterse.**

Dec. 10. Martial law was imposed amid strikes and protests over the execution of 15 opposition leaders by government security forces.

1983, Feb. 28. Bouterse named a new cabinet headed by **Errol Alibux,** a Marxist political leader.

1986, Dec. 1. Martial law was reimposed because of widespread guerrilla activity. The insurgent **Surinamese Liberation Army (SLA)**, led by **Ronnie Brunswijk,** called for democracy, respect for human rights, and development of the interior.

1987, Sept. 30. A new constitution created a five-year presidency and council of ministers, both to be chosen by an elected National Assembly.

Nov. 25. The opposition **Front for Democracy and Development (FDD)** won by a landslide in the first elections since the military takeover.

1988, Jan. 25–26. Ramesewak Shankar was sworn in as president, and Henk Arron became prime minister. The new government faced a severe economic crisis, made worse by repeated guerrilla attacks on major bauxite plants.

Feb. An international report accused the Surinamese army of murdering between 120 and 200 civilians during the 1986–87 civil war.

1990. The population reached 447,000.

Dec. 24–30. Army chief Bouterse deposed Pres. Shankar, who favored a peaceful settlement with the SLA, and replaced him with **Johan Kraag.**

1991, May 25. In the general election, the antimilitary FDD won a majority in the National Assembly.

Sept. 7. Antimilitary politician **Ronald Venetiaan** was elected president by the **United People's Assembly.**

1992, Aug. 1. After suspension of hostilities in Surinam's civil war, the SLA signed a peace accord that included an OAS-supervised surrender of weapons.

1999, June. Surinam president Jules Wijdenbosch, pressured by the National Assembly and widespread public discontent over the poor economy, agreed to resign but remain in office until after the May 2000 election. Seventy percent inflation and territorial disputes with neighboring Guyana continued to thwart the Surinam economy.

2000, May 25. Pres. Wijdenbosch was defeated in the executive elections by former president Ronald Venetiaan of the New Front for Democracy and Development. The four-party, labor-supported coalition secured 33 of the 52 seats in elections for the legislature, one seat shy of a two-thirds majority.

3. CENTRAL AMERICA, 1945–2000

a. PANAMA

(From p. 744)

1945. Panamanian women received the vote.

1948, Feb. 15. In response to widespread protests in Panama, **the U.S. announced the final withdrawal of troops from its wartime bases.**

May 9. Presidential elections produced a close and contested decision between former president **Arnulfo Arias** and the Liberal **Domingo Díaz Arosemena.** The latter finally won and on Oct. 1 succeeded Enrique Jiménez as president of Panama.

1949, Aug. 25–Nov. 24. The death of Pres. Arosemena on Aug. 23 touched off a struggle for his succession, from which Arnulfo Arias emerged victorious.

1951, May 9. Rioting in Panama City followed the dissolution of the National Assembly and the **suspension of the constitution** by Pres. Arias. On the next day **the president was impeached and replaced by First V.P. Arosemena.**

1952, May 11. The government's candidate, former police chief **José A. Remón Cantera,** won the presidential elections, described by the opposition candidate as a "dangerous burlesque of democratic principles." **Remón renegotiated the 1903 canal treaty,** resulting in wage equalizations between Panamanians and North Americans and **an increase in the annual lease payment** for the canal to $1.93 million.

1955, Jan. 15. Following the National Assembly's dismissal of **Pres. José Ramón Guizado** for being implicated in former president Remón's assassination (Jan. 2), **Ricardo Arias Espinoza** was installed as president.

1956, June 15. Returns from the May 13 election indicated that **Ernesto de la Guardia** had won the presidency.

1960, May 8. Roberto F. Chiari, the Liberal Party candidate, won the presidential election.

Sept. 17. U.S. president Dwight D. Eisenhower ordered that the Panamanian flag be flown with the U.S. flag in the canal zone.

1964, Jan. 9. Rioting erupted when U.S. students in the canal zone ignored the order that U.S. and Panamanian flags should fly side by side. Panamanian students invaded the canal zone, and soon after the government broke relations with the U.S. and denounced the canal treaties. Both Panama and the U.S. agreed to let the Inter-American Peace Committee settle the dispute. In the following days, Pres. Chiari demanded a revision of the canal treaty. U.S. president Lyndon Johnson refused to commit himself, although he later (Jan. 23) declared that the U.S. would engage in a "full and frank" review of all controversial issues.

April 3. After Pres. Johnson, in a public statement to the OAS council (March 21), expressed U.S. willingness to "review every issue" involved in the rift with Panama, **diplomatic relations were resumed.**

May 10. Marco A. Robles, government candidate and advocate of a tough policy toward the U.S., was elected president.

1965, Sept.–1967, June. Negotiation of new agreements with the U.S. Final drafts provided for **abrogation of the 1903 treaty, recognition of Panamanian sovereignty over the canal zone,** and Panama's right to a share in the management of the canal, as well as the right of the U.S. to ensure defense.

1968, March 14. The National Assembly voted to **impeach Pres. Robles** on charges of misuse of public funds. Robles called on the National Guard for support. **Clashes between the guard and the populace** followed (March 24–29).

May 12. In presidential elections, David Samudio, Robles's candidate, was defeated by former president **Arnulfo Arias.**

Oct. 11–12. Arias was ousted by the National Guard. Brig. Gen. **OMAR TORRIJOS HERRERA** (1929–81), commander of the guard, emerged as the provisional junta's dominant figure. Torrijos, a nationalist and populist, sought to stir up sentiment over the canal and unite diverse Panamanian classes behind his regime. Torrijos first jailed numerous Communists, but later he invited several members of leftist movements into his cabinet. The regime also decreed banking and tax laws that attracted numerous banks to the country, as did Torrijos's retention of the U.S. dollar as the official currency.

1969, Feb. All political parties were declared abolished by the junta.

1970. The National Confederation of Peasant Settlements (CONAC) was founded. This organization facilitated the dispersal of 4.4 percent of the nation's agricultural lands.

Sept. 1. Torrijos rejected the 1967 **draft agreements with the U.S.** as falling short of complete control of the canal. Under the nationalist banner, the Panamanians continued to push for a treaty that would guarantee the full repatriation of the canal.

1972. Torrijos passed a **new labor code,** which granted new rights to urban slum dwellers, peasants, and workers. Elite opposition stifled its implementation.

1974. Panama reestablished diplomatic relations with Cuba.

1975. Panama joined the nonaligned movement. This, along with Torrijos's quiet support of the Sandinistas in Nicaragua, signaled a shift from Panama's previous pro-U.S. position.

1978, April. After four years of negotiations, the U.S. **Senate ratified a new canal treaty** hammered out by U.S. president Jimmy Carter and Panamanian president Torrijos. The new treaty called for full repatriation of the canal by the year 2000, but gave the U.S. the right to intervene to ensure operation of the canal.

1981, Aug. 1. Gen. Torrijos was killed in a plane crash.

1982, July 30. Civilian president Aristides Royo resigned, forced out by the National Guard under Gen. MANUEL ANTONIO NORIEGA and replaced by his vice president.

1984, May 6. Nicolas Ardito Barletta, of the **National Democratic Union (UNADE),** won the presidential election under charges that the election was fixed by Noriega, head of the newly renamed National Defense Forces (NDF).

1985. In an effort to undermine Noriega's power in Panama, the U.S. Central Intelligence Agency released reports that he was involved in drug trafficking. A long-time informant for the CIA, **Noriega was, at this time, becoming a liability to U.S. interests.** At the same time, Noriega was under pressure in Panama from an official investigation into torture and murder launched by Pres. Barletta.

Sept. 28. Noriega forced Pres. Barletta to resign, replacing him with V.P. Eric Arturo del Valle of the Republican Party (PR).

Dec. Noriega refused U.S. National Security Adviser John Poindexter's request to use Panama as a staging ground for an invasion of Nicaragua.

1986. With unemployment reaching 45 percent and a foreign debt of $3.7 billion, **del Valle was forced to accept IMF austerity measures** in order to receive aid.

June–July. A broad-based alliance of academics, businesspeople, students, and opposition parties held a series of **three general strikes,** demanding the resignations of del Valle and Noriega, who held the key to power in Panama as head of the NDF. In response, **Noriega arrested several military and civilian leaders** and declared a state of emergency. The U.S. closed its embassy and suspended aid to Panama.

1987. Relations with the U.S. continued to deteriorate. Noriega sought, with some success, to blame unrest in Panama on the U.S.

1988. U.S. president Ronald Reagan announced his intention to remove Noriega from power. After the Noriega-controlled Congress removed Pres. del Valle, the U.S. continued to recognize him as the legitimate leader, froze Panamanian assets in the U.S., stopped payments for use of the canal, and increased the U.S. military presence in the canal zone by 1,300.

April 8. Pres. Reagan announced **economic sanctions** against the Noriega regime.

1989. Panama's population reached 2,373,000.

April 27. U.S. president George Bush extended the sanctions against Panama.

May 7. In presidential elections, **the government candidate was declared the winner, but the results were annulled** three days later (May 10) when international observers complained of massive fraud and intimidation.

Dec. After a two-year campaign to oust Noriega, **U.S. FORCES INVADED PANAMA,** ostensibly to protect American lives, defend democracy, arrest Noriega on drug charges, and protect the canal. The invasion was broadly **condemned as a violation of the U.N. Charter and the OAS treaty,** and it led to the deaths of approximately 3,000 to 4,000 Panamanians, mostly civilians living in poor urban neighborhoods. After the invasion, U.S. forces installed **Guillermo Endara** as president. Many observers were skeptical about the stated motives for the invasion, arguing that U.S. intelligence had long known of Noriega's involvement in drug trafficking. Instead, they argued that the invasion was prompted by the Bush administration's fear of being unable to control Noriega, and enmity on the part of the Republican administration to the Carter-Torrijos treaties.

Dec. 29. The U.N. General Assembly voted 75–20 (with 40 abstentions) to condemn the U.S. invasion as a flagrant violation of international law.

1990, Jan. 3. Gen. Noriega surrendered to U.S. forces and was taken to the U.S. to stand trial on drug trafficking charges.

1994, May 8. Businessman **Ernesto Pérez Balladares won the presidency;** his victory marked the reemergence of Manuel Noriega's left-of-Center **Revolutionary Democratic Party.**

1997, Dec. 24. Panamanian and U.S. governments announced an accord that would allow U.S. troops to stay in Panama after the U.S. relinquished control of the Panama Canal at end of 1999.

1998, Aug. 30. Voters rejected a constitutional change that would have allowed Pres. Ernesto Perez Balladares to run for reelection in 1999.

1999, May 2. Panama elected its first woman president, Mireya Moscoso de Grubar, the widow of former president Arnulfo Arias.

Dec. 31. The United States formally passed control of the Panama Canal to Panama.

2000, June. The Financial Action Task Force, comprised of the seven leading industrialized nations of the world, blacklisted Panama as one of fifteen nations that recycle money made by international criminal activity.

b. GUATEMALA

(From p. 745)

1945. Guatemalan women gained the vote.

1950, Nov. 10–12. COL. JACOBO ARBENZ GUZMÁN (1913–71), a consistent supporter of Arévalo's liberal program, **was elected president.**

1952, June 17. Pres. Arbenz signed a **land reform bill.** Arbenz reiterated his commitment to capitalism, but the reform was **supported by a variety of labor and left-wing organizations** active in the subsequently formed peasant leagues. Under the reform, **holdings of over 223 acres were to be expropriated** and given to the landless, paid for with 25-year bonds.

1953, Feb. 25. The United Fruit Company (UFCO) was told of a plan to expropriate 225,000 of its 550,000 acres in holdings, only 15 percent of which were under cultivation. **The UFCO immediately began a public relations campaign in the U.S. to portray Arbenz as a Communist.**

Oct. 14. The U.S. State Department declared that Guatemala, **"openly playing the Communist game,"** could expect no U.S. help or cooperation. **UFCO executives requested CIA help in overthrowing the Arbenz regime.**

1954, Jan. 29. Guatemala accused Nicaragua of planning an invasion of Guatemala with the "tacit assent" of the U.S. During this time the CIA, with Pres. Dwight D. Eisenhower's approval, was preparing to install **Col. Carlos Castillo Armas,** then exiled in Honduras, as president.

March 17. The U.S. State Department, reporting a major shipment of Czech-made arms to Guatemala, condemned Communist influence in the region.

June. The CIA launched **"Operation Success"** to overthrow the Arbenz government. A rebel army under Castillo Armas entered the country from Honduras and waited while CIA planes bombed and dropped leaflets on the capital and jammed radio communications. The army refused to enter the conflict but hoarded weapons so that workers and peasants could not fight.

June 28. A military junta, headed by **Col. Castillo Armas, ousted Pres. Arbenz,** but on the following day yielded power to a government under **Col. Elfego Monzón,** which arranged a cease-fire and ordered the arrest of all Communist leaders in the country. The new regime began a **counterrevolution that reversed the land and social reforms,** and bloodily repressed the opposition.

July 8. Castillo Armas was made president of the ruling junta.

1957, July 26. Col. Castillo Armas was assassinated, and **V.P. Luís Arturo González** was installed as provisional president.

Oct. 24. Electoral fraud touched off a **national crisis,** which brought a three-man junta to power. The junta installed a provisional president, Guillermo Flores Avendaño.

1958, March 2. Gen. Miguel Ydígoras Fuentes was inaugurated as president for a six-year term.

1960, Nov. Supported by students and other democratic movements, a group of **reformist military officers rebelled.** CIA-trained Cuban exiles were used to suppress the revolt while U.S. warships waited off the coast. The survivors fell back to the countryside and began a low-intensity guerrilla war.

1963, March. Arévalo returned to Guatemala to run in the November presidential elections. His return prompted renewed political activity, raising alarm in the military.

March 30. The government of Pres. Ydígoras Fuentes was overthrown by a rightist anti-Fidelista rebel group, led by **Defense Minister Col. Enrique Peralta Azurdia.**

April 10. The new military government issued an interim **decree giving public power to the army.** The U.S. recognized the government on April 17.

1966, July 1. Inauguration of **Julio César Méndez Montenegro,** a civilian, as **president.** He was allowed to take power only after agreeing to let the military control internal security. **The Constitution of Sept. 15, 1965,** restored a democratic regime, but led to further polarization between the Left and the Right. Guatemala's notorious right-wing death squads, known as the **Mano Blanca,** emerged at this time.

Nov. 2. Proclamation of a **state of siege,** due to the rapid spread of guerrilla activity. Under the leadership of figures such as **Yon Sosa,** the guerrillas called for agrarian and social reform, and a return to democracy. In response to the guerrilla activity, **thousands of peasants in northern Guatemala were killed** by Guatemalan, Mexican, and American troops. Kidnapping, murder, and torture became government staples.

1968, Jan. 16. Two U.S. military attachés were slain by guerrillas. On Aug. 28, the U.S. ambassador, **John G. Mein,** was kidnapped and executed. Urban terrorism proliferated.

1970, Feb. 26. Kidnapping of the Guatemalan foreign minister, **Alberto Fuentes Mohr.**

March 31. Kidnapping of the West German ambassador. The ambassador was executed after negotiations broke down, and West Germany broke off diplomatic relations (April 6).

July 1. Col. Carlos Arana Osorio, a conservative, was inaugurated as president.

Nov. 13. In the struggle against guerrillas, a state of siege was again imposed.

1972. Guerrillas in northern Guatemala founded **the Guerrilla Army of the Poor (EGP).** Building a base among highland Indians, this movement numbered over 6,000 by 1980.

1974–78. Gen. Kjell Langerud García became president.

1977. Citing **massive human rights violations,** the Carter administration refused further military aid to Guatemala. By this point Guatemala was noted as one of the worst violators of human rights in the hemisphere.

1978–82. Gen. Romeo Lucas García was sworn in as president. His **"pacification program"** involved forced relocations and **a massive increase in death squad activity,** destroying an estimated 500 Indian villages.

1980, May 27. The secretary-general of the Coca-Cola workers' union was murdered by rightists linked to the plant's U.S. owner. The third union member murdered in 18 months, he had led a strike in April. **An international outcry** followed, and after a brief troop occupation of the plant, the union was recognized, and some concessions were granted.

1981. Three major guerrilla organizations agreed to unify their military command under the **Guatemalan National Revolutionary Union (URNG).**

1982, March. After Lucas García tried to impose a successor in fraudulent elections, an ultrarightist coup installed **Gen. Efrain Ríos Montt,** an evangelical Christian, as head of a junta. Ríos Montt instituted a scorched-earth policy against rebel areas, murdering all inhabitants of villages suspected of pro-rebel sympathies.

April. The U.S. National Security Council decided to circumvent a congressional ban on military aid to Guatemala and provided the regime with **$22 million in counterinsurgency aid.**

July 16. Over 300 Indians were massacred in Huehuetenango after being driven from a church by government troops. By the end of the Ríos Montt regime, over 30,000 Indian villagers had been killed in the counterinsurgency war.

1983, Aug. Ríos Montt was overthrown in a coup headed by his defense minister, **Gen. Oscar Mejía Victores.** The new junta escalated the violence, but under pressure from the U.S., it agreed to hold elections in 1985.

1984, July 1. In elections for a constituent assembly, the reformist **Christian Democratic Party (DCG)** won a plurality.

1985, Nov. 3. Marco Vinicio Cerezo Arévalo, DCG candidate, won the presidential elections, but the military maintained its massive program of repression. Hundreds of thousands of Indians were forced into civil defense patrols, which kept a tight grip over the countryside. Refugees fleeing these measures amounted to 10 percent of the population by the late 1980s.

1989, April. Peace negotiations opened between the URNG and the Cerezo government. Concurrently, death squad violence increased, and

little progress was made. Guatemalan police came under attack after reports indicated that they had been involved in the **murder of dozens of street children in Guatemala City.**

1991, Jan. 6. Conservative Christian Jorge **Serrano Elias** won runoff presidential elections. Serrano promised peace and an end to human rights abuses, but his regime seemed unable to produce either.

1992, Oct. 16. Rigoberta Menchú, the Quiche Maya author and Indian rights activist, was awarded the Nobel Peace Prize for her decade-long struggle to expose human rights abuses against Guatemalan Indians.

1993, May 25. Citing social and economic problems, Pres. Serrano initiated executive rule by decree, imprisoning opponents and dismissing the Congress and the Supreme Court.

June 1. Pres. Serrano was ousted by the military amidst widespread popular protests.

June 6. After the military allowed Congress to hold elections, **Ramiro de León Carpio,** the minister for human rights, was elected president.

June 7. Pres. de León **fired the defense minister and reassigned several top military officers** in order to diffuse their power and challenge the political role of the military.

1994, Jan. The Guatemalan **government resumed peace talks with leftist rebels aimed at ending the 33-year-old civil war.** They were the first talks since **Ramiro de León Carpio** assumed the presidency.

March 29. The Guatemalan government and the Guatemalan National Revolutionary Union (an umbrella organization for four leftist guerrilla groups) reached a **breakthrough agreement,** including a **human rights accord** and an **agenda for ending the civil war by the end of 1994.** The key obstacle to the accord had been the government's refusal to allow a full human rights probe, but officials agreed to allow an investigation by a United Nations verification commission.

June 23. A **mass grave** containing the charred remains of about 1,000 men, women, and children **was unearthed by heavy rains** in Quiche Province. The remains were widely assumed to be those of Indian peasants killed in early 1980s by the government-sponsored counterinsurgency program.

1995, March 10. The U.S. State Department suspended its military aid program to Guatemala, citing the government's ongoing failure to end human rights abuses.

March 13. The UN mission issued its first report on human rights abuses; the document cited the government as responsible for the great majority of violations.

1996, Jan. 7. A **presidential runoff was won by Alvaro Arzú Irigoyen** of the Center-Right National Advancement Party.

Jan. 19. Pres. Irigoyen dismissed many military leaders for their involvement in human rights abuses.

Sept. 19. The Guatemalan government signed a major treaty with rebels in an effort to end the 36-year civil war, Central America's longest running armed conflict. On Dec. 29 **the two sides signed a final peace agreement.**

1998, Jan. 16. Guatemala reestablished diplomatic relations with Cuba, ending 37 years of no contact with Castro's regime.

April 26. Human rights advocate and Catholic bishop Juan José Gerardi was murdered. In a situation of rampant politically motivated violence, the case remained unsolved. One year later, the chief prosecutor and two judges resigned because of repeated death threats.

1999, Feb. 25. In a report independent of Bishop Gerardi's investigations, a Guatemalan truth commission attributed over 93 percent of the nation's civil rights abuses to the army and only 3 percent to paramilitary groups such as the Guatemalan National Revolutionary Union.

March 10. U.S. president Bill Clinton visited Guatemala, apologizing for the aid given by the U.S. to right-wing military governments during the past decade.

Nov. 7. The right-wing Guatemalan Republican Front won a majority in the nation's congressional elections.

Dec. 26. Alfonso Portillo Cabrera won the presidential election for the Guatemalan Republican Front and took office in January 2000. Portillo was victorious despite his campaign connections with former president Efrain Rios Montt, whose administration committed some of Guatemala's most severe human rights atrocities during the years of civil war.

2000, June. Guatemala, Honduras, and El Salvador signed a free trade agreement with Mexico.

c. EL SALVADOR

(From p. 745)

1948, Dec. 14. Pres. Salvador Castañeda was forced to resign. A provisional government restored full constitutional liberties and called for free elections.

1950, March 26–28. In the first free elections since 1931, **Maj. Oscar Osorio was elected president.** Osorio introduced a constitution that allowed urban unions but banned rural organizing.

1956, Sept. 14. Gen. José María Lemus became president.

1961, Jan. 26. After a three-month junta was overthrown on Jan. 25, the new five-member **Military-Civilian Directorate** took control amid a rash of urban violence that left 96 dead.

Feb. 15. U.S. president John F. Kennedy recognized the junta, which could then receive aid from the **Alliance for Progress.** Aid seemed crucial to dealing with the explosive social problems stemming from El Salvador's massive population growth and booming coffee industry. The population was 2.5 million by 1961. Along with the **"fifty families"** (the country's economic elite), the government sought to promote **foreign-sponsored light industry.** With the creation of the **Central American Common Market (CACM),** Salvadoran officials saw a solution to social problems, but these enterprises **did little to alleviate population and unemployment pressures.** Meanwhile, mechanization increased in cotton, cattle, and coffee, driving peasants off the land.

1962, Jan. 5. The constituent assembly approved a constitution to replace the 1950 document, and on Jan. 25, **Eusebia Rodolfo Cordón was inaugurated as provisional president.**

April 29. With opposition parties boycotting the presidential election, **Lt. Col. Julio Adalberto Rivera** ran unopposed and on July 1 was inaugurated for a five-year term.

1964. JOSÉ NAPOLEÓN DUARTE (1925–90), a **Christian Democrat,** won the mayoral election in San Salvador. Duarte was one of the few reformist politicians tolerated by the military.

1967, March 5. Election of **Col. Fidel Sánchez Hernández,** of the ruling National Conciliation Party, as president.

1968. In an atmosphere of increasing political violence, **the National Guard tortured and murdered two labor leaders.** These tactics were intensified by the **creation of ORDEN by Gen. José Alberto Medrano.** A right-wing paramilitary squad, ORDEN was reputed to carry out summary executions of alleged peasant subversives. It received training from U.S. military advisers.

1969, July. Suffering from an economic crisis, Honduras expelled 80,000 Salvadoran refugees, causing war between the two countries (p. 956). Known as the **"soccer war"** because it erupted after a series of heated soccer matches, it resulted in victory for El Salvador, which invaded and bombed the Honduran capital (July 14). After some 3,000 deaths, the OAS proclaimed a truce. The victory soured, however, as the Salvadorans were faced with the loss of the Honduran market and the return of nearly 100,000 migrants.

1972, Sept.–Oct. With the economy in recession and opposition coalescing behind Christian Democrat José Napoleón Duarte, **the military used electoral fraud to install Col. Arturo Molina as president.** Dissidents in the military revolted, and protests erupted at the National University, but both groups were quickly suppressed by troops loyal to Molina. **ORDEN death squads scoured the countryside** to punish Duarte supporters. Duarte himself was imprisoned, tortured, and then exiled. The U.S. quickly recognized the Molina government.

1975. With over 80 percent of the land in El Salvador owned by a few families, Pres. Molina initiated a **minor agrarian reform,** redistributing 150,000 acres of public land.

July 30. University students, protesting peacefully, **were massacred by the army.** In the aftermath, several new organizations, such as **the Popular Revolutionary Bloc (BPR),** were founded.

1977, Feb. Due to fraudulent elections during which ORDEN bands terrorized opponents, **Gen. Carlos Humberto Romero became president.** He raised the brutal tactics of earlier regimes to new levels. As the Left and the Right mobilized for civil war, Romero intensified repression and made radical priests a major target.

Feb. 15. During a rally of over 50,000 people protesting the election in San Salvador, **police and ORDEN soldiers opened fire, killing 100.**

Nov. Romero introduced the **Law for the Defense and Guarantee of Public Order,** which banned public assembly and gave the army broad repressive powers. The law led to increased ORDEN death squad activity and political murders. At the same time, repression increased support for leftist movements such as **the Front for United Popular Action (FAPU).**

1979, Oct. 15. Following a series of successful strikes that seemed to foreshadow victory for popular forces, **Gen. Romero was overthrown** by the **"COLONELS' COUP."** He was replaced by a military-civilian junta that promised the dissolution of ORDEN, political freedoms, and agrarian reform. The first junta included moderates **Román Mayorga Quiroz** and **Guillermo Ungo** and military leaders **Col. Adolfo Majano** and **Col. Jaime Abdul Gutiérrez,** but the power structure changed with the addition of the conservative **Col. Guillermo García.** The junta also **allowed Duarte to return from exile.**

Oct. 28. National security forces **massacred 25 protesters.** This case was one of many in which the military used violent repression despite the change in government.

1980, Jan. 1. In a dispute over the junta's authority over the military, **Ungo and Mayorga resigned.** In the turmoil that followed, the military made a secret deal with the Christian Democrats to form a **new junta under the nominal leadership of José Napoleón Duarte,** and to accept agrarian reform and an end to repression. Just weeks later, however, troops opened fire on a demonstration, killing 20.

Feb. 23. Christian Democrat **Attorney General Mario Zamora,** one of the few remaining civilians in the government, **was assassinated.**

March 24. ARCHBISHOP OSCAR ROMERO, a strong opponent of the government and proponent of popular resistance, **was assassinated.** At his funeral, attended by over 80,000 protesters, another massacre occurred, resulting in 39 dead and 200 injured. These events marked a **radical increase in military violence during 1980,** with thousands murdered by troops.

April 18. Popular opposition groups coalesced into the **Democratic Revolutionary Front (FDR).** The FDR called for genuine democracy, social reforms, and economic independence.

Nov. Duarte was proclaimed president of the military-civilian junta. He was allowed to assume the leadership because his presence ensured ever larger aid packages from the U.S.

Dec. Four American churchwomen were kidnapped, raped, and murdered by government soldiers, provoking a public outcry in El Salvador and the U.S.

1981, Jan. After losing six leaders in a kidnap-assassination plot, the FDR, under **Guillermo Ungo,** set up a **government-in-exile.** During the same month the **Farabundo Martí National Liberation Front (FMLN),** which had formed the previous summer as a coalition of guerrilla groups, launched the **"Final Offensive."** The offensive failed, but the guerrilla movement remained strong, in spite of massive military aid from the U.S. for government forces. By the mid-1980s the number of guerrillas had risen to over 10,000.

Jan. 17. Alarmed by the successes of the FMLN offensive, outgoing U.S. president Jimmy Carter sent a $5 million **military aid package** to El Salvador and leased the government several attack helicopters. Later, Pres. Ronald Reagan **increased that amount by $25 million for 1981, and doubled it in subsequent years.**

Dec. The U.S.-trained Atlacatl army battalion **massacred 794 men, women, and children** in the village of El Mozote.

1981–82. The war settled into a stalemate, but by mid-1982 it seemed that the **guerrilla forces were making major advances.** At the **Battle of Escandón** (June), rebel forces defeated a battalion of elite troops. Rebel offensives were destroying the economic infrastructure and making the situation of the government tenuous.

1982, Aug. After U.S.-backed Christian Democrats failed to win a majority in congressional elections boycotted by the Left, the Christian Democratic Party (PDC), the **Party of National Reconciliation (PCN),** and the **Nationalist Republic Alliance (ARENA)** agreed on moderate **Alvaro Magaña** as president. In a concession to the far Right, ARENA's **Roberto d'Aubuisson** (the man widely believed to have orchestrated the murder of Archbishop Romero) was made president of the constituent assembly.

1983, Jan. A military mutiny demanded the removal of Defense Minister García, who was replaced by Gen. Carlos Vides Casanova.

1984, May. PDC candidate **Duarte won presidential elections,** defeating extreme right-wing ARENA candidate d'Aubuisson. Heavily backed with U.S. funds, Duarte promised some reforms and negotiations with the rebels. He did initiate talks with the FMLN that year, but they soon broke off. After the elections, the U.S. Congress voted an immediate increase in military aid.

1986, Jan. Presiding over a devastated economy and unable to initiate any social reform, Duarte announced an **austerity program** to help pay the costs of the war.

Oct. 10. An **earthquake** hit El Salvador, killing over 1,000 and leaving nearly half a million people homeless.

1987, April. Rebel forces attacked the second largest military base in the nation at El Paraíso, destroying the base and killing dozens of soldiers.

1989. El Salvador's population reached 5,125,000.

March 19. In elections boycotted by the Left, **ARENA's Alfredo Cristiani was elected president.** The results marked a severe repudiation of Duarte's inability to end the war. Cristiani, a coffee grower, initiated talks with the FMLN but insisted on their total surrender. Talks soon broke off.

Oct. 31. The National Federation of Salvadoran Workers (FENESTRAS) headquarters was bombed, leaving ten dead. Among those killed was FENESTRAS president **Elizabeth Velásquez.** The FMLN broke off talks two days later.

Nov. 11. The **FMLN launched its largest offensive since 1981,** aimed mainly at working-class neighborhoods in the cities. Rebel troops held parts of San Salvador for two weeks before withdrawing.

Nov. 16. Six Jesuit priests and two female employees were murdered by a military death squad. The Salvadoran government was condemned internationally for the murders.

1990, May. Alarmed by FMLN successes and fearing an end to U.S. military aid, **Cristiani agreed to go back to the peace table,** setting a cease-fire for September. Talks broke down quickly, and fighting resumed by winter.

1992, Jan. 16. After 21 months of negotiations, the FMLN and the government signed a **peace treaty** in Mexico City. Under the agreement the FMLN would disarm and become a political party, the military would be cut in half, human rights violators would be purged, a national civilian police force would be created, U.S.-trained counterinsurgency forces would be disbanded, political prisoners would be freed, and land would be granted to combatants in the conflict.

Jan. 23. An **amnesty law** was passed for most combatants, excluding the most serious human rights violators.

Feb. 1. An **armed truce** went into effect.

Dec. 15. Peace was formally proclaimed to end the 12-year civil war. Seventy-five thousand people had perished in the conflict.

1993, March 12. On the eve of the release of the **UN Truth Commission Report** detailing human rights abuses during the civil war, **Defense Minister Gen. René Emilio Ponce resigned,** prompted by information that linked him to the 1989 murder of the Jesuit priests. The report (released on March 15) attributed 85 percent of the human rights atrocities during the war to the military and right-wing death squads.

May 1. Months behind schedule, Pres. Cristiani began a purge of the military to rid it of human rights violators.

1994, April 24. In a runoff election, **Armando Calderón Sol** of the ruling right-wing party, Arena, **won the presidency** with 68 percent of the vote. Arena had already gained a strong parliamentary majority (March 20) in legislative elections.

1997, March 16. The left-wing **FMLN made major gains in midterm elections.** Violence, however, marred the electoral campaign; two FMLN campaign workers were killed and three others injured in a machine gun attack, presumably by right-wing gunmen, in the town of Nejapa (Feb. 20).

1999, March 7. Francisco Flores Pérez of the reigning ARENA party was elected president of El Salvador. The FMLN carried almost as many seats as ARENA in the National Assembly, but its presidential candidate won only 29 percent of the vote.

March 10. U.S. president Clinton visited San Salvador, the capital

of El Salvador, speaking publicly about illegal immigration issues and the need to lessen El Salvador's economic disparity between rich and poor. Though opposed by leftist politicians, Pres. Flores gained legislative approval for a U.S. military base in El Salvador. This fortification would replace the drug trafficking facilities given up when the Panama Canal was turned over to Panama on Dec. 31, 1999.

2000, June. El Salvador, Guatemala, and Honduras signed a free trade agreement with Mexico.

d. NICARAGUA

(From p. 746)

1947, Feb 2. Leonardo Argüello was elected president to succeed **Anastasio Somoza.** The new president was removed (May 27) when he showed signs of independence; in September, Somoza made **Victor Román Reyes** president. Under Reyes the new labor code went unenforced, and strikes were completely forbidden.

1950, March 25. Gen. Somoza resumed the presidency. During subsequent years the Somoza "kleptocracy" dominated the economy. The Somozas appeased elites by splitting profits from economic ventures and foreign aid with a small number of families.

1955. Nicaraguan women were given the vote.

1956, Sept. 29. Pres. Somoza died of gunshot wounds inflicted on Sept. 22. He was succeeded by his son **Luis,** elected to serve until May 1957, and then reelected for a six-year term. Luis, with the help of his brother **ANASTASIO SOMOZA DEBAYLE** (1925–80), known as Tachito, who controlled the National Guard, continued the graft and terror initiated by his father. The cotton boom drew large capital investments, driving peasants off their land. Among the only sources of opposition allowed was the mildly critical paper *La Prensa*, published by conservative **Pedro Joaquín Chamorro.**

1961. Carlos Fonseca, Silvio Mayorga, and Tomás Borge founded the FRENTE SANDINISTA DE LIBERACIÓN NACIONAL (FSLN), composed largely of students, which sought to overthrow the Somozas through guerrilla warfare. The **Sandinistas** were almost wiped out by the late 1960s.

1963, Feb. 3. René Schick Gutiérrez, the candidate selected by retiring president Somoza, defeated Diego Chamorro in the presidential election.

1966, Aug. 3. Lorenzo Guerrero was elected president.

1967, April 13. Luis Somoza died. His massive holdings reflected the **expansion of cattle ranches,** which bred cattle for U.S. markets. Peasants who had lost their land to cotton were now driven off by large-scale cattle ranching. Deforestation occurred, **60 percent of the peasants were left landless, and urban slums swelled.**

Feb. Gen. Anastasio Somoza Debayle was elected president, prolonging the Somoza dynasty.

1972, Dec. 23. A devastating **earthquake** hit Managua, killing over 10,000 and leaving approximately 200,000 homeless. Somoza pocketed millions in emergency aid.

1974, Dec. 27. During a Christmas party held to honor the U.S. ambassador, **FSLN guerrillas stormed in and took 40 hostages,** including high-ranking officials. The raid brought worldwide recognition to the FSLN. Somoza announced a state of siege, leading to brutal repression in rural areas.

1976, Nov. FSLN founder and leading ideologue **Carlos Fonseca was ambushed and killed.**

1978, Jan. 10. PEDRO JOAQUÍN CHAMORRO WAS ASSASSINATED, allegedly by Somoza gunmen. The murder touched off demonstrations, strikes, and widespread violence. It moved many middle-class and elite groups to join the movement to end the dictatorship. **The Catholic Church also withdrew its support of the government.** The FSLN, meanwhile, had moderated its platform and was seeking to ally itself with all opponents of the Somoza regime.

Feb. Indians in Monimbo, Masaya, rose up in support of the FSLN but were bombed into submission.

Aug. 22. An FSLN unit stormed the National Palace during a session of Congress, taking over 2,000 prisoners and demanding the release of political prisoners and publication of their agenda. Numerous Latin American countries, including Costa Rica, Panama, Venezuela, and

Cuba, had extended offers of both material aid and safe haven to the FSLN.

Sept. 8. **The FSLN launched insurrections in five cities, but was defeated** by National Guard assaults preceded by extremely heavy bombing of urban areas. In the "cleanup" operation, government forces killed over 5,000 persons. In the aftermath the FSLN grew radically, as grassroots groups emerged to oppose Somoza. In the U.S., the Carter administration announced an arms freeze against Nicaragua.

1979, June. As Somoza bombed several major cities, Sandinista forces called for a **general strike and final offensive to overthrow the dictator.** A broad insurrection, including all classes of Nicaraguans, rallied behind the Sandinista forces to overthrow Somoza.

June 8. The FSLN launched an attack on Managua, whereupon Somoza used National Guard planes to bomb the capital. The capital was completely encircled within a month. During this time U.S. secretary of state Cyrus Vance proposed that an OAS peacekeeping force be sent to Nicaragua, but he was rebuffed by all sides.

July 16. Under pressure from **Archbishop Miguel Obando y Bravo** and the U.S. government, **Somoza agreed to go into exile** in the U.S., clearing the way for **revolutionary victory.**

July 18. The new ruling junta, composed of three Sandinistas but including moderates **Alfonso Robelo and Violeta Chamorro,** entered Managua in triumph. **The toll of the war was an estimated 50,000 dead, over $1.3 billion in damages,** and a foreign debt totaling $1.6 billion. The five-member junta, along with a legislative and consultative assembly, was responsible to the nine-member FSLN directorate.

1979–84. Led by FSLN leader **DANIEL ORTEGA SAAVEDRA** (b. 1945), **the government engaged in a series of important economic and social reforms.** During the fall of 1979, Sandinista Defense Committees tackled the damage done by nearly a decade of war and the 1972 earthquake. In 1980–81, a literacy crusade swept through the countryside, doubling the literacy rate. **The Sandinistas nationalized the Somoza holdings,** creating state enterprises and a land base for **agrarian reform,** which eventually placed one-third of the arable land in the public sector. Many large landowners remained but faced new labor and commercial regulations. **The Luisa Amanda Espinosa Association of Nicaraguan Women (AMNLAE),** an FSLN affiliate, also pushed through numerous initiatives for women. The government introduced social welfare programs, bringing medical care to almost 80 percent of the population. The FSLN sought to consolidate its hold on the state, putting the military under Sandinista control and centralizing authority in the FSLN Directorate.

1980. Angry over Sandinista power in the government, moderates **Alfonso Robelo and Violeta Chamorro resigned** from the five-person Governing Junta of National Reconstruction.

July. U.S. president Jimmy Carter, who had cut off aid to Somoza, promised a $125 million aid package to the new Nicaraguan government.

1981, Jan. Evidence of Sandinista arms shipments to rebels in El Salvador moved outgoing **U.S. president Carter to suspend aid to Nicaragua.** Upon assuming office, Pres. Ronald Reagan canceled it altogether.

April–Nov. After months of meetings with right-wing Nicaraguans and ex–National Guardsmen, the Reagan administration decided to create a counterrevolutionary guerrilla group to be known as the **CONTRAS.** This marked the beginning of the Nicaraguan civil war.

1983, March. Ex-Somocistas and mercenaries invaded Nicaragua from Honduras, supported by Honduran troops. U.S. warships were stationed off the Nicaraguan coast.

1984, March 13. The first of several mines in Nicaraguan harbors, planted by U.S. agents, was detonated. The measure proved to be a major blunder by the Reagan administration, drawing international condemnation.

Nov. Under pressure from the international community, **the government held elections** for a president, vice president, and a 90-member National Assembly. Although the elections were boycotted by certain right-wing groups, seven parties won representation in the election. Eighty-four percent of eligible voters cast ballots, awarding the FSLN 67 percent of the vote and electing Sandinista **Daniel Ortega Saavedra as president.**

1985, Jan. 10. Ortega was sworn in as president.

April. In an effort to promote Nicaragua in the eastern bloc, Ortega visited the Soviet Union.

May. The U.S., Nicaragua's main trade partner, **announced a trade embargo of Nicaragua.**

1986, June. At Pres. Reagan's urging, **the U.S. Congress voted $100 million in aid for the Contra rebels.** Though military victory for the Contras was viewed as impossible, an ongoing guerrilla war seemed likely to harm the Sandinistas. The economy had been declining since 1983, with the GNP falling by over 30 percent in 1985 alone and inflation growing at an alarming rate. By the mid-1980s, the Contras were attacking Sandinista economic and social projects as fast as they could be built.

1987. The government promulgated **the first constitution since the Sandinistas took power.** The document promised a pluralistic democracy, a mixed economy, basic human and social rights, and autonomy for ethnic minorities. This last feature reflected the struggles of the **Miskito Indians** against the abusive treatment they had received from the FSLN in the early 1980s.

Aug. Pres. Ortega signed the **ARIAS PEACE PLAN,** pledging to end outside military interference, to release some 1,000 political prisoners, and to hold fair elections.

1988. After approximately 60,000 deaths during the war and serious shortages in basic foodstuffs, the country suffered from an annual inflation rate of 30,000 percent.

1989. Nicaragua's population reached 3,503,000.

1990, Feb. In national elections, **VIOLETA CHAMORRO, CANDIDATE OF THE NATIONAL OPPOSITION UNION (UNO), defeated FSLN candidate Ortega.** With the nation in severe economic crisis and fearful of renewed U.S. support for the Contras in the event of a Sandinista victory, Chamorro took 55 percent of the vote to Ortega's 41 percent. UNO also won a narrow majority in the National Assembly. Chamorro quickly announced a severe austerity program. The FSLN kept control of the military and the unions.

July. The first major confrontation between Sandinista unions and Chamorro occurred with a ten-day general strike, which brought the unions wage increases and political concessions.

Oct. 26. Chamorro announced plans for **economic reconstruction and social reconciliation.** Although embarking on a private sector–oriented plan, the government promised to respect all previous labor agreements and protect those who had benefited from urban and rural reform prior to Feb. 25, 1990.

1992, Dec.–1993, Jan. Disgruntled by the Chamorro government's conciliatory policies and claiming that they were in danger from Sandinista soldiers, numerous ex-Contras rearmed and began new military actions.

1994, Feb. 24. **The last remaining band of former contra rebels agreed to disarm.**

1996, Oct. 21. Rightist **José Arnoldo Alemán Lacayo** of the Liberal Alliance Party declared **winner of Nicaragua's presidential elections.** Although himself a conservative, he called for unity among all of the country's political factions.

1998, June 15. Former Nicaraguan president and Sec. Gen. Daniel Ortega of the leftist opposition party FSLN invoked immunity in the face of May 27 charges by his stepdaughter of sexual abuse.

Oct. 30. Hurricane Mitch ravaged Nicaragua, leaving economic and societal scars that would take years to heal. With over 9,000 dead and more than 2 million homeless, Nicaragua was left with $10 billion in hurricane damages.

1999, May 4. Nationwide student protests and transport worker strikes forced the Nicaraguan government to increase university funding, to stop bus line deregulation, and to cut fuel taxes.

Dec. 30. Nicaragua and Honduras agreed to a military pact that included Nicaragua in negotiations over a 12,000 sq. mi. piece of coastal territory that was already shared between Colombia and Honduras.

e. COSTA RICA

(From p. 746)

1944–48. A National Republican-Vanguardia Alliance under Pres. Teodoro Picado ruled Costa Rica. The "Calderonista" coalition government introduced social security, high income taxes, an eight-hour workday, and a social welfare system.

1948, Feb. 8. **Otilio Ulate Blanco** of the National Union Party was elected president. When the government declared the election invalid because of irregularities, **JOSÉ (PEPE) FERRER FIGUERES's** (1906–90) anti-Communist **Army of National Liberation** openly revolted, with U.S. military and economic assistance.

April 17. The U.S. put its military forces in the Panama Canal zone on alert, allegedly prepared to rid Costa Rica of Communist influence in the government. In the aftermath, **the overpowered populist government negotiated a surrender** with Figueres's forces.

May 8. Figueres headed a **military junta** that embarked on a program of political and economic reforms. Although he had promoted rightist ideology during his opposition, much of Figueres's programs were clearly populist. **He dismantled the army, introduced new taxes, nationalized the banking system, and called a constituent assembly.**

Dec. 10. Costa Rica was invaded from Nicaragua by Costa Rican exiles. Charges of Nicaraguan complicity were examined by a commission of the Organization of American States and dismissed.

1949. Women received the vote in Costa Rica.

Feb. 21. Costa Rica and Nicaragua signed a pact of friendship.

Nov. 8. Twenty-one months after his election, **Otilio Ulate was inaugurated as president.**

1953, July 26. Socialist **José (Pepe) Figueres won a sweeping victory** over his Conservative opponent **in presidential elections.** During the next five years, the Figueres government took control of banking, insurance, and public utilities. Figueres also introduced **widespread literacy and social welfare programs.** In order to pay for these programs, the government negotiated a new contract with the United Fruit Company that increased the Costa Rican share of profits. Despite these reforms, Figueres and his new party, the **Partido de Liberación Nacional (PLN)**, remained staunchly anti-Communist and closely tied to the U.S. from the 1950s to the 1970s. This election also signaled the beginning of a **long period of relative economic and political stability.**

Jan. 20. Costa Rica and Nicaragua accepted the OAS plan to set up a buffer zone.

1958. Opposition candidate **Mario Echandi Jiménez** won the presidential elections. In an effort to demonstrate the democratic base of the PLN, Figueres gave up power peacefully.

1961. Fearful of the leftist reforms in Cuba, the Costa Rican government supported the U.S.-organized Bay of Pigs invasion.

1962, Feb. 4. Francisco José Orlich Bolmarcich, PLN candidate, was elected president.

1965. At the height of anti-Communist fervor in Costa Rica, the government sent troops to the Dominican Republic to help with the U.S.-backed overthrow of Juan Bosch's elected government.

1966, Feb. José Joaquín Trejos was elected president. During his term, **foreign investors,** mostly from the U.S., **increased their holdings in Costa Rica by approximately 3,000 percent.** Investment moved from fruit and small-scale manufacturing to cattle and lumber, which expanded at an alarming rate, **clearing the countryside of many rural dwellers** and sending them into growing urban slums.

1970, Feb. 1. Figueres returned to the presidency. He continued to promote foreign investment in Costa Rica and supported U.S. initiatives against Cuba.

1974. Daniel Oduber was elected president. As the Sandinista revolution gained momentum in Nicaragua, Oduber's government gave support to the FSLN and provided sanctuary to Sandinistas.

1978–82. Rodrigo Carazao became president. During his term the **growth rate declined** from 10 percent to −2.4 percent as the price of Costa Rican exports declined. In an effort to revive the economy, **Carazao increased Costa Rica's foreign debt to over $4 billion.** Inflation soared, and wages fell sharply. During the same period, U.S. aid increased after Carazao agreed to join a U.S.-sponsored organization aimed at isolating the Nicaraguan revolution.

1980. Due to the decline in living standards among workers, **over 60 labor strikes** took place. In one incident the Civil Guard fired upon striking banana workers. Widening gaps between the rich and the poor, and cutbacks on government price supports fueled discontent.

1981, Sept. Deep in crisis, **the government suspended interest payments on the foreign debt.** In the International Monetary Fund (IMF) accord that followed, wages were frozen, the currency devalued, social welfare programs cut, and price supports for basic foods ended.

1982. Amid widespread discontent, **Luis Alberto Monge Alvarez was elected president.** The **economic crisis continued to deepen,** and Costa Rica became increasingly dependent on IMF-approved aid. Monge allowed U.S. Special Forces advisers into Costa Rica, who used it as a base to support Nicaraguan Contra forces.

1986. In an atmosphere of continued economic crisis, including a $4.5 billion debt, PLN candidate **OSCAR ARIAS SANCHEZ** narrowly won the election. One of his key pledges was to **protect Costa Rica's social welfare programs** while adhering to IMF demands. Regarding the Contra war, Arias ended the past policy of tacit Contra support.

1987, July. Arias was joined by four other **Central American presidents in signing his peace accord,** which called for cease-fires, peace talks, amnesties, an end to direct aid from foreign military forces, political pluralism, and guarantees for democratic rights and freedoms. Arias was awarded the **Nobel Peace Prize** for his efforts.

1989. Costa Rica's population reached 2,954,000.

1990, Feb. 4. Rafael Angel Calderón, of the opposition **Social Christian Unity Party (PUSC),** was elected president. Calderón promised income redistribution and housing for the poor.

June. Costa Rica began an **IMF-endorsed austerity program,** designed to reduce the public debt and ensure access to foreign loans. The program incited numerous strikes and protests.

1991, April 8. Citing Costa Rica's efforts at debt reduction, the IMF agreed to a new financial package, with disbursements of $119 million.

1994, Feb. 6. José Maria Figueres Olsen of the National Liberation Party **won the presidency** over a conservative candidate from the incumbent Social Christian Unity Party.

1998, Feb. 1. Miguel Angel Rodriguez was elected president and his PUSC captured a majority in the Legislative Assembly. He defeated José Miguel Corrales of the PLN.

March 19. The trade ministers of the Western Hemisphere met in San José, Costa Rica, to discuss the development of the Free Trade Area of the Americas (FTAA).

Oct. 8. Costa Rica was elected as one of five new nonpermanent members on the UN Security Council.

1999, May. Talks began between Costa Rica and Nicaragua concerning the border crisis over the San Juan River Valley.

2000, April. Pres. Rodriguez's plan to partially privatize the Costa Rican electricity and telecommunications industries failed in court because of strong union opposition.

f. HONDURAS

(From p. 746)

1948, Oct. 10. Pres. Tiburcio Carías, after 15 years of dictatorship, supported the election of Nationalist candidate **Juan Manuel Gálvez.**

1954, April 30. In response to United Fruit's refusal to pay dock workers for overtime, **50,000 laborers under the leadership of banana workers launched a 69-day strike that paralyzed the nation.** They gained the right to unionize and wage concessions. However, strike leaders were arrested, and the banana companies began to mechanize, thereby laying off workers.

In the aftermath of the strike, the Honduran government signed a treaty with the U.S. that allowed for **U.S. military exercises on Honduran soil.**

Dec. 5. Control of the country was taken over by **acting president Julio Lozano Días.**

1955. Honduran women were given the vote.

1956, Oct. 21. The first **bloodless coup** in the nation's history took place as a group of military officers forced the resignation of Lozano Días as chief of state. On Oct. 22, all political parties endorsed the military junta, led by **Col. Hector Caraccioli.**

1957, Sept. 22. In elections for a constituent assembly, the Liberal Party, led by **Ramón Villeda Morales,** won a majority. The assembly elected him president on Nov. 15.

1960, Nov. 18. The International Court of Justice awarded border areas, claimed by Nicaragua, to Honduras.

1963, Oct. 3. Armed forces, led by **Col. Osvaldo López Arellano,** overthrew Villeda Morales.

1965, June 5. Under the presidency of **Gen. Osvaldo López Arellano,** the country returned to a constitutional regime, and a **new constitution** was put forth.

1969, July. An undeclared **war between Honduras and El Salvador** was precipitated by demonstrations against Salvadoran migrant workers in Honduras following Honduras's defeat in a **soccer match** with El Salvador (p. 952). Of the 300,000 Salvadoran workers in Honduras, some 80,000 were expelled, prompting a **Salvadoran invasion** (July 14). The OAS negotiated an armistice (July 18) and induced Salvadoran forces to withdraw (July 30). Despite the opening of peace negotiations in Costa Rica (Jan. 26, 1970), sporadic hostilities continued. The war resulted in a **humiliating defeat for Honduras.**

1970. Peasants who had gained land from agrarian reforms created the **Federation of Agrarian Reform Cooperatives (FECORAH).** They represented only 10 percent of rural dwellers, most of whom continued to live in deep poverty.

1972, Nov. Gen. Oswaldo López Arellano seized power. He initiated a small agrarian reform.

1975. Despite the "bananagate" scandal, in which United Brands was caught giving a $1.2 million bribe to the Honduran finance minister, López's regime was replaced by the similarly corrupt and repressive right-wing government **of Col. Juan Alberto Melgar Castro.** The new government gave **tax and wage concessions to U.S. firms** and helped businesspeople suppress labor and peasant unrest.

1978, Aug. 7. Melgar Castro was overthrown by a bloodless military coup. The new ruling junta was headed by **Gen. Policarpo Paz García.**

1980, May 14. Honduran troops aided Salvadoran troops in the **massacre of 600 Salvadoran refugees** while they were attempting to cross the Sampul River into Honduras.

1981. Workers founded the **United Federation of Workers of Honduras (FUTH).** Strikes during 1981 **prevented the government from implementing an IMF-imposed austerity program.**

1982. U.S. ambassador **John Negroponte** arrived in Honduras, marking the **acceleration of Honduran involvement in the Contra war** in Nicaragua. Negroponte oversaw the explosion of U.S. military aid to Honduras, which grew from $2 million in 1980 to $144 million in 1982–83.

 Jan. 27. Roberto Suazo Córdova assumed the presidency, the first civilian to hold that post in nine years. The military, however, continued to play a dominant political role.

1984, March 31. Col. Gustavo Alvarez, notorious for his corruption and rabid anti-Communism, was **removed as commander in chief** of the military in a coup d'etat.

1986. José Simeón Azcona Hoyo was elected president. He faced a stagnant economy, restless peasant and labor groups, and serious threats from emergent guerrilla groups.

 Feb. Two U.S. officials and a Honduran military officer admitted **CIA collusion in the murder and disappearance of over 200 Hondurans** during the early 1980s. These admissions fed anti-U.S. sentiment, already growing because of Contra atrocities committed on Honduran soil.

1988, April. Alarmed at the U.S. military presence in Honduras, thousands took to the streets of Tegucigalpa in **anti-U.S. protests.**

1989. The population of Honduras reached 5,104,000.

 Nov. 26. Rafael Leonardo Callejas, a millionaire agricultural economist and candidate of the **National Party (PN),** was elected president.

1990, June. The Callejas government succeeded in implementing an **IMF-imposed free market program** but in the process generated social unrest.

 Aug. 4. In a climate of unrest due to austerity programs and economic conditions, **500 troops were used to end a 42-day banana workers' strike.**

1993, Nov. 28. Carlos Roberto Reina, of the Center-Right Liberal Party, was elected president.

1994, Jan. 22. Carlos Roberto Reina of the Center-Right Liberal Party **assumed the presidency** of Honduras, saying that he would target corruption and human rights violations.

1997, Nov. 30. Carlos Roberto Flores Facusse of the ruling Liberal Party **won the presidential elections.**

1998, Jan. 27. Carlos Roberto Flores Facusse of the Liberal Party took office as president. Flores immediately began measures to modernize the Honduran economy and government in an effort to raise the standard of living for the poor and increase international competitiveness.

 Sept. 22. Pres. Flores further stifled the influence of the Honduran military by quickly passing legislation through Congress that gave control of the military to the presidentially appointed minister of defense, making military autonomy a much smaller problem in the national political equation.

 Oct. 26. Hurricane Mitch demolished much of Honduras. The $5 billion in damage and 2 million homeless caused a precipitous economic decline as 70 percent of Honduran crops were lost for the year.

2000, June. Honduras, El Salvador, and Guatemala signed a free trade agreement with Mexico to stimulate their battered economies.

4. MEXICO, 1946–2000

(From p. 749)

1946, July 7. MIGUEL ALEMÁN (1900–83) **WAS ELECTED PRESIDENT.** Even more conservative than Avila Camacho, he embarked on an extensive program to develop industry and infrastructure. **Foreign capital was welcomed, though under government control.** Alemán's presidency initiated a period of **rapid economic growth.** He used all government resources, including the military, to promote the economy and to suppress dissent. Relations with the U.S. were cordial, and the first exchange of presidential visits took place in 1947.

1946–52. Using the power of the Mexican state, Alemán solidified the **monopolization of the political process by the PRI (Party of the Institutionalized Revolution).** Amid rampant corruption, Alemán continued the tradition of lip service to the Revolution of 1910 while **supporting capital projects and working against labor and peasant groups.** Workers' movements were co-opted or crushed. Leftist union leaders were replaced with corrupt party loyalists, known as *charros.* The *ejido* (agrarian cooperative) program and rural education were ignored in favor of middle-class and upper-class interests.

1947, Sept. 30. A final settlement was made by the Mexican government for the **1938 expropriation of U.S. oil properties.**

1952, July 6. The PRI candidate, **Adolfo Ruiz Cortines, was elected president.** Distancing himself from the Alemán regime's corruption, Ruiz Cortines **ordered all public officials to publicize their finances** and fired a number of notoriously corrupt officials. Otherwise, he continued Alemán's policy of encouraging foreign investment and capital-driven growth.

1953. Thirty-six years after the constitution declared universal male suffrage, **Mexican women received the vote.**

 Rubén Jaramillo, veteran Zapatista, member of the Communist Party, and ordained minister, **rose in armed revolt** against the government. His combination of Marxism and Christianity eventually became a powerful social force.

1958. The national population reached 32 million, having doubled in the previous 25 years. Mexico's cities were also growing at 5 to 10 percent per year, with the population of Mexico City reaching 4.5 million.

 July 6. Adolfo López Mateos, candidate for the PRI and minister of labor and social security, **was elected president.**

1958–59. After a **national railway strike** grew to include teachers, farmers, and factory workers, the government used the military to suppress the strike and jail labor leaders. Many remained in prison long after peace was restored, including railway union leader **Demetrio Vallejo, imprisoned until 1971.**

1959, Feb. 19–20. Pres. Mateos and U.S. president Dwight D. Eisenhower, conferring in Acapulco, Mexico, agreed on **construction of the Diablo Dam** and on U.S.-Mexico economic collaboration.

1964, July. Election of Gustavo Díaz Ordaz (PRI candidate) **as president.**

1968, Sept. Major **STUDENT DEMONSTRATIONS** took place on the eve of the international Olympic Games in Mexico City. Demanding a more democratic government and the release of political prisoners, **students occupied the National University and proclaimed a strike.**

The government, wanting to ensure peace for the Olympics, **called out the army to suppress the protests.**

Oct. 2. During a protest by unarmed demonstrators in the Plaza Tlatelolco, **the army opened fire, killing approximately 500** and injuring an additional 2,500. **Over 1,500** students, professors, and other intellectuals **were arrested,** and over 100 were held without trial.

1969, Sept.–Oct. A recurrence of student protests was punctuated by **bombings of public offices.** Many activists took to **guerrilla warfare** as the only possible means of struggle against a repressive regime. Rightists also turned to more violent means, attacking and harassing dissidents.

1970, July 6. Luis Echeverría Alvarez, candidate of the PRI and former secretary of the interior, was **elected president.** In response to the bloodshed of the late 1960s, Echeverría changed the tone of government rhetoric to indicate that Mexico was undergoing a **"democratic opening."** The labor movement was especially important to Echeverría since movements for union democracy were posing a strong challenge to government authority.

1971–74. In the aftermath of the 1968 riots, a series of **guerrilla movements emerged in rural Mexico.** In response, the Echeverría government dispatched troops to affected regions and suppressed most rural dissent. Echeverría also promised aid to Mexico's 6 million landless peasants, but in the end provided little help. More and more rural Mexicans moved to the slums of Mexico City and other urban centers, rapidly changing the face of Mexican society.

1974. The Mexican government announced the **discovery of large oil reserves in the states of Tabasco and Chiapas,** as well as offshore in the Gulf of Mexico.

1976, July 6. Amid widespread charges of fraud and corruption, PRI candidate **José López Portillo was elected president.** López Portillo was more conservative than Echeverría, but he did propose constitutional reforms that allowed opposition groups to have a greater voice in the Congress.

Sept. Deficit problems and economic stagnation led to a **60 percent devaluation of the Mexican peso** vis-à-vis the American dollar.

Nov. Thousands of **landless peasants seized privately owned lands in the Yaqui Valley** in Sonora. Pres. Echeverría, with only a few weeks remaining in his term, stepped in to declare the seizures legal and **granted the peasants 250,000 acres** for development.

Dec. 1. López Portillo took office amid optimism that recent oil discoveries in Mexico would lead to an era of prosperity.

1976–80. López Portillo gradually increased Mexican oil production to over 2 million barrels per day. Due to rising oil prices, the net result was a **twelvefold increase in earnings from $500 million in 1976 to $6 billion in 1980.** This led to **grandiose public spending programs,** but the capital-intensive oil sector created few jobs for the 800,000 people who entered the Mexican workforce each year.

1980, March. With unemployment and underemployment in Mexico growing rapidly, the government introduced the **Mexican Food System (SAM).** SAM called for **intensive growth in the agricultural sector** and was funded by a $325 million loan from the World Bank.

1981. Due to a world oil glut, **PEMEX was forced to lower the price for Mexican oil,** creating enormous fiscal problems for the government. Mexico's foreign public debt had risen to $57 billion.

1982, Feb. With foreign exchange reserves running out, López Portillo allowed the peso to drop by 60 percent vis-à-vis the U.S. dollar.

July 6. The economist **Miguel de la Madrid,** candidate of the PRI, **was elected president.** Because of massive opposition to de la Madrid in some areas, **several local opposition candidates were "permitted" to win elections.**

Sept. With the peso and oil prices falling, inflation rising, and Mexicans racing to take their money out of the country, López Portillo announced the **nationalization of 59 Mexican banks.** Foreign creditors then rushed to negotiate a debt agreement with the Mexican government to cover their loans, which totaled over $80 billion. The **"rescue" loan** package that Mexico received from the IMF included an austerity program to reduce public spending.

Dec. 1. Pres. de la Madrid took office, challenged to address the extensive corruption perpetrated by the outgoing administration.

1982–88. De la Madrid prosecuted a number of López Portillo's appointees, including PEMEX director **Jorge Díaz Serrano.** He was also forced to implement unpopular fiscal measures. Between 1982 and 1985, real

wages fell by 40 percent as the peso continued its fall and Mexico's foreign debt grew to over $100 billion. By the late 1980s it was estimated that the **dismal economic conditions in Mexico had driven between 4 million and 6 million workers** over the border into the U.S. to work illegally.

1985, Sept. 19. An earthquake measuring higher than 8 on the Richter scale hit Mexico City, leading to over 20,000 deaths and $4 billion in damage. In the midst of recession, the massive problems created by the earthquake made regular debt payments impossible.

1988, July 6. CARLOS SALINAS DE GORTARI (b. 1948), PRI candidate, **was elected president** with a reported 50.1 percent of the vote. **Many believed that the election was actually won by Cuauhtemoc Cárdenas,** an ex-PRI official who had formed the **National Democratic Front (FDN),** calling for renegotiation of the debt and more government help to the lower classes.

Dec. 1. Salinas took office as president. A Harvard-trained economist, Salinas embarked on a **neoliberal program of privatization** of Mexico's 600 state-owned industries and trade liberalization. One important result of these policies was the explosive growth of *maquiladoras*, plants established mostly by foreign-owned firms in the border towns of northern Mexico because of the lure of low wages and the reduction of tariff barriers. By Nov. 1989 there were over 1,700 *maquiladoras* in northern Mexico employing nearly 500,000 mostly female workers.

1989. Mexico's population reached 86,366,000.

July. Salinas accepted the victory of the **National Action Party (PAN)** in Baja California gubernatorial elections, but he used fraud and violence to impose PRI candidates in Michoacán and Guerrero, two states won by Cárdenas's newly formed **Democratic Revolutionary Party (PRD).** The move was meant to engender cooperation with PAN, which had an economic agenda similar to that of the PRI, and to isolate the PRD, which was largely supported by popular groups.

1990, June. Pres. Salinas created **the National Commission on Human Rights** to deal with the widespread problem of police brutality.

1992, April 22. One hundred ninety people were killed and another 1,400 injured when a **sewer blast destroyed 20 blocks in Guadalajara.** In the aftermath of the explosion, the city's mayor resigned from his post, and a number of PEMEX executives were charged with negligent homicide.

Nov. 28. The PRI selected **Donaldo Colosio Murrieta,** head of the government antipoverty program Solidaridad, as its presidential candidate to succeed Salinas de Gortari.

Dec. 17. After having come to an agreement with Canada and the U.S. in August, Mexico signed the **North American Free Trade Agreement (NAFTA).** The treaty, creating a massive free trade area, was a victory for the neoliberal administration of Pres. Salinas, but met with mixed reactions in all three countries. It took effect on Jan. 1, 1994.

1994, Jan. The **Zapatista Army for National Liberation (EZLN) seized four towns in the southern state of Chiapas** in opposition to the North Atlantic Free Trade Agreement, whose free-trade policies they claimed would increase poverty and insecurity of poorer Mexicans. **Pres. Carlos Salinas de Gortari pressed for formal peace talks** with the rebels, asking for a cease-fire and promising amnesty for all combatants. The rebels continued to take a defiant stance against the government and gained widespread popular sympathy.

March 2. The Zapatistas accepted a tentative reform pact with the government, but later (June 16) rejected the proposed peace agreement, citing the government's narrow approach to the peace talks and refusal to discuss wider democratic reforms. The insurgents, however, vowed to continue to observe the cease-fire.

March. A Tijuana mechanic **assassinated leading presidential candidate Luis Donaldo Colosio Murrieta** of the Institutional Revolutionary Party (PRI) after a campaign speech. Despite identifying several suspects and making several arrests, the government failed to prove there was a conspiracy to kill Colosio.

Aug. 21. Ernesto Zedillo Ponce de León of the PRI was elected president by a comfortable majority. Foreign observers noted the absence of visible fraud, in contrast to the 1988 presidential vote.

Sept. 28. José Francisco Ruíz Massieu, second-ranking official in the PRI, was killed by a single gunshot in Mexico City. A suspected assassin was arrested; allegations linked him either to drug traffickers or antireform factions in the PRI.

Nov. 23. Deputy Attorney General Mario Ruíz Massieu resigned, charging that PRI officials were blocking his investigation into the murder of his brother, José Francisco Ruíz Massieu.

Dec. 20. Mexico devalued the peso by 13 percent, and it then suffered another drop of 15 percent, **precipitating a massive financial crisis** that continued into the next year.

1995, Jan. 15. The U.S. sent a loan guarantee to assist with the financial crisis.

Jan. 31. U.S. president Clinton authorized an emergency loan of $20 billion to Mexico. The International Monetary Fund added $10 billion to the loan package. On Feb. 20 Mexico and the U.S. finished negotiating the loan; Mexico prepared for a recession.

Feb. 12. The conservative **National Action Party (PAN)** dealt a major blow to PRI's virtual monopoly on political power with a **near sweep of state elections on Jalisco.** This trend continued when the PAN gubernatorial candidate won in Guanajuato (May 28); elections in Baja (Aug. 6) yielded similar results.

Feb. 20. The government's National Commission on Human Rights confirmed that army personnel tortured guerrillas who had been taken captive during a police action against the Zapatistas (Feb. 9–14).

Feb. 28. Raúl Salinas de Gortari, brother of the former president, was arrested and charged with planning and arranging the Sept. 1994 assassination of José Francisco Ruíz Massieu. Later in the year (Dec. 2) federal prosecutors charged Salinas with falsifying bank documents and with illicit enrichment.

March 9. Pres. Zedillo announced a new plan to stabilize the economy. It consisted of a series of austerity measures that promised recession-level economic hardships for virtually all Mexicans.

July 25. Peace talks resumed between the Zapatistas and the Mexican government.

1996, Jan. 10. Four state government officials and 17 police officers in the western state of Guerrero were arrested in connection with a June 1995 massacre of 17 peasants who had been on their way to a leftist antigovernment rally.

Feb. 16. The government signed the first of six formal peace accords with Chiapas rebels to resolve the two-year-old uprising. The first accord mainly dealt with Indian political rights.

May 1. Some 200,000 union members staged a May Day march in Mexico City despite official cancellation of the march by the government-allied Confederation of Mexican Workers.

Aug. 28–29. Rebel gunmen from the Popular Revolutionary Party launched attacks in the states of Oaxaca, Guerrero, and Mexico, in at least seven different locations, killing more than thirteen people.

Dec. 2. Pres. Zedillo fired Attorney General Antonio Lozano Gracia for his failure to solve a number of assassination and corruption cases involving high-level politicians.

1997, Jan. 15. Mexico finished repaying its loan from the U.S.

Feb. 6. Jesús Gutiérrez Rebollo was forced to resign as head of the National Institute to Combat Drugs and detained by police amid allegations that he accepted bribes from one of Mexico's top drug lords. The institute itself was subsequently abolished (April 30).

July 6. The ruling Institutional Revolutionary Party (PRI) lost its majority in the Chamber of Deputies. **For the first time since the revolution of 1910, opposition parties would exercise significant influence in the federal government.** Also in the balloting, Cuauhtémoc Cardenas of the left-leaning Democratic Revolutionary Party (PRD) won the mayoralty of Mexico City by a landslide.

Dec. 22. Gunmen raided the Tzotzil Indian village of Acteal in Chiapas, killing 45 men, women, and children. The victims of the attack reportedly sympathized with, but were not members of, the Zapatista army (EZLN).

1998. Gubernatorial elections throughout the year indicated the waning influence of the dominant Partido Revolucionario Institucional (PRI) that had maintained power for 70 years. In 1998 Mexico became the second-largest trading partner of the United States, behind Canada and ahead of Japan.

1999, Jan. 21. Brother of former Mexican president Carlos Salinas de Gortari, Raúl Salinas de Gortari was convicted of plotting the political murder of José Francisco Ruíz Massieu in 1994. Raúl Salinas de Gortari received the maximum sentence for his crime: 50 years of imprisonment without parole.

March 4. Pres. Ernesto Zedillo vowed that he would not continue the practice of *dedazo* by which the president chooses his party's candidate for the upcoming election.

March 21. A referendum on the rights of Mexican Indians was held nationwide by the EZLN. The vote was intended to generate support for the EZLN cause; more than 800,000 ballots were cast.

Nov. 7. The PRI held its first presidential primary, won by former interior secretary **Francisco Labastida Ochoa.**

2000, July 2. The PRI was defeated for the first time since 1929 in the presidential election: VICENTE FOX QUESADA of the PAN prevailed over Labastida of the PRI. However, the PAN failed to win a majority in either the Chamber of Deputies or the Senate.

5. THE WEST INDIES, 1946–2000

a. CUBA

(From p. 749)

1948, June 1. In an economy prospering from high sugar prices, **Carlos Prío Socorras** was elected president. Prío was a member of Grau San Martín's Auténtico Party and an anti-Communist.

1952, March 10. With elections approaching and victory for the opposition likely, **Gen. Fulgencio Batista overthrew Prío Socorras** and assumed power. During the next seven years, Batista allowed U.S. influence to pervade the entire Cuban economy, including public utilities, petroleum, sugar, and tourism. Famous for its African-Cuban music and freewheeling nightlife, Havana became the tourism capital of the Americas.

1953, July 26. FIDEL CASTRO RUZ (b. 1926), a student activist, led an abortive **attack on the Moncada garrison in Santiago.** Castro's eloquent defense of his actions at his trial brought him national prestige. He was imprisoned but allowed to go into exile in Mexico in 1955.

1954, Oct. 30. On the eve of presidential elections, Gen. Batista's only rival for the presidency, Ramón Grau San Martin, withdrew, charging that the election was rigged.

1956, Nov. 24. Castro and 81 followers, including his brother **Raúl** and **ERNESTO "CHE" GUEVARA,** sailed for Cuba from Mexico to renew the struggle. After a difficult landing, Castro and a handful of survivors barely made it to the Sierra Maestra in Oriente.

1957, May 20. Castro appealed to the U.S. to stop sending arms to Batista. He led many raids in Oriente Province, gaining sympathy from peasants. Guerrilla actions and strikes had paralyzed the region's economy by the end of 1957. Repression only generated more support for his **26th of July Movement.**

1958, March 17. Castro issued a manifesto calling for "total war" against the Batista regime.

April. Castro's call for a general strike failed, largely because of the lukewarm support of the Communist Popular Socialist Party (PSP) for Castro. After the strike, Communist leader **Carlos Rafael Rodríguez** went to Oriente to try to repair relations with Castro.

1959, Jan. 1. After Castro's capture of Santa Clara, capital of Las Villas Province (Dec. 31, 1958), Pres. Batista resigned and fled, taking most of the treasury with him. Two days later, Castro's forces took Havana.

Jan. 5. Manuel Urrutia, named provisional president by Castro (Jan. 3), named **José Miro Cardona** premier, and the following day announced rule by decree for 18 months. The U.S. recognized the new regime on Jan. 7.

Feb. 16. Castro took office as premier because of the sudden resignation of Miro Cardona and his cabinet. Following his takeover, he proclaimed the **Fundamental Law of the Republic,** which concentrated power in the executive.

April. Castro introduced the first wave of major reforms, including wage hikes and rent cuts.

April 15. Castro arrived in Washington, D.C., for an unofficial visit.

On April 17 he declared that his regime was not Communist and characterized his revolution as "humanistic."

June 4. An agrarian reform law was promulgated, providing for appropriation (with remuneration) of large landholdings. U.S. sugar companies, expecting to lose 1,666,000 acres, responded by demanding full and prompt payment in cash.

July 17. Pres. Urrutia resigned in a dispute with Premier Castro over growing Communist influence in the government. **Osvaldo Dórticos Torrado took over the presidency.**

Oct. Maj. Huber Matos, revolutionary leader and virulent anti-Communist, **was arrested for treason.** His trial, which resulted in a 20-year prison sentence on little evidence, indicated the direction of the revolution. This occurred as **Castro was moving toward an alliance with the PSP,** as well as assuming **an increasingly nationalist stance vis-à-vis the U.S.** Right-wingers and moderates were pushed out of the government and the unions.

Nov. 3. The U.S. State Department declared it would not tolerate the establishment, by anti-Castro Cuban refugees, of an exiled, provisional government in the U.S.

1960, Feb. 13. Premier Castro signed an agreement in Havana for the **Soviet purchase of 5 million tons of sugar and for $100 million of Soviet credit to Cuba.**

March 17. The Eisenhower administration approved **plans for a future invasion of Cuba.**

June 23. After American-owned oil companies (on the advice of the U.S. State Department) refused to process Soviet crude oil, Castro seized the refineries.

July 6. In retaliation for the oil refinery incident, **Pres. Eisenhower cut Cuba's sugar quota by 95 percent.** Eisenhower declared economic war on Cuba, stating that the U.S. would never allow a regime "dominated by international Communism" in the Western Hemisphere. Following this, the **CUBAN GOVERNMENT BEGAN EXPROPRIATING ALL U.S.-OWNED PROPERTY** in Cuba, without compensation.

July 9. Soviet premier Nikita Khrushchev, in a Moscow address, threatened Soviet use of rockets if the U.S. intervened militarily in Cuba.

Sept. 28. After a right-wing bomb attack on a Castroite rally in Havana, Castro announced the creation of **Committees for the Defense of the Revolution,** local groups armed and prepared against attack and invasion. By the time of the Bay of Pigs invasion, there were 8,000 such committees. These groups, along with organizations such as the **Cuban Federation of Women,** founded in 1960 by **Vilma Espín** (wife of Raúl Castro), also became important foci for grassroots political organization.

Oct. 14. The Cuban government nationalized all banks and all large enterprises.

Oct. 19. The U.S. imposed an embargo on all exports to Cuba except for medical supplies and most foodstuffs.

1961. Declared as the **Year of Education,** 1961 saw almost 250,000 Cuban students and teachers working in rural areas to teach literacy.

Jan. 3. The U.S. severed diplomatic relations with Cuba after Castro demanded that the U.S. cut its embassy personnel.

March 22. In New York, **the Democratic Front and the Revolutionary Movement of the People,** two major Cuban opposition groups, announced agreement on setting up a **revolutionary council** with ex-premier **José Miro Cardona as president.** He urged all Cubans to revolt against Castro.

April. Rumors became rife of anti-Castro forces led by the Cuban revolutionary council. At the UN on April 15, **Cuban foreign minister Raúl Roa accused the U.S. and the Latin American nations of preparing an invasion.**

April 17–20. A CUBAN REBEL FORCE of about 1,600 men, funded and trained by the CIA, INVADED SOUTHERN CUBA and established a beachhead near the **Bay of Pigs,** but it was driven off with heavy losses. The force had been directed by CIA officials, but at the last moment the U.S. government withdrew air support, effectively guaranteeing a massive defeat. In the aftermath of the invasion, **popular support for Castro in Cuba reached new heights,** and Castro began to refer to the revolution as a socialist one. Members of the former PSP also assumed more prominent roles in his government.

Dec. 2. PREMIER CASTRO DECLARED HIMSELF A MARXIST-LENINIST and announced the formation of a vanguard party to bring communism to Cuba.

1962–70. Castro initiated a major restructuring of the economy. A brief experiment with diversification and industrialization failed because of poor planning. **By 1963 Castro decided to reemphasize the sugar economy,** realizing that the capital for industrialization could only be generated by sugar. Rural production actually fell by 7 percent between 1962 and 1969, but as early as Oct. 1963 the government began efforts to revitalize agriculture. **The Agrarian Law of 1963** expropriated thousands of medium-size farms, making centralized state farms dominant. During the subsequent period of **Communist construction,** Castro concentrated economic authority in the government. Working closely with Che Guevara, in 1965 Castro introduced **moral incentives** and promoted the idea of the **new Socialist man** in order to increase productivity. Cuba became dependent on Soviet subsidies as production targets were missed and absenteeism became endemic. In 1969, Castro launched a **revolutionary offensive** aimed at producing a **ten-million-ton sugar harvest.** This campaign severely disrupted the national economy, draining manpower and resources from other sectors before falling short with a harvest of 8.5 million tons. Following this failure, Castro's economic policies became more eclectic and his dependency on Soviet aid more pronounced. Despite these problems, the Cuban government was able to achieve **noteworthy improvements in education, social services, and health care.**

1962, Sept. 11. The USSR accused the U.S. of preparing aggression against Cuba and warned that this would mean war. Khrushchev declared that Soviet arms were being sent to Cuba "exclusively for defensive purposes."

Oct. 10. The U.S. government agreed to help pay the $60 million ransom set by Castro for the release of 1,113 Cuban prisoners.

Oct. 22–Nov. 20. THE CUBAN MISSILE CRISIS came to a head in a U.S.-USSR confrontation over the installation in Cuba of Soviet offensive missile and bomber bases (p. 920). Pres. Kennedy announced a U.S. air and naval "quarantine" to prevent arms shipments and proceeded to negotiate for the removal of Soviet offensive weapons from Cuba. **Kennedy and Premier Khrushchev reached agreement** on Oct. 28 that (1) the Soviets would halt construction of missile bases in Cuba and remove weapons under UN supervision, and (2) the U.S. would end the quarantine and give assurances that it would not invade Cuba. The U.S. blockade was ended on Nov. 20.

Dec. 23–24. The remaining 1,113 Cuban rebels were returned to the U.S. in return for food and medicines valued at $53 million.

1964, Jan. 22. Concluding a visit by Castro to Moscow, Cuba and the Soviet Union signed a **long-term trade agreement** calling for increased Soviet purchase of Cuban sugar.

Feb. 26. Minister of Industry Ernesto "Che" Guevara announced a **reduction in industrial investments** to allow for more production of consumer items.

July 21–26. Cuba was condemned by the Organization of American States for supplying pro-Communist Venezuelan guerrillas with arms. The OAS invoked sanctions and called on members to sever diplomatic and trade relations. Only Mexico and Jamaica refused.

1965, Oct. Castro announced that Cubans were free to leave. On Nov. 6 **an agreement was reached with the U.S. government to airlift 3,000–4,000 Cuban refugees monthly.** In the next five years several hundred thousand, many from the educated classes, left the island, joining those who had left during the first great wave of out-migration from 1959 to 1961.

Oct. 3. Che Guevara departed for an unspecified destination. During his time in the revolutionary government, Guevara had been second in command in Cuba, serving as president of the National Bank, minister of industry, and architect of the policy of exporting the Cuban revolution. Guevara went on to lead a failed guerrilla war in Bolivia and was killed on Oct. 8, 1967, by Bolivian troops.

1966, Feb. A new trade agreement was signed with the USSR. Cuba was increasingly dependent on Soviet Russia for both direct and indirect aid. Serious friction developed between the two countries, however, leading to savage attacks on the Cuban ideology in *Pravda* and a cooling of relations in 1967.

1968, Jan. Eleven old-guard Communist leaders were tried for treason and sentenced to long prison terms, apparently because of their objections to Cuban revolutionary activity abroad.

1970, July 26. Castro admitted the **failure of the sugar harvest** to achieve its goal. After the failure, moral incentives were abandoned in favor of material ones, including minor **wage differentials, production quotas, and material rewards** for high productivity.

1970–75. Despite economic problems and poor productivity, the Castro government made **advances in housing, employment, health care, and education.** In part as a result of Soviet aid, rural income jumped, and hunger was largely eradicated.

1971, March. Prominent Cuban poet **Herberto Padilla was arrested,** put on trial for treason, and forced to make a public confession. The move reflected growing government intolerance and provoked widespread international condemnation.

1974. Under pressure from the Cuban Federation of Women, the government introduced the national **Family Code.** The code gave equal rights to women, as well as legal rights to children, but was never aggressively enforced. The year 1974 also saw the inauguration of **Assemblies of Popular Power,** meant to counter the central state's style of governing from the top down. Real power remained in the higher echelons of the Cuban Communist Party (PCC) and Castro's inner circle, but these assemblies did express some popular concerns.

1975, July. The OAS lifted a trade embargo that it had imposed on Cuba in 1964.

Oct. Castro sent troops to Angola to help defend the Socialist government against invading South African soldiers. At the peak of its involvement, Cuba fielded 32,000 troops there. Along with troops, during the 1970s and 1980s **Cuba sent nearly 30,000 professionals to 22 Third World countries.**

Dec. The first Communist Party Congress was held. The PCC had a membership of over half a million. The Congress adopted a **new constitution.**

1976, Feb. The new constitution was approved in a national referendum.

1978. At the Soviet Union's urging, **11,000 Cuban troops were sent to Ethiopia** to help defend the country against a Somalian invasion.

1979, July. The FSLN came to power in Nicaragua after years of Cuban assistance. The Cuban government immediately pledged aid to the regime. By June 1982 there were over 2,000 Cuban military advisers in Nicaragua.

1980–85. The Cuban economy grew at an average rate of 7 percent per year, reflecting some economic liberalization and tourism. Castro introduced a free market for agricultural products and housing, allowing a parallel market to emerge.

1980, April–Sept. After the Peruvian embassy refused to turn over six refugees, Castro declared that all those who wished to could leave Cuba. Ten thousand Cubans swamped the embassy grounds, seeking asylum. Over the following months, some 125,000 fled Cuba in the **Mariel boatlift** to Florida. Some of those who left were criminals released from Cuban prisons.

1981, Jan. Cuba provided military assistance to the major guerrilla offensive in El Salvador.

1986, April 19. With oil, nickel, and sugar prices plummeting and the economy in deep trouble, Castro announced a partial return to the **moral incentives** of the late 1960s. The free market was closed, supposedly to combat corruption.

Dec. At the PCC Congress, Castro announced **major economic reforms** designed to correct the errors caused by economic liberalization.

1989, July 13. Maj. Gen. Arnaldo Ochoa Sánchez and three others were executed on charges of drug trafficking.

1989–92. With the collapse of the Soviet Union and dramatic disruptions in Cuba's trading relationships, **the Cuban economy contracted by 45 percent.** The resulting shortages and rationing brought the standard of living back down to pre-1959 levels and threatened to wipe out most revolutionary gains.

1990. After a period of tense Soviet-Cuban relations because of Castro's heavy criticism of perestroika, the two countries signed a **trade agreement** to increase trade by 7.5 percent. Tourism also became an important source of foreign exchange earnings, bringing 360,000 visitors who spent over $200 million in Cuba during 1990, and reviving prostitution, which had been nearly wiped out after 1959.

Sept. Rationing was extended to 63 food items and 180 consumer goods.

1991, Jan. Cuban-Soviet trade relations (excepting oil shipments) were

halted because the two nations lacked the hard currency needed to trade. Relations were resumed six months later (June 12) under a new barter agreement.

1992, Jan. After the execution of **Eduardo Díaz Betancourt** (amid widespread international condemnation) for acts of terrorism against Cuba, Castro initiated a crackdown on dissidents. This raised **human rights abuses** in Cuba to their worst level in over a decade.

Sept. 18. The U.S. tightened its trade embargo by forbidding foreign subsidiaries of U.S. companies from trading with Cuba.

1994, April 22–24. In a Havana conference the Cuban government held its first dialogue with exiles since 1978. The exiles requested relaxation of various restrictions.

July 26–Aug. 4. A new exodus of Cubans to the U.S. began as the Cuban government allowed people to leave at will; widely seen as a move by Pres. Fidel Castro to pressure a U.S. government fearful of a repeat of the 1980 Mariel boatlift.

Aug. 19. U.S. president Clinton announced that **Cuban refugees** intercepted at sea by the U.S. Coast Guard or navy **would be transferred to holding camps in the U.S.'s Guantánamo Bay naval base** and other locations. Immediately following the announcement more than 7,000 Cubans were intercepted at sea.

Oct. 26. Cuba made a move toward a more mixed economy by implementing **economic reforms** that opened some new markets. As part of this initiative, the government announced (Dec. 20) a "convertible peso" with a fixed value of one U.S. dollar, placed in circulation for international transactions.

1996, Feb. 24. Two civilian U.S. planes were shot down in Cuban airspace by Cuban jets; the U.S. called for international sanctions against Cuba and heightened its own embargo.

1997, Oct. 8–10. Some 1,500 delegates attended the fifth Communist Party Congress in Havana. No major changes in economic or political policy emerged. Pres. Castro reaffirmed supremacy of the Communist state, anointed his brother Raúl Castro as his successor, and called for Cubans to stand by revolutionary ideals in the face of adversity and outside pressure for change.

1998, Jan. 11. A new National Assembly was elected.

Jan. 21–25. Pope John Paul II visited Cuba to call for an end to U.S. trade sanctions and for Castro to release political prisoners and afford political and religious freedom to his citizens. In preparation for the Pope's visit, Christmas was declared a national holiday for the first time in Communist Cuba's history.

Feb. 24. In the opening session of the National Assembly, **Fidel Castro was elected to another five-year term as president of the Ruling Council of State.** Ricardo Alarcon was reelected as the president of the National Assembly.

1999, Jan. 5. The United States modified its embargo on Cuba to encourage communication with Cuba and ease poverty without supporting the Cuban government.

Jan. 15–18. Venezuelan president Chavez and Colombian president Pastrana visited and discussed with Fidel Castro peace and prosperity between Latin American nations.

2000, June 28. After seven months of deliberation, the U.S. government rejected the pleas of members of the U.S. Cuban community that six-year-old Elian Gonzalez be granted refugee status. The government's order that the boy be returned to his father in Cuba ended a legal battle that began with the child's rescue after his fleeing mother died in a shipwreck off the coast of Florida.

b. PUERTO RICO

(From p. 750)

1948, Nov. 2. Popular Party candidate **Luis Muñoz Marín** (1898–1980) became the first elected governor of Puerto Rico. He would win repeated elections until he left power in 1964. Muñoz Marín oversaw **OPERATION BOOTSTRAP,** begun in 1948, which was designed to industrialize and urbanize the island by utilizing low wages and tax concessions to promote investment. For the next 20 years, the economy boomed. Operation Bootstrap promoted out-migration to the mainland (particularly New York) to provide labor for U.S. industry. After 1945, over a million Puerto Ricans, including many women, immigrated to the U.S.

1950, July 3. An act of the U.S. Congress permitted Puerto Rico to draft its own constitution.

Nov. 1. The attempt on U.S. president Harry Truman's life by two Puerto Ricans led to the arrest of large numbers of Communists and nationalists on the island. Support for the nationalists dwindled.

1952, March 3. By popular vote, Puerto Rico ratified its **new constitution.** It made the island a **"free state in association with the United States."**

July 4. Gov. Muñoz Marín proclaimed the **Commonwealth of Puerto Rico** one day after Pres. Truman had signed a congressional resolution approving its constitution.

1960, Nov. 8. Gov. Muñoz Marín and his **Popular Democratic Party (PPD) won** all but one of 83 precincts.

1964, Feb. 24. U.S. president Lyndon Johnson signed a bill creating a 13-member committee to study the political future of Puerto Rico. The island continued to experience **both rapid population and economic growth.**

1967, July 16. In the largest political rally in Puerto Rican history, **thousands protested the upcoming statehood referendum.** It represented an upsurge of the reinvigorated nationalist Left. Composed mostly of students, the **Pro-Independence Movement (the precursor to the Puerto Rican Socialist Party)** had ties with leftist movements in the U.S., where approximately 40 percent of Puerto Ricans resided. The large U.S.-based population retained strong cultural ties to the island.

July 23. In a popular referendum on the future status of the island, over 60 percent voted for continuance as a commonwealth associated with the U.S. The vote for independence was negligible.

1968, Nov. 5. Luis A. Ferré, right-wing leader of the New Progressive Party (PNP) and advocate of statehood, **was elected as governor.**

1972, Nov. 7. PPD candidate Rafael Hernández Colón was elected as governor. During his term the economy stagnated as U.S. firms contemplated leaving the island because of unionization and increasing taxes; proindependence terrorism in Puerto Rico and on the mainland increased.

1976, Nov. 2. Carlos Romero Barceló, PNP candidate, won the election for governor. The outgoing administration was blamed for economic collapse, corruption, and repression.

1978, July. Two young **nationalist militants were executed by police at Cerro Maravilla,** with the apparent complicity of Gov. Romero. Widely believed to be an ambush, the incident mobilized opposition to the government.

1980, Nov. 5. Carlos Romero Barceló was reelected governor. In a worsening economic climate, U.S. federal assistance had grown to $2.3 billion by 1980. Unemployment was reaching 25 percent, and over half the island's residents qualified for federal aid.

1981, Jan. 12. Members of the **Boricua People's Army (EPB)** attacked a U.S. Air National Guard installation and bombed nine jet fighters.

1984, Nov. 6. With the Romero Barceló government under pressure for corruption and general economic crisis, **Rafael Hernández Colón was elected as governor.** Hernández Colón promised to abandon efforts to achieve more complete autonomy and to continue tax exemptions for foreign companies. He introduced the **twin plant initiative,** in which U.S. companies could use Puerto Rican labor for final assembly of products produced in Caribbean nations with cheaper labor, thereby evading trade barriers.

1985, July 4. Thousands of Puerto Ricans rallied in San Juan, calling for complete independence. Protesters decried Puerto Rico's "colonial" status, which made the island more dependent on the U.S. than any other region of Latin America. Unemployment was over 30 percent, and more than half the population received welfare benefits. Thus, many believed that full independence would be disastrous.

1988, Nov. 8. Rafael Hernández Colón was reelected as governor. Favoring greater autonomy for Puerto Rico, he **promised a referendum on the island's status.**

1990. The island's population reached 3.5 million.

1991, Dec. A referendum on the status question produced **no clear majority** in favor of closer integration with the U.S.

1992, Jan. Politically defeated in the referendum, **Gov. Hernández resigned.**

Nov. 3. Pedro Rosselló of the pro-statehood **New Progressive Party (PNP)** won the gubernatorial election. He promised health, educational, and police reforms, as well as a referendum on statehood for 1993.

1993, Nov. 14. In the referendum, **voters rejected statehood:** 48.4 percent favored current commonwealth status, 46.2 percent supported statehood, and only 4.4 percent voted for independence.

1996, Nov. 5. Gov. Pedro Rosselló won reelection on the New Progressive Party ticket with 57 percent of the vote.

1998, March 4. The U.S. House of Representatives passed legislation that would provide a referendum to determine Puerto Rico's permanent political status with regard to statehood. A vote in favor of statehood would have enabled the Congress to legislate for a 51st state in 1999, possibly admitting Puerto Rico to the union within the following ten years.

Dec. The Puerto Rican electorate voted against statehood by a margin of 50.2 percent to 46.5 percent.

1999, April. A Puerto Rican civilian security guard was accidentally killed on the small offshore island of Vieques, which the U.S. Navy was using for ammunition testing. This incident gave rise to protests, supported by the pro-independence PIP, that escalated into an occupation of the island by campers who aimed to inhibit use of the area by the U.S. military. In May 2000 the year-long protest was ended through forcible removal of the civilians from Vieques.

c. THE DOMINICAN REPUBLIC

(From p. 750)

1947, May 16. Rafael Leonidas Trujillo, who had controlled the country since 1930, was reelected as president. His reign of corruption and terror, which included seven different intelligence agencies and required all citizens to carry passes, continued unabated.

1947–50. The Dominican Republic **accused its neighbors, notably Cuba and Guatemala, of abetting subversive activities** directed against Trujillo. The OAS council considered the matter and condemned the Dominican Republic, as well as Cuba and Guatemala, for engaging in conspiracies and attempted invasions.

1952. A bilateral agreement with Haiti was signed, providing 20,000 Haitian laborers per year for work on state-owned Dominican sugar estates. Because of the U.S. market, **Dominican sugar was booming** at this time, but workers were forced to live in slavelike conditions.

1960, Feb. Weary of the brutal Trujillo regime and preparing for the Bay of Pigs invasion, **U.S. president Dwight D. Eisenhower approved Central Intelligence Agency (CIA) plans to start aiding opponents of the regime.**

Aug. 3. Trujillo supporter **V.P. Joaquín Balaguer** (b. 1907) was sworn in as president, succeeding Hector Trujillo Molina, who resigned on Aug. 2. **Popular unrest continued,** and the OAS maintained sanctions in August and September.

1961, May 30. Gen. Trujillo was assassinated in Ciudad Trujillo by a group led by **Gen. Juan Tomas Dias.** The group used CIA-supplied weapons.

Sept. 21. Yielding to popular pressure, Pres. Balaguer initiated steps toward more democratic government.

Nov. 18–19. Gen. Rafael L. Trujillo, Jr., and other members of the Trujillo family left the country amid labor strikes and reports of a threatened military coup. They took with them a substantial portion of the treasury.

Dec. 19–20. After prolonged strikes and demonstrations, Pres. Balaguer and the opposition National Civic Union reached a political agreement, pledging to hold **general elections no later than Dec. 20, 1962.** U.S. president John F. Kennedy praised the settlement on Dec. 20 and promised U.S. support.

1962, Jan. 1. A council of state was inaugurated, which pledged to restore civil liberties.

Jan. 4. The OAS removed sanctions imposed in Aug. 1960. The U.S. resumed diplomatic ties with the country on Jan. 6.

Jan. 18. A military countercoup deposed the military junta that had overthrown the ruling council of state on Jan. 16. The council was reinstated, and **V.P. Rafael Bonnelly was appointed president.**

Dec. 20. JUAN BOSCH GAVINO (b. 1909) was elected president.

1963, Feb. 27. Bosch took office as the country's first constitutionally elected president since 1924. He was a well-known anti-Trujillo journalist and reformer who had **pledged agrarian reform.** Bosch immediately went to work on a **new constitution,** providing for a democratic system. He was opposed by traditional elites who, fearing their country would become "another Cuba," quickly began to work for his removal.

Sept. 25. Military leaders overthrew the government of Pres. Bosch in a bloodless coup. The U.S. suspended diplomatic ties and economic aid. In the following months, conflict between pro-Bosch constitutionalists (mainly students and laborers) and the military escalated to the point of civil war.

1965, April 24–25. The ruling junta was overthrown by a coup in favor of ex-president Bosch. Opposition to Bosch was organized by conservative **Gen. Elias Wessin y Wessin.** Factional fighting led to defeat of the Bosch forces, and the former junta resumed control. The U.S. began to fear results similar to those in Cuba in 1959 and decided to **intervene with 22,000 marines** on behalf of the anti-Bosch forces (April 27–28). Although the U.S. government claimed this was intended to protect American lives, there was no evidence of a threat to U.S. citizens. A truce was arranged by the OAS (May 5), but fighting continued. More American forces were landed and were eventually merged with the **INTER-AMERICAN ARMED FORCE,** approved in a vote by the OAS (May 6). The force went into operation on May 23 with contingents from Brazil, Paraguay, Honduras, and Costa Rica.

May 7. The Wessin forces formed the National Government of Reconstruction, headed by **Gen. Antonio Imbert Barreras.** In the ensuing heavy fighting, his forces made considerable gains.

Aug. 30. The Imbert junta resigned, and both sides agreed to the **OAS RECONCILIATION ACT,** which provided for a provisional government and gradual withdrawal of foreign forces.

Sept. 3. Hector García-Godoy, former foreign minister, was accepted by both factions as **president of the provisional government.**

Sept. 25. Return of Juan Bosch from abroad. He called at once for withdrawal of OAS forces.

1966, Feb. 9–13. Riots and proclamation of a general strike were fomented by constitutionalists who demanded that rightist army officers accept diplomatic appointments and leave the country.

June 3. In the presidential elections, the U.S.-supported candidate **Joaquín Balaguer** of the **Reform Party (PR),** an ex-Trujillista, was victorious over Juan Bosch. During the elections Bosch was kept at home under virtual house arrest; many of his supporters were murdered, tortured, or deported.

June 24. The OAS decided to withdraw armed forces. The withdrawal was completed by October.

July 1. INAUGURATION OF PRES. BALAGUER, whose regime was supported by the U.S. During the next 12 years Balaguer opened the door for **massive foreign investment** in the Dominican Republic, removing limits on land ownership by foreigners and revising tax and legal codes to give incentives to foreign business. He used murder and repression to quiet dissent. His economic policies generated **considerable growth,** some of which was used for housing for the poor and for education. During these years **the population grew at an alarming rate,** swelling the urban slums and aggravating rural poverty.

1970, March 24–26. Kidnapping of U.S. air attaché Donald J. Crowley by guerrillas. He was released when the government agreed to free 20 political prisoners.

May 17. Election of Pres. Balaguer to a second four-year term.

Aug. 16. Inauguration of Pres. Balaguer, who now took **drastic action against leftist elements,** including Bosch's Dominican Revolutionary Party. Balaguer continued promoting foreign investment in the republic, advertising the country as a low-wage haven for American and other investors. Little was done to ensure decent wages, and many poorer Dominicans began migrating to the U.S.

1973. Col. Francisco Camano, leader of the 1965 pro-Bosch forces, headed a **guerrilla landing in the Dominican Republic.** He was hunted down and executed, and in the aftermath some 1,400 people were detained. This incident and the subsequent repression resulted in a **massive boycott of the 1974 elections.**

1974, May 16. Balaguer was reelected president over Juan Bosch amid a widespread electoral boycott.

1978, May 16. Antonio Guzmán, a wealthy rancher and candidate of the **Dominican Revolutionary Party (PRD),** won heavily contested presidential elections. Results were held back for seven weeks while Balaguer and the military considered intervening. Only when U.S. president Jimmy Carter threatened to cut off U.S. aid was Guzmán declared the winner.

1982, May 16. Salvador Jorge-Blanco, candidate of the PRD, won presidential elections over Balaguer and Bosch. Faced with **IMF-imposed austerity programs** in 1984, he was forced to walk a tightrope between demands for reform and IMF-required wage freezes and price hikes.

1983. Dissatisfied with the pace of agrarian reform, **peasants briefly occupied the Ministry of Agriculture.**

1984, Jan. Fearing unrest if he complied with aid-related demands from the IMF and the U.S., Pres. Jorge-Blanco appealed to U.S. president Ronald Reagan for help. He received none and was forced to meet the IMF requirements in April. **Popular protests** led to clashes with the police, who killed over 100 people.

1986, May 16. With unemployment over 30 percent, **Balaguer was reelected.** He faced an economy in severe crisis. Sugar, accounting for one-third of Dominican exports, had fallen from almost 80 cents per pound in the mid-1970s to less than 10 cents by the mid-1980s. This led to **huge deficits and an escalating debt.** By 1986, nearly **1 million Dominicans had migrated to the U.S.**

1989. The population of the Dominican Republic reached 7 million.

1990, May 16. Balaguer, now age 83 and blind, was reelected over Juan Bosch.

Nov. 20–21. Labor launched its third **general strike** since Balaguer's reelection, protesting government austerity measures and demanding his resignation.

1991. Some economic recovery occurred as the inflation rate dropped from 100 percent to less than 5 percent. Tourism in 1991 earned $880 million.

1992, June. The U.S. Drug Enforcement Agency released charges that **two senior government officials were involved in a trafficking ring.** The charges confirmed beliefs that the Dominican Republic had become a drug conduit.

1994, Aug. 2. Results of the presidential election showed an aging conservative leader, **Joaquín Balaguer,** narrowly defeating José Francisco Peña Gomez amid widespread charges of fraud. Peña Gomez had sought to become the first black Dominican president, and racism had been a major issue in the campaign.

Aug. 16. Balaguer inaugurated as president, but his term was reduced to two years by an accord with five opposition parties who alleged that the incumbent president had gained reelection through fraud.

1996, June 30. In a runoff election, **Leonel Fernandez Reyna** of the Dominican Revolutionary Party **became the new president.**

1998, May 16. Elections for the Senate and the Chamber of Deputies resulted in heavy majorities for the PRD. The death of party leader José Peña Gómez one week before the vote was seen to have benefited the PRD during the election.

2000, May 16. Dominican Revolutionary Party candidate **Hipolito Mejía was elected president.** The Center-Left politician was sworn in during August. He faced substantial public dissatisfaction with the government over recent privatization of the electric industry in the Dominican Republic.

d. HAITI

(From p. 751)

1946, Jan. 11. A military group under **Col. Paul Magliore** ousted Pres. Elie Lescot, took over the government, and installed **Dumarsais Estimé as president.** Estimé replaced mulatto civil servants with blacks and initiated reforms for urban and rural workers.

1948, Feb. 11. Pres. Estimé was overthrown by a military junta under Col. Paul Magliore.

1950. Electoral suffrage was extended to women.

1956, Dec. 12. His regime weakened by a general strike, Magliore gave up the presidency.

1957, Feb. 7. The legislature elected **Franck Sylvain** as provisional president.

April 2. Accused of trying to fix upcoming elections, provisional president Sylvain resigned, and a provisional executive council took over.

May 26. Following a flare-up of civil war between the executive council and the forces of army Chief of Staff León Cantave, **Daniel Fignolé** took over as provisional president.

June 14. The army, led by Brig. Gen. Antonio Kebreau, ousted provisional president Fignolé and proclaimed a **state of emergency.**

Sept. 22. The presidential election resulted in victory for **FRANÇOIS DUVALIER** (1907–71).

Oct. 22. Amid a crisis with the U.S. over the fatal beating of an American by police, **Duvalier became president,** and the military junta resigned. Duvalier, known as **"Papa Doc,"** would rule the country until his death in 1971. He mixed mystic populist symbols, such as vodun (voodoo), with brutal repression. Duvalier expelled all mulattos from the civil service and made the army and police responsible only to him. To secure control he created the **Tonton Macoutes,** the most feared repressive arm of his regime. His **"kleptocracy"** enriched a small number of favorites while it impoverished the rest of the nation. Human rights were ignored, but at the same time Duvalier tried to maintain relations with the U.S. in order to ensure continued aid.

1963, May 2. An OAS commission began investigating the Haitian-Dominican conflict, which concerned the violation of diplomatic immunity after armed soldiers surrounded the Dominican embassy in Port-au-Prince in April. Haiti refused to grant safe-conduct exits for some of the 22 foes of Duvalier who had taken refuge in the Dominican embassy.

May 15. Pres. Duvalier's legal term expired.

May 17. The U.S. suspended diplomatic ties with Haiti.

Aug. 5–7. An invasion by a small force of Haitian exiles, attempting to overthrow Pres. Duvalier, failed.

1964, April 1. François Duvalier became president for life.

June. A new constitution, although providing for universal suffrage and an elected one-chamber legislature, concentrated all executive power in a president elected for life. Duvalier, who posed as the champion of the poverty-stricken black masses, had broken the power of the army and was loyally protected by a personal guard.

1968, May. Another attempt to invade Haiti, staged by opposition elements in exile, was easily defeated, as had been previous efforts.

1971, April 21. After the death of "Papa Doc" Duvalier, Jean-Claude "Baby Doc" Duvalier was named president for life. Although less brutal than his father, "Baby Doc" continued the corrupt practices of his father's regime, diverting foreign aid and investment into his own pockets. The younger Duvalier maintained the Tonton Macoutes, the most despised symbol of the regime's repression.

1980–86. As the **economy shrank by 10 percent,** the situation in Haiti gradually worsened. Unemployment and hunger grew, and Haiti was widely cited as the poorest nation in the hemisphere.

1986, Jan. Worried about the inflow of Haitian refugees into the U.S. and unable to justify supporting such a repressive and corrupt dictatorship, **the Reagan administration suspended aid to Haiti.**

Feb. Fearing Communist threats in Haiti, the Reagan administration agreed to help **engineer a coup.** Amid demonstrations and the threat of civil war, U.S. military transport was arranged to take Jean-Claude Duvalier to exile in France. A civilian-military government headed by Duvalier's chief of staff, **Lt. Gen. Henri Namphy,** took over. Namphy failed to fulfill promises of an end to repression.

1987, Nov. 29. Presidential elections collapsed in heavy violence, as opposition voters and candidates were ruthlessly attacked by paramilitary forces. **Thirty-four were killed** in right-wing attacks on polling stations. Subsequent balloting led to the election of Leslie Manigat, but he was quickly deposed by Gen. Namphy.

1989, Sept. Gen. **Namphy was overthrown** by lower military officers in a bloodless coup. The new junta called for democracy, social reform, and an end to repression. **Gen. Prosper Anvil,** a long-time Duvalier supporter and friend of the U.S., was installed as president. He promised free elections for 1990.

1990. Haiti's population reached 6.5 million.

March. Faced with numerous strikes and social protests, Anvil was

forced to resign and was replaced by **Supreme Court Justice Ertha Pascal-Trouillot,** the first woman president in Haitian history. She promised elections for that year.

Dec. 16. JEAN-BERTRAND ARISTIDE (b. 1953), a left-wing populist priest, **was elected president** with 70 percent of the vote.

1991, Feb. 7. Aristide was inaugurated. He promised justice for Duvalier's victims, social and land reform, an end to corruption, and protection of Haiti's national industries.

Sept. 30. Aristide was ousted in a coup led by **Brig. Gen. Raoul Cedras.** Thousands fled the country in the aftermath.

Oct. 8. Supreme Court Justice **Joseph Nerette** was named president by Parliament.

1992, Jan. Haitian refugees at the U.S. naval base at Guantánamo Bay numbered 7,000 (out of a total 15,000). Pres. George Bush, claiming the refugees left Haiti for economic reasons, ordered their forced repatriation.

June 19. Pres. Nerette stepped down, leaving the presidency vacant pending Aristide's return and inaugurating **Marc L. Bazin** as premier.

June 25. After initiating an open sea interdiction policy (May 24) and effectively ending refugee movements, American forces completed the forcible return of over 27,000 refugees.

1993, June 23. The UN issued an oil embargo of Haiti, demanding Aristide's return.

June 27–July. Talks between Aristide and Cedras in New York established Oct. 30 as the date for Aristide's return to power.

Oct. 14. After the collapse of the agreement for Aristide's return and the murder of **Justice Minister Guy Malary** (Oct. 11), the UN reissued the oil embargo against Haiti.

1994, Jan. Exiled Haitian president Jean-Bertrand Aristide held a conference of 500 Haitians in Miami, Fla., **calling for a return of democratic government in Haiti** and **asking for foreign intervention to remove the military regime there.**

May 6. The UN imposed a **trade embargo** on Haiti in protest against the military regime. The U.S. backed this measure and announced its willingness to grant asylum to Haitian refugees.

July 31. The UN endorsed an **invasion of Haiti by U.S. troops** in order to **oust the military regime and restore Aristide to power.**

Sept. 18. The ruling junta in Haiti said it would step down. A date was set for the reinstatement of Aristide. On Sept. 19 U.S. forces began to arrive in Haiti to pave the way for Aristide's return. On Oct. 3 U.S. troops raided various sites in order to stop violence. The chief of police went into exile.

Oct. 15. Artistide returned to Haiti and resumed his position as president. Raoul Cedras, head of the military government, left for exile in Panama.

1995, Feb. 21. Pres. Aristide announced that he ordered the forced retirement of 43 senior army officers, including all of the army's generals and lieutenants. The purge removed all remaining senior military personnel who had served under the regime that ousted Aristide.

March 31. Responsibility for peacekeeping in Haiti was formally transferred from U.S.-led troops to forces of the UN mission.

Oct. 16. Haitian premier Smarck Michel resigned due to ongoing differences with Aristide over economic reforms.

1996, Feb. 7. René Preval became the new president of Haiti, marking the first peaceful shift in democratically elected leadership since Haiti won its independence in 1804.

1999, Jan. 1. Pres. René Preval, who had split from the Lavalas Political Organization in mid-1997, appointed a prime minister and other governmental officials in an attempt to end his deadlock with Parliament over political power. After Jan. 1, there was no Chamber of Deputies and only a partially filled Senate. The government was virtually paralyzed.

2000, May 21–June 9. The Lavalas Family Party swept the Parliamentary elections in Haiti. Many opposition party and international observers, however, deemed the elections fraudulent due to glaring irregularities.

Nov. 26. Former president Jean-Bertrand Aristide was reelected, running on the Lavalas Family Party ticket. There was no serious opposition because the major parties withdrew, saying the election was rigged to favor the ruling Lavalas. In congressional elections, the Lavalas Family Party won all nine contested seats. Again, controversy surrounded the legitimacy of the vote.

e. BRITISH CARIBBEAN TERRITORIES AND GUYANA (BRITISH GUIANA)

1953, Oct. 6. Britain dispatched troops and warships to Guiana to handle a suspected attempt to set up a Communist regime there.

1956, Feb. 23. Delegates from **Jamaica, Trinidad, Tobago, Barbados, the Windward Islands, and the Leeward Islands came to a preliminary agreement for a Caribbean federation.**

1957, Aug. 12. Cheddi Jagan's (b. 1918) left-wing party won 9 of the 14 elective seats in the Guiana legislative council. On Aug. 16, Gov. Patrick Renison invited Jagan to participate in, but not to form, a new cabinet.

1958, Jan. 3. The Federation of the West Indies came into being. The 77,000-square-mile federation, with a population of 3 million, was composed of ten units: Trinidad, Tobago, Jamaica, Barbados, St. Lucia, St. Vincent, Grenada, Montserrat, St. Kitts-Nevis-Anguilla, Dominica, and Antigua.

1960, March 31. The British colonial office announced that if a new constitution was accepted for British Guiana, it would go into effect in Aug. 1961. Two years after the general election, full independence would be considered.

Aug. 21. The People's Progressive Party in Guiana, headed by Cheddi Jagan, won 20 of the 35 seats in the legislative council.

Sept. 19. Jamaica voted to withdraw from the West Indies Federation.

1962, Jan. 15. The People's National Movement announced that the colony of Trinidad and Tobago would seek independence outside the West Indies Federation.

Feb. 6. The British government announced its decision to dissolve the West Indies Federation in view of the recent withdrawals.

April 10. Legislative elections in Jamaica gave **Sir Alexander Bustamente's** Labor Party a majority. He took office as premier on April 24.

May 24. Eight small colonies in the West Indies announced plans for a new federation without Jamaica or Trinidad and Tobago.

Aug. 6. Jamaica became an independent dominion within the British Commonwealth.

Aug. 31. The independence of Trinidad and Tobago within the Commonwealth was celebrated under its first prime minister, the noted historian **ERIC WILLIAMS** (1911–81). Originally a sugar exporter, over the next 20 years Trinidad and Tobago developed into an important oil-refining nation and the economic center of the British Caribbean.

1963, July 22. The colonial office announced British Honduras would attain internal self-government on Jan. 1, 1964.

1964, May 24. More British troops arrived in Guiana to preserve order amid continuing race riots between East Indians and blacks.

June 14. Gov. Sir Richard Luyt of British Guiana assumed full emergency powers for an indefinite period in order to end violence stemming from Indian-black racial conflicts.

Dec. 7. Elections by proportional representation gave Dr. Jagan's People's Progressive Party 24 seats in the legislature and Forbes Burnham's People's National Congress 22 seats. Burnham and a minor party formed a ruling coalition, despite Jagan's protests.

1965, Dec. The British government proposed that Antigua, Dominica, St. Lucia, St. Vincent, Grenada, and St. Kitts-Nevis-Anguilla each become a state associated with the U.K., with complete autonomy and the power to declare for independence. The British government was to provide defense and control foreign relations. This culminated in the establishment of the Associated States of the United Kingdom.

1966, May 26. BRITISH GUIANA BECAME AN INDEPENDENT STATE within the British Commonwealth, assuming the name **Guyana.** Forbes Burnham became the first prime minister.

1967, April 11. Death of Prime Minister Sir Donald Sangster, of Jamaica. He was succeeded by **Hugh Shearer.**

May 30. The island of Anguilla declared its independence, leaving the Associated Territories of St. Kitts-Nevis-Anguilla. Though this act

was supported by a popular vote (July 11), it was disapproved by the British government.

Oct. The heads of Commonwealth Caribbean governments at Barbados met with representatives of the U.K., the U.S., and Canada. They agreed to establish the Regional Development Bank and the Caribbean Population Research Center, and to adopt measures securing freedom of trade.

1968, Jan. The new Guyana government was confronted by Surinam's claims to the Corentyne area, rich in bauxite, and by Venezuelan claims (July) to frontier areas rich in oil.

June 27. Jamaica joined the Caribbean Free Trade Area, which provided for early abolition of interstate tariffs among members of the British Commonwealth.

1969, March. In Anguilla, which was temporarily administered by a British official, the British under secretary for foreign and Commonwealth affairs was driven out while trying to solve the question of the island's status. British paratroopers and police forces then took over. **Ronald Webster** was deposed as acting president.

1970, Feb. 23. Guyana was proclaimed a cooperative republic within the British Commonwealth by Prime Minister Burnham.

April 21–24. An attempted rebellion in Trinidad and Tobago was defeated. All political activities were then banned.

Nov. 24. When the ban on political activity was lifted in Trinidad and Tobago, black militancy was renewed.

1972, Feb. 29. Michael Manley (b. 1924) of the People's National Party (PNP) was elected prime minister of Jamaica. Facing opposition from businesspeople and the banking community, Manley attempted over the next eight years to introduce a democratic social welfare state.

1974, Feb. 7. Grenada, under the leadership of Eric Gairy, gained independence from Britain amid unrest and strikes.

1978, Nov. 2. Dominica, with a population of 75,000, gained independence. It elected the first woman prime minister in the British Caribbean, **Eugenia Charles.**

1979, Feb. 21. St. Lucia gained independence from Britain.

March. Maurice Bishop (1944–1983) of the New Jewel Movement took power in Grenada, overthrowing the dictatorship of the U.S.-backed eccentric, Sir Eric Gairy. Bishop immediately began social reforms, building housing and expanding literacy, and he established closer ties with Cuba.

Oct. 30. St. Vincent and the Grenadines gained independence.

1980. Edward Seaga (b. 1930) of the Jamaica Labor Party (JLP) defeated Manley in violence-plagued general elections. After his election, the IMF and the U.S. government agreed to increase aid and to refinance the Jamaican debt.

1981, Sept. 21. Belize (formerly British Honduras) gained independence.

Nov. 1. Antigua and Barbuda gained independence from Britain. The nation, with a population of approximately 77,000, was heavily dependent on tourism for economic survival.

1983, Sept. 19. St. Kitts-Nevis gained independence. Facing low sugar prices, the nation was soon besieged by crises.

Oct. 12. Prime Minister Maurice Bishop of Grenada was overthrown and assassinated (Oct. 19) in a coup led by **Bernard Coard,** of his own party.

Oct. 25. Claiming that U.S. medical students there were in danger, **American forces invaded Grenada,** overthrowing the government. The Reagan administration was alarmed at the close relations between Cuba and Grenada.

1993. Anguilla, Bermuda, the Cayman Islands, Montserrat, Turks and Caicos, and the British Virgin Islands remained as British possessions. Like their independent neighbors, these colonies were heavily dependent on tourism for survival, but because of direct aid from Britain they tended to be somewhat more prosperous.

1994, Sep. 6. The Barbados Labour Party won control of Parliament under leader Owen Arthur.

1995, June 14. Edison James of the United Workers' Party was sworn in as new **prime minister of Dominica.**

June 22. Keith Mitchell of the New National Party was sworn in as new **prime minister of Grenada.**

Aug. 16. Bermuda voters in referendum rejected independence from Great Britain. Prime Minister John Swan announced his plans to step down because of the result.

Nov. 9. Basdeo Panday became the new **prime minister of Trinidad and Tobago** after his party, the United National Congress, formed several strong coalitions. Panday was the nation's first prime minister of South Asian descent.

1997, March 6. Prime Minister **Cheddi Jagan of Guyana,** founder and leader of the People's Progressive Party and **a major figure in Guyanese politics** since the 1950s, **died.** In subsequent elections (Dec. 15) his widow, **Janet Jagan, was elected** to succeed him.

March 19. Prime minister of Bermuda, David Saul, unexpectedly **resigned.** The ruling United Bermuda Party elected **Pamela Gordon** as his replacement, making her the **first woman to serve as Bermuda's political leader.**

Dec. 18. The ruling People's National Party of Jamaica won 49 of 60 seats in parliamentary elections; victory gave the PNP control of the government for an unprecedented third term.

1999, Jan. Barbados prime minister Owen Arthur, whose administration helped the unemployment level in Barbados drop from 22 percent to 11 percent, **was reelected** by an overwhelming majority to the head of state position. The Labor Party of Barbados took 26 of 28 seats in Parliament.

March. The Antigua and Barbuda Labor Party won its sixth consecutive victory in parliamentary elections. However, in April Antigua and Barbuda's offshore banking industry was disrupted by warnings from the United States Treasury that lax procedures on the islands were making Antigua and Barbuda's banking industry very susceptible to money laundering.

Aug. 11. Guyana president Janet Jagan of the People's Progressive Party (PPP) faced civil unrest in the opposition People's National Congress (PNC) and resigned her position for health reasons. The two parties were divided mostly along racial lines, the PNC being composed primarily of blacks and the PPP of East Indians. Jagan's replacement was 35-year-old **Bharrat Jagdeo,** who became the **youngest head of state in the Western Hemisphere.**

E. THE MIDDLE EAST AND NORTH AFRICA, 1945–2000

1. OVERVIEW

(From p. 752)

The postwar period saw the **end of foreign rule and the achievement of independence** by all countries in the region. The old colonial masters, Britain and France, lost their position of dominance, to be replaced by **the U.S. and the USSR,** whose competition for allies and resources embroiled the area in the **cold war.** From the 1970s, and especially after the dissolution of the Soviet Union, the **U.S. emerged as the supreme foreign power.**

Much **domestic turbulence** accompanied independence. Military coups in the Arab world during the 1950s and 1960s **brought down the old ruling elites** based on great landowners and installed **new regimes** in which military officers and senior bureaucrats predominated. The new political order embraced **radical ideologies,** notably **pan-Arabism and socialism,** and implemented populist programs such as **land reform.** By the 1970s these ideologies had lost their appeal, giving way to a certain **economic liberalization** as well as pragmatism in foreign policy. There was, however, **no democratization of the region's regimes,** most of which developed into **highly authoritarian structures** intolerant of opposition.

A number of **major wars,** both within and between states, shook the region, causing immense loss of life and treasure. The **Arab-Israeli conflict** emerged as a seemingly permanent condition after 1948, when the Arab states and the Palestinians vowed to destroy the newly created state of Israel and put an **Arab Palestinian state** in its place. After four bloody wars failed to dislodge the Israelis (who actually gained territory), fatigue and realism prompted **three historic breakthroughs: the Egyptian-Israeli peace treaty (1979), the Israeli-Palestinian Declaration of Principles (1993), and the Jordanian-Israeli peace treaty (1994).**

Several other major conflicts convulsed the region during this period: **the Algerian War for independence** (1954–62), **the civil war in North Yemen** (1962–70), **the Turkish invasion of Cyprus** (1974), **the civil war in Lebanon** (beginning in 1975), Morocco's long **war in the Western Sahara** (beginning in 1976), **the Soviet invasion of Afghanistan** (1979), the long **Iran-Iraq War** (1980–88), and the **Iraqi invasion of Kuwait** (1990). Other conflicts involved **separatists,** the most notable of whom were **Kurdish nationalists,** who staged revolts throughout the postwar period against regimes in Iraq, Iran, and Turkey.

Alongside this turmoil, the Middle East experienced **rapid demographic and economic growth.** The region's population grew at an astonishing rate, accelerating from about 2 percent per year (1945–60) to almost 3 percent per year (1960–93). The total population rose from about 101 million in 1945 (61 million in the Middle East and 20 million in North Africa) to about 314 million (255 million and 59 million, respectively). The proportion of urban people climbed from one-quarter to about one-half, the product of **massive rural-urban migration,** primarily to the capital cities. This **population explosion** undermined development plans and prompted the first family-planning programs.

From the 1950s onward, the region was swept up in an **economic boom.** The standard of living improved everywhere. The economy was becoming **more diversified and less dependent on agriculture.** Though agricultural production expanded, it represented a diminishing share of total output. **Industry made considerable advances despite only a modest level of development** by world standards. Most states took an active (sometimes exclusive) role in directing their national economies. Their **bureaucracies and public sectors swelled** to unprecedented dimensions, especially as a high proportion of their budgets went into the military and internal security forces, which expanded tremendously.

The region's **oil industry** gained world importance, and especially when oil prices soared in the 1970s, **an immense amount of wealth flowed into the oil states** from the West. The **oil boom** set in motion several regional trends: large-scale **investment** in development schemes; a **massive migration** of workers to the oil states; a growing gap between rich and poor countries; increasing dependence of the oil states on the West for goods, expertise, and investment opportunities; and economic liberalization in the poorer states as a way of sharing in the boom.

The position of women changed with the great socioeconomic transformations of the period. Women entered the educational system and the workforce in unprecedented numbers. Several countries passed laws to reduce social inequalities and to provide women with a greater measure of security within the family. The feminist cause gained some ground, although conservative elements insisted on keeping women in more traditional social roles.

The cultural scene was also transformed, especially by **the expansion of education and the spread of the mass media.** The number of schools and students increased dramatically at all levels, and **illiteracy rates declined** (from about 75 percent to 40 percent). **Radio and then television** became commonplace and, together with the cinema, formed the prime sources of popular entertainment as well as exposure to the wider world. The output of novels and poetry increased, and two regional writers, S. Y. Agnon of Israel and Najib Mahfuz of Egypt, won Nobel Prizes for their literary accomplishments.

A remarkable phenomenon amid these changes was the **emergence** of militant Islamic opposition movements throughout the region. The programs of the various "fundamentalist" groups differed in methods and demands, but all shared a rejection of secular government and the desire to impose an Islamic identity on state and society. Although only in Iran was a government overthrown by Muslim opposition, movements everywhere won wide appeal among the disaffected. Their clashes with the authorities, often violent, intensified a long-standing, bitter debate over the nature and future of Muslim societies. The rise of fundamentalism also triggered bitter cultural disputes among intellectuals in countries such as Egypt between the fundamentalists and the defenders of more pluralist traditions and secular outlooks.

2. MILITARY, DIPLOMATIC, AND SOCIAL DEVELOPMENTS

1945–90. Steep rise in average life expectancy throughout the region, from about 35 years to nearly 60 years. Most of these gains came from a **reduction in mortality rates,** which declined as people improved their diets, acquired better medical care, raised their standard of living, and became more educated.

1945–70. Emigration of approximately **1 million North Africans** (almost entirely from Morocco, Algeria, and Tunisia) to France. Most worked in semiskilled or unskilled occupations such as construction, mining, and the service sector.

1945, March 22. Proclamation of the covenant of the **ARAB LEAGUE** (Egypt, Iraq, Jordan, Lebanon, Saudi Arabia, Syria, and Yemen). The league soon founded committees to oppose Israel and to support North African independence movements. It added North African states, including Sudan, in the 1950s and 1960s.

1947–49. The uprooting of 700,000 Palestinians (of a prewar population of 1.3 million) from the territory that became the state of Israel. All Arabs who fled during the war of 1948 were later **barred by Israeli authorities from returning to their homes.** The refugees eventually settled in Jordan (400,000, mainly in the West Bank), the Gaza Strip (150,000), and Syria and Lebanon (150,000). The other 600,000 Palestinians who did not relocate were distributed among Israel (150,000), the Gaza Strip (50,000), and the West Bank (400,000).

1947, March 12. Announcement of **the Truman Doctrine** by the U.S., which pledged to provide **economic and military assistance** to Greece and Turkey to help these countries resist Soviet pressures and encroachments. The **U.S. thereby replaced Britain,** which was facing financial difficulties, as the chief source of foreign aid to these countries.

1948, May 15. ARAB ATTACK ON ISRAEL, which had proclaimed its independence on the previous day. **Five Arab armies** engaged Israeli forces: Egyptian troops (about 10,000) from the south moved into the Negev desert, the Arab Legion of Transjordan (about 4,500) into the West Bank, Iraqis (about 3,000) alongside the Arab Legion, and token forces from Syria and Lebanon into the north. The **Israelis had an estimated strength of 62,500:** the Hagana at 55,000, the Palmach (regular troops) at 3,000, and the Irgun at around 4,000.

Of the Arab armies, only the **Arab Legion,** which **captured the West Bank and eastern Jerusalem,** achieved any significant successes. The Syrians turned away after inconsequential border skirmishes. The Egyptians performed badly and held on to only the Gaza Strip. **Israeli troops overall were more disciplined and better supplied** and, unlike the Arabs, had the additional advantage of fighting under a unified command. The combat was fierce, and casualty rates were high. Israeli forces suffered over 6,000 dead. The Arabs lost over 2,000 men from the regular armies, together with an unknown number of Palestinian irregulars.

By the end of the war, **Israel held 80 percent of the territory from the original Palestine mandate.** In contrast to international wishes expressed in the UN plan of 1947, no Arab Palestinian state had come into existence. All land not held by Israel was either in the possession of Jordan (the West Bank) or under Egyptian administration (the Gaza Strip). Hostilities came to an end through a **series of armistices,** which disengaged the combatants without terminating the technical state of war between them. Israel first concluded a **cease-fire with Egypt** (Feb. 24, 1949), then with **Lebanon** (March 23, 1949), **Jordan** (April 3, 1949), and **Syria** (July 20, 1949). Yet the peace was fragile. Incidents along the borders were frequent, mainly caused by the activities of **Palestinian guerrillas,** who received encouragement from the Arab countries that hosted them. Even the most explicit terms of the armistices were not always observed. The most flagrant case was the **Jordanian refusal to admit Israelis into east Jerusalem** for visits to the Jewish holy places.

Sept. Creation by the Arab League of the **Government of All Pales-**tine, based in Gaza. It was set up ostensibly to govern the Palestinian territory still under Arab control. In reality, its chief purpose was to thwart the Jordanian absorption of the West Bank, occupied by the Arab Legion.

Sept. 17. Assassination of UN mediator Count Folke Bernadotte by Zionist terrorists.

1948–53. MASS MIGRATION OF JEWS FROM ARAB COUNTRIES, mostly to Israel. The movement came in the wake of **widespread anti-Jewish attacks** during the late 1940s and quickly gained in size and momentum after the foundation of Israel in May 1948. Emigration most severely drained the **Jewish communities in Libya** (31,000 out of some 35,000 Jews between April 1949 and Dec. 1951), **Yemen** (44,000 of some 45,000 between June 1949 and Sept. 1950), **Syria** (about 10,000 of 15,000 between 1948 and 1953), and above all, **Iraq** (134,000 from about 140,000 during 1950–51). In most of **North Africa,** the Jewish exodus took place over a somewhat longer period and at a slower rate. The Jewish population of **Morocco** dwindled from a quarter of a million after World War II to about 25,000 in the early 1970s. Nearly all of **Algeria's** Jews (140,000 in 1950) departed before 1962. Fewer than 8,000 Jews (of a postwar population of about 50,000) remained in **Tunisia** after 1967. During 1949–67, **Egypt** lost all but some 3,000 of its original Jewish enclave of 80,000. **Lebanon** was the only Arab country in which the Jewish population increased after 1948 (eventually reaching about 11,000).

1950–73. The share of **Middle Eastern oil** in total world production rose from 17 percent to approximately 40 percent. From this peak, it dropped by 1980 to about 35 percent.

1950. The UN Relief and Works Agency (UNRWA) took over the task of administering the **Palestinian refugee camps** and providing their inhabitants and nearby villagers with basic care. By establishing an educational system for the refugees, UNRWA played a pivotal role, albeit an indirect one, in the creation of the **Palestinian national identity.** In 1950, UNRWA listed 950,000 Palestinian refugees on its records. The number had risen to 2.2 million by 1987 (mainly because of natural increase), about one-third of whom lived in UN camps.

1955. Egyptian blockade of the Straits of Tiran. The action effectively closed the Israeli port of Eilat in the Gulf of Aqaba.

Feb. 24. Signing of the **BAGHDAD PACT** by Iraq and Turkey. The treaty eventually came to include Britain (April), Pakistan (Sept.), and Iran (Oct.). **The purpose of the pact** was to provide **mutual defense and a unified shield against Soviet influence.** Britain agreed to supply equipment and advice, and to take military measures in the event of an attack. The treaty firmly aligned the signatories with the Western powers. Among Arab countries, the signing caused a **deep rift between Iraq and Egypt.** The latter viewed Iraq's foreign policy not merely as a capitulation to the West, but also as a challenge to Egyptian leadership of the Arab world.

1956, Oct. 29. Opening of the **SUEZ WAR.** The war was planned in advance by **Britain, France, and Israel,** each of which wanted to overthrow the regime of Gamal Abdel Nasser in Egypt. The British were incensed with the **nationalization of the Suez Canal.** The French resented **Nasser's support for the Algerian independence movement.** The Israelis were exasperated by the incessant **guerrilla raids from the Gaza Strip,** launched with Egyptian backing.

Israel started the war by attacking Egypt in the Sinai. According to the plan, **Britain and France then delivered an ultimatum** (Oct. 30) to both sides to stop fighting and stay clear of the canal zone. When **Egypt refused to comply,** the British and French dropped troops by air and sea (Nov. 5–6) into the canal zone. But Britain and France had not reckoned on the active **opposition of the U.S.,** which arranged a **UN cease-fire** (Nov. 7) and demanded a full Anglo-French withdrawal. The

British and French had no alternative but to back down and leave. Far from removing **Nasser,** the war had served only **to enhance his prestige** around the world. On the other hand, the **Israelis obtained two concessions** that proved to be highly consequential in 1967: **the demilitarization of the Sinai and the deployment of UN troops** along the Egyptian-Israeli border, and a U.S. commitment to keep the **Straits of Tiran** open to Israeli shipping.

1957, March 9. The U.S. government announced the **Eisenhower Doctrine** (p. 919). The U.S. pledged economic and military aid, upon request, to any Middle Eastern country threatened by communism.

1958, Feb. 1. Establishment of the **UNITED ARAB REPUBLIC, which united Egypt and Syria.** Impetus for the union came mainly from the **Syrians,** who **faced a political crisis** in which the notables and mainstream politicians were unable to form stable governments. Though hopelessly at odds with one another, they all shared a fear of a political takeover by left-wing parties and sought an outside solution. Believing the Syrians to be unready for the union, **Pres. Nasser** of Egypt was cautious, but finally **consented on three conditions:** the creation of a **powerful central government** based in Cairo, the **abolition of all political parties,** and the **exclusion of the Syrian army** from all political activity. While the two countries were joined, Syria became subject to many of the same socialist and populist policies (such as land reform and the shift to a centralized economy) that the Egyptians were beginning to implement in their own country.

The union was never stable. It was not long before the Syrians grew unhappy with Egyptian domination of the central government. Moreover, resentment over Egyptian control of the army was rife among Syrian officers. Indeed, **the union was finally dissolved** by rebellious Syrian army units (Sept. 28, 1961) who marched on Damascus. Unwilling to spill blood, Nasser let them **restore Syrian independence.** In the end, the experiment with Arab unity left bad memories in both Egypt and Syria.

1959, March 24. Iraqi repudiation of the **Baghdad Pact,** which effectively ended the organization. In its place Britain (with informal U.S. backing) organized **CENTO (Central Treaty Organization),** which included Turkey, Iran, and Pakistan.

1960, Sept. 10–14. Formation of OPEC (Organization of Petroleum Exporting Countries). The founding members were Venezuela, Iran, Iraq, and Saudi Arabia. They banded together **to fight Western oil companies,** which, in the midst of an oil glut on the world market, were trying to force down prices. The **early success of OPEC** was not in raising the price of oil per barrel (though prices did rise gradually throughout the 1960s), but in increasing each country's "take," or share of profit, per barrel. Spectacular price rises did not occur until the 1970s, particularly after 1973.

1961. Founding of the **Kuwaiti Fund for Arab Economic Development,** the first attempt to divert a portion of the oil proceeds to poorer Middle Eastern states. Abu Dhabi, Iraq, and Saudi Arabia all followed with similar projects in the 1970s. **The Arab Fund and the Islamic Development Bank** also were created for the same purpose. Total disbursements for the period 1973–77 reached $24.2 billion, two-thirds of which flowed to Arab states.

1964. Formation of **the Arab Common Market,** consisting of Egypt, Iraq, Jordan, and Syria. Libya and Sudan joined in 1977. The organization sought to promote inter-Arab trade and development.

Founding of the **PALESTINE LIBERATION ORGANIZATION (PLO)** in east Jerusalem. The PLO claimed to represent all Palestinians, denied the legitimacy of Israel, and worked for the creation of an Arab Palestinian state within the boundaries of the former British mandate. The first chairman of the organization was **Ahmad Shuqayri.**

1967, June 5. Outbreak of **THE SIX-DAY WAR** (the June War) between Israel and neighboring Arab states. The war followed weeks of rising tensions on both sides. **Border skirmishes** between Israel and Syria, mostly involving guerrilla raids, led to **air battles** between the two states (April 7). **Arab governments** were subsequently alarmed by a mistaken Soviet report (May 12–13) that Israel was preparing to attack. **Egypt and Syria** responded by mobilizing their armies (May 16–17). Pres. Nasser of Egypt requested (May 18) and obtained the **removal of UN peacekeeping forces** from the Sinai. **The Egyptian army** then reoccupied the Sinai and promptly **closed the Straits of Tiran** to Israeli shipping (May 22). In Israel, a national government was formed (June

1). Israeli leaders decided that, under the circumstances, war was imminent and that Israel ought to take the initiative.

In a **surprise attack** (June 5), the **Israeli air force struck** at 25 Arab airfields in Egypt, Jordan, Syria, and Iraq, and destroyed nearly all the Arab aircraft, most of them on the ground. Meanwhile Jordan failed to heed an Israeli warning to stay out of the war. **After Jordanian troops opened an assault on Jerusalem, the Israeli army counterattacked** and rapidly drove them from east Jerusalem and the West Bank (June 7). Farther south, the Israelis had little trouble pushing the Egyptian army out of the Gaza Strip and Sinai, and they quickly **reached the Suez Canal** (June 8). In one final action, Israeli forces bombed Damascus and occupied the Golan Heights (June 9). All sides accepted a **UN ceasefire** on June 10. The war ended in **total victory for Israel,** which emerged with an area over three times its pre-1967 size, as well as an added **Arab population** of about 1 million (about 450,000 Palestinians had fled). **The Arab states were severely demoralized** by the defeat, which cost over 18,000 Arab lives (compared to some 700 for Israel) and inflicted immense damage on the Arab armed forces. Afterward, the Arab regimes insisted on Israel's complete evacuation of all occupied territory as a precondition to any settlement. Flushed with confidence from their military successes, the Israelis felt little inclination to negotiate and were willing to withdraw only to secure mutually recognized borders that served their strategic needs.

June 6. Declaration by 10 Arab states of an **oil embargo against the U.S. and Britain,** which were accused of aiding Israeli attacks on Arab countries. It was the first attempt to use oil as an economic and diplomatic weapon. The boycott, however, lasted only until Aug. 1967 and had no perceptible effect on the Western economies.

Aug. 29. The Khartoum Conference was convened by the leaders of 13 Arab states following the Arab defeat in the June War. The Arab governments defiantly vowed not to make peace or to negotiate with Israel. At the same time, the Egyptians and the Saudis concluded a settlement to evacuate Egyptian troops from Yemen.

Nov. 22. Passage by the UN Security Council of **RESOLUTION 242,** which called for "the establishment of a just and lasting peace" and the "withdrawal of Israeli armed forces from territories occupied" during the June War. The resolution also **called for free navigation** in international waterways, for the **independence and territorial integrity of every state** in the region, and for a **solution to the refugee problem.** Israel, Egypt, Jordan, and Lebanon accepted the resolution. The PLO and radical Arab states, led by Syria, denounced it.

1968, Jan. 9. Formation of the **Organization of Arab Petroleum Exporting Countries (OAPEC),** a parallel organization to OPEC that consisted of only Arab countries. The members were Kuwait, Libya, Saudi Arabia, Algeria, Bahrain, Egypt, Iraq, Qatar, Syria, the United Arab Emirates, and Tunisia.

July. Amendment of the PLO Charter to emphasize the role of **armed struggle** as the PLO's chief strategy. At the same time, **al-Fatah** emerged as the supreme faction. Its leader, **Yasir Arafat,** was later elected as PLO chairman (Jan. 3, 1969). Over the next decade, the **Palestinians conducted a worldwide terrorist campaign** against Israeli targets and citizens. The PLO believed that violent methods were necessary to keep the world from forgetting the plight of the Palestinians and to maintain pressure on Israel.

1969, March. Opening of the **War of Attrition between Egypt and Israel.** The war consisted mainly of **bombardments along the Suez Canal.** The Egyptian government mistakenly hoped that the heavy expense of maintaining constant preparation for war would induce the Israelis to accept a peace settlement. The war was finally halted in Aug. 1970 because Egyptian losses from Israeli attacks exceeded the damage inflicted on the Israeli economy.

Dec. Announcement of the **"Rogers Plan,"** a U.S. initiative **to resolve the Arab-Israeli conflict,** by U.S. secretary of state William Rogers. It essentially called for **Israel to withdraw behind its 1949 borders,** with minor modifications to accommodate Israeli concerns about security. Israel and the radical Arab states, notably Syria, rejected the plan. Only Egypt and Jordan showed any interest. By the end of 1970, the proposal was dead.

1971. Founding of the **Islamic Conference Organization (ICO),** which brought together top officials from Muslim states to foster solidarity and cooperation. In the late 1960s, **Saudi Arabia** was the most active promoter of the organization. The ICO received even greater attention after a Christian fundamentalist set a destructive fire in al-Aqsa Mosque in Jerusalem (Aug. 1969). Despite the existence of the ICO, **pan-Islamism remained a negligible force** in Middle Eastern politics.

1973, Oct. 6–22. THE YOM KIPPUR WAR (also called the October War and the Ramadan War) was launched by Egypt and Syria against Israel. The war came about largely as a result of Egyptian frustrations with Israel, which showed little desire for a formal peace settlement. During the first three days of the war, **the Egyptian army** successfully attained its primary objective—namely, to **breach Israeli fortifications** (the Bar-Lev line) and establish a bridgehead on the east bank of the Suez Canal. Meanwhile, **Syrian troops advanced into the Golan Heights,** approaching Israel itself. Over the next week, however, the tide turned against the Arabs, thanks partly to the American resupply of the Israeli army. First, the Syrians were turned back (Oct. 11). **Israeli forces then crossed to the west bank of the Suez Canal** (Oct. 15), where they were poised (Oct. 18) to trap the entire Egyptian Third Army in the Sinai. Egypt and Israel obeyed a **UN cease-fire** (Oct. 22), and Syria stopped fighting two days later. An agreement arranged by the U.S. and the USSR allowed Egyptian forces in the Sinai to be resupplied (Oct. 27), saving them from surrender.

Both the Arabs and the Israelis suffered **heavy casualties** in the fighting. Egypt lost some 15,000 soldiers, Syria 3,500, and Israel 2,700. In the end, **neither side could claim a clear-cut victory**.

Oct. The ARAB OIL EMBARGO, which lasted until March 18, 1974. To support the Arab cause in the October War, the Arab oil states (OAPEC), led by Saudi Arabia, scaled back production and refused to export oil to the U.S. Unlike the earlier attempt to use oil as political leverage (1967), this one was relatively successful. By 1973, new international conditions had made the oil states more powerful than ever. The 1970s ushered in an **oil shortage** at the same time that **U.S. production was markedly falling**. Moreover, the rate of **world consumption** was for the first time outstripping additions to the world's oil reserves, of which the Middle East held more than half, thereby drawing attention both to the ultimate limits of oil as a resource and to the growing economic importance of Arab oil. **The boycott was highly disruptive** to the industrial economies. By the end of 1973, **oil prices had risen** from $3.00 to $11.65 per barrel, **peaking** in the mid-1970s at around **$40 per barrel**. The greatest political effect of the boycott was to make European countries more sympathetic to the Arab side of the Arab-Israeli dispute.

Nov. The Algiers Arab Summit Conference recognized the PLO as the sole legitimate representative of the Palestinian people.

Dec. 17. Palestinian terrorists killed 31 people at the Rome airport.

1974–75. U.S. secretary of state Henry Kissinger embarked on several rounds of "**shuttle diplomacy**" in an effort to disengage Arab and Israeli military forces. Israel and Egypt came to terms on Jan. 18, 1974. A second accord, signed on Sept. 4, 1975, reopened the Suez Canal to traffic. The Syrians and Israelis agreed to disengage forces in the Golan Heights on May 29, 1974.

1975, March 6. Signing of an **Iran-Iraq agreement** at an OPEC summit in Algiers. **Iran pledged to cut off aid to Kurdish rebels** in Iraq. In exchange, **Iraq relinquished its claim to full possession of the Shatt al-Arab,** the waterway extending from the confluence of the Tigris and Euphrates to the Persian Gulf. Henceforth, the boundary between Iraq and Iran would run through the middle of the deepest channel. The concession remained a source of deep resentment to Iraq, and the issue contributed to the outbreak of the Iran-Iraq War in 1980.

Nov. 10. The UN General Assembly passed a resolution declaring that "**Zionism is a form of racism.**" The resolution was repealed on Dec. 16, 1991.

1975–90. MASSIVE IMMIGRATION BY ARAB WORKERS (particularly Egyptians, Yemenis, and Palestinians) **TO THE PERSIAN GULF, where** oil-rich states required an **influx of labor** to compensate for their own internal shortages. Most immigrants worked as unskilled or semi-skilled laborers in fields such as construction. The **proportion of immigrants** in these societies reached extremely high levels: the United Arab Emirates, 85 percent; Qatar, 80 percent; Kuwait, 69 percent; Saudi Arabia, 43 percent; Libya, 42 percent; and Oman, 34 percent. The best available estimates have put the total number of Arab immigrants in the Gulf region at about 5 million. The guest workers have made **vital contributions to their home economies** outside the Gulf

through remittances from their wages (in the case of Egypt, for example, as much as 10 percent of the annual GNP originated from this source alone by the late 1980s).

1977, Oct. 1. In Geneva, an international peace conference opened concerning the Arab-Israeli conflict, sponsored jointly by the U.S. and the USSR. Discussions made little progress.

Nov. 19. Egyptian president **Anwar Sadat made a dramatic and unexpected visit to Jerusalem,** where he declared Egypt's willingness to negotiate a "permanent peace based on justice." In an address before the Israeli Knesset, he insisted that Palestinian participation was essential for any peace settlement.

1978, Sept. Signing of the **CAMP DAVID ACCORDS** between Israel and Egypt, mediated by U.S. president Jimmy Carter. The main points of the treaty concerned a gradual **Israeli withdrawal from the Sinai Peninsula** and the establishment of **normal Egyptian-Israeli relations.** Further provisions dealt with the status of the West Bank and the Gaza Strip but were never implemented because the PLO and Jordan, who were expected to take part, rejected them out of hand. The peace treaty between Egypt and Israel was formally signed on March 26, 1979.

Dec. 10. Prime Minister Menachem Begin of Israel and **Pres. Anwar Sadat** of Egypt were jointly awarded the **Nobel Peace Prize.**

1979, March 27. The Arab League expelled Egypt and transferred its headquarters from Cairo to Tunis.

1980–87. Sharp drop in oil prices from the range of $30 to $35 per barrel of crude oil to $16 to $18.

1980, Sept. 22. Start of the **IRAN-IRAQ WAR,** which lasted for nearly eight years. Iraq invaded Iran primarily to secure **territorial claims** related to the Shatt al-Arab, the waterway to the Persian Gulf. **Other Iraqi motives** were the desire for greater **prestige** and the **ambition** to become the leading state in the Arab world. Iraq also hoped to topple the revolutionary **regime in Iran,** fearing that Tehran would incite Shi'ites in southern Iraq to rebellion.

The scale of the war, the costliest and most murderous since World War II, was enormous: 1 million casualties (60 percent of them Iranian), $200 billion in direct costs, and another $1 trillion in indirect costs. Each side conscripted between 1.3 and 1.6 million men, a figure equivalent to more than half the males of military age in Iraq and about one-sixth of them in Iran.

Iraq held the advantage for the first two years and penetrated far into southwestern Iran, even capturing the city of Khuramshahr. But drawing on their superior numbers, **Iranians assumed the offensive after 1982** and over the next four years pushed the war back to Iraqi soil. Early in 1988 a series of **successful Iraqi counteroffensives,** in which chemical weapons were used extensively, compelled the Iranians to accept a **UN cease-fire** (July 20, 1988). The war ended in an exhausting, bloody draw and significantly impoverished both nations.

1982, June 6. ISRAELI INVASION OF LEBANON. The Israelis had grown weary of constant **Palestinian raids** from southern Lebanon and worried about the presence (since 1981) of **Syrian missiles** on Lebanese soil. The purpose of the invasion was to expel the Syrians and permanently eliminate the PLO's bases inside Lebanon. **Israeli forces advanced as far north as Beirut.** The Syrians chose to avoid contact with the Israelis after suffering heavy losses in air battles over Beirut. To the satisfaction of the Israelis, **the PLO evacuated** the country in August. Yet in the succeeding months, **Israel** was unable to organize a stable Lebanese government to maintain order. Unwilling to stay permanently, **the Israeli army withdrew** in stages between July 1983 and June 1985, and kept only a **security zone** in southern Lebanon. As the Israelis fell back, the Syrians resumed their former position of paramountcy in Lebanon.

1983, Oct. 23. A suicide attack blew up U.S.-French headquarters in Beirut, killing 241 U.S. Marines and 58 French soldiers. The bombing was in retaliation for U.S. naval shelling of areas outside Beirut in Sept. 1983. The U.S. withdrew from Lebanon in Feb. 1984.

Dec. Syrian forces and PLO rebels **expelled Yasir Arafat** and other Palestinian officials of al-Fatah from northern Lebanon. PLO headquarters was transferred to Tunis.

1985. Launching of **Arabsat,** two medium-size **space satellites operated by the Arab League.** On the second mission, the satellite was accompanied by the first Arab astronaut, Saudi prince Sultan ibn Salman. Arabsat has served primarily as a communications network for pan-Arab broadcasting.

Oct. 1. Israeli jets attacked PLO headquarters in Tunis, killing between 30 and 50 people. The raid was in retaliation for a PLO terrorist strike against a yacht in Cyprus.

Oct. 7. PLO commandos hijacked the Italian cruise ship *Achille Lauro* off the coast of Egypt, killing one American. U.S. fighter planes forced the Egyptian jet carrying the surrendered hijackers to land in Italy.

Dec. 27. Palestinian terrorists killed 16 people in attacks at the Rome and Vienna airports.

By the 1980s, **PLO officials** were becoming increasingly **divided over the wisdom of terrorism. Mainstream groups** in the PLO began to see **diplomacy** as the only realistic option for achieving universal recognition and a Palestinian state. But **Palestinian extremists,** such as **Abu Nidal,** vowed never to compromise and continued to carry out **terrorist strikes** in Europe and the Middle East, often against moderate officials within the PLO itself.

1987, May 17. An Iraqi jet fired on the USS *Stark* off the coast of Bahrain. Thirty-seven sailors were killed. Iraq later issued an apology.

May 29. Responding to pleas from the Kuwaiti government, the **U.S. announced** that it would provide **naval escorts** for all Kuwaiti ships sailing under the U.S. flag in the **Persian Gulf. Kuwait** had requested U.S. protection after several Iranian attacks on Arab shipping in the Gulf. The Iranian actions had been provoked by previous Iraqi attacks (1986) on ships calling in Iranian ports.

Nov. The Amman Summit, at which most Arab states restored diplomatic ties with Egypt.

1988, Nov. 15. Announcement by the **Palestine National Council (PNC)** that it would henceforth honor **UN Resolution 242** and renounce terrorism. The Palestinian leadership also proclaimed its willingness to participate in an **international peace conference** to settle the Arab-Israeli dispute. The immediate consequence was the opening of discussions between U.S. and Palestinian officials in Tunis. At the same time, the PNC officially proclaimed the state of Palestine, which won widespread international recognition. **Yasir Arafat** became its president in April 1989.

Dec. 21. Pan Am Flight 103 exploded over Lockerbie, Scotland. All 258 people on board died. The U.S. blamed Libyan agents for staging the attack, but a later investigation also raised questions about the possible involvement of Syria and Iran.

1989, Feb. 14. Ayatollah Khomeini (p. 975) formally authorized the murder of **Salman Rushdie,** author of *The Satanic Verses,* for **allegedly defaming Islam.** Khomeini called for a worldwide ban on the book's publication. Rushdie immediately went into hiding. The Iranian government later put a bounty of $1 million on the novelist's head.

1990, Jan. 13. Turkey began diverting water from the Euphrates River to a reservoir behind the Ataturk Dam in southeastern Anatolia. The flow of water beneath the dam dropped by 75 percent for nearly one month, angering the governments of Syria and Iraq. The Turkish action highlighted the **scarcity of water** throughout the wider region and the delicate diplomatic problems that it posed. As countries worked to raise agricultural output, squabbling intensified over rights to river water and underground aquifers (especially between Israel and Jordan).

Aug. 2. IRAQI INVASION OF KUWAIT, which succumbed within hours after offering feeble resistance. The attack followed a **Kuwaiti refusal to cancel** billions of dollars in **Iraqi war debt** accumulated during the Iran-Iraq War. Iraq also charged Kuwait with **stealing oil** from the Rumayla oil field, shared by Iraq and Kuwait, and with illegally **exceeding** its OPEC-assigned **production quota,** thereby depressing world oil prices to the detriment of Iraq. After the invasion, **Kuwait was annexed** and converted into Iraq's 19th province.

Acting under the authority of the UN, the **U.S.** assembled an **international military coalition** during the late summer and autumn of 1990. Most of the troops and equipment were supplied by the **U.S. and Britain,** but the coalition also included token forces from many **Arab states,** notably Saudi Arabia, the various Gulf states, Egypt, and Syria. As leader of the coalition, **the U.S. insisted on an unconditional Iraqi pullout** from Kuwait and refused to link Iraqi compliance with other regional disputes such as the Palestinian question. On Nov. 30, Iraq formally rejected UN Resolution 678, which demanded a complete withdrawal by Jan. 15, 1991.

1991, Jan. 16. The coalition forces, under the command of U.S. general **Norman Schwarzkopf,** began bombing raids on Baghdad and military

sites elsewhere in Iraq. **The ground offensive,** involving 700,000 troops, commenced on Feb. 23 and quickly **overcame Iraqi resistance** in Kuwait and southern Iraq. After four days of fighting, the U.S. and allied troops halted their advance and allowed the remnants of the Iraqi army to escape into central Iraq.

April 6. The U.S. and its allies established a safe haven for **Kurds** in northern Iraq.

Sept. 10. The Arab League moved its headquarters back to Cairo.

Oct. 30. Opening of the **Madrid peace conference.** For the first time in the history of the Arab-Israeli conflict, **Israeli and Arab negotiators** (Palestinians, Lebanese, Syrians, and Jordanians) met face-to-face to discuss the terms of a peace settlement. Israel still refused to meet with representatives of the PLO, and Palestinian delegates were not allowed to have official ties to the organization.

1993, Oct. 2. An international conference in Washington raised $3 billion in financial pledges to help Palestinian authorities establish self-rule in the occupied territories.

1994, Sept. 30. Six Persian Gulf nations of the Gulf Cooperation Council announced a lessening of the 46-year trade boycott of Israel.

1998, Aug. 8–11. In attempts to take the last 10 percent of Afghani territory from opposition forces, the Taliban government launched massive offensives in Mazar-e Sharif and Taloquan as fighting spread to many areas along the Uzbekistan border. Heavy fighting resumed on July 28, 1999, because the Taliban still did not have control over the entire country.

Sept. 10. Iran sent some 200,000 troops to the Afghanistan border in response to the Aug. 8 killings of several Iranian diplomats, presumably by Taliban forces.

Oct. 23. In a historic peace agreement, Israeli prime minister Netanyahu, Palestinian National Authority (PNA) president Yasir Arafat, King Hussein of Jordan, and U.S. president Bill Clinton convened to sign the Wye River Peace Accords. The agreement established a preliminary plan for the gradual transfer of the West Bank to Palestinian control, and the freeing of some 750 Palestinian prisoners in the process. In exchange, the PNC agreed to remove clauses from the PLO charter that called for the destruction of Israel, and both sides agreed to halt the persistent violence that had plagued the region.

Dec. 16–19. After a year of broken promises by Saddam Hussein to allow UN inspections teams into Iraqi weapons facilities, the U.S. and Britain began a bombing campaign that would last for the next two years, regularly attacking Iraq's missile factories, command centers, and airfields in order to continually thwart Iraqi attempts to build up arms supplies. Although the UN renamed its inspections team, now called UNMOVIC (United Nations Monitoring Verification and Inspection Commission), Iraq continued to be noncompliant to its demands.

1999, Feb. 7. In a day of mourning for diplomats across the world, many world leaders came together to grieve the death of King Hussein of Jordan, whose death came during his 46th year as ruler of Jordan.

Feb. 16. Leader of the Kurdish terrorist group, the Kurdistan Workers Party (PKK), Abdullah Ocalan was captured, tried, and convicted of treason for his militant leadership role. Ocalan was sentenced on June 29 to death for his war crimes. Attributing a desire for peace to the wishes of Ocalan himself, the PKK announced on Aug. 5 that it would cease its 14-year armed rebellion against the Turkish government.

March 6. Bahrain's ruler for 40 years, Sheik Isa ibn-Sulman al-Khalifah died and was succeeded by his son.

March 8. In Qatar municipal elections, women were enfranchised for the first time. Qatar and Oman were the only Gulf States to uphold a woman's right to vote. Massive protests erupted in Morocco over a similar attempt to advance as women's rights supporters and Islamic fundamentalists clashed over proposed reforms.

April 5. The international embargo of Libya was ended when Pres. Qaddafi handed over two men suspected of perpetrating the 1988 bombing of a Pan American World Airways aircraft, which exploded over Lockerbie, Scotland during flight 103, leaving over 270 dead.

May 17. Benjamin Netanyahu lost the premiership to Ehud Barak, head of the Center-Left One Israel coalition.

July 23. King Hassan II, who had reigned in Morocco since 1961, died and was succeeded by his son, Sidi Muhammad VI.

Nov. 14. Refusing to turn over ex-Saudi millionaire and terrorist leader Osama bin Laden to the U.S. for prosecution, Taliban-led Afghanistan faced increased U.S. and UN economic sanctions; the two partners froze all of Afghanistan's foreign assets and tightened an embargo against the nation.

Dec. 15. Newly elected Israeli prime minister Ehud Barak met with Syrian foreign minister Farouk al-Sharon in Washington, D.C. In this summit, Syrian talks with Israel resumed after four years of silence between the nations and focused on the peaceful return of Golan Heights to Syrian control.

2000, Jan. 13. The Algerian government, although suspected to be exaggerating, claimed that some 80 percent of the rebels who had been prolonging Algeria's bloody civil war had surrendered. Over 100,000 people had died in the seven-year-old war.

Jan. 20. Turkish foreign minister Ismail Cem and Greek foreign minister George Papandreou signed six peace accords, greatly improving foreign relations between Turkey and Greece. This marked the first visit by a Greek foreign minister to Turkey in 38 years.

April 23–27. The Iranian Supreme Court began shutting down reformist newspapers throughout the country after the rebel spirit had enveloped the nation following parliamentary elections where almost two-thirds of the available seats went to progressive candidates. By late July the conservative judiciary had succeeded in closing all 16 moderate newspapers in Iran, extending the crackdown on free press to include numerous arrests of liberal writers and artists.

May 24. Southern Lebanon came suddenly under Hizbollah control as Israeli forces and 3,000 Christian militiamen withdrew from the area after 22 years of occupation.

June 10. Pres. Hafez al-Assad, who had dictatorially ruled Syria since 1971, died and was succeeded by his son, Bashar al-Assad. Assad, 34, had previously been the armed forces commander.

Sept. 28. After Palestinian-Israeli talks had failed in late July due to disagreement over the issue of East Jerusalem, the worst violence seen in the region since 1996 erupted and continued through the end of the year.

Oct. 21–22. In Cairo, Egypt, the members of the Arab League held an emergency summit to discuss the recent Israeli-Palestinian violence outbreaks. At the conference, 21 of 22 league members signed a document that accused Israel of committing recent atrocities against the Palestinians. A $1 billion fund was devoted by the league to aid injured Palestinians and their families during the continuing crisis.

Dec. 31. The trial proceedings of the fugitive Osama bin Laden began in New York City. Several suspected international terrorists, many of whom were still at large, were designated to be put on trial for their violent human rights crimes. Still believed to be living in Afghanistan, bin Laden was the foremost of several Islamic militants facing prosecution in the U.S.

3. THE MIDDLE EAST AND EGYPT, 1943-2000

a. TURKEY

(From p. 754)

1945, May 19. Pres. Ismet Inönü announced the switch to a **multiparty state** and relaxed the restrictions on party formation. Between 1946 and 1950, 27 new political parties came into being. Only two of them had any real significance: **the Democratic Party** (1946) and **the Nation Party** (1948).

June 11. Land reform measures. The state began to parcel out unowned land and unused state and community land to peasants. In addition, the new laws called for the **expropriation** of all private holdings over 500 donums (123.5 hectares), though the **ceiling** was raised to 5,000 donums in 1950. By 1960, the program had dispensed some 1.7 million hectares of arable land and 1.5 million of pasture land to 360,000 families. Despite the effort to redistribute land, the position of the **great landowners** remained strong. Even in 1960, only 15 percent of all landowners still owned about half the land. **Great estates** were most common in **eastern Anatolia.**

1946, Jan. 7. Formation of **the Democratic Party,** which became the **first legal opposition party** in the history of the republic. It quickly asserted itself as a vigorous challenger to the ruling **Republican People's Party (RPP).** The chairman of the party was Celal Bayar, who had once served as prime minister (1937–39). Other prominent members of the party were **Adnan Menderes, Refik Koraltan, and Fuat Köprülü.** In July elections, the young party made an impressive showing by capturing 61 seats in Parliament.

Aug. 3. Appointment of **Recep Peker** as prime minister. He soon lost support within the RPP and was replaced by **Hasan Saka** (Sept. 10, 1947), who backed a more tolerant policy toward opposition parties.

1947, Feb. 20. Legalization of trade unions, which nonetheless remained barred from participating in politics and subject to close government supervision. Workers did not win the **right to strike** until 1963. A large confederation of unions, **Türk Iş,** was formed in 1952 and became the biggest labor organization in the country. It maintained a steadfast policy of **political neutrality.** More radical was **DISK,** an openly leftist union founded in 1967. **The Turkish Workers' Party,** a Marxist organization, appeared in 1962 but appealed only to a tiny constituency of industrial workers and Kurds.

Dec. End of martial law imposed during World War II. All restrictions on freedom of the press were lifted.

1948, July. Formation of **the Nation Party,** which attracted religious conservatives who were dissatisfied with both the ruling Republican People's Party and the opposition Democratic Party. **Fevzi Çakmak,** for-

mer commander of the armed forces, assumed leadership of the new party.

1949, Oct. Opening of the faculty of divinity at the University of Ankara. The act was a government gesture to appease the mounting sentiment around the country to restore a religious presence to public life.

1950–86. Dramatic growth in population. The number of Turks rose from about 21 million to 52 million. **The percentage of urban dwellers increased** from around 25 percent to an estimated 46 percent. **Istanbul** remained the biggest city (up from 1 million in 1950 to 5.5 million in 1985) and was followed by **Ankara** (up from 290,000 to 2.2 million in the same period) and **Izmir** (230,000 to 1.5 million).

1950–90. Rapid growth of the Turkish economy, which expanded at an average rate of 6 percent per year. **Industrial production** climbed to unprecedented levels (from 16.5 percent of GNP in 1950 to 27 percent in 1986), and the economy as a whole became less dependent on agriculture (from 37 percent down to 20 percent of GNP, 1950–86).

Dramatic improvement in literacy rates. The proportion of literate Turks rose from about one-third (1950) to one-half (1970) to three-quarters (1990). **Literacy rates among women jumped** from about 20 percent to well over 50 percent. Most of the gains were achieved among the younger generations and not through the education of adults.

1950–57. Relaxation of restrictions on religious activities. Responding to widespread popular sentiment, the new **Democratic government** permitted religious broadcasting and public prayers in Arabic (1950) and the founding of secondary schools (1952) and later of middle schools (1956), which included religious teaching along with the standard curriculum. Schools that offered only religious instruction were legalized in 1957. In the wake of RPP's thoroughgoing secularization program, the entire decade of the 1950s was marked by a **revival in religious activity and expression.**

1950–52. About 400,000 **Bulgarian Muslims** migrated to and settled in Turkey.

1950, May 14. OPPOSITION VICTORY IN ELECTIONS. For the first time in the history of the Turkish Republic, **the Republican People's Party relinquished power** to another party. In elections that were remarkable for their freedom and openness, **the Democratic Party** came to office with a substantial majority of the vote (53 percent, compared to 39 percent for the RPP). The transfer of power was smooth and peaceful. **Celal Bayar** became the new president, and **Adnan Menderes** was appointed prime minister.

1951–54. Campaign by the Democratic Party **to depoliticize state institutions.** During the more than quarter-century of rule by the Republican People's Party, the **separation between the party and the state**

had become somewhat blurred, owing to the presence of active RPP partisans in the judiciary, the army, the state economic sector, the bureaucracy, and the educational system. To eliminate the influence of the RPP within the state apparatus, **the Democratic government enacted a series of reforms.** In 1951, it shut down the **People's Houses** (founded in 1932 to disseminate Republican ideology), which in effect had become branches of the larger RPP organization. The second attack on the RPP was the confiscation of all **party property,** including its newspaper *Ulus,* deemed unessential to normal operations (1953). The next year the government took the further measure of **retiring a number of judges, officials, and teachers** and implementing laws that tightly regulated political conduct in these occupations. In addition, the new laws **reduced freedom of the press and public assembly.** Critics accused the government of orchestrating a campaign of political repression.

1952. Suppression of the **Tijani Sufi** order. The government feared that it might become a focal point for political unrest, especially in the countryside.

Feb. 18. **Turkish membership in NATO** (p. 838) was ensured by Turkey's enthusiastic participation in the Korean War.

1954. Riding on economic prosperity during the Korean War, the **Democratic Party** achieved an overwhelming **victory in elections** for the National Assembly. The **Democrats won again** in Oct. 1957, but with a smaller margin of the vote (47.2 percent, compared to 40.6 percent for the RPP).

March 7. **Denationalization** of the Turkish **oil industry** to attract foreign investment.

1960. Death of **Saidi Nursi** (b. 1873), founder of the conservative Nurist movement, which demanded a larger role for religion in Turkish politics and society.

May 27. **ARMY COUP.** The political situation rapidly deteriorated early in 1960. **The government closed the universities** in response to student demonstrations. Most domestic **newspapers were suspended** for printing harsh criticism of government policies. Many complaints concerned the **economy,** which had recently been subjected to austerity measures from the International Monetary Fund to curb inflation and reduce the government deficit. Many **military officers were upset** with what they regarded as civilian **neglect of the military** and the government's use of the army to suppress political opposition. The government further antagonized its opposition by launching an investigation into the RPP's internal affairs. Both **the army and the RPP** believed that the Democrats had overstepped their authority. After ignoring an ultimatum (May 3) from the army for political reforms and the resignation of the president, **the Democratic government was overthrown.** The army soon **restored civilian rule** (Nov. 13) and resumed its self-appointed role as guardian of Republican values. **The Democratic Party was outlawed,** former prime minister **Menderes** was executed, and a number of Democratic officials were thrown into jail.

1961, May 26. Promulgation of a **new constitution.** Among the most significant changes were the addition of a second chamber (the Senate) to the Turkish Parliament, the establishment of a constitutional court, guarantees for individual rights, and political protections for the courts and universities. The army designed the constitution to prevent the rise of another powerful opposition party similar to the Democrats.

In elections for the new government (Oct. 1961), the **RPP** emerged as the winner but lacked a majority within the Parliament. Its chief rival was the **Justice Party,** which was more or less the reincarnation of the Democratic Party. Over the next four years, power was exercised by a series of **coalition governments** led by the RPP. The new president was **Cemal Gürsel.** Veteran politician **Ismet Inönü** assumed the office of prime minister and worked hard to restore stability to the system of civilian rule.

Oct. A Turkish–West German labor agreement allowed "guest workers," working immigrants excluded from formal citizenship, to settle legally inside West Germany (p. 872). From 1963 to 1973 the number of legal **Turkish immigrants** rose from approximately 22,000 to over 600,000 (another 100,000 or so also resided in Germany). Most of these workers found jobs in the service sector or positions requiring unskilled labor.

1963. Turkey won associate membership in the **European Economic Community.**

Founding of the **National Action Party (NAP),** a reorganized version of the Republican Peasants Nation Party. The party drew its support from hard-line conservatives and espoused a **mixture of Islam and Turkish nationalism. Alparslan Türkeş,** a former military officer, was the dominant figure and organized the party in a manner resembling the Fascist groups of the 1930s. Attached to the party were **paramilitary squads** known as the **Gray Wolves.** The NAP never achieved widespread popularity (it received no more than 3 percent of the vote in 1969) and was confined almost entirely to the large cities.

1964. Death of **Halide Edip Adivar** (b. 1884), a prominent writer and journalist. She was also a vocal advocate of women's rights.

Release of jailed Democratic politicians from prison. They won back their political rights in 1969.

Aug. 7. The Turkish air force launched **attacks** on the western coast of **Cyprus** in retaliation for the Greek Cypriot persecution of the Turkish minority.

1965, Oct. Victory of **Justice Party** in national elections. Capturing a solid majority of the vote, the Justice government was able to rule single-handedly with **Süleyman Demirel** as prime minister. Elections in Oct. 1969 returned the party to power. Unlike the RPP, the Justice Party had little use for central economic planning. Demirel's government **encouraged foreign investment,** which was funneled into an aggressive **industrialization policy** aimed at private firms. In political affairs, too, the Justice Party tended to favor **a more open system** than the one that the RPP had historically maintained.

1970. Outbreak of **armed revolt in the Kurdish areas** of eastern Anatolia.

Founding of the **National Order Party,** which was banned the following year and later reemerged as the **National Salvation Party.** Organized by **Necmettin Erbakan,** the party adhered to a **conservative religious program** and opposed the unchecked secularization of Turkish society. Its popularity among conservative voters split the constituencies of the major parties, particularly the Justice Party, and helped lead to a succession of weak governments (1973–80).

Feb. A permanent split in the ruling Justice Party left Prime Minister Demirel in command of a minority government. Demirel was further hampered by a rising wave of **civil unrest** fed by political violence from the extreme Left and Right.

1971. A Turkish-American agreement to eliminate the production of opium in Turkey. The American-financed program had little effect on this lucrative industry.

1971–73. MILITARY INTERVENTION IN POLITICS. On March 12, the army **deposed Prime Minister Demirel,** whom it judged unable to maintain law and order, and **replaced his government with a council of conservative politicians** who were held responsible for leading the country back to stability. Although civilian institutions were retained, a series of measures restricted civil liberties, abolished the Turkish Workers Party, imposed martial law on a number of provinces, and unleashed the security forces on extremists. For the next two years, the government was managed by **an unstable succession of coalition governments. The army restored full civilian rule in Oct. 1973,** but the military's intervention had done nothing to strengthen the political system, which was still afflicted by factionalism and violence.

1972. Inauguration of Turkish television broadcasts.

1973–80. ECONOMIC INSTABILITY. A steep **rise in oil prices** threw the Turkish economy into disarray as the government struggled to pay higher energy bills. Difficulties with the balance of trade payments led to **increased borrowing** from foreign sources. The crisis was further aggravated by a **decline in remittances** from Turkish workers in Europe. **Inflation,** too, was a chronic problem and reached levels as high as 50 percent in 1978.

1973–80. WEAK COALITION GOVERNMENTS. The two largest parties, **the Justice Party and the RPP,** controlled most of the vote (at least two-thirds) but were unable to forge stable parliamentary alliances with fringe parties. One of the most consequential developments was the emergence of the **National Salvation Party** (it received 12 percent of the vote in 1973), which undermined the Justice Party in particular by depriving it of a large share of its conservative constituency.

1973. Death of **Aşik Veysel** (b. 1894), perhaps the most renowned Turkish minstrel of the 20th century. He was a blind Alevi from Sivas whose songs dwelt on themes of tolerance and humanity.

Aug. 30. Opening of the Bosphoros Bridge to automobile traffic.

Dec. 25. Death of **ISMET INÖNÜ** (b. 1884), one of the most important figures in the history of the Turkish Republic. He first came to prominence as one of the leaders of the **Kemalist resistance** in the Turkish War for Independence (1918–23). After the war he served as **prime minister under Atatürk** until 1937, and upon Atatürk's death, became **president**. In the postwar era, he was the politician chiefly responsible for introducing a **multiparty political system**. Though his own party, the RPP, suffered a massive and unprecedented defeat in the national elections of 1950, he personally oversaw the **first transfer of power** to the opposition in the history of the republic. Throughout the 1950s and 1960s, he remained active as one of the RPP's leaders and worked to keep the military out of politics.

1974, July 20. INVASION OF CYPRUS (p. 973). A coup in Cyprus brought a **right-wing government** to power. The regime's avowed intention to **unite with Greece** and **massacres of Turkish-speaking Cypriots** provoked a Turkish invasion of the northern part of the island. The Turks refused to withdraw until they had secured **full autonomy for the Turkish minority and recognition of the Turkish Federated State of Cyprus.**

1977–78. Thawing of Turkish-Soviet relations. In 1977, the government of **Bülent Ecevit** certified that the USSR was no longer a threat to Turkey. A **treaty of friendship** was signed the next year.

1980, Sept. 12. ARMY COUP, in which leading politicians were arrested. Martial law was declared throughout the country (Sept. 18), and Parliament was dismissed. The provisional government under **Bülent Ulusu** sent security squads after political extremists of the Left and the Right to eliminate terrorism and restore political order. In 1981, all existing **political parties** (including the RPP) **were banned.**

1981, Dec. 7. The Ministry of Education banned the wearing of headscarves by female students and teachers. The law, which generated considerable controversy on campuses and in the courts, was finally repealed in Dec. 1989.

1982, April 24. The 1936 Montreux Convention, originally providing for unrestricted international access to the Straits in peacetime, **was amended** to allow Turkey to close them at its discretion.

Nov. 7. Approval of a **new constitution.** Turkey reverted to a unicameral legislature, but this time under a strong **presidential system.** The president was given the authority to appoint the prime minister and all upper-echelon judges, to dissolve Parliament, and to declare a state of emergency. To avoid the paralysis of coalition politics that had afflicted Turkey over the preceding 30 years, **parties were required to win at least 10 percent of the vote** to qualify for seats in the Parliament. **Kenan Evren,** commander of the armed forces, assumed office as president.

1983, Oct. A law was passed forbidding student, teacher, and soldier associations; Marxist organizations; and groups promoting religious or cultural differences.

Nov. First **national elections** under the new constitution. **The Motherland Party,** a coalition of liberal and Islamicist groups, won a majority in Parliament (211 of 400 seats), and its leader, **Turgut Özal,** became prime minister. The major policy of the new government was to encourage private industry and scale back the public sector of the economy.

1986. Death of **Haldun Taner** (b. 1916), a pioneer in the development of Turkish fiction.

1987. Permission for banned politicians to reenter politics. Among the most prominent figures excluded from political life in 1980 were **Süleyman Demirel, Bülent Ecevit, Necmettin Erbakan, and Alparslan Türkeş.** Most of the old political parties resurfaced under new names. **Erdal Inönü,** son of Ismet Inönü, appeared at the head of **the Social Democratic Populist Party,** which retained the core of the former RPP. Demirel formed the **True Path Party,** the reincarnation of the Justice Party. **The Welfare Party,** under the direction of Erbakan, was not much different from the former National Salvation Party. Türkeş assembled **the National Work Party,** essentially a replication of the National Action Party.

1989, Aug. 22. The Turkish government **closed its border** with Bulgaria to stem a tide of **Muslim refugees** fleeing religious and ethnic persecution. Before the Turkish action, the total number of refugees had reached 279,000.

Oct. 31. Election of **Turgut Özal** as president.

Dec. 17. Reopening in Istanbul of the Greek Orthodox Fener Patriarchate, which had burned down in 1941.

1990, July 6. A law permitted women to serve in top civil service posts.

1993, Jan. 27. Demonstrations in Ankara against religious extremism occurred after the murder of Ugur Mumcu, a journalist and outspoken critic of Islamic fundamentalists.

April 17. Death of president Turgut Özal, who was succeeded by **Süleyman Demirel.** On June 14, he named **Tansu Çiller** prime minister, the first woman ever to hold this position.

1995, March 20. The Turkish military invaded Iraq in order to assault Kurds.

July 5. Turkey sent approximately 3,000 troops to northern Iraq to continue this assault.

Sept. 20. Tansu Çiller resigned because of a split within the ruling coalition party.

1996, June 28. The Turkish Islamic Welfare Party, led by Necmettin Erbakan, formed a coalition government with a secular party, making **Erbakan** the **new premier.**

1997, Feb. 15. More than 8,000 people, most of them women, protested in Ankara against governmental actions to enforce Islamic law. On April 26 Premier Erbakan agreed to retain secularism in Turkey.

June 18. Erbakan resigned as premier under pressure from the military. On June 30 the president appointed **Mesut Yilmaz the new premier** and approved a secular government.

1998, Jan. 16. Turkey's highest court ruled that the religion-based Welfare Party violated the Turkish constitution, which upholds a strictly secular state. The Welfare Party, dissolved on Feb. 23, was one of Turkey's oldest Islamic groups.

March 30. The European Union (EU) rejected Turkey's application for inclusion in the organization (p. 844).

Oct. 21. Turkey and Syria signed an agreement to halt Syrian military aid to Kurdish rebels in Turkey.

Nov. 25. Turkish premier Yilmaz lost a parliamentary vote of confidence and was removed from office after his alleged links to organized crime were made public.

1999, Feb. 16. Abdullah Ocalan, the leader of the Kurdish militant group the Kurdistan Workers Party (PKK), was captured, tried, and convicted of treason and separatism. In June Ocalan was sentenced to death.

April 18. Deputy Premier Bulent Ecevit, temporarily the head of state after Yilmaz's resignation, saw a victory for his Democratic Left Party, which won 136 seats in Turkey's parliamentary elections.

Aug. 5. The PKK announced that it would cease its 14-year armed rebellion, following the wishes of the imprisoned leader, Ocalan. Officials worried that should his death sentence be carried out, Ocalan's supporters would renew hostilities.

Nov. 18. Representatives attending a summit of the Organization for Security and Cooperation in Europe (OSCE) approved a 1000-mile oil pipeline to run from Azerbaijan to the Mediterranean city of Ceyhan. The estimated cost of the international pipeline was more than $2.4 billion; the accord was seen as a major foreign policy victory.

Aug. 17. An earthquake of Richter magnitude 7.4 hit Izmit, Turkey. The entire country was without electric power for several days; deaths were estimated at between 30,000 and 40,000. This was the largest recorded earthquake to have struck an industrialized area since the 1906 San Francisco and the 1923 Tokyo events.

2000, Jan. 20. Turkish foreign minister Ismail Cem and Greek foreign minister George Papandreou signed six peace accords that greatly improved Turkey's relations with Greece. This marked the first trip to Turkey by a Greek foreign minister in 38 years.

Feb. 9. The leadership of the PKK again renounced all violence in a pledge of peace. There was no indication, however, that Premier Bulent Ecevit intended to accept Kurdish leaders as contributors to the Turkish political system.

May 5. Chief Justice Ahmet Necdet Sezer was elected president by the Parliament. He succeeded Demirel, who was prohibited from serving a second term because Parliament refused to amend the constitution, which limited the presidency to one term.

Dec. 10. Turkey was tentatively invited to join the EU after an international conference in Helsinki, Finland. Conditions of Turkey's admittance included improving its human rights record, settling disputes with Greece, and modernizing its political and economic systems.

b. CYPRUS

1945. Agitation among Greek Cypriots for **Enosis,** union with Greece. The ethnic Turks on the island, who constituted about 20 percent of the population, adamantly opposed it.

1946, Aug. Cyprus began to play an important role as a way station for Jews immigrating to Palestine.

1948, May. British submission of the **Winster Constitution,** which granted greater autonomy to Cyprus. It was **rejected** outright by the Greek Cypriot community under the leadership of the Greek Orthodox Church.

1950, Jan. 15. Greek Orthodox officials conducted a **referendum** on Cyprus's future in which 95.7 percent of the Greek Cypriot electorate **voted for Enosis.** The Greek government made the absorption of Cyprus an official national policy (Feb. 11, 1951).

Oct. 18. Election of Michael Mouskos, bishop of Citium, as **Archbishop MAKARIOS III.** He quickly became the central figure in the struggle for Cypriot independence. After his election as **the first president of Cyprus** (1961), he pursued pragmatic policies that aimed to preserve the binational character of the Cypriot state and peaceful relations among the island's communities.

1955, April 1. Opening of **guerrilla warfare by EOKA, the National Organization of Cypriot Fighters,** which demanded union with Greece. **Col. George Grivas,** a native Cypriot who had become a Greek citizen, emerged as the organization's leader. EOKA originally confined itself to British targets but struck against Turkish Cypriots after they actively sided with the British. The terrorist campaign lasted until 1959.

Aug. 29–Sept. 7. A London conference, attended by British, Turkish, and Greek representatives, reached a deadlock on the future of Cyprus.

Dec. 7. Archbishop Makarios, spokesman for the Greek Cypriots, demanded immediate internal sovereignty. On March 9, 1956, the British **deported** him to the Seychelles Islands. He was released (March 28, 1957) after denouncing terrorism, but he boycotted negotiations until he was allowed to return to Cyprus (March 1, 1959).

1959, Feb. 19. An international agreement in London set a timetable for Cypriot independence. **A constitution forbade both union with Greece and ethnic partition** of the island, provided **guarantees for the Turkish minority,** and established a formula for proportional representation. **A Greek Cypriot would serve as president** of the republic, an **ethnic Turk would be the vice president,** and both would hold veto power over legislation. Other provisions set aside 30 percent of the legislature and civil service, as well as 40 percent of the army, for Turkish Cypriots. The British received two military bases. A Treaty of Guarantee gave Britain, Turkey, and Greece the right to intervene, collectively or individually, in Cypriot affairs to maintain the constitution or the island's independence.

Dec. 13. Election of **Archbishop Makarios as president** of Cyprus. Fazil Küçük was chosen as vice president.

1960, Aug. 16. FORMAL INDEPENDENCE FOR CYPRUS, which became a republic.

1963, Dec. 21. Armed clashes between Greek and Turkish Cypriots followed an attempt by Greek Cypriots to amend the constitution. **Ethnic Turks stopped participating** in the Cypriot government.

1964, March 14. Arrival of a **UN peacekeeping force.** Despite the international presence, **sporadic battles** between ethnic Greeks and Turks continued until mid-August.

1967, Nov. Communal fighting led to escalating tensions between Turkey and Greece, whose armies were supplying, training, and sometimes joining the Cypriot combatants. After Turkey threatened to go to war (Nov. 14), the Greek government recalled EOKA leader Gen. Grivas and began withdrawing its 20,000 troops (Dec. 8).

1968, Feb. 25. Reelection of Pres. Makarios. The Cypriot government **lifted all economic sanctions** against the Turkish minority and removed roadblocks to the northern part of the island. Yet, in effect, the island remained partitioned.

1974, Jan. 27. Death by heart attack of **Gen. George Grivas,** the leading advocate of Enosis.

June 10. Fearing a revolt by radical Greek Cypriots, Makarios re-

quested that Greece reduce the number of its officers in the National Guard from 650 to 50. Simultaneously, Makarios opened a campaign to stamp out EOKA.

July 15. A MILITARY COUP, led by Greek officers in the National Guard, ousted Pres. Makarios. **Nicos Samson,** a former EOKA leader, became the new president.

July 20. THE TURKISH INVASION (pp. 898, 972). **Turkish troops rapidly occupied the northern portion of the island,** where ethnic Turks predominated. The invaders eventually extended their **control over 37 percent** of the island's territory. In the aftermath of the landing, some **180,000 Greek Cypriot refugees fled** southward from the Turkish-held region. Approximately **27,000 Turkish troops remained** behind to protect Cyprus's 115,000 ethnic Turks and maintain their separate status.

Dec. 7. Upon his return to Cyprus, Makarios rejected all proposals to partition the island permanently.

1975, Feb. 13. Formation of the **Turkish Federated State of Cyprus** in the northern part of the island. The Turkish minority proposed to link it to the Greek portion of the island by federation. A **constitution** was approved (June 8), and **Rauf Denktaş** was elected president (June 20, 1976).

1977, Aug. 3. Death of **Archbishop Makarios** (b. 1913). **Spyros Kiprianou,** president of the House of Representatives, became the new president.

1978, Feb. 10. Disbandment of EOKA, the secret terrorist organization run by Greek Cypriots.

1981, June 28. Reelection of **Rauf Denktaş** as president of northern Cyprus.

1983, Nov. The Turkish Cypriot state unilaterally declared itself independent and became the **Turkish Republic of North Cyprus.** Turkey was the only country to recognize the new state and exchange ambassadors with it. The **U.N.** Security Council issued a condemnation (May 11, 1984).

1985, May 5. Turkish Cypriots approved a new constitution. Denktaş was reelected as president (June 9).

July 5. The Turkish government rejected a UN proposal to reunite Cyprus despite Greek Cypriot approval (June 12) because it had not been consulted earlier. The UN presented a second plan (June 11, 1986), but this time it was scotched by the Greek Cypriots.

1988, Feb. 21. Independent leftist **Georgios Vassiliou** became president of Greek Cyprus.

1993, Feb. 15. Glavkos Clerides, an opponent of the UN plan to unify Cyprus, was elected president of the Greek government.

1997, Nov. Greek premier Costas Simitis and Turkish premier Mesut Yilmaz signed a pact aimed at improving Turkish–Greek relations on the island of Cyprus.

1998, Feb. 15. Pres. Glafcos Clerides was reelected to his second five-year term.

June 16–18. Both Greece and Turkey sent aircraft to Cyprus when the island nation attempted to purchase S-300 anti-aircraft missiles from Russia. Through the influence of Greek premier Simitis, deployment of the weapons was canceled on Dec. 29.

Dec. The EU decided to invite Cyprus to apply for membership after it had rejected Turkey earlier in the year. This heightened international tensions between Turkey and Cyprus.

1999, April 22. Conflicts with Turkey resumed over the issue of missile deployment plans and the increased military capability of Cyprus because of its surface-to-air missile purchases from Russia. Turkey considered further arming its territory in northern Cyprus.

2000, Jan. 20. Peace accords were signed between Turkey and Greece two days after the nations agreed on plans for a pipeline that would supply fresh water to Turkish and Greek areas on Cyprus.

April 15. Rauf Denktash, president of the Turkish Republic of Northern Cyprus, was reelected to a fourth five-year term.

c. IRAN

(From p. 757)

1945. Founding of the Fada'iyan-i Islam by Navvab Safavi. It became the first religious organization to advocate the creation of an **Islamic state.** The movement involved itself in **political violence,** including the assassinations of writer **Ahmad Kasravi** (1946) and the shah's minister of court, **Abd al-Husayn Hazhir** (1949). It gradually faded from the scene in the 1950s, especially after the arrest and execution of Safavi (1956).

Oct. Outbreak of a **revolt in Azerbaijan.** The insurrection was organized by the **Democratic Party of Azerbaijan,** founded in Sept. 1945 and led by **Ja'far Pishavari,** who became prime minister in Dec.

The Azeri government proposed **radical reforms,** including land and labor reforms, and made **Azeri** the official language of government and education. The young regime rapidly collapsed after the return of Iranian troops to Azerbaijan (Dec. 1946).

1946, Jan. 22. Proclamation of the **Kurdish Republic of Mahabad** in Kurdistan. The Kurdish government was led by **the Democratic Party of Kurdistan,** formed in 1945 under **Qazi Muhammad.** Iranian troops reentered Kurdistan in December and quickly crushed the secessionist regime.

April. Soviet-Iranian agreement. The Soviets promised to **withdraw their troops** from northern Iran (completed on May 9) in return for a large oil concession. The Iranian government under **Prime Minister Ahmad Qavam** (who took office in Jan. 1946) avoided its part of the bargain by cleverly insisting on ratification by the Majlis (Parliament), which had been dissolved in March 1946. The next **Majlis,** which did not meet until the following year, **refused to sanction** the pact (Oct. 1947).

1949, Oct. Formation of the **NATIONAL FRONT** under the leadership of **MUHAMMAD MUSADDIQ.** The front was composed of **three main groups:** political factions opposed to the shah, politicians connected to the bazaars and the religious establishment, and Western-educated intellectuals who for the most part were young and radical. The original program of the coalition called for freedom of the press, free and honest elections, and the promotion of social justice. The National Front later became identified with Musaddiq's **nationalization of the oil industry.**

1950–75. Growth of the bureaucracy from 130,000 to approximately 500,000 civil servants.

1951. Death of **Sadiq Hidayat** (b. 1903), one of the founders of modern Persian literature. He was celebrated for his innovative novels and short stories, particularly *The Blind Owl.*

March 20. NATIONALIZATION OF THE OIL INDUSTRY by the Majlis, which then appointed **MUHAMMAD MUSADDIQ** as the new prime minister. In retaliation, the **Anglo-Iranian Oil Company suspended** production at the Abadan refinery (Oct. 1951).

1952, July. The shah reinstated Musaddiq as prime minister, following massive demonstrations protesting Musaddiq's earlier resignation.

1953, Aug. 16. The shah again tried to remove Musaddiq from office and appointed **Gen. Fazlallah Zahdi** as the new prime minister. Musaddiq refused to step down. After huge **pro-Musaddiq demonstrations** filled the streets, **the shah fled the country.**

Aug. 19. OVERTHROW OF MUSADDIQ, whose government was toppled by a combination of widespread **popular protests** (arranged partly through CIA funding) and the intervention of the army. Other factors in the coup included Musaddiq's **alienation of the religious establishment,** his unpopularity among many **tribal leaders,** his inept handling of **landowners and army officers,** and crumbling support from within **the National Front.** In the aftermath of the coup, **the shah** emerged as the major figure on the political scene.

1955. Widespread **persecution of Baha'is.**

1956. Piped water available to Tehran for the first time.

1957. Creation of **SAVAK,** the shah's **secret police.** The organization functioned above the law, arresting suspects as it saw fit and often in secret. Torture, execution, and assassination were other methods that SAVAK did not hesitate to use.

1958. Beginning of television broadcasts, on a privately owned station. Television was later nationalized in 1969.

1960–89. Growth of the population from 23 million to 50 million. The proportion of urban dwellers rose from one-third to about three-quarters of the total population. Tehran's population tripled from 2 million to 6 million (1986).

1960–79. Improvement in general literacy, from around 20 percent of the population up to 40 percent.

1960–63. THE WHITE REVOLUTION, a program of sweeping **social and economic reforms,** became the central doctrine of the shah's regime. The goal of the White Revolution was to **transform Iran into a modern society and a great Asian power.**

In the forefront of the White Revolution was **LAND REFORM,** which was certainly the shah's most publicized measure. Like other land reforms in the Middle East, the chief effect of the shah's program was **to smash the power of the great landowners,** who had previously owned about half the cultivated land and dominated the countryside. **Landlords were restricted** to ownership of one village. They were awarded **compensation** for sequestered land, which was then distributed to peasants. **Small absentee landlords** retained about half the arable land and continued to thrive, but their survival did not prevent the emergence by the early 1970s of nearly 2 million **small-scale independent cultivators.** The performance of the new rural order fell far below expectations. Agricultural production steadily sank during the 1970s despite the widespread availability of fertilizers and tractors.

Other reforms included the nationalization of forests and pastures (1963), **the literacy corps** (1963), **the health corps** (1964), and **the reconstruction and development corps** (1964). **The religious corps** (1971), in spite of its name, was founded to promote the ideals of modern secular culture and was staffed by graduates of secular universities.

The main **opponents of the White Revolution were the religious establishment, wealthy landowners, and tribal leaders.** The first and second groups were stripped of substantial property and wealth. The religious establishment was also apprehensive about cultural and religious reforms. All three groups **resented the rise of the state** and their consequent loss of power and prestige.

1960. Death of **Nima Yushij** (b. 1897), generally considered Iran's first modernist poet.

1962. Women received the right to vote.

1963, June. Popular opposition to the shah. A disparate **coalition** of shopkeepers, religious officials, students, and unemployed workers staged **violent demonstrations** against the policies of the shah's regime, particularly the programs of the **White Revolution.** Led by the **Ayatollah Khomeini,** the opposition demanded the **reform** of the government, but had not yet reached the point of calling for a revolution. **Rioting** soon spread to all of Iran's major cities. The authorities put down the protests with great severity. It is estimated that over 1,000 people may have died in clashes with police.

1969. Death of **JALAL AL-E AHMAD** (b. 1923), literary author and social commentator. He was especially known for his criticism of blind and excessive westernization.

1971. Founding of the **Sazman-i Mujahidin-i al-Khalq,** a guerrilla organization that staged attacks against the shah's regime. Its ideology was an eclectic mixture of Islam and left-wing doctrines.

1975, March 2. Replacement of the official two-party system with **the Resurgence Party,** which embraced the principles of the **White Revolution.** People were expected to join the party to show support for the government and its programs. By 1977 party officials claimed a membership of some 5 million.

1976, March 15. Switch to a new **Persian calendar,** which was calculated from the founding of the Persian Empire in the 6th century B.C.E. As of March 21, the new year was dated 2535.

May 15. Ratification of a treaty that fixed the boundaries with Iraq.

1977, June 19. Death of **ALI SHARI'ATI** (b. 1933), a writer and political activist who combined Islamic and Western thought to produce a radical critique of contemporary Iranian society. His polemics were simultaneously directed at both conservative elements in the religious establishment and reckless modernizers in the state.

Aug. 6. Resignation of Prime Minister Amir Abbas Huvayda, who was replaced by **Jamshid Amuzgar,** a technocrat who had been educated in the U.S.

1978. Founding of the **Islamic Republican Party,** controlled by **radical religious figures** and committed to toppling the shah's regime. It became the **major political party after the Islamic Revolution.**

Aug. 19. A fire at a cinema in Abadan took the lives of over 400 moviegoers who were locked inside. The following day, tens of thousands of protesters gathered in the streets to denounce SAVAK, which was accused of setting the blaze.

1978–79. THE ISLAMIC REVOLUTION eventually overthrew the shah's regime. The opening stage of the revolution was characterized by **massive street protests,** which involved hundreds of thousands of demonstrators. Marches early in 1978 had primarily drawn agitators from the **middle classes,** notably students. But during the summer of 1978 the **urban poor,** goaded by inflation, high unemployment, and spiraling rents, began turning out in large numbers to voice their own grievances. From Sept. 1978 the protests, though confined mainly to the cities, became a true mass phenomenon, **aligning the middle and working classes** against the shah's government. In the face of such a broad and hostile movement, **the shah vacillated.** He first declared **martial law** (Sept. 7), then later passed **conciliatory decrees** (Nov.), which the opposition ignored. Civil order began to break down as the violence of the demonstrations intensified (Dec.). The shah appointed **Shahpur Bakhtiyar,** a leader of **the National Front,** as prime minister, but the move failed to mollify the opposition. Unable to hold out any longer, **the shah finally went into exile** on Jan. 16, 1979. He died in Cairo on July 27, 1980. His son proclaimed himself Riza II.

1979, Feb. 1. Return from exile of the **AYATOLLAH KHOMEINI** (p. 974). On Feb. 5, he named **Mahdi Bazargan** prime minister of a provisional government. The remnants of the shah's government, under **Bakhtiyar,** resigned (Feb. 11) after the army withdrew its support.

Feb. 15. Four generals were shot in the first round of **political executions,** which, by 1984, had taken the lives of over 5,000 civilian and military officials from the shah's regime. On March 16, **Khomeini** placed all political trials under the supervision of **the Revolutionary Islamic Council,** which made the tribunals more regular and systematic.

March 31. Voters approved a referendum to establish the **Islamic Republic.**

May. Founding of the **REVOLUTIONARY GUARDS (PASDARAN).** The organization first functioned as a **militia** serving the radical *ulama* (men of religion), but later became, in essence, a branch of the national army. By 1987, the force had grown to about 450,000. Besides acting as a mainstay of the Islamic Republic, it remained one of the centers of religious fervor and revolutionary ideology.

Nov. 4. Seizure of the U.S. embassy by armed students (p. 924). **The U.S. government** immediately halted the shipment of spare parts to Iran (Nov. 9) and **froze some $11 billion in Iranian assets** (Nov. 11). The militants holding the embassy staff released all women, African Americans, and non-U.S. personnel (Dec. 26), leaving 52 diplomats in custody. **A secret U.S. mission** to rescue the hostages (April 24, 1980) ended in failure and the death of eight U.S. servicemen. **The hostages,** who were accused of being spies, **were finally freed on Jan. 20, 1981,** after 444 days in captivity. Iran immediately received one-quarter of its frozen assets abroad; another $3.2 billion of the frozen assets was designated for arbitration. The remaining portion was earmarked to repay outstanding loans.

Nov. 6. Resignation of Mehdi Bazargan as prime minister. All power was transferred to **the Islamic Revolutionary Council,** which had been operating as a parallel government under the direction of the radical ulama since Feb. 1979.

Nov. 15. Approval of a **constitution for the Islamic Republic.** Like all republican governments, the Iranian state would be governed by a president, a cabinet, and a parliament. In addition, there were **three "Islamic" institutions: the revolutionary guards, a council of experts** to examine legislation and if necessary to veto it, and **a vali faqih** who nominated candidates for high offices and had the option of taking control of the government. All legislation had to conform to Islamic law.

1980, Jan. 25. Election of **Abu al-Hasan Bani Sadr** as president of the new Islamic Republic. He later displeased Khomeini, who removed him from office (June 22, 1981).

1981, June 28. Bombing of the Islamic Republican Party's headquarters in Tehran **by the Mujahidin,** leaving 120 dead, including **Muhammad Husayni Bihishti,** the leader of the party. A second attack, in which the prime minister's office was bombed (Aug. 31), claimed the lives of **Pres. Muhammad Ali Rajai** (elected on July 25) and **Prime Minister Muhammad Javad Bahunar,** among others. Over the next 18 months, the government conducted extensive counterterrorist operations. The most notable victim was **Musa Khaybani,** leader of the Mujahidin-i Khalq, assassinated by Iranian security forces on Feb. 8, 1982.

Oct. 2. Election of **Ali Khameni** as president.

1982, Dec. Election of **the Assembly of Experts** to discuss who would be the future successor to Ayatollah Khomeini.

1983, April 16. Passage of a law that required all women to meet **"Islamic standards of dress."** Headscarves became mandatory, and tight-fitting clothing was prohibited. The maximum penalty for non-compliance was one year in prison.

Sept. Reopening of the universities for the first time since 1980.

1985, Aug. 19. Reelection of **Ali Khameni** as president.

Nov. Ayatollah Khomeini chose Hasan Ali Muntazari as his future successor for the office of spiritual head of state. But in March 1989, the Assembly of Experts forced Muntazari out and replaced him with **Ali Khameni,** who officially became an ayatollah.

1987, June 2. Dismantling of the Islamic Republican Party, under orders from Ayatollah Khomeini, who claimed that the party had served its purpose and was no longer needed.

1988, July 3. The U.S. warship *Vincennes* shot down an Iranian passenger plane over the Persian Gulf, killing all 290 people aboard.

Dec. 31. Eighteen political groups filed for official recognition under a law that **legalized political parties.** Among the parties were the Freedom Movement, led by former prime minister Mehdi Bazargan, and the Mujahidin-i Khalq.

1989, Feb. 28. Forced **resignation of Ayatollah Montazeri** as Khomeini's successor on account of Montazeri's support for Mehdi Bazargan.

June 3. Death of AYATOLLAH KHOMEINI (b. 1899), who was succeeded as vali faqih by **Pres. Ali Khameni.**

Khomeini first emerged on the political scene during the 1960s as the chief spokesman for the **protests of June 1963.** After his exile by the shah, he settled down in Iraq, where his thinking turned truly radical. He had displayed an early interest in **the theory of an Islamic state** (1940s) and now urged its immediate establishment. He was a shrewd and charismatic politician who blended Islamic themes with populist rhetoric. Through **taped sermons** distributed all over Iran, he positioned himself during the 1970s as the **leading opponent of the shah's regime** despite living in exile. During the Islamic Revolution of 1978–79, his prestige was so great that a broad array of political groups readily accepted his authority. From the beginning, he loomed as the defining figure of the Islamic Republic, occupying the supreme office of **vali faqih.** Though he tended to remain aloof from the routine business of government, his mere presence guaranteed the stability of the political system. Indeed, one of the central preoccupations of Iranian politics during the 1980s was the question of his successor.

July 18. Election of **Ali Akbar Hashimi Rafsanjani** as president.

1991, Aug. 8. Assassination of former prime minister **Shahpur Bakhtiyar** in Paris.

1993, June 11. Election of **Pres. Rafsanjani** to a second term.

1994, Feb. 1. A member of an anti-Islamic group launched an unsuccessful assassination attempt on Iranian president Ali Akbar Hashemi.

Feb. 23–24. Iran and Russia signed an agreement providing Iran with a nuclear reactor for commercial purposes in spite of objections from the U.S.

1997, May 23. Iran elected moderate **Mohammed Khatami** the **new president** against a more religiously conservative opponent. **Khatami called for a more open and tolerant society.**

1998, Sept. 10. Iran sent several thousand troops to its border with Afghanistan after the Taliban government admitted responsibility for the Aug. 8 murder of eight Iranian diplomats and a journalist. With a majority of Shi'ite Muslims composing its population, Iran had openly supported the rebels fighting against the Sunni Taliban.

Oct. 23. Elections for the Assembly of Experts gave overwhelming governmental power to the ruling conservatives.

1999, Feb. 26. Religious leaders allowed the first local elections since 1979. Pres. Muhammad Khatami's new moderate party, begun only three months earlier, carried the vote in several cities and won large victories nationwide.

July 8–13. Pro-democracy students in Tehran were attacked by a militant Islamic group that killed eight and injured dozens more. During six more days, student protests swept across cities throughout Iran; the uprisings were violently suppressed by national police forces. Pres. Khatami condemned the riots, and many questioned his devotion to continued calls for greater democracy in the Iranian government.

2000. Amid signs of a loosening of social constraints in Iran—for example, more opportunities for women to appear unveiled—conservatives blocked most formal reform legislation, such as a proposal to raise women's marriage age from 9 to 14 years.

2000, Feb. 18 and May 5. Elections to the Majlis, the Iranian parliament, resulted in nearly two-thirds of the seats going to reformers and Khatami supporters. Hard-line conservatives won only 44 of the 290 seats.

April 23–27. In an effort to crush the rebel spirit, the government closed more than 16 moderate reform newspapers through rulings by the conservative high courts. By August, the judiciary had succeeded in closing every one of Iran's reformist newspapers that had supported the moderate agenda of Pres. Khatami. A severe crackdown on the liberal press ensued, and writers throughout Iran were arrested.

d. AFGHANISTAN

(From p. 757)

1946. Official opening of the **University of Kabul.** The various schools associated with it were not grouped into a single campus until 1964.

May. Resignation of Prime Minister Hashim Khan, who was succeeded by his brother, **Mahmud Shah Khan.**

1949, July. Formal **abrogation of all treaties signed with Britain defining the Durand Line,** which after 1947 had become the border between Afghanistan and Pakistan. Afghanistan had long coveted Pakistan's northwest border region, which was inhabited by **Pashtun tribes.** The Afghan government now demanded that Pakistan hold elections in the territory for self-determination. Afghan-Pakistani relations became further strained after Pakistani planes bombed the village of Moghol-gai, just inside the border of Afghanistan. In August, Pashtun tribal leaders inside Pakistan declared the independent state of Pashtunistan, which was recognized by Afghanistan. Pashtunistan never came into existence, but the issue remained an irritant to Afghan-Pakistani relations for many years to come.

1953, Sept. 20. A PALACE COUP was carried out without bloodshed. **MUHAMMAD DAOUD KHAN,** former commander of the Central Forces in Kabul, became the new prime minister. His government ushered in a series of **moderate social and economic reforms** and drew the country away from a pro-Western foreign policy and toward **neutrality.** Among the major accomplishments during his tenure were the **upgrading of the country's infrastructure** (better communications, more roads and airfields) and the **strengthening of the armed forces.**

1955, Dec. 18. Signing of a ten-year extension to the **Soviet-Afghan treaty** of nonaggression.

1956, March. Implementation of the first Afghan Five-Year Plan for economic development.

1959. A government decree made **veiling optional for women.** In practice, female employees in the state bureaucracy and female relatives of high government officials had to give up the custom.

Suppression of tribal revolts in eastern Afghanistan.

1960, Sept. Entry of irregular Afghan troops into Pakistan to assist **Pashtun tribesmen** who were resisting government troops. Subsequently, **escalating tensions between Afghanistan and Pakistan led to a break in relations** (Sept. 6, 1961). Normal ties were not restored until May 29, 1963.

1963, March 9. Resignation of Prime Minister Muhammad Daoud. KING MUHAMMAD ZAHIR SHAH emerged as the leader of the government, in fact as well as in name, thereby ending some 30 years of rule by a succession of relatives in the office of prime minister. The king appointed **Muhammad Yousef** as the new premier.

1964, Oct. 2. Promulgation of a new **constitution,** which created a bicameral legislature responsible for appointing a cabinet. **The king still retained extensive powers.** One of the major innovations of the constitution was the enfranchisement of women. The first parliamentary elections were held Aug. 26–Sept. 24, 1965, and took place without the activities of political parties.

1965, Jan. 1. Founding of **the People's Democratic Party of Afghanistan,** the first Communist political organization. Among its leading figures were **Nur Muhammad Taraki and Babrak Karmal.**

Oct. 29. Appointment of **Muhammad Hashim Maiwandwal** as the new prime minister, replacing the outgoing premier, Muhammad Yousef.

1967, Nov. Nur Ahmad Etemadi became the new prime minister.

1971–72. The worst **drought** in Afghanistan's recorded history. In spite of extensive international aid, some 100,000 people died during the resulting famine.

1973, July 17. A bloodless **MILITARY COUP** was organized by former prime minister **MUHAMMAD DAOUD,** who became the new head of state. The new government, which declared itself a republic, immediately suspended the constitution of 1964. The king, **Zahir Shah,** officially **abdicated** on Aug. 24.

1975, May 1. Nationalization of the country's banks.

1977, Jan. 30. Promulgation of a new **constitution. Muhammad Daoud** was elected president on Feb. 14.

1978, April 27. A MILITARY COUP installed the left-wing regime of **Nur Muhammad Taraki,** who became president and prime minister. **Muhammad Daoud** and several other leaders of the fallen government were **executed.**

1979, Sept. 16. Resignation of Pres. Taraki. **Prime Minister Hafizullah Amin** became the new president.

Dec. 21. THE SOVIET INVASION OF AFGHANISTAN immediately ignited a civil war (p. 905). The Soviet force consisted of 85,000 troops, rising to 120,000 by 1983. The war uprooted more than **3 million civilian refugees,** who fled across the border to Pakistan and Iran. Six days later, **Pres. Amin was overthrown** and executed. **BABRAK KARMAL** succeeded to the presidency.

1981, Aug. 22. Formation of an alliance among five **Afghan resistance groups** who became known as **mujahidin.**

1986, Nov. 20. Resignation of Babrak Karmal as president. His replacement was Najib Ahmadzai, known as **Najibullah,** the secretary-general of the Communist Party.

1988, April 8. In an **international agreement** involving the U.S., the USSR, Pakistan, and Afghanistan, the signatories pledged that Afghanistan would become a **nonaligned country** whose neutral status would be guaranteed by the U.S. and the USSR.

Fighting continued in the countryside between the leftist government and the U.S.-supplied guerrillas.

1989, Feb. 15. Completion of the **Soviet military withdrawal,** which had begun in May.

1991, Sept. 13. Agreement by the U.S. and the USSR to halt all shipments of arms to the combatants in the civil war.

1992, April 16. Resignation of Pres. Najibullah, who was forced out of office by an **alliance of rebel leaders and disaffected army officers.** Rebel forces later occupied Kabul without resistance (April 22–24). An interim government took power until **Burhanuddin Rabbani** was elected president (June 28) by a supreme council of rebel leaders. An electoral assembly confirmed his appointment (Dec. 30), but opponents charged that the election had been rigged.

1993, June 17. Gulbuddin Hekmatyar, leader of the mujahidin, became prime minister. His first step was the announcement of a program to **unite and pacify the countryside,** which was effectively split into **three regions:** the Tajik and Uzbek north, controlled by Gen. Abdul Dostam; the south and east (including Kabul), in the hands of Pashtun tribesmen; and the west, lying within the Iranian sphere of influence.

1994, Jan. A series of **bombing raids** was launched **against government forces in Kabul** in an **attempt to oust the president, Burhanuddin Rabbani.**

1995, Feb. 22. The peace efforts in Afghanistan led by the UN lagged when the Afghan president Rabbini refused to relinquish power to an interim council.

Sept. 5. The conservative Muslim **Taliban militia** captured the important city of Herat in a newly launched oppositional offensive.

1996, Sept. 27. The Taliban forces took control of Kabul after a two-day siege during which hundreds were killed.

1998, Aug. 8–12. The Taliban fundamentalist Islamic faction that had control of Afghanistan's government won control of more than 90 percent of the country with victories in Mazar-e Sharif and Taloqan on Aug. 8 and 11, respectively. Further territory along the Uzbekistan border was taken by Taliban forces on Aug. 12. The conflicts caused the deaths of dozens, including several Iranian diplomats.

Aug. 20. Terrorist training camps, allegedly run by ex-Saudi businessman and Islamic extremist Osama bin Laden, were struck by U.S. cruise missiles southeast of Kabul. This strike was one of a series of air attacks by the U.S. in response to the Aug. 2 bombing of embassies in Kenya and Tanzania.

Sept. 10. As tensions rose following the August murders of several Iranian diplomats in Afghanistan, Iran sent 200,000 troops to the Afghani border.

1999, March 14. Secret UN talks in Turkmenistan ended with an accord "in principle" that Afghanistan would soon be ruled by a coalition government. The Taliban retained control, however, and the civil war raged through 1999.

July 28. Taliban forces deployed a major offensive in an attempt to gain control of the last 10 percent of the nation's territory.

Nov. 14. Because Afghanistan refused to turn over Osama bin Laden to the U.S. for prosecution, the U.S. and UN imposed stricter economic sanctions on the country, freezing foreign assets and as a result inciting anti-UN riots across Afghanistan.

Dec. 24. The Taliban improved its international image slightly by successfully mediating an agreement between the Indian government and Muslim extremist hijackers who had commandeered an Indian Airlines plane.

2000, Sept. 6. The Taliban won a key victory by taking the town of Taloqan, where the opposing Northern Alliance was headquartered. Headed by Ahmed Shah Massoud, the Northern Alliance was the primary rebel force that had withheld the last 10 percent of Afghani soil from Taliban control. The following day the Taliban requested that the UN recognize it as Afghanistan's official and sovereign government.

Dec. 19. The UN Security Council voted to tighten diplomatic sanctions on Afghanistan by imposing an arms embargo on the Taliban government. The UN also repeated its demands for extradition of bin Laden, but the Taliban continued to avoid cooperation.

e. SYRIA

(From p. 761)

1945, May. Fighting between French and Syrian forces. The French demanded a treaty giving them autonomy within Syria and guaranteeing their economic and military interests. They further announced that they would not withdraw their troops until the Syrians agreed to these terms. **Anti-French demonstrations** immediately broke out, and Syrian police skirmished with French units. The French backed down and dropped their demands after the diplomatic intercession of Britain.

1946. Death of Shakib Arslan, one of the most prominent Syrian political activists during the Mandate. Permanently at odds with French authorities, he spent most of his political career as an exile in Europe. He was the ultimate **representative of the older generation** of Syrian politicians who received their education in Ottoman schools and remained nostalgic for the Ottoman Empire. Apart from his anti-French activities, he was best known as an ardent spokesman for the pan-Islamic political movement.

Official formation of the **BA'TH PARTY,** whose program espoused **Arab unity and socialism.** The leading figures in the early years were **Michel Aflaq and Salah al-Din al-Bitar.** By the mid-1950s the party had become a major contender on the political scene.

Aug. SYRIAN INDEPENDENCE and the withdrawal of all Allied troops.

1948, April 17. Reelection of **Shukri al-Quwatli** as president.

1949. Three successive **MILITARY COUPS.** The first one (March) was conducted by the commander in chief of the army, **Husni al-Za'im,** who became president in July. Za'im expanded the army from 5,000 to 27,000 men but failed to secure his own position, and as a result, **he was deposed** the following month (Aug. 14) **by Col. Muhammad Sami al-Hinnawi.** The latter was in turn brought down (Dec. 19) by yet **another coup, organized by Col. Adib al-Shishakli,** who briefly stabilized the political situation. At first, he attempted to restore civilian government. But in Nov. 1951 he moved entirely to **military rule** after failing to work out a satisfactory arrangement with the politicians.

1950. Dissolution of the Syrian-Lebanese Customs and Monetary Union.

1952, Nov. 26. Death of Ali al-Darwish (b. 1884), one of the great specialists in traditional Middle Eastern music. He trained numerous musicians and put together an extensive collection of material on melodic modes and rhythmic patterns.

1953. Abolition of minority law. The special legal codes relating to Alawi and Druze personal law were eliminated.

1954, Feb. 25. Resignation of Shishakli, following widespread protests against his regime. The disturbances began with a **tribal revolt in Jabal Druze** (July 1953). Soon afterward, strikes and demonstrations erupted throughout the country. The final blow to Shishakli was a **military rebellion** centered originally in Aleppo and spreading to the other large towns in Syria outside Damascus. Rather than plunge the country into civil war, Shishakli stepped down as president. Civilian government was immediately reinstated, and **Faris al-Khuri** assumed office as prime minister.

1954–58. PARTY POLITICS AND WEAK GOVERNMENTS. The leading parties were **the National Party and the People's Party,** dominated by the preindependence class of notables and the emerging Ba'th Party. Few of the parties were willing to cooperate with one another. **Political paralysis** was heightened by the Suez War (1956), which drew Syria ever closer to Egypt. By 1958, **union with Egypt** was regarded as the only solution to Syria's ineffectual system of government.

1955. Signing of a **defense pact with Egypt.** Syrian foreign policy began to favor the Soviet bloc.

1960–80. Rapid urbanization of Syrian society. The percentage of urban dwellers rose from 30 to 50 percent of the population.

1961, Nov. RESTORATION OF CIVILIAN GOVERNMENT. The military officers who had revolted against Egyptian rule (in the form of the United Arab Republic [p. 967], 1958–61) issued a constitution and organized elections (Dec. 1). **Nazim al-Qudsi** won the vote for the presidency (Dec. 14). Like the civilian regimes of 1954–58, the governments of the next two years were riven by factional rivalries and were unable to exercise effective power.

1962, March 28. A bloodless **COUP** was organized **by army officers.** The army ordered changes in the government (retaining al-Qudsi as president) and then quickly **returned to the barracks** (April 13).

Sept. 13. Appointment of **Khalid al-Azm** as prime minister. He **dissolved Parliament** (Sept. 24) and announced that he would govern by decree until the next elections, to be staged within one year.

1963. Outlawing of the MUSLIM BROTHERHOOD. Over the next 20 years, Muslim groups (mostly factions of the proscribed Brotherhood) emerged as the most active and vocal opponents of the Syrian government.

March 8. MILITARY COUP. The regime that succeeded it was controlled mainly by members of the **BA'TH PARTY.** The early years of the regime were a time of rapid growth for the Ba'th Party, which had only about 400 civilian members in 1963. Another significant development unfolding during the remaining years of the decade was the gradual **eclipse of the Sunni Muslims** as a political force and the **ascendency of the Alawi community.** Overall, the men who ruled Syria were no longer drawn from the class of urban notables from Damascus and Aleppo. The new political elite, besides its marked military component, tended to incorporate men of a younger and more radical generation whose social roots lay in the countryside.

1965, Jan. Nationalization of Syrian industry.

1966, Feb. 23. A **MILITARY COUP** brought down the military government of **Salah al-Din al-Bitar,** who was also leader of the Ba'th Party. The victorious faction of the state and military was predominantly Alawi. The two major figures who emerged in the new government were **Salah Jadid and Hafez al-Assad.**

1970. Opening of the port of Tartus, which became the largest port in the country.

Nov. 13. A **MILITARY COUP** toppled the government. **HAFEZ AL-ASSAD,** the defense minister and mastermind of the coup, became president (Feb. 1971). His chief rival, **Salah Jadid,** was eliminated from the government. Assad also **seized control of the Ba'th Party** and took the further precaution of placing only trusted friends and clients in the high echelons of the armed forces. **The army benefited** immensely from Assad's benevolence (and anxiety), growing from 50,000 men in 1968 to 500,000 in 1986. Another feature of Assad's regime was the wild growth of the **security apparatus,** composed mainly of Alawis. By the late 1980s, 12 separate security forces were in operation, all carefully counterbalancing one another.

Dec. Proclamation of **the Tripoli Charter,** a proposed federation of Syria, Egypt, Libya, and Sudan. Though the plan never materialized, Arab unity remained an ideological priority of Assad's regime. Similar schemes followed throughout the 1970s, and all of them fell apart before they were realized. Among these failed attempts were a tenuous federation with Egypt and Libya (1971), an effort to merge with Iraq (1978), and preparations to unite with Libya (1980).

1973. Unveiling of a **new constitution,** which granted the president enormous power, including the veto of legislation and the appointment of all senior executive and judicial officials.

1976, June. The Syrian army entered Lebanon. The pretext of the occupation was to bolster the position of Christian forces and prevent a takeover by Palestinian radicals. Excepting the interlude of the Israeli invasion (1982–83) (p. 968), **Syria** established itself as the **dominant outside power in Lebanon** into the 1990s.

1979, Feb. 24. Opening of the Banias oil terminal, which served as an outlet for Iraqi oil.

June. Islamic militants murdered 60 Alawi cadets at the Aleppo artillery school.

1980, March. Strikes and demonstrations paralyzed Aleppo, and many dissidents openly called for an end to Assad's regime. The government sent in the army, which surrounded the city. The Aleppines resisted, and hundreds died in the fighting. A wave of arrests followed, and the government executed a large number of dissidents.

1982, Feb. Brutal suppression of a REVOLT IN HAMA, which was organized by **the Muslim Brotherhood.** The uprising was by far the most serious challenge that Assad's regime had ever faced. Rebels held out for three weeks until the **armed forces overran the city,** killing some 20,000 people.

1983, Nov. As Pres. Assad lay gravely ill, rival Alawi factions began maneuvering to contest the succession. The most prominent claimant was Assad's brother, **Rif'at.** After Assad's recovery, there was a silent confrontation in the streets of Damascus between Rif'at's troops and those loyal to the president. A **compromise** was reached, but the public quarreling deeply embarrassed the regime.

1986. Syria officially became the largest purchaser of Soviet arms in the Third World.

1987, June 4. Syria closed the Damascus offices of the Abu Nidal group, its erstwhile ally within the PLO.

1989, June 23. Death of MICHEL AFLAQ (b. 1910), a Syrian Christian writer and political activist. Aflaq argued that the Arabs, regardless of religion and local affiliations, were an indivisible nation kept apart only by imperialist forces. During the 1940s he helped to organize the **Ba'th Party,** which attracted a substantial number of adherents in Syria and founded a branch in Iraq. The party espoused **socialist policies** and played a leading role in forging the brief political **union between Egypt and Syria** (1958–61). Aflaq was ousted from the Syrian Ba'th after an internal dispute (1966) and spent most of his remaining years in Baghdad as a guest of the other Ba'thist regime.

1991, June. Enactment of "Law 10," a package of tax exemptions offered to a wide spectrum of private companies, by which the government hoped to stimulate the faltering national economy.

1993, Dec. Syria's 850 Jews were permitted to apply for emigration papers in response to an American request. Similar permission had been given in April 1992, allowing some Jews to leave.

1994, Jan. After meeting with U.S. president Clinton, **Pres. Assad signaled his readiness to negotiate a peace treaty with Israel after the return of the Golan Heights to Syria.** Israel said it would take the return of the Golan to a national referendum.

1998, Oct. 21. With 10,000 Turkish troops assembled at its border, Syria signed an agreement with Turkey to halt its aid to Kurdish rebels.

Dec. 4. Pres. Assad's National Progressive Front won all 167 seats in the Syrian legislative elections.

1999, Feb. 10. Pres. Assad was reelected by an overwhelming majority to his fifth seven-year term as president of Syria.

June 24. Israel invaded Lebanon with air strikes against the Syria-backed Hizballah rebel group.

Dec. 15. Israeli prime minister Ehud Barak met Syrian foreign minister Farouk al-Sharan in Washington, D.C.; the meeting marked the continuation of talks between the two nations after four years of silence. Progress was made in discussions about the peaceful resumption

of Syrian control over Golan Heights, a long-disputed area between the two countries.

June 10. Pres. Hafez al-Assad, who had ruled Syria since a 1970 military coup, died and was succeeded by his son, Bashar al-Assad.

f. LEBANON

(From p. 762)

1943–64. MINISTERIAL INSTABILITY. Thirty-five cabinets held power during this span of only 21 years.

1946, March 10. INDEPENDENCE was proclaimed, and the last French troops departed from Lebanese soil.

1948, May 27. Reelection of **Bishara al-Khuri** as president.

1949. Execution of **Antun al-Sa'ada,** the Greek Orthodox radical, for fomenting a rebellion to overthrow the Lebanese state.

Formation of the **Progressive Socialist Party** by **KAMAL JANBULAT,** a Druze chieftain. The party espoused leftist ideology, but functioned essentially as a **Druze organization.**

1952, Sept. 23. Election of **KAMIL SHAM'UN (Camille Chamoun)** as president. He replaced outgoing president **Khuri,** who resigned (Sept. 18) in the face of a general strike.

1953. Women won the right to vote. Lebanon became the first Arab country to grant women this privilege.

1958, July 15–19. LANDING OF U.S. MARINES. The National Front, a broad antigovernment coalition that wished to unseat Pres. Sham'un, fared badly in earlier **parliamentary elections.** Frustrated at the polls, they resorted to **street violence and strikes.** The **Lebanese Army,** under the command of **FU'AD SHIHAB,** refused to intercede. Sham'un thereupon turned to the U.S. for help. The **American government** immediately dispatched 10,000 marines as an application of the so-called **Eisenhower Doctrine.** The crisis was defused by the selection (July 31) of **Shihab** as the new president. **Rashid Karami,** a Sunni Muslim leader of the National Front, was installed as prime minister. No changes were made in the sectarian structure of the national political system.

1964, Aug. 18. Election of **Charles Hilu** as president.

1969, Nov. THE CAIRO AGREEMENT. After meeting with **PLO officials** in Cairo, the **Lebanese government** pledged not to harass Palestinian guerrillas operating out of southern Lebanon. In return, the Palestinians were to keep out of Lebanese affairs. The settlement was an **uneasy compromise** between Christian politicians, who wanted strict controls on the Palestinians, and Muslim representatives, who fully backed the guerrilla activities. The problem became even more acute with the influx of additional **Palestinian refugees** after the Jordanian expulsion of the PLO (Sept. 1970). The number of Palestinians living in Lebanon at this time stood roughly at 300,000.

1970, Aug. 17. Election of **Sulayman Faranjiyya** as president.

1972, July 8. Assassination in Beirut of **Ghassan Kanafani,** renowned Palestinian author and journalist, and leader of the Popular Front for the Liberation of Palestine.

1975. Establishment of **AMAL, a Shi'ite militia** that drew its recruits primarily from the heavily Shi'ite districts of southern Lebanon. Another Shi'ite organization, **HIZBOLLAH,** was founded in 1978 but came to prominence during the 1980s. Hizbollah represented a **coalition of factions** closely allied with Iran and adhering to the ideology of the Iranian Revolution. It was largely responsible for the **campaign of kidnappings** aimed at westerners during the 1980s.

April 13. OUTBREAK OF CIVIL WAR. Christian Phalangist militiamen massacred 27 Palestinians at Ain el-Roumaneh. Over the following weeks, skirmishes erupted throughout the country between **Christian and Palestinian forces. Muslim militias** soon entered the fray and aligned themselves with the Palestinians.

1976, Feb. 14. Attempt to revise the political system. **Pres. Faranjiyya** offered **equal representation** in Parliament to Muslims. He also promised to do away with the **sectarian allocation** of jobs in the civil service, except at the highest levels.

March. COLLAPSE OF THE LEBANESE ARMY, which fell prey to factional disputes and large-scale desertions. The national government lost the only means of enforcing its will.

May. ENTRY OF SYRIAN TROOPS INTO THE CIVIL WAR.

Syria thereby became the paramount power (briefly interrupted, 1982–85) in Lebanese politics.

May 8. Election of **Ilyas Sarkis** as president.

Sept. Creation of the **Lebanese Forces,** an overarching militia that comprised all the Christian military factions (excepting that of the Greek Orthodox).

Oct. Temporary truce in the civil war. The war had so far claimed about 35,000 lives and uprooted a large portion of the population. Lebanese industry was devastated.

1977, March 16. Assassination of Kamal Janbalat, leader of the Lebanese Druze community. The Syrian government was widely suspected of carrying out the murder. Janbulat's son, Walid, became the new Druze leader.

1978. Israeli invasion of southern Lebanon up to the Litani River. To maintain the security of their border, the Israelis left behind a peace-keeping force from the UN and a Greek Catholic militia.

Aug. Disappearance of prominent Shi'ite spokesman and cleric **Musa al-Sadr** during a trip to Libya.

1980. Rapid urbanization was accelerated by the civil war. Nearly 80 percent of Lebanese were now living in cities or large towns; half of the entire population resided in Beirut. A second demographic trend sprang entirely from the civil war. Whereas in the past the population was intermixed to various degrees, **religious sects now tended to concentrate** in particular areas. **Christians** held east Beirut and the northern section of Mt. Lebanon. **Muslims** predominated in west Beirut and the (mostly Shi'ite) southern and (mostly Sunni) northern ends of the country. The **Druze** took over the Shuf, the southern half of Mt. Lebanon.

1982, Aug. 23. Election of **Bashir Jumayyil** as president. After his **assassination** (Sept. 14), his brother Amin succeeded him.

Sept. 16–18. Massacre of at least 300 unarmed Palestinians at the Sabra and Shatila refugee camps in Beirut. The attacks, conducted by **Christian militiamen** with the connivance of Israeli forces, were apparently in revenge for the assassination of president-elect Bashir Jumayyil.

1982–92. Western hostages in Lebanon. Radical groups staged about 25 kidnappings of westerners residing in Lebanon in an effort to apply pressure to Western governments. Most of the kidnappers had ties to the Iranian government.

1985, Dec. Signing of the **Damascus Accord** by Christian, Druze, and Shi'ite representatives. It laid down the framework for a new political system in which Christians and Muslims had equal representation in Parliament, and the power of the Muslim prime minister was raised at the expense of the Christian president. Few Lebanese politicians rallied behind **the treaty, which remained a dead letter.**

1988, Sept. Appointment of **Michel Awn** (Aoun), a Christian militia commander, as prime minister. The acting Muslim prime minister, **Salim al-Huss,** refused to step down. Meanwhile, **Parliament** was unable to decide on a successor to outgoing president **Amin Jumayyil.** In the ensuing crisis, Lebanon was left with no president and two competing prime ministers.

1989, Sept. 30. THE TA'IF CONFERENCE. The surviving 62 members of the last official Parliament, elected in 1972, agreed **to amend the National Pact.** The number of seats in Parliament was divided evenly between Christians and Muslims, and the power of the president (a Christian) was reduced and that of the prime minister (a Muslim) was correspondingly raised. Command of the armed forces was to be shared by the president and the cabinet.

Nov. 5. Parliament elected **Rene Mu'awwad** as president. He was **assassinated** on Nov. 22, and **Ilyas Hrawi** was chosen to replace him.

1990, Oct. 13. Surrender of troops loyal to Gen. Michel Awn, who took refuge in the French embassy. The decisive factor that tipped the balance was Syria's offer (Oct. 10) to use its troops against Awn.

1991, May 22. Signing of a **Syrian-Lebanese treaty,** which coordinated defense, foreign policy, and economic policy between the two countries. The pact effectively, if not officially, reduced Lebanon to an appendage of Syria (excepting the Israeli security zone in the extreme south).

Nov. 5. Signing of a **peace accord by the rival Shi'ite militias,** Amal and Hizbollah.

1992, Jan. 15. Assassination of **Abbas Musawi,** leader of Hizballah, by Israeli troops.

Sept. 9. The first **parliamentary elections** in 20 years were conducted according to the terms of the Ta'if Conference.

1994, Feb. Lebanese and other Arabs agreed to invest $926 million to establish a company called Soldiere to develop the commercial district of Beirut.

1996, April 26. The U.S. brokered a cease-fire between Israel and Lebanon following an Israeli offensive against guerrillas in Southern Lebanon.

1998, Oct. 15. The pro-Syrian National Assembly unanimously elected Gen. Emile Lahoud as the new president. Salim al-Hoss became his appointed prime minister.

1999, June 24. Following the May 17 election in Israel where Prime Minister Netanyahu lost his position, the lame-duck leader opened the most severe Israeli attacks on southern Lebanon since 1996. The increased bombing and continued warfare was between Hizbollah militants and Israeli troops.

2000, May 24. Southern Lebanon came suddenly under Hizbollah control as Israeli forces and 3,000 Christian militiamen withdrew from the area after 22 years of occupation.

Aug. 27 and Sept. 3. The Syrian-backed Hizbollah and Amal parties won all 23 parliamentary seats in elections for the zone formerly occupied by Israel. In alliance with opposition party candidates, former prime minister Rafik Hariri won a substantial victory in parliamentary elections. The results removed Prime Minister Salim al-Hoss from office. Hoss agreed to support Hariri on Sept. 12 but Pres. Lahoud continued to resist cooperating with the new coalition. Hariri was a construction billionaire with significant holdings and influence in Syria and a personal friend of Syria's president Assad. Syria was unlikely to oppose a potential Hariri government.

g. PALESTINE AND ISRAEL

(From p. 764)

1946, May 1. Report of the **Anglo-American Commission.** The committee called for the admission of 100,000 Jewish refugees and the creation of a single Arab-Jewish state under the trusteeship of the UN.

July 22. Zionist terrorists blew up the King David Hotel in Jerusalem, which housed British headquarters.

Oct. 4. U.S. president Harry S. Truman announced **American support for the partition of Palestine.** The American position doomed all attempts to construct a binational state.

1947, Feb. Britain put the Palestine question before the UN and requested advice on the administration of the mandate. On Aug. 31, **the UN. Special Committee on Palestine** declared its support for a three-sided partition: a **Jewish zone** (half Jewish and half Arab in population), an **Arab zone** (fully Arab), and an **international zone** around Jerusalem. A **minority** on the committee endorsed a proposal for a single federal state. The UN ultimately **approved the majority's recommendation** (Nov. 29).

Dec. 11. The British announced the timetable for their withdrawal, which was scheduled to be completed on May 15, 1948. A full-blown **CIVIL WAR** immediately erupted **between the Palestinians and the Zionists.** Over the following months, **the British refused to intervene** on behalf of either side and prohibited outside forces from entering Palestine.

During the first months of the civil war, **Zionist forces stayed on the defensive,** protecting Jewish villages from Arab attacks. By April 1948, the **tide had turned** and **the Zionists had seized the offensive,** wresting towns of mixed population, such as Haifa and Jaffa, from Arab control. Throughout the fighting before May 1948, the two sides enjoyed a rough equality in the number of men under arms. But **the Zionists built a far better military organization** and were therefore able to co-ordinate their attacks more effectively. **Palestinian fighters were further weakened by factional squabbles,** which, in a few notable cases, led to battles among their own forces.

1948, April 9. The Dayr Yasin Massacre, in which Jewish terrorists killed 254 Palestinian villagers. Fearing similar incidents, thousands of Palestinians began streaming out of areas under Zionist control.

May 14. Official establishment of the **STATE OF ISRAEL.**

June 30. Departure of the last British troops.

Creation of the **Israeli Defense Forces,** which grew largely out of the **Hagana,** the main Zionist militia during the Mandate. All Israeli men were required to serve for two years of active duty, followed by a long period of reserve duty. Israeli women were subject to a one-year obligation. Terms of active service were later extended by one year (1975) for both sexes.

Founding of **Herut,** the political party of the **Revisionists,** who sought to establish the Jewish state on both banks of the Jordan River. The party, led by **MENACHEM BEGIN,** primarily attracted conservative voters.

1948–49. Flight of approximately **750,000 Arabs** from Israeli territory to surrounding Arab countries.

1948–51. Seven hundred thousand immigrants arrived in Israel, mostly from Eastern Europe and elsewhere in the Middle East. Over the following 40 years, 1951–91, over **1 million more immigrants** entered Israel. **Nearly half** of those who arrived after Israeli independence **came from Asia or Africa,** a far higher percentage than during the interwar period. Ultimately this shift in immigration gave non-Western Jews a greater prominence in Israeli society.

1948–70. AN ECONOMIC BOOM gave Israel the most prosperous economy in the Middle East. During this period, **the GNP rose** at an average rate of 10 percent per year, and **economic growth** was steady, at about 5 percent per year. **Outside contributions** were a major factor in Israel's extraordinary performance and provided nearly all of the funds available for investment (representing about one-quarter of national income annually). Up to 1967, Israel received about $200 million every year from **donations and foreign aid.** The figure jumped to $700 million per year during 1967–73. The **large influx of immigrants,** which kept wages low and the demand for goods and services high, was another stimulus to economic growth. Israel was also blessed with an abundance of highly skilled and educated workers, who boosted the productivity of the economy.

1949. Meeting of **the National Constituent Assembly,** which set up the Israeli political system. The assembly chose not to adopt a constitution, passing only a few founding laws. The major institution was the **KNESSET,** the 120-seat parliament that selected the prime minister and effectively held power. The presidency was a ceremonial office. Voters cast ballots for party lists rather than individual candidates. **Seats in the Knesset** were then distributed to parties according to their percentage of the national vote. All parties that received at least **1 percent of the vote** were entitled to representation. Under such a system, **all governments were necessarily coalitions.**

Jan. 25. Victory of **THE MAPAI PARTY** in Israel's first national elections. **DAVID BEN-GURION** became the first prime minister. He occupied the office for the next 14 years (except for one brief interlude, 1954–55). Until his retirement in 1963, he was unquestionably the most important figure on the political scene. His Mapai Party (founded in 1930) modeled itself after the **socialist parties** of Western Europe.

1950. Passage of the **LAW OF RETURN,** which guaranteed **unimpeded entry and citizenship** to all Jews who wished to immigrate to Israel.

1952, Nov. 9. Death of CHAIM WEIZMANN, one of the founding fathers of the Zionist movement in Palestine and the first president of Israel.

1953, Sept. Passage of the **Rabbinical Courts Jurisdiction Law,** which placed all matters pertaining to **marriage and divorce** under the jurisdiction of rabbinical courts. All Jews, regardless of personal beliefs, were subject to the new law.

1954. Appointment of **Moshe Sharrett** of Mapai as prime minister. He lost his position to Ben-Gurion the following year.

1956. Suez War (p. 966).

1959. Riots broke out among Moroccan Jews **in Haifa,** protesting chronic unemployment and economic neglect. This episode typified the **divisions among Jews** within Israeli society. Jews of European descent **(Ashkenazim)** tended to be wealthier and better educated than "Oriental" Jews of Middle Eastern extraction **(Sephardim).** The latter, on the whole, had lower status and less influence within the wider society.

Creation of the **National Land Authority,** which received all the land formerly held by the Jewish National Fund. The new organiza-

tion, which was operated by the state, managed 92 percent of Israel's land.

1961, April 11. The trial of Nazi war criminal ADOLF EICHMANN opened in Jerusalem after his abduction in Argentina. He was convicted (Dec. 15) of crimes against Jews during World War II and later executed (May 21, 1962).

1963. Appointment of **Levi Eshkol** of Mapai as prime minister.

1964. Formation of **GAHAL,** a conservative alliance built around Herut and the Liberal Party. It quickly emerged as the **principal opposition party.** In 1973, it became known as **LIKUD.**

1966. S. Y. Agnon received the Nobel Prize for literature. He was the first writer of fiction in Hebrew to win the award.

End of West German war reparations, which had provided $125 million per year to the economy.

1967. Six-Day War (p. 967).

June 28. Formal **ANNEXATION OF EAST JERUSALEM,** which was predominantly Arab.

1968, Jan. 21. Formation of the **Israeli LABOR PARTY,** which was built around the old Mapai Party.

1969, March 17. Golda Meir of the Labor Party became Israel's fourth prime minister, after the death of Prime Minister Eshkol (Feb. 26).

1972, May 30. Three Japanese terrorists hired by Palestinian guerrillas killed 28 people at Tel Aviv airport.

Sept. 5. Palestinian terrorists stormed the Israeli dormitory at the Olympic Games in Munich. Eleven Israelis and five terrorists died in the attack and later confrontation with West German police.

1973. October War (p. 967).

1974. Founding of **GUSH EMUNIM,** an ultraconservative political movement that urged the **complete absorption and settlement by Jews of the occupied West Bank.**

April 22. Appointment of **YITZHAK RABIN** of the Labor Party as prime minister.

1976, June 27. A civilian El-Al airliner bound for Tel Aviv **was diverted to Entebbe** (Uganda) by **Palestinian hijackers** who demanded the release of 53 Arab prisoners in Israeli jails. **Israeli commandos** raided the airport (July 4) and liberated the 103 hostages whom the terrorists had not already freed. Four Israelis, seven guerrillas, and 20 Ugandans died during the operation.

1977, June 7. Formation of the **first non-Labor government** in Israeli history. After the triumph of **Likud** in national elections, **MENACHEM BEGIN** became prime minister.

1978. Formation of the **National Guidance Committee** by Palestinian mayors from the West Bank. The organization actively opposed the **Camp David Accords** (p. 924). It was outlawed by Israeli authorities in 1981.

1981, Dec. 14. ANNEXATION OF THE GOLAN HEIGHTS after the Knesset extended Israeli civilian law to the region.

1983, Sept. 21. Formation of a new **Likud government** under **YITZHAK SHAMIR** after Menachem Begin resigned (Sept. 15).

1984, Sept. 14. Formation of a **government of national unity between Likud and the Labor Party.** Shimon Peres and Yitzhak Shamir agreed to split the term for prime minister. Peres took office for the first half. Shamir assumed the duties of premier on Oct. 10, 1986.

1987, Dec. 9. Beginning of the **INTIFADA,** a widespread **movement of protests by Palestinians in the West Bank and Gaza Strip.** The harsh treatment of demonstrators by Israeli authorities won worldwide sympathy for the Palestinian cause.

1988, April 18. An Israeli court convicted John Demjanjuk—who was believed to be the Nazi death-camp executioner "Ivan the Terrible"—of war crimes and sentenced him to death. After years of appeals, the Israeli Supreme Court overturned the verdict (April 1993).

Aug. 18. Public announcement of the formation of **HAMAS, a radical Palestinian group** in the occupied territories. Hamas, which espoused an Islamic ideology, opposed negotiations with Israel and quickly established itself as **the PLO's most dangerous rival.**

Nov. 1. General elections returned a **government of national unity** to power. However, the balance within the Knesset tilted slightly in favor of the Likud bloc over Labor. **Yitzhak Shamir** remained as prime minister.

Dec. 7. Yasir Arafat publicly announced **the PLO's recognition of Israel.**

1990, March 21. Shimon Peres became prime minister of the government of national unity but soon relinquished the post to his Likud rival **Yitzhak Shamir** (April 26).

1991, Oct. 27. Israeli authorities granted free access to scholars who wished to study the **Dead Sea Scrolls,** but retained some restrictions on the use of the documents.

1992, June 23. The Labor coalition won national elections that were widely viewed as an **endorsement of peace talks** with the PLO. The new leader of the Labor Party, **Yitzhak Rabin,** took office as prime minister on July 2.

1993, Sept. 13. Formal signing by Israeli and PLO officials of THE DECLARATION OF PRINCIPLES AND MUTUAL RECOGNITION. The accord was worked out in **secret negotiations** in Norway during the spring and summer of 1993. It called for **interim self-rule** (originally scheduled for Dec. 13, but later delayed) for **the Gaza Strip and** the West Bank town of **Jericho.** Both sides agreed to determine the final status of the occupied territories in negotiations over the next five years.

Oct. 2. Meeting in Washington, D.C., in which Foreign Minister Peres and Crown Prince Hassan of Jordan announced the establishment of a joint economic committee.

1994, Jan. 10. Israel and the PLO resumed peace talks regarding the West Bank and the Gaza Strip. The PLO signed an economic pact with Jordan providing for a Jordanian financial role in developing the Palestinian regions. The **Syrian president Hafez al-Assad** also **endorsed the Israel-PLO accord.** On Feb. 9 **Israel and the PLO signed accords to further implement Arab self-rule on the Gaza Strip** and the West Bank city of Jericho.

Feb. 24. An Israeli settler launched a rifle attack in a mosque in Hebron, killing 40 Muslims and wounding 150.

March 21. The PLO and Israel agreed to reopen their talks. They set terms for the release of Palestinian prisoners and allowed for Palestinian police in the Gaza Strip and Jericho.

May 4. Israel and the PLO ratified an accord implementing some Palestinian self rule in the Gaza Strip and Jericho. They also signed an economic accord giving these territories some economic autonomy.

May 18. Israel totally withdrew from Gaza and Jericho and Palestinian police came in.

May 20. Muslim militants killed a group of Israeli soldiers at a Gaza checkpoint. Arafat announced that Israeli laws no longer applied in Jericho or the Gaza Strip.

June 6. The **peace talks between Israel and Jordan,** which had stopped because of the massacre at Hebron, **resumed.**

July 1. Arafat visited the Gaza Strip and Jericho for the first time in 27 years.

Oct. 14. Arafat, Rabin, and Israeli foreign minister Shimon Peres won the Nobel Peace Prize.

Nov. 30. The World Bank and 22 countries met in Belgium and decided to give more than 200 million dollars in economic aid to the **Palestinian National Authority (PNA).**

1995, March 14. Israel resumed formal peace talks with Syria in Washington, D.C. at the urging of U.S. secretary of state Warren Christopher.

April 9. After two terrorist car bombs in the Gaza Strip killed 8, Arafat called for a crackdown on terrorism.

Sept. 24. Israel and the PLO reached an agreement for Israeli withdrawal from additional territories in the West Bank. **On Oct. 10 Israel released approximately 900 Palestinian prisoners and began to withdraw from Palestinian towns.**

Nov. 4. Yitzhak Rabin was assassinated by Yigal Amir, a Jewish right-wing extremist opposing the peace process. The assassination occurred at a peace rally in Tel-Aviv. Shimon Peres stepped in as the acting prime minister.

Dec. 11. Israeli troops pulled out of Nablus, the West Bank's largest city. On Dec. 27 Israel and Syria reopened peace talks.

1996, Jan. 20. Arafat won the Palestinian presidency in what was considered an **affirmation of the peace process.** On Feb. 11 Peres called for early elections for Israel's prime minister and Parliament. On Feb. 27 two suicide bombings by Hamas killed 27 Israelis. A summit of 27 world leaders met in Egypt (March 13) to lend support to the peace process and condemn terrorism; 14 Arab nations participated. On April

24 the PLO's parliamentary body eliminated the specifically anti-Israel clauses in its charter.

May 29. Benjamin Netanyahu of the right-wing Likud Party became the new **prime minister of Israel.** Netanyahu visited the U.S. (July 9) and delivered a speech emphasizing his concern with security in the peace negotiations. On Aug. 27 the Israeli government approved plans to **expand Jewish settlement in the West Bank, precipitating an Aug. 29 strike by Palestinians across that area.**

Sept. 4. Netanyahu met with Arafat in a symbolic gesture to reopen PLO-Israeli talks.

Sept. 25–26. **Riots in the West Bank and Gaza Strip** were precipitated by the opening of a tunnel in Jerusalem by Israelis, marking the **worst Palestinian-Israeli violence in three years.**

Oct. 2. Netanyahu and Arafat conducted a 2-week emergency summit in Washington, setting dates for new talks but leaving important issues unresolved.

1997, Jan. 5. Israel and the Palestinians reached an accord on the Israeli pullout from Hebron with the help of King Hussein of Jordan.

Feb. 26. The Israeli cabinet approved the development of a Jewish neighborhood in East Jerusalem, despite Palestinian and international protest. Israeli-Palestinian **talks reached an impasse** over the issue (April 3). Netanyahu refused to compromise. King Hussein of Jordan asked the U.S. to intervene. On May 6 Israeli president **Weizman met with Arafat** in an attempt to put an end to the impasse.

July 30. Thirteen Israelis were killed in suicide bombings by Hamas in West Jerusalem. Netanyahu declared his refusal to comply with American and Jordanian appeals to ease sanctions on Palestinians.

Aug. 20. Israeli war planes launched attacks against sites in Lebanon.

Sept. 4. Three suicide bombers killed four Jewish civilians in West Jerusalem. Hamas claimed responsibility. The Palestinian National Authority decried the attack.

Sept. 25. Israel attempted to assassinate a Hamas leader in Jordan, sparking international outrage. To appease Jordan, Israel released 20 Palestinian and Jordanian prisoners.

Oct. 21. Israel resumed talks with the Palestine National Authority.

1998, Feb. 24. In a sharp setback for Jordanian-Israeli relations, Israel's central intelligence chief Maj. Gen. Danny Yatom resigned after admitting serious mistakes made during the Sept. 1997 mission to assassinate Palestinian Islamic leader Khaled Meshal while he was on Jordanian soil.

Oct. 23. Israel and the Palestinian National Authority signed the Wye River Accords as U.S. president Clinton, Netanyahu, King Hussein of Jordan, and Yasir Arafat met to discuss peace in the Middle East. Approved by the Israeli parliament (known as the Knesset) in a Nov. 17 vote, the accords established that Israel would free 750 Palestinian prisoners and that the PNA would remove clauses from the PLO charter that called for the destruction of Israel. Following the agreement, Israeli military forces withdrew from 13.1 percent of the West Bank. This was the first step in a year-long plan to gradually transfer control of the area to Palestinian leadership.

Dec. 21. Israel's parliament voted to dissolve itself and called for early elections in the spring of 1999. The collapse of Netanyahu's government had been impending throughout 1998.

1999, March 26. The EU declared in a summit that in due course the Palestinians had a right to a future state.

May 17. Netanyahu lost to Ehud Barak, the head of the Center-Left One Israel coalition of parties.

Sept. 5. In an attempt to revive the Oct. 1998 accords brokered in the U.S. by Pres. Clinton at Wye River, Md., it was planned that 40 percent of the West Bank was to be handed over to Palestinians by Jan. 2000. The accord was signed and revived peace talks between Israel and Palestine. It established a Sept. 2000 deadline for a final peace agreement; simultaneously, 200 Palestinian prisoners were released.

Nov. 2. Barak, Arafat, and Clinton met in Oslo, Norway. This was the first meeting in 11 months for Israel, the Palestinian National Authority, and the United States.

2000, May 24. With the initiative of Barak's new government, Israel completed its withdrawal from Lebanon after occupying the southern part of that country for 22 years.

July 11–25. A two-week-long summit was arranged by Pres. Clinton at Camp David, Maryland, but the talks ended without a final peace agreement. The unresolved conflict was over the status of Jerusalem, which Israel claimed in its entirety. Palestinians demanded East Jerusalem as the capital of a future Palestinian state.

Sept. 6–8. More than 150 world leaders met at the Millennium Summit, where Middle East peace was a primary topic of discussion. This conference marked the largest gathering of heads of state in world history.

Sept. 28. The worst Israeli-Palestinian violence since 1996 erupted after right-wing Israeli politician Ariel Sharon visited the Temple Mount in old Jerusalem, considered sacred by Israelis and Palestinians.

Nov. 9. Arafat, Barak, and Clinton met in Washington, D.C. to discuss violence that had escalated since September. No substantial progress was made in the discussions. As the talks closed, veteran U.S. Middle East mediator Dennis Ross announced that he would resign in January 2001. The fall 2000 violence was among the worst seen in the region for several years. By late December, over 340 had died in the fighting.

Nov. 28. After only 17 months of his four-year term, Prime Minister Ehud Barak told Israel's parliament that he was prepared to dissolve the government and hold new elections in the spring of 2001. Five related motions passed through the Knesset, and Barak's idea was carried out. His government had failed as a result of renewed violence with the PNA and a subsequent drop in popular support. Palestinian leader Yasir Arafat rejected a new peace deal two days later because it did not address the problems of East Jerusalem and the right of return for Palestinian refugees.

h. JORDAN

(From p. 764)

1946, March 22. A treaty between Britain and Transjordan ensured the continued dependence of Transjordan on Britain. The terms of the pact guaranteed **British command of the Arab Legion** and the maintenance of **bases for British forces.** In return, the British agreed to pay **financial subsidies** to the Transjordanian government.

May 25. Proclamation of the kingdom of Transjordan. It was renamed **THE HASHEMITE KINGDOM OF JORDAN** on June 2, 1949.

1948–67. Expansion of the Arab Legion from 6,000 to 65,000 soldiers.

1948, March 15. Another **Anglo-Jordanian treaty** established a joint defense board and further restricted British influence within the Jordanian government.

1949–61. Decline of nomadism. The beduin population fell from about 200,000 to 56,000.

1950, April 25. Opening session of the **Jordanian Parliament,** half of whose delegates represented constituencies from the West Bank. One of the first acts of the assembly was to **merge the West Bank with Jordan.** By this one stroke, **the Jordanian population nearly tripled** to 1.5 million. Only half a million of the population was properly Jordanian, residing east of the Jordan River; the remainder consisted of Palestinians, one half of whom were refugees from Israeli territory. Abdullah's government made the additional gesture of **offering Jordanian citizenship to Palestinians** everywhere. Jordan was the only Arab state to do so.

1951, July 20. ASSASSINATION OF KING ABDULLAH by a Palestinian in Jerusalem outside al-Aqsa Mosque. He was succeeded by his son, **Talal.**

1952. Promulgation of a **constitution.** Jordan received a bicameral legislature: a lower house of 40 elected deputies (half from the West Bank) and an upper house appointed by the king. The cabinet was responsible only to Parliament. In practice, most members of Parliament invariably stood behind the king, who retained considerable influence.

Aug. 11. Parliament declared **Talal unfit to rule** due to his poor mental health. His son, **HUSAYN,** was designated the successor upon reaching adulthood.

1953, May 2. On his 18th birthday, **Husayn** officially became **king of Jordan.**

1956, March 1. Dismissal of **GEN. JOHN GLUBB,** commander of the **Arab Legion.** The move was an attempt to pacify opposition groups that had staged violent demonstrations (Jan. 1956).

1957, Feb. 12. Termination of the Anglo-Jordanian treaty.

April. Dismissal of the government (elected in Oct. 1956) of **Sulayman al-Nablusi,** a prominent opposition figure. Political parties were outlawed, and the new government decreed martial law. **King Husayn** quickly conducted a **purge** of pro-Egyptian and pro-Syrian officers from **the army.**

1962. Opening of the **University of Amman.**

1967, June. About 350,000 **Palestinian refugees** arrived in the aftermath of **the second Arab-Israeli War.** Another 65,000 immigrated to Jordan (1967–89).

1970, Sept. 16. CIVIL WAR began after the **Jordanian army** attacked **Palestinian guerrilla camps** inside Jordan. The Jordanian government had been growing increasingly nervous about the disruptive role that the Palestinians might be willing to play in Jordanian politics. **The guerrillas,** who received active support from Syria, **were gradually defeated** and by July 1971 had been completely expelled.

1971. King Husayn declared the **Jordanian National Union** as the only legal political party.

1972. Jordan became the first Arab state to broadcast on two television channels.

1974. Indefinite suspension of Parliament.

1978. Creation of the **National Consultative Council** (60 appointed members), which took the place of the dissolved Parliament.

Sept. 23. Following a meeting between King Husayn and PLO chairman Yasir Arafat, the PLO was allowed to reopen its Jordanian offices.

1980. Jordan publicly backed Iraq in the Iran-Iraq War (p. 968). Throughout the 1980s, Jordan benefited immensely from its economic ties with Iraq. In particular, Jordan's port of **Aqaba** served Iraq as a vital outlet to the outside world.

1984, Jan. 5. Restoration of Parliament.

1988, July 31. Jordan formally agreed to sever all legal and administrative links with the Israeli-occupied West Bank. The move paved the way for Jordanian recognition of the **PLO's ambition to set up an independent Palestinian state** in the region.

1989, April. Violent protests swept through Jordanian cities after the announcement of price increases.

Nov. 8. First general elections since 1967. Islamic groups, led by **the Muslim Brotherhood,** won 37 of the 80 available seats.

1990, Dec. 26. Passage of a new law that made male and female inheritance shares equal.

1990–91. Jordan took a precarious diplomatic stand during **THE GULF WAR** (p. 969). **It opposed the Iraqi invasion** and annexation of Kuwait but insisted that the crisis be resolved through **diplomatic means.** In the West, the Jordanian position was generally perceived as sympathetic to Iraq. The Jordanian public overwhelmingly supported the Iraqi cause and saw the war as an attempt to humiliate the Arabs.

1992, July 5. Parliament formally lifted the ban on political parties imposed by King Husayn 36 years earlier.

1993, Sept. 14. Jordanian and Israeli officials concluded a framework for peace in Washington, D.C. The signing paved the way for the eventual establishment of normal ties between the two countries, which technically remained at war with each other.

1994, July 25. King Hussein signed a pact with Premier Yitzhak Rabin of Israel declaring the official end of the 46-year state of war between their countries and a move toward the establishment of peace.

Aug. 8. Jordan and Israel opened a border crossing north of the Gulf of Aqaba.

Oct. 17. Israel and Jordan signed an informal pact establishing full and normal diplomatic relations and increased commercial ties.

Oct. 26. The two countries **signed a formal peace treaty.**

1995, May 4. Jordan signed a pact with the Palestinian National Authority to increase trade between Jordan and the Palestinian territories.

1998, July 5. Jordan's king Hussein met with Egyptian president Hosui Mubarak and Palestinian leader Yasir Arafat in Cairo, Egypt, to discuss unilateral boundary changes in the Middle East.

Oct. 20–23. Jordan's king Hussein was invited to Camp David in Maryland to discuss peace issues and intervene in the talks between Israel and the Palestinian National Authority that had been unraveling during the previous week. Hussein helped Israeli prime minister Benjamin Netanyahu and PNA president Yasir Arafat to complete the signing of the Wye Memorandum, an accord aimed at establishing compromises between the PNA and Israel.

1999, Feb. 7. King Hussein died in his 46th year as Jordan's monarch. Hussein's eldest son, Abdullah, took the monarch's oath before Parliament just hours after his father's death.

July. The IAF won a majority of council seats in three of Jordan's major cities. The IAF was a political extension of the pan-Arab Muslim Brotherhood.

i. IRAQ

(From p. 766)

1945–46. An attempt at **political liberalization.** The government tolerated the **formation of opposition parties,** the most notable of which were **the Istiqlal Party and the National Democratic Party.** Both parties were left-wing organizations whose constituencies, confined to urban and educated classes, left them with a narrow base of support. Labor unrest and, above all, the wariness and insecurity of the political establishment led ultimately to the **failure of the liberalization policy.**

1948, Jan. Widespread **popular demonstrations,** known as the *wathba* (uprising). The protests were sparked by the announcement of **the Portsmouth Treaty** with Britain (Jan. 15), a renegotiated version of the 1930 treaty. **The British agreed to remove their troops** from Iraq and **gave up** sovereignty over their **two air bases** in Iraq, but they still retained a voice in Iraqi military planning and remained as the sole supplier of training and equipment to the Iraqi army. Together with Britain's role in the escalating Palestine crisis, **the treaty roused nationalist opposition** in Iraq and failed to win popular approval. The political crisis was compounded by **economic difficulties** in the wake of a bad harvest, bread shortages, and accelerating inflation. In the end, the cabinet fell, and **the treaty was never ratified.**

1949. Failure of negotiations to unify Iraq and Syria. The attempt was largely inspired by the ambitions of the regent, Abd al-Ilah. An attempt to revive the project in 1953 came to nothing.

1950. Establishment of the **Development Board,** made possible by the recent increase in oil revenues. Most projects were devoted to **agricultural improvements.** Communications and transportation were of secondary priority, and industry received the least amount of funding.

1950–52. New agreements with the **Iraq Petroleum Company.** The first (1950) substantially raised Iraqi royalties, and the second (1952) gave Iraq half the profits.

1951. **Flight of nearly the entire Jewish community** (over 130,000) **to Israel.** The emigrés were forced to leave their assets behind (estimated at over $150 million).

1952. Formation of **THE BA'TH PARTY,** which was committed to the cause of **pan-Arabism.** Before 1958 the party attracted only a handful of political activists.

Nov. 23. Appointment of a **military government** and the outlawing of all political parties. A series of strikes and riots earlier in the year had led to the breakdown of order. The military regime organized **new elections** and stepped down on Jan. 22, 1953.

1954, Aug. A series of decrees issued by the cabinet under **NURI AL-SA'ID** effectively outlawed all organized opposition, which was driven underground until the revolution of 1958.

1956, May 2. The first Middle Eastern television station began broadcasting to the Baghdad area.

1958, May 12. Ratification of a **union between Jordan and Iraq,** modeled on the United Arab Republic, comprising Egypt and Syria.

July 14. THE IRAQI REVOLUTION. An **army coup brought GEN. ABD AL-KARIM QASIM to power.** The revolutionaries **dissolved the monarchy** and executed the royal family, including the king, **Faysal II.** Other notables, such as **Nuri al-Sa'id,** were rounded up and put to death.

Qasim's government was confined to a tight circle of **military officers.** Outside the army, his **only reliable ally** was the **Iraqi Communist Party,** which never received any appreciable power. His enemies generally came from the ranks of Arab nationalists, Nasserite groups, and the Ba'th Party.

1958. LAND REFORM and social programs. Among the permanent achievements of the revolution was a large **shift in government spending** from agricultural projects to urban programs. Expenditures on health, education, and housing all rose rapidly (if taken together, their

portion of the budget doubled). The government also imposed controls on prices and ceilings on rents, enormously boosting its popularity among the urban poor.

The most dramatic policy of Qasim's government was **LAND REFORM** (2 percent of all landowners possessed 68 percent of the land in 1958). In broad outline, Iraqi policy imitated the earlier Egyptian example. The government capped the amount of land an individual could own at 250 hectares for irrigated land and 500 for rain-fed tracts. Owners received compensation for expropriated land (over 1 million hectares by 1964), which was parceled out to peasants in small plots (12 hectares for irrigated land, 23 for rain-fed). As in Egypt, peasants were required to join **agricultural cooperatives,** but the government originally lacked the means to implement this measure. Later regimes passed further reforms. In 1969–70, ceilings on land ownership were lowered, and compensation was no longer offered. During the following decade, the government encouraged the establishment of **collectivized farms.** Disillusioned with the results of state farming, **policy in the 1980s veered back to support for private cultivation.** All state-owned farms were subsequently liquidated (1987).

In the long term, the **biggest success** of land reform was the **massive redistribution of the land.** Whereas only 15 percent of the agricultural population had owned land in 1958, the figure had reached 95 percent as early as 1971. Regarding production, however, land reform was a disappointment. An exporter of food in 1958, Iraq was devoting 15 percent of its imports by 1982 to purchases of food. Moreover, agriculture's share of GNP declined from 17 percent (1960) to 8 percent (1980).

1958–83. Doubling of the population, from 7 million to 14 million. During the same period, the percentage of Iraqis residing in towns soared from about 37 percent to 75 percent. Baghdad swelled from 1 million to 4 million inhabitants, and Mosul and Basra each acquired populations of over 1 million.

1958–83. Expansion of the educational system overall registered huge gains. The number of elementary school students rose from 500,000 to 2.6 million. For secondary schools, the figures leaped from 74,000 to 1 million; and for higher education, the number of students increased from 8,500 to over 120,000. By 1980, nearly all eligible Iraqi children attended elementary school, and about 60 percent of them moved on to secondary school. **Literacy rates** reflected the advances in education, rising from 15 percent (1958) to 50 percent (1977).

1958–88. Expansion of the army. From 1958 to 1974, military spending rose from 7 percent to 19 percent of GNP, and the size of the army grew from 50,000 to 200,000. The **Iran-Iraq War** (1980–88) generated another wave of expansion, and at the close of the war Iraq claimed a regular army of 950,000, supplemented by a popular army of 250,000.

1959. Appointment of **Naziha Dulaymi** as minister of municipalities. She became the **first Arab woman to hold a ministerial position** in government. Most Arab countries later adopted the practice of including at least one woman in government cabinets, usually in posts for education, health, and social welfare.

Dec. 30. Promulgation of **a code of Personal Status** that was much more radical than drafts proposed intermittently since 1947. Among its chief provisions were laws improving the **status of women,** new regulations for **marriage and divorce,** and reforms of **inheritance laws.**

1961, Sept. Iraqi offensive against **KURDISH REBELS** in northern Iraq. The Kurds, represented by **the Kurdish Democratic Party (KDP),** had demanded economic and cultural concessions from Baghdad (e.g., more investment in the north and official status for the Kurdish language). After repeated failures to reach a negotiated settlement, **the government outlawed the KDP** and sent troops to Kurdistan, where tribal rebels under **MUSTAFA AL-BARZANI** had declared a Kurdish state. A split appeared among Kurdish ranks after the formation of the **Patriotic Union of Kurdistan** (1964) by the former leaders of the KDP. Nevertheless, with the help of arms supplied from Iran, **Barzani's forces** retained their position as the **strongest Kurdish faction.** Hostilities temporarily ended after the negotiation (1970) of limited autonomy, the recognition of Kurdish as an official language, and political concessions such as the appointment of a Kurdish vice president.

1963, Feb. 8–9. MILITARY COUP. Qasim was **overthrown and executed by an alliance of discontented army officers and radicals from the Ba'th Party.** An uneasy coalition, in which the Ba'th had a large and somewhat exaggerated presence, governed the country for another nine months.

Nov. 18. A SECOND COUP, led by PRES. ABD AL-SALAM ARIF, overthrew the government and reduced the power of the Ba'th Party. **Few political institutions were established.** No constitution was issued, no parliament was created, and few political parties were tolerated. Arif's power depended mainly on support from army officers (less so after Sept. 1965), government officials, and friends and relatives who were appointed to high positions. He died in an airplane crash (April 13, 1966) and was succeeded as president by his brother, **Abd al-Rahman Arif,** who exercised power in roughly the same manner.

1964. Death of poet Badr Shakir al-Sayyid (b. 1926), one of the originators of Arabic free verse.

July. Announcement of a large-scale **NATIONALIZATION PROGRAM** in which **the state seized all banks and insurance companies.** The state also nationalized several industries, including tobacco processing and cement, and partly extended its control into textile and flour production. **The switch to a planned economy** was designed to encourage rapid development, meet the high demand for public sector jobs, and mold Iraq in Egypt's image in order to facilitate a desired union. Despite the public transition to a socialist economy in 1964, the movement did not gather speed until the **Ba'th regime** came to power in 1968. By 1977, the **state sector** was responsible for creating 80 percent of Iraq's gross domestic product (up from 31 percent in 1968). In addition, the state employed 261,000 Iraqis by 1973 (compared to a mere 27,000 in 1957); by 1978, over 20 percent of the country's workers held jobs with the state.

July 17. A MILITARY COUP deposed Pres. Arif. The main plotters were army officers and members of **the Ba'th Party. A second coup** (July 30) eliminated the army officers from the government. The Ba'th Party—a small, exclusive, and secretive organization—emerged as the sole master of the regime. **Ahmad Hasan al-Bakr** assumed office as president, prime minister, and commander in chief. The Ba'th announced a **constitution** (1970) that advocated Arab socialism and Islam, though in practice the latter was neglected until the outbreak of the Iran-Iraq War (1980). Within the party, leadership became increasingly concentrated in the hands of a **small clique** originating from the town of **Takrit** along the Tigris River.

1969. Founding of **al-Da'wa al-Islamiyya,** a Shi'ite religious party hostile to the Ba'th regime. Backed by Iran, the party in 1982 helped to carry out armed operations against the government. A number of party leaders who had not yet fled Iraq were arrested, and some were executed.

1972. Signing of 15-year **treaty of friendship** with the **Soviet Union.**

June 1. NATIONALIZATION OF THE OIL INDUSTRY. The move came after more than a decade of wrangling between the Iraqi government and Western oil companies, in particular, **the Iraq Petroleum Company.** Until the start of the Iran-Iraq War, Iraq enjoyed a **tremendous oil boom** and became highly dependent upon its earnings from oil. Most of the additional revenues were channeled into **heavy industries,** such as steel, iron, and petrochemicals, and into the development of Iraq's infrastructure. The **service sector** was another favored area of the economy. By 1979, Iraq ranked second in production of oil among Gulf states. Oil revenues provided 98 percent of foreign exchange and 90 percent of total revenues. The Iran-Iraq War (p. 968) cut these revenues in half.

1974. Resumption of **fighting in Kurdistan.** The agreement of 1970 was undermined by disputes between Baghdad and Kurdish insurgents over the precise boundaries of the Kurdish autonomous zone, the status of the Kirkuk oil fields, and the scheduled integration of Kurdish forces into the Iraqi army. The **Kurdish resistance received a severe setback when Iran cut its flow of weapons** to the rebels following the **Algiers agreement** of 1975. Government troops occupied most of Kurdistan, implemented the 1970 accord on its own terms, and opened the region to economic reform and development. **Kurdish separatism** revived during the Iran-Iraq War but was again smothered once that conflict came to a close.

1979, July 16. Resignation of **Pres. Ahmad Hasan al-Bakr,** ostensibly due to poor health. His successor was **SADDAM HUSSEIN.**

1980. Formation of the National Assembly. Kurdish regions in the north were granted an additional assembly.

1981, June 7. Destruction of Iraq's Osirak nuclear reactor by Israeli jets.

1984, Jan. 31. Agreement with Jordan to build an **oil pipeline** costing $1 billion. Iraq began exporting oil from Aqaba in April.

March 19. Signing of a treaty that permanently fixed the border with Jordan.

1990, April 2. Iraq admitted to possessing binary chemical weapons.

1991, Oct. The Iraqi Kurdish Front, allied with Turkey, staged an offensive against PKK forces (Kurdish rebels from Turkey) stationed in northern Iraq. The PKK retreated to Iranian territory.

1992, Aug. 26. The U.S. imposed a **"no-fly zone"** in Iraqi territory south of the 32d parallel. Iraq was barred from flying fixed-wing aircraft into the designated area. The U.S. justified the measure as necessary for the protection of Iraq's **Shi'ite population** in the south. Since the U.S. had already carved out a haven for the **Kurds** in the north (p. 969), the authority of the Baghdad regime was now confined essentially to central Iraq.

1994, May 9. Saddam Hussein fired the Iraqi premier and appointed himself to the position, saying he wanted to help alleviate the economic crisis.

Oct. 15. The UN voted to condemn the buildup of Iraqi troops along the Kuwaiti border. **U.S. troops were put in place to defend Kuwait.**

1995, Aug. 8. Two top Iraqi military leaders, both sons-in-law of Saddam, defected to Jordan because of **turmoil within Saddam's government.** They called for his ousting.

1996, May 20. Iraq signed a **deal with the UN allowing Iraq to export oil** in hopes of **alleviating its tremendous food shortage;** this represents the **first easing of sanctions since 1990.**

Sept. 3–4. The **U.S. launched missile attacks on Iraqi military sites** to counter Iraq's recent moves against the Kurds in northern Iraq.

Dec. 9. The UN trade embargo on Iraq was eased, and **Iraq reentered the global oil market.**

1997, Nov. 20. After a threat of military action by the U.S. and Britain, Iraq allowed UN arms inspectors to return to inspect various weapons manufacturing sites.

1998, Feb. 22. Under substantial military pressure from the U.S., Iraq accepted UN terms of peace brought to Baghdad by UN Sec. Gen. Kofi Annan. However, over the course of the following months, Iraq continued to impede UN weapons inspections teams. Saddam completely terminated the inspections in August; Iraqi cooperation came only after an Oct. 31 threat of military retaliation by the U.S. and Britain.

Nov. 14. Iraq agreed to cooperate unconditionally with UN inspectors if the U.S. and Britain would agree to call off military strikes.

Dec. 16–19. Conflict between the UN and Iraq resumed as Iraq once again resisted weapons inspections. This culminated in severe U.S. and British air attacks and bombing of Iraqi military targets. During the next two years, U.S. and British warplanes recurrently carried out air strikes on Iraq. Attacks focused on command centers, missile factories, airfields, and other targets which, if destroyed, would deplete an Iraqi weapons buildup. The goal of low-level warfare was to injure Iraq's military capabilities and possibly instigate an overthrow of Saddam.

2000, March 27. National Assembly elections were held, but the only candidates allowed to run were members of the National Progressive Front and non-partisans supporting the Ba'th government.

Sept. 4. Iraq committed the first violation in 10 years of Saudi air space with its planes. It was suspected that Saddam was trying to provoke a U.S. response. Iraq was still uncooperative and continued to resist the new UN Monitoring Verification and Inspection Commission (UNMOVIC) inspections team of the UN, claiming that the U.S. and Britain would have to cease air attacks before inspectors would be allowed into the country. Severe economic sanctions continued, but oil-for-food trading resumed in 2000.

j. SAUDI ARABIA

(From p. 766)

1953, Nov. 9. Death of **ABD AL-AZIZ IBN SA'UD.** His oldest son, **Sa'ud,** ascended the throne.

Creation of a full-fledged **cabinet.** Before World War II, there had been only two government ministers, one for foreign affairs and the other for finance. Posts for defense (1944) and the interior (1952) later appeared, and in 1953 the number of ministers was expanded to ten.

Princes from the **royal family** assumed nearly all the positions, confirming **Saudi dominance** over the central government.

1958–64. STRUGGLE FOR POWER between KING SA'UD and his brother, FAYSAL. The latter held effective power for most of this period (1958–60 and 1962–64) as the prime minister. The rivalry centered on the **future direction of the Saudi government.** Sa'ud believed that a loose confederation of tribes, as in the past, was the best system. Faysal, on the other hand, argued that the Saudi government had to be radically reorganized into a modern state, which would be better able to manage the economy and society in an era of abundant oil wealth.

1964–86. Expansion of the armed forces. The army grew from 12,000 to 40,000 and was complemented by the National Guard, primarily recruited from among tribesmen and standing at around 23,000 in 1982. The government also built a highly trained **air force** whose membership reached 14,000.

1964–89. Expansion of the educational system. The total number of students increased from a little over 200,000 to about 2.2 million.

1964, Nov. ABDICATION OF SA'UD. After a palace revolution, his brother, **FAYSAL, became the new Saudi king.** Faysal embarked on policies that transformed the Saudi government into a **modern state.** One of the peculiar features of the Saudi state was the overwhelming presence of the **Saudi royal family**, which numbered some 20,000 individuals by the 1980s. Saudi princes and their relatives filled the central and provincial governments, the upper echelons of the bureaucracy, and the armed forces.

1975, March 25. ASSASSINATION OF KING FAYSAL by his nephew. He was succeeded by his half brother **KHALID IBN ABD AL-AZIZ.**

1979, Nov. 20. Occupation of the Great Mosque in Mecca by religious militants and Utayba tribesmen. The protesters wanted an Islamic state on the Iranian model and objected to the loose and ostentatious lifestyle of the royal family. **Rioting** broke out concurrently in the Province of **Hasa**, which held a large portion of Saudi oil reserves and a substantial population of Shi'ites. These disturbances were quelled with little violence. In Mecca, **security forces** besieged the Great Mosque for over two weeks before the surviving insurgents finally surrendered (Dec. 5).

1982. Death of King Khalid, who was succeeded by his half brother **FAHD.**

1987, July 30. Death in Mecca of over 400 Muslim pilgrims, most of them Iranian. The pilgrims lost their lives in political demonstrations that degenerated into violent clashes with Saudi security forces.

1989, Dec. 23. An agreement between Saudi Arabia and Oman formally fixed the border between the two countries. The settlement followed armed clashes along the border in October.

1993, Aug. 20. A royal decree established a **consultative council,** the first legislative institution in the history of the Saudi kingdom. The 60-seat council, whose members were appointed by the king, was granted no real power and could not pass legislation.

1996, June 25. A bomb exploded in Saudi Arabia, killing 19 U.S. troops.

1998. The first recession in 6 years occurred as Saudi Arabia's oil income fell by 40 percent following a worldwide petroleum price reduction.

2000, Sept. At $35 per barrel, world oil prices reached their highest level in ten years. Throughout the year 2000, OPEC nations had limited their supply of petroleum worldwide.

k. NORTH AND SOUTH YEMEN

(From p. 766)

1948. ASSASSINATION OF THE IMAM YAHYA in North Yemen, as part of an attempted coup. The insurgents failed to seize power after about a month of fighting. Afterward, the shaken government, led by Yahya's son **AHMAD,** promulgated a **constitution.**

1950. Founding of the **Aden Association.** The leaders of this movement called for a transition to self-government within the **Aden Colony.** The leadership was drawn mainly from the prosperous merchant class of the port of Aden, which was flourishing because of greatly increased commercial traffic.

1952. Founding of the **South Arabian League,** consisting of notables from South Yemen who desired a greater measure of autonomy from the British.

1955. Attempted coup in North Yemen. A **coalition of opposition factions** drawn from sections of the military, the sayyids (descendants of the prophet Muhammad), and radical dissidents tried to take power. Their defeat was largely a result of a **military alliance** between the tribes and the imam.

1956. Creation of the **Aden Trades Union Congress.** This organization had its roots among the middle and working classes of the colony of Aden. Its program demanded the independence of South Yemen and its unification with North Yemen.

1959. Introduction of a **legislative council** in Aden. Membership was dominated by the great merchant families.

Creation of an **11-state federation of local tribal rulers** in the western portion of South Yemen. Aden itself joined the union (1962), which was named the Protectorate of Southern Arabia.

1959–60. Suppression of tribal rebellion among northern tribes in North Yemen. Several leaders were executed, permanently antagonizing the vanquished tribes.

1962. Appearance in South Yemen of the **People's Socialist Party,** which drew its strength from trade union activism. In 1965, this party lost its leading role among workers to the **Organization for the Liberation of the Occupied South.**

Sept. CIVIL WAR and the end of the Imamate. Imam Ahmad died (Sept. 18), and several days later (Sept. 26) a **MILITARY COUP** took place. The leaders, who had belonged to the **Free Officers' Association,** overthrew Ahmad's successor, **Imam Muhammad al-Badr,** and announced the establishment of a republic.

The civil war was fought by **two main factions,** both of which received outside assistance. The **republican side** consisted primarily of army officers, intellectuals, townsmen, and the majority of the Shafi'i population. Arrayed against them were the **royalists:** the Hamid al Din family under Imam Muhammad al-Badr, a large number of sayyids, and most of the Zaydi tribes. Royalist forces were able to rely on large amounts of **Saudi financial assistance** and the expertise of **military advisers sent from Jordan.** The republicans countered with **Egyptian troops,** which first arrived in Nov. 1964 (later peaking at 60,000). The war lasted over six years during which the royalists held the advantage, particularly after the **Egyptian withdrawal** (completed in Dec. 1967). But the tide turned at the very end when San'a, the capital, survived a protracted siege (1968) from royalist tribes. The republican government then negotiated a **settlement** with tribal leaders (1970).

1963. Founding of **the National Liberation Front (NLF) in South Yemen.** This party originally was an alliance of tribal groups and members of the radicalized urban population. Its ideology was pan-Arab, socialist, and anti-imperialist. From the time of a rural uprising in Radfan in 1963, the NLF was able to establish itself as the dominant political group in the countryside.

1964. British promise of independence to South Yemen by 1968. In Feb. 1966, the British reaffirmed this pledge and promised also to close their military base in Aden.

1966. Formation of **the Federation for the Liberation of South Yemen (FLOSY),** a brief alliance between the NLF and the Organization for the Liberation of the Occupied South. FLOSY's main goal was the independence of South Yemen. The NLF left the alliance at the end of 1966.

1967–86. Growth of the South Yemeni population from 1.5 million to 2.4 million. Aden was the biggest city and held some 350,000 inhabitants by the mid-1980s. About 38 percent of the total population was urban, and another 10 percent remained nomadic.

1967–80. Expansion of the educational system in South Yemen. The number of schools increased from 65,000 to 270,000. General literacy similarly improved from 20 percent to 40 percent of the population.

1967–73. Severe drought in North and South Yemen.

1967. During the summer and autumn, **the NLF** essentially **seized power in the countryside** and militarily defeated its main rival, FLOSY. On Nov. 6, negotiations began between Britain and the NLF over the terms of withdrawal.

Nov. 5. A MILITARY COUP in North Yemen ousted Pres. **Abdallah al-Sallal. Abd al-Rahman al-Iryani** seized power as the new president.

Nov. 29. Completion of **British withdrawal from South Yemen.** On the next day, **THE PEOPLE'S REPUBLIC OF SOUTH YEMEN** was founded. The first president was **Qahtan al-Sha'bi,** leader of the NLF.

Dec. 28. Publication of South Yemen's first newspaper, *al-Thawri.*

1968–86. Expansion of the armed forces in South Yemen. The number of troops was raised from 10,000 to 27,500. To supplement the army, the National Liberation Front established a sizable militia of 15,000 (1973). Other units included a police force of 30,000 at the disposal of the ministry of the interior. In addition, the ministry of state security had its own special forces (1974).

1968–70. Antitribal laws in South Yemen. The Tribal Reconciliation Decree (1968) forbade tribal quarreling or any open expression of tribal rivalry. The next year, the government imposed a ban on the wearing of arms. The final step in the antitribal campaign was the abolition of tribal associations (1970). Though tribes were never as prominent in South Yemen as in North Yemen, **tribal affiliations persisted** and sometimes surfaced in the political struggles that wracked the country after independence.

1968, March. Party congress for the National Liberation Front in South Yemen. Radicals overthrew the moderate leadership and pushed for a program of rapid change.

1969. Removal of the president, **Qahtan al-Sha'bi,** by the National Liberation Front, which then organized a purge of the army. **All foreign property was nationalized,** except the oil refinery owned by British Petroleum, which was seized in 1977. In 1970, the government implemented **land reform.** Peasants were forbidden to hold more than 8.5 hectares of irrigated land and 17 hectares of rain-fed land (the limit was doubled for family holdings). All farmers had to join **cooperatives** run by the government, which held exclusive management of the water supplies. The new law severely undermined the position of tribal sheiks and other rural notables.

1970–85. Expansion of the educational system in North Yemen. The number of schools climbed from about 700 to 5,000. Literacy rates, which had stood at under 3 percent in 1962, rose to 13 percent by 1985.

1970. South Yemen was renamed **the People's Democratic Republic of Yemen** to suit the leftist ideology of the new regime. **Salim Rubayi Ali** became president.

1971. Inauguration of the **University of San'a.**

Promulgation of a new **constitution for North Yemen and elections** for its consultative assembly. The government was controlled by the **tribes,** whose members occupied most of the important positions and formed the bulk of the army. **The central government under Pres. Abd al-Rahman al-Iryani was weak** and possessed few means to assert itself.

1972. The National Liberation Front in South Yemen acquired a politburo, secretariat, and central committee, and it effectively became a Communist-style party. It took the name **Yemeni Socialist Party** in 1978. Membership remained exclusive (about 26,000).

Sept. 30. A border dispute between North and South Yemen escalated into a brief war, lasting through most of October. Incidents along the border continued into the following year.

1974–83. Replacement, in South Yemen, of Islamic and tribal law with **secular codes** on family law (1974), personal law (1976), and civil law (1983). The reforms significantly reduced the jurisdiction and influence of the religious establishment.

1974, June 13. A MILITARY COUP in North Yemen overthrew Pres. Iryani and replaced him with **Lt. Col. Ibrahim Muhammad al-Hamdi.** Hamdi suspended the constitution of 1971 and presided over an executive council that came to function as the new government.

1975. Introduction of a **commercial code** in North Yemen. **Secular courts** were created to administer the new code the following year. The reform helped to undercut the power of the religious establishment.

Founding of the **University of Aden.**

1977, Oct. 11. Murder of North Yemeni president **Hamdi** under mysterious circumstances. The next president was **Ahmad Husayn al-Ghashmi,** the former deputy commander of the army. **Ghashmi** himself was **assassinated** in June 1978. **Lt. Col. Ali Abdallah Salih** emerged as the new president.

1978. A MILITARY COUP overthrew Pres. Rubayi Ali in South Yemen. **Abd al-Fattah Isma'il** was installed as his successor. Two years later, a **power struggle** led to the dismissal of Isma'il. **Ali Nasir Muhammad** became the new president and also assumed the office of prime minister and general secretary of the Yemeni Socialist Party.

1979. Introduction of **military conscription** in North Yemen. The chief

significance of this step was to enlarge the army (to 37,000 troops by 1986) and reduce its dependence on tribal levies. The net effect was to increase the state's power and freedom of action.

Feb. Resumption of **fighting between North and South Yemen.** By the time peace was restored in 1982, the North Yemeni government had secured its border and decisively defeated rebels who had been operating in its southern provinces with assistance from South Yemen.

Dec. 27. Election of **Abd al-Fattah Isma'il** as president of South Yemen.

1984. Discovery of oil in the eastern part of North Yemen. Export began in 1988.

1986, Jan. 13. A shootout at a politburo meeting left four prominent South Yemeni politicians dead, including former president **Abd al-Fattah Isma'il** and former army commander **Ali Ahmad Nasir Antar.** The incident was planned by **Pres. Ali Nasir,** who thereby provoked a brief **civil war** in which he was ousted from power. **Haydar Abu Bakr al-Attas** emerged as the new president.

1990, May 22. UNIFICATION OF NORTH AND SOUTH YEMEN. Yemen thereby became the most populous country on the Arabian Peninsula (9.5 million from North Yemen, 2.5 million from South Yemen). **Ali Abdallah Saleh,** former president of North Yemen, became the first president of the new country. **Haydar Abu Bakr al-Attas,** former president of South Yemen, was appointed prime minister.

1994, May 5. Civil war broke out in Yemen between northerners loyal to Pres. Ali Abdullah Saleh and southerners supporting V.P. Ali Salem al-Baidh. The southerners sought a redivision of the state, which had united in 1990. The northern forces prevailed and the union was preserved.

1998, Dec. 28. The militant Islamic faction known as the Aden-Abyan Islamic Army abducted several Western tourist groups; four members of the groups were killed after a muddled rescue plan was put into action. Faction leader Zein Al-Abidine al-Mihdar promised more attacks with the overall goal of turning Yemen into an Islamic state.

1999, Sept. 23. Pres. Ali Abdullah Saleh was elected for a third term and claimed 96.3% of the votes cast. The Socialist Party was not allowed to enter a candidate; this explained Saleh's great victory.

2000, Oct. 12. The *U.S.S. Cole* was bombed by terrorists while it was refueling in Aden. Seventeen soldiers were killed and dozens injured in the attack. Saudi exile Osama bin Laden was suspected of organizing the attack.

1. THE GULF STATES

(From p. 766)

1946. Beginning of **oil exports from Kuwait. Qatar** followed in 1949, **Abu Dhabi** in 1962, and **Dubayy** in 1969.

1950. Death of **Sheik Ahmad,** ruler of Kuwait. His cousin, **Sheik Abdallah,** succeeded him as emir.

1955. Establishment of the **Muscat and Oman Field Force,** an expanded version (approximately 400 men) of the existing military unit in Oman.

1959. The sultan of Oman suppressed a tribal uprising in Jabal al-Akhdar and for the first time enjoyed direct rule over the district.

1960. Ahmad ibn Ali became ruler of Qatar. His government began a broad **program of modernization** under the direction of Prime Minister **Khalifa ibn Ahmad.**

1961–85. Growth in the Kuwaiti population from 250,000 to about 1.7 million. In 1985, **native Kuwaitis** made up approximately 43 percent of the population (but only one-seventh of them qualified for full political rights as male descendants of Kuwaitis who resided in the country prior to 1920). The next largest group was the **Palestinians,** at about 25 percent of the total.

1961, June 19. INDEPENDENCE OF KUWAIT. The government published a **constitution** in 1962 providing for a **national legislature and a council of ministers,** but the effective functioning of this system soon broke down due to persistent conflicts between the legislature and the council.

June 25. Iraq asserted that Kuwait was historically part of the Ottoman province of Basra and that it therefore **ought to be ceded to Iraq.** In accordance with a Kuwaiti-British defense pact, **British troops** arrived in Kuwait to deter a possible Iraqi attack. The Iraqi government finally relinquished its claims and recognized Kuwaiti independence on Oct. 4, 1963.

1963–75. A tribal revolt in Dhafur, in the interior of Oman. As it came under the South Yemeni influence in the early 1970s, the movement acquired a revolutionary character and aimed at the overthrow of the sultanate itself. The rebels' most prominent organization was **the Popular Front for the Liberation of the Occupied Arab Gulf** (formerly, until Nov. 1968, the Dhafur Liberation Front). The government emerged victorious in 1975 with assistance from Iran.

1965, Nov. 24. Death of the Kuwaiti emir **Abdallah,** who was succeeded by his younger brother, **Sabah.**

1966, Aug. 6. Deposal of Sheik Shakbut ibn Sultan, ruler of Abu Dhabi. He was replaced by **Sheik Zayd,** his younger brother.

1967. Start of **oil exports in Oman.**

1968. Iran claimed Bahrain, a revival of an old claim to the island from the 17th century. With Iran's acquiesence, the matter was placed before the UN, which ruled against the Iranians.

1970, July 23. MILITARY COUP IN OMAN. Sultan Sa'id was deposed and exiled by his son, **QABUS,** who subsequently began to reorganize the Omani government to cope with the country's newfound oil wealth.

1970–85. Construction of an educational system in Oman. Only 16 schools were open in 1970; the country had almost 600 by 1985 and established its own university, **Sultan Qabus University,** the next year.

1971, Aug. 14. INDEPENDENCE OF BAHRAIN from British rule.

Sept. 1. INDEPENDENCE OF QATAR from British rule.

Dec. 2. CREATION OF THE UNITED ARAB EMIRATES, a collection of small sheikdoms that emerged from the territory known as Trucial Oman under British rule. The political system consisted of a president (**Sheik Zayd** of Abu Dhabi at independence), a council of ministers, and a consultative assembly. But the most important institution was the **Supreme Council of Rulers,** on which Abu Dhabi and Dubayy alone held veto power. Within the federation, the dominant state was **Abu Dhabi,** which held most of the wealth and population. The lesser sheikdoms resisted attempts to strengthen the union but were irresistably drawn together by acts such as the establishment of a common currency board (1973), an army (1976), a judicial system (1978), and a central bank (1980). Only two other sheikdoms, **Dubayy and Sharja,** possessed significant **reserves of oil.**

1971–88. Increase in population throughout the Gulf. In Qatar, the population rose from about 100,000 to 230,000, more than half of whom were resident aliens. The number of inhabitants of **Bahrain** nearly doubled, from 216,000 to 416,000. In the **United Arab Emirates,** the population grew rapidly from 320,000 to 1.6 million, about two-thirds of whom were foreign workers.

1972. Palace revolution in Qatar. Sheik Ahmad was deposed as emir. His cousin, **Sheik Khalifa,** came to power as the new ruler.

1975. Dismissal of the National Assembly in Bahrain. The Sunni regime had grown uneasy from the public opposition voiced by the Shi'ite majority.

1976. Dissolution of the Kuwaiti National Assembly, which had shown more independence than the government was willing to tolerate. The constitution was subsequently revised, and new elections were finally held in 1981.

1977, Dec. 31. Death of Kuwaiti emir Sabah. Next in line as ruler was his nephew **JABIR.**

1979. Introduction in Kuwait of **military conscription.** By 1986, the army stood at 12,000 members.

1981. Establishment of the Gulf Cooperation Council. The organization was intended to promote the common economic interests of the Gulf; but in the shadow of the **Iran-Iraq War,** it assumed more importance as a political and military alliance.

1986, July 3. Dissolution of the Kuwaiti National Assembly, which had again proven to be much less pliable than the government had hoped. By the 1980s, **religious fundamentalists** had replaced radical secularists as the main opponents of the regime.

Nov. 26. Opening of a causeway linking Bahrain to Saudi Arabia. The primary purpose of the road, a four-lane highway wide enough to accommodate tanks, was **defense.** The Sunni authorities in Bahrain, who had quelled an attempted coup in 1981, had little confidence in

the island's Shi'ites, who made up 70 percent of the population. The causeway was designed as a ready channel of Saudi assistance during emergencies.

1990, Oct. 7. Death of Sheik Rashid, ruler of Dubayy. He was succeeded by Sheik Maktum.

1990–91. Iraqi invasion and Gulf War (p. 969).

1992, Oct. 20. Opening session of the **reinstated Kuwaiti National Assembly.**

1995, June 27. A bloodless coup in Qatar allowed **Hamad bin Khalifa al-Thani to take the position of emir** from his father, Khalifa bin Hamad al-Thani. The move was recognized by the U.S. and the five other countries of the Gulf Cooperation Council.

1999, March 6. Bahrain's ruler for 40 years, Sheik Isa ibn-Sulman al-Khalifah, died and was succeeded by his son.

March 8. In Qatar municipal elections, women were enfranchised for the first time, participating as candidates and voters. A similar ruling passed by the emir of Kuwait was repealed later in the year by Parliament. Qatar and Oman remained the only Gulf States to uphold a woman's right to vote.

2000, Sept. 27. The UN Security Council ruled that Iraq had to pay the Kuwait Petroleum Corp. $15.9 billion for oil field damage caused during the Persian Gulf War.

2000. One of the largest arms trades in world history took place: the United Arab Emirates bought 80 fighter jets and accompanying missiles from Lockheed Martin at a cost of $8 million.

m. EGYPT

(From p. 760)

1946. Reform of religious endowments *(waqfs).* Though charitable *(khayri)* endowments dedicated to public causes could still be funded in perpetuity, private *(ahli)* endowments that served as family trusts had to be designated for a specific period. After the revolution of 1952, private endowments were abolished altogether. In 1957, **all waqfs came under state administration.**

Jan. Failure of negotiations between Britain and Egypt to revise the Treaty of 1936. In response, violent street demonstrations organized by students shook Cairo over the next two months.

1947. Currency reform. The Egyptian pound, formerly tied to the British pound sterling, became an independent currency.

1947–78. Expansion of the bureaucracy, from 310,000 functionaries to over 1 million (1967) and then up to 1.9 million (1978). By 1978, an additional 1.3 million employees worked in state-owned companies. After 1962, the runaway growth of the bureaucracy was fed by a **government promise that guaranteed a job to every university graduate** (approximately 100,000 per year by the 1970s). Bloated far beyond its needs and capacities, the bureaucracy operated as an unwieldy instrument of the state's social policy.

1948. Introduction of the **Egyptian Civil Code,** which was drawn up by a committee under the leadership of **Abd al-Razzaq al-Sanhuri.**

May. Imposition of martial law. On May 15, Egyptian troops entered **the war in Palestine** against the newly formed state of Israel.

Dec. 8. Outlawing of the Muslim Brotherhood. Retaliation was swift. A member of the Brotherhood **assassinated Prime Minister Mahmud Fahmi al-Nuqrashi** in January.

1949. The government responded in kind and with equal alacrity. On Feb. 12, Brotherhood leader **HASAN AL-BANNA** himself **was killed,** most likely by members of the security forces.

Formation of the **FREE OFFICERS' MOVEMENT,** a revolutionary cell within the army composed of young officers hostile to and suspicious of the reigning political order. **GAMAL ABDEL NASSER** became chairman of the organization in Jan. 1950. One of its members, **GEN. MUHAMMAD NAGUIB,** was elected president of the army's Officers' Club in Dec. 1951.

Death of Khalil Mutran (b. 1872), who invented the narrative poem in Arabic. He was also associated with the romantic movement in Arabic literature, which flourished during the interwar period.

1950. Minister of Education **TAHA HUSAYN** declared education to be **free at all levels.**

Creation of **Ayn Shams University** in Cairo. The school specialized primarily in language training.

Jan. Last victory of the Wafd at the polls. **Mustafa al-Nahhas** again became prime minister and immediately resumed negotiations with the British over possible revisions to the Treaty of 1936.

1951, Oct. 8. Prime Minister Nahhas abrogated the Anglo-Egyptian Treaty of 1936. From Nov. 1951 until Jan. 1952, **attacks by guerrilla groups** on British troops stationed in the **canal zone** steadily mounted.

1952, Jan. 26. Black Saturday Riots in Cairo, in response to events in the canal zone on the previous day, when British troops had attacked an Egyptian police station. **Violent demonstrations** left 30 dead while angry crowds burned and looted commercial districts in the city.

Jan. 27. Resignation of the last Wafdist government, under Mustafa al-Nahhas. Paralysis completely overcame the political system. A few independent governments that possessed no real power briefly held office through the spring and early summer.

July 23. THE EGYPTIAN REVOLUTION. A group of army officers, officially led by **Gen. Muhammad Naguib,** deposed the government. The revolution represented a true watershed in Egyptian history, bringing about the **downfall of the old class of political notables** drawn primarily from the landed elite and paving the way for a new elite composed of military officers and high-ranking bureaucrats. In the early days of the revolution, power was vested in the **Revolutionary Command Council (RCC)**, staffed by members of the **Free Officers' Society**, which had carried out the coup. With the exception of Gen. Naguib, all the conspirators were young (average age of 33), held middling military ranks (mostly lieutenant colonel and major), and hailed from modest circumstances. The dominant personality on the RCC was unquestionably **NASSER**, who soon emerged as the real power in the country.

July 26. ABDICATION OF KING FARUQ (Farouk). His young son, Ahmad Fu'ad, stayed behind as the new king under a regency. **The monarchy itself was terminated** on June 18, 1953. Egypt thereafter became a republic.

Sept. 9. First **LAND REFORM** law, directed primarily against the 4,000 or so families (1 percent of the population) who owned about 70 percent of Egypt's arable land. **Landholders were forbidden to own more than 200 feddans** (1 feddan = 1.038 acres) and were compensated for sequestered land. **Further reductions** were introduced in 1961 (maximum holdings of 100 feddans) and again in 1969 (an even lower ceiling of 50 feddans). **The state distributed the expropriated land** in small plots to peasants, who had to join **agricultural cooperatives** from which they received credit, seed, fertilizer, and other forms of assistance. By 1970, it was estimated that more than 800,000 feddans of confiscated land and some 200,000 feddans of state land had been turned over to 400,000 families (constituting about 10 percent of the rural population).

The **chief effect** of the land reforms **was to smash the political power of the great landowners.** The social consequences were far less revolutionary. Although many landless peasants received their own plots for the first time, the **main beneficiaries were the rural notables** who typically owned 20–50 feddans and dominated their local villages. Over half the rural population still worked as landless laborers. As the population grew, moreover, the proportion of land to cultivators actually dropped from 1.3 hectares for a family of five (1947) to 0.8 hectares (1971).

Dec. 10. Abolition of the constitution. All political parties were banned in Jan. 1953. After the monarchy was suppressed in June, **Muhammad Naguib** became prime minister and president of the republic.

1952. The banning of all honorific titles (pasha, bey, and so on) by the revolutionary government.

1952–86. Population boom. The number of Egyptians rose from 20 million in 1952 to 50 million by 1986. The urban population grew dramatically. Cairo's population alone increased from about 2.2 million inhabitants in 1950 to 14 million in 1986.

1953. Establishment of **Sawt al-Arab (Voice of the Arabs),** the radio station that became one of the regime's most effective propaganda tools, particularly for the cause of pan-Arabism.

Feb. Organization of **the Liberation Rally,** created as the political party of the new government. Its function was to generate grassroots support for the policies and reforms that the regime sought to implement. It was superseded in 1956 by **the National Union,** which soon became preoccupied with selecting candidates for the new Parliament.

Feb. Anglo-Egyptian settlement on the question of Sudan. It was announced that Sudan would achieve its independence in 1956, at which time Sudanese voters would choose either union with Egypt or separate status (they eventually opted for the latter).

June. Appointment of **Abd al-Hakim Amir** as commander in chief of the armed forces. A close ally of Nasser, he soon became the second most powerful person in the country. He kept the army loyal to Nasser, who looked to it as the mainstay of his regime. In return, the grateful president **raised military expenditures** until by 1965 they were consuming 12 percent of the GNP (in comparison to 4 percent in 1950).

1954. The government organized **political purges** of provincial and local governments and the press. In Jan. 1955, the Bar Association was also purged.

Jan. 14. Official suppression of the MUSLIM BROTHERHOOD, including the arrest of 78 leading figures. In November, the government foiled a plot hatched by Brotherhood sympathizers in the army. Afterward, the remnants of the organization went underground.

April 15. A decree deprived all members of government cabinets of their political rights for ten years, from Feb. 1942 to July 1952.

April 17. An internal **power struggle** in the early part of 1954 ended with the appointment of **Nasser** as prime minister. **Naguib** stayed on as president, though without any effective power, until his dismissal and arrest in Nov. 1954.

Nasser (1918–70) became the most pivotal political figure in 20th-century Egyptian history. During his political career, **he was closely identified with three causes: the Egyptian Revolution of 1952, the pan-Arab political movement of the 1950s and 1960s, and the policy of nonalignment** among Third World countries. Within Egypt, he was a highly charismatic figure who enjoyed immense popularity. His appeal was further heightened by the **populist socialism** that became the domestic agenda of his regime. He achieved international celebrity for his leadership in the nonaligned movement following the **Bandung Conference** (1955) and the **Suez War** (1956), and for his outspoken pan-Arabism, an ideology that advocated the unification of the Arab world into one state. His extravagant rhetoric and pan-Arab ambitions led him into a disastrous **war with Israel** in June 1967. Though pan-Arabism suffered an irreparable setback, Nasser managed to fight off challengers and retain power until his death in Sept. 1970.

Oct. 19. Anglo-Egyptian Agreement, by which British troops were to withdraw from the canal zone in 20 months. The last British troops left on June 13, 1955.

Oct. 26. Failed attempt by a member of the Muslim Brotherhood to assassinate Nasser in Alexandria.

1955. First steps in the **dismantling of the Islamic courts.** By the following year, the process was complete.

March. Israeli raid on Gaza, which was under Egyptian administration. Egyptian-Israeli relations steadily worsened.

Sept. Nasser appeared at the **Bandung Conference,** attended by African and Asian countries, and became one of the leaders of the nonaligned movement, which sought to establish a foreign policy that was neither pro-Western nor pro-Soviet. At the same time, Nasser aroused concern in the West when he struck **a deal with Czechoslovakia,** exchanging cotton for arms.

1956. A law made public education free. The measure was extended to higher education in 1962.

Jan. 16. Promulgation of a **new constitution.** Under the new system of government, the president was invested with broad powers. **Nasser became the first president** in June.

June 23. Universal male suffrage for all men age 21 and older. **Women also obtained the right to vote.**

July. The **U.S. and Great Britain withdrew offers of financial aid** for the planned construction of the Aswan High Dam. In response, **EGYPT NATIONALIZED THE SUEZ CANAL** on July 26.

Nov. Nationalization of all British and French companies in Egypt. In response to the Suez War (p. 966), **the government seized all British, French, and Jewish property.** The measure was extended in Jan. 1957 to all foreign-owned insurance companies, commercial houses, and banks. Later, in 1960, came the expropriation of all Belgian property.

By this time, Egypt had committed itself to a **centrally planned economy.**

1957, Oct. Opening of **Asyut University.**

1958. Abolition of foreign schools, which were restructured as Egyptian private schools under the supervision of the Ministry of Education.

1959. A new labor code established a minimum wage and maximum number of working hours per day. Employees won the right to form labor associations (though only under government supervision) and were to receive a share of profits. Women secured additional benefits including exemption from night work and protection against firing if they married or had children.

1960, Jan. Start of construction on the **HIGH DAM AT ASWAN** with Soviet assistance. The project was eventually completed in Jan. 1968.

Feb. Nationalization of **Bank Misr and the National Bank.** In May, the press was also put under government control. By July 1961, the entire import trade of the country and most of the export trade had been nationalized.

July. Start of television broadcasting in Cairo. Egypt became the first Arab state to operate its own television station.

1961. New labor law. Employees were required to work no more than 42 hours per week (six days per week).

Reform at al-Azhar. A government decree ordered the university's curriculum and administration to be modernized. The measure ended over a century of resistance from faculty and students to attempted reforms.

Suppression of the Sufi orders by government decree. Yet Sufism continued to thrive. In 1964, it was reported that 60 different Sufi orders were still operating.

1962. Founding of the Arab Socialist Union (ASU), an attempt to create a mass political party to generate enthusiasm and motivate people to support the government's programs. The party had over 7,000 local chapters in villages, neighborhoods, schools, and workplaces. In practice, it functioned as a patchwork of wards controlled by political bosses and rural notables. Serving as secretary-general of the ASU (1965-67, 1968-69), **ALI SABRI** became one of the most prominent politicians in the country.

1963. Guarantee of university admission to all secondary school graduates.

Founding of the Middle East's first Islamic bank, the Mit Cham Savings Bank in Cairo. The leading organizer was the Egyptian economist Ahmad al-Najjar.

In some Islamic circles, modern banking was viewed as problematic because Islamic law forbade lending at interest, though not lending itself or profit sharing. In Islamic banking, **depositors enter into long-term or short-term contracts with a bank and receive a portion of the bank's profits,** instead of earning interest.

1966, Aug. 29. Execution of **SAYYID QUTB** (b. 1903), the leading intellectual of the Muslim Brotherhood, for political activities against the state. In his writings, he condemned the corruption of the modern world and accused contemporary Muslim societies of abandoning the principles of Islam. He encouraged true believers to withdraw from their societies in order to attain spiritual purification and regeneration.

1967, June 9. Nasser publicly assumed responsibility for Egypt's defeat in the war against Israel. He promised to resign as president, but changed his mind after huge crowds filled the streets throughout the country and expressed their support for him. In the following months, **he organized a purge of the army and security forces, and quashed an attempted coup** by disgruntled military leaders who had been blamed for Egypt's poor performance in the war.

1970, Sept. 28. Death of Pres. Nasser of a heart attack at Cairo airport. He was succeeded in office by **V.P. ANWAR EL-SADAT.**

1970-81. Era of SADAT. He had first come to prominence as a member of the Free Officers' Society in the Revolution of 1952, and subsequently remained one of Nasser's most trusted associates. At the time of his ascension to the presidency, he was widely regarded as a mere **interim figure.** But he surprised everyone by successfully outmaneuvering and eliminating his rivals. **His style of rule was autocratic,** and in many respects he held more power than his predecessor. His major domestic achievement, yielding both good and bad results, was the *infitah* (opening) of the Egyptian economy to private enterprise and outside investment. Sadat also abandoned the legacy of Nasser in **foreign policy.** He showed little interest in pan-Arabism, soon spurned the Soviet alliance, and aligned Egypt with the West. After redeeming Egyptian honor in the 1973 war with Israel—which was neither a victory nor a defeat—he boldly opened **direct negotiations with Israel.** These talks eventually produced the **Camp David Accords** (1978) (p. 924) and formal peace between the two countries. During the last years of his rule, he became increasingly **unpopular at home,** particularly among leftists, Coptic Christians, and religious extremists. Soldiers belonging to the latter group assassinated him (1981) but failed to shake the political system that he bequeathed to his country.

1971, March 7. Egypt stopped renewing its cease-fire agreement with Israel.

May 14. The "corrective revolution." Sadat organized a **purge** of his rivals in the state and the army. His most notable victim was the chairman of the ASU, **Ali Sabri.** Henceforth Sadat's position as president was secure.

May 27. Egyptian-Soviet treaty of friendship, by which Egypt continued to obtain large amounts of Soviet military aid.

Sept. 2. Egypt officially changed its name from the United Arab Republic to the **Arab Republic of Egypt.**

1972, July 18. Expulsion of Soviet military advisers, who numbered about 18,000. Egypt took over all the Soviet military bases inside the country.

1973, Oct. 28. Death of TAHA HUSAYN (b. 1889), one of the greatest literary figures of 20th-century Egypt. Despite his early training in the traditional Muslim educational system, he later became Egypt's foremost exponent of modern literary techniques in both fiction and criticism. He was closely identified with the **Egyptianist movement** of the 1920s, which sought to construct a unique national identity persisting throughout history. Because of his modernist leanings and daring scholarship, he became embroiled in **religious controversy** with conservatives, who accused him of undermining conventional Muslim scholarship and even Islam itself. He also served briefly as minister of education (1950-52).

1974, Oct. Declaration of the *infitah*, the "open-door" economic policy that **encouraged foreign investment and private enterprise.** The new program represented a complete and **radical reversal of Nasser's state-planned socialism.** Sadat probably had several motives for introducing the new policy. The sudden **pro-Western tilt in foreign policy** and the wish to strengthen **ties with conservative Arab regimes** generated external pressures for Egypt to retreat from, or if possible completely break with, its socialist policies. An additional spur to a more open economy was the **need to attract foreign investment,** particularly from wealthy Arab oil states, to stimulate economic growth. It is also likely that the government wanted to **improve Egypt's system of foreign exchange** so that Egyptians working abroad could more easily inject their remittances into the domestic economy.

Although economic investment rose markedly, it rarely entered vital sectors of the economy such as industry. **Tourism, oil, and construction** received the overwhelming share of investors' attention. Rapid economic expansion (an average of 7 percent per year, 1973-80) was counterbalanced by **severe inflation** (reaching 30 percent at times), an enormous **trade deficit,** and a crushing **foreign debt.** A further problem was the new **social tensions** generated by the *infitah*. Almost overnight a new class of **entrepreneurs** sprang up, whose ostentatious behavior offered a sharp and provocative contrast to the more austere lifestyle of the socialist era.

1975, Feb. 3. Death of UMM KULTHUM (b. 1898), popular singer adored throughout the Arab world. Her career began at the age of 5. Winning early acclaim for her mastery of classical and religious songs, she later broke into popular music and established herself as the preeminent singer in the region.

1976. Gradual abandonment of the one-party system. In a small move toward political pluralism, **the Arab Socialist Union,** still the only recognized party in Egypt, created three internal "platforms"—roughly corresponding to leftist, moderate, and conservative positions—to encourage debate within the party and to offer a larger number of candidates for parliamentary elections. The centrist bloc evolved into the Arab Socialist Party of Egypt, which was soon renamed **the National Democratic Party.** It quickly replaced the ASU, abolished in 1980, as the party of the government. Genuine opposition groups took longer to establish themselves. The New Wafd existed briefly in 1978.

March. Egypt canceled its treaty with the Soviet Union. The next month Soviet ships were barred from calling in Egyptian ports.

1977, Jan. Bread riots in Cairo followed a government announcement that food subsidies, which had already increased tenfold since 1972, would be curtailed. The government restored order but canceled the proposed price hikes.

March 30. Death of Abd al-Halim Hafiz, one of the most celebrated singers in the Arab world. He also acted in a number of Egyptian films.

July 3. Islamic extremists kidnapped and murdered **Hasan al-Dhahabi,** the minister of *waqf*s.

1980, Dec. 16. Official opening of the Suez Canal to supertankers.

1981, Sept. 3–7. Arrest of over 1,500 critics of the government. Among those detained were religious extremists, intellectuals, and leftist and conservative political leaders. The government banned the publications of the Muslim Brotherhood and all Coptic organizations. On Sept. 5, Sadat deposed Coptic pope Shenuda III and outlawed the Muslim Brotherhood.

Oct. 6. ASSASSINATION OF PRES. SADAT in Alexandria by members of a radical Muslim organization inside the army. His successor was **V.P. HOSNI MUBARAK.**

Death of Salah Abd al-Sabur (b. 1931), one of Egypt's leading poets.

1982, April 25. Completion of the **Israeli withdrawal** from the Sinai Peninsula.

1986, April 22. Death of Umar Talmasani, head of the Muslim Brotherhood.

1987. Death of TAWFIQ AL-HAKIM (b. 1898), the greatest playwright in the modern Arab world. More than any other author, he made drama a respected and vibrant field of modern Arabic letters.

Sept. 27. Opening of the Cairo Metro.

Oct. 5. Pres. Mubarak was officially elected to a second term.

1988, Oct. 13. The Nobel Prize for literature was awarded to NAGUIB MAHFUZ (b. 1911), the most famous novelist in modern Arabic literature and the author primarily responsible for developing the novel as a literary form in Arabic. He was the **first Arab author to win the prize.**

1991. Death of Yusuf Idris, one of the great Arab literary figures of the 20th century. Educated as a doctor, he achieved distinction for his novels, short stories, plays, and journalism.

Nov. 21. Nomination of **BOUTROS BOUTROS-GHALI,** deputy prime minister, to succeed Javier Perez de Cuellar (Jan. 1, 1992) as secretary-general of the U.N.

1992, June 10. Murder of prominent journalist **Farag Foda** by religious extremists upset with his criticism of conservative Islamicist movements. By the early 1990s, a number of **extreme religious groups** such as al-Jama 'a al-Islamiya had **declared open war on the government.** Among their targets were government officials, police, secularist authors, and Western tourists. They demanded the establishment of an Islamic state and the elimination of Western influences from Egyptian society.

Death of **Muhammad Abd al-Wahhab,** famous singer and composer. He led the movement to transform Egyptian music by incorporating Western orchestration, instruments, and themes.

1995, June 26. In a **failed assassination attempt,** several gunmen believed to be associated with militant Islamic groups opened fire on a motorcade carrying Pres. Hosni Mubarak.

Dec. 6. The last of two rounds of legislative elections to the People's Assembly gave the ruling National Democratic Party an overwhelming majority of the vote. This was promptly contested by opposition parties accusing the NDP of fraud.

1997, Nov. 17. Islamic militants attacked two tourist buses near the ancient city of Luxor, leaving 68 dead and 17 wounded. Pres. Mubarak demanded stronger security measures.

1998, Aug. 22–23. Palestinian National Authority (PNA) leader Yasir Arafat met in Cairo with the Democratic Front for the Liberation of Palestine leader Nayef Hawatmeh. It was the first union of these organizations in six years. Hawatmeh's group was one of several extremist factions that split from the PLO in 1993, opposing a peace accord with Israel. The Aug. 1998 meeting was intended to unite the PLO in hopes of a broader final peace agreement with Israel in the near future.

1999, March 25. Islamic Group, a Muslim extremist organization in Egypt, announced a permanent cease-fire. On April 26 the Egyptian government freed nearly 1,000 imprisoned group members.

Sept. 6. An attempt was made to assassinate Pres. Mubarak, but he was only slightly injured by the knife-wielding attacker.

Sept. 26. A referendum was held as the People's Assembly's nominee, Hosni Mubarak, was elected to a fourth presidential term.

2000, Oct. 21–22. In Cairo the members of the Arab League held an emergency summit to discuss recent Israeli-Palestinian violence. Of the 22 league members present, 21 signed an accord that accused Israel of committing atrocities against the Palestinians in the renewed conflict. The agreement also installed a trade boycott against Israel and established a $1 billion fund to help Palestinians who were injured or killed in the confrontations.

Nov. 15. The National Democratic Party (NDP) won 388 out of 444 seats in legislative elections. Though diminishing his majority, this maintained Pres. Mubarak's grip on governmental power inasmuch as his party retained a two-thirds majority in the Parliament.

4. NORTH AFRICA, 1945–2000

a. MOROCCO

(From p. 767)

1946. Erik Labonne became French resident-general, replacing **Gen. Gabriel Puaux.** Labonne's conciliatory policies attracted little support from the Moroccan leadership. Consequently, Labonne lost his position to **Gen. Alphonse Juin** the next year.

1951. Formation of the **National Front,** combining the Maghrib Unity and Islah Parties in Spanish Morocco, and the Istiqlal and Democratic Parties in the French zone.

1952, Dec. 7–8. Rioting in Casablanca (38 dead) in protest over the murder of Tunisian labor activist Ferhat Hached.

1953, Aug. French authorities deposed King **Muhammad Ben Yusuf and installed Muhammad Ben Arafa** as the new monarch. The former king was exiled to Madagascar. Over the next two years, French authorities had to contend with a campaign of **urban guerrilla warfare.** In Casablanca alone, attacks took the lives of 406 Moroccans and Europeans up to the autumn of 1955.

1955. Founding of the **Union Marocaine du Travail,** the first Moroccan trade union, by the labor activists **Tayyib Bouazza** and **Mahjoub Ben Seddiq.**

Aug. At the **conference of Aix-les-Bains,** French officials and Moroccan representatives concluded an agreement that paved the way for Moroccan independence. The French promised to remove Ben Arafa as king before withdrawing. **Muhammad Ben Yusuf (Muhammad V) officially returned** to the throne on Oct. 29, 1955.

1956, March 2. Formal French recognition of **MOROCCAN INDEPENDENCE.** Spain withdrew from its portion of Morocco on April 7 and recognized the unity of the Moroccan state. The international administration of Tangier was dismantled on Oct. 29.

1958, May 1. Morocco joined the **Arab League.**

1961, Feb. 26. Death of Muhammad V, who was succeeded by his son, **HASSAN II.**

1962, Nov. 18. Promulgation of a **new constitution.** Morocco received a bicameral legislature and a prime minister who was responsible to the king.

1963, Oct.–Nov. Skirmishes along the frontier between Morocco and Algeria.

1965, June 7. Amid widespread disturbances, **Hassan II suspended the**

constitution and declared a state of emergency. The king governed by decree up to July 1967 and then through his appointees to the cabinet until the unveiling of the new constitution in 1970.

Oct. 29. Assassination of exiled opposition leader **Mehdi Ben Barka** in Paris, presumably on orders from the Moroccan government.

1970, July 24. Voters overwhelmingly approved a referendum on a **new constitution,** which restored Parliament. The king retained the right to veto all legislation.

1971, July 10. Failure of a military coup that involved an equally unsuccessful attempt to assassinate the king.

1972, March 1. Approval of a referendum on a **new constitution,** which stipulated that two-thirds of Parliament was to be popularly elected. After a **second attempt to assassinate the king** (Aug. 16), the government decided to suspend the constitution.

1973, March. Defeat of a third attempt to overthrow the government. Radical activists infiltrated the country in armed bands and staged attacks on strategic targets. The plot failed to shake the regime.

1975, June 25. Morocco and Mauritania presented their **claims to the Spanish Sahara** before the World Court (p. 1055), which ruled (Oct. 16) in favor of self-determination for the inhabitants. **Fighting** was reported (Nov. 7) **between the Moroccan army and the Polisario,** the nationalist organization representing the inhabitants of the Spanish Sahara. **Morocco and Mauritania officially divided the territory** and annexed their respective shares on April 14, 1976. Morocco prized the territory, which was little more than barren wasteland, for its large phosphate deposits.

Nov. 6. With encouragement from King Hassan, thousands of marchers crossed the border into Spanish Sahara to demonstrate support for Morocco's claims to the territory.

1978, Oct. 10. King Hassan named Abdel-Latif Jouhari as prime minister.

1981, June 23. Price increases touched off **rioting in Casablanca,** resulting in the deaths of 66 people.

Nov. 4. Appointment of Maati Bouabid as prime minister.

1983, June 10. Pro-government parties won 58 percent of the vote in national elections.

Nov. 30. Appointment of Karim Lamrani as prime minister.

1985, Nov. 11. Morocco formally withdrew from the Organization of African Unity, which had consistently backed the Polisario movement.

1986, Sept. 30. Appointment of Azzedine Laraki as prime minister.

1991, Sept. 6. The UN helped to arrange the **first cease-fire** in the 15-year struggle **between Morocco and the Polisario.** Preparations commenced for a **referendum on self-determination** for Western Sahara (the former Spanish Sahara), but bickering over the terms of the referendum frustrated all attempts to hold it over the next two years.

1992, Aug. 11. Appointment of veteran politician Muhammad Karim Lamrani as prime minister.

1993, June 25. The ruling coalition won a majority of parliamentary seats (116 of 222) in national elections.

1999, July 23. King Hassan II, who had reigned since 1961, died and was succeeded by his son Sidi Muhammad VI.

2000, March 12. Some 500,000 Islamic fundamentalists protested in Casablanca, and nearly 300,000 women's rights advocates rallied in the capital city of Rabat when a government plan was presented to grant more rights to women. The proposed reforms would have banned polygamy, raised the legal marriage age from 14 to 18 years, and reserved one-third of Morocco's parliamentary seats for female candidates. The plan, set forth by King Muhammad VI, also included reforms in divorce legislation and assertions of greater property rights for women. A council of Islamic scholars was arranged to solve the problem through compromise.

b. ALGERIA

(From p. 768)

1945, Aug. Muslim Algerians received the right to elect 13 members to the French constituent assembly (the same number of seats granted to the colonists).

1946, June. Formation of the **Mouvement pour le Triomphe des Libertés Democratiques (MTLD)** under the leadership of **Messali al-Hajj.** Before the war for independence, Hajj's party had been the most extreme Muslim party that the colonial regime tolerated. It split up in 1955 over the question of violent resistance, which Messali originally denounced. He then formed a new party, the **Mouvement National Algérien (MNA).**

1947, Sept. 20. The Algerian Statute, passed in France by the first National Assembly of the Fourth Republic. The act provided for an **Algerian assembly in which power was unequally distributed between the colonists** (60 seats for 60,000 electors) **and Muslims** (60 seats for 1.3 million electors). The Algerian administration remained under the control of the governor-general, who was responsible to the French ministry of the interior and not to the Algerian assembly.

Unhappiness with the Algerian Statute, combined with the rigging of elections for the Algerian assembly, once and for all turned the Muslim political parties away from compromise and toward a policy of armed struggle.

1954, Oct. Formation of the **FRONT DE LIBÉRATION NATIONALE (FLN),** which became the leading party in the armed struggle against the French authorities.

1954–62. THE ALGERIAN WAR FOR INDEPENDENCE (p. 813) started (Oct. 31, 1954) with a series of raids organized by the FLN. The war exacted a **heavy toll in casualties.** The Algerian government later estimated that over 1 million Algerians perished during the conflict. French authorities listed their own casualties at 26,000. **The Algerian countryside was particularly scarred** by the war. The French uprooted about one-third of the rural population (2.3 million peasants) and transferred them to "regroupment villages" where they lived under close supervision.

1956, June 13. Rejection by Ferhat Abbas of a French offer for a **cease-fire** unless France conceded Algerian sovereignty and independence beforehand.

Oct. 22. French operatives kidnapped Ben Bella, Ait Ahmad, Muhammad Khidar, and Muhammad Boudiaf, four of the most important leaders in the FLN. They had boarded a plane in Rabat that, in midflight, was forced to land in Algiers, where they were arrested.

1957, Jan. 28. Opening of an **eight-day national strike,** called by the Algerian rebels. The demonstration provoked the BATTLE OF ALGIERS with French authorities. Over the next six months, troops under Gen. Jacques Massu systematically uprooted the organized resistance within Algiers, particularly in the Qasbah, the old section of the city.

March 22. Announcement by the FLN that it was forming a provisional government, which was ready to negotiate independence from France.

1958, Feb. 5. The French National Assembly declared Algeria an integral part of France.

April 27–30. The Tangier Conference, attended by representatives from the Moroccan Istiqlal Party, the Algerian FLN, and the Tunisian Neo-Destour Party. Morocco and Tunisia pledged their support for Algerian independence.

May 19. Formation of the **Algiers Committee of Public Safety** under the leadership of **Gen. Jacques Massu.** The committee was dominated by high-ranking military officers stationed in Algeria and sympathetic to the demands of the French colonists. **The generals assumed direction of the colonial government** in Algiers until Charles de Gaulle appointed their superior, **Gen. Raoul Salan,** as delegate-general (June 6).

Sept. 19. Establishment of the provisional government of the Algerian Republic, which operated in exile, first from Cairo and later from Tunis. **Ferhat Abbas** was named the **first president.**

1960, June 25–29. Abortive talks in Paris between France and members of the provisional Algerian government. The latter balked after being informed that they would have to lay down their arms before negotiations could begin.

1961, April 22–26. THE GENERALS' INSURRECTION in Algiers (p. 857). Four top-ranking commanders in the French army organized a mutiny **to protest de Gaulle's policy of accommodation** toward the Algerian rebels. The coup failed when most of France's armed forces refused to take part in it.

April. Formation of the **Organisation de l'Armée Secrète (O.A.S.)** by extremist settlers, who mounted a fierce **guerrilla campaign against French officials and Muslim Algerians.** The organization suspended operations on June 26, 1962, more than three months after Algerian independence.

Aug. 27. Replacement of Ferhat Abbas by **Ben Youssef Ben Khedda** as prime minister of the Algerian provisional government.

1962, March 18. ALGERIAN INDEPENDENCE, as recognized by the **Evian Accords, which arranged a cease-fire and a referendum** to decide the ultimate fate of Algeria. French negotiators pledged **economic and technical assistance** and the removal of French troops from Algerian soil. In exchange, France retained its privileged role in developing and transporting Algerian oil.

The settlement was a **complete triumph for the Algerian provisional government.** The French had failed to impose special legal and political protections for the Europeans resident in Algeria. They had also been unable to wrest the oil-rich Saharan provinces from Algerian control. Moreover, they had recognized the provisional government as the only legitimate voice of the Algerian people.

1962–66. Emigration of most of the French population in Algeria. Previously just under 1 million (1954), the French population dropped to about 90,000 in 1966.

1962, May. The Tripoli conference, at which Algerian delegates elected a national politburo and committed independent Algeria to a socialist economy.

July 1. In a **nationwide referendum,** Algerians overwhelmingly voted for complete independence from France.

Aug. 16. Algeria joined the **Arab League.**

Sept. 20. Elections for the National Assembly selected **AHMAD BEN BELLA** as president.

1963. Nationalization of French estates in the countryside.

1964, April 16–21. First congress of the FLN, the only legal political party. **Pres. Ben Bella** was elected secretary-general.

1965. Death of Ahmad Rida Huhu (b. 1911), generally considered the pioneer of the Arabic short story among Algerian writers.

June 19. A MILITARY COUP deposed **Ben Bella.** The new president was **HOUARI BOUMEDIENNE,** the commander of the army.

1971, Feb. Nationalization of the oil industry.

Feb. Land reform. The government **redistributed public lands** (including property from religious endowments) and **seized estates** held by absentee owners. The new laws **set ceilings** (scaled to the productivity of the soil) on the amount of land that individuals were permitted to hold.

The attention given to land reform marked a **shift in state policy,** which had formerly emphasized industrial projects. In view of Algeria's rapidly expanding population, the government decided to intensify agricultural development.

1978, Dec. 27. Death of Pres. Houari Boumedienne. His successor was **CHADLI BENJEDID** (Jan. 31, 1979).

1984. Adoption of a **new family code,** which eliminated polygamy and granted women the right to divorce under certain conditions.

Jan. Reelection of **Pres. Benjedid** to a second term.

1985, Dec. 24. Death of FERHAT ABBAS (b. 1899), one of the central figures in 20th-century Algerian politics. During the 1930s, he was an outspoken **champion of assimilation** and wished for Algeria to become merely one more province of France. By 1955, he had given up these hopes and **aligned himself with the FLN.** He became a **moderate leader** within the resistance and served (1958–61) as president of the Algerian provisional government. After independence, he clashed with government leaders, and he abandoned politics altogether following his arrest and brief detention (1964).

1988, Dec. 22. Reelection of **Pres. Benjedid** to a third term.

1989. Death of Kateb Yacine (b. 1923), one of Algeria's greatest authors. His early work appeared in French, but after 1970 he concentrated on producing plays in colloquial Arabic. His name is often associated with the **"generation of 1952,"** a group of Algerian authors who came to prominence during the 1950s and, publishing in French, won critical accolades throughout the Francophone world. Among the most illustrious of these writers were **Muhammad Dib, Mouloud Feraoun, and Mouloud Mammeri.**

Feb. 23. Voters approved a **referendum that created a multiparty political system,** granted the right to strike (within limits), and extended freedom of expression.

July 19. As part of an aggressive **Arabization program,** Arabic was declared the only language for general publications. In Dec. 1990, **demonstrations against the act** drew more than 100,000 people. Arabic was later made the required language for public and commercial transactions (Feb. 11, 1991).

1990, April 20. Tens of thousands, demanding early elections and full application of Islamic law, marched in Algiers under the banner of the **ISLAMIC SALVATION FRONT (FIS).**

June 12. The FIS won a majority of provincial and municipal councils in national elections.

1991, June 5. The government declared a four-month state of emergency due to FIS agitation for early elections.

Dec. 26. The first round of **parliamentary elections** in which the FIS emerged as the leading party.

1992, Jan. 11. Pres. Benjedid resigned his office amid widespread turmoil and political uncertainty. **The Higher State Council,** headed by **Muhammad Boudiaf,** assumed power with the backing of the military and **nullified the results of the Dec. elections.** Over the next month, the FIS and other Islamicist groups sponsored **nationwide protests** that often entailed violent clashes with police.

June 29. ASSASSINATION OF PRES. BOUDIAF by one of his bodyguards. The new president was **Ali Kafi.**

1993, March 1. Algerian police arrested **Ikhlef Cherati,** Islamic militant and director of terrorist operations that had resulted in the deaths of nearly 600 people.

1994, Jan. 30. The Algerian Council appointed defense minister **Gen. Liamine Zeroual president.**

1995, Jan. 13. The Algerian government attempted to negotiate a truce with Islamic opposition groups in the country, but without success.

March 30. Algeria announced a major offensive against the Islamic fundamentalists seeking to overthrow the government.

1997, Jan. 24. Pres. Zeroual vowed to destroy Islamic fundamentalist groups attempting to overthrow his government.

1998. Bloody assassinations continued, with civil strife and political murders claiming the lives of over 40,000 people in 7 years. From attacks on government officials and intellectuals, violence escalated to include the indiscriminate killing of defenseless villagers. The widespread and startlingly random violence remained largely out of the hands of the ineffectual military and government. Algeria's government continued to refuse international help, and its civil war, which had remained hidden from most other nations, raged on.

Sept. 11. Algerian president Gen. Liamine Zeroual announced that he would retire early from his position as head of state.

1999, April 15. Though allegations that he had been involved in fraud were widespread, Abdelaziz Bouteflika was elected president of Algeria.

July 5. Thousands of militant Muslims were freed by the Algerian government in connection with the country's celebration of a national holiday.

Sept. 16. Pres. Bouteflika made peace with the rebel AIS as an amnesty plan won overwhelming support in a national referendum. Since 1992, an estimated 100,000 persons had died in Algeria's civil war.

c. TUNISIA

(From p. 768)

1946, Jan. Founding of the **Union Générale des Travailleurs Tunisiens (UGTT),** under the direction of **FERHAT HACHED.** It was the first major trade union in Tunisian history. Membership soon reached over 150,000 workers.

1951, Oct. Tunisian prime minister **Muhammad Shanniq** traveled to Paris to demand independence tempered by close economic, cultural, and military ties with France. **The French officially rejected his proposal** on Dec. 15.

1952. Formation of **Tunisian guerrilla bands** in the mountains. In response, the settlers organized **the Red Hand,** their own terrorist organization, which attacked Tunisian political leaders. The most famous victim of the settlers was **Ferhat Hached** (assassinated on Dec. 12, 1954), leader of the UGTT.

Jan. 18. Arrest of neo-Destour leaders, including **Habib Bourguiba,** after extensive rioting (Jan. 15). The French resident-general had provoked demonstrations by ordering **al-Amin Bey** to dismiss the Tunisian government. When the bey refused, **French authorities arrested Prime Minister Shanniq** (March 25).

1954, July 30. The French government granted complete **internal independence** to Tunisia. The terms of Tunisian sovereignty were spelled out in a French-Tunisian agreement (June 3, 1955).

1956–62. French exodus. The size of the French population shrank from about 180,000 (1956) to 30,000 six years later.

1956. Enactment of a **new code of personal status,** which was phased into effect over the next seven years. Among the revisions were **the abolition of polygamy, equal divorce rights for men and women, the outlawing of unilateral divorce by men, more balanced custody laws, a minimum age for marriage, and the requirement of both partners' consent before the marriage ceremony.**

March 20. TUNISIAN INDEPENDENCE. The NEO-DESTOUR PARTY under HABIB BOURGUIBA won national elections (March 25), and Bourguiba became the first prime minister (April 10).

1957, July 25. The National Assembly deposed the bey of Tunis and ended the monarchy. TUNISIA WAS PROCLAIMED A REPUBLIC.

1958, Feb. 8. A French air attack on the village of **Saqiat Sidi Yusuf** killed 69 Tunisian villagers. The French planes had been chasing **FLN guerrillas** from Algerian territory.

June 17. A French-Tunisian agreement arranged for the **withdrawal of French troops** from Tunisia (except Bizerte).

Oct. 1. Tunisia became a member of **the Arab League.**

1959–71. Expansion of the educational system. All levels registered increases in enrollment: from 362,000 to 935,000 in primary schools (from 44 percent to 72 percent of the eligible population); from 36,000 to 184,000 in secondary schools; and from 2,100 to 11,000 at the universities.

1959, June 1. A new constitution switched Tunisia from a parliamentary to a presidential system of government.

1961. Appointment of **Ahmad Ben Salah** as secretary of state for planning and finance. Ben Salah became responsible for overseeing the **transition of the economy to a system of central planning.**

1961–63. THE BIZERTE ISSUE. The French attempted to expand their only remaining military base in Tunisia (June 1961) but encountered opposition from the Tunisian government, which surrounded the base with troops. **Fighting erupted** (July 19), and French troops eventually took control of the entire city, killing some 1,300 Tunisians in the process. **Tunisia broke off diplomatic relations with France** but opened negotiations in July 1962. **The French finally withdrew** from Bizerte in Oct. 1963.

1964, May 11. A new agrarian law resulted in the seizure of about half of all French-owned land.

1970, March 24. Arrest and disgrace of Ahmad Ben Salah, architect of the planned economy. Tunisia rapidly moved toward a more open economy and sought to attract foreign investment.

1974, Jan. 12. Announcement of political union with Libya. The Tunisian government backed out of the scheme soon afterward.

Sept. 14. The Socialist Destour Party (formerly the neo-Destour) elected **Habib Bourguiba** as president for life.

1978, Jan. 26. A general strike escalated into violent antigovernment demonstrations throughout Tunisia.

1981, Sept. 22. The government **prohibited women from veiling** in schools and government buildings.

Nov. 1. Candidates from a coalition of the Socialist Destour Party and the UGTT swept parliamentary elections.

1983, Nov. 1. Two women, **Fethia Mzali and Souad Yaacoubi,** became Tunisia's first female cabinet members.

Dec. 29. Outbreak of bread riots, lasting over a week. The protests came on the heels of price increases arising from cuts in state subsidies. After troops brutally restored order (killing 89), the government ordered prices to be lowered (they were quietly raised a second time in July 1984).

1986, Nov. 1. Opposition groups boycotted nationwide parliamentary elections.

1987, Nov. 7. Prime Minister Zine El Abidine Ben Ali deposed Pres. Habib Bourguiba and assumed office as the new president.

1988, July 12. The constitution was amended to limit the president to a maximum of two terms in office.

1989, April 2. In nationwide elections, **Pres. Ben Ali** received 99 percent of the vote. The ruling party, the Constitutional Democratic Rally (renamed in Feb. 1988), won every seat in the Parliament. Municipal elections, boycotted by the opposition, resulted in a similar landslide.

1992, Jan. 3. Tunisia's major Islamicist movement, **al-Nahda,** formed a political wing, **the National Rally for Protecting the People's Choice.**

1999, Oct. 24. Tunisian president Zine El Abidine Ben Ali was reelected to his third 5-year presidential term. In the first multiparty elections in Tunisian history, the ruling Constitutional Democratic Assembly (CDA) won 148 of 182 available seats in the National Assembly.

d. LIBYA

(From p. 769)

1947, March. Formation of the **Libyan Liberation Committee** in Cairo under the leadership of **Bashir al-Sa'dawi.** The organization proposed a union between Tripolitania and Cyrenaica under Sanusi rule.

1949, May 17. Defeat of the Bevin-Sforza Plan in the UN. The British-Italian scheme would have split Libya into three trusteeships: Cyrenaica for the British, Tripolitania for the Italians, and Fezzan for the French. **The UN** instead adopted a **resolution calling for Libyan independence** by 1952 (Nov. 21, 1949).

1950, Dec. 2. The Libyan National Assembly recognized **IDRIS** as king of Libya.

1952, Jan. 1. Official **INDEPENDENCE OF LIBYA.** The country emerged as a federal monarchy dominated by a clique of conservative notables. It essentially retained the administrative divisions (Tripolitania, Cyrenaica, and Fezzan) inherited from the colonial period.

1953, Feb. Libya became a member of **the Arab League.**

1955, Nov. Granting of the **first oil concessions.** The first strike was at Bir Zelten in 1959. **The oil industry** was primarily developed during 1961–69 as foreign firms, especially independent companies, moved into the country to conduct intensive exploration.

1962, June. Libyan entry into **OPEC.**

1967, June 15. The government requested that the U.S. and Britain withdraw their remaining forces at the earliest possible date.

1969, Sept 1. MILITARY COUP against the monarchy. The plot was organized by a group of army officers directed by **MU'AMMAR AL-QADHAFI.** One of the first acts of the new regime was to **abolish the monarchy.** In its place emerged **the Libyan Arab Republic.** Effective authority was vested in a **Revolutionary Command Council** headed by Qadhafi, who officially became prime minister on Jan. 16, 1970.

1970, March 28. Completion of the British military withdrawal, as demanded by the Libyan government. **The U.S. pulled out** the last of its troops less than three months later (June 11).

July 21. Confiscation of all Italian and Jewish property.

1971, June. Founding of **the Arab Socialist Union,** which served as the regime's political party. It was the only legal party in the country.

1972, Feb. Announcement of plans to unite with Egypt. The proposed federation was officially rejected by Egypt in Aug. 1973.

1973, Sept. 1. Libya seized a majority share of all foreign oil companies operating inside the country and **completely nationalized** three American firms.

1975, Sept. 7. Official **annexation** of a belt of territory along the border with **Chad.** The area contained significant deposits of uranium.

1976, Jan. Publication of the first volume of Qadhafi's ***Green Book,*** by which he sought to explain the principles that guided his regime.

1977, July 21–29. Skirmishes along the border with Egypt.

1981, Aug. 19. U.S. fighter planes shot down two Libyan jets that fired on them as U.S. ships carried out maneuvers in the Gulf of Sidra.

1986, April 15. U.S. bombing of Tripoli and Benghazi. The raids killed at least 100 people. Among the sites selected by the U.S. military was Qadhafi's personal compound.

1987, Aug.–Sept. Launching of a major Libyan offensive against Chadian troops.

1990, Aug. 31. Libya and Chad submitted their border dispute to the International Court of Justice.

1991, March 11. Opening of **the Great Man-Made River,** a pipeline carrying water from wells deep in the interior to the heavily populated coastal regions.

1992, April 15. The **UN imposed economic sanctions against Libya,** which had refused to extradite six Libyans wanted in connection with two airline bombings (Pan Am flight 103 and UTA flight 772).

1993, Oct. 11–15. The government quashed an **attempted coup** by units in the army.

1994, Feb. 3. The World Court dismissed Libya's claim to a piece of land in northern Chad that had been the object of 20 years of periodic violence.

1995, Sept. 1. Libya announced plans to expel Palestinians in protest against the PLO for working toward peace with Israel.

1999, April 5. Although U.S. sanctions remained in effect, the international embargo against Libya ended after Libya handed over Abdel Basset Ali al-Megrahi and Lamen Khalifa Fhimah; the two suspects were connected with the 1988 bombing of a Pan American Airways plane during flight 103; the aircraft had exploded over Lockerbie, Scotland.

F. SOUTH AND SOUTHEAST ASIA, 1945–2000

1. SOUTH ASIA, 1945–2000

a. OVERVIEW

(From p. 772)

This period witnessed the **independence of South Asia from direct imperial control** and the struggle by the resulting nation-states of the subcontinent to create viable civil societies and to find appropriate places in a world becoming increasingly interdependent economically, geopolitically, and culturally. Britain's withdrawal marked not only independence but also **partition,** as it handed over power in 1947 to the new, separate nation-states of **India and Pakistan.** (Sri Lanka and Maldives achieved independence later.) This decision to divide the subcontinent conceded the impossibility of devising a federal system sufficiently loose in nature to reassure Muslim activists who felt their voices and interests would be brushed aside by the nationalist Congress Party, which was often incapable of recognizing the extent to which it conflated the terms *Hindu* and *nationalist* in its rhetoric and policies. The new states' boundary lines did not bode well for the future, however, as they demarcated a "moth-eaten" Pakistan (as Mohammed Ali Jinnah put it) carved out of two distinct pieces of territory in the east and west, with India in between. (Significantly, the dividing line in the east followed virtually the identical line drawn during the partition of Bengal in 1905 [p. 556]—a boundary protested at the time as "unnatural.")

Although at first the two nations mainly strove to find appropriate roles in a world sharply bifurcated by the cold war, more recent events have underscored their continuing struggle to resolve a much larger conundrum that has long affected the region: how to create shared understandings on which to build a civil society and how to determine the role of the state within it, in a way that makes room for the diverse groups that make up pluralistic societies. In part, this conundrum resulted from the legacy of imperialism, particularly the British Indian state's predilection to deal with groups rather than individuals. (The tension between the nation's need to deal directly with individuals, a basic foundation stone of national integration, and the state's desire to prove to different groups its ability to protect group interests, is the most pronounced characteristic of contemporary society in South Asia.) The conundrum also reflected a fundamental challenge faced by all modern nation-states: the need to create viable political systems that do not depend on cultural and ethnic homogeneity to succeed. Dealing with this problem has been exacerbated in postcolonial states by the accompanying need to create economic development strategies that minimize dependence on the industrialized world while achieving as much financial self-sufficiency as possible. These issues influenced the debate concerning the formation of an independent, postcolonial society and the role the state should play in directing it.

Certainly the implications of **demographic growth** have complicated these attempts to gain self-sufficiency; from a population base in 1941 of 389 million, numbers had increased by 1961 to 439.2 million in India and an additional 93.8 million in Pakistan. But the **population growth rate** for the region, after peaking in 1971–81 (at a decade rate of 26.4 percent) **seems to be slowly decreasing** now; for the decade 1981–91, the rate of growth has been 25.2 percent.

The position of **women** in independent India, if measured by standards such as **literacy** rates, has improved. The female workforce in the independent sector, for instance, has also been organized to exercise some political clout (through **SEWA, the Self-Employed Women's Association**). But issues such as the spate of **dowry deaths** (the murder of young wives for their dowries) in urban areas—especially in Delhi in the late 1980s and early 1990s—serve as symbols for the continuing disadvantages experienced by women in middle-class and extended family contexts.

b. BRITISH INDIA, TO INDEPENDENCE AND PARTITION

From independence into the 1970s, Pandit Nehru's vision of a secular Indian state with strong central planning processes still left room for the influence of business leaders who dominated and shaped the relationship among the state, communities, and individuals. But the increasing acrimony among those making demands on the state (especially communities invoking regional, religious, or ethnic identities, such as the Kashmiris or the Sikhs); Congress's growing reliance on ethnic, religious, and class-defined communities of "vote banks"; and the shift toward **economic liberalization policies** (which downplayed central planning and opened up new opportunities for Indian entrepreneurs as well as multinational corporations) have created in the 1980s and 1990s an increasingly unstable and doubt-riven civil society. For instance, the number of deaths in **communal (religious) riots** in the 1980s quadrupled those of the 1970s. Although supporters of partition had asserted that a shared Islamic identity would unite Pakistan, from its earliest days the state has been unable to resolve the tension between the attempt to use Islam to integrate very different regional cultures and the need to accede countering identities constructed around regional and ethnic identities. The fact that Pakistan began with a truncated institutional infrastructure (since most of the integrative institutions, such as the civil service and communication networks, went to India) has exacerbated the problem, at times leading the military to intervene in governance in order to maintain stability and efficiency.

1945, June 29. The **All-India Congress** failed to agree on a common list of ministers for the new government, and the **deadlock between Muslim leaders and Congress leaders** continued.

Sept. 19. The new British Labour government proposed to discuss with Indian representatives the offer for Indian autonomy made in 1942.

Sept. 20–23. The **All-India Congress,** meeting in Bombay, declared this plan to be unsatisfactory and called on Great Britain to "quit India."

Dec. 27. Elections to the **central legislative assembly** gave the largest number of seats to the **Congress Party and the Muslim League.**

1946. Hindu-Muslim differences over the future of India, combined with a serious food shortage, led to frequent riots, causing thousands of deaths.

March 14. The British government offered **full independence to India.**

March–June. Negotiations between British and Indian leaders failed to draw up a plan that satisfied both the Congress Party and the Muslim League. The latter, under **Mohammed Ali Jinnah,** insisted on a separate Muslim state of **Pakistan** and decided on "direct action" to achieve its goal.

Aug. 24. A new **executive council** (boycotted by the Muslim League) was formed as an interim government, including seven Congress members and five non-League Muslims. The Muslim League finally decided to join on Oct. 25.

Dec. 9. The constituent assembly, elected earlier, began its deliberations on the future of India. The Muslim League refused to participate.

1947, Feb. 20. To hasten developments, the British government declared its intention to transfer power into Indian hands not later than June 1948.

May 29. The constituent assembly outlawed "untouchability."

June 3. Following negotiations with Hindu and Muslim leaders, the British government announced the new constitutional plan, which called for **partition between India and Pakistan.** This plan was endorsed by the Muslim League on June 9 and the All-India Congress on June 16.

July 5. The Indian Independence Bill was introduced into Parliament. It called for two dominions, **India and Pakistan,** and the termination of British authority over the remaining **Indian states.** Both India and Pakistan were to remain members of the British Commonwealth. The bill became law on July 18.

Aug. 15. THE INDEPENDENCE OF INDIA went into effect. The process of partition was accompanied by terrible acts of violence, notably in the Punjab region, among Muslims, Hindus, and Sikhs. By the end of September, close to 2 million refugees had been exchanged between India and Pakistan.

Sept. 21. The two new governments issued a joint statement stressing their readiness to remove all causes of conflict.

c. THE REPUBLIC OF INDIA

1947, Aug. 15. The Dominion of India was inaugurated in Delhi, with **Pandit Jawaherlal Nehru** as prime minister and **Lord Mountbatten** as governor-general. Most of the **Indian states** (princely and chiefly), notably excepting Hyderabad, Kashmir, and Junagadh, acceded to the new dominion for defense, external affairs, and communications, while retaining their internal sovereignties.

Oct. 26. The government of India admitted **Kashmir** into the Indian Union, thus precipitating a crisis with Pakistan, since Kashmir contained a majority of Muslims.

Nov. 9. The Indian government assumed control over the administration of the state of **Junagadh.**

Dec. 30. After vain attempts to solve the conflict over **Kashmir,** the dispute was referred to the **UN.** Sporadic fighting continued in Kashmir between Indian and Muslim forces.

1948–49. The integration of states began. The rulers, in response to an appeal to consolidate the country, agreed to form regional unions of states or to merge their states with the dominion. While renouncing their ruling powers, they retained their personal privileges, private properties, and privy purses. Ultimately, the government had to invade to force accession.

1948, Jan. 30. Mahatma Gandhi was assassinated by a Hindu for his part in the partition of India, on the grounds that he had not created a militant enough vision for Hindus in India.

June 21. Chakravarti Rajagopalachari succeeded Earl Mountbatten as governor-general.

1949–50. A constitution-drafting committee, chaired by **B. R. Ambedkar** (an Untouchable leader) created a new constitution that was adopted on Jan. 26, 1950 (a date later celebrated as **Republic Day**). In this constitution, much emphasis was placed on the relationship between the individual and the state. Universal franchise made India the world's largest democracy, with 173 million people able to vote in 1951. Many of the provisions in the constitution carried over the institutional arrangements established in the 1935 Government of India Act.

1949, Jan. 1. Following the mediation attempts of a UN commission set up by the security council on Jan. 20, 1948, India and Pakistan agreed on a **cease-fire order for Kashmir.** India rejected a subsequent arbitration scheme submitted by the U.N.

Nov. 26. The Indian constituent assembly adopted a new **constitution,** which **made India a federal republic.** The British king continued to be recognized, however, as symbol of the free association of Commonwealth members.

1950s. This decade was marked especially by India's emerging leadership of what came to be called the **"nonaligned nations,"** composed primarily of postcolonial nations anxious to remain independent of cold war bipolarity (p. 814). (Nehru worked with Gamal Abdal Nasser of Egypt and Pres. Sukarno of Indonesia in forging these ties among developing countries.) These efforts were accompanied by resolution of several still-ambiguous relationships with imperial powers, especially with France and Portugal (who still retained control over pockets of territory in the subcontinent) and with the U.S. and the USSR.

1950s–1960s. The Tamil film industry became closely aligned with the Tamil language movement. Tamil linguistic pride translated into pro-Tamil, anti-Brahman, anti–North India political sentiments. The key symbol of this ideological stance was **MGR,** the main film star of the Tamil cinema industry, who was first used to draw crowds for the **DMK (Dravida Munnetra Kazhagam)** political party. Eventually, MGR gained such a strong following that he served three terms as chief minister of Tamilnadu (1977, 1980, and 1985).

1950, Jan. 26. INAUGURATION OF THE REPUBLIC OF INDIA and election of **Rajendra Prasad** as its first president.

April 8. Mounting tension between India and Pakistan was eased by an agreement (**Delhi Pact**) between Prime Ministers Pandit Nehru and Liaqat Ali Khan, promising fair treatment to each other's minorities. The continued **deadlock over Kashmir,** on the other hand, made any really close relations between the two countries impossible.

Nov. 20. Nehru declared that India accepted the 1941 **McMahon boundary with Tibet,** and not the line indicated on Chinese maps.

1951, Feb. 24. A trade block, existing since 1949, was broken when India and Pakistan reached agreement on a full trade pact.

June 3. After months of famine, the Indian Socialist Party staged a giant demonstration in Delhi to protest the government's failure to solve the **food and housing problems.**

July 3. Prime Minister Nehru lodged a formal **complaint against Pakistan** with the UN Security Council. He charged repeated violations of the cease-fire agreement in Kashmir.

Nov. 28. The Colombo Plan to aid India, Pakistan, Ceylon, Sarawak, and Borneo was presented to the British Commonwealth Parliament. It envisaged £8 billion over six years, beginning in 1951. Colombo Plan nations, adding new members, continued Asian economic development planning.

1952, March 1. Final results of the **first national elections** gave Prime Minister Nehru's Congress Party 364 of 489 seats in the National Assembly. Pro-Soviet parties won only 28 seats but showed surprising strength in the local assemblies.

May 13. Formal installation of Rajendra Prasad as the first president elected under the republican constitution.

Aug. 7. Parliament approved legislation to give **Jammu and Kashmir** greater autonomy than other Indian states.

1953, Dec. 2. The government signed a five-year trade agreement with the USSR.

1954. Nehru denounced U.S. policies in Parliament early in the year. Later that year he concluded a **trade agreement with China** and got **France to transfer its four settlements** to India (concluded in 1956).

1955. The first **Backwards Classes Commission,** under the direction of Kaka Kalelkar, submitted a report to the government about special privileges to be extended to Untouchables and others by the state. Although sharply divided among themselves, the commissioners ultimately recommended that special "reservations of places" in education and government employment be awarded not simply on the basis of group membership, but by calculating individual economic need. This decision maintained the constitution's original emphasis on the relationship between state and individual, and it was sharply resisted by those advocating the extension of reservations to entire groups (identified by caste name and listed on the "schedules" of castes and tribes inherited from the British and maintained by the independent government).

June 7–22. During a **visit of Nehru to Moscow,** the USSR and India concluded an agreement for Soviet economic and technical assistance to India. In November the visit was reciprocated by Marshal Nikolay Bulganin and Nikita Khrushchev.

July 25. The government ordered the **closure of the Portuguese legation** in New Delhi because of Portugal's unwillingness to negotiate on Goa's integration into the Indian republic. On Aug. 15 **Indian demonstrators marched on Goa and Damao.** Portuguese police killed 21 and wounded over 100. India broke relations with Portugal on Aug. 19.

Oct. A **States Reorganization Commission** submitted its report recommending that many British-imposed administrative boundaries be redrawn to recognize certain regional, cultural, and linguistic configurations. Although this change was justified on the basis of administrative efficiency (the use of a single language in a given state), the emergence the following year of 14 states and 6 centrally administered territories legitimized community identities based on linguistic (and therefore regional, cultural, and often ethnic) affinities. The commission explicitly rejected the demands for redrawn boundaries in the **Punjab,** however, arguing that although these demands claimed to accommodate Punjabi, they really aimed to satisfy Sikh (therefore religious, not linguistic) identity claims.

The remainder of the decade illustrated that the redrawing of some boundaries did not defuse the demands of communities that resisted the pull of national identity. In addition to the **Sikhs,** another major regional challenge emerged in South India concerning **Tamil** identity. This movement combined language (Tamil), kinship, and religious claims (Tamil was represented as the goddess Tamilttay) to resist what Tamils felt was a colonizing effort to force Hindi and Gangetic Plains identity on the South.

1956–61. The **second Five-Year Plan** aimed quickly to create, through central planning, an economy supported by state investment in heavy industry and military strength. But this strategy demanded a short-run reliance on imports, foreign exchange, and foreign aid (which India cleverly attracted from both the Communist and capitalist blocs). It also gave short shrift to agrarian development and the agrarian self-sufficiency that could have come from investment in that sector.

1957, April 5. Kerala, a coastal state in southwest India, installed its recently elected **Communist government.**

July 11. The Aga Khan, the spiritual and temporal leader of 20 million Ismailis, died and was succeeded by his oldest grandson, Prince Karim Khan, with the title **Aga Khan IV.**

1958, Jan. 10. Former Kashmiri prime minister **Sheik Muhammad Abdullah,** who was released on Jan. 8 after four and a half years of detention, charged that India had set up an illegal regime in Kashmir. On Jan. 13 he asked for a plebiscite to settle the Indian-Pakistani dispute over Kashmir.

1959, June 30. The **government refused to recognize Tibet's Dalai Lama** as heading a "separate" government of Tibet functioning in India.

July 31. Pres. Rajendra Prasad issued a **proclamation taking over the state government of Kerala** and ousting its Communist regime.

Oct. 26. Indian border police and a Chinese Communist force clashed in Ladakh.

1960s. New form of **neocolonialism,** based on economic relationships between the industrial world and the developing world, began to emerge. Postcolonial areas continued to produce cash crops and minerals for export to a world market in order to earn the capital they needed to invest in industrialization at home. But because the prices of primary products fluctuated dramatically, however, Third World countries suffered severe disadvantages. This neocolonialism has been extended through development policies, especially the **Green Revolution,** wherein ex-colonies become dependent on Western benefactors for supply of fertilizers and new kinds of seeds even when they achieve **self-sufficiency in food production,** as India managed to do in this decade.

1960–64. Uneven development marked **industrial growth: steel production,** stagnating at 1 million tons per year in the early postwar period, increased to 3 million tons in 1960 and 6 million tons in 1964. By contrast, **cotton textile production** in the same period remained the same (5 billion yards of cloth). **Agricultural production** increased, but only because the amount of arable land was extended. The ability of the internal market to consume manufactured goods, however, stag-

nated; two-thirds of the average household income continued to be spent on food. (Consequently, when food prices rose dramatically in 1965, consumption of other durable goods dropped sharply.)

1961, Feb. 14. The government maintained that China was in "unlawful occupation of about 12,000 square miles of Indian territory," and (May 2) charged China with intrusion on the Indian border and fomenting tensions among Asian nations.

Dec. 18–19. Indian troops invaded and conquered the Portuguese territories of Goa, Damao, and Diu.

1962, Oct. 20. INVASION OF INDIA BY CHINESE COMMUNIST TROOPS (p. 1023). On Oct. 29 Prime Minister Nehru asked for U.S. military aid.

Oct. 31. Nehru dismissed V. K. Krishna Menon as minister of defense, in the wake of a Chinese military advance, and assumed the post himself.

Nov. 19. Since Indian troops were retreating in the face of a massive Chinese attack, **Nehru asked U.S. president Kennedy for further military aid.** Two days later the U.S. responded by sending India transport planes with U.S. crews.

Nov. 21. Communist China unexpectedly ordered a **cease-fire along the Indian border** and offered to draw its troops back of the "lines of actual control" that existed as of Nov. 7, 1959. Fighting ceased the next day.

Dec. 14. Although Nehru had rejected the Chinese offer of a cease-fire and negotiations, India announced the beginning of a **massive Chinese troop withdrawal** from the northeastern frontier area.

1964, April 8. Sheik Muhammad Abdullah, the "Lion of Kashmir" (again in detention since April 1958), was released from prison. Upon his release, he denounced the Indian policy toward Kashmir, but on April 29 arrived in Delhi to discuss the future of Kashmir with Nehru.

May 27. Jawaharlal Nehru died suddenly.

June 1. The National Congress Party chose **Lal Bahadur Shastri** to succeed Nehru.

Aug. Sheik Abdullah's talks with Shastri, after consultations with Pres. Ayub Khan of Pakistan.

Oct. 12. Meeting of Shastri and Ayub at Karachi, ending in agreement to work for better understanding.

Nov. 15. According to a government statement, 775,000 refugees had entered India from East Pakistan since January.

Dec. 30–31. Arrest of members of the pro-Chinese wing of the Communist Party, charged with plotting a violent revolution to be timed with another Chinese attack on India.

1965–66. Great drought underscored the weakness of Indian agricultural development and its reliance on productivity of marginal lands. The drought exercised a staggering impact on food prices, the ability of the state to plan and follow through on its five-year budget plans, and voter behavior. (Planning processes were resumed only after the **Green Revolution** had succeeded [p. 820].)

1965, Jan. 26. Hindi became India's official language, despite violent opposition in southern India. On Feb. 24 it was decided that English should be an associate language in dealings between the central government and non-Hindi-speaking states.

May 8. Arrest and confinement of Sheik Abdullah for agitation in behalf of self-determination for Kashmir.

May 12–19. Visit of Prime Minister Shastri to Moscow in the interest of further Soviet economic aid.

Aug.–Dec. India suffered an **acute food shortage,** which was relieved only by huge shipments from the U.S. and Australia.

Aug. 5. NEW KASHMIR CRISIS. Indian forces, charging infiltration of Kashmir by Pakistani irregulars, crossed the cease-fire line (Aug. 16) and launched an offensive in the direction of Lahore. An undeclared war ensued. Britain banned arms supplies to India (Sept. 8), and the U.S. terminated military aid to both sides. On Sept. 20 the UN Security Council called for a cease-fire, which both sides accepted (Sept. 22). Nonetheless, truce violations occurred frequently in the following months.

1966, Jan. 4–10. Conferences at Tashkent between the Indian and Pakistani prime ministers, under the auspices of Soviet premier Aleksey Kosygin. They agreed to restore normal relations and withdraw troops to the lines of Aug. 1965, but without a settlement of the Kashmir issue.

Jan. 11. Death of Prime Minister Shastri, of a heart attack.

Jan. 19. Mrs. Indira Gandhi, daughter of Nehru, was elected leader of the Congress Party and prime minister.

March 28–29. Mrs. Gandhi's visit to Washington, London (April 1), **and Moscow** (April 2). She continued the policy of nonalignment and acceptance of economic aid wherever possible. The acute food shortage continued throughout the year.

June 5. Devaluation of the rupee by 36.5 percent.

Oct. An epidemic of **student riots and strikes.** Several universities were closed.

Nov. 1. Creation of two Sikh states, one Punjabi-speaking, the other (Hariana) Hindi-speaking.

1967, Feb. 15–21. National elections. The Congress Party secured a small majority in the lower house, but lost in many of the state assemblies, while the Communists gained. In 9 of the 16 Indian states, **coalition governments** became necessary. Growth of regional parties, in part the reflection of tension over the language question, formed part of this significant **shift in the nature of the Congress Party.** The shared vision shaped by the independence movement receded; in its place, Congress began to form other kinds of alliances and strategies to keep "interest groups" within the fold. Under the leadership of **Indira Gandhi** (especially after she returned to power in 1980), Congress began to treat Muslims, Sikhs, and Untouchables as minority interest **"voting blocs";** the appeasement strategies devised by the party worked directly against state and civil society interests in maintaining relationships with individuals.

Rich peasants, who had benefited from steep rises in food prices after the 1966–67 drought, achieved greater autonomy and state support under the new regime. They consequently invested in Green Revolution approaches that significantly improved agricultural production.

1968, Jan. Further tension with China and with Pakistan over their support of Naga and Mizo rebels.

Student and communal disturbances increased greatly. In some areas, Communists tried to start peasant revolts.

Sheik Abdullah was again released.

Jan. 25–31. Visit of Premier Kosygin to India. A joint Indian-Soviet declaration called for unconditional cessation of the U.S. bombing of North Vietnam.

Feb. Disintegration of the non–Congress Party coalition in West Bengal and (April) in Uttar Pradesh and other states. In these areas, where the Congress Party did not control a majority in the assembly, presidential rule had to be instituted.

1969, May 3. Death of Pres. Zakir Husain.

July 9. The Congress Party accepted Mrs. Gandhi's program for nationalization of banks, restrictions on foreign capital, ceiling on incomes, and so on, representing a policy of socialization to forestall further gains by the Communists.

Aug. 16. Election of V. V. Giri as president, by a narrow margin. He was the candidate of Mrs. Gandhi and the left wing of the Congress Party.

Nov. 12. Congress Party leaders of the right wing (the Syndicate) expelled Mrs. Gandhi for indiscipline, but the lower house of Parliament gave her overwhelming support. The Syndicate then formed the **Congress Parliamentary Party** under **Ram Subhag Singh,** as opposition to Mrs. Gandhi.

1970, Aug. "Land Grab" campaigns by Communist and Socialist parties as symbolic seizure of large holdings and redistribution to needy peasants. The leaders of the movement were arrested.

Sept. 2. Abolition of the allowances and privileges of the former princes was voted by the lower house, with the support of Socialists and Communists. The bill was then rejected by the upper house, but put into effect by presidential fiat (Sept. 6).

Oct. 2. Suspension of the Uttar Pradesh government by decree of the prime minister. Under pressure and criticism, Mrs. Gandhi reversed her decision (Oct. 17) and permitted the formation of a coalition government under old Congress Party leadership.

Dec. 15. The Indian Supreme Court ruled that the presidential orders abolishing the privileges of former rulers were illegal. Mrs. Gandhi stated that her government nonetheless remained committed to their abolition.

1971, March 1. Indian elections resulted in success for Indira Gandhi and her wing of Congress, **Congress (R).** They won 350 out of 520 Lok Sabha (lower house) seats, reducing the Congress opposition to 16 members.

March 31. India intervened in the **civil war between East and West Pakistan:** Indira Gandhi appealed to the UN regarding the plight of civilians in East Pakistan. This was a subcontinentwide issue, as East Pakistan's military attacks on peasants in the West Bengali countryside prompted more than 1 million refugees to flood into India, beginning in April. Thousands of young Bangladeshis joined guerrilla bands of **"Liberation Forces" (Mukti Bahini),** which received arms and support from Indian troops.

Aug. 9. Indira Gandhi signed the 20-year **Treaty of Peace, Friendship, and Cooperation with the Soviet Union.**

Nov. 23. Troops of three Indian divisions, with armor and air support, attacked Jessore, Rangpur, Chittagong Hill Tracts, and Sylhet.

Dec. 15. After India made rapid advances in East Pakistan, the banner of the **new nation of Bangladesh** was unfurled in every town and village. The Instrument of Surrender was signed on this date by India's chief of staff Gen. Sam Manekshaw and Pakistani general Niazi.

Dec. 22. Refugees began to return to Bangladesh. By March nearly all of the almost 10 million people had returned to their homeland.

1972. State elections strengthened Indira Gandhi's position.

SEWA (meaning "service," also stands for the Self-Employed Women's Association) was organized. Based first in the city of Ahmedabad, in Gujarat, it worked with women with no fixed place of employment (homes, streets, or fields) and with no fixed employers. Within two decades SEWA gained 30,000 members and succeeded in forcing employers to provide the minimum wages stipulated by law. Using cooperatives, SEWA functioned as a union while also providing banking and health services.

July. India's Gandhi and president of Pakistan Zulfiqar Ali Bhutto signed the **Simla Agreement.** Both countries renounced the use of force and agreed to respect the cease-fire line in Kashmir and international borders elsewhere.

1973–74. Drought brought severe hardship to West and Central India. This was exacerbated by inflation and the worldwide petroleum crisis, leading to a reduced standard of living.

Riots in a number of states protested these conditions. For instance, in Gujarat, street fighting led to resignation of the state government and the imposition of presidential rule.

A strike of railway staff was suppressed by the army.

In Bihar, the veteran socialist **Jayaprakash Narayan (JP)** headed a popular campaign against the local Congress government. During 1974 he sought allies outside Bihar and began to attack the central government. He posed a Gandhian vision of a nation of self-sufficient villagers against the multinational development philosophy of Nehru and Indira Gandhi.

1974, May. Explosion of India's first nuclear device set back relations with Pakistan and provoked worldwide criticism.

1975. L. N. Mishra, central minister for railways, was assassinated.

April. Inclusion of Sikkim (an Indian protectorate since 1950) in the Indian Union strained relations with Nepal.

June. The Janata Front (organized by JP Narayan) contested and won the election in Gujarat that followed the ending of presidential rule.

The Allahabad High Court found **Indira Gandhi guilty** of election malpractices. She then proclaimed a **state of emergency** and arrested large numbers of her opponents. The houses of Parliament were recalled and, in the absence of nongovernment members, rapidly approved constitutional amendments to strengthen the executive and legislative branches and to protect the prime minister.

New policies implemented during the state of emergency demonstrated the **abrogation of individual rights** that was under way; **forced sterilization** (to reduce the birthrate) became the most publicized example.

1976. An agreement was reached with Pakistan on exchange of ambassadors and restoration of air links; relations improved with China to the point of exchange of ambassadors.

1977, Jan. Indira Gandhi announced that the postponed **general elections** would be held in March, at which time the state of emergency would be terminated. Widespread fears that democratic institutions had

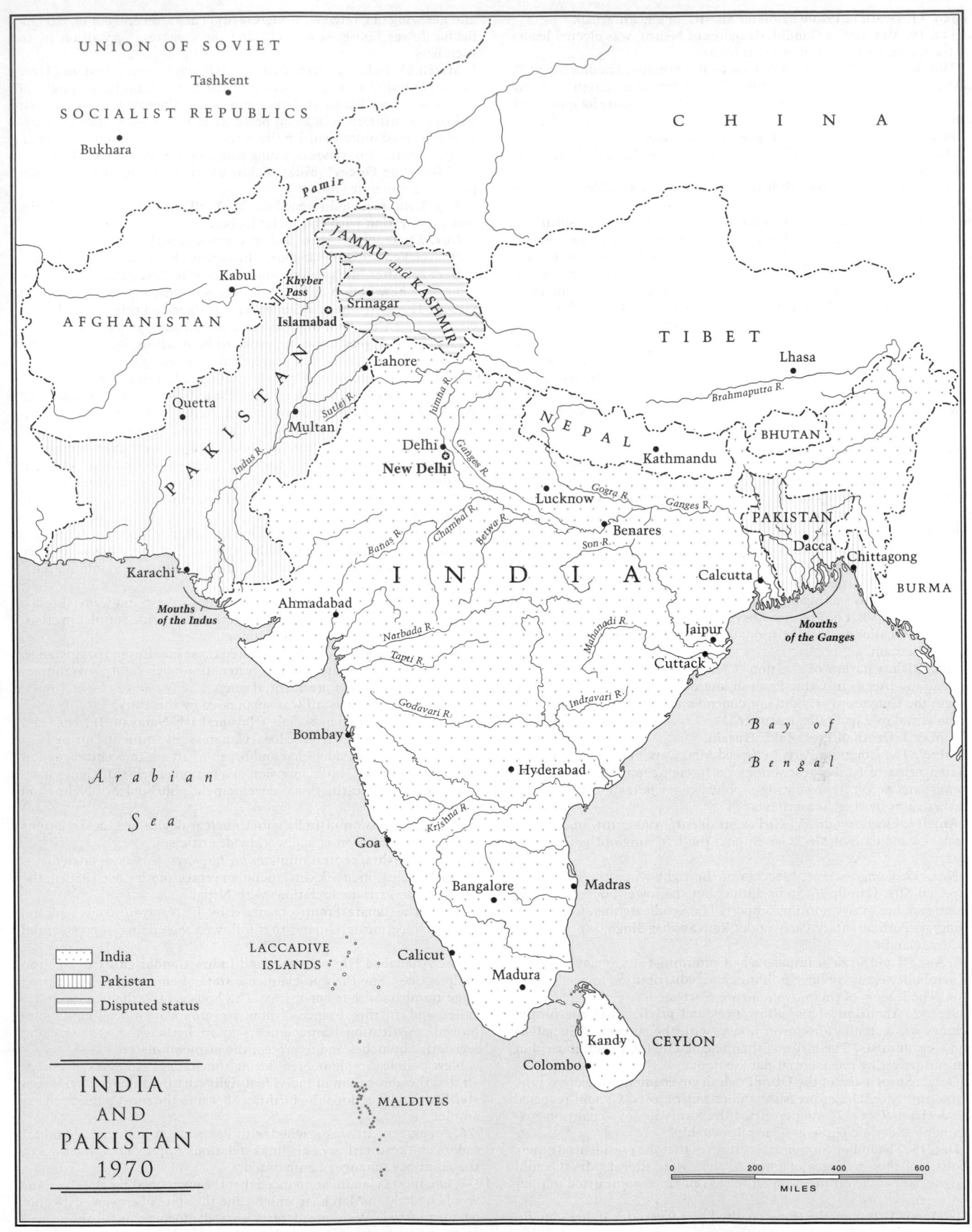

UNION OF SOVIET

Tashkent

SOCIALIST REPUBLICS

Bukhara

CHINA

Pamir

JAMMU and KASHMIR

Kabul

Khyber Pass

Islamabad

Srinagar

AFGHANISTAN

PAKISTAN

Lahore

TIBET

Lhasa

Brahmaputra R.

Quetta

Sutlej R.

Multan

Indus R.

Delhi

Jumna R.

NEPAL

BHUTAN

New Delhi

Ganges R.

Kathmandu

Lucknow

Gogra R.

Ganges R.

PAKISTAN

Banas R.

Chambal R.

Betwa R.

Benares

Son R.

Dacca

Chittagong

Karachi

I N D I A

Calcutta

BURMA

Mouths of the Indus

Ahmadabad

Jaipur

Mouths of the Ganges

Narbada R.

Mahanadi R.

Cuttack

Tapti R.

Indravari R.

Godavari R.

Bay of Bengal

Bombay

Arabian

Hyderabad

Sea

Krishna R.

Goa

Bangalore

Madras

India

LACCADIVE ISLANDS

Pakistan

Calicut

Disputed status

Madura

INDIA

AND

PAKISTAN

1970

Kandy

CEYLON

Colombo

MALDIVES

0   200   400   600

MILES

ceased to function were disproved in the extraordinary elections that took place.

March. Indira Gandhi lost her own seat in the Lok Sabha, and the Congress was defeated throughout North India. In the South, Congress and its allies improved their position. Congress (R) retired from the field and allowed the winners (the Janata Party) to establish a new government.

The first tasks of the **Janata government,** under the leadership of Morarji Desai, were to dismantle the machinery of the state of emergency and to repair the constitution.

July. Neelim Sanjiva Reddy was named president, but rifts quickly appeared in the Janata government.

1978, Nov. Indira Gandhi won a Lok Sabha by-election in Karnataka.

Dec. Indira Gandhi was imprisoned for a week by the government. Her followers protested in India's major cities, even hijacking an Indian Airlines plane.

The Congress faction led by Indira Gandhi became known as Congress (I) (for Indira).

1979, July 19. Morarji Desai resigned as the Janata leader, on the eve of a no-confidence motion.

Pres. Reddy, unable to pull a majority coalition government together, instead dissolved Parliament and called for a new general election in Jan. 1980.

1979–80. Unrest spread across northeastern India's seven tribal states—Assam, Arunachal Pradesh, Nagaland, Manipur, Meghalaya, Mizoram, and Tripura. Starting as nonviolent responses to the mounting influx of Bengali immigrants from Bangladesh, these protests became increasingly violent, popular, and ideological.

1980s. Economic policies had made it possible for the government to rely on the political support of urban populations and the rural rich. Policy emphasis on regressive indirect taxation, and refusal to levy progressive direct taxation, had encouraged the redistribution of income in favor of the rich peasants in the countryside and relatively privileged urban populations.

1980, Jan. Elections to the Lok Sabha brought Indira Gandhi back to the political center. Indira's son **Sanjay Gandhi** entered the Lok Sabha. (Much of his political clout came from his leadership in **Shiv Sena,** a conservative Hindu youth organization.)

June. Sanjay Gandhi was killed in a plane crash.

1981, June. Indira's other son, **Rajiv Gandhi,** won Sanjay's former seat in the Lok Sabha, although he had previously avoided political life.

A mass conversion ceremony by Untouchables (to become Muslims, rather than Buddhists, which had generally been their previous preference) in South India provoked riots that killed large numbers. At much the same time, the **Mandal Commission Report** called for job reservations for a much-increased number of people on the basis of their caste status, rather than individual economic conditions ("Mandalization"). This **expansion of the reservations policy** reinforced the shift by Congress government to reliance on relationship with communities rather than individuals. Uneasiness about the policy was reinforced by the fact that a number of groups included in the Backward Classes classification actually exercised considerable power in the localities (for example, Yadavs in Uttar Pradesh, Lingayats in Mysore).

1983, Feb. Rajiv Gandhi became general secretary of the All-India Congress Committee.

Resurgence of caste and communal feeling led to uncommonly violent **rioting,** the most notable conflict emerging between low castes and Harijans (Untouchables). Protests focused on Harijans' statutory and constitutional guarantees, and so lower-caste protest had some high-caste backing as well. Additional conflict developed between low-class sections of the Muslims and Hindus.

This socioeconomic conflict also translated into political developments. The Backward Classes had supported the Janata Party but became disillusioned with it after Indira Gandhi's victory in the 1980 general election, even though Congress (I) had, to secure their support as a voting bloc, intermittently extended special considerations to buy their loyalty. At the same time, resentment of the economic benefits thus granted to Untouchables began to be expressed in **Hindu fundamentalist** ideology by other castes.

1984. Civil unrest indicated that civil society was undergoing severe stress. Increasingly broad-scale riots measured the seriousness of

Hindu-Muslim confrontation, particularly in Maharashtra. In Assam and northeastern India, feelings against Bengali residents and immigrants were expressed in murders, bomb outrages, strikes, and a campaign of noncooperation. In Punjab, a militant Sikh secessionist movement had been smouldering for some years and now began to find systematic expression in terrorism.

The Vishva Hindu Parishad (VHP), a fundamentalist organization of Hindu religious leaders, organized a **march** through Uttar Pradesh and on to Delhi to dramatize their campaign at a religious site in **Ayodhya,** considered the birthplace of the god-avatar, Ram. Under dispute was a small mosque (which came to be known as the **Babri Masjid**), built in 1556 by the first Mughal, Babur, ostensibly on the site of a temple dedicated to Ram. The VHP campaign demanded that the mosque be torn down to make room for the construction of a new temple. Public opinion mounted quickly in favor of this campaign.

May. Sikh followers of **Jarnail Singh Bhindrawale,** a leader originally supported by the Congress government in opposition to the more militant Sikhs, turned the Golden Temple of Amritsar into a terrorist stronghold. The public was horrified at this politicization of a sacred space, but then turned against the state when the **Indian army stormed the temple,** killing Bhindrawale and hundreds of supporters. Sacred buildings were damaged.

Oct. 31. Indira Gandhi was assassinated by Sikh members of her personal guard, Beant Singh and Satwant Singh. Rajiv Gandhi was sworn in as India's new prime minister.

Nov. 1–3. Massacres of Sikhs were launched in Delhi and other cities; the police and India's army ignored them. By official count, more than 1,000 Sikhs were murdered in Delhi alone.

Nov. Rajiv Gandhi called for national elections.

Bhopal tragedy. Defective valves in Union Carbide's insecticide storage tanks let deadly invisible gas escape. Within hours, 2,000 people were dead and hundreds of thousands injured by the worst industrial accident in recent history.

Dec. 24. Landslide victory for Rajiv Gandhi. The national opposition was reduced to 19 seats.

1985–90. Food grain production remained remarkably stable, despite uneven monsoon patterns, undoubtedly as a result of the rapid expansion achieved during the Green Revolution. **Punjab and Haryana** increased their share of agricultural production from 13 percent in 1975 to 21 percent in 1985 and retained this share through 1990. Such financial success doubtless explained part of the strong sense held among Punjabi **Sikhs** that the national government "owed" them more recognition.

1985. Rajiv Gandhi and Minister of Finance V. P. Singh **shifted economic policy** toward fiscal rather than direct government controls. They lowered taxes to stimulate investment.

The focus on the place of Muslims in Indian civil society was increased by the ruling in the case of **Shah Bano,** an elderly Muslim woman who sought recourse through civil law when her husband divorced her and refused to pay alimony. The court ruled in her favor, arguing that even though separate civil law structures applied to Hindus and Muslims, all citizens should be treated equally. In 1986, to appease conservative Muslim agitators, the Congress government introduced legislation (ironically entitled the **Muslim Women Protection of Rights on Divorce Act**) that not only denied equal protection to Muslim women, but also did so retroactively, so that Shah Bano lost her award.

July. The Punjab Accord was signed by Rajiv Gandhi and Akali Dal leader Sant Longowal. It promised the transfer of Chandigarh to Punjab on Jan. 26, 1986. New elections were to be held in Punjab, and some concessions made to other Sikh demands. **Sant Longowal was assassinated** by Sikh terrorists in his own village.

Sept. Elections in Punjab gave victory to the Akali Dal and its new leader, S. S. Barnaloo, who became chief minister.

1986. "Honeymoon" ended for Rajiv Gandhi; early 1986 was marked by increased **Sikh extremism,** including the temporary recapture of the Golden Temple; by mid-1986, militant Sikh factions had broken away from the ruling Akali Dal Party. **A Hindu backlash** emerged because many saw Rajiv's policies toward Sikhs as too conciliatory.

Feb. The Hindu backlash was strengthened when a judge ruled that the **Babri Masjid site in Ayodhya** (see 1984) should be **opened to the**

public. The lock on a gate erected 50 years earlier was removed. Agitations by politicized Hindu groups (especially the **Bharatiya Janata Party [BJP]**, the political party supported by other militant Hindu groups) escalated, using Ayodhya as the focal point.

In Haryana, the second state carved out of the territory that had originally formed the Punjab, the chief minister resigned and was replaced according to timing that jeopardized the Haryana elections. In an attempt to save the elections, Rajiv suspended the government, thus shutting out future cooperation by moderate Sikhs. In the June elections, Congress (I) was defeated by the Lok Dal (B).

1987. India expanded its number of states: Mizoram and Arunachal were admitted as the 23rd and 24th states of India in February; Goa became the 25th state in May.

New regionalist movements also began to emerge in other parts of India. The Tribal National Volunteers (TNV) had begun demanding an autonomous state in part of Tripura; in late 1986 more than 100 people had been killed by TNV guerrillas, and in Jan. 1987 the TNV was declared illegal. The central government sent paramilitary troops to Tripura in Jan. 1988, and order returned in the wake of the general elections, won by Congress (I).

The Gurkha National Liberation Front (GNLF) emerged in Darjeeling and West Bengal, and it organized violent disturbances and a general strike. Rajiv met with the GNLF leader but dismissed their demand for a separate Gurkha state. (Agitation collapsed in July 1988.)

May, June. Communal (Hindu-Muslim) riots in Old Delhi and Meerut marked further advances of fundamentalist Hindu political agitation. (This political philosophy was called **Hindutva.**)

1988, Jan. Congress (I) was defeated decisively by the **Dravida Munnetra Kazhagam (DMK)** in state elections in Tamil Nadu. The DMK demonstrated effective campaigning to promote an ideology of regional identity expressed through linguistic, cultural, kin-based rhetoric.

March. The opposition to Congress called a **general strike,** which proved most effective in West Bengal, Kerala, and Karnataka. Severe drought in northwest India exacerbated opposition to the Congress (I) government. Both the opposition and Congress (I) were affected by increased Hindu-Muslim tension. Relations were worsened by the controversy over the religious site in Ayodhya (p. 999).

1989, Nov. 22–26. Rajiv Gandhi called an election several weeks ahead of schedule. Congress (I) won only 193 seats; **the BJP won control of four states,** including Uttar Pradesh and Bihar, the Bhojpuri heartland (a linguistic cultural area in the eastern Gangetic Plain), center for Hindu fundamentalist political agitations.

Dec. V. P. Singh was elected leader of the Janata Dal Parliamentary Party and became prime minister. Devi Lal, the populist chief minister of Haryana and a powerful rural leader, was named deputy prime minister. (But by July of following year, competition between V. P. Singh and Devi Lal led to the dismissal of Devi Lal.)

1990. In a decade of **industrial growth** (1980–90), coal production had doubled, and oil and automobile production had tripled. This advance had doubtless been facilitated by economic liberalization, but was challenged to the point of economic crisis in 1990 because of the country's political instability.

Sept. V. P. Singh's government announced that it would implement **Mandalization** (p. 999) in a bid to win support of the Backward Classes. Widespread unrest within the middle classes (especially among traders, owners of small businesses, and white-collar workers) followed the announcement; some 40 students immolated themselves in a form of protest new to India.

Oct.–Nov. A procession to Ayodhya by Hindus was halted by the government. A major confrontation ensued, and a large number of people were killed. V. P. Singh was given a vote of no confidence, a new government was formed by Chandra Shekhar, and fresh elections were scheduled for May 1991.

1991, May 21. Rajiv Gandhi was assassinated after the first days of polling while he was campaigning in Tamil Nadu. His assassination was most likely the work of Liberation Tigers of Tamil Eelam (LTTE), who suffered as result of India's intervention in the Sri Lankan civil war between Sinhalese and Sri Lankan Tamils (p. 1007).

Elections were postponed to mid-June. Congress (I) won 227 of 511 seats, probably some out of sympathy. P. V. Narasimha Rao was chosen as interim party president of Congress (I).

Sikh terrorism continued at high levels in the Punjab area.

1992, Feb. 29. The government introduced a "revolutionary" budget for 1992–93, calling for **economic liberalization.** Its policies removed the block on sending rupees out of India, encouraged private entrepreneurship and investment from overseas (for multinational corporations as well as diasporic Indians), and removed large areas of the economy from government control.

Dec. 7. Under encouragement from the BJP state government in Uttar Pradesh, **Hindu activists destroyed the Babri Masjid in Ayodhya** and began building a new temple. After an embarrassing period of inaction, the central government finally condemned the action and took four BJP state governments under control.

1993. New revelations of tensions over marriage dowries cited several incidents in which men killed their wives to protest what they judged to be inadequate payments.

March 12–19. Amid growing **Hindu fundamentalism,** urban riots convulsed Bombay and Calcutta in the aftermath of the Ayodhya mosque destruction; 1,200 were killed.

1996, May 15. After shaky election results, the **Indian president Shanksar Dayal Sharma asked the Hindu Nationalist Party, or BJP,** now growing in popularity, **to form a coalition government** and take power. On May 28 the BJP resigned in anticipation of an imminent no-confidence vote. The president appointed a new prime minister, centrist H. D. Deve Gowda, and asked him to form a new government. This new government pledged a more free-market economy to spur economic growth. Training in computer science and software development continued to expand in the middle classes.

1997, April 11. The ten-month-old coalition government collapsed due to a no-confidence vote. On April 19 former finance minister Inder Kumar Gujral was named the new prime minister.

Sept. 5. Nobel Peace Prize–winner Mother Theresa died. She was given a state funeral on Sept. 13.

1998, Feb. 16–March 15. In parliamentary elections the **Hindu nationalists, or Baratiya Janata Party (BJP), won a major victory;** Atal Bihari Vajpayee was chosen as the new prime minister, to serve for a five-year term. He was the first Hindu nationalist to assume that position in India; moderates and Muslims worried that the chauvinism characteristic of previous Hindu nationalists in the government would bias his rule.

May 11–13. To the dismay of the world's industrialized nations India ignited international controversy **by conducting five nuclear tests.** Two weeks later, India's rival Pakistan responded with several of its own nuclear tests, causing even more concern in the international community. Though ridiculed and sparking sanctions from the United States, the UN, and other countries, India had refused to sign the Comprehensive Test Ban Treaty for nuclear weapons; in the popular opinion, "the bomb" was evidence that India was at last a "real power."

Oct. 16–18. The foreign secretaries of India and Pakistan met in Pakistan's capital city of Islamabad to discuss an agreement regarding the international dispute over the Kashmir and Jammu, but no accord was reached during the talks.

1999, Feb. 20. Prime Minister Vajpayee met with Pakistani prime minister Nawaz Sharif in talks aimed at reducing Indian-Pakistani aggressions and curbing the threat of nuclear war between the two countries.

April 17. Prime Minister Vajpayee's government lost a confidence vote, leaving India's system in a state of turmoil and uncertainty.

Vajpayee remained in power after the reelection of the BJP in the third general referendum in as many years, which was held Sept. 4–Oct. 1. The alliance led by the prime minister secured a parliamentary majority for the BJP and assured Vajpayee another chance to serve as prime minister. He was the first to be reelected to the position since Indira Gandhi in 1972.

May 26. As the conflict that had prompted the recent nuclear displays between India and Pakistan refocused on the disputed territory of Kashmir, international peace talks concerning the predominantly Muslim territory stalled. The Indian Air Force launched air strikes over Kashmir and sent ground troops to subdue Islamic guerrilla forces in the area. Substantial evidence suggested that Pakistan was arming and aiding the Kashmiri rebels, and by July 26 Pakistan was forced to withdraw troops from the area. Intermittent fighting between Indian forces and rebels continued.

2000, June 26. The Provincial Assembly of Jammu and Kashmir approved a controversial resolution for autonomy in all government matters except defense, foreign policy, and communications. This proposal was rejected by the Indian cabinet on July 4.

July 24. A surprising unilateral cease-fire was supported by the anti-India militant group, Hizbul Mujahideen. Pakistan was excluded from peace negotiations, and the cease-fire ended a few weeks later when rebels favoring Pakistan's annexation of Kashmir resumed fighting.

d. PAKISTAN

Many of the issues facing independent India loomed large for the new state of Pakistan as well. The legacy of a state that often preferred to deal with groups rather than individuals became exacerbated in Pakistan, where the need to explain the **place of Islam** in the state tempted policy makers to talk about the *'umma* (community) rather than citizenry. This tension further confused the newly forged relationship of the five separate regional cultures (ranging from the Balochi and Sindhi-based communities in the west to that of the Bengalis in the east) that existed just beneath the surface of this new nation. In addition, Pakistan inherited considerably less of the infrastructure of a working state than did India; it therefore faced much larger problems in terms of communication networks and national integration, intensified by the fact that its two very distinct wings were separated by an often-hostile India.

The continuing power of large landlords also made the formation of economic policy and central planning much more problematic in Pakistan. No significant shift in the distribution of resources was achieved in Pakistan, nor did an overarching vision of socioeconomic change guide the use of development aid. Stagnant economic policies and irresolute ideological vision made the state vulnerable to control by the military, which aimed simply for efficient government and political stability. This, in turn, made the development of an independent civil society much more difficult to achieve.

1947, Aug. 15. The Dominion of Pakistan was inaugurated, with **Liaqat Ali Khan** as prime minister and **Mohammed Ali Jinnah** as governor-general. Pakistan, the Islamic provinces of India, consisted of West Pakistan (formerly the western part of Punjab with Sind, the Northwest Frontier Province [NWFP], and other muslim-majority areas) on the northwest side of India, and East Pakistan (formerly the eastern part of Bengal). The East wing had only 15 percent of the territory, but 55 percent of the population.

1948, Sept. 11. Mohammed Ali Jinnah died and was succeeded by **Khwaja Nazimuddin** as governor-general.

1949, June 4. The Awami League was formed in Dhaka.

1950, April 8. The Delhi Pact between India and Pakistan substantially reduced friction between the two dominions.

June–Dec. Pakistan supported the UN cause in the **Korean War,** profiting economically from the sudden demand for its raw materials brought on by the war.

1951, Oct. 16. Prime Minister Liaqat Ali Khan was assassinated while addressing a public meeting. On the next day Governor-General Khwaja Nazimuddin assumed leadership of the dominion.

1953, April 17. In the face of a growing **economic crisis** of famine proportions, **Governor-General Ghulam Mohammed** dismissed the cabinet and Prime Minister Nazimuddin, and named **Mohammed Ali,** leader of the progressives in the Muslim League Party, as prime minister.

Nov. 2. The constituent assembly voted to make Pakistan a republic within the Commonwealth.

1954, March 19. In elections, voters in East Pakistan turned the administration of the large province over to the opposition, a major setback for the Muslim League Party.

May 19. The government signed an **agreement with the U.S.** for American military and technical assistance, specified for defensive purposes only.

May 30. The central government dismissed East Pakistan's chief minister for having engaged in "treasonable activities" and sent 10,000 troops to the province to suppress labor riots and restore order.

1956, March 23. As the **new constitution** went into effect, Pakistan officially became the **ISLAMIC REPUBLIC OF PAKISTAN.**

Sept. 12. Hussein Shaheed Suhrawardy became prime minister, succeeding Mohammed Ali, who had resigned on Sept. 8.

1958, Oct. 7. Pres. Iskander Mirza dismissed the prime minister, annulled the constitution, and declared martial law. He appointed the commander in chief of the army, **Gen. Mohammed Ayub Khan,** as administrator of martial law.

Oct. 27. GEN. MOHAMMED AYUB KHAN BECAME PRESIDENT (to 1970), after forcing the resignation of Iskander Mirza. Military government was introduced for the first of several times, in the interest of maintaining stability and achieving effective rule.

1960, Aug. 1. By presidential order, **Rawalpindi,** an industrial center and military station, was **declared to be Pakistan's only capital,** thus replacing Karachi.

Sept. 19. Indian prime minister Pandit Nehru and Pakistani president Mohammed Ayub Khan signed **agreements on the joint use of Indus River waters.**

1962, June 7. The cabinet of the military government resigned after 44 months. On June 8 Pres. Ayub Khan announced a **return to constitutional government.** On July 16, when he signed legislation permitting the reestablishment of political parties, the Jamaat-i-Islami, the strongest orthodox Muslim party, and later the Muslim League announced their revival.

1963, March 12. The foreign office published the text of a provisional **Pakistani-Chinese agreement** revealing the tentative cession to Pakistan of 750 sq. mi. of territory held by China. There was to be no corresponding territorial loss to Pakistan.

Aug. 29. The government signed a treaty to provide scheduled **air service with Communist China.** Pakistan was the first Western-oriented nation to sign such a pact.

1964, Jan. 6. The government outlawed **Jamaat-i-Islami** and jailed 60 of its leaders. The ban was lifted by order of the Supreme Court (Sept. 25).

Jan. 20. Pakistan called for an immediate meeting of the UN Security Council to consider the worsening **situation in Kashmir.** On Jan. 24, India blamed Pakistan for stirring up trouble and asked for direct negotiations.

Feb. 17. The Security Council suspended debate on Kashmir at the request of Pakistani foreign minister Zulfikar Ali Bhutto.

1965, March. Elections to the National Assembly gave the government party (Pakistan Muslim League) more than a two-thirds majority.

Aug. Undeclared war with India, over Kashmir (p. 996).

Loan agreement with Communist China, which thenceforth became the chief source of Pakistani military supplies.

Dec. 14–15. Visit of Pres. Ayub Khan to Washington, D.C.

1966. Growing agitation in East Pakistan for autonomy.

Dec. 23. Agreement with the U.S. for huge grain shipments to relieve the food shortage.

1967. Continuance of the drought and food shortage obliged the government to revise its economic plan and give greater emphasis to development of agriculture. The introduction of new and greatly improved strains of wheat and rice was to prove of great value.

April. Emergence of the **Pakistan Democratic Movement,** working for direct elections and the extension of provincial autonomy. The movement was supported by most opposition groups.

1968, Oct. Student outbreaks culminated in the arrest of Bhutto, leader of the Pakistan People's Party, and other leftist leaders.

1969, Jan. Formation of the **Direct Action Committee,** composed of eight parties of the Right and Center under **Nasrullah Khan.** It demanded release of political prisoners and a return to parliamentary government.

Feb. 21. Pres. Ayub Khan announced that he would not run for reelection. The news was met with widespread student riots and strikes.

March 25. RESIGNATION OF PRES. AYUB KHAN. He was succeeded by **Gen. Agha Mohammed Yahya Khan.** Martial law was proclaimed as a result of student and worker unrest.

Nov. 28. The new president announced **constitutional reforms** designed to assuage unrest in Bengal. West Pakistan was to be divided into provinces (thus loosening its impact vis-à-vis the East wing and providing more recognition and room for regional groups to achieve self-regulation in Sind and other western provinces). Maximum autonomy was to be given local government in both parts of the state.

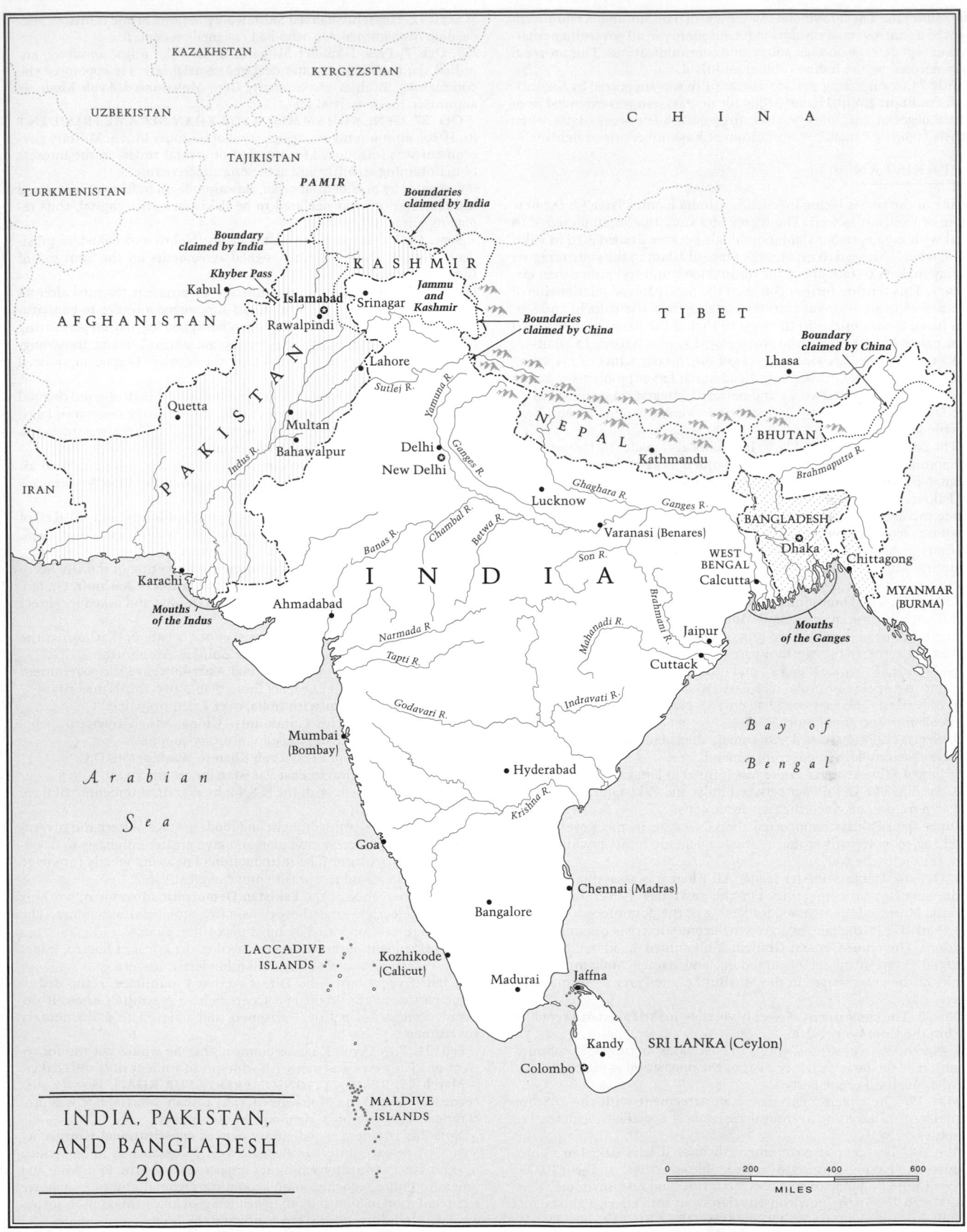

INDIA, PAKISTAN,
AND BANGLADESH
2000

0   200   400   600
MILES

Sheik Mujibur Rahman (Mujib), leader of the Awami League (AL), was imprisoned. Mujib was released with the fall of Pres. Khan.

1970, Nov. 12–13. A southwesterly cyclone with winds of 100–150 mi. per hour struck the Ganges-Brahmaputra deltas in East Pakistan, raising the tides as much as 25 ft. and sweeping over thickly populated delta islands. The dead numbered in the hundreds of thousands in what was probably the worst natural disaster of the century.

Dec. 7. In the **national elections, Sheik Mujibur Rahman** and his East Pakistani **Awami League** won an absolute majority of the 300 seats in the assembly. In West Pakistan, **Bhutto's Pakistan People's Party (PPP)** (Marxist) dominated with 82 seats. There could then be no further question that fundamental changes in the state would be undertaken, chiefly in favor of East Pakistan.

1971, March 1. Although the newly elected **National Assembly** was scheduled to meet, Bhutto demanded that it be postponed, and Yahya Khan agreed. In protest, Mujib in early March called upon the people of East Pakistan to strike.

March 23. On Pakistan Day, the Bangladesh flag was raised, setting the stage for secession (p. 1004).

March 25–26. Talks broke down between Pakistan's leader Yahya Khan and Mujibur Rahman; the Pakistani military moved into East Pakistan.

Dacca University students were killed. **Mujibur Rahman** was arrested and brought to West Pakistan. In his absence, and to protest his imprisonment, Maj. Ziaur Rahman announced on the radio the **formation of the provisional government of Bangladesh.** An underground army, the **Mukti Bahini,** supplied with arms from India, began operating from across the Indian border. In the face of large numbers of civilian deaths, almost 10 million refugees flooded into India.

Nov. The Indian army invaded East Pakistan (p. 997).

Dec. 15. The Instrument of Surrender was signed by India's chief of staff Gen. Sam Manekshaw and Pakistani general, Niazi. Ninety thousand troops were captured.

Dec. 20. Pakistan emerged from the war with less than half its population and its army and economy on the brink of collapse. When president of Pakistan Yahya resigned, **Bhutto** took over as **president** and chief martial law administrator.

Dec. 21. Mujibur Rahman was released from jail in Pakistan and allowed to return to Bangladesh two weeks later.

1972, Oct. The National Assembly was convened. A federal parliamentary system of government was agreed upon, with four units and two houses of legislature.

1973, Feb. Tribal fighting in Balochistan, followed by the imposition of direct presidential rule and the invocation of emergency powers, raised fears that the new constitution would give too much power to the prime minister and central government.

April. Pakistan inaugurated a **new democratic constitution,** framed by a directly elected assembly, on April 14. **Pres. Bhutto became the prime minister** of Pakistan.

1975, Feb. The National Awami Party (NAP) was banned, and many of its leading members were arrested following the murder of the NWFP's most senior minister, Hayat Mohammed Sherpao. Although boycotted by opposition parties, the National Assembly adopted a constitution bill empowering the government to extend the state of emergency beyond six months without parliamentary approval. The bill designated a Third Pakistan, or "New" Pakistan. Elections confirmed Bhutto as leader.

Nov. The **National Democratic Party (NDP)** was launched, with Sherbaz Khan Mazari, leader of the Independent Group in the National Assembly, as leader. It claimed the adherence of most former NAP leaders.

1977, Jan. Elections were announced for March. Nine parties formed a broadly based opposition front called the Pakistan National Alliance (PNA).

March 7. The main **electoral contest** emerged between the PNA and the ruling PPP, led by Bhutto. Bhutto's PPP won the election, controlling 155 seats and conceding only 36 seats to the PNA and 1 to the Qayyum Muslim League. This result, however, was disputed by the PNA, which insisted the elections had been rigged and called for a boycott of the provincial assembly elections scheduled for March 9 as well as a countrywide strike on the following day.

The PNA charge that the elections had been rigged was later confirmed by the chief election commissioner and the findings of the Election Commission.

March 14. Civil disobedience movement launched. Leaders were arrested, but the movement continued to gain momentum, causing a breakdown of law and order in several places and interrupting economic life in the major industrial centers. The armed forces were called in, with martial law imposed on Karachi, Lahore, and Hyderabad through June 7. A curfew was imposed. Official sources put the death toll at 275 and the injured at 2,000, but the unofficial figures were over 1,000 dead and several thousand injured. Some 40,000 people were arrested.

March 26. The National Assembly met and reelected Bhutto as the leader of the house.

June. Saudi Arabia was brought in to mediate, suggesting a larger strategy of identifying Pakistan with other Muslim countries in contradistinction to other countries in the subcontinent. Although elections were scheduled for Oct. 7, the negotiations broke down again, resulting in armed clashes between PPP and PNA supporters.

July 5. Armed forces intervened once more, taking top PPP and PNA leaders into "protective custody" (including Bhutto). The constitution was not abrogated, but some of its clauses were put in abeyance as the armed forces took over the administration.

Gen. Zia ul-Huq took over as martial law administrator. In August, PPP and PNA leaders were released.

Sept. 15. The state of emergency was lifted. The election campaign officially began three days later.

Oct. 1. Gen. Zia postponed elections indefinitely, arguing that only after those holding public offices during the past seven years were brought to account for their misdeeds could meaningful elections be held. The Lahore high court convicted Bhutto and four others of instigating political murders and sentenced them to death.

1978, Sept. Pres. Fazal Elahi Chaudhri resigned for "health reasons." Gen. Zia became president.

1979, Feb. The Pakistan Supreme Court confirmed the verdict on Bhutto.

April 4. Bhutto was hanged, which led to commotion and disturbances in the major cities, but the government controlled protests within three days.

1979–88. The Zia regime used **Islamization** of Pakistan as a way to underscore the shared identities of Pakistanis in the face of increasing demands by Sindhis, Muhajirs (originally Urdu-speaking refugee Muslims from North India), Pathans (from the Northwest Frontier Province area), and others.

1979. The Soviet Union occupied Afghanistan (p. 976), causing a massive influx of Afghan refugees into Pakistan.

Zia announced elections for Nov. 17, but with a series of **amendments to the Political Parties Act** of 1962, arguing that political parties led to factious tendencies in the populace. Major parties refused to register by the Sept. 30 deadline. Zia then postponed the elections indefinitely, dissolved political parties, and reinforced martial law.

1980, May. Article 199 of the constitution was amended so that high courts could no longer rule on the validity or effect of martial law. The legal community became disaffected, despite earlier support for Zia's supplanting of the Bhutto regime. Nevertheless, the Zia regime lasted for several more years because no major challenger emerged to provide a viable alternative.

1983, Aug. 12. Zia announced a new political framework, promising provincial and national elections by March 1985.

Aug. When the Movement for the Restoration of Democracy (MRD) (originally organized in March 1981) launched a nonviolent civil disobedience movement in response to Zia's announcement, a **mass uprising** resulted **in Sind.** Rural violence focused on government property, banks, trains, and the police.

1984, Dec. 1. A national referendum was called by Zia to seek popular approval for a five-year term and to ensure the process of Islamization. The 11-party opposition urged a boycott; the results claimed a 64 percent turnout and a 97.7 percent confirmation of Zia as president.

1985, Feb. 25–28. National and provincial elections were held on a nonparty basis. Public meetings and processions were forbidden, and the press was monitored closely.

March. The National Assembly elected Fakhr Imam as speaker, defeating the government-backed candidate.

Dec. Martial law and the state of emergency (continuously in effect from March 1969) were finally **lifted.** Fundamental rights were restored.

1986. Political parties were again permitted.

April. Bhutto's daughter, **Benazir Bhutto,** returned to Pakistan from Britain to revive the PPP. Her tumultuous welcome in Lahore was followed by a four-week tour. Although she attracted huge crowds, her unilateral appeal for the observance of "Black Day" (the anniversary of the day when Zia overthrew her father and seized power in 1977) proved to be unsuccessful in July, doubtless because she was keeping her distance from the other antigovernment leaders in the MRD. In August she was placed under house arrest.

Aug. Benazir Bhutto achieved rapprochement with the leaders of the MRD.

1988, May 29. Zia dissolved the National Assembly, the four provincial assemblies, and the cabinet, citing a "complete breakdown" in morality and law and order. Elections were announced for November.

Aug. 17. Pres. Zia was killed in a plane crash at Bahawalpur in eastern Pakistan amid widespread rumors of sabotage. A new state of emergency was declared. The acting president announced that elections would still proceed as planned.

Nov. 16. A general election for the new National Assembly netted 93 of the 207 directly elected seats for the PPP; the PPP was the only party to secure seats in each of the four provinces. Benazir Bhutto declared results to be a "mandate" for the PPP government.

Dec. Although Bhutto's chief rival, Mian Nawaz Sharif, was elected as Punjab's chief minister, she was appointed prime minister, becoming the **first female leader of a Muslim country.** The state of emergency was repealed. Ghulam Ishaq Khan was elected president.

A crisis in Balochistan was provoked by the dissolution of the provincial assembly by the state's governor. Opposition demands for restoration of the assembly were supported when the Balochistan High Court ruled that the dissolution was unconstitutional.

1989, March. A group of fundamentalist Islamic religious leaders ruled that the PPP must dismiss Benazir Bhutto and elect a male leader.

1990, Aug. 6. The president used his constitutional powers to dissolve the National Assembly and then dismissed Bhutto as prime minister, along with her cabinet. He declared a state of emergency and announced a fresh general election for October.

Sept. Benazir Bhutto was charged with ten counts of corruption and misuse of power. Immigration authorities were given a list of 32 people, including Benazir and her husband, to prevent from leaving the country.

Oct. 24. In new elections, a coalition led by Mian Nawaz Sharif won; he was sworn in as prime minister; the state of emergency was lifted.

1994, Jan. 2–3. A meeting occurred in Islamabad, Pakistan, between India and Pakistan over the regions of Jammu and Kashmir. In a conflict continuing from 1947, Kashmir, a mostly Muslim region, wanted independence from Hindu India, protesting rights violations. The talk ended in a stalemate.

1995, June 22–25. The militant Muslim group Mohajir Quami Movement ravaged the commercial hub of Karachi, killing approximately 75 people.

July 19. At least 30 were killed in an ethnic battle in Karachi.

1996, Nov. 5. Prime Minister Benazir Bhutto was ousted on charges of corruption. New elections were scheduled for February.

1998, May 28–30. Pakistan carried out nuclear tests in response to India's testing from earlier that month. Economic sanctions were imposed on Pakistan and India by the United States; international concern heightened over the nuclear capability of both nations, particularly in light of their ongoing dispute over the Jammu-Kashmir territory in northern India.

1999, April 15. Although in exile, former prime minister Benazir Bhutto was convicted of political corruption for receiving extorted funds and was sentenced to five years in prison.

May 26–June 10. India sent troops and air strikes into Kashmir to battle radical Muslim insurgents. Pakistani troops apparently aided the Muslim rebels in the territory with a predominately Muslim population. Pakistan's military shot down two Indian jet fighters that had

allegedly flown over Pakistani-controlled territory in Kashmir. Conflict continued to heighten.

July 4. U.S. president Clinton met with Nawaz Sharif to discuss international peace and safety with regard to Pakistan's and India's recent successes with nuclear weapons. Pakistan's forces withdrew from the disputed Kashmir territory soon after the talks had ended.

Oct. 12. Pakistan's government was taken over by a **bloodless coup** as Prime Minister Nawaz Sharif attempted to fire his army chief of staff, Gen. Pervez Musharraf. Musharraf took control through martial law and suspended the powers of the Pakistani constitution. **This coup marked the first time in world history that a military regime had taken over an affirmed nuclear power,** but the pattern of a military takeover in reaction to perceived corruption by a civil government was long-standing in Pakistan.

2000, April 6. The former prime minister, Nawaz Sharif, was sentenced to two life imprisonment terms for hijacking and terrorism. Sharif had tried to prevent a commercial airliner, containing Gen. Musharraf and 200 other passengers, from landing in Pakistan. This action had precipitated the 1999 military coup.

May 12. Pakistan's supreme court legalized Musharraf's government overthrow by recognizing his as the legitimate government. Musharraf promised to return the country to civilian rule within three years.

e. BANGLADESH

Bangladesh, literally meaning "land of the Bangla [Bengali] speakers," was born out of the civil war in Pakistan in 1971–72 (p. 1003). Pakistan's very creation had been rooted in its claim to serve as a homeland for Muslim South Asians, but it proved unable to incorporate Muslim Bengalis into the polity. The major sources of conflict included language—Bangla bore little resemblance to the ideological, conceptual frameworks created for Urdu and Punjabi, the main languages used in the West wing—and rather different cultural understandings of the practice of Islam. Muslim reformists had acquired significant influence in the West wing, whereas the East still revolved around certain shared Bengali assumptions about devotionalism and related emphases on saints and goddesses. As the Muslim League of Pakistan and the state itself (dominated especially by Urdu-speaking, reformist Muhajirs) pushed the Urdu language and strove for a purist definition of Islam as the basis of the Pakistani state, Bengali speakers turned to their own language and regional identity as the foundation for a separate nation.

These cultural and linguistic conflicts were aggravated by severe economic inequality between East and West Pakistan. Development policies, framed by leaders in the West wing, generally favored the West. Moreover, although significant support for the state of Pakistan resulted from exports cultivated in the East, almost none of these remittances were devoted to economic development of that wing.

As a result of the civil war, in which India intervened decisively on the side of Bangladesh, the new state faced overwhelming needs in rebuilding itself and creating a new infrastructure to support an independent nation-state.

1971, March 26. Declaration of Bangladeshi independence, in direct response to a fierce army crackdown on the previous day. Large numbers of Bengalis were massacred. Mujibur Rahman was arrested and taken to West Pakistan. Many of his colleagues fled to India and established a government in exile. Millions of refugees flooded into India.

Dec. 4. India invaded in support of the **Mukti Bahini** ("freedom fighters") and other irregular Bengali groups operating inside East Pakistan (p. 997). The successful campaign led Pakistan's military and civilian authorities to surrender on Dec. 16.

1972. Bangladesh enacted a new constitution.

With the seventh largest population in the world (growing at a rate of 2.5 percent per annum), the new nation was economically the poorest and most vulnerable of the larger economies of the region. It lacked a functional infrastructure, its minimal industrialization left it heavily dependent on imports, and it could not attract commercial credit. In addition, little artificial irrigation existed, making the country subject to severe climatic instability (cyclones, floods, and so on). It had a weaker administrative service than did India or Pakistan. Finally, it was the nation most dependent on a continuous flow of aid ($2.5 billion in its first three years). Together, these characteristics fed a political instability that precluded any real control over economic and social change.

1973, March. Bangladesh **elections** gave **Sheik Mujib** and the **Awami League** a large majority. Sheik Mujib became Bangladesh's first prime minister.

Oct. The Awami League formed an alliance with the Communist Party and the pro-Soviet wing of the National Awami Party with a joint policy of suppressing terrorism. A militia, the Rakkhi Bahini, was formed to assist the police.

The Awami League's economic policy, **socialist reconstruction,** recognized the limitations of central planning; it took over banks and similar institutions but had to leave much to the private sector.

1974, Feb. 22. Bangladesh was recognized by Pakistan.

July–Aug. Disastrous **floods** intensified an already desperate situation, leading to famine. Fifty thousand people died.

Despite massive infusions of foreign aid, the cost-of-living index rose by 400–500 percent; starvation and death claimed thousands of people. The Awami League was seen as ineffectual and soon came under attack by leftist groups.

Dec. The government declared a **state of emergency,** and all fundamental rights guaranteed by the constitution were suspended.

The **Jatiya Sangsad** (Parliament) adopted a constitution bill that replaced the parliamentary government with a **presidential form of government** and provided for the introduction of a one-party system. Mujib became president, assuming absolute powers, and created the **Bangladesh Krishak-Sramik** (Peasants and Workers) Awami League, excluding all other parties from government.

1975, Aug. 15. Young army officers, dissatisfied with political developments, assassinated Mujib and staged a **military coup;** they brought to power Khandakar Mushtaq Ahmed, the former minister of commerce.

Nov. An expected countercoup briefly installed Khalid Musharaf, a pro-Mujib figure. When he and many of his supporters were killed, Mushtaq Ahmed resigned as president in favor of the chief justice of the Supreme Court, Abu Sadat Mohammad Sayem. Real power was assumed by **Maj. Gen. Ziaur Rahman** (Gen. Zia), one of the most famous of the Liberation War heroes and the army chief of staff. The general election was postponed indefinitely, and Mushtaq Ahmed and Zia's other possible electoral opponents were arrested.

1977, Feb. District elections were finally held.

April. Gen. Zia took over as president, following the resignation of Pres. Sayem. An Islamic amendment to the constitution was introduced.

1978, June. Gen. Zia won a massive majority in the presidential election.

Dec. The president's "undemocratic" powers were abolished.

Burma expelled thousands of illegal Bangladeshi immigrants.

1979. A number of political prisoners were released in January; the next month the delayed elections to the Jatiya Sangsad were finally held. Although the opposition parties took part, Zia's Bangladesh National Party (BNP) gained a majority.

March–April. Azizur Rahman took over as prime minister, and martial law was lifted.

1981, May 30. Pres. Zia was assassinated. A presidential election selected the ailing Abdus Sattar to replace him. Within a year, this weak arrangement prompted a coup; **Gen. Ershad** became martial law administrator in Bangladesh. By the end of the year, Ershad proclaimed himself president of Bangladesh.

1984. Talks occurred concerning the relaxation of martial law.

1985. Although a general election was announced for April, in March Ershad banned all political activity and canceled the election. A referendum in support of the presidency was held instead. In the fall, a new five-party alliance was created to promote government policies.

1986. The ten-month ban on political activity was revoked, and Ershad's Jatiya Party won the parliamentary election. The National Front became the Jatiya Dal (National Party). In a presidential election fraught with violence and intimidation, Ershad defeated Mujib's daughter, Sheik Hasina Wajed. Through 1987 a stalemate resulted, in which the opposition could not defeat Ershad, and Ershad could not succeed in legitimizing his regime.

1988, Jan. Clashes between agitators and police marred local elections to the Union Parishads (150 people were killed) and the general elec-

tions in March. The opposition succeeded in convincing many voters to boycott the elections, although Ershad won reelection. In April, Ershad repealed the state of emergency, and in July protests resumed.

Sept. Monsoon floods hit on a massive scale. Emergency supplies and development aid contracts flowed in behind the floodwaters. One dramatic result, the megaproject known as the **Bangladesh Flood Alteration Plan,** put the World Bank in charge of a group of 15 donor countries coordinating the construction of nearly 5,000 mi. of embankments along Bangladesh's three major rivers. The controversial scheme has since been brought into question all of the fundamental assumptions underlying development aid.

1990, Oct.–Dec. Demonstrations against the government, particularly at Dhaka University, led Ershad to impose a new state of emergency. This failed to stop an overwhelming wave of strikes and violent demonstrations, leading Ershad to resign (he was then placed under house arrest). Chief Justice Shahabuddin Ahmed assumed the post of acting president.

1991, Feb. In elections, the BNP won an overall majority, and **Begum Khaleda Zia** assumed office as prime minister.

May 1. A **cyclone** killed 250,000 people and caused extensive economic damage. Many criticized the government's slow response. This disaster replicated an established pattern: a climatic catastrophe reveals the country's organizational and economic disarray, fomenting protest and political instability, which augment the painful effects of the disaster.

1995, Jan. 24. Bombs were thrown at Bangladeshi prime minister Khaleda Zia; she escaped injury.

1996, March 27. The premier stepped down because of ongoing political violence.

1998, July–Sept. Floodwaters devastated Bangladesh by covering most of the country, killing over 1,400 people and stranding up to 30 million. This number accounted for nearly one-fourth of the total population.

Nov. 8. Fifteen former members of the Bangladesh military were sentenced to death for their role in the 1975 assassinations of the family of Sheik Hasina Wazed, whose Awami League was restored to power in 1996.

f. SRI LANKA (CEYLON)

After gaining **independence from Great Britain in 1948,** Sri Lanka experienced escalating ethnic conflict between the majority Sinhalese and the Tamil minority. The antagonism dated to the struggle to choose a national language. Two propositions were considered: "Sinhala only" or "parity of status for Sinhala and Tamil." As the majority language (nearly 70 percent of Sri Lankans speak Sinhala), Sinhala could also be used to stand in for a range of related identities that emphasize the uniqueness of Sinhalese Buddhist culture—particularly to differentiate it from Tamil Hindu culture with its uncomfortably close connections to South India, which loomed large above the island.

Language thus became interpreted as a test of national loyalty. Nevertheless, Tamils rejected the victory of the "Sinhala only" proposition in the general election of 1956; they feared that that policy would place them in a disadvantageous position with respect to employment and higher education. Although the extent of protections for the use of Tamil has varied from 1956 to the present, the contentiousness of the debate has only escalated.

By 1975, the language question had evolved to include the complex issue of national and territorial rights; a powerful Tamil secessionist movement had emerged. Both sides in the developing civil war have grown increasingly intransigent, and the conflict has drawn in Sri Lanka's large neighbor to the north (it is likely that Rajiv Gandhi's assassination [p. 1000] was directly connected to this conflict).

1946, May 15. Ceylon was granted a **new constitution,** which gave it almost complete self-government in domestic affairs.

1947, Sept. 26. The first cabinet under the new constitution took office, with **Stephen Senanayaki** as prime minister. The new Parliament opened on Nov. 24. A series of agreements with the U.K. (Nov. 11) further reduced British influence in Ceylon.

1948, Feb. 4. CEYLON BECAME A SELF-GOVERNING DOMINION in the British Commonwealth, the first non-European colony to achieve this status.

1950, Nov. 7. Ceylon was the second to sign **an agreement with the U.S.,** providing assistance under the Point Four Program.

1952, May 24. Despite vigorous Marxist efforts to win control, the Conservative government won a majority in parliamentary elections.

1956, April 12. After the neutralist **People's United Front** was victorious in parliamentary elections, **Sirimavo Bandaranaike** was appointed to head a leftist coalition cabinet made up of Democratic Socialists, Trotsky-Marxists, and orthodox Buddhists.

June 15. Parliament approved the **Sinhalese Language Bill** to make Sinhalese the sole official language of Ceylon, despite rioting by the Tamil-speaking minority. The Senate, on July 6, approved the language bill. Language became the basis of nationalism; Sinhala nationalism became equated with Sri Lankan nationalism, which Tamils rejected.

1957, June 7. An agreement, concluded in Colombo, provided for Ceylon's payment of $50 million to Britain over a five-year period for **British bases in Ceylon.** The Trincomalee naval base was scheduled for transfer on Oct. 1, and the Katunayaka base, Nov. 1.

July 26. Negotiations from both the government and from the Federal Party successfully compromised on the language problem by agreeing to the use of both the Tamil and Sinhalese languages.

Sept. 19. Ceylon and Communist China concluded a five-year trade pact.

1959, Sept. 26. Prime Minister Bandaranaike died in Colombo of wounds inflicted by an assassin. **Education Minister Wijayananda Dahanayake** was named to replace him.

1960, July 20. In parliamentary elections, the opposition **Sri Lanka Freedom Party** and its allies won an overwhelming victory over the ruling United National Party. On July 21 **Mrs. Sirimavo Bandaranaike** was sworn in as prime minister.

1961, April. The Tamil Federal Party touched off an emergency situation because of its disobedience **campaign for a separate Tamil-speaking state.**

1963, May 1. Emergency rule ended after 743 days.

1964, Feb. 27. Chinese premier **Zhou Enlai** began a three-day visit to discuss the Chinese-Indian border dispute.

Oct. 30. An agreement with India provided for the **repatriation of 525,000 Indians** over the next 15 years; Ceylon was to grant citizenship to 300,000 others of Indian origin.

1965, March 22. Elections. The ruling **Freedom Party** of Mrs. Bandaranaike was **defeated by the National United Party,** which formed a new coalition government under **Dudley Senanayake.**

July. A consortium of powers (Britain, the U.S., Canada, Australia, and Japan) extended a credit of $50 million to help meet the cost of import requirements.

1966, Jan. 11. An act was passed allowing more extensive **use of the Tamil language** in the northern and eastern provinces. Sinhalese factions were violently opposed to this measure.

July. World Buddhist Congress in Colombo.

1967, June 5. An Indo-Ceylonese agreement provided for repatriation of Indian plantation workers.

Nov. 22. Devaluation of the rupee followed the devaluation of the British pound sterling.

1969, Dec. Widespread **student unrest** and an effort to open a "free" university in Colombo. The universities were closed after a general student strike.

1970, May 28. Resignation of Premier Senanayake, following a setback in the elections. **Mrs. Sirimavo Bandaranaike** formed a new coalition government.

1971, April. A leftist insurrection led by the **Janatha Vimukthi Peramuna (JVP,** or People's Liberation Front), fueled by disappointment with the new United Front, was suppressed with considerable ruthlessness.

1972, May. Ceylon was renamed **Sri Lanka.** The United Front government introduced a new republican constitution, advancing Sinhalese-Buddhist interests and downgrading minority rights. Protections of the use of Tamil guaranteed under the Tamil Language (Special Provisions) Act, approved in 1966, were undermined. Departing from its policy of religious neutrality, the state became more closely identified with Buddhism. The upper house of the legislature (Senate), which previously had acted as a deterrent to hasty legislation, was abolished.

1974. Mrs. Sirimavo Bandaranaike negotiated an amicable settlement regarding the status of Indians in Sri Lanka. Nearly half a million Indians eventually were integrated into the Sri Lankan polity as citizens, conferring on them a political legitimacy that, as an ethnic group, they had not enjoyed on the island since 1948.

The government extended control over newspapers, especially the Lake House Group; another group, the Davasa Group, was closed down.

University admission policies were changed to reduce the "overrepresentation" of Tamils in higher education, an act that radicalized Tamil youth.

1975. Internal disputes over how to nationalize foreign-owned plantations led to expulsion of the Lanka Sama Samaja Party (LSSP) from the government.

Tamils, frustrated by reduced access to employment and higher education, formed a **youth movement named Liberation Tigers of Tamil Eelam (LTTE)** to carry out an armed struggle that would establish a separate Tamil state in the island's northern and eastern provinces.

1976. Tamils organized the Tamil United Liberation Front (TULF). In the Vadukkodai resolution, they proposed to wage a separatist struggle.

Aug. A nonaligned nations' conference was held in Colombo.

1977, Feb. Sri Lanka's worst wave of **strikes** in 20 years.

July. Mrs. Bandaranaike and the Sri Lanka Freedom Party (SLFP) were defeated in elections by the United National Party (UNP), led by J. R. Jayawardene. When Tamil Appapillai Amirthalingam became leader of the opposition, ethnic and language rights became the basis of opposition to the government.

Sept. The National State Assembly adopted a constitutional amendment establishing a presidential form of government.

Dec. Voting restrictions on plantation workers, mostly of Indian origin, were lifted.

1978, Feb. 4. Prime Minister Junius Jayawardene became the first executive president in February; the National State Assembly was renamed Parliament in August.

Sept. A new constitution offered minorities a more secure position; it rejected many of the authoritarian features of the constitution of 1972 and emphasized individual rights and the rights of minorities. Article 19 declared that Sinhala and Tamil were to be the national languages of Sri Lanka (with Sinhala remaining the sole official language). Tamils benefited by the removal of distinctions between citizens by descent and citizens by registration, and by extension of civil rights to stateless persons. S. Thondaman, leader of the Ceylon Worker's Congress (CWC), the main political party cum trade union of the Indian plantation workers, entered the cabinet. These changes brought the Indian Tamils within Sri Lanka's "political nation" for the first time since the 1930s.

1980, Oct. 16. Mrs. Sirimavo Bandaranaike, leader of the SLFP, was expelled from Parliament after a presidential commission of inquiry found her guilty on charges of abuse of power.

Despite attempts to accommodate minorities, the Jayawardene government faced increasing ethnic conflict between the Sinhalese majority and the Tamil minority. Tamil separatists (including a number of guerrilla groups) continued to operate in the north and east.

1982, Oct. The presidential **election** gave Jayawardene a massive majority, making him the first head of government to win two consecutive terms.

Dec. 22. A referendum asked for a mandate for Jayawardene to extend the life of the 1977 Parliament for six more years; the electorate endorsed this, thus guaranteeing the UNP a huge majority in Parliament until 1989. Through four sets of national elections, held between Oct. 1982 and June 1983, the UNP consolidated its hold on the electorate.

1983. Violence organized by **terrorist groups** marred local elections in the Jaffna peninsula. The army clashed with Tamil Tigers, leading to an anti-Tamil pogrom in Colombo.

May. A state of emergency was declared in response to heightened political tension provoked by the long period of electioneering, but ethnic violence erupted anyway.

May–July. Pressure from India on behalf of the Tamils. Indira Gandhi's government attempted to mediate between the Sri Lankan government and Tamil groups.

July. **Worst eruption of anti-Tamil violence** since 1958. The most severely affected was the city of Colombo and its suburbs. In an unprecedented breakdown in law enforcement, the government took nearly a week to reestablish control.

Aug. **A ban on the advocacy of separatism** was imposed with the passage through Parliament of the sixth amendment to the constitution. All TULF members lost their seats in Parliament. Anura Bandaranaike, the son of Sirimavo Bandaranaike, took over from Appapillai Amirthalingam as leader of the parliamentary opposition.

1983–85. A political settlement was attempted while the insurgent struggle continued in the north and the east.

1986. Mrs. Sirimavo Bandaranaike received a presidential pardon, which restored her civic and political rights. Head of SLFP, she remained outside Parliament while her son continued as leader of the parliamentary opposition.

Autonomy for the Tamil north was promised by Jayawardene.

1987. Siege of Tamils in Jaffna by the Sri Lankan army. India intervened, responding to Tamil protests concerning the number of Tamil casualties.

July 29. Prime Minister Rajiv Gandhi of India and Pres. J. R. Jayawardene of Sri Lanka sign a peace agreement recognizing the Tamil language as a national official language along with Sinhala.

Oct. 7. The government introduced bills to recognize Tamil along with Sinhala as an official language, with English designated as a "link language," and to provide for provincial councils, thus giving constitutional recognition to a devolution of power to the localities.

Nov. 12. The 13th amendment was passed.

The presence of an Indian peacekeeping force led to political changes in Tamilnad (India) as well as in Sri Lanka. The Tamilnad government retreated from support of terrorist groups and encouraged the peace accord. Although extremist Tamils felt betrayed, more moderate Tamils expressed satisfaction with the accord, since it guaranteed devolution of power to the northern and eastern provincial units. Many Sinhalese expressed dissatisfaction, feeling that too much power and land had been granted to Tamils. Thus the conflict still remained largely unresolved.

1994, Oct. 15. The Sri Lankan **government released 13 rebel prisoners and started peace talks with Tamil rebel groups.**

Oct. 23. A bomb killed Gamini Dissanayake, a presidential candidate who had been running in opposition to the incumbent leader.

Nov. 9. Chandrika Bandaranaike Kumaratunga of the People's Alliance won the Sri Lankan presidency, ousting the former ruling party.

1995, Jan. 8. A **truce went into effect** in Sri Lanka between government and rebel groups.

1996, Jan. 31. **Rebels bombed Colombo,** the capital, killing dozens.

1999, Dec. 18. Pres. Chandrika Bandaranaike Kumaratunga was injured by a bomb attack at a campaign rally three days before elections in which she won a second year in office.

2000, Aug. 8. Pres. Kumaratunga tried to pass a new constitution in hopes of ending the ongoing civil war by giving more autonomy to the minority Hindu Tamils. She postponed the referendum when it became apparent that the constitution would not receive the necessary two-thirds vote.

Aug. 10. Sirimavo Ratwatte Dias Bandaranaike, who in 1960 had become the world's first elected female prime minister, resigned from that position due to ill health. She died one month later.

Oct. 10. In parliamentary elections the People's Alliance Party, backed by President Kumaratunga, was returned to power. However, the coalition did not secure the majority needed for passage of her Tamil autonomy plan.

g. MALDIVES

1953–54. The islands, a British protectorate, temporarily replaced the sultanate with a **republican form of government.**

1954–68. The sultanate was restored.

1960. The islands were granted **local self-government.**

1965, July 26. The British government accorded the islands **complete independence,** on condition of retaining an air base on Gan Island until 1986.

Sept. 21. **Maldives was admitted to the UN.**

1968, March. A referendum selected a republican form of government.

Nov. 11. **The Republic of Maldives** was proclaimed. **Ibrahim Nasir,** former premier, became president.

1969, April. **The country was renamed Maldives.**

1975, March. Acting on rumors of a coup conspiracy, Pres. Nasir invoked emergency powers, dismissing and banishing the prime minister, Ahmed Zaki, and abolishing the office of prime minister.

1978. Nasir announced that his health prohibited seeking reelection. Maumoon Abdul Gayoom, minister of transport in Nasir's cabinet and a former representative of Maldives to the UN, succeeded Nasir as president. Nasir left Maldives for Singapore.

1980, April. Pres. Gayoom discovered an attempted coup, which implicated Nasir.

1981, April. Ahmed Naseem, former deputy fisheries minister and brother-in-law of Nasir, was sentenced to life imprisonment for plotting to overthrow Pres. Gayoom. Nasir denied involvement. Attempts to extradite him from Singapore were unsuccessful.

1983, Sept. Gayoom was reelected as president for another five years, by a national referendum in which he obtained 95.6 percent of the vote.

1988, Sept. Gayoom was again reelected unopposed, for a third five-year term, obtaining 96.4 percent of the vote.

Nov. Another, more serious, attempt to depose Pres. Gayoom. In hiding, Gayoom successfully appealed to the Indian government, whose troops quickly suppressed the insurrection. Mercenaries, said to be Sri Lankan members of the Tamil separatist group the People's Liberation Organization of Tamil Eelam (PLOTE), allegedly were recruited by a disaffected Maldivian businessman, Abdullah Luthufi, acting in concert with the leader of PLOTE, Kadirkaman Uma Maheswaran.

1989, Sept. The president commuted to life imprisonment the death sentences of the 12 Sri Lankans and 4 Maldivians who took part in the aborted coup. In November, the Indian government withdrew its remaining troops.

Nov. Maldives hosted an **international conference,** with delegates from other small islands, to discuss the threat posed by the predicted rise in sea level caused by the "greenhouse effect."

1990, Feb. Pres. Gayoom announced a broad new policy of liberalization and democratic reform.

May. Pres. Gayoom dismissed the minister of state for Defense and National Security, Ilyas Ibrahim, following the latter's abrupt and unannounced departure from the country. The government later disclosed that Ibrahim was to have appeared before a presidential special commission investigating alleged embezzlement and misappropriation of government funds.

July. Pres. Gayoom officially pardoned Nasir in absentia in recognition of his role in gaining national independence.

The government's new policy of press liberalization was reversed, in order to control outspoken political magazines; all publications not sanctioned by the government were banned, and leading writers and publishers were arrested.

Aug. Ibrahim returned to Maldives and was placed under house arrest.

1991, April. The president founded an anticorruption board.

h. NEPAL

1994, Nov. 15. Nepalese parliamentary elections were won by the Communist Party, defeating the ruling party, which had lately faced charges of corruption.

1995, Sept. 10. The Nepalese **Parliament passes a no-confidence vote, ousting the ruling Communist Party.**

2. SOUTHEAST ASIA, 1941–2000

a. OVERVIEW

(From p. 772)

In Southeast Asia, the **struggle for independence** from the European colonial powers held center stage during the period immediately following World War II. Most of these struggles were completed by 1954, except for those of Malaysia (1957), Singapore (1965), and Brunei (which did not occur until 1984, largely because of the lack of strong internal pressure for independence). During the period 1954–67, the Western powers and many Southeast Asians experienced fears of Communism that were directly related to the worldwide implications of the cold war. These concerns led to **fresh intrusions by the West into Southeast Asian life and politics.** During 1965–75, American involvement in the Vietnam War (Second Indochina War) dramatically affected mainland Southeast Asia. After the Americans withdrew, the Communists triumphed in Vietnam, Cambodia, and Laos. **The Association of Southeast Asian Nations (ASEAN)** was formed (Aug. 6, 1967) by the non-Communist Southeast Asian countries (Malaysia, the Philippines, Indonesia, Thailand, and Singapore) to deal with the threat of further Communist encroachments, especially in the face of China's increasing power. Informal neocolonial influences, in the form of multinational involvement in local economies, continued in this period. One of the most significant ongoing tensions during this recent phase of Southeast Asian history concerns the place of immigrant groups, primarily Chinese, who dominate economic activities in many Southeast Asian countries.

In the 1950s and 1960s, all the governments in the region, excepting that of Laos, launched **ambitious industrialization programs** to lessen their dependencies on the export of primary commodities and the import of manufactured goods. **By the 1970s, the initial focus on import substitution industries shifted to export-oriented industrialization in the ASEAN countries, with Singapore leading the way.**

In Thailand, economic growth has been consistently high. In Malaysia, the economy has prospered, in large measure because of the abundance of natural resources and the ability to take advantage of foreign investments to advance industrialization. In Indonesia, oil export earnings and political stability have provided for stable, unprecedented, and, by world standards, remarkable economic growth; but the benefits have not been equally shared. The lower classes' exclusion from these economic advances and the uneven levels of development on Java and the outer islands have led to labor unrest.

Burma (Myanmar) experienced a slower rate of economic expansion than the ASEAN states. The structure of its economy has changed little because, after 1962, the government followed a strict policy of autarky in order to maintain economic independence and increase equality among all classes. Laos remained one of the world's poorest countries, but in the early 1990s it instituted reforms to establish a more market-driven economy in an effort to attract potential foreign investors. Cambodia's economic development was devastated by the chaos the nation experienced until a new political structure was introduced in 1993.

Demographically, at the end of World War II, the **population** in Southeast Asia just surpassed **150 million.** By 1990, well over **400 million** people lived in the region. From 1950 to the 1980s, the population doubled in the urban centers, and one out of four people resided in a city.

The reactions of leaders to the population explosion varied. Indonesia's Sukarno initially boasted that his country would welcome a population of 250 million. After 1970, resultant economic problems changed this attitude; although Indonesia's family-planning program gained much international acclaim, by 1992 some 2.5 million new job seekers every year joined a labor force that already suffered from serious rates of unemployment and underemployment. In the early 1980s, the Malaysian leader Mahatir announced an ultimate target population of 70 million people in the hope of expanding the internal economic market and also for political reasons—as he wanted to capitalize on the fact that the Malays were reproducing faster than other

Malaysian ethnic groups. At the time, the Malaysian population had reached 15 million, and by 1992 it stood at about 18.5 million. Although the Burman (Myanmar) government introduced population control programs, they floundered because of the government's contradictory and confusing policies. Because of its unique situation, Singapore adopted the most draconian state intervention in family planning, and in the 1980s fertility actually fell below replacement levels. After 1970, Thailand was unambiguously committed to population control, which did reduce birthrates by the late 1980s. Throughout Southeast Asia, fertility fell substantially after 1960; but because of declining mortality rates, Southeast Asia still faced the problems of rising population rates in the 1990s.

On Dec. 15, 1995 the Association of Southeast Asian Nations signed a **nuclear-free-zone pact** for their region, including Brunei, Indonesia, Malaysia, the Philippines, Singapore, Thailand, and Vietnam.

1996, Nov. 25. The Asian-Pacific Economic Cooperation (APEC) leaders endorsed a declaration to eliminate tariffs on computers and other high-technology products by the year 2000.

1997, Nov. 24–25. APEC convened in Vancouver, Canada, to discuss the economic turmoil brewing in Southeast Asia.

b. MAINLAND SOUTHEAST ASIA

1. MYANMAR (BURMA)
(From p. 773)

1946, Dec. 20. The British government invited a Burmese delegation to meet in **London** and discuss the early achievement of **self-government** for Burma.

1947, Jan. 28. An agreement between British and Burmese leaders called for a constituent assembly.

April 9. Election of constituent assembly. The Anti-Fascist People's Freedom League (AFPFL), founded in World War II in opposition to cooperation with the Japanese, was headed by **U Aung San** and received an overwhelming majority.

June 17. The constituent assembly unanimously adopted a resolution calling for an "**independent sovereign republic to be known as the Union of Burma.**"

July 19. U Aung San and several members of his provisional government **were assassinated** by political opponents under the direction of former premier **U Saw.**

U Aung San had been the single political figure capable of bridging differences between the various warring political factions: he had the allegiance of the army, the trust of the Communists, and the support of the various ethnolinguistic communities, who in the preindependence "excluded areas" had remained relatively unaffected by colonial Burma's nationalist politics and modern economy. The assassins were tried and executed (May 8, 1948).

July, 20. Thakin Nu, vice president of the AFPFL, formed a new government.

Sept. 24–25. The new constitution was adopted by the constituent assembly, and Sao Shwe Thaik, the sawbwa (ruler) of **Yawnghwe** (one of the largest of the Shan states), was elected provisional president.

1948, Jan. 4. The UNION OF BURMA, an independent republic free from any ties with the British Commonwealth, was officially proclaimed. **Sao Shwe Thaik** continued as president, and **Thakin Nu** as prime minister. The new state immediately embarked on a program of radical nationalization of resources and industries. Its program was not radical enough, however, to satisfy the two Communist parties of Burma.

March. A Communist rebellion broke out in Southern Burma. The situation was further aggravated by the Karens.

Aug. The Karens started a rebellion to achieve an autonomous Karen state. Both Karens and Communists succeeded in occupying large parts of southern and central Burma. At the same time, an element of the "**People's Volunteer Organization**" (part of the AFPFL's old army) fought government forces for control of central Burma.

1949, June 14. The Karen rebels proclaimed a separate state, with headquarters at Toungoo.

1950, March 19. Government forces captured **Toungoo.**

May 19. The main center of Communist resistance at **Prome** was taken by the army. The government was thus able to regain some control over the major towns and means of communication. **Rebel activity,** however, continued, and elections, already postponed several times, had to be postponed for another year. In the meantime the economic condition of the country, already seriously affected by the war, was steadily growing worse.

1953, March 3. The army announced **a major offensive** in northern Burma, to suppress a strong force of **Chinese Nationalists** in operation there since 1949. On March 25, the government called on the UN to condemn Nationalist China for aggression.

April 22. The UN political committee adopted a resolution that called for removal or internment of "foreign troops" in operation in Burma. Burma and Nationalist China abstained.

1956, April 27. In parliamentary elections, victory was secured by the Anti-Fascist People's Freedom League, which had become dependent upon the charisma of the devoutly Buddhist prime minister, U Nu. He found himself under pressure to satisfy various special interest groups. In order to raise morale and strengthen his following, he tried to combine Buddhist and Marxist values in a new national ideology, "**Buddhist socialism,**" a return to fundamental ethical principles that would avoid the abuses of capitalism.

June 5. Former defense minister **U Ba Swe became premier,** after Premier U Nu resigned for one year in order to reorganize his party, the Anti-Fascist People's Freedom League.

Oct. 2. Premier U Ba Swe announced a **Communist Chinese agreement to withdraw the troops** that had penetrated Burma in July, and to respect the boundary established by treaty in 1941.

1957, Feb. 28. Parliament voted unanimously to approve **U Nu's assumption of the premiership.**

1958, May. A split in the ruling AFPFL Party ushered in a period of political instability.

July 23. More than 1,100 insurgents of the minority Mon racial group surrendered in a mass ceremony that marked the **end of a ten-year rebellion.**

Sept. 26. The army took over power in Burma, as **Gen. Ne Win** agreed to head a new government at the request of Premier U Nu, who resigned in favor of Ne Win on Oct. 28.

1960, Jan. 28. Communist China and Burma signed a ten-year nonaggression treaty and border agreement.

Feb.–March. In the elections, U Nu's faction, now called the **Union Party,** won a decisive victory.

April 4. Parliament elected **U Nu as premier,** succeeding Gen. Ne Win.

1961, Oct. 13. Communist China and Burma signed a protocol, as an annex to their boundary agreement of 1960, stating that a joint border committee had successfully defined and marked off the boundaries.

1962, March 2. Ne Win led an **army coup** that deposed U Nu's civilian government. U Nu and other leaders of the Union Party were arrested. Parliament was abolished, and the small **Revolutionary Council** was put in its place. The council on March 8 named **Ne Win chief of state.**

July 4. The new regime sponsored the **Burmese Socialist Program Party,** committed to "the Burmese Way to Socialism." All other parties were banned.

1964, Feb. 14. Chinese premier **Zhou Enlai arrived in Rangoon** on a visit.

Despite the military regime, troubles continued especially in the north, where the Chinese Communists were suspected of encouraging and supporting the rebellious Karen, Kachin, and Shan tribes.

1966, Oct. Release of U Nu and U Ba Swe from captivity.

1967, June. Serious anti-Chinese riots in Rangoon, in response to greatly increased insurgency in the north.

Oct. Recall of Chinese technicians by the Beijing government. Relations between the two countries became strained.

1968, April. First Central People's Workers' Council met in Rangoon. This was an attempt to stimulate economic life by the appointment of agricultural and industrial workers' councils.

1969. Growing dissatisfaction with the government's Socialist policy and one-party rule. **U Nu,** from London, **called for overthrow of the regime,** by force if necessary, and the restoration of parliamentary democracy (Aug. 29).

June 2. Report of an advisory body on the **drafting of a new constitution** and return to civilian rule.

Aug. U Nu announced plans to set up a revolutionary movement in Thailand.

1970, March. Communist guerrillas, supported by Beijing, seized the northern town of Kyokuk. Government troops at first won a victory over them at **Lushio,** but this was followed by severe fighting and heavy casualties (July 21).

Aug. 15. Further battles between Nankham and Kutbar. The government felt obliged to set up an independent **Strategic Command Headquarters** at Lushio to coordinate large-scale operations.

Early 1970s. Chinese aid to the antigovernment insurgents, both the Burmese Communist Party and the Kachin Independence Army, **decreased** as relations with Rangoon improved. The Burmese government succeeded in exerting its authority over much of the country because at the same time the Karen National Liberation Army was in decline.

1974. A new constitution replaced the Revolutionary Council with a one-party state, the Socialist Republic of the Union of Burma, ending 12 years of military rule. Gen. Ne Win remained chairman of the Burma Socialist Programme Party. The Security and Administration Committees in local government were replaced with elected People's Councils. The government, however, continued to endorse centralized economic development.

Early 1980s. Although some signs of opening up to foreign investment and aid appeared, the country remained largely closed to the outside world. The resulting stagnation of what had once been a prosperous export economy caused growing political unrest.

1988. Violence erupted, fueled by the combination of poverty and the alienation of youth. Although **Gen. Ne Win** was forced to step down from office, he continued to manipulate the government and repress the opposition (including the most effective **leader for prodemocracy opposition** to Burma's military government, **Aung San Suu Kyi,** the daughter of Aung San and the head of the National League for Democracy [NLD]).

1989. The country's name was changed again, this time to the Union of **Myanmar,** which is the Burmese literary style for "Burma." The opposition to the military regime continued to use the name "Burma"; the issue has become a political one, with the name "Myanmar" associated with the military and its supporters.

July. Aung San Suu Kyi, while many of her party members were jailed, **was placed under house arrest.**

1990, May 27. The National League for Democracy (NLD) won a resounding victory in the general election, but the party was not allowed to take office.

July. A decree issued by the military regime's ruling State Law and Order Restoration Council (SLORC) confirmed its retention of executive, legislative, and judicial powers.

1991, Dec. Aung San Suu Kyi was awarded the Nobel Peace Prize in absentia. She had continued to be held under house arrest since July 1989, refusing to voluntarily leave the country.

1992, spring. The SLORC of the military regime showed signs of finally responding to increasingly strong international pressures to institute reforms and to introduce new policies of liberalization.

April 24. Gen. Than Shwe replaced Gen. Saw Maung as the head of the SLORC. Gen. Ne Win was still believed to have veto power over the most important matters of state, even though he no longer handled day-to-day matters.

Gen. Than Shwe became prime minister.

April 28. The SLORC declared a cease-fire on the Karen insurrection front.

Aug. 24. Colleges and universities reopened.

Sept. 26. Martial law was ended, after having been in effect since July 18, 1989.

1993, Jan. 9. The national convention, consisting of delegates from the 135 ethnic and functional groups in the country, opened with the stated purpose of determining principles on which a new constitution would be based.

1998, Aug. 21. The NLD pressed the ruling junta (SPDC) to reconvene Myanmar's parliament.

Sept. 16. The NLD, led by Suu Kyi, declared itself to be the legal parliament of Myanmar and claimed null and void all junta legislation passed since 1990. After this uprising, the ruling **State Peace and Development Council (SPDC)** incarcerated hundreds of opposition-party members. While the UN increased sanctions against the junta government on Oct. 27, the number of imprisoned NLD members rose to over 220.

2000, Jan. 24. Led by twin 12-year-old boys, a fundamentalist Christian offshoot of the Karen National Union known as God's Army seized a Thai hospital along the Myanmar border. Leaders Johnny and Luther Htoo guided the mob into taking some 800 prisoners in the locality of Ratchaburi Thailand. The twins lost their lives days later in a standoff.

Sept. 2. Though denounced by various world powers, the ruling junta withheld pro-democracy NLD leader Aung San Suu Kyi under house arrest in Rangoon, preventing her from rallying her supporters as the government sought to suppress them.

2. THAILAND
(From p. 773)

1941, Dec. 21. Siam concluded a ten-year **treaty of alliance with Japan.**

1942, Jan. 25. Siam declared war on Great Britain and the U.S.

1946, Jan. 1. The state of war between Great Britain and Siam was officially ended. The U.S. resumed diplomatic relations with Siam on Jan. 4.

June 9. King Ananda Mahidol was found dead from a bullet wound. His brother, **Phumiphol Adulyadet,** succeeded him.

Oct. 13. The Siamese government accepted the UN verdict to return to **Indochina** the provinces acquired in 1941.

1947, Nov. 8. In a bloodless **coup d'état,** an army group under **Marshal Luang Pibul Songgram** overthrew the government.

1948, Jan. 29. A general election resulted in a victory for the new government, and on April 8, **Luang Pibul Songgram** became premier. There was considerable resistance, however, notably from the followers of **Nai Pridi Panomyang,** wartime resistance leader.

1949, May 11. Siam henceforth was to be known as **Thailand.**

1950. The rise of communism in Southeast Asia found Thailand on the anti-Communist side. On March 1, it recognized the **South Korean government,** and later sent a contingent to participate in the **Korean War** on the UN side.

March 24. King Phumiphol Adulyadet returned from Switzerland, where he had been studying.

May 5. Phumiphol Adulyadet was crowned **King RAMA IX.**

1951, June 30. A naval revolt against the government of Premier Pibul Songgram was suppressed by loyal army and air force units.

1954, May 29. The government requested action by the UN Security Council to prevent the Indochinese War from spreading to Thailand, and to send observers.

June 18. The Soviet Union vetoed the **plan for a UN peace-observation team in Thailand.**

Oct. 5. A conference in Canada of the Colombo Plan nations admitted Thailand to membership.

1955, Aug. 6. Premier Pibul Songgram ousted some of the country's most powerful men in a successful attempt to regain exclusive control of the government.

1957, Sept. 17. In a military but bloodless coup, **Commander in Chief Sarit Thanarat took control of the country.** On Sept. 18, King Phumiphol Adulyadet appointed Sarit as military governor of Bangkok. Dissolving Parliament, the king appointed 123 members, pending new elections within 90 days. On Sept. 21, **SEATO's secretary-general Pote Sarasin** was unanimously chosen as premier.

1958, Oct. 20. Field Marshal Sarit Thanarat, supreme commander of the armed forces, in a quiet coup established **military rule.** On Oct. 21, Sarit abolished political parties and began arresting persons engaged in Communist activity.

1962, Nov. 24. The U.S. began the **withdrawal of 2,300 U.S. soldiers** from Thailand.

1963, Dec. 8. Premier Marshal Sarit Thanarat died. **Gen. Thanom Kittikachorn,** former senior deputy premier, succeeded him and promised to follow the policies of Marshal Sarit.

1965–75. In the **Vietnam War** (p. 1038) the Thai government took its

stand with the U.S. and the anti-Communist governments. Thailand obtained U.S. assurances of support if it was seriously threatened.

Sept. A Thai contingent was sent to Vietnam, while some 35,000 **American troops were based in Thailand,** mostly to service air attacks on North Vietnam. Massive U.S. financial aid helped to develop Thailand's communications. Although the Thanom regime spent vast sums on social and economic development, by the late 1960s there was serious rural unrest, largely due to the activities of the Communist Party of Thailand.

1968, June 20. A new constitution provided limited parliamentary government. An appointed senate (composed largely of military and police officers) was to wield power until election of a house of representatives.

1969, Feb. 11. The first general election in ten years. The ruling **United Thai People's Party** secured 75 of the 219 seats in the lower house, and the related **Independents** another 72, but the opposition **Democratic Party** garnered all the seats in Bangkok and other cities.

March 7. Marshal Thanom was reappointed premier.

July 28. Visit of Pres. Richard Nixon. There were now 48,000 U.S. troops in Thailand. The president repeated assurances of U.S. support in the event of an attack on Thailand.

1970, Aug. 18. The Thai government notified the U.S. of its **intention to withdraw its 11,000-man contingent from South Vietnam,** in consonance with the U.S. policy of withdrawal.

1971. Thanom reimposed military rule in response to fears regarding the first signs of American withdrawal from Vietnam.

1973, Oct. Student unrest and violent mass demonstrations protested the lack of an elected government, forcing Thanom to flee. A civilian government was formed.

1973–76. In this period of turbulent civilian rule, various coalition governments succeeded one another; since 1932, Thai politics had been dominated by the military and the bureaucrats. Groups of Thai professionals, intellectuals, students, and workers struggled to establish a new political order during an era of radical worldwide change that was prompted by a slump in commodity prices, a world oil crisis, and the Communist victories in Indochina.

1975. Having common frontiers with Cambodia and Laos, Thailand was the country most affected by the Communist victories, especially in regard to the thousands of refugees who fled into Thailand.

Dec. Thailand closed its borders for a time because of clashes with Lao Communists on the Mekong River.

1976, July. In continuation of the civilian government's attempt to distance itself from its alliance with the Americans (begun in Oct. 1973), Thailand ordered an American military pullout, completed by July. The Thai also forced Malaysia to withdraw a police field force from southern Thailand, which had been allowed under a 1964 Malaysian-Thai agreement. As a result of these various actions, Thailand was able to establish full diplomatic relations with Hanoi.

Oct. The army intervened to suppress student riots at Thammasat University. As a result, the secretary-general of the National Reform Advisory Council, Gen. Kriangsak Chomanand, installed a new regime under Prime Minister Thanin Krivichien, to replace the inept Seni Pramoj government. He toured the member countries of ASEAN, calling for closer regional cooperation against communism.

1977, Oct. Gen. Kriangsak took over direct control of the government, calling for strong regional cooperation. Although military rule dominated Thailand until 1988, it was less autocratic than in the days of Phibun, Sarit, and Thanom.

1988, July. Civilian rule returned to Thailand under the elected prime minister, **Chatichai Choonhavan,** although the Thai army remained in a strong position. Economic development became the first priority, but the civilian government lasted for only 18 months.

1990. Thailand was experiencing steady economic growth. Negative side effects of the rapid transition to an industrial economy included rampant property speculation, urban crowding, rapid deterioration of the environment, and a clash between long- versus short-term priorities of resource users.

1991, Feb. 23. A military coup ended parliamentary democracy. Despite tensions between Prime Minister Gen. Chatichai and the military, the coup surprised observers. Unlike previous coups, no large-scale protests emerged.

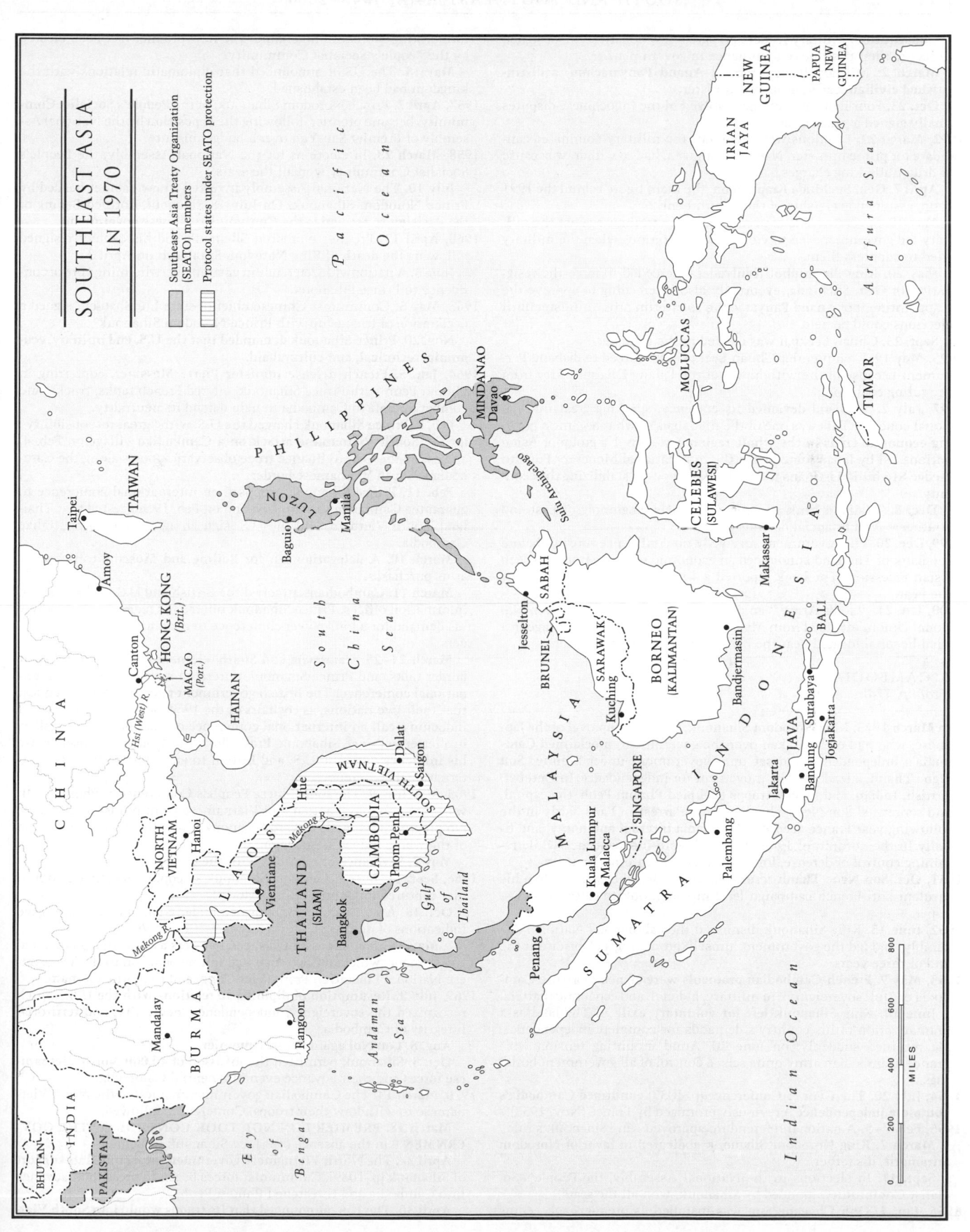

SOUTHEAST ASIA
IN 1970

Southeast Asia Treaty Organization
(SEATO) members

Protocol states under SEATO protection

Constitution. Military leaders prepared new constitution, designed to secure their position of dominance in government.

March 2. Military leaders named **Anand Panyarachun, a distinguished civilian leader, as prime minister.**

Oct. 23. Four fighting factions involved in the Indochinese disputes finally signed a peace treaty.

1992, March 22. Elections were held, but the military-nominated candidate for prime minister, **Narong Wongwan,** had to withdraw because of drug-trafficking charges.

April 7. Gen. Suchinda Kraprayoon, the main figure behind the 1991 coup, assumed leadership of the government.

May 18. Several weeks of peaceful demonstrations against the military-led government led to violent confrontations when the military tried to suppress them.

May 20. King Phumiphol Adulyadet interceded to force the resignation of **Gen. Suchinda,** eventually also interceding to approve the reappointment of **Anand Panyarachun** as interim prime minister until elections could be held.

Sept. 23. Chuan Leekpai was elected prime minister.

1995, May 19. Thai premier Chuan Leekpai was forced to disband Parliament because of the withdrawal of the Palang Dharma Party from the ruling coalition.

1997, July 2. Thailand devalued its currency, sparking great international concern. This was one of the first signs of what became a **growing economic crisis in the whole region.** On Aug. 1 a group of Asian nations led by Japan joined with the International Monetary Fund to pledge $16 billion in loans to Thailand in hopes of stabilizing the economy.

Dec. 8. Thailand bank and currency crisis. Beginning of East and Southeast Asia financial decline.

1999, Dec. 20. The government survived a no-confidence vote just before the Bank of Thailand announced an economic recovery from the deep Asian recession. The bank reported a 4 percent increase in GDP for the year.

2000, Jan. 24. "God's Army," an offshoot group of the rebel Karen National Union, intruded from Myanmar to take 800 people hostage in a Thai hospital located near the border between the two nations.

3. CAMBODIA
(From p. 774)

In **March 1945, King Norodom Sihanouk,** with the approval of the Japanese, who had earlier taken over the government, **proclaimed Cambodia's independence** and set up a government under **Premier Son Ngoc Thanh,** a leader in the movement for independence. In October, **British, Indian, and French troops occupied Phnom Penh,** the capital, and sentenced Son Ngoc Thanh to house arrest in Paris. Early in the following year **France accorded Cambodia internal autonomy,** and finally in the autumn of 1949 granted de jure **independence** while retaining control of defense, foreign affairs, and internal security.

1951, Oct. Son Ngoc Thanh returned, but he fled the capital when his virulent anti-French campaign led King Sihanouk to close his newspaper.

1952, June 15. King Sihanouk dismissed the cabinet and National Assembly, and led the government himself, promising a plebiscite at the end of three years.

1953, May 9. French-Cambodian protocols were signed to assure Cambodia of "full sovereignty" in military, judicial, and economic matters.

June 14. King Sihanouk left for voluntary exile in Thailand as a dramatization of his country's demands for complete independence. He returned suddenly, on June 20. Amid mounting tension with France, Cambodian army units seized control of all government buildings.

1954, July 20. The Geneva Conference (p. 1037) **confirmed Cambodia's complete independence,** previously promised by France (Nov. 1953).

1955, Feb. 7–9. A national referendum approved King Sihanouk's rule.

March 2. King Norodom Sihanouk abdicated in favor of Norodom Suramarit, his father.

Sept. 11. In elections to the National Assembly, the People's Socialist Community, founded by Sihanouk, won all the seats.

1956, Jan. 4. Oun Cheeang Sun was installed as premier, succeeding

former king Norodom Sihanouk. The new premier had been elected by the People's Socialist Community.

May 18. The USSR announced that diplomatic relations with the kingdom had been established.

1957, April 7. Prince Norodom Sihanouk, of the **People's Socialist Community,** became premier, following the **deposition** by the National Assembly of **Premier San Yun** over a budget dispute.

1958, March 23. In elections for the National Assembly, the People's Socialist Community won all the seats.

July 10. The National Assembly invested a new cabinet headed by Prince Norodom Sihanouk. On July 18 Sihanouk notified Beijing of the **decision to recognize the Communist Chinese government.**

1960, April 12. Premier Norodom Sihanouk and his cabinet resigned following the **death of King Norodom Suramarit** on April 3.

June 5. A nationwide referendum gave an overwhelming vote of confidence to Prince Sihanouk.

1963, May 5. Communist Chinese chief of state Liu Shao-chi signed a declaration of friendship with Prince Norodom Sihanouk.

Nov. 20. Prince Sihanouk demanded that the U.S. end military, economic, technical, and cultural aid.

1964, Jan. 5. French defense minister Pierre Messmer, conferring in Phnom Penh with Prince Sihanouk, offered French tanks, trucks, and combat aircraft to Cambodia to help defend its neutrality.

Feb. 8. Prince Sihanouk charged the U.S. with "great responsibility" for the **South Vietnamese attack on a Cambodian village** on Feb. 4, and asked the U.S. to finance truce observation posts along the Cambodian–South Vietnamese border.

Feb. 11. Prince Sihanouk proposed an international conference to guarantee Cambodia's neutrality, and on Feb. 19 suggested that Thailand, South Vietnam, and the U.S. sign an agreement to neutralize Cambodia.

March 10. A delegation left for Beijing and Moscow to negotiate arms purchases.

March 11. Cambodians attacked the British and U.S. embassies and information offices. Prince Sihanouk offered his regrets and withdrew his demand for a four-power conference to guarantee Cambodia's borders.

March 24–25. Cambodia and South Vietnam formally ended their border talks, and Prince Sihanouk reiterated his demand for an international conference. The British government rejected a Soviet request that their two nations, as cochairs of the 1954 Geneva Conference on Indochina, call an international conference on Cambodian neutrality. In a letter to Prince Sihanouk, **Pres. Charles de Gaulle promised to use his influence** with the U.S. and Britain to effect the calling of an international conference.

1965, March 1–9. The Indochinese People's Conference at Phonm Penh was dominated by Laotian and Vietnamese Communist delegations. No progress was made toward Sihanouk's plan for the neutralization of the whole Indochinese region.

May 3. Severance of relations with the U.S.

1966, Sept. 11. In the elections, Sihanouk's People's Socialist Community captured four-fifths of the seats.

Oct. 18. A new cabinet was formed **under Gen. Lon Nol,** who gave indications of desiring better relations with the West.

1967, May 2. Sihanouk assumed special powers as head of a provisional government, which at once accorded full recognition to the Vietnamese National Liberation Front (Viet Cong) and to North Vietnam.

1969, July 2. Resumption of diplomatic relations with the U.S., which recognized the sovereignty, independence, neutrality, and territorial integrity of Cambodia.

Aug. 8. Lon Nol again became premier.

Oct. 8. Sihanouk permitted the **invasion of 40,000 North Vietnamese forces** and their advance even into central Cambodia.

1970, March 13. The Cambodian government requested the North Vietnamese to withdraw their troops. Conferences followed.

March 18. PREMIER LON NOL TOOK CONTROL OF THE GOVERNMENT in the absence of Prince Sihanouk in Beijing.

April 27. The North Vietnamese government proclaimed its support of Sihanouk (p. 1039). Communist forces began to press their advance into Cambodia and threatened Phnom Penh.

April 30. The U.S. announced that its troops would join South Viet-

namese forces in an invasion of Cambodia (p. 922) to destroy North Vietnamese and Viet Cong bases near the border of South Vietnam. This news caused a furor in the U.S., where opinion ran strongly against any escalation of the war. U.S. troops were withdrawn by June 29.

Oct. 9. PROCLAMATION OF THE KHMER REPUBLIC as the new name for Cambodia. Initially, some party politics were allowed: **Son Ngoc Thanh** even served as prime minister for several months. But as the war began to go very badly for the republic forces, **Gen. Lon Nol** became repressive.

1973. Early in the year, in an effort to prop up the Khmer Republic, the U.S. dropped twice as many bombs on Cambodia as had been dropped on Japan in World War II. This bombing was politically unpopular in the U.S., and by the end of 1973, the U.S. Congress forced an end to the bombing. Rather than help the war effort, the bombing alienated the Cambodian populace and enhanced the appeal of the Communists as they recruited followers to their cause.

By the end of the year, Communist forces of the **Khmer Rouge,** largely trained and equipped by Vietnam, controlled two-thirds of Cambodia, including the ruins at Angkor.

Public services broke down in Phnom Penh under the combined stress of the Lon Nol regime's ineptness and the 2 million refugees who fled to the city from the rural areas.

1975. As the year opened, **Phnom Penh was surrounded by the Communists.** When they seized control, Lon Nol, a few advisers, and the U.S. embassy staff abandoned the city and flew to safety.

Aug. Kampuchea, the name adopted by the Khmer Rouge to refer to the state, signed a cooperation **agreement with China,** planning to use this as a check on Vietnam's long history of intrusions in Cambodian affairs.

The Khmer Rouge, under the leadership of **Pol Pot** (pseudonym of Saloth Sar), are believed to have **executed** tens of thousands once they gained power. Initially, the executions focused on the so-called "exploiting classes": army officers, civil servants, teachers, and so on. This first wave of executions subsided by mid-1976.

1976, Sept.–Nov. Events prompted Pol Pot to disappear—to "retire" from public view—for one month. Hundreds of party members were targeted for execution.

Cambodian forces attacked Vietnam targets along the border early in the year, in order to regain territory taken by Vietnam several hundred years earlier in which sizable numbers of Cambodian minorities still resided. Until the end of 1976, relations between the two countries remained chilly but correct.

1976–78. More than 4,000 "confessions" were extracted from individuals who were then tortured and put to death. The entire population was drafted. **A complete restructuring of society** included the nationalization of private property, the abolition of money, suppression of the Buddhist church, and enforcement of communal living for everyone.

1978. Now engaged in open hostilities, the Vietnamese began to support Cambodian forces hostile to Pol Pot, especially in eastern Cambodia on the Vietnam border (p. 1040).

By **mid-1978,** Cambodia was involved in a **civil war** as well as an **international war.** Pol Pot responded by instituting a policy of terror. In addition to many deaths from political executions, over a million people are believed to have died from disease, overwork, and malnutrition. All this served to delegitimize Pol Pot's rule in the eyes of the people.

1979, Jan. Phnom Penh fell. Within one month a pro-Vietnamese regime, the People's Republic of Kampuchea, was installed. Pol Pot's forces fled to the forests along the Thai border. Hundreds of thousands of Cambodians fled the country as refugees to France, Canada, the U.S., and other destinations. Pol Pot received support from Thailand and China.

When the Vietnamese attacked early in the year, they met with no resistance except from the retreating Khmer Rouge army.

March. China launched an attack in the northern provinces of Vietnam (p. 1040), which lasted only a few weeks but was costly to both sides and worsened relations between the countries. It also affected Sino-Soviet relations because the Soviets supported Vietnam.

1982. Various anti-Communist groups formed a coalition. For many

years it was the only government in exile recognized by the UN; Prince Sihanouk nominally served as its head. (Since 1941, he had never been completely out of power except for two and a half years.)

The Vietnamese-backed People's Republic of Kampuchea was slow to exert economic or political control. **The Vietnamese set domestic and international policies.** More than 100,000 Vietnamese "volunteers" in the country helped maintain control. At first, those named to be Cambodian leaders were required to have Vietnamese or pre-1979 Communist affiliations.

1984. The Vietnamese began an offensive against the Cambodian opposition late in the year.

1985. Violent and sustained military action continued, resulting in scarcity of food, forced military service, continued displacement of refugees, and factionalism among Cambodians. Although a flurry of diplomatic efforts attempted to resolve the conflict, they failed.

1986. The Vietnamese began to loosen their hold. As in Laos, they encouraged Buddhism, but monitored it closely.

Both sides began to tire by the end of the year, realizing that time might not be on their side. Although the Vietnamese were militarily predominant in Cambodia, their own disastrous economy put them in a weakened political and diplomatic position.

For Cambodians, Khmer resistance received the backing of both the ASEAN and China; the 1984–85 mauling it had suffered at the hands of the Vietnamese army had been costly in both lost bases and supply routes. Moreover, serious internecine conflict crippled efforts to mount coherent strategies and policies.

1987. Serious bargaining to resolve the issues was commenced. Difficult economic conditions and Vietnamese soldiers' discontent at being away from home prompted a sustained break in guerrilla warfare. Relaxation of the cold war, reflected in a USSR–U.S. summit and improved Sino-Soviet relations, also affected the situation in Cambodia.

Sihanouk surprised even his supporters and put himself in the limelight by taking a leave of absence from the coalition government of Kampuchea, a move interpreted as an attempt to distance himself from the brutality and excesses of the Khmer Rouge.

1990. The People's Republic of Kampuchea became the state of Cambodia. Numerous indications of trouble emerged: sharp cuts in Soviet aid, deepening dissension among leaders, economic stagnation, public dissatisfaction, and widespread corruption. The eastern half of the country was controlled by the antigovernment guerrillas. **Altercations arose between indigenous Cambodians and Vietnamese soldiers.** In Vietnam, Cambodian students were targeted, and Vietnamese student dissidents were detained in South Vietnam.

Sept. The four warring factions in Cambodia agreed to the UN's participation in setting up free elections.

1991, Oct. 23. After significant delays, a draft **peace plan** was signed by all the parties involved at the Paris International Conference on Cambodia. The Agreements on a Comprehensive Political Settlement of the Cambodia Conflict laid out a plan for a pluralistic political system and prospects for a viable economy, but it depended for success on the good-faith adherence by all the Cambodian parties and the support of the international community.

1993, May 28. UN–sponsored elections.

June 18. The leading parties agreed to share power until a new constitution could be drafted (after a lengthy period of **Khmer Rouge** noncompliance with UN efforts to enforce the agreements leading up to elections).

Sept. 24. The new constitution went into effect, following its adoption by the National Assembly on Sept. 21. It created a constitutional monarchy; **King Norodom Sihanouk** became the **head of state, and First Prime Minister Prince Norodom Ranariddeh** became **head of government.**

1994, Jan. The Cambodian government dispatched more than a thousand soldiers in an **attack against the Khmer Rouge rebel forces** because they refused to agree to a cease-fire before starting peace talks.

March 25. The Cambodian army captured Pailin, an important town for the Khmer Rouge rebel forces. Many Cambodian civilians began to flee to Thailand.

1997, July 6. The Cambodian second premier Hun Sen ousted the first premier, Prince Norodom Ranariddeh, from power after two days of fighting in the capital, Phnom Penh.

1998, April 15. Pol Pot, the Khmer Rouge tyrannical leader of the late-1970s, died. His infamous reign sponsored the extermination of between one and two million Cambodian citizens who were either massacred or worked to death in forced labor camps. The Marxist extremist wiped out nearly every member of the professional–technical class in Cambodia between 1975 and 1979.

July 26. Hun Sen's Cambodian People's Party (CPP) won a victory in parliamentary elections. Hun Sen agreed to form a coalition government that would divide power as he became the "sole premier" and Ranariddh became the president of the National Assembly.

Dec. 25. The last Khmer Rouge troops surrendered; all the group's leaders were captured by March 1999, including Ta Mok and Kang Kech Iev, who ran the infamous Tuol Sleng prison.

1999, April 30. Cambodia was formally admitted to ASEAN.

4. LAOS
(From p. 774)

Like the other Indochinese states, **Laos was occupied by the Japanese** (1945), who supported a declaration of independence on April 15. Since 1945, the political history of Laos reflected the struggle of various Laotian and foreign groups to create a national entity where none had previously existed. Strong factors worked against these efforts: deeply embedded traditions of regionalism, family rivalries among the Laotian elite, poor communications systems and economic backwardness throughout the country, and, finally, the political pressures and physical devastation created by the Vietnam War.

Following Japan's capitulation, Chinese troops, allotted the task of disarming the Japanese north of the 16th parallel, occupied most of the country. Concurrently a **rebel Laotian government,** acting in collaboration with the Viet Minh, deposed the king. In 1946, however, the French slowly reoccupied the country and on Aug. 27 signed an agreement with the king, providing for the unity and independence of Laos. A **national constituent assembly** met in Jan. 1947, and on May 11 the king proclaimed a constitution providing for a parliamentary constitutional monarchy.

1949, July 19. By a treaty signed in Paris, **Laos became an Associated State within the French Union.**

1953, Oct. 22. France and Laos signed a treaty making **Laos "fully independent and sovereign"** within the French Union.

1954, Feb. 1. Viet Minh forces, after launching an invasion from the Dien Bien Phu region, **crossed the Laotian border** and moved 35 miles into the country.

Nov. 1. Premier Souvanna Phouma's cabinet decided to take the Communist-backed Pathet Lao ("Land of Lao") movement into the government. On Nov. 19 the central government assumed control of the administration of two Pathet Lao provinces in northern Laos.

1959, Jan. Premier Phoui Sananikone, aided by an expanded **U.S. program of military and economic aid,** began an attempt to wipe out the Pathet Lao, which had continued to receive Communist help.

Sept. 2. The rebels, aided by regular troops from North Vietnam, opened a **major offensive** and captured 80 northern villages.

Sept. 4. The government asked the UN to send an emergency force to help defend Laos against "aggression" by North Vietnam. On Sept. 16 the UN subcommittee on Laos began its investigation in Vientiane.

Nov. 4. Prince Regent Savang Vathana was named king, succeeding **King Sisavang Vong,** who had died on Oct. 29.

Nov. 6. A UN investigating subcommittee revealed that it had found no clear evidence indicating direct participation by North Vietnamese troops in Laotian fighting.

On Dec. 31 King Savang Vathana finally accepted Sananikone's resignation and placed the country under army control. **Gen. Phoumi Nosavan** headed the new government.

1960, Aug. 9. After several cabinet shifts since Jan. 1959, a **military coup,** led by **Capt. Kong Le,** ousted the current pro-Western government. On Aug. 15 the king asked Prince Souvanna Phouma to form a new government.

Sept. 2–Dec. 16. Civil strife over the composition of the government involved the Communist Pathet Lao, the neutralists around Prince Souvanna Phouma, and anti-Communists under **Prince Boun Oum** and Gen. Nosavan.

Dec. 16. After defeating **Kong Le,** Gen. Nosavan installed a **pro-Western government under Prince Boun Oum;** Souvanna Phouma had fled into exile in Cambodia (Dec. 9), and Kong Le joined the Pathet Lao. War with the Pathet Lao continued.

1961, Feb. 19. King Savang Vathana asked for an impartial three-man commission of Cambodia, Burma, and Malaya to help restore peace in Laos. He affirmed Laos's neutrality and declared that Premier Boun Oum would effect a policy of nonalignment.

On Feb. 20, the U.S. voiced approval and urged the USSR to support the king's neutrality statement and cooperate with the three-man commission.

May 3. The Laotian **cease-fire agreement** between the government and the pro-Communist rebels went into effect.

May 16. A 14-nation conference on Laos, under the joint chairmanship of Britain and the USSR, met in Geneva. The most troublesome issues were (1) the establishment of an effective cease-fire, for frequent reports revealed continuing advances of the Pathet Lao; and (2) the formation of a Laotian government acceptable to the three factions.

June 22. The three rival princes—rightist **Boun Oum,** neutralist **Souvanna Phouma,** and leftist **Souphanouvong,** meeting in Zürich, announced **agreement upon a coalition government,** without revealing details.

July 30. The National Assembly amended the constitution to empower the king to name a government without assembly approval.

1962, June 22. King Savang Vathana installed the new coalition government, and the new premier, Souvanna Phouma, declared that Laos no longer recognized the protection of SEATO.

Sept. 17–Oct. 5. The U.S. withdrew its military personnel from Laos in accord with the Geneva agreement on Laotian neutrality.

1963, March–May. Sporadic fighting between the Pathet Lao and neutralist forces occurred.

1964, Feb. 27. The Pathet Lao captured strategic positions in the Plaine des Jarres.

March 16. Representatives of the neutralist, rightist, and pro-Communist factions agreed to halt "all military activities" in the Plaine des Jarres.

April 19. A rightist coup, led by two generals, sought to expand rightist representation in the cabinet. The Western powers, the USSR, and China protested such a modification of the Geneva agreement of 1962. Premier Souvanna Phouma agreed to reorganize and enlarge the coalition government. The Pathet Lao denounced the revolutionary committee as illegal and refused to recognize any agreement between it and the premier.

May 16. Premier Souvanna Phouma announced that the Pathet Lao, with the aid of the North Vietnamese, had opened a **general offensive on the Plaine des Jarres.**

June 1. The Pathet Lao withdrew its government officials from Vientiane, thus **severing its last ties with the neutralist government** of Premier Souvanna Phouma.

June 12. U.S. reconnaissance flights over Laotian territory, approved by the Laotian government, provided photographic proof of the presence of North Vietnamese troops. **Laos,** despite all recognitions of its neutrality, was **deeply involved in the Vietnam War.** Pathet Lao and North Vietnamese troops occupied much of the northern section of the country and staged advances on the Plaine des Jarres as required. The eastern section of the country contained the network of trails known as the **Hô Chi Minh Trail,** over which the North Vietnamese transported most of their supplies to South Vietnam. The U.S. provided the Laotian army with needed supplies and armed and trained the Meo tribesmen, who offered the most effective resistance to the advance of the Pathet Lao.

1965, Oct. The Pathet Lao was officially renamed the **Lao People's Liberation Army.**

1968. A new vigorous offensive by the Liberation Army, supported by the North Vietnamese, resulted in a substantial advance.

1969, Dec. 14. Souvanna Phouma admitted the presence of four or five battalions of **Chinese Communists in north Laos,** while the North Vietnamese were also advancing. The Communists were eventually driven back from the Plaine des Jarres by Laotian forces and Meo tribesmen, operating with U.S. air support.

1970, Feb. 13–21. In what was really the **Laotian war,** the North Viet-

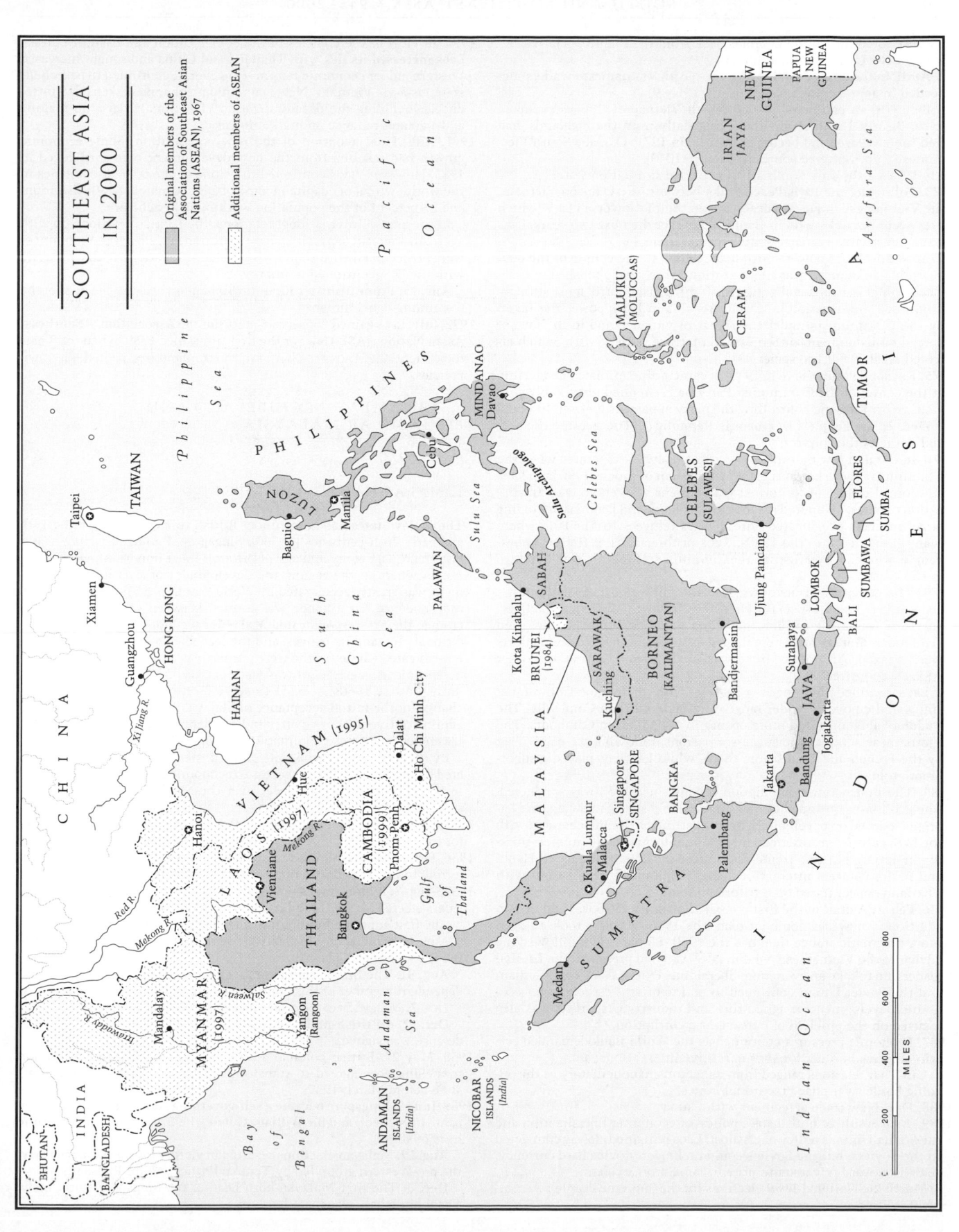

SOUTHEAST ASIA
IN 2000

Original members of the
Association of Southeast Asian
Nations (ASEAN), 1967

Additional members of ASEAN

namese forces drove the Laotians back from the Plaine des Jarres, despite heavy U.S. air bombardment.

April. In the continued fighting, the North Vietnamese invaders succeeded in approaching **Luang Prahang** (May 9).

By 1970, an estimated 70,000 North Vietnamese troops occupied Laos. Nearly 1 million civilians, especially from the highlands, had fled their villages and become refugees. In 1971, U.S. and South Vietnamese forces entered southern Laos (p. 1040).

Early 1970s. Laos only nominally functioned as a nation-state.

1973. Following the **Paris Peace Talks** between the U.S. and Vietnam, the Vietnamese imposed a cease-fire on their followers in Laos (which they were not able to do in Cambodia). Over the next two years, Laos remained relatively free from full-scale warfare, but the erosion of non-Communist state power continued, leading to the **eclipse of the 600-year-old Lao monarchy** as an institution, which was abolished in 1975. The gradual institutionalization of Communist control most strongly resembled the situation in Czechoslovakia in 1948: power was taken by the Communists under the threat of violence and in the face of deep disillusionment, bitterness, and fatigue with warfare, which affected all strata of Lao society.

1975. Kaysone Phomvihan (b. 1920) became prime minister. Leadership at the center of the Communist Party had remained remarkably constant, with Kaysone controlling the party apparatus for over 40 years.

Dec. 2. Lao People's Democratic Republic (LPDR) became the official name of the country.

1976. In the first few months of the year, goodwill evaporated when the Communist cadre began the **collectivization** of much of lowland Laos and forced thousands of former government workers to take "reeducation courses." Hundreds of thousands of lowland Laotians, including large numbers of educated elite, fled as refugees to Thailand where many remained into the 1980s. Tens of thousands of **Hmong tribespeople,** who had been fighting the Communists for years, sought refuge in the West.

1979. The government acknowledged the failure of doctrinally purist economic policies. Especially after 1979, following Vietnamese advice, an effort was made to bind Indochina together: Vietnam, Laos, and Cambodia. **Market forces** reemerged as failing collectivization efforts were relaxed. An uneasy truce was made with Thailand and other ASEAN countries.

Laos retained diplomatic relations with many non-Communist states and enjoyed a wider range of foreign aid than Cambodia. **The Buddha Sabha** operated more openly in Laos than in Cambodia. The Vietnamese acted as the successor patrons, following the pattern set by the French and Thai before them, while Laotians played a subordinate role.

1985. The first national population **census** since 1953 was conducted. The economy continued to make a relatively strong showing, and Laotians focused on developing a new constitution. Rapprochement with the U.S. grew from American interest in information on soldiers missing in action, but this trend was limited by Laos obeisance to Hanoi and to "proletarian internationalism." Diplomatic negotiations with Thailand concentrated on territorial issues.

1986, Feb. 1. A draft of the first constitution since 1975 was adopted. In addition, a new development plan, the 1986–90 plan, took an even more pragmatic stance than had the 1980–85 plan. This followed the advice of the Vietnamese, who in late 1985 had pressured the Laotian leadership to take an even more liberal line. External aid from Vietnam and the Soviet Union continued to be important, especially for economic development in agriculture and industry. Attention was also focused on the problem of bureaucratic corruption.

1987. Economic pressures continued as the **World Bank** demanded certain changes in order for Laos to receive international aid.

Lao-Thai relations ranged from dangerous to conciliatory as the ongoing border war raised territorial issues.

1988, Dec. New trade agreement with China.

1989. As a result of both Laos's policy of economic liberalization and the Soviet Union's policy of glasnost, Laos remained closely connected to the Soviets, but the Soviets could no longer provide hard currency. A trend toward private enterprise became more evident.

March 26. National-level elections for the Supreme People's Assembly (SPA).

1990. In view of the changes in the Soviet Union and Eastern Europe, **Laos increased its ties with Thailand and China** and sought increased Western aid for economic reform. However, it continued to be a client state vis-à-vis Vietnam. New economic mechanisms were also introduced, including the decentralization of economic decision making and a greater reliance on market forces.

1991, Aug. Final adoption of the new constitution. Some economic growth had resulted from the new development plan introduced in 1985. However, Laos continued to be one of the poorest countries in the world, with a per capita income of approximately $180 per annum and 85 percent of the population working in agriculture.

In the area of international relations, the Laotian relationship with Vietnam was still "special" but less substantial, since the Vietnamese were preoccupied with their own problems. Relations with China and with the U.S. continued to improve.

Aug. 15. Prime Minister Khamtai Siphandon became the head of the Communist government.

1992, July. Laos gained "observer" status in the **Association of Southeast Asian Nations (ASEAN).** For the first time since 1789, when the Thais took Vientiane, Laos was without a patron and free to make its own policies.

c. THE MALAY ARCHIPELAGO AND PENINSULAR MALAYSIA

(From p. 774)

1. MALAYSIA AND SINGAPORE

The Malay States had come under British rule or control in the 19th and early 20th centuries (p. 560). **Singapore,** founded in 1819, was a British crown colony and one of Britain's most important naval bases. As elsewhere in the region, the development of a nationalist movement was greatly accelerated by World War II (p. 813). In order to gain independence, an alliance was formed between the leaders of two groups: the **Western-educated Malay leadership,** drawn from the traditional elite and its fringes, and the leaders of a small group of **Western-educated Chinese,** who were primarily wealthy, Malaya-born businesspeople. An agreement was made between these two factions that, until the late 1960s, seemed to serve both of their interests: in exchange for the initial acceptance of Malay domination of political and administrative authority after independence, there would be noninterference in Chinese domination of economic activities.

By the late 1960s, racial riots erupted, stemming from tensions created by the Malays' lack of access to economic power; the Chinese had in fact accrued political power over time and now dominated both spheres.

1955, July 27. The first **national elections in Malaya** resulted in victory for the **Alliance Party.**

1956, Feb. 8. A **British-Malayan agreement** was signed in London, transferring to Malaya control of internal security and defense.

1957, Aug. 3. In preparation for Malayan independence, a conference of rulers elected **Sir Abdul Rahman,** ruler of the Negri Sembilan state, to be the first supreme head of the federation for a five-year term.

Aug. 15. The federal legislative council ratified the constitution of the **federation of Malaya.**

Aug. 31. The British protectorate ended, and **Malaya became an independent member of the Commonwealth.**

Oct. 7. Malaya became **a member of the Colombo Plan** (p. 995).

Oct. 12. A British-Malayan treaty of mutual assistance and external defense was signed.

1958, May 27. British colonial authorities and an all-party delegation from Singapore agreed to transform Singapore into a self-governing state before March 1959.

1959, June 3. Singapore became a self-governing state as the constitution came into effect, and **Sir William Goode,** the British governor, became head of state.

Aug. 19. Malayan elections resulted in **victory for the Alliance Party,** the pro-Western group led by Tengku (Prince) Abdul Rahman.

Dec. 3. The first Malayan-born head of the Singapore state, **Inche Yusof bin Ishak,** was installed.

1961, Oct. 16. Malayan prime minister Prince Abdul Rahman told Parliament that Britain would not be allowed to use Singapore as a SEATO defense base after the merger of Malaya and Singapore.

1962, July 31. The agreement to establish the **federation of Malaysia,** comprising Malaya, Singapore, Sarawak, Brunei, and British Borneo, was signed in London.

1963, June 11. Foreign ministers of Malaya, Indonesia, and the Philippines announced a **proposed mutual defense treaty** to protect their countries from subversion. They urged a "confederation of nations of Malay origin," and they expressed agreement on their conflict over the projected federation of Malaysia.

Aug. 12. In accordance with a request by the presidents of Indonesia and the Philippines, and the prime minister of Malaya, Secretary-General U Thant named a **UN fact-finding mission** to survey the wishes of the people of North Borneo and Sarawak. But on Aug. 29 the Malayan government proclaimed that the federation of Malaysia would be formed regardless of the UN mission report, which was expected to be issued on Sept. 14.

Sept. 16. THE FEDERATION OF MALAYSIA, comprising Malaya, Singapore, Sarawak, and North Borneo, **was formally established.**

Sept. 17. Malaysia severed ties with Indonesia and the Philippines because of their **opposition to the new federation.**

1964, Feb. 5–10. The foreign ministers of the Philippines, Indonesia, and Malaysia conferred in Thailand on the Malaysian situation. On Feb. 6 they advised UN Secretary-General U Thant that they had asked Thailand to police a cease-fire along the Malaysian-Indonesian border.

Feb. 17. Indonesia's **Foreign Minister Subandrio** declared that Indonesian guerrillas, who had infiltrated into the Malaysian territories of Saba and Sarawak, would not be withdrawn until the Malaysian question was settled. Efforts to reach a settlement continued without success, while guerrilla warfare went on.

June 20. The Tokyo "summit conference" of Malaysia, Indonesia, and the Philippines broke up without result, and renewed Indonesian guerrilla attacks in Sarawak followed.

July, Sept. Repeated outbreaks of **hostilities in Singapore** between the Chinese and the Malays.

Aug.–Sept. Indonesian landings and paratrooper **attacks on the coast of mainland Malaysia.** These were successfully contained by Malaysian troops, assisted by British, Australian, and New Zealander contingents. These raids diminished in the course of 1965 as the revolution developed in Indonesia.

1965, Aug. 7. Agreement between the governments of Malaysia and **Singapore** for the latter's **withdrawal from the federation.** The initiative came from the Malaysian government, which was disturbed by the efforts of the Singapore Chinese organization **(the People's Action Party, led by Lee Kuan Yew)** to extend its influence elsewhere in Malaysia.

Sept. 20. The sultan of Trengganu succeeded the raja of Perlis as **paramount ruler** of Malaysia, chosen by the Conference of Rulers for a term of five years.

1966, June 1. Agreement between Malaysia and Indonesia to end hostilities. Details were worked out in conferences at Bangkok (Aug.), and the final agreement was signed at Jakarta (Aug. 11).

Sept. 1. Malay was declared the only official language in mainland Malaysia.

Nov. Strikes and racial conflicts involving considerable loss of life grew out of economic and other grievances.

1968, June. Revival of Communist guerrilla activity in northern Malaysia.

June–July. A **Malaysian-Philippine discussion** at Bangkok dealt with **Philippine claims to Saba** on historical grounds. These talks having proved abortive, the Philippine government on Sept. 18 passed a law incorporating Saba. Thereupon Malaysia broke off diplomatic relations.

1969, May 10. The **elections in Malaysia** revealed losses to the ruling Malay Alliance and a growing threat to Malay dominance. Communal riots broke out in Kuala Lumpur and lasted for five days. To meet the emergency, the paramilitary **National Operations Council** took over executive power.

Nov. Agreement of the Malaysian and Thai governments to set up an antiguerrilla command, following guerrilla activities on the Thai frontier.

1970, Sept. 6. Abdul Razak was designated successor to Prime Minister Prince Abdul Rahman on the latter's retirement (Sept. 21). The new premier announced a future policy of nonalignment.

Sept. 20. Abdul Halim Muazzam, sultan of Kedah, became paramount ruler for a five-year term.

Sept. 22. Abdul Razak succeeded Prince Abdul Rahman as prime minister, with a program of rapprochement to Communist China and other Communist states.

1971, Feb. Parliamentary government resumed, but pursued markedly different policies than had existed before. Passage of the **Constitution (Amendment) Act** made nonnegotiable the special position of the Malays and the status of the rulers. It also sought to increase Malay access to university education.

The establishment of the Department of National Unity set forth a new ideological basis for the nation in the **"Principles of State" ("Rukunegara").** Formal and informal institutional means promoted a shared sense of national identity and purpose, including the strengthening of the position of Malay as the sole national language and medium of instruction at all school levels.

In the economic sphere, the **New Economic Policy (NEP),** set out in successive four-year Malaysia Plans, had two main objectives: elimination of poverty for all communities and the restructuring of society so that economic function was not identified with community.

1980s. Changes in Malaysia led to a significantly more urbanized society (especially important was the higher proportion of Malays living in towns) and an expanded industrial sector (although most of Malaysia's income still came from primary production). Rubber had been displaced by petroleum products as the main source of revenue. Although rural poverty persisted, Malaysia fared better economically during the recession of the early 1980s than did many other Southeast Asian countries.

1984. The White Paper addressed the threat of Islamic extremism and violence to national unity. Near the end of 1985, this potential threat was realized when 18 deaths resulted from a police action against an "Islamic" group in Baling. Problems of unemployment due to the economic recession exacerbated the situation.

1986. Except for concerns about the ongoing situation in Kampuchea, foreign affairs remained calm. Internally, Malay and non-Malay acrimony continued to rise. The tensions in Sabah resulted in bomb blasts and rioting. The troubled Malaysian economy was rocked by scandals connecting government officials with business fiascos, including questionable stock dealings.

Aug. Delayed elections took place. Although Dr. Mahathir retained control due to the loyalty of the rural Malay vote, a strong showing in the urban vote favored the opposition, interpreted as a reflection of increasing ethnic polarization.

1987. The United Malays National Organization (UMNO) continued as the dominant party, but a no-holds-barred political battle was reflected in detentions for "security reasons" and in the passage of laws to repress the free press. The Chinese school issue and the rally of the UMNO served to inflame ethnic tensions.

1989, Dec. 2. The Communist Party of Malaysia (CPM), a predominantly ethnic Chinese revolutionary organization, formally ended its 41-year armed struggle to overthrow the government (initially the British colonial authority).

1994, Feb. 25. Malaysia announced **trade sanctions against Great Britain** because of reports of bribery and corruption in Britain involving trade with Malaysia.

1998, Sept. 20. After dismissing popular deputy prime minister and finance minister Anwar bin Ibrahim on Sept. 2, Prime Minister Mahathir bin Mohamad had Anwar arrested and later convicted of corruption. Anwar received a further conviction of sodomy on Aug. 8, 2000, establishing his total prison sentence at 15 years. Anwar's trumped-up trial brought international condemnation and domestic unrest. It was the longest trial in Malaysian history. Anwar alleged that his firing and subsequent charges stemmed from a disagreement between the two leaders concerning measures to repair the ailing economy.

Nov. 14–18. Malaysia hosted a 21-nation meeting of APEC (the

Asia-Pacific Economic Cooperation). At this conference, U.S. vice president Al Gore strongly criticized Mahathir in a speech, pointing out human rights violations and the unfair trial of Anwar.

1999, April 26. Paramount Ruler Sultan Salahuddin Abdul Aziz Shah Alhaj took his place as the constitutional monarch.

Nov. 28–29. The 14-party ruling coalition known as the National Front gained 148 of 193 seats in the legislature. However, the 45 seats that went to opposition parties was twice as many as in the 1995 election.

2. SINGAPORE

1965, Aug. 9. SINGAPORE BECAME AN INDEPENDENT NATION. It was admitted to the UN (Sept. 21) and became a member of the British Commonwealth (Oct. 16).

Dec. 22. Singapore adopted a republican form of government.

1966, Oct. The Chinese People's Action Party (PAP) emerged victorious in the Singapore elections under the continuing leadership of **Lee Kuan Yew.** Under his direction, government policies consistently enhanced economic development while emphasizing **social control,** social planning, and governmental authoritarianism, at the expense of the individual.

1968. Britain announced it would close its Singapore military base, a major element of Singapore's economy, as part of the dismantling of its "East of Suez" military role. In response, the dominant political party, the People's Action Party, sought economic growth by attracting foreign capital for industrial development in electronics, petroleum processing, global and regional communications, and shipbuilding and ship repair.

Politically, the PAP pursued policies of social mobilization and social control through heavy investment in urban renewal; infrastructural development in transport, communications, and public utilities; and land-use planning and reclamation. Singapore has built one of Asia's most successful economies and has achieved a standard of living second only to that of Japan among Asian countries. Although the rate of growth slowed down with the recession of the 1980s, Singapore continued to thrive.

1990, Nov. 20. Goh Chok Tong succeeded **Lee Kuan Yew** as prime minister and head of government.

1991, Aug. 31. In the general election, the PAP was victorious, but Prime Minister Goh did not receive a strong enough mandate to supplant **Lee Kuan Yew's** domination of the PAP as party head.

1992, Dec. Lee Kuan Yew relinquished leadership of the PAP to **Prime Minister Goh** by passing to him the role of **secretary-general of the PAP.**

1993, Sept. 2. Ong Teng Cheong became president and head of state, while **Prime Minister Goh** maintained his role as head of government.

1999, Aug. 28. Sellapan Rama (SR) Nathan became president at the time of elections because he was declared the only candidate eligible to run for the office.

3. BRUNEI

1984, Jan. 1. Brunei became a **fully independent** state under Sultan Hassanal Bolkiah, though without a fully elected legislature or a government responsible to the people. Previously a British colonial protectorate, it was an extremely rich nation because of the Seris oil fields.

1980s. As a result of its oil revenues, Brunei had accrued foreign reserves of more than $9 billion. Even among other oil-rich states, it stood as one of the wealthiest in the world on a per capita basis.

1991. As a result of the events surrounding the Gulf War, Brunei decided to increase its own security and defense. It was, like Kuwait, a small, oil-rich Islamic state ruled by an absolute monarchy. Although the ruler of Brunei supported the U.S.-led coalition against Iraq, he also felt that the coalition's actions overstepped the mandate of the UN resolution. As an Islamic nation, Brunei expressed discomfort with the level of destruction that was wrought on another Islamic nation, Iraq. A trend toward the re-Islamicization of the country's institutions emerged in this context. In addition, diplomatic relations with China and the former Soviet Union were established—Brunei's first diplomatic links with Communist states. As a member of ASEAN, Brunei was influenced by other members' rhetoric concerning development.

1998, July 29. Sultan Hassanal Bolkiah dismissed his brother and former finance minister, Prince Jefri Bolkiah, from his position as chairman of the Brunei Investment Agency (BIA). Replacing Prince Jefri as heir to the 500-year-old monarchy was Oxford-educated prince Al Muhtadee, the sultan's 24-year-old son. Amedo Development Corp., run by Prince Jefri and his son, collapsed earlier in July with apparent losses of some $16 billion.

2000, Feb. 24. After misappropriating the funds of his brother, the sultan, whose petroleum empire had made him the second-richest man in the world, Prince Jefri was charged with stealing state funds. Jefri allegedly squandered $15 billion on personal expenditures. There was a trial settlement on May 12.

Nov. 15. Brunei hosted 21 representatives from APEC member nations. In a new round of global trade discussions, heated debate arose between industrialized and developing nations. The meeting was attended by important world leaders such as Bill Clinton of the U.S., Ernesto Zedillo of Mexico, Alberto Fujimori of Peru, and Jean Chrétien of Canada.

4. INDONESIA
(From p. 775)

1946, Feb. 19. Negotiations began between Dutch and Indonesian representatives (p. 775), while Dutch and British troops slowly pushed back the Indonesian forces into central and eastern Java.

Nov. 15. Following the conclusion of a military truce, the Dutch and Indonesians initialed the **CHERIBON AGREEMENT** providing for **Dutch recognition of the Indonesian Republic** (Java, Sumatra, and Madura) and the establishment of the **United States of Indonesia,** to include, besides the Indonesian Republic, the states of **Borneo and the Great East** (Celebes, the Sunda Islands, and the Moluccas). The whole was to be joined with the Netherlands in equal partnership under the Dutch crown. The agreement was signed on March 25, 1947.

Nov. 29. The last British troops left Indonesia.

1947, May–July. Attempts to carry out the **Cheribon Agreement** revealed far-reaching differences in its interpretation between Dutch and Indonesian authorities.

June 26. Prime Minister Sjahrir resigned, but his successor, **Amir Sjarifoeddin,** was no more successful in solving the deadlock in the negotiations. Both sides continued to violate the cease-fire agreement, and the republic rejected a Dutch proposal for joint police action against the disruptive Indonesian forces.

July 20. The Dutch launched a full-scale offensive in central and eastern Java, making rapid advances.

Aug. 1. A resolution of the **UN Security Council** called for a **cease-fire** and formed a **committee of good offices.** Both sides accepted the action but did not strictly observe the cease-fire.

Dec. 8. Negotiations between Dutch and Indonesian leaders were resumed under the auspices of the **UN Committee of Good Offices.**

1948, Jan. 17. The Netherlands and the Republic of Indonesia signed a **truce agreement on board the** USS *Renville,* which laid down the principles to serve as a basis for future negotiations. Immediately, however, differences arose as to the interpretation of these principles.

Jan. 31. A new Indonesian cabinet was formed under **Mohammed Hatta.**

Sept. 18. Indonesian Communists, under the leadership of **Muso,** a veteran Communist recently returned from Moscow, **set up a "soviet government" at Madioen (Java).** The government intervened successfully, and the Communists withdrew to the jungle.

1949, Dec. 16. Sukarno was elected first president and **Mohammed Hatta** became first prime minister of the United States of Indonesia.

Dec. 27. As the result of UN efforts, **the Netherlands and the Republic of Indonesia formally transferred sovereignty to the UNITED STATES OF INDONESIA,** a federal republic of 16 states, whose independence was proclaimed simultaneously at its capital of Jakarta (Batavia). The status of **Dutch New Guinea,** which remained outside the new federation, was to be determined in future negotiations.

1950. Local uprisings and guerrilla warfare continued in many parts of the new state, notably in East Indonesia.

May 19. A conference between the federal government and the states decided to substitute a **unitary state** for the United States of Indonesia.

Aug. 17. A provisional constitution was drawn up, establishing the **REPUBLIC OF INDONESIA.**

Sept. 6. Mohammed Natsir formed a new cabinet.

Sept. 28. The Republic of Indonesia was admitted to the UN.

1951, March 19. A government spokesman revealed that 25,000 troops had been sent (March 1) to suppress the **extremist Muslim movement** Darul Islam and armed bands of Communists and outlaws in Java.

1952, Dec. 31. The government announced its decision to participate in the **Colombo Plan** (p. 995) but declared that its decision to join "does not and will not obligate Indonesia either politically or militarily."

1953, March 16. A major outburst of violence occurred when the government attempted to enforce its **land redistribution program,** affecting illegal squatters.

July 30. Pres. Sukarno announced the formation of a primarily leftist government, headed by **Ali Sastroamidjojo.** The Muslim Party for the first time since 1949 was not represented in the cabinet.

1954, Aug. 11. The formal dissolution of the Netherlands-Indonesian union took place without resolving the problem of New Guinea, which Indonesia referred to the UN.

1955, Sept. 29. The first national elections began.

1956, Sept. 12–17. Sukarno made a **state visit to Moscow.** On Sept. 15 the government announced a Soviet loan of $100 million.

1957, Feb. 21. Sukarno issued an appeal to the people to replace the Western democratic method with a **system of mutual help,** which would allow Communist participation in the cabinet.

March 2. A military coup occurred in the four provinces of eastern Indonesia when the Celebes army commander and a 51-man council declared a state of war there. The rebels demanded **complete autonomy** for the region and urged that 70 percent of the revenues collected there be used for local development.

March 5. Sukarno invited the firm anti-Communist former vice president, Mohammed Hatta, to meet with him.

March 9. Another military coup occurred when **Lt. Col. Barlian** took control of South Sumatra. On March 12 **Borneo repudiated the central government** and set up its own council.

March 14. Premier Sastroamidjojo and his cabinet **resigned,** and Pres. Sukarno declared a **state of war and siege.** In order to break a deadlock among competing parties in the formation of a new government, Sukarno, on March 25, called for a cabinet composed of non-political experts.

April 9. In the face of continuing rebellion in the outer islands, an emergency **extraparliamentary cabinet** of experts was installed under a new premier, **Djuanda Kartawidjaja.** The new cabinet of experts contained no Communists.

June 27. Without consulting the central government, officials of North Celebes established a separate province, with **D. Manopo** as governor.

July 6. Lt. Col. Ventje Sumual, on his own authority, assumed military command of the whole of East Indonesia. By July 24 defiance was so widespread that the central government was left in control only of Java.

Aug. 22. In a major move to reunify the country, Indonesia's emergency cabinet invited representatives of the rebellious outer regions to a **round-table conference** with representatives of the central government.

Oct. 28. The government threatened to seize West New Guinea from the Netherlands by force if the UN refused to take up its appeal.

Dec. 1–9. To protest continued Dutch rule of West New Guinea, the government, on Dec. 1, ordered a 24-hour **strike against Dutch businesses.** On Dec. 5 the government asked the Netherlands to close all consular missions except the one in Jakarta and announced the **expulsion of all Dutch nationals** from the country. On Dec. 9 the government expropriated Dutch agricultural properties.

1958, Jan. 9. The government refused to accept UN mediation in its dispute with the Netherlands over the territory of West New Guinea.

Feb. 15. A rebel regime was proclaimed in central Sumatra.

1959, July 5. Pres. Sukarno decreed the **restoration of the 1945 constitution** and dissolved the constituent assembly. On July 6 Premier Kartawidjaja's cabinet resigned. On July 8 a new ten-person "inner" cab-

inet with Sukarno in the premiership was announced. On July 22 Parliament voted to continue under the 1945 constitution.

Dec. 11. Following the government's **prohibition of trade in rural areas by the Chinese,** Communist China protested Indonesia's "most cruel treatment" of Chinese residents, regarded as "nationals of a hostile country." In a formal reply, Indonesia charged Beijing's diplomats with inciting Chinese residents to defy presidential regulations.

1960, Feb. 28. Pres. Sukarno and Soviet premier Nikita Khrushchev signed an agreement for **a Soviet credit** of $250 million.

March 28. After dissolving Parliament on March 5, Sukarno named a 261-person **"mutual help" parliament** and promised parliamentary elections in 1962 if conditions permitted.

1961, April 5. In Netherlands New Guinea, after the first elected legislative council was sworn in, the Netherlands government told its 28 members to work out a date and method for self-determination within a year.

1962, Aug. 15. Dutch and Indonesian negotiators signed an **agreement in New York to transfer the administration of West New Guinea** (West Irian) from the Netherlands to the UN on Oct. 1, 1962, and to Indonesia on May 1, 1963. Indonesia ratified the agreement on Sept. 1, and the Netherlands on Sept. 13. The UN General Assembly approved the settlement on Sept. 31.

1963, Feb. 13. Sukarno announced Indonesia's opposition to the British-sponsored **federation of Malaysia** and voiced support for the rebel troops in British Borneo.

May 18. The 623-person congress unanimously named **Sukarno president for life.** Congress members had been appointed by Sukarno.

1964, Jan. 8. Sukarno, conferring in Manila with **Pres. Macapagal,** was unable to persuade the Philippines to join Indonesia in an **economic boycott of Malaysia.**

April 1–3. Foreign Minister Subandrio visited the Netherlands for talks with Dutch leaders. Subandrio and the **Dutch foreign minister Joseph Luns** signed a technical cooperation agreement.

1965, Jan. 2. Indonesia withdrew from the UN, the first nation to do so.

April 24. The government seized all remaining foreign-owned properties.

Sept. 30. THE COMMUNIST CRISIS. The army defeated an attempt by the Communists to seize control. The army chief of staff and five generals had been kidnapped. Pres. Sukarno then named **Gen. T. N. J. Suharto** as temporary chief of the army.

Oct. 8. Beginning of a general **assault on Communists,** of whom tens of thousands or more were massacred throughout the country.

1966, Feb. 21. Sukarno, in an effort to regain power, replaced the anti-Communist defense minister **Gen. Abdul Haris Nasution** and other anti-Communist officers and cabinet ministers with Leftists. This move led to vast **student riots** and demonstrations (Feb. 25).

March 11. Sukarno was obliged to surrender the powers of government to Gen. Suharto.

March 12. The Communist Party was banned.

May 29–June 1. Peace conference in Bangkok and **termination of hostilities between Indonesia and Malaysia.**

1967, Feb. 20. Sukarno, who retained the titles of president and supreme commander, was obliged to surrender his remaining powers to Gen. Suharto. The latter dismissed many officials of the old regime and did his utmost to **undo Sukarno's economic policies:** drastic measures were introduced to check the almost fantastic inflation, foreign debts were renegotiated, and foreign-owned properties were restored to their owners. At the same time a drive was launched on every form of corruption, in the army as well as the administration.

1968, March 27. Gen. Suharto was given full presidential powers for five years by the **People's Consultative Congress.**

1969, July–Aug. The UN–supervised **referendum in West Irian** (West New Guinea) led to annexation of that territory by Indonesia (approval of UN General Assembly, Nov. 19, 1969).

Oct. 5. Reorganization and **amalgamation of the military services** to reduce duplication and factional rivalries. At the same time the police forces were demilitarized.

1970s. Indonesia's leaders sought closer ties to the West, abandoning their former left-wing orientation. Whereas Sukarno had championed anticolonial revolution, Suharto stressed anti-Communism and development. His regime, under the slogan **"national resilience,"** consolidated the New Order. Its emphasis on stability endowed the **army** with a dominant political and economic role.

Suharto's policies favored political passivity by the populace; his political structures, unlike Sukarno's, were designed to reduce political mobilization. Political parties were seen as too divisive. Instead he formed an organization known as **Golkar,** which organized the population by function—agglomerations of civil servants, the armed forces, intellectuals, women, youth, workers, farmers, veterans, and so on.

The New Order's foreign policy also reflected its goals of internal stability and economic growth. It broke with the Soviet Union and China. Instead, Suharto successfully allied his country with Japan and the West to acquire the aid and technical assistance needed.

1971. In elections, **Suharto's party**—dominated by bureaucrats, technocrats, and the military—**won** landslide victories.

July. The Golkar won 236 out of a total of 360 seats in the country's second national election.

1983. The MPR (parliament) enacted a **formal separation of religion and politics** by requiring all political organizations to adopt the **Pancasila** (the five basic principles of independent Indonesia as outlined by Sukarno in 1945: nationalism, internationalism, democracy, social justice, and belief in one God).

All political groups were significantly affected by this emphasis on secularism because it separated them from their traditional sources of power. But the implications for Muslim groups were particularly threatening, given that the population was 90 percent Muslim. Suharto shared his predecessor's bias against Islam, especially its militant version, and he played Muslims off against the nationalist parties.

1985, Aug. 17. At the celebration of the 40th anniversary of the proclamation of independence from the Dutch, Pres. Suharto warned the nation that it must still be on guard against neocolonialism and internal divisions.

1987. Suharto instituted an even stronger policy to instill political passivity; all societies, not only political parties, were required to declare as their sole guiding principle the state ideology of the **Pancasila.** Violent opposition to these limits was once again expressed by Muslim groups. Islamic parties had commanded about 30 percent of the vote, making them the largest sector in opposition to Suharto's New Order. Suharto's policies of defining the "Indonesian soul" in primarily secular terms left Muslims feeling extremely threatened; they perceived themselves a majority treated like a minority in their own country.

1990s. Concerns were growing about corruption in government and its adverse impact on economic development. In addition, the role of the military and its involvement in these issues were also questioned. The argument that autocratic government is inherently necessary for economic growth began to be challenged by more vocal groups.

1991. Regional divisions continued to plague the country, especially in **Aceh and East Timor.** Although from a military standpoint the two-year, separatist rebellion in **Aceh** was over, the Acehnese grievances about Javanese political and economic domination continued, along with allegations against the Indonesian military of torture and execution.

Nov. In **East Timor,** the Indonesian military's violent response to proindependence protests undermined the government's 15-year rule in East Timor and its efforts to gain the support of the inhabitants for the de facto unification with Indonesia.

1993. Gen. Suharto (originally named president in 1968) was reelected to his sixth five-year term.

1995, Aug. 16. Pres. Suharto ordered the release of three political prisoners who had been arrested in 1965 for participating in a coup.

1996, July 27. Riots broke out in Jakarta because of government raids on the headquarters of an opposition party.

1998, Feb. 20. Pres. Suharto cancelled a plan to reform the currency system when the IMF threatened to withhold $40 billion in aid from Indonesia.

March 10. With an impending economic crisis injuring his popular support, Gen. Suharto was elected by Parliament to his seventh five-year presidential term. Following Suharto's reelection, protests erupted, and he was charged with massive corruption and widespread human rights violations. Meanwhile, Indonesia was the country hit hardest by the worldwide economic crisis: one in five Indonesians lost their jobs.

May 2. Government price hikes in fuel costs set off nationwide student riots; tens-of-thousands protested in various Indonesian cities. These uprisings were similar to the Jan. 1998 riots against ethnic Chinese in Indonesia.

May 21. After ruling for 32 years as a military leader and head of state, Gen. Suharto resigned his presidential position and was succeeded by his vice president, Bacharuddin Jusuf Habibie.

Nov.–Dec. Student demonstrations were staged every day for two months, calling for prosecution of Suharto on corruption and human rights charges. Protestors also called for the resignation of Pres. Habibie.

1999, June 7. Indonesia had its first free parliamentary elections in 44 years. Led by Megawati Sukarnoputri, the Indonesian Democracy Party-Struggle (PDI-P) made great gains on the ruling Golkar Party.

Aug. 30. In a UN-led referendum, the **people of East Timor voted overwhelmingly for independence** (by 79 percent). The vote resulted in numerous bloody rebellions by pro-Indonesian militia forces and Indonesian soldiers. Many thousands were killed in the fighting, and international intervention was considered.

Sept. 12. International pressure was placed on the Indonesian government to allow peacekeeping forces into East Timor.

Oct. 20. Abdurrahman Wahid (commonly known as Gus Dur), the leader of Indonesia's largest Muslim organization, was elected president, which surprised many observers.

Oct. 26. In an effort to quell continuing violence, a UN interim government took command in East Timor, temporarily replacing the existing administration.

2000, Feb. 13. Pres. Wahid suspended the influential Gen. Wiranto from the Indonesian cabinet due to allegations that Wiranto engaged in war crimes during the East Timor crisis.

June 4. Separatists declared West Papua, formally called Irian Jaya, an independent state. Because West Papua was an area rich in natural resources such as copper and gold it was blankly denied independence by Pres. Wahid. Similar calls for independence emerged in the oil-rich province of Aceh, a devoutly Muslim area seeking Islamic law and political autonomy. Riots and violence resulted in Indonesia.

Aug. 9. Pressed by the legislature, Pres. Wahid agreed to share executive power with V.P. Megawati Sukarnoputri, the daughter of former president Sukarno.

G. EAST ASIA, 1945–2000

1. CHINA, 1945–2000

(From p. 781)

a. THE CIVIL WAR

The immediate postwar years witnessed various efforts to keep the Guomindang (GMD) and the Chinese Communist Party (CCP) from returning to the bloody civil war that had preceded the anti-Japanese united front. Within a year, however, those efforts had gone for naught, and the second civil war broke out. The Communists' victory came with stunning rapidity, and by 1949 there were two Chinas.

1945, Aug. 26–Oct. 10. Negotiations between **JIANG JIESHI** (Chiang Kai-shek) (1888–1975) and **MAO ZEDONG** (Mao Tse-tung) (1893–1976) failed to settle their differences, and before the end of October, heavy fighting was in progress between Nationalists and Communists in northern China. Each side aimed at the control of Manchuria, which was being evacuated by Soviet forces.

Nov. Jiang sent a large force north of the Great Wall against the Communist forces in Manchuria. Late in the month, Patrick Hurley, U.S. ambassador to China, resigned.

Dec. 14. The U.S. sent **Gen. George Marshall** (1880–1959) as mediator.

1946, Jan. 10. Marshall was able to effect a **truce between the Nationalist and Communist forces,** followed by an agreement to create a national army, form a coalition government, and draw up a new constitution.

Jan. 11. A political consultative conference in Nanjing, representing the main political groups in postwar China, eventually came to naught.

Feb. 17. The Communists demanded joint control with the Nationalists over Manchuria, a request ignored by the GMD.

April 14. All-out civil war resumed, interrupted by another uneasy truce (May 12–June 30) and intermittent peace overtures from both sides. During the initial campaigns, GMD forces advanced steadily.

Summer. A GMD program of intimidation of leftists and centrists led to assassinations, as in the case of famed poet **Wen Yiduo** (b. 1899). In July, the GMD again violated the cease-fire and attacked CCP forces in Manchuria. That summer, Soviet troops began withdrawing from Manchuria, and many of the area's richest industrial sites fell to the GMD.

Aug. 10. U.S. president Harry Truman warned Jiang Jieshi that his recent actions might undermine U.S. assistance.

Oct. 10. Jiang Jieshi was reelected president of China by the GMD.

Nov. 15. The National Assembly met (with Communist participation) and on Dec. 25 adopted a **new constitution,** which guaranteed political equality and civil rights to all citizens and vested supreme authority in the National Assembly. The government was to consist of a legislative *yuan* (Parliament) and an executive *yuan* (cabinet). The constitution **went into effect on Dec. 25, 1946.** It ultimately failed.

1946–47. The CCP began to undertake land reform in the areas of China under their control. Peasant associations were formed; landlords were publicly tried, and many were killed.

1947, Jan. 29. The U.S. officially abandoned its mediation efforts. Gen. Marshall, in his final report, criticized both the reactionaries in the GMD and the extremists in the Communist camp, who prevented a compromise.

Feb. Jiang Jieshi's men, having begun preparations to make his base of operations in Taiwan as early as late 1945 and having appointed a crew of corrupt officials, found public anger exploding there. The GMD troops killed as many as 10,000, including many respected citizens.

March 19. GMD military successes against the Communists culminated in the capture of the Communist capital of **Yan'an.** An almost immediate reversal resulted in **Communist control over Manchuria by the end of 1947.**

Nov. 21–23. Elections for the National Assembly aroused little popular interest. Most of the candidates belonged to the GMD, because the Communists and the Democratic League had been excluded.

On the eve of defeat in the war (Aug. 1945), Japanese scientists in Harbin, working on chemical and biological weapons and having already committed unspeakable atrocities on thousands of live Chinese subjects, released (rather than killed) plague-infested rats. In the year 1947, 30,000 people died of bubonic plague.

Inflation and popular discontent were becoming widespread. Strikes among workers increased. Rice, cooking oil, and flour prices skyrocketed.

1948. In the course of the year, **the decline of Jiang Jieshi's forces,** already evident in 1947, **proceeded rapidly,** and by the end of the year most of **northern China was in Communist hands.** The Nationalists by now had lost most of their best troops, and corruption among their provincial leaders had led to the surrender or sale of vast amounts of U.S. equipment. The GMD economy, badly in need of reform and shaken by growing inflation, had long depended on U.S. aid, which, since the defeat of Japan, was estimated at more than $2 billion. In early 1948

an additional $400 million was allocated, but as time went on and the Nationalist government failed to liberalize and reform itself, U.S. aid was drastically curtailed.

March. CCP forces under the command of Peng Dehuai retook Yan'an.

March 29. The National Assembly convened at Nanjing. After severely criticizing the government and its conduct of the war, it reelected Jiang Jieshi as president of China (April 19) and gave him virtual dictatorial powers during the national emergency.

April. Luoyang finally fell to CCP forces after long being fiercely contested.

Aug. 28. Jiang declared a number of financial and economic emergency measures to cope with hyperinflation.

Sept. 1. The Communists announced the formation of a **North China People's Government.**

Sept.–Oct. CCP troops under the command of **Lin Biao** (1908–71) captured Mukden (Shenyang) and Changchun, and decimated the GMD forces sent against them.

1949. The rapid decomposition of the GMD armies; the capture of Tianjin (Jan. 15) and Beijing (Jan. 21) by the Communists; and the imminent Communist advance into the lower Yangzi valley brought about a temporary change in the GMD government.

Jan. 21. Gen. Jiang Jieshi resigned the presidency, leaving V.P. Li Zongren (1891–1969) in charge of peace talks with the Communists. These negotiations broke down.

April 20. Communist demands, including the formation of a coalition cabinet under Mao Zedong and the punishment of "war criminals" (notably, Jiang Jieshi), proved unacceptable to the Nationalists. The Communists thereupon resumed their offensive, and in the course of the year they **drove the Nationalist armies off the Chinese mainland.**

July 16. The GMD organized a supreme council under Jiang Jieshi and began to prepare for withdrawal to the island of Taiwan, a plan that was completed by Dec. 8.

Aug. 5. The U.S. issued the White Paper, announcing the cessation of all aid to Nationalist China. The latter's collapse was attributed to the military, political, and economic incompetence of GMD leaders, who had come to rely on the U.S. to win the war and keep them in power.

Oct. 1. THE PEOPLE'S REPUBLIC OF CHINA was officially proclaimed in Beijing, with MAO ZEDONG as chairman of the central people's administrative council and **ZHOU ENLAI** (1899–1976) as premier and foreign minister. The new regime was immediately recognized by the Soviet Union and the eastern bloc countries, and later by Burma, India, and Great Britain (Jan. 6, 1950).

Dec. 8. The UN General Assembly called upon all states to respect the political independence of China and the right of the Chinese people to choose their own political institutions.

b. THE PEOPLE'S REPUBLIC OF CHINA (PRC)

1950. The unification of the country, together with a program of reconstruction and deflation, brought considerable **economic improvement** to the PRC. Although some changes were introduced in agriculture as land reform went into effect, no radical innovations were set in motion, other than overall state planning in industry. Landlords were publicly condemned in mass denunciations; many perished. Land was redistributed to those who had had the least; private property in land disappeared. A new **marriage law** accorded women equal rights in marriage and divorce, and enabled women of any marital status to hold land in their own names. **The People's Liberation Army (PLA)** carried on continued warfare against anti-Communist guerrillas. Party membership topped 5 million.

Feb. 14. Mao Zedong traveled to Moscow, his first trip beyond China's borders, and signed the 30-year **Treaty of Friendship, Alliance, and Mutual Assistance with the Soviet Union.** It was followed by a series of economic agreements for joint exploitation of Chinese resources.

May 2. Communist forces completed the occupation of Hainan Island.

Oct. Chinese Communist "volunteers" intervened in the **Korean War** (p. 1029) on the North Korean side. Ultimately, over 700,000 Chinese troops would be involved. Over the course of the war, China suffered between 700,000 and 900,000 casualties.

Nov. 10. Following a **Chinese invasion, Tibet** appealed to the UN to bring about a peaceful settlement of Chinese-Tibetan relations.

1951–52. The government of the PRC commenced the **"three-anti" campaign** to wipe out waste, corruption, and bureaucratism. This was seen as a housecleaning operation by the much enlarged CCP, resulting from Communist victories. Similarly, a **"five-anti" campaign** against bribery, tax evasion, fraud, stealing of state property, and theft of economic secrets was launched. A later campaign was aimed at ridding China of rats, sparrows, flies, and mosquitoes—"four pests" responsible for carrying disease and whose elimination improved public health greatly.

1951, March 5. The government reportedly reached an **agreement with Tibet,** under which the latter was granted internal autonomy; China retained control of the defense and foreign affairs of the Dalai Lama's realm.

1952, Dec. 31. In accordance with their 1950 treaty, the PRC and the Soviet Union ended their joint administration of the Changchun Railway; the USSR yielded its rights in the partnership.

1953, Sept. 15. The Chinese Communist radio announced the negotiation of an "unprecedented" **economic aid program** with the USSR to enable China to build up its heavy industry.

The first Five-Year Plan commenced (1953–57), following Soviet models and with Soviet assistance: 28,000 Chinese technicians went to study in the USSR, and 11,000 Soviet technicians came to China. The state invested widely in heavy industry, with only a tiny fraction of the money coming from Soviet loans.

From late 1953 into early 1954, the first purge of high-level CCP members took place. **Gao Gang** (1902–54), with his power base in Manchuria, and **Rao Shushi,** with his base in Shanghai, had apparently disagreed with Mao over economic policy; they were accused of establishing their own "independent kingdoms" and accordingly driven from the party. Gao allegedly committed suicide; Rao simply disappeared.

The first PRC **census** listed the total mainland Chinese population as 582,600,000.

1954, Aug. 13. Zhou Enlai's call for a determined **drive to win Taiwan** was approved.

Oct. 11. A Sino-Soviet agreement provided for the Soviet Union's **evacuation of the Lüshun** (Port Arthur) **naval base** by June 1955 and arranged for a substantial extension of Soviet credit to help build up Chinese industry. The agreement also called for the "occupation" of Taiwan.

Oct. 15. The Soviet Union called on the UN General Assembly to condemn the U.S. for aggression against China by its conversion of Taiwan into a "breeding ground for war."

Nov. 23. A military court sentenced to long prison terms the 13 **U.S. airmen** who disappeared on anti-Communist missions during the Korean War.

Dec. 10. The UN General Assembly, voting 47–5, condemned the PRC's conviction of the U.S. airmen for spying. On Dec. 11, **Secretary-General Dag Hammarskjöld** (1905–61) conferred with Premier Zhou Enlai in Beijing about the release of the prisoners. Zhou accepted the proposal on Dec. 17.

1955, Jan.–Feb. Communist and Nationalist forces battled over the **offshore islands** in the Taiwan Strait. Premier Zhou Enlai refused (Feb. 3) a UN Security Council invitation to talk about a cease-fire.

Feb. 5. The U.S. Seventh Fleet was ordered to help evacuate Nationalist Chinese from the Dazhen Islands, which were taken over by the Communists (Feb. 11).

April 23. Premier Zhou Enlai announced to the participants at the **Bandung Conference** in Indonesia that his country did not want war with the U.S. and expressed his willingness to negotiate on East Asian issues, including that of Taiwan. The offer was renewed on May 16.

July. Mao announced that China would move more rapidly toward **agricultural collectivization,** a means of streamlining agricultural production, which was needed to support industrial growth. Over the course of the next year, Chinese agricultural organization was largely transformed, a process completed in 1957.

During 1955, **Hu Feng,** a former friend of Lu Xun and activist in left-

wing literary affairs from the 1930s, became the object of a fierce campaign of invective, all of it seemingly fabricated. He was imprisoned almost continuously until 1979.

1956, Aug. 6. The government **lifted the seven-year ban on visits from U.S. newsmen,** but on Aug. 20, the U.S. State Department reaffirmed its ban on travel to the PRC.

Sept. 15. Mao Zedong proclaimed to the 8th Party Congress of the CCP, opening in Beijing, that there was "a trend toward relaxation of tension in the international situation." On Sept. 16, Premier Zhou Enlai announced a plan to increase by 50 percent total national income during the **second Five-Year Plan** (1958–62).

Sept. 24. A Chinese-Nepalese treaty, by which Nepal surrendered extraterritorial rights in Tibet and recognized Chinese sovereignty there, was made public.

1957, May 1–June 7. Mao stated that even in a Communist state, "contradictions" existed between rulers and the ruled. Calling for freer expression, he also declared, "Let a hundred flowers bloom, let a hundred schools of thought contend." The **Hundred Flowers Campaign** commenced. Numerous intellectuals voiced widespread grievances against the state and were largely critical of interference by state and party functionaries in academic, literary, and artistic realms.

The response was so forceful that Mao and the CCP immediately began an **"anti-rightist" campaign** to punish those who had spoken out. Many disappeared into labor camps or the countryside. By December, this campaign became a full-fledged movement.

May 11. The foreign ministry declared that future installations of Matador missile units in Taiwan by the U.S. were to be interpreted as an "act of war."

June 12. The government press printed the partial texts of **Mao Zedong's speeches** delivered in February and March. Mao had reported the "liquidation" of 800,000 persons in the PRC from 1949 to 1954.

June 17. The government revealed its tentative decision to withdraw its cadres from Tibet.

1958, Jan. The commencement of the GREAT LEAP FORWARD. It lasted in full force for about a year, then slowed up from the fall of the following year until it was discontinued in Jan. 1961. Through it, Mao attempted to radically speed up the transformation to socialism through mass mobilization, in order to thoroughly imbue the nation with Communist ideology.

May 10. The government notified Japan of the **cancellation of all trade** between the two countries, because of Japanese prime minister Kishi Nobusuke's "hostile attitude."

Aug. 23. The Chinese Communists began a heavy **bombardment of Quemoy Island,** off the coast of Xiamen (Amoy), precipitating a crisis.

Aug. 27. U.S. president Dwight D. Eisenhower declared that the islands of Quemoy and Matsu were more important to the defense of Taiwan than they had been three years before, at which time an earlier crisis had been averted. The U.S. Navy announced the dispatch of an aircraft carrier and four destroyers from the Mediterranean Sea to the Seventh Fleet in the waters around Taiwan.

Aug. 29. The CCP politburo adopted a resolution approving the widespread **formation of "people's communes,"** a basic element of the Great Leap Forward, to advance the country's economic development. By the end of the year, there were 26,000 communes, home to 98–99 percent of the rural population. Many farmers were pulled out of agriculture to join in the campaign to build "backyard furnaces" and thus localize industry by producing iron and steel locally. It was a disastrous failure. Production statistics were both flawed and grossly exaggerated. Mass starvation ensued, and millions died.

Sept. 4. U.S. secretary of state John Foster Dulles declared that U.S. forces would come to the aid of the Chinese Nationalists defending Quemoy and Matsu, if Pres. Eisenhower considered such action necessary for the defense of Taiwan. He also declared that the U.S. would not respect the 12-mile offshore territorial limit claimed by the Chinese Communists. When ships of the U.S. Seventh Fleet escorted a Chinese Nationalist convoy carrying supplies to Quemoy (Sept. 7), the Chinese Communists held their fire.

Sept. 11. Pres. Eisenhower, in an address to the nation, said the U.S. must be ready to fight to prevent the Chinese Communist capture of Quemoy and Matsu, but he urged negotiations. The British government declared that it was under no obligation to support the U.S. in the Quemoy-Matsu crisis.

Sept. 15. Ambassadorial talks between the U.S. and the PRC on the Taiwan issue opened in Warsaw, Poland.

Oct. 6. The Chinese Communists began a week-long cease-fire. The PRC's defense minister called for talks between the two Chinese governments, to settle their "internal differences." On Oct. 8, the U.S. announced that convoy operations had stopped but would be resumed if the Communists reopened fire.

Oct. 17. Jiang Jieshi reasserted his determination to keep the offshore islands, and on Oct. 20, the Chinese Communists renewed their shelling of those islands, thereby breaking their extended cease-fire. But the bombardments gradually dwindled over the following months.

Dec. 18. The Central Committee of the CCP passed a resolution ordering a slowdown in the establishment of communes in large cities and improvement in the operation of the 26,000 communes. Intended to create entirely new self-contained communities, the plan to create communes had created unwieldy groupings, too large to be managed efficiently; by the end of the Great Leap Forward, the communes had been subdivided, forming a total of 74,000, in an effort to build smaller, more workable collectives. Poor planning, bad harvests, and social dislocations led to mass starvation. In December, Mao resigned his post as head of the Chinese government, largely because of the disasters of the Great Leap Forward.

1959, March 13. Fighting broke out in Lhasa, Tibet, between the populace and PLA forces.

March 28. Premier Zhou Enlai dissolved the Tibetan government, headed by the Dalai Lama, and put the Panchen Lama at the head of a preparatory committee for the Tibetan Autonomous Region. On March 31, **the Dalai Lama crossed the border into India,** seeking asylum.

April 23. The government claimed to have dispersed the rebels in southeastern Tibet and sealed the border to India.

April 27. Liu Shaoqi (1898–1969) succeeded Mao Zedong as chief of state of the PRC. Mao retained his position as chairman of the CCP. Liu decreased the breakneck pace of social change and turned away from stress on ideology to greater emphasis on expertise. Incentives were reintroduced to boost production.

July. At a party plenum held in the city of **Lushan** (Jiangxi Province), **Gen. Peng Dehuai** (1898–1974) sharply **criticized Mao's policies in the Great Leap Forward.** Mao retaliated by having Peng removed from his post as minister of defense (a job that was then given to **Lin Biao**) and publicly lambasting him.

Sept. 9. The Dalai Lama called for UN action against Chinese Communist oppression in Tibet.

Sept. Historian of the Ming period and deputy mayor of Beijing, **Wu Han** (d. 1969) published in the *People's Daily* a play about the official Hai Rui (1513–87), who had risked personal safety to excoriate the Ming emperor for wasting public funds while the population starved and who was dismissed from office for his efforts. This clear morality play about Mao (represented by the Ming emperor) and Peng Dehuai (Hai Rui) was first staged in Beijing in Feb. 1961. When it was reprinted in 1965, it set off the **Cultural Revolution** (p. 1023).

Oct. 21. In a letter to Pres. Eisenhower, Premier Nikita Khrushchev voiced his support of the Chinese Communist claim to the Nationalist-controlled islands, which he termed an "internal" Chinese matter.

Dec. 19. In the first instance of aerial combat activity since Nov. 1958, **Quemoy was shelled** by the Chinese Communists, and MiG fighters flew over the island.

1960, March 21. China and Nepal signed an agreement by which they set up a committee to demarcate their common border.

April 26. Shortly before his departure from India, after six days of border talks, Premier Zhou Enlai declared that his government would not recognize the McMahon Line as the Indian-Chinese border.

May 31. Xinhua, the PRC news agency, reported the signing of a treaty with Outer Mongolia, hitherto within the Soviet sphere of influence.

June 10. Reports reached New Delhi that fierce fighting had been raging for ten days between Tibetans and PLA troops near the Nepalese frontier. On June 19, an international commission of jurists asserted

that the Chinese Communists were guilty of genocide in attempting a systematic extermination of the Buddhist religion in Tibet.

Aug. The Soviet Union withdrew all of its technicians and specialists from China.

Dec. 29. Beijing newspapers and radio broadcasts reported that during 1960 some 148 million acres of farmland had been affected by disastrous "natural calamities" such as drought and floods.

1962, Oct. 21–Nov. 22. A border war with India was fought (p. 996).

During the relaxation following recognition of the Great Leap's failures, the spirit of the Hundred Flowers Campaign briefly returned to intellectual life.

1963, Feb. 27. The Chinese Communist Party harshly criticized the Soviet Union for supplying India with planes and for having stopped economic and military aid to China in 1960. Differences between the two Communist giants led to constant acrimonious dispute and divided the entire Communist world.

May. The Socialist Education Campaign began, aimed at reviving vigorous interest in socialist ideology.

Dec.–Jan. 1964. For seven weeks, Zhou Enlai toured ten African nations, returning to Beijing on Feb. 5.

1964, Feb. 25. Diplomatic sources disclosed that **Sino-Soviet consultations** regarding border disputes were in progress.

March 1. Zhou Enlai returned from a goodwill tour of Burma, Pakistan, and Ceylon.

April 19. An agreement with Japan was concluded, calling for the exchange of foreign correspondents and the establishment of unofficial trade relations offices.

June 15. China and Yemen signed a ten-year friendship treaty.

Oct. 16. China exploded its **first atomic bomb.**

Nov. 5–13. Zhou Enlai visited Moscow, evidently in hope of improving relations with the Soviet Union following the downfall of Khrushchev. The discussions proved fruitless, if not actually damaging, because of conflicting territorial claims. Many border clashes followed.

1965, March. A dispute with the Soviet Union erupted over the proposed convocation of a world congress of Communist parties.

Border conflicts with India broke out on the Sikkim front.

Sept. 1. Tibet became an autonomous region of the PRC.

1965–68. THE GREAT PROLETARIAN CULTURAL REVOLUTION was launched by Chairman Mao. This movement attempted to transform radically the very consciousness of the Chinese people, to keep alive the revolution begun by Mao, to attack bureaucratism and complacency among Communist cadres and officials, and ultimately to revolutionize the nature of China's state and society. At the broadest level, it was Mao's effort to transform complacency with an ever-present revolutionary ethic. Mao and his many supporters also sought to retaliate against his critics, who had proliferated since the disastrous days of the Great Leap Forward. To accomplish these goals, Mao was prepared, if necessary, to demolish the very party and state institutions he had built up. The cataclysmic results of this movement—including the shutting down of all institutions of higher education for several years, the dislocations of large numbers of people, and the widespread abuses of marauding Red Guards—would unfold in the ensuing three years.

Mao's first salvo comprised an attack on "reactionary bourgeois ideology" and bureaucrats whom he described as the "Beijing Black Gang." A duel resulted, in which **Lin Biao** and the army supported Mao, while **Liu Shaoqi** (head of state of the PRC) and **Deng Tuo** (deputy mayor of Beijing) retained control of the party apparatus and did not side with Mao.

1966, March 26. Liu departed on a trip to Pakistan. On the same day, **Peng Zhen** (b. 1899), mayor of Beijing and vice premier, **disappeared**—an early victim of the purge.

April 18. The PLA newspaper called for a "great cultural socialist revolution" directed against "persons in authority in the Communist Party who have taken the capitalist road," namely, those who relied too heavily on expertise and incentives in industry and not sufficiently on ideological purity. This stance represented the culmination of a conflict between the Military Affairs Committee of the CCP (led by Lin Biao, who supported Mao, emphasized ideology, and believed in popular mass action) and the Party Secretariat (led by **Deng Xiaoping**

[b. 1904], and supported by Liu Shaoqi, who advocated more cautious, traditional approaches to both internal and foreign issues].

May. Mao's supporters designated his thought, codified in *Quotations from Chairman Mao* (or *The Little Red Book*), as the ideological weapon of choice for the Cultural Revolution.

June 1. The Maoists seized control of the *People's Daily* and on June 4 took over the Beijing Municipal Party Committee. On July 18, **Mao returned to Beijing.**

Aug. 1. In the Central Committee of the CCP, Mao engineered the **promotion of Lin Biao** as first vice chairman and demoted Liu Shaoqi. The party announced the **FORMATION OF THE RED GUARDS**, who would implement the assault on dissidents and target institutions throughout the country. The Cultural Revolution had come to fruition. The Red Guards, mostly younger students, soon brought the country to the verge of chaos: they fought pitched battles, carried out summary executions, drove thousands to suicide, and forced tens of thousands into labor camps, usually far from home. Intellectuals were sent to the countryside to learn the virtues of peasant life. Countless art and cultural treasures as well as books were destroyed, and universities were shut down. Insulting posters and other personal attacks, often motivated by blind revenge, were mounted against educators, experts in all fields, and other alleged proponents of "old thought" or "old culture," namely, anything pre-Maoist. Liu Shaoqi (among others) was forced to undergo "self-criticism," placed under house arrest, ultimately deprived of all power (Oct. 1968), and driven to his death through lack of adequate health care after mistreatment in prison. Many other high officials were humiliated, including **Zhu De,** the founder of the Red Army. Eventually the turmoil and confusion reached such a state that **factional fighting** among contending cliques of Red Guards took place in many parts of the country, requiring measures to check the disorder.

Nov. 22. Mao's secretary, **Chen Boda** (b. 1904), was appointed chairman of the **Central Cultural Revolutionary Committee,** of which Mao's wife, **Jiang Qing** (1914–91), was vice chair. This committee, together with Lin Biao's **Military Affairs Committee** and Zhou Enlai's **State Council,** constituted a ruling triumvirate.

1967, Jan. Revolutionary committees, largely under PLA control, were established at central and provincial levels. Mao ordered the Red Guards to desist from attacks on government officials.

Feb. 5. As the Cultural Revolution reached high tide, a workers' movement in Shanghai toppled the party leadership and established the **Shanghai People's Commune,** which fell after 19 days. Even Mao believed this movement to be too radical.

June 17. China set off its **first hydrogen bomb.**

Summer. Many thousands of students in Beijing demonstrated against Liu Shaoqi and Zhou Enlai. PLA arrests of some 500 or more Red Guards in Wuhan led to mass protests and eventually to armed battles, in which over 1,000 demonstrators were killed. The city came under siege in July.

July. The PLA cracked down on attackers of government officials outside of Beijing. The following month, Mao ordered the army, the only stable institution in the country now that the CCP was in shambles, to return the country to order.

1968. The army took over administrative control at many levels, resulting in a **gradual restoration of order.** In the spring and summer, many violent clashes occurred between the Red Guards and the workers and peasants organized by local authorities to resist them; but by the fall, progress had been made in getting the Red Guard students back to school or assigned to farm labor. Throughout local government, revolutionary committees, increasingly dominated by the military, made their appearance.

1969, March–June. China's internal crisis was aggravated by a series of **clashes along the Sino-Soviet frontier,** both in the east and in Central Asia (p. 904). The two governments embarked on long, controversial debates, culminating in the interview of Zhou Enlai with Soviet premier Aleksey Kosygin at the Beijing Airport (Sept.) during the latter's return from the funeral of Hô Chi Minh.

April 1–24. THE 9TH PARTY CONGRESS (the first since 1958) met in secrecy and officially marked the **end of the Cultural Revolution,** formally declaring the victory of Mao's thought over the "revisionists." About 40 percent of the new Central Committee was drawn from

the military, and **Lin Biao,** who reported on the "success" of the Cultural Revolution, **was officially designated as Mao's eventual successor.** Lin celebrated Mao as the "great teacher of the world proletariat of our time." Although Mao had indeed (with the support of the army) purged the bureaucracy of the more moderate elements, he had done so at the expense of countless deaths, destruction of property, wastage of much of China's cultural heritage, and the dislocation and demoralization of its people. Moreover, the conflict greatly enhanced the influence of the military, who came to dominate the revolutionary committees that had taken control. Many former Red Guards were now sent down to the countryside, as the objects of their attacks had earlier been, to work in the fields.

Oct. 19. Soviet-Chinese border discussions began in Beijing.

Dec. 19. The U.S. relaxed restrictions on trade with the PRC, marking the beginning of a slow and cautious policy of friendlier relations between the two countries.

1970, Jan. At the regular Sino-U.S. meetings in Warsaw, both sides agreed to try to elevate the talks to "a higher level or through other channels."

April 28. China launched its first space satellite.

July 22. Qinghua University was reopened in Beijing, having been closed by Red Guards since 1966. Other university openings followed, though admission was based on class background and the recommendations of one's work unit. Academic criteria were reintroduced in 1972.

1971, April. Following a competition in Japan, **the U.S. table tennis team was invited by the Chinese for a goodwill visit.**

July. U.S. secretary of state Henry Kissinger secretly traveled to China and met with Zhou Enlai. The planned visit of Pres. Richard Nixon for the following year was announced (July 15).

Sept. 13. Lin Biao perished, allegedly in a plane crash in Outer Mongolia. He had reportedly clashed with Mao about continued use of the military to run the country and then planned a coup that had failed. His death occurred as he attempted to escape to the Soviet Union. The truth about the incident has never been conclusively revealed. The other leaders of the Cultural Revolution Group remained highly influential, even as the strident tone of the revolution was subdued.

The UN voted to admit the PRC to the General Assembly and to remove the Republic of China (Taiwan).

1972, Feb. 21–27. U.S. president **Richard Nixon visited the PRC and met with Zhou Enlai and Mao Zedong.** Together they issued the **Shanghai Communiqué,** setting the stage for eventual resumption of diplomatic ties (1979).

Normalization of foreign relations with Japan began.

1973, Aug. The 10th Congress of the CCP met in Beijing. The Cultural Revolution Group still maintained control, and many military leaders, former allies of Lin Biao, had been ousted. In addition, some 40 former members of the Central Committee, who had been disgraced during the Cultural Revolution, returned to power, including **Deng Xiaoping.** Party membership soared to 28 million. At this meeting Zhou Enlai officially denounced Lin Biao in a public forum, the first time this was done by a high-level CCP official.

Late in the year and continuing well into the next, a **mass campaign** highly reminiscent of the Cultural Revolution was launched **to vilify** the unlikely twosome of **Confucius and Lin Biao.** As well, thinly veiled attacks on Zhou Enlai were contained in some of the published material from the campaign, printed in March 1974.

1975, Oct. At an important meeting in Shanxi, **Hua Guofeng** (b. 1920), a little-known party bureaucrat from Mao's native province of Hunan who had only recently been promoted to vice premier of the State Council, gave the keynote address. He had been appointed minister of public security (Jan.) after his investigations into Lin Biao's "plans" to assassinate Mao.

1976, Jan. 8. Zhou Enlai died. His opponents outlawed all public demonstrations of mourning, in spite of which a mass demonstration erupted in Beijing on April 4–5 to pay final tribute to him. **Deng Xiaoping** delivered the official eulogy (Jan. 15).

Feb. After Mao, who was severely ailing, appointed Hua Guofeng to be Zhou's successor as premier, another campaign against Deng Xiaoping (murmurings of which had been heard in late 1975) grew stronger.

July. Zhu De, founder of the Red Army who was disgraced during the Cultural Revolution but was later rehabilitated, **died.**

July 28. China's worst **earthquake** in many centuries occurred in **Tangshan.** The death toll was close to one-quarter million.

Sept. 9. MAO ZEDONG DIED.

Oct. 6. On the orders of Hua Guofeng, the **four top leaders of the Cultural Revolution Group, including Mao's widow, were arrested.** They were to become known as the **Gang of Four.**

Oct. 7. Hua Guofeng was named chairman of the Central Committee of the CCP and head of the Military Affairs Committee.

Nov. Building of a new mausoleum for Mao in Tiananmen Square was commenced.

1977, July. Deng Xiaoping returned to power a second time, gaining back his position as vice premier as well as his seats on the politburo and the Military Affairs Committee. Beginning in the following year, he would grow to be the most powerful man in China.

U.S. president Jimmy Carter proposed normalizing Sino-U.S. relations; the next year bilateral meetings were held in Beijing.

1978. China began gearing up for a major reform program, known as the **"Four Modernizations."** In addition to building new educational and technical institutions in China, students were selected for overseas study in the U.S., Japan, and Europe, primarily in technical fields.

Oct. 23. Japan and China signed the Treaty of Peace and Friendship.

Nov.–Dec. The "Democracy Wall" movement began. Large wall posters called for democratization of the political system to accompany modernizations in other areas. On Dec. 5, a poster written by **Wei Jingsheng** (b. 1949) on Democracy Wall explicitly called for a **"fifth modernization": democracy.** The government retaliated in Jan. 1979. Wei was arrested, tried (March 1979), and sentenced to 15 years in prison.

1979, Jan. 1. Diplomatic relations were established between China and the U.S. The U.S. broke relations with the Republic of China.

Jan. 28. Deng Xiaoping visited the U.S., sealing the new Sino-U.S. ties.

Feb. 17. After several years of increasingly tense relations with Vietnam, combined with support for the Cambodian regime of Pol Pot, Chinese troops invaded northern Vietnam (p. 1040). After a difficult and expensive mission, Chinese troops were withdrawn (by March 16).

July. Four special economic zones were created along the southeast China coast—the most famous being at Shenzhen, near Hong Kong— which looked much like Taiwan's export processing zones. Capitalism was given liberties within these zones that it was not (as yet) given elsewhere.

Nov. 15. It was announced that all those improperly denounced during the campaigns from 1957 forward were to be rehabilitated.

Dec. The Third Plenum of the 11th Central Committee of the CCP met. The Gang of Four was vilified, and the Four Modernizations were elaborated in somewhat more detail. They entailed reforms and development in agriculture, science and technology, industry, and national defense, marking a return to stress on expertise and incentive based on performance, not ideological purity.

1980, Sept. Hua Guofeng announced that the Chinese, excepting minority peoples, should limit the size of their families to one child. Soon thereafter, a revised marriage law was issued setting slightly older minimum ages for marriage: 22 for men and 20 for women, though recommendations had been made for higher minimums.

Nov. The Gang of Four was put on trial by the Deng regime, together with Chen Boda and five top army officers long held for complicity in the Lin Biao affair. Jiang Qing and one other Cultural Revolution leader were given death sentences (Jan. 25, 1981), later commuted to life imprisonment. Others received assorted prison terms. Hua Guofeng soon all but disappeared from any important government role.

1982. A census revealed that China's population had topped the 1 billion mark. The government became even more serious about population control; earlier, under Mao, the Chinese had derided Malthusianism as propaganda. Now the **one-child-per-family policy** was more strongly encouraged, with strong disincentives for those who bore more than one. Large-scale female infanticide, it is believed, was carried out in the mid-1980s. Even with a reduced birthrate, China continued to face an immense population problem, and as the countryside grew wealthy, fears of financial sanctions for producing more than a

single child abated. Critics voiced the fear that the one-child policy would produce a new generation of spoiled and doted-upon children.

Communes were dismantled as the sociopolitical basis for rural life in China. They were replaced by a "responsibility system," which afforded farmers more control over the land they were contracted to till.

Many foreign firms were encouraged to invest in Chinese industry, and the number of joint ventures rose appreciably. Thousands of foreign tourists began flocking to China, and countless new hotels (many of them joint ventures) were built to house them. These efforts to forge foreign ties contrasted sharply with the earlier emphasis on self-reliance at almost all costs.

Mao Zedong was now openly criticized in the PRC. However, the rapid changes in China over the previous few years had renewed intellectual life in the nation, raising questions about its future direction that particularly irked the leadership; also, rapid industrial and agricultural development was undermining the earlier egalitarian aims of the regime. In response to these trends, a new campaign was taking shape to eradicate "spiritual pollution," meaning the influence of the West. Some spectacular cases of corruption within the Chinese government were exposed by the Chinese press as well.

1983–84. Premier Zhao Ziyang (b. 1919) in 1983 called for increased modernization, and this trend continued into 1984. Foreign investment continued to soar. Ever larger numbers of Chinese students were studying overseas. Accompanying the dizzying pace of economic change was a concomitant rise in crimes of theft, personal injury, and corruption. **Hu Yaobang** (1915–89) calmed people's fears by saying, "Do not fear prosperity."

1985, Jan. 5. The CCP announced a new bill of rights for writers, promising greater freedom of expression. Later that month, Hu Yaobang noted that writers needed to be guided by the CCP and Marxism-Leninism.

March. Forty-seven thousand older officers in the PLA retired. The next month, officials announced plans to lay off some 1 million members of the Chinese armed forces and transfer them into the workforce.

April. Several hundred men and women, who had been sent down to do rural work some 17 years earlier and had largely been forgotten, returned illegally to Beijing, and on behalf of many thousands more they protested their ill treatment before the CCP headquarters.

Mikhail Gorbachev called for alleviation of Sino-Soviet tensions through greater bilateral trade and cultural exchanges; the Chinese responded warmly.

1986, Dec. Student demonstrators in Hefei, Anhui Province (Dec. 5, 9), and later in Wuhan, called for greater democratization. Posters soon went up on several campuses in Beijing. The government banned all such activities, but the students continued undaunted. On Dec. 20, some 30,000 marched in Shanghai. Later demonstrations occurred in Tianjin and Nanjing. Over 1 million students were sent down to the countryside for summer vacation.

1987, Jan. An immense **demonstration** and rally took place in **Tiananmen Square.** The intellectuals who supported the students, such as **Fang Lizhi** (b. 1936) and **Liu Binyan** (b. 1925), were attacked by the government for **"bourgeois liberalism."** On Jan. 16, **Hu Yaobang himself resigned as party secretary-general,** allegedly for having been the cause of the discord.

Oct. 25. The 13th Congress of the CCP met in Beijing. Pernicious Western influences notwithstanding, Zhao Ziyang called for keeping the development of a market economy on track. On Nov. 1, it was announced that old-timers **Deng Xiaoping, Peng Zhen, and Chen Yun** (b. 1900) **would step down from the Central Committee** of the party. **Zhao Ziyang was elected secretary-general of the party** (Nov. 2), and he named **Li Peng** (b. 1928) **acting premier** (late November).

1988. Reforms continued apace, and the economy was developing so rapidly that Chinese inflation soared to 20 percent early in the year. This and other problems resulting from the Four Modernizations program were discussed intently late in the year at the Central Committee plenum and the National People's Congress (early 1989).

1989, April 15. Hu Yaobang died suddenly of a heart attack.

April 17. A massive demonstration of students from various Beijing campuses was held **in Tiananmen Square** to eulogize Hu Yaobang. A sit-in took place nearby (April 18) at the Great Hall of the People.

April 24. A widespread strike of university classes began in Beijing, demanding that the government listen to the students' demands.

May 4. On the 70th anniversary of the May Fourth Incident (1919), over 100,000 students gathered peacefully at Tiananmen Square.

May 19. Zhao Ziyang went out to talk with students and exhorted those of them enduring a hunger strike (about 300) to put an end to it. Li Peng denounced the demonstrators—nearly 1 million at this point—as "counterrevolutionaries." On the next day (May 20), **martial law** was declared. When troops attempted to enter the square (May 21), the students blocked them.

May 30. A statue of the Goddess of Democracy and Freedom was brought into Tiananmen Square.

June 3–4. PLA TROOPS ENTERED TIANANMEN SQUARE DURING THE NIGHT AND FIRED DIRECTLY INTO THE SLEEPING CROWD. Even more were killed at Muxidi, west of the square. In all, several thousand died. Sympathy demonstrations erupted elsewhere. **Deng Xiaoping lambasted the students** (June 9) and praised the army.

1990, Jan. 2. Some 10,000 demonstrators marched in Hong Kong for democratization in China.

Jan. 11. The government lifted martial law.

Feb. Early signs prefigured a return to the eased economic policies that had preceded June 4, 1989.

March 12. U.S. president George Bush criticized China for continued political repression.

April 25. China signed a ten-year agreement with the Soviet Union for economic and high-tech cooperation.

May 11. Two hundred ten people arrested for roles played in the demonstrations of 1989 were released from jail.

May 25. Pres. Bush renewed most-favored-nation status for China.

June 26. Fang Lizhi, the Chinese astrophysicist and dissident leader, was allowed to **leave China** with his wife, Li Shuxian, for the U.S. They had been living in the U.S. Embassy in Beijing since June 4, 1989.

Sept. 23. China convened the Asian Games, in an effort to regain international respect.

1991, Jan. 27. Eight leading dissidents involved in the events of 1989 were sentenced to prison terms, the stiffest being seven years.

Feb. 13. Two major prodemocracy dissidents, **Wang Juntao and Chen Ziming,** were sentenced to 13 years in prison.

May 28. Pres. Bush extended most-favored-nation status to China for another year, despite troubling human rights problems.

June 5. Jiang Qing, Mao's widow and former leader of the Cultural Revolution, died in prison, an alleged suicide.

July 23. Signs hinted that **Lin Biao** might be rehabilitated, for reasons that remain unclear.

Nov. In continuing talks with U.S. officials, Chinese remained intransigent on human rights issues.

1992, Feb. 1. Pres. Bush and Premier Li Peng had a brief meeting, their first since the events of 1989.

Feb. 25. The Chinese press began calling for an end to the hard-line policies in effect since 1989 and encouraged a return to relaxed economic programs.

Oct. 10. The U.S. and China reached accords on trade after years of acrimony. China dropped some of its barriers to imports.

Oct. 20. In a reshuffling of the politburo, some older leaders were replaced by younger appointees who supported free markets.

Oct. 24. Japanese emperor Akihito visited China and admitted wartime guilt for the "great suffering" caused by Japan, though he stopped short of actually apologizing.

Investments by foreign enterprises grew steadily throughout the year in China.

1993, April 5. China and South Korea signed a series of trade accords.

May 28. U.S. president Bill Clinton renewed most-favored-nation status for China.

Sept. 14. Dissident Wei Jingsheng was released from prison one year early in China's effort to curry favor with the Olympic Organizing Committee. China wanted to host the 2000 Summer Games.

Sept. 24. The Olympic Games for the year 2000 were awarded not to China, but to Sydney, Australia.

A panic in the mid-1980s about the **reversion of Hong Kong** to the People's Republic of China in 1997 switched to considerable calm by the early 1990s, with a brief scare following the crackdown on the demonstrations in Beijing in 1989. Although some discord marked the

planning of a new international airport for Hong Kong, by the early 1990s, Hong Kong had become the effective banker for the entire country and a major funnel for investment money from Taiwan into the People's Republic; even the newly rich in China frequently did their banking there.

1994, Jan. China signed a pact with the U.S. setting trade quotas and agreeing to periodic inspections of Chinese companies. **China also promised to make an effort at improving human rights,** releasing two Tibetan dissidents who were arrested in May 1993.

May 26. U.S. president Clinton granted most favored nation trading status to China despite its alleged continued record of human rights violations. Clinton said that China ended prisoner-made exports to the U.S. and freed dissidents' family members to leave the country, allowing the U.S. to make this move, which economists applauded.

Sept. 2–5. Chinese president **Jiang Zemin visited Russia,** signing a pact with Yeltsin to **alleviate tensions** remaining between the two countries in hopes of allowing for **future economic and political cooperation.**

Nov. 14. The Chinese government **banned the sex-screening of fetuses.**

1995, Feb. 4. The U.S. imposed huge tariffs on imports from China in an effort to punish the Chinese government for its continued manufacture of pirated goods. On Feb. 26 The U.S. and China signed a negotiation pact because China agreed to crack down on piracy. The pact was expected to be a big boost to trade. The U.S. and China signed trade accords on March 12.

June 7–10. Taiwan president Lee Teng-hui made his first presidential visit to the U.S., angering China. He was the first president of Taiwan to visit the U.S. since 1979.

1996, March 23. Lee Teng-hui won the first democratic elections in Taiwan; his win was seen as a blow to mainland China.

June 8. China announced plans to carry out nuclear tests despite an earlier agreement not to. On July 29 China conducted a nuclear test and then declared it to be its last one.

1997, Feb. 19. Chinese paramount leader **Deng Xiaoping died at the age of 92** in Beijing. He had been responsible for negotiating many of the market-opening reforms in China. Chinese president Jiang Zemin vowed to continue Deng's reforms.

April 21. The first Chinese troops in 150 years arrived in Hong Kong and began taking over the positions held by the British army.

July 1. Hong Kong reverted officially to Chinese sovereignty after 156 years of British colonial rule.

July 1. Tung Chee-hwa was sworn in as its first chief executive.

1998, March 17. China's parliament (the National People's Congress) elected **Zhu Rongji** as the country's new premier.

June 25–July 3. U.S. president Clinton made a prolonged visit to China and appeared on national television as he criticized China for human rights abuses and asked leader Jiang Zemin to open up and democratize Chinese society.

Sept. 10–19. The Chinese government extinguished the fledgling China Democracy Party, sentencing three party leaders to prison terms on charges of subversion.

May. In a measure praised by Western economists, Prime Minister Zhu Rongji installed a broad program to liberalize China's economy by privatizing state-run businesses.

1999, May 1. The U.S. Congress accused China of stealing nuclear secrets from its classified reports during the past 20 years.

May 7. Sino-American relations deteriorated as U.S. forces mistakenly bombed the Chinese embassy in Belgrade, Yugoslavia. Three died and twenty-seven others were wounded in the bombing strike that was part of Operation Allied Force.

July 9. Japan reached a comprehensive trade agreement with China, lowering duties on various important commodities between the two nations. This agreement won Japanese backing for China's application to join the World Trade Organization (WTO). The U.S. agreed upon a similar pact with China on Nov. 15 in a landmark trade agreement to significantly reduce obstacles to imported goods and foreign investments and to give China a normal status as a trading partner with the U.S.

July 10. New military missile threats faced Taiwan as tensions mounted when Taiwan's president **Lee Teng-hui** said publicly that his country was a separate state from China; the announcement abandoned the long-standing "One China" policy in an indirect declaration of Taiwan's independence.

July 22. Another human rights issue developed in China: the government banned the Falun Gong religious movement, a combination of Buddhism, Daoism, and martial arts. The group was publicly persecuted by actions of the national government, which was reported to have responded so violently because of suspicions that the incredibly popular group encouraged beliefs contrary to the Chinese communist philosophy. Thousands protested in Beijing's largest unauthorized demonstration since 1989.

Dec. 20. Macao was returned to Chinese sovereignty after 442 years as a Portuguese colony.

2000, March 18. Chen Shui-bian, a pro-independence Democratic Progressive Party leader, was elected president of Taiwan. Though armed conflict with China seemed imminent, Chen stabilized the growing threat of violence by softening his revolutionary stance shortly before the election. His rise to power marked the end of five decades of Nationalist Party rule in Taiwan.

Sept. 19. In a move vigorously supported by Pres. Clinton, the U.S. House of Representatives voted to grant Beijing permanent normal trading relations. This historic agreement reduced Chinese tariffs on many products and gave the U.S. access to some previously restricted Chinese markets.

c. THE REPUBLIC OF CHINA (TAIWAN, NATIONALIST CHINA)

(From p. 1021)

1950. The Nationalist government in Taiwan at last began to introduce some of the **reforms** it had promised while still in control of the mainland. It had wiped out a major sector of the local elite in the repressions of 1947. Some 2 million GMD leaders, their families, and their supporters had flocked to Taiwan in 1948–49 and soon dominated politics completely.

March 1. Jiang Jieshi (Chiang Kai-shek) resumed the presidency.

1953, Feb. 3. U.S. president Eisenhower relieved the Seventh Fleet from its duties of "neutralization" around Taiwan.

Feb. 24. The legislative *yuan* **abrogated the treaty signed with the USSR** in 1945 and reserved the right to sue the Soviet Union for indemnities.

1954, March 14. K. C. Wu, a former governor of Taiwan, broke with the Nationalist government for its increasingly dictatorial character.

Sept. 3. The Nationalist government reported heavy artillery fire by the Chinese Communists against the **offshore island of Quemoy.**

Dec. 2. A mutual defense pact with the U.S. was concluded. The treaty was confined to Taiwan and the Pescadores and not the offshore islands in Taiwan's possession.

1958, June 30. V.P. Chen Cheng became premier.

Oct. 21–23. U.S. secretary of state John Foster Dulles and Chinese Nationalist president Jiang Jieshi, after conferring in Taibei, issued a communiqué stating that the **Nationalists would not attempt to return to the mainland by force.** They also indicated that Nationalist forces on the offshore islands might be reduced if Communist aggression ceased (p. 1023).

Oct. 31. The U.S. State Department revealed that Jiang Jieshi had reserved the right to use force in the event of a "large-scale" anti-Communist revolt on the mainland.

1959, Oct. 7. U.S. undersecretary of state Douglas C. Dillon stated that if the Chinese Communists attacked Taiwan and the offshore islands, they would be risking "total" world war.

Over the course of the 1950s, help from the U.S., particularly via the Joint Commission on Rural Reconstruction, facilitated a program of land reform whereby rents were reduced and land was sold to those who could till it. Extreme inflation from the 1940s was brought under control by the early 1950s. These undertakings helped lay the groundwork for **rapid development in the 1970s and 1980s.** In the 1960s, the government moved to reorient the domestic economy to produce for export markets. Electronics, textiles, and chemicals, among other products, dominated Taiwan's industry.

1960, March 21. Gen. Jiang Jieshi was reelected for his third presidential term by the National Assembly.

1961, March 19. At the urging of the U.S., the Nationalist government announced the opening of **Operation Hurricane** to remove Chinese irregulars from the Thailand, Burma, and Laos border regions. These irregulars had fled from China in 1948–49, at the time of the Communist takeover.

1962, June 27. U.S. president **John F. Kennedy** stated that the U.S. "would not remain inactive" if a Communist Chinese attack on Quemoy and Matsu appeared to threaten Taiwan. On June 10, a large buildup of troops and planes had begun in Fujian Province, opposite the offshore islands of Quemoy and Matsu.

1962–71. The Republic of China, with its 13 million inhabitants, remained throughout this period the representative of China in the UN, occupying a permanent seat on the Security Council and claiming authority over all mainland China, with its 600 million people. Year after year the effort was made to have the PRC elected to the UN, and indeed the vote in favor grew from year to year. But a solution was all but impossible because Communist China would hear nothing of a "two Chinas" solution. It demanded that Nationalist China be expelled and the permanent seat assigned to the Beijing government. The U.S., bound by treaty to the Republic of China, was unwilling to desert an ally, so the situation, although less tense in 1970 than it had been a decade before, remained open. It was finally resolved in the next year (1971).

Because of the greater newsworthiness of both the rift between the Soviet Union and the Communist Chinese regime, and the Cultural Revolution in China (1965–68), developments in Nationalist China were often overlooked and received little international attention. However, great progress was being made along economic and social lines: important land reforms, notable advances in popular education, development of industrialization, introduction of family planning, and the like were instituted. Politically, affairs remained basically unchanged.

1966. The Nationalist government established **Export Processing Zones** (the first one at Gaoxiong [Kaohsiung]) with special economic privileges, to enhance growth and industry. Two more such zones were introduced in 1969.

1969, June. Jiang Jingguo (1909–88), the son of the president, was appointed vice premier and was thus informally designated as the probable successor to his father.

1971–72. Riots erupted against both the U.S. and the harshly undemocratic, rigid Jiang government. Tensions grew as well between the native population of Chinese on the island and those who had come with Jiang Jieshi in the late 1940s. The emerging movement for an independent Taiwan was anathema to the Nationalist regime. It was recurrently crushed by the government.

1973–74. The international oil crisis (p. 968) temporarily undermined Taiwan's economy, which was heavily dependent on oil imports. The problem did not reach destructive proportions because the government controlled imports closely to protect domestic industry and produce, and it forcefully encouraged exports, to build foreign reserves.

1975. Jiang Jingguo succeeded his father as president of the Republic of China.

1979. When the U.S. and the PRC normalized relations and those between the U.S. and Taiwan were broken off (p. 1025), contacts between the latter were carried on through two "institutes" (in Taibei and Washington, D.C.). Military ties were also scaled back. In April, the Taiwan Relations Act was passed by the U.S. Congress; it promised effectively to protect Taiwan from being overrun by the PRC. The economy of Taiwan continued to develop without interruption.

1980. The government built an industrial park devoted to scientific development. Taiwan's per capita income was in Asia second only to Japan. The International Monetary Fund and the World Bank took their "China" seats from Taiwan and gave them to the PRC.

As PRC policy shifted from engendering change through radical ideology to stressing rapid economic development, Taiwan's great economic successes seemed to temper PRC rhetoric. Both sides' earlier shared belief in reunification was beginning to be rethought.

1987. After many years, **martial law was lifted.** Censorship was relaxed, and signs hinted that some measure of democracy might be allowed. Travel to the PRC (outlawed since 1949) became legal.

1988, Jan. Upon the death of Jiang Jingguo, **Lee Teng-hui** (b. 1923) became premier. Moves encouraging democratization increased. When travel restrictions were removed, numerous Chinese began traveling to the PRC to see their relatives. By May the number had climbed to 10,000 per month. Open PRC-Taiwan joint ventures began to appear. The new openness also put a damper on Taiwan's exuberance about rapid reunification, which, it became clear, would have to be paid for by Taiwan. The reunification problems experienced by Germany in the next year exacerbated these concerns.

1998. Taiwan revived its recent interests in establishing a separate seat in the UN. As it had been in the past, the idea was stifled by the Beijing government.

Dec. 5. The legislative majority held by the ruling Nationalist Party grew by a substantial margin in parliamentary elections.

1999, July 10. In a public declaration of Taiwanese autonomy Pres. Lee announced Taiwan's abandonment of the long-standing "One China" policy. A possible threat to international peace, Pres. Lee's new policy with regard to Chinese relations held that Taiwan would work with China on a state-to-state basis.

Aug. 18. Pres. Lee's Taiwan government expressed interest in being included in a proposed anti-missile defense system with its Asian allies. This public defiance of Beijing was reported to have infuriated the Chinese government.

2000, March 18. Democratic Progressive Party leader **Chen Shui-bian** was elected president; Taiwan-China tensions mounted over the opposing faction's new rise to power. A few days before the election, Chen subdued fears of armed conflict by softening his pro-independence political stance. Mainland China reiterated, however, that it would never allow Taiwanese independence in any form. The election of a Democratic Progressive Party leader to the presidency ended 50 years of political control by the Nationalist Party (KMT) in Taiwan.

Oct. 4. Vice-Premier Chang Chun-hsiung was named prime minister after the resignation of Tang Fei.

2. THE REPUBLIC OF MONGOLIA (THE MONGOLIAN PEOPLE'S REPUBLIC), 1945-2000

(From p. 782)

Alliance with the Soviet Union. The Mongolian People's Republic entered into formal alliance with the Soviet Union with the signing of a ten-year assistance treaty in 1936 and its renewal in 1946. It supported the Soviet Union in its ideological conflict with China in the 1960s. A 20-year treaty of friendship, cooperation, and mutual assistance was signed in 1964, and an agreement eliciting Soviet economic aid was completed in 1970.

1945. Independence of Mongolia. A national plebiscite on Oct. 20 voted for independence, and China thereafter recognized the Mongolian People's Republic (MPR) as an independent state. On Feb. 14, 1950, China and the Soviet Union signed a treaty that guaranteed the MPR's independence. A new boundary agreement with China was signed in 1987.

1960. A new constitution stated that the construction of socialism was the country's basic task.

1961, Oct. 27. Admission to UN membership.

1980s–1990s. Some reforms were initiated to parallel glasnost and perestroika in the Soviet Union in the late 1980s. In July 1990, the first

multiparty elections were held, in which the Mongolian People's Revolutionary Party (MPRP) won 85 percent of the vote. Economic reforms moved toward privatization and market economy in the 1990s. Trade with China increased by over 40 percent in the early 1990s.

1991, Nov. The Grand People's Hural voted to change the country's name from the Mongolian People's Republic to the **Republic of Mongolia.** It has been a multiparty democracy since July 1990.

1998, April 23. Discord over proposed market reforms spread within Mongolia's ruling coalition. As a result, Tsakhiagiyn Elbegdorj was suddenly given the position of prime minister. However, further parliamentary disagreement led to his resignation on July 24.

Oct. 2. A political crisis spread following the murder of cabinet member and potential prime minister Sanjaasuregiyn Zorig.

2000, July 2. The formerly Communist MPRP won 72 of 76 seats in parliamentary elections. MPRP leader Nambariin Enkhbayar announced that although he planned to slow privatization in the economy, Mongolia would not revert to communism.

3. KOREA (NORTH AND SOUTH), 1945-2000

(From p. 784)

1945. Japan's defeat in World War II led to the dismantling of its colonial regime in Korea. Koreans quickly began imagining what their new liberty would entail, and the issue of earlier collaboration with the Japanese loomed large. In the last days of the war, the Japanese turned to **Song Chin-u** (1890–1945) to form a transition regime and keep order until the Allies arrived; he turned them down. On Aug. 15, the Japanese asked **Yŏ Un-hyŏng** (1886–1947), and he accepted with the proviso that all political prisoners be freed, that food be provided for the next three months, and that there be no Japanese interference of any kind. Yŏ next set up the **Committee for the Preparation of Korean Independence,** and soon numerous **"people's committees"** emerged nationwide, 145 of them by late August. By the end of the year, every village throughout the country had one. A representative council met (Sept. 6) in Seoul to create the **Korean People's Republic (KPR),** which was leftist-controlled but not necessarily a Communist front. **SYNGMAN RHEE (YI SŬNG-MAN)** (1875–1965) became chairman. Famed for his fidelity to the cause of Korean independence, Rhee, upon his return to Korea in the fall of 1945, attacked both the Soviets and the KPR for willingness to cooperate with Korean Communists.

Sept. 14. A platform of the KPR called for confiscation of all lands owned by the Japanese and collaborators for redistribution and the nationalization of major industries. All Koreans were to get the vote.

Having arrived on Sept. 8, the U.S. forces under the command of Gen. John Hodge refused to recognize the KPR and soon banned it. In its stead, they established the **U.S. Army Military Government in Korea (USAMGIK),** using the much-hated colonial bureaucratic structure.

Sept. 16. The **Korean Democratic Party** was founded by **Kim Sŏng-su** (1891–1955) and **Song Chin-u;** it was a moderate-to-conservative group that sharply criticized the KPR.

Dec. 27. The Moscow Conference, held by Great Britain, the U.S., and the Soviet Union, called for a **provisional Korean democratic government** under a five-year trusteeship of the three powers and of China. A joint Soviet-U.S. commission subsequently attempted to put this agreement into force but failed because of basic differences between the two parties concerning the definition of democracy. **Korea thus remained divided** into a largely agricultural south and a largely industrial north, with disastrous consequences to its economy.

1946, Feb. The Interim People's Committee was set up in P'yŏngyang, under the leadership of **KIM IL-SŎNG** (b. 1912). Kim had been a guerrilla fighter against the Japanese in Manchuria during the war. Non-Communists, such as **Cho Man-sik** (b. 1882), were forced out of power in the north.

At the same time, **Syngman Rhee** established the Representative

Democratic Council. Both north and south were moving toward the formation of their own governments.

March. By this time, the Soviet-led program in the north had completely transformed the social structure and ousted the colonial regime. In this month a profound land reform was implemented that eliminated land as a form of wealth. Industries were subsequently nationalized. Women's equal rights were ensured by law.

Sept. A general strike in Pusan of railway workers was touched off by the violent destruction of the people's committees. It spread but was soon mercilessly crushed by Korean police and U.S. forces. By the end of the year, most of the people's committees had ceased to exist. Thousands of people were killed in the process, and countless villages were decimated.

Land reform in the south was repeatedly put off both by USAMGIK and its right-wing Korean advisers. It finally was accomplished (March 1948) but was not far-reaching.

Dec. 12. The South Korean Interim Legislative Assembly, half popularly elected and half nominated, was opened in the U.S. zone. Its functions, at the start, were largely advisory. This was another step toward creating a separate regime in the south.

1947, Sept. Following another futile attempt to settle the future of Korea by negotiations with the Soviet Union, **the U.S. referred the Korean problem to the UN.** The UN supported elections, but when the north prohibited UN access there, the elections were scheduled only for the south. The Soviets in turn proposed the simultaneous withdrawal of U.S. and Soviet occupation forces.

Nov. 14. The UN General Assembly recognized **Korea's claim to independence** and laid plans for the establishment of a government and the withdrawal of occupation forces.

1948, Jan. 8. A UN commission arrived in Seoul to supervise elections for the **National Assembly.**

May 10. Elections were held in South Korea for the new National Assembly. The parties of the right gained a majority. The **National Assembly** met at Seoul (May 28).

Aug. 15. THE REPUBLIC OF KOREA (ROK) was founded, with **Syngman Rhee** as president. USAMGIK was officially terminated, and the new government entered into an agreement with the U.S. for the training of Korean military forces.

Aug. 25. The north held its own elections, and the DEMOCRATIC PEOPLE'S REPUBLIC OF KOREA (DPRK) was proclaimed in P'yŏngyang (Sept. 9) with **Kim Il-sŏng** as premier. Both it and the ROK claimed to be the only legitimate Korean government.

Nov. The National Security Law was passed by the National Assembly. It was used by Syngman Rhee to silence his opposition by defining as Communist (or "seditious") thousands of people who opposed his autocratic designs. The judicial establishment went along with Rhee's plans; by spring 1950, almost 60,000 persons were in jail, well over half for violating the National Security Law.

Dec. 12. The UN General Assembly endorsed the government of South Korea as the only lawfully elected one and set up a commission to aid in the unification of the country.

Dec. 25. The Soviet Union announced the complete withdrawal of its forces from North Korea.

1949, June 29. The U.S. completed its withdrawal of occupation forces from South Korea.

Sept. 2. The UN commission, reporting on its failure to mediate between North and South Korea, **warned of a possible civil war.** Sporadic fighting was occurring along the 38th parallel, sometimes assuming the proportions of major battles.

Oct. For alleged violations of the National Security Law, the Rhee regime arrested 16 assemblymen for overriding his veto on a land reform measure and for demanding his cabinet's resignation.

1950, May 30. Elections for the **National Assembly of South Korea** gave the majority to more **moderate forces** rather than to the extreme rightwing supporters of Syngman Rhee.

June 5. North Korea proposed negotiations for an all-Korea assembly but refused to deal with the government of Syngman Rhee.

June 25. The KOREAN WAR erupted, as North Korean troops crossed the 38th parallel at 11 points. A leftist guerrilla movement in the South had just been squelched after two years of bloody warfare. **The UN Security Council** called for an immediate cessation of hostilities and the withdrawal of North Korean troops. By the end of June, the DPRK had taken Seoul.

June 27. The Security Council, in the temporary absence of the Soviet representative, asked members of the UN to furnish assistance to the ROK. **The U.S. intervened** immediately to help stem the North Korean advance (p. 918).

July 8. Following a request of the Security Council, which had set up a Korean command under the U.S. (July 7), Pres. Harry S. Truman designated **Gen. Douglas MacArthur** (1880–1964) as commanding general of the UN forces in Korea.

Sept. 8. At its farthest advance, North Korea held most of the Korean peninsula except for a **UN beachhead around Pusan** in the southeast.

Sept. 13. U.S. and South Korean forces launched a counteroffensive, coordinating with an amphibious landing at Inch'on (Sept. 15). **Seoul was soon retaken** (Sept. 28), and by the end of the month, **UN forces reached the 38th parallel.** Gen. MacArthur asked for the surrender of the North Korean forces; he was ignored.

Oct. 7. The UN General Assembly adopted a resolution for a unified, independent, and democratic Korea, and set up a commission for the unification and rehabilitation of Korea.

Oct. 9. Gen. MacArthur ordered the crossing of the 38th parallel, acting on the implicit authority of the UN General Assembly. Within three weeks, **UN forces were approaching the Manchurian border,** reaching the Yalu River at several points.

Nov. 1. A North Korean counteroffensive halted and in some places **drove back UN forces.** The first Chinese prisoners were taken by MacArthur's forces; troops from the People's Republic of China had been coming into Korea since mid-October.

Nov. 24. Gen. MacArthur launched a general assault to end the Korean War.

Nov. 26. Massive numbers of **CHINESE FORCES INTERVENED** (p. 1021), and by the end of the year they had **driven the UN and ROK forces back to the vicinity of the 38th parallel.**

1951, Jan. 1. North Korean and Chinese forces attacked and broke through UN lines along the 38th parallel. **Seoul fell again** on Jan. 4.

Jan. 11. The UN truce commission proposed a five-point peace plan for East Asia. After the People's Republic of China rejected the proposal (Jan. 17), the U.S. submitted a resolution that China be found guilty of aggression in Korea. The UN General Assembly so resolved on Feb. 1.

Feb. South Korean military forces murdered some 500 local people in South Kyongsang Province for, the government claimed, harboring Communist guerrillas.

Feb. 12. Prime Minister Clement Attlee announced Great Britain's opposition to sanctions against China as long as any possibility of a negotiated settlement remained.

March 12. UN forces reoccupied Seoul, sending the North Koreans and Chinese into retreat.

March 24. Gen. MacArthur announced his readiness to meet in the field the commander of the North Korean and Chinese forces for a discussion of means to end the bloodshed. The Beijing government rejected his offer on March 29. The governments of India (March 31) and Great Britain (April 2) urged that a truce be arranged.

April 3. UN forces, having contained the Communists' first spring offensive, **counterattacked** across the 38th parallel.

April 10. Pres. Truman replaced Gen. MacArthur with **Gen. Matthew B. Ridgway** (p. 918).

May 15. Chinese and North Korean armies launched their **second spring offensive.** After one week of heavy losses, they were halted and forced into a general withdrawal.

May 18. The UN General Assembly embargoed arms, munitions, and critical raw materials to Communist China.

June 23. On a UN radio program, Soviet representative **Jacob A. Malik** made a vaguely worded call for a cease-fire and armistice talks in Korea. Two days later, Pres. Truman replied that the U.S. was willing to engage in such talks. On June 29, Gen. Ridgway broadcasted to the commander in chief of Communist forces in Korea an **offer to negotiate an armistice.** The Communist forces agreed to a meeting to discuss a cease-fire (July 1).

July 8. Truce negotiations commenced at Kaesŏng.

Aug. 5. Gen. Ridgway broke off armistice talks, charging that Communist troops had violated the demilitarization regulations in Kaesŏng. Talks resumed five days later, but they were deadlocked on the question of a truce demarcation line. On Aug. 23, the Communists suspended negotiations because of an alleged bombing of Kaesŏng by UN planes.

Sept. 23. UN forces in Korea captured "Heartbreak Ridge" after 37 days of hard fighting to secure strategic heights north of Yanggu.

Oct. 8. The high command of the Communist forces in Korea agreed to resume **armistice talks at a new site—P'anmunjŏm.** UN and Communist liaison officers held a series of meetings from Oct. 10 to Oct. 22 to resolve procedural issues. Formal negotiations were renewed on Oct. 25 for the first time since August.

Nov. 27. Truce delegates from both sides met in plenary session and approved a **provisional cease-fire line** to go into effect if armistice terms could be negotiated within 30 days.

Dec. 27. The 30-day armistice "trial period" lapsed, with neither side proposing an extension. **Armistice talks** remained stalled on two issues: prisoner exchanges and the building of airfields in North Korea during the prospective armistice.

Late in the year, Rhee created his own political party, the **Liberal Party,** and he used it to control the National Assembly and amend the constitution. He also used assassination to dispatch dissenting voices: Song Chin-u in 1945, Yŏ Un-hyŏng in 1947, and Kim Ku (1876–1949); other critics of Rhee, such as Pak Hŏn-yŏng (1900–55), had fled to the North (Oct. 1946), and still others had died of illness. Thus Rhee's power remained secure.

1952, March 4. The U.S. proposed an inquiry into Chinese Communist accusations that U.S. forces were using germ warfare in North Korea. On March 14, the Soviets repeated the charges but failed to acknowledge an offer by the International Red Cross to investigate.

April 4. The Korean armistice talks at staff-officer level recessed for six days as each side moved to break the deadlock on the question of prisoner exchange.

April 28. Gen. Mark W. Clark was appointed to succeed Gen. Ridgway as UN commander.

June 23. The **South Korean assembly,** boycotted by an aroused opposition, **reelected Pres. Rhee** for an indefinite term.

Aug. 5. In the country's first popular presidential election, Syngman Rhee was reelected for another four-year term.

Oct. 8. The Communists broke off armistice talks.

1953, Jan. 5. Prime Minister Winston Churchill, at the beginning of a visit in the U.S., declared his government's **opposition to any "indefinite extension"** of the Korean War into Communist China.

Feb. 25. The new U.S. delegate to the UN, **Henry Cabot Lodge,** told the UN political committee that the Eisenhower administration firmly accepted **India's truce proposal** for Korea.

March 2. Soviet foreign minister Andrei Vishinsky announced to the UN political committee that no Korean armistice except on the Communists' terms would be acceptable.

April 26. After agreements in March and April on prisoner exchanges, **truce talks were resumed** at P'anmunjŏm.

June 9. South Korea's assembly, rejecting the impending armistice, adopted a resolution calling for preparation to "advance north to unify Korea," but the government was persuaded (July 11) in talks with the U.S. to accept the proposed armistice terms.

July 26. The armistice was signed at P'anmunjŏm, to go into effect the next day. It provided for a **demilitarized zone** along the North and South Korean boundary, a joint UN-Communist **military armistice commission, and a neutral nations supervisory commission** to enforce the armistice terms.

July 27. The 16 nations that fought in Korea under the UN signed a declaration made public on Aug. 7, promising to resume fighting in the event of any new aggression there.

Oct. 25. Talks opened in P'anmunjŏm between UN delegates Arthur H. Dean and Communist representatives to arrange for the time and locations of a **Korean peace conference.**

Korean casualties in the war numbered 1.3 million in the South and about 1.5 million in the North; massive destruction of homes, factories, roads, and fields was sustained; many cities were demolished.

1954, Jan. 19. Despite bitter protests by the Communists, the Neutral Nations Repatriation Commission began the transfer of some 22,000 non-Communist prisoners of war to the UN command. The prisoners were then freed on Jan. 22.

Jan. 26. The U.S. Senate ratified the **Mutual Security Treaty** with South Korea. The pact obligated the U.S. to support South Korea in the event of attack, but not if South Korea attempted unification by force.

May 20. Parliamentary elections gave Pres. Rhee's Liberal Party a narrow majority.

June 5. At Geneva, Communist China urged that the Neutral Nations Advisory Commission, which had supervised the Korean armistice, also supervise the proposed elections in Korea. The U.S. termed the plan "completely fraudulent."

June 15. Sixteen non-Communist delegates at Geneva declared that since the Communists rejected the two fundamental principles for Korean unification and independence—the full power of the UN to repel aggression and to establish peace and "genuinely free elections"—further discussion "would serve no useful purpose."

1955. The Democratic Party was founded in opposition to Rhee's Liberal Party. Although factionalized itself, in 1956 its vice presidential candidate, **Chang Myŏn** (1899–1966), was elected.

1957, May 15. Syngman Rhee was reelected to a third term as president.

June 21. The UN command in Korea declared that it was no longer bound by the 1953 armistice ban against the introduction of new equipment because of North Korea's continued disregard of the provisions of the armistice.

1958, Oct. 22. Beijing reported the **withdrawal of the last Chinese forces** from Korea.

1959. Cho Pong-am, a socialist who ran for the presidency in 1952 and 1956, and who did extremely well in 1956, was executed for violating the National Security Law.

1960, March 15. Syngman Rhee, running for his fourth term, was **reelected president.** He ran unopposed, largely because the main opposition candidate, **Cho Pyŏng-ok,** died just prior to the election. Chang Myŏn resigned in protest at the corruption used by the Liberal Party in the elections.

April 19. Police and troops fired on some 30,000 demonstrators—initially students and later other citizens—protesting the rigged elections; 127 were reported killed and about 1,000 wounded. This became known as the **April Revolution. Syngman Rhee resigned** as president on April 26. The reins of government fell to **Hŏ Chŏng,** who moved to lift many of Rhee's repressive measures, rewrite the constitution (promulgated on June 15), and establish a parliament with two houses.

July 29. Parliamentary elections gave the Democratic Party a clear victory. The National Assembly elected **Yun Po-sŏn** (b. 1897) president and approved his appointment of **Chang Myŏn** as premier.

Dec. Local elections were held at the provincial level.

1961, Feb. In the ranks of the South Korean army, dissatisfaction with the corruption among officers led **Kim Chong-p'il** (b. 1926) to persuade Chang Myŏn to institute reforms; but instead, Kim was cashiered.

May 16. In South Korea, an **anti-Communist military junta,** led by Kim and **Maj. Gen. Pak Chŏng-hŭi** (Park Chung Hee, 1917–79), overthrew the government and arrested Pres. Yun Po-sŏn.

June 6. The military junta decreed an absolute **military dictatorship** with power concentrated in the hands of a few officers.

July 3. Maj. Gen. Pak Chŏng-hŭi became chairman of the military junta.

1961–79. The **MILITARY DICTATORSHIP OF PAK CHŎNG-HŬI** witnessed great changes and growth in Korean society, but without a hint of democracy. The Pak regime set South Korea on the path to rapid economic development. Trained by the Japanese military during the colonial period, Pak had no time for political power-sharing and made his rule ever more authoritarian.

1961–63. Pak governed through a junta, which ruled above the civilian apparatus of government. His regime declared martial law and eliminated all undesirable elements from state, society, and the military. Thousands were arrested. The National Assembly was closed down, political action was itself prohibited, and rigorous censorship was invoked. In June 1961, the **Korean CIA (KCIA) was established under Kim Chong-p'il.** In March 1962, over 4,000 former political figures were prohibited from participating in politics for six years.

1963–72. Pak and his fellows in the armed forces tried to use "democratic" political forms to rule. The U.S. was providing large sums of money to the regime and pressuring for a return to civilian rule. Pak had announced (Aug. 12, 1961) that the junta would relinquish authority to civilian control in 1963, followed by the end of martial law (Dec. 1962) and the approval of a constitutional referendum.

1963, Jan. A measure of political freedom was allowed, as the country prepared for elections.

March 22. Marchers demonstrated in Seoul against Pak's statement of March 16 in which he withdrew his promise of elections to a new government, claiming the necessity of four more years of military government. On March 26, civilian politicians refused Pak's compromise offer of a civilian-military junta. The U.S. government also claimed it would withdraw $25 million in aid if he went through with his plans.

April 1. Civilian leaders, insisting that the ruling junta honor its promise to hold elections, agreed to meet with the junta to discuss a coalition government. Pak agreed (April 6) to hold elections in the fall and to form an **interim coalition government** of military and civilian leaders to prepare the country for the election.

Aug. 31. The junta's **Democratic Republican Party (DRP)** nominated Pak as its presidential candidate in the Oct. 15 elections. Pak had just retired (Aug. 30) from the military. The other parties learned of the Oct. 15 election date only in mid-August, thus having but a month to pick candidates and launch campaigns.

Oct. 15-18. The presidential elections resulted in a victory for Pak, with 47 percent of the vote.

1964, June 3-July 28. Martial law was again proclaimed in Seoul, following a long series of **student demonstrations** and charges of corruption in government. A number of ministers were obliged to resign.

1965, April 13-17. Student protests, supported by the opposition in the National Assembly, erupted against the government policy of normalizing relations with Japan. Protests by the opposition became chronic and were matched by scenes of violence in Parliament.

June 22. Diplomatic relations with Japan were restored, and Japan promised extensive economic aid.

Aug. 26. Martial law was again proclaimed. Hundreds were arrested, and the universities were occupied by the police.

Sept. 25. Martial law was revoked.

1965-73. ROK troops were involved on the U.S. side in the war in Vietnam (p. 1038). South Korea at an early date sent a contingent and by 1966 had fielded 143,000 troops in Vietnam. In all, some 300,000 ROK troops fought in the war.

1966, Oct. North Korea, which at first had sided with Communist China in its dispute with the Soviet Union, tended to return to its old allegiance following the deposition of Nikita Khrushchev and the onset of the Cultural Revolution in China.

1967, March 3. Presidential elections in South Korea turned out a victory for Pak.

Tensions grew in the relations between North and South Korea. **North Korean border raids** and guerrilla operations became common and often assumed major dimensions.

1968, Jan. 23. North Korean gunboats seized the U.S. intelligence ship *Pueblo* and its crew of 82 outside the 12-mile limit in the Sea of Japan. Despite U.S. naval and air demonstrations and a momentary danger of war, the ship and crew were held by the North Koreans until Dec. 22, when they were released.

Also in January, a North Korean paramilitary unit assaulted Pak's presidential home; a similar assassination attempt in Aug. 1974 killed Pak's wife.

April 15. The North Koreans shot down a U.S. intelligence plane 90 miles off the Korean coast. The government made no secret of its hatred of "U.S. imperialism" nor of its determination to effect the reunification of Korea under Communist auspices in the near future, despite the continued presence in South Korea of some 60,000 U.S. troops.

1969, Aug. 21-22. In a **meeting between U.S. president Richard Nixon and Pres. Pak,** Nixon explained the new U.S. policy of letting friendly nations solve their own problems supported by U.S. economic and military aid but without the involvement of U.S. forces.

Sept. 13. The South Korean National Assembly met in a secret session called by the DRP and passed an amendment permitting Pak to stand for a third term. This amendment was approved by popular referendum (Oct. 17).

1970, July 8. The U.S. announced that it intended to reduce its forces in South Korea. The ROK government opposed this decision, in view of the increasing threat from North Korea, and demanded large quantities of modern military equipment and more intensive training of the South Korean army. Some 20,000 troops were withdrawn.

Nov. 13. In an act of self-immolation, a laborer by the name of Chŏn T'ae-il protested the exploitation of labor in the name of economic growth. Later in the decade, labor union memberships mushroomed.

1971. In the **presidential elections,** the **New Democratic Party,** a vibrant opposition party, ran **KIM TAE-JUNG** (Kim Dae Jung, b. 1925); he earned 45 percent of the vote. Pak remained in power, but the opposition forces were growing stronger nationally and locally.

Dec. Pak declared a **state of emergency** because of alleged domestic and international disorder. This was followed on Oct. 17, 1972, with yet another proclamation of martial law, bringing all political activity to an end and restricting most freedoms. The U.S. was reluctant to pressure Pak against taking such actions, especially after his willingness to commit troops to the Vietnam War.

1972, Nov. The Yusin Constitution was to institute new rejuvenating reforms, from the top down. The period 1972-79 is often considered the Yusin era. Student opposition grew in force as Pak continually abandoned his promises to liberalize the political system.

The economic plan of the Pak regime from 1972 forward greatly stressed heavy industry and exports, but during 1971-72 efforts were also made to shore up support for the regime among the conservative farming populace with the New Village movement, in which the government paid greater heed to rural development.

1973, Aug. 8. Kim Tae-jung was kidnapped from his hotel in Tokyo **by agents of the KCIA** who planned to assassinate him. After the case exploded internationally, he was taken back to his home in Seoul and released on Aug. 13.

1975, May. Like the National Security Law and similar acts used to stifle opposition, **Emergency Measure No. 9** was issued. Henceforth, any criticism of the president was a criminal act.

In the spring, the "Koreagate" scandal reached the headlines. High-level KCIA agents were trying to buy influence within the U.S. government.

1976. Over the previous 30-year period, the U.S. had provided South Korea with economic and military aid to the amount of $12.6 billion.

1979, Oct. A more visibly antigovernment wing of the NDP, led by **KIM YŎNG-SAM** (Kim Young Sam, b. 1927), took control of the NDP. The DRP (Oct. 4) voted to oust Kim from the National Assembly. Demonstrations and protests exploded, calling for Kim's rehabilitation and Pak's resignation.

Oct. 26. As the demonstrations grew in the Pusan area, a disagreement emerged between Pak and the head of the KCIA, **Kim Chae-gyu** (1926-80). Pak wanted to send in the army; Kim sought a compromise. Kim assassinated Pak and his main bodyguard, Ch'a Chi-ch'ol.

Dec. 7. Emergency Measure No. 9 was canceled; hundreds were released from jail (Dec. 7-8). Kim regained his civil rights on Feb. 29, 1980.

Dec. 12-13. A new junta began to seize power when Maj. Gen. Chŏn Tu-hwan (Chŭn Doo Hwan, b. 1931) **arrested the army's chief of staff** for a link to the Pak assassination. Then, Chŭn's ally, **Maj. Gen. No T'ae-u** (Roh Tae Woo, b. 1932), sealed off the city of Seoul with troops and armaments. In a protracted battle, they overcame the army headquarters. Roh took over as head of the Capital Garrison Command. The third main collaborator, **Maj. Gen. Chŏng Ho-yong,** became special forces commander.

1980, April. With the army under his control, Chŭn seized control over the KCIA. This illegal action set off demonstrations that continued to grow until they culminated in a mass protest in Seoul of some 70,000–100,000 students on May 15.

May 17. Chŭn promulgated Martial Law Decree No. 10, which closed down all colleges and the National Assembly, and prohibited all political action.

May 18. Students in Kwangju began a demonstration demanding an end to martial law. They were decimated by military paratroopers who killed indiscriminately. By May 21, the city was in rebellion. Troops crushed the rebels, beginning on May 27. Hundreds were killed, possibly more.

May 31. Chŭn established the joint civil-military Special Committee for National Security Measures.

Aug. 16. The puppet president stepped down; Chŭn resigned his army post on Aug. 22 and within about ten days became president.

1981, Feb. Under the new constitution of Oct. 1980, Chŭn was elected president again. His constitution limited an individual to one term as president.

Feb. 2. Chŭn was the first head of state to be a guest at the White House under Pres. Ronald Reagan, an honor seen as U.S. sanctioning of his presidency.

As punishment for allegedly inciting the Kwangju riots, Kim Tae-jung had been sentenced to death; this was commuted to life, and later to a 20-year term (1982).

1982. The Japanese government of Prime Minister Nakasone Yasuhiro floated a $4 billion loan to the Chŭn regime. Japanese business interests in Korea mushroomed.

1983. At this point in time, North Korea had a population of 19.2 million; South Korea had a population of 59.1 million.

1986, May. Massive antigovernment demonstrations and violence among students, workers, and the police erupted in Inch'on. They were followed by similar protests in Seoul (late October).

1987, Jan. A student at Seoul National University was tortured to death by the police, and the police actually admitted it, the first time in Korea's history that law enforcement had publicly stated its involvement in a crime.

April 13. Chŭn barred all public discussion of constitutional emendation; he had in the previous year (April) agreed to a dialogue on this issue, but then pulled an about-face. That action and the announcement on June 10 of the DRP candidate for president, No T'ae-u, set off more popular protests. Street fighting ensued in Seoul.

June 29. In a surprise move, **No promulgated an eight-point plan of reform,** with Kim Tae-jung's rights restored, human rights for all, freedom for many political prisoners, and an end to press censorship. Chŭn accepted this plan (July 1). Part of the background of this sharp change of direction and opening up of the political system had to do with South Korea's hosting of the Summer Olympic Games in the next year, which was intended to strengthen Korea's reputation and role in the international community.

Oct. 27. The National Assembly ratified a new constitution with provisions for direct presidential elections, which were to be held on Dec. 16. However, the two opposition leaders, Kim Tae-jung and Kim Yŏng-sam, could not agree between themselves and thus split the opposition vote. No T'ae-u was elected with 37 percent of the vote; Kim Yŏng-sam received 28 percent and Kim Tae-jung 27 percent.

Following the model of Japan, South Korea sought economic development through acquiring international markets. Exports reached $47 billion in 1987, as compared with $33 million in 1960. The huge Korean conglomerates (chaebol), such as Hyundai and Samsung, fueled the economic expansion. Through the 1980s, South Korea's trade surplus with the U.S. soared, like Japan's.

1988, Feb. 25. No T'ae-u became president of the ROK.

April. The National Assembly elections gave the opposition a majority, and with its newfound powers it opposed some of the administration's measures.

June. No endorsed a new relationship with North Korea, offering talks that might reunite the two countries.

Summer. South Korea hosted the Summer Olympic Games in Seoul, a source of great pride for the regime and many Koreans. It forced the government to open its doors to the international media and accordingly to introduce certain liberalizing reforms.

1990, Jan. 23. Pres. No's party and two opposition parties merged to gain a majority in the South Korean legislature.

March 15. Jiang Zemin, leader of the Chinese Communist Party, visited North Korea to meet with aging dictator **Kim Il-sŏng.**

May 10. Major demonstrations in Seoul protested No's new power bloc.

June 5. Soviet president Mikhail Gorbachev met with No in San Francisco and said diplomatic relations were to be opened (effected on Oct. 1).

July–Aug. New hopes for North-South relations were sparked. For five days in early August, the South Korean government eased restrictions on travel to the North.

Sept. 5–7. Prime ministers from North and South Korea met for two days for talks, the highest level of contact since the Korean War.

Sept. 29. Japan and North Korea finished a series of meetings and resolved to engage in talks about opening diplomatic relations. Negative repercussions in Japan greeted government officials' mention of paying reparations to Korean victims of Japanese colonialism.

Dec. 29. After two years of voluntary internal exile for the abuses of his regime, former president **Chŭn Tu-hwan** returned home to Seoul.

1991. Talks continued on reunification on and off throughout the year.

May. Big demonstrations and several public suicides (by self-immolation) by opponents of the No government took place. No continued his reforms toward democracy.

Sept. 25. Pres. No addressed the UN. He proposed a three-stage North-South reunification, with North Korea abandoning nuclear weapons.

Dec. 13. North and South Korean leaders signed a treaty ending the Korean War, after 38 years.

Dec. 26. Kim Jong Il, son of Kim Il-sŏng, was made head of the North Korean military, heir to his father's mantle.

1992, Jan. 6. U.S. president George Bush traveled to South Korea for talks.

Aug. 23. China and South Korea announced that they would commence diplomatic relations.

Dec. 19. Kim Yŏng-sam won the presidential elections.

Reports continued to appear that North Korea was trying to develop nuclear weapons, a source of conflict with the U.S.

1993, Feb. 25. Kim Yŏng-sam was inaugurated as president, South Korea's first nonmilitary president in over 30 years.

March 7. Pres. Kim granted amnesty to thousands of prisoners.

March 12. Angry at international pressure, North Korea announced that it would withdraw from the Nuclear Non-Proliferation Treaty. Tensions continued to mount. North Korea changed its mind (June 12).

June 11. U.S. president Bill Clinton went to Seoul. He further pressured North Korea to end its nuclear program.

Nov. 8. Pres. Clinton issued another sharp warning on nuclear weapons to North Korea.

Per capita GNP in South Korea was roughly $5,000, as compared with roughly $100 in 1963. Like postwar Japan, the ROK was soaring economically.

1994, Jan. North Korea signed an agreement with the U.S. to allow for inspection of seven nuclear facilities; some South Koreans found this agreement too lenient.

Jan. 27. South Korea announced an agreement to deploy a Patriot antimissile system, indicating the lingering high tensions regarding the nuclear situation in North Korea.

Feb. 15. North Korea agreed to limited inspections of all nuclear sites.

March 21. The UN Atomic Energy Agency **demanded** that North Korea allow **full inspections. North Korea threatened to withdraw from the Nuclear Non-Proliferation Treaty.**

May 14. Disclosure that North Korea had been refueling their Yongbyon nuclear reactor along with their continued refusal to allow full inspection of its nuclear sites caused increased tension.

June 15–18. Former U.S. president Jimmy Carter paid a visit to North Korea, doing a great deal to ease tensions there. On June 28 North and South Korean leaders set a date for a **summit at P'yŏngyang,** which would be their first since World War II.

July 8. North Korea's leader, Kim Il-sŏng, died of a heart attack in P'yŏngyang at the age of 82. His son Kim Jong Il took over, assuaging fears of a power struggle. Having ruled from 1948–94, Kim Il-sŏng was, at his death, the world's longest serving leader.

Aug. 12. The U.S. signed a pact with North Korea allowing for inspections of more nuclear sites.

Oct. 21. The U.S. and North Korea **signed a pact to dismantle North Korea's program of nuclear development,** reducing tension regarding a potential nuclear crisis.

1995, Feb. 15. North Korea **threatened to withdraw from the nuclear pact.**

1996. Signs of food shortage and famine proliferated in North Korea. Discussions of humanitarian aid included some new contacts between the two Koreas.

1997, Nov. 21. Amid a serious economic crisis, South Korea requested aid from the IMF.

Dec. 18. South Korea elected opposition leader **Kim Tae-jung** to replace Kim Yŏng-sam as president of South Korea. Kim Tae-jung's reformist policies, however, were for the most part rejected by the National Assembly until mid-1999.

1998, Aug. 23. Approximately 2.3 million people died in North Korea due to massive famine in the previous three years; international aid agencies warned that North Korea's system for national food distribution had virtually shut down. Only 10 percent of North Korea's rice fields were cultivated in 1998.

Aug. 31. North Korea launched an experimental missile over Japan, later claiming that it was simply a scientific satellite. Following the launch international concern was expressed about possible North Korean intentions to reenter the nuclear arms race.

1999, June. Open conflict erupted for the second time since Dec. 1998 between North and South Korea when two North Korean ships were sunk and another disabled after trespassing in South Korean waters.

Sept. 17. In exchange for food and economic aid, North Korea agreed to allow U.S. inspections teams into Kumchangri, which was suspected of being a nuclear development site. In addition, North Korea agreed to suspend long-range missile testing.

2000, March. Peace talks in Geneva and secret meetings between leaders of South Korea and several Western powers took place, leading up to further negotiations.

May 19. South Korean prime minister Park Tae Joon resigned his position after a financial scandal involving him was uncovered soon after he had taken office.

June 13–15. South Korean president Kim and North Korean president Kim Jong Il met for peace and unification talks in Pyongyang. Greatly calming tensions between north and south, the historic summit marked the first meeting of the countries' two heads of state. Pres. Kim Tae-jung was subsequently named to be awarded the 2000 Nobel Peace Prize.

July 21. Russian president Vladimir Putin met with North Korean president Kim in a conference in the course of which Kim pledged to discontinue North Korea's long-range missile program. In exchange, North Korea would require help from other nations that would enable it to secure rockets with which to send satellites into space.

Aug. 15–18. Following a summer of peace conferences, dozens of North and South Korean families that had been separated because of war were reunited with their relatives in Seoul, South Korea.

4. JAPAN, 1946–2000

(From p. 787)

With the formal surrender of Japan at the end of World War II, supreme authority passed into the hands of **Gen. Douglas MacArthur** as supreme commander for the Allied powers (**SCAP**). Though aided by an Allied control council and subject to the general directions of the 11-nation Far Eastern Commission with headquarters in Washington, D.C., MacArthur pursued an independent policy. To facilitate his task, Japan's governmental structure was left intact and put under the direction of **Prime Minister Shidehara Kijūrō** (1872–1951) and a nonpartisan cabinet. The most immediate task of the occupation authorities was to rid Japan of its imperialist customs, institutions, and mind-set. In a series of decrees, Gen. MacArthur restored civil liberties, liberated political prisoners, liberalized the educational curriculum, granted the franchise to all adults, encouraged the formation of labor unions and the abolition of older land tenure systems, and ended the compulsory adherence to state Shinto. The climax of these moves to break with the past came on Jan. 1, 1946, when **Emperor Hirohito**, in a New Year's message, disclaimed the divinity that was traditionally accredited to him by the Japanese people.

Among the most important initiatives of the occupation was land reform. Absentee landlordism was eliminated, as were large landholdings. The amount of land worked by tenants dropped from 46 percent to 10 percent; rents were regulated. Japan thus rapidly changed to a country of small farmers who owned their own land.

1946, April 10. The first general election favored the moderate parties. Communist returns were negligible. A new government under **Yoshida Shigeru** (1878–1967) took office on May 16.

A series of **purges**, initiated by SCAP, was directed against all "active exponents" of aggressive nationalism, including intellectuals and businessmen, and ultimately involved more than 1.5 million people. In addition, an **international military tribunal** in Tokyo began the trials of major war criminals, while separate British and Australian tribunals were set up in Southeast Asia and the South Pacific, respectively.

Nov. 3. A new constitution provided for an elected upper house, transferred sovereignty from the emperor to the people, **safeguarded individual rights and equal rights for women,** and introduced a broad measure of local self-government. It also renounced war for all time and became effective on May 3, 1947.

1947–48. The postwar **economic recovery** of Japan was extremely slow and heavily dependent on U.S. aid. To improve matters, the initial Allied policy of dissolving the large industrial combines was abandoned in 1948, and **reparations** from capital equipment were drastically reduced. Japan's future **standard of living** was set at the 1930–34 level. Beginning in April 1947, a limited resumption of private **foreign trade** was authorized, though by the end of 1948 Japan had regained only a small fraction of its former trade volume. To counteract the economic loss incurred from numerous strikes, Gen. MacArthur repeatedly imposed a ban on strikes. On Dec. 23, 1948, **the Diet prohibited all strikes** and collective bargaining **by government employees.** The initiative for Japan's economic revival came from the U.S., seconded by Great Britain. It met with opposition from Australia and China; they feared a powerful Japan as a threat to their future security.

1947, April. Elections for both houses of the Diet returned a right-wing majority for the **House of Councilors.** In the **House of Representatives,** the Social Democrats received the largest number of seats. On May 23, the Diet elected Socialist **Katayama Tetsu** to head a coalition government.

1948, Feb. 7. The Katayama government resigned because of friction within the Socialist Party. A new coalition was formed by Democratic Party leader **Ashida Hitoshi** on March 9.

March 15. A new right-wing opposition party, the **Democratic Liberals,** was formed under the leadership of former prime minister **Yoshida.**

Oct. 7. When **Prime Minister Ashida resigned** following a scandal involving members of his cabinet, **Yoshida Shigeru** formed a Democratic Liberal government on Oct. 14.

Nov. 12. The international military tribunal sentenced to death **Tōjō Hideki** and six others for major war crimes. Sixteen others were given life sentences.

1949, Jan. 23. The U.S. representative on the Far Eastern Commission announced the **termination of reparation removals** to aid Japan's economic recovery. The inflationary tendencies of Japan's economy were gradually being overcome through a strict program of economic stabilization imposed by Gen. MacArthur.

1950. Largely under the impact of the Korean War (p. 1029), severe restrictions were imposed on **Japanese Communists,** most of whose overt activities were suppressed and many of whose presence in labor unions came to an end. In the economic field, the war brought a much-needed increase in Japanese exports. The Korean War provided Japan with an opportunity to produce for the U.S. military, and the economic boom proved critical to the postwar recovery.

The creation of the **National Police Reserve** of 75,000 officers, to be used against domestic disturbances, was seen by some as the beginnings of a new Japanese army.

Sept. More than 10,000 prominent figures who had been dismissed at the beginning of the occupation were readmitted to public life.

1951, Jan. 29. Prime Minister Yoshida and John Foster Dulles opened **talks concerning a peace treaty,** as the Liberal Party issued a call for the restoration to Japan of the Soviet-held **Kuril Islands** and the U.S.-held **Ryūkyū Islands,** which included **Okinawa.**

March 29. The U.S. completed the draft of a peace treaty with Japan and communicated it to the 14 cobelligerent powers, including the Soviet Union.

May 19. The U.S. officially rejected a **Soviet proposal for a Japanese peace treaty** to be drawn up by the U.S., Great Britain, the USSR, and Communist China.

Sept. 4. The Japanese **peace treaty conference opened at San Francisco.** Four days later the treaty was approved and signed by delegates from Japan and 48 other powers. Defeated in their efforts at obstruction, the Soviet and other Communist delegates boycotted the final session. The treaty deprived Japan of its overseas possessions but levied no reparations and permitted rearmament. Japan ratified the treaty on Nov. 18.

Sept. 8. Japan signed a **mutual security pact with the U.S.,** permitting U.S. troops to remain indefinitely in Japan and to assist UN action in East Asia. The arrangement required Japan not to permit any other nation to impose bases or military authority there without U.S. consent.

1952, Feb. 25. The peace treaty negotiations with Nationalist China came to a deadlock over Japan's refusal to recognize Chinese Nationalist sovereignty over Communist-held territory and over Chinese insistence that 1937 be acknowledged as the date when hostilities broke out, rather than 1941, as Japan claimed.

April 28. A peace treaty with Nationalist China was signed, under which Japan renounced title to Taiwan, the Pescadores, and its former assets in China. On the same date **the war in the Pacific formally ended,** and the U.S.-Japanese Mutual Security Pact went into effect.

Aug. 5. Diplomatic relations resumed with Nationalist China.

Oct. 1. In general elections, the conservative **Liberal Party,** led by Prime Minister Yoshida Shigeru, won 240 out of 466 seats in the Diet. Not a single Communist Party candidate was elected.

Nov. 12. In the first formal step toward **defensive rearmament,** the U.S. agreed to lend Japan 18 frigates and 50 landing craft.

1953, April 19. In **national elections,** the Liberals' majority in the Diet was substantially narrowed.

July 29. The House of Representatives unanimously voted to adopt a resolution favoring an **increase of trade with the People's Republic of China.**

Oct. 30. A **U.S.-Japanese agreement** was concluded for the enlargement of Japan's "Self-Defense Forces," to protect it from possible aggression and to reduce the U.S. burden in the defense of Japan.

1954, June 7. Liberals overcame a Socialist boycott and pushed through the Diet legislation to end autonomous local police forces and to establish centralized controls.

Oct. 5. A conference of the Colombo Plan nations admitted Japan to membership (p. 995).

Oct. 12. Acting Prime Minister Ogata Taketora (1888–1956) rejected the PRC's offer of normalized relations. He termed it "bait" aimed at weakening Japan's ties to the U.S.

Dec. 9. The Diet elected **Hatoyama Ichirō** (1883–1959) of the Japan Democratic Party as interim prime minister, pending new elections in the spring.

1955, Feb. 27. Prime Minister Hatoyama's government won the elections.

Nov. 15. The two conservative parties, the Liberals and the Democrats, merged to form the **Liberal Democratic Party (LDP). The LDP won every election through the summer of 1993.**

1956, May 15. A Soviet-Japanese fishing and sea-rescue agreement was signed in Moscow.

Sept. 28. When **Soviet-Japanese peace negotiations** reached an impasse over the disposition of the Kurile Islands, the two powers agreed to postpone discussion of the issue and to proceed with the negotiation of a peace treaty.

Oct. 19. A Soviet-Japanese peace declaration ended the 11-year state of war. The treaty left unresolved the question of the **Kurile Islands.**

The USSR recognized Japanese sovereignty over Habomai and Shikotan Islands. Other provisions of the settlement included establishing diplomatic relations, Soviet support of Japanese application for UN membership, repatriation of Japanese prisoners of war, and the relinquishing of reparations from Japan.

1957, Feb. 25. Foreign Minister and Liberal Democrat **Kishi Nobusuke** (1896–1987) was elected prime minister, succeeding **Prime Minister Ishibashi Tanzan** (1884–1973), who resigned on Feb. 23 because of poor health.

June 21. The U.S. agreed to the immediate withdrawal of its ground combat forces and to a reduction in strength of other U.S. units stationed in Japan.

July 16. The government announced an **easing of trade restrictions with Communist China.**

1958, May 22. Prime Minister Kishi and his Liberal Democratic Party won in the national elections.

1960, Jan. 19. The U.S.-Japanese Treaty of Mutual Security was signed in Washington, D.C.

June 16. Following three weeks of **demonstrations opposed to the treaty,** Prime Minister Kishi requested that Pres. Eisenhower postpone his scheduled visit to Japan.

June 19. The U.S.-Japanese Treaty of Mutual Security was passed by the Japanese House of Representatives despite violent riots opposed to it. The treaty became effective on June 23.

July 18. Ikeda Hayato (1899–1965) was elected prime minister. A pro-Western former minister of international trade and industry, Ikeda became Japan's ninth postwar prime minister.

1962, April 26. Some 6,000 university students staged a protest march on the Japanese Diet, where the new Japanese-U.S. Treaty of Mutual Security was being considered for ratification.

July 18. After the governing Liberal Democratic Party retained its majority in the July 1 elections, Prime Minister Ikeda Hayato replaced 13 of his 16 cabinet members. **Foreign Minister Kōsaka Zentarō** was replaced by **Ōhira Masayoshi,** former chief secretary of the cabinet.

1963, May 14. The new Franco-Japanese Trade Agreement was signed, which provided that France would free or liberalize import quotas on over 60 Japanese products.

1964, March 24. U.S. ambassador **Edwin O. Reischauer** was stabbed by an allegedly deranged young Japanese.

March 27. Soviet Deputy Premier Anastas Mikoyan, with a 290-member parliamentary mission, ended a two-week visit made at the invitation of Japanese parliamentary leaders.

The Summer Olympic Games were held in Tokyo; hosting the Olympics became an important symbol of the country's emergence into the world arena.

Nov. 19. Satō Eisaku (1901–75) **became prime minister,** succeeding the ailing Prime Minister Ikeda.

1965, Jan. 12–13. Prime Minister Satō visited the U.S. Discussions were held on relations with the PRC and plans for the return of Okinawa to Japan.

June 22. Diplomatic relations with South Korea were established, along with agreements favoring Korea in matters of fishing rights.

1967. Relations with the Soviet Union and the Communist countries of Eastern Europe developed. A trade protocol (March) provided for a 16 percent increase in trade. Air service between Japan and the Soviet Union was opened in April. An agreement for scientific and technological cooperation was signed on June 22.

At the same time, agitation and pressure increased for the return of the Bonin and Ryūkyū Islands.

Nov. The second visit of Prime Minister Satō to Washington led to the U.S. promise to return the **Bonin Islands,** which was done in 1968.

1968. Repeated **demonstrations** and clashes by students and other radical elements agitated against the renewal of the 1960 **security treaty** with the U.S. and against the visit to Japan by U.S. nuclear-powered or nuclear-equipped vessels.

The novelist **Kawabata Yasunari** (1899–1972) was awarded the **Nobel Prize for literature,** the first East Asian author so acclaimed. He committed suicide in 1972. Other famed postwar novelists included **Tanizaki Jun'ichirō** (1886–1965) whose career really dated to the prewar era, **Mishima Yukio, Dazai Osamu,** and **Ariyoshi Sawako.** The postwar years produced a spate of brilliant writers.

1969, Oct. 21. Anti-War Day was celebrated, marked by huge student disturbances and drastic police actions.

Nov. 19–21. Prime Minister Satō visited the U.S. The "reversion" of Okinawa to Japan was promised for 1972; the U.S. base on the island would then have the same status as other U.S. bases in Japan. Nuclear weapons were to be removed before reversion, and the **security treaty was to continue in effect indefinitely,** subject to termination on one year's notice.

1970. The Ōsaka Exposition brought visitors from around the world to Japan. The Self-Defense Forces reached 250,000 in number, the most rapidly growing military force in the world.

1972, May. Okinawa was returned to Japanese control.

July 7. Tanaka Kakuei (1918–93) became prime minister.

Aug. Tanaka met with U.S. president Richard Nixon; the following month, he went to Beijing to meet with Premier Zhou Enlai. Diplomatic relations were established between Japan and the People's Republic of China. Ambassadors were soon exchanged.

1974, April. China and Japan signed an airlines agreement, a maritime pact (Nov.), and a fisheries treaty (Aug. 1975). Although Taiwan denounced all of these moves, trade between Japan and the People's Republic of China continued and grew.

Dec. Tanaka stepped down as prime minister.

1975. By this time, **the Japanese economy had been growing rapidly for over two decades.** It was the third largest in the world, behind only the U.S. and the Soviet Union. Japanese laborers became famous for their industriousness, frugality, and willingness to work closely with management to ensure success. Technologies supplied by the U.S. aided this growth, as did the low domestic spending on the military (1 percent of GNP). In addition, the Japanese government played a critical role in the development of the economy, through the **Finance Ministry and the Ministry of International Trade and Industry (MITI).**

Japanese **agriculture** also became more productive, indeed becoming the most efficient in the world. Prices on domestically produced essential foodstuffs, such as rice, were kept artificially high by government supports; in return, the agrarian populace and those dependent on them for a livelihood supported the ruling conservative Liberal Democratic Party.

Trade also exploded, increasing from $2 billion in 1955 to $55.75 billion in 1975. The U.S. consumed 22 percent of Japanese exports (1975). Japan largely imported raw materials in exchange, mainly from the Middle East (oil), Southeast Asia, and Australia (Japan's largest supplier). Japanese protectionism became a topic of heated negotiations from the 1970s, and the government was compelled partially to open certain markets to foreign goods; but by that time foreign producers were usually in no position to compete with their Japanese counterparts. High-quality Japanese products—especially electronic equipment, automobiles, shipping lines, and other products of the **immense industrial combines** (zaibatsu)—were by the 1970s to be found everywhere in the world.

It should also be noted that, following the Arab oil boycott of 1973 and the great increase in the price of oil, the Japanese economy went into a major recession during 1974–76.

A negative effect of rapid industrial growth was insufficient attention to environmental problems. Forest lands were wiped out, and Japanese industrialists began importing wood from Southeast Asia thereafter. There was considerable **industrial pollution,** the most famous case (early 1970s) being that of **Minamata** (Kyushu), where a chemical plant spewed mercury waste into the local water supply, poisoned the fish, and brought havoc to the local populace, some of whom died. Similar cases cropped up elsewhere.

By 1975 the **rate of population growth had slowed down** because of family planning and the paucity of living spaces for families. In 1945, the population was 72 million; by 1965, it had reached 98 million; ten years later, it was only 112 million. In 1985, it numbered 121 million. The social position of women rose slowly, too, as many attended school and began to opt for careers of their own. Some became active in politics, both in the long governing LDP and in opposition parties. But **relative pay levels and employment rates for women** lagged behind comparable Western figures.

Compulsory education, initiated by the occupation, drove up the numbers of students enrolled in middle and high schools. University students also increased in number dramatically. This development helped close the divide between elite and commoner. At the same time, schools became exceedingly competitive in entrance requirements.

From the latter half of the 1970s, a new attitude became more generally visible in Japan, as many more Japanese began to take advantage of their great economic successes. Japan massed immense export surpluses and was no longer in the position of "catching up" even though the annual growth rate slowed down considerably.

1976. Early in the year, the **Lockheed scandal** stunned the Japanese and others. Former prime minister Tanaka was charged with corruption, found guilty in 1983, and found guilty on appeal in 1987.

1978. China and Japan signed a peace treaty. The 1972–75 agreements and this treaty paved the way for bilateral trade in immense volume.

1982. Nakasone Yasuhiro (b. 1918) became prime minister, a post he held until 1987.

1987, April. Prime Minister Nakasone visited Washington, D.C., and met with Pres. Ronald Reagan.

Nov. Takeshita Noboru (b. 1924) became prime minister. He was forced to resign (June 1989) in a cloud of scandal concerning money funneled his way by the Recruit Company.

1988. The Dai-ichi Kangyō Bank of Japan was ranked the largest in the world.

1989, Jan. Emperor Hirohito died. He was succeeded by his son, **Akihito,** and the new reign period was to be called **Heisei** (Complete Peace).

Aug. Kaifu Toshiki (b. 1931) became prime minister. The Socialist Party had been gaining ground against the LDP, but was unable to capitalize in the Feb. 1990 elections.

1990, Jan. 18. The mayor of Nagasaki, **Motoshima Hitoshi,** was shot by a right-wing extremist for saying that Emperor Hirohito was partially to blame for World War II.

June 30. Prince Aya, second son of Akihito, married a commoner, Kawashima Kiko.

Nov. 12. Akihito was enthroned as Japan's 125th emperor.

1991, April 17. Soviet president Mikhail Gorbachev traveled to Japan for talks with Prime Minister Kaifu concerning economic aid, the Kurile Islands, and the like. Sovereignty over the islands remained unresolved.

Aug. Prime Minister Kaifu became the first head of state to visit the People's Republic of China in the aftermath of the massacres at Tiananmen Square in June 1989.

Nov. 6. Miyazawa Kiichi (b. 1919), an old LDP faithful, became prime minister, despite the fact that he had had to resign from the cabinet earlier because of the Recruit Company scandal. His cabinet was full of politicians long suspected of corruption and influence peddling.

1992, Jan. 21. The speaker of the lower house of the Diet, Sakurauchi Yoshio, claimed that U.S. workers were "too lazy" to compete with Japan and that half of them were illiterate.

Feb. 4. Prime Minister Miyazawa said that the U.S. "might lack a work ethic," implying that the economic problems in the U.S. were fundamental to the country and its people, not the result of unfair Japanese trade or business practices.

March–April. There were continuing signs of a slump in the Japanese economy.

June 16. The Diet passed a bill allowing Japanese "peacekeeping forces" overseas under UN control, the first time since World War II that Japanese troops might go abroad.

Oct. 15. Kanemaru Shin, a leader of the LDP, resigned from the Diet under an immense cloud of corruption, subsequently substantiated. He was later brought to trial.

1993. The slump continued as the yen grew ever stronger on international markets. As a result, Japanese goods became more difficult to sell overseas, which further hurt the domestic economy. There were major layoffs, heretofore considered a U.S. industrial phenomenon to which Japan was immune, the first since the end of the war. The "lifetime employment" ideal of Japanese management was in a state of havoc.

June 9. Crown Prince Naruhito married commoner **Owada Masako.**

June 19. Miyazawa received a vote of no confidence; the LDP was in shambles.

July 7. The Group of Seven held a summit in Tokyo.

Aug. 5. The Miyazawa government resigned.

Aug. 7. After the LDP lost control of the Diet, through a coalition of parties **Hosokawa Morihiro** was elected prime minister by the Diet. **Doi Takako** (b. 1928), former head of the Socialist Party and possibly the strongest woman political figure in Japan, became Speaker of the House. Hosokawa promised extensive political and economic reforms. Hosokawa proved extremely popular with the public but not with the entrenched politicians and bureaucracy he wished to shake up.

Japan was now the most densely populated country in the world; land values made Japan more valuable than the entire U.S.; Japanese men and women looked forward to a longer life expectancy than any people in the world; and a new conservatism could be felt in the air, a pride or satisfaction in Japan's great postwar economic turnaround.

In film, Japanese directors such as **Akira Kurosawa** (b. 1910), **Itami Jūzō**, and others ranked with the finest in the world, although they frequently had to seek funding outside Japan. Esteemed writers such as **Endō Shūsaku** (b. 1923), **Ōe Kenzaburō** (b. 1935), **Abe Kōbō**, and many others were widely read throughout the world.

1994, Jan. The Japanese Diet rejected a plan proposed by Prime Minister Hosokawa Morihiro to limit political corruption and corporate campaign funding; the failure disappointed the Japanese public as well as foreign governments. On Jan. 29 the Diet agreed to a compromise package.

Feb. 11. Trade talks between Japan and the U.S. collapsed because Japan refused to open its markets to help even out a huge trade imbalance; Hosokawa and Clinton both faced domestic pressures not to compromise.

April 8. Prime Minister Hosokawa resigned because of charges of financial impropriety.

April 25. Japan named its new prime minister, Hata Tsutomu. On June 29 Hata quit in order to avoid a no-confidence vote; he was replaced by Murayama Tomiichi of the Social Democratic Party. On July 30 Murayama named his cabinet. Japan came to an agreement with the U.S. (Oct. 1) to open Japanese markets in insurance, glass, telecommunications, and medical equipment to foreign competition.

Dec. Ōe Kenzaburō received the Nobel Prize for literature.

1995, March 23. Ten were killed in a nerve gas attack on the Tokyo subway system by the Aum Shinrikyo religious sect.

April 19. Three hundred more were injured by poisonous gas in Yokohama.

May 16. A cult leader, Asahara Shōkō, was arrested because of his links to the Tokyo subway gassing.

1996, Jan. 5. Murayama resigned as prime minister of Japan, saying that the country needed new leadership. The Parliament subsequently voted in Hashimoto Ryūtarō of the Liberal Democratic Party to be his successor.

April 1. Two Japanese banks merged to form the **largest bank in the world in terms of assets.** It was called the **Bank of Tokyo-Mitsubishi Ltd.**

Oct. 2. In elections, **Hashimoto was reelected as prime minister,** and his Liberal Democratic Party almost won the majority in the Diet.

1998, Feb. 7–22. Nagano hosted the Winter Olympics.

July 12. When the Asian economic crisis invaded Japan, the LDP saw a drastic popular decline in Japanese elections for the upper house. Prime Minister Hashimoto Ryūtarō resigned and was replaced on July 24 by Obuchi Keizo, also of the LDP. The recession facing Japan in 1998 was the worst to strike the nation since World War II.

1999, April 20. The IMF reported that several signals pointed to a limited recovery of the Japanese economy.

Aug. 11. The Obuchi government survived a no confidence vote although some liberals threatened to abandon their current coalition support.

2000, April 3. Prime Minister Obuchi suffered a stroke and was replaced two days later by LDP leader Mori Yoshiro. Obuchi died on May 14.

June 25. In parliamentary elections the LDP and its allies held a reduced majority in the lower house by successfully forming a coalition government with two other parties, New Komeitō and the Conservatives.

Aug. 2. As successive government scandals involving the cabinet secretary, finance minister, and former construction minister emerged during the year 2000, the Mori government faced strong criticism and a decline in popular support.

5. VIETNAM, 1945–2000

(From p. 788)

1945, Sept. 2. With U.S. support, **HÔ CHI MINH** (1890–1969) **proclaimed an independent Democratic Republic of Vietnam** in Hanoi.

The surrender of Japanese forces was taken north of the 16th parallel by the Chinese and south of it by the British. In the north the Viêt Minh, under Nationalist Chinese auspices, continued to operate with Chinese support, in spite of usually tacit French desires to the contrary. The British in the south supported the Free French, with some 20,000 French civilians still in Saigon concerned that French imperial glory not be completely undone. With British help, **the French militarily recaptured Saigon** (Sept. 23) and by Jan. 1946 had retaken much of Cochin China. The British withdrew in Jan. 1946, the Chinese in the spring.

Nov. To gain wider support domestically from the educated elite and also internationally (especially from the Nationalists in China), the Viêt Minh claimed to disband the Indochinese Communist Party. Elections were held, and many non-Communist nationalists were brought into the government under the banner of the **Lien Viêt** popular front group.

1946, March 6. The Viêt Minh were unable to keep the French completely out of their homeland, though. **France recognized Vietnam as a free state within the French Union and the Indochinese Federation,** but this did not deter Hô Chi Minh and his faction from carrying on hostilities aimed at driving out the French and uniting all Indochina in one Vietnamese state. In retaliation, the French proclaimed the "autonomous Republic of Cochin China" (June 1).

July–Sept. In protracted **conferences at Fontainebleau,** Hô Chi Minh was unable to persuade the French to accept his program. The French dispatched troops to Hanoi and Haiphong.

Nov. 23. The French bombardment of Haiphong left 6,000 civilians dead and effectively marked the beginning of the drawn-out and unsuccessful French struggle to retain control over Indochina, better known as the First Indochina War. The Viêt Minh retaliated (Dec.), and full-fledged war commenced. Over the course of the next eight years, France would commit some 420,000 troops to the field (including 200,000 Vietnamese).

1947, April. The Viêt Minh, having been forced out of all urban areas, became a guerrilla army. The French, far better equipped for conventional warfare, were unable to root them out of the countryside. Over the course of time, the Viêt Minh became stronger, but not strong enough to force the French out of the cities.

1949, March 8. On the eve of the Communist victory in China, the French made an agreement with non-Communist nationalist forces under **Bao Dai** (b. 1914), the former emperor of Annam, by which they recognized the independence of Vietnam (including Cochin China) within the French Union. A government was established in Huê and Saigon, with Bao Dai as head of state. France retained the right to keep military bases in the country. This move only strengthened the determination of the Viêt Minh, who drew added encouragement and support when the Chinese Communists were victorious in their revolution. By 1950, the conflict had taken on the appearance of a regular war.

1950, Jan.–Feb. Communist China and the Soviet Union both recognized the Communist regime of Hô Chi Minh in Vietnam. On the other hand, **the U.S. and Great Britain recognized Vietnam,** along with Cambodia and Laos, as associated states within the French Union. Bao Dai's former chief lieutenant, the anti-Communist Catholic **Ngô Dinh**

Diem (1901–63), refused to join his French-backed regime. Although initially cool to French efforts to rebuild their prewar empire, the U.S. was influenced by cold war anti-Communist political trends—the victory of the Communists in China and the commencement of the Korean War—toward recognition of the Bao Dai regime.

1951, Jan.–Feb. The French general Jean De Lattre de Tassigny (1889–1952) repulsed Communist attacks on Hanoi, and the Communists for the time being reverted to guerrilla tactics.

Feb. The disbanded Indochinese Communist Party reemerged as the Vietnamese Workers' Party.

1953. By this time, the Communists had built an army of some 125,000 men and women, to whom 230,000 French troops stood in opposition. In November, the French began construction of a huge **entrenched camp at Dien Bien Phu.**

1954, March 13–May 7. As a result of the **BATTLE OF DIEN BIEN PHU,** the French, gradually surrounded and cut off by forces under the command of **Gen. Vo Nguyên Giap,** appealed for help to the U.S.; but Pres. Eisenhower, although he declared (March 24) that the defeat of "Communist aggression" in Indochina, Burma, Thailand, or elsewhere in Southeast Asia was of crucial importance to the U.S., declined to use U.S. air forces to relieve the siege of Dien Bien Phu. Meanwhile (March 9) the French had indicated a readiness to discuss a peace settlement.

April 26–July 21. THE GENEVA CONFERENCE debated the Korean situation and in addition the problems of Cambodia and Laos as well as those of Vietnam. Much of the time the conference was deadlocked, especially on the questions of a cease-fire, a truce line, and an enforcement commission. On June 4, a Vietnamese prince serving as premier and French premier Joseph Laniel signed accords providing for South Vietnam's "complete independence" in "free association" with France. The new French premier **Pierre Mendès-France,** who was intent on making peace, conferred with Chinese Communist premier **Zhou Enlai** at Berne (June 23) and came to an agreement on the basic lines of a settlement (p. 857). The Geneva Conference (July 20) agreed to an armistice in Indochina that divided Vietnam just north of Huê into northern and southern halves at the 17th parallel. The Communist-led Democratic Republic of Vietnam ruled in Hanoi in the north, while Bao Dai's regime, now with Ngô Dinh Diem as premier (as of June 14) but without the French, continued in the south.

July 21. In addition to the division of Vietnam, the **GENEVA AC-CORDS** provided for elections to be held nationwide within two years, under international supervision. The Soviet Union, Great Britain, and the People's Republic of China signed the accords, but Pres. Eisenhower refused to accept responsibility for the armistice, to be bound by its terms, or to try to upset them. Diem, too, refused to participate in the election plan.

Sept. 8. The Manila Pact (or Southeast Asia Treaty Organization, SEATO) was engineered by the U.S. in an effort to forestall further Communist gains after the defeat of France. The U.S. was joined by Great Britain, France, Australia, New Zealand, the Philippines, Thailand, and Pakistan, with the objective of contributing to peace and security in Southeast Asia through mutual aid. Cambodia, Laos, and South Vietnam, precluded by the Geneva Accords from formally joining, signed a protocol bringing them within the scope of the treaty's military and economic terms. The treaty became effective on Feb. 19, 1955.

1955, March 21. Three armed **opposition religious groups** gave Premier Diem a five-day ultimatum to reorganize the government to suit them. Diem rejected the ultimatum on March 24, and on March 29 heavy fighting broke out between government forces and well-armed religious groups. A cease-fire was negotiated on March 30, and the next day one of the groups switched to the government's support.

April 28. Civil war broke out in Saigon. Premier Diem declared all-out war against the Bing Xuyen rebels. After five days of heavy fighting, **government troops forced the rebels out of the capital** (May 2).

May 1. Diem won a 15-hour **struggle for power** with the supporters of **Bao Dai** over control of the army.

May 5. Diem gained backing when a political congress in Vietnam called for Bao Dai's ouster and the establishment of a republic. Another congress urged that all of Bao Dai's powers be transferred to Diem until the National Assembly decided on a government. Diem indicated

(May 8) that the **French plan**—wherein Bao Dai would return under a reorganized system of government—would be unacceptable.

May 12. The government asked France either to move its troops to where the Viêt Minh threat existed (in the north) or withdraw them completely. **France agreed** (May 20) **to move its troops to the northern border.**

July 7. Pres. Hô Chi Minh of **North Vietnam concluded an agreement with Chinese Communist leaders,** providing for $338 million worth of Chinese economic aid.

Oct. 18. Bao Dai dismissed Diem, but Diem refused to resign. The Oct. 23 referendum was held as scheduled, with an overwhelming vote for Diem and against Bao Dai. On Oct. 26, **Ngô Dinh Diem proclaimed a republic.** As South Vietnam's first president, he promised early elections for a national legislature. He drew most of his backing from the 900,000 Catholics, an anti-Communist group, many of whom had fled the regime in the north.

1956, Jan. 23. The cabinet, meeting with Pres. Diem, gave final approval to ordinances setting up new electoral rules and creating an assembly to discuss and approve a new constitution.

Oct. 26. A new constitution was issued.

1959. Communist forces who had remained in the south after the partition became more politically active. Diem moved to suppress them, and soon the Vietnam War (Second Indochinese War) had begun. Hanoi agreed to the formation of a **National Liberation Front (NLF);** various dissident groups in the south, called collectively the **Viêt Cong** (Vietnamese Communists) formed this organization (Dec. 20, 1960). The Viêt Cong (or NLF) continued to organize among the rural populace despite efforts to root them out, and guerrilla warfare ensued.

Nov. The Nghe An rebellion erupted out of discontent with land reform measures begun the previous year in North Vietnam. Hô Chi Minh saw to it that forced collectivization of land ceased thereafter.

1960, Jan. 1. A new constitution was promulgated in North Vietnam. It effectively enshrined Hô Chi Minh as president with extensive powers.

Nov. 12. Diem was restored to power by the army, following a coup on Nov. 11 by the paratroop brigade in Saigon.

1961, April 9. Diem was reelected president.

June 16. South Vietnam's chief cabinet minister, **Nguyên Ding Thuan,** and U.S. officials under Pres. John F. Kennedy completed three days of **conferences in Washington, D.C.** The U.S. agreed to increase its 685-person military advisory group, to assign training specialists, and to send U.S. officers into the field to observe troops in action. In addition to the $40 million in arms previously promised, the U.S. agreed to pay salaries and supply arms for 20,000 troops to be added to the army of 150,000.

Sept. Hô Chi Minh turned over his position as secretary-general of the Vietnamese Workers' Party (Communist Party) to **Lê Duan.**

1962, March 22. Troops began Operation Sunrise to eliminate **NLF** guerrillas.

June 2. The international control commission on Indochina (composed of Canada, India, and Poland) reported that North Vietnam was supplying the NLF in the south in violation of the Geneva Accords. Poland did not sign the report.

1963, May 9. South Vietnam agreed to pay for all the costs ($17 million) of the "strategic hamlet program," deemed essential to its fight against the NLF.

Aug. 21. South Vietnamese **security forces occupied Buddhist pagodas** and arrested many priests. A UN mission to investigate charges of persecution arrived on Oct. 24.

Nov. 1–2. The Diem government was overthrown by Gen. Duong Van Minh and other officers. Diem and his security chief were killed. NLF military successes and the lack of political reforms under Diem led to the coup, with the complicity of the U.S. The new regime proved no better. More and more U.S. troops were committed to the war in South Vietnam.

1964, Jan. 6. A power realignment placed the country under the rule of three generals.

Jan. 30. Gen. Nguyên Khanh led a bloodless coup against the ruling junta and proclaimed himself chief of state.

Feb. 25. *Tass* released an "authorized statement" warning the U.S. not to carry the war into North Vietnam.

March 7. Premier Khanh announced a **one-year reform program** to improve the standard of living, increase government stability, and strengthen the anti-Communist military effort.

March 8–12. U.S. defense secretary Robert McNamara, leading a fact-finding mission, declared that the U.S. would aid Vietnam as long as necessary to defeat the NLF. In a speech (March 26), he later outlined U.S. goals in South Vietnam: to support its independence and prevent a Communist takeover. He rejected neutralization as opening the door to Communism.

March 18. Khanh declared his willingness to restore **diplomatic ties with Laos** and named a mission to Cambodia to discuss border problems.

April 15. The council of SEATO (p. 1037), meeting in Manila, affirmed support for South Vietnam against the NLF.

June–July. Further NLF successes brought increased U.S. efforts to help the Khanh regime stem the tide. Agitation grew for extending the war to North Vietnam to destroy the supply bases for the NLF.

July 8. UN secretary-general U Thant proposed reconvening the Geneva Conference to end the war.

July 24. The U.S. rejected a proposal by Charles de Gaulle (1890–1970) for international neutralization of Vietnam, Cambodia, and Laos. De Gaulle doubted the possibility of a military victory.

Aug. 2. Following South Vietnamese coastal raids (July 30–31), three North Vietnamese torpedo boats pursued and attacked the U.S. destroyer *Maddox* in international waters. The *Maddox,* supported by U.S. airplanes from the carrier *Ticonderoga,* returned fire, disabling one attacker. A second North Vietnamese naval attack (Aug. 4) on the *Maddox* and the *Turner Joy* followed. In retaliation, U.S. planes destroyed oil and naval installations on the North Vietnamese coast. The matter was brought to the UN Security Council, which invited both North and South Vietnam to appear to present evidence.

Aug. 5. At Pres. Lyndon B. Johnson's request, Congress passed overwhelmingly (with only two senators opposed) the **TONKIN GULF RESOLUTION** (p. 920), authorizing him to "take all necessary measures to repel any armed attack against the U.S. and to prevent further aggression." Congress also approved "all necessary steps, including the use of armed force, to assist any member or protocol state" of SEATO.

Aug. 16. A new constitution was adopted in South Vietnam. **Premier Khanh was elected president,** invested with nearly dictatorial powers. Riots by students and Buddhists (Aug. 19) led the government to withdraw the constitution (Aug. 25). Khanh then joined **Gen. Duong Van Minh and Gen. Trân Thieu Khiem in the Committee of Unification** (Aug. 27). But on Sept. 3, **Khanh resumed the premiership,** dissolved the triumvirate, and restored Minh as chief of state.

Sept. 13. A military coup failed against Khanh.

Sept. 26. The High National Council of civilians began to draft a new constitution. It provided (Oct. 20) for civilian rule, with the cabinet responsible to the assembly.

Nov. 4. Trân Van Huong succeeded Khanh as premier; Khanh remained as commander in chief of the army. The new arrangements were supported by U.S. ambassador Maxwell Taylor but led to much Buddhist protest and army intrigue.

Dec. 11. Vastly **increased U.S. aid** was announced. Its purpose was "to restrain the mounting infiltration of men and equipment by the Hanoi regime" for the NLF. By the next year there were 75,000 U.S. troops in South Vietnam.

Dec. 19. A military coup, associated with Khanh, overthrew the High National Council and canceled certain provisions of the constitution. **The Armed Forces Council** now took control, despite the disapproval of the U.S. authorities and their demand for a return to civilian government.

1965, Jan. 26. The government of Trân Van Huong was forced out by the military, following Buddhist demonstrations. **Gen. Khanh returned to power.**

Feb. 7, 8, 11. Air bombardments of North Vietnam were inaugurated by U.S. forces in retaliation for an NLF attack on the barracks in Pleiku. The Soviets warned that they would take stronger measures to strengthen North Vietnam's defense capability. Premier Aleksey Kosygin visited Hanoi.

Feb. 16. Khanh supported a civilian government under Phan Huy Quat, which enjoyed the favor of the Buddhists.

The Soviets proposed a new conference on Indochina, as suggested

by Pres. de Gaulle (Feb. 10). U Thant worked hard to get talks started, but U.S. president Lyndon Johnson (Feb. 25) rejected negotiations so long as North Vietnam failed to respect the independence and security of South Vietnam.

Feb. 20. The Armed Forces Council, led by **Gen. Nguyên Cao Ky and Gen. Nguyên Van Thieu,** deposed Khanh as commander of the armed forces. Thieu soon became the leader of the Armed Forces Council.

March 2. A severe **bombing campaign against North Vietnam** began.

March 7–9. Two battalions of U.S. Marines arrived to defend the air base at Danang (p. 921).

March 22. The NLF issued its five-point manifesto: no negotiations until after the withdrawal of U.S. troops.

March 30. The U.S. Embassy in Saigon was bombed by the NLF, demonstrating their pervasive power.

April 7. In a Baltimore speech, Pres. Johnson declared the readiness of the U.S. government to embark on "unconditional discussions of peace." At the same time, he outlined a vast plan for the economic development of all Southeast Asia.

April 13. As though in reply to Johnson, **the North Vietnamese stated their terms for peace,** which were basic to later developments: withdrawal of all U.S. troops from South Vietnam, cessation of U.S. hostilities against North Vietnam, settlement of South Vietnamese affairs in accordance with the NLF program, and peaceful reunification of North and South Vietnam by the people of both zones, without foreign interference.

June 12. Premier Quat was forced out of office by Generals Ky and Thieu, who (June 18) became respectively premier and president of the **National Leadership Committee.**

July. Detachments from Australia and New Zealand arrived in South Vietnam (p. 1044). A South Korean contingent had arrived earlier. Pres. Johnson announced (July 28) that U.S. forces would be increased to 125,000 and that the draft would be doubled. He appealed to the UN (July 30) for aid in arriving at a settlement.

Nov. 28–29. Defense Secretary McNamara visited Saigon. Military leaders argued for the need of 350,000 to 400,000 men to bring the war to a victorious end.

Dec. 15. U.S. airplanes bombed a power plant on the outskirts of Haiphong, a port thus far spared in view of the heavy Soviet shipping there.

Dec. 24. A Christmas truce began, and bombing over North Vietnam was suspended. Efforts by the U.S. to initiate peace talks were rejected by Hô Chi Minh.

1966, Jan. 31. U.S. bombing of North Vietnam resumed.

Feb. 6–8. Pres. Johnson conferred with Ky and Thieu in Honolulu. Social reforms needed in South Vietnam were discussed.

March 10–April 5. Widespread **Buddhist protests** and demonstrations were directed against the Ky regime. The unrest ended when the government (April 14) promised early elections for a constituent assembly.

May 15–June 23. Armed intervention against Buddhist rebels took place in Danang and Huê, where Buddhists had burned the U.S. consulate (May 31). Buddhist leader **Thich Tri Quang was arrested** (June 19), which was followed by the seizure of the Secular Affairs Institute, the last Buddhist stronghold, in Saigon (June 23).

June 29–July 5. U.S. planes repeatedly hit oil storage tanks near Hanoi and Haiphong.

July 12. The North Vietnamese threatened to try imprisoned U.S. pilots as war criminals. Pres. Johnson warned against it (July 20).

July 25. Ky urged the invasion of North Vietnam even at the cost of Chinese Communist intervention. The U.S. government was never willing to take this risk, though at the time the air war was being carried right up to the Chinese border with Vietnam.

Sept. 1. Pres. de Gaulle, on a visit to Cambodia, insisted that the U.S. would have to withdraw its forces before a negotiated settlement could become possible. Hanoi rejected a U.S. proposal for mutual withdrawal (Sept. 11).

Sept. 11–12. Elections for a constituent assembly were held. Despite NLF threats, over 80 percent of the eligible voters went to the polls.

Oct. 24–25. At the **Manila Conference,** the powers allied in support of South Vietnam pledged to withdraw as their opponents withdrew. Hanoi and Beijing rejected the idea (Oct. 27).

Dec. 2–5. The U.S. led intensive bombing of targets around Hanoi.

Dec. 31. U.S. troop strength in South Vietnam reached 389,000.

1967, Jan. 3. Hanoi offered to negotiate in return for an unconditional cessation of bombing.

Feb. 8. An exchange of letters between Lyndon Johnson and Hô Chi Minh proved fruitless.

Feb. 8–14. Bombing paused during the Tet (Vietnamese New Year) holiday. British prime minister Harold Wilson and Soviet premier Kosygin tried to persuade the U.S. to cease its bombing as a prelude to negotiations.

March 18. The constituent assembly unanimously approved the draft of the new constitution. It went into effect on April 1.

March 22. Thailand agreed to let U.S. bombers use its bases in attacks on targets in Vietnam.

May 18–19. U.S. troops moved into the demilitarized zone dividing North and South Vietnam. Heavy bombing of the power plant at Hanoi ensued.

June. By midyear, **U.S. forces numbered 463,000,** to which the allied powers added many more. The South Vietnamese army counted 600,000. The North Vietnamese had 50,000 regulars and 294,000 NLF and other irregulars. The North also had the support of some 50,000 Chinese laborers who repaired the damage done by bombing. Furthermore, they had the advantage of terrain (infiltration of troops over the jungle **Ho Chi Minh Trail** in eastern Laos) and of the reluctance of the U.S. to provoke Chinese or Soviet intervention through the invasion of North Vietnam or through outright attack on Haiphong or Hanoi. Despite the acute antagonism that had developed between the USSR and China, the Chinese throughout the Vietnamese War allowed Soviet supply trains to cross Chinese territory to reach their destination.

July 6–11. While in Vietnam, Secretary McNamara heard Gen. William Westmoreland's request for an additional 70,000 troops.

Sept. 3. In **South Vietnamese elections,** Generals Thieu and Ky became president and vice president, securing about 35 percent of the vote.

Dec. 26. The South Vietnamese threatened to pursue Communist troops into Cambodia if they used that country as a base for infiltrating South Vietnam. In reply, Beijing promised (Dec. 29) Cambodia support if the U.S. extended hostilities to that country.

1968, Jan.–June 27. The siege of Khe Sanh by the Communists ensued. This base, commanding an important road junction, was finally evacuated without serious losses.

Jan. 31. THE TET OFFENSIVE was launched (p. 921), involving coordinated NLF and North Vietnamese attacks on numerous South Vietnamese cities—a contrast to earlier fighting, which had been largely confined to the countryside. Saigon and Huê were scenes of desperate fighting. Operations continued until Feb. 24, when South Vietnamese troops recaptured the palace grounds at Huê. The Communist forces had counted on a mass supportive rising of the population in the south; this did not transpire, and countless NLF forces were slaughtered in the fighting. Thereafter, Communist forces primarily consisted of North Vietnamese regulars. While the Tet offensive failed to attain its objective, it did make a profound impression on U.S. and world opinion; all parties were astounded by the power of the Communist forces. It proved to be a major turning point in the war.

Feb. 24. U Thant, returning from an extended mission in the interest of peace, reported his conviction that a cessation of the bombing would soon lead to meaningful peace talks.

March 9. Gen. Westmoreland was reportedly asking for 206,000 additional men.

March 31. Johnson announced the **cessation of air and naval bombardment north of the 20th parallel,** which meant relief for some 90 percent of the North Vietnamese population.

April 3. North Vietnam offered to meet to discuss unconditional cessation of bombing.

May 5–June. Communist attacks on cities in South Vietnam were renewed; shelling and fighting near Saigon entailed heavy civilian casualties and a stream of countless refugees.

May 10. PEACE TALKS began in Paris with W. Averill Harriman as chief U.S. delegate and Xuan Thuy representing North Vietnam. North Vietnam immediately demanded unconditional cessation of the bombing.

June 10. Gen. Creighton W. Abrams succeeded Gen. Westmoreland as commander of the U.S. forces in South Vietnam.

July 18–20. Presidents Johnson and Thieu met in Honolulu. Johnson promised that in peace talks the U.S. would not impose a coalition government on Saigon.

Oct. 31. Johnson announced the **complete cessation of U.S. naval, air, and artillery bombing of North Vietnam.** The U.S. later claimed that this was part of an unwritten understanding in which North Vietnam promised to respect the demilitarized zone, abstain from bombing southern cities, and embark on meaningful negotiations. Hanoi denied that there was any such understanding.

Nov. The Paris Peace Talks made no progress, stymied by squabbling over procedural matters and over the status of the NLF in the negotiations.

1969, Jan. 5. Henry Cabot Lodge replaced Harriman as chief U.S. negotiator at Paris.

Jan. 25. The first plenary session of the expanded Paris conference was held, with both the Saigon government and the NLF represented. After extensive arguments, agreement was finally reached on seating arrangements and procedural matters.

March 6. It was announced that **U.S. troops in South Vietnam had increased to 541,000.**

May 8. Heavy Communist attacks left numerous casualties.

May 14. U.S. president Richard Nixon outlined peace proposals involving the withdrawal of the major part of all foreign forces from South Vietnam within a year. The basic U.S. peace requirement, he said, was a guarantee of freedom for South Vietnam.

June 8. Presidents Nixon and Thieu met at Midway. Nixon announced the beginning of U.S. withdrawal and the new policy of **"Vietnamization,"** that is, helping the Vietnamese in every way to deal with their own problems.

Sept. 3. Death of HÔ CHI MINH. He was succeeded as president by Ton Duc Thong. Real power remained in the hands of four men: **Lê Duan** (first secretary of the Workers' Party), **Pham Van Dong** (prime minister), **Truong Chinh** (chair of the Standing Committee of the National Assembly), and **Vo Nguyên Giap** (defense minister).

Nov. 3. Nixon announced that 60,000 U.S. troops would be withdrawn from South Vietnam by Dec. 15. A more precipitate withdrawal, he argued, would allow the Communists to massacre their opponents.

Nov. 20. Lodge resigned as chief delegate in Paris, in part to protest the lack of progress in the talks. Soon, the North Vietnamese delegate went on an extended leave, so that the talks remained stagnant for months.

1970, Jan. 29. As a warning against attacks on U.S. reconnaissance planes, **a North Vietnamese antiaircraft missile base was bombed.**

March 18. In a U.S.-supported uprising, **Lon Nol ousted Prince Sihanouk** (p. 1012) from power in Cambodia. Soon thereafter, U.S. and South Vietnamese troops extended the war to Cambodia. Sihanouk joined forces with the leftist **Khmer Rouge** in guerrilla fighting.

April 22. Nixon promised to withdraw 150,000 more troops over the ensuing year.

April 30. When Pres. Nixon announced that U.S. combat troops would join South Vietnamese troops in invading Cambodia to destroy enemy supply bases and concentrations, he precipitated the **Cambodian crisis.**

June 24. The U.S. Senate voted to repeal the ill-fated Tonkin Gulf Resolution, which had given the two administrations carte blanche to conduct their policies in Vietnam.

June 30. The Senate passed the **Cooper-Church Amendment,** barring the use of U.S. troops in Cambodia. At the same time, Nixon announced the end of combat operations in Cambodia and promised that in the future the U.S. would provide only air support for South Vietnamese operations.

Sept. 17. An **eight-point statement of terms** was submitted to the Paris conference by the NLF delegate. The statement seemed designed to commit the U.S. to withdrawal of all foreign troops from South Vietnam by June 30, 1971, and to the replacement of the existing South Vietnamese government by a coalition in which the NLF would share power.

Oct. 7. Pres. Nixon outlined a "major new initiative for peace": a general cease-fire throughout all Indochina, with international supervision; an international conference to settle Indochinese problems; negotiations of a timetable for complete withdrawal of forces from South Vietnam; a South Vietnamese settlement reflecting the will of the people and the existing relationships of political forces; and immediate and unconditional release of all prisoners of war.

Oct. 14. Hanoi rejected the Nixon proposals as "fraud."

Nov. 21. Heavy U.S. bombing of North Vietnamese antiaircraft and other targets retaliated for attacks on U.S. reconnaissance planes.

A U.S. helicopter raid on a prisoner of war camp 23 miles from Hanoi failed when the camp was found to be empty.

1971, Feb. U.S. and South Vietnamese troops entered southern Laotian territory in an effort to sever the communications route between the NLF and the North Vietnamese regulars (p. 1016). These U.S.-engineered moves of 1970–71 effectively enlarged the theater of war to all of former Indochina.

1972, Dec. Late in the month, Hanoi and Haiphong came under heavy bombardment from U.S. warplanes, eliciting sharp international censure.

1973, Jan. The Paris Peace Accords were signed (p. 923). A cease-fire went into effect (Jan. 28), and U.S. forces were guaranteed safe withdrawal. South Vietnam lost the superior U.S. air power.

1975, April 30. Surrounded by Communist forces, Saigon accepted unconditional surrender, and South Vietnam's military forces were finally defeated by North Vietnam and the NLF. The U.S. embassy staff left the country. A provisional revolutionary government took over in South Vietnam. In a blow to the NLF, North Vietnam dispatched its own people to take over administration of the southern half of the country. Saigon was renamed Hô Chi Minh City.

The pre-1975 regime in the south had never secured a meaningful mandate from its populace; its rulers were extraordinarily corrupt military men, with little following outside the armed forces and related industries. Although better armed and possessing greater troop strength than the north, South Vietnam's anti-Communist rulers were not able to keep the trust of even the traditional anti-Communist elites, such as the Buddhist and Catholic clergy. All the billions of dollars in U.S. aid, hundreds of thousands of U.S. (and allied) troops, millions of tons of bombs, and threatening pronouncements made little difference on the field of battle, where North Vietnam and its Viêt Cong allies were willing to make countless sacrifices in the interest of ultimate victory. The U.S. lost 57,939 men and women; the Vietnamese lost 10 to 20 times that number.

Nov. A political consultative council met in Saigon to discuss reunification of the country.

1976, June. After elections were held, a national assembly was convened.

July 12. NORTH AND SOUTH VIETNAM WERE PEACEFULLY REUNITED, and the Socialist Republic of Vietnam was born. The postliberation government began to rebuild the wartorn country, collectivize agriculture, and institute a five-year economic plan.

1977, Sept. Vietnam joined the UN. Participation in the International Monetary Fund and the Asian Development Bank followed.

1978, March. In measures aimed at rebuilding the economy, Vietnam nationalized all private trade. This move adversely affected the ethnic Chinese community in Vietnam. Dual citizenship was revoked.

June. Vietnam joined COMECON (Council for Mutual Economic Assistance), the Communist trading group controlled largely by the USSR. The next month the Chinese ceased all aid to Vietnam.

Dec. Vietnamese forces invaded Cambodia (p. 1013). In 1975 the Khmer Rouge, a Communist organization in Cambodia, came to power after ousting the U.S.-backed regime of Lon Nol. They then began to unleash a horrific holocaust on their own populace that left over 1 million—perhaps as many as 2 million—dead, including countless ethnic Chinese and Vietnamese living in Cambodia. The Vietnamese military ousted the Khmer Rouge and installed a puppet regime in Phnom Penh under Heng Samrin and Hun Sen, both Cambodian Communists opposed to Pol Pot. As long as ten years later, and in the face of worldwide criticism, 140,000 Vietnamese troops remained in Cambodia.

The People's Republic of China sided with Cambodia and disgorged venomous attacks on Vietnam. The Soviet Union and Vietnam had signed a 25-year treaty of friendship (Nov.). Although China and the USSR had both supported North Vietnam in its struggle against the U.S. and South Vietnam—specifically, long after the Sino-Soviet split—postliberation Vietnam chose to side with the Soviets against its historical enemy to the north. The treaty gave the USSR the former base at Cam Ranh Bay, and Vietnam received various forms of aid.

North Vietnam had never been happy with China for inviting Pres. Nixon to visit the People's Republic while U.S. troops were still on Vietnamese soil. China would have liked to see a more grateful Vietnam, and it was angered by the treatment meted out to ethnic Chinese in Vietnam, the so-called "boat people" who fled the country in 1977–78.

1979, Feb.–March. China invaded the northern provinces of Vietnam (p. 1013) to "punish" it. Casualties were heavy on both sides, but Vietnam fought off the Chinese attack.

1980, Dec. A constitution was promulgated; it announced that Vietnam was at present a proletarian dictatorship "in transition to socialism."

1981–85. The third five-year plan finally began to show efficacious results in the economy, but major problems remained in agriculture and industry. Increased autonomy in both sectors contributed to growth.

1986. Celebrating ten years of reunification, the Vietnamese Communist Party held its 6th Congress late in the year. Support was reaffirmed for construction of a Socialist state as laid out by Secretary-General **Lê Duan,** who had died that July. The country was in the throes of a serious inflation (1,000 percent). The congress recognized that it would take a "comparatively long period of time" to realize socialism. Calls were made for greater emphasis on the production of consumer goods and agriculture—and less on heavy industry—as well as developing the untapped capacity of private enterprise and for establishing economic ties with the international community. Nguyên Van Linh, who had lost out at the previous congress, was selected as secretary-general, and he launched a series of popular, bold reforms.

As of this time, 112 nations had established diplomatic relations with Vietnam or had decided to do so in the near future.

1987–88. New reform-minded officials were appointed with the aim of jump-starting the Vietnamese economic revival, a policy known as *doi moi.* Aside from government sponsorship of several large national power projects, centralized economic planning was curtailed; subsidies to national industries were abandoned to encourage the development of financial independence.

1988, Jan. New laws on foreign investment allowed the establishment of joint Vietnamese-foreign enterprises and others based on 100 percent foreign capitalization.

April. New laws on national enterprises gradually eased restrictions on individual and private economic ventures. In order to boost rural production, a plan was put forward to divide all commune lands of the subsequent 15 years among the farming households and thus instill greater freedom of production through a contract system. As in China, comparable far-reaching reforms were not forthcoming in the political realm; the Communist Party still was completely in charge. The Linh regime did try to use mass communications to launch an attack on corruption in party and government bureaus; but the leadership feared that criticism from these sources might extend to the party leadership itself, so restrictions on speech were imposed late in 1988.

Despite major economic reforms, the Linh government proved unable to rebuild the economy. Both the continued cost of troops deployed to prop up the Cambodian government and the trade embargo imposed by the U.S. and other Western nations took their toll on the Vietnamese economy.

1989, Aug. The 7th Central Committee meeting was held late in the month. In the face of democracy movements throughout the Communist world and China's crushing of demonstrators (June 3–4) in Tiananmen Square, Nguyên Van Linh, secretary-general of the Vietnamese Communist Party, continued to take a comparatively hard line, dismissing the idea of a multiparty state or a move toward democratic reform in Vietnam. He denounced the democracy movements elsewhere as counterrevolutionary. He wished to avoid the economic disorder that student demonstrators in China and elsewhere had caused.

Still seriously afflicted with economic problems at home and faced with international censure for its continued occupation of Cambodia ("Vietnam's Vietnam"), the Linh regime began to move toward a political resolution of the Cambodia situation. In September, after nearly 11 years of involvement, the last Vietnamese troops were withdrawn from Cambodia.

1990. The national census listed a population of 66.2 million.

April 1. A purge of politburo member **Tran Xuan Bach** was announced; he had called for more rapid political reforms in the manner of Eastern Europe and the USSR.

Sept. 20. Vo Nguyên Giap, deputy prime minister, visited the People's Republic of China to attend the Asian Games and received a warm welcome.

Sept. 30. The U.S. and Vietnam were observed to be moving toward the resumption of diplomatic ties.

1991. Calls for more openness were heard steadily from within the Vietnamese Communist Party.

April 26. The U.S. announced that it would provide $1 million, a small but symbolic amount, in aid to Vietnam, for providing artificial limbs to those maimed in the Vietnam War.

June 25. Leader **Nguyên Van Linh** reaffirmed the Vietnamese Communist Party's monopoly of political power, stating that Vietnam would not follow Eastern Europe's path of reform.

Aug. 11. China and Vietnam announced the mutual desire to normalize diplomatic relations. Talks in Beijing (November) formalized ties, and the border was clarified.

1992, Feb. 16. Hô Chi Minh City (Saigon) hosted an international marathon, using sports as a medium for gaining international recognition and easing of relations (as China had done with the U.S. table tennis team [p. 1024] in 1971 and in the 1990 Asian Games, as Japan had done in the 1964 Summer Olympic Games, and as Korea had done in the 1988 Summer Olympic Games).

April 30. The U.S. eased its 28-year economic embargo on Vietnam. More goods flooded into Vietnam through many channels.

1993, Feb. 10. French president François Mitterrand traveled to Vietnam, the first Western leader to do so since 1975.

July 18. The U.S. announced plans to post diplomats in Vietnam to assist U.S. families resident there.

Sept. Measures were taken by the Clinton administration to further relax the U.S. embargo. Many called to end it altogether. By year's end, the embargo was all but dissolved, and the pace of economic change in Vietnam was accelerating.

1994, Jan. The U.S. lifted its trade embargo against Vietnam. It had been in place for 19 years because of allegations of MIAs (Missing In Action) from the war.

1995, Jan. 28. The U.S. signed an agreement with Vietnam to exchange diplomats and to open offices in each other's capitals. On July 11 **Pres. Clinton formally reestablished diplomatic ties with Vietnam.**

July 28. Vietnam was admitted to the Association of Southeast Asian Nations as its seventh and only Communist member.

1998, March 10. Pres. Clinton waived the cold war trade regulations stipulated in the Jackson-Vanik amendment in order to permit U.S. firms in Vietnam to borrow from the Import-Export Bank.

2000, July 13. The United States and Vietnam signed a comprehensive trade agreement.

H. THE PACIFIC REGION, 1944–2000

1. THE ISLANDS, 1946–2000

(From p. 789)

The postwar years brought a period of significant change to the islands. They saw the dismantling of colonial rule through peaceful negotiation, except in Vanuatu; by the 1990s, only France and the U.S. remained "colonial powers" in the Pacific. They saw generally successful attempts at regional cooperation among independent island states, but they also witnessed the steadily growing dependence of the small, resource-poor, isolated islands on metropolitan countries. At the close of the 20th century, real political or economic independence appears to be a vanishing dream for most island communities.

1946, July 1, 25. The U.S., under **Operation Crossroads,** carried out the first of its atomic tests at **Bikini Atoll** in the Marshall Islands.

1947. Former (Japanese) mandated territories of the Marianas and the Marshall and Caroline Islands were given by the UN to the U.S. as the **Trust Territory of the Pacific Islands (TTPI).** The TTPI was designated a **strategic trusteeship,** which meant (1) that its political status could not be altered without the agreement of the governing power; (2) its affairs were to be supervised by the UN Security Council, where the U.S. (not the Trusteeship Council) had veto powers; and (3) the U.S. could close off any part of it for strategic purposes. Initially under the U.S. Navy, the administration of the TTPI was assumed by the Department of the Interior in 1951.

The creation of the **South Pacific Commission (SPC)** resulted at the signing of the Canberra Agreement by six colonial powers: Australia, France, the Netherlands, New Zealand, the U.K., and the U.S. The first regional body of its kind, the SPC was intended primarily to secure Western political and military interests in the postwar Pacific.

1949. The territories of **Papua and New Guinea** were merged into one administrative unit by Australia.

1954, March 1. The U.S. exploded its first **hydrogen bomb,** code-named **Bravo,** at Bikini Atoll, with long-term environmental and political consequences.

1958. An independence referendum in the French territories was ordered by **Pres. Charles de Gaulle.** It returned majority support for the continuing presence of France in the islands.

1959. The Hawaiian Islands, a territory of the U.S. since the turn of the century, became the 50th state of the U.S.A.

1962, Nov. 4. The U.S. carried out its last **nuclear test (Tightrope)** in the Pacific.

Western Samoa became the first Pacific island to gain independence.

1963. The first South Pacific Games were held at Backhurst Park in Suva.

Dutch New Guinea (Iriyan Jaya) became a part of Indonesia.

Anthony Solomon, a Harvard economics professor appointed by Pres. John F. Kennedy to carry out a survey of political, social, and economic problems in Micronesia, recommended an "integrated plan of action" to increase the islands' dependence on the U.S.

1964. The Cook Islands gained self-government from New Zealand; a constitutional conference in London moved **Fiji** further along the path of internal self-government.

1966, March. The University of Papua New Guinea opened and rapidly became the center for debating national issues by an emerging Papua New Guinean elite.

1968. Nauru became an independent nation. The **University of the South Pacific** opened in Suva, Fiji.

1970, Oct. 10. Fiji gained its independence from Britain as a dominion within the British Commonwealth. Ratu Sir Kamisese Mara became its first prime minister.

1971. The South Pacific Forum was launched at Wellington, New Zealand, in August, to provide heads of independent and self-governing island states (and Australia and New Zealand) the opportunity to discuss matters of mutual interest and promote regional cooperation.

1974, Oct. 19. Niue attained self-government in free association with New Zealand, which assumed responsibility for its defense.

1975, Sept. 16. Papua New Guinea gained its independence from Australia.

1976. The Northern Mariana Islands, which opted for U.S. citizenship and commonwealth status in 1975, became fully incorporated into the U.S. Its government was instituted in 1978.

1978. Ellice Island became independent as **Tuvalu** after it separated from the Gilbert Islands in 1976.

The Solomon Islands also gained independence from Britain.

1979. The Gilbert Islands, together with **Line and Phoenix groups and Ocean Island,** achieved independence as the **Republic of Kiribati.**

May 1. The Marshall Islands became an independent republic.

May 10. The Federated States of Micronesia (Yap, Pohnpei, Truk, and Kosrae) came into existence.

1980. The Condominium of New Hebrides became independent under a new name, **Vanuatu.**

1981. The Micronesian island of Palau became the self-governing **Republic of Palau (Belau).**

1985. The South Pacific Nuclear Free Zone Treaty (the Treaty of Rarotonga) was signed by nine forum countries.

1987, May 14. Col. Sitiveni Rabuka, in a **military coup** (the first in modern Pacific history) overthrew the democratically elected National Federation–Fiji Labour Party Coalition government in Fiji. In September he executed another coup, leading to Fiji's expulsion from the British Commonwealth and the creation of the **Republic of Fiji.**

1988, Aug. 20. The Matignon Accord was signed in Paris to defuse a political crisis in **New Caledonia,** put some power back into the hands of the Kanaks, and provide for a new **referendum on independence to be held in 1998.** In December, the **Bougainville Republican Army,** committed to Bougainville's separation from Papua New Guinea, began attacks on government officials and installations.

1992, May. Fiji held its **first postcoup election.** Sitiveni Rabuka became prime minister with the support of the Fiji Labour Party, which he had ousted from power in 1987.

1997, May. The South Pacific Commission changed its name to Pacific Islands Commission at a meeting in Noumea on May 19–23.

July. The Legislative Assembly of Western Samoa passed a constitutional amendment to change the country's name to **Samoa.**

1998, July. The Fijian parliament unanimously adopted a new multiracial constitution based mainly on the report of the three-member Constitution Review Commission appointed by Pres. Ratu Sir Kamisese Mara in March 1995.

Nov. 8. By a 72 percent majority, voters in New Caledonia approved a plan for 15 to 20 years of shared sovereignty with France. This was one in a series of measures to increase New Caledonian autonomy.

1999, Feb. The leader of Vanuatu's independence movement and its first prime minister, Father Walter Lini, died on Feb. 2. Lini served as prime minister from 1980–91.

2000, Jan. 10. Kessai Note became the new president of the Marshall Islands.

Feb. The UN formally admitted Tuvalu as the 189th full member.

March. The Fiji Court of Appeal, comprising judges from Australia, New Zealand, Tonga, and Papua New Guinea, upheld a Fiji high court ruling that the 1997 constitution had not been abrogated.

May. George Speight and six armed gunmen stormed the Fiji parliament and held the government hostage for 50 days.

May. Papua New Guinea's first stock exchange, the Port Moresby Stock Exchange (POMOX), opened for business.

May. A Labour Party–led coalition won Fiji's general election, with Mahendra Chaudhry becoming the first Fijian of Indian descent to become prime minister.

May 19. Fiji's first Indian prime minister, Mahendra Chaudhry, took office.

June 5. A coup attempt in the Solomon Islands ignited factional fighting in the country's capital of Honiara.

Aug. 4. A military takeover of the Fiji government that began with the May 19 abduction of Prime Minister Chaudhry ended when rebel leader George Speight was charged with treason.

Sept. 14. Kiribati, Nauru, and Tonga were admitted to the UN.

Oct. The Pacific Islands Forum met in Tarawa, the capital of Kiribati, and endorsed the Biketawa Declaration, outlining measures member states could take to preserve democracy in the islands.

Oct. A peace monitoring contingent from Fiji and Vanuatu arrived in Honiara, the capital of the Solomon Islands, to oversee the surrender of arms by militants who had caused ethnic unrest.

2. THE PHILIPPINES, 1945–2000

(From p. 791)

The history of the postindependence Philippines has been characterized by complex social, economic, and political problems. Population increases led to internal migration, most notably to Manila and to Mindanao, creating serious urban problems in the former and exacerbating tensions between Muslims and non-Muslims in the latter. In addition, many Filipinos left the country to work overseas during this period.

Initial economic growth gave way to stagnation in the 1980s. Rural poverty has been a persistent problem; all attempts at land reform have proved ineffective. Bureaucratic inefficiency, political corruption, and the dominance of the elite in almost all areas of national life contributed to popular discontent. Guerrilla insurgencies, involving leftist groups and also Muslim separatists, have continued with varying intensity from the time of independence to the 1990s. Political life has been volatile, marked by a long period of dictatorship under Ferdinand Marcos in the 1970s and 1980s. Military interference in politics has been a further complicating factor. Relations with the U.S. have also been problematic, especially over the question of military bases: nationalistic Filipinos often categorized the relationship as neocolonial.

1945. The commonwealth government was officially restored under Osmena. Manila was liberated in March. The war had seriously damaged the Philippine economy, and disillusionment with the elites who had collaborated with the Japanese was prevalent. Antagonism between landlords and tenants also increased during the war.

1946, April 23. Manuel Roxas became president, against the background of the **Hukbalahap (Huk) insurrection,** a Marxist guerrilla movement that had been active during the war and sought redress of social inequalities.

The Bell Trade Relations Act gave the Philippines free trade access to U.S. markets until 1954. This measure was designed to help economic recovery after the war.

July 4. The Philippines was formally declared an independent republic.

1947, March 11. The Parity Amendment to the constitution gave U.S. citizens the right to equal access to Philippine resources. The amendment passed partly because of the propagandizing of Roxas.

March 14. The U.S. was given the right to military bases in the Philippines on a 99-year lease. Nationalists were upset by these actions.

1948, April 16. Roxas died in office and was succeeded by **Elpidio Quirino.** An amnesty for Huk guerrillas was negotiated, resulting in temporary peace.

1949, Nov. 8. Quirino won the election, and the populist **Ramon Magsaysay** became secretary of defense. The Central Bank was established to increase Philippine control over financial affairs.

1950. In the midst of a fiscal crisis, the Central Bank had to borrow to pay government servants. Magsaysay arrested the leaders of the Communist Party. By negotiating with the army to ensure that the 1951 election would be free of corruption, Magsaysay increased public confidence in the political system.

1953, Nov. 10. Magsaysay won the presidential election. The Huk insurgency began to decline as a result of a government policy combining reconciliation and military force. Magsaysay attempted to improve the situation of the poor with a series of reforms. However, land redistribution was obstructed by lack of funds, and the problems of poverty remained unsolved.

1957, March. Magsaysay was killed in a plane crash, bringing to an end his populist political program. **Carlos Garcia** was elected president and embarked on a program of austerity and economic nationalism.

1963. Diplomatic tension flared between the Philippines and Malaysia over North Borneo, which the Philippines claimed as the former territory of Sulu. **Ferdinand Marcos** became leader of the Senate.

1964. Involvement in the retail trade was restricted to Philippine nationals, a move symptomatic of Philippine **anxieties about foreign control of the economy.**

1965, Nov. 9. Marcos was elected president, pledging to reform the "old order" by removing bureaucratic inefficiency and corruption.

1966. Amid great political controversy, Marcos sent troops to Vietnam.

1967. The Philippines joined the Association of Southeast Asian Nations (ASEAN) (p. 1008).

1968. The Moro National Liberation Front was established to fight for **independence for Muslims** in Mindanao. Muslim guerrilla activity reached its peak in the early 1970s. The insurgency has continued into the 1990s, but its intensity diminished during the 1980s, in part because of increased government spending in Mindanao and divisions in the movement about their goal: independence or autonomy.

1969. Marcos won the election, promising a policy of liberal government expenditure and initiating a period of authoritarian rule in the name of national rejuvenation. The Communist Party of the Philippines was reestablished. The Communist **New People's Army (NPA)** was set up.

1970. Economic crisis and civil unrest.

1971. Students took control of the University of the Philippines, forming the **Diliman commune.** Although suppressed by the government, it was a catalyst for leftist political action.

1972. Marcos proclaimed **martial law.** Rallies were banned, Marcos's opponents were arrested (including the journalist and politician **Benigno Aquino,** who had been Marcos's rival for the presidency), and the country was ruled by presidential decree. Marcos justified martial law because of the purported risk of Maoist revolution under the NPA. However, he was also attempting to safeguard his own position against challenges by other members of the oligarchy.

1973. Land reforms were proclaimed, but sugar and coconut plantations were exempted, and little change occurred. In the first years of martial law, economic growth was strong, but **by 1975, disillusionment with Marcos** was already considerable.

1974. The parity arrangement and tariff-free access to the U.S. market for Philippine products ended.

1976. Marcos amended the constitution to give himself supreme power.

1980. Aquino was released from jail and went to the U.S.

1981, Jan. Marcos lifted martial law in response to internal and external criticism, but kept the power to rule by decree. Marcos won an election in June that was widely regarded as fraudulent. Corruption and abuses of power by the army were widespread.

1983. Benigno Aquino was assassinated on returning to the Philippines from exile in the U.S.; the Marcos regime was implicated in the killing. In October, Marcos established a commission of inquiry into the death of Aquino. Popular resentment was expressed in continual anti-Marcos rallies. The peso was devalued, symptomatic of an economic crisis accompanying huge national debts.

1984, Feb. Marcos called elections for the Assembly. **The National Movement for Free Elections, led by Corazon Aquino,** widow of Benigno Aquino, was successful in the election, despite widespread voting fraud. The International Monetary Fund (IMF) imposed strict financial controls on the government in response to the national debt problem, leading to an internal economic crisis.

1985. Guerrilla activity by the NPA increased. A thousand NPA members were killed in internal party purges in Mindanao. Senior military officers, including **Gen. Fabian Ver,** were accused of killing Aquino. In November, Marcos called immediate presidential elections in response to growing public dissatisfaction. In December, Ver and other military officials were acquitted of involvement in Benigno Aquino's murder. Many Filipinos regarded the verdict as a coverup.

1986, Feb. 7. Elections were held. The National Movement for Free Elections won the popular vote, but Marcos proclaimed victory. Election fraud caused popular resentment, and mass demonstrations took place. The military sided with demonstrators in the **"PEOPLE POWER REVOLUTION."** Marcos and his family went into exile in Hawaii. Corazon Aquino took power, releasing political prisoners and sacking Marcos appointees in the judiciary and government, including all local officials elected in 1980. **A new constitution** was drafted, and a cease-fire with the NPA was called. Coup attempts against Aquino were defeated. New credit from the IMF was arranged, but the economy remained stagnant.

1987. A number of attempted coups occurred. The new constitution was ratified, reintroducing the government structure contained in the 1935 constitution. Elections for the House of Representatives and Senate were held in May. Political life was tumultuous; politicians maneuvered for power in constantly changing alliances and factional struggles, a feature that has continued throughout the post-Marcos era. The government engaged in negotiations with the Mindanao Muslims over the question of autonomy.

1988. Ferdinand and Imelda Marcos were indicted by a New York grand jury for fraud and embezzlement. Provincial elections were held. The U.S. agreed to pay rent for military bases.

1989. Death of Ferdinand Marcos in Hawaii. Imelda Marcos was found not guilty of fraud in New York. A coup attempt against the Aquino government in December was defeated with U.S. assistance.

1990. Negotiations were held with the U.S. concerning the question of military bases. Despite power shortages, economic stagnation, and political violence, the Aquino government remained relatively stable.

1991. Imelda Marcos was permitted to return to the Philippines.

The eruption of Mt. Pinatubo caused widespread damage.

The Senate voted for the **removal of U.S. bases.**

1992. Elections were held in May for the offices of president and vice president as well as for the Senate and House of Representatives. Aquino did not seek a further term. **Fidel Ramos,** Aquino's defense secretary and a former general who had played a key role in the overthrow of Marcos, became president. American forces withdrew from their Philippine bases.

1993. José Maria Sison, leader of the NPA, called for the organization to reaffirm its allegiance to Maoist principles, while Ramos sought means to end the insurgency.

1994, Jan. 30. The government signed a cease-fire agreement with the Muslim Separatist group known as the Moro National Liberation Front.

May 31–June 4. A conference on human rights abuses in East Timor was held in the Philippines. The Indonesian and Filipino governments tried to prevent the conference. A Filipino coalition to stop the abuses was formed.

1995, April 4. Muslim separatists attacked the town of Ipil. They wanted a Muslim state on the island of Mindanao. About 52 were killed in the attacks.

1998, May 11. Former action film star Joseph Estrada was elected president after Gen. Ramos declined the opportunity to run for reelection. The ruling LAKAS Party, however, won a majority of the seats in the lower house elections.

1999, Nov. 24. A pact resolving the conflict of the Philippines with China over the Spratly Islands was signed.

2000, March 20–July 16. The Philippines government clashed with the rebel group the Moro Islamic Liberation Front, which battled the army and took hostages in several incidents. A number of deaths occurred.

Sept. 16. Estrada's government began a military assault against the Muslim guerrilla group Abu Sayyaf that was holding 21 international tourists hostage on Jolo Island. Abu Sayyaf demanded monetary compensation and declared itself to be fighting for an independent Islamic state. Fishing rights issues also played a part in sparking the rebel activity. Estrada's massive military offensive, aimed at rescuing the hostages, proved unsuccessful; his public support plummeted amid charges of rampant corruption.

3. AUSTRALIA, 1944–2000

(From p. 792)

Large-scale immigration—until the 1970s chiefly from Europe, thereafter increasingly from Asia—transformed British Australia. New and old migrants shared expectations of material prosperity, but after the very prosperous 1950s and 1960s, living standards declined. In the 1990s, the challenges of multiculturalism, unemployment, environmental degradation, and an aging population have raised for Australians new questions about their future. U.S. investments in Australia have increased and, during the cold war alliance with the U.S., reduced traditional ties with Britain. Agricultural and mineral exports to Japan increasingly defined Australia as a major supplier of the Pacific Rim.

1944, Dec. The Liberal Party was formed, with R.G. Menzies as leader.

1945, July 5. Prime Minister John Curtin died, after holding office since Oct. 1941. **Joseph B. Chifley** was elected leader of the Federal Labour Party and became **prime minister on July 12.**

Sept. 23–Dec. 12. A strike of coal workers in New South Wales seriously crippled Australian industry before it was settled by arbitration. To counteract absenteeism and strikes, and to improve coal production in general, Parliament, in Aug. 1946, adopted the **Coal Industry Act,** setting up a coal board with wide powers of control over every aspect of the coal industry.

1946, Sept. 28. Parliamentary elections maintained the Labour government's majority in both houses.

Oct. 31. A governmental ordinance called for radical improvements in the working conditions of natives in **Papua and New Guinea.**

1947, Jan. 27–Feb. 6. A meeting of representatives from Great Britain, France, the U.S., the Netherlands, Australia, and New Zealand at **Canberra** established the **South Pacific Commission** to deal with all common questions concerning the treatment and general improvement of the native peoples.

March 11. Sir William McKell, an Australian citizen and member of the Labour Party, took office as **governor-general.**

July 22. To help alleviate the manpower shortage, Australia agreed to admit 12,000 displaced persons per year from Europe.

Nov. 27. The **Banking Act,** calling for the nationalization of the banks, was passed after bitter political debate. Intended to aid in the prevention of depression and inflation, opponents of the bill branded its adoption as dictatorial and unconstitutional.

1949, June 26–Aug. 15. A coal strike almost stopped all industrial activity. It was settled, amid misleading claims of Communist instigation, with the aid of emergency legislation and the use of troops in operating the mines.

Dec. 10. The general election brought a decisive victory to the anti-Labour coalition of the Liberal and Country Parties. In preelection campaigns, they had opposed the government's socialist measures, especially the Banking Act, and had promised effective action against Communism. A new coalition government was formed by Liberal leader **Robert G. Menzies** (Dec. 17). The Labour Party did maintain its majority in the Senate, where most of the new government's legislation was vetoed.

1950, June. Australia participated in UN action against **North Korea** and took measures to strengthen its armed forces.

June 29. The Menzies government announced the dispatch of warships to the Korean War (troops were sent on July 26).

Oct. 20. The Communist Party Dissolution Act became law. After being overturned by the High Court, the measure was rejected at a referendum on Sept. 22, 1951.

Sept. 1. The U.S., Australia, and New Zealand signed a **tripartite security treaty (ANZUS).**

1954, Feb. 3. Queen Elizabeth II began the first tour of Australia by a reigning monarch (until April 1).

April 13. Prime Minister Menzies announced that a Soviet diplomat, Vladimir Petrov, had been granted political asylum. "The Petrov Affair" became a major political controversy and led in 1955–56 to a Labour Party split and the formation of the Democratic Labour Party.

1955, Dec. 10. Menzies's coalition government was victorious in national elections.

1956, Sept. 16. Australia's first regular TV service began in Sydney.

Nov. 22–Dec. 8. The Olympic Games were held in Melbourne.

1960, Oct. 17. The Papua New Guinea Act provided for the election of Papua New Guineans to the territory's legislative council for the first time.

1962, July. Thirty military advisers were sent to help train the South Vietnamese army.

1963, May 9. The U.S. and Australia signed an agreement permitting the U.S. to establish a major **navy communications center** in Western Australia, gaining sole operational rights for at least 25 years.

1964, Nov. 10. Adoption of **compulsory military training,** with liability to service overseas. In 1964–66, Australia sent supplies and professional troops to southern Malaysia to help resist the operations of Indonesian guerrillas.

1965, April. Decision to send troops to South Vietnam, in collaboration with the U.S. The first conscripts in Australia's history to be sent outside Australian territory to fight in war went to Vietnam on April 18, 1966. As in the U.S., the policy of involvement in Southeast Asia met with increasing popular protest.

Dec. An act was passed, similar to the English one, to limit and control monopolies.

1966, Jan. 20. Retirement of Sir Robert Menzies, who was succeeded as prime minister by **Harold Holt.**

Feb. 14. Conversion of the currency from the British system to that of Australian dollars and cents.

March. The contingent sent to Vietnam was raised to 4,500, despite the opposition of the Labour Party to the use of conscripts overseas.

Aug. 18. Australian troops defeated a larger enemy force at Long Tan, Vietnam.

Oct. 20–23. Visit of Pres. Johnson, the first visit of an American executive. He was met with hostile demonstrations in Sydney, Melbourne, and other places.

Gurindji people walked off Wave Hill and Newcastle Waters cattle stations, Northern Territory, demanding the return of traditional land. After a seven-year struggle, they won. This was seen as the beginning of the Aboriginal land rights movement.

1967, May 27. By a record 91 percent, a referendum voted to give Aborigines the rights of citizens.

Dec. 17. Prime Minister Harold Holt was accidentally drowned. John G. Gorton (Liberal Party leader) was appointed to succeed him on Jan. 10, 1968.

1970, May 8. Australia's largest demonstration was held in all capital cities to **protest involvement in the Vietnam War.**

Nov. Pope Paul VI made the first papal visit to Australia.

1972, Feb. 19. The last military units, from the air force, were withdrawn from Vietnam.

Sept. Conversion was begun to the metric system of measurement.

Dec. 2. The Labour Party under Edward Gough Whitlam won federal office, ending 23 years of Liberal-Country Party government.

1974, April 8. "Advance Australia Fair" replaced "God Save the Queen" as the national anthem.

Dec. 24–25. Cyclone Tracy destroyed Darwin, Northern Territory.

1975, Sept. 16. Papua New Guinea, self-governing since Dec. 1973, became **independent of Australia.**

Nov. 11. The governor-general, Sir John Kerr, dismissed the Whitlam Labour government and appointed **Liberal Party leader Malcolm Fraser** as caretaker prime minister. Fraser's government was returned at a federal election on Dec. 13.

1978, July 1. The Northern Territory, a Commonwealth territory, was granted self-government.

1980, June. The world's oldest known fossil, a 3.5 billion-year-old bacterium, was found near Marble Bar, Western Australia.

1983, Feb. 16. In Australia's worst natural disaster, "Ash Wednesday" bush fires killed 71 people and destroyed $400 million worth of property in Victoria and South Australia.

March 5. The Labour Party under Bob Hawke defeated Malcolm Fraser's Liberal-National Party coalition in a federal election.

1989, March 4. The Australian Capital Territory held its first election under self-government.

1990, Aug. 13–14. Three navy ships, the first commitment to the Persian Gulf crisis, left Sydney.

1991, Dec. 19. In a Labour Party ballot, **Paul Keating** replaced Bob Hawke as leader, and later as prime minister.

1992, June 3. In the **Mabo case,** the High Court conceded limited traditional land rights to Aborigines and Torres Strait Islanders, denied since European settlement in 1788.

In **Mabo and others v. Queensland,** the High Court recognized that the peoples of Murray Island in Torres Straits legally owned their land. This overturned the *terra nullius* (empty land) doctrine that had underwritten white Australian law since 1788 and implied for the first time that, unless it had been specifically alienated, Aborigines own their land.

1993, Aug. The Labour Government–appointed Republican Advisory Committee, headed by investment banker and lawyer Malcolm Turnbull, submitted its report outlining various options for amending the constitution to make Australia a republic. **Republicans wanted to make Australia a republic** by the centenary of federation in 2001.

Nov. The federal Labour government introduced a bill in Parliament to effect the High Court's Mabo decision.

1994, Oct. 9. Right wing parties gained many parliamentary seats in elections in Australia.

1996, March 2. National elections were won by **John Howard of the Liberal Party–National Party Coalition,** who was sworn in as prime minister on March 11. Thus ended a 13-year rule of the Labor Party.

1998, July 8. The Native Title Bill, a major piece of land-rights legislation, was passed in regard to aboriginal claims on Australian land. The bill gave Australian state governments the authority to rule on the issue.

Oct. 3. Prime Minister John Howard and his Liberal Nationalist Coalition retained power in parliamentary elections. The majority it enjoyed in the House of Representatives decreased when the Liberal Nationalists carried only 79 of 148 seats.

1999, Sept. Australia was the leading foreign power among international peacekeeping forces that entered East Timor to help quell the massacres in progress there.

Nov. 6. In a national referendum, voters rejected a proposal to make Australia a republic. Since 55 percent of the vote was against the transition, Australia failed to sever its remaining ties to the British Crown. The proposed constitution had called for a parliament-chosen head executive instead of a popularly elected president.

2000, Sept. 15–Oct. 1. Sydney, Australia, hosted the XXVII Summer Olympic Games. The Australian theme for the event was modernization and conservation, which emphasized Australia's commitment to preserving the environment. In a symbolic event, Cathy Freeman, an Australian sprinter of aboriginal descent, was chosen to light the torch that began the games.

4. NEW ZEALAND, 1945–2000

(From p. 793)

New Zealand enjoyed relative prosperity and security in the decades following World War II, bolstered by high prices for its agricultural exports and shielded by economic protectionism. The political landscape was dominated by the National Party (p. 793). Socially, the country tended to be conservative, with the nuclear family being the main unit of social identification for most Pakeha people. A fondness for sport and other outdoor activities was a distinctive feature of the country's culture. In the 1970s the economy began to falter, as the world market for agricultural products declined and Britain consumed less of New Zealand's exports. Social and political movements, in particular feminism, questioned the existing order. Immigration, from the Pacific islands and later from East Asia, contributed to social diversification. Maori, whose population had grown considerably since the 1950s and had become urbanized, displayed greater cultural and political assertiveness. From the middle 1980s, economic problems led governments to dismantle the earlier protectionist and interventionist economic structure in a bid to make the country more internationally competitive. Social welfare programs and the civil service also underwent radical changes. Maori social and economic problems, in particular the question of redressing historical injustices in the alienation of land and other resources, were also major issues in national politics during the 1980s and 1990s. In foreign policy, New Zealand's ties to Britain weakened after World War II, leading at first to closer links with the U.S. and later to an attempt to strengthen New Zealand's identification with the South Pacific. New Zealand's opposition to nuclear weapons led to conflict with the U.S. and France.

1945. The Maori Social and Economic Advancement Act established tribal executives and committees.

The Bank of New Zealand was nationalized, along with other enterprises. Self-government was granted to Samoa.

1946. The government began to provide universal child subsidies.

Nov. 26. Labour was reelected under Fraser.

1947. Ratification of the Statute of Westminster (passed in Britain in 1931) **confirmed New Zealand's independent status.**

1949. Reflecting cold war concerns, Labour imposed national service conscription, after a referendum (Aug. 3) in which a large number of people did not vote.

The **National Party took charge of the government,** with Sidney Holland as prime minister. National dominated postwar politics, although it did not substantially change the institutions set up by the first Labour government.

1950. The government removed controls on rents and land prices, as well as on imports. The Korean War increased wool prices, leading to an economic boom. The Legislative Council was abolished, leaving New Zealand with a single-chamber Parliament.

1951. Signing of the **ANZUS treaty**—a mutual defense pact between New Zealand, Australia, and the U.S. A **waterfront dispute** led to major conflict between unions and government, and in February the government declared a state of emergency, which lasted until July. A snap election was won by the National Party.

Creation of the **Maori Women's Welfare League,** one of the first national Maori organizations.

1954. In the general election, National was reelected. New Zealand joined the Southeast Asia Treaty Organization (SEATO). This committed the country to security involvement in Southeast Asia. Involvement in SEATO was important in foreign policy in the 1950s and 1960s, but it was no longer operative in the late 1970s.

1957. Labour won the election, led by **Walter Nash,** instituting tax rebates and housing loans; but an austere budget in 1958, which sought to reduce imports with higher sales taxes, damaged its political fortunes.

1960. The exclusion of Maoris from the New Zealand rugby tour to South Africa caused protests.

Nov. 26. Reflecting public discontent at Labour's economic policies, National won the general election, and **Keith Holyoake** became prime minister. **National stayed in power throughout the 1960s,** being reelected in 1963, 1966, and 1969. New Zealand enjoyed comparative prosperity and stability during the 1960s.

1961. The Hunn report highlighted economic and social inequalities between Maori and Pakeha (people of European origin). After World War II the Maori population grew and became increasingly urbanized, leading to social dislocation.

1962, Jan. 1. Western Samoa became independent.

1964. The Cook Islands gained self-government in all spheres except defense and some aspects of foreign policy (p. 1041).

1965. A small contingent of New Zealand soldiers was sent to Vietnam.

Some were withdrawn in 1971; the last contingent was withdrawn in 1972. The New Zealand–Australia Free Trade Agreement strengthened trade across the Tasman.

1960s–70s. Immigration of labor from the Pacific islands, mostly into low-wage work in the cities.

1971. New Zealand joined the South Pacific Forum.

1972. Equal pay for men and women doing the same work was brought into force. **Labour won the election** under the leadership of **Norman Kirk.**

1973. New Zealand's protests at French nuclear testing in the South Pacific included an unsuccessful application to the International Court of Justice to halt the tests and the dispatch of frigates to the test site.

Britain's entry into the European Economic Community adversely affected New Zealand's external trade situation, contributing to New Zealand's poor economic performance in the 1970s and 1980s.

1975. In the general election, the **National Party** came to power under **Robert Muldoon,** a populist conservative leader. The Muldoon years coincided with a period of **economic decline,** extensive state interference in the economy, and, in the early 1980s, investment in expensive development projects.

In the 1975 **Maori Land March,** activists walked through the North Island to protest injustices relating to land. This was one of a series of protest actions relating to Maori rights in the 1970s and 1980s, including the occupation of former Maori land at **Bastion Point** in Auckland, which culminated in the arrest of protesters in 1978 and annual protests on the anniversary of the Treaty of Waitangi. **Mana Motuhake,** a Maori political party seeking greater Maori self-determination, was formed in 1980.

1976. New Zealand's rugby team toured South Africa, and several African nations boycotted the Olympic Games in protest. The government established a **scheme of universal superannuation,** under which all retired individuals received 80 percent of the average wage. Coinciding with an aging population and low economic growth, this scheme was a substantial financial burden. Dawn raids and random street checks were carried out on Pacific islanders suspected of staying in the country past the time limits of their visas.

1981. A tour of New Zealand by the South African Springbok rugby team led to protests and civil disruption throughout the country.

1982. Establishment of the first **Kohanga Reo** (Language Nest), a system of Maori language preschools, in an attempt to revive the Maori language. This movement symbolized a wider Maori cultural revival in the 1980s. The **Te Maori exhibition** of Maori art treasures, which toured in the U.S. and New Zealand between 1984 and 1987, was an important expression of this movement. Writing and art produced by Maori people also burgeoned in this period.

1983. The Closer Economic Relations (CER) Agreement was signed with Australia. CER was designed to strengthen economic ties and to lower trade barriers between the two countries.

1984. A Labour government was elected under **David Lange.** This government **deregulated the economy,** transformed the civil service, and enacted a radical foreign policy program. These were the most significant reforms of New Zealand institutions since those of the 1935 Labour government. The Labour government empowered the **Waitangi Tribunal,** a legal body, to investigate Maori land claims dating back to 1840.

1985. The policy of **refusing entry to nuclear-powered or armed vessels,** which enjoyed broad domestic support, caused **diplomatic tension with the U.S.** The ANZUS alliance ceased to function as a result.

French government agents bombed the Greenpeace vessel *Rainbow Warrior* in Auckland Harbor, leading to tensions with France.

Paul Reeves was appointed New Zealand's first Maori governor-general.

1986. The State-Owned Enterprises Bill established principles of **free market management for government enterprises,** including the need to make a profit. Post and telephone services, airlines, and forestry and coal were organized into corporations.

1987. Labour was reelected under David Lange's leadership. The government pressed ahead with deregulation, including the sale of state-owned assets and cuts in welfare funding. Economic conditions, particularly unemployment, remained bad.

1989. Catherine Tizard was appointed New Zealand's first woman governor-general.

1990. Lange resigned as prime minister. In a general election, **National** under **Jim Bolger** won a landslide victory, reflecting public discontent with Labour's deregulatory policies.

1991. Despite public opposition, National continued with radical economic deregulation and instituted changes in health care and industrial relations. Charges for hospital care were introduced, and wage awards were replaced with a system of individual contracts between employer and employees. Welfare benefits were reduced, and unemployment levels remained high.

1992. The government and some Maori tribes negotiated an agreement to establish Maori ownership of commercial fishing enterprises in response to claims for fishing rights under the Treaty of Waitangi. This was hailed as a potential solution to other Maori claims.

Public discontent with the political system was manifested in a referendum to change the electoral system to incorporate proportional representation. This referendum was not binding, being subject to reconfirmation in a plebiscite to be held in 1993.

1993, Nov. 6. In one of the most closely contested elections in New Zealand history, Jim Bolger's National Party was returned to power with a narrow majority. The electorate also voted (53.8 percent of the vote) to replace the British-style first-past-the-post electoral system with a mixed-member proportional representation system, similar to the one used in Germany.

1994, Feb. 18. The U.S. restored ties with New Zealand; relations had been curbed in 1987 because of a ban on U.S. nuclear-powered armed ships docking there, since New Zealand is a nuclear-free zone.

1997, Nov. 3. The prime minister of New Zealand, **Jim Bolger** of the National Party, was **forced to resign** due to pressure from within his party.

Dec. 8. Jenny Shipley became New Zealand's **first female prime minister.**

1999, Feb. 23. Shipley's government survived its second confidence vote in six months.

Nov. 27. Nine years of National Party rule ended as the Labour Party won the general elections, securing a majority in a coalition with the Alliance. **Helen Clark, of the Labour Party, was elected prime minister.**

2000, July 25. Prime Minister Helen Clark announced that the Labour caucus had elected **Hon Parekura Horomia** as the next minister of Maori affairs.

July 28. The UN established a new permanent forum on indigenous issues. **Maoris** of New Zealand played an active role in the negotiations.

I. AFRICA, 1941–2000

1. OVERVIEW

(From p. 794)

World War II reinforced the importance of colonies to metropolitan economies. Even more than during the previous world war, **Africa's** reserves of essential minerals—including uranium, magnesium, cobalt, gold, and copper—as well as its agricultural resources, made the colonies crucial to the war effort. **The war raised world commodity prices,** and Africans actively participated in the expanding colonial economies. After the war, metropolitan governments coveted the huge cash reserves controlled by the colonial commodity marketing boards, which were drawn on for postwar reconstruction in Europe.

World War II also spawned the new **geopolitical realities of the cold war.** Both the U.S. and the Soviet Union employed anticolonial rhetoric even as they sought to create informal empires of their own. The Atlantic Charter of 1941 underscored the Allies' commitment to national self-determination. Like Woodrow Wilson's Fourteen Points following World War I, the Atlantic Charter was not intended for colonial Africans. However, the Chinese revolution, the Malaysian peasant rebellion, and the independence of India provided Africans with important examples of **anticolonial and liberation movements.**

After the war, the British and the French, if not yet the Belgians and the Portuguese, began to think of the **eventual decolonization of Africa.** Their time horizon was long. Few officials thought of independence for any but the most "advanced" colonies in less than 50 years. As a result, European governments made some important concessions to Africans in terms of representation in the advisory legislative councils, but planning for decolonization was lackadaisical. Central to the European timetable for decolonization was the recognition that colonial powers had not nurtured a managerial middle class prepared to run a modern nation-state. Until the 1940s and 1950s, only a tiny handful of institutions of higher education existed on the African continent. Up to the end of World War II, most primary education and nearly all secondary education was in the hands of missionaries. Whenever they could afford it, Africans sent their children to universities in Europe and the U.S. Thus, the first tangible step on the route of gradual independence was to **establish universities in Africa and expand primary education.**

Planned decolonization hinged on the assumption that European colonial powers would determine the pace of change in Africa; it took no account of the actions of Africans. Instead, **the Africans determined the pace of decolonization in Africa.** By 1948, **waves of strikes** by dockworkers, railway workers, and miners swept through Africa. Protests by African veterans and soldiers, who had served the mother country faithfully during the war, shocked colonial administrations. Kwame Nkrumah, a student activist and later an organizer for the Pan-African Congress who had spent half of his life in the U.S. and England, returned home as a political organizer for the United Gold Coast Convention, a moderate nationalist party. In 1949, he led his followers to form a mass political party, Convention People's Party, which agitated for immediate self-government (although not yet for independence). **Mass political parties** had also emerged in the postwar period in French West Africa, following the Brazzaville reforms, and in Nigeria, following the Richards Constitution. Mass political parties were slower to emerge in East and Central Africa.

Not all African protest and resistance to colonial rule took the form of strikes and mobilization through political parties. The Mau Mau rebellion in Kenya, which broke out in 1952 and persisted until 1956, reflected the specific outcomes of the economic and political deprivation of Africans within a white settler colony. With economic and political avenues barred to them, Kikuyu took to the forests and launched a **peasant revolution** informed by ethnic nationalism. The British responded ambivalently at first, then with crushing force. More than 50,000 British troops were needed to contain the small bands of African freedom fighters. The scale of British military involvement worried British strategic planners, who began to understand the high costs of protecting the interests of a handful of white settlers.

White settlers were not quiescent during this time of emergent African nationalism. In 1948, **the whites of South Africa staged a counterrevolution** by electing to power the Afrikaner-dominated Nationalist Party, with a mandate to establish **apartheid** as a political and economic strategy (p. 1070). The Nationalist victory in South Africa stood in sharp contrast to the postwar imperial policy of gradual implementation of majority rule. The Nationalist victory, however, strengthened the resolve of white settlers in East and Central Africa, in the Belgian Congo, and in Portuguese Africa. Indeed, white immigration to settler colonies actually increased during the years immediately following the war.

Black South Africans responded to the Nationalist victory by **reviving the African National Congress (ANC).** Already in 1944, a number of young intellectuals, including Nelson Mandela, Oliver Tambo, Walter Sisulu, and Anton Lemebede formed the youth wing of the ANC in an effort to promote more direct action. In 1949, this group had seized control of the ANC and launched it firmly in the direction of civil disobedience, noncooperation, and strikes. The ANC's main tactic was nonviolent direct action, and by 1952 its campaigns had resulted in over 8,000 arrests. By 1955, the leaders were either under arrest and facing a long treason trial, or in exile.

In 1956, Sudan, which had been increasing the numbers of Sudanese in the colonial administration, became independent. In 1957, Nkrumah led Ghana to independence (p. 1053). Precisely because Ghana's independence was based on mass political mobilization, it became a **model for nationalists across the continent.**

The 25 years from 1955 to 1980 witnessed the rapid end of European empires in Africa. Only Namibia remained a "trust territory" of South Africa and would become independent only in 1990. Angola, Guinea-Bissau, and Mozambique became independent in 1975, following 20-year guerrilla wars. Zimbabwe became independent in 1980 in the face of guerrilla advances, the crumbling of white regimes in neighboring colonies, and the economic collapse of Ian Smith's white settler regime, which had unilaterally declared itself independent of Britain in 1965 in an attempt to implement a South African model.

Most African nations became independent in the 1960s. Despite the persistence of the recalcitrant white settler colonies still remaining, this was a **decade of great enthusiasm and promise.** Africans were freed from the shackles of nearly a century of colonialism. They believed that their economies and their cultures would blossom. World commodity prices continued to favor African producers of primary products in the early 1960s. But by the end of the decade, world demand was slowing, and by the 1970s, commodity prices began a gradual descent. The rapid escalation of oil prices drained the little cash reserves remaining in African economies.

Independence also ushered in a **flourishing of arts and culture.** Most dramatic were changes in **African music.** Of all the arts, music was the most "democratic," since it was the cheapest and most easily available. **The revolution in consumer electronics** largely coincided with the independence decades of the 1960s and 1970s and provided African musicians with unique opportunities. Since World War II, West Africa had been the site of important **musical innovations involving syntheses of traditional African instruments and idioms with Western ensemble structures and beats. West African Highlife** originated in the Gold Coast out of a marriage between local African music and American and British big band sounds. Highlife spread rapidly through the **mushrooming cities** of the continent. In the 1950s, **Nigerian juju music** emerged out of a local response to rock 'n' roll. Wide varieties of traditional, history-telling (the art of the West African griot), neotraditional, and modern African music can be heard from the windows or courtyards of houses everywhere.

Besides cassette recordings, **national radio broadcasting** has contributed to the diffusion of both traditional and new forms of African music. Many countries also have **annual cultural festivals,** which promote both neotraditional and innovative music and dance. Nightlife is often lively in urban Africa, with nightclubs providing opportunities for aspiring musicians.

In the nearly complete absence of public transportation in most of Africa, privately owned taxis and vans are the premier form of urban transportation. **Elaborate decorations of these taxis** are an important popular art form. The exterior walls of shops and kiosks became the canvases of popular representational art, also providing inexpensive commercial advertising. Urban and rural Africans are also consumers of **neotraditional African arts.** Craftworkers produce objects using traditional tools and techniques, but such art is often used in new ways. Instead of functioning primarily within religious ceremonies, this neotraditional African sculpture is used more widely as decoration. Larger even than the market for neotraditional sculpture is the demand for cloth and clothing. African tailors use locally produced or imported textiles to meet a nearly **inexhaustible demand for fashion.** Often based on local traditions, these tailors produce couture for the rapidly changing fashion worlds of urban Africa. Weavers, using traditional looms and machine-made yarns, produce cloth for ordinary use and festive occasions. Particularly when incomes are low, cloth provides an inexpensive luxury.

The period after World War II also witnessed the **flowering of African literature.** Most African literature is written in **European languages,** and the literature in these languages has become widely known throughout Africa and abroad. Written in French, Camara Laye's *The Dark Child* (1953) fit within the wider **négritude** traditions celebrating traditional Africa. Some years later, Ousmane Sembene's *The Black Docker* (1956) and his more widely acclaimed *God's Bits of Wood* (1960) challenged the romanticism of négritude by depicting the gritty world of urban work. *God's Bits of Wood* is a historical novel set against the 1947–48 railway strike along the Dakar-Bamako rail line. Sembene also turned to filmmaking as a means of capturing the bitter satires of modern urban life. His early film, *Barom Sarett,* won a prize at the Tours Film Festival in 1961. Filmmaking in former French West Africa remains a vital form of artistic creativity, and Burkinabe (Burkina Faso) filmmakers are among the avant-garde.

A somewhat analogous pattern is discernible among **West African anglophone writers.** Written on the eve of independence, **Chinua Achebe's *Things Fall Apart*** (1957) reflected on colonialism's rupture of traditional Igbo society. Very quickly, however, the glow of independence faded in the face of the very real difficulties of the 1960s and 1970s. Achebe's satirical *A Man of the People* (1967) showed politics to be a means of accumulation of personal wealth and a tool for personal vendettas. The Ghanaian Ayi Kwei Armah's hero in *The Beautyful Ones Are Not Yet Born* (1968) represented the impotent rage of independent Africans thrust into a world of sudden, deep decay.

South African writers, particularly black writers, could not escape the realities of **apartheid.** The poet Dennis Brutus wrote lyrical verse juxtaposed with themes of apartheid's oppressiveness. Peter Abrahams and Alex La Guma reflect the thematic shifts over the late 1940s to the 1960s as apartheid more deeply penetrated daily life. Abrahams's *Mine Boy* (1946) dramatized the harsh world of the South African mines, but closed with an optimistic expectation of nonracial worker solidarity. In the mid-1950s, Abrahams's *A Wreath for Udomo* (1956) extolled revolutionary struggles. By the time of Alex La Guma's *A Walk in the Night* (1962), a deep despair had set in. La Guma's South Africa was an urban world of vagabonds, beggars, prostitutes, and delinquents. Even white South Africans could not escape the negative realities of apartheid. Nadine Gordimer's *July's People* (1981) captured the very real dependency of privileged white society upon impoverished black South Africa.

In this world of Europhone literature, the Kenyan writer Ngugi wa Thiong'o, who had produced major novels in English in the 1970s, made a **dramatic anti-neocolonial gesture** in the 1980s by writing in Kikuyu, his native language. Claiming that writing in Kikuyu reached a wider audience in Kenya than writing in English, Ngugi wrote both a play and a novel in Kikuyu. Literature in Swahili and in Hausa, for example, have deep precolonial roots. Particularly after independence, significant efforts have been made to produce phonetic alphabets for many African languages. A **considerable literature in African languages**—including newspapers, magazines, poetry, and school primers—now exists. Plays and local television shows are often produced in local languages as well as in the national European language. Aspiring novelists, however, will continue to grapple with the choice about the language in which they write and the audience they wish to address. In independent Africa, language has a politics of its own.

Independent Africans emerged into a world where **managed political economies** were favored and most initiated ambitious economic development programs designed to modernize their economies as rapidly as possible. Declining world commodity prices played havoc with these plans. Economic mismanagement and ill-advised international loans led to profound balance-of-payments problems. Even for oil-rich Nigeria, mismanagement, corruption, and overly ambitious and poorly designed economic and social development led to the squandering of national wealth. Through much of the West African Sahel, ecological crises in the late 1960s and early 1970s yielded a massive refugee problem, devastated the livestock economies, and added to the general economic woes of the new states.

Newly independent African states also proved remarkably prone to political instability. Between 1966 and 1970, waves of **military coups** and the emergence of one-party political systems firmly ended the early experiments in political democracy. Political instability in Africa owed much to the legacy of the colonial period. Under colonial rule, Africans had few opportunities for training in democratic political processes; they had limited opportunities to pursue higher education; and few had well-developed commitments to the idea of a "nation."

Other factors contributed to Africa's political and economic troubles. Many African politicians saw state institutions as a means for accumulation of personal wealth, which had been closed to most of them under colonial rule. It is not surprising, then, that the military emerged as the most stable "national" institution during this period. Military regimes are rarely noted for their commitment to democratic processes.

The Nigerian Civil War of 1967–70 (p. 1056) represented the **prominence of the military** in the independence period, the legacy of the ethnic politics of the colonial era, and the remarkable efforts to forge a new federal community in the aftermath of the war. Nigeria, the most populous country of sub-Saharan Africa, came to independence in 1960, administered by an awkward system of federal and regional governments. The three regional governments reflected the most important ethnic groups: the **Hausa** in the north, the **Yoruba** in the west, and the **Igbo** in the southeast. The system was unstable, and federal leadership weak and corrupt. In 1966, a coup instituted a military regime, which appeared to be dominated by Igbo officers. Another coup sought to balance the ethnic composition of the military regime and to divide the three regions into 12 states. These actions infuriated the Igbo of the eastern region, who began a movement for secession. The region's leader, Col. Chukwuemeka Odumegwu-Ojukwu, was motivated to secede by the presence of offshore oil reserves in the eastern region. The secessionists called their new state Biafra. When war broke out in May 1967, it pitted two factions of the best-trained military in Africa against each other.

The war lasted for two and a half years, perhaps longer than militarily justified because of the role of various competing international groups, including international aid charities, supporting one or the other side. By 1970, about 1 million Biafrans had died, and the Biafran secession was over. The reintegration of the Igbo back into the federal fold of Nigeria was the one shining success of this story. Although Nigeria survived this secession intact, its future as a unified country remains doubtful in the context of growing religious intolerance, persistent economic decline, and the military's refusal to yield to popular democratic sentiments.

Civil wars and attendant ecological crises stalked the continent in the decade of the 1980s and continue into the 1990s. Old enmities, fostered by colonial policies, were fueled by mendacious African rulers of independent states. Regional aspirations of neighboring countries and rival superpowers seeking narrowly conceived geopolitical advantages fed civil wars in Ethiopia, Uganda, Sudan, Somalia, Angola, Mozambique, Chad, Liberia, and the Western Sahara. Civil wars yielded both refugees and declining agricultural and livestock production, thus creating a huge need for international humanitarian assistance and contributing to the crisis of state power.

The 1980s and 1990s witnessed the sustained crisis of inadequate state institutions in Africa, most of which were inherited from the colonial era. Africans voraciously sought higher education, but universities in Africa were badly overcrowded and underfunded. Yet investment in human capital remains crucial for Africa's future.

Despite significant advances in public health since independence, **poverty and inequality** have been on the rise. Increased **public health** has contributed to long-term decline in African infant mortality rates. Contrary to widely accepted assumptions, African birthrates have not declined as rapidly as expected, thus contributing to severe food shortages and poverty. As African populations have increased, **inequalities between classes and between sexes have grown.** The gaps in income between urban and rural areas and between high-level government employees and successful entrepreneurs, and the mass of poorly educated, underemployed urban dwellers has increased over the past two decades. Especially in rural areas of Central and southern Africa where male migration is prevalent, women, children, and the elderly have borne the brunt of increased labor and declining standards of living.

Women, who have had fewer educational and employment options than men, have been doubly burdened by having to support larger surviving families and increased labor obligations. In regions where **clitoridectomy** (female circumcision) is practiced, women have significantly increased medical problems.

To further complicate the current situation of poverty and inequality, an **epidemic of AIDS** swept through East and Central Africa. There was intense speculation concerning the origins of the virus, and much more research will be required before any definite conclusion can emerge. AIDS was identified in Africa only in the early 1980s, where it was commonly referred to as "slim" because of the general wasting away of the infected person. Spread largely by heterosexual intercourse, **AIDS has spread unevenly throughout the continent,** even in the most seriously affected regions. HIV-1 was concentrated in Central, eastern, and southern Africa; HIV-2 was limited to West Africa. It was largely an urban disease. In Lusaka, Zambia, one in four male and female adults had been infected by the 1990s. However, in certain rural areas, including the Rakai District of southwestern Uganda, even higher rates of infection have been documented. Unlike most other diseases on the continent, which affect mostly the very young or the very old, AIDS struck sexually active young and middle-aged adults. There is no doubt that AIDS will have a significant impact on the human capital of the continent. In the Rakai District, the epidemic left a large pool of orphaned children to the care of aged grandparents and eventually to the state. Although AIDS has been found in all socioeconomic groups, the AIDS infection rate among the Rwandan elite and middle class has been disproportionately high. Most African nations have mounted **energetic public health campaigns** to combat the spread of the infection. Nonetheless, the impact of AIDS on Africa will be felt for generations to come.

Despite this bleak situation, Africans have engaged in **exciting experiments in political and economic liberalization.** The end of white minority rule in Namibia in 1990 and the transition to majority rule in South Africa held out great promise for equity and opportunity for all Africans. The end of the civil wars in Ethiopia (leading to the creation of the new state of Eritrea) and the promised end of civil wars in Mozambique and in Angola were hopeful signs that Africans might turn to political processes to resolve their grievances and that new investment might flow not to the military, but to economic and social development.

Despite the anemic world economy of the early 1990s, Africans engaged in shedding state-managed policies, and expensive state enterprises embarked on economic liberalization programs. The World Bank and the International Monetary Fund devised programs called "**structural adjustment**," which promised long-term benefits but called for devastating cuts in social spending in the short term. A poor economic performer for the past two decades, Ghana emerged as an example of the economic benefits of such programs. On the other hand, studies of Africa's **informal economies** showed them to be robust, dynamic sectors. Urban areas, which had grown dramatically since independence, have been crucibles for new, informal, smaller-scale enterprises catering to local and regional demand. **These informal economies were often many times larger than the formal sectors.** Despite the problems caused by lack of services, urban areas also have been sites for experimentation in new forms of community, providing opportunities for changing economic, social, and political processes.

The final years of the 20th century saw additional gains for democracy in several regions, but also a proliferation of civil wars in a number of nations. Concerns about poverty and disease continued, particularly in the regions of the AIDS epidemic. United Nations efforts, often in combination with the **Organization for African Unity (OAU),** persisted, with mixed results.

2. REGIONS

The following entries are organized by broad region until around 1960. After 1960, entries are organized country by country for each region.

a. WEST AFRICA

(From p. 795, 797)

1944. Toward the end of World War II, the Free French administration under Charles de Gaulle agreed to implement a series of major reforms in its West African colonies. These reforms, announced at the **1944 conference at Brazzaville,** were largely designed to recognize African support for the Free French during World War II. **The accords granted Africans representation in the French National Assembly and outlined a program of economic, social, and legal reforms.** The French never intended the Brazzaville Accords to lead to colonial self-government; rather, the reforms were designed to strengthen the relationship between France and its West African colonies and to reward Africans for siding with the Free French.

1945. The Richards Constitution for Nigeria led to the development of political parties. Named after the current governor, the new constitution brought northern Nigeria into the central government, extended Nigerian representation in the legislative and executive councils, and established three subregions with their own representative bodies. African nationalists criticized the constitution because it had been imposed without their consultation and provided for only indirect elections. New African political groups began to coalesce in the late 1940s, including the National Council of Nigeria and Cameroon, and the Northern People's Congress.

1946. Election of African representation at the French constituent assembly resulted from the Brazzaville Accords. The most important political reform resulting from the Brazzaville conference was the agreement that the colonies should be represented in the constituent assembly charged with drawing up the constitution of the French Fourth Republic. The first constituent assembly was held in April 1946, but the liberal reforms it proposed for the colonies went down to defeat. The second constituent assembly framed a new French constitution and placed the colonies within the framework of a unitary republic. Africans participated in both constituent assemblies.

The enactment of the **première loi Lamine Gueye,** named after the first Senegalese deputy to the French National Assembly, offered French citizenship to all African subjects within the context of the Fourth Republic. In 1946, forced labor and the hated **indigénat,** a summary code of administrative justice exercised arbitrarily by colonial officials, were abolished.

March. New constitution for the Gold Coast, which became the first British colony to have an African majority in its legislature.

1947. *Présence Africaine,* a major French African intellectual publication, was founded by Alioune Diop.

University College of the Gold Coast was founded.

1948. Ex-servicemen triggered a public disturbance in Accra under the leadership of **Kwame Nkrumah.**

Shortly after his return to the Gold Coast from Britain in 1947, Nkrumah began a campaign to organize the African masses in support of self-government. In 1948, African ex-servicemen loyal to Nkrumah staged a mass demonstration in Accra to protest against poor living conditions. The rioting that followed led to the deaths of 29 people. Following the unrest, an official inquiry recommended a "rapid advance" toward self-government in the Gold Coast. **A boycott of European imports** in the Gold Coast occurred during January and February.

Ibadan University admitted its first students.

Nov. Léopold Sédar Senghor founded Bloc Démocratique Sénégalais.

1949, Nov. 18. Serious labor disturbance at the Enugu Colliery, Nigeria. **Riots** at Aba, Calabar, Onitsha, and Port Harcourt followed.

1950. Enactment of the **deuxième loi Lamine Gueye,** designed to equalize the pay scales and employment codes for African and French civil servants.

Jan.–Feb. Political demonstration in the Ivory Coast. **Institut des hautes études** was established in Dakar, to become the University of Dakar in 1957.

1951. In June 1949, **Nkrumah had split with the United Gold Coast Convention to form the Convention People's Party.** Adopting the slogan

"Self-Government Now," the **Convention People's Party (CPP)** threatened to take "positive action" unless the British took concrete steps to give the Gold Coast autonomy. The colonial authorities jailed Nkrumah and other CPP leaders in 1950. The following year, an election was held as part of the government's reform proposals. After the CPP won an overwhelming victory, Nkrumah was released from prison to become leader of government business.

1950s. Sekou Touré, a former postal clerk with little formal schooling, became head of the Parti Démocratique de Guinée in the early 1950s. His work on behalf of striking workers made him especially popular among urban trade unionists. In regional elections in the mid-1950s, Touré's emphasis on Marxism, Islam, and anticolonialism gained him a national following. In 1958, he was the only leader in French West Africa to push for immediate independence when others chose to continue their association with France. Elected as the first president of independent Guinea in 1958 (p. 1053), Touré embarked on a program of radical socioeconomic change. He early on distanced himself from France and sought ties with Eastern European countries.

1951. Sierra Leone People's Party gained overwhelming victory in the National Council elections in Sierra Leone.

The British-sponsored **Yundum Egg Scheme** in the Gambia collapsed despite the investment of £900,000. As part of the Colonial Development Corp.'s economic development program, the scheme was meant to transform the Gambia into a major exporter of eggs and dressed chickens. Its failure demonstrated the high costs of ill-suited development plans.

1953. Serious ethnic riots in Kano. Northerners attacked Yoruba and Igbo. Alhajji Muhammad Sanusi succeeded as emir of Kano and introduced a program of land reform and other improvements.

1954. A new constitution was established for Nigeria, organizing the country as a federation. British Northern Cameroon and Southern Cameroon separated. General elections were held in the Gambia.

1955-58. Nicholas Grunitzky served as premier of Togo.

1956. Discovery of **Nigeria's offshore oil reserves** at Oloibiri. Production began in 1958. Control over oil revenues exacerbated Nigeria's rocky route to independence.

Queen Elizabeth II visited Nigeria.

1957. Independence of Ghana. The CPP achieved another victory in the 1956 elections, which immediately preceded independence negotiations. In 1957, Nkrumah became the first prime minister of independent Ghana. Ghana thus became the first West African colony to achieve independence in the decolonization era.

The College of Technology opened in Kumasi.

In elections throughout French West Africa, the **Rassemblement Démocratique Africain** won an overwhelming majority in French Sudan, Guinea, and Ivory Coast.

Alhajji Abubakar Tafawa Balewa became first federal prime minister of Nigeria.

Sept. The Fifth French Republic offered a **referendum,** giving its African territories the option of continuing their association with France under self-government or becoming totally independent. France's recognition that its colonies might want independence signaled an entirely new attitude. French president Charles de Gaulle made it clear that if a colony chose to become independent, it would face a complete cutoff of French aid. Those colonies opting for self-government would gain control over their domestic affairs, whereas France would control economic, defense, and foreign policies. Of the 12 territories voting in the referendum on self-government versus independence, **only Guinea opted for immediate independence.** The 11 colonies voting for self-government joined the French Community; their leaders favored independence in principle, but feared the effects of a cutoff of French aid. During 1959-60, these **African leaders successfully pressed for complete independence.** France, preoccupied with a costly war in Algeria (p. 857), relented in the face of African pressure but continued to maintain its influence in the region.

1959-60. In 1959, **Léopold Sédar Senghor of Senegal and Modibo Keita of French Sudan sought to merge** their two countries into what became known as the **Mali Federation,** in an effort to increase their region's political and economic power. In Aug. 1960, France granted independence to the Mali Federation. But Senghor became increasingly wary of Sudanese interference in Senegalese politics, and the fed-

eration collapsed in Dec. 1960. French Sudan then changed its name to Mali and closed its border with Senegal, leaving it landlocked.

1960. France granted independence to all its West African colonies, including Cameroon, Dahomey, Ivory Coast, Mali, Niger, Senegal, Togo, and Upper Volta. All joined the UN as full members. The advent of political independence in French West Africa, however, did not mean that the ex-colonies had achieved real economic independence.

Nigerian independence was achieved more through negotiation than mass mobilization. The Africans to whom power was transferred inherited a deeply divided country. These divisions—including north versus south, Muslim versus Christian, Yoruba versus Igbo, educated versus uneducated—would severely challenge the Nigerian state in the years to come.

1960-93. Sub-Saharan Africa witnessed rapid urbanization. Africans began migrating to the cities in increasing numbers after World War II. During the first 15 years of independence, urbanization proceeded at an even faster pace. The population influx placed great strains on housing, health, and infrastructure in African cities and towns. Unfortunately, the urban expansion was not accompanied by similar economic growth, and unemployment in the cities skyrocketed. Without sufficient job opportunities in the formal sector, many Africans became part of an urban underclass.

1969-74. Six years of insufficient rainfall in the Sahel led to a **drought** that devastated agricultural production in Chad, Mali, Mauritania, Niger, Senegal, and Upper Volta. Food shortages took a heavy toll on livestock and civilian populations and increased an already high rate of urbanization. In many West African nations, the drought aggravated economic problems that had been developing since independence.

1960s-1970s. Expansion of national culture through radio and television. Radio and television spread to the African masses in this era, symbolizing the increased penetration of international cultures into the continent. Those Africans who sought to use the communications media to develop a uniquely African popular culture faced heavy competition from foreign influences.

Pan-African festivals were held to develop cultural awareness and exchange. Dakar hosted a conference on African literature in 1963 and an arts festival in 1966, thus celebrating the culture of black Africa and the African diaspora. Lagos hosted an African arts festival of its own in 1977. UNESCO organized a conference on the influence of colonialism on African cultures, held at Dar es Salaam in 1972. Two years later, the Tanzanian capital hosted the 6th Pan-African Congress.

1970s-the present. Impact of liberalization and structural adjustment on African economies and the influence of the World Bank. By the late 1970s, African countries faced shortages of hard currency because of balance-of-payment deficits. The World Bank agreed to make funding available on the condition that African countries adjusted the structure of their economies. These adjustment programs, begun in the 1980s, often required recipient countries to ease price controls, reduce public expenditure and budget deficits, encourage private enterprise and investment, and liberalize trade and payment policies. Some, both in and outside of Africa, viewed the World Bank's measures as unwelcome intrusions on African economic autonomy.

1994 ff. The gradual and uneven trend of democratization continued in several countries, especially in the west and south. A number of countries, including Uganda and Botswana, also recorded industrial growth.

Jan. Under significant domestic pressure and scrutiny from the EEC, France negotiated a devaluation of the African franc (CFA), which it had artificially supported through bilateral banking agreements with members of the former French West African Federation. The devaluation of the CFA effectively doubled the external debt of former French West African nations and led to significant economic crises throughout the region. France agreed to bilateral negotiations with individual countries for debt relief, including the cancellation and rescheduling of debt.

1996, April 11. Forty-three African countries signed a ban on nuclear arms proliferation in Africa. Other nuclear powers agreed not to do any tests on the African continent.

1998, Feb. 13. Nigerian troops defeated Sierra Leone's military government, previously led by rebel militant Lt. Col. Johnny Paul Koromah, and ousted it from power. This Nigerian intervention helped restore

Pres. Kabbah to power after ten months of exile. Yet the Armed Forces Revolutionary Council (AFRC) and the Fodaj Sankoh–led Revolutionary United Front (RUF), Sierra Leone's two main rebel factions in its civil war, continued fighting the government. Sankoh was captured twice in recent years (Jan. 6, 1999 and May 17, 2000); both times he escaped prosecution from Sierra Leone or the UN Security Council (p. 1057). As civil war raged in Sierra Leone, some 300,000 refugees poured into neighboring Guinea.

March 23. U.S. president Bill Clinton spoke to more than 250,000 people in Ghana's capital city of Accra (p. 1053) as he began his 12-day tour of six African nations: Ghana, Uganda, Rwanda, South Africa, Botswana, and Senegal. Clinton pledged greater aid and support in all the nations he visited during the trip.

June 8. Military tyrant and acting president Gen. Sani Abacha of Nigeria died of a heart attack, leaving the transitional military government to Abdusdem Abubakar. On May 29 of the following year, **Nigeria's first popularly elected president in fifteen years, Olusegun Obasanjo,** took office (p. 1056).

1999. Pres. Charles Taylor of Liberia was internationally exposed by the UN as a supporter of rebels in Sierra Leone's civil war through his illegal diamonds-for-arms trading (p. 1054). Taylor's Liberia was the greatest offender, supplying arms, staging grounds, safe havens, and even training to Sierra Leonese rebels. Other nations implicated as possibly involved were The Gambia, Uganda, Central African Republic, Ghana, Namibia, Republic of the Congo, Mali, and Zambia. This widespread international crime led the UN to impose stiff sanctions against Sierra Leone's diamond trade in Dec. 2000 (p. 1055).

Jan. 13. In a huge international victory for human rights advocates, **Senegal banned female circumcision.**

April 9. The **president of Niger, Gen. Ibrahim Bare Mainassara, was assassinated** by members of his own security squad in a military coup led by the National Reconciliation Council (p. 1055).

May 7. The Vieira regime in Guinea-Bissau was defeated by rebel troops paying no heed to the peace accord signed on Nov. 1 of the previous year (p. 1054).

July 18. Niger ratified a new constitution by legislative vote in an attempt to return its political control to civilian rule. The nation's army had ruled the government for several years.

Dec. 24. Ivory Coast president Bedie was overthrown by the forces of Gen. Robert Guei in the country's first military coup since its independence in 1960 (p. 1054).

2000, March 19. Abdoulaye Wade won a presidential runoff election in Senegal and peacefully took power, ending forty years of Socialist Party rule in that country (p. 1057).

May 7. RUF rebel forces in Sierra Leone's civil war took 500 UN peacekeeping troops hostage; it was not until July 15 that the last of these hostages were rescued (p. 1057). The UN created an international tribunal to begin trying war criminals in Sierra Leone on Aug. 14 (p. 1058).

West Africa, country by country, from 1960:

1. BENIN (DAHOMEY)

1960, Aug. Dahomey gained independence from France. Northerner Hubert Maga became president after his Parti Dahoméen de l'Unité won national elections.

1967. Lt. Col. Alphonse Alley led a successful **coup** and formed the Comité Révolutionnaire Militaire. Alley assumed the presidency.

1972–74. Following a successful **coup**, Maj. Mathieu Kerekou implemented a program of "scientific socialism" in Dahomey. Key sectors of the economy were nationalized.

1975. Dahomey was renamed Benin.

1979. Transition to civilian rule occurred.

1985. Kerekou was reelected to a five-year term. A shift toward favoring the West continued.

1988, March and June. Foes of Kerekou made **two unsuccessful coup attempts.**

1996, March 24. Presidential runoffs in Benin were won by former Marxist military ruler **Mathieu Kerekou.** At his inauguration (April 4), Kerekou pledged national reconciliation and appointed his rival, former president Nicéphore Soglo, as minister of finance.

1999, March 30. In legislative elections Nicephore Soglo's Renaissance of Benin Party gained seats in the National Assembly, securing a majority.

2000, July. The World Bank and the International Monetary Fund (IMF) qualified Benin for $460 million in debt relief under the Heavily Indebted Poor Countries Initiative, legitimating the loan by citing Benin's increased economic growth and stability.

2. BURKINA FASO

1960, Aug. 5. Upper Volta gained independence from France. Maurice Yameogo and his Mouvement Démocratique Voltaique formed the country's first government.

1965. Civil servants and trade unionists staged mass demonstrations to **protest government austerity measures.**

1966, Jan. The military seized power and suspended the constitution, forming a new government under Lt. Col. Sangoule Lamizana.

1970, Dec. After **countrywide elections,** Gerard Ouedraogo became the head of a civilian government.

1974. The military retook power and placed Lamizana at the helm of a new government. A border dispute with Mali led to inconclusive bouts of armed conflict.

1977–78. A new constitution was drafted, and political parties were allowed to operate freely. The Union Démocratique Voltaique won a plurality of seats in the legislative assembly.

1980, Nov. 25. Forces loyal to Col. Saye Zerbo overthrew Lamizana. **The new regime dissolved the National Assembly and banned all political parties.**

1982, Nov. 7. Following a successful **coup,** Maj. Jean-Baptiste Ouedraogo was installed as the leader of a new military regime.

1983, Jan. Former information minister Thomas Sankara was appointed prime minister. Sankara gained strong support from the military and left-wing activists. He sought to **strengthen the role of peasants in the government and the economy.**

1984. Upper Volta was renamed Burkina Faso, meaning "the Land of Free Men," by Sankara.

1987, Oct. 15. Sankara was assassinated in a coup that claimed at least 100 lives. The Burkinabe government fell under the control of the Popular Front.

1998, Sept. 16. The UN announced that a treaty banning the production and use of land mines would go into effect in March 2000. Burkina Faso was the fortieth nation to ratify the treaty, fulfilling an established provision that the UN would begin enforcing the stipulations of the treaty six months after 40 countries had signed it.

2000, July. Burkina Faso qualified for $700 million in debt relief under the Heavily Indebted Poor Countries Initiative of the IMF and the World Bank.

3. CAMEROON

1960, Jan. 1. The portion of **Cameroon under French mandate became independent.**

1961, June 1. The new **Federal Republic of Cameroon was formed,** linking former British-controlled Western Cameroon with the Republic of Cameroon.

1972, May. The United Republic of Cameroon was established, following approval of a new constitution by referendum.

1982, Nov. Pres. Ahmadou Ahidjo resigned after 22 years in power. Prime Minister Paul Biya became the new president.

1984, April. The republican guard staged an **unsuccessful coup,** during which many lives were lost. Rivalries between followers of Ahidjo and Biya, as well as those between northerners and the rest of the country, continued to plague the country.

1986. Lake Nyos disaster. An explosion of volcanic gases in northwest Cameroon killed 1,700 people and thousands of livestock. A massive international relief operation provided food and medical care to the survivors.

1987. Electoral reforms led to a greater choice of candidates and increased voter turnout in municipal elections. The arrest of journalists, however, signaled continuing government authoritarianism.

1988, April. Biya, running unopposed, was reelected president.

2000, June 14. The World Bank agreed to give over $200 million toward a $3.7 billion oil pipeline connecting Cameroon with its inland neighboring nation, Chad. Its principal export, petroleum, accounts for more than 60 percent of Cameroon's export revenue.

4. CENTRAL AFRICAN REPUBLIC

1960, Aug. 13. The Central African Republic gained independence from France.

1962. Pres. David Dacko declared the Central African Republic to be a **one-party state.**

1965, Dec. 31. Army chief of staff Jean-Bedel Bokassa staged a **coup,** toppling the Dacko regime. Bokassa dissolved the National Assembly, nullified the constitution, and placed Dacko under house arrest. Bokassa's dictatorship began.

1972. Bokassa declared himself president for life.

1977. Bokassa was crowned emperor in a lavish ceremony.

1979, Jan. Students staged violent demonstrations to protest compulsory uniforms. In the ensuing government crackdown, large groups of students were arrested, and approximately 100 of them were killed in prison. Some charged Bokassa with participating in student killings.

 Sept. 20. Former leader Dacko seized power while Bokassa was on a trip to Libya. His coup was supported by French troops flown in from Gabon.

1981. Widespread violence followed the March elections. Dacko's opponents accused him of rigging the elections and laid siege to Bangui, the capital city. After Dacko fled, Andre Kolingba formed the Comité Militaire pour le Redressement National (CMRN).

1985, Sept. 21. Kolingba dissolved the CMRN and formed a new government, which included several civilian ministers. The military continued to wield power behind the scenes.

1986, March. A French Jaguar aircraft crashed in Bangui, killing 35. Anti-French feeling surged, but Kolingba continued to allow the French to operate military bases in the country.

 Oct. Bokassa returned to the Central African Republic, where he was put on trial.

1987, June. Bokassa was sentenced to death.

1988, Feb. Kolingba commuted Bokassa's sentence to life imprisonment.

1998, Nov. 22–Dec. 13. Loyalists to Pres. Age-Felix Patasse won a slight majority in legislative elections.

1999, Sept. 19. Amid widespread charges of fraud, Pres. Patasse was reelected to serve another six-year term.

5. CHAD

1960. Chad gained independence from France.

1968. The French helped quell a three-year rebellion in the northern region of Tibesti.

1975, April 13. Pres. François Tombalbaye was killed in a **military coup.** A new regime headed by Gen. Félix Malloum took power. Ethnic, religious, and regional differences continued to divide the country.

1979, April. Conferences in Kano, Nigeria, failed to unite Chad's warring factions.

1980, March. Civil war broke out between followers of Goukouni Oueddei and Hissène Habré. Oueddei gained Libyan support and established control over the capital and the northern two-thirds of Chad.

1983. With help from France, Egypt, and the U.S., Habré gained the upper hand in the military conflict with Oueddei's forces. Continued fighting failed to resolve the military stalemate between the country's French- and Libyan-backed factions.

1987, Sept. A cease-fire ended hostilities between Chad's warring factions. Habré, backed by France, retained power.

1988, Oct. Chad and Libya restored diplomatic relations.

 April 20. U.S. Peace Corps personnel evacuated Chad because of violence between rebels and Chad government forces.

2000, June 14. The World Bank pledged $200 million toward a $3.7 billion oil pipeline connecting Chad oil fields with coastal Cameroon.

6. EQUATORIAL GUINEA

1968, Oct. 12. After 190 years of Spanish rule, **Equatorial Guinea became independent.** The nation consisted of the Bioko Islands (Fernando Po,

Corisco, Great Elobey, Small Elobey, and Annobón) and the mainland territory of Rio Muni. **Francisco Macias became the first president** of a coalition government formed of all political parties.

1969, March. A failed coup attempt resulted in the death of Foreign Minister Atanasio Ndongo.

1970, Feb. After winning multiparty elections, **Pres. Macias Nguema outlawed all political parties.**

1972. Nguema declared himself president for life.

1973. A new constitution **prohibited citizens from leaving the country.**

1979, Aug. Nguema was overthrown by a **military coup, led by Lt. Col. Teodoro Obiang Nguema Mbasogo.**

1981, Dec. Obiang Nguema appointed civilians to his government.

1982, Aug. Obiang Nguema was reappointed president and introduced constitutional changes leading to a return to popular elections.

1983, Aug. Elections were held within a single-party platform.

1989, June. The first presidential elections resulted in a return of Obiang Nguema to power.

1991, April. Opposition parties in exile formed a coalition and forced constitutional changes.

1999, March 6. Legislative elections took place and were deemed fraudulent by various opposition parties. Of the 80 open seats 75 went to the ruling Democratic Party of Equatorial Guinea.

7. GABON

1957. Formerly part of French Equatorial Africa, **Gabon gained internal autonomy.**

1958, Nov. The country gained self-government within the French Community, under the leadership of **Léon M'Ba,** leader of the Bloc Démocratique Gabonaise.

1960, Aug. 7. Gabon became independent.

1961, Feb. M'Ba was elected president.

1964, Feb. Five days before scheduled elections, M'Ba was overthrown by **a military coup** staged by supporters of his rival, **Jean-Hilaire Aubame. The French military immediately intervened** and restored M'Ba to power.

1967, Feb. In failing health, M'Ba was reelected president, with **Albert-Bernard Bongo** as vice president.

 Nov. M'Ba died, and Bongo succeeded as president.

1968, March. Bongo declared one-party rule, led by Parti Démocratique Gabonaise (PDG).

1973, Feb. Bongo was reelected president, announced that he had converted to Islam, and changed his name to Omar Bongo.

1975. The constitution was reorganized and gave significant political autonomy to the provinces.

1980. Under a new constitution, municipal elections took place with considerable electoral competition. Nonetheless, the Bongo regime repressed political dissent.

1982, Nov. Thirty-two members of the illegal opposition were imprisoned.

1990, Jan. Students at Omar Bongo University **demonstrated against inadequate facilities** and were violently suppressed by government forces.

 Feb. Imposition of **economic austerity programs led to waves of strikes.**

 May 22. The Central Committee of the PDG changed its constitution to permit a multiparty political system.

 Sept.–Nov. New elections were marred by fraud, but led to a new government of national unity, under Casimir Oye Mba.

1998, Dec. 6. Pres. Omar Bongo, who had already ruled the country for thirty-one years, **was elected to an additional seven-year term.** The election was tainted by charges of voter fraud and irregularities related to Bongo's Gabonese Democratic Party. The U.S.-based International Foundation for Electoral Systems denounced and discredited the election procedures and results.

8. GAMBIA

1960–65. African nationalists in Gambia expressed **little desire for independence prior to 1960** because they felt their colony was too small and poor to survive on its own. By the mid-1950s, Gambia had its own legislative council, which provided for African representation. When independence was finally negotiated with Britain in 1965, no major difficulties arose on either side.

1965, Feb. 18. Gambia gained independence from Britain. Dawda Jawara, leader of the People's Progressive Party, became prime minister.

1970, April. Gambia became a republic within the British Commonwealth.

1980, Oct. Disaffected groups undertook an **unsuccessful mutiny** in a paramilitary unit. Jawara quelled the revolt by summoning Senegalese aid.

1981, July. A left-wing **coup failed** after Jawara received backing from 3,000 Senegalese troops. Violence left over 1,000 Gambians dead. Jawara declared a state of emergency.

1982, Feb. 1. The Senegambian Federation was established. Gambia retained its sovereignty but became more economically integrated with Senegal.

1985, Feb. Jawara lifted the state of emergency in Gambia.

1987. Jawara's People's Progressive Party won 31 out of 35 seats in elections to the Gambian House of Representatives. Jawara continued to receive support from rural voters and the Mandinka ethnic group.

1994, July 22. Soldiers in Gambia staged a coup, ousting the president, Sir Dawda Jawara, and establishing a military government. The EU and the U.S. suspended most of their aid to Gambia and pressed for civilian rule. A counter-coup led by L. Basian Barrow failed in November.

1995, Nov. A government decree accorded unlimited power of arrest and detention without charge to the minister of the interior. Taiwan and Libya emerged as primary providers of foreign assistance.

2000, Jan. Pres. Jammeh quelled a coup attempt led by some of his own bodyguards. Student protests and nationwide violence followed the insurrection.

9. GHANA

1957, March 6. Ghana gained independence from Britain under the leadership of **Kwame Nkrumah.**

1960, July 1. Ghana became a republic within the British Commonwealth. Nkrumah and his Convention People's Party moved further to the left, embracing the Soviet Union, Cuba, and China.

1964. Nkrumah's growing authoritarianism resulted in the formation of a **one-party state** in Ghana. The country's dependence on cocoa exports created an unstable economy.

1966, Feb. 23. While out of the country, **Nkrumah was overthrown by a right-wing coup.** Lt. Gen. Joseph Ankrah headed the new government under the banner of the National Liberation Council.

1969, Sept. The military transferred power to a civilian government led by Kofi Busia. Busia's government failed to stem economic crises, and it too became increasingly authoritarian.

1972, Jan. The military retook power, this time under Lt. Col. I. Kuta Acheampong. His National Redemption Council embarked on an economic austerity program but failed to turn the country around. Corruption and inflation worsened.

1978, July 5. Gen. Frederick Akuffo replaced Acheampong at the head of Ghana's government. Despite Akuffo's statements to the contrary, the country failed to move toward civilian rule.

1979, June 4. Flight Lt. Jerry Rawlings and his supporters seized power in Ghana. Many of the country's previous leaders were put on trial and executed. The Rawlings regime soon held elections that set the stage for the temporary **return to civilian rule.**

1981, Dec. 31. Rawlings returned to power in a second coup. After flirting with the Eastern bloc, the Rawlings government tilted toward the West. New austerity measures strengthened the Ghanaian economy somewhat.

1987. Rawlings and his Provisional National Defense Council encouraged electoral registration and made plans for local elections, signaling a **move toward civilian rule.**

1998, March 23. In the capital of Accra, U.S. president Bill Clinton gave a speech to more than 250,000 people as he began a 12-day African tour of six nations: Ghana, Uganda, Rwanda, South Africa, Botswana, and Senegal. Pres. Clinton pledged $67 million in aid to purchase two natural gas power plants for Ghana.

2000, July. Farmers in Ghana and the surrounding cocoa-dependent countries began destroying massive amounts of cocoa in an effort to drive up the crop's price in a floundering world market.

10. GUINEA

1958, Sept. 28. Guinea declared independence from France. Ahmed Sekou Touré became Guinea's first president.

Nov. 10. Touré declared Guinea to be a **one-party state.**

1965. Guinea broke off diplomatic relations with France.

1970, Nov. Portuguese troops attempted to invade Guinea because of Touré's support of the liberation movement in neighboring Guinea-Bissau. The Portuguese invasion failed.

1971, July. In a **crackdown against internal dissent,** 91 Guineans were sentenced to death by government courts.

1976. Guinea restored diplomatic relations with France.

1978, Nov. Touré renamed Guinea the People's Revolutionary Republic of Guinea.

1980, March. A new investment code in Guinea offered inducements to foreign investors.

1984, Feb. Peasants staged **protests** against government tax policies. A plot to overthrow Touré failed.

March 26. Touré died in the U.S. while receiving treatment for a heart attack.

April 3. The military seized control of the Guinean government before a successor to Touré could be chosen. Many restrictions on trade unions, banks, and internal movement were eased, and hundreds of political prisoners were released.

1985, July 4. A coup attempt led by Col. Diarra Traore failed. Sixty government opponents, including 9 former ministers and 30 military officers, were eventually sentenced to death and executed.

1988, Jan. Student riots in Conarky forced the Guinean government to reverse recent price hikes springing from the devaluation of the country's currency.

1994, Dec. The government announced measures to **combat organized crime and other serious offenses** that were sweeping the capital and outlying regions. Government also introduced legislation to curb the influence of Islamic fundamentalism.

1995, March. Elections for the national assembly were planned for June. Parties for the opposition denounced the date, claiming that they would not have enough time to organize.

June 11. A total of 848 candidates from 21 parties competed for 114 seats. The government's Parti de l'unité et du progrès won 70 of the seats.

July. Three radical opposition parties joined forces with nine other parties to form a new front for the opposition.

1996, Jan. Elements of the **army** demanding improved pay and allowances **seized control of the airport and shelled the presidential palace,** causing severe damage. In April **Pres. Conte announced a reorganizing of the armed forces.**

Nov. Offices of the opposition political parties were ransacked. Rumors spread of political dissidents forming alliances with rebels from neighboring Sierra Leone.

1997, April. Three Belgian nationals were arrested and charged with plotting to overthrow the president. Belgium vehemently denied the accusation and claimed that its nationals were arrested following a commercial dispute.

1998, Dec. 14. Gen. Lansana Conte was again voted into the presidency; outside monitoring officials questioned the validity of the election.

2000, Aug. Military conflict continued in Sierra Leone, adding refugees to the more than 300,000 already residing in Guinea as a result of the neighboring country's civil war.

11. GUINEA-BISSAU

1974. Assassination of Amilcar Cabral, leader of the Guinea-Bissau liberation struggle.

1975. Portugal recognized the **independence of Guinea-Bissau.**

1980, Nov. 14. Prime minister and army commander João Bernardo Vieira led a successful **coup** against Pres. Luiz Cabral (Amilcar's brother).

1985, Nov. V.P. Paulo Correia attempted to overthrow Vieira, but failed. Correia and his co-conspirators were later executed.

1998, May. Serious fighting broke out in the capital between forces loyal to Pres. Vieira and rebels—apparently affiliated with Casamance separatists—fighting against Senegal. Fighting led to widespread disruption of services in the city, and a majority of the inhabitants of Bissau, the capital, fled.

June 7. A military revolt, led by former army chief of staff Gen. Ansumane Mane, incited civil war in Guinea-Bissau. The reigning Vieira regime was supported by adjacent states Senegal and Guinea. Hundreds of thousands fled the capital, Bissau, as the Senegalese army bombed the city.

Nov. 1. An ineffectual peace accord was signed; rebel activity increased in Guinea-Bissau. The peace accord was intended to end a five-month civil war and was signed by Pres. Vieira and Gen. Mane. Under the treaty, a peacekeeping force of the Economic Community of West African States (ECOWAS) would replace troops from Senegal and Guinea.

1999, May 7. Rebel troops defeated the Vieira regime and took control of the government. Gen. Vieira sought political asylum with the Portuguese; the leader of the National Popular Assembly, Malam Bacai Sanha, was installed as the new president. The nation was largely controlled at this time by the victorious coup leader, Gen. Mane.

2000, Jan. 16. Interim president Sanha was defeated by the leader of Guinea-Bissau's popular independence movement, Kumba Yala, who received nearly 72 percent of the vote. This second round of presidential voting and a Nov. 1999 legislative election restored the government to civilian rule.

12. IVORY COAST

1960, Aug. 7. Ivory Coast gained independence from France. Félix Houphouët-Boigny became the country's first prime minister and remained in power for over 30 years.

1968–69. Student leaders were arrested after staging a series of protests against government policies.

1970. Authorities quelled antigovernment unrest in the city of Gagnoa.

1971. Houphouët-Boigny began **secret communications with the South African government.** Other African leaders criticized the move.

1974–75. Houphouët-Boigny traveled to South Africa and met with government officials.

1980. The government began to **open up the political system** and held the country's first free elections. Over 600 candidates vied for 147 seats in the National Assembly.

1981. Unemployment in Ivory Coast reached a record high of 100,000. Inflation began to rise faster than wages, prompting a series of strikes in 1982–83. Questions about the Ivory Coast's reliance on export-oriented economy were raised.

1986, Jan. Henri Konan Bédié was reelected president of the National Assembly, strengthening his claim to be Houphouët-Boigny's successor.

1993, Nov. Houphouët-Boigny died.

1998, Sept. Thousands protested as Pres. Henri Konan Bedie passed a constitutional revision that would increase substantially his powers as chief executive. Pres. Bedie was further criticized for his political support of "ivoirite," a concept that roughly translates as "pure Ivoirian pride" and that was used to disqualify Bedie's main political rival, Alassane D. Ouattara, from running in elections. Ouattara was allegedly born in Burkina Faso, and his political backing lay mainly in support from northern Muslims.

1999, Sept. Pres. Bedie ordered the arrest of hundreds of members of the Rally of the Republicans (RDR), an opposition party. Political unrest stemmed from their subsequent incarceration.

Dec. 24. Pres. Bedie was overthrown by Gen. Robert Guei in the Ivory Coast's first military coup since gaining independence in 1960. Guei suspended the constitution; his dictatorial rule that followed encouraged a virtual halt in foreign economic aid to Ivory Coast.

2000, July 23. A national referendum favored a new constitution and elections that would reestablish civilian rule in Ivory Coast, but in August the September elections were postponed.

Oct. 6. Ivory Coast's Supreme Court disqualified two main opposition party contenders from running in the presidential election scheduled for Oct. 22. Alassane Ouattara and Emile Bombet were removed from the race by a Court favoring the incumbent leader, Gen. Robert

Guei, who remained in hiding until Nov. 13. In further pursuing office, Ouattara was ruled ineligible to run for a parliamentary position on Nov. 30.

Dec. 4–5. Riots protesting Ouattara's exclusion from elections and opposing newly elected president Laurent Gbagbo erupted throughout Ivory Coast.

Dec. 10. Gbagbo broke his public promise to postpone parliamentary elections for a week so that Ouattara could attempt to qualify himself through the courts. The Dec. 10 election went on as originally scheduled. The RDR boycotted the election; therefore most of the seats went to Gbagbo's Ivorian Popular Front (FPI).

13. LIBERIA

1971. William Tubman, president of Liberia since the 1940s, died and was succeeded by William Tolbert.

1973. The Mano River Union was signed, promoting economic cooperation between Liberia and Sierra Leone.

1979. The climbing price of rice triggered **widespread rioting.** Over 100 people were killed.

1980, March. Opposition leader Gabriel Baccus Matthews called for a **general strike to protest government policies.** He and a number of his supporters were arrested.

1980, April 12. Forces loyal to Master Sgt. Samuel K. Doe **assassinated Pres. Tolbert** and overthrew the Liberian government. Leading members of the Tolbert regime were executed.

1984, July. A new constitution was approved by national referendum. The ban on political activity was lifted.

1985, Oct. Doe was elected president in national elections. Opponents accused the government of **rigging the vote** and refused to take their seats in the National Assembly.

Nov. Former army commander Thomas Quiwonkpa returned from exile and staged an **unsuccessful coup attempt.** He and many of his supporters were killed in clashes with government forces.

1987. Doe appointed 17 Americans to his administration as economic advisers. Critics protested the move as compromising Liberian sovereignty.

1988, March. The government arrested opponents after discovering evidence of a **planned coup.**

April. William Gabriel Kopolleh, head of the banned Liberia Unification Party, was charged with treason, along with 13 others.

July. Government forces killed 12 rebels during efforts to quell **another coup.** While under arrest, two Americans admitted their involvement in the coup attempt.

1989, Dec. 24. Armed rebels belonging to the National Patriotic Front of Liberia crossed into the country from the Ivory Coast, hoping to overthrow the Doe government. The rebel group, led by Charles Taylor, accused the Doe administration of widespread corruption and human rights abuses.

1990, Jan.–May. Taylor's rebel army took control of large portions of Liberia and began to move toward the capital. **Fighting between government and troops escalated.** Thousands of civilians were caught in the crossfire.

July. A rebel group under the control of Prince Johnson advanced into Monrovia, which was already partly controlled by forces loyal to Taylor.

Sept. 10. Pres. Doe was shot by Johnson's forces. **The civil war continued** following Doe's death. A stalemate developed between former Doe loyalists, Johnson's and Taylor's backers, and a **five-nation West African peacekeeping force.**

Nov. 28. The factions in Liberia signed a **cease-fire agreement.** An interim government under Amos Sawyer assumed power temporarily.

1996, April 6. Fighting broke out in Monrovia, the Liberian capital, despite a peace plan brokered in Aug. 1995. U.S. forces began to evacuate. On April 18 Liberia announced a cease-fire. Nigeria played an active role in peacekeeping.

1997, July 19. Thirteen candidates competed in peaceful presidential elections. More than 500 international observers were present.

Aug. 2. Former warlord **Charles G. Taylor** of the National Patriotic Party was sworn in as the new **president of Liberia.**

1999, Feb. 13. Nigerian forces captured almost 50 high-level officials of the rebel military junta of Sierra Leone in Monrovia, Liberia. The rebels had fled there after being ousted from power the previous day. Because of his aid to rebels in war-torn Sierra Leone, Liberian president Charles Taylor received widespread international criticism. Rebel leaders from the Revolutionary United Front (RUF) of Sierra Leone continued to give Taylor a huge cut from its illegal diamond trade in return for money and arms.

July 7. The United Nations agreed to Taylor's proposal for ongoing international monitors along Liberia's border with Sierra Leone, although cooperation was limited. The UN approved various international restrictions on Liberia and its role in the Sierra Leone diamond trade.

2000, Dec. 20. Pres. Taylor, the Liberian government, and Gambia were implicated in a UN Security Council report that recommended sanctions against various diamond-trading nations for supplying millions of dollars through illegal diamond exchanges with Sierra Leone and for supplying the Revolutionary United Front (RUF) of that nation with military training, weapons, and an area to stage attacks. Other countries potentially involved in the diamonds-for-arms trading were Uganda, Central African Republic, Ghana, Namibia, Republic of Congo, Mali, and Zambia.

14. MALI

1960, June 20. Following the dissolution of the Mali Federation, **Mali became an independent nation.** Mobido Keita became the country's first president and declared the formation of a **one-party state.**

1968, Nov. Keita was overthrown in a bloodless **coup.** Lt. Moussa Traore became president, and Capt. Yoro Diakite prime minister.

1969, Aug. An unsuccessful coup attempt ended in the arrest of 20 army officers. Traore's military regime remained in place.

1974. A new constitution was approved in a nationwide referendum. The constitution outlined a five-year transition to civilian rule.

1977, May. Former president **Keita died in detention.** Students began to stage a series of protests against continued military rule. Opposition leaders were detained later in the year.

1980, Dec. A coup attempt by junior officers was thwarted, resulting in the execution of three people.

1985, June. Traore won reelection to a second six-year term as president. He received 98 percent of the vote in a tightly controlled electoral process.

Dec. Malian forces clashed with troops from Burkina Faso in a territorial dispute. A ruling from the International Court of Justice the following year ended hostilities.

1988, June. In an act designed to further consolidate his power, Traore abolished the position of prime minister.

1990. Students and workers protested Traore's policies. Government reprisals led to mass protests and collapse of the government. Free elections were held. Alpha Konare was elected president.

1995, Nov. Clashes between students and security forces in Bamako marked the end of the honeymoon phase of the Konare presidency. New elections were scheduled for Jan. 1997, but these were postponed when opposition parties threatened to boycott them.

1996, Feb. Three thousand Tuareg separatist fighters surrendered their weapons under a planned integration of former rebels into the national army. This demilitarization marked the **end of a major regional rebellion** in the western desert region of West Africa.

1997, April. Elections were held amid considerable confusion and complaints of intimidation. Election results were annulled by the constitutional court.

July. Voting proceeded fairly among 17 parties standing for legislative seats.

1999, Sept. Former president Moussa Traore's death sentence for war crimes was reduced to life imprisonment.

15. MAURITANIA

1960, Nov. Mauritania gained **independence from France.** Moktar Ould Daddah continued as head of state.

1966. The government announced that **Arabic was to become a compulsory subject** in Mauritanian secondary schools. The new policy aggravated hostilities between the country's African and Arab population groups.

1969–74. Sahelian **drought** hit Mauritania, devastating the country's nomadic population and livestock herds.

1975. The Spanish government gave Mauritania territorial rights over a portion of the Western Sahara (p. 991). Troops from the **Polisario Front, a Western Saharan rebel group,** reacted by commencing a four-year campaign of cross-border raids into Mauritanian territory.

1978, July. Daddah was overthrown in a **military coup** led by Lt. Col. Moustapha Ould Salek.

1979. Mauritania signed the **Algiers Agreement,** thus relinquishing control over its territory in Western Sahara.

1981. The Parti Islamique, backed by Morocco, launched an **unsuccessful coup** attempt against the Mauritanian government.

1984. The government of **Mohammed Khouna Haidalla was overthrown** by forces loyal to the army chief of staff, Sid'Ahmed Taya. Taya's policies led to an economic upturn.

1986. The government imposed a **stricter code of Islamic law** on the country, angering black Mauritanian groups and leading to **racial clashes.** Prominent African political activists were arrested after publishing the "Oppressed Black African Manifesto."

1998–2000. Mauritania persisted as one of the poorest countries in the world; further human rights issues were exposed regarding the apparent slave trade that still existed in the impoverished nation.

1998, April 17. In Senate elections the ruling Democratic and Socialist Republican Party (PRDS) obtained 54 of 56 available seats.

16. NIGER

1960, Aug. Niger gained independence from France. Hamani Diori became the first head of state.

1974, April. Diori was overthrown in a **coup** led by army chief of staff Lt. Col. Seyni Kountche.

1976. The government reacted to an **unsuccessful coup** attempt by executing several alleged ringleaders.

1982–83. The Kountche government began to open up Niger's political system. **Civilians were brought into the government.** New elections were held, and a civilian prime minister, Oumarou Mamane, was appointed.

1983, Oct. Following a **failed coup attempt,** Kountche dismissed Prime Minister Mamane.

1983–85. Nigeria embarked on a mass expulsion of Niger nationals, thus placing a great strain on Niger's economy.

1985. American **vice president George Bush** visited Niger, signaling a warming of relations between the U.S. and Niger.

1987, Nov. Death of Kountche, who was succeeded by Col. Ali Seibou, the military chief of staff. Although Seibou agreed to preside over the **drafting of a new constitution,** he continued to support military rule.

1996, Jan. 27. The **first democratically elected president of Niger, Mahamaue Ousmane,** was overthrown and placed under house arrest in a military coup.

1999, April 9. After surviving an attempt on his life in Jan. 1998, Niger's president, Gen. Ibrahim Bare Mainassara, was assassinated by members of his own security squad. This coup was led by the NRC; surviving prime minister Ibrahim Mayaki promised to hold fall elections. Military leader Daouda Malam Wanke assumed temporary control of the government after the assassination.

July 18. A new constitution returning political control to civilians was passed by legislative vote.

Nov. 25. In the first democratic election since 1993, Tandja Mamadou was chosen to become the new president of Niger.

17. NIGERIA

1960, Oct. 1. Nigeria gained independence from Britain. Having learned from its experiences in Ghana, the **British sought to avoid mass political agitation** by negotiating with Nigerian political leaders. However, the Nigerian political leaders inherited a deeply divided and politically unstable country. Abubakar Tafawa Balewa became the country's first prime minister; Dr. Nnamdi Azikiwe was named governor-general.

1966, Jan. 15. Igbo army officers staged an **unsuccessful coup** in which

Prime Minister Balewa was assassinated. Army commander Gen. Johnson Aguiya-Ironsi restored order by putting a military regime in place.

May. Northerners overthrew the military government and replaced it with a new one, killing Aguiya-Ironsi and others in the process. Army chief of staff Lt. Col. Yakubu Gowon was chosen to head the new regime.

1967–70. Nigerian Civil War (also known as the Biafran War). The Nigerian federation was unstable from the outset. Northerners and southerners disagreed over the composition of the federal House of Representatives, with those from the south greatly fearing northern domination. In May 1967, Igbos (from the south) proclaimed the independent state of Biafra, thus provoking civil war. During the next two and a half years of fighting, northern-based federalists battled southern-based secessionists. The war claimed at least 1 million lives, most lost through starvation and disease rather than military action. The war ended in 1970 when the federal government defeated the breakaway state of Biafra.

1967, May 30. Lt. Col. Chukwuemeka Odumegwu-Ojukwu announced the **formation of the state of Biafra,** marking the secession of the country's Igbo-dominated eastern region. During the next three years, Nigeria was plagued by **civil war** as federal troops fought to regain control over Biafra. The war left 100,000 soldiers and more than 1 million civilians dead. In the end, the Biafran secessionists were defeated.

1975, July 29. Gen. Murtala Muhammad ousted Gowon in a **successful coup.** The Muhammad government trimmed the country's bureaucracy and announced plans for an eventual return to civilian rule.

1976, Feb. 13. Head of state Muhammad was assassinated in Lagos. Chief of staff Gen. Olasegan Obasanjo was named to succeed Muhammad.

1979. The Obasanjo government **lifted the ban on independent political activity.** Fifty new political parties were formed.

July–Aug. In nationwide elections held over a period of six weeks, **Shehu Shagari's National Party of Nigeria won** a plurality of votes.

Oct. 1. Shagari was sworn in as head of state. His rule coincided with a **severe economic slump and rise in corruption.**

1984, Jan. 1. Maj. Gen. Muhammad Buhari led a **successful coup** against the Shagari government.

1985, April–May. Buhari expelled almost 800,000 immigrants in Nigeria as part of an economic austerity program. Approximately half of those expelled were Ghanaians.

Aug. 27. Army chief of staff **Maj. Gen. Ibrahim Babangida seized power.** He announced plans for the return of civilian rule.

Nigeria moved uneasily toward civilian rule. Babangida seized power with the goal of eventually restoring civilian rule. Early in his administration he improved human rights conditions and lifted government restrictions on the opposition. In May 1988, the swearing in of a constituent assembly signaled a definite swing toward elective government. But outbreaks of unrest later in the year indefinitely postponed the implementation of full civilian rule.

1988, May. A new constituent assembly was given the task of **drafting a new constitution** for Nigeria. Babangida called for the introduction of a two-party system based on civilian participation.

The government closed universities after student protests against rising fuel prices turned violent. Demonstrations staged by **trade unions** prompted the government to arrest a number of labor leaders.

Nov. Babangida disregarded local feeling and appointed Ibrahim Dasuki as sultan of Sokoto, sparking **violent protests in the north.**

1993. Elections were held, employing the two-party system created by the government; the presidential race offered two handpicked candidates. Moshood Abiola, a Yoruba businessman, apparently won the election, but **Babangida annulled the returns. Massive protests took place in Nigeria, and a general strike was called. Babangida was overthrown by Gen. Sani Abacha.**

1994, June 11. Moshood Abiola declared himself president of Nigeria, defying Sani Abacha, the current ruler. Abiola was arrested for treason on July 6, a major setback for democracy.

1996, Oct. Ken Saro-Wiwa and eight other Ogoni activists were sentenced to death. They were executed on Nov. 10 despite pleas from the British Commonwealth and from South Africa. **Nigeria was suspended from the Commonwealth as a result.**

June. Kudriat Abiola, wife of Moshood Abiola and a prominent critic of the Abacha military government, was killed by unidentified assailants.

1997. Escalating tensions between Ijaw and Itsekiri ethnic groups severely disrupted petroleum production in the region. Economic conditions in Nigeria continued to deteriorate, and shortages of petroleum products caused widespread power outages and transportation delays.

July. Gen. Abacha announced that presidential elections would be held in Aug. 1998. Abacha said that he would stand for election at that time.

1998, June 8. Military tyrant and acting president Gen. Sani Abacha died of a heart attack. The resultant transitional military government was led by army chief Abdusdem Abubakar. Pres. Abubakar freed political prisoners in an act of reconciliation, but foul play was suspected when former opposition leader Moshood Abiola mysteriously died just before his scheduled release.

1999, May 29. The first popularly elected president in over 15 years, Olusegun Obasanjo took power. The former general and military ruler faced increased civil violence between Muslims and Christians, who were fighting over the spread of Islamic Law (*shari'a*) in the densely Muslim northern part of the country. This conflict was compounded by social and economic disorder due to rising fuel prices and billions of dollars having been stolen by past regimes.

2000, Jan.–March. Muslim-Christian clashes caused the death of more than 800 people in Northern Nigeria.

Aug. 26. The first U.S. head of state to visit Nigeria in 22 years, Pres. Bill Clinton spoke in response to increased religious and political violence and to encourage the economic success of Nigeria.

Sept.–Oct. The Ogoni people and international environmentalists continued to protest the drilling of wells along the southern coast of Nigeria. Petroleum from these wells represented a substantial portion of the estimated 22.5 billion barrels of oil available as a natural resource in Nigeria.

18. SÃO TOMÉ AND PRÍNCIPE

1960. The nationalist group Comissão de Liberaça de São Tomé and Príncipe was formed.

1972. The Comissão became the Movimento de Liberaça de São Tomé and Príncipe (MLSTP) under the leadership of **Dr. Manuel Pinto da Costa.**

1973. The islands were given autonomy by Portugal.

1974, Nov. Following the military coup in Portugal, the islands were given the right to be independent, and the MLSTP was recognized as the sole political party.

1975, July 12. Independence was granted, and Dr. da Costa became the first president.

1978, March. Dr. da Costa alleged a coup had been planned and imprisoned his opponents.

1982. Worsening economic conditions contributed to a political and economic reevaluation and led in 1984 to a **declaration of nonaligned status.**

1987, Oct. Constitutional changes were introduced and free elections planned.

1988, May. Police stopped an attempted **coup** by a small band of armed dissidents.

1990. Presidential elections were scheduled, but were postponed. In October, MLSTP voted to oust Pres. da Costa.

1991, Oct. Elections led to the defeat of MLSTP candidates.

Feb. A transitional government was headed by **Daniel dos Santos Daio.**

1995, Aug. 15. Rebel soldiers in São Tomé and Príncipe **arrested Pres. Miguel Trovoada** and **took control of the government.** Trovoada had been the country's first freely elected leader, chosen in 1991.

Aug. 22. The coup ended and the **president resumed power.**

1996, June. In a contested election, Trovoada was returned to office with 52 percent of the votes.

1998, Nov. 8. The Center-Left Liberation Movement of São Tomé and Príncipe (MLSTP) secured a majority of parliamentary seats; party leader Guilherma Posser da Costa became the new prime minister.

19. SENEGAL

1960, June. Senegal gained independence from France. Senegal joined with Mali to form the Mali Federation.

Aug. The Republic of Senegal was established in the wake of the Mali Federation's collapse. Léopold Sédar Senghor became Senegal's first president; socialist Mamdou Dia became prime minister.

1962. Senghor dismissed Dia after uncovering a **coup plot.**

1963. After Senghor and his Union Progressive Sénégalaise won national elections, government opponents accused the authorities of rigging the vote. **Widespread rioting occurred. Senghor banned opposition parties.**

1968. When **students at Dakar University** staged a walkout to protest government policies and the country's trade unions mounted a general strike, authorities promised reforms. Senghor was returned to power after national elections.

1970. Abdou Diouf was appointed prime minister as part of a program of **constitutional reform.** Diouf was given major responsibility for reviving Senegal's **troubled economy.** International donors underwrote aid programs on the condition that Senegal undertake economic austerity measures.

1980. Senghor retired and was succeeded by Diouf, who embarked upon a major campaign to weed out corruption.

1982, Feb. Senegal joined the Confederation of Senegambia. Senegal and Gambia eventually forged agreements on issues relating to defense, foreign policy, transportation, and communications. Agreements relating to financial and monetary cooperation proved harder to establish.

1982–83. Unrest plagued the Province of Casamance; separatists clashed with police on several occasions.

1988, Feb. Forty percent of Senegalese voters refrained from casting ballots in nationwide elections to **protest government policies.** When violence broke out during protests in Dakar, the government declared a **state of emergency.** Opposition leaders were rounded up, charged with subversion, and put on trial in April. Protests waged by students and workers mounted. Diouf reacted by embarking on further reforms.

May. Diouf lifted the state of emergency.

1993. Separatist violence in the Casamance intensified.

1998, June 9. Senegal sent military forces to help the reigning Vieira government of Guinea-Bissau quell an army insurrection (p. 1054).

Sept. Parliament was so thoroughly controlled by Pres. Adbou Diouf's Socialist Party that the legislature passed a law allowing him to become president for life.

1999, Jan. 13. In a great victory for human rights advocates, Senegal banned the practice of female circumcision.

Jan. 24. Diouf's administration created an "upper house," or senate, for the legislative branch of the Senegal government. Despite protests of opposition parties, Diouf's Socialist Party carried all 45 new seats.

Nov. 1. Senegal signed a peace accord with Guinea-Bissau.

2000, Feb. 3. In a Senegal court former Chad ruler Hisseue Habre was charged with torture and barbarity.

March 19. Leader of the Senegalese Democratic Party Abdoulaye Wade won a presidential runoff election with 60 percent of the vote. This peaceful shift of power, rare in Western Africa, ended 40 years of Socialist Party rule in Senegal. Separatists in the southern Casamance region rioted on the first day of balloting, Feb. 27.

20. SIERRA LEONE

1961, April 27. Sierra Leone gained independence from Britain. As leader of the Sierra Leone People's Party, **Dr. Milton Margai** spearheaded Sierra Leone's drive for independence. In 1951, Margai became the leader of government business in the colony's new Executive Council. Though conservative, he enjoyed the support of most of Sierra Leone's Creoles and other ethnic groups. His 1960 request that Sierra Leone be given independence was granted by Britain in 1961.

1967. Siaka Stevens and his All-People's Congress Party won the **national elections.** Military officers failed in their attempt to nullify the election results.

1971. Brig. Gen. John Bangura led an **unsuccessful coup** attempt and was executed. Stevens survived two assassination attempts that year.

1973. General elections sparked widespread unrest. Authorities reacted by jailing and executing opponents.

1977. The House of Representatives declared Sierra Leone to be a **one-party state.**

1982, May. Violence marred the first one-party election. Rumors of Stevens's impending retirement spread.

1985, Nov. Stevens stepped down from the presidency in favor of Maj. Gen. Joseph Saidu Momoh. The Momoh government secured aid from Western donors, but proved **unable to establish domestic tranquility.**

1995, Jan. 25. A **rebel attack** occurred in the town of Kambia. Approximately 30,000 refugees fled to Guinea. Several were left unprotected by the government and were **killed in the attacks.**

1996, Jan. 16. The leader of Sierra Leone's military government, Capt. Valentine E. M. Strasser, was overthrown by army officials and replaced by second-in-command Brig. Gen. Julius Maada Bio. On April 23 the junta and rebels agreed to a cease-fire.

Feb. 26. Thirteen political parties competed in elections for president and national legislature. The elections were monitored by international observers, but violence in some areas led to the annullment of results. A second round of presidential elections was held on March 15, and **Ahmed Tejan Kabbah was elected** with a 59.5 percent majority. In September, Kabbah ordered the retirement of 20 leading military officers. Rumors of coup plots spread throughout the capital. Kabbah sought Nigerian assistance in reorganizing the armed forces.

1997, May 25. Dissident members of the armed forces, led by Maj. Johnny Paul Koroma, seized power and **deposed Pres. Kabbah.** Widespread looting in Freetown followed the coup, and most foreign nationals were evacuated. On June 2 rebels in Sierra Leone seized power in a coup. The Nigerian government demanded that the junta relinquish power and began a naval bombardment of the capital. Instability in Sierra Leone was linked to the outbreak of a regional crisis centered in Liberia. Still in power in mid-July, the Koroma junta formed a new government, comprising members of the military and the rebel group Revolutionary United Front (RUF). Civilians, however, continued to observe a campaign of civil disobedience organized by the Sierra Leone labor congress. Kabbah remained in neighboring Guinea.

1998, Feb. 13. Nigerian troops defeated the ruling military government and ousted Lt. Col. Johnny Paul Koromah from power.

March 10. Pres. Kabbah resumed his rule over Sierra Leone after ten months in exile due to ongoing junta and other rebel violence against the military and civilians. Nigerian military intervention helped Kabbah regain power, but ARFC leader Johnny Paul Koromah continued to pursue his reign of terror, though his power was temporarily compromised.

Oct. 23. Foday Sankoh, founder of the RUF, was sentenced to die for treason by a Sierra Leonean court.

1999, Jan. 6. Though protected by the Nigerian-led troops known as ECOMOG, the government in the capital of Freetown fell briefly to a Liberian coup in which rebels called for the release of imprisoned leader Foday Sankoh and the deposing of Pres. Kabbah. The ECOMOG restored order, but Sankoh was released to participate in negotiations between rebels and the government.

July 7. A cease-fire was called when RUF and ARFC control over the government increased after RUF leader Sankoh was given amnesty and the groups agreed to share loyalty to the government of Sierra Leone. Unfortunately, the RUF failed to disarm, and fighting continued into the year 2000. Koromah's AFRC remained loyal to the government in which it shared power, but RUF conflicts persisted in the north.

2000, May. The RUF took more than 500 UN peacekeepers hostage in an international military situation embarrassing for the UN during the first week of May (p. 1051).

May 17. Sankoh was captured in Freetown and faced the possibility of standing trial for his role in rebel leadership. However, the influence of Liberian president Charles Taylor was thought likely to prevent serious prosecution inasmuch as Taylor and Sankoh were partners in an illegal diamond-trading agreement.

May 29. The last of the UN hostages were released by the RUF.

July 5. The UN Security Council instituted a worldwide ban on trade in diamonds from Sierra Leone.

July 15. In another successful mission, 233 additional UN employees were rescued from behind rebel lines.

Aug. 14. At the request of Pres. Kabbah, the UN Security Council agreed to create an international court of justice to investigate and prosecute accused war criminals in Sierra Leone.

Nov. 10. A cease-fire that was to last for at least 30 days was signed between the Sierra Leone government and the RUF.

21. TOGO

1960, April 27. Togo gained independence from France. Sylvanus Olympio was elected as the country's first president.

1963, Jan. Olympio was assassinated by rebels in the army. Nicholas Grunitsky became head of a coalition government.

1967, Jan. 13. Lt. Col. Étienne Gnassingbe Eyedema took power in a **successful coup and banned all political parties.**

1969, Aug. Eyedema formed the Rassemblement du Peuple Togolais (RPT) to bolster his style of personal rule. The influence of the military on government policy faded as Eyedema appointed civilians to serve under him.

1970, 1977, 1978. Coup plots failed to oust Eyedema from power.

1972, 1979. National referendums endorsed Eyedema's leadership.

1974. Eyedema embarked on a **program of "authenticity"** to encourage the use of African names and languages in Togo, rather than those from Europe.

1985, March. In **nationwide elections,** RPT members vied for seats in the National Assembly. These elections marked the first time in which more than one candidate could compete for an individual seat.

1986, Dec. Eyedema was reelected to another seven-year term as Togo's president.

1987, Oct. Eyedema formed the Human Rights Commission and pardoned 230 detainees.

1994, Jan. 5. One hundred Ghanaian gunmen allegedly made an assassination attempt on Togo president Gnassingbe Eyadema, probably because of the recent closure of border crossings with Ghana and the institution of a dusk-to-dawn curfew in Lome, the capital. A battle followed in which 40 people were killed.

Feb. Elections for the national assembly were held, despite some isolated incidences of violence, under international observation. A total of 381 candidates competed for 81 seats. Observers declared themselves satisfied with the elections.

June. France, which had withdrawn most economic assistance during the political crisis of 1992–93, resumed cooperation with Togo.

Nov. Members of the opposition Comité d'action pour le renouveau (CAR) boycotted the national assembly, demanding new by-elections.

Dec. The government issued general amnesty to all persons charged with political offenses prior to Dec. 15.

1996, Aug. Pres. Eyadema proposed a government of national unity, but members of the opposition parties, including CAR, refused to join.

July. In efforts to promote economic development, the **government established a free trade zone** in the country and some 30 companies began operation; 20 more followed.

1997, May. In a **protest of government efforts to stifle the opposition,** 100,000 people attended a rally organized by CAR.

1998, June 24. Pres. Gnassingbe Eyadema was elected to serve another five-year term. As in previous elections, the vote was widely disputed and rioters claimed that opposition leaders were subjected to military intimidation and harassment.

2000, Aug. The Togolese government, short of funds, had been unable to pay employee wages for several months.

b. NORTHEAST AFRICA (HORN)

(From p. 798)

1941–52. Restoration and rebuilding of central powers of the Ethiopian Empire under **Haile Selassie.** The emperor continued to hold most power, but some bureaucratic reform occurred. Britain remained in control of the Horn outside Ethiopia.

1945. Senior civil servants in Sudan formed a moderate nationalist group, the **Umma Party.**

1946. Formation of the **nationalist, modernist Somali Youth League.**

1948. Umma dominated the national legislature established by British in Sudan; most members of this legislature came from **northern areas.**

1949, Nov. The UN placed **Somalia** in a ten-year trusteeship under Italy.

1950. University College was founded in Addis Ababa. In **British Somaliland,** clan leaders were made into "local authorities."

Dec. The UN placed **Eritrea** in federation with Ethiopia, with limited autonomy, under the Ethiopian Empire.

1953, Jan. A renegotiation of the Anglo-Egyptian relationship concerning Sudan led to an agreement for **Sudanization of administration** within three years, followed by independence.

1955–72. A civil war between southern and northern Sudan was set in motion by the alienation of south from the north and its Islam-oriented capital, by population transfers, and by the destruction of the southern economy.

1956. The Somali Youth League won two-thirds of the seats in the newly elected Somali legislature.

1998, May 6. An Eritrean border war with Ethiopia began over territorial conflicts that originated with Eritrean separation from Ethiopia and independence in 1993.

Aug. 20. The U.S. destroyed a pharmaceutical manufacturing facility in Khartoum, Sudan, that was allegedly producing chemical weapons. This international strike against suspected orchestrator Osama bin Laden, Islamic militant and wealthy businessman, was sparked by the bombing of U.S. embassies in Kenya and Tanzania on Aug. 7, when more than 250 people were killed (p. 1063).

1999, Dec. 12. Sudan president Bashir declared a state of emergency, fighting against Muslim military leader Hassan al-Turabi, head of the powerful National Islamic Front. By Jan. 2000 Bashir had dissolved the entire Sudanese government, replacing it with his own supporters.

Arabs from northern Sudan were found to be enslaving southern Dinkas (p. 1061).

2000, Aug. A Somalian parliament met in the neighboring nation of Djibouti and elected Abdulkassim Salat Hassana as Somalia's new president. Although recognized internationally, this first Somalian government in almost ten years was opposed by various Somali warlords, and it was unclear if the new government would be permitted to govern freely.

Northeast Africa, country by country, from 1960:

1. DJIBOUTI

1967. The Afars ethnic group (Ethiopian in origin) in the north, with French support, **won a referendum to retain ties to France rather than seek independence,** as wished by the Issas group (of Somali origin).

1977, June. Continued Somali immigration resulted in pressure leading to **independence under Pres. Hassan Gouled,** of the Ligue Populaire Africaine pour l'Indépendence (LPAI).

1987. Pres. Gouled was elected to a third term. His rule also continued to be endorsed in legislative elections. Djibouti maintained close links with France.

1999, May 8. Hassan Gouled Aptidon, the head of state who had ruled the Djibouti government since its 1977 independence, stepped aside peacefully when **Ishma'il Omar Gulleh was elected as the new president.**

2. ERITREA

1962. Eritrea lost its autonomous status within Ethiopia.

1965. The Eritrean People's Liberation Front began a guerrilla war against Ethiopian rule.

1974, Nov. Severe famine in Wollo and Eritrea led to a **military coup in Ethiopia.** The military regime sent more troops to Eritrea.

1984–85. Widespread famine in Ethiopia, due to wars of secession in Tigre and Eritrea, was compounded by severe drought, led to as many as **1 million deaths,** and sparked massive international relief efforts, including the July 1985 internationally televised Live Aid concert.

1991, May 24. The EPLF defeated the Ethiopian army and captured Asmara, Eritrea.

1993, May 24. Eritrea declared its independence, with Issaias Aferki of the EPLF as president.

1998, May 6. A brutal border war broke out between Ethiopia and Eritrea as conflicts concerning the 150-mile border area known as Badame carried over from Eritrean independence in 1993. The war lasted through June 2000, when peace was reached and UN peacekeepers entered the area to regulate the border.

1999, Sept. 4. OAU peace talks intent upon ending the border war with Ethiopia broke down as Ethiopian officials refused to go along with the terms. The bloody war continued with an ever-mounting death toll.

2000, May 26. The war with Ethiopia heightened as Ethiopian troops flooded into Western Eritrea.

June 18. United Nations peacekeepers were sent to patrol the Ethiopian-Eritrean border as national leaders signed a cease-fire that created a buffer zone on Eritrean soil. The border established on Dec. 12, 2000, was returned to its May 1998 location. Millions of dollars were spent reinforcing the 600-mile border, and many thousands of lives were lost in the two-year conflict.

3. ETHIOPIA

1962. Eritrea, which was a semiautonomous province within Ethiopia, was more fully integrated into the Ethiopian state.

1972–74. Severe drought in the eastern and southern Horn led to famine and thousands of deaths, mainly in Eritrea and the Wollo sections of Ethiopia.

1974. The Ethiopian revolution ended imperial rule with a revolt of armed forces led by the **Dergue,** after months of general discontent marked by strikes and demonstrations. The revolutionary regime in Ethiopia **nationalized land.**

Sept. 10. Haile Selassie was driven from office and died in prison the following year.

Nov. Maj. Mengistu Haile Mariam defeated rivals in the Dergue, established a social revolutionary regime, executed officials of the old regime, and sent more troops to Eritrea.

1977. The U.S. and the USSR traded places with respect to support of Somalia and Ethiopia in a war over the Ogaden region; the latter was aided by the USSR and Cuba in the war with U.S.-backed Somalia (1977–78).

1984–85. Widespread famine in Ethiopia, due to wars of liberation in Tigre and Eritrea, was compounded by severe drought, led to as many as 1 million deaths, and sparked massive international relief efforts, including the July 1985 internationally televised Live Aid concerts.

1987, Sept. The Ethiopian legislature passed a bill to grant some **autonomy to rebellious provinces,** but this failed to end the wars of secession.

1991, May 21. Lt. Col. Mengistu Haile Mariam **quit the presidency and fled the country** as the Tigrean People's Liberation Front (TPLF) advanced on the capital and other rebel groups made advances against the Ethiopian army.

May 24. The EPLF defeated the Ethiopian army and captured Asmara, Eritrea.

1994, summer. More than 5,000 Ethiopians died because of a terrible **drought in the south** that recalled the famine of a decade past.

1995, Aug. 22. Ethiopia swore in a **newly elected Parliament under Premier Meles Zenawi. Armed opposition to the new government** appeared in several regions, including Afar, Benishangul-Gumuz, and in the Ogaden region, site of sustained fighting between Ethiopia and Somalia in the 1980s.

1996, Oct. The deputy prime minister and minister of defense, Tamisrat Layne, was dismissed for corruption, and concerns about widespread abuses of government swept the country.

1997. The **government's decision to continue state ownership of all land resulted in peasant unrest** in the Amhara and Tigrean regions.

Jan. A monk was shot while trying to assassinate the Ethiopian Orthodox Patriarch, indicating dissension within the church.

1998, May 6. Armed conflict ignited along the Ethiopian border with Eritrea, a province that had declared its independence in 1993. The war continued for two years, escalating throughout 1999 and exploding in May 2000 when Ethiopian troops invaded Eritrea.

1999, Sept. 4. Peace negotiations with Eritrea failed, and the border war continued. In 1999 some 8 million Ethiopians were threatened with starvation due to massive famine from years of drought. Many lives were saved through international food aid and relief.

2000, June 18. The Ethiopian and Eritrean foreign ministers signed a cease-fire, returning the border to its original May 1998 location. Tens of thousands of soldiers on both sides died in the struggle. UN peacekeeping troops arrived to temporarily patrol the Ethiopian-Eritrean border.

Dec. 12. Ethiopia and Eritrea finalized a peace agreement to formally end the border war; the OAU functioned as a mediator in the proceedings.

4. SOMALIA

1960, June 26. Independence of British Somaliland.

July. The former British and Italian colonies were joined as the independent Somali Republic.

1964. The Somali Youth League (SYL), the nationalist movement that pursued independence, won the country's first elections.

1969, Oct. Clan rivalry for political power led to the assassination of Prime Minister Abdirashid Ali Shirmake and the accession of a military council under Maj. Gen. Muhammad Siad Barre.

1976. Siad Barre became president following one-party elections. Siad Barre allied Somalia with the Soviet Union and adopted centralized socialist policies.

1977–78. Superpower rivalries influenced events in the Ogaden region. In a war for control over Ogaden, Ethiopia was aided by the USSR and Cuba, Somalia by the U.S. By the end of 1978, Ethiopia had regained Ogaden with the aid of Soviet and Cuban troops.

1978. Guerrilla movements representing clan groups were excluded from Barre's government; especially the Isaq (which formed the Somali National Movement [SNM] in 1981), Somalia's largest clan, began to oppose the government.

1979–82. The government responded to guerrilla movements with a **state of emergency.**

1986. Siad Barre was severely injured in an automobile accident, raising the issue of succession. **The government was heavily dominated by Siad Barre's immediate family.**

1988, April. Somalia renounced its claims to Ogaden and concluded a **treaty with Ethiopia,** depriving the SNM of bases in Ethiopia and freeing the latter to concentrate on its fight with the EPLF. The SNM thereupon launched an **invasion of northern Somalia.** The government response left 15,000 dead, using South African and Zimbabwean mercenaries against the civilian population. The Isaq were purged and detained in the capital, Mogadishu.

1991, Jan. 26. Pres. Siad Barre was ousted and forced into exile, but war among contending factions continued.

1992, Dec. The U.S. sent troops to Somalia to assist in famine relief.

1993, June 12–16. U.S. and UN forces attacked those of Somali general Mohammed Farah Aidid in an abortive attempt to capture him, in response to an earlier attack on UN soldiers. UN soldiers fired on a crowd, killing 20 civilians.

1994, Jan. Following a series of **attacks on humanitarian agencies** in Somalia, two UN relief groups pulled out; the U.S. said it would maintain standby troops. UN secretary general Boutros Boutros-Ghali recommended that 16,000 UN troops remain in Somalia after the scheduled withdrawal of U.S. forces.

Jan. 16. Two factions in the Somali capital, **Mogadishu, reached a peace accord.**

March 25. U.S. forces officially pulled out of Somalia; the success of their mission was questionable.

Nov. 4. The UN voted to withdraw its troops from Somalia because of their inability to help.

1995, Jan. 28. U.S. troops arrived in Somalia to assist with the UN withdrawal. On March 3 **the UN occupation of Somalia officially ended.**

Dec.–Jan. 1996. Fighting between rival militias was renewed in Mogadishu and in Hoddur, the third largest city of southern Somalia.

1996, Dec. Representatives of 26 Somali factions held protracted talks **in Ethiopia** under the auspices of the Ethiopian government. Talks **culminated in** Jan. 1997 in the **creation of the 41-member National Salvation Council.** The NSC contained representatives from each of the four major and five minor Somali clans.

1997, Jan. Due to years of fighting, increasing banditry, and erratic climatic conditions, the **traditional agricultural foundation of Somalia**

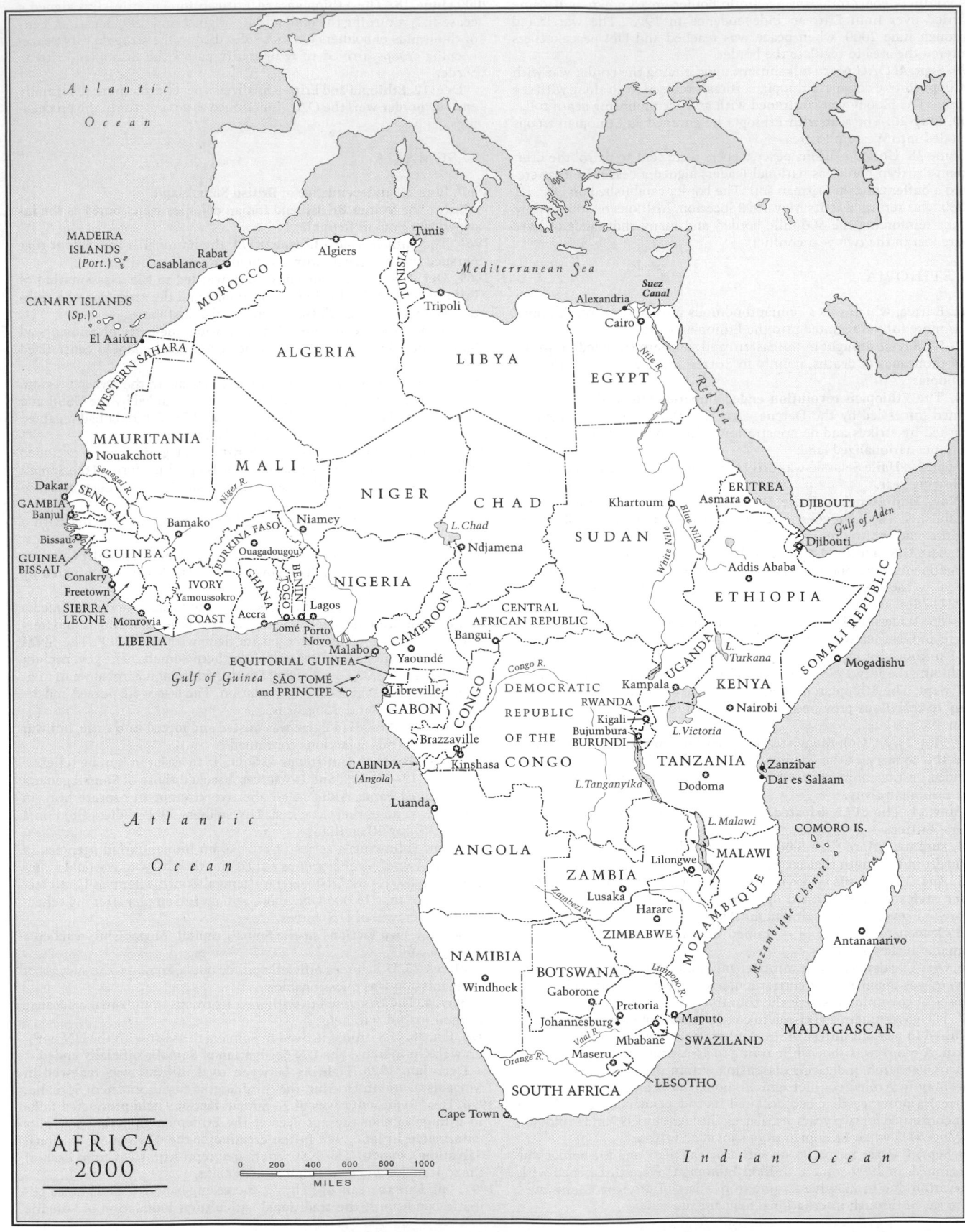

Atlantic Ocean

MADEIRA ISLANDS *(Port.)*

CANARY ISLANDS *(Sp.)*

El Aaiún

WESTERN SAHARA

Rabat
Casablanca
MOROCCO

Algiers
TUNISIA
Tunis

Mediterranean Sea

Tripoli

Alexandria
Suez Canal
Cairo

ALGERIA

LIBYA

EGYPT

Red Sea

MAURITANIA
Nouakchott

MALI

NIGER

CHAD

Khartoum

ERITREA
Asmara
DJIBOUTI
Djibouti
Gulf of Aden

Dakar
Senegal R.
GAMBIA
SENEGAL
Banjul
Bissau
GUINEA BISSAU
Conakry
Freetown
SIERRA LEONE
Monrovia
LIBERIA

Bamako
Niger R.
BURKINA FASO
Ouagadougou
GUINEA
IVORY COAST
Yamoussokro
Accra
GHANA
TOGO
BENIN

Niamey

NIGERIA

Lagos
Lomé
Porto Novo
Malabo
EQUITORIAL GUINEA
Gulf of Guinea
SÃO TOMÉ and PRINCIPE

L. Chad
Ndjamena

SUDAN

White Nile
Blue Nile

Addis Ababa

ETHIOPIA

SOMALI REPUBLIC

CAMEROON
Yaoundé
Libreville
GABON
Brazzaville
CONGO
CABINDA *(Angola)*
Kinshasa

CENTRAL AFRICAN REPUBLIC
Bangui

Congo R.
DEMOCRATIC REPUBLIC OF THE CONGO

UGANDA
Kampala
L. Turkana

RWANDA
Kigali
Bujumbura
BURUNDI
L. Victoria

KENYA
Nairobi

Mogadishu

TANZANIA
Dodoma
Zanzibar
Dar es Salaam
L. Tanganyika

Luanda

Atlantic Ocean

ANGOLA

ZAMBIA
Lusaka
Zambezi R.

L. Malawi
Lilongwe
MALAWI

COMORO IS.

Mozambique Channel

Antananarivo

MADAGASCAR

NAMIBIA
Windhoek

BOTSWANA
Gaborone

Harare
ZIMBABWE

MOZAMBIQUE
Limpopo R.

Pretoria
Johannesburg
Vaal R.
Maputo
Mbabane
SWAZILAND

Maseru
LESOTHO

Orange R.

SOUTH AFRICA

Cape Town

Indian Ocean

AFRICA 2000

0 200 400 600 800 1000
MILES

became profoundly threatened. The U.S. released a study indicating a serious food emergency.

2000, Aug. A Somalian parliament met in the neighboring nation of Djibouti and elected **Abdulkassim Salat Hassana as the new president.** Although recognized internationally, this first Somalian government in almost ten years was opposed by various Somali warloads, and it was unclear if the new leaders would be permitted to govern freely.

5. SUDAN

1956, July. Sudan gained independence with Umma's 'Abd allah Khalil as prime minister, but the ruling coalition was composed of religious parties.

1958. The military, led by Gen. Ibrahim Abbud, took power in a **bloodless coup in Sudan, repeated in 1969,** as power shifted among factions within religious parties.

1963. **Southern Sudanese resistance movements** in the Christian and traditionalist south united as the Land Freedom Army, later called Anyanya (snake venom); a rise in guerrilla attacks coincided with intensification of the government military campaign and repression.

1964. Gen. Abbud was overthrown, leading to the installation of a democratic government.

1969, May. A military coup in Sudan was led by Col. Ja'fer Nimeiry, who became president under a new constitution in 1972. **Nimeiry followed a Nasserist line** and aligned his government with the radical Arab states.

1971. Nimeiry founded the Sudan Socialist Union as the **only legal party** and was elected to a six-year term as president.

1972. The Addis Ababa Agreement gave southern Sudan regional autonomy, recognition of Christianity and the English language, cessation of the war, and the repatriation of 300,000 refugees.

1981. Oil was discovered in southern Sudan. Because the revenues did not benefit the south, rebel activity increased.

1983. The Nimeiry regime broke the Addis Ababa Agreement by announcing a plan to divide the south into three regions. The introduction of Sharia (Islamic law) throughout the nation ensured **renewed civil war.**

1985. The military assumed power under Gen. Abdul Rahman Siwar al-Dahhab, after large-scale protests had erupted, prompted by the ending of food and fuel subsidies required by the International Monetary Fund. The new government had to contend with a **disastrous drought** affecting half of Sudan's people.

1986, April. Sadiq al-Mahdi was elected prime minister. **His government remained unable to defeat the rebels** in the south; nor did it implement the agreement reached at Koka Dam in April 1986 to repeal the Sharia, lift the state of emergency, and call a constitutional conference.

1988. Sadiq al-Mahdi was reelected at the head of a government of national unity. Severe floods struck the south, killing thousands. In November, **the government began talks with the SPLA** (Sudanese People's Liberation Army).

1994, Feb. 4. The Islamic fundamentalist government in Sudan launched an attack against the rebel group Sudanese People's Liberation Army. This group had been fighting against the government in southern Sudan since 1983. On March 17 the Sudanese **government met with the rebels for peace talks,** and on March 27 the government announced a **cease-fire** with rebels.

1996, March 6–17. Sudanese **president Omar Hassan al-Bashir** won reelection and his supporters won election to the legislature, amid allegations regarding the unfairness of the elections.

Aug. Opponents of the government claimed that 11 military officers were executed for an alleged coup plot.

1997, March. Sudanese People's Armed Forces were reported to be rounding up young men in Khartoum for obligatory military service. By the end of May, Pres. al-Bashir announced that all male secondary school leavers were subject to mandatory military service. By April, the Sudanese People's Liberation Army was in control of most of southern Sudan and was within 40 km of Juba, the government's major stronghold in the region.

1998, July 15. The Sudan People's Liberation Army, a separatist group, signed a three-month cease-fire with the government. In 1998 the U.S. sent 10,000 tons of food to fight ongoing famine in Sudan.

Aug. 20. The U.S. destroyed a pharmaceutical manufacturing facility in Khartoum that was allegedly making chemical weapons. A retaliatory strike for U.S. embassy bombings in Kenya and Tanzania, the cruise missile attack came in light of Sudanese ties with Iraq, repeatedly resistant to UN inspections for biological weapons. The U.S. postulated that the factory in Khartoum was financed by wealthy **Islamic militant Osama bin Laden.**

1999. International investigation revealed evidence that slavery was prevalent throughout Sudan. Arab raiders from northern Sudan had enslaved thousands of southern Sudanese, particularly the Dinka people. An international human and civil rights debate ensued following these discoveries. Most of the controversy surrounded the actions of several human rights organizations in rescuing enslaved Sudanese by buying them back from traders. Some argued that this indirectly encouraged the continuance of the slave trade, but with no political resolution in sight, many activists were left with few immediate alternatives.

Dec. 12. Pres. Bashir declared a state of emergency, protesting against Muslim military leader Hassan al-Turabi, head of the powerful National Islamic Front. Bashir dissolved Parliament and by Jan. 2000 had dismissed the entire government, replacing it with his own supporters.

c. EAST AFRICA

(From p. 798)

1944–49. Britain created multiracial legislative councils in Kenya (1944), Tanganyika and Uganda (1945), Northern Rhodesia (1948), and Nyasaland (1949). They had the opposite of their intended effect, spurring African nationalism as **Africans rejected the colonial concept of multiracialism.**

1945–56. Waves of strikes and urban protest in East and Central Africa, including Mombassa, Dar, Zanzibar, Southern Rhodesia, and Copperbelt (1956).

1946. Jomo Kenyatta returned to Kenya after an absence of 15 years.

1947. The Groundnut Scheme, a colonial development project designed to introduce large-scale mechanized agriculture, began at Kingwa, Tanganyika.

The Zanzibar Legislative Council was reformed and included two Africans, two Indians, three Arabs, and one European.

1949–60. Beginning of university education in region. The pace of university construction was still too slow. **Makerere University** was founded in 1949. By 1960, many more Africans from the region were seeking higher education abroad.

1949. The Groundnut Scheme harvest proved to be very disappointing. Similar big development projects were being funded throughout the continent, but results were rarely positive.

The Zanzibar Legislative Council demanded elections as a step toward self-government.

1951. The Matthew Commission reported on constitutional developments in Tanganyika. A legislative council was proposed, to include seven African, seven Asian, and seven European members.

1952–59. The Mau Mau rebellion broke out on Sept. 11, 1952, and a state of emergency in Kenya was declared in 1953. Rebellion was sparked by discontent among the Kikuyu over land lost to Europeans and was heightened by general discontent over government regulation of peasant farming and urban nationalist aspirations. In 1953, **Jomo Kenyatta** and five others were convicted of "managing" the Mau Mau, but the conviction was overturned by the Kenya Supreme Court. Then the East African Court of Appeals upheld the conviction. Political associations were prohibited during the state of emergency. Thousands of Africans died in the rebellion and the British military campaign to crush it.

1953. Julius Nyrere was elected president of the **Tanganyika African Association.**

1954. The Tanganyika African National Union (TANU) was established and became a mass party representing urban and rural grievances.

A state of emergency was declared in Buganda.

1955. The kabaka (traditional ruler) of Buganda returned from abroad.

1956. Bibi Titi binti Mohamed, a woman nationalist leader, entered Tanganyikan politics.

1959. Jomo Kenyatta was released from prison but placed under house arrest.

Zinjanthropus skull discovered by Mary Leakey, at Olduvai, resulting in a major reevaluation of the chronology of human origins.

Nov. Ethnic violence erupted in Rwanda, with Hutu attacks on Tutsi villagers, followed by the assassination of Hutu leaders by the Tutsis.

1961. Kenya African National Union (KANU) leader Jomo Kenyatta was released from detention.

1961–64. Independence of Tanganyika (1961); Uganda (1962); Kenya (1963); Malawi and Zambia (1964).

1990s. Widespread HIV virus in East and Southeast Africa. Over a quarter of the population was infected in several countries by the 1990s, including many pregnant women.

1998, June 21. A temporary cease-fire was called in the fifth year of Burundi's civil war, which again flared up as the death toll rose to over 200,000 by late in the year 2000 (p. 1062). On Aug. 28 of that year, a peace accord, witnessed by South African president Nelson Mandela and U.S. president Bill Clinton, was signed by most of the major combatants, but Tutsi-Hutu conflicts resumed in late September.

Aug. 2. Rwanda and Uganda aided rebels in the civil war of the Democratic Republic of the Congo (formerly Zaire). Congo was aided by Angola, Namibia, and Zimbabwe in what some experts deemed as Africa's first world war (p. 1067).

Aug. 7. Bombings of U.S. embassies in Nairobi, Kenya and in Dar es Salaam, Tanzania (pp. 1063, 1064) killed 243 and 10, respectively, in what was thought to be an attack by the forces of Islamic terrorist and wealthy businessman Osama bin Laden.

Sept. 4. Former prime minister of Rwanda Jean Kambanda received a life sentence from a UN tribunal for his role between 1994 and 1999 in the Rwandan genocide that saw the death of over half a million people (p. 1063).

Nov. 6. Comoros president Muhammad Taki Abdoulkarim died in office and was replaced by interim president Tradjidine Ben Said Massoundi (p. 1063).

1999, April 30. A military coup led by Col. Azzaly Assoumani on Grande Comore Island resulted from ongoing attempts of the Anjouan islanders to secede from Comoros (p. 1063). The anti-Anjouan demonstrators overthrew Pres. Massoundi, and Assoumani assumed full executive, legislative, and military power. OAU sanctions and calls for return to civilian rule followed in Feb. 2000.

Aug. 31. Rwanda and Uganda signed a cease-fire for the civil war in Congo (p. 1064), but conflicts between formerly allied rebel groups led Rwanda and Uganda to war fought mostly on Congolese soil (p. 1063). The conflict persisted until the following year, when on June 19 at the request of the UN the two nations withdrew from the Congo capital of Kisangani and agreed to halt fighting. Rwandan forces had already gained the upper hand and were said to have exited the war with a victory (p. 1064).

East Africa, country by country, from 1960:

1. BURUNDI

1961. The Union pour le Progrés National (UPRONA), founded in 1958 by Ganwa Rwagasore, son of Mwami Mwambutsa IV, **won the elections held prior to independence.** Rwagasore campaigned for unity between the Hutu peasantry and the elite Tutsi minority until his assassination in 1962.

1962. Burundi gained independence under conditions of ethnic polarization between Tutsi and Hutu factions of the ruling UPRONA Party. Rwagasore was assassinated, but the monarchy continued to maintain a balance between Hutu and Tutsi until the abolition of the monarchy in 1966.

1963, June. The intervention of the Burundi king, Mwami Mwambutsa IV, in the political situation led to the resignation of Prime Minister Muhirwa and to increasing royal domination of politics.

1965. An attempted coup by Hutu officers in Burundi led to a purge and the execution of Hutu leaders and the **massacre of thousands of Hutu peasants by the Tutsi military and Tutsi mobs.** After this date, the Hutu played only a nominal role in the central government.

1966. Mwami Mwambutsa was deposed and **a republic was declared,**

ending the balance between ethnic groups and between regions; the new ruling bloc was dominated by southern Tutsi.

1972. Hutu were blamed for a coup attempt in which Mwami Ntare V was killed. Perhaps **5 percent of the Burundi population** (50,000–100,000) died in **mass ethnic violence** against the Hutu by the Tutsi, hardening the Tutsi ruling class's determination to exclude the Hutu. The Tutsi were left in undisputed control of the army and government.

1974. UPRONA became the sole legal party.

1987, Sept. Maj. Pierre Buyoya assumed power with a military council.

1988. Hutu rioting killed more than 1,000 Tutsi, leading to army reprisals in which at least 100,000 Hutu were killed. **A massive flight of refugees** to Rwanda followed.

1993, Oct. The president was ousted and killed three months after the newly elected government had taken office in Burundi, leading to a **severe outbreak of ethnic violence** and a flood of refugees to neighboring countries.

1994, Jan. 13. The Burundi **Parliament elected Cyprien Ntaryamir as president,** in order to replace Melchiar Ndadaya, who was assassinated in Oct. 1993.

Sept. 30. The assembly **elected Sylvestre Ntibantunganya president,** replacing Ntaryamir, who had died in an airplane crash.

1996, March 26. The government announced a recent **escalation in fighting between the Hutus and the Tutsis,** causing many to flee from Bujumbura, the capital.

July 25. The Burundi **army,** dominated by Tutsis, announced that it had **seized power in a coup** amid continuing ethnic strife. **Former president Maj. Pierre Buyoya was declared the new president.**

July 31. At a meeting of regional East African powers in Arusha, the assembled nations declared their intention to **impose severe economic sanctions against the new regime.**

Aug. Military events in eastern Zaire resulted in a shift in the balance of power in the region. Burundi managed to export and import goods through Goma, the major city of that region.

Sept. 12. Pres. Boyoya announced that political parties could resume their activities if they were prepared to make a "positive contribution" to the life of the nation.

Dec. The government began to enforce a policy of **"regroupment,"** leading to the **massive transfer of populations from one region to another.** The UN estimated that **more than 10 percent of the entire population consisted of internally displaced persons.** Another 800,000 Burundians lived as refugees in neighboring countries.

1998, June 21. A temporary truce was called for Burundi's five-year-long civil war as peace talks commenced between Burundi president Pierre Buyoya and Hutu rebel leader Leonard Nyangoma. The civil war continued to use up Burundi lives and resources, and by the end of 2000, the war between Tutsis and Hutus had brought death to over 200,000 Burundians.

1999, Dec. Mediated by former South African president Nelson Mandela, more peace negotiations took place with most of Burundi's warring factions in attendance.

2000, Aug. 28. Most of the major militants in the Burundi civil war signed a peace treaty in Arusha, Tanzania. The agreement was witnessed by Mandela and U.S. president Bill Clinton.

Sept. 20. At another peace summit in Nairobi, Kenya, three Tutsi representatives signed further peace accords; two of the major Hutu representatives refused, threatening to again intensify fighting in Burundi.

2. COMOROS

1975, July. Comoros, formerly a French dominion, became **independent under Pres. Ahmed Abdallah.** The island of Mayotte remained a French dependency.

Aug. French mercenaries ousted Abdallah and installed Ali Soilih, whose socialist tendencies led to a withdrawal of French aid. The government then pursued a Maoist cultural revolution.

1978. French mercenaries restored Abdallah to power. Abdallah's reliance on white mercenaries led to his ouster from the Organization of African Unity (OAU). He pursued a program of development financed by Gulf state allies.

1985–90. Comoros drew closer to South Africa, and Comoros mercenaries were accused of providing arms to RENAMO (Movimento Nacional da Resistencia de Mozambique) in Mozambique.

1998, Nov. 6. Pres. Muhammad Taki Abdoulkarim died and was replaced by Tradjidine Ben Said Massoundi.

1999, April 30. A military coup led by Col. Azzaly Assoumani on the island of Grande Comore stemmed from opposition to continuing attempts of the Anjouan islanders to secede from Comoros. Anjouan originally declared its independence on Aug. 3, 1997. The anti-Anjouan demonstrators overthrew interim president Massoundi as Assoumani assumed full executive, legislative, and military power. The coup was condemned by the OAU, which responded with harsh economic sanctions.

2000, Jan. 23. In a disputed referendum, Anjouans (the island is also called Nzwani) endorsed secession.

Feb. 1. The OAU enforced economic sanctions and ceased communications with Anjouan in an effort to end the rebellion. The OAU insisted that Assoumani return Comoros to civilian rule.

3. KENYA

1960. A constitution leading to independence was put in place, and the Kenyan African National Union (KANU), led by Oginga Odinga, Tom Mboya, and Daniel arap Moi, became the leading party. Moi, however, left KANU to form the Kenyan African Democratic Union (KADU), a party to represent smaller Kenyan ethnic groups distinct from the large Luo and Kikuyu blocs that supported KANU.

1961, Aug. Jomo Kenyatta was released from detention and assumed the leadership of KANU.

1963, Dec. 12. Kenya became independent following May elections won by KANU.

1964. Kenyatta brought Moi back into the KANU fold, and KADU was dissolved.

1966. Kenyan vice president Oginga Odinga and 30 other KANU members of Parliament left KANU to form a leftist opposition party, the Kenyan People's Union (KPU). Moi then became vice president.

1969, July 5. Kenyan labor leader and politician **Tom Mboya was assassinated;** this fueled **ethnic conflict** as Mboya, a Luo, had been killed by a Kikuyu. The resulting unrest led to the banning of opposition KPU and the detention of Odinga.

1970–80. Kenya's government became **increasingly authoritarian and repressive** while its foreign policy was pro-Western.

1975, March. Member of Parliament and former Mau Mau detainee J. M. Kariuki, who had challenged corruption and wealth accumulation by the powerful elite, was assassinated, signaling a more class-oriented politics.

1978, Aug. 23. Kenyatta died. Moi became president and brought more non-Kikuyus into government, but otherwise continued the previous regime's policies.

1982, May. Kenya became a **one-party state** following the second expulsion of Odinga from KANU.

Aug. 1. An attempted coup by air force junior officers failed.

1986–87. Moi's government carried out a **wave of detentions against opposition group MwaKenya,** which claimed to uphold the ideals of the Mau Mau fighters.

1992, Dec. Multiparty elections in Kenya resulted in the reelection of Pres. Daniel arap Moi and the KANU Party, but the opposition charged electoral fraud.

1998, Jan. 1. In another disputed election, it was confirmed that Pres. Moi won reelection in a close race between several candidates. His party, KANU, secured 107 of the 210 seats in the national legislature.

Aug. 7. In an attack blamed on Islamic terrorists, a truck bomb devastated the U.S. embassy in Nairobi, killing some 243 people and injuring thousands more. U.S. officials believed wealthy Saudi businessman and terrorist leader Osama bin Laden responsible for the explosion; that same day in Tanzania ten people were killed when another U.S. embassy was bombed.

2000, July. After a three year suspension, the World Bank recommended loaning funds to Kenya's government.

4. RWANDA

1959, Nov. Ethnic violence erupted in Rwanda with Hutu attacks on Tutsi villagers, followed by the assassination of Hutu leaders by Tutsis.

1961, Jan. 28. The Hutu party in Rwanda (Parmehutu) declared **independence and abolition of the monarchy,** leading to Belgian recognition of independence under Hutu domination on July 1, 1962.

1963. Ethnic violence flared up again in retaliation against Tutsi raids from neighboring Burundi.

1973. Northern officers staged a **coup against Pres. Grégoire Kayibanda** and brought to power a military government under Maj. Gen. Juvenal Habyarimana.

1975. A new party, the MRND (Mouvement Révolutionaire Nationale pour le Développement), dedicated to eliminating ethnic conflict, replaced Parmehutu.

1981. Despite the MRND's stated policies, only two Tutsi candidates stood in the legislative elections, and Tutsi refugees (1 million) were not readmitted to the country. However, the north-south split was from this time more pronounced than the ethnic divide.

1992, Aug. 18. A peace accord ending the 22-month civil war was signed by the rebel Rwandan Patriotic Front (which had invaded from Uganda to protect Tutsis against persecution) and the government of Rwanda, calling for a multiparty interim government.

1994, April 6. The **presidents of Burundi and Rwanda were killed in a plane that crashed while landing in Kigali,** Rwanda. Rwandans claimed this was an assassination of Rwandan president Juvenal Habyarimana. **Violence between the Hutu and Tutsi people broke out over the deaths.** Rioting delayed the installation of a transitional government. Much ethnic violence continued, and **thousands were massacred.** Tens of thousands fled Rwanda for Tanzania and other places.

June 23. France sent troops to protect civilians in Rwanda.

July 4. Rwandan rebels captured major sections of Kigali, the capital.

July 18–19. The rebels proclaimed victory, precipitating the **flight of 2 million refugees to Zaire.**

July 21–Aug. 3. Thousands of Rwandan refugees died of cholera. The U.S. started a relief operation with the UN.

Aug. 21. French troops fully withdrew from Rwanda; **refugees were still afraid to return from Zaire.**

1995, April 22. More than 2,000 refugees, most of them Hutus, were killed when **government soldiers fired on refugee camps** in Zaire.

Nov. 9. Five Central African nations agreed to send the approximately 1.8 million refugees back to Rwanda.

Aug. The **security** situation **in the refugee camps** along the Zairean border **continued to deteriorate.** The Zairean government forcibly repatriated 15,000 refugees to Rwanda. Hutu militia launched an attack on the border village of Kanama, killing 100 civilians.

1996. During the course of the year, more than 1.3 million refugees were repatriated to Rwanda.

1997. The **UN-sponsored war crimes tribunals,** concerning the **alleged Hutu genocide of Tutsis in 1994,** began its operations from a base in neighboring Arusha, Tanzania.

1998, April 24. Twenty-two people convicted of genocide committed during the mid-1990s were publicly executed by firing squads in various Rwanda localities, though international human rights activists had discouraged the Rwanda government from doing so.

Aug. 2. Rwanda joined forces with Uganda to assist rebel forces in an attempted overthrow of Democratic Republic of the Congo (formerly Zaire) president Laurent Kabila. Although both nations had supported his rise to power in 1997, they opposed Kabila within a year of his taking office.

Sept. 4. Former prime minister Jean Kambanda was sentenced by a UN tribunal to life imprisonment for genocide. Kambanda became the first person in history to plead guilty and be officially convicted of genocide as defined by the 1948 Genocide Convention (following World War II). Refugee problems and ethnic massacres continued in Rwanda and neighboring nations through 1999, despite a cease-fire in August of that year in the Congo.

1999, Aug. 31. Rwanda signed the Congo peace agreement, but the cease-fire was generally disobeyed by the anti-Congo factions involved, including Rwanda and Uganda. A split in Congolese rebels led to war between Rwanda and Uganda, formerly allies; most of the fighting occurred on Congolese soil.

Dec. An independent UN-commissioned report questioned Kofi Annan and other UN officials for not effectively responding to the Rwandan genocide with countermeasures between 1994 and 1998.

2000, April 22. Following the resignation of Pres. Bizimungu, Maj. Gen.

Paul Kagame, rebel leader of the Rwandan Patriotic Front (RPF), became the first Tutsi president in Rwanda's history.

June 19. Rwanda and Uganda withdrew from the Congolese capital city of Kisangani as demanded by the UN. At least 150 dead and 1,100 injured were left in their wake. Most of the fighting occurred between the two nations as a result of rebel divisions after the Congolese civil war, yet many civilians in Congo died as the fighting took place in their country. Rwanda was the definitive victor in the conflict.

5. TANZANIA

1961, Dec. 9. Tanganyika became **independent, with TANU (Tanganyika African National Union) as the ruling party and Julius Nyerere as prime minister.**

1962, Dec. Tanganyika became a republic, and Nyerere was elected president.

1963, Dec. 10. Zanzibar gained independence.

1964, April. Following a revolution on Zanzibar, **Tanganyika and Zanzibar united as the United Republic of Tanzania,** with Nyerere as president and Abeid Karume of Zanzibar as vice president. **Zanzibar retained substantial autonomy.**

1965. Tanzania implemented **one-party rule** under TANU.

1967, Feb. 5. Pres. Julius Nyerere of Tanzania issued the **Arusha Declaration, inaugurating the Ujaama Movement** for independent socialist development, based on a concept of an African-derived variant of socialism, rooted in communalism. *Ujaama* is a Swahili word meaning "familyhood" and has since taken the general meaning of African socialism.

1975, June. Pres. Nyerere announced that **65 percent of the population had been moved into ujaama villages.** However, collective control of distribution, combined with a severe drought in 1974–75 and a steep rise in oil prices, produced considerable economic problems.

1979, April 11. A force of **Tanzanian and Ugandan soldiers deposed Gen. Idi Amin of Uganda,** ending an eight-year reign of terror that resulted in perhaps 300,000 deaths.

1980. Tanzania joined the **Southern African Development Coordination Conference (SADCC),** designed to reduce dependence on South Africa.

1985, Oct. Nyerere retired as president, and Ali Hassan Mwinyi was elected. He quickly concluded an agreement with the International Monetary Fund, though Nyerere, as party chairman, opposed its austerity and liberalization measures.

1987, Oct. Nyerere was reelected, with Mwinyi's support, as chair of Chama Cha Mapinduzi (CCM—the Revolutionary Party of Tanzania—the successor to TANU after unity with the Zanzibar Party).

1995, Oct. 29. Tanzania held its first multiparty elections, choosing as **president Benjamin W. Mkapa** of Chama Chu Mapinduzi, or the Revolutionary Party, which had already been in power.

1998, Aug. 7. Terrorists, thought to be connected to Islamic militant and wealthy businessman Osama bin Laden, bombed the U.S. embassy in Dar es Salaam. Paired with an attack on the U.S. embassy in Nairobi, Kenya, the bombing in Tanzania killed ten and injured dozens more.

2000, Aug. 28. Often the host of peace talks for Burundi and other East African nations, Tanzania mediated a peace agreement between Burundian opposing factions in hopes of ending the Burundi civil war.

Oct. 29. Incumbent president Benjamin William Mkapa of the ruling Chama Cha Mapinduzi (CCM) Party won reelection against three other major opponents. On the same day, allegedly tainted elections for the semi-autonomous island of Zanzibar resulted in Amani Abeid Karume securing a position in the presidency.

6. UGANDA

1962, April. Preindependence **elections were won by the Uganda People's Congress,** led by the socialist-nationalist **Milton Obote,** in alliance with Buganda royalists.

Oct 9. Uganda became independent, with Obote as prime minister and Bugandan Kabaka Mutesa as head of state.

1963, Oct 9. Uganda became a republic with Mutesa II, the kabaka (king), as nonexecutive president.

1966, April. A new constitution made Obote executive president and removed the kabaka as head of state. **Obote suppressed a Bugandan rebellion** against this constitution and abolished the monarchy in Buganda.

1966–71. Obote instituted **increasingly authoritarian rule.** The kabaka fled to London. The army became more powerful, and **Gen. Idi Amin** was promoted to army commander.

1971. Ugandan army commander **Gen. Idi Amin seized power** from Obote, leading to a kleptocratic, anarchic military regime.

1972. Amin ordered all noncitizen Asians to leave and took actions that resulted in the departure of most of the remaining Asian community in Uganda. He seized their property to enrich himself and his supporters. Amin also **nationalized property held by British companies and expelled Israeli advisers,** turning to the PLO, Libya, East Germany, and the Soviet Union for military assistance.

1976–77. Student and church groups protested against the Amin regime and were brutally repressed. The university was destroyed, and Anglican archbishop Janine Luwum was assassinated.

1979, April 11. After several attacks by Uganda on Tanzania, **Gen. Idi Amin was deposed** by a force of Tanzanian and Ugandan soldiers, ending his eight-year reign, which resulted in perhaps 300,000 deaths. The Tanzanians installed Yusufu Lule, but he was deposed by June and replaced by conservative former attorney general Godfrey Binaisa.

1980. A period of anarchy ensued, but general elections held in December led to the **victory of Milton Obote's Uganda People's Party.** Obote was opposed by **Yoweri Museveni,** who led the more radical Uganda Patriotic Movement. Museveni denounced the elections as rigged.

1981. Museveni launched a guerrilla war against the Obote government.

1985, July 27. Milton Obote was overthrown in a Ugandan **military coup** brought about by the National Resistance Movement's (NRM) guerrilla campaign, led by Museveni.

1986, Jan. Yoweri Museveni became president of Uganda after the NRM won its guerrilla struggle. The NRM was composed mainly of Bantu-speaking southwesterners; it ended the domination of government and army by the northern Nilotic-speakers. The NRM, however, promised an end to ethnic conflict and government abuse but faced several rebel movements in its first two years in power.

1988. An amnesty program failed to end ongoing **armed rebellions** in the country. However, Museveni's government achieved a degree of stability and order, while reducing corruption.

1998, March 24. Pres. Bill Clinton visited Uganda, praising the nation's growing economy and making a controversial apology for U.S. policies of the past concerning slavery and for neglect during the cold war.

Aug. 2. Uganda joined forces with Rwanda in assisting Congolese rebels in an attempted overthrow of Congo (formerly Zaire) president Laurent Kabila, the successor of Mobutu Sese Seko. Both nations had supported Kabila's rise to power but came to oppose him less than a year after he took office.

1999, Aug. 31. Uganda and Rwanda signed the Congo peace agreement, as did Congo president Laurent Kabila, his international supporters, and some of the rebel groups who had opposed the Kabila government. However, disputes between the once-united rebels in Congo led to war between Uganda and Rwanda, most of which was fought in the Congo capital of Kisangani.

2000, March 17. Concluding a series of cult uprisings that claimed the lives of at least 924 Ugandans, some 330 members of the Movement for the Restoration of the Ten Commandments of God died in a church fire in Kanungu.

June 19. Having lost the war with Rwanda that had broken out in the Congolese city of Kisangani, Uganda withdrew from the area, leaving more than 150 dead and 1,100 injured.

June 29. Pres. Museveni won a victory for his "no party" system (a form of one-party rule) inasmuch as it was supported by voters in a national referendum.

d. WEST CENTRAL AFRICA

(From p. 798)

1945–57. Rapid economic growth in Congo was especially stimulated by the mining of copper and other minerals.

1948. Colonato, a form of state encouragement for "progressive" African farmers, was introduced in Angola.

1949. The University of Louvanium was established by decree. The first students were admitted to only a preuniversity course in 1954.

1949–50. Beginning of the Movement of Young Intellectuals in Angola, founded by Viriato da Cruz. This group proclaimed the importance of Angolan culture.

1949–57. Belgium began to plan for gradual **decolonization** of Congo through ten-year plans for economic development, aided by the commodity boom. The first plan was introduced in 1949. The pace of reform, however, remained very slow, and was **overtaken by emerging nationalist movements.**

1950. The Nationalist Alliance de Bakongo (ABAKO) was founded.

Sixty percent of the doctors in the Cameroon were Africans. The Portuguese program of assimilating "Westernized" Africans into Portuguese citizenship proved a failure. Out of a population of 3 million, only 30,000 fit the Portuguese category of *assimilado*, which entitled them to escape the harsh labor and legal regime for Africans.

1951, Dec. Municipal elections were held in the Belgian Congo; **Joseph Kasavubu's ABAKO won** in Kinshasa.

1953. The Kitawala Movement, originally based on an Africanized version of the apocalyptic doctrine of the American Watch Tower movement, spread in the lower Congo.

1954. A university was established at Elisabethville.

1954–55. A wave of **strikes** broke out in Cameroon.

1955. Oil was discovered near Luanda.

1956. The Comité national d'organisation (CNO) was founded in Cameroon; it engaged in a campaign of violence, including attacks on missions. The CNO ordered a boycott of elections.

Dec. The Movimento Popular de Libertação de Angola (MPLA) was formed to challenge colonial rule.

1957, Dec. Municipal elections in Leopoldville (Kinshasa); Elizabethville (Lubumbashi); and Jadotville (Likasi) gave a vast majority to the **Nationalist Alliance de Bakongo (ABAKO),** which demanded **"immediate independence."**

1958. Gen. Charles de Gaulle announced the independence of all of French Africa at Brazzaville.

1958–59. Foreign investment in Congo dried up, and **capital quickly flowed out as the tide of nationalism rose higher.**

1959. Belgium was forced to abandon its slow pace of reform by popular mobilization in Congo and agreed to immediate independence.

1960–64. The Congo crisis continued, including the division and collapse of the **central government;** intervention of Belgian and UN forces, the U.S., and the USSR; the death of Lumumba; and the secession of Katanga and other provinces before the restoration of central government could be effected.

1998. War raged in Angola between the Popular Movement for the Liberation of Angola (MPLA) and the National Union for the Total Independence of Angola (UNITA) (p. 1066). Although the UN spent some $1.6 billion between 1994 and 1998 in peacekeeping activities, the fighting continued as UN forces withdrew substantially in 1999. The ongoing war directly affected more than one-third of Angolan citizens, some 2 million of whom fled as refugees.

Aug. 2. Fighting in the Congo civil war escalated to the international level when Rwanda and Uganda sent 20,000 troops to the Democratic Republic of the Congo (formerly Zaire) in support of Tutsi opposition to the government of Pres. Laurent Kabila. Kabila was backed by Hutu support and by the Mayi-Mayi, a group of indigenous warriors who were mainly allied with the Hutu in a shared hatred of the Tutsi (p. 1067).

Oct. 21. Angola agreed to send 2,000 troops (along with Zimbabwe, 10,000, and Namibia, 2,000) in support of Pres. Kabila in the Congo civil war (p. 1066).

1999, Aug. 31. After the signing of a weak peace accord by the six involved nations, fighting increased in the Democratic Republic of the Congo war and conflict erupted between Rwanda and Uganda on Congolese soil. The Rwandan-Ugandan violence lasted until July 19, 2000 (p. 1067).

2000. Early in the year, the UN increased its commitment to seeking peace in the Congo civil war. Seven UN Security Council members visited the area in May and met with leaders from the nations involved, gaining a rough peace agreement by the end of the month. After his substantial resistance to UN occupation just a few weeks earlier,

Pres. Kabila accepted an agreement for 5,500 UN peacekeeping troops to begin monitoring the area on Aug. 24.

Sept. 22–25. The Angolan government won a substantial set of victories over the rebel forces of Jonas Savimbi's UNITA rebels. Taking military bases back from the valuable diamond-mining areas of Lunda Norte and Lunda Sul, Angolan troops severely limited Savimbi's ability to continue funding his army.

West Central Africa, country by country, from 1960:

1. ANGOLA

1961. Uprisings in Angola, beginning with a religious millenarian movement in Luanda and later spreading in the name of the **MPLA,** marked the beginning of armed struggle against the Portuguese, leading to independence in 1975.

1974, April. A military coup in Portugal (p. 863) led to the end of its colonial wars and the independence of Mozambique, Angola, and other Portuguese territories in the following year.

1974–75. A power struggle occurred in Angola among three liberation armies: the MPLA (Movimento Popular de Libertação de Angola), supported by the USSR and Yugoslavia; Jonas Savimbi's UNITA (União Nacional para a Independência Total de Angola), supported by South Africa, Portugal, and the U.S. CIA; and the FNLA (Frente Nacional de Libertação de Angola), likewise supported by the CIA, Zaire, and China.

1975, Oct. 23. South Africa invaded Angola in support of UNITA and the FNLA (p. 1071).

Nov. 11. The MPLA, controlling the capital at Luanda, **declared the independence of Angola, with Agostinho Neto as president.** The MPLA brought in **13,000 Cuban troops** to stop the South African advance and drive out the FNLA.

1976, Feb. South Africa withdrew from Angola to Namibia as result of opposition by the U.S. Congress to further military activity in Angola.

March. MPLA and Cuban forces secured the defeat of FNLA-Zaire forces and pushed back UNITA–South African forces.

1979, Sept. 10. Pres. Neto died, and José Eduardo dos Santos became president.

1980. The Southern African Development Coordination Conference (SADCC) was founded by Angola, Botswana, Lesotho, Malawi, Mozambique, Swaziland, Tanzania, Zambia, and Zimbabwe to reduce dependence on South Africa. In the struggle against white supremacy in South Africa, these states called themselves the **Frontline States** because of their proximity to South Africa.

1981–87. South Africa repeatedly intervened in support of UNITA, culminating in major battles at the end of 1987.

1988, Jan. South African forces failed to capture the town of Cuito Cuanavale, defended by combined Angolan and Cuban forces.

Dec. 22. Angola, Cuba, and South Africa agreed to the withdrawal of foreign troops (including 50,000 Cuban troops) from Angola and **independence for Namibia.**

1992, Oct. 3. UNITA's **Jonas Savimbi** rejected the results of the Angolan election, in which he trailed the MPLA's Eduardo dos Santos, leading to a renewed civil war 16 months after the signing of the peace accord.

1993. Up to 1,000 people per day were dying in the civil war between UNITA and the government forces; UNITA held most of the territory.

1994. Angola's petroleum output was 560,000 barrels per day. It was expected to rise to 780,000 barrels per day in 1998. The major portion was exported to the United States.

Nov. 20. The Angolan **government signed a peace treaty with the rebel group** UNITA, ending 19 years of civil wars and giving UNITA some governmental power.

1995, Feb. 8. The UN agreed to send peacekeeping forces to Angola.

Aug. Peace talks between Pres. dos Santos and UNITA rebel leader Jonas Savimbi resumed in Gabon. Savimbi agreed to the offer of the vice presidency and to a timetable for demobilizing rebel forces.

1996, Feb. 8. The UN decided to extend its peacekeeping mission.

March. Further talks between dos Santos and Savimbi resulted in the **agreement** on paper **to form a government of national unity and reconciliation. Actual peace process and demobilization of rebel forces**

barely proceeded. In June there was public protest of the continuing deterioration of economic conditions.

1997, March. UN officials reported the involvement of both government and UNITA troops in the civil war in Zaire. It was reported that UNITA supported forces loyal to Mobutu, and the government supported rebel forces allied with **Laurent Kabila.** Savimbi was accused of resuming military action against the government despite his agreement to the peace process.

April. Chevron Oil Company announced a major new offshore oil discovery.

May. The government officially recognized the new government of the Democratic Republic of the Congo (formerly Zaire) and welcomed Kabila's victory.

1998. Fighting continued between the Popular Movement for the Liberation of Angola (MPLA) and the National Union for the Total Independence of Angola (UNITA). This conflict stemmed from the 1994 victory of MPLA candidate Jose Eduardo dos Santos over UNITA leader Jonas Savimbi in the presidential elections. Although the UN spent some $1.6 billion between 1994 and 1998 in peacekeeping activities, the fighting raged on, claiming approximately 100,000 lives by 1999.

Oct. 21. Angola agreed with Zimbabwe and Namibia to send thousands of troops into the Democratic Republic of the Congo (formerly Zaire) in support of Congo president Laurent Kabila's regime.

1999, March 4. The UN ended its largely ineffectual implementation of the 1994 Lusaka Peace Accord as rebel forces of Savimbi now controlled as much as 70 percent of the country. This control included nearly all of Angola's valuable diamond resources, which greatly helped to provide funding for rebel weapons and supplies.

July 10. Angola signed the Congo peace agreement, along with Congo, Namibia, Zimbabwe, Rwanda, and Uganda.

2000, Sept. 25. Measures to curb the illegal Angolan diamond trade were taken by Angola's government, aiming to use federal agencies to oversee legal trade. On Sept. 22 and 25 Angolan forces in a major victory won back military bases from the rebel UNITA forces in Lunda Norte and Lunda Sul. These were two of the major diamond-mining areas that had been funding UNITA armed conflicts and the various activities of Jonas Savimbi.

2. REPUBLIC OF THE CONGO (BRAZZAVILLE)

1958, Nov. Republic of the Congo became autonomous within the French community under Prime Minister Abbé Fulbert Youlou.

1960, Aug. 15. Congo became independent.

1961, March. Youlou elected president and new constitution adopted giving the president extensive powers.

1963, Aug. General strike **forced Youlou to resign** and established a **provisional government under Alphonse Massambe-Débat,** who was elected president the following year.

1964. The Mouvement national de la révolution became the sole political party based on Marxist-Leninist principles.

1968. Capt. Marien Ngoubai seized power in a coup.

1969. Ngoubai was elected president. He created a new political party, Parti congolais du travail, and the following year **changed the name of the country to the People's Republic of the Congo (PCT).**

1977. Following the **exacerbation of ethnic tensions and power struggles among the elite, Ngoubai was assassinated** during an attempted coup organized by supporters of Massambe-Débat, who was subsequently arrested and executed. **Brig. Gen. Jacques-Joachim Yhombi-Opango was named head of state.**

1979, Feb. Yhombi-Opango surrendered power to the president of the PCT, Col. Denis Sassou-Nguesso, who became president of the Republic. Sassou-Nguesso pursued a pro-Western foreign policy, which led to the marginalization of some left-wing factions.

1987. Twenty army officers, mostly belonging to the northern Kouyou ethnic group, were arrested and charged with sedition. These arrests reflected **increasing ethnic tensions.**

1989, July. Following the national election in which **Sassou-Nguesso was reelected** to another five-year term, the president introduced **political reforms** and released some political prisoners, including former president Yhombi-Opango.

1991, Feb. A national **conference on the future of the country was ad-**

journed because of serious disputes over the representation of opposition movements.

1992. Armed clashes occurred in Brazzaville following the demands by army officers loyal to Sassou-Nguesso to have their positions reinstated.

1993, May. Serious irregularities marred legislative elections and led to **fighting by militias** owing loyalty to rival candidates.

1995, Oct. The government announced efforts to reform the government, to provide more balanced representation in the armed forces, and to slash state expenditures to meet IMF requirements. Former president Sassou-Nguesso left the country. Later that year, political parties signed a peace pact only to see the renewal of factional fighting by early 1996.

1997, Jan. Former president Sassou-Nguesso returned to the Congo for the first time since 1995, in preparation for the upcoming presidential elections.

Feb. 19. Opposition parties called for an expedited establishment of republican institutions, the establishment of an independent electoral commission, and the disarming of civilian militias.

May. Violent skirmishes broke out between the supporters of Sassou-Nguesso and former prime minister Yhombi-Opango. Barricades were erected in the capital, Brazzaville, and the city was effectively split into three competing camps.

June. French troops assisted with the evacuation of foreign residents of Brazzaville.

July 13. A **cease-fire was signed** between supporters of the two rivals and by July 16, fighting had stopped. **Between 1,000 and 3,000 people were reported killed** in the fighting in June and July.

Oct. 15. The forces of former Marxist dictator Denis Sassou-Nguesso, assisted by Angolan troops, took control of the capital city, Brazzaville. Ousting the government of Pres. Pascal Lissouba, Sassou-Nguesso prevailed through military overthrow.

1998, Dec. Full-scale war ensued in the Republic of the Congo as rebel forces battled to take control of Brazzaville.

1999, Nov. 17. A peace agreement was reached between Pres. Sassou-Nguesso's government and the militias of the south that had been loyal to the exiled opposition leaders, former president Lissouba and Bernard Kolelas.

3. ZAIRE (CONGO)

1959. Belgium was forced to abandon its slow pace of reform by the popular mobilization in Congo; it moved toward **immediate independence.**

1960, Jan. 25. The Round Table Conference in Belgium agreed to independence for Congo in June 1960; an election campaign stoked ethnic and rural mobilization.

May. The Congo national election gave the advantage to the Mouvement National Congolais-Lumumba (MNC/L); Patrice Lumumba became prime minister at the head of a precariously divided coalition, with **Joseph Kasavubu** as president (June 1960).

July 4. The Congo crisis began with the revolt of the army against the all-European officer corps; the army remained in anarchic rebellion for several weeks.

July 10. Belgian troops intervened to protect whites but also to support the Katanga secession; the Congo government appealed to the UN, which sent troops that remained until 1964. **The U.S. opposed and the USSR supported Lumumba.**

July 11. Moise Tshombe and the Confédération des Association Tribales du Katanga (CONAKAT), in alliance with European mining interests and Belgian colonists, led the **secession of Katanga Province.**

Sept. Pres. Kasavubu and Prime Minister Lumumba attempted to dismiss one another, leading to a **collapse of central government.**

Nov. 27. Lumumba escaped UN confinement, was captured, and was killed in Katanga.

1961. UN Secretary-General Dag Hammarskjöld died in a plane crash en route to negotiate a cease-fire with Tshombe.

1963, Jan. 14. Tshombe ended the Katanga secession following a UN military onslaught.

1965, Nov. 25. A military coup put army commander Gen. Joseph Désiré Mobutu in power in Congo; he quickly banned opposition politics and consolidated power.

1965–75. Mobutu succeeded in reuniting the Congo but presided over a corrupt, authoritarian regime.

1967. Mobutu institutionalized his power in a one-party state, under the Mouvement Populaire de la Révolution (MPR) and through sweeping presidential powers.

1977–78. Serious rebellions were suppressed in Shaba Province with the aid of France and Belgium. Moves toward democracy were halted, and a new constitution made Mobutu chair of the ruling MPR Party.

1986. Zaire denied Zambian allegations that Zaire was funneling arms from the U.S. to South African–backed UNITA in Angola.

1987, April. Zaire, Angola, and Zambia agreed to restore the Benguela railway, which had not functioned since the mid-1970s due to UNITA action.

1988. The U.S. threatened to discontinue aid—$46 million annually—because of human rights abuses in Zaire, including the recent disruption of opposition meetings and the arrest of leaders.

1991, Oct. A crisis in Zaire included widespread violence by soldiers and civilians. Pres. Mobutu Sese Seko (formerly Joseph Désiré Mobutu) fired recently named premier Étienne Tshisekedi.

1995, May 26. In a report issued by the World Health Organization the death toll from a recent **outbreak of the Ebola virus** in Zaire was 153. On Aug. 28 WHO declared the end to this outbreak.

1996, Aug. 9. Zaire followed several other African countries in imposing trade sanctions on neighboring Burundi because of the military takeover by the Tutsis.

Oct. 30. The Zairean army began fighting Tutsi rebels and dissidents of diverse origins who had formed the Alliance des forces démocratiques pour la libération du Congo-Zaire (AFDL). Many Rwandan Hutu refugees remained stranded in eastern Zaire.

Nov. 13. Canada proposed a UN plan to provide a relief mission to Rwandan refugees in Zaire; Africans requested a UN presence.

Nov. 15–18. Hundreds of thousands of refugees left Zaire and returned to Rwanda.

1997, March 15. Rebels in Zaire (supported by troops from several neighboring countries) captured the third largest city, Kisangani, threatening the rule of **Mobutu Sese Seko,** who had **ruled for 31 years and faced severe charges of corruption.** On April 9 Mobutu imposed military rule throughout the country.

April 14–15. The Zairean opposition began a general strike in the capital city of Kinshasa, essentially shutting the city down.

May 16. Pres. Mobutu relinquished power and guerrilla Laurent Kabila declared himself the country's new leader.

Mobutu fled Kinshasa, en route to Morocco. Many of his supporters and family fled across the border to Brazzaville, in the Republic of the Congo. Speaking from Lubumbashi, **Laurent Kabila declared himself president of the Democratic Republic of the Congo** (May 17). On May 20, Kabila arrived in Kinshasa and announced on May 23 the formation of the new government, composed mostly of his Alliance des forces démocratiques pour la libération du Congo-Zaire.

May 29. Zaire was renamed the Democratic Republic of the Congo and Kabila was sworn in officially as its leader.

June. Arrests of several high-ranking officials from the Mobutu era were announced. Étienne Tshisekedi, the leading government figure opposing Mobutu, was placed in preventive detention following a speech to students that was critical of the new government.

June. The UN withdrew its commission charged with inquiring into the disappearance of thousands of Hutu refugees during the AFDL's military campaign against Mobutu's forces. UN officials claimed that the Kabila government had thwarted their efforts.

1998, Aug. 2. With the military aid of Rwanda and Uganda, rebels threatened to overthrow dictatorial president Laurent Kabila. The insurrection was suppressed with the help of Angolan, Namibian, and Zimbabwean troops (p. 1069). The continued conflict involved seven nations and various rival factions and ethnic divisions, especially pro-Kabila Hutus and anti-Kabila Tutsis, whose conflicts resulted in the 1994 genocide in Rwanda and in massacres that followed throughout the surrounding nations. Engulfing most of Central Africa, the crisis was referred to by some diplomats as Africa's first world war.

1999, July 12–14. An OAU summit in Algeria was held to address the great devastation of the Congo civil war and possible peace measures.

Aug. 31. A cease-fire was reached as Congo, Angola, Namibia, Uganda, Rwanda, and Zimbabwe signed an accord to begin peace processes in the region. However, divisions within Tutsi rebel factions led Uganda and Rwanda into opposition in late August. A small war was begun between those two nations, with most of the fighting occurring in Congo's capital city, Kisangani; among those killed were many Congolese civilians. Rwanda and Uganda did not withdraw until June 19, 2000.

Dec. Pres. Kabila rejected former president of Botswana Sir Ketumile Masire as a political mediator in the Congo conflict, saying he was biased against Kabila's interests. Central Africa had become one of the UN's most active areas of concern as the war in Congo continued into 2000.

2000, Feb. 24. The UN approved the deployment of more than 5,500 peacekeeping troops to the Democratic Republic of the Congo.

May. Seven members of the UN Security Council met in Congo for peace discussions with Pres. Kabila and traveled to the capitals of several of the other countries involved in the fighting. Though Kabila signed a rough agreement for UN intervention, he hampered the UN's ability to send peacekeeping troops into the country, blocking their movement and encouraging attacks on UN forces.

Aug. 24. In a sudden reversal of his lack of cooperation, Pres. Kabila attended peace talks in Lusaka, Zambia, and agreed to allow UN peacekeeping troops to monitor a cease-fire in the Congo civil war.

e. SOUTHERN AFRICA

(From p. 800)

1. NORTH OF THE LIMPOPO

1945–60. Economic development led to **large-scale urbanization and wage labor** in Zambia and Rhodesia, leading to the development of a stable urban population of workers and families, accompanied by the rise of bureaucratic and professional elites.

1947. African trade unions were first formed in Northern Rhodesia.

1948. Seretse Khama married Ruth Williams in London, but the Ngwato people refused to accept him as their chief because of his marriage to an Englishwoman.

Constitutional reforms in Northern Rhodesia extended appointments on the legislative council to five years.

1950. Out of a population of about 5 million, only **4,353** assimilados lived in Mozambique.

1950–56. Successful organization by Copperbelt miners in Northern Rhodesia (Zambia) led to a **wave of strikes** in 1956.

1951. Six white members of the Southwest Africa House of Assembly took seats in the South African Parliament.

1953. Increased political activity in opposition to the proposed federation of Central Africa between Nyasaland and the two Rhodesias. Rev. Michael Scott preached nonviolent opposition to the federation.

1954. Rhodesian University College was founded.

1955. Africans were admitted to the legislative council in Nyasaland.

1956. A state of emergency was declared in Northern Rhodesia, following miners' strikes.

Pres. Craveiro Lopes of Portugal visited Mozambique. Its administrative districts were reorganized.

1957. The Constitutional Party was founded in Northern Rhodesia. In the next year, **the Zambian African Congress Party** was founded.

1958. Hastings Banda returned to Nyasaland and became president of Nyasaland African Congress.

1959. A state of emergency was declared in Nyasaland. Banda was arrested in Southern Rhodesia, and the **Malawi Congress Party** was formed to replace the banned Nyasaland African Congress (NAC).

Tshkedi Khama, regent of the Ngwato people and leader of the nationalist opposition in Bechuanaland (Botswana), died, leading to the accession of his nephew **Seretse Khama,** who later became the **first president of independent Botswana.**

1998, Oct. 21. Zimbabwe involved itself in the Congo civil war by sending 11,000 troops to support Pres. Laurent Kabila of the Democratic Republic of the Congo (p. 1069).

Nov. 4–18. Riots and protests led by the Zimbabwe Congress of Trade Unions (ZCTU) shut down almost all of Zimbabwe's business and industry; citizens objected to Pres. Robert Gabriel Mugabe's handling of the economy, his controversial land redistribution program, and his costly military commitment to the Congo civil war.

1999, Sept. 12–16. Zambia hosted the Eleventh International Conference on AIDS and Sexually Transmitted Diseases in the capital city of Lusaka (p. 1069). Southern Africa continued to be the region most devastated by HIV/AIDS in the world, with UN estimates citing Botswana as the world's most afflicted country, 36 percent of its population having been infected with the AIDS virus. One-fifth to one-fourth of the populations of Zambia, Mozambique, Malawi, and Zimbabwe were also infected, according to UN estimates.

2000, Feb. 12. Taking into consideration a nationwide fuel crisis, 50 percent unemployment, and 60 percent inflation, voters in Zimbabwe rejected a new constitution that would have given Pres. Mugabe a 12-year term in office. New elections were planned for 2002 (p. 1070).

Dec. 1. Because violence had continued to rise against white landowners due to Zimbabwe's land redistribution policies, South African and Nigerian presidents Thabo Mbeki and Olusegun Obasanjo met with Pres. Mugabe to discuss possible monetary compensation for white landowners. UN representatives also visited in order to urge Mugabe to change his land program unless he was prepared to face greater economic sanctions and international discord (p. 1070).

Southern Africa north of the Limpopo, country by country, from 1960:

a. Botswana

1966, Sept. 30. Botswana became independent as a republic under **Pres. Sir Seretse Khama.** Khama's Botswana Democratic Party (BDP) won 28 of 31 seats in the legislature. The Botswana National Front (BNF), more Socialist in orientation than the ruling BDP, was formed as the main opposition party.

1970–1980. Botswana declared support for the Nationalist Patriotic Front in Rhodesia and served as a sanctuary for Nationalist guerrillas.

1980, July 13. Pres. Khama died and was succeeded by his vice president, Quett Masire.

1980–90. Botswana accepted refugees from South Africa while refusing to allow South African liberation groups to operate on its soil; it suffered **numerous cross-border raids by the South African Defence Forces,** including a 1985 attack in the capital, Gaberone, that killed 15.

1984, Sept. Pres. Masire won reelection, and the BDP continued to hold 29 of 34 elective seats in the legislature.

1998. According to UN estimates, Botswana became the most HIV/AIDS-threatened country in the world, with as much as 36 percent of its adult population being infected with the disease.

1999, Oct. 16. National Assembly elections saw 33 of 40 open seats go to the Botswana Democratic Party, which had ruled the nation's politics since 1966.

2000, Aug. Pres. Festus Mogae announced a plan for the near future to enable health facilities around the nation to provide free AIDS medications for Botswana's infected citizens.

b. Malawi

1960, April. Dr. Hastings Banda (who had returned from London in 1958), leader of the Nyasaland National Congress (which in 1966 became the Malawi Congress Party), was released from detention, and constitutional negotiations were opened in London.

1961, Aug. Banda and the MCP won by a **landslide in the preindependence election.**

1964, July 6. Malawi became independent. Banda quickly showed that his policies would be strikingly **conservative,** including slow Africanization of the civil service and cooperation with the Portuguese and South Africans.

1966. Malawi became a **one-party state** under Pres. Banda's Malawi Congress Party (MCP).

1967, Oct. Banda **defeated an uprising** led by a former cabinet minister and consolidated his power.

1980. Malawi joined the **Southern African Development Coordination Conference (SADCC),** which aimed to reduce dependence on South Africa.

1986, Oct. As a result of pressure from neighboring countries after the death of Mozambique's president, Samora Machel, Malawi developed **better relations with Mozambique** and stationed 500 troops there to guard a railway line against RENAMO, which Malawi had previously been suspected of supporting.

1988. Malawi was plunged into **economic crisis** as a result of food shortages, the presence of more than 400,000 refugees from the war in Mozambique, and growing dissent against Banda's repressive government.

1994, May 17. Malawi held its first multiparty elections, electing **Bakili Muluzi** after a voting process thought to be handled fairly and peacefully.

1995, Jan. Following an independent commission of inquiry into several deaths in 1993, former president Banda was arrested for his role in the alleged murders.

1996, Jan. Banda released a statement in which he **admitted that he may have unknowingly been responsible for brutalities committed under his regime** and apologized to Malawians for the pain and suffering inflicted during his presidency.

1997, April and May. A strike by civil servants caused considerable disruption. A government-appointed commission recommended increases of as much as 300 percent in the salaries of public sector employees.

Nov. 25. Former Malawi president Hastings Kamuzu Banda, who ruled from 1964 to 1994, died.

1999, June 15. Pres. Bakili Muluzi, only the second president since Malawi's independence, was reelected over the opposition's candidate, Gwanda Chakuamba.

c. Mozambique

1962. Frente de Libertação de Mozambique (FRELIMO), led by **Eduardo Mondlane,** was founded to fight against colonial rule.

1966. FRELIMO captured control of most of the rural north, while the Portuguese continued to hold the urban centers.

1969. FRELIMO leader **Eduardo Mondlane was assassinated and was succeeded by Samora Machel,** who promoted a more revolutionary Socialist line.

1970–80. Liberated zones, and after 1975 the independence of Mozambique under FRELIMO, provided a **base of operations for Rhodesian (Zimbabwean) and South African liberation movements.** The liberated zones were also a target for the Rhodesian security forces until Zimbabwean independence in 1980. After independence, the Rhodesian security forces shaped a Mozambiquan **rebel army that became known as Movimento Nacional da Resistencia de Mozambique (MNR, or RENAMO).**

1974. A military coup in Portugal (p. 863) forced the end of its colonial wars. Mozambique, Angola, and other Portuguese territories became independent the following year.

1975, June 25. Mozambique attained **independence** under the ruling party, FRELIMO. Upon independence, skilled Portuguese managers left, leaving much of the economic infrastructure in shambles. Moreover, financial difficulties resulted from the struggle against colonialism in Rhodesia and South Africa.

1977. FRELIMO expressed its revolutionary commitment by declaring itself a Marxist-Leninist party.

1980. Mozambique joined the Southern African Development Coordination Conference (SADCC), organized to reduce dependence on South Africa.

1983. By this time **RENAMO,** which had been taken over by South African agents after Zimbabwean independence, **was disrupting life in large areas of the countryside.**

1984. South Africa agreed to stop aiding RENAMO, and Mozambique agreed not to aid ANC guerrillas, in the Nkomati Accord. Mozambique did curb ANC activities, but South African assistance continued to come to RENAMO. As a result, Mozambique relied on aid from surrounding countries, including 10,000 troops from Zimbabwe, to guard its vital installations and communications.

1986, Oct. Pres. Samora Machel was killed when his airplane crashed just over the South African border, leading to suspicion of foul play by South Africa. **Joaquim Alberto Chissano,** the foreign minister, succeeded to the presidency.

1993, Oct. 4. A peace accord with the FRELIMO government of Pres. Chissano ended the 16-year rebellion by South African–backed RENAMO in Mozambique. Elections were planned.

1994, Nov. 19. Mozambique held its **first multiparty elections.** Incumbent president **Joaquim A. Chissano** of the FRELIMO Party won.

Dec. 9. Chissano was sworn in as president. All major ministerial positions went to members of FRELIMO.

1995, May. Opposition parties held an extra-parliamentary conference at Inhambane to voice their concerns about the new constitution and government.

1996, Feb. The government postponed municipal elections from October to the following year. The postponement was due to a dispute with opposition parties regarding the scope of the election and what constituted a municipality.

1997, May. The government signed an agreement with South Africa for the **joint management of the agriculturally rich Lugenda valley.** A wave of anti-government demonstrations spread in response to the limitations on municipal elections. Chissano was reelected the leader of FRELIMO at the first party congress since the introduction of multiparty democracy.

1999, Dec. 3. Pres. Joaquim Chissano was reelected, and his Mozambique Liberation Front (FRELIMO) Party won a majority in the Parliament (133 of 250 seats). This was the second free election in Mozambique since its 16-year-long civil war ended in 1992.

d. Zambia

1964. Zambia became independent under the leadership of Kenneth Kaunda of the United National Independence Party (UNIP).

1964–90. Zambia suffered from continual **economic and political crisis as a result of the poor price performance of copper,** its main resource. Zambia was a **one-party state,** but debate occurred within the party, and the unions were a separate center of political power.

1966–80. Zambia supported liberation movements in Zimbabwe and Mozambique and consequently suffered from sanctions and military attacks.

1973, July. A one-party state was declared in Zambia under Kenneth Kaunda's UNIP, after the **radical United Progressive Party (UPP)** opposition was banned and its leaders were detained, in 1972.

1980. Zambia joined the Southern African Development Coordination Conference (SADCC), designed to reduce dependence on South Africa.

1980–90. Zambia continued to support the liberation movements in Namibia and South Africa. **South African raids** created a suspicious attitude toward foreigners.

1983. Kaunda was reelected, ensuring his dominance within UNIP.

1987, Dec. Violent riots broke out in the Copperbelt in the midst of economic crisis. Kaunda blamed outside agitators and arrested three foreigners as South African agents.

1991, Oct. 31. Multiparty elections resulted in an overwhelming victory for union leader Frederick Chiluba of the opposition Movement for Multiparty Democracy; Pres. Kenneth Kaunda and UNIP were ousted.

1999, Sept. 12–16. The Eleventh International Conference on AIDS and Sexually Transmitted Diseases was held in Lusaka, Zambia's capital. At the conference, $3 billion was pledged by the World Bank to further AIDS research and treatment developments.

1999, Feb. Angola accused Zambia of helping the UNITA rebels fight the Angolan government in its civil war. Bombings in Lusaka on Feb. 28 were suspected of being a retaliatory strike by Angola.

March 31. Kenneth Kaunda was stripped of his Zambian citizenship by the country's highest court. In a legal struggle between Zambian political leaders to disqualify each other from running in elections, the court found that Kaunda could not be a citizen because although he was born in Zambia, his parents were Malawian missionaries. Though never having been convicted of any charges, Kaunda had been accused on Jan. 10, 1998, of plotting to overthrow Pres. Frederick T.J. Chiluba.

e. Zimbabwe

1959. The revived national movement, the African National Congress (ANC), led by **Joshua Nkomo, was banned, and 500 leaders were detained.**

1960. Former ANC militants formed the National Democratic Party (NDP), led by Nkomo.

1961. The NDP was banned, and the Zimbabwean African People's Union (ZAPU) was organized.

1962, Sept. ZAPU was banned, and nationalist activity went underground.

1963. The Zimbabwean African National Union (ZANU) was formed by ZAPU members who disagreed with Nkomo's policies. ZANU organized the Zimbabwean African National Liberation Army (ZANLA) and **sent recruits to China for training.**

1964, July. ZANLA guerrillas killed a Rhodesian Front official, signaling the **beginning of the liberation war.**

Aug. Several top nationalist leaders, including ZAPU's Nkomo and ZANU's Robert Mugabe, were detained.

1965, Nov. 11. Reactionary white settlers in Southern Rhodesia, led by Ian Smith's Rhodesian Front, made a **Unilateral Declaration of Independence (UDI).** Britain imposed some sanctions.

Zimbabwe African People's Revolutionary Army (ZIPRA) guerrillas began to infiltrate the country. ZIPRA was the military wing of ZAPU.

1966, April. The first large military encounter of the war occurred in Sinoia.

1972, Dec. ZANU began a **new phase of the war** in northeastern Rhodesia (Zimbabwe), using bases in liberated zones in Mozambique controlled by FRELIMO. ZAPU operated from Zambia.

1974. South African détente talks resulted in the release of the nationalist leaders from detention but failed to reach a settlement.

1975. Mugabe deposed Reverend Ndabaningi Sithole and assumed undisputed leadership of ZANU.

1978. Sithole and Bishop Abel Muzorewa, without the support of the nationalist movements and guerrilla armies, signed an internal settlement with Smith to form a black government under white control.

1979. Muzorewa was elected prime minister of Zimbabwe-Rhodesia, widely considered a puppet regime, under the internal settlement. The **Lancaster House Conference,** facilitated by Britain and the U.S., reached a **negotiated settlement** of the Zimbabwean War, leading to elections and independence.

1980, April 18. Zimbabwe became independent under Prime Minister Robert Mugabe after an electoral victory of his ZANU-PF (Patriotic Front) Party. Smith's party won all the 20 seats to be reserved for whites. Nkomo's ZAPU was in coalition with ZANU.

Zimbabwe joined the Southern African Development Coordination Conference (SADCC), designed to reduce dependence on South Africa.

1980–85. Despite an official policy of reconciliation, there was initial strain, soon followed by violence, between the Patriotic Front partners ZANU (mostly Shona) and ZAPU (mostly Ndebele). **ZAPU dissidents renewed the guerrilla war against Mugabe's government,** and Matabeleland was heavily repressed by the North Korean–trained Fifth Brigade, leading to thousands of civilian deaths.

1987. After unity talks, ZANU and ZAPU merged, and Nkomo, returned from exile, joined the cabinet. **Mugabe began to remove the constitutional restrictions** imposed by the Lancaster House Accords, abolishing the 20 reserved white seats in Parliament and becoming executive president.

1995, April 8–9. Despite widespread popular discontent, the **government won a decisive fourth election,** although **eight opposition parties boycotted the election.** Six opposition parties participated and election turnout was estimated at 57 percent. The opposition accused the Mugabe regime of election violation, but the international observers were favorably impressed by the open elections.

1996, March 17. Pres. **Mugabe was returned to office** in a presidential election, winning 92 percent of the votes cast. Joshua Nkomo announced that he would resign as one of the two vice presidents because of ill health.

Aug. and Sept. Thousands of civil servants organized a **national strike** and called for higher pay to offset the declining standard of living. Further strikes by nurses and junior doctors took place in October and November.

1996–97. The **IMF suspended assistance** to Zimbabwe for failing to attain targets for economic reform and failing to reduce the budgetary deficits.

1997. Allegations of high-level government corruption fanned popular protests. Peasants seized 450,000 hectares in protest of the slow pace of land reform.

1998, Oct. 21. Zimbabwe joined Namibia and Angola in supporting Pres. Laurent Kabila of the Democratic Republic of the Congo as he battled rebel Tutsi forces and troops from Rwanda and Uganda. Zimbabwe supplied more than 11,000 soldiers to the Congo civil war.

Nov. 4, 11, 18. Riots and protests led by the Zimbabwe Congress of Trade Unions (ZCTU) shut down almost all the country's business and industry in objection to Pres. Robert Gabriel Mugabe's handling of the economy, his controversial land redistribution program, and his costly military commitment to the Congo civil war.

1999. Court rulings pulled back from full legal equality for women, arguing that tradition gave primacy in property ownership to men.

2000, Feb. 12. In light of a nationwide fuel crisis, 50 percent unemployment, and 60 percent inflation, voters in Zimbabwe rejected a new constitution that would have given Mugabe more power by extending his time in office by 12 years. Out of the referendum came plans for elections in 2002 and opposition to Mugabe's plan allowing landless blacks to seize lands owned by whites.

April. Violence stirred against white farmers after a land redistribution campaign by Pres. Mugabe that opposed many Zimbabwean white landowners, who made up 1 percent of the population but owned more than 70 percent of the land. Mugabe's support for belligerent squatters on white land has led to foreign sanctions against Zimbabwe.

June 24–25. Legislative elections resulted in 57 of 120 seats being won by the opposition party.

Dec. 1. Pres. Mugabe met with South African president Thabo Mbeki and Nigerian president Olusegun Obasanjo to discuss the political and economic turmoil that had resulted from Mugabe's land redistribution program. These talks, and a discussion with UN representatives, were aimed at encouraging Mugabe to consider compensating white landowners whose property was being taken over.

2. SOUTH OF THE LIMPOPO

1948. The Afrikaner National Party, under the leadership of D. F. Malan, won the white general election under an ill-defined **slogan of apartheid** (separateness), an intensification of existing structures of segregation.

1950. The Population Registration Act in South Africa required classification of all South Africans on racial lines, especially for the purpose of dividing white and mixed-race (coloured) populations, but more generally as the basis of **strategy of Grand Apartheid**, involving rigid political, territorial, and economic segregation by race in order to entrench white domination and Afrikaner nationalist power. **The Groups Areas Act** furthered this concept by rigidifying urban segregation and excluding black traders from central business districts. **The Suppression of Communism Act** gave the government broad powers to ban and detain opposition leaders; it drove the Communist Party of South Africa to underground reformation as the South African Communist Party (SACP) in 1952.

1953. The Bantu Education Act placed the Department of Native Affairs in charge of African education (in place of mission churches and provincial administrations) and adopted a syllabus that **emphasized training for servitude and downplayed academics**.

1955. The Congress of the People, led by the African National Congress, the Indian Congresses, and white liberal and leftist groups, adopted the **Freedom Charter** as a consensus statement of **opposition to denial of political freedom and wealth to the majority**.

1956. One hundred fifty-six Freedom Charter proponents were charged with treason, leading to dismissals and acquittals after a four-year trial.

1957. Herman Toivo ja Tovio founded the Ovamboland People's Organization.

1959, Dec. 10. Police fired on unarmed demonstrators in Katatura, outside Windhoek, Namibia, killing 11. This event led to the transformation of the Ovamboland People's Organization into a broad nationalist alliance known as **South West African People's Organization (SWAPO),** under the leadership of **Sam Nujoma,** who established SWAPO's headquarters in exile in Dar es Salaam.

1998, Feb. 23. Former South African leaders P. W. Botha and F. W. de Klerk appeared before the South African Truth and Reconciliation Commission created by Pres. Nelson Mandela to review the apartheid system (p. 1072).

Oct. 21. Namibia entered the Congo civil war in support of Pres. Laurent Kabila's regime.

1999, June 2. Nelson R. Mandela retired from the presidency of South Africa, having established himself as one of the world's most recognized and revered statesmen. In parliamentary and presidential elections in South Africa, the ANC won a huge victory, gaining 266 of 400 available seats in the Assembly and a two-thirds majority through al-

liance with another party. The ANC leader **Thabo Mbeki became South Africa's second popularly elected president** (p. 1072).

Oct. 11. South Africa signed a free trade agreement with the European Union (p. 1072).

2000, July 8–14. The Thirteenth International AIDS Conference was held in Durban, South Africa. Southern Africa was the hardest-hit region by HIV/AIDS in the world, with 20 to 25 percent of the populations of Namibia, South Africa, and Swaziland suffering infection from the disease (p. 1072).

Dec. 10. Pursuing the goals of the 1997 Kyoto Protocol, delegates from 122 nations met in Johannesburg, South Africa, to discuss a treaty that would ban 12 highly toxic chemicals that have been proved detrimental to humans and the environment (p. 1072).

South of the Limpopo, country by country, from 1960:

a. Lesotho

1960–66. The Basutoland African Congress (later renamed the Basotho Congress Party or BCP), led by Ntsu Mokhehle, campaigned for independence. More conservative parties, such as Chief Leabua Jonathan's Basutoland National Party (renamed, on independence, the Basotho National Party or BNP), supported by chiefs and elders, also supported independence.

1966, Oct. 4. Lesotho became independent. The BCP led the opposition to incorporation into South Africa, which had been posed as an alternative. The BNP, however, won 31 seats to the BCP's 25, and Chief Jonathan became prime minister.

1966–67. Jonathan reduced King Moshoeshoe II's influence to a ceremonial role, pursued good relations with South Africa, and was antisocialist.

1970, Jan. Jonathan banned opposition parties and put the king under house arrest to prevent an electoral victory by the BCP. The move was supported by South Africa.

1980. After years of pro–South African policies, Jonathan made Lesotho a member of the Southern African Development Coordination Conference (SADCC) and started to take an **antiapartheid stance.** South Africa, in return, began to support guerrilla opposition to Jonathan's government by the Lesotho Liberation Army (LLA), the armed wing of the banned BCP.

1982, Dec. 9. The South African Defence Force launched a raid into the capital, Maseru, killing 37 people. South Africa had accused Lesotho of harboring ANC guerrillas.

1983. Lesotho agreed to expel the ANC from the country as a result of a South African blockade.

1986, Jan. Maj. Gen. Justin Lekhanya seized power after another blockade by South Africa. Lekhanya banned political parties, restored the role of the monarchy, and adopted a pro–South African stance.

1990. Increasing conflict between Lekhanya and King Moshoeshoe resulted in a political and legislative stalemate. Moshoeshoe went into exile in England. Lekhanya invited Moshoeshoe to return, but he refused until reforms were implemented.

1991, April 30. Col. Elias Phitsoome Ramaema led a coup that ousted Lekhanya from office.

1992. King Moshoeshoe promised to return but failed to.

1993. Junior officers rose in mutiny against senior military. Tensions remained high throughout the country.

1994, Aug. 17. King Letsie III announced the dissolution of the elected government due to apparent popular dissatisfaction. Other African leaders denounced this action.

1995, Jan. 25. Letsie III abdicated, and exiled king Moshoeshoe returned to the throne.

1996, Feb. 7. Letsie David Mohato assumed the throne. Political instability continued.

1997, Oct. 31. Following dissolution of the national assembly earlier that year, King Letsie III was returned to the throne.

1998, Sept. 22. After widespread disputation of the May 23 vote that put Prime Minister Pakalitha Mosisili back in power and prolonged the dominance of his party, the Lesotho Congress for Democracy, in Parliament, protestors across Lesotho demanded that the government step down and that new elections be held. South African and Botswanan troops entered the country to put down an army mutiny and stop riots.

b. Namibia

1959, Dec. 10. A police incident outside of Windhoek led to the formation of a broad nationalist alliance known as the South West African People's Organization (SWAPO).

1960–65. SWAPO concentrated on petitioning the UN and organizing within Namibia. It gained considerable support among Ovambo migrant workers. It pursued independence, nationalization of mines and fisheries, and nonracialism.

1965. SWAPO was recognized by the Organization of African Unity as the sole representative of Namibians.

1966, Aug. The International Court of Justice (ICJ) refused to rule on the validity of South African rule of Namibia.

Aug. 26. The first armed clashes between South African forces and SWAPO occurred in Namibia.

1968. South Africa introduced a "homeland" plan for Namibia, assigning each ethnic group to a "homeland" with its own legislative council.

1971. The ICJ ruled that South Africa's claims to Namibia were invalid. South Africa ignored the ruling, but the UN stepped up efforts to secure Namibian independence.

1975. The independence of Angola under its allies, the MPLA, provided SWAPO with a base of operations over Namibia's northern border. South Africa countered by fighting against the MPLA and SWAPO in Angola, in alliance with UNITA.

1979. By this time **South Africa had 60,000 troops in Namibia**, especially in Ovamboland in the north. This increased in the early 1980s, when South Africa occupied part of southern Angola, to perhaps 100,000.

1980–90. South Africa continued to step up its presence in Namibia, pursued an internal settlement plan independent of the UN, and incurred increasing casualties and expenses fighting SWAPO's 10,000 troops.

1988, Dec. 22. Angola, Cuba, and South Africa (in talks brokered by the U.S.) agreed to withdrawal of foreign forces (including 50,000 Cuban troops) from Angola and **independence for Namibia.**

1990, March 21. Independence of Namibia. Sam Nujoma became president at the head of the ruling party, SWAPO.

1998, Oct. 21. Namibia sent troops to the Democratic Republic of the Congo (formerly Zaire) in support of Pres. Laurent Kabila in the Congo civil war.

1999, Nov. 30. Pres. Sam Nujoma was reelected, and his party, SWAPO, won a major victory after the constitution was amended to allow Nujoma to run for a third term. The SWAPO secured 76 percent of the seats in the National Assembly.

Sept. Namibian troops battled separatist uprisings from the Caprivi Strip, a narrow tract of land that connects Namibia with the Zambezi River.

c. South Africa

1960, March 21. Demonstrations against passes, organized by the Pan-Africanist Congress (PAC), led to the Sharpeville massacre in which police fired on unarmed demonstrators, killing 67. Disturbances following this event led to a **state of emergency** and the banning of the African National Congress (ANC) and the PAC, terminating all possibility of legal opposition in the country.

1961. The ANC formed an underground armed wing, Umkhonto we Sizwe, under the leadership of Nelson Mandela, to carry out a campaign of sabotage against government installations. **The PAC formed an underground armed wing, Poqo.**

South Africa became a republic, terminating ties to Britain and dropping out of the Commonwealth.

1963. Arrest of the Umkhonto we Sizwe high command. **The "Rivonia Trial," charging the group with sabotage, led to life terms (imposed in 1964) for Nelson Mandela and much of the ANC top leadership.** Oliver Tambo escaped into exile.

1968. The South African Students Organization (SASO) was founded by Steve Biko, separating from the white-led National Union of South African Students (NUSAS) under the emergent **doctrine of black consciousness.**

1973. A wave of strikes in Durban marked the **new militancy of African labor unions.**

Legislation was passed to regularize industrial action, giving new legitimacy to unions.

1975, March 22. Inkatha was revived under the leadership of KwaZulu chief minister Mangasuthu Gatsha Buthelezi.

Oct. 23. South Africa invaded Angola in support of UNITA and the FNLA (p. 1072).

1976, Feb. South Africa withdrew from Angola to Namibia as a result of opposition by the U.S. Congress to further military activity in Angola.

June 16. Beginning of Soweto uprising. Initiated by African high school students' objections to the use of the Afrikaans language as a medium of instruction, the movement spread in a wave of discontent and violent repression throughout the country, resulting in 700 deaths and the flight of thousands of youths across borders and into the military camps of liberation movements.

1977, Sept. 12. Steve Biko was killed in police custody.

Oct. Black consciousness organizations were banned and their leaders detained.

The UN imposed an arms embargo against South Africa.

1983, Aug. The United Democratic Front (UDF), a coalition of groups opposing apartheid, was founded to oppose tricameral parliament (which continued to exclude Africans from central government while attempting to incorporate Indians and mixed-race "coloureds") and persisted as the principal opposition movement until it was dissolved after the unbanning of the ANC in 1990.

1984. South Africa agreed to stop aiding RENAMO rebels, and Mozambique agreed not to aid ANC guerrillas in the **Nkomati Accord.** South African assistance continued to flow to RENAMO.

1984–86. Uprisings in South African townships were marked by violent repression by the state and violent struggle among contending groups in townships. The UDF, in support of the rebellion, was opposed in Natal by Chief Buthelezi's Inkatha movement.

1985, Nov. The Congress of South African Trade Unions (COSATU) was founded, with 500,000 members.

1986, June 12. A nationwide state of emergency was declared in South Africa.

Oct. The U.S. Congress overrode a presidential veto to impose comprehensive sanctions on South Africa.

1990, Feb. 2. South African president F. W. de Klerck announced the unbanning of the ANC, the PAC, the SACP, and other opposition groups, beginning the process of negotiations for a transition to majority rule.

Feb. 11. Nelson Mandela was released from prison and informally assumed the leadership of the ANC.

Aug. Violence broke out on the Rand between Inkatha-supporting migrant workers and township residents, resulting in more than 500 deaths. The violence was seen as the spread of the ANC-Inkatha rivalry in Natal Province, which had killed more than 3,000 since 1987.

1991, Dec. 20–21. At the first session of the Convention for a Democratic South Africa (CODESA), multiparty negotiations for a majority-rule constitution began. Negotiations lapsed in May 1992 but were restarted in March 1993.

1993, April 10. Assassination of SACP and ANC leader Chris Hani led to widespread rioting.

Sept. 7. Multiparty negotiations in South Africa reached an **agreement for the installation of the Transitional Executive Council (TEC),** involving all major parties, to oversee the period leading to universal franchise. **National elections were planned for April 27, 1994.** The Inkatha Freedom Party (IFP) and the Conservative Party (CP) continued to boycott the talks and threatened to boycott the elections.

Sept. 24. Nelson Mandela, president of the ANC, called for an end to the UN sanctions against South Africa.

1994, Jan. 16. The Pan-Africanist Congress, a radical black group in South Africa, announced an end to its armed struggles against whites, announcing instead its plans to register as an official party to be included in the upcoming elections.

March 13. The leader of the semi-independent black homeland of Bophuthatswana, **Lucas Mangope, was deposed** after a revolt demanding reincorporation with South Africa. South Africa imposed direct rule over Bophuthatswana.

April 19. The leader of the predominantly Zulu Inkatha Freedom

Party announced that the party could participate in upcoming elections.

April 26–28. South Africa announced election dates. De Klerk announced that he would run.

May 2. ANC president **Nelson Mandela claimed a huge victory in South Africa's first elections with universal suffrage,** representing the dissolution of whatever was left of apartheid. A new flag was raised in South Africa, and the new constitution, bill of rights, and national anthems went into effect. On May 10, Mandela was inaugurated and the new cabinet was sworn in.

1995, April 8. The Inkatha Party withdrew from the constituent assembly.

June 6. South Africa's highest court **abolished the death penalty** on the grounds that it is a violation of human rights.

1996, May 8. South Africa voted in a **new constitution** providing **majority rule and broad civil rights.**

Aug. The **Truth and Reconciliation Commission,** established in Dec. 1995 under the chairmanship of **Desmond Tutu,** began conducting public hearings throughout the country. Former victims of human rights violations gave evidence and the commission considered applications for amnesty from perpetrators of such abuses. Former president de Klerk apologized for the policy of apartheid, but denied that he or other members of the previous government had ordered or condoned violations of human rights. Buthelezi refused to cooperate with the commission.

1997. Mandela announced that he would resign as leader of the ANC at the end of the year and that he would not seek reelection when his term ended in 1999.

Dec. Thabo Mbeki was elected president of the ANC and would become heir apparent if the ANC maintained its political prominence in the next elections.

1998, Feb. 23. Former National Party leader P. W. Botha pleaded not guilty to contempt charges by the South African Truth and Reconciliation Commission created by Pres. Nelson Mandela to review the apartheid system. The commission partially promised amnesty to those National Party members and other leaders who confessed their crimes during the prior political regime. Botha's contempt charge was in response to his prior refusals to testify; he was found guilty on Aug. 21. Another leader who appeared before the Truth and Reconciliation Commission in 1998 was F. W. de Klerk.

April 6. Gen. Georg Meiring resigned his position as head of the South African army after accusations of conspiracy arose concerning a report he gave Pres. Mandela warning of an impending coup against the government. The report was allegedly a hoax, falsely naming various ANC party leaders, including the president's ex-wife, Winnie Madikizela-Mandela, as conspirators in a plan to overthrow the Mandela government.

1999, June 2. Pres. Mandela retired from office, establishing himself as one of the world's most recognized and revered statesmen. In parliamentary and presidential elections, the ANC gained 266 of 400 Assembly seats. ANC leader Thabo Mbeki became South Africa's second popularly elected president, and an alliance with the Minority Front gave the ANC a two-thirds majority that could permit them to amend the constitution in the future.

Oct. 11. South Africa signed a free trade agreement with the European Union to eliminate most tariffs on trade between the two partners.

2000, July 8–14. The Thirteenth International AIDS Conference was held in Durban, South Africa, with discussions focusing on treatment plans and ways of controlling the spread of the disease. Pres. Mbeki softened earlier criticism of Western medical assessments of AIDS. In a related development on Dec. 1, Pfizer Inc. of the U.S. promised to provide $50 million in AIDS medications for treatment of the disease in South African clinics.

Dec. 5. In South Africa's local elections, the ruling ANC won only 59 percent of the vote while the newly formed Democratic Alliance (DA) carried 23 percent. The significant success of the DA indicates the possible emergence of a true two-party system in South Africa.

Dec. 10. Continuing the international pursuance of the 1997 Kyoto Protocol, delegates from 122 nations met in Johannesburg, South Africa, and agreed to a treaty that would ban 12 highly toxic chemicals that have historically proved detrimental to humans and the environment. While many industrialized countries had already imposed bans on some of the discussed substances, this was the first globally collaborative effort to ban them worldwide. In order to take effect, the treaty was to require ratification by 50 countries.

d. Swaziland

1968. Swaziland became independent under a constitutional monarchy headed by King Sobhuza. The royal family retained considerable influence over Parliament.

1980. Swaziland joined the Southern African Development Coordination Conference (SADCC), aimed at reducing dependence on South Africa. However, Swaziland signed a secret nonaggression accord with South Africa soon thereafter and has remained under considerable South African influence.

1982. King Sobhuza died after a 61-year rule, setting in motion conflict between the queen mother regent and Parliament during the minority of his successor, Prince Makhosetive.

1986. Prince Makhosetive was crowned as King Mswati III.

Aug. South Africa raided Swaziland in pursuit of ANC activists, and many ANC members were killed in Swaziland in 1986 and 1987.

1987–88. Several former leaders were tried for treason and sentenced to terms of 3–15 years. All were released by July 1988 except Prince Mfansibili, who was to be held for a further six years.

f. MADAGASCAR

(From p. 800)

1943–45. Wartime impositions, including conscription and forced labor, and the 1944 forced sale of the rice crop, led to **widespread discontent** with French rule.

1956. Several political parties emerged to campaign for independence.

1958, Aug. Madagascar voted in favor of the de Gaulle proposal for autonomy within the French sphere.

1960, June 26. Full independence was gained under the leadership of Philibert Tsiranana and his Parti Social Démocrat (PSD).

1971–74. A revolt of Antandroy peasants led to strikes and demonstrations, followed by the installation of a **military government under Gen. Gabriel Ramanatsoa,** who was initially popular with the Left.

1975, Feb. Ramanatsoa was forced from power after violent **anti-Merina riots against the political and ethnic elite and spreading popular revolt;** he was replaced by the Conseil Suprême Révolutionnaire (CSR) led by **Capt. Didier Ratsiraka.** The CSR pursued a radical Socialist line, including widespread nationalization of industry. These policies led to economic stagnation, loss of foreign investment, and food shortages.

1982. By this time Madagascar was heavily reliant on **aid from the Soviet bloc and China,** and was importing 350,000 metric tons of rice per year, which consumed 20 percent of the country's foreign exchange. **Pres. Ratsiraka** was returned to office in fraudulent elections, and the government signed a **structural adjustment** agreement with the International Monetary Fund (IMF).

1983–89. Austerity measures introduced by the IMF agreement led to a resumption of foreign aid and the return of market policies for agriculture. Incomes fell sharply. Poverty and banditry in the countryside led to rapid urbanization.

1987. Drought in the south resulted in **famine,** killing 47,500 and resulting in 200,000 refugees.

1993, Feb. 10. Albert Zafy led the opposition to electoral victory over Pres. Didier Ratsiraka in multiparty elections.

1999, April 19–23. An interisland conference was held in Madagascar with the Comoros and other surrounding islands in attendance.

APPENDIXES

I. ROMAN EMPERORS

27 B.C.–14 C.E.	Augustus (Gaius Julius Caesar Octavianus)
14–37	Tiberius (Tiberius Claudius Nero Caesar)
37–41	Caligula (Gaius Claudius Nero Caesar Germanicus)
41–54	Claudius (Tiberius Claudius Nero Caesar Drusus)
54–68	Nero (Lucius Domitius Ahenobarbus Claudius Drusus)
68–69	Galba (Servius Sulpicius Galba)
69	Otho (Marcus Salvius Otho)
69	Vitellius (Aulus Vitellius Germanicus)
69–79	Vespasian (Titus Flavius Vespasianus)
79–81	Titus (Titus Flavius Vespasianus)
81–96	Domitian (Titus Flavius Domitianus)
96–98	Nerva (Marcus Cocceius Nerva)
98–117	Trajan (Marcus Ulpius Nerva Traianus)
117–38	Hadrian (Publius Aelius Traianus Hadrianus)
138–61	Antoninus Pius (Titus Aurelius Fulvius Boionius Arrius Antoninus Pius)
161 (146)–80	Marcus Aurelius (Marcus Annius Aurelius Verus)
161–69	Lucius Aurelius Verus (Lucius Ceionius Commodus Verus)
180 (177)–92	Commodus (Lucius Aelius Marcus Aurelius Antoninus Commodus)
193	Pertinax (Publius Helvius Pertinax)
193	Didius Julian (Marcus Didius Salvius Julianus Severus)
193–211	Septimius Severus (Lucius Septimius Severus)
211 (198)–17	Caracalla (Marcus Aurelius Antoninus Bassianus Caracallus)
209–11	Geta (Publius Septimius Geta)
217–18	Macrinus (Marcus Opellius Severus Macrinus)
218–22	Elagabalus (Marcus Varius Avitus Bassianus Aurelius Antoninus Heliogabalus)
222–35	Alexander Severus (Marcus Alexianus Bassianus Aurelius Severus Alexander)
235–38	Maximin (Gaius Julius Verus Maximinus "Thrax")
238	Gordian I (Marcus Antonius Gordianus)
238	Gordian II
238	Pupienus (Marcus Clodius Pupienus Maximus)
238	Balbinus (Decimus Caelius Balbinus)
238–44	Gordian III (Marcus Antonius Gordianus)
244–49	Philipp "Arabs" (Marcus Julius Philippus "Arabs")
249–51	Decius (Gaius Messius Quintus Traianus Decius)
251	Hostilian (Gaius Valens Hostilianus Messius Quintus)
251–53	Gallus (Gaius Vibius Trebonianus Gallus)
253	Aemilian (Marcus Julius Aemilius Aemilianus)
253–59	Valerian (Gaius Publius Licinius Valerianus)
259 (253)–68	Gallienus (Publius Licinius Egnatius Gallienus)
268–70	Claudius II (Marcus Aurelius Claudius Gothicus)
270	Quintillus (Marcus Aurelius Claudius Quintillus)
270–75	Aurelian (Lucius Domitius Aurelianus)
275–76	Tacitus (Marcus Claudius Tacitus)
276	Florian (Marcus Annius Florianus)
276–82	Probus (Marcus Aurelius Probus)
282–83	Carus (Marcus Aurelius Carus)
283–84	Numerian (Marcus Aurelius Numerius Numerianus)
283–85	Carinus (Marcus Aurelius Carinus)
284–305	Diocletian (Gaius Aurelius Valerius Diocles Jovius)
286–305	Maximian (Marcus Aurelius Valerius Maximianus Herculius)
305 (293)–306	Constantius I (Flavius Valerius Constantius Chlorus)
305 (293)–311	Galerius (Gaius Galerius Valerius Maximianus)
306–7	Severus (Flavius Valerius Severus)
306–8	Maximian (second reign)
306–12	Maxentius (Marcus Aurelius Valerius Maxentius)
308–13	Maximinus Daia (Galerius Valerius Maximinus Daia)
311 (307)–24	Licinius (Gaius Flavius Valerius Licinianus Licinius)
311 (306)–37	Constantine I, the Great (Flavius Valerius Constantinus)
337–40	Constantine II (Flavius Valerius Claudius Constantinus)
337–61	Constantius II (Flavius Valerius Julius Constantius)
337–50	Constans (Flavius Valerius Julius Constans)
361–63	Julian, the Apostate (Flavius Claudius Julianus)
363–64	Jovian (Flavius Jovianus)
364–75	Valentinian I (Flavius Valentinianus, in the West)
364–78	Valens (in the East)
375 (367)–83	Gratian (Flavius Graatianus Augustus, in the West)
375–92	Valentinian II (Flavius Valentinianus, in the West)
379–95	Theodosius, the Great (Flavius Theodosius, in the East, and, after 392, in the West)
383–88	Maximus (Magnus Clemens Maximus)
392–94	Eugenius
395 (383)–408	Arcadius (in the East)
395 (393)–423	Honorius (Flavius Honorius, in the West)
421	Constantius III
423–25	Johannes
408 (402)–50	Theodosius II (in the East)
425–55	Valentinian III (Flavius Placidius Valentinianus, in the West)
450–57	Marcian (Marcianus, in the East)
455	Petronius (Flavius Ancius Petronius Maximus, in the West)
455–56	Avitus (Flavius Maecilius Eparchus Avitus, in the West)
457–61	Majorian (Julius Valerius Maioranus, in the West)
457–74	Leo I (Leo Thrax, Magnus, in the East)
461–65	Severus (Libius Severianus Severus, in the West)
467–72	Anthemius (Procopius Anthemius, in the West)

472	Olybrius (Anicius Olybrius, in the West)
473	Glycerius (in the West)
473–75	Julius Nepos (in the West)
473–74	Leo II (in the East)

| 474–91 | Zeno (in the East) |
| 475–76 | Romulus Augustulus (Flavius Momyllus Romulus Augustus, in the West) |

II. BYZANTINE EMPERORS

474–91	Zeno
475–76	Basiliscus
491–518	Anastasius I
518–27	Justin I (Flavius Justinus)
527 (518) –65	Justinian the Great (Flavius Justinianus)
565–78	Justin II (Flavius Justinus)
578 (574) –82	Tiberius II (Flavius Constantinus Tiberius)
582–602	Maurice (Maurikios)
602–10	Phocas I
610–41	Heraclius I
641	Constantine III (Constantinus)
641	Heracleon (Heracleonas)
641–68	Constans II
668–85	Constantine IV (Pogonatus)
685–95	Justinian II (Rhinotmetus)
695–98	Leontius
698–705	Tiberius II (Apsimar)
705–11	Justinian II (restored)
711–13	Philippicus
713–15	Anastasius II
715–17	Theodosius III
717–41	Leo III (the Isaurican)
741–75	Constantine V (Kopronymos)
775–80	Leo IV
780–97	Constantine VI (Porphyrogenetos)
797–802	Irene (empress)
802–11	Nicephorus I
811	Stauracius (Staurakios)
811–13	Michael I (Rhangabé)
813–20	Leo V (the Armenian)
820–29	Michael II (Balbus)
829 (820) –42	Theophilus I
842–67	Michael III
867 (866) –86	Basil I (the Macedonian)
886–912	Leo VI (the Wise)
912–13	Alexander II
912–59	Constantine VII (Porphyrogenetos)
920–44	Romanus I (Lekcapenus)
959–63	Romanus II
963 (976) –1025	Basil II (Bulgaroktonos)
963–69	Nicephorus II (Phocas)
969–76	John I (Tzimisces)
1025 (976) –28	Constantine VIII
1028–50	Zoë (empress)
1028–34	Romanus III (Argyropulos)
1034–41	Michael IV (the Paphlagonian)
1041–42	Michael V (Kalaphates)
1042–55	Constantine IX (Monomachus)

1055–56	Theodora (empress)
1056–57	Michael VI (Stratioticos)
1057–59	Isaac I (Komnenos)
1059–67	Constantine X (Dukas)
1068–71	Romanus IV (Diogenes)
1071–78	Michael VII (Parapinakes)
1078–81	Nicephorus III (Botaniates)
1081–1118	Alexius I (Comnenus)
1118–43	John II (Comnenus)
1143–80	Manuel I (Comnenus)
1180–83	Alexius II (Comnenus)
1183–85	Andronicus I (Comnenus)
1185–95	Isaac II (Angelus)
1195–1203	Alexius III (Angelus)
1203–4	Isaac II (restored)
1203–4	Alexius IV
1204	Alexius V (Dukas)

Latin Emperors

1204–5	Baldwin I
1205–16	Henry
1216–17	Peter of Courtenay
1217–19	Yolande
1219–28	Robert of Courtenay
1228–61	Baldwin II
1231–37	John of Brienne (co-emperor)

Nicaean Emperors

1204–22	Theodore I (Lascaris)
1222–54	John III (Dukas Vatatzes)
1254–58	Theodore II (Lascaris)
1258–61	John IV (Lascaris)
1259–61 (1282)	Michael VIII (Paleologos)

The Paleologi

1261 (1259) –82	Michael VIII
1282–1328	Andronicus II (the Elder)
1295–1320	Michael IX (co-emperor)
1328–41	Andronicus III (the Younger)
1341–47	John V (Paleologos)
1347 (1341) –54	John VI (Kantakuzenos)
1355–76	John V (restored)
1376–79	Andronicus IV
1379–91	John V (restored)
1390	John VII
1391–1425	Manuel II
1425–48	John VIII
1448–53	Constantine XI

III. CALIPHS, TO 1256

| 622 (570) –32 | MUHAMMAD IBN ABDALLAH |

The Orthodox Caliphate

| 632–34 | Abu Bakr |
| 634–44 | Umar ibn al-Khattab |

| 644–56 | Uthman ibn Affan |
| 656–61 | Ali ibn Abi Talib |

The Umayyad Caliphate

| 661–80 | Mu'awiya I (Mu'awiya ibn Abi Sufyan) |
| 680–82 | Yazid I |

683	Mu'awiya II
684–85	Marwan I
685–705	Abd al-Malik
705–15	Walid I
715–17	Sulaiman
717–20	Umar ibn Abdul-Aziz
720–24	Yazid II
724–43	Hisham
743–44	Walid II
744	Yazid III
744	Ibrahim
744–50	Marwan II

The Abbasid Caliphate

750–54	Abu al Abbas al-Saffah
754–75	Al-Mansur
775–85	Al-Mahdi
785–86	Al-Hadi
786–809	Harun Al-Rashid
809–13	Al-Amin
813–33	Al-Ma'mun (Mamun the Great)
833–42	Al-Mu'tasim
842–47	Al-Wathiq
847–61	Al-Mutawakkil
861–62	Al-Muntasir
862–66	Al-Musta'in
866–69	Al-Mu'tazz
869–70	Al-Muqtadi
870–92	Al-Mu'tamid
892–902	Al-Mu'tadid
902–8	Al-Muqtafi
908–32	Al-Muqtadir
932–34	Al-Qahir
934–40	Al-Radi
940–44	Al-Muttaqi
944–46	Al-Mustaqfi
946–74	Al-Muti
974–91	Al-Ta'i
991–1031	Al-Qadir
1031–75	Al-Qa'im
1075–94	Al-Muqtadi
1094–1118	Al-Mustazhir
1118–35	Al-Mustarshid
1135–36	Al-Rashid
1136–60	Al-Muqtafi
1160–70	Al-Mustanjid

1170–80	Al-Mustadi
1180–1225	Al-Nasir
1225–26	Al-Zahir
1226–42	Al-Mustansir
1242–56	Al-Musta'sim

The Umayyad Caliphate of Córdoba

756–88	Abd ar-Rahman I
788–96	Hisham I
796–822	Al-Hakam I
822–52	Abd ar-Rahman II
852–86	Muhammad I
886–88	Al Mundhir
888–912	Abdallah
912–61	Abd ar-Rahman III
961–76	Al-Hakam II al Mustansir
976–1009	Hisham II al Muayyad
1009–10	Muhammad II al-Mahdi
1009–10	Sulaiman al-Mustain
1010–13	Hisham II (restored)
1013–16	Sulaiman (restored)
1016–18	Ali ben Hammud
1018	Abd ar-Rahman IV
1018–21	Al-Qasim
1021–22	Yahya
1022–23	Al-Qasim (restored)
1023–24	Abd ar-Rahman V
1024–25	Muhammad III
1025–27	Yahya (restored)
1027–31	Hisham III

The Fatimid Caliphate of Egypt

909–34	Al-Mahdi
934–45	Al-Qaim
945–52	Al-Mansur
952–75	Al-Muizz
975–96	Al-Aziz
996–1021	Al-Hakim
1021–36	Az-Zahir
1036–94	Al-Mustansir
1094–1101	Al-Mustadi
1101–30	Al-Amir
1130–49	Al-Hafiz
1149–54	Az-Zafir
1154–60	Al-Faiz
1160–71	Al-Adid

IV. ROMAN POPES

33–?67	*Peter
?67–?76	*Linus
?76–?88	*Anacletus I
?88–?97	*Clement I
?97–?105	*Evaristus
?105–?15	*Alexander I
?115–?25	*Sixtus I
?125–?36	*Telesphorus
?136–?40	*Hyginus
?140–?55	*Pius I
?155–?66	*Anicetus
?166–?75	*Soter
?175–89	*Eleuterus
189–99	*Victor I
199–217	*Zephyrinus
217–22	*Calixtus I
222–30	*Urban I

222–35	*Hippolytus*
230–35	*Pontian
235–36	*Anterus
236–50	*Fabian
250–51	(Vacancy)
251–53	*Cornelius
251–?58	*Novatian*
253–54	*Lucius I
254–57	*Stephen I
257–58	*Sixtus II
258–60	(Vacancy)
260–68	*Dionysius
269–74	*Felix I
275–83	*Eutychian
283–96	*Caius
296–304	*Marcellinus
304–8	(Vacancy)

---

* Names marked with an asterisk indicate popes sainted by the Church. Names in italics are those of anti-popes.

308–9	*Marcellus I	767	*Constantine*
309–10	*Eusebius	767	*Philip*
311–14	*Miltiades	767–72	Stephen III
314–35	*Sylvester I	772–95	Adrian I
335–36	*Marcus	795–816	*Leo III
337–52	*Julius I	816–17	Stephen IV
352–66	*Liberius	817–24	Paschal I
353–65	*Felix II*	824–27	Eugene II
366–83	Damasus I	827	Valentine
366–67	*Ursinus*	827–44	Gregory IV
384–99	*Siricius	*844*	*John VIII*
399–401	*Anastasius I	844–47	Sergius II
401–17	*Innocent I	847–55	*Leo IV
417–18	*Zosimus	855–58	Benedict III
418–22	*Boniface I	*855*	*Anastasius III*
418–19	*Eulalius*	858–67	*Nicholas I
422–32	*Celestine I	867–72	Adrian II
432–40	*Sixtus III	872–82	John VIII
440–61	*Leo I	882–84	Marinus I
461–68	*Hilarius	884–85	Adrian III
468–83	*Simplicius	885–91	Stephen V
483–92	*Felix III	891–96	Formosus
492–96	*Gelasius I	896	Boniface VI
496–98	*Anastasius II	896–97	Stephen VI
498–514	*Symmachus	897	Romanus
498–505	*Laurentius*	897	Theodore II
514–23	*Hormisdas	898–900	John IX
523–26	*John I	900–903	Benedict IV
526–30	*Felix IV	903	Leo V
530–32	Boniface II	903–4	Christopher
530	*Dioscurus*	904–11	Sergius III
533–35	John II	911–13	Anastasius III
535–36	*Agapetus I	913–14	Lando
536–37	*Silverius	914–28	John X
537–55	Vigilius	928–29	Leo VI
556–61	Pelagius I	929–31	Stephen VII
561–74	John III	931–35	John XI
575–79	Benedict I	936–39	Leo VII
579–90	Pelagius II	939–42	Stephen IX (VIII)
590–604	*Gregory I	942–46	Marinus II
604–6	Sabinian	946–55	Agapetus II
607	Boniface III	955–63	John XII
608–15	*Boniface IV	963–64	Leo VIII
615–18	*Deusdedit	964	Benedict V
619–25	Boniface V	965–72	John XIII
625–38	Honorius I	973–74	Benedict VI
638–40	(Vacancy)	974–83	Benedict VII
640	Severinus	983–84	John XIV
640–42	John IV	984–85	Boniface VII
642–49	Theodore I	985–96	John XV
649–55	*Martin I	996–99	Gregory V
655–57	*Eugene I	*996–98*	*John XVI*
657–72	*Vitalian	999–1003	Sylvester II
672–76	Adeodatus	1003	John XVII
676–78	Donus	1003–9	John XVIII
678–81	*Agatho	1009–12	Sergius IV
681–83	*Leo II	1012–24	Benedict VIII
684–85	*Benedict II	*1012*	*Gregory VI*
685–86	John V	1024–33	John XIX
686–87	Conon	1033–45	Benedict IX
687	*Theodore II*	1045	Sylvester III
687–92	*Paschal I*	1045–46	Gregory VI (John Gratian Pierleoni)
687–701	*Sergius I	1046–47	Clement II (Suitgar, Count of Morsleben)
701–5	John VI	1048	Damasus II (Count Poppo)
705–7	John VII	1049–54	*Leo IX (Bruno, Count of Toul)
708	Sisinnius	1055–57	Victor II (Gebhard, Count of Hirschberg)
708–15	Constantine	1057–58	Stephen IX (Frederick of Lorraine)
715–31	*Gregory II	1058	Benedict X (John, Count of Tusculum)
731–41	*Gregory III	1058–61	Nicholas II (Gerhard of Burgundy)
741–52	*Zacharias	1061–73	Alexander II (Anselmo da Baggio)
752–57	Stephen II	*1061–64*	*Honorius II*
757–67	*Paul I	1073–85	*Gregory VII (Hildebrand of Soana)

1080–1100	*Clement III*
1086–87	Victor III (Desiderius, Prince of Beneventum)
1088–99	Urban II (Odo of Chatillon)
1099–1118	Paschal II (Ranieri da Bieda)
1100–1102	*Theodoric*
1102	*Albert*
1105	*Sylvester IV*
1118–19	Gelasius II (John Coniolo)
1118–21	*Gregory VIII*
1119–24	Calixtus II (Guido, Count of Burgundy)
1124–30	Honorius II (Lamberto dei Fagnani)
1124	*Celestine II*
1130–43	Innocent II (Gregorio Papareschi)
1130–38	*Anacletus II (Cardinal Pierleone)*
1138	*Victor IV*
1143–44	Celestine II (Guido di Castello)
1144–45	Lucius II (Gherardo Caccianemici)
1145–53	Eugene III (Bernardo Paganelli)
1153–54	Anastasius IV (Corrado della Subarra)
1154–59	Adrian IV (Nicholas Breakspear)
1159–81	Alexander III (Orlando Bandinelli)
1159–64	*Victor IV*
1164–68	*Paschal III*
1168–78	*Calixtus III*
1179–80	*Innocent III (Lando da Sessa)*
1181–85	Lucius III (Ubaldo Allucingoli)
1185–87	Urban III (Uberto Crivelli)
1187	Gregory VIII (Alberto del Morra)
1187–91	Clement III (Paolo Scolari)
1191–98	Celestine III (Giacinto Boboni-Orsini)
1198–1216	Innocent III (Lotario de' Conti di Segni)
1216–27	Honorius III (Cencio Savelli)
1227–41	Gregory IX (Ugolino di Segni)
1241	Celestine IV (Goffredo Castiglione)
1243–54	Innocent IV (Sinibaldo de' Fieschi)
1254–61	Alexander IV (Rinaldo di Segni)
1261–64	Urban IV (Jacques Pantaléon)
1265–68	Clement IV (Guy le Gros Foulques)
1268–71	(Vacancy)
1271–76	*Gregory X (Tebaldo Visconti)
1276	Innocent V (Pierre de Champagni)
1276	Adrian V (Ottobono Fieschi)
1276–77	John XXI (Pietro Rebuli-Giuliani)
1277–80	Nicholas III (Giovanni Gaetano Orsini)
1281–85	Martin IV (Simon Mompitie)
1285–87	Honorius IV (Giacomo Savelli)
1288–92	Nicholas IV (Girolamo Masci)
1294	*Celestine V (Pietro Angelari da Murrone)
1294–1303	Boniface VIII (Benedetto Gaetani)
1303–4	Benedict XI (Niccolò Boccasini)
1305–14	Clement V (Raimond Bertrand de Got)
1316–34	John XXII (Jacques Duèze)
1328–30	*Nicholas V (Pietro di Corbara)*
1334–42	Benedict XII (Jacques Fournier)
1342–52	Clement VI (Pierre Roger de Beaufort)
1352–62	Innocent VI (Étienne Aubert)
1362–70	Urban V (Guillaume de Grimord)
1370–78	Gregory XI (Pierre Roger de Beaufort, the Younger)
1378–89	Urban VI (Bartolomeo Prignano)
1378–94	*Clement VII (Robert of Geneva)*
1389–1404	Boniface IX (Pietro Tomacelli)
1394–1423	*Benedict XIII (Pedro de Luna)*
1404–6	Innocent VII (Cosmato de' Migliorati)
1406–15	Gregory XII (Angelo Correr)

1409–10	*Alexander V (Petros Philargi)*
1410–15	*John XXIII (Baldassare Cossa)*
1415–17	(Vacancy)
1417–31	Martin V (Ottone Colonna)
1423–29	*Clement VIII*
1424	*Benedict XIV*
1431–47	Eugene IV (Gabriele Condulmer)
1439–49	*Felix V (Amadeus of Savoy)*
1447–55	Nicholas V (Tommaso Parentucelli)
1455–58	Calixtus III (Alonso Borgia)
1458–64	Pius II (Aeneas Silvio de' Piccolomini)
1464–71	Paul II (Pietro Barbo)
1471–84	Sixtus IV (Francesco della Rovere)
1484–92	Innocent VIII (Giovanni Battista Cibo)
1492–1503	Alexander VI (Rodrigo Lanzol y Borgia)
1503	Pius III (Francesco Todoeschini-Piccolomini)
1503–13	Julius II (Giuliano della Rovere)
1513–21	Leo X (Giovanni de' Medici)
1522–23	Adrian VI (Hadrian Florensz)
1523–34	Clement VII (Giulio de' Medici)
1534–49	Paul III (Alessandro Farnese)
1550–55	Julius III (Giovanni Maria Ciocchi del Monte)
1555	Marcellus II (Marcello Cervini)
1555–59	Paul IV (Gian Pietro Caraffa)
1559–65	Pius IV (Giovanni Angelo de' Medici)
1566–72	*Pius V (Antonio Michele Ghislieri)
1572–85	Gregory XIII (Ugo Buoncompagni)
1585–90	Sixtus V (Felice Peretti)
1590	Urban VII (Giambattista Castagna)
1590–91	Gregory XIV (Niccolò Sfondrati)
1591	Innocent IX (Gian Antonio Facchinetti)
1592–1605	Clement VIII (Ippolito Aldobrandini)
1605	Leo XI (Alessandro de' Medici-Ottaiano)
1605–21	Paul V (Camillo Borghese)
1621–23	Gregory XV (Alessandro Ludovisi)
1623–44	Urban VIII (Maffeo Barberini)
1644–55	Innocent X (Giambattista Pamfili)
1655–67	Alexander VII (Fabio Chigi)
1667–69	Clement IX (Giulio Rospigliosi)
1670–76	Clement X (Emilio Altieri)
1676–89	Innocent XI (Benedetto Odescalchi)
1689–91	Alexander VIII (Pietro Ottoboni)
1691–1700	Innocent XII (Antonio Pignatelli)
1700–21	Clement XI (Gian Francesco Albani)
1721–24	Innocent XIII (Michelangelo dei Conti)
1724–30	Benedict XIII (Pietro Francesco Orsini)
1730–40	Clement XII (Lorenzo Corsini)
1740–58	Benedict XIV (Prospero Lambertini)
1758–69	Clement XIII (Carlo Rezzonico)
1769–74	Clement XIV (Lorenzo Ganganelli)
1775–99	Pius VI (Gianangelo Braschi)
1800–1823	Pius VII (Barnaba Chiaramonti)
1823–29	Leo XII (Annibale della Genga)
1829–30	Pius VIII (Francesco Saverio Gastiglioni)
1831–46	Gregory XVI (Bartolomeo Alberto Cappellari)
1846–78	Pius IX (Giovanni Mastai-Ferretti)
1878–1903	Leo XIII (Gioacchino Pecci)
1903–14	Pius X (Giuseppe Sarto)
1914–22	Benedict XV (Giacomo della Chiesa)
1922–39	Pius XI (Achille Ratti)
1939–58	Pius XII (Eugenio Pacelli)
1958–63	John XXIII (Angelo Roncalli)
1963–78	Paul VI (Giovanni Battista Montini)
1978–	John Paul II (Karol Jozef Wojtyla)

V. PRESIDENTS OF THE UNITED STATES

George Washington, 1789–97
John Adams, 1797–1801
Thomas Jefferson, 1801–9
James Madison, 1809–17

James Monroe, 1817–25
John Quincy Adams, 1825–29
Andrew Jackson, 1829–37
Martin Van Buren, 1837–41

William Henry Harrison, 1841
John Tyler, 1841–45
James Knox Polk, 1845–49
Zachary Taylor, 1849–50
Millard Fillmore, 1850–53
Franklin Pierce, 1853–57
James Buchanan, 1857–61
Abraham Lincoln, 1861–65
Andrew Johnson, 1865–69
Ulysses Simpson Grant, 1869–77
Rutherford Birchard Hayes, 1877–81
James Abram Garfield, 1881
Chester Alan Arthur, 1881–85
Grover Cleveland, 1885–89
Benjamin Harrison, 1889–93
Grover Cleveland, 1893–97
William McKinley, 1897–1901
Theodore Roosevelt, 1901–9

William Howard Taft, 1909–13
Woodrow Wilson, 1913–21
Warren Gamaliel Harding, 1921–23
Calvin Coolidge, 1923–29
Herbert Clark Hoover, 1929–33
Franklin Delano Roosevelt, 1933–45
Harry S. Truman, 1945–53
Dwight D. Eisenhower, 1953–61
John F. Kennedy, 1961–63
Lyndon B. Johnson, 1963–69
Richard M. Nixon, 1969–74
Gerald Ford, 1974–77
Jimmy Carter, 1977–81
Ronald Reagan, 1981–89
George Bush, 1989–93
Bill Clinton, 1993–2001
George W. Bush, Jr., 2001–

VI. MEMBERS OF THE UNITED NATIONS IN ORDER OF ADMISSION

1.	Argentina	24 Oct. 1945
2.	Brazil	24 Oct. 1945
3.	Belarus (Byelorussia)	24 Oct. 1945
4.	Chile	24 Oct. 1945
5.	China (Nationalist)	24 Oct. 1945
6.	Cuba	24 Oct. 1945
7.	Denmark	24 Oct. 1945
8.	Dominican Republic	24 Oct. 1945
9.	El Salvador	24 Oct. 1945
10.	France	24 Oct. 1945
11.	Haiti	24 Oct. 1945
12.	Iran	24 Oct. 1945
13.	Lebanon	24 Oct. 1945
14.	Luxembourg	24 Oct. 1945
15.	New Zealand	24 Oct. 1945
16.	Nicaragua	24 Oct. 1945
17.	Paraguay	24 Oct. 1945
18.	Philippines	24 Oct. 1945
19.	Poland	24 Oct. 1945
20.	Saudi Arabia	24 Oct. 1945
21.	Syria (Syrian Arab Republic)*	24 Oct. 1945
22.	Turkey	24 Oct. 1945
23.	Ukraine	24 Oct. 1945
24.	Russian Federation (U.S.S.R.)	24 Oct. 1945
25.	Arab Republic of Egypt (United Arab Republic)*	24 Oct. 1945
26.	United Kingdom	24 Oct. 1945
27.	United States	24 Oct. 1945
28.	Greece	25 Oct. 1945
29.	India	30 Oct. 1945
30.	Peru	31 Oct. 1945
31.	Australia	1 Nov. 1945
32.	Costa Rica	2 Nov. 1945
33.	Liberia	2 Nov. 1945
34.	Colombia	5 Nov. 1945
35.	Mexico	7 Nov. 1945
36.	South Africa	7 Nov. 1945
37.	Canada	9 Nov. 1945
38.	Ethiopia	13 Nov. 1945
39.	Panama	13 Nov. 1945
40.	Bolivia	14 Nov. 1945
41.	Venezuela	15 Nov. 1945
42.	Guatemala	21 Nov. 1945
43.	Norway	27 Nov. 1945
44.	Netherlands	10 Dec. 1945
45.	Honduras	17 Dec. 1945
46.	Uruguay	18 Dec. 1945
47.	Ecuador	21 Dec. 1945
48.	Iraq	21 Dec. 1945
49.	Belgium	27 Dec. 1945
50.	Afghanistan	19 Nov. 1946
51.	Iceland	19 Nov. 1946
52.	Sweden	19 Nov. 1946
53.	Thailand	16 Dec. 1946
54.	Pakistan	30 Sep. 1947
55.	Yemen†	30 Sep. 1947
56.	Myanmar (Burma)	19 Apr. 1948
57.	Israel	11 May 1949
58.	Indonesia	28 Sep. 1950
59.	Albania	14 Dec. 1955
60.	Austria	14 Dec. 1955
61.	Bulgaria	14 Dec. 1955
62.	Cambodia	14 Dec. 1955
63.	Sri Lanka (Ceylon)	14 Dec. 1955
64.	Finland	14 Dec. 1955
65.	Hungary	14 Dec. 1955
66.	Ireland	14 Dec. 1955
67.	Italy	14 Dec. 1955
68.	Jordan	14 Dec. 1955
69.	Laos (Lao People's Democratic Republic)	14 Dec. 1955
70.	Libya (Libyan Arab Jamahiriya)	14 Dec. 1955
71.	Nepal	14 Dec. 1955
72.	Portugal	14 Dec. 1955
73.	Romania	14 Dec. 1955
74.	Spain	14 Dec. 1955
75.	Morocco	12 Nov. 1956
76.	Sudan	12 Nov. 1956
77.	Tunisia	12 Nov. 1956
78.	Japan	18 Dec. 1956
79.	Ghana	8 Mar. 1957
80.	Malaysia (Federation of Malaya)	17 Sep. 1957
81.	Guinea	12 Dec. 1958
82.	Cameroon	20 Sep. 1960
83.	Central African Republic	20 Sep. 1960
84.	Chad	20 Sep. 1960
85.	Congo (capital: Brazzaville)	20 Sep. 1960
86.	Democratic Republic of the Congo	20 Sep. 1960
87.	Cyprus	20 Sep. 1960
88.	Benin (Dahomey)	20 Sep. 1960
89.	Gabon	20 Sep. 1960
90.	Ivory Coast (Côte d'Ivoire)	20 Sep. 1960
91.	Republic of Madagascar (Malagasy Republic)	20 Sep. 1960
92.	Niger	20 Sep. 1960
93.	Somalia	20 Sep. 1960
94.	Togo	20 Sep. 1960
95.	Burkina Faso (Upper Volta)	20 Sep. 1960
96.	Mali	28 Sep. 1960
97.	Senegal	28 Sep. 1960

98.	Nigeria	7 Oct. 1960
99.	Sierra Leone	27 Sep. 1961
100.	Mauritania	27 Oct. 1961
101.	Mongolia	27 Oct. 1961
102.	United Republic of Tanzania (Tanganyika)	14 Dec. 1961
103.	Burundi	18 Sep. 1962
104.	Jamaica	18 Sep. 1962
105.	Rwanda	18 Sep. 1962
106.	Trinidad and Tobago	18 Sep. 1962
107.	Algeria	8 Oct. 1962
108.	Uganda	25 Oct. 1962
109.	Kuwait	14 May 1963
110.	Kenya	16 Dec. 1963
111.	Zanzibar‡	16 Dec. 1963
112.	Malawi	1 Dec. 1964
113.	Malta	1 Dec. 1964
114.	Zambia	1 Dec. 1964
115.	Gambia	21 Sep. 1965
116.	Maldives	21 Sep. 1965
117.	Singapore	21 Sep. 1965
118.	Guyana	20 Sep. 1966
119.	Botswana	17 Oct. 1966
120.	Lesotho	17 Oct. 1966
121.	Barbados	9 Dec. 1966
122.	Democratic Yemen†	14 Dec. 1967
123.	Mauritius	24 Apr. 1968
124.	Swaziland	24 Sep. 1968
125.	Equatorial Guinea	12 Nov. 1968
126.	Fiji	13 Oct. 1970
127.	Bahrain	21 Sep. 1971
128.	Bhutan	21 Sep. 1971
129.	Qatar	21 Sep. 1971
130.	Oman	7 Oct. 1971
131.	United Arab Emirates	9 Dec. 1971
132.	Bahamas	18 Sep. 1973
133.	Germany (Federal Republic of Germany and German Democratic Republic)	18 Sep. 1973
134.	Bangladesh	17 Sep. 1974
135.	Grenada	17 Sep. 1974
136.	Guinea Bissau	17 Sep. 1974
137.	Cape Verde	16 Sep. 1975
138.	Mozambique	16 Sep. 1975
139.	Sao Tome and Principe	16 Sep. 1975
140.	Papua New Guinea	10 Oct. 1975
141.	Comoros	12 Nov. 1975
142.	Suriname	4 Dec. 1975
143.	Seychelles	21 Sep. 1976
144.	Angola	1 Dec. 1976
145.	Samoa	15 Dec. 1976
146.	Viet Nam	20 Sep. 1977
147.	Djibouti	29 Sep. 1977
148.	Solomon Islands	19 Sep. 1978
149.	Dominica	18 Dec. 1978
150.	Saint Lucia	18 Sep. 1979
151.	Zimbabwe	25 Aug. 1980
152.	Saint Vincent and the Grenadines	16 Sep. 1980
153.	Vanuatu	15 Sep. 1981
154.	Belize	25 Sep. 1981
155.	Antigua and Barbuda	11 Nov. 1981
156.	Saint Kitts and Nevis	23 Sep. 1983
157.	Brunei Darussalam	21 Sep. 1984
158.	Namibia	23 Apr. 1990
159.	Liechtenstein	18 Sep. 1990
160.	Democratic People's Republic of Korea	17 Sep. 1991
161.	Estonia	17 Sep. 1991
162.	Latvia	17 Sep. 1991
163.	Lithuania	17 Sep. 1991
164.	Marshall Islands	17 Sep. 1991
165.	Micronesia (Federated States of)	17 Sep. 1991
166.	Republic of Korea	17 Sep. 1991
167.	Armenia	2 Mar. 1992
168.	Kazakhstan	2 Mar. 1992
169.	Kyrgyzstan	2 Mar. 1992
170.	Republic of Moldova	2 Mar. 1992
171.	San Marino	2 Mar. 1992
172.	Tajikistan	2 Mar. 1992
173.	Turkmenistan	2 Mar. 1992
174.	Uzbekistan	2 Mar. 1992
175.	Azerbaijan	9 Mar. 1992
176.	Bosnia and Herzegovina**	22 May 1992
177.	Croatia**	22 May 1992
178.	Slovenia**	22 May 1992
179.	Georgia	31 Jul. 1992
180.	Czech Republic§	19 Jan. 1993
181.	Slovak Republic§	19 Jan. 1993
182.	The Former Yugoslav Republic of Macedonia**	8 Apr. 1993
183.	Eritrea	28 May 1993
184.	Monaco	28 May 1993
185.	Andorra	28 Jul. 1993
186.	Palau	15 Dec. 1994
187.	Kiribati	14 Sep. 1999
188.	Nauru	14 Sep. 1999
189.	Tonga	14 Sep. 1999
190.	Tuvalu	5 Sep. 2000
191.	Yugoslavia**	1 Nov. 2000

*Egypt and Syria were original members of the United Nations. In 1958, a union of the two countries established the United Arab Republic. On October 3, 1961, Syria resumed its status as an independent state. On September 2, 1971, the United Arab Republic became the Arab Republic of Egypt.

†Democratic Yemen and Yemen merged on May 22, 1990.

‡Zanzibar's seat was given up on May 13, 1964, following the union of Zanzibar with Tanzania.

**The Socialist Federal Republic of Yugoslavia was admitted to the United Nations on October 19, 1945. Between 1991 and 1992, the republic split into the following countries, which were admitted to the United Nations as new members: Bosnia, Herzegovina, the Republic of Croatia, the Republic of Slovenia, the Former Yugoslav Republic of Macedonia, and the Federal Republic of Yugoslavia.

§Czechoslovakia was admitted to the United Nations on October 24, 1945. In 1992, Czechoslovakia split into the Czech Republic and the Slovak Republic.

INDEX

B

D

E

F

G

H

K

L

M

V

W

X

Y

Z

The Encyclopedia of
WORLD HISTORY
CD-ROM

The Encyclopedia of World History CD-ROM

- features the complete text of *The Encyclopedia of World History*

- allows users to search for information by keyword (proper name, event, place, or date) or browse through a detailed outline of the entire book

- features 52 color maps

- features 66 genealogical tables

- can be used with any Microsoft Office application: click on a word in MS Word, for example, and the *Encylopedia*'s relevant entry pops up instantly!

Installation Instructions

- Close any open programs.

- Insert the CD into your CD-ROM drive.

- Click the Start button and select Run.

- Type D:\SETUP.EXE and click OK. Then follow the interactive prompts issued by the setup program.
  Note: Substitute the correct CD-ROM drive letter in place of D if necessary.

Minimal System Requirements

PC with Pentium® 200 or higher processor • Windows® 95, Windows® 98, Windows NT®, Windows® 2000 or Windows® Me
32 megabytes of RAM • Hard disk with at least 40 megabytes of free space • CD-ROM drive (or DVD-ROM drive)
SVGA 800 × 600 or higher resolution monitor • Mouse (or other pointing device) and keyboard

This CD is PC compatible only. Customer Service: 617-351-3836